Who's Who in America®

Who's Who in America®

Who's Who in America®
2005

59th Edition
Volume 2 • M-Z
Geographic Index • Professional Index

MARQUIS Who'sWho®

562 Central Avenue
New Providence, NJ 07974 U.S.A.
www.marquiswhoswho.com

Who's Who in America®
Marquis Who's Who®

Chief Executive Officer	Gene M. McGovern	**Chairman**	Wilbur L. Ross, Jr.
Senior Managing Director	Fred Marks	**President**	James A. Finkelstein
Managing Director, Special Projects	Jon Gelberg		
Director, Editorial & Product Development	Robert Docherty		

Editorial

Managing Editor	Karen Chassie
Senior Editors	Danielle Netta
	Alison Perruso
Associate Editor	LeighAnne Helfmann
	Laura Koserowski
	Holli Kurdes
	Deanna Richmond
	Sandy Sauchelli
	Kate Spirito

Editorial Services

Production Manager	Paul Zema
Production Editor	Robert Lovas
Freelance Manager	Mary SanGiovanni
Editorial Services Assistant	Ann Chavis
Systems Engineer	Ben McCullough
Mail Processing Manager	Kara A. Seitz
Mail Processing Staff	Hattie Walker

Creative Services

Director, Marketing & Creative Services	Michael Noerr
Creative Services Manager	Rose Butkiewicz
Production Manager	Jeanne Danzig
Marketing Specialist	Jill Tarbell

Research

Managing Editor	Kerry Nugent Morrison
Senior Research Editors	Patricia Delli Santi
	Todd Kineavy
Research Editor	Eric Amato
Assistant Research Editor	Gayle Childers

Editorial Systems

Director	Jack Zimmerman
Technical Project Leader	Ben Loh
Composition Programmer	Tom Haggerty

Published by Marquis Who's Who LLC.

For information, contact:
Marquis Who's Who
562 Central Avenue
New Providence, New Jersey 07974
1-908-673-1001
www.marquiswhoswho.com

WHO'S WHO IN AMERICA is a registered trademark of Marquis Who's Who LLC.

International Standard Book Number	0-8379-6982-4	(Set, Classic Edition)
	0-8379-6984-0	(Volume 2, Classic Edition)
	0-8379-6986-7	(Set, Deluxe Edition)
	0-8379-6988-3	(Volume 2, Deluxe Edition)
International Standard Serial Number	0083-9841	

Manufactured in the United States of America.

Table of Contents

Preface

"WHO'S WHO IN AMERICA *shall endeavor to list those individuals who are of current national reference interest and inquiry either because of meritorious achievement or because of the position they hold."*

Albert Nelson Marquis
Founder, 1899

Marquis Who's Who is proud to present the 2005 Edition of *Who's Who in America*. The 59th edition features over 100,000 profiles of prominent individuals representing virtually every major field of endeavor.

In 1899, our first year of publication, Marquis biographees numbered 8,602. While the number of individuals profiled in *Who's Who in America* has grown substantially, our selection standards remain stringent. Fewer than one in 2,900 Americans are included in the 2005 edition of *Who's Who in America*.

While the vast majority of the individuals profiled on the following pages are American, *Who's Who in America* also includes the biographies of select individuals from around the world whose lives have had considerable impact and influence in America.

On the pages that follow, you will find Olympic champions, Nobel and Pulitzer Prize winners, university presidents, accomplished artists, renowned entertainers, entrepreneurs, and leaders representing hundreds of industries. Our 2005 Edition includes some of the most recognizable names in the world. Here you will find President George W. Bush, Microsoft CEO Bill Gates, and novelist Stephen King. *Who's Who in America* also includes the profiles of thousands of remarkable achievers who, despite extraordinary accomplishments in everything from breakthrough medical research to cutting-edge technological innovations, have not as yet become household names.

Our profiles provide you with critical biographical information, including educational background, family history, work history, civic activity, memberships, honors, and awards. In many cases, hobbies and special interests are also listed.

One Principle Governs Selection

As in all Marquis Who's Who biographical volumes, the individuals profiled in *Who's Who in America* are selected on the basis of current reference value. Factors such as position, noteworthy accomplishments, visibility, and prominence in a field are all taken into account. An individual's desire to be listed is not sufficient reason for inclusion. Similarly, wealth and social position are not relevant criteria. Of course, Marquis Who's Who has never charged a fee for publishing a biography, nor is purchase of the book ever a factor in the selection of biographees. Final decisions concerning inclusion or exclusion are made following extensive discussion, evaluation, and deliberation.

Biographical information is gathered in a variety of manners. In most cases, we invite our biographees to submit their biographical details. In many cases, though, the information is collected independently by our research and editorial staffs, which use a wide assortment of tools to gather the most complete, accurate, and up-to-date information available. Sketches researched by Marquis Who's Who are followed by an asterisk (*).

Responding to Your Reference Needs

As a complement to the biographical profiles, the Geographic and Professional Indexes, featured in volume 2, make *Who's Who in America* an even more productive research tool. Through these indexes, users can identify and locate individuals in any of thirty-eight professional categories, as well as by country, state, or city. Each entry contains name and occupation description.

The Geographic Index lists names in the United States under state and city designations, as well as biographees in American territories. Canadian listings include provinces and cities. Names in Mexico and other countries appear by city. Biographees whose addresses are not published in their sketches are found under Address Unpublished.

The Professional Index includes categories ranging alphabetically from Agriculture to Social Science. Within each area, the names appear under geographic subheadings. Names without published addresses appear at the end of each professional area listing under Address Unpublished. If the occupation does not fall within one of the specified areas, the name is listed under Unclassified.

Some biographees have professions encompassing more than one area; each of these appears under the field best suited to the biographee's occupation. Thus, while most bankers are listed under Finance: Banking Services, investment bankers are found in Finance: Investment Services. A biographee with two or more diverse occupations is found under the area that best fits his or her professional profile.

Our Challenge

While the Marquis Who's Who editors exercise the utmost care in preparing each biographical sketch for publication, it is inevitable in a publication involving so many profiles that occasional errors will appear. Users of this publication are urged to notify the publisher of any issues so that adjustments can be made, which will not only be reflected in all subsequent editions of the book but which can now be immediately displayed via Marquis Who's Who on the Web.

We sincerely hope that this volume will be an indispensable reference tool for you. We are always looking for ways to better serve you and welcome your ideas for improvements. In addition, we continue to welcome your Marquis Who's Who nominations. Feel free to submit these via our Web site (www.marquiswhoswho.com) or by e-mail and postal mail.

Our Utmost Thanks

Without the cooperation and assistance of those profiled on the pages that follow, *Who's Who in America* would not be possible. We would like to specifically thank our biographees for reviewing and editing their profiles. As a consequence, *Who's Who in America* remains the unchallenged leader in the field of biographical reference works. For this we are truly grateful.

Standards of Admission

The foremost consideration in determining who will be admitted to the pages of *Who's Who in America* is the extent of an individual's reference interest. Reference value is based on either of two factors: (1) the position of responsibility held or (2) the level of significant achievement attained in a career of noteworthy activity. The majority of biographees qualify for admission on the basis of the first factor, a specific position of responsibility. Incumbency in the position makes the person someone of high reference interest. The factor of position includes the following categories:

1. High-ranking members of the executive, legislative, and judicial branches of the United States government. This group includes, for example, the President of the United States, members of Congress, cabinet secretaries, chief administrators of selected federal agencies and commissions, and justices of the federal courts.

2. Military officers on active duty with the rank of Lieutenant General or higher in the Army, Air Force, and Marine Corps, and of Rear Admiral or higher in the U.S. Navy.

3. Specified state government officials. Among these are governors, lieutenant governors, secretaries of state, attorneys general, and treasurers. Also included under this standard are presidents of state senates, state university system administrators, chief state health officers, and officials of American territories.

4. Judges of state and territorial courts of the highest appellate jurisdiction.

5. High-level officials of principal cities, based on population. These officials include mayors, police chiefs, school superintendents, and other selected positions.

6. Leading government officials of Canada and Mexico. In Canada, this group includes the prime minister, premiers of the provinces, ministers of departments of the federal government, and justices of the highest courts. Examples in the Mexican government are the president of the country and cabinet secretaries of the national government.

7. Principal officers of major national and international businesses as defined by several quantitative criteria.

8. Ranking administrative officials of major universities and colleges. Some of the officers included in this category are president, provost, dean, and selected department heads.

9. Heads of leading philanthropic, cultural, educational, professional, and scientific institutions and associations. These institutions include, for example, selected foundations, museums, symphony orchestras, libraries, and research laboratories.

10. Selected members of certain honorary and professional organizations, such as the National Academy of Sciences, the National Academy of Design, the American College of Trial Lawyers, and the Institute of Medicine.

11. Chief ecclesiastics of the principal religious denominations.

12. Recipients of major national and international awards, such as the Nobel and Pulitzer Prizes, MacArthur Fellows, the Academy Awards, Lasker Awards, and the Antoinette Perry or Tony Awards. Also included are winners of important professional awards, such as the American Institute of Architecture's Gold Medal for Architecture.

Admission by the second factor—significant achievement—is based on the application of objective criteria established for each field. An artist whose works are included in major museums qualifies for admission for noteworthy accomplishment. The professor who has made important research contributions in his field is of reference interest because of his outstanding achievements. Qualitative standards determine eligibility for every field.

In many instances there is considerable overlap between the two factors used for inclusion in *Who's Who in America*. For example, the head of a major library is in the book because of position, but reaching that responsibility also signifies important achievement. Similarly, a state governor not only holds a position that warrants inclusion; attaining that post also represents significant achievement in the political world. In both cases, the reference value of the biographical sketch is significant. Whether the person has been selected because of position or as a mark of achievement, the biographee in *Who's Who in America* has noteworthy accomplishments beyond those of the vast majority of contemporaries.

Key to Information

[1] **GIBSON, OSCAR JULIUS,** [2] physician, medical educator; [3] b. Syracuse, N.Y., Aug. 31, 1937; [4] s. Paul Oliver and Elizabeth H. (Thrun) G.; [5] m. Judith S. Gonzalez, Apr. 28, 1968; [6] children: Richard Gary, Matthew Cary, Samuel Perry. [7] BA magna cum laude, U. Pa., 1960; MD, Harvard U., 1964. [8] Diplomate Am. Bd. Internal Medicine, Am. Bd. Preventive Medicine. [9] Intern Barnes Hosp., St. Louis, 1964-65, resident, 1965-66; clin. assoc. Nat. Heart Inst., NIH, Bethesda, Md., 1966-68; chief resident medicine U. Okla. Hosps., 1968-69; asst. prof. cmty. health Okla. Med. Ctr., 1969-70, assoc. prof., 1970-74, prof., chmn. dept., 1974-80; dean Coll. Medicine U. Okla., 1978-82; v.p. med. staff affairs Bapt. Med. Ctr., Oklahoma City, 1982-86, exec. v.p., 1986-88, chmn., 1988-95, chmn, CEO, 1995—; [10] mem. governing bd. Ambulatory Health Care Consortium, Inc., 1979-80; mem. Okla. Bd. Medicolegal Examiners, 1985—; mem. Okla. Bd. of Med. Ethics, 1994—. [11] Contrb. articles to profl. jours. [12] Bd. dirs., v.p. Okla. Arthritis Found., 1982—; trustee N. Ctrl. Mental Health Ctr., 1985—. [13] Served U.S. Army, 1955-56. [14] Recipient R.T. Chadwick award Overlook Hosp., 1968; Am. Heart Assn. grantee, 1985-86, 88, 1995-96. [15] Fellow Assn. Tchrs. Preventive Medicine; mem. AAAS, AMA, Am. Fedn. Clin. Rsch., Assn. Med. Colls., Masons, Shriners, Sigma Xi. [16] Republican. [17] Roman Catholic. [18] Avocations: swimming, weight lifting, travelling. [19] Home: 6060 N Ridge Ave Oklahoma City OK 73126 [20] Office: Bapt Med Ctr 1986 Cuba Hwy Oklahoma City OK 73120*

KEY

[1]	Name
[2]	Occupation
[3]	Vital statistics
[4]	Parents
[5]	Marriage
[6]	Children
[7]	Education
[8]	Professional certifications
[9]	Career
[10]	Career-related
[11]	Writings and creative works
[12]	Civic and political activities
[13]	Military
[14]	Awards and fellowships
[15]	Professional and association memberships, clubs and lodges
[16]	Political affiliation
[17]	Religion
[18]	Avocations
[19]	Home address
[20]	Office address
[*]	Researched by Marquis Who's Who

Table of Abbreviations

The following abbreviations and symbols are frequently used in this book.

An asterisk following a sketch indicates that it was researched by the Marquis Who's Who editorial staff and has not been verified by the biographee.

A

A Associate (used with academic degrees only)

AA, A.A. Associate in Arts, Associate of Arts

AAAL American Academy of Arts and Letters

AAAS American Association for the Advancement of Science

AACD American Association for Counseling and Development

AACN American Association of Critical Care Nurses

AAHA American Academy of Health Administrators

AAHP American Association of Hospital Planners

AAHPERD American Alliance for Health, Physical Education, Recreation, and Dance

AAS Associate of Applied Science

AASL American Association of School Librarians

AASPA American Association of School Personnel Administrators

AAU Amateur Athletic Union

AAUP American Association of University Professors

AAUW American Association of University Women

AB, A.B. Arts, Bachelor of

AB Alberta

ABA American Bar Association

ABC American Broadcasting Company

AC Air Corps

acad. academy, academic

acct. accountant

acctg. accounting

ACDA Arms Control and Disarmament Agency

ACHA American College of Hospital Administrators

ACLS Advanced Cardiac Life Support

ACLU American Civil Liberties Union

ACOG American College of Ob-Gyn

ACP American College of Physicians

ACS American College of Surgeons

ADA American Dental Association

a.d.c. aide-de-camp

adj. adjunct, adjutant

adj. gen. adjutant general

adm. admiral

adminstr. administrator

adminstrn. administration

adminstrv. administrative

ADN Associate's Degree in Nursing

ADP Automatic Data Processing

adv. advocate, advisory

advt. advertising

AE, A.E. Agricultural Engineer

A.E. and P. Ambassador Extraordinary and Plenipotentiary

AEC Atomic Energy Commission

aero. aeronautical, aeronautic

aerodyn. aerodynamic

AFB Air Force Base

AFL-CIO American Federation of Labor and Congress of Industrial Organizations

AFTRA American Federation of TV and Radio Artists

AFSCME American Federation of State, County and Municipal Employees

agr. agriculture

agrl. agricultural

agt. agent

AGVA American Guild of Variety Artists

agy. agency

A&I Agricultural and Industrial

AIA American Institute of Architects

AIAA American Institute of Aeronautics and Astronautics

AIChE American Institute of Chemical Engineers

AICPA American Institute of Certified Public Accountants

AID Agency for International Development

AIDS Acquired Immune Deficiency Syndrome

AIEE American Institute of Electrical Engineers

AIM American Institute of Management

AIME American Institute of Mining, Metallurgy, and Petroleum Engineers

AK Alaska

AL Alabama

ALA American Library Association

Ala. Alabama

alt. alternate

Alta. Alberta

A&M Agricultural and Mechanical

AM, A.M. Arts, Master of

Am. American, America

AMA American Medical Association

amb. ambassador

A.M.E. African Methodist Episcopal

Amtrak National Railroad Passenger Corporation

AMVETS American Veterans of World War II, Korea, Vietnam

ANA American Nurses Association

anat. anatomical

ANCC American Nurses Credentialing Center

ann. annual

ANTA American National Theatre and Academy

anthrop. anthropological

AP Associated Press

APA American Psychological Association

APGA American Personnel Guidance Association

APHA American Public Health Association

APO Army Post Office

apptd. appointed

Apr. April

apt. apartment

AR Arkansas

ARC American Red Cross

arch. architect

archeol. archeological

archtl. architectural

Ariz. Arizona

Ark. Arkansas

ArtsD, ArtsD. Arts, Doctor of

arty. artillery

AS American Samoa

AS Associate in Science

ASCAP American Society of Composers, Authors and Publishers

ASCD Association for Supervision and Curriculum Development

ASCE American Society of Civil Engineers

ASHRAE American Society of Heating, Refrigeration, and Air Conditioning Engineers

ASME American Society of Mechanical Engineers

ASNSA American Society for Nursing Service Administrators

ASPA American Society for Public Administration

ASPCA American Society for the Prevention of Cruelty to Animals

assn. association

assoc. associate

asst. assistant

ASTD American Society for Training and Development

ASTM American Society for Testing and Materials

astron. astronomical

astrophys. astrophysical

ATLA Association of Trial Lawyers of America

ATSC Air Technical Service Command

AT&T American Telephone & Telegraph Company

atty. attorney

Aug. August

AUS Army of the United States

aux. auxiliary

Ave. Avenue

AVMA American Veterinary Medical Association

AZ Arizona

AWHONN Association of Women's Health Obstetric and Neonatal Nurses

B

B. Bachelor

b. born

BA, B.A. Bachelor of Arts

BAgr, B.Agr. Bachelor of Agriculture

Balt. Baltimore
Bapt. Baptist
BArch, B.Arch. Bachelor of Architecture
BAS, B.A.S. Bachelor of Agricultural Science
BBA, B.B.A. Bachelor of Business Administration
BBB Better Business Bureau
BBC British Broadcasting Corporation
BC, B.C. British Columbia
BCE, B.C.E. Bachelor of Civil Engineering
BChir, B.Chir. Bachelor of Surgery
BCL, B.C.L. Bachelor of Civil Law
BCLS Basic Cardiac Life Support
BCS, B.C.S. Bachelor of Commercial Science
BD, B.D. Bachelor of Divinity
bd. board
BE, B.E. Bachelor of Education
BEE, B.E.E. Bachelor of Electrical Engineering
BFA, B.F.A. Bachelor of Fine Arts
bibl. biblical
bibliog. bibliographical
biog. biographical
biol. biological
BJ, B.J. Bachelor of Journalism
Bklyn. Brooklyn
BL, B.L. Bachelor of Letters
bldg. building
BLS, B.L.S. Bachelor of Library Science
BLS Basic Life Support
Blvd. Boulevard
BMI Broadcast Music, Inc.
BMW Bavarian Motor Works (Bayerische Motoren Werke)
bn. battalion
B.&O.R.R. Baltimore & Ohio Railroad
bot. botanical
BPE, B.P.E. Bachelor of Physical Education
BPhil, B.Phil. Bachelor of Philosophy
br. branch
BRE, B.R.E. Bachelor of Religious Education
brig. gen. brigadier general
Brit. British, Brittanica
Bros. Brothers
BS, B.S. Bachelor of Science
BSA, B.S.A. Bachelor of Agricultural Science
BSBA Bachelor of Science in Business Administration
BSChemE Bachelor of Science in Chemical Engineering
BSD, B.S.D. Bachelor of Didactic Science
BSEE Bachelor of Science in Electrical Engineering
BSN Bachelor of Science in Nursing
BST, B.S.T. Bachelor of Sacred Theology
BTh, B.Th. Bachelor of Theology
bull. bulletin
bur. bureau
bus. business
B.W.I. British West Indies

C

CA California
CAA Civil Aeronautics Administration
CAB Civil Aeronautics Board
CAD-CAM Computer Aided Design– Computer Aided Model
Calif. California
C.Am. Central America
Can. Canada, Canadian
CAP Civil Air Patrol
capt. captain
cardiol. cardiological
cardiovasc. cardiovascular
CARE Cooperative American Relief Everywhere
Cath. Catholic
cav. cavalry
CBC Canadian Broadcasting Company
CBI China, Burma, India Theatre of Operations
CBS Columbia Broadcasting Company
C.C. Community College
CCC Commodity Credit Corporation
CCNY City College of New York
CCRN Critical Care Registered Nurse
CCU Cardiac Care Unit
CD Civil Defense
CE, C.E. Corps of Engineers, Civil Engineer
CEN Certified Emergency Nurse
CENTO Central Treaty Organization
CEO chief executive officer
CERN European Organization of Nuclear Research
cert. certificate, certification, certified
CETA Comprehensive Employment Training Act
CFA Chartered Financial Analyst
CFL Canadian Football League
CFO chief financial officer
CFP Certified Financial Planner
ch. church
ChD, Ch.D. Doctor of Chemistry
chem. chemical
ChemE, Chem.E. Chemical Engineer
ChFC Chartered Financial Consultant
Chgo. Chicago
chirurg. chirurgical
chmn. chairman
chpt. chapter
CIA Central Intelligence Agency
Cin. Cincinnati
cir. circle, circuit
CLE Continuing Legal Education
Cleve. Cleveland
climatol. climatological
clin. clinical
clk. clerk
C.L.U. Chartered Life Underwriter
CM, C.M. Master in Surgery
CM Northern Mariana Islands
CMA Certified Medical Assistant
cmty. community
CNA Certified Nurse's Aide
CNOR Certified Nurse (Operating Room)
C.&N.W.Ry. Chicago & North Western Railway
CO Colorado
Co. Company
COF Catholic Order of Foresters
C. of C. Chamber of Commerce
col. colonel
coll. college

Colo. Colorado
com. committee
comd. commanded
comdg. commanding
comdr. commander
comdt. commandant
comm. communications
commd. commissioned
comml. commercial
commn. commission
commr. commissioner
compt. comptroller
condr. conductor
Conf. Conference
Congl. Congregational, Congressional
Conglist. Congregationalist
Conn. Connecticut
cons. consultant, consulting
consol. consolidated
constl. constitutional
constn. constitution
constrn. construction
contbd. contributed
contbg. contributing
contbn. contribution
contbr. contributor
contr. controller
Conv. Convention
COO chief operating officer
coop. cooperative
coord. coordinator
CORDS Civil Operations and Revolutionary Development Support
CORE Congress of Racial Equality
corp. corporation, corporate
corr. correspondent, corresponding, correspondence
C.&O.Ry. Chesapeake & Ohio Railway
coun. council
CPA Certified Public Accountant
CPCU Chartered Property and Casualty Underwriter
CPH, C.P.H. Certificate of Public Health
cpl. corporal
CPR Cardio-Pulmonary Resuscitation
C.P.Ry. Canadian Pacific Railway
CRT Cathode Ray Terminal
C.S. Christian Science
CSB, C.S.B. Bachelor of Christian Science
C.S.C. Civil Service Commission
CT Connecticut
ct. court
ctr. center
ctrl. central
CWS Chemical Warfare Service
C.Z. Canal Zone

D

D. Doctor
d. daughter
DAgr, D.Agr. Doctor of Agriculture
DAR Daughters of the American Revolution
dau. daughter
DAV Disabled American Veterans
DC, D.C. District of Columbia
DCL, D.C.L. Doctor of Civil Law
DCS, D.C.S. Doctor of Commercial Science
DD, D.D. Doctor of Divinity

DDS, D.D.S. Doctor of Dental Surgery
DE Delaware
Dec. December
dec. deceased
def. defense
Del. Delaware
del. delegate, delegation
Dem. Democrat, Democratic
DEng, D.Eng. Doctor of Engineering
denom. denomination, denominational
dep. deputy
dept. department
dermatol. dermatological
desc. descendant
devel. development, developmental
DFA, D.F.A. Doctor of Fine Arts
D.F.C. Distinguished Flying Cross
DHL, D.H.L. Doctor of Hebrew Literature
dir. director
dist. district
distbg. distributing
distbn. distribution
distbr. distributor
disting. distinguished
div. division, divinity, divorce
divsn. division
DLitt, D.Litt. Doctor of Literature
DMD, D.M.D. Doctor of Dental Medicine
DMS, D.M.S. Doctor of Medical Science
DO, D.O. Doctor of Osteopathy
docs. documents
DON Director of Nursing
DPH, D.P.H. Diploma in Public Health
DPhil, D.Phil. Doctor of Philosophy
D.R. Daughters of the Revolution
Dr. Drive, Doctor
DRE, D.R.E. Doctor of Religious Education
DrPH, Dr.P.H. Doctor of Public Health,
    Doctor of Public Hygiene
D.S.C. Distinguished Service Cross
DSc, D.Sc. Doctor of Science
DSChemE Doctor of Science in Chemical
    Engineering
D.S.M. Distinguished Service Medal
DST, D.S.T. Doctor of Sacred Theology
DTM, D.T.M. Doctor of Tropical Medicine
DVM, D.V.M. Doctor of Veterinary
    Medicine
DVS, D.V.S. Doctor of Veterinary Surgery

E

E, E. East
ea. eastern
E. and P. Extraordinary and Plenipotentiary
Eccles. Ecclesiastical
ecol. ecological
econ. economic
ECOSOC Economic and Social Council (of
    the UN)
ED, E.D. Doctor of Engineering
ed. educated
EdB, Ed.B. Bachelor of Education
EdD, Ed.D. Doctor of Education
edit. edition
editl. editorial
EdM, Ed.M. Master of Education
edn. education
ednl. educational

EDP Electronic Data Processing
EdS, Ed.S. Specialist in Education
EE, E.E. Electrical Engineer
E.E. and M.P. Envoy Extraordinary and
    Minister Plenipotentiary
EEC European Economic Community
EEG Electroencephalogram
EEO Equal Employment Opportunity
EEOC Equal Employment Opportunity
    Commission
E.Ger. German Democratic Republic
EKG Electrocardiogram
elec. electrical
electrochem. electrochemical
electrophys. electrophysical
elem. elementary
EM, E.M. Engineer of Mines
EMT Emergency Medical Technician
ency. encyclopedia
Eng. England
engr. engineer
engring. engineering
entomol. entomological
environ. environmental
EPA Environmental Protection Agency
epidemiol. epidemiological
Episc. Episcopalian
ERA Equal Rights Amendment
ERDA Energy Research and Development
    Administration
ESEA Elementary and Secondary Education
    Act
ESL English as Second Language
ESPN Entertainment and Sports
    Programming Network
ESSA Environmental Science Services
    Administration
ethnol. ethnological
ETO European Theatre of Operations
Evang. Evangelical
exam. examination, examining
Exch. Exchange
exec. executive
exhbn. exhibition
expdn. expedition
expn. exposition
expt. experiment
exptl. experimental
Expy. Expressway
Ext. Extension

F

F.A. Field Artillery
FAA Federal Aviation Administration
FAO Food and Agriculture Organization (of
    the UN)
FBA Federal Bar Association
FBI Federal Bureau of Investigation
FCA Farm Credit Administration
FCC Federal Communications Commission
FCDA Federal Civil Defense Administration
FDA Food and Drug Administration
FDIA Federal Deposit Insurance
    Administration
FDIC Federal Deposit Insurance Corporation
FE, F.E. Forest Engineer
FEA Federal Energy Administration
Feb. February

fed. federal
fedn. federation
FERC Federal Energy Regulatory
    Commission
fgn. foreign
FHA Federal Housing Administration
fin. financial, finance
FL Florida
Fl. Floor
Fla. Florida
FMC Federal Maritime Commission
FNP Family Nurse Practitioner
FOA Foreign Operations Administration
found. foundation
FPC Federal Power Commission
FPO Fleet Post Office
frat. fraternity
FRS Federal Reserve System
FSA Federal Security Agency
Ft. Fort
FTC Federal Trade Commission
Fwy. Freeway

G

G-1 (or other number) Division of General
    Staff
GA, Ga. Georgia
GAO General Accounting Office
gastroent. gastroenterological
GATE Gifted and Talented Educators
GATT General Agreement on Tariffs and
    Trade
GE General Electric Company
gen. general
geneal. genealogical
geod. geodetic
geog. geographic, geographical
geol. geological
geophys. geophysical
geriat. geriatrics
gerontol. gerontological
G.H.Q. General Headquarters
GM General Motors Corporation
GMAC General Motors Acceptance
    Corporation
G.N.Ry. Great Northern Railway
gov. governor
govt. government
govtl. governmental
GPO Government Printing Office
grad. graduate, graduated
GSA General Services Administration
Gt. Great
GTE General Telephone and
    Electric Company
GU Guam
gynecol. gynecological

H

HBO Home Box Office
hdqs. headquarters
HEW Department of Health, Education and
    Welfare
HHD, H.H.D. Doctor of Humanities
HHFA Housing and Home Finance Agency
HHS Department of Health and Human
    Services

HI   Hawaii
hist.   historical, historic
HM, H.M.   Master of Humanities
HMO   Health Maintenance Organization
homeo.   homeopathic
hon.   honorary, honorable
Ho. of Dels.   House of Delegates
Ho. of Reps.   House of Representatives
hort.   horticultural
hosp.   hospital
H.S.   High School
HUD   Department of Housing and Urban
    Development
Hwy.   Highway
hydrog.   hydrographic

I

IA   Iowa
IAEA   International Atomic Energy Agency
IATSE   International Alliance of Theatrical
    and Stage Employees and Moving Picture
    Operators of the United States and Canada
IBM   International Business Machines
    Corporation
IBRD   International Bank for Reconstruction
    and Development
ICA   International Cooperation
    Administration
ICC   Interstate Commerce Commission
ICCE   International Council for Computers in
    Education
ICU   Intensive Care Unit
ID   Idaho
IEEE   Institute of Electrical and Electronics
    Engineers
IFC   International Finance Corporation
IGY   International Geophysical Year
IL   Illinois
Ill.   Illinois
illus.   illustrated
ILO   International Labor Organization
IMF   International Monetary Fund
IN   Indiana
Inc.   Incorporated
Ind.   Indiana
ind.   independent
Indpls.   Indianapolis
indsl.   industrial
inf.   infantry
info.   information
ins.   insurance
insp.   inspector
insp. gen.   inspector general
inst.   institute
instl.   institutional
instn.   institution
instr.   instructor
instrn.   instruction
instrnl.   instructional
internat.   international
intro.   introduction
IRE   Institute of Radio Engineers
IRS   Internal Revenue Service
ITT   International Telephone & Telegraph
    Corporation

J

JAG   Judge Advocate General

JAGC   Judge Advocate General Corps
Jan.   January
Jaycees   Junior Chamber of Commerce
JB, J.B.   Jurum Baccalaureus
JCB, J.C.B.   Juris Canoni Baccalaureus
JCD, J.C.D.   Juris Canonici Doctor, Juris
    Civilis Doctor
JCL, J.C.L.   Juris Canonici Licentiatus
JD, J.D.   Juris Doctor
jg.   junior grade
jour.   journal
jr.   junior
JSD, J.S.D.   Juris Scientiae Doctor
JUD, J.U.D.   Juris Utriusque Doctor
jud.   judicial

K

Kans.   Kansas
K.C.   Knights of Columbus
K.P.   Knights of Pythias
KS   Kansas
K.T.   Knight Templar
KY, Ky.   Kentucky

L

LA, La.   Louisiana
L.A.   Los Angeles
lab.   laboratory
L.Am.   Latin America
lang.   language
laryngol.   laryngological
LB   Labrador
LDS   Latter Day Saints
LDS Church   Church of Jesus Christ of
    Latter Day Saints
lectr.   lecturer
legis.   legislation, legislative
LHD, L.H.D.   Doctor of Humane Letters
L.I.   Long Island
libr.   librarian, library
lic.   licensed, license
L.I.R.R.   Long Island Railroad
lit.   literature
litig.   litigation
LittB, Litt.B.   Bachelor of Letters
LittD, Litt.D.   Doctor of Letters
LLB, LL.B.   Bachelor of Laws
LLD, L.L.D.   Doctor of Laws
LLM, L.L.M.   Master of Laws
Ln.   Lane
L.&N.R.R.   Louisville & Nashville Railroad
LPGA   Ladies Professional Golf Association
LPN   Licensed Practical Nurse
LS, L.S.   Library Science (in degree)
lt.   lieutenant
Ltd.   Limited
Luth.   Lutheran
LWV   League of Women Voters

M

M.   Master
m.   married
MA, M.A.   Master of Arts
MA   Massachusetts
MADD   Mothers Against Drunk Driving
mag.   magazine

MAgr, M.Agr.   Master of Agriculture
maj.   major
Man.   Manitoba
Mar.   March
MArch, M.Arch.   Master in Architecture
Mass.   Massachusetts
math.   mathematics, mathematical
MATS   Military Air Transport Service
MB, M.B.   Bachelor of Medicine
MB   Manitoba
MBA, M.B.A.   Master of Business
    Administration
MBS   Mutual Broadcasting System
M.C.   Medical Corps
MCE, M.C.E.   Master of Civil Engineering
mcht.   merchant
mcpl.   municipal
MCS, M.C.S.   Master of Commercial Science
MD, M.D.   Doctor of Medicine
MD, Md.   Maryland
MDiv   Master of Divinity
MDip, M.Dip.   Master in Diplomacy
mdse.   merchandise
MDV, M.D.V.   Doctor of Veterinary
    Medicine
ME, M.E.   Mechanical Engineer
ME   Maine
M.E.Ch.   Methodist Episcopal Church
mech.   mechanical
MEd., M.Ed.   Master of Education
med.   medical
MEE, M.E.E.   Master of Electrical
    Engineering
mem.   member
meml.   memorial
merc.   mercantile
met.   metropolitan
metall.   metallurgical
MetE, Met.E.   Metallurgical Engineer
meteorol.   meteorological
Meth.   Methodist
Mex.   Mexico
MF, M.F.   Master of Forestry
MFA, M.F.A.   Master of Fine Arts
mfg.   manufacturing
mfr.   manufacturer
mgmt.   management
mgr.   manager
MHA, M.H.A.   Master of Hospital
    Administration
M.I.   Military Intelligence
MI   Michigan
Mich.   Michigan
micros.   microscopic, microscopical
mid.   middle
mil.   military
Milw.   Milwaukee
Min.   Minister
mineral.   mineralogical
Minn.   Minnesota
MIS   Management Information Systems
Miss.   Mississippi
MIT   Massachusetts Institute of Technology
mktg.   marketing
ML, M.L.   Master of Laws
MLA   Modern Language Association
M.L.D.   Magister Legnum Diplomatic
MLitt, M.Litt.   Master of Literature, Master
    of Letters

MLS, M.L.S. Master of Library Science
MME, M.M.E. Master of Mechanical Engineering
MN Minnesota
mng. managing
MO, Mo. Missouri
moblzn. mobilization
Mont. Montana
MP Northern Mariana Islands
M.P. Member of Parliament
MPA Master of Public Administration
MPE, M.P.E. Master of Physical Education
MPH, M.P.H. Master of Public Health
MPhil, M.Phil. Master of Philosophy
MPL, M.P.L. Master of Patent Law
Mpls. Minneapolis
MRE, M.R.E. Master of Religious Education
MRI Magnetic Resonance Imaging
MS, M.S. Master of Science
MS, Ms. Mississippi
MSc, M.Sc. Master of Science
MSChemE Master of Science in Chemical Engineering
MSEE Master of Science in Electrical Engineering
MSF, M.S.F. Master of Science of Forestry
MSN Master of Science in Nursing
MST, M.S.T. Master of Sacred Theology
MSW, M.S.W. Master of Social Work
MT Montana
Mt. Mount
MTO Mediterranean Theatre of Operation
MTV Music Television
mus. museum, musical
MusB, Mus.B. Bachelor of Music
MusD, Mus.D. Doctor of Music
MusM, Mus.M. Master of Music
mut. mutual
MVP Most Valuable Player
mycol. mycological

N

N. North
NAACOG Nurses Association of the American College of Obstetricians and Gynecologists
NAACP National Association for the Advancement of Colored People
NACA National Advisory Committee for Aeronautics
NACDL National Association of Criminal Defense Lawyers
NACU National Association of Colleges and Universities
NAD National Academy of Design
NAE National Academy of Engineering, National Association of Educators
NAESP National Association of Elementary School Principals
NAFE National Association of Female Executives
N.Am. North America
NAM National Association of Manufacturers
NAMH National Association for Mental Health
NAPA National Association of Performing Artists

NARAS National Academy of Recording Arts and Sciences
NAREB National Association of Real Estate Boards
NARS National Archives and Record Service
NAS National Academy of Sciences
NASA National Aeronautics and Space Administration
NASP National Association of School Psychologists
NASW National Association of Social Workers
nat. national
NATAS National Academy of Television Arts and Sciences
NATO North Atlantic Treaty Organization
NATOUSA North African Theatre of Operations, United States Army
nav. navigation
NB, N.B. New Brunswick
NBA National Basketball Association
NBC National Broadcasting Company
NC, N.C. North Carolina
NCAA National College Athletic Association
NCCJ National Conference of Christians and Jews
ND, N.D. North Dakota
NDEA National Defense Education Act
NE Nebraska
NE, N.E. Northeast
NEA National Education Association
Nebr. Nebraska
NEH National Endowment for Humanities
neurol. neurological
Nev. Nevada
NF Newfoundland
NFL National Football League
Nfld. Newfoundland
NG National Guard
NH, N.H. New Hampshire
NHL National Hockey League
NIH National Institutes of Health
NIMH National Institute of Mental Health
NJ, N.J. New Jersey
NLRB National Labor Relations Board
NM New Mexico
N.Mex. New Mexico
No. Northern
NOAA National Oceanographic and Atmospheric Administration
NORAD North America Air Defense
Nov. November
NOW National Organization for Women
N.P.Ry. Northern Pacific Railway
nr. near
NRA National Rifle Association
NRC National Research Council
NS, N.S. Nova Scotia
NSC National Security Council
NSF National Science Foundation
NSTA National Science Teachers Association
NSW New South Wales
N.T. New Testament
NT Northwest Territories
nuc. nuclear
numis. numismatic
NV Nevada

NW, N.W. Northwest
N.W.T. Northwest Territories
NY, N.Y. New York
N.Y.C. New York City
NYU New York University
N.Z. New Zealand

O

OAS Organization of American States
ob-gyn obstetrics-gynecology
obs. observatory
obstet. obstetrical
occupl. occupational
oceanog. oceanographic
Oct. October
OD, O.D. Doctor of Optometry
OECD Organization for Economic Cooperation and Development
OEEC Organization of European Economic Cooperation
OEO Office of Economic Opportunity
ofcl. official
OH Ohio
OK Oklahoma
Okla. Oklahoma
ON Ontario
Ont. Ontario
oper. operating
ophthal. ophthalmological
ops. operations
OR Oregon
orch. orchestra
Oreg. Oregon
orgn. organization
orgnl. organizational
ornithol. ornithological
orthop. orthopedic
OSHA Occupational Safety and Health Administration
OSRD Office of Scientific Research and Development
OSS Office of Strategic Services
osteo. osteopathic
otol. otological
otolaryn. otolaryngological

P

PA, Pa. Pennsylvania
P.A. Professional Association
paleontol. paleontological
path. pathological
PBS Public Broadcasting System
P.C. Professional Corporation
PE Prince Edward Island
pediat. pediatrics
P.E.I. Prince Edward Island
PEN Poets, Playwrights, Editors, Essayists and Novelists (international association)
penol. penological
P.E.O. women's organization (full name not disclosed)
pers. personnel
pfc. private first class
PGA Professional Golfers' Association of America
PHA Public Housing Administration
pharm. pharmaceutical

PharmD, Pharm.D. Doctor of Pharmacy
PharmM, Pharm.M. Master of Pharmacy
PhB, Ph.B. Bachelor of Philosophy
PhD, Ph.D. Doctor of Philosophy
PhDChemE Doctor of Science in Chemical Engineering
PhM, Ph.M. Master of Philosophy
Phila. Philadelphia
philharm. philharmonic
philol. philological
philos. philosophical
photog. photographic
phys. physical
physiol. physiological
Pitts. Pittsburgh
Pk. Park
Pky. Parkway
Pl. Place
P.&L.E.R.R. Pittsburgh & Lake Erie Railroad
Plz. Plaza
PNP Pediatric Nurse Practitioner
P.O. Post Office
PO Box Post Office Box
polit. political
poly. polytechnic, polytechnical
PQ Province of Quebec
PR, P.R. Puerto Rico
prep. preparatory
pres. president
Presbyn. Presbyterian
presdl. presidential
prin. principal
procs. proceedings
prod. produced (play production)
prodn. production
prodr. producer
prof. professor
profl. professional
prog. progressive
propr. proprietor
pros. atty. prosecuting attorney
pro tem. pro tempore
PSRO Professional Services Review Organization
psychiat. psychiatric
psychol. psychological
PTA Parent-Teachers Association
ptnr. partner
PTO Pacific Theatre of Operations, Parent Teacher Organization
pub. publisher, publishing, published
pub. public
publ. publication
pvt. private

Q

quar. quarterly
qm. quartermaster
Q.M.C. Quartermaster Corps
Que. Quebec

R

radiol. radiological
RAF Royal Air Force
RCA Radio Corporation of America
RCAF Royal Canadian Air Force

RD Rural Delivery
Rd. Road
R&D Research & Development
REA Rural Electrification Administration
rec. recording
ref. reformed
regt. regiment
regtl. regimental
rehab. rehabilitation
rels. relations
Rep. Republican
rep. representative
Res. Reserve
ret. retired
Rev. Reverend
rev. review, revised
RFC Reconstruction Finance Corporation
RFD Rural Free Delivery
rhinol. rhinological
RI, R.I. Rhode Island
RISD Rhode Island School of Design
Rlwy. Railway
Rm. Room
RN, R.N. Registered Nurse
roentgenol. roentgenological
ROTC Reserve Officers Training Corps
RR Rural Route
R.R. Railroad
rsch. research
rschr. researcher
Rt. Route

S

S. South
s. son
SAC Strategic Air Command
SAG Screen Actors Guild
SALT Strategic Arms Limitation Talks
S.Am. South America
san. sanitary
SAR Sons of the American Revolution
Sask. Saskatchewan
savs. savings
SB, S.B. Bachelor of Science
SBA Small Business Administration
SC, S.C. South Carolina
SCAP Supreme Command Allies Pacific
ScB, Sc.B. Bachelor of Science
SCD, S.C.D. Doctor of Commercial Science
ScD, Sc.D. Doctor of Science
sch. school
sci. science, scientific
SCLC Southern Christian Leadership Conference
SCV Sons of Confederate Veterans
SD, S.D. South Dakota
SE, S.E. Southeast
SEATO Southeast Asia Treaty Organization
SEC Securities and Exchange Commission
sec. secretary
sect. section
seismol. seismological
sem. seminary
Sept. September
s.g. senior grade
sgt. sergeant
SHAEF Supreme Headquarters Allied Expeditionary Forces

SHAPE Supreme Headquarters Allied Powers in Europe
S.I. Staten Island
S.J. Society of Jesus (Jesuit)
SJD Scientiae Juridicae Doctor
SK Saskatchewan
SM, S.M. Master of Science
SNP Society of Nursing Professionals
So. Southern
soc. society
sociol. sociological
S.P.Co. Southern Pacific Company
spkr. speaker
spl. special
splty. specialty
Sq. Square
S.R. Sons of the Revolution
sr. senior
S S Steamship
S S S Selective Service System
St. Saint, Street
sta. station
stats. statistics
statis. statistical
STB, S.T.B. Bachelor of Sacred Theology
stblzn. stabilization
STD, S.T.D. Doctor of Sacred Theology
std. standard
Ste. Suite
subs. subsidiary
SUNY State University of New York
supr. supervisor
supt. superintendent
surg. surgical
svc. service
SW, S.W. Southwest
sys. system

T

TAPPI Technical Association of the Pulp and Paper Industry
tb. tuberculosis
tchg. teaching
tchr. teacher
tech. technical, technology
technol. technological
tel. telephone
Tel. & Tel. Telephone & Telegraph
telecom. telecommunications
temp. temporary
Tenn. Tennessee
Ter. Territory
Ter. Terrace
TESOL Teachers of English to Speakers of Other Languages
Tex. Texas
ThD, Th.D. Doctor of Theology
theol. theological
ThM, Th.M. Master of Theology
TN Tennessee
tng. training
topog. topographical
trans. transaction, transferred
transl. translation, translated
transp. transportation
treas. treasurer
TT Trust Territory
TV television

TVA Tennessee Valley Authority
TWA Trans World Airlines
twp. township
TX Texas
typog. typographical

U

U. University
UAW United Auto Workers
UCLA University of California at Los Angeles
UDC United Daughters of the Confederacy
U.K. United Kingdom
UN United Nations
UNESCO United Nations Educational, Scientific
    and Cultural Organization
UNICEF United Nations International Children's   Emergency Fund
univ. university
UNRRA United Nations Relief and
    Rehabilitation Administration
UPI United Press International
U.P.R.R. United Pacific Railroad
urol. urological
U.S. United States
U.S.A. United States of America
USAAF United States Army Air Force
USAF United States Air Force
USAFR United States Air Force Reserve
USAR United States Army Reserve
USCG United States Coast Guard
USCGR United States Coast Guard Reserve
USES United States Employment Service
USIA United States Information Agency
USMC United States Marine Corps

USMCR United States Marine Corps Reserve
USN United States Navy
USNG United States National Guard
USNR United States Naval Reserve
USO United Service Organizations
USPHS United States Public Health Service
USS United States Ship
USSR Union of the Soviet Socialist Republics
USTA United States Tennis Association
USV United States Volunteers
UT Utah

V

VA Veterans Administration
VA, Va. Virginia
vet. veteran, veterinary
VFW Veterans of Foreign Wars
VI, V.I. Virgin Islands
vice pres. vice president
vis. visiting
VISTA Volunteers in Service to America
VITA Volunteers in Technical Assistance
vocat. vocational
vol. volunteer, volume
v.p. vice president
vs. versus
VT, Vt. Vermont

W

W, W. West
WA Washington (state)
WAC Women's Army Corps

Wash. Washington (state)
WATS Wide Area Telecommunications Service
WAVES Women's Reserve, US Naval Reserve
WCTU Women's Christian Temperance Union
we. western
W. Ger. Germany, Federal Republic of
WHO World Health Organization
WI Wisconsin
W.I. West Indies
Wis. Wisconsin
WSB Wage Stabilization Board
WV West Virginia
W.Va. West Virginia
WWI World War I
WWII World War II
WY Wyoming
Wyo. Wyoming

X, Y

YK Yukon Territory
YMCA Young Men's Christian Association
YMHA Young Men's Hebrew Association
YM & YWHA Young Men's and Young Women's Hebrew Association
yr. year
YT, Y.T. Yukon Territory
YWCA Young Women's Christian
    Association

Z

zool. zoological

Alphabetical Practices

Names are arranged alphabetically according to the surnames, and under identical surnames according to the first given name. If both surname and first given name are identical, names are arranged alphabetically according to the second given name.

Surnames beginning with De, Des, Du, however capitalized or spaced, are recorded with the prefix preceding the surname and arranged alphabetically under the letter D.

Surnames beginning with Mac and Mc are arranged alphabetically under M.

Surnames beginning with Saint or St. appear after names that begin Sains, and are arranged according to the second part of the name, e.g., St. Clair before Saint Dennis.

Surnames beginning with Van, Von, or von are arranged alphabetically under the letter V.

Compound surnames are arranged according to the first member of the compound.

Many hyphenated Arabic names begin Al-, El-, or al-. These names are alphabetized according to each biographee's designation of last name. Thus Al-Bahar, Neta may be listed either under Al- or under Bahar, depending on the preference of the listee.

Also, Arabic names have a variety of possible spellings when transposed to English. Spelling of these names is always based on the practice of the biographee. Some biographees use a Western form of word order, while others prefer the Arabic word sequence.

Similarly, Asian names may have no comma between family and given names, but some biographees have chosen to add the comma. In each case, punctuation follows the preference of the biographee.

Parentheses used in connection with a name indicate which part of the full name is usually omitted in common usage. Hence, Chambers, E(lizabeth) Anne indicates that the first name, Elizabeth, is generally recorded as an initial. In such a case, the parentheses are ignored in alphabetizing and the name would be arranged as Chambers, Elizabeth Anne.

However, if the entire first name appears in parentheses, for example, Chambers, (Elizabeth) Anne, the first name is not commonly used, and the alphabetizing is therefore arranged as though the name were Chambers, Anne.

If the entire middle name is in parentheses, it is still used in alphabetical sorting. Hence, Belamy, Katherine (Lucille) would sort as Belamy, Katherine Lucille. The same occurs if the entire last name is in parentheses, e.g., (Brandenberg), Howard Keith would sort as Brandenberg, Howard Keith.

For visual clarification:

Smith, H(enry) George: Sorts as Smith, Henry George
Smith, (Henry) George: Sorts as Smith, George
Smith, Henry (George): Sorts as Smith, Henry George
(Smith), Henry George: Sorts as Smith, Henry George

Who'sWho in America®

Biographies M - Z

MA, CHUNG-PEI MICHELLE, astronomer, educator; BS, PhD, MIT, 1993. From asst. prof. to assoc. prof. physics and astronomy U. Pa., Phila., 1996—2001; assoc. prof. astronomy U. Calif., Berkeley, 2001—. Contbr. articles to profl. jours. Recipient Annie J. Cannon award, 1997, 1st prize Taiwan Nat. Violin Competition, 1983, Cottrell Scholars award Rsch. Corp., 1999, Lindback award for Disting. Tchg., U. Pa., 1999; Alfred P. Sloan fellow, 1999; Sherman Fairchild fellow, 1993. Mem. Phi Beta Kappa. Achievements include research in the formation and evolution of galaxies and large scale structure in the Universe; performed numerical simulations of the clustering of dark matter in various cosmological models of structure formation from the Early Universe until the present day; computation of the temperature variations imprinted on the cosmic microwave background radiation which provides a snapshot of the infant Universe. Office: U Calif Berkeley Dept Astronomy 601 Campbell Hall Berkeley CA 94720

MA, HENGWEI, music educator; b. Souzhou, China, Mar. 8, 1955; arrived in U.S., 1996; s. Jiazhang Ma and Feng Huang. BA, Nanjing Fine Arts Coll., 1981. Cert. violin Music Tchrs. Nat. Assn. 1st violinist Shenzheng (China) Symphony Orch., 1985—86, Westerville Symphony, Columbus, Ohio, 2000—; violin/music dir. Suzhou Juvenile Activity Ctr., 1987—88; owner, music dir. Ma's Violin Sch., Suzhou, 1989—96; owner Ma's Violin Studio, Columbus, 1997—; 2d violin Capital U. Orch., Columbus, 1998—2000. Mem. internat. bd. Shanghai Conservatory of Music, 1995—96. Author: Ma's Violin Studio Violin Practice Pieces, 1990 (Excellence award, 93). Trustee mgmt. bd. Columbus Music Tchrs. Assn., 1999—2000. Home and Office: Ma's Violin Studio 5649 Wendy Trail Ln Dublin OH 43017 E-mail: otcrpg@yahoo.com.

MA, JINGJING, mathematician; b. Beijing, Mar. 7, 1955; m. Li Liu, Oct. 8, 1988; children: Cheng, Elisa. PhD in math., U. of Toledo, 1993—99, MA in math., 1993—96; MS in math., Jiangxi U., 1985—87. Grad. tchg. asst. U. of Toledo, 1993—99; vis. asst. prof. of math. U. of Tex. at El Paso, 1999—2001; asst. prof. of math. U. of Houston-Clear Lake, 2001—. Contbr. articles to profl. jours. Mem.: Am. Math. Soc. Home: 1620 Bay Area Blvd #1304 Houston TX 77058 Office: U of Houston at Clear Lake 2700 Bay Area Blvd Houston TX 77058 E-mail: ma@cl.uh.edu.

MA, JINPENG, economics and business educator; b. Xishui, Hubei, China, Apr. 10, 1962; came to U.S., 1989; s. Degui and Yongjun (Li) M.; m. Mei Han, July 18, 1987; 1 child, Lynn. BA in Engring., Huzhong Agrl. U., Wuhan, China, 1984; MSc in Engring., Beijing Agrl. Engring. U., 1987; PhD in Econs., SUNY, Stony Brook, 1993. Postdoctoral fellow Hebrew U., Jerusalem, Israel, 1994; assoc. prof. econs. and bus. Rutgers U., Camden, N.J., 1994—. Contbr. articles to profl. jours. Mem. Am. Econ. Assn., Econometric Soc. Home: 21 Corbin Dr Exton PA 19341

MA, KOUGEN, engineering educator, researcher; b. Jianhu, Jiangsu Province, China, Feb. 24, 1965; arrived in US, 2001; s. Guoxian Ma and Guilan Xu; m. Yang Tian, Aug. 28, 1992; 1 child, Zhengyuan. PhD, Nanjing U. Aeronautics and Astronautics, China, 1992. Assoc. prof. Nanjing U. Aeronautics and Astronautics, China, 1992—99; sr. scientist German Aerospace Ctr., Braunschweig, 1999—2001; assoc. rschr. U. Hawaii, Honolulu, 2001—. Recipient 2nd award Advancement of Sci. and Tech., China Aviation Industry, 1995, 3d award Advancement of Sci. and Tech., 1996, 1998, 1st award Advancement of Sci. and Tech., Jiangsu Province, 1995, 4th award Advancement of Sci. and Tech., 1996, Outstanding Young Core Faculty, 1996, 3d award Advancement of Sci. and Tech., Ministry of Edn., China, 1998, 1st in Advancement of Sci. and Tech., Nanjing U. Aeronautics and Astronautics, 1998, 3d prize article in natural sci., Nanjing Mcpl. Govt., 1999. Office: Univ of Hawaii Dept ME Holmes 302 2540 Dole St Honolulu HI 96822 Personal E-mail: kougen@wiliki.eng.hawaii.edu.

MA, O. JOHN, emergency physician, editor; m. Elizabeth Ma, Feb. 6, 1997. BA, U. Colo., 1986. MD George Wash. U., 1990. Prof., vice chair UMKC Sch. of Medicine, Kans. City, Mo., 1997—; asst. prof. UNC Sch. of Medicine, Chapel Hill, NC, 1994—97. Emergency physician, rschr. Truman Med. Ctr., Kans. City, Mo., 1997—2004. Editor: (med. textbook) Manual of Emergency Medicine, 6th edit., (medical textbook) Emergency Ultrasound, Geriatric Emergency Medicine, Just the Facts in Emergency Medicine, 2nd edit., A Companion Handbook of Emergency Medicine, 5th edit., A Companion Handbook of Emergency Medicine, 4th edit., Just the Facts in Emergency Medicine, 1st edit. Full voting mem. Am. Emergency Ultrasonographic Soc., Augusta, Ga., 2001—04. Recipient Tchr. of Yr., Truman Med. Ctr. Emergency Dept., 1999, 2000, 2001, 2003. Fellow: Am. Acad. of Emergency Medicine (life); mem.: Soc. for Acad. Emergency Medicine (life). Achievements include research in Utility and accuracy of ultrasonography in evaluating trauma patients. Office: Truman Med Ctr Emergency Dept 2301 Holmes St Kansas City MO 00008 E-mail: john.ma@tmcmed.org.

MA, QINGLI, environmental hydrologist; b. Chengwu, Shandong, China, Sept. 3, 1964; came to U.S., 1991; s. Hanying Ma and Meilian Feng; m. Qun Zhang, Oct. 24, 1991; children: Yan, David. BSc, Shandong U., Jinan, 1985; MSc, Zhejiang U., Hangzhou, Zhejiang, China, 1988; PhD, U. Ga., 1998. Vis. scientist USDA Agrl. Rsch. Svcs., Ft. Collins, Colo., 1991-94; rsch. scientist U. Ga., Athens, 1995-98; vis. scientist AgResearch, Hamilton, New Zealand, 1998-99; soil scientist USDA-Agrl. Rsch. Svcs.-U.S. Salinity Labs./U. Calif.-Riverside, 1999—2000; sr. environ. hydrologist, cons. Environ. and Turf Svc., Inc., Wheaton, Md., 2000—. Author: (book) Root Zone Water Quality Model, 1992; contbr. articles to periodicals. USDA-Office of Internat. Corp. and Devel. Rsch. fellow, 1991, U. Ga. fellow, 1995, AgResearch rsch. fellow, 1998, U.S. Salinity Lab. rsch. fellow USDA-Agrl. Rsch. Svcs., 1999. Mem. AAAS, Am. Soc. Agronomy, Soil Sci. Am., New Zealand Plant Protection Soc. Office: Environ and Turf Svc Inc # 208 11144 Georgia Ave Wheaton MD 20902 E-mail: qinglima@aol.com.

MA, TSU SHENG, chemist, educator, consultant; b. Guangdong, China, Oct. 15, 1911; came to U.S., 1934, naturalized 1956; s. Shao-ching and Sze (Mai) M.; m. Gioh-Fang Dju, Aug. 27, 1942; children: Chopo, Mei-Mei. BS, Tsinghua U., Peking, 1931; PhD, U. Chgo., 1938. Faculty U. Chgo., 1938-46; prof. Peking U., 1946-49; sr. lectr. U. Otago, New Zealand, 1949-51; mem. faculty NYU, 1951-54, CUNY, 1954—, prof. chemistry, 1958—, prof. emeritus, 1980—. Vis. prof. Tsinghua U., 1947, Lingnan, 1949, NYU, 1954-60, Taiwan U., 1961, Chiangmei U., 1968, Singapore U., 1975; hon. prof. Hangzhou Tchrs. Coll., 1998—; specialist Bur. Ednl. and Cultural Affairs State Dept., 1964, Hong Kong, Philippines, Burma, Sri Lanka; Fulbright lectr., 1961-62, 68-69. Author: Small-Scale Experiments in Chemistry, 1962, Organic Functional Group Analysis, 1964, Microscale Manipulations in Chemistry, 1976, Organic Functional Group Analysis by Gas Chromatography, 1976, Quantitative Analysis of Organic Mixtures, 1979, Modern Organic Elemental Analysis, 1979, Organic Analysis Using Ion-Selective Electrodes, 1982, Trace Element Determination in Organic Materials, 1988; editor: Mikrochimica Acta, 1965-89; contbr. articles to profl. jours., chpts. to 10 books. Recipient Benedetti-Pichler award in microchemistry, 1976. Fellow N.Y. Acad. Sci., AAAS, Royal Soc. Chemistry, Am. Inst. Chemists; mem. Am. Chem. Soc., Soc. Applied Spectroscopy, Am. Microchem. Soc., Sigma Xi. Achievements include 1 patent; research in trace element analysis, microchemical investigation of medicinal plants, organic analysis and synthesis in the milligram to microgram range, and the use of small-scale, inexpensive equipment to teach chemistry. Office: CUNY Dept Chemistry Brooklyn NY 11210 Home: 7900 Creedmoor Road #224 Raleigh NC 27613

MA, XIAOLIANG, research scientist; b. Fuzhou, Fujian, China, Mar. 18, 1957; s. Hongxiang Ma and Xuan Lin; m. Xiuna Jiang; children: Ruilong, Toby. B in Engring. Sci., Zhejiang U., Hangzhou, China, 1982; M in Engring. Sci., China Coal Rsch. Inst., Beijing, 1987; D in Engring. Sci., Kyushu U., Fukuoka, Japan, 1995. Asst. engr. China Coal Rsch. Inst., Beijing, 1982—84, engr., 1987—91; vis. rschr. Nat. Inst. for Resources and Environment, Tsukuba, Japan, 1991—92; rsch. assoc. dept. materials sci. and engring. Pa. State U., University Park, 1993—97, group leader Energy Inst., 2000—, sr. rsch. assoc., 2003—. Contbr. chapters to books, articles to profl. jours. Mem.: Am. Chem. Soc. (reviewer 1996—, mem. divsn. fuel chemistry 1995—, mem. divsn. petroleum chemistry 1995—). Avocation: photography. Office: The Energy Inst 409 Academic Activities Building University Park PA 16802-2308 Office Phone: 814-863-8744. Office Fax: 814-863-8892. Business E-Mail: mxx2@psu.edu.

MA, XIN-LIANG, biomedical researcher, educator; b. Taiyuan, China, Aug. 21, 1957; came to U.S., 1989; s. Ren-Chen Ma and Yu-Lang Wang; m. Yaping Guo, Jan. 28, 1986; children: Jeffrey, Joanna. MMed, Shangxi Med. U., Taiyuan, China, 1982; PhD, 4th Mil. Med. U., Xian, China, 1988. Asst. prof. Thomas Jefferson U., Phila., 1993-97, rsch. dir. emergency medicine, 1993—, assoc. prof. surgery, 1997—2002, prof. surgery, 2002—. Presenter over 100 abstracts at nat. and internat. confs. Rschr. in myocardial apoptosis after reprefusion, opposite role of nitric oxide and nitroxyl in myocardial reprefusion injury; contbr. over 100 articles to profl. jours. Fellow Soc. for Acad. Emergency Medicine (Best Basic Sci. award 1998, 2000); mem. Am. Heart Assn. Home: 12 Kyle Ct Mount Laurel NJ 08054 Office: Thomas Jefferson U 1020 Sansom St Philadelphia PA 19107 Fax: (215) 923-6225. E-mail: Xin.Ma@mail.tju.edu.

MA, YEMING, statistician, medical researcher; b. Jinan, Shandong, China, Apr. 23, 1964; s. XiJiu Ma and Qin Wei; m. Wei Zhu, June 1, 1990; 1 child, Victor Donglin. PhD, Stanford U., Palo Alto, Calif., 1997. Certified JAVA Programmer Sun Microsystems Inc., 2001. Sr. process engr. Applied Materials Inc., Santa Clara, Calif., 1997—2000; computer arch. Speedia LLC, Brooklyn, NY, 2001—02. Scholar 2nd Rank Grad. Scholarship, Shandong U., 1988, Shanghai Inst. Ceramics, Chinese Acad. of Sci., 1989. Mem.: Am. Stats. Assn. (assoc.). Achievements include discovery of Proteomics applied to cancer diagnostics. Office: Nat Inst Health 30 Bell Ave Upton NY 11973 Business E-Mail: jimma@bnl.gov.

MA, YO-YO, cellist; b. Paris, 1955; m. Jill; children: Nicholas, Emily. Studied with Janos Scholz; studied with Leonard Rose, Juilliard Sch. Music, N.Y.C., 1962; AB, Harvard U., 1976, MusD (hon.), 1991. Debut at age 9, Carnegie Hall, N.Y.C.; appeared with Pablo Casals, Isaac Stern, Leonard Bernstein, Emanuel Ax, Jaime Laredo, performs throughout world with maj. orchs.; rec. artist Sony Classical; recs. include Portrait of Yo-Yo Ma, Japanese Melodies, Anything Goes (with Stephanie Grapelli), Hush (with Bobby McFerrin), Yo-Yo Ma at Tanglewood, The New York Album, Cello Suites Inspired By Bach, Great Cello Concertos, Made in America, Portrait of Cello Works, Premieres, Simply Baroque, Simply Baroque 2, Solo, Soul of The Tango, Tavener-Protecting Veil/Wake Up. Recipient Avery Fisher prize, 1978, 14-time Grammy award winning artist. Office: ICM Artists 40 W 57th St Fl 16 New York NY 10019

MA, ZHENKUI, remote sensing applications scientist, consultant; b. Shenyang, Liaoning, China, Nov. 4, 1955; arrived in U.S., 1983; s. Deshan Ma and Shuxuan Zhang; m. Shufang Zhao; children: Bin, Jeanne. BS, Beijing Forestry Coll., 1982; MS, U. Mich., 1985, PhD, 1990. Sr. specialist Weyerhaeuser, Federal Way, Wash., 1996—2002, info. tech. cons., 2002—. Internat. cons. UN, Beijing, 1994—96. Mem.: Am. Soc. for Photogrammetry and Remote Sensing (bd. dirs. Seattle 2001, Puget Sound region). Achievements include research in mapping large geographic areas biodiversity protection. Home: 21745 113th Place SE Kent WA 98031 Office: Weyerhaeuser 33405 Eighth Ave South Federal Way WA 98003 Office Phone: 253-924-4772. Personal E-mail: zhenkui_ma@yahoo.com. Business E-Mail: zhenkui.ma@weyerhaeuser.com.

MAAG, URS RICHARD, statistics educator; b. Winterthur, Switzerland, Jan. 20, 1938; m. Tannis Yvonne Arbuckle, July 31, 1965; children: Liane, Karin, Eric Diploma in Math, Swiss Fed. Inst. Tech., Zurich, 1961; M.Sc., U. Toronto, Can., 1962, PhD, 1965. Asst. prof. U. Montreal, Canada, 1965—72, assoc. prof., 1972-78, prof., 1978—2001, adj. prof., 2001. Contbr. articles to profl. jours. Mem. Statis. Soc. Can. (sec. 1973-77, pres. 1980, Founder Recognition award 1998), Am. Statis. Assn. (pres. Montreal chpt. 1975-77), Internat. Statis. Inst., Can. Assn. Rd. Safety Profls., Inst. Math. Stats. Home: 545 St Laurent Blvd Ste 705 Ottawa ON Canada K1K 4H9 Office: U Montreal Dept Math and Stats CP 6128 Succ Centre-ville Montreal QC Canada H3C 3J7

MAAR, ROSINA, medical organization executive; BS, Ga. Inst. Tech., 1984; MD, Morehouse Sch. Medicine, 1988. Cert. internal medicine Ga., N.C. Intern and resident in internal medicine Emory U. Sch. Medicine, Atlanta, 1991; physics lab. instr. Ga. Inst. Tech., Atlanta, 1981-84; rsch. asst. Emory U., Atlanta, 1985-86; med. evaluator maternal and infant project Grady Meml. Hosp., Atlanta, 1987-88; contract physician Wesley Woods Geriatric Hosp., Atlanta, 1989-90; contract physician, program dir. Piedmont Hosp./Spinal Shepard Ctr., Atlanta, 1989-91; med. dir. Cellcor, Inc., Atlanta, 1991-92, corp. med. dir. Newton, Mass., 1992-93; med. scientist med./regulatory svcs. Quintiles, Inc., Research Triangle Park, N.C., 1993-94, dir. med. svcs., 1994-95, v.p. clin. ops., 1995—, sr. v.p. strategic mgmt., until 1999; COO Clinicor, Inc., Austin, Tex., 1999—. Contbr. articles and abstracts to med. jours. Mem.: AMA, ACP, Am. Bd. Internal Medicine (diplomat). Office: Clinicor Inc 1717 W 6th St Austin TX 78703-4773

MAARBJERG, MARY PENZOLD, office equipment company executive; b. Oct. 2, 1943; d. Edmund Theodore and Lucy Adelaide (Singleton) Penzold; m. John Peder Maarbjerg, Oct. 20, 1966; 1 child, Martin Peder. AB, Hollins Coll., 1965; MBA, Wharton Sch., Pa., 1969. Cons. bus. and fin., Stamford, Conn., 1977-78; corp. staff analyst Pitney Bowes, Inc., Stamford, 1978-80, mgr. pension and benefit fin., 1980-81, dir. investor rels., 1981-85; v.p. planning and devel. Pitney Bowes Credit Corp., Norwalk, Conn., 1985-86, treas., v.p. planning, 1986-94; v.p. mktg. devel. and mng. dir. Asia Pacific Bowes Fin. Svcs., 1994-95, v.p. ops. and mng. dir., 1995-97; v.p. corp. svcs. Pitney Bowes, Inc., Stamford, 1997-99, v.p. real estate and adminstrn., 1999-2001, v.p. adminstrn. and process integration, 2001—. Bd. dirs. Stanford Dental Ctr., 2003—; mem. cmty. bd. U. Conn., Stanford, 2003—; bd. dirs. Person-to-Person, 2004—. Mem. adv. com. City of Stamford Mcpl. Employees Retirement Fund, 1980-85; mem. fin. adv. com. YWCA, Stamford, 1982-86; bd. dirs. Stamford Symphony, 1985-95, Vis. Nurses Assn., 1984-86, Am. Recorder Soc., 1986-98, Am. Classical Orch., 1999-2002; bd. dirs. Stamford Partnership, chmn., 1998—; bd. dirs., treas. Amherst Early Music, 2000—. Fellow Royal Statis. Soc.; mem. Fin. Execs. Inst., Phi Beta Kappa. Office: Pitney Bowes Inc 1 Elmcroft Rd Stamford CT 06926-0700

MAAS, DUANE HARRIS, distilling company executive; b. Tilleda, Wis., Aug. 26, 1927; s. John William and Adela (Giessel) M.; m. Sonja Johnson, Mar. 11, 1950; children: Jon Kermit, Duane Arthur, Thomas Ervin. BS, U. Wis., 1951. With Shell Chem. Corp., 1951-59; plant mgr. Fleischmann Distilling Corp., Owensboro, Ky., 1959-63, Plainfield, Ill., 1963-65; asst. to v.p. Barton Distilling Co., Chgo., 1965-68, exec. asst. to pres., 1968, v.p. adminstrn., 1968; v.p., gen. mgr. Barton Brands, Inc., Chgo., 1968— 72; pres. Leaf Confectionery div. W.R. Grace, Chgo., 1972-74; v.p., gen. mgr. Romano Bros., Chgo., 1974 79; v.p., sec.-treas. Marketing Directions Inc., Chgo., 1974-77; pres. Associated Wine Producers, Inc., 1979-80; exec. v.p., chief exec. officer Mohawk Liqueur, Detroit, 1980-86; v.p. McKesson Wine & Spirits Group of N.Y., Detroit, 1982-86; pres. Mgmt. Cons. Services Co., Chgo., 1986—, U.S. Distilled Products Co., Princeton, Minn., 1996-99, Am. Distilled Products Corp., 2001—. Chmn. Qingdao Johnson Distiller Co. Ltd., Qingdao, China, 1996-99; past pres. Bart on Distilling (Can.), Ltd.; past mng. dir. Barton Distilling (Scotland), Ltd.; past dir. Barton Distillers Europe, Barton Internat., Ltd. Sec.-treas. Plainfield Twp. Park Dist., 1967-70; chmn. Plainfield Planning and Zoning Commn., 1965-70. Served with USAAF, 1945-47. Mem.: Wis. Alumni Assn. Lutheran. Home and Office: 13264 W Highway 29 Bowler WI 54416 E-mail: dhm@mcservices.com.

MAAS, JANE BROWN, advertising executive; b. Jersey City; d. Charles E and Margaret (Beck) Brown; m. Michael Maas, Aug. 30, 1957; children: Katherine, Jennifer. BA, Bucknell U., 1953; postgrad., U. Dijon, France, 1954; MA, Cornell U., 1955; LittD, Ramapo Coll., 1986, St. John's U., 1988. Assoc. producer Name That Tune TV Program, N.Y.C., 1957-64; v.p. Ogilvy and Mather Inc., N.Y.C., 1964-76; sr. v.p. Wells, Rich, Greene, Inc., N.Y.C., 1976-82; pres. Muller Jordan Weiss Inc., N.Y.C., 1982-89, Earle Palmer Brown Cos., N.Y.C., 1989-92, chmn., 1992-94, chmn. emeritus, 1994—. Co-author: (book) How to Advertise, 1975, Better Brochures, 1981, Adventures of a Advertising Woman, 1986, The New How to Advertise, 1992, Christmas in Wales: A Homecoming, 1994. Bd govs comt Scholastic Achievement, 1985—92; active Girl Scouts US, NY, 1970—76; mem adv bd William E Simon Grad Sch Bus, Univ Rochester, 1989—; pub dir AIA, 1993—95; trustee Bucknell Univ, Lewisburg, 1976—86, Fordham Univ, NY, 1983—91. Named Woman of the Yr, NY Advert, 1986; recipient Matrix Award, Women in Communications, 1980. Mem.: AIA (hon.), Am Assn. Advt. Agys. (bd govs), Am Archtl. Found (regent 1993—2000), Phi Beta Kappa. Avocations: creative writing, jogging. Home: 3 Meadow Way Westhampton Beach NY 11978 Office Phone: 631-288-5881. E-mail: janemaas@att.net.

MAAS, JOE (MELVIN JOSEPH MAAS), retired federal agency administrator; b. Washington, Feb. 29, 1940; s. Melvin Joseph and Katherine (Endress) M.; m. Constance Mary Haile, June 13, 1965; children: Christine, Michael, Kevin. BS, U. Md., 1965; postgrad., Stanford U., 1972—73. Dir. career edn. U.S. Dept. Labor, Washington, 1969-73; dep. dir. pers. SBA, Washington, 1973-76, dir. pers., 1976-82, asst. adminstr., 1982-95; founder, prin. Advancement Power, 2003—. Sr. v.p. Crave Entertainment Group, Inc., 2000; mem. Internat. Pers. Assn., 1981-83, chairperson, 1982. Bd. dirs., treas. Snowden Mill Assn., Silver Spring, Md., 1994-2002, pres. 2002-04; Wash. rep. Ind. Charities of Am., 1995-96; bd. dirs. Amen Found., 1998—, Pres. Amen Found., 2003—. With USMCR, 1957-64. Mem. Fed. Exec. Adminstrs. Assn., Sr. Exec. Assn., Pub. Employee Roundtable (bd. dirs. 1994—, chair Pub. Svc. Excellence awards 1996-98, treas. 1998-2002), Coun. Former Fed. Execs. (pres., bd. dirs. 1995-2002), Nat. Assn. Ret. Fed. Employees (chpt. pres. 1996-98, v.p. 1998-2000, state tng. officer 1997-01), Volkswagen Club (pres. Washington chpt. 1988-95). Roman Catholic. Home: 2213 Aventurine Way Silver Spring MD 20904-5253 E-mail: jmaas@advancementpower.com.

MAAS, WERNER KARL, microbiology educator; b. Kaiserslautern, Germany, Apr. 27, 1921; came to U.S., 1936, naturalized, 1945; s. Albert and Esther (Meyer) M.; m. Renata Diringer, Oct. 15, 1960; children— Peter, Andrew, Helen. AB, Harvard U., 1943; PhD, Columbia U., 1948. Postdoctoral fellow Calif. Inst. Tech., Pasadena, 1946-48; commd. officer USPHS, Tb Research Lab., Cornell U. Sch., N.Y.C., 1948-54; asst. prof. pharmacology NYU, 1954-57, assoc. prof. microbiology, 1957-63, prof., 1963-94, prof. emeritus, 1994—, chmn. dept. basic med. scis., 1974-81. Career grantee USPHS, 1962-94. Mem. Am. Soc. Biol. Chemists, Genetics Soc. Am., Am. Soc. Microbiology. Home: 86 Villard Ave Hastings On Hudson NY 10706-1821 Office: 550 1st Ave New York NY 10016-6402 Office Phone: 212-263-5322. E-mail: miaasw01@endeavor.med.nyu.edu.

MAASS, ARTHUR, political science and environmental studies educator; b. Balt., July 24, 1917; s. Arthur Leopold and Selma (Rosenheim) M. AB, Johns Hopkins, 1939; M.P.A., Harvard, 1941, PhD, 1949. Adminstrv. asst. Bur. Budget, 1939-40; intern Nat. Inst. Pub. Affairs, 1939-40; research technician Nat. Resources Planning Bd., 1941-42; budget analyst Dept. Navy, 1946; water resources analyst Natural Resources Task Force, Hoover Commn., 1948; faculty Harvard, 1949—, prof. govt., 1959-67, Frank G. Thomson prof. govt., 1967-84, prof. emeritus, 1984—, chmn. dept., 1963-67. Cons. Office Dir. Budget, 1949, Office Sec. Interior, 1950-52, Pres.'s Materials Policy Commn., 1951-52, TVA, 1952, C.E., 1961—, Bur. Reclamation, 1971, Ministry Water Conservancy, People's Republic China, 1980—; vis. prof. polit. sci. U. Calif. at Berkeley, 1951, U. P.R., 1955, El Colegio de México, 1986, U. Internat. Menendez y Pelayo, Valencia, Spain, 1990. Author: Muddy Waters, The Army Engineers and the Nation's Rivers, 1951, Congress and the Common Good, 1983, Water Law and Institutions in the Western U.S.: Comparisons with Early Developments in California and Australia, Contemporary Developments in Australia and Recent Legislation Worldwide, 1990; co-author: Area and Power, 1959, Design of Water-Resource Systems: New Techniques for Relating Economic Objectives, Engineering Analysis and Governmental Planning, 1962, A Simulation of Irrigation Systems, 1971, rev., 1974, 78, 87, Chinese edit., 1980, . . . and the Desert Shall Rejoice: Conflict, Growth and Justice in Arid Environments, 1978, rev. edit., 1986, Un Modelo de Simulacion Para Sistemas de Regadio, 1985; contbr. articles to profl. jours. Served to lt. comdr. USNR, 1942-46. Guggenheim fellow, 1955; Fulbright research fellow Spain, 1960-61; Faculty research fellow Social Sci. Research Council, 1961 Mem.: Harvard (N.Y.C.). Home: 63 Atlantic Ave Boston MA 02110-3722 Office: Harvard U Littauer Ctr Cambridge MA 02138

MAATMAN, GERALD LEONARD, insurance company executive; b. Chgo., Mar. 11, 1930; s. Leonard Raymond and Cora Mae (Van Der Laag) M.; children: Gerald L. Jr., Mary Ellen; m. Bernice Catherine Brummer, June 3, 1971. BS, Ill. Inst. Tech., 1951. Asst. chief engineer Ill. Inspection & Rating Bur., Chgo., 1951-58; prof., dept. chmn. Ill. Inst. Tech., Chgo., 1959-65; v.p. engring. Kemper Group, Chgo., 1966-68, pres. Nat. Loss Control Svc. Corp., 1969-74, v.p. corp. planning Long Grove, Ill., 1974-79, sr. v.p. info. svcs. group, 1979-85, exec. v.p. ins. ops., 1985-87; pres. Kemper Nat. Ins. Co., Long Grove, Ill., 1987-92, CEO, 1989-95, also bd. dirs., chmn. bd. dirs., 1991-95. Bd. dirs. Advs. for Auto and Hwy. Safety, 1992-98; chmn. bd. trustees Underwriters Labs., 1991-2002. Lt. (j.g.) USCGR, 1952-54. Mem. Knollwood Golf Club, Springs Club, Tau Beta Pi. Republican.

MAATSCH, DEBORAH JOAN, manufacturing executive; b. Lincoln, Nebr., Mar. 26, 1950; d. Leon F. Forst and Jarolyn J. Hoffman Forst Conrad; m. Gordon F. Maatsch, Mar. 14, 1969; children: Jason, Diana. BS, U. Nebr., 1976; MBA, U. Phoenix, 1997. Accredited tax advisor; IRS enrolled agt. Acct., supr. US Civil Svc., Heidelberg, Germany, 1971—73; paralegal Mattson Rickets Davies et al, Lincoln, Nebr., 1976—87; tax cons., 1981—; paralegal Wade Ash Woods & Hill, P.C., 1986—94; sr. trust adminstr. Investment Trust Co., 1994—96; compliance officer Nelson, Benson and Zellmer, Inc., 1995—96; pres. DGJD Inc., 1993—; contr. Arena Devel., Inc., 1996—2000; pres. Boyd Industries, Inc., 2001—. Mem. Park County Sr. Wellness Team, 1999—; mem. bus. adv. bd. Ponderosa HS, 1994-98. Contbr. articles to profl. jour. Event chmn., vol. Jefferson Cty. Ctr., 1999—; bd. dirs. JCCA, 2001-03, pres., 2002-03; bd. dirs. Kids Roundup, 2002—; coord.

Jefferson Hist. Preservation Fund; mem. Women's C. of C. Mem. Doane Coll. Alumni Assn. (dir. 1989-93). Avocations: travel, outdoor activities, horses. Office: DGJD Inc PO Box 267 Jefferson CO 80456-0267 also: Boyd Industries Inc PO Box 315 Boyd TX 76023 E-mail: dgjdinc@bemail.com.

MAAZEL, LORIN, conductor, composer, violinist; b. Neuilly, France, Mar. 6, 1930; s. Lincoln and Marie (Varencove) M.; m. Dietlinde Turban, 1986; 3 children; 4 children from previous marriages. Studies with, Vladimir Bakaleinikoff; student, U. Pitts., Mus. D. (hon.), 1968; H.H.D., Beaver Coll., 1973. Debut as condr., 1938; condr. Am. symphony orchs., 1939—; violin recitalist; European debut, 1953; festivals include Bayreuth, Salzburg, Edinburgh; tours include S.Am., Australia, USSR, Japan, Korea, People's Republic China; artistic dir. Deutsche Opera Berlin, 1965-71; assoc. prin. condr. New Philharm. Orch., London, 1970-72; dir. Cleve. Orch., 1972-82, condr. emeritus, 1982-86; dir. Vienna State Opera, 1982-84; music dir. Pitts. Symphony Orch., 1988-96, Orchestre Nat. de France, 1988-90, Bavarian Radio Symphony Orch., Munich, 1993-2001; music dir. NY Philharmonic, 2002-. Decorated officer Legion d'Honneur 1981; Finnish Commdr. of the Lion; Portuguese Commdr.; Bundesverdienstkreuz, Germany. Office: NY Philharmonic Avery Fisher Hall 10 Lincoln Center Plaza New York NY 10023-6990*

MABASA, TERESA ALBAR, social welfare association administrator; b. Roxas City, Capiz, The Philippines, Oct. 2, 1935; d. Catalino Martelino Mabasa and Antonia Andrada Albar. BE, U. The Philippines, Diliman, Quezon City, 1956; MA in Social Work, St. Louis U., 1968; PhD in Orgn. & Devel. and Planning Inst., S.E. Asia Interdisciplinary Devel., Antipolo, The Philippines, 1981. Registered social worker. Acad. dean La. Salette U., Santiago City, The Philippines, 1982-85; pres., superior Coll. of Sacred Heart, Iloilo City, The Philippines, 1985-88; dir. Devel. Ctr. of Nazareth, Aklan, The Philippines, 1988-91; ministry coord. for social svcs. Daus. of Charity of St. Vincent de Paul, Paranaque, The Philippines, 1991-94, asst. visitatrix, 1994-97, CEO, 1997—2003. Program dir. CARITAS Manila, 1978-81; cons. planning Manila Archdiocese, 1996-97. Vol. Nat. Movement Free Election, Indonesia and The Philippines, co-chair Parañaque chpt., 1996-2004; mem. Konsyensyang Pilipino, 1996-2004. Recipient Most Outstanding Adminstr. in Western Visayas Region award Dept. of Edn., Iloilo, 1987, Most Outstanding Profl. Social Worker award Profl. Regulation Com., Manila, 2000; scholar U. The Philippines, 1952. Mem. AMRSP (bd. dirs. 1999-2003), Philippine Assn. Social Workers Inc. (life, pres. Iloilo chpt. 1987-88, cons. 1998-99) Roman Catholic. Avocations: reading, swimming, museums, plays. Home and Office: Daus of Charity St Vincent 8486 E Service Rd Km 18S NCR Paranaque 1700 MM Philippines Fax: 63.2.838.8987. Office Phone: 632-838-3961.

MABEE, CARLETON, historian, educator; b. Shanghai, Dec. 25, 1914; s. Fred Carleton and Miriam (Bentley) M.; m. Norma Dierking, Dec. 20, 1945; children: Timothy I., Susan (Mrs. Paul Newhouse). AB, Bates Coll., 1936; MA (Perkins scholar), Columbia U., 1938, PhD, 1942. With Civilian Pub. Svc., 1941-45; instr. history Swarthmore (Pa.) Coll., 1944; tutor Olivet (Mich.) Coll., 1947-49; asst. prof. liberal studies Clarkson Coll. Tech., Potsdam, NY, 1949-51, asso. prof., 1951-55; prof., 1955-61; dir. social studies divsn. Delta Coll., University Center, Mich., 1961-64; prof., chmn. dept. humanities and social scis. Rose Poly. Inst., Terre Haute, Ind., 1964-65; prof. history State U. Coll. at New Paltz, NY, 1965-80, prof. emeritus, 1980—. Participant in projects for Am. Friends Svc. Com., 1941-47, 53, 63; Fulbright prof. Keio U., Tokyo, 1953-54 Author: The American Leonardo, A Life of Samuel F.B. Morse, 1943, The Seaway Story, 1961, Black Freedom: The Nonviolent Abolitionists from 1830 through the Civil War, 1970, Black Education in New York State: From Colonial to Modern Times, 1979, (with Susan Mabee Newhouse) Sojourner Truth: Slave, Prophet, Legend, 1993, Listen to the Whistle: An Ancedotal History of the Wallkill Valley Railroad in Ulster and Orange Counties, N.Y., 1995; editor: (with James A. Fletcher) A Quaker Speaks from the Black Experience: The Life and Selected Writings of Barrington Dunbar, 1979, Bridging the Hudson: The Poughkeepsie Railroad Bridge and its Connecting Rail Lines, a Many-Faceted History, 2001, Gardiner and Lake Minnewaska, 2003; contbr. articles to profl. jours. Trustee Young-Morse Hist. Site, Poughkeepsie, N.Y., 1991-2002; ofcl. town historian, Gardiner, N.Y. Recipient Pulitzer prize in biography, 1944, Bergstein award for excellence in tchg. Delta Coll., 1963, Anisfield-Wolf award race rels., 1971, Gustavus Myers award for outstanding book on human rights, 1994; rsch. grantee Rsch. Found. SUNY, 1965, 67, 68, 80, Am. Philos. Soc., 1970, Nat. Inst. Edn., 1973-76, NSF, 1982-83. Mem. N.Y. State Hist. Assn., Phi Beta Kappa, Delta Sigma Rho. Methodist. Home: 2121 Route 44-55 Gardiner NY 12525-5808

MABEE, KEITH V. communications/investor relations executive; BS in Journalism, Bowling Green State U., 1969; MEd in Sociology, Wayne State U., 1972; MBA, Pepperdine U., 1980. Comm. specialist Internat. Paper Co., N.Y.C., 1969-70, 73; pub. affairs officer, U.S. Army NATO, Europe, 1970-72; sr. lectr. Coll. Mgmt., Queensland U. Tech., Australia, 1973-77; organizational/effectiveness officer U.S. Army, Pacific, 1978-80; sr. v.p., corp. comm. AMFAC, Inc., San Francisco, 1980-89; v.p. comm. Indsl. Indemnity, San Francisco, 1989-93; v.p. corp. rels. Figgie Internat. Inc., 1993-98; sr. exec. v.p. Dix & Eaton, 1997-98, pres., 1998—2001, pres., COO, 2001—. Former pres. San Francisco chpt. Nat. Investor Rels. Inst., former officer, former dir. nat. bd., chmn. sr. roundtable; founding trustee, lectr. San Francisco Acad.; vice chmn. bd. dirs. Ohio Tuition Trust Authority. Accredited mem. Pub. Rels. Soc. Am. Office: The Galleria and Tower at Erieview 1301 E 9th St Ste 1300 Cleveland OH 44114-1882 Fax: 216-241-3070. Office Phone: 216-241-3068.

MABEY, RALPH R. lawyer; b. Salt Lake City, May 20, 1944; s. Rendell Noel and Rachel (Wilson) M.; m. Sylvia States, June 5, 1968; children: Kathryn, Rachel, Elizabeth, Emily, Sara. BA, U. Utah, 1968; JD, Columbia U., 1972. Bar: Utah 1972, U.S. Dist. Ct. Utah 1972, U.S. Ct. Appeals (10th cir.) 1976, N.Y. 1985, U.S. Supreme Ct. 1988, U.S. Ct. Appeals (4th cir.) 1988, U.S. Ct. Appeals (3d cir.) 1993. Law clk. Atty. Gen., Salt Lake City, 1970, U.S. Dist. Ct., Salt Lake City, 1972-73; ptnr. Irvine, Smith & Mabey, Salt Lake City, 1973-79; U.S. bankruptcy judge U.S. Ct., Salt Lake City, 1979-83; ptnr. LeBoeuf, Lamb, Greene & MacRae, Salt Lake City and N.Y.C., 1983—. Sr. lectr. Brigham Young U. Sch. Law, Provo, Utah, 1983—, U. Utah Coll. Law, Salt Lake City, 1983-85. Mng. editor Norton Bankruptcy Law Adviser, 1983-85; contbg. author: Collier Bankruptcy Manual, 1986—, Collier on Bankruptcy, 15th Edition. With USAR, 1968-74. Mem. ABA (bus. bankruptcy com., select adv. com. on bus. reorgns.), Nat. Bankruptcy Conf., Am. Law Inst., Am. Bankruptcy Inst., Am. Coll. Bankruptcy (chmn.). Republican. Mem. Lds Ch. Avocations: running, fly fishing. Home: 253 S 1550 E Bountiful UT 84010-1350 Office: LeBoeuf Lamb Greene & MacRae 1000 Kearns Bldg 136 S Main St Salt Lake City UT 84101-1601 also: 125 W 55th St New York NY 10019-5369 Office Phone: 801-320-6721. Business E-Mail: mabey@LLGM.com.

MABILANGAN, FELIPE HUGO, JR., Philippine diplomat; b. Manila, Feb. 15, 1936; s. Felipe and Felisa (Hugo) M.; m. Ada Ledesma, Dec. 8, 1943; children: Jose Antonio, Anne Marie, Lisa. BA, Balliol Coll., U. Oxford, Eng., 1959; MA, Balliol Coll., U. Oxford, 1964; diploma in internat. rels., U. Geneva, 1965. Fgn. svc. officer Philippines Ministry Fgn. Affairs, 1962-75, dir. gen., 1975-79, permanent del. to UNESCO, 1980-82, amb. to France and Portugal, 1979; amb. to People's Republic of China, 1990-94; permanent rep. of The Philippines to the UN, 1994. Mem. adv. com. on adminstrv. and budgetary questions UN. Decorated Order Diplomatic Merit (Republic of Korea); Nat. Order of Merit (France); recipient Outstanding Young Men award for govt. svc. Manila Jaycees, 1975; Carnegie fellow U. Geneva, 1964-65. Mem. Manila Polo Club, Racing Club France (Paris). Office: 117 Gamboa St Le Gaspi Village Makati Philippines

MABLEY, JACK, newspaper columnist, communications consultant; b. Binghamton, N.Y., Oct. 26, 1915; s. Clarence Ware and Mabelle (Howe) M.; m. Frances Habeck, Aug. 29, 1940; children: Mike, Jill, Ann, Pat, Robert. BS, U. Ill., 1938. With Chgo. Daily News, 1938-61, reporter, writer, columnist, 1957-61; columnist Chgo.'s Am., 1961-69, asst. mng. editor, 1966-69; asso. editor Chgo. Today, 1969-73; columnist Chgo. Today, Chgo. Tribune, 1973-74, Chgo. Tribune, 1974-82; pres. Mabley & Assocs., Corp. Communications, Glenview, Ill., 1982; columnist Daily Herald, Arlington Heights, Ill., 1987—. Lectr. journalism Northwestern U., 1949-50 Pres. Village of Glenview, Ill., 1957-61, Skokie Valley Community Hosp., Skokie, Ill., 1977-79. Served from ensign to lt. USNR, 1941-45. Recipient Media award Nat. Assn. for Retarded Citizens, 1977 Home and Office: 2601 Chestnut St Apt 3413 Glenview IL 60025 E-mail: jmabley@dailyherald.com.

MABREY, VICKI, news correspondent, anchor; b. St. Louis; BA in Polit. Sci. cum laude, Howard U., 1977. AFTRA tng. reporter Sta. WUSA-TV, Washington, 1982-84; gen. assignment reporter Sta. WBAL-TV, Balt., 1984-92; corr. CBS News, Dallas, 1992-95, London, 1995-98, 60 Minutes II, N.Y.C., 1998—. Recipient 2 Emmy awards, 1996, 2 Emmy awards, 1997. Office: c/o 60 Minutes II 524 W 57th St New York NY 10019-2902

MABRY, DONALD JOSEPH, university administrator, history educator; b. Atlanta, Apr. 21, 1941; s. Jerry Leon and Eunice Leigh (Harris) M.; m. Susan Strong Johnston, July 28, 1962 (div. Oct. 1986); children: Scott, Mark; m. Paula Ann Crockett, Dec. 18, 1992. BA, Kenyon Coll., Gambier, Ohio, 1963; MEd, Bowling Green State U., 1964; PhD, Syracuse U., 1970. Instr. St. Johns River Community Coll., Palatka, Fla., 1964—67; rsch. asst. fin. aid Syracuse U., NY, 1967—68, teaching fellow in history, 1968—69, Maxwell fellow, 1969—70, vis. lectr. dept. history, 1969—70; asst. to chancellor U. Kans., Lawrence, 1978—79; from. asst. prof. to prof. dept. history Miss. State U., Mississippi State, 1970—, asst. to pres., 1979—81, assoc. dean for budget and rsch., 1991—2001; now dir., assoc. dean Biol. Physical Sciences Rsch. Inst., Mississippi State, Miss. Sr. fellow Ctr. for Internat. Security and Strategic Studies, Miss. State U., 1981-91. Author: Mexico's Accion Nacional, 1973, The Mexican University and the State, 1982, (with others) Neighbors--Mexico and the United States, 1981; editor: The Latin American Narcotics Trade and U.S. National Security, 1989; contbr. articles to profl. jours. Mem. Am. Coun. on Edn. (exec. com. Coun. of Fellows 1980-83), South Ea. Coun. on Latin Am. Studies, The Hist. Text Archive (founding editor). Avocation: computer telecommunications. Home: 206 Hiwassee Dr Starkville MS 39759-2105 Office: Miss State U Drawer H Mississippi State MS 39762 E-mail: djm1@ra.msstate.edu.

MABRY, EARL W. military officer; m. Mary Ann Morton; 4 children. BA, Dartmouth Coll., 1967; MD, U. Okla., 1971; medicine primary course, Sch. Aerospace, 1973; student, Air War Coll., 1991; physician in mgmt. courses I, II, III, Am. Coll. Physician Execs., 1992-94; student, George Washington U., 1993, Nat. Def. U., 1996. Bd. cert. in adult and pediat. urology Am. Bd. Urology, 1982; cert. Nat. Bd. Med. Examiners; cert. ATLS instr. Surgery intern, resident Duke U. Med. Ctr., Durham, N.C., 1973, urology resident, 1980; capt. USAF, 1973, advanced through grades to maj. gen., 1997; chief aeromed. svcs. Reese USAF Hosp., Reese AFB, Tex., 1973-75; chief flight medicine Torrejon USAF Hosp., Torrejon Air Base, Spain, 1975-77; chief urology David Grant Med. Ctr., Travis AFB, Calif., 1980-83; comdr. Bitburg USAF Hosp., Bitburg Air Base, West Germany, 1985-88, Ehrling Bergquist Hosp., Offutt AFB, Nebr., 1988-90; dep. command surgeon Scott AFB, Ill., 1991-92; dir. med. pers. Air Force Manpower and Pers. Ctr., Randolph AFB, Tex., 1992-94; command surgeon Hdqs. Air Force Materiel Command, Wright-Patterson AFB, Ohio, 1994-95; comdr. 74th Med. Group, lead agt. Dept. Def. Health Svc. Region 5, Wright-Patterson AFB, 1995-96; comdr., dir. Air Force Med. Ops. Agy., Bolling AFB, D.C., 1996—; comdr. 74th Med Group, Lead Agt. DOD Health Svc. Region 5, Wright Patterson AFB, 1996-99. Comdr. Air Force Med. Ops. Agey., Office of Surgeon Ge., Bolling AFB, Washington, 1999—. Assoc. dean Air Force affairs Wright State U. Sch. Medicine. Decorated Def. Superior Svc. medal, Legion of Merit, Meritorious Svc. medal with 3 oak leaf clusters. Mem. Am. Urologic Assn., Soc. Med. Cons. to the Armed Forces, Soc. Govt. Svc. Urologists, Soc. Air Force Clin. Surgeons, Assn. Mil. Surgeons of U.S., Air Force Assn., Alpha Omega Alpha. Office: Comdr 59th Med Wing Region 6 TRICARE SW USAF 2200 Bergquist Dr Ste 1 Lackland A F B TX 78236-5322

MABRY, PAUL DAVIS, psychobiologist, educator, researcher; b. Meridian, Miss., Sept. 28, 1943; s. Paul Davis and Frances Elizabeth (Thigpen) M.; m. Celia Elaine Hales, 1986. BS, Millsaps Coll., Jackson, Miss., 1965; MS, U. Miss., 1967, PhD, 1970. Rsch. trainee dept. neurosurgery U. Miss. Med. Ctr., 1966, predoctoral rsch. fellow, 1969-70; rsch. assoc. neurosci. and behavior program Princeton U., N.J., 1970-76; chair dept. psychology, head div. behavioral & natural scis. Sacred Heart Coll., Belmont, N.C., 1976-86; chair dept. Psychology U. St. Thomas, St. Paul, 1986-91, assoc. prof., 1986—, dir. behavioral neurosci. program, 1991—. Contbr. articles to profl. jours. NIMH fellow, 1969. Mem. AAAS, Soc. for Neurosci., Am. Psychol. Assn., Internat. Brain Rsch. Orgn., Sigma Xi. Home: 28 Mississippi River Blvd N Saint Paul MN 55104-5713 Office: Dept Psychology U St Thomas 2115 Summit Ave Saint Paul MN 55105-1048 E-mail: pdmabry@stthomas.edu.

MABRY, PHILIP T. political consultant; b. Spartanburg, SC, Feb. 29, 1940; s. Roy T. and Eleanor Eva (Waddell) Mabry; m. Mary E. Byars, July 3, 1961 (div. Mar. 1980); children: Tammy Kay Waldrop, Phyllis Dianne Gibbons, Sonya Kowalski; m. Amy D. Mabry, June 18. Founder Ams. for Human Rights, Greenville, SC, 1975—79; pres. Western Rsch. Cons., Euless, Tex., 1982—; dir. Western Rsch., Euless, Tex., 2000—. Cons. U.S. Dept. State, Washington, 1982—87. Contbr. news articles, interviews on Iran/Contra and Iran hostage af. Polit. activist Rep. Party, Washington, 1962—. Recipient Cert. of Appreciation, Nat. Rep. Party, 2001, Cert. of Membership, Acad. Polit. Sci., 2001. Republican. Avocations: golf, coins, reading, American history. Home: 125 Wanda Way Apt 119 Hurst TX 76056 Office: Western Rsch Cons 605 Del Paso St Euless TX 76040

MACADAMS, WILLIAM, writer; b. Richmond, Ind., Dec. 3, 1944; s. Ira Lloyd Stout and Gertrude Catherine MacAdams; m. Susan Merriam MacAdams; 1 child, Mark Barr; m. Kathy Cronkite; 1 child, Rob Slan. MA, NYU, 1972. Author: Anxious to Please, 1972, Ben Hecht: The Man Behind the Legend, 1990, 701 Toughest Movie Trivia Questions of All Time, 1995, Ben Hecht: A Biography, 1995, The Life and Death of a Book, 2003. Sec. Student Peace Union, N.Y.C., 1967—68. Avocations: chess, bicycling, book collecting, films. Home: 311 North 9th St Richmond IN 47374 Office Phone: 765-965-4834.

MACAFEE, SUSAN DIANE, reporter; b. Feb. 1944; Attended, Foothill Coll. Disc jockey with news, pub. affairs; engr., editor, prodr. Sta. KZSU-Stanford U., Calif., 1975-80; freelance reporter, broadcast journalist, 1975—. Writer, prodr., engr. editor, narrator 25 original nationwide news stories and furnished story material for numerous radio stas. and networks, TV stas. including NPR, Pacifica, ABC, NBC and CBS networks, BBC radio and TV, Channel 9 Australia, numerous newspapers and magazines; rschr., documentor and author: Agent Orange Pilot Nutritional Detox Program, 1986, (5-part series) Food-Diet-Crime, Behavior and Learning Disability Connection, 1986; author, prodr., engr., editor and narrator: Treatment of Refractory Eosinophilia Myalgia Syndrome Associated with the Injestion of L-Tryptophan Containing Products, Parts I and II, 1990; interviewer, recorder, transcriber: A Historical Prospective of Vitamin C With Linus Pauling, 1991; researcher, documentor, writer Postscipt: Interactions of Glutathione, Ascorbic Acid HIV and AIDS, 1992, Neural Tube Defects and Folic Acid, 1995, Chromium - A New Treatment for Adult Type II (Maturity Onset) Diabetes, 1996. The Legality and Use of Bone Wax, 1997, 1999. V.p. Calif. Coll. Young Reps., 1967; sec., asst. to Nat. Field Dir. Coll. Young Reps., Rep. Nat. Com., Washington, 1968; dir. precinct orgn. Calif. State Assembly Campaign, San Francisco Rep. Ctrl. Com., 1968. Recipient 3 Nat. awards Young Rep. Nat. Com., 1967-68. Home and Office: 334 Paseo De Golf Green Valley AZ 85614-3319

MACAL, ZDENEK, conductor; b. Jan. 8, 1936; Ed., Janacek Music Acad. Music dir. Milw. Symphony Orch., 1986-96; chief condr. Cologne Radio Orch., 1970-74; former chief condr. Prague Symphony, Hannover Radio Orch., Sydney Symphony Orch.; music dir. N.J. Symphony, Newark, 1993—. Office: NJ Symphony 2 Central Ave Newark NJ 07102-3119

MACALISTER, ROBERT STUART, oil industry executive, consultant; b. L.A., May 22, 1924; s. Robert Stuart and Iris Grace (Doman) MacAlister; m. Catherine Vera Willby, Nov. 15, 1947 (dec. 1994); children: Rodney James, Sara Marjorie; m. Grace V. LeClerc, Dec. 2, 1995. Student, Brighton Coll., Sussex, Eng., 1945; BSME, Calif. Inst. Tech., 1947. Registered profl. engr., Tex. Petroleum engr. Shell Oil Co., 1947-56; mgmt. trainee Royal Dutch Shell, The Hague, Netherlands, 1956-57; with exec. staff, mgr. Shell Oil Co., U.S.A., 1957-68; v.p., ops. mgr. Occidental Petroleum Corp., Tripoli, Libya, 1968-71, mng. dir. various subs. London, 1971-76; mng. dir., pres. Occidental Internat. Oil, Inc., London, 1976—78; pres., chmn. bd. Can. Occidental Petroleum Ltd., Calgary, 1978-81; mng. dir. Australian Occidental Petroleum Ltd., Sydney, 1982-83, Hamilton Bros. Oil & Gas Ltd., London, 1983-86; petroleum cons. Camarillo, Calif., 1986—. Exe. U.K. Offshore Operators, London, 1972—78, London, 1983—86. Cubmaster Boy Scouts Am., Larchmont, NY, 1964—65, scoutmaster Houston, 1965—68. Sgt. U.S. Army, 1944—45, ETO. Mem.: Can. Petroleum Assn. (bd. govs. 1978—81), Soc. Petroleum Engrs., Am. Assn. Petroleum Geologists, Caltech Torchbearer, Las Posas Country Club, Gold Coast Srs. Republican. Episcopalian. Avocations: carpentry, crafts, watercolor painting, golf, gardening. Home and Office: 78 Lopaco Ct Camarillo CA 93010-8846

MACALLASTER, ARCHIE, investment company executive; Grad., U.S. Naval Acad., 1953. Pres. Pitfield MacKay Ross (now MacAllaster Pitfield MacKay), 1984—; CEO MacAllaster Pitfield MacKay, N.Y., chmn. Trustee emeritus St. Lawrence U.; trustee Clark Fedn. Mem.: The Clark Found. Office: MacAllaster Pitfield MacKay 30 Broad St New York NY 10004 Office Phone: 212-422-9250.

MACALPINE, MICHELLE LEWIS, neuroscientist; b. Colorado Springs, Colo., Dec. 19, 1954; d. Arthur and Erma Lewis; m. J. David MacAlpine; children: Kira, Caylan. BA, Colo. State U., 1976; MA, U. Colo., 1983; PhD, U. Tex.-Dallas, Richardson, 1998. Owner Lariat, Ft. Collins, Colo., 1983-87, Brain Tng., Plano, Tex., 1995—; trainer Lectra, Richardson, 1987-89. Author: Word Master, 1996, Treating Developmental Delays and Autistic Spectrum Disorders, 1997, 2d edit., 1998, Brain Training: New Hope for Children with Developmental Delays, 2004. Mem.: Mensa. Democrat. Achievements include obtaining of 100% recovery rate in group of autistic children by promoting their cognitive development. Office: Brain Tng 6913 K Ave Ste 309 Plano TX 75074 Office Phone: 972-578-8150. E-mail: braintrain@aol.com.

MACALUSO, CHRISTIE A. bishop; b. June 12, 1945; M. in Sacred Theology, St. Mary's Seminary, Balt.; MA in philosophy, Trinity U., Hartford; MA in psychology, NYU; Doctoral Studies, New Sch. for Social Rsch., N.Y.C. Ordained priest Roman Cath. Ch., 1971. Priest Archiodecese of Hartford, Conn., 1971, consecrated aux. bishop, 1997, aux. bishop, 1997, consecrated bishop, 1997—. Office: 134 Farmington Ave Hartford CT 06105-3723

MACAN, WILLIAM ALEXANDER, IV, lawyer; b. Boston, Nov. 21, 1942; s. William A. and Carol (Whitten) M.; m. Jane Mitchell Ahern, Sept. 3, 1965; children: Sandi, Andrew. BS, Haverford Coll., 1964; LLB, U. Pa., 1967. Bar: Pa. 1968, U.S. Tax Ct. 1970, N.Y. 1999. Law clk. to judge U.S. Tax Ct., Washington, 1967-69; assoc. firm Morgan, Lewis & Bockius, Phila., 1969-76; ptnr. Morgan, Lewis & Bockius L.L.P., 1976-2000, Allen & Overy, N.Y.C., 2000—. Lectr. legal instns., seminars. Author publs. on tax-oriented equipment leasing, other tax subjects. Mem. ABA. Presbyterian. Office: Allen & Overy 1221 Ave of the Americas New York NY 10020 Office Phone: 212-610-6413. Business E-Mail: william.macan@newyork.allenovery.com.

MACARIO, ALBERTO JUAN LORENZO, physician; b. Naschel, Argentina, Dec. 1, 1935; came to the U.S., 1974, naturalized, 1980; s. Alberto Carlos and Maria Elena (Giraudi) M.; m. Everly Conway, Mar. 16, 1963; children: Alex, Everly. MD, Nat. U. Buenos Aires, 1961. Intern Ramos Mejia Hosp., Buenos Aires, 1958-60, resident, 1960, Rivadavia Hosp., Buenos Aires, 1961-62, physician-hematologist, 1962-64; fellow NRC Argentina, Buenos Aires, 1964-69; head dept. radioactive isotopes Inst. Hematol. Investigations, Nat. Acad. Medicine, Buenos Aires, 1967-69; Eleanor Roosevelt fellow Internat. Union Against Cancer, Dept. Tumorbiology, Karolinska Inst., Stockholm, 1969-71; mem. sci. staff Lab. Cell Biology NRC Italy, Rome, 1971-73; head lab. immunology Internat. Agy. Rsch. on Cancer, WHO, Lyons, France, 1973-74; rsch. scientist Brown U., Providence, 1974-76; rsch. scientist divsn. labs. and rsch. N.Y. State Dept. Health, Albany, 1976-79, chief hematology clin. lab. ctr., 1979-81; dir. clin. and exptl. immunology sect. Lab. Medicine Inst., 1981-83, rsch. physician, 1981—, Wadsworth Ctr. N.Y. State Dept. Health. Prof. dept. biomed. scis. Sch. Pub. Health, SUNY, Albany, 1985—, mem. senate, 1989-94; adj. prof. pathology and lab. medicine Albany Med. Coll., 1991—; mem. structural and cell biology program Albany Univs. and Colls.; grant reviewer for nat. and internat. agys.; manuscript reviewer for sci. jours. Editor multivolume treatise Monoclonal Antibodies Against Bacteria and treatise Gene Probes for Bacteria; contbr. chpts. to books and encys. and articles to profl. jours. Recipient Diploma de Honor prize Nat. U. Buenos Aires, 1961, Bernardino Rivadavia prize Nat. Acad. Medicine Argentina, 1967, Ciencia e Investigation prize Argentinian Soc. Advancement Sci., 1967; Ford Found.-NAS travel fellow, 1968, Eleanor Roosevelt fellow, 1969. Mem. Internat. Soc. Microbial Ecology, Cell Stress Soc. Internat., Scandinavian Soc. Immunology, Italian Assn. Immunologists, French Soc. Immunology, Am. Assn. Immunologists, Am. Soc. Microbiology (sect. editor Manual of Clin. Lab. Immunology 4th and 5th edits. 1989-97), Am. Soc. Investigative Pathology, Assn. Internat. Union Against Cancer. Achievements include patents in field; discovered primary myeloperoxydase deficiency in leucocytes, and oscillations of antibody affinity during maturation of immune responses; developed method for immunologic identification of bacteria (archaea) that produce methane gas; discovered antigenic diversity of these microbes in natural and manufactured ecosystems; described structural topography of methanogenic archaea and population dynamics in granular microbial consortia; found novel multicellular forms of archaea; isolated for the first time ABC-transporter genes and the genes in the hsp70(dnak) locus from an archaebacterium (archaeon); devised and constructed the first integration vector for genetically engineering a methanogen useful for waste bioconversion; discovered a uni-celled organism with the main four chaperoning systems in its cytosol, found two new chaperonins in archaea; developed concept of sick chaperone or chaperonepathy as a factor contributing to the aging process and disease. Office: NY State Dept Health Wadsworth Ctr Empire State Plz PO Box 509 Albany NY 12201-0509 E-mail: macario@wadsworth.org. *I am capable of walking alone, but with my wife by me, I fly. We can both ascend toward the sky and together we reach the stars. Separately, alone, who knows, we might never have been able to rise above the mountains, perhaps not even the hills, we have conquered, flapping our wings in unison.*

MACARTHUR, CAROL JEANNE, pediatric otolaryngology educator; b. Glendale, Calif., Aug. 23, 1957; d. Seth Gerald and Barbara Jeanne (Shaw) MacA.; m. Geoffrey Buncke, Dec. 14, 1990; children: Keith Davis, Michelle Jeanne. BS, Occidental Coll., 1979; MD, UCLA, 1984. Diplomate Am. Bd. Otolaryngology. Intern U. Calif., Davis, 1984-85, resident in otolaryngology, 1985-90; fellow in pediatric otolaryngology Boston Children's Hosp., 1990-91; instr. dept. otolaryngology U. Calif.-Davis, Sacramemto, 1989-90; clin. fellow in otology and laryngology Harvard U. Med. Sch., Boston, 1990-91; asst. prof. U. Calif., Irvine, 1991—2002, asst. prof. dept. pediatrics, 1993-98, program dir. dept. otolaryngology-head and neck surgery, 1992-95; staff dept. otolaryngology Oreg. Health Scis. U., Portland, 2002—. Recipient investigator devel. award Am. Acad. Facial Plastic and Reconstructive Surgery, 1993. Fellow ACS, Am. Acad. Pediatrics; mem. Am. Soc. Pediat. Otolaryngology, Soc. for Ear, Nose and Throat Advances in Children, Am. Acad. Otorhinolaryngology-Head and Neck Surgery, Alpha Omega Alpha. Home: 4018 Canal Woods Ct Lake Oswego OR 97034 Office: Oreg Health Scis U Dept Otolaryngology 3131 SW Sam Jackson Park Rd Portland OR 97201-3011

MACARTHUR, DIANA TAYLOR, advanced technology executive; b. Santa Fe, July 7, 1933; widowed; children: Elizabeth Tschursin, Alexander Tschursin. BA, Vassar Coll., 1955. Cons. economist Checchi & Co., 1957-61;

v.p., dir. Thomas J. Deegan Co., 1961-62; dep. chief West Africa Peace Corps, 1963, reg. program officer for North Africa, Near East, South Asia, 1964, dir. divsn. pvt. and internat. orgns., 1965-66; pvt. cons., 1966-74; program mgr. Aerospace Divsn. Gen Elec. Co., 1974-76; pres. Consumer Dynamics, 1977-80; v.p., dir. Dynamac Internat. Inc., 1980-88, chmn., pres., CEO, 1988—; chmn., CEO Rsch. Analysis and Mgmt. Corp., 1988-92. Pres. Fgn. Traders, Inc., 1980—86. Trustee Menninger Found., Topeka, 1972—, Lady Bird Johnson Wildflower Ctr., 1985-; mem. Pres.'s Com. of Adv. on Sci. and Tech., 1994-01; citizens adv. bd. to the Pres. Coun. on Youth Opportunity, 1966-70; served on CSIS Strengthening of Amer. Com., 1992, Nat. Benefits from Nat. Lab. Com., 1993, Sr. Policy on Nat. Challenges, 1996, Geopolitics of Energy Com., 2000; mem. The Chancellor's Adv. Coun. U. System of Md.; bd. visitors U. Md. Biotech. Inst.; adv. com. Ctr. Strategic & Internat. Studies; bd. dirs. Atlantic Coun. USA; bus. adv. coun. Ctr. for China-U.S. Coop., U. Denver. Mem. Coun. on Competitiveness, Business-Higher Edn. Forum (mem. exec. com.), Tech. Coun. Md. (mem. exec. com.), Los Alamos Nat. Lab. Found. (bd. mem.), Phi Beta Kappa. Office: Dynamac Internat Inc 2275 Research Blvd Rockville MD 20850-3268 E-mail: dmacarthur@dynamac.com

MACASKILL, BRIDGET, finance company executive; b. Aug. 5, 1948; M in Bus., U. Edinburgh. Joined Oppenheimer Funds, Inc., N.Y.C., 1983, pres./CEO, 1995—2001, chmn., 2000—01; ind. consultant Merrill Lynch, 2003—. Non-exec. dir. J Sainsbury plc, Prudential plc, 1999—2001, 2003—.

MACAULAY, DAVID (ALEXANDER), author, illustrator; b. Burton-on-Trent, Eng., Dec. 2, 1946; s. James and Joan (Lowe) M.; m. Janice Elizabeth Michel, 1970 (div.); 1 child, Elizabeth Alexandra; m. Ruth Marris, 1978 (div.); 1 child, Charlotte Valerie; m. Ruth Ellen Murray, 1997. BArch, R.I. Sch. Design, 1969. Instr. interior design R.I. Sch. Design, Providence, 1969-73, instr. two-dimensional design, 1974-76, adj. faculty dept. illustration, 1977-79; tchr. art Central Falls (R.I.) Pub. Schs., 1969-70, Newton, Mass., 1972-74; designer Morris Nathanson Design, 1969-72. Author, illustrator: Cathedral: The Story of Its Construction, 1973 (Caldecott Honor book 1973), City, 1974, Pyramid, 1975 (Christopher medal 1975), Underground, 1976, Castle, 1977 (Caldecott Honor book 1977), Great Moments in Architecture, 1978, Motel of the Mysteries, 1979, Unbuilding, 1980, Mill, 1983, Baaa, 1985, Why the Chicken Crossed the Road, 1987, The Way Things Work: From Levers to Lasers, Cars to Computers- A Visual Guide to the World of Machines, 1988, Black and White, 1990 (Caldecott medal 1991), Ship, 1993, Shortcut, 1995, Rome Antics, 1997, The New Way Things Work, 1998, Angelo, 2002; illustrator: Help! Let Me Out!, 1982, Electricity, 1983, The Amazing Brain, 1984, David Macaulay, 1997; cons., presenter various TV projects. Recipient Wash. Children's Book Guild award, 1977, AIA medal, 1978, Bradford Washburn meda. Boston Mus. Sci., 1993, Charles Frankel prize NEH, 1995, Chevalier of Order of Arts and Letters, France, 1995.

MACAULAY, LAWRENCE A. Canadian government official, member of Parliament; b. St. Peters Bay, Sept. 9, 1946; s. Archibald and Bernadette MacAulay; m. Frances Elaine O'Connell, Aug. 16, 1972; children: Carolyn, Rita, Lynn. Mem. House of Commons, 1988—, apptd. assoc. critic for fisheries and oceans, 1989, apptd. critic for srs. and assoc. critic for fisheries, 1990; sec. of state for vets. Govt. of Can., 1993—96, min. labour, solicitor gen. of Can., 1998—2002. Mem. standing com. on forestry and fisheries, caucus com. on health and social devel.; acclaimed chair Atlantic Caucus, 1992. Roman Catholic. Office: House of Commons 556 Confederation Bldg Ottawa ON Canada K1A OA6

MACAULAY, WILLIAM EDWARD, financial executive; b. N.Y.C., Sept. 2, 1945; s. John H. and Ella M. (Cook) M.; m. Linda L. Rodger, June 17, 1967; children: Elizabeth R., Anne R. BBA cum laude, CCNY, 1966; MBA, U. Pa., 1968. Asst. v.p. Dominick & Dominick/Parker Advisory, N.Y.C., 1968—71; v.p. Midlantic Bank, Newark, 1971—73, Oppenheimer Mgmt. Corp., N.Y.C., 1973—75, exec. v.p., 1976—79; gen. ptnr. Century Capital Assocs., N.Y.C., 1975—76; dir. corp. fin. Oppenheimer & Co., Inc., N.Y.C., 1979—81, ptnr., 1976-81; gen. ptnr. Meridien Capital Co., Greenwich, Conn., 1981-92. Pres., CEO, dir. First Res. Corp., Greenwich, 1982—; bd. dirs. Weatherford, Inc.; chmn. Pride Internat., Houston, Nat. Oilwell, Houston; chmn. Dresser, Inc., Dallas. Mem.: Indian Harbor Yacht Club, Beta Sigma Gamma. Presbyterian. Office: First Reserve Corp One Lafayette Pl Greenwich CT 06830-7165

MACAULEY, EDWARD C. retired company executive; b. St. Louis, Mar. 22, 1928; s. Charles J. and Josephine (Durkin) M.; m. Jacqueline Combs, July 12, 1952; children: Mary Ann, Robert, Teresa, Michael, Kathleen, Margaret. BS, St. Louis U., 1949. Basketball player Boston Celtics, 1950-56, St. Louis Hawks, 1957-58, coach, 1959-60; sports dir. Stas. KTVI-TV and KSDK-TV, St. Louis, 1960-70; stockbroker A.G. Edwards-Shearson Lehman, St. Louis, 1970-81; pres. Macauley Kremjet, St. Louis, 1981—, Eagle Communications, St. Louis, 1982-86. Bd. dirs. Color Art Printing Co., St. Louis. Trustee Basketball Hall of Fame, Springfield, Mass., 1980—, Mo. Basketball Hall of Fame, Columbia, 1988—, Marianist Apostolic Ctr., St. Louis, 1988—; mem. St. Liborius Food Pantry, St. Louis, 1988-89; organizer St. Nicholas Food Pantry, St. Louis, 1989; ordained deacon Archdiocese of St. Louis, Roman Cath. Ch., 1989—. Named to All Am. Basketball Team, AP, UP, Life, Colliers mag., 1948, 49, All Pro Team, NBA, 1951, 52, 53; inducted into Basketball Hall of Fame, 1961. Avocations: golf, travel, preaching. Home and Office: 13277 Barrett Chase Cir Ballwin MO 63021-3825

MACAVERY, TRISTAN ALEXANDER (TRISTAN BLACK WOLF), small business owner, writer, actor; b. Petersburg, Va., Aug. 16, 1958; s. Carroll Alden and Mildred Harriet (Leon) Peabody. BA, Sam Houston State U., 1979. Editl. assoc Internat. Fire Svc. Tng. Assn., Stillwater, Okla., 1983—84; pub. Aegis Unicorne, Davis, Calif., 1985—92; exec. assoc. Okla. Ctr. Integrated Design and Mfg., Stillwater, 1993—95; Houston bur. chief Tex. Triangle newspaper, 1995; actor, writer, dir., prodr. ADV Films, Houston, 1996—99; owner Intangible Plastics, Houston, 1999—. Spkr. numerous Japanese anime convs., 1996—; founding mem. Third Coast Comedy, Houston. Voice actor: Neon Genesis Evangelion, 1996—2001; author: Divine Intervention, 2001, Lion Dance, 2002, Tea for Twenty, 2003, Remnant Stew, 2004, over 100 articles and short stories. Democrat. Native Am. Shaman. Avocations: piano, voice. Home: 5114 Torchlight Dr Houston TX 77035 Office: PO Box 310575 Houston TX 77231-0575 Fax: 713-729-6811. Business E-Mail: tristan@intangibleplastics.com.

MACAVINTA-TENAZAS, GEMORSITA, family physician; b. Numancia, Aklan, Phillippines, Dec. 18, 1938; came to U.S., 1967; d. Dominador Zalazar and Georgina Estrada (Tabanera) Macavinta; m. Salvador Torrefiel Tenazas Jr., Apr. 18, 1963; children: Alan, Alex, Albert, Alfred. BA, Far Ea. U., Manila, 1959, MD, 1964. Diplomate Am. Bd. Family Practice. Intern North Gen. Hosp., Manila, 1963-64; pvt. practice Manila, 1965-67; extern Chinese Gen. Hosp., Manila, 1965-67; with St. Joseph Med. Ctr., Burbank, Calif., 1967-69; chief cytotechnologist Cancer Screening Svcs., North Hollywood, Calif., 1969-73; resident in family practice medicine Health Scis. Ctr., Tex. Tech. U., Lubbock, 1974-75; staff physician VA Outpatient Clinic, L.A., 1975—. Recipient physician recognition awards AMA, 1973-85, 92-94; named Mrs. Aklan, 1986, Disting. Alumna, Aklan Acad., Philippines, 1991, Most Outstanding Parent award Builders Lions Club, 1995, Citizen of Yr. Builders Lions Club, 1996, Outstanding Physician Club Filipino, 1996, one of 10 Outstanding Women of Nation, Uliran, 1997, Mrs. Philippine Am., 2000. Fellow Am. Acad. Family Physicians; mem. Philippine-Am. Assn. Family Physicians (bd. govs. 1996, 2002—, sec. 1998, outstanding leader award 2000, sec. 1998-2002), Am. Assn. Family Physicians (named Mrs. Philippine, bd. govs. 2004—), Calif. Acad. Family Physicians, Filipino Asian-Pacific VA Employees Soc. (pres. L.A. chpt. 1988—), Assn. Philippine Physicians in Am. (named Mrs. Mindanao, 2002), Aklanons of Am. (pres. 1988—, bd. govs. 1998-2000, 1st Mrs. Aklan 1986-89, bd. dirs. 2000—), Far Ea. U. Med. Alumni Assn. (asst. sec. 1988—); life mem. FEUDNR Med. Alumni Found. Roman Catholic. Avocations: dance, singing, sewing, piano playing, gardening. Office: VA Outpatient Clinic 425 S Hill St Los Angeles CA 90013-1110 Office Phone: 213-253-2677 4417.

MACAVOY, THOMAS COLEMAN, manufacturing executive, educator; b. Jamaica, N.Y., Apr. 24, 1928; s. Joseph V. and Edna M. Mac A.; m. Margaret M. Walsh, Dec. 27, 1952; children: Moira Mac Avoy Brown, Ellen Mac Avoy Jennings, Christopher, Neil. BS in Chemistry, Queens Coll., 1950; MS in Chemistry, St. John's U., 1952, DSc (hon.), 1973; PhD in Chemistry, U. Cin., 1952. Chemist, Charles Pfizer & Co., Bklyn., 1957-60; mgr. electronics rsch. Corning Glass Works, N.Y., 1960-64, dir. phys. rsch., 1964-66, v.p. electronic products divsn., 1966-69, v.p. tech. products divsn., 1969-71, pres., 1971-83, vice-chmn., 1983-87; prof. mgmt. grad. sch. U. Va., 1988—. Patentee in field; contbr. articles to tech. jours. Trustee Corning Mus. Glass; past pres. Boy Scouts Am. With USN, 1946; with USAF, 1952-53. Recipient Silver Antelope award Boy Scouts Am., 1976, Silver Beaver award, 1975, Silver Buffalo award, 1982, Bronze Wolf award, 1988. Roman Catholic. E-mail: tcm2m@virginia.edu.

MACBAIN, LOUISE T. BLOUIN, publishing executive; b. Can., 1958; m. David Stewart (div.); m. John H. McBain (div.); 3 children. Grad., Harvard U. With various investment banking firms, 1977—87; co-founder, CEO ops Hebdo Mag Group (now Trader Classified Media), Montreal, Canada, 1987—2000; CEO Phillips, de Pury & Luxembourg, 2002; chmn. LTB Holdings, 2003—; owner Art & Auction Mag., 2003—, Art Knowledge Corp., 2004—, Spoon mag., Paris, 2004—. Office: Art & Auction Mag 9th Fl 11 E 36th St New York NY 10016*

MACBAIN, WILLIAM HALLEY, minister, theology educator, seminary chancellor; b. Cambridge, Ont., Can., Aug. 12, 1916; s. George Alexander and Grace Ann (Wilkins) MacB.; m. Mary Ann Munday, Aug. 20, 1941; children: Grace Elizabeth MacBain Silvester, Constance Marilyn MacBain Parker. Licentiate in Theology, Toronto Baptist Sem., Ont., 1939; DD (hon.), Cen. Bapt. Sem., Toronto, 1962. Ordained to ministry Bapt. Ch., 1940. Pastor, founder Temple Bapt. Ch., Sarnia, Ont., 1937-64; pastor Forward Bapt. Ch., Toronto, 1964-73; dir., gen. sec. Fellowship Fgn. Missions, Toronto, 1973-81; chancellor Cen. Bapt. Sem., 1981-93, Heritage Bapt. Bible Coll. and Theol. Sem., Cambridge, Ont., Can., 1993—. Pastor emeritus Forward Bapt. Ch., Toronto, 1994—; chmn. Can. Bd. Greater Europe Mission, 1963-73. Mem. Fellowship Evang. Bapt. Chs. in Can. (pres. 1953-54, 83-84) Conservative. Home: 1540 Kipling Ave Apt 903 Etobicoke ON Canada M9R 4C6 Office: Heritage Bapt Bible Coll and Theol Sem 175 Holiday Inn Dr Cambridge ON Canada N3C 3T2

MACBETH, ANGUS, lawyer; b. L.A., May 9, 1942; BA, Yale U., 1964, LLB, 1969. Bar: N.Y. 1970, D.C. 1981. Law clk. to Hon. Harold R. Tyler, Jr. U.S. Dist. Ct. (so. dist.) N.Y., 1969-70, asst. U.S. atty. criminal divsn., 1975-77; chief pollution control sect. Land and Natural Resources Divsn., U.S. Dept. Justice, 1977-79, dep. asst. atty. gen., 1979-81; ptnr. Sidley, Austin, Brown & Wood, Washington. Adj. prof. law N.Y. Law Sch., 1985—; spl. counsel Wartime Relocation and Internment Civilians Commn., 1981-83. Mem. D.C. Bar (steering com. energy and natural resources divsn. 1982-84), N.Y. State Bar Assn., Phi Beta Kappa. Office: Sidley Austin Brown & Wood 1501 K St Washington DC 20005

MACCABY, RIVKAH, writer, interpreter; b. Bloomington, Ind., Jan. 7, 1967; d. Darrell P. and Louise B. Hammer; m. Benjamin S. Maccaby, June 25, 1971. Student, Gallaudet U., 1987—88; BA in English, Ind. U., 1990. Interpreter; slc/slf Options for Better Living, Bloomington, Ind., 1997—2003. Tchr. Bloomington Jewish Cmty., 1998—2000. Author: Happy Families Are Not Alike. Jewish. Avocations: reading, writing. Home: 3609 Woodyard Rd Bloomington IN 47404 Personal E-mail: rvkhmcbi@insightbb.com.

MACCALLUM, MARTHA, correspondent; BA, St. Lawrence U. Anchor, reporter Sta. WBIS-TV, N.Y.C.; anchor, reporter, prodr. Wall St. Jour. T.V., N.Y.C., 1992-96; corr. Bus. News, CNBC, Ft. Lee, N.J. Office: CNBC 2200 Fletcher Ave Fort Lee NJ 07024-5005

MACCARIO, MAURICE MALCOLM, oral and maxillofacial surgeon, consultant; b. Newark, Jan. 17, 1942; s. Melchiorre Malcolm and Susan (Bocchino) M.; m. Rosemarie Agnes Nocera; children: Lenora, Marcus. BA, Villanova U., 1964; DDMedicine, Fairleigh Dickinson U., 1968. Diplomate Am. Bd. Oral and Maxillo Facial Surgery. Intern Bklyn. Jewish Hosp., 1969; resident Bklyn. Vets. Hosp., 1970; chief resident Bklyn. Cumberland Med. Ctr., 1971; sr. registrar North Staffordshire Royal Infirmary, Eng., 1971-72; tchr. oral surgery Bklyn. Hosp., 1972-82; pvt. practice, Oakland, N.J., 1972—; mem. staff Valley Hosp., Ridgewood, N.J., 1971—, dir. oral surgery, 1980—87, chief and dir. oral surgery, 1999—. Cons. St. Joseph Hosp., Paterson, N.J., 1971—. Contbr. articles to profl. jours. V.p. Oakland (N.J.) Rep. Club., 1986-88. Fellow Am. Assn. Oral and Maxillofacial Surgeons, Oral Surgery Soc. N.J., Am. Mensa Soc. Roman Catholic. Avocation: private pilot. Home: 160 Long Hill Rd Oakland NJ 07436-3113 Office: 180 Ramapo Valley Rd Oakland NJ 07436-2524 Address: 103 St Martin Dr Palm Beach Gardens FL

MACCARTHY, TALBOT LELAND, civic volunteer; b. St. Louis, Jan. 28, 1936; d. Austin Porter Leland and Dorothy (Lund) Follansbee; m. John Peters MacCarthy, June 21, 1958; children: John Leland MacCarthy, Talbot MacCarthy Payne. BA, Vassar Coll., 1958. Sec., treas. Station List Pub. Co., St. Louis, 1975-85, pres., 1985-90. Hon. trustee Robert E. Lee Meml. Assn., Arts and Edn. Coun. Greater St. Louis, pres., 1978-80, emerita; past vestry mem. St. Michael and St. George Ch., 1997-00; past trustee St. Louis Art Mus., St. Louis Merc. Libr. Assn., Family & Children's Svc. Greater St. Louis, Health and Welfare Coun., Greater St. Louis, Jr. Kindergarten St. Louis Page Park YMCA, Scholarship Found. St. Louis, Friends St. Louis Art Mus. Bd., Ch. St. Michael and St. George Sch. Bd., Mid-Am. Arts Alliance; chmn. Mo. Arts Coun., 1980-85; past chmn. Vol. Action Ctr. Greater St. Louis; past vice chmn. bd. dirs. Mary Inst.; past pres. Jr. League St. Louis; mem. Nat. Coun. Arts, 1985-91; mem. nat. coun. for Sch. of Art Washington U.; bd. dirs. Sheldon Art Galleries; trustee Seabury-Western Theol. Sem. Recipient Woman of Achievement citation St. Louis Globe Democrat, 1979, Mo. Citizens for Arts/Arts Advocacy award, 1987, Mo. Arts Award, 1993. Mem. Vassar Club St. Louis (past pres.), Mary Inst. Alumnae Assn. (past pres.), Colonial Dames Am., Garden Club St. Louis, Belvedere Club (Charlevoix, Mich.; bd. dirs.). Republican. Episcopalian. Avocations: tennis, visual arts, performing arts.

MACCARTHY, TERENCE FRANCIS, lawyer; b. Chgo., Feb. 5, 1934; s. Frank E. and Catherine (McIntyre) MacC.; m. Marian Fulton, Nov. 25, 1961; children— Daniel Fulton, Sean Patrick, Terence Fulton, Megan Catherine BA in Philosophy, St. Joseph's Coll., 1955; JD, DePaul U., 1960. Bar: Ill. 1960, U.S. Dist. Ct. (no. dist.) Ill. 1961, U.S. Ct. Appeals (7th cir.) 1961, U.S. Supreme Ct. 1966. Assoc. prof. law Chase Coll. Law, Cin., 1960-61; law clk. to chief judge U.S. Dist. Ct., 1961-66; spl. asst. atty. gen. Ill., 1965-67; exec. dir. Fed. Defender Program, U.S. Dist. Ct. (no. dist.) Ill., Chgo., 1966—. Mem. nat. adv. com. on criminal rules; 7th cir. criminal jury instrn. com.; chmn. Nat. Defender Com.; chmn. bd. regents Nat. Coll. Criminal Def.; faculty Fed. Jud. Ctr., Nat. Coll. Criminal Def., Nat. Inst. Trial Advocacy, U. Va. Trial Advocacy Inst., Harvard Law Sch. Trial Advocacy Program, Western Trial Advocacy Inst., Northwestern U., U. Ill. Defender Trial Advocacy course, Nat. Criminal Def. Coll., Loyola U. Trial Advocacy Program; lectr. in field Contbr. articles on criminal law to profl. jours. Bd. dirs. U.S.O. Served as 1st lt. USMC, 1955-57 Recipient Nat. Legal Aid and Defender Assn./ABA Reginald Heber Smith award, 1986, Alumni Merit award St. Joseph Coll., 1970, Cert. of Distinction USO, 1977, Harrison Tweed Spl. Merit award Am. Law Inst./ABA, 1987, Bill of Rights award Ga. chpt. ACLU, 1986, William J. Brennan award U. Va., 1989, Alumni Svc. award DePaul U. Coll. Law, 1994, Ann. Significant Contbns. award Calif. Attys. for Criminal Justice, Defender of the Century Fed. Defenders Assn., Inns of Ct. and Ct. of Appeals (7th cir.) Professionalism award; named to Outstanding Young Men of Am., 1970. Mem. ABA (past chmn. criminal justice sect., ho. of dels., bd. govs., Charles English award criminal justice sect.), Ill. Bar Assn., Chgo. Bar Assn., 7th Cir. Bar Assn., Nat. Assn. Criminal Def. Lawyers (Disting. Svc. award 1993), Nat. Legal Aid and Defender Assn., Nat. Coll. Criminal Def. (chair), Union League of Chgo. (pres.). Democrat. Roman Catholic. Office: US Dist Ct No Dist Ill 55 E Monroe St Ste 2800 Chicago IL 60603-5802

MACCHIA, DAVID ALAN, management consultant; s. Edmund Joseph and Anna Alice Macchia; m. Robin Cynthia Haley, Mar. 8, 1997; children: Spencer David, Ava Haley. Pres. Donahue-Macchia Ins. Agy., Inc., Braintree, Mass., 1985—2000; pres., CEO Wealth2k, Inc., Hingham, Mass., 2000—. Cons. PaineWebber, N.Y.C., 1987—89, Aviva Life Ins. Co., North Quincy, Mass., 1988—2001, Nat. Life, Montpelier, Vt., 1998—2000, Keyport Life Ins. Co., Boston, 1999—2000, ING U.S., DesMoines. Author: (seminar selling program) The Alternative Plan, (video series) Generations. Mem.: Soc. Cert. Sr. Advisors. Achievements include design of unique utilization of a life insurance policy. Office: Wealth2k Inc 50 Derby St Hingham MA 02043 Office Phone: 781-740-9777. E-mail: dmacchia@wealth2k.com.

MACCHIA, VINCENT MICHAEL, lawyer; b. Bklyn., Dec. 30, 1933; s. Vincent and Lina Rose (Cewll) M.; m. Irene Janet Audino, Feb. 27, 1965; children: Lauren, Michele, Michael. BS, Fordham U., 1955, LLB, 1958; LLM, NYU, 1967. Bar: N.Y. 1958. Assoc. Bernard Remsen Millham & Bowdish, N.Y.C., 1959-60; atty. Equity Corp., N.Y.C., 1961-63, Pfizer Inc., N.Y.C., 1964, TWA, N.Y.C., 1964-66; mem. Gifford, Woody, Palmer & Serles, N.Y.C., 1966-85, Townley & Updike, N.Y.C., 1985-90; of counsel Smith, Don, Alampi, Scala & D'Argenio, Ft. Lee, N.J., 1990-91; counsel Tenzer, Greenblatt, LLP, N.Y.C., 1991-2000, Diamant, Katz Kahn & Co. LLP, N.Y.C., 2000—02, Amper, Politziner & Mattia, P.C., N.Y.C., 2002—. Dir. Hudson Rev., Inc. Mem. editl. staff Fordham Law Rev., 1956-58. With USAR, 1958-64. Mem. ABA, N.Y. State Bar Assn. Republican. Roman Catholic. Home: 4 Greentree Dr Scarsdale NY 10583-7014

MACCHIAROLA, FRANK JOSEPH, academic administrator, educator; b. N.Y.C., Apr. 7, 1941; s. Joseph John and Lucy (Bernardo) M.; m. Mary Teresa Collins, June 13, 1970; children: Joseph John, Michael Collins, Frank Joseph. BA, St. Francis Coll., 1962, L.H.D. (hon.), 1981; LL.B., Columbia U., 1965, PhD, 1970; L.H.D. (hon.), Coll. S.I., 1983; LL.D. (hon.), Dominican Coll., 1983, Manhattan Coll., 1983, St. Joseph's Coll., Molloy Coll., 1999. From fellow to prof. polit. sci. CUNY, 1964-83, v.p., 1977-78; asst. v.p. Columbia U., N.Y.C., 1973-74; dep. dir. N.Y. State Emergency Fin. Control Bd. for N.Y.C., 1976-77; chancellor of schs. N.Y.C. Public Sch. System, 1978-83; pres., chief exec. officer N.Y.C. Partnership, Inc., 1983-87; pres. Acad. of Polit. Sci., 1987-91; prof. bus. Columbia U., N.Y.C., 1987-91; dean Benjamin N. Cardozo Sch. of Law, Yeshiva U., N.Y.C., 1991-96; of counsel Tannenbaum, Helpern, Syracuse and Hirschtritt, N.Y.C., 1991—; pres. St. Francis Coll., N.Y., 1996—. Bd. dirs. Jeffries Group Inc.; trustee Manville Personal Injury Settlement Trust. Decorated cavalieri Order of Merit Italy; recipient cert. of merit Dirigible Soc. Am., 1976 Democrat. Roman Catholic. Office: 900 3rd Ave New York NY 10022-4728 also: 180 Remsen St Brooklyn NY 11201-4305 Office Phone: 718-489-5345. E-mail: fmacchia@stfranciscollege.edu.

MACCINI, LOUIS JOHN, economic educator; b. Cambirdge, Mass., Aug. 3, 1942; s. Joseph and Jennie (Leccacorvi) M.; m. Carol Monterisi, June 25, 1965; children: Michael S., Sharon L. BS in Economics, Boston Coll., 1965; PhD in Economics, Northwestern U., 1970. From asst. prof. to assoc. prof. economics The Johns Hopkins U., Balt., 1969-86, prof., 1986—, chair, 1992—. Ad hoc com. mem. graduate fin. aid, Johns Hopkins U., editorial bd., public interest investment adv. com., law sch. com., med. sch. com., and other coms.; mem. recruting chair dept. grad. student advisor dept., and other depts. Referee Am. Econ. Review, Jour. Econ. Dynamics and Control, Oxford Econ. Papers, and others; contbr. articles to profl. jours. Grantee NSF. Mem. Am. Econ. Assn., The Econometric Soc., Internat Soc. Inventory Rsch. Office: Johns Hopkins U 3400 N Charles St Baltimore MD 21218-2680 Office Phone: 410-516-7607. E-mail: maccini@jhu.edu.

MACCLEAN, WALTER LEE, dentist; b. Sheridan, Wyo., July 10, 1935; s. Edward Satterlee and Eleanor Elizabeth (Weir) Mac.; m. Nancy Lee Strale, Sept. 4, 1965 (div. 1975); children: David Satterlee, Carrie Lynn. BS with honors, U. Wyo., 1957, postgrad., 1958; DMD, U. Oreg., Portland, 1962. Mil. dental adv. Korean Mil. Adv. Group, Wonju, 1962-63; chief dental svc. Dugway Chem. Testing Ctr., Utah, 1965-68; pvt. dental practice Cheyenne, Wyo., 1968-70; assoc. prof. Sheridan Coll., Wyo., 1970-76; staff dentist VA Hosp. Med. Ctr., Ft. Meade, S.D., 1976-93; ret., 1993. Cons., lectr. Health Edn. Program Svc., Ft. Meade, 1984-93. With U.S. Army 1962-68. Mem. ADA. Seventh-Day Adventist. also: Highbourne House 13 15 Marylebone High St London W1M 3PE England Home: PO Box 3046 Sheridan WY 82801-1146

MACCOBY, ELEANOR EMMONS, psychology educator; b. Tacoma, May 15, 1917; d. Harry Eugene and Viva May (Johnson) Emmons; m. Nathan Maccoby, Sept. 16, 1938 (dec. Apr. 1992); children: Janice Carmichael, Sarah Maccoby Blunt, Mark. BS, U. Wash., 1939; MA, U. Mich., 1949, PhD, 1950. Study dir. div. program surveys USDA, Washington, 1942-46; study dir. Survey Rsch. Ctr. U. Mich., Ann Arbor, 1946-48; lectr., rsch. assoc. dept. social rels. Harvard U., Cambridge, Mass., 1950-58; from assoc. to full prof. Stanford (Calif.) U., 1958-87, Barbara Kimball Browning prof., 1979, chmn. dept. psychology, 1973-76, prof. emeritus, 1987—. Author: (with R. Sears and H. Levin) Patterns of Child-Rearing, 1957, (with Carol Jacklin) Psychology of Sex Differences, 1974, Social Development, 1980, (with R.H. Mnookin) Dividing the Child: Social and Legal Dilemmas of Custody, 1992, (with Buchanan and Dombusch) Adolescents after Divorce, 1996, The Two Sexes: Growing Up Apart, Coming Together, 1998; editor: (with Newcomb and Hartley) Readings in Social Psychology, 1957, The Development of Sex Differences, 1966. Recipient Gores award for Excellence in Tchg., Stanford U., 1981, Disting. Contbn. to Ednl. Research award Am. Ednl. Rsch. Assn., 1984, Lectureship award Soc. for Devel. and Behavioral Pediats., 2002. Fellow APA (pres. Divsn. 7, 1971-72, G. Stanley Hall award 1982), Soc. for Rsch. in Child Devel. (pres. 1981-83, mem. governing coun. 1963-66, Disting. Sci. Contbn. award 1987), Am. Psychol. Soc. (Disting. Sci. Contbns. award 1988); mem. NAS, AAAS, Am. Acad. Arts and Scis., Inst. Medicine, Western Psychol. Assn. (pres. 1974-75, Lifetime Achievement award 2004), Inst. for Rsch. on Women and Gender, Social Sci. Rsch. Coun. (chmn. 1984-85), Consortium of Social Sci. Assns. (pres. 1997-98), Am. Psychol. Found. (Life Achievement award 1996). Democrat. Home: 729 Mayfield Ave Palo Alto CA 94305-1016 Office: Stanford U Dept Psychology Stanford CA 94305-2130 E-mail: Maccoby@psych.stanford.edu.

MAC CORMAC, EARL RONALD, retired education educator; b. N.Y.C., Apr. 26, 1935; s. Earl Copeland and Katherine Kissel MacC.; m. Nancy Hamilton, Aug. 23, 1958; children: Ann F., Susan H. B Engring., Yale U., 1955, MA, 1959, PhD, 1961, Karlsruke U., Germany, 2003. Adminstrv. asst. Hazen Found., New Haven, Conn., 1958-61; Charles A. Dana Prof. of Philosophy Davidson (N.C.) Coll., 1961-86; Fulbright Prof. U. Madras, India, 1985-86; sci. advisor to gov. Gov.'s Office, Raleigh, N.C., 1986-92; pres. N.C. Quality Leadership Found., Raleigh, 1992-94; cons. prof. of radiology Duke U. med. Ctr., Durham, N.C., 1994—. Adj. prof. indsl. engring. N.C. State U., Raleigh, 1986-92; exec. dir. N.C. Bd. Sci. and Technology, Raleigh, 1986-92; mem. kuratorium Wissenschaftszentrum, North-Rhine Westphalia, 1991—; nat. Fulbright selection com. Inst. of Internat. Edn., N.Y., 1984-87. Author: (books) Metaphor and Myth in Science and Religion, 1976, A Cognitive Theory of Metaphor, 1985, Myths of Science and Technology, 1986; co-author: Decision Analysis Applied to Electrical Rate Design, 1985; co-editor: (book) Fractals in Brain, Fractals in Mind, 1995; editl. bd. John Benjamins Pubs., 1998—. Bd. dirs. Alt. Energy Corp., N.C., 1989-92; adv. bd. N.C. Solar Ctr., Raleigh. Named Outstanding Engring. Student, ASME, 1955; recipient Jefferson award for Tchg., McConnell Found., Davidson, 1971. Mem. N.C. Soc. for Electron Microscopy and Microbeam Analysis (hon.), Tau Beta Pi, Sigma Xi. Presbyterian. Avocations: tennis, golf. Home: 4413 Keswick Dr Raleigh NC 27609-6325 E-mail: ermnhm@earthlink.net.

MACCORMACK, GEORGE F. pharmaceutical executive; b. Mass., 1943; m. Deborah MacCormack. BS, Northeastern U., 1966, MS in Chem. Engring., 1968; MBA, U. Del., 1973. Dir. ops. for Specialty Chemicals DuPont, 1995—96; v.p., gen. mgr. DuPont Specialty Chemicals, 1996—98, DuPont White Pigment & Mineral Products, 1998—99; group v.p. polyester enterprise DuPont, 1999—2000, group v.p. chemicals and polyester, 2000—02; group v.p. DuPont Textiles & Interiors, 2002—. Office: DuPont Corp Info Ctr Barley Mill Plz PIO Wilmington DE 19880-0010

MACCORMACK, JEAN F. academic administrator; d. George and Helen MacCormack. BA, Emmanuel Coll., Boston, 1969; MEd, U. Mass., Amherst, 1978, EdD, 1979. Assoc. dean Coll. of Edn. U. Mass, Boston, 1984—87, acting dean Coll. of Edn., 1984—85, assoc. chancellor, 1987—88, vice chancellor arts and fin., 1988—95, interim chancellor, 1995—96, dep. chancellor and vice chancellor arts and fin., 1996—99, chancellor Dartmouth, 1999—. Mem. South Coast Econ. Devel. Partnership, 1999, Joint CEO Group, 2000, Racial and Ethnic Access and Fairness Adv. Bd., 2001; chair South Coast Edn. Compact, 2000; mem. vis. com. U. So. Maine New Eng. Assoc. of Sch. and Coll., 2000—01; ex-officio mem. U. Mass. Dartmouth Libr. Archive Campaign, 2001; bd. mem. South Coast Health Sys., Inc., 2002; mem. marine sci. com. Fall River CEO Group, 2003, mem. med. device com., 03, mem. south coast edn. com., 03; mem. Regional Competitiveness Coun., 2003. Vice chair bd. govs. New Bedford Oceanariun, 1999, chair edn and rsch. com., 1999, trustee, chair edn. com., 2000; trustee Artworks! at Dover St., 2000, mem. edn. com, 2000, mem. pers. com., 2000; trustee Global Learning Charter Sch., 2000; bd. mem. Greater New Bedford Workforce Investment Bd., 2000, mem. legis. affairs and pub. info. com., 2000, mem. youth coun., 2000; mem. New Bedford Econ. Devel. Coun., 2000; corporator Child and Family Svcs., Inc., 2002; incorporator Home Aged People in Fall river, 2003; corporator Narragansett Fin. Corp. Citizens - Union Savs. Bank, 2003; mem. pres.'s coun. New Bedford Symphony Orch., 2003; mem. leadership coun. New Bedford Whaling Mus. Mem.: YMCA of Southeastern Mass., WHALE, Am. Assn. of State Coll. and U., U. Mass. Dartmouth Libr. Assoc. E-mail: jmaccormack@umassd.edu.

MACCRACKEN, THOMAS GREGG, musicologist; b. Norwalk, Connecticut, May 15, 1951; s. Constable and Eleanor (Dickson) MacCracken; m. Alexandra Jane (Moore-Robinson), May 28, 1988. BA, Yale Univ., 1973; PhD, Univ. of Chgo., 1985. Asst. prof. of music U. of Va., Charlottesville, 1986—90. Trustee Kinhaven Music Sch., Weston, Vt., 1974—80, 1993—98. Co-editor: (musical score) Mathurin Forestier Opera Omnia; musician: (CD recording) Pour 2 Clavecins; contbr. articles to profl. journals. Rsch. fellow, Smithsonian Instn., 1991—93. Mem.: Am. Musical Instrument Soc. (editl. bd. 1996), Am. Musicological Soc. (rev. editor 1991—96), Am. Recorder Soc. (bd. mem. 1990—94), Early Music Am., Southeastern His. Keyboard Soc., Viola da Gamba Soc. of Am. (editor 1996). Presbyterian. Home: 12108 Vale Rd Oakton VA 22124

MACCRATE, ROBERT, lawyer; b. Bklyn., July 18, 1921; s. John and Flora (MacNicholl) MacC.; m. Constance Trapp, May 4, 1946; children: Christopher Robert, Barbara Constance MacCrate Gatti, Thomas John. BA, Haverford Coll., 1943, LLD (hon.), 1987; LLB (hon.), Harvard U., 1948; LLD (hon.), Union U., 1986, Dickinson Sch. Law, 1987, William Mitchell Coll. Law, 1994, Quinnipiac Coll. Law, 1995, CUNY, 2002, U. S.C., 2003. Bar: N.Y. 1949, U.S. Supreme Ct. 1955, D.C. 1965. Assoc. Sullivan & Cromwell, N.Y.C., 1948-51, 51-55, ptnr., 1956-59, 62-91, ret., 1991—96, sr. counsel, 1997—; law sec. N.Y. Appelate Divsn. Presiding Justice David W. Peck, 1951; counsel N.Y. Gov. Nelson A. Rockefeller, 1959-62; spl. counsel U.S. Army for Investigation Mylai incident, 1969-70; counsel N.Y. State Ct. on Judiciary, 1971; mem. jud. selection com. for fed. judgeships Senator Jacob K. Javits, 1972-80; mem. jud. nominating com. N.Y. 2d Jud. Dept., 1975-82. Trustee Lawyers Com. for Civil Rights Under Law, 1976—; chmn. emeritus Fund for Modern Cts., 1978—; cons. N.Y. Profl. Edn. Project, 1994-96. Co-author: Appellate Justice in New York, 1982, Legal Education and Professional Development--an Educational Continuum, 1992, Preserving the Core Values of the American Legal Profession, 2000; contbr. articles to profl. jours. Bd. mgrs. Haverford Coll., 1971-85, emeritus 1986—. Lt. USNR, 1943-46. Recipient Justice System Improvement award Coun. for Ct. Excellence, 1988, Gold medal Nat. Inst. Social Scis., 1989. Fellow Am. Bar Found. (chmn. N.Y. state 1973-80, bd. dirs. 1989—, sec. 1992-94, v.p. 1994-96, pres. 1996-98); mem. ABA (pres. 1987-88, del. 1972-78, 89—, N.Y. State del. 1979-81, bd. govs. 1981-84, 86-89, chair task force law schs. and the profession 1989-92, chair spl. adv. com. internat. activities 1988-89, 2d cir. mem. standing com. on fed. judiciary 1984-86, mem. commn. on opportunities in profession 1993-96, mem. coun. sect. individual rights and responsibilities 1997-2000, medal 2002), N.Y. State Bar Assn. (pres. 1972-73, del. 1972—, chair com. law governing firm structure and operation 1999-2002), Assn. of Bar of City of N.Y. (v.p. 1969-71, chmn. exec. com. 1968-69, chmn. libr. com. 1977-80, chmn. 2d century com. 1989-92), Bar Assn. Nassau County, D.C. Bar Assn., N.Y. County Lawyers Assn. (Disting. Svc. award 1991), Nat. Bar Assn., Am. Coll. Trial Lawyers, Am. Soc. Internat. Law (exec. coun. 1975-80), Union Internationale des Avocats, Acad. Polit. Sci. (bd. dirs. 1975-94), Am. Judicature Soc. (pres. 1979-81, bd. dirs. and mem. exec. com. 1974-83, Justice award 1989), Practising Law Inst. (trustee and mem. exec. com. 1972-95, emeritus trustee 1995—, Seligson award 1995), Am. Law Inst. (coun. 1975—, ABA com. on continuing profl. edn. 1994-97, chair subcom. on future 1994-97), N.Y. Bar Found. (pres. 1976-91), Phi Beta Kappa. Home: 40 The Terrace Plandome NY 11030-1349 Office: Sullivan & Cromwell Rm 2421 125 Broad St New York NY 10004-2498 Office Phone: 212-558-3614. Personal E-mail: maccrate@sullcom.com.

MACDIARMID, ALAN GRAHAM, metallurgist, educator; b. Masterton, New Zealand, Apr. 14, 1927; married, 1954; 4 children. BSc, U. New Zealand, 1948, MSc, 1950; MS, U. Wis., 1952, PhD in Chemistry, 1953, Cambridge U., 1955. Asst. lectr. in chemistry St. Andrews U., 1955; from instr. to assoc. prof. U. Pa., Phila., 1955-64, Sloan fellowship, 1959-63, prof. chemistry, 1964—, Blanchard prof. chemistry, 1998—. Recipient Frederic Stanley Kipping award, 1970, Marshall award, 1982, Doolittle award, 1982, Chemical Pioneer award, 1984, Royal Soc. of Chem. Centenary Medal, Francis J. Clamer medal, Franklin Inst., 1993, Nobel Prize in Chemistry, 2000. Mem.: Royal Soc. Chemistry, Am. Chem. Soc. Achievements include preparation and characterization of organosilicon compounds; preparation and charachterization of derivatives of sulfur nitrides and quasi one-dimensional semiconducting and metallic covalent polymers such as polyacetylene and its derivatives. Office: U Pa Dept Chemistry Rm 343 231 S 34th St Philadelphia PA 19104-3803

MACDONALD, ALAN HUGH, librarian, university administrator; b. Ottawa, Ont., Can., Mar. 3, 1943; s. Vincent C. and Hilda C. (Durney) MacD.; children: Eric Paul Henry, Nigel Alan Christopher. BA, Dalhousie U., Halifax N.S., 1963; BLS, U. Toronto, Ont., 1964. With Dalhousie U., 1964-78, law libr., 1965-67, 69-71, asst. univ. libr., 1970-72, health sci. libr., 1972-78, lectr. Sch. Libr. Svcs., 1969-78; with U. Calgary, Canada, 1979—2003, sr. advisor Info. Resources, 1999—2003, asst. to provost, 1999—2003, adj. prof. faculty comm. and culture, 2000—03, dir. Info Svcs., 1988—99, dir. librs., 1979-92, univ. orator, 1989—2003; dir. U. Calgary Press, 1984—90. Chair editl. bd. U. Calgary Press, 2001—03; libr. N.S. Barristers Soc., 1969—74; mem. adv. bd. Nat. Libr. Can., 1972—76, Health Scis. Resource Ctr., Can. Inst. Sci. and Tech. Info., 1977—79; mem. Coun. of Prairie Univ. Librs., 1979—92, 1997—98, chair, 1984—85, 1989, 91; Bassam lectr. U. Toronto Faculty Info. Studies, 1994; Lorne MacRae lectr. Libr. Assn. Alta., 1996; mem. steering com. Alta. Libr. Knowledge Network, 1999—2002; steering com. Can. Digital Libr. Rsch. Initiative, 1999—2000. Mem. editl. bd. America: History and Life (ABC-CLIO), 1985-93. Pres. TELED Cmty. Media Access Orgn., Halifax, 1972—74; mem. Minister's Com. on Univ. Affairs, Alta., 1979—83; bd. dirs. Alta. Found. for Can. Music Ctr., 1985—92, Can. Inst. for Hist. Microreprodn., 1990—98, pres., 1996—97; bd. dirs. Calgary Learning Ctr., 1997—2004, vice-chair, 2000—04. Coun. Libr. Resources fellow, 1975; exec. fellow Univ. Microfilms Internat., 1986; recipient Disting. Acad. Librarian award Can. Assn. of Coll. and Univ. Libraries, 1988, U. Toronto Faculty of Info. Studies Alumni Jubilee award, 1999. Mem.: Order of U. Calgary, Calgary Cmty. Network Assn. (bd. dirs. 1994—99, chair 1996—99), Can. Assn. Rsch. Librs. (bd. dirs. 1981—86, v.p. 1985—86, Disting. Svc. award to rsch. librarianship 2003), Can. Assn. Info. Sci. (pres. 1979—80), Foothills Libr. Assn., Libr. Assn. Alta. (v.p. 1988—89, Pres.' award 1992), Atlantic Provinces Libr. Assn. (pres. 1977—78), Can. Libr. Assn. (treas. 1977—79, pres. 1980—81, Award for Outstanding Svc. to Librarianship 1997), Australian Libr. and Info. Assn. (assoc.), Can. Health Libr. Assn. (life; treas. 1977—79), AeroSpace Mus. Assn. Calgary (bd. dirs. 2002—, exec. dir. 2003—04, curator 2004—). Office: Calgary AeroSpace Mus 4629 McCall Way NE Calgary AB Canada T2E 8A5 E-mail: ahmacdon@ucalgary.ca.

MACDONALD, ALAN S. diversified financial services company executive; BS, Drexel U.; MS, London Sch. Econs.; PhD in Econs., Cambridge (Eng.) U. Economist UN Econ. Commn. for Europe, Geneva; fin. mgmt. assoc. GM, Wilmington, Del.; co-head global markets Citigroup, head corp. and investment banking U.S. and Can., head corp. banking in emerging markets, head info. bus. group, head Banco de Investimento Crefisul, head Banco Internacional de Colombia; vice chmn., head global relationship banking Citibank and Citicorp, 2000—04; COO global banking Citigroup, 2004—. Bd. dirs. Liberty Brokerage Co. Trustee NY Philharm. Orch., Hosp. for Spl. Surgery, NY. Mem.: NY Partnership (mem. high tech. com.), Am. Bankers Assn. (bd. dirs.), Am. Inst. Contemporary German Studies (trustee), Conf. Bd., Nat. Policy Assn. (trustee, mem. exec. com. new Am. realities com.), Econ. Club NY. Office: Citigroup Inc 399 Park Ave New York NY 10043*

MACDONALD, ALEXANDER EDWARD, meteorologist; b. Fort Snelling, Minn., Mar. 29, 1945; s. Alexander Colin and Marie Christine (Peterson) MacD.; m. Susan Hayes, June 17, 1969; children: Lee Alexander, Ann Elizabeth, Michael Hayes. BS, Mont. State U., 1967; MS, U. Utah, 1973, PhD, 1975. Meteorologist Nat. Weather Svc., Salt Lake City, 1973-80, NOAA/Forecast Systems Lab., Boulder, Colo., 1980—. Dir. NOAA Forecast Systems Lab., 1988—. Capt. USAF, 1967-71. Fellow Am. Meteorol. Soc. (exec. com. 1993-96). Home: 8554 Thunderhead Dr Boulder CO 80302-9381 Office: NOAA/FSL 325 S Broadway St Boulder CO 80305-3464 E-mail: alexander.e.macdonald@noaa.gov.

MACDONALD, ANDREW STEPHEN, management consulting firm executive; b. Fairbanks, Alaska, July 15, 1953; s. Bernard L. and Rosemary (Unger) MacD.; m. Josephine A. Joanne, Aug. 4, 1972; children: Peter, Stephen, Charles. BA in Acctg., Seattle U., 1974. CPA, cert. mgmt. cons. Acct. Boeing Aerospace, Seattle, 1976-79; owner, pres. Triak Corp., Seattle, 1977—; pres. Exec. Cons. Group, Inc., Seattle, 1979—. Mem. AICPA, Inst. Mgmt. Cons., Wash. Soc. CPAs, Columbia Tower Club. Home: 10030 Lake Shore Blvd NE Seattle WA 98125-8158

MACDONALD, BARBARA KATIC, secondary school educator; b. Pittsburgh, Pa., May 2, 1952; d. Louis A and Charlotte Katic; m. H. Jeffrey Tipton (div. 1984); 1 child, Toby; m. Lyle L. MacDonald, 1986 (div. 1994). BS, Clarion U., 1973; MEd, U. Pitts., 1977; studied at, Penn State, 1980—2000, math edn. doctoral courses, 2001—02. Tchr. No. Allegheny Sch., Pitts., 1974—. Math dept. leader No. Allegheny, Pitts., 1980—2002; bd. math. coun. western Pa., Pitts., 1999—; bd. Pa. coun. of teachers of math., 2003—; steering com. Math and Sci. Collaboration, 2000—; spkr. at various math. meetings, 1984—. Mem.: Delta Kappa Gamma (fin. com. 2002—). Avocations: dance, reading, bowling, golf, camping. Home: 160 Fox Run Rd Cranberry Township PA 16066

MACDONALD, DAVID ROBERT, lawyer, fund administrator; b. Chgo., Nov. 1, 1930; s. James Wear and Frances Esther (Wine) M.; m. Verna Joy Odell, Feb. 17, 1962; children: Martha, Emily, David, Rachel, Rebecca. BS, Cornell U., 1952; JD, U. Mich., 1955. Bar: Ill. 1955, Mich. 1955, D.C. 1983. Practiced in Chgo., 1957-74; mem. firm Kirkland, Ellis, Hodson, Chaffetz & Masters, Chgo., 1957-62, ptnr., 1962, Baker & McKenzie, Chgo., 1962-74, 77-81; asst. sec. of Treasury for enforcement, ops. and tariff affairs Dept. Treasury, Washington, 1974-76; undersec. of Navy, 1976-77; dep. U.S. Trade Rep., 1981-83; ptnr. Baker & McKenzie, Chgo., 1983-96. Bd. dirs. Mestek, Inc. (N.Y. Stock Exch.). Pres. David R. Macdonald Found., 1996—. Mem. ABA, D.C. Bar Assn., Chgo. Assn. Commerce and Industry (bd. dirs. 1977-81), Order of Coif, Econ. Club (Chgo.), Cosmos Club (Washington), Grolier Club (N.Y.C.). Home: 6605 Radnor Rd Bethesda MD 20817-6324 Office: 815 Connecticut Ave NW Washington DC 20006-4004

MACDONALD, DONALD ARTHUR, JR., physician, surgeon; b. Englewood, NJ, May 9, 1955; s. Donald Arthur and Ruth Moran M.; m. Florence Twombly Childs, June 14, 1980; children: Donald, Alexandra, Margaret, Ian. BA with highest honors, Williams Coll., 1977; MD, Dartmouth U., 1980. Diplomate Am. Bd. Ophthalmology. Intern Mary Imogene Bassett Hosp., Cooperstown, N.Y., 1980-81; resident Manhattan Eye Ear & Throat Hosp., N.Y.C., 1981-84, attending physician, 1985—; fellow N.Y. Eye Ear & Throat Hosp., 1984-85; attending physician Riverview Med. Ctr., Red Bank, N.J., 1985—, chief dept. ophthalmology, 1995-97. Trustee Rumson (NJ) Country Day Sch., 1990-96, Monmouth County Vol. Ctr., 1996-98, Horizons Program, Rumson, 1996-98; trustee, bd. dirs. ALS Assn. Greater NY chpt.; bd. dirs. Burden Ctr. for the Aging, 2000-03. Mem. Lions, Rumson Country Club (commodore 1996-2003), Seabright Lawn Tennis and Cricket Club, St. Andrews Soc. N.Y. Roman Catholic. Office: 43 N Gilbert St Red Bank NJ 07701-4913 Office Phone: 732-741-1902. E-mail: Drdonaldmadonald@mac.com.

MACDONALD, DONALD STOVEL, corporate director; b. Ottawa, Ont., Can., Mar. 1, 1932; s. Donald Angus and Marjorie (Stovel) M.; m. Ruth Hutchison, Mar. 4, 1961 (dec.); children: Leigh, Nikki, Althea, Sonja; m. Adrian Merchant Lang, Sept. 10, 1988; stepchildren: Maria (dec.), Timothy, Gregory, Andrew, Elisabeth, Amanda, Adrian. Student, Ashbury Coll., Ottawa; BA, U. Toronto, Ont., 1951; LLB, Osgoode Hall Law Sch., 1955; LLM, Harvard, 1956; diploma internat. law, Cambridge U., 1957; LLD, St. Lawrence U., U N.B. Saint John, 1990, U. Toronto, 2000, Carleton U., 2003; DEng, Colo. Sch. Mines. Bar: Called to Ont. bar 1955. Assoc. McCarthy & McCarthy, Toronto, 1957-62; M.P. for Toronto-Rosedale, 1962; reelected, 1963, 65, 68, 72, 74; parliamentary sec. to Min. of Justice, 1963-65, to Min. of Finance, 1965, to Sec. of State for External Affairs, 1966-68, to Min. of Industry, 1968; pres. Privy Coun. and Govt. House Leader, 1968-70; min. of nat. def., 1970-72; min. energy, mines and resources, 1972-75; min. of fin., 1975-77; ptnr. firm McCarthy & McCarthy, Toronto, 1977-88; high commr. for Can. to U.K., 1988-91; counsel McCarthy Tetrault, Toronto, 1991-2000. Sr. advisor UBS Bunting Warburg, Toronto, 2000-02; sr. advisor pub. policy Lang Michener Barristers and Solicitors, 2002—; spl. lectr. U. Toronto Law Sch., 1978-82, 86-88; chmn. Royal Commn. on Econ. Union and Devel. Prospects for Can., 1982-85; chmn. adv. com. competition Ont. Electricity Sys., 1995-96; chmn. Inst. for Rsch. on Pub. Policy, Montreal, 1991-97, Siemens Can. Inc., 1991-2004, Atlantic Coun. of Can., 1998-2002; bd. dirs. Boise Cascade Corp., Idaho, The Clan Donald Lands Trust, Skye, Scotland; chmn., trustee IPC US REIT, 2001—; trustee Clean Power Clean Power Operating Trust, 2001—. Named Freeman of the City of London, 1990, hon. fellow Trinity Hall, Cambridge U., 1994, Companion of the Order of Can., 1994. Mem. Queen's Privy Coun. Can., Delta Kappa Epsilon. Liberal. Baptist. Office: Lang Michener Toronto Office Box 747 ste 2500 BCE place 181 Bay st Toronto ON Canada m5j 2t7 Office Phone: 416-307-4241. Personal E-mail: hondon@merchantmac.com. Business E-Mail: dmacdonald@langmichener.ca.

MACDONALD, DOUGLAS ANDREW, psychologist, educator; b. Barrie, Ontario, Canada, June 2, 1967; s. David James and Rachel Marie MacDonald; m. Clementina Iampietro, Mar. 15, 1995; children: Moriah, Sarah. BA in Psychology(hon.), U. Windsor, Ont., Can., 1990, MA in Psychology, 1992, PhD in Clin. Psychology, 1998. Practicum student Guelph Assessment and Treatment Unit, Guelph, Ont., Canada, 1991; intern U of Windsor Psychol. Svc. Clinic, Winsor, Ont., Canada, 1992—93, Windsor Regional Hosp., Windsor, Ont., Canada, 1994—95; behavioral cons. Essex County Dist. Sch. Bd., Essex, Ont., Canada, 1995—97; psychologist Greater Essex County Dist. Sch. Bd., Windsor, Ont., Canada, 1997—2004; part-time faculty Saybrook Grad. Sch., San Francisco, 2001—; prof. of psychology U. Detroit, 2000—; dir. clin. MA program U. Detroit Mercy, Detroit, 2003—. Rsch. assist. U of Windsor, Windsor, Ont., Canada, 1987—88. Co-editor: (novels) Approaches to Transpersonal Measurement and Assessment, 2002; editor (rsch. assoc.): (jour.) Jour. of Humanistic Psychology, 2002; co-editor (guest): The Humanistic Psychologist, 2003; co-editor: Internat. Jour. Transpersonal Studies, 2003—; assoc. editor: Jour. Transpersonal Psychology, 2001, consulting editor: jour. Australian Gestalt Jour. Mem. bd. of dir. Glengarda Child & Family Svc., Windsor, Ont., Canada, 2000—. Grantee Rsch. Devel. Grant, Floraglades Found./Fl, 2000—04. Mem.: Can. Psychol. Assoc., Am. Psychol. Assoc. Achievements include research in Numerous publ. on rsch. of expression, measurement, and devel. of spirituality and the tools to assess it; editor for three academic jour. Avocations: gardening, music, martial arts. Home: 470 Frontenac Ave N9E1M1 Windsor ON Canada Office: Univ Detroit Mercy Dept Psycol 4001 W McNichols Rd Detroit MI 48219-0900 Office Phone: 313-578-0388.

MACDONALD, ELIZABETH HELEN, bassoonist, educator; b. Lancaster, Pa., July 5, 1942; d. Joseph Harold and Verna Elizabeth (Schaeffer) Bishop; m. William Dallas MacDonald, Aug. 17, 1968. MusB in Music Edn., Eastman Sch. Music, Rochester, N.Y., 1964; MusM in Music Lit. and Performance, Eastman Sch. Music, 1966. Bassoonist Music in Maine Woodwind Quintet, Bangor, Maine, 1966—67; dir. jr. h.s. band and elem instrumental music Brewer, Maine, 1967—69; instr. music history, woodwind class and bassoon No. Conservatory Music, Bangor, 1967—69; tchr. jr. h.s. gen. and instrumental music Orono, Maine, 1969—72; tutor bassoon and oboe Colby Coll., Waterville, Maine, 1972—75; instr. bassoon, woodwind ensemble coach U. Maine, Orono, 1977—; prin. bassoonist Portland Symphony Orch., Maine, 1967—91; pvt. woodwind instr., 1972—. Recitalist, soloist, music adjudicator, 1966—. Mem.: Internat. Double Reed Soc. Republican. Methodist. Office: U Maine Lord Hall Orono ME 04473

MACDONALD, ERIN E. healthcare company executive; With Sierra Health Svcs. Inc. and predecessor firms, 1978—, ops. mgr. Southwest Med. Assocs.; dir. ops. HPN Sierra Health Svcs. Inc., Reno, Nev., v.p. HMO Ops., pres. HPN, 1984, v.p. HMO and ins. ops., 1989-92, pres. SHL, 1990, sr. v.p. ops. Office: Sierra Health Svcs 2724 N Tenaya Way Las Vegas NV 89128

MACDONALD, FLORA ISABEL, Canadian government official; b. North Sydney, N.S., Can., June 3, 1926; d. George Frederick and Mary Isabel (Royle) MacD. Attended Empire Bus. Coll.; grad., Nat. Def. Coll., 1972; DHL (hon.), Mt. St. Vincent U., 1979, various univs., Can., U.S. and U.K. Exec. dir. Progressive Conservative Party Hdqs., Ottawa, Ont., Can., 1957-66; adminstrv. officer, tutor dept. polit. studies Queen's U., 1966-72; mem. Can. Parliament for Kingston and the Islands, Ont., 1972-88; Progressive Conservative spokesman for Indian affairs and no. devel. Can. Parliament, 1972; for housing and urban devel., 1974; chmn. Progressive Conservative Caucus Com. on Fed.-Provincial Relations, 1976; sec. of state for external affairs, 1979-80; minister employment and immigration, 1984-86; min. comms., 1986-89; chairperson Internat. Developmental Rsch. Ctr., 1992-97; spl. adv. Commonwealth of Learning, 1990-91. Vis. fellow Ctr. for Can. Studies, U. Edinburgh, 1989; host T.V. series North South Vision T.V., 1990-94. Bd. dirs. Carnegie Commn. Re-preventing Deadly Conflict, 1994-99, Friends of the Nat. Libr., Shashtri Indo-Can. Adv. Coun., pres., 1996-2004; program advisor CARE Can., Helpage Internat., London, 1996-2001; chmn. Partnership Africa-Can., 2001-04, Ottawa, Can., Future Generations, 2001—, Franklin, W.Va.; co-chair Can Coord. Com. UN Yr. of Older Persons, 1999; hon. pres. Assn. Can. Clubs, World Federalists, Can., 2000-04; patron Commonwealth Human Rights Initiative. Decorated Companion Order of Can., Order of Ont. Mem. Nat. Mus. Scotland (hon. patron Can.), UN (Eminent Persons to study Trans-Nat. Corps. in South Africa 1989). Mem. United Ch. of Canada. Office: Ste 1103 350 Queen Elizabeth Drivewy Ottawa ON Canada K1S 3N1 E-mail: flora@intlanet.ca.

MACDONALD, GORDON CHALMERS, management consultant; b. Boston, Sept. 27, 1928; s. Frank C. and Anna E. (MacLean) MacD.; m. Eileen T. Harkins, May 25, 1952; children: Brian P., Peter G., Keith A., Audrey A. AA, Boston U., 1950, BBA, 1952; grad. advanced mgmt. program, Harvard U., 1979. Grad. tng. program Westinghouse Electric Corp., Pitts., 1952-64, regional/zone mgr., 1953-60, nat. mdse. mgr. Metuchen, N.J., 1960-64; asst. to v.p. sales mgr. Magnavox Co., N.Y.C., 1964-68; v.p. mktg. GTE Corp., Batavia, N.Y., 1968-69; dir. mktg. Mitsubishi Internat. Corp., Lincolnwood, Ill., 1969-75, v.p. N.Y.C., 1975-88, sec., 1984-88, advisor, 1989-91, bd. dirs., 1976-88; prin., mgmt. cons. G.C. MacDonald & Assocs., Greenwich, Conn., 1988—. Chmn. Sea Explorers com. Boy Scouts Am., Greenwich, 1976-81. With U.S. Army, 1946-48. Mem.: U.S. Power Squadron (comdr. 1981-82, exec. com. 1987—) (Greenwich). Avocations: sailing, skiing, bridge. Home: 11 Highgate Rd Riverside CT 06878-2610 E-mail: Grampymac@snet.net.

MACDONALD, HUGH IAN, university president emeritus, economist, educator; b. Toronto, Ont., Can., June 27, 1929; s. Hugh and Winnifred (Mitchell) M.; m. Dorothy Marion Vernon, June 4, 1960; 5 children. B.Com., U. Toronto, 1952; MA, Oxford (Eng.) U., 1954, B.Phil., 1955; LLD (hon.), U. Toronto, 1974; D Univ. (hon.), Open U., U.K., 1998; DLitt (hon.), Open U., Sri Lanka, 1999, Open U., Hyderabad, India, 2001. Lectr. U. Toronto, 1955-62, asst. prof., 1962-65; dean of men U. Toronto (Univ. Coll.), 1956-65; chief economist Govt. Ont., Toronto, 1965-67, dep. treas., 1967, dep. treas., dep. minister econs., 1968, dep. treas., dep. minister econs. and intergovtl. affairs, 1972; pres. York U., Toronto, Ont., 1974-84; prof., dir. York Internat., 1984-94, prof., pres. emeritus, 1984—. Past pres. World U., Univ. Svc. Can.; past chmn. Hockey Can.; past chmn. The Commonwealth of Learning. Named Officer, Order of Can., 1977; recipient Can. Centennial medal, 1967, Queen's Silver Jubilee medal, 1977, Commemorative medal, 125th Anniversary Can. Confedn., 1992, Vanier medal for distinction in pub. svc. and excellence in pub. adminstrn., 2000, Queen's Golden Jubilee medal, 2002; Rhodes scholar, 1952. Office: York U Rm N207 SSB 4700 Keele St Toronto ON Canada M3J 1P3 E-mail: yorkmpa@yorku.ca.

MACDONALD, J. RANDALL, information technology executive, human resources specialist; B in Polit. Sci., M in Indsl. Rels., St. Francis Coll. Human resources position Ingersoll-Rand Co., Sterling Drug Inc.; various human resources positions including exec. v.p. human resources and adminstrn. GTE (now Verizon Comm.), 1983—2000; sr. v.p. human resouces IBM, 2000—. Bd. dirs. Covance (formerly Corning Pharm. Svcs.); mem. Cornell U. Ctr. for Advanced Human Resources Study, chmn. exec. bd. Bd. trustees St. Francis Coll., Pa. Fellow: Nat. Acad. Human Resources (bd. dirs. 2000—); mem.: Labor Policy Assn. (vice chmn. bd. dirs.), Pers. Roundtable, Cowdrick Group. Office: IBM 1133 Westchester Ave White Plains NY 10604 Office Phone: 800-426-4968.

MACDONALD, JAMES ROSS, physicist, researcher; b. Savannah, Ga., Feb. 27, 1923; s. John Elwood and Antonina Jones (Hansell) M.; m. Margaret Milward Taylor, Aug. 3, 1946; children: Antonina Hansell, James Ross IV, William Taylor. BA, Williams Coll., 1944; SB, MIT, 1944, SM, 1947; PhD, Oxford (Eng.) U., 1950, DSc, 1967. Staff Digital Computer Lab., MIT, 1946-47; physicist Armour Rsch. Found., Chgo., 1950-52; assoc. physicist Argonne Nat. Lab., 1952-53; with Tex. Instruments Inc., Dallas, 1953-74, v.p. corp. rsch. and engring., 1968-73, v.p. corp. R & D, 1973-74; cons., 1974—; dir. Simmonds Precision Products Inc., 1979-83; William Rand Kenan Jr. prof. physics U. N.C., Chapel Hill, 1974-91, prof. emeritus, 1991—. Adj. prof. biophysics U. Tex. Med. Sch., Dallas, 1954-74; solid state sci. panel NRC, 1965-73; adv. com. for sci. edn. NSF, 1971-73; vis. com. physics MIT, 1971-74; external adv. com. Engring. Expt. Sta., Ga. Inst. Tech., 1976-79 Editor, contbr.: Impedance Spectroscopy-Emphasizing Solid Materials and Systems, 1987; mem. editl. bd. Jour. Applied Physics, 1984-86; contbr. over 230 articles to profl. jours. Mem. Dallas Radio Comm., 1967-71; mem. sci. adv. coun. Callier Hearing and Speech Ctr., Dallas, 1974-78; bd. dirs. League for Ednl. Advancement in Dallas, 1965-70; adv. com. Weber Rsch. Inst., 1985-90. Rhodes scholar, Oxford U., 1948—50. Fellow Am. Phys. Soc. (mem. com. on edn 1973-75, mem. com. on applications of physics 1975-78, George E. Pake prize 1985), IEEE (awards 1962, 74, assoc. editor Transactions of

Profl. Group on Audio 1961-66, Transactions on Audio and Electroacoustics 1966-73, Edison Gold medal 1988), AAAS; mem. NAE (exec. com. assembly of engring. 1975-78, coun. 1971-74), NAS (chmn. numerical data adv. bd. 1970-74, mem. com. on motor vehicle emissions 1971-74, chmn. com. on motor vehicle emissions 1973-74, mem. com. on satellite power sys. 1979-81, mem. com. on sci., engring., and pub. policy 1981-83, mem. commn. on phys. scis., math., and applications 1985-88, mem. report rev. com. 1990-97), Am. Inst. Physics (mem. governing bd. 1975-78, chmn. com. on profl. concerns 1976-78), Electrochem. Soc., Audio Engring. Soc., Phi Beta Kappa, Sigma Xi, Tau Beta Pi. Achievements include 10 patents in field. Office: Univ NC Dept Physics And Astronomy Chapel Hill NC 27599-3255 Business E-Mail: macd@email.unc.edu.

MACDONALD, JOHN, marketing executive; V.p. mktg. Chrysler Corp., Auburn Hills, Mich., 1996-98, v.p. sales and svc., 1997-99; sr. v.p. sales and svc. DaimlerChrysler Corp., Auburn Hills, 1999—. Office: DaimlerChrysler Corp 1000 Chrysler Dr Auburn Hills MI 48326-2766

MACDONALD, JOHN L. chemical company executive; b. 1943; Pres., CEO JLM Industries, Inc., Tampa. Recipient Fla. Internat. Businessperson of Yr. award Fla. Coun. of Internat. Devel., 1998. Office: JLM Industries Inc 8675 Hidden River Pkwy Tampa FL 33637 Fax: 813-632-3301. E-mail: john.macdonald@jlmindustries.com., info@jlmindustries.com.

MACDONALD, JOHN STEPHEN, oncologist, educator; b. Bklyn., June 2, 1943; s. John Stephen and Margaret (Martin) M.; m. Mary Suzanne Stock, July 11, 1964; children: Margaret Wilson, John Stephen, Kathleen Lenore, Frederick Stock. AB, Dartmouth Coll., 1965, BMS, 1967; MD, Harvard U., 1969. Diplomate Am. Bd. Internal Medicine (mem. med. oncology com. 1989-93, chmn. med. oncology self edn. process com. 1993-95). Intern and resident in medicine Beth Israel Hosp., Boston, 1969-71; clin. assoc. immunology and med. oncology Nat. Cancer Inst., Bethesda, Md., 1971-74, assoc. dir. cancer therapy evaluation program, div. cancer treatment, 1979-82, med. oncologist Washington Clin., 1982-84; instr., asst. prof., then assoc. prof. medicine Georgetown U., Washington, 1974-79, clin. assoc. prof., 1979-84, George Washington U., 1980-84; prof. medicine, chief div. hematology-oncology U. Ky., Lexington, 1984-89, assoc. dir. Markey Cancer Center, 1984-89; prof. medicine, chief sect. med. oncology, dir. cancer ctr. Temple U., Phila., 1989-97; dir. gastrointestinal oncology St. Vincent's Comprehensive Cancer Ctr., N.Y.C., 1997—; nat. dir. physician orgns. Salick Health Care, Inc., L.A., 1997-98, exec. v.p. med. affairs, 1998—, chief med. officer, 1999—. Chmn. gastrointestinal cancer com. S.W. Oncology Group, 1985—. Editor-in-chief: Cancer Treatment Reports, 1979-82; co-editor: Gastrointestinal Oncology, 1992; mem. editorial bd. Jour. Clin. Oncology, 1988-91; contbr. more than 250 articles to med. jours. Bd. mgmt. YMCA, 1979-84; bd. dirs. CYO, 1979-84. Served with USPHS, 1971-74. Jr. faculty clin. fellow Am. Cancer Soc., 1974-76 Fellow ACP; mem. Am. Fedn. Clin. Research, Am. Soc. Clin. Oncology, Am. Assn. for Cancer Research, Am. Cancer Soc. (bd. dirs. Phila. chpt. 1994—). Roman Catholic. Home: # 705 666 Greenwich St Apt 705 New York NY 10014-6329 Office: St Vincent's Comprehensive Cancer Ctr 325 W 15th St New York NY 10011-5903

MACDONALD, JOHN THOMAS, educational administrator; b. Utica, N.Y., Nov. 21, 1932; s. Gerald Clement and Mildred (Hayes) MacD.; m. Marcia Sprague Gallup; children: Terrence (dec.), Anthony, Elizabeth, Michele, Elise, Denise. BS, Northeastern U., 1958, EdM, 1960; PhD, U. Conn., 1970. Cert. elem. and secondary sch. tchr., prin., supt., Mass., Conn. Supervising prin. Noank, Ft. Hill. and Poquonnock Elem. Schs., Groton, Conn., 1962-66, Robert E. Fitch Jr. H.S., Groton, 1966-70; rsch. asst. Ednl. Resources and Devel. Ctr. U. Conn., Storrs, 1969-70; supt. schs. Wallingford (Conn.) Pub. Schs., 1970-73, Walpole (Mass.) Pub. Schs., 1973-78, Dartmouth (Mass.) Pub. Schs., 1978-86; commr. edn. State Dept. Edn., Concord, NH, 1986-90; asst. sec. for elem. and secondary edn. U.S. Dept. Edn., Washington, 1990-93; dir. state leadership ctr. Coun. of Chief State Sch. Officers, Washington, 1993-99, sr. advisor, 2000-01; prof. of ednl. policy and leadership Neag Sch. Edn., U. Conn., 2001—; dir. NE Ctr. for Ednl. Policy and Leadership. Mem. Postsecondary Edn. Commn., Concord, 1986-90, Coun. for Tchr. Edn., Concord, 1986-90, Profl. Stds. Bd., Concord, 1986-90; trustee Univ. System of N.H., Durham, 1986-90; mem. Surgeon Gen's Task Force, 1990-93; mem. White House Conf. on Indian Edn., 1990-93; mem. Interagy. Com. on Sch. Health, 1990-93, others; mem. dean's adv. coun. U. Conn., 1999—, Coll. Arts and Scis., Northeastern U., 1999—; mem. adv. coun. Va. Edn. Policy Inst., Va. Commonwealth U., 2000—; mem. adv. bd. ERIC, Washington, 1998—. Contbr. articles to profl. jours. Co-chmn. Emergency Sch.-Aide Proposals, U.S. Office Edn., 1973—75; mem. adv. com. external program rev. CDC, 1992—; mem. nat. adv. bd. ERIC Clearinghouse, 1999—; mem. Mass. Adv. Commn. for Ednl. TV, 1983—86, N.H. Task Force on Child Abuse, 1987—90; mem. Nat. Adv. Coun. Northeastern U., 1990—; mem. Galaxy Classroom Nat. Adv. Coun. Galaxy Inst. for Edn., 1992—; mem. sch. health policy initiative Ctr. for Population & Family Health Columbia U., 1992—; mem. Packard roundtable to children Ctr. for Health Policy George Washington U., 1992—; mem. adv. bd. Va. Commonwealth Policy Inst., 1999—; mem. Dean's adv. coun. Neag Sch. Edn. U. Conn., 1999—, Coll. Arts & Scis. Northeastern U., 1999—. Recipient Sears B. Condit award, 1958, Alumni award Northwestern U., 1973, Recognition award Coun. of Chief State Sch. Officers, 1990. Fellow Phi Delta Kappa, Phi Alpha Theta; mem. N.H. Sch. Bldg. Authority, Mass. Assn. Sch. Supts. (pres. 1985-86). Office: U Conn Neag Sch Edn Dept Ednl Leadership 249 Glenbrook Rd Box U-2093 Storrs Mansfield CT 06269-2064 Office Phone: 860-486-4029. Business E-Mail: John.MacDonald@uconn.edu. E-mail: macmarjack@aol.com.

MACDONALD, KAREN CRANE, occupational therapist, geriatric counselor; b. Denville, N.J., Feb. 24, 1955; d. Robert William and Jeanette Wilcox (Crane) M.; m. Geno Piacentini, Oct. 22, 1993. BS, Quinnipiac U., 1977; MS, U. Bridgeport, 1982; PhD, NYU, 1998. Cert. occupl. therapist. Occupational therapist, coord. of spl. care unit Jewish Home for the Elderly, Conn., 1987-92, N.Y. Inst., N.Y.C., 1984-86; pvt. practice Fairfield County, Conn., 1977-88; occupl. therapist Rehab. Assocs., Fairfield, Conn., 1993-96; instr. Housatonic Cmty. Coll., Conn. Instr. NYU, 1985—89, Quinnipiac Coll., 1986—92, Housatonic CC, Bridgeport, Conn., 2002; lectr., cons. in field. Contbr. articles to profl. jours. Youth leader, deacon Union Meml. Ch., Stamford, Conn., 1980-88; deacon Southport Congl. Ch., 1992-94; chair consumer com. Alzheimer's Coalition of Conn., 1991-92. Teaching fellow NYU, 1983-86. Mem. AAAS, P.E.O., World Fedn. Occupl. Therapy, Am. Occupl. Therapy Assn. (scholar 1985, coun. edn.), Conn. Occupl. Therapy Assn. (gerontology liaison 1980-83), Am. Bd. Disability Analysts, NY Acad. Scis., Grange, Pi Lambda Theta. Avocations: poetry writing, quilting. Home: 198 Glenbrook Rd Bridgeport CT 06610-1149

MACDONALD, KEN CRAIG, geophysicist; b. San Francisco, Oct. 14, 1947; m. Rachel Haymon, 1984. BS in Engring. Geoscis., U. Calif., Berkeley, 1970; PhD in Marine Geophysics, MIT/Woods Hole, 1975. Cecil H. and Ida Green postdoctoral scholar Scripps Instn. of Oceanography, 1975-76, asst. rsch. geophysicist, lectr., 1976-80; assoc. prof. U. Calif., Santa Barbara, 1980-83, prof., 1983—. Chief scientist on over 30 deep sea expeditions; prin. ALVIN diver on over 40 dives to the mid-ocean ridge. Assoc. editor Jour. of Geophys. Rsch., 1979-82, Earth and Planetary Sci. Letters, 1978-88; mem. editorial bd. Marine Sci. Revs., 1986—; editor Marine Geophys. Rschs., 1986-90; contbr. over 100 articles to profl. jours. Mem. ALVIN Rev. Com., 1979-82; mem. Ocean Sci. Bd. of NAS, 1980-83, Lithosphere Panel Advanced Ocean Drilling Project, 1983-85, Ocean Scis. Panel, NSF, 1984-86, COSOD II planning com.; mem. various RIDGE coms., RIDGE steering com., 1987-90; mem. NSF Ocean Scis. Strategic Plan for Rsch. and Edn. Com., 1993-94, U.S. Geodynamics Comm., 1997—. Regents scholar U. Calif., Berkeley, 1966-70, Mineral Tech. scholar, 1967-70, Cecil H. and Ida Green scholar Inst. Geophysics and Planetary Physics/U. Calif., San Diego, 1975-76; NSF Grad. fellow, 1970-73;recipient AAAS Newcomb-Cleveland prize, 1980, Robert L. and Bettie P. Cody prize and medal Scripps Instn. Oceanography, 1994; named U. Hawaii SOEST Disting. lectr., 1990. Fellow Am. Geophys. Union, Geol. Soc. Am.; mem. Phi Beta Kappa, Sigma Psi. Avocations: windsurfing, fly fishing. Office: U Calif Santa Barbara Dept Geol Sci Santa Barbara CA 93106 E-mail: macdonald@geol.ucsb.edu.

MACDONALD, KENNETH R., JR., author, artist; b. N.Y.C., Apr. 14, 1944; s. Kenneth R. and Wilma Christine (Lange) M. BA, Lehigh U., 1967; MA, W.Va. U., 1970, PhD, 1976. Instr. W.Va. U., Morgantown, 1980-81. Author: The Destiny of Man, 1978, The Gods, 1993, The Palace of Time: The Proof of God and Immortality, 1999, Henry Lange: Master Painter, 2001; exhbns. include Art's Alive (fifty Vt. artists) Festival of Fine Art, Burlington, 2003; commd. portraits KMacD Art, 2003—. Home and Studio: PO Box 1027 Middlebury VT 05753-5027

MACDONALD, KIRK STEWART, lawyer; b. Glendale, Calif., Oct. 24, 1948; s. Bruce Mace and Phyllis Jeanne MacDonald. BSCE, U. So. Calif., 1970; JD, Western State U., 1982. Bar: Calif. 1982, U.S. Dist. Ct. (cen. dist.) Calif. 1982, U.S. Ct. Appeals (9th cir.) 1982, U.S. Dist. Ct. (no. dist.) Calif. 1984, U.S. Dist. Ct. (so. dist.) Calif. 1985, U.S. Dist. Ct. (ea. dist.) Calif. 1987. Dist. engr. Pacific Clay Products, Corona, Calif., 1971-76, Nat. Clay Pipe Inst., La Mirada, Calif., 1976-82; ptnr. Gill and Baldwin, Glendale, Calif., 1982—. Mem. ABA, L.A. County Bar Assn., Water Environ. Assn., Calif. Water Environ. Assn. Avocations: travel, woodworking. Office: Gill & Baldwin Ste 405 130 N Brand Blvd Glendale CA 91203-2646 E-mail: kirk@gillandbaldwin.com.

MACDONALD, LAURIE, film company executive; m. Walter Parks, prodr., 1983; 2 children. BA in English Lit., Sonoma State U., Calif. Documentary and news prodr. K-RON, NBC affiliate, San Francisco; creative exec. Columbia Pictures, 1984—85, v.p. prodn., 1985—88; head Aerial Pictures, 1988—94; exec. prodr. Amblin Entertainment, 1994—; co-head motion pictures divsn. DreamWorks Pictures, 1994—. Prodr.: (films) Hayseed, 1997, Men in Black, 1997 (nominated Golden Globe best musical or comedy), Men in Black II, 2002, The Ring, 2002; (TV series) SFO; exec. prodr.: (films) How to Make an American Quilt, 1995, The Trigger Effect, 1996, Twister, 1996, The Mask of Zorro, 1998, Gladiator, 2000, The Time Machine, 2002, The Tuxedo, 2002, Catch Me If You Can, 2002. Named one of 100 Most Powerful Women in Hollywood, Hollywood Reporter, 2003; recipient Women in Hollywood Icon award, Premiere Mag., 1999. Office: DreamWorks SKG 100 Flower St Glendale CA 91201 Office Phone: 818-733-7000. Office Fax: 818-695-7574.*

MACDONALD, LELAND LLOYD, lawyer; b. Marfa, Tex., July 19, 1931; s. John Edward and Nannye Myrtle (Barnett) M.; m. Juanice L. Koen, Nov. 22, 1958; children: David Allen, Kathryn Ann. BBA, Baylor U., 1952, LLB, 1957. Bar: Tex. 1957, U.S. Dist. Ct. (we. dist.) Tex. 1960, U.S. Ct. Appeals (5th cir.). Title analyst Shell Oil Co., Midland, Tex., 1957—60; pvt. practice Midland, 1960—64; ptnr. Kerr, Fitz-Gerald & Kerr, Midland, 1964—73, Turpin, Smith, Dyer, Saxe & MacDonald, Midland, 1973—2003; pvt. practice, 2004—. Mem. admissions com. Tex. State Bar, 1978—80, grievance com., 1976—78. Past chmn. adv. bd. Salvation Army, 1962—82. Lt. USAF, 1952—54. Fellow: Tex. Bar Found. (life); mem.: Midland County Bar Assn. (pres. 1973—74), Baylor Law Alumni Assn. (bd. dirs. 1980—86), Tex. Assn. Def. Counsel, Tex. State Bar Assn., Midland County Jr. Bar Assn. (pres. 1964—65), Midland Jaycees (v.p. 1960), Green Tree Country Club (bd. dirs. 1983), Rotary (pres. 1972—73), Masons (writer). Baptist. Home: 1515 Community Ln Midland TX 79701-4011 Office: Ste 1310 500 W Texas Midland TX 79701-4289 Office Phone: 432-684-9990.

MAC DONALD, MARGARET CLARK, retired real estate agent; b. Lewiston, Maine, Dec. 20, 1929; d. Arthur Bailey and Blanche (Plummer) Clark; m. John Edward Mac Donald, June 16, 1951 (dec. July 1988); children: Cornelia Ann Roberts (dec.), Edward Clark, Susan Mac Donald Moynahan. BS, Skidmore Coll., 1951. Bus. rep. N.Y. Bell Co., N.Y.C., 1951-52; show room mgr. Bonnie Doone, N.Y.C., 1952-53; interior decorator Susan Wang, N.Y.C., 1953-54; designer Maggie Mac Donald Interiors, Miami, Fla., 1960-64; owner, sec. Atlantic Millwork, Inc., Miami, 1964-88; assoc. realtor Keyes Co. Realtors, Miami, 1995-98. Pres. Homemaker Svc. Dade County, Cmty. Vol. Svc. Bur., 1967-68; pres. Jr. League Miami, Inc., 1969-70, chmn. sustaining mems., 1982; pres. Vis. Nurse Assn. Dade County, Fla., Inc., 1975-77; pres., past treas. Metropolitans, 1983-84; second v.p., spl. events chmn. The Vizcayans, 1984-85; pres. Dade County Nat. Soc. Colonial Dame Am., 1988-89; pres. Colonial Dame of Am. XVII, 1989-90, rec. sec., 1998-99. Mem. Nat. DAR (Biscayne chpt., del. conf. Washington, corr. 1998-99), Daus. Colonial Wars, Founders and Patriots (v.p. 2000). Avocations: reading, tennis. Home: 13480 Wansteadt Pl Bristow VA 20136-5728

MACDONALD, MICHAEL C. consumer products company executive; b. Philadephia, July 5, 1953; BA in Polit. Sci., Rutgers U., 1975. Dist. sales mgr. Xerox Corp., Stamford, Conn., 1977, pres. North Am. solutions group, 2000—, sr. v.p., 2000—. Bd. dirs. Xerox Capital Svcs. Bd. trustees overseers Rutgers U.; mem. US C. of C. Mem.: HealthRite (bd. dirs.), Jimmy V Found. (bd. dirs.). Office: Xerox Corp 800 Long Ridge Rd Stamford CT 06904

MACDONALD, MICHAEL PATRICK, humanities educator; b. Portland, Oreg., July 29, 1945; s. Rodney Franklyn and Virginia Lee (Jackson) MacDonald; m. Carol Wilson Dickerman, May 26, 1979 (div. June 1999). BA, Reed Coll., 1968; MA in English, SUNY, 1970; PhD in History, Stanford U., 1979. Asst. prof. humanities Reed Coll., Portland, 1975—77; from asst. prof. to prof. history U. Wis., Madison, 1977—88; prof. history U. Mich., Ann Arbor, 1988—. Author: Mystical Bedlam: Madness, Anxiety and Healing in 17th Century England, 1981, Sleepless Souls: Suicide in Early Modern England, 1990. Fellow, Guggenheim Found., 1985. Fellow: Royal Hist. Soc.; mem.: Midwest Conf. on British Studies (pres. 1992—94), N.Am. Conf. on British Studies (exec. sec. 1993—95, Love prize 1986). Office: Univ Mich Dept History 1029 Tisch Hall Ann Arbor MI 48109

MACDONALD, PATRICIA GENEVE, theater director; b. Mt. Vernon, Wash., July 10, 1926; d. Malcolm Livingston MacDonald and Anna Geneve Leech. BA, UCLA, 1947. Usher and phone operator So. Calif. Theatre Assn., Los Angeles, 1961—66, asst. house mgr., 1966—71, house mgr., 1971—84, 1984—2000, 2000—01. Recipient Lucy Jordan award, Actors Equity Assn. Mem.: Assn. of Theatrical Press Agents and Mgrs. Avocations: theater, music, animals. Home: 3901 Livingston Dr #304 Long Beach CA 90803

MACDONALD, PURIFICACION O. statistician, researcher; m. Warren MacDonald, Oct. 28, 1942; children: Mark W., Michelle O. Steiner, Melissa A. PhD in Agrl. Econs./Econometrics, Pa. State U., 1972. Sr. planning analyst Pa. State U., University Park, 1980—95; prin. statistician U.S. Postal Svc., 1998—2001; math. statistician Bur. Transp. Stats. U.S. Dept. Transp., Washington, 2001—. Rsch. statistician Md. Dept. of Edn., Balt., 1995—98. Advisor for racial/ethnic diversity Pa. State U., University Park, 1990—95. East West Ctr. fellow, U.S. Govt., 1963—65, Ford Found. fellow, 1967—69. Mem.: Am. Statis. Assn. Achievements include research in multivariate analyses. Avocations: travel, gardening, music, cooking. Office: US Dept Transp Bur Transp Stats 400 7th Street SW Washington DC 20590

MACDONALD, R. FULTON SMITH, venture capitalist, advertising executive, consultant, finance educator; b. Monmouth County, NJ, Dec. 24, 1940; s. James Fleming Smith Macdonald and Jane Macfarlane Barnes Abbott; m. Carol Jean Archer (div.); 1 child, Paige Brubaker Smith; m. Laura Boswell; children: George Dewey Boswell, James Fleming Smith Macdonald II. AB, U. Pa., 1963, MBA, 1969; postgrad. sr. mktg. mgmt., Stanford U., 1979. Systems mgr., mcht. John Wanamaker, Inc., Phila., 1969-74; prin. Booz, Allen & Hamilton, N.Y.C., 1974-79; pres. Irwill Industries, N.Y.C., 1979-82, Internat. Bus. Devel. Corp., N.Y.C., 1982—; chmn. IBEX Mktg. Corp., N.Y.C., 1988—. Adj. prof. grad. Bus. Sch., Columbia U., N.Y.C., 1984-85, Mgmt. Inst. NYU, 1992-98, chmn. globalization adv. bd., 1993-94; pres. Simfer Operational Internat., Inc., N.Y.C., 1984; vice chmn. Neusteter Co., Denver, 1984-85; mng. dir. Stuyvesant Group Internat., Dutch Am. Bus. Advisors, N.Y.C. and Amsterdam, 1987-88; chmn. Am. Bus. Media, Inc., 1989-90, One Ams., Inc., Washington, 1990—; mng. dir. Synoptics Devel. Corp., N.Y.C., 1992—; bd. dirs. C4SI, Inc., Ill., First Fin M&A, Fla., Nisco Sys., Inc., Ga., Data Treasury Inc., NY, Vispron, Inc., Fla., 2002-; vice chmn., dir. CloseOut-Now.com, N.Y., 1999-2001; vice chmn. World Brand Management.com, Jacksonville, Fla., 2000-01; pres., CEO, bd. dirs., Asia Am. Investments.com, Holdings Ltd., N.Y., 2000—; chmn., CEO Casa Caribe Devel. Corp., NY and Dominican Rep., 2002—, www.casacaribe.com. Designer Manpower Mgmt. Concepts computer system, 1972—; author, pub. The IBD Quarterly Report, 1996—; contbr. articles to bus. publs. Capt. inf. U.S. Army, 1963-67, Vietnam. Decorated Bronze Star Mem. Inst. Mgmt. Consultants (cert. mgmt. cons. 1989), Global Econ. Action Inst., Soc. Mayflower Descendants, Soc. Coll. Alumni U. Pa. (pres. 1973-74, bd. mgrs. 1975—), Ripon Soc. (Washington), Penn Club (N.Y.), Princeton Club (N.Y.). Republican. Christian Scientist. Avocation: squash. Home: 40 Central Park S Ph A New York NY 10019-1633 Office: Internat Bus Devel Corp Ste 1700 300 Park Ave New York NY 10022 E-mail: fultonm@aol.com., ibdcorpny@aol.com.

MACDONALD, ROBERT RIGG, JR., retired museum director; b. Pitts., May 11, 1942; s. Robert Rigg and Ruth (Johnson) M.; m. Catherine Ronan, Nov. 27, 1965; children: Matthew, Robert, Catherine. BA, U. Notre Dame, 1964, MA, 1965, U. Pa., 1970. Asst. curator Smithsonian Instn., Washington, 1965; curator Mercer Mus., Doylestown, Pa., 1966-70; dir. New Haven Colony Hist. Soc., 1970-74, La. State Mus., New Orleans, 1974-85; dir., CEO Mus. of City of N.Y., 1985—2002; ret., 2002. Adj. prof. mus. studies NYU, 1989—; mem. Commn. on Mus. for a New Century; bd. dirs. SC Aquarium. *Forty years as an innovative museum executive and consultant designing and managing strategic plans and capital projects advancing the missions of major public and private museums. Created acclaimed national and international exhibitions, award winning educational programs, and noted publications. Raised millions of dollars to support museum operations and capital projects. Held leadership positions in local, national, and international museum associations and published extensively on museum related issues. Recipient of national and international citations for service to the community and the museum profession.* Editor: Editor: New Haven Colony Furniture, 1973, Louisiana Images 1880-1920, 1975, Louisiana Black Heritage, 1977 Louisiana Portraitures, 1979, Louisiana Legal Heritage, 1981, The Sun King: Louis XIV and the New World, On Being Homeless, A Community of Many Worlds: Arab American New Society, 2002; organizer (children's art, photographs) The Day Our World Changed: Children's Art of 9/11, The City Resilient: Photographs by Joel Meyerowitz. Decorated chevalier de l'Ordre des Arts et des Lettres (France), cruz de Caballero de la Orden de Isabel La Catolica (Spain); assoc. fellow Berkeley Coll., Yale U., 1978; Hagley fellow U. Del., 1970-71; Univ. scholar U. Notre Dame, 1964-65 Mem.: Mus. City N.Y. (dir. emeritus 2002—), Am. Assn. Mus. (pres. 1985—88, chmn. ethics task force 1988—91, Disting. Svc. award 2003), Am. Assn. State and Local History (coun.), Century Assn. Roman Catholic. Home: 602 Island Walk East Mount Pleasant SC 29464 Office Phone: 843-670-7440. E-mail: robertrm2@aol.com.

MACDONALD, RONALD FRANCIS, diversified financial services company executive; b. Detroit, July 23, 1946; s. Alfred and Marianne Dorothy (Paddock) MacDonald; m. Harriet Pratt Higgins, Dec. 18, 1982 (div. 1997); children: John Higgins, Peter Brewer. BS, U. Detroit, 1968; MBA, Mich. State U., 1970. V.p. No. Trust Co., Chgo., 1970—84, Bankers Trust Co., NYC, 1984—89; mng. dir. CapMAC Holdings, Inc., NYC, 1989—97, MBIA Ins. Corp., Armonk, NY, 1998—2000, Chubb Fin. Solutions Inc., NYC, 2001—02, FCS Advisors, NYC, 2002—. Mem.: Ins. Industry Planning Forum, NY Athletic Club, Royal Oak Soc. Roman Catholic. Avocations: skiing, running, art history, reading. Home: # 5-E 64 E 94th St New York NY 10128-0773

MACDONALD, SCOTT, real estate company executive; Realtor Gladstone and Assocs., Washington, BartonAschman, Evanston, Ill.; pres., CEO Plaza Properties Am.; exec. v.p., COO Hahn Co.; CEO CenterAmerica Property Trust; pres. New Plan Excel Realty Trust, N.Y., 2002—, COO, 2002—. Office: New Plan Excel Realty Trust 1120 Avenue of the Americas New York NY 10036*

MACDONALD, SHEILA DE MARILLAC, company executive; MBA, Harvard U. Prin. Tex. Transaction Mgmt. Co., Fair Winds Corp., Houston, 1990—. Chpt. 11 trustee, 1997-99; pres., CEO Bristol Resources Corp., 2000. Office Phone: 713-528-7309. E-mail: sheilamacdonald@sbcglobal.net.

MACDONALD, THOMAS COOK, JR., lawyer, mediator; b. Atlanta, Oct. 11, 1929; s. Thomas Cook and Mary (Morgan) MacD.; m. Gay Anne Everiss, June 30, 1956; children: Margaret Anne, Thomas William. BS with high honors, U. Fla., 1951, LLB with high honors, 1953. Bar: Fla. 1953. Practice law, Tampa, Fla., 1953—; mem. firm Shackleford, Farrior, Stallings & Evans, 1953-97; mem. Cook & MacDonald, Tampa, 1997—2002; pvt. practice law Tampa, 2003—. Spl. counsel Gov. of Fla., 1963, U. Fla., 1972-98; del. 5th cir. Jud. Conf., 1970-81; mem. adv. com. U.S. Ct. Appeals (5th cir.), 1975-78, (11th cir.), 1988-93; mem. Fla. Jud. Qualifications Commn., 1983-88, vice chmn., 1987, chmn., 1988, gen. counsel, 1997—; mem. jud. nominating com. Fla. Supreme Ct., 1995-99. Mem. Fla. Student Scholarship and Loan Commn., 1963-67; bd. dirs. Univ. Cmty. Hosp., Tampa, 1968-78, Fla. West Coast Sports Assn., 1965-80, Hall of Fame Bowl (now Outback Bowl) Assn., 1989-93, Jim Walter Corp., 1979-87; mem. Hillsborough County Pub. Edn. Study Commn., 1965; lic. lay eucharistic min. Episcopal Ch., 1961—; chancellor Episcopal Diocese of S.W. Fla., 1990-93, 2000—, ch. atty. for ecclesiastical ct., 1998-2000; bd. dirs. U. Fla. Found., 1978-86, Shands Tchg. Hosp., U. Fla., 1981-95; counsel Tampa Sports Authority, 1983-94. Recipient George Carr award FBA, 1991, Herbert Goldburg award Hillsborough County Bar Assn., 1995. Fellow Am. Coll. Trial Lawyers (chmn. state com. 1990-91), Am. Bar Found., Fla. Bar (chmn. com. profl. ethics 1966-70, bd. govs. 1970-74, bar mem. Supreme Ct. com. on stds. conduct governing judges 1976, Presdl. award of merit 1995); mem. ABA (com. on ethics and prof. responsibility 1970-76), Am. Law Inst. (life), 11th Cir. Hist. Soc. (trustee 1982-95, pres. 1989-95), U. Fla. Nat. Alumni Assn. (pres. 1973), Phi Kappa Phi, Phi Delta Phi, Fla. Blue Key, Kappa Alpha. Episcopalian. Home: 1904 S Holly Ln Tampa FL 33629-7004 Office Phone: 813-254-9871.

MACDOUGAL, GARY EDWARD, corporate director, foundation trustee; b. Chgo., July 3, 1936; s. Thomas William and Lorna Lee (McDougall) MacD.; children: Gary Edward, Michael Scott; m. Charlene Gehm, June 15, 1992. BS in Engring., UCLA, 1958; MBA with distinction, Harvard U., 1962. Cons. McKinsey & Co., L.A., 1963-68, ptnr., 1968-69; chmn. bd., chief exec. officer Mark Controls Corp. (formerly Clayton Mark & Co.), Evanston, Ill., 1969-87; gen. dir. N.Y.C. Ballet, 1993-94; chmn. Gov. Task Force on Human Svcs. Reform State of Ill., 1993-97; chmn. Ill. Rep. Party, 2002. Sr. advisor and asst. campaign mgr. George Bush for Pres., Washington, 1988; chmn. Ill. Rep. Party, 2002; chmn. Bulgarian-Am. Enterprise Fund, Chgo. and Sophia, Bulgaria, 1991-93, bd. dirs., 1991—; apptd. to U.S. Commn. on Effectiveness of UN, 1992-93; bd. dirs. United Parcel Svc. Am., Inc., Atlanta; adv. dir. Saratoga Ptnrs., N.Y.; instr. UCLA, 1969. Author: Make a Difference: How One Man Helped Solve America's Poverty Problem, 2000; contbr. articles to Harvard Bus. Rev., Wall St. Jour., N.Y. Times, Chgo. Tribune, other publs., chpts. to books. Trustee Annie E. Casey Found., UCLA Found., 1973-79, W.T. Grant Found., 1992-94, Russell Sage Found., 1981-91, chair, 1987-90; apptd. by Pres. Bush as pub. del., alt. rep., U.S. Del. UN 44th Gen. Assembly, 1989-90; commr. Sec. Labor's Commn. on Workforce Quality and Productivity, Washington, 1988-89; chmn. Ill. Rep. Party, 2002. Lt. USN, 1958-61. Mem. Coun. Fgn. Rels., Author's Guild, Harvard Club, Kappa Sigma. Episcopalian. Home: 505 N Lake Shore Dr Apt 2711 Chicago IL 60611-3406

MACDOUGALL, SIR DONALD (SIR GEORGE DONALD ALASTAIR MACDOUGALL), economist; b. Glasgow, Scotland, Oct. 26, 1912; s. Daniel Douglas and Beatrice Amy (Miller) MacD.; m. Bridget Christabel Bartrum, 1937 (dissolved 1977); children: John Douglas, Mary Jean; m. Laura Margaret Hall, 1977 (dec. 1995). MA, Oxford U., 1938; LLD (hon.), U. Strathclyde, 1968; LittD (hon.), U. Leeds, 1971; DSc (hon.), U. Aston, 1979. Asst. lectr., then lectr. econs. U. Leeds, 1936-39; with statis. br. Office First Lord

Admiralty, 1939-40, Office Prime Min., 1940-45; ofcl. fellow Wadham Coll. Oxford U., 1945-50, domestic bursar, 1946-48, hon. fellow, 1964—, faculty fellow Nuffield Coll., 1947-50, professorial fellow, 1950-52, ofcl. fellow, 1952-64, first bursar, 1958-64, hon. fellow, 1967—, univ. Nuffield reader internat. econs., 1950-52; hon. fellow Balliol Coll., Oxford U., 1992—. Econ. dir. Orgn. European Econ. Cooperation, Paris, 1948-49; chief adv. statis. br. Office Prime Min., 1951-53; vis. prof. Australian Nat. U., Canberra, 1959, MIT Ctr. Internat. STudies, New Delhi, 1961; econ. dir. Nat. Econ. Devel. Office, 1962-64; mem. Turnover Tax Com., 1963-64; dir. gen. Dept. Econ. Affairs, 1964-68; head govt. econ. svc., chief econ. adv. Treasury, 1969-73; chief econ. adv. Confedn. Brit. Industry, 1973-84. Author: The World Dollar Problem, 1957, The Dollar Problem: A Reappraisal, 1960, Studies in Political Economy, 2 vols., 1975, Don and Mandarin: Memoirs of an Economist, 1987; co-author: Measures for International Economic Stability, 1951, The Fiscal System of Venezuela, 1959; chmn. EEC Report of Study Group on Role of Public Finance in European Integration, 1977; contbr. articles to profl. publs. Decorated Knight, Officer Order Brit. Empire, commdr.; scholar George Webb Medley Jr., 1934, George Webb Medley Sr., 1935. Fellow Brit. Acad.; mem. Coun. Royal Econ. Soc. (pres. 1972-74), Nat. Inst. Econ. and Social Rsch. (chmn. exec. com. 1974-87), Soc. Strategic and Long-Range Planning (pres. 1977-85), Soc. Bus. Eocnomists (v.p. 1978—), Reform Club (London). E-mail: donald.mac@virgin.net.

MACDOUGALL, GORDON PIER, lawyer; b. Bethlehem, Pa., May 31, 1930; s. Curtis Daniel and Elizabeth (Pier) MacD. AB, U. Mich., 1952; postgrad., Columbia U., 1952-55. Bar: Wis. 1955, N.Y. 1958, D.C. 1960. Atty. N.Y. Cen. R.R. Co., N.Y.C., 1957-59; assoc. LaRoe, Winn & Moerman, Washington, 1959-66; pvt. practice, Washington, 1966—. Spl. asst. atty. gen. Commonwealth Pa., Washington, 1971-78; asst. counsel Pa. Pub. Utility Commn., Washington, 1975-80. Named Disting. Hoosier Gov. Edgar D. Whitcomb, Inpls., 1972. Mem. Assn. Transp. Law, Logistics and Policy, Transp. Lawyers Assn., Maritime Adminstrv. Bar Assn., Transp. Research Forum (gen. counsel). Office: 1025 Connecticut Ave NW Ste 410 Washington DC 20036-5423

MACDOUGALL, HARTLAND MOLSON, trust company executive, retired bank executive; b. Montreal, Que., Can., Jan. 28, 1931; s. Hartland Campbell and Dorothy (Molson) MacD.; m. Eve Gordon, Oct. 29, 1954; children: Cynthia, Wendy, Keith, Willa, Tania. Ed., LeRosey, Switzerland, 1947-48, McGill U., 1949-53, Advanced Mgmt. Program, Harvard U., 1976. With Bank Montreal, various locations, 1953-84, dir., 1974, vice chmn., 1981; chmn., dir. Royal Trustco Ltd., Toronto, 1984-93. Dep. chmn. London Ins. Group, Inc., London Life Ins. Co., 1985-97; dep. chmn., dir. Robert T. Jones Jr. Can. Scholarship Found.; dir. Conros Corp. Founding chmn. Heritage Can., St. Michael's Hosp. Found., The Japan Soc.; past chmn. Can.-Japan Bus. Com.; gov., past pres. Coun. Can. Unity; dir. Friends of the Youth Awards Inc., U.S.; past pres. Royal Agrl. Winter Fair; mem. Internat. Coun. Music Ctr. L.A., Can. Sports Hall of Fame; bd. govs. Can. Olympic Found.; sen. Stratford Shakespearean Found.; former chmn. The Duke of Edinburgh Awards Internat. Coun.; v.p., dir. The Macdonald Stewart Found. Decorated Order of Can., comdr. Royal Victorian Order, Order of the Rising Sun, Gold and Silver Star (Japan); recipient Gabrielle Leger medal, 1978. Avocations: golf, gardening, skiing, tennis, farming. Home: 16978 Shaws Creek Rd Belfountain ON Canada L0N 1B0 Office: BCE Place 181 Bay St Ste 300 PO Box 771 Toronto ON Canada M5J 2T3

MACDOUGALL, JOHN DUNCAN, surgeon; b. Indpls., Mar. 4, 1925; s. Duncan Campbell and Beulah Stewart (Ward) MacD.; m. Inga Margaretha Tranberg, Oct. 6, 1951 (div. 1980); children: Duncan Campbell, Stewart Andrew, Eric Matthew, Victoria Suzanne MacDougall Oehmen; m. Barbara Lee Mayse, Nov. 1, 1980; children: Katherine Jane, James William. BS, Ind. U., 1948; MD, Ind. U., Indpl., 1951. Diplomate Am. Bd. Surgery, Am. Bd. Thoracic Surgery. Pvt. practice, Indpls., 1957-93; pres. med. staff St. Francis Hosp., Beech Grove, Ind., 1975, pres. adv. bd., 1993-95, mem. governing bd. trustees, 2003—, chmn. governing bd. trustees, 1995—2003. Chmn. bd. dirs. Med. Assurance of Ind., Indpls., 1987-2000, med. cons., 1993-. Exec. com. dean's coun. Ind. U. Sch. Medicine, Indpls., 1988—, adv. com., 1989-96, pres. dean's coun., 1992-95; mem. Ind. Govs. Task Force on Organ Transplantation, Indpls., 1986-89; pres. Ind. Med. Polit. Action Com., Indpls., 1992-98; bd. dirs. Ind. Med. History Mus., 1989-2000; active Ind. Hist. Soc., Indpls. Mus. Art; pres. Indpls. English Speaking Union, 1997-2001. With U.S. Army, 1943-46, ETO. Decorated Bronze Star medal. Fellow ACS; mem. AMA (del., chmn. Ind. delegation 1994-2003), Ind. State Med. Assn. (pres. 1987-88), Indpls. Med. Soc. (pres. 1978-79), Orgn. State Med. Assn. Pres. (pres. 1994-95), Nat. Med. Vets. Assn. (bd. dirs. 1992—), Am. Legion (comdr. Paul Coble Post # 26 1999-2001), Masons (33d degree), Indpls. Lit. Club, Contemporary Club, Meridian Hills Country Club, Univ. Club Indpls. Republican. Episcopalian. Avocations: woodworking, golf, fishing. Home: 7202 Dean Rd Indianapolis IN 46240-3628 Office: ProAssurance Profl Liability Group Castle Creek VI 5975 Castle Creek Pky North Dr Ste 300 Indianapolis IN 46250 Office Phone: 317-558-2536. E-mail: jmacdougall@proassurance.com.

MACDOUGALL, PETER, lawyer; b. Boston, Sept. 22, 1937; s. Duncan Peck and Hildegard (Moebius) MacD. AB, Harvard U., 1958, LLB, 1963. Assoc. Ropes & Gray, Boston, 1964-73, ptnr., 1973-97, ret., 1997—. Sheldon fellow Harvard U., 1963-64. Mem.: Harvard (Boston). Avocations: concert and opera going, gardening, reading, travel. Home: 1720 Washington St Key West FL 33040-4916 also: 542 River Rd Westport MA 02790-5161 E-mail: pmacdougall@earthlink.net.

MACDOUGALL, PRISCILLA RUTH, lawyer; b. Evanston, Ill., Jan. 20, 1944; d. Curtis Daniel and Genevieve Maurine (Rockwood) MacDougall; m. Lester H. Brownlee, July 5, 1987. BA, Barnard Coll., 1965; grad. with honors, U. Paris, 1967; JD, U. Mich., 1970. Bar: Wis. 1970, Ill. 1970. Asst. atty. gen. State of Wis., 1970-74; instr. Law Sch. and undergrad. campuses U. Wis., 1973-75; staff counsel Wis. Edn. Assn. Council, Madison, 1975—; instr. Columbia Coll., Chgo., 1988—; litigator, writer, speaker, educator women's and children's names and women's rights and employment issues. Mem. ABA, Wis. State Bar (co-founder sect. on individual rights and responsibilities, chairperson, 1973-75, 78-79), Legal Assn. Women Wis. (co-founder). Author: Married Women's Common Law Right to Their Own Surnames, 1972; co-author: Booklet for Women Who Wish to Determine Their Own Names After Marriage, 1974, supplement, 1975; The Right of Women to Name Their Children, 1985; contbr. articles to profl. jours. Home: 502 Engelhart Dr Madison WI 53713-4742 Office: 33 Nob Hill Dr Madison WI 53713-2198 Office Phone: 608-276-7711. E-mail: macdougallp@weac.org.

MACDOUGALL, WILLIAM LOWELL, magazine editor; b. Des Moines, July 24, 1931; s. David Gregory and Elizabeth Jeanette (Dugan) MacD. AB, Willamette U., Salem, Oreg., 1952; M.J. in Journalism (Pulitzer scholar 1953-54), Columbia U., 1953. Reporter Washington Star, 1958-62; corr. Los Angeles Times, 1962-63; asso. editor, then London corr. U.S. News & World Report, 1964-68, asst. mng. editor, 1978-86; mng. editor Artsreview mag. NEA, 1987; pres. Atlantic Media Co., Arlington, Va., 1989—. Author: American Revolutionary: A Biography of General Alexander McDougall, 1977. Served with USAF, 1954-57. Recipient George Washington medal Freedoms Found., 1978, citation U.S. Bicentennial Commn., 1976 Methodist. Office: Mid-Atlantic Media Co 5000 37th St N Arlington VA 22207-1823

MAC DOWELL, ANDIE (ROSE ANDERSON MAC DOWELL), actress; b. Gaffney, S.C., Apr. 21, 1958; m. Paul Qualley (div.); 3 children; m. Rhett Hartzog, 2001. Spokesmodel L'Oreal cosmetics and haircare. Films include: Greystoke, 1984, St. Elmo's Fire, 1985, sex, lies and videotape, 1989, Green Card, 1990, Hudson Hawk, 1991, The Object of Beauty, 1991, The Player, 1992, Ruby, 1992, Groundhog Day, 1993, Luck, Trust and Ketchup, 1994, Short Cuts, 1993, Four Weddings and a Funeral, 1994, Bad Girls, 1994, Unstrung Heroes, 1995, Michael, 1996, Multiplicity, 1996, The End of Violence, 1997, Town and Country, 1998, Shadrack, 1998, The Scalper, 1998, The Muse, 1999, Muppets From Space, 1999, Just the Ticket, 1999, Harrison's Flowers, 2000, Town & Country, 2001, Crush, 2001, Ginostra, 2002; TV movies include The Secret of the Sahara, 1988, Women and Men 2: In Love There Are No Rules, 1991, On the Edge, 2000, Dinner With Friends, 2001, Jo, 2002; prodr. Just the Ticket, 1999; TV guest appearances include Spenser: For Hire, 1985, Clive Anderson All Talk, 1996, Muppets Tonight!, 1997, The Practice, 2003. Office: ICM 8942 Wilshire Blvd Beverly Hills CA 90211-1934

MACDOWELL, RICHARD T. surgeon, educator; b. Albany, N.Y., Jan. 23, 1948; s. Robert L. and Madah (Taylor) M.; m. Geraldin Roberta Goetchis, Aug. 25, 1973 (dec.); children: Shannon T., Katherine F., Jennifer R.; m. Barbara Jean Yanko, Sept. 14, 2002. BS, Rensselaer Poly. Inst., 1968; MD, Albany Med. Coll., 1972. Diplomate Am. Bd. Surgery. Intern Albany Med. Coll., 1972-73, resident in surgery, 1973-76; practice medicine specializing in surgery Albany, 1976—. Mem. faculty Albany Med. Coll., 1972—, assoc. prof., 1980—, pres. Faculty Orgn., 1984-88, chmn. accelerated admissions com. 1982-88; cons. VA Hosp., 1976—, N.Y. State Health Care Consortium, 1983—, St. Peter's Hosp., 1986, vice chmn. med. staff Albany Med. Ctr. Hosp., 1999-2003, chmn. med. staff, 2003—. Contbr. articles to profl. jours. Bd. dirs. Mental Health Assn. Albany, 1978-82; v.p. Eastern N.Y. bd. dirs. Am. Cancer Soc. Fellow ACS (coun. 1983—, field liaison, cancer com. 1986, pres. Upstate chpt. 1994, gov. 1999—); mem. Assn. Acad. Surgeons, Soc. Oncology Edn. Avocations: tennis, skiing, running, diving. Office: 319 S Manning Blvd Albany NY 12208-1742 Office Phone: 518-446-0391.

MACDUFF, ILONE MARGARET, music educator; b. Berwyn, Ill., Jan. 30, 1938; d. Albert Kenneth Hinckle and Dorothy Lydia Ardina Lange; m. James Donald Macduff, Jr., Apr. 2, 1959; children: Gordon Scott, James Alexander, Charles Colin. MusB, U. Idaho, 1976. Internat. rep. Boy Scouts Am., 1983—93; mem. Thurston County (Wash.) Hist. Commrs., 1984—98; active Boy Scouts Am., Tumwater, Wash., 1968—93, dist. Cub Scout program chmn., 1973—75, mem. coun. Pow Wow staff, 1973—76; founder Cub Scout Day Camp, Tumwater Area Coun., 1973; chmn. Coun. Scout-O-Rama, 1979, 1980, 1981; mem. coun. Eagle bd. Boy Scouts Am., 1985—90; dir. monthly musicales State Captial Mus., 1970—74. Recipient Single and Double awards, Nat. Fedn. Music Clubs, 1969, 1977, Silver Beaver award, Boy Scouts Am., 1981, Disting. Commr. award, 1981, Lamb award, 1987. Mem.: Olympia Music Tchrs. Assn. (pres. 2003—04), Music Tchrs. Nat. Assn. (Olympia chpt. voice auditions chair 2001, 2004), Gordon Setter Club Am. (chmn. nat. dog show 2003), Puget Sound Gordon Setter Club (treas. 1998—2000, show chmn. 2003—04). Lutheran. Avocation: photography. Home: 8524 Delphi Rd SW Olympia WA 98512

MACE, ARNETT CLAY, JR., university administrator; b. Hackers Valley, W.Va., Nov. 18, 1937; s. Arnett C. and Ruth L. (Duke) M.; m. Barbara J. Hawks, June 5, 1993; children: Lisa D., Bradley C. BSF, W.Va. U., Morgantown, 1960; MS, U. Ariz., Tucson, 1962, PhD, 1968. Rsch. asst. U. Ariz., Tucson, 1960-62; rsch. forester U.S. Forest Service, Tempe, Ariz., 1962-64; from asst. prof. to prof. U. Minn., St. Paul, 1967-78, head of Forestry Resources and Conservation dept., 1974-78; dir. Sch. Forest Resources and Conservation, U. Fla., Gainesville, 1978-91; dean Daniel B. Warnell Sch. Forest Resources, U. Ga., Athens, 1991—. Cons. Peace Corps., Rabat, Morocco, 1969-71, Winrock Internat., New Delhi, 1987. Recipient Horace T. Morse Award U. Minn. Fellow Soc. Am. Foresters (chmn. accreditation com. 1984—); mem. Am. Geophys. Union, Nat. Assn. Profl. Forestry Schs. and Colls. (nat. research chmn. 1985—), Sigma Xi. Clubs: Heritage (Gainesville). Avocations: golf, bicycling. Office: U Ga Forest Resources Bldg Athens GA 30602

MACE, JERILEE MARIE, opera company executive; BA in Speech Comm. and Mgmt. magna cum l, Simpson Coll., 1991. Mem. adminstrv. staff Des Moines Metro Opera, 1976, dir. mktg., exec. dir., 1988—. Developer OPERA Iowa, Des Moines Metro Opera; cons. various opera cos. On-site evaluator NEA; grad., bd. dirs. Greater Des Moines Leadership Inst.; founding mem. Warren County Leadership Com. Named Iowa Arts Orgn. of Yr., 2000, Employee of Yr., Indianola C. of C., 2004; recipient Outstanding Achiever award, Ft. Dodge C. of C., 1994, Best Kept Secret award for bus. excellence, Greater Des Moines Partnership 2001, Women of Influence award, Des Moines Bus. Record, 2001; fellow exec., OPERA Am., 1993. Office: Des Moines Metro Opera 106 W Boston Ave Indianola IA 50125-1836 E-mail: jerimace@aol.com.

MACE, JOHN WELDON, pediatrician; b. Buena Vista, Va., July 9, 1938; s. John Henry and Gladys Elizabeth (Edwards) M.; m. Janice Mace, Jan. 28, 1962; children: Karin E., John E., James E. BA, Columbia Union Coll., 1960; MD, Loma Linda U., 1964. Diplomate: Am. Bd. Pediatrics, Sub-bd. Pediatric Endocrinology. Intern U.S. Naval Hosp., San Diego, 1964-65, resident in pediatrics, 1966-68; fellow in endocrinology and metabolism U. Colo., 1970-72; asst. prof. pediatrics Loma Linda (Calif.) U. Med. Ctr., 1972-75, prof., chmn. dept., 1975—2003. Med. dir. Loma Linda U. Children's Hosp., 1990-92, physician-in-chief, 1992—2003. Contbr. articles to profl. jours. Treas. Found. for Med. Care San Bernardino County, 1979-80, pres., 1980-82; mem. Congl. Adv. Bd., 1984-87; pres. So. Calif. affiliate Am. Diabetes Assn., 1985-86, dir., 1987-89; chmn. adv. bd. State Calif. Children's Svcs., 1986—; bd. dirs. So. Calif. Children's Cancer Svcs., 1993-94, Loma Linda Ronald McDonald House, 1991—2003, Aetna Health Plans of Calif., 1993-95; bd. dirs. Loma Linda U. Health Care, 1995—2003. Named Alumnist of Yr., Loma Linda U. Sch. Medicine, 1994; recipient Shirley N. Pettis award, 2002, Contrbn. to Medicine award, San Bernardino County Med. Soc., 2003. Mem. AAAS, N.Y. Acad. Sci., Calif. Med. Soc. (adv. panel genetic diseases State Calif., 1975—, chmn. acad. practice forum 1997—), Western Soc. Pediatric Rsch., Lawson Wilkens Pediatric Endocrine Soc., Assn. Med. Pediatric Dept. Chmn., Am. Acad. Pediatrics, Sigma Xi, Alpha Omega Alpha. Office: Loma Linda U Childrens Hosp 11234 Anderson St Loma Linda CA 92354-2870 Office Phone: 909-558-4861.

MACE, STEPHEN ALAN, investment advisor; b. Springfield, Mo., Dec. 30, 1957; s. Leslie Jasper and Virginia Sue (Dunaway) M.; m. Deborah Marie Smith, Dec. 3, 1983; children: Andrew Stephen, Ashley Marie, Alexander Edward. BA, William Jewell Coll., 1979; JD, U. Mo., 1982. Bar: Mo. 1982; CPA, Mo.; CFP; CFA Assn. Investment Mgmt. and Rsch. Tax specialist Coopers & Lybrand, St. Louis, 1982-85; atty. Blumenfeld, Sandweiss, et al, St. Louis, 1985-86; sr. trust officer Boatmen's Nat. Bank, St. Louis, 1986-89; prin. Moneta Group, Inc., St. Louis, 1989-94; v.p., portfolio cons. Templeton Portfolio Adv., Carmel, Calif., 1994-2000; mng. dir., gen. counsel Centurion Alliance, Inc., Carmel, 2000—. Mem. estate planning bd. Make-A-Wish Found., 2004—; mem. Sports Crusaders Bd., 2004—. Mem. Mo. Bar, Bar Assn. Met. St. Louis, Fin. Planning Assn. (nat. bd. dirs., chair audit com. 1993, mem. practitioner adv. coun. 1991-93), Kiwanis Internat. (charter pres. chpt. 1982-83, Disting. Club pres. 1983). Republican. Baptist. Avocations: scuba diving, big-game hunting, fly fishing, skiing, tae kwon do (2d degree black belt).

MACEDO DE LA CONCHA, RAFAEL, attorney general of Mexico; b. Mexico City, May 6, 1950; Grad., Heroic Mil. Coll.; law degree, U. Nacional Autónoma Mex., Mexico City; Dr Degree (hon.), Nat. Inst. Criminal Sci., Mex., 2003. With Mexican Army, advanced through grades to brig. gen.; legal, fiduciary and asst. dir. Nat. Bank of the Army, Air Force and Navy; judge, 1st magistrate Supreme Mil. Ct.; legal coun. fed. exec. br. Govt. of Mex., asst. chief legal counsel Presdl. staff, atty. gen. mil. justice, legal counsel Secretariat Nat. Def., atty. gen., 2000—; prof. various subjects including Mexican positive law, polit., econ. and social problems of Mex., constl. law U. Nacional Autónoma Mex., Lat. Am. U., dir. law program. Rep. of Govt. of Mex. and Secretariat of Nat. Def. regarding arms and drug trafficking U.S. Dept. of State; rep. Secretariat of Nat. Def. before the Jt. Secretariat Com.; pres. drug abuse control commn. CICAD, 2002—03. Decorated great cross Order of Isabella the Cath. Spain, Army 5th, 4th, 3d, 2d and 1st class medals, Army Spl. Class medal; recipient Mil. Tchg. award, Mexican Army, 1992. Office: Office Atty Gen Reforma No 211-213 Cuauhtemoc 06500 Mexico City Mexico

MACER, GEORGE ARMEN, JR., orthopedic hand surgeon; b. Pasadena, Calif., Oct. 17, 1948; s. George A. and Nevart Akullian M.; m. Celeste Angelle Lyons, Mar. 26, 1983; children: Christiana Marilu, Marina Lynn, Emily Sue. BA, U. So. Calif., 1971, MD, 1976. Diplomate Am. Bd. Med. Examiners; diplomate in orthop. surgery and hand surgery Am. Bd. Orthop. Surgery. Intern Meml. Hosp. Med. Ctr., Long Beach, Calif., 1976; resident Orthop. Hosp./U. So. Calif., 1977-81; pvt. practice Long Beach, 1983—; vol. clin. faculty orthops. U. So. Calif., L.A., 1983-89, 90—; cons. hand surgery svc. Rancho Los Amigos Hosp. Downey, 1990—. Cons. Harbor UCLA Med. Ctr., Torrance, 1983—. Joseph Boyes hand fellow, 1982. Mem. AMA, Calif. Med. Assn., Los Angeles County Med. Assn., Calif. Orthop. Assn., Western Orthop. Assn., Am. Soc. for Surgery of Hand, Am. Acad. Orthop. Surgery, So. Calif. Soc. Surgery of Hand (pres. 2004). Republican. Avocations: boating, skiing, scuba diving, carpentry. Office: 3550 Linden Ave Ste 2 Long Beach CA 90807-4577 Office Phone: 562-424-2600. E-mail: macer4337@aol.com.

MACER-STORY, EUGENIA ANN, writer; b. Mpls., Jan. 20, 1945; d. Dan Johnstone and Eugenia Loretta (Andrews) Macer; divorced; 1 child, Ezra Arthur Story. BS in Speech, Northwestern U., 1965; MFA, Columbia U., 1968. Writing instr. Polyarts, Boston, 1970-72; theater instr. Joy of Movement, Boston, 1972-75; artistic dir. Magik Mirror, Salem, Mass., 1975-76, Magick Mirror Comm., 1977—. Author: Congratulations: The UFO Reality, 1978, Angels of Time, 1982, Project Midas, 1986, 2d edit., 2004, Dr. Fu Man Chu Meets the Lonesome Cowboy: Sorcery and the UFO Experience, 1991, 3d edit., 1994, Gypsy Fair, 1991, The Strawberry Man, 1991, Sea Condor/Dusty Sun, 1994, Awakening to the Light-After the Longest Night, 1995, Battles with Dragons: Certain Tales of Political Yoga, 1993, 2d edit., 1994, Legacy of Daedulus, 1995, The Dark Frontier, 1997, Troll and Other Interdimensional Invasions, 1999, Congratulations: The UFO Reality, 2000, Vanishing Questions, 2000, Carrying Thunder, 2002, Crossing Jungle River, 1998, Doing Business in the Adirondacks; True Tales of the Bizarre and Supernatural, 2003, Struck By Green Lightning aka Project Midas, 2004, (poetry book) The Merry Piper's Hollow Hills, 2003; (plays) Fetching the Tree, Archaeological Politics, 1986, Strange Inquiries, Divine Appliance, 1989, The Zig Zag Wall, 1990, The Only Qualified Huntress, 1990, Telephone Taps Written Up for Tabloids, 1991, Wars with Pigeons, 1992, Conquest of the Asteroids, 1993, Commander Galacticon, 1993, Meister Hemmelin, 1994, Six Way Time Play, 1994, Radish, 1996, Setting Up for the World Trade Centaur, 1996, Mister Shooting Star, 1998, Wild Dog Casino, 1999, Magic Mirror Space Installation at 515 Greenwich Street, 1999-2001, The Old Gaffer From Boise (at Gallery 113), 2000, The Redecoration According to Currier (at Gallery 113), 2001, (play) Ars Chronicon Sylvestre (at Theatre for the New City), 2002, Swords of the Equinox, 2003, New Life Expo, New Yorker Hotel, N.Y.C., 2003, Sayeed/Sayeeda, New Yorker Hotel, N.Y.C., 2003, Just 45 Minutes From Paradise, 2004, others; philosophy writer; contbr. articles to profl. jours.; author (poetry): in Woodstock Times, Lamia Ink!, Manhattan Poetry Rev., Sensations, Kore, The Rift mag., Poet's House, Poetry Publ. Showcase, Poetry.com Anthology, 2000, Theatre for the New City Festivals, 1997—, others; feature writer: Newspeak Pubs., 1995, Paranoia Mag., 2002; editor Yankee Oracle Gazette, 1999; personal appearance as profl. clairvoyant (TV documentary) Haunted Houses, 1996, UFO Desk, Sta. WBAI radio shows, 1996-2001, Star People Confs., 1998—; interviewer: Interview and Occult Investigations, Magonia Mag. Online, 1998, Paranoia Mag., 2000, Infinity Factory: exhbn. paintings Barcelona, Spain, 1999, 2000, 02, Magick Mirror Comm. Installation, 1999-2001, 515 Greenwich Gallery, So-Ho, N.Y., 1999, City Art Gallery, Stockholm, 2000, 04, Gam'Art Diffusion, Port Frejus, France, 2003, Kelikian Gallery, Beirut, 2002, 03, Holland Art Fair, The Hague, 2003, BCN Art-Directe Gallery, Barcelona, Spain, 2003. Shubert fellow, 1968. Mem. Am. Soc. Dowsers, Dramatists Guild (spkr., interviewer on radio shows and internet confs.), Theosophical Soc. Democrat. Avocations: swimming, outdoor activities, hiking. Office: Magick Mirror Comm PO Box 741 New York NY 10116-0741 Personal E-mail: MagickMirr@aol.com.

MACEVA, CAROL ANN, accountant; b. Louisville, Dec. 28, 1946; d. A. B. Pearson and Eva Bernice Byerley Pearson; m. Albert William Schneider, Apr. 29, 1967 (div. Dec. 1994); children: Janine, Kathleen, Michael; m. Edward Woodford Brashear, Sept. 13, 1997. Grad., Corydon (Ind.) Ctrl., 1964. Adminstrv. asst. P.I. Burks, Louisville, 1966—67; acctg. clk. Citizen Fidelity, Louisville, 1967—68; sec., bookkeeper Jefferson Med., Louisville, 1979—83; office mgr., head acctg. Melaney Plum, Louisville, 1983—90; office mgr. 21st Century Rehab., Floyds Knobs, Ind., 1990—94; acctg. mgr. asst. Nat. Distributors, Sellersburg, Ind., 1994—. Bookkeeper Jefferson County Juvenile Divsn. Program, Louisville, 1984—90. Mem.: Am. Inst. Profl. Bookkeeper. Office: Nat Distributors 1517 Avco Blvd Sellersburg IN 47172

MACEWAN, NIGEL SAVAGE, merchant banker; b. Balt., Mar. 21, 1933; s. Nigel Savage and Ellen (Wharton) MacE.; children: Alison, Nigel, Pamela, Elizabeth; m. Judith Sperry, Sept. 2, 1995. BA, Yale U., 1955; MBA, Harvard U., 1959. Assoc. Morgan Stanley & Co., N.Y.C., 1959-62, White, Weld & Co., N.Y.C., 1962-63; v.p. R.S. Dickson & Co., Charlotte, N.C., 1963-68; chmn. Fin. Cons. Internat. Ltd., Brussels, 1965-68; successively gen. ptnr., exec. v.p., pres., dir. White, Weld & Co., N.Y.C., 1968-78; sr. v.p., dir. Merrill Lynch, Pierce, Fenner & Smith, N.Y.C., 1978-87; chmn. Merrill Lynch Capital Ptnrs., N.Y.C., 1985-87; pres., CEO Kleinwort Benson, N.Am. Inc., N.Y.C., 1987-93, also bd. dirs. Chmn. Kleinwort Benson North Am., Inc., Kleinworth Benson Holdings, Inc., Alex Brown Kleinwort Benson Realty Advs.; bd. dirs. Kleinwort Benson Group plc, Kleinwort Benson Ltd., 1987-93, Kleinworth Benson Australian Income Fund, 1992-99; adj. prof. bus. adminstrn. NYU, 1973-75. Pres. Tokeneke Tax Dist., Darien, 1978-80, later treas.; bd. dirs. Islesboro (Maine) Health Ctr., 1994—, Sailors Mus. and Lighthouse, Islesboro, 1993-2000; trustee coun. Island Inst., 1997-02; adv. coun. Islesboro Island Trust, 1997-2000, Conservation Law Found., 1998—. Served with USN, 1955-57. Mem. Securities Industry Assn. (chmn. N.Y. group 1975-76), N.Y. Yacht Club, Yale Club N.Y., Wee Burn Country Club, Tokeneke Club, Tarrantine Club (Dark Harbor, Maine), Cruising Club Am., Clyde Cruising Club (Scotland). Republican. Episcopalian. Home: 153 Oenoke Ln New Canaan CT 06840-4518 E-mail: nsmace@msn.com.

MACEY, JONATHAN R. law educator; b. 1955; BA, Harvard U., 1977; JD, Yale U., 1982; PhD (hon.), Stockholm Sch. Econs., 1996. Bar: Ga. 1986. Law clk. to Hon. Henry J. Friendly U.S. Ct. Appeals (2nd cir.), N.Y.C., 1982-83; asst. prof. Emory U., 1983-86, assoc. prof., 1986-87; vis. assoc. prof. U. Va., 1986-87; prof. Cornell U., 1987-90; vis. prof. U. Chgo., fall 1989, prof., 1990-92; J. Dupratt White prof. law Cornell U., Ithaca, NY, 1993—2004; dir. John M. Olin program in law and econs. Cornell U. Law Sch., Ithaca, 1992—2004; vis. prof., spring Harvard, 1999; vis. prof. Yale, 2003—04; prof. Yale U. Law Sch., New Haven, 2004—. Vis. prof. Harvard U., 1999, Bocconi, Milan, 2000. Recipient Paul M. Bator prize Federalist Soc. for Law and Pub. Policy, 1995, D.P. Jacobs prize. Mem. ABA (bus. assn. and corp. gov.), Am. Law Inst., Assn. Am. Law Schs. (com. corp. law), NY Stock Exchange (legal adv. bd.), Nat. Assn. Securties Dealers (economic adv. bd.). Office: Yale U Law Sch 127 Wall St New Haven CT 06511 Office Phone: 203-432-7913.

MACEY, WILLIAM BLACKMORE, oil company executive; b. Buffalo, Aug. 1, 1920; s. Richard Charles and Doris (Bourne) M.; m. Jean Olive Mullins, Oct. 6, 1945; 1 dau., Barbara Jean. BS in Petroleum Engring, N.Mex. Sch. Mines, 1942; D.Engring. (hon.), N.Mex. Inst. Mining and Tech., 1984. Dist. engr. N.Mex. Oil Conservation Commn., 1946-48; dist. supt. Am. Republics Corp., 1948-52; chief engr. N.Mex. Oil Conservation Commn., 1952-54, state geologist, dir., 1954-56; v.p. Internat. Oil & Gas Corp. (and predecessor co., developers mineral properties), Denver, 1956-60, then pres., 1960-67; pres. Nielson Enterprises Inc., oil and gas prodn. and pipelines, livestock ranching, 1967-74; v.p., dir. Y-Tex Corp. (mfr. livestock identification tags), 1972-73; pres. GEN Oil Inc. (oil and gas prodn.), 1972-75, Col. Cody Inn (real estate and golf course devel.), 1970-73; pres., dir. Macey & Mershon Oil, Inc., 1974-93; dir. Juniper Oil and Gas Corp., Denver, 1981-83, Ruidoso (N.Mex.) State Bank Holding Co., 1987—; pres. The Macey Corp., Denver, 1985—. Chmn. Pres.'s N.Mex. Inst. Mines and Tech., 1980-82; mem. adv. bd. U. Ariz. Heart Ctr., 1997—; mem. Pres.'s U. Ariz. Found. Served from 2d lt. to capt. USAAF, 1942-45. Mem.: N.Mex. Oil and Gas Assn. (exec. com. 1949—52, 1960—61), Popejoy & Pres.'s Club (U. N.Mex.), N.Mex.

Jockey Club (bd. dirs. 1985—88, 1991—93, pres. 1993), Ruidoso, Tucson Country Club, Altolakes Golf and Country Club, Skyline Country Club (Tucson) (dir., treas. 1980—82, pres. 1982—83), Garden of the Gods. Episcopalian. Home: 7010 N Javelina Dr Tucson AZ 85718-1850 also: 10153 Masters Dr NE Albuquerque NM 87111-5894 Office: PO Box 2210 Denver CO 80201-2210

MACFARLAND, MIRIAM KATHERINE (MIMI MACFARLAND), writer; b. Trenton, NJ, June 21, 1949; d. James and Merrianne (Collins) MacF.; children: Bridget Lorraine MacFarland, Chloe Merrianne Griffin. Attended, Rutgers U., 1976-78, U. Pa., 1981-83, Oxford U., Eng., 1988; B in Liberal studies with distinction, U. Okla., 2000; MFA, L.I. Univ., 2002. Programmer analyst R&D Computer Sci. Corp., Naval Air Devel. Ctr., Warminster, Pa., 1977-81; programmer analyst NASA Ames Rsch. Ctr., Moffett Field, Calif., 1978; staff writer Aydin Controls, Inc., Ft. Washington, Pa., 1981-82; writer Banc Tec, Inc., Okla. City and Dallas, 1983-95; cons. engr. MCI Comm. Internat., Rye Brook, NY, 1984-86, Western Union Internat., N.Y.C., 1984, RCA Global Comm., Ft. Lee, NJ, 1985; cons. engr., writer Siemens Med. Sys., Iselin, NJ, 1988-98; adj. asst. prof. English and writing Southampton Coll. L.I. Univ., 2001—02. Guest spkr. U. Ctrl. Okla., Edmond, 1994, Americorp Patch project, Okla. City, 1995; mem. dean's student adv. com. U. Okla., 1999-2000. Author plays, journalism, numerous lit. rev.; CONTACT II, Hightimes Mag., The Bloomsbury Rev.; Another Chgo. Mag.; Renovated Lighthouse; author: 14 books, numerous poems; contbr. chpts. to books, articles to profl. jours. Mem. Dem. Nat. Com. L.I. U. fellow in writing, Grad. Acad. Performance award, 2000—02. Mem.: Associated Writing Programs, Southampton Coll. Alumni Assn., Phi Kappa Phi. Home and Office: PO Box 1669 Norman OK 73070-1669 E-mail: mimimac621@aol.com.

MACFARLANE, ALASTAIR IAIN ROBERT, manufacturing executive; b. Sydney, Australia, Mar. 7, 1940; arrived in U.S., 1978; s. Alexander Dunlop and Margaret Elizabeth (Swan) M.; m. Madge McCleary, Sept. 24, 1966, children: Douglas, Dennis, Robert, Jeffrey. B in Econs. with honors, U. Sydney, 1961; MBA, U. Hawaii, 1964; postgrad., Columbia U., 1964; AMP, Harvard U., 1977. Comml. cadet B.H.P. Ltd., Australia, 1958-62; product mgr. H.J. Heinz Co., Pitts., 1965-66, gen. mgr. new products divsn. Melbourne, Australia, 1967-72; ptnr., dir., gen. mgr. Singleton, Palmer & Strauss McAllan Pty. Ltd., Sydney, 1972-73; dir., gen. mgr. successor co. Doyle Dane Bernbach Internat. Inc., Sydney, 1973-77, group sr. v.p. N.Y.C., 1978-84; pres., CEO PowerBase Systems, Inc., 1984-85, Productivity Software Internat. L.P., N.Y.C., 1985-86; divsn. pres., pub. Whittle Comm. L.P., Knoxville, Tenn., 1987-88; chmn., CEO Phyton Techs. Inc., Knoxville, 1988-94; pres., CEO Knox Internat. Corp., Knoxville, 1988-94; chmn., CEO Mich. Bulb Co., Grand Rapids, 1988-94; dir. Univ. of Sydney USA Found., 1994—; chmn., CEO Creative Pub. Internat., Inc., Minnetonka, Minn., 1997-99; sr. v.p. Pleasant Co., Middleton, Wis., 2000-2001; CEO Centric Strategies Internat., Inc., Mpls., 2001—02; sr. v.p. The Middleton Doll Co., Waukesha, Wis., 2002—04; CEO Lee Middleton Original Dolls, Inc., Columbus, Ohio, 2002—04; pres. Biz Coaching & Assocs., LLC, Madison, Wis., 2004—. Chmn., CEO Lansinoh, Labs., Inc., Oak Ridge, Tenn., 1994—96; lectr. Monash U., Melbourne, 1970—71; ind. mgmt. cons., Melbourne, 1970—72. Author papers in field. V.p. Waverley Dist. Cricket Club, 1975-77. East-West Ctr. fellow, 1962-64; Australian Commonwealth scholar, Australian Steel Industry scholar, 1958-61. Fellow Australian Inst. Mgmt. (assoc.); mem. Australian Soc. Accts. (assoc.), Harvard Club N.Y.C., Blackhawk Country Club (Madison). Home: 6219 S Highlands Ave Madison WI 53705 Office: 6219 S Highlands Ave Madison WI 53705 Office Phone: 608-238-7844. Business E-Mail: iainmacfarlane@action-international.com.

MACFARLANE, JOHN ALEXANDER, former federal housing agency administrator; b. Winnipeg, Man., Can., Sept. 6, 1916; s. John MacKay and Annie Catherine (Smith) MacF.; m. Gladys Valda Church, Dec. 20, 1941; children: John Lane, Elizabeth Ann, Janet Christine. BA with honours, U. Man., Winnipeg, 1939. With stats. br. Wartime Prices and Trade Bd., Ottawa, Ont., Can., 1940-46; supr. stats. dept. Cn. Mortgage and Housing Corp., Ottawa, 1946-65, asst. dir. econs. and stats. div., 1965-69, asst. dir. secretariat div., 1969-78; ret., 1978; treas. Caribbean and N.Am. area coun. World Alliance Ref. Chs., 1984—2002. Treas. Ottawa Valley Cricket Coun., 1946-70, 73-80, pres., 1970-73, 83-88; moderator Presbytery of Ottawa, Presbyn. Ch. Can., 1994-96, rep. elder, 1961-97. Recipient Long Svc. medal Boy Scouts Assn., 1945, Centennial medal Govt. of Can., 1967, spl. achievement award for amateur sport Govt. of Ont., 1991. Mem. Def. Cricket Club (sec.-treas. 1944-46, pres. 1951-76, 78-92). Avocation: stamp collecting/philately. Address: 1216 Foxborough Private Ottawa ON Canada K1J 1E2 E-mail: jamacf@sympatico.ca. *I have touched many people as the years have passed; if I have helped one for the better I shall rest content.*

MACFARLANE, JOHN CHARLES, utility company executive; b. Hallock, Minn., Nov. 8, 1939; s. Ernest Edward and Mary Bell (Yates) MacF.; m. Eunice Darlene Axvig, Apr. 13, 1963; children: Charles, James, William. BSEE, U. N.D., 1961. Staff engr. Otter Tail Power Co., Fergus Falls, Mn., 1961-64, div. engr. Jamestown, N.D., 1964-71, div. mgr. Langdon, N.D., 1972-78, v.p. planning and control Fergus Falls, 1978-80, exec. v.p., 1981-82, pres. and chief exec. officer, 1982—, also bd. dirs., now chmn. Bd. dirs. Wells Fargo, Fergus Falls, Pioneer Mut. Ins. Co. Pres. Langdon City Commn., 1974-78; chmn. Fergus Falls Port Authority, 1985-86; bd. dirs. Minn. Assn. Commerce and Industry, Minn. Safety Coun., Edison Electric Inst., Village Family Svcs., Fargo; bd. dirs. U. N.D. Energy Rsch. Adv. Coun. Served with U.S. Army, 1962-64. Mem. Am. Mgmt. Assn., IEEE (chmn. Red River chpt.), U. N.D. Alumni Assn., Fergus Falls C. of C. Lodges: Rotary, Masons. Republican. Presbyterian. Office: Otter Tail Power Co 215 S Cascade St Fergus Falls MN 56537-2897

MACGHEE, DAVID F. retired military officer, air transportation executive; BS, USAF Acad., 1970; grad., Squadron Officer Sch., 1975, Air Command and Staff Coll., 1980; MS, Vanderbilt U., 1981; MS in Strategic and Tactical Scis., Air Force Inst. Tech., 1983; grad., Air War Coll., 1985, Nat. War Coll., 1991. Commd. 2d lt. USAF, 1970, advanced through grades to maj. gen., 2001; air staff officer Tactical Forces Divsn., Directorate Plans Hdqs. USAF, Washington, 1983-85; aide-de-camp to chief of staff Supreme Hdqs. Allied Powers Europe, Mons, Belgium, 1985-86; chief of safety 20th Tactical Fighter Wing RAF, Upper Heyford, Eng., 1987-88, comdr. 77th Tactical Fighter Squadron, 1988-90; asst. dep. comdr. for ops. 20th Tactical Fighter Wing, Upper Heyford, Eng., 1990; chief strategy and policy divsn. Directorate Plans & Policy US Cen. Command, MacDill AFB, Fla., 1990-92; exec. officer to chief of staff Hdqs. USAF, Washington, 1992-94; comdr. 48th Fighter Wing, RAF, Lakenheath, Eng., 1994-96; inspector gen. Hdqs. Air Combat Command, Langley AFB, Va., 1996-98, dir. air and space ops., 1998-2000; comdt., Air War Coll., vice comdr. Air U., Maxwell AFB, Ala., 2000—01; comdr. (ret.) Air Force Doctrine Ctr., Maxwell AFB, Ala., 2001—04; sr. v.p. flight ops. NetJets, Inc., Columbus, Ohio, 2004—. Decorated Disting. Svc. medal, Legion of Merit with oak leaf cluster, Def. Meritorious Svc. medal with 2 oak leaf clusters. Office: SVP Flight Ops NetJets Inc. 4111 Bridgeway Ave Columbus OH 43219-1882*

MACGILLIVRAY, LOIS ANN, organization executive; b. Phila., July 8, 1937; d. Alexander and Mary Ethel (Crosby) MacG. BA in History, Holy Names Coll., 1966; MA in Sociology, U. N.C., 1971, PhD in Sociology, 1973. Joined Sisters of Holy Names of Jesus and Mary, 1955. Research asst. U. N.C., Chapel Hill, 1969-70, 71-72, instr. sociology, 1970-71; sociologist Rsch. Triangle Inst., Durham, N.C., 1973-75, sr. sociologist, 1975-81; dir. Ctr. for Population and Urban-Rural Studies, Research Triangle Inst., Durham, 1976-81; pres. Holy Names Coll., Oakland, Calif., 1982-92, mem. steering com. Symposium for Bus. Leaders, 1982-92; prin. owner Svc. Orgns.: Planning and Evaluation, Chapel Hill, 1994—. Vis. scholar dept. sociology U. N.C., Chapel Hill, 1992-94; mem. policy bd. U. Oakland Met. Forum, co-convenor panel on edn. and youth. Bd. dirs. Oakland Coun. Econ. Devel., 1984-86; bd. dirs. Bay Area Biosci. Ctr., 1990-92, mem. adv. com., 1992-94. Mem. Am. Sociol. Assn., Assn. Ind. Calif. Colls. and Univs. (exec. com. 1985-92, vice chmn. 1989-92), Regional Assn. East Bay Colls. and Univs. (past pres., bd. dirs. 1982-92). Avocation: birding. Home and Office: 101 N Hamilton Rd Chapel Hill NC 27517-5627

MACGINITIE, WALTER HAROLD, psychologist, educator; b. Carmel, Calif., Aug. 14, 1928; s. George Eber and Nettie Lorene (Murray) MacG.; m. Ruth Olive Kilpatrick, Sept. 2, 1950; children: Mary Catherine, Laura Anne. BA, UCLA, 1949; A.M., Stanford U., 1950; PhD, Columbia U., 1960. Tchr. Long Beach (Calif.) Unified Sch. Dist., 1950, 1955-56; mem. faculty Columbia U. Tchrs. Coll., 1959-80, prof. psychology and edn., 1970-80; Lansdowne scholar, prof. edn. U. Victoria, B.C., Can., 1980-84. Research assoc. Lexington Sch. Deaf, N.Y.C., 1963-69; mem. sci. adv. bd. Ctr. for Study of Reading, 1977-80, chmn. 1979-80. Co-author: Gates-MacGinitie Reading Tests, 1965, 78, 89, 2000, Psychological Foundations of Education, 1968; Editor: Assessment Problems in Reading, 1972; co-editor: Verbal Behavior of the Deaf Child, 1969. Life mem. Calif. PTA. Served with USAF, 1950-54. Fellow APA, AAAS, Am. Psychol. Soc., Nat. Conf. on Rsch. on Language and Literacy, N.Y. Acad. Scis.; mem. Internat. Reading Assn. (pres. 1976-77, Spl. Svc. award 1981), Reading Hall of Fame (pres. 1989-90). Home and Office: PO Box 1789 Friday Harbor WA 98250-1789

MACGOWAN, EUGENIA, lawyer; b. Turlock, Calif., Aug. 4, 1928; d. William Ray and Mary Bolling (Gilbert) Kern; m. Gordon Scott Millar, Jan. 2, 1970 (dec. Jan. 1997); 1 dau., Heather Mary. AB, U. Calif., Berkeley, 1950; JD, U. Calif., San Francisco, 1953. Bar: Calif. 1953; cert. family law specialist Calif. State Bar Bd. Legal Specialization. Research atty. Supreme Ct. Calif., 1954, Calif. Ct. Appeals, 1955; partner firm MacGowan & MacGowan, Calif., 1956-68; pvt. practice, San Francisco, 1968-99. Bd. dirs. San Francisco Speech and Hearing Center, San Francisco Legal Aid Soc., J.A.C.K.I.E. Mem. Am., Calif., San Francisco bar assns., Queen's Bench. Clubs: San Francisco Lawyers, Forest Hill Garden. Office: 236 W Portal Ave San Francisco CA 94127-1423

MACGOWAN, SANDRA FIRELLI, publishing executive, publishing educator; b. Phila., Nov. 9, 1951; d. William Firelli and Barbara (Gimbel) Kapalcik. BS in Biology, BA in English, Pa. State U., 1973, MA in English Lit., 1978. Cert. supervisory analyst N.Y. Stock Exchange. Editor McGraw-Hill Pub. Co., N.Y.C., 1979-81; sr. acquisitions editor Harcourt Brace Jovanovich, Inc., N.Y.C., 1981-82; sr. editor The Coll. Bd., N.Y.C., 1982-88; v.p., head editorial CS First Boston Corp., N.Y.C., 1988-94; v.p. supervisory analyst internat. rsch. SBC Warburg, N.Y.C., 1994-96; v.p., supervisory analyst internat. rsch. Arnhold and S. Bleichroeder, N.Y.C., 1996—2003; sr. v.p. Natexis Bleichroeder Inc. (formerly Arnhold and S. Bleichroeder), N.Y.C., 2003—, mgr. Rsch. Dept., 2003—. Part time assoc. prof. pub. NYU Sch. Continuing Edn., N.Y.C., 1985—. Author: 50 College Admission Directors Speak to Parents, 1988. Democrat. Avocations: art, reading, travel. Office: Natexis Bleichroeder Fl 44 1345 Avenue Of The Americas New York NY 10105-4300 Office Phone: 212-698-3219.

MACGRAW, ALI, actress; b. Pound Ridge, N.Y., Apr. 1, 1939; m. Robert Evans, 1970 (div.); 1 child, Joshua; m. Steve McQueen, 1973 (div.). Ed., Wellesley Coll. Former editorial asst. Harper's Bazaar Mag.; former asst. to photographer Melvin Sokolsky. Actress in films including Goodbye, Columbus, 1969, Love Story, 1971, The Getaway, 1973, Convoy, 1978, Players, 1979, Just Tell Me What You Want, 1979, Natural Causes, 1994, Glam, 2001; TV mini-series The Winds of War, 1983, China Rose, 1983, Dynasty, 1985, Falcon Crest; TV movies Survive the Savage Sea, 1992, Gunsmoke, The Hollywood Fashion Machine, 1995: the Long Ride, 1993; author: (autobiography) Moving Pictures, 1991. Address: PO Box 284 Tesuque NM 87574-0284

MACGREGOR, DAVID LEE, lawyer; b. Cedar Rapids, Iowa, Sept. 17, 1932; s. John H. and Beulah A. (Morris) MacG.; m. Helen Jean Kolberg, Aug. 7, 1954; children— Scott J., William M., Brian K., Thomas D. BBA, U. Wis., 1954, LL.B., 1956. Assoc. Quarles & Brady and predecessor firms, Milw., 1959-64, ptnr., 1964-99, retired, 1999—. Pres. Nat. Assn. Estate Planning Coun., 1979-80, pres. Milw. chpt. 1972-73; mem. adv. bd. CCH Fin. and Estate Planning, N.Y.C., 1982-87 Mem. State Bar Wis. (chmn. taxation sect. 1977-78), Regency House Condominium Assn. (treas., dir.), Stackner Family Found. Inc. (asst. sec., dir.). Home: 929 N Astor St Unit 1608 Milwaukee WI 53202-3486 Office: Quarles & Brady 411 E Wisconsin Ave Milwaukee WI 53202-4497

MACGREGOR, GEORGE LESCHER, JR., freelance writer; b. Dallas, Sept. 15, 1936; s. George Lescher and Jean (Edge) MacG.; divorced; children: George Lescher III (dec.), Michael Fordtran. BBA, U. Tex., 1958. Asst. cashier First Nat. Bank in Dallas, 1960-64, asst. v.p., 1964-68; v.p. Nat. Bank of Commerce of Dallas, 1968-70, sr. v.p., 1970-73, exec. v.p., 1973-74; pres., chief exec. officer Mountain Banks Ltd., Colorado Springs, 1974-77; chief exec. officer Highfield Fin. (U.S.A.) Ltd., 1978-83; chmn. bd., chief exec. officer, dir. Dominion Nat. Bank, Denver, 1981-84; chmn. bd., chief exec. officer Royal Dominion Ltd., Denver; chmn. bd., chief exec. officer, dir. Market Bank of Denver, 1983-84; vice chmn., dir. Bank of Aurora, Denver, 1983-84; chmn., pres., chief exec. officer Alamosa Bancorp. of Colo., Denver, 1983-84; pres., chief exec. officer Am. Interstate Bancorp., 1984-88; pres. Banco, Inc., 1984-89; sr. mng. ptnr. Scotland Co., Denver, London, 1988-91; free-lance writer, 1992—. Served with M.C. AUS, 1958-60. Mem. Am. Inst. Banking (hon.), Young Pres.'s Orgn., Koon Kreek Club, Broadmoore Golf Club, Oxford Club, Phi Gamma Delta. Anglican Catholic. Home and Office: 1736 Blake St Denver CO 80202-1226 Home Fax: 303-292-9794. Personal E-mail: twotatertotts@aol.com.

MACGREGOR, JAMES GRIERSON, retired civil engineering educator, structural engineering consultant; b. Vegreville, Alta., Can., Feb. 14, 1934; s. James Grierson and Marjorie Annette (Woodside) MacG.; m. Barbara Ann Dawson, Sept. 1, 1956; children: Robert J.G. (dec.), Joan P., David J. BSc, U. Alta., 1956, DSc (hon.), 1999; MS, U. Ill., 1958, PhD, 1960; DEng. (hon.), Lakehead U., 1998. Registered profl. engr., Alta., B.C. Research assoc. U. Ill., Urbana, 1958-60; asst. prof. U. Alta., Edmonton, 1960-63, assoc. prof., 1963-68, prof. civil engring., 1968-85, univ. prof., 1985-93, univ. prof. emeritus, 1993—, chmn. dept. civil engring., 1987-90; pres. Adams and MacGregor Cons. Engrs. Ltd., 1976-81, MKM Engring. Cons., 1981-99. Recipient Gold medal Assn. Profl. Engrs. Alta., 1956, Alta. Achievement award Province of Alta., 1972, G.J. Kaplin rsch. prize U. Alta., 1990. Fellow Can. Acad. Engring., Royal Soc. Can., ASCE (State of Art of Civil Engring. award 1968, 74, Raymond C. Reese rsch. prize 1976, 79, Can.-Am. Civil Engring. Amity award 1979, Norman medal 1983), Am. Concrete Inst. (dir. 1972-75, v.p. 1990-92, pres., 1992-93, hon. mem. 2001, Wason medal, 1972, 99, Raymond C. Reese medal 1972, 87, Delmar L. Bloem disting. service award 1974, J. Kelly award 1986, A. Lindau award 2001, Structural Rsch. award 2004), Can. Soc. Civil Engring. (cert. appreciation 1978, A.B. Sanderson award 1994); mem. Assn. Profl. Engrs. Geologists and Geophysicists Alta. (dir. 1972-75, Centennial award 1986), Reinforced Concrete Rsch. Coun. (A.J. Boase medal 1985), Can. Standards Assn. (Merit award 1991, John Jenkins award 1997), Engring. Inst. Can. (Julian C. Smith medal 1997). E-mail: bjmacgr@dccnet.com.

MACH, MICHAEL J. state agency administrator; BA, U. Wis. - Superior; MA, Grad. Sch. Banking, U. Wis. - Madison; MBA, U. Wis. - Oshkosh. Bank examiner Divsn. Fin. Insts., Oshkosh, Wis., 1971—78, field office supr. La Crosse, Wis., 1978—84, various positions Madison, Wis., adminstr., divsn. banking. Instr. Grad. Sch. Banking, U. Wis., Madison, Wis.; bd. dirs. Am. Coun. State Savings Suprs., Conf. State Bank Suprs. Regulatory Com.; co-chair fin. com. Gov.'s Blue Ribbon Commn. on Year 2000 Preparedness; fin. cons. and speaker. Contbr. articles to profl. jours. Vol. Boy Scouts Am. Office: PO Box 8861 Madison WI 53707-8861

MACH, RUTH, principal; m. Stan Mach; 2 children. Grad., Truman State U., 1958; M, U. Mo.; PhD, St. Louis U. Cert. elem. sch. adminstr., reading specialist, tchr. of learning disabled, tchr. behaviorally disturbed. Tchr. Affton Sch. Dist., Lindbergh Sch. Dist.; elem. sch. prin. Mehlville Sch. Dist.; prin. Meramec Elem. Sch., Clayton, Mo. Bd. dirs. Truman State U. Found.; apptd. bd. govs. Truman State U., 1995—. Mem.: ASCD, St. Louis Suburban Prins. Assn. (past pres., Disting. Prin. award), Conf. on Edn., Mo. Assn. Elem. Sch. Prins. (Disting. Elem. Prin. award), Nat. Assn. Elem. Sch. Prins. Office: Meramec Elem Sch 400 S Meramec Clayton MO 63105

MACHADO, CAROLYN FRANCES, political consultant; b. Providence, Mar. 13, 1967; d. Edward Steven and Patricia Ann Machado; m. Eugene Christopher Ulm, Feb. 14, 1998. BA in Polit. Sci., Boston U., 1990; postgrad., Georgetown U. Legis. rschr. Environ. and Energy Study Inst., Washington, 1988; fin. dir. Rep. Claudine Schneider Senate Campaign, Providence, 1990, Steve Duprey Congl. Campaign, Concord, N.H., 1992, Rep. Bill Zeliff Congl. Campaign, Manchester, N.H., 1992; media dir. Renew Am., Washington, 1991-92; dir. Am. Cons. Engrs./Polit. Action Com. and grassroots programs Am. Cons. Engrs. Coun., Washington, 1992-95; prin., founder Machado & Co., Washington, 1994—; Washington corr. to overseas radio stas. Australia, New Zealand, 1996—. Vol. cons./trainer Internat. Rep. inst., Washington, 1998—, Women's Campaign Fund, Washington, 1997—; mem. polit. adv. bd. Voter.com, Boston, 1999—. Named Rising Star of Politics, Campaigns and Elections mag., 1996. Mem. Am. Assn. Polit. Cons., U.S. House and Senate Press Gallery, New Zealand Nat. Press Club (hon.). Republican. Roman Catholic. Avocations: travel, photography, writing. Office: Machado & Co 6111 Newman Rd Fairfax VA 22030-5918 Fax: 703-266-5873.

MACHASKEE, ALEX, newspaper publishing company executive; b. Warren, Ohio; m. Carol Machaskee. BA in Mktg., Cleve. State U., 1972, LHD (hon.), 1995, U. Akron, 1998. Sports reporter The Warren (Ohio) Tribune; asst. to pub., promo dir. to dir. labor rels. & pers. to v.p., gen. mgr. The Plain Dealer, Cleve., 1985—90, pres., pub., 1990—. V.p. Mus. Arts Assn. (Cleve. Orch.); chmn. United Way Campaign, 2000; mem. bd. governance, fin. and adminstrn. com. Cleve. Found.; bd. dirs. Univ. Cir. Inc., Greater Cleve. Partnership, Cleve. Tomorrow, Gt. Lakes Sci. Mus., Leadership Cleve., Urban League of Greater Cleve., St. Vladimir's Orthodox Theol. Sem., Crime Stoppers of Cuyahoga County; chmn. bd. dirs. United Way Svcs., 2002—03; bd. trustees Cleve. Mus. Art; nat. bd. dirs. IOCC. Named to N.E. Ohio Bus. Hall of Fame, 2001. Mem.: Corp. mem. of the Holden Arboretum, Am. Soc. Newspaper Editors, Newspaper Assn. Am. (mem. labor rels. subcom.). Office: Plain Dealer Pub Co 1801 Superior Ave E Cleveland OH 44114-2198 E-mail: publisher@plaind.com.

MACHEN, JAMES BERNARD, academic administrator; m. Chris; children: Maggie, Michael, Lee. DDS, St. Louis U., 1968; MS, U. Iowa, 1972, PhD in Edn. Psychology, 1974. Prof., assoc. dean U. N.C., 1983-89; pres. Am. Assn. Dental Schs., 1987; dean U. Mich. Sch. Dentistry, 1989-95; provost, exec. v.p. acad. affairs U. Mich., 1995-97; pres. U. Utah, 1998—2003, U. Fla., Gainesville, 2004—. Mem. Inst. Medicine Com. in Future Dental Edn. Nat. Acad. Scis., 1993-95. Office: U Fla Office of the Pres 226 Tigert Hall PO Box 113150 Gainesville FL 32611-3150*

MACHER, FRANK E. automotive executive; b. Detroit, Mar. 1, 1941; BSME, GMI Engring & Mgmt. Inst., Flint, Mich., 1963; MBA, Mich. State U., 1975. Mfg. engr. mgr. Ford Motor Co., Saline, Mich., 1971, prodn. mgr., 1972, mfg. mgr., 1973, mgr. plastics, paint and vinyl div. Saline Plastics and Instrumentation Plant, 1975—. Office: Plastics Paint and Vinyl Div Ford Motor Co 7700 E Michigan Ave Saline MI 48176-1721

MACHIN, BARBARA E. lawyer; b. Kansas City, Mo., Mar. 26, 1947; d. Roger H. and Doris D. (Dunkel) Elliott; m. Peter A. Machin, June 1, 1969; 1 child, Andrew D. BS in Sec. Edn., U. Kans., 1969, MA in Curriculum Devel./Anthropology, 1973; JD, U. Toledo Coll., 1978. Bar: Ohio 1978, U.S. Dist. Ct. (no. dist.) Ohio 1978, U.S. Ct. Appeals (6th cir.) 1981, U.S. Supreme Ct. 1987. Instr. rsch. and writing U. Toledo Coll. of Law, 1978-79; law clerk Lucas County Ct. of Common Pleas, Toledo, 1979-80; assoc., ptnr. Doyle, Lewis & Warner, Toledo, 1980-87; assoc. Shumaker, Loop & Kendrick, Toledo, 1987-92; gen. counsel U. Toledo, 1993—. Pres., v.p., mem. bd. trustees Toledo Legal Aid Soc., 1983-93; pres. Toledo Civil Trial Attys., 1990-93; trustee Esworth Found., 1993-96. Contbr. articles to profl. jours. Mem. house corp. bd. Gamma Phi Beta Sorority, 1985—; mem. bd. trustees Epworth Found., 1993—, St. Luke's Hosp., 1994—. Mem. Ohio State Bar Assn., Toledo Bar Assn., Toledo Women's Bar Assn., Toledo Civil Trial Attys. (pres. 1983-92). Home: 414 Grenelefe Ct Holland OH 43528-9232 Office: U of Toledo Office of the Gen Counsel 3620 University Hall 2801 W Bancroft Toledo OH 43606

MACHINA, MARK JOSEPH, economist; b. Detroit, Oct. 27, 1954; BA in Econs., BA in Math., Mich. State U., 1975; PhD in Econs., MIT, 1979. Asst. prof. econs. U. Calif., San Diego, 1979—84, assoc. prof. econs., 1984—88, prof. econs., 1988—. Vis. prof. econs. Duke U., Durham, NC, 1996; jr. rsch. officer Cambridge U., 1980—81; vis. asst. prof. econs. Princeton (N.J.) U., 1981—82; instr. People's U. China, Beijing, 1987, 90, 91, 93; Kaiser vis. prof. econs. Stanford (Calif.) U., 1999. Assoc. editor: Jour. Econ. Theory, 1983—91, Econometrica, 1984—91, Quarterly Jour. Econs., 1985—91, Jour. Econ. Perspectives, 1987—90, Jour. Econ. Surveys, 1987—91; co-editor: Theory and Decision, 1986—, Jour. Math. Econs., 1999—; founding co-editor: Jour. Risk and Uncertainty, 1988—90; contbr. articles to profl. jours. Trustee U. Calif. San Diego Found., 2001—03. Fellow, Ctr. for Advanced Study in the Behavioral Scis., 1987—88; grantee, NSF, 1983—86, 1992—95, 1998—2001; Grad. fellow, 1975—78, Vis. fellow, Australian Nat. U., Canberra, 1983, Rsch. fellow, Alfred P. Sloan Found., 1984—86, Erskine fellow, U. Canterbury, Christchurch, New Zealand, 1994. Fellow: Econometric Soc., Am. Acad. Arts and Scis.; mem.: Phi Beta Kappa. Office: Univ Calif San Diego 9500 Gilman Dr La Jolla CA 92093-0508 E-mail: mmachina@ucsd.edu.

MACHLE, EDWARD JOHNSTONE, theology educator, retired; b. Canton, China, Sept. 29, 1918; s. Edward Charles and Jean (Mawson) M.; m. Neva Hull, Aug. 29, 1942; children— Stewart, Douglas, Kathi; m. Mary Lou Reynolds, Dec. 15, 1970; 1 child, Michelle; stepchildren— Rebecca, Richard, Harvey, Robin. Student, Pacific Lutheran Jr. Coll., 1937; BA, Whitworth Coll., 1939; B.D., San Francisco Theol. Sem., 1942, MA, 1944; PhD, Columbia U., 1952. Ordained to ministry Presbyn. Ch., 1942; minister Concrete, Wash., 1942-43; asst. minister San Francisco, 1943-44, Mineola, N.Y., 1944-46; instr. Columbia, 1946-47; asst. prof. U. Colo., 1947-53, assoc. prof., 1953-63, prof., 1963-80, emeritus, 1981—, chmn. dept., 1951-52, 56-58, 66-69. Vis. lectr. U. Alta., summer 1960, Iliff Sch. Theology, 1962, Evergreen State, 1981, Peninsula Coll., 1985-86; in-parish research dir. San Francisco Theol. Sem.; dir. music St. Andrew Presbyn. Ch., Boulder, Colo., 1961-70; guest lectr. ch. music U. Colo. Sch. Music, 1950-65; disting. faculty fellow Sheldon Jackson Coll., 1986-88. Author: Nature and Heaven in the Xunzi, 1993. Mem. Am. Phil. Assn., Soc. Asian and Comparative Philosophy, Acad. Religion. Presbyterian. Home: 11 Silver Canyon Place The Woodlands TX 77381 E-mail: machle@wt.net. *Faith is largely willingness to learn of what can destroy us. Idolatry feeds on our fear of having faith. Research methods spring from the soil of our cultured idolatries. Thus, to learn, faith must at times be a traitor to "learning.".*

MACHLEIDT, RUPRECHT, physicist; b. Kiel, Germany, Dec. 18, 1943; came to U.S., 1985; s. Dietrich and Erika (Eber) M.; m. Francesca Sammarruca; children: Dario Alexander, Helga Julia. MS in Physics, U. Bonn, Germany, 1971, PhD in Physics, 1973. Postdoctoral rsch. assoc. U. Bonn, Germany, 1974-75, SUNY, Stony Brook, 1976-77; asst. prof. U. Bonn, Germany, 1978-83; vis. sr. scientist Tri-Univ. Meson Facility, Vancouver, 1983-85; vis. rsch. physicist LAMPF, Los Alamos, N.Mex., 1986-88; adj. assoc. prof. UCLA, 1986-88; assoc. prof. U. Idaho, Moscow, 1988-91, prof. physics, 1991—. Cons. Los Alamos (N.Mex.) Nat. Lab., 1986-88. Author: (chpt. book) The Meson Theory of Nuclear Forces and Nuclear Structure;

contbr. numerous articles to profl. jours. Recipient Fellowship Deutsche Forschungs-Gemeinschaft, 1976-77, 83-85. Fellow Am. Phys. Soc. Achievements include co-development of Bonn Meson-Exchange Model for the Nucleon-Nucleon Interaction; research on nuclear matter theory with subnuclear degrees of freedom and relativity, relativistic few-nucleon physics; chiral symmetry and the nucleon-nucleon interaction. Office: U Idaho Dept Physics Moscow ID 83844

MACHOR, JAMES LAWRENCE, language educator; b. Cleve., Oct. 13, 1950; s. Lawrence Joseph and Helen Machor; m. Nancy Ann Taylor, May 13, 1972; 1 child, Travis James. BA, Ohio U., 1972; MA, U. Idaho, 1974; PhD, U. Ill., 1980. Asst. to assoc. prof. Ohio State U., Lima, 1980—90; assoc. prof. Kans. State U., Manhattan, 1990—95, prof., 1995—. Vis. sr. lectr. U. Brussels, Belgium, 1991; mem. adv. bd. Studies in the Novel, 1994—. Author: Pastoral Cities, 1987; editor: Readers in History, 1993, Reception Study, 2001. Fellow, Fulbright Found., 1991; grantee, NEH, 1986. Mem.: Am. Studies Assn., Modern Lang. Assn. Office: Kans State Univ Dept English Manhattan KS 66506

MACHOVER, CARL, computer graphics consultant; b. Bklyn., Mar. 26, 1927; s. John Herman and Rose (Alter) M.; m. Wilma Doris Simon, June 18, 1950; children: Tod, Julie, Linda. BEE, Rensselaer Poly. Inst., 1951; postgrad., NYU, 1953-56. Mgr. applied engring. Norden div. United A/C Corp., 1951-59; mgr. sales Skiatron Electronics & TV, N.Y.C., 1959-60; v.p. mktg., dir. Info. Displays, Inc., Mount Kisco, N.Y., 1960-73, v.p., gen. mgr., 1973-76; pres. Machover Assocs. Corp., White Plains, N.Y., 1976—. Adj. prof. Rensselaer Poly. Inst.; mem. RPI H&SS adv. bd. Bradford EIMC Indsl. Adv. Bd. Author: Gyro Primer, 1957, Basics of Gyroscopes, 1958; mem. editl. bd., new products editor IEEE Computer Graphics and Applications; mem. editl. bd. Computers and Graphics; editor C4 Handbook, 1989, 2d edit., 1995, The CAD/CAM Handbook, 1996; co-editor Computer Graphics Rev.; co-exec. prodr. The Story of Computer Graphics, 1999; contbr. articles to profl. jours. Mem. adv. bd. Pratt Ctr. for Computer Graphics in Design. With USNR, 1945-46. Named to Computer Graphics Hall of Fame, Fine Arts Mus. of L.I., Hempstead, N.Y., 1988; recipient Frank Oppenheimer award, Am. Soc. Engring. Edn., 1971, Orthagonal award, N.C. State U., 1988, Vanguard award, Nat. Computer Graphics Assn., 1993, Industry Lifetime Achievement award, CAD Soc., 2003. Fellow Soc. for Info. Display (pres. 1968-70), Eurographics Assn.; mem. IEEE, Assn. for Computing Machinery, Am. Inst. Design and Drafting, Soc. Mfg. Engrs., Nat. Computer Graphics Assn. (bd. dir., pres. 1989-90), Computer Graphics Pioneer, Art and Sci. Collaborators Inc. (pres. 1995—), Sigma Xi, Tau Beta Pi, Eta Kappa Nu. Home: 152 Longview Ave White Plains NY 10605-2314 Office: Machover Assocs Corp PO Box 308 152A Longview Ave White Plains NY 10605-2314 E-mail: cmachover@aol.com.

MACHTIGER, HARRIET GORDON, retired psychoanalyst; b. N.Y.C., July 27, 1927; d. Michael J. and Miriam D. (Rand) Gordon; m. Sidney Machtiger, Feb. 7, 1948; children: Avram Coleman, Marcia Gordon, Bennett Rand. BA, Bklyn. Coll., 1947; diploma with distinction, U. London, 1966, PhD, 1974. Cert. psychologist, Pa. Tchr. Phila. Pub. Schs., 1962-64; ednl. therapist Child Guidance Tng. Ctr., London, 1966-68, Sch. Psychol. Svc./Inner London Edn. Authority, 1968-70; therapist Paddington Day Hosp., London, 1970-71, London Ctr. for Psychotherapy, 1971-74, Staunton Clinic U. Pitts., 1974-78; pvt. practice Pitts., 1976-2000; ret., 2000. Pres. C.G. Jung Ctr., Pitts., 1976-81; cons. in field. Active S.W. Pitts. Cmty. Mental Health, 1976-78; dir. Pitts. program Inter-Regional Soc. Jungian Analysts, 1975-85. Recipient Pa. Dept. Edn. award for disting. contributions to advancement in edn., 1962, Social Sci. Rsch. Coun. award, 1973. Mem. Pa. Psychol. Assn., Brit. Psychol. Soc., Brit. Assn. Psychotherapists. Home: 6562 Jog Palm Dr Boynton Beach FL 33437-3925

MACHUCA, CARLOS R. management consultant; b. Santiago, Chile, May 25, 1948; came to U.S., 1969; s. Carlos Enrique Machuca and Maria Luisa Canales; m. Amelia M. Jones, Nov. 2001; children from previous marriage: Jorge, Carlos, Jennifer. BFA magna cum laude, N.Y. Inst. Tech., 1974; MBA in Mktg. and Internat. Bus., NYU, 1981. Lic. ins. agt., real estate agt., securities, N.C.; cert. mgmt. cons. Ptnr. M-Graphic Co., Santiago, 1966-69; exec. v.p. Alexander Proudfoot Co., West Palm Beach, Fla., 1976-96; pres. L.Am. Inst. Mgmt. Resources, Las Vegas, Nev., 1996-98; pres. CRM Internat., LLC, Raleigh, N.C., 1998—, Global Bus. Ptnrs., LLC, Wilmington, Del., 1998-99; fin. cons. Merrill Lynch, Raleigh, 1999—2001; exec. v.p. Prondfoot Cons., West Palm Beach, Fla., 2001—02, Global Bus. Ptnrs., LLC, Wilmington, Del., 2002—. Haskins ptnr. mem. NYU, N.Y.C., 1986—. Author: Completeness Management System, 1998, The Making of a Successful Entrepreneur, 2003; patent publishing Confederate Treasure, 1998. Life mem. Rep. Nat. Com. Mem. Inst. Mgmt. Cons., N.C. Mus. History, Person's House Preservation Assn. Avocations: soccer, camping, history, teaching, travel. Address: 2-2030 Brentwood Blvd Sherwood Park AB Canada T8A 4P6

MACHUGA, THOMAS RICHARD, music educator; b. Oswego, NY, May 5, 1966; s. Richard George Machuga and Gloria Jean Bickel; children: Holly Katelyn, Scott Richard. MusM in edn., Crane Sch. of Music, 1990—93. Profl. Teaching Cert. NY State Edn. Dept., 1991. Instrumental music tchr. Watertown City Sch. Dist., Watertown, NY, 1988—. Mem.: Internat. Trumpet Guild, NY State Band Directors Assn., NY State Sch. Music Assn. Home: 317 Richardson Rd Parish NY 13131 Office: Watertown City Schools Wiley School Washington St Watertown NY 13131 Personal E-mail: tomminny@aol.com.

MACIA, NANETTE, social worker, secondary school educator; b. NYC, Sept. 23, 1950; d. Conrado Macia and Charlotte Jean McCullough; m. Oswald Salcedo, 1970 (div. 1972); 1 child, Ozzy Salcedo. AA, CUNY, 1977; BFA., NYU, 1978; MSW, Yeshiva U., 1997; M in Sch. Adminstrn. and Supervision, Touro Coll., 2003. LCSW NY. Paralegal Queens Dist. Atty., Kew Gardens, NY, 1989—95; ESL instr. York Coll. CUNY, Jamaica, NY, 1989—91, Victim Svcs., Jackson Heights, NY, 1989—91, caseworker, 1996—98; bi-lingual social worker NYC Bd. Edn. Manhattan HS, 1998—. Dir.: (films) Dream at Dawn, 1978. Scholar, NYC Bd. Edn., 1994—97. Mem.: NASW (assoc.), Nat. Assn. U. Women (assoc.), Queens Womens Network (assoc.). Home: 71-20 34th Ave Apt 2B Jackson Heights NY 11372

MACIAS, E. JAMES, utilities executive; BA in Mech. Engring., Calif. Polytech State U., 1976; grad, Harvard U., 1998. Sr. v.p. Pacific Gas & Elec., 1987—2000; sr. v.p. power and indsl. mktg. Calpine Corp., 2001—02, exec. v.p., CEO power and indsl. mktg., 2002, exec. v.p., 2002—. Office: Calpine 50 W San Fernanco St 5th Fl San Jose CA 95113

MACIAS, EDWARD S. chemistry educator, university official and dean; b. Milw., Feb. 21, 1944; s. Arturo C. Macias and Minette (Schwenger) Wiederhold; m. Paula Wiederhold, June 17, 1967; children: Matthew Edward, Julia Katherine. AB, Colgate U., 1966; PhD, MIT, 1970. Asst. prof. Washington U., St. Louis, 1970-76, assoc. prof., 1976-84, prof. chemistry, 1984—, chmn. dept., 1984-88, provost, 1988-95, interim dean Faculty Arts and Scis., 1994-95, exec. vice chancellor and dean Faculty Arts and Scis., 1995—. Cons. Meteorology Rsch., Inc., Altadina, Calif., 1978-81, Salt River Project, Phoenix, 1980-83, Santa Fe Rsch., Bloomington, Minn., 1985-88, AeroVironment, Inc., Monrovia, Calif., 1986-88. Author: Nuclear and Radiochemistry, 1981; editor: Atmospheric Aerosol, 1981; contbr. numerous articles to profl. jours. Bd. dirs. Mark Twain Summer Inst., St. Louis, 1984-87, 88-90, The Coll. Sch., St. Louis, 1984-88, Colgate U., 1997—. Grantee NSF, EPA, Electric Power Rsch. Inst., So. Calif. Edison Co., Dept. Energy, AEC. Mem. Am. Chem. Soc., Am. Assn. Aerosol Rsch. (editorial bd.), Am. Phys. Soc., AAAS. Home: 6907 Waterman Ave Saint Louis MO 63130-4333 Office: Washington U Campus Box 1094 One Brookings Dr Saint Louis MO 63130 Office Phone: 314-935-6800.

MACILVAINE, CHALMERS ACHESON, retired financial executive, former association executive; b. Bklyn., Oct. 25, 1921; s. James Andrew and Helen Marguerite (Acheson) MacI.; m. Elizabeth Jean Babcock, Mar. 26, 1943; children: Judith Anne, Joseph Chad, Martha Elizabeth. AB, Stanford U., 1943. With Kaiser Steel Corp., 1946-73, asst. controller, 1953-62, treas., 1962-70, v.p., 1967-70, v.p. finance and planning, 1970-73; also v.p., dir. subsidiaries; v.p. project financing group Bank of Am., San Francisco, 1973-74, sr. v.p., dep. head Asia div., 1974-77; sr. v.p.-fin. Peabody Coal Co., St. Louis, 1978-80; sr. v.p., dir. Stifel, Nicolaus & Co., Inc., St. Louis, 1980-83; exec. dir. Japan Am. Soc. of St. Louis, 1983-85. Pres. Bamerical Internat. Fin. Corp., 1973-74 Served to lt. (j.g.) USNR, 1943-46. Mem. Phi Beta Kappa, Sigma Chi. Clubs: Tokyo Lawn Tennis, Burns Club of St. Louis. Home: PO Box 99 Friendship ME 04547-0099

MACILWAINE, MARY JARRATT, public relations executive; b. Clifton Forge, Va., Oct. 29, 1942; d. Robert Bell and Mary Louise (Wood) J. BA, Mary Baldwin Coll., Staunton, Va., 1964; cert. bus., Katharine Gibbs Sch., Boston, 1965. Staff asst. com. on agr. U.S. Ho. of Reps., 1975-81; asst. sec. food and consumer services Dept. Agr., 1981-85; v.p. Wampler & Assocs. Inc., Washington, 1985-86; pres. Jarratt & Assocs., Inc., Washington, 1986-90; asst. to pres and CEO Va. Nat. Bank, Charlottesville, 2000—. Editor various legis. reports. Republican. Episcopalian. Home: 1149 Marion Dr Charlottesville VA 22903-4649 E-mail: mmacilwaine@virginianb.com.

MACINNES, DONALD A. automotive executive; CFO Ed Morse Automotive Group, Fort Lauderdale, Fla., until 1999. Office: Ed Morse Automotive Group 6363 NW 6th Way Ste 400 Fort Lauderdale FL 33309-6188

MACINNIS, AL, professional hockey player; b. Inverness, N.S., Can., July 11, 1963; Hockey player Calgary (Can.) Flames, 1981-94, St. Louis Blues, 1994—, Team Canada Olympic Hockey Team, 2002. Recipient Max Kaminsky trophy, 1982-83, Conn Smythe trophy, 1988-89; played in NHL All-Star Game, 1985, 88, 90-92, 94; named to The Sporting News All-Star first team, 1989-90, 90-91, NHL All-Star first team, 1989-90, 90-91, Stanley Cup championship team, 1989, Gold medal, Olympic Games, 2002. Office: care St Louis Blues Kiel Ctr 1401 Clark Ave Saint Louis MO 63103-2700

MACINNIS, FRANK T. construction executive, securities trader, holding company executive; b. Camrose, Alta., Can., Nov. 10, 1946; came to U.S., 1978; s. H. Frank and Adele M. (Irving) MacI.; m. Beverley J. McAndrews, Nov. 3, 1977; children: Christopher, Katrina, Lauren, Robbie. BA, U. Alta., Edmonton, Can., 1968, LLB, 1971. Assoc. Liden, Ackroyd & Co., Edmonton, 1971-75; gen. counsel Banister-Price Internat., Tehran, Iran, 1975-77; dir. Banister-Price Overseas, London, 1977-78; exec. v.p. H.C. Price Co., Bartlesville, Okla., 1978-80; chmn., chief exec. officer H.C. Price Constrn. Co., Dallas, 1980-84; pres. Spie Group, Inc., Dallas, 1984—; exec. v.p. Comstock Group, Inc., Danbury, Conn., 1986—; chmn,pres., ceo Emcor Group Inc, Norwalk, Conn. Mem. exec. com. Spie Batignolles, Paris, 1985—; bd. dirs. The Williams Companies, ITT Industries, Inc. Served to lt. Royal Can. Navy, 1964-68; bd. dirs. Greater New York Chapter of the March of Dimes. Roman Catholic. Avocations: sports, coin collecting/numismatics, music. Office: EMCOR Croup Inc 301 Merritt Seven Corporate Park 6th Fl Norwalk CT 06851-1060 Office Phone: 203-849-7800. Office Fax: 203-849-7900.*

MACIOCE, FRANK MICHAEL, lawyer, financial services company executive; b. N.Y.C., Oct. 3, 1945; s. Frank Michael and Sylvia Maria (Morea) M.; children: Michael Peter, Lauren Decker, Theodore Kenneth; m. Helen Latourette Duffin, July 9, 1988. BS, Purdue U., 1967; JD, Vanderbilt U., 1972. Bar: N.Y. 1973, U.S. Dist. Ct. (so. dist.) N.Y. 1973, U.S. Ct. Appeals (2d cir.) 1975, U.S. Supreme Ct. 1976. Mem. law dept. Merrill Lynch, Pierce, Fenner & Smith Inc., N.Y.C., 1972-80, v.p., 1978-88, 1st v.p., 1988-2000, Merrill Lynch Investment Mgrs., Plainsboro, NJ, 2000—03; councilman-at-large Summit, NJ, 2004—. Mgr. corp. law dept. Merrill Lynch & Co., Inc., N.Y.C., 1980-93, asst. gen. counsel, 1982-2000; gen. counsel investment banking group, 1993-95, ops., svcs. and tech. counsel, 1995-2000, sec. of audit, compensation and nominating coms. bd. dirs., 1978-83, sec. exec. com., 1981-83; mng. dir. Merrill Lynch Overseas Capital, N.V., Netherlands Antilles, 1980-85; sec., dir. Merrill Lynch Employees Fed. Credit Union, N.Y.C., 1978-82; dir. Merrill Lynch Pvt. Capital Inc., N.Y.C., 1981-87, Teleport Comm. Group Inc., N.Y.C., 1987-92, Enhance Fin. Services Inc, N.Y.C., 1988-92; fin. planning adv. bd. Purdue U., 1996-2000. Pres. pro tem City of Summit Common Coun., 2004--; served with U.S. Army, 1969-70. Mem. ABA, Assn. of Bar of City of N.Y. Home: 22 Essex Rd Summit NJ 07901-2802 Personal E-mail: fmacioce@comcast.net.

MACIOCH, JAMES EDWARD, investment consultant, financial planner; b. Cleve., Mar. 30, 1947; Cert. fin. planner, Coll. for Fin. Planning, Denver, 1992; BS, U. Dayton, 1969; MBA, Olivet Nazarene U., 1997. Lic. series 7, Nat. Assn. Securities Dealers. Registered floor broker Mid-Am. Commodity Exch., 1988-90; registered floor broker, mem. Chgo. Bd. Trade, 1990-2000; investment cons. Montano Securities Corp., Chgo., 1993-94, Dickinson & Co., Rosemont, Ill., 1995-96, Rosemont Investment Corp., 1996—. Mem. Fin. Planning Assn. Office: Rosemont Investment Corp 5600 N River Rd Ste 180 Rosemont IL 60018-5184

MACISAAC, JOHN ANTHONY, retired municipal official; b. Albany, N.Y., Feb. 16, 1935; s. Joseph Leonard and Josephine MacIsaac. Grad. high sch., Schenectady, N.Y. Cert. assessor profl., assessor advanced, real estate appraiser, N.Y. Real property appraisal technician trainer dept. assessment City of Schenectady, 1979-81, real property appraisal, 1981-91, sole assessor, 1991-97; ret., 1997-98; town assessor Town of Rotterdam, 1998—2001, ret., 2001. Active Rep. polit. campaign. With U.S. Army, 1957, 61-62. Named on Ronald Reagan Eternal Flame of Freedom, Washington, 1994; represented in Nat. Rep. Victory Monument, Washington, 1995; recipient Rep. Presdl. award, 1994, Rep. Congl. Order of Freedom, 1995, Presdl. Order of Merit, Nat. Rep. Senatorial Com.; inducted into Presdl. Legion of Merit Honor Roll. Mem. Inst. Assessing Officers (cert. profl. assessor), Albany-Schenectady Assessors Assn., N.Y. State Assessors Assn., Schoharie County Hist. Soc. (life), Clan Donald U.S.A. (life), Am. Legion. Avocations: stamps and coins, antiques, gardening, wood walks, acadian genealogy.

MACISAAC, RONALD FRANCES THÉRÈS, lawyer; b. Prince Albert, Sask., Can., Oct. 29, 1925; s. John Francis and Marie (MacNair) M.; children: Carol, Daniel, Elizabeth, Hugh, Melanie, Juliette, Bruce; stepchildren: Frank, Maria, Tara, Brad, Nicola, Peter, Russell, Tami, Monique, Todd, Michelle. LLB, U. Sask., 1948. Bar: B.C. 1949, Grand Cayman Island, 1975. Sr. ptnr. MacIsaac & Mac Isaac, Victoria, B.C., Can., 1949—. Book rev. editor: magazines Verdict, Barrister, Sask Advocate; contbr. articles to profl. jours. Mem. Trial Lawyers Assn., Mediator Assn., Holistic Law Assn. Roman Catholic. Office: MacIsaac 2227 Sooke Rd Victoria BC Canada V9B 1W8 Business E-Mail: ron@macisaacandmacisaac.bc.ca.

MACIUSZKO, KATHLEEN LYNN, librarian, educator; b. Nogales, Ariz., Apr. 8, 1947; d. Thomas and Stephanie (Horowski) Mart; m. Jerzy Janusz Maciuszko, Dec. 11, 1976; 1 child, Christina Aleksandra. BA, Ea. Mich. U., 1969; MLS, Kent State U., 1974; PhD, Case Western Res. U., 1987. Reference libr. Baldwin-Wallace Coll. Libr., Berea, Ohio, 1974-77, dir. Conservatory of Music Libr., 1977-85; dir. bus. info. svcs. Harcourt Brace Jovanovich, Inc., Cleve., 1985-89; staff asst. to exec. dir. Cuyahoga County Pub. Libr., Cleve., 1989-90; dir. Cleve. Area Met. Library System, Beachwood, Ohio, 1990; media specialist Cleve. Pub. Schs., 1991-93, Berea (Ohio) City Sch. Dist., 1993—. Author: OCLC: A Decade of Development, 1967-77, 1984; contbr. articles to profl. jours. Named Plenum Pub. scholar, 1986. Mem. Spl. Librs. Assn. (pres. Cleve. chpt. 1989-90, v.p. 1988-89, editor newsletter 1988-89), Baldwin-Wallace Coll. Faculty Women's Club (pres. 1975), Avocation: music. Office: Midpark HS 7000 Paula Dr Middleburg Heights OH 44130

MACK, ARTHUR NEAL, emergency medicine and family practice physician; b. Abiline, Tex., Dec. 3, 1955; s. Alonzo Vandever and Mary Elizabeth (Milner) M.; m. Teresa Ann Wehrheim, Nov. 29, 1987; children: Aaron Matthew, Andrew Nathan, Abram Daniel, Hannah Michele, Abby Lynn. BS in Biology, Graceland Coll., 1978; MD, U. Ill., 1983. Pvt. practice family medicine Richland Meml. Hosp., Olney, Ill., 1986-90; dir. emergency svcs. Harrisburg (Ill.) Med. Ctr., 1990-91; staff emergency physician St. Mary's Med. Ctr., Evansville, Ind., 1991-94; assoc. dir. Family Practice Residency, Evansville, 1995-96; dir. St. Mary's Med. Ctr., Evansville, 1996-98; clin. asst. prof. of family medicine Ind. U., Evansville, 1995-98; preceptor of family nurse practitioners U. So. Ind., Evansville, 1996-98; dir. TPI Ctr. for Med. Studies, 1996—. Contbr. articles to profl. jours. Mem. Am. Acad. of Family Physicians (grad. nat. inst. for program dir. devel. 1996), Ind. Acad. of Family Physicians. Avocations: God, family, medicine, writing. Office: 119 Oakfield Dr Brandon FL 33594 Home: 5723 Eaglemount cir Lithia FL 33547-3852 E-mail: anmack55@aol.com.

MACK, CHARLES DANIEL, III, labor union executive; b. Oakland, Calif., Apr. 16, 1942; s. Marlene Helen Fagundes, Oct. 15, 1960; children: Tammy, Kelly, Kerry, Shannon. BA, San Francisco State Coll., 1964. Truck driver Garrett Freight Lines, Emeryville, Calif., 1962-66; bus. agt. Teamsters Local No. 70, Oakland, 1966-70, sec.-treas., 1972—. Legis. rep. Calif. Teamsters Pub. Affairs Coun., Sacramento, 1970-71; trustee Western Conf. Teamsters Pension Trust Fund, 1980—, pres. Teamsters' Joint Coun., San Francisco, 1982—, v.p. western region, 1998—; mem. Calif. Inst. for Fed. Policy Rsch., 1993—. Bd. dirs. Econ. Devel. Corp. Oakland, 1980-90, Calif. Compensation Ins. Fund, San Francisco, 1980-86, Calif. Coun. Econ. and Environ. Balance, Calif. Found. on Environ. and the Economy. E-mail: wrvpmack@aol.com., ibt70@aol.com.

MACK, CONNIE, III, (CORNELIUS MACK), former senator; b. Phila., Oct. 29, 1940; s. Cornelius Mack and Susan (Sheppard) McGillicuddy; children: Debra Lynn, Cornelius Harvey. Degree in bus., U. Fla., 1966. Mgmt. tng. Sun Bank, Cape Coral, Fla., 1966-68; v.p. bus. devel. First Nat. Bank, Ft. Myers, 1968-71; sr. v.p., dir. Sun Bank, Cape Coral, Fla., 1971-75; pres., dir. Fla. Nat. Bank, Cape Coral, 1975-82; mem. U.S. Ho. of Reps. from 13th Dist. Fla., Washington, 1983-89; former Senator from Fla U.S. Senate, Washington, 1989-2001; sr. policy advisor Shaw Pittman LLP, Washington, 2001—. Former chmn. joint econ. com.; former mem. com. on fin., com. on banking, housing and urban affairs, former chmn. subcom. on econ. policy; bd. dirs LNR Property Corp. Bd. dirs., chmn. Palmer Drug Abuse Program, Cape Coral; bd. dirs. Cape Coral Hosp. Mem. Exact Scis. Corp. (dir. 2001-), Met. Ft. Myers C. of C., Cape Coral C. of C. Republican. Roman Catholic. Office: Shaw Pittman LLP 2300 N St NW Washington DC 20037

MACK, DENNIS WAYNE, lawyer; b. Chgo., Sept. 11, 1943; s. Walter Andrew and Betty Jane (Klimek) M. BA, Yale U., 1965; JD, Harvard U., 1969. Bar: N.Y. 1970. Assoc. firm Curtis Mallet-Prevost Colt & Mosle, N.Y.C. and Paris, 1969-78; sec., gen. counsel Dominion Textile (USA) Inc., N.Y.C., 1978-91, v.p., 1986-91; pvt. practice N.Y.C., 1991—; gen. counsel Knoa Corp., 2000—02. Alt. rep. Internat. Lesbian and Gay Assn. at ECOSOC of UN, 1994. Mem. dept. fin. Presbytery N.Y., 1978-83. Mem. ABA, N.Y. State Bar Assn., Bar Assn. City N.Y. (spl. com. on AIDS and the law 1996-2001). Home: 180 Riverside Dr New York NY 10024-1021

MACK, EDWARD GIBSON, retired business executive; b. Toronto, Ont., Can., Dec. 4, 1917; s. Edward Gibson and Marion Margaret (Ward) M.; m. Ruth Harriet Davies, Aug. 3, 1940 (dec.); children: Edward Davies Mack (dec. May 2002), Carol Mack Fuller, Susan Mack Vassel; m. Isolde Maderson, Sept. 30, 1978. Grad., Pickering Coll., 1938; student, Syracuse U., 1938-40, U. Pa., 1945-46. Investment analyst trust dept. Syracuse (N.Y.) Trust Co., 1939-43; acct. Hurdman & Cranstoun CPA's, Syracuse, 1943-44; from dist. sales mgr. to dir. mktg. and product research Easy Washing Machine Corp., Syracuse, 1948-55; dir. research Avco Corp., Connersville, Ind., 1955-58; exec. sec. planning and policy bd. Aeronca Mfg. Corp., Middletown, Ohio, 1958-60; pres. E.D.I., State College, Pa., 1960-62; pres., dir. Sherman Indsl. Electronics Inc., Eutectics Inc.; exec. Richards Musical Instruments, Inc., Elkhart, Ind., 1962-65; mgr. supply and distbn. plastic products Union Carbide Ltd., Lindsay, Ont., 1965-68; corp. sec. Dominion Dairies Ltd., Toronto, 1968-73, v.p., sec., 1973-81. Sec., dir. Sealtest (Can.) Ltd., 1968-81 Bd. mgmt. Pickering Coll., 1980-88. Served with U.S. Army, World War II. Mem. Inst. Chartered Secs. and Adminstrs., Can. Inst. Chartered Secs. (assoc.), Pickering Coll. Alumni Assn. (chmn. 1981-86), Am. Legion, Elks, Sigma Chi. Democrat. Home: 217-5 Selby Ranch Rd Sacramento CA 95864-5826

MACK, GREGORY JOHN, financial executive and consultant; b. Buffalo, Oct. 11, 1954; m. Rosemary Lynn Testa, Aug. 17, 1979; children: Lindsey Marie, Stephanie Kaitlyn. BS in Polit. Sci., SUNY, Buffalo, 1978. Cert. tchr., N.Y. Police officer Town of Amherst, N.Y., 1978-81; fin. cons., regional v.p. Cigna Individual Fin. Advisors, Amherst, 1981-94; dir. new bus. devel. Manulife Fin., U.S., Williamsville, N.Y., 1997—. Host radio show Fin. Forum, Sta. WXBX; speaker in field. Host daily radio show Fin. Forum, Sta. WWWS. Mem. Buffalo Life Underwriters Assn., Buffalo C. of C., Gen. Agts. and Mgrs. Assn. (Agt. of Yr. award 1987-92), Cigna's President's Club (life, pres. 1990-91), Cigna's Honor Table (pres. 1987-89), Cigna's Gold Key (chmn. 1988), Cigna's Excalibur (life). Republican. Roman Catholic. Avocations: hockey, golf, tennis, baseball, skiing. Home: 241 Halston Pky East Amherst NY 14051-1856 Office: Manulife Fin 6225 Sheridan Dr Ste 203 Williamsville NY 14221-4800

MACK, J. CURTIS, II, civic organization administrator; b. Los Angeles, Dec. 22, 1944; s. James Curtis and Ahli Christina (Youngren) M.; m. Tamara Jo Kriner, Jan. 23, 1988; children: James Curtis III, Robert Lee, Edward Albert. BA cum laude, U. So. Calif., 1967, M in Pub. Adminstrn., 1969, MA, 1976. Asst. to regional dir. VA, Los Angeles, 1973-79; exec. dir. Citizens for the Republic, Santa Monica, Calif., 1979-85; asst. sec. oceans and atmosphere U.S. Dept. Commerce, Washington, 1985-88; pres. Los Angeles World Affairs Coun., 1988—. Adj. prof. Pepperdine U. Grad. Sch. Pub. Policy, 1999—; bd. dirs. Brentwood Bank of Calif. Mem. Pres.'s Commn. on White House Fellowships, 1984-85; mem. exec. adv. bd. European Union Ctr. Calif. Col. USAFR, 1969-99. Mem. Coun. Fgn. Rels., Nat. Space Club (bd. dirs. 1987-88). Republican. Episcopalian. Avocation: philatelist. Office: LA World Affairs Coun 345 S Figueroa St Ste 313 Los Angeles CA 90071-1002

MACK, JAMES A. health products executive; BSChemE, Mich. Tech. U.; MBMA, Western New Eng. Coll. V.p. Olin Corp., 1985—90; exec. v.p. Oakite Products., Inc., 1982—84; various positions, most recently pres., gen. mgr. chem. divisn. The Sherwin-Williams Co., 1977—81; pres. Cambrex Corp., East Rutherford, NJ, 1990—, CEO, 1995—, chmn. bd., 1999—. Bd. trustees Mich. Tech Alumni Fund. Mem.: Synthetic Organic Chem. Mfg. Assn. (past chmn. bd. govs.). Office: Cambrex Corp 1 Meadowlands Plz East Rutherford NJ 07073 E-mail: communications@cambrex.com.

MACK, JIM, advertising executive; With Frankel & Co., Chgo., 1979-89, pres., 1989-98, pres., CEO, 1998—2002, Chmn., 2002—. Office: Frankel and Co 111 E Wacker Dr Chicago IL 60601-3713

MACK, JOHN EDWARD, III, utility company executive; b. Poughkeepsie, N.Y., Feb. 20, 1934; s. John Edward Jr. and Agnes D. (Albrecht) M.; m. Maureen Whitworth, Sept. 12, 1970; children: John, Todd, Ellen, David. BS, Siena Coll., 1956, MBA, 1966; LHD (hon.), Mt. St. Mary Coll., 1994. With Ctrl. Hudson Gas & Electric Corp., Poughkeepsie, 1958—, v.p. corp. svcs., 1974-76, v.p. customer svcs., 1976-79, exec. v.p., 1979-82, pres., 1982—, CEO, 1986—, also chmn. bd. dirs. Pres. Empire State Electric Energy Rsch. Corp.; bd. dirs. Mid Hudson Med. Ctr.; mem. exec. com. N.Y. Power Pool. Pres. Hudson Valley coun. Boy Scouts Am.; bd. dirs. Astor Home for Children, Rhineback, N.Y., Marist Coll., N.Y. Bus. Devel. Corp. With U.S. Army, 1956-58. Recipient Alexis de Tocqueville Volunteerism award United Way, Poughkeepsie, 1988, Americanism award Anti Defamation League, 1988, Citizenship award Hudson-Del. Boy Scouts, 1987, Disting. Citizen award Dutchess County Boy Scouts Am. Mem. Am. Gas Assn., Edison Electric Inst. (bd. dirs.), Energy Assn. N.Y. State (chmn.). Roman Catholic. Office: Cen Hudson Gas & Electric 284 South Ave Poughkeepsie NY 12601-4838

MACK, JOHN J. diversified financial services company executive; b. Mooresville, NC, 1944; m. Christy King. Grad., Duke U., 1968. Municipal bond trader and salesman Smith Barney; mem. bond dept. Morgan Stanley &

Co., 1972, v.p., 1976—77, principal, 1977, mng. dir., 1979, head Worldwide Taxable Fixed Income Divsn., 1985—92; mem. bd. dirs. Morgan Stanley Group, NYC, 1987-97, chmn. operating com., 1992-97, pres., 1993-97; pres., COO Morgan Stanley Dean Witter & Co., NYC, 1997—2001; CEO Credit Suisse First Boston, 2001—04; co-CEO Credit Suisse Group, NYC, 2003—04. Bd. dirs. Catalyst, Inc., Celiant Corp., Cousins Properties Inc.; bd. exec. NYSE; mem. internat. adv. panel Monetary Authority, Singapore; mem. chmn. adv. com. Nat. Assn. Securities Dealers (NASD); past mem. Beijing's Advisory Coun.; past dir. CICC (first investment bank in China), India Bus. Sch.; past bd. visitors Fuqua Sch. Bus., Duke U. Serves numerous positions of leadership for bus., civic and philanthropic org.; chmn. bd. trustees NY Presbyn. Hosp., U. Hosp. Columbia, Cornell; mem. bd. trustees Duke U.; trustee Doris Duke Charitable Found.; vice chmn. NYC2012; co-founder CJ Mack Found. Recipient Thomas F. Keller Disting. Leadership award, Fuqua Sch. Bus., Duke U., 1998.*

MACK, JUDITH COLE SCHRIM, political scientist, educator; b. Cin., Aug. 9, 1938; d. James Douglas and Cathleen (Cole) Schrim; m. Thomas H. Mack, Jan. 3, 1968; children: Robert Michael, Cathleen Cole. AB with high distinction, U. Ky., 1960; AM, Radcliffe Grad. Sch., 1962; MPhil, Columbia U., 1988, postgrad., 1986—. Tchr. Lexington (Ky.) Sch., 1962-63; instr. Russian Emory U., Atlanta, 1963-64, Kent (Ohio) State U., 1964-65; instr. Hunter Coll., N.Y.C., 1988-90; adj. lectr. Barnard Coll., N.Y.C., spring 1991, 92; instr. Douglass Coll. Rutgers U., New Brunswick, NJ, 1992—93. Rsch. asst. sociology dept. U. Ky., 1961; rsch. asst. Russian and E. European Studies Ctr. UCLA, 1965—67, rsch. asst. Security Studies Ctr., 1967—68, adj. lectr. Hunter Coll., N.Y.C., 1988; presenter in field. Chmn. state pub. affairs com. N.J. Jr. Leagues, 1979—80, bd. dirs. Children's Aide Adoption Soc., Hackensack, NJ, 1979—90, v.p., 1985—90; bd. dirs. Assn. Children N.J., Newark, 1982—, v.p., 1983—88, chair spl. events, 1999; trustee Divsn. Youth and Family Svcs., Trenton, NJ, 1982—91, v.p., 1983—88; others; trustee Dumbarton Ho., Washington; mem. Millburn-ShortHills County Rep. Com., 1994—, corr. sec., 1994—96, chmn., 1996—98. Woodrow Wilson fellow, Radcliffe Coll., 1960—61, Nat. Def. fellow, 1961—62. Mem.: Mortar Bd., Nat. Soc. Colonial Dames Am. (N.J. treas. 1995—2001), Phi Sigma Iota, Phi Beta Kappa. Episcopalian. Avocations: bridge, cooking, ballet, theater, movies. Home: 657C Del Parque Dr Santa Barbara CA 93103

MACK, JULIA COOPER, retired judge; b. Fayetteville, N.C., July 17, 1920; d. Dallas L. and Emily (McKay) Perry; m. Jerry S. Cooper, July 30, 1943; 1 dau., Cheryl; m. Clifford S. Mack, Nov. 21, 1957. BS, Hampton Inst., 1940; LL.B., Howard U., 1951; JD (hon.), U. D.C., 1999. Bar: D.C. 1952. Legal cons. OPS, Washington, 1952-53; atty.-advisor office gen. counsel Gen. Svcs. Adminstrn., Washington, 1953-54; trial appellate atty. criminal div. Dept. Justice, Washington, 1954-68; civil rights atty. Office Gen. Counsel, Equal Employment Opportunity Commn., Washington, 1968-75; assoc. judge Ct. Appeals, Washington, 1975-89; sr. judge DC Ct. of Appeals, Washington, 1989—2001. Mem. Am., Fed., Washington, Nat. Bar Assns., Nat. Assn. Women Judges. Home: 1610 Varnum St NW Washington DC 20011-4206

MACK, KELLY, newscaster; BA magna cum laude, U. Announcer / prodr. "Public Radio in Mississippi", affiliate of Nat. Public Radio, Jackson, Miss., 1984; anchor, reporter WAPT-TV & WLBT-TV, 1985—87; anchor WXIA-TV, Atlanta, 1987—91; gen. assignment reporter, fill-in anchor WNBC-TV, New York, 1993—94; gen. assignment reporter NBC 4, Los Angeles, 1994—97, co-anchor, Channel 4 News at 6pm, 1997—2001, co-anchor, Today in LA, 2001—. Office: NBC4 3000 W Alameda Ave Burbank CA 91523

MACK, MARK PHILIP, chemical company executive; b. Buffalo, Jan. 14, 1950; s. Stanley Joseph and Florence M. (Kopacz) M.; m. Jean Ann Merrick, June 2, 1984; 1 child, Hannah Elizabeth. BS in Chemistry, Buffalo State Coll., 1971; PhD in Chemistry, SUNY, Buffalo, 1976. Rsch. assoc. Duke U., Durham, N.C., 1975-77; rsch. chemist Conoco Inc., Ponca City, Okla., 1977-80, group supr., 1980-81; group leader Conoco/DuPont, Ponca City, 1982-85; sr. supr. DuPont Polymer Products, Wilmington, Del., 1985-89; rsch. mgr. OxyChem, Houston, 1989-90; dir. tech. Occidental Chem. Corp., Houston, 1990-95, Lyondell Petrochem. Co., Houston, 1995-97, v.p. licensing, 1996-97; dir. R&D Equistar Chems., LP, 1997-99, dir. catalyst R&D, analytical chemistry and polymer sci., 1999—2002; chief scientist Lyondell/Equistar, Cin., 2002—. *Invented polymer technology that speeds crude oil transportation through pipelines by reducing turbulence or drag. Material was named " CDR" or "Conoco Drag Reducer" and introduced in 1979 at Pump Station #1, in the Alyeska Pipeline, Prudhoe Bay, Alaska. Brought Nissan process technology to North America in the 80's and modified it to produce plastic containers and flexible packing with step-out performance called "ALATHON" polyethylene. Discovered a class of unique polymerization catalysts at EQUISTAR to produce new polymers and plastic called "STAR" SSC.* Patentee in field; contbr. articles to profl. jours. Mem. Am. Indian Relief Coun.; mem. adv. bd. Black Am. PAC; mem. World Affairs Coun. Greater Cin., Ctr. for Sci. in the Pub. Interest; mem. nat. bd. The Lincoln Inst. Recipient Linus Pauling award SUNY-Buffalo, 1971, Outstanding Student in Chemistry award Western N.Y. Sect. Am. Chem. Soc., 1971, Samuel B. Silbert Fellowship SUNY-Buffalo, 1974-75, Conoco Patent award, 1983, Equistar/Lyondell Inventor award, 2001, St. Labre Indian Sch. Ednl. Assn. award, 2002. Mem. AAAS, Am. Chem. Soc., Soc. Plastics Engrs., N.Y. Acad. Sci., Am. Mgmt. Assn., Product Devel. and Mgmt. Assn., Sierra Club, Nat. Wildlife Fedn., The Wilderness Soc., World Wildlife's Fund's Living Planet Soc., The Humane Soc., The Nature Conservancy, Sigma Xi. Home: 8483 Beckett Pointe Dr West Chester OH 45069-6440 Office Phone: 513-530-4096. Office Fax: 513-530-4267.

MACK, ROBERT E. lawyer; B, Havard U., 1972; JD, Harvard U., 1975. Prin. Smith Alling Lane, P.S., Tacoma. Instr. U. Wash., U. Puget Sound (name now Seattle U.). Office: 1102 Broadway Ste 403 Tacoma WA 98402-3526 Business E-Mail: rmack@smithallinglane.com.

MACK, THOMAS RUSSELL, foundation administrator, management consultant; b. Independence, Iowa, May 22, 1955; s. Russell John and A. Catherine M.; children: Christopher E., Stephen A. BA, Morningside Coll., 1978; MBA, U. S.D., 1988. CEO, dir. Whitestone Found. Rsch., Inc., Sioux City, Iowa, 1981—; tax splst. Commerce Clearing House, 1991-95; v.p., controller Grand Prairie Cos., 1996-98; pres. Greenway-Infinity Internat., Inc., 1998—. Staff instr. Upper Iowa U., 1989-90; vis. prof. Mont. Coll. Mineral Sci. & Tech., 1988-89, auditor, examiner Iowa Dept. Revenue. Bd. dirs. The Exodus Counseling Ctr., Lombard, Ill., 1998—, Iowa Bapt. Mission Inc, West Des Moines, 1998—, Shepherd Ministries, Milo, Iowa, 1981—. Home: 1513 S Rustin St Sioux City IA 51106-2240

MACK, TOM, retired professional football player; b. Cleve., Nov. 1, 1943; Guard L.A. Rams, 1966—78. Named to Pro Football Hall of Fame, 1999. Achievements include Rams No. 1 draft pick, 1966; player 4 NFC championship games; player 3 NFL Pro Bowls; 8 AFC-NFC Pro Bowls; All-Pro 1970, 71, 73, 84; All-NFL, 1969; All-NFC, 1970, 71, 72, 73, 74, 75, 77, 78; All-Am., Mich., 1965; playing in 184 consecutive games; never missed a game in 13-season career. Office: Pro Football Hall of Fame 2121 George Halas Dr NW Canton OH 44708

MACK, VALERIE LIPPOLDT, music educator, performing arts educator, freelance/self-employed choreographer; b. Wichita, Kans., Aug. 30; d. Vaughn Lippoldt and Velma Miller; m. Tom M. Mack, Aug. 7, 1987; children: Stevie, Zane. BA, Bethany Coll., Lindsborg, Kan., 1983; BME, Wichita State Univ., Wichita, Kan., 1987, MME, 1993. Dance instr. Bethany Coll., Lindsberg, Kans., 1981—83; aerobics instr. Mary Mayt Fitness, Wichita, Kans., 1984—86; ballet, tap instr. Kans. Dance Acad., Wichita, Kans., 1986—87; choreographer Wichita State Univ., Wichita, Kans., 1987—95; vocal music H.S. instr. Maize H.S., Maize, Kans., 1986—87; lead vocal and dance instr. Butler C.C., El Dorado, Kans., 1987—. Clinician Emporia State Univ., Emporia, Kans., 1998—2003; producer, bd. mem. Miss Wichita, Miss Butler, Wichita, Kans., 1983—2003; artistic dir. Butler Showchair Showcase, El Dorado, Kans., 1993—2003. Choreographer (plays) 100 Years Of Broadway, Carnegie Hall, 2000, (video) Mary Mayta Fitness for Life, 1986; performer: (video) Mary Mayta Fitness for Life, 1986; contbr.: chpt. Warm-Ups for Choral Directors, 2003. Praise choir, praise team dir. Risen Savior Luth. Ch., Wichita, Kans., 1994—, bells, chimes, Sunday sch., 1994—; prod., bd. mem. Miss Wichita, Wichita, Kans., 1988—2002; bd. mem. Alzheimer Assn., Wichita, Kans., 1995. Mem.: Music Educators Nat. Conf. Republican. Luth. Avocations: dance, travel, Broadway shows. Home: 4104 Plum Tree St Wichita KS 67226 Office: Butler Cmty Coll 901 S Haverhill Rd El Dorado KS 67042

MACKAIG, JANET BROWNLEE, artist, printmaker, educator; b. Santa Monica, Calif., July 16, 1931; d. Roy Edward and Lorna (Feckler) Murphy; m. Richard Allaire Mackaig, Dec. 15, 1950; children: Janet (Mrs. William Chadwick), Steven Richard. AA, Pasadena City Coll., 1964; BA, Calif. State U., Los Angeles, 1969, MA, 1971, postgrad., 1975, UCLA, 1975. Tchr. Creative Arts Group, Sierra Madre, Calif., 1965-75, Duarte (Calif.) Unified Sch. Dist., 1973-76, Otis Art Inst., Los Angeles, 1975-76, Saddleback Coll., Mission Viejo, Calif., 1976-78, Laguna Beach Sch. Art, 1980—. Solo shows at Upstairs Gallery, Claremont, Calif., 1969, U. Oreg., 1976, Fine Arts Gallery, Laguna Beach, Calif., 1981, Minot (N.D.) State Coll., 1981, Merced Coll., Calif., 2000, Mt. San Jacinto Coll., Calif., 2001, L.A. Artcore at Union Ctr., 2002, Maturango Mus., Ridgecrest, Calif., 2003, Mt. San Antonio Coll., Walnut, Calif., 2004; group shows include Colorprint U.S.A., Tex. Tech. U., 1975, U. Ala., 1975, Pioneer Press Traveling Print Show, Africa, 1975-76, Art-A-Multi-Cultural Show, Calif. Mus. Sci. and Industry, 1978, Contemporary Korean Printmakers Assn. Print Show, 1978, Coos Art Mus., Coos Bay, Oreg., 1979, La Grange (Ga.) Coll., 1980, Trenton (N.J.) State Coll., 1980, Internat. Print Biennial, Miami, Fla., 1982, Nat. Printmaking Invitational, San Bernardino, Calif., 1983, Fukuoka Prevecture Mus., 2001, L.A. Artcore, 2000, Angeles Gate Cultural Ctr., San Pedro, Calif.; represented in permanent collections. Bd. dirs. Womanspace. Recipient Calif. Purchase awards Santa Monical Coll., 1973, Calif. State U., Los Angeles, 1976, Calif. Poly. U., Pomona, 1979. Mem. Laguna Beach Art Assn., Calif. Soc. Printmakers, L.A. Printmaking Soc. (pres. 1977-78), L.A. Inst. Contemporary Art, Print Club Phila., Pasadena Artists Concernm Pioneer Press Club. Home: 23821 Salvador Bay Monarch Beach CA 92629-4207

MACKALL, HENRY CLINTON, lawyer; b. Ft. Lauderdale, Fla., Apr. 6, 1927; s. Douglass Sorrel and Mildred (Parker) M.; m. Mary Margaret Sullivan, June 21, 1952 (dec. Dec. 23, 2002); children: Caroline Clark, Nancy Sorrel, Lucy Parker. BA, U. Va., 1950, LLB, 1952. Bar: Va. 1951. Ptnr. Mackall, Mackall & Gibb, P.C. and predecessors, Fairfax, Va., 1952—. Asst. commr. accounts Fairfax County (Va.), 1963—; spl. commr. in chancery for audit functions for Cir. Ct. Fairfax County, 1976—; substitute judge Fairfax County Ct., Juvenile and Domestic Rels. Ct. Fairfax County, 1964-69. Trustee Fairfax Hosp. Assn., 1966-75; with Va. State Bar Client Security Fund Bd., 1976-88, chmn., 1977-78; past bd. dirs. F&M Bank, No. Va. Served with AUS, 1945-46. Fellow Am. Coll. Trusts & Estate Counsel, Am. Coll. Real Estate Lawyers, Va. Law Found.; mem. ABA, Va. Bar Assn. (regional v.p. 1963-64), Fairfax County Bar Assn. (pres. 1966-67), Hist. Soc. Fairfax County (pres. 1970-72), Jamestowne Soc. (gov. 1995-97), River Bend Country Club (Gt. Falls, Va., pres. 1967-68), Georgetown Assembly (Washington). Democrat. Episcopalian. Home: 1032 Towlston Rd Mc Lean VA 22102-1111 Office: 4031 Chain Bridge Rd Fairfax VA 22030-4103 Office Phone: 703-273-0320. E-mail: mackmarhen@aol.com., mackgibb@aol.com.

MACKALL, LAIDLER BOWIE, lawyer; b. Washington, Aug. 8, 1916; s. Laidler and Evelyn (Bowie) M.; m. Nancy M. Taylor, Aug. 28, 1942; children: Nancy Taylor Mackall Lurton (dec.), Christie Beall Mackall Connard, Susan Somervell Mackall Smythe, Bruce Bowie Mackall McConihe; m. Prudence Robertson Colbert, July 26, 1978. AB, Princeton U., 1938; postgrad., Georgetown U., 1938-40, JD, 1947. Bar: D.C. bar 1947, ICC bar 1951, U.S. Supreme Ct. bar 1958. Law clk. to chief judge of predecessor to D.C. Ct. Appeals, 1946-47; assoc. Minor, Gatley & Drury, Washington, 1947-49, Steptoe & Johnson, Washington, 1949-51, ptnr., 1952-86, of counsel, 1986-98. Mem. D.C. Ct. Appeals Com. on Admissions, 1974-78, D.C. Circuit Jud. Conf., 1983, 85, 86; bd. mgrs. Nat. Conf. Bar Examiners, 1974-77 Served to col. USAAF, 1940-46, 51. Decorated Silver Star, 2 D.F.C.s, 5 Air medals, 3 Presdl. unit citations. Fellow Am. Coll. Trial Lawyers (emeritus); mem. ABA (past vice chmn. standing com. aviation ins. law), D.C. Bar, Bar Assn. D.C. (past chmn. com. on negligence, motor vehicle and compensation law), Barristers Club (v.p. 1964), Chevy Chase Country Club, Met. Club (Washington), Hawk's Nest Golf Club of Fla. Episcopalian. Home (Summer): 3809 Village Park Dr Chevy Chase MD 20815-5746 Home: 151 Passage Island Vero Beach FL 32963-4265 E-mail: lbmackall@webtv.net.

MACKAY, A.D. DAVID, food products executive; b. Hamilton, New Zealand, Aug. 16, 1955; m. Michelle Mackay; 2 children. B of Bus., Charles Stuart U., Australia. Group product mgr. Kellogg Australia, 1985—87; category dir. ready-to-eat cereals corp. hdqs. Kellogg, Battle Creek, Mich., 1987—91; mng. dir. Sara Lee Bakery, Australia, 1992—98; mng. dir. Kellogg Australia Kellogg, Battle Creek, 1998, mng. dir. U.K. and Republic of Ireland, 1998—2000, sr. v.p. Kellogg Co., 2000—03, pres. Kellogg USA, 2000—03, exec. v.p. Kellogg Co., 2000—03, pres., COO Kellogg Co., 2003—. Mem.: Biscuit and Cracker Mfrs.' Assn. (mem. exec. com.), Grocery Mfrs. of Am. (mem. industry affairs coun.), Australian Food Coun. (former dir., bd. dirs.), Grocery Mfrs. of Australian (former dir., bd. dirs.). Office: Kellogg PO Box 3599 1 Kellogg Sq Battle Creek MI 49016-3599

MACKAY, ALFRED F. dean, philosophy educator; b. Ocala, Fla., Oct. 1, 1938; s. Kenneth Hood and Julia Horsey (Farnum) MacK.; m. Ann Nadine Wilson, Feb. 4, 1962; children: Douglas Kevin, Robert Wilson. AB, Davidson Coll., 1960; PhD, U. N.C., 1967. Prof. philosophy Oberlin (Ohio) Coll., 1967-84, 96—, dean Coll. Arts and Scis., 1984-95, acting pres., 1991. Vis. asst. prof. philosophy dept. U. Ill., Urbana/Champaign, 1970-71; vis. prof. philosophy dept. Wayne State U., Detroit, 1983. Author: Arrow's Theorem: The Paradox of Social Choice, 1980; editor: Society: Revolution and Reform, 1971, Issues in the Philosophy of Language, 1976. Campaign cons. Buddy MacKay for U.S. Senate, Fla., 1988. 1st lt. U.S. Army, Airborne, 1961-63. Fellow Woodrow Wilson Found., 1963-66, Am. Coun. of Learned Socs., 1973, Humanities fellow Rockefeller Found., 1981. Democrat. Avocations: choral singing, automobiles. Office: Oberlin Coll Dept Philosophy King Bldg Oberlin OH 44074

MACKAY, CHARLES ROBERT, federal official, consultant; b. Waterbury, Conn., Nov. 26, 1935; s. Charles Anselm and Marie Carmella MacKay; m. Maria Giovanna Pillon, Mar. 28, 1967; children: Daniel Brian, Lawrence Frank. STL, St. Mary's Sem. and U., Balt., 1961; MA, U. Notre Dame, South Bend, Ind., 1961; PhD, Urban U., Rome, 1966. Dean Keystone Coll., LaPlume, Pa., 1969—73; exec. dir. Pub. Com. for the Humanities, Lewisburg, Pa., 1973—74; vis. faculty U. Pa., Phila., 1974—75; sr. policy analyst and acting staff dir. President's Biomed. Rsch. Panel, Washington, 1975—76; dep. dir. comm. control of Huntington's disease NIH, Bethesda, Md., 1976—78, dep. dir. office protection from rsch. risks, 1978—90, project clearance officer, 1990—; adj. faculty Georgetown U. Sch. of Medicine, Washington, 1995—. Cons. Uniformed Svcs. U. of Health Scis., Bethesda, 1981—, Nat. Inst. of Neurol. Disorders and Stroke, Bethesda, 1990—, GeneLogic, Inc., Gaithersburg, 1995—, Nat. Inst. of Stds. and Tech., Gaithersburg, 1997—, Nat. Inst. Child Health and Human Devel., Bethesda, 2001—; inaugural keynote spkr. plenary address Internat. Dimensions of Bioethics, 1988; invited lectr. Holroyd Lectr., 1989; Regents lectr. U. Calif., Berkeley, 1988—89; mem. adv. bd. Partnership for Human Rsch. Protection, Washington, 2000—03. Prodr.: (videotape series) Protecting Human Subjects (CINE Golden Eagle award, 1989); contbr. articles to profl. jours. (Nellie Westerman prize Rsch. in Ethics, 1975). Recipient Outstanding Svc. awards, U.S. Dept. Health and Human Svcs., 1975—2003; fellow Biomedical Ethics, NEH, 1974—75. Office: NIH 9000 Rockville Pike Bethesda MD 20892-7974

MACKAY, DAVID B. finance educator; b. Yonkers, N.Y., May 1, 1944; s. Norman A. and Katherine D. MacK.; m. Carole E. Bartlett, Aug. 9, 1945; children: Deborah, Jonathan. BS, Cornell U., Ithaca, NY, 1966; PhD, Northwestern U., Evanston, Ill., 1971. Mktg. educator Ind. U., Bloomington, 1971—. Pres. PROSCAL, Bloomington, 2000—; vis. prof. Norwegian Sch. Econs., Bergen, 1987—88. Mem. adv. com. U.S. Census. Probabilistic Scaling grantee, NSF, 1976—95. Mem.: Psychometric Soc., Assn. Computing Machinery, Am. Statistical Assn., Am. Mktg. Assn. Office: Ind U 1309 E 10th St Bloomington IN 47405 Office Phone: 812 855 1009. Office Fax: 812 855 6440. Business E-Mail: mackay@indiana.edu.

MACKAY, HAROLD HUGH, lawyer; b. Regina, Sask., Can., Aug. 1, 1940; s. John Royden and Grace Madeliene (Irwin) MacK.; m. Jean Elizabeth Hutchison, Dec. 27, 1963; children: Carol, Donald. BA, U. Sask., 1960; LLB, Dalhousie U., Halifax, N.S., 1963; LLD (hon.), U. Regina, 2002. Bar: Sask. 1964, Queen's Counsel 1981. Assoc. MacPherson Leslie & Tyerman, Regina, 1963-69, ptnr., 1969-75, 76—, mng. ptnr., 1989-96, chmn., 1997—2003. Bd. dirs. IMC Global Inc.; chmn. task force Future of the Can. Fin. Svcs. Sector, 1997-98; chair Saskatchewan Inst. Pub. Policy; Clifford Clark vis. economist Dept. of Fin., Gov't. of Canada, 2002-04. Recipient Officer Order of Can., 2002. Mem. Internat. Bar Assn., Can. Bar Assn., Law Soc. Sask. Mem. United Ch. Office: 1500 1874 Scarth St Regina SK Canada S4P 4E9 Office Phone: 306-347-8417.

MACKAY, JAMES ROBERT, psychiatric social worker, mayor, educator, state legislator; b. Medford, Mass., May 8, 1930; s. James Alexander and Julia (MacNaught) MacK. BA, Tufts U., 1952, MA, 1954; MSW, Boston U., 1958; PhD, Union Inst., 1987. Social worker Peter Bent Brigham Hosp., Boston, 1958-60; dir. alcoholism N.H. Dept. Health and Welfare, Concord, 1960-63; dir. cmty. mental health State of N.H., Concord, 1963-64; pvt. practice psychotherapy Concord, 1964-97; exec. dir. Merrimack Valley Assistance Program, Concord, 2002; adj. faculty U. N.H., Durham, 1995—2001; mem. N.H. State Ho. of Reps., 1995—96, 2001—, chmn. com. on legis. adminstrn., clk. com. on health and human svcs. Mem. bd. examiners mental health practice State of N.H., 1995-97; mayor City of Concord, N.H., 1986-88, 90-91; sr. lectr. psychotherapy Franklin Pierce Law Center, Concord, 1978; lectr. U. Conn. Grad. Sch. Social Work, 1981-88; adv. com. City of Concord Airport, 1992—. Contbr. articles on alcoholism, addiction, and juvenile delinquency to profl. jours. Chmn. N.H. Coun. Aging, 1969-83; chmn. Merrimack Valley AIDS Program, 2000-2002, treas., 2003—; pres. N.H. Social Welfare Coun.; chmn. N.H. del. to White House Conf. Aging, 1974, 80; chmn. N.H. Com. Older Am. Act, 1968-69; mem. Concord City Coun., 1980-91; chmn. Concord Pub. Transp. Adv. Bd., 1982-86; del. N.H. Rep. Conv., 1982; del. N.H. Constl. Conv., 1984; chmn. City of Concord Rep. Com.; mem. exec. com. State Rep. Com.; pres. Concord Outright Inc., 2000-02; commr. Christa McAuliffe Planetarium, 2001-. Recipient Ann. award N.H. Social Welfare Coun., 1970, Vaughn award Activities in Aging, N.H., 1974; named Social Worker of Yr., State of N.H., 1997. Mem. NASW (pres. N.H. chpt. 1995-97), AAUP, Nat. League Cities (human devel. policy com. 1986). Office: 139 N State St Concord NH 03301-6414

MACKAY, KENNETH HOOD, JR., (BUDDY MACKAY), federal official; b. Ocala, Fl, Mar. 22, 1933; m. Anne Selph; children: Ken, John, Ben, Andy. BS, BA, U. Fla., 1954, LL.B. with honors, 1961. Bar: Fla. 1961. Mem. Fla. Ho. of Reps. state of Fla., 1968-74; mem. Fla. State Senate, 1974-80; mem. U.S. Ho. Reps. from 6th dist. Fla., 1982-88; lt. gov. State of Fla., 1990-98, gov., 1998-99; spl. envoy for the Americas The White House, Washington, 1999—. With USAF 1955-58. Recipient Nat. Legis. Leadership award, 1976; named Most Valuable Legislator St. Petersburg Times, 7 times; recipient Allen Morris award. Mem. ABA, Kiwanis. Democrat. Office: Office of Spl Envoy for the Americas White House Oeob Rm 176A Washington DC 20502-0001

MACKAY, LEO SIDNEY, JR., federal agency administrator; b. San Antonio, Tex., Aug. 15, 1961; s. Leo Sidney Sr. and Barbara Jean (Hodge) MacK.; m. Heather Lee Deebel, Jan. 9, 1993; children: Sarah Bley, Josiah Edward Earl. BS, U.S. Naval Acad., 1983; M Pub. Policy, J.F. Kennedy Sch. Govt., 1991; PhD, Harvard U., 1993. Commd. ensign USN, 1983, advanced through grades to lt. comdr., 1993; flight student Naval Aviation Tng. Comd., Pensacola, Fla., 1983-85; F-14 fighter pilot U.S. Navy, Virginia Beach, Va., 1985-89; grad./doctoral student Harvard U., Cambridge, Mass., 1989-92; instr. history dept. U.S. Naval Acad., Annapolis, Md., 1992-93; mil. asst. office of sec. of def. Dept. of Def., Washington, 1993-95; ret., 1995; dir. market devel. Lockheed Martin Corp., Bethesda, Md., 1995-97; v.p. bus. devel. and strategic planning Bell Helicopter Textron, Inc., Ft. Worth, 1997—2001; dep. secy. U.S. Dept. Veterans Affairs, Washington, 2001—. Contbr. articles to profl. jours.; article reviewer Internat. Security Jour., Cambridge, Mass., 1991-94. Pres. congregation St. Martin's Luth. Ch., Annapolis, 1996-97. Kennedy fellow J.F. Kennedy Sch. Govt., Cambridge, 1989-90, guest fellow Brookings Inst., Washington, 1992-93, Internat. Affairs fellow Coun. Fgn. Rels., N.Y.C., 1995-96; MacArthur scholar MacArthur Found., Cambridge, 1991-92. Mem. Internat. Inst. Strategic Studies, U.S. Naval Inst., Coun. Fgn. Rels., Arlington C. of C. (bd. dirs.), U.S. Naval Acad. Alumni Assn. (nat. trustee 1995-98), Army and Navy Club. Republican. Lutheran. Avocations: reading, golf. Office: US Dept Veterans Affairs Off of the Secy 810 Vermont Ave NW Washington DC 20420-0001

MACKAY, NEIL DUNCAN, plastics company executive; b. Chelsea, Mass., Nov. 5, 1931; s. Allan Foster and Helen May (Smith) MacKay; m. Marcia Ann McCarthy, Aug. 22, 1953 (dec. 1979); children: Duncan, Jerry, Alan, Neil, Bonnie; m. Beverly J. Burke, May 31, 1991. BS, BA, Northeastern U., Boston, 1954. Gen. mgr. Plastic Molding Corp., Newtown, Conn., 1954-67; market specialist Chem. div. Uniroyal, N.Y.C., 1967-70; project mgr. Colt Ind. Korean Project, N.Y.C., 1970-76; pres. Automatic Injection Molding Corp., Berkeley Heights, NJ, 1976-87, Diamond Mgmt. Cons., Inc., Winchester, NH, 1988—. Bd. dirs. Frazier & Son, Inc., Lor-Tech Plastics, Inc. Author: Korean Plastics, 1973. Mem. Rep. Nat. Com., Washington, 1986—92. Recipient Outstanding Performance award, Ministry Nat. Def. Republic of Korea, 1974. Mem.: Plastic Pioneers Assn., Soc. Plastics Engrs. (sec. 1963—70, treas. 1983—86), Am. Profl. Capt.'s Assn., Scottish-Am. Cultural Soc., Am. Yacht Club, Stuyvesant Yacht Club, St. Andrews Soc. N.Y. Republican. Presbyterian. Avocation: sailing. Home: 19 Lovely Ln Winchester NH 03470-2916 Office: Diamond Mgmt Cons Inc PO Box 40 Winchester NH 03470-0040

MACKAY, RAYMOND ARTHUR, chemist; b. N.Y.C., Oct. 30, 1939; s. Theodore Henry and Helen Marie (Cusack) M.; m. Mary Dilberian, Aug. 13, 1966; 1 child, Chelsea Christine; children by previous marriage: Brett, Edward. BS in Chemistry, Rensselaer Poly. Inst., 1961; PhD in Chemistry, SUNY-Stony Brook, 1966. Rsch. assoc. Brookhaven Nat. Lab., Upton, N.Y., 1966-67; prof. Drexel U., Phila., 1969-83; chief chem. div. Chem. Research and Devel. Ctr., Aberdeen Proving Ground, Md., 1983-91; prof. chemistry, dir. ctr. advanced materials processing Clarkson U., Potsdam, N.Y., 1991—, currently on leave as dir. of Rsch. & Tech., U.S. Army Edgewood Chem. Biological Ctr. Contbr. articles to profl. jours. Served to capt. U.S. Army, 1967-69. Grantee U.S. Army, Dept. Energy, Army Rsch. Office, NSF, Acad. Applied Scis., 1972-83, 95—, NATO, 1982-86, NYSSTF, 1991—. Mem. Am. Chem. Soc., Am. Oil Chemists Soc. (assoc. editor), Sigma Xi. Office: Clarkson U PO Box 5665 Potsdam NY 13699-0001

MACKAY, ROBERT BATTIN, museum director; b. Bklyn., Jan. 24, 1945; s. John French and Helen (Pflug) Mack; m. Anna V.; 1 child, Hale V. BS, Boston U., 1968, PhD in Am. Studies, 1980; MEd, Harvard U., 1972. With Archtl. Heritage, Inc., Boston, 1967-71; dir. Soc. Preservation of L.I. Antiquities, Cold Spring Harbor, NY, 1974—. Chmn. N.Y. State Bd. Hist. Preservation; mem. N.Y. State Coun. Parks, N.Y. State Heritage Areas. Editor: Long Island: An Illustrated History, 2000, AIA Architectural Guide of L.I., L.I. Country Houses and Their Architects, 1997. Treas. St. Giles Found.; v.p. Homeland Found.; adv. Gerry Charitable Trust; trustee Seatuck Enrivon. Assn., I.Y.R.S. Mem. N.Y. Yacht Club (chmn. fine arts com.). Home: 59 Midland St Cold Spring Harbor NY 11724-1805 Office: Soc Preservation of LI Antiquities PO Box 148 Cold Spring Harbor NY 11724-0148

MACKAY, WILLIAM ANDREW, judge; b. Halifax, N.S., Can., Mar. 20, 1929; s. Robert Alexander and Mary Kathleen (Junkin) MacK.; m. Alexa Eaton Wright, July 7, 1954; 1 dau., Margaret Kathleen. BA, Dalhousie U., 1950, LL.B., 1953, LL.M., 1954, Harvard U., 1970; LL.D. (hon.), Meml. U. Nfld., St. F.X. Univ., N.S. Bar: N.S.; Named queen's counsel. Fgn. service officer Dept. External Affairs, Ottawa, Ont., Can., 1954-57; asst. sec. Royal Com., Ottawa, 1955-57; sucessively asst. prof., assoc. prof., prof. law, dean Faculty of law Dalhousie U. (Halifax), N.S., Can., 1957-69, v.p., 1969-80, pres., vice-chancellor, 1980-86; ombudsman N.S., 1986-88; judge Fed. Ct. Can., trial div., Ottawa, Ont., Can., 1988—. Chmn. Assn. Atlantic Univs., Halifax, 1981-83; v.p. Assn. Univs. and Colls. Can., 1982-83, pres., 1983-85; pres. Conf. Gov. Bodies Legal Profession Can., 1968-69, Assn. Can. Law Tchrs., 1964-65 Chmn. N.S. Human Rights Com., Halifax, 1967-86; chmn. N.S. Commns. on Salary and Allowances of Elected Provincial Ofcls., 1974, 78, 81, 83, 84, 85; chmn. N.S. Task Force on AIDS, 1987-88. Mem. Can. Bar Assn. Home: 4-433 Besserer St Ottawa ON Canada K1N 6B9 Office: Fed Ct of Canada Ottawa ON Canada K1A 0H9

MACKEITH, PETER, architecture educator; BA in Lit. and Internat. Rels., U. Va.; MArch, Yale U. Dean Yale U., Trumbull Coll.; archtl. design critic Yale U. Sch. Arch.; asst. prof. U. Va. Sch. Arch.; dir. internat. master program for dept. arch. Helsinki (Finland) U. Tech., 1994—99; assoc. dean, dir. grad. admissions Washington U., St. Louis, 1999—. Vis. prof. faculty arch. U. Llubljana, Slovenia, 1988. Author: The Finland Pavilions, 1992. Recipient Merit award, Va. AIA, 1993; Fulbright scholar, Finland. Achievements include analytical drawings of Alvar Aalt's buildings included in the 1998 MoMA (Museum of Modern Art) Aalto retrospective. Office: Washington Univ Sch Arch Givens Hall Campus Box 1079 One Brookings Dr Saint Louis MO 63130*

MACKEN, DANIEL LOOS, physician, educator; b. Rochester, NY, May 7, 1933; s. Daniel Edward and Mary Frances (Loos) M.; children: Elizabeth Redford, Diana Loos; m. Maria Luisa (Medina de Palma), Nov. 16, 1979. BA, Holy Cross Coll., Worcester, Mass., 1955; post grad., Yale U., 1956-57; MD, U. Mass, Boston, 1960. Resident Roosevelt and Columbia-Presbyn. Hosp., N.Y.C., 1960-63; fellow Am. Heart Assn., 1964-65; dir., coronary care unit Walter Reed Gen. Hosp., Washington, 1968; staff rsch. physician Walter Reed Army Inst. of Rsch., Washington, 1970; instr. Columbia U., N.Y.C., 1966-78, asst. clin. prof., 1979—. Pres. Medica Found., Inc., N.Y.C., 1971—; bd. dir. Medica Endowment Fund, N.Y.C.; vis. lectr. U. saigon, Vietnam, 1969. Contbr. chpts. in book and articles to profl. jours.; student editor Jour. of History of Medicine and Allied Scis., 1956-57. Lt. Col., U.S. Army Med. Corp, 1967-70; Vietnam. Decorated Bronze Star and Vietnam Cross. Fellow Am. Coll. Cardiology; Royal Soc. Medicine; N.Y. Acad. Medicine; Harvey Soc.; mem. AMA; Assn. Mil. Surgeons of U.S.; Am. Heart Assn.; Met. Gov. Island Officers Club. Roman Catholic. Office: Columbia-Presbyn Med Ctr 161 Ft Washington Ave New York NY 10032-3713

MACKENBACH, FREDERICK W. welding products manufacturing company executive; b. St. Marys, Ohio, Mar. 10, 1931; s. Frederick Jacob and Mabel (Tangeman) M.; m. Jo Ann Dietrich, Oct. 21, 1953; children: John Frederick, David Dietrich. BS in Econs., Wharton Sch. Fin. & Commerce, 1953. Various sales engr. positions The Lincoln Electric Co., Indpls., Ft. Wayne, L.A., 1956-64, asst. dist. mgr. L.A., 1973-76, dist. mgr., 1976-88; pres. Lincoln Electric Mexicana, 1988-91, Lincoln Electric Latin Am., 1991-92; pres., COO The Lincoln Electric Co., Cleve., 1992-96, ret., 1996. Mem. Com. on Fgn. Rels. Mayor City of Palos Verdes Estates (Calif.) City Coun. With U.S. Army 1953-55. Mem. Econ. Roundtable in L.A., Am. Welding Soc. Office: Lincoln Electric Co 732 Via Somonte Palos Verdes Estates CA 90274-1629 E-mail: mackenbach@aol.com.

MACKENZIE, CHARLES RUDD, lawyer; b. Boston, Dec. 19, 1964; s. Alan Eno Mackenzie and Susan Taylor Menges; m. Jessica Stretton, Sept. 2, 2000. BA, Bowdoin Coll., 1987; JD, Western New Eng. Coll., 1993; M of Studies in Environ. Law cum laude, Vt. Law Sch., 1994. Rsch. dir. Senator Chafee Com., Cranston, R.I., 1988; fgn. policy aide U.S. Senator John Chafee, Washington, 1989-90; pvt. practice law Hastings on Hudson, N.Y., 1995—. Bd. dirs. Vols. for Peace Internat. Vol. Svc., Belmont, Vt. Pres. Gitt-Moul Historic Properties, Inc., Hanover, Pa. Mem. N.Y. State Bar Assn., 1995, U.S. Dist. Court (so. and ea. dist. of N.Y. 1995), Westchester County Bar Assn., Yonkers Lawyers Assn., Estate Planning Coun. Westchester, Delta Kappa Epsilon (v.p. chpt. 1985, 86), Yale Club N.Y.C. Office: 230 Park Ave 10th Fl New York NY 10169

MACKENZIE, CHARLES SHERRARD, academic administrator; b. Quincy, Mass., Aug. 21, 1924; s. Charles Sherrard and Dorothy MacKenzie; m. Florence Evelyn Phelps Meyer, Aug. 28, 1964 (dec. 1981); 1 child, Robert Walter Meyer; m. Lavonne Rudolph Gaiser, Mar. 30, 1985. Student, Boston U., 1942-43; BA, Gordon Coll., 1946; M.Div., Princeton Theol. Sem., 1949, Th.D., 1955, PhD, 1957; LHD, Grove City Coll., 1997; postgrad., U. Paris, 1953. Ordained to ministry Congl. Christian Ch., 1949. Pastor Carversville (Pa.) Christian Ch., 1948-51; fellow faculty Princeton Theol. Sem., 1949-51, 53-54, Princeton U., 1954-64; pastor First Presbyn. Ch., Avenel, N.J., 1954-64, Broadway Presbyn. Ch., Columbia U., N.Y.C., 1964-67, First Presbyn. Ch., Stanford U., San Mateo, Calif., 1967-71; pres. Grove City (Pa.) Coll., 1971-91, chancellor, 1991-92; advisor to pres., prof. philosphy Reformed Seminary, Orlando, Fla., 1992—; sr. min. Eastminster Presbyn. Ch., Wichita, Kans., 1993. Bd. dirs. Covenant Life Ins. Co., C.S. Lewis Inst.; cons. Oxford Project, 1992—, Provident Mutual Ins. Co.; lectr. Oxford U., 1965, U. Hamburg, 1968, Columbia U., 1964-67, Stanford U., 1967-71, U. Pitts., 1990-93; adv. Provident Mutual Ins. Co. Author: The Anguish and Joy of Pascal, 1973, Freedom, Equality, Justice, 1980, The Trinity and Culture, 1985. Bd. dirs. Knox Fellowship, Frontline, Orlando; mem. Human Relations Commn., San Mateo, 1968-70; mem. Indsl. Devel. Council, Grove City, 1972-75. Served with USAF, 1951-53. Mem. Presbyn. Coll. Union, Am. Assn. Pres.'s Ind. Colls. and Univs. (dir., pres.), Nat. Assn. Ind. Colls. and Univs. (mem. secretariat 1985-91), Freedoms Found. (nat. jury), Soc. Christian Philosphers, Duquesne Club (Pitts.), Univ. Club Boston, Citrus Club (Orlando), Evangelical initiative Notre Dame U., Rockford Inst. Main St. com. (De Toqueville award 1998). Republican. Address: 1231 Reformation Dr Oviedo FL 32765-7197

MACKENZIE, DONALD MURRAY, healthcare administrator; b. Toronto, Ont., Can., June 5, 1947; s. Donald Alexander and June Cameron MacKenzie; m. Marilyn Adele McNaughton, Jan. 3, 1970; children: Jennifer, Katherine, Kenneth. BA in Econs., U. Toronto, 1968, MA in Polit. Sci., 1970, D Health Adminstr., 1974. Exec. asst. Mt. Sinai Hosp., Toronto, 1974-76, successively asst. exec. dir., assoc. exec. dir., v.p., 1974-89; pres. North York Gen. Hosp., Toronto, 1989—2002; asst. prof. U. Toronto, 1989—; internat. healthcare cons., 2002—. Chair Cardiac Care Network Ont., 2001-2002; bd. dirs. Neuchâtel Jr. Coll. Editor: History of Canadian Hospitals, 1972; contbr. articles to profl. jours. Bd. dirs. Cancer Care Ont., 1989-99. Mem. Can. Coll. Health Svc. Execs. (cert., various coms.), Can. Cancer Soc. (hon. life, pres. Ont. div. 1989-91, award of merit 1988), Ont. Hosp. Assn. (chmn. 1999-2000), York Club, Toronto Bd. Trade, Parkview Golf Club (bd. dirs.). Anglican. Avocations: golf, tennis, canoe tripping.

MACKENZIE, GEORGE ALLAN, medical products executive; s. George Adam and Annette Louise MacKenzie; m. Valerie Ann Marchand, June 30, 1971; children from previous marriage: Richard Michael, Barbara Wynne. Student, Jamaica Coll., Kingston, 1944-48. Commd. flying officer Canadian Air Force, 1951, advanced through grades to lt. gen., 1978; comdr. Canadian Forces Air Command, Winnipeg, Man., 1978-80, resigned, 1980; exec. v.p., COO Gendis Inc., 1980-89, pres., COO, 1989-99, pres., CEO, 1999—2002; bd. dirs. Sony of Can. Ltd., Willowdale, Ont., Can.; pres., CEO CANUSA MedExpress Ltd., 2003—. Mem. regional adv. bd. Carleton U. Decorated comdr. Order of Mil. Merit, Order St. Johns, Can. Decoration, Knight of St. Lazarus of Jerusalem. Mem. United Services Inst. Can. (hon. v.p.), Can. Corps Commissionaires (gov.), Police Chiefs Rsch. Found. (co-chmn.), Lakewood Country Club (Delta), Manitoba Club, Royal Mil. Inst. of Manitoba. Home: 383 Christie Rd Winnipeg MB Canada R2N 4A5 Office Phone: 204-487-6555. E-mail: gallanmac@hotmail.com.

MAC KENZIE, JAMES DONALD, clergyman; b. Detroit, Mich., Nov. 17, 1924; s. James and Ida Catherine (Conklin) M.; m. Elsie Joan Kerr, May 7, 1960; children: Janet Eileen, Kayly Kathleen, Christy Carol, Kenneth Kerr. Student, Moody Bible Inst., 1946-49, Union Theol. Sem., 1952. Ordained to ministry Presbyn. Ch., 1953. Pastor Calvary Ch., Swan Quarter, NC, Edenton (N.C.) Presbyn. Ch., 1952-60, Kirkwood Ch., Kannapolis, 1960-64, Barbecue and Olivia Ch., Olivia, 1964-71, Elise Ch., Robbins, 1971-92, Horseshoe Presbyn. Ch., Carbonton, 1971—. Co-founder, Rehoboth Gospel Fellowship, Chicago, 1949. tchr. North Moore High School, 1977-87.; instr. Sandhills Comm Coll., 1986. Columnist The Chowan Herald, Edenton, N.C., 1952-60, The Robbins (N.C.) Record, 1971-86, The Pilot, Southern Pines, N.C., 1987—. Historian Fayetteville Presbytery, 1975—, chmn. hist. com., 1983—, moderator, 1978. Founder Conf. on Celtic Studies, Campbell Coll. (now Campbell U.), Buies Creek, N.C., 1972—; councillor Conf. on Scottish Studies (Can.), 1968-75; co-founder Rehoboth Gospel Fellowship, Chgo., 1949. With AUS, 1943-45, ETO. Decorated Purple Heart, Bronze Star, Combat Inf. Badge; recipient Disting. Citizen award, Robbins, 1983, Disting. Pastor award, 1988, Scottish Heritage Ctr. award St. Andrews Presbyn. Coll., Laurinburg, N.C., 1999. Mem. N.C. Presbyn. Hist. Soc. (pres. 1972-74, Author's award 1970, 75, Cert. Merit 1975), Harnett Hist. Soc. (pres. 1968-71, Distinguished Service award 1970, Scottish Heritage award 1999), Irish Uillean Pipers Soc., Gaelic Soc. of Inverness, An Comunn Gaidhelach (life). Author: Colorful Heritage, 1970; editor: The Uilleann Piper, 1974—; contbr. articles to profl. jours. Home and Office: PO Box 867 Robbins NC 27325-0867

MACKENZIE, JOHN, retired oil industry executive; b. 1919; BS, N.Y. U., 1948. Accountant S.Am. Devel. Co., N.Y.C., 1938-41; financial comptroller French Oil Ind. Agy.-Groupment D'Achat des Carburants, N.Y., 1946-53; v.p., treas. George Hall Corp., 1954-56; asst. treas. Am. Petrofina, Inc., 1956-61, sec., 1961-64, v.p., sec., 1964-68, sr. v.p., sec., 1968-84; ret., 1984. Decorated comdr. Order of Crown (Belgium) Address: 3861 Frio Way Frisco TX 75034-8469

MACKENZIE, KENNETH DONALD, management consultant, educator; b. Salem, Oreg., Dec. 20, 1937; s. Kenneth Victor and Dorothy Vernon (Minaker) M.; m. Sally Jane McHenry, June 16, 1957; children: Dorothy Jane Rivette, Carolyn M. McFarland, Susan M. Treber, Nancy M. Murphy. AB in Math, U. Calif., Berkeley, 1960, PhD in Bus. Adminstrn, 1964. Cert. mgmt. cons. Asst. prof. indsl. adminstrn. Carnegie Mellon U., 1964-67; assoc. prof. industry Wharton Sch. U. Pa., 1967-71; prof. mgmt. scis. U. Waterloo, Ont., 1969-72; Edmund P. Learned disting. prof. Sch. Bus. U. Kans., Lawrence, 1971—; pres. Organizational Systems, Inc., Lawrence, 1976-84; founder, pres. Mackenzie And Co. Inc., Lawrence, 1983—, EMAC Assessments, LLC, Lawrence, 2000—. Author: An Introduction to Continuous Probability, 1969, A Theory of Group Structures, 2 vols., 1976, Basic Theory, 1976, A Theory of Group Structures, vol. II: Empirical Tests, 1976, Organizational Structures, 1978, Organizational Design: The Organizational Audit and Analysis Technology, 1986, The Organizational Hologram: The Effective Management of Organizational Change, 1991, Practitioner's Guide for Improving an Organization, 1995, Practitioner's Guide for Organizing an Organization, 2004; co-editor: Current Topics in Management, Vol. 4-9, 1999-2004; editor: Organization Behavior series; mem. editl. bd. profl. jours. Served with USMCR, 1957-60, with Army N.G., 1960-64. Fellow AAAS; mem. Inst. Mgmt. Scis. (chmn. coll. on orgns. 1983-93), Internat. Conf. on Advances in Mgmt., Meso Orgnl. Studies Group. Republican. Home: 502 Millstone Dr Lawrence KS 66049-2350 Office: Mackenzie And Co Inc 3d Fl 700 Massachusetts St 3rd Fl Lawrence KS 66044-2344 also: U Kans Sch Bus Lawrence KS 66045-0001 E-mail: hologram@orgdesign.com., survey@emacassessments.com. *While the pursuit of a better theory of organizations has led me from the classroom to the laboratory and then into the boardrooms of corporations, the thrust of all these many activities has been to develop the science of organizations.*

MACKENZIE, MAUREEN L, insurance company executive; d. Mary and Dennis P Kenny; m. Donald K Mackenzie; children: Sean Michael, Megan Maureen. PhD, LI U., 2003. Shared market divsnl. mgr. Allstate Ins. Co., Farmingville, NY, 1990—96, regional mktg. mgr., 1996—98. Tng. and devel. divisional mgr. Allstate Ins. Co., 1988—90. Academic researcher (various profl. jours.) (A. R. Zipf Fellowship In Info. Mgmt., 1998). Mem.: Am. Soc. for Info. Sci. and Tech. (assoc.). Right To Life Party. Office: Dowling Coll Idle Hour Blvd Oakdale NY 11769-1999 E-mail: mackenzm@dowling.edu.

MACKENZIE, NANCI, gas company executive; m. Len Mackenzie, 1988. Co-founder (with Sue Palmer) Lucky Lady Oil Co., 1976—82; founder, pres. USGT/Aquila (formerly U.S. Gas Transp. before sale to Aquila), Dallas, 1986—2001. Office: USGT/Aquila 2711 N Haskell Ave Ste 2050 Dallas TX 75204-2965

MACKENZIE, RONALD ALEXANDER, anesthesiologist; b. Detroit, Mar. 31, 1938; s. James and Elizabeth Mackenzie; m. Nancy Lee Vogan, Aug. 25, 1962; children: Margaret, James. BS, Alma Coll., 1961; DO, Kansas City Coll., 1967. Diplomate Am. Bd. Anesthesiology. Resident in anesthesiology Detroit Osteo. Hosp., 1970-72, Cleve. Clinic, 1972-73, Mayo Clinic, Rochester, Minn., 1973-74, cons. in anesthesia, 1974—87, vice-chmn. anesthesiology, 1988—99, chmn. GYN/ENT anesthesia, 1998—99; pres. ceo Am. Soc. Anesthesiologists. Vice-chmn. dept. anesthesiology Mayo Clinic, 1988-98. Pres. Minn. Orch., Rochester, 1987-89. Fellow Am. Coll. Anesthesiologists; mem. Am. Soc. Anesthesiologists (bd. dirs. 1983-87, sec. 1991-97, 1st v.p. 1998, pres.-elect 1999), Sigma Xi. Avocations: sailing, photography. Office: Mayo Clinic 200 1st St SW Rochester MN 55905-0002

MACKENZIE-SMITH, SYDNEY (LORD WHITFORD), marketing and financial executive; b. Sheffield, Eng., June 25, 1937; s. Sydney and Amy Laura (Brown) Mac; m. Jutta Von Zitzewitz, Apr. 19, 1963; children: Sigrid, Oliver. FCA, Brit. Inst. of Chartered Accts., London, 1958; ATII, Brit. Inst. of Taxation, London, 1959; F. Inst. SMM, Brit. Inst. of Sales, Mktg. and Mgmt., London, 1982; PhD, U. London, 1998. Dep. mng. dir. S. Casket, P.L.C., Manchester, Eng., 1963-85; dir. Eltec Svcs., Ltd., Bradford, Eng., 1984-89; chmn. Pathfinder Mktg., Chester, Eng., 1982—. Cons. to Can. Govt.; underwriting mem. Lloyds of London, 1977—. Author: How to Stop Smoking the American Way, 1984, The Profit Program, 1994, Kitchens of the World, 1995. Treas. various charities. Mem. Mensa. Avocations: bridge, golf, travel, writing financial articles for canadian mags.

MACKERETH, BEVERLY D. state representative; b. Wash., DC, Jan. 27, 1958; m. Michael Mackereth; children: Casey, David, Nicholas, Shannon. BA, Frostburg State U., 1979. Dir. Office of Dist. Atty's. Child Abuse Unit/Victim/Witness Program, 1987—95; programs mgr. Office of the Dist. Atty., York County, Pa., 1987—97; dep. dir. Govs. Cmty. Partnership for Safe Children, 1997—99; exec. dir. Healthy York County Coalition, York Health Sys.; Pa. state rep., 2001—. Com. woman Spring Grove Borough, 1993—94, planning commn., 1994, borough coun., 1994—97, mayor, 1997—. Mem. Spring Grove Scholarship Found., 1997—. Mem.: Rep. Club of York, Rotary Club of York. Republican. Office: 52B E Wing Harrisburg PA 17120-2020 E-mail: bmackere@pahousegop.com.

MACKERODT, FRED, public relations specialist; b. Bklyn., Sept. 17, 1938; s. Leroy and Margaret (Murphy) M.; m. Christy Woods, June 7, 1987. Student, NYU, 1958-59. Freelance writer, photographer, N.Y.C. and Barcelona, Spain, 1968-73; editor Cars Mag., Popular Publs. Inc., N.Y.C., 1973-76; pres. Fred Mackerodt, Inc. (pub. relations and publicity), N.Y.C., 1976—, Stone House Farm, Inc., 2001—. Contbr. articles to popular mags.; contbg. editor, sci. and tech.: Popular Mechanics, 1987—. Spl. dep. sheriff Indian River County, Fla., 1994—2001. Mem. Aviation and Space Writers Am., Internat. Motor Press Assn., Publicity Club N.Y., Wings Club, N.Y. Zool. Soc. (aquarium field assoc. 1971—) Home: 940 Craigville Rd Chester NY 10918 Address: Apt 612 205 W 86th St New York NY 10024-3362 E-mail: fmackerodt@fredmackerodt.com.

MACKERRAS, SIR CHARLES (ALAN MACLAURIN), conductor; b. Schenectady, N.Y., Nov. 17, 1925; s. Alan Patrick and Catherine Mackerras; m. Helena Judith Wilkins, 1947; 2 children. Student, Sydney Conservatorium Music, Australia, 1938-42; student with Vaclav Talich, Prague Acad. Music, 1947-48; DMus (hon.), U. Hull, 1990, U. Nottingham, 1991, U. Brno, Czech Republic, 1994, York (Eng.) U., 1994, Griffith U., Brisbane, Australia, 1994, Oxford (Eng.) U., 1997, Prague Acad. Music, 1999, Napier U., Scotland, 2000, U. Sydney, 2003, U. Melbourne, 2003, Janácek Acad. Music, Brno, 2004. Prin. oboist Sydney (Australia) Symphony Orch., 1943-46; staff condr. English Nat. Opera (formerly Sadler's Wells Opera), London, 1948-54, musical dir., 1970-77; prin. condr. BBC Concert Orch., 1954-56; first condr. Hamburg Opera, 1966-69; chief guest condr. BBC Symphony Orch., 1976-79; chief condr. Sydney Symphony Orch., Australian Broadcasting Commn., 1982-85; prin. guest condr. Royal Liverpool Philharm. Orch., 1986-88, Scottish Chamber Orch., 1992-95, condr. laureate, 1995—; music dir. Orch. of St. Luke's, 1998-2001, music dir. emeritus; pres. Trinity Coll. Music, London, 2000. Freelance condr. with most Brit. and many continental orchs.,c oncert tours, Russia, South Africa, N. Am., Australia, 1957—66, U.S. coast-to-coast, 1983; prin. guest condr. San Francisco Opera, 1993—96, prin. guest condr. emeritus, 1996—; prin. guest condr. Royal Philharm. Orch., 1993—96, Czech Philharm. Orch., 1997—2003, Philharmonia Orch., 2002—; mus. dir. Welsh Nat. Opera, 1987—92, condr. emeritus, 1993—; appearances at internat. festivals and opera houses, frequent radio and TV broadcasts; condr. comml. recordings, notably Handel, Mozart operas and symphonies, Janácek, Brahms, Beethoven and Schubert. Published ballet arrangements Pineapple Poll (Sullivan), Lady and the Fool (Verdi), reconstrn. Sullivan's Lost Cello Concerto, contbr. appendices to book A Musicians' Musician, articles to Opera Mag., Charles MacKerras: A Musicians' Musician, other jours. Decorated comdr. Order of Brit. Empire, 1974, knight bachelor Companion Order of Australia, 1997, comdr. Companion of Honor, 2003; recipient Evening Std. award for opera, 1977, Janacek medal, 1978, Gramophone Record of Yr. award, 1977, 1980, 1999, Grammy award for best opera recording, 1981, Gramophone Best Opera Recording award, 1983, 1984, 1994, 1999, prix, Fondation Jacques Ibert, 1983, Record of Yr. award, Stereo Rev., 1983, Medal of Merit, Czech Republic, 1996, Chocs de l'Année award, 1998, Edison award, Preis der Deutschen Schallplattenkritik, Prix Caecilia, 1999, Conducting award, Royal Philharm. Soc., 1999, Chopin prize and lifetime achievement award, Cannes Classical awards at Midem, 2000, award, Assn. Brit. Orchs., 2001, Disting. Musician award, Inc. Soc. Musicians, 2002. Fellow: St. Peter's Coll., Trinity Coll. Music, Cardiff U., Royal Acad. Music, Royal No. Coll. Music (hon.), Royal Coll. Music; mem.: Oxford. Office: Askonas Holt Ltd Lonsdale Chambers 27 Chancery Ln London WC2A 1PF England

MACKEY, GEORGE WHITELAW, mathematician, educator; b. St. Louis, Feb. 1, 1916; s. William Sturges and Dorothy Frances (Allison) M.; m. Alice Willard, Dec. 9, 1960; 1 child, Ann Sturges Mackey. BA, Rice Inst., 1938; A.M., Harvard U., 1939, PhD, 1942; MA, Oxford, 1966. Instr. math. Ill. Inst. Tech., 1942-43; faculty instr. math. Harvard U., 1943-46, asst. prof., 1946-48, assoc. prof., 1948-56, prof. math., 1956-69, Landon T. Clay prof. math. and theoretical sci., 1969-85, prof. emeritus, 1985—. Vis. prof. U. Chgo., summer, 1955, UCLA, Summer, 1959, Tata Inst. Fundamental Rsch., Bombay, 1970-71, U. Calif., Berkeley, 1984; Walker Ames vis. prof. U. Wash., summer, 1961; Eastman vis. prof. Oxford (Eng.) U., 1966-67; assoc. prof. U. Paris, 1978; vis. rschr. Math. Sci. Inst., Berkeley, 1983; lectr. U. Heidelberg, Germany, 1988, CUNY, 1987, U. Iowa, 1988, Kings Coll. of U. London, 1991; invited lectr. U. Munich, Germany, 1994, U. Heidelberg, 1995; vis. lectr. U. Tainjin, U. Beijing, U. Shanghai,. U. Hong Kong, 19911 mem. Inst. Advanced Study Princeton U., 1978. Author: Mathematical Foundations of Quantum Mechanics, 1963, Lectures on the Theory of Functions of a Complex Variable, 1967, Induced Representations and Quantum Mechanics, 1968, The Theory of Unitary Group Representations, 1976, Unitary Group Representations in Physics, Probability and Number Theory, 1978, The Scope and History of Commutative and Noncommutative Harmonic Analysis, 1992; contbr. articles math. jours. Served as civilian, operational research sect. 8th Air Force, 1944; applied math. panel NDRC, 1945. Recipient Humboldt prize Max Planck Inst., Bonn, Fed. Republic of Germany, 1985-86; Guggenheim fellow, 1949-50, 61-62, 70-71; Vis. scholar Catalan U., Bellaterra, Spain, 2000. Mem. Am. Math. Soc. (v.p. 1964-65, Steele prize 1974), Nat. Acad. Scis., Am. Philos. Soc., Am. Acad. Arts and Scis., Phi Beta Kappa, Sigma Xi. Office: Harvard U Dept Math 1 Oxford St Cambridge MA 02138-2901

MACKEY, JEFFREY ALLEN, priest; b. Kingston, N.Y., July 12, 1952; s. Allen William and Vivian Mathilda (Hornbeck) M.; m. Martha LaVonne Webster, Dec. 18, 1971; children: Guy Linwood, Kenyon Paul, Geoffrey Joel. BS, Nyack Coll., 1974; D of Sacred Lit., Ridgedale Theol. Sem., 1975; MDiv, Macon (Ga.) Baptist Sem., 1976; DHL, Macon (Ga.) Bible Inst., 1978; D Ministry, Mansfield Sch. Div., 1985, Grad. Theol. Found., 1990; cert. of theol. studies, Gen. Theol. Sem., 1993; postgrad., Grad. Theol. Found., 1991—, U. of the South; DHL, St. Paul Theol. Sem., 2000; DLitt, Evangel U., 2003. Ordained to ministry Congl. Christian Ch., 1974; ordained priest Episcopal Ch., 1993. Min. music Neversink Valley Bapt. Ch., Huguenot, N.Y., 1969-70; pastor Ponckhockie Congl. Ch., Kingston, 1971-74, The Alliance Ch., Andover, 1974-76; acad. dean Macon (Ga.) Bible Inst., 1976-78; min. Oak Grove Gospel Tabernacle, Williamsport, Pa., 1977-80, 69th St. Alliance Ch., Phila., 1980-83; sr. min. Vestavia Alliance Ch., Birmingham, Ala., 1983-87, Hope Alliance Ch., New Hartford, N.Y., 1987-91; assoc. rector Grace Ch., Utica, N.Y, 1991-96, vicar Waterville, N.Y., 1995-96; rector Trinity Episcopal Ch., DeRidder, La., 1996-97; vicar Polk Meml. Episcopal Ch., Leesville, La., 1996-97; rector St. Mark the Evangelist Ch., North Bellmore, N.Y., 1997-99; registrar/Bible faculty Nyack Coll., Manhattan Campus, N.Y.C., 1999-2000, assoc. dean for acad. affairs, 2000-2001, acad. dean, 2001—. Adj. prof. Cranmer Theol. House, Sheveort, La., 1997, Nyack (N.Y.) Coll., 1998-99; assisting priest St. John's Episcoal Ch., Kingston, N.Y., 2000—02; interim rector St. John's Ch., Kingston, N.Y., 2002-03. Author: A Worship Manifesto, 1986, Indicatives and Imperatives, 1987, Christ's Centripetal Cross, 1990; co-author: Where Love and People Are, 1990; contbg. author: Prophet of Justice, Prophet of Life: Essays on William Stringfellow, 1997, A Diary of Three Decades: Grace Church, Utica, N.Y. 1963-96, 1999, And Jesus Everything: Conversations with A.B. Simpson, 2000; contbr. numerous articles to profl. jours. Mem. Alcohol and Drug Abuse Prevention Treatment Program, Birmingham, 1987—88; chaplain N. Bellmore Vol. Fire Dept., 1998—99; trustee Cathedral of St. John the Divine, N.Y.C., 2002—. Mem. Fellowship Christian Sch. Adminstrs., Evang. Theol. Soc., Am. Assn. Sch. Adminstrs., Am. Guild Organists, Anglican Assn. of Biblical Scholars, Order of Preachers (Anglican), Inst. for Advanced Theology, Soc. Biblical Lit. Avocations: organ and piano playing, collecting art and statues, hymn writing, walking, restoring antique automobiles. E-mail: mackeyj@ncmc.nyack.edu.

MACKEY, JOHN P. food company executive; Owner Safer Way Natural Foods, Austin; co-founder, CEO Whole Foods Market Inc., Austin, 1980—. Office: Whole Foods Market Inc 601 N Lamar Blvd Ste 300 Austin TX 78703-5424

MACKEY, LOUIS HENRY, philosophy educator; b. Sidney, Ohio, Sept. 24, 1926; s. Louis Henry and Clara Emma (Maurer) M.; children: Stephen Louis, Thomas Adam, Jacob Louis, Eva Maria. BA, Capital U., 1948; student, Duke, 1948-50; MA, Yale, 1953, PhD, 1954. Instr. philosophy Yale U., 1953-55, asst. prof., Morse fellow, 1955-59; assoc. prof. philosophy Rice U., Houston, 1959-65, prof., 1965-67, U. Tex., Austin, 1967—2002. Author: Kierkegaard: A Kind of Poet, 1971, Points of View: Readings of Kierkegaard, 1986, Fact, Fiction, and Representation, 1997, Peregrinations of the Word: Essays on Medieval Philosophy, 1997, An Ancient Quarrel Continued: The Troubled Marriage of Philosophy and Literature, 2002; contbr. articles to profl. jours. Recipient Harry Ransom award for Tchng. Excellence, 1987, Pres.'s Assocs. award for Tchng. Excellence, 1991, Grad. Tchng. award 1994; NEH fellow, 1976-77. Episcopalian. Home: 4105 Victory Dr Apt A108 Austin TX 78704-7552 Office: 405A Devereux Ave Princeton NJ 08540-5645

MACKEY, PAMELA ROBILLARD, lawyer; b. Harlingen, Tex., July 16, 1956; d. Gregory Leo and Rosanne Elizabeth (Niland) Robillard; m. Craig W. Mackey, Dec. 30, 1983. BS in Journalism, U. Colo., 1981; JD, George Wash. U., 1985. Bar: Colo. 1985, U.S. Dist. Ct. Colo. 1985. Assoc. Davis, Graham & Stubbs, Denver, 1985-87, Haddon, Morgan & Foreman, P.C., Denver, 1987—, shareholder, 1997—. Pub. defender Colo., 1989-94. Exec. editor George Wash. Law Review, 1984-85. Mem. ABA, Colo. Bar Assn., Denver Bar Assn., Colo. Women's Bar Assn. (bd. dirs. 1988-96; pres. 1995-96), Colo. Criminal Def. Bar (newsletter editor 1988—). Democrat. Roman Catholic. Avocations: skiing, golf. Office: Haddon Morgan Mueller Jordan Mackey & Foreman PC 150 E Tenth Ave Denver CO 80203 Office Phone: 303-831-7364.

MACKEY, PATRICIA ELAINE, university librarian; b. Balt., July 29, 1941; d. Timothy and Hazel Mozelle (Davis) M. BA in Anthropology, CUNY, 1978; MLS, Columbia U., 1981. Asst. libr. I, European Exch. Sys., Mainz-Kastel, Germany, 1966-68; interlibr. loan asst. Poly. U., Bklyn., 1968-72, Rockefeller U., N.Y.C., 1972-73, sr. libr. asst., 1974-80, libr., 1981-91, univ. libr., 1991—. Mem. various libr. coms., N.Y.C., 1991—. Chair pub. svc. scholars program Hunter Coll. CUNY, 1992—; trustee Met. N.Y. Libr. Coun., 2000—, also 1st v.p. Named to, Hunter Coll. Hall of Fame, 2002. Mem.: ALA, Assn. Coll. and Rsch. Librs., N.Y. State Libr. Assn., Hunter Coll. Alumni Assn. (bd. dirs. 1998—, 2d v.p. 1998—2002). Democrat. Roman Catholic. Avocations: reading, chess, gardening. Office: Rockefeller U Libr RU Box 263 1230 York Ave New York NY 10021-6307 Office Phone: 212-327-8909. Business E-Mail: rmackey@mail.rockefeller.edu.

MACKEY, TERRENCE WAYNE, lawyer; b. Denver, Nov. 20, 1942; s. Harold E. Mackey and Dorothy E. (Newville) Brand; m. Catherine Marie Long, Sept. 4, 1966; children: Shawna, Brian, Kristin. AA, Casper (Wyo.) Coll., 1966; BA, U. Wyo., 1968, JD, 1970. Bar: Wyo. 1970, Colo. 1993, U.S. Dist. Ct. Wyo. 1970, U.S. Ct. Appeals (10th cir.) 1970, U.S. Ct. Appeals (9th cir.) 1992, U.S. Supreme Ct. 1973. Mem. firm King & Mackey, Jackson, Wyo., 1970-73, Urbigkit, Mackey & Whitehead, Cheyenne, Wyo., 1973-79; pvt. practice Cheyenne, 1979-82; pres. Terry W. Mackey P.C., Cheyenne, 1982-94, Hickey & Mackey, Cheyenne, 1994—. Mem. Drafting Com. Fed. Local Rules, Cheyenne, 1991—, Standing Com. Local Rule, Cheyenne, 1992—; appellate counsel most significant constl. cases, 1977. Mem. grounds com. Cheyenne Frontier Days, 1986—; mem. coun. Ascension Luth. Ch., Cheyenne, 1989-91; mem. adv. coun. Foster Grandparents, Cheyenne, 1987-89; bd. dir. Wyo. Children's Soc., 1999—, Attention Wyo., 2004—. With USN, 1960-63. Fellow Internat. Soc. Barristers, Am. Coll. Trial Lawyers; mem. ABA, Am. Trial Lawyers Assn. (judge student trial competition 1991), Wyo. State Bar, Wyo. Trial Lawyers (pres. bd. 1977, dir. 1971—), Laramie County Bar. Avocations: hunting, fishing, golf, reading. Office: PO Box 467 1800 Carey Ave Ste 700 Cheyenne WY 82001-4420 Office Phone: 307-634-1525.

MACKEY, THOMAS B. health facility administrator; COO Tenet Healthcare Corp., Santa Barbara, Calif., 1998—. Office: Tenet Healthcare Corp PO Box 31907 Santa Barbara CA 93130-1907

MACKICHAN, MARGARET ANNA, artist, art educator; b. Charleston, W.Va., Feb. 27, 1948; d. Kenneth Allen and Lois Alma (Deyton) MacK.; 1 child, Jemma Moccasin. BFA, U. Nebr., 1970; MA, U. N.Mex., 1974, MFA, 1977. Assoc. VISTA, Ky., 1966-67; photographer Ky., 1968—87, Rosebud (S.D.) Reservation, 1987-92; founding dir. Great Plains Art Inst., Sinte Gleska U., Rosebud Reservation, SD, 1987. Curatorial intern Internat. Mus. of Photography, George Eastman House, Rochester, N.Y., 1971-72; artist-in-community Western Nebr. Art Ctr., Scottsbluff, 1978-79; instr. Nebr. Western Coll., Scottsbluff, 1978-79; vis. prof. Nebr. Wesleyan U., Lincoln, 1980-87; participant Annual Plains Indian Seminar, 1987-98. Co-author: In the Kingdom of Grass, 1992. Recipient 1st prize photography Mademoiselle Mag., 1970, Vreeland award U. Nebr., 1970, Artist grant Nebr. Arts Coun./Nebr. Com. on Humanities, 1978, Artist fellowship Mid-Am. Arts Alliance, 1983, Outstanding Svc. in Art Edn. award S.D. Gov., 2003. Fellow Ctr. for Great Plains Study; mem. Soc. for Photographic Edn., Nat. Am. Art Studies Assn., Scottish Soc. Artists. Presbyterian. Avocations: walker horses, Lakota arts, Scottish dancing, banjo, bagpipes. Home: PO Box 6 Mission SD 57555-0006 Office: Sinte Gleska Univ PO Box 490 Rosebud SD 57570-0490

MACKIE, JERRY, state legislator, business owner; b. Ketchikan, Alaska, Jan. 10, 1962; s. Ralph P. Mackie and Marge (Thompson) Young; divorced; 1 child, John. Grad. high sch., Ketchikan. Chmn. bd. Shaan Seet Inc., Craig, Alaska, 1981-90; comml. fisherman Craig, 1985—; rep. Alaska State Legislature, Juneau, 1990-96; owner fishing lodge Craig, 1985—; mem. State Senate AK, Juneau, AK, 1996—. Bd. dirs. Alaska Fed. Natives, Anchorage. Recipient Pub. Svc. commendation USCG, 1987. Mem. Alaska Native Brotherhood, Moose. Democrat. Avocations: fishing, basketball, racquetball, skiing. Office: Alaska State Legislature State Capitol St Juneau AK 99801-1182 Home: 2100 Belmont Dr Anchorage AK 99517-1374

MACKIE, RICHARD H. orchestra executive; married; 3 children. Grad., Tulane U.; M in Arts Adminstrn., U. Wis., Madison. Jazz musician New Hyperion Oriental Foxtrot Orch.; pres. Friends of WHA-TV; dir. devel. Edgewood Coll.; exec. dir. Madison (Wis.) Symphony Orch., 1999—. Office: Madison Symphony Orch 6314 Odana Rd Madison WI 53719

MACKIE, ROBERT GORDON, costume and fashion designer; b. Monterey Park, Calif., Mar. 24, 1940; s. Charles Robert and Mildred Agnes (Smith) M.; m. Marianne Wolford, Mar. 14, 1960 (div.); 1 son, Robin Gordon. Student, Chouinard Art Inst., 1958-61. Sketch for Jean Louis, 1962-63; mem. staff Edith Head, 1962-63; pres. ptnr. Bob Mackie Originals, N.Y.C.; costume designer: (films) Brigadoon, 1954, Divorce, American Style, 1967, ...All the Marbles, 1981, Pennies from Heaven, 1981 (Academy award nomination best costume design 1981), Max Dugan Returns, 1983, (TV movies) Fresno, 1986, (TV series) The Carol Burnett Show, 1967-78, The Sonny and Cher Comedy Hour, 1971-74, Cher, 1975-76, The Diahann Carroll Show, 1976, The Sonny and Cher Show, 1976-77, Donny and Marie, 1976-79, Mama's Family, 1983-85, (TV spls.) Alice Through the Looking Glass, 1967, Carousel, 1967, Kismet, 1967, Fred Astaire Show, 1968, Diana Ross and the Supremes, 1969, Of Thee I Sing, 1972, Once Upon a Mattress, 1973, (theatrical prodns.) The Best Little Whorehouse Goes Public, 1994; co-costume designer: (films) Lady Sings the Blues, 1972 (Academy award nomination best costume design 1972), Funny Lady, 1975 (Academy award nomination best costume design 1975), The Villain, 1979, Butterfly, 1981, ... All the Marbles, 1983, Staying Alive, 1983, Brenda Starr, 1987, (theatrical prodns.) On the Town, 1971, Lorelei, 1972; author: Dressing for Glamour, 1969; appeared on Broadway and in TV prodn. Night of 100 Stars II, 1985. Recipient Emmy awards for outstanding costume design, 1966, 67, 69, 70, 76, 78, 84, 88, 95, Emmy award nominations for outstanding costume design, 1972, 74, 75, 76, 77, 79, 80, 83, 86, 87, Costume Designers Guild award, 1968, Fashion Achievement award Otis/Parsons Sch. Design, 1987; named most creative fashion designer in Am. US mag., 1982, 83; honored by Costume Inst. Fine Arts, Houston, 1987, AIDS Project L.A., 1989. Democrat. Address: Bob Mackie Ltd 530 7th Ave Frnt 3D New York NY 10018-4878

MACKIEWICZ, LAURA, advertising agency executive; Formerly with D'Arcy Advt.; with BBDO, Chgo., 1973—, now sr. v.p., dir. broadcast and print svcs. Office: BBDO Chgo 410 N Michigan Ave Ste 8 Chicago IL 60611-4273

MACKIEWICZ, THERESA ANN, special education educator; b. Boston, Mar. 16, 1976; d. Joseph James and Angelina Marie Mangiaratti; m. Theresa Ann Mangiaratti, Dec. 21, 2002. AAS, Dean Coll., Franklin, Mass., 1996; BS, Bridgewater State Coll., 2000. Cert. presch. tchr. The Commonwealth of Mass. Office for Children, 1996. Asst. tchr. Walker Home and Sch., Needham, Mass., 1999—2001; spl. needs parent specialist Home Health and Child Care, Brockton, Mass., 2001—01; long term permanent substitute for spl. edn. Southeastern Regional Vocat.-Tech. H.S., South Easton, Mass., 2001—03; spl. edn. tchr. for a 45 day assessment program South Shore Ednl. Collaborative, Hingham, Mass., 2003—. Mem.: Kappa Delta Pi (life). Avocations: writing childrens' books, poetry, ceramics, excercising, baking cookies and Italian desserts. Home: 6 Bachant Way Wareham MA 02571 Office: South Shore Ednl Collaborative 90 Industrial Park Rd Hingham MA 02043 Personal E-mail: bandtmac@cape.com.

MACKIN, CHARLES PHILIP, JR., lawyer; b. Boston, Dec. 13, 1947; s. Charles Philip and Mary Patricia (Sparkes) M.; m. Deborah Ann Huey, Oct. 18, 1980; children: Emily K., Claire E.S. BA, St. Anselm Coll., 1969; JD, Loyola U., New Orleans, 1972; MGA, U. Pa., 1987; grad., U.S. Army War Coll., 1990. Bar: Pa. 1972, U.S. Ct. Mil. Appeals 1973, U.S. Ct. Appeals (D.C. cir.) 1977, U.S. Supreme Ct. 1977, U.S. Ct. Appeals (3rd cir.) 1985. Asst. dist. atty., Coudersport, Pa., 1978-81; sr. dep. atty. gen. Office of Atty. Gen. of Pa., Harrisburg, 1982-86, chief dep. atty. gen., 1986-89; dep. chief counsel for investigations Dept. Auditor Gen. of Pa., Harrisburg, 1989-91, dep. auditor gen., 1991-96. Capt. USMC, 1972-77. Mem. Pa. Bar Assn., Army Navy Club (Washington). Office: 3344 Trindle Rd Camp Hill PA 17011-4432

MACKIN, JEANNE ANN, journalist, educator; b. Waterloo, N.Y., June 9, 1948; d. Richard J. and Helen (Campfield) M.; m. Stephen Poleskie. BA in English, Ithaca Coll., 1970; MFA in Creative Writing, Bennington Coll., 1986. Columnist Ithaca (N.Y.) Times, 1974—; sci. writer Cornell U., Ithaca, 1979—; writing instr. Ithaca Coll., 1991—; MFA faculty mem. Goddard Coll., 2001—. Cons. Strong Mus., Rochester, 1994; cons., auditor N.Y. State Coun. on Arts, N.Y.C., 1984—; writing tchr. State Coun. on Arts, Hawaii, 1992; spkr. in field. Author: The Frenchwoman, 1989, The Queen's War, 1991, Dreams of Empire, 1996, The Sweet By and By, 2001, The Cornell Book of Herbs, 1993; editor: Book of Love, 1998. Recipient Excellence in Newswriting award Coun. for Advancement and Support of Edn., 1986, Writing Scholarship award Wesleyan U., 1989; rsch. fellow Am. Antiquarian Soc., 1999. Mem. Author's Guild. Home: PO Box 849 Ithaca NY 14851-0849

MACKINNEY, ARCHIE ALLEN, JR., physician; b. St. Paul, Aug. 16, 1929; s. Archie Allen and Doris (Hoops) MacK.; m. Shirley Schaefer, Apr. 9, 1955; children— Julianne, Theodore, John. BA, Wheaton (Ill.) Coll., 1951; MD, U. Rochester, 1955. Intern, resident in medicine U. Wis. Hosp., 1955-59; clin. assoc. NIH, 1959-61; clin. investigator VA, 1961-64; asst. prof. medicine U. Wis., Madison, 1964-68, assoc. prof., 1968-74, prof., 1974-98, med. alumni prof., 1987. Mentor class of '03 U. Wis. Med. Sch.; chief hematology VA Hosp., Madison, 1964-98, chief nuclear medicine, 1964-73, 78-79 Author (editor): Pathophysiology of Blood, 1984, Hematology for Students, 2002; contbr. articles to profl. jours. Trustee Intervarsity Christian Fellowship, 1985-88. Served with USPHS, 1959-61. Danforth assoc., 1962 Mem. Am. Soc. Hematology, Am. Fedn. Clin. Research, Central Soc. Clin. Research. Republican. Baptist. Home: 190 N Prospect Ave Madison WI 53705-4071 Office: 2500 Overlook Ter Madison WI 53705-2254

MACKINNIS, ANN PHELPS, municipal government and land use management executive; b. Hartford, Conn., Sept. 3, 1936; d. George Henry and Margaret Louise (Stewart) Phelps; m. Frank Reader MacKinnis, Mar. 15, 1957 (div. Dec. 1980); children: Robert Phelps, John Stewart. AS in Retailing summa cum laude, Lasell Jr. Coll., 1956; BSBA summa cum laude, Coll. of St. Elizabeth, 1988. Acctg. clk. Washington Aluminum Co., Balt., 1975—76; adminstrv. aide Town of Morristown, NJ, 1978—, adminstrv. officer planning and zoning bd., 1986—, mgr. divsn. land use adminstrn., zoning officer, 1986—. Trustee Christmas on the Green, Morristown, 1978-86; adj. prof. Rutgers U. Editor: Morristown Master Plan, 1978-79; also author of ordinances and pamplets. Mem. Morris County Bldg. Ofcls. Assn., Dover, N.J., 1995—, Rutgers Club, New Brunswick, 1998—, Calvert Marine Mus., Solomons Island, Md., 1997—; mem. Mayor's Design Rev. Com., Morristown, N.J., 2001—. Recipient Women of Accomplishment, Outstanding Acad. Achievement, Coll. of St. Elizabeth, 1985, Scholastic Achievement award, 1988. Mem. N.J. Planning Ofcls. (Achievement in Planning award 1997), N.J. Assn. Planning and Zoning Adminstrs. (pres. 1996-99, bd. dirs. 1992—, chmn. edn. and cert. commn. 1999—), Morristown Town Coun. (Achievement in Planning award 1997), Rutgers Club, Calvert Marine Mus. Republican. Protestant. Avocations: sailing, travel, reading, jigsaw and word puzzles. Home: 14 Cromwell Dr Morristown NJ 07960-4602 Office: Town of Morristown 200 South St Morristown NJ 07960-0914 E-mail: A-Mackinnis@TownofMorristown.org.

MACKINNON, CATHARINE ALICE, lawyer, law educator, legal scholar, writer; d. George E. and Elizabeth V. (Davis) MacKinnon. BA in Govt. magna cum laude with distinction, Smith Coll., 1969; JD, Yale U., 1977, PhD in Polit. Sci., 1987. Vis. prof. Harvard U., Stanford U., Yale U., others, Osgoode Hall, York U., Canada, U. Basel, Switzerland; prof. of law U. Mich., 1990—. Long term vis. prof. U. Chgo., 1997—; co-dir. project Equality Now, Legal Alliance Women, 2001—. Author: Sexual Harassment of Working Women, 1979, Feminism Unmodified, 1987, Toward a Feminist Theory of the State, 1989, Only Words, 1993, Sex Equality, 2001, Women's Lives, Men's Laws, 2004; co-author: In Harm's Way, 1997, Directions in Sexual Harassment Law, 2003. Office: U Michigan Law School Ann Arbor MI 48109-1215

MACKINNON, JAMES GORDON, economist, educator; b. Charlottetown, P.E.I., Can., Jan. 4, 1951; s. James William and Marion Elizabeth MacKinnon; m. Susan Gentleman, Nov. 23, 1985. BA with honors, York U., 1971; MA, Princeton U., 1974, PhD, 1975. Asst. prof. Queen's U., Kingston, Canada, 1975—78, assoc. prof., 1978—82, prof., 1982—, Sir Edward Peacock prof. econometrics, 1991—. Mem. editl. bd. Can. Jour. Econs., 1984—87, assoc. editor Jour. Applied Econometrics, 1989—91, software rev. editor, 1991—, assoc. editor Jour. Econometrics, 1991—. Fellow: Royal Soc. Can., Econometric Soc.; mem.: Can. Econs. Assn. (pres.-elect 2000—01, pres. 2001—02, past pres. 2002—03). Office: Queen's U Dept Econs Kingston ON Canada K7L 3N6 Office Phone: 613-533-2293. E-mail: jgm@qed.econ.queensu.ca.

MACKINNON, JOHN ALEXANDER, lawyer; b. Glen Ridge, N.J., Feb. 5, 1949; s. John and Carol McNeir (Cox) M.; m. Anne Rider Patterson, Aug. 19, 1972; children: Lindsay Rider, John William. BA, Williams Coll., 1971; JD, U. Va., Charlottesville, 1974. Assoc. Brown & Wood, N.Y.C., 1974-82, ptnr., 1983-2001, Sidley Austin Brown & Wood, N.Y.C., 2001—. Trustee, Tuxedo Park Libr., N.Y., 1982-89; mem. chmn., bd. zoning appeals, Tuxedo Park, 1987-89. Mem. The Tuxedo Club.

MACKINNON, MALCOLM D(AVID), retired insurance company executive; b. Guelph, Ont., Can., Mar. 9, 1931; came to U.S., 1955; s. A.L. and Jean (Butchart) MacK.; m. Betty Campbell, June 18, 1955; children: Sandra, Katherine, Donald. BA, U. Toronto, 1953. CLU; chartered fin. analyst. With Prudential Ins. Co., 1954-94, v.p., 1979-81, sr. v.p., 1981—94; ret., 1994. Commentator pub. radio. Trustee Kean Coll., Union, N.J., 1990-93, Millburn Free Pub. Libr., 1996—, pres., 1997-2000; chmn. Milburn Short Hills chpt. ARC, 1992-94. Fellow Soc. Actuaries; mem. Canoe Brook Country Club (Summit, N.J.). Home: 23 Grosvenor Rd Short Hills NJ 07078-1639

MACKINNON, PEGGY LOUISE, public relations executive; b. Florence, Ariz., June 18, 1945; d. Lacy Donald Gay and Goldie Louise (Trotter) Martin; m. Ian Dixon Mackinnon, Oct. 20, 1973. BA, San Jose State U., 1967, postgrad., 1968. Cert. secondary tchr., Calif. Tchr. Las Lomas H.S., Walnut Creek, Calif., 1968-69; edn. officer Ormond Sch., Sydney, Australia, 1970-72; tchr. Belconnen H.S., Canberra, Australia, 1972-73; temp. exec. sec. various orgns., London, 1973-75; mktg. mgr. Roadtown Wholesale, Tortola, British Virgin Islands, 1975-80; sr. v.p., gen. mgr. Hill & Knowlton Inc., Denver, 1981-96; pres. Peggy Mackinnon Inc., Denver, 1996—. Bd. dirs. Rocky Mountain Poison and Drug Found., Denver, 1984-87, Denver C. of C., Boy Scouts Am., Denver coun. Avocations: tennis, skiiing, fishing, travel. Home and Office: Apt 21 9200 Cherry Creek South Dr Denver CO 80231-4018

MACKINNON, RODERICK, neuroscientist, educator; b. Burlington, Mass., 1956; BA, Brandeis U., 1978; MD, Tufts U., 1982, PhD (hon.), 2002. Postdoctoral fellow Beth Israel Hosp., Harvard U., 1985—86, Brandeis U., 1986—89; from asst. to prof. dept. neurobiology Harvard Med. Sch., 1989—96; John D. Rockefeller Jr. prof. lab. molecular neurobiology and biophysics Rockefeller U., 1996—. Recipient Young Investigator award, Biophysical Soc., 1995, Newcomb Cleveland prize, AAAS, 1998, Albert Lasker Basic Med. Rsch. award, 1999, Lewis S. Rosentiel award, 2000, Gairdner Found. Internat. award, 2001, Nobel prize for chemistry, 2003; grantee, Howard Hughes Med. Inst. Chevy Chase, Md., 1997—. Mem.: NAS. Office: Rockefeller Univ 1230 York Ave New York NY 10021 also: Howard Hughes Med Inst 4000 Jones Bridge Rd Chevy Chase MD 20815-6789*

MACKINNON, ROGER ALAN, psychiatrist, educator; b. Feb. 13, 1927; Student, Princeton U., 1944-46; MD, Columbia U., 1950, cert. in psycoanalytic medicine, 1957. Diplomate Am. Bd. Psychiatry and Neurology. Intern E.W. Sparrow Hosp., Lansing, Mich., 1950-51; resident in psychiatry N.Y. State Psychiatric Inst., N.Y.C., 1951-52, 52-54; chief psychiatry Vanderbilt Clinic, Presbyn. Hosp., N.Y.C., 1959-77; prof. clin. psychiatry Coll. Physicians & Surgeons, Columbia U., N.Y.C., 1986-97, prof. emeritus, 1997—; tng., supervising analyst Columbia U. Psychoanalytic Ctr., 1970—, asst. dir. for selection, 1981-91, dir., 1991-97; attending psychiatrist Presbyn. Hosp., N.Y.C., 1972—, N.Y. State Psychiatric Inst., N.Y.C., 1972—. Asst. examiner Am. Bd. Psychiatry and Neurology, 1960-70; cons., lectr. in field. Co-author textbook: The Psychiatric Interview, 1971, The Psychiatric Evaluation, 1986; contbr. articles to profl. jours., chpts. to books. Lt. USNR, 1952-54. Fellow Am. Psychiat. Assn. (life), N.Y. Acad. Medicine; mem. Am. Psychoanalytic Assn., Assn. Psychoanalytic Medicine (George E. Daniels Merit award 1995), N.Y. Psychiat. Soc. (pres. 1987-88), N.Y. Psychiat. Inst. (Centennial award 1996). Avocations: woodworking, boating, hiking. Home: 11 Edgewood St Tenafly NJ 07670-2909 Office: 11 E 87th St New York NY 10128-0527

MACKINNON, SALLY ANNE, retired fast food company executive; b. Chgo., Apr. 20, 1938; d. Eugene and Anne Elizabeth (Jones) MacK. BA, Smith Coll., 1960; postgrad., U. Ark., 1961-62. Brand mgr. Speidel div. of Textron, Providence, 1967-70; mktg. mgr. Candy Corp. Am., Bklyn., 1970-72; v.p. account service William Esty Advt., N.Y.C., 1972-76; mktg. mgr. R.J. Reynolds Tobacco, Winston-Salem, N.C., 1976-84, v.p. new brands, 1984-86; v.p. new products mktg. Ky. Fried Chicken, Louisville, 1986-88; ret., 1988. Democrat. Episcopalian. Avocations: photography, travel. Home: 7500 E Boulders Pkwy # 20 Scottsdale AZ 85262

MACKINNON, STEPHEN R. Asian studies administrator, educator; b. Columbus, Nebr., Dec. 2, 1940; s. Cyrus Leland and Helen (Wigglesworth) MacK.; m. Janice Carolyn Rachie, July 15, 1967 (dec. Sept. 1999); children: Rebecca, Cyrus R. BA, Yale U., 1963, MA, 1964; PhD, U. Calif., Davis, 1971. Acting instr. Chinese U., Hong Kong, 1968-69; dir. Asian Studies, prof. history Ariz. State U., Tempe, 1971—; vis. assoc. Chinese Acad. Social Sci., Beijing, 1979-81, 85. Mem. U.S. State Dept. Selection Bd., Washington, 1991, Nat. Com. on U.S.-China Rels., N.Y.C., 1991—; cons. PBS film documentary "Dragon and Eagle." Author: Power/Politics China, 1980; co-author: Agnes Smedley, 1988, China Reporting, 1987; co-editor: Chinese Women Revolution, 1976 (ALA notable book 1976), Scars of War, 2001; lectr. on China to local orgns. and TV, 1981—. Commr. Phoenix Sister Cities, 1986-91; bd. dirs. Com. on Fgn. Rels., Phoenix, 1988—; bd. dirs. Marshall Fund Ariz., 1995—. Rsch. fellow Am. Coun. Learned Socs., Hong Kong, 1978, Fulbright Found., India, 1977-78; rsch. sr. Com. on Scholarly Com. People's Republic China, Washington-Beijing, 1992, Pacific Cultural Found., 1999, Am. Inst. Indian Studies, 2003. Mem. Assn. Asian Studies (bd. dirs. 1990-91), Am. Hist. Assn. (program com. 1990-91). Avocations: tennis, hiking, jazz. Office: Ariz State U Dept History Tempe AZ 85287-2501 Office Phone: 480-965-6692. E-mail: stephen.mackinnon@asu.edu.

MACKINTOSH, CAMERON, musical theater producer; b. Enfield, Middlesex, Eng., Oct. 17, 1946; s. Ian Robert and Diana Gladys (Tonna) M. Student, Prior Pk. Coll., Somerset, Eng., Cen. Sch. for Speech and Drama. §st. stage mgr. Oliver! tour, British cities, 1965; N.Y. debut as producer, deviser Tomfoolery, Top of the Gate, 1981; London debut producer Little Women, Jeanetta Cochrane, 1967; producer, deviser musicals Anything Goes, Saville, London, 1969, Trelawney, Sadler Wells, Prince of Wales, 1972, The Card, Queens, 1973, Winnie the Pooh, Phoenix, 1974, 75, Owl and the Pussycat Went To See, Westminster, 1975, Side By Side By Sondheim, Wyndhams and Garrick, 1976, Oliver!, Albery, 1977-80, Aldwych, 1983, Godspell, Phoenix, 1975, Her Majesty's P.O.W., Shaftsbury, 1977, Duke of York, 1978, Diary of a Madam, Phoenix, 1977, After Shave, Apollo, 1977, Out On a Limb, Vaudeville, 1977, Gingerbread Man, Old Vic, 1978, 79, Royalty, 1980, Westminster, 1981, My Fair Lady, Adelphi, 1979, Tomfoolery, Criterion, 1980, Jeeves Takes Charge, Fortune, 1981, Cats, New London, 1981, Song and Dance, Palace, 1982, Blondel, Old Vic, Aldwych, 1983, Little Shop of Horrors, Comedy, 1983, Abbacadabra, Lyric Hammersmith, 1983, The Boyfriend, Old Vic. and Albery, 1985, Les Misérables, 1985, The Phantom of the Opera, 1987, Follies, 1989, Miss Saigon, 1989, Five Guys Named Moe, 1990, Moby Dick: Putting It Together, 1992, Carousel, 1993 (Tony award, 1994), Oliver!, 1994, Martin Guerre, 1996, Oklahoma, 1999, The Witches of Eastwick, 2000, My Fair Lady, 2001, Mary Poppins, 2004; major tours in Britian include Little Women, 1967, Murder at the Vicarage, 1969, Rebecca, 1969, At Home with the Dales, 1970, Salad Days, 1972, Butley, 1973, Winnie the Pooh, 1973-74, Time and Time Again, 1974, Godspell, 1974-80, The Owl and The Pussycat Went To See, 1974, 75, 76, Relativeley Speaking, 1974-75, An Inspector Calls, 1974, Private Lives, 1974, Bell, Book and Candle, 1974, A Merry Whiff of Windsor, 1975, So Who Needs Marriage. 1975, John, Paul, George and Ringo, 1975-76, Rock Nativity, 1975-76, Touch of Spring, 1976, Virginia Woolf, 1976, Lauder, 1976, Oliver!, 1977, 83, Side By Side By Sondheim, 1978-79, My Fair Lady, 1978, 81-82, Rocky Horror Show, 1979-80, Gingerbread Man, 1979, Oklahoma, 1980; also tours various shows to Can., Republic S. Africa, Ireland, Scandinavia, Australia, U.S.A. Decorated knight of the Brit. Empire. Fellow St. Catherine's Coll. (hon., Oxford); mem. Soc. West End Theatres (exec. officer), Dramatists League, League Am. Theaters, Am. Dramatists Guild. Office: Cameron Mackintosh Ltd Number One Bedford Sq London England WC1B 3RB also: 1650 Broadway Ste 800 New York NY 10019-6833

MACKINTOSH, FREDERICK ROY, oncologist; b. Miami, Fla., Oct. 4, 1943; s. John Harris and Mary Carlotta (King) MacK.; m. Judith Jane Parnell, Oct. 12, 1961 (div. Aug. 1977); children: Lisa Lynn, Wendy Sue; m. Claudia Lizanne Flournoy, Jan. 7, 1984; 1 child, Gregory Warren. BS, MIT, 1964, PhD, 1968; MD, U. Miami, 1976. Intern then resident in gen. medicine Stanford (Calif.) U., 1976-78, fellow in oncology, 1978-81; asst. prof. med. U. Nev., Reno, 1981-85, assoc. prof., 1985-92, prof. medicine, 1992—. Contbr. articles to profl. jours. Fellow ACP; mem. Am. Soc. Clin. Oncology, Am. Cancer Soc. (pres. Nev. chpt. 1987-89, Washoe chpt. 1988-90), No. Nev. Cancer Coun. (bd. dirs. 1981-92), No. Calif. Cancer Program (bd. dirs. alt. 1983-87, bd. dirs. 1987-91). Avocation: bicycling. Office: Med Sch Assocs North Ste 302 1500 E 2nd St Reno NV 89502

MACKLEM, MICHAEL KIRKPATRICK, publisher; b. Toronto, Ont., Can., July 12, 1928; s. Hedley Clark and Mary Eileen (Kirkpatrick) M.; m. Anne Woodburne Hardy, Dec. 30, 1950; children— Timothy Street, Nicholas Hardy. BA, U. Toronto, 1950; AM (Charles Scribner fellow), Princeton U., 1952, PhD (Porter Ogden Jacobus fellow, Royal Soc. Can. fellow), 1954. Instr., English Yale U., New Haven, 1954-55; staff editor Ency. Canadiana, 1955-58; asst. to dir. Humanities Research Council of Can., 1958-60; gen. mgr. Oberon Press, Ottawa, Ont., 1966-85. Pres. Michael, Hardy, Ltd., Ottawa, 1972— Author: The Anatomy of the World: Relations Between Natural and Moral Law from Donne to Pope, 1958, God Have Mercy: The Life of John Fisher of Rochester, 1967, Cinderella, 1969, Voyages to New France 1615-1618, 1970, Voyages to New France 1599-1603, 1971, The Sleeping Beauty, 1973, Jacques the Woodcutter, 1977, Liberty and the Holy City, 1978, The Oberon Reader, 1991, The Oberon Poetry Collection, 1992. Can. Council fellow, 1964-65 Home: 555 Maple Ln Ottawa ON Canada K1M 0N7 Office: Oberon Press 400-350 Sparks St Ottawa ON Canada K1R 7S8 E-mail: oberon@sympatico.ca.

MACKLIN, CROFFORD JOHNSON, JR., lawyer; b. Columbus, Ohio, Sept. 10, 1947; S. Crofford Johnson, Sr. and Dorothy Ann (Stevens) M.; m. Mary Carole Ward, July 5, 1969; children: Carrie E., David J. BA, Ohio State

U., 1969; BA summa cum laude, U. West Fla., 1974; JD cum laude, Ohio State U., 1976. Bar: Ohio 1977, U.S. Tax Ct. 1978. Acct. Touche Ross, Columbus, 1976-77; assoc. Smith & Schnacke, Dayton, 1977-81; ptnr. Porter, Wright, Morris & Arthur, Dayton, 1983-88; shareholder Smith & Schnacke, 1988-89; ptnr. Thompson, Hine LLP, 1989—, practice group leader pers. and succession planning, 2001—; sole practice Dayton, 1981-82. Adj. faculty Franklin U., 1977; adj. prof. U. Dayton Law Sch., 1981. Contbr. articles to profl. jours. Bd. dirs. Great Lakes Nat. Bank Ohio, 1997, Easter Seals, 1984-86. Served to capt. USMCR, 1969-74. Fellow Am. Coll. Trust and Estate Counsel; mem. ABA, Dayton Bar Assn. (chmn. probate com. 1981-83), Dayton Trust & Estate Planning (pres. 1983-84), Ohio Bar Assn. Presbyterian. Home: 7276 Wetherington Dr West Chester OH 45069 Office: Thompson Hine LLP 2000 Courthouse Pla NE PO Box 8801 Dayton OH 45401-8801 Office Phone: 937-443-6730.

MACKLIN, PHILIP ALAN, physics educator; b. Richmond Hill, N.Y., Apr. 13, 1925; s. Egbert Chalmer and Margaret Griswold (Collins) M.; m. Cora Baldwin Galindo, Sept. 5, 1953; children: Susan, Steven, Peter. BS cum laude, Yale U., 1944; MA, Columbia U., 1949, PhD, 1956. Physicist Carbide & Carbon Chems. Corp., Oak Ridge, 1946-47; research scientist AEC, Columbia U., 1949-51; instr. physics Middlebury Coll., Vt., 1951-54, acting chmn. dept., 1953-54; mem. faculty Miami U., Oxford, Ohio, 1954—, prof. physics, 1961-93, chmn. dept., 1972-85, prof. emeritus, 1993—. Research scientist Armco Steel Co., summers 1955-56; vis. prof. U. N.Mex., summers 1957-68, Boston U., fall 1985-86; physicist Los Alamos Sci. Labs., summers 1960-62; participant NSF summer insts., 1970-71; vis. scientist MIT, 1985-86 Author publs. in field; patentee in field. Vestryman Holy Trinity Episcopal Ch., Oxford, 1959-61, 67, 71-73, 75-77, mem. fin. com., chmn. blood assurance program, 1980—, lector, 1989—. With USN, 1944-46. Mem. AAAS, AAUP, LWV of Oxford (treas. 1986-88, dir. governance 1997—), Am. Phys. soc., Forum Physics and Soc., Am. Assn. Physics Tchrs., Kiwanis (bd. dirs. 1994-97), Torch Club of Butler County (pres. 1982-83, 96-97, mem. editl. adv. com. The Torch), 1809 Club (pres. 1964-65), Campus Ministry Ctr. (trustee 1994-2002), Union of Concerned Scientists, Ctr. for Voting and Democracy (charter), Membership Assn. Miami U. Art Mus. (exec. com. 1999-2002), Phi Beta Kappa (pres. Iota of Ohio chpt. 1987-88), Sigma Xi, Sigma Pi Sigma, Omicron Delta Kappa. Democrat. Home: 211 Oakhill Dr Oxford OH 45056-2710 Office: Culler Hall Miami Univ Oxford OH 45056 E-mail: macklipa@muohio.edu.

MACKLIN, RUTH, bioethics educator; b. Newark, Mar. 27, 1938; d. Hyman and Frieda (Yaruss) Chimacoff; m. Martin Macklin, Sept. 1, 1957 (div. June 1969); children: Meryl, Shelley Macklin Taylor. BA with distinction, Cornell U., 1958; MA in Philosophy, Case Western Res. U., 1966, PhD in Philosophy, 1968. Instr. in philosophy Case Western Res. U., Cleve., 1967—68, asst. prof., 1968—71, assoc. prof., 1971—76; assoc. for behavioral studies The Hastings Ctr., Hastings-on-Hudson, NY, 1976—80; vis. assoc. prof. Albert Einstein Coll. Medicine, Bronx, NY, 1977—78, assoc. prof., 1978—84, prof. dept. epidemiology and social medicine, 1984—. Cons. NIH, 1986—; advisor WHO, Geneva, 1989—; mem. White House Adv. Com. on Human Radiation Experiments, Washington1994; chair ethical rev. com. UNAIDS, Geneva, 1996—2001. Author: Man, Mind and Morality, 1982, Mortal Choices, 1987, Enemies of Patients, 1993, Surrogates and Other Mothers, 1994, Against Relativism, 1999, Double Standards in Medical Research, 2004; contbr. articles to ethics, law and med. jours. Fellow: APHA, Am. Soc. Law, Medicine and Ethics, Inst. Medicine NAS, The Hastings Ctr., Am. Philosophys. Assn. (life); mem.: Am. Soc. Bioethics and Humanities (bd. dirs. 1997—99), Internat. Assn. Bioethics (bd. dirs., pres. 1999—2001). Democrat. Office: A Einstein Coll Medicine Dept Epidemiology Population Health 1300 Morris Park Ave Bronx NY 10461-1926

MACKLIS, ROGER MILTON, physician, educator, researcher; b. Stratford, Conn., Mar. 12, 1956; m. Carol Clark, July 25, 1987; children: Andrew Clark, Paul Clark. BS, MS, Yale U., 1978; MD, Harvard U., 1983. Diplomate Am Bd Radiation Oncology. Instr. Harvard Med. Sch., Boston, 1988-89, asst. prof. radiation oncology, 1989-93; dep. div. chief Children's Hosp., Boston, 1990-93; chmn. dept. radiation oncology Cleve. Clinic Found., 1993—. Biomedical consult, Boston, 1989—; assoc prof hist med Case Western Res Univ, 1995—; prof. medicine Cleve. Clin. Lerner Coll. of Medicine, 2004—. Author: (book) Manual of Introductory Clinical Medicine, 1984; contbr. articles to profl jours. Recipient Resident Research Award, ASTRO, 1988, Jr Faculty Research Award, Am Cancer Soc, 1990. Mem.: Soc Chairs of Acad Radiation Oncology Programs (treas, vpres, pres), Am Soc Therapeutic Radiology and Oncology, Am Soc Clin Oncology (Young Investigator Award 1987), Radiation Research Soc. Achievements include research in research on new approaches to cancer treatment involving radioactively labeled molecules and novel technologies for minimizing medical errors in oncology. Office: Cleve Clinic Found Dept Radiation Oncology 9500 Euclid Ave Cleveland OH 44195-0001 Office Phone: 216-444-5576. Business E-Mail: macklis@ccf.org.

MACKNIGHT, WILLIAM JOHN, chemist, educator; b. N.Y.C., May 5, 1936; s. William John and Margaret Ann (Stuart) M.; m. Carol Marie Bernier, Aug. 19, 1967 BS, Rochester U., N.Y., 1958; MA, Princeton U., N.J., 1963, PhD, 1964. Research assoc. Princeton U., N.J., 1964-65; asst. prof. chemistry U. Mass., Amherst, 1965-69, assoc. prof. chemistry, 1969-74, prof. chemistry, 1974-76, dept. head polymer sci., 1976-85, prof. polymer sci. and engring., 1985-88, 95-96, head dept. polymer sci. & engring., 1988-95, disting. univ. prof., 1996-98, Wilmer D. Barret disting. prof., 1998-99, Wilmer D. Barret Disting. prof. emeritus, 1999—. Mem. sci. and tech. adv. bd. Alcoa, Pitts., 1984-86, Diversitech Gen., Akron, Ohio, 1985-89; mem. panel for materials sci. Nat. Bur. Standards, Washington, 1983-89. Author: Polymeric Sulfur and Related Polymers, 1965; Introduction to Polymer Viscoelasticity, 2d edit., 1983 Served to lt. USN, 1958-61 Recipient Ford prize in high polymer physics Am. Phys. Soc., 1984, award for disting. svc. in the advancement of polymer sci. Japan Soc. for Polymer Sci., 1998; Guggenheim fellow, 1985 Fellow: AAAS, Am. Phys. Soc. (exec. com. 1975—76); mem.: Am. Chem. Soc. (award in polymer chemistry 1997, Herman F. Mark award polymers chemistry divsn. 2002), Nat. Acad. Engring., Cosmos Club. Avocations: music, sports. Home: 127 Sunset Ave Amherst MA 01002-2019 Office: U Mass Polymer Sci & Engring Dept Conte Bldg Amherst MA 01003 Office Phone: 413-577-1412. Business E-Mail: wmacknight@polysci.umass.edu.

MACKORELL, JAMES THEODORE, JR., entrepreneur, small business owner; b. Chapel Hill, N.C., Nov. 6, 1959; s. James Theodore and June (Andrews) M.; m. Wendy LeVeau, June 25, 1983 (div.); children: Andrew James, Ashley Nicole; m. Stacy Conn, Oct. 5, 1996. BS, Appalachian State U., 1982. Owner Makoto's of Boone, N.C., 1981-87; treas. Mendenmack, Inc., Boone, 1985-86; sec., treas. Mackenall Enterprises, Inc., Boone, 1986-87; owner Makato's of Tenn., 1987-91; founder, owner, mgr. Mackorell Group, Inc., Boone, 1989—, pres., 1996. Cons. Food Mgmt., Inc., Boone, 1982-86. Organizer fund raising Boone Citizens Com. for Legal Control, 1986; chmn. Emily B. Andrews Meml. Found., 2003; mem. chancellors com., alumni corp. com. Appalachian State U.; chmn. Emily B Andrews Meml. Found., 1998. Recipient Eagle Scout award Boy Scouts Am., 1976. Mem. Nat. Restaurant Assn. (Cert. of Achievement 1984), N.C. Restaurant Assn., High Country Host, Boone Area C. of C., Nat. Eagle Scout Assn. (life), Chancellors Club (Appalachian State U. com.), Yosef Club (Boone). Republican. Mem. Church of Christ. Avocations: basketball, skiing, travel. Home: 626 Windwood Ln Boone NC 28607-7090 Office: The Mackorell Group Inc 2124 Blowing Rock Rd Boone NC 28607-6154 E-mail: ted@makotos-boone.com.

MACKOWSKI, JOHN JOSEPH, retired insurance company executive; b. Westport, Mass., Feb. 1, 1926; s. John J. and Victoria K. (Skript) Mieczkowski; m. Ruth Williams, Feb. 3, 1951; children: Martha, John Matthew, Daniel, Joan. AB, Duke U., 1948; student, Harvard Advanced Mgmt. Program, 1970, 71. With Ins. Co. of N.Am., Boston, Phila., Chgo., 1948-51; with Atlantic Mut. Ins. Co., N.Y.C., 1951-88, chmn., CEO, to 1988. Bd. dirs. Transatlantic Holdings, Inc. 1st lt. USMCR, 1943-46. Mem. Sawgrass Club (Ponte Vedra Beach, Fla.), Acoaxet Country Club (Westport Harbor, Mass.), Spindle Rock Yacht Club, Sigma Chi, Beta Lambda. Episcopalian. Home: 19 Village Walk Cir Ponte Vedra Beach FL 32082-3500 also: 33 Widgeon Ln Little Compton RI 02837-1960 E-mail: jmackowski@aol.com.

MACKUS, ELOISE L. food products company executive; Asst. gen. counsel J.M. Smucker Co., Orrville, Ohio, 1994-99, dir. internat., 1999, v.p., gen. mgr. internat. market, 2000—. Office: 1 Strawberry Ln Orrville OH 44667-1241

MACKWELL, STEPHEN JOSEPH, geophysicist, educator; b. Christchurch, New Zealand, June 5, 1956; arrived in U.S., 1984; s. Alan Gordon Mackwell and Mary Veronica (Carter) Francis; m. Carmen Yevette Sykes, Dec. 31, 1994. BSc in Physics and Math., U. Canterbury, Christchurch, New Zealand, 1978, MSc in Physics, 1979; diploma of edn., Christchurch Tchrs. Coll., New Zealand, 1979; PhD in Geophysics, Australian Nat. U., Canberra, 1985. Postdoctoral assoc. Cornell U., Ithaca, NY, 1984—86, rsch. fellow, 1984—87; asst. prof. Pa. State U., University Park, 1987—92, assoc. prof., 1992—98; prof. exptl. geophysics Bayerisches Geoinst., Germany, 1998—2000, dir., 2000—02, Lunar and Planetary Inst., Houston, 2002—. Program dir. for geophysics, div. of earth sci., NSF, Washington, 1993-94, expert cons., 1995; panelist proposal rev. NASA, Houston, 1994-95; expert rev. Geoscis. Rsch. program, Dept. Energy, 1993; mem. rev. panel Planetary Geology and Geophysics program, NASA, 1994-96, 2002-, group chief, 1996-98. Assoc. editor Jour. Geophys. Rsch. - Solid Earth, 1992—97, mem. editl. bd. Physics of the Earth and Planetary Interiors, 1992—98, Tectonophysics, 2002; editor: (Solid Earth) Geophys. Rsch. Letters, 2000—01; editor-in-chief Geophys. Rsch. Letters, 2002—; contbr. articles to profl. jours. Recipient Stipendiat der Alexander von Humboldt-Stiftung, Bayreuth, Germany, 1996; grantee, NSF, 1988—98, NASA, 1993—98. Fellow: Mineral. Soc. Am.; mem.: AAAS, Am. Geophys. Union (mem. meetings program com. 1988—91, mem. mineral acquisition and distbn. subcom. 1989—90, mem. phys. properties of Earth materials com., tectonophysics section 1989—91, mem. mineral physics com. 1990—92, mem. 75th anniversary com. 1992—94, mem. meetings com. 1992—96, mem. mineral and rock physics com. 2000—03, mineral physics editor for EOS trans. 1990—92, editor-in-chief, frontiers in mineral physics 1988), Am. Ceramic Soc. Office: Lunar and Planetary Inst 3600 Bay Area Blvd Houston TX 77058

MACLACHLAN, DOUGLAS LEE, marketing educator; b. Hollywood, Calif., Aug. 27, 1940; s. Alexander D. and Patricia E. (Culver) MacL.; m. Natalie Bowditch Knauth, July 23, 1966; children: Heather Bowditch, Trevor Douglas. AB in Physics, U. Calif., Berkeley, 1962, MBA, 1965, MA in Stats., 1970, PhD in Bus. Adminstrn., 1971; student, Hastings Sch. Law, 1965—66. Instr. bus. adminstrn. U. Calif., Berkeley, 1969-70; v.p. Hartec Corp., Newport Beach, Calif., 1965-70; acting asst. prof. U. Wash., Seattle, 1970-71, asst. prof., 1971-74, assoc. prof., 1974-78, prof., chmn. dept. mktg. and internat. bus., 1978-86, prof., acting chair dept. mktg. and internat. bus., 1993-94, Affiliate Program Disting. prof. mktg. and internat. bus., 1986-88, Nordstrom prof. retail mktg., 1988-89, Ford Motor Co. prof. mktg., 1989-90, assoc. dean Sch. Bus., 1995-99, prof. mktg., 1999—, faculty dir. Internat. Alliances, 2003—. Vis. prof. bus. adminstrn. U. Calif., Berkeley, 1974; vis. prof. Institut Europeen des Affaires, Fontainebleau, France, 1982—83, Cath. U. Leuven, Belgium, 1991—92, Koc U., Istanbul, 2001; dir. Univ. Book Store, 1985—2002. Contbr. articles to profl. jours.; mem. editl. bd.: Jour. Mktg. Rsch., 1975-81. Mem. Am. Mktg. Assn. (dir. Puget Sound chpt. 1975-77, 90-91, pres. 1978-79), Informs, Am. Statis. Assn., Decision Scis. Inst., Assn. Consumer Rsch., Clan MacLachlan Soc. (pres. n.w. br. 1995—), Alpha Kappa Psi, Kappa Delta Rho. Home: 16305 Inglewood Rd NE Kenmore WA 98028-3908 Office: U Washington Box 353200 Seattle WA 98195-3200 E-mail: macl@u.washington.edu.

MACLACHLAN, GORDON ALISTAIR, biology professor, researcher; b. Saskatoon, Sask., Can., June 30, 1930; s. Hector Ross and Nellie (Glass) M.; m. Sarah Dangerfield, June 26, 1959; children: Mary, Anna. BA, U. Sask., 1952, MA, 1954; PhD, U. Man., 1956. Nat. Rsch. Coun. Can. postdoctoral fellow Imperial Coll., London, 1956—58, Agrl. Rsch. Coun. Gt. Britain fellow, 1959; asst. prof. U. Alta., Edmonton, 1960-62; assoc. prof. biology McGill U., Montreal, 1962-69, prof., 1970-98, emeritus prof., 1998—, chmn. dept., 1970-75, 95, dean. grad. studies, vice prin. rsch., 1980-90. Commonwealth prof. Australia, 1975. Home: #2104 1088 Quebec St Vancouver BC Canada V6A 4H2 E-mail: g.maclac@telus.net.

MACLACHLAN, KYLE, actor; b. Yakima, WA, Feb. 22, 1960; m. Desiree Gruber, 2002. BFA, U. Wash., Seattle, 1981. Actor: (films) Dune, 1984, Blue Velvet, 1986, The Hidden, 1987, Don't Tell Her It's Me, 1990, The Doors, 1991, Twin Peaks: Fire Walk with Me, 1992, Where the Day Takes You, 1992, Rich in Love, 1993, The Trial, 1993, The Flintstones, 1994, Showgirls, 1995, The Trigger Effect, 1996, Mad Dog Time, 1996, One Night Stand, 1997, Hamlet, 1999, Perfume, 2001, Me Without You, 2001, Miranda, 2002, Northfork, 2003, Touch of Pink, 2004; TV series Twin Peaks, 1990-91 (Golden Globe award, 1991), Sex and the City, 2000; TV movies: Against the Wall, 1994, Roswell, 1994, Moonshine Highway, 1996, Thunder Point, 1996, Route 9, 1998, The Spring, 2000; dir. (TV series) Tales from the Crypt, 1989; TV guest appearance Miami Vice, 1988. Address: Industry Entertainment Ste 300 955 S Carrillo Dr Los Angeles CA 90048 also: ICM 8942 Wilshire Blvd Beverly Hills CA 90211*

MACLACHLAN, PATRICIA, author; b. Cheyenne, Wyo., Mar. 3, 1938; d. Philo and Madonna (Moss) Pritzkau; m. Robert MacLachlan, Apr. 14, 1962; children: John, Jamie, Emily. BA, U. Conn., 1962. Tchr. English Bennett Jr. High Sch., Manchester, Conn., 1963-79. Vis. lectr. Smith Coll., Northampton, Mass., 1986—. Author: The Sick Day, 1979, Arthur, for the Very First Time, 1980 (Golden Kite award Soc. Children's Book Writers 1980), Moon, Stars, Frogs, and Friends, 1980, Through Grandpa's Eyes, 1980, Cassie Binegar, 1982, Mama One, Mama Two, 1982, Tomorrow's Wizard, 1982, Seven Kisses in a Row, 1983, Unclaimed Treasures, 1984 (Boston Globe/Horn Book award 1984), Sarah, Plain and Tall, 1985 (Golden Kite award 1985, Scott O'Dell Historical Fiction award 1985, John Newbery medal 1986, Jefferson Cup award Va. Libr. Assn. 1986, Christopher award 1986, Garden State Children's Book award N.J. Libr. Assn. 1988), The Facts and Fictions of Minna Pratt, 1988 (Parent's Choice award Parent's Choice Found. 1988), Three Names, 1991, Journey, 1991, All the Places to Love, 1993, Baby, 1993, Skylark, 1994, What You Know First, 1995, Caleb's Story, 2001; author (screenplays): Sarah Plain and Tall, 1988, Skylark, 1992, Journey, 1992. Bd. dirs. Children's Aid Family Svc. Agency, 1970-80. Recipient numerous awards for children's fiction. Office: Curts Brown Ltd c/o Marilyn Marlow 10 Astor Pl Fl 3D New York NY 10003-6935*

MACLAINE, SHIRLEY, actress; b. Richmond, Va., Apr. 24, 1934; d. Ira O. and Kathlyn (MacLean) Beatty; m. Steve Parker, Sept. 17, 1954 (div.); 1 child, Stephanie Sachiko. Ed. high sch. Broadway appearances include Me and Juliet, 1953, Pajama Game, 1954, films appearances The Trouble With Harry, 1954, Artists and Models, 1954, Around the World in 80 Days, 1955-56, Hot Spell, 1957, The Matchmaker, 1957, The Sheepman, 1957, Some Came Running, 1958 (Fgn. Press award 1959), Ask Any Girl, 1959 (Silver Bear award as best actress Internat. Berlin Film Festival), Career, 1959, Can-Can, 1959, The Apartment, 1959 (Best Actress prize Venice Film Festival), Children's Hour, 1960, The Apartment, 1960, Two for the Seesaw, 1962, Irma La Douce, 1963, What A Way to Go, The Yellow Rolls Royce, 1964, John Goldfarb Please Come Home, 1965, Gambit and Woman Times Seven, 1967, The Bliss of Mrs. Blossom, Sweet Charity, 1969, Two Mules for Sister Sara, 1969, Desperate Characters, 1971, The Possession of Joel Delaney, 1972, The Other Half of the Sky: A China Memoir, 1975, The Turning Point, 1977, Being There, 1979, A Change of Seasons, 1980, Loving Couples, 1980, Terms of Endearment, 1983 (Acad. award 1984, Golden Globe-Best Actress), Cannonball Run II, 1984, Madame Sousatzka, 1988 (Best Actress Venice Film Festival, Golden Globe-Best Actress), Steel Magnolias, 1989, Waiting For the Light, 1990, Postcards From the Edge, 1990, Defending Your Life, 1991, Used People, 1992, Wrestling Ernest Hemingway, 1993, Guarding Tess, 1994, Evening Star, 1995, Mrs. Winterbourne, 1996, Carolina, 2003; TV appearances Shirley's World, 1971-72, Shirley MacLaine: If They Could See Me Now, 1974-75, Gypsy in My Soul, 1975-76, Where Do We Go From Here?, 1976-77, Shirley MacLaine at the Lido, 1979, Shirley MacLaine...Every Little Movement, 1980 (Emmy award 1980), TV movie appearances Out On A Limb, 1987, (directorial debut) Bruno, 2000, TV mini-series Joan of Arc, Salem Witch Trials, 2002; prodr., TV movies These Old Broads, 2001; co-dir. documentary: China The Other Half of the Sky; star U.S. tour stage musical Out There Tonight, 1990; author: Don't Fall Off the Mountain, 1970, The New Celebrity Cookbook, 1973, You Can Get There From Here, 1975, Out on a Limb, 1983, Dancing in the Light, 1985, It's All in the Playing, 1987, Going Within: A Guide for Inner Transformation, 1989, Dance While You Can, 1991; editor: McGovern: The Man and His Beliefs, 1972, My Lucky Stars, 1995, The Camino, 2000, Out On A Leash: Exploring The Nature of Reality and Love, 2003. Address: C/O ICM 8942 Wilshire Blvd Beverly Hills CA 90211-1934*

MACLANE, SAUNDERS, mathematician, educator; b. Taftville, Conn., Aug. 4, 1909; s. Donald Bradford and Winifred (Saunders) MacLane; m. Dorothy M. Jones, July 21, 1933 (dec. Feb. 1985); children: Margaret Ferguson, Cynthia M. Hay; m. Osa Segal, Aug. 16, 1986. PhB, Yale U., 1930; AM, U. Chgo., 1931; DPhil, Goettingen, Fed. Republic Germany, 1934; DSc (hon.), Purdue U., 1965; DSc (hon.), Yale U., 1969, Coe Coll., 1973; DSc (hon.), U. Pa., 1977; DSc (hon.), Union Coll., 1990, Notre Dame U., 1998; LLD (hon.), Glasgow (Scotland) U., 1971. Sterling Research fellow Yale U., 1933—34; Benjamin Peirce instr. Harvard U., 1934—36; instr. Cornell U., 1936—37, U. Chgo., 1937—38; asst. prof. Harvard U., 1938—41, assoc. prof., 1941—46, prof., 1946—47; prof. math. U. Chgo., 1947—63, chmn. dept., 1952—58, Max Mason Disting. Service prof. of math., 1963—82, prof. emeritus, 1982—. Exec. com. mem.Internat. Math. Union, 1954—58; rsch. mathematician Applied Math. Group, Columbia, 1943—44, dir., 1944—45; mem. Nat. Sci. Bd., 1974—80. Author (with Garrett Birkhoff): Survey of Modern Algebra, 1942; author: Homology, 1963, Algebra, 1967, Categories for the Working Mathematician, 1971, Mathematics: Form and Function, 1985; author: (with I. Moerdijk) Sheaves in Geometry and Logic, A First Introduction to Topos Theory, 1992; editor: Bull. Am. Math. Soc.1943, mng. editor Bull. Am. Math. Soc.1943, 1946—47; editor: Trans. Am. Math. Soc., 1949—54; chmn. editl. com., editor Carus Math. Monographs, 1940—45, contbr. articles to Annals Math., other jours. Recipient Nat. medal of Sci., NSF, 1989; fellow John Simon Guggenheim, 1947—48, 1972—73. Mem.: NAS (coun. mem. 1958—61, 1969—72, v.p. 1968—71, chmn. editl. bd. prpocs. 1960—68), Am. Acad. Arts and Sci. (coun. mem. 1981—85), Assn. for Symbolic Logic (exec. com. 1945—47), Royal Soc. Edinburgh, Akademie der Wissenschaften (Heidelberg), Am. Philos. Soc. (mem. coun. 1960—63, v.p. 1968—71), Royal Danish Acad. Scis. (fgn. mem.), Math. Assn. Am. (v.p. 1948—49, pres. 1950—52, Chauvenet prize for math. expn. 1941, Disting. Svc. award 1975, Proctor prize 1979), Am. Math. Soc. (coun. mem. 1939—41, v.p. 1946—47, pres. 1973—74, Leroy P. Steele prize 1986), Sigma Xi, Phi Beta Kappa. Congregationalist.

MAC LAREN, DAVID SERGEANT, manufacturing corporation executive, inventor; b. Cleve., Jan. 4, 1941; s. Albert Sergeant and Theadora Beidler (Potter) MacL.; children: Alison, Catherine, Carolyn. AB in Econs., Miami U., Oxford, Ohio, 1964. Chmn. bd., pres., Jet Inc., Cleve., 1967—; founder, chmn. bd., pres. Air Injector Corp., Cleve., 1966-78; founder, pres., chmn. bd. Fluid Equipment, Inc., Cleve., 1966-72; founder, chmn. bd., pres. T&M Co., Cleve., 1966-71, Alison Realty Co., Cleve., 1966—; chmn. bd., pres. Sergeant Realty, Inc., 1979-86; bd. dirs. Gilmore Industries, Cleve., 1975-77, MWL Systems, L.A., 1979-85; mem. tech. com. Nat. Sanitation Found., Ann Arbor, Mich., 1967-90. Patentee in field. Mem. Rep. State Cen. Com., 1968-72; bd. dirs. Cleve. State U. Found., 1986-90. Served with arty. AUS, 1964-66. Fellow Royal Soc. Health (London); mem. Nat. Environ. Health Assn., Am. Pub. Health Assn., Nat. Water Pollution Control Fedn., Cen. Taekwondo Assn. (2d Dan), Jiu-Jitsu/Karati Black Belt Fedn. (black belt instr.), Mercedes Benz Club N.Am. (pres. 1968), H.B. Leadership Soc. (sch. headmaster soc., devel. com. 1976-78), SAR, Soc. Mayflower Descendants, Delta Kappa Epsilon (nat. bd. dirs. 1974-86, dir. Kappa chpt. 1969—), Mentor Harbor Yachting Club, The Country Club, Cotillion Soc., Union League Club (N.Y.C.), Yale Club (N.Y.C.), Deke Club (N.Y.C.), N.Y. Acad. Scis. Office: Jet Inc 750 Alpha Dr Cleveland OH 44143-2167

MACLAREN, ROBERT IAN, II, lawyer; b. West Palm Beach, Fla., Aug. 5, 1947; s. Robert Ian and Gertrude Lilly (Carson) MacL.; m. Linda Carl Olson, Dec. 19, 1970; children: Eleonora Olson, Robert Ian III, Carson Hunt, Marylinda Pierce-Mills. BA, U. Fla., 1969, JD, 1972. Assoc. Gunster, Yoakley, Criser, Stewart & Hersey P.A., Palm Beach, Fla., 1973-76; ptnr. Osborne, Hankins & MacLaren, Boca Raton, Fla., 1977—. Adminstrv. asst. to Ho. minority leader Fla. Ho. of Reps., Tallahassee, 1970; bd. dirs. Hospice By The Sea, Inc. Chmn. bd. dirs. Boca Raton Hist. Soc., 1980, 82, YMCA of Boca Raton, Inc., 1981. Served with USMC, 1966-68. Mem. ABA, Fla. Bar Assn., Palm Beach County Bar Assn., South County Bar Assn., Assn. Trial Lawyers Am. Republican. Episcopalian. Office Phone: 561-395-1000.

MACLAREN, ROY, retired federal official; b. Vancouver, B.C., Can., Oct. 26, 1934; s. Wilbur and Anne (Graham) MacLaren; m. Alethea Mitchell, June 25, 1959; children: Ian, Vanessa, Malcolm. BA, U. B.C., 1955; MA, U. Cambridge, Eng., 1957; postgrad., Harvard U., 1974; MDiv, U. Toronto, 1991, DCL (hon.), 1996; DHL (hon.), U. N. Ala.; LLD (hon.), U. N.B., U. P.E.I. Fgn. svc. officer Can. Diplomatic Svc., 1957-69; dir. corporate pub. affairs Massey-Ferguson Ltd., Toronto, 1969-74; chmn., CEO Ogilvy & Mather, Toronto, 1974-76; chmn. C .B. Media Ltd., 1976-93; mem. Parliament of Can., 1979-84, 88-96, parliamentary sec. to min. of energy, mines and resources, 1980-82, min. of state (fin.), 1983-84, min. of nat. revenue, 1984, min. of internat. trade, 1993-96; high commr. for Can. to U.K. of Gt. Britain and No. Ireland, 1996-2000; ret., 2000. Bd. dirs. Std. Life, Brascan, Patheon, Algoma Ctrl. Author: (book) Canadians in Russia: 1918-19, 1976, Canadians on the Nile, 1882-1898, 1978, Canadians Behind Enemy Lines, 1939-1945, 1981, Honourable Mentions, 1986, African Exploits: The Diaries of William Stairs, 1998; contbr. articles to profl. jours. Commr. Trilateral Commn.; chmn. Can. Inst. Internat. Affairs, Can.-India Bus. Coun.; coun. mem. Internat. Inst. Strategic Studies. Hon. col. 7th Toronto Rgt. Royal Can. Arty. Mem.: Pratt's (London), White's (London), Rideau Club (Ottawa), Toronto Club, Royal Can. Yacht Club. Address: 425 Russell Hill Rd Toronto ON Canada M5P 2S4

MACLAUCHLIN, ROBERT KERWIN, communications artist, educator; b. Framingham, Mass., Oct. 8, 1931; s. Charles Lewis and Elinor Frances (Kerwin) MacL.; m. Elizabeth D'Ann Willson, June 13, 1964. BA in Sociology, U. Mass., Amherst, 1954; MEd, Bridgewater State Coll., 1958; MS in Radio and TV, Syracuse U., 1959; PhD in Speech, Radio, TV, Mich. State U., 1969. 54personnel trainee Nat. Security Agy., Washington, 1954—55; elem. sch. tchr. Mattapoisett (Mass.) Pub. Schs., 1957-58; asst. prof., dir. programming Maine Ednl. TV Network, Orono, 1959-66; assoc. prof. speech communications, dir. TV-Radio instrn. Colo. State U., Ft. Collins, 1969-76, prof., dir. TV-Radio instrn., 1976-98, prof. emeritus, 1998—. Cons. U. Maine, Orono, 1968, Ft. Collins Presbyn. Ch., 1976-78, Sta. KCOL-AM-FM Ft. Collins, 1978, Pub. Health Assn., Ft. Collins, 1985; archives program guest Maine Pub. Broadcast, Orono, 1983; adv. team NASA, 2000; lectr. Met. State Coll., Denver, 2001, Metro State Coll., Denver, 2001-02. Festival luncheon spkr. dist. convention Rotary Club, 1998; layman's Sunday spkr. First Presbyn. Ch., Ft. Collins, 2002-03. With U.S. Army, 1955-57. Recipient Excellence in Teaching award Mich. State U., 1969, Friend of Broadcasting award Colo. Broadcasters Assn., 1985, Resolution award Colo. Broadcasters Assn., 1997, Oliver P. Pennock Disting. Svc. award Colo. State U., 1997; named Disting. Vis. Prof. U. Vt., Burlington, 1983, A Teacher Who Makes A Difference Denver's Rocky Mountain News, KCNC-TV, 1987; endowed scholarship named in his honor Colo. State U., 2000. Mem. NATA (panel Colo. chpt. 1989—), Broadcast Edn. Assn. (Industry State chmn. 1981-86, panel 1991—, chmn. faculty internship com. 1991—), Colo. Broadcasters Assn. (edn. com. 1972—, Hall of Fame com. 1980—, human resources com. 1991, Friend of Broadcast award 1985, panelist summer conv. 1994, panelist summer conv. 1995), Broadcast Pioneers (charter mem. Colo. chpt.), Kiwanis (Disting. past pres. 1979-80, Legion of Honor award 2000, Ring of Honor award 2003). Republican. Avocation: outdoor activities. Home: 1407 Country

Club Rd Fort Collins CO 80524-1907 E-mail: bobmacl@lamar.colostate.edu. *Personal philosophy: Set high goals, enjoy people and laughter, and always seek to give back more to society than you take from it.*

MACLAUGHLIN, FRANCIS JOSEPH, lawyer; b. Davenport, Iowa, Oct. 5, 1933; s. Francis Joseph and Sylvia (Boone) MacL.; m. Joan Elizabeth Pfeiffer, Oct. 17, 1959; children: Lisa Ann, Christine Ann, Francis Joseph BA, Yale U., 1955; JD, U. Mich., 1958. Bar: Ill. 1958, Calif. 1963. Assoc. Graham, Califf, Harper & Benson, Moline, Ill., 1958-59, Lillick, McHose & Charles, Los Angeles, 1963-70, ptnr. L.A., 1970-90, White and Case, 1990—. Lt. USN, 1959-63 Mem. ABA, Calif. Bar Assn., Los Angeles County Bar Assn., Maritime Law Assn. U.S. Republican. Office: White & Case 633 W 5th St Ste 1900 Los Angeles CA 90071-2087

MACLAUGHLIN, HARRY HUNTER, federal judge; b. Breckenridge, Minn., Aug. 9, 1927; s. Harry Hunter and Grace (Swank) MacL.; m. Mary Jean Shaffer, June 25, 1958; children: David, Douglas. BBA with distinction, U. Minn., 1949, JD, 1956 Bar: Minn. 1956. Law clk. to justice Minn. Supreme Ct.; ptnr. MacLaughlin & Mondale, MacLaughlin & Harstad, Mpls., 1956-72; assoc. justice Minn. Supreme Ct., 1972-77; U.S. sr. dist. judge Dist. of Minn., Mpls., 1977—. Part-time instr. William Mitchell Coll. Law, St. Paul, 1958-63; lectr. U. Minn. Law Sch., 1973-86; mem. 8th Cir. Jud. Council, 1981-83. Bd. editors: Minn. Law Rev, 1954-55. Mem. Mpls. Charter Commn., 1967-72, Minn. State Coll. Bd., 1971-72, Minn. Jud. Council, 1972; mem. nat. adv. council Small Bus. Adminstrn., 1967-69. Served with USNR, 1945-46. Recipient U. Minn. Outstanding Achievement award, 1995, named Best Fed. Dist. Ct. Judge in 8th Cir., Am. Lawyer mag., 1983. Mem. ABA, Minn. Bar Assn., Hennepin County Bar Assn., Beta Gamma Sigma, Phi Delta Phi. Congregationalist. Office: US Dist Ct 8E US Courthouse 300 S Fourth St Minneapolis MN 55415

MACLAURY, BRUCE KING, financial institution executive; b. Mount Kisco, N.Y., May 7, 1931; s. Bruce King and Edith Mae (Wills) MacL.; m. Virginia Doris Naef, Jan. 8, 1955; children— John, David. BA, Princeton, 1953; MA, Harvard, 1958, PhD, 1961. Successively mgr., v.p. fgn. dept. Fed. Res. Bank N.Y., N.Y.C., 1958-69; dep. under sec. for monetary affairs U.S. Treasury Dept., Washington, 1969-71; pres. Fed. Res. Bank of Mpls., 1971-77, Brookings Instn., Washington, 1977-95, pres. emeritus, 1995—. Bd. dirs. Am. Express Bank Ltd., Nat. Steel Corp., St. Paul Cos., The Vanguard Group. Trustee Nat. Com. for Econ. Devel., 1978—; mem. Coun. on Fgn. Rels., N.Y.C., 1962,; chair emergency trustees D.C. Pub. Schs., 1996-98. Recipient Exceptional Service award U.S. Treasury Dept., 1971 Mem. Phi Beta Kappa, Cosmos. Home: 5109 Yuma Pl NW Washington DC 20016-4309 Office: Brookings Instn 1775 Massachusetts Ave NW Washington DC 20036-2103

MACLAY, DONALD MERLE, retired lawyer; b. Belleville, Pa., Feb. 16, 1934; s. Robert Barr and Grace Virginia (Royer) M.; m. Nancy Margaret Hixenbaugh, Sept. 13, 1958; children: Susan Jo (dec.), Timothy Dean. AB magna cum laude, Grove City Coll., 1956; LLB, U. Pa., 1961. Bar: D.C. 1968, Pa. 1970. Commd. fgn. svc. officer U.S. Dept. State, 1961; assigned Am. embassy, Cotonou, Dahomey (Benin), 1962-64, Am. Consulate Gen., Frankfurt, Fed. Republic Germany, 1964-66, U.S. Dept. State, Washington, 1966-69; dir. courses of study Am. Law Inst.-ABA Com. on Continuing Profl. Edn., Phila., 1969-87, dep. exec. dir., 1987-99, ret., 1999. Served with U.S. Army, 1956-58. Mem. Am. Law Inst. Democrat. Presbyterian. Home: 936 Church Rd Springfield PA 19064-3935

MACLEAN, ALEX STOKES, aerial photographer; b. Seattle, Jan. 8, 1947; s. Paul D. and Alison (Stokes) MacL. BA, Harvard Coll., 1969; M of Architecture, Harvard U., 1973. Lic. pilot. Aerial photographer, artist, Boston, 1972—. Book credits: Look of the Land: Aerial Reflections on America, 1993. One-man shows include North Street Gallery, Boston, 1977, Alfred Stieglitz Gallery, Bank of Am. Office Hdqrs., 1984, Bain and Co., Boston, 1987; exhibited in group shows including Soho Photo Gallery, N.Y.C., 1977, Boston Visual Arts Union, 1980, Wilhelm Gallery, Houston, The Berkshire Mus., Pittsfield, Mass., 1986, N.D. Mus. Art, Grand Forks, 1987, Harvard U. Grad. Sch. Design, Cambridge, 1988, 93, Westport (Conn.) Arts Ctr., 1989, others. Mem. Am. Soc. Mag. Profls., Am. Soc. Picture Profls., Aircraft Owners and Pilot Assn., Harvard Club (Boston). Office: 25 Bay State Rd 3rd Fl Boston MA 02215

MACLEAN, BABCOCK, lawyer; b. N.Y.C., Jan. 26, 1946; s. Charles Chalmers and Lee Selden (Howe) MacL.; m. Cynthia Gannon, Feb. 15, 1983. BA, Yale U., 1967; MA, Columbia U., 1970; JD, Case Western Res. U., 1975; LLM in Taxation, NYU, 1987. Bar: Ohio 1975, N.Y. 1983. Assoc. Hadley, Matia, Mills & MacLean, Cleve., 1976-77, mem., 1977-83; tax editor Rsch. Inst. Am., N.Y.C., 1983-85; assoc. Robinson Brog, N.Y.C., 1985-86, mem., 1987—. Adj. asst. prof. taxation Pace U., N.Y.C., 1983-84; adv. bd. Rsch. Inst. Am., 1992-97. Trustee Soc. for the Preservation of Long Is. Antiquities, 2003—. Mem. ABA (sect. taxation), N.Y. State Bar Assn. (sect. taxation), Assn. Bar City N.Y. (personal income taxation com.), Yale Club, St. Anthony Club, N.Y. Yacht Club, Seawanhaka Corinthian Yacht Club, St. Andrew's Soc. N.Y., Pilgrims of the U.S. Home: 40 Lloyd Lane Lloyd Harbor NY 11743 Office: Robinson Brog 1345 Avenue Of The Americas New York NY 10105-0143 Office Phone: 212-603-6315.

MACLEAN, BARBARA HUTMACHER, author, retired journalist; b. Toledo, Ohio, Dec. 16, 1926; d. Norman Eugene and Betty Lucille Price; div. 1971; m. E. Fraser MacLean, Aug. 30, 1977; children: Beth, Jessica, Cary, David, Clay. Student, Rockford Coll., 1945, Western Mich. Coll., 1946. Reporter News-Leader, Richmond, Va., 1962; editor-writer News-Chronicle, Thousand Oaks, Calif., 1963-70, Star-Free Press, Ventura, Calif., 1971-75, Daily Dispatch, East London, South Africa, 1974-78, Wenatchee (Wash.) World, 1980-92, ret., 1992. Exchange journalist The Examiner, Huddersfield, Eng., 1983, China Daily, Beijing, 1988, The Times, Windhoek, Namibia, 1991. Author: In Black and White: Voices of Apartheid, 1980 (Eng.), 1983, I Can't Do What? Voices of Pathfinding Women, 1997, South African Women, 2003, Africa World Press, 2003, Strike A Woman, Strike A Rock: Fighting for Freedom in South Africa, 2003. Named Woman of Achievement AAUW, 1997; recipient Nat. Headliners award, 1968, 1st Social Issues Reporting award Soc. of Profl. Journalists, 1989. Home: 40 Hemlock Ct Port Townsend WA 98368-9446

MACLEAN, JUDITH E. writer, editor; b. L.A., May 13, 1946; d. Fred M. and Dorothy C. (Schmidt) MacL. BA, Rice U., 1969; postgrad., Duquesne U., 1970-71; postgrad. lang. study, Sorbonne U., 1966. Family therapist Families Together, Pitts., 1974-76; reporter In These Times, Chgo., 1976-77; co-chmn. New Am. Movement, Chgo., 1977-79; editor Am. Soc. on Aging, San Francisco, 1980-85; freelance writer, editor San Francisco, 1986—99, Berkeley, Calif., 1999—. Instr. U. Calif. Berkeley ext., San Francisco, 1994-95, Support Ctr., San Francisco, 1992-93. Co-author: (book) Women Take Care, 1986; author: Rosemary and Juliet, 2004; contbr. articles/stories to publs. Newsletter editor: Harvey Milk Lesbian and Gay Dem. Club, San Francisco, 1982-85, polit. action chmn., 1986-87; mem. nat. com. New Am. Movement, Pitts., 1972-76; mem. Nicaragua Solidarity Brigarde, Leon, Nicaragua, 1986. Named Vol. of Yr. Harvey Milk Lesbian and Gay Dem. Club, San Francisco, 1986. Avocations: cross country skiing, backpacking, hiking, sea kayaking.

MAC LEAN, LLOYD DOUGLAS, surgeon; b. Calgary, Alta., Can., June 15, 1924; s. Fred Hugh and Azilda (Trudel) MacL.; m. Eleanor Colle, June 30, 1954; children— Hugh, Charles, Ian, James, Martha. B.Sc. (Viscount Bennett scholar), U. Alta., 1947, MD (Viscount Bennett scholar), 1949; PhD, U. Minn., 1957. Resident U. Minn. Hosp., Mpls., 1950-56; instr. dept. surgery U. Minn., Mpls., 1956-58, asst. prof. surgery, 1958-59, asso. prof., 1959-62; prof. McGill U., Montreal, Que., Can., 1962—, chmn. dept. surgery, 1968-73, 77-82, 87-88. Surgeon-in-chief Ancker Hosp., St. Paul, 1957-62, Royal Victoria Hosp., Montreal, 1962-88; Edward Archibald prof. surgery McGill U., 1988-93, prof. surgery 1993—. Contbr. numerous articles on surgery, shock, host resistance and transplantation to profl. jours. Decorated officer Order Can. Fellow Royal Soc. Can.; mem. ACS (pres. 1993-94), Am. Surg. Assn. (pres. 1993), Ctrl. Surg. Assn. (pres. 1982-83), Am. Physiol. Soc., Am. Assn. Thoracic and Cardiovasc. Surgery, Soc. Surgery of Alimentary Tract. Home: # 1402-80 Berlioz Montreal QC Canada H3E 1N9 E-mail: lloydm@citenet.net.

MACLEAN, PAUL DONALD, government institute medical research official; b. Phelps, N.Y., May 1, 1913; s. Charles Chalmers and Elizabeth (Dreyfus) MacL.; m. Alison Stokes, July 16, 1942; children— Paul, David, Alexander, James, Alison. BA, Yale U., 1935; postgrad., U. Edinburgh, Scotland, 1935-36; MD cum laude, Yale U., 1940; DSci (hon.), SUNY, Binghamton, 1986. Intern in medicine Johns Hopkins U., 1940-41; asst. resident medicine New Haven Hosp., Yale Sch. Medicine, 1941-42, research asst. pathology, 1942, asst. prof. physiology, 1949-51, asst. prof. psychiatry, physiology and neurology, 1951-53, assoc. prof. physiology, 1956-57; clin. instr. medicine U. Wash. Med. Sch., Seattle, 1946-47; USPHS research fellow Harvard U. Med. Sch., also Mass. Gen. Hosp., 1947-49; dir. EEG lab. New Haven Hosp., 1951-52; assoc. prof. psychiatry, physiology and neurology, attending physician Grace-New Haven Hosp., 1953-56; sr. postdoctoral fellow NSF dept. physiology U. Zurich, 1956-57; chief sect. limbic integration and behavior Lab. Neurophysiology Intramural Research, NIMH, USPHS, Dept. Health and Human Services, Bethesda, Md., 1957-71; chief lab. brain evolution and behavior Intramural Research, Bethesda, Md., 1971-85; sr. research scientist Intramural Research Program, NIMH, 1985—. Author: The Triune Brain in Evolution, 1990; mem. editorial bd.: Jour. Nervous and Mental Disease. Emeritus trustee L.S.B. Leakey Found. Served to maj. M.C. AUS, 1942-46, PTO. Recipient award for disting. research Assn. for Research in Nervous and Mental Disease, 1964; Salmon medal and Lectureship award, 1966; Superior Service award HEW, 1967; Hincks Meml. lectr. Ont.; Spl. award Am. Psychopathol. Assn., 1971; G. Burroughs Mider NIH Lectureship award, 1972; Karl Spencer Lashley award Am. Philos. Soc., 1972; Adolph Meyer Lectureship award Am. Psychiat. Assn., 1982, Anokhin medal P.K. Anokhin Inst. Normal Physiology USSR Acad. Med. Scis., 1986; hon. Fulton fellow Yale U. Med. Sch., 1990. Mem. Am. Neurol. Assn., Am. Physiol. Soc., Am. Assn. Electroencephalographers, Am. Assn. Neurol. Surgeons, Soc. Neurosci., Am. Assn. Anatomists, Sigma Xi, Alpha Omega Alpha. Office: NIMH Intramural Rsch Prog 9000 Rockville Pike Bethesda MD 20892-0001 Home: PO Box 35 Clayton NY 13624-0035

MACLEAN, RHONDA, information technology executive; m. Lynn Maclean. Various positions to sr. mgr. computer and comm. security The Boeing Co., 1982—96; dir. corp. info. security Nations Bank (now Bank of Am.), 1996; sr. v.p. Bank of Am., 1998—. Tech. adv. Pres. Nat. Security Telecom. Adv. Com. Fin. Services Risk Assessing, 1997; private sector coord. for fin. services industry public/private partnership on critical infostructure protection and homeland security Dept. of Treasury, 2002—. Mem. bd. adv. U. NC, Charlotte Coll. of Info. Tech. Named Women of Vision, Information Security mag., 2003, one of the 50 Most Powerful People in Networking, Networking World mag., 2003. Mem.: Fin. Services Info. Security Analysis Ctr. (FS/ISAC) (adv. to bd. dirs.), Internat. Inst. Info. Integrity (vice chmn. mem. Adv. Com.), Banking Industry Tech. Secretariat (elected mem. of Security Laboratory Governance Bd.). Office: Bank of Am Corp 100 N Tryon St Charlotte NC 28255

MACLEISH, RODERICK, novelist, screenwriter, television producer; b. Bryn Mawr, Pa., Jan. 15, 1926; s. Norman Hillard and Lenore (McCall) MacL.; m. Diana S. Chapin, May 1, 1950 (div. June 1971); children: Cynthia Sumner, Roderick Jr. Student, U. Chgo., 1944-45; DHL (hon.), Washington-Jefferson Coll., 1958. Copy boy, TV script editor ABC, N.Y.C., 1945-51; news dir. WBZ-Westinghouse Broadcasting Co., Boston, 1951-57; Washington bur. chief Westinghouse Broadcasting Co., 1957-59, chief fgn. corr., 1959-66, sr. commentator Washington, 1966-71; commentator CBS, Washington, 1971-76, NPR, Washington, 1976-90; commentator, TV prodr. Monitor Radio-TV, Washington, 1990-97; ret., 1997. Writer, narrator (PBS 3-hr. spl.) The Hermitage, 1994-95; author: The First Book of Eppe, 1985, Prince Ombra, 1987, Crossing At Ivalo, 1989. Pres. Assn. Am. Corrs. in London, 1964. Mem. Cosmos Club (Washington). Episcopalian. Home: 4000 Cathedral Ave NW Washington DC 20016-5249

MACLENNAN, AMY MARIE, poet; b. San Mateo, Calif., Jan. 11, 1967; d. Hugh William MacLennan and Barbara Jean Tompkins. BS in psychology, U. Calif., 1989; MA in English, Notre Dame de Namur U., 2003. Bd. dir. Sat. Poets. Co-author: So Luminous the Wildflowers, 2003, An Anthology of California Poets, 2003; contbr. poetry to mags. Featured reader San Luis Obispo (Calif.) Poetry Festival, 2003, 2001, Petaluma (Calif.) Poetry Walk, 2002, Sacramento (Calif.) Poetry Ctr., 2003. Recipient 1st pl., Ina Coolbrith Cir. Poetry Contest, 2003. Mem.: MLA, Tchrs. & Writers, Poetry Soc. Am., Acad. Am. Poets, PEN Ctr. USA, Calif. Writers Club, Delta Epsilon Sigma. Home: 2130 Valparaiso Dr # 4 Belmont CA 94002 Personal E-mail: amaclennan@earthlink.net.

MACLENNAN, BERYCE WINIFRED, psychologist; b. Aberdeen, Scotland, Mar. 14, 1920; came to U.S., 1949, naturalized, 1965; d. William and Beatrice (MacRae) Mellis; m. John Duncan MacLennan, Nov. 29, 1944. BSc with honors, London Sch. Econs., 1947; PhD, London U., 1960. Diplomate Am. Bd. Clin. Psychology; cert. group therapist, trauma specialist. Group psychotherapist, youth specialist cons., N.Y.C. and Washington, 1949-63; dir. Ctr. for Prevention Juvenile Delinquency and New Careers, Washington, 1963-66; sect. chief NIMH, Mental Health Study Ctr., Adelphi, Md., 1967-70, chief, 1971-74; regional adminstr. Mass. Dept. Mental Health, Springfield, 1974-75; sr. mental health adv. GAO, Washington, 1976-90; pvt. practice, specialist psychotherapy Bethesda, Md., 1990—. Clin. prof. George Washington U., 1970—; group therapy cons. D.C. Mental Health Svcs., 1993-2002, Washington Assessement and Therapy Svcs., 1992—; lectr. Montgomery C.C., 1988-91, Washington Sch. Psychiatry Geropsychiatric Program, 1997—; mem. tech. adv. com. Prince George's County Mental Health Assn., 1968-84; cons. Washington Bus. Group on Health, 1990-91, KOBA, 1991; leader Trauma Psychotherapy Groups, 2002-03, Hebrew Home Rsch. Inst. Elder Housing Socialization and Memory Improvement Groups, 2000-02. Mem. NIMH Prevention Intervention Rsch. Task Force, 1990-91, Montgomery County Victims Assistance Programs, 1990-95; v.p. Compliance, Federally Employed Women, 1979-81; pres. Glenecho chpt. Older Women's League, 1993-94. Fellow APA, Am. Orthopsychiat. Assn.; disting. fellow Am. Group Psychotherapy Assn.; mem. Washington Mushroom Club. Democrat. Office Phone: 301-320-4151.

MACLENNAN, DAVID HERMAN, research scientist, educator; b. Swan River, Man., Can., July 3, 1937; s. Douglas Henry and Sigridur (Sigurdson) MacL.; m. Linda Carol Vass, Aug. 18, 1965; children: Jessica Lynn (dec.), Jeremy Douglas, Jonathan David. BSA, U. Man., 1959; MS, Purdue U., 1961, PhD, 1963; DSc (hon.), U. Man., 2001. Postdoctoral fellow Inst. Enzyme Research, U. Wis., Madison, 1963-64; asst. prof. U. Wis., Madison, 1964-68; assoc. prof. U. Toronto, 1969-74, prof., 1974-93, J.W. Billes prof. med. rsch., 1987—, Univ. prof., 1993—, acting chmn., 1978-80, chmn., 1980-90; prin. investigator Can. Genetic Diseases Network of Ctrs. of Excellence, 1991—. Med. adv. bd. Muscular Dystrophy Assn. Can., 1976-87; scientists' rev. panel Med. Rsch. Coun. Can., 1988-90; chmn. molecular biology and pathology grants com. Heart and Stroke Found. Can., 1995-99; rsch. rev. panel U. Ottawa Heart Inst., 1991-95; med. rev. panel Gairdner Found., 1999-2001, med. adv. bd., 2001—; cons. Merck, Sharp and Dohme, West Point, Pa., 1992-98. Assoc. editor Can. Jour. Biochemistry, 1972-76; mem. editl. bd. Jour. Biol. Chemistry, 1975-80, 82-87; contbr. articles on muscle membrane biochemistry to profl. jours. Decorated Officer Order of Can.; recipient Gairdner Found. Internat. award, 1991; Can. Med. Rsch. Coun. scholar, 1969-71, I.W. Killam Meml. scholar, 1977-78; recipient I.W. Killam Meml. prize Health Scis., 1997, Jonas Salk award Ont. March of Dimes, 1998, Salute to the City award, City of Toronto, 2002, Rick Gallop award Heart and Stroke Found. Ont., 2002. Fellow Royal Soc. Can., Royal Soc. London (Glaxo-Wellcome prize 2000), NAS (fgn. assoc.); mem. Can. Biochem. Soc. (Ayerst award 1974), Am. Soc. Biol. Chemists, Biophys. Soc. (Nat. Lectr. award 1990). Home: 293 Lytton Blvd Toronto ON Canada M5N 1R7 Office: U Toronto-Banting & Best Med Rsch 112 College St Toronto ON Canada M5G 1L6 E-mail: david.maclennan@utoronto.ca.

MACLEOD, ALEX, newspaper editor; b. Seattle; Student, Whitman Coll. Night reporter to city editor to asst. mng. editor-news Seattle Times, 1976-84, assoc. mng. editor, 1984-86, mng. editor, 1986—. Office: Seattle Times PO Box 70 Seattle WA 98111-0070

MACLEOD, ANGUS, retired internist; b. Romford, Essex, U.K., Apr. 24, 1943; came to U.S., 1967; s. Malcolm Macleod and Jean (Littlefair) McKean; m. Gwynne Louise Grellner, May 23, 1969 (div. Aug. 1987); children: Kenneth, Anne, Stephen. MB, ChB, Glasgow (Scotland) U., 1967. Diplomate Am. Bd. Internal Medicine. Intern Lutheran Hosp., St. Louis, 1967-68; resident in internal medicine St. Louis U., 1969, 71-73, fellow in cardiology, 1973-74; physician Grandel Med. Group, St. Louis, 1974—2000, ret., 2000. Instr., then asst. prof. medicine St. Louis U.; chmn. dept. medicine Lutheran Hosp., St. Louis; pres. Grandel Med. Group, St. Louis. Capt. U.S. Army, 1969-71. Decorated Bronze Star. Fellow: ACP; mem.: St. Louis Met. Med. Soc., Mo. State Med. Soc. E-mail: corvus24@aol.com.

MACLEOD, DONALD WILLIAM, secondary school educator; b. Stornoway, Scotland, Oct. 3, 1935; s. Angus and Mary (MacArthur) MacL.; m. Theresa Plaskon, Aug. 25, 1973; children: Heather Anne, Robert Angus. BS, Fairleigh Dickinson U., 1964; MA, Seton Hall U., 1968, Kean U., 1977. Tchr. English and pub. speaking Hawthorne (N.J.) H.S., 1964-97, head soccer coach, 1977-79, asst. soccer coach, 1988-94, tchr. English and pub. spkg., 1995-98. Adj. prof. comms. Ramapo Coll. of N.J., Mahwah, N.J., 1981-84; tchr. English Englewood (N.J.) Adult H.S., 1987-94, adj. prof. English Ramapo Coll. N.J., 1998. With U.S. Army, 1958-60. Mem. NEA, N.J. Edn. Assn., Hawthorne Tchrs. Assn. (past v.p.). Presbyterian. Avocations: soccer, Scottish Gaelic lang., bagpipe music, jogging.

MACLEOD, GORDON C. surgeon; b. Quincy, Mass., July 12, 1930; AB, Harvard U., 1952, MD, 1956. Diplomate Am. Bd. Surgery. Intern Madigan Army Hosp., Tacoma, 1956-57; resident Brigham-Childrens Hosps., Boston, 1957-59; surg. resident Boston Univ. Hosps., Boston, 1959-61; staff surgeon USAF Hosp., Tachi-Kawa AB, Japan, 1961-64, surgeon Westover AFB, Mass., 1964-68, David Grant USAF Med. Ctr., Calif., 1968-74; chmn. surgery USAF Med. Ctr., Scott AFB, Ill., 1974-76, active staff Washington Hosp., Fremont, Calif., 1976—2002, med. dir. oper. rm., 1998-2000. Instr. surgery Boston U., 1960-61; instr. U. Calif., Davis, 1969-71, asst. clin. prof. surgery, 1971-74. Mem. ACS, AMA. E-mail: gcmacleodmd56@post.harvard.edu.

MACLEOD, GORDON KENNETH, physician, educator; b. Boston, Jan. 30, 1929; s. Gordon Kenneth and Margaret J. MacL.; m. Janet B., Aug. 17, 1957; children: Gordon K. III, Alexander B. AB, Blackburn Coll., 1954; MD, U. Cin., 1960. Indsl. engr. Procter & Gamble Co., Cin., 1954-56; intern Boston City Hosp., 1960-61; resident, clin. fellow Mass. Gen. Hosp., Boston, 1961-64; rsch. fellow Harvard U., 1962-64; sr. resident, sr. physician Boston VA Hosp., 1964-66; asst. clin. prof. medicine Yale U., 1966-69, assoc. clin. prof. medicine and pub. health, 1969-71; dir. HMO Svc., HEW, 1971-73; prof. emeritus health svcs. adminstrn. Grad. Sch. Pub. Health, U. Pitts., 1974—, chmn. dept., 1974-83, assoc. clin. prof. medicine, 1976-86, clin. prof. medicine, 1986—; pres. senate U. Pitts., 1997-98. Sec. health, State of Pa., 1979; academic dean Semester at Sea, 1999, interim dir. MD/MPH program, 2000—; mem. staff West Penn Hosp.; mem. nat. adv. coun. divsn. rsch. resources NIH, 1983-87; bd. dirs. Inst. Rsch., Edn. and Tng., 2004—; cons. Shadyside Hosp.; cons. in field. Editor: (with Mark Perlman) Health Care Capital: Competition and Control, 1978; contbr. articles to profl. jours. Served with U.S. Army, 1948-49. Ford Found. travel grantee, 1973 Fellow ACP; mem. Allegheny County Med. Soc., AMA (editl. bd. jour. 1986-94), Am. Pub. Health Assn., Med. Adminstrs. Conf., Pa. Pub. Health Assn., Pa. State Med. Soc. (pres.), Pitts. Acad. Medicine. Office: 130 Desoto St Pittsburgh PA 15213-2535 Business E-Mail: gmacleod@pitt.edu. *My first job was an industrial engineer with later training in internal medicine; it uniquely prepared me for an academic career in health management with intervals as a government executive at federal and state levels. My most challenging assignments were in initiating the federal Health Maintenance Organization program nationally, in managing the health aspects of the nuclear accident at Three Mile Island, and in training young persons for careers in internal medicine and health management.*

MACLEOD, JAMES L. minister, finance company executive, art gallery owner; b. Oakdale, La., Apr. 27, 1937; s. William Lasater and Sara Louise (Macaulay) MacLeod. BA, Washington and Lee U., 1959; MA, Emory U., 1968, BD, 1968; D, Miss. State U., 1972. Ordained to ministry Presbyn. Ch., 1963. Minister U.S.-So. Presbyn. Ch., 1963-85, minister assoc. reform synod, 1985—; educator Ga. State Schs., 1972-91; pres. Brunswick (Ga.) Fin., 1991—, Brunswick Gallery, 1993—; min. First Assoc. Reformed Pres. Ch., Augusta, Ga., 1988—99. Author: (book) Great Dr. Waddel, 1985, A Season of Grace, 1974, Presbyterian Tradition in the South, 1978. Councilman City of Brunswick, 1994—, mayor pro tem, 1996—; mem. Soc. Cin., Washington, 1970. Scholar, NEH, 1986. Fellow: Soc. Antiquaries Scotland; mem.: NEA, Ga. Assn. Edn., Fulbright Alumni Assn., Pinnacle Club, Phi Delta Kappa. Democrat. Presbyterian. Home: 508 Walker St Augusta GA 30901-2316

MACLEOD, JOHN AMEND, lawyer; b. Manila, June 5, 1942; s. Anthony Macaulay and Dorothy Lillian (Amend) M.; m. Ann Klee; children: Kerry, Jack. BBA, U. Notre Dame, 1963, JD, 1969. Bar: D.C. 1969, U.S. Supreme Ct. 1980. Assoc. Jones, Day, Reavis & Pogue, Washington, 1969-73, ptnr., 1974-79, Crowell & Moring, Washington, 1979—; CEO C&M Capitolink, 2004—, also bd. dirs. Mem. mgmt. com., 1979-82, 83-86, 91-94, 99-2000, chmn., 1984-85, 93-94. mem. mgmt. bd. and exec. com., 2000—, chmn. of the firm, 2000—. Editor-in-chief Notre Dame Law Rev., 1968-69; contbr. articles to profl. jours. Trustee Energy Mineral and Law Found., 1979—2002; bd. dirs. St. Francis Ctr., 1982—91, C&M Internat., 1991—94, 1999—, C&M Capitalink, 2004—. Served to lt. U.S. Army, 1963—65. Recipient disting. mining lawyer award Nat. Mining Assn., 1995, forest industry victory of yr. award Am. Forest and Paper Assn., 1994. Mem. ABA, D.C. Bar Assn., Notre Dame Law Assn. (dir., exec. bd.), Ptnrs. Leadership Forum, Metro. Club (Washington). Home: 4040 Swartz Rd Maurertown VA 22644-2320 Office: Crowell & Moring 1000 Pennsylvania Ave NW Washington DC 20004-2595

MACLEOD, ROBERT ANGUS, microbiology educator, researcher; b. Athabasca, Alta., Can., July 13, 1921; s. Norman John and Eleonora Pauline Bertha (Westerhoff) MacL.; m. Patricia Rosemarie Robertson, Sept. 1, 1948; children— Douglas John, Alexander Robert, Kathleen Mary, David Gordon, Michael Norman, Susan Joan BA with honors in Chemistry, U. B.C., Vancouver, Can., 1943, MA in Chemistry and Biology, 1945; PhD in Biochemistry, U. Wis., Madison, 1949. Asst. prof. Queen's U., Kingston, Ont., Can., 1949-52; sr. biochemist Fisheries Research Bd. Can., Vancouver, B.C., 1952-60; assoc. prof. to prof., chmn. dept. microbiology Macdonald Coll., McGill U., Ste. Anne de Bellevue, Que., Can., 1960-86, prof. emeritus, 1986—. Cons. Def. Research Bd., Ottawa, Ont., 1965-75; assoc. editor Can. Jour. Microbiology, Ottawa, 1965-70 Author tech. papers. Recipient Harrison prize, Royal Soc. Can., 1960. Fellow: Royal Soc. Can.; mem.: Am. Soc. Microbiology (hon.), Can. Soc. Microbiologists (hon.; pres. 1976—77, award 1973). Avocations: swimming, fishing. Home: 10 Slate St Stittsville ON Canada K2S 1Y5 E-mail: ramacl@sympatico.ca.

MACLEOD, WILLIAM BENTLEY, economics and law educator; b. Iserlohn, Germany, 1954; came to U.S., 1995; m. Raisa Nones (div.); children: Raisa, Gabriela; m. Janet Marion Currie, May 18, 1997; children: Joana, Daniel. BA magna cum laude, Queen's U., Kingston, Ont., Can., 1975, MSc in Math., 1979; PhD in Econs., U. B.C., Vancouver, Can., 1984. From asst. prof. to assoc. prof. Queen's U., 1982-90; assoc. prof. U. Montreal, 1990-92, prof. econs., 1992-96, Boston Coll., 1996-97; prof. econs. and law U. So. Calif., L.A., 1997—, dir. Ctr. for Law, Econs. and Orgn., 1997—, chair jr. recruiting, 2000—03; program dir., personnel and behavioral econs. IZA, Bonn, Germany, 2003—. Cons. Ind. Power Producers Ont., Toronto, 1990-92, Human Resources Can., Ottawa, Ont., 1993-95; Harold Innis Meml. lectr., 1996; vis. prof. econs. and law Calif. Inst. Tech., 2002, Princeton U., 2003-04; bd. dirs. We. Econs. Assn. Assoc. editor: Jour. Econ. Behavior and Orgn.,

2002—; editor: Jour. Labor Econs., 2003—; contbr. articles to profl. jours. NSF grantee, 1997-2003. Mem. AAAS, Am. Econs. Assn., Econometric Soc., Soc. Labor Economists (H. Gregg Lewis prize 2002), Assn. for Comparative Systems, Econ. Sci. Assn., Am. Law and Econs. Assn., Western Econs. Assn. (bd. dirs. 2003—). Office: U So Calif 3620 S Vermont Ave Los Angeles CA 90089-0253

MACLIN, ERNEST, biomedical diagnostics company executive; b. N.Y.C., Jan. 25, 1931; s. Samuel and Dora (Sonsky) M.; m. Edith Samuel, Feb. 18, 1956; children: Alan David, Deborah Ellen, Julie Anne. BME, CCNY, 1952, M Engring., 1969. Registered profl. engr., N.Y., N.J. Engr. Reeves Instrument Corp., N.Y.C., 1952-54, Adrian Wilson Assocs., Nagoya, Japan, 1956-57, Ford Instrument Co., L.I., N.Y., 1957-58, Technicon, Tarrytown, N.Y., 1968-69; engr., unit head Kearfott divsn. Singer Corp., Little Falls, N.J., 1958-68; v.p. R & D, Electro-Nucleonics Inc., Fairfield, N.J., 1969-90; pres. The Product Devel. Group, Paramus, N.J., 1990—. Bd. dirs. Nat. Com. for Clin. Lab. Stds., Villanova, Pa., 1981-87. Contbr. articles to profl. jours.; patentee various instruments. Capt. USAF, 1954-57; mem. USAFR ret. Fellow ASME; mem. Am. Assn. Clin. Chemistry. Jewish. Home and Office: 659 Rutgers Pl Paramus NJ 07652-4207 Office Phone: 201-261-4180.

MAC LOW, MORDECAI-MARK, astrophysicist; b. N.Y.C., Mar. 9, 1963; s. Jackson Mac Low and Iris Lezak. BA, Princeton U., 1983; PhD, U. Colo., 1989. Rsch. asst. U. Colo., Boulder, 1983-88; NRC fellow NASA Ames Rsch. Ctr., Moffett Field, Calif., 1989-90; rsch. assoc. U. Calif., Berkeley, 1991-92, U. Chgo., 1992-95; sci. Max-Planck-Inst. für Astronomie, Heidelberg, Germany, 1995-99; asst. curator of astrophysics Am. Mus. Natural History, N.Y.C., 1999—2002, assoc. curator astrophysics, 2002—. Adj. asst. prof. Columbia U., 1999—2002, adj. assoc. prof., 2002—; mem. grant rev. panels NASA; chair panels NSF and NASA; mem. adv. com. tchr. renewal for urban sci. tchg. program Am. Mus. Natural History and CUNY; mem. several conf. sci. organizing coms.; spkr. in field; reviewer in field. Contbr. articles to popular mags. and profl. jours. Grantee, NSF, 1999—, NASA, 1999—. Mem. Am. Astron. Soc. (com. on employment 2001-04), Am. Phys. Soc., Internat. Astron. Union. Office: Am Mus Natural History Dept Astrophysics CPW & 79th St New York NY 10024-5192 Office Phone: 212-496-3443. E-mail: mordecai@amnh.org.

MACMAHON, THOMAS P. healthcare company executive; B in mktg., St. Peter's Coll., NJ; MBA, Fairleigh Dickinson U., 1975. Joined Roche Bio-Med. Labs. as mktg. rsch. analyst, 1969; v.p. pub. affairs and planning Hoffman-La Roche Inc., Nutley, NJ, 1982—83, v.p. and gen. mgr. diagnostics systems unit, 1983—86, pres. Roche Diagnostics Group, 1988—96, mem. exec. com., 1988—96, sr. v.p., 1993—96; vice chmn. Lab. Corp. Am. Holdings, Burlington, NC, 1995—96, chmn., 1996—, CEO, pres., 1997—. Named to The Pinnacle (highest award), Fairleigh Dickinson U., 2001. Office: Lab Corp Am Holdings 358 S Main St Burlington NC 27215*

MACMANUS, SUSAN ANN, political science educator, researcher; b. Tampa, Fla., Aug. 22, 1947; d. Harold Cameron and Elizabeth (Riegler) MacM. BA cum laude, Fla. State U., 1968, PhD, 1975; MA, U. Mich., 1969. Instr. Valencia C.C., Orlando, Fla., 1969-73; rsch. asst. Fla. State U., 1973-75; asst. prof. U. Houston, 1975-79, assoc. prof., 1979-85, dir. MPA program, 1983-85; rsch. assoc. Ctr. Pub. Policy, 1982-85; prof., dir. PhD progam Cleve. State U., 1985-87; prof. pub. adminstrn. and polit. sci. U. South Fla., Tampa, 1987—, chair dept. govt. and internat. affairs, 1987-93, disting. univ. prof., 1999. Vis. prof. U. Okla., Norman, 1981—; field rsch. assoc. Brookings Inst., Washington, 1977—82, Princeton (N.J.) U., 1979—, Cleve. State U., 1982—83, Westat, Inc., Washington, 1983—; summer field rsch. assoc. Columbia U., N.Y.C., 1979, Nat. Acad. Pub. Adminstrn., Washington, 1980. Author: Revenue Patterns in U.S. Cities and Suburbs: A Comparative Analysis, 1978, Federal Aid to Houston, 1993; author: (with others) Governing A Changing America, 1984; author: (with Francis T. Borkowski) Visions for the Future: Creating New Institutional Relationships Among Academia, Business, Government, and Community, 1989; author: Reapportionment and Representation in Florida: A Historical Collection, 1991, Doing Business with Government: Federal, State, Local and Foreign Government Purchasing Practices for Every Business and Public Institution, 1992, Young v. Old: Generational Combat in the 21st Century, 1996; author: (with Elizabeth R. MacManus) Citrus, Sawmills, Critters & Crackers: Life in Early Lutz and Central Pasco County, 1998; author: Targeting Senior Voters, 2000; author: (with Elizabeth R. MacManus) The Lutz Depot, 2000; editor: Mapping Florida's Political Landscape: The Changing Art and Politics of Reapportionment and Redistricting, 2002; editor: (with Thomas R. Dye) Politics in States and Communities, 11th edit., 2003; writer: manuals in field, mem. editl. bd.: various jours; contbr. articles to jours., chpts. to books. Bd. dirs. Houston Area Women's Ctr., 1977, past pres., v.p. fin., treas.; mem. LWV, Gov.'s Coun. Econ. Advisers, 1988-90, Harris County (Tex.) Women's Polit. Caucus, Houston; bd. dirs. USF Rsch. Found., Inc.; chair Fla. Elections Commn., 1999-2003; mem. Fla. Gov.'s Coun. Econ. Advisers, 2000—. Recipient U. Houston Coll. Social Scis. Tchg. Excellence award, 1977, Herbert J. Simon award for best article in 3d vol., Internat. Jour. Pub. Adminstrn., 1981, Theodore & Venette Askounes-Ashford Disting Scholar award U. South Fla., 1991, Disting. Rsch. Scholar award, 1991, Tchg. Excellence award, 1999; Ford Found. fellow, 1967-68; grantee Valencia C. C. Faculty, 1972, U. Houston, 1976-77, 79, 83; Fulbright Rsch. scholar, Korea, 1989; Choice mag. award, 1996; named Disting. Univ. Prof., 1999; rsch. fellow Fla. Inst. of Govt., 2000—. Mem. Am. Polit. Sci. Assn. (program com. 1983-84, chair sect. intergovtl. rels., award 1989, mem. exec. coun. 1994—, pres.-elect sec. urban politics 1994-95, pres. sect. urban politics 1995-96), So. Polit. Sci. Assn. (v.p. 1990-91, pres.-elect 1992-93, pres. 1993-94, V.O. key award com. 1983-84, best paper on women and politics 1988, Diane Blair award 2001), Midwest Polit. Sci. Assn., Western Polit. Sci. Assn., Southwestern Polit. Sci. Assn. (local arrangements com. 1982-83, profession com. 1977-80), ASPA (nominating com. Houston chpt. 1983, bd. mem. Suncoast chpt., pres.-elect 1991, Lilly award 1992), Policy Studies Orgn. (mem. editl. bd. jour. 1981—, exec. coun. 1983-85), Women's Caucus Polit. Sci. (portfolio pre-decision rev. com. 1982-83, projects and programs com. 1981, fin.-budget com. 1980-81), Fla. Polit. Sci. Assn. (pres. 1997-98, Manning Dauer Disting. Fla. Polit. Sci. award 2001), Acad. Polit. Sci., Mcpl. Fin. Officers Assn., Phi Kappa Phi (Artist/Scholar award U. South Fla. 1997), Phi Beta Kappa, Pi Sigma Alpha (mem. exec. coun. 1994-96, pres. 2000-02), Pi Alpha Alpha. Methodist. Home: 2506 Collier Pky Land O Lakes FL 34639-5228 Office: U South Fla Dept Polit Sci Tampa FL 33620 E-mail: samacmanus@aol.com.

MACMASTER, DANIEL MILLER, retired museum official; b. Chgo., Feb. 11, 1913; s. Daniel Howard and Charlotte Louise (Miller) MacM.; m. Sylvia Jane Hill, Feb. 22, 1935; children— Daniel Miller, Jane Irene (Mrs. Robert W. Lightell). Student, Lakeside Press Tng. Sch., 1930-31, U. Chgo., 1931-34; L.H.D., Lincoln Coll., 1970; D.H.L., DePaul U., 1978. Mem. staff Mus. Sci. and Industry, Chgo., 1933—, acting dir., 1950, dir., 1951-72, pres., 1968-78, pres. emeritus, 1978—, life trustee, 1968—. Gen. mgr. Chgo. R.R. Fair, 1948-49 Author: (with others) Exploring the Mysteries of Physics and Chemistry, 1938; book reviewer; contbr. to newspapers, mags., encys. Mem. Homewood (Ill.) Bd. Edn., 1945-49, pres., 1948-49; mem. U. Ill. Citizen' Adv. Com., 1945—; sec. Higher Edn. Commn. Ill., 1955-59; dir. Hyde Park Bank and Trust Co., 1965-86; U.S. State Dept. Specialist to Ireland, Germany, Sweden, 1963; dir. Floating Seminar to Greece, 1960; guest mus. cons. Fed. Republic Germany, 1961, Iran, 1973, 74, 76, Hong Kong, 1978, 89, 90, 91, Singapore, Chili and Peru, 1978, Poland, Czechoslovakia and Hungary, 1979, Mexico, 1980, 81, Saudi Arabia, 1981, 82, 84, Columbia, Ecuador and Bolivia, 1983, Taiwan 1986-90, 92, 94; mem. Nat. 4-H Svc. Com.; hon. dir. Chgo. Chamber Orch. Soc., pres., 1969-70; bd. dirs. Sears Roebuck Found., 1970-73, Internat. Coll. Surgeons Hall of Fame; mem. Lincoln Acad. Ill.; hon. trustee U. Chgo. Cancer Rsch. Found.; life trustee Adler Planetarium; dir. emeritus Monmouth Coll.; bd. govs. Chgo. Heart Assn., vice chmn., 1972-73; founder Scotish Heritage Libr., 1999. Decorated Golden Cross Royal Order Phoenix Greece; Officer's Cross Polonia Restituta Poland; Grand Badge of Honor Austria; Grand Badge of Honor of Burgenland Austria; Golden Badge of Honor Vienna; Officer's Cross 1st class Order of Merit Germany; Officer Order of Merit Luxembourg; Order Cultural Merit Poland; Royal Swedish Order North Star; recipient Patriotic Civilian Service award U.S. Army, St. Andrews Soc. Citizen of Yr. award, 1978 Fellow Assn. Sci. and Tech. Centers; mem. Kappa Sigma. Clubs: Tavern, Quadrangle, Commercial. Home: 3633 Breakers Dr Apt 237 Olympia Fields IL 60461-1051

MACMASTER, ROBERT ELLSWORTH, historian, educator; b. Winthrop, Mass., Oct. 10, 1919; s. Joseph Oscar and Ruby (Slocomb) MacM.; m. Ann Elizabeth Lynch, Apr. 28, 1942; children— Angus Michael, Martha Ann, David Joseph. AB, Harvard, 1941, A.M., 1948, PhD, 1952. Mem. faculty MIT, 1952-90, prof. history and lit., 1967-90, prof. emeritus, 1990—, chmn. history faculty, 1970-72. Author: Danilevsky: A Russian Totalitarian Philosopher, 1967; contbr. articles on L.N. Tolstoi to publs. Served with AUS, 1941-46. Mem. Am. Assn. Advancement Slavic Studies. Home: 461 Main St Hingham MA 02043-4701 Office: MIT Dept History Cambridge MA 02139

MACMEEKEN, JOHN PEEBLES, foundation executive, educator; b. Aug. 15, 1924; s. John West and Esther (Strong) M.; m. Mary Swanberg, Nov. 26, 1949; children: Carol B. Macmeeken Luther, John W., Susan G. Student, U. Calif., Berkeley, 1941-43, Ind. U., 1943-44; JD, Harvard U., 1948. Bar: Calif. 1948. Assoc. Chickering & Gregory, San Francisco, 1948-60, ptnr., 1960-82, Pettit & Martin, San Francisco, 1982-93; v.p. Zynk Indsl. Corp., 1995-98; pres. Found. for Books to China, 1993—, SOAR Bus. Inst., 1998—. Bd. dirs. Lanark West Corp.; pres. Clinton U., San Francisco, 1995-97; lectr. law Fudan U., Shanghai, China, East China Normal U., Shanghai, Nanking U., China, Zhongshan U., Guangzhou; sec. Zynk Internat. Corp., Twan Co. LLC, Siam Tien Dao Yuan. Sgt. U.S. Army, 1943-45. Mem. ABA, Calif. Bar Assn., Outlook Club Calif., World Trade Club. Republican. Congregationalist. Home: 5708 Glenbrook Dr Oakland CA 94618-1724 Office Phone: 510-428-2145. E-mail: jmacmeeken@aol.com.

MACMILLAN, DAVID PAUL, retired oil company executive; b. East Orange, N.J., Nov. 16, 1943; s. Hugh Dame and Marie Ann (Hahn) MacM.; m. Rosemary Longo, Nov. 16, 1969; children: Melanie, Hugh. With Exxon Rsch. and Engring. Co., various locations, 1969-85, sect. head Florham Park, N.J., 1978-80, project mgr. Denver, 1980-82, spl. assignment to sr. gen. mgr. Florham Park, 1982-83, project mgr.-Belgium, 1983-85, engring. mgr., 1993-95, mgr. spl. projects divsn., 1996-97, mgr. project mgmt. divsn., 1996-97, project dir. Japan, 1997-99. Staff advisor controllers dept., Exxon Co. Internat., Florham Park, N.J., 1986-88, sr. advisor materials dept., 1991-93; materials mgr. Exxon Cen. Svcs., Florham Park, 1989-91. Served with USMC, 1961-65. Mem. Nat. Assn. Purchasing Mgrs., Am. Soc. Quality Control, Tokyo Am. Club, Kyokawa Country Club, Tau Beta Pi, Pi Tau Sigma. Republican. Presbyterian. Home: PO Box 101 Florham Park NJ 07932-0101

MACMILLAN, HOKE, former state attorney general; m. Becky Klemt; children: Ryan Klemt, Christopher Klemt. BA, U. Wyo., 1967, JD, 1970. Bar: Wyo., Colo., Nebr., U.S. Ct. Appeals (10th cir.), U.S. Ct. Mil. Appeals, U.S. Supreme Ct. Capt. U.S. Army JAG, 1970—74; mem. Pence and Millett, Laramie, Wyo., 1974—2001, sr. ptnr., 1982—2001; atty. gen. State of Wyo., 2001—02. Fellow: Am. Bar Found.; mem.: Albany County Bar Assn., Nebr. State Bar, Wyo. State Bar (pres. 1996—97). Home: 41438 N Cedar Chase Ct Anthem AZ 85086-1067

MACMILLAN, ROBERT SMITH, electronics engineer; b. L.A., Aug. 28, 1924; s. Andrew James and Moneta (Smith) M.; m. Barbara Macmillan, Aug. 18, 1962; 1 child, Robert G. BS in Physics, Calif. Inst. Tech., 1948, MS in Elec. Engring., 1949, PhD in Elec. Engring./Physics cum laude, 1954. Rsch. engr. Jet Propulsion Lab., Calif. Inst. Tech., Pasadena, 1951-55, asst. prof. elec. engring., 1955-58; assoc. prof. elec. engring. U. So. Calif., L.A., 1958-70; mem. sr. tech. staff Litton Sys., Inc., Van nuys, Calif., 1969-79; dir. sys. engring. Litton Data Command Sys., Agoura Hills, Calif., 1979-89; pres. The Macmillan Group, La Canada Flintridge, Calif., 1989—. Treas., v.p. Video Color Corp., Inglewood, 1965-66; cons. fgn. tech. div. USAF, Wright-Patterson AFB, Ohio, 1957-74, Space Tech. Labs., Inglewood, Calif., 1956-60, Space Gen. Corp., El Monte, Calif., 1960-63. With USAAF, 1943-46. Recipient Nat. Patriot's medal, Nat. Rifle Assn., 2002, Rep. Senatorial medal of freedom, 2004. Mem. IEEE, Am. Inst. Physics, Am. Phys. Soc., Sigma Xi, Tau Beta Pi, Eta Kappa Nu. Achievements include research in ionospheric, radio-wave, propagation; very low frequency radio-transmitting antennas; optical coherence and statistical optics. Home: 350 Starlight Crest Dr La Canada Flintridge CA 91011-2839 Office: The Macmillan Group 350 Starlight Crest Dr La Canada Flintridge CA 91011-2839 Office Phone: 818-790-4809. Personal E-mail: rsmacmillan08@aol.com.

MACMILLAN, SHANNON ANN, professional soccer player; b. Syosset, N.Y., Oct. 7, 1974; Student in social work, U. Portland. Profl. soccer player San Diego Spirit, 2001—03. Mem. U.S. Nat. Women's Soccer Team, 1993—, including silver medal World Univ. Games team, 1993, gold medal U.S. Olympic Team, 96; mem. U.S. Women's Under-20 Nat. Team, 1993—94, including championship Internat. Women's Tournament, France, 1993; mem. LaJolla (Calif.) Nomads club soccer team, winning state club championship, 1991, 92, Japanese Women's Profl. League, 1996, 97. Named 1995 Soccer Am. Player of Yr., Female Athlete of Yr., 1993, 1995, U. Portland, World Cup Champion, 1999; named to San Diego Union Tribune All-Acad. team; recipient Mo. Athletic Club award, 1995, Hermann award, U. Portland, 1995, Bill Hayward award, 1995, Silver medal, Sydney Olympic Games, 2000. Office: US Soccer Fedn 1801-1811 S Prairie Ave Chicago IL 60616

MACMILLAN, STEPHEN P. health products executive; married; 2 children. BA in econ., Davidson Coll.; grad. advanced mgmt. program, Harvard Bus. Sch. Mktg. Procter & Gamble; mgr. dir. subsidiary of Johnson & Johnson MSD (Merck); v.p., mtg. and profl. sales McNeil Consumer and Specialty Pharm.; sector v.p. Pharmacia Corp., Global Specialty Oper., 1988—99; pres. Pharmacia, 1999—2003; pres., Chief Oper. Officer Stryker, Kalamazoo, 2003—. Office: Stryker 2725 Fairfield Rd Portage MI 49002

MACMILLAN, WHITNEY, food products and import/export company executive; Chmn., CEO Cargill, Wayzata, Minn., chmn. emeritus, 1996—. Mem., bd. dirs. Deluxe Corp., Minn. Office: Cargill PO Box 9300 Minneapolis MN 55440-9300

MACMILLAN, WILLIAM HOOPER, dean, educator; b. Boston, Oct. 21, 1923; s. Alexander Stewart and Leslie (Hooper) M.; m. Anne Stearns, May 29, 1948; children: Leslie Jean, Robert Bruce, William Ian. BA, McGill U., 1948; PhD, Yale U., 1954. From instr. pharmacology to assoc. prof. U. Vt. Coll. Medicine, 1954—64, chmn. dept. pharmacology, 1962-63, prof. pharmacology, 1964-76, dean Grad. Coll., 1963-69, 71-76; rsch. fellow USPHS, U. Oxford, Eng., 1958-59; cons. New Eng. Assn. Schs. and Colls., 1967-76; Ford Found. project specialist, sci. adv. to Haile Sellassie U., Addis Ababa., Ethiopia, 1969-71; prof. biology, dean Grad. Sch. U. Ala., 1976-91, prof. biology emeritus, dean emeritus, 1991—; cons. So. Assn. Colls. and Schs., 1976-91. Exec. com. African grad. Fellowship Program, African-Am. Inst., N.Y.C., 1971-92; chmn. com. biomed. scis. Coun. of Grad. Schs., Washington, 1973-77, bd. dirs., 1985-88; exec. com. N.E. Assn. Grad. Schs., 1975-76; v.p. Conf. So. Grad. Schs., 1981, pres., 1982; pres., v.p. New Eng. Assn. Grad. Schs., 1971; bd. dirs. Oak Ridge Associated Univs., 1987-93. Cmty. activator, chair, bd. dirs., vol. various regional non-profit agencies, 1992—. With USNR, 1944—46. Mem. Am. Soc. Pharmacology and Exptl. Therapeutics, AAAS, N.Y. Acad. Sci., AAUP, Sigma Xi.

MACMILLEN, RICHARD EDWARD, biological sciences educator, researcher; b. Upland, Calif., Apr. 19, 1932; s. Hesper Nichols and Ruth Henrietta (Golder) MacM.; m. Ann Gray, June 12, 1953 (div. 1975); children: Jennifer Kathleen, Douglas Michael; m. Barbara Jean Morgan, Oct. 23, 1980; 1 child, Ian Richard. BA, Pomona Coll., 1954; MS, U. Mich., 1956; PhD, UCLA, 1961. From instr. to assoc. prof. Pomona Coll., Claremont, Calif., 1960-68, Wig Disting. prof., 1965; assoc. prof., then prof. U. Calif., Irvine, 1968—, chair dept. population and environ. biology, 1972-74, chair dept. ecology and evolutionary biology, 1984-90, prof. emeritus, 1993—. Mem. award panel NSF, Washington, 1976-80; coord. U. Calif. Multi-Campus Supercourse in Environ. Biology, White Mountain Rsch. Sta., spring 1996, 97, tchg. participant, 1998—; mem. rev. panel, EPA Star grad. fellowship program, 2002, 04; mem. budget com., Jackson County Fire Dist. 5, 2001-2004; Alumni Admissions vol., Pomona Coll., 2001—; vol. morphologist U.S. Fish and Wildlife Svc. Forensics Lab., 2004—. Contbr. numerous articles to profl. jours. Chair sci. adv. bd. Endangered Habitats League, 1991-93. Recipient rsch. awards NSF, 1961-83; Fulbright-Hays advanced rsch. fellow Monash U., Australia, 1966-67. Fellow AAAS; mem. Am. Soc. Mammalogists (life), Ecol. Soc. Am. (cert. sr. ecologist), Am. Ornithologists Union, Cooper Ornithol. Soc. (life, bd. dirs. 1982-84). Democrat. Avocations: fly fishing, camping, hiking, nature photography. Home: 705 Foss Rd Talent OR 97540-9758 Business E-Mail: bidmac@jeffnet.org. *As world human populations continue to increase, our natural world continues to degrade. It is incumbent upon all of us to accept the responsibility of stewarding our land and its biota as precious and renewable resources.*

MACMINN, PAMELA LEE See KOPACK, PAMELA

MACMULLEN, JEAN ALEXANDRIA STEWART, nurse, administrator; b. N.Y.C., Feb. 21, 1945; d. John Douglas and Isabella Stewart (Park) MacM. Diploma in nursing, Lenox Hill Hosp., N.Y.C., 1965; BSN, Adelphi U., 1969, MSN, 1971; MA in Anthropology, U. South Fla., 1978. Nurse renal disease unit N.Y. Hosp., N.Y.C., 1971-72; clin. nurse specialist VA Hosp., Tampa, Fla., 1972-76, med.-surg. coord., 1976-82; assoc. chief nurse VA Med. Ctr., Gainesville, Fla., 1982-93, assoc. med. ctr. dir. patient support svcs. Montgomery, Ala., 1993-98; pvt. practice Inverness, Fla., 1998—. Editor Am. Assn. Nephrology Nurses, Pitman, N.J., 1980-82, referee, adviser, 1983—; contbr. articles to profl. jours. Mem.: Fla. Nurses Assn., Am. Nephrology Nurses Assn., Order Eastern Star. Republican. Episcopalian. Avocations: gardening, raising orchids.

MACMULLEN, RAMSAY, retired history educator; b. NYC, Mar. 3, 1928; s. Charles William and Margaret (Richmond) MacM.; m. Edith Merriman Nye, Aug. 7, 1954 (div. 1991); children: John A., Priscilla N., William R., Lucinda S.; m. Margaret McNeill, Aug. 1, 1992. AB, Harvard U., 1950, AM, 1953, PhD, 1957. Instr., asst. prof. U. Oreg., 1956-61; asso. prof., prof. Brandeis U., 1961-67, chmn. dept. classics, 1965-66; prof. Yale U., 1967-93, Dunham prof. history and classics, 1979-93, chmn. dept. history, 1970-72, master Calhoun Coll., 1984-90. Author: 12 books on ancient history, Cicero to 6th Century A.D., 1963-2001, Sisters of the Brush, 1997, Sarah's Choice, 2001, Feelings in History Ancient and Modern, 2003. Recipient Porter prize Coll. Art Assn., 1964; Fulbright fellow, 1960-61; Guggenheim fellow, 1964; Princeton Inst. for Advanced Study fellow, 1964-65; Nat. Endowment for Humanities sr. fellow, 1974-75; Lifetime award Scholarly Distinction, Am. Hist. Assn., 2001. Mem. Soc. for Promotion Roman Studies, Assn. Ancient Historians (pres. 1978-81) Home: 25 Temple Ct New Haven CT 06511 Office: Yale U Dept History New Haven CT 06520 E-mail: ramsay.macmullen@yale.edu.

MACMURREN, HAROLD HENRY, JR., psychologist, lawyer; b. Jersey City, Sept. 18, 1942; s. Harold Sr. and Evelyn (Almone) MacM.; m. Margaret Bartro, Nov. 21, 1970. BA, William Paterson Coll., Wayne, N.J., 1965; MA, Jersey City Coll., 1973; EdD, St. Johns U., N.Y.C., 1985; JD, Rutgers U., 1989. Cert. secondary tchr., N.J.; Bar: N.J. 1989. Instr. Wanaque (N.J.) Bd. Edn., 1965-66, cons. psychologist, 1983-84; instr. Elmwood Park (N.J.) Bd. Edn., 1967-70; coll. faculty mem., psychologist Assoc. Clinic, Jersey City, 1971-72; cons. psychologist Rockaway (N.J.) Bd. Edn., 1972-83; intern lawyer Environ. Law Clinic, Newark, N.J., 1988-89; cons. psychologist Pequannock (N.J.) Bd. Edn., 1984—; pvt. practice law, 2000—. Coord. child study team Sandyston Walpack Sch. Sys.; adj. prof. William Paterson U.; spkr., writer in field. Mem. ABA, NEA, N.J. Edn. Assn., N.J. Psychologist Assn., N.J. Bar Assn., Sierra Club, Phi Delta Kappa. Avocations: reading, travel, skiing, hiking. Home: 4 Systema Pl Sussex NJ 07461-2833

MACMURREN, MARGARET PATRICIA, secondary education educator, consultant; b. Newark, Nov. 4, 1947; d. Kenneth F. and Doris E. (Lounsberry) Bartro; m. Harold MacMurren, Nov. 21, 1970. BA, Paterson State U., 1969; MA, William Paterson Coll., 1976; postgrad., Jersey City State Coll., 1976—. Tchr. Byram (N.J.) Twp. Schs., 1969-77; learning cons., child study team coord. Andover Regional Schs., Newton, N.J., 1977—. Mem.: NEA, Andover Regional Edn. Assn. (pres. 1986—87), Sussex County Assn. Learning Cons. (pres. 1982—83, 1993—94, sec.-treas. 1991—92, v.p. 1992—93), N.J. Learning Assn., N.J. Edn. Assn. Avocations: skiing, dance, weightlifting, travel, reading. Home: 4 Systema Pl Sussex NJ 07461-2833 Office: Andover Regional Schs 707 Limecrest Rd Newton NJ 07860-8801 Office Phone: 973-940-1234 246. Business E-Mail: haroldm@nac.net.

MACNAMARA, BRIAN SCOTT, veterinarian, law educator; b. N.Y.C., Apr. 5, 1954; s. Donal Eoin Joseph and Margaret Scott MacNamara; m. Laura Burchill, May 14, 1999; children: Sean, Frendon; m. Carol MacNamara, July 14, 1991 (div. Oct. 1998). BS, Cornell U., Ithaca, N.Y., 1976; DVM, Cornell U., 1980; JD, Pace U., White Plains, N.Y., 2000. Bar: N.Y., N.J.; lic. veterinarian N.Y., N.J. Veterinarian Warwick Equine Clinic, Warwick, NY, 1982—2003; asst. prof. law John Jay Coll. of Criminal Justice, N.Y.C., 2001—. Pvt. practice law, Goshen, NY, 2001—. Contbr. articles to profl. jours. Mem.: N.Y. County Lawyers Assn., Nat. Assn. Criminal Def. Lawyers, N.Y. Defenders Assn., N.Y. State Assn. Criminal Def. Lawyers. Democrat. Avocations: flying, horseback riding. Office: John Jay Coll Criminal Justice 899 Tenth Ave New York NY 10019

MACNAUGHTON, ANGUS ATHOLE, finance company executive; b. Montreal, July 15, 1931; s. Athole Austin and Emily Kidder (MacLean) MacN.; children: Gillian Heather, Angus Andrew. Student, Lakefield Coll. Sch., 1941-47, McGill U., 1949-54. Auditor Coopers & Lybrand, Montreal, 1949-55; acct. Genstar Ltd., Montreal, 1955, asst. treas., 1956-61, treas., 1961-64, v.p., 1964-70, exec. v.p., 1970-73, pres., 1973-76, vice chmn., chief exec. officer, 1976-81, chmn. or pres., chief exec. officer, 1981-86; pres. Genstar Investment Corp., 1987—. Bd. dirs. Barrick Gold Corp., Diversified Collection Svcs., Inc., Genstar Investment Corp., Varian Semicondr. Assocs., Inc., San Ramon Med. Ctr.; past pres. Montreal chpt. Tax Execs. Inst. Bd. govs. Lakefield Coll. Sch.; past chmn. San Francisco Bay Area coun. Boy Scouts Am.; bd. dirs. San Francisco Opera; trustee World Affairs Coun. of No. Calif. Mem. Pacific Union Club, World Trade Club, Villa Taverna (San Francisco), Mt. Royal Club (Montreal), Toronto Club. Office: 4 Embarcadero Ctr Ste 1900 San Francisco CA 94111-4191

MACNEAL, EDWARD ARTHUR, economic consultant; b. Winona Lake, Ind., Apr. 19, 1925; s. Kenneth Forsythe and Marguerite Josephine (Giroud) MacN.; m. Priscilla Creed Perry, Dec. 27, 1952; children: Catherine Wright, Madeleine Creed. Student, Harvard, 1943; BA, U. Chgo., 1948, MA, 1951. Exec. sec. Internat. Soc. Gen. Semantics, Chgo., 1947-50; staff cons. James C. Buckley, Inc., N.Y.C., 1951-55; market researcher Socony Mobil Oil Co., N.Y.C., 1955-58; research dir. O.E. McIntyre, Inc., N.Y.C., 1958-61; econ. cons. N.Y., 1956-66, 1966—. Adv. local govt. agys. Author: The Semantics of Air Passenger Transportation, 1981, MacNeal's Master Atlas of Decision Making, 1988, Mathsemantics: Making Numbers Talk Sense, 1994. Served with AUS, 1943-46, ETO. Mem. ABA, Am. Statis. Assn., Am. Econ. Assn., Am. Math. Soc., Inst. Gen. Semantics, Am. Sociol. Assn., Am. Psychol. Soc., Travel Rsch. Forum, Harvard Club Phila. Home: 348 Louella Ave Wayne PA 19087-4855 Office: PO Box 249 Wayne PA 19087-0249 Personal E-mail: macneal@erols.com.

MACNEIL, IAN RODERICK, lawyer, educator; b. N.Y.C., June 20, 1929; s. Robert Lister and Kathleen Gertrude (Metcalf) Macneil; m. Nancy Carol Wilson, Mar. 29, 1952; children: Roderick, Jennifer, Duncan (dec.), Andrew. BA magna cum laude, U. Vt., 1950; LLB magna cum laude, Harvard U., 1955. Bar: N.H. 1956-02. Law clk. Hon. Peter Woodbury, 1955-56; asso. Sulloway Hollis Godfrey & Soden, Concord, N.H., 1956-59; mem. faculty Cornell U. Law Sch., Ithaca, N.Y., 1959-72, 74-80, Ingersoll prof. law, 1976-80; Wigmore prof. law Northwestern U. Sch. Law, Chgo., 1980-99, prof. emeritus,

1999—. Vis. prof. U. East Africa, 1965-67, Duke U., 1971-72; prof. law, mem. Inst. Advanced Studies, U. Va., 1972-74; vis. fellow Centre for Socio-legal Studies and Wolfson Coll., Oxford U., 1979; hon. vis. fellow faculty law U. Edinburgh, 1979, 87; Rosenthal lectr. Northwestern U. Sch. Law, 1979; Braucher vis. prof. Harvard U., 1988-89. Author: Bankruptcy Law in East Africa, 1966, Contracts: Exchange Transactions and Relations, 3d edit., with Paul J. Gudel, 2001. The New Social Contract, 1980, American Arbitration Law: Reformation Nationalization Internationalization, 1992; co-author: Federal Arbitration Law, 1994. Served with U.S. Army, 1951-53. Guggenheim fellow, 1978-79. Fellow Royal Soc. Antiquaries (Scotland); mem. ABA, Am. Law Inst., Am. Acad. Arts and Scis., Scottish Soc. No. Studies, The Scottish Medievalists, Carlton Cricket Club (dir.). Home: 95/6 Grange Loan Edinburgh EH9 2ED Scotland

MAC NEIL, JOSEPH NEIL, archbishop; b. Sydney, N.S., Can., Apr. 15, 1924; s. John Martin and Kate (Mac Lean) Mac N. BA, St. Francis Xavier U., Antigonish, N.S., 1944; postgrad., Holy Heart Sem., Halifax, N.S., 1944-48, U. Perugia, 1956, U. Chgo., 1964; JCD, U. St. Thomas, Rome, 1958. Ordained priest Roman Cath. Ch., 1948. Pastor parishes in N.S., 1948-55, officialis Chancery Office, Antigonish, 1958-59; adminstrn. Diocese of Antigonish, 1959-60; rector Cathedral Antigonish, 1961; dir. extension dept. St. Francis Xavier U., Antigonish, 1961-69, v.p., 1962-69; bishop St. John, N.B., Can., 1969-73; chancellor U. St. Thomas, Fredericton, N.B., 1969-73; archbishop of Edmonton, Alta., 1973-99; ret., 1999. Chmn. Alta Bishops' Conf., 1973-99; chmn. bd. Newman Theol. Coll., Edmonton, 1973-99, St. Joseph's Coll. U. Alta., Edmonton, 1973-99. Vice chmn. N.S. Voluntary Econ. Planning Bd., 1965-69; bd. dirs. Program and Planning Agy., Govt. of N.S., 1969; exec. Atlantic Provinces Econ. Coun., 1968-73, Can. Coun. Rural Devel., 1965-75, bd. dirs. Futures Secretariat, 1981, Ctr. for Human Devel., Toronto, Ont., Can., 1985-95; mem. bd. mgmt. Edmonton Gen. Hosp., 1983-92, Edmonton Caritas Health Group, 1992-99; mem. Nat. Com. for Can. Participation in Habitat, 1976. Mem. Can. Assn. Adult Edn. (past pres. N.S.), Can. Assn. Dirs. Univ. Extension and Summer Schs. (past pres.), Inst. Rsch. on Pub. Policy (founding mem.), Can. Conf. Cath. Bishops (pres. 1979-81, mem. com. on ecumenism 1985-91, com. on missions 1991-96, mem. permanent coun. 1993-95). Roman Catholic. Office: Archbishop Emeritus Edmonton 8421 101st Ave Edmonton AB Canada T6A 0L1

MACNEIL, ROBERT BRECKENRIDGE WARE, retired broadcast journalist, writer; b. Montreal, Que., Can., Jan. 19, 1931; came to U.S., 1963; s. Robert A.S. and Margaret Virginia (Oxner) MacN.; m. Rosemarie Anne Copland, 1956 (div. 1964); children: Catherine Anne, Ian B.; m. Jane J. Doherty, May 29, 1965 (div. 1983); children: Alison N., William H.; m. Donna P. Richards, Oct. 20, 1984. Student, Dalhousie U., 1949-51; BA, Carleton U., 1955; LHD (hon.), William Patterson Coll., 1977, Beaver Coll., Bates Coll., 1979, Lawrence U., 1980, Bucknell U., 1982, George Washington U., Kings Coll., Trinity Coll., U. Maine, 1983, Brown U., 1984, Colby Coll., Carleton Coll., U. S.C., 1985, Franklin and Marshall Coll., 1987, Nazareth Coll., Washington Coll., 1988, Kenyon Coll., 1990, U. Western Ont., 1992, U. Miami, Clark U., 1994, U. L.I., 1995, Columbia U., 1995, Princeton U., 1995, The Cooper Union, 1996, U. Toronto, 1997, Mt. Allison U., 1998; LHD (hon.), Dalhousie U., 2000. Radio actor CBC, Halifax, N.S., Can., 1950-52, radio/TV announcer, 1954-55; announcer Sta.-CJCH, Halifax, 1951-52; announcer, news writer Sta. CFRA, Ottawa, Ont., Can., 1952-54; sub-editor to filing editor Reuters News Agy., London, 1955-60; news corr. NBC, London, 1960-63, Washington, 1963-65, N.Y.C., 1965-67; corr. Panorama program BBC, London, 1967-71, 73-75; sr. corr. Nat. Public Affairs Center for TV, Washington, 1971-73; exec. editor, co-anchor MacNeil/Lehrer Report, Sta. -WNET-TV, N.Y.C., 1975—, MacNeil/Lehrer News Hour, PBS, 1983-95, ret., 1995. Author: The People Machine, The Influence of Television on American Politics, 1968, The Right Place at the Right Time, 1982, Wordstruck, 1989, Burden of Desire, 1992, The Voyage, 1995, Breaking News, 1998; co-author: The Story of English, 1986; editor The Way We Were 1963, 1988. Trustee Freedom Forum Newseum. Decorated Officer Order of Can., 1998; inductee TV Acad. Hall of Fame, 1999; recipient Lifetime Achievement award Overseas Press Club, 1995, Broadcaster of Yr. Internat. Radio and TV Soc., 1991, Paul White award Radio TV News Dirs. Assn., 1990, Medal of Honor U. Mo. Sch. Journalism, 1980; Catto fellow The Aspen Inst. Fellow AAAS, The MacDowell Colony (chmn. 1993); mem. AFTRA, Assn. Radio and TV News Analysts, Japan Soc. (trustee), Writers Guild Am., Century Club (N.Y.C.). Office: c/o MacNeil-Lehrer Prodns 2700 S Quincy St Ste 240 Arlington VA 22206-2226

MACNEILL, JAMES WILLIAM, international environment management consultant; b. Sask., Can., Apr. 22, 1928; s. Leslie William and Helga Ingeborg (Nohlgren) MacN.; m. Phyllis Beryl Ferguson, Nov. 30, 1953; children: Catherine Anne, Robin Lynne. BA, U. Sask., 1949, BE Mech., 1958, LLD (hon.), 1988; Diplome, U. Stockholm, 1951; DSc (hon.), McGill U., 1992; D of Environ. Studies (hon.), U. Waterloo, 1993; LHD (hon.), Lakehead U., 1994. Spl. adv. on constl. rev. Privy Council Office, Govt. Can., Ottawa, Ont., 1969-70; asst. sec. Can. Ministry of State for Urban Affairs, Ottawa, 1970-73, permanent sec., 1973-76; Can. AEP, Can. commr.-gen. UN Human Settlements Conf., Vancouver, B.C., 1975-78; dir. environ. directorate OECD, Paris, 1978-84; sec. gen. World Commn. Environment and Devel., Geneva, 1984-87; sr. fellow Inst. Research Pub. Policy, Ottawa, 1987-93; pres. J.W. MacNeill and Assocs., 1987-98; chmn. Internat. Inst. for Sustainable Devel., 1994-99. Spl. advisor to adminstrn. UN Devel. Program, 1994-97; chmn. ind. insp. panel World Bank, 1997-2002; mem. adv. panel BP Caspian Devel., 2003--. Author: Environmental Management, 1971, Beyond Interdependence, 1991. Apptd. officer Order of Can., 1995. Recipient Saskatchewan Achievement award, 1985, Silver medal City of Paris, 1984, Climate Inst. award, 1991, Swedish WASA award, 1991, Lifetime Achievement award Govt. of Can., 1993. Mem. Assn. Profl. Engrs. Ont., Assn. Profl. Engrs. Sask. E-mail: jwmacneill@hotmail.com.

MACO, PAUL STEPHEN, securities and exchange administrator; s. Paul and Rose Mary (McFadden) M.; m. Lisa M. Griglack, Aug. 23, 1997; 1 child, Claire Fiona. BA, Lehigh U., 1974; JD, NYU, 1977. Ptnr. Mintz, Levin, Cohn, Ferris, Glovesky & Popeo, Boston, 1988-94; faculty law Morin Ctr. for Internat. Banking Law Boston U., 1992-96, 99—; atty. fellow Office of Gen. Counsel SEC, Washington, 1994, dir. Office of Mcpl. Securities, 1995—. Adj. assoc. prof. Washington Coll. Law Am. U., 1999. Author: (with others) Bond Markets, Law and Regulation, 1999; bd. editors Jour. of Mcpl. Fin. Dir. Traditions for Tomorrow, Inc. Mem. ABA (co-reporter disclosure rules of counsel 1994), Nat. Assn. Bond Lawyers (dir. 1989-92, chair spl. com. on securities laws and disclosure 1987-89). Office: Office of Mcpl Securities SEC 450 5th St NW Washington DC 20549-0001

MACOMBER, JOHN D. investment company executive; b. Rochester, N.Y., Jan. 13, 1928; s. William Butts and Elizabeth Currie (Ranlet) M.; m. Caroline Morgan, Oct. 21, 1955; children: Janet Morgan, Elizabeth Currie, William Butts II. BA, Yale U., 1950; MBA, Harvard U., 1952. Mng. dir. McKinsey & Co., N.Y.C., France and Switzerland, 1954-73; chmn., CEO Celanese Corp., N.Y.C., 1973-87; chmn. J.D. Macomber & Co., N.Y.C., 1987-89; pres., chmn. Export-Import Bank of U.S., Washington, 1989-92; prin. JDM Investment Group, Washington, 1992—. Bd. dirs. Lehman Brothers Holdings, Inc., 1994—. 1st lt. USAF, 1952-54. Mem. Links (N.Y.C.), River Club (N.Y.C.), Union Club (N.Y.C.), Metropolitan (Washington). Office: JDM Investment Group 2806 N St NW Washington DC 20007-3339*

MACON, IRENE ELIZABETH, interior designer, consultant; b. East St. Louis, Ill., May 11, 1935; d. David and Thelma (Eastlen) Dunn; m. Robert Teco Macon, Feb. 12, 1954; children: Leland Sean, Walter Edwin, Gary Keith, Jill Renee Macon Martin, Robin Jeffrey, Lamont. Student Forest Park Coll., Washington U., St. Louis, 1970, Bailey Tech. Coll., 1975, Lindenwood Coll., 1981. Office mgr. Cardinal Glennon Hosp., St. Louis, 1965-72; interior designer J.C. Penney Co., Jennings, Mo., 1972-73; entrepreneur Irene Designs Unltd., St. Louis, 1974—; vol. liaison Pub. Sch. System, St. Louis, 1980-82; cons. in field. Inventor venetian blinds for autos, 1981, T-blouse and diaper wrap, 1986, owner, partner, mgr., Black Ball Inc., St. Louis, 1996—; cons., bus. mgr. Anything and Everything Store, St. Louis; Author 26th Word newsletter, 1986, (songs) My God's Child Teach Free Will, God is Hiring Now, 1993. Committeewoman Republican party, St. Louis, 1984; vice chair 4th Senatorial Dist. of Mo., 1984, vol. St. Louis Assn. Community Orgns., 1983; instr. first aid Bi-State chpt. ARC, St. Louis, 1984, mem. speakers bur., 1991; cubmaster pack #80 Keystone dist. Boy Scouts Am.; block capt. Operation Brightside, St. Louis, 1984; co-chair status and role of women Union Meml. United Meth. Ch., 1986—, program resource sec., 1990—; trustee Wofit Found., 1989; spokesperson Minority Affairs Initiative Program Am. Assn. Retired Persons, 1991; sec. to block Fedn. Block Units St. Louis Urban League, 1994; mem. Notary Pub. Commn., 1994—; Rep. election judge 26.8 pct Ward, 1994; pub. speaker, story teller prayer breakfast Grace Chapel Ministries, 1994; gospel radio program host Sta. KSTL Radio; transl. bible stories Old Testament and New Testament, It's Gospel Time; volunteer Northside Preservation Commission 1996; speaker at Black Alcoholic/Drug Svc. Info. Center, 1996. Composer religious music, The Ball Point, monthly newsletter and weekly talk radio prog., WGNU Radio, 1998, special guest and player relations, Old Negro Sports Hist. Biographies. Named One of Top Ladies of Distinction St. Louis, 1983. Mem. NAACP, Am. Soc. Interior Designers (assoc.), Nat. Mus. Women in the Arts (charter), Nat. Stroke Assn., Internat. Platform Assn., Nat. Coun. Negro Women (1st v.p. 1984), Invention Assn. of St. Louis (subcom. head 1985), Coalition of 100 Black Women, St. Louis Assn. Fashion Designers, Pres. Club. Methodist. Achievements include invention of Irene's Autoshade, an accordian type of pleated material designed to adhere to automobile windows for the purpose of protecting it from the sun. Avocations: reading, designing personal wardrobe, modeling, horseback riding, boating.

MACON, JANE HAUN, lawyer; b. Corpus Christi, Tex., Sept. 26, 1946; d. E.H. and Johnnie Mae (De Mauri) Haun; m. R. Laurence Macon, Sept. 6, 1969. BA in Internat. Studies, U. Tex., 1967, JD, 1970. Bar: Tex. 1971, Ga. 1971, U.S. Dist. Ct. (we. dist.) Tex. 1973, U.S. Ct. Appeals (5th and 11th cirs.) 1973. Legal staff Office Econ. Opportunity, Atlanta, 1970-71; trial atty. City of San Antonio, 1972-77, city atty., 1977-83; ptnr. Fulbright & Jaworski, LLP, San Antonio, 1983—. Pres. Internat. Women's Forum, Washington, 1987-89; mem. Com. of 200, 1988—; bd. dirs. Siebert Fin. Corp., N.Y. Legal counsel Nat. Women's Polit. Caucus, 1981—. Named to San Antonio Hall of Fame, 1984; named one of Rising Stars, 1984. Fellow Tex. Bar Found., Tex. Bar Assn. (chmn. women and the law 1984-85, client security fund com.), Southwest Research Found.; mem. San Antonio Bar Assn., San Antonio Young Lawyers Assn., Women Lawyers Tex. (pres. 1984-85), Tex. Banking Bd., Bexar County Women's Bar Assn. Democrat. Baptist. Home: 230 W Elsmere Pl San Antonio TX 78212-2349 Office: Fulbright & Jaworski LLP 300 Convent St Ste 2200 San Antonio TX 78205-3720

MACOUL, MICHAEL K. business executive, recruiter; s. Kenneth L. and Carole A. Macoul. BSBA, Boston U., 1989; MBA, Suffolk U., 1992. Registered investment advisor, fin. cons. Merrill Lynch, Andover, Mass., 1992—97; fin. cons., broker Olde Investments/Brokerage, Boston, 1997—99; pres., CEO, MKM Recruiting Specialists, Hollywood, Calif., 1999—2002; CEO, Kendall Recuriting, Internat., L.A., 2000—. Actor: (TV series) The Young and The Restless, 1990—. Mem.: Am. Fedn. of Radio and TV Artists (assoc.), SAG (assoc.). Personal E-mail: mike@kendallinternational.com.

MACOVSKI, ALBERT, electrical engineer, educator; b. N.Y.C., May 2, 1929; s. Philip and Rose (Winogr) Macovski; m. Adelaide Paris, Aug. 5, 1950; children: Michael, Nancy. BEE, City Coll. N.Y., 1950; MEE, Poly. Inst. Bklyn., 1953; PhD, Stanford U., 1968. Mem. tech. staff RCA Labs., Princeton, NJ, 1950—57; asst. prof., then assoc. prof. Poly. Inst. Bklyn., 1957—60; staff scientist Stanford Rsch. Inst., Menlo Park, Calif., 1960—71; fellow U. Calif. Med. Center San Francisco, 1971—72; prof. elec. engring. and radiology Stanford U., 1972—, endowed chair, Canon USA prof. engring., 1991—. Dir. Magnetic Resonance Sys. Rsch. Lab.; cons. to industry. Author. Recipient award for color TV cirs., Inst. Radio Engrs., 1958; spl. fellow, NIH, 1971. Fellow: IEEE (Zworykin award 1973), Internat. Soc. Magnetic Resonance in Medicine (trustee 1991—94, gold medal 1997), Optical Soc. Am., Am. Inst. Med. Biol. Engring.; mem.: NAE, Am. Assn. Physicists in Medicine, Inst. Medicine, Eta Kappa Nu, Sigma Xi. Jewish. Achievements include patents in field. Home: 2505 Alpine Rd Menlo Park CA 94025-6314 Office: Stanford U Dept Elec Engring Stanford CA 94305 Business E-Mail: macovski@stanford.edu.

MACPHEE, CRAIG ROBERT, economist, educator; b. Annapolis Royal, N.S., Can., July 10, 1944; came to U.S., 1950; s. Craig and Dorothy (Seney) MacP.; m. Kathleen Gray McCown, Feb. 6, 1966 (div. 1981); children: Paul, Heather, Rob; m. Andrea Joy Sime, June 26, 1983. BS, U. Idaho, 1966; MA, Mich. State U., 1968, PhD, 1970. Asst. prof., then assoc. prof. econs. U. Nebr., Lincoln, 1969-89, prof., 1989—, chmn. econs. dept., 1980—83, 1989—98. Econ. affairs officer UN, Geneva, 1975-77; internat. economist U.S. Dept. Labor, Washington, 1983-84; cons. in field; econ. adv. Republic of Ga., 1998-2001, Republic of Montenegro, 2001. Author: Economics of Medical Equipment and Supply, 1973, Restrictions on International Trade in Steel, 1974. Mem. Am. Econ. Assn., Midwest Econ. Assn., Nebr. Econ. and Bus. Assn., Delta Sigma Pi (faculty adviser 1982-95), Phi Eta Sigma, Omicron Delta Epsilon. Avocations: running, skiing, sailing, reading. Home: 631 Hazelwood Dr Lincoln NE 68510-4325 Office: U Nebr Coll Bus Dept Econs Lincoln NE 68588-0489

MACPHERSON, ELLE, model; b. Sydney, Australia, Mar. 29, 1964; m. Gilles Bensimon, May 24, 1986 (div.) Appeared on covers of Sports Illustrated swimsuit edit., 1986, 87, 88, 94, Elle, Cosmopolitan, Self; film appearences include Husbands and Wives, 1992, Sirens, 1994, If Lucy Fell, 1996, Jane Eyre, 1996, The Mirror Has Two Faces, 1996, The Edge, 1997, Batman and Robin, 1997, Beautopia, 1998, With Friends Like These, 1998, South Kensington, 2001; TV mini-series, A Girl Thing, 2001; TV appearance in Friends, 1999-2000. Office: Artist Mgmt Penn House B 414 E 52d St New York NY 10022

MACQUEEN, CHER, interior designer, retired newscaster, sportscaster; b. Kansas City, Mo., Mar. 20, 1952; d. Ira Raymond and Peggy Estelle (Turner) Milks. AA in Liberal Arts, L.A. Valley Coll., 1982; BS in Liberal Studies, Excelsior Coll., Albany, N.Y., 1993; grad., Barbizon Sch. Modeling, 1996; postgrad., Calif. State U., San Bernardino, 1998—; cert. in Interior Design, U. Calif., Riverside, 2002. Lic. radio-TV operator. Personnel specialist U.S. Army, Honolulu, 1973-75, adminstrv. specialist San Francisco, 1975-77, broadcast journalist Vicenza, Italy, 1977-80; radio traffic specialist Armed Forces Radio and TV, L.A., 1980-84, radio prodn. specialist, 1984-86, supr. broadcast support specialist Sun Valley, 1986-90, broadcast support mgr, 1990-91, internal info. mgr., 1991-94, news and sports specialist, 1994-99; owner The Keilani Co., Highland, 2003—. Mem.: DAV (life), Am. Soc. Interior Designers (allied mem., co-chair (Inland/Palm Springs chpt.), bd. dirs. Inland/Palm Springs chpt. 2003—04), Pacific Pioneer Broadcasters, Women in Mil. Svc. for Am. (charter), Armed Forces Broadcasters Assn. (v.p. L.A. chpt. 1991—93). Avocations: crafts, crocheting. Home: PO Box 276 Highland CA 92346-0276

MAC RAE, ALFRED URQUHART, physicist, electrical engineer; b. N.Y.C., Apr. 14, 1932; s. Farquhar and Eliza J. (Urquhart) Mac R.; m. Peggy M. Hazard, May 13, 1967; children: Susan, Pamela. BS in Physics, Syracuse U., 1954, PhD in Physics, 1960. Dir. integrated circuit devel. Bell Labs., Murray Hill, N.J., 1979-83, dir. satellite communications systems Homdel, N.J., 1983-95; pres. Mac Tech., Berkeley Heights, N.J., 1995—. Chair NASA Internat. Technology Studies, 1997-98; mem. adv. com. to bd. trustees N.J. Inst. Tech., 1981-85. Bd. editor: Vacuum Sci. and Tech, 1965-67, Rev. Sci. Instruments, 1969-71; contbr. articles to jours.; patentee in field. Bd. dirs. Summit Area ARC, 1996-2004, chmn., 2001-02. Fellow IEEE (mem., chmn. numerous coms. 1969—), Am. Phys. Soc., Nat. Acad. Engring.; mem. Bohmische Phys. Soc., IEEE Electron Devices Soc. (pres. 1986-87, chmn. field awards coun. 1989-93, Ebers award 1994). Office: 72 Sherbrook Dr Berkeley Heights NJ 07922-2346

MACRAE, CAMERON FARQUHAR, III, lawyer; b. N.Y.C., Mar. 21, 1942; s. Cameron F. and Jane B. (Miller) MacR.; m. Ann Wooster Bedell, Nov. 30, 1974; children: Catherine Fairfax, Ann Cameron. AB, Princeton U., 1963; LLB, Yale U., 1966. Bar: N.Y. 1966, D.C. 1967, U.S. Dist. Ct. (so. dist.) N.Y. 1975. Atty.-advisor Office of Gen. Counsel to Sec. Air Force, Washington, 1966-69; assoc. Davis, Polk & Wardell, N.Y.C., 1970-72; dep. supt. and counsel N.Y. State Banking Dept., N.Y.C., 1972-74; sr. ptnr. LeBoeuf, Lamb, Greene & MacRae, N.Y.C., 1975—. Dir. Nat. Integrity Life Ins. Co., 2000—. Note and comment editor Yale Law Jour., 1965-66. Trustee, sec. St. Andrew's Dune Ch., 1982—; hon. chmn. Clear Pool Inc., 1990-94. Capt. USAF, 1966-69. Mem. Assn. of Bar of City of N.Y. (past mem. securities regulation com., banking law com.), D.C. Bar Assn., Racquet and Tennis Club, Union Club (N.Y.C.), Meadow Club (v.p., bd. govs.), Bathing Corp. Southampton, Shinnecock Hills Golf Club (Southampton), Cottage Club (Princeton, N.J.), Jupiter Island Club. Independent. Episcopalian. Office: LeBoeuf Lamb Greene & MacRae LLP 125 W 55th St New York NY 10019-5369 Office Phone: 212-424-8080. E-mail: cfmacrae@llgm.com.

MACRI, THEODORE WILLIAM, book publisher; b. N.Y.C. s. Francis Carl and Emma Julia (Fantini) M.; m. Joan Michele Damato; children: Alicia, Theodore William AB, Villanova U.; MA, NYU. With Doubleday & Co. Inc., N.Y.C., dir. domestic rights, 1978-82, editorial group dir., 1982-83, asst. to pres., 1983; v.p., pub. R.R. Bowker Co., 1983-85; v.p., dir. subs. rights Contemporary Books, Inc., 1985-90; v.p. Carol Pub. Group, Inc., N.Y.C., 1990-94; pres. Ted Macri Assocs., 1994—. Bd. dirs. CUNY Ctr. for Pub., Nat. Book Awards Mem. N.Y. County Republican Com.; mem. men's com. Mus. Natural History, N.Y.C. Served to lt. (j.g.) USNR. Named Disting. Alumnus Villanova U. Mem. Assn. Am. Pubs. (edn. com.), Am. Bookseller's Assn. Clubs: N.Y. Athletic (N.Y.C.). Republican. Roman Catholic. Office: 180 Central Park S Ste 441 New York NY 10019-1562 E-mail: papatwm@aol.com.

MACRIS, MICHAEL, lawyer; b. Jackson Heights, N.Y., July 12, 1949; Student, Cornell U.; BA with distinction, Stanford U., 1971; JD, Columbia U., 1974. Bar: N.Y. 1975, Conn. 1976. Mem. Cahill Gordon & Reindel LLP, N.Y.C. Bd. editors Columbia Law Rev., 1973-74; co-editor ERISA & Benefits Law Jour., 1992-99. Harlan Fiske Stone scholar. Fellow Am. Coll. Employee Benefits Counsel (charter); mem. ABA (chmn. com. on fiduciary responsibility, real property, probate and trust law sect. 1993—), Phi Beta Kappa. Office: Cahill Gordon & Reindel LLP 80 Pine St Fl 19 New York NY 10005-1790 Office Phone: 212-701-3409. E-mail: mmacris@cahill.com.

MACRURY, KING, management counselor; b. Manchester, N.H., Oct. 14, 1915; s. Colin H. and Lauretta C. (Shea) MacR.; 1 son, Colin C. AB, Rollins Coll., 1938; postgrad., St. Anselms Coll., L.I. Coll. Medicine, Princeton. Asst. personnel dir. Lily-Tulip Cup Corp., 1939; asst. dir. market research Ward Baking Co., 1940-41; staff mem. Nat. Indsl. Conf. Bd., 1941-43; cons. indsl. relations and orgn. planning McKinsey & Co., 1946-48; internal cons. Oxford Paper Co., 1949-50; installer, dir. indsl. relations Champion Internat. Co., 1950-51; pvt. practice mgmt. counselor, 1951—. Lectr. Indsl. Edn. Inst., 1962-68, Mgmt. Center, Cambridge, 1968-71, Dun & Bradstreet, 1979—; extension div. U. N.H., 1968—; extension program U. Maine, 1978—; also U. Bridgeport, extension program U. Conn.; coordinator mgmt. edn. extension div. U. Conn., 1964-68, Philippine Council Mgmt., 1969—, Econ. Devel. Found. Philippines, 1969—, Am. Metal Stamping Assn., 1969—; condr. mgmt. seminars for Asian Assn. Mgmt. Orgns. C.I.O.S., 1972; Mem. Indsl. Devel. Commn. Andover, 1957-58; manpower com. U.S. Dept. Labor Bus. Adv. Council, 1958-61. Author: Developing Your People Potential; Contbr. numerous articles in field to profl. jours. Served to lt. USNR, 1943-46. Mem. N.H. Dental Soc. (hon.), Smaller Bus. Assn. N.E., Res. Officers Assn. Office: PO Box 215 Rye NH 03870-0215 *As individuals or as corporations, we derive our vitality from the responsiveness of those to whom we are bound in interest or effort. So it becomes, necessarily, our primary goal to inspire and to nurture this elemental source of strength.*

MACSAI, JOHN, architect; b. Budapest, Hungary, May 20, 1926; came to U.S., 1947, naturalized, 1954; s. Ferenc and Margit (Rosenfeld) Lusztig; m. Geraldine Marcus, May 7, 1950; children: Pamela, Aaron, Marian, Gwen. Baccalaureate summa cum laude, Kolcsey Gimnasium, Budapest, 1944; student, Atelier Art Sch., Budapest, 1941-43, Poly. U., 1945-47; BArch magna cum laude, Miami U., Oxford, Ohio, 1949. Archtl. designer Skidmore, Owings & Merrill, Chgo., Pace Assos., Chgo., Raymond Loewy Assos., Chgo., 1949-55; ptnr. Hausner & Macsai, Chgo., 1955-71, Campbell & Macsai, Chgo., 1971-74; prin. John Macsai & Assocs. Architects, Inc., Chgo., 1975-90, O'Donnell Wicklund Pigozzi & Peterson, Chgo., 1991-2000, ret., 2000. Prof. architecture U. Ill., Chgo., 1970-76, prof. emeritus, 1997—. Author: High Rise Apartment Buildings: A Design Primer, 1972, Housing, 1976, Housing, 2d edit., 1982, Housing, Russian edit., 1980, Housing, Mexican edit., 1984; co-author: Designing Environments for the Aged, 1977, Housing for a Maturing Population, 1983, (ency.) Highrise Apartment Buildings, 1988, East European Modernism, 1996; contbr. articles to profl. jours.; prin. works include Nat. Opinion Rsch. Ctr., U.Chgo., 1967, High Energy Physics Bldg., 1968, Social Svcs. Ctr., 1970, Harbor House, 1965, Malibu East, 1972, Waterford apt. bldg., 1976, U. Chgo. faculty townhouses, 1986, Fairfield Ct. housing for the elderly, 1988, Evanston Pl. apt. bldg and city garage, 1991, 2960 N. Lake Shore Dr. Housing for the Elderly, 1991; staff arch. Tel Tanninim Archaeol. Project, Israel, 1996—2000, Elike Archaeol. Project, Greece, 2001; exhibitions include watercolors at Gallery 1756, Chgo., 1991—2003, Chgo. Cultural Ctr., 2000, Cliffdwellers Club, 2002. Fellow AIA (13 design award citations Chgo. chpt.). Jewish. Home: 1501 Hinman Ave Apt 3B Evanston IL 60201-4675 Business E-Mail: jgmacsai@uic.edu.

MACTAGGART, TERRENCE JOSEPH, professor, former university chancellor; b. Buffalo, Sept. 20, 1946; s. Joseph Carol and Genieve Mary (Quinn) MacT. BA in English and Philosophy, Canisius Coll., Buffalo, 1967; MA in Lit., St. Louis U., 1971, PhD in Lit., 1976; MBA, St. Cloud (Minn.) State U., 1986. Prof. Blackburn Coll., Carlinville, Ill., 1973-74; dir. Webster U., St. Louis, 1974-77; acting dean U. Alaska, Fairbanks, 1977-79; dean St. Cloud (Minn.) State U., 1979-83; v.p. Met. State U., St. Paul, 1983-86; vice chancellor Minn. State U. System, St. Paul, 1986-87; chancellor U. Wis., Superior, 1987-91, Minn. State U. System, Saint Paul, 1991-95; prof. English Minn. State U., Saint Paul, 1991-95; chancellor U. Maine System, Bangor, 1996—2001; prof. Univ. of Maine, 2002—. Fulbright Scholar in Thailand, 1996. Editor: Cost Effective Assessment of Prior Learning, 1983; contbr. articles on higher edn. to profl. jours. Sgt. U.S. Army, 1969-71, Viet Nam. NDEA fellow, 1968-72. Mem. Phi Beta Kappa. Avocations: cross country skiing, sailing. Office: Univ Maine System Office 107 Maine Ave Bangor ME 04401-4380

MACTAS, MARK V. diversified financial services company executive; Former mng. dir. global health and welfare bus. Towers Perrin, N.Y.C., 1997, former v.p., former pres., chmn., CEO, 2001—. Office: Towers Perrin One Stamford Plaza Stamford CT 06901

MACTAVISH, CRAIG, professional hockey coach, former hockey player; b. London, Ont., Can., Aug. 15, 1958; Hockey player Boston Bruins Nat. Hockey League, 1980-85, hockey player Edmonton Oilers, 1985-94, hockey player N.Y. Rangers, 1994, hockey player Phila. Flyers, 1994-96, hockey player St. Louis Blues, 1996-97; asst. coach N.Y. Rangers, 1997-98, Edmonton Oilers, 1998—. Mem. Stanley Cup championship team 1987, 88, 90, 94; capt. Edmonton Oilers, 1992-93, 93-94. Office: Edmonton Oilers 11230 110 St Edmonton AB Canada T5G 3GB

MACURDY, JOHN EDWARD, bass; b. Detroit, Mar. 18, 1929; s. Blanchard Archibald and Dorathea Rosalie (Radtke) Macurdy; m. Justine May Votypka, Apr. 12, 1958; children: Allison Anne, John Blanchard. Student, Wayne State U., 1947; student of Avery Crew, Detroit, 1946. Mem. N.Y.C. Opera, 1959-62, Met. Opera, 1962—. Appeared in U.S., Europe, including San Francisco Opera, La Scala; performances include world premieres Mourning Becomes Electra, Met. Opera, 1967, opening night Anthony and Cleopatra, Met. Opera,

1966, Wuthering Heights, Santa Fe Opera, 1958, Six Characters in Search of an Author, N.Y.C. Opera, 1959, Griffalkin, Tanglewood Festival, 1957; Am. premieres Capriccio, Santa Fe Opera, 1958, Murder in the Cathedral, Empire State Music Festival, Bear Mountain Park, N.Y., 1959, Inspector General, N.Y.C. Opera, 1960; appeared with numerous orchs.; film Don Giovanni, 1979; participant 40th Anniversary Sud-Deutsche Rundfunk, 100th Anniversary Gala Met. Opera, 1983. Served with USAF, 1950-54. Recipient medal for artistic merit during Mich. Week City of Detroit, 1969, Arts Achievement award Wayne State U., 2003; inducted into Acad. Vocal Hall of Fame, 1985. Mem.: Bohemian Club of San Francisco. Presbyterian. Office: Met Opera Lincoln Ctr New York NY 10023

MAC WATTERS, VIRGINIA ELIZABETH, singer, music educator, actress; b. Phila. d. Frederick-Kennedy and Idoleein (Hallowell) Mac W.; m. Paul Abée, June 10, 1960. Grad., Phila. Normal Sch. for Tchrs., 1933; student, Curtis Inst. Music, Phila., 1936. With New Opera Co., N.Y.C., 1941-42; artist-in-residence Ind. U. Sch. Music, 1957-58; assoc. prof. U. Ind. Sch. Music, 1958-68, prof. voice, 1968-82, prof. emeritus, 1982—. Singer: leading roles Broadway mus. Rosalinda, 1942-44, Mr. Strauss Goes to Boston, 1945, leading opera roles New Opera Co., N.Y.C., 1941-42, San Francisco, 1944, N.Y.C. Ctr., 1946-51; leading soprano for reopening of Royal Opera House, Covent Garden, London, 1947-48, Guatemala, El Salvador, Cen. Am., 1948-49; debut at Met. Opera, N.Y.C., 1952; TV spls. on NBC include Menotti's Old Maid and the Thief, 1949, Would-be Gentleman (R. Strauss), 1955; leading singer with Met. Opera Co. on coast to coast tour of Die Fledermaus, 1951-52, Met. Opera debut, N.Y.C., 1952, leading soprano Cen. City Opera Festival, Colo., 1952-56; performed with symphony orchs. in U.S., Can., S.Am.; concert recitalist U.S., Can., 1950-62; opened N.Y. Empire State Music Festival in Ariadne auf Naxos (Strauss), 1959; soloist Mozart Festival, Ann Arbor, Mich. Recipient Mile award Album Familiar Music, 1949, Ind. U. Disting. Tchg. award, 1979; named One of 10 Outstanding Women of the Yr.; Zeckwer Hahn Phila. Mus. Acad. scholar, 1941-42; MacWatters chair donated by New Auer Grand Concert Hall, U. Ind. Sch. Music. Mem. Nat. Fedn. of Music Clubs, Nat. Soc. Arts and Letters, Nat. Soc. Lit. and Arts, Soc. Am. Musicians, Nat. Assn. Tchrs. of Singing, Internat. Platform Assn., Sigma Alpha Iota. Clubs: Matinee Musical (hon. mem. Phila., Indpls. chpts.). Achievements include having only original recorded version of Zerbinetta aria from Ariadne auf Naxos (Strauss). Home: 3800 Arlington Rd Bloomington IN 47404-1347 Office: Ind U Sch Music Bloomington IN 47405

MACWILLIAMS, DIANE, communications executive; m. Bill MacWilliams. Degree in Fine and Applied Arts, U. Ill. Designer Arthur Andersen & Co.; pres., CEO, founder Quicksilver Assocs., Inc., Chgo., 1976—. Office: Quicksilver Assocs Inc 18 W Ontario St Chicago IL 60610-3809

MACWILLIAMS, KENNETH EDWARD, investment banker; b. Newburyport, Mass., Aug. 21, 1936; s. Harold Freeman and Helen (Melia) MacW.; m. Angelyn Wishnack, July 16, 1960 (div. 1975); children: Robert Hovey, James Stuart. BA, Harvard U., 1958, MBA, 1962. V.p. Morgan Guaranty Trust Co., N.Y.C., 1962-71; sr. assoc. Goldman Sachs & Co., N.Y.C., 1971-74; mng. dir., domestic merchant banking group Manfacturers Hanover Trust Co., N.Y.C., 1975-82; chmn., chief exec. officer Prudential Capital Corp. subs. Prudential Ins. Co. Am., Newark, 1982-90; pres. Prudential Equity Mgmt. Assn. subs. Prudential Ins. Co. Am., Newark, 1990-92; founder, pres. Woodrow Wilson Assocs., Chapel Hill, NC, 1993—. Office: Apt 6B 319 E 50th St New York NY 10022

MACY, WILLIAM H. actor; b. Miami, Mar. 13, 1950; m. Felicity Huffman, 1997. Actor: (TV series) The Awakening Land, 1978, Kate & Allie, 1984, Spenser: For Hire, 1985, The Equalizer, 1985, L.A. Law, 1986, Law & Order, 1990, Civil Wars, 1991, Bakersfield P.D., 1993, Frasier, 1993, ER, 1994, Superman, 1996, King of the Hill, 1997, The Lionhearts, 1998, Hercules, 1998, Sports Night, 1998, Batman Beyond, 1999, Out of Order, 2003; writer: thirtysomething, 1987; writer, actor Above Suspicion, 1995; dir., actor: Lip Service, 1988; actor: (TV films) The Cradle Will Fall, 1983, The Boy Who Loved Trolls, 1984, The Dining Room, 1984, The Murder of Mary Phagan, 1988, In the Line of Duty: Siege at Marion, 1992, A Private Matter, 1992, The Water Engine, 1992, The Heart of Justice, 1993, Texan, 1994, The Writing on the Wall, 1994, In the Shadow of Evil, 1995, Andersonville, 1996, The Night of the Headless Horseman, 1999, It's a Very Merry Muppet Christmas Movie, 2002; writer, actor: The Con, 1998; A Slight Case of Murder, 1999; Door to Door, 2002 (Screen Actors Guild award best actor, 2003, Emmy award best actor in a TV movie, 2003, Emmy award best writing TV movie, 2003); writer Every Woman's Dream, 1996; Just a Walk in the Park, 2002; actor: (films) Foolin' Around, 1980, Somewhere in Time, 1980, Without a Trace, 1983, The Last Dragon, 1985, Radio Days, 1987, House of Games, 1987, Things Change, 1988, Homicide, 1991, Shadows and Fog, 1992, Benny & Joon, 1993, Searching for Bobby Fischer, 1993, Twenty Bucks, 1993, Being Human, 1993, The Client, 1994, Oleanna, 1994, Murder in the First, 1995, Roommates, 1995, Tall Tale, 1995, Evolver, 1995, Mr. Holland's Opus, 1995, Down Periscope, 1996, Fargo, 1996, Hit Me, 1996, Ghosts of Mississippi, 1996, Colin Fitz, 1996, Air Force One, 1997, Boogie Nights, 1997, Wag the Dog, 1997, Jerry and Tom, 1998, Pleasantville, 1998, Psycho, 1998, The Secret of NIMH 2: Timmy to the Rescue, 1998, A Civil Action, 1998, Happy, Texas, 1999, Mystery Men, 1999, Magnolia, 1999, Panic, 2000, State and Main, 2000, Jurassic Park III, 2001, Focus, 2001, Welcome to Collinwood, 2002, The Cooler, 2003, Seabiscuit, 2003, Cellular, 2004. Office: Ste 550 8383 Wilshire Blvd Beverly Hills CA 90211

MACZULSKI, MARGARET LOUISE, event marketing professional, meeting manager; b. Detroit, Apr. 01; d. Bohdan Alexander and Olga Louise (Martinuick) M. BS, Mich. State U.; cert. E-Commerce Mgmt., DePaul U., 2000. Cert. meeting mgr. Mgr. meetings Nat. Assn. Realtors, Mktg. Inst., Chgo., 1977-82, mgr. mktg., 1982-83; regional sales mgr. Fairmont Hotels, Chgo., 1982; dir., mgr. trade shows and confs. Capital Cities Am. Broadcasting Co./Pub. Div., Wheaton, Ill., 1983-85; mgr. meeting and conf. planning Soc. Human Resource Mgmt., Alexandria, Va., 1985-90; mgr. meeting and conv. planning Kraft Foods, Glenview, Ill., 1990-95; cons. meetings and spl. events Chgo., 1996-98; sr. mgr. meeting and travel svcs. Coll. Am. Pathologists, Northfield, Ill., 1998-2000; conv. mgr. Common, A User Group, 2001—02, cons. spl. events, 2002—. Mem. Meeting Planners Internat., Greater Washington Soc. Assn. Execs. (past chmn. site inspection com.), Soc. Corporate Meeting Planners, Am. Soc. Assn. Execs., Mich. State U. Alumni Assn. (treas. D.C. chpt. 1987-90), Soc. for Corp. Mtg. Planners, Assn. Forum, Profl. Conf. Mgmt. Assn. Republican. Roman Catholic. Avocations: piano, swimming, skiing. Home: 849 W Lakeside Pl 3 East Chicago IL 60640-6693 E-mail: gwenraz@hotmail.com.

MADAN, DEEPAK S. engineering executive; came to U.S., 1982; s. S. M. and K. S. Madan; m. A. P. Madan; 1 child, N. S. B Technology/Metall. Engr., Indian Inst. Technology, Kanpur, India, 1982; MS Materials Engr., Rensselaer Polytechnic Inst., 1986, PhD Materials Engr., 1988. Rsch. fellow Rensselaer Polytechnic Inst., Troy, NY, 1982-87; sr. materials engr. Elkem Metals Co., Pitts., 1987-95; exec. v.p. F.W. Winter, Inc. & Co., Camden, NJ, 1995—. Patentee in field; contbr. articles to profl. jours. Mem.: Am. Powder Metallurgy Inst., Am. Soc. Metals. Avocations: photography, travel, computers. Office: FW Winter Inc & Co Delaware Ave and Elm St Camden NJ 08102

MADANSKY, ALBERT, statistics educator; b. Chgo., May 16, 1934; s. Harry and Anna (Meidenberg) M.; m. Paula Barkan, June 10, 1990; children from previous marriage: Susan, Cynthia, Noreen, Michele. AB, U. Chgo., 1952, MS, 1955, PhD, 1958. Mathematician Rand Corp., Santa Monica, Calif., 1957-65; sr. v.p. Interpub. Group of Companies, N.Y.C., 1965-68; pres. Dataplan Inc, N.Y.C., 1968-70; prof. computer scis. CCNY, 1970-74; prof. bus. adminstrn. grad. sch. U. Chgo., 1974—, assoc. dean, 1985-90, dep. dean, 1990-93, H.G.B. Alexander prof. bus. adminstrn., 1996-99, H.G.B. Alexander emeritus bus. adminstrn., 1999—. Bd. dirs. Analytic Services, Washington, 1975—. Author: Foundations of Econometrics, 1975, Prescriptions for Working Statisticians, 1988. Fellow: Ctr. for Advanced Study in Behavioral Scis., Am. Statis. Assn., Inst. Math. Stats., Econometric Soc. Home: 200 E Delaware Pl Apt 23F Chicago IL 60611-5799 Office: U of Chicago Grad Sch Business Chicago IL 60637 E-mail: albert.madansky@gsb.uchicago.edu.

MADARA, JAMES LEE, dean, pathologist, educator, epitheliologist; b. Altoona, Pa., Sept. 16, 1950; s. Daniel Rodman and Margaret Jane (Hauser) M.; m. Victoria Mollenkopf, May 14, 1975; children: J. Maxwell, Alexis Lindsy. BA, Juniata Coll., 1971; MD, Hahnemann Med., 1975. Cert. anatomic and clin. pathology. Intern Deaconess Hosp., Boston, 1975—76, resident in pathology, 1976—78; fellow in internal medicine Harvard Med. Ctr., Boston, 1978—80; instr. pathology Harvard Med. Sch., Boston, 1980-81, asst. prof. pathology, 1981-85, assoc. prof. pathology, 1985-91, prof. pathology, 1993-97; assoc. prof. of health scis. and tech. Harvard-M.I.T., Boston, 1986-91; Timmie prof., chmn. dept. pathology & lab. medicine Emory U. Sch. Medicine, Atlanta, 1997—2002; dean, v.p. for medical affairs Pritzker Sch. of Med. and Div. of Biological Sciences, U. of Chicago, Chicago, Ill., 2002—. Assoc. editor Gastroenterology, 1986-91; mem. editl. bd. Jour. Clin. Investigation, 1987—; editor-in-chief Am. Jour. Pathology, 2000; contbr. over 160 articles to profl. jours. Grantee NIH, 1980—. Mem. Am. Soc. for Clin. Investigation (elected), Am. Soc. for Cell Biology, Am. Gastroenterological Assn. (rsch. coun. 1988-90, Ross Rsch. scholar award 1982), Am. Physiol. Soc., Am. Assn. Pathology (Parke/Davis award 1990), Assn. Am. Physicians. Achievements include description of functional sequellae of neutrophil-epithelial cell interactions; recognition that tight junctions between epithelial cells are regulated under physiological conditions. Office: Pritzker Sch Med U Chicago 5841 S Maryland Ave Chicago IL 60637*

MADDALONI, MARTIN J. labor union administrator; Bus. mgr. Steamfitters Local 420; v.p., Phila. internat. rep. United Assn. Journeyman and Apprentices Plumbing and Pipe Fitting Industry U.S. and Can., Wash., DC, 1988—97, gen. pres., 1997—. Office: United Assn 901 Massachusetts Ave NW Washington DC 20001-4307 also: 1717 K St NW Ste 207 Washington DC 20036 Office Phone: 202-628-5823.

MADDEN, ALICE DONNELLY, lawyer; b. St. Louis, Dec. 9, 1958; d. William Joseph and Katherine (Kinsella) Donnelly; m. Peter Gerard Madden, Aug. 3, 1985; children: Thomas Joseph, Jackson Joseph. BA in Psychology, U. Colo., 1981, JD, 1989. Bar: Colo. 1989, U.S. Dist. Ct. Colo. 1989, U.S. Ct. Appeals (10th cir.) 1989. Assoc. Fairfield & Woods, P.C., Denver, 1989-94, Clayton & Stone, Boulder, Colo., 1994-96. Bd. dirs. Boulder County (Colo.) Land Trust, 1991-96, sec., 1992, pres., 1994; bd. dirs. Shannon Estates Homeowners Assn., Boulder, Colo., 1989-92; dir. alumni rels. U. Colo. Sch. of Law, 1997—. Mem. ABA, Colo. Bar Assn., Denver Bar Assn. (ct. reform com. 1991), Boulder County Bar Assn., Colo. Women's Bar Assn. Democrat. Avocations: skiing, hiking, reading. Office: U Colo Sch of Law PO Box 401 Boulder CO 80309-0401

MADDEN, CHERYL BETH, state legislator; b. Burke, S.D., Nov. 15, 1948; d. Herman and Ida Denker; m. Michael K. Madden, 1977; children: Pamela, Jessica, Rachel. Grad. high sch. Mem. S.D. Ho. of Reps., Pierre, 1992-98, mem. edn., health and human svc. coms.; mem. S.D. Senate from 35th dist., Pierre, 1999—. Chaplain, chmn. Fedn. Rep. Women. Address: 63 Langdon Rd Buffalo WY 82834-9341

MADDEN, DAVID, author; b. Knoxville, Tenn., July 25, 1933; s. James Helvy and Emile (Merritt) M.; m. Roberta Margaret Young, Sept. 6, 1956; 1 son, Blake Dana. BS, U. Tenn., 1957; MA, San Francisco State Coll., 1958; postgrad., Yale Drama Sch., 1959-60. Faculty Appalachian State Tchrs. Coll., Boone, N.C., 1957-58, Centre Coll., Danville, Ky., 1960-62, U. Louisville, 1962-64, Kenyon Coll., Gambier, O., 1964-66, Ohio U., Athens, 1966-68; writer-in-residence La. State U., Baton Rouge, 1968-92, dir. creative writing program, 1992-94, dir. U.S. Civil War Ctr., 1992-99, Donald and Velvia Crumbley prof. creative writing, 1999—. Alumni prof. La. State U., 1994. Author: (novels) Cassandra Singing, 1969, Bijou, 1974, The Suicide's Wife, 1978, Pleasure Dome, 1979, On the Big Wind, 1980, Sharpshooter: A Novel of the Civil War, 1996, (stories) The Shadow Knows (Nat. Coun. on Arts selection), 1970, The New Orleans of Possibilities (lit. criticism) Wright Morris, 1964, Poetic Image in Six Genres, 1969, James M. Cain, 1970, A Primer of the Novel, 1980, Writers' Revisions, 1981, Cain's Craft, 1985, Revising Fiction, 1988, Rediscoveries II, 1988; asst. editor: The Kenyon Rev., 1964-66; editor: Remembering James Agee, 1974; co-editor: (with P. Bach) Classics of Civil War Fiction, 1991, Beyond the Battlefield, 2000, The Legacy of Robert Penn Warren, 2000, Thomas Wolfe's Civil War, 2004, Losses of the Sultana, 2004. Served with AUS, 1953-55. Recipient Rockefeller grant in fiction, 1969; John Golden fellow in playwriting, 1959 Mem. Authors League, Associated Writing Programs (bd. dirs.). Democrat. Office: La State U Dept English Baton Rouge LA 70803-0001 Office Phone: 225-578-3156.

MADDEN, EDWARD GEORGE, JR., lawyer; b. Newark, Feb. 21, 1924; s. Edward and Catherine (Mahon) M.; m. Mary B. Haveron, June 20, 1959; children: Maurica, Margaret, Thomas, Mary, Jane. BS, St. Peter's Coll., 1950; JD, U. Mich., 1953. Bar: N.J. 1954, U.S. Dist. Ct. N.J. 1954, U.S. Ct. Appeals (3d cir.) 1981, U.S. Supreme Ct. 1959. Assoc. McCarter & English, Newark, 1954-56, Donohue & Donohue, Nutley, N.J., 1956-61; ptnr. Troast, Mattson & Madden, Newark, 1961-65, Mattson & Madden, Newark, 1965—. Mem. N.J. State Legislature, 1960-62. With USN 1943-46. Fellow Am. Bar Found.; mem. ABA, N.J. Bar Assn. (trustee, treas. 1972-78), Essex County Bar Assn. (trustee 1971-75), Internat. Assn. Def. Counsel, Transp. Lawyers Assn. Democrat. Roman Catholic. Office: 33 Bleeker St Millburn NJ 07041-1414

MADDEN, EDWARD HARRY, philosopher, retired educator; b. Gary, Ind., May 18, 1925; s. Harry Albert and Amelia Dorothy (Schepper) M.; m. Marian Sue Canaday, Sept. 15, 1946; children: Kerry Arthur, Dennis William. AB, Oberlin Coll., 1946, A.M., 1947; PhD, U. Iowa, 1950. Prof. philosophy U. Conn., 1950-59, San Jose State Coll., 1959-64, SUNY, Buffalo, 1964-80, prof. emeritus, 1980, U. Ky., 1982-95, ret., 1995. Vis. prof. Brown U., 1954-55, Amherst Coll., 1962, U. Toronto, 1967, Am. U. Beirut, Lebanon, 1969-70; sr. research fellow Linacre Coll., Oxford U., 1978, Inst. Advanced Study, Princeton, 1980-81, The John Dewey Summer Inst., 2002. Author: Philosophical Problems of Psychology, 1962, Chauncey Wright and the Foundations of Pragmatism, 1963, Evil and the Concept of God, 1968, Civil Disobedience and Moral Law, 1968, The Structure of Scientific Thought, 1960, Causal Powers, 1975, Causing, Perceiving and Believing, 1975, Freedom and Grace, 1982; co-author, editor: Theories of Scientific Method, 1960, Philosophical Perspectives on Punishment, 1968, The Idea of God, 1968; gen. editor: Harvard U. Press Source Books in History Sci.; mem. editl. bd.: The Works of William James, Thoreau Quar., History of Philosophy Quar., Philosophy of Sci., 1960-76; mem. adv. bd.: A Critical Edition of the Correspondence of William James (Am. Coun. Learned Socs.). Served with USNR, 1943-45. Recipient Am. Philos. Soc. research grant, 1961, Fulbright-Hays award, 1969-70, Herbert W. Schneider award Soc. for Advancement Am. Philosophy, 1991. Fellow Asa Mahan Soc.; mem. C.S. Peirce Soc. (pres. 1962-63, sec.-treas., editorial bd. Transactions of Soc.), Am. Council Learned Socs. (selection com.), Am. Philos. Assn. (co-chmn. com. publs. 1960-77), Phi Kappa Phi. Home: 4 Sanctuary Cir White River Junction VT 05001-2960

MADDEN, ELISABETH ANNE, theater director; b. Cleveland, Apr. 27, 1976; d. Susan Marie and Thomas Michael Madden. BA, Baldwin-Wallace Coll., 1994—99. Dir. theatre publicity Baldwin-Wallace Coll. Theatre Dept., Berea, Ohio, 1995—99; audience devel. coord. Cleve. Signstage Theatre, 1999—2000; bus. mgr. Cleve. Shakespeare Festival, 1999; ho. mgr. Tony N' Tina's Wedding, Cleveland, 2000—01, prodn. asst.; mktg. assoc. Porthouse Theatre, Kent, Ohio, 2001; mng. dir. Kent State U. Sch. Theatre & Dance and Porthouse Theatre, Ohio, 2001—. Bd. mem. Cleve. Shakespeare Festival, 2000—01. Actor(assistant): (plays) Tony N' Tina's Wedding; dir.: Bye, Bye Birdie, Meet Me In St. Louis; asst. to dir. (plays) The Tempest, stage mgr. On Golden Pond. Office: Kent State Univ Sch Theatre and Dance PO Box 5190 Kent OH 44242-0001 Office Phone: 330-672-0103. Office Fax: 330-672-2889. E-mail: emadden@kent.edu.

MADDEN, GLENDA GAIL, sales professional; b. Norman, Okla., Aug. 30, 1949; d. John Samuel Jr. and Z. June (Pence) M. BA in Polit. Sci., Okla. Coll. Liberal Arts, 1970. Account clk. U. Okla. Press, Norman, 1977-78, advt. asst., 1978-80, asst. supr., 1980-81, sales mgr., 1981-98, asst. dir. mktg., 1998—. Avocations: home renovation, antiques, reading, genealogy. Office: Univ Okla Press 4100 28th Ave NW Norman OK 73069-8218

MADDEN, JAMES COOPER, V, management consultant; b. Glen Cove, N.Y., June 18, 1961; s. James Cooper IV and Linda Marie (Lizza) M.; m. Heather Madden; 1 child, Jennifer Louise. Student, Webb Inst. Naval Architecture, Glen Cove, 1979-80; BA cum laude, BBA magna cum laude, So. Meth. U., 1983. Cert. Soc. Naval Architects and Marine Engrs. Cons. Andersen Cons./Arthur Andersen, Houston, 1983-85, sr. cons., 1985-87, mgr. L.A., 1987-90, sr. mgr., 1990-91; prin. Booz-Allen & Hamilton, L.A., 1991-93; v.p. mng. dir. MCI Systemhouse, L.A., 1993-95, pres. U.S. and Mexico ops., 1995-97, CFO, 1997-98; chmn., pres. Exult, Inc., Irvine, Calif., 1998—. Contbr. articles to profl. jours. Bd. dirs. Exolt. Webb Inst. Naval Architecture scholar, 1979-80. Avocations: sailing, skiing, travel, reading. Office: Exult Inc 121 Innovation Dr #200 Irvine CA 92612-3094

MADDEN, JAMES D. forensic engineer; b. Jersey City; s. Louis A. and Ann Madden. BSChemE, U. S.C., 1963, ME, 1966. Lic. profl. engr., Ohio; cert. diplomate forensic engr. Process engr. Monsanto Co., Alvin, Tex., 1966-67; process and project engr. Union Carbide Corp., Houston, 1967-70; systems engr. M.W. Kellogg Co., Houston, 1970-73, prin. systems engr., 1974-77; sr. process engr. Litwin Co., Houston, 1973-74; sr. project engr. Davy Powergas, Houston, 1977-78, supervising project engr., 1978-79; mgr. equipment engring. DM Internat., Houston, 1979-80, project engring. mgr., 1980-83; owner, forensic engr. Madden Forensic Engring., Parma, Parma Heights and Brecksville, Ohio, 1983—. Pres. Houston Young Adult Rep. Club, 1970-73; chmn. Tex. Young Adult Rep. Clubs, 1973. NSF rsch. grantee, 1963; NASA fellow, 1963-65; named to Outstanding Young Men Am., 1973. Mem. ASME, NSPE, AIChE, Soc. Automotive Engrs., Nat. Fire Protection Assn., Inst. Transp. Engrs., Am. Soc. Agrl. Engrs., Bldg. Ofcls. and Code Adminstrs. Internat., Nat. Acad. Forensic Engrs., Sigma Xi, Sigma Pi Sigma, Tau Beta Pi, Omicron Delta Kappa. Office: 10175 Brecksville Rd Cleveland OH 44141-3205

MADDEN, JOHN, television sports commentator, former professional football coach; b. Austin, Minn., Apr. 10, 1936; s. Earl and Mary O'Flaherty M.; m. Virginia Madden; children: Mike, Joe. BS, Calif. Poly. U., 1959, MA, 1961. Player Phila. Eagles (NFL team), 1959; asst. coach Hancock Jr. Coll., Santa Maria, Calif., 1960-62, head coach, 1962-64; defensive coordinator Calif. State U., San Diego, 1964-66; with Oakland Raiders, Am. Football League (now Am. Football Conf., Nat. Football League), 1967-79, linebacker coach, 1967-69, head coach, 1969-79; head coach NFL Pro Bowl team Am. Football Conf., 1971, 73, 74, 75; head coach 6 Western div. Am. Football Conf. championship teams, Super Bowl champions, 1976; sports commentator, football analyst CBS Sports, 1979-93; appears in TV and radio comms.; sports commentator, football analyst Fox Sports, 1994—2002, Monday Night Football (ABC), 2002—. Author: Hey, Wait a Minute, I Wrote a Book!, 1984; One Knee Equals Two Feet, 1986; developer (software) John Madden Football, 1988, John Madden Football II, 1993. Named Coach of Year Am. Football League, 1969, Sports Personality of the Yr., Am. Sportscasters Assn., 1985; recipient Emmy awards for sports broadcasting, 1982, 83, 85, 86, 87, 88. Office: care Sandy Montag 1211 Ave of Americas New York NY 10021-4911

MADDEN, JOHN J. lawyer; b. N.Y.C., May 27, 1946; s. John L. and Bertha M.; m. Mary A. O'Neill, June 19, 1976; children: Elisabeth, Samuel. BA, U. Pa., 1968; JD, Fordham U., 1975. Bar: N.Y. 1976, U.S. Dist. Ct. (so. dist.) N.Y. 1976; avocat a la cour de Paris 1994. From assoc. to ptnr. Shearman & Sterling, N.Y.C., 1975—83, ptnr., 1983—, mng. ptnr. European Offices Paris, 1991-95. Mem. policy com. Mergers and Acquisitions Group Shearman & Sterling, mem. exec. group, head Mergers and Acquisitions Group, 1986—91, 1995—2001. Trustee St. David's Sch., N.Y.C., 1981-91. Served to 1st lt. U.S. Army, 1969-71, Vietnam. Mem. ABA, N.Y. Bar Assn., Assn. of Bar of City of N.Y., Internat. Bar Assn., Cercle de l'Union Interalliee (Paris). Business E-Mail: jmadden@shearman.com.

MADDEN, JOHN PATRICK, lawyer; b. N.Y.C., Sept. 9, 1945; s. Eugene Patrick and Eileen Mary (Gaughan) M.; m. Sally Williams, Apr. 21, 1984; children: Samuel, Christopher. Student in Mechanical Engineering, U. Maine, 1966; student in Structural Engineering, U. Wash., 1967, Purdue Univ., 1968; student in Environmental Engineering, George Washington Univ., 1975; BCE, Manhattan Coll., 1967; MSCE, NYU, 1969; JD, St. John's U. Sch. Law, NYC, 1978; EC Trade Law, Trinity Coll., Cambridge Univ., England, 1976; Comecon Trade Law, Univ. Warsaw, Poland, 1976. Bar: US Patent and Trademark Office 1978, NY State Ct. 1979, NJ State Ct. 1982, US Dist. Ct. (so. and ea. dists.) NY 1982, US Dist. Ct. NJ 1982, US Supreme Ct. 1985; solicitor Law Soc. England and Wales, 2003; cert. Accredited Mediator Chartered Inst. Arbitrators, London, 2002; accredited mediator, CEDR, London, 2002; Large Complex Case Panel, Am. Arbitration Assn., 1996; constrn. arbitrator, 1983, Am. Arbitration Assn., comml. mediator, 1990, internat. arbitrator, 1993; US D.O.D. qualified instr., Nuclear Def. Design, 1967. Engr., 1966—75; law clk., assoc. Buckley, Treacy, Shaffel Mackey & Abbate, N.Y.C., 1977-80; cons. Contractors Consulting Svcs. Inc., Greatneck, N.Y., 1980-81; ptnr. Madden, Sciarra & Muirhead, N.Y., N.J., 1981-82, Canfield, Venusti, Madden & Rossi, N.Y.C., 1979—. Lectr. in field; arbitrator and mediator conciliator in field. Contbr. articles to profl. jours. V.p. N.Y.C. Jaycees, 1975-95. ROTC USAF, 1963-65. Mem. ABA (pub. contract law sect., forum com. on constrn. industry), Internat. Bar Assn. (mem. alternative dispute resolution com., internat. constrn. projects com.), London Ct. Internat. Arbitration, Swiss Arbitration Assn., Am. Trial Lawyers Assn., NY State Bar Assn., NY State Trial Lawyers Assn., Assn. of Bar of City of NY, Chartered Inst. Arbitrators, Union Internationale Des Avocats, Am. Arbitration Assn., NJ State Bar Assn., Nat. Arts Club, Fidelity & Surety Law com. Office: Canfield Venusti Madden & Rossi 230 Park Ave Rm 2525 New York NY 10169-2599

MADDEN, JOSEPH DANIEL, trade association executive; b. Bayside, N.Y., Dec. 25, 1921; s. Thomas A. and Margaret (McFadden) M.; m. Eileen M. MacDonnell, Sept. 8, 1951; children: Joseph Daniel, Jr., Maureen A. BS, Fordham U., 1951; MBA, N.Y. U., 1956. Credit investigator Dun & Bradstreet, N.Y.C., 1947-48; credit mgr. Devoe & Raynolds Co., N.Y.C., 1948-50, Admiral Corp., N.Y.C., 1950-51; nat. credit mgr. Standard Toch Chems., Inc., S.I., N.Y., 1951-52; with chems. and plastics div. Union Carbide Corp., Midland, Mich., 1952-62; mgr. Detroit sales office, 1958-60; sr. staff adminstr. Soc. Plastics Industry, Washington, 1962-69; exec. v.p. Drug, Chem. and Assoc. Techs. Assn., Robbinsville, NJ, 1969-88, cons. assn. mgmt., 1988—. With U.S. Army, 1942-43. Mem. Am. Soc. Assn. Execs. (cert.), N.Y. Soc. Assn. Execs. (past bd. dirs., Exec. of Yr. award 1988), Soc. Friendly Sons of St. Patrick, Kiwanis (past pres. Bayside, sec.), Am. Legion, Am. Assn. Ret. Persons (past pres. local chpt.), Toastmasters Internat. (past pres. local club). Home: 211-37 18th Ave Bayside NY 11360-1529 E-mail: josephdmaddensr@att.net.

MADDEN, LAURENCE VINCENT, plant pathology educator; b. Ashland, Pa., Oct. 10, 1953; s. Lawrence Vincent and Janet Elizabeth (Wewer) M.; m. Susan Elizabeth Heady, July 7, 1984. BS, Pa. State U., 1975, MS, 1977, PhD, 1980. Research scientist Ohio State U., Wooster, 1980-82, asst. prof., 1983-86, assoc. prof., 1986-91, prof., 1991—. Invited univ. lectr. on plant disease epidemiology in more than 10 countries. Author: Introduction to Plant Disease Epidemiology; sr. editor Phytopathology, 1988-90, APS Press, 1988-90; editor-in-chief Phytopathology, 1991-93; contbr. 140articles to profl. jours. U.S. Dept. Rsch. grantee, 1984, 85, 86, 87, 89, 90, 91, 95, 99, 2000; Disting. scholar Ohio State U., 1991,; recipient Outstanding Alumni award Pa. State U. Coll. Agrl. Scis. Fellow AAAS, The Linnean Soc. of London, Am. Phytopathol. Soc. (chmn. com. 1983, 86, coun. 1991-93, Ciba Geigy Agrl. Achievement award 1990, v.p. 1994-95, pres.-elect 1995-96, pres. 1996-97); mem. Biometric Soc., Brit. Soc. Plant Pathology, Sigma Xi (chpt. pres. 1985). Achievements include development of statistical and mathematical models for

understanding, predicting and comparing botanical epidemics and assessing crop losses. Home: 1295 Briarcrest Cir Wooster OH 44691 Office: Ohio State U OARDC Dept Plant Pathology Wooster OH 44691 E-mail: madden.1@osu.edu.

MADDEN, M. STUART, lawyer, educator; b. Washington, Dec. 1, 1948; s. Murdaugh Stuart and Louise (Mann) M. BA, U. Pa., 1971; MA, London Sch. Econs., 1972; JD, Georgetown U., 1976. Bar: D.C. 1976, U.S. Ct. Appeals (D.C. cir.) 1977, U.S. Ct. Internat. Trade 1982, U.S. Cts. Appeals (5th and 11th cirs.) 1982. Assoc. Reed, Smith, Shaw & McClay, Washington, 1976-78, Weil, Gotshal & Manges, Washington, 1978-80, Santarelli & Gimer, Washington, 1980-83; ptnr. Santarelli & Bond, Washington, 1983-85; Disting. Prof. Law, Pace U. Sch. Law, White Plains, N.Y., 1986—; vis. prof. William Mitchell Coll. Law, St. Paul, 1985. Co-editor Jour. Products and Toxics Liability, 1981—95; Author: Madden and Owen on Products Liability, 3d edit, 2000; contbr. articles to profl. jours. Mem. ALI, ABA, Assn. Trial Lawyers Am., Phi Delta Phi. Episcopalian. Home: 2 Westchester Ave #62 White Plains NY 10601 Office: Pace U Sch Law 78 N Broadway White Plains NY 10603-3710 Business E-Mail: smadden@law.pace.edu.

MADDEN, MARTIN GERARD, former state legislator; b. Washington, May 24, 1949; s. Anthony M. and Catherine W. Madden; m. Julia Gatewood Spangler, July 29, 1988; children: Donald Gerard, Thomas Martin, Christina Lynne, Marguerite Allen Spangler. BA in Econs., Iona Coll., 1971. Mem. Md. Ho. of Dels., Annapolis, 1991-94, Md. Senate, Annapolis, 1995—2002; senate minority leader State of Md. Gen. Assembly, Annapolis, 1999—2001, mem. Senate Budget and Taxation com. Mem. Budget and Tax com.; co-chmn. joint com. on welfare reform. Chmn. Critical Area Commn. for Atlantic and Chesapeake Bays, 2003—. Republican. Roman Catholic. Avocation: folk art collector. Office: 1804 West St Annapolis MD 21401 Personal E-mail: themaddens@hotmail.com.

MADDEN, MICHAEL DANIEL, finance company executive; b. Buffalo, Feb. 16, 1949; s. Daniel Francis and Miriam (Catron) M.; m. Mary Madden, May 1, 1976; children: Daniel, Kristina, Megan, Michael. BA in Econs. magna cum laude, Le Moyne Coll., 1971; MBA with distinction, U. Pa., 1973. Assoc. Kidder, Peabody & Co., N.Y.C., 1973-77, v.p., 1977 80, mng. dir., 1980 85, global head investment banking, 1985-88; head investment banking Lehman Bros., NYC, 1989—93; exec. mng. dir. Global Capital Markets Kidder, Peabody Co., N.Y.C., 1993-94; vice chmn., chief origination officer Paine Webber Inc., N.Y.C., 1995-96; chmn., CEO Hanover Capital LLC, N.Y.C., 1996—; ptnr. Beacon Group, N.Y.C.; sr. ptnr. Questor Mgmt., N.Y.C., 1999—. Bd. dirs. Geologistics Corp., Transonic Sys. Inc., Chef Solutions Inc., Pinn Oak Mining, Freeport Properties, Inc. Bd. dirs. Cath. TV Ctr., NYC, 1981-85, Canisius Prep. Sch., Buffalo, 1992—; chmn. bd. trustees LeMoyne Coll., Syracuse, NY, 1987—. Mem. Am. Petroleum Inst., MBA Assn., Univ. Club, The Creek, Longboat Key Club. Republican. Roman Catholic. Avocations: boxing, hunting, tennis, coin collecting/numismatics, fishing. Office: Questor Mgmt 9 W 57th St New York NY 10019 E-mail: mmadden@questorfund.com.

MADDEN, MURDAUGH STUART, lawyer; b. Morgantown, W.Va., Feb. 26, 1922; s. Joseph Warren and Margaret (Liddell) M.; m. Constance Viens McKenna, May 12, 1999; children by previous marriage: Liddell Louise, Murdaugh Stuart Jr., Michael Mann. Student, Oberlin Coll., 1939-40; BA, George Washington U., 1942; JD, Harvard U., 1948. Bar: D.C. 1948, Va. 1948, U.S. Supreme Ct. 1953. Asst. counsel Bur. Aero., Washington, 1948-50; sole practice Washington, 1950-61, 71—; sr. ptnr. Shaw, Pittman, Potts, Trowbridge & Madden, Washington, 1961-71. Sr. counsel Humane Soc. U.S., Atlantic Devel. Co. and related corps. Author: (with Sherman L. Cohn) The Legal Status and Problems of the American Abroad, 1966. Trustee Inst. for Study Nat. Behavior, Princeton, N.J., Friends of India Com., Washington; pres. World Fedn. for Protection Animals, The Netherlands; v.p. World Soc. forProtection Animals, London. With USAAF, 1942-45, ETO. Mem. ABA (past chmn. internat. and comparative law com. internat. transp., chmn. subcom. on charitable orgns. internat. law sect. 1985—), D.C. Bar Assn., (past dir., past chmn. com. bar ethics), Va. Bar Assn., The Barristers, Am. Soc. Internat. Law, Harvard Law Sch. Assn., Oberlin Alumni Assn., Metropolitan Club, Harvard Club N.Y., Internat. Lawn Tennis Club U.S., Chevy Chase Club, Phi Sigma Kappa. Episcopalian. Home: 2530 Queen Annes Ln NW Washington DC 20037-2148 Office: 2100 L St NW Washington DC 20037-1525

MADDEN, PALMER BROWN, lawyer; b. Milw., Sept. 19, 1945; m. Susan L. Paulus, Mar. 31, 1984. BA, Stanford U., 1968; JD, U. Calif., Berkeley, 1973. Bar: Calif. 1973, U.S. Dist. Ct. (no. dist.) Calif. 1973, U.S. Supreme Ct. 1982. Ptnr. McCutchen, Doyle Brown & Enersen, Walnut Creek, 1985-98; prin. ADR Svcs., Alamo, Calif., 1999—. Pres. State Bar Bd. Govs., 2000-01. Chair bd. govs. Continuing Edn. of the Bar, 1997; judge pro tem Contra Costa Superior Ct., 1991-98; pres. Contra Costa Coun., 1995, Kennedy-King Found., 1994; bd. dirs. Episcopal Homes Found., 2001. Mem. Contra Costa County Bar Assn. (pres. 1996-97). Democrat. Episcopalian. Office: ADR Svcs 3000 Danville Blvd # 543 Alamo CA 94507 Office Phone: 925-838-8593.

MADDEN, PAUL ROBERT, lawyer, director; b. St. Paul, Nov. 13, 1926; s. Ray Joseph and Margaret (Meyer) Madden; m. Rosemary R. Sorel, Aug. 7, 1974; children: Margaret Jane, James Patrick, Derek R. Sorel, Lisa T. Schoutsen. Student, St. Thomas Coll., 1944; AB, U. Minn., 1948; JD, Georgetown U., 1951. Bar: Ariz. 1957, Minn. 1951, D.C. 1951. Assoc. Hamilton & Hamilton, Washington, 1951-55; legal asst. to commr. SEC, Washington, 1955-56; assoc. Lewis and Roca, Phoenix, 1957-59, ptnr., 1959-90, Beus, Gilbert & Morrill, Phoenix, 1991-94, Chapman and Cutler, Phoenix, 1994-97; of counsel Gallagher & Kennedy, Phoenix, 1997—. Mem. nat. bd. visitors U. Ariz. Law Sch.; mem. adv. bd. Cath. Cmty. Found., Cath. Social Svcs. No. Ariz., 2002—; bd. dirs. Ind. Devel. Authority of City of Prescott, 2002—, Yavapai Coll. Dist. Governing Bd., Prescott, 2003—, Found. Jr. Achievement Ctr. Ariz., Phoenix, Yavapai Symphony Assocs., Prescott, 2004—, Prescott People Who Care, 2001—, Hidden Valley Homeowners Assn., Prescott, 2003—; past bd. dirs., past chmn. Mesa Air Group, Inc., Camelback Charitable Trust, Found. for Sr. Living; bd. dirs., pres. Ariz. Club, Phoenix, 1990—93; past bd. dirs., vice chmn. Ctrl. Ariz. chpt. ARC; past bd. dirs., past pres. Jr. Achievement Ctrl. Ariz., Inc.; past bd. dirs. The Samaritan Found., Phoenix, St. Joseph the Worker, Phoenix; bd. visitors Embry Riddle Aero. U., Prescott, 2002—; Prescott Ambs., 2002—; nat. co-chmn. Youth for Eisenhower, 1951—52; sec. Minn. Fedn. Coll. Rep. Clubs, 1947—48; chmn. 4th dist. Minn. Young Rep. Club, 1948; mem. Ariz. Rep. Com., 1960—62. Served with USNR, 1946—48. Mem. ABA, Ariz. Bar Assn., Maricopa County Bar Assn., Yauapai County Bar Assn., The Barristers Club (Washington), Phi Delta Phi. Home: 1565 Range Rd Prescott AZ 86303 Office: Gallagher & Kennedy PA 101 E Gurley Ste 214 Prescott AZ 86301 Office Phone: 928-445-5800. E-mail: prm@gknet.com.

MADDEN, RICHARD BLAINE, forest products executive; b. Short Hills, N.J., Apr. 27, 1929; s. James L. and Irma (Twining) M.; m. Joan Fairbairn, May 24, 1958; children: John Richard, Lynne Marie, Kathryn Ann, Andrew Twining. BS, Princeton U., 1951; JD, U. Mich., 1956; MBA, NYU, 1959; PhD (hon.), St. Scholastica Coll., 1994. Bar: Mich. 1956, N.Y. 1958. Gen. asst. treas.'s dept. Socony Mobil Oil Corp., N.Y.C., 1956-57, spl. asst., 1958-59, fin. rep., 1960; asst. to pres. Mobil Chem. Co.; also dir. Mobil Chems. Ltd. of Eng., 1960-63; exec. v.p., gen. mgr. Kordite Corp.; also v.p. Mobil Plastics, 1963-66; v.p. Mobil Chem. Co., N.Y.C., 1966-68, group v.p., 1968-70; asst. treas. Mobil Oil Corp., 1970-71; chmn. Mobil Oil Estates Ltd., 1970-71; pres., chief exec. Potlatch Corp., San Francisco, 1971-77, chmn. chief exec. officer, 1977-94; ret., 1994. Bd. dirs. URS Corp.; former bd. dirs. Potlatch Corp., PG&E Corp., CNF Inc., Del Monte Corp., AMFAC Inc., Bank Calif. N.A. and BankCal Tri-State Corp.; from lectr. to adj. assoc. prof. fin. NYU, 1960-63; bd. dirs., pres., Knight Grand Cross Magistral Grace in Obedience Order of Malta, Western Assn.; bd. govs., chmn. audit com., mem. adminstrv. compensation and labor rels. com. San Francisco Symphony. Bd. dirs. Smith-Kettlewell Eye Rsch. Inst., trustee emeritus, former chmn. Am. Enterprise Inst.; former mem. bd. Nat. Park Found.; hon. trustee Com. for Econ. Devel. Lt. (j.g.) USNR, 1951-54. Mem. N.Y. Bar Assn., Mich. Bar Assn. Clubs: Bohemian (San Francisco); Lagunitas (Ross, Calif.); Metropolitan (Washington). Roman Catholic.

MADDEN, ROBERT EDWARD, surgeon, educator; b. Oak Park, Ill., Sept. 16, 1925; s. Joseph Edward and Gertrude Celelia (McGowan) M.; m. Susan Ann Hale, May 24, 1958; children: Robert Joseph, Lisa Marie, Karen Louise, Kevin Francis. BS in Medicine, U. Ill., Chgo., 1950, MS in Biochemistry, MD, U. Ill., Chgo., 1952. Diplomate Am. Bd. Surgery, Bd. Thoracic Surgery. Assoc. in surgery U. Ill. Coll. Medicine, Chgo., 1957-58; sr. surgeon Nat. Cancer Inst., Bethesda, Md., 1959-60; asst. prof. surgery N.Y. Med. Coll., N.Y.C., 1961-66, assoc. prof., 1966-71, prof. Valahlla, 1971—. Mem. N.Y. State Health Rsch. Coun., Albany, 1976—; med. coord. N.Y. State Dept. Health, 1990—. Author: (with Lippincott) Problems in General Surgery, 1988; editor: Gastrointestinal Bleeding, 1987; editor-in-chief N.Y. Med. Quarterly, 1979-90; contbr. articles to profl. jours. With U.S. Army, 1943-46. Recipient Borden Undergrad. Rsch. award Borden Corp., 1952; postdoctoral fellow Am. Cancer Soc., 1958-59. Fellow ACS (com. on cancer 1993-97); mem. Am. Soc. for Vascular Surgery, Soc. Internat. Chirurgie, Am. Assn. Cancer Edn. (pres. 1979), N.Y. Cancer Soc. (pres. 1975-76), N.Y. State Cancer Programs Assn. (pres. 1975-76), Knights of Holy Sepulchre, Knights of the Order of Malta, Pi Gamma Mu. Republican. Roman Catholic. Home: 6 Crows Nest Rd Bronxville NY 10708-4802 Office: NY Med Coll Munger Pavilion Valhalla NY 10595 Office Phone: 914-493-7615. E-mail: remadden@bellatlantic.net.

MADDEN, THOMAS F. medieval history educator, author; b. Phoenix, June 10, 1960; s. Thomas J. and Joyce L. (Parsons) M.; m. Page A. Ettle, Oct. 15, 1994; children: Helena, Melinda. BA, U. N.Mex., 1986; MA, U. Ill., 1990, PhD, 1993. Asst. prof. history St. Louis U., 1992-96, assoc. prof., 1996—2004, chmn. dept., 1996-98, 2001—, prof., 2004—. Co-author: The Fourth Crusade: The Conquest of Constantinople, 1997 (History Book Club selection 1998); author: A Concise History of the Crusades, 1999 (Washington Post Book World Raves selection 2000), Enrico Dandolo and the Rise of Venice, 2003 (Book of Month, BBC History Mag.); co-editor: Medieval and Renaissance Venice, 1999; editor: The Crusades: The Essential Readings, 2002. Rsch. grantee Gladys Krieble Delmas Found., 1990, 98, 2004. Mem. Medieval Acad. Am., The Hist. Soc., Cath. Hist. Assn., Soc. for Study Crusades and Latin East, Midwest Medieval History Conf. (pres. 1999-2000). Roman Catholic. Office: 3800 Lindell Blvd Saint Louis MO 63108-3414 Fax: 314-977-1603. E-mail: maddentf@slu.edu.

MADDEN, THOMAS JAMES, lawyer, educator; b. Trenton, NJ, Sept. 13, 1941; s. Jerry A. and Minerva (Quigley) M.; m. Irene Lyons, June 17, 1967; children: Jay, Beth. BEE, Villanova U., 1964; JD with honors, Cath. U., 1968. Bar: N.J. 1968, D.C. 1968, U.S. Patent Office 1968. Atty. adv. Naval Air Sys Command, 1968-69; dep. gen. counsel Dept. Justice Law Enforcement Assistance Adminstrn., 1970-71, gen. counsel, 1972-79; dir. Nat. Adv. Commn. on Criminal Justice Stds. and Goals, 1971-73; adv. U.S. Office Mgmt. and Budget on Fed. Assistance Programs, Washington, 1979-80; gen. counsel Dept. Justice Office Justice Assistance Rsch. and Stats., 1980; from assoc. to ptnr. Kay Scholer, Fierman, Hays and Handler, Washington, 1980-84; ptnr. Venable, Baetjer, Howard & Civiletti, Washington, 1984—. Adj. prof. contract law American U., 1980-85; gen. counsel Nat. Coun. Juvenile and Family Ct. Judges; adv. panel on streamlining and codifying fed. acquisition laws Dept. Def., 1991-93; mem. Procurement Round Table, 1998—, vice chmn., 2002—. Contbr. articles to profl. jours. Pres. U.S. Ct. Fed. Claims Bar Assn., 1999-2000. Recipient Louis Brownlow award Am. Soc. for Pub. Adminstrn., 1982, Disting. Svc. award Dept. Justice Law Enforcement Assistance Adminstr., 1973, Wilson Cowen award US Ct. Fed. Claims, 1998. Fellow Am. Bar Found.; mem. ABA (chmn. pub. contract law sect. 1988-89, pres. fellows of pub. contract law sect. 1992-93), D.C. Bar Assn., Fed. Bar Assn. (pres. D.C. chpt. 1982-83). Office: Venable LLP 575 7th St N W Washington DC 20004 Office Phone: 202-344-4803.

MADDEN, WALES HENDRIX, JR., lawyer; b. Amarillo, Tex., Sept. 1, 1927; s. Wales Hendrix and Kathryn (Nash) Madden; m. Alma Faye Cowden, Nov. 8, 1952; children: Wales Hendrix III, Straughn. BA, U. Tex., 1950, LLB, 1952. Bar: Tex. 1952. Pvt. practice, Amarillo. Mem. Tex. Constl. Revision Commn., 1973. Mem. Tex. Coll. and Univ. Sys. Coord. Bd., 1964—69, Amarillo Area Found., Cal Farley's Boys Ranch, Pres.'s Export Coun., 1981, Select Com. Higher Edn., 1985, 1987; chmn. SWST regional panel Pres.'s Commn. White Ho. Fellowships, 1989—90; chmn. Tex. Water Devel. Bd., 2002; mem. Gov.'s Com. Ad Valorem Taxes, 1996; bd. regents Amarillo Coll., 1958—59, U. Tex., 1959—65; trustee Trinity U., San Antonio; chmn. bd. Internat. Food and Agrl. Devel., 1990—94. With USNR. Named Outstanding Man of Amarillo, 1972, Disting. Alumnus, U. Tex., 1979, U. Tex. Law Sch., 1986. Mem.: ABA, State Jr. Bar Tex. (pres. 1956), State Bar Tex., Amarillo Bar Assn. (pres. 1956), Friar Soc., Amarillo C. of C. (pres. 1968), Tex. Philos. Soc., Sigma Alpha, Phi Eta Sigma, Phi Delta Theta, Phi Alpha Delta. Presbyterian. Home and Office: PO Box 15288 Amarillo TX 79105-5288

MADDEN, WANDA LOIS, nurse; b. Augusta, Kans., Apr. 26, 1929; d. George W. and Lillian B. (Dobyns) Provost; m. Laurence R. Madden, June 3, 1947 (div. 1961); children: Matthew, Mark, Luke, John, Michele. ADN, Pasadena City Coll., 1970; postgrad., Calif. State U. Consortium, 1986. RN, Calif.; ordained to ministry Am. Fellowship Ch., 1995. CCU nurse Huntington Meml. Hosp., Pasadena, Calif., 1970-71; ICU Community Hosp., Pico Rivera, Calif., 1971-72; CCU nurse Queen of the Valley Hosp., West Covina, Calif., 1973-74; ICU supr. Visalia (Calif.) Community Hosp., 1974-77, 89-90, ICU nurse, 1978, San Miguel Hosp. Assn., San Diego, 1978-79; supr. Casa Blanca Corp., San Diego, 1979-80; dir. nursing Visalia Convalescence Hosp., 1981-89, Westgate Gardens Convalescent Ctr., Visalia, 1990; psychiat. staff nurse Mill Creek Hosp., Visalia, 1990-91; AIDS case mgr. Tulare County Health Svcs., 1993-95; assoc. lay pastor Met. Cmty. Ch. of Sequoias, Visalia, 1994-95; pastor Tulare County Rainbow Cmty. Ch., 1995—. Mem. Tulare County HIV Care Consortium, Tulare County HIV-AIDS Edn. and Prevention Planning Com.; gay and AIDS activist, Tulare County; mem. AIDS Outreach Ministry in Home & Hosp. and Outreach to Gay/Lesbian and Transgender Cmty. Home and Office: 332 Pleasant St Roseville CA 95678-1555

MADDERN, DAVID, artist; b. Gill, Mass., Oct. 23, 1933; BM, U. Miami, 1973, MM, 1974. Music instr. Barry U., Miami, 1977—. Contbr. The Best of Watercolor, 1995, vol. III, 1999, The Best of Flowers, 1996, The Best of Watercolor Painting Color, 1997, Floral Inspirations, 1997, The Best of Watercolors Vol. III, 1999, The One-Hour Watercolorist, 2002; exhibited in shows at Ft. Lauderdale (Fla.) Festival of Arts, Artists' Showcase Bapt. Hosp., Banyan Festival, Coconut Grove, Fla., South Miami Art Festival, Key Biscayne (Fla.) Art Festival, Mus. Sci., Miami, Riveria Country Club, Miami; featured in The One Hour Watercolorist, 2001. Named Best in Flora Cultural Coun., Inc., Miami, 1991, Best in Show, Ft. Lauderdale Festival of Arts, 1993, Miami Watercolor Soc., 1993, Goldcoast Watercolor Soc., Ft. Lauderdale, 1995, 97, Fla. Flora Art Exhibit, Miami, 1996; First Place Watercolor, Key Biscayne Art Festival, 1995, Baptist Hosp. Artists Showcase, Miami, 1995; Best of Show, 58th Anniversary Juried Exhibit Fla. Artists, 1999, 1st pl. Miami Watercolor Soc. 26th ann. fall exhibit, 1999, 1st Place Watercolor Pembroke Pines (Fla.) Fine Arts, 2000, Best of Show Cauley Square (Fla.) Fine and Arts Show, 2000, 1st Pl. Internat. Watercolor Biennial, Miami, 2000. Mem.: Miami Watercolor Soc. (1st v.p. 1993—95), Fla. Watercolor Soc. (signature), La. Watercolor Soc. (signature), Watercolor West (signature), N.W. Watercolor Soc. (signature). Home: 6492 SW 22nd St Miami FL 33155-1945

MADDIN, ROBERT, metallurgist, educator; b. Hartford, Conn., Oct. 20, 1918; s. Isadore I. and Mae (Jacobs) Levine; married, July 8, 1945; children: Leslie, Jill. BS in Metall. Engring., Purdue U., 1942; DEng., Yale U., 1948. Registered profl. engr., Pa. Asst., assoc. prof. Johns Hopkins U., Balt., 1949-55; prof. U. Pa., phila., 1955-73, univ. prof., 1973-83; vis. prof. Harvard U., Cambridge, Mass., 1983-87, curator, 1987—; vis. prof. Oxford (Eng.) U., 1970, vis. fellow Wolfson Coll., 1987. Vis. prof. U. Birmingham, Eng., 1953-54; vis. scholar Hebrew U., Jerusalem, 1976; hon. prof. Beijing Sci. and Engring. U., 1986; hon. mem. Japan Metals. Editor-in-chief Math., Sci., and Engring, 1965-82; contbr. more than 250 publs. to profl. jours. 1st Lt. USAF, 1942-45. Disting. Sr. Sci. fellow A. von Humboldt Found., Germany, 1989-90, Disting. Alumnus Purdue U., 1974; recipient Pomerance award Archaeol. Inst. Am., 1994, medal of merit U. Pa. Fellow Am. Soc. Metallurgists, TMS. Avocation: history early metallurgy. E-mail: robertmaddin@comcast.net.

MADDING, BRUCE WALLACE, foundation executive; b. San Angelo, Tex., Oct. 2, 1951; s. Gordon Francis and Rebecca Garrison (Waldron) M.; m. Margaret Stearns Quintrell, Aug. 7, 1982; children: Thomas, Sara, Ann. BS, U. Calif., Berkeley, 1972; MBA, U. So. Calif., L.A., 1974. CPA, Calif. Sr. mgr. Price Waterhouse, San Francisco and London, 1974-86, sr. mgr., dir. Tech. Centre Menlo Park, Calif., 1986-88; sr. v.p., CFO, chief adminstrv. officer The Henry J. Kaiser Family Found., Menlo Park, 1988—. Chmn. Found. Fin. Officers Group, 1995-98, ARC Investment Com. and Endowment Fund, 2003-, bd. trustees. Bd. dirs. Menlo Atherton Edn. Found., Menlo Park, 1994-98; mem. Not-for-Profit Adv. Task Bd. of Fin. Acctg. Standards Bd. Mem. AICPAs, Fin. Execs. Inst., Calif. Inst. CPAs. Avocations: tennis, skiing, music, art. Office: Henry J Kaiser Family Found 2400 Sand Hill Rd Menlo Park CA 94025-6941

MADDING, CLAUDIA, agricultural products executive; b. Detroit, Dec. 27, 1950; d. Clarence Irving and Theresa Flemming; m. John Eldon Madding, Apr. 4, 1979; children: Jonathan, Bryan, Collin. Student, Millikin U., 1969, Richland C.C., Decatur, Ill., 1979-80. Stenographer State of Ill., Springfield, 1968-74; adminstrv. asst. Archer Daniels Midland Co., Decatur, 1979-93, asst. sec., 1993—2001, exec. asst. to chmn. bd., 1994—2001, pres. ADM found., asst. sec., 1997—, exec. asst. to chmn. emeritus, exec. asst. to chmn. bd., 1999—, sec. to exec. com., 1999—2001. Bd. dirs. Hickory Point Bank, Decatur, Ill. Bd. dirs. United Way of Decatur, Decatur Club; past bd. dirs. Jr. Achievement Decatur, Holy Family Sch.; adv. bd. The Parent Project for Duchenne, Muscular Dystrophy Rsch., Inc., Middletown, Ohio; bd. St. Teresa H.S. Mem.: Country Decatur. Roman Catholic. Avocations: reading biographies, watching 1930-40's movies, foreign stamp collecting. Home: 16 Oakridge Dr Decatur IL 62521-4600 Office: Archer Daniels Midland Co 4666 E Faries Pkwy Decatur IL 62526-5666

MADDOCK, JEROME TORRENCE, information services specialist; b. Darby, Pa., Feb. 7, 1940; s. Richard Cotton and Isobel Louise (Mezger) M.; m. Karen Rhueama Weygand, Oct. 2, 1965. BS in Biology, Muhlenberg Coll., 1961; MS in Info. Sci., Drexel U., 1968. Editl. assoc. Biol. Abstracts, Phila., 1962—63; mgr. rsch. info. Merck & Co., West Point, Pa., 1963—72; sr. cons. Auerbach Assocs., Inc., Phila., 1972—79; mgr. libr. and info. svcs. Solar Energy Rsch. Inst., Golden, Colo., 1979—88; mgr. info. svcs. Transp. Rsch. Bd., Washington, 1988—99; project mgr. IHS Enterprise, Boulder, Colo., 1999—2001; ind. cons., 2002—; faculty online U. Phoenix, 1999—. Del. Gov.'s Conf. on Libr. and Info. Svc., Pa., 1978; mem. blue ribbon panel to select archivist of U.S., Washington, 1979; U.S. del. to ops. com. on transp. rsch. info. Orgn. for Econ. Cooperation and Devel., 1988-99. Bd. dirs. Paoli (Pa.) Pub. Libr., 1976-77, Boulder Friends of Jazz, 2003-; bd. trustees Louisville County Pub. Libr., 2002-, pres. 2004-. With USAFR, 1962-68. Mem. AAAS, Am. Soc. Info. Sci. (chmn. 1974-75), Elks, Beta Phi Mu, Pi Delta Epsilon. Republican. Episcopalian. Achievements include projection of information science operations 10 years into the future. Home: 545 W Laurel Ct Louisville CO 80027-1116

MADDOCK, LAWRENCE HILL, retired language educator; b. Ogden, Utah, July 14, 1923; s. Lawrence J. and Nellie (Hill) Maddock. Student, U. Fla., 1941-42; BA, George Peabody Coll., 1946, PhD, 1965; MA, U. So. Calif., 1949. Tchr. pub. schs., Jacksonville, Fla., 1949-52; instr. U. Fla., Gainesville, 1952-53; asst. prof. California (Pa.) State Coll., 1955-56, assoc. prof., 1956-64, N.E. La. State Coll., Monroe, 1964-67, U. West Fla., Pensacola, 1967-90. Author: The Door of Memory, 1974, revised, 2003, John Maddock: Mormon Pioneer, 1996; contbr. chpts. to books and articles to profl. jours. Mem. MLA (bibliographer 1978-93), Thomas Wolfe Soc., Mormon History Assn. Republican. Mem. Lds Ch. Home: 1012 Gerhardt Dr Pensacola FL 32503-3222

MADDOCKS, ROBERT ALLEN, lawyer, manufacturing executive; b. Missouri Valley, Iowa, Dec. 25, 1933; s. Clarence A. and Helen Louise (Unger) M.; m. JoAnn Skaggs, June 2, 1956; children— Todd Duncan, Susan Colette, Amy Annette. BS, Drake U., 1956, JD, 1958. Bar: Iowa 1958, U.S. Supreme Ct. 1969, Ohio 1970, Mo. 1972, Colo. 1992. Pvt. practice law, Clarion, Ia., 1958-67; atty. Massey Ferguson, Inc., Des Moines, 1967-68; div. gen. counsel Akron, Ohio, 1968-69; asst. sec., gen. counsel, dir. corp. relations Kellwood Co., St. Louis, 1970-73, sec., gen. counsel, 1973-90, v.p., 1978-90, also bd. dirs. subs. cos. Dep. chmn., dir. Smart Shirts Ltd., Hong Kong, 1980-90; sec. Midwest Credit Corp.; Wright County atty., Clarion, 1961-65; chmn., dir. Appt. Zone., 1998-99. Trustee Maryville Coll., St. Louis, 1975-78, Drake U., 1987-94; bd. dirs. Kellwood Found., 1975-90. Mem. Am. Bar Assn., Inter-Am., Ia., Ohio, Mo., Colo. bar assns., Am. Trial Lawyers Assn., Nat. Corporate Secs. Assn., Comml. Law League, Licensing Execs. Soc., Am. Apparel Mfrs. Assn. (legal com. 1972-90). Home: 5605 Southern Hills Ct Flower Mound TX 75022-9738 E-mail: bmadox@earthlink.net.

MADDOX, ALVA HUGH, retired state supreme court justice; b. Andalusia, Ala., Apr. 17, 1930; s. Christopher Columbus and Audie Lodella Maddox; m. Virginia Roberts, June 14, 1958; children: Robert Hugh, Jane Maddox. AB in Journalism, U. Ala., Tuscaloosa, 1952, JD, 1957. Bar: Ala. 1957. Law clk. to Judge Aubrey Cates, Ala. Ct. Appeals, Montgomery, 1957-58; field examiner Chief Atty.'s Office, VA, Montgomery, 1958-59; law clk. to Judge Frank M. Johnson, U.S. Dist. Ct., Montgomery, 1959-61; pvt. practice Montgomery, 1961-65; cir. judge, spl. cir. judge Montgomery Cir. Ct., 1963, asst. dist. atty., 1964; legal advisor to govs. including George C. Wallace, Lurleen B. Wallace, Albert P. Brewer, State of Ala., Montgomery, 1965-69; assoc. justice Supreme Ct. Ala., Montgomery, 1969-2001; ret., 2001. Author: Billy Boll Weevil: A Pest Becomes A Hero, 1976, Alabama Rules of Criminal Procedure, 1991, supplements, 1992—. Founder youth jud. program YMCA, Montgomery, 1979, also mem. metro. bd. dirs. 2d lt. USAF, 1952-54, col. USAF Res. ret. Recipient Man of Yr. award YMCA, 1988, Disting. Program Svc. award, 1989, Srs. of Achievement award Montgomery Coun. on Aging, 1999. Mem.: ABA, Am. Inns of Ct. (former trustee), Hugh Maddox Inn of Ct. Montgomery (charter, founding mem.), Christian Legal Soc. (bd. dirs.), Inst. Jud. Adminstrn., Ala. Bar Assn. (Jud. award of merit 1997), Order of Samaritan/U. Ala. Law Sch., Kiwanis (bd. dirs. Montgomery). Baptist. Office: 3137 Hathaway Pl Montgomery AL 36111-1707

MADDOX, JERRY AVEN, retired catalog management executive; b. Atlanta, Sept. 27, 1935; s. George Ernest and Emilie Marion (Peeples) Maddox; m. Roberta Ann Eddy; children: Lamont Edward, Ryan Allen, Jolie Aven. BBA in Fin. and Acctg., Emory U. Bus. Sch., Atlanta, 1957; JD, Emory U. Law Sch., 1964. Catalog Mgmt. Exec. Sears, Roebuck & Co., Atlanta, 1957—89; Substitute Tchr. DeKalb County Sch. System, Atlanta, 1992—2000. Author: (geneology books) Descendants of John Allen, 1997, The Peeples Family, Descendants of William Peeples, 1999, (historical fiction) Song of the Ogeechee, 2002, From Salacoa to Tahlequah, 2004. Page Congressman James C. Davis, Washington, 1951; adminstrv. bd. Dunwoody United Meth. Ch., 1972—81, mem., 1972—2003; coach nat. age group U.S. Swimming, 1978—88; mem. Nat. Assn. of Purchasing Mgrs. (NAPM), Ga., 1989—92; v.p., sec. DeKalb County Jaycees, Ga., 1964—70; mem. Purchasing Mgrs. Assn. of Georgia (PMAG), 1989—92; life mem. Dunwoody Preservation Trust, Inc., 2004. With U.S. Marine Corps. active duty and reserves, 1957—63. Mem.: Mil. Order Stars and Bars (Lt. Comdr. Gen. William J. Hardee chpt. 2002—03, The Jackson medal 2000), St. Andrews Soc., Clan Hay/Clan Irwin, Ft. Delaware Soc. (life), Nat. Eagle Scout Assn. (life), Eddy Family Assn. (life; rec. sec. 1995—2000), Dunwoody Preservation Trust Inc. (life), Belle Meade Hunt Club (equestrian), SCV (Comdr. Maj. Charles A. Dunwoody Camp 2002—), St. David's Welch Soc. of Georgia, Phi Alpha Delta, Pi Kappa Alpha, Alpha Kappa Psi. Republican. Achievements

include distance running: competed in numerous 5K and 10K races, including 5 Peachtree Road Races; listed in "Outstanding Atlantans," by Heritage Publishing Co., 1977-1978. Home: 4917 Cambridge Dr Dunwoody GA 30338-5007

MADDOX, KEN, state official; b. Long Beach, Calif. m. Crystal Maddox; 2 children. BS in Comm. Arts, Calif. Poly. State U., Pomona; MA in Mgmt., Nat. U., 2000. Police officer; coun. mem. Garden Grove City Coun., Calif., 1996; state assembly mem. Dist. 68 Calif. State Assembly, 1998—. Mem. agr. com.; mem. environ. safety and toxic materials com.; mem. govtl. orgn. com.; vice-chair ins. com.; mem. utilities and commerce com. Chair Garden Grove Housing Authority, Garden Grove Indsl. Devel. Authority; commr. El Toro Citizens Adv. Commn.; mem. Orange County Libr. Adv. Bd.; mem. adv. bd. Breast Cancer Survivors; hon. bd. mem. Doris Tate Crime Victims Bur. 1st. lt. N.G. U.S. Army, 1981—89. Mem.: C. of C., Elks. Republican. Mailing: Rm 4167 PO Box 942849 Sacramento CA 94249 Office: Rm 205 1503 S Coast Dr Costa Mesa CA 92626

MADDOX, LYNDELL E. utilities company executive; BS, MBA in bus. admin., Wichita State U. Fin. analyst NCR Corp.; gas acquisitions rep. No. Natural Gas Co.; dir., supplemental supplies Peoples Natural Gas Co.; sr. v.p., operations Aquila Energy Inc.; pres., COO Brooklyn Interstate Natural Gas Corp. (formerly Brooklyn Union Gas and subsidiary of Keyspan); pres. PennUnion Energy Services (subsidiary of Pennzoil), 1995—97; pres., CEO PG&E Energy Trading, 1997; sr. v.p. PG&E Corp., San Francisco. Office: PG&E Corp Spear Tower Ste 2400 1 Market San Francisco CA 94105

MADDOX, RICHARD, manufacturing executive; Pres. Blue Bird, Macon, Ga., 1999, CEO, 1999—. Office: Blue Bird Corporation PO Box 938 Fort Valley GA 31030-0938

MADDOX, ROBERT NOTT, chemical engineer, educator; b. Winslow, Ark., Sept. 29, 1925; s. R.L. and Mabel (Nott) M.; m. Paula Robinson, Oct. 6, 1951 (dec. Apr. 1984); children: Deirdre O'Neil, Robert Dozier; m. Pauline Razook, Nov. 30, 1987. Student, Iowa State Coll., 1944-45; BS, U. Ark., 1948; MS, U. Okla., 1950; PhD, Okla. State U., 1955; Sc.D. (hon.), U. Ark., 1991. Registered profl. engr., Okla. Mem. faculty Sch. Chem. Engring., Okla. State U., 1950-51, 52-58, prof., head dept., 1958-77, Leonard F. Sheerar prof., 1976-86, dir. phys. properties lab., 1976-86. Design engr. process div. Black, Sivalls & Bryson, Inc., Oklahoma City, 1951-52; adminstrv. v.p., tech. dir. Fluid Properties Research, Inc., 1972-85; chem. engring. cons. Author: Gas and Liquid Sweetening, 1971, rev. ed. 1978, 83, (with J. Erbar) Gas Conditioning and Processing Vol. 3 - Computer Techniques and Applications, 1981, rev. ed. (with L. Lilly), 1988, (with A. Hines) Mass Transfer - Fundamentals and Applications, 1985; also numerous tech. papers. Served with USNR, 1944-45. Recipient award for personal achievement Chem. Engring. mag., 1988; Phillips lectr. in chem. engring. edn., Oklahoma State U., 1989; inducted into Engring. Hall of Fame, U. Ark., 1989, Okla. Higher Edn. Hall of Fame, 1996; Dr. Robert N. Maddox Professorship in Chem. Engring. established in his honor by Gas Processors Suppliers Assn. at Okla. State U., 1989, Founders award Am. Inst. of Chemical Engineers, 1994 Fellow AIChE (chpt. pres. 1956-57, André Wilkins Meml. award 1981, Founder's award 1994); mem. NSPE, Okla. Soc. Profl. Engrs. (chpt. pres. 1961-62, dir. 1966-68, Engr. of Yr. 1972), Am. Inst. Mining Engrs., Soc. Petroleum Engrs., Am. Chem. Soc. (treas. indsl. and engring. chemistry div. 1966-68, chmn. div. 1970, Stewart award 1971), Gas Processors Assn. (Hanlon award 1985, Svc. citation 1987, Meritorious Svc. award 1998), Gas Processors Suppliers Assn. (editorial adv. bd. Engring. Data Book 1972—), Sigma Xi, Omega Chi Epsilon (nat. pres. 1968-70), Tau Beta Pi, Alpha Chi Sigma, Omicron Delta Kappa, Sigma Nu (high coun. 1966-70, regent 1972-74, Hall of Honor 1988). Episcopalian (lay reader, vestryman). Clubs: Elks, Masons. Home: 1710 Davinbrook Ln Stillwater OK 74074-2339 Office Phone: 405-744-5280.

MADDOX, WILMA, health facility administrator; Grad., Truman State U., 1979. Bus. mgr. Vision Care Assocs., Macon, Maine. Bd. govs. Truman State U., 1994—; mem. Ko. K-16 Coalition; mem. bd. edn. Macon County R-I Sch. Dist.; vol. aftersch. program Macon United Meth. Ch. Mem.: Am. Found. for Vision Awareness (past pres. Mo. affiliate). Office: Vision Care Associates 1705 Prospect Drive Macon MO 63552

MADDOX-ADAMS, SHERRY, secondary school educator; Tchr. E.L. Connally Sch., Atlanta. Recipient Excellence Tchg. award, Nat. Coun. Negro Women, 2001, Chevy Malibu Tchg. Excellence award, Atlanta Jour.-Constitution Honor Roll Tchr. award; fellow, Earth Watch Inst.; Fulbright Meml. Fund Tchr. scholar, Japan. Mem.: Nat. Bd. for Profl. Tchg. Stds. (bd. mem.). Office: EL Connally Sch 1654 S Alvarado Terr SW Atlanta GA 30311

MADDREY, WILLIS CROCKER, medical educator, internist, academic administrator, consultant, researcher; b. Roanoke Rapids, N.C., Mar. 29, 1939; s. Milner Crocker and Sara Jean (Willis) M.; m. Ann Marie Matt; children: Jeffrey, Gregory, Thomas. BS, Wake Forest U., 1960; MD, Johns Hopkins U., 1964. Diplomate: Am. Bd. Internal Medicine. Intern Osler Med. Service Johns Hopkins Hosp., Balt., 1964-65, asst. resident, 1965-66, 68-69, chief resident, 1969-70; fellow in liver disease Yale U., 1970-71; asst. prof. medicine Johns Hopkins U., Balt., 1971-75, assoc. prof., 1975-79, prof., 1980—82, asst. dean Sch. Medicine, 1975-79, assoc. dir. dept. medicine, 1979-82; prof., chmn. dept. medicine Jefferson Med. Coll., Phila., 1982-90; v.p. clin. affairs U. Tex. Southwestern Med. Ctr., Dallas, 1990-93, exec. v.p. clin. affairs, 1993—. Assoc. editor: Medicine, 1972-82, Hepatology, 1988-95, mem. editl. bd., 1981-84, 86-87, Gastroenterology, 1982-87, Am. Jour. Medicine, 1978-88; contbr. articles to profl. jours. Bd. dirs. Am. Liver Found., 1978-81, Dallas County Med. Soc., 1996-98; trustee Magee Rehab. Hosp., Phila., 1982-87. With USPHS, 1966-68. Mem. ACP (bd. regents 1986-92, pres. 92-93), Am. Soc. Clin. Investigation, Am. Gastroenterol. Assn., Am. Assn. Study Liver Disease (pres. 1981). Republican. Office: U Tex Southwestern Med Ctr 5323 Harry Hines Blvd Dallas TX 75390-8570

MADDUX, CAROLYN L. writer, educator; b. Aug. 13, 1943; d. Stanford and Rachel (Flint) Freelin; m. Donald J. Maddux, Dec. 30, 1968; 1 child, Michael Joseph Robert. BA, U. Wash., 1965; MA, McGregor Coll., 1998. Tchr. Aberdeen (Wash.) HS, 1965—67, Annie Wright Sch., Tacoma, 1968—70; from reporter to mng. editor Shelton (Wash.)-Mason County Jour., 1978—2002; co-owner Very Ltd. Antiques, Shelton, 2000—. Adj. faculty Olympic Coll., Shelton, 1990—, co-convenor, co-founder Shelton Writers Conf., 1999—. Author: (poems) Remembering Water, 1996, numerous poems; book reviewer Antioch Rev., 1997—2003. Co-founder Olympic Poets & Writers Workshop Reading Series, Shelton, 1991—2003. Episcopalian. Home: 706 W Birch St Shelton WA 98584

MADDUX, GREGORY (GREGORY ALAN MADDUX), professional baseball player; b. San Angelo, Tex., Apr. 14, 1966; Grad., H.S., Las Vegas. Baseball player Chgo. Cubs, 1986—92, 2004—, Atlanta Braves, 1992—2003. Named Nat. League Pitcher of Yr., Sporting News, 1993, Nat. League Innings Pitched Leader, 1991—95, Nat. League Earned Run Avg. Leader, 1993—95, 1998; named to All-Star team, 1988, 1992, 1994—98, 2000; recipient Cy Young award, Baseball Writers Assn. Am., 1992, 1993, 1994, 1995, Gold Glove award, 1990—2002. Achievements include being a mem. of World Series Championship team, 1995. Office: c/o Chicago Cubs 1060 W Addison Chicago IL 60613-4397*

MADEIRA, FRANCIS KING CAREY, conductor, educator; b. Jenkintown, Pa., Feb. 21, 1917; s. Percy Childs and Margaret (Carey) M.; m. Jean E. Browning, June 17, 1947. Grad., Avon Old Farms, 1934; student, Julliard Grad. Sch., 1937-43; DFA (hon.), Providence Coll., 1966; DHL, R.I. Coll., 1969; MusD (hon.), Brown U., 1976. Instr. music Brown U., 1943-46, asst. prof. music, 1946-56, assoc. prof. music, 1956-66. Founder, condr. R.I. Philharm. Orch., 1945-78; concert pianist recitals and condr. concerts, U.S. and Europe; also guest condr. U.S. and fgn. orchs. World premiere Trilogy (JFK-MLK-RFK) (by Ron Nelson), R.I. Philharmonic Orch., 1969. Mem. music panel Maine State Arts Commn., 1987-90; bd. trustees Saco River Festival Assn., 1988-94; mem. adv. bd., trustee Portland (Maine) Symphony Orch., 1996—. Recipient Gov.'s award for excellence in arts, 1972; John F. Kennedy award for svc. to cmty., 1978, Maestro award R.I. Philharm. Orch., 1998, Millennium Reflections award R.I. Philharm. Orch., 1999, John Hazen White Sr. Leadership award R.I. Philharm. Orch., 2003, Citizen Citation award Mayor or Providence, R.I., 2003.

MADEIRA, ROBERT LEHMAN, professional society administrator; b. Elizabethtown, Pa., Aug. 30, 1915; s. Isaac Titus and Elsie Hernley (Lehman) M.; m. Mary Elizabeth Evans, Feb. 5, 1938; children: Terry Madeira Harsney, Chase Landre. Student, Juniata Coll., 1933-34; BS in Econs, Elizabethtown Coll., 1937; postgrad., Mpls. Honeywell Sch. Aero. Engring., U. Minn., 1945. Pianist, tchr., Elizabethtown, 1935-41; automobile salesman Packard Lancaster Co., Lancaster, Pa., 1937; owner, mgr. Conewago Foods, Elizabethtown, 1938-39; aircraft technician U.S. Air Force Middletown, Pa. and Columbia, 1941-42; project engr. Mpls. Honeywell, Chgo. and Mpls., 1942-45; mgr. Iceland, Inc., Elizabethtown, 1945-51; exec. sec. Nat. Frozen Food Locker Inst., Elizabethtown, 1951-55; exec. dir. Nat. Inst. Locker and Freezer Provisioners, Elizabethtown, 1955-73, Am. Assn. Meat Processors, Elizabethtown, 1973-80, exec. dir. emeritus, 1980-85. Tchr. course in assn. mgmt. Yale U., Mich. State U., Syracuse U.,,966-70; condr. internat. meat processing seminars, Europe, S.Am., Australia, New Zealand, The Orient, Africa, 1962-85. Chmn. Elizabethtown ARC, 1948-49, Elizabethtown Community Chest, 1952-53, Elizabethtown Park Dr., 1950; bd. dirs. Lancaster Com. of 100, 1953-57, Elizabethtown Music Found., 1951-57; bd. dirs. Norlanco Med. Center, Elizabethtown, 1972-75, chmn. fund dr., 1972-73. Recipient Man of Yr. award Nat. Inst. Locker and Freezer Provisioners, 1955; honor cert. Freedoms Found. at Valley Forge, 1976 Mem. Am. Soc. Assn. Execs. (Key award 1971, chartered assn. exec.), C. of C. U.S., Nat. Assn. Exhbn. Mgrs., Nat. Fedn. Ind. Bus., Gideons Internat., Nat. Right-to-Work Com. Republican. Presbyterian. Home: 660 Willow Valley Sq Apt M102 Lancaster PA 17602-4874 Office: Am Assn Meat Processors PO Box 269 Elizabethtown PA 17022-0269 E-mail: bobmadeira@webtv.net.

MADER, CHARLES LAVERN, chemist; b. Dewey, Okla., Aug. 8, 1930; s. George Edgar and Naomia Jane (Harer) M.; m. Emma Jean Sinclair, June 12, 1960; 1 child, Charles L. II. BS, Okla. State U., 1952, MS, 1954; PhD, Pacific Western U., 1980. Fellow Los Alamos (N.Mex.) Nat. Lab., 1955—; JIMAR sr. fellow U. Hawaii, Honolulu, 1985-94; pres. Mader Cons. Co., Honolulu, 1985—. Author: Numerical Modeling of Detonation, 1979, Numerical Modeling of Water Waves, 1988, Numerical Modeling of Explosives and Propellants, 1997, Numerical Modeling of Water, 2d edit., 2004; editor: Los Alamos Explosives Performance Data, 1982, LASL Phermex Data, vol. 1, 1980, vol. 2, 1980, vol. 3, 1981; contbr. numerous articles to profl. jours.; author 70 reports. Scoutmaster Boys Scouts Am., Los Alamos, 1971-85. Fellow Am. Inst. Chemists; mem. Am. Chem. Soc., Combustion Inst., Tsunami Soc. (editor 1985—), Marine Tech. Soc., Sigma Xi, Pi Mu Epsilon, Phi Lambda Upsilon. Methodist. Achievements include development and definition of field of numerical modeling of explosives and water waves. Office: Mader Consulting Co 1049 Kamehame Dr Honolulu HI 96825-2860 also: 214 Barranca Rd Los Alamos NM 87544-2410 also: PO Box 5930 Avon CO 81620-5930 Office Phone: 808-396-9855. E-mail: mccohi@aol.com.

MADERER, WILLIAM. F. lawyer; b. N.Y.C., Apr. 16, 1947; s. Paul S. and Miriam (Flexner) M.; m. Marlene D. Richer, Dec. 28, 1969; children: Jill, Paige. AB, Washington U., St. Louis, 1969; JD, N.Y. U., 1973. Bar: N.Y. 1973, N.J. 1977, U.S. Ct. Appeals (2d cir.) 1974, U.S. Ct. Appeals (3rd cir.) 1977, U.S. Supreme Ct. 1985. Assoc. Weil, Gotshal & Manges, N.Y.C., 1973-74; asst. U.S. atty. U.S. Atty.'s Office, Newark, 1974-80, chief spl. prosecutions div., 1978-80; ptnr. Saiber Schlesinger Satz & Goldstein LLC, Newark, 1980—. Office: Saiber Schlesinger Satz & Goldstein LLC 1 Gateway Ctr Ste 1300 Newark NJ 07102-5315

MADESKA, VALERIE GAY, research scientist; b. Bethpage, N.Y., Mar. 1, 1959; d. Arthur Lincoln and Theresa Van Dyke; m. Christopher Joseph Madeska, Aug. 24, 1982; children: Christopher Arthur, Thomas Michael, Joseph Daniel. AS, SUNY, Farmingdale, 1979. Cert. Nat. Credentialing Agy. for Lab. Pers. Part-time tech. asst. SUNY, Farmingdale, 1981—83, full time tech. asst., 1983—88, instrnl. support tech., 1988—2001, instrnl. support specialist, 2001—, lab. mgr., 2001—. Sec. med. lab. tech. dept. adv. bd. SUNY, Farmingdale, 1997—; v.p. for profls. United Univ. Professions, Farmingdale, 2000—. Mem.: N.Y. State Soc. Med. Techs. (Chancellor's award Profl. Svc. 1999). Democrat. Methodist. Office: Farmingdale State Univ NY 2350 Broadhollow Rd Farmingdale NY 11735 Office Phone: 631-420-2511. E-mail: valerie.madeska@farmingdale.edu.

MADEWELL, JOHN EDWARD, radiologist; Student, Ctrl. State Coll., Oklahoma City, 1960-69; MD, U. Okla., 1969. Intern Madigen Gen. Hosp., Tacoma, 1969-70; resident in diagnostic radiology Walter Reed Med. Ctr., Washington, 1970-73; fellow in radiol. pathology Armed Forces Inst. Pathology, Washington, 1973-74; radiologist Pa. State Geisinger Health Sys.; prof., chmn. dept. radiology Milton S. Hershey Med. Ctr./Pa. State U., 1987—; exec. dir. Univ. Physicians/Pa. State U., Hershey, 1996-97. Mem. Am. Coll. Radiology, Am. Roentgen Ray Soc., Assn. Univ. Radiologists, Internat. Skeletal Soc., Radiologic Soc. N.Am. Office: Pa State U Coll Medicine Hershey MC Dept Radiol H066 PO Box 850 Hershey PA 17033-0850

MADGALENE, DAVID, editor, writer; b. Wilmington, Del., Oct. 26, 1959; s. David James Randolph and Anita Ferland; m. Judy Marie Irwin, June 2, 1998. BA, Middle Tenn. State U., 1992; MA, Naropa Inst., Boulder, Colo., 1998. Editor New Way Media, Albany, Calif., 2000—. Author: Resurrected and Still In Love, 1988, Robin Ildebrandt, 2002, The Music of Michael Breaking-Down, 2003. With USN, 1980—84, 6th Fleet. Avocations: songwriting, performance, reading, hiking, travel. Home: 10987 Rio Ruso Dr Windsor CA 95492 Office: New Way Media 535 Pierce St # 5400 Albany CA 94706

MADGETT, NAOMI LONG, poet, editor, publisher, educator; b. Norfolk, Va., July 5, 1923; d. Clarence Marcellus and Maude Selena (Hilton) Long; m. Julian F. Witherspoon, Mar. 31, 1946 (div. Apr. 1949); 1 child, Jill Witherspoon Boyer; m. William H. Madgett, July 29, 1954 (div. Dec. 1960); m. Leonard P. Andrews, Mar. 31, 1972 (dec. May 1996). BA, Va. State Coll., 1945; MEd, Wayne State U., 1955; PhD, Internat. Inst. for Advanced Studies, 1980; LHD (hon.), Siena Heights Coll., 1991, Loyola U., 1993; DFA (hon.), Mich. State U., 1994. Reporter, copyreader Mich. Chronicle, Detroit, 1946; svc. rep. Mich. Bell Telephone Co., Detroit, 1948-54; tchr. English pub. high schs. Detroit, 1955-65, 66-68; rsch. assoc. Oakland U., Rochester, Mich., 1965-66; mem. staff Detroit Women Writers Conf. Ann. Writers Conf., 1968—; lectr. English U. Mich., 1970-71; assoc. prof. English Eastern Mich. U., Ypsilanti, 1968-73, prof., 1973-84, prof. emeritus, 1984—; editor-pub. Lotus Press, 1974—. Editor Lotus Poetry Series, Mich. State U. Press, 1993-98. Author: (poetry) Songs to a Phantom Nightingale (under name Naomi Cornelia Long), 1941, One and the Many, 1956, Star by Star, 1965, 70, Pink Ladies in the Afternoon, 1972, 90, Exits and Entrances, 1978, Phantom Nightingale: Juvenilia, 1981, Octavia and other Poems (Creative Achievement award Coll. Lang. Assn.), 1988, Remembrances of Spring: Collected Early Poems, 1993; Octavia: Guthrie and Beyond, 2002Connected Islands, 2004; (textbook) (with Ethel Tincher and Henry B. Maloney) Success in Language and Literature B, 1967, A Student's Guide to Creative Writing, 1980; editor: (anthology) A Milestone Sampler: 15th Anniversary Anthology, 1988, Adam of Ife: Black Women in Praise of Black Men, 1992; In Her Lifetime tribute Afrikan Poets Theatre, 1989. Participant Creative Writers in Schs. program. Recipient Esther R. Beer Poetry award Nat. Writers Club, 1957, Disting. English Tchr. of Yr. award, 1967; Josephine Nevins Keal award, 1979; Mott fellow in English, 1965, Robert Hayden Runagate award, 1985, Creative Artist award Mich. Coun. for the Arts, 1987, award Nat. Coalition 100 Black Women, 1984, award Nat. Coun. Tchrs. English Black Caucus, 1984, award Chesapeake/Virginia Beach chpt. Links, Inc., 1981, Arts Found. Mich. award, 1990, Creative Achievement award Coll. Lang. Assn., 1988; Arts Achievement award Wayne State U., 1985, The Black Scholar Award of Excellence, 1992; Am. Book award, 1993, Mich. Artist award, 1993; Creative Contbrs. award Gwendolyn Brooks Ctr. Black Lit. and Creative Writing Chgo. State U., 1993, Lifetime Achievement award Furious Flower, 1994, George Kent award, 1995, Lifetime Achievement award Gwendolyn Brooks Ctr., 2003; Naomi Long Madgett Poetry award named for her, 1993—, Alain Locke award Detroit Inst. Arts, Friends of African and African Am. Art, 2003; inducted Sumner H.S. Hall of Fame, St. Louis, 1997, Nat. Lit. Hall Fame for Writers of African Descent, Chgo. State U., 1999, Mich. Women's Hall of Fame, 2002; named Poet Laureate, City of Detroit, 2001—, Alain Locke award, 2003. Mem. NAACP, Coll. Lang. Assn., So. Poetry Law Ctr., Langston Hughes Soc., Detroit Women Writers, Charles H. Wright Mus. of African Am. History, Detroit Inst. of Arts, Fred Hart Williams Geneal. Soc., Alpha Kappa Alpha. Congregationalist. Home: 18080 Santa Barbara Dr Detroit MI 48221-2531 Office: PO Box 21607 Detroit MI 48221-0607 Office Phone: 313-861-1280. E-mail: nlmadgett@aol.com. *I have tried to set an example of excellence in the use of language, especially the language of poetry. If I can leave behind some enduring work—my own words and the words of others I have published—I will consider myself amply rewarded for my labors. The truly great people I have known have given a great deal of themselves in the service of others, have not been puffed up by their own importance, and have maintained integrity in their personal and professional lives. They have been my models.*

MADHAVAN, GURUPRASAD, biomedical engineer; b. Tamilnadu, India, July 19, 1979; BE with honors, U. of Madras, India, 2001; MSBME, SUNY, Stony Brook, 2002; PhD/MBA, SUNY, 2002—. Rsch. fellow Sri Ramachandra Med. Coll. and Rsch. Inst. (Deemed U.), Chennai, India, 1998—2004; rsch. scientist AFx Inc, Fremont, Calif., 2002—04; tech. corr., columnist ISA Asia Pacific Jour. for Measurement and Control, Bombay, 2002—; cons. Guidant Coop., Fremont, 2004—. Cons. engr. Kenafric Industries, Nairobi, Kenya, 1999—2000; book reviewer various orgns.; program chmn. NorCal Tech. 2004-Instrumentation Systems and Automation, Inc., San Francisco, 2003—. Contbr. more than 90 sci. articles to profl. jours. and mags.; assoc. editor IEEE Potentials, 2004. Recipient Youth Leadership award, Rotary Club, 1996, Leadership award, AT&T, 2001, Award of Achievement, Nat. Scholars Honor Soc., 2001, Chancellor's Promising Inventor award, SUNY, 2003, Pres.'s Vol. Svc. award (Silver & Bronze medals), 2004; Grad. fellow, SUNY at Stony Brook, 2001—, Ednl. Found. scholar, ISA, 2001, Biosystems fellow, SUNY Binghamton, 2004—. Fellow: Royal Soc. of Medicine (assoc.), NY Acad. of Medicine (assoc.); mem.: Australasian Coll. Phys. Scientists and Engrs. in Medicine, Binghamton Bioengrs. IEEE-EMBS (founding pres.), Royal Soc. New Zealand, Am. Heart Assn., AAMI, BMES, Biomed. Engring. Soc. (life), ISA, IEEE (Coulter award 2002), ASME, Inst. Elec. Engrs. U.K., N.Y. Acad. Sci., Can. Med. and Biol. Engring. Soc., Nat. Scholars Honor Soc. (life). Achievements include patents pending for Microwave ablation monitoring. E-mail: guru@binghamton.edu.

MADHAVAN, MURUGAPPA CHETTIAR, economics educator, international consultant; b. Kandramanickam, Tamilnadu, India, Dec. 17, 1932; came to U.S., 1960; s. L. Murugappa Chettiar and Adaikkammai Achi (Meyyappan) M.; m. Nachammai Manickam, May 3, 1953; children: Nachiappa, Nataraj. BA with honors, Annamalai U., India, 1955, MA, 1958; MS, U. Wis., 1963, PhD, 1969. Lectr. in econs. Annamalai U., 1955-60; economist Europe and Mid. East World Bank, Washington, 1963-66, asst. sec. econ. com., 1966-68; dir. Ctr. for Rsch. in Econ. Devel. San Diego State U., 1969-85, prof. econs., 1974—, dir. Asian Studies, 1991-2000, chmn. dept. Asian Studies, 1999-2000. Prof. econs. Nat. Inst. Bank Mgmt., Bombay, 1971—72; vis. prof. econs. Indian Inst. Tech., Madras, 1979—80, Madras Sch. Econs., 1996, U. Putra, Malaysia, 2002; Father Carty Meml. lectr. U. Madras, 1980; vis. Fulbright prof. U. of the Philippines, 1987—88; cons. UN Devel. Program, N.Y.C., 1987—88, Gen. Atomics, San Diego, 1993—99; advisor Gov. Sim Grinio, Philippines, 1988; vis. scholar IMF Inst., Washington, 2002; Fulbright sr. specialist Faculty of Law and Econs., Phnom Penh, Cambodia, summer, 2001. Co-author: The Transfer of Knowledge Through Expatriate Nationals, 1988. Chmn. World Affairs Coun. San Diego, 1991-93; pres. Tamil Nadu Found., Inc., Chgo., 1985-87, life mem.; advisor Mingei Internat. Mus., San Diego, 1985—; pres. San Diego Indian Am. Soc., 1984-99. Fulbright fellow, 1960; recipient Hon. Am. award Ams. by Choice, 1987, Leadership and Contbn. award Tamil Nadu Found., 1994; Fulbright sr. scholar Fulbright Program in Ho Chi Minh City, U. Econs., 2000, U. Putra Malaysia, 2000. Mem.: Am. Econ. Assn., Assn. Indian Econ. Studies (life), Indian Econ. Assn. (life), San Diego Indian Am. Soc. (life), Tamilnadu Found. (life), Fulbright Assn. (life). Democrat. Avocations: reading, walking, organizational activities. Home: 8727 Verlane Dr San Diego CA 92119-2033 Office: San Diego State U Coll Arts & Letters Ctr Asian Studies San Diego CA 92182 E-mail: madhavan@mail.sdsu.edu.

MADHOK, ASHISH BRIJ, pediatrician, cardiologist; b. New Delhi, Jan. 5, 1973; arrived in U.S., 1997; s. Brij Dev and Promila Madhok; m. Shailee Ashish Madhok, Oct. 12, 1997; 1 child, Akshat. MB, BChir, Seth G.S. Med. Coll., Bombay, 1996. House officer pediat. Bandra Bhabha Hosp., Bombay, 1996, Lokmanya Tilak Med. Coll. Sion Hosp., Bombay, 1996—97; resident pediat. Bklyn. Hosp. Ctr., 1997—2000; fellow pediat. cardiology North Shore-Long Island Jewish Health Sys., Manhasset, NY, 2000—02; chief fellow pediat. cardiology North Shore Univ. Hosp. Long Island Jewish, Schneider Children's Hosp., Manhasset, NY, 2002—03; dir. pediat. cardiology Claxton Hepburn Med. Ctr., Ogdensburg, NY, 2003—. Mem.: AMA, Am. Coll. Cardiology, Am. Acad. Pediat. Avocations: tennis, hiking, reading, travel. Office: Claxton Hepburn Med Ctr Dept Cardiology 214 King St Ogdensburg NY 13669 E-mail: ashishdoc1973@yahoo.com.

MADHUSOODANAN, SUBRAMONIAM, psychiatrist, educator; b. Trivandrum, India, Sept. 7, 1947; came to U.S., 1976; s. Subramoniam Pillai and Leelavathi K. Amma; m. Rama Sivathanu, Feb. 5, 1976 (div. Feb. 1991); children: Leena, Deepa; m. Gunjan Jain, Sept. 12, 1991; 1 child, Neha. MBBS, Trivandrum Med. Coll., 1971; Diploma in Otorhinolaryngology, Kurnool (India) Med. Coll., 1975; MD, SUNY, 1992. Diplomate in psychiatry and geriatric psychiatry Am. Bd. Psychiatry and Neurology, Am. Bd. Quality Assurance and Utilization Physicians, Am. Soc. clin. Psychopharmacology, Inc. Instr. Mt. Sinai Sch. Medicine, CUNY, 1978—82; asst. attending psychiatrist Mt. Sinai Svcs., City Hosp. Ctr. at Elmhurst, NY, 1979—81; med. dir. outpatient alcohol program St. John's Episcopal Hosp., Far Rockaway, NY, 1981—83, acting dir. psychiatry, 1984—86, assoc. chair psychiatry, 1986—, program dir. geriatric psychiatry fellowship program, 1993—; dir. psychiatry Peninsula Hosp., Far Rockaway, 1983—; clin. instr. SUNY Downstate Med. Ctr., Bklyn., 1993—2002, clin. assoc. prof. dept. psychiatry, 1997—2002, clin. prof., 2002—. Cons. psychiatrist St. John's Nursing Home, Peninsula Nurses Home, Far Rockaway Nursing Home, Brookhaven Nursing Home Haven Manor, 1981—. Fellow Am. Psychiat. Assn. (disting.); mem. Am. Geriatric Psychiatry Assn., Queens County Psychiat. Soc., Lawrence Assn. Democrat. Hindu. Avocations: gardening, photography, travel. Home: 249 Broadway Lawrence NY 11559-1511 Office: St John's Episcopal Hosp 327 B 19th St Far Rockaway NY 11691

MADIA, WILLIAM JUUL, chemist; b. Pitts., May 20, 1947; s. William Anthony and Joanna (VanKerchkoven) M.; m. Audrey Marie Madia, May 23, 1970; children: Joseph Anthony, Benjamin Paul, William Byron. BS in Chemistry, Ind. U. of Pa., 1969, MS in Nuclear Chemistry, 1970; PhD in Radiochemistry, Va. Polytech. Inst., 1975. With Battelle, 1975—; chemist, researcher Battelle Columbus (Ohio) div., 1975-77, assoc. sect. mgr., 1977-80, sect. mgr., 1980-83, mgr. office of nuclear waste isolation, 1983-85; pres. Battelle Project Mgmt. div., 1985-86; sr. v.p. Battelle Meml. Inst., 1988-89, 89—; pres. Battelle Tech. Internat., 1988-89, corp. sr. v.p., 1990-91, gen. mgr. environ. systems and tech. divsn., corp. sr. v.p., 1992-94; dir. Pacific Northwest Nat. Lab., 1994—99, Oak Ridge Nat. Lab., Tenn., 2000—03; pres., CEO UT- Battelle, Oak Ridge, Tenn., exec. v.p., 2003—. Mem. adv. bd. Ohio State U. Coll. Engring.; bd. dirs. Mason & Hanger. Mem. editl. bd. R&D Mag.; contbr. articles to profl. jours. Bd. dirs. Franklin U., 1987-94, Franklin County Children Svcs., 1988-94; editorial adv. bd. High Tech. Bus., 1988—; bd. dirs. Tri-City Indsl. Devel. Coun., Washington Roundtable; hon. bd. dirs. Mid-Columbia Edn. Alliance; adv. bd. Jr. Achievement Greater Tri-Cities; bd. dirs. Reading Found.; co-chair Tri-Cities Corp. Coun. Arts; mem. exec. com. Children's Ctr. Capital Campaign. With U.S. Army, 1970-72. Mem. AAAS,

Indsl. Rsch. Inst. (fed. sci. and tech. com.), Midwest Rsch. Inst. (trustee), Nat. Renewable Energy Lab. (bd. govs.), Brookhaven Sci. Assocs. (bd. dirs.), U.S. Dept. Energy Lab. Ops. Bd., Washington Tech. Alliance. Roman Catholic. Office: Battelle 505 King Ave Columbus OH 43201

MADIAN, ALAN LEONARD, economist, management consultant; b. N.Y.C., May 25, 1938; s. Sydney and Anna (Lieber) M.; m. Susan R. Kneller, Apr. 20, 1986; children: Nicholas James Kneller, Antonia Chloe Kneller. AB, U. Calif., Berkeley, 1959; MA, Yale U., 1961; postgrad., Oxford (Eng.) U., 1963-65. Sr. rsch. scientist econs. Columbia U., 1963; asst. prof. U. Rochester, N.Y., 1964-65; from asst. prof. to assoc. prof. London Sch. Econs., 1965-70; sr. economist Inst. Pub. Adminstrn., N.Y.C., 1971-74; pres. Econ. Strategies, Inc., N.Y.C., 1975, 78; econ. advisor to gov. State of N.Y., 1976-77; prin. assoc. Robert R. Nathan Assocs., Washington, 1979-80, cons. U.S. Senate Antitrust Subcom., 1980; dir. econ. studies Hamilton, Rabinovitz & Szanton, Inc., Washington, 1981; pres. Madian Econ. Assocs., 1981-97; mng. dir. Erb & Madian, Inc., 1984-97; CEO Lafayette Capital Corp., 1987—; from prin. to sr. v.p. Hagler Bailly Inc., 1997-2000, v.p., 1997-99, sr. v.p., 1999-2000; mem. mgmt. group PA Consulting Group, 2000—01; dir. LECG, Washington, 2001—. Cons. World Bank, Goldman Sachs, others. Contbr. to books, articles to profl. jours. Exec. com. Young Dems. Calif., 1958-59; dir. Children's Found., 1985-96; No.-Calif./gov. campaign mgr. Edmund G. Brown, 1962. Served with AUS, 1955. Woodrow Wilson fellow, 1959-60, Falk Found. fellow, 1960. Mem. Am. Econ. Assn., Royal Econ. Soc., Internat. Assn. Energy Economists, Nat. Assn. Bus. Economists, Phi Beta Kappa. Office: 1725 Eye St NW Washington DC 20006-3700 Home: 1919 Franklin Ave Mc Lean VA 22101-5309 Personal E-mail: almlafcap@aol.com. Business E-Mail: amadian@lecg.com.

MADIGAN, JENNIFER CAROLINE, education educator; d. John Robert Erskine Booker and Roberta Marie Louise Carlson; m. Michael Jarad Madigan, Aug. 21, 1978; children: Jerome Jacob, Ashley May. BA in Sociology, U. Mass., Boston, 1977; MA in Tchg., Notre Dame de Namur U., Belmont, Calif., 1980; EdD in Learning and Instrn., U. San Francisco, 2002. Asst. prof. Bethany Coll., Scotts Valley, Calif., 1997—2002; instr. U. San Francisco, 2000—02; asst. prof. San Jose (Calif.) State U., 2002—. Mem. adv. bd. Nat. Assn. Single Sex Pub. Schooling, Washington, 2002—, U. San Francisco, 2000—; rsch. assoc. Project LASER, U. South Fla., 2002—03. Contbr. articles to profl. jours. Grantee, Office of Spl. Edn., U.S. Dept. Edn., Washington, 2001—02. Mem.: Coun. Exceptional Children (pres. state chpt. 2003—). Avocations: hiking, snorkeling, jogging, gardening, travel. Office: San Jose State U Dept Spl Edn 1 Washington Sq San Jose CA 95192-0078 Office Phone: 408-924-3313. Business E-Mail: jennifer.madigan@sjsu.edu.

MADIGAN, JOHN WILLIAM, publishing executive; b. Chgo., June 7, 1937; s. Edward P. and Olive D. Madigan; m. Holly Williams, Nov. 24, 1962; children: Mark W., Griffith E., Melanie L. BBA, U. Mich., 1958, MBA, 1959. Fin. analyst Duff & Phelps, Chgo., 1960—62; audit mgr. Arthur Andersen & Co., Chgo., 1962—67; v.p. investment banking Paine, Webber, Jackson & Curtis, Chgo., 1967—69; v.p. corp. fin. Salomon Bros., Chgo., 1969—74; v.p., CFO, dir. Tribune Co., Chgo., 1975—81, exec. v.p., 1981—91; pub. Chgo. Tribune, 1990—94; pres., CEO Tribune Pub. Co., Chgo., 1991—94; pres., COO Tribune Co., Chgo., 1994—95, pres., 1994—2001, CEO, 1995—2002, chmn., 1996—. Bd. dirs. AP, Morgan Stanley, AT&T Wireless Svcs. Trustee Rush-Presbyn.-St. Luke's Med. Ctr., Mus. TV and Radio in N.Y., Northwestern U., Ill. Inst. Tech.; mem. bd. overseers Hoover Instn. Mem.: Chgo. Coun. on Fgn. Rels. (chmn.), Robert R. McCormick Tribune Found. Office: Tribune Co 435 N Michigan Ave Chicago IL 60611-4066

MADIGAN, JOSEPH EDWARD, financial executive, consultant, director; b. Bklyn., June 26, 1932; s. James Peter and Mary (Goldman) M.; m. Catherine Cashman, July 26, 1980; children: Kerri Ann, Kimberly Ann Burquest, Elizabeth Ann Laginess. BBA cum laude, Baruch Coll., CUNY, 1958; MBA, NYU, 1963. Adminstrv. asst. Assoc. Metals & Minerals Corp., 1961-63; fin. analyst, fgn. exch. trader, corp. portfolio trader AMAX, Inc., 1963-65; mgr. corp. portfolio, dir. cash mgmt., asst. treas. TWA, Inc., 1965-68; treas. Borden, Inc., 1968-76, v.p., treas., 1976-80; exec. v.p., chief fin. officer, dir. Wendy's Internat., Inc., Dublin, Ohio, 1980-87. Bd. dirs Frank Gates Holding, Columbus Show Case Co., Scioto Properties LLC. Chmn. bd. Lexford Residential Properties, 1997-99. With USN, 1951-55. Mem. Fin. Execs. Inst., Nat. Investor Rels. Inst., Baruch Coll.-CUNY Alumni Assn., NYU Alumni Assn., Imperial Golf Club (Naples, Fla.), Beta Gamma Sigma. Republican. Roman Catholic. Home: 5555 Heron Point Dr # 2102 Naples FL 34108

MADIGAN, LAURIE ANNE, municipal official; b. Alhambra, Ca., Dec. 26, 1950; d. Harold Steven and Kathe (Roehl) Jencks; m. Michael D. Madigan, Oct. 7, 2001; m. D. Kirk McKinley, 1971 (div. 1995); 1 child, Erin Jencks McKinley. BA in Comparative Lit., U. Calif., Berkeley, 1971, BA in Theater, 1972; MPA, San Diego State U., 1980. Planner County of San Diego, San Diego, 1974—75; exec. dir. San Diego County Local Agy. Formation Commn., San Diego, 1975—80; v.p., planning and govt. rels. A. Cal Rossi Co., San Francisco, 1980—82; owner The McKinley Group (pub. policy cons.), San Diego, 1983—85; prin. asst. to mayor for policy and program devel. City of San Diego, 1985—86; v.p. Presley Homes of San Diego, 1986—88; owner/sr. ptnr. San Diego MNA Consulting-Pub. Policy and Planning, 1988—2002; dir. cmty. devel. (redevel., econ. devel., and housing) City of Chula Vista, Calif., 2003—; apptd. Spl. Task Force on Fire Dist. Post Proposition Financing State of Calif., 1979; mem. Mayor's Blue Ribbon Task Force on Park Bonds City of San Diego, 1987. Mem. local govt. San Diego C. of C.; com. mem. San Diego Adv. Coun.; mem. legis. and comm. com. San Diego Bldg. Industry Assn. Leader Girl Scouts of Am., San Diego, 1985—94, mem. adv. coun. Mem.: Westpark Cmty. Assn. (founding mem.), Lambda Alpha Internat., Phi Beta Kappa. Office: City of Chula Vista Comm Devel Dept 276 4th Ave Chula Vista CA 91910

MADIGAN, LISA, state attorney general; BA, Georgetown U., 1988; attended, Loyola U. Asst. dean adult, continuing edn., dir. Sr. Acad. Lifelong Learning Wrights Family Coll. Wilbur Wright Coll., with positive alts. project; mem. Ill. Senate, Springfield, 1999—2003, mem. appropriations, local govt. coms., mem. senate appropriations com., joint com. adminstrv. rules; litigator Sachnoff & Weaver, Ltd., Chgo.; served as Dem. Senate Edn. Com., 1998; atty. gen. State of Ill., 2003—, co-chmn. Bd. dirs. AIDS Living Remembrance Com. Mem. Ill. Bar Assn., Women's Bar Assn. Ill., Chgo. Bar Assn. Democrat. Office: Atty Gen James R Thompson Ctr 100 W Randolph St Chicago IL 60601

MADIGAN, RITA DUFFY, career education coordinator; b. N.Y.C., Jan. 22, 1919; d. Anthony E. and Mary (Feichter) Duffy; m. John Callanan Madigan, May 1, 1943; children: John C., James A., Paul F. BA in English History, Our Lady of Good Counsel Coll., 1940; M of Adminstrn., U. Bridgeport, 1963, postgrad., 1970. Tchr. English City of Bridgeport (Conn.), 1961-63, Birkshire Jr. High Sch., Birmingham, Mich., 1963-66; career counselor East Side Mid. Sch., Bridgeport, 1969-71; coord. career edn. Ctrl. HS, Bridgeport, 1972—99, ret., 1999. Recipient State SCOVE award, 1986, CCCA Meritorious award, 1993, Meritorious award Teikyo Post Univ, 1993, Meritorious award for svc. to cmty. Girl Scouts of Am., 1996. Mem. AAUW, NEA, Conn. Edn. Assn., Conn. Career Counselors Assn., Bridgeport Edn. Assn., St. Joseph's Ladies League (bd. dirs. 1992-94), Bridgeport U. Alumnae Assn. Republican. Roman Catholic. Avocations: skiing, golf, tennis, sailing, travel. Home: 44 Chatham Dr Trumbull CT 06611-3262

MADISON, ANNE CONWAY, public relations and marketing professional; b. Balt., Mar. 13, 1963; d. Earl Cranston Jr. and Nancy (Schucker) C.; 1 child, Ryan Douglas. BS in Comm., Wittenberg U., 1985. Pub. rels. specialist Springfield (Ohio) Met. Housing Authority, 1984-85; account rep. CT Corp. Sys., Washington, 1985-86; pub. rels. asst. Ryland, Columbia, Md., 1986-88, comm. coord., 1988-90, mgr. mktg. comm., 1990-92, dir. mktg. comm., 1992-94, v.p. comm., 1994—2003; v.p. mktg. and comm. ESIC, Inc., Columbia, 2003—. Bd. dirs., officer Domestic Violence Cr. of Howard County, Columbia, 1987-96; bd. dirs. Norbel Sch., Nat. Family Resiliency Ctr. Named Vol. of Yr. Domestic Violence Ctr., 1988, recipient Spirit award, 1992; named one of Top 100 Women in Md., The Daily Record, 1996. Mem. Pub. Rels. Soc. Am., Nat. Investor Rels. Inst. Republican. Roman Catholic. Office: 10227 Wincopin Cir Columbia MD 21044 Office Phone: 410-772-3050. Personal E-mail: acmadison@comcast.net. Business E-Mail: amadison@esic.org.

MADISON, EDDIE LAWRENCE, JR., public relations consultant, editor, writer; b. Tulsa, Sept. 8, 1930; s. Eddie Lawrence Sr. and Laverta (Pyle) M.; m. Davetta Jayn Cooksey, Nov. 17, 1956; children: Eddie Lawrence III, Karyn Devette, David Cooksey. B in Journalism, Lincoln U., Jefferson City, Mo., 1952; MA, U. Tulsa, 1959. Editor-in-chief Okla. Eagle, Tulsa, 1954-59; assoc. editor Chgo. Daily Defender, 1959-61; dep. editor Assoc. Negro Press, Chgo., 1961-63; sect. editor Chgo. Tribune, 1963-65; dep. dir. publs. divsn. Domestic and Internat. Bus., U.S. Dept. Commerce, Washington, 1965-69; mgr. cmty. svcs. Evening Star Broadcasting Co., Washington, 1969-78; asst. editor Bus. Am. Mag., Washington, 1978-81; press asst. Ho. of Reps., Washington, 1981-82; pub. affairs specialist U.S. Dept. HHS, Washington, 1982-92, mgr. HHS radio, 1991-92; asst. prof., chmn. dept. comm. Lincoln U., 1992-99; exec. editor Okla. Eagle, Tulsa, 2001—; pres., CEO Three Elms & Assoc., Inc., Tulsa, 2001—. Founder Nat. Broadcast Assn. for Cmty. Affairs, Washington, 1974, 1st pres., 1974-77; adj. prof. Tulsa C.C. Corres. Native Am. Times. Pres. Brightwood Civic Assn., Washington, 1969-72; mem. media adv. com. Mo. Arts Coun., 1996-99; mem. tobacco coalition and assist coms. Am. Cancer Soc., 1993-99; Hist. Preservation Commn., 1997-99, bd. dirs. Opportunities Industrialization Ctr., Washington, 1971-77, D.C. United Way, 1972-77, Boy Scouts Am., Washington, 1972-77. With U.S. Army, 1952-54; corr., Army Times, columnits, Recon Observer, Ellsworth AFB, S.D. Mem. Alpha Phi Alpha (pres. Washington chpt. 1969-72, nat. dir. pub. rels. 1985-91, co-chair nat. pub. policy com. 1973, v.p. Montgomery County chpt. 1987-89, pres. Jefferson City Beta Zeta Lambda chpt. 1993, assoc. editor Sphinx mag., award of merit Ea. region 1992). Methodist. Avocations: photography, aerobics, jogging. Home: 4355 S Braden Ave Tulsa OK 74135-6337 Office: The Okla Eagle 624 E Archer St Tulsa OK 74120-1000 Address: Native Am Times 12833 E 41st St Tulsa OK 74146 also: Three Elms & Assocs PO Box 161 Tulsa OK 74101-0161 Fax: 918-852-8905. E-mail: emadsept@aol.com., threeelms1@aol.com.

MADISON, GEORGE W. lawyer; b. 1953; BS, NYU; MBA, JD, Columbia U. Law clk. to Hon. Nathaniel R. Jones U.S. Ct. Appeals (6th cir.) Ohio, Cin., 1980-81; assoc. Shearman & Sterling, N.Y.C., 1981-87; with Mayer, Brown & Platt, N.Y.C., 1987-89, ptnr., 1989-96; exec. v.p., corp. sec., gen. counsel Comerica Inc., Detroit, 1996—2003; exec. v.p., gen. counsel TIAA-CREF, 2003—. Bd. visitors Law Sch. Columbia U. Recipient Learned Hand award, Am. Jewish Com., 2003. Mem. ABA (chmn. com. corp. gen. counsel), Am. Judicative Soc. (mem. exec. com.), Am. Law Inst., Assn. of Bar of City of N.Y. Office: TIAA-CREF 730 Third Ave New York NY 10017 Office Phone: 212-916-4750. Business E-Mail: gmadison@tiaa-cref.org.

MADISON, JAMES RAYMOND, lawyer; b. White Plains, N.Y., Apr. 27, 1931; s. Raymond S. and Katherine (Sherwin) M.; m. Mary Massey, Sept. 19, 1953; children: Michael, Matthew, Molly. BS, Stanford U., 1953, LLB, 1959. Bar: Calif. 1960, U.S. Dist. Ct. (no. dist.) Calif. 1960, U.S. Ct. Appeals (9th cir.) 1960, U.S. Dist. Ct. (ctrl. dist.) Calif. 1970, U.S. Supreme Ct. 1973, U.S. Dist. Ct. (ea. dist.) Calif. 1981, U.S. Dist. Ct. (so. dist.) Calif. 1988. Assoc. Orrick, Herrington & Sutcliffe, San Francisco, 1959-67, ptnr., 1968-95; pvt. practice Menlo Park, Calif., 1996—. Trustee Antioch U., Yellow Springs, Ohio, 1980-87; bd. dirs. Planned Parenthood Alameda/San Francisco, 1984-89; pres. Calif. Dispute Resolution Coun., 2001. Lt. (j.g.) USN, 1953-56. Mem. ABA, ASCE, State Bar Calif., Bar Assn. San Francisco, San Mateo County Bar Assn., Am. Arbitration Assn. (large complex case panel arbitrators and mediators, No. Calif. regional adv. coun.), Mediation Soc., Calif. Dispute Resolution Coun., Dispute Rev. Bd. Found., Coll. Comml. Arbitrators. Democrat. Episcopalian. Avocation: soccer. Office: 750 Menlo Ave Ste 250 Menlo Park CA 94025-4758 Office Phone: 650-614-0160. E-mail: jrmcoach@aol.com.

MADISON, PAULA, broadcast executive; b. N.Y.C. married; 1 child. Grad., Vassar Coll., 1974. Asst. city editor Dallas Times Herald; investigative bur. reporter Ft. Worth Star - Telegram, 1980; reporter Syracuse Herald Jour.; cmty. affairs dir. WFAA-TV, Dallas, 1982—84, news mgr., 1984—86; news dir. KOTV-TV, Tulsa, 1986—87; exec. news dir. KHOU-TV, Houston, 1987—89; asst. news dir. WNBC, N.Y.C., 1989—96, v.p., news dir., 1996—2000; v.p., sr. v.p. diversity NBC, N.Y.C., 2000—02; pres., gen. mgr. KNBC, L.A., 2000—. Bd. trustees Vassar Coll. Named Disting. African-Am. New Yorker, N.Y.C. Comptroller Alan Hevesi; recipient Ida B. Wells award, Nat. Assn. Black Journalists', 1998, Ellis Island medal of honor, Nat. Ethnic Coalition of Orgns., 1999, President's award, NAACP, 2001, Frederick C. Patterson award, United Negro College Fund, 2001, Diversity award, Nat. Assoc. Minority Media Execs., 2002, Woman of the Year, Los Angeles County Commn. for Women, 2002, Excellence in Media Award, Calif. NOW Chap., 2003, TRISCCORT award, Tri-State Catholic Com. on Radio and TV, Asian-Pacific Am. Corp. Impact award, Org. Chinese Americans Greater Los Angeles Chap. Image award Corp. Achievement. Mem.: N.Y. Assn. Black Journalists, Nat. Assn. Black Journalists. Office: NBC 4 3000 West Alameda Ave Burbank CA 91523*

MADISON, ROBERT PRINCE, architect; b. Cleve., July 28, 1923; s. Robert J. and Nettie (Brown) M.; m. Leatrice L. Branch, Apr. 16, 1949; children: Jeanne Marie, Juliette Branch. Student, Howard U., 1940—43, HHD, 1987; BArch, Western Res. U., 1948; MArch, Harvard U., 1952; DFA (hon.), Cleveland State U., 2000; HHD (hon.), Kent State U., 2001. Mem. various archtl. firms, 1948-52; instr. Howard U., Washington, 1952-54; chmn., CEO Robert P. Madison Internat., architects, engrs. and planners, Cleve., 1954—. Trustee Am. Automobile Assn.; vis. prof. Howard U., 1961-62; lectr. Western Res. U., 1964-65; mem. U.S. architects del. Peoples Repub. China, 1974 Prin. works include U.S. Embassy Dakar, Senegal, West Africa, 1966, State of Ohio Computer Ctr., 1988, Cuyahoga County Jail, 1990, Continental Airlines Hub Concourse, Cleve. Internat. Airport, 1991. Mem. tech. adv. com. Cleve. Bd. Edn., 1960—; mem. adv. com. Cleve. Urban Renewal, 1963—; mem. fine arts adv. com. to mayor, Cleve.; mem. archtl. adv. coun. Cornell U.; trustee Case Western Res. U., Cleve. Opera, 1990, NCCJ, 1990, Commn. on Higher Edn., 1990; bd. dirs. Jr. Achievement Greater Cleve.; trustee Cuyahoga County Hosp. Found., 1983—, Univ. Circle Inc., Midtown Corridor Inc.; mem. Ohio Bd. Bldg. Standards, 1986, Cleveland Heights City Planning Commn., 1987. 1st lt., inf. AUS, 1943-46. Decorated Purple Heart; Fulbright fellow, 1952-53; recipient Disting. Svc. award Case Western Res. U., 1989, Disting. Archtl. Firm award Howard U., 1989, Entrepreneur of Yt. award Ernst Young, Inc., Merrill Lynch, 1991, Arch. of Yr. Nat. Tech. Assn., 1996, Martin Luther King Jr. Corp. award African-Am. Archives Aux. Western Res. Hist. Soc., 1997, Disting. Alumni award Case We. Res. U., 1997; named to Corp. Hall of Fame, Ohio Assembly of Couns., 1991, Pres. award Kent State U., 1999; named to Cleve. Bus. Hall of Fame, 2002. Fellow AIA (chpt. pres., nat. task force for creative econs. 1976, mem. jury of fellows 1983-85, mem. nat. judicial coun. 1993, Gold Medal Firm award Ohio 1994, Gold Medal award Ohio 1997); mem. Architects Soc. Ohio, Epsilon Delta Rho, Alpha Phi Alpha, Sigma Pi Phi. Office: Robert P Madison Internat Inc 2930 Euclid Ave Cleveland OH 44115-2416 Home: 18975 Van Aken Blvd Apt 410 Shaker Heights OH 44122-3539 Office Phone: 216-861-8195. E-mail: rmadison@rpmadison.com.

MADISON, SAM A., JR., professional football player; b. Thomasville, Ga., Apr. 23, 1974; Student, Louisville. Cornerback Miami Dolphins, 1997—. Active Habitat for Humanity, Prudential/No Passing Zone. Named first-team All-Pro, Sports Illustrated, 1998, second-team AP All-Pro, 1998, first-team All-AFC selection Football News, 1998, second-team All-Pro Choice, Football Digest, 1998, first-team All-Pro selection AP, USA Today, Sports Illustrated, The Sporting News, Pro Football Weekly, Football Digest, 1999, NFL Alumni Assn. Defensive Back of Yr., 1999, Dolphins' MVP, 1999; named to AFC Pro Bowl squad, 1999. Office: Miami Dolphins Tng Facility 7500 SW 30th St Davie FL 33314

MADISON, SUE WOOD, state legislator; b. Uchitomari, Okinawa, Feb. 10, 1948; d. Roy and Lyda (Camille) Wood; m. Bernard L. Madison; children: Eva, Blair. BS, La. State U., 1970, MS, 1976. Planning commr. City of Fayetteville, Ark., 1984-88; justice of peace Washington County, Ark., 1991-94; state rep., 1995—2000; state senator, 2003—. Property mgr., owner. Democrat. Presbyterian. Avocation: gardening. Home: 573 N Rockcliff Rd Fayetteville AR 72701-3809

MADISON, T. JEROME, business executive; b. N.Y.C., June 2, 1940; s. Theodore H. and Eleanor E. (Eveland) M.; m. Marsha A. Heeb, Sept. 26, 1964 (dec.); children: Jillian, Kimberly, Ryan. BS, U. Pa., 1962; MBA, Monmouth U., 1975. CPA NJ. Mgr. KPMG, Newark and Princeton, NJ, 1970-75, Abbott Labs., North Chicago, Ill., 1976; asst. corp. contr. Rhone-Poulenc Rorer (now Aventis), Ft. Washington, Pa., 1977-78; corp. contr. Aventis, Ft. Washington, Pa., 1979-82; v.p. fin. Cytogen Corp., Princeton, 1982-86; pres., CEO, dir. Outwater & Wells Ventures, Inc., 1981-85, Atlantic Capital Resources Group, Inc., 1985-87, Founders Ct. Inc., 1986—, Montgomery Ptnrs., 1991—. Chmn, CEO Pilling Co., 1986—91, AxCell Bioscis. Corp., 1996—97, Trinity Tech. Ptnrs., 1997—, Trinity Ptnrs., S.A.; chmn. Somerset Ctrl. Corp.; bd. dirs. ProMed Sys., ProTech. Flight Officer USN, 1962-66.

MADISON, WILLIE CLARENCE, park administrator; b. Winchester, Ky., Aug. 20, 1942; s. Horace James Clark and Ella Louise (Madison) Cosby; m. Edna Marie Kennedy, June 23, 1965; children: Chandra Monique, Thalassa Mont. BS, Western Ky. U., 1974, MPS, 1977. Asst. corpsman supv. Great Onyx Job Corps Nat. Park Svc., Mammoth Cave, Ky., 1972-75, corpsman supv. Great Onyx Job Corps, 1975-84, supt. Tuskegee Inst. (Ala.) Nat. Hist. Site, 1984—, supt. Horshoe Bend Nat. Mil. Pk., Selma to Montgomery Nat. Historic Trail, 1997—. Chmn. adv. coun. Tuskeegee Inst., 1984—. Active Phoenix Consistory # 23, 1978, Rajah Temple # 92, Solomon Commandment # 25. With U.S. Army, 1962—65. Mem.: African Am. Mus. Assn., NAACP (past pres. 1983—84), Ky. Col., Bowling Green Shrine Club (past pres. 1982—83), Ancient Landmark Lodge, Am. Legion, Omega Psi Phi. Democrat. Baptist. Office: National Park Service Tuskegee Inst Nat Hist Site PO Drawer 10 Tuskegee Institute AL 36087-0010

MADIX, ROBERT JAMES, chemical engineer, educator; b. Beach Grove, Ind., June 22, 1938; s. James L. and Marjorie A. (Strohl) M.; children: Bradley Alan, David Eric, Micella Lynn, Evan Scott. BS, U. Ill., 1961; PhD, U. Calif., 1964. NSF postdoctoral fellow Max Planck Inst., Göttingen, Fed. Republic of Germany, 1964-65; asst. prof, chem. engr. Stanford (Calif.) U., 1965-72, assoc. prof., chem. engr., 1972-77; prof. chem. engring. Stanford U., 1977—, chmn., chem. engr., 1983-87, prof. chemistry, 1981—. Cons. Monsanto Chem., St. Louis, 1975-84, Shell Oil Co., Houston, 1985-86; Peter Debye lectureship Cornell U., 1985; Eyring lectr. chemistry Ariz. State U., 1990; Barnett Dodge lectr. Yale U., 1996; disting. prof. lectr. U. Tex., Austin, 1980; Walter Robb Disting. lectr. Penn State U., 1996; chmn. Gordon Rsch. Conf. on Reactions on Surfaces, 1995. Assoc. editor Catalysis Rev., 1986—, Catalysis Letters, 1992—, Rsch. on Chem. Intermediates, 1994—; contbr. articles to profl. jours. Recipient Alpha Chi Sigma award AIChemE, 1990, Paul Emmett award Catalysis Soc. N.Am., 1984, Humboldt U.S. Sr. Scientist prize, 1978; Ford Found. fellow, 1969-72. Mem. AIChE, Internat. Precious Metal Inst. (Henry J. Alber award 1997), Am. Chem. Soc. (Irving Langmuir Disting. Lectr. award 1981, Arthur Adamson award 1997, Am. Phys. Soc., Am. Vacuum Soc., Calif. Catalysis Soc.

MADJID, A. HAMID, retired science educator; b. Tashkent, Russia, Aug. 16, 1922; arrived in US, 1966; s. A. Madjid and Emilia (Madjid) Zabuli; m. Anni Neukomm-Madjid, Dec. 31, 1958; children: Torai, A. Hamid Jr. BA, Cornell U.; DSc, Swiss Fed. Inst. of Tech., Switzerland. Sec., sci. adv. to pres., coord. Afghan scholarships, head indsl. planning Afghan Nat. Bank, Munich, 1948—55; sr. rsch. assoc. The Swiss Fed. Inst. of Tech., Zurich, Switzerland, 1955—66; asst. assoc. prof., dir. thermionic emission lab, co-head of sci. program Pa. State U., U. Park, 1966—90; retired, 1990. Chair various com. Pa. State U., 1977—86. Contbr. articles various profl. jours. Mem. Am. European Swiss Phys. Soc., 1966—90; chair Harris Twp. Planning Commn., Pa., 1982—86; mem. State Coll. Area Sch. Dist. Curriculum Coun., 1987; dir. A.M. Zabuli Charitable Found., 1998, Renaissance Charitable Found., 1999. Mem.: AAAS, Am. Assn. of Naval Engrs., US Holocaust Meml. Mus., Heritage Found., Nat. Rifle Assn. Achievements include research in electron emission from metal, semi conductor and insulator surfaces and the transport and optical properties of such substances; patents for layer structured switching and negative resistance devices; development of methods of involving undergraduate students in basic scientific rsch. Avocation: growing bonsai trees. Home: 326 Harris Dr State College PA 16801 Office Phone: 814-466-7127.

MADLA, FRANK, JR., insurance and real estate broker, state legislator; b. Helotes, Tex. BA in Govt., St. Mary's U., San Antonio, 1959, MA in Govt., 1963. Tchr. Jr. H.S.; home health provider, ins. and real estate broker; mem. Tex. Ho. of Reps., 1973-92, Tex. Senate, 1993—, chair nominations com., mem. intergovtl. rels. com., mem. health and human svcs. com., mem. econ. devel. com., mem. com. of the whole on legis. and congl. redistricting. Part-time instr. Incarnate Word U. Recipient Tex. Medicine's Best Legislator award, Tex. Senate Crime Fighter of the Yr. award, Tex. Police Chiefs Assn.'s Outstanding Legislators award; named Outstanding Legislator of Yr., Tex. Acad. Family Physicians, Legislator of Yr., Am. Subcontractors Assn. Democrat. Office: PO Box 12068 Austin TX 78711-2068 also: 1313 SE Military Dr Ste 101 San Antonio TX 78214-2850

MADLE, ROBERT ALBERT, writer; b. Phila., June 2, 1920; s. Vincent Robert and Mary Virginia (Kidwell) M.; m. Billie Franklin Lindsay, Nov. 7, 1943 (dec. Dec. 1997); children: Robert, Richard, Jane, Mary Anne; m. Ana Lisseth Martinez, Feb. 28, 2002. BS, Drexel U., 1951, MBA, 1953. Asst. to sales mgr. Masland Duraleather, Phila., 1951-53; asst. to dir. indsl. rels. Chadbourne Hosiery, Charlotte, N.C., 1953-54; pers. and credit mgr. Shaw Mfg. Co., Charlotte, 1954-56; pers. rsch. specialist U.S. Army, Washington, 1956-59; rsch. psychologist, program mgr. USN, Washington, 1959-80. Guest speaker sci. fiction confs.; sci. fiction rsch. cons. Paramount Prodns., other film cos.; rsch. cons. projects Yesterday's Tomorrows and Study on Hugo Gernsback, Smithsonian Inst.; developed first survey on science fiction's predictions of atomic energy. Co-author: Science Fiction Fandom, 1994; contbr. articles to sci. fiction and sports mags.; specialist in field of sci. fiction and fantasy lit.; condr. search svcs. rare books in field of sci. fiction and fantasy lit.; cons. editor profl. fantasy mags., including Mag. of Horror, Bizarre Mystery, Startling Mystery, Famous Sci. Fiction. With U.S. Army, 1942-46. Nominated for Hugo, 1956; guest of honor World Sci. Fiction Conv., Miami, 1977, U. Md. Sci. Fiction Conv., 1982, Boston Sci. Fiction Conv., 1996; rep. Am. sci. fiction Brit. Worldcon., 1957. Mem.: Phila. Sci. Fiction Soc. (founding mem.), First Fandom (pres. 1959—82, 1st Fandom Hall of Fame award 1990, E.E. Evans Sci. Fiction Achievement award 1974, Sam Moskowitz Achievement award for sci. fiction collection 2002), Washington Sci. Fiction Assn., Sci. Fiction Writers Am. Achievements include one of largest science fiction and fantasy collections extant. Home: 4406 Bestor Dr Rockville MD 20853-2137 Office Phone: 301-460-4712.

MADLOCK, YVONNE, city health department administrator; m. Lawrence Madlock; 3 children. BS, Wellesley Coll.; MAT, Wesleyan U., Middletown, Conn.; studied, U. Tex. Sch. Pub. Health. Adminstr., bur. personal health svcs. Shelby Co. Divsn. Health Svcs., Memphis, dir., 1995—. Bd. pres. Cmty. Inst. for Early Childhood; bd. dirs. W. Tenn. Area Health Edn. Ctr., Memphis Leadership Inst., Cmty. Found. of Greater Memphis, Shelby Co. Ground Water Quality Control Bd. Mem.: Nat. Assn. City and County Health Officials (bd. dirs.). Office: Shelby Co Divsn Health Svcs 814 Jefferson Ave Memphis TN 38103*

MADNI, ASAD MOHAMED, engineering executive; b. Bombay, Sept. 8, 1947; came to U.S., 1966; s. Mohamed Taher and Sara Taher (Wadiwalla) M.; Gowhartaj Shahnawaz, Nov. 11, 1976; 1 child, Jamal Asad. Gen. cert. edn., U. Cambridge, Eng., 1964; AAS in Electronics, RCA Insts., Inc., 1968; BS in Engring., UCLA, 1969, MS in Engring., 1972; postgrad. exec. inst., Stanford U., 1984; cert. in engring. mgmt., Calif. Inst. Tech., 1987; PhD in Engring., Calif. Coast U., 1987; sr. exec. program, MIT, 1990. chartered engr. Engring. Coun., U.K. Sr. instr. Pacific States U., LA, 1969-71; sr. electronics auditor Pertec Corp., Chatsworth, Calif., 1973-75; project engr., sr. engr., program mgr., dir. advanced programs Microwave divsn. Systron Donner, Van Nuys, Calif., 1975-82, dir. engring., 1982-92; gen. mgr. Microwave and Instrument divsn. Systron Donner, Van Nuys, Calif., 1985-90; chmn., pres., CEO Systron Donner Corp., 1990-92; pres., CEO Sensors and Controls Group BEI Electronics, Inc., 1992-93, BEI Sensors & Sys. Co., 1993—; pres., COO BEI Techs. Inc., 2000—. Vice-chmn. IEEE-MTTS, San Fernando Valley chpt., 1991-92, chmn., 1992-94; tech. advisor Test and Measurement World, Boston, 1982-90; adv. Calif. State U. Northridge; bd. adv. UCLA Mech. and Aerospace Engring. Dept., UCLA WINMEC, UCLA Elec. Engring. Dept., chmn.; mem. adv. bd. UCLA RFID Group; chmn. adv. bd. elec. engring. dept. U. So. Calif. Named George Washington Engr. of Yr., LA Coun. of Engrs. and Scientists, 2003; recipient Joseph F. Engelberger Best Paper award, World Automation Congress, 2000, Disting. Alumni award, Calif. Coast U., 2001, Profl. Achievement award, UCLA, 2002, Disting. Engring. Achievement award, San Fernando Valley Engrs. Coun., 2004. Fellow: AAAS, IEEE (adv. bd. MTT-S San Fernando Valley chpt. 1993—2001, tech. review com. aerospace conf. 1994—, 3d Millennium medal), NY Acad. Scis., Inst. Advancement Engring., Instn. Elec. Engrs. U.K. (chartered elec. engr.); mem.: AIAA (vice chair honors and awards L.A. sect. 2000—01, sr. life mem.), NRA (life), Soc. Automotive Engrs., MIT Soc. Sr. Execs. (life), Assn. Old Crows (life gold cert. of merit 1992), UCLA Engring. Alumni Assn. (life), MIT Alumni Assn. (life), UCLA Alumni Assn. (life), Calif. Rifle and Pistol Assn. (life). Home: 3281 Woodbine St Los Angeles CA 90064-4836 Office: BEI Techs Inc 13100 Telfair Ave Sylmar CA 91342-3576 E-mail: bei1madni@aol.com. *Personal philosophy: There is no substitute for talent and vision complemented by perseverance, dedication and integrity.*

MADONNA, JON C. accounting firm executive; Chmn., CEO KPMG Peat Marwick, N.Y.C.; vice chmn. Travelers Group, N.Y.C., 1997-98; pres., CEO Carlson Wagonlit Travel Worldwide, Plymouth, MA, 1998—. Trustee Kenan Inst. Pvt. Enterprise, U. N.C., Chapel Hill, Fin. Acctg. Found., N.Y.C. Partnership, Lincoln Ctr. Leadership Com.; bd. dirs. INROADS, Inc.; campaign vice chmn. Tri-State chpt. United Way. Mem. Brit.-Am. C. of C. (internat. adv. bd.), N.Y. State Soc. CPAs. Office: Carlson Wagonlit Travel Worldwide 1405 Xenium Ln MS 8214 Plymouth MA 55441

MADONNA, (MADONNA LOUISE VERONICA CICCONE), singer, actress, producer; b. Bay City, Mich., Aug. 16, 1958; d. Sylvio and Madonna Ciccone; m. Sean Penn, Aug. 16, 1985 (div. 1989); m. Guy Ritchie, 2000; 2 children, Lourdes, Rocco. Student, U. Mich., 1976-78. Dancer Alvin Ailey Dance Co., N.Y.C., 1979; CEO Maverick Records, L.A., 1992—. Albums include Madonna, 1983, Like a Virgin, 1985, True Blue, 1986, (soundtrack) Who's That Girl, 1987, (with others) Vision Quest Soundtrack, 1983, You Can Dance, 1987, Like a Prayer, 1989, I'm Breathless: Music From and Inspired by the Film Dick Tracy, 1990, The Immaculate Collection, 1990, Erotica, 1992, Bedtime Stories, 1994, Something to Remember, 1995, (soundtrack) Evita, 1996, Ray of Light, 1998 (Grammy award for Best Pop Album 1999), (with others) Austin Powers, The Spy Who Shagged Me soundtrack, 1999, Music, 2000, GHV2: Greatest Hits Volume II, 2002, American Life, 2003; film appearances include A Certain Sacrifice, 1980, Vision Quest, 1985, Desperately Seeking Susan, 1985, Shanghai Surprise, 1986, Who's That Girl, 1987, Bloodhounds of Broadway, 1989, Dick Tracy, 1990, Shadows and Fog, 1992, Truth or Dare, 1991, Body of Evidence, 1992, A League of Their Own, 1992, Dangerous Game, 1993, Blue in the Face, 1995, Four Rooms, 1996, Girl 6, 1996, Evita, 1996 (Golden Globe, 1997), The Next Best Thing, 2000, Swept Away, 2002; Broadway theater debut in Speed-the-Plow, 1987, stage appearance in Up for Grabs, 2002; TV appearances include Happy Birthday Elizabeth: A Celebration of a Life, 1997, Will & Grace, 2003; author: Sex, 1992, (children's books) The English Roses, 2003, Mr. Peabody's Apples, 2003, Yakov and the Seven Thieves, 2004. Office: 8491 W Sunset Blvd Ste 485 West Hollywood CA 90069-1911*

MADORI, JAN, art gallery director; Founder, CEO Personal Preference Inc., Bolingbrook, Ill., 1979—. Named Illinois/Northwest Indiana Entrepreneur of the Year, Ernst & Young; named to U. Illinois Entrepreneurship Hall of Fame. Office: Personal Preference Inc 800 Remington Blvd Bolingbrook IL 60440-4800

MADORY, RICHARD EUGENE, lawyer; b. Kenton, Ohio, May 14, 1931; s. Harold Richard and Hilda (Strictland) Madory; m. Barbara Jean Madory, Sept. 25, 1955; children: Richard Eugene, Terry Dean, Michael Wesly. BS in Edn., Ohio State, Columbus, 1952; JD, Southwestern U., 1961. Bar: Calif. 1961, U.S. Ct. Mil. Appeals, U.S. Supreme Ct., U.S. Dist. Ct. (ctrl. dist.) Calif. With Madory, Booth, Zell & Pleiss, Santa Ana, Calif., 1962—, now pres., v.p., sec.-treas. Lectr. continuing edn. Bar of State of Calif. Col. USMC. Fellow: Am. Coll. Trial Lawyers; mem.: ABA, Nat. Bd. Trial Advocacy, Am. Bd. Trial Advs., So. Calif. Def. Counsel Assn., LA County Bar Assn., Orange County Bar Assn. Office: Ste 205 17822 17th St Tustin CA 92780-2152 Office Phone: 714-832-3772.

MADOW, LEO, psychiatrist, educator; b. Cleve., Oct. 18, 1915; s. Solomon Martin and Anna (Meyers) Madow; m. Jean Antoinette Weisman, Apr. 16, 1942 (dec.); children: Michael, Robert; m. Barbara N. Young, Dec. 26, 2000. AB, Western Res. U., 1937, MD, 1942; MA, Ohio State U., 1938. Diplomate Am. Bd. Psychiatry and Neurology. Intern Phila. Gen. Hosp., 1942-43; resident Phila. Gen. Hosp., Jefferson Hosp., Inst. Pa. Hosp., 1943-46; practice medicine specializing in psychiatry Phila., 1948—; prof., chmn. dept. neurology Med. Coll. Pa., Phila., 1958-65, prof., chmn. dept. psychiatry and neurology, 1965-70, prof., chmn. dept. psychiatry, 1970-81, clin. prof. psychiatry Hershey Med. Ctr., 1982—; sr. cons. psychiatry Inst. Pa. Hosp., Phila., 1975—. Tng. analyst, past pres. Phila. Psychoanalytic Inst.; past pres., mem. med. staff Inst. Pa. Hosp. Author: Anger, 1972, Love, 1983, Guilt, 1989; editor: Dreams, 1970, Sensory Deprivation, 1970, Psychomimetic Drugs, 1971, Integration of Child Psychiatry with Basic Resident Program, 1975. Served to capt. U.S. Army, 1944—46. Named Outstanding Educator, Am. Med. Coll. Pa., 1972. Fellow: ACP, Am. Coll. Psychoanalysts (pres. 1989—90, Laughlin award 1990), Am. Coll. Psychiatrists, Am. Psychiat. Assn. (life), Phila. Psychiat. Soc. (past pres., Lifetime Achievement award 1991); mem.: Phila. Psychoanalytic Soc. (past pres.), Am. Neurol. Assn., Am. Psychoanalytic Assn., Phi Soc., Alpha Omega Alpha. Home and Office: 2401 Pennsylvania Ave Philadelphia PA 19130 Office Phone: 215-235-5253. Personal E-mail: leomadow@aol.com.

MADRAS, BERTHA KALIFON, neuroscientist, educator, consultant; b. Montreal, Quebec, Canada, Dec. 9, 1942; m. Peter Madras, June 21, 1964; children: Cynthia Gumbert, Claudine D. BSc, McGill U., 1963, PhD, 1967. Postdoctoral fellow Tufts U., Boston, 1966-67; postdoctoral fellow rsch. assoc. MIT, Cambridge, 1967-69, 72-74; asst. prof. U. Toronto, 1979—80, Harvard Med. Sch., Boston, 1986-90, assoc. prof., 1990-99, prof., 1999—, assoc. dir. pub. edn. divsn. addictions, 1998—. Sci. adv. com. Brookhaven Nat. Lab., Upton, N.Y., 1998—; rev. com., cons. Nat. Inst. Drug Abuse, chair B study sect., 1998-99; MDCN-5 MNPS rev. com.; cons. Ont. Mental Health Found., 1984-90, chmn. fellowships and awards com., 1988-90; chmn. radiation safety Harvard U., 1995-99, acting dir. Primate Ctr., 1998-99; chmn. faculty affairs Harvard Med. Sch.; mem. Dana Alliance for Brain Initiatives. Author: (book chpt.) Dopamine, 1984; editor: Neurosci.; mem. editl. bd. Synapse, 1991-2004; contbr. articles to profl. jours. Sci. fair judge. Recipient Rsch. grants Nat. Inst. Drug Abuse, 1992—, 94—, Sci. Edn. Partnership award grant, 1992-94, Parkinson's Disease Found., 1990-91, Nat. Inst. Neurol. Disease and Stroke, 1994, 99—, NIMH, Dana Alliance for Brain Initiatives, Merit award NIH, Sr. Scientist award. Mem. Soc. for Neuroscience, Coll. Probs. Drug Dependence. Achievements include development of a marker for Parkinson's disease and attention deficit hyperactivity disorder, a probe for cocaine binding sites in brain; developed a PET imaging SPECT for living brain; developed a PET and SPECT imaging drug to monitor Parkinsonism in brain; rsch. in how drugs work in brain; co-developer of CD-ROM on how drugs affect brain. Office: Harvard Medical Sch 1 Pine Hill Rd Southborough MA 01772-1312 E-mail: bertha-madras@hms.harvard.edu.

MADRICK, JEFFREY G. writer, editor, economic consultant; b. N.Y.C., July 15, 1947; s. Milton and Corazon (De Arego) M.; m. Gloria Jean Adrian, June 29, 1969 (div. 1975); 1 child, Matina. BS salutatorian, NYU, 1969; MBA, Harvard U., 1971. Writer, columnist Money Mag., N.Y.C., 1972-75; fin. editor, columnist Bus. Week, N.Y.C., 1975-78; exec. asst. to pres. Columbia Pictures, N.Y.C., 1979-80; writer, cons. N.Y.C., 1980-82; TV corr., commentator ESPN, N.Y.C., 1982-85, NBC News, N.Y.C., 1985-93; writer N.Y.C., 1993—; contbr. columnist New York Times, 2000—. Adj. prof. social sci. Cooper Union, N.Y.; sr. fellow World Policy Inst., N.Y.; fellow Shorenstein Ctr. for Peace, Politics and Policy, Harvard U.; NASDAQ vis. prof. New Sch. U. Author: Taking America, 1987 (Bus. Week award 1987), The End of Affluence, 1995 (N.Y. Times Notable Book award), Why Economies Grow, 2002; editor Challenge mag., 1996-. Recipient Emmy award, 1986, Page One award Newspaper Guild, 1979. Mem. Beta Gamma Sigma.

MADRID, DON, electronics executive; CFO Fry's Electronics, San Jose, Calif. Office: Fry's Electronics 600 E Brokaw Rd San Jose CA 95112-1006

MADRID, OLGA HILDA GONZALEZ, retired elementary education educator, associate executive; b. San Antonio, May 4, 1928; d. Victor A. and Elvira Ardilla Gonzalez; m. Sam Madrid, Jr., June 29, 1952; children: Ninette Marie, Samuel James. Student, U. Mex., San Antonio, St. Mary's U.; BA, Our Lady of Lake U., 1956, MEd, 1963. Cert. bilingual tchr., adminstr., Tex. Sec. Lanier HS San Antonio Ind. Sch. Dist., San Antonio, 1945-52; tchr. Collins Garden Elem. Sch., Storm Elem. Sch., San Antonio Ind. Sch. Dist., San Antonio, 1963-92; tutor Dayton, Ohio, 1952-54. Bd. dir., sch. rep. San Antonio Tchr. Coun., 1970-90; chair various coms. Collins Garden Elem., 1970-92. Elected dep. precinct, senatorial and state Dem. Conv., San Antonio, 1968—; apptd. commr. Keep San Antonio Beautiful, 1985; life mem., past pres. San Antonio YWCA; bd. dir. Luth. Gen. Hosp., Nat. Conf. Christians and Jews, Cath. Family and Children's Svc., St. Luke's Luth. Hosp.; nat. bd. dir. YWCA, 1985-96, also mem. exec. com.; mem. edn. commn. Holy Rosary Parish, 1994—; mem. bus. assoc. com. Our Lady of the Lake U., 1995—. Recipient Outstanding Our Lady Lake Alumni award Our Lady Lake U., 1975, Guadalupana medal San Antonio Cath. Archdiocese, 1975, Yellow Rose Tex. citation Gov. Briscoe, 1977; Olga H. Madrid Ctr. named in her honor, YWCA San Antonio and San Antonio City Coun., 1983; Lo Mejor De Lo Nuestro honoree San Antonio Light, 1991, honoree San Antonio Women's History Month Coalition, 1996; named Our Lady of Lake Outstanding Alumna, 1999, one of five women honored for promoting literacy and cultural hertiage with a sch. wall mural titled "Mis Palabras, Mi Poder", 2002. Mem. San Antonio Bus. and Profl. Women, Inc. (mem. exec. com.), Salute Quality Edn. (honoree 1993), Delta Kappa Gamma (Theta Beta chpt., mem. exec. com.). Avocations: reading, gardening. Home: 2726 Benrus Blvd San Antonio TX 78228-2319

MADRID, PATRICIA A. state attorney general; BA in English and Philosophy, U. N.Mex., 1969, JD, 1973; cert., Nat. Jud. Coll., U. Nev., 1978. Bar: N.Mex. N.Mex. State Dist. Judge, 1978—84; atty. gen. State of N.Mex., 1999—. Named Latina Atty. of Yr., Nat. Hispanic Bar Assn., 2001. Democrat. Office: Atty Gens Office PO Drawer 1508 Santa Fe NM 87504-1508

MADSEN, BARBARA A, state supreme court justice; BA, U. Wash., 1974; JD, Gonzaga U., 1977. Pub. defender King and Snohomish Counties, 1977—82; staff atty. Seattle City Atty.'s Office, 1982—84, spl. prosecutor, 1984—88; judge Seattle Mcpl. Ct., 1988—92; justice Washington Supreme Ct., Olympia, 1993—. Office: Wash Supreme Ct PO Box 40929 Olympia WA 98504-0929

MADSEN, DOROTHY LOUISE (MEG MADSEN), writer; b. Rochester, N.Y. d. Charles Robert and Louise Anna Agnes Meyer; m. Frederick George Madsen, Feb. 17, 1945 (dec.). BA, Mundelein Coll., Chgo., 1978; grad., US Army Command and Genl. Staff Coll., 1960. Feature writer Gannett Newspapers, Rochester Democrat & Chronicle, 1937—41; pub. rels. rep. Rochester Tel. Corp., 1941-42; exec. dir. LaPorte (Ind.) chpt. ARC, 1964; dir. adminstrv. svcs. Bank Mktg. Assn., Chgo., 1971-74; exec. dir. Eleanor Women's Found., Chgo., 1974-84; founder Meg Madsen Assocs., Chgo., 1984-88, women's career counselor; founder Clearinghouse Internat. Newsletter, Eleanor Women's Forum, Clearinghouse Internat., Eleanor Intern Program Coll. Students and Returning Women, Radiotelephone and Teletype Conf. Ctr. Chief global radiotelephone and radioteletype top secret encrypted conf. ctr. War dept. Staff Pentagon, Washington, 1944—46; conf. aide to Pres. Harry S Truman, Washington, 1945. Lt. col. WAC, 1942-47, 67-70. Decorated Legion of Merit, Meritorious Svc. award. Mem.: Res. Officers Assn. (life), Mundelein Alumnae Assn., Ret. Officers Assn. (life), Phi Sigma Tau (charter mem. Ill. Kappa chpt.). Achievements include Aide to Pres. Truman during Sigsaly encoded phone conf. with Prime Min. Winston Churchill and U.S. Joint Chiefs Staff concerning terms of German surrender, WWII, Apr. 25, 1945. Home and Office: 1030 N State St Apt 25H Chicago IL 60610-2831

MADSEN, GEORGE FRANK, lawyer; b. Sioux City, Iowa, Mar. 24, 1933; s. Frank O. and Agnes (Cuhel) M.; m. Magnhild Norstog; 1 child, Michelle Marie. BA, St. Olaf Coll., 1954; LLB, Harvard U., 1959. Bar: Ohio 1960, Iowa 1961, U.S. Dist. Ct. (no. and so. dists.) Iowa, U.S. Ct. Appeals (8th cir.), U.S. Supreme Ct. 1991. Trainee Cargill, Inc., Mpls., 1954; assoc. Durfey, Martin, Browne & Hull, Springfield, Ohio, 1959-61; assoc., then ptnr. Shull, Marshall & Marks, Sioux City, 1961-85; ptnr. Marks & Madsen, Sioux City, 1985-97, Marks, Madsen & Hirschbach, Sioux City, 1998-99, Mayne, Marks, Madsen & Hirschbach, LLP, Sioux City, 1999-2001. Author, editor: Iowa Title Opinions and Standards, 1978; contbg. author: The American Law of Real Property, 1991. Sec., bd.dirs. Sioux City Boys Club, 1969-76; mem. Sioux City Zoning Bd. Adjustment, 1963-65; active Iowa Mo. River Preservation and Land Use Authority, 1992-2001, pres., 1997-2001. Lt. USAF, 1954-56. Fellow Iowa State Bar Found.; mem. ABA, Iowa Bar Assn., Woodbury County Bar Assn., Nat. Wildlife Assn., Mont. Wildlife Assn., Pheasants Forever, Phi Beta Kappa (past pres. Siouxland chpt.), Rotary Internat. Avocations: skiing, hunting, swimming, reading. Office: PO Box 3661 Sioux City IA 51102-3661

MADSEN, H(ENRY) STEPHEN, retired lawyer; b. Momence, Ill., Feb. 5, 1924; s. Frederick and Christine (Landgren) Madsen; m. Carol Ruth Olmstead, Dec. 30, 1967; children: Stephen Stewart, Christie Morgan, Kelly Ann. MBA, U. Chgo., 1948; LLB, Yale U., 1951. Bar: Wash. 1951, Ohio 1953, U.S. Supreme Ct. 1975. Rsch. asst. Wash. Water Power Co., Spokane, 1951; assoc. Baker, Hostetler & Paterson, Cleve., 1952-59, ptnr., 1960-88, sr. ptnr., 1989-92; ret., 1992. Danish consul for Ohio, 1973—98. Active Bus. Advisers Cleve.; trustee Ohio Presbyn. Ret. Svcs. With AC U.S. Army, 1943—46. Decorated Knight Queen of Denmark. Fellow: ABA (life); mem.: Cleve. Bar Assn., Am. Law Inst., Am. Coll. Trial Lawyers (life), Country Club Cleve.

MADSEN, LIBBE HURVITZ, clinical social worker; d. Nathan and Faye Avrunin Hurvitz; m. Loren Wakefield Madsen, June 30, 1968; children: Anne Lea, Nora Karin. MSW, UCLA, 1977. Certified Social Worker NY, 1978. Dir. staff devel., trauma ctr. Jewish Bd. Family Children's Svcs., N.Y.C., 1999—. Adj. assoc. prof. NYU Sch. Social Work, N.Y.C., NY, 1991—2001. Office: Jewish Bd Family & Children's Svcs 120 W 57 St New York NY 10019 E-mail: lmadsen@jbfcs.org.

MADSEN, LOREN WAKEFIELD, sculptor; b. Oakland, Calif., Mar. 29, 1943; s. Roy Sondergaard and Kathryn O. (Finerty) M.; m. Libbe Hurvitz, June 30, 1968; children: Anne Lea, Nora Karin. Student, Reed Coll., Portland, 1961-63; BA, UCLA, 1966, MA, 1970. One-man shows include Riko Mizuno Gallery, L.A., 1973, 74, McKee Gallery, N.Y.C., 1976, 77, 82, 84, 86, 90, 92, 96, 98, L.A. Louver Gallery, Venice, Calif., 1976, 78, Hansen Fuller Goldeen Gallery, San Francisco, 1980, Wright State U., Dayton, 1980, U. Mass., 1981, Cheryl Haines Gallery, San Francisco, 1991, Art First Gallery, London, 1998, Mus. Contemporary Art, San Diego, 2000; group shows include Los Angeles County Mus. Art, 1974, 76, 83, Hayward Gallery, London, 1975, Walker Art Ctr., Mpls., 1976, Biennale of Sculpture, Sydney, Australia, 1976, Ft. Worth Mus. Art, 1977, Joslyn Art Mus., Omaha, 1979, Hirshhorn Mus., Washington, 1979, Newport Harbor Art Mus., 1982, Freedman Gallery, Albright Coll., 1987, Art First Gallery, London, 1998, SUNY, Stony Brook, 1999, Drury Coll., Mo., 1999, MCA, San Diego, 2000, others. Nat. Endowment for Arts grantee, 1975-76, 1980-81, 87-88; Pollock-Krasner grantee, 2004. Office: 426 Broome St New York NY 10013-3251 E-mail: lmadsen@bellatlantic.net.

MADSEN, MICHAEL, actor; b. Chicago, IL, Sept. 25, 1959; m. Jeannine Bisignano; 1 child, Christian. Films include: Wargames, 1983, The Natural, 1984, Racing with the Moon, 1984, The Killing Time, 1987, Shadows in the Storm, 1988, Iguana, 1988, Blood Red, 1989, Kill Me Again, 1990, The Doors, 1991, The End of Innocence, 1991, Thelma and Louise, 1991, Fatal Instinct, 1992, Inside Edge, 1992, Reservoir Dogs, 1992, Straight Talk, 1992, Almost Blue, 1992, Free Willy, 1993, A House in the Hills, 1993, Money for Nothing, 1993, Trouble Bound, 1993, Wyatt Earp, 1993, The Getaway, 1994, Dead Connection, 1994, Species, 1995, Free Willy II: The Adventure Home, 1995, The Winner, 1996, Red Line, 1996, Mullholland Falls, 1996, Man With a Gun, 1996, The Last Days of Frankie the Fly, 1996, Rough Draft, 1997, The Maker, 1997, Donnie Brasco, 1997, Catherine's Grove, 1997, Papertrail, 1997, The Girl Gets Moe, 1997, Executive Target, 1997, The Thief and the Stripper, 1998, Supreme Sanction, 1998, The Florentine, 1998, Species II, 1998, Fait Accompli, 1998, The Thief & the Stripper, 1998, Flat Out, 1998, Ballad of the Nightingale, 1998, The Florentine, 1999, Detour, 1999, The Stray, 1999, Luck of the Draw, 2002, The Alternate, 2000, The Price of Air, 2000, Love.com, 2000, Ides of March, 2000, The Ghost, 2000, Fall, 2000, Choke, 2000, Bad Guys, 2000, Extreme Honor, 2001, Pressure Point, 2001, Outlaw, 2001, L.A.P.D.: To Protect and to Serve, 2001, Die Another Day, 2002, Welcome to America, 2002, The Real Deal, 2002, Where's Angelo, 2003, My Boss's Daughter, 2003, Kill Bill: Vol. 1, 2003, Vampires Anonymous, 2003, Hunt for the Devil, 2003, Blueberry, 2004, Kill Bill: Vol. 2, 2004; TV movies include: Special Bulletin, 1983, War and Remembrance, 1988, Montana, 1990, Baby Snatcher, 1992, Beyond the Law, 1994; TV series include: Our Family Honor, 1985-86, Vengeance Unlimited, 1998. also: CAA Michael Manchal 9830 Wilshire Blvd Beverly Hills CA 90212-1804

MADSEN, RICHARD PAUL, sociology educator, writer; b. Alameda, Calif., Apr. 2, 1941; s. Harold Paul Madsen and Gazella Marie Matjasic; m. Judith Ann Rosselli, Jan. 12, 1974; 1 child, Susan Sooyoung. BA, Maryknoll Coll., 1963; MTh, Maryknoll Sem., 1968; PhD, Harvard U., 1977. Cath. priest Maryknoll Fathers, Taiwan, 1968—73; lectr. Harvard U., Cambridge, Mass., 1977—78; prof. U. of Calif. - San Diego, La Jolla, 1978—. Bd. dirs. U.S. Cath. China Bur., South Orange, NJ; editl. bd. Jour. of Critical Asian Studies, London, 1998—, Jour. of Contemporary China, London, 1995—; asst. editor Jour. of Asian Studies, Ann Arbor, Mich., 1987—90. Co-author: (nonfiction book) Chen Village, 1984; author: Morality and Power in a Chinese Village, 1984 (C. Wright Mills award, 1986); co-author: Habits of the Heart, 1985 (L.A. Times Book award, 1986, Pulitzer Prize jury nominee, 1986); co-editor: Unofficial China, 1989; co-author: The Good Society, 1991; author: China and the American Dream, 1995, China's Catholics, 1998; co-editor: Meaning and Modernity, 2002, Popular China, 2002, The Many and the One: Perspectives on Ethical Pluralism, 2003. Bd. dirs. U. City Found. for Pub. Schs., San Diego, Burke Lectureship on Religion and Soc., La Jolla, Calif., 1993. Named Hume Lectr., Yale U., 1997; grantee, Ford Found., 1980—84, NEH, 1987—89, SSRC, 1987—89, Luce Found., 1992—95. Mem.: Assn. for Asian Studies (China and Inner Asia coun. rep. 1988), Am. Sociol. Assn. Democrat. Roman Catholic. Office: U Calif - San Diego Dept of Sociology 9500 Gilman Dr La Jolla CA 92093-0533 Personal E-mail: rmadsen@ucsd.edu. Business E-Mail: rmadsen@ucsd.edu.

MADSEN, ROY I., JR., language educator; b. L.A., Jan. 12, 1940; s. Roy I and Beulah Lee Madsen; m. Linda Sue Madsen, July 10, 1966; 1 child, Laura Danielle. BA French, U of Redlands, Redlands, CA, 1961; MA French, Middlebury Coll., Middlebury, VT, 1963; PhD French, UCLA, Los Angeles, Ca., 1978; studied flute with, Jean-Perre Rampal. Cert. sec. and CC tchr., lang. devel. specialist. Tchr.-French Palmer Twp. Elem. Sch., Easton, Pa., 1961—62; French/Latin tchr. Chatsworth HS, L.A., 1963—65; French tchg. asst. UCLA, 1965—66; asst. prof.-French Oakland U, Rochester, Mich., 1970—73; asst. prof. -French Cal. State Coll., San Bernardino, Calif., 1973—76; instr. French San Bernardino C.C., Calif., 1977—78, Monterey C.C., 1986, 1988; entrepreneur fin. svcs. AL Williams, Mapbook, Calif., Oreg., and Wash., 1984—87; tchr. French Santa Catalina Sch., Monterey, Calif., 1980—86; French/world his. tchr. Salinas HS, Salinas, Calif., 1987—2003. Creator self-paced French program Calif. State Coll.; workshop dir. French Advanced Placement, 1985. Active ACLU, 1999—, Human Rights Watch, 1999—, Alliance Francaise of Monterey County, 1980—; VP Walton Housing Homeowners Assoc., Rochester, Mich., 1970—73; flutist Orch. Soc. Westchester; Bd. dirs. San Bernardino Symphony, Calif., 1975—76. Recipient first place in tchr. placement exam, Los Angeles City Sch., 1963. Mem.: NAACP, NEA, Calif. Lang. Tchr. Assoc., Fgn. Lang. Assoc. Monterey County (charter mem, v.p., pres.), Fgn. Lang. Assoc. North Calif., Am. Fedn. of Tchr., Am. Assoc. Tchrs. French, Am. Soc. for Eighteenth-Century Studies, So. Poverty Law Ctr. Avocations: flute, tennis. Home: 3108 Fehring Place Marina CA 93933

MADSEN, STEPHEN STEWART, lawyer; b. Spokane, Wash., Oct. 13, 1951; s. H. Stephen Madsen and Sarah Pope (Stewart) Ruth; m. Rebecca Wetherill Howard, July 28, 1984; children: Stephen Stewart Jr., Lawrence Washington, Christina Wetherill, Benton Howard. BA, Harvard U., 1973; JD, Columbia U., 1980. Bar: N.Y. 1981, U.S. Dist. Ct. (so. dist.) N.Y. 1981, U.S. Ct. Appeals (6th cir.) 1983, U.S. Ct. Appeals (8th cir.) 1985, U.S. Ct. Appeals (2d, 7th and D.C. cirs.) 1994, U.S. Supreme Ct. 1996. Law clk. to presiding judge U.S. Ct. Appeals 2d cir., N.Y.C., 1980-81; assoc. Cravath, Swaine & Moore, N.Y.C., 1981-88, ptnr., 1988—. Bd. vis. Columbia U. Sch. Law, 1991—; bd. govs. Hill-Stead Mus., 1995-2002; mem. vestry St. Bartholomew's Ch., 1995-2004; bd. trustees La Scuola d'Italia, 2004—. Mem. ABA, N.Y. State Bar Assn. (exec. com. antitrust law sect. 1998—), New York County Lawyers Assn., London Ct. Internat. Arbitration, Fedn. Bar Coun. Office: Cravath Swaine & Moore LLP Worldwide Pla 825 8th Ave Fl 38 New York NY 10019-7475 Office Phone: 212-474-1886.

MADSEN, SUSAN ARRINGTON, writer; b. Logan, Utah, Aug. 25, 1954; d. Leonard J. and Grace F. Arrington; m. Dean Madsen, Aug. 20, 1974; children: Emily, Rebecca, Sarah, Rachel. BS in Journalism, Utah State U., 1975. Mem. adj. faculty Logan Latter-day Saints Inst. Religion, 1991-95. Author: Christmas: A Joyful Heritage, 1984, The Lord Needs a Prophet, 1990, I Walked to Zion: True Stories of Young Pioneers on the Mormon Trail, 1994, Growing Up in Zion: True Stories of Young Pioneers Building the Kingdom, 1996, The Second Rescue: The Story of the Spiritual Rescue of the Willie and Martin Handcart Pioneers, 1998, (with Leonard J. Arrington) Sunbonnet Sisters: True Stories of Mormon Women and Frontier Life, 1984, Mothers of the Prophets, 1987; contbr. numerous articles to Collier's Ency. Yearbooks. Chair Hyde Pk. (Utah) Bd. Adjustments, 1985-94. Honoree Utah State U. Nat. Women's History Week, 1985; recipient Cmty. Svc. award Nat. Daus. Utah Pioneers, 1990. Mem. Lds Ch. Avocations: horseback riding, skiing, genealogy, family activities.

MADSON, DAVID JOHN, fundraising executive; b. Mpls., 1955; s. John Richard and K. Rae Madson; m. Helen M. DeMichiel; children: Antonia, Nathan. BS in Comm. magna cum laude, U. Minn., Mpls., 1979. Advanced cert. fund raiser exec. Assoc. dir. devel. Film in the Cities, St. Paul, 1981-84; assoc. devel. officer propsect rsch. U. Minn. Found., 1985-86; chief devel. officer Coll. Edn. U. Minn., Mpls., 1987-93, chief devel. officer Cancer Ctr., 1993-95; dir. devel. Sch. Nursing U. Calif., San Francisco, 1995-98, dir. devel. Sch. Dentistry, 1998-00, sr. regional devel. dir. univ. rels. Berkeley, 2000—02, dir. devel. neurosci. San Francisco, 2002—. Adv. panels Minn. State Arts Bd., St. Paul, 1993-95, Nat. Endowment Arts, Washington, 1991, 93-94; panelist photography fellowships Minn. State Arts Bd., 1985, NEA, 1994; panelist

McKnight Found./Mpls. Arts Commn., 1986-88; media grants rev. panelist Minn. Humanities Commn., 1991; program com. Minn. Coun. on Planned Giving Conf., 1992. Treas. Univ. Film Soc., Mpls., 1981-84, 89-95, KFAI Cmty. Radio, Mpls., 1989-92; pres. Seward Cmty. Coop., Mpls., 1993-95, United Cerebral Palsy, San Francisco, 1996-99, Red Eye Collaboration Theater, Mpls., 1986-91; bd. dirs. Lowertown Cmty. Coun., 1981-83, Palace Theater Co., 1982-84, So. Theater, 1986-89, Minn. Span Assn., 1988-93; arts adv. com. City of St. Paul Planning Dept., 1982-84; mem. Chain of Lakes planning com. City of Mpls. Park Bd., 1989; bd. dirs. Powderhorn Cmty. Coun., 1985-90, treas., 1986-88; co-founder, treas. Lowertown Lofts Artist Housing Coop., 1982-90; facilities com. Minn. chpt. Am. Youth Hostels, 1990-93; devel. com. Headwaters Fund, 1990-93, sec. Film in the Cities, 1993-95; pres. Berkeley Montessori Sch., 1998-2000; bd. dirs., pres. Friends of Photography, Ansel Adams Ctr., San Francisco, 1999-2002; bd. dirs. Golden Gate Coun. Am. Youth Hostels, 2002—, Mechanics' Inst. Libr., 1999—, Berkeley Pub. Libr. Found., 2002—; bd. dirs. Hasteling Internat. USA, 2003—. Mem. Assn. Fundraising Profls. (v.p. Golden Gate chpt. 1996-99, bd. dirs. Minn. chpt. 1993-95, v.p. external affairs 1999-2001, nat. govt. rels. com. 2000—, nat. edn. com. 2001—), U. Minn. Alumni Assn. (nat. bd. 1996-2002, pres. San Francisco charter 1995-98). Avocations: cross country skiing, bicycling. Office: U Calif San Francisco Box 0248 San Francisco CA 94143-0248 E-mail: dmadson@support.ucsf.edu.

MADSON, PHILIP WARD, engineering executive, consultant; b. Atlantic, Iowa, Aug. 27, 1948; s. Philip Ward and Pearl Elaine (Thomson) M.; m. Maria Concepcion Casamitjana, Aug. 11, 1968; children: Peter Wesley, David Philip. BSChemE, Iowa State U., 1969, MSChemE, 1970. Registered profl. engr., Ohio. Process engr. Procter & Gamble, Cin., 1971-74, tech. brand mgr., 1974-76, sect. head, 1976-77, assoc. dir., 1977-79; cons. engr. Raphael Katzen Assocs., Cin., 1979-84, v.p., 1984-90, sr. v.p. tech. and mktg., 1990-92, pres., 1993-98; pres., CEO, COO Katzen Internat., Inc., Cin., 1999—. Guest lectr. Alltech's Annual Internat. Short Course, 1983—. Chmn. Police/Community Rels. Com. Kennedy Heights, 1978-84; chmn. media response team S.W. Ohio Sportsmen's Assn., 1990—; chmn. pub. rels. com. Firearms Facts Com., 1991—; founder, chmn. Kennedy Heights Concerned Citizens, Cin., 1979-85; mem. exec. bd. dirs. Kennedy Heights Community Coun., 1979-84. Recipient Spl. award Kennedy Heights Community Coun., 1984, Recognition Hamilton County Crime Prevention Assn., 1983, Ky. Col. Fellow Am. Inst. Chemists; mem. AIChE, Tech. Assn. Pulp and Paper Industry, New Uses Coun., Clean Fuels Devel. Coalition (chmn. mem. com. 1999—), Am. Chem. Soc., Internat. Inst. of Distillers (founding bd. dirs., v.p.), Internat. Exec. Svc. Corp. Avocations: music, hunting, target shooting. Home: 3749 Davenant Ave Cincinnati OH 45213-2218 Office: Katzen Internat Inc 2300 Wall St Ste K Cincinnati OH 45212-2789 E-mail: madson@katzen.com.

MADU, LEONARD EKWUGHA, lawyer, human rights advocate, columnist; b. Ibadan, Nigeria, Mar. 17, 1953; came to U.S., 1977; s. Luke E. and Grace (Dureke) M.; m. Jaculine Stephanie Turner, June 4, 1980; children: Christine, Oscar. BA, Marshall U., 1980; JD, U. Tenn., 1988; MA, Am. U. Rsch. assoc. Lamberts Publs., Washington, 1980-82; data specialist Govt. Employees Ins. Co., Washington, 1982-85; law intern Knoxville (Tenn.) Urban League, 1986-88; cons. Morris Brown Coll., Atlanta, 1988; staff atty. East Carolina Legal Svc., Wilson, N.C., 1989-90; cons. youth devel. Nat. Crime Prevention Coun., Washington, 1990; contract compliance officer Walters State C.C., Morristown, Tenn., 1990; examiner Dept. of Human Svc., Nashville, 1990-93; human rights officer Human Rights Commn., Nashville, 1993—; pres. Panafrica, Nashville, 1994—; CEO Madu and Assoc. Internat. Bus. Cons., 1996—; with Bus. Forum & Banquet, 1994—; 1st v.p. Nashville Multicultural Partnership, Inc., 2000—. Polit. cons. Embassy of Nigeria, Washington, 1995; cons. Embassy of Sierra Leone, Washington, 1995, Healthcare Internat. Mgmt. Co., 1996-2001, Embassy of Mozambique, 2000-01, Embassy of Togo, 2001—; bd. dirs. Peace and Justice Ctr., Nashville; pres. African Conglomerates Internat., Inc. Editor: African Nations Handbook, 1994, Directory of African Universities and Colleges, 1994; editor-in-chief Panafrican Digest, 1994, Panafrican Jour. of World Affairs, 1994; columnist Met. Times, Nashville, 1991—, The African Herald, Dallas, 1995—, U.S./African Voice, Balt., 1995—, African Sun Times, 1995—, The Nigerian and African, 1995—, The African Press, N.Y. Co-chmn. Clergy and Laity Concerned, Nashville, 1992-95; mem. curriculum and character com. Met. Sch. Bd., Nashville, 1994-97; co-coordinator The Haitian Project, 1991-94; vice-chmn. Nigerian Network Leadership awards N.Y., 1996; chmn. Internat. Women's Expo, Knoxville, 1996; co-chair Miss Nigeria Internat. Beauty Pageant, Washington, 1995, Miss Africa Internat. Beauty Pageant, Nashville, 1996, Igbo Union Chieftaincy Coronation Ceremony, Nashville, 1995; chmn. Nigerian Patriotic Front, 1997—; coord. United Nigeria Congress Party, 1997-98, Southeast U.S.; recruiter internat. students Tenn. State U., 1998-99; chmn. bd. dirs. Africa Found., Washington, 2001—2002. Recipient World Hunger Devel. Program award Marshall U., 1978-79, Hall of Nations scholar Am. U., 1980, 82, Mary Strohbel award United Way, 1994-95, Non-profit Vol. award Nat. Conf. of Christians and Jews, 1994. Mem. NAACP, U.S. Com. on Fgn. Rels., Soc. Profl. Journalists, UN Assn., Orgn. African Natonals (pres. 1994), African C. of C. (pres. 2000—). Avocations: reading, travel, soccer, ping-pong, tennis. Office: Panafrica 1016 18th Ave S Nashville TN 37212-2105

MADUKA, CHIKEZIE, journalist; b. Umuahia, Abia, Nigeria, Apr. 25, 1963; arrived in U.S., 1993; s. Frank Chijioke and Comfort Ehichanya Maduka; m. Ngozi Nwanyisunday Enwere, Mar. 15, 1988; children: Chikerenma, Chibuisi, Chinomnso, Chijiaku, Chiamaka. BA in Journalism, St. Petersburg State U., Russia, 1989; MA in Internat. Journalism, MA in Russian Lang., St. Petersburg State U., 1991; Rsch. Cert., St. Petersburg Humanitarian U., 1993. Pres. Chyke Dimensions Inc., Landover, Md., 2000—, Chykes Gift Gallery, Landover, 2000—. Author: International Information Relations in the New Millennium: Interrelationship with the Common Heritage of Mankind, 2001. Gen. sec. Prince George's Head Start Policy Coun., Prince George's, Md., 1996, 1997—98, Judge Sylvannia Woods Sch. PTA, Glenarden, Md., 2002—. Avocations: photography, travel, reading, sports. Home: 2416 Greeley Pl Landover MD 20785

MADURA, JAMES ANTHONY, surgical educator; b. Campbell, Ohio, June 10, 1938; s. Anthony Peter and Margaret Ethel (Sebest) M.; m. Loretta Jayne Sovak, Aug. 8, 1959; children: Debra Jean, James Anthony II, Vikki Sue. BA, Cogate U., 1959; MD, Western Res. U., 1963. Diplomate Am. Bd. Surgery. Intern in surgery Ohio State U., Columbus, 1963—64, resident in surgery, 1966—71; asst. prof. surgery Ind. U., Indpls., 1971—76, assoc. prof. surgery, 1976—80, prof. surgery, 1980—, J.S. Battersby prof. surgery, 2001—. Dir. gen. surgery Ind. U. Sch. Medicine, Indpls., 1985—, vice-chmn., 1985—. Contbr. articles to profl. jours. Capt. U.S. Army, 1964-66, Vietnam. Fellow Am. Coll. Surgeons; mem. Cen. Surg. Assn., Western Surg. Assn., Soc. Surgery Alimentary Tract, Midwest Surg. Assn., Internat. Biliary Assn., Acad. Surgeons, The Columbia Club. Republican. Roman Catholic. Home: 9525 Copley Dr Indianapolis IN 46260-1422 Personal E-mail: jmadura1@comcast.net. Business E-Mail: jmadura@iupui.edu.

MADURGA, GONZALO F. artistic director, actor, singer; b. Havana, Cuba, Jan. 21, 1932; arrived in U.S., 1953; s. Bernabé Madurga and Matilda Barrena. MS, L.I. U., 1977. Cert. bilingual tchr., NY. Artistic dir. Counterpoint Theatre, N.Y.C., 1972-75, Operatic, Concert & Theatre Artists, Inc., Miami, Fla., 1996—. Acting appearances include Carmelina, N.Y.C., 1979, La Verbena de la Paloma, Queens, NY, 1985 (Best Actor, Assn. Cronistas de Espectaculos 1985), Romeo and Juliet, NYC, 1994, Coimbra, Miami, 1994 (Best Actor Assn. Críticos y Cronistas de las Artes 1994), The Fantasticks, Miami, 1996, Macbeth, NY, 1997, The Merchant of Venice, 1997, NY, Drama, Death and the Maiden, Coconut Grove, Fla., 1999, Praying with the Enemy, Coconut Grove, 2000, Hamlet, Fla., 2000, Anna in the Tropics, Fla., 2000, The Man of La Mancha, NJ, The Most Happy Fella. With U.S. Army, infantry, 1956-58. Mem. Actors' Equity, Screen Actors' Guild, Am. Fed. T.V. Radio Artists, Nat. Acad. T.V. & Sciences, Home and Office: Operatic Concert & Theatre Artists Inc 1315 SW 21st St Miami FL 33145 Fax: (305) 858-0365. E-mail: gonzalomadurga@msn.com.

MADUROS, JOHN, real estate company executive; BS in Acctg., No. Ill. U. CFO The Shidler Group, Shamrock Co.; sr. v.p., chief acctg. officer HSA Comml. Real Estate, Chgo., 2001—04, exec. v.p., CFO, 2004—. Office: HSA Comml Ste 500 180 N Wacker Dr Chicago IL 60606*

MADVA, STEPHEN ALAN, lawyer; b. Pitts., July 27, 1948; s. Joseph Edward and Mary (Zulick) M.; children: Alexander, Elizabeth. BA cum laude, Yale U., 1970; JD, U. Pa., 1973. Bar: Pa. 1973, U.S. Dist. Ct. (ea. dist.) Pa. 1975, U.S. Ct. Appeals (3d cir.) 1976, U.S. Ct. Appeals (11th cir.) 1987, U.S. Supreme Ct. 1985, N.Y. 1990. Asst. defender Defender Assn. Phila., 1973-75, fed. defender, 1975-77, also bd. dirs., 1985—; assoc. Montgomery, McCracken, Walker & Rhoads, Phila., 1977-81, ptnr., 1981—, mem. mgmt. com., 1993—, chmn. litig. sect., 1993—2002, vice chmn., 2002—03, chmn., 2003—. Bd. dirs. Ferag-Ams., LLC, chmn. 2004-; bd. dirs. WRH Mktg. Ams., LLC., chmn. 2004- . Bd. dirs. Ctrl. Phila. Devel. Corp., 1995—; bd. dirs. St. Christopher's Hosp. for Children, 2000—, chmn., 2004-; bd. dirs. Opera Co. of Phila., 2000—, v.p., 2002-04, chmn., 2004—; bd. dirs. Police Athletic League, 2003-, bd. dirs Phila. C. of C., 2003-. Fellow Internat. Soc. Barristers, Am. Coll. Trial Lawyers; mem. ABA, Internat. Assn. Def. Counsel, Pa. Bar Assn. (mem. ho. of dels.), Phila. Bar Assn. (bd. govs. 2002-, fed. cts. com., chmn. commn. on jud. selection and retention,), Def. Rsch. Inst., Hist. Soc. Pa., Phila. C. of C. (bd. dirs. 2003-), Yale Alumni Assn. (schs. com.), Yale Rowing Assn., Union League of Phila., Sunday Breakfast Club. Democrat. Avocations: tennis, distance running, opera, classical music. Home: 523 Delancey St Philadelphia PA 19106 Office: Montgomery McCracken Walker & Rhoads LLP 123 S Broad St Fl 24 Philadelphia PA 19109-1099 Office Phone: 215-772-7600. E-mail: smadva@mmwr.com.

MAECHLING, CHARLES, JR., lawyer, diplomat, educator, writer; b. N.Y.C., Apr. 18, 1920; s. Charles and Eugenie H. M.; m. Janet Leighton, Sept. 2, 1944; children: Philip Leighton and Eugenie Elisabeth (Mrs. David Buchan). Attended, Birch Wathen Sch., N.Y.C., 1924 37; BA with honors, Yale U., 1941; JD, U. Va., 1949. Bar: N.Y. 1949, D.C. 1957. Assoc. Sullivan & Cromwell, N.Y.C., 1949-51; atty. Office Sec. Air Force, 1951-52; counsel Electronics Industries Assn., Washington, 1953-56; founding ptnr. Shaw, Pittman, Potts & Maechling, 1956-61; dir. for internal def. Dept. State, Washington, 1961-63, staff dir. cabinet level spl. group and spl. asst. to undersec. Averell Harriman, 1963-66; dep. and acting gen. counsel NSF, 1966-71, spl. asst. to dir., 1972-74; prof. law U. Va., 1974-76; spl. counsel N.Y. law firms, 1976-81; sr. assoc. Carnegie Endowment for Internat. Peace, 1981-85; vis. fellow, mem. law faculty Cambridge U. (Wolfson Coll.), Eng., 1985-88; guest scholar internat. law Brookings Inst., Washington, 1989-93; internat. arbitrator and cons., 1993—. Legal adviser internat. matters NAS, 1970-73, mem. ocean policy com.; mem. law-of-sea and other adv. coms. Dept. State; gen. counsel Fairways Corp., 1959-61; adj. prof. Georgetown Univ. Law Sch., Sch. Internat. Svc., Am. U.; mem. adv. bd. Internat. Peace Acad.; lectr. U.S. Def. Schs., also Hague Acad. Internat. Law; arbitrator complex internat. cases Am. Arbitration Assn. Editor-in-chief Va. Law Rev., 1948-49; contbr. articles to N.Y. Times, Internat. Herald Tribune, Boston Globe, L.A. Times, Miami Herald, profl. and lit. jours. Bd. dirs. Coun. for Ocean Law, Washington Inst. Fgn. Affairs; mem. U.S. Com. for IIASA, adv. bd.; outside counsel to CIA, 1957-60. From ensign to lt. comdr. USNR, 1941-47, at sea and secretariat Joint Chiefs Staff, 1943-44, del. 1943 Cairo Conf., UN Law of Sea Conf., 1971-82; asst. naval attache Peru, 1945-47. Mem.: ABA (Ross Essay award 1969), Am. Soc. Internat. Law, Yale Club (Washington), Cosmos Club (Washington), City Tavern Club (Washington). Avocation: languages. Home: 3403 Lowell St NW Washington DC 20016-5024 Office Phone: 202-244-8923.

MAEDA, J. A. data processing executive, consultant; b. Mansfield, Ohio, Aug. 24, 1940; d. James Shunso and Doris Lucille Maeda; m. Robert Lee Hayes; 1 child, Brian Sentaro Hayes. BS in Math., Purdue U., 1962, postgrad., 1962-63, Calif. State U., Northridge, 1968-75; cert. profl. designation in tech. of computer operating systems and tech. of info. processing, UCLA, 1971. Cons., rsch. asst. computer ctr. Purdue U., West Lafayette, Ind., 1962-63; computer operator, sr. tab operator, mem. faculty Calif. State U., Northridge, 1969, programmer cons., tech. asst. II, 1969-70, supr. acad. applicatons, EDP supr. II, 1970-72, project tech. support coord. programmer II, office of the chancellor, 1972-73, tech. support coord. statewide timesharing tech. support, programmer II, 1973-74, acad. coord., tech. support coord. instrn., computer cons. III, 1974-83; coord. user svcs. info. ctr., mem. tech. staff IV CADAM INC subs. Lockheed Corp., Burbank, Calif., 1983-86, coord. user svcs., tech. specialist computing dept., 1986-87; v.p., bd. dirs. Rainbow Computing, Inc., Northridge, 1976-85; dir. Aki Tech/Design, Northridge, 1976—. Mgr. mktg. thaumaturge Taro Quipu Cons., Northridge, 1987—; tech. cons. Digital Computer Cons., Chatsworth, Calif., 1988; computer tech., fin. and bus. mgmt., sys. integration, 1988—90; tech. customer software support Collection Data Sys., Westlake, Calif., 1991; sr. tech. writer info mgmt. divsn. Sterling Software, 1992—2000; sr. tech. writer, quality analyst Computer Assocs. Internat., Inc., 2000—. Contbr. articles and photos to profl. jours. Mem.: DECUS (ednl. spl. interest group 1977—83, ednl. steering com. RSTS/E 1979—82), SHARE, IEEE, Soc. for Tech. Comm. Avocations: photography, photojournalism, vintage automobiles. Office Phone: 818-593-0345.

MAEDA, KENJI, medical educator; b. Tsu-City, Japan, Apr. 1, 1939; s. Tamotsu and Sumi (Kubo) M.; m. Mayuko Matsunaga, Mar. 30, 1975; children: Kayaho, Mayuho. MD, Nagoya U., 1965, PhD, 1978. Intern Nagoya U. Br. Hosp., 1965-66, asst., 1973-79, assoc. prof., 1979-91, prof. dept. medicine, 1991—, dir., 1992-96; prof. medicine Daiko-Med. Ctr. Nagoya U. Editor: Contributions to Nephrology, 1993, 94; contbr. articles to profl. jours. Recipient Jinkenkyukai award Japan Kidney Found., Tokyo, 1993. Mem. N.Y. Acad. Sci., AAAS, Am. Soc. Nephrology. Home: 20-1 5 chome Fujimidai Chikusa-ku Nagoya Aichi 464-0015 Japan Office: Nagoya U Daiko Med Ctr 20-1-1 Daiko Higashi-Ku Nagoya 461-0047 Japan Office Phone: 81 52 741 2133. E-mail: kmaeda@tsuru.med.nagoya-u.ac.jp.

MAEHL, JANE CECILIA, social worker, administrator; b. Summit, N.J., Nov. 2, 1967; d. Donald Kenneth and Ruth Louise Maehl. BA, BSW, Juniata Coll., 1989; MSW, Marywood Coll., 1992. Lic. social worker, Pa. Social worker Cornell Hall Convalescent Ctr., Union, N.J., 1989-91, Presbyn. Children's Village, Rosemont, Pa., 1992-94, social worker II, 1994-95, supr., 1995-97, supr. II, 1997-98, dir. clin. svcs., 1998-2000, dir. residential treatment, 2000—. Adj. instr. Widener U., Chester, Pa., 2000—, Edn. Consortium, Phila., 2000—; adj. musician, 1997—. Head cook homeless project St. Paul's Luth. Ch., Ardmore, Pa., 1999—. Mem. NASW, NAWCC, AMC. Avocations: playing flute, music, hiking, bicycling, sports. Office: Presbyn Childrens Village 452 S Roberts Rd Bryn Mawr PA 19010 Home: 803 Andover Ct West Chester PA 19382-6662

MAEHL, WILLIAM HARVEY, historian, educator; b. Bklyn., May 28, 1915; s. William Henry and Antoinette Rose (Salamone) M.; m. Josephine Scholl McAllister, Dec. 29, 1941; children: Madeleine, Kathleen. BSc, Northwestern U., 1937, MA, 1939; PhD, U. Chgo., 1946. Asst. prof. history St. Louis U., 1941-42, Tex. A&M U., College Sta., 1943, De Paul U., Chgo., 1944-49; historian Dept. of Def., Karlsruhe, Stuttgart, Fed. Rep. Germany, 1950-52; chief briefing office U.S. hdqrs. U.S. Hdqs. European Command, Frankfurt, Germany, 1952-53; chief historian Arty. Sch., Okla., 1954; with War Plans Office, Hdqs. No. Air Materiel Area for Europe, Burtonwood, Eng., 1954-55; assoc. prof. European history Nebr. Wesleyan U., Lincoln, 1955-57, prof., 1958-62, 65-68; prof. German history Auburn (Ala.) U., 1968-81, prof. emeritus, 1981—. Vis. prof. U. Nebr., 1962, U. Auckland, New Zealand, 1963-64, Midwestern U., Wichita Falls, Tex., 1965. Author: German Militarism and Socialism, 1968, History of Germany in Western Civilization, 1979, A World History Syllabus, 3 vols., 1980, August Bebel, Shadow Emperor of the German Workers, 1980, The German Socialist Party: Champion of the First Republic, 1918-33, 1986; author monographs for U.S. Army in Europe, chpts. in books, atomic, biol. and emergency war plans for No. Air Materiel Area for Europe; contbr. poetry to Question of Balance, Tears of Fire, Disting. Poets Am., Best Poems of 1995, Journey of Mind; contbr. articles to profl. jours. Grantee Nebr. Wesleyan U., 1959, Auburn U., 1969-73, 79-80, Am. Philosophical Soc., 1973-74, Deutscher Akademischer Austauschdienst, 1978. Mem. Am. Hist. Assn., Phi Kappa Phi, Phi Alpha Theta.

MAEHL, WILLIAM HENRY, historian, university administrator, educational consultant; b. Chicago Heights, Ill., June 13, 1930; s. William Henry and Marvel Lillian (Carlson) M.; m. Audrey Mae Ellsworth, Aug. 25, 1962; 1 child, Christine Amanda. BA, U. Minn., 1950, MA, 1951; postgrad., King's Coll., U. Durham, Eng., 1955—56; PhD, U. Chgo., 1957; LHD (hon.), Fielding Inst., 1993. Asst. prof. Montclair (N.J.) State Coll., 1957-58, Washington Coll., Chestertown, Md., 1958-59, U. Okla., Norman, 1959-64, assoc. prof., 1964-70, prof. English history, 1970-86; dean Coll. Liberal Studies, 1976-86, vice provost for continuing edn. and public service, 1979-86; pres. The Fielding Inst., Santa Barbara, Calif., 1987-93, pres. emeritus, 1993—. Prin. investigator Project for a Nation of Lifelong Learners, Regents Coll., Albany, N.Y., 1994-97; vis. prof. U. Nebr., summer 1965; vis. fellow Wolfson Coll. Oxford (Eng.) U., spring 1975; fellow Salzburg Seminar in Am. Studies, 1976. Author: The Reform Bill of 1832, 1967, Lifelong Learning at Its Best: Innovative Practices in Adult Credit Programs, 2000; contbg. author: Encyclopedia of Education, 2d edit., 2003, Encyclopedia of Distributed Learning, 2004; editor: R.G. Gammage, Chartist Reminiscences, 1981, Continuum: Jour. of the Nat. Continuing Edn. Assn., 1980-83, also articles. Mem. coun. Nat. Ctr. for Adult Learning, 1990—2001; bd. dirs. Alliance for Alternative Degree Programs, 1988—90; trustee Coun. for Adult and Exptl. Learning, 1990—94, Southwestern Coll., 2000—02. Fulbright fellow, 1955-56; Leverhulme Rsch. fellow, 1961-62; grantee Am. Philos. Soc., 1961-62, 67-68, 71, 76. Fellow: Assn. Grad. Liberal Studies Programs, Royal Hist. Soc.; mem.: Adult Higher Edn. Alliance. Office: PO Box 31757 Santa Fe NM 87594-1757 E-mail: wmaehl2@cs.com.

MAEHR, MARTIN LOUIS, psychology educator; b. Guthrie, Okla., June 25, 1932; s. Martin J. and Regina (Meier) M.; m. Jane M. Pfeil, Aug. 9, 1959; children— Martin, Michael, Katherine BA, Concordia Coll., 1953, MA, 1959; PhD, U. Nebr., 1960. Counselor U. Nebr., Lincoln, 1959-60; asst. prof. to assoc. prof. Concordia Sr. Coll., Fort Wayne, Ind., 1960-67; assoc. prof. ednl. psychology U. Ill., Urbana, 1967-70, prof., 1970—, chmn. dept. ednl. psychology, 1970-75, assoc. dean grad. and internat. programs prof., 1975-77, research prof., dir. Inst. Research on Human Devel., prof. ednl. psychology, 1977-88, assoc. dir. Office Gerontology and Aging Studies, 1980-82; prof. edn. and psychology U. Mich., Ann Arbor, 1988—, chair combined program edn. and psychology, 1988-92. Vis. prof. U. Queensland, Australia, 1981; vis. prof., cons. to dean Faculty Edn. U. Tehran, Iran, 1973-74 Author: Sociocultural Origins of Achievement, 1974, (with Jane Maehr) Being a Parent in Today's World, 1980, (with L.A. Braskamp) The Motivation Factor, 1986, (with Carol Midgley) Transforming School Cultures, 1996; editor: Advancement in Motivation and Achievement series; contbr. articles to profl. jours. Lutheran. Office Phone: 734-647-0627.

MAEKAWA, KOJI OGURA, technology company administrator; b. Fukui, Japan, Sept. 11, 1954; s. Eiji and Toshiko M.; m. Yukiko Ogura, Nov. 30, 1995. BSChemE, Tokyo U. of Agr. & Tech., 1979; MBA, U. St. Thomas, St. Paul, 1992. Analytical engr., Analytical Lab. Sumitomo 3M, Sagamihara, Japan, 1979-81, chem. engr., Corporate Lab., 1982-87; process engr., Optical Storage Divsn. Minn. Mining Mfg., St. Paul, 1988-92, sr. process devel. engr., 1993-96; technical team leader Imation Corp. Adv. Imaging Technology, St. Paul, 1997-98, bus. devel. mgr., 1998-99, program mgr., 1999—. Intellectual property translator (English/Japanese), language soc. Minn. Mining Mfg., 1993—; cons. Expert Magnetics Corp., Chiba, Japan, 1993—. Patentee in field. Mem. Am. Japanese Soc. Avocations: golf, gardening. Office: Imation Corp Advanced Imaging Tech Mercury Bldg 1 Imation Pl Oakdale MN 55128-3414 Home: Apt 3309 4515 Carlyle Ct Santa Clara CA 95054-3962 Fax: 651-704-5840. E-mail: kjom1@mn.mediaone.net., kmaekawa@imation.com.

MAELAND, ARNULF JULIUS, research scientist; b. Aakrehamn, Norway, Apr. 21, 1933; came to U.S., 1952; s. Erling Magnus and Dagny Marie M.; m. Gunhild Olaug, June 18, 1955; children: Lynn Solveig, David Erling, Kerry Brynhild. BS, Augsburg Coll., 1955; MS, Tufts U., 1959; PhD, U. Vt., 1965. NATO postdoctoral fellow NRC Inst. Atomic Energy, Kjeller, Norway, 1965-66; NAS-NRC postdoctoral rsch. assoc. NRC Army Materials Rsch. Ctr., Watertown, Mass., 1966-68; prof. Worcester (Mass.) Polytechnic Inst., 1968-75; adj. prof. N.J. Inst. Tech., Newark, 1981—84; sr. rsch. assoc. Allied Corp., Morristown, N.J., 1975-90; vis. sr. rsch. fellow Inst. Energy Tech., Lillestrom, Norway, 1992—. Chmn. Gordon Rsch. Confs., Kingston, R.I., 1999; advisor Internat. Sci. and Tech. Ctr., Moscow, 1998—; program evaluator Norwegian Rsch. Coun., Oslo, Norway, 1998-99; cons. Norsk Hydro, Oslo, 2000—. Editor: Hydrides for Energy Storage, 1977; patentee in field; contbr. articles to profl. jours. Rsch. grantee Aluminum Assn., 1969-75. Lutheran. Avocations: stamp collecting/philately, travel, classical music. Home: 305 Cactus Hill Ct Royal Palm Beach FL 33411 Office: Inst Energy Tech Kjeller N-2027 Norway

MAEROFF, GENE I. academic administrator, journalist; b. Cleve., Jan. 8, 1939; s. Harry B. and Charlotte (Szabo) Maeroff; children: Janine Amanda, Adam Jonathan, Rachel Judith. BS, Ohio U., 1961; MS, Boston U., 1962. Tchg. fellow Boston U., 1961-62; news bur. dir. R.I. Coll., 1962-64; religion editor Akron (Ohio) Beacon Jour., 1964-65; with Cleve. Plain Dealer, 1965-71, assoc. editor, 1969-71; edn. writer N.Y. Times, N.Y.C., 1971-86; sr. fellow Carnegie Found. Advancement Tchg., Princeton, NJ, 1986-97; dir. Hechinger Inst. Tchr.'s Coll. Columbia U., N.Y.C., 1997—. Author: (book) Don't Blame the Kids, 1981, School and College, 1983, The Empowerment of Teachers, 1988, The School-Smart Parent, 1989, Sources of Inspiration, 1992, Team Building for School Change, 1993, Altered Destinies, 1998, Imaging Education, 1998, The Learning Connection, 2001, A Classroom of One, 2003; author: (with others) The New York Times Guide to Suburban Public Schools, 1976, Scholarship Assessed, 1997; co-author: The Human Encounter: Readings in Education, 1976, Human Dynamics in Psychology and Education, 1977, Social Problems, 1978, Education Reform in the 90's, 1992, Teachers as Leaders, 1994; contbr. articles to mags. Trustee Guild-Times Scholarship Fund, Ed Bang Journalism Scholarship Found.; mem. adv. bd. Nat. Ctr. Postsecondary Governance, Inst. Ednl. Mgmt., Harvard U., Ednl. Resources Info. Ctr., U.S. Dept. Edn. Recipient Writing award, Press Club Cleve., A.P. Soc. Ohio, Edn. Writers Assn., AAUP, Internat. Reading Assn. Mem.: Blue Key, Phi Sigma Delta, Kappa Tau Alpha, Omicron Delta Kappa. Office: 23 Carriage Pl Edison NJ 08820-4023

MAERSCH, NANCY KAY, health facility administrator; b. Norfolk, Nebr., May 11, 1942; d. Ambrose Pryor and Angela Gertrude (Goergen) Jordan; m. Frank C. Maersch, May 11, 1968; 1 child, Todd F. BS in Med. Tech., Mt. Marty Coll., 1963; MA in Health Care Adminstrn., Cen. Mich. U., 1981. Diplomate in lab mgmt.; cert. med. technologist, hematology specialist. From med. technologist to mgr. adminstrv. svc. and mktg. Madison (Wis.) Gen. Hosp. Lab., 1963-85; from mgr. mobile diagnostics to mgr. lab. ops. Meriter Gen. Med. Labs., 1985-96; dir. regional devel. Meriter Hosp., 1997—. Bd. dirs. Dane County Cytology Ctr., Madison, Wis. chpt. of Clin. Lab. Mgmt. Assn. Chair Edgefest event Edgewood H.S. Aux., 1987—92; vol. Ronald McDonald House, mem. house adv. com., 2001—; mem. RMH Gala Planning Com., 2001—03, Bus. Forum, Madison, 1989—95; bd. dir. Parents Assn. Marquette U., 1993—97. Mem. Am. Soc. Clin. Lab. Sci., Wis. Soc. Clin. Lab. Sci. (sec. 1967-70, 76-80), Clin. Lab. Mgmt. Assn. (Wis. chpt. bd. dirs., pres. 1997-98, chair bi-state conf. 1999, 2001, chair CLMA-WI/WMGMA Joint Conf. 2000), Women in Healthcare Mgmt., Med. Group Mgmt. Assn., Madison Civics Club. Roman Catholic. Avocations: sailing, cross country skiing, reading, walking. Home: 6413 Keelson Dr Madison WI 53705-4370 Office: Meriter Hosp McConnell Hall 1010 Mound St Madison WI 53715-1532 E-mail: nmaersch@meriter.com.

MAES, JOHN LEOPOLD, theologian, psychologist, educator; b. Watertown, Mich., Aug. 6, 1923; s. John and Mary (Cornwell) M; m. Mary M. Johnson, Aug. 28, 1942; children: Barbara (dec.), John David. BTh, Owosso Coll., 1948; AB, Mich. State U., 1954, MA, 1957, PhD, 1963. Ordained to

ministry United Meth. Ch., 1963, United Ch. Christ, 1976; lic. health care provider in psychology Nat. Registry Health Care Providers in Psychology, Mass., Maine, lic. psychologist, Mass., Maine. Pastor, Houghton Lake, Mich., 1948-52, Francestown, N.H., 1977-80; assoc. prof. Sch. Theology Boston U., 1963-72, adj. prof. Colls. Liberal Arts, Edn. and Theology, exec. dir. Danielsen Inst., 1982-89, prof. emeritus, cons., 1989—; prof., acad. dean Franklin Pierce Coll., Rindge, N.H., 1972-75; cons., pvt. practice, 1975-82; bd. govs. Danielsen Inst., 1967-82; min. couns. 1st Congl. United Ch. Christ, Bradenton, Fla., 1999—. Dir. counseling ctr. Boston U., 1967—72, acting assoc. dean student affairs, 1970—72; writer pastoral counselor's licensure exam. State of Maine, 1991; guest lectr., vis. prof. Caribbean Grad. Sch. Theology, 2001. Author: Suffering: A Caregiver's Guide, 1990; (with others) Fathering: Fact or Fable, 1977, Maturity and the Quest for Spiritual Meaning, 1988, Psychological Perspectives and the Religious Quest, 1999; contbr. articles to profl. jours. John L. Maes grad. scholar established in honor Boston U., 2001. Mem. APA, Am. Assn. Pastoral Counselors (diplomate, bd. govs. 1966-71, chmn. ctrs. and tng. com. 1967-71, mem. pastoral counselors exam. bd. 1994-98), Am. Mental Health Counselors Assn. Democrat. Home: 391 Main Rd Islesboro ME 04848-4503 also: 4419 56th St W Bradenton FL 34210-2715 *In the long run it doesn't matter what the causes of suffering are; the unavoidable personal task is to put life back together, making meaning of the environment in which it is lived, and to go on from there.*

MAES, PETRA JIMENEZ, state supreme court justice; widowed; 4 children. BA, U. N.Mex., 1970, JD, 1973. Bar: N.Mex. 1973. Pvt. pratice law, Albuquerque, 1973-75; rep., then office mgr. No. N.Mex. Legal Svcs., 1975-81; dist. judge 1st Jud. Dist. Ct., Santa Fe, Los Alamos, 1981-98; chief judge, 1984-87, 92-95; chief justice Supreme Ct. N.Mex., 1998—. Active S.W. coun. Boy Scouts Am., mem. dist. coms.; presenter pre cana St. John's Cath. Ch.; bd. dirs. Nat. Ctr. on Women and Family Law; chairperson Tri-County Gang Task Force; mem. Gov.'s Task Force on Children and Families, 1991-92; mem. adv. com. Santa Fe County Jail, 1996. Mem. N.Mex. Bar Assn. (elderly law com. 1980-81, alternative dispute resolution com. 1987-92, code of jud. conduct com. 1992—, juvenile cmty. corrections svcs. com. chairperson), Hispanic Women's Coun. (charter). Office: Supreme Court NMex PO Box 848 Santa Fe NM 87504-0848

MAESCHEN, DAVID MICHAEL, software engineer; b. Mitchell, SD, May 31, 1957; s. Lawrence Roy and Dorothy Cora Maeschen. AB Physics 1980, U. of Chgo., 1975—80. Real estate broker's lic. Calif. DRE, 2003, Certificate in Real Estate Santiago Canyon Coll., 2003. Sr. staff software engr. Toshiba Am., Irvine, Calif., 1999—2001; prin. software engr. Calcomp, Anaheim, 1995—98, Ascendant Enlightenment, Tustin, Calif., 1995, SRS Imaging, Newport Beach, 1991—94, SRS Technologies, Newport Beach, 1984—91; assoc. rsch. scientist Dynamics Tech., Torrance, Calif., 1980—84. Scholar Nat. Merit Scholar, U. of Chgo., 1975-1980. Home: 1411 Windemere Lane Tustin CA 92780-5729 Personal E-mail: aenlighten@hotmail.com.

MAESTRONE, FRANK EUSEBIO, diplomat; b. Springfield, Mass., Dec. 20, 1922; s. John Battista and Margaret Carlotta (Villanova) M.; m. Jo Colwell, Jan. 20, 1951; children: Mark, Anne. BA, Yale U., 1943; grad., Naval War Coll., 1963. With Fgn. Svc., Dept. State, 1948-84; assigned to Vienna and Salzburg, Austria, 1948, 1954, Hamburg, Germany, 1949, Khorramshahr, Iran, 1960; with NATO, Paris, 1963, dep. asst. sec. gen. Brussels, 1968—71; counselor of embassy for polit. affairs Am. Embassy, Manila, 1971-73; Dept. State adviser to pres. Naval War Coll., 1973; min.-counselor Am. Embassy, Cairo, 1974, amb. to Kuwait, 1976-79; diplomat-in-residence U. Calif., San Diego, 1979; spl. rep. of Pres., dir. U.S. Sinai Support Mission, 1980; exec. dir. World Affairs Coun., San Diego, 1984-86; adj. prof. internat. rels., amb.-in-residence U.S. Internat. U., San Diego, 1986-90. Mem. adv. bd. Hansen Inst. for World Peace, San Diego State U. Found. With AUS, 1943-46. Decorated chevalier du Merite Agricole (France). Mem. Internat. Inst. Strategic Studies. E-mail: fmaestrone@juno.com.

MAFFEO, ALPHONSE A. anesthesiologist; b. 1947; MD, SUNY Syracuse, 1972. Diplomate Am. Bd. Anesthesiology. Intern Harrisburg Hosp., 1972-73; res. anesthesiology Mass Gen. Hosp., Boston, 1973-75; physician Lehigh Valley Hosp., Allentown, Pa., 1977—, chmn. anesthesiology, 1990-2001. Clin. assoc. prof., assoc. chmn. anesthesiology Pa. St. U. Hershey Med. Ctr., 1994—2001. Fellow ABA, Am. Coll. Anesthesiologists, mem. Am. Soc. Anesthesiologists. Office: Allentown Anesthes Assn Inc 1245 S Cedar Crest Blvd Ste 301 Allentown PA 18103-6258

MAFFEO, VINCENT ANTHONY, lawyer, executive; b. Jan. 22, 1951; s. Michael Anthony and Marie Maffeo; m. Debra Maffeo, Dec. 16, 1972. BA summa cum laude, Bklyn. Coll., 1971; JD, Harvard U., 1974. Bar: NY 1975, Calif. 1982, Va. 1988, DC 1988, Mich. 1994. Assoc. Simpson Thacher & Bartlett, N.Y.C., NY, 1974—77; legal counsel Comms. Sys. divsn. ITT, Hartford, Conn., 1977—79; v.p., gen. counsel Bus. Comms. divsn. ITT, Des Plaines, Ill., 1979—80; asst. counsel western region ITT, 1980—83; group counsel ITT Europe, Inc., 1983—86; v.p. gen. coun. ITT Defense Inc., 1987—91; v.p., gen. coun. ITT Automotive, Inc., 1992—95; sr. v.p., gen. counsel ITT Industries, Inc., 1995—. Lt. Judge Adv. Gen. Corps. USNR, 1975. Mem.: ABA, N.Y.State Bar Assn., Calif. State Bar, Phi Beta Kappa. Office: ITT Industries Inc 4 W Red Oak Ln Ste 2 White Plains NY 10604-3617

MAFFIA, CHRISTINA, elementary school educator, consultant; b. Astoria, N.Y.C., Dec. 3, 1953; d. Edward and Madeline Maffia; m. Joseph Dunn, Sept. 20, 1975 (div. June 1993); children: Lisa Dunn, Joseph Dunn III; life ptnr. Donna J. Crinnian. BA, Iona Coll., 1975; MS with distinction, Hofstra U., 1991. Nat. bd. cert. tchr., 1999. Tchr. 4th grade N.Y.C. Bd. Edn., Cambria Hts., NY, 1994—97, Deer Park, NY, 1997—2000, 3 Village Sch. Dist., E. Setauket, NY, 2000—, mem. profl. devel. and diversity coms., 2000—. Ednl. advisor Bronx Zoo, NY, 1993—97, Columbia U. Tchr.'s Coll., NY, 1998, Nat. Wildlife Fedn., Wash., 2002—, Suffolk County BOCES, 2002—, NY State Dept. Edn., 2004. Author articles and essays. Mem. 3 Village Civic Assn., Setauket, NY, 2001—, 3 Village Hist. Soc., Setauket, 2001—, 3 Village Sch. Dist. Grantee, Impact, N.Y.C., 1995, Western Suffolk Boces, Dix Hills, N.Y., 1997, 1998, 1999, Suffolk County Math Assn., N.Y., 1998, 1999, 2002, Newsday Future Corp., 2000, McDonald's Corp., 2002—03, MESTRACT, 2003—04. Mem.: Kappa Delta Phi. Avocations: hiking, photography, cooking, kayaking, adventure travel. Home: 175 Quaker Path Setauket NY 11733 Office: Arrowhead Elem Sch 62 Arrowhead Ln East Setauket NY 11733 Office Phone: 631-730-4100. Personal E-mail: cmaffia58@aol.com.

MAFFIA, ROMA, actress; b. Brooklyn, May 31, 1958; Actress: (films) Smithereens, 1982, Stuck on You!, 1984, Married to the Mob, 1988, American Blue Note, 1989, The Paper, 1994, Disclosure, 1994, Nick Of Time, 1995, Eraser, 1996, Kiss the Girls, 1997, Double Jeopardy, 1999, Things You Can Tell Just By Looking at Her, 2000, The New Women, 2001, I Am Sam, 2001, Treading Water, 2002, Holes, 2003; (TV movies) Internal Affairs, 1988, Her Deadly Rival, 1995, The Heidi Chronicles, 1995, Her Costly Affair, 1996, Mistrial, 1996, The Defenders: Payback, 1997, Route 9, 1998, The David Cassidy Story, 2000; (TV series) Chicago Hope, 1994-95, Profiler, 1996, Nip/Tuck, 2003-.*

MAFFITT, JAMES STRAWBRIDGE, lawyer; b. Raleigh, N.C., Oct. 29, 1942; s. James Strawbridge III and Lois (Handy) M.; children: Amy Maffitt Barkley, Margaret Maffitt Kramer; m. Frances Holton, Aug. 15, 1981. BA, Washington and Lee U., 1964, LLB, 1966. Bar: Va. 1966, Md. 1969. Assoc. Apostolou, Place & Thomas, Roanoke, Va., 1966-67; trust officer Mercantile-Safe Deposit & Trust Co., Balt., 1967-71; from assoc. to ptnr. Cable, McDaniel, Bowie & Bond, Balt., 1971-82; ptnr. Maffit & Rothschild, Balt., 1982-85, Anderson, Coe & King, Balt., 1986-90, Miles & Stockbridge, Easton, Balt., 1990—. Chmn. Acad. Art Mus., 1994—97, bd. dirs., 1993—99; trustee Grayce B. Kerr Fund, Inc., 1998—; bd. dirs. Chesapeake Coll., 2002—, Leadership Md., 2002—, United Fund of Talbot County, 1994—98, pres., 1997—98. Fellow Md. Bar Found.; mem. ABA (ho. dels. 1986-88), Md. Bar Assn. (bd. govs. 1989-91), Va. Bar Assn., Balt. City Bar Assn. (pres. 1985-86), Wednesday Law Club, Talbot Country Club. Republican. Episcopal. Avocation: golf. Home: 6272 Country Club Dr Easton MD 21601 Office: Miles & Stockbridge 101 Bay St Easton MD 21601-2748 also: Miles & Stockbridge 10 Light St Baltimore MD 21202-1407 Office Phone: 410-820-0222. E-mail: jmaffitt@milesstockbridge.com.

MAFFLY, ROY HERRICK, internist, educator, retired dean; b. Berkeley, Calif., Nov. 26, 1927; s. Alfred Emil and Frances Elizabeth (Henderson) M.; m. Marilyn Miles, Feb. 2, 1952; children: Robert, Nancy, Laurie. AB, U. Calif.-Berkeley, 1949; MD, U. Calif.-San Francisco, 1952. Intern U. Calif.-San Francisco, 1952-53, resident in medicine, 1953-54, research fellow in medicine, 1959-61; resident in medicine Herrick Meml. Hosp., Berkeley, 1954-55; research fellow in medicine Mass. Gen. Hosp., Boston, 1957-59; asst. prof. medicine Stanford U., Palo Alto, Calif., 1961-65, assoc. prof., 1965-70, prof., 1970-92, assoc. dean students Sch. Medicine, 1983-92, chmn. dept. physiology, 1986-88; ret., 1992. Chief renal service VA Med. Ctr., Palo Alto, Calif., 1968-83; mem. adv. com. on renal dialysis ctrs. State of Calif., 1966-70; mem. gen. med. B study sect. NIH, 1967-71; dir. Health Edn. Network, 1980-83; mem. medicine test com. Nat. Bd. Med. Examiners, 1981-88, chmn. medicine test com., 1983-88, mem. com. for comprehensive part II exam., 1987-89; established investigator Am. Heart Assn., 1961-66, mem. rsch. study com., 1972-82, rsch. com., 1976-82. Served to lt. USNR, 1955-57, PTO. Recipient Kaiser award for teaching Stanford U. Sch. Medicine, 1970, 72, 77, 79, 86, 87; recipient Bloomfield award for teaching Stanford U. Sch. Medicine, 1977, Gores award for teaching Stanford U., 1982; Disting. Achievement award Am. Heart Assn. Sci. Council, 1984; Gift of Life award Nat. Kidney Found. No. Calif., 1985. Mem. Am. Heart Assn., Am. Physiol. Soc., Am. Soc. Clin. Investigation (editorial com. 1970-75), Nat. Kidney Found. (sci. adv. bd. 1970-77). Home: 1401 Webster St Palo Alto CA 94301-3649 Business E-Mail: rmaffly@stanford.edu.

MAFFRE, MURIEL, ballet dancer; b. Enghien, Val D'Oise, France, Mar. 19, 1966; came to U.S., 1990; d. Bernard and Monique (Berteaux) M. Diploma, Paris Opera Ballet Sch., 1981; Baccalauréat (hon.), France, 1984; BA (hon.), St. Marys Coll., 2002. Dancer Hamburg Ballet, Fed. Republic Germany, 1983-84; soloist Sarragoza Ballet, Spain; premiere danseuse Monte Carlo Ballet, Monaco, 1985-90; prin. dancer San Francisco Ballet, 1990—. Guest artist with Berlinor Staatsoper and Lines Contemporary Ballet. Recipient 1st prize Nat. Conservatory, Paris, 1983, Grand prize and Gold medal Paris Internat. Ballet Competition, 1984, Isadora Duncan award, 1990. Office: San Francisco Ballet 455 Franklin St San Francisco CA 94102-4471

MAFFUCCI, DAVID G. paper company executive; b. Stamford, Conn., 1950; Degree, Sacred Heart U., 1972. Cert. CPA. Asst. contr. Bowater, Inc., 1977, v.p., treas., exec. v.p., CFO, 1995—. Office: Bowater Inc 55 E Camperdown Way Greenville SC 29602

MAGADAN, DAVID JOSEPH, professional baseball player; b. Tampa, Fla., Sept. 30, 1962; m. Monique Magadan; children: Jordan, Christian. Student, U. Ala. 1st baseman-3d baseman N.Y. Mets, N.Y.C., 1986—92, Fla. Marlins, Miami, 1993; 1st-baseman-3d-baseman-designated hitter Seattle Mariners, 1993; 1st baseman-3d baseman Fla. Marlins, 1994, Houston Astros, 1995; 1st baseman-3d baseman-designated hitter Oakland Athletics, Calif., 1997—99, San Diego Padres, 1999—. Drafted Boston Red Sox, declined, 1980. Chmn. No Small Affair-South. Named Coll. Player of Yr., Baseball Am., 1983, All-Southeast Conf., 1983; recipient Payson award for humanitarian svc., N.Y. chpt. Baseball Writers' Assn. Am., Golden Spikes award, USA Baseball, 1983. Achievements include leading U. Ala. to championship game 1983 Coll. World Series, 1983; leading NCAA divsn. 1 with .525 batting average, 1983. Office: c/o San Diego Padres PO Box 2000 San Diego CA 92112-2000

MAGANA, JORGE CARLOS, pediatrician; b. Merida, Yucatan, Mexico; married; 4 children. MD, U. Mexico, 1956. Diplomate Am. Bd. Pediat. Rotating intern El Paso (Tex.) Gen. Hosp., 1957-58; resident in pediat. R.E. Thomason Gen. Hosp., El Paso, 1960-61, Children's Hosp. Denver, 1961-63; pvt. practice Mexico City, 1963-64, Cleburne, Tex., 1965-68, El Paso, 1969-89; dir. pediat. R.E. Thomason Gen. Hosp., El Paso, 1969-70; chief pediat. Providence Meml. Hosp., 1971, 75, 82,83, vice chief med. staff, 1984, chief med. staff, 1985; chief pediat. Hotel Dieu Hosp., 1983-84; med. dir. Border Children's Health Ctr., 1985-89, Pediat. Arthritis Clinic, 1986—; interim pub. health physician Health Authority El Paso City-County Health & Environ. Health Dist., 1995—. Pediat. cons. El Paso County Health and Environ. Dist., 1989-95; chmn. El Paso City-County Health and Environ. Dist. Lead Task Force. V.p. bd. El Paso Guidance Ctr., 1976, pres., 1977. Mem. Am. Acad. Pediat., Southwestern Assn. Hispanic Am. Physicians, Tex. Med. Assn., El Paso Pediat. Soc. (pres. 1972), El Paso County Med. Soc. (alt. del. 1985, del. 1986-87, v.p. 1988). Office: Health Dist Adminstrn 1148 Airway Blvd El Paso TX 79925-3628

MAGAOAY, MICHAEL Y. state representative; b. Waialua, Hawaii, Aug. 13, 1953; m. Felimar C. Visaya; children: Chanel, Michael. BEE, U. of Hawaii, 1976. Chief elec. engr., estimator, project mgr. George S. Okano Elec. Contracting Corp., 1976—86; mgr., chief engr. of facilities and bldg. svcs. Queen's Med. Ctr., 1986—89; dir. engring. and sales Am. Techs., Inc., 1989—94; project mgr., estimator Am. Electric Co., 1994—96; sr. project engr. A-1 A-lectrician, Inc., 1997—. Chairperson St. Michael's Sch. Bd., Waialua, Hawaii, 1995—98; elected mem. C. of C. of Hononlulu Neighborhood Bd. #27, 1998, 2000, chmn., 1999—2000; pres., bd. dirs. Aloha Ke Akua HS, 1996—; mem. pastoral coun. St. Michael's Ch., 1995—98; corp. bd. mem. Cath. Charities, 1998—2003. Mem.: Engring. Alumni Assn. (treas. 1992, sec. 1993, v.p. 1994, pres. 1995, bd. dirs. 2003—), Hawaii Soc. of Hosp. Engrs. (pres. 1989), IEEE, Mililani Lions Club (1st v.p. 1994, pres. 1995, 2d v.p. 1993, 3d v.p. 1992). Democrat. Office: State Capitol Rm 418 415 S Beretania St Honolulu HI 96813 E-mail: repmagaoay@Capitol.hawaii.gov.

MAGARGEE, W(ILLIAM) SCOTT, III, lawyer; b. Abington, Pa., Sept. 3, 1940; m. Annette Bruno, July 6, 1963; children: Scott, Todd, Ashley. AB, Princeton U., 1962; LLB, Yale U., 1966. Bar: Pa. 1966, U.S. Dist. Ct. (ea. dist.) Pa. 1966, U.S. Tax Ct. 1973. Assoc. Dechert LLP, Phila., 1966-75, ptnr., 1975—. Bd. dirs. United Way Southeastern Pa., 1994—, C.C. Phila. Found., pres., 2000-04. Fellow Am. Coll. Employee Benefits Counsel; mem. ABA (sect. taxation, real estate, probate, trust law, bus. law), Phila. Bar Assn., Princeton Club Phila., Princeton Univ. Alumni Coun. (chmn. 1985-87). Office: Dechert LLP 4000 Bell Atlantic Tower 1717 Arch St Philadelphia PA 19103-2793 Office Phone: 215-994-2609.

MAGARIAN, ROBERT ARMEN, medicinal chemist, researcher, educator, author, inventor; b. East St. Louis, Ill., July 27, 1930; s. Leon and Pauline Mary (Struel) M.; m. Charmaine Virginia Kugler, June 24, 1950; children: Paula, Cindy, Leslie, Robert. Student, Washington U., St. Louis, 1951-52, Bellville Jr. Coll., 1948—50; BA, U. Miss., 1956, BS in Pharmacy with highest honors, 1960, PhD, 1966. Registered pharmacist, Miss., Ill. Am. Found. for Pharm. Edn. fellow, 1961-66; NIH postdoctoral research fellow U. Kans., Lawrence, 1966-67; asst. prof. St. Louis Coll. Pharmacy, 1966-70; assoc. prof. U. Okla. Coll. Pharmacy, Norman, 1970-76; prof. U. Okla., Oklahoma City, 1978-96, prof. emeritus, 1996—. Exec. dir. Kappa Psi, pharm. frat., 1980-2000. Assoc. editor Current Medicinal Chemistry, 1995-97; patentee in field. Served with U.S. Army, 1952-54, Korea. Recipient teaching awards Coll. Pharmacy, U. Okla., 1974, 78, 86, 89, Excellence in Rsch. and Svc. award, 1985, Baldwin study-travel award, 1978, Assocs. Disting. Lectureship award, 1988; named Outstanding Prof. Okla. Soc. Hosp. Pharmacists, 1987, Alumni Teaching Excellence award, 1989, Outstanding Teaching award Gamma Omicron, 1990, 91, 92; Mead-Johnson grantee Am. Assn. Colls. Pharmacy, 1968, NSF grantee, 1968-70, Nat. Cancer Inst. grantee, 1987-93. Mem. Am. Assn. Colls. Pharmacy, Am. chem. soc., Sigma Xi, Phi Kappa Phi, Kappa Psi (Tchr. Excellence award 1990, 92), Rho Chi (chpt. Rsch. award 1981). Episcopalian. Office: 311 N Mercedes Dr Norman OK 73069-6447

MAGASANIK, BORIS, microbiology educator; b. Kharkoff, U.S.S.R., Dec. 19, 1919; came to U.S., 1938; s. Naum and Charlotte (Schreiber) M. BS, CCNY, 1941; PhD, Columbia U., 1948; MS (hon.), Harvard U., 1958. Tech. asst. Mt. Sinai Hosp., N.Y.C., 1939-41; rsch. asst. Columbia U., N.Y.C., 1948-49; Ernst fellow Harvard U. Med. Sch., Boston, 1949-51, assoc. to assoc. prof., 1951-59; prof. microbiology MIT, Cambridge, 1960-77, Jacques Monod prof., 1977—, head dept. biology, 1967-77. Tutor in biochem. scis. Harvard U., 1951—. Contbr. over 250 sci. articles and revs. to profl. publs. With M.C., U.S. Army, 1942-45, ETO. Guggenheim fellow, 1959; Markle scholar in med. scis., 1951-56; recipient SelmanA. Waksman Award in Microbiology Nat. Acad. of Sciences, 1994, Lifetime Achievement award Abbott-ASM, 2000. Mem. NAS, Am. Acad. Arts and Scis., Am. Soc. Microbiology, Am. Soc. Biol. Chemists. Home: 54 Garfield St Cambridge MA 02138-1802 Office: MIT Dept Biology Rm 68625 77 Massachusetts Ave Cambridge MA 02139-4301 E-mail: bmag@mit.edu.

MAGAW, JOHN W. former federal agency administrator; b. Columbus, Ohio; m. Helen Mahley; 5 children. BA in Edn., Otterbein Coll., 1957. Patrolman State of Ohio, Columbus, 1958-66; joined U.S. Secret Svc., Columbus, 1967, spl. agt., 1967, former head protection for U.S. President and First Lady Washington, until 1992, 17th dir., 1992-93; dir. Bur. Alcohol, Tobacco & Firearms, Washington, 1993—99; spl. advisor to Dir. FEMA, Washington, 1999—2001; under secy. security U.S. Dept. Transp., Washington, 2002. Bd. trustees Otterbein Coll., Westerville, Ohio. Recipient Presdl. Rank Meritorious award, 1991. Mem. Fed. Investigators Assn., Internat. Assn. Chiefs of Police (exec. com. adv. com. for internat. policy). Office: US Dept Transp Transp Security Admin 400 7th St SW Washington DC 20590

MAGAZINE, ALAN HARRISON, association executive, consultant; b. Cambridge, Mass., May 16, 1944; s. Arnold Lloyd and Ruth Magazine; m. June Ann O'Donohue, June 20, 1971 (div. Feb. 1984); children: Sarah Elizabeth, David Michael; m. Cynthia Louise Cordiner, Aug. 30, 1984. BA, Monmouth Coll., 1966; MPA, Kent State U., 1968; PhD, U. Md., 1976. Sr. cons. Real Estate Rsch. Corp., Washington, 1969-72; exec. dir. Nat. Ctr. for Pub. Svc. Internships, Washington, 1972-75; nat. policy coord. Internat. City Mgmt. Assn., Washington, 1973-76; dep. asst. dir. U.S. Commn. on Fed. Paperwork, Washington, 1976-78; dir. office of intergovernmental rels. EPA, Washington, 1978-81; dir. Bus.-Higher Edn. Forum, Washington, 1981-86; pres. Coun. on Competitiveness adv. com. Congl. Tech. Policy Task Force, 1986-89; adv. bd. George Mason U. Ctr. Conflict Resolution, 1986-89; pres. Health Industry Mfgs. Assn., 1990-99; cons. in field, 1999—2001; sr. advisor Coun. on Competitiveness, 1999—2003; prin., sr. advisor New Economy Strategies, 2003—. Bd. dirs. Dickinson Coll., Clark Ctr. Pub. Policy, Congrl. Econ. Leadership Inst., Healthcare Tech. Inst. Bd. Advisors, Sunrise Techs. Internat., Inc., Eyetel Corp., PLC Med. Inc., Innotech, USA; mem. adv. bd. Brookings Inst. Ctr. Econ. Progress and Employment, 1986-89; mem. U.S. China Joint Commn. on Commerce and Trade, 1996-97 Author: Environmental Management in Local Government, 1977. Bd. dirs. Met. Washington Coun. of Govts., 1972-79; mem. Fairfax County Bd. Suprs., Va., 1972-79; chmn. No. Va. Transp. Commn., 1974-75; mem. No. Va. Planning Dist. Commn., Fairfax, 1976-79; mem. Dickinson Coll. Parents Coun., 1994-98, bd. dirs. Clark Ctr. for the Study of Contemporary Issues. With USAFR, 1968-71. Ford Found. fellow, 1970-71. Democrat. Jewish. Avocations: jogging, reading, photography. Home: 322 S Fayette St Alexandria VA 22314-5903 Personal E-mail: amagazine@comcast.net.

MAGAZINER, ELLIOT ALBERT, musician, conductor, educator; b. Springfield, Mass., Dec. 25, 1921; m. Sari Fromkin; 2 children. Student, Nat. Orch. Assn., 1937-40, Princeton U., 1943, Juilliard School of Music, 1946-50. Music dir., prof. music Manhattanville Coll., Purchase, N.Y., 1970—. Faculty Westchester Conservatory Music, Summit Music Festival, 2001. Debut: Town Hall, NYC, 1952; staff artist, concertmaster CBS-TV and Radio; Networks: condrs. Reiner, Ansermet, Beecham, Stokowski; condr., sr. violin instr. Westchester Conservatory of Music; vis. condr. Dubuque Symphony; soloist N.Y. Philharm. Symphony, Symphony of the Air, Kol Visrael, symphonies in Chgo., Ft. Myers, Dubuque, York, St. Petersburg, Lincoln Ctr., NYC, 2002; recitals in N.Y.C., Washington, Detroit, Amsterdam, Paris, Jerusalem; star of CBS-TV, The Violin. Recs.: Charles Ives Sonata #2, Charles Ives Trio (with Frank Glazer and David Weber); Vivaldi Concerto in C and Concerto in B (with orchestre Symphonique de Paris); conductor Westchester All County Festival Orch. Mem. AAUP, N.Y. TV Musicians (pres.), CBS Musicians Fund (sec.) Avocation: collecting unique and ancient instruments. Home: 250 Garth Rd Apt 2b3 Scarsdale NY 10583-3954 Office: Manhattanville Coll 2900 Purchase St Purchase NY 10577-2131 Office Phone: 914-694-2200 ext 6267.

MAGAZINER, FRED THOMAS, lawyer; b. Phila., July 4, 1947; s. Henry Jonas and Reba (Henken) M.; m. Phyllis Heller, June 28, 1970; children: Daniel, Andrew. BA, Columbia U., 1969, JD, 1976. Bar: Pa., U.S. Dist. Ct. (ea. dist.) Pa., U.S. Ct. Appeals (3rd cir.), U.S. Claims Ct. Law clk. to judge Max Rosenn U.S. Ct. Appeals (3rd cir.), Phila., 1976-77; assoc. Dechert, Price & Rhoads, Phila., 1977-84, ptnr., 1984—. Mem. ABA, Pa. Bar Assn., Phila. Bar Assn., Am. Law Inst. Democrat. Jewish. Home: 1021 W Cliveden St Philadelphia PA 19119-3702 Office: Dechert Price & Rhoads 4000 Bell Atlantic Tower 1717 Arch St Philadelphia PA 19103-2713 E-mail: fred.magaziner@dechert.com.

MAGAZINER, HENRY JONAS, architect, writer; b. Phila., Sept. 13, 1911; s. Louis and Selma (Jonas) M.; m. Reba Henken, June 19, 1938; children: Ellen Louise (Mrs. Alan I. Widiss), Fred Thomas. BArch, U. Pa., 1936. Cert. Nat. Coun. Arch. and Registration Bds. Draftsman Phila. City Planning Project, 1936-37; draftsman Louis Magaziner (Architect), Phila., 1937-39, architect, 1946-48; chief Architects' Squad, Day & Zimmermann, Inc., Burlington, Iowa, 1940-41; architect Albert Kahn (Architect), Detroit, 1942; designer Wright Aero. Corp., Wood Ridge, N.J., 1943-45; ptnr. Louis & Henry Magaziner, Phila., 1948-56; architect, planner pvt. practice, 1956-72; regional hist. architect, archtl. historian Mid-Atlantic region Nat. Pk. Svc., Phila., 1972-87; pvt. practice architecture, 1987—. Archtl. adviser Phila. Hist. Commn., 1970-75, mem. archtl. com., 1979-85, chmn. archtl. com., 1972-75. Author: The Golden Age of Ironwork, 2000. Mem. Carpenters' Co. of City and County of Phila., mem. mng. com. historic Carpenters' Hall, 2000-02; v.p. Phila. Health and Welfare Coun., 1957-61, Phila. chpt. Victorian Soc. Am., 1975; v.p. city planning Germantown Comty. Coun., 1957-62; bd. dirs. Downtown Children's (day care) Ctr., 1956-73, v.p., 1960-61; bd. dirs. Allens Ln. Art Ctr., 1945-67, Neighborhood Ctr. Phila., 1956-74, Hist. Soc. Pa., 1970-74, Chestnut Hill Hist. Soc., 1970-80, Phila. chpt. Assn. for Preservation Tech., 1991-98, Clean Air Coun., 1980-92, Center City Residents Assn., 1995-96; bd. dirs. Maxwell Mansion Mus., pres., 1964-67; trustee Stewardsom Meml. Fellowship in Arch., 1958-90. Recipient Presdl. award for Excellence in Design for the Govt., 1988, James Biddle award Preservation Alliance for Greater Phila., 1999; named to Germantown Hall of Fame, 1994. Fellow AIA (mem. com. on hist. resources, John Harbeson award 2000); mem. ASTM (mem. com. on hist. preservation stds. 1981-90), Am. Inst. Conservation, Assn. for Preservation Tech., Ea. Nat. Pk. and Monument Assn., Fellows in Am. Studies (pres. 1983-84), Nat. Trust for Hist. Preservation, Soc. Archtl. Historians (bd. dirs. 1977-80, mem. editl. bd. 58 vol. Buildings of the United States 1992-98), Bldg. Conservation Internat., Victorian Soc. Am., T-Square Atelier (pres. 1963-65), Pa. Soc. Architects, Pa. Acad. Fine Arts, Libr. Co. Phila., Sierra Club, Athenaeum of Phila., Preservation Action. Home: 2 Franklin Town Blvd Apt 2404 Philadelphia PA 19103-1237 Office Fax: 215-545-8397. *I do hope that we can pass on to future generations a prejudice-free America having a natural environment without pollution and a man-made environment with its best elements both preserved and appreciated. Achieving these objectives is an unending struggle but one certainly worth winning. God willing, I expect to continue to fight for these ends.*

MAGDOL, MICHAEL ORIN, bank executive; b. N.Y.C., May 18, 1937; s. David Aaron and Ruth (Wein) M.; m. Alice Jane Gates, Aug. 29, 1940 (div. Sept. 1974); 1 child, David; m. Patricia Elizabeth Marshall, Feb. 1, 1943; 1 child, Jennifer. BSE, U. Pa., 1959. Internat. officer Mfrs. Hanover Trust Co., N.Y.C., 1959-65; exec. v.p. J. Henry Schroder Bank, N.Y.C., 1965-87; vice chmn., chief fin. officer, dir. Fiduciary Trust Co. Internat., N.Y.C., 1987—. Bd.

dirs. Arch Chems. Inc. Bd. dirs. Boy Scouts Am., N.Y.C., 1975—, Children Oncology Soc. N.Y., Lingnan Found. Mem. Univ. Econs. Club, Onteora Club (Tannersville, N.Y.). Office: Fiduciary Trust Co Internat 600 5th Ave New York NY 10020 E-mail: mmagdol@ftci.com.

MAGEE, ALAN, artist; b. Newtown, Pa., May 26, 1947; s. Richard Forrest and Rena (Cook) M.; m. Monika Gabriele Ruth Siekmann, Jan. 4, 1969. Student, Tyler Sch. of Art, 1965-66, Phila. Coll. Art, 1967-69. Contbr. articles to profl. jours.; one-person shows include Allport Assocs. Gallery, Larkspur, Calif., 1978, 81, Clark Gallery, Lincoln, Mass., 1979, Staempfli Gallery, N.Y.C., 1980, 82, 90, FIAC Grand Palais, Paris, 1983, Norton Gallery and Sch. of Art, West Palm Beach, Fla., 1983, San Jose Mus. of Art, 1983, Newport Art Mus., 1984, Farnsworth Art Mus., Rockland, Maine, 1984, Ark. Art Ctr., Columbus Mus. of Art, Ohio Chgo. Art Inst., U. Maine, 1985, Fresno Art Ctr., 1985, L.A., 1986, Schmidt-Bingham Gallery, N.Y.C., 1986, 88, 89, Allport Assocs. Gallery, San Francisco, 1986, Joan Whitney Payson Gallery at Westbrook Coll., Portland, Maine, 1990, Farnsworth Art Mus., 1991, James A. Michener Art Mus., Bucks County, Pa., 1991, Ringling Sch. Art & Design, Sarasota, Fla., 1992, Fine Arts Ctr. at Cheekwood, Nashville, 1992, Edith Caldwell Gallery, San Francisco, 1992, 93, 95, 96, 97, Edith Lambert Gallery, Santa Fe, 1995, Hollis Taggart Gallery, N.Y.C., 2000, San Francisco, 2000, Berlin Philharm. Hall, 2000, Forum Gallery, L.A., 2001, 02, Forum Gallery, N.Y., 2003, James A. Michener Art Mus., 2003; 30-Yr. Retrospective traveling exhbn. James A. Michener Art Mus., 2003, Farnsworth Art Mus., 2004, Mus. of Tex. Tech U., 2004, Frye Art Mus., 2005; group shows include Farnsworth Art Mus., Rockland, Maine, 1985, Akron (Ohio) Mus. of Art, 1985, Maine Coast Artists, Rockport, 1985, Ark. Art Ctr, Little Rock, 1985, Smithsonian Instn., Nat. Air and Space Mus., Washington, 1985, Wunderlich & Co., N.Y.C., 1986, Light Gallery, N.Y.C., 1986, Schmidt-Bingham Gallery, N.Y.C., 1986, 88, Mus. Fine Arts, Springfield, 1986, Butler Inst. Am. Art, Youngstown, Ohio, 1987, Am. Acad. and Inst. Arts and Letters, N.Y.C., 1987, Nat. Invitationnal Drawing Exhbn., 1989, Staempfli Gallery, N.Y.C., 1990, Albrecht Art Mus., St. Joseph, 1990, NAD, N.Y.C., 1990, Edith Caldwell Gallery, San Francisco, 1993, 94, 95, 96, Nora Eccles Harrison Mus. of Art, Logan Utah, 1992, Portland Mus. of Art, 1993, Creiger Dane Gallery, Boston, Mass., 1995, Phila. Art Mus., 1995, Forum Gallery, N.Y.C, 1996, Nat. Mus. Am. Art, Washington, 1997, Hollis Taggart Gallery, N.Y., 1998, Hackett, Feedman Gallery, San Francisco, 1998, Portland Mus. Art, 1998, Farnsworth Art Mus., 1998, Art Inst. Chgo., 1999, Katonah Mus. Art, 1999, U. Rochester, 1999, O.P. FotoGalery, Hong Kong, 1999, others; pub. collections include Farnsworth Art Mus., Rockland, Arco Collection, Lucasfilm, Bank of Japan, Mobil Oil, Janss Collection, L.A., Achenbach Collection, Palace of the Legion of Honour, San Francisco, Art Inst. Chgo., Portland (Maine) Mus. of Art, Rutgers U. Art Mus., Tapestry for Riverview Psychiat. Ctr., ME, and others; commns. include mural U. Maine, 1997, Maine State House, 1999; author: Stones and Other Works, 1987, Alan Magee 1981-91, Archive, Monotypes, Alan Magee, 2000, 03, Alan Magee - paintings, sculpture, graphics, 2003; prin. commd. works include portrait of Senate Majority Leader George Mitchell 2003 and Alan Mapee, Maine, 2002; TV: Visions of Darkness and Light, 1988. Recipient Richard and Hinda Rosenthal Found. award N.Y.C., Am. Book award, Nevelson award, 1982; The Leo Meissner Prize, Nat. Acad. of Design, 1990. Home: 476 Pleasant Point Rd Cushing ME 04563-3422

MAGEE, CHARLES THOMAS, international consultant, retired diplomat; b. Clifton Forge, Va., Mar. 6, 1932; s. Charles Thomas and Dorothy Elizabeth (McPherson) M.; m. Maideh Mazda, May 30, 1959; 1 child, Maya. BA, Harvard U., 1953. Vice consul Am. Consulate, Windsor, Can., 1961-63; polit.-mil. affairs officer Am. Emb., Paris, 1964-66; polit. officer Soviet desk Dept. State, 1966-68; adv. Russian language and area studies Garmisch, Germany, 1968—69; polit. officer Am. Embassy, Moscow, 1969—71; dep. dir. for ops. Exec. Secretariat Dept. State, Washington, 1971-72, officer-in-charge French desk, 1972-74; chief internal polit. affairs, exec. asst. to amb. Am. Embassy, Paris, 1974—77, dep. chief mission Sofia, Bulgaria, 1977-80; chief jr. officer div. Bur. Pers. Dept. State, 1980-82, fgn. svc. insp., 1982-83; cons. gen. U.S. Consulate Gen., Leningrad, USSR, 1984-86; spl. asst. to mayor City of San Francisco, 1986-87; dir. Russian lang. ops. U.S. Del. to Negotiations on Nuclear and Space Arms with USSR, Geneva, 1988-91; sr. program officer for Russia Citizens Democracy Corps, Washington, 1992—93; amb. mission to Latvia Orgn. Security and Coop. Europe, 1994-97, amb. mission to Ukraine, 1998-99. Ofcl. election observer, Ukraine, 1998, 2002, Russia, 2000, 03, 04, Latvia, 2002; polling supr., Bosnia and Herzegovina, 2000; head Orgn. for Security and Coop. in Europe election observation mission to Former Yugoslav Republic of Macedonia, Azerbaijan, 2000, Moldova, Bulgaria, 2001; cons. Acad. Arrangements Abroad, N.Y.C., 1987—, Dept. of State, 1989—, Seabourn Cruise Line, San Francisco, 1989-92, Acad. Travel Abroad, Washington, 1995; asst. prof. Dept Navy, 1959-61. Active duty USN, 1953—59, lt. comdr. USNR. Mem. Am. Fgn. Svc. Assn., Harvard Club. Home and Office: 4518 Albemarle St NW Washington DC 20016-2016 Personal E-mail: ctmagee32@aol.com.

MAGEE, CHRISTOPHER L. systems engineer; PhD in Metallurgy and Materials Sci., Carnegie Inst. Tech. Exec. dir. Ford/MIT Strategic Tech. Partnership MIT, Cambridge. Lectr. in field; prof. MIT. Ford Tech. fellow, 1996. Mem. NAE. Achievements include vehicle design, concepts and processes, systems engineering, application of computer-aided engineering and vehicle crashworthiness. Office: Engring Sys Div MIT Bldg E40-293 77 Massachusetts Ave Cambridge MA 02139-4307 Fax: 617-452-3760. E-mail: cmagee@MIT.edu.

MAGEE, DONALD EDWARD, retired national park service administrator; b. Trenton, N.J., Sept. 24, 1937; s. Donald A. and Anna C. (Bocskowics) M.; m. Linda Kimball, June 27, 1964; children: Kevin, Bonnie Magee Burch, Gale. BS in Forestry Mgmt., U. Mass., 1964. Pk. ranger Bryce Canyon (Utah) Nat. Pk., 1966-68; area mgr. Sunset Crater Nat. Monument, Flagstaff, Ariz., 1968-73; mgmt. analyst Nat. Capital Region, Washington, 1973-80; supt. Stones River Nat. Battlefield, Murfreesboro, Tenn., 1980-89, USS Ariz. Meml., Pearl Harbor, Hawaii, 1989-95; ret., 1995. With USN, 1956-58. Recipient Excellence of Svc. award Dept. of Interior, 1991. Home: 95-457 Kaukoe St Mililani HI 96789-1865

MAGEE, JOHN FRANCIS, research company executive; b. Bangor, Maine, Dec. 3, 1926; s. John Henry and Marie (Frawley) M.; m. Dorothy Elma Hundley, Nov. 19, 1949; children: Catherine Anne, John Hundley, Andrew Stephen. AB, Bowdoin Coll., 1947; MS, U. Maine, 1952; MBA, Harvard U., 1948; LLD, Bowdoin Coll., 1996. With Arthur D. Little, Inc., Cambridge, Mass., 1950-98, v.p., 1961-72, pres., 1972-86, chief exec. officer, 1974-88, chmn., 1986-98, also dir., 1968-98. Author: Physical Distribution Systems, 1967, Industrial Logistics: Analysis and Management of Physical Supply and Distribution Systems, 1968, (with D. M. Boodman) Production Planning and Inventory Control, 1968; (with W. Capacino and W. Rosenfield) Modern Logistics Management, 1985. Trustee Emerson Hosp., Thompson Island Outward Bound Edn. Ctr., chair, 1995—2000; emeritus trustee Bowdoin Coll.; hon. trustee Woods Hole Oceanographic Instn.; mem. dean's coun. Harvard U. Grad. Sch. Edn.; chmn. trustees Bowdoin Coll., 1990—94; overseer emeritus Mus. Sci., Boston. Recipient Disting. Leadership award, MIT, 1977. Fellow: Inst. for Ops. Rsch. and Mgmt. Sci., Phi Beta Kappa (life); mem.: Am. Soc. Metals (disting. life mem.), Inst. Mgmt. Scis. (pres. 1971—72), Ops. Rsch. Soc. Am. (pres. 1966—67, Kimball medal 1978), Comml. Club (pres. 1992—94), Somerset Club (Boston), The Country Club (Brookline, Mass.), Concord (Mass.) Country Club (gov. 1971—74), Phi Kappa Psi. Personal E-mail: magjfmagee@netscape.net.

MAGEE, THOMAS HUGH, lawyer; b. Rochester, NY, Aug. 15, 1943; s. Edward Charles and Jane Kathleen (Cranmer) M.; m. Judith Joy Stone, Oct. 2, 1982; 1 child, Michael Julian. BSME, U. Rochester, N.Y., 1965; JD, Syracuse U., 1973. Bar: N.J. 1974, U.S. Dist. Ct. N.J. 1974, U.S. Ct. Appeals (D.C. cir.) 1975, N.Y. 1981, U.S. Supreme Ct. 1978, U.S. Patent and Trademark Office. Sr. patent counsel RCA Corp., Princeton, N.J., 1973-86, GE/RCA Licensing Operation, Princeton, 1986-88; corp. counsel E.I. duPont de Nemours & Co., Wilmington, Del., 1988—. Lt. USN, 1965-70, Capt. USNR (ret.), 1991. Navy commendation medal with combat V, Vietnam, 1969. Mem. Am. Intellectual Property Law Assn. (com. chair 1974—), Phila. Intellectual Property Law Assn. (com. chmn. 1974—), N.J. Patent Law Assn., Justinian hon. law soc., Phi Alpha Delta. Republican. Presbyterian. Avocations: tennis, handball, coin-collecting. Home: 721 Severn Rd Wilmington DE 19803-1724 Office: E I duPont de Nemours & Co Barley Mill Plz BMP 25-1372 Wilmington DE 19880 Office Phone: 302-892-0795. Business E-Mail: thomas.h.magee@usa.dupont.com.

MAGEE, WAYNE EDWARD, biochemistry educator, researcher; b. Big Rapids, Mich., Apr. 11, 1929; s. William Fredrick and Elsie E. (Gifford) M.; m. Nannette A. Pierce, June 11, 1951; children: Lawrence, William, John. BA magna cum laude in Chemistry, Kalamazoo Coll., 1951; MS in Biochemistry, U. Wis., 1953, PhD in Biochemistry, 1955. Sci., then sr. sci. Upjohn Co., Kalamazoo, 1955-71; prof. life sci. Ind. State U., 1971-74; prof. biology, head divsn. allied health and life sci. U. Tex., San Antonio, 1975-80; prof. biochemistry, head dept. bacteriology and biochemistry U. Idaho, 1981-85; dir. divsn. Life. Scis., prof., head dept. biosci./biotech. Drexel U., Phila., 1985-92, prof. biosci., 1985-95, W.R. Nes prof. bioscience, 1995-99; prof. emeritus, 1999— Adj. prof. biology Western Mich. U., 1970 71; adj. prof. molecular and cellular biology U. Ariz., 2000—. Contbr. articles and abstracts to profl. jours., chpts. in books. Wis. Alumni Found. Grad. fellow, 1951-52; Predoctoral fellow NSF, 1952-55. Fellow AAAS, Am. Chem. Soc., Am. Inst. Biol. Sci., Am. Soc. Biochemistry and Molecular Biology, Am. Soc. Microbiology. Achievements include research in phospholipid membranes, liposomes as drug carriers, immune modulation, monoclonal antibodies; improving under grad. edn. Home: 7672 S Galileo Ln Tucson AZ 85747 Office: U of Ariz Dept Molec and Cell Biology PO Box 210106 Tucson AZ 85721-0106 E-mail: mageewe@aol.com.

MAGEE-EGAN, PAULINE CECILIA, psychology and management educator; b. N.Y.C., Feb. 27, 1934; d. John Joseph and Rosina (Sweeney) Magee; m. Patrick Joseph Egan, Aug. 5, 1967; children: Anne, Patrick, Deirdre, John. BS, Fordham U., 1956, MS, 1957, PhD, 1963. Cert. psychologist, N.Y. Rsch. asst. Fordham U., N.Y.C., 1956-58; asst. dir. Bur. Testing and Guidance St. John's U., Jamaica, N.Y., 1958-62, asst. prof. psychology, 1962-78, assoc. prof. mgmt., 1978-98, prof., 1998—, assoc. dean external rels. Coll. Bus. Adminstrn., 1997-2000. Cons. in field, 1962—. Contbr. articles to profl. publs. Bd. dirs. Winston Prep. Sch., N.Y.C., 1989—, St. Vincent's Hosp., Harrison, N.Y. Mem. APA, N.Y. State Psychol. Assn. (past pres. pers., indsl. and orgnl. div.). Avocations: gourmet cooking, trap shooting, tennis. Home: 321 Avenue C New York NY 10009-1628 E-mail: eganpm@pipeline.com.

MAGELITZ, LARRY L. construction company executive; CFO Dillingham Constrn. Corp., Pleasanton, Calif. Office: Dillingham Constrn Corp 1020 Serpentine Ln Ste 110 Pleasanton CA 94566-4758

MAGEN, MYRON SHIMIN, osteopathic physician, educator, university dean; b. Bklyn., Mar. 1, 1926; s. Barney and Gertrude Beatrice (Cohen) M.; m. Ruth Sherman, July 6, 1952; children— Jed, Ned, Randy D.O., Coll. Osteo. Medicine and Surgery, 1951; Sc.D. (hon.), U. Osteo. Medicine and Health Scis., Des Moines, 1981. Rotating intern Coll. Hosp., Des Moines, 1951-52, resident in pediatrics, 1953-54; chmn. dept. pediatrics Coll. Osteo. Medicine and Surgery, Des Moines, 1958-62, Riverside Osteo. Hosp., Trenton, Mich., 1962-68, Detroit Osteo. Hosp., 1965-67; med. dir., dir. med. edn. Zieger-Botsford Hosps., Farmington, Mich., 1968-70; prof. pediatrics Mich. State Coll. Osteo. Medicine, East Lansing, 1970—, dean, 1970-98, dean emeritus, 1998—. Mem. spl. med. adv. group to chief med. dir. VA, 1973-77; mem. grad med. edn. nat. div. com. HHS, Washington, 1978-80; James Watson disting. lectr. Ohio Ostio Assn., 1974, Grad. Med. Edn. Nat. Adv. Com.; Watson Meml. lectr. Am. Coll. Osteo. Pediatricians, 1987; chair Mich. Med. Schs. Coun. Deans, 1979-84, 90-91; mem. PEW Health Professions Com., 1991—. Contbr. articles to profl. jours. Served with USN, 1943-45 Recipient Disting. Service award Okla. Coll. Osteo. Medicine and Surgery, 1975; Founder's medal Tex. Coll. Osteo. Medicine, 1978 Mem. NAS, Am. Assn. Colls. Osteo. Medicine (pres. 1977), Am. Osteo. Assn. (com. edn., chair com. on colls. 1987-90, La. Burns lectr. 1977, chair bur. profl. edn. 1990-92), Am. Coll. Osteo. Pediats. (pres. 1965-66), Inst. of Medicine, Mich. Assn. Osteo. Physicians and Surgeons. Home: 1251 Farwood Dr East Lansing MI 48823-1831 Office: Mich State Univ Coll Osteopathic Medicine 541 W Fee Hall East Lansing MI 48824-1315

MAGENDANTZ, HENRY GUENTHER, physician; b. Boston, 1939; s. Heinz Herbert Max Richard and Melitta Lissy (Hey) M.; m. Nancy Storrow Rotch, July 15, 1960; children: Eric, Christopher, Nicholas, Elisa. AB, Harvard Coll., 1958; MD, Duke U., 1962. Diplomate Am. Bd. Ob-Gyn. Intern Phila. Gen. Hosp., 1962-63; resident in ob-gyn. U. Hosps., Cleve., 1964-68; fellow in endocrinology Case Western Res. U., Cleve., 1963-64; mem. staff Women Infants Hosp., Providence, 1979—, R.I. Hosp., 1981—, Miriam Hosp., 1987—; assoc. clin. prof. ob-gyn. Brown U., Providence, 1985—; asst. clin. prof. ob-gyn. Tufts U., Boston, 1982—. Contbr. more than 20 articles to profl. jours. Deacon Ctrl. Congl. Ch., Providence, 1985. Fellow Am. Coll. Ob-Gyn., Am. Soc. Reproductive Medicine, Bayard Carter Soc. Ob-Gyn. Office: Ob-Gyn Assocs 1 Randall Sq Providence RI 02904 Office Phone: 401-331-6980. Personal E-mail: magendantzh@cox.net.

MAGENHEIM, MARK JOSEPH, physician, epidemiologist, educator; b. Deland, Fla., Nov. 1, 1947; s. Milton David and Dolores Ella (Raithel) M. BA cum laude, Wash. U., 1969; MPH, Yale U., 1971; MD with honors, McMaster U., 1974. Diplomate Am. Bd. Preventive Medicine, Am. Bd. Pub. Health, Am. Bd. Family Medicine. Health officer, prof. Oreg. State U., Corvallis, 1976-78; prof. cmty. health U. Sierra Leone, Freetown, West Africa, 1978-81; asst. prof. McMaster U., Hamilton, Ont., Can., 1978-83; asst. state health officer State of Fla., Tallahassee, 1989-91; health officer, dir. County Health Dept., Sarasota, Fla., 1984—2003; med. dir. Hospice of S.W. Fla., Sarasota, 1994-99; CEO, med. dir. Suncoast Cmtys. Blood Bank, 2003—. Author, editor Clinics in Geriatric Medicine, 1986, (with others) Practice of Geriatrics, 1986; contbr. articles to profl. jours. Med. dir., instnl. rev. bd. Sarasota Meml. Hosp., 1992—. Recipient Surgeon Gen.'s medallion of excellence, USPHS, 1989, award of commendation, CDC, 1989, Leadership award, 1991—92, numerous grants. Fellow: Royal Soc. Tropical Medicine and Hygiene; mem.: Sarasota County Med. Soc. (chair pub. health com. 1987—), Fla. Soc. Preventive Medicine, Fla. Med. Assn. (Roy Baker Leadership award 2000), Fla. Pub. Health Assn., Fla. Pub. Health Leadership Inst., Pub. Health Leadership Soc. (chair 1993—95). Avocations: tennis, music, bicycling, international travel. Home: 4571 Robin Hood Trail W Sarasota FL 34232-2640 Office: Suncoast Communities Blood Bank 1760 Mound St Sarasota FL 34236 Office Phone: 941-954-1600 x229. E-mail: mmagenheim@scbb.org., markomag@comcast.net.

MAGER, ARTUR, retired aerospace company executive, consultant; b. Nieglowice, Poland, Sept. 21, 1919; arrived in U.S., 1939, naturalized, 1944; s. Herman and Ella (Kornbluh) M.; m. Phyllis R. Weisman, Aug. 19, 1942; 1 child, Ilana Gail. BS, U. Mich., 1943; MS, Case Inst. Tech., 1951; PhD in Aeros., Calif. Inst. Tech., 1953. Aero. rsch. scientist NASA Lewis Labs., Cleve., 1946-51; rsch. scientist Marquardt Corp., Van Nuys, Calif., 1954-60; dir. Nat. Engring. Sci. Co., Pasadena, Calif., 1960-61; dir. spacecraft scis. Aerospace Corp., El Segundo, Calif., 1961-64, gen. mgr. applied mechanics divsn., 1964-68, v.p., gen. mgr. engring. sci. ops., 1968-78, v.p. engring. group, 1978-82, cons., 1982—. Mem. BSD Re-entry Panel, 1961—63; mem. NASA com. missile and space vehicle aerodynamics, 1963—65; mem. adv. com. AFML, 1971—72; mem. NASA Adv. Coun., 1982—86; chmn. NASA Space Applications Adv. Com., 1982—86; mem. Aeros. and Space Engring. Bd. NRC, 1982—87; mem. Space Sta. Task Force NRC, 1983—87, mem. Shuttle Critically and Hazard Analysts Rev. Bd., 1986—88; mem. DSB NASP Task Force, 1987—88, AFSB Hypersonic Task Force, 1987—88. Contbr. articles to profl. jours. Mem. alumni fund coun. Calif. Inst. Tech., 1972—74; trustee West Coast U., 1980—92; mem. devel. disabilities bd. Area X, 1976—80, chmn., 1976—78; 1st v.p. Calif. Assn. Retarded, 1983—85; pres. Exceptional Children's Found., 1970—72; bd. councilors U. So. Calif. Sch. Engring., 1976—86. Recipient Disting. Alumni award, U. Mich., 1969, Golden Rule award, Calif. Assn. Retarded, 1977, 1989. Fellow: AAAS, AIAA (chmn. L.A. sect. 1967—68, bd. dirs. 1975—77, pres. 1980—81), Inst. Advanced Engring.; mem.: Nat. Acad. Engring., Technion Soc., Sigma Xi. Home and Office: 1353 Woodruff Ave Los Angeles CA 90024-5129 Personal E-mail: ap.mager@verizon.net.

MAGER, EZRA PASCAL, investment management company executive; b. N.Y.C., Nov. 1, 1941; s. Harold and Naomi (Levinson) M.; m. Sarah Johnson, Mar. 25, 1964 9div.); 1 child, Emma Rachel; m. Reeva Starkman, May 14, 1972; children: Camilla Elizabeth, Michael Johanon. BA, Cornell U., 1963; MBA, Harvard, 1966. Successively v.p., sr. v.p., exec. v.p. and dir. Seiden & DeCuevas, Inc., N.Y.C., 1966-73; exec. v.p., dir. Furman Selz Mager Dietz & Birney, Inc., N.Y.C., 1973-90; vice chmn. United Auto Group, Inc., N.Y.C., 1990-96, Cross Continent Auto Retailers, Inc., N.Y.C., 1996-97, First Team Auto Corp., N.Y.C., 1997-98; pres. Torrey Funds Mgmt., N.Y.C., 1998—. Trustee Baron de Hirsch Fund. Mem. N.Y. Soc. Security Analysts, Alpha Delta Phi. Clubs: Harvard (N.Y.C.). Democrat. Home: 141 E 72d St New York NY 10021-4315 Office: Torrey Funds Mgmt 505 Park Ave New York NY 10022

MAGER, INGRID IRINA, artist; b. San Luis Obispo, Calif., Dec. 16, 1955; d. Hans and Irina Mager; life ptnr. Daniel Elidege Renault. BS, No. Ariz. U., 1996. Designer Carpenter & Stringham Archs., Salt Lake City, 1983—2000, Madonna Constrn. Co., San Luis Obispo, Calif., 1994—2000. Personal artist & designer Essam Khashoggi Family & Estate, Lake Tahoe, Nev., 1989—90. Winner of final design for estate, Estate for Essam Khashoggi. Healer/student Heart Awakening Project, Sedona, Ariz., 1998—2002. Moller scholarship, No. Ariz. U., 1995, Art and Design scholarship, 1995. Achievements include design of Designer of spearhead project for the State of California; Designer for spearhead project for the State of California DSS/EDA. Avocations: skiing, camping, glass etching, painting, photography. Office: IIM Design Ltd 224 Laurel Mountain Rd #13 Mammoth Lakes CA 93546 E-mail: imaeger@netscape.net.

MAGERKO, MAGGIE HARDY, lumber company executive; b. Pitts., Dec. 7, 1965; d. Joseph Hardy; m. Peter Magerko. Student, W.Va. U. Pres. Nemacolin Woodlands Resort & Spa, 1987—, 84 Lumber Co., Eighty Four, Pa., 1994—. Office: 84 Lumber Co 1019 Route 519 Eighty Four PA 15330 Business E-Mail: magerkom@84lumber.com.

MAGFORD, MARY, investment company executive; BA with honors, U. Wales, 1966. Ptnr. Mogford Campbell Inc.; com. chair bd. dirs. Ont. SuperBuild Corp., Toronto, Canada, 2000—. Bd. dirs. Falconbridge Ltd., MDS Inc., Potash Corp. Saskatchewan, Sears Can., Teranet Inc., Altamira Adv. Coun.; hon. gov. Trent U.; assoc. mem. Bd. Can. Policy Rsch. Network; former dep. minister of fin., Ont.; former minister natural resources. Vol. Hosp. Sick Children Foun., Toronto Symphony Found.; former vice chair Hosp. Sick Children; former mem. Econ. Coun. Can., Bd. Nature Conservancy Can., Premier's Jobs and Investment Bd. Scholar Lady Astor scholar, Coll. William and Mary. Office: Ont SuperBuild Corp 6th Flr Frost Bldg S 7 Queen's Park Crescent Toronto ON M7A 1Y7 Canada E-mail: Info@SuperBuild.gov.on.ca.

MAGGARD, WOODROW WILSON, JR., management consultant; b. Quincy, Ill., Feb. 5, 1947; s. Woodrow Wilson and Claire Lorraine (Lyons) M.; m. Linda Margaret Davis, Dec. 30, 1967; children: Jared Isaac, Erin Leigh-Taylor, Solveig Kirsten, Christian Heinrich, Anica May, Kayla Margaret. BA, Brigham Young U., 1971; postgrad., Ventura Coll. Law, 1975; MPA, Consortium of Calif. State U., 1978. Cert. rev. appraiser; registered mortgage underwriter. Divsn. mgr. Sears, Roebuck & Co., Provo, Utah and Ventura, Calif., 1967-74; adminstrv. officer County of Ventura, 1974-78; founding ptnr. Maggard, Maughan, Gress and Assocs., Ventura, 1976-83; founder Intermountain Property Svcs., Ventura, 1974—; pres., CEO Ariz. Tech. Incubator, Inc., 2000—. Bd. dirs. EmisCo Internat. Corp., Phoenix, Qameleon, Inc., Scottsdale, Ariz.; v.p. econ./bus. devel. Dineh Coops., Inc., Chinle, Navaho Nation Ariz., 1978-80; dir. econ. devel. City of Scottsdale, Ariz., 1980-81; exec. dir., CEO Fairbanks (Alaska) Devel. Authority, 1981-87; co-founder Pacific Rim Inst., 1984—; founder Maggard & Maggard, Fairbanks and Orlando, 1983—; pres., co-founder So. Global Trading Co., Tex. and Orlando, 1991-98; sr. v.p. Cookies N' Cream, Inc., Tex. and Fla., 1990-91; exec. dir., CEO Reichenbach Techs, Provo, Utah, 1975—, pres., 1999—; exec. dir., CEO Ctrl. Fla. Rsch. Park, Orlando, 1988-91, Reichenbach Maegert Internat., Provo, 1997—; chmn. NETeXc, Inc., Wilmington, Del. and Provo, 1998-2000, bd. dirs. 1998—; co-founder LearnDaily.com, Provo, 1999—; pres., CEO Del. Tech. Park, Inc., Newark, 1993-98; chmn. Calif. Mission Days Food, Altaloma, Calif., 1996-99, Ariz. Mfg. Ext. Partnership, Scottsdale, 2000-02, Rural Incubator Bd. Ariz., 2000—; exec. dir., CEO Inst. Applied Composites Tech., Newark, 1993-98; instr. real estate econs./appraisal Oxnard (Calif.) Coll., 1975-78; instr. bus. Utah Tech. Coll., Provo, 1978. Contbr. articles to profl. jours. and books. Active Boy Scouts Am.; high priest Ch. of LDS; econ. dir. City of Dover, N.H., 1988; exec. dir. Dover Indsl. Devel. Authority; exec. dir. Del. Tech. Park and Inst. for Applied Composites Tech.; office of vice provost U. Del., Newark, 1993-98; bd. dirs. WMFE-TV, Fla. Hosp. Found.; bd. dirs. Next Level Found., 2002—; interim dir., Miller Bus. Innovation Ctr., Salt Lake City, 2002—. Recipient Nat. Merit award for excellence in comml. devel., 1987, Dixwell Pierce award, 1975, Alaska Environ. Enhancement award, 1983; one of Top 10 Sci. Parks in the World Cen. Fla. Rsch. Park, 1991. Mem. Nat. Assn. Seed and Venture Funds (sec.), Am. Soc. Pub. Adminstrn., Internat. Right-of-Way Assn. (internat. property mgmt. com.), Nat. Assn. Rev. Appraisers and Mortgage Underwriters (sr.), Nat. Coun. on Urban Econ. Devel., Am. Econ. Devel. Coun. (internat. com.), Nat. Bus. Incubation Assn., So. Indsl. Devel. Coun., Assn. Univ.-Related Rsch. Parks (bd. dirs.), Del. Innovation Fund (bd. dirs.), Urban Land Inst., Nat. Assn. Indsl. and Office Parks, Am. C. of C. Rschrs. Assn., Acad. Polit. Sci., United Indian Planners, Japan-Am. Soc. Cen Fla. (bd. dirs.), Inst. Internal Auditors, Assn. U. Tech. Mgrs., Sci. and Tech. Coun. of the States, Soc. Profl. Composite Engrs. (charter), Suppliers Advanced Composite Materials Assn., Soc. for Advancement of Materials and Process Engring., Assn. Tech. Transfer Soc., Licensing Execs. Soc., Rotary, Phi Alpha Theta. Independent. Home: 4006 N Canyon Rd Provo UT 84604-5018 Office: 1435 N Hayden Rd Scottsdale AZ 85257-3773

MAGGERT, JEFFREY ALLAN, professional golfer; b. Columbia, Mo., Feb. 20, 1964, m. Michelle., Tex. A&M U. Profl. golfer, 1986—; winner Malaysian Open, 1989, Vines Classic, Australia, 1990, Knoxville (Tenn.) Open (NIKE Tour), 1990, Buffalo (N.Y.) Open (NIKE Tour), 1990; mem. PGA Tour, 1991—; winner Walt Disney World/Oldsmobile Classic, 1993, WGC Andersen Cons. Match Play, 1999. Mem. Pres. Cup Nat. Team, 1994, Ryder Cup Nat. Team, 1995, 97, PGA Tour Charity Team, Buick Open, 1999. Avocations: fishing, hunting, camping, sporting events. Office: c/o PGA Box 109601 100 Ave of Champions Palm Beach Gardens FL 33410

MAGGIOLO, ALLISON JOSEPH, lawyer; b. New River, N.C., Aug. 29, 1943; s. Allison and Florence Celeste (Vago) M. Cert., U. Paris-Sorbonne, 1965; AB, Brown U., 1966; JD, U. Louisville, 1975. Bar: Ky. 1976, U.S. Dist. Ct. (we. dist.) Ky. 1981. Ops. mgr., stockbroker Bache & Co., Louisville, 1970-73; ptnr. Reisz, Blackburn, Manly & Treitz, Louisville, 1976-78, Greenebaum Boone Treitz Maggiolo & Brown, Louisville, 1978-91, Wyatt, Tarrant & Combs, LLP, Louisville, 1991—. Workshop panelist Fin. Adv. Coun., 1994; panelist Seminar on Defaulted Bond Issues, 1987-89, Bond Counsel and the Corp. Trustee, 1990-92, Defaults and Workouts, 1993. Author: Indenture Trustee Liability and Defaulted Bond Issues, 1987, Minimizing Indenture Trustee Liability and Defaulted Bond Issues, 1991, Bond Default Resolution, 1993; co-author: The legal Aspects of Doing International Business in Kentucky, 1990. Mem. exec. com. St. Louis Com. Fgn. Rels., 1979—, chmn., 1991—96; bd. dirs. Ky. Show, Louisville, 1978—91, Ky. Opera, Louisville, 1978—91, mem. hon. coun., 1991—; bd. dirs. Glassworks Found., 2002—03. Decorated Bronze Star. Mem. Internat. Bar Assn., Nat. Assn. Bond Lawyers, Bond Attys. Workshop (planning com. 1991-93), Pendennis Club, Wynn Stay Club, Jefferson Club. Office: Wyatt Tarrant & Combs LLP PNC Plz Louisville KY 40202-2823

MAGGIOTTO, ROCCO J. financial company executive; Vice chmn., Coopers & Lybrand, N.Y.C, chmn. nat. banking practice N.Y.C., global mktg. leader. Office: Coopers and Lybrand 1177 Avenue Of The Americas New York NY 10036

MAGGIPINTO, V. ANTHONY, lawyer; b. Tucson, Apr. 15, 1943; s. William Vito and Elizabeth Maria (Rice) M.; m. Maria Teresa Zequeira, Aug. 31, 1976; children: Marshall Albert Nicholas, Spencer William Jonathan. AB cum laude, Southampton Coll., 1970; JD, Fordham U., 1976. Bar: Fla. 1977, N.Y. 1978, U.S. Dist. Ct. (ea. and so. dists.) N.Y. 1979, U.S. Ct. Appeals (2d cir.) 1980. Asst. to pres. Interpub. Group of Cos., N.Y.C., 1965-66; asst. dean of admission Southampton (N.Y.) Coll., 1971-73; investigative aide N.Y. State Com. on Jud. Conduct, N.Y.C., 1974-76; asst. state atty. Dade County State Atty., Miami, Fla., 1977-78; asst. dist. atty. Suffolk Dist. Atty., Hauppauge, N.Y., 1978-80; asst. county atty. Suffolk County Atty., Hauppauge, 1980-84; sole practice Riverhead and St. James, N.Y., 1982—. Mem. spl. coms. on discovery, civil litigation U.S. Dist. Ct. (ea. dist.) N.Y., Bklyn., 1983-90, 95—, arbitrator, 1986—, Civil Justice Reform Act adv. group, 1990-95, chair jury task force, 1993—, commendation U.S. Dist. Ct., 1997. Mem. appeals bd. SSS, 1982—2001, vice chmn., 1986—97, chmn., 1997—2001. Served with submarine svc. USN, 1961—65. Recipient Disting. Alumni award L.I. U., 1990. Mem.: Southampton Coll. Alumni Assn. (exec. com. 1997—2004, pres. 2001—02), Navy League (judge adv. L.I. coun. 1992—), U.S. Naval Inst., Fla. Bar Assn., Suffolk County Bar Assn., N.Y. State Bar Assn. (exec. com. real property sect. 1997—2002), Nissequogue Golf Club (counsel 1980—, bd. govs.). Republican. Roman Catholic. Avocations: hiking, horseback riding. Office: 1212 Roanoke Ave Riverhead NY 11901-2740

MAGGS, PETER BLOUNT, lawyer, educator; b. Durham, N.C., July 24, 1936; s. Douglas Blount and Dorothy (Mackay) M.; m. Barbara Ann Widenor, Feb. 27, 1960; children: Bruce MacDowell, Gregory Eaton, Stephanie Ann, Katherine Ellen. AB, Harvard U., 1957, JD, 1961; postgrad. (exchange student), Leningrad (USSR) State U., 1961-62. Bar: D.C. 1962. Research assoc. Law Sch. Harvard U., 1963-64; asst. prof. law U. Ill., 1964-67, assoc. prof., 1967-69, prof., 1969-88, William and Marie Corman prof., 1988-98, Peer & Sarah Pedersen prof., 1998—2002, acting dean, 1990, Clifford M. and Bette A. Carney chair in law, 2002—; dir. Rule of Law program Washington, 1994. Fulbright lectr. Moscow State U., 1977; reporter Uniform Simplification of Land Transfers Act.; vis. prof. George Washington U., 1998. Author: (with others) The Mandelstam File, 1996; co-translator Civil Code of the Russian Federation, translation, 2003, Civil Code of the Republic of Armenia, translation, 1999, Intellectual Property (in Russian), 2000, Internet and Computer Law, 2001, Trademark and Unfair Competition, 2002; designer talking computers for the blind. Fulbright rsch. scholar, Yugoslavia, 1967; Fulbright disting. chair, Trento, 2002; East-West Ctr. fellow, 1972, Guggenheim fellow, 1979. Mem. ABA, D.C. Bar, Am. Assn. Advancement Slavic Studies, Assn. Am. Law Schs., Am. Law Inst. (consultative group, UCC Article 2), Internat. Acad. Comparative Law. Office: U Ill Coll Law 504 E Pennsylvania Ave Champaign IL 61820-6909 E-mail: p-maggs@uiuc.edu.

MAGID, GAIL AVRUM, neurosurgeon, neurosurgery educator; b. Chgo., Oct. 15, 1934; s. Harry M. and Henrietta (Busch) M.; m. Janet Louise Reinhardt, June 15, 1962 (div.); children: Allison Magid London, Jonathan Alward; m. Roseanne Cipra Muirhead, Sept. 4, 1982. BSc, U. Ill., 1954; MD, Chgo. Med. Sch., 1958. Diplomate Am. Bd. Neurol. Surgery. Intern Cook County Hosp., Chgo., 1958-59; resident, then fellow neurol. surgery Mayo Clinic, Rochester, Minn., 1959-61, 63-65; clin. instr. neurosurgery U. Calif., San Francisco, 1965-70, asst. clin. prof., 1970-79, assoc. prof., 1979—. Chmn. Dominican Neurol. Inst., Santa Cruz, Calif., 1975; bd. dirs. Dominican Found.; cons. neurosurgery U.S. Army, San Francisco Gen. Hosp. Assoc. editor: Clinical Neurosurgery, 1974. Bd. dirs. Santa Cruz Symphony Assn., 1983-85, U. Calif. Friends of Arts, Santa Cruz, 1985-86. Served to lt. comdr. USN, 1961-63. Fellow ACS, Internat. Coll. Surgeons; mem. AMA, Calif. Med. Assn., Internat. Soc. Pediatric Neurosurgeons, Am. Assn. Neurol. Surgeons, We. Neurosurg. Soc. (v.p. 1996), Cong. Neurol. Surgeons, San Francisco Neurol. Soc. (pres.-elect 1991, pres. 1992), St. Francis Yacht Club (San Francisco). Republican. Home: 241 4th Ave Santa Cruz CA 95062-3815 Office: 241 4th Ave Santa Cruz CA 95062-3815 E-mail: gamagid@itsa.ucsf.edu.

MAGIELNICKI, ROBERT L. lawyer; b. Perth Amboy, N.J., Mar. 28, 1947; s. Leon C. and Dorothy M. (Hudanish) M.; m. Kathleen J. Urban, June 14, 1969; children: Robert Jr., Kimberly, Peter, Matthew. AB with honors, Rutgers U., 1967; JD with distinction, Cornell U., 1970. Bar: N.Y. 1971, U.S. Supreme Ct. 1974, D.C. 1990. Commd. lt. USN, 1968; assoc. Donovan Leisure Newton & Irvine, N.Y.C., 1970-71, 74-80; asst. staff judge advocate U.S. Naval Base Subic Bay, Republic of Philippines, 1971-73; asst. prof. law U.S. Naval Acad., Annapolis, Md., 1973-74; assoc. litigation and antitrust counsel Gen. Electric Co. Hdqrs., Fairfield, Conn., 1980-83, counsel, 1989-90; divsn. gen. counsel Gen. Electric Factory Automation Products, Charlottesville, Va., 1983-88; ptnr. Kutak Rock, Washington, 1990-2000, Schnader Harrison Segal & Lewis LLP, Washington, 2000—03, Sheppard Mullin Richter & Hampton LLP, Washington, 2003—. Avocations: tennis, golf, swimming, reading. Office: Sheppard Mullin Richter & Hampton LLP 11th Fl East 1300 I St NW Washington DC 20005-3314 Office Phone: 202-218-0002.

MAGILL, DODIE BURNS, early childhood education educator; b. Greenwood, S.C., July 10, 1952; d. Byron Bernard and Dora Curry B.; children: Charles Towner II, Emily Curry. BA, Furman U., 1974; MEd, U. S.C., 1978. Cert. tchr., early childhood, elementary, elementary principal, supv., S.C. Kindergarten tchr. Sch. Dist. Greenville County, 1974-83; early childhood edn. instr. Valdosta (Ga.) State Univ., 1983-84; dir. lower sch. Valwood Sch., Valdosta, 1984-86; kindergarten tchr. Sch. Dist. Greenville County, 1986—. Tchr.-in-residence S.C. Ctr. for Tchr. Recruitment, Rock Hill, 1993, mem. policy bd.; workshop presenter and lectr. in various schs. and sch. dists. throughout U.S., 1974—; chmn. S.C. Pub. Kindergarten Celebration, 1994; giv. S.C. State Readiness Policy Group; mem. Southeastern Region Vision for Edn. Adv. Bd., S.C. Coun. Ednl. Collaboration. Demonstration tchr. S.C. ETV (TV show) Sch. Begins with Kindergarten. Mem. Gov. of S.C.'s State Readiness Policy Group, Southeastern Regional Vision for Edn. Adv. Bd., South Carolina Ctr. Tchr. Recruitment Policy Bd. Recipient Ralph Witherspoon award S.C. Assn. for Children Under Six; named Tchr. of Yr., Greenville County, 1992, 93, State of S.C., 1993, S.C. Tchr. of Yr. Coun. of Chief State Sch. Officers, 1993, 94. Mem. Assn. for Childhood Edn. Internat., S.C. Tchr. Forum (chmn. 1993-94), S.C. Early Childhood Assn., Alpha Delta Kappa. Presbyterian. Office: Partee Elem Sch 4350 Campbell Rd Snellville GA 30039-6922 Fax: 770-982-6923.

MAGILL, FRANK JOHN, federal judge; b. Verona, N.D., June 3, 1927; s. Thomas Charles and Viola Magill; m. Mary Louise Timlin, Nov. 22, 1955; children: Frank Jr., Marguerite Connolly, R. Daniel, Mary Elizabeth, Robert, John. BS in Fgn. Svc., Georgetown U., 1951, LLB, 1955; MA, Columbia U., 1952. Ptnr. Nilles, Hansen, Magill & Davies, Ltd., Fargo, ND, 1955—86; judge U.S. Ct. Appeals (8th cir.), Fargo, 1986—. Chmn. fin. disclosure com. U.S. Jud. Conf., 1993—98. Fellow: Am. Coll. Trial Lawyers; mem.: Cass County Bar Assn. (Pres. 1970). Republican. Avocations: tennis, sailing, skiing. Home: 501 7th St S Apt 301 Fargo ND 58103-2761 Office: Quentin N Burdick US Courthouse 655 1st Ave N Ste 320 Fargo ND 58102-4932 Fax: 701 297-7255. Office Phone: 701-297-7250. E-mail: frank_magill@ca8.uscourts.gov.

MAGILL, SAMUEL HAYS, academic administrator, higher education consultant; b. Decatur, Ga., July 19, 1928; s. Orrin Rankin and Ellen Howe (Bell) M.; children: Samuel Hays Jr., Katherine Magill Walters, Suzanne Magill Weintraub. AB, U. N.C., 1950; BD, Yale U., 1953; PhD, Duke U., 1962; LHD (hon.), Stockton State Coll., 1990. Ordained to ministry Congl. Christian Ch., 1953; gen. sec. Davidson Coll. YMCA, 1953-55; dir. student activities U. N.C., Chapel Hill, 1955-58, asst. dean student affairs, 1958-59; chaplain Dickinson Coll., 1962-63, asst. prof. religion, 1962-66, asso. prof. religion, 1966-68, dean coll., 1963-68; pres. Council Protestant Colls. and Univs., Washington, 1968-70; exec. asso., chief office acad. affairs Assn. Am. Colls., 1971-76; pres. Simon's Rock Early Coll., Great Barrington, Mass., 1976-79, Monmouth U., West Long Branch, N.J., 1980-93, pres. emeritus, 1993—; higher edn. cons., 1993-98; assoc. dir. gift planning U. N.C., 1999—2004, major gifts officer, 2004—. Adj. prof. Duke U., 1996. Trustee Jersey Shore Med. Ctr., 1985-93; bd. overseers N.J. Gov.'s Sch., 1986-93. Guerney Harris Kearns fellow in religion, 1960-61; Danforth Found. spl. grad. fellow, 1959-61. Fellow Soc. Values in Higher Edn. (dir. 1969-81); mem. Am. Assembly Collegiate Sch. Bus. (accreditation task force 1989-90), NCAA (pres.'s commn. 1990-93), Am. Coun. Edn. (commn. leadership devel. 1982-85, commn. on minority affairs 1986-89), Harvard Inst. Ednl. Mgmt., Assn. Ind. Colls. and Univs. N.J. (dir. 1980-93, exec. com. 1983—, chair 1987-89), Order of Golden Fleece U. N.C., Fearrington Dem. Club (co-chair 1997-98). Home: 1 Weybridge Pl Chapel Hill NC 27517-8938 E-mail: Smagill@nc.rr.com.

MAGILL, SHERRY, foundation administrator; m. Robert J. Willis. BA, U. Ala., 1974, MA, 1976; PhD, Syracuse U., 1984. V.p., dep. to pres. Washington Coll., Md.; program officer for edn. Jessie Ball duPont Fund, Jacksonville, Fla., 1991-93, exec. dir., 1993-2000, pres., 2000—. Sr. moderator Aspen Inst.; founding exec. dir. Wye Faculty Seminar. Former chair Fla. Funders Group, state bd. dirs. P.A.C.E. Ctr. for Girls; former bd. dirs. Leadership Jacksonville; former chair jud. nominating commn. Fla. State Supreme Ct. Mem. Southeastern Coun. Founds. (bd. dirs.), Jacksonville Women's Network (bd. dirs.). Office: Jessie Ball DuPont Fund One Independent Dr Ste 1400 Jacksonville FL 32202-5011 E-mail: smagill@dupontfund.org.

MAGINN, JOHN LEO, retired insurance company executive; b. Omaha, Feb. 17, 1940; s. Walter J. and Ruth C. (Sawtelle) M.; m. Carol Varnes, Aug. 3, 1963; children: Mary Kay, Karen, Colleen, Matthew. BSBA, Creighton U., 1961; MS, U. Minn., 1962. Chartered fin. analyst. Investment analyst Continental Casualty, Chgo., 1962-64, Mut. Omaha Ins. Co., 1964-68, asst. v.p., 1968-69, 2d v.p., 1969-76, v.p., asst. treas., 1976-82, exec. v.p., 1982-87, treas., 1982-2000, exec. v.p., chief ins. officer, 1987-2000; sr. advisor Summit Strategies, Inc.; pres. Maginn Assocs. Pres. Mut. Asset Mgmt. Co.; bd. dirs. Companion Life Ins. Co., Rye, N.Y., Kirkpatrick, Pettis, Smith, Polian, Omaha. Editor, author: Managing Investment Portfolios, 1983, 2d edit., 1990. Sgt. U.S. Army, 1957-65. Mem. Assn. for Investment Mgmt. and Rsch. (bd. dirs. 1991, chmn. bd. govs.), Inst. Chartered Fin. Analysts (C. Steward Sheppard award 1990). Republican. Roman Catholic.

MAGINNIS, JOHN C., III, lawyer; b. Balt., Aug. 24, 1948; BBA, U. Mich., 1970, JD, 1973. Bar: DC 1974, Va. 1978, Md. 1984. Pvt. practice, Washington. Mem.: Md. State Bar Assn., Va. State Bar Assn., DC Bar Assn. Office: 1350 Connecticut Ave NW Ste 301 Washington DC 20036

MAGINNIS, ROBERT P. bishop; b. Phila., Dec. 22, 1933; Student, St. Charles Borromeo Sem., Overbrook, Pa. Ordained priest Roman Cath. Ch. 1961. Titular bishop Diocese of Siminina, 1996—; auxiliary bishop Diocese of Phila., 1996—.

MAGISON, DEBORAH HELEN, elementary school educator; b. Abington, Pa., Aug. 9, 1969; d. Ernest C. and Doris K. (Ko) M. BS in Elem. Edn./Early Childhood, Kutztown (Pa.) U., 1991; postgrad, Bloomsburg U., 1997—. Cert. tchr. instrnl. I, Pa. Tchr. asst. summer camp Ardsley (Pa.) Day Care Ctr., 1989-91, tchr. summer camp, summer 1991, tchr., supr., 1991-98; long-term sub. tchr. Abington (Pa.) Sch. Dist., 1998—. Jr. ch. tchr., Bible Sch. tchr. Faith Cmty. Ch., Roslyn, Pa., 1996—; strategic planner Abington Sch. Dist., 1995. Mem. Del. Valley Assocs. Edn. Young Children. Avocations: art, crafts, writing, exercise. Home: 2131 Curtis Ave Abington PA 19001-2523 Office: Overlook Elem Sch 2001 Old Welsh Rd Abington PA 19001-1215

MAGLACAS, A. MANGAY, nursing researcher, educator; BSN, Vanderbilt U.; MPH, U. Minn.; DPH, Johns Hopkins U.; DSc (hon.), U. Ill. Former chief sci. for nursing devel. health manpower divsn. WHO, Geneva, Switzerland, 1976-89, regional nurse adviser Southeast Asia Office Delhi, India, 1972-75. Internat. health/nursing cons., 1989—; adj. prof. Coll. Nursing, U. Ill., Chgo., 1990-2000; various vis. prof. positions in several countries, 1990—. Former mem., bd. dirs. Internat. Coun. Nurses, 1989-93; fgn. assoc. NAS Inst. Medicine, 1988—. Rockefeller fellow, 1964-67; Fulbright-Smith-Mundt scholar, 1952-54; recipient Outstanding alumni award Vanderbilt U., 1986, Internat. Pub. Health Leadership award Johns Hopkins U., 1992, Outstanding Profl. award for Nursing, Profl. Regulation Commn. of Philippines, 2000, Profl. Recognition award U. Philippines, 1989, Disting. Achievement award Philippine Nurses Assn., 1989, Outstanding Alumni award U. Philippines Sch. Nursing, 1987, Disting. Leadership award USA Commn. on Grads. of Fgn. Nursing Schs., 2002; named Woman of Yr. Am. Rsch. Inst. Bd. Internat. Rsch., 1988, named Most Outstanding Paulinian St. Paul's U., Philippines, 2002. Fellow Royal Coll. Nursing U.K. (hon.). Office: 70 Rue De La Prulay CH-1217 Meyrin Geneva Switzerland E-mail: hjm@firsteurasian.com.

MAGLICH, BOGDAN CASTLE, physicist; b. Yugoslavia; came to U.S., 1956, naturalized, 1972; s. Cveta and Ivanka (Bingulac) M.; children: Marko Castle, Ivanka Taylor, Roberta Cveta, Angelica Dara, Aleksandra Mara Nadine. Diploma physics, U. Belgrade, 1951; MS, U. Liverpool, Eng., 1955; PhD, MIT, 1959. Staff mem. Lawrence Berkeley Lab., 1959-62; dep. group leader Brit. group, 1962-63; leader Swiss group CERN European Orgn. Particle Rsch., 1964-67; vis. prof., joint faculty mem. Princeton U.-U. Pa. accelerator U. Pa., 1967-69; prof. physics, prin. investigator high energy physics Rutgers U., 1969-74; pres., chmn. Fusion Energy Corp., Princeton, N.J., 1972-81, Aneutronix, Inc., 1982-83, Sci. Transfer Assocs., Inc., 1981-84, United Scis., Inc., 1984-87, Aneutronic Energy Lab., Inc., 1986-88; pres. Advanced Physics Corp., 1988-94; chmn. Advanced Projects Group, Inc., 1994—, HiEnergy Microdevices, Inc., 1995—, HiEnergy Tech., Inc., 2002—, Maglich Innovation Fund, Inc., 2002—, Maglich Family Holdings, 1997—. Chmn. The Tesla Found., 1985—; resident scientist UN-ILO Seminar Econ. Devel. East Africa, Kenya, 1967; lectr. Postdoctoral Sch. Physics, Yerevan, USSR, 1965, Internat. Sch. Majorana, Italy, 1969; mem. U.S. delegation Internat. Conf. High Energy Physics, Vienna, 1968, Kiev, 1970; spl. rep. of U.S. Pres. to Yugoslavia, 1976; sci. project dir. Univ. Research Ctr., King Abdulaziz U., Saudi Arabia, 1981-82; prin. investigator for aneutronic energy USAF Weapons Lab., 1985-87, USAF Space Tech. Ctr., 1988-89. Editor: Adventures in Exptl. Physics, 1972-80. Chmn. Yugoslav-Am. Bicentennial Com., 1975-76; co-chmn. Serbian-Am. Com. for a Dem. Yugoslavia, 1989-92; pres. World Serbian Union, Geneva, 1990-92. Recipient White House citation, 1961; Bourgeois d'honneur de Lens Switzerland, 1973; UNESCO fellow, 1957-58 Fellow Am. Phys. Soc.; mem. Serbian Acad. Scis. and Arts (Yugoslavia), Ripon Soc., Nassau Club, MIT Club, Sigma Xi. Mem. Serbian Orthodox Ch. Achievements include discovering omega-meson, filmless spark chamber, missing-mass spectrometer, delta g, S, T and U-mesons, precetron, self collider migma, aneutronic energy process, supersenzor and microsenzor atometry, and neutron microscope; patentee in field. E-mail: maglich2@hienergyinc.com.

MAGLIOCCO, JOHN, wholesale distribution executive; b. 1942; BS in Econs., U. Pa., 1963. With Peerless Importers Inc., 1963—, v.p., 1965-77, pres., 1978-85, chmn., 1986, CEO. Office: 16 Bridgewater St Brooklyn NY 11222-3804

MAGNABOSCO, LOUIS MARIO, chemical engineer, researcher, consultant; b. Glarus, Switzerland, Nov. 29, 1938; s. Josef and Maria (Schlittler) M.; m. Vreni S. Zentner, Mar. 18, 1966 (div. Sept. 1985); 1 child, Henry Louis; m. D'Ella P. Phelon, Apr. 25, 1990; 1 child, Deon M. BSChemE, Swiss Fed. Inst. Tech., Zurich, 1961, MSChemE, 1963, ScD, 1967. Sr. scientist FMC Corp., Santa Clara, Calif., 1967-68; from engr. to project engr. Shell Devel. Co., Emeryville, Calif., 1968-72, sr. engr. Houston, 1972-74, staff engr., 1974-76; processing specialist ARCO, Harvey, Ill., 1976-79, mgr. process devel., 1979-85; cons. Magna Assocs., Olympia Fields, Ill., 1985-87; mgr. processes and catalysis Enimont, Zurich, 1987-90; pres. Chem. Engring. Ptnrs., Newport Beach, Calif., 1990-93; v.p. R&D Intercat, Sea Girt, N.J., 1993-94; cons. Magna Assocs., 1994—. Cons. to maj. corps. Contbr. articles to internat. profl. jours.; conducted seminars and gave lectures on hydroprocessing internationally in petroleum field. Mem. AIChE, AAAS, Am. Chem. Soc. Catalysis Club. Achievements include: invention and development of Fluid Catalytic Cracking Sulfur Oxide Reduction Tech. (DESOX and NOSOX technologies); developer of math. models for: hydrotreating, hydrocracking, other petroleum processes, recycling tech. used motor oils, semi-synthetic lube oil process (H-H process). Personal E-mail: LouisMag@aol.com.

MAGNABOSCO-BOWER, JENNIFER LYNN, mental health professional; b. Champaign, Ill., Aug. 14, 1963; d. Peter Thomas and Gail Gwendolyn Magnabosco; m. Anthony G. Bower, July 12, 1997. BA, MA, U. Chgo., 1985; MPhil, Columbia U., 1995, PhD, 2001. Staff therapist Postgrad. Ctr. for Mental Health, N.Y.C., 1988-90; rsch. assoc. Grad. Sch. Bus. Decision Rsch. Lab., U. Chgo., 1985—86, 1993—94, Ctr. for Psychiat. Rehab., U. Chgo., 1994; adminstr., rsch. assoc. Ctr. for the Study of Social Work Practice, N.Y.C., 1991-92, project mgr., 1995-96, dir. adminstrn. and ops., 1994-97; mental health cons. Wayne, Pa., Redwood City and L.A., Calif., 1998—2000; assoc. policy rschr. RAND, Santa Monica, Calif., 2001—. Ad hoc tech. rev. com. Dept. of Health and Human Svcs., Substance Abuse and Mental Health Svcs. Adminstrn., Ctr. for Mental Health Svcs., Rockville, 1997-99. Author, co-editor: Outcomes Measurement in the Human Services: Cross Cutting Issues and Methods (NASW Press Best Seller 1997-98); co-author: Cultural Contingencies: Behavior Analytic Perspectives, 1997; manuscript reviewer Jour. Behavioral Health Svcs. and Rsch., 2001—; book reviewer Adminstn. in Social Work, 2001—. Mem. AAAS, Am. Psychol. Assn., Am. Pub. Health Assn., U. Chgo. Alumni Assn. (bd. govs., v.p., Young Alumni Citation 1997, Vol. Leadership All Univ. award). Democrat. Avocations: tennis, piano playing, doll and fan collecting, fundraising, history ancient civilizations. Office: 1700 Main St PO Box 2138 Santa Monica CA 90407-2138 Home: 807 18th St Apt 4 Santa Monica CA 90403-1950

MAGNAN, SALLY SIELOFF, language educator; b. Cleve., May 7, 1951; d. Francis Xavier and Wilma Lois Sieloff; m. Robert Pierce, July 30, 1944; children: Nicholas Paul, Elizabeth Marianne. PhD, Ind. U., 1981. Pickard-Bascom prof. French U. Wis., Madison, 1981—. Editor: Modern Lang. Jour., 1994—; author: Paroles, 1999. Recipient Disting. French Educator award, Wis. Assn. of Tchrs. of French, 1986, Wis. Assn. of Fgn. Lang. Tchrs., 1996, Chevalier Dans, l'Ordre des Palmes Académiques, 2003. Home: 22 Oxwood Cir Madison WI 53717 Office: U of Wis Madison 1220 Linden Dr 618 Van Hise Madison WI 53706 E-mail: ssmagnan@wisc.edu.

MAGNANO, SALVATORE PAUL, retired financial executive, treasurer; b. Portland, Conn., Jan. 10, 1934; s. Salvatore and Lucy (Dimodica) M.; m. Lois Jewel Johnson, July 16, 1955; children: Paul C., Mark J., Peter E. B.Metall. Engring., Rensselaer Poly. Inst., Troy, N.Y., 1955; MBA, Northwestern U., Chgo., 1959. Div. controller Sanders Assocs., Inc., Nashua, N.H., 1962-73; v.p., controller Teledyne Mec, Palo Alto, Calif., 1973-75; div. controller Sanders Assocs., Inc., Nashua, 1975-79, grp. controller, 1979-81, grp. v.p., controller, 1981-86, v.p. fin. and treas., 1986-96; ind. fin. and adminstrv. cons., 1996—. Pres. Boys and Girls Club of Greater Nashua, 1988-89, bd. dirs., 1981—; bd. dirs. Boys and Girls Club of Greater Nashua Charitable Found., 1991—; trustee Daniel Webster Coll., Nashua, 1993—, Congl. Ch. of Hollis, 2002-. Lt. USN, 1955-57. Mem. Fin. Execs. Inst., Beta Gamma Sigma (award for excellence 1959).

MAGNANTI, THOMAS L. management educator, engineering educator; b. Omaha, Oct. 7, 1945; s. Leo A. and Florence L. Magnanti; m. Beverly A. McVinney, June 10, 1967; 1 child, R. Randall. BS in Chem. Engring., Syracuse U., 1967; MS in Stats., Stanford U., 1969, MS in Math., 1971, PhD in Ops. Rsch., 1972; Doktor honoris causa, Linköping U., 1995. Asst. prof. Alfred P. Sloan Sch. Mgmt. MIT, Cambridge, Mass., 1971-75; rsch. fellow, vis. prof. Ctr. for Ops. Rsch. and Econometrics Univ. Catholique de Louvain, 1976-77, 89; assoc. prof. Alfred P. Sloan Sch. Mgmt. MIT, 1975-79, prof., 1979-85, George Eastman prof. of mgmt. sci., 1985—, head mgmt. sci. area, 1982-88, co-dir. Ops. Rsch. Ctr., 1986—, founding co-dir. Leaders for Mfg. Program, 1988-94, prof. dept. elec. engring. and computer sci., 1995—; founding co-dir. System Design and Mgmt. Program, 1995—; now dean Sch. Engring., Inst. prof. MIT. Vis. scientist Bell Labs., 1977, GTE Labs., 1989; vis. scholar Grad. Sch. Bus. Adminstrn., Harvard U., 1980-81; mem. corp. mfg. staff Digital Equipment Corp., 1990; mem. editl. bd. Jour. Computational Optimization and Applications; mem. adv. bd. North Holland Handbooks in Ops. Rsch. and Mgmt. Sci. Author: Applied Mathematical Programming, 1977, Network Flows, 1993; editor: Jour. Ops. Rsch., 1983-87; co-editor: Math. Programming, 1981-83; assoc. editor SIAM Jour. Algebraic and Discrete Methods, 1981-83, Mgmt. Sci., 1978-81, Ops. Rsch., 1978-81, SIAM Jour. Applied Math., 1976-81, Math. Programming, 1988—; adv. editor Transp. Sci., 1985—, Mktg. Sci., Math. of Artificial Intelligence, 1987-91; contbr. numerous articles to profl. jours. Mem. NSF Sci. and Tech. Exchange Delegation to Soviet Union, 1977, NSF Rsch. Initiation Grant panels, 1985, 90; advisor NSF program on decision, risk and mgmt. sci., 1988, 89; mem. mfg. studies bd. Nat. Rsch. Coun., 1993—. Recipient Gordon Billard award MIT, 1992; Mgmt. Program Exch. grantee IREX, Curriculum Devel. grantee Sloan Found., 1990-94. Mem. IEEE (com. on large scale systems 1979-83), TIMS (mem. and chmn. various coms.), Nat. Acad. Engring., Ops. Rsch. Soc. Am. (pres. 1988-89, mem. and chmn. various coms., coun. mem. computer sci. tech. sect. 1983-87, co-organizer 1st doctoral consortium 1983, plenary speaker conf. on telecom. 1983, Lanchester prize 1993, Kimball medal 1994), Tau Beta Pi, Pi Mu Epsilon, Phi Kappa Phi. Achievements include research in network analysis and optimization, network design and combinatorial optimization, and applications in manufacturing, telecommunications, and transportation; development of new engineering/management programs. Home: 33 School St Hopkinton MA 01748-2003 Office: MIT Ops Rsch Ctr 77 Massachusetts Ave Cambridge MA 02139-4307

MAGNEE, TOM, federal agency administrator; Various tech., mgmt. and exec. positions NASA, dir. program planning and devel. Office Earth Sci., 2000—. Office: NASA Hdqrs Mail Code Y 300 E St SW Washington DC 20546

MAGNER, JEROME ALLEN, entertainment company executive; b. Bklyn., Mar. 14, 1929; s. Herman and Evelyn I. (Wolfe) M.; m. Frances Ogens, Mar. 22, 1953; children: Merrill, Steven. BBA cum laude, CCNY, 1951. Asst. to treas., chief acct. Grayson-Robinson Stores, Inc., S. Klein Dept. Stores, Inc., N.Y.C., 1951-59; contr. Food Fair Properties, N.Y.C., 1959-61; v.p., contr. Am. Leisure Products Corp., N.Y.C. and Providence, 1961-69; sr. v.p. fin., treas., CFO, Nat. Amusements Inc., NE Theatre Corp., Dedham, Mass., 1969—. Mem. Nat. Assn. Theatre Owners (bd. dirs.), CCNY Alumni Assn. Office: Nat Amusements Inc 200 Elm St Dedham MA 02026-4536 Business E-Mail: jmagner@nationalamusements.com.

MAGNER, MARJORIE, bank executive; b. Brooklyn; BS in Psychology, Brooklyn Coll., NY, 1968; MS, Purdue U., 1974; D of Mgmt. (hon.), Purdue University, 2004. Mng. dir. Chem. Tech. Divsn. Chemical Bank; from mem. staff Commercial Credit to chmn., CEO Citigroup, N.Y.C., 1987—2003, chmn., CEO Global Consumer Group, 2003—. Bd. trustees Bklyn. (N.Y.) Coll.; mem. dean's adv. coun. Krannert Sch. Mgmt. Purdue U. Bd. dirs. Welfare to Work Partnership, Dress for Success Worldwide, Port Discovery Children's Mus., Balt., Md. Bus. Roundtable Edn. Named One of 50 Most Powerful Women in Am. Bus., Fortune Mag., 2001, 2002, 2003, One of 25 Most Power Women in Banking, US Banker mag., 2003; recipient Am. Found. for the Blind Helen Keller Achievement award, 2001. Office: Citigroup 399 Park Ave New York NY 10022*

MAGNER, RACHEL HARRIS, retired banker; b. Aug. 05; d. Garner Greer and Catherine Alice (Cloaninger) Harris; m. Fredric Michael Magner, May 14, 1972. BS in Fin., U. S.C., 1972; postgrad, UCLA, 1974, Calif. State U., 1975. Mgmt. trainee Union Bank, L.A., 1972-75, comml. loan officer, 1975-77; asst. v.p. comml. fin. Crocker Bank, L.A., 1978, v.p. comml. svcs. divsn., 1981-82,

v.p., sr. account mgr. bus. banking divsn., 1982-83; v.p. and mgr. corp. banking Office of Pres. Sumitomo Bank Calif., L.A., 1983-00; ret., 2000—. Investment cons., 2000—. Home: 2200 Pine Ave Manhattan Beach CA 90266-2833

MAGNES, HARRY ALAN, physician; b. Orange, N.J., Dec. 3, 1948; s. Sam and Shirley (Daniels) M.; m. Patricia Bruce, Mar. 25, 1989; 1 child, Carlos Fontiveros. AB in Biology magna cum laude, Brown U., 1970; MD, Yale U., 1974; M in Med. Mgmt., Tulane U., 1998; cert. in med. mgmt., Am. Coll. Physician Execs., 1997. Diplomate Am. Bd. Internal Medicine, Am. Bd. Med. Mgmt. Intern, resident internal medicine U. Iowa Hosps. and Clinics, 1974-77; ptnr., med. dir., pres., CEO Gallatin Med. Clinic, Downey, Calif., 1977-2001; pres., CEO Gallatin Med. Corp., Downey, Calif., 1992-94; med. dir., bd. dirs. Gallatin Med. Found., Downey, Calif., 1993-2001; chief med. officer Gallatin Med. Group, 2000-2001, Physician Assocs of Greater San Gabriel Valley, Pasadena, Calif., 2001—; staff physician Downey Cmty. Hosp., 1977—96, Presbyn. Intercmty. Hosp., 1992—2001; clin. instr. Rancho Los Amigos Hosp., Downey, 1981—83; chairperson bd. dirs. Primehealth of So. Calif., 1997—99; bd. dirs. Calif. Health Network, sec.-treas., 1998—99; project adv. bd. VA/UCLA/RAND Calif. Med. Group, IPA Governance Project, 1997—98; prin. investigator Reach Asthma Rsch. Project, 2002. Author: Rheumatic Fever in Connecticut, 1974. James Manning scholar Brown U., 1968. Mem.: Med. Group Mgmt. Assn., Am. Med. Group Assn. (policy com. 1994—98, legis. com. 1997—2000), Calif. Assn. Physician Groups, Healthcare Assn. So. Calif. (chmn. med. dirs. forum 1997—98), Am. Coll. Physician Execs., Delta Omega, Sigma Xi, Phi Beta Kappa. Avocation: racquetball. Office: Physician Assocs 199 S Los Robles Ave Ste 300 Pasadena CA 91101 Office Phone: 626-817-8472.

MAGNESS, RHONDA ANN, microbiologist; b. Stockton, Calif., Jan. 30, 1946; d. John Pershing and Dorothy Waneta (Kelley) Wetter; m. Barney LeRoy Bender, Aug. 26, 1965 (div. Jan. 1977); m. Gary D. Magness, Mar. 5, 1977; children: Jay D.(dec.), Troy D. BS, Calif. State U., 1977. Med. asst. C. Fred Wilcox, MD, Stockton, 1965-66; clk. typist Dept. of U.S. Army, Ft. Eustis, Va., 1967, Def. Supply Agy., New Orleans, 1967-68; med. asst. James G. Cross, MD, Lodi, Calif., 1969, Arthur A. Kemalyan, MD, Lodi, 1969-71, 72-77; med. sec. Lodi Meml. Hosp., 1972; lab. aide Calif. State U., Sacramento, 1977; phlebotomist St. Joseph's Hosp., Stockton, 1978-79; microbiologist Dameron Hosp. Assn., Stockton, 1980—. Active Concerned Women Am., Washington, 1987—. Mem.: San Joaquin County Med. Assts. Assn., Calif. Assn. Clin. Lab. Technologists, San Francisco Offshore, Nat. Geog. Soc., Nat. Audubon Soc., Jobs. Daus. (chaplain 1962—63). Baptist. Avocations: boating, birdwatching, sewing, reading. Home: 9627 Knight Ln Stockton CA 95209-1961 Office: Dameron Hosp Lab 525 W Acacia St Stockton CA 95203-2405

MAGNESS-EUBANK, KAREN ANN, writer, educator; d. Samuel Herbert and Beatrice Virginia Magness; m. Eric Magness-Eubank, May 29, 1999. BS, U. Louisville, Ky., 1981; MS, Ill. State U., Bloomington, 1992; PhD, Tex. Tech U., Lubbock, 2001. Acting instr. Tex. Tech U., Lubbock, 1992—93, ethics instr., 1995—96; acting adj. lectr. U. Louisville, 1997—98; lectr., humanities Ind. U. S.E., New Albany, 1997—. Author: (books) Gangs, 1992, The Italian Renaissance, 1996. Mem.: Am. Philosophical Assn., Am. Soc. for Aesthetics, Phi Kappa Phi. E-mail: kareneri@peoplepc.com.

MAGNUS, LENNEA D. community development planner; b. Washington, Mar. 25, 1953; d. Richard Neal Magnus and Lanna Lee Pierson; m. Thomas John Peters, Sept. 15, 1977 (div. Dec. 8, 1992); children: Joshua Peters, Stefan Peters, Raissa Larson, Adena Peters, Natalie Peters; m. John Robert Paulk, Dec. 28, 1992; children: Robert Paulk, Stephanie Paulk, Gina Paulk. BA in Health Svcs. Mgmt. magna cum laude, Whitworth Coll., 1989. Coord. N.W. Regional Food Network, Spokane, Wash., 1987—88; fund devel. mgr. Big Bros./Big Sisters of Tacoma-Pierce County, 1990—96; planning mgr. South Puget Intertribal Planning Agy., Shelton, Wash., 1996—98; grantwriter/planner Confederated Tribes of the Chehalis Reservation, Oakville, Wash., 1997—98, dir. of planning, 2000—; grant specialist City of Tacoma, 1998—2000. Prin. DLM Consulting, Tacoma, 1990—2000. Mem. Thurston Regional Planning Coun., Olympia, Wash., 2001—03, vice chair, 2004; commr. Tacoma Arts Commn., 1993—96, pres., 1994, 1995; mem. Coalition for the Prevention of Adolescent Pregnancy, Tacoma, 1990—97; mem., procedures and operation com. chair Family Opportunity Coun., Spokane, 1987—89; mem. Arts Together, Tacoma, 1996—97; chair Pierce County N.W. Devel. Officers Assn., 1996—99; mem. N.W. Devel. Officers Assn., Seattle, 1989—99; founding mem. Pierce County N.W. Devel. Officers Assn., Tacoma, 1992—99. Democrat. Avocations: quilting, cooking, travel. Office: Confederated Tribes of the Chehalis 420 Howanut Rd Oakville WA 98568 Personal E-mail: lenneam@comcast.net. E-mail: lmagnus@chehalistribe.org.

MAGNUSON, HAROLD JOSEPH, physician; b. Halstead, Kans., Mar. 31, 1913; s. Joseph Simeon and Margaret Ethel (Matson) M.; m. Ruth Prusia, Feb. 16, 1935 (dec. 1941); children: Karen Margaret Magnuson Mauro, Ruth Ellen; m. Kathryne I. Bause, Dec. 20, 1941 (dec. 1993). AB, U. So. Calif., 1934, MD, 1938; MPH, Johns Hopkins U., 1942. Diplomate: Am. Bd. Preventive Medicine (mem. bd. 1964-75, vice chmn. occupational medicine 1968-75). Intern Los Angeles County Gen. Hosp., 1937-39; research fellow A.C.P., 1939-40; instr. medicine U. So. Calif., 1939-41; commd. asst. surgeon USPHS, 1941, med. dir., 1952; instr. medicine Johns Hopkins, 1943-46; research prof. exptl. medicine U. N.C., 1946-55; chief div. occupational health USPHS, 1956-62; ret., 1962; prof. internal medicine U. Mich. Sch. Medicine, prof. indsl. health, 1962-76, prof. emeritus, 1976—; chmn. dept. U. Mich. Sch. Pub. Health; also dir. U. Mich. Sch. Pub. Health (Inst. Indsl. Health), 1962-69; asso. dean U. Mich. Sch. Pub. Health (Sch. Pub. Health), 1969-76. Mem. U.S. delegation ILO Conf., 1958, 59; Chmn. U.S. indsl. toxicology delegation to, USSR, 1963 Fellow A.C.P., A.A.A.S., A.M.A. (chmn. sect. preventive medicine 1966, Hektoen bronze medal 1956), Am. Acad. Occupational Medicine, Am. Pub. Health Assn. (chmn. sect. occupational health 1966, Indsl. Med. Assn., Knudsen award 1970); mem. Soc. Clin. Investigation, Soc. Exptl. Biology and Medicine, Soc. Exptl. Pathology, Mich. Indsl. Med. Assn. (pres. 1965-66), Internat. Congress Indsl. Medicine (v.p. 1969), Rammazzini Soc., Phi Beta Kappa, Sigma Xi, Alpha Omega Alpha, Delta Omega. Home: 18755 W Bernardo Dr Apt 1125 San Diego CA 92127-3023

MAGNUSON, KAREN M. editor; m. Tod Myers. City editor Sturgis (Mich.) Daily News; writer, bur. mgr. UP Internat., Ill., Iowa, Utah and Calif.; various mgmt. positions Daily News, L.A.; editor Oxnard (Calif.) Press-Courier, Calif.; mng. editor Valley Times, Pleasanton, Calif., 1994—97, Wichita (Kans.) Eagle, 1997—99, Rochester (NY) Dem. and Chronicle, 1999—2001, editor, v.p. news, 2001—. Mem.: AP Mng. Editors (vice chmn. journalism studies 2002—). Office: Rochester Dem and Chronicle 55 Exchange Blvd Rochester NY 14614-2001

MAGNUSON, NANCY, librarian; b. Seattle, Aug. 15, 1944; d. James Leslie and Jeanette (Thomas) M.; 2 sons, Daniel Johnson, Erik Johnson. BA in History, 1977; MLS, U. Wash., 1978. With. King County Libr. System, Seattle, 1973-80; rsch. asst. Free Libr. Phila., 1980-81; asst. libr. Haverford (Pa.) Coll., 1981-87; libr. dir. Goucher Coll., Balt., Md., 1987—. Contbr. to profl. publs. Mem. ALA (com. on status of women in librarianship, various others), Online Computer Libr. Ctr. Users Coun., Md. Libr. Assn., Congress Acad. Libr. Dirs., NOW, Women's Internat. League for Peace and Freedom, Balt. Bibliophiles, Jane Austen Soc. N.Am. Democrat. Office: Goucher Coll Julia Rogers Libr 1021 Dulaney Valley Rd Baltimore MD 21204-2753

MAGNUSON, PAUL ARTHUR, federal judge; b. Carthage, S.D., Feb. 9, 1937; s. Arthur and Emma Elleda (Paulson) Magnuson; m. Sharon Schultz Magnuson, Dec. 21, 1959; children: Marlene Peterson, Margaret(dec.), Kevin, Kara Berger. BA, Gustavus Adolphus Coll, 1959; JD honors causa, William Mitchell Coll., 1963; DLL (hon.), Wm. Mitchell Coll., 1991; DLL (hon.), Gustavus Adolphus Coll., 1982. Bar: Minn. 1963, U.S. Dist. Ct. Minn. 1968. Asst. registrar William Mitchell Coll. of Law, 1959-60; claim adjuster Agrl. Ins. Co., 1960-62; clk. Bertie & Bettenberg, 1962-63; ptnr. LeVander, Gillen, Miller & Magnuson, South St. Paul, Minn., 1963-81; judge U.S. Dist. Ct. Minn., St. Paul, 1981—, chief judge, 1994—2001. Jurist-in-residence Hamline U., 1985, Augsberg Coll., 1986, Bethel Coll., 1986, Concordia Coll., St. Paul, 1987, U. Minn., Morris, 1987; instr. William Mitchell Coll. Law, 1984-92, Corcordia Coll., Moorhead, 1988, St. John's U., 1988, Coll. of St. Benedict, 1988; mem. jud. conf. com. on adminstrn. of Bankruptcy Sys., 1987-96; mem. Eighth Cir. Edn. Com., 1992-97, chmn. 1994-97; mem. jud. conf. com. on Internat. Jud. Rels., 1996—, chair, 1999—; mem. com. on dist. judges edn. Fed. Jud. Ctr., 1998—; mem 8th cir. Edn. com., 1992-97, chmn. 1994-97. Mem. Met. Health Bd., St. Paul, 1970-72; legal counsel Ind. Rep. Party Minn., St. Paul, 1979-81. Recipient Disting. Alumnus award Gustavus Adolphus Coll., 1982; First Disting. Svc. award William Mitchell Coll. Law, 1999, Dr. of Laws Honors Causa, William Mitchell Coll. of Law, 1991. Mem. Minn. State Bar Assn., 1st Dist. Bar Assn. (pres. 1974-75), Dakota County Bar Assn., 10th Jud. Dist. Bar Assn., Am. Judicature Soc., Fed. Bar Assn., Fed. Cir. Bar Assn., Fed. Judges Assn. (bd. dirs., treas. 1997-2001, v.p. 2001-). E-mail: PAMagnuson@mnd.uscourts.gov.

MAGNUSON, ROBERT G. former communications executive; BA in Polit. Sci., U. Calif. Berkeley; M in Econ., U. Mass.; M in Journalism, Columbia U. Bus. editor L.A. Times, 1990—96, pres. Orange County Edit., 1996—97, sr. v.p., 1997—2000; pres., CEO InfoWorld Pub., San Mateo, Calif., 2000—02. Exec. bd. mem. Coll. of Letters and Sci. U. Calif. Berkeley; bd. dirs. Daily Californian Found. Bd.; corp. adv. bd. mem. Pacific Coun. on Internat. Policy. Recipient Pulitzer prize, 1993, 1995. Office: Infoworld Media Group 501 2nd St #120 San Francisco CA 94107-1431

MAGNUSON, ROBERT MARTIN, retired health facility administrator; b. Chgo., June 28, 1927; s. Martin David and Adena Marie (Hallberg) M.; m. Patricia Ann McNaughton, Dec. 30, 1960; children: Thomas Martin, Dana Caroline. BS cum laude, Lake Forest (Ill.) Coll., 1951; MBA, Harvard U., 1955. Factory budget mgr., asst. budget dir. Zenith Radio Corp., Chgo., 1955-57; asst. adminstr., controller Elmhurst Meml. Hosp., (Ill.), 1957-64, asso. adminstr., 1964-66, pres., 1966-92. Officer, dir. Chgo. Hosp. Coun., 1972-79, chmn. bd. dirs., 1983; mem. hosp. adv. council Ill. Dept. Pub. Health, 1972-76; faculty preceptor U. Chgo. Program in Hosp. Adminstrn., 1971-92, Northwestern U. Program in Hosp. and Health Sci. Adminstrn., 1972-92; dir. DuPage County Comty. Nursing Service, 1964-67, Health Chgo. HMO, 1984-92; pres. Meml. Health Services, Inc., 1980-92. Pres. Elmhurst Meml. Hosp. Found., 1980-92. Served with USN, 1945-48, 51-52. Mem. Am. Coll. Health Care Execs., Ill. Hosp. Assn. (dist. pres. 1967-69, bd. dirs. 1985-90), Inter-Hosp. Planning Assn. of Western Suburbs (pres., dir.) Clubs: Medinah (Ill.) Country. Republican.

MAGNUSON, ROGER JAMES, lawyer; b. St. Paul, Jan. 25, 1945; s. Roy Gustaf and Ruth Lily (Edlund) M.; m. Elizabeth Cunningham Shaw, Sept. 11, 1982; children: James Roger, Peter Cunningham, Mary Kerstin, Sarah Ruth, Elizabeth Camilla, Anna Clara, John Edlund, Britta Kristina. BA, Stanford U., 1967; JD, Harvard U., 1971; BCL, Oxford U., 1972. Bar: Minn. 1973, U.S. Dist. Ct. Minn. 1973, U.S Ct. Appeals (8th, 9th, 10th cirs.) 1974, U.S. Supreme Ct. 1978. Chief pub. defender Hennepin County Pub. Defender's Office, Mpls., 1973; ptnr. Dorsey & Whitney, Mpls., 1972—. Dean Oak Brook Coll. of Law and Govt. Policy, 1995—; chancellor Magdalen Coll., 1999—. Author: Shareholder Litigation, 1981, Are Gay Rights Right, The White-Collar Crime Explosion, 1992, Informed Answers to Gay Rights Questions, 1994; Internat. Judicial Asst. in Civil Matters (1999), contbr. articles to profl. jours. Elder, Straitgate Ch., Mpls., 1980—. Fellow, Ctr. of Internat. Legal Studies, Mem. Christian Legal Soc., The Am. Soc. Writers of Legal Subjects, Mpls. Club, White Bear Yacht Club. Republican. Home: 625 Park Ave Saint Paul MN 55115-1663 Office: Dorsey & Whitney LLP 50 S 6th St Ste 1500 Minneapolis MN 55402-1498 Business E-Mail: magnuson.roger@dorsey.com.

MAGONI, DESPO, artist; b. Feb. 17, 1943; MFA, Polytechnion of Athens, 1967. One-person shows include Henry-Hicks Gallery, Bklyn., 1976, Nonson Gallery, N.Y.C., 1976, 78, Ora Gallery, Athens, 1978, 81, 83, Kouros GAllery, N.Y.C., 1984, Alternative Mus., N.Y.C., 1986, New Forms Gallery, Athens, 1988, 99, Bklyn. Coll. Art Gallery, 1994, Robeson Gallery, Rutgers U., Newark, 1994, André Zarre Gallery, N.Y.C., 1997, Parsons Sch. of Design, N.Y.C., 1999, John Jay Coll. Art Gallery, N.Y.C., 1999; exhibited in group shows at Kouros Gallery, 1983, Mint Mus., Charlotte, N.C., 1989, Mitchell Mus., Mt. Vernon, Ill., 1989, Haggerty Mus. Art, Marquette U., Milw., 1990, Pratt Inst. Gallery, N.Y.C., 1990, André Zarre Gallery, 1997, Islip Mus., Oakdale, N.Y., 1997; pub. collections include Vorres Mus., Paiania, Greece, Mus. Modern Art, Guadalajara, Mexico, Mint Mus., Charlotte, N.C., Alternative Mus., N.Y.C., Pratt Inst. Libr., N.Y.C.

MAGOON, DONALD W. retired business educator; b. Big Rapids, Mich., Mar. 1, 1910; s. Elbert Elvin Magoon and Edith Marie Whitsey; widowed, 1994; children: Elbert, Louise Libii, Carol Feakins. BSME, U. Mich., 1932, MS, 1934, MBA, 1941. Grad. gemologist Gemological Inst. Am. Instr. U. Findlay, 1932-33, asst. prof., 1934-37; rschr. L.A. Examiner, 1938-39; asst. prof. bus. La. State U., Baton Rouge, 1940-41; treas. Meijer Supermkts., Grand Rapids, Mich., 1946-60; cons. U.S. State Dept., Israel, Mex., 1961-64; prof. bus. Ea. Mich. U., Ypsilanti, 1965-80; prof. emeritus, 1980—. Tutor, Canton (Ohio) City Schs., 1996—. Capt., statis. officer, U.S. Army Signal Corps, 1941-46. Mem.: Rotary (com. mem. 1995—2001). Achievements include at 93 yrs. of age has sent out hundreds of letters with article 'World Scientists Warning to Humanity' on protecting the world environ. Avocation: gemology. Home: 1238 Lorrell Ave SW North Canton OH 44720-3447

MAGOR, LOUIS ROLAND, conductor; b. Auburn, Nebr., May 16, 1945; s. John William and Eleanor Lucille (Niemann) M. B.Mus. Edn., Northwestern U., 1967, Mus.M., 1974. Choral dir. Avoca Jr. High Sch., Wilmette, Ill., 1968-70; choral dir. Niles North High Sch., Skokie, Ill., 1970-73; dir. San Francisco Symphony Chorus, 1974-82, Schola Cantorum, 1982-85, San Francisco Boys Chorus, 1985-88; artistic dir. Seattle Bach Choir, 1990—2001. Founder The Louis Magor Singers; mem. faculty San Francisco Conservatory of Music, 1976-78, San Francisco State U., 1979-80 Founder West Seattle Children's Chorus, 1990—; condr. Sing-It-Yourself Messiah, 1979-91, Calif. Symphony Chorus, 1990-92; exec. prodr. Sandy Bradley's Potluck, 1995-96; co-founder, mng. dir. Hokum Hall, 1993—. Mem. Pi Kappa Lambda. E-mail: louis@magor.com.

MAGORIAN, JAMES, poet, writer; b. Palisade, Nebr., Apr. 24, 1942; s. Jack and Dorothy (Gorthey) M. BS, U. Nebr., 1965; MS, Ill. State U., 1969; postgrad., Oxford U., 1972, Harvard U., 1973. Author children's books: School Daze, 1978, 17%, 1978, The Magic Pretzel, 1979, Ketchup Bottles, 1979, Imaginary Radishes, 1980, Plucked Chickens, 1980, Fimperings and Torples, 1981, The Witches' Olympics, 1983, At the City Limits, 1987, The Beautiful Music, 1988, Magic Spell #207, 1988; author numerous books of poetry, including: Ideas for a Bridal Shower, 1980, The Edge of the Forest, 1980, Spiritual Rodeo, 1980, Tap Dancing on a Tight Rope, 1981, Training at Home to Be A Locksmith, 1981, The Emily Dickinson Jogging Book, 1984, Keeper of Fire, 1984, Weighing the Sun's Light, 1985, Summer Snow, 1985, The Magician's Handbook, 1986, Squall Line, 1986, The Hideout of the Sigmund Freud Gang, 1987, Haymarket Square, 1998, Dragon Bones, 1999, Millennial Journal, 2000, (novels) America First, 1992, Hearts of Gold, 1996; contbr. poems and stories to numerous publs. Home and Office: 1225 N 46th St Lincoln NE 68503-2308

MAGOUN, HAROLD IVES, JR., osteopath; b. Scottsbluff, Nebr., June 11, 1927; s. Harold Ives Magoun, Sr. and Helen Louise Couse; m. Winifred Linsenmaier, Aug. 25, 1953 (div. July 1989); children: Daniel Richard, David Allen, Scott Frederick, Michael James. DO, Kirksville Coll. Osteo. Medicine, 1950, D of Osteo. Edn., 2000. Pvt. practice osteo. medicine, Denver, 1951—; founder, pres. Rocky Mountain Acad. Osteopathy, Denver, 1992—98. Lectr. in field. Author: Structural Healing, 2001. With USN, 1944—46. Fellow: Cranial Acad. (bd. dirs. 1992—, Exceptional Svc. award 2001), Am. Osteo. Assn., Am. Acad. Osteopathy (trustee 1976—83, pres. 1981—82, bd. govs. 1983—2002, A.T. Still Medallion of Honor 1999). Republican. Lutheran. Avocations: skiing, reading, home workshop. Address: PO Box 1509 Vail CO 81658 Home: 6413 S Dallas Ct Englewood CO 80111 Office: 5340 S Quebec St # 220-S Greenwood Village CO 80111

MAGOVERN, JAMES ANTHONY, thoracic surgeon; b. San Antonio, June 8, 1954; MD, U. Pitts., 1980. Diplomate Am. Bd. Thoracic Surgery, Am. Bd. Surgery. Intern Johns Hopkins, Balt., 1980-81, resident in surgery, 1981-82, Pa. State U. Coll. Medicine, Hershey, 1982-89; fellow in rsch. cardiothoracic surgery Milton S. Hershey Med. Ctr., 1985-87; with Allegheny Gen. Hosp., Pitts. Asst. prof. surgery Med. Coll. Pa. Mem. Assn. Acad. Surgery, Am. Coll. Cardiology, Am. Coll. Surgeons, Am. Heart Assn., People's Med. Soc. Office: 490 E North Ave Ste 302 Pittsburgh PA 15212-4740

MAGOWAN, PETER ALDEN, professional sports team executive, retail executive; b. N.Y.C., Apr. 5, 1942; s. Robert Anderson and Doris (Merrill) Magowan; m. Jill Tarlau (dec. July 1982); children: Kimberley, Margot, Hilary; m. Deborah Johnston, Aug. 14, 1982. BA, Stanford U., 1964; MA, Oxford U., Eng., 1966; postgrad., Johns Hopkins U., 1967—68. Store mgr. Safeway Stores Inc., Washington, 1968—70, dist. mgr. Houston, 1970—71, retail ops. mgr. Phoenix, 1971—72, divsn. mgr. Tulsa, 1973—76, mgr. internat. divsn. Toronto, Canada, 1976—78, mgr. western region San Francisco, 1978—79, CEO Oakland, Calif., 1980—93, chmn. bd. dirs., 1980—98; pres., mng. gen. ptnr. San Francisco Giants, 1993—. Bd. dirs. Daimler Chrysler Corp, Caterpillar, Safeway Inc. Office: San Francisco Giants 24 Willie Mays Plz San Francisco CA 94107-2199 Office Phone: 415-972-1950. E-mail: schasabat@sfgiants.com.

MAGRASS, YALE ROBERT, sociology educator, writer; b. Boston, Jan. 15, 1950; s. Harold B. and Evelyn P. (Sandler) M.; m. Ana M. Matos, Aug. 13, 1989; children: Jose, Miguel, David. BA magna cum laude, Brandeis U., 1971; postgrad., Columbia U., 1971-72; PhD in Sociology, U. Calif., Santa Barbara, 1978. Instr. U. Calif., Santa Barbara, 1975-77, U. Lowell, Mass., 1977-78; chancellor prof. U. Mass., North Dartmouth, 1978—. Cons. Profl. as Workers NIMH Grant, Boston, 1982-90; dir. Holocaust Oral History Project, New Bedford, 1980-84. Author: Thus Spake the Moguls, 1982, Power in the Highest Degree, 1990, Branded on My Arm and in My Soul, 2003; mem. editl. bd. Humanity and Soc., 1983—, Quar. Jour. of Ideology, 1992—, Bimonthly review of law books, 2003—; book reviewer, 2001-. Del. New Jewish Agenda, Israel, 1983, Cultural Exch. Program, China, 1986, Economist Tour of Eastern Europe, USSR, Hungary, Bulgaria, 1987, North Am. & Cuban Philosophers, Havana, 1995, Congress on Human Co-Existence, 2000. Columbia U. fellow, 1972, U. Calif. fellow, 1973. Mem. Am. Sociol. Assn., Assn. Humanist Sociologists, Radical Philosophers Assn., New Mobilization for Survival, Mass Pirg. Avocations: computers, hiking, video, travel. Office: U Mass North Dartmouth MA 02747

MAGRATH, C. PETER, educational association executive; b. NYC, Apr. 23, 1933; s. Laurence Wilfrid and Giulia Maria (Dentice) M.; m. Deborah C. Howell, 1988; children: Valerie Ruth, Monette Fay. BA summa cum laude, U. N.H., 1955; PhD, Cornell U., 1962. Faculty Brown U., Providence, 1961-68, prof. polit. sci., 1967-68, assoc. dean grad. sch., 1965-66; dean coll. Arts and Scis. U. Nebr., Lincoln, 1968-69, dean faculties Coll. Arts and Scis., 1969-72, interim chancellor, 1971-72, prof. polit. sci., 1968-72, vice-chancellor for acad. affairs, 1972; pres. SUNY, Binghamton, 1972-74, prof. polit. sci., 1972-74; pres. U. Minn., Mpls., 1974-84, U. Mo. System, 1985-91, Nat. Assn. State Univs. and Land Grant Colls., Washington, 1991—. Bd. dirs. Salzburg Seminar. Author: The Triumph of Character, 1963, Yazoo: Law and Politics in the New Republic, The Case of Fletcher v. Peck, 1966, Constitutionalism and Politics: Conflict and Consensus, 1968, Issues and Perspectives in American Government, 1971; (with others) The American Democracy, 2d edit., 1973; (with Robert L. Egbert) Strengthening Teacher Education, 1987; contbr. articles to profl. jours. Served with AUS, 1955—57. Mem. Assn. Am. Univs. (chmn. 1985-86, bd. dirs. Salzburg Sem. 2002—), Phi Beta Kappa, Phi Kappa Phi, Pi Gamma Mu, Pi Sigma Alpha, Kappa Tau Alpha. Office: Nat Assn State U and Land Grant Colls 1307 New York Ave NW Ste 400 Washington DC 20005-4722 E-mail: cmagrath@nasulgc.org. *True personal success cannot be measured by public acclaim, recognition, or status. It grows out of an ability to recognize right from wrong, and to maintain principles of fairness and understanding in all human relationships - regardless of one's role in life. In my case I have tried to fulfill this ideal; I have been willing to exercise leadership by asserting my judgements and views openly and directly on the educational and human issues that came my way.*

MAGRATH, JANE, music educator; b. Conway, SC, Dec. 27, 1949; MusB, Wesleyan Coll., 1972; MusM, U. N.C., 1974; MusD, Northwestern U., 1982. Prof. U. Okla., Norman, 1981—; author, editor Alfred Publishing, Inc., Van Nuys, Calif., 1985—. Lectr. in field. Author: Pianist's Guide to Standard Literature, 1995; editor (music series) Masterwork Classics, 1988, 89, 92, 2000, Encore, 1990; editl. bd. Piano Forum; Masterpieces with Flair, 1993, Melodious Masterpieces, 1993. Office: Univ Okla Sch Music 500 W Boyd St Norman OK 73019-2070 E-mail: jmagrath@ou.edu.

MAGRILL, JOE RICHARD, JR., religious organization administrator, minister; b. Marshall, Tex., Aug. 7, 1946; s. Joe Richard and Mary Belle (Chadwick) M. BA summa cum laude, East Tex. State U., 1967; MDiv, Princeton Theol. Sem., 1970, MTh, 1972; MLS, Rutgers U., 1971. Ordained to ministry Cumberland Presbyn. Ch., 1970. Stated supply min. Newsome (Tex.) Cumberland Presbyn. Ch., 1966-67; Christian edn. asst. United Presbyn. Ch., Carlstadt, N.J., 1967-70; order libr. Princeton (N.J.) Theol. Sem., 1969-72; head libr., prof. Memphis Theol. Sem., 1972-79; pastor Brookhaven Cumberland Presbyn. Ch., Nashville, 1987-89; asst. to stated clk. Gen. Assembly Office, Cumberland Presbyn. Ch., Memphis, 1979-83, supr. ctrl. acctg. div., 1980-87, editor The Cumberland Presbyn., 1984-87, chief exec. bd. stewardship, 1989—, mem. Gen. Assembly Coun., 1993—, chief exec. Cumberland Presbyn. Investment Loan Program, Inc., 1999—. Mem. Trinity Presbytery of Cumberland Presbyn. Ch., 1970—; sec.-treas. Hist. Found. Cumberland Presbyn. Ch., Memphis, 1974—; bd. dirs. Hist. Found. Presbyn. Ch. U.S., Montreat, N.C., 1980-83. Editor: In the Valley of the Cauca, 1981, One Family Under God, 1982, Family of Faith, 1998. Recipient achievement award Hist. Found. Cumberland Presbyn. Ch., 1980; scholar Phi Alpha Theta, 1967, Am. Theol. Libr. Assn., 1970. Democrat. Avocations: computers, historical research. Office: Cumberland Presbyn Ch 1978 Union Ave Memphis TN 38104-4134 E-mail: jrm@cumberland.org.

MAGRILL, ROSE MARY, library director; b. Marshall, Tex., June 8, 1939; d. Joe Richard and Mary Belle (Chadwick) M. BS, E. Tex. State U., 1960, MA, 1961; MS, U. Ill., 1964, PhD, 1969. Asst. to dean women E. Tex. State U., Commerce, 1960-61, librarian II, 1961-63; teaching asst. U. Ill., Urbana, 1963-64; instr. to asst. prof. E. Tex. State U., Commerce, 1964-67; asst. prof. Ball State U., Muncie, 1969-70; asst. prof. to prof. U. Mich., Ann Arbor, 1970-81; prof. U. N. Tex., Denton, 1981-99; dir. libr. E. Tex. Bapt. U., Marshall, 1987-2001. Accreditation site visitor ALA, Chgo., 1975—; cons. in field. Co-author: Building Library Collections, 4th edit. 1974, Library Technical Services, 1977, Building Library Collections, 5th edit. 1979, Acquisition Management and Collection Development in Libraries, 2d edit. 1989; author: Family of Faith, 1998. Trustee Memphis Theol. Sem., 1988-98; treas. Mission Synod of Cumberland Presbyn. Ch., 1989—; mem. bd. fin. Trinity Presbytery, 1989—; sec.-treas. Harrison County Hist. Commn., 1995—; trustee Hist. Found., 1999—; sec. Nat. Conv. Cumberland Presbyn. Women, 2000—02, chmn. bd., 2003—; bd. dirs. Presbyn. Hist. Soc. of S.W., 2000—. Recipient award Cumberland Presbyn. History, 1995. Mem. ALA (RTSD Resources Sect. pub. award 1978), Tex. Libr. Assn. Home: 804 Caddo St Marshall TX 75672-2414

MAGRO, CYNTHIA MARIA, pathologist; BS, U. Man., MD, 1985. Medical diplomate, diplomate Am. Bd. Cytopathology, Am. Bd. Dermatopathology, Am. Bd. Anotomic Pathology. Intern Harvard Med. Sch., Boston, 1985—87, resident, 1987—89, fellow, 1989—91; asst. prof. U. Winnipeg, 1991—93; asst. clin. prof. pathology Harvard Med. Sch., Boston, 1995—98;

assoc. clin. prof. dermatology U. Hosps., Case Western Res. U., Cleve., 1998—99; assoc. prof. pathology Thomas Jefferson U., Phila., 1999—2000; prof. Ohio State U., Columbus, 2000—, dir. dermatopathology, 2000—. Author: (textbook) The Melanocytic Proliferations: A Comprehensive Textbook of Pigmented Lesions (Am. Assn. Pubs. award for Excellence, 2001). Mem.: Am. Soc. Dermatopathology (chair edn. com. 2000—02). Achievements include research in inflammatory and malignant disorders of skin; inflammatory lung disease. Office: Ohio State U Pathology Dept N305 Doan Hall 410 W 10th Ave Columbus OH 43210-1218 Business E-Mail: magro-1@medctr.osu.edu.

MAGUIRE, CHARLOTTE EDWARDS, retired pediatrician; b. Richmond, Ind., Sept. 1, 1918; d. Joel Blaine and Lydia (Betscher) Edwards; m. Raymer Francis Maguire, Sept. 1, 1948 (dec.); children: Barbara, Thomas Clair II (dec.). Student, Stetson U., 1936—38, U. Wichita, 1938—39; BS, Memphis Tchrs. Coll., 1940; MD, U. Ark., 1944; LHD (hon.), Fla. State U., 2002. Intern, resident Orange Meml. Hosp., Orlando, Fla., 1944-46, med. staff., 1944—69, instr. nurses, 1947-57; resident Bellevue Hosp. and Med. Ctr., NYU, NYC, 1954—55; staff mem. Fla. Santarium and Hosp., Orlando, 1946-56, Holiday House and Hosp., Orlando, 1950-62; mem. courtesy and cons. staff West Orange Meml. Hosp., Winter Garden, Fla., 1952-67; active staff, chief dept. pediat. Mercy Hosp., Orlando, 1965-68; med. dir. childrens med. svcs., asst. sec. Fla. Dept. Health and Rehab. Svcs., 1969—71, med. dir. med. svcs. and basic care, 1975-84; med. exec. dir., med. svcs. divsn. worker's compensation Fla. Dept. Labor, Tallahassee, 1984-87; chief of staff physicians and dentists Ctrl. Fla. divsn. Children's Home Soc. Fla., 1947-56; dir. Orlando Child Health Clinic, 1949-58; pvt. practice Orlando, 1946—68; asst. regional dir. HEW, 1970-72; ret., 1987. Asst. dir. health and sci. affairs Dept. Health Edn. & Welfare, Atlanta, 1971-72, Washington, 1972-75; pediat. cons. Fla. Crippled Children's Commn., 1952-70, dir., 1968-70; med. dir. Office Med. Svcs. and Basic Care, sr. physician Office of Asst. Sec. Ops., Fla. Dept. Health and Rehab. Svcs.; clin. prof. dept. pediat. U. Fla. Coll. Medicine, Gainesville, 1980-87; mem. Fla. Drug Utilization Rev., 1983-87; real estate salesperson Investors Realty, 1982-2003; bd. dirs. Stavros Econ. Ctr. Fla. State U., Tallahassee; pres.'s coun. Fla. State U., U. Fla., Gainesville; Charlotte Edwards Maguire eminent scholar chair and scholarships for qualified students, 1999. Mem. profl. adv. com. Fla. Ctr. for Clin. Svcs. at U. Fla., 1952-60; del. to Mid-century White House Conf. on Children and Youth, 1950; U.S. del from Nat. Soc. for Crippled Children to World Congress for Welfare of Cripples, Inc., London, 1957; pres. of corp. Eccleston-Callahan Hosp. for Colored Crippled Children, 1956-58; sec. Fla. chpt. Nat. Doctor's Com. for Improved Med. Svcs., 1951-52; med. adv. com. Gateway Sch. for Mentally Retarded, 1959-62; bd. dirs. Forest Park Sch. for Spl. Edn. Crippled Children, 1949-54, mem. med. adv. com., 1955-68, chmn., 1957-68; mem. Fla. Adv. Coun. for Mentally Retarded, 1965-70; dir. ctrl. Fla. poison control Orange Meml. Hosp.; mem. orgn. com., chmn. com. for admissions and selection policies Camp Challenge; participant 12th session Fed. Exec. Inst., 1971; del. White House Conf. on Aging, 1980; dir. Stavros Econ. Ctr. Fla. State U.; trustee Fla. State U. Found., 1998—, mem. campaign com. Charlotte Edwards Maguire Eminent Scholarship named in her honor Fla. State U.; named Outstanding Woman in Our Cmty. AAUW, Tallahassee, 2002. Mem. AMA (life), Nat. Rehab. Assn., Am. Congress Phys. Medicine and Rehab., Fla. Soc. Crippled Children and Adults, Ctrl. Fla. Soc. Crippled Children and Adults (dir. 1949-58, pres. 1956-57), Am. Assn. Cleft Palate, Fla. Soc. Crippled Children (trustee 1951-57, v.p. 1956-57, profl. adv. com. 1957-68), Mental Health Assn. Orange County (charter mem.; pres. 1949-50, dir. 1947-52, chmn. exec. com. 1950-52, dir. 1963-65), Fla. Orange County Heart Assn., Am. Med. Women's Assn., Am. Acad. Med. Dirs., Fla. Med. Assn. (life, chmn. com. on mental retardation), Orange County Med. Assn., Orange Med. Soc. (life), Fla. Pediat. Soc. (pres. 1952-53), Fla. Cleft Palate Assn. (counselor-at-large, sec.), Nat. Inst. Geneal. Rsch., Nat. Geneal. Soc., Assn. Profl. Genealogists, Tallahassee Geneal. Soc., Fla. State U. Found. Inc. (bd. dirs. Stavoris Ctr. for Econ. Edn.), Capital City Tiger Bay Club, Fla. Econs. Club, Francis Eppes Soc. Fla. State U., Econ. Club Fla., Governors Club. Home: 4158 Covenant Ln Tallahassee FL 32308-5765

MAGUIRE, D. E. electronics executive; b. Sept. 27, 1934; BS in Math. and Indsl. Engring., Mich. U., 1959. Various positions Kemet, 1959—87; CEO, dir. Kemet Electronic Corp., Fountain Inn, SC, 1990—, chmn., 2002—. Mem.: Electronics Industry Assn. (gov.). Office: Kemet Electronic Corp 2835 Kemet Way Simpsonville SC 29681-6298

MAGUIRE, GREGORY, writer; PhD in English and Am. Lit., Tufts U., 1990. Fellow Bread Load Writers Conf., Middlebury, Vt., 1978; prof., assoc. dir. Ctr. for the Study of Children's Lit., Simmons Coll., 1979—86; co-dir., founding bd. mem. Children's Lit. New England, Inc., 1986—; artist-in-residence Isabella Stewart Gardner Mus., Boston, 1994; fellow Blue Mountain Ctr., NY, The Hambridge Ctr., Ga., 1998, The Va. Ctr. for the Creative Arts, 1999. Author: (children's novels) The Dream Stealer, 1983 (named one of the Children's Books of the Yr., Child Study Children's Books Com., 1983, named a Nat. Coun. Tchrs. of English Tchr.'s Choice, 1984), Missing Sisters, 1994 (named a Parents Choice Hon. book, 1994), Wicked: The Life and Times of the Wicked Witch of the West, 1995, Confessions of an Ugly Stepsister, 1999, Lost, 2001, Mirror Mirror, 2003, The Hamlet Chronicles, Seven Spiders Spinning (named an ALA Notable book, 1994, Judy Lopez Meml. Award Hon. book, 1995), Six Haunted Hairdos, Five Alien Elves, Four Stupid Cupids, Three Rotten Eggs, A Couple of April Fools; contbr. articles to profl. mags. including the Boston Rev., Christian Sci. Monitor, The Horn Book Mag., others. Office: William Reiss - Literary Agt John Hawkins and Assocs 71 W 23rd St Ste 1600 New York NY 10010 Address: Jennifer Suitor - Publicist HarperCollins 10 E 53rd St New York NY 10022

MAGUIRE, JAMES HARVEY, physician; b. Easton, Pa., Nov. 25, 1948; s. James I and Elizabeth C (Updegrove) Maguire. AB, Princeton U., 1970; MD, Harvard U., 1974, MPH, 1978. Cert. internal med, infectious disease. Rsch. assoc. Harvard Sch. Pub. Health, Boston, 1978-81; instr. in medicine Harvard Med. Sch. Pub. Health, 1982-85; asst. prof. Medicine Tropical Pub. Health, Boston, 1985-92, assoc. prof. medicine, 1992-2001; physician, clin. dir. infectious disease Brigham Womens Hosp., Boston, 1992-2001; chief parasitic disease br. Ctrs. for Disease Control & Prevention, Atlanta, 2001—. Editor: Parasitic Diseases, 1993; sect. editor: Am. Jour. Tropical Medicine and Hygiene, 2002—. Mem.: Infectious Disease Soc. Am., Am. Soc. Tropical Medicine and Hygiene (councillor 2000—, Ben Kean medal 2001). Avocation: tennis. E-mail: jmaguire@cdc.gov.

MAGUIRE, JOHN DAVID, academic administrator, educator, writer; b. Montgomery, Ala., Aug. 7, 1932; s. John Henry and Clyde (Merrill) M.; m. Lillian Louise Parrish, Aug. 29, 1953; children: Catherine Merrill, Mary Elizabeth, Anne King. AB magna cum laude, Washington and Lee U., 1953, Litt.D. (hon.), 1979; Fulbright scholar, Edinburgh (Scotland) U., 1953-54; B.D. summa cum laude, Yale, 1956, PhD, 1960; postdoctoral research, Yale U. and U. Tübingen, Germany, 1964-65, U. Calif., Berkeley, 1968-69, Silliman U., Philippines, 1976-77; HLD (hon.), Transylvania U., 1990. Dir. Internat. Student Ctr., New Haven, 1956-58; mem. faculty Wesleyan U., Middletown, Conn., 1960-70, asso. provost, 1967-68; vis. lectr. Pacific Sch. Religion and Grad. Theol. Union, Berkeley, 1968-69; pres. SUNY Coll. at Old Westbury, 1970-81, Claremont (Calif.) Grad. U., 1981-98. Sr. fellow Claremont Grad. U. Sch. Politics and Econs.; dir. nat. project Renewing Democracy through Interracial/Multicultural Comty. Bldg., 1998—. Author: The Dance of the Pilgrim: A Christian Style of Life for Today, 1967; also numerous articles. Mem. Conn. adv. comt. US Comn. Civil Rights, 1961—70; participant White House Conf. on Civil Rights, 1966; advisor Martin Luther King Cent. Social Change, Atlanta, 1968—, permanent trustee, 1968—, 1st chmn. bd. dirs., 1968—; bd. dirs. Nassau County Health and Welfare Coun., 1971—81, pres., 1974—76; trustee United Bd. Christian Higher Ed in Asia, 1975—81, Inst. Int. Ed., 1980—86; charter trustee Tomas Rivera Policy Inst., Claremont, Calif., 1984—, vice chmn., 1987—94, treas., 1995—; with Asn. Ind. Calif. Cols. and Univs., 1985—98; chmn. Asn. Ind. Calif. Cols. and Univs., 1990—92, mem. exec. comt., 1992—98; with Calif. Achievement Coun., 1985—94, chmn., 1990—94; with Transylvania Univ. Bingham Trust, 1987—, Lincoln Found. and Lincoln Inst. Land Policy, Inc., 1987—94; The JL Found., 1988—; with Bus. Enterprise Trust, 1989—99; with Educ. Found. African Ams., 1991—99; bd. dirs. Asn. Am. Cols. and Univs., 1981—86, chmn., 1984—85; bd. dirs. Legal Def. and Edu. Fund NAACP, 1991—, west coast div., 1981—91, Thacher Sch., Ojai, Calif., 1982—94, vice chmn., 1986—90; with Salzburg Seminar, 1992—96; charter mem. Pacific Coun. Int. Policy, 1995—; mem. Am. Comt. US-Soviet Rels., 1981—92, Blue Ribbon Calif. Comn. Teaching Profession, 1984—86; mem. gov. coun. Aspen Inst. Wye Faculty Seminar, 1984—94; mem. Coun. Fgn. Rels., 1983—; mem. adv. bd. RAND Cent. Research Immigration Policy, 1994—97, Peter F. Drucker Found. Non-Profit Mgt, 1990—, Andrew Young Sch. Policy Ga. State Univ., 1999—, The Eureka Communities, 1998—; mem. Pres.'s Adv. Coun. Comn. on Calif. Master Plan Higher Educ., 1986—87, Los Angeles Educ. Alliance Restructuring Now, 1992—98, Calif. Bus. Higher Educ. Forum, 1992—98; leader Idyllwild Sch. Summer Poetry Festival, 1998—. Recipient Julia A. Archibald High Scholarship award Yale Div. Sch., 1956; Day fellow Yale Grad. Sch., 1956-57; Kent fellow, 1957-60; Howard Found. postdoctoral fellow Brown U. Grad. Sch., 1964-65; Fenn lectr., 7 Asian countries, 1976-77; recipient Conn. Prince Hall Masons' award outstanding contbns. human rights in Conn., 1965; E. Harris Harbison Gt. Tchr. prize Danforth Found., 1968 Fellow Soc. Values Higher Edn. (pres. 1974-81, bd. dirs. 1972-88); mem. Phi Beta Kappa, Omicron Delta Kappa Democrat. Office: Claremont Grad U Inst for Dem Renewal 170 E 10th St Claremont CA 91711-5909 Office Phone: 909-607-9220.

MAGUIRE, JOHN PATRICK, investment company executive; b. New Britain, Conn., Apr. 1, 1917; s. John Patrick and Edna Frances (Cashen) M.; m. Mary-Emily Jones, Sept. 8, 1945; children: Peter Dunbar (dec.), Joan Guilford. Student, Holy Cross Coll., 1933-34; degree in bus. adminstrn. with distinction, Babson Inst., 1936; AB cum laude, Princeton U., 1941; BS (hon.), Babson Inst., 1995, Babson Coll., 1995; JD, Yale U., 1943; PhD (hon.), St. Bonaventure U., 1965. Bar: Conn. 1943, N.Y. 1944. Assoc. Cravath, Swaine & Moore (and predecessor), N.Y.C., 1943-50, 52-54; v.p., dir. Forbes, Inc.; also mng. editor Investors Adv. Inst., 1951-52; asst. counsel Gen. Dynamics Corp., 1954-60, sec., 1962-87, v.p., 1981-87; sec., gen. counsel Tex. Butadiene and Chem. Corp., 1960-62; with J.P. Maguire Investment Advisors, 1987-95; exec. v.p. Fiduciary Asset Mgmt. Co., 1995—2002. Mem. bd. govs. N.Y. Young Rep. Club, 1951-52; chmn. fin. and investment coms. St. Louis Art Mus., 1984-94; trustee St. Bonaventure U., 1965-71, Webster U., 1983-85, John Burroughs Sch. (chmn. investment com.) 1976-85. Mem. ABA. Clubs: Piping Rock (Locust Valley, L.I.); Yale (St. Louis); St. Louis Country; Princeton (St. Louis); Tiger Inn (Princeton). Home: PO Box 1088 Boca Grande FL 33921-1088 E-mail: jmaguire@sbcglobal.net.

MAGUIRE, KIM D. retail executive; With Target, 1981—2001, sr. v.p. hardlines; exec. v.p., chief merchanising officer Circuit City, Richmond, Va., 2001—. Office: Circuit City 9950 Mayland Dr Richmond VA 23233-1464

MAGUIRE, LAMBERT, social worker, educator; b. Chgo., Oct. 26, 1946; s. Lambert and Mary Ann (Murphy) Maguire; m. Barbara Ann Magnusson, June 11, 1971; children: Amy, Mandy. BS, Loyola U., Chgo., 1968; AM, U. Chgo., 1971; MA, U. Mich., 1976, PhD, 1979. Lic. social worker Pa. Dir. Treatment Outcome Rsch., Ann Arbor, Mich., 1976—78; chmn. direct practice U. Pitts., 1979—, asst. prof., 1979—84, assoc. prof., 1984—90, prof., 1990—. Chair direct practice U. Pitts. Sch. Social Work, 1980—; prin. investigator NIMH, Pitts., 1980—81, 1981—83. Author: Understanding Social Networks, 1983, Il Lavoro Sociale Di Rete, 1991, Social Support Systems in Practice, 1991, Japanese edit., 1995, Clinical Social Work, 2002. Capt. USPHS, 1971—74. Fellow, U. Chgo., NIMH, 1969—71. Mem.: NASW, Soc. Social Work Rsch., Acad. Cert. Social Workers. Roman Catholic. Avocations: swimming, travel, opera. Office: U Pitts Sch Social Work 2012 C of L Pittsburgh PA 15260

MAGUIRE, MARTHA ELENOR ERWIN (MARTIE MAGUIRE), musician; b. York, Pa., Oct. 12, 1969; d. Paul and Barbara Erwin; m. Ted Seidel, 1995 (div.); m. Gareth MaGuire, Aug. 10, 2001. Student, So. Meth. U. Performer Blue Night Express, 1984—89; fiddle player, violinist, vocalist Dixie Chicks, 1989—. Performer: (albums) LIttle Ol' Cowgirl, 1992, Thank Heavens for Dale Evans, 1992, Shouldn't a Told You That, 1993, Wide Open Spaces, 1998 (Album of Yr., Acad. Country Music, 1998, Best Country Album, Grammy Awards, 1998, Best Country Artist Clip of Yr., Billboard Awards, 1998, Maximum Vision Clif of Yr., Billboard Awards, 1998, Best Selling Album, Can. Country Music Award, 1999, Song of Yr. (Country), WB Radio Music Awards, 1999, Album of Yr., Acad. Country Music, 1999), Fly, 1999 (Best Country Album, Grammy Awards, 1999, Best Selling Album, Can. Country Music Awards, 2000, Internat. Album, British Country Music Awards, 2000, Country Album of Yr., Billboard Awards, 2000, Album of Yr., Acad. Country Music, 2000, Album of Yr., CMA, 2000), Home, 2002 (Favorite Country Album, Am. Music Awards, 2002, Best Recording Package, Grammy Awards, 2002, Best Country Album, Grammy Awards, 2002), Top of the World Tour: Live, 2003. Named Top New Country Artist, Billboard, 1998, Most Significant New Country Act, Country Monitor, 1998, Group of Yr., CMA, 1998, Top Vocal Group, Acad. Country Music, 1998, Internat. Rising Star, British Country Music Awards, 1999, Country Artist of Yr., Rolling Stone, 1999, Artist of Yr. (Country), WB Radio Music Awards, 1999, Favorite New Artist (Country), AMA, 1999, Vocal Group of Yr., CMA, 1999, Country Artist of Yr., Billboard, 1999, 2000, Vocal Group of Yr., CMA, 2000, Entertainer of Yr., 2000, ACM, 2000, 2001, Vocal Group of Yr., 2001, Favorite Musical Group or Band, People's Choice Awards, 2001, Favorite Country Band, Am. Music Award, 2002, Vocal Group of Yr., Country Music Assn. Award, 2002, Country Duo/Group of Yr., Billboard, 2002; recipient Horizon award, CMA, 1998, others. Office: Monument Sony Nashville 34 Music Sq East Nashville TN 37203

MAGUIRE, MILDRED MAY, chemistry educator, magnetic resonance researcher; b. Leetsdale, Pa., May 7, 1933; d. John and Mildred (Sklarsky) Magura. BS in Chemistry, Carnegie-Mellon U., 1955; MS in Phys. Chemistry, U. Wis., 1960; PhD in Phys. Chemistry, Pa. State U., 1967. Devel. chemist Koppers Co., Monaca, Pa., 1955-58; rsch. chemist Am. Cyanamid Co., Stamford, Conn., 1960-63; asst. prof. chemistry Waynesburg (Pa.) Coll., 1967-70, assoc. prof., 1970-74, prof., 1974—. Leverhulme vis. prof. U. Leicester, Eng., 1980-81, summer 1989; cons. Pitts. Energy Tech. Ctr., summers 1978-86; faculty rsch. participant Oak Ridge Assoc. Univs., 1978-80, 82-85; U.S. del. Internat. Conf. Phys. Chemists, China, 1996, Sci. and Tech. Conf., India, 1997. Contbr. articles to sci. jours., chpt. to book. Sec. Waynesburg Women's Club, 1981-82; citizen amb. People to People Program, 1996, 97. Recipient Woman of the Yr. award AAUW, Waynesburg, 1983; Cottrell grantee Rsch. Corp. N.Y., 1970-71; Leverhulme vis. fellow U.K., 1980-81; Curie Internat. fellow AAUW, U.K., 1980-81; Robert West Superconductor Rsch. Grantee, Univ. Wis., 2001-02. Mem. AAUP, AAAS, Am. Chem. Soc.; Spectroscopy Soc. of Pitts.; Pitts. Soc. of Analytical Chemists. Avocations: gardening, painting, swimming, classical music, reading. Home: 1550 Crescent Hills Waynesburg PA 15370-1654 Office: Waynesburg Coll College St Waynesburg PA 15370 E-mail: mmaguire@waynesburg.edu.

MAGUIRE, RAYMER F., JR., lawyer; b. Orlando, Fla., Oct. 20, 1921; s. Raymer F. Sr. and Ruth (McCullough) M.; m. Sara Corry, Aug. 13, 1951; children: Craig Corry, Raymer F. III, Sara Maguire LeMone, Edmund Corry. BA, U. Fla., 1943, JD, 1948. Bar: Fla. 1948, U.S. Dist. Ct. (so. dist.) 1948, U.S. Supreme Ct. 1969. Assoc. Maguire, Voorhis & Wells, P.A., Orlando, 1948-53, mem., 1953—. Bd. dirs. Sun Bank, N.A.; bd. dirs. and trustee various corps. and trusts. Elder First Presbyn. Ch., 1961—; mem., chmn. community coll. coun. State of Fla., 1976-79, mem. community coll. coordinating bd., 1979-83, vice chmn. 1979-81, chmn. 1981-82; trustee Valencia Community Coll., 1967-86, chmn. 1967-72; bd. dirs. Orange County Hist. Soc., 1982—, pres., 1987-88; chmn. bd. Cen. Fla. chpt. Am. Heart Assn., 1966-67; bd. dirs. Valencia Community Coll. Found., pres., 1974-75; chmn. citizens com. Orange County Sch. Bd. Referendum, 1964. Named in honor of Raymer F. Maguire Jr. Learning Resource Ctr., Valencia Community Coll., 1977. Mem. ABA, Fla. Bar Assn. U. Fla. Alumni Assn. (bd. dirs. 1954—, pres. 1959-60, Disting. Alumnus award 1975), Kiwanis (pres. 1962), U. Fla. Found. Republican.

MAGUIRE, ROBERT FRANCIS, III, real estate investor; b. Portland, Oreg., Apr. 18, 1935; s. Robert Francis Jr. and Jean (Shepard) M. BA, UCLA, 1960. Vice pres. Security Pacific Nat. Bank, L.A., 1960-64; chmn. Maguire Thomas Ptnrs., L.A., 1964—. Exec. bd. med. scis. UCLA. Bd. dirs. Los Angeles County Mus. Art; trustee UCLA Found., Bard Coll.; bd. dirs. St. John's Hosp., Music Ctr. Bd. Govs., Calif. Mem.: California (Los Angeles); Valley (Montecito, Calif.), L.A. Country. E-mail: robert.maguire@maguirepartners.com.

MAGUIRE, TOBEY (TOBIAS VINCENT MAGUIRE), actor; b. Santa Monica, Calif., June 27, 1975; s. Vincent and Wendy Maguire. Actor: (films) The Wizard, 1989, This Boy's Life, 1993, Healer, 1994, SFW, 1994, Revenge of the Red Baron, 1994, Joyride, 1996, The Ice Storm, 1997, Deconstructing Harry, 1997, Pleasantville, 1998 (Saturn Award for best performance by a younger actor, 1999), Fear and Loathing in Las Vegas, 1998, Ride with the Devil, 1999, The Cider House Rules, 1999, Wonder Boys, 2000 (Toronto Film Critics Assn. Award for best male supporting performance, 2000), Don's Plum, 2001, Spider-Man, 2002, Spider-Man 2, 2004; voice (films) Cats & Dogs, 2001; actor: (TV films) Tales from the Whoop: Hot Rod Brown Class Clown, 1990, Spoils of War, 1994, A Child's Cry for Help, 1994, Seduced by Madness: The Diane Borchardt Story, 1996, (short film) Duke of Groove, 1996 (Oscar nomination for best short film, 1996); (TV series) Great Scott!, 1992; actor, exec. prodr.: (films) Seabiscuit, 2003; (TV films) Rock of Ages, 2003; prodr.: (films) 25th Hour, 2002, Whatever We Do, 2003; guest appearences on: Blossom, 1991, Roseanne, 1991, Eerie, Indiana, 1991, Wild & Crazy Kids, 1992, Walker, Texas Ranger, 1994, Tracey Takes On, 1996. Office: c/o SFM 1122 S Robertson Blvd Los Angeles CA 90036 also: c/o Creative Artists Agency 9830 Wilshire Blvd Beverly Hills CA 90212-1825*

MAGURNO, RICHARD PETER, lawyer; b. Suffern, N.Y., June 29, 1943; s. Eugene and Rose (Foresta) M. BS, Georgetown U., 1964; MS, U. Wis., 1965; JD, Fordham U., 1968. Bar: N.Y. 1970, Fla. 1982, U.S. Supreme Ct. 1974, U.S. Ct. Appeals (2d, 5th, 11th cirs.) 1976, U.S. Dist. Ct. (so. and ea. dists.) N.Y. 1979. Atty. Eastern Air Lines, N.Y.C., 1970-73, sr. atty., 1973-76, gen. atty., 1976-79, dir. legal Miami, Fla., 1980, v.p. legal, asst. sec., 1980-84, gen. counsel, sr. v.p. legal, sec., 1984-88; ptnr. Lord Day & Lord, Barrett Smith, 1989-94; gen. counsel, sr. v.p. legal Trans World Airlines, St. Louis, 1994-98; aviation cons., 1998-2000; gen. counsel, sr. v.p., sec. AirTran Airways, 2000—. Author: Romantic Suffern, 1773-1973, 1973. Served in Peace Corps, 1968-69. Mem. ABA, Fla. Bar Assn. Democrat. Roman Catholic.

MAGWOOD, WILLIAM D. federal agency administrator; BS in Physics, BA in English, Carnegie-Mellon U.; MFA, U. Pitts. Scientist Westinghouse Electric Corp., Pitts., 1984—94; with Edison Electric Inst., Washington, 1984—94; exec. sec. highly enriched uranium oversight com. Office Nuc. Energy, Sci. and Tech., Washington, assoc. dir. tech. and program planning, 1994—95, acting dir., 1996—98, dir., 1998—. Office: US Dept Energy NE-10 Office Nuc Energy Sci and Tech 1000 Independence Ave SW Washington DC 20585-1290*

MAHADEVA, KUMAR, information technology executive; b. Colombo, Sri Lanka; MEE, Cambridge U., England; MBA, Harvard Bus. Sch. Rsch. devel. British Broadcasting Corp., London; consultant McKinsey and Co.; dir. strategy corp. devel. AT&T; chmn. Dun & Bradstreet India China; founder, chmn., CEO Cognizant Tech. Solutions, 1994—. Office: 500 Glenpointe Ctr W Teaneck NJ 07666

MAHADEVAN, KUMAR, marine laboratory administrator, researcher; b. Madras, Tamilnadu, India, Sept. 29, 1948; came to U.S., 1971; s. Sockalingam Ponnusamy and Pankajam (Nadar) M.; m. Linda Claire Goggin, Sept. 27, 1980; children: Andrew, Alexander, Chad, Vijayan. BS, Madras U., 1967; MS, Annamalai U., Chidambaram, India, 1971; PhD, Fla. State U., 1977. Instr. Chingleput (India) Med. Coll., 1967-68, Lakshman's Coll., Madras, 1968-69; rsch. asst. Fla. State U., Tallahassee, 1971-75; staff scientist Conservation Cons., Inc., Palmetto, Fla., 1975-78; sr. scientist Mote Marine Lab., Sarasota, Fla., 1978-79, dir. divsn., 1979—86, interim co-dir., 1984, pres., 1986—. Mem. Coun. on Ocean Affairs, Washington, 1989-91, steering com. Gulf of Mex. Program, Atlanta, 1988-96; mem. South Atlantic and Gulf States Coastal Protection Commn., 1990-93; vice chmn. NOAA Marine Rsch. Bd., Gulf of Mex., 1992-96. Contbr. articles to profl. jours. Mem. sch. adv. bd., Sarasota, 1988-89; mem. tech. adv. bd. Myakka River, Sarasota, 1987-90; legis. liason Parents Assn. of Sarasota Schs., 1988-89; bd. dirs. Jason Found. for Edn., 1991—, Health Care Sarasota, 1997-98; vice chmn. Fla. Ocean Alliance, 2000—; mem. Fla. Gov.'s Ocean Com., 1997-98; mem. adv. bd. Harte Inst. for Gulf of Mex. Studies, 2001—. Nat. Merit scholar Univ. Grants Commn., India, 1969-71. Fellow Explorers Club (nat.); mem. N.Am. Benthological Soc., Oceanographic Soc., World Aquaculture Soc., Deep Sea Biol. Soc. (hon.), Fla. Acad. Scis. (councillor 1975), So. Assn. Marine Labs (pres. 1990, exec. bd. 1986-91, treas. 1995—), Assn. Marine Labs Caribbean (pres. 1987-88, exec. bd. 1984—), Nat. Assn. Marine Labs. (pres. 1994-95), Sigma Xi. Republican. Avocations: racquetball, fishing, gardening. Office: Mote Marine Lab 1600 Ken Thompson Pkwy Sarasota FL 34236-1096 Office Phone: 941-388-4441. Business E-Mail: kumar@mote.org.

MAHADY, JOSEPH M. former pharmacy products company executive; Pres. Am. Home Products Corp., Madison, N.J. Office: Am Home Products Corp 5 Giralda Farms Madison NJ 07940-1027

MAHAFFEY, JOHN CHRISTOPHER, professional society administrator; b. Jefferson City, Mo., July 20, 1953; s. Fred Turner and Betty Cord (Woodfill) Mahaffey; children: Michael, Katherine. BA, Western Ill. U., Macomb, 1975; MS, DePaul U., 1999. Legis. aide Congressman Harold R. Collier, Washington, 1972-73; legis. asst. Nat. Assn. Retail Druggists, Washington, 1975-76; dir. Commn. and Meetings Nat. Assn. Bds. of Pharmacy, Chgo., 1976-80; pres., CEO Assn. Forum, Chgo., 1980—2002; exec. dir. Am. Coll. Foot and Ankle Surgeons, Park Ridge, Ill., 2002—. Bd. dirs. Healthcare Assocs. Credit Union, 2003—. Commr. City of Park Ridge (Ill.) Econ. Devel. Commn., 1990—94, 1996—2000; mem. exec. com. Chgo. Convention and Tourism Bur., Chgo., 1993—. Recipient Disting. Alumni award, Western Ill. U., Macomb, 1993. Fellow: Am. Soc. Assn. Execs. (mem. cert. commn. 1989—91, Key award 1994); mem.: U.S. C. of C., Assn. Com. 1000. Presbyterian. Office: Am Coll Foot and Ankle Surgeons 8725 W Higgins Rd Chicago IL 60603 Office Phone: 773-693-9300. Business E-Mail: mahaffey@acfas.org.

MAHAFFEY, KATHRYN ROSE, risk assessor; b. Johnstown, Pa., Dec. 24, 1943; d. William T. and Harriet L. Mahaffey; m. Samuel Nelson Kramer, June 1977 (div. 1984); children: Harriet Mahaffey Kramer, Charles Herbert Kramer; m. David Ernst Jacobs, Oct. 13, 1996. BS, Pa. State U., 1965; PhD, Rutgers U., 1968. Sr. environ. scientist Nat. Inst. Environ. Health Sci., Research Triangle Park, N.C., 1987-93, Nat. Ctr. for Environ. Assessment, U.S. EPA, Cin., 1993-99, br. chief, 1983-87; dir. divsn. exposure assessment Office of Prevention, Pesticides, Toxic Substances, U.S. EPA, Washington, 1999—. Asst. prof. dept. pathology U. N.C. Sch. Medicine, Chapel Hill, 1969-71. Editor: Dietary and Environmental Lead: Human Health Effects, 1985, (with others) Clinical Effects of Environmental Chemicals, 1989; contbg. author books and reports; author articles. Mem. Am. Soc. for Nutritional Scis., Am. Soc. for Clin. Nutrition, Soc. for Internat. Nutrition Rsch. Office: 1200 Pennsylvania Ave NW MC 7203 Washington DC 20460 E-mail: mahaffey.kate@epa.gov.

MAHAFFEY, MARYANN, councilwoman; b. Burlington, Iowa, Jan. 18, 1925; m. Herman Dooha; 1 child, Susan. BA, Cornell Coll., 1946, LHD (hon.), 1995; MSW, U. So. Calif., 1951. Legis. rep., chair Mich. Social Work Coun., 1965-68; founder, chair City of Detroit Task Force on Hunger & Malnutrition, 1969-74; council member, pres. pro tem City of Detroit, 1974—; emeritus prof. Wayne State U., Detroit, 1990—. Pres. Detroit City Coun., 1991-98. Del. founding conv. Nat. Women's Polit. Caucus, 1971-73; chair, founder Mich. Statewide Nutrition Commn., 1973-83; designer, initiator Detroit Police Dept. Rape Crisis Ctr. and Family Trouble Clinic of Detroit,

Family Svc. and Police, 1974-75; del. IWY, Mexico City, 1975, Houston, 1978; dep. chair U.S. Conf. on Families, 1979-81; chair human devel. com. Nat. League of Cities, 1992, chair Mich. del. to UN Conf. Women, Beijing, 1995; summer recreation dir. Nat. Intercollegiate Christian Coun. in Concentration Camp for Japanese Ams., 1945; trainer, integrator Brownie Troop Indpls. Girl Scouts, 1951-52; organizer Welfare Rights, Detroit, 1961; founder Nat. Peace and Disarmament Com. NASW, 1962-69, pres., 1975-77; founder Women in Social Welfare, 1972-74; author policy of women's rights, Internat. Fedn. Social Workers, 1987; mem. exec. com. Internat. Fedn. Social Workers, 1984-86. Mem. NAACP (life), Am. Orthopsychiat. Assn. (pres. 1984-85), Japanese Am. Citizens League, Women in Mcpl. Govt. (pres. 1995, adv. bd. 1996—, mem. NLC policy adv. coun. 1997—), Nat. Coun. Negro Women (life). Office: 1340 City County Bldg Detroit MI 48226

MAHAFFEY, REDGE ALLAN, movie producer, director, writer, actor, scientist; b. Bethesda, Md., Dec. 15, 1949; s. George Newton and Lila Katherine (Drum) M.; m. Ellen Cecilia Cranston, May 30, 1973 (div. Dec. 1980); m. Patricia Jane Guy, Apr. 29, 1984 (div. Sept. 1994); children: Travis Guy, Morgan Nicole; m. Veronica Bird, Sept. 24, 1994; children: Ryan Alexander, Ramsey Blake. BS, U. Md., 1971, MS, 1973, PhD, 1976. NRC postdoctoral fellow Nat. Acad. of Scis., Washington, 1976-77; research physicist Naval Research Lab., Washington, 1977-78; sr. research physicist Sachs/Freeman Assocs., Bladensburg, Md., 1978-79, dir. research Bowie, Md., 1979-81, exec. v.p., chief scientist Largo, Md., 1981-91, 1999—, also bd. dirs. Landover, Md., 1985—; mng. ptnr. Ramsway Pictures, 1991—; pres. WHOH, Largo, Md., 1993—. Instr. George Washington U., Washington, 1979-80, Prince George's Coll., 1987; pres. Capitol Contracts, Bowie, 1981-83. Author: A Higher Education, 1989, Me, Myself and I, 1992, Deadly Rivals, 1992; exec. prodr., writer Deadly Rivals, 1992, Quest of the Delta Knights, 1993; prodr., actor, writer, dir. Life 101, 1995 (hon. mention Atlantic City Film Festival 1997), First Encounter, 1997; prodr., actor, dir., writer She's Too Tall, 1998 (Best Comedy award Atlantic City Film Festival 1998); contbr. articles on lasers and particle beams to sci. jours., also short stories, essays and poems to mags.; patentee laser, x-rays and particle beams. Recipient Research Publ. award Naval Research Lab., 1978, 1st Place Novel Internat. Lit. Awards, 1988, award of merit Internat. Soc. for Advancement of Poetry, 1990. Mem. IEEE, Am. Phys. Soc., Mensa, Intertel, Nat. Writer's Club, Internat. Platform Assn., Internat. Soc. Phil. Enquiry, Writer's Assn. Anne Arundel County, Bethesda Writer's Ctr., Inst. Noetic Scis. Clubs: Sea Dragons Martial Arts(Washington) (treas. 1984-85, instr. 1987-91). Republican. Avocations: martial arts, softball, basketball. Office: SFA Inc 9315 Largo Dr W Largo MD 20774-4755

MAHAFFY, TELFAIR, safety scientist; b. Jacksonville, Fla., Jan. 26, 1936; s. Conrad Brickwedel and Mary Willard (Telfair) M.; m. Nancy A. Scheurer, Oct. 23, 1959 (div.); children: Anne, Michael. AB in English, U. N.C., 1958; postgrad., Yale U., 1958-60. Mortgage broker The Travelers, Jacksonville, Fla., 1960-64, Norton Realty, Jacksonville, Fla., 1964-68; v.p. Haughton & Co., Jacksonville, Fla., 1968-72; pres., onwer Fla. Mortgage Exch., Jacksonville, 1972-87; safety dir. Holmes Lumber Co., Jacksonville, 1987-99. Bd. dirs. Jacksonville Athletic Charities, 1988-93, v.p. Mem. Fla. Hunter-Jumper Assn. (pres. 1978), North Fla. Hunter-Jumper Assn. (pres. 1976), Osprey Club (bd. dirs. 1998—). Republican. Episcopalian. Avocations: swimming, horse show jumping. Home: 4944 Arapahoe Ave Jacksonville FL 32210-8336 Office: Builders First Source 6550 Roosevelt Blvd Jacksonville FL 32244-4098

MAHAJAN, ROOP L. engineering educator; b. Jassar, Punjab, India, Mar. 15, 1943; arrived in U.S., 1972; s. Buta Mal and Krishana Devi Mahajan; m. Kavita D. Mahajan, Jan. 7, 1978; children: Neha, Shreya, Parag. BSME, Punjab U., 1964, MSME, 1969; PhD in Mech. Engring., Cornell U., 1977. Mem. tech. staff Bell Labs., Princeton, NJ, 1976—79, supr., 1979—91; prof., dir. mech. engring. Colo. U., Boulder, 1991—2001, interim dean Coll. Engring., 2001—. Author: (book) Buoyancy-Induced Flows and Transport, 1988; chief editor: Jour. Microelectronics Packaging. Founder, condr. Bal-Vihar, Boulder, 1991—. Recipient Bell Labs. fellowship, AT&T, 1989. Fellow: ASME (Heat Transfer Meml. award 2002, Charles Russ Richards Meml. award 2003). Achievements include patents in field; development of condensation soldering technology; new artificial neural network software; innovative metal foam heat sinks; cellular engineering microsystems. Home: 1158 Pintail Cir Boulder CO 80303 Office: Colo U Boulder CO 80309-0427 E-mail: mahajan@spot.colorado.edu.

MAHAJAN, SANJIV RAI, entrepreneur; b. Delhi, India; s. Swaran and Amrit Rai M.; m. Pratima Kaushik, Jan. 22, 1980; children: Payal, Sushaen. BA in Econs. with honors, Shri Ram Coll. Commerce, Delhi, 1978. Mktg. dir. SanSun Electronics P. Ltd., Madras, India, 1984-85; pres. MARRS Inc., New Delhi, 1985-90; mng. dir. SPSS South Asia, New Delhi, 1993-96; internat. dir. SPSS Internat., Woking, 1996-98; dir. SPSS Inc., Chgo., 1998-2000; CEO IGPartner.Net Corp., North Brunswick, N.J., 2000—. Pres. Fedn. of Asian Am. Tech. Cos., Woodbridge, N.J., 2000—; chmn. STATSIG, New Delhi, 1993-96; co-founder 6 cos.; expert worldwide markets for tech. products and svcs. Contbr. articles to profl. jours. Mem. Am. Mktg. Assn., Himalayan Mountaineering Assn. Office: IGPartner Net Corp 64 Timber Ridge Rd North Brunswick NJ 08902-5515 E-mail: srmahajan@igpartner.net.

MAHAJAN, SUBHASH, electronic materials educator; b. Gurdaspur, India; m. Sushma Sondhi, Sept. 3, 1965; children: Sanjoy, Sunit, Ashish. BS with highest honors, Panjab U., India, 1959; BE in Metallyrgy with highest honors, Indian Inst. Sci., 1961; PhD in Materials Sci. and Engring., U. Calif., 1965. Rsch. asst. U. Calif., Berkeley, 1961-65; rsch. metallurgist U. Denver, 1965-68; Harwell fellow Atomic Energy Rsch. Establishment, Harwell, Eng., 1968-71; mem. tech. staff AT&T Bell Labs., Murray Hill, N.J., 1971-83, rsch. mgr., 1981-83; prof. electronic materials dept. material sci. and engring. Carnegie Mellon U., Pitts., 1983-97; prof. electronic materials Ariz. State U., Tempe, 1997—, assoc. chair, 1999, interim chair and chair dept. chem. and materials engring., 2000—. Mem. site panel Materials Rsch. Lab., 1993; vis. prof. U. Antwerp, Belgium, 1991, Ecole Ctrl. Lyon, Ecully, France, 1993; lectr., spkr., patentee, cons. in field. Editor: Handbook on Semiconductors, vol. 3, 1994, Acta Materialia, 2001; editor: (with V.G. Keramidas) Electrochemical Society Symposium Volume, 1983; editor: (with L.C. Kimerling) The Concise Encyclopedia of Semiconducting Materials and Related Technologies, 1992; editor: (with D. Bloor, R.J. Brook and M.C. Flemings) The Encyclopedia of Advanced Materials, 1994; editor: (with K.H. Jurgen Buschow, Robert W. Cahn et al) Encyclopedia of Materials: Science and Technology, 2001; coordinating editor: The Acta Materiala Jours., 2004; contbr. more than 200 articles to profl. jours. Mem. materials rsch. adv. com. divsn. materials rsch. NSF, 1989-92. Fellow TMS, Am. Soc. Metals Internat. (Albert Sauveur Achievement award); mem. Materials Rsch. Soc. (editor symposium volume 1983, organizer symposium Am. Assn. Crystal Growers), Electrochem. Soc. (mem. electronics divsn. 1973-86, divisional editor 1976-86), Minerals, Metals and Materials Soc. (mem. phys. metallurgy com. 1976-83, vice chmn. mech. metallurgy com. 1978-79, mem. 1975-80, mem. electronic materials com. 1990-94, chmn. electronic, magnetic and photonic materials com. 1984-86, tech. dir. bd., John Bardeen award, The Educator award), Sigma Xi. Home: 8824 S Poplar St Tempe AZ 85284-4521 Office: Ariz State U Dept Chem and Materials Engring Tempe AZ 85287-6006 Office Phone: 480-965-9710. E-mail: smahajan@asu.edu.

MAHAMMAD, RIYAZ BASHA, biomedical researcher; arrived in US, 2000; s. Abdul Rahim and Ravufunnisa Begum Mahammad; m. Shabrin Shaik, Aug. 9, 1998. BSc, S.V. U., India, 1989; MSc, S.V.U., 1991, PhD, 1999. Sr. rsch. fellow S.V. U., Tirupati, India, 1996—99; rschr. U. RI, Kingston, RI, 2000—. Contbr. articles various profl. jours. Sec. Rsch. Scholar's Forum, S.V.U., Tirupati, India, 1994—95; chmn. Rsch. Scholar's Forum, 1995—98. Named Young Scientist Travel award, Asian Pacific Soc. for Neurochemistry, Korea, 1998; recipient 2nd Pl. award, Neurotoxicology Splty. Sect., Soc. of Toxicology, 2001, 3rd Pl. award, 2002, Monsanto 1st Pl. award, 2003. Mem.: NY Acad. of Sci., Internat. Brain Rsch. Organ., Soc. of Toxicology, Indian Soc. for Comparative Animal Physiology (life). Avocations: poem writing, reading, cricket, scientific mtgs. Office: U RI Biomedical Scis 41 Lower Coll Rd Kingston RI 02881 Office Phone: 401-874-5368. Office Fax: 401-574-5048. E-mail: riyaz@uri.edu.

MAHAN, CHARLES SAMUEL, public health educator; b. Pitts., Nov. 4, 1938; AB, W.Va. U., 1960; MD, Northwestern U., 1964. Diplomate Am. Bd. Ob-Gyn. Intern Hennepin County Gen. Hosp., Mpls., 1964-65; med. fellow in obstetrics and gynecology U. Minn. Hosp., Mpls., 1965-68; staff physician Shands Teaching Hosp., Coll. Medicine U. Fla., Gainesville, 1974-95, dir. divsn. ambulatory svcs. women, 1974-87, assoc. prof. dept. obstetrics and gynecology, 1974-80, prof., 1980—, acting chmn. dept. obstetrics and gynecology, 1978-79; asst. and assoc. prof. dept. obstetrics and gynecology med. sch. U. Minn., Mpls., 1970-74; dir. maternal and child health State of Fla., 1982-86; dep. sec. health, state health officer Fla. Dept. Health and Rehabilitative Svcs., 1988-95; prof. dept. cmty. and family health, maternal health program U. South Fla. Coll. Pub. Health, Tampa, 1995—, dean, 1995—2002. Sr. assoc. physician ob-gyn. Pilot City Health Ctr., Mpls., 1970-74, med. dir. Red Door Venereal Disease Clinic, Mpls., 1972-74; dir. North Ctrl. Fla. Maternity and Infant Care, Family Planning, Teen-Age Pregnancy Team Projects, and WIC Program, 1974-87; assoc. dir. Tech. Assistance Health Rsch. Group, Gainesville, 1975-82; chmn. med. care evaluation com. Shands Teaching Hosp., 1976-80; mem. faculty senate U. Fla., 1976-78, 79-80, 87-88, mem. outpatient clinics com., 1978-86, mem. health policy task force, 1992—, mem. promotion and tenure com. coll. medicine, 1978-81, dir. undergrad. edn. dept. ob-gyn., 1980-85, pres. faculty, 1982-83, mem. faculty coun., 1982-85, dir. Fla. midwifery resource ctr., 1992—, mem. nurse-midwife tng. program adv. com. coll. nursing, 1982—, mem. adv. com. inst. HIV rsch. and edn., 1992—; mem. State of Fla. Family Planning Coun., 1976-79; chmn. 1st ann. med. alumni sci. seminar Hennepin County Med. Ctr., Minn., 1976; mem. Alachua County Child Advocacy Coun., 1977-79; mem. adv. bd. Rape Info. and Counseling Ctr., 1977-79; mem. nat. adv. coun. maternal, fetal and infant nutrition USDA, 1978-81; chmn. health com. Alachua County Human Svcs. Planning Coun., 1980-82, acting pres. coun., 1982; mem. adv. bd. Nat. Cesarean/Support, Edn. and Concern, 1984-89; gov.'s rep. Healthy Mothers/Healthy Babies Steering Com., 1985—; chmn. rsch. adv. com. nat. study freestanding birth ctrs. Nat. Assn. Childbearing Ctrs., 1986-88; chmn. Gov.'s Task Force AIDS, 1988-90; mem. child health initiative nat. adv. com. Robert Wood Johnson Found., 1992—, dir. healthy futures: a program to imporve maternal and infant care in the South, 1987-92; mem. adv. com. to dir. Ctrs. Disease Control and Prevention, 1994—, chair, 1995--; mem. secy. adv. com. on Infant Mortality Health and Human Svcs., 1996--, Bright Futures for Women Commn., 2000--; vis. prof. various instns.; lectr. in field. Editor: Generally Funny: A Monograph of Medical Ancedotes and Cartoons, 1976; contbr. chpts. and revs. to books and articles to profl. jours. Active Nat. Found.-Mar. Dimes, 1978-88, chmn. edn. adv. com., 1978-82, 85-87; active Leadership Gainesville, 1978; mem. ob-gyn. alumni coun. med. sch. Northwestern U., 1986—; mem. Gov.'s Adv. Coun. Farmworkers Affairs, 1988—; mem. innovation coun. Ounce Prevention Fund Fla., 1994—. With USN, 1957-70, res. Recipient Cmty. Svc. award Gainesville Women's Health Ctr., 1976, Spl. MCH award Fla. Coun. Primary Care, 1984, Spl. Award for Mother-Infant Health, Coalition Fla. Childbirth Educators, 1984, Award for MCH Leadership, So. Health Assn., 1991, Mary E. Switzer award Assn. Schs. Applied Health Professions, 1992, State of Fla. Cabinet Disting. Svc. award, 1992; Rsch. fellow USN, Aviation Med. Acceleration Lab., 1961. Mem. AMA, APHA (mem. coun. maternal and child health 1985-88), Am. Coll. Ob-Gyn. (chmn. spl. interest group ambulatory reproductive health care 1978-80, chmn. dist. IV maternity mortality com. 1979-81, mem. com. health care underserved women 1988—, chmn. 1992, chmn. nat. fetal-infant mortality rev. steering com. 1990—), Nat. Assn. Childbearing Ctrs. (bd. dirs. 1983—), Nat. Perinatal Assn. (bd. dirs. 1996—), Fla. Ctr. Children and Youth, Fla. Healthy Mothers/Healthy Babies Coalition (Spl. Award for MCH Leadership 1985), Fla. Med. Assn. (mem. com. pub. health 1988—, mem. com. AIDS 1988-96), Fla. Obstet. and Gynecol. Soc., Fla. Perinatal Assn. (bd. dirs. 1993—), Fla. Pub. Health Assn. (chmn. maternal and child health sect. 1987-88, mem. jour. editl. bd. 1987—), Fla. Soc. Childbirth Educators, Assn. State and Territorial Health Ofcls. (mem. exec. com. 1991—, pres. 1993-94), Inst. Women's Health (founding mem.), W.Va. U. Alumni Assn. (life), Rotary Club Tallahassee (bd. dirs. 1989-90). Home: 1001 N Riverhills Dr Tampa FL 33617-4241 Office: MDC 056 13201 Bruce B Downs Blvd Tampa FL 33612-3805

MAHAN, CLARENCE, retired govenment official, writer; b. Dayton, Ohio, Jan. 1, 1939; s. Clarence Mahan and Elsie (Crouch) Dlitz; m. Suky Mahan, May 27, 1962; children: Sean M., Christiane Elizabeth. BA, U. Md., 1963; MA, Am. U., 1968; MBA, Syracuse U., 1969. Dep. comptroller U.S. Army, Japan, 1974-76; dep. chief program and budget Defense Commn. Agy., Arlington, Va., 1976; aide Asst. Sec. Army, Washington, 1976-77; chief operating appropriations Dept. AF, Washington, 1979-80; dir. fin. and acctg. Dept. Energy, Washington, 1980-81, dep. comptroller, 1981-82; dir. fiscal and contracts mgmt. EPA, Washington, 1982-83, dep. comptroller, 1983-85, dir. Rsch. Program Mgmt. Office, 1985-95. Instr., lectr. in field. Contbr. articles to profl. jours. and hort. mags. With U.S. Army, 1959-62, Korea. Mem. Am. Iris Soc. (bd. dirs., 2d v.p. 1991-95, 1st v.p. 1995-98, pres. 1998-2001), Hist. Iris Preservation Soc. (pres. 1991-93), Soc. Japanese Irises (pres. 1989-92), Reblooming Iris Soc. (bd. dirs. 1986-94, pres. 2002--). Democrat. Home and Office: 7311 Churchill Rd Mc Lean VA 22101-2001

MAHAN, DAVID JAMES, retired university official; b. St. Louis, May 29, 1934; s. John William and Eleanor (Johnson) M.; m. Jane E. Pyle, Nov. 28, 1957; children: Elizabeth Mahan-Shaw, Kathryn Goodman. BA, Okla. Baptist Coll., 1956; MA, Washington U., St. Louis, 1962, EdD, 1968. Cert. elem., secondary English tchr., Mo., cert. elem. prin., Mo., cert. supt., Mo. Adminstr., tchr. St. Louis Pub. Schs., 1958-90, supt., 1990-96; supt. in residence U. Mo., St. Louis, 1996-99. Co-author: The Faculty Team: School Organization for Results, 1971. Bd. dirs. Commerce and Growth Assn., St. Louis, 1990—, Asthma and Allergy Found. Am., St. Louis, 1990—, St. Louis Symphony Soc., 1992—, Boy Scouts Am., 1992—. Home: 5 Portland Ct Saint Louis MO 63108-1293

MAHAN, GERALD DENNIS, physics educator, researcher; s. Thomas Finley and Julia Kay (Swails) M.; m. Sally Ann Spaugh, Feb. 20, 1965; children— Christopher Parker, Susan Thayer, Roy Finley AB, Harvard U., 1959; PhD in Physics, U. Calif.-Berkeley, 1964. Rsch. physicist GE, Schenectady, 1963-67, part-time, 1967-84; assoc. prof. physics U. Oreg., Eugene, 1967-73; prof. physics Ind. U., Bloomington, 1973-82, disting. prof., 1982-84; disting. prof. physics U. Tenn., Knoxville, 1984—2001, Penn State U., University Park. Guest prof. Niels Bohr Inst., Copenhagen, 1977-78 Author: Many-Particle Physics, 1981; contbr. numerous articles on physics to profl. jours. Alfred Sloan fellow, 1968-70. Fellow Am. Phys. Soc.; mem. NAS. Office: Penn State U 104 Davey Lab University Park PA 16802 E-mail: gmahan@psu.edu.

MAHAN, JAMES CAMERON, judge; b. El Paso, Tex., Dec. 16, 1943; m. Eileen Agnes Casale, Jan. 13, 1968; 1 child, James Cameron Jr. BA, U. Charleston, 1965; JD, Vanderbilt U., 1973. Bar: Nev. 1974, U.S. Dist. Ct. Nev. 1974, U.S. Ct. Appeals (9th cir.) 1975, U.S. Tax Ct. 1980, U.S. Supreme Ct. 1980. Assoc. Lee & Beasey, Las Vegas, Nev., 1974-75; mem. firm John Peter Lee Ltd., Las Vegas, 1975-82; sr. ptnr. Mahan & Ellis, Chartered, Las Vegas, 1982-99; dist. ct. judge 8th Jud. Dist. Nev., Las Vegas, 1999—2002; U.S. dist. judge, 2002—. With USN, 1966-69. Office: 333 Las Vegas Blvd S Las Vegas NV 89101 Office Phone: 702-464-5520. E-mail: james_mahan@nvd.uscourts.gov.

MAHAN, JAMES S. communications company executive; BA in Econs., Washington & Lee U. V.p. Wachovia Bank & Trust Co., Winston-Salem, N.C.; co-founder Cardinal Bancshares, Lexington, Ky.; pres., COO, vice chmn. Citizens Union Nat. Bank & Trust Co., Lexington; CEO Security First Techs, Atlanta, 1995-99, S1 Corp., Atlanta, 1999—. Office: S1 Corp 3500 Lenox Rd Ste 200 Atlanta GA 30326

MAHAN, JAMES T. manufacturing executive; V.p., engineered adhesives divsn. 3M Co., gen. mgr., bonding sys. divsn., exec. v.p., engring., mfg., and logistics, 2003—. Mem. Engring. Coll. Indsl. Adv. Coun., Iowa State U. Office: 3M Co 3M Ctr Saint Paul MN 55144

MAHANES, DAVID JAMES, JR., retired distillery executive; b. Lexington, Ky., June 19, 1923; s. David James and Ethel (Brock) M.; m. Dorothy Jean Richardson, Oct. 28, 1950; 1 child, David James III. BS, U. Ky., 1947; MBA, Harvard U., 1950. Regional mgr. Jack Daniel Distillery, Nashville, 1960-65, v.p., 1965-70, sr. v.p., 1970-71, exec. v.p., 1971-85, pres., 1985-88, chmn. bd. dirs. Chmn. bd. dirs. Early Times Distillery Co., Can. Mist Distilling Co., Thoroughbred Plastics Co. Lt. inf. AUS, 1943-46, ETO; lt. col. AG ret. Recipient Bronze Star; Runnerup as outstanding sales exec. Gallagher Report, 1982. Mem. SAR (pres. Andrew Jackson chpt.), Soc. Colonial Wars in Tenn. (gov., dep. gov. gen., sec.), English Speaking Union (dir.), Res. Officers Assn., The 200 Club, Belle Meade Country Club, Beaver Creek Club, Exch. Club, Tenn. Profl. Golfers Assn. (hon.), Nashville Srs. Golf Assn., Kappa Alpha, Beta Gamma Sigma. Republican. Presbyterian. E-mail: djmandot@aol.com.

MAHANTHAPPA, KALYANA THIPPERUDRAIAH, physicist, researcher; b. Hirehalli, Mysore, India, Oct. 29, 1934; s. Kalyana and Thippamma (Maddanappa) T.; m. Prameela Talkerappa, Oct. 30, 1961; children: Nagesh, Rudresh, Mahesh. BSc, Ctrl. Coll. Bangalore, India, 1954; MSc, Delhi U., 1956; PhD (Faculty Arts and Scis. fellow), Harvard, 1961. Research assoc. U. Cal. at Los Angeles, 1961-63; asst. prof. U. Pa., Phila., 1963-66; mem. Inst. Advanced Study, Princeton, N.J., 1964-65; assoc. prof. physics U. Colo., Boulder, 1966-69, prof., 1969—, faculty research fellow, 1970-71, 76-77, 83-84, 93-94. Vis. prof./scientist U. Rome, 1970, Internat. Ctr. for Theoretical Physics, 1971, Cambridge U., 1976-77; cons. Aerojet-Gen., L.A., 1962-63; dir. Summer Inst. Theoretical Physics, Boulder, 1968-69, NATO Advanced Study Inst. in Elem. Particles, 1979, NATO Advanced Rsch. Workshop on Superstrings, 1987; gen. dir. Theoretical Advanced Study Inst. in Particle Physics, 1989—; sr. vis. rsch. fellow Imperial Coll., London, 1983-84. Contbr. articles to profl. jours. Fellow Am. Phys. Soc.; mem. AAAS, Sigma Xi. Achievements include research theoretical high energy and elementary particle physics. Home: 4760 Lee Cir Boulder CO 80303-1111 Office Phone: 303-492-8780. E-mail: ktm@verb.colorado.edu.

MAHAR, ELLEN PATRICIA, law librarian; b. Washington, Jan. 15, 1938; d. Richard A. and Lina Mahar. BA, St. Joseph Coll., Emmitsburg, Md., 1959; MLS, U. Md., 1968. Asst. librarian Covington & Burling, Washington, 1971-73, libr. dir., 1978-92; librarian Shea & Gardner, Washington, 1974-78; mgr. info. ctr. Assn. Comml. Real Estate, Herndon, Va., 1992-94; head libr. Caplin & Drysdale Chtd., Washington, 1994—. Co-editor: Legislative History of the Securities Act of 1933 and the Securities Act of 1934, 11 vols., 1973. Mem. Am. Assn. Law Libraries, Spl. Libraries Assn., Law Librarians' Soc. Washington. Office: Caplin & Drysdale Chtd 1 Thomas Cir NW Fl 11 Washington DC 20005-5802

MAHAR, JASON, education educator; s. Philip and Laurel Mahar. BS Math, SUNY, Binghamton, N.Y., 1994; MS Applied Math., M Engring. in Ops. Rsch. and Stats., Rensselaer Poly. Inst., Troy, N.Y., 2001. Customer svc. mgr. OfficeMax, Inc., Rotterdam, NY, 1996—97; tchg. asst. Rensselaer Poly. Inst., Troy, NY, 1997—2001; instr. Monroe C.C., Rochester, NY, 2001—. Mem.: Am. Math. Assn., Math. Assn. of Am., NY State Math. Assn. of Two Yr. Colleges. Conservative. Christian. Avocations: bowling, golf. Office: Monroe C C 1000 East Henrietta Rd Rochester NY 14623 Business E-Mail: jmahar@monroecc.edu.

MAHARIDGE, DALE DIMITRO, journalist, educator, writer; b. Cleve., Oct. 24, 1956; s. Steve and Joan (Kopfstein) Maharidge. Student, Cleve. State U., 1974—75. Freelance reporter various publs., Cleve., 1976, Cleve. Plain Dealer, 1978—80; reporter The Gazette, Medina, Ohio, 1977—78, Sacramento Bee, 1980—91; vis. prof. Stanford U., Palo Alto, Calif., 1992—2002; asst. prof. Columbia U. Grad. Sch. Journalism, NYC, 2002—. Author: Journey to Nowhere: The Saga of the New Underclass, 1985, Journey to Nowhere: The Saga of the New Underclass repub. with introduction by Bruce Springsteen, 1996, And Their Children After Them, 1989 (Pulitzer Prize for gen. nonfiction, 1990), The Last Great American Hobo, 1993, The Coming White Minority: California, Multiculturism and the Nation's Future, 1996, The Coming White Minority: California's Eruptions and the Nation's Future, Vintage Books edit., 1999, Homeland, 2004; contbr. articles to profl. jours. Nieman fellow, Harvard U., 1988, Pope Found. grantee, 1994, Freedom Forum grantee, 1995. Democrat. E-mail: dmaharidge@yahoo.com.

MAHATO, RAM ISHWAR, pharmacist, educator; b. Janakpur, Nepal, Jan. 11, 1963; s. Srinarayan and Sarswati Mahato; m. Subhashini Mahto, Jan. 18, 1993; 1 child, Kalika. PhD, U. of Strathclyde, Scotland, 1992; B.S., China Pharm. U., 1989; Diploma in Chinese, Beijing Lang. Inst., 1985. PhD in Pharm. Sciences U. of Strathclyde, 1992. Rsch. assoc. U. of So. Calif., Dept of Pharm. Sciences, Los Angeles, Calif., 1992—92; postdoctoral fellow Wash. U., St Louis, Mont., 1993—93; guest scholar Kyoto U., Faculty of Pharm. Sciences, Kyoto, 1994—96; sr. scientist GeneMedicine, Inc., The Woodland, 1996—99; mgr., pharm. drug devel. Copernicus, Inc., Cleve., 1999—99; rsch. asst. prof. U. of Utah, Dept of Pharmaceutics and Pharm. Chemistry, Salt Lake City, 1999—2001; asst. prof. U. of Tenn. Health Sci. Ctr., Memphis, 2001—. Ad hoc grant reviewer NIH, Bethesda, Md., 2002—04, Am. Inst. of Biol. Sciences, 2002; session chair Controlled Release Soc., 2002—. Editor: (book on nucelic acid delivery) Pharmaceutical Perspectives of Nucleic Acid-Based Therapeutics. Fellow, Goho and Uehara Foundations of Japan, 1995—96. Mem.: Assn. for the Advancement of Sci., NY Acad. of Sci., Am. Assn. of Pharm. Sciences, Am. Chem. Soc., Am. Soc. of Gene Therapy, Controlled Release Soc. (assoc.). Achievements include research in Pharmaceutical Perspectives of Oligonucleotides and Genes. Office: Univ of Tenn Dept of Pharm Sci 26 S Dunlap St Feurt Bldg RM 406 Memphis TN 38103-4909 Home Fax: (901)448-6092. Personal E-mail: rmahato@utmem.edu. E-mail: rmahato@utmem.edu.

MAHDAVI, KAMAL B. writer, researcher; b. Esfahan, Iran, Sept. 1, 1933; came to U.S., 1958, naturalized. s. Ebrahim B. and Ghamar (Jalilian) M. BA, U. Calif., Berkeley, 1964; MA, U Toronto, 1965; postgrad., U. Cambridge, Eng., 1965—69. Cert. coll. tchr., Calif. R&D rschr. U. Stockholm, 1969-71; freelance rschr., writer self-employed, San Francisco, San Diego, 1972—. Ind. legal rschr. San Francisco, San Diego, 1980—. Author (as K.M.B. Writer): Technological Innovation: An Efficiency Investigation, 1972; contbr. articles to profl. jours. Civil rights litigant. Avocations: swimming, chess. Office: PO Box 121164 San Diego CA 92112-1164

MAHDAVIANI, MIRIAM, choreographer, educator; Student, Sch. Am. Ballet, 1968. Past mem., instr. Balanchine Co. Choreographer Jacob's Pillow Dance Festival, 1986, 87, Am. Music Festival N.Y.C. Ballet, 1988. Choreographer (ballets) N.Y.C. Ballet's Am. Music Festival, 1988, Dance Preludes Dancer's Emergency Fund Benefit, N.Y.C., 1991, Images, N.Y.C., 1992, Images Maggio Danza Festival, Florence, Italy, 1994, Correlazione N.Y.C. Ballet, 1994; dancer over 40 ballets including Ballo Della Regina, Coppelia, Donizetti Variations, Jewels, Raymonda Variations, La Valse. Office: Pacific Northwest Ballet 301 Mercer St Seattle WA 98109-4600

MAHER, BILL, talk show host, comedian, producer; b. N.Y.C., Jan. 20, 1956; s. Bill and Julie (Berman) M. BA, Cornell U., 1978. Creator, host Politically Incorrect, (HBO), N.Y.C., 1993-96, Politically Incorrect, ABC, 1996—2002; host Real Time With Bill Maher, HBO, 2003—. Performances include (theatre) Seymour Glick is Alive But Sick (Steve Allen); (stand-up) The Bob Monkhouse Show, Late Night with David Letterman, The Tonight Show Anniversary Show, The Tonight Show, HBO Spl., 1989, 92; (TV shows) Steve Allen's Music Room, Alice, Sara, Max Headroom, Hard Knocks, Newhart, Murder, She Wrote, The Midnight Hour, Say What?; (TV movies) Out of Time, Rags to Riches, Club Med; (films) D.C. Cab, Rat Boy, House II, Cannibal Women in the Avocado Jungle of Death, Pizza Man; author: (novel) True Story, 1994, Does Anybody Have a Problem With That? Politically

Incorrect's Greatest Hits, When You Ride Alone You Ride with bin Laden, 2002. Recipient Cableace award Nat. Acad. Cable Programming, 1990, Cableace award for best talk show series, 1995, Cableace award for best talk show host, 1995. Office: Brillstein Grey Entertainment Ste 350 9150 Wilshire Blvd Beverly Hills CA 90212*

MAHER, BRENDAN ARNOLD, psychology educator, editor; b. Widnes, Eng., Oct. 31, 1924; came to US, 1955; s. Thomas F. and Agnes (Power) M.; m. Winifred Barbara Brown, Aug. 27, 1952; children: Rebecca, Thomas, Nicholas, Liam, Niall. BA with honours, U. Manchester, Eng., 1950; MA, Ohio State U., 1951, PhD, 1954; student, U. Ill. Med. Sch., 1952-53; AM (hon.), Harvard, 1972; DPhil (hon.), U. Copenhagen, 1998. Diplomate Am. Bd. Examiners in Profl. Psychology. Psychologist Her Majesty's Prison, Wakefield, England, 1954-55; instr. Ohio State U., Ohio, 1955-56; asst. prof. Northwestern U., 1956-58; asso. prof. La. State U., La., 1958-60; lectr. Harvard, 1960-64; chmn. Ctr. Rsch. Personality, 1962-64; prof. U. Wis., 1964-67, 71-72; vis. fellow U. Copenhagen, 1966-67, vis. fellow and rsch. scientist, 1979, 96-98; prof. psychology Brandeis U., 1967-72; dean Brandeis U. (Grad. Sch.), 1969-71, dean faculty, 1971-72; E. C. Henderson prof. psychology Harvard U., 1983-99, E.C. Henderson rsch. prof., 1999—, prof., 1972—, chmn. dept. psychology and social relations, 1973-78, chmn. dept. psychology, 1987-89, dean Grad. Sch. Arts and Scis., 1989-92; assoc. psychologist McLean Hosp., Belmont, Mass., 1968-77, psychologist, 1977-84. Cons. in medicine Peter Bent Brigham Hosp., Boston, 1977-85; cons. in psychology Mass. Gen. Hosp., 1977-2002. Author: Principles of Psychopathology, 1966, Introduction to Research in Psychopathology, 1970, A Passage to Sword Beach, 1996; co-editor: National Research Council: Rsch. Doctorate Programs in the United States, 1995; editor Progress in Exptl. Personality Rsch., 1964-87, Jour. Cons. and Clin. Psychology, 1972-78; cons. editor Rev. Personality and Social Psychology, Clin. Psychology Rev. Served with Brit. Royal Navy, 1943-47. Recipient Zubin award for rsch. in psychopathology, 1998. Fellow AAAS, Am. Psychol. Soc.; mem. Brit. Psychol. Assn. (chartered psychologist UK), Soc. Rsch. in Psychopathology (pres. 1985-87), Phi Beta Kappa. Office: Harvard U William James Hall Cambridge MA 02138 also: Giffords Island Mahone Bay NS Canada E-mail: bam@wjh.harvard.edu.

MAHER, CORNELIUS CREEDON, III, neurologist, toxicologist, army officer; b. N.Y.C., Jan. 30, 1949; s. Cornelius Creedon Jr. and Hester Maher; m. Lynn Marie Elliott, July 15, 1972; children: Christa, Cornelius IV, Kimberley. BS in Chemistry, Boston Coll., 1969; MS in Chemistry, U. Mich., 1973, PhD in Chemistry and Environ. Health, 1976; MD, St. Louis U., 1986. Diplomate Am. Bd. Psychiatry and Neurology. Rsch. fellow Brookhaven Nat. Lab., Upton, N.Y., 1969; rsch. fellow then lectr. U. Mich., Ann Arbor, 1969-76; rsch. assoc. Children's Hosp. Med. Ctr., Boston, 1976-77; indsl. toxicologist West Allis (Wis.) Meml. Hosp., 1977-82; commd. 2d lt. U.S. Army, 1982, advanced through grades to col., 2001; intern in neurology Letterman Army Med. Ctr., San Francisco, 1986-87, resident in neurology, 1987-90; staff neurologist William Beaumont Army Med. Ctr., El Paso, 1990-94; asst. chief neurology dept. Walter Reed Army Med. Ctr., Washington, 1994-98; chief operational neurology Madigan Army Med. Ctr., Tacoma, 1998—2001; staff dir. Joint Readiness Clin. Adv. Bd., Ft. Detrick, Md., 2001—; neurology cons. to surgeon gen. U.S. Army, 2003—. Mem. neurology faculty Tex. Tech. U., 1991—, Uniformed Svcs. U. of Health Scis., 1995—, U. Wash., 1999—. Contbr. articles to profl. jours. Mem. AMA, Am. Acad. Neurology, Am. Chem. Soc., Assn. Mil. Surgeons, N.Y. Acad. Scis., Sigma Xi, Phi Lambda Upsilon, Alpha Chi Sigma. Office: JRCAB 1423 Sultan Dr Fort Detrick MD 21702 Business E-Mail: cornelius.maher@us.army.mil.

MAHER, DAVID L. drug store company executive; b. Iowa City, 1939; Grad., U. Iowa, 1964. Pres., vice chmn., COO Am. Stores Co., Salt Lake City, vice chmn., COO, 1997-99. Office: American Stores Co 299 S Main St Salt Lake City UT 84111-2263

MAHER, DAVID WILLARD, lawyer; b. Chgo., Aug. 14, 1934; s. Chauncey Carter and Martha (Peppers) M.; m. Jill Waid Armagnac, Dec. 20, 1954; children: Philip Armagnac, Julia Armagnac. BA, Harvard, 1955, LLB, 1959. Bar: N.Y. 1960, Ill. 1961, Wis. 1996, U.S. Patent Office 1961. Pvt. practice, Boston, N.Y.C., 1958-60; assoc. Kirkland & Ellis, and predecessor firm, 1960-65, ptnr., 1966-78, Reuben & Proctor, 1978-86, Isham, Lincoln and Beale, 1986-88, Sonnenschein, Nath & Rosenthal, Chgo., 1988—2003; ret., 2003; chmn. bd. dirs. Publ. Interest Registry, 2003—04, sr. v.p law and policy, 2003—. Dir. BBB Chgo. and No. Ill., 2004—; lectr. DePaul U. Sch. Law, 1973—79, Loyola U. Law Sch., Chgo., 1980—84. Vis. com. U. Chgo. Div. Sch., 1986—. 2d lt. USAF, 1955-56. Fellow Am. Bar Found. (life); mem. ABA, Am. Law Inst., Wis. State Bar, Chgo. Bar Assn., Chgo. Lit. Club. Roman Catholic. Home: 501 N Clinton St Apt 1503 Chicago IL 60610-8886 Office: Sonnenschein Nath & Rosenthal 233 S Wacker Dr Ste 8000 Chicago IL 60606-6491 Office Phone: 312-876-8055. E-mail: dmaher@pir.org.

MAHER, EDWARD JOSEPH, lawyer; b. Cleve., Sept. 18, 1939; s. Richard Leo and Lucile (Thompson) M.; m. Marilyn K. Maher, Oct. 8, 1966; children: Richard A., David C., Michael E, Colleen Therese. B.S., Georgetown U., 1961, LL.B., 1964; student U. Fribourg, Switzerland, 1959-61. Bar: Ohio 1964, U.S. dist. ct. (no. dist.) Ohio 1964. Assoc., Sweeney, Maher & Vlad, Cleve., 1964-71; sole practice, Cleve., 1971— . Pres. parish council St. Raphael's Ch., Bay Village, Ohio, 1983-84; former adv. bd. Catholic Family and Children's Services; adv. bd. Cath. Youth Orgn., 1973-79, pres., 1975-76; chmn. Elyria Cursillo Ctr., 1974-75; lay del. to Ohio Cath. Conf., Diocese of Cleve., 1973-75; chmn. adv. bd. Cath. Social Services of Cuyahoga County, 1978-79; trustee Cath. Charities Corp., 1977—2001, hon. trustee, 2002-, treas., 1979, sec., 1981, 1st v.p., 1983, gen. chmn. campaign, 1983, 84, pres., 1985-86; pres. Diocesan adv. bd. Cath. Youth Orgn., 1980-82; team capt. United Way Services Agy. Team Group, 1981, nominating com., 1983; mem. Tabor House, The Consultation Ctr. of the Diocese of Cleve., pres., 1992-94; mem. bd. regents St. Ignatius High Sch., 1997—. Recipient Cardinal Robert Bellarmine S.J. award St. Ignatius High Sch., 1990, Cath. Man of the Year award, 1995. Mem. ABA, Ohio Bar Assn., Cuyahoga County Bar Assn., Cleve. Bar Assn., Cath. Lawyers Guild Cleve. (pres. 1970). Clubs: Irish Good Fellowship (pres.), First Friday of Cleve. (pres. 1990). Office: 1548 Standard Bldg Cleveland OH 44113

MAHER, FRANCESCA MARCINIAK, lawyer, former air transportation executive; b. Chgo., Oct. 27, 1957; BA, Loyola U., 1978, JD, 1981. Ptnr. Mayer, Brown & Platt, Chgo., 1981—84, 1987—93; v.p. law, corp. sec. UAL Corp., Elk Grove Village, Ill., 1993-97, v.p., gen. counsel, sec., 1997-98, sr. v.p., gen. counsel, sec., 1998—2003; spl. counsel Mayer, Brown, Rowe & Maw, Chgo., 2003—. Bd. dirs. YMCA Met. Chgo., Lincoln Park Zool. Soc. Mem. Ill. Humane Soc. (pres. 1996-98). Office: Mayer Brown Rowe & Maw LLP 190 S LaSalle St Chicago IL 60603-3441 E-mail: fmmaher@mayerbrownrowe.com.*

MAHER, FRANK J. former communications executive; V.p., mgmt. dir. Foote, Cone & Belding, Chgo.; pres., CEO Creswell, Munsell, Fultz & Zirbel, Des Moines, 2002—03.

MAHER, IRENE, newscaster; b. Hampton, Va. married. BA in Theatre and Speech, Coll. of William and Mary. Weekend weather anchor, med. reporter WAVY-TV, Portsmouth/Norfolk, Va.; health reporter WFLA-TV, Tampa, Fla., 1985, co-anchor, med. editor. Named Health Communicator of Yr., Fla. Hosp. Assn., 1994; recipient award, Am. Cancer Soc., Am. Heart Assn., Fla. Dietetic Assn., Tampa Bay Soc. Profl. Journalists, Fla. Dental Assn., Mental Health Assn. Hillsborough County, Comm. Media award, Fla. Nurses Assn. Office: WFLA-TV PO Box 1410 Tampa FL 33601

MAHER, JAMES VINCENT, JR., physics educator; b. N.Y.C., Aug. 25, 1942; s. James Vincent and Anne (Cunneen) M.; m. Angela Beth Braunstein, Aug. 13, 1966; children: Robin, James. BS in Physics, U. Notre Dame, 1964; MS in Physics, Yale U., 1965, PhD in Physics, 1969. Postdoctoral fellow Argonne (Ill.) Nat. Lab., 1968-70; asst. prof. U. Pitts., 1970-74, assoc. prof., 1974-80, prof., 1980—, dept. chair physics and astronomy, 1991-94, provost and sr. vice-chancellor, 1994—. Dir. Scaife nuclear physics lab., 1979-80. Contbr. over 100 articles to profl. jours. Grantee Dept. Energy, NSF. Fellow AAAS, Am. Phys. Soc.; mem. Am. Crystal Growth Assn. (pres. Pitts. chpt. 1989-92, exec. com. 1988-93), Sigma Xi. Democrat. Roman Catholic. Home: 1313 Denniston Ave Pittsburgh PA 15217-1330 Office: U Pitts Dept Physics And Astro Pittsburgh PA 15260

MAHER, JOHN, adult education educator, writer; b. Cedar Rapids, Iowa, Apr. 25, 1945; s. Rose F. (Hopkins) Maher. BS, So. Ill. U., 1972; MA, Ariz. State U., 1976; PhD, Pacific W. U., 1992. Tchg. asst. So. Ill. U., 1972; tchr. Phoenix Union H.S. Dist., Ariz., 1976—82, Mesa Sch. Dist., 1982—97; adj. prof. Ctrl. Ariz. Coll., 1990—2002; ret., 2002. Author: (book) Twentieth Century Campfire Culture, 1999. Mem. Pinal County Transp. Adv. Com., 1990—2004, Gov. Task Force on Transp., 2001. With U.S. Army, 1963—65. Mem.: C.A.A.R.S. Corvette Club (dir. 1992—2004, founder). Democrat. Roman Catholic. Avocation: hiking. Home: 131 W Canyon St Apache Junction AZ 85220

MAHER, JOHN A. lawyer, law educator; b. Bklyn., Dec. 3, 1930; s. John A. and Helen D. (Stack) M.; m. Joan Dawley, July 31, 1954; children: Jeanne M., John A. III, James A., Helen D., Thérèse. AB, U. Notre Dame, 1951; LLB, NYU, 1956, LLM in Trade Regulation, 1957; cert. bus. adminstrn., U. Va., 1969; cert. fgn. and comparative law, Columbia U., 1974; LLD (hon.), Pa. State U., 1998. Bar: N.Y. 1957, D.C. 1960, Pa. 1986. Assoc. Healy & Baillie, N.Y.C., 1957-59; staff atty. Swift & Co., N.Y.C, 1959-62; asst. gen. counsel Celanese Corp., N.Y.C., 1962-70; v.p. law Blount, Inc., Montgomery, Ala., 1970-73; prof. Dickinson Sch. of Law, Carlisle, Pa., 1973—2002, dean, 1989-94, dean and prof. emeritus, 2002—, Montague prof. law, 2000—02; commr. Pa. Securities Commn., 1997—2004. Bd. dirs. Atlantic Liberty Savs., Bklyn., 1960-2001, vice chmn., 1984-96, chmn., 1996-2001; counsel Eaton & Van Winkle, N.Y.C., 1974-87; trustee Food and Drug Law Inst., Washington, 1984-96; mem. lawyers' adv. com. Pa. Securities Com., 1994-97. Author: Survey of Robinson-Patman Act, 1969; co-author: Export Opportunities and The Export Trading Act of 1982, periodically supplemented; bd. editors Food Drug Cosmetic Law Jour., 1987-84, Jour. Financial Crime (U.K.), 1994—, Internat. Corp. Law Bull. (U.K.), 1998—; contbr. articles to profl. jours. Mem. Pres.'s Adv. Com. on Textile Info., Washington, 1967-68; bd. visitors John Marshall Law Sch., 1995—; N.Am. corr. Amicus Curiae, U.K., 1997—; bd. govs. Witan Hall, U.K., 2001—03, vice chmn. 2003-; bd. dir. Dickinson Sch. Law Alumni Assn., 2003—; trustee U.S. Army War Coll. Found., 2002—. Served with USNR, 1951-55, ret. lt. comdr., 1974. Food Law Inst. fellow NYU Law Ctr., 1956-57, hon. fellow Soc. for Advancement Legal Studies, U. London, 1997; named to Wall of Fame, U. Notre Dame, 1994. Fellow Am. Bar Found. (life), Pa. Bar Found. (charter, life); mem. Pa. Bar Assn. (chmn. corp. banking and bus. sect. 1987-89, Ho. of Dels. 1989—, Disting. Svc. award 1988, pres.'s award 1994), Dickinson Sch. Law Gen. Alumni Assn. (Disting. Svc. award and Honor Alumnus 1989). Roman Catholic. Avocations: reading, travel.

MAHER, L. JAMES, III, molecular biologist; b. Mpls., Nov. 28, 1960; s. Louis James and Elizabeth Jane (Crawford) M.; m. Laura Lee Moseng, July 2, 1983; children: Elizabeth Lillian, Christina Ailene. BS in Molecular Biology, U. Wis., 1983, PhD in Molecular Biology, 1988. Fellow U. Wis., Madison, 1983-84, rsch. asst., 1984-88; postdoctoral fellow Calif. Inst. Tech., Pasadena, 1988-91; asst. prof. molecular biology Eppley Inst., U. Nebr. Med. Ctr., Omaha, 1991-95; assoc. prof. biochem. molecular biology Mayo Found., Rochester, Minn., 1995-2000, prof., 2000—02, vice chmn., 2002—; assoc. dean for academic affairs Mayo Clinic Coll. of Med., 2003—. Editorial bd. Antisense and Nuclear Acid Drug Design, 1991—, Nucleic Acids Rsch. Jour., 1988—; contbr. articles to profl. jours. Musician, Madison Symphony Orch., 1983-88, Calif. Inst. Tech. Symphony Orch., L.A., 1988-91. Gosney fellow, 1988; Am. Cancer Soc. postdoctoral fellow, 1988. Mem. AAAS, Phi Beta Kappa. Evangelical Christian Ch. Achievements include research in chemical and biochemical agents designed to artificially regulate the flow of genetic information in biological systems. Office: Mayo Found Dept Biochem and Molec Biol 200 1st St SW Rochester MN 55905-0001 Office Phone: 507-284-9041.

MAHER, LISA KRUG, editor; b. N.Y.C., Nov. 11, 1952; d. George William and Rita (Earle) Krug; m. Barney Rosset, Nov. 5, 1980 (div. Dec. 1990); 1 child, Chantal; m. Richard Maher, July 29, 2000. BA magna cum laude, Smith Coll., 1974; MA, Columbia U., 1976. Editor Latin Am. Series, N.Y.C., 1976-86; gen. editor Grove Press, N.Y.C., 1987-89; mng. editor Aperture, N.Y.C., 1987-90; pvt. practice N.Y.C., 1990—. Writer and editor UNICEF, N.Y.C., 1995—. Author: James Baldwin, 1989, Thurgood Marshall, 1993 (Outstanding Book For Teenagers award 1994). Mem. Phi Beta Kappa

MAHER, LOUIS JAMES, JR., geologist, educator; b. Iowa City, Iowa, Dec. 18, 1933; s. Louis James and Edith Marie (Ham) M.; m. Elizabeth Jane Crawford, June 7, 1956; children: Louis James, Robert Crawford, Barbara Ruth. BA, U. Iowa, 1955, MS, 1959; PhD, U. Minn., 1961. Mem. faculty dept. geology and geophysics U. Wis.-Madison, 1962—, prof., 1970—2003, chmn. dept., 1980-84, prof. emeritus, 2003—. Contbr. articles to profl. jours. Served with U.S. Army, 1956-58. Danforth fellow, 1955-61; NSF fellow, 1959-61; NATO fellow, 1961-62 Fellow AAAS, Geol. Soc. Am.; mem. Am. Quaternary Assn., Ecol. Soc. Am., Wis. Acad. Sci., Arts and Letters, Sigma Xi. Episcopalian. Office: U Wis Dept Geology and Geoph 1215 W Dayton St Madison WI 53706-1600 Office Phone: 608-262-9595. E-mail: maher@geology.wisc.edu.

MAHER, PATRICK JOSEPH, retired utility company executive; b. Dublin, Apr. 20, 1936; came to U.S., 1946, naturalized, 1955; s. Pierce Albeus and Mary (Brady) M.; children: Kathy, Kevin, Erin, Megan. BBA, Iona Coll., 1959; MBA, N.Y. U., 1965. With spl. devel. program Chase Manhattan Bank, N.Y.C., 1961-64, 2d v.p. fiduciary dept., 1964-68; asst. v.p. Nat. Comml. Bank, Albany, N.Y., 1968-70; chief sect. utility fin. N.Y. State Pub. Svc. Commn., Albany, 1970-74; v.p., chief fin. officer Washington Gas Light Co., 1974-80, exec. v.p. fin. and adminstrn., 1980-87, pres., 1987-92, 1992-99, chmn. bd. dirs., CEO, 1993-98, chmn. bd. dirs., 1998-99. Served with USAR, 1960-61. Mem. Am. Gas Assn., Nat. Soc. Rate of Return Analysts, Natural Gas Men's Roundtable, Inst. Gas Tech., Associated Electric and Gas Ins. Svcs., U.S. C. of C., Rotary, N.Y. Athletic Club, Washington City Club. Roman Catholic.

MAHER, STEPHEN TRIVETT, lawyer, educator; b. N.Y.C., Nov. 21, 1949; s. William John and Jean Dorothy (Trivett) M.; m. Sharon Leslie Wolfe, Nov. 22, 1981 (dec.); children: Meaghan Wolfe, Caitlin Wolfe. BA, NYU, 1971; JD, U. Miami, Coral Gables, Fla., 1975. Bar: Fla. 1975, U.S. Dist. Ct. (so. dist.) Fla. 1976, D.C. 1979, U.S. Dist. Ct. (no. dist.) Fla. 1979, U.S. Supreme Ct. 1980, U.S. Ct. Appeals (5th and 11th cirs.) 1981, U.S. Dist. Ct. (so. dist.) Fla. 1982, U.S. Dist. Ct. (mid. dist.) Fla. 1983. Assoc. Chonin & Levey, Miami, 1975; staff atty. Legal Svcs. of Greater Miami, Inc., 1975-81; assoc. Finley, Kumble, Wagner et al, Miami, 1981-84; dir. clin. program Sch. of Law U. Miami, Coral Gables, 1984-90, assoc. prof. law Sch. of Law, 1984-92; pvt. practice Stephen T. Maher, P.A., Miami, Fla., 1992—2003; ptnr. Shutts & Bowen LLP, 2003—, chair adminstrv. and appellate practice group, 2003—. Mem. Fla. Bar/Fla. Bar Found. Joint Commn. on Delivery Legal Svcs. to the Indigent, Tallahassee, 1990-91; chmn. organizer Seventh Adminstrv. Law Conf., Tallahassee, 1990, Conf. on the Fla. Constn., 1995; cons. on in-house legal edn. Contbr. articles to profl. jours. Fellow Fla. Bar Found. (bd. dirs. 1984-91); mem. ABA, Fla. Bar (chair adminstrv. law sect. 1993-94, chair coun. of sects. 1996-97), Dade County Bar Assn. Home: 1015 Sevilla Ave Miami FL 33134-6328 Office: 1500 Miami Ctr 201 S Biscayne Blvd Miami FL 33131-4332 Office Phone: 305-373-2211. Business E-Mail: smaher@shutts-law.com.

MAHER, SUSAN MARGUERITE, language educator; b. Summit, N.J., Mar. 31, 1955; d. Edward Franklin Naramore and Nancy Louise Kenny; m. Harmon D. Maher, Dec. 23, 1977 (div. June 1995); children: Dana Craig, Anna Turi. BA, SUNY Albany, 1977; MA, U. S.C., 1979; PhD, U. Wis., 1985. From asst. to prof. U. Nebr., Omaha, 1991—. Gov. Ctr. Great Plains Studies, Lincoln, Nebr., 1998—2000. Author (editor): Coming Into McPhee Country, 2002. Recipient Outstanding Tchr. Humanities award, Alumni Assn. U. Nebr., 2001. Mem.: We. Lit. Assn. (pres. 2001), Children's Lit Assn. (conf. coord.), Assn. Study Lit. and Environment. Democrat. Presbyterian. Avocations: eco-travel, dog breeding, art. Office: Dept English AS 192 Univ Nebr Omaha Omaha NE 68182

MAHER, THOMAS GEORGE, academic administrator, producer, media educator; b. St. Louis, Feb. 18, 1947; s. Dale Russel and Dorothy Leone M.; m. (div.). AB, St. Louis U., 1969, MA, 1971; PhD, U. So. Calif., 1985. Cert. C.C. tchr. and supr., Calif. Tchg. fellow St. Louis U., 1969-71; assoc. prof. Chaffey Coll., Rancho Cucamonga, Calif., 1974-79, media dir., 1980-84; assoc. producer Corp. for C.C. TV, Orange, Calif., 1979-80; assoc. dir. instrnl. tech. Calif. State Poly. U., Pomona, 1984-89; dir. office media svcs. U. Ill., Chgo., 1989-94; dir. office instrnl. svcs. Colo. State U., Ft. Collins, 1994—, interim v.p. divsn. ednl. outreach, 2000—02. Cons. Rsch. Comm., Ltd., Boston, 1984—; book reviewer Focal Press, Inc., Boston, 1985—. Writer: (TV series) Project: Universe, 1978 (Emmy award nomination 1979), The Business of Management, 1981; assoc. producer, dir., writer (TV series) Oceanus: The Marine Environment, 1979 (Emmy award 1980); exec. producer (TV program) For the People: Local Gov. Budget Making, 1992 (Cert. Merit, Chgo. Internat. Film/Video Festival 1992); producer, dir. numerous refereed ednl. TV shows, 1974—. 1st lt. USAF, 1971-74. Mary Clemens scholar St. Louis U., 1965-67, Educare scholar U. So. Calif., 1983-84; grantee numerous competitive contracts. Mem. Acad. TV Arts and Scis., Am. Ednl. Research Assn., Assn. for Ednl. Comm. and Tech. Democrat. Roman Catholic. Avocations: reading spy novels, computers, running, theater. Office: Colo State U A 71 Clark Bldg Fort Collins CO 80523-2023 Office Phone: 970-491-1325. Business E-Mail: thomas.maher@colostate.edu.

MAHERAS, THOMAS G. finance company executive; b. Chgo. BBA in Fin., U. Notre Dame. Various positions including head mortgage-backed securities, head high yield trading desk Salomon Smith Barney (Citigroup), 1984—96, vice chmn., head global fixed income, 1996—2004; CEO Global Capital Markets, Global Corp. and Investment Banking Group Citigroup, N.Y.C., 2004—. Mem. borrowing adv. com. U.S. Treasury Dept. Mem.: Bond Market Assn. (bd. dirs., mem. exec. com.). Office: Citigroup Global corp and Investment Banking Group 390 Greenwich St 4th Fl New York NY 10013*

MAHESH, VIRENDRA BHUSHAN, endocrinologist; b. India, Apr. 25, 1932; came to U.S., 1958, naturalized, 1968; s. Narinjan Prasad and Sobhagyawati; m. Sushila Kumari Aggarwal, June 29, 1955; children: Anita Rani, Vinit Kumar. BSc with honors, Patna U., India, 1951; MSc in Chemistry, Delhi U., India, 1953, PhD, 1955; DPhil in Biol. Sci, Oxford U., 1958. James Hudson Brown Meml. fellow Yale U., 1958-59; asst. prof. endocrinology Med. Coll. Ga., Augusta, 1959-63, assoc. rsch. prof., 1963-66, prof., 1966-70, Regents prof., 1970-86, Robert B. Greenblatt prof., 1979-99, chmn. endocrinology, 1972-86, chmn., Regents prof. physiology and endocrinology, 1986-99, chmn. physiology and endocrinology, 1986-99, regents prof., chmn. emeritus physiology and endocrinology, 1999—, Robert B. Greenblatt prof. emeritus endocrinology, 1999—. Dir. Ctr. for Population Studies, 1971-99; mem. reproductive biology study sect. NIH, 1977-81, mem. human embryology and devel. study sect. NIH, 1982-86, 90-93, chmn., 1991-93. Contbr. articles to profl. jours., chpts. to books; editor: The Pituitary, a Current Review, Functional Correlates of Hormone Receptors in Reproduction, Recent Advances in Fertility Research, Hirsuitism and Virilism, Regulation of Ovarian and Testicular Function, Excitatory Amino Acids: Their Role in Neuroendocrine Function; mem. editl. bd. Steroids, 1963—, Jour. of Clin. Endocrinology and Metabolism, 1976-81, Jour. Steroid Biochemistry and Molecular Biology, 1991—, Assisted Reproductive Tech./Andrology, 1993-98, Endocrinology, 1999-2003; mem. adv. bd. Maturitas, 1977-81; editor-in-chief Biology of Reprodn., 1999-2004, cons. editor, 2004—. Recipient Rubin award Am. Soc. Study Sterility, 1962, Billings Silver medal, 1965, Best Tchr. award freshman class Sch. Medicine, Med. Coll. Ga., 1969, Outstanding Faculty award Sch. Medicine, 1992, Outstanding Faculty award Sch. Grad. Studies, 1981, 94, Disting. Teaching award, 1988, Excellence in Rsch. award Grad. Faculty Assembly, 1987-91, 93-95, Disting. Scientist award Assn. Scientist Indian Origin in Am., 1989, Lifetime Achievement award Sch. Medicine, 1997; rsch. grantee NIH, 1960—. Mem. Chem. Soc. (Eng.), Soc. Biochem. and Molecular Biol., Soc. Neurosci., Endocrine Soc., Soc. for Gynecologic Investigation, Internat. Soc. Neuroendocrinology, Soc. for Study Reproduction (Carl G. Hartman award 1996), Am. Physiol. Soc. (chmn. endocrinology and metabolism sect. 2004—), Internat. Soc. Reproductive Medicine (pres. 1980-82), Soc. Exptl. Biology and Medicine, Am. Fertility Soc., Am. Assn. Lab. Animal Sci., N.Y. Acad. Scis., AAUP, FASEB (bd. dirs., 2004—), Sigma Xi. Office: Med Coll of Ga Dept Physiology & Endocrinology Augusta GA 30912-3000 Office Phone: 706-721-6257. Business E-Mail: vmahesh@mail.mcg.edu.

MAHEU, SHIRLEY, Canadian legislator; b. Montreal, Que., Can., Oct. 7, 1931; d. George William Johnson and Bertha Hunt; m. René Albert Maheu, Sept. 5, 1953; children: Ronadl, Richard, Daniel, Marc. Diploma, O'Sullivan Bus. Coll. Cert. ins. broker. Ins. broker; mcpl. councillor City of Saint-Laurent, Canada, 1982-88; mem. City of Saint-Laurent Mcpl. Coun., 1982—86; mem. from Saint-Laurent Cartierville Ho. of Commons, Canada, 1988-96; mem. Can. Senate, Ottawa, Canada, 1996—. Pres. Saint-Laurent br. Red Cross Soc. Mem.: Saint-Laurent C. of C. Roman Catholic. Office: Canadian Senate Wellington St EB Rm 263 Ottawa ON Canada K1A 0A4*

MAHEY, JOHN ANDREW, retired museum director; b. DuBois, Pa., Mar. 30, 1932; s. Manasseh A. and Bernyce (Holdar) M. Student, Columbia U., 1950-52; BA, Pa. State U., 1959, MA, 1962. Asst. dir. Peale Mus., Balt., 1964-69; dir. E.B. Crocker Art Gallery, 1969-72, Cummer Gallery of Art, 1972-75, Meml. Art Gallery of U. Rochester, 1975-79; chief curator Philbrook Art Center, Tulsa, 1979-84; dir. San Antonio Mus. Art, 1984-89, Flint (Mich.) Inst. of Arts, 1989-96; ret., 1996. Contbr. articles on artists to art his. jours.; author exhbn. catalogs. Fulbright scholar, 1962 Mem. Phi Beta Kappa, Phi Alpha Theta. Home: 4645 N Progress Ave Harrisburg PA 17119 E-mail: mahey@aol.com.

MAHFOOD, STEPHEN MICHAEL, governmental agency executive; b. Evansville, Ind., Feb. 12, 1949; s. George Mahfood and Bonnie Short Morse; m. Kathleen Kas; children: Nadia Joan, Leila Emma, Toni Henzler. BS, Rutgers U., 1971; grad. environ. leadership program, Yale U., 1992. Vol. dir. YMCA, Beirut, 1974; environ. dir. Project Hope, Tunisia, 1975-77; dir. prin. asst. Dept. of Health Mo. State Health Planning and Devel. Agy., Jefferson City, 1977-78, dir., 1978-81; gen. mgr. Chimney Rock (N.C.) Co., 1982-84; dir. Mo. Environ. Improvement and Energy Resources Authority, Jefferson City, 1984-97, Mo. Dept. Natural Resources, Jefferson City, 1998—. Chmn. govt. adv. bd. to coun. for environ. corp. N. Am. Free Trade Assn.; mem. EPA Environ. Fin. Adv. Bd.; apptd. Congressman Anthony's Ho. Ways and Means Task Force on Pub. Fin.; past pres. Mo. Waste Control Coalition; mem., co-founder Coun. Infrastructure Fin. Authorities; past pres. Coun. of Pollution Control Fin. Agys., mem. Environ. Coun. of States; chmn. Gov.'s Commn. on Total Compensation; mem. Gov.'s Adv. Com. on Chip Mills. Recipient Achievement award Mo. Waste Control Coalition, 1986, 88, Presdl. Environ. Challenge award, 1992, Govs. Leadership Excellence award, 2003. Mem. Am. Mgmt. Assn., Am. Planning Assn., Nat. Assn. Environ. Profls., Missouri River Basin Assn. (bd. dirs.), Upper Miss.River Basin Assn. (bd. dirs.), Mo. Soil and Water Commn. Avocations: canoeing, cross country skiing, hiking, motorcycling, horseback riding. Home: 7311 North Shore Dr Hartsburg MO 65039-9211 Office: Mo Dept Natural Resources PO Box 176 Jefferson City MO 65102-0176

MAHL, GEORGE FRANKLIN, psychoanalyst, psychologist, educator; b. Akron, Ohio, Nov. 27, 1917; s. Floyd Alexander and Margaret (Strecker) M.; m. Martha Jane Fenn, Jan. 10, 1944; 1 dau., Barbara Jessica. A. B., Oberlin Coll., 1939, MA, 1941; PhD, Yale U., 1948; certificate, Western New Eng. Inst. Psychoanalysis, 1962. Asst. psychology Oberlin Coll., 1939-41; rsch. asst. in psychology Yale U., New Haven, 1941-42, mem. faculty, 1947—, prof. psychiatry and psychology, 1964-88, prof. emeritus, 1988—; tchr. Western New Eng. Inst. Psychoanalysis, 1961-85, pres., 1972-74. Served to 1st lt.

AUS, 1942-46. Fellow AAAS, APA; mem. Ea. Psychol. Assn., Western New Eng. Inst. Psychoanalysis, Western New Eng. Psychoanalytic Soc., Internat. Psychoanalytical Assn., Inst. Psychoanalytic Tng. and Rsch. (N.Y.). Home: 106 Bayard Ave North Haven CT 06473-4303

MAHLA, MICHAEL E. anesthesiologist, educator; b. Wilmington, Del., Mar. 8, 1953; s. Elbert Myron and Mary Pauline (Tice) M.; m. Sno Ellen White, June 8, 1979; 1 child, Melody Joy. BS in Chemistry, Davidson Coll., 1975; MD, Jefferson Med. Coll., 1979. Diplomate Am. Bd. Anesthesiology. Intern Walter Reed AMC, Washington, 1979-80, resident in anesthesiology, 1980-83; fellow in neuroanesthesiology Johns Hopkins Med. Inst., Balt., 1983; mem. staff Shands Teaching Hosp., Gainesville, Fla.; assoc. prof. anesthesiology/neurosurgery U. Fla. Coll. Medicine. Program dir. anesthesiology residency Walter Reed AMC, Washington, 1986-88; assoc. prof., assoc. chair edn. dept. anesthesiology U. Fla. Coll. Medicine, Gainesville, 1995—. Author: (with others) Clinical Anesthesiology Practice, 1994, Clinical Neuroanesthesia, 1997. Fellow Am. Soc. Neurologic Monitoring; mem. AMA, Am. Soc. Anesthesiologists, Soc. Neurosurg. Anesthesia and Critical Care. Office: Box 100254 Dept Anesthesiology Gainesville FL 32610-0254

MAHLE, CHRISTOPH ERHARD, electrical engineer; b. Stuttgart, Germany, Mar. 7, 1938; came to U.S., 1968; s. Ernst Johannes and Else (Wurth) M.; m. Mary Heavenrich, Mar. 23, 1975; children: Lisa, Charles. Diploma engring., Swiss Fed. Inst. Polytech., Zurich, 1961, D of Sci. Tech., 1966. Rsch. asst. Swiss Fed. Inst. Tech., Zurich, Switzerland, 1961-67; with tech. staff Comsat Labs., Clarksburg, Md., 1968-71, sect. head, 1971-73, dept. mgr., 1973-81, dir., 1981-83, exec. dir., 1983-94, v.p., 1995-96; ret., 1996. Patentee in field; contbr. articles to profl. jours. Fellow IEEE. Avocations: music, mountain climbing. E-mail: chrismahle@usa.net.

MAHLENDORF, URSULA RENATE, literature educator; b. Strehlen, Silesia, Germany, Oct. 24, 1929; came to U.S., 1953; Student, Oberschule an der Hamburgerstraße, Bremen, Fed. Republic Germany, 1950, U. Tübingen, Fed. Republic Germany, 1950 52, Brown U., 1953-57, MA in English Lit., 1956, PhD in German Lit., 1958; student, Bonn (Fed. Republic Germany) U., 1953, London U. Teaching asst. Brown U., Providence, 1953-57; from acting instr. to prof. German U. Calif., Santa Barbara, 1957—93, assoc. dir., campus coord. edn. abroad program, 1967—69, chmn. dept. Germanic and Slavic langs. and lits., 1980 83, assoc. dean Coll. Letters and Sci., 1986-89, emeritus, 1993—. Chmn. symposium in honor of Harry Slochower, 1977; campus coord. edn. abroad program U. Calif., 1967-69, assoc. dir., 1969-72; co-chair Nietzsche symposium Dept. Germanic and Slavic Langs. and Lits., U. Calif., Santa Barbara, 1981. Author: The Wellsprings of Literary Creation, 1985; editor: (with John L. Carleton) Man for Man: A Multi-Disciplinary Workshop on Affecting Man's Social and Psychological Nature through Community Action (Charles C. Thomas), 1973, Dimensions of Social Psychiatry, 1979, (with Arthur Lerner) Life Guidance through Literature, 1992; assoc. editor Am. Imago, Am. Jour. Social Psychiatry, Jour. Evolutionary Psychology; contbr. more than 90 articles to profl. jours. Recipient Alumni award, 1981; rsch. grantee U. Calif., 1974—; Fulbright fellow, 1951-52. Mem. MLA, Am. Assn. for Aesthetics and Art Criticism (past pres. Calif. div.), Assn. for applied Psychoanalysis (profl. mem.), Am. Assn. Social Psychiatry (councillor 1977-81), Internat. Assn. Social Psychiatry (treas. 1978-83). Avocations: sculpting, woodcarving. Home: 1505 Portesuello Ave Santa Barbara CA 93105-4626 Office: U Calif Dept Dept Germanic Semitic Slavic Studie Santa Barbara CA 93106 Office Phone: 805-682-6863.

MAHLER, HALFDAN THEODOR, physician, health organization executive; b. Vivild, Denmark, Apr. 21, 1923; s. Magnus and Benedicte (Suadicani) M.; m. Ebba Fischer-Simonsen, Aug. 31, 1957; children: Per Bo, Finn. MD, U. Copenhagen, 1948, postgrad. degree in pub. health; LLD (hon.), U. Nottingham, Eng., 1975; MD (hon.), Karolinska Inst., Stockholm, 1977; Docteur, de l'Universite des Scis. Sociales de Toulouse, France, 1977; DPH (hon.), Seoul Nat. U., 1979; ScD (hon.), U. Lagos, Nigeria, 1979, Emory U., 1989; MD (hon.), Warsaw Med. Acad., 1980; LHD, U. Nacional Federico Villareal, Lima, Peru, 1980; LHD (hon.), U. Gand, Belgium, 1983, CUNY, 1989; MD (hon.), Charles U., Prague, 1982, Mahidol U., Bangkok, Thailand, 1982, Aarhus U., Denmark, 1988, U. Copenhagen, 1988, Aga Khan U., Pakistan, 1989; LHD (hon.), U. Nacional Autonoma de Nicaragua, 1983; PhD (hon.), The Semmelweis U., Budapest, Hungary, 1987; LLD (hon.), McMaster U., Can., 1989; DSc (hon.), SUNY, 1990; MD (hon.), U. Newcastle Upon Tyne, 1990; LLD (hon.), U. Exeter, 1990, U. Toronto, 1990. Specialized tng. in TB; active field of internat. pub. health work; planning officer mass Tb campaign, 1950-51; sr. officer nat. Tb program WHO, India, 1951-61, chief Tb unit, Hdqrs., 1962-69, sec. to expert adv. panel on Tb, 1962-69, dir. project systems analysis, 1969-70, asst. dir.-gen. div. health services and div. family health, 1970-73, dir.-gen., 1973-88, dir. gen. emeritus, 1988; sec. gen. Internat. Planned Parenthood Fedn., 1989-95. Contbr. articles on epidemiology and control of Tb, polit., social, econ, and technol. priorities in health sector, application of systems analysis to health care problems to profl. jours. Decorated Grand Officier de l'Ordre Nat. du Benin, 1975, Grand Officier de l'Ordre Nat. du Voltaique, Upper Volta, 1978, comdr. de l'Ordre Nat. du Mali, 1982, Grand Officer de l'Ordre du Merite de la Rep. du Senegal, 1982, comdr. 1st class Order White Rose (Finland), Grand Officier de l'Ordre nat. malgache, Madagascar, 1987, Grand Cross Icelandic Order of the Falcon, 1988, Grand Cordon of Order Sacred Treasure, Japan, 1988, Bourgeoisie d'Honneur, Geneva, Switzererland, Grand Croix De L'Ordre De Merite, Luxenbourg, 1990, Grand Cross Ordem do Merito Medico, Brazil, 2003; recipient Jana Evangelisty Purkyne medal (Presdl. award) Prague, 1974, Comenius U. gold medal Bratislava, 1974, Carlo Forlanini gold medal Federazione Italiana contro la Tubercolosi et le Malattie Polmonari Sociali Rome, 1975, Ernest Carlsens Found. Prize Copenhagen, 1980, Georg Barfred-Pedersen prize Copenhagen, 1982, Hagedorn medal and prize Denmark, 1986, Freedom From Want medal Roosevelt Inst., 1988, Storkors Af Dannebrogsordenen, Denmark, 1988; hon. prof. U. Nacional Mayor de San Marcos, Lima, Peru, U. Chile Faculty of Medicine, Beijing Med. Coll., Rep. of China, Shanghai Med. U.; Bartel World Affairs fellow Cornell U., 1988; U.N. Population award, 1995, Andrija Stampar award, 1995. Fellow Royal Coll. Physicians (London), Faculty Community Medicine of Royal Colls. Physicians U.K. (hon.), Indian Soc. for Malaria and other Communicable Diseases (hon.), Royal Soc. Medicine (London) (hon., U.K.-U.S. Hewitt award 1992), London Sch. Hygiene and Tropical Medicine (hon.); mem. Med. Assn. Argentina (hon.), Latin Am. Med. Assn. (hon.), Italian Soc. Tropical Medicine (hon.), Belgium Soc. Tropical Medicine (assoc.), Societe medicale de Geneve (hon.), Union internationale contre la Tuberculose (hon.), Societe francaise d'Hygiene, de Medecine sociale et de Genie sanitaire (hon.), Uganda Med. Assn. (hon. life), Coll. Physicians and Surgeons, Bangladesh Royal Coll. Gen. Practitioners (ad eundem), List of Honour of the Internat. Dental Fedn., Am. Pub. Health Assn. (hon.), Nat. Acad. Medicine Mex. (hon.), Nat. Acad. Medicine Buenos Aires (hon.), Swedish Soc. Medicine (hon.), Brit. Medal Assn. (hon. fgn. corr. 1990), Inst. Medicine (NAS U.S.A.). Home and Office: Chemin de Pont-Céard 12 CH-1290 Versoix Switzerland Fax: 022-755 26 10. E-mail: halfdan.mahler@bluewin.ch.

MAHLER, HOWARD SAMUEL, psychiatrist; b. Bklyn., July 21, 1952; s. Eugene and Mildred (Winnick) M. BS, SUNY, Albany, 1974; MD, Med. Coll. Wis., 1979. Diplomate Am. Bd. Psychiatry and Neurology. Intern and resident sch. medicine Wash. U., St. Louis, 1979-83; Staff psychiatrist Malcolm Bliss Mental Health Ctr., St. Louis, 1983-84; psychiatrist II Kingsboro Psychiat. Ctr., Bklyn., 1986—2001; med. dir. Kingsboro Addiction Treatment Ctr., 2001—; psychiatrist II CK post ATC, 2003—. Mem. Am. Psychiat. Assn., Phi Beta Kappa. Office: Kingsboro Addiction Treatmt Ctr 754 Lexington Avenue Brooklyn NY 11221

MAHLER, RICHARD JOSEPH, internist; b. N.Y.C., Mar. 4, 1934; s. Jacob and Naomi (Feder) M.; m. Ida May Adler, Aug. 23, 1960; children: Susan Toba, Jonathan David. BA, NYU, 1955; MD, N.Y. Med. Coll., 1959. Diplomate Am. Bd. Internal Medicine. Intern New Rochelle (N.Y.) Hosp., 1960; resident in internal medicine N.Y. Med. Coll., N.Y.C., 1960-63, metabolic rsch. fellow, 1962-63, instr. medicine, 1964-67, asst. prof., 1967-70, assoc. prof., 1970-71; traveling fellow N.Y. Acad. Medicine, 1963-64; practice medicine specializing in internal medicine N.Y.C., 1964-71; chief sect. diabetes Met. Hosp., N.Y.C., 1968-71; assoc. dir. dept. metabolism and endocrinology City Hope Med. Ctr., 1971-73; dir. dept. metabolism and endocrinology Eisenhower Med. Ctr., Palm Desert, Calif., 1973 88, mem. med. staff, 1973-88, pres., 1976-79; clin. assoc. prof. medicine Cornell U. Med. Coll. Dept. Medicine, Section Endocrinology, 1988—; assoc. attending physician N.Y. Hosp., 1988—. Med. cons. to Merck and Co., Rahway, N.J., 1971-74, U.S. Vitamin Corp., N.Y.C., 1973-76; spl. cons. to FDA, 1972. Assoc. editor Hormone and Metabolic Rsch., 1969-76, co-editor, 1976—; assoc. editor Jour. Clin. Endocrinology and Metabolism, 1997-2000; contbr. articles on metabolic rsch. and diabetes to profl. jours., chpts. to med. books. Fellow ACP; mem. Endocrine Soc., Am. Diabetes Assn. (Devel. award 1966-67), Am. Fedn. Clin. Research, Diabetes Assn. So. Calif., Western Soc. Clin. Research, Am. Physiol. Soc., N.Y. Acad. Scis., Royal Soc. Medicine, Assn. Am. Med. Colls., Alpha Omega Alpha. Jewish. Home: 165 E 72d St New York NY 10021-4335 Office: 220 E 69th St New York NY 10021 Office Phone: 212-879-4073.

MAHLEY, ROBERT W. health facility administrator, PhD, Vanderbilt U., 1968, MD, 1970. Dir., sr. investigator Gladstone Inst. of Cardiovascular Disease, San Francisco; prof. pathology and medicine U. Calif., San Francisco. Mem.: Inst. of Medicine of NAS. Office: Gladstone Inst Cardiovascular Disease 365 Vermont St San Francisco CA 94103

MAHLMAN, JERRY DAVID, climate and atmospheric scientist; b. Crawford, Nebr., Feb. 21, 1940; s. Earl Lewis and Ruth Margaret (Callendar) M.; m. Janet Kay Hilgenberg, June 10, 1962, children: Gary Martin, Julie Kay. AB, Chadron State Coll., Nebr., 1962, LHD (hon.), 2000; MS, Colo. State U., 1964, PhD, 1967. Instr. Colo. State U., Ft. Collins, 1964-67; from asst. prof. to assoc. prof. Naval Postgrad. Sch., Monterey, Calif., 1967-70; rsch. meteorologist NOAA Geophys. Fluid Dynamics Lab., Princeton, NJ, 1970-84, lab. dir., 1984-2000; lectr. with rank of prof. Princeton U., NJ, 1980—2002; sr. rsch. fellow Nat. Ctr. for Atmospheric Rsch., Boulder, Colo., 2001—. Chmn. panel on mid-atmosphere program NAS-NRC, 1982-84, mem. climate rsch. com., 1986-89, mem. panel on dynamic extended range forecasting, 1987-90; mem. U.S.-USSR Commn. on Global Ecology, 1989-92; mem. Bd. on Global Change, 1991-95, Bd. on Sustainable Devel., 1995 2000, Commn. to Review U.S. Climate Change Program Strategic Plan, 2002-03; U.S. rep. world climate rsch. program Joint Sci. Commn., 1991-96. Contbr. over 100 articles to profl. jours. Bd. dirs. Lawrence Non-Profit Housing Inc., 1978-88. Recipient Disting. Authorship award Dept. Commerce, 1980, 81, Gold medal, 1986, Disting. Svc. award Chadron State Coll., 1984, Presdl. Rank award disting. exec. 1994, Honor Alumnus award Colo. State U. 1995, Climate Protection award EPA, 2000. Fellow Am. Geophys. Union (Jule Charney lectr. 1993), Am. Meterol. Soc. (awards com. 1984, 95, chmn. 2000, chmn. upper atmosphere com. 1979, assoc. editor Jour. Atmospheric Sci. 1979-86, councilor 1991-94, Editor's award 1978, Carl-Gustaf Rossby Rsch. medal 1994, disting. lectr. 1999). Home: 460 Golden Ln Longmont CO 80501 Office: Nat Ctr for Atmospheric Rsch PO Box 300 Boulder CO 80307-3000 Office Phone: 303-497-1608. Business E-Mail: jmahlman@ucar.edu.

MAHLMANN, JOHN JAMES, music education association administrator; b. Washington, Jan. 21, 1942; s. Charles Victor and Mary Elizabeth (Deye) M.; m. Ning Ning Chang, Feb. 5, 1972; 1 son, Justin Geeng Ming. BFA, Boston U., 1962, MFA, 1963; postgrad., U. Notre Dame, summer 1962; EdD, Pa. State U., 1970; DM (hon.), Duquesne U., 1997. Grad. asst. Boston U., 1962-63, instr., supr. student tchrs., dir. masters degree candidates, 1964-66; grad. asst., research asst. Pa. State U., 1963-64, instr., 1966-67, dir. gallery, art edn. dept., 1966-67; asst. prof. Tex. Tech U., 1967-69; chmn. tenure and promotions com.; dir. publs., asst. exec. sec. Nat. Art Edn. Assn., Washington, 1969-71, exec. sec., 1971-82, also tour dir. to Japan and Orient; exec. dir. Music Educators Nat. Conf., 1983—. Instr. drawing Lubbock Art Assn.; asst. debate coach, asst. coord. forensics Boston U.; vis. instr., mem. staff George Washington U., No. Va. C.C., Tchrs. Coll. N.Y. Exhibited at, Boston U., Pa. State U., Harvard U., Tex. Tech. U., Salem (Mass.) State Coll., Botolph Gallery, Boston, Inst. Contemporary Art, Boston, Barncellar Gallery, Orleans, Mass., State Gallery, State College, Pa., Halls Gallery, Lubbock, Lubbock Art Assn., Loft Gallery, San Antonio, Llano Estacado Art Assn., Hobbs, N.Mex., Purdue U., Cushing Gallery, Dallas, Religious Art Exhbn., Cranbrook Acad. Art, Bloomfield Hills, Mich., Upstairs Gallery, Arlington, Tex., S.W. Tex. State Coll., San Marcos.; Editor: Art Edn., 1970-81, Art Tchr., 1971-80; contbr. articles to mags. Mem. adv. bd. Hartt Sch., 1997—. Mem. Music Educators Nat. Conf., Nat. Art Edn. Assn., Am. Soc. Assn. Execs., Washington Soc. Assn. Execs., Phi Delta Kappa. Home: 10703 Cross School Rd Reston VA 20191-5105 Office: Music Ed Nat Conf 1806 Robert Fulton Dr Reston VA 20191-4348

MAHLUM, DALE DUANE, state legislator, small business owner; b. Bowman, N.D., June 12, 1930; s. Lloyd S. and Ragna (Paulson) M.; m. Sandra Sue Little, Dec. 21, 1956; children: Douglas, Connie, Thomas, Dee Ann, Michele. BS, U. Mont, 1956. Mgr. Super Foods, Kalispell, Mont., 1954-58; store owner Missoula, Mont., 1959-93; thoroughbred farm owner, breeder Coast to Coast, Missoula, Mont.; mem. Mont. Senate, Dist. 35, Helena, 1996—. Chmn. Mont. Bank Bd., Missoula, 1974—; bd. dirs. Mont. Hardware Implement, Helena, St. Patricks Hosp., Missoula; chmn. adv. bd. sch. bus U. Mont., Missoula, 1985-88. Mem. Western Mont. Fair Commn., Missoula, 1974-94. With USN, 1950-54. Mem. Mont. Thoroughbreds Breeders Assn. (pres.), Thoroughbred Owners/Breeders Assn. Republican. Lutheran. Home: 10955 Us Highway 93 N Missoula MT 59808-9227 Office: Mont Legislature PO Box 201706 Helena MT 59620-1706 Office Phone: 406-549-3115.

MAHMOUD, ADEL A. infectious disease and tropical medicine physician, educator, pharmaceutical executive; b. Cairo, Aug. 24, 1941; arrived in U.S., 1972; s. Abdel Fattah and Fathia (Osman) Mahmoud; m. Sally L. Hodder, Jan. 31, 1993. Grad., Cairo U., 1958, MD, 1963; PhD, U. London, 1971. Asst. lectr. Ain Shams U., Cairo, 1965—68; WHO fellow U. London, 1969—72; rsch. assoc., prof. Case Western Res. U., Cleve., 1973—87; physician-in-chief Univ. Hosps., Cleve., 1987—98; prof., chmn. dept. medicine Case Western Res. U., Cleve., 1987—98; pres. vaccines Merck & Co. Inc., Whitehouse Sta., NJ, 1998—. Editor: The Eosinophil in Health and Disease, 1979, Tropical and Geographical Medicine, 1990, Schistosomiasis, Tropical Medicine Sci. and Practice, Vol. 1, 2001, Biological Threats and Terrorism: Assessing the Science and Response Capabilities, 2002. Fellow: Infectious Diseases Soc. Am.; mem.: Inst. Medicine, Assn. Am. Physicians, Am. Soc. Clin. Investigations. Office: Merck & Co One Merck Dr Whitehouse Station NJ 08889

MAHMOUD, AHMED MOHAMED, information technology executive; b. Tripoli, Libya, June 6, 1964; s. Mohamed R. and Nadia A. (El Boury) M.; m. Michele A. Mobley, May 26, 1990; children: Maryam, Adam, Sami. BS, Tex. A&M U., 1987, MS, 1990. Rsch. asst. Tex. A&M U., College Station, 1986-90; computational programmer U. Houston, 1990-91; database analyst Eastman Kodak Co., Rochester, N.Y., 1991-95; sr. mgr. corp. info. tech. Dell Computer Corp., Austin, Tex., 1995-99, dir. corp. info. tech., 1999—. E-mail: ahmed_mahmoud@dell.com.

MAHMUD, SHIREEN DIANNE, photographer; b. Chittagong, Pakistan, Oct. 4, 1949; came to U.S., 1974; d. Mohammed Mazhurul Qudus and Mumtaz Mahal Begum; m. Abdul Wazed Mahmud, Apr. 10, 1966 (div. 1996); children: Sharmin, Anita. BA in Mass Comm., U. Hartford, 1982. Part-time med. sec., Middletown, Conn., 1979-82; freelance photographer, 1985—; typist Aetna Ins. Co., Middletown, 1991; freelance photographer Conn. Post. Prodr. feature program Storer Cable Comm., Clinton, Conn., 1991-95; freelance photojournalist Middletown Press, Durham Gazette, Middletown, 1991-95; mem. Bridgeport Regional Bus. Coun., 1997. Literacy vol. Russell Libr., Middletown, Conn. Mem. AAUW, Nat. League Am. Pen Women, Internat. Soc. Poets (Hall of Fame award 1997), Conn. Soc. Poets, Conn. Songwriter's Assn., Internat. Platform Assn.

MAHN, TIMOTHY WAYNE, music educator; b. Vancouver, Wash., Apr. 15, 1972; s. Richard W. and Pamela J. Mahn; m. Angie A. Armstrong, June 21, 1997; 1 child, Elijah. BA, Milligan Coll., 1995. Dir. of choral activities Mountain Mission Sch., Grundy, Va., 1997—2000; prof. of music Ozark Christian Coll., Joplin, Mo., 2000—. Deacon Pk. Plz. Christian Ch., Joplin, Mo., 2001—. Mem.: Nat. Assn. of Teachers of Singing (assoc.). Republican. Home: 604 S Oronago St Webb City MO 64870 Office: Ozark Christian Coll 1111 N Main Joplin MO 64801

MAHOMED, YOUSUF, physician, cardiothoracic surgeon; b. Pretoria, South Africa, Dec. 23, 1945; s. Moosa Kara and Fatima Mahomed (Ahmed) M.; m. Lorraine S. Mahomed, Jan. 26, 1980; children: Julie M., Adam J. MD, Royal Coll. Surgeons Ireland, 1970. Diplomate Am. Bd. Surgery, Am. Bd. Thoracic Surgery. Resident in surgery St. Joseph Hosp./U. Mich., Ann Arbor, 1971-75; staff surgeon U. Calif., Davis, 1975-76; resident in plastic surgery Case Western Res. U., Cleve., 1976-78, staff in plastic surgery/oncology, 1978-79; staff cardiothoracic surgeon Ind. U./Clarian Cardiovasc. Ctr. at Meth. Hosp., Indpls., 1981—; resident in cardiothoracic surgery Ind. U., Indpls., 1979-81, prof. surgery, 1991—, dir. adult cardiac surgery, 1995—. Cons. Ethicon; Guidant, St. Jude Med., Medtronic, Inc.; mem. cardiothoracic core team Clarian Health. Contbr. chpts. to books, articles to profl. jours. Bd. dirs. Park Tudor Sch., Indpls., 1992—. Fellow ACS, Am. Coll. Cardiology, Am. Coll. Chest Physicians, Internat. Coll. Surgeons; mem. Am. Assn. Thoracic Surgery, Internat. Soc. Minimally Invasive Cardiac Surgery, Soc. Vascular Surgery, Soc. Thoracic Surgeons, Am. Heart Assn., Internat. Soc. for Heart and Lung Transplantation, Internat. Soc. of Cardiovascular Surgery. Islamic. Office: Ind U Sch Medicine Clarian Cardiovascular Ctr 1801 N Senate Blvd MPC 2 Ste 3550 Indianapolis IN 46202-5112

MAHON, ARTHUR J. lawyer; b. N.Y.C., Jan. 13, 1934; s. Arthur Logan and Mary Agnes (Craine) M.; m. Myra E. Murphy, Aug. 10, 1957; children: Maura, Madonna, Arthur, Nancy. BA, Manhattan Coll., 1955; JD, NYU, 1958. Bar: N.Y., Fla., D.C. Adj. prof. law NYU Sch. of Law, N.Y.C., 1964-78; ptnr. Mudge, Rose, Guthrie, Alexander & Ferdon, N.Y.C., 1970-94; counsel Donovan Leisure Newton & Irvine, N.Y.C., 1994-98, McDermott, Will & Emery, 1998—. Trustee Manhattan Coll., N.Y.C., 1988-2003, Adrian and Jesse Archbold Charitable Trust, N.Y.C., 1976—, N.Y. Presbyn. Hosp., N.Y.C., 1994—, Alvin Ailey Am. Dance Theatre, 1998—; mem. joint bd. N.Y. Hosp.-Cornell Med. Ctr., N.Y.C., 1990-98; com. on trust and estate gift plans Rockefeller U., N.Y.C., 1984—; bd. dirs. United Way Internat., 1988-94, Alexandria, Va., chmn. planned giving and endowments com. Archdiocese, N.Y.C., 1982-97; bd. overseers Cornell Med. Coll., N.Y.C., 1986—, chmn., 1992-95, vice chmn., 1990-91, 96-; dir. Am. Skin Assn., N.Y.C., 1989—; v.p., dir. Cath. Communal Fund, Archdiocese of N.Y., 1997—, trustee Inner City Scholarship Fund, 1998—. Served to capt. USAF, 1958-60. Root-Tilden scholar NYU. Mem. N.Y. State Bar Assn., Bar Assn. City of N.Y., Fla. Bar Assn., D.C. Bar Assn. Home: 16 Cambridge Dr Madison CT 06443-3016 Office: McDermott Will & Emery 50 Rockefeller Plz Fl 12 New York NY 10020-1600 E-mail: amahon@mwe.com.

MAHON, MALACHY THOMAS, SR., lawyer, educator; b. N.Y.C., Jan. 4, 1934; s. James and Alice (Rooney) M.; m. Margaret Phyllis Kirwan, Jan. 25, 1958 (dec. 1993); children: Veronica Mahon Grover, Laura Mahon Chandonnet, Malachy. BA, Manhattan Coll., 1954; JD, Fordham U., 1960. Bar: N.Y. 1960. Law clk. to chief magistrate John M. Murtagh, N.Y.C., 1959-60; law clk. to justice Tom C. Clark U.S. Supreme Ct., 1960-61; assoc. Hale Russell & Stentzel, N.Y.C., 1961-62, Mudge Rose Guthrie & Alexander, N.Y.C., 1979-80; of counsel Farrell, Fritz, Caemmerer, Cleary, Barnosky & Armentano, Mineola, NY, 1982-83, Havens & Lombard, Flushing, N.Y., 1994-95; prof. Fordham U. Law Sch., 1962-68; prof. law Hofstra U. Law Sch., 1968—, founding dean, 1968-73, S.B. Wilzig disting. prof. banking, 1985—. Vis. prof. U. Tex. Law Sch., 1973-74; exec. dir., spl. N.Y. State asst. atty. gen. Meyer Investigation of State Police Murder Coverup Charges Against the Spl. Attica Prison Riot Prosecutor's Office, 1975; chief counsel N.Y. Gov.'s Spl. Com. on Criminal Offenders, 1966; mem. Nassau County Bd. Ethics, 1983-96, chmn., 1989-96; chmn. merit selection com. EDNY Bankruptcy Judges, 1985-88. Staff author: Mental Illness, Due Process and the Criminal Defendant, 1968; monthly comml. law columnist: N.Y. Law Jour, 1976-78. Served with U.S. Army, 1954-56. Mem. ABA, N.Y. State Bar Assn., Assn. Bar City N.Y., Am. Law Inst. Home: 14 Duke Of Gloucester Manhasset NY 11030-3210 Office: Hofstra U Law Sch Hempstead NY 11550 Office Phone: 516-463-5868. Business E-Mail: lawmtm@hofstra.edu.

MAHON, MAXINE, performing company executive; BA in Sociology, San Diego (Calif.) State U. Dancer Starlight Opera, San Diego (Calif.) Ballet, Calif. Ballet Co., Nat. Ballet, Washington; dir., founder Calif. Ballet Co., San Diego, 1968—. Choreographer (films) Being John Malkovich, (plays) The Masked Ball, Seattle (Wash.) Opera Co., 2002, Toronto (Can.) Opera Co., 2003. Recipient Headliner of Yr. in Arts award, San Diego (Calif.) Press Club; grantee, NEA. Office: California Ballet Company 4819 Ronson Ct San Diego CA 92111

MAHON, ROBERT, photographer; b. Wilmington, Del., Dec. 28, 1949; s. Clifton and Mary Veronica (Figash) M.; m. Carol Joyce, Apr. 24, 1983. BA in Am. Studies, U. Del., 1971. One-man shows include Twining Gallery, N.Y.C., 1985, Mercer Coll., Trenton, N.J., 1993, Anne Reid Gallery, Princeton, 1996, N.J. State Mus., 1997, Dana Libr. Rutgers U., Newark, 1998, RVC Coll., N.J., 2001, PhilosophyBox, N.Y.C., 2004, exhibited in group shows at Whitney Mus. Am. Art, 1982, Phila. Mus. Art, 1982, 1995, Am. Ctr., Paris, 1982, Mus. Modern Art, N.Y.C., 1983, 1984—85, 1993, Kolnischer Kunstverein, 1983, Art Inst., Chgo., 1985, Twining Gallery, 1985—86, 1988, 1989, N.J. State Mus., 1990, 1997, 2002, 1999, Guggenheim Soho, 1994, Sandra Gering Gallery, N.Y.C., 1996, Newark Mus., 1997, 2002, Korn Gallery Drew U., Madison, N.J., 1999, N.Y. Pub. Libr., 1999, Guild Hall, East Hampton, N.Y., 1999, also others, Represented in permanent collections Phila. Mus. Art, Mus. Modern Art, Met. Mus. Art, N.Y. Pub. Libr., Humanities Rsch. Ctr., U. Tex., Austin, Princeton U. Libr., Princeton U. Art Mus., Harvard U. Art Mus., N.J. State Mus., Newark Mus., Montclair Art Mus., Rutgers U., Dana Libr., Zimmerli Mus., Noyes Mus., also pvt. collections, exhibitions include 100 NJ Artists Nat. Tour, 2002—03. Guggenheim grantee, 1985; RCIP Printmaking fellow, 1996. Home: PO Box Q Stockton NJ 08559-0390 E-mail: mailbox@robertmahon.net.

MAHONE, BARBARA JEAN, automotive company executive; b. Notasulga, Ala., Apr. 19, 1946; BS, Ohio State U., 1968; MBA, U. Mich., 1972; program for mgmt. devel., Harvard U., 1981. Sys. analyst GM, Detroit, 1968-71, sr. staff asst., 1972-74, mgr. career planning, 1975-78, dir. pers. adminstrn. Rochester, N.Y., 1979-81, mgr. indsl. rels. Warren, Ohio, 1982-83, dir. human resources mgmt. Chevrolet-Pontiac-Can. group, 1984-86, dir. gen. pers. and pub. affairs Inland divsn., 1986-88, gen. dir. pers. Indland Fisher Guide divsn. Detroit, 1989-91, gen. dir. employee benefits, 1991-93, dir. human resources truck group Pontiac, Mich., 1994—2000, exec. dir. human resources, 2001—. Chmn. Fed. Labor Rels. Authority, Washington, 1983-84, Spl. Panel on Appeals; dir. Metro Youth; mem. govs. U. Mich. Alumni. Bd. dirs. ARC, Rochester, 1979-82, Urban League Rochester, 1979-82, Rochester Aea Multiple Sclerosis; mem. human resources com. YMCA, Rochester, 1980-82; mem. exec. bd. Nat. Coun. Negro Women; mem. allocations com. United Way Greater Rochester. Recipient Pub. Rels. award Nat. Assn. Bus. and Profl. Women, 1976, Mary McLeod Bethune award Nat. Coun. Negro Women, 1977, Senate resolution Mich. State Legislature, 1980; named Outstanding Woman, Mich. Chronicle, 1975, Woman of Yr., Nat. Assn. Bus. and Profl. Women, 1978, Disting. Bus. Person, U. Mich., 1978, one of 11 Mich. Women, Redbook mag., 1978. Mem. Nat. Black MBA Assn. (bd. dirs., nat. pres. Disting. Svc. award, bd. dirs., nat. pres. Outstanding MBA), Women Econ. Club (bd. dirs.), Indsl. Rels. Rsch. Assn., Internat. Assn. for Pers. Women, Engring. Soc. Detroit. Republican. Home: 175 Kirkwood Ct Bloomfield Hills MI 48304-2927 Office: 30001 Van Dyke Ave Mail Code 480-210-1 Warren MI 48090

MAHONE, GLENN, federal agency administrator; B Commn. and Speeck, U. Ctrl. Ark. Mgmt. cons. to pres., CEO Stephens Engring. Co., Inc., Lanham, Md.; cons. employment and tng. U.S. Dept. Labor, Washington; v.p., dir. sales tng. and devel. FirstSouth Savs. and Loan, Little Rock; dir. info. svcs., press sec. Office Ark. Sec. of State, Little Rock; comml. sales and mktg. mgr. ADT Security Svcs., Balt.; key advisor U.S. EEOC, 1999—2000; sr. advisor, press sec. NASA, Washington, 2000, acting assoc. adminstr. pub. affairs, 2001—02, asst. adminstr. pub. affairs, 2002—. Office: NASA Hdqrs Mail Code P 300 E St SW Washington DC 20546

MAHONEY, ANN DICKINSON, fundraiser; b. Topeka, Sept. 12, 1961; d. Jacob Alan II and Ruth (Curd) Dickinson; m. Michael James Mahoney, May 29, 1993; children: James Junius Castle, Catherine Lane, Grace Dickinson, Christopher Michael Hayes. AB in History, Grinnell Coll., 1983; postgrad., McGill U., Montreal, Que., Can., 1985. Analyst, corp. fin. dept. E.F. Hutton & Co., Inc., NYC, 1983-85; pres., owner The Dark Side, NYC, 1985-87; asst. dir. individual giving Meml. Sloan-Kettering Cancer Ctr., NYC, 1987-88, dir. spl. gifts, 1988-91; assoc. dir. devel. Sch. Humanities and Scis. Stanford (Calif.) U., 1991-96; ind. fundraising cons., 1996—. Devel. asst. regional office Brandeis U., NYC, 1987. Vol. interviewer Grinnell Coll., NYC, San Francisco, 1983—; chair No. Calif. adv. bd. Nat. Found. for Tchg. Entrepreneurship, 2000-02. Mem.: Peninsula Assn. Retarded Children and Adults Aux. (bd. dirs. 1998—2002, pres. 2000), Pacific Rsch. Inst. for Pub. Policy, Nat. Soc. Fund Raising Execs., San Francisco Ballet Aux., Friends of Filoli (Woodside, Calif.), Jr. League San Francisco (com. chmn. 1996—98), Hist. Topeka Assn., Hayden Lake (Idaho) Country Club, Spokane Club, Villa Taverna (San Francisco). Republican. Episcopalian. E-mail: admahone@pacbell.net.

MAHONEY, CATHERINE ANN, artist, educator; b. Macon, Mo., Nov. 18, 1948; d. Joe H. and Berneice Joyce (Garnett) Dickson; m. Michael W. Mahoney, July 19, 1969; children: Karin Lynn Mahoney Broeker, Ryan Michael. BS in Edn. with honors, Truman U., Kirksville, 1969. Mo. state life cert. for tchg. art. Elem./secondary art instr. Bucklin (Mo.) R-I Schs., 1970-74; pvt. art instr. Groom (Tex.) Artist's Assn., 1974-75; substitute tchr. Gasconade R-I Schs., Hermann, Mo., 1977-89; pvt. art instr. Colorful Brushes Studio, Hermann, Mo., 1987—; elem./secondary art instr. Crosspoint Christian Schs., Union, Mo., 1994-98. Pres. City of Hermann Arts Coun., 1983-87, membership chmn., 1980-82; dir. Summertime Children's Watercolor Workshops, Colorful Brushes, Hermann, 1987—. One-woman shows at Truman U., Kirksville, 1969, Capitol City Art Guild, Jefferson City, Mo., 1983, Kolbe Gallery of Art, Hermann, 1984, Colorful Brushes Studio, Hermann, 1987-94; designer Sister Cities Emblem City of Hermann/Arolsen, Germany, 1989, 20 ft. histl. mural, Gasconade County; works published in: Best of Watercolor: Texture, 1998, The Artful Home 2, 2004. Pres. Hermann Parent-Tchr. Orgn., 1985—87; leader 4-H, Girl and Boy Scouts, Hermann, 1982—95; organist, pianist, tchr. Hermann Cath. and Bapt. Chs., 1977—97, E. Free Ch., 1997—. Named Outstanding Young Woman of Yr., Hermann Jaycees, 1984, 1st place award Mo. Artists Collection, Mo. Pub. Svc., Sedalia, Mo., 1992, 3d place award and purchase prize Watercolor USA, Springfield (Mo.) Art Mus., 1995, 1st place award Arts Rolla Art Show, 1999. Mem.: Mo. Watercolor Soc. (bd. mem. 1998—2004, signature, M. Graham Mdse. award 2003), Oil Painters Am., St. Louis Artist Guild (mem. art sect., Hon. Mention 1993, 1998, 2002), Watercolor USA Honor Soc. (hon. Art Show award 1995), Okla. Watercolor Assn. (assoc. included Art Show 1989), Nat. Watercolor Soc. (assoc. included Nat. Art Show 1995). Avocations: piano, reading, embroidery, sewing, knitting. Home: 1058 Old Stonehill Hermann MO 65041 Office: Colorful Brushes Studio 126 E 4th St Hermann MO 65041-1130 E-mail: camahoney@ktis.net.

MAHONEY, DAVID L. former pharmaceutical wholesale and healthcare management company executive; b. Brighton, Mass., June 24, 1954; s. Thomas H.D. and K. Phyllis (Norton); m. Winn Canning Ellis, Sept. 26, 1992. AB in English, Princeton U., 1975; MBA, Harvard U., 1981. Asst. gen. mgr. Ogden Food Svc. Corp., L.A., 1975-76, concessions mgr. East Boston, Mass., 1976-77, gen. mgr., 1977-78, ops. analyst, 1978-79; assoc. McKinsey & Co., San Francisco, 1981-86, prin., 1986-90; v.p. strategic planning McKesson Corp., San Francisco, 1990-94, pres. HDS, Inc., 1994-95, pres. pharm. svcs., 1995-97, group pres. pharm svcs. & internat. group, 1997-99; exec. v.p., CEO pharm. svcs. bus. McKesson HBOC, 1999, co-CEO, 1999-2001; CEO iMcKesson, 2000-01. Bd. dirs. Symantec Corp., KQED, Live Oak Sch. Mem.: Young Pres. Orgn., City Club of San Francisco. Avocations: outdoor activities, photography. Office: 235 Montgomery St Ste 820 San Francisco CA 94104-5292

MAHONEY, DONNA MARIE, psychotherapist; b. Oak Park, Ill., Mar. 13, 1961; d. Thomas Joseph and Eileen Mary Mahoney. MA, Loyola U., 1989; PhD, Inst. Clin. Social Work, 2000. Acad. advisor Triton Coll., River Grove, Ill., 1984-87; psychotherapist Centrum Clinic, Oak Park, 1989—97; psychotherapist, case mgr. Kenneth Young Ctrs., Elk Grove, Ill., 1989-96; psychotherapist Anxiety and Stress Ctr., Orland Park, Ill., 1996—. Adj. faculty Argosy U., Rolling Meadows, Ill., 2002, Loyola U., 2003. Contbr. articles to profl. jours. Mem. Anxiety Disorders Assn. Am., Obsessive Compulsive Fedn., Ill. Soc. Clin. Social Work, Chgo. Assn. Psychoanalytic Psychology. Democrat. Avocations: aerobics, music. Home: 712 Bell Ave La Grange IL 60525

MAHONEY, GERALD FRANCIS, manufacturing executive; b. Bklyn., July 31, 1943; s. Francis B. and Leona (Gray) M.; m. JoAnne A. Maselli, May 2, 1971; children: G. Scott, Ryan J. BA, Adelphi U., 1965; MBA, Northeastern U., 1966. CPA, N.Y. Mgr. Arthur Andersen & Co., N.Y.C., 1966-73; asst. contr. Bairnco Corp., N.Y.C., 1973-78, v.p. fin., 1980-81, gen. mgr. Pensauken, N.J., 1979-80, v.p., div. pres. Union, N.J., 1981-83; sr. v.p. fin. and adminstrn. Polychrome Corp., Yonkers, N.Y., 1984-87; pres. Transcrit Corp., Brewster, N.Y., 1987-90, Pavey Envelope & Tag Corp., Jersey City, 1991-94; chmn., CEO Mail-Well, Inc., Englewood, Colo., 1994—. Mem. AICPA, N.Y. State Soc. CPA's, Noyac Country Club (Sag Harbor, N.Y., bd. dirs. 1980-83), Glenmoor Country Club (Englewood, Colo.), Ridgewood Country Club (N.J.). Republican. Roman Catholic. Avocations: golf, tennis. Office: Mail Well Inc 8310 S Valley Hwy # 400 Englewood CO 80112 Home: 266 Cook St Denver CO 80206

MAHONEY, JAMES R. federal agency administrator; b. Syracuse, N.Y. D in Meteorology, MIT. Faculty pub. health Harvard U.; co-founder Environ. Rsch. and Tech., Inc.; sr. exec. Bechtel Group, San Francisco, Internat. Tech. Corp., L.A., Washington; dir. Nat. Acid Precipitation Assessement Program, 1988; asst. adminstrv. for oceanic and atmospheric rsch. Dept. Commerce, Silver Springs, Md., 2001—; pres. Consulting and Ventures Group. Mem.: NAS (com. mem., co-chmn. bd. on atmospheric sci. and climate), Am. Meteorol. Soc. (pres. 1990—91). Office: Dept Commerce Oceanic and Atmospheric Rsch 1315 East-West Hwy Silver Spring MD 20910-3279

MAHONEY, JOAN, law educator; AB, AM, U. Chgo.; JD, Wayne State U.; PhD, Cambridge U. Assoc. Honigman Miller Schwartz and Cohn, Detroit; mem. law faculty U. Mo., Kansas City, 1980—94; mem. faculty, dean Western New Eng. Coll. Law, 1994—96; mem. faculty Wayne State U. Law Sch., Detroit, 1994—, dean, 1996—. Contbr. articles to profl. jours., chpts. to books. Office: Wayne U Law Sch 471 W Palmer Detroit MI 48202

MAHONEY, JOHN, actor; b. Blackpool, Eng., June 20, 1940; MA in English, Western Ill. U.; student, Quincy Coll.; trained for the theater, St. Nicholas Theatre, Chgo. Stage performances include The Water Engine, 1977, The Hothouse, Taking Steps, Death of a Salesman, Orphans, 1985 (Theater World award), The House of Blue Leaves, 1986 (Tony award, Clarence Derwent award), The Subject Was Roses, 1991; films include Mission Hill, 1982, Voyeur, 1984, Code of Silence, 1985, The Manhattan Project, 1986, Streets of Gold, 1987, Tin Men, 1987, Suspect, 1987, Moonstruck, 1987, Frantic, 1988, Betrayed, 1988, Eight Men Out, 1988, Say Anything, 1989, Love Hurts, 1990, The Russia House, 1990, Barton Fink, 1991, Article 99, 1992, In the Line of Fire, 1993, Striking Distance, 1993, Reality Bites, 1994, The Hudsucker Proxy, 1994, The American President, 1995, Mariette in Ecstasy, 1996, Primal Fear, 1996, She's the One, 1996, Antz (voice), 1998, The Iron Giant (voice), 1999, The Broken Hearts Club, 2000, Almost Salinas, 2001, Atlantis: The Lost Empire (voice), 2001, Atlantis: Milo's Return (voice), 2003; TV series: Lady Blue, 1985-86, H.E.L.P., The Human Factor, 1991, Frasier, 1993-2004; TV movies Chicago Story, 1981, Listen to your Heart, 1983, Dance of the Phoenix,, 1984, The Killing Floor, 1984, First Steps, 1985, Trapped in Silence, 1986, Favorite Son, 1988, (TNT) Dinner at Eight, 1989, (HBO) The Image, 1990, The 10 Million Dollar Getaway, 1991, The Secret Passion of Robert Clayton, 1992; TV special The House of Blue Leaves, 1987. Served AUS Recipient award SAG, 2000.

MAHONEY, JOHN J. office supply company executive; Degree, College of Holy Cross; MBA, Northeastern U. Ptnr. Ernst & Young; CFO Staples Inc., Framingham, Mass., 1996—, exec v.p., 1996—, chief administrative officer, 1997—. Office: Staples Inc 500 Staples Dr Framingham MA 01701

MAHONEY, JOHN JOSEPH, business executive, educator; b. Chattanooga, Nov. 9, 1921; s. John J. and Helen M. (Armstrong) M.; m. Elizabeth DuBose Porcher, June 25, 1949. BS in Commerce, The Citadel, 1946; MS in Indsl. Mgmt., Ga. Inst. Tech., 1967. Ordained deacon Roman Cath. Ch., 1979. Instr. dept. bus. adminstrn. The Citadel, Charleston, S.C., 1947-50, asst. prof., 1967-92; founder, pres., gen. mgr. Carolinga Vending Inc., 1947-67, Shamrock Sys., Inc., 1960-67. Dir. Charles F. Cates & Sons, Inc. Pickle Co., Faison, N.C., also mem. exec. com.; v.p., treas., dir. Cons. to Bus., Inc. (formerly Mahoney Cons., Inc.); dir., pres. Associated Distbrs., Inc., Metro Stylists, Inc.; dir. Aunt Jane Foods, Inc.; S.C. editor Diaconal Quar.; founder, bd. dirs. Isnt. Organizational Excellence, Charleston. S.C., 1998—. Procurator, advocate diocesan tribunal Diocese of Charleston; mem. Bishop's Com. on Vocations: pres. Cath. Charities, 1958-60; bd. dirs. Charleston Devel. Bd., 1957-60, Charleston C. of C., United Fund, Charleston, 1955-57, Family Agy., Charleston, 1956-60; chmn. Pres.'s Export Expansion Coun. Atlanta Region; initiator, planner Ctr. for Entrepreneurship, Charleston Coll. Served to lt. AUS, 1943-46, capt. Res. Recipient Disting. Svc. award Jaycees, 1956. Mem. So. Mgmt. Assn., Fellowship Cath. Scholars, Hibernian Soc. (life), Confederate Hist. Assn., SCV (former mem. gen. staff, chaplain-in-the-field S.C. divsn.), O'Mahoney Records Soc., Assn. Pvt. Enterprise Edn. (former mem. exec. com.), Fund for Conservative Majority (bd. dirs.), Irish Am. Cultural Inst. (life). Home: 1602 Porchers Bluff Rd Mount Pleasant SC 29466-8942 Office: 276 E Bay St Charleston SC 29401-2600

MAHONEY, JOHN L. English literature educator; b. Somerville, Mass., Feb. 4, 1928; AB, Boston Coll., 1950, AM, 1952, DHL (hon.), 2003; PhD, Harvard U., 1957. From instr. of English to prof. emeritus Boston Coll., 1955—2002, Rattigan prof. English emeritus, 2002—. Chmn. dept. English, Boston Coll., 1962-67, 69-70, dir. PhD program in English, 1970-75, 82-85, mem. ednl. policy com. Grad. Sch. Arts and Scis., 1985-87; vis. prof. of English Harvard U. summer sch., 1963, 65, 67, 71, 80, 83, 86; cons. for self-study Weston Coll. Schs. of Philosophy and Theology, Boston Coll., 1965; sem. leader programs for women, Boston Coll., Newton Coll., 1976, 78, 79; mem. numerous acad. coms. and couns.; cons., mem. English adv. com. Commonwealth of Mass., 1968-70; mem. acad. coun. Coll. of Advancing Studies, Boston Coll., 1969—, univ. core curriculum devel. com., 1991-97; bd. trustees St. John's Sem., Brighton, Mass., com. on acad. affairs, 1980-86; sec. bd. trustees Katharine Gibbs Sch., Boston, 1982-90; mem. adv. bd. Jesuit Inst., Boston Coll., 1987—; mem. Boston Coll. Coun. the Arts, 1997—. Author: The Whole Internal Universe: Imitation and the New Defense of Literature in British Criticism, 1660-1830, 1985, The Persistence of Tragedy: Episodes in the History of Drama, 1985, The Logic of Passion: The Literary Criticism of William Hazlitt, rev. edit., 1981, Wordsworth: A Poetic Life, 1997, Wordsworth and the Critics, 2001, Wordsworth of Rydal: Religious Experience and Religious Practice, 2003; editor, author intro. and notes: The Enlightenment and English Literature, 1980, The English Romantics: Major Poetry and Critical Theory, 1978, An Essay of Dramatic Poetry and Other Critical Writings by John Dryden, 1965, William Duff's Essay on Original Genius, 1964; contbr. Imagination and the Ways of Genius (in Approaches to Hazlitt), 1986, Teaching the Immortality Ode with Coleridge's Dejection: An Ode (in Approaches to Teaching Wordsworth's Poetry), 1986, Teaching Shelley's Skylark and the Defence of Poetry (in Approaches to Teaching Shelley's Poetry), 1990, and others; editor: (with J. Robert Barth, S.J.) Coleridge, Keats, and the Imagination: Romanticism and Adam's Dream, 1990, Seeing Into the Life of Things: Essays on Literature and Religion, 1998; mem. editl. bd. Boston Coll. Mag., 1981-90; author articles, papers delivered at profl. confs.; reviewer for Studies in Romanticism, The Wordsworth Circle, Nineteenth Century Contexts, So. Humanities Rev., Coll. Lit.; series editor Fordham U. Press Series on Religion and Lit., 1997—. Active Sacred Heart Parish, Lexington, Mass., del. to Lexington Coun. Chs., 1968, chmn. parish coun., 1969-72, mem. parish coun., 1995-98, vice chmn., 1996-98, mem. religious edn. commn., 1974-79, 90-93, sem. leader Christian Youth Edn., 1969-73, lector, 1972—; mem. Archdiocese of Boston Commn. for Promotion of Parish Couns., 1969-74, Benjamin Mays Mentor Ahana program, 1993—. Boston Coll. Grad. Sch. fellow, 1950-52; Boston Coll. Faculty rsch. grantee, 1964, 68, 86, 92, 96, 97, 98, Mellon Found. grantee for rsch. and faculty devel., 1981-82; grantee rsch. Am. Philos. Soc., 1987; recipient Boston Coll. Campus Coun. Tchr. of Yr. award, 1966, Boston Coll. alumni award for excellence in edn., 1978, Andre Favat award Mass. Coun. Tchrs. English, 1988, Prof. of Yr. award Coun. for Advancement and Support of Edn. Mass., 1989, Ann. Wordsworth Meml. Lectr., Rydal Ch., 2003. Mem. AAUP (pres. Boston Coll. chpt. 1962), MLA, N.E. Soc. Eighteenth Century Studies, Wordsworth-Coleridge Assn. Am., Keats-Shelley Assn. Am., The Johnsonians, Alpha Sigma Nu, Phi Beta Kappa (Tchg. award Boston Coll. 1994). E-mail: mahoneyj@bc.edu.

MAHONEY, JOSEPH FRANCIS, historian, educator; b. Jersey City, N.J., July 4, 1927; s. Daniel Joseph and Margaret Cecilia Mahoney; m. Natalie Helen Krolovich, May 9, 1953; children: Joseph, Natalie, Cecilia, Claire. AB, Duns Scotus Coll., 1949; AM, Seton Hall U., 1958; PhD, Columbia U., 1964. From instr. to prof. history dept. Seton Hall U., South Orange, NJ, 1958—99; ret., 1999. Dir. N.J. Cath. Hist. Rec. Commn., Newark, 1976—. Author: The Healing Touch, 1992; co-editor (with P. Wosh): Diocesan Journal of M.A. Corrigan, 1987; editor: N.J. Hist. Soc. Jour., 1969—79. Col. U.S. Army, 1952—82. Recipient Scroll of Achievement, N.J. Hist. Soc., 1981, Award of Recognition, N.J. Hist. Commn., 1978; fellow, N.J. Hist. Soc., 1970. Mem.: Orgn. Am. Historians, Am. Cath. Hist. Assn., Am. Hist. Assn. Roman Catholic. Avocations: reading, walking. Home: 639 Sayre Ln Paramus NJ 07652-1908

MAHONEY, KIMBERLY LYNNE, event and facility executive; b. Johnson City, N.Y., Nov. 1969; d. Dewitt Duncan and Selina Faye Smith; m. Michael Mahoney, June 24, 2000. BA, U. of Ky., 1992; Med, U. of Ga., 1994. Cert. Diversity Trainer Soc. for Human Resource Mgmt., 2002, instr. Techniques for Effective Alcohol Mgmt. Tng. Program, 1999. Facility mgmt. intern Charlotte Coliseum, NC, 1994; event coord. Charlotte Conv. Ctr., NC, 1994—95; account mgr. Show Pros Entertainment Svcs., Inc., Charlotte, NC, 1995—97, regional mgr. Greensboro, NC, 1997—98; guest services mgr. Schottenstein Ctr., Ohio State U., Columbus, 1998—2000, asst. dir. event svcs. and adminstrn., 2000—03; asst. commr. Ohio High Sch. Athletic Assn., 2003—. Cons., trainer NFL Jacksonville Jaguars, 2002—03; lectr. Ohio State U., 2003—. Vol. events dir. Ga. Spl. Olympics, Athens, 1993; vol. NCAA YES (Youth Edn. through Sport) Clinic, Atlanta, 1993; vol. youth soccer coach Charlotte, NC, 1995—96. Mem.: North Am. Soc. for Sport Mgmt. (student rep. for exec. coun. 2002—03), Ohio Assn. for Health, Phys. Edn., Recreation, and Dance, Acad. of Mgmt., Sport Mktg. Assn., Phi Kappa Phi. Office: Ohio High School 4080 Roselea Pl Columbus OH 43214 Office Phone: 614-267-2502. E-mail: kmahoney@ohsaa.org.

MAHONEY, MARGARET ELLERBE, foundation executive; d. Charles Hallam and Leslie Nelson (Savage) M. BS magna cum laude, Vanderbilt U., 1946; LHD (hon.), Meharry Med. Coll., 1977, U. Fla., 1980, Med. Coll. Pa., 1982, Williams Coll., 1983, Smith Coll., 1985, Beaver Coll., 1985, Brandeis U., 1989, Marymount Coll., 1990, Mt. Sinai Sch. Medicine, 1992, Rush U., 1993, SUNY, Bklyn., 1994, N.Y. Med. Coll., 1995. Fgn. affairs officer State Dept., Washington, 1946-53; exec. assoc., assoc. sec. Carnegie Corp., N.Y.C., 1953-72; v.p. Robert Wood Johnson Found., Princeton, NJ, 1972-80; pres. Commonwealth Fund, N.Y.C., 1980-94, MEM Assocs., Inc., N.Y.C., 1995—. Spkr. in field. Contbr. articles to profl. jours. Trustee John D. and Catherine T. MacArthur Found., 1985—2002, Smith Coll., 1988—93, Columbia U., 1991—96, Carnegie Found. Advancement of Tchg., 1963—2001, Arthur Ashe Found., 1997—; vis. fellow Sch. Archtl. and Urban Planning, Princeton U., 1973—80; bd. dirs. Coun. on Found., 1982—88; mem. N.Y.C. Commn. on the Yr. 2000, 1985—87, MIT Corp., 1984—89; bd. govs. Am. Stock Exch., 1987—92, Skillbuilders Fund, 1993—, Am. Skin Assn., 1994—, Classroom Inc., 1996—; mem. adv. bd. Office of Med. Examiner, N.Y.C., 1987—; vice chmn. N.Y.C. Mayor's Com. for Pub./Pvt. Partnerships, 1990—93; bd. dirs. Alliance for Aging Rsch., 1987—, Overseas Devel. Coun., 1988—2001, Nat. Found. Ctrs. for Disease Control and Prevention, Inc., 1994—, chmn., 1996—98; mem. vestry Parish of Trinity Ch., 1982—89, 1991—95. Recipient Frank H. Lahey Meml. award, 1984, Women's Forum award, 1989, Walsh McDermott award, 1992, Disting. Grantmaker award Coun. Founds., 1993, Edward R. Loveland award ACP, 1994, Spl. Recognition award AAMC, 1994, Merit medal Lotos Club, 1994, Terrance Keenan Leadership award in health philanthropy Grantmakers in health, 1995, Distinction award Am. Skin Assn., 1998, Rsch. Am. award, 1999, Hon. Classmate Class of 1976 award Princeton U., 2001, Picker Inst. award, 2003. Mem. AAAS, Inst. Medicine of NAS, Am. Acad. Arts and Scis., Am. Philos. Soc., Coun. Fgn. Rels., Fin. Women's Assn. N.Y., N.Y. Acad. Medicine, N.Y. Acad. Scis., Alpha Omega Alpha. Office: MEM Assocs Inc 521 5th Ave Rm 1801 New York NY 10175-0088 Office Phone: 212-297-0500.

MAHONEY, MARGARET ELLIS, accountant; b. Detroit, Mar. 17, 1929; d. Seth Wiley and Mildred Elizabeth (Hill) Ellis; m. Stephen Bedell Smith, Mar. 15, 1956 (div. Oct. 1962); 1 child, Laura Elizabeth; m. Patrick John Mahoney, Sept. 1, 1972 (dec.). BA, Butler U., 1953. Copywriter Hook Drugs Inc., Indpls., 1953; continuity dir. Sta. WXLW, Indpls., 1954-57; ptnr. Steve Smith and Assocs. Advt., Indpls., 1956-62; account mgr. Sive Advt., Cin., 1963-64, Associated Advt., Cin., 1964-65; copywriter SupeRX Drugs Inc., Cin., 1965-72; promotion writer U.S. News and World Report, Washington, 1974; asst. mgr. advt. Drug Fair, Alexandria, Va., 1975-82; dir. advt. Cosmetic and Fragrance Concepts Inc./DBA Cosmetic Ctrs., Beltsville, Md., 1982-89; advt., prodn. cons. Nat. Red Cross, Galladet U., Washington, 1989-94; asst. to real estate agt. Carmel, Ind., 1994-96; editl. cons., mem. svc. rep., acctg. clk. Angie's List, Carmel, Ind., 1996—. Vestrywoman St. Matthews Episcopal Ch., Cin., 1969-71; vol. jr. achievement hosp. chmn. Sleepy Hollow Citizens Assn., Falls Church, Va., 1973; vol. resident assoc. program Smithsonian Instn., Washington, 1989-94; chmn. membership and pub. rels. Friends Chinn Park Regional Libr., Woodbridge, Va., 1991-94; vol. Indpls. Art Ctr. Gift Shop, 1997—, Prince William Symphony Orch., Prince William County Voter Registration Bd. Mem. Potomac Valley Aquarium Soc. (past treas., past sec., editor jour.), Am. Cichlid Assn. (nat. pub. rels. chair 1985-90), Delta Delta Delta. Avocations: swimming, reading, needlecrafts, travel, computers. Home: 9850 Greentree Dr Carmel IN 46032-9099 Office Phone: 317-803-3961. E-mail: mmah317@aol.com.

MAHONEY, MARY, hotel executive; b. Orlando, Fla., Dec. 20, 1959; Various positions Days Inn of Am., Inc., 1980—90; founder Targa Internat., Inc, 1990—94; dir. preferred vendor mktg. Cendant Corp., dir. market devel., 1994—96, v.p. mktg., Howard Johnson, 1996-98, pres., CEO, Howard Johnson Internat. Inc., 1998—2003, sr. v.p., member relations and customer support, Fairfield Resorts, 2003—. Adv. bd. William F. Harrah Coll. Hotel Admin., UNLV. Mem. state bd. Junior Achievement, NJ; bd. dirs. Nat. Academy's Found. Travel & Tourism. Named Most Powerful Women in Travel Travel Agt. mag., 1997, 98, 99, Next Generation of Hot New Marketers list Brandweek. Mem.: Am Hotel & Lodging Assoc. Coun. Inns & Suites (audit com., fin. com.), Hospitality Industry Hall of Honor. Office: Fairfield Resorts 8669 Commodity Cir Orlando FL 32819

MAHONEY, MAUREEN A. academic administrator; PhD in Human Devel. and Family Studies, Cornell U., 1977. Prof. psychology Hampshire Coll., Amherst, Mass.; dean Smith Coll., Northampton, Mass., 1996—. Office: Smith Coll Dean of the College College Hall 21 Northampton MA 01063*

MAHONEY, MICHAEL J. science administrator, educator; b. Streator, Ill., Feb. 22, 1946; s. Zita E. Fitzgibbons; children: Sean M., Maureen E. AA, Joliet Jr. Coll., 1967; BA, Ariz. State U., 1969; PhD, Stanford U., 1972. Prof. Pa. State U., State College, 1972—84; resident sport psychology U. S. Olympic Tng. Ctr., Colorado Springs, 1983—84; prof. U. of Calif., Santa Barbara, 1985—90, U. of North Tex., Denton, 1990—; exec. dir. Soc. for Constructivism in the Human Scis., Denton, 1996—. Disting. adj. faculty mem. Saybrook Grad. Sch., San Francisco, 1998—. Author: (text) Human Chage Processes. Fellow: AAAS.

MAHONEY, MICHAEL JAMES, investment and software executive; b. Spokane, Wash., July 18, 1960; s. James Lyle and Frances Edith (Castle) Mahoney; m. Ann Dickinson, May 29, 1993; children: James Junius Castle, Catherine Lane, Grace Dickinson, Christopher Michael Hayes. BA in History cum laude, Whitman Coll., 1982; MBA, Stanford U., 1991. Analyst corp. fin. dept. E.F. Hutton & Co., Inc., N.Y.C., 1982-85; assoc. cons. Bain & Co., Inc., Boston, 1985-87, cons., 1987-89; summer assoc. Goldman, Sachs & Co., N.Y.C., 1990; investment analyst G.T. Global (acquired by AIM Funds), San Francisco, 1991-93; portfolio mgr., lead mgr. G.T. Global Telecom. Fund, 1993-99; sr. portfolio mgr. AIM Funds, San Francisco, 1998-99; founding ptnr. J&M Investments, Menlo Park, Calif., 1996—; sr. analyst, portfolio mgr., dir. Dresdner RCM Global Investors, San Francisco, 1999-2000; chief strategy officer Neon Yoyo, Inc. (acquired by Interwoven, Inc.), San Francisco, 2000; dir. Interwoven, Inc., Sunnyvale, Calif., 2000—01; mng. dir., sr. portfolio mgr., bd. dirs. EGM Capital, LLC, San Francisco, 2001—. Guest lectr. in investments Stanford Grad. Sch. of Bus., 1994—; frequent print and TV commentator on the telecomms. industry and investing, 1993—; profiled in Investment Visionaries by Peter Tanous, 2003. Pres. Spokane County Young Reps., 1976-78; campaign mgr. Malone for U.S. Senate, Boston, 1988; bd. overseers Whitman Coll., investment com. 1999—. Recipient Pete Reid award Whitman Coll., 1997. Mem. O'Mahony Records Soc., Ea. Wash. Geneal. Soc., Pacific Rsch. Inst. for Pub. Policy (mem. tech. adv. bd.), Stanford Alumni Assn. (life), Guardsmen, Villa Taverna (San Francisco), Spokane Club (Washington), Lincoln Club of No. Calif., Hayden Lake Country Club (Idaho), Phi Beta Kappa, Sigma Chi (com. chmn. 1979-80). Office: EGM Capital LLC Two Embarcadero Ctr Ste 1300 San Francisco CA 94111 Business E-Mail: mmahoney@egm.com.

MAHONEY, MICHAEL ROBERT TAYLOR, art historian, educator; b. Worcester, Mass., Jan. 24, 1935; s. Michael J. and Mary (Taylor) M. Grad., Phillips Acad., 1953; BA, Yale U., 1959; PhD, Courtauld Inst., U. London, 1965. Finley fellow Nat. Gallery Art, 1962-64; fellow Harvard Center Italian Studies, Villa I Tatti, 1963; museum curator Nat. Gallery Art, 1964-69; prof. fine arts, chmn. dept. Trinity Coll., Hartford, Conn., 1969-86, Genevieve Harlow Goodwin prof. fine arts, 1974-99. Incorporator Hartford Pub. Library, 1970-99; elector Wadsworth Atheneum, Hartford, 1974-85 Author: The Drawings of Salvator Rosa, 1977, (with Jean Cadogan) Wadsworth Atheneum Paintings II: Italy and Spain; editor: National Gallery of Art Report and Studies in the History of Art, 1968-69. Trustee Cesare Barbieri Found., Trinity Coll., 1977-99, Watkinson Libr., Trinity Coll., 1985-99, Somerset House Art History Found., N.Y.C., 1985—; bd. govs. Hill-Stead Mus., Farmington, Conn., 1992-95; mem. adv. coun. Am. Friends of Georgian Group, 1996—.

MAHONEY, THOMAS HENRY, IV, finance executive; b. Cambridge, May 27, 1952; s. Thomas Henry Donald and Kathrine Phyllis (Norton) M.; m. Emily A. Chien, Nov . 11, 1989. AB, Harvard Coll., 1973; MBA, U. Pa., 1976. Assoc. corp. fin. Dillon, Read & Co. Inc., N.Y.C., 1976-80, v.p. corp. fin., 1981-84, Oppenheimer & Co., Inc., N.Y.C., 1984-86; v.p. debt fin. Merrill Lynch Capital Markets, N.Y.C., 1986-87, dir. product devel., 1988-89, mng. dir., 1989-96; mng. dir., group head Capital Group, Deutsche Morgan Grenfell, N.Y.C., 1996-98; mng. dir., group head Pvt. Equity Group, PaineWebber Inc., N.Y.C., 1998-2000; v.p. fin., CFO Molecular OptoElectronics Corp., Watervliet, NY, 2000—02; mng. dir., co-head Pvt. Capital Markets Group, Capital Markets N.Am., N.Y.C., 2002—03; mng. dir., COO, Gabelli & Ptnrs., Rye,

NY, 2003—. Bd. dirs. N.Y.C. Opera. Mem. Coun. Fgn. Rels., Doubles Club, Harvard Club (N.Y.C.), Harvard Club (Boston), Univ. Club, Meadow Club Southampton. Republican. Office: Gabelli & Ptnrs LLC One Corporate Ctr Rye NY 10580 E-mail: tmahoney@gabelli.com.

MAHONEY, WILLIAM FRANCIS, editor, writer; b. Joliet, Ill., Jan. 24, 1935; s. Cletus George and Mildred Marie (Ochs) Mahoney; m. Carroll Frances Johnson, June 28, 1958; children: Erin Michele Alderfer, Kevin William, Megan Ann, Sheila Marie Startup, Nora Aileen Petchkofski. BS in Journalism, Marquette U., 1957. Reporter Ft. Wayne (Ind.) News Sentinel, 1958-59; pub. rels. mgr. Motorola, Inc., Franklin Park, Ill., 1959-66; sr. acct. exec. Young & Rubicam, Inc., Chgo., 1966-68; pub. info. dir. ABA, Chgo., 1969-71; investor rels. mgr. Chemetron Corp., Chgo., 1971-76; corp. comm. dir. Scott Paper Co., Phila., 1976-80; pub. rels. dir. Esmark Inc., Chgo., 1980-81; prin. Mahoney & Mitchell Incorp., Phila., 1981-89, Investor Rels. Ptnrs., Livingston, NJ, 1993—, prin., editl. dir. VI LLC, 2004—. Author: Investor Relations: The Professional's Guide to Financial and Marketing Communications, 1991, The Active Shareholder, 1993, The Strategy and Practice of Investor Relations, 1997; author, editor: The Investor Relations Guide, 1999, The IR Book, Capital Markets and Valuation, 2003; exec. editor Shareholder Value Mag., 2000-2003; Investor Rels. Update, 1981-99, Valuation Issues. Mem. Nat. Investor Rels. Inst., Vesper Club. Republican. Roman Catholic. Home and Office: 716 S Brandywine St West Chester PA 19382-3511 E-mail: wfmahoney@csi.com.

MAHONY, EDWARD B. corporate financial executive; BS in Acctg., Manhattan Coll.; MBA in Fin., NYU. CPA 1977. With Price Waterhouse, Touche Ross & Co.; v.p., controller consumer products divsn. Bristol Myers Squibb, 1978—93; v.p., chief fin. officer The Purdur Frederick Co., 1993—99; v.p. Purdue Pharma, 1993—99, exec. v.p., chief fin. officer, 1999—. Office: Purdue Pharma 1 Stamford Forum Stamford CT 06901

MAHONY, ROGER MICHAEL, archbishop; b. Hollywood, Calif., Feb. 27, 1936; s. Victor James and Loretta Marie (Baron) Mahony. AA, Our Lady Queen of Angels Sem., 1956; BA, St. John's Sem. Coll., 1958, BST, 1962; MSW, Cath. U. Am., 1964. Priest Roman Cath. Ch., 1962, ordained bishop, 1975, created cardinal priest, 1991. Asst. pastor St. John's Cathedral, Fresno, Calif., 1962, 1968—73, rector, 1973—80; adminstr. St. Genevieve's Parish, Fresno, Calif., 1964—67, pastor, 1967—68; titular bishop of Tamascani, aux. bishop of Fresno Fresno, Calif., 1975—80; chancellor Diocese of Fresno, 1970—77, vicar gen., 1975—80; bishop Diocese of Stockton, Calif., 1980—85; archbishop Archdiocese of L.A., 1985—, cardinal priest, 1991—; diocesan dir. Cath. Charities and Social Svc., Fresno, 1964—70; exec. dir. Infant of Prague Adoption Svc., Cath. Welfare Bur., Fresno, 1964—70. Faculty extension divsn. Fresno State U., 1965—67; sec. U.S. Cath. bishops ad hoc com. on farm labor Nat. Conf. Bishops, 1970—75; chmn. com. on pub. welfare and income maintenance Nat. Conf. Cath. Charities, 1969—70; adminstrv. com. Nat. Conf. Cath. Bishops, 1976—79, 1982—85, 1987—90, 1992—95, 1998—2001, com. migration and refugees, 1976—95, chmn. com. farm labor, 1981—92, com. moral evaluation of deterrence, 1986—88, cons. com., chmn. for prolife activities, 1990—95; com. social devel. and world peace U.S. Cath. Conf., 1985—93, chmn. internat. policy sect., 1987—93; com. justice and peace Pontifical Couns., 1984—98, chmn. com. domestic policy, 1998—2001, pastoral care of migrants and itinerant people, 1986—91, social comms., 1989—. Active Mexican-Am. Coun. for Better Housing, 1968—72, Fed. Commn. Agrl. Workers, 1987—93, Urban Coalition of Fresno, Calif., 1968—72, Fresno County Econ. Opportunities Commn., Calif., 1964—65, Fresno County Alcoholic Rehab. Com., Calif., 1966—67, Fresno City Charter Rev. Com., 1968—70, Fresno Redevel. Agy., 1970—75, L.A. 2000 Com., 1985—88, Blue Ribbon Com. Affordable Housing City of L.A., L.A., 1988; mem. commn. to draft an ethics code L.A. City Govt., 1989—90; trustee St. Agnes Hosp., Fresno, 1969—73, Cath. U. Am., 1984—88, 1998—; named chaplain to Pope Paul VI, 1967; chaplain St. Vincent de Paul Soc., 1964—70; bd. dirs. West Coast Regional Office Bishops Com. for Spanish-Speaking, 1967—70; chmn. Calif. Assn. Cath. Charities Dirs., 1965—69; trustee St. Patrick's Sem., Archdiocese of San Francisco, 1974—75; bd. dirs. Fresno Cmty. Workshop, 1965—67, Rebuild L.A., 1992—95. Named Young Man of Yr., Fresno Jr. C. of C., 1967. Mem.: Canon Law Soc. Roman Catholic. Office: Archdiocese LA 3424 Wilshire Blvd Los Angeles CA 90010-2241

MAHONY, SHEILA ANNE, broadcast executive; b. Yonkers, N.Y., Jan. 30, 1942; d. Paul Ambrose and Grace (Sullivan) M.; m. Charles A. Riggs, July 7, 1983; stepchildren: Charles Riggs, Julia Riggs. BA, Newton Coll. Sacred Heart, Mass., 1963; JD, Fordham U., 1967. Asst. corp. counsel Law Dept. City of N.Y., N.Y.C., 1967-72; regional dir. Cable TV Info. Ctr., The Urban Inst., Washington, 1972-74, gen. counsel, 1974-75, exec. dir., 1976-77, Carnegie Commn. on Future of Pub. Broadcasting, N.Y.C., 1977-79; v.p. govt. rels. Cablevision Systems Corp., Woodbury, N.Y., 1980-95, sr. v.p. comm. and pub. affairs, 1995-99, exec. v.p. comm., govt. and pub. affairs, 1999—, dir., 1988—. Mem. exec. com. CSPAN, 2000—. Author: Keeping PACE With the New Television, 1979. Dir. C-SPAN, Washington, 1990—, Found. for Minority Interests in Media, N.Y.C., 1992—; bd. dirs. Lustgarten found., 2000—, Legal Aid Soc. of N.Y., 2000—. Mem.: Legal Aid Soc. (bd. dirs. 2000—), Cable TV and Telecom. Assn. N.Y. (dir. 1995—, 1st vice chair 1997—2001, chair 2001—03), Cable TV Pub. Affairs Assn. (dir. 1994—98), Lustgarten Found. for Pancreatic Cancer Rsch. (bd. dirs. 1999—). Office: Cablevision Systems Corp 1111 Stewart Ave Bethpage NY 11714-3581

MAHOOD, KEN, music educator; s. Kenneth Mahood Sr. and Helen Mahood; children: Jonathan Scott, Jason Kenneth. BS Music, The King's Coll., 1969; MusM, Manhattan Sch. Music, 1971; PhD of Music Theory, Met. Coll., 1981; PhD of Music, Concordia Coll., 1999; EdD, Am. U., 2001. Assoc. dir. music Christian Fellowship Ch., Ashburn, Va., 1981—; exec. dir. edn. KME, Inc., Leesburg, Va., 1983—. Adj. faculty prof. No. Va. C.C.; mem. internat. adv. bd. Validsites.com, Inspectedsites.com. Recipient 20 yr. Achievement Award, Assn. Of Music Students, 2001. Mem.: Music Educators Nat. Conf., Am. Coll. Musicians, Music Tchrs. Nat. Assn. Office: KME Internat Inc PO Box 1616 Leesburg VA 20177 Personal E-mail: drken@musikdok.com.

MAHOOD, WILLIAM H. gastroenterologist; b. Charleston, W.Va., July 28, 1934; m. Perry Mahood; 1 child, Tessa. BA, W.Va. U.; MD, Jefferson Med. Coll., 1960. Diplomate Am. Bd. Internal Medicine, Am. Bd. Gastroenterology. Intern Jefferson Hosp., Phila., 1960-61, resident in internal medicine, 1961-63; resident in gastroenterology Grad. Hosp. Pa., Phila., 1963-64; chief gastroenterology Abington Meml. Hosp., Pa.; pvt. practice. Hosp. staff Holy Redeemer Hosp., Meadowbrook, Pa.; co-chair task force on health Dept. of Health; pres. Digestive Disease Nat. Coalition, Washington. Fellow ACP, Am. Coll. Gastroenterology, Am. Gastroenterol. Assn., Am. Soc. of Gastrointestinal Endoscopy, Am. Soc. Internal Medicine; mem. AMA (bd. trustees 1996, mem. coun. med. svc. 1991, vice chair coun. 1995, mem. task force on credentialing and privileges), Pa. Med. Soc. (com. on health care reform and access, chair coun. med. econs.), Am. Soc. of Gastrointestinal Endoscopy (governing bd.), Pa. Soc. of Gastroenterology (pres.), Montgomery County Med. Soc. (bd. dirs.). Address: AMA 515 N State St Chicago IL 60610-4325 Fax: 215-947-4316.

MAHORNER, JAMES M. lawyer; b. DeLand, Fla., Jan. 28, 1932; s. James Glennon and Sue Mahorner; m. Brenda Johnson (div. May 0, 1992); children: John G., James G., Mary Christine Gore, Amy Caprice, Ted G. JD, Stetson U., DeLand, FL; BSEE, US Naval Acad., Annapolis, MD. Bar: Fla. Atty. Pvt. Practice, Fla., 1975—; gen. counsel Dept. of HRS, Fla., 1970—74; trial counsel Dept. of Agr., Fla., 1965; ptnr. Dickens, Linn, and Mahorner, Tallahassee, Fla., 1967—70, White, Phipps, Linn, Furnell and Mahorner, Tallahassee, Fla., 1965—67; atty. State Attorney's Gen. Office, Fla., 1960—65. Mem.: Mensa. Democrat-Npl. Avocations: chess, bridge, tennis. Office: 234 9th Avenue South Jacksonville Beach FL 32250 Home: PO Box 50774 Jacksonville Beach FL 32240-0774 E-mail: jgmahorner@netzero.net.

MAHR, AARON LEE, retired government executive; b. Canton, Ill., Jan. 4, 1947; s. Ivan Lee and Nina Berniece Mahr; m. Nicole Adrienne Bourque, June 30, 1987; children: Jennifer Ward, David Abba, Timothy. BA, Emory U., 1969; Sr. Ofcls. in Nat. Security, Harvard U., 1991. Cert. Army Acquisitions Corps. Inventory mgmt. specialist U.S. Army Weapons Command, Rock Island, Ill., 1969-70; supply sys. analyst Frankford Arsenal, Phila., 1970-71, U.S. Army Gen. Materiel & Petroleum Ctr., New Cumberland, Pa., 1971-74; Jordan/Kuwait country desk officer U.S. Army Internat. Logistics Command, Alexandria, Va., 1974-76; Mid-East program mgr. U.S. Army Security Assistance Command, Alexandria, 1976-82; Mid-East program mgr. Office Dep. Chief Staff for Logistics Hdqs. Dept. of the Army, Pentagon, Washington, 1982-83; chief Israel and Turkey divsn. U.S. Army Security Assistance Command, Alexandria, 1983-85; dir. Internat. Coop. Programs Activity, Alexandria, 1986—2000. Diabetes hotline cons. Inst. for Peripheral Nerve Surgery, Balt., 2000—. Chmn. fund raising Children's House by the Sea, Believe in Tomorrow Nat. Children's Found. Mem. Assn. U.S. Army (assoc.), Am. Def. Preparedness Assn. (internat. subcom. 1987-97), Worcester County Fire Police Assn., Ocean Pines Vol. Fire Dept., Kiwanis Internat., Order of DeMolay, Delta Tau Delta. Avocations: videography, photography, travel, fishing. Home: 1228 Vista Hills Dr Lakeland FL 33813-5641 E-mail: opfp26@aol.com.

MAHR, JOE, journalist; Reporter The State Jour.-Register, Copley News Svc., Ill., 1995; statehouse reporter Copley News Svc., Ill., 1998—2000; gen. assignment/projects reporter Block News Alliance (The Blade and The Pitts. Post-Gazette), 2000—. Recipient Pulitzer Prize for investigative reporting, 2004, medal winner, Investigative Reporters and Editors, Inc., 2004. Office: The Blade 541 N Superior St Toledo OH 43660*

MAHSMAN, DAVID LAWRENCE, religious publications editor; b. Quincy, Ill., Aug. 16, 1950; s. Alvin Henry and Dorothy Marie (Schnack) M.; m. Lois Jean Mohn, July 27, 1975. BS in Journalism, So. Ill. U., 1972; MDiv, Concordia Theol. Seminary, Fort Wayne, Ind., 1983; STM, Concordia Sem., St. Louis, 1995. Staff writer Paddock Publs., Arlington Heights, Ill., 1972-73, Decatur (Ill.) Herald & Rev., 1973-76; press asst. Hon. Tom Railsback U.S. Ho. Reps., Washington, 1976-79, campaign press sec. Hon. Dan Coats Ft. Wayne, Ind., 1979-80, 82; pastor Trinity Luth. Ch., Glen Cove, N.Y., 1983-85; dir. news and info. Luth. Ch. Mo. Synod, St. Louis, 1985—, exec. editor, contbr. Luth. Witness, St. Louis, 1985—; exec. editor Reporter, St. Louis, 1985—. Mem. Inter-Luth. task force on pornography Luth. Coun. U.S.A., 1986; mem. Washington adv. coun. Mo. Synod, Office of Govt. Info., Washington, 1987-2000. Editor: Augsburg Today: This We Believe, Teach and Confess, 1997. Recipient Jacob Scher Investigative Reporting award Women in Comm., 1974, Commendation award Concordia Hist. Inst., 1988, 98. Mem. Concordia Hist. Inst. (life). Republican. Lutheran. Avocations: travel, photography. Office: Luth Ch-Mo Synod 1333 S Kirkwood Rd Saint Louis MO 63122-7226 E-mail: david.mahsman@lcms.org.

MAI, CHAO CHEN, engineer; b. Kwangchow, Canton, China, Feb. 26, 1936; came to U.S., 1962, naturalized, 1973; m. Shao Shen Yam; children: Glenn, Kenneth. MSEE, Oreg. State U., 1964; PhD in Elec. Engring., Utah State U., 1968. Project engr. Sylvania Electric Co., Woburn, Mass., 1967-70; mgr. R&D Mostek Corp., Carrollton, Tex., 1970-76, v.p. R&D, 1976-84; founder, sr. v.p. Dallas Semiconductor Corp., 1984-2000, pres. and COO, 2000—. Mem. IEEE, Electrochem. Soc. Achievements include patent for Silicon gate combined with depletion load process, method for making a semiconductor device, MOSFET Fabrication Process; research advanced processing technology in integrated circuits; subspecialty integrated circuits, microchip technology.

MAI, DAVID E. biotechnology company executive; BS in Biology, U. Hawaii. Sales engr.Hewlett-Packard Med. Electronics; v.p. Stanco Med.; dir. strategic mktg. Advanced Technologies divsn. Boston Sci. Corp.; dir. Intravascular Ultrasound divsn. Diasonics Corp., 1988—89; new product program mgr. Miravant Med. Technologies, Santa Barbara, Calif., 1991—92, clin. rsch. mgr., 1992, v.p. corp. devel., 1992—96, Miravant Cardiovascular, Inc., 1994—96, pres., 1992—2001, Miravant Systems, Inc., 1997—, Miravant Pharms., Inc., 1996—, Miravant Med. Technologies, Santa Barbara, 1996—. Office: Miravant Med Technologies 336 Bollay Dr Santa Barbara CA 93117

MAI, HAROLD LEVERNE, retired judge; b. Casper, Wyo., Apr. 5, 1928. BA, U. Wyo., 1950, JD, 1952. Bar: Wyo. 1952, U.S. Supreme Ct. 1963. Sole practice, Cheyenne, Wyo., 1953-62, 67-71; judge Juvenile Ct., Cheyenne, 1962-67; U.S. bankruptcy judge, Cheyenne, 1971-93, ret., 1993. Mem. ABA, Wyo. Bar Assn., Laramie County Bar Assn., Nat. Conf. Bankruptcy Judges.

MAI, WILLIAM FREDERICK, plant nematologist, educator; b. Greenwood, Del., July 23, 1916; s. William Frederick and Laurana (Owens) M.; m. Barbara Lee Morrell, June 2, 1941; children: Virginia Mai Abrams, William Howard Mai, Eliabeth Hardy Mai. BS, U. Del., 1939; PhD, Cornell U., 1945. Asst. prof. Cornell U., Ithaca, N.Y., 1946-49, assoc. prof., 1949-52, prof., 1952-81, Liberty Hyde prof. plant pathology, 1981-83, prof. emeritus, 1983—. Cons. Nat. Acad. Scis., Internat. Potato Ctr., Brands Co., AID Author (with H.H. Lyon), Pictoral Key to Genera of Plant Parasitic Nemtodes, 1960, 5th edit. 1993, Plant Parasitic Nematodes, 1971; editor: Control of Plant Parasitic Nematodes, 1968. Coach Little League Baseball and Football, Ithaca, 1955-60; chmn. Community Orgn., 1960-65. Recipient award of distinction Internat. Plant Protection Conf., 1979; Paul Harris fellow Rotary Found., 1997. Fellow Am. Phytopath. Soc. (pres. Northeastern div. 1968-69 award of merit Northeastern div); mem. AAAS, Soc. Nematologists (pres. 1969 hon. life), Helminthological Soc. Washington, Soc. European Nematologists, Potato Assn. Am. Lodges: Rotary. Home: Apt 203 103 Bundy Rd Ithaca NY 14850 Office: Cornell U Dept Plant Pathology Ithaca NY 14853

MAIBACH, BEN C., JR., service executive; b. Bay City, Mich., 1920; With Barton-Malow Co., Detroit, 1938—, v.p., dir.-in-charge field ops., 1949-53, exec. v.p., 1953-60, pres., 1960-76, chmn. bd., 1976; chmn. and dir. Barton-Malow Ent.; chmn. bd. Cloverdale Equipment Co. Trustee Barton-Malow Found, Maibach Found., 1967—; chmn. Apostolic Christian Woodhaven, Detroit; bishop Apostolic Christian Ch., Mich., Ont., Fla.; bd. dirs. S.E. Mich. chpt. ARC, Rural Gospel and Med. Missions of India. Home: 29711 Wentworth St Apt 207 Livonia MI 48154-3887 also: 5525 Azure Way Sarasota FL 34242-1857

MAIBACH, BEN C., III, construction company executive; b. May 5, 1946; BS, Mich. State U., 1969. With Barton-Malow Corp., Oak Park, Mich., 1964—, v.p. field ops., 1964-68, systems analyst, programmer, 1968-70, project adminstr., 1970-72, officer mgr., purchasing agt., 1972-73, v.p., 1973-76, exec. v.p., 1976-81, pres., 1981—. Office: Barton Malow Co 26500 American Dr Southfield MI 48034

MAICKEL, ROGER PHILIP, pharmacologist, educator; b. Floral Park, N.Y., Sept. 8, 1933; s. Philip Vincent and Margaret Mary (Rose) M.; m. Lois Louise Pivonka, Sept. 8, 1956; children: Nancy Ellen Maickel Ward, Carolyn Sue Maickel Anderson. BS, Manhattan (N.Y.) Coll., 1954; postgrad., Poly. Inst. Bklyn., 1954-55; MS, Georgetown U., 1957, PhD, 1960. Biochemist Nat. Heart Inst., Bethesda, Md., 1955-65; asso. prof. pharmacology Ind. U., 1965-69, prof., 1969—, head sect. pharmacology med. scis. program, 1971-77; prof. pharmacology and toxicology, head dept. Sch. Pharmacy and Pharmacal Scis. Purdue U., West Lafayette, Ind., 1977-83; dir. lab. animal program Purdue U., West Lafayette, 1988-98, emeritus prof., 1999—; acting v.p. product acquisition and devel. BetaMED Pharms., Inc., Indpls., 1983-84. Adv. editor: Pergamon Press, 1970-88; adv. editorial bd.: Neuropharmacology, 1974-88. Bd. dirs. TEAMS, Inc., 1981-87, Am. Coun. on Sci. and Health, 1993-2000; trustee AAALAC, 1992—. Recipient Alumni award in medicine Manhattan Coll., 1972 Fellow: AAAS, Collegium Internat. de Neuro-Psychopharmacologicum, Royal Soc. Chemistry, Am. Coll. Neuropsychopharmacology, Am. Inst. Chemists (bd. dirs. 1989—92, 2001—, pres.-elect 1992—94, pres. 1994—96, chmn. 1996—98); mem.: ASTM, Soc. Toxicology, Soc. Neurosci., N.Y. Acad. Scis., Internat. Soc. Psychoneuroendocrinology, Internat. Assn. Chiefs Police, Soc. Forensic Toxicologists, Am. Soc. Clin. Pharmacology and Therapeutics, Am. Soc. Pharmacology and Exptl. Therapeutics, Am. Chem. Soc., Rho Chi, Sigma Xi. Home: 3567 Canterbury Dr Lafayette IN 47909-3714 E-mail: maickel@pharmacy.purdue.edu. *As a human being, I hope to be able to do my best in the roles of scientist, teacher, and citizen by fulfilling the academic criteria of teaching, research, and service to the utmost degree humanly possible.*

MAICKI, G. CAROL, former state senator, consultant; b. Holden, Mass., July 16, 1936; d. John Arne and Mary Emily (Bumpus) Mannisto; m. Henry J. Maicki, May 4, 1957; children: Henry III, Matthew, Scott, Julia, Mary. BA, U. Mich., 1978. Exec. dir. Sweetwater County Task Force/Sexual Assault, Rocksprings, Wyo., 1978-81; program mgr. Family Violence/Sexual Assault, Cheyenne, Wyo., 1981-85; coord. S.D. Coalition Against Domestic Violence and Sexual Assault, Black Hawk, 1985-90; state senator S.D. Legislature, Pierre, 1990-92. Cons. Black Hawk, 1990—, Nat. Coalition Against Domestic Violence, 1987; spkr. Nat. Coalition Against Sexual Assault, Portland, Oreg., 1987, 96, Rutger Ctr. for Women in Politics, San Diego, 1991, Gov.'s Conf., Las Vegas, Nev., 1997; mem. planning com. Office for Victims of Crime, U.S. Justice, Phoenix, 1989; expert witness state and fed. cts., 1990—. Author: (manuals) Operating Standards, 1984, Rules and Regulations, 1986, Shelter Procedures, 1987, Administrative Procedures, 1995, Responders to Rope, 1996, Cultural Competency, 2001. Com. mem. Health and Human Svc. State Legislature, Pierre, 1990-92, local govt., 1990-92; commn. mem. local govt. study commn., Pierre, 1990-92; bd. dirs. Crisis Intervention Svcs., 1991-99, Dakotah territory, 1996 —; apptd. def. adv. com. on women in svcs. Sec. of Def., 1995-97; apptd. exec. com. def. adv. com. on women in the svcs., 1996-97; founder Women's Connection, Inc., 1996; mem. Dacotah Terr. Youth Devel., Inc. Recipient award Gov. Wyo., 1985, Spirit of Peace award Women Against Violence, Rapid City, 1993, U.S. Dept. of Justice award, 1994, fellowship Share Our Strength, 1996-98, Equity award S.D. chpt. AAUW, 1996, Failure is Impossible award Rapid City, 1998. Mem. S.D. Alliance for Mentally Ill, Rapid City Womens Network, S.D. Advocacy Network for Women. Democrat. Avocations: reading, crosswords, gardening. Home: PO Box 375 Black Hawk SD 57718-0375 E-mail: gcarol@starband.net.

MAIDA, ADAM JOSEPH CARDINAL, archbishop; b. East Vandergrift, Pa., Mar. 18, 1930; Student, St. Vincent Coll., Latrobe, Pa., St. Mary's U., Balt., Lateran U., Rome, Duquesne U. Ordained priest Roman Cath. Ch., 1956, consecrated bishop Roman Cath. Ch., 1984. Bishop, Green Bay, Wis., 1984—89; archbishop Detroit, 1990—; elevated to cardinal, 1994—. Home: 75 E Boston Blvd Detroit MI 48202-1318 Office: Archdiocese of Detroit Ste 1 1234 Washington Blvd Detroit MI 48226-1825

MAIDIQUE, MODESTO ALEX, academic administrator; b. Havana, Cuba, Mar. 20, 1940; s. Modesto Maidique and Hilda Rodriguez; children: Ana Teresa, Mark Alex. BS, MIT, 1962, MS, 1964, PhD, 1970. Instr. MIT, Boston, 1976-79; v.p., gen. mgr. Analog Devices Semiconductor, Boston, 1970-76; asst. prof. Harvard U., Boston, 1976-81; assoc. prof. Stanford U., Palo Alto, Calif., 1981-84; sr. ptnr. Hambrecht and Quist Venture Ptnrs., Palo Alto, Calif., 1981-86; co-founder, dir. U. Miami (Fla.) Innovation and Entepreneurship Inst., 1984-86; pres. Fla. Internat. U., Miami, 1986—. Mem. Pres.'s Edn. Policy Adv. Com.; chmn. Beacon Coun., 1992-93. Recipient Citizenship award HEW, 1973, Teaching award Stanford U., 1983 Mem. IEEE, Assn. Cuban Engrs. Republican. Roman Catholic. Office: Fla Internat U Office of Pres Univ Park PC 528 Miami FL 33199-0001 Fax: 305-348-3660. E-mail: maidique@fiu.edu.

MAIDMAN, RICHARD HARVEY MORTIMER, lawyer; b. NYC, Nov. 17, 1933; s. William and Ada (Seegle) M.; m. Lynne Rochelle Lateiner, Apr. 3, 1960 (div. Sept. 1987); m. Gail Lowe Haymes, Sept. 27, 1998; children: Patrick, Mitchel, Dagny. BA, Williams Coll., 1955; JD, Yale U., 1959; postgrad., NYU Grad. Sch. Bus., 1957, NYU Grad. Sch. Law, 1960, 77. Bar: N.Y. 1961, Fla. 1961, U.S. Dist. Ct. 1962, 79, U.S. Ct. Appeals 1966, U.S. Supreme Ct. 1978. Assoc. Saxe, Bacon & O'Shea, N.Y.C., 1962-64; ptnr. Weiner, Maidman & Goldman, N.Y.C., 1964-67; pvt. practice N.Y.C. and Fla., 1968—. Of counsel Shwal, Thompson & Bloch, NYC and Geneva, 1976-87, Maidman and Mittelman, LLP, 1996—; pres. MBS Equities, Inc., 1970-88, Fashion Wear Realty Co., Inc., NYC, 1975—; mng. gen. ptnr. Richard and David Maidman, NYC, 1972—, Barcelona Hotel Ltd., Miami Beach, Fla., 1975-84, New Haven Projects Co., 1987—; dir., gen counsel The Farr Companies, Washington, 1990-92; legis. counsel Theodore R. Kupferman, 17th Congl. Dist. NY, 1966-68; receiver Halloran House Hotel, NYC, 1981; chmn. Townhouse Mgmt. Co., 1998—; prin. Manhattan Parking Sys. Group, NYC, 2000—. Contbr. articles to profl. jours. Mem. ABA, N.Y. State Bar Assn., Fla. Bar Assn., Assn. of the Bar of the City of N.Y., Bankruptcy Lawyers Assn., N.Y.C. Real Estate Bd. N.Y. Home: Stamboat Landing 27 Astor Ln Sands Point NY 11050-2602 also: 9 E 79th St New York NY 10021-0123 Office: 70 E 55th St New York NY 10022-3222 Office Phone: 212-755-0500. Personal E-mail: rhmm59@aya.yale.edu. Business E-Mail: richard@maidman.org.

MAIDMAN, STEPHEN PAUL, lawyer; b. Hartford, Conn., Feb. 8, 1954; s. Harry and Roslyn (Mandell) M.; m. Mari Rosenberg, Oct. 13, 1996. AB summa cum laude, Bowdoin Coll., 1976; MBA, U. Pa., 1979, JD, 1980. Bar: Pa. 1980, Mass. 1996, U.S. Dist. Ct. (ea. dist.) Pa. 1980, U.S. Ct. Appeals (3d cir.) 1980, U.S. Dist. Ct. Mass. 1996, U.S. Ct. Appeals (1st cir.) 1996, U.S. Supreme Ct. 1997. Assoc. Drinker, Biddle & Reath, Phila., 1980-81; atty. IBM, Boca Raton, Fla., 1981-84, N.Y.C., 1984-85, staff atty., 1985-87, Rye Brook, N.Y., 1987-88, lab. counsel Poughkeepsie, N.Y., 1988-92, site counsel Hopewell Junction, N.Y., 1992-95; pvt. practice, Springfield, Mass., 1996—. Adj. faculty U. Conn Law Sch., 2001—. Co-class agt. Bowdoin Coll. Alumni Fund. Mem. Nat. Assn. Criminal Def. Lawyers, Mass. Bar Assn., Mass. Assn. Criminal Def. Lawyers, Hampden County Bar Assn., Phi Beta Kappa. Avocations: running, black Labradors. Office: 1145 Main St Ste 417 Springfield MA 01103-2123 Office Phone: 413-731-7300. Personal E-mail: maidman@prodigy.net.

MAIDMENT, PAUL, publishing executive; m. Lisa Martineau; 2 children. Grad., St. Catherine's Coll. Sr. editor Newsweek, 1992—95; editor FT.com, 1995—2001; exec. editor Forbes.com, 2001—, Forbes, 2001—. Author: (online publ.) A Middlesex Cricket Gazetteer, The Plain Words Glossary of Financial and Economic Terms. Office: Forbes 60 Fifth Ave New York NY 10011

MAIDON, CAROLYN HOWSER, director; b. Chgo., May 13, 1946; d. Lloyd Earl and Esther Lillian (Beck) Howser; m. Charles Randall Maidon, Nov. 21, 1970; children: Randall Scott, April Janel. BS in Edn., Okla. State U., 1968; MS in Edn., N.C. State U., 1984, postgrad., 1987—. Tchr. biology and English Cary (N.C.) High Sch., 1968-71; grad. instr. N.C. State U., Raleigh, 1984-85, asst. affirmative action officer, 1985-89, asst. dir. univ. undesignated program, 1989-95; dir. tchr. edn., 1995-99; coord. MentorNet N.C. State U., Raleigh, 2000—; chief, tchr. edn. sect. N.C. Dept. Pub. Instrn., 1999-2000. Home: 4204 Belnap Dr Apex NC 27502-5378 Office: NC State U PO Box 7632 Raleigh NC 27695-7632

MAIENSCHEIN, FRED, retired physicist; b. Belleville, Ill., Oct. 28, 1925; s. Fred and Ethel (Forsythe) M.; m. Joyce Kylander, Aug. 14, 1948; children: Jane, Jon. BS in Chem. Engring, Rose Hulman Inst. Tech., 1945; MS in Physics, Ind. U., 1948, PhD in Physics, 1949. Physicist Oak Ridge Nat. Lab., 1951-60, assoc. dir. engring. physics div., 1960-66; co-dir. Oak Ridge Electron Linear Accelerator, 1965-74, dir. engring. physics div., 1966-90, ret., 1990. Mem. com. reactor physics Nuclear Energy Agy., 1962-89; mem. adv. com. radiation aspects of SST, FAA, 1969-74; mem. subcoms. Nat. Com. Radiation Protection, 1959-71. Contbr. articles to profl. jours., chpts. in books. Fellow Am. Nuclear Soc.; mem. Am. Phys. Soc., AAAS, Soc. Neurosci., Tau Beta Pi. Home: 838 W Outer Dr Oak Ridge TN 37830-8402

MAIER, GERALD JAMES, corporate executive; b. Regina, Sask., Can., Sept. 22, 1928; s. John Joseph and Mary M. Student, Notre Dame Coll. (Wilcox), U. Man., U. Alta., U. Western Ont.; LLD (hon.), U. Alta., 1999. With petroleum and mining industries Can., U.S., Australia, U.K.; responsible for petroleum ops. Africa, United Arab Emirates, S.E. Asia; past chmn., pres., CEO TransCan. PipeLines, Calgary, Canada, 1985-99; vice-chmn. NOVA Chems. Corp., Calgary, 1998-2000. Bd. dirs. Stream-Flo Industries, Ltd., Master Flo Valve Inc., Can. Superior Energy Inc., Vintage Petroleum, Inc.; chmn. Can. Nat. Com. for World Petroleum Congresses, 1991-94, Van Horne Inst. for Internat. Transp., 1992-2000. Chmn. bd. dirs. Notre Dame Coll. Named Hon. Col. (ret.) King's Own Calgary Rgt., Resource Man of Yr. Alta. Chamber of Resources, 1990, named Officer Order of Can., 2004; recipient Can. Engr.'s Gold medal Can. Coun. Profl. Engrs., 1990, Disting. Alumni award U. Alta., 1992, Mgmt. award McGill U., 1993, Centennial award Alta. Assn. Engrs., Geologists and Geophysicists, 1994, Hal Godwin award U. Calgary, 1999, Can. Bus. Leader award U. Alta., 1999, Can. Engring. Leader award U. Calgary, 2003; named to Can. Petroleum Hall of Fame, 1999. Fellow Can. Acad. Engring.; mem. Assn. Profl. Engrs., Geologists and Geophysicists Alta. (past pres.), Can. Inst. Mining and Metallurgy (Past Pres.'s Meml. medal 1971). Avocations: golf, downhill skiing, shooting, fishing. Office: Granmar Investments Ltd 400 3rd Ave SW Ste 3300 Calgary AB Canada T2P 4H2

MAIER, HAROLD GEISTWEIT, law educator, lawyer; b. Cin., Mar. 25, 1937; s. Alfred F. and Alberta (Wilmes) M.; divorced; children: Marc L., Kurt S. BA in English Lit., U. Cin., 1959, JD, 1963; postgrad., Free U., Berlin, 1959-60; LLM, U. Mich., 1964; postgrad., U. Munich, 1964-65. Bar: Ohio 1963. Mem. law faculty Vanderbilt U., Nashville, 1965—, prof., 1970—, David Daniels Allen prof. law, 1988—, dir. Transnat. Legal Studies program, 1973-99. Faculty San Diego Internat and Comparative Law Inst., King's Coll., U. London, 1986-87, Regent's Coll., 1989, 91, 96; vis. prof. law U. Pa., 1985, U. NC, Chapel Hill, 1987; vis. Lyle T. Alverson prof. law George Washington U., Washington, 1987-88; vis. Woodruff prof. internat. law U. Ga., Atlanta, 1995; prof. law LSU, Aix-en-Provence, France, 1995; vis. Straus disting. prof. law Pepperdine U., Malibu, Calif., 2000-01; cons. Office of Sec. Army, Panama Canal Treaty Negotiations, 1976; guest scholar Brookings Instn., Washington, 1976-77; dir. PDS Patrons, Inc. U. Sch. Nashville, 1975-87, pres., 1978-79; counselor on internat. law Office of Legal Adviser, US Dept. State, 1983-84; Blain Sloan disting. lectr. internat. law Pace U. Sch. Law, White Plains, NY, 2001 Mem. editl. bd. Am. Jour. Internat. Law, 1984-88, Academic Coun., Inst. Transnational Arbitration, 1996—, Am. Jour. Comparative Law, 1997—, U.S. Assoc. Constitutional Law, 1997-2002, Am. Br. Internat. Law Assn., 2001—; author: (with T. Buergenthal) Public International Law in a Nutshell, 1985, 2d edit., 1989, (with T. Buergenthal, K. Doehring, J. Kokott) Grundzüge des Völkerrechts, 1987, Manual de Derecho Internacional Publico, 1994; contbr. articles to profl. jours. Recipient Luftbrucke Dankstipendium, Free U. Berlin, 1959-60; Ford internat. studies fellow U. Mich., 1964-65, Vanderbilt U. faculty fellow, 1976-77. Mem. Am. Soc. Internat. Law (exec. coun. 1974-78, 84-87, steering com. pvt. internat. law working group 2003--), Am. Soc. Comparative Law (bd. dirs. 1984-2001), Am. Law Inst., Order of Coif, Omicron Delta Kappa, Phi Alpha Delta, Tau Kappa Alpha, Pi Delta Epsilon, Nashville Symphony Guild, 2002-. Office: Vanderbilt U Law School 131 21st Ave S Nashville TN 37203 Home: 225 West chase Dr Nashville TN 37205 Office Phone: 615-322-2587.

MAIER, HOWARD ROBERT, urban planner, government agency administrator; b. Cleve., Oct. 10, 1944; s. Ernest and Florence B. Maier; m. Sue A. Maier, February 4, 1973; children: Matthew A., Abigail F., Michael C. BA in Econs., Ohio State U., Columbus, 1966, M in City Planning, 1972; MS in Pub. Mgmt., Case Western Res. U., 1974. Assoc. planner Met. Health Planning Corp., Cleve., 1970-71; prin. planner Cuyahoga County Regional Planning Commn., Cleve., 1971-75; dir. planning and devel., asst. dir., cmty. planner City of Cleveland Heights, Ohio, 1975-85; exec. staff Jewish Cmty. Fedn., Cleve., 1985-88; dir. spl. projects N.E. Ohio Areawide Coord. Agy., Cleve., 1988-89; acting exec. dir. Northea. Ohio Areawide Coord. Agy., Cleve., 1989-91, exec. dir., 1991—. Mem. adj. faculty and adv. coms. Cleve. State U., 1974—. Editl. cartoonist Sun Newspapers, 1975-77. Active Leadership Cleve., Gov. Regional Econ. Devel. Adv. Bd., Build Up Greater Cleve., Greater Cleve. Growth Assn., Ohio Canal Corridor Adv. Bd.; pres., bd. dirs. Planned Lifetime Assistance Network N.E. Ohio; mem. adv. bd. No. Ohio divsn. March of Dimes; mem. Ohio State U. Advocates. Named Hall of Fame, Mayfield H.S. Alumni Assn. Fellow Am. Inst. Cert. Planners; mem. Am. Planning Assn., Nat. Assn. Regional Couns. (exec. dirs. com.), Ohio Planning Conf. (Excellence in Planning Leadership award), Ohio Assn. Regional Couns. (bd. dirs.). Avocations: family activities, art, cartooning. Office: NE Ohio Areawide Coord Agy 1299 Superior Ave Cleveland OH 44114 Office Phone: 216-241-2414.

MAIER, JACK C. food products company executive; Chmn. Frisch's Restaurants, Inc., Cin. Office: Frisch's Restaurants Inc 2800 Gilbert Ave Cincinnati OH 45206-1206

MAIER, PAUL VICTOR, pharmaceutical executive; b. Seattle, Nov. 6, 1947; s. Norman Alvin and Rosalie (Godek) M.; m. Shirley Diehl, Aug. 11, 1979. BS, Pa. State U., 1969; MBA, Harvard U., 1975. Fin. analyst Greyhound Corp, Phoenix, 1975-76; asst. mgr. Wells Service Wells Fargo Bank, San Francisco, 1976-78; v.p. Fin. Cummins Service and Sales, Los Angeles, 1978-84; v.p., treas. ICN Pharms, Inc., Costa Mesa, Calif., 1984-90; v.p. fin. DFS West, 1990-92; sr. v.p., CFO Ligand Pharmaceuticals, Inc., San Diego, 1992—. Chmn. audit com. Entropin Inc., 2000—, also bd. dirs. Chmn. hosp. div. United Way Region V, L.A., 1983-84; bd. dirs. The Wellness Community, San Diego, 1993-2003. Served with USNR, 1969-95. Mem. Fin. Execs. Inst., The Athletic Congress, Pa. State Club of S.D., Harvard Bus. Sch. Assn. So. Calif., Ctr. for Non-Profit Mgmt., Vis. Nurse Assn. L.A. (bd. dirs. 1979-92, chmn.), Protection Mut. Inst. (West Coast adv. bd. 1985-90). Republican. Roman Catholic. Office: Ligand Pharmaceuticals 10275 Science Center Dr San Diego CA 92121-1117 E-mail: pmaier@ligand.com.

MAIER, PAULINE, history educator; b. Apr. 27, 1938; d. Irvin Louis and Charlotte (Winterer) Rubbelke; m. Charles Steven Maier, June 17, 1961; children: Andrea Nicole, Nicholas Winterer, Jessica Elizabeth Heine. AB, Radcliffe Coll., 1960; postgrad., London Sch. Econs., 1960-61; PhD in History, Harvard U., 1968; LLD (hon.), Regis Coll., 1987; DHL (hon.), Williams Coll., 1993. Asst. prof. then assoc. prof. history U. Mass., Boston, 1968-77; Robinson-Edwards prof. history U. Wis., Madison, 1977-78; prof. history MIT, Cambridge, Mass., 1978—, William R. Kenan Jr. prof. history, 1990—. Dept. head, MIT, 1979-88, mem. coun. Inst. Early Am. History, 1982-84; trustee Regis Coll., 1988-93; trustee Commonwealth Sch., 1991-96; bd. mgrs. Old South Meeting House, 1987-97, bd. advisors Internat. Ctr. Jefferson Studies, 2000-. Author: From Resistance to Revolution: Colonial Radicals and the Development of American Opposition to Britain, 1765-1766, 1972, The Old Revolutionaries: Political Lives in the Age of Samuel Adams, 1980, The American People: A History, 1986, American Scripture: Making the Declaration of Independence, 1997; co-author: Inventing America, 2002. Recipient Douglass Adair award Claremont Grad. Sch.-Inst. Early Am. History, 1976, Kidger award New Eng. History Tchrs. Assn., 1981; fellow Nat. Endowment Humanities, 1974-75, 88-89, Charles Warren fellow, 1974-75, Guggenheim fellow, 1990. Mem. Orgn. Am. Historians (mem. exec. bd. 1978-82), Am. Hist. Assn. (mem. nominations com. 1983-85, chmn. 1985), Soc. Am. Historians, Am. Antiquarian Soc. (mem. exec. coun. 1984-89), Colonial Soc. Mass. (mem. exec. coun. 1990-93), Mass. Hist. Soc., Am. Acad. Arts and Scis., The Hist. Soc. (bd. govs. 1998—). Home: 60 Larchwood Dr Cambridge MA 02138-4639 Office: MIT E51-279 77 Massachusetts Ave Cambridge MA 02139-4307 Office Phone: 617-253-2646. E-mail: pmaier@mit.edu.

MAIER, PETER KLAUS, lawyer; b. Wurzburg, Germany, Nov. 20, 1929; came to U.S., 1939, naturalized, 1945; s. Bernard and Joan (Sonder) M.; m. Melanie L. Stoff, Dec. 15, 1963; children: Michele Margaret, Diana Lynn. BA cum laude, Claremont McKenna Coll., 1949; JD, U. Calif., Berkeley, 1952; LLM in Taxation, NYU, 1953. Bar: Calif. 1953, U.S. Supreme Ct. 1957; cert. specialist in taxation law, Calif. Atty. tax div. U.S. Dept Justice, Washington, 1956-59; pvt. practice tax law San Francisco, 1959-81. Prof. law Hastings Coll. Law, U. Calif., San Francisco, 1967-95; vis. prof. U. Calif. Boalt Sch. Law, Berkeley, 1988-89, Stanford U. Sch. Law, 1996-98; chmn. Maier, Siebel. Baber, Inc., San Francisco, 1981—; mng. dir. U.S. Trust Co. NA, San Francisco, 1998—; chmn. Fromm Inst. for Lifelong Learning, U. San Francisco, 1997—; pres. John B. Huntington Found., 1996—, Alfred and Hanna Fromm Found., 1974—. Author books on taxation; contbr. articles to profl. jours. Chmn. Property Resources Inc., San Jose, Calif., 1968-77; pres. Calif. Property Devel. Corp., San Francisco, 1974-81. Capt. USAF, 1953-56. Mem. San Francisco Bar Assn. (chmn. sect. taxation 1970-71), Order of Coif. Home: 2559 Clay St San Francisco CA 94115 Office: Maier Siebel & BaberInc 1 Embarcadero Ctr 20th Fl San Francisco CA 94111 E-mail: pmaier@ustrust.com.

MAIER, ROBERT HENRY, real estate executive; b. Greenville, Tex., Nov. 19, 1932; s. William Lokey and Charlsie Lorraine (Nation) M.; m. Ruth Jean Chapman, Mar. 1, 1968; children: Alice, Joy Kupp. BA, So. Meth. U., 1964. Pers. dir. Atlantic Richfield Co., Dallas, 1954-69; v.p. adminstrn. ETMF Freight System, Dallas, 1969-78; chief pers. officer Varo, Inc., Garland, Tex., 1978-80; corp. v.p. adminstrn. Comml. Metals Co., Dallas, 1980-88; pres., COO The Staubach Co., Dallas, 1988-93; pres., CEO, bd. dirs. Cornerstone Mgmt. Co., 1993-96; pres., CEO ProblemSolvers, Inc., 1996—.

MAIER, ROBERT J. microbiologist, educator; b. Detroit, July 1, 1951; married; 4 children. BS in Microbiology, Mich. State U., 1973; MS in Bacteriology, U. Wis., 1975, PhD in Bacteriology, 1977. Offered and declined William D. Gill endowed chair in biochemistry Johns Hopkins U., 1997. Contbr. articles to profl. jours. and conf. procs.; patentee in field. Office: U Ga Dept Microbiology 815 Biol Scis Bldg Athens GA 30602-2605

MAIER, ROMULUS, journalist; b. Bucharest, Romania, May 5, 1961; arrived in U.S., 1998; s. Romulus and Victoria Maier; m. Irena Maier, July 20, 1990. BSc in Engring., Polytech. Inst., Bucharest, Romania, 1987; Grad. degree in Journalism, Superior Sch. Journalism, Bucharest, Romania, 1993; MA in Polit. Sci., U.Conn., Storrs, 2001. Reporter Romanian Reality, Bucharest, Romania, 1991—92, chief editor, 1992—93; econ. chief editor Free Romania, Bucharest, 1993—97, dep. chief editor, 1997, press corr., 1997—; grad. asst. U. Conn. T. Dodd Rsch. Ctr., Storrs, 2000—. Exec. prod. mgr. Rsch. Eqipment Factory, Bucharest, 1990—91; polit. and econ. advisor CDR Campaign 1996, Bucharest, 1995—96; vis. prof. Superior Sch. Journalism, Bucharest, 1994—95. Mem.: Internat. Orgn. Journalists, Acad. Polit. Sci., Am. Polit. Sci. Assn. Eastern Orthodox. Home: 1250 Farmington Ave Apt B8 Hartford CT 06107 Office: Univ Conn 541 Mansfield Rd Storrs Mansfield CT 06269 E-mail: irerom@msn.com.

MAIER, RONALD VITT, surgeon; b. Wheeling, W.Va., Oct. 23, 1947; BS, U. Notre Dame, 1969; MD, Duke U., 1973. Intern Parkland Meml. Hosp., Dallas, 1973-74; resident U. Wash. Hosps., Seattle, 1974-78; rsch. assoc. Scripps Rsch. Found., La Jolla, Calif., 1978-81; surgeon-in-chief HMC, Seattle, 1993—; prof., vice chair surgery U. Wash., Seattle, 1994—. Office: Dept Surgery 359796 Harborview Med Ctr 325 9th Ave Seattle WA 98104-2499 Office Phone: 206-731-3299. Business E-Mail: ronmaier@u.washington.edu.

MAIER-LORENTZ, MADELINE MARIE, nurse educator; b. Boulder City, Nev., Oct. 7, 1952; d. William J. and Madeline A. (Menegus) Maier; m. John F. Lorentz, May 22, 1982; 1 child, William Charles Lorentz. BA in Psychology, U. San Francisco, 1974, BSN, 1979; MSN, U. Phoenix, 1998; postgrad., Grad. Sch. Am., 1998—. RN, Calif.; cert. pub. health nurse, Calif. Nurse Davies Med. Ctr., San Francisco, 1979-81; nurse to pvt. practice plastic reconstructive surgeon San Francisco, 1979-81; nurse Richland Meml. Hosp., Columbia, S.C., 1981-82; dir. clin. svcs. OccuPoint Med. Corp., 2000—. Vol. election dist. congressman, San Diego, 1993-98. Mem. ANA, ACA, Nat. League Nursing, Am. Acad. Bereavement, Calif. Advocates Nursing Home Reform, Psi Chi, Sigma Theta Tau. Republican. Roman Catholic. Avocation: reading. Home: 11539 Keisha Cv San Diego CA 92126-6604 E-mail: mlorentzrn@aol.com., cupoint@earthlink.net.

MAIERS, MICHAEL ALBERT, librarian; b. Sandusky, Ohio, Oct. 7, 1960; s. Richard Edward and Carol Evelyn (Davie) M.; m. Pamela Helen Haskett, June 17, 1995; 1 stepchild, Thomas A. Fernando. AA, Tallahassee C.C., 1982; BA in Am. History, Fla. State U., 1984; MS in LS, Wayne State U., 1994. Cert. in archives adminstrn. Asst. mgr. Seafood Bay Restaurants Pan Foods Inc., 1985-86; clk. for food svcs. dept. Electronic Data Sys., Troy, Mich., 1986-91, libr. for mfg. competitiveness group, 1991-96, Libr. Network, Wayne, Mich., 1997—99; head info. svcs. Palm Harbor (Fla.) Libr., 1999—2000; libr. ITT Tech. Inst., Tampa, Fla., 2000—. Mem. ALA, Spl. Librs. Assn., Soc. Am. Archivists. Roman Catholic. Home: 7608 Laurel Oak Ct Port Richey FL 34668-5829 Office: ITT Tech Inst 4809 Memorial Hwy Tampa FL 33634

MAIESE, KENNETH, neurologist, neuroscientist; b. Audubon, NJ, Dec. 5, 1958; s. Charles and Margaret (Fioretti) M. BA summa cum laude, U. Pa., 1981; MD, Cornell U., 1985. Intern N.Y. Hosp., 1985-86, resident in neurology, 1986-89, asst. attending physician, 1989-94; asst. prof. Cornell U. Med. Coll., N.Y.C., 1989-94; assoc. prof. dept. neurology, anatomy and cell biology Wayne State U. Ctr. for Molecular Toxicology & Medicine, Detroit, 1994—; dir. lab. molecular and cellular cerebral ischemia Wayne State U. Ctr. for Molecular Toxicology, Detroit, 1994—, prof. dept. neurology, anatomy, cell biology, 1999—. Dir. neurol. diagnosis NY Hosp., 1991—94; chmn. nat. brain/stroke consortium Am. Heart Assn., 2000—01, exec. coun., 2001—, nat peer rev. steering com., 2002—, mem. rsch. com., 2003—; mem. minority edn. tng. NIH, 2002—; mem. study sect. cell death and injury NIH/CDIN, 2003—. Author: Neurology and General Medicine, 1989, Neurological and Neurosurgical ICU Medicine, 1988; editor-in-chief Current Neurovascular Rsch., 2002—; editor: Neuronal and Vascular Plasticity, 2003; assoc. editor, mem. editl. bd. Letters in Drug Design and Discovery, 2002—, Histology and Histopathology, 2002—, Jour. Histological Histopathology, 2002—; mem. editl. bd. Drug Design Revs., 2003—, Medicinal Chemistry, 2004—, Current Drug Targets-Heme Agts.; contbr. articles to profl. jours. Joseph Collins scholar, 1981-85, Grupe Found. scholar, 1985; grantee NIH, 1990—, Nat. Stroke Assn., 1992-94, Alzheimer's Assn., 1994—, Am. Heart Assn., 1995—, United Cerebral Palsy Found., 1995—, Janssen Found., 1995—; recipient Young Scientist award Jours. Cerebral Blood Flow, 1991, Hoechst Investigator award, 1993, Robert G. Siekert award in stroke, 1994, Johnson and Johnson Disting. Investigator award, 1996-98, Maiese Lab. Neurosci. Tng. award J & J/Janssen, 1998, Boehringer Investigator award, 1999, NIH/NIEHS award, Learn Found. award, 2002, 2003, MI Challenge award. Mem. Am. Acad. Neurology, N.Y. Acad. Scis., Assn. for Rsch. in Nervous and Mental Diseases, Am. Neurol. Assn. (elected), Soc. Neurosci., Internat. Acad. Cardiology (sci. com. 2003—). Roman Catholic. Achievements include rsch. in imidazole receptors, cerebral ischemia, nitric oxide toxicity, growth factor neuroprotection, signal cellular transduction mechanisms, metabotropic glutamate receptors, gene regulation, and gene therapy. Office: Wayne State U Sch Medicine 8C-1 U Health Ctr Dept Neur 4201 Saint Antoine St Detroit MI 48201-2153 Business E-Mail: kmaiese@med.wayne.edu.

MAIKON, MARC STEVEN, podiatrist; BA, Grinnell Coll., 1980; BS, U. Iowa, 1982; DPM, U. Osteo. Medicine, Des Moines, 1989. Cert. Am. Coun. Cert. Podiatric Physicians and Surgeons. Podiatrist, owner Family Foot Care Ctr. PLC, Cedar Rapids, Iowa, 1991—. Mem. Am. Coll. Foot Surgeons, Am. Podiatric Med. Assn., Iowa Podiatric Med. Soc., C. of C. Cedar Rapids, Rotary Internat. Office: Family Foot Ctr 3359 Center Point Rd NE Cedar Rapids IA 52402-5568 Home: 1750 Emerald Ct Robins IA 52328-9651

MAIL, PATRICIA DAVISON, public health specialist; b. Kamloops, B.C., Can., Dec. 10, 1940; d. George Allen and Constance (Davison) M. BS, U. Ariz., 1963, MA, 1970; MS, Smith Coll., 1965; MPH, Yale U., 1967; postgrad., Seattle U., 1974; PhD, U. Md., 1996. Cert. health edn. specialist. Commd. officer USPHS, 1970-97; chief health edn. br. Portland Indian Health Svc., 1979-86; dep. chief field ops. Nat. Health Svc. Corps., 1986-87, dep. chief clin., prof. activities bd., 1987-88, br. chief Health Resources and Svcs. Adminstrn., 1988; dep. staff dir. Office Pub. Health Svc. Surgeon Gen., 1989; officer pers. specialist Alcohol, Drug Abuse and Mental Health Adminstrn., 1990—92; staff mem., divsn. clin. and prevention rsch. Nat. Inst. Alcohol Abuse and Alcoholism, 1991—93, extramural sci. adminstr., 1993-97; faculty Medicine Creek Tribal Coll., 1998—99. Mem. faculty Seattle U., 1974-78; commr. Nat. Commn. Health Edn. Credentialing, chair, 1993-94; accreditation site visitor Coun. on Edn. in Pub. Health, 1996—; vis. scientist Addictive Behaviors Rsch. Ctr., U. Wash., 1998-99, rsch. scientist, 1999—; pres. Dragon-Archer Cons., 1997—; asst. prof. Oreg. Health Scis. U., 1998-99. Author: (with D.R. McDonald) Tulapai to Tokay, 1980; editor: (with Heurtin-Roberts, Martin and Howard) American Indian Alcoholism: Multiple Perspectives on a Complex Problem, 2002; editor Soc. for Pub. Health Edn. Sounds, 1976-86; assoc. editor Health Promotion Practice; contbr. articles to profl. jours. Recipient Meritorious Svc. award Uniformed Svcs. U. Health Scis., 1991; USPHS traineeship, 1965-67; grantee NDEA, 1968-70. Fellow Am. Sch. Health Assn., Soc. Applied Anthropology; mem. AAAS (life), APHA (chair pub. health edn. sect. 1995-96, chmn. continuing profl. edn. com. 1997, 98, exec. bd. 2001-2004, Early Career award Pub. Health Edn. sect. 1979, Judith Miller award 1998, Exec. Dir.'s citation 1999), Wash. State Public Health Assn. (Tom Drummey award, 2002), Mil. Officers Assn. Am. (life), Commd. Officers Assn. USPHS (life), Am. Assn. Health Edn. (life), Am. Acad. Health Behavior (bd. dirs. 2001), Soc. Pub. Health Edn., Med. Anthropology Soc., Assn. Mil. Surgeons U.S. (life), Res. Officers Assn. (life), Smith Coll. Alumnae Assn., Delta Psi Kappa, Eta Sigma Gamma. Episcopalian. Home: 35214 28th Ave S Federal Way WA 98003-7120 E-mail: pmail@sprynet.com.

MAILER, NORMAN, author; b. Long Branch, N.J., Jan. 31, 1923; s. Issac Barnett and Fanny (Schneider) M.; m. Beatrice Silverman, 1944 (div. 1952); 1 dau., Susan; m. Adele Morales, 1954 (div. 1962); children: Danielle, Elizabeth; m. Jeanne Campbell, 1962 (div. 1963); 1 dau., Kate; m. Beverly Bentley, 1963 (div. 1980); children: Michael, Steven; m. Carol Stevens, 1980 (div. 1980); 1 dau., Maggie; m. Norris Church, 1980; 1 son, John Buffalo. SB cum laude, Harvard U., 1943; postgrad., Sorbonne, Paris, France, 1947-48. Columnist Village Voice, 1946, Commentary, 1962-63, Esquire, 1962-63; contbg. editor Dissent, 1953-69; co-founding editor Village Voice, 1955. Author: No Percentage, 1941, The Naked and the Dead, 1948, Barbary Shore, 1951, The Deer Park, 1955, The White Negro: Superficial Reflections on the Hipster, 1957, Advertisements for Myself, 1959, Deaths for the Ladies and Other Disasters, 1962, The Presidential Papers, 1963, An American Dream, 1965, Cannibals and Christians, 1966, Why Are We in Vietnam?, 1967 (Nat. Book award nomination 1967), The Short Fiction of Norman Mailer, 1967, The Bullfight, 1967, The Armies of the Night, 1968 (Pulitzer prize for non-fiction 1969, George Polk award 1969), Miami and the Siege of Chicago, 1968 (Nat. Book award for non-fiction 1968), The Idol and the Octopus, 1968, Of a Fire On The Moon, 1970, King of the Hill, 1971, The Prisoner of Sex, 1971, The Long Patrol, 1971, Existential Errands, 1972, St. George and the Godfather, 1972, Marilyn, 1973, The Faith of Graffiti, 1974, The Fight, 1975, Some Honorable Men, 1975, Genius and Lust, 1976, A Transit to Narcissus, 1978, The Executioner's Song, 1979 (Pulitzer Prize for fiction 1980, Nat. Book Critics Circle award nomination 1979, Am. Book award nomination 1980), Of a Small and Modest Malignancy, Wicked and Bristling with Dots, 1980, Of Women and Their Elegance, 1980, Pieces and Pontifications, 1982, Ancient Evenings, 1983, Tough Guys Don't Dance, 1984, The Last Night, 1984, Harlot's Ghost, 1991, How the Wimp Won the War, 1991, Oswald's Tale, 1995, Portrait of Picasso as a Young Man, 1995, The Gospel According to the Son, 1997, The Spooky Art: Thoughts on Writing, 2003; (plays) The Deer Park: A Play, 1967, Strawhead, 1985; editor: Genius and Lust: A Journey Through the Major Writings of Henry Miller, 1976; screenwriter: (films) The Executioner's Song, 1982 (Emmy award nomination outstanding adapted screenplay 1983); screenwriter, prodr., dir., actor: (films) Wild 90, 1967, Maidstone: A Mystery, 1971; screenwriter, prodr.: (films) Beyond the Law, 1968; screenwriter, dir.: (films) Tough Guys Don't Dance, 1987; actor: (films) Ragtime, 1981. Served with AUS, 1944-46. Recipient Edward MacDowell medal MacDowell Colony, 1973, Nat. Arts Club Gold medal, 1976, Emerson-Thoreau Medal for lifetime of literary achievement, 1989; Nat. Inst. and Am. Acad. grantee, 1960; Pappas fellow U. Pa., 1983. Mem. PEN Am. Ctr. (pres. 1984-86), Nat. Inst. Arts and Letters.

MAILLE, BRENDA PATRICIA, lawyer; b. Lowell, Mass., Oct. 1, 1956; BS, U. Lowell, 1978; JD, New Eng. Sch. Law, 1982. Bar: Mass. Atty. Zaroulis & Maille, Lowell, 1983-95; pvt. practice Lowell, 1995—. Bd. dirs. Big Bros./Big Sisters Greater Lowell, 1988-97, 2000-, former pres.; coach, advisor City Magnet Sch. Mock Trial Team, Lowell, 1996. Mem. Mass. Bar Assn., Greater Lowell Bar Assn. (dir. 1990-93, Lawyer Yr. award 1994). Avocations: skiing, travel. Office: 9 Middlesex St Lowell MA 01852-2110 Office Phone: 978-452-4504.

MAILLET, LUCIENNE, humanities educator; b. Lewiston, Maine, Apr. 16, 1934; d. Leon J. and Alice (Lizotte) Thibault; m. Daniel J. Maillet, July 14, 1956; 1 child, Daniel Jr. BA in Chemistry, Bates Coll., 1956; MA in Edn., George Washington U., 1963; MLS, Cath. U., 1969; cert. of profl. devel. and library and info. scis., CUNY, 1975; DLS, Columbia U., 1982; MBA, L.I. U., 1999. Librarian Conn. Park Elem. Sch., 1965-69, Southwoods Jr. High Sch., 1969-70; head curriculum materials and audiovisual ctr. CUNY, York Coll., Jamaica, NY, 1970-75; asst. prof. Palmer Sch., Long Island U., Brookville, NY, 1975-84, dean, 1984-89, prof., 1975—. Mem. Am. Library Assn., Am. Soc. Info. Sci., Assn. Colls. and Rsch. Libraries, Spl. Libraries Assn., N.Y. Library Club, Assn. Library and Info. Sci. Edn., Beta Phi Mu. Home: 77 Andrew St Manhasset NY 11030-2309 Office: Long Island Univ Palmer Sch Libr & Info Sci CW Post Campus Brookville NY 11548 Office Phone: 516-299-2175. E-mail: lmaillet@liu.edu.

MAILLET, MARTIN JOSEPH, SR., retired police captain; b. Lynn, Mass., Jan. 2, 1933; s. Joseph Maximum and Mary Agnes (Deveau) M.; m. Elizabeth Ann Kasprzyk, June 16, 1957; children: Martin Joseph Jr., Lawrence James, Jayne Marie. Student, Bloomberg's Sch. Law, Boston, 1958-63, Boston U., 1970, North Shore Community Coll., 1974-76; grad., Linotype Sch., Boston, 1954. Cert. secondary tchr., Mass. Linotype operator Willimantic (Conn.) Chronicle, 1954-55; police officer Saugus (Mass.) Police Dept., 1957-64, police sergeant, 1964-73, police capt., exec. officer to chief, 1973-95; ret., 1995. Dep. sheriff Essex County Sheriffs, 1987—, Mass Police Assn., 1957—. Cpl. U.S. Army, 1950-52, Korea. Democrat. Roman Catholic. Avocations: health club fitness, jogging, swimming, travel. Home: PO Box 1471 Saugus MA 01906-0771

MAILLOUX, ROBERT JOSEPH, physicist; b. Lynn, Mass., June 20, 1938; s. Joseph H. and Nora S. M.; m. Marlene Schirf, Jan. 14, 1967; children: Patrice, Julie, Denise. BS, Northeastern U., 1961; SM, Harvard U., 1962, PhD, 1965. Physicist NASA Electronics Rsch. Ctr., Cambridge, Mass., 1965-70, Air Force Cambridge Rsch. Labs., Bedford, Mass., 1970-77, Rome Air Devel. Ctr., Bedford, 1977-80, chief antennas and components div., electromagnetic directorate, 1980-91; sr. scientist Air Force Rsch. Lab., 1992—2004. Lectr. Tufts U., Boston, 1985—. Author: Phased Array Antenna Handbook; guest editor IEEE/AP-S Transactions Spl. Issue on Phased Array Antennas, 1999; contbr. chpts. to 8 textbooks, articles to sci. jours. Served with C.E. U.S. Army, 1966-68. Recipient Air Force Marcus O'Day paper award, 1971, Engineer of Yr. award RADC, 1988; RADC fellow, 1988. Fellow IEEE (chmn. tech. com. 1997 phased array symposium, spl. achievement award 1969, 76, nat. lectr., assoc. editor Transactions on Antennas and Propagation 1984-92, Harry Diamond award 1991, Fred Diamond award 1997, IEEE Third Millenium medal, 2000); mem. Antenna and Propagation Soc. (chmn. Boston chpt. 1968, nat. meetings chmn. 1977-80, adcom mem. 1977-80, v.p. 1982, pres. 1983), Internat. Sci. Radio Union (Commn. B. tech. activities chmn. 1980—), Sigma Xi (pres. Hanscom chpt. 1980-81), Eta Kappa Nu, Tau Beta Pi. Achievements include 12 patents in field. Office: AFRL/SNH 31 Grenier St Hanscom AFB MA 01731-3008

MAILO, TOETAGATA ALBERT, territory attorney general; b. Utulei, Am. Samoa; married; 2 children. BA, Brigham Young U., 1972, JD, 1976. Bar: Hawaii 1977, Samoa 1977. Asst. atty. gen. Am. Samoa, 1977—79; pvt.

practice, 1979—89, 1993—97; legal counsel Gov. of Am. Samoa, 1989—92; atty. gen. Am. Samoa, Pago Pago, 1997—. Mem.: Am. Samoa Bar Assn., Hawaii State Bar Assn. Office: Office of Attorney General PO Box 7 Pago Pago AS 96799-0007

MAIMAN, MITCHELL, oncologist, gynecologist; b. Bklyn., 1957; s. Inwin Maiman; m. Judith E. Levy, 1985. MD, SUNY-Health Sci. Ctr., 1981. Diplomate Am. Bd. Obstetrics and Gynecology with subspecialty in gynecologic oncology. Resident Einstein Coll. Medicine, Bronx, 1981—85; fellow Univ. Hosp., Bklyn., 1985—87; pvt. practice oncology, gynecology S.I., NY, 1987—. Chmn. dept. ob-gyn. S.I. Univ. Hosp., 1999—; assoc. prof. SUNY, Bklyn. Office: 256 Mason Ave Staten Island NY 10305-3408

MAIMON, ELAINE PLASKOW, academic administrator; b. Phila., July 28, 1944; d. Louis J. and Gertrude (Canter) Plaskow; m. Morton A. Maimon, Sept. 30, 1967; children: Gillian Blanche, Alan Marcus. AB, U. Pa., 1966, MA, 1967, PhD, 1970. Asst. prof. Haverford (Pa.) Coll., 1971-73; lectr. Arcadia U., Glenside, Pa., 1973-75, asst. prof., dir. writing, 1975-77, assoc. prof., 1977-83, assoc. dean, 1980-84, assoc. v.p., prof. English, 1984-86; adj. assoc. prof. U. Pa., Phila., 1982-83; assoc. dean of coll. Brown U., Providence, 1986-88; dean, prof. English Queens Coll. CUNY, Flushing, N.Y., 1988-96; campus CEO, provost Ariz. State U. West, Phoenix, 1996—2004; v.p. Ariz. State U., 1996—2004; chancellor U. Alaska, Anchorage, 2004—. Nat. bd. cons. NEH, 1977-81; mem. adv. bd. Cox Comm., 1997-2001; bd. dirs. Arrowhed Cmty. Bank. Co-author: Writing in the Arts and Sciences, 1981, A Writer's Resource, 2003; co-editor: Readings in the Arts and Sciences, 1984, Thinking, Reasoning and Writing, 1989, A Writer's Resource, 2003. Trustee Heard Mus., Phoenix, 1999—. Recipient Golden Heart award, Today's Ariz. Woman, 2000, Women of Distinction award, YMCA, Maricopa County, 2001, YWCA award in Edn., 2002, World award, Girl Scouts Am., Ariz. Cactus-Pine Coun., 2002, Woman of Vision award, Phoenix Bus. Jour.; Elaine Maimon award for Excellence in Writing named in her honor, Arcadia U., 1994. Mem.: MLA (exec. com., tchg. of writing divsn.), Am. Assn. Colls. and Univs. (exec. bd. 2002—), Conf. on Coll. Composition Comm. (exec. com. 1985—87), ACE Nat. Commn. Women, Nat. Coun. Tchrs. English (nominating com. 1986—87, teaching of writing divsn. 1991), Phi Beta Kappa. Office: U Alaska 3211 Providence Dr Anchorage AK 99508-8060 Home: 2831 UAA Dr Unit B Anchorage AK 99508 Office Phone: 907-786-1437. E-mail: elaine.maimon@uaa.alaska.edu.

MAIN, EDNA DEWEY (JUNE MAIN), education educator; b. Hyannis, Mass., Sept. 1, 1940; d. Seth Bradford and Edna Wilhelmina (Wright) Dewey; m. Donald John Main, Sept. 9, 1961 (div. Dec. 1989); children: Alison Teresa Main Ronzon, Susan Christine Main Leddy, Steven Donald. Degree in merchandising, Tobe-Coburn Sch., 1960; BA in Edn., U. North Fla., 1974, MA in Edn., 1979, M in Adminstrn. and Supervision, 1983; PhD in Curriculum and Instrn., U. Fla., 1990. Asst. buyer Abraham & Straus, Bklyn., 1960-61; asst. mdse. mgr. Interstate Dept. Stores, NYC, 1962-63; tchr. Holiday Hill Elem. Sch., Jacksonville, Fla., 1974-86; instr. summer sci. inst., 1984-92; prof. edn. Jacksonville U., 1992—, dir. masters program in integrated learning and ednl. tech. Instr. U. Fla., 1987—90, U. North Fla., 1990—92; cons. Assn. Internat. Schs. Africa, 1994—97. Co-author: (book) Developing Critical Thinking Through Science, Book I, 2001, Developing Critical Thinking Through Science, Book II, 2002. Rep. United Way, 1981—86; tchr. rep., chpt. leader White Ho. Young Astronaut Program, 1984—85; team leader NSF Shells Elem. Sci. Project. Named Fla. Prof. of the Yr., Carnegie Found., 2002; recipient Innovative Excellence in Tchg., Learning and Tech. award, Internat. Coll. Conf., 1999, Outstanding Alumni award, U. North Fla., 1999, Eve award for Edn., 2001, Apple Disting. Educator award, 2003—04. Mem.: Internat. Soc. Tech. Edn., Soc. Info. Tech. and Tchr. Edn., ASCD, NSTA (Sci. Tchrs. Achievement Recognition award 1983), Kappa Delta Pi, Phi Delta Kappa, Phi Kappa Phi. Episcopalian. Office: Jacksonville U 2800 University Blvd N Jacksonville FL 32211-3394 E-mail: main750@bellsouth.net.

MAIN, PATRICIA ENGLANDER, investor; b. London, Apr. 8, 1931; d. Harry Norman and Eve (Roth) Englander; m. Arnold M. Singer, June 11, 1950 (div. May 1963); m. Frank Graham Main, Apr. 30, 1966 (div. Apr. 1981); m. Franklin Walter Mohney, Aug. 10, 1981 (dec. May 1991); children: Lisa Nicole Kelly, Susan Jennifer Kerschner, Jacqueline Eve Singer. Student, Mt. Holyoke Coll., 1948-50. Dir. pub. rels. Contemporary Arts Mus., Houston, 1962-64; relocation sales assoc. Paul Reinke Corp., Cherry Hill, N.J., 1964-69; account exec. Relocation Realty Svc. Corp., N.Y.C., 1972-76, v.p. ops., 1976-79; owner Patricia Mohney Gallery, Reading, Pa., 1981-84; v.p. Venture Components Corp., N.Y.C., 1984-92; pvt. investor N.Y.C., 1992—. Trustee, bd. mem. Reading Art Mus., 1980-83; mem. bus. and profl. com. N.Y.C. Ballet, 1985-95; mem. com. denominational affairs All Souls Ch., N.Y.C., 1998—. Mem. Mt. Holyoke Coll. Alumnae Club (bd. dirs. 1969-77, pres. 1977-79). Office: 65 E 76th St Ste 3B New York NY 10021-1844

MAIN, PHILIP DAVID, lawyer, probate judge; b. New Britain, Conn., Apr. 10, 1936; s. George Lawrence Main and Nancy Elia; m. Patricia Ann Baker, Sept. 10, 1960; children: Linda S. Erwin, William G. BA in History, Bates Coll., 1958; LLB, George Washington U., 1961. Bar: Conn. 1962. Staff atty. CIGNA, Bloomfield, Conn., 1961-63; ptnr. Pease & Main, Simsbury, Conn., 1963—. Judge Granby (Conn.) Probate Ct., 1990—. Town com. chmn., Granby. Mem. Granby Lions Club (pres. 1966-68). Office: Pease & Main PO Box 544 Simsbury CT 06070-0544 E-mail: peasemain@aol.com.

MAIN, ROBERT GAIL, communications educator, training consultant, television and film producer, former army officer; b. Bucklin, Mo., Sept. 30, 1932; s. Raymond M. and Inez L. (Olinger) M.; m. Anita Sue Thoroughman, Jan. 31, 1955; children: Robert Bruce, David Keith, Leslie Lorraine. BS magna cum laude, U. Mo., 1954; grad. with honors, Army Commd. Gen. Staff Coll., 1967; MA magna cum laude in Comm., Stanford U., 1968; PhD, U. Md., 1978. Commd. 2d lt. U.S. Army, 1954, advanced through grades to lt. col., 1968; mem. faculty Army Commd. Gen. Staff Coll., 1968-70; chief speech-writing and info. materials divsn. U.S. Army Info. Office, 1971, chief broadcast and film divsn., 1972-73; dir. def. audiovisual activities Office of Info. for Armed Forces, 1973-76; ret., 1976; prof. instrnl. tech. Calif. State U., Chico, 1976—, dept. chair, 1993-98. Cons. in field. Author: Rogues, Saints and Ordinary People, 1988; prodr. (TV documentary) Walking Wounded, 1983, Army Info. Films, Army Radio Series, 1972-73; contbr. articles on computer based tng. and telecoms. to scientific and profl. jours. Decorated Legion of Merit, Meritorious Svc. medal, Commendation medal with oak leaf cluster, combat Inf. Badge; Vietnamese Cross of Gallantry; recipient Freedom Found. awards, 1972, 73, 74; Bronze medal Atlanta Film Festival, 1972; Best of Show award Balt. Film Festival, 1973; Creativity award Chgo. Indsl. Film Festival, 1973; Cine gold award Internat. Film Prodrs. Assn., 1974; named an Outstanding Prof. Calif. State U., 1987-88. Mem. Phi Eta Sigma, Alpha Zeta, Phi Delta Gamma, Omicron Delta Kappa, Alpha Gamma Rho.

MAIN, TIMOTHY L. electronics executive; BS, Mich. State U.; M in Internat. Mgmt., Am. Grad. Sch. Internat. Mgmt. Comml. lending officer internat. divsn. Nat. Bank Detroit; mgr. prodn. control Jabil Cir., St. Petersburg, Fla., 1987; ops. mgr., 1987-89; project mgr., 1989-91; v.p. bus. devel., 1991; sr. v.p. bus. devel.; pres., 1999—; CEO, 2000—; also bd. dirs. Office: Jabil Cir 10560 9th St N Saint Petersburg FL 33716

MAINE, DOUGLAS L. computer company executive; b. Lancaster, Pa. m. Fran Maine; children: Alison, Steven. BA, Temple U.; MBA, Hofstra U. Contr., sr. v.p. fin., pres. 14-state operating div. MCI Comm. Corp., CFO, exec. v.p., 1992-98; sr. v.p., CFO, IBM, Armonk, N.Y., 1998-99; gen. mgr. ibm.com, 1999—. Bd. dirs. WolfTrap Found. for Performing Arts, Pvt. Sector Coun.; former mem. bd. dirs. Mus. Sci. and Tech., Atlanta, Woodruff Arts Ctr., Atlanta. Mem. Zeta Beta Tau (past bd. dirs.). Office: IBM New Orchard Rd Armonk NY 10504

MAINE, MICHAEL ROLAND, lawyer; b. Anderson, Ind., Feb. 22, 1940; s. Roland Dwight and Vivian Louise (Browning) M.; m. Suzanne Bauman, Aug. 25, 1962; children: Christopher Michael (dec.), Melinda Louise. AB with high distinction, DePauw U.; JD with distinction, U. Mich. Bar: Ind., D.C., U.S. Dist. Ct. (so. dist.) Ind., U.S. Ct. Appeals (7th cir.), U.S. Supreme Ct. Assoc. Baker & Daniels, Indpls., 1964-71, ptnr., 1972—. Contbr. articles to profl. jours. Bd. dirs. Ind. Repertory Theatre, Indpls., 1986—2003, Cmty. Hosp. N., 1988—91, Japan-Am. Soc. Ind. Inc., 1988—2003; pres. Mental Health Assn. Ind., Indpls., 1985; bd. visitors Sch. Law Ind. U., Indpls.; trustee De Pauw U., Greencastle, Ind., 1990—; bd. dirs. U.S.-China Bus. Coun. Legal Cooperation Fund, 2002—. Capt. USAF, 1965—68. Named Sagamore of Wabash, Gov. Ind., 1986. Fellow: Indpls. Bar Found., Ind. Bar Found.; mem.: Indpls. Bar Assn. (sec. 1983, pres. 1985, extraordinary svc. award 1985), Ind. Bar Assn. (chmn. fed. judiciary com. 1986—88), Kiwanis (lt. gov. Ind. club 1972, pres. Indpls. club 1969), Masons, Kiwanis (lt. gov. Ind. club 1972, pres. Indpls. club 1969), Masons, Phi Beta Kappa, Order of Coif. Avocation: golf. Home: 13100 Joseffa Ct Placida FL 33946 Office: Baker & Daniels 300 N Meridian St Ste 2700 Indianapolis IN 46204-1782

MAINELIS, GEDIMINAS, research scientist, educator; s. Zita Maineliene and Jonas Mainelis; m. Rimute Gaidyte. MS in Physics, Vilnius U., Lithuania, 1994; PhD in Environ. Health, U. Cin., 2000. Grad. asst. U. Cin., 1994—2000, postdoctoral scientist, 2000—01; asst. prof. Rutgers U., New Brunswick, NJ, 2001—; dir. Bioaerosol Rsch. and Tech. Lab. New Brunswick, 2001., Govt. of Salzburg Land scholar, 1992-1993, Am. Indsl. Hygiene Found. scholar, 1997, travel grantee, Am. Assn. for Aerosol Rsch., 2003, Rsch. awardee, Charles and Johanna Busch Meml. Fund, 2003. Mem.: Am. Geohysical Union, Inst. for Occupl. Safety and Health, Ctr. for Environ. Prediction, Am. Soc. for Microbiology, Am. Assn. for Aerosol Rsch. Achievements include research in instruments and techniques to collect, determine, inactivate and analyze airborne microorganisms; application of electrostatic techniques to collect airborne microorganisms. Avocations: science fiction, travel, hiking, reading. Office: Rutgers U 14 Coll Farm Rd New Brunswick NJ 08901 Office Phone: 732-932-7166. E-mail: mainelis@envsci.rutgers.edu.

MAINELLA, FRANCES P. federal agency administrator; b. Groton, Conn. BS cum laude, U. Conn.; MS cum laude in Counseling, Ctrl. Conn. State Coll.; PhD in Pub. Svc. (hon.), Ctrl. Conn. State U., 2002. H.S. phys. edn. tchr. Vernon Pub. Sch., Rockville, Conn., 1969—77; asst. ctr. dir. Tallahassee Parks and Recreation Dept., 1977—78; dir. recreation Town of Lake Park, Fla., 1978—83; exec. dir. Fla. Recreation and Park Assn., Tallahassee, 1983—89; dir. divsn. Recreation and Parks Fla. Dept. Environ. Protection, 1989—2001; dir. Nat. Park Svc., U.S. Dept. Interior, Washington, 2001—. Spkr. in field. Contbr. numerous articles to profl. publs. Co-chair Com. for Preservation of the White House, mem. adv. coun. on hist. preservation; bd. trustees John F. Kennedy Ctr. for Performing Arts; liaison White House Hist. Soc.; sec., treas. Nat. Park Found.; mem. Am. Folklife Bd.; past pres. Nat. Assn. State Park Dirs.; past bd. mem. Am. Acad. Park and Recreation Adminstr.; past mem. Fla. Commn. Ttourism; past officio bd. mem. Fla. Recreation and Park Assn.; past mem. Gov.'s Mansion adv. com.; past bd. mem. Fla. Gov.'s Coun. on Phys. Fitness and Sports; past sec., bd. dirs. Spl. Olympics; past pres. Tallahassee Soc. Assn. Execs.; past chair United Way Drive for Tallahassee Soc. Assn. Execs.; past bd. dirs. Tallahassee Leon County Convention and Visitors Bur.; bd. dirs. Ford's Theatre Soc., Wolf Trap Found. for Performing Arts. Recipient Disting. Svc. award, Nat. Assn. Recreation Resource Planners, 1996, Woman of Distinction award, Girl Scout Coun. of Apalachee Bend, 1998, Pugsley medal, Am. Acad. Park and Recreation Adminstrn., 1998, Disting. Svc. award, Nat. Assn. State Park Dirs., 1999, Senator Bob Williams award, State of Fla., 2001, Sheldon Coleman Outdoors award, 2002, Walter T. Cox Pub. Svc. Achievement award, Clemson U., 2002. Mem.: Nat. Recreation and Park Assn. (congress planning com. 1984, 1987, past chair coun. exec. dirs., pres. 1997—, Harold D. Meyer Profl. award 2000). Office: US Dept Interior Nat Park Svc 1849 C St NW Washington DC 20240*

MAINES, NATALIE LOUISE, musician; b. Lubbock, Tex., Oct. 14, 1974; d. Lloyd Maines and Tina; m. Michael Tarabay, May 1997 (div. Jan. 1999); m. Adrian Pasdar, June 24, 2000; children: Jack Slade Pasdar, Beckett Finn. Student, Tex. Tech., Berklee Sch. Music. Performer Dixie Chicks, 1995—. Performer: (albums) Wide Open Spaces, 1998 (Maximum Vision Clip of Yr., Billboard, 1998, Best New Country Artist Clip of Yr., Billboard, 1998, Best Country Album, Grammy Awards, 1998, Album of Yr., Acad. Country Music, 1998, Best Selling Album, Can. Country Music Awards, 1999, Song of Yr. (Country), WB Radio Music Awards, 1999, Album of Yr., ACM, 1999), Fly, 1999 (Best Country Album, Grammy Awards, 1999, Best Selling Album, Can. Country Music Awards, 2000, Internat. Album, British Country Music Awards, 2000, Country Album of Yr., Billboard, 2000, Album of Yr., ACM, 2000, Album of Yr., CMA, 2000), Home, 2002 (Favorite Country Album, Am. Music Awards, 2002, Best Recording Package, Grammy Awards, 2002, Best Country Album, Grammy Awards, 2002). Named Most Significant New Country Act, Country Monitor, 1998, Top New Country Artist, Billboard, 1998, Group of Yr., CMA, 1998, Top Vocal Group, Acad. Country Music, 1998, Country Artist of Yr., Rolling Stone, 1999, Top Country Artist, Billboard, 1999, Internat. Rising Star, British Country Music Awards, 1999, Artist of Yr., WB Radio Music Awards, 1999, Favorite New Artist (Country), AMA, 1999, Vocal Group of Yr., CMA, 1999, Country Artist of Yr., Billboard, 1999, Entertainer of Yr., CMA, 2000, ACM, 2000, 2001, Vocal Group of Yr., 2001, Favorite Musical Group or Band, People's Choice Award, 2002, Vocal Group of Yr., Country Music Assn. Awards, 2002, others; recipient Horizon award, CMA, 1998. Office: Monument Sony Nashville 34 Music Sq East Nashville TN 37203

MAINPRIZE, DONALD CHARLES, minister, writer; b. Coleman, Mich., Aug. 28, 1930; s. James Raymond and Ople Belle Mainprize; m. Doris Olive Humphrey, July 27, 1952; children: Daniel Andrew, Debra Ann, Susan Lynn, Edward Raymond. Pastor's diploma, Grand Rapids Sch. Bible & Music, 1953; student, Dallas Theol. Sem., 1957; BA in Profl. Writing, U. Okla., Norman, 1960; MA in English and Am. Lit., Ctrl. Mich. U., 1967. Pastor Dildine Comty. Ch., Ionia, Mich., 1953—56; pastor First Presbyn. Ch., Minco, Okla., 1958—60; mng. editor Scripture Press, Wheaton, Ill., 1960—64; freelance writer Houghton Lake, Mich., 1965; 5th grade tchr. Houghton Lake Elem. Sch., 1965—66; grad. asst. Ctrl. Mich. U., Mt. Pleasant, 1966—67, instr. journalism, advt., composition, 1967—68; English tchr. Houghton Lake Schs., 1965—94. Writing cons. Writing Doctor, Roscommon, Mich., 1994—2002; supply pastor various denominations, Mich., 1965—2001. Author: Enjoy The Christian Life, 1966, 2d edit., 1971, Meditations for Teachers, 1974 (1st prize humorous poetry, Poetry Soc. Mich.), Christian Heroes of Today, 1964, Happy Anniversary, with Wife, 1975, Your Journey into Joy, 2002, (poetry) ABC's for Educators, Fragments of Faith and Failure, 2003; editor: Pure Mountain Air, 1979, (student poems) STARS STARS STARS, 1977. Mem. Kiwanis, Minco, Okla., 1958—60. Mem.: Mich. Edn. Soc., Nat. Edn. Assn., Kappa Tau Alpha. Republican. Episcopalian. Achievements include first to introduce rollercoaster poems in Language Arts and the English Jour. Avocations: travel, writing, walking, reading. Home: 519 W Higgins Lake Dr Roscommon MI 48653

MAINWARING, SCOTT PATTERSON, political scientist, educator; b. July 18, 1954; s. William Thomas and Camille Brent Mainwaring; m. Susan M. Elfin, Aug. 9, 1986; children: Benjamin E., Grace E. BA in Polit. Sci., MA in Polit. Sci. magna cum laude, Yale U., 1976; PhD in Polit. Sci., Stanford U., 1983. Asst. prof. govt. & internat. studies U. Notre Dame, Notre Dame, Ind., 1983—88, assoc. prof. govt. & internat. studies, 1988—93, prof. govt. & internat. studies, 1993—96, Eugene Conley prof. polit. sci., 1996—, chair polit. sci., 1996—97; dir. Kellogg Inst. Internat. Studies, 1997—2004. Mem. Coun. on Fgn. Rels., 1986-91; mem. rsch. coun. Internat. Fourm for Dem. Studies, Nat. Endowment for Democracy, Washington, 1994—; cons. The Ford Found., N.Y., Inter-Am. Dialogue, Washington, MacArthur Found., Chgo., Woodrow Wilson Ctr. for Scholars, Washington. Author: The Cath. Ch. and Politics in Brazil, 1986; co-editor: The Progressive Church in Latin America, 1989, Issues in Democratic Consolidation, 1992, Building Democratic Institutions: Party Systems in Latin America, 1995, Presidentialism and Democracy in Latin America, 1997; author: Rethinking Party Systems in the Third Wave of Democratization: The Case of Brazil, 1999; co-editor: Christian Democracy in Latin America, 2003, Democratic Accountability in Latin America, 2003. Recipient Hubert Herring prize Pacific Coast Coun. on Lat. Am. Studies, 1983-84; fellow Hoover Inst., 1990-91, Woodrow Wilson Ctr., 1995-96, Guggenheim, 2000. Mem. Am. Polit. Sci. Assn., Latin Am. Studies Assn. (treas. 1997-2000), Phi Beta Kappa. Office: Kellogg Inst 231 Hesburgh Ctr Notre Dame IN 46556-5677 Office Phone: 574-631-8530. Business E-Mail. SMainwaring@nd.edu.

MAINWARING, THOMAS LLOYD, management consultant, former motor freight company executive; b. Cleve., Aug. 25, 1928; s. Hugh Trevor and Mary Beatrice (Ottman) M.; m. Gladys Fraser Mehr, June 10, 1983; children by previous marriage— Kevin, James, Eileen, Scott, Bruce BA, Albion Coll., 1950; MBA, Western Res. U., 1958. C.P.A., Ohio. Controller Cleve. Cartage Co., 1959-61, v.p., treas., 1961-64; controller Associated Truck Lines, Inc., Vandenberg Ctr., Grand Rapids, Mich., 1964-69; v.p. fin. Associated Transport, Inc., N.Y.C., 1969-70, exec. v.p. fin. and adminstrn., 1970-72; pres. Ryder Truck Lines Inc., Jacksonville, Fla., 1972-78, exec. v.p., chief operating officer, 1978-81, chief exec. officer, 1981-84; pres. Freight System div. Ryder System Inc., Miami, Fla., 1984-86; cons. trucking industry affairs Arlington, Va., 1986-88; pres., chief oper. officer H & M Internat. Transp., Inc., 1989-91, vice chmn., 1991-92; transp. cons., 1992-93; pres., gen. mgr. E.I. Kane Intermodal Transport, Inc., Balt., 1993-95, vice chmn., 1995, transp. cons., 1996—99; COO, Am. C. of C. Execs., 0200—2001; mgmt. cons., 2002—03; treas. & CFO AICHI-USA 2005 World Expn., Inc., 2003—. Bd. dirs. Trucking Mgmt., Inc. Mem. exec. com. United Way Jacksonville, 1981-84; trustee Albion Coll., 1977; bd. dirs. Goodwill Industries North Fla. Served with AUS, 1950-53. Mem. Am. Trucking Assn. (nat. acctg. and fin. council 1964, pres. 1971, chmn. ATA Found. 1986-88, exec. com. 1985-88), Fla. Trucking Assn. (bd. dirs. 1973, pres. 1979), Am. Mgmt. Assn. (lectr. seminars), Jacksonville Area C. of C. (bd. govs., com. of 100, v.p. internat. 1984), Cen. and So. Motor Freight Tariff Assn. (bd. dirs. 1981-84, pres. 1983, exec. com. transp. rsch. bd. 1987-89), Sigma Nu. Home: Apt 334 South 1600 S Eads St Arlington VA 22202

MAINWARING, WILLIAM LEWIS, publishing company executive, author; b. Portland, Oreg., Jan. 17, 1935; s. Bernard and Jennie (Lewis) M.; m. Mary E. Bell, Aug. 18, 1962; children: Anne Marie, Julia Kathleen, Douglas Bernard. BS, U. Oreg., 1957; postgrad., Stanford U., 1957-58. With Salem (Oreg.) Capital Jour., 1958-76, editor, pub., 1962-76; pub. Oreg. Statesman, 1974-76; pres. Statesman-Jour. Co., Inc., Salem, 1974-76, Westridge Press, Ltd., 1977—, MediAmerica, Inc., Portland, 1981-96, CEO, 1988—91. Bd. dirs. MediAmerica, Inc. Author: Exploring the Oregon Coast, 1977, Exploring Oregon's Central and Southern Cascades, 1979, Exploring the Mount Hood Loop, 1992, Government, Oregon-Style, 1996, rev. edit., 1997, 99. Pres. Salem Beautification Coun., 1968, Marion-Polk County United Good Neighbors, 1970, Salem Social Svcs. Commn., 1978-79, Salem Hosp. Found., 1978-81, Maricou Hist. Found., 2002-03. 2d lt. AUS, 1958; capt. Res. Ret. Mem. Salem Area C. of C. (pres. 1972-73), Oreg. Symphony Soc. Salem (pres. 1973-75), Salem City Club (pres. 1977-78), Sigma Chi. Republican. Presbyterian. Home and Office: 1090 Southridge Pl S Salem OR 97302-5947 E-mail: Billmain00@aol.com.

MAIOLINI, GLORIA J. nurse case manager, poet, writer; d. Harriet Yvonne and Matthew Boyd; 1 child, Galen R. Young Jr. Assoc. in Sci. in Nursing, C.C. Allegheny County, 1990—94; BS in health arts, U. St. Frances, 1998—2000. Case mgr., Commn. Case Mgr. Cert./Ill., 2002, gerontol. nurse, Am. Nurses Credentialing Ctr./Washington DC, 1997. RN FMC Carswell, Bur. Prisons, Fort Worth, Tex., 1995—95, Heritage Shadyside Nursing Rehab Ctr., Pitts., 1996—99; unit mgr. St. Joseph's Nursing Rehab Ctr., Pitts., 1997—98; RN case mgr. Highmark Blue Shield, Pitts., 1998—. Author numerous poems in anthologies. Coord. United Way, Pittsburgh, 2000—03. Recipient Editor's Choice award/Outstanding Achievement Poetry, Poetry.com, 2001, Editor's Choice award/Internat. Poet Merit award, Internat. Libr. Poetry, 2002, Editor's Choice award/Outstanding Achievement Poetry, 2003, 2004, merit award, outstanding achievement award. Mem.: Acad. Cert. Case Mgr., Wis. Songwriter Assn. Internat., Internat. Soc. Poets, Broadcast Music (BMI), Internat. Songwriters Assn. Achievements include copyrights for 200 original songs and poems. Avocation: exercise. Office: Gz Jamz Recordz PO Box 22214 Pittsburgh PA 15222-3000 Office Phone: 412-496-7628. Personal E-mail: iwrktolive1@cs.com. E-mail: iwrktolive1@hotmail.com.

MAIORIELLO, RICHARD PATRICK, retired otolaryngologist; b. Mar. 17, 1936; s. Gesumino Theodore and Angelina (Del Rossi) M.; m. Susan Hemenway, Mar. 6, 1979; children: Gabriel, Angela, Richard. AB, U. Pa., 1960; MD, Jefferson Med. Coll., 1964; MS, Thomas Jefferson U., 1972. Diplomate Nat. Bd. Med. Examiners, Am. Bd. Otolaryngology. Commd. 2d lt. USAF, 1963, advanced through grades to col., 1977, ret., 1979; intern Keesler Hosp., 1965-67; chief flight medicine USAF Base, Bitburg, Fed. Republic Germany, 1965-68; resident in otolaryngology Thomas Jefferson Hosp., Phila., 1968-71, 72-73; dir. med. edn. Andrews AFB, 1974-78; assoc. prof. uniformed svcs. Univ. Health Scis., 1978-79; assoc. prof. Northeastern Ohio U. of Medicine, 1983—; mem. staff Aultman Hosp., 1979—; assoc. staff Timken Mercy Med. Ctr., 1981—, Union Hosp., 1988—; retired, 2001. Cons. otolaryngology to Surgeon Gen., 1977—; pres. Mid-Ohio Dressage Assn. With USNR, 1954-58. Decorated Air Force Commendation medal. Fellow ACS, Am. Soc. Head and Neck Surgery; mem. Am. Acad. Otolaryngology, Am. Acad. Facial Plastic and Reconstructive Surgery, Am. Assn. Cosmetic Surgery, Vail Cosmetic Surg. Soc., Hanoverian Soc. (exec. v.p.), U.S. Dressage Fedn. (chmn. all-breeds coun.), Centurion Club. Republican. Roman Catholic.

MAIR, BRUCE LOGAN, interior designer, company executive; b. Chgo., June 5, 1951; s. William Logan and Josephine (Lee) M. BFA, Drake U., 1973; postgrad., Ind. Wesleyan U., 1990—. Mgr., head designer Reifers of Indpls., 1973-79; pres. Interiors Internat., Indpls., 1979-87; sr. designer Kasler Group, Indpls., 1987-89; dir. devel. Tillery Interiors and Imports, Greenwood, Ind., 1990, v.p. Indpls., 1990-92; owner Mair Interior Design Group, Indpls., 1992—. Pres. Tokens Inc., Indpls., 1982-88, Meg-A-Watt Enterprises Inc., Indpls., 1985-87, Luxury Ice Creams Inc., Indpls., 1986-87. Cover designer Indpls. Home and Garden mag., 1978, feature designer 1980; feature designer Builder mag., 1979; co-designer feature Indpls. At Home mag., 1979. Campaigner Anderson for Pres., 1980. Mem. Am. Soc. Interior Designers (profl., treas. Ind. chpt. 1982-83, Pres. awards 1981-82), U.S. Rowing Assn. (master 1987—), St. Joseph Hist. Neighborhood Assn., Columbia Club (rowing crew coxswain 1986—), Highland Model A Club, Tower Harbor Yacht Club (Douglas, Mich.), Royal Palm Yacht Club Ft. Myers, Alpha Epsilon Pi. Avocations: sculling, historic preservation, model a ford restoration, fishing, farming. Office: Mair Interior Design Group 1716 Fowler St Fort Myers FL 33901 E-mail: BruceMairID@aol.com.

MAIR, CHARLES, social studies educator; b. Evansville, Ind., Jan. 14, 1953; s. Charles David Mair and Alvetta Rose Ricker; m. Debra Lee Sharp-Mair, Aug. 10, 1973; children: Ashley Brocke Mair-Davis, McKenzie Nicole. BA in Social Studies, Ky. Wesleyan, 1975; MA in Social Studies, U. Evansville, 1980. Life lic. social sci. tchr., Ind. Tchr. social studies New Hon. H.S., New Harmony, Ind., 1975—77, North Posey H.S., Poseyville, Ind., 1977—2003. Mem. Ind. Basketball Coaches Assn., named Dist. Five Coach of Yr., 1987, Ind. Coaches Girls Sports Assn.; Nat. Edn. Assoc. Ind. State Tchrs. Assn. Republican. Protestant. Achievements include 25 years varsity girls basketball coach: 7 sectional: 1-Regional and 8 Conference Championships, 309 Career wins; Baseball-1 sectional championship, football one sectional, one regional and 2 conference championships.

MAISANO, PHILLIP NICHOLAS, investment company executive; b. Newark, May 15, 1947; s. Salvatore and Mary (Vella) M.; m. Mary-Alice Yanch, Aug. 10, 1968; children: Phillip, Matthew. BA, Belmont (N.C.) Abbey Coll., 1969; MBA, Iona Coll., 1976; postgrad., NYU Law Sch., 1972-73, Columbia U., summer 1987; LLD (hon.), Belmont Abbey Coll., 1999. CLU. Asst. v.p. The Equitable, N.Y.C., 1969-79; v.p. Manhattan Life Ins. Co., N.Y.C., 1979-81, MONY Fin. Svcs., Purchase, N.Y., 1981-88, sr. v.p., 1989—; pres. EACM Advisors, A Mellon Fin. Co., Norwalk, Conn., 1988—; chmn., CEO Evaluation Assocs. Inc., 1996; incorporator New Dartmouth Bank, Hanover, N.H., 1991—. Trustee Belmont Abbey Coll., 1992—; bd. advisors Hagan Sch. of Bus. Iona Coll. Contbr. articles to profl. publs. 1st lt. USAR.

Mem.: Mem. Investment Mgmt. Cons. Assn. (chmn. adv. bd. 2000—). Roman Catholic. Avocations: football coaching, softball, running, golf, skiing. Home: 6 Charlotte Ct Montvale NJ 07645-1005 Office: 200 Connecticut Ave Norwalk CT 06854-1940

MAISEL, SHERMAN JOSEPH, economist, educator; b. Buffalo, July 8, 1918; s. Louis and Sophia (Beck) M.; m. Lucy Cowdin, Sept. 26, 1942; children: Lawrence C., Margaret L. AB, Harvard U., 1939, M.P.A., 1947, PhD, 1949. Mem. bd. govs. FRS, 1965-72; economist, fgn. service res. officer Dept. State, 1945-46; teaching fellow Harvard U., 1947-48; asst. prof., assoc. prof., prof. bus. adminstrn. U. Calif. at Berkeley, 1948-65, 72-86; sr. economist Nat. Bur. Econ. Research-West, 1973-78; chmn., bd. dirs. Farmers Savings & Loan, 1986-88; pres. Sherman J. Maisel & Asscs. Inc., 1986—. Fellow Fund For Advancement Edn., 1952-53, Inst. Basic Math. with Application to Bus., 1959-60, Center for Advanced Study in Behavioral Scis., 1972; mem. adv. coms. to Bur. Census, FHA, State of Calif., Ford Found., Social Sci. Research Council; mem. bldg. research adv. bd. NRC. Author: Housebuilding in Transition, 1953, Fluctuations, Growth, and Forecasting, 1957, Managing the Dollar, 1973, Real Estate Investment and Finance, 1976, Risk and Capital Adequacy in Commercial Banks, 1981, Macroeconomics: Theories and Policies, 1982, Real Estate Finance, 1987, 2d edit., 1992. Bd. dirs. Berkeley Unified Sch. Dist., 1962-65. Served to capt. AUS, 1941-45. Mem. Am. Fin. Assn. (pres. 1973), Am. Econ. Assn. Home: 2164 Hyde St San Francisco CA 94109-1788 Office: U Calif Haas Bus Sch Berkeley CA 94720-1900

MAISTO, JOHN F. ambassador; b. Braddock, Pa., Aug. 28, 1938; married; 3 children. BSFS, Georgetown U., 1961; MA, San Carlos Coll., Guatemala, 1962. With BiNational Ctr., Cordoba, Argentina, 1963-66; asst. cultural affairs officer USIA, Cochabamba, Bolivia, 1966-68; with Fgn. Svc., 1968—; adminstrv. asst. Fgn. Svc. Inst. Dept. State, 1968-69; econ. and comml. officer U.S. Embassy, La Paz, Bolivia, 1969-71; internat. rels. officer Ops. Ctr., 1971-72; spl. asst. Office of Counselor, 1972-73; internat. rels. officer office Andean affairs, bur. inter-Am. affairs Dept. State, 1973-75; polit. officer U.S. Embassy, San Jose, Costa Rica, 1975-78, Manila, 1978-82; dep. dir. office Philippine affairs, bur. East Asian and Pacific affairs Dept. State, 1982-84, dir., 1984-86; dep. chief of mission and charge d'affaires Am. Embassy, Panama, 1986-89; dep. permanent U.S. rep. to OAS, 1989-92; dep. asst. sec. state for Ctrl. Am. and Panama U.S. Dept. State, 1992-93; U.S. amb. to Nicaragua, 1993-96; U.S. amb. to Venezuela, 1997—2000; fgn. policy advisor U.S. so. commd., 2000—01; spl. asst. to Pres., sr. dir. for western hemisphere affairs Nat. Security Coun., 2001—03; U.S. permanent rep. to OAS U.S. Dept. State, Washington, 2003—. Office: Harry S Truman Bldg 2201 C St NW Rm 5914 Washington DC 20520

MAIT, JOSEPH N. electrical engineer, educator; b. N.Y.C., Nov. 16, 1958; s. Martin Benjamin and Lila Mait; m. Elisabeth Anna Bauer, Mar. 3, 1960; children: Sonja Miriam Bauer, Simon Adler, Leon Jakob. BSEE, U. Va., 1979; MSEE, Ga. Inst. Tech., 1980, PhD, 1985. Asst. prof. U. Va., Charlottesville, 1984—89; sr. rschr. US Army Rsch. Lab., Adelphi, Md., 1988—. Vis. prof. U. Erlangen-Nuremburg, Germany, 1986, 90; adj. assoc. prof. U. Md., College Park, 1997—; sr. rsch. fellow Nat. Def. U., Washington, 2001—. Fellow: SPIE, Optical Soc. Am. Office: US Army Rsch Lab 2800 Powder Mill Rd Adelphi MD 20783-1197 E-mail: jmait@arl.army.mil.

MAITLAND, GUY EDISON CLAY, lawyer; b. London, Dec. 28, 1942; (mother Am. citizen); s. Paul and Virginia Francesca (Carver) M. BA, Columbia U., 1964; JD, N.Y. Law Sch., 1968. Bar: N.Y. 1969, U.S. Dist. Ct. (so. and ea. dists.) N.Y. 1969, U.S. Ct. Appeals (2d and D.C. cirs.) 1969. Assoc. Burlingham, Underwood & Lord, N.Y.C., 1969-74; admiralty counsel Union Carbide Corp., N.Y.C., 1974-76; exec. v.p., gen. counsel, officer Liberian Svcs., Inc., N.Y.C. and Reston, Va., 1976-99; pres. Trust Co. of the Marshall Islands, Inc., 1990—; mng. ptnr. Internat. Registries, Inc., 2000—. Del. UN Conf. on Trade and Devel., Manila, 1979, Belgrade, 1983; participant London Conf. on Limitation of Maritime Liability, 1976; mem. legal com. Internat. Maritime Orgn. (UN) London, 1980—; del. UN Conf. on Law of the Sea, 1976-82, London UN Maritime Law Conf., 1984; co-founder The Admiralty-Fin. Forum, N.Y.C., 1986; mng. ptnr. Internat. Registries, Inc. Contbr. articles on maritime law, U.S. shipping policy. Mem. N.Y. Rep. State Exec. Com., 1974-76; del. Rep. Nat. Conv., Kansas City, 1976; sec. N.Y. Rep. County Com., 1976-87, vice chmn., 1988—, mem. exec. com., 1974-76; co-chmn. Citizens for Reagan, N.Y. State, 1979-80; trustee Am. Mcht. Marine Mus. Found. at U.S. Mcht. Marine Acad., King's Point, Nat. Maritime Hist. Soc., chmn., 2000-01; trustee N.Y. Maritime Coll. at Ft. Schuyler Found., Inc.; bd. dirs. Coast Guard Found.; del. UN Geneva Conf. on Arrest of Vessels, 1999; bd. dirs. Seamen's Ch. Inst., N.Y.C., Ctr. for Seafarers Rights; mem. adv. com. Am. Maritime History Project. Named Outstanding Young Man of Am. U.S. Jaycees, 1975; hon. del Rep. Nat. Conv., Dallas, 1984. Mem. ABA, Assn. of Bar of City of N.Y. (chmn. admiralty com. 1982-85), Maritime Law Assn. U.S. (chmn. com. on intergovtl. orgns. 1987-95), Ctr. for Seafarer's Rights Seamen's Ch. Inst. (bd. dirs. 1995—), Maritime Assn. Port of N.Y. (dir. 1984-87, 98—, pres. 1999-2001). Office: Internat Registries Inc 11495 Commerce Park Dr Reston VA 20191-1507

MAITLAND, MARGARET TODD, editor; b. Madison, Wis., Nov. 18, 1947; d. David Johnston Maitland and Daniel Francis Green; m. Daniel Francis Bachhuber, Sept. 11, 1982; 1 child, Peter Bachhuber. BA, Lawrence U., 1969; postgrad., Mpls. Coll. Art & Design, 1972—74; MFA, Bennington Coll., 1999. Registrar, cataloguer Rianegol's Inst. Arts, Mpls., 1974—83; freelance writer, 1983—88; mng. editor Hungry Mind Rev., St. Paul, 1989—99; editor Ruminator Rev., 2000—03. Fellow, Bush Found., St. Paul, 1989, 1999, Minn. State Arts Bd., 1981, 1985. Mem.: Nat. Book Critics Cir. Office: Ruminator Rev 1648 Grand Ave Saint Paul MN 55105 E-mail: todd@ruminator.com.

MAITLAND-LEWIS, STEPHEN, writer; b. London, Nov. 22; s. Philip and Esther Maitland-Lewis; m. Stephanie Helen Caplan, July 30, 1966 (div.); m. Monika Charlotte Datzmann, May 14, 1982 (div.); children: Victoria, Benjamin Felix, Toby James. LLB with honors, Sheffield U., Eng., 1966, LLM, 1970. Solicitor of Supreme Ct.: Gt. Britain 1969. Gen. mgr. Internat. Fin. Advisors, Kuwait City, Kuwait, 1980—82; chmn. Fine Art Funds Inc., N.Y.C., 1982—85, Basford & Davis, Inc., N.Y.C., 1982—2000; v.p. Salomon Bros., N.Y.C., 1987—88, Security Pacific Mcht. Bank, N.Y.C., 1988—91; dir. AMIFS, N.Y.C., 1988—91; chmn. European Country Inns, Inc., Palm Springs, Calif., 1990—94; writer The Daily Jour., L.A., 2001—. Cons. Lazard Freres & Co., N.Y.C., 1984—87. Author: (novel) Hero on Three Continents, Enemies on Three Continents; contbr. articles on jazz and banking. Various positions Conservative Party, Westminster, 1969—80. Mem.: The Law Soc. (Eng.), Friars Club (Calif.). Jewish. Avocations: music (jazz), biography, art, theater, history. Home: 9903 Santa Monica Blvd Ste # 493 Beverly Hills CA 90212 Address: 100 S Sunrise Way # 500 Palm Springs CA 92262

MAITOZA, COLLEEN, professional sports team executive; Gen. mgr., co-owner Sacramento (Calif.) Sirens, 2001—. Achievements include an undefeated 2003 season in the Independent Women's Football League; the Sacramento Sirens won the 2003 Independent Women's Football League Championship against the New York Sharks. Office: Sacramento Sirens PO Box 15920 Sacramento CA 95813-9998

MAIWURM, JAMES JOHN, lawyer; b. Wooster, Ohio, Dec. 5, 1948; s. James Frederick and Virginia Anne (Jones) M.; m. Wendy S. Leeper, July 31, 1971; children: James G., Michelle K. BA, Coll. Wooster, 1971; JD, U. Mich., 1974. Bar: Ohio 1974, D.C. 1986, Md. 1987, N.Y., 1987. Ptnr. Squire, Sanders & Dempsey, Cleve. and Washington, 1974-90; ptnr., group head Crowell & Moring, Washington, 1990-98; ptnr. Squire, Sanders & Dempsey, Washington, 1998-99; chmn., CEO Kaiser Group Internat., Inc., Fairfax, Va., 1999-2000; mng. ptnr. Squire, Sanders & Dempsey, Washington, 2001—03, firmwide mng. ptnr., 2003—. Bd. dirs. Kaiser-Hill Co., LLC, Kaiser Group Holdings Inc., George Mason U. Coll. Visual and Performing Arts, Trax Internat., Inc. Contbr. articles to profl. jours. Mem. ABA, D.C. Bar Assn., Leadership Washington, The Tower Club (bd. govs. 2003—). Home: 9419 Brian Jac Ln Great Falls VA 22066-2002 Office: Squire Sanders & Dempsey LLP 14th fl 8000 Towers Crescent Vienna VA 22182

MAIZE, JOHN CHRISTOPHER, dermatologist, educator; b. Elizabeth, N.J., July 23, 1943; s. Donald Adam and Caroline Marie (Costanzo) Maize; m. Janice Lee Bentley, May 21, 1966; children: Sandra Kristine Tolly, John C. Jr., Jennifer Lee. MD, U. Mich., 1968. Cert. Am. Bd. Dermatology. Intern U. Mich., Ann Arbor, 1968—69, residency in dermatology, 1968—72; asst. prof. dermatology SUNY, Buffalo, 1972—77, assoc. prof., 1977—80, Med. U. of S.C., Charleston, 1980—83, prof., 1983—89, prof., chmn. dept. dermatology, 1989—. Author: Pigmented Lesions of the Skin, 1987, Cutaneous Pathology, 1998. Fellow: Am. Soc. Dermapathology (pres. 1995), Am. Acad. Dermatology; mem.: Am. Bd. Dermatology (dir. 1990—99, pres. 1999), S.C. Dermatol. Assn. (pres. 2001), S.C. Med. Assn., Internat. Soc. Dermatopathology (sec. 1987—89, pres. 1989—91), Am. Dermatol. Assn. Roman Catholic. Avocations: fishing, golf, travel. Office: Med U SC 171 Ashley Ave Charleston SC 29425-0001

MAIZEL, ROY, federal agency administrator; BA in Polit. Sci., U. Rochester, 1979, MS in Pub. Policy Analysis, 1981. Dir. resource mgmt. divsn. Office of Space Sci. NASA, Washington, 1997—, presdl. mgmt. intern Office Space Flight, 1981, various program analyst positions, 1981—87, various mgmt. positions space shuttle, space sta. and mission to planet earth programs, 1988—97. Office: NASA Hdqrs Mail Code S 300 E St SW Washington DC 20546

MAJAK, ROGER, administration executive; b. Hammond, Ind., July 14, 1941; BS in Journalism, Northwestern U., 1964; MA in Internat. Rels., Ohio U., 1967; postgrad., Ohio State, 1964-67. Chief of staff Janathan B. Bingham, Washington, 1969-74; staff dir. House subcom. on internat. econ. policy and trade House Fgn. Affairs, Washington, 1975-85; mgr. fed. govt. affairs office Tektronix, Inc., 1985-90; legis. dir. Powell, Goldstein, Frazer & Murphy, 1990-96; asst. sec. of commerce for export adminstrn. Dept. Commerce, Washington, 1997—. Congl. fellow Am. Polit. Sci. Assn. Office: Dept of Commerce Bur Export Adminstrn 14th And Constitution NW Washington DC 20230-0001

MAJDALANI, BRENDA J. prosecutor, educator; d. Ralph and Sharon Skinkiss; m. Badih John Majdalani (div.); 1 child, Amy; m. Mel J. Siedlecki Jr., Apr. 12, 2003; children: Mike Siedlecki, Melanie Siedlecki. EdB magna cum laude, U. Toledo, 1983, MBA, JD, 1988. Bar: Ohio 1989, U.S. Ct. Appeals (6th cir.) 1993, U.S. Supreme Ct. 1995. Litig. support clk. Owens-Ill. Inc., Toledo, 1986—90; pvt. practice Toledo, 1990—96; staff atty. U.S. Ct. Appeals (6th cir.), Toledo, 1993; asst. prosecutor Lucas County, Toledo, 1996—. Adj. instr. law U. Toledo Coll. Law, 2001—. Mem.: Ohio Bar Assn. Avocations: golf, bowling. Office: Lucas County Prosecutor's Office 700 Adams St Ste 250 Toledo OH 43624 Office Phone: 419-213-2001.

MAJDIC, MICHAEL JAMES, film producer, director; b. Peoria, Ill., Jan. 18, 1960; s. James Berwyn Majdic and Judy Kay Thompson. BA, U. of Ill., 1983; MA, U. of Ill. at Springfield, Springfield, Illinois, 1988. Producer-director (documentary) Roll on Columbia: Woody Guthrie and the Bonneville Power Administration (First Pl. Gold Camera Award, 33rd US Internat. Film & Video Festival, 2000). Pres., treas. Mid-Oregon Prodn. Arts network, Eugene, Oreg., 2001—04. Office: University of Oregon 1299 University of Oregon Eugene OR 97403 Office Phone: 541-346-1945. Personal E-mail: bkmaj@teleport.com. Business E-Mail: majdic@uoregon.edu.

MAJERS, ELIZABETH LOUISE, lawyer; b. Chgo., Sept. 25, 1958; m. Roger Daniel Majers Bonds; children: Katelyn Christine Majers, Kellyanne Louise Majers. BS, U. Ill., 1979; JD, Ind. U., 1982. Bar: Tex. 1982, Ill. 1983; CPA, Ill. Tax atty. Exxon Co., U.S.A., Houston, 1982-83; assoc. Chapman and Cutler, Chgo., 1983-90, ptnr., 1990-92, capital ptnr., 1992-97, McDermott, Will & Emery, Chgo., 1998—. Spkr. in field, 1983—. Fellow Am. Coll. Investment Counsel (past pres. 1995-97, pres., v.p. 1993-95, trustee 1991—). Avocations: golf, cooking, photography, travel. Office: McDermott Will & Emery 227 W Monroe St Ste 4400 Chicago IL 60606-5096 E-mail: emajers@mwe.com.

MAJERUS, PHILIP WARREN, physician; b. Chgo., July 10, 1936; s. Clarence Nicholas and Helen Louise (Mathis) Majerus; m. Janet Sue Brakensiek, Dec. 28, 1957; children: Suzanne, David, Juliet, Karen; m. Elaine Michelle Flansburg, 1996. BS, Notre Dame U., 1958; MD, Washington U., 1961. Resident in Medicine Mass. Gen. Hosp., Boston, 1961—63; research assoc. NIH, Bethesda, Md., 1963—66; asst. prof. biochemistry Washington U., St. Louis, 1966—75, asst. prof. medicine, 1966—69, assoc. prof. medicine, 1969—71, prof. medicine, 1971—, dir. div. hematology, 1973—, prof. biochemistry, 1976—. Mem. editl. bd. numerous jours. and profl. mags.; contbr. articles to profl. jours. Recipient Faculty Rsch. Assoc. award, Am. Cancer Soc., 1966—75, Disting. Career award for contbns. to hemostasis, Internat. Soc. for Thrombosis and Hemostasis, 1985, Alumni Faculty award, Washington U. Sch. Medicine, 1986, The Robert J. and Claire Pasarow Found. award, 1994, Bristol-Myers Squibb prize for cardiovascular rsch., 1998, numerous others. Fellow: ACP; mem.: Inst. of Medicine of NAS, Am. Soc. Clin. Investigation (pres. 1981—82), Am. Soc. Biol. Chemists, Am. Fedn. Clin. Rsch., Am. Soc. Hematology (pres. 1991), Assn. Am. Physicians, Am. Acad. Arts and Scis., Alpha Omega Alpha, Sigma Xi. Home: 7220 Pershing Ave Saint Louis MO 63130-4248 Office: Wash Univ Sch of Med Dept Int Med Saint Louis MO 63110

MAJESTY, MELVIN SIDNEY, psychologist, consultant; b. New Orleans, June 6, 1928; s. Sidney Joseph and Marcella Cecilia (Kieffer) M.; m. Bettye Newanda Gordon, Dec. 18, 1955; 1 child, Diana Sue. BA, La. State U., 1949; MS, Western Res. U., 1951; PhD (USAF Inst. Tech. fellow), Case-Western Res. U., 1967. Commd. 2d lt. USAF, 1951, advanced through grades to lt. col., 1968; program mgr., ast. dir. tng. rsch. Air Force Human Resources Lab., 1967-69; dir. faculty and profl. ednl. rsch. USAF Acad., 1969-72; dir. plot tng. candidate selection program Officer Tng. Sch., Air Tng.Command, 1972-76; ret. USAF, 1976; personnel selection cons. to Calif. State Pers. Bd., Sacramento, 1976-92. Patentee listening center; founded pers. testing for ballistic missile and space systems; directed largest study of fighter pilot selection since World War II; pioneered use of phys. testing as replacement for the maximum age requirement in law enforcement jobs; developed phys. fitness tests and established psychol. screening standards for state highway patrol officer and police officers; contbr. numerous articles to profl. publs. With U.S. Army, WWII, 1944-46, Korea, Vietnam, USAF, 1951-76. Decorated Commendation medal (2), Meritorious Svc. medal (2), Am. Campaign medal, WWII Victory medal, WWII Overseas Occupation medal, Ballistic Missile badge, numerous others. Mem.: DAV, VFW, APA, Mil. Officers Assn. Am., Am. Family Assn., Am. Legion, Mil. Order Fgn. Wars, Vietnam Vets. Am., Amvets, Bible Soc., Nat. Assn. Uniformed Svc. Avocation: being a grandfather. Office: 801 Capitol Mall Sacramento CA 95814-4806

MAJETTE, DENISE, congresswoman; b. Bklyn., May 18, 1955; d. Voyd and Olivia Majette; m. Rogers Mitchell Majette; 2 children. BA, Yale U., 1976; JD, Duke U., 1979. Atty. Legal Aid Soc. Winston-Salem, NC, 1981—83; law asst. Ga. Ct. Appeals, 1984—89; ptnr. Jenkins Nelson & Welch, 1989—92; spl. asst. atty. gen. State of Ga., 1991—92; adminstrv. law juste Ga. State Bd. Workers' Compensation, 1992; judge State Ct. of DeKalb County, 1993—2002; congresswoman 4th Dist. Ga. U.S. Ho. Reps., 2003—; mem. budget, edn. and workforce, and small bus. ho. coms. Grad. Leadership DeKalb, 1992; mem. Kidney Caucus; former com. mem. Miller Grove PTA; past mem. vestry Episcopal Ch. of Holy Cross; former pres. DeKalb Lawyers Assn.; mem. Childcare Com. YMCA, Decatur; mem. adv. bd. Jr. League DeKalb County; mem. Congl. Black Caucus, Congl. Caucus on India and Indian Ams.; mem. steward bd. Antioch AME Ch. Recipient Judge's Cmty. Recognition award, Black Law Students' Assn., Ga. State U. Coll. Law, 2001, You Go Girl award, Ga. Assn. Black Women Attys., 2003. Democrat. Office: 1517 Longworth House Office Bldg Washington DC 20515-1004*

MAJEV, HOWARD RUDOLPH, lawyer; b. N.Y.C., Dec. 10, 1952; s. Benny and Hela (Wolnowicz) M.; m. Janet Brandt; children: Brendan Joshua, Collin Campbell. BA, Johns Hopkins U., 1973; JD, U. Md., 1976. Bar: Md. 1978, D.C. 1995. Exec. asst. to city coun. pres. City of Balt., Balt., 1976-79; assoc. Weinberg and Green, Balt., 1979-84; ptnr. Weinberg & Green, Balt., 1985-94, Piper Rudnick LLP (formerly Rudnick & Wolfe), Washington, 1994—2001, Winston & Strawn LLP, Washington, 2001—. Author: (with K.S. Koenig) How to be a Legal Eagle: A Checklist for Remodelers, 1988; dir. Lex Mundi, 1992-94. Dir. Citizens Planning and Housing Assn., Balt., 1985-95, pres., 1990-92; bd. dirs. Md. Food Bank, Inc., 1988-92, Florence Crittenton Svcs. Balt., 1986-87, Sinai Hosp. Balt., 1990-92, Levindale Hebrew Geriat. Home and Hosp., 1991; devel. coun. The Kennedy Krieger Inst., 1988-92; participant Leadership-Greater Balt. Com., 1986. Mem. ABA, D.C. Bar Assn., Md. State Bar Assn. Avocations: tennis, reading. Office: Winston & Strawn LLP 1400 L St NW Washington DC 20005 Office Phone: 202-371-5781. Business E-Mail: hmajev@winston.com.

MAJEWSKI, ANTHONY, brokerage house executive; b. Detroit, Jan. 11, 1976; s. Lech and Patricia Majewski; m. Julie Reaume, Aug. 10, 2002. BS in Psychology, Western Mich. U., 2000. Lic. life, health and accident ins. NASD. Ind. fin. advisor Gt. Lakes Fin. Advisors, Grosse Pointe Woods, Mich., 2000—02; nat. dir. Gt. Lakes Distbn. & Brokerage, LLC, Algonac, Mich., 2002—. Author: America on the Move. Home: 7776 Farnsworth Dr Clay Twp MI 48001 Office: Gt Lakes Distbn & Brokerage LLC 9303 Stone Rd PO Box 444 Algonac MI 48001 Office Phone: 810-794-1300.

MAJMUDAR, BHAGIRATH, medical educator; b. Nadiad, India, Jan. 29, 1938; came to U.S., 1967; s. Nanubhai and Pramilaben (Trivedi) M.; m. Uma Mehta, May 24, 1962; children: Nija, Sangini. MB BS, B.J. Med. Coll., Ahmedabad, India, 1962, MD, 1966. Diplomate Am. Bd. Pathology; ordained Hindu priest, 1976. Asst. prof. pathology B.J. Med. Coll., 1966-67; chief resident in pathology Salem (Mass.) Hosp., 1967-69; instr. in pathology Ohio State U., Columbus, 1971-75; asst. prof. pathology Emory U., Atlanta, 1971-75, assoc. prof. pathology, 1975-85, assoc. prof. ob-gyn, 1978—, prof. pathology, 1985—. Lectr., trainer S.E. Regional Tng. Ctr., Atlanta, 1988-; lectr. in field. Contbr. articles to profl. publs. Mem. Interfaith Com., State of Ga., 1991-94, Interfaith Com. for Olympic Games, Atlanta, 1992-96; pres. India Am. Cultural Assn., Atlanta, 1976, chmn. bd. dirs., 1979. Recipient Outstanding Cmty. Svc. award India-Am. Cultural Assn., 1982. Fellow Coll. Am. Pathology, Internat. Acad. Pathology; mem. Soc. Med. Assn. (sec., chmn. 1992-95), Internat. Soc. for Study of Vulvovaginal Diseases, Arthur P. Soc. Surg. Pathologists, Internat. Soc. Gynecol. Pathology, Alpha Omega Alpha. Avocations: acting, directing and writing plays, writing, interfaith spirituality, global travel. Home: 3220 Olde Dekalb Way Atlanta GA 30340-4531 Office: Grady Health Sys Pathology Dept 80 Butler St SE Atlanta GA 30303-3031 Office Phone: 404-616-7445. E-mail: bmajmud@emory.edu.

MAJOR, CLARENCE LEE, poet, novelist, educator, artist; b. Atlanta, Dec. 31, 1936; s. Clarence and Inez (Huff) M.; m. Pamela Ritter, May 8, 1980. BS, SUNY, Albany; PhD, Union Inst. Prof. U. Colo., Boulder, 1977-89, U. Calif., Davis, 1989—. Author: All-Night Visitors, 1969, 2d version, 1998, Dictionary of Afro-American Slang, 1970, No, 1973, Reflex and Bone Structure, 1975, rev. edit., 1996, Emergency Exit, 1979, My Amputations, 1986, Such Was the Season, 1987, Painted Turtle: Woman with Guitar, 1987, Fun and Games, 1990, Calling the Wind, 1993, Juba to Jive: A Dictionary of African American Slang, 1994, Dirty Bird Blues, 1996; poetry: Swallow the Lake, 1970, Symptoms & Madness, 1971, Private Line, 1971, The Cotton Club, 1972, Inside Diameter: The France Poems, 1985, Painted Turtle, 1988, Surfaces and Masks, 1988, Some Observations of a Stranger at Zuni in the Latter Part of the Century, 1989, Parking Lots, 1992, The Garden Thrives, 1996, Configurations: New and Selected Poems, 1958-1998, 1998 (Nat. Book Award finalist 1999), Clarence Major and His Art: Portraits of an African American Postmodernist, 2001, Necessary Distance, 2001, Come By Here: My Mother's Life, 2002, Waiting for Sweet Betty, 2002, Conversations with Clarence Major, 2002, One Flesh, 2003; group shows include Kresge Mus., Mich., 2001, Schacknow Mus. Fine Art, Plantation, Fla., 2003; contbr. articles to Washington Post Book World, L.A. Times Book Rev., N.Y. Times Book Rev. Recipient Nat. Council on Arts award, Washington, 1970; Western States Book award, Western States Found., Santa Fe, 1986; Fulbright grantee, 1981-83. Office: U Calif Dept English 281 Voorhies Hall Davis CA 95616

MAJOR, COLEMAN JOSEPH, chemical engineer; b. Detroit, Sept. 7, 1915; s. Coleman I. and Anna (Galik) M.; m. Marjorie Lois Shenk, Nov. 21, 1941; children: Roy Coleman, Marilyn M. Phillips Bever. BS, U. Ill., 1937; PhD, Cornell U., 1941. Chief prodn. engr., supt. services Sharples Chems., Inc., Wyandotte, Mich., 1941-50; assoc. prof. chem. engring. U. Iowa, 1950-56; head high energy chems. Am. Potash & Chem. Corp., Whittier, Calif. and Henderson, Nev., 1956-59; prof. chem. engring. U. Iowa, 1959-64; prof., head dept. chem. engring. U. Akron, 1964-70; dean Coll. Engring., also dir. Inst. Technol. Assistance, 1970-80; dir. Inst. Biomed. Engring. Rsch., 1979-80; cons. computers. Contbr. articles to tech. jours.; patentee in field. Named Chem. Engr. of Yr., 1979; C.J. Major Scholarship award established in his honor, 1990; recipient Disting. Svc. award U. Akron, 1993. Fellow Am. Inst. Chem. Engrs.; mem. Am. Chem. Soc., Sigma Xi, Tau Beta Pi. Home: 7838 Jaymes St Dublin OH 43017-8812 *A few guidelines that I have used: 1. Work very hard but find time to relax. 2. Push yourself ahead, but don't hold anyone else back. 3. When gathering facts, be rigorous and unrelenting but when making decisions involving people, use the art of compromise.*

MAJOR, JOHN CHARLES, judge; s. William and Elsie M.; m. Hélène Provencher, 1959; children: Suzan, Peter, Paul, Steven. BComm, Loyola Coll., Montreal, 1953; LLB, U. Toronto, 1957. Bar: Alta. 1958, Queen's Counsel, 1972. With Bennett, Jones & Verchere, Calgary, 1957-91, sr. ptnr., 1967; sr. counsel City of Calgary Police Svc., 1975-85; counsel McDonald Commn., 1978-82; sr. counsel Province of Alta., 1987, Alta. Ct. Appeal, 1991; mem. Supreme Ct. of Can., Ottawa, Ont., 1992—. Fellow Am. Coll. Trial Lawyers; mem. Can. Bar Assn., Can. Inst. of the Adminstrn. of Justice, Can. Judges Conf., The Glencoe Club (Calgary), Calgary Golf and Country Club, Ottawa Hunt and Golf Club. Avocation: golf. Office: Supreme Court of Can Wellington St Ottawa ON Canada K1A 0J1

MAJOR, PATRICK WEBB, III, principal; b. Wai, Maharastra, India, Mar. 12, 1947; s. Patrick W. Jr. and Alice (Seeland) M.; m. Daphnelynn Jantz, June 26, 1971; children: Mindy Joy, Matthew Patrick Webb. BA in BE, Columbia Internat. U., 1969; BA, Biola U., 1972; MA, Point Loma Nazarene U., 1979; postgrad., U. Calif., Irvine. Cert. secondary tchr., adminstr., Calif. Prin. Omega High Sch., Bakersfield, Calif., 1980-84; headmaster Bakersfield Christian Life Schs., 1984-86; prin. North Kern Christian Sch., Wasco, Calif., 1986-88; prin., adminstr. Yucaipa (Calif.) Christian Schs., 1988-2000; prin. Christian H.S., El Cajon, Calif., 2000—03; adminstr. First Bapt. Ch. of Lakewood (Calif.) Schs., 2003—. Chmn. ACSI So. Calif. Accreditation Commn., 1998-2003. Mem. ASCD, Assn. Christian Schs. Internat. (former dist. rep., exec. bd. 1992-2001), Ctrl. Redwood League (pres. 1985-86), CIF Ctrl Sect., Internat. Fellowship Christian Sch. Adminstrs.

MAJORE, FRANK, artist; b. Richmond Hill, NY, Feb. 9, 1948; s. Frank John and Anna Majore; life ptnr. Beverly Weinstein. BS, Phila. Coll. Art, 1965—69. One-man shows include Between Heaven and Earth, Internat. Ctr Photography, NY, Frank Majore: Dreamsville, John and Mable Ringling Mus. Art, Sarasota, Fla., Biennial Exhbn., Whitney Mus. Am. Art, exhibited in group shows at Pleasures and Terrors of Domestic Comfort, Mus. Modern Art, NY, The Photography of Invention: Am. Pictures of the 1980's, Nat. Mus. of Am. Art, Washington. Recipient Tiffany award, Louis Comfort Tiffany Found., 1993; fellow Photography Fellowship, NY Found. Arts, 1985, Aaron Siskind Found., 1993, John Simon Guggenheim Found., 1996. Personal E-mail: fmajore@verizon.net.

MAJORKUMAR, GOVINDARAJU, human factors engineer; b. Bangalore, Karnataka, India, Apr. 20, 1964; s. Govindaraju Mallappan and Sarada Ramasamy; m. Anitha Anithabose Subashchandrabose, June 8, 1995; 1 child,

Nikhil Amarnath Kumar. PhD, U. Cin., 1993—99; MTech, Indian Inst. Tech., New Delhi, 1988; B in Engring., Nat. Inst. Tech., Trichirapalli, India, 1985. Engring. cons. Tech. Mgmt. Services, Cleve., 1999—2000; sr. human factors engr. Intel Corp., Folsom, Calif., 2000—; tchg. and rsch. asst. U. of Cin., 1993—99; rsch. scholar Indian Inst. of Tech., Chennai, India, 1989—93. Editl. bd. mem. Internat. Jour. of Indsl. Engineering-Theory, Applications and Practice, Cin., 1999—; jour. reviewer Internat. Jour. of Indsl. Ergonomics, Elsevier Publications, NY, 1993—; book reviewer Internat. Jour. of Indsl. Engring. - Theory, Applications and Practice, 1993—; reviewer, jour. of applied ergonomics Internat. Ergonomics Assn., United Kingdom; reviewer, disability and rehab. jour. Taylor and Francis, London; vice-chairman, autofact conf. Soc. of Mfg. Engineers, Detroit, 1997; reviewer, advances in occupl. ergonomics and safety Internat. Soc. for Occupational Health and Safety, Zurich, Switzerland, 1995. Author: (book chapter) Effects of exercise on physical and psychological preparedness of chronic heart disease patients for work: A review (in Perspectives in Rehabilitation, pp. 95-123, Taylor and Francis, UK), Reach design data for the elderly (in Designing for an Aging Population: Ten Years of Human Factors/Ergonomics Research, Human Factors and Ergonomics Society, pp. 65-69, 1997), Rehabilitation in International Journal of Industrial Engineering: Users' Encyclopedia (CD ROM), Industrial Inspection in Industrial and Occupational Ergonomics: Users' Encyclopedia (CD ROM). Blood donor BloodSource, Sacramento, Calif., 2003. Recipient Nat. Merit Scholarship, Govt. of India, 1981-1988, Gold Medalist, Bd. of Secondary Edn., Chennai, India, 1979, PCS Recognition Award, Intel Corp., 2003, Employee Svc. Achievement Award, 2002; scholar U. Grad. Scholarship, U. of Cin., 1993-1998, Rsch. and Tchg. Assistantship, 1993-1997. Mem.. Soc. of Mfg. Engineers, Human Factors and Ergonomics Soc., Alpha Pi Mu Honor Soc. Achievements include developing a new methodolgy using Rate Pressure Product Measurments (RPP) to evaluate the mental and physical load of worker stress; developing a new framework to evaluate the bus. value of investments in info. tech. in a co; conducting a unique job-simulated cardiac rehab. program that improved the return-to-work ratio from a value of 62% for conventional programs to 100% for the new program, performing a field study on elderly population and obtained functional reach design data that could be used for designing safe and accessible work and home environments for the aged; developing a new procedure for designing and developing usable consumer products by linking the usability and manufacturing attributes; making several presentations in the reputed internat. and nat. confs. in the field of Human Factors Engring. and Ergonomics; publishing articles in various journals and magazines. Home: 1162 Scheidegger Cir Folsom CA 95630 Office: Intel Corporation 1900 Prairie City Road ML: FM7-186 Folsom CA 95630 Office Phone: 916-356-5027. Personal E-mail: majorkumar@hotmail.com. E-mail: majorkumar.govindaraju@intel.com.

MAJORS, JAMES EDWARD, electrical engineer; b. Honolulu, Hawaii, Sept. 25, 1959; s. Edward Thomas and Shirley Anne Majors. Elec. designer The Boeing Co., Seattle, 1979—93, 1996—. Recipient Editors Choice award, Modern Poetry Soc., 1995, Silver Bowl Merit award, Internat. Soc. Poets, 2002, Bronze Medallion award, 2002. Avocations: song writing, instrumental performance, music recording. Home: 125 Wells Ave N Renton WA 98055

MAJORS, NELDA FAYE, physical therapist; b. Houston, Aug. 3, 1938; d. Columbus Edward and Mary (Mills) M. Cert. in Phys. Therapy, Hermann Sch. Phys. Therapy, Houston, 1960; BS, U. Houston, 1963. Lic. phys. therapist, Tex. Staff therapist Tex. Med. Ctr. Hermann Hosp., Houston, 1960-61; phys. therapist Chelsea Orthopedic Clinic, Houston, 1961-63; dir. phys. therapy Meml. Hosp. Southwest, Houston, 1963-75; owner, pres. Nelda Majors, Inc., Houston, 1975—. Mem. profl. adv. bd. Logos Home Health Agy., Houston, 1985-86; adv. dir. Prime Bank, Houston; sec.-treas., bd. dirs. Dominion Media Corp. Ptnr. Houston Proud Ptnr., 1986—; founder, pres. Instnl. Safety Advs. Inc., 1994—; bd. dirs. Texans for the Improvement of Long Term Care Facilities, 1995—; active St. Stephens Episcopal Ch., 2001—; trustee St. Stephen's Episc. Sch., Houston. Named All Am. Softball Pitcher, Amateur Softball Assn., 1964, All-Regional and All-State Pitcher, Tex. Amateur Softball Assn., 1954-70; named to Houston Amateur Softball Assn. Softball Hall of Fame, 1994, Houston Softball Legends Hall of Fame, 2002. Mem. Am. Phys. Therapy Assn. (pvt. practice sect.), Ams. for Separation of Ch. and State, Tex. Phys. Therapy Assn., U. Houston Alumni Assn., E. Cullen Soc. (U. Houston), Rotary Club (Houston, Meml. Spring br.), Phi Kappa Phi. Clubs: U. Houston Cougar. Republican. Avocations: softball, bicycling, travel, golf, reading.

MAJUMDER, SABIR AHMED, process engineer; b. Chandpur, Bangladesh, July 15, 1957; came to U.S., 1986; s. Quashem Majumder and Momtaz Begum; m. Hamida Khanam, Dec. 15, 1985; children: Faryha, Nabilah, Abir. BS in Chemistry with honors, U. Dhaka, Bangladesh, 1981, MS, 1983, Duquesne U., 1988; PhD, U. N.Mex., 1994. Corr. The Daily Janapad, Dhaka, Bangladesh, 1973-74; rsch. fellow U. Dhaka, 1983-84, lectr. in Chemistry, 1984-86; teaching asst. Duquesne U., Pitts., 1986-88, U. N.Mex., Albuquerque, 1988-90; Assoc. Western Univs. grad. lab. fellow Sandia Nat. Labs., Albuquerque, 1991-93, postdoctoral fellow, 1994-96, U. Minn., Mpls., 1997-98; sr. process engr. Aplex Inc., Sunnyvale, Calif., 1998—; rsch. scientist Strasbaugh, San Luis Obispo, Calif., 1999—; sr. process engr. Lam Rsch. Corp., Fremont, Calif., 2000. Contbr. articles to profl. jours. Gen. Sec. Bangladesh Youth Coun., Dhaka, 1982; mem. Nat. Student League Ctrl., Dhaka, 1983. Trainee Youth Leadership Tng. Inst., Singapore, 1981; recipient Link Energy Fellowship Link Found., Rochester, N.Y., 1987. Mem. Am. Chem. Soc., Bangladesh Chem. and Biol. Soc. N.Am. (elected gen. sec. 1993-94, pres. 1997-98, advisor 1999—), Electrochem. Soc. Democrat. Moslem. Achievements include patent disclosure: photocatalytic degradation of aromatic compounds by metalloporhyrins adsorbed into alumina using visible light. Home: 43964 Cerro Ct Fremont CA 94539-6301

MAJZIK, WILLIAM, accountant, writer; BSBA, Youngstown State U., 1989. Author: (fiction/novel) The Renewal, First Encounter (First of a trilogy); contbr. articles to profl. jours. With USAF, 1975—79. Scholarships, Youngstown Found., 1980-1984, Grad. Assistantship, youngstown State U., 1987-1988. Achievements include assisting Donald Gacura with research and writing of a geology text. Home: PO Box 90134 Youngstown OH 44509 Personal E-mail: ian@ianjcue.com.

MAK, BEN BOHDAN, engineer; b. Chortkiw, Ukraine, June 11, 1926; s. Iwan and Antonya (Smerechynská) M. Student, U. Cracow (Poland) Poly., Friburg U., Ukrainian Tech. Husbandry Inst, U. Miami, War Coll.; MSME, MS in Mgmt. Engring., MS in Ordnance Engring., MBA, MS in Value Engring., N.J. Inst. Tech. Registered profl. engr.; cert. plant engr. Design engr., engring. mgr. Bernard & Burk-Huston Corp., Miami, Fla., 1956-60; instr. value engring. U. Miami, Fla., 1959-60; prof. ordnance engring., logistic armament Air Force Inst. Tech.; gen. engr., mgr. Wiz Kids; engring. mgr. Sec. Def. Office Dept. Def., 1961-69; v.p. engring. Metal Improvement Co. and Valiant Metal Products Co., 1969-78; engring. mgr. Coll. Medicine and Dentistry N.J., 1978-82; dean facilities, engr., arch. Dutchess C.C., 1982-89; pvt. practice cons. mgmt., engring., mktg., 1970—. Author: Value Engineering, 1963, Bomb Fragmentation, 1964, Value Analysis for Industry, 1965, Sydor-Shelest, 1996, UPA Officer School, 1998; contbr. articles to profl. jours. 1st lt. army USSR, WWII, Ukrainian Insurgent Army, 1945-48. Recipient awards and merit citations U.S. Army, USN, USAF, Sec. of Def., Pres.'s office, univs. Mem. NSPE, ASME, Assn. Phys. Plant Adminstrs. of Univs., Soc. Cert. Plant Engrs., Ukrainian Engrs. Soc. Am., Assn. Energy Engrs., Ordnance Assn., APPA, others. Avocations: architecture, history.

MAK, WING KWONG TONY, life insurance executive, training consultant; b. Hong Kong, Mar. 2, 1952; s. Man Mak and Jun Poon; m. Kam Amy Tse, Dec. 25, 1979; children: Emily Sui Wo, Fiona Sui Wah. B of Social Sci. (hon.), Chinese U. of Hong Kong, 1976. Tchr. St. Joannes Coll., Hong Kong, 1976-77; dist. dir. Am. Internat. Assurance (Bermuda) Ltd., Hong Kong, 1977—. Chmn. Tony Cons. Ltd., Hong Kong, 1994—; bd. dirs. Faith Asia Cons. Ltd.; cons. Consultancy De Excel, Kuala Lumpur, Malaysia, 1992—; hon. advisor Elite Children Tng. Ctr., Kuala Lumpur, 1997—. Chmn. Ins. Tng. Bd. of Hong Kong Govt., 1992—; vice chmn. Hong Kong Amateur Handball Assn., 1984-88, Lion's Club of Hong Kong, 1987; mem. adv. com. Humanities Program Hong Kong Baptist U., 2000—. Mem. Life Underwriters Assn. of Hong Kong (pres. 1988-89), Life Underwriters Assn. Charitable Found. (vice chmn.), 4th Asia Pacific Life Ins. Congress (chmn. 1997). Office: 701 Island Pl Tower 510 King's Rd Hong Kong Hong Kong

MAKADOK, STANLEY, management consultant; b. N.Y.C., Mar. 30, 1941; s. Jack and Pauline (Speciner) Makadok; m. Neilia A. David, Nov. 12, 1989; 1 child from previous marriage, Richard. BME, CCNY, 1962; MS in sci. mgmt., Rutgers U., 1964. Bus. sys. analyst Westinghouse Electric Corp., Balt., 1964—65; project engr., corp. cons. Am. Cyanamid Corp., Pearl River, NY, Wayne, NJ, 1965—68; v.p., bus. devel. and planning Pepsico Inc. and affiliates, Purchase, NY, Miami, Fla., 1968—75; mgr. fin. and planning cons. Coopers & Lybrand, N.Y.C., 1975—77, pres. Century Mgmt. Cons., Inc., Princeton, NJ, 1977—. Contbr. articles to profl. jours. Office: Century Mgmt Cons Inc 32 Nassau St Princeton NJ 08542-4503

MAKALOU, OUMAR, economic advisor; b. Kita, Mali, 1934; s. Sambou and Coumba (Tounkara) M.; m. Morimoussou Koite, July 30, 1944; children: Modibo Mao, Kalle, Mamaye, Sambou, Coumba. BA in Law (Polit. Economy), Paris U., 1960, MA in Econs., 1968; PhD in Econs., U. Paris-Sorbonne, 1970. Insp. Fin. Services, Paris, 1956-60; pres. Devel. Bank, Bamako, Mali, 1961-63; state controller Office of Pres., Koulouba, Mali, 1963-68; dir. gen. Treasury Banks and Ins., Koulouba, 1968-71, Internat. Coop., Koulouba, 1971-73; chmn. bd. dirs. Cen. Bank, Bamako, Mali, 1973-77; chief of staff Office of Pres., Bamako; dep. dir. African dept. IMF, Washington, 1977 84; sr. advisor IMF Inst., Washington, 1984—; ret., 1993. Vis. prof. U. Montreal, Que., Canada, 1983; dir. gen. taxes, investments and credit Ministry of Fin., Mali, 1984—91; spl. advisor to Pres. of Mali, 1991—93; pres. Ctr. of Studies and Rsch. for Democracy, Econ. and Social Devel., 1993—2002; sr. fellow, disting. vis. prof. Sch. Pub. Policy George Mason U., 1997—2002. Author: Budget Equilibrium in Developing Countries, 1970, Privatization in Africa: A Critical Analysis, 1999. Named Grand Officer of the Cross of Merit, Fed. Republic of Germany, Officer of Merit Order of France, Officer and Knight of the Nat. Order of Mali. Fellow: Asian Inst. Mgmt. (Manila), Asian Inst. Tech. (Bangkok), mem. Soc. for Internat. Devel. (bd. dirs. 1986 90), Internat. Profl. Bankers' Assn., Nat. Economists Club (Washington). Avocations: reading, music, the arts. Home: 5915 Bradley Blvd Bethesda MD 20814-1106 Office: IMF 700 19th St NW Washington DC 20431-0001

MAKANSI, MUNZER, chemical engineer, researcher; b. Aleppo, Syria, Dec. 23, 1923; arrived in U.S., 1949; s. Ismail Makansi and Amina Khudari; m. Nellie M. Kotsakis, Jan. 2, 1951; children: Delal, Antar, Jason, Tarek. BS in Chemistry, U. Egypt, 1947; MA in Indsl. Chemistry, Columbia U., 1950, MS in Chem. Engring., 1951, PhD in Engring. Sci., 1957. Rsch. and tech. asst. Columbia U., N.Y.C., 1951—54; rsch. engr. E.I. Dupont DeNemours & Co., Wilmington, Del., 1954—62, sr. rsch. engr., 1962—64, rsch. supr., 1964—66, rsch. and devel. supr. Chattanooga, 1966—76, rsch. assoc., 1976—93; pres., founder Fiber Engring., Inc., Signal Mt., Tenn., 1994—. Author: (book) Periodic Classification of Elements, 1949, (tech. papers in jours.) Jour. Physical Soc., Textile Res. Jour., Textile Chems. and Colorists. Recipient Inventor of Yr., Chattanooga Engring. Soc., 1993. Achievements include patents for 11 inventions including; invention of True holographic fabrics, with colored holograms diffracted from fabric surface while maintaining inherent fabric properties intact; product for removing stubborn mildew stains without scrubbing; Remay non woven fabric. Home: 106 Stratford Way Signal Mountain TN 37377 Office: Fiber Engring Inc 106 Stratford Way Signal Mountain TN 37377

MAKARUK, HANNA EWA, theoretical physicist; b. Warsaw; d. Leszek Henryk and Halina (Wojnowska) M.; m. Robert Michal Owczarek. MSc, U. Warsaw, 1989; PhD summa cum laude, Polish Acad. Scis., 1994. Rsch. asst. Polish Acad. Scis. Inst. Fundamental Technol. Rsch., Warsaw, 1989—94, assoc. prof., 1994—; postdoctoral fellow Los Alamos Nat. Lab., 1996-98, tech. staff mem., 1999—. Lecturing prof. Polish Acad. of Scis., 1995—96. Referee Classical and Quantum Gravity, Jour. of Physics, Jour. of Tech. Physics, Reports on Math. Physics; reviewer Math. Revs.; contbr. articles to profl. jours. Fellowship Kosciuszko Found., N.Y.C., 1996, Japanese Soc. for the Promotion of Sci., 1995; rsch. grant Polish State Com. for Sci., Warsaw, 1995. Mem.: IEEE Computer Soc., IEEE, Inst. of Physics U.K., Am. Math. Soc., Polish Phys. Soc., Soc. for Indsl. and Applied Math., Polish Soc. for Applied Electromagnetics, Internat. Soc. for Interaction between Math. and Mechanics. Achievements include research in the description of conductivity in conducting polymers by multidimensional Dirac equation, spinor structure methods; new algebraic methods in strongly nonlinear problems and field theory; math. methods in theory of neural networks. Office: Los Alamos Nat Lab RRES-CE M 319 Los Alamos NM 87545-0001

MAKAU, JOHN, artist; b. Amsterdam, Jan. 27, 1927; s. Victor and Elisabeth (van Gyzelen) M.; m. Corry Saakes, 1962 (div. 1967); children: Desiree, Sandra, Petra; m. Lydia Catharina Amman, Apr. 1977. Owner Lyra Art Gallery & Studio, Sarasota, Fla., 1977—. Home: 5216 Creekside Trail Sarasota FL 34243

MAKEPEACE, MARY LOU, former mayor; 2 children. BA in Journalism, U. N.D.; MPA, U. Colo., Colorado Springs. Tchr. Am. Sch., Tananarive, Madagascar; asst. to Def. Attaché Am. Embassy, Prague, Czechoslavakia; adult edn. officer Ramstein AFB, Germany; case worker, adminstr. El Paso County Dept. Social Svcs., 1974-82; exec. dir. Cmty. Coun. Pikes Peak Region, 1982-84; dist. 1 rep. City Colorado Springs, 1985-97, vice mayor, 1997, mayor, 1997—2003; exec. dir. Leadership Pike's Peak, Colo. Springs, 2003—. Exofficio mem. Econ. Devel. Coun. Bd. Dirs.; chair Econ. Devel. Com., Task Force City Svcs. to Srs., urban affairs com. Pikes Peak Area Coun. Govts.; apptd. Colo. Space Adv. Coun.; adj. prof. U. Colo.; ex-dir. leadership Pikes Peak Mem. steering com. Imagination Celebration; sr. advisor Palmer Found., Pikes Peak Partnership; mem. Nat. League Cities Leadership Tng. Coun.; past mem. Colo. Mcpl. League Exec. Bd., 1st United Meth. Ch. Gates Found. fellow, 1992; recipient Svc. Mankind award Centennial Sertoma Club, 1985, Mary Jean Larson Cmty. Svc. award Girl Scouts Wagon Wheel Coun., 2002, Spence Vanderlin Pub. Ofcl. award Am. Pub. Power Assn., 2002, Outstanding Cmty. award Econ. Devel. Corp., 2003; named Super Woman Women's Health Ctr., 1988, Best City Councilmem. Springs Mag., 1991; honored Women in Your Life dinner Women's Found. Colo., 2002. Mem. Am. Soc. Pub. Adminstrn., Pi Alpha Alpha. Office: Leadership Pikes Peak 219 W Colorado Ave Colorado Springs CO 80903

MAKI, ALAN WALTER, biologist, environmental scientist; b. Winchendon, Mass., Aug. 8, 1947; s. Walter John and Lila Irene (Hackler) Maki; m. Ann Whitaker, Sept. 28, 1968; children: Geoffrey, Benjamin, Travis. BS, U of Mass., Amherst, Mass., 1969; MS, U of No. Tx, Denton, TX, 1971; PhD, MI State U, Ea. Lansing, MI, 1974. Cert. Fisheries Sci. Am. Fisheries Soc. Rsch. sci. Procter & Gamble, Cincinnati, Ohio, 1974—80; Environ. adv. Exxon Mobil, Ea. Milstone, NJ, 1980—, Anchorage, Ala., 1980—, Houston, 1980—. Pres./ bd. mem. Soc. of Environ. Toxicology and Chemistry, 1980—85; sci. adv. bd. US EPA, Wash., DC, 1991—. Author: (novels) (6 books, over 200 pub.) Environ. Sci., 1970—. Mem.: Soc. of Environ. Toxicology & Chemistry, Am. Fisheries Soc. Avocations: hunting, fishing. Office: Exxon Mobil 3301 "C" St Anchorage AK 99503 also: Exxon Co 800 Bell St Houston TX 77002-7497

MAKI, ATSUSHI, economics professor; b. Kanagawa, Japan, Jan. 14, 1948; s. Sadao and Eiko (Yamaguchi) M.; m. Michie Yabu, Feb. 28, 1975; children: Chiori, Hisashi. BA, Keio U., 1971, MA, 1973, PhD, 1993. Asst. prof. Keio U., Tokyo, 1973-79, assoc. prof., 1979-87, prof., 1987—. Guest rsch. officer Ministry Posts and Telecom., 1988-90; vis. scholar Harvard U., Cambridge, Mass., 1982-84, 2001, George Washington U., 2001, U. Sydney, Australia, 2002; vis. prof. Osaka (Japan) U., 1989, Ecole Superieure des Scis. Econs. et Commls., France, 1994; vis. fellow Australian Nat. U., Canberra, 1990, Massey U., New Zealand, 1991, U. Western Australia, Perth, 1993, Victoria U., Wellington, New Zealand, 1997, Bur. Labor Stats., Washington, 2001. Author: Consumer Preferences and Measurement of Demand, 1983, Japanese Consumer Behavior, 1998, Applied Econometrics, 2001. Recipient award Japan Found., 1996; Abe fellow SSRC, 2001; Ministry of Edn. grant-in-aid, 1997-99, 2003-04. Mem. Am. Econ. Assn., Econometric Soc., Japanese Econ. Assn., Japan Assn. Stats., Japan Soc. Household Econs., Royal Econ. Soc. Home: 107-8 Terao Kawagoe-shi Saitama 350-1141 Japan Office: Keio U 2-15-45 Mita Minato-ku Tokyo 108-8345 Japan E-mail: maki@fbc.keio.ac.jp.

MAKI, DENNIS G. medical educator, researcher, clinician; b. River Falls, Wis., May 8, 1940; m. Gail Dawson, 1962; children: Kimberly, Sarah, Daniel. BS in Physics with honors, U. Wis., 1962, MS in Physics, 1964, MD, 1967. Diplomate Am. Bd. Internal Medicine, Am. Bd. Infectious Diseases, Am. Bd. Critical Care Medicine. Physicist, computer programmer Lawrence Radiation Lab., AEC, Livermore, Calif., 1962; intern, asst. resident Harvard Med. unit Boston City Hosp., 1967-69, chief resident, 1972-73; with Hosp. Infections sect. Ctrs. for Disease Control, USPHS, Atlanta, 1969-71; acting chief nat. nosocomial infections study Ctr. for Disease Control, USPHS, Atlanta, 1970-71; sr. resident dept. medicine Mass. Gen. Hosp., 1971-72, clin. and research fellow infectious disease unit, 1973-74; asst. prof. medicine U. Wis., Madison, 1974-78, assoc. prof., 1978-82, prof., 1982—; hosp. epidemiologist, U. Wis. Hosp. and Clinic, Madison, 1974—; Ovid O. Meyer chair in medicine U. Wis., Madison, 1975—, head sec. infectious diseases, 1979—, attending physician Ctr. for Trauma and Life Support, 1976—. Clinician, rschr., educator in field; mem. program com. Intersci. Conf. on Antimicrobial Agts. and Chemotherapy, 1987-94; mem. Am. Bd. Critical Care Medicine, 1989-95, Sr. assoc. editor Infection Control and Hosp. Epidemiology, 1979 93; mem. editl. bd. Jour. Lab. and Clin. Investigation, 1980-86, Jour. Critical Care, 1985-96, Jour. Infectious Diseases, 1988-90, Critical Care Medicine, 1989-94, 97—; contbr. articles to med. jours. Recipient 1st award for disting. rsch. in Antibiotic Rev., 1980, Internat. CIPI award, 1994, SHEA lectr., 1999, numerous tchg. awards and hon. lectrs. Master ACP; fellow Infectious Diseases Soc. Am. (coun. 1993-96, citation 2000), Am. Acad. Microbiology, Soc. for Critical Care Medicine, Surg. Infection Soc.; mem. Soc. Hosp. Epidemiologists Am. (pres. 1990), Ctrl. Soc. for Clin. Rsch., Am. Soc. Microbiology, Am. Fedn. Clin. Rsch., Alpha Omega Alpha (nat. bd. dirs. 1983-89). Office: U Wis Hosp and Clinics H4/574 Madison WI 53792 Fax: 608-231-3896. E-mail: dgmaki@facstaff.wisc.edu.

MAKI, KAZUMI, physicist, researcher; b. Takamatsu, Japan, Jan. 27, 1936; s. Toshio and Hideko M.; m. Masako Tanaka, Sept. 21, 1969. BS, Kyoto U., 1959, PhD, 1964. Research asso. Inst. for Math. Scis., Kyoto U., 1964; research asso. Fermi Inst., U. Chgo., 1964-65; asst. prof. physics U. Calif., San Diego, 1965-67; prof. Tohoku U., Sendai, Japan, 1967-74; vis. prof. Universite Paris-Sud, Orsay, France, 1969-70; prof. physics U. So. Calif., Los Angeles, 1974—. Vis. prof. Inst. Laue-Langevin, U. Paris-Sud, France, 1979-80, Max Planck Inst. fur Festkorper Forschung, Stuttgart, Germany, 1986-87, U. Paris-7, 1990, Hokkaido U., Sapporo, Japan, 1993, Centre de Recherche sur Tres Basses Temperatures, Grenoble, France, 1993-94, Instituto de Ciencia de Materiales, Madrid, Spain, 1994, Max Planck Inst. Phys. Complex Sys., Dresden, Germany, 2001-02. Assoc. editor Jour. Low Temperature Physics, 1969-91; contbr. articles to profl. jours. Guggenheim fellow, 1979-80, Japan Soc. Promotion of Sci. fellow, 1993; Fulbright scholar, 1964-65; recipient Nishina prize, 1972, Alexander von Humboldt award, 1986-87. Fellow Japan Soc. Promotion of Sci., Am. Phys. Soc.; mem. AAAS, Phys. Soc. Japan. Office: U So Calif Dept Physics and Astronomy Los Angeles CA 90089-0484 E-mail: kmaki@usc.edu.

MAKIHARA, MINORU, diversified corporation executive; b. London, Jan. 12, 1930; BA, Harvard U., 1954. With Mitsubishi Corp., Tokyo, 1956-59, London, 1959-67, with Marine Products dept. Tokyo, 1967-70, dep. gen. mgr., 1976-80, gen. mgr. Marine Products dept., 1980-83, gen. mgr. mktg. and coordination dept., 1983-85, bd. dirs., 1986-88, mng. dir., 1988-90, sr. mng. dir., 1990-92, pres., chmn., 1992-98, 1998—; with, then gen. mgr. Mitsubishi Internat. Corp., Seattle, 1970-71, v.p., gen. mgr., 1980-83, gen. mgr. Washington, 1971-76, exec. v.p., gen. mgr., 1985-86, pres. N.Y.C., 1987-90, chmn., 1990-92; pres. Mitsubishi Corp., Tokyo, 1992—98, chmn., 1998—. Vice chmn. the Keidanren (Japan Fedn. of Econ. Orgns.); mem. exec. com. Trilateral Comm. (Japan, NAm., Europe); vice chmn. Japan U.S. Bus. Coun. Office: Mitsubishi Corp Office of the Chmn 6-3 Marunouchi 2-chome Chiyoda-ku Tokyo 100 8086 Japan Office Phone: +81-3-3210-2121. Office Fax: +81-3-3210-8935.

MAKINEN, MARVIN WILLIAM, biophysicist, educator; b. Chassell, Mich., Aug. 19, 1939; s. William John and Milga Katarina (Myllyla) M.; m. Michele de Groot, July 30, 1966; children: Eric William, Stephen Matthew. AB, U. Pa., 1961; postgrad., Free U. Berlin, 1960-61; MD, U. Pa., 1968; DPhil, U. Oxford, Eng., 1976. Diplomate Am. Bd. Med. Examiners. Intern Columbia-Presbyn. Med. Ctr., N.Y.C., 1968-69; rsch. assoc. NIH, Bethesda, Md., 1969-71; vis. fellow U. Oxford, Eng., 1971-74; asst. prof. biophysics U. Chgo., 1974-80, assoc. prof., 1980-86, prof. biochemistry and molecular biology, 1986—, chmn. dept., 1988-93. Established investigator Am. Heart Assn., 1975-80; lectr. in field. Contbr. numerous articles to profl. jours. Sr. surgeon USPHS, 1969-71. John Simon Guggenheim fellow 1997-98, John E. Fogarty Sr. Internat. fellow, 1984-85, European Molecular Biology Orgn. sr. fellow, 1984-85, NIH spl. fellow, 1971-74, Berquist fellow Am. Scandinavian Found., 1970. Fellow Am. Inst. Chemists; mem. Am. Chem. Soc., Biophys. Soc., Am. Soc. Biochemistry and Molecular Biology, The Protein Soc., AAAS. Office: U Chgo Dept Biochemistry/Mol Biol 920 E 58th St Chicago IL 60637-5415 Office Phone: 773-702-1080. E-mail: makinen@uchicago.edu.

MAKINS, CHRISTOPHER JAMES, foreign policy institute administrator; b. Southampton, N.Y., July 23, 1942; s. Roger Mellor and Alice Brooks (Davis) M.; m. Wendy Whitney, July 26, 1975; 1 child, Marian Whitney. BA, Oxford U., Eng., 1963; MA, Oxford U., 1971. From 3rd to 1st sec. Her Majesty Diplomatic Svc., London, Paris, Washington, 1964-75; dep. dir. Trilateral Commn., N.Y.C., 1975-76; sr. assoc. Carnegie Endowment for Internat. Peace, Washington, 1977-79; sr. scientist, asst. v.p. Sci. Applications Internat. Corp., Washington, 1979-89; dir. internat. security programs Roosevelt Ctr. Am. Policy Studies, Washington, 1985-89; v.p., exec. v.p. Aspen Inst., Washington, 1989-97; pres. Atlantic Coun. U.S., Washington, 1999—. Sr. adviser German Marshall Fund U.S., Washington, 1997—99; mem. internat. adv. bd. ICL Ltd., London, 1999—2000; bd. dirs. New Star Enhanced Income Trust, 2001—03. Contbr. articles to profl. jours. Mem. coun. Non-Profit Sector Rsch. Fund, Washington, 1997—2001; bd. dirs. Washington Concert Opera, 1987—, chmn., 1993—97; trustee The Phillips Collection, Washington, 1991—98, Greater Washington Ednl. Telecomms. Assn., 1980—88, Gov. Ditchley Found., 2004—. Fellow All Souls Coll., Oxford, 1963-70; mem. Coun. Fgn. Rels., Internat. Inst. Strategic Studies, Pratts Club, Met. Club, Alibi. Avocations: tennis, squash, boating, opera. Home: 3034 P St NW Washington DC 20007-3052 Office: 1024 29th St NW Washington DC 20007-3831

MAKISHI, YASUKO, securities trader, writer; m. Kevin Shuppert, July 8, 1977. BA in Econs., Ind. U., 1981. Commodity futures trader, Shreveport, La., 1995—97; stock trader, 1998—2004; founder of marketreadings.com Fortuna Prodns., LLC, Shreveport, La., 2003—. Author: America 2003 Predictions: Timing the Sectors of the Economy, Fortuna System I: Reading is Fundamental - Power to Control Your Own Destiny for an Independent Life, 2004; creator: astrology course and seminar The Fortuna System of Business and Financial Astrology, 2004. Office: Fortuna Prodns LLC 5737 S Lakeshore Dr Shreveport LA 71119 Personal E-mail: makishiy@bellsouth.net. Business E-Mail: yasuko@marketreadings.com.

MAKKAY, ALBERT, broadcast executive; b. Carteret, N.J., Apr. 13, 1934; s. John E., and Helen (Fetyko) M.; Maureen Monaghan, Oct. 29, 1962; children: Allison, Albert, Colleen. BS in Mktg., U. Ariz., 1961. Gen. sales mgr. Sta. KTAN, Tucson, 1961-66; gen. mgr. Sta. WPST, Trenton, 1966-70; v.p. gen. mgr. Sta. WLKW, Providence, 1970-75; v.p., gen. mgr. Sta. WEZE, Boston, 1975-79; owner Sta. WKPE, Orleans, Mass., 1979-83, Sta. WKFM, Syracuse, N.Y., 1983-86, Stas. WPXC, WRZE, WCIB, Hyannis, Mass., 1986—; pres.

Makkay Group Broadcasting. Dep. sheriff (hon.) Barnstable County Sheriff's Office. Sgt. U.S. Army, 1953-56. Mem. KC, Nat. Assn. Broadcasters, New Eng. Broadcasters Assn., Mass. Broadcasters Assn., Korean Vets. Assn., Korean War Vets., Nam Vets of Cape Cod (Mass.) Assn. (hon.), Otis (mem. adv. bd.), Knights Columbus. Roman Catholic. Avocations: travel, golf, swimming. Office: 154 Barnstable Rd Hyannis MA 02601-2930 Home: 15 Meadow Farm Rd Centerville MA 02632-3161 E-mail: capemo@aol.com.

MAKKAY, MAUREEN ANN, broadcast executive; b. Chgo. d. John Paul and Bernice Ann (Williams) Monaghan; m. Albert Makkay, Oct. 20, 1962; children: Allison, Albert Jr., Colleen. BA, U. R.I., 1974. Cert. secondary sch. tchr., Mass. Adminstr. Ednl. Records Bur., Wellesley, Mass., 1979-81; local sales mgr. Sta. WKZE, Orleans, Mass., 1981-83; nat. sales mgr. Sta. WKFM, Syracuse, N.Y., 1983-85; pres. Sta. WPXC-FM, Hyannis, Mass., 1987—; v.p. Sta. WRZE, Nantucket, Mass., Sta. WCIB-FM, Falmouth, Mass. Corporator Cape Code Five Cents Savings Bank, 1998—. Pres. Cape and Islands unit Am. Cancer Soc., 1988-91, bd. dirs., 1989-95; mem. pers. bd. Town of Barnstable, Mass., 1989-94, chmn., 1990-91; bd. dirs. Cape Cod Alcoholism Intervention and Rehab., Inc., 1995—. Mem. Bus. and Profl. Women Cape Cod (bd. dirs. 1989—), Am. Women in Radio and TV, Nat. Assn. Braodcasters. Office: Sta WPXC-FM Radio 154 Barnstable Rd Hyannis MA 02601-2930 Home: 15 Meadow Farm Rd Centerville MA 02632-3161

MAKOUS, BRUCE B. fundraiser; b. Phila., June 24, 1953; s. Norman and Dorothy Makous; m. Barbara H. Makous, Oct. 17, 1981; children: Dyani, Kacie. BA in Lit., Oberlin Coll., 1976; MA in Cultural Adminstrn., NYU, 1986. CLU, ChFC. Gen. mgr. 78th Street Theatre Lab., N.Y.C., 1979-81; comm. cons. Price Waterhouse Nat. Offices, N.Y.C., 1981-84; dir. info. svcs. Theatre Comm. Group, N.Y.C., 1984-86; mng. dir. Attic Theatre, Detroit, 1986-89, Players Theatre Columbus, Ohio, 1989-90; founder, pres. Makous Mktg. & Fundraising, Phila., 1990-93; dir. devel. Am. Coll., Bryn Mawr, Pa., 1993-98, dir. planned giving, 1998-99; dir. major and planned gifts Drexel U., Phila., 1999-2000, asst. v.p. for major and planned gifts, 2000—01; maj. gifts and planned giving officer Am. Assn. for Cancer Rsch., 2001—. Lectr. Wayne State U., Detroit, 1998-89, Assn. Fundraising Profls.-Villanova (Pa.) U., 1998—. Co-prodr. Back in the World, 1987 (award for best play outside N.Y. Nat. Theatre Critics Assn. 1987); assoc. editor Boulevard lit. mag., 1991—. Grad. Leadership, Inc. Class of 1992, 1991-92; co-chmn. bd. dirs. Prints in Progress, Phila., 1993-95. Mgmt. for Arts Rev. scholar NYU, 1983-86. Mem. Assn. Fundraising Profls. (cert., internat. bd. dirs., pres. Greater Phila. chpt. 2001-02), Nat. Com. on Planned Giving. Democrat. Roman Catholic. Avocation: writing novels. Home: 7905 Cadillac Ln Philadelphia PA 19128 Office: Am Assn Cancer Rsch Ste 826 150 S Independence Hall W Philadelphia PA 19106-3483 Fax: 215-895-4966. E-mail: makous@aacr.org., bmakous@aol.com.

MAKOUS, NORMAN, internist, cardiologist, educator; b. Chgo., July 22, 1924; s. Lawrence Alonzo and Ruth (Luehring) M.; m. Dorothy Murl Bowlin, Sept. 25, 1948 (dec. July 25, 2003); children: David, Bruce, Catherine, Monte, Joseph, Martin, John, Virginia, Dorothy, Margaret; m. Elanor B. Sullivan Feb. 21, 2004. BS, U. Wis., 1945, MD, 1947. Diplomate in internal medicine and cardiovascular diseases Am. Bd. Internal Medicine. Mixed intern Rsch. Hosp., Kansas City, Mo., 1947—48, resident in internal medicine, 1948—50; fellow in cardiovasc. disease U. Vt., Burlington, 1950—51; resident in internal medicine U.S. Naval Hosp., Camp Lejeune, NC, 1951—52; dir. cardiac catheterization lab. Kansas City, Mo., 1955—56; fellow in cardiovasc. disease Pa. Hosp., Phila., 1953—54, assoc. cardiologist, assoc. physician to hosp., 1960—72, cardiologist, physician to hosp., 1972—2000, cons., 2000—01; pvt. practice Kansas City and Independence, Mo., 1956—59, Phila., 1959—2001; assoc. in medicine U. Pa., Phila., 1959—71, asst. prof. clin. medicine, 1971—74, clin. asst. prof. medicine, 1974—, Thomas Jefferson U., Phila., 1994—. Physician advisor Keystone Profl. Rev. Orgn., 1986-93; mem. cons. Pa. Bur. Disability Determination, 1981-2001; cardiology cons. Phila. City Solicitor's Office, 1986-; mem. peer rev. panel Jour. Cardiopulmonary Rehab., 1990; mem. adv. group Greater Delaware Valley Regional Med. Program, 1971-75. Contbr. articles to med. jours., chpts. to books. Founder, acting chmn. Southeastern Pa. Regional High Blood Pressure Control Program, 1978-80; mem. interim bd. Health Sys. Agy. Southeastern Pa., 1975-77, chmn. adv. coun., 1979-80; trustee Edna B. Kynett Meml. Found., Phila., 1963—, v.p., 1994-96, pres., 1997—; pres. Home and Sch. Assn., Our Lady of Lourdes Parish, Phila., 1972-73, mem. parish pastoral coun., 1991-95, co-chmn., 1993-95; trustee Vis. Nurse Assn. Greater Phila., 1997-2000. Lt. USNR, 1943-45, 50-52, Res., 1952-62. Recipient Legion of Honor, Chapel of Four Chaplains, 1980, Spl. Achievement award Southeastern Pa. Regional High Blood Pressure Control Program. Fellow ACP, Am. Coll. Cardiology, Am. Soc. Internal Medicine; mem. AMA, Pa. Med. Soc. (chmn. profl. liability ins. appeals com. 1986-91), Phila. County Med. Soc. (standing com. Med. Econs., 1979-86, pres. Center City br. 1980-81, sec. 1990-91, chmn. membership and orgn. com. 1991-2000, Cristol award 1994), Am. Heart Assn. (fellow coun. clin. cardiology, pres. Southeastern Pa. affiliate 1988-89, bd. govs., program chmn. 1988-92, pres. Pa. affiliate 1981-82, Disting. Svc. award Pa. affiliate 1982, Disting. Achievement award Pa. affiliate, 1986, Disting. Achievement award Southeastern Pa. affiliate 1988, Vol. of Yr. award Southeastern Pa. affiliate 1988), Pa. Soc. Internal Medicine (pres. 1983-84). Avocations: tennis, cinematography. Office: 243 Freedom Blvd Coatesville PA 19320 Personal E-mail: drnmakous@aol.com.

MAKOUS, WALTER LEON, visual scientist, educator; s. Lawrence and Ruth Lorraine (Luehring) Makous; m. Marilyn Ann Carlson, Feb. 2, 1958 (div. 1973); children: Ann, James, Matthew; m. Joyce Brown Menconi, 1974 (div. 1981); m. Barbara Anne Duggins, Apr. 29, 1982. BS, U. Wis., 1958; M.Sc., Brown U., 1961, PhD, 1964. Mem. staff IBM, Yorktown Heights, N.Y., 1963-66; asst. prof. psychology U. Wash., 1966-69, lectr. in physiology and biophysics, 1966-69, assoc. prof. psychology, 1969-74, prof. psychology, 1974-79; prof. psychology, ophthalmology and visual sci. U. Rochester, 1979-95; prof. brain and cognitive sci., ophthalmology & visual sci., 1995—; dir. Ctr. for Visual Sci. U. Rochester, 1979-90. Northwest rep, charter mem steering comt West Coast Regional Consortium Univs in Neurosciences, 1976—79; mem coun on energy saving through more efficient lighting NAS-NRC, 1978—79, night vision coun, 1985—86; chmn ctr symp Univ Rochester, 1981—82; sensory processes panelist NSF, Washington, 1977—82, mem adv comt applied sci and research applicaitons policy, 1978—81; rev comt Presidential Young Investigator Award Program, 1984; vis scientist IBM Research, 1970—71. Editor (consult ed): Sensory Processes, 1977—79, Jour of the Optical Soc Am, 1982—86; contbr. articles to profl jours. With USNR, 1953—55. Grantee, Nat Eye Inst, 1969—, NSF, 1959—62, 1981—82. Fellow: AAAS, Optical Soc Am (mem coord vision and physiological optics comt 1983—89, coord vision and med optics comt 1983—89, publs comt 1985—89, chmn fellows and hon mems comt 1986, ed vision and color 1982—86, feature ed applied vision 1989—90), Am Psychol Soc; mem.: Am Nat Standards Inst/Human Factor & Ergonomics Soc-100 (rev comt 1992—), Human Factors and Ergonomics, Psychonomic Soc, Soc Neuroscience, Asn Research in Vision and Ophthalmology (chmn sect psycho-physics 1977). Office: U Rochester Ctr for Visual Sci Rochester NY 14627 Business E-Mail: walt@cvs.rochester.edu.

MAKOVSKY, KENNETH DALE, public relations executive; b. St. Louis, Oct. 3, 1940; s. Jack and Minnie (Freedman) Makovsky; m. Phyllis Ann Peck, Oct. 15, 1972; children: Evan, Matthew. BA, Washington U., St. Louis, 1962, JD, 1965. Asst. account exec. Curtis Hoxter Inc., N.Y.C., 1965—66; account exec. Ruder & Finn Inc., N.Y.C., 1966—69, Harshe-Rotman & Druck, N.Y.C., 1970—72, v.p., 1973—75, sr. v.p., 1975—79, sr. v.p., dep. gen. mgr. N.Y. office, 1978—79; founder, pres. Makovsky & Co., Inc., N.Y.C., 1979—; founder, past pres. Internat. Pub. Rels. Exch.; chmn. Makovsky & Co., Inc., N.Y.C. Contbr. articles to profl. pubs. Nat. bd. govs. Am. Jewish Com. N.Y., 1999—, nat. pub. rels. com. chmn., 1981—; speechwriter 17th Dist. Congl. Campaign, N.Y.C., 1972; v.p. Am. Jewish Com. N.Y., N.Y.C., 1985—, N.Y. bd. dirs., 1978—; adv. com. S.I. Newhouse Sch. Pub. Commn., 1996—, Washington U. Nat. Arts and Sci. Coun., 1998—; bd. trustees Inst. PR, 2000—. Recipient Gold Quill IABC, 1990, Cipra award Inside Pub. Rels., 1994, PRSA's Silver Anvil, PRSA-NY's Big Apple award; named Pub. Rels. All Star, Inside Pub. Rels., 1992; co. named one of ten fastest growing pub. rels. firms in U.S., O'Dwyer Rankings, 1985, 86, 87, 89, 90, 91, one of four top pub. rels. firms in N.Y.C., Small Agy. Yr. Inside Pub. Rels., 1990, among 12 Best Managed Firms in U.S., 1993, 94, among the 12 top strategic counseling firms in U.S., 1995, one of the 8 hot bus.-to-bus. agys., 1996, one of the 8 best managed agys., 1997, one of the 12 top investor relations agys., 1997, among the 15 top tech. agys., 1997, best managed PR agy. in U.S., 1998, among 16 top investor relations agys., 1998, among 9 top bus.-to-bus., 1998, 16 nat. capabilities agys., 1998, among 12 best managed agys., 1999, one of 12 top bus.-to-bus. mktg., 1999, among 12 top investor relations agys., 1999, one of 15 top agys. in N.Y.C., 1999, among top 8 bus.-to-bus. mktg., 1999. Mem.: Inst. Pub. Rels., Arthur Page Soc., Nat. Investors Rels. Inst., Pub. Rels. Soc. Am. (Silver Anvil award for Chem. Spltys. Mfrs. Assn. 1978, award for Am. Superconductor 1994), India House, Washington U. Alumni Club N.Y.C. (pres. 1970). Avocations: theater, movies, travel. Office: Makovsky & Co Inc 575 Lexington Ave Fl 15 New York NY 10022-6104 E-mail: kmakovsky@makovsky.com.

MAKOWSKI, EDGAR LEONARD, obstetrician and gynecologist; b. Milw., Oct. 27, 1927; s. Adam and Ernestine (Horn) M.; m. Patricia M. Nock, Nov. 1, 1952; children: Peter, James, Ann, Mary, Thomas, Paul. BS, Marquette U., 1951, MD, 1954. Intern Deaconess Hosp., Milw., 1954-55; resident in Ob/Gyn U. Minn., Mpls., 1955-59, asst. prof., 1959-66, asso. prof., 1966; asso. prof. Ob/Gyn U. Colo., Denver, 1966-69, prof., 1969-93, chmn. dept., 1976-88, prof. emeritus, 1993—. Contbr. articles to sci. jours., chpts. to books. Served with AUS, 1946-47. NIH spl. fellow in physiology Yale U., 1963 Mem. Am. Gynecol. and Obstet. Soc. (pres.), Am. Coll. Obstetricians and Gynecologists, Soc. Gynecol. Investigators, Central Assn. Obstetricians and Gynecologists, Colo. Soc. Ob/Gyn., Perinatal Research Soc. (pres.). Roman Catholic. Achievements include radioactive microsphere technique for determination of organ blood flow. Home: 1900 E Girard Pl Unit 408 Englewood CO 80113 E-mail: EdPat124@msn.com.

MAKRI, NANCY, chemistry educator; b. Athens, Greece, Sept. 5, 1962; came to the U.S., 1985; d. John and Vallie (Tsakona) M.; m. Martin Gruebele, July 9, 1992; children: Alexander Makris Gruebele, Valerie Gruebele Makri. BS, U. Athens, 1985; PhD, U. Calif., Berkeley, 1989. Jr. fellow Harvard U., Cambridge, Mass., 1989-91; from asst. prof. to assoc. prof. U. Ill., Urbana, 1992-99, prof., 1999—. Recipient Beckman Young Investigator award Arnold & Mabel Beckman Found., 1993, Ann. medal Internat. Acad. Quantum Molecular Sci., 1995, Camille Dreyfus Tchr.-Scholar award The Camille and Henry Dreyfus Found., 1997, Agnes Fay Morgan award Iota Sigma Pi, 1999, physics prize Bodossaki Found., 1999; named NSF Young Investigator, 1993; Packard fellow for sci. and engring. David and Lucile Packard Found., 1993, Sloan Rsch. fellow Alfred Sloan Found., 1994, Cottrell scholar Rsch. Corp., 1994; univ. scholar U. Ill., 1999. Fellow: AAAS, Am. Phys. Soc. Home: 2722 Valley Brook Dr Champaign IL 61822-7634 Office: U Ill Urbana Dept Chem 601 S Goodwin Ave Urbana IL 61801-3709 E-mail: nancy@makri.scs.uiuc.edu.

MAKRIS, ANDREAS, composer; b. Salonica, Greece, Mar. 7, 1930; came to U.S., 1950, naturalized, 1962; s. Christos and Kallitza (Andreou) M.; m. Margaret Lubbe, June 12, 1959; children: Christos, Myron. Grad. with highest honors, Nat. Conservatory, Salonica, 1950; postgrad., Kansas City (Mo.) Conservatory, 1953, Mannes Coll. Music, 1956, Aspen Music Festival, 1956-57, Fontainbleau (France) Sch., 1958; pupil of Nadia Boulanger. Adv. to Maestro Rostropovich for new music, 1979-90. Composer: compositions permiered and performed in U.S., Can., S.Am., Europe, Japan, USSR; composer-in-residence Nat. Symphony Orch., 1979—90; composer: prin. works include Scherzo for Violins, 1966, Concerto for Strings, 1966, (for Orch. or Band) Aegean Festival, 1967, (Chamber Orch.) Anamnesis, 1970, Viola Concerto, 1970, Concertino for Trombone, 1970, Efthymia, 1972, Five Miniatures, 1972, Mediterranean Holiday, 1974, Fantasy and Dance for Saxophone and Piano, 1974, Saxophone and Concert Band or Saxophone Strings and Harp, 1974, (for Orch. or Band) Chromatokinesis, 1978, In Memory, 1979, Variations and Song for Orchestra, 1979, Fanfare Alexander, 1980, (for Orch. or Band) Fourth of July March, 1982, Violin Concerto, 1983, Nature-Life Symphonic Poem, 1983, (for Violin Alone) Caprice "Tonatonal", 1986, Intrigues for Solo Clarinet and Wind Ensemble, 1987, Concertante for Violin, Cello, Clarinet, French Horn, Percussion and Orchestra, 1988, Trilogy for Orchestra, 1990, Polychronion Chorus and Orchestra, 1990, Procession Chorus and Brass Quintet, 1990, Intrigues for Solo Clarinet, Strings, Brass and Percussion, 1991, Concertino for Organ, Flute and Strings, 1992, A Symphony for Soprano and Strings, 1992, Woodwind Quintet, 1993, Decalog (ten songs for young students), 1995, Antithesis for Orch., 1995, J.F.K. Commemorative Fanfare For Strings and Snare Drum, 1996, Introduction and Kalamatianos for solo trumpet, strings, snare and bass drums, 1997, Sonatina for Solo Violin, 1997, Sextet for Woodwind Quintet and Piano in 3 Movements, 1999, Concertino for Flute or Violin and Piano, 1999, Serenade for Voice and Violin, 2001, Voyage Caprice for Violin and Piano, 2003, Concertino for solo flute and chamber ensemble, 2003, Hellenic Odyssey for Orch., 2003, Strathmre Overture for Orch., 2004, also works for violin, string quartets, voice quintets, duets and arrangements of Paganini, Bach, Corelli and Fiorillo. Recipient citation Greek Govt., 1980; Student Program grantee Phillips U., Enid, Okla., 1950, grantee Nat. Endowment Arts, 1967, grantee Martha Baird Rockefeller Fund, 1970, grantee Damrosh Found., 1958 Mem. ASCAP (ann. awards 1980-2004), Internat. Platform Assn. Greek Orthodox. Home: 11204 Oak Leaf Dr Silver Spring MD 20901-1313 Office: Nat Symphony Orch Kennedy Ctr Washington DC 20566-0001 *Two important elements have contributed tremendously to my composing: As a child I was in the midst of war in Greece, and, while all wars are terrible, it taught me both self-discipline and an appreciation for simplicity. Just being alive and able to compose makes me very happy. As a student I was not able to have a piano, the most valuable instrument for a composer. I learned to write with only a pencil and paper for full orchestra, and this liberated me both musically and practically.*

MAKRIS, CONSTANTINE JOHN, computer engineer; b. Chalkis, Greece, Nov. 16, 1927; arrived in US, 1952, naturalized, 1960; s. John Constantine and Chryso Makris; m. Helen Loukaides, 1956; children: John, Nicholas, Dorothy. Diploma in radio engring., Inst. Electronic Tech., Athens, Greece, 1951; BEE, NYU, 1958, MEE, 1962. Rsch. scientist NYU, NYC, 1958—62; product mgr. computer R & D Mergenthaler divsn. Eltra, Plainview, NY, 1962—69; mgr. advt. devel. Harris-Intertype, Watchung, NJ, 1969—73; pres. Orthodata Inc., Glen Cove, NY, 1973—75; sr. staff mem., project mgr. Network Analysis Corp., Gt. Neck, NY, 1976—78; sr. sys. engr., asst. sec. Mfrs. Hanover Trust Co., NYC, 1978—88; sr. comm. planner networks and telecomm. Grumman Data Sys. div. Grumman Corp., Bethpage, NY, 1988—92; comm. cons. Glen Cove, 1993—. Lectr.; cons. Contbr. articles to profl. jours. V.p. High Elms Civic Assn., 1968—69, Ch. Coun., 1976—77. With Greek Air Force, 1946—51. Mem.: IEEE, Comm. Soc., Computer Soc., Krikos Inc. (chmn. LI chpt. 1981—83, v.p. bd. dirs. 1983—86). Home and Office: 42 Old Tappan Rd Glen Cove NY 11542-1248

MAKTOUF, SAMIR, education company executive; b. Sousse, Tunisia, June 25, 1957; s. Salem Bechir and Douja (Zaabouri) M.; m. Raja Khabcheche, Apr. 3, 1995 (div. Feb. 1997); 1 child, Ameen. grad., pilot cert., Tunisian Air Force Acad. Pilot Tunisian Air Force, Bizerta, 1979-83; sales mgr. Sorena, Tunis, Tunisia, 1983-84; pilot Aeroclub Herault, Montpellier, France, 1984-86; asst. chief flight instr. Pro-flite, Vero Beach, Fla., 1986-89; pres., owner Fla. Pilot Sch. Inc., Fort Pierce, Fla., 1990—; tchr. Indian River Cmty. Coll., Fort Pierce, Fla., 1992—. Cons. aviation degree Palm Beach Cmty. Coll., 1997-99; cons. Training Piper Aircraft Corp., Pratt & Whitney and Sikorsky Aircraft; aviation safety counsellor, FAA, 1997—. Author: Radio Communication, 1989, Economic Growth of General Aviation in South Fla., 1989. Mem. Aircraft Owner & Pilot Assn., Nat. Assn. Flight Instr. Avocations: reading, boating, travel. Office: Florida Pilot Sch Inc PO Box 258 Stuart FL 34995-0258 Home: 2888 Tennis Club Dr #701 Port Saint Lucie FL 34953

MAKUPSON, AMYRE PORTER, television station executive; b. River Rouge, Mich., Sept. 30, 1947; d. Rudolph Hannibal and Amyre Ann (Porche) Porter; m. Walter H. Makupson, Nov. 1, 1975; children: Rudolph Porter, Amyre Nisi. BA, Fisk U., 1970; MA, Am. U., Washington, 1972. Asst. dir. news Sta. WGPR-TV, Detroit, 1975-76; dir. pub. rels. Mich. Health Maintenance Orgn., Detroit, 1976-77; mgr. pub. affairs, news anchor Sta. WKBD-TV, Southfield, Mich., 1977—. Children's Miracle Network Telethon, 1989—. Mem. Co-Ette Club, Inc., Met. Detroit Teen Conf. Coalition; mem. adv. com., bd. dirs. Alzheimers Assn.; bd. dirs. com. March of Dimes; pres. bd. dirs. Detroit Wheelchair Athletic Assn.; bd. dirs. Providence Hosp. Found., Sickle Cell Assn., Kids In Need of Direction, Drop-out Prevention Collaborative, Merrill Palmer Inst., Skillman Found. Recipient 5 Emmy awards 3 Best Commentary/Best Anchor, Best Interview/Discussion Show, 24 Emmy nominations NATAS, Editl. Best Feature award AP, Media award UPI, Oakland County Bar Assn., TV Documentary award, Detroit Press Club, Bishop Gallagher award Mental Illness Rsch. Assn., Svc. award Arthritis Found. Mich., Mich. Mchts. Assn., DAV, Jr. Achievement, City of Detroit, Salvation Army, Spirit award City of Detroit, Spirit award City of Pontiac, Golden Heritage award Little Rock Bapt. Ch., 1993, Neal Shine award outstanding contbn. Nat. Soc. Fundraising Execs., Virginia Merrick award outstanding contbn. Christ Child Soc., Outstanding Achievement award Tuskegee Airmen, Best Feature Story award Mich. Assn. Broadcasters; named Media Person of the Yr., So. Christian Leadership Conf., 1994, Humanitarian of the Yr., March of Dimes, 1995. Mem. Pub. Rels. Soc. Am., Am. Women in Radio and TV (Outstanding Achievement award 1981, Outstanding Woman in TV Top Mgmt. 1993, Mentor award 1993), Women in Comm., Nat. Acad. TV Arts and Scis., Detroit Press Club, Ad-Craft, Howard U. Nat. Gold Key Honor Soc. (hon.). Roman Catholic. Office: 26955 W 11 Mile Rd Southfield MI 48034-2292

MALA, THEODORE ANTHONY, physician, consultant; b. Santa Monica, Calif., Feb. 3, 1946; s. Ray and Galina (Liss) M.; children: Theodore S., Galina T.; 1 adopted child, Christine A. Lindholm. BA in Philosophy, DePaul U., 1972; MD, Autonomous U., Guadalajara, Mex., 1976; MPH, Harvard U., 1980. Spl. asst. for health affairs Alaska Fedn. Natives, Anchorage, 1977-78; chief health svcs. Alaska State Divsn. Corrections, Anchorage, 1978-79; assoc. prof., founder, dir. Inst. for Circumpolar Health Studies, U. Alaska, Anchorage, 1982-90; founder Siberian med. rsch. program U. Alaska, Anchorage, 1982, founder Magadan (USSR) med. rsch. program, 1988; commr. Health and Social Svcs. State of Alaska, Juneau, 1990-93; pres., CEO Ted Mala, Inc., Anchorage, 1993-97; pres., ptnr. Mexican-Siberian Trading Co., Monterrey, Mex., 1994-96; CEO, Confederated Tribes of Grand Ronde, Oreg., 1998-99; dir. tribal rels. Southcentral Found., Anchorage, 1999—, 2000—. Traditional healing dir. Southcentral Found., Anchorage, 2000—; Alaska rsch. and publs. com. Indian Health Svc., USPHS, 1987-90; advisor Nordic Coun. Meeting, WHO, Greenland, 1985; mem. Internat. Organizing Com., Circumpolar Health Congress, Iceland, 1992-93; chmn. bd. govs. Alaska Psychiat. Inst., Anchorage, 1990-93; cabinet mem. Gov. Walter J. Hickel, Juneau, 1990-93; advisor humanitarian aid to Russian Far East U.S. Dept. State, 1992-96; cons. USAID on U.S.-Russian Health Programs, 1994; apptd. adv. com. Sec. of Health and Human Svc. on Minority Health for the U.S., 2000—; mem. coun. pub. reps. NIH, 2002—. Past columnist Tundra Times; contbr. articles to profl. jours. Trustee United Way Anchorage, 1978-79; chmn. bd. trustees Alaska Native Coll., 1993-96. Recipient Gov.'s award, 1988, Outstanding Svc. award Alaska Commr. Health, 1979, Ministry of Health citation USSR Govt., 1989, Citation award Alaska State Legislature, 1989-90, 94, Commendation award State of Alaska, 1990, Alaska State Legislature, 1994, Honor Kempton Svc. to Humanity award, 1989, citation Med. Cmty. of Magadan region, USSR, 1989; Nat. Indian fellow U.S. Dept. Edn., 1979. Mem. Assn. Am. Indian Physicians (pres.), N.Y. Acad. Scis., Internat. Union for Circumpolar Health (permanent sec.-gen. 1987-90, organizing com. 8th Internat. Congress on Circumpolar Health 1987-90), Russian Acad. Polar Medicine (elected). Avocations: cross country skiing, hiking, photography, travel. Office Phone: 907-729-4955. E-mail: tmala@post.harvard.edu. *Personal philosophy: Progress in the North will come only when circumpolar countries put aside their geopolitical thinking and work together as one northern family.*

MALACH, MONTE, physician; b. Jersey City, Aug. 15, 1926; s. Charles and Yetta (Pascher) M.; m. Ann Elaine Glazer, June 15, 1952 (dec. June 1989); children: Barbara Sandra, Cathie Tara, Matthew David; m. Barbara Meryl Lipstein, Dec. 24, 1994; stepchildren: Heather Ilene, Jennifer Beth, Matthew Howard. BA, MD, U. Mich., 1949. Diplomate Am. Bd. Internal Medicine, Nat. Bd. Med. Examiners. Intern Beth Israel Hosp., Boston, 1949-50, resident, 1950-51, chief resident, 1951-52, Kings County Hosp., Bklyn., 1954-55; practice medicine specializing in internal medicine and cardiology Bklyn., 1955-97; dir. CCU Bklyn. Hosp., 1965-91, dir. emeritus CCU, 1991—; med. dir., clin. coord. Medicare IPRO Downstate N.Y., 1990—. Pres. profl. staff Bklyn. Hosp., 1966-69, chmn. med. bd., 1971-72; attending staff Caledonian Hosp., pres. profl. staff, 1984-85; pres. profl. staff Bklyn. Hosp.-Caledonian Hosp., 1987-89, chmn. med. bd., 1988-89; cons. Kings County Hosp.; tchg. fellow Tufts U. Med. Sch., 1951-52; instr. medicine Downstate Med. Ctr., Bklyn., 1955-59, clin. asst. prof. medicine, 1959-68, clin. assoc. prof., 1969-76, clin. prof., 1976—; clin. prof. medicine NYU Med. Ctr., 1994—; bd. dirs. Bay St. Landing One Owners Corp., 1985-87; v.p. Ocean View Condos, 1989-90, pres., 1990-95; med. dir. IPRO Medicare Rev., N.Y. State, 1990—, IPRO N.Y. State Peer Rev., 1990—. Kings County committeeman Democratic Party, 1964, 65. Served with USNR, 1944-46, to 1st lt. M.C. U.S. Army, 1952-54. Recipient 1st Prize for Crisis Mgmt. Habitat Mag., 1987. Fellow Am. Coll. Chest Physicians, ACP (master, Laureate award 2000), Am. Coll. Cardiology (task force Health Care Quality Improvement Initiative 1996—); mem. AMA (chmn. sect. coun. internal medicine 1980), N.Y. Heart Assn., Am. Soc. Internal Medicine (master, trustee 1975-79, sec.-treas. 1979—, pres. elect 1981, pres. 1982-83, chmn. investment com. 1985-93), N.Y. State Soc. Internal Medicine (pres. 1973-74, dir. 1966-84, chmn. Bklyn. chpt., v.p. 1971, award of merit 1978), Bklyn. Soc. Internal Medicine (mem. council 1965, pres. 1969-72), Med. Soc. State of N.Y. (chmn. sect. internal medicine 1976, chmn. med. care ins. com. 1988-93), Federated Council for Internal Medicine (chmn. 1979-80), Med. Soc. County Kings (censor 1985-91). Office Phone: 718-494-9245. E-mail: nypro.mmalach@sdps.org. *There is a place for hard work, scrupulous ethics and pride of accomplishment. A great marriage and a fine close family are buffers against adversity.*

MALACHOWSKY, CHRIS ALAN, electrical engineer; b. Danville, Pa., May 2, 1959; s. Martin Norman and Zelda Luba (Rutenberg) M.; m. Melody Ann Connella, Oct. 10, 1981; children: Ryan David, Spencer Gordon. BSEE with high honors, U. Fla., 1980; MS in Computer Sci., Santa Clara U., 1986. Mem. tech., staff Hewlett-Packard Co., Cupertino, Calif., 1980-87; sr. mem. tech. staff Sun Microsystems Computer Corp., Mountain View, Calif., 1987-89, staff engr., 1989-90, sr. staff engr., 1991—. Instr. grad. extension program U. Calif., Berkeley, 1990—. Patentee in electronic circuit designs for computer graphics; contbr. articles to profl. publs. Avocations: woodworking, basketball, tennis, salt-water aquariums. Office: Sun Microsystems Computer Corp MS MTV 18-112 2550 Garcia Ave Mountain View CA 94043

MALAFA, MOKENGE PETER, surgeon; b. Lagos, Nigeria, Oct. 10, 1958; came to U.S., 1978; Grad., U. Wis., MD, 1986. Intern Med. Ctr. Ohio, Toledo, 1986-87, resident, 1987-91; with Meml. Med. Ctr., St. Johns Hosp., 1994—2003, H. Lee Moffitt Cancer Ctr., Tampa, Fla., 2003—. Surg.-Oncology fellow City of Hope, Duarte, Calif., 1991-94. Mem. AMA, AAAS, Am. Assn. for Cancer Rsch., Am. Coll. Surgeons, Soc. Surg. Oncology, Am. Soc. of Clin. Oncology. Office: H Lee Moffitt Cancer Center 12902 Magnolia Drive Tampa FL 33612 Office Phone: 813-632-1432.

MALAFRONTE, DONALD, health executive; b. Bklyn., Dec. 16, 1931; s. Pasquale and Amalia (Castaldo) M.; m. Diane Freedenberg, Jan. 7, 1960 (dec. Nov. 14, 1970); children: Philip, Victor.; m. Hillary Demby, Oct. 30, 1982. BS, NYU, 1954. Reporter L.I. Daily Press, 1956-58; reporter, editor Newark Star-Ledger, 1958-65, art columnist, 1963-70; adminstrv. asst. to mayor of Newark, 1965-70; dir. Newark Model Cities Program, 1967-70, Newark Community Devel. Adminstrn., 1968-70; chief urban field operations N.J. Regional Med. Program, 1970-73; pres. Urban Health Inst., Roseland, N.J.,

1973—. Cons. to hosps., local govts., 1970— Author articles in field. Served with AUS, 1954-56. Recipient Joyce Kilmer fiction prize NYU, 1953 Office: Urban Health Inst 101 Eisenhower Pky Roseland NJ 07068-1028 Home: 1056 5th Ave New York NY 10028-0112

MALAKHOV, VLADIMIR, dancer; b. Krivoy Rog, Ukraine, USSR, Jan. 7, 1968; arrived in Can., 1994; s. Anatoly and Elena Malakhov. Grad., Bolshoi Ballet Acad., Moscow, 1986. Prin. dancer Vienna State Opera, 1992-94, Nat. Ballet Can., 1994-97, guest artist, 1997-98; prin. dancer Am. Ballet Theatre, N.Y.C., 1995—; artistic dir. & principal dancer Deutsche Straatsoper, Berlin, 2002—. Guest artist Am. Ballet Theatre, 1994. Appeared in Giselle, Swan Lake, Nutcracker, Manon, Romeo and Juliette, others; performed in major opera houses worldwide. Recipient Gold medal Varna Ballet Competition, 1986, Gold medal Moscow Ballet Competition, 1986, Serge Lifar prize, 1991, Nijinsky prize, 2002, Benois Prix de la Dance, London, 2001. Address: Am Ballet Theatre 890 Broadway New York NY 10003-1211*

MALAMUD, ALEXANDER, lawyer, consultant; b. Beltz, Moldova, Jan. 4, 1971; came to U.S. s. Yafim and Haya Urman M. BS in Criminal Justice, U. Ariz., 1996; postgrad., UCLA, 1996-2000. CEO, pres. Orient Express, Inc., Bklyn., 1995—. Bus. cons. N.Y. Transporters Assn., 1994; mem. adv. bd. Metro, Inc., Phoenix, 1994-96; cons. Mass. Transp. Mem. N.Y. Transp. Assn. Republican. Avocations: reading books, basketball, practicing law. Home: 29 Park View Pl Fair Lawn NJ 07410-4353 Office: 177 Sargeant Ave Clifton NJ 07013-1934

MALAMUD, DANIEL, biochemistry educator; b. Detroit, June 5, 1939; s. Jack and Jennie (Ashe) M.; m. Judith Disner, Mar. 7, 1961; children: Randy, Lisa. BS, U. Mich., 1961; MA, Western Mich. U., 1962; PhD, U. Cin., 1965; MA, U. Pa., 1983. Postdoctoral fellow Temple U., Phila., 1966-68, asst. prof. pathology, 1968-69; asst. biologist Mass. Gen. Hosp., Boston, 1969-72, assoc. biologist, 1972-77; assoc. prof. biochemistry Sch. Dental Medicine, U. Pa., Phila., 1977-84, prof. biochemistry, 1984—, chmn. dept., 1985-92. Asst. prof. pathology Harvard U., Boston, 1970-77; vis. assoc. prof., Fulbright lectr. U. Philippines, Manila, 1975; vis. scientist Wistar Inst., Phila., 1985; affiliated scientist Monell Chem. Senses Ctr., Phila., 1985—; exch. scientist Hebrew U., Jerusalem, 1982. Author: Autoradiography, 1969, Saliva As a Diagnostic Fluid, 1993; contbr. over 120 articles to profl. jours., chpts. to books. Recipient Career Devel. award NIH, 1972-77. Mem. Am. Soc. Biol. Chemists, Am. Soc. Cell Biologists, Am. Soc. Microbiologists, Am. Soc. Biochem. Molecular Biology, N.Y. Acad. Scis. Office: U Pa Sch Dental Medicine 240 S 40th St Philadelphia PA 19104-4118 Office Phone: 215-898-6576. E-mail: malamud@pobox.upenn.edu.

MALAMUTH, NEIL MOSHE, psychology and communication educator; BA in Psychology summa cum laude, MA in Psychology, UCLA, 1972, PhD in Social Psychology and Personality, 1975. Lectr. dept. psychology, UCLA and postdoctoral fellow Ctr. for Behavioral Therapy, Beverly Hills, Calif., 1975-77; asst. prof. psychology U. Man., Winnipeg, Can., 1977-80, assoc. prof., 1980-82; prof. comm. and psychology, chairperson dept. comm. U. Mich., Ann Arbor, 1991-94; tchg. asst. dept. psychology UCLA, 1971-73, rsch. assoc. Ctr. for Computer-Based Behavioral Studies, 1973-75, assoc. prof., 1982-86, assoc. dir. Ctr. for Study of Women, 1986-87, prof. comm. and psychology, 1982-91, 94—, chairperson comm. studies program and speech dept., 1984-91, 94—. Vis. scholar Stanford (Calif.) U., fall 1988; mem. rev. com. on violence and stress NIMH, 1989-93; Lady Davis sr. fellow Hebrew U. Jerusalem, spring 1995; participant leadership inst. Freedom Forum, Columbia U., summer 1992; participant workshop for deans and chairpersons Annenberg Programs, Washington, winter 1993; presenter various profl. and ednl. confs., most recently Oakland (Mich.) U., 1994, Nat. Assn. for Devel. of Work with Sex Offenders, Durham (Eng.) U., 1994, Soc. for Sci. Study of Sex., Miami, Fla., 1994, Ctr. for Study of Evolution and Origins of Life, UCLA, 1994, Ctr. for Evolutionary Psychology, Santa Barbara, Calif., 1995, Tel Aviv U., 1995, Bar-Ilan U., Israel, 1995, Hebrew U. Jerusalem, 1995, NRC, Washington, 1995, Soc. Exptl. Social Psychology, Washington, 1995, Nat. Assn. for Treatment of Sexual Aggression, New Orleans, 1995, Polish Nat. Acad. Sci., Warsaw U., 1995. Co-author: An Instructor's Manual and Guide for Teaching a Course in Social Psychology, 1976, Pornography, 1993; co-editor Sites and Insights in Psychology, 1976; co-editor, contbr. chpt. to: Pornography and Sexual Aggression, 1984, Sex, Power, Conflict: Evolutionary Feminist Perspectives, 1996; contbr. chpt. to: Aggression in Children and Youth, 1984, Handbook of Research on Rape and Sexual Assault, 1984, Media Violence and Pornography: An International Perspective, 1984, The psychology of Women: Ongoing Debates, 1987, Public Communication and Behavior, Vol. 2, 1989; contbr. or co-contbr. various chpts., also numerous articles; mem. editl. bd. Motivation and Emotion, 1983-89, Comm. Rsch., 1986-92, Jour. Sex Rsch., 1982-99, Sexual Abuse: A Jour. and Treatment, 1995-99; assoc. editor Comm. Concepts Series, 1989-98, Jour. Rsch. in Personality, 1990-93; co-editor issue Jour. Social Issues, 1986. Recipient John Kendall award for Outstanding Contbns. to Psychology, Gustavus Coll., Minn., 1987; rsch. grantee Social Sci. and Humanities Rsch. Coun. Can., 1979-81, NIMH, 1986-89, 89-91, 91-92; named one of 7 scholars among top 100 rschrs. in 4 categories of eminence Personality and Social Psychology Bull., 1992. Fellow APA, Am. Psychol. Soc.; mem. Internat. Comm. Assn. (presenter 1994, Top 5 Conf. Paper award mass comm. divsn. 1987), Internat. Soc. for Rsch. on Aggression, Soc. for Psychol. Study of Social Issues, Soc. for Sci. Study of Sex, Phi Beta Kappa. Office: UCLA Comm Studies Program 334 Kinsey Hall Los Angeles CA 90095-0001

MALANGONI, MARK ALAN, surgeon, educator; b. East Chicago, Ind., Nov. 3, 1949; s. Roland G. and Cornelia (Marza) M.; m. Nancy Knapp, Aug. 12, 1972; children: Joseph, Michael, Jonathan. AB in Zoology cum laude, Ind. U., 1971, MD, 1975. MD; diplomate Am. Bd. Surgery. Asst. prof. surgery Med. Coll. Wis., Milw., 1980-84, assoc. program dir., gen. surgery, 1981-84; assoc. prof. Surgery U. Louisville, 1984-90, chief surgery Humana Hosp., 1985-90; prof. surgery Case Western Res. U., Cleve., 1990—. Chmn. dept. surgery MetroHealth Med. Ctr., Cleve., 1990—. Merit Rev. grantee VA, Louisville, 1985-88. Fellow Am. Coll. Surgeons; mem. Cen. Surg. Assn., So. Surg. Assn., Am. Surg. Assn., Phi Beta Kappa, Alpha Omega Alpha. Office: MetroHealth Med Ctr 2500 Metrohealth Dr # 914 Cleveland OH 44109-1998

MALANY, LE GRAND LYNN, lawyer, engineer, bank executive; b. May 14, 1941; s. LeGrand Franklin and Marion (Jaynes) M.; m. Barbara Bumgarner, June 26, 1965; children: LeGrand Karl, Siobhan, Carleen. BS in Engring. Physics, U. Ill., 1964, JD, 1970. Registered profl. engr., Ill.; bar: Ill. 1970, U.S. Dist. Ct. (cen. dist.) Ill. 1970, Ill. Supreme Ct. 1970, U.S. Ct. Mil. Appeals 1971, U.S. Ct. Appeals (7th cir.) 1972, U.S. Dist. Ct. (so. dist.) Ill. 1974, U.S. Supreme Ct. 1975, U.S. Dist. Ct. (no. dist.) Ill. 1982; lic. real estate broker, bldg. inspector, mgmt. planner, and asbestos project designer Ill. Asst. astronomer Adler Planetarium, Chgo., 1960-63; rsch. asst. Portland Cement Rsch. Assn., Skokie, Ill., 1964; instr. dept. gen. engring. U. Ill., 1965-70; instr. Office Instrn. Resources, 1967-68; lectr. Police Tng. Inst., Urbana, Ill., 1969-70; project dir. driver control program U.S. Dept. Transp., 1971-73, project dir., author driver license examiner tng. curriculum, 1973; assoc. drivers license adminstr. State of Ill., Springfield, 1973-74, asst. auditor gen., 1977-83, asst. atty. gen., dir. policy, planning and tech., 1983-85, chief internal auditor office of atty. gen., 1985-86, spl. asst. atty. gen., 1986—, spl. asst. auditor gen. and gen. counsel office auditor gen., 1986-92, gen. counsel state comptroller Cusas II project, 1986-88; ptnr. Kabumoto and Malany, Springfield, 1986—97; emergency and disaster engr. U.S. Office of Fgn. Disaster Assistance, 2003—. Commr. Williamsville-Sherman Water Commn., 1997—; pres. Microgeneral Ltd., 1983—, assoc. ptnr. Johnson & Assoc., 1990-93, Mgmt. Control Sys., Inc., 1986; chmn. bd. Flowers LaGrand Ltd., 1985—; founder, dir. Foster Bank, Chgo., 1988-90; expert U.S. Fed. Energy Adminstrn., 1974; counsel juvenile divsn. Cir. Ct., Sangamon County, Ill., 1973-75; chief counsel Ill. Dept. Motor Vehicles, Springfield, 1974; trustee Meret Ctr., Inc., 1973-75; internat. dir. construction Shelter Now Internat., HQ Oshkosh, Wis., 1999—. Dem. candidate for States Atty., Sangamon County, Ill., 1980; program dir. sch. renovation projects, Macedonia, 2000, Housing Renovations for Refugees, Macedonia, 1999; bd. dirs. J. Keil Braid Leadership Found., Villagrove, Colo., 1997—, Home Ownership Program for Equity, Springfield, Ill., 1998-2001, Springfield Heritage Found., 1999—; country dir. Macedonia for Shelter Now Internat., 2000—. Recipient Midwest Intergovtl. Audit Forum Recognition award, 1981. Mem. ABA, Am. Phys. Soc., Nat. Soc. Profl. Engrs., Ill. Socs. Profl. Engrs., Ill. Farm Bur., Ill. Christmas Tree Growers Assn., Ill. Foster parents Assn., Rotary (Springfield chpt. sec. 1983-85, pres. 1986-87, trustee Rotary South Found. 1986-93), Habitat for Humanity-Sangamon County (bd. dirs. 1996-2001, dir. constr. 1998-2000). Achievements include development statewide motorcycle driver licensing program. Home: 600 S Rose Hill Ave Springfield IL 62704-1560 Office: 631 E Adams St Springfield IL 62701-1947 Office Phone: 217-525-1132.

MALASANOS, LOIS JULANNE FOSSE, nursing educator; b. LaPorte City, Iowa, Sept. 1, 1928; d. Lewis Reginald and Henrietta Marie Fosse; widowed; 1 child, Toree. BSN, U. Tex., 1948; BA in Gen. Sci., U. Iowa, 1952; MA in Nursing Edn., U. Chgo., 1959; PhD in Physiology, U. Ill., 1973. Assoc. dir. nursing U. Iowa Hosps., Iowa City, 1950-51, staff charge nurse, 1951; instr. operating room Sch. Nursing, Michael Reese Hosp., Chgo., 1951-58; charge nurse, med.-surg. U. Chgo., Billings Hosp., 1952-59; pvt. duty nurse Ill., 1959 63; charge nurse, maternal-infant nursing Weiss Meml. Hosp., Chgo., 1963-66; asst. prof. Loyola U., Chgo., 1966-69; teaching asst. in physiology U. Ill., Chgo., 1969-73, assoc. prof., assoc. head gen. nursing dept. Coll. Nursing, 1973-76, prof., assoc. head gen. nursing dept., 1976-80; prof., dean Coll. Nursing U. Fla., Gainesville, 1980-95, Disting. Svc. prof., 1995—. Instr. anatomy and physiology Cook County Hosp., Chgo., 1973; lectr. endocrinology Chgo. Coll. Osteopathic Medicine, 1973-80; active Pres. Clinton's Task Force on Health Care, 1993; cons. Am. Assn. Med. Colls., 1977-78, Am. Heart Assn., 1977-94, Am. Jour. Nursing, 1978-79, Gainesville (Fla.) Vets. Ctr., 1980-95, Lake Butler Receiving Ctr., 1980—; chair Deans and Dirs. of Fla. Colls. Nursing, 1981-89; chair edn. com. State Bd. Nursing, 1983-87, chair probable course com., 1984—; vis. prof. Dokuz Eylul U., Izmir, Turkey, 1995-96; cons., presenter in field. Co-author, editor: Manual of Medical Surgical Nursing, 1983, Translating Comitment to Reality, 1986, Health Assessment, 1977 (Am. Jour. Nursing Book of Yr. award 1977), 4th edit., 1989; editor: Vital Signs, 1981-90, Fla. Cancer Nursing News, 1983-84; co-editor: Fla. Nursing Rev., 1986-90; mem. editl. rev. bd. Image, 1980-96; editl. cons. Nursing, 1982-94; manuscript referee Rsch. in Nursing and Health, 1980-94, Jour. Profl. Nursing, 1985-94, Turkish Jour. Nurse Rsch.; chairperson adv. com. Nursing Outlook, 1986-91, Peer Rev., 1986-94; contbr. more than 100 articles, revs. to profl. jours. Nursing com., scholarship com. and rsch. rev. com. Am. Cancer Soc., Tampa, Fla., 1980-94. Recipient Bronze medal Fla. Heart Assn., 1986, Silver medal Fla. Heart Assn., 1989, 93; named Disting. Alumnus U. Tex. Med. Br., 1985; named to Disting. Faculty, Albany State U., 1988, Hall of Fame, U. Tex. Med. Br., 1992; NEH fellow, 1981; Fulbright awardee to Turkey, 1995-96, 2001-02. Mem. ANA (mem. coun. nurse rschrs.), AACN, AAAS, AAUP, Am. Acad. Nursing (mem. pub. com. 1986-89) Am. Assn. Higher Edn., Am. Assn. Colls. Nursing, Fla. Nurses Assn. (mem. dist. 10), N.Y. Acad. Sci., Fla. League Nursing, Nat. League Nursing (chair, mem. coun. baccalaureate and higher degree program, Dirs. award 1995, site visitor for program rev. 1980—, bd. rev. for accreditation 1993-2002, Outstanding Leadership in Nursing Edn. award 2002), Fla. State Bd. Nursing (probable cause com.), So. Regional Edn. Bd., Sigma Xi, Sigma Theta Tau (Outstanding Leadership award 2003), Phi Kappa Phi (pres. 1987-88). Office: U Fla Coll Nursing PO Box 100187 Gainesville FL 32610-0187 E-mail: malaslj@nursing.ufl.edu.

MALAVE, ANDRES, pharmacologist, educator; b. San Juan, Puerto Rico, Nov. 18, 1949; s. Andres Malave, Adela Nevarez; m. Lillian Arce, July 28, 1972; children: Jose A., Jaime E., Josue I., Jessica M. BS in Pharmacy, U. P.R., 1972; MS, Purdue U., 1981, PhD of Pharmacology, 1983. Registered pharmacist P.R. Instr. U. P.R., San Juan, 1975—78, asst. prof., 1984—87, assoc. prof., 1988—91; prof., chmn. Nova Southeastern U., Ft. Lauderdale, Fla., 1992—2001, assoc. dean, 2001—. CEO Malave Consulting Svcs., Inc., Ft. Lauderdale, 2001—; dean coll. pharmacy U. P.R., 1987—91. Recipient Bristol Meyers/Squibb Faculty Devel. award, 1991—92; scholar, Fulbright, 2001. Mem.: Peruvian Acad. of Pharmacy, N.Y. Acad. Sci., Soc. Neurosci., Am. Assn. Coll. Pharmacy. Achievements include development of simple non-radioactive assay for estimating protein kinase C and protein phosphatase-1. Avocations: sports, racquetball, basketball, music, guitar. Home: 224 La Costa Way Weston FL 33326 Office Phone: 954-262-1384.

MALBON, CRAIG CURTIS, pharmacology educator, university official; b. Providence, June 1, 1950; s. Elroy Willis and Edith Roberta (Curtis) M.; children: Lindsey Gei Sook, Hailey Sook Yee; m. Hsien-yu Wang, June 26, 1993. BA, Mass. State Coll., Worcester, 1972; PhD, Case Western Reserve U., 1976. NIH postdoctoral fellow sect. physiological chemistry Brown U., Providence, 1976-77, research assoc. sect. physiological chemistry, 1977, asst. prof. research sect. physiological chemistry, 1978; asst. prof. dept. pharmacology SUNY Sch. Medicine, Stony Brook, 1978-83, assoc. prof., 1983-90, prof., 1990—; leading univ. prof. Sch. Medicine SUNY, Stony Brook, 1993—, vice chmn. dept. pharmacology, 1988-89, prof. dept. pharmacology, 1990—, assoc. dean biomed. scis. Sch. Medicine, 1989-93, v.p. rsch., 1993-97; vice dean Univ. Hosp. and Med. Ctr. SUNY, Stony Brook, 1993—. Bd. dir. diabetes & metabolic diseases rsch. program NIH, Stony Brook, NY, mem. cell biology & physiology study sect., Bethesda, Md., 1981—86; bd. dir. LI High Tech. Incubator; mem. sci. adv. bd. Brookhaven Nat. Lab. DOE, 1998—. Mem. editl. bd. Am. Jour. Physiology, 1985—, assoc. editor, 1993-99; mem. editl. bd. Jour. Biol. Chemistry, 1988-93; contbr. articles to profl. jours. Mem. Marine Biol. Lab., Inc., Woods Hole, Mass., 1986; bd. dirs. Faculty/Student Assn., Inc., Stony Brook, 1979-82. Recipient nat. rsch. Svc. award NIH, 1976-80, career devel. award, 1981-86; rsch. award Am. Cancer Soc., 1998. Mem. Biophys. Soc., N.Y. Acad. Scis., Am. Physiol. Soc. (editl. bd. 1986, assoc. editor 1990), Am. Soc. for Biochemistry and Molecular Biology (editl. bd. 1988), Biochem. Soc. (U.K.) (hon.), Sigma Xi. Home: PO Box 2726 East Setauket NY 11733-0852 E-mail: craig@pharm.sunysb.edu.

MALBON, LOUISE, nursing educator, hypnotherapist; b. Fayetteville, N.C., Feb. 13, 1956; d. Margaret Bess and John Bullard, Fletcher Bess (Stepfather); children: Lessel Malbon, III, Lawrence A., Leslie. Assoc. Applied Scis., Excelsior Coll., 1987. Cert. CPR instr., ACLS instr.; RN; cert. clin. hypnotherapist. Clin. resource nurse educator DC Gen. Hosp., Washington, 2001—02; ambulatory svs. coord. Wash. Hosp. Ctr., Washington, 2002. ACLS instr. Wash. Adventist Hosp. Tng. Ctr., Takoma Park, 2002—. Author: Caring Enough to Change, 2002. Cmty. activist 8th Precinct Civic Assn., Chillum, 1987—2002. Named 100 Extra Ordinary Nurses, Sigma Theta Tau Internat. Honor Soc. Nursing, 2001. Mem.: Emergency Nurses Assn. Democrat. Baptist. Home and Office: Fresh Start Hypnotherapy and Pub 5405 13th Avenue Chillum MD 20783 Personal E-mail: LSMLB@AOL.COM. Business E-Mail: Freshstarthypnotherapy.com.

MALCHOW, THOMAS A, Olympic athlete; b. St. Paul, Minn., Aug. 18, 1976; Student, U. Mich. Winner Silver medal Pan Am. Games, 1995, 200 meter butterfly swimming Atlanta Olympics, 1996, Gold medal World Univ. Games, 1995. Office: US Swimming Inc One Olympic Plz Colorado Springs CO 80909

MALCOLM, CHRISTINE ANNE, university hospital administrator; b. St. Paul, Jan. 25, 1950; d. Harold Thomas and Velma Lucille (Kuefler) Lehto; m. Mark Justin Malcolm, Sept. 18, 1971; children: Justine Emily, Benjamin Alexander. AB with hons., U. Chgo., 1972, MBA in Hosp. Adminstrn., 1978. Clinic mgr. Hennepin County Med. Ctr., Mpls., 1972-76; adminstrv. resident Ingalls Meml. Hosp., Harvey, Ill., 1977-78; cons. A.T. Kearney, Chgo., 1977, Coopers & Lybrand, Chgo., 1978-80; mgr. Amherst Assocs., Chgo., 1980-81; dir. Coopers & Lybrand, Chgo., 1981-86; v.p. planning and corp. devel. U. Chgo. Hosps., 1986—93; v.p. managed care and network devel. U. Health-System Consortium, Chgo.; v.p. provider solutions Global Health Solutions Group Computer Sci. Corp.; sr. v.p. strategic planning, mktg. and program devel. Rush U. Med. Ctr., Chgo., 2002—. V.p. Q.V., Inc., Chgo., 1987—. Author: (Digital Perspectives column) Healthcare Fin. Mgmt. mag. Sec., treas. and bd. dirs. Chgo. Child Care Soc., 1978—. Recipient Am. Mktg. Assn. Innovator award, 1988; named one of Chicago's 100 Most Influential Women, Crain's Chgo. Bus., 2004; NSF grantee, 1971. Mem. U. Hosp. Consortium, Am. Coll. Healthcare Execs., Am. Mktg. Assn. Lutheran. Avocations: gardening, canoeing, cooking. Office: Rush Univ Med Ctr 1653 W Congress Pkwy Chicago IL 60612*

MALCOLM, DAWN GRACE, family physician; b. L.A., Nov. 3, 1936; d. Thomas N. and Grace S. (Salisian) M. BA, UCLA, 1959; MD, Med. Coll. Pa., 1973. Diplomate Am. Bd. Family Practice. Tchr. elem. music Fullerton (Calif.) Sch. Dist., 1960-61; tchr. Ahlman Acad., Kabul, Afghanistan, 1961-65; intern and resident in family practice Kaiser Found. Hosp., L.A., 1973-76; family physician So. Calif. Permanente Med. Group, L.A., 1976—. Mem. faculty family practice residency program Kaiser Found. Hosp., L.A., 1976—. Fellow Am. Acad. Family Physicians. Office: So Calif Permanente Med Grp 4747 Sunset Blvd Los Angeles CA 90027-6021

MALCOLM, MOLLY BETH, political party official, counselor; BAS in Elem. Edn. with high honors, So. Meth. U., 1976; MS in Counseling and Guidance, Tex. A&M U.-Texarkana, 1988. Lic. profl. counselor, lic. chem. dependency counselor, Tex. Tchr. pub. schs., Ark., Tex., Okla., 1977-87; elem. counselor Texarkana (Ark.) Schs., 1987-89; drug. abuse prevention and counseling specialist Region VII Edn. Svc. Ctr., Kilgore, Tex., 1989-90; drug free schs. student assistance coord. Longview (Tex.) Ind. Sch. Dist., 1990-92; counseling and student svcs. coord. Texarkana (Tex.) Ind. Schs., 1992-93; owner, counselor Malcolm Cons., 1993—; field dir. Max Sandlin for Congress Campaign, 1996; dist. cmty. outreach coord. Congress Max Sandlin, Tex. 1st Dist., 1997-98; state chair Tex. Dem. Party, 1998—2003. Contbr. publs. and curricula. Active Dem. Nat. Com., 1998-2003, exec. com., 2000-2003; active Presbytery of the Pines, Synod of the Sun Presbyn. Ch. USA, Pine Street Middle Sch. PTA; pres. Texarkana Ind. Sch. Dist., 1993-94; deacon First Presbyn. Ch., Texarkana; advisor career devel. U. Tex. Chi Omega, 1999-2001; Texarkana bd. dirs. Susan G. Komen Race for the Cure. Named one of Rising Stars in Politics, Campaigns and Elections Mag., 2000, Pres.' award Ark. Counseling Assn., 1989, Hon. Bill Clinton Gov. Ark. Traveler award, 1989, Texarkana Alumni Achievement award Tex. A&M U., 1989, Winnsboro ISD Disting. Alumni award, 2003, Tex. Women's Polit. Caucus Blazing New Trails award Tex. Lyceum Assn., Inc., 2001-. Mem. NAACP (life), Tex. Counseling Assn. (Disting. Svc. award 1993, 96), Tex. Mental Health Counselors Assn., Tex. Sch. Counselors Assn., Tex. Assn. for Multicultural Counseling and Devel. (chair awards com. 1994), N.E. Tex. Counseling Assn., Assn. State Dem. Chairs (co-chair resolution com. 1999-2001, exec. com., treas. exec. com. 2001-2004), Tex. Rural Cmtys. Bd., Clinton Birthplace Found. Bd., Texarkana Mus. Sys. Bd., Texarkana Hist. Landmark Preservation Commn., Texarkana Regional Arts and Humanities Coun., Inc.(mem. AMAX adv. bd. 2004-), Better Orgn. New Downtown Bd., Tex. Dem. Women (pres. 1997-99, Mem. of Yr. 1998), Leadership Texarkana Alumi Assn. (adv. bd. 1996-99), Jr. League Texarkana, Leadership Tex. Alumnae Assn. (life, adv. bd. 1996-99), Ark. PTA (life), DAR, Tex. A&M U. at Texarkana Alumni Assn. (life, Achievement award 1989), So. Meth. U. Alumni Assn. (life), Rotary Internat., Psi Chi (v.p. 1987-89), Delta Kappa Gamma (pres. chpt. 1988-89), Chi Omega (pres. chpt. alumni assn. 1998-99), Dem. Nat. Com., Texarkana C. of C. (mil. affairs com.), Tex. Lyceum Assn. (bd. dirs.), Am. Legion. Office: Malcolm Consulting PO Box 6282 Texarkana TX 75505

MALCOLM, STEVEN J. petroleum pipeline company executive; b. St. Louis, Sept. 1948; m. Gwen Malcolm; 1 child. BCE, U. Mo.-Rolla, 1970. Sr. v.p., gen. mgr. Williams Field Svcs. Co., 1994—98; pres., CEO Williams Energy Svcs. LLC, 1998—2001; pres., COO Williams Companies, Tulsa, Okla., 2001—02, chmn., pres., CEO, 2002—. Office: Williams 1 Williams Ctr Tulsa OK 74172*

MALCOM, SHAWNA L. journalist; b. Hamburg, Iowa, July 9, 1975; BSJ, Northwestern U., Evanston, IL, 1993—97. Editl. asst. Entertainment Weekly, New York, NY, 1997—99; staff writer TV Guide, Los Angeles, Calif., 1999—. Freelance work In Style, Rolling Stone, Cosmopolitan, Teen People, Los Angeles, Calif. Mem.: NUEA West, Alpha Chi Omega. Avocations: travel, volunteer. Office: TV Guide 6922 Hollywood Blvd 11th Fl Hollywood CA 90028 E-mail: shawna.malcom@tvguide.com.

MALDE, HAROLD EDWIN, retired federal government geologist; b. Reedsport, Oreg., July 9, 1923; s. Emil and Bessie May (Alspaugh) M.; m. Caroline Elizabeth Rose, Dec. 21, 1954; children; Margaret Jean, Melissa Ruth. AB, Willamette U., 1947; postgrad., Harvard U., 1947-48, U. Colo., 1948-51. Geologist U.S. Geol. Survey, Denver, 1951-87, emeritus, 1987—; affiliate prof. U. Idaho, 1968—76, 1987—91. Mem. Colo. com. for Nat. Register Hist. Places, 1972-80; vol. photographer Nature Conservancy, 1987—; mem. paleoanthropology del. to Peoples Republic China, Nat. Acad. Scis., 1975, mem. various coms. for study surface mining, 1973-79; mem. oil shale environ. adv. panel U.S. Dept. Interior, 1976-80. Contbr. numerous sci. papers to profl. lit. Served to ensign USNR, 1942-44. Recipient Meritorious Service award U.S. Dept. Interior, 1979, Oak Leaf award Nature Conservancy, 1993. Fellow Geol. Soc. Am. (Kirk Bryan award 1970, assoc. editor 1982-88), AAAS, Ariz.-Nev. Acad. Sci.; mem. Am. Quaternary Assn., Explorers Club, Assn. Earth Sci. Editors. Democrat. Unitarian Universalist. Home: 842 Grant Pl Boulder CO 80302-7415 E-mail: halmalde@msn.com.

MALDEN, KARL (MALDEN SEKULOVICH), actor; b. Chgo., Mar. 22, 1912; s. Peter and Minnie (Sebera) Sekulovich; m. Mona Graham, Dec. 18, 1938; children— Mila, Carla. Student, Goodman Theatre, Chgo., 1935-38. Pres. Acad. of Motion Arts and Scis., 1989-92; mem. Citizens Stamp Com., U.S. Govt., Washington. Actor, 1935—; stage plays include Golden Boy, 1938, Gentle People, 1939, Key Largo, 1940, Flight to the West, 1942, Uncle Harry, 1940, All My Sons, 1949, A Streetcar Named Desire, 1950, Desire Under the Elms, 1952, Desperate Hours, 1954; in motion pictures, 1940 films include: Boomerang, Gunfighter, 1945, Halls of Montezuma, 1950, A Streetcar Named Desire (Acad. award for best supporting actor), 1951, Ruby Gentry, 1952, I Confess, 1953, On the Waterfront, 1954, Baby Doll, 1956, Desperate Hours, 1957, Fear Strikes Out, 1957, The Hanging Tree, 1959, Pollyanna, 1960, One Eyed Jacks, 1961, Parrish, The Adventures of Bullwhip Griffin, 1967, Patton, 1970, Beyond the Poseidon Affair, 1978, Meteor, 1979, Sting II, 1982, Twilight Time, 1982, Billy Galvin, 1987, Nuts, 1987; TV films include: Word of Honor, 1981, Miracle on Ice, 1981, Intent to Kill, 1983, Fatal Vision, 1984 (Emmy award), My Father My Son, 1988, The Hijacking of the Achille Lauro, 1989, Call Me Anna, 1990, Absolute Strangers, 1991, Back to the Streets of San Francisco, 1992; dir.: Time Limit, 1957, Billion Dollar Brain, 1967, Hot Millions, 1968, Hotel, Cat O'Nine Tails, 1971, Wild Rovers, 1971, Summertime Killer, 1973, Nuts, 1987; star TV series Streets of San Francisco, 1972-77, Skag, 1980. Recipient Donaldson award, 1950, Critic's award, 1950, Lifetime Achievement Award, Screen Actors Guild, 2003. Address: 1845 Mandeville Canyon Rd Los Angeles CA 90049-2222

MALDONADO, CARLOS MANUEL, surgeon; b. Barcelona, Sept. 25, 1938; came to U.S., 1964. MD, U. Barcelona, 1964. Diplomate Am. Bd. Surgery. Intern Columbia Hosp., Milw., 1964-65; resident in gen. surgery Marquette Affiliatee Hosps., Milw., 1966-68; fellow in thoracic cardiac surgery Newark Beth Israel Med. Ctr., 1969-70, resident in gen. surgery, 1972-75. Mem. staff Martin Meml. Hosp., Stuart, Fla., Martin Meml. Hosp. South, Ft. Salerno, Fla., 1975—, chief of surgery, 1983-85, chmn. quality coun., 1994—. Fellow ACS; mem. AMA, Fla. Med. Assn., Internat. Soc. Cardiovascular Surgery, Southeastern Surg. Congress, Martin County Med. Soc. (pres. 1999). Address: 421 SE Osceola St Stuart FL 34994-2505 Office Phone: 772-286-0050. Business E-Mail: carlosmmaldonado@cs.com.

MALDONADO, F. CÉSAR, priest, educator; b. Itapaya-Cochabamba, Bolivia, Jan. 6, 1962; arrived in U.S., 1998; s. Benigno Maldonado, Pastora Sanabria. Philosophy Licenciatura, Cochabamba, 1986; B. Theology, U. Catolica, 1990; M.Anthropology, FLACSO, Quito, Ecuador, 1992; postgrad., Georgetown U., Washington, 1999—. Ordained priest, Roman Cath. Ch.; entered Soc. of Jesus. Tchr. Juan XXIII H.S., Cochabamba, Bolivia, 1987—88; prof. Pontificia U. Católica, Quito, Ecuador, 1991—92; cons. Acción Cultural Loyola, Sucre, Bolivia, 1993—95; prof. U. Catolica, Col-

hambamba, Bolivia, 1995—97; prin. Juan XXIII H.S., Colhambamba, 1996—97; cons. Centro de Investigacion y Promociōn Campesinado, Santa Cruz, Bolivia, 1997—98; prof. U. Gabriel Renē Moreno, Santa Cruz, 1997—98. Contbr. articles to profl. jours. Mem.: Spanish Masses Arlington. Roman Catholic. Avocations: sports, meditation, poetry. Mailing: 37th and O Sts NW Washington DC 20057-0001 E-mail: fcm@georgetown.edu.

MALDONADO, GRAZIANO, management consultant, educator; b. San Juan, P.R., Dec. 5, 1955; s. Graziano Maldonado and Virginia Martínez; 1 child, Gabriel. MBA, Bloomsburg State U. of Pa., 1985; ABD, Argosy U. at Sarasota, Fla., 2004. Sr. auditor Price WaterhouseCoopers (Formerly Price Waterhouse & Co), San Juan, PR, 1978—81; CEO Gen. Mgmt. Assistance Corp., San Juan, PR, 1984—91; dir. adminstrn. and contr. Retail Mgmt., Inc., Caguas, PR, 1995—96; contr. Ana G. Mendez U. System, San Juan, 1997—99; prin. ptnr. and mng. dir. Synectics for Mgmt. Decisions, Inc., San Juan, 1991—93; contr. GM Co LLP, Orlando, Fla., 1999. Recipient Disting. Info. Sciences award - Svc. Sector, Assn. of Info. Systems Profls., 1993; grantee Grad. Assistanship award, Bloomsburg State U. of PA, 1994—95. Mem.: Am. Acctg. Assn. (assoc.), Soc. for Human Resource Mgmt. (assoc.), P.R. C. of C. (assoc.). Democrat-Npl. Catholic. Avocation: travel. Home: 246 St No HV-20 Carolina PR 00982 Office: GM Co LLP 7380 Sand Lake Rd Orlando FL 32819 Office Phone: 407-352-3980. E-mail: graziano.maldonado@gmcollp.com.

MALDONADO, KIRK FRANCIS, lawyer; b. Omaha, Mar. 7, 1950; s. Manuel and Orpha Mae (Kovar) Maldonado. BA, U. Nebr.-Omaha, 1975; JD, Creighton U., 1978; MLT, Georgetown U., 1981. Bar: Nebr. 1981, Calif. 1982. Atty. Employee Plans and Exempt Orgns. Divsn. Office of Chief Counsel IRS, Washington, 1978—81; assoc. Gibson, Dunn & Crutcher, Newport Beach, Calif., 1982—85; prin. Stradling, Yocca, Carlson & Rauth, Newport Beach, 1985—89, Riordan & McKinzie, Costa Mesa, Calif., 1989—2001; ptnr. Bobeck Phleger & Harrison LLP, 2001—03, Sherman & Howard, LLC, Denver, 2003—. Contbr. articles to profl. jours. Mem.: ABA (employee benfits com.), State Bar Calif. Office: Sherman & Howard LLC 633 17th St Ste 3000 Denver CO 80202 E-mail: kmaldonado@sah.com.

MALDONADO, NORMAN I. physician, educator; b. Adjuntas, P.R., Nov. 3, 1935; s. Herminio and Esther (Simon) M.; m. Mary Anne Maldonado, July 2, 1960; children: Norman H., Michael A., Maria B., Luis F., Ana E. BA, Inter Am. U., San Germán, P.R., 1955; MD, U. P.R., San Juan, 1959; D Honoris Causa, U. West Indies, 1999. Intern D.C. Gen. Hosp., Washington, 1959-60; resident in internal medicine Univ. Hosp. of San Juan, 1960-61, 64, fellow in hematology, 1964-65, New Eng. Ctr. Hosp., 1966; chief hematology sect. U. P.R. Med. Sch., San Juan, 1966-73; med. dir. San Juan City Hosp., 1973-76; undersec. health Commonwealth of P.R., San Juan, 1977-78; chancellor med. scis. campus U. P.R., San Juan, 1978-85, prof. medicine, 1985—; pres. U P.R. Sys., San Juan, 1994—2001. Cons. hematology VA Hosp., Tchrs. Hosp., San Juan, 1968- Contbr. articles to profl. jours. Bd. dirs. P.R. chpt. ARC, San Juan, 1973-; pres. fund raising Soc. for Crippled Children and Adults, San Juan, 1980; pres. adv. bd. Antiaddiction Services Dept., San Juan, 1982-84; mem. adv. bd. P.R. Planning Bd., San Juan, 1983-84. Served to capt. U.S. Army, 1962-63 Named Outstanding Young Man in Medicine, P.R. Jr. C. of C., 1972, Outstanding Man in Medicine, P.R. Jr. C. of C., 1983, hon. prof. U. Madre Maestra, Dominican Republic, 1985 Fellow ACP; mem. Am. Soc. Hematology, Internat. Soc. Hematology, P.R. Soc. Hematology (pres. 1983-85), Alpha Omega Alpha Roman Catholic. Avocations: reading; sports. Home: 16-10 Calle Granada Guaynabo PR 00966-3116 Office: U PR Sys Office of the Pres PO Box 364984 San Juan PR 00936-4984

MALDONADO-BEAR, RITA MARINITA, economist, educator; b. Vega Alta, P.R., June 14, 1938; d. Victor and Marina (Davila) Maldonado; m. Larry Alan Bear, Mar. 29, 1975. BA, Auburn U., 1960; PhD, NYU, 1969. With Min. Wage Bd. & Econ. Devel. Adminstr., Govt. of P.R., 1969-70; asst. prof. econs. Manhattan Coll., 1970-72; assoc. prof. econs. Bklyn. Coll., 1972-75; assoc. prof. fin. & econs., undergrad./grad. divsn. Stern Sch. Bus. NYU, 1975-81, prof., 1981—2004, prof. emerita, 2004—. Vis. assoc. prof. fin. Stanford (Calif.) Grad. Bus. Sch., 1973-74; acting dir. markets, ethics & law, NYU, 1993-94; cons. Morgan Guaranty Trust Co., N.Y.C., 1972-77, Bank of Am., N.Y.C., 1982-84, Res. City Bankers, N.Y.C., 1978-87, Swedish Inst. Mgmt., Stockholm, 1982-91, Empresas Master of P.R., 1985-90. Author: Role of the Financial Sector in the Economic Development of Puerto Rico, 1970; co-author: Free Markets, Finance, Ethics and Law, 1994; contbr. articles to profl. jours. Bd. dirs. Medallion Funding Corp., 1985-87; mem. NYU Senate and Faculty Coun., 1995—2003, chair fin. com., 1996—2000; apptd. adv. bd. dirs. equity & diversity in ednl. environs. Mid. States Commn. Higher Edn., 1991—; trustee Securities Industry Assn., N.Y. Dist. Econ. Edn. Found., 1994—; chair NSF, Nat. Vis. Com. Curriculum Devel. Project Networked Fin. Simulation, 1995—; econ. cons. Inst. Women of Color, Nat. Coun. Black Women Cmty. Svcs. Fund, 2000—; trustee Bd. Edn., Twp. Mahwah, N.J., 1991-92. P.R. Econ. Devel. Adminstrn. fellow, 1960-65, Marcus Nadler fellow, NYU, 1966-67, Phillips Lods Dissertation fellow, 1967-68. Mem. Am. Econs. Assn., Am. Fin. Assn., Metro. Econ. Assn. N.Y., Assn. Social Econs. (trustee exec. coun. 1994-96). Home: 95 Tam O Shanter Dr Mahwah NJ 07430-1526 Office: Mgmt Edn Ctr 44 W 4th St Ste 9-190 New York NY 10012-1106

MALDONADO-DEOLIVEIRA, DÉBORA, classicist, researcher; d. Angel A. and Clara E. Maldonado; m. Manoel L. DeOliveira, June 6, 1996. LittB in Comparative Lit., U. P.R., Río Piedras, 1989; MLitt in Comparative Lit., U. Rochester, 1994, PhD in Comparative Lit., 2000. Spanish instr. Durham Tech. C.C., Durham, NC, 2000; asst. libr. U. P.R., Río Piedras; grad. tchg. asst. U. Rochester, 1990—96; asst. prof. Spanish Wayne State U., Detroit, 1997—99, Meredith Coll., Raleigh, NC, 2000—. Mem.: MLA, Rocky Mountain Lang. Assn., Fgn. Lang. Assn. N.C., Am. Assn. Tchrs. Spanish and Portuguese, So. Humanities, Feministas Unidas. Office: Meredith Coll Joyner Hall Dept Fgn Lang & Lit 3800 Hillsborough St Raleigh NC 27607

MALE, ALAN THOMAS, engineering educator, association executive; b. Birmingham, England, Sept. 3, 1937; came to U.S., 1968; s. Albert Leslie and Olive (Caddel) M.; m. Beryl Glover, Sept. 20, 1958; children: Andrew James, Christopher John. BSc, U. Birmingham, 1958, PhD, 1962. Registered profl. engr. Pa., Ky.; chartered engr. U.K. Lectr. U. Birmingham, 1960-67; supr. Westinghouse Astronuclear Lab., Pitts., 1968-70; from mgr. metals processing to mgr. processing rsch. Westinghouse Rsch. Labs., Pitts., 1970-83; mgr. advanced processing Westinghouse Sci. & Tech. Ctr., Pitts., 1990-91; prin., tech. mgr. Concurrent Techs. Corp., Johnstown, Pa., 1992-96; dir. Ctr. for Robotics and Mfg. Systems U. Ky., assoc. dean rsch. and grad. studies College of Engring., 1996—, prof. mech. engring. Holder 16 patents in field. Fellow Inst. Materials (award 1977), Soc. Mfg. Engrs. (life, internat. dir. 1991-99, pres. N.Am. mfg. rsch. inst. 1988-89, Frederick W. Taylor Rsch. medal 1989, internat. pres. 1997-98), ASM Internat. (life); mem. ASME, Am. Welding Soc. Republican. Methodist. Avocations: freemasonry, carpentry, fishing. Home: 3390 Mantilla Dr Lexington KY 40513-1039

MALE, ROY RAYMOND, English language educator; b. Bklyn., Mar. 15, 1919; s. Roy Raymond and Mary Edwards (Brooks) M.; m. Carolyn Kate Conlisk, Aug. 19, 1944; children: Marilyn, Frank. BS, Hamilton Coll., 1939; MA, Columbia U., 1940; PhD, U. Tex., 1950. Instr. English U. Tex., 1946-50; asst. prof. Tex. Tech. Coll., 1950-55; mem. faculty U. Okla., 1955-84, Boyd prof. English emeritus. Vis. prof. Bowling Green U., 1962, U. Wash., 1968, U. Tex. at Arlington, 1971 Author: Hawthorne's Tragic Vision, 1957, Enter, Mysterious Stranger, 1979; editor: Types of Short Fiction, 2d edit, 1970, Money Talks, 1981; co-editor: Am. Literary Masters, 1974. Served with AUS, 1940-45. Ford Found. fellow, 1954-55; Recipient Regents award excellence teaching U. Okla., 1968 Mem. Modern Lang. Assn., South Central Modern Lang. Assn. (pres. 1968) Home: Hilton Head Plantation 40 Field Sparrow Rd Hilton Head Island SC 29926-1813 E-mail: RoyMale@aol.com.

MALEC, WILLIAM FRANK, utilities company executive; b. Broadalbin, N.Y., June 22, 1940; s. Henry and Anna Frances M.; m. Sarah Powell, Sept. 11, 1965; children: Charles A., Mariah E. BS cum laude, Niagara U., 1962; MBA, Ind. U., 1967; AMP, Harvard U., 1987. Mgmt. trainee Marine Midland Bank, Buffalo, 1962-63; project budget analyst Cleve. Electric Illuminating Co., 1967-68; asst. treas. Mid-Continent Telephone Co., Hudson, Ohio, 1968-75; v.p., treas. Gulf States Utilities, Beaumont, Tex., 1975-78; treas. Cen. and S.W. Corp., C&W Leasing Inc., CSW Energy Inc., CSW Fin., Inc., Dallas; v.p., treas. Cen. and S.W. Services, Inc., Dallas, 1978-89; pres. C&W Credit, Inc., 1985-89; exec. v.p., CFO TVA, Knoxville, 1989-95. Pres. Paradise Ranch Homeowners Assn.; founder Fredericksburg New Comers Club. Served with U.S. Army, 1963-65. Mem. Nat. Mgmt. Assn., Leading Chief Fin. Officers. Republican. Roman Catholic. Office: 110 N Nilam St No PMB 123 Fredericksburg TX 78624

MALECHA, MARVIN JOHN, architect, academic administrator; b. Lonsdale, Minn., June 26, 1949; s. George and Barbara Malecha; m. Cynthia Marie Miller, Aug. 8, 1970; children: Peter, Michelle. Student, St. Thomas Coll.; BArch, U. Minn.; MArch, Harvard U. Registered architect, Calif. Designer Wallace and Mundt Architects, Edina, Minn., 1969-73, Hugh Stubbins and Assocs., Cambridge, Mass., 1973-76; instr. Cambridge Urban Awareness Program, 1973-76, Boston Archtl. Ctr., 1974-76; asst. chmn., asst. prof. dept. arch. Coll. Environ. Design Calif. State Poly. U., Pomona, 1976-77, chmn., assoc. prof., 1979-82, prof., dean Coll. Environ. Design, 1982-94; dean Coll. Design N.C. State U., 1994—. Chmn. Univ. Fall Conf. com. Calif. State Poly. U., 1984; mem. steering com. Architects for Social Responsibility; mem. bd. advisors Tchrs. cert. program City Bldg. Edn. Program, planning com. So. Calif. Assn. Govts.; vis. critic UCLA, 1985, U., Minn., 1981-83, 87, U. So. Calif., 1980-87, Calif. Poly. State U., San Luis Obispo, 1979-87, Clemson U., 1988, Columbia U., 1993, U. Tenn., 1994, U. Md., 1995, Miss. State U., 1995, U. Wis., Milw., 1996, Roger Williams U., 1997; lectr. to schs. and archtl. assns.; cons. in architecture and research, Claremont, Calif., 1976—; master juror Nat. Council Archtl. Registration Bds.; mem. edn. equity com. Calif. State U. System, 1985-86; pres. Calif. Coun. Archtl. Edn., 1986-88; mem. accreditation vis. team for collegiate programs in landscape architecture, 1988—; bd. dirs. Nat. Archtl. Accreditation Bd.; campus architect cons. U. Calif., Riverside, 1990-94. Author: Reconfiguration in the Study and Practice of Architecture, Form of Performance, The Fabric of Architecture, The Pomona Method; co-sgner, author internat. protocol for internat. exch. in arch. edn.; contbr. articles to profl. jours. Mem. Art and Liturgy com. Our Lady Assumption Ch., Claremont, Calif., 1982-94; mem. bldg. and real estate com. Archdiocese of Raleigh; bd. dirs. United Arts Raleigh, City Gallery Raleigh, 1995—. Recipient Ellerbe Archtl. award, 1972, Hon. Mention Mass. Housing Dept., 1976, Topaz medallion for excellence in archtl. edn., 2003, Prize for Creative Integration of Practice and Edn. in the Acad., Nat. Coun. Archtl. Registration, 2002; Rotch scholar, 1980. Fellow AIA (bd. dirs. L.A. chpt. 1982-83, chmn. state and nat. awards coms. 1983-85, chmn. Monterey design conf. com., Henry Adams award 1973, mem. steering com. archs. in edn. com. 1991, chair archs. in edn. com. 1994-95, adv. bd. ArchVoices, co-chmn. case study workgroup Downtown Raleigh Alliance, presdl. citation L.A. chpt. 1987, mem. Calif. coun. 1994, Excellence in Arch. Edn. award), European Assn. for Arch. Educators (hon.), Soc. Am. Registered Archs., Assn. Collegiate Schs. Arch. (v.p. 1988-89, chair ann. meeting, pres. 1988-89, adminstrs. conf. Washington 1985, Disting. Prof. 2002), Calif. Coun. Archtl. Edn. (pres. 1988-89), Golden Key (hon. mem. N.C. chpt.). Office: NC State U Coll Design PO Box 7701 Raleigh NC 27695-0001

MALECKI, EDWARD STANLEY, JR., political science educator; b. Chgo., Nov. 16, 1938; s. Edward Stanley and Lucille Clara (May) M.; m. Judith Evelyn Sobczak, Aug. 24, 1962; children: Stephen, Robert. BA, U. Ill., 1961, LL.B., 1963, MA, 1965, PhD (Charles Merriam fellow), 1969. Bar: Ill. 1963. Asst. prof. polit. sci. Calif. State U., L.A., 1967-71, assoc. prof., 1971-76, prof., 1976—, chair dept. Polit. Sci., 1993-99, acting dir. curriculum and instrn., 1998-99, dir. curriculum and instrn., 1999, acting assoc. dean, 1999—2002; dean Coll. Arts and Scis., Met. State U., Mpls./St. Paul, 2002—. Author: (with H.R. Mahood) Group Politics: A New Emphasis, 1972; contbr. articles to profl. jours.; patentee in field for kneading paddle extraction device. Chmn. Caucus for a New Polit. Sci., 1970-71; ednl. cons. Foothill Urban League, 1969-70; bd. dirs. Pasadena Area Democratic Council, 1974. Calif. State U. Los Angeles Found. grantee, 1971-72, 84-85; HEW-Urban League grantee, 1969-70; NEH fellow, 1987. Mem. Ill. Bar Assn., Am. Polit. Sci. Assn. (Outstanding Tchg. in Polit. Sci. award with Pi Sigma Alpha 1998), Am. Sociol. Assn., United Profs. Calif. (chpt. sec. 1974), ACLU (chpt. pres. 1974, 85-86, bd. dirs. So. Calif. 1981), Phi Kappa Phi. Home: 2556 Oakridge Ct E Maplewood MN 55119-6793 Office: 708 F Seventh St Saint Paul MN 55106-5000

MALEK, FREDERIC VINCENT, finance company executive; b. Oak Park, Ill., Dec. 22, 1936; s. Fred W. and Martha (Smickilas) M.; m. Marlene A. McArthur, Aug. 5, 1961; children: Fred W., Michelle A. BS, U.S. Mil. Acad., 1959; MBA, Harvard U., 1964; D of Humanities (hon.), St. Leo Coll., St. Petersburg, Fla., 1970. Assoc. McKinsey & Co., Inc., L.A., 1964-67; chmn. exec. com. Triangle Corp., Columbia, S.C., 1967-69; dep. under sec. HEW, Washington, 1969-70; spl. asst. to Pres. U.S., Washington, 1970-73; dep. dir. U.S. Office of Mgmt. and Budget, Washington, 1973-75; with Marriott Corp., Washington, 1975-88, sr. v.p., 1975-77, exec. v.p., 1978-88; pres. Marriott Hotels and Resorts, 1981-88, Northwest Airlines, Mpls., 1989-90, vice chmn., 1990-91, also bd. dirs.; campaign mgr. Bush-Quayle '92, 1991-92; co-chmn. CB Richard Ellis, 1989-96; chmn. Lodging Opportunities Fund, 1991—, Thayer Capital Ptnrs., 1992—, Thayer Hotel Investors, 1994—. Chmn. 1996 Rep. Presdl. Trust, 1995-96; bd. dirs. Automated Data Processing Corp., Fannie Mae, N.W. Airlines, FPL Group Inc., Manor Care Inc., CB Richard Ellis; dir. with rank of amb., 1990 Econ. Summit, 1989—; adj. prof. U. S.C., 1986-89; lectr. Kennedy Sch. Govt., Harvard U., 1976. Mem. Pres.'s Commn. on White House Fellows, 1971-75, White House Domestic Coun., 1974-75, Pres.'s Commn. on Pers. Interchange, 1974-76; dep. dir. com. for Re-election of Pres., 1972; Pres.'s Commn. on Pvt. Sector Initiatives, 1982-85, dir. conv. Bush for Pres., 1988; mem. Nat. Coun. on Surface Transp. Rsch., 1993-95; nat. adv. bd. Nat. Ctr. Econ. Edn. of Children, 1980-82; mem. Pres.'s Coun. on Phys. Fitness and Sports, 1986-91. Named Bus. Statesman of Yr. Harvard Bus. Sch. Club Washington, 2000, Citizen of Yr. Boy Scouts Am. Nat. Capitol Coun., 2000, Am. Friends of Czech Republic Civil Soc. Vision award, Woodrow Wilson award for corp. citizenship. Mem. Am.-Israel Friendship League (bd. trustees 1991—), Aspen Inst. (bd. trustees 1996—). Episcopalian. Avocations: bicycling, skiing. Office: 1455 Pennsylvania Ave NW Washington DC 20004-1008 Office Phone: 202-371-0150.

MALEK, M. MIKE, medical association administrator; Diplomate Am. Bd. Surgery. Resident Hamot Med. Ctr., Duke U. Ctr., Shriners Hosp. Sys.; dir. Washington Orthop. and Knee Clinic. Lectr. Contbr. articles to profl. jours. Founder Nat. Knee Rsch. Edn. Found. Fellow Sports Medicine, U. Cin. Med. Ctr. Fellow: ACS, Soc. Knee, Internat. Arthoscopy Assn., Am. Orthop. Soc. Sports Medicine, Am. Acad. Orthop. Surgeons, Anthroscopic and Reconstructive Knee Surgery; mem.: Arthroscopy Assn. N.Am. (pres.), European Soc. Sports Traumatology, Knee Surgery and Antrhoscopy, Internat. Soc. Anthroscopy, Knee Surgery, and Orthop. Sports Medicine, Am. Assn. Hip and Knee Surgeons. Office: Washington Orthop & Knee Clinic 7777 Leesburg Pike Ste 3025 Falls Church VA 22043-2403

MALEK, MARLENE ANNE, healthcare advocate, foundation administrator; b. Oakland, Calif., June 22, 1939; d. William and Yolanda (Stella) McArthur; m. Frederic Malek; children: Frederic William, Michelle A. duPont. Degree in nursing, Marymount U. Vice chmn. bd. dirs. Marymount U., Arlington, Va.; presdl. appointee bd. dirs. Kennedy Ctr., 2002—; mem. adv. bd. Second Genesis, Bethesda, Md.; bd. dirs. Nat. Mus. Women in Arts, World Wildlife Found. Coun.; mem. collectors com. Nat. Gallery of Art; pres. Friends of Cancer Rsch., Washington; presdl. appointment to Nat. Cancer Adv. Bd., 1991-96; mem. bd. overseers Duke U. Cancer Ctr.; mem. Nat. Dialogue on Cancer. Episcopalian. Avocations: cross country skiing, road biking.

MALEK, REZA SAID, urological surgeon; b. Aug. 22, 1940; s. Said and Banoo (Rais) M.; m. Haleh F. Rassa, Feb. 9, 1980. MB, BS, U. London, 1964; MS in Urology, U. Minn., 1971. Diplomate Am. Bd. Urology. Intern St. Mary's Hosp., Eastbourne, Eng., 1964-65, Lister Hosp., Hitchin, Eng., 1964-65; resident, sr. house officer St. Thomas's Hosp., U. London, 1965-66, Mayo Grad. Sch. Medicine, Rochester, Minn., 1967-71; rsch. fellow in calculous disease of urinary tract, vis. clin. surgeon Bowman-Gray Sch. Medicine, Winston-Salem, N.C., 1971-72; instr. urology Mayo Clinic, Rochester, 1972-74, asst. prof., 1974-76, assoc. prof., 1976-91, prof., 1991—. Adviser to regional dir. WHO, 1972; cons. urology Mayo Clinic, 1972—; mem. Am. Bd. Urology Examiners commn., 1978-81. Mem. editl. bd. Mayo Clin. Proceedings, 1994-96. Fellow ACS, Royal Coll. Physicians and Surgeons of Can., Am. Soc. for Laser Medicine and Surgery; mem. AMA, Am. Urological Assn. Home: 1523 Camelback Ct NE Rochester MN 55906-8960 Office: Mayo Clinic 200 1st St SW Rochester MN 55905-0002

MALEKOFF, ANDREW, social services administrator, writer; b. Newark, May 14, 1951; s. Isadore and Evelyn Malekoff; m. Dale Hashkowitz, July 27, 1980; children: Jamie, Darren. BA, Rutgers Coll., 1973; MSW, Adelphi U. Sch. of Social Work, 1976—78. Cert. social worker NY State, 1979; credentialed alcoholism and substance abuse counselor NY, 1992. Social worker/ assoc. exec. dir. North Shore Child and Family Guidance Ctr., Roslyn Heights, NY, 1977—; vista vol. VISTA, Grand Island, Nebr., 1974. Author: Groan Up: from Newark to Nebraska- A True Story (sort of), 2003, Nightcrawlers: after hours in the ER, Group Work with Adolescents: Principles and Practice; editor: Group Work with Suburbia's Children: Difference, Acceptance, and Belonging, Stories Celebrating Group Work, Haworth Press, 1992—; editor, author 9/11 Memorial Issue of REFLECTIONS. Commr. civil svc. City of Long Beach, NY, 2004—. Mem.: NASW, Assn. Advancement Social Work with Groups. Home: 9 Kirkwood St Long Beach NY 11561 Office: N Shore Child and Family Guidance Ctr 480 Old Westbury Rd Roslyn Heights NY 11577 Office Phone: 516-626-1971 ext 326. Personal E-mail: anjru@aol.com. Business E-Mail: amalekoff@northshorechildguidance.org.

MALEN, BETTY, education policy and leadership educator; b. Fargo, N.D., July 6, 1946; d. Harold Martin and Lucille Gudrun (Larson) Malen. BA in Speech Comm., Concordia Coll., Moorhead, Minn., 1964; MA in Ednl. Adminstrn., U. N.D., 1973; PhD in Ednl. Policy and Adminstrn., U. Minn., 1983. Cert. adminstr. K-12 schs. N.D. Tchr. Huron H.S., Ann Arbor, Mich., 1968—72; adminstrv. staff Ann Arbor (Mich.) Pub. Schs., 1971—72; dir. dropout prevention program South H.S., Fargo, ND, 1972—79; asst. prin. North H.S., Fargo, ND, 1983—84; asst. prof. ednl. adminstrn. U. Utah, Salt Lake City, 1984—89, assoc. prof., 1989—90; assoc. prof. ednl. leadership and policy studies U. Wash., Seattle, 1990—94; prof. edn. policy and leadership U. Md., College Park, 1994—. Contbr. chapters to books, articles to profl. jours. Mem.: EDPA (Outstanding Faculty Mentor award 1999), Am. Edn. Fin. Assn. (Disting. Svc. award 1990), Politics of Edn. Assn. (pres. 1992—), Phi Kappa Phi. Office: Edn Policy and Leadership U Md Coll of Edn College Park MD 20742

MALENG, NORM, prosecutor; b. Acme, Wash., 1938; m. Judy Maleng; 1 child. BS in Econs., U. Wash., 1960, JD, 1966. Bar: Wash. State 1967, U.S. Supreme Ct. 1983, USOC Wash. 1973. Staff atty. U.S. Senate Com. on Commerce; pvt. practice Seattle; chief dep. civil divsn. King County, Seattle, prosecutor, 1978—. Chair Gov.'s Task Force on Cmty. Protection, 1989; vice chair Wash. Sentencing Guidelines Commn. Named Outstanding Pub. Ofcl. in King County, Mcpl. League, 1986. Mem. Wash. Assn. Pros. Attys. (pres.), Nat. Dist. Attys. Assn. (v.p., mem. exec. bd.), Wash. Assn. County Ofcls. (pres.). Office: W554 KC Courthouse 516 3d Ave Seattle WA 98104 Office Phone: 206-296-9067.

MALENKA, BERTRAM JULIAN, physicist, researcher; b. N.Y.C., June 8, 1923; s. Morris and Mollie (Wichtel) M.; m. Ruth D. Stolper, Mar. 28, 1948; children: David Jonathan, Robert Charles. AB, Columbia, 1947; MA, Harvard, 1949, PhD, 1951. Research fellow Harvard, 1951-54; asst. prof. physics Washington U., St. Louis, 1954-56; asso. prof. Tufts U., Medford, Mass., 1956-60; faculty Northeastern U., Boston, 1960—, prof. physics, 1962-93, prof. emeritus, 1993—. Mem. sci. adv. group Harvard-Mass. Inst. Tech. Cambridge Electron Accelerator, 1956— Mem. vis. com. dept. conservation Mus. Fine Arts, Boston, 1997—. Mem. Am., Italian phys. socs., N.Y. Acad. Scis., Phi Beta Kappa, Sigma Xi. Achievements include research and publications on theory of nuclear forces and structure of nucleus, explanation polarization phenomena in high-energy scattering, gamma radiation, electric polarization deuteron, accelerator design. Home: 16 Rutledge Rd Belmont MA 02478-3323 Office: Northeastern Univ Dept Of Physics Boston MA 02115

MALENKA, ROBERT C. psychiatrist, educator; PhD in Neuroscis., MD, Stanford U., 1983. Resident in psychiatry Stanford Sch. Medicine; postdoctoral work U. Calif., San Francisco, asst. prof. psychiatry and physiology, prof. psychiatry and physiology; dir. Ctr. for Neurobiology of Addiction; assoc. dir. Ctr. for Neurobiology and Psychiatry; Pritzker prof. psychiatry and behavioral scis., dir. Pritzker Lab. Stanford U. Sch. Medicine, 1999—; lectr. in field. Wendy and Stanley Marsh lectr., 2002. Mem. editl. bd. jours.:; co-author: (textbook) Molecular Neuropharmacology: A Foundation for Clinical Neuroscience, 2001; contbr. articles to profl. jours. Mem. Nat. Adv. Coun. on Drug Abuse. Recipient Soc. for Neurosci. Young Investigator award, 1993, Daniel H. Efron award, Am. Coll. Neuropsychopharmacology, 1998, Dargut and Milena Kemali Found. Internat. prize in neurosci., 2000, MERIT award, NIMH, 2001—11, Scholars award in neurosci., McKnight Endowment Fund for Neurosci., 1990, Investigator award in neurosci., 1997, Young Investigator award, Nat. Alliance for Rsch. in Schizophrenia and Depression, 1990, 1992, Alfred P. Sloan rsch. fellowship, 1990. Mem.: Soc. for Neurosci. (program com.). Office: Stanford U Sch Medicine Psychiatry and Behavioral Scis MSLS P104 Mail Code 5485 Stanford CA 94305-5485

MALERNEE, JAMES KENT, JR., finance and securities consultant; b. Durango, Colo., June 15, 1947; s. James Kent and Norma Virginia (Calhoon) M.; m. Charlean Ann Born, Aug. 21, 1971 (div. May 1, 1992). BS in Engring., U. Tex., Austin, 1970; PhD in Bus. Adminstrn., U. Tex., 1977; MBA, So. Meth. U., 1972. Petroleum engr. Tex. R.R. Commn., 1970-71; instr. fin. U. Tex., 1973-75; lectr. fin. U. Tulsa, 1975-76; assoc. Mgmt. Analysis Ctr., Northbrook, Ill., 1977-80, v.p., 1980—; sr. v.p. The MAC Group, 1987-89; also dir. MAC Rsch.; mng. dir. Cornerstone Rsch., N.Y.C., 1989-2000, pres., CEO, 2000—. Lectr. mgmt. Stanford GSB, 1983; leader seminars on mergers and acquisitions and corp. strategy; guest speaker in field of strategy; speaker on damages in securities litigation P.L.I. and ABA; expert witness in securities and fin.; bd. dirs. Real Page. Contbr. articles to profl. jours. Named one of Outstanding Young Men Am. U.S. Jaycees, 1977. Mem. Fin. Mgmt. Assn. (v.p. 1981-82, bd. dirs. 1983-85), Assn. Corp. Growth. Home: 208 E 51st St # 123 New York NY 10022-6557 Office: Cornerstone Rsch 599 Lexington Ave New York NY 10022-6030

MALES, MICHAEL ARNOLD, sociologist, educator, writer, consultant; b. Oklahoma City, Oct. 13, 1950; s. Morris Ogden and Ruth Lair Males, Benjamin Edwin Males (Stepfather). BA, Occidental Coll., 1972; PhD, U. Calif., Irvine, 1999. Sr. rsch. fellow Ctr. on Juvenile and Criminal Justice, San Francisco, 1996—; sociology lectr. U. Calif., Santa Cruz, 2000—. Bd. mem. Calif. Wellness Found. Teen Pregnancy Adv. Bd., Sacramento. Author: The Scapegoat Generation: America's War on Adolescents, 1996 (1997 award for the advancement of human rights, The Gustavus Myers Ctr. for the Study of Human Rights in N.Am., 1997), Framing Youth: 10 Myths about the Next Generation, 1998, Smoked: Why Joe Camel Is Still Smiling, 1999. Dir. Nat. Youth Rights Assn., Washington. Mem.: Am. Fedn. Tchrs. (assoc.). Green Party. Agnostic. Achievements include research in Montana Student Tobacco Referendum, 1991. Avocation: wilderness hiking. Home and Office: PO Box 7842 Santa Cruz CA 95061-7842 Personal E-mail: mmales@earthlink.net. E-mail: mmales@earthlink.net.

MALESKI, CYNTHIA MARIA, lawyer; b. July 4, 1951; d. Richard Anthony and Helen Elizabeth (Palovcak) Maleski; m. Andrzej G. Groch, Aug. 7, 1982; 1 child, Elizabeth Maria. Student, U. Rouen, France, 1970; BA summa cum laude, U. Pitts., 1973; JD, Duquesne U., 1976. Bar: Pa. 1976, U.S. Dist. Ct. (we. dist.) Pa. 1976, U.S. Supreme Ct. 1980, U.S. Ct. Appeals (3d cir.) 1984. Indsl. rels. adminstr. Allegheny Ludlum Industries, Inc., Brackenridge, Pa., 1972—74; law clk. Conte, Courtney, Tarasi & Price, Pitts., 1974, Paul Hammer, Pitts., 1974—76; solo practice Natrona Heights, Pa., 1978—92, 1995—. Adj. prof. law Sch. Law Duquesne U., Pitts., 1998—; ins. commnr. Penna, 1992—; mem. Gov.'s cabinet, 1992—95; v.p., regulatory coun. Highmark Blue Cross/Blue Shield, 1995—99; assoc. dir. pers. Mercy Hosp., Pitts., 1976—77, dir. legal affairs, 1977—81, gen. counsel, 1981—92; spl. master Allegheny County Ct. Common Pleas, 1989; bd. dirs. legal adv. bd. Cath. Health Assn., 1980—82; gen. counsel, vice chmn. nat. assembly of reps. Nat. Confedn. Am. Ethnic Groups, 1980—; health law cons. and lectr. Co-author: The Legal Dimensions of Nursing Practice, 1982 (Nurses' Book of Month Club award, 1982); contbr. articles to publs. Mem. Allegheny-Kiski Hist. Soc., 1995—; elected mem. Allegheny County Dem. Com., 1986—89; corp. sec., pres. Duquesne U. Tamburitzans, Pitts., 1985—92; vice chmn. Czechoslovak room com. Nationality Rooms Program, U. Pitts., Pitts., 1983; v.p. Slovak League Am., 1990—; mem. adv. bd. Children's and Youth Svcs., Allegheny County, 1984—92; soloist, spkr. various groups Pitts. Slovakians. Named Disting. Alumnus, 1993; recipient Acad. Excellence award, Duquesne U., 1976; scholar, U. Rouen, 1970; Allegheny Ludlum Industries scholar, 1969—73, Andrew Mellon scholar, 1969—73, tuition scholar, U. Pitts., 1969—73, tuition remission grantee, Duquesne U., 1975, 1976. Mem.: ABA, St. Thomas More Soc. (bd. govs. 1980—), Slavic Edn. Assn. (nat. treas. 1981—86), Allegheny County Bar Assn., Pa. Bar Assn. (commn. on women 1996—, exec. women's coun.), Soc. Hosp. Attys. We. Pa., Soc. Hosp. Attys. of Hosp. Assn. Pa. (v.p.), Women Execs. in State Govt. (mem. nat. bd. 1994), Nat. Health Lawyers Assn., Am. Soc. Hosp. Attys., Nat. Slovak Soc., 1st Cath. Slovak Ladies' Assn., First Cath. Slovak Union (nat. trustee, bd. dirs.), Polish Falcons, Phi Beta Kappa. Roman Catholic. Home: 137 Oak Manor Dr Natrona Heights PA 15065-1949 Office: 2413B Freeport Rd Box 263 Natrona Heights PA 15065-0046 Office Phone: 724-224-6800.

MALETSKY, ALFRED F. sculptor, engraver; b. Easton, Pa., 1943; Cert., Pa. Acad. Fine Arts; student, John Hussian Sch. Art, Phila. Advt. art dept. Phila. Evening Bull., 1969—75; sculptor Franklin Mint, 1976—92; sculptor, engraver U.S. Mint, Phila., 1993—. Recipient Watercolor prize, Franklin Mint Found Arts Show, 1992, Coin of Yr., 1998, Excellent Work award, Japan Min. Fin. Internat. Coin Competition, 1999, Coin of Yr. award, 2001. Office: 801 9th St NW Washington DC 20220

MALEWITZ, JOAN, elementary school educator, multi-media specialist; b. Dec. 15, 1947; d. Benjamin and Minnie Malewitz. B in Elem. Edn., Queens Coll., 1968, M in Elem. Edn., 1972, MLS, 1992. Cert. tchr. N-6 N.Y. Tchr., sch. libr. media specialist Pub. Sch. 160Q, Jamaica, NY, 1968—. Children's book reviewer Kirkus Revs., N.Y.C., 2000—. Recipient Success award, Citibank, N.Y.C., 1994. Mem.: ALA, Beta Phi Mu. Avocations: reading, travel, New York City history. Home: 62-95 Saunders St Rego Park NY 11374 Office: PS 160Q 109-59 Inwood St Jamaica NY 11435

MALEY, PATRICIA ANN, preservation planner; b. Wilmington, Del., Dec. 25, 1955; d. James Alfred and Frances Louise (Fenimore) M.; m. Scott A. Stone, Dec. 7, 1991 (div. June 1994). AA, Cecil C.C., 1973; BA, U. Del., 1975, MA, 1981. Cert. secondary tchr., Del. Analyst econ. devel. City of Wilmington, 1977-78, evaluation specialist, 1978-80, planner II mayor's office, 1980-86, cons. preservation, 1986-87; dir. Belle Meade Mansion, Nashville, 1987-88; dir. planning, devel. Children's Bur. of Del., Wilmington, 1988; prin. preservation planner Environ. Mgmt. Ctr., Brandywine Conservancy, Chadds Ford, Pa., 1988-92; planning cons., 1992-95; design review and preservation commn. coord. Wilmington Dept. Planning, 1995—, code enforcement constable, 1997—. Cons. cultural resources M.A.A.R. Inc., Newark, Del., 1987, ITC Cons., Wilmington, 1985-86; mem. Planned Approach to Comty. Health, Wilmington, task force for Wilmington Enterprise Comty. Health Benchmarking Project. Contbg. photographer America's City Halls, 1984; author numerous Nat. Register nominations, 1980-86; 88—. Pres., founder Haynes Park Civic Assn., Wilmington, 1977-80; photographer Biden U.S. Senate Campaign, New Castle County, Del., 1984; sec. parish coun. Our Lady Fatima Roman Cath. Ch., 1985-86, choir dir., 1983-87; mem. com. on design & renovation of worship spaces Diocese of Wilmington, also mem. Diocesan com. on music; bd. dirs. Del. Children's Theatre; music dir. St. Elizabeth Ann Seton parish, Bear, Del., 1988—, mem. long range planning com./demographics. U. Del. fellow, 1976-77. Mem.: Del. Inst. for Planning and Design (bd. dirs. 2002—, v.p. 2004), New Castle County (Del.) Bd. Realtors, Am. Planning Assn. (exec. com. Del. chpt. 1997, elected state chpt. treas. 1997, 1999, 2001), Am. Inst. Cert. Planners (cert. planner), Nat. Trust Hist. Preservation, Del. Hist. Soc., Nat. Pastoral Musicians Assn., Pi Sigma Alpha. Democrat. Avocations: photography, choral, piano, cello, organ music. Office: City of Wilmington Dept Planning 800 N French St Fl 7 Wilmington DE 19801-3590 Office Phone: 302-576-3113.

MALGIERI, NICK, chef, author, educator; b. Newark, Sept. 30, 1947; s. Nufre and Antoinette (LoConte) M. BA in French, Seton Hall U., 1970; AOS in Culinary Arts, Culinary Inst., Hyde Park, N.Y., 1973. Pastrycook Seehotel Meierhof, Zurich, 1973-74, Hotel de Paris, Monte Carlo, 1974, Sporting Club, Monte Carlo, 1974-76, Hotel la Reserve, Beaulieu, France, 1974; pastry chef Windows on the World, N.Y.C., 1976-79; asst. pastry chef Hotel Waldorf Astoria, N.Y.C., 1979; chmn. baking dept. N.Y. Restaurant Sch., N.Y.C., 1979-83; dir. baking curriculum Inst. of Culinary Edn., N.Y.C., 1984—; founder, owner Total Heaven Baking Co. Exec. chef Paine Webber; pastry chef Board Room; cons. Inhilco, Inc.; guest lectr. Smithsonian Instn.; Am. spokesperson for Switzerland tourism. Author: Nick Malgieri's Perfect Pastry, 1989, Great Italian Desserts, 1990, How to Bake, 1995 (James Beard Found. Cookbook award/Best Book on Baking/Desserts of 1995), Chocolate, 1998 (IACP/Julia Child cookbook award 1998, Salon Internat. du Livre award), Cookies Unlimited, 2000, Perfect Cakes, 2002 (100 Best Books of 2002 Pub. Weekly); contbr. articles and recipes to newspapers and profl. jours. Named One of 10 Best Pastry Chefs in USA, Pastry Art & Design Mag., 1998, 99. Mem. Internat. Assn. Culinary Profls. Found. (former trustee), Internat. Assn. Culinary Profls. (cert. culinary profl., chmn. certification 1989-91), Amicale Culinaire de Monaco, Societe Culinaire Philanthropique N.Y., Federazione Italiana dei Cuochi, James Beard Found. (coord. competitions 1991-95), N.Y. Assn. Cooking Tchrs. (former bd. dirs., Ann. honor 2000), Bakers Dozen East (founding mem.). Home: 277 W 10th St New York NY 10014-2562 Office: Inst of Culinary Education 50 W 23d St New York NY 10010 Personal E-mail: nickmalg@ix.netcom.com.

MALHAM, JOSEPH MARIO, artist, writer; b. Gary, Ind., Sept. 10, 1961; s. Howell J and Martha Karas Malham. BA in hist., Loyola U., 1985—87. Dir. commn. Port Ministries, Chgo., 1999—2000; dir. ops. Imago Icons, Chgo., 2000—; artist in residence St. Gregory the Gt. Ch., Chgo., 2002—. Cons. Arts Alliance, Chgo., 2003—. Author: (book) By Fire into Light, 2002; contbr. articles. Home: 4220 N Sheridan Rd Chicago IL 60613

MALHERBE, ABRAHAM JOHANNES, VI, religion educator, writer; b. Pretoria, South Africa, May 15, 1930; arrived in US, 1951; s. Abraham Johannes and Cornelia Aletta (Meyer) Malherbe; m. Phyllis Melton, May 28, 1953; children: Selina, Cornelia, Abraham Johannes VII. BA, Abilene Christian U., 1954; STB, Harvard U., 1957; student, U. Utrecht, The Netherlands, 1960-61; ThD, Harvard U., 1963; LLD (hon.), Pepperdine U., 1981; LHD (hon.), Centre Coll., 1990; STD (hon.), Providence Coll., 1994; DD (hon.), U. Pretoria, 2000. Minister Ch. of Christ, Lexington, Mass., 1956-63; asst. and assoc. prof. Abilene (Tex.) Christian U., 1963-67; vis. scholar Harvard Divinity Sch., Cambridge, Mass., 1967-68; assoc. prof. Abilene Christian U., 1968-69, Dartmouth Coll., Hanover, N.H., 1969-70, Yale Divinity Sch., New Haven, 1970-77, prof., 1977-81, Buckingham prof., 1981-94, assoc. dean acad. affairs, 1987-89, prof. emeritus, 1994—. Guest prof. U. Pretoria, South Africa, 1989, 98. Author: (book) Social Aspects of Early Christianity, 1983, Moral Exhortation, 1986, Paul and the Thessalonians, 1987, Ancient Epistolary Theorists, 1988, Paul and the Popular Philosophers, 1989, Commentary on Thessalonian Letters, 2000; cons.: Anchor Bible Dictionary, 1992; inspiration for books Greeks, Romans and Christians: Essays in Honor of Abraham J. Malherbe, 1990, Early Christianity and Classical Culture: Comparative Studies in Honor of Abraham J. Malherbe, 2003; mem. editl. bd.: Bible Rev., 1986—, Novum Testamentum, 1991—, Religious Studies Rev., 1980—, co-founder: Restoration Quar., 1957; contbr. articles to profl. jours. Recipient Teaching Award, Abilene Christian U., 1965, 1967, Outstanding Alumni Citation, 1996, NEH award, 1973; Abraham J. Malherbe scholar developed in his honor, Yale Divinity Sch., 1997—, Abraham J. Malherbe Doctoral fellow developed in his honor, classics dept. U. Tex., Austin, 2002—. Mem.: Novum Testamentum, N.Am. Patristic Soc., Soc. Bibl. Lit., South African New Testament Soc. (hon.). Ch Of Christ. Home: 71 Spring Garden St Hamden CT 06517-1913 Office: Yale Divinity Sch 409 Prospect St New Haven CT 06511-2167 E-mail: abraham.malherbe@yale.edu.

MALHI, GURBAX SINGH, legislator; b. India; m. Devinder Brar, Mar. 16, 1976; children: Gurinder, Harinder. BA in Polit. Sci., English, History, Punjab U., India; BA in Polit. Sci., English and History. Prior com. appts. Ho. of Commons Standing Com. for Govt. Ops., Standing Com. on Procedure and Ho. Affairs, Spl. Com. on Code of Conduct for MPs and Senators, Subcom. on Bus. of Supply, Pearson Airport Subcom., Limousine Subcom.; assoc. mem. Com. for Fgn. Affairs, 0000—00; with Justice, Legal Affairs, Human Rights, Industry Coms.; mem. Scrutiny of Regulations Com.; chmn. Ho. of Commons Standing Com. for Libr. of Parliament; former pres. Bramalea-Gore-Malton Fed. Liberal Assn.; elected Ho. of Commons, 1993, re-elected, 1997, 2000, 2004, apptd. parliamentary sec. to min. of industry with spl. emphasis on entrepreneurs and new Canadians, 2003—; mem. Standing Com. on Human Resources Devel. Founder, chair Canada-South Asia Parliamentary Friendship Group. Active Toronto Real Estate Bd., Canadian Real Estate Assn.; former dir. Malton Neighborhood Svcs., 2004; appointed parliamentary sec. to min. of human resources. Office: Unit 4-2565 Steeles Ave E Brampton ON L6T 4L6 Canada E-mail: malhig@parl.gc.ca.

MALHOTRA, ASHOK KUMAR, philosophy educator; b. Ferozepur, India, 1940; came to the U.S., 1963, naturalized, 1977. s. Nihal Chand and Vidya (Wanti) M.; m. Nina Judith Finestone, Oct. 24, 1966 (dec.); children: Raj Kumar, Ravi Kumar. BA, U. Rajasthan, 1961, MA, 1963; PhD, U. Hawaii, 1969. Asst. prof. SUNY, Oneonta, 1967-70, assoc. prof., 1970-80, prof., 1980—, chmn. philosophy dept., 1975-80. Vis. prof. SUNY-Buffalo, summer 1970, Kurukshetra U. and Birla Inst., Pilani, India, spring 1980; grants reviewer NEH, 1978—; bd. dirs. SUNY Press editorial, 1989-93, dir. SUNY study abroad, program to India, 1980—; cons. TV series Kung Fu: The Legend Continues., 1992. Author: Sartre's Existentialism in Nausea and Being and Nothingness, 1978, Sartre's Existentialsim as Literature and Philosophy, 1995, Pathways to Philosophy: A Multidisciplinary Approach, 1996, Culture and Self, 1997, Transcreation of the Bhagavad Gita, 1998, Instant Nirvana, 1999, An Introduction to Yoga Philosophy, 2001; TV appearances include ABC World News Now, NBC News, JAIN TV, Doordarshan TV, ZEE TV (India), Natraj TV (Holland), All India Radio, NPR. Founder Ninash Found. Oneonta; established Indo-Internat. Sch., Dundlod, Rajasthan and Kuran, Gujarat, India. Recipient Excellence in Tchg. award and Disting. Tchg. Prof. award United Univ. Profession; Friend of Ednl. award City of Oneonta, 1998, Disting. Alumni award East-West Ctr., 2000, Jewel of India award 2002, Bharat Excellence award Friendship Forum of India, 2002; East-West Ctr. fellow, 1963-65, 66-67; N.Y. State Dept. Edn. grantee, 1967-69, NEH grantee, 1979. Mem. Am. Philos. Assn., Soc. Asian and Comparative Philosophy, Assn. Asian Studies, N.Y. State Asian Studies Soc., Internat. Phenomenol. Soc. Home: 17 Center St Oneonta NY 13820-1445 Office Phone: 607-436-3220. E-mail: malhotak@oneonta.edu.

MALHOTRA, DAVINDER KUMAR, finance educator, consultant, researcher; b. New Delhi, Delhi, India, May 25, 1961; came to U.S., 1988; s. Jagat Ram and Sushila (Vohra) M.; m. Rashmi Nagpal, July 1, 1990; 1 child, Kunal. B in Commerce, U. Delhi, India, 1980, M in Commerce, 1982; MA in Fin., U. Ala., 1991, PhD in Fin., 1993. Sr. lectr. in commerce U. Delhi, Delhi, India, 1982-88; asst. prof. fin. Phila Coll. Textiles and Sci., 1993—. Advisor MBA program Phila. Coll., 1993—; cons. Ctr. for Internat. Bus. Excellence, 1995—. Contbr. articles to profl jours. including Jour. Fin. Rsch., Advance in Futures and Options, Jour. of Retail Banking, Jour. of Comml. Lending, Jour. of Global Bus., Banker's Mag. Recipient various rsch. and best paper awards at fin. confs. Mem. Fin. Mgmt. Assn., Ea. Fin. Assn., Midwest Fin. Assn., So. Fin. Assn., Acad. Fin. Svcs., Acad. Internat. Bus. Home: 2991 W School House Ln # 24E Philadelphia PA 19144-5357 Office: Phila Coll Sch of Bus School House Lane And Henry Av Philadelphia PA 19144-5444

MALHOTRA, NARESH KUMAR, management educator; b. Ambala, Punjab, India, Nov. 23, 1949; arrived in U.S., 1975; s. Har Narian and Satya (Kakkar) M.; m. Veena Bahl, Aug. 13, 1980; children: Ruth Veena, Paul Naresh. *Dr. Malhorta converted from Hinduism to Christianity on March 19, 1978. He is a Bible preacher, teacher, and evangelist. He has preached the Gospel in 24 countries and has been blessed to see more than 110,000 people pray to accept the Lord Jesus Christ as their personal Savior. He frequently travels overseas to share his faith in the Lord Jesus Christ. He is a Deacon and member of the First Baptist Church, Atlanta. He has been married to Veena for over 24 years and they have two children, Ruth and Paul.* BTech with honors, Indian Inst. Tech., Bombay, 1971; MBA, I.I.M., Ahmedabad, India, 1973; MS, SUNY, Buffalo, 1978, PhD, 1979. Mgmt. cons. ASCI, Hyderabad, India, 1971-73; asst. prof. Ga. Tech. Inst., Atlanta, 1979—, assoc. prof. mgmt., coord. mktg., 1982-87, 89—, prof., 1988, Regents' prof., 1992—. Organizer several nat. and internat. mktg. mgmt. confs. *Malhotra is ranked the number one researcher in the country based on four different rankings; articles published in: Journal of Marketing Research, 1980-1985; Journal of Health Care Marketing, Journal of the Academy of Marketing Science,since 1986-1995, Journal of the Academy of Marketing Science since inception through volume 23, 1995, International Marketing Review, 1992-2002.* Author: Marketing Research: An Applied Orientation (N.Am., European, Internat., Australia and New Zealand, Spanish, Portuguese, Chinese, Russian, French and Hungarian edits.), Basic Marketing Research: Application to Contemporary Issues; contbr. articles to profl. jours. Lay preacher of the Gospel. Fellow Acad. Mktg. Sci. (disting., program chmn. 1984-85, 85-86, v.p. programs 1988-90, chmn. bd. 1990-92, pres. 1994-96, chmn. found. 1996-98, Top Rsch. Jour., Jour. Mktg. Rsch., Jour. Acad. Mktg. Sci., Jour. Healthcare Mktg., Internat. Mktg. Rev.), Decision Scis. Inst. (track chmn. 1984-86); mem. Am. Mktg. Assn. (track chmn. 1983-84), Am. Statis. Assn. Republican. Baptist. Avocations: reading, writing, ch. activities, outdoor activities. Home: 1956 Lenox Rd NE Atlanta GA 30306-3035 Office: Ga Tech Inst Coll Mgmt Atlanta GA 30332-0520 Office Phone: 404-894-4358. Business E-Mail: naresh.malhotra@mgt.gatech.edu.

MALHOTRA, PULIN, financial infrastructure consultant; b. Simla, India, Nov. 24, 1964; s. Kulwant Rai and Urmil (Khanna) M. BS in Biomed. Engring., U. Bombay, 1987; MBA in Fin. and Investments, George Washington U., 1991. NASD. Export mgr. Mascot Enterprises, Bombay, 1982-84; mgr. internat. bus. markets U.K. Marines Shipping, Internat., Bombay, 1984-87; fin. trainee Metlife and Fin. Svcs., N.Y.C., 1987-89; fin. planning svcs. Fin. Cons., Tarrytown, N.Y., 1989-90; sr. fin. analyst ICMA Retirement Corp., Washington, 1991-92, mgr. bus. devel., 1992-94; v.p. product devel. 1st Union Bank, Evergreen Asset Mgmt., 1994-95; gen. ptnr., sr. cons. Ingress Assocs., Washington, 1995—. Recipient scholarship NYU, 1988. Avocations: windsurfing, golf, squash, tennis, dance.

MALHOTRA, VIVEK, medical educator; BS with honors, Stirling U., 1982; DPhil in Biochemistry, Oxford U., 1985. Asst. prof. biology U. Calif., San Diego, 1990-95, assoc. prof. biology, 1995-99, prof. biology, 1999—. Contbr. articles to profl. jours. Recipient Established Investigator award Am. Heart Assn., 1995; postdoctoral fellow Stanford U., 1985-90, Am. Cancer Soc., Calif., 1988-90; Pirie-Reid scholar, Oxford U., 1982-85, Basil O'Connor Starter scholar, March of Dimes, 1992-95. Office: U Calif Dept Biology 9500 Gilman Dr # 0347 La Jolla CA 92093-5004

MALHOTRA, YOGESH, former computer scientist, management educator, corporate and national consultant, entrepreneur, former computer engineer; b. India, Jan. 11, 1964; B in Engring. with distinction, U. Delhi, India, 1984; MBA Phi Kappa Phi and Beta Gamma Sigma honors, U. Nev., Las Vegas, 1993; PhD in Bus. Adminstrn./Info. Sys. and Knowledge Mgmt. with honors, U. Pitts., 1998. Cert. computing profl.; chartered engr. Exec. engr. Suzuki Maruti Udyog Ltd., Gurgaon, India, 1984—87; sys. analyst Tata Unisys Ltd., New Delhi, 1987—89; sr. sys. analyst JK Technosoft, Neepz, India, 1989; sr. cons. info. sys. Bank Am., Nev., 1990—91; prin. founder, knowledge architect @BRINT.COM, The Biztech Network, Pitts., 1994—98; founder, chmn., chief knowledge officer Brint.com L.L.C., 1998—2001, Fla. Atlantic U.; founding chmn., chief knowledge architect BRINT Inst. LLLC, 2001—. Coun. ptnr., Inter-Agency Benchmarking & Best Practices Coun. US Fed. Govt., 1995—99; advisor, cons. Intel, Br. Telecom, Ziff Davis, Hewlett Packard, Arthur Andersen, South Korean, Vision Korea Nat. Campaign, Govt. of Netherlands, U.S. Fed. Govt, and, Govt. of Mex., 1995—2001; founder, editor-in-chief, pub. WWW Virtual Libr. on Knowledge Mgmt., 1996—2001; founder, editor-in-chief The Knowledge Mgmt. Think Tank, 1997—2001; plenary keynote presenter, spkr. Conf. Bd., Maeil Bus. TV Network and Bus. Newspaper Vision Korea Campaign (South Korea), Govt. of Mex., Silicon Valley based tech. entrepreneurs global orgn., KMWorld, others, 1998—2001; cons., advisor Govt. of Netherlands, 1998; internat. advisory bd. Knowledge Mgmt. Jour., London, 1998—2004; disting. faculty, advisory bd. mem. BrainTrust, San Francisco, 1998; knowledge mgmt. spl. issues editor Expert Sys. with Applications Jour. (Elsevier Science), Info. Strategy: The Executive's Jour. (CRC Press), Info. Resources Mgmt. Jour. (IRMA), Jour. of Global Info. Mgmt. (IRMA), 1998—2001; assoc. editor e Svc. Jour. (Ind. U. Press), Bloomington, 1999—2001; founding mem., contbg. editor Ziff Davis Internet Commerce Standard, 1999—2000; mem. adv. bd., Most Admired Knowledge Leaders study Teleos, London, 2000; bd. dirs. Knowledge Mgmt. Consortium Internat., Vt., 2001—02; assoc. editor Info. Resources Mgmt. Jour., Hershey, Pa., 2001—; conf. bd. Intel Corp., 2001; mem. adv. bd. on leading new economy workplaces conf. Conf. Bd., N.Y.C., 2001; cons., advisor Intel Corp., 2002, NSF, 2002; founder The Knowledge Mgmt. Network, 2002—; cons., advisor UN, 2003, NSF, 2004, Philips (Netherlands), 2004; editl. adv. bd. The Learning Orgn., 2004—; bd. dirs. Commonwealth Centre for e-Governance, India, 2004; scif./editl. com. World Coun. of Nuc. Workers, France, 2004; spkr. in field. Lead author, editor: Books Knowledge Mgt. and Virtual Orgns., 2000 (5-Star award for Strategy Web Site for Managers by Accreditation Board of Anbar Electronic Intelligence (UK), 1999); author: Knowledge Mgmt. and Bus. Model Innovation, 2001 (Computerworld 'Best Web Site' Award, 1997); editor: (Spl. Issue on Knowledge Mgmt.) Expert Sys. with Applications Jour. (Elsevier Sci.), 2001 (Top Nominee, Industry.Net Online Achievement Awards, 1996), Info. Strategy: The Executive' s Jour. (CRC Press), 2000 (Academy of Management 'Best Reviewer Award', 1997), Jour. of Global Info. Mgmt., Info. Resources Mgmt. Assn., 2000, Info. Resources Mgmt. Jour., Info. Resources Mgmt. Assn., 2000; author: (Refereed and Invited Articles and Papers) Comm. of the ACM, Ednl. Tech., Expert Systems With Applications, IEEE Engring. Mgmt. Rev., Indsl. Mgmt. & Data Systems, Info. and Mgmt., Info. Resources Mgmt. Jour., Info. Strategy: The Executive's Jour., Jour. of Global Info. Mgmt., Jour. of High Tech. Mgmt. Rsch., Jour. of Informatics Edn. and Rsch., Jour. of Systems Mgmt., Jour. for Quality & Participation, Knowledge Mgmt. (UK), UNESCO Ency. of Life Support Systems, E-Business: A Monthly E-Bus. Digest (Inst. of Chartered Fin. Analysts of India), Jour. of Prodn. Engring. (Korea), Asian Strategy & Leadership Inst. Rev. (Malaysia), (Refereed Conf. Proceedings Articles) 2000 Info. Resource Mgmt. Assn. Internat. Conf., 1999 Hawaii Internat. Conf. on Sys. Sciences, 1997 Acad. of Mgmt. Meeting, 1997 Americas Conf. on Info. Systems, First INFORMS Conf. on Info. Systems and Tech., Inaugural Americas Conf. on Info. Systems, and Ednl. Multimedia and Hypermedia Ann. 1993, (BRINT.com e-learning knowledge portals) Consistently featured as benchmarks and reviewed in Bus. Week, Wall St. Jour., Fortune, CIO Mag., Computerworld, Fast Co., Info. Week, KM World and hundreds of other worldwide TV, print and media channels.; contbr. rschd. articles to profl. jours.; reviewer: info. tech. publs. and e-commerce and knowledge mgmt. books. Expert interviews analyses featured in Business Week, Wall Street Journal, Forbes, Fortune, Inc., CIO Magazine, Information Week, Computerworld, etc. BRINT Institute, Syracuse, NY, 1998—2001, As thought leader, advice and opinion quoted in strategy and policy documents of pre-eminent worldwide governments, corporations, and institutions. Recipient Top Rank cert., Am. Inst. Banking, Kaizen Quality Improvement award, Japanese Car Mfg. Co., 1984—87, Japanese Lang. award, Largest car mfr. India, Gurgaon, 1984—87, Online Achievement award, Industyr.Net, 1996, Top Two Practitioner Experts in Knowledge Mgmt., ISWorld Survey, 2000; grantee, UN, 2003, SAP Univ. Alliance, 2003, Kaufman Found., 2003; Rsch. Grant, Inst. for Indsl. Competitiveness, U. Pitts., 1996, Doctoral Consortium Fellow, Acad. Mgmt., 1997, Americas Conf. Info. Systems (AIS), 1997. Mem.: Academy Mgmt., Inst. Certification Computing Profls. (Certified Computing Professional 1993-current), Inst. Engrs. (life Chartered Engineer 1987-current), Phi Kappa Phi, Beta Gamma Sigma. Avocations: information systems, e-business, knowledge management. Office: School of Management Syracuse University Syracuse NY 13244 Office Phone: 315-443-3571. E-mail: yogesh.malhotra@brint.com.

MALIA, ELIZABETH A. state representative, state legislator; Degree, Boston Coll. State rep. legis., Mass., 1998—. Com. mem. Ward 11 Dem. Com., Pub. Svc., ho. vice-chair; com. mem. Pub. Safety, transp. Mem.: Network for Women in Polit. and Govt. Democrat. Office: State Ho Rm 540 Boston MA 02133 also: Dist Office 72 Child St Jamaica Plain MA 02130

MALICK, TERRENCE (DAVID WHITNEY II), film director; b. Waco, Tex., Nov. 30, 1943; m. Jill Jakes (div. 1978); m. Michele Malick, 1985 (div. 1998); m. Alexandra Wallace, 1998. Student, Harvard U., Oxford U.; MFA, Am. Film Inst. Motion picture director, writer, prodr. Films include Dirty Harry, 1971, Pocket Money, 1972, Deadhead Miles, 1972, Badlands, 1973 (Golden Seashell award 1974), The Gravy Train, 1974, Days of Heaven, 1978 (Best Dir. award Cannes Film Festival 1979, nominee Golden Globe award 1979, N.Y. Film Critics Circle award 1978), The Thin Red Line, 1998 (nominee Best Dir. Oscar 1999, nominee Best Writing Oscar 1999, Golden Berlin Bear award 1999, Chgo. Film Critics Assn. award 1999, Golden Satellite award 1999, others), Bear's Kiss, 2002; prodr. The Endurance, Shackleton's Legendary Antartic Expedition, 2000. Office: c/o DGA 7920 W Sunset Blvd Los Angeles CA 90046-3300 also: c/o Harley Williams 1900 Ave of the Stars Fl 17 Los Angeles CA 90067

MALIFRANDO, FRANK, foundation executive director, theater producer, consultant; b. NYC, Feb. 16, 1954; s. Frank Malifando and Michele Michelin Kuhn. BS, S.W. U., LA, 1986; MS in health scis., S.W. Univ, LA, 2004. Cert. Media Comm. Boston U., 1991. CEO Spring Fed Corp., 1982—88, Thunder Key Inc., 1982—89; mktg. dir. Mus. Edits. West, LA, 1988—91; dir. of devel. No. Calif. Svc. League, 1997—99; exec. dir. Keith Haring AIDS Interfaith Chapel, 1994—2000; dir. devel. Life Lines Ministries, San Francisco, 1997—98; dir. of career svcs. Computer Learning Ctr., 1999—2001; project dir., designer Career Acceleration Mentor Program, 2000—01; exec. dir. Seton Health Svcs. Found., Daly City, Calif., 2001—, Marin Gen. Hosp. Found., 2004—. Dir. of programs Alma DelFina Group, San Francisco, 1995—2000; CEO Artist Alliance Against AIDS, 1996; mem. bd. Seton Found., 2001—. Prodr.: Red Shoes, Kenn Duncan, 1984, (fine art reproductions) Hula Kahiko Series, 1986 (Pele Award of Excellence, 1986), Dance Cos., 1984 (Nat. Ann. Print award and Comm. Arts award, 1984); prodr./dir.: (Film-Documentary) "Awakening New Futures" (behind bars), 1997; Charity Ball-150 Years for Daughters of Charity Seton Medical Center, 2001. Recipient Radiant Baby Gold Pin, Keith Haring Found., 1995, Canon Pastor award, Grace Cathedral, San Francisco, 1995, Pele award for excellence, Advertising Assn. of Hawaii, 1984, Cert. of Design Excellence, Print's Regional Design Annual, 1986, Black and White award, Assn. Honolulu Artist, 1987, Resolution recognition, state of Calif., 2003. Mem.: San Francisco C. of C., Seniors RSVP/San Francisco (adv. bd.), Seton Health Svcs. Found. (bd. mem.), Brishane C. of C., Half Moon Bay C. of C., Daly City C. of C. Achievements include creator and founder of the AIDS Interfaith Chapel in Grace Cathedral, San Francisco. Office: Seton Med Ctr 1900 Sullivan Ave Daly City CA 94015

MALIK, DAVID JOSEPH, chemist, educator; b. Pittsburg, Calif., July 24, 1945; s. Joseph Elois and Marguerite Barbara (Jacopetti) M.; m. Sandra Louise Funk, Oct. 10, 1986; children: Stephanie Lauren, Stephen David, Michael Josef. BS, Calif. State U., Hayward, 1968; MS, Calif. State U., 1969; PhD, U. Calif., La Jolla, 1976. Post-doctoral rsch. chemist Dept. of Chemistry, U. Calif., La Jolla, Calif., 1976-77; post-doctoral rsch. assoc. Dept. of Chemistry, U. Ill., Urbana, 1977-80; asst. prof. dept. chemistry Ind. U.-Purdue U., Indpls., 1980-86, assoc. prof., 1986-95, prof., 1995—, dept. chmn., 1990-2000, Chancellor's prof. of chemistry, 2002—. Organizer Midwest Theoretical Chemistry Conf., Indpls., 1989, 96. Contbr. articles to profl. jours. Grantee Rsch. Corp., 1981, Petroleum Rsch. Fund, U.S. Dept. Edn.; P.A. Mack founding fellow, 2002-03. Mem.: Am. Chem. Soc. (chmn. Ind. sect. 1986, tech. program chmn. joint Cen.-Great Lakes regional mtg. Indpls. 1991, councilor 1996—, com. on edn. 1998—, gen. chmn. 36th ctrl. reg. meeting 2004), Am. Assn. Higher Edn., Am. Phys. Soc. (life), Sigma Xi. Democrat. Home: 30 Danbury Ct Zionsville IN 46077-3825 Office: Ind U Purdue U Sch Sci-Dept Chemistry 402 N Blackford St Indianapolis IN 46202-3274 Office Phone: 317-274-6884. Business E-Mail: malik@chem.iupui.edu.

MALIK, GHAUS MUHAMMAD, neurosurgeon; b. Mar. 1, 1946; MD, King Edward Med. Coll., Lahore, Pakistan, 1968. Sr. staff neurosurgeon Henry Ford Hosp., Detroit, 1975—; vice chmn. dept. neurosurgery Henry Ford Health Sys., Detroit, 1983—; John R. Davis chair neurosurgery Henry Ford Health Systems, 2004—; chair divsn. neurosurgery William Beaumont Hosp., Royal Oak, 2000—. Office: 3577 W 13 Mile Rd Ste 206 Royal Oak MI 48073 Office Phone: 248-551-2500.

MALIK, OM PARKASH, electrical engineering educator, researcher; b. Sargodha, Punjab, India, Apr. 20, 1932; arrived in Can., 1966; s. Arjan Dass and Kesar Bai (Ahuja) M.; m. Margareta Fagerstrom, Dec. 22, 1968; children: Ola Parkash, Mira, Maya. Nat. Diploma in Elec. Engring., Delhi (India) Poly., 1952; M in Engring., Roorkee (India) U., 1962; PhD, London U., 1965; D.I.C., Imperial Coll., London, 1966. Registered profl. engr., Ont., Alta. Asst. engr. Punjab State Elec. Bd., 1953-61, asst. to chief engr., 1957-59; rsch. engr. English Elec. Co., Eng., 1965-66; asst. prof. U. Windsor, Ont., Can., 1966-68; assoc. prof. U. Calgary, Alta., Can., 1968-74, prof., 1974-97, faculty prof., 1997—2000, assoc. dean student affairs, faculty engring., 1995-98, assoc. acad. dean faculty engring., 1979-90, acting dean, 1981, prof. emeritus, 1997—. Cons. prof. Huazhong U. Sci. and Tech., Wuhan, People's Republic China, 1986—. Assoc. editor Can. Elec. and Computer Engring. Jour., 1988-97, mng. editor, 1998-2003; contbr. 400 articles to profl. jours. Indsl. tng. scholar Govt. India, 1952-53, sr. indsl. tng. scholar Confedn. Brit. Industries, 1959-60; recipient Can. Pacific Rwy. engring. medal Engring. Inst. Can., 1997, Alberta Ingenuity Fund Rsch. Excellence award, 2002. Fellow IEEE (life, chmn. life mems. com. 2004, chmn. Western Can. coun. 1983-84, chmn. student activities Can. region 1979-82, chmn. life mems. com., mem. Found., Centenniel medal 1984, Merit award 1986, Third Millennium medal 2000, A.G.L. McNaughton award 2001), EIC, Inst. Elec. Engrs., Can. Acad. Engring.; mem. IEEE Power Engring. Soc. (machine theory subcom. 1979—, excitation sys. subcom. 1988—, chmn. 2004-, sys. dynamic performance com. 1988—, energy devel. and power generation com. 1990—), Assn. Profl. Engrs., Geologists and Geophysicists Alta. (Vol. Svc. award 1990, Alta. Ingenuity Rsch. Excellence award), Assn. Profl. Engrs. Ont., Am. Soc. Engring. Edn., Can. Elec. Assn. (assoc., controls com. 1977-92, chmn. digital control com. 1977-85, chmn. edn. com. 1983-85, mem. expert sys. com. 1989-94), Confederacion Panamericana de Ingenieria Mecanica, Electica y Ramas Afines (v.p. 1987-2000, bd. dirs. region I, 1991-93), Univ. of Calgary Emeritus Assn. (v.p. 2002-03, pres. 2003-04), Internat. Fed. Automatic Control (chmn. power plants and power sys. control commn. 2002-). Hindu. Home: 4 6841 Coach Hill Rd SW Calgary AB Canada T3H 3T9 Office: U Calgary Dept Elec & Computer Engring 2500 University Dr NW Calgary AB Canada T2N 1N4 E-mail: maliko@ieee.org.

MALIK, THOMAS WARREN, lawyer; b. Chgo., Mar. 2, 1948; s. Russell R. and Virginia L. M.; m. Karen L. Coy, June 21, 1975. BA, Northwestern U., 1970; JD, Duke U., 1973. Bar: Ill. 1973, U.S. Dist. Ct. (no. dist.) Ill. 1973, U.S. Ct. Appeals (7th cir.) 1976, U.S. Supreme Ct. 1976. Gen. counsel, asst. gen. counsel, atty. Sun Elec. Corp., Chgo., 1973-78; atty. Trans Union Corp., Lincolnshire, Ill., 1978-79; pvt. practice, Barrington and Wauconda, Ill., 1979—. Arbitrator Cir. Ct. Cook County, Chgo., 1990—, Cir. Ct. 19th Jud. Cir., Waukegan, Ill., 1990—, agent Chgo. Title Ins. Co. and Ticor Title Ins. Co. Mem. Ill. Bar Assn., Lake County Bar Assn., Chgo. Bar Assn. Office: 211 S Main St Wauconda IL 60084-1868 Office Phone: 847-526-3310. E-mail: thomas@malik.lawoffice.com.

MALIN, AMIR, former film company executive; BS, Brandeis U.; JD, Boston U. Founder, pres., co-CEO Cinecom Entertainment Group, 1982-88; former pres., CEO Millennim Pictures; former co-pres. October Films; pres., then CEO Artisan Entertainment, Santa Monica, Calif., 1997—2003. Office: Artisan Entertainment 2700 Colorado Ave Fl 2 Santa Monica CA 90404-5502*

MALIN, HAROLD MARTIN, JR., sexologist, educator; b. Colorado Springs, Aug. 26, 1945; s. Harold M. and Harriett Anne (Heyer) M.; m. Janice Karen Atkins. BA in Chemistry and Biology, Cornell Coll., 1967; postgrad., U. Iowa Med. Sch., 1968; PhD in Human Sexuality, Inst. for Advanced Study of Human Sexuality, 1986; postgrad. med. sch., Johns Hopkins U., 1986-87; MA in Psychology/Counseling, Western Inst. for Social Rsch., 1996. Diplomate Am. Coll. Sexologists. Clin. sexologist Sexology Assocs., Inc., 1985-90; cons. clin. sexologist Johns Hopkins Hosp. Sexual Disorders Clinic Johns Hopkins U. Med. Sch., 1987-89, mgr. Johns Hopkins Hosp. Sexual Disorders Clinic, 1989-91, cons. clin. sexologist Johns Hopkins Hosp. Sexual Disorders Clinic, 1991-92, instr. clin. sexology dept. psychiatry and behavioral scis., 1992-95; assoc. prof. clin. sexology, chair clin. studies dept. Inst. for Advanced Study of Human Sexuality, 1992-96; MET intern Child and Family Inst., Sacramento, 1996-97; pres., chmn. bd. dirs. Skolos, 1997—; pres. Planetsex, 1997—. Cons. clin. sexologist, corp. sec. Nat. Ctr. for Study and Treatment of Pathol. Gambling, Balt., 1986-95; cons. clin. sexologist Nat. Inst. for Study, Prevention and Treatment of Sexual Trauma, Balt., 1991-99, Drug and Alcohol Prevention Program, Inc., Ocean City, Md., 1991-95; cons. clin. sexologist for program devel. Nat. Ctr. on Instns. and Alternatives, Alexandria, Va. and Balt., 1991-94; sr. case mgmt. supr. Planned Parenthood Shasta-Diablo, Fairfield, Calif., 1994-96. Cons. editor Jour. of Sex and Marital Therapy; peer reviewer Jour. Sex Rsch.; contbr. articles to profl. jours. Mem. Solano County Adolescent Resource Network, Solano County Ryan White Consortium, Solano County Cmty. Health Outreach Sys., Solano Cmty. Svcs. Task Force. Mem. Am. Profl. Soc. on the Abuse of Children, Calif. Assn. Marriage and Family Therapists, Am. Bd. Sexology (bd. clin. examiners, diplomate, cert. sex therapist, cert. clin. supr., cert. sex rschr.), Assn. Sexologists, Am. Acad. Clin. Sexologists (founding, life, clin. fellow), Soc. for Sci. Study of Sexuality, World Assn. for Sexology, Harry Benjamin Internat. Gender Dysphoria Assn., Inst. for Advanced Study of Sexuality Alumni Assn. Inc. (pres., bd. dirs. 1994-98), Adolescent Perpetrators Network, Intersex Soc. of N.Am. (bd. dirs.), Calif. Coalition on Sexual Offending (bd. dirs., pres. bay area network). E-mail: mmalin@skolos.org.

MALIN, HOWARD GERALD, podiatrist; b. Providence, Dec. 2, 1941; s. Leon Nathan and Rena Rose (Shapiro) M. AB, U. R.I., 1964; MA, Brigham Young U., 1969; BSc, Calif. Coll. Podiatric Medicine, 1969, DPM, 1972; MSC, Pepperdine U., 1978; MD (hon.), Internat. U. Sch. Medicine, Winnipeg, Man., Can., 2001. Diplomate Am. Bd. Podiatric Pub. Health, Am. Bd. Podiatric Orthopedics, Am. Acad. of Wound Care Mgmt. Extern in podiatry VA Med. Ctr., Wadsworth, Kans., 1971-72, Marine Corps Res. Dept., San Diego, 1972; resident in podiatric medicine and surgery N.Y. Coll. Podiatric-Medicine, N.Y.C., 1972-73; resident in podiatric surgery, instr. in podiatric surgery N.Y. Coll. Podiatric Medicine, N.Y.C., 1973-74; pvt. practitioner in podiatric medicine and surgery Bklyn., 1974-77; mem. staff Prospect Hosp., Bronx, N.Y., 1974-77; chief podiatry service, mem. staff, cons. sports medicine David Grant U.S. Air Force Med. Ctr., Travis AFB, Calif., 1977-80; chief podiatric sect., mem. staff VA Med. Ctr., Martinsburg, W.Va., 1980—. Instr. ednl. devel. program VA Med. Ctr., Martinsburg, W.Va., 1980—; clin. prof. med. sci. Alderson-Broaddus Coll., U. Osteopathic Medicine and Health Scis.; adj. faculty Barry U. Sch. Podiatric Medicine; adj. clin. prof. Ohio Coll. Podiatric Medicine, dir. extern program; clin. assoc. prof. W.Va. U. Sch. Medicine. Editorial rev. bd. Jour. Contemporary Podiatric Physician, 1991—. Lt. col. USAFR, ret. Fellow Am. Soc. Podiatric Dermatology, Am. Coll. Foot Orthopedics, Am. Coll. Podiatric Physicians, Am. Coll. Podiatric Radiology (archivist, past pres.), Am. Soc. Podiatric Medicine (past pres., archivist), Am. Podiatric Med. Writers Assn. (pres., archivist), Am. Coll. Foot and Ankle Pediatrics (pres., archivist, historian), Am. Profl. Wound Care Assn., Royal Soc. Health; mem. Am. Acad. Podiatric Sports Medicine (assoc.), Assn. Mil. Surgeons U.S. (life), Am. Coll. Podiatric Surgery (assoc.), Phi Kappa Theta, Phi Kappa Psi. Home and Office: 118 Trooper Dr Apt 2D Martinsburg WV 25401-5428 Office Phone: 304-263-0811 3770.

MALIN, IRVING, English literature educator, literary critic; b. N.Y.C., Mar. 18, 1934; s. Morris and Bertha (Silverman) M.; m. Ruth Lief, Dec. 18, 1955; 1 child, Mark. BA, Queens Coll., 1955; PhD, Stanford U., 1958. Acting instr. English Stanford U., 1955-58; instr. Ind. U., 1958-60; from instr. to prof. CCNY, 1960-72, prof., 1972—. Cons. Jewish Publ. Soc., 1964, Am. Quar., 1964, NEH, 1972, 79, 80, 81, 82, B'nai B'rith, 1974-75, Yaddo, 1975-77, Jewish Book Coun., 1976, 79, PEN, 1978-82, Princeton U. Press, 1979, Fairleigh Dickinson Press, 1980, Wayne State U. Press, 1980, Internat. Coun. Exch. of Scholars, 1980-81, Duke U. Press, 1981, Jewish Daily Forward, 1981, U. Pitts. Press, 1981, Papers on Lang. and Lit., 1981, U. Ga. Press, 1983, UMI Rsch., 1989, Gordian Press, 1990, Ctr. for Study of Higher Edn., 1990, Mosiac, 1991, MacArthur Found., 1996, U. of S.C. Press, 1998, Purdue U. Press, Lafayette, Ind., 1999. Author: William Faulkner: An Interpretation, 1957, New American Gothic, 1962, Jews and Americans, 1965, Saul Bellow's Fiction, 1969, Nathanael West's Novels, 1972, Isaac Bashevis Singer, 1972; co-editor: Breakthrough: A Treasury of Contemporary American Jewish Literature, 1964, William Styron's The Confessions of Nat Turner: A Critical Handbook, 1970, The Achievement of William Styron, 1975, William Goyen, 1997, Into the Tunnel, 1998, Garrett's Elizabethan Trilogy, 1998; editor: Psychoanalysis and American Fiction, 1965, Saul Bellow and the Critics, 1967, Truman Capote's in Cold Blood: A Critical Handbook, 1968, Critical Views of Isaac Bashevis Singer, 1969, Contemporary American-Jewish Literature: Critical Essays, 1973, Conrad Alken's Prose, 1982; co-editor: Underwords: Perspectives on Don DeLillo's Underworld, 2002; adv. editor: Studies in American Jewish Literature, Jour. Modern Literature, Review of Contemporary Fiction, Saul Bellow Jour., 20th Century Literature; reviewer: Hollins Critic, So. Quar.; co-editor Paul Bowles, 1986, Spl. Issue of 20th Century Lit., James Dickey Spl. Issue of S.C. Rev., 1994, Pynchon and Mason and Dixon, 2000, So. Novelists on Stage and Screen So. Quar., 1995, James Dickey's Fiction Spl. Tex. Rev., 1996, Leslie Fiedler and American Culture, 1999, Torpid Smoke: The Stories of Vladimir Nabokov, 2000. Fellow Yaddo, 1963, Nat. Found. for Jewish Culture, 1963-64, Huntington Libr., 1978. Mem. MLA, AAUP, Am. Studies Assn., Am. Jewish Hist. Soc., Melville Soc., Authors League Am., Soc. Study of So. Lit., Poe Studies Assn., English Inst., Nathaniel Hawthorne Soc., N.Y. Acad. Scis., Poetry Soc. Am., Popular Culture Assn., Nat. Book Critics Circle, Sherwood Anderson Soc., Internat. Assn. Univ. Prof. English, Kafka Soc., English-Speaking Union, Multi-Ethnic Lit. U.S. Soc., Hastings Ctr., Am. Jewish Congress, Assoc. Writing Programs, Nat. Coun. Tchrs. of English, Vladimir Nabokov Soc., Phi Beta Kappa. Jewish. Home: 96-13 68th Ave Forest Hills NY 11375-5039 Office: CCNY Dept English New York NY 10031

MALIN, ROBERT ABERNETHY, investment management executive; b. Mt. Vernon, N.Y., Dec. 13, 1931; s. Patrick Murphy and Caroline Cooper (Biddle) M.; m. Gail Lassiter, Nov. 5, 1960; children: Alison Campbell, Robert Lassiter. AB, Dartmouth Coll., 1953, MBA, 1954. Asst. to comptr. Biddle Purchasing Co., N.Y.C., 1958-59; with Blyth & Co., Inc., N.Y.C., 1960-71, v.p., 1965-71, dir., 1968-71, sr. v.p., mem. exec. com., 1971-72; sr. v.p. corp. fin. Reynolds Securities Inc., N.Y.C., 1972-74, dir., 1973-74; mng. dir. First Boston Corp., N.Y.C., 1974-90; gen. ptnr. Tiedemann Investment Group, N.Y.C., 1991-96; mng. dir. SeaBridge Investment Advisors, Summit, NJ, 1997—. Mem. adv. coun. Fin. Acctg. Stds. Bd., 1973-78. Served as lt. (j.g.) USNR, 1954-57. Mem.: Securities Industry Assn. (acctg. com.), Investment Bankers Assn. Am., The Moorings Club, Morris County Club, Beacon Hill Club. Republican. Home: 233 Binnacle Point Vero Beach FL 32963-2905 Office: SeaBridge Investment Advisors 450 Springfield Ave Ste 301 Summit NJ 07901-2610 Office Phone: 908-273-5763. Personal E-mail: malinrobta@aol.com. Business E-Mail: bobmalin@seabridge.com.

MALINDA, PAUL F. emergency physician; b. Balt., Dec. 21, 1961; s. Adam Frank and Diane Mary Malinda; m. Maria C. Sam, May 20, 1989; children: James, Benjaman, Ann. BS cum laude, Loyola Coll., Balt., 1983; MD, U. Md., Balt., 1987. Diplomate Am. Coll. Forensic Examiners, Am. Bd. Family Practice, Emergency Medicine. Intern, resident U. Md., Balt., 1987—90; emergency rm. physician St. Joseph's Hosp., Buckhannoy, W.Va., 1990—93, Olmsted Cmty. Hosp., Rochester, 1993—96, Annie Penn Meml. Hosp., Reidsville, NC, 1996, Wesley Long Cmty. Hosp., Greensboro, NC, 1997—2000, Moses Cone Meml. Hosp., Greensboro, 1997—2000, Alamance Regional med. Ctr., Burlington, NC, 1997—. Dir. physicians asst. program, interim emergency rm. dir. Upshur County, Buckhannon, 1992—93. Vol. Our Lady Mercy Sch., Winston-Salem, 2002—; adult leader Boy Scouts Am., Kernersville, NC, 2003—. Cpt. USAR, 1996—97, maj. USAR, 1997—2004, lt. USAR, 2004—. Fellow: Am. Acad. Emergency Physicians (gov. 2002—), Am. Acad. Family Physicians; mem.: AMA, Am. Assn. Physician Specialists, N.C. Med. Soc. Avocations: travel, reading, swimming, hiking. Office: Alamance Regional Med Ctr Hoffman Mill Rd Burlington NC 27215

MALING, GEORGE CROSWELL, JR., physicist; b. Boston, Feb. 24, 1931; s. George Croswell and Marjory Maling; m. Norah J. Horsfield, Dec. 29, 1960; children: Ellen P., Barbara J., Jeffrey C. AB, Bowdoin Coll., 1954; SB, MIT, 1954, SM, 1954, PhD in Physics, 1963. Rsch. asst., postdoctoral fellow MIT, 1957—65; adv. physicist IBM Corp., Poughkeepsie, NY, 1965—71, sr. physicist, 1971—92; pres. Empire State Software Sys., Ltd., 1992—93; dir. Noise Control Found., Inc., Poughkeepsie, 1975—; chmn. com. SI-acoustics Am. Nat. Std. Com., 1976—79; dir. Internat. Noise Control Engring. Found., Inc., 1993—; mng. dir. Inst. of Noise Control Engring., 1994—2001. Pres. Internat. Noise Control Engring. Found., 1999—. Editor: Noise/News, 1972—92; mng. editor: Noise/News Internat., 1993—, assoc. editor: Jour. Acoustical Soc. Am., 1976—83, editor tech. proc.; contbr. articles to profl. jours. Recipient Raleigh medal, Inst. Acoustics U.K., 1999, Dist. Noise Ctrl. Eng., INCE, 2001. Fellow: AAAS, IEEE, Audio Engring. Soc., Acoustical Soc. Am. (exec. coun. 1980—83, Silver medal in noise 1992); mem.: Nat. Acad. Engring., Internat. Inst. Noise Control Engring. (editor-in-chief 2002—, bd. dirs. 1980—86, v.p. comms. 1997—, bd. dirs.), Inst. Noise Control Engring. (bd. dirs. 1972—77, pres. 1975, award 2001). Business E-Mail: maling@alum.mit.edu.

MALINOWSKI, ARTHUR ANTHONY, lawyer, labor arbitrator; b. Chgo., Apr. 4, 1929; s. Ignatius and Sophie (Data) M. BS in Econs., DePaul U., 1956, JD, 1960; MS in Indsl. Rels., Loyola U., 1958; PhD, Ill. Inst. Tech., 1972; LLM in Labor Law, Chgo. Kent Coll. Law, 1981. Bar: Ill. 1960. Instr. indsl. rels. Loyola U., Chgo., 1963-69, prof., 1969-94; prof. emeritus, 1994—; mem. Ill. Office Collective Bargaining, Chgo., 1973-83. Lectr. dept. econs. Ill. Inst. Tech., Chgo., 1965-68. Mem. Ill. Bar Assn., Indsl. Rels. Rsch. Assn., Nat. Acad. Arbitrators, Knights Malta, Phi Alpha Delta, Alpha Sigma Nu, Pi Gamma Mu, Iota Sigma Epsilon, Beta Gamma Epsilon. Home: 9240 Major Ave Morton Grove IL 60053-1552 Office: Loyola U of Chgo 25 E Pearson Ste 1250 Chicago IL 60611-2147

MALINOWSKI, MICHAEL E. ambassador; b. Chgo., Nov. 1948; m. Karen Gerlach Malinowski, 1975. Polit. affairs analyst on South Asia Dept. of State, 1983—85, prin. officer U.S. Consulates in Maracaibo, Venezuela, 1985—86, prin. officer U.S. Consulates in Peshawar, Pakistan, 1987—89, dep. to Pres. Envoy to the Afghan Resistance, 1989, spl. asst. for counterterrorism to under sec. for polit. affairs, 1989—91, spl. asst. for Near East and South Asian Affairs, 1989—91, dep. chief of mission Am. Embassies in Mbabane, Swaziland, and Kathmandu, Nepal, 1994—97, office dir. for Pakistan, Afghanistan and Bangladesh Bur. South Asian Affairs, 1997—98, dep. chief mission Am. Embassy Manila, 2000—01, U.S. amb. to Nepal Washington, 2001—. Office: DOS Amb 6190 Kathmandu Pl Washington DC 20521

MALINS, DONALD CLIVE, biochemistry, researcher; b. Lima, Peru, May 19, 1931; came to U.S., 1947; s. Richard Henry and Mabel (Madeline) M.; m. Mary Louise Leiren, 1962; children: Christopher W., Gregory S., Timothy J. BA, U. Washington, 1953; BS in Chemistry, Seattle U., 1954; PhD in Biochemistry, U. Aberdeen, 1967, DSc, 1976. Dir. environ. conservation div. Nat. Marine Fisheries Svc., Seattle, 1974-87; sr. scientific cons. U.S. Dept. Justice, Washington, 1989-91; sci. cons. NOAA, 1990-92; prin. scientist, dir. molecular epidemiology program Pacific N.W. Rsch. Inst., Seattle, 1992—; rsch. prof. dept. chemistry Seattle U., 1972-95. Affiliate prof. dept. environ. health U. Washington, 1984—, Coll. Ocean & Fishery Scis. U. Washington, 1974-91; editor-in-chief Aquatic Toxicology, 1980-95; lectr., speaker in field. Contbr. articles to profl. jours.; inventor in field. Bd. dirs. Am. Oceans Campaign, 1989-91; adv. bd. Internat. Jt. Commn., 1990-91. Recipient U.S. Dept. Commerce Gold medal, 1982. Mem. NAS, Am. Soc. Biochemistry and Molecular Biology, Am. Assn. for Cancer Rsch. Office: Pacific Northwest Rsch Inst Biochem Oncology Program 720 Broadway Seattle WA 98122-4302 Office Phone: 206-726-1200. E-mail: dmalins@pnri.org.

MALIS, ANDREW GARY, telecommunications company executive; b. Boston, Aug. 20, 1953; s. Irving and Nora Malis; m. Leslie Seaton, July 30, 1978; 1 child, Jonathan. ScB in Computer Sci., Brown U., 1975; ScM in Applied Math. and Computer Sci., Harvard U., 1979. Mem. tech. staff Mitre Corp., Bedford, Mass., 1975-78; divsn. engr. Bolt Beranek and Newman, Cambridge, Mass., 1979-93; cons. engr. Ascom Nexion, Acton, Mass., 1993-96; sr. cons. engr. Cascade Comm./Ascend Comm./Lucent Techs., Westford, Mass., 1996-2000; chief technologist Vivace Networks, Inc., San Jose, Calif., 2000—03, Tellabs, San Jose, 2003—. Chmn. working group Internet Engring. Task Force, Reston, Va., 1993—, ATM Forum, St. Louis, 1998-2000; mem. tech. adv. bd. Megisto Sys., Inc., Germantown, Md., 2000—; cons. Coun. Tech. Advisors, Gerson Lehrman Group, N.Y.C., 2000—; pres., chmn. Multi-Protocol Label Switching Forum, Fremont, Calif., 2002-03; chmn., pres. Mpls. and Frame Relay Alliance, Fremont, 2003—; spkr., chmn. numerous telecom.-related confs. Contbr. articles to sci. jours., including Procs. IEEE, IEEE Comm.; author telecom. stds. documents, 1981—. Bd. dirs., past pres. Temple Emanuel, Andover, Mass., 1986—. Recipient spl. tech. achievement award Frame Relay Forum, 1994, Disting. Svc. award, 1999; Spotlight award ATM Forum, 2000. Mem. IEEE, Internet Soc., Sigma Xi. Democrat. Jewish. Achievements include patent for method and apparatus for enabling flow control over multiple networks having disparate flow control capability. Office: Tellabs 90 Rio Rubles Dr San Jose CA 95134 Office Phone: 408-273-8723. Business E-Mail: andy.malis@tellabs.com.

MALIS, LEONARD IRVING, neurosurgeon; b. Phila., Nov. 23, 1919; s. Morris Melvin and Dorothy (Brodsky) M.; m. Ruth Gornstein, June 24, 1942; children: Larry Alan, Lynne Paula. MD, U. Va., 1943. Intern Phila. Gen. Hosp., 1943-44; resident in neurology Mt. Sinai Hosp., N.Y.C., 1947, resident in neurosurgery, 1948-50, neurosurgeon in chief, dir. dept. neurol. surgery, 1970-92; prof., chmn. dept. neurosurgery Mt. Sinai Sch. Medicine, 1970—92; prof. emeritus dept. neurosurgery Mt. Sinai Sch. Medicine, CUNY, 1993—; fellow in neurophysiology Med. Sch., Yale U., 1951; practice medicine specializing in neurosurgery N.Y.C., 1951-95. Cons. in field. Contbr. numerous articles to profl. jours.; developer various surg. and electronic instruments. Capt. M.C., U.S. Army, World War II. Mem. ACS, Am. Assn. Neurol. Surgery, Congress Neurol. Surgeons, Am. Physiol. Soc., Soc. Neuroscis., Am. Acad. Neurol. Surgery, Soc. Neurol. Surgeons, Alpha Omega Alpha. Home: 219-44 Peck Ave Hollis Hills NY 11427 Office Phone: 718-479-9326. Personal E-mail: nsdoclen@aol.com.

MALISHENKO, TIMOTHY PETER, communications executive; b. Reading, Eng., Nov. 4, 1944; s. John and Myra Phillys (Morris) M.; m. Jane Baxter, Mar. 17, 1968; 1 child, Andrew. BSBA, Ohio State U., 1968; MBA in Supply Chain Mgmt., Mich. State U., 1969; MS in Sys. Mgmt., U. So. Calif., 1972; postgrad., Squadron Officer Sch., Maxwell AFB, Ala., 1973, Armed Forces Staff Coll., Norfolk, Va., 1979, Nat. War Coll., Washington, 1986. Commd. 2d lt. USAF, 1968, advanced through grades to maj. gen., 1998, adminstrv. contracting officer, rep. Hughes Aircraft Co., 1969-73, procurement staff mgmt. officer, Air Staff Tng. Program Washington, 1973-74, from dep. plant rep. to plant rep. Sec. Air Force Spl. Proj. Sunnyvale, Calif., 1974-76, chief contracts and acquisition NATO E-3A Early Warning Sy. Brunssum, The Netherlands, 1979-82, dep. dir. R&D contracting Aero. Sys. Divsn. Wright-Patterson AFB, Ohio, 1982-84, dir. contracting, dep. aero. equipment, 1984-86, chief contract support divsn. Office Asst. Sec. Washington, 1987-88, chief, sys. and logistics contracting divsn., 1988-89, asst. dep. asst. sec. for contracting, 1989-90, dir. contracting Electronic Sys. Ctr. Hanscom AFB, Mass., 1990-93, dep. dir. contracting Hdqrs. Air Force Materiel Command Wright-Patterson AFB, Ohio, 1993-94, dir. contracting Hdqrs. Air Force Materiel Command, 1994-95; dep. asst. sec. for contracting USAF, Pentagon, Washington, 1995-97, dir. def. contract mgmt. agy., 1997—2001; v.p., contracts and pricing, integrated def. sys. Boeing Co., Seal Beach, Calif., 2001—03, corp. v.p., contracts and pricing Chgo., 2003—. Maj. gen. USAF. Contbr. articles to profl. jours. Decorated Legion of Merit with oak leaf cluster, Def. Meritorious Svc. medal, Meritorious Svc. medal with two oak leaf clusters. Personal E-mail: tim@malishenko.com. Business E-Mail: timothy.p.malishenko@boeing.com.

MALKANI, PRAKASH, medical educator, neuroradiologist; b. New Delhi, July 16, 1956; came to the U.S., 1990; s. Kotumal D. and Parpati K. (Abichandani) M.; m. Sonia N. Jiandani, Sept. 15, 1986; children: Natasha, Alisha. Student, U. Delhi, 1973; MB, BChir, All India Inst. Med. Sci., Delhi, 1979, MD, 1983. Diplomate Am. Bd. Radiology, Am. Bd. Neuroradiology. Intern All India Inst. Med. Sci., 1978; resident in radiology N.Y. Med. Coll., 1990-93, fellow in neuroradiology, 1990-91; head dept. imaging Hinduja Hosp., Bombay, 1985-90; clin. asst. prof. Mich. State U., East Lansing, 1993—2003; pres. Advanced Diagnostic Imaging, Saginaw, Mich., 2001—02, Saginaw County Med. Soc., 2002—03. Mem. MRI adv. bd. GE Asia Pacific, Singapore, 1986-90; chmn. radiology Covenant Health Sys., 1998-2001, Berkshire Med. Ctr., 2003—. Merit scholar Bd. Secondary Edn., New Delhi, 1972. Mem. Am. Soc. Neuroradiology, Saginaw Med. Radiology (treas. 1994-98). Home: 50 Meadow Ridge Pittsfield MA 01201 Office: Advanced Berkshire Med Imaging Dept Radiology Berkshire Med Ctr 725 North St Pittsfield MA 01201 E-mail: malkani@aol.com.

MALKASIAN, GEORGE DURAND, JR., physician, educator; b. Springfield, Mass., Oct. 26, 1927; s. George Dur and Gladys Mildred (Trombley) M.; m. Mary Ellen Koch, Oct. 16, 1954; children: Linda Jeanne, Karen Diane, Martha Ellen. AB, Yale U., 1950; MD, Boston U., 1954; MS, U. Minn., 1963. Diplomate Am. Bd. Ob-Gyn. Intern Worcester (Mass.) City Hosp., 1954-55; resident in ob-gyn Mayo Grad. Sch. Hosp., Rochester, Minn., 1955-58, 60-61; mem. faculty Mayo Med. Sch., 1962—, prof. ob-gyn, 1976—, chmn. dept. ob-gyn, 1976-86. Author articles in field. Served to lt. comdr. M.C., USNR, 1958-60. Named Tchr. of Yr., Mayo Grad. Sch. Medicine, 1973, 77, Alumnus of Yr., Boston U. Sch. Med., 1990. Fellow Royal Coll. Obstetricians and Gynecologists (ad eundum); mem. ACS, Am. Coll. Ob-Gyn (pres. 1989-90), Am. Ob-Gyn Soc., Am. Radium Soc., Soc. Ob-Gyn, Assn. Profs. Ob-Gyn, N.Am. Ob-Gyn. Soc., Ctrl. Assn. Ob-Gyn, Minn. Soc. Ob-Gyn, Internat. Fedn. Ob-Gyn (v.p. 1997-2000), Zumbro Valley Med. Soc. (exec. dir. 1996-2002). Home: 1750 11th Ave NE Rochester MN 55906-4215 Office: Mayo Clinic 200 1st St SW Rochester MN 55905-0001

MALKASIAN, WILLIAM, real estate company executive; BS in Polit. Sci., U. Wis.; diploma in Mgmt. Designation, Notre Dame U. Cert. assn. exec. From legis. dir. to exec. v.p. Wis. Realtors Assn., Madison, Wis., 1975—78, pres., 1978—. Treas. Wis. Ednl. Found.; sec., treas. On Common Ground Land Use Found.; dir. Wis. Environ. Initiative; chmn. Realtors Polit. Action Com. Mem.: Nat. Assn. Realtors (vice chmn. task force smart growth, William R. Magel award 2001). Office: Wisconsin Realtors Association 4801 Forest Run Rd Ste 201 Madison WI 53704*

MALKIEL, BURTON GORDON, economist, educator; b. Boston, Aug. 28, 1932; s. Sol and Celia (Gordon) Malkiel; m. Judith Ann Atherton, July 16, 1954 (dec. 1987); 1 child, Jonathan; m. Nancy Weiss, July 31, 1988. BA, Harvard, 1953, MBA, 1955; PhD, Princeton, 1964. Assoc. Smith Barney & Co., N.Y.C., 1958—60; asst. prof. dept. econs. Princeton U., 1964—66, assoc. prof., 1966—68, prof., 1968—81, Rentschler prof. econs., 1969—81, chmn. dept. econs., 1974—75, 1977—81, Chem. Bank chmn.'s prof. econs., 1988—; dean Sch. Orgn. and Mgmt., Yale U., 1981—87. Mem. Pres.'s Coun. Econ. Advisors, 1975—77; dir. Jeffrey Co., Prudential Fin., BKF Capital, Vanguard Group. Author: The Term Structure of Interest Rates, 1966; author: (with others) Strategies and Rational Decisions in the Securities Options Market, 1969; author: The Inflation-Beater's Investment Guide, 1980, Global Bargain Hunting, 1998; author: (with others) The Index Fund Solution, 1999; author: A Random Walk Down Wall Street, 8th edit., 2003, The Random Walk Guide to Investing, 2003. 1st lt. U.S. Army, 1955—58. Mem.: Am. Fin. Assn. (dir., pres. 1978). Home: 76 North Rd Princeton NJ 08540-2430 Office: Princeton U Dept Econs Princeton NJ 08544-0001 E-mail: bmalkiel@princeton.edu.

MALKIEL, NANCY WEISS, dean, historian, educator; b. Newark, Feb. 14, 1944; d. William and Ruth Sylvia (Puder) Weiss; m. Burton G. Malkiel, July 31, 1988. BA summa cum laude, Smith Coll., 1965; MA, Harvard U., 1966, PhD, 1970. From asst. to assoc. prof. history Princeton (N.J.) U., 1969-82, prof., 1982—, master Dean Mathey Coll., 1982-86, dean coll., 1987—. Author (as Nancy J. Weiss): (book) Charles Francis Murphy, 1858-1924: Respectability and Responsibility in Tammany Politics, 1968; author: (with others) Blacks in America: Bibliographical Essays, 1971, The National Urban League, 1910-1940, 1974, Farewell to the Party of Lincoln: Black Politics in the Age of FDR, 1983 (Berkshire Conf. of Women Historians prize, 1984), Whitney M. Young Jr., and the Struggle for Civil Rights, 1989. Trustee Woodrow Wilson Nat. Fellowship Found., 1975—, chmn. bd. trustees, 1999—; trustee Smith Coll., Northampton, Mass., 1984—94. Fellow, Woodrow Wilson Found., 1965, Charles Warren Ctr. Studies in Am. History, 1976—77, Radcliffe Inst., 1976—77, Ctr. Advanced Study Behavioral Scis., 1986—87. Mem.: So. Hist. Assn., Orgn. Am. Historians (chmn. status women hist. profession 1972—75), Am. Hist. Assn., Phi Beta Kappa. Democrat. Jewish. Office: Princeton U Office Dean Of College Princeton NJ 08544-0001

MALKIN, BARRY, film editor, consultant; b. N.Y.C., Oct. 26, 1938; s. Richard and Helen (Kandix) M.; m. Stephanie Byer, 1 child, Sacha Janine. BA, Adelphi U., 1960. Freelance film editor Sacha Prodns., Inc., N.Y.C., 1964—. Editor: (films) The Rain People, 1969, Cotton Comes to Harlem, 1970, They Might Be Giants, 1971, Who is Harry Kellerman?, 1971, Cops and Robbers, 1973, The Godfather Part 2, 1974, One Summer Love, 1976, Somebody Killed Her Husband, 1978, Last Embrace, 1979, One Trick Pony, 1980, Windows, 1980, Four Friends, 1981, Hammett, 1982, Rumble Fish, 1983, The Cotton Club, 1984 (Acad. award nominee for best film editing 1984), Peggy Sue Got Married, 1986, Gardens of Stone, 1987, Big, 1988, New York Stories ("Life Without Zoe"), 1989, The Freshman, 1990, The Godfather Part III, 1990 (Acad. award nominee for best film editing 1990), Honeymoon in Vegas, 1992, It Could Happen to You, 1994, Jack, 1996, The Rainmaker, 1997, Isn't She Great, 1999, Lucky Numbers, 2000, The Big Bounce, 2003. Mem. Acad. Motion Picture Arts and Scis., Motion Picture Editors Guild, Am. Cinema Editors. Home and Office: 275 Central Park W New York NY 10024-3015 E-mail: cpwblackie@aol.com.

MALKIN, CARY JAY, lawyer; b. Chgo., Oct. 6, 1949; s. Arthur D. and Perle (Slavin) Malkin; m. Lisa Kimley, Oct. 27, 1976; children: Dorothy R., Victoria S., Lydia R. BA, George Washington U., 1971; JD, Northwestern U., 1974. Bar: Ill. 1974, U.S. Dist. Ct. (no. dist.) Ill. 1974, N.Y. 2001. Assoc. Mayer, Brown & Platt, Chgo., 1974—80, ptnr., 1991—2002, Mayer, Brown, Rowe & Maw LLP, Chgo., 2002—. Chmn. spl. events com. Mental Health Assn., 1984—85; mem. steering com. Endowment Campaign Latin Sch. Chgo., 1990—91, trustee, 1991—2000, nat. trustee, 2000—02, sr. trustee, 2002—; mem. exec. com. Friends Prentice Women's Hosp., 1991—92; bd. dirs. SOS Children's Village Ill., 1992—96; mem. M. S. Weiss fund bd. Children's Meml. Hosp., 1993—96, mem. Graziano fund bd., 1993—96, mem. steering com., 1995—; trustee Field Mus., 1999—, mem. fin. com., 2002—, mem. investment com., 2003—. Mem.: Std. Club, Arts Club, Saddle and Cycle Club, Chgo. Club, Phi Beta Kappa, Order of Coif. Home: 233 E Walton St Chicago IL 60611-1526 Office: Mayer Brown Rowe & Maw LLP 190 S La Salle St Ste 3100 Chicago IL 60603-3441

MALKIN, HAROLD MARSHALL, medical researcher; b. San Francisco, Calif., Oct. 9, 1923; s. Charles Herman and Dorothy Levin Malkin; m. Joanne Clark (div.); m. Sonja Sandeman (div.); children: Alison, Dinah, Aaron, Miriam, Richard. AB, U. Calif., Berkeley, 1947, MA, 1949; MD, U. Chgo., Chicago, 1951. Dir. MML Diagnostic Labs, Palo Alto, Calif., 1954—72, Solano Clin. Labs, Berkeley, Calif., 1972—78, Oslerwelch Laboratories, San Leandro, Calif., 1978—86; cons. Smith Kline Laboratories, Dublin, Calif., 1986—93, Quest Diagnostic Labs, Dublin, Calif., 1993—. Instr. Stanford U. Sch. Medicine, Palo Alto, Calif., 1954—60, intern in pathology, 1960—62. Author: (pathology book) Out of the Mist; contbr. articles to profl. jours. Sgt. U.S. Army, 1943—46, PTO. Fellow, Nat. Found. Infantile Paralysis, 1951—53, Am. Cancer Soc., 1953—54. D-Liberal. Achievements include research in Protein and Nucleic Acid Metabolism. Avocation: medical history. Home: 9 Rio Porto Court Sacramento CA 95831

MALKIN, MICHAEL M. lawyer; b. New Haven, Nov. 1, 1944; s. Eli B. and Gladys (Pollak) M.; children: Andrea, Lisa, Daniel. BA, U. N.Mex., 1966; JD, NYU, 1969. Bar: N.Y. 1970, U.S. Dist. Ct. (so. dist.) N.Y. 1971, U.S. Dist. Ct. (ea. dist.) N.Y. 1971, U.S. Ct. Appeals (2d cir.) 1972, U.S. Supreme Ct. 1984. Assoc. Weil, Lee & Bergin, N.Y.C., 1970-76, Weil, Guttman & Davis, N.Y.C., 1976-77, ptnr., 1977-82, Weil, Guttman, Davis & Malkin, N.Y.C., 1982-86, Weil, Guttman & Malkin, N.Y.C., 1986-95, Weil, Guttman & Malkin, LLP, N.Y.C., 1995—2001. Judge Giles Sutherland Rich Moot Ct. Competition, N.Y.C., 1982; arbitrator Civil Ct. of City N.Y., 1984-88. Mem. editl. bd. Trademark Reporter, 1973-75, 88-90, contbg. editor, 1974-75. Mem. N.Y. State Bar Assn., U.S. Trademark Assn., Phi Delta Phi, Alpha Epsilon Pi. Office Phone: 480-513-2859. Business E-Mail: mikemalkin@cox.net.

MALKIN, MOSES MONTEFIORE, employee benefits administration company executive; b. Revere, Mass., Sept. 18, 1919; s. Irving and Annie (Helfant) M.; m. Hannah Lacob, Oct. 11, 1941. AB, U. N.C., 1941; BSME, Columbia U., 1948. Enrolled actuary; CLU. Engr. GE, Schenectady, N.Y., 1948-50; engr. Gen Bronze, Inc., Jersey City, 1950-51; v.p. Malkin Warehouse, Inc., New Haven, 1951-57; pvt. practice actuary New Haven, 1957-72; chmn., actuary Profl. Pensions, Inc., Middletown, Conn., 1973—93; ret., 1993. Presenter pension issues at numerous confs., 1970-80. Pres., founder Milford, Conn., 1962, Milford Child Guidance Clinic, 1966; pres. Clifford Beers Child Guidance, New Haven, 1971, Jewish Family Svc., New Haven, 1973. With U.S. Army, 1941-45, ETO. Mem. Am. Acad. Actuaries, Am. Soc. Pension Actuaries (instr. 1984), Am. Soc. CLUs, Phi Beta Kappa, Tau Beta Pi. Jewish. Office: Profl Pensions Inc 245 Long Hill Rd Middletown CT 06457 Address: 1514 Heron Dr Sun City Center FL 33573-4707

MALKIN, PETER LAURENCE, lawyer, real estate investor; b. N.Y.C., Jan. 14, 1934; s. Samuel and Gertrude (Greenberger) Malkin; m. Isabel L. Wien, July 10, 1955. Grad. cum laude, Poly. Prep. Country Day Sch., 1951; AB summa cum laude, Harvard Coll., 1955; LLB magna cum laude, Harvard U. Law Sch., 1958. Bar: N.Y. 1958, Conn. 1976, Fla. 1977. Sr. ptnr., chmn. Wien & Malkin LLP, N.Y.C., 1958—; mng. Empire State Bldg. Assocs. L.L.C., 1961—; chmn. W & M Properties, Inc., N.Y.C., 1965—. Bd. dirs. U.S. Trust Corp.; ptnr. N.Y.C. Partnership and C. of C., 2001—; founding chmn. Grand Ctrl. Partnership Inc. & 34th Street Partnership, Inc.; dir., sec. Fashion Ctr. Bus. Improvement Dist.; dir. Realty Found. N.Y., 1981—, v.p., 1995—; mem. adv. com. Greenwich (Conn.) Japanese Sch., 1992—; mem. N.Y.C. Mayor's Bus. Adv. Coun., 1997—2002; gov. Real Estate Bd., NYC, 1993—2000, NYC, 2001—; co-founder, hon. co-chmn. Com. to Encourage Corp. Philanthropy, 1998—. Nat. vice-chmn. Harvard Law Sch. Fund, 1967-71, chmn. nat. scholarship com., 1975-76, chmn. N.Y.C. com., 1981-83; founder, bd. dirs. Urban League Southwestern Fairfield County, 1969-73, treas., 1969-71; bd. dirs., mem. exec. com. Lincoln Ctr. for Performing Arts, 1979—; bd. dirs. Inst. Internat. Edn., 1983-89, hon. 1994—; trustee Nat. Trust for Hist. Preservation, 1988-91, mem. adv. coun., 1997—; founding chmn. Greenwich (Conn.) Green & Clean, Inc., 1986—, Greenwich Adopt-A-Road, 1996 , founding co-chmn., Merritt Pkwy. Conservancy, 2002—; v.p., mem. exec. com. Greenwich chpt. NAACP, 1967-69; trustee Citizens Budget Commn., N.Y.C., 1971-91, Jewish Communal Fund, N.Y., 1976-81; dean's coun., Harvard U., 1987-95; chmn. capital campaign and chmn. dean's coun. Kennedy Sch. Govt., 1995—, mem. overseers com. to visit Kennedy Sch. Govt., 1976-82, 83-89, 90—, to visit Harvard Law Sch. 1977-83; exec. com. Program for Ctr. for Jewish Studies, 1974-80; bd. overseers Harvard Coll., 1989-95, overseers com. univ resources, 1972—, exec. com., 1985—; dean's adv. com., Harvard Law Sch., 1988-90; elected dir. Harvard Alumni Assn., 1981-83; chmn. schs. and scholarship com. Harvard Coll., Greenwich, 1973-79; exec. com. Assn. Better N.Y., 1972—. Recipient Nat. Preservation Honor award Nat. Trust Hist. Preservation, 1987, President's award Grad. Sch. and Univ. Ctr. CCNY, 1989, Crain's All-Star award, 1994, Nacore Disting. Man of Yr. award, 1995; named Outstanding Young Man, N.Y.C. Jaycees, 1969, fellow Brandeis U., 1970—, Man of Yr., Hist. Soc. Greenwich, Conn., 1993, Murray Hill Archl. award, 1996, PENCIL award for outstanding commitment to N.Y.C. Pub. Schs., 2003, Lincoln Ctr. Outstanding Vol. Leader award, 2004. Mem. Harvard Law Sch. Assn. N.Y.C. (trustee 1968-70, v.p. 1973-74), Assn. Bar City N.Y., Century Assn., The Links N.Y., The Hasty Pudding Inst. 1770, AD Hon., Harvard Varsity Club (Cambridge), Harvard Club N.Y.C. (bd. mgrs. 1979-81), Harvard Club (Fairfield County, Conn., v.p. 1974-75, bd. dirs. 1976-80), Bailwick Club (hon. life mem., founding pres.), Blind Brook Club, Conn. Golf Club, Phi Beta Kappa. Office: 60 E 42d St New York NY 10165-0015 E-mail: plmalkin@wienmalkinllp.com.

MALKIN, STANLEY LEE, neurologist; b. Pitts., Pa., Nov. 11, 1942; s. Maurice and Bessie Beatrice (Serbin) M.; m. Candace N. Conard; children: Justin Ross, Keith Richard. BA with honors, U. Pa., 1964; MD, U. Pitts., 1968. Diplomate Am. Bd. Psychiatry and Neurology, Nat. Bd. Med. Examiners. Intern Montefiore Hosp., Pitts., 1968-69; resident in neurology Columbia-Presbyn. Med. Ctr., N.Y.C., 1969-72; chief neurology svc., Wright-Patterson AFB, Dayton, 1972-74; practice medicine specializing in neurology N.Y.C.; attending staff Mt. Sinai Hosp.; former dir. Neuro Diagnostic Lab., Englewood; asst. clin. prof. neurology Mt. Sinai Sch. Medicine; founder Bergen-Passaic Tomography Ctr., Fairlawn, N.J. Neurology cons. Regent Hosp.; med. dir. Pain Suppression Labs., Inc.; med. dir. Efficient Health Systems, Inc.-N.Y.C. Healthline; founder, med. dir., exec. v.p. Hosp. Diagnostic Equipment Corp., 1987—; pres. Cancer Treatment Holdings, Inc, 1993-95, dir. 1993-94, sr. med. dir. 1995-97; founder Montvale Med. Imaging Assocs. (N.J.), N.Y. Med. Imaging, N.Y.C., Hosp. Diagnostic Equipment Corp. Co-mcpl. coord. Ft. Lee Citizens for McGovern, 1972; ptnr. Sall/Myers Med. Assocs., prin. 1995—; mem. Edgewater Rent Control Bd., 1978. Maj. M.C. USAF, 1972-74. Recipient Comdr.'s Recognition award for care of repatriated prisoners of war, 1973. Fellow Royal Soc. Medicine; mem. Am. Acad. Neurology, Am. Assn. Electrodiagnostic Medicine, Am. Soc. Neuro-Imaging (charter), EEG and Clin. Neurosci. Soc., Am. Headache Soc. (rev. bd.), Nat. Headache Found., Internat. Headache Soc., Nat. Neurotrauma Soc., N.Y. Acad. Scis., NYU Bellevue Psychiat. Soc., European Fedn. Neurol. Socs. Office: 100 Hamilton Plaza 3d Fl Paterson NJ 07509 also: Ste 601 10 W 44th St New York NY 10036

MALKINE-FALVEY, FERN SYLVIE, writer, journalist, painter; b. Bklyn., Apr. 11, 1950; d. Georges Alexandre and Sonia May Malkine; m. Peter Anthony Falvey, June 20, 1992. MS Spl. Edn., Fordham U., New York, New York, 1976; BS History/English Lit., NYU, New York, New York, 1974; AA History/English, Ulster County CC, Stone Ridge, New York, 1972. Rschr., writer Editions de la Difference, Paris, 1976—78; copy editor Elle Mag., Paris, 1983—85; painter, freelance journalist Woodstock, NY, 1985—89; gallery dir. Isidore Ducasse Fine Arts, Manhattan, NY, 1989—92; art cons. Pavillon des Arts Mus., Paris, 1998—99; copy editor Look Mag., New York, NY, 1978—79; curator On-line Gallery, Woodstock, NY, 2001—; fgn. correspondant Paris Match, New York, NY, 1979—81. Author: Georges Malkine: An Arbitrary Destiny; co-author: Georges Malkine: Le Vagabond du Surrealism; exhibitions include Tom Fletcher Gallery, Woodstock, 2001, The Art Gallery-Western New Eng. Coll., Springield, Mass., 2002—. Vol. Congressman Matt McHugh, Kingston, NY, 1981, Justice of the Peace Sid Slayton, Woodstock, 1982, Oglala Sioux Emergency Svcs., 1987, ARC, 2001—. Mem.: Hist. Soc. of Woodstock. Avocations: guitar, historical post cards, designing moccasins, designing tapestries. Home: PO Box 261 Shady NY 12409 Personal E-mail: fernmf@hotmail.com.

MALKINSON, FREDERICK DAVID, dermatologist, educator; b. Hartford, Conn., Feb. 26, 1924; s. John Walter and Rose Malkinson; m. Una Zwick, June 15, 1979; children by previous marriage: Philip, Carol, John. Student, Loomis Inst., 1937-41; 3 yr. cert. cum laude, Harvard U., 1943, DMD, 1947, MD, 1949. Intern Harvard-Beth Israel Hosp., Boston, 1949-50; resident in dermatology U. Chgo., 1950-54, from instr. to assoc. prof. dept. dermatology, 1954-68; prof. medicine and dermatology U. Ill., Chgo., 1968-71; chmn. dept. dermatology Rush Med. Coll. and Rush-Presbyn.-St. Luke's Med. Ctr., Chgo., 1968-92, Clark W. Finnerud, M.D. prof. dept. dermatology, 1981-95, 95—; trustee Sulzberger Inst. Dermatol. Comm. and Edn., 1976-96; pres. Sulzberger Inst. Dermatol. Communication and Edn., 1983-88, 93-96; prof. emeritus Rush Presbyn.-St. Luke's Med. Ctr., Chgo., 2000—. Editor: Year Book of Dermatology, 1971-78; chief editor: AMA Archives of Dermatology, 1979-83; bd. editors, 1976-84, Jour. AMA, 1979-83; editorial cons. World Book Medical Encyclopedia, 1991—; contbr. articles and abstracts to profl. jours., chpts. to books. Active Evanston (Ill.) Libr. Bd., 1988-94, pres., 1993-94. With M.C. USN, 1950-52. Grantee U.S. Army, 1955-61, USPHS, 1962-73 Fellow AAAS; mem. Am. Acad. Dermatology (v.p. 1987-89, dir. 1964-67), Am. Dermatol. Assn., Soc. Investigative Dermatology (v.p. 1978-79, dir. 1963-68), Am. Fedn. Med. Rsch., Cen. Soc. Clin. Rsch., Radiation Rsch. Soc., Assn. Profs. of Dermatology (dir. 1982-85), Dermatology Found. (trustee 1980-93, pres. 1983-85), Nat. Coun. on Radiation Protection and Measurements (mem. com. on cutaneous radiobiology 1986-92), Chgo. Dermatol. Soc. (pres. 1964-65, Gold Medal award 1992, established ann. lectureship, 2004), Chgo. Lit. Club (v.p. 1997-99, 2000-03, pres. 1999-2000). Office: Rush-Presbyn-St Luke's Med Ctr Kidston 507b 1653 Congress Street Pkwy Chicago IL 60612 Office Fax: 312-942-7778.

MALKOVICH, JOHN, actor; b. Christopher, Ill., Dec. 9, 1953; m. Glenne Headley, 1982 (div.); children: Amandine and Loewy, with Nicoletta Peyran. Student, Eastern Ill. U., Ill. State U. Co-founder Steppenwolf Theatre, Chgo., 1976 Made N.Y.C. theatrical debut in True West, 1982 (Obie award, Clarence Derwent award); other theatrical appearances include: Death of a Salesman, 1984, Burn This, 1987, States of Shock; dir. Balm in Gilead, 1984-85, Arms and the Man, 1985, The Caretaker, 1986, Coyote Ugly, (Chgo., Kennedy Ctr. for Performing Arts, Washington) 1985, Libra, 1994, Steppenwolf, 1994; appeared in films Places in the Heart, 1984, The Killing Fields, 1984, Eleni, 1985, Making Mr. Right, 1987, Glass Menagerie, 1987, Empire of the Sun, 1987, Miles From Home, 1988, Dangerous Liaisons, 1988, The Sheltering Sky, 1990, Queen's Logic, 1991, The Object of Beauty, 1991, Shadows and Fog, 1992, Jennifer 8, 1992, Of Mice and Men, 1992, In The Line Of Fire, 1993 (Academy award nomination best supporting actor 1993), Alive, 1993, Touchstone, 1994, Para De La Nuages, 1994, Mary Reilly, 1994, Mulholland Falls, 1996, Der Unhold, 1996, The Portrait of a Lady, 1996, Primary Colors, 1997, Con Air, 1997, The Man in the Iron Mask, 1998, Rounders, 1998, Le Temps retrouvé, 1999, The Libertine, 1999, Ladies Room, 1999, Joan of Arc, 1999, Being John Malkovich, 1999 (American Comedy Award, 2000), Shadow of the Vampire, 2000, Les Ames Forte, 2001, Knockaround Guys, 2001, Je rentre a la Maison, 2001, Ripley's Game, 2002, Hotel, 2001, The Dancer Upstairs, 2002, Johnny English, 2003; exec. prodr. The Accidental Tourist, 1988, Somewhere Else, 2000; prodr. Ghost World, 2000, The Loner, 2001, Found in the Street, 2001, The Dancer Upstairs, 2002; co-exec. prodr. The Accidental Tourist, 1988; dir. The Libertine, 1999, The Dancer Upstairs, 2002; appeared in TV films Word of Honor, 1981, American Dream, 1981, Death of a Salesman, 1985 (Emmy award 1986), Heart of Darkness, 1994, RKO 281, 1999, Les Miserables, 2000, Napoleon, 2002. Office: William Morris Agency One William Morris Place Beverly Hills CA 90212

MALKOVICH, MARK PAUL, III, musician, artistic director, scientist, sports agent; b. Eveleth, Minn., July 10, 1930; s. Mark II and Mary Frances (Greben) M.; m. Joan Shewring, Feb. 7, 1959; children: Mark IV, Erik, Kent, Kara. BS in Chemistry, Columbia U., 1952, MS, 1953; studied piano with Dorothy Crost Bourgin, Chgo. Mus. Coll., 1947-50; William Beller ch. Piano Dept., Columbia U., 1951-54; Adele Marcus, Juilliard Sch., 1959-62; MusD (hon.), Salve Regina, 1993; DFA, U. R.I., 1994; MusD, Cath. U. Am., 1999. Pres. Chem. Gum Industries, Ltd., N.Y.C., 1964—69. Artistic and gen. dir. Newport Music Festival, 1975—; exec. dir. Palm Beach Festival, Fla., 1984-86; guest lectr. TV and radio appearances and adjudicator at music competitions; pres. Chopin Found. of U.S., Miami, Fla., 1985; presented N.Am. debuts of Bella Davidovich, Jean-Philippe Collard, Dmitry Sitkovetsky, Andrei Gavrilov, others; founder Sports US*A*SR; negotiator/agt. for USSR leading hockey players Fetisov, Krutov, Larionov, Makarov, 1989. Recipient Individual Achievement award Bus. Vols. for the Arts, R.I., 1998; named to R.I. Heritage Hall of Fame, 2000. Mem. Harvard Mus. Assn., Newport Reading Rm., Spouting Rock Beach Assn., Clambake Club. Office: care Newport Music Festival PO Box 3300 Newport RI 02840-0992

MALKOWICZ, STANLEY BRUCE, urologist; b. Passaic, NJ; s. Stanley Jacob and Jeanne (iracki) M.; m. Denise Elaine Ewald, Sept. 22, 1985. BA, U. Vt., 1977; MD, U. Pa., Phila., 1981. Intern in surgery Hosp. U. Pa., Phila., 1981-82, resident in surgery, 1982-83, resident in urology, 1983-86, chief resident in urology, 1986-87; fellow in urologic oncology U. So. Calif., LA, 1987-88, Hosp. U. Pa., Phila., 1988-90, asst. prof. surgery, 1990-95, assoc. prof., 1995—2003, prof. urology, 2003—; chief urology Phila. VA Med. Ctr. Assoc. scientist Wistar Inst. Anatomy and Biology, Phila., 1988—; Nat. Kidney Found. rsch. fellow, 1983-84; Am. Found. Urologic Disease rsch. scholar, 1988-90. Contbr. articles to profl. jours. Mem. AAAS, Am. Urologic Assn., Am. Soc. Clin. Oncology, Soc. Univ. Urologists, Urodynamics Soc., Assn. Academic Surgeons, Soc. Pelvic Surgeons, Soc. Urologic Oncology, Urol. Rsch. Soc., Phila. Urol. Soc. (pres.), S.E. Pa. Am. Cancer Soc. (pres.), Sigma Xi. Presbyterian. Avocations: camping, reading, cooking. Office: Hosp U Pa 3400 Spruce St Philadelphia PA 19104-4206 Office Phone: 215-662-7330.

MALKUS, DAVID STARR, mathematician; b. Chgo., June 30, 1945; s. Willem V.R. Malkus and Joanne (Gerould) Simpson; m. Evelyn R. (div.); children: Christopher, Annelise, Byron, Renata. AB, Yale U., 1968; PhD, Boston U., 1976. Mathematician U.S. Nat. Bur. Standards, Gaithersburg, Md., 1975-77; asst. prof. math. Ill. Inst. Tech., Chgo., 1977-83, assoc. prof., 1983-84; assoc. prof. mechanics U. Wis., Madison, 1984-87, prof., 1987—2002, chmn. Rheology Rsch. Ctr., 1991-94, prof. emeritus, 2002—. Chair prof. Nanjing (People's Republic China) Aero. Inst., 1986. Co-author: Concepts and Applications of Finite Element Analysis, 1989; contbr. articles to Computer Methods Applied Mech. Engring., Jour. Computational Physics. Achievements include research on finite element methods--reduced and selective integration techniques, a unification of concepts. Home: 2710 Mason St Madison WI 53705-3716 Office: U Wis Dept Engring Physics 1500 Engineering Dr Madison WI 53706-1609 E-mail: malkus@engr.wisc.edu.

MALL, WILLIAM JOHN, JR., aerospace executive, retired Air Force general; b. Pitts., Jan. 13, 1933; s. William John and Margaret (Henry) M.; m. Vivian Lea Fenton; children— Michele, William, Catherine BBA, U. Pitts., 1954; MBA, George Washington U., 1966; sr. mgrs. in govt. program, Harvard U., 1980. Commd. officer USAF, 1954, advanced through grades to maj. gen., 1981; insp. gen. Mil. Airlift Command., Scott AFB, Ill., 1978, comdr. 436 wing Dover AFB, Del., 1979; DCS personnel Mil. Airlift Command, Scott AFB, Ill., 1979-81; comdr. Air Rescue Service, Scott AFB, Ill., 1981-83, 23d AF/MAC, Scott AFB, Ill., 1983-85; assigned to Hdqrs USAF, Bolling AFB, D.C., 1985-86; ret.; dir. integrated logistics support div. Douglas Aircraft Co., Long Beach, Calif., 1987-89, gen. mgr. human resources, 1989-91; exec. dir. LAX Two Corp., L.A., 1991-99. Decorated Legion of Merit, Bronze Star, Air medal Mem. Airlift Assn., Daedalians, Jolly Green Pilots Assn. Avocations: tennis, sailing. Office: LAX Two Corp 200 World Way Los Angeles CA 90045-5859

MALLAK, JAMES A. auto parts company executive; BS in Acctg., Mich. StateU.; MBA, Mich. State U. Numerous fin. mgmt. positions ITT Automotive, 1977—98; v.p. fin. Heavy Vehivle Systems divsn. Arvin/Meritor, 1998—99; exec. v.p., chief fin. officer Textron Automotive Corp., 1999—2001; chief fin. officer Tower Automotive Inc, Novi, Mich., 2004—. Mem. adv. bd. acctg. and fin. dept. Oakland U., Mich. Office: Tower Automotive Inc 27175 Haggarty Rd Novi MI 48377

MALLARD, STEPHEN ANTHONY, retired utility company executive; b. Jersey City, Sept. 15, 1924; s. Stephen F. and Gertrude V. (Donahue) M.; m. Winifred Anne Carey, June 7, 1947; children: Stephen Kevin, Catherine Anne, Eileen Rosemary Mallard McClenahan. M.E., Stevens Inst. Tech, Hoboken, N.J., 1948, MSE.E., 1951. Registered profl. engr. With elec. distbn., system planning and devel. Pub. Service Electric and Gas Co., Newark, 1951-77, v.p. system planning, 1977-80, sr. v.p. planning and research, 1980-88, sr. v.p. transmission systems, 1989; pvt. practice engring. Nutley, N.J., 1990—. Advisor Brookhave Nat. Lab.; cons. Manhattan Coll. Bd. dirs. Met. chpt. ARC, Fairfield, N.J., 1985—, bd. dirs. No. N.J. chpt., 1988—; bd. dirs. Essex County Grand Jury Assn., 1978-87. With USN, 1944-46, PTO. Fellow IEEE; mem. Nat. Soc. Profl. Engrs.,, Conf. Internationale des Grands Reseaux Electriques a Haute Tension, Eta Kappa Nu, Tau Beta Pi Roman Catholic. Home and Office: 68 High St Nutley NJ 07110-1134 E-mail: samallardnj@aol.com.

MALLERY, DAVID, education association executive, consultant; b. Sugar Hill, N.H., Aug. 3, 1923; s. Otto Tod and Louise Marshall Mallery; m. Judith Chappell Mallery, June 15, 1956; children: Roger, Diane Mallery Cusick. BA, Haverford (Pa.) Coll., 1945, PhD (hon.), 1995; MA, Middlebury (Vt.) Coll., 1950. Tchr. English Germantown Friends Sch., Phila., 1946-58; seminar leader Friends Coun. on Edn., Phila., 1959-94; dir. profl. devel. Nat. Assn. Ind. Schs., Washington, 1959—. Edn. cons., 1959—; tchr. Bell Tel./U. Pa. Inst. for Humanistic Studies for Execs., 1960's. Author: High School Students Speak Out, 1960's, Ferment on the Campus, 1960's. Edn. advisor Tracy S. Voorhees, Pres. Eisenhower's rep. on Cuban refugee crisis, 1959-60; founding trustee Am. Film Inst., 1967-79. Lt. (j.g.) USNR, 1943-46, WW II. Recipient Klingenstein award Columbia U. Tchrs. Coll., 1996. Avocations: film, theater, music, international networking. Home: 9006 Crefeld St Philadelphia PA 19118-3607 Office: Nat Assn Ind Schs Sugar Loaf Conf Ctr 9230 Germantown Ave Philadelphia PA 19118-2603

MALLET, JACQUES ROBERT, art dealer; b. Paris, Feb. 19, 1945; came to U.S., 1972; s. Jean-Pierre Theodore and Christiane Claire (De Watteville-Berckheim) M.; m. Laurie Helene Belhassen, May 30, 1973 (div. 1985); children: Clementine, Arthur. B in Maths., Lycee Louis-Le-Grand, Paris, 1966; M in Econs., U. Paris, 1971; MBA, Columbia U., 1973. Salesman mut. funds Banque De Neuflize, Schlumberger, Mallet, Paris, 1969; asst. v.p. Kuhn Loeb & Co. Inc., N.Y.C., 1973-78; sr. assoc. corp. fin. ABD Securities Corp., N.Y.C., 1978-80; pres. Mallet Fine Art Ltd., N.Y.C., 1982—. Mem.: Nat. Arts (N.Y.C.); Brooks's (London). Office: Mallet Fine Art Ltd 220 Park Ave S Apt 9B New York NY 10003-1519

MALLETT, CONRAD LEROY, JR., former state supreme court chief justice, hospital administrator; b. Detroit, Oct. 12, 1953; s. Conrad LeRoy and Claudia Gwendolyn (Jones) M.; m. Barbara Straughn, Dec. 22, 1984; children: Alex Conrad, Mio Thomas, Kristan Claudia. BA, UCLA, 1975; MPA, JD, U. So. Calif., 1979; MBA, Oakland U. Bar: Mich. 1979. Legal asst. to congressman, Detroit, 1979-80; dep. pol. dir. Dem. Nat. Com., Washington, 1980-81; assoc. Miller, Canfield, Paddock & Stone, Detroit, 1981-82; legal counsel, dir. to gov. State of Mich., Lansing, 1983-84; sr. exec. asst. to Mayor

City of Detroit, 1985-86; ptnr. Jaffe, Raitt, Heuer & Weiss, Detroit, 1987-90; justice Mich. Supreme Ct., Lansing, 1990—98, chief justice, 1997—98; pvt. practice Miller Canfield, Detroit, 1999; gen. counsel, chief adminstrv. officer Detroit Med. Ctr., 1999—2001, exec. v.p., chief adminstrv. officer, 2003—; COO City of Detroit, 2002; pres., gen. counsel Hawkins Food Group, 2002—03; interim pres. Sinai Grace Hosp., Detroit, 2003—. Bd. mem. Lear Corp., TechTeam Global, Inc. Mem. NAACP, Kappa Alpha Psi. Democrat. Roman Catholic. Avocations: writing, fiction. Office: Sinai-Grace Hosp 6071 W Outer Dr Detroit MI 48235-2624*

MALLETTE, DAVID, performing company executive; Exec. dir. Ft. Worth Ballet, Ft. Worth/Dallas Ballet, 1990—. Office: Ft Worth Dallas Ballet 6845 Green Oaks Rd Fort Worth TX 76116

MALLEY, RAYMOND CHARLES, retired foreign service officer, industrial executive; b. Cambridge, Mass., Dec. 22, 1930; s. William and Evangeline (Vautour) M.; m. Rita Ann Masse, May 26, 1951 (dec. June 1989); children: Keith, Bruce, Gregory; m. Josette Lucile Vidril Murphy, Aug. 11, 1995. AA, Boston U., 1950, BS, 1952; MA Equivalent, U. Geneva, 1955; MA, PhD, ABD, Fletcher Sch. Law & Diplomacy, Tufts U. and Harvard U., Mass., 1956. Economist, fin. analyst Texaco, Inc., NYC, 1957—61; fgn. svc. officer U.S. Dept. State, AID, Washington & fgn. posts, 1961—82; dir. U.S. Trade and Devel. Program, Washington, 1980; v.p. Silopress, Inc., Sioux City, Iowa, 1982—87; pres. Silopress Can., 1985—87; cons., advisor Labat-Anderson Internat., Arlington, Va., 1988—93; sr. group advisor, N.Am. and S.Am. rep. Halla Bus. Group, Seoul, Republic of Korea, NYC, Washington, 1991—. Chmn. Halla Am. Inc., 1996-2001. Mem. exec. bd. Coll. of Mgmt., L.I. U., Brookville, NY, 1994—. 2nd lt., 1st lt., capt. then maj. USAFR. Recipient Nat. Def. Svc. medal, USAFR, Korean War. Mem. Acadian Cultural Soc., Am. Fgn. Svc. Assn., Diplomatic and Consular Officers Ret., U.S. Profl. Tennis Registry, Harvard Club. Roman Catholic. Avocation: tennis. Home: 10 Berrill Farms Ln Hanover NH 03755-3205 Office: Halla America Inc 6224 Loch Raven Dr Mc Lean VA 22101-3133 E-mail: Rcmalley@aol.com.

MALLIA-HUGHES, MARIANNE, medical writer; b. Davenport, Iowa, Feb. 14, 1948; d. Norman Bramblett and Mary Jane (Hilkemeyer) Hagar; m. Michael L. Hughes; 1 child from previous marriage, Lindsay Sharyn Mallia. BA in English, U. Iowa, 1970. Cert. tchr. Tchr. tech. writing Houston Ind. Sch. Dist., 1970—76; med. writer Tex. Heart Inst., Houston, 1976—; editl. cons. Tex. Heart Inst. Jour., Houston, 1977—87, head sci. publ., 1986—, sr. med. writer, 1994—. Instr. Sch. Allied Health Sci. and Sch. Pub. Health U. Tex., 1990—94. Editor: Techniques in Cardiac Surgery, 1984; editor: (with Denton A. Cooley) Surg. Treatment of Aortic Aneurysms, 1985; editor: (essays) Reflections and Observation, Denton A. Cooley, MD, 1985, (handbook) Heart Owner's Handbook, 1995; bd. editors: Life Sci., 2002. Fellow: Am. Med. Writers Assn. (core curriculum cert. 1984, instr. 1985—, advanced curriculum cert. 1989, honor roll workshop leader 1992—, bd. dir., exec. com. 1996—, pres. 2002—03, writer and advanced core curriculum); mem.: Women in Comm. (cert. editor in life sci., Matrix Aaward 1996—2000), Coun. Biology Editors, Pi Beta Phi. Office: Tex Heart Inst PO Box 20345 Houston TX 77225-0345 Home: 3779 Tangley St Houston TX 77005-2031 Business E-Mail: mmallia@heart.thi.tmc.edu.

MALLIK, MUHAMMAD ABDUL-BARI, soil microbiologist; b. Pabna, Bangladesh, Mar. 15, 1927; s. Monsur Ali and Ataharun-Nisa Mallik; m. Rowshan Jahan Hamida, Sept. 24, 1966; 1 child, Abds-Sami. BSc, Rajshahi (Bangladesh) Coll., 1949; MSc, Dhaka (Bangladesh) U., 1952; MS, Minn. U., 1961; PhD, Okla. U., 1964. Lectr. botany U. Karachi, Pakistan, 1956-59, asst. prof., 1964-68, 69-72; vis. scholar dept. botany Baghdad (Iraq) U., 1968-69; asst. prof. Dhaka (Bangladesh) U., 1973-74; rsch. assoc. dept. botany and microbiology u. Okla., Norman, 1974-75; assoc. rsch. prof. agrl. rsch. program Langston (Okla.) U., 1975-82, rsch. prof. agrl. rsch. program, 1982—. Author: Introduction to Fungi, 1973; contbr. articles to profl. and popular publs. Fulbright scholar Minn. U., St. Paul, 1961; rsch. grantee Pakistan Agrl. Rsch. Coun., Karachi, 1968-69, USDA, Langston, 1982—. Mem. Am. Soc. Agronomy, Internat. Allelopathy Soc., Okla. Acad. Sci., Bangladesh Bot. Soc. Democrat. Moslem. Avocation: gardening. Home: 2611 S Oxford Dr Stillwater OK 74074-2276 Office: Langston Univ Agrl Rsch Program PO Box 730 Langston OK 73050-0730

MALLINSON, RICHARD GREGORY, chemical engineering educator; b. Indpls., Apr. 9, 1954; s. Harry and Susan Louise (Keckler) M. BSChemE, BS in Biomed. Engring., Tulane U., 1977; MSChemE, Purdue U., 1979, PhD, 1983. Rsch. asst. Purdue U., West Lafayette, Ind., 1977-83, Argonne Nat. Lab., Chgo., 1978; asst. prof. chem. engring. U. Okla., Norman, 1983-89, assoc. prof., 1989-99, dir. Inst. for Gas Utilization Techs., 1995—, prof., 1999—. Faculty fellow Lawrence Livermore Nat. Lab., Livermore, Calif., 1990; vis. prof. Tianjin (China) U., 1994—, Chulalongkorn U., Bangkok, 1994—; ptnr. OKKINETICS, Norman, 1996-2000; prin. investigator Univ. Technologists, Inc., Norman, 1988-91; Kerr McGee Disting. lectr. Kerr-McGee Found./U. Okla., 1989-94. Contbr. many articles on Energy. Bd. dirs. C.D. Mallory Found., Inc., Ala., 1994-99, Heartland Found., Inc., Okla., 1995—; mem. Okla. Found. for Excellence, 1993—. 1st lt. USAR, 1977-85. Mem. AIChE (dir. local sect. 1989, symposia organizer 1986-89), Am. Chem. Soc. (symposia organizer 1985-91), Am. Soc. Engring. Edn., Sigma Xi. Achievements include patents pending and patents in field for high density natural gas storage at high temperature, and chemical conversion of natural gas at low temperatures; other areas of exoertise such as natural gas utilization, clean production of N204, emulsion polymerization modeling, alkane cracking modeling, coal conversion modeling. Home: 4631 Ridgeline Dr Norman OK 73072-1700 Office: U Okla 100 E Boyd St Rm T335 Norman OK 73019-1028 Office Phone: 405-325-4378. Business E-Mail: mallinson@ou.edu.

MALLIS, MELISSA MERCEDES, research psychologist; b. Kingston, Pa., Apr. 24, 1972; d. Thomas John and Paulette Mary Mallis. BS in Physics, Villanova U., 1994; PhD in Biomed. Sci., Drexel U., 1999. Rsch. psychologist NASA Ames Rsch. Ctr., Moffett Field, Calif., 1999—. Roman Catholic. Avocations: swimming, travel. Office: NASA Ames Rsch Ctr Fatigue Countermeasures Group MS 262-4 Moffett Field CA 94035 Office Phone: 650-604-3654.

MALLO, LUIS, artist, art director, photographer; b. Havana, Cuba, Sept. 14, 1962; s. Braulio Luis Mallo and Rosa Candida Barber; m. Ana Nery Fragoso, June 26, 1995. AAS, Fashion Inst. of Tech., N.Y., 1983. Installation, Passengers (Cintas Fellowship, 1991), exhibitions include Laminas (Art Matters Fellowship, 1994), In Camera, Reliquiarium (inside the cave), eros and civilization, Passersby. Portfolio reviews SE Mus. of Photography, Daytona Beach; photographer Smithsonian Inst., Washington. Recipient Best of Show, Mus. of Fine Arts, 1994. Mem.: Woodstock Ctr. for Photography. Personal E-mail: luis@lmallo.com.

MALLO-GARRIDO, JOSEPHINE ANN, advertising executive; b. Agana, Guam, Mar. 20, 1955; d. Benjamin Corneja and Salvacion (Lacuesta) Mallo; m. John Marco Haniu Garrido, Feb. 16, 1980; children: Josiah Michael (dec.), Jordan Thaddeus. Student, U. Guam, Agana, 1972-74; BA in Journalism, Seattle U., 1976; MBA, Pepperdine U., 1982. Reporter Pacific Daily News, Agana, 1976, features editor, 1977-78, asst. city editor, 1978-79; copy editor features Honolulu Star-Bull., 1979-81; advt. copywriter Advt. Factors, Honolulu, 1981-83; communications specialist Liberty House, Honolulu, 1983-84; editor, advt. copywriter Safeway Stores Inc., Oakland, Calif., 1984-88; features writer Tracy (Calif.) Press, 1988-91; mktg. mgr. ComputerLand of Guam, Maite, 1992-93; mktg. officer Citibank, Agana, 1993-94; owner JMG Advt., 1994—. Newspaper graphics cons. Pacific Daily News, 1984. Editor/writer Foods Unltd., 1984-88, Tracy Community Hosp. Health Beat and Update, 1988-91; editor Pacific Voice, 1977-78; contbr. articles to profl. jours. Vol. Engaged Encounter, Honolulu, 1989, Trans-Pacific Yacht Race, Honolulu, 1983, United Way, Oakland, 1986; advt. coord. Easter Seals, Oakland, 1987; organist St. Patrick's Ch., Honolulu, 1980—84, Immaculate Heart of Mary Ch., Toto, Guam, 1994—; mem. adv. bd. Cath. Social Svcs., Agana, Guam, 1993—97, bd. dirs., 1997—, bd. trustees, 2002—. Recipient Cert. Achievement award Advt. Age Mag., 1985, Cert Appreciation award Am. Heart Food Festival, 1985, Best in the West award Am. Advt. Fedn., 1986, Retail Nutrition award Nat. Potato Promotion Bd., 1986, Spl. Achievement award Newspaper Spl. Sect. Mother's Day/Father's Day Coun., 1989, 90, Best Feature Story 2d place Calif. Newspaper Pubs. Assn., 1989, 1st place Classified Advt. Assn., 1989, 1st place appetizer Spam Food Festival, 1991. Mem. Guam C. of C. (media coord. 1993-95), Citiclub (exec. sec. 1994-95). Roman Catholic. Avocations: piano, travel, Karate (black belt).

MALLON, CHARLES J. management consultant executive; BS in Acctg., Bus. Admin., Drexel U. CPA. With Ernst & Young; CFO ACS Enterprises, Inc.; exec. v.p., CFO Right Mgmt. Consultants, 1996—. Mem.: Am. Inst. CPAs, Pa. Inst.CPAs. Office: World Headquarters 1818 Market St 33rd Fl Philadelphia PA 19103-3614

MALLON, FRANCIS J. health science association administrator; Chief exec. officer Am. Physical Therapy Assn., Alexandria, Va. Office: Am Physical Therapy Assn 1111 N Fairfax St Alexandria VA 22314-1436 Office Phone: 703-684-2782.

MALLON, MEG, professional golfer; b. Natick, Mass., Apr. 14, 1963; Student, Ohio State U., 1983-87. Prof. Golfer LPGA Tour, 1987—. Mem. Solheim Cup Team, 1992, 94, 96, 98, 2000, 2002, 2003 Named Female Player of Year, Golf Writers Assn. of Am., 1991, one of the LPGA's top 50 players and tchrs., LPGA's 50th Anniversary, 2000. Achievements include winner 15 career LPGA victories including: Mazda LPGA Championship, 1991, U.S. Women's Open, 1991. Avocations: music, sports, travel. Office: care LPGA 100 International Golf Dr Daytona Beach FL 32124-1082

MALLOR, ANDREW C. lawyer; b. Newark, Jan. 19, 1949; AB, Ind. U., 1971, JD, 1974. Bar: Ind. 1974, U.S. Dist. Ct. (so. dist.) Ind. 1974, U.S. Tax Ct. 1981, U.S. Supreme Ct. 1981. Ptnr. Andrew C. Mallor Assocs., P.C., Bloomington, Ind. Contbr. articles to legal jours. Fellow: Am. Acad. Matrimonial Lawyers; mem.: ATLA, Ind. Trial Lawyers Assn. Office: Andrew C Mallor Assocs PC PO Box 5787 Bloomington IN 47407-5787

MALLORY, ARTHUR LEE, university dean, retired state official; b. Springfield, Mo., Dec. 26, 1932; s. Dillard A. and Ferrell (Claxton) M.; m. Joann Peters, June 6, 1954; children: Dennis Arthur (dec.), Christopher Lee, Stephanie Ann, Jennifer Lyn. BS, S.W. Mo. State Coll., 1954; MEd, U. Mo., 1957, EdD, 1959; HHD, S.W. Bapt. Coll., Mo., 1972. History supr. U. Mo. Lab. Sch., Columbia, 1956-57; asst. to supt. schs. Columbia, 1957-59; asst. supt. schs. Parkway Sch. Dist., St. Louis County, Mo., 1959-64; dean evening div. U. Mo., St. Louis, 1964; pres. S.W. Mo. State U., Springfield, 1964-70, dean Coll. Edn., 1991-94; commr. edn. Mo. Dept. Edn., Jefferson City, 1971-87. Dir. Internat. House, U. Mo., Columbia, 1956-59; chmn. bd. Mo. Coun. on Econ. Edn., 2000—. V.p. Ozarks coun. Boy Scouts Am., 1967, pres. Gt. Rivers coun., 1972-73, Greene County Assn. for Retarded Citizens, 1989—, pres., 1991-96, mem. north ctrl. region exec. bd., 1984—; bd. dirs. Meml. Cmty. Hosp., Mid-Continent Regional Ednl. Lab., Ozark Pub. Telecoms. Inc., 1989—; chmn. bd. Mo. Coun. on Econ. Edn.; bd. regents Mo. State Univs.; trustee Pub. Sch. Retirement, William Jewell Coll., 1972-74; chmn. com. bds. So. Bapt. Conv., 1972-73, mem. com. or bds., 1981—; mem .exec. bd. Mo. Bapt. Conv., 1972-75, 77-80, 2d v.p., 1995-96, pres., 1996-97; trustee Southwestern Bapt. Theol. Sem., Fort Worth, 1995—; mem. adv. com. Young Audiences, Inc., 1986, ARC Bd., Greene County, 1986, Children's Svcs. Commn., chmn., 1986—, Edn. Commn. U.S.; bd. dirs. Ozark Pub. TV; chmn. bd. advisors Windemere Bapt. Assembly, 1992—, chmn. bd. trustees, 2000–; pres. Gt. River coun. Boy Scouts Am., 1972, 73; chmn. Mo. Coun. for Econ. Edn., 2000–. With U.S. Army, 1954-56. Recipient Disting. Service award Mo. Jr. C. of C., 1966; Distinguished Service award U. Mo., 1976; Faculty/Alumni award U. Mo., 1976; Silver Beaver award Boy Scouts Am., 1983, Good Shepherd and Cross, 1986, Disting. Citizen award, 1986; hon. life mem. Mo. Congress Parents and Tchrs.; named Springfield's Outstanding Young Man of Yr., 1965; Champion of Excellence PUSH, 1978 Mem. Am. Assn. State Colls. and Univs., N. Central Assn. Colls. and Secondary Schs., Council Chief State Sch. Officers, Mo. Assn. Sch. Adminstrs., NEA, Mo. Tchrs. Assn. So. Baptist (deacon). Clubs: Masons (33 deg.), Rotary.

MALLORY, BRUCE, academic administrator; Dean Grad. Sch. U. N.H., Durham, prof. edn., sr. vice provost, provost, 2003—. Office: Office Acad Affairs Thompson Hall 207 Univ NH Durham NH 03824*

MALLORY, FRANK LINUS, lawyer; b. Calgary, Alta., Can., May 5, 1920; s. Frank Louis and Anna Amy (Allstrum) M.; m. Jean Ellen (Lindsey), Jan. 29, 1944; children: Susan Mallory Remund, Ann, Bruce R. AB, Stanford U., 1941, LLB, 1947. Bar: Calif., 1948. Assoc. Gibson, Dunn, and Crutcher, L.A., 1947-54; ptnr. L.A. and Orange County, 1955-88. Cert. specialist taxation law Calif. Bd. Legal Splty., 1973-89. Pres. town hall of L.A., 1970; Boys Republic, Chino, Calif., 1962-64; pres. Braille Inst. Am., L.A., 1988-92; Lt.(j.g.), USNR, 1942-46. Mem. ABA, Los Angeles County Bar Assn., Orange County Bar Assn., Newport Harbor Yacht Club, Big Canyon Country Club, Transpacific Yacht Club (staff commodore), Order of Coif, Phi Beta Kappa. Republican. Home: 633 Bayside Dr Newport Beach CA 92660-7213 E-mail: flmallory@cs.com.

MALLORY, ROBERT MARK, controller, finance executive; b. Mattoon, Ill., Apr. 15, 1950; s. Robert Monroe and Betty Ann (Mudd) M.; m. Diana Marie Burde, Aug. 19, 1972; 1 child, Laura Elizabeth. BS in Accountancy, U. Ill., 1972; MBA, Northwestern U., 1985. CPA, Ill. Staff acct. Price Waterhouse, Chgo., 1972-74, sr. acct., 1974-77, mgr., 1977-79; dir. internal audit Mark Controls Corp., Skokie, Ill., 1979-81, corp. contr., 1981-86, v.p., contr., 1986-88; contr., dir. planning Tribune Co., Chgo., 1988-91, v.p., contr., 1991—. Bd. dirs. Met. Family Svcs. Mem. AICPA (Elijah Watts Sells award 1972), Ill. CPA Soc., Fin. Execs. Internat. (bd. dirs.), Internat. Newspaper Fin. Execs. (bd. dirs.), Beta Gamma Sigma. Methodist. Home: 3312 Lakewood Ct Glenview IL 60025-2505 Office: Tribune Co 435 N Michigan Ave Chicago IL 60611-4066 E-mail: mallory435@aol.com.

MALLORY, TROY L. accountant; b. Sesser, Ill., July 30, 1923; s. Theodore E. and Alice (Mitchell) M.; m. Magdalene Richter, Jan. 26, 1963. Student, So. Ill. U., 1941-43, Washington and Jefferson Coll., 1943-44; BS, U. Ill., 1947, MS, 1948. Staff sr. supr. Scovell, Wellington & Co., CPAs, Chgo., 1948-58; mgr. Gray Hunter Stenn CPAs, Quincy, Ill., 1959-62, ptnr., 1962-99. Mem. fin. com. United Fund, Adams County, 1961-64; bd. dirs. Woodland Home for Orphans and Friendless, 1970—, pres., 1981-84, 87-90. Served with 84th Inf. Divsn. AUS, 1942-45. Decorated Purple Heart, Bronze Star. Mem. AICPA, Ill. CPA Soc., Quincy C. of C. (bd. dirs. 1970-76), Rotary (bd. dirs. Quincy 1967-70, pres. 1978-79), Shriners (bd. dirs. Quincy 1982-85, pres. 1988), Royal Order Jesters (Ct. 20 dir. 1997), Railsplitters Soc. (pres. 1993). Home: 2229 Jersey St Quincy IL 62301-4341

MALLOY, CRAIG RIGGS, physician, educator; b. Pasadena, Calif., Feb. 8, 1952; s. John Atherton and Frances Dwight (Riggs) M.; m. Deborah Finger, May 24, 1980; children: William Atherton, Mary Margaret, George Joseph. BS, Stanford U., 1973; MD, U. Calif., San Francisco, 1977. From asst. to prof. U. Tex., Dallas, 1984—; dir. Mary Nell and Ralph B. Rogers Magnetic Resonance Ctr., 1984—. Dir. Southwestern Biomedical Magnetic Resonance Ctr., Dallas, 1993. Contbr. articles to profl. jours.

MALLOY, DANNEL PATRICK, mayor; m. Cathy Malloy; children: Dan, Ben, Sam. LLB, Boston Coll. Bar: Conn., Mass., N.Y., U.S. Dist. Ct. Conn., U.S. Dist. Ct. (ea. and so. dists.) N.Y. Asst. dist. atty. Bklyn., N.Y. Dist. Atty.'s Office, 1980-84; ptnr. Abate & Fox, Stamford, Conn., 1984-95; mayor City of Stamford, 1995—. Mem. bd. fin. City of Stamford, 1983-94, Stamford Bd. Edn., 1994-95; spl. master Conn. Superior Ct.; lectr. Family Law Tng. Seminar. Past bd. dirs. Teen Life Ctr., Liberation Programs, Inc., CTE; treas. Conn. Conf. Municipalities, 1997-98, v.p.; vice chair mayors and pub. schs. task force U.S. Conf. Mayors; mem. fair policy steering com. Nat. League of Cities, 1997-98, mem. task force on youth and edn; chmn. Dem. Mcpl. Ofcls. Orgn.; mem. Dem. Nat. Com., mem. exec. com.; mem. adv. bd. U.S. Conf. Mayors. Mem. ABA, ATLA, Nat. Trial Lawyers Assn., Conn. Bar Assn., Conn. Trial Lawyers Assn. Democrat. Office: 10th Fl Govt Center 888 Washington Blvd Stamford CT 06902

MALLOY, EDWARD ALOYSIUS, academic administrator; b. Washington, D.C., May 3, 1941; s. Edward Aloysius and Elizabeth (Clark) Malloy. BA, U. Notre Dame, 1963, MA, 1967, ThM, 1969; PhD, Vanderbilt U., 1975. Ordained to ministry Cath. Ch., 1970. Instr. U. Notre Dame, South Bend, Ind., 1974—75, asst. prof., 1975—81, assoc. prof., 1981—88, prof. theology, 1988—, assoc. provost, 1982—86, pres. elect, 1986, pres., 1987—. Established chair Cath. Studes in name of Edward A. Malloy Vanderbilt U., 1997; bd. regents U. Portland, 1985—; editl. adv. bd. The Presidency mag.; bd. dir. Nat. Com. on Higher Edn. and Health of Youth; co-chmn. Nat. Inst. on Alcohol Abuse and Alcoholism; chmn. Nat. Commn. on Substance Abuse and Sports. Author: (books) Culture & Commitment: The Challenge of Today's University, 1992, Notre Dame: The Unfolding Vision, 1994, Monk's Reflection: A View from the Dome, 1999; co-author: Colleges and Universities as Citizens, 1999. Chmn. Am. Coun. Edn.; bd. dirs. NCAA Found., 1989—; mem. Pres. Adv. Coun. on Drugs, 1989—; mem. adv. bd. AmeriCorps and Nat. Civilian Cmty. Corps, 1994—97; interim chmn. Ind. Commn. Cmty. Svc., 1994—97; mem. Boys and Girls Clubs Am., 1997—; trustee St. Thomas U., 1967—, Vanderbilt U., 1999; bd. advisors Bernnadin Ctr., 1997—; founding dir., bd. dir. Points of Light Found.; past chmn. Campus Impact; mem. Bishopps and pres. com. Assn. Cath. Colls. and Univs., 1988—; bd. dirs. Internat. Fedn. Cath. Univs., 1988—. Mem.: Nat. Assn. Ind. Colls. and Univs. (bd. dirs. 1997), The Conf. Bd., Assn. Governing Bds. of Univs. and Colls. (vice chair 1996—), Bus.-Higher Edn. Forum, Am. Soc. Christian Ethics, Cath. Theol. Soc. Roman Catholic. Office: U Notre Dame Office Pres Notre Dame IN 46556

MALLOY, JAMES MATTHEW, health management executive, healthcare consultant; b. N.Y.C., Aug. 26, 1939; s. Peter Joseph and Catherine (Cunningham) M.; m. Joan Elizabeth Wagner, Sept. 9, 1967; children— Stephen, Christopher BS, Manhattan Coll., 1961; MPH, Yale U., 1967. Asst. to dir. Yale New Haven Hosp., New Haven, Conn., 1967-69; assoc. adminstr. Waterbury Hosp., Conn., 1969-75; exec. dir., CEO Jersey City Med. Ctr., N.J., 1975-77; dir., CEO U. Conn. Hosp., Farmington, 1977-82; CEO U. Ill. Hosp. and Clinics, Chgo., 1982-87; exec. v.p. Our Lady of the Resurrection Med. Ctr., Chgo., 1988-89; pres., CEO, St. Dominic Jackson Meml. Hosp., Jackson, Miss., 1989-91; sr. v.p. health affairs Miss. and La. Blue Cross/Blue Shield, Jackson, Miss., 1991-92; health care cons., pres. Malloy Assocs., Jackson, 1992—; pres., CEO S.E. Managed Care Orgn., Jackson, 1993-95. Cons. NIH, Bethesda, Md., 1976-84; dir. Univ. Health Consortium; chmn. Compass Health Plan, Chgo., 1983-87; dir. Hosp. Fund, Inc., New Haven; lectr. Yale U. Sch. Medicine; asst. prof. U. Miss. Sch. Nursing; assoc. prof. U. Ill. Sch. Pub. Health Contbr. articles to profl. jours. Past chmn. Miss. chpt. Nat. Multiple Sclerosis Assn.; mem. Wilson Rsch. Found. (chmn. 1999—). Fellow: Am. Coll. Healthcare Execs.; mem.: Am. Assn. Healthcare Cons., Pub. Health Alumni Assn., Yale U. Assoc. Pub. Health Alumni Assn. (dir. 1996—), Yale Club (pres. Miss. chpt.). Avocations: golf, jogging. Home and Office: 177 Saint Andrews Dr Jackson MS 39211-2532 Business E-Mail: jmalloy@son.umsmed.edu.

MALLOY, JOHN RICHARD, lawyer, chemical company executive; b. Boston, Nov. 26, 1932; s. Thomas Francis and Mary (Field) M.; m. Maraleta Ellerson, May 24, 1960; children: Maureen, John, Megan, Elizabeth. BA, St. John's Sem., Brighton, Mass., 1954; LLB, Boston Coll., 1957. Bar: Mass. 1957. V.p., dir. fin. Remington Arms Co., Inc., Bridgeport, Conn., 1975-78; chief counsel, energy and raw materials E. I. du Pont de Nemours and Co., Wilmington, Del., 1978-79, asst. gen. counsel legal, 1979-83, dir. pub. affairs, 1983-85, v.p. pub. affairs, 1983-85, sr. v.p. external affairs, 1985-92, v.p., spl. counsel to chmn. bd., 1992-93; ret., 1993. Chmn. Jobs for Del. Grads, Wilmington, 1985-97, Del. Compensation Commn., 1988-96; trustee Med. Ctr. of Del., Christiana, 1985—, Del. Pension Fund, 1993-99; bd. dirs. Del. Cmty. Found., 1996-2000, Children's Beach House, 1993-2000; mem. Minner Commn., Del., 1993-96; chmn. Del. Coun. on Transp., 1994-2001, Riverfront Devel. Corp., 2002—; trustee Archmere Acad., 2001—. Mem. ABA, Fed. Bar Assn. Democrat. Roman Catholic. Avocations: tennis, golf, skiing.

MALLOY, JOHNN EDWARD, media artist, writer; b. Superior, Wis., Jan. 1, 1940; s. Robert Francis and Celestine Marie (Evenson) M. BS, U. Wis., LaCrosse, 1962; MS, Winona (Minn.) State U., 1967; MEd, Chgo. State U., 1970; EdS, Ea. Ill. U., 1977; D Arts, U. No. Colo., 1982. Cert. K-14 tchr., Ill., Wis., Colo. Tchr. speech and English Merrill (Wis.) Pub. Schs., 1962-65; tchr. radio and TV Harvey (Ill.) Sch. Dist., 1965-94; instr. speech and theatre, set designer So. Suburban Coll., South Holland, Ill., 1968-70, 75-77, 85; media lectr. Chgo. State U., 1970-72; supr. media lab. U. No. Colo., Greeley, 1980-82; news anchor Colo. Radio Info. Svc., Greeley, 1981-82. Actor College Street Players, LaCrosse, 1964, Summer Theatre Co., Charleston, Ill., 1974-78; actor, dir. Theatre 21 Co., South Holland, 1974-78; scene painter Sedona (Ariz.) Art Ctr. Theatre, 1996; tech. asst. Red Barn Playhouse, Saugatuck, Mich., 1996—2002; theater mgr. Thornton Auditorium, Harvey, Ill., 1976-96; art assoc. You'nique Internat. Gallery, Douglas, Mich., 1999—, Art Assoc. Discovery Art Ctr., Saugatuck, Mich., 2000—; stage designer, cons. Saugatuck Ctr. for the Arts, 2001—; cons. Mason St. Warehouse Theatre, 2003—. Author: Communication in the High School: Speaking and Listening, 1972, Instructional Guides to Media Communication, 1982; prodr. TV mag. series Getting Around, 1981-94. Active CAP, Chgo., 1965—; participant in tchr.-in-space program NASA, 1985-86; charter sponsor, USAF Meml., Washington. Recipient degree of Diamond Key Coach, Nat. Forensic League, Ripon, Wis., 1994, Silver Medalist Canon USA Photo Contest, 1985, Publ. award Internat. Libr. Photography, 1999; Cert. of Recognition in CBS TV Worth Teaching Program, 1987. Mem. NEA, Ill. Speech and Theatre Assn., Ill. Edn. Assn., Am. Air Mus. Britain (founding mem.), Challenger Ctr. (founding mem.), Air Force Assn., Nat. Air & Space Soc. (founding mem.), Libr. of Congress Assocs. (founding mem.), Saugatuck-Douglas Hist. Soc. (Mich. chpt.), Brit. Interplanetary Soc., Saugatuck-Douglas Art Club. Lutheran.

MALLOY, MICHAEL PATRICK, law educator, consultant; b. Haddon Heights, N.J., Sept. 23, 1951; s. Francis Edward and Marie Grace (Nardi) Malloy; divorced; 1 child, Elizabeth; m. Susie Pieratos, Jan. 1992; children: Michael Emil, Nicholas Charles, Edward Francis, Theodora Marie, Sophia Grace. BA magna cum laude (scholar), Georgetown U., 1973, PhD, 1983; JD (scholar), U. Pa., 1976. Bar: N.J. 1976, U.S. Supreme Ct. 1991. Rsch. assoc. Inst. Internat. Law and Econ. Devel., Washington, 1976—77; atty. advisor Office Fgn. Assets Control U.S. Dept. Treasury, Washington, 1977—80, spl. asst. Office Gen. Counsel, 1985; atty. advisor Office Comptr. Currency, Washington, 1981; spl. counsel SEC, Washington, 1981—82; asst. prof. N.Y. Law Sch., N.Y.C., 1982—83; assoc. prof. Seton Hall U. Sch. Law, Newark, 1983—86, prof., assoc. dean, 1986—87; prof. Fordham U. Sch. Law, N.Y.C., 1987—96, dir. grad. studies, 1990—94; prof. U. Pacific McGeorge Law Sch., Sacramento, 1996—2002, disting. prof. and scholar, 2003—. Law lectr. Morin Ctr. Banking and Fin. Law Studies Boston U. Law Sch., 1986—90, 1995—96, 2001; vis. prof. U. Salzburg, Austria, 2000, Suffolk U. Sch. Law, 2001—02, 2004—; cons. bank regulation and pvt. internat. law matters; dir. Pacific/McGeorge Ctr. for Global and Bus. Develop., 2004—. Author: (book) Corporate Law of Banks, 2 vols., 1988, Economic Sanctions and U.S. Trade, 1990, The Regulation of Banking, 1992, Banking Law and Regulation, 3 vols., 1994, Fundamentals of Banking Regulation, 1998, International Banking, 2004, Banking and Financial Services Law, 2004, Hornbook on Bank Regulation, 1999, 2d edit., 2003, U.S. Economic Sanctions: Theory and Practice, 2001; contbr. articles, revs. and comments to profl. jours. Mem.: L'Association des Auditeurs et Anciens Auditeurs de l'Academie de Droit International de la Haye, Hegel Soc. Am., Assn. Am. Law Schs. (chair-elect and program chair 2001—02, chair sect. fin. insts. and consumer fin. svcs. 2002—03), Internat. Law Assn. (com. chair Am. br. 1995—97), Am. Soc. Internat. Law (exec. coun. 1986—89), Phi Beta Kappa. Office: U of Pacific McGeorge Sch Law 3200 5th Ave Sacramento CA 95817-2705 Office Phone: 916-739-7338., 916-481-3250. E-mail: malloympm@aol.com.

MALLOY, MICHAEL TERRENCE, journalist, newspaper editor; b. Chgo., Feb. 26, 1936; s. Medard Valentine and Lucille (Zehrol)M.; m. Ruth Gwendolyn Lor, June 5, 1965; children: Linda Jo, Terrence. Student, Reed Coll., 1953-54, Columbia U., 1966-67; BA, U. Toronto, 2001. Police reporter City News Bur. Chgo., 1956-58; reporter, then bur. chief and chief corr. S.E. Asia UPI, Japan, Laos, India, Vietnam and Thailand, 1960-66; reporter Nat. Observer, Washington, 1968-76, mng. editor, 1976-77; reporter Asian Wall St. Jour., Manila, 1977-80, mng. editor, Hong Kong, 1980-84; mng. editor Dow Jones Can., Toronto, Ont., 1984-94; chief corr. Dow Jones India Report, 1995-97. Author: Racing Today, 1967, The Art of Retirement, 1967. With U.S. Army, 1958-60. E-mail: mikemalloy@idirect.ca.

MALLOY, WILLIAM G. entertainment company executive; Mem. corp. staff Bally Mfg., v.p., treas., CFO; dir., chmn. bd. Scientific Games Holdings Corp., Altpharetta, Ga., 1991—, pres., CEO, 1990—. Bd. dirs. MDI Entertainment, Inc. Office: Scientific Games Holdings Corp 1500 Bluegrass Lakes Pkwy Alpharetta GA 30004-7754

MALM, MIA, actress; b. Ann Arbor, Mich., Oct. 18, 1962; d. William P. and Joyce A. (Rutherford) M. Student, San Francisco Sch. of the Arts, Herbert Berghof Studios, N.Y.C.; studied with Maria Vegh. Dance instr. Marin Ballet Sch., 1978-79. Appeared in (stage prodns.) Make Mine Disco, 1979, Dancin', 1981-83, 42nd Street, The Showgirl Musical, 1986, (films) Moscow on the Hudson, Curtain Call, 1984, Joan-Lui, A Chorus Line, 1985, Ishtar, (TV) Dance Through Time, 1978. Mem. Actors' Equity Assn., Screen Actors Guild, AFTRA, NOW, Planned Parenthood. Avocations: drawing, watercoloring, reading. Office: care Landslide Mgmt 928 Broadway New York NY 10010-6008

MALM, RITA H. securities executive; d. George Peter and Helen Marie (Woodward) Pellegrini; m. Robert J. Malm, Apr. 19, 1970. Student, Packard Jr. Coll., 1950-52, N.Y. Inst. Fin., 1958, Wagner Coll., 1955. Sales asst. Dean Witter & Co., N.Y.C., 1959-63, asst. v.p., compliance dir., 1964-74; v.p., dir. Securities Ind. Assocs., N.Y.C., 1969-72; CEO Muriel Siebert & Co., Inc., N.Y.C., 1981-83; pres., founder Madison-Chapin Assocs., N.Y.C., 1984-89; pres. Hayward Malm Securities, Ltd., 1989-93; pres., founder Concord Stuart, Inc., 1993—. Art mktg. cons. Author: Dying On Wall Street, 1996; author NASD Series 63 Blue Sky Uniform Securities Agent State Law Exam for Potential Stock Brokers, NASD Stockbroker Examination, NASD Series 6 primer. Bd. dirs. Head Start, 1996—. Mem. NAFE (bd. dirs.), Am. Caner Soc. (bd. dirs. Jupiter/Tequesta chpt. 1992-95), Profl. Women's Network (founder Palm Beach and Martin Counties 1991), Women's Bond Club N.Y. (dir., v.p. program chmn., pres. 1980-82), Cornell U. Club Ea. Fla. (bd. dirs. 1995). Address: PO Box 8603 Jupiter FL 33468-8603

MALM, ROGER CHARLES, lawyer; b. Hot Springs, S.D., July 8, 1949; s. Harry Milton and Angeline Mae (Johnson) M.; m. Sandra M. Metz, July 15, 1972; children: Andrew, Elliott, Nicholas. BA, St. Olaf Coll., 1971; JD, U. N.D., 1974. Bar: N.D. 1974, Ariz. 1975, Minn. 1980, U.S. Dist. Ct. N.D. 1974, U.S. Dist. Ct. Ariz. 1976, U.S. Ct. Appeals (9th cir.) 1981, U.S. Supreme Ct. 1981, U.S. Ct. Appeals (8th cir) 1982, U.S. Dist. Ct. Minn. 1985, U.S. Claims Ct. 1985, U.S. Tax Ct. 1988. Ptnr. Brink, Sobolik, Severson, Malm & Albrecht, P.A., Hallock, Minn., 1980—; county atty. Kittson County, Minn., 1995—. Pres. N.W. Minn. County Atty.'s Coun. Hospice dir. Kittson County Hospice, Inc., 1984—; bd. dirs. Cmty. Theatre, Hallock, 1987—, Greater Grand Forks Cmty. Theater, 1991-95, N.W. Minn. Found., 2004—. Mem. ABA, Ariz. Bar Assn., N.D. Bar Assn., Minn. Bar Assn. (mem. bd. govs. 1993-2000). Lutheran. Avocations: skiing, sailing. Office: Brink Sobolik Severson Malm & Albrecht PO Box 790 Hallock MN 56728-0790

MALM, SCOTT, lawyer; BA magna cum laude, Brigham Young U., 1975, JD, 1978. Bar: Calif. 1978, U.S. Dist. Ct. (ea. dist.) Calif. 1978, U.S. Claims Ct. 1991, U.S. Supreme Ct., 1994, U.S. Dist. Ct. (no. dist.) Calif. 1998; cert. Nev. 2d Jud. Dist. 1986. Assoc. Steinheimer, Riggio, Haydel & Mordaunt, Stockton, Calif., 1978-84, prin., 1984-99, Cassel Malm Fagundes, Stockton, Calif., 2000—. Judge pro tem San Joaquin County Mcpl. Ct.; arbitrator San Joaquin County Superior Ct.; spkr. and presenter in field. Contbr. articles to profl. jours. Mem. San Joaquin County Bar Assn. (chair mandatory fee arbitration com. 1983-87, 2001—, chair client rels. com. 1988-89, mem. bus. litig. sect. 1997—). Office: 6 S El Dorado Ste 601 Stockton CA 95202 Office Phone: 209-870-7900. Fax: 209-870-7922. E-mail: scottm@cmf-law.com.

MALMGREN, HARALD BERNARD, economist; b. Boston, July 13, 1935; s. Berndt Birger and Magda Helena (Nilsson) M.; m. Patricia A. Malmgren, 1959 (div. 1975); children: Karen Philippa, Britt Patricia, Erika Nina; m. Linda V. Einberg, Oct. 3, 1987; children: Markus Harald, Liivia Linda, Viivianne Vaike. BA summa cum laude, Yale U., 1957; postgrad., Harvard U., 1959; PhD, Oxford U., 1961. Asst. prof. dept. engring. and econs. Cornell U., Ithaca, NY, 1961-62; head, econ. group Inst. for Def. Analyses, Washington, 1962-64; asst. U.S. trade rep. Exec. Office Pres. The White House, Washington, 1964-69; sr. fellow Overseas Devel. Coun., 1969-71; amb., dep. U.S. trade rep., 1972-75; sr. fellow Woodrow Wilson Internat. Ctr. for Scholars, Washington, 1975-76; prof. George Washington U., Washington, 1976-77; pres. Malmgren, Inc., Washington, 1977—; mng. dir. Malmgren, Golt, Kingston, Ltd., London, 1979-99; chmn. Malmgren O'Donnell, London, 1998-2001; vice-chmn. Cordell Hull Inst., Washington. Adv. coun. Ctr. Strategic and Internat. Studies, Washington, 1987-97; adv. Senate Fin. Com., Washington, 1970-71, 75-76, Interaction Coun., 1985—. Author: International Economic Peace Keeping, 1972; co-author: Assisting Developing Countries, 1972; editor: Pacific Basin Development, 1972; bd. editors: The International Economy, 1987—, The Washington Quarterly, 1987-95, The World Economy, 1980-90; contbr. articles to profl. jours. Mem. Am. Econ. Assn., Met. Club, Reform Club. Home: Summerfield Farm 7620 Cannonball Gate Rd Warrenton VA 20186-7304 Office Phone: 202-466-8740. E-mail: hm@malmgrenglobal.com.

MALMO, JOHN, advertising executive; m. Betty Malmo, 1961. BA, Boston U. Sales and promotions mgr. E.L. Bruce Co., Nat. Cotton Coun.; mktg. dir. Gem Inc.; founder, prin. John Malmo Advt., Memphis, 1967-91; ptnr. Archer/Malmo (merger John Malmo Advt. and Ward Archer Advt.), Memphis, 1991—; pres. Koenig Cons., Memphis; chmn. Archer/Malmo Advt. Inc., Memphis. Chmn. Park Commn., Memphis, 1971-78, 92—. With U.S. Army. Office: Archer/Malmo Adv Inc 65 Union Ave Ste 500 Memphis TN 38103

MALMQUIST, CARL PHILLIP, psychiatrist; b. St. Paul, Mar. 10, 1934; s. Phillip C. and Lillian Viola (Kahler) M.; m. Arlyn Virginia Bodal (dec. 1984); children: Derek, Jay. BA summa cum laude, U. Minn., 1954, MD, 1958, MS in Philosophy of Sci., 1961. Diplomate Am. Bd. Psychiatry and Neurology, Am. Bd. Child Psychiatry, Am. Bd. Adult Psychiatry; cert. forensic psychiatry, added qualification in forensic psychiatry. Intern U. Minn., 1962-63, Columbia Med. Ctr., N.Y.C., 1963-64; assoc. prof. dept. psychiatry U. Mich., 1965-67; assoc. prof. Inst. Child Devel. U. Minn., Mpls., 1967-70, prof., dir. child and adolescent psychiatry, 1971-72, prof. criminal justice, 1972-80, prof. social psychiatry, dept. sociology, 1980—. Cons. Hennepin County Dist. Ct., Mpls., 1967—; mem. commn. of mentally disabled ABA, 1985. Author: Handbook of Adolescence, 1980, Homicide: Psychiatric Perspectives, 1996; mem. editl. bd. Psychiat. Anns., 1981; contbr. articles to profl. jours. Fellow Am. Psychiat. Assn. (mem. commn. on jud. action 1994—), Am. Coll. Psychiatrists, Am. Orthopsychiat. Assn., Am. Acad. Child Psychiatry, Am. Acad. Psychiatry and Law, Am. Coll. Forensic Psychiatry; mem. Group for Advancement Psychiatry, Am. Psychopathol. Assn. Episcopalian. Home: 5010 Bruce Ave Minneapolis MN 55424-1318 Office: U Minn 6600 France Ave S Ste 545 Minneapolis MN 55435-1804

MALMSTAD, JOHN EARL, Slavic languages and literatures educator; b. Bismarck, N.D., June 25, 1941; s. Manley Ellsworth and Joyce Evelyn (David) M. BA summa cum laude with distinction and departmental honors in Russian Lang. and Lit., Northwestern U., 1963; MA in Slavic Langs. and Lits., Princeton U., 1965, PhD in Slavic Langs. and Lits., 1969; AM (hon.), Harvard U., 1985. Instr. Columbia U., N.Y.C., 1968-69, asst. prof. Russian Lit., 1969-73, assoc. prof., 1973-79, prof. dept. slavic langs. and lits., 1979-85; Samuel Hazzard Cross prof. Slavic langs. and lits. Harvard U., Cambridge, Mass., 1985—, assoc. dean, 1993-94. Vis. assoc. prof. Stanford U., 1977-79, U. Calif. Berkeley, 1977-78; vis. prof. Harvard U., fall 1982; cons., referee NEH translation awards; lectr. in field; attendee internat. symposia. Editor: (with others) The Poetry of Mikhail Kuzmin (3 vols.), 1977, The Poetry of Andrei Bely (3 vols.), 1982-85, Gibel Senatora, 1986, Vladislav Khodasevich Sobranie sochinenii, 1983, Andrei Bely, Spirit of Symbolism, 1987, Readings in Russian Modernism to Honor Vladimir Markov, 1993, Mikhail Kuzmin: Zhizn' Tvorchestvo, Epokha, 1996, Andrey Bely-Ivanov-Razumnik Perepiska, 1998, Mikhail Kuzmin: A Life in Art, 1999, K.N. Bugaeva Vospominaniia o Belom, 2001; Russian book rev. editor Slavic Rev., 1975-86; assoc. editor Russian Rev., 1986-88; mem. editl. bd. Feniks, Opyty, Novoe Literaturnoe obozrenie, Experiment, Philologica, Diaspora; manuscript rev. profl. jours., univ. presses; contbr. articles to profl. jours. Woodrow Wilson fellow, 1963, NDFL fellow Columbia U., 1963-66, Princeton U., 1967-68, Fulbright-Hays fellow, 1966-67, spring 1981, spring 1987, Woodrow Wilson Dissertation fellow, 1966, ACLS rsch. fellow, 1972, Rsch. fellow Russian Inst. Columbia U., summer 1977, 79, 83, 84, IREX fellow, 1975, John Simon Guggenheim fellow, 1980-81; ACLS grant-in-aid, summer, 1980, IREX/ACLS grantee exch. Acad. Scis. USSR, fall 1981, spring 1987, 91, IREX travel grantee Moscow, 1992, Am. Coun. Internat. Edn. grantee, Moscow, 2003. Mem. MLA, Am. Assn. Advancement of Slavic Studies, Assn. Tchrs. of Slavic and East European Langs., Inst. d'Etudes Slaves (Paris), Phi Beta Kappa. Avocations: fine arts, ballet, reading. Home: 8A Cogswell Ave Cambridge MA 02140-2001 Office: Harvard U Dept Slavic Langs/Lit Barker Ctr, 12 Quincy St Cambridge MA 02138 E-mail: malmstad@fas.harvard.edu.

MALMSTADT, MARY JANE, music educator; b. Milwaukee, Wis., Apr. 12, 1923; d. Daniel Monte and Angela Marie LaFata; m. Robert Guy, June 25, 1949 (dec. Apr. 1998); children: Keith Robert, Deborah Jean. BS in Music Edn., U. Wis., 1945; postgrad., U. Wis., Marinette and Madison, 1950—83. Music tchr. K-12 NeKoosa (Wis.) Pub. Schs., 1945—46; music tchr. 9-12 Marinette (Wis.) H.S., 1946—51; music tchr. K-6 Elem. Schs., Marinette, 1965—85; organist, pianist Pioneer Presbyn. Ch., Marinette, 1970—2004; pvt. piano tchr. Marinette, 1955—2004. Bd. dirs. Tri-City Cmty. Concerts, Wis. Mem.: Golden Soc. of Alumni/U. Wis. Milw., Gen. Fedn. of Women's Club (pres. 1988). Presbyterian. Avocation: oil painting, gardening, reading, travel, floral arrangements. Home: 1303 Elizabeth Ave Marinette WI 54143

MALMUTH, NORMAN DAVID, research scientist, program manager; b. Bklyn., Jan. 22, 1931; s. Jacob and Selma Malmuth; m. Constance Nelson, 1970; children: Kenneth, Jill. AE, U. Cin., 1953; MA in Aero. Engring., Polytech. Inst. of N.Y., 1956; PhD in Aeronautics, Calif. Inst. Tech., 1962. Rsch. engr. Grumman Aircraft Engring. Corp., 1953-56; preliminary design engr. N.A. Aviation Div., L.A., 1956-68; teaching asst. Calif. Inst. Tech., L.A., 1961; mem. maths. sci. group Rockwell Internat. Sci. Ctr., 1968-75, project mgr. fluid dynamics rsch., 1975-80, mgr. fluid dynamics group, 1980-82, sr. scientist, project mgr., 1982—. Cons. Aerojet Gen., 1986—89; lectr. UCLA, 1971—72; mem. adv. group for aerospace R&D Fluid Dynamics Panel, 1995; vis. scientist Rensselaer Poly. Inst.; vis. assoc. Calif. Inst. Tech., 2003. Referee AIAA Jour.; bd. editors Jour. Aircraft; contbr. articles to Jour. of Heat Transfer, Internat. Jour. Heat Mass Transfer, and others. Named Calif. Inst. Tech. fellow; recipient Outstanding Alumnus award Univ. Cin., 1990. Fellow AIAA (Aerodynamics award 1991), Am. Phys. Soc.; mem. Am. Acad. Mechanics, Am. Inst. Physics (fluid dynamics divsn.), Soc. Indsl. and Applied Math. Achievements include patent in Methods and Apparatus for Controlling Laser Welding, hypersonic transition delay; pioneering development of high aerodynamic efficiency of hypersonic delta wing body combinations, hypersonic boundary layer stability, transonic wind tunnel interference, plasma aerodynamics, flow control web dynamics, combined asymptotic and numerical methods in fluid dynamics and aerodynamics. Home: 182 Maple Rd Newbury Park CA 91320-4718 Office: Rockwell Sci Co PO Box 1085 1049 Camino Dos Rios Thousand Oaks CA 91360-2362 E-mail: nmalmuth@rwsc.com.

MALONE, CLAUDINE BERKELEY, financial and management consultant; b. Louisville, May 9, 1936; d. Claude McDowell and Mary Katharine (Smith) M.; BA, Wellesley Coll., 1963; MBA, Harvard U., 1972. CPA, Md. Systems engr. IBM Corp., Washington, 1964; sr. systems analyst Crane Co., Chgo., 1966; contr., mgr. data processing Raleigh Stores, Washington, 1967-70; asst. prof. Harvard U., 1972-76, assoc. prof., 1977-81; pres., CEO, Fin. and Mgmt. Consulting Inc., Bethesda, Md., 1981-; vis. prof., Georgetown U., 1982-84, U. Va., 1984-87; dir. Scott Paper Co., Houghton Mifflin Co., Campbell Soup Co., Boston Co., Dart Group Inc., Hasbro Inc., 1994-, Novell Inc., 2003-; trustee Penn Mut. Life Ins. Co. Chmn. Bus. for Reagan-Bush Com. Mass., 1980; trustee Wellesley Coll., 1982-. Recipient Candace award, 1982. Mem. Assn. Women CPA's, UN Assn., Wellesley Coll. Alumnae Assn., Washington Wellesley Club. Episcopalian. Office Phone: 703-821-8861.

MALONE, DAN F. journalist; b. Dallas, Jan. 22, 1955; s. Charles Ted and Ela Grace (Darden) Malone; m. Kathryn Jones, June 27, 1981. BJ, U. Tex., 1978. Editor-in-chief The Daily Texan, Austin, Tex., 1977—78; intern Harte-Hanks Austin Bur., 1978—79; staff writer Corpus Christi (Tex.) Caller-Times, 1979—81, Ft. Worth Star-Telegram, 1981—85, Dallas Morning News, 1985—, Ft. Worth bureau chief, 1992—98. Recipient Pulitzer Prize for investigative reporting, 1992, 1st Pl. Freedom of Info. Category award, Tex. AP Mng. Editors Assn., 1992, 1st Pl. Investigative Reporting, Inst. Southern Studies, 1992; fellow Fox fellow, Nat. News Coun., N.Y.C., summer, 1978. Office: Dallas Morning News PO Box 655237 Dallas TX 75265-5237

MALONE, DAVID MICHAEL, diplomat, educator; b. Ottawa, Canada, Feb. 7, 1954; s. Paul Thomas Malone and Deirdre Lavalette Ingram. BA, Univ. Montreal, Montreal, Can., 1972; MPA, Kennedy Sch. of Govt., Harvard U., Cambridge, MA, 1980; DPhil, Oxford U., Eng., 1997. Various positions in can. fgn. min. and at can. diplomatic missions in cairo, amman and kuwait Govt. of Can., 1975—90; can. rep. to the un's ecosoc N. Y. and Geneva, NY, 1990—92; amb., dep. permanent rep. Can. Permanent Mission to the UN, N. Y., NY, 1992—94; dir. gen., policy, internat. orgn. and global issues bureaus Can. Ministry of Fgn. Affairs and Internat. Trade, Ottawa, Canada, 1994—98; pres. Internat. Peace Acad., N.Y., NY, 1998—2004. Adj. prof. law N.Y. U. Sch. of Law, 1999; adj. prof. internat. rels. Institut des Etudes Politiques (Sciences Po), Paris, 2001. Author: The UN Security Council aftert the Cold War and into the Twenty First Century; contbr. articles to profl. jour. Office: Internat Peace Acad 777 UN Plaza New York NY 10017 Business E-Mail: malone@ipacademy.org.

MALONE, DAVID ROY, educational association administrator, director; b. Beebe, Ark., Nov. 4, 1943; s. James Roy and Ila Mae (Griffin) M.; m. Judith Kaye Huff, June 20, 1965 (div. Feb. 1990); m. Deborah W. Thomas, Jan. 23, 2004; 1 child, Michael David. BSBA, U. Ark., 1965, JD, 1969, MBA, 1982. Bar: Ark. 1969, U.S. Dist. Ct. (we. dist.) Ark. 1969, U.S. Tax Ct. 1972, U.S. Ct. Appeals (8th cir.) 1972, U.S. Supreme Ct. 1972. Pvt. practice, Fayetteville, Ark., 1969-72; atty. City of Fayetteville, 1969-72; asst. prof. bus. U. Ark., Fayetteville, 1972-76, asst. dean law, 1976-91; mem. Ark. Ho. of Reps., 1980-84, Ark. Senate, 1984—2002; exec. dir. U. Ark. Found., 1991—2002, Ark. Tchr. Ret. Sys., 2003—. Chair Senate edn. com., 1997-2002, co-chair legis. coun., 1999-2000; bd. dirs. Bank of Elkins, 1976-98, S.W. Edn. Devel. Lab., Austin, Tex., 1988-94; legal adv. coun. So. Regional Edn. Bd., Atlanta, 1991-2002. Contbr. articles to profl. jours.; bd. dirs. Ark. Law Rev., 1978-92; contbg. author U. Ark. Press, 1989. Mayor City of Fayetteville, 1979-80; mem. Jud. Article Task Force, Little Rock, 1989-91; chair Motor Voter task force, 1994-95; bd. dirs. Music Festival Ark., 1989-91, Washington County Hist. Soc., 1993-96; bd. dirs. Walton Arts Ctr. Found., 1994-2000, chmn., 1994-98; chmn. bd. dirs. Washington County Law Libr., 1970-84; chmn. Ark. Tuition Trust Authority, 1997-99. Recipient Svc. award, Ark. Mcpl. League, 1980, Disting. Svc. award, U. Ark., 1988, Lucas Svc. award, Ark. Alumni Assn., 1998, award, Walton Coll. Bus., U. Ark., 2004. Mem. Ark. Bar Assn. (ho. of dels. 1977-81, award of merit 1980, exec. 1981-82, Outstanding Lawyer-Citizen award 1990), Washington County Bar Assn., Ark. Inst. Continuing Legal Edn. (bd. dirs. 1979-88), Fayetteville C. of C. (bd. dirs. 1984-99), Ark. Genealogy Soc. (bd. dirs. 1990-99). Democrat. Methodist. Avocations: genealogy, stamp collecting/philately. Home: 804 N Arthur St Little Rock AR 72205-2902 Office: 1400 W Third St Little Rock AR 72201 E-mail: david_malone@atrs.state.ar.us.

MALONE, EMBRY, property manager, advocate; b. Louisville, Mar. 9, 1954; BA in European History, Pepperdine U., 1977. Mgr. Pelican Properties, Stone Mountain, Ga., 1988—; owner ABA Franchise/The Gwinnett Gwizzlies. Cmty. activist Nat. Assn. Cmty. Devel., Atlanta, 1993—2003. AWP scholar, Pepperdine U., Malibu, 1976—77. Mem.: Pepperdine U. Alumni Assocs. (assoc.). Office: PO Box 870273 Stone Mountain GA 30087 Personal E-mail: palucanx@aol.com.

MALONE, JAMES HIRAM, graphic artist, painter, writer; b. Winterville, Ga., Mar. 24, 1930; s. Ralph and Sarah Lena (Echols) M.; m. Mary Louise Liebaert, 1972 (div. 1982); children: Andrew Ralph, Matthew Martin. Student, Morehouse Coll., 1949-50, Coll. Art and Design, 1959-62. Art dir., prodn. mgr. Better Brochures, Inc., Detroit, 1963-65; graphics mgr. Fed. Dept. Stores, Detroit, 1965-69; sr. art cons. Northgate Ad Agy., Detroit, 1969-75; sr. graphics designer Montgomery Ward Regional Hdqs., Southfield, Mich., 1975-80; layout/prodn. designer K-Mart Internat. Hdqs., Troy, Mich., 1980-83; ad/promotions creative dir. Atlanta Jour./Constitution, 1983-90; fine art prodr., painter Bianco Art Collections of Atlanta, Marietta, Ga., 1990-92; cartoonist, newspaper columnist/reporter Atlanta News Leader, Union City, Ga., 1992—. Author, artist: Ralph cartoon strip, 1998, Here and There Poetry, Blues Poetry, 1954, Grandma Sarah's Closet, 1960, Brother, 1970, Malone's Atlanta, 1986, No-Job Dad, 1992, The Cart, 1994, April Mae Jones Coloring Book, 1999; contbr. The Total Cartoonist, 1983, Lure of the Local, 1997, Landscape Narratives, 1998, If I Live (novel), 2003; co-authored songs, Talk to Your Child, Willie Lives in the Streets, 1986, Homeless Hope, 1987, The TAP Song, 1995, artist: (literacy drawings) Say (Simply Apply Yourself), 1988, contbr. Word-Up Anthology, 1990, (paintings) BIG (Black Inventors Gifts), 1991, one-man shows include AAA Art Gallery, Detroit, 1963-67, Richard Russell Hall Gallery, Atlanta, 1985, C.W. Hill Gallery, Atlanta, 1990, Walker St. Gallery, Atlanta, 1992, Alma Simmons Gallery, 1986-94, The Atlanta Project Collaboration Ctr., 1994, Atlanta's Auburn Ave. Rsch. Libr., African Am. Culture and History Gallery, 1999, Tchg. Mus. South, 1999-2001, Decatur Bapt. Ch., 2000; exhibited in group shows at Red Cross European Exchange Touring Art Exhbn., 1949, Atlanta U., 1949, 53-55, Contemporary Art Studio Gallery, Detroit, 1962, 64-67, 75, Detroit Mus. Art, 1968, Wayne State Coll. Cmty. Gallery, Detroit, 1969, Kumarsi Mart Art Gallery, Detroit, 1970, Scarab Club Mus., Detroit, 1974, United Auto Workers, Detroit, 1977, Salon Internat. De La Caricature, Montreal, Can., 1980-83, 85-86, 88, Artistic Directions Gallery, Atlanta, 1983, Nexus Gallery, Atlanta, 1984, 89, Ctr. Creative Studies Coll. Art and Design Alumni Exhibits, Detroit, 1986-92, Spelman Coll., Atlanta, 1987, Mattress Factory, 1987, 89, Nat. Black Arts Festival, Atlanta, 1988-92, Ga. State U., 1989, Ruth Hall Hodges Gallery, Atlanta, 1990-93, TULA Galleries, Atlanta, 1990, Seven Stages, 1990, 96, EarthFactory, Atlanta, 1991, Art Station, Atlanta, 1991, Atlanta Life, 1992, Trinity Art Gallery, 1992, Samari Art Gallery, 1993, Mobile (Ala.) Coll., 1993-94, Albany Mus. Art, 1994, Alma Simmons Gallery, Atlanta, 1994, Atlanta Project Hdqs., 1994, Avery Gallery, 1995; Buttermilk Bottom Art Proj., 1995-96, Atlanta's Civic Ctr., 1995-96, Alma Simmons Gallery, 1995-96, Atlanta's Auburn Ave Rsch. Libr., African Am. Culture and History Gallery, 1996, City Hall East Gallery, 1996-97, Atlanta Olympic Park, 1997, Eddies' Alley, 1997, Miles Gallery, 1997, House of Colors, 1998, Annie McPheeters Art Gallery, 1999, Tchg. Mus. South, 1999-2003, Atlanta Hartsfield Airport, 2000, New Orleans Art Galleries, 2000, Kennesaw State U. Gallery, 2000, Walt Disney's movie screening, 2001-, Motion Through Art, 2002, Pilgrimage to Paradise, Gallery on Greene, 2002, Youth Gallery, 2003, Atlanta Biennial, 2003, Mills Srs. Ctr. Collection, 2003, Habersham Gardens, 2004; represented in permanent collections including Atlanta U., Hatch-Billups, N.Y., Ga. Artists Register, Atlanta, Bianco Collections, Ga. Rsch. libr. African-Am. culture and history, 1995, RepoHistory Assn., 1996, neighborhood schs. mentor Fed. Dept. Stores, Detroit, 1964-69; motivator, sch. lectr. Atlanta Jour./Constitution, 1983-90, minority job fairs guide, 1985; bd. dirs. Neighborhood Planning Unit J, Atlanta, 1984—, Bankhead Hwy. Revitalization Project, Atlanta, 1990—; arts cons. Fulton County Arts Task Force, Atlanta, 1990—; com. chmn. Jimmie Carter's West Fulton and Douglass Atlanta Cluster Project, 1992—; active Feed The Homeless, Inc., Atlanta Olympics Com., Atlanta Mayor's Bicycle Paths Commn., 1995; com. chmn. Atlanta-Fulton County Action Authority Assn., 1994, North Ave Civic League Assn., 2002, The Atlanta Contemporary Studios, 2003. Recipient George H. Clapp Meml. Found. award Art Inst. Pitts., 1949, Nat. Art award, Scholastic Art Awards Contest, Atlanta U. Nat. Art award, 1949, Nat. Cartoonist Soc. scholar, 1958, Editorial Cartoon award Nat. Newspapers Pubs. Assn., 1973, Bronze Jubilee Cmty. award WPBA TV, Atlanta, 1986, Alumni Art award Ctr. Creative Studies, Coll. Art and Design, Detroit, 1986, Atlanta Symphony Art award, 1986, Youth Motivation award Merit Employment Assn., 1987-89, So. Drawl Art Exhbn. award, 1993, Atlanta's Centennial Olympic Park Art award, 1997, Annie L. McPheeters Cmty. Medallion award, 1998, Million Man March Srs. award, 1998, Cmty. award Together Atlanta, 1999; grantee Atlanta Jour./Constitution, 1986, Nexus Family History Artbook Project, 1994, Avant Gardening Tour 2000, Daimler/Chrysler Art award, 2002. Mem. Assn. Am. Cultures, 1980, High Mus. Art, 1st World Writers (v.p. 1993-94), Internat. Black Writers (cons., pres. 1996), Atlanta Writing Resource Ctr., Nat. Conf. Artists, Friends of Atlanta/Fulton County Libr., Buttermilk Bottom Cmty. Assn. (cons., v.p. 1996, pres. 1998), Individual Visual Artists' Coalition, Laughing Trees Assn. (pres. 2000). Democrat. Baptist. Avocations: poetry, photography, tennis, rummage sales, reading. Home: 1796 North Ave NW Atlanta GA 30318-6441 Office: 1796 North Ave NW Atlanta GA 30318-6441 Office Phone: 404-794-0948. E-mail: j.l.t.malone@att.net.

MALONE, JOHN C. telecommunications executive; b. 1941; m. Leslie. Attended Yale U., Johns Hopkins U. Formerly pres. Jerrold Electronics Corp.; pres. Tele-Comms., Inc., Denver, 1994—97; CEO Tele-Comms.,Inc, 1994—99; chmn. Tele-Comms., Inc., Denver, 1996-99, Liberty Satellite, 1996—2000, Liberty Media Corp., Denver, 1990—. Office: Liberty Media Corp 12300 Liberty Blvd Englewood CO 80112*

MALONE, JOHN I. pediatrics educator, biomedical researcher; b. Altoona, Pa., Oct. 10, 1941; s. W. Paul and Olive (Romine) M.; m. Gloria Joyce Cromer, Sept. 5, 1964; children: John Irvin Jr., Michael A., Jennifer A., W. Andrew. BS, Pa. State U., 1963; MD, U. Pa., 1967. Diplomate Am. Bd. Pediatrics, Am. Bd. Pediatric Endocrinology; cert. diabetes educator. Straight pediatric intern Children's Hosp. Phila., 1967-68, resident, 1968-69, research fellow div. biochem. devel. and molecular diseases, 1969-71; instr. pediatrics U. Pa. Sch. Medicine, Phila., 1971-72; chief resident Hosp. of U. Pa., 1971-72; asst. prof. U. South Fla. Coll. Medicine, Tampa, 1972-76, assoc. prof., 1976-80, chief divsn. pediatric diabetes & metalbolic diseases, 1976—, prof., 1980—, co-dir. Diabetes Ctr., 1979—. Co-dir. Fla. Camp for Children and Youth with Diabetes, Tampa, 1973—, pres., 1990; mem. clin. and sci. adv. bd. Children's Diabetes Found. at Denver, 1976-86; dir. Suncoast Regional PKU Program, 1976—, Suncoast Regional Diabetes Program, 1976—, chief pediat. endocrinology, diabetes and metabolism, 1995—; mem. Fla. Gov.'s Diabetes Adv. Coun., 1979—; mem. Internat. Study Group Diabetes in Children and Adolescents, Paris, 1982—; vis. prof., cons. in pediatric endocrinology Uniformed Svcs. U. Health Scis., Bethesda, Md., 1990-98; mem. staff various hosps. Contbr. over 110 articles Sci., New Eng. Jour. Medicine, Jour. Pediatrics, Am. Jour. Human Genetics, Am. Jour. Diseases of Children, Diabetes, Jour. Fla. Med. Assn., Diabetes Care, Jour. Clin. Investigation, Jour. Clin. Psychiatry, European Jour. Pediatrics, Proc. NAS, Pediatrics Rsch., Pediatrician, Diabetes Care, Pediatrics, Am. Jour. Med. Scis., Am. Jour. Med. Genetics, Clin. Pediatrics, also chpts. to books. Bd. dir. Diabetes Trust Fund, Birmingham, Ala., 2002—. Mem. AAAS, Am. Acad. Pediatrics, Am. Diabetes Assn. (program chmn. youth coun. 1987-88), Lawson Wilkins Pediatric Endocrine Soc., So. Soc. for Pediatric Rsch. (pres. 1986-87), Am. Fedn. for Clin. Rsch., Soc. for Pediatric Rsch., N.Y. Acad. Sci., Am. Inst. Nutrition, Am. Pediatric Soc., Am. Soc. for Clin. Nutrition, Soc. for Inherited Metabolic Disorders. Achievements include research on the metabolic causes of diabetes

associated complications and research on the development and prevention of diabetes in relatives of patients with insulin-dependent diabetes. Office: U South Fla Coll Medicine 12901 Bruce B Downs Blvd Tampa FL 33612-4742 E-mail: jmalone@hsc.usf.edu.

MALONE, JOSEPH JAMES, mathematics educator, researcher; b. St. Louis, Sept. 9, 1932; s. Joseph James and Aurelia Theresa (Schomaker) M.; m. Dorothy Sue Cleary, Nov. 24, 1960; children: Michael, Barbara, Philip, Patrick. BS, St. Louis U., 1954, MS, 1958, PhD, 1962. Instr. math. Rockhurst Coll., Kansas City, Mo., 1960-62; asst. prof. U. Houston, 1962-67; assoc. prof. Tex. A&M U., College Station, 1967-70, prof., 1970-71, Worcester (Mass.) Poly. Inst., 1971-2000, prof. emeritus, 2000—, chmn. dept. math., 1971-78. Contbr. articles to profl. jours. Mem. pub. schs. bd. Town of Westborough (Mass.), 1974-83, 84-87, fin. com., 1992-98, selectman, 1998-2001, fin. com., 2001—. With U.S. Army, 1954-56. Mem. Am. Math. Soc., Math. Assn. Am. Democrat. Roman Catholic. Achievements include research in near-ring theory and group theory. Home: 45 Adams St Westborough MA 01581-3610 Office: Worcester Poly Inst 100 Institute Rd Worcester MA 01609-2280 E-mail: jjmalone@wpi.edu.

MALONE, KARL, professional basketball player; b. Summerfield, La., July 24, 1963; m. Kay Malone; 4 children; 1 child, Cheryl Ford (Plays in WNBA). Student, La. Tech. U., 1981—85. Basketball player Utah Jazz, Salt Lake City, 1985—2003, Los Angeles Lakers, 2004—. Mem. U.S. Olympic Basketball Team, 1992, 96. Founder Karl Malone Foundation for Kid's; works with Utah Special Olympics. Named NBA Most Valuable Player, 1997, 1999; named one of 50 Greatest Players in NBA History, 1996; named to NBA All-Rookie team, 1986, NBA All-Star team, 1988—89, 1991—2001, 2003, All-NBA 1st team, 1989—99, All-NBA 2d team, 1988, NBA All-Defensive 1st team, 1997—99; recipient All-Star Game Most Valuable Player award, NBA, 1989, All-Star game Most Valuable Player award co-recipient, 1993, Gold medal, U.S. Olympic Basketball Team, 1992, 1996. Achievements include being co-leader most seasons (11) with 2000 points, 1987-95. Office: c/o Los Angeles Lakers 555 N Nash St El Segundo CA 90245*

MALONE, LISA A. federal agency administrator; b. Mobile, Ala. BJ, U. Ala., 1984; M in Mgmt., Fla. Inst. Tech., 1995. Accredited pub. rels. profl. Fla. Pub. Rels. Assn., 1992, cert. pub. rels. counselor Fla. Pub. Rels. Assn., 1996. With NASA Kennedy Space Ctr., Fla., 1984—, news chief media svc. br., 1993—95, chief media svcs. br., spokeswoman, 1995—, dir. external relations and bus. development, 2004—. Recipient Exceptional Service Medal, NASA, 2001. Office: NASA Kennedy Space Ctr Mail Code XA-E Kennedy Space Center FL 32899

MALONE, NANCY, actress; b. Queens Village, N.Y. d. James and Bridget (Sheilds) M. Freelance actress, dir., producer, writer. Performer (TV series) The First Hundred Years, Naked City, The Long, Hot Summer (Best Performance by an Actress award); Broadway debut in Time Out For Ginger, other stage performances include Major Barbara, The Makropoulis Secret, A Touch of the Poet, The Trial of the Catonsville Nine; touring performances include The Chalk Garden, The Seven Yr. Itch, A Place For Dolly; actress (films) The Violators, I Cast No Shadow, An Affair of the Skin, Intimacy, The Trial of the Cantonsville Nine, The Man Who Loved Cat Dancing, Capricorn One; producer (TV series) including Bionic Woman, 1978, Husbands, Wives and Lovers, 1978, The Great Pretender, 1984, (special) Bob Hope: The First 90 Years, 1993 (Emmy award, Outstanding Variety, Musical or Comedy Special, 1993), Womanspeak, 1983; dir. (TV series) Dynasty, 1984-87, Hotel, 1984-87, Colbys, 1985, Cagney and Lacey, 1987, Star Trek Voyager, 1997, Burning Zone, 1997, Fame I.A. 1997-98, Rosie O'Niel (Emmy nomination), Sisters (Emmy nomination), Melrose Place, 1992-99, Beverly Hills, 1990-2000, Picket Fences, Judging Amy, 1999-, Resurrection Blvd., 2000-02; producer, dir. (film) There Were Times Dear, 1986 (John Muir Trustees award, Cine Golden Eagle, Blue Ribbon); founder Nancy Malone Prodns., 1975, Lilac Prodns., 1979. Fellow Leaky Found.; mem. Am. Film Inst. (mem. founder), Women in Film (trustee, Chrystal award, Founders award 1996). Office: Guild Mgmt PHA 9911 W Pico Blvd Los Angeles CA 90035-2703 Home: 4604 Ledge Ave Toluca Lake CA 91602-1536

MALONE, RICHARD P. psychiatrist; b. Mount Pleasant, Pa. BA, U. Pitts., 1974; MD, Hahnemann U., 1983. Psychiatry intern Med. Coll. Pa., 1983, resident in psychiatry, 1983-87, fellow in child and adolescent psychiatry, 1986-88, fellow in child psychopharmacology rsch., 1988-90; dir. child and adolescent psychiatry rsch. MCP Hahnemann U., Phila., 1990—.

MALONE, ROBERT ROY, artist, art educator; b. McColl, S.C., Aug. 8, 1933; s. Robert Roy and Anne (Matthews) M.; m. Cynthia Enid Taylor, Feb. 26, 1956; 1 child, Brendan Trevor. BA, U. N.C., 1955; MFA, U. Chgo., 1958; postgrad., U. Iowa, 1959. Instr. art Union U., Jackson, Tenn., 1959-60, Lambuth Coll., 1959-61; asst. prof. art Wesleyan Coll., Macon, Ga., 1961-67, assoc. prof., 1967-68, W.Va. U., 1968-70, So. Ill. U., Edwardsville, 1970-75, prof., 1975—2000, prof. emeritus, 2000—. One-man shows at Gallery Illien, Atlanta, 1969, De Cinque Gallery, Miami, 1968, 71, Ill. State Mus., Springfield, 1974, U. Del., Newark, 1978, Elliot Smith Gallery, St. Louis, 1985, Merida Galleries, Louisville, 1985, Yvonne Rapp Gallery, Louisville, 1990, 92, 93, 96, 98, 2000, 04, St. John's Coll., Santa Fe, 1991, Uzelac Gallery, Pontiac, Mich., 1997, others; group shows include Bklyn. Mus., 1966, Assoc. Am. Artists Gallery, N.Y.C., 1968, Musée d'Art Modern, Paris, 1970, DeCordova Mus., 1973, 74, St. Louis Art Mus., 1985, Wake Forest U., 1985, New Orleans Mus. Art, 1990, Dakota Internat., Vermillion, 1994, Springfield Art Mus., Mo., 2004; represented in numerous permanent collections including Smithsonian Instn., Washington, USIA, Washington, Library of Congress, Calif. Palace of Legion of Honor, San Francisco, N.Y. Pub. Library, N.Y.C., Victoria and Albert Mus., London, Chgo. Art Inst., Indpls. Mus. Art, Humana Inc., Louisville, State of Ill. Ctr., Chgo., Speed Mus., Louisville, N. Ill. Univ., Capital Devel. Bd., Ill.; co-editor: Contemporary American Printmakers, 1999 (English and Chinese edits.). Recipient numerous regional, nat. awards in competitive exhbns.; Ford fellow, 1977; So. Ill. U. at Edwardsville sr. research scholar, 1976, 84 Home: 600 Chapman St Edwardsville IL 62025-1260

MALONE, ROBERT WALLACE, surgeon; s. Edgar Wallace and Nancy Adams Malone; m. Jill Glasspool, Feb. 17, 1979; children: William Zachary, Spencer James. AA, Santa Barbara C.C., Calif., 1982; BS in Biochemistry, U. of Calif., Davis, 1984; MS in Biology, U. of Calif., La Jolla, 1989; MD, Northwestern U., Chgo., 1991. Rsch. scientist Vical, Inc, San Diego, 1989; pathology resident U. of Calif., Davis, 1991—92, rsch. fellow, 1992—93, asst. prof. pathology, 1993—97; asst. prof, pathology U. of Md., Sch. of Medicine, Balt., 1997—2000; chief of lab. sci., dir. of tissue banking USUHS Clin. Breast Care Program, Bethesda, Md., 2000—01; pres. and founder Gene Delivery Alliance, Inc, Rockville, Md., 2001; assoc. dir, clin. rsch. Dynport Vaccine Co., LLC, Frederick, Md., 2002—; assoc. prof. of surgery Uniformed Services U. of the Health Sci., Bethesda, Md., 2001. Cons. Inovio, Oslo, 2001—02; sr. cons. Mgmt. Systems Designers, Inc, Vienna, 2001—02; med. dir. Molecular Histology, Montgomery Village, Md., 2002. Contbr. chpts. to books. Recipient Trainee Investigator award, Am. Fedn. for Clin. Rsch., 1993, Svc. to the Coll. award, Santa Barbara C.C., 1981—82, Giannini Found. fellow, Bank of Am., Giannini Found., 1992—93, Henry Christian Award for Excellence in Rsch., Am. Fedn. for Clin. Rsch., 1992, 1st Pl., Northwestern AOA Rsch. Symposium competition for Med. Students, Northwestern U. AOA, 1989; fellow Edmonson Summer fellow, UC Davis Dept. of Med. Pathology, 1984, Pre-Doctoral fellow, USPHS, 1986—88; grantee Pres.'s Undergraduate Fellowship grantee, U. Calif.-Davis, 1983—84, Med. Scholars Program grantee, Univ of Calif. Davis Med. Ctr., 1992—93, Grant for RNA structure modeling, San Diego Supercomputer Ctr., 1988; scholar MD./Ph.D. scholar, Northwestern U., 1984—86. Mem.: AAAS, European Gene Therapy Soc., Bioelectrochem. Soc., NY Acad. of Sci., Gene Therapy/Molecular Biology Internat. Soc. Achievements include invention of electroporative gene delivery into lung; patents for direct DNA delivery; genetic (DNA) vaccination; mucosal polynucleotide vaccination; invention of nuclease inhibitors for non-viral gene therapy; patents pending for nuclease inhibitors fo non-viral gene therapy; invention of skin electroporation for genetic vaccination. Avocations: carpentry, kayacking, animal husbandry, mountain climbing. Office: Dynport Vaccine Co LLC 64 Thomas Johnson Dr Frederick MD 21702 Personal E-mail: gtinventor@hotmail.com. E-mail: maloner@dynport.com.

MALONE, ROXANNE ENYEART, artist, educator; b. Topeka, Kans. d. Clarence J. and Audrey (Wiss) Malone; m. James L. Enyeart, Sept. 7., 1964; children: Mara, Sascha, Megan. BFA, Kans. City Art Inst., 1965; MFA, U. Ariz., 1984. Prof. Pima Coll., Tucson, 1987-89, Rochester (N.Y.) Inst. Tech., 1991-92, Cornell U., Ithaca, N.Y., 1994, Coll. of Santa Fe, N. Mex., 1995-00. Mem. advisory com. MIT, Boston, 1993. Artist: Kirlian Photograms, Androgyne Series, 1986 (award 1986), video art, Zen Trilogy, 1987 (award 1987), Plant and Geometric Series, Cibachromes, 1991, Mixed Media, 1997 (award 1997), (photo montage) Power Grid/Off Grid, 2000, (photo jet prints) Ironic Feminity, 2001, (video/photo/montage) Survival Series, 2002. Mem. art com. Rochester, N.Y. Diocese, 1993-94, arts advocate Women, Montage, Rochester, 1994. Art award Woman's Gallery, Tucson, 1992. Mem. Soc. for Photographic Edn., George Eastman House, Ctr. for Creative Photography Avocation: horticulture. Office: Coll of Santa Fe 1600 Saint Michaels Dr Santa Fe NM 87508-7615

MALONE, THOMAS FRANCIS, academic administrator, meteorologist; b. Sioux City, Iowa, May 3, 1917; s. John and Mary (Hourigan) M.; m. Rosalie Doran, Dec. 30, 1942; children: John H., Thomas Francis, Mary E., James K., Richard K., Dennis P. BS, S.D. Sch. Mines, 1940, D.Eng., 1962; Sc.D., MIT, 1946; L.H.D., St. Joseph Coll., West Hartford, Conn., 1965; Sc.D. (hon.), Bates Coll., 1988. Instr. MIT, 1942-43, asst. prof., 1943-51, assoc. prof., 1951-56; dir. Travelers Rsch. Ctr., Travelers Ins. Co., Hartford, Conn., 1955-56, dir. rsch., 1956-69, sr. v.p., 1968-70, chmn. bd., 1961-70; dean Grad. Sch., U. Conn., Storrs, 1970-73; chmn. bd. Ctr. for Environment and Men, 1970-71; dir. emeritus Holcomb Rsch. Inst., Butler U., Indpls., 1983—; scholar in residence St. Joseph Coll., 1983-91; Nat. Scis. fellow Resources for Future, 1983-84; Univ. Disting. scholar N.C. State U., 1991—98. Chmn. bd. Univ. Corp. for Atmospheric Rsch., 1973—76; mem. Conn. Weather Control Bd., 1959—73; mem. panel on sci. and tech. com. on sci. and astronautics U.S. Ho. of Reps., 1960—70; nat. adv. com. cmty. air pollution HEW, 1962—66; mem. sci. info. coun. NSF, 1962—66; rep. Am. Geophys. Union to U.S. Nat. Commn. for UNESCO, 1963—73, chmn. U.S. Nat. Commn., 1965—67; mem. nat. adv. com. on oceans and atmosphere, 1972—75; mem. Conn. Rsch. Commn., 1965—71; mem. com. application sci. and tech. New Eng. Coun.; chmn. Nat. Motor Vehicle Safety Adv. Coun., 1967—70; mem. sci. adv. com. climate impact assessment and response program UN Environ. Program, 1992—; mem. adv. com. on accreditation Conn. Dept. Higher Edn., 2000—02; mem. acad. adv. bd. S.D. Sch. Mines and Tech., 1991—2002; bd. dirs. Conn. Acad. for Edn., 2001—02. Editor: Compendium of Meteorology, 1951; contbg. editor: Environment, 1992-99; bd. editors: Jour. of the Marine Tech. Soc., 1995-99. Bd. dirs. Engrs. Joint Coun., 1968-70; bd. govs. Ins. Inst. Hwy. Safety, 1968-70; mem. oversight rev. bd. Nat. Acid Precipitation Assessment Program, 1990-96; corporator Hartford Sem., 2003—. Recipient Robert M. Losey award Inst. Aero. Sci., 1960, Charter Oak Leadership medal Greater Hartford C. of C., 1962, Charles Franklin Brooks award, 1964, Cleveland Abbe award Am. Meteorol. Soc., 1968, Conn. Conservationist of Yr. award, 1966, Guy E. March Silver medal S.D. Sch. Mines, 1976, Internat. Meteorol. Orgn. prize, 1984, Internat. St. Francis Assissi prize for environment, 1991, AAAS Internat. prize, 1994, Irving award Distance Edn. Consortium, 1997, Disting. Alumni award S.D. Sch. Mines, 1998, named to S.D. Hall of Fame, 2003; N.C. State U. disting. scholar, 1990-99, emeritus, 1999—. Fellow AAAS (internat. sci. coop., 1994), N.Y. Acad. Scis., Am. Meteorol. Soc. (pres. 1960-62), Am. Geophys. Union (past pres., sec. internat. participation 1964, Waldo E. Smith award 1986); mem. NAS (chmn. geophysics rsch. bd. 1969-76, chmn. bd. on internat. orgns. and programs, dep. fgn. sec. 1969-73, fgn. sec. 1978-82), NRC (space application bd. 1973-77), Am. Acad. Arts and Scis., Internat. Coun. Sci. Unions (v.p., sec.-gen. sci. com. problems environ. 1970-76, treas. 1978-82) Am. Geog. Soc. (coun. 1971-77), Royal Irish Acad. (hon.), Conn. Acad. Sci. and Engring. (exec. scientist 1987-91, 97-2000), Acad. Polit. Scis., Sigma Xi (bd. dirs. 1983-96, pres. 1988-89, dir. Sigma Xi Ctr. 1992-95, chief scientist 1996-98). Home: 275 Steele Rd Apt 504B West Hartford CT 06119 E-mail: tfmalone@aol.com.

MALONE, THOMAS J. textile company executive; Grad., Yale U.; numerous hon. degrees, various colls. and univs. With Milliken & Co., W. LaGrange, Ga., 1966—, pres., COO, 1983—. Bd. dirs. Am. Textile Mfrs. Inst., Crafted with Pride in the U.S.A. Coun., Ludwig von Mises Inst. Entrepreneurs Coun. Chmn. nat. adv. bd. Ga. Inst. Tech. Recipient Quality award Textile & Needle Trade Divsn., 1991, Silver medal No. Textile Assn., 1989, Lifetime Achievement award No. Textile Assn., 1999; named 29th on 50 Most Influential List, Textile World, Leader of Yr., Textile World, 1994; named to S.C. Bus. Hall of Fame, 1985. Mem. NAE, NSF (mem. adv. com. for directorate of engring.), S.C. Textile Mfrs. Assn. (bd. dirs.), Coun. Competitiveness, Chief Execs. Orgn., World Bus. Coun. Office: Milliken Design Ctr 201 Lukken Industrial Dr W Lagrange GA 30240 Fax: 706-880-5448. E-mail: mccservice@milliken.com.

MALONE, WALLACE D., JR., bank executive; b. Dothan, Ala., 1936; married. BS, U. Ala., 1957; MBA, U. Pa., 1960. With First Nat. Bank, 1959-71, SouthTrust Corp., Birmingham, Ala., 1972—, now chmn., CEO & pres. Office: SouthTrust Corp 420 N 20th St PO Box 2554 Birmingham AL 35290-0001

MALONE, WILLIAM GRADY, retired lawyer; b. Minden, La., Feb. 19, 1915; s. William Gordon and Minnie Lucie (Hortman) M.; m. Marion Rowe Whitfield, Sept. 26, 1943; children: William Grady, Gordon Whitfield, Marion Elizabeth, Helen Ann, Margaret Catherine. BS, La. State U., 1941; JD, George Washington U., 1952. Bar: Va. 1952, U.S. Supreme Ct 1971. Statis. analyst Dept. Agr., Baton Rouge, 1941; investigator VA, Washington, 1946-59, legal officer, dep., gen. counsel, asst. gen. counsel, 1959-79; pvt. practice law Arlington, Va., 1979-97. Editor: Fed. Bar News, 1972-73. Pres. Aurora Hills Civic Assn., 1948-49; spl. asst. to treas. Com. of 100, 1979-81, chmn., 1982-83; pres. Children's Theater, 1968-69; trustee St. George's Episc. Ch., 1979—; chmn. Arlington County Fair Assn., 1979-83. Lt. col. AUS, 1941-46, ETO. Decorated Legion of Merit; recipient Disting. Svc. award, 1979, 3 Superior Performance awards, 1952-72, Outstanding Alumni award George Washington Law Sch., 1978 Mem. Fed. Bar Assn. (pres. D.C. chpt. 1970-71, nat. pres. 1978-79), Va. Bar Assn., Arlington County Bar Assn., Nat. Lawyers Club (dir.), Arlington Host Lions, Ft. Myer Officers Club. Home: Apt 1523 900 N Taylor St Arlington VA 22203 E-mail: wgmalone@juno.com. *Success is not measured by dollars accumulated but by service to others.*

MALONE, WILLIAM ROBERT, lawyer; b. Terre Haute, Ind., Apr. 15, 1936; s. Leander Alonso and Dorothy Alice (Reveal) M.; m. Jane H. Foulkes, June 25, 1959 (dec.); children: Elizabeth, David, Christina. AB, Harvard U., 1958, JD, 1962. Bar: Ind. 1962, D.C. 1963, Conn. 1981. Law clk. to presiding justice U.S. Ct. Appeals, D.C., 1962-63; assoc. Covington & Burling, Washington, 1963-70; atty. Gen. Tel. & Electronics Corp., Washington, 1970-72; v.p., assoc. gen. counsel GTE Corp., Stamford, Conn., 1981-86; of counsel Miller & Holbrooke, Washington, 1989-94, Miller, Canfield, Paddock & Stone, Washington, 1994—96; ptnr. Miller & Van Eaton, PLLC, Washington, 1996—. Author: Broadcast Regulation in Can., 1962. Served with signal corps U.S. Army, 1959 Mem. ABA, Fed. Bar Assn., Fed. Communications Bar Assn., Computer Law Assn. (bd. dirs.). Republican. Presbyterian. Home: 9117 Vendome Dr Bethesda MD 20817-4022 Office: Miller & Van Eaton PLLC 1155 Connecticut Ave NW Ste 1000 Washington DC 20036-4306 Office Phone: 202-785-0600.

MALONE, WINFRED FRANCIS, health scientist; b. Revere, Mass., Feb. 10, 1935; s. Winfred and Margurite (Meehan) M.; m. Eleanor Malone, Aug. 1974. BS, U. Mass., 1957, MS, 1961, Rutgers U., 1963; PhD, U. Mich., 1970. Health scientist Nat. Cancer Inst., Bethesda, Md., 1970-81, chief chemoprevention br., 1981-95, acting assoc. dir., 1991-93, program dir., 1995—. Author articles on drug devel. Mem. AAAS, N.Y. Acad. Scis., Drug Info. Assn. Home: 3209 Wake Dr Kensington MD 20895-3216 Office: Nat Cancer Inst EPN # 2122 Bethesda MD 20892-0001 E-mail: wm22@nih.gov.

MALONEY, CAROLYN BOSHER, congresswoman; b. Feb. 19, 1948; d. R.G. and Christine (Clegg) Bosher; m. C.H.W. Maloney, 1976; children: Christina, Virginia. Student, Greensboro Coll. Various sr. staff positions N.Y. State Assembly and Senate, 1977-82; mem. N.Y.C Council dist. 8, 1983-93, U.S. Congress from 14th N.Y. dist., Washington, 1993—; mem. fin. svcs. com., ranking mem. subcom. domestic monetary policy, tech. and econ. growth; mem. fin. instns. and consumer credit subcom., internat. monetary policy and trade subcom.; mem. govt. reform and oversight com.; mem. joint economic com. Past chmn. Common Cause; active Assn. for a Better N.Y., Manahattan Women's Polit. Caucus. Mem. NAACP, Nat. Orgn. Women, Hadassah. Democrat. Home: 49 E 92nd St Apt 1A New York NY 10128-1326 Office: US Ho of Reps 2331 Rayburn HOB Washington DC 20515-0001

MALONEY, CHARLES WAYNE, gunsmith; b. Washington, June 5, 1945; s. Nicholas and Madeline Atkins Maloney; m. Lee J. Mullikin; m. Sue Vleck; m. Patricia Ann Mostad Maloney, Sept. 9, 1988 (dec. Feb. 1996); 1 child, Nicholas George. BFA, Va. Commonwealth U., 1973, MFA, 1976; cert., U.S. Nat. Match Firearms Sch. Owner, mgr. Firing Pin Gunshop, Catonsville, Md., 1976-80; armorer D.I.O. Weapons Br., Ft. Meade, Md., 1980-82; nat. match gunsmith U.S. Army Marksmanship Unit, Ft. Meade, 1982-89; chief gunsmith Fulton Armory, Savage, Md., 1989-96; owner, gunsmith Gunning Arts, Inc., Balt., 1986—. Author (screenplay): House Divided, 1997, (stage play) Nine Scenes in the Lives of Two Call Girls. Artistic dir. Pasadena Theatre Co., Millersville, Md., 1994-98; active profl. and comty. theater; dir./actor numerous theatrical prodns. and films. With USNR, 1964-70, Vietnam, 1965-68. Mem. NRA (life). Avocations: guitar, photography, collecting coins and books. Home: 1920 Edmondson Ave Catonsville MD 21228-4232 Office: Gunning Arts Inc 5305 East Dr Arbutus MD 21227-2687 E-mail: charliesarts@comcast.net.

MALONEY, GERALD P. retired utilities executive; b. Lawrence, Mass., Mar. 9, 1933; s. Thomas P. and Concetta Maloney; m. Dorothea Ames. BSEE, BSBA, MIT, 1955; MBA, Rutgers U., 1962. With Am. Electric Power Co., Inc., Columbus, Ohio, 1955-98, contr., 1965-70, v.p. fin., 1970-75, sr. v.p. fin., 1975—91, exec. v.p., CFO, 1992—98, vice chmn., 1998; ret., 1998. Mem.: Beta Gamma Sigma. Home: 275 S Parkview Ave Bexley OH 43209-1649

MALONEY, JAMES HENRY, community development executive, former congressman; b. Quincy, Mass., Sept. 17, 1948; s. James Henry Jr. and Katherine Smith (Murphy) M.; m. Mary Angela Draper, Aug. 16, 1980; children: Adele, Anna, Ellen. BA cum laude, Harvard U., 1972; JD, Boston U., 1980. Vol. VISTA, Gary, Ind., 1969-70; exec. dir. Community Action Com. Danbury, Conn., 1974-78; atty. Pinney, Payne, VanLenten, Burrell, Wolfe & Dillman, P.C., Danbury, 1980-86; ptnr. Dice, Maloney & Lenz, P.C., Danbury, 1986-93, Maloney, Leaphart & Assocs., PC, Danbury, 1995-97; mem. Conn. Senate, Hartford, 1987-95, 105-107th Congresses from 5th Conn. dist., 1997—2003, mem. armed svcs. com., mem. fin. svcs. com.; pres., gen. counsel Conn. Resource Devel. Corp., 2003—; COO, Main St. Devel. Corp., 2003—. Democrat. Roman Catholic. Avocation: sailing. E-mail: JamesHMaloney@aol.com.

MALONEY, JOHN JOSEPH, writer; b. N.Y.C., Jan. 15, 1929; s. John J. and Breda T. (O'Leary) M.; m. Helen Martin; children: Peter, Elizabeth, Mary Ellen. BA, Fordham Coll., 1951. City editor Patent Trader, Mt. Kisco, N.Y., 1953-59; news bureau mgr. N.Y. Stock Exchange, N.Y.C., 1959-63; dir. pub. rels. Lehman Bros., N.Y.C., 1963-71, Warnaco, Inc., Bridgeport, Conn., 1971-77; v.p. charge of media rels. Citigroup (formerly Citicorp/Citibank), N.Y.C., 1977-91; writer Easton, Conn., 1991—. Cons. capital formation markets Kenyan govt., 1991, Bulgarian govt., 1999. With U.S. Army, 1951-53. Avocation: sailing. Home: 65 Sport Hill Pkwy Easton CT 06612-2239 E-mail: johnhelenmaloney@cs.com.

MALONEY, KRISTEN, gymnast; b. Hacketstown, N.J., Mar. 10, 1981; d. Richard and Linda. Mem. U.S. Gymnastics Team, 1994—2001, UCLA Gymnastics Team, 2000—. Mem. U.S. World Championships Team, 1997, 99, U.S. Gymnastics Team Sydney Olympics, 2000. Recipient numerous awards, 1st pl. Am. Classic, 1997, 98, 1st pl. (3) Foxsport Challenge, Sydney, 1997, 1st team, 1st balance beam, 1st floor exercise 1st AA, Internat. Team Championships, 1998, 1st team, 1st AA, Pacific Alliance Champaionships, Winnipeg, Can., 1998, 1st balance beam Goodwill Games, 1998, others. Mem. Parketts Club. Avocations: reading, music, movies, shopping. Office: UCLA Women's Gymnastics PO Box 24044 Los Angeles CA 90024

MALONEY, MARILYN C. lawyer; b. New Orleans, Nov. 24, 1950; BA, La. State U., 1972, JD, 1975. Bar: La. 1975, U.S. Dist. Ct. (ea. dist.) La. Ptnr. Liskow & Lewis, New Orleans, 1975—. Contbr. articles to profl. jours. Fellow Am. Coll. Real Estate Lawyers; mem. La. State Law Inst. (v.p.), La. Bar Found. (bd. dirs.), Order of Coif, Omicron Delta Kappa. Office: Liskow & Lewis 1 Shell Sq Fl 50 New Orleans LA 70139

MALONEY, MARY D. lawyer; BA, U. Akron, 1984; JD summa cum laude, Cleve. State U., 1987; LLM, Case Wester Res. U., 1995. Bar: Ohio 1987. With Jones Day, Cleve., 1987—, ptnr., 2001—. Mem.: Ohio State Bar Assn. Office: Jones Day North Point 901 Lakeside Ave Cleveland OH 44114-1190

MALONEY, MARYNELL, lawyer; b. Hutchinson, Kans., Jan. 14, 1955; d. Robert Edgar and Marian Ellen (Benson) Baker; m. Michael D. Maloney, Nov. 30, 1977; children: Michelle M., Erica O., Dennis Jr. BA, Oberlin Coll., 1975; MA, Trinity U., San Antonio, 1978; JD, St. Mary's U., San Antonio, 1980. Cert. by Tex. bd. of legal specialization. Assoc. Law Offices Pat Maloney, P.C., San Antonio, 1981-82; ptnr., owner Maloney & Maloney, San Antonio, 1982—. Bd. dirs. San Antonio Internat. Keyboard Competition, 1988-90; bd. govs. St. Peters/St. Joseph's Children's Home, San Antonio, 1989-92. Mem. ACLU of Tex. (bd. dirs. 1990—, v.p. 1995-96, SACLU 1990—), Am. Trial Lawyers Assn., State Bar Tex., Tex. Trial Lawyers Assn. (assoc. bd. dirs. 1989-90, bd. dirs. 1991-2002, dir. emeritus 2002—, cert. personal injury trial law), San Antonio Bar Assn., San Antonio Trial Lawyers Assn. (pres. 1991-92). Democrat. Avocations: reading, writing, film. Office: Maloney & Maloney PC 2000 Milam 115 E Travis San Antonio TX 78205

MALONEY, MAUREEN MURPHY, social sciences educator; b. N.Y.C., Nov. 16, 1941; d. Cyril Bernard Murphy and Monique Louissiane Jacques; m. Paul K. Maloney, Dec. 5, 1964; children: Jennifer, Paula, Edward. Diploma, Holy Name Sch. Nursing, 1962; BS in Psychology, Sacred Heart U., 1982; M in Applied Psychology, Fairfield U., 1986; D summa cum laude of Ednl. Leadership, U. Bridgeport, 2003. RN N.J. Head nurse neurosurgery Columbia Presbyn. Med. Ctr., N.Y.C., 1962—65; prof. Housatonic C.C., Bridgeport, Conn., 1993—. Adj. prof. Norwalk C.C., 1987—93, chmn. dept. behavioral scis., 2000—02. Mem.: ASCD, APA, AAUP, Am. Psychological Soc. Roman Catholic. Avocations: reading, skiing, tennis. Office: Housatonic CC 900 Lafayette Ave Bridgeport CT 06608

MALONEY, MICHAEL PATRICK, lawyer, mediator, arbitrator; b. Syracuse, N.Y., June 1, 1944; s. Randolph Bartholomew and Alice Mary (Loban) M.; m. Jane McBurney, May 21, 1977; children: Christopher, Kara. AB, Georgetown U., 1966; MBA, Cornell U., 1968, JD, 1971. Bar: N.Y. 1972. Assoc. Donovan Leisure Newton and Irvine, N.Y.C., 1971-78; asst. dir. div. market regulation SEC, Washington, 1978-79; sr. v.p., gen. counsel, sec. Orion Capital Corp., N.Y.C., 1979-98; pres. OSOWA Enterprises, LLC, 1998—. Sec., bd. dirs. Carden Sch. Maui; pres., dir. Seabury Hall Parents Orgn. Mem.: Am. Corp. Counsel Counsel Assn., Am. Soc. Corp. Secs., The Kapalua Club. Home: 891 Holopuni Rd Kula HI 96790

MALONEY, MILFORD CHARLES, retired internal medicine educator; b. Buffalo, Mar. 15, 1927; s. John Angelus Maloney and Winifred Hill; m. Dione Ethyl Sheppard. BS, Canisius Coll., 1947, postgrad., 1947-49; MD, U. Buffalo, 1953. Diplomate Am. Bd. Internal Medicine. Rsch. chemist Buffalo Electrochem. Co., 1947-49; intership Mercy Hosp./Georgetown U., 1953-54; med. residency Buffalo VA Hosp., 1954-56; cardiology fellow Buffalo Gen. Hosp., 1956-57; chmn. dept. medicine Mercy Hosp., 1969-94, program dir.,

internal medicine residency, 1972-89; with steering com. Assn. Program Dirs. in Internal Medicine, 1976, coun. mem., 1977-80; clin. prof. medicine SUNY, Buffalo, 1981-94; trustee Am. Soc. Internal Medicine, 1984-90, edn. leader, European seminar, 1987, edn. leader, So. Am. seminar, 1988; faculty instr. Christopher Wren Assn. Coll. William and Mary, Williamsburg, Va., 1997—. Bd. dirs. Internal Medicine Ctr. for Advancement and Rsch. Edn.; pres. Heart Assn. Western N.Y., Buffalo, 1969; sr. cancer rsch. physician Roswell Park Meml. Cancer Inst., 1959-62; mem. internal medicine liaison com. N.Y. State, 1980-90; faculty instr., mem. curriculum com. Christopher Wren Assn. Coll. William & Mary, Williamsburg, Va., 1997-99. Editor newsletter N.Y. State Soc. Internal Medicine, 1972-78. Bd. dirs. Health Sys. Agy. Western N.Y., Buffalo, 1981; mem. exec. com., bd. dirs. Blue Cross Western N.Y., Buffalo, 1987; mem. bd. regents Canisius Coll., Buffalo, 1987—; mem. pres. assocs. SUNY, Buffalo; founding mem. Greater Williamsburg Va. Symphony Soc., 1998; bd. dirs. Va. Symphony, Norfolk, 2001; dir. devel. Williamsburg Ctr. Excellence in Aging and Geriatric Health, 2004. Capt. M.C., U.S. Army, 1957-59. Recipient award of merit N.Y. State Soc. Internal Medicine, 1980, Man of Yr. award Heart Assn. Western N.Y., 1982, ann. honoree award Trocaire Coll., 1986, Disting. Alumni award Canisius Coll., 1991, Berkson Excellence award in tchg. and art of medicine, SUNY at Buffalo, 1992, Outstanding Med. Tchg. Attending award Mercy Hosp./SUNY Med. Residents, 1994, Lifetime Career Achievement award Med. Alumni Assn. SUNY, Buffalo, 1998; named to Sports Hall of Fame, Canisius Coll., 1978. Fellow ACP (Upstate Physician Recognition award 1989), fellow Am. Coll. Cardiology; mem. AMA (SUNY rep. 1986-94, rep. to sect. med. schs. at ann. meetings 1984-94, chmn. sect. on internal medicine 1990-91), Am. Soc. Internal Medicine (bd. dirs. Internal Medicine Ctr. for Advancement of Rsch. Edn. 1988-91, trustee 1984-90, pres. 1990-91, chmn. long range planning com., rep. to Federated Coun. on Internal Medicine 1990-91, rep. to AMA nat. practice parameters and guidelines com. 1989-91, Scroll of Honor benefactor for Internal Medicine Ctr. for Advancement of Rsch. and Edn. 1991), N.Y. State Soc. Internal Medicine (pres. 1974-75), Alumni Assn. SUNY (pres. 1975), Med. Soc. County Erie (pres. 1991-82), Va. Soc. Internal Medicine (hon.), Greater Williamsburg Va. Symphony Soc. (founding mem. 1998, editor newsletter 1998-2003). Home: 116 Cove Point Ln Williamsburg VA 23185-8613 E-mail: mcmaloney@widomaker.com.

MALONEY, PAMELA, minister; b. Fostoria, Ohio, July 30, 1945; d. Raymond and L. Maurine (Risser) Yeager; m. Rev. William James Maloney (dec.); children: Heather, James. BS in Music Edn. cum laude, Bowling Green State U., 1967; MDiv cum laude, Pitts. Theol. Sem., 1971. Asst. pastor Pleasant Hills Cmty. Presbyn. Ch., Pitts., 1971—74; organist, choir dir., asst. pastor Dormont Presbyn. Ch., 1975—83; interim asst. pastor Corssroads Presbyn. Ch., Monroeville, 1983—84; asst., assoc. pastor, organist, choir dir. Glenshaw Presbyn. Ch., 1984—99; interim pastor Hillside Presbyn. Ch., Greenville, 1999—2000, Slippery Rock Presbyn. Ch., Ellwood City, 2000—02; assoc. pastor 1st Presbyn. Ch., Sharon, 2003—. Vice moderator Pitts. Presbytery, 1983, Shenango Presbytery, 2002—03, moderator, 2003—04; mem. the Pitts. Cleric, 1985—. Tchr. Dormont New Century Club, Pitts., 1976—83. Mem.: New Wilmington Missionary Conf. (bd. mgrs. 2000—), Hamton-Shaler-Etna Clergy Assn. (sec., pres.). Avocations: singing, piano, organ, reading.

MALONEY, PAT, SR., lawyer; b. Dallas, Tex., Aug. 9, 1924; s. James Edward and Flora Agnes (Kessler) M.; m. Olive Boger, May 20, 1950; children: Patricia, Pat Jr., Michael, Janice, Tim. BJ, U. Tex., 1948, LLB, 1950. Bar: Tex. 1950, U.S. Dist. Ct. (we. dist.) Tex. 1955, U.S. Supreme Ct. 1951; cert. civil law and personal injury trial law, Tex. Bd. Legal Specialization, civil trial advocacy Nat. Bd. Trial Advocacy. 1st asst. trial chief Dist. Atty.'s Office, San Antonio, Tex., 1950-53; pvt. practice Law Offices of Pat Maloney P.C., San Antonio, 1953—. Moderator, founder annual seminar Anatomy of a Lawsuit, St. Mary's U., San Antonio; frequent lectr. throughout U.S. in areas of product liability and personal injury law. Author: Winning the Million Dollar Law Suit, 1980; co-author: Trials and Deliberations: Inside the Jury Room, 1992. With USMC, 1942-45, PTO. Recipient Warhorse award So. Trial Lawyers Assn., 1992. Fellow Law Sci. Acad. Am., Am. Bd. Trial Advocates, mem. Inner Circle of Trial Advocates, ATLA, Internat. Soc. Barristers, Internat. Acad. Trial Lawyers, San Antonio Trial Lawyers Assn. (co-founder, pres. 1967, 72, bd. dirs. 1967-73,) San Antonio Bar Assn., State Bar of Tex., Tex. Trial Lawyers Assn. (director emeritus) Democrat. Roman Catholic. Achievements include 1977 personal injury verdict awarding his client $26,510,800.00. At that time the largest personal injury verdict in the history of the U.S. He has obtained verdicts and settlements in excess of a million dollars more than fifty times. Office: 239 E Commerce St San Antonio TX 78205-2931 Office Phone: 210-226-8888.

MALONEY, PATRICK RAYMOND, retired judge; b. Tacoma, Wash., Feb. 8, 1928; s. Thomas Emmett and Celia Margaret (Joyce) M.; m. Mary Anne Christnacht, July 2, 1955; children: Martin, Kathleen, John, Michael, James. BSS, Seattle U., 1951; JD, U. San Francisco, 1954. Bar: Calif. 1955, U.S. Dist. Ct. (no. dist.) Calif. 1955, U.S. Dist. Ct. (no. dist.) Tex. 1979, U.S. Ct. Appeals (9th cir.) 1955. Assoc. Lyons & Reisch, South San Francisco, Calif., 1955-57; claims atty. Indsl. Imdemnity Co., San Francisco, 1957-61; sr. counsel State Compensation Ins. Fund, Sacramento, 1961-63; referee, referee in charge Calif. Workments Compensation Appeal Bd., Bakersfield, 1963-72; adminstrv. law judge HHS, San Jose, Calif., 1972-96; ret., 1996. Night law faculty Bakersfield Adult Sch., Calif., 1966-71. Pres. Santa Clara St. Vincent DePaul Assn., San Jose, 1979-81, Peninsula Toastmasters, San Mateo, Calif., 1959. Sgt. U.S. Army, 1950-52. Mem. ABA (adminstrv. law sect. 1963-2000, jud. adminstrv. divsn. 1976-96), Serra Club (pres. 1970-71), K.C. Republican. Roman Catholic. Home: 2244 Glenkirk Ct San Jose CA 95124-1220

MALONEY, RITA, radio personality; With Sta. WBVP, Pitts., news dir.; radio host Sta. WCCO radio, Mpls. Named one of Pitts. 50 Finest Young Profls.; recipient Best Regularly Scheduled Newscast award, 3 AIR awards for Best Traffic Reporter, Best Spot News Coverage award, Pa. AP. Office: WCCO 625 2nd Ave S Minneapolis MN 55402

MALONEY, ROBERT E., JR., lawyer; b. San Francisco, Sept. 17, 1942; s. Robert E. and Mara A. (Murphy) M.; children: Michael, Sarah, Paul. BA magna cum laude, U. Portland, 1964; JD summa cum laude, Willamette U., Salem, Oreg., 1967. Bar: Oreg., Wash., U.S. Dist. Ct. Oreg., U.S. Dist. Ct. (we. dist.) Wash., U.S. Dist. Ct. (ea. dist.) Wash., U.S. Ct. Appeals (9th cir.). Ptnr. Lane Powell Spears Lubersky, LLP, Portland, 1967—; chmn., profl. svcs. counsel Bounce Back Oreg., 2003. Bd. dirs., sec. Norm Thompson Outfitters, Inc., Portland; chmn. bd. visitors Willamette U. Law Sch., 1993-95, bd. dirs. emeritus, 1998—; past chair, mem. exec. com. Portland Trial Dept.; lawyers del. 9th Cir. Jud. Conf., 1995-97; pres. adv. coun. U. Portland, 2001—. Bd. dirs. Oreg. chpt. Multiple Sclerosis Soc., 1995-2002, Children's Cancer Assn., 2001—, Oreg. Independent Coll. Found., 2001—, Oreg. Lawyers Against Hunger, 1997-99; judge pro tem Multnomah County Cir. Ct., 1994-99. Mem. ABA (co-chair products liability com., trial practice com. 1990-94), Nat. Assn. R.R. Trial Counsel, Fedn. Ins. Corp. Counsel, Oreg. Assn. Def. Counsel (bd. dirs. 1987-94, sec. 1991-92, v.p. 1993-94, pres. 1994), Fed. Bar Assn. (exec. com. Oreg. divsn. 1988-96, pres. 1994-95), Multnomah Athletic Club. Republican. Roman Catholic. Office: Lane Powell Spears Lubersky LLP 601 SW Second Ave Ste 2100 Portland OR 97204-3158 Fax: 503-778-2200. Office Phone: 503-778-2105. Business E-Mail: maloneyr@lanepowell.com.

MALONEY, ROBERT KELLER, ophthalmologist, medical educator; b. May 1, 1958; AB in Mathematics summa cum laude, Harvard U., 1979; MA in Philosophy, Politics and Econs., Oxford (Eng.) U., 1981; MD, U. Calif., San Francisco, 1985. Diplomate Am. Bd. Ophthalmology. Rsch fellow dept. physiology Cambridge (Eng.) U., 1985; intern U. Calif., L.A., 1985-86; resident Wilmer Ophthal. Inst. Johns Hopkins Hosp., Balt., 1986-89; Heed fellow cornea and refractive surgery Emory U., Dept. Ophthalmology, Atlanta, 1989-91; assoc. prof. ophthalmology UCLA Sch. Medicine, Jules Stein Eye Inst., 1991-98. Bd. dirs. Lasik Inst., Calhoun Vision. Contbr. numerous articles to profl. jours.; presenter and spkr. in field; assoc. editor (N.Am.) Jour. Refractive and Corneal Surgery, 1991-95; internat. editl. bd. European Jour. Implant and Refractive Surgery, 1995; reviewer Am. Jour. Ophthalmology, Ophthalmology, Archives of Ophthalmology, Jour. Cataract and Refractive Surgery, Ophthalmic Surgery and Lasers; editl. bd. Ophthalmology Times. Rhodes scholar, 1979, Heed Found. fellow, 1989-90, Heed/Knapp fellow, 1990-91, John Harvard scholar, 1978; recipient Retur and Edward Whitaker prizes, Harvard U., Rsch. to Prevent Blindness Career Devel. award, 1992, Mericos Whittier award, 1997, VISX Star Surgeon award, 1999, 2000. Mem. Am. Acad. Ophthalmology (long-range planning com. 1989-92, quality of care com. 1987-91, retina preferred practice pattern subcom., refractive errors preferred practice pattern subcom.; chmn. ann. meeting program com. for young ophthalmologists, 1990-92; adv. group to ad hoc com. on orgnl. design 1991, young ophthalmologists' com. 1992-94; Honor award 1993, 97, Sr. Achievement award 2002, Secretariat award 2003), Assn. Rsch. in Vision and Ophthalmology, Internat. Soc. Refractive Surgery (Disting. Lans Refractive Surgery award 2001), Calif. Assn. Ophthalmology, Max Fine Corneal Soc., Phi Beta Kappa. Office: Maloney Vision Inst 10921 Wilshire Blvd Ste 900 Los Angeles CA 90024 Office Phone: 310-208-3937.

MALONEY, SEAN M. computer company executive; Mgr. applications engring. Intel U.K. Intel Corp., country mgr. Intel U.K., dir. mktg. Intel Europe, gen. mgr. Asia Pacific ops., tech. asst. to chmn. and chief exec., 1992—95, mgr. sales and mktg. activities Asia Pacific, 1995—99, sr. v.p., 1999—2001, exec. v.p. and dir. sales and mktg. group, exec. v.p., gen. mgr. Intel Comm. Group, 2001—. Bd. dirs. Cadence Design Sys., U.S./China Bus. Coun. Office: 2200 Mission College Blvd Santa Clara CA 95052

MALONEY, SEAN ROBERT, physician, biomedical engineer; b. L.A., Feb. 21, 1949; s. Robert Edward and Virginia Elizabeth (Walsh) M.; m. Susan Marie Howard, Aug. 15, 1981; children: Michael Patrick, Matthew Robert, John Howard. BSChemE, BS in Phys. Scis., U. Calif., Davis, 1975; MD, Emory U., 1980; MSME, Stanford U., 1984. Diplomate Am. Bd. Electrodiagnostic Medicine, Nat. Bd. Med. Examiners, Am. Bd. Phys. Medicine and Rehab. Process control engr. Atlantic Richfield and Hanford (Wash.) Co., 1975-76; intern/resident phys. medicine and rehab. Stanford (Calif.) U., 1980-83; asst. med. dir., dir. spinal cord injury unit Thoms Rehab. Hosp., Asheville, N.C., 1984-85; pvt. med. practice Asheville, 1985—; sole proprietor, biomedical engr. Sean R. Maloney & Co., Asheville, 1989—; asst. clin. prof. surgery orthop./rehab. Bowman Gray Sch. Medicine, 1995—. Presenter in field. Article reviewer Archives Phys. Medicine & Rehab., 1988—; patentee intraoral controller. Col. Asheville Buncombe County Christian Mission Free Med. Clinic, 1992—. With U.S. Army, 1968-72. Grantee Nat. Inst. Neurol. Disorders and Stroke, 1990, 92-93, 96-98, Bapt. Hosp. Inc., 1995-98. Fellow AIChE, So. Soc. Phys. Medicine and Rehab., Am. Med. Soc., Buncombe County Med. Soc. Democrat. Roman Catholic. Avocations: dixieland jazz, tennis. Home: 2036 Rossmore Road Clemmons NC 27012

MALONEY, SIMONE, accountant; b. Manchester, NH, Sept. 11, 1936; d. Henri and Emilia Carignan; m. Anthony Maloney, Aug. 30, 1958; children: Paul, Charles, James. BS in Acctg., So. Univ. N.H., 1981. Cert. tax profl., practitioner of taxation. Receptionist, telephone operator, acctg. supr. Travelers Ins. Co., Manchester, 1966-76, auditor, 1976-79; pvt. practice as acct. and bookkeeper, also tax svcs. Manchester, 1981—. Vol. Boy Scouts Am., campaign to reelect Robert Shaw Mayor City of Manchester, 1985, presdl. campaign Congressman Phil Crane, 1980, Congressman Bill Zeliff, 1990; candidate for alderman City of Manchester, 1983; office mgr. campaign Congressman Bob Smith, 1983-84, treas., 1985-86; elected Selectman Ward 2, Manchester, 1992-95, appointed moderator, 1996, elected moderator, 1997—; sec. Greater Manchester Federated Rep. Women's Club, 1987; treas. Manchester Rep. Com., 1989-92, 96—, sec., chmn. Ward 2 Rep. Com., 1987-88. Recipient Bella Duperron award, Manchester Rep. Party, 2003, Clarence Ferry Appreciation award, Manchester Ward 2 Rep. Com., 2004. Mem.: Nat. Soc. Tex. Profls., Nat. Federated Rep. Women, Smithsonian Inst. Roman Catholic. Avocations: sewing, reading, travel, swimming. Home and Office: 171 Russell St Manchester NH 03104-3770

MALONEY, TERRY, horticulturist, educator; b. Corning, N.Y., June 15, 1955; s. Robert Frances Maloney Sr. and Shirley Lucille (Borden) Maloney; m. Sylvaine Marie Senechal, Oct. 26, 1991. Student, Cornell U., 1973—75. Rm. mgr. Corning Hilton Inn., 1975—80; horticulturist cons. Corning, 1979—84; ops. cons. various orgns., 1984—2002; owner, advisor Earth Centre, North Myrtle Beach, SC, 1998—2004. Educator, advisor, owner Spiritual Growth Horticulture, North Mrytle Beach, 2002—; horticulturist Surf Golf and Beach Country Club, North Myrtle Beach, 2003—; cons. Mkt. St. Restoration Agy., Corning, 1979—84, City of Corning, 1980—84. Author: Rewriting Religion, 2004; contbr. articles to profl. jours. Recipient Citizen award for Volunteer Work, Mkt. St. Assn., Corning, 1983. Avocations: gardening, theology, string theory, writing. Home: 81 Princess Dr North Myrtle Beach SC 29582 Office: Earth Centre 81 Princess Dr North Myrtle Beach SC 29582

MALONEY, THERESE ADELE, insurance company executive; b. Sept. 15, 1929; d. James Henry and F. Adele (Powers) M. BA in Econs., Coll. St. Elizabeth, Convent Station, N.J., 1951; AMP, Harvard U., 1981. CPCU. With Liberty Mut. Ins. Co., Boston, 1951-94, asst. v.p., asst. mgr. nat risks, 1974-77, v.p., asst. mgr. nat. risks, 1977-79, v.p., mgr. nat. risks, 1979-86, sr. v.p. underwriting mktg. and adminstrn., 1986-87, exec. v.p. underwriting, policy decision, 1987-94, also bd. dirs.; pres. and bd. dirs. subs. Liberty Mus. (Bermuda) Ltd., 1981-94, LEXCO Ltd.; cons. Exec. Svc. Corp., 1994—2002. Bd. dirs., dep. chmn. Liberty Mut. (U.K.) Ltd., London; bd. dirs. Liberty Mut. Ins. Co., Liberty Mut. Fire Ins. Co., Liberty Mut. Life Assurance Co., Liberty Fin. Cos.; mem. faculty Inst. Northeastern U., Boston, 1969—74; mem. adv. bd., risk mgmt. studies Ins. Inst. Am., 1977—83; mem. adv. coun. Suffolk U. Sch. Mgmt., 1984—96; mem. adv. coun. to program in internat. bus. rels. Fletcher Sch. Law and Diplomacy, 1985—94; cons. Exec. Svc. Corp., Boston, 1994—2002. Trustee Coll. St. Elizabeth, N.J., 1993-02. Mem. Soc. CPCUs (past pres. Boston chpt.), Univ. Club, Boston Club, Neighborhood Club of Quincy.

MALONEY, THOMAS E. insurance executive; CFO John Hancock Fin. Svc., Boston. Office: John Hancock Fin Svc John Hancock Pl Boston MA 02117

MALONEY, WILLIAM JAMES, dentist, educator; b. White Plains, NY, Feb. 16, 1967; BS, Siena Coll., Loudonville, N.Y., 1989; DDS, NYU, 1992. Faculty NYU Coll. Dentistry, NY, 2000—. Contbr. articles to profl. jours. Mem.: ADA. Office: 12 Ellis Pl Ossining NY 10562

MALOOF, GILES WILSON, academic administrator, educator, author; b. San Bernardino, Calif., Jan. 4, 1932; s. Joseph Peters and Georgia (Wilson) M.; m. Mary Anne Ziniker, Sept. 5, 1958 (dec. Oct. 1976); children: Mary Jane, Margery Jo. BA, U. Calif., Berkeley, 1953; MA, U. Oreg., 1958; PhD, Oreg. State U., 1962. Petroleum reservoir engr. Creole Petroleum Corp., Venezuela, 1953-54; mathematician electronics divsn. rsch. dept. U.S. Naval Ordnance Rsch. Lab., Corona, Calif., 1958-59; asst. prof. math. Oreg. State U., Corvallis, 1962-68, rsch. assoc. dept. oceanography, 1963-68, vis. prof. math., 1977-78; prof. math. Boise (Idaho) State U., 1968—, head dept., 1968-75, dean grad. sch., 1970-75. Author, reviewer of coll. textbooks; contbr. to profl. jours. Served with Ordnance Corps, AUS, 1950, 54-56. Recipient Carter award, 1963, Mosser prize, 1966, Oreg. State U., Alumni Found. scholar Teaching award Boise State U., 2000. Mem. Math. Assn. Am., Am. Math. Soc., Soc. Indsl. and Applied Math., N.W. Coll. and Univ. Assn. for Sci. (dir. 1973—, pres. 1990-92), N.W. Sci. Assn. (trustee 1977-80), Assn. Western Univs. (mem. edn. and rsch. com. 1993-2001), Sigma Xi, Pi Mu Epsilon, Phi Kappa Phi. Home: 1400 Longmont Ave Boise ID 83706-3730 E-mail: giles@diamond.boisestate.edu.

MALOOLEY, DAVID JOSEPH, electronics and computer technology educator; b. Terre Haute, Ind., Aug. 20, 1951; s. Edward Joseph and Vula (Starn) Malooley. BS, Ind. State U., 1975; MS, Ind. U., 1981. Supr. Zenith Radio Corp., Paris, Ill., 1978—79; assoc. prof., electronics and computer tech. Ind. State U., Terre Haute, 1979—; cons. in field. Served to 1st lt. U.S. Army, 1975—78. Mem.: Nat. Fire Protection Assn., Nat. Assn. Indsl. Tech., Soc. Mfg. Engrs., Instrument Soc. Am. (sr.), Epsilon Pi Tau, Pi Lambda Theta, Phi Delta Kappa. Democrat. Home: 11420 Spring Creek Rd Terre Haute IN 47805-9679 Office: Ind State U Dept Electronics and Computer Tech Terre Haute IN 47809-0001 Office Phone: 812-237-3395. Business E-Mail: etmaloo@isugw.indstate.edu.

MALOON, JERRY L. trial lawyer, physician, medico legal consultant; b. Union City, Ind., June 23, 1938; s. Charles Elias and Bertha Lucille (Creviston) M.; children: Jeffrey Lee, Jerry Lee II. BS, Ohio State U., 1960, MD, 1964; JD, Capital U. Law Sch., 1974. Intern Santa Monica (Calif.) Hosp., 1964-65; tng. psychiatry Ctrl. Ohio Psychiat. Hosp., 1969, Menninger Clinic, Topeka, 1970; clin. dir. Orient (Ohio) Devel. Ctr., 1967-69, med. dir., 1971-83; assoc. med. dir. Western Electric, Inc., Columbus, 1969-71; cons. State Med. Bd. Ohio, 1974-80; pvt. practice law Columbus, 1978—; pres. Jerry L. Maloon Co., L.P.A., 1981—. Medicolegal cons., 1972—; pres. Maloon, Maloon & Barclay Co., L.P.A., 1990-95; guest lectr. law and medicine Orient Devel. Ctr. and Columbus Devel. Ctr., 1969-71; dep. coroner Franklin County (Ohio), 1978-84. Dean's coun. Capital U. Law Sch. Capt. M.C., AUS, 1965-67. Fellow: Columbus Bar Found., Am. Coll. Legal Medicine; mem.: ATLA, AMA, ABA, Am. Profl. Practice Assn., Columbus Trial Lawyers Assn., Ohio Trial Lawyers Assn., Columbus Bar Assn., Ohio Bar Assn., Ohio State U. Alumni Assn., U.S. Trotting Assn., The Country Club at Muirfield Village, Ohio State U. Pres.'s Buckeye Club. Home: 2140 Cambridge Blvd Upper Arlington OH 43221-4104 Office: 9155 Moors Pl North Dublin OH 43017 Office Phone: 614-798-1616. E-mail: maloonmdjd@columbus.rr.com.

MALORATSKY, LEO G. electrical engineer; b. Zaporoghe, U.S.S.R., Apr. 28, 1939; arrived in U.S., 1989; s. German M. Maloratsky and Slava I. Grinberg; m. Helena A. Vinitsky, Oct. 3, 1968; children: Artem, Anna. MSEE, Moscow Aviation Inst., 1962; PhD, Moscow Int. Telecomm., 1967. Rsch. scientist Electrotech. Inst., Moscow, 1962—79; asst. prof. Moscow Inst. Radio, Electronics and Automation, 1969—88; sr. rsch. scientist Automation Lab., Moscow, 1979—89; vis. scholar Northeastern U., Boston, 1989; sr. engr. M/A-COM, Boston, 1990; v.p. REC, Boston, 1991—92; staff engr. Allied Signal, Ft. Lauderdale, Fla., 1992—97; prin. engr. Rockwell Collins, Melbourne, Fla., 1997—. Author: Microminiaturization of Microwave Components and Devices, 1976, Passive RF and Microwave Integrated Circuits, 2003; co-author: Design and Calculation of Microwave Stripline Elements, 1972, Design of Microwave Devices, 1983, Microwave Devices and Screens, 1990. Mem.: IEEE. Home: 2160 N Hwy A1A Apt 205 Indialantic FL 32903 Office: Rockwell Collins PO Box 1080 Melbourne FL 32902 Personal E-mail: lhmal@earthlink.net.

MALORZO, THOMAS VINCENT, lawyer; b. Rome, N.Y., Jan. 10, 1947; s. Vincent T. and Helene Adeline Malorzo; m. Catherine Marie Malorzo, Dec. 28, 1968; children: Amy, Craig, Mary, Thomas Jr. BA, Walsh U., Canton, Ohio, 1969; JD, Cleve. State U., 1979. Bar: Ohio 1979, U.S. Dist. Ct. (no. dist.) Ohio 1980, U.S. Patent Office 1980, Tex. 1981, U.S. Dist. Ct. (no. dist.) Tex. 1981, U.S. Ct. Appeals (7th cir.) 1994, U.S. Dist. Ct. (ea. dist.) Tex., 1998, U.S. Dist. Ct. (so. dist.) Tex., 2000. Analytical chemist Glidden-Durkee divsn. SCM Corp., 1969—79; environ. regulations analyst Diamond Shamrock Corp., Dallas, 1979-81; ind. counsel, agt. Southwestern Life Ins. Co., Dallas, 1981-83; staff atty. NCH Corp., Irving, Tex., 1983-89; gen. counsel Wormald US, Inc., Dallas, 1989-90; patent atty. Otis Engring. Corp., Carrollton, Tex., 1990-93; pvt. practice Addison, Tex., 1993-95; ptnr. Falk, Vestal & Fish LLP, 1995; pvt. practice Dallas, 1996-97; of counsel Bennett & Weston P.C., 1997—2002; prin. atty. Malorzo & Tapscott, 2002; sole practitioner Dallas, 2002—. Asst. prof. law Dallas/Ft. Worth Sch. Law, Irving, Tex., 1990-92. Dist. com. Circle 10 Boy Scouts Am., Dallas, 1985-2003; first aid team ARC, Cleve., 1972-80. Recipient Dist. Award of Merit, Boy Scouts Am., 1990, Silver Beaver award Boy Scouts Am., 1997. Mem. State Bar Tex. (chmn. trademark com. intellectual property sect. 1989). Office: Law Office of Thomas V Malorzo PO Box 59283 Dallas TX 75229-1283 Office Phone: 214-597-3247. E-mail: patents@prodigy.net.

MALOTT, ADELE RENEE, editor; b. St. Paul, July 19, 1935; d. Clarence R. and Julia Anne (Christensen) Lindgren; m. Gene E. Malott, Oct. 24, 1957 BS, Northwestern U., 1957. Coordinator news KGB Radio, San Diego, 1958-60; asst. pub. relations dir. St. Paul C. of C., 1961-63; night editor Daily Local News, West Chester, Pa., 1963-65; editor, co-pub. Boutique and Villager, Burlingame, Calif., 1966-76; sr. editor mag. The Webb Co., St. Paul, 1978-84; editor GEM Pub. Group, Reno, 1985-2001. Faculty Reader's Digest Writers' Workshops. Co-author: Get Up and Go: A Guide for the Mature Traveler, 1989, The Mature Traveler's Book of Deals, 1997; columnist The Mature Traveler, 1989—. Recipient numerous awards Soc. Am. Travel Writers, Nat. Fedn. Press Women, Calif. Newspaper Pubs. Assn., San Francisco Press Club, Calif. Taxpayers Assn., White House Citations. Mem. Internat. Assn. Bus. Communicators (Merit award 1984), Press Women Minn. (numerous awards), Press Women Nev., Soc. Am. Travel Writers (v.p. 1999, chair Western chpt. 1996-98, pres. 2002-03). Avocations: historical research, golf, travel, photography, reading. E-mail: maturetrav@aol.com.

MALOTT, FRANK STEPHEN, foreign service officer; b. Pasadena, Tex., Nov. 29, 1949; s. Frank Barhum and Mary Margaret (Williams) M.; m. Leslie Irene Hale, Jan. 14, 1984; B.S. in Bus. Adminstrn., Georgetown U., 1971; M.P.A., U. So. Calif., 1979. Asst. dean Georgetown U., Washington, 1971-73, 78-79; bus. mgr. Coll. and Univ. Personnel, Washington, 1974-77; prin. Hay Assocs., Phila., 1977-78; dir. compensation U. Alaska, Fairbanks, 1980-82; fgn. service officer Dept. State, Washington 1982—, consul, Curaçao, 1984— . Treas., Coll. Young Democratic Clubs Am., 1969-70; v.p. U.S. Youth Council, 1970-71. Mem. Georgetown U. Alumni Assn. (bd. dirs. 1978-84). Am. Fgn. Service Assn., Am. Assn. Higher Edn. Presbyterian. Home: Choncorogaiweg 2 Willemstad Curaçao Netherlands West Indies Office: Am Consul Curaçao Dept State Washington DC 20520-0001

MALOTT, JOHN RAYMOND, writer, consultant; b. Kankakee, Ill., Nov. 5, 1946; s. Raymond Roderick and Ruth Pearl (Jacobs) M.; m. Hiroko Iwami, Nov. 23, 1971; children: David Iwami, Rumi Justine. BA, Northwestern U., 1967; grad., Nat. War Coll., 1983. Civilian advisor U.S. Dept. State, Vietnam, 1969-70, China desk officer, 1970-71, am. consul Kobe, Japan, 1971-73, 1st sec. Am. Embassy Tokyo, 1974-77, Sri Lanka desk officer Washington, 1977-78, India desk officer, 1978-80; Am. consul &, Bombay, 1980-82, with Nat. War Coll. Washington, 1982-83, dep. dir. Japan Affairs, 1983-85, spl. asst. to Under Sec. State Econ. Affairs, 1985-86, Am. consul gen. Osaka, Japan, 1986-89, dir. Japan Affairs Washington, 1989-91, sr. seminar, 1991-92, dep. asst. sec. state South Asian Affairs, 1992-93; sr. advisor to Undersec. State for Econ. Affairs, Washington, 1993-95; U.S. amb. to Malaysia Dept. State, 1995-98; exec. chmn. Malott & Assocs., 1999—; pres. World Affairs/Coun. of Orange County, 2000—02; mng. dir. Manatt Jones Global Strategies, 2003—; sr. advisor Manatt, Phelps & Phillips, LLP, 2003—. Author: Partners, 1992. Recipient Vietnam Svc. award, 1970, Meritorious Honor award Dept. State, 1982, Superior honor award, 1991. Presbyterian. Home: 5911 Reservoir Heights Ave Alexandria VA 22311-1017 Office Phone: 202-463-4314. E-mail: jmalott@manatt.com.

MALOUF, WALDY, food service executive; m. Meg Malouf; children: Max, Merrill. Grad., Culinary Inst. Am., 1975. With The Four Seasons, La Côte Basque, St. Regis Hotel, La Cremaillere, Banksville, NY, Hudson River Club, The Rainbow Rm.; chef, owner Beacon Restaurant, N.Y.C. Tchr. The New Sch., Macy's DeGustibis; judge various culinary competitions; trading chef N.Y. State Dept. Econ. Devel., N.Y. Wine and Grape Found.; guest chef numerous host countries; active James Beard Found.; regional chef-cons. N.W./KLM Airlines; bd. dirs. Culinary Inst. Am. Alumni Assn. Author: (books) The Hudson River Valley Cookbook: A Leading American Chef Savors the Region's Bounty, 1995 (One of Yr.'s Ten Best, N.Y. Times), Magnificent Meats, 2000; featured House Beautiful, Met. Home, N.Y. mag., Ladies' Home Jour., Food and Wine, Paper, numerous Japanese mags. and guide books, appeared Time Out New Morning, CNN, The Food Network, CBS Latin Am., CBS Saturday Morning, Brazilian TV, N.Y. 1 News. Active Share Our Strength, God's Love We Deliver, Culinary Inst. Am., City

Meals-on-Wheels, Green Chimneys; pres. bd. dirs. Ballet Sch. Stamford, Conn. Named Great Chef N.Y., James Beard Found.; recipient 1st prize, 3rd Ann. Cointreau Recipe Contest, 1992, Golden Ann. Gala honors, Culinary Inst. Am., 1996. Mem.: Am. Inst. Wine and Food (co-chair ann. marketplace tasting, bd. dirs. N.Y. chpt.). Office: Beacon Restaurant 25 West 56th St New York NY 10019 Office Phone: 212-332-0500. E-mail: waldyny@aol.com.

MALOUFF, FRANK JOSEPH, health care association executive; s. Phillip Francis and Lillian Aileen Malouff; m. Virginia Lynn Frye, Aug. 24, 1968; children: Lynnea, Joseph, J. Daniel, David. BS in Journalism, U. Colo., Boulder, 1969; MS in Health Adminstrn., U. Colo., Denver, 1974; LLD (hon.), Ohio Coll. Podiatric Medicine, 1988. Program adminstr. U. Colo. Health Scis. Ctr., Denver, 1974-83; exec. dir. Ohio Podiatric Med. Assn., Columbus, 1983-89, Am. Podiatric Med. Assn., Bethesda, Md., 1989-98, Am. Soc. Therapeutic Radiology and Oncology, Fairfax, Va., 1998—2002; prin. JVF Mgmt., Chantilly, Va., 2002—. Dir. Fund for Podiatric Med. Edn., Bethesda, 1986-98, Foothealth Found. Am., Bethesda, 1991-98. Contbg. author: Handbook of Healthcare Human Resources Management, 1981; co-author: Pursuing Mastery: Professional Development Tools and Techniques, 1991; columnist in field. Leader Boy Scouts Am., various locations. 1st lt. U.S. Army, 1969-72, Korea. Mem. Am. Soc. Healthcare Edn. and Tng. (officer 1977-81, Disting. Svc. award 1982, past dir.), Am. Soc. Assn. Execs., Area 26 Coun., Spl. Olympics Va. Roman Catholic. Avocation: lay church ministry. Office: JVF Mgmt PO Box 2234 Centreville VA 20122

MALOUIN, JEAN-LOUIS, university educator; b. Three-Rivers, Que., Can., Oct. 5, 1943; m. Hélène Pépin; children: Pascale, Philippe. B in Commerce, Université Laval, Que., 1965, MSc, 1966; PhD, UCLA, 1970. Prof. Bus. Sch., U. Laval, 1966-89, dir. OSD dept., 1971-75, 78-79, assoc. dean acad. affairs, 1979-84, dean, 1984-89; dean faculty of bus. U. Alta., Edmonton, Alta., Can., 1989-92; dean faculty of adminstrn. U. Ottawa, Ottawa, Ont., Can., 1992-2000. Coord. Can. Consortium for the Support of the Sea PhD program; bd. dirs. Corel Corp., 1997—2003, Acerra Corp. Editor: The Generation of Scientific Administrative Knowledge, 1986; co-author: L'Innovation Technologique dans les PME Manufacturières: études de cas enquête, 1992. Bd. dirs. Centre québécois de Productivité, du Vêtement, Montréal, 1983-86, Nat. Rsch. Ctr., London, 1986-87, Banff Sch. Advancement Mgmt., 1989-92. Mem. Can. Fedn. Deans (v.p. 1987), Edmonton C. of C. (bd. dirs. 1989-92). Home: 1410 Clay Ct Gloucester ON Canada K1C 4T2 E-mail: malouin@uottawa.ca.

MALOY, FRANCES, librarian; MLS, SUNY Albany. Leader of the access services divsn. Emory U. Gen. Libraries, 1992—; v.p. Assoc. Rsch. and Coll. Libraries, 2003—; dir., pub. services Hamilton Coll. Mem. bd. dirs. ACRL; chmn. ACRL Nominations Com. and ACRL Com. on Ethics. Office: 50 East Huron St Chicago IL 60611

MALOY, STUART, materials scientist, engineer; BS, Case Western Res. U., 1989, MS, 1991, PhD, 1994. Postdoc. fellow Los Alamos (N.Mex.) Nat. Lab., 1994—95, mem. tech. staff, 1995—. Contbr. more than 70 articles to profl. jours. Office: Los Alamos Nat Lab MST-8 MS H816 PO Box 1663 Los Alamos NM 87545

MALPHURS, ROGER EDWARD, biomedical marketing executive; b. Lake Worth, Fla., Dec. 15, 1933; s. Cecil Edward and Muriel Thelma (Ward) M.; m. Carolyn Sue Calapp, Feb. 2, 1963(div. 1993); children: Steven, Brian, Darren, Regina, Victoria. BS, U. Utah, 1961; D of Chiropractic, Palmer Coll. Chiropractic West, 1990. Cert. med. technologist; lic. chiropractor, Calif., Ariz. Supr. spl. chemistry Cen. Pathology Lab., Santa Rosa, Calif., 1968-73; mgr. lab. Cmty. Hosp., Santa Rosa, 1973-76; supr. chem., staff asst. Meml. Hosp., Santa Rosa, 1976-85; pres., CEO R.E. Malphurs Co., Sunnyvale, Calif., 1972—. Owner, developer REMCO Mktg. Assocs., Santa Rosa, 1970—71; pvt. commodity trader, 1974—; owner Better Bus. Forms and Typeset, Santa Rosa, Calif., 1977—81; commodity pool operator, 1979—81; dept. mgr. immunochemistry Spectra Labs, Fremont, Calif., 1990—95; clin. trials cons. hematology, tech. writer Abbott Diagnostics, Santa Clara, Calif., 1995—2000; tech. writer Healtheon/WebMD, Santa Clara, Calif., 2000—01; tech. writer, project mgr. Hewlett-Packard, Roseville, Calif., 2000—04. Author: A New, Simple Way to Win at Blackjack, 1972. Served as squadron commdr. CAP USAF Aux., 1982-84. Mem. APHA, Am. Chiropractic Assn., Calif. Chiropractic Assn., Optimists Internat. (youth awards chmn. 1969-74), Toastmasters (sec./treas. 1988-89), Rep. Senatorial Inner Circle. Republican. Avocations: flying, computers, pistol shooting, painting, writing.

MALSACK, JAMES THOMAS, retired manufacturing company executive; b. Milw., Apr. 4, 1921; s. Leonard Henry and Florence Alice (Webb) M.; widowed; children: Thomas James, Claudia Irene, Robert Richard, Thomas John, Pamela Joyce. BSBA, Marquette U., 1946; D Pub. Svc. (hon.), No. Mich. U., 1990. Acct. Price Waterhouse & Co., Milw., 1946-51; with Lake Shore, Inc., Iron Mountain, Mich., 1951-88, exec. v.p., 1959-72, pres., chief exec. officer, 1972-84, chmn., 1984-88. Bd. control No. Mich. U., trustee emeritus. With USN, 1942-45. Mem. Masons, Shriners. Republican. Episcopalian.

MALT, RONALD BRADFORD, lawyer; b. Boston, Aug. 1, 1954; s. Ronald A. and Geraldine (Sutton) M.; m. Sharon Lynn Harford, Feb. 14, 1981; 2 children. AB, Harvard U., 1976, JD, 1979. Bar: Mass. 1979. Assoc. Ropes & Gray, Boston, 1979-86, ptnr., 1987—, chmn. policy com., 2004—; dir. Fenway Ptnrs., Inc., N.Y.C., 1999—. Asst. treas. Butler Capital Corp., N.Y.C., 1983—; sec. to adv. bd. Mezzanine Lending Assocs., N.Y.C., 1983—. Mem. corp. Mass. Gen. Hosp., Boston, 1989—; trustee Butler Found., 1989—, Butler Fund for the Environment, 2004—, Black River Environ. Improvement Assn., Inc., 1991—. Republican. Episcopalian. Office: Ropes & Gray One International Pl Boston MA 02110 Office Phone: 617-951-7318. E-mail: bmalt@ropesgray.com.

MALTBY, FLORENCE HELEN, library science educator; b. Sumner, Iowa, Mar. 2, 1933; d. Harold George and Blanche Theresa (Gritzner) Garland; m. George Robert Maltby, June 3, 1964 (dec. Oct. 1985); 1 child, Patricia Garland Maltby Clark. BA, U. No. Iowa, Cedar Falls, 1954; MS in Libr. Sci., U. Ill., 1960, cert. advanced study librarianship, 1967. Cert. literary braille transcriber. Elem. sch. libr. Barrington (Ill.) Pub. Sch., 1954-57, USAF Dependent Sch. Europe, Sculthorpe, Eng., 1957-58, Ramstein, Fed. Republic of Germany, 1958-59, Wiesbaden, Fed. Republic of Germany, 1960-61; grad. asst. U. Ill., Champaign, 1959-60; reference asst., instr. Libr. Cen. Mich. U., Mt. Pleasant, 1961-63; asst. prof. libr. sci. Southwest Mo. State U., Springfield, 1963-66, 67-80, assoc. prof. libr. sci., 1980-97; instr. libr. sci. U. Ill., Champaign, 1966-67; archivist Diocese of Springfield-Cape Girardeau, 2001—. Evaluator North Cen. Assn., Springfield, 1989, Dept. Elem. and Secondary Edn., Mo. Sch. Improvement, 1989; com. mem. Children's Lit. Festival, Springfield, 1990, treas., 1991. Contbr. to Masterplots II: Juvenile and Young Adult Fiction, 1991, 97. Mem. AAUP, ALA, Assn. Libr. and Info. Sci. Edn., Mo. Assn. Sch. Librs. (mem. standards rev. com. for state sch. libr. media standards 1994), Assn. Cath. Diocesan Archivists, Beta Phi Mu, Alpha Beta Alpha, Kappa Delta Pi. Roman Catholic. Avocations: reading, playing organ and piano.

MALTER, JAMES SAMUEL, pathologist, educator; b. Tooele, Utah, May 18, 1956; s. Robert Henry Malter and Evvajean (Harris) Mintz; m. Elaine Gadzicki, May 26, 1988. AB, Dartmouth Coll., 1979; MD, Washington U., 1983. Diplomate Am. Bd. Clin. Pathology. Resident in pathology U. Pa., Phila., 1983-88, chief resident, 1987-88; asst. prof. pathology Tulane U., New Orleans, 1988-91; dir. exptl. pathology Tulane Med. Ctr., New Orleans, 1988-91, dir. Blood Ctr., 1989-91; asst. prof. pathology Sch. Medicine U. Wis., Madison, 1991-97; med. dir. Blood Bank U. Wis. Hosp. & Clinic, Madison, 1991—; prof. pathology Sch. Medicine U. Wis., Madison, 1997—. Mem. editl. bd. Hepatology jour., 1991—. Recipient Nat. Rsch. Svc. award NIH, 1986-88, Clin. Investigator award NCI-NIH, 1988-91, Ind. Investigator award NIH, 1991—. Mem. Am. Assn. Blood Banks, Am. Assn. Pathologists, Am. Coll. Pathologists (diplomate). Office: U Wis Hosp & Clinic Dept of Pathology 600 Highland Ave # B4 263 Madison WI 53792-0001

MALTESE, SERPHIN RALPH, state legislator, lawyer; b. N.Y.C., Dec. 7, 1932; s. Paul and Frances (Scafidi) Maltese; m. Constance Mary Del Vecchio, Aug. 27, 1955; children: Andrea Constance, Leslie Serphine, Serphin Ralph(dec.). BA, Manhattan Coll., 1958; LL.B., JD (War Service scholar 1958-62), Fordham U., 1962. Bar: N.Y. 1963. Trial atty. for ins. cos., 1963-66; asst. dist. atty., dep. chief homicide bur. Queens County, N.Y., 1966-69; asso. counsel N.Y. State Com. Campus Disorders, 1969-70; counsel N.Y. State Com. Deaf and Multiple Impaired, 1970; chmn. law com. Buckley for U.S. Senator, 1970; counsel N.Y. State Assembly, 1972-76, N.Y. State Senate, Albany, 1976-88, state senator, 1988—, chmn. senate standing com. on cities, mem. com. on civil svc. and pensions, codes, elections, fin., judiciary, higher edn., investigations and govt. ops. com. Past pres. N.Y. Conf. Italian Am. Legislators. Chmn. bd. trustees Christ the King Regional HS, 1976—; mem. exec. bd. Stuyvesant HS Alumni; exec. dir. N.Y. State Conservative Party, 1971—86, exec. vice chmn., 1978—86, state chmn., 1986—88; N.Y. state chmn. Conservatives for Ronald Reagan, 1980; chmn. Queens (N.Y.) Reps. With U.S. Army, 1952—54, Korea. Named Man of the Yr., Commn. Social Justice, 1998; recipient Charles Edison Meml. award, N.Y. State Conservative Party, 1977, Pres.'s medal, St. John's U., 1994, Pres.'s award, LaGuardia CC, 1998. Mem.: VFW, Queens Asst. Dist. Attys. Assn., N.Y. State Bar Assn., Italian Am. Profl. Bus. Assn. (hon. chmn.), Queens C. of C., Young Ams. for Freedom (nat. sr. adv. bd.), Christopher Columbus Assn. (chmn. 1970—), Am. Conservative Union (nat. bd. dirs.), Harold Gray Collectors Soc. (pres.), Internat. Assn. Space Philatelists, Am. Legion, Cath. War Vets., Alpha Phi Delta. Roman Catholic. Office: 71-04 Myrtle Ave Glendale NY 11385-7254 also: 413 Capitol Albany NY 12247 Office Phone: 518-455-3281. Business E-Mail: maltese@senate.state.ny.us.

MALTIN, LEONARD, television commentator, writer; b. N.Y.C., Dec. 18, 1950; s. Aaron Isaac and Jacqueline (Gould) M.; m. Alice Tlusty, Mar. 15, 1975; 1 child, Jessica Bennett. BA, NYU, 1972. Mem. faculty New Sch. for Social Rsch., N.Y.C., 1973-81; curator Am. Acad. Humor, N.Y.C., 1975-76; guest curator dept. film Mus. Modern Art, N.Y.C., 1976; film critic and corr. Entertainment Tonight, Hollywood, Calif., 1982—; columnist Modern Maturity, 1996-99; film critic Playboy mag., 1998—. Adj. prof. Sch. Cinema & TV, U. So. Calif., 1998—. Author: Movie Comedy Teams, 1970, rev. edit., 1985, Behind the Camera (reprinted as The Art of the Cinematographer), 1971, The Great Movie Shorts (reprinted as Selected Short Subjects), 1971, The Disney Films, 1973, rev. edit., 2000, The Great Movie Comedians, 1978, Of Mice and Magic: A History of American Animated Cartoons, 1980, rev. edit., 1987, The Great American Broadcast, 1997; co-author: Our Gang: The Life and Times of the Little Rascals, 1977, reprinted as The Little Rascals: The Life and Times of Our Gang, 1992; editor: Leonard Maltin's Movie & Video Guide, 1969, rev. annually, Leonard Maltin's Movie Encyclopedia, 1994, Leonard Maltin's Family Film Guide, 1999; producer, writer, host (video) Cartoons for Big Kids, 1989; writer (TV spl.) Fantasia: The Making of a Disney Classic, 1990; writer, host (video) The Making of The Quiet Man, 1992, The Making of High Noon, 1992, Cartoon Madness: The Fantastic Max Fleischer Cartoons, 1993, Cliffhanger!, 1993; co-host Hot Ticket, 2001—. Mem. steering com. Hollywood Entertainment Mus., 1989—. Mem. Authors Guild, Soc. for Cinephiles (pres. 1990-91, Man of Yr. 1973), L.A. Film Critics Assn. (pres. 1995-96). Office: c/o Entertainment Tonight Paramount TV 5555 Melrose Ave Los Angeles CA 90038-3112

MALTSEV, NIKOLAI ELYSEEVICH, research scientist; s. Elysey Dmitrievich Maltsev and Natalia Fedorovna Maltseva; m. Vera Vasilievna Dementieva, Apr. 30, 1968; 1 child, Marina Maltseva. DSc, Inst. Acoustics, Moscow, Russia, 1985; degree in Engring. Physics-Acoustics, Moscow Inst. Physics & Tech., 1968. Rsch. scientist Inst. of Acoustics, Moscow, Russia, 1968—88; head of dept. Pacific Oceanog. Inst., Vladivostok, Russia, 1988—90. Sr. tech. staff Superconductor Technologies, Santa Barbara, Calif., 2001—. Contbr. articles to profl. jours. Recipient Can. award for Bus. Excellence, Govt. of Can., 1994. Mem.: IEEE, Acoustical Soc. Am. Achievements include patents for algorithm for automatic filter tuning. Business E-Mail: nmaltsev@suptech.com. E-mail: nmaltsev@sv.suptech.com.

MALTZ, ROBERT, surgeon; b. Cin., July 21, 1935; s. William and Sarah (Goldberg) M.; m. Sylvia Moskowitz, Aug 24, 1958; children: Mark Edward, Deborah Lynn, Steven Alan, David Stuart. BS in Zoology, U. Cin., 1958, MD, 1962. Diplomate Am. Bd. Otolaryngology. Intern Cin. Gen. Hosp., 1962-63; resident Barnes Hosp., St. Louis, 1965-69; asst. prof. surgery Stanford U. Med. Ctr., Palo Alto, Calif., 1969-71; asst. prof. otolaryngology U. Cin. Med. Ctr., 1971-75, assoc. prof. otolaryngology, 1975—; dir. dept. otolaryngology Jewish Hosp., Cin., 1992—. Chief, divsn. head and neck surgery, dept. otolaryngology and maxillofacial surgery U. Cin. Med. Ctr., 1972-76; bd. dirs. Cancer Control Council, U. Cin. Med. Cntr.; cons. Bur. Crippled Children's Svcs., State of Ohio; on staff Univ. Hosp., Cin., Jewish Hosp., Cin., Children's Hosp. Med. Ctr., Bethesda Hosp., Cin., Christ Hosp., Our Lady of Mercy Hosp.; del. to numerous profl. confs.; mem. health affairs adv. com. Cmty. Mut. Ins. Co.; mem. mng. bd. PIE Mut. Ins. Co.; bd. dirs. UCATS, 1995-98; trustee Health Found. Greater Cin., 1997—, vice-chmn., 2000-01, chmn. 2001-03, chmn. program com., 2000-01; instr. short term courses in field; pres.-elect alumni exec. coun. U. Cin. Coll. Medicine, 1998-2000, pres., 2000-2002. Contbr. articles to profl. jours. Bd. dirs. Jewish Cmty. Rels. Coun.; bd. trustees Cin. Art Acad., 1998—; faculty adv. com. U. Cin.; trustee Health Found. Fund, 2002-, vice-chmn., 2002-03, chmn., 2003—. Capt. USAF, 1963-65, PTO. USPHS fellow, 1968-69; Eli Lilly Co. grantee, 1971-76, Burroughs Wellcome Co., 1972. Fellow ACS, Am. Acad. Facial and Reconstructive Surgery (edn. com. 1972, future plans com. 1973-75, sci. program com., budget and fin. com. 1975, chmn. credentials com., no. sect. 1980-85), Royal Soc. Health, Internat. Cosmetic Surgeons, Am. Acad. Cosmetic Surgeons, Am. Assn. Cosmetic Surgeons (sec.-treas. 1976-81); mem. Am. Acad. Otolaryngology and Head and Neck Surgery, Am. Coun. Otolaryngology, Soc. Univ. Otolaryngologists, Pan-Am. Assn. Oto-Rhino-Laryngology and Broncho-Esophagology, Ohio State Med. Assn., Cin. Acad. Medicine (trustee 1992-95, treas. 1993-95, pres. 1996-97, chmn. pub. rels. com. 1980, chmn. comm. com. 1994-96, chmn. sply. soc. com. 1995, legis. com. 1985, editl. bd. 1994-96, jud. com. 1995—2004, chmn. managed care med. dirs. com. 1997-2002), U. Cin. Alumni Assn. (bd. govs., sec. 1994, fin. v.p. 1995, 1st v.p. 1996, pres. 1997-98), Acad. Medicine Found. (bd. dirs., v.p., pres. 2002—2004), Cin. Ear, Nose and Throat Soc., Losantiville Country Club (bd. govs. 1996-2002, pres. 1999-2001), Omicron Delta Kappa, Sigma Sigma, Sigma Alpha Mu. Avocations: tennis, golf, travel. Home: 2601 Willowbrook Dr Cincinnati OH 45237-3725 Office: 10496 Montgomery Rd Cincinnati OH 45242-5223 Office Phone: 513-984-1190. E-mail: maltz@cinci.rr.com.

MALTZAN, MICHAEL THOMAS, architect; b. Roslyn Heights, N.Y., Oct. 10, 1959; s. William George and Jacqueline (Cain) M.; m. Amy Louise Murphy, Sept. 25, 1988. Student, Wentworth Inst. Tech., 1977-79; BFA, RISD, 1984, BArch, 1985; MArch with letter of distinction, Harvard U., 1988. Lic. architect, Calif. Architect The Architects, Glastonbury, Conn., 1978-80, Williamd D. Warner Assocs., Exeter, R.I., 1980-83, Steven Lerner Assocs., Providence, 1983-84, Schwartz/Silver Assocs., Boston, 1984-86, Machado-Silvetti Assocs., Boston, 1986-88, Frank O. Gehry Assocs., L.A., 1988-95; pvt. practice architecture L.A., 1995—. Prof. RISD, Providence, 1987, Harvard U., Cambridge, Mass., 1988; co-instr. UCLA, 1989, U. Waterloo, 1993, RISD, 1995, Harvard U., 1999, USC, 2002; vis. prof. GSD, 2003; invited jury critic Harvard U., RISD, Ariz. State U., Tempe, Calif. Coll. Arts and Crafts, San Francisco, U. So. Calif., L.A., UCLA, Iowa State U., Ames, Miami (Ohio) U. Prin. works include Inner-City Arts, L.A., 1994 (PA award), Getty Digital Lab., 1997, Feldman-Horn Ctr. Arts, 1997 (AIA award), Hergott-Shepard Residence, 1998 (AIA awards), Kidspace Mus., Pasadena, Calif., 1998 (PA award), UCLA Hammer Mus., 1999, MOMA ONS, 2002 (AIA awards), World Trade Ctr. Team, 2002, Fresno (Calif.) Met. Mus., 2002 (AIA award), Giardini Di Porta Nuova, Milan, Italy, 2004, Vancouver (Can.) Art Gallery, 2004. Recipient Collegiate Gold medal AIA, Young Archs. award. Office: 2801 Hyperion Ave # 107 Los Angeles CA 90027-2571 Office Phone: 323-913-3098.

MALTZMAN, IRVING MYRON, psychology educator; b. Bklyn., May 9, 1924; s. Israel and Lillian (Mass) M.; m. Diane Seiden, Aug. 21, 1949; children— Sara, Kenneth, Ilaine. BA, NYU, 1946; PhD, State U. Iowa, 1949. Mem. faculty UCLA, 1949—, assoc. prof., 1957—60, prof. psychology, 1961—94, chmn. dept., 1970—77, prof. emeritus, 1994—. Co-author: Handbook of Contemporary Soviet Psychology, 1969, Alcoholism: A Review of it Characteristics, Etiology, Treatments, and Controversies, 2000. Fellow: APA, AAAS; mem.: Psychonomic Soc., APS, Phi Beta Kappa, Sigma Xi. Home: 11260-22B Overland Ave Culver City CA 90230-5559 Office Phone: 310-825-2909.

MALVEAUX, FLOYD JOSEPH, dean; BS, Creighton U., 1961; MS, Loyola U.; PhD in Microbiology and Pub. Health, Mich. State U., 1968; MD, Howard U., 1974; postgrad., Washington Hosp. Ctr., 1974—76, Johns Hopkins U., 1976—78. Asst. prof. microbiology Howard U. Med. Sch., Washington, 1968—70, chmn. microbiology, assoc. prof. microbiology and medicine, 1989—94, dean, v.p. health affairs, prof. microbiology and medicine, 1995—; mem. faculty Johns Hopkins U., Balt., 1984—89. Founder, pres. Urban Asthma and Allergy Ctr., Balt., 1986—89; mem. numerous med. panels; lectr. in field. Contbr. articles to profl. jours. Recipient Nat. Rsch. Svc. award, NIH, Clemens von Pirquet Rsch. award, Georgetown U. Sch. Medicine, 1991; grantee, Nat. Inst. Allergy and Infectious Diseases, Nat. Heart, Lung and Blood Inst. of NIH, Hasbro Children's Found., Robert Wood Johnson Found.; Vivian B. Allen Found. fellow. Mem.: NAACP (life), Kappa Alpha Psi, Sigma Pi Phi, Sigma Xi, Alpha Omega Alpha. Office: Howard U Med Sch 520 W St NW Washington DC 20059-0001

MALVERN, DONALD, retired aircraft manufacturing company executive; b. Sterling, Okla., Apr. 22, 1921; s. George Michael and Anna Francesca (Elsass) M.; m. Ruth Marie Vogler, June 4, 1949; 1 son, Michael John. BSME, U. Okla., 1946. Engr. Victory Architects and Engrs., Clinton, Okla., 1943, Douglas Aircraft Co., Santa Monica, Calif., 1943; with McDonnell Aircraft Co., St. Louis, 1946-88, exec. v.p., 1973-82, pres., 1982-86; v.p. McDonnell Douglas Corp., 1973-88; aerospace cons. St. Louis, 1988—; pres. McDonnell Douglas Services, Inc., 1978-82. Trustee Falcon Found., 1983—; bd. visitors Def. Sys. Mgmt. Coll., 1983-86, U. Okla. Coll. Engring., 1988-91; pres. Wings of Hope, 1989-92, chmn., 1992-2004, dir. emeritus, 2004—. 1st lt. USAAF, 1943-46; capt. Mo. Air NG, 1946-51. Inducted into Okla. Aviation and Space Mus.'s Hall of Fame, 1987; recipient Disting. Alumni award U. Okla., 1999, Unsung Hero award United Way of St. Louis, 2000. Fellow AIAA (Tech. Mgmt. award 1968, Reed Aeros. medal 1980); mem. Am. Def. Preparedness Assn. (pres. St. Louis chpt. 1979-80), Navy League U.S. (life), Nat. Aeros. Assn., Air Force Assn., Armed Forces Mgmt. Assn., Pi Tau Sigma, Tau Beta Pi, Tau Omega, Sigma Tau Beta. Clubs: Bellerive Country, St. Louis. Home: 213 Grand Banks Ct Chesterfield MO 63017-9507

MALY, KURT JOHN, computer science educator; b. Modling, Austria, Aug. 20, 1944; came to U.S., 1969; s. Anton and Editha (Gneist) M.; m. Christiana Peterlik, Mar. 18, 1972; 1 child, Angela Claudia. Diplom Ingenieur summa cum laude, U. Tech., Austria, 1968; MS, Courant Inst. NYU, 1970, PhD, 1973. Asst. prof. U. Minn., Mpls., 1972-78, assoc. prof., 1978-85, acting head, 1980-82, head, 1982-85; eminent prof., chmn. computer sci. Old Dominion U., Norfolk, Va., 1985—, Kaufman prof., 1991—. Hon. prof. Chengdu U. of Sci. and Tech., People's Republic of China, 1986—, Hefei U., People's Republic of China, 1991—, Guangxi Computer Inst., People's Republic of China, 1993—; bd. dirs. Inst. of Info. Tech., Ctr. for Innovative Tech., Blacksburg, Va., 1988-92; bd. dirs., exec. co-dir. Microelectronic and Info. Scis. Ctr., Mpls., 1980-85. Author: Fundamentals of the Computing Sciences, 1978; assoc. editor: Jour. for Microcomputer Application Tech., PRC; contbr. articles to profl. jours. Served with Austrian Air Force, 1963-64. Fellow Sorbonne U., Paris, 1966, Courant Inst., N.Y.C., 1968-72. Mem. Assn. Computing Machinery, IEEE, Sigma Xi. Roman Catholic. Office: Old Dominion U Norfolk VA 23529 Office Phone: 757-683-4817. E-mail: maly@cs.odu.edu.

MAMAT, FRANK TRUSTICK, lawyer; b. Syracuse, N.Y., Sept. 4, 1949; s. Harvey Sanford and Annette (Trustick) M.; m. Kathy Lou Winters, June 23, 1975; children: Jonathan Adam, Steven Kenneth. BA, U. Rochester, 1971; JD, Syracuse U., 1974. Bar: D.C. 1976, U.S. Ct. Appeals (D.C. cir.) 1976, Fla. 1977, U.S. Supreme Ct. 1979, U.S. Dist. Ct. (ea. dist.) 1983, U.S. Ct. Appeals (6th cir.) 1983, Mich. 1984, U.S. Dist. Ct. (no. dist.) Ind. 1984. Atty. NLRB, Washington, 1975—79; assoc. Proskauer, Rose, Goetz & Mendelsohn, Washington, N.Y.C. and L.A., 1979—83, Fishman Group, Bloomfield Hills, Mich., 1983—85, ptnr., 1985—87; sr. ptnr. Honigman, Miller, Schwartz and Cohn, 1987—94; pres., CEO Morgan Daniels Co., Inc., West Bloomfield, Mich., 1994—; ptnr. Clark Klein & Beaumont, P.L.C., Detroit, 1995—96, Clark Hill, P.L.C., Detroit, 1996—2003, mem. exec. com., 1999—2001; ptnr. Dickinson Wright PLLC, 2003—. Bd. dirs. Mich. Food and Beverage Assn., Air Conditioning Contractors of Am., Air Conditioning Contractors of Mich., Am. Subcontractors Assn., Mich. Mfrs. Assn. Labor Counsel, Jewish Vocat. Svcs., Constrn. Fin. Mgmt. Assn., Mich. Assn. Home Bldg. Gen. counsel Rep. Com. of Oakland County, 1986—; chmn. Constrn. Code Commn. Mich., 1993—; bd. dirs. 300 Club, Mich., 1984-90; pres. 400 Club, 1990-93, chmn., 1993—, chmn. bd., Am. Soc. of Employers, 2003-; mem. Associated Gen. Contractors Labor Lawyers Coun.; mem. Rep. Nat. Com. Nat. Rep. Senatorial Com., Presdl. Task Force, Rep. Labor Coun., Washington; city dir. West Bloomfield, 1985-87; pres. West Bloomfield Rep. CLub, 1985-87; fin. com. Rep. Com. of Oakland County, 1984-93; pres. Oakland County Lincoln Rep. Club, 1989-90; bd. dirs. camping svcs. and human resources com. YMCA, 1989-93, Anti-Defamation League, 1989—; vice chmn. Lawyers for Reagan-Bush, 1984; v.p. Fruehauf Farms, West Bloomfield, Mich., 1985-88; mem. staff Exec. Office of Pres. of U.S. Inquiries/Comments, Washington, 1981-83. Fellow Coll. Labor and Employment Attys.; mem. ABA, FBA, Mich. Bar Assn., Fla. Bar Assn. (labor com. 1977—), Rep. Nat. Lawyers Assn., Mich. Bus. and Profl. Assn., Am. Acad. Constrn. and Labor Attys. (exec. dir. 1998—), Am. Subcontractors Assn. (Southeastern Mich., bd. dirs.), Founders Soc. Detroit Bar Assn., Oakland County Bar Assn., B'nai B'rith (v.p. 1982-83, trustee 1987-88, bd. dirs. Detroit Barristers unit 1983-91, pres. 1985-87), Am. Soc. Employers (chmn. 2003—), Oakpointe Country Club, Detroit Soc. Clubs, Skyline Club, Fairlane Club, Detroit Athletic Club, Renaissance Club, Econ. Club Detroit. Office: Dickinson Wright PLLC 500 Woodward Ave Ste 4000 Detroit MI 48226 also: Morgan Daniels Co Inc 5484 Crispin Way Rd West Bloomfield MI 48323-3402 Office Phone: 313-223-3169. E-mail: fmamat@aol.com., fmamat@dickinsonwright.com.

MAMATEY, VICTOR SAMUEL, history educator; b. North Braddock, Pa., Feb. 19, 1917; s. Albert Paul and Olga (Darmek) M.; m. Denise M. Perrone, Nov. 20, 1945; children: Albert R., Peter V. Student, Wittenberg Coll., 1938-39, U. Chgo., 1939-40; AM, Harvard U., 1941; PhD, U. Paris, 1949. Asst. prof. history Fla. State U., Tallahassee, 1949-55, assoc. prof., 1955-58, prof., 1958-67, chmn. dept. history, 1964-67; rsch. prof. hist. U. Ga., Athens, 1967-82, acting dean Coll. Arts and Scis., 1972-73. Vis. prof. Columbia U., 1961, Tulane U., 1963. Author: The United States and East Central Europe, 1914-18, 1957, Soviet RussianImperialism, 1964, (with Geoffrey Brunn) The World in the Twentieth Century, 1967, The Rise of the Hapsburg Empire, 1526-1815, 1971, (with Radomir Luza) History of the Czechoslovak Republic, 1918-1948, 1973. With U.S. Army, 1942-46. Guggenheim fellow, 1959. Mem. Am. Hist. Assn. (George Louis Beer prize for best book on internat. history 1958), Am. Assn. For Advancement Slavic Studies. Home: 142 Spruce Valley Rd Athens GA 30605-3332

MAMAYEK, TELLY, radio personality; married; children: Emily, Nathan. BA Journalism, U. Wis., 1985. With Stas. WBIZ/WJJK Radio, Eau Claire, Wis., Stas. KZIO/WDSM Radio, Duluth, Minn., Sta. WNIU Pub. Radio, DeKalb, Ill., Sta. WCKY Radio, Cin., Sta. WCCO Radio, Mpls., 1991—, morning news editor, anchor. Mem.: Minn. AP Broadcast Bd., Minn. Chpt. Profl. Journalists (pres.). Avocation: bicycling. Office: WCCO 625 2nd Ave S Minneapolis MN 55402

MAMER, JAMES MICHAEL, secondary school educator; b. L.A., Oct. 8, 1948; s. James Robert and Annette (Babue) M.; m. Jessica Puma, Aug. 31, 1963. BA in Polit. Sci., Calif. Poly. U., Pomona, 1970; MA in Internat.

Studies, Immaculate Heart Coll., 1990. Tchr. Irvine (Calif.) Unified Sch. Dist., 1978—. Mentor tchr. Irvine Sch. Dist., 1988-95. Mem. editl. bd. Global Pages, L.A., 1991-96. Recipient Global Teaching award Western Internat. Studies Consortium, L.A., 1991, Am. Coun. Internat. Edn. award, 1998; Fulbright-Hays grantee, India, 1977; Coe fellow, 1984. Mem. Nat. Coun. Social Studies (Nat. Social Studies Tchr. of Yr. 1992), Irvine Tchrs. Assn. Democrat. Avocation: reading. Home: 29102 Kommers Ln Silverado CA 92676-9726

MAMER, JOHN WILLIAM, business educator; b. July 4, 1954; BA, BS, U. Calif., Davis, 1975; MS, U. Calif., Berkeley, 1978, PhD, 1982. Analyst Manalytics Inc., 1977-78; rsch. intern Xerox Corp., 1979-80; from asst. prof. to prof. U. Calif., L.A., 1981-96, prof., 1996—. Lectr. in field. Referee Mgmt. Sci., 1982—, Ops. Rsch., 1984—, Jour. Econ. Dynamics and Control, 1984, 88; contbr. over 15 articles to profl. jours. Mem. Inst. Mgmt. Sci. (organizing chmn. 1994, arangements chmn. 1995), Ops. Rsch. Soc. Am. Office: The Anderson School UCLA PO Box 951481 Los Angeles CA 90095-1481

MAMER, STUART MIES, lawyer; b. East Hardin, Ill., Feb. 23, 1921; s. Louis H. and Anna (Mies) M.; m. Donna E. Jordan, Sept. 10, 1944; children: Richard A., John S., Bruce J. AB, U. Ill., 1942, JD, 1947. Bar: Ill. bar 1947. Assoc. Thomas & Mulliken, Champaign, 1947-55; partner firm Thomas, Mamer & Haughey, Champaign, 1955—. Lectr. U. Ill. Coll. Law, Urbana, 1965-85; Mem. Atty. Registration and Disciplinary Commn. Ill., 1976-82 Chmn. fund drive Champaign County Community Chest, 1955; 1st pres. Champaign County United Fund, 1957; Pres., dir. U. Ill. McKinley Found., Champaign, 1957-69; trustee Children's Home and Aid Soc. of Ill., v.p., 1977-96. Served as pilot USAAF, 1943-45. Mem. Am. Coll. Trust and Estate Counsel (bd. regents 1984-90), Phi Beta Kappa, Phi Gamma Delta. Republican. Presbyterian. Home: 101 W Windsor Rd # 3105 Urbana IL 61802-6663 Office: Thomas Mamer & Haughey 30 E Main St Fl 5 Champaign IL 61820-3629 E-mail: smamer@tmh-law.com.

MAMET, DAVID ALAN, playwright, director, essayist; b. Chgo., Nov. 30, 1947; s. Bernard Morris and Lenore June (Silver) Mamet; m. Lindsay Crouse, Dec. 1977 (div.); m. Rebecca Pidgeon, Sept. 22, 1991. BA, Goddard Coll., Plainfield, Vt., 1969; DLitt (hon.), Dartmouth Coll., 1996. Artist-in-residence Goddard Coll., 1971-73; artistic dir. St. Nicholas Theatre Co., Chgo., 1973-75; guest lectr. U. Chgo., 1975, 79, NYU, 1981; assoc. artistic dir. Goodman Theater, Chgo., 1978; assoc. prof. film Columbia U., 1988. Chmn. bd. Atlantic Theater Co. Author: (plays) The Duck Variations, 1971, Sexual Perversity in Chicago, 1973 (Village Voice Obie award, N.Y. Drama Critics Cir. award), Reunion, 1973, Squirrels, 1974, American Buffalo, 1976, A Life in the Theatre, 1976, The Water Engine, 1976, The Woods, 1977, Lone Canoe, 1978, Prairie du Chien, 1978, Lakeboat, 1980, Donny March, 1981, Edmond, 1982 (Village Voice Obie award, 1983), The Disappearance of the Jews, 1983, The Shawl, 1985, Glengarry Glen Ross, 1984 (Pulitzer prize for drama, N.Y. Drama Critics Cir. award), Speed-the-Plow, 1987, Bobby Gould in Hell, 1989, The Old Neighborhood, 1991, Oleanna, 1992, The Cryptogram, 1994, Ricky Jay and His 52 Assistants, 1994; author: (one act) Death Defying Acts, 1995; author: Boston Marriage, 1999, (screenplays) The Postman Always Rings Twice, 1979, The Verdict, 1980, The Untouchables, 1986, House of Games, 1986; author: (with Shel Silverstein) Things Change, 1987; author: We're No Angels, 1987, Homicide, 1991, Hoffa, 1991, Oleanna, 1994, The Edge, 1996, The Spanish Prisoner, 1996, Wag the Dog, 1997, Ronin, 1998, The Winslow Boy, 1999, State & Main, 2000, Lakeboat, 2001, Hannibal, 2001, (children's books) Warm and Cold with drawings by Donald Sultan, 1985, The Duck and the Goat, Jafsie & John Henry, 1999, Bar Mitzvah, 1999, (essays) Writing In Restaurants, 1986, SomeFreaks, 1989, on Directing Film, 1990, The Cabin, 1992; actor: (essays) Make-Believe-Town, 1996; author: (novels) The Village, 1994, The Old Religion, 1996, True and False, 1996, 3 Uses of the Knife, 1996, Wilson, 2001, Passover, The Duck and the Goat, 1996, Henrietta, 1999, the Hero Pony, 1990, (poetry) The China Man, 1999, Wilson, 2000; dir.: (films) House of Games, 1986, Oleanna, 1994, The Spanish Prisoner, 1996, The Winslow Boy, 1988, State and Main, 2000, Catastrophe, 2000, Homicide, 1991, Things Change, 1988; assoc. prodr. (films) Hoffa, 1992; dir.: (plays) Dangerous Corner, 1995; exec. prodr.: (TV films) Lansky, 1999, A Life in the Theater, 1993; prodr.: Lip Service, 1988; writer, dir. (films) Heist, 2001. Recipient Outer Critics Circle award for contbn. to Am. theater, 1978, Acad. award nominee for best screenplay adaptation, 1983, 1998; Rockefeller grantee, 1977, CBS Creative Writing fellow, Yale U. Drama Sch, 1976—77. Office: 8707 Skokie Blvd Ste 400 Skokie IL 60077-2283

MAMLOK, URSULA, composer, educator; b. Berlin, Feb. 1, 1928; d. John and Dorothy Lewis; m. Dwight G. Mamlok, Nov. 27, 1947. Student, Mannes Coll. Music, 1942-45; MusB, Manhattan Sch. Music, 1955, MusM, 1958. Faculty dept. music NYU, 1967-74, CUNY, 1971-74; prof. composition Manhattan Sch. Music, N.Y.C., 1968—2003. Composer numerous works including Variations and Interludes for 4 percussionists, 1973, Sextet, 1977, Festive Sounds, 1978, When Summer Sang, 1980, piano trio Panta rhei, 1981, 5 recital pieces for young pianists, 1983, From My Garden for solo viola or solo violin, 1983, Concertino for wind quintet, strings and percussion, 1984, Der Andreas Garten for voice, flute and harp, 1986, Alariana for recorder, clarinet, bassoon, violin and cello, 1986, 3 Bagatelles for harpsichord, 1987, 5 Bagatelles for clarinet, violin, cello, 1988, Rhapsody for clarinet, viola, piano Inward Journey for Piano, 1989, Sonata for violin and piano, 1989, Music for flute, violin, cello, 1990, Girasol, a sextet for flute, violin, viola, cello and piano, 1991, Constellations for orch., 1993, Polarities for flute, violin, cello, piano, 1995, Festive Sounds for Organ, String Quartet II, 1996-97, Two Thousan Notes for Piano, 2000-01, Confluencies for Clarinet, Violin, Cello, Piano, 2002, Rückblick for Saxophone and Piano, 2002. Recipient Opus One Rec. award Am. Composers Alliance, 1987, Serge Koussevitzky Found. commn., 1988, Walter Hinrichsen award Acad. Inst. Arts and Letters, 1989, commn. San Francisco Symphony, 1990; Nat. Endowment Arts grantee, 1974, Am. Inst. Acad. Arts and Letters grantee, 1981, 89, Martha Baird Rockefeller grantee, 1982; John Simon Gugenheim fellow, 1995. Mem. Am. Soc. Univ. Composers, Am. Women Composers, N.Y. Women Composers, Internat. League Women Composers, Am. Music Ctr., Internat. Soc Contemporary Music (bd. dirs.), Fromm Found. Commn., Am. Guild Organists Continuum Commn. Address: 315 E 86th St New York NY 10028-4714 *In my music, I have never striven for novelty nor originality for its own sake. Rather, my primary concern as a composer has been the consolidation of older and newer techniques, as they best serve the work at hand.*

MAMMEL, RUSSELL NORMAN, retired food distribution company executive; b. Hutchinson, Kans., Apr. 28, 1926; s. Vyvian E. and Mabel Edwina (Hursh) M.; m. Betty Crawford, Oct. 29, 1949 (dec. Oct. 1994); children: Mark, Christopher, Elizabeth, Nancy. BS, U. Kans., 1949. With Mammel's Inc., Hutchinson, 1949-57, pres., 1957-59; retail gen. mgr. Kans. divsn. Nash Finch Co., Hutchinson, 1959-61, retail gen. mgr. Iowa divsn. Cedar Rapids, 1961-66, dir. store devel. Mpls., 1966-75, v.p., 1975-83, exec. v.p., 1983-85, pres., COO, 1985-91, also bd. dirs., 1991-97; pvt. investments, 1991—. With AUS, 1944-46. Office: Nash Finch Co 7600 France Ave S Ste 200 Minneapolis MN 55435-5920 Home: c/o B Howard 155 Gleason Lake Rd Apt 205 Wayzata MN 55391-1350

MAMMONE, RICHARD JAMES, engineering educator; b. N.Y.C., Sept. 3, 1953; s. Anthony Anth and Helen (Kowalski) M.; m. Christine Podilchuk, Aug. 19, 1989; children: Robert, Jason, Richard, James Jr. BE, CCNY, 1975, ME, 1977; PhD, CUNY, 1981. Computer systems analyst Picatinny Arsenal, Dover, N.J., 1975-77; rsch. fellow CCNY, 1977-81; asst. prof. Manhattan Coll., Riverdale, N.Y., 1981-82; assoc. prof. engring. Rutgers U., Piscataway, N.J., 1981-93, prof., 1993—. Co-founder Computed Anatonomy Inc., N.Y.C., 1982; founder SpeakEZ, Inc., N.J., 1992, chmn. of bd., 1995—; chief tech. advisor, bd. dirs T-NETIX, Inc., Colo., 1995—; founder, CEO Visionary Systems Inc. (VSI), 1999; cons. in field. Co-author: Image Recovery: Theory and Applications, Acad. Press Pubs., 1987, Computational Methods of Signal Recovery and Recognition, 1992; co-editor: Neural Networks: Theory and Applications, 1991; editor: Artificial Neural Networks for Speech and Vision, 1993; editor Pattern Recognition Jour., 1989—; series editor Chapman-Hall on Neural Networks, 1991—; editor artificial neural networks speech and vision Chapman-Hall Pubs., 1993—; asst. editor IEEE Transactions on Speech and Audio Processing, IEEE Transactions on Neural Networks; contbr. articles to profl. jours.; patentee in filed. Assoc. Whitaker Found. grant, 1982, NSF grant, 1992; Internat. Tel. & Tel. grant, 1984; CAIP Rsch. Ctr. grant, 1985; Henry Rutgers fellow, 1985-87, U.S. Nat. Security Agy. grant, 1986—, USAF grant, 1986—, Temeplex grant, 1986—. Mem. IEEE (sr., editor Comms. Jour. 1983-89), N.Y. Acad. Scis. Office: Rutgers U Dept Elec Engring Piscataway NJ 08854 Office Phone: 732-445-5554. Business E-Mail: mammone@caip.rutgers.edu.

MAMPRE, VIRGINIA ELIZABETH, communications executive; b. Chgo., Sept. 12, 1949; d. Albert Leon and Virginia S. (Joboul) M. BA with honors, U. Iowa, 1971; Masters degree, Ind. U., 1972; spl. cert., Harvard U., 1981. Cert. tchr. Harris Intern WTTW-TV Sta., Chgo., 1972, asst. dir., 1972-73; prod. and dir. WSIU/WUSI-TV Sta., Carbondale, Ill., 1973-74; instr. So. Ill. U., Carbondale, 1972-77; prog. and prod. mgr. WSIU/WUSI-TV, Carbondale, 1974-77; prog. dir. KUHT-TV Sta., Houston, 1977-83; pres. Victory Media, Inc., Houston, 1984-89, Mampre Media Internat., Houston, 1984—. Cons. Corp. Pub. Broadcasting, Washington, 1981—83; bd. dirs. TVPC; program bd. Ea. Ednl. Network; spkr., presenter in field Europe, Asia, Australia, S. Am. Contbg. author/editor to mags. including Focus, 1989, News & Views, 1987-88, In the Black, 1984-93, Festivals; creator: (report card campaign) Multi-media, U.S., 1985—; exec. prodr. TV spls., pub. affairs and info., 1977-83 (awards 1978-91). Pres. Child Abuse Prevention Coun., Houston, 1984—97; chmn. exhbns. Mayor's 1st Hearing, Children and Youth, Houston, 1985—88; rep. Houston 2nd World Conf. on Mayors, Japan, 1989; bd. govs. Houston Read Commn., pres., 1995—2001; mem. nat. faculty Ctr. Children's Issues, 1995—97; v.p. Episcopal Ch. Women; chair adv. bd. Houston Read Commn., 1993—2001; pres. bd. dirs. Houston Fin. Coun., 1983—; bd. dirs. Child Abuse Prevention Network, 1990—97; chmn. bd. dirs., gala chair Crime Stoppers Houston, 1984—99; founder, bd. dirs. Friends of WSIU-TV, 1974—77; chmn. St. Kevork/ACYO Nat. Sports Fair, St. John the Divine, 1990; mem. exec. bd. Nat. Com. To Prevent Child Abuse, 1990—97; pres., bd. dirs. Fedn. Houston Profl. Women Found., 1996; bd. dirs. Humanities Tex., 1998—, Tex. Coun. Humanities, Operation Rainbow, 1997—, pres. bd. gala chair; bd. dirs. Kellogg Fellows Leadership Alliance; adv. bd. Southwest Area Media Project. Fellow W.K. Kellogg Found., Battle Creek, Mich., 1987-90; recipient award for Excellence Pres. Pvt. Sector, White House, Washington, 1987, Ohio State U., Columbus, 1983, Feddersen award for excellence in Pub. TV Ind. U., Bloomington, 1981, Heritage award Child Abuse Prevention Coun., 1990, Dona J. Stone Founders award Nat. Assn. for Prevention of Child Abuse, 1990; named among Outstanding Women Vols. for community, civic and profl. contbns., Fedn. Houston Profl. Women, 1989; honoree Woman on Move, 1997. Mem.: Culinary Guild Houston, Internat. Festivals Events. Assn. (sec. 1994—, bd. dirs., creator Mampre Media Internat. Leadership Devel.), Profls. in Culinary Arts (pres. 2002—), TV Program Conf. (sec. bd. 1990—), Ctr. Bus. Women's Devel., Nat. Assn. Programming TV Execs., Nat. Assn. Ednl. Broadcasters (presenter nat. conv. 1975—76), Houston Fed. Profl. Women (del. 1986—93, chmn. 1994—, pres.), Am. Women in Radio and TV (bd. dirs. 1985—, nat. v.p. 1986—90, award 1987, pres. Houston chpt. 1990), Dau. of the King, Christ in the Arts (chair), Dephians, Tex. Lyceum (v.p., bd. dirs. 1990—96). Republican. Episcopalian. Avocations: photography, swimming, sailing, languages, travel. Office: Mampre Media Internat 5123 Del Monte Dr Houston TX 77056-4391 Personal E-mail: vemampre@aol.com.

MAMRACK, WILLIAM H. tax specialist; b. Canonsburg, Pa., June 7, 1943; BBA, U. Mich., 1965. Tax mgr. Arthur Andersen and Co., 1971—77, tax ptnr., 1978—84, head Memphis tax divsn., 1984—89; v.p. taxes Ga. Pacific, Atlanta, 1992—. Active Salvation Army; mem. adv. coun. Boys and Girls Clubs; mem. Tex. Execs. Inst. Mem.: AICPA, Pa. Inst. CPA's, Ga. Soc. CPA's, Am. Forest & Paper Assn. (tax subcom.). Office: Ga Pacific 133 Peachtree St NE Atlanta GA 30303

MAMUT, MARY CATHERINE, retired entrepreneur; b. Calabria, Italy, Oct. 17, 1923; came to U.S., 1928; d. Carmelo Charles and Caterina (Tripodi) Cogliandro; m. Michael Matthew Mamut, May 15, 1954; children: Anthony Carl, Charles Terrance. Student, Stenotype Comml. Coll., 1946-50. Sec. to pres. Thomas Goodfellow, Inc., Detroit, 1942-50; asst. to v.p. R.G. Moeller Co., Detroit, 1951-52; sec. to pres. United Steel Supply Co., Detroit, 1952-54; sec. to libr. Farmington (Mich.) Schs., 1962-68; real estate agt., 1969; owner, mgr. Crystal Fair, Birmingham, Mich., 1969-88, ret. Tchr. Stenotype Comml. Coll., Detroit, 1952-54. Vol. Henry Ford Mus., Dearborn, Mich., 1989-90, Greenfield Village, 1989-90, West Bloomfield Libr., 1993-95. Recipient World Lifetime Achievement award Am. Biog. Inst. U.S.A., 1993. Mem. Am. Bus. Women's Assn., Birmingham-Bloomfield C. of C., Profl. Secs. Internat, NAFE. Roman Catholic. Avocations: reading, music, art, theater. Home: 7423 Coach Ln West Bloomfield MI 48322-4022

MAN, LAWRENCE KONG, architect, art dealer; b. Kowloon, Hong Kong, July 4, 1953; s. Hon-Kwong Man and Sau-Ching Luk. Student, U. Redlands, 1971-72; BArch, U. Oreg., 1977; MArch, Harvard U., 1978. Registered architect, Mass., Calif. Designer, project architect Shepley Bulfinch Richardson & Abbott, Boston, 1978-86; project designer, project architect E. Verner Johnson & Assoc., Boston, 1987-91; owner Lawrence Man Architect, Cambridge, Mass., 1992-95, L.A., 1994—. Prin. works include LMAN studio, Chu House, Downey, Calif., Fong House, San Marino, Calif., Tighe Summer House, Sagamore Beach, Mass, Frozen Fusion Juice Bar, L.A. schs., Fed. Credit Union, L.A., Pub. Mus. Grand Rapids, Mich. (AIA Grand Valley Disting. Bldg. award 1997), LCP Studio, Somerville, Mass., New Asia Restaurants, Danvers and Arlington, Mass., Tai Pan Restaurant, Cambridge, Mass. (Honor award AIA 1993, New Eng. award Excellence in Architecture 1993, Design Excellence award Nat. Orgn. Minority Architects 1993), Ti-Sales Office, Sudbury, Mass. (Design Excellence award Nat. Orgn. Minority Architects 1993), Dental Clinic, Reading, Mass. (AIA Interior Architecture award 1992, Interior Design Project award Am. Soc. Interior Designers 1991, Boston Exports citation AIA 1990, Boston Soc. of Architects/New Eng. Healthcare Assembly honor award, 1994), Mus. Ctr. Union Terminal, Cin. (Reconstrn. award 1991), Ramesses Pavilion Boston Mus. Sci. (Double Vision award/Double Silver Soc. Environ. Graphics 1990), Smithsonian South Quadrangle Mus., Washington (Boston Exports award/citation AIA 1990, Honor award AIA 1989), U. Vt. Student Ctr., Burlington, Campus Ctr. Study and Libr. addition Franklin & Marshall Coll., Andover (Mass.) Co. Corp. Hdqs., Emerson Hosp., Concord, Mass., pvt. residences, others. Avocations: dance, travel, music. Office: 949 Chung King Rd Los Angeles CA 90012 E-mail: info@lawrencemanarchitects.com. *There are ups and downs in life. It is more rewarding to experience them all, no matter how hard it may get sometimes. It allows you to become a more complete person. That is, in my view, a true achievement.*

MANABE, SYUKURO, climatologist; b. Shingu-Mura, Uma-Gun, Ehime-ken, Japan, Sept. 21, 1931; came to U.S., 1958; s. Seiichi and Sueko (Akashi) M.; m. Nobuko Nakamura, Jan. 21, 1962; children: Nagisa M., Yukari C. BS, Tokyo U., 1953, MS, 1955, DS, 1958; DSc (hon.), McGill U., 2004. Rsch. meteorologist U.S. Weather Bur., Washington, 1958-63; sr. rsch. meteorologist Geophys. Fluid Dynamics Lab. NOAA, Washington, 1963-68, sr. rsch. meterologist geophys. fluid dynamics lab. Princeton, N.J., 1968-95, mem. sr. exec. svc. of U.S., 1979-95, sr. scientist, 1995-97; dir. global warming rsch. program Frontier Rsch. Sys. for Global Change, Yokohama, Japan, 1997—2001; vis. rsch. collaborator, Program in Atmospheric and Oceanic Scis. Princeton U., 2002—. Lectr. with rank of prof. Princeton U., 1968-98; joint sci. com. World Climate Rsch. Program, 1981-87; bd. atmospheric sci. and climate NRC, 1988-91; com. on Geoscis., Environ. and Resources, NRC, 1990-93, climate rsch. com., 2001-03; panel on climate and global change NOAA, 1988-97. Recipient Gold medal U.S. Dept. Commerce, 1970, Presdl. Rank Meritorious Exec. award Pres. of U.S., 1989, Blue Planet prize Asahi Glass Found., 1992, Asahi prize Asahi Daily Found., 1996, Volvo Environ. prize Volvo Found., 1997, Milankovitch medal European Geophys. Soc., 1998. Fellow AAAS, Am. Geophys. Union (Revelle medal 1993), Am. Meteorol. Soc. (hon.; Meisinger award 1967, 2d half century award 1977, Rossby medal 1992), Japan Meteorol. Soc. (hon.; Fujiwara award 1966); mem. NAS, Acad. Europaea (fgn.), Royal Soc. Can. (fgn.). Achievements include the first numerical modeling study of global warming. Home: 6 Governors Ln Princeton NJ 08540-3666 Office: Princeton U Sayre Hall Forrestal Campus PO Box CN710 Princeton NJ 08544-0710

MANAFETTE, MICHAEL, writer; b. New York, Aug. 20, 1971; s. Richard Robert Manfetano, Sr. and Christine Mary Mathews. AA, Rutgers U., 1995; BA, SUNY Oneonta, 1998. Author: (short story collection) New Jersey Stories, 2002, Darklands, 2004. Independent Thinkers. Avocation: graphic art. Office: Thomas Heineman Publishing PO Box 29 Harrington Park NJ 07640 Personal E-mail: manfo999_@hotmail.com.

MANAHAN, ANNA, actress; b. Ireland, Oct. 18, 1924; Student, Gaiety Sch. Acting. Actress Edwards/MacLiammoir Co., Nat. Theatre, London, Walter Kerr Theatre, N.Y.C. Appeared in numerous theatrical prodns., including The Rose Tattoo, Moon for the Misbegotten, Bloomsday, Entertaining Mr. Sloane, The Killing of Sister George, Cat on a Hot Tin Roof, the Gingerbread Lady, Lovers (Tony nomination), Live Like Pits, The Plough and the Stars (Oliver award nomination), The Leenana Trilogy, the Loves of Cass Maguire, I do Not Like Thee Dr. Fell, the Shaughraun, the Matchmaker, The Taylor, Ansty, Dr. Fell, The Beauty Queen of Leenane (Tony award 1998), The Matchmaker, 2002, Sive, 2002, numerous others; TV appearances include Me Mammy, The riordans, Leave it to Mrs. O'Brien, the Irish RM, (TV/films) the Bill, Lovejoy, 1986, Young Indiana Jones Chronicles, 1992, the Treaty, Blind Justice, Hear My Songs, 1991, Clash of the Titans, 1981, A Man of No Importance, 1994, Woman Found Dead in Elevator, 2000, On the Edge, 2000, Black Day at Black Rock, 2001, others. Recipient Tony award, Theatre World award, Freedom of City award, 2002. Office: Walter Kerr Theatre 219 W 48th St New York NY 10036-1423

MANAHAN, JOAN ELSIE, health and physical education educator; b. Haskell, N.J., Jan. 18, 1940; d. Edward A. and Elsie G. (Beckmann) M. BA, Trenton State Coll., 1962; MA, Columbia U., 1966, EdD, 1975. Tchr., coach Bloomfield (N.J.) Bd. Edn., 1962-97. Cons. Nat. Dairy Coun., 1970s. Cons. (book): Basic Stuff: Motor Learning and Performance; contbr. articles to profl. jours. Grantee A+ For Kids Tchr. Network, Inc., 1992-93; recipient Proclamation, N.J. State Legislature, 1997. Mem. NEA, AAHPER (cons. 1980s, 1990s), Am. Archery Assn., N.J. AHPER, N.J. Athletic Assn. (treas. 1966-67, co-editor newsletter 1967-68, archery tournament chairperson 1965-75), N.J. Edn. Assn., Essex County Coaches Assn., Kappa Delta Pi, Pi Lambda Theta. Roman Catholic. Avocations: collecting playing cards and swizzle sticks, life master bridge.

MANAS, GERALD BENNETT, information technology manager; b. Phila., Mar. 15, 1960; s. Sidney Ralph and Barbara M. Manas; m. Sharon Erica Olson, Sept. 10, 1989; 1 child, Elizabeth Rose. Student, Temple U., 1978-79. Cert. project mgmt. Am. Mgmt. Assn., project mgmt. profl. Project Mgmt. Inst., Microsoft Project Users Group. Programmer Alfred Angelo, Inc., Willow Grove, Pa., 1978-81, Pepper, Hamilton & Scheetz, Phila., 1981-82; programmer, analyst Hurst Performance, Warminster, Pa., 1982-85; sys. analyst C&D Power Sys., Plymouth Meeting, Pa., 1985-87; mgr. product devel. Centennial Sys., Wayne, Pa., 1987-89; mgr. edn. Responsive Software Solutions, Wayne, 1989-90; client mgr. Alliance Cons., Phila., 1990—2003, Rohm and Haas, Phila., 2003—. Pres. Manas Comm., Inc., Phila., 1994—96; chmn. round table Del. Valley Computer Users Group, Phila., 1987—88. Author: (articles) Project Mgmt. According to Napoleon, 2002, Lessons Learned from Napoleon, 2002, Lessons From the Rise and Fall of the Roman Empire; songwriter Sept. Forever, 1996. Vol. contr. Project Mgmt. Inst. Mem.: Nat. Acad. Songwriters, Alliance Francaise Phila., Delaware Valley Entrepreneur's Club (pres., founder 1994—96). Democrat. Jewish. Avocations: music, art, photography, writing, french studies. Office: Rohm and Haas 7th Fl E-Bus 100 Independence Mall W Philadelphia PA 19106 Office Phone: 215-592-3279.

MANASSAH, EDWARD E. publishing executive; b. Sharon, Pa., Mar. 8, 1947; BS, BA, Youngstown State Univ.; MA, U. Fla. Copy editor TODAY, Brevard County, Fla., 1972—83; mng. editor Battle Creek (Mich.) Enquirer, 1983—84; editor Lansing (Mich.) State Jour., 1984—86; exec. editor Fla. Today, 1986—88; pub., editor The Desert Sun, Palm Springs, Calif., 1988—93; pres., publ. The Courier-Journal, Louisville, 1993—. Office: The Courier Journal 525 W Broadway Louisville KY 40202-2137

MANASSAH, JAMAL TEWFEK, electrical engineer, educator, management consultant; b. Haifa, Palestine, Feb. 23, 1945; s. Tewfek George and Alia Nasrallah (Kardoush) M.; m. Azza Tarek H.I. Mikdadi, Mar. 16, 1979; children: Tala, Nigh. BSc, Am. U., Beirut, Lebanon, 1966; MA, Columbia U., 1968, PhD, 1970. Mem. Inst. Advanced Study, Princeton, N.J., 1970-72, 74-79; asst. prof. Am. U. Beirut, 1972-75; chief sci. adviser Kuwait Inst. Sci. Rsch., 1976-81; COO Kuwait Found., 1979-81; prof. dept. elec. engring. CUNY, N.Y.C., 1981—. Cons. Columbia Radiation Labs., N.Y.C., 1970-73, Ford Found., N.Y.C., 1973-79, NSF, Washington, 1978-83; chmn. Internat. Symposium Series, Kuwait, 1979-81; mng. dir. Khayatt and Co., Inc., N.Y.C., 1982; organizing com. Chem. Rsch. Applied to World Needs II, 1980-83; mem. Welfare Assn., Geneva, 1984-92; steering com. Internat. Workshop on Laser Physics, 1993-2000. Editor: Alternate Energy Sources (2 vols.) 1981; (with others) Advances in Food Producing Systems for Arid and Semiarid Lands (2 vols.), 1981, Innovations in Telecommunication (2 vols.), 1982, (with others) Transient Coherent Phenomena, 1995, Elementary Mathematical and Computational Tools for Electrical and Computer Engineering Using MATLAR, 2001, (with others) Coherent and Nonlinear Optics and Spectroscopy, 2002; mem. editl. bd. Internat. Jour. Laser Physics, 1994—, Laser Physics Letters, 2004—; contbr. over 150 articles on statis. field theory, nonlinear and quantum optics, photonics, ultrafast phenomena and new techs. assessment. Commr. Lebanese Boy Scouts Assn., Beirut, 1972-75; adviser internat. program NSF, 1979-83; bd. dirs. CUNY Rsch. Found., 2001-03. Columbia U. faculty fellow, 1966-68, Pfister fellow, 1968-70; grantee NSF, 1982-87; recipient ABI Key award, 1987, Commemorative medal of honor, 1988; named Man of Yr., 1990. Mem. Assn. Mems. of Inst. for Advanced Study, Princeton Club. Christian Orthodox. Achievements include the theoretical discovery or co-discovery of resonant absorption coefficient frequency shift, collective Lamb shift, pion minus condensation in nuclear matter, blackbody frequency shift, dynamical Lorenz shift, reflectivity frequency shift, induced coherent pulse compression, induced spectral broadening, induced frequency shift, three-photons frequency shift, twin peaks in second harmonics generation, induced waveguiding and focusing, time-space superspike, non-linear compression of noise correlation time, soliton phases, coherently inhibited amplification, induced channeling, delayed reflectivity, two-color photon echos, superradiance without inversion, pressure induced optical cavities, periodicity enhanced precocious superradiant transition. Home: 55 E 87th St Apt 15G New York NY 10128-1051 Office: CUNY Dept Elec Engring Convent Ave New York NY 10031 E-mail: manassah@ccny.cuny.edu.

MANASSE, HENRI RICHARD, JR., pharmaceutical executive; b. Amsterdam, The Netherlands, Nov. 27, 1945; came to U.S., 1954, naturalized, 1963; s. Henri David and Janny Lynn (Borst) M.; m. Arlynn Hem, Aug. 9, 1969; children: Bryan, Sheralynn. BS in Pharmacy, U. Ill., Chgo., 1968; MA, Loyola U., Chgo., 1972; PhD, U. Minn., 1974; DSc (hon.), Campbell U., 1997, Union U., 1997, Mercer U., 1998, L.I. (N.Y.) U., 2004. Lic. pharmacist, Ill. Rsch. pharmacist Xttrium Labs., Chgo., 1968-69; asst. to dean Coll. Pharmacy U. Ill., Chgo., 1969-72, asst. prof. pharmacy adminstrn., 1974-77, assoc. dean, 1977-80, acting dean, 1980-81, dean, prof., 1981-93, interim vice chancellor for health affairs, 1983-84, 1991-93; prof. coll. pharmacy and medicine U. Iowa, v.p. for health scis., 1993-96; exec. v.p.-designate Am. Soc. Health-Sys. Pharmacists, 1996—, CEO, exec. v.p., 1997—. Sr. policy fellow Ctr. on Drugs and Pub. Policy, U. Md., 1988—; mem. Ill. Bd. Pharmacy, Springfield, 1982-94; pub. mem. Am. Soc. Hosp. Pharmacists Commn. on Credentialling, Bethesda, Md., 1984-86; chair bd. dirs. Nat. Patient Safety Found. AMA, 1999-2001; mem. adv. bd. PEW Found. Health Professions Edn. Reform Commn.; bd. dirs. Am. Soc. Cons. Pharmacists Rsch. and Edn. Found.; pres. Coun. on Credentialing in Pharmacy, 1998—02; mem. quality quest prize selection com. Am. Hosp. Assn.; co-chair safe practices steering com. Nat. Quality Forum, 2001—04; mem. sentinel events adv. com. JCAHO Sentinel, 2002—; cons. FDA Adv.

Com. on Risk Mgmt. and Drug Safety; mem. com. on the future of emergency care in the U.S. health sys. Inst. of Medicine, 2004—. Mem. editl. bd. Am. Jour. Hosp. Pharmacy, 1990-92; contbr. chpts. to books and articles to profl. jours. Pres. Downers Grove Sch. Bd. Caucus, Ill., 1984-85; bd. dirs. med. svc. Westside Holistic Ctr., Chgo., 1979-89. Recipient Lederle Faculty award Lederle Pharm. Co., 1975, Outstanding Achievement award U. Minn., 1998; named Alumnus of Yr., U. Ill. Alumni Assn., 1983. Jesse E Stewart Svc. award, U. of Illinois, 2004. Fellow Inst. Medicine Chgo.; mem. Am. Assn. Colls. Pharmacy (pres., adminstrv. bd. 1982-86, bd. dirs. 1984-86, pres. 1988-89), Am. Soc. Health Sys. Pharmacists, Nat. Acad. Scis., Inst. Medicine, Am. Pharm. Assn., Am. Soc. Assn. Execs. Baptist. Avocations: computers, international travel. Home: 10118 Vanderbilt Cir Rockville MD 20850-4674 Office Phone: 301-657-3000. Business E-Mail: hrmjr@ashp.org.

MANATOS, ANDREW E. public relations executive; b. Washington, July 7, 1944; m. Tina G. Weber, June 25, 1967; children: Mike A., Nick A., Tom A., George A. BA, Am. U., 1968, MA, 1969. Staff post office and civil service com. U.S. Senate, Washington, 1969-73; assoc. staff dir. of Senate Senator Thomas Eagleton, 1973-77; asst. sec. congl. affairs Dept. Commerce, Washington, 1977-81; owner Manatos & Manatos Inc., Washington, 1981—. Creator White House Conf. on Productivity, U.S. Senate Productivity Award, Greek Independence Day Resolution, (videotapes) U.S. Congress and You, Your Court System and You, The Executive Branch and You, Where We Stand; bd. dirs. Washington Coord. Coun. Productivity, 1981-88, Com. for Citizen Awareness, 1985—. Contbr. articles to N.Y. Times, Washington Post, Indianapolis Star. Bd. dirs., mem. nat. fin. com., co-chmn. Dukakis for Pres., 1987-88; mem. Archdiocesan Coun. & Leadership 100 Greek Orthodox Ch. Recipient Cross of Holy Sepulcher, Medal of St. Andrew, Ellis Island Medal of Honor Nat. Ethnic Coalition of Orgns.; named Archon, Greek Orthodox Ch. Office: Manatos & Manatos 601 13th St NW Ste 1150S Washington DC 20005-3883

MANATT, CHARLES TAYLOR, lawyer; b. Chgo., June 9, 1936; BS, Iowa State U., 1958; JD, George Washington U., 1962. Bar: Calif. 1962, U.S. Supreme Ct. 1967, D.C. 1985. Ptnr. Manatt, Phelps & Phillips, Washington, now chmn.; U.S. ambassador Dominican Republic, 1999—2001. Bd. editors George Washington Law Rev., 1960-62. Pres. Calif. Bankers Assn.; chmn. Nat. Democratic Inst., Calif. Dem. Com., Nat. Dem. Com., Internat. Found. for Election Sys.; chmn. bd. trustees George Washington U.; bd. dirs. Mayo Clinic. Mem. ABA, Calif. State Bar, L.A. County Bar Assn., San Fernando Valley Bar Assn. (pres. 1971-72), Century City Bar Assn., Phi Delta Phi, Delta Sigma Rho. Office: Manatt Phelps & Phillips 1501 M St NW Ste 700 Washington DC 20005-1737 also: Manatt Phelps & Phillips Trident Ctr E Tower 11355 W Olympic Blvd Los Angeles CA 90064-1614

MANATT, RICHARD, retired education educator; b. Odebolt, Iowa, Dec. 13, 1931; s. William Price and Lucille (Taylor) M.; m. Sally Jo Johnson, Aug. 20, 1952; children— Tamra Jo, Ann Lea, Joel Price; m. Jacquelyn M. Nesset, Feb. 25, 1970; 1 child, Megan Sue. BSc, Iowa State U., 1953, MS, 1956; PhD, U. Iowa, 1964. Prin. Oskloosa (Iowa) Schs., 1959-62; rsch. assoc. U. Iowa, Iowa City, 1962-64; mem. faculty Iowa State U., Ames, 1964—, prof., 1972—, chmn. dept. ednl. adminstrn., 1970-80, 93-98, dir. Sch. Improvement Model Projects, 1980—, prof., 1998—2002, prof. emeritus, 2002—. Cons. performance evaluation for public and independent schs.; disting. vis. prof. Calif. State U., L.A. Author: Educator's Guide to the New Design, When Right is Wrong, Fundamentalists and the Public Schools, Clinical Manual for Teacher Performance Evaluation Compendias of Professional Growth Plans, (computer software program) Computer Assisted Teach Evaluation/Supervision. Served with AUS, 1953-55. Named Disting. Prof., Nat. Acad. Sch. Execs., 1979, Regents' Prof. Edn., 1994; recipient faculty citation Iowa State U. Alumni Assn., 1998, Margaret White Grad. Faculty award, 2001, Pres.'s award NAACP, 2002. Mem. NEA, NASSP, ASCD (Outstanding Cons. 1981), Am. Assn. Sch. Adminstrs., Phi Kappa Phi, Phi Delta Kappa, Phi Delta Chi. Democrat. Methodist. Home: 2926 Monroe Dr Ames IA 50010-4362 Office Phone: 515-232-0202. E-mail: rmanatt@iastate.edu.

MANBECK, HARVEY B. agricultural and biological engineer, educator; b. Reading, Pa., Jan. 11, 1942; m. Glenda Manbeck; children: Eric, Christina. BS, Pa. State U., 1963, MS in Agrl. Engring., 1965; PhD in Engring., Okla. State U., 1970. Rsch. assoc. agrl. engring. dept. Pa. State U., 1965, instr. agrl. engring. dept., 1966, prof. agrl. engring., 1980-96; asst. prof. agrl engring. dept. U. Ga., 1970-75, assoc. prof. agrl. engring. dept., 1977-80; assoc. prof., extension agrl. engr. Ohio State U., 1975-77; adminstrv. intern rsch. office Pa. Agrl. Experiment Sta., 1991-92; Disting. prof. agrl. engring. Pa. State U., 1996—2004, Disting. prof. emeritus, 2004—, interim head agrl. and biol. engring. dept., 1996—98. Vis. prof. agrl. engring. U. Manitoba, 1986-87, Shenyang Agrl. U., 1988; interim dir. Housing Rsch. Ctr., Pa. State U., 1995. Contbr. chpts. to books and articles to profl. jours. Coach Little League Baseball, 1981-84, leader YMCA Indian Princess Longhouse, 1983-85, Webelo's Cub Scouts 1984, com. mem. Troop 31 Boy Scouts of Am. 1985—. Recipient Outstanding and Premier Tchg. award, Outstanding Rsch. award Coll. of Engring., Pa. State U., Atherton Excellence in Tchg. award Pa. State U., Black award for rsch. excellence Coll. Agrl. Scis., Pa. State U. Mem. ASCE, Am. Soc. Agrl. Engrs. (mem. structures group, vice chair 1978-79, chair, 1979-81, Pa. State sect. sec.-treas. 1983-84, chair 1985-86, trustee 1992-94, tech. dir. S.E. divsn. 1993-95, Henry Giese S & E award 1990), Nat. Frame Builders Assn. (mem. editl. rev. com. for the post-frame profl., chair 1998—), Ga. Soc. Profl. Engrs (state dir. at large 1974-75, named Outstanding Young Engr. of the Year, 1972, recipient Outstanding Chpt. Pres. award, 1974, various other coms.), Ohio Soc. Profl. Engrs., Forest Products Rsch. Soc., Gamma Sigma Delta (internat. sec. 1998—), Alpha Epsilon, Sigma Xi, numerous others. Achievements include development of standard designs and specs for hardwood glulam highway bridges, authorship of national engineering practice for post-frame structural diaphragm design, development of FEM for predicting thermal pressures in grain bins, development of FEM for predicting structural performance of wood-framed, metal-clad diaphagm evaluation of creep response of wood I-joist floor systems, lateral stability of composite wood I-joists and development of standards for ventilation of confined space storage systems in agriculture. Home: 912 Anna St Boalsburg PA 16827-1214 Office: Penn State U 210 Agr Engring Bldg University Park PA 16802 Business E-Mail: Hmanbeck@psu.edu.

MANCALL, ELLIOTT LEE, neurologist, educator; b. Hartford, Conn., July 31, 1927; s. Nicholas and Bess Tuch M.; m. Jacqueline Sue Cooper, Dec. 27, 1953; children: Andrew Cooper, Peter Cooper. BS, Trinity Coll., Hartford, 1948; MD, U. Pa., 1952. Diplomate Am. Bd. Psychiatry and Neurology. Intern Hartford Hosp., 1952-54; clk. in neurology Nat. Hosp. Nervous Disease, London, 1954-55; asst. resident neurology Neurol. Inst. NY, 1955-56; resident in neuropathology Mass. Gen. Hosp., 1956-57, clin. and rsch. fellow, 1957-58; tchg. fellow neuropathology Harvard Med. Sch., 1956-57; from asst. prof. neurology to assoc. prof. Jefferson Med. Coll., 1958-65; prof. medicine Hahnemann Med. Coll. and Hosp., 1965-76; prof. neurology Med. Coll. Pa.-Hahnemann U., 1993-95; prof. neurology, chmn. dept. Hahnemann Med. Coll. and Hosp., 1976-93; prof. neurology Jefferson Med. Coll., Phila., 1995—, interim chmn. dept. neurology, 1997—2003. Dir. Hahnemann U. ALS Clinic, 1985-95; chmn. bd. dirs. Phila. Profl. Stds. Rev. Orgn., 1981-84. Author: (with others) The Human Cerebellum: A Topographical Atlas, 1961; (with B.J. Alpers) Clinical Neurology, 1971, Essentials of the Neurological Examination, 1971, 81; contbr. articles to profl. jours. With USN, 1945-47. Recipient Christian R. and Mary F. Lindback award, 1969, Oliver Meml. prize ophthalmology U. Pa., 1952. Fellow Am. Acad. Neurology (alt. del. to AMA 1982-86, gen. editor CONTINUUM 1991-2003, A.B. Baker award for excellence in neurol. edn. 1997, Presdl. award 2003); mem. Am. Neurol. Assn., Am. Assn. Neuropathology, Assn. Rsch. in Nervous and Mental Diseases, Soc. Neurosci., AAUP, Pa. Med. Peer Rev. Orgn. (dir. 1979-84), Phila. Neurol. Soc., Alpers Soc. Clin. Neurology, Coll. Physicians Phila., Sydenham Coterie, Phila. County Med. Soc., Pa. State Med. Soc., AMA (sec.-treas. sect. coun. neurology 1983-86), Am. Med. Soc. on Alcoholism, Neurology Intersoc. Liaison Group, Intersoc. Com. Neurol. Resources, Assn. Univ. Prof. Neurology (pres. 1988-90), Soc. for Exptl. Neuropathology, Am. Bd. Med. Specialities (exec. bd., chmn. com. study of evaluation procedures, 1992-99, rep. accreditation com. continuing med. edn. 1998—, chair accreditation coun., 2003-), Am. Bd. Psychiatry and Neurology (v.p. 1990, del. to Am. Bd. Med. Spltys., dir. 1983-91, emeritus dir. 1991—), Pa. Blue Shield (profl. adv. coun. 1991-98). Home: PO Box 498 Lafayette Hill PA 19444-0498 Office: Ste 200 900 Walnut St Philadelphia PA 19107 Office Phone: 215-955-0707. Business E-Mail: elliottmancall@jefferson.edu.

MANCHESTER, CRAIG, construction executive; Pres. Western Pacific Homes, El Segundo, Calif., 1998—. Office: 300 Continental Blvd Ste 390 El Segundo CA 90245

MANCHESTER, KENNETH EDWARD, electronics executive, consultant; b. Winona, Minn., Mar. 22, 1925; s. Laurence Edwin and Daisy Idel (Finley) M.; m. Bonnie Lee Hardgrave, June 24, 1946; children: Cynthia Lee, David Scott. AB, San Jose State Coll., 1949; MS, Stanford U., 1950, PhD, 1955. Sr. chemist Shell Devel. Co., Emeryville, Calif., 1955-62; head chemistry sect. Sprague Electric Co., North Adams, Mass., 1962-63, head chemistry dept., 1963-69, dir. semiconductor rsch., devel. and engring., 1969-79, dir. quality assurance and reliability Worcester, Mass., 1979-85, v.p. corp. R & D North Adams, 1985-89, Sprague fellow, 1985; cons. semiconductor industry, 1989—. Lectr. Rensselaer Poly. Inst., Troy, N.Y., 1967. Contbr. articles to profl. jours.; patentee in field. Chmn. com. Troop 70 Boy Scouts Am. Sgt. U.S. Army Ground Forces, 1943-46, ETO. Mem. Am. Chem. Soc., AIME, Optimist Club, Sigma Xi. Democrat. Avocations: woodworking, golf. E-mail: kmbucko@netzero.com.

MANCHESTER, PAUL BRUNSON, economist; b. Winsted, Conn., Oct. 7, 1942; s. Elbert Grant and Eleanor Elizabeth (Jones) M.; m. Ruth Elaine Garbisch, Oct. 25, 1969; children: Sarah H., Daniel P. BA, Yale U., 1964; PhD, U. Minn., 1973. Vol. Peace Corps, Colombia, 1964-66; teaching assoc. U. Minn., Mpls., 1966-69; asst. prof. Mary Washington Coll., Fredericksburg, Va., 1971-74; cons. U.S. Dept. Treasury, Washington, 1974-75; asst. prof. Cath. U. Am., Washington, 1974-78; cons. Robert R. Nathan Assocs., Washington, 1975-78; economist joint econ. com. U.S. Congress, Washington, 1978-89; econ. adviser to Tenn. senator U.S. Senate, Washington, 1988; sr. economist U.S. League Savs. Insts., Washington, 1989-90; economist Office Thrift Supervision, Washington, 1990-91; fin. economist U.S. Dept. HUD, Washington, 1991—. Contbr. articles to profl. jours. Pres. Woodmoor-Pinecrest Citizens' Assn., Silver Spring, Md.; del. Allied Civic Group, Silver Spring. Mem. Am. Econ. Assn., Soc. Govt. Economists, Nat. Economists Club (v.p. 1985, 87, bd. dirs. 1989-92). Lutheran. Avocations: tennis, skiing, bowling. Home: 105 Lexington Dr Silver Spring MD 20901-2546 Office: US Dept HUD 451 7th St SW Rm 8212 Washington DC 20410-0001

MANCHESTER, STEVEN HERBERT, writer, educator; b. Fall River, Mass., Nov. 4, 1967; s. William and Nancy Ann Manchester; children: Evan Steven, Jacob Alexander. AA, Bristol C.C., Fall River, Mass., 1987—89. Prison investigator Mass. Dept. Corrections, Bridgewater, 1989—98. Writing instr. Southcoast Learning Network, New Bedford, Mass., 2002—03. Author: (novels) The Unexpected Storm - The Gulf War Legacy, At The Stroke of Midnight, Jacob Evans, A Father's Love, 6-5; A Different Shade of Blue, (movie) Gooseberry Island. Vol. lectr. Straight Ahead Ministry, Taunton, Mass., 2000—03. Sgt. U.S. Army, 1990—91, Operation Desert Storm. Decorated SW Asia Svc., Liberation of Kuwait, Nat. Def. citations U.S. Army. Mem.: VFW (assoc.). Independent. Avocations: reading, running, travel, weightlifting. Home and Office: 55 Summerfield Ave Somerset MA 02725 Personal E-mail: shmanchester@statestreet.com. E-mail: paula1271@attbi.com.

MANCHEVSKI, MILCHO, film director, scriptwriter; b. Skopje, Macedonia, Yugoslavia, Oct. 18, 1959; s. Aleksandar and Vasilka Mančevski. Student, U. Kiril i Metodij, Skopje, 1978—79; BA in Film & Photography, So. Ill. U., 1983. Prof. N.Y. U., N.Y.C., 2001—. Screenwriter, dir.: Before the Rain, 1994 (Venice Golden Lion for Best Film award, 1994, Venice Internat. Critics prize, 1994, Venice UNICEF prize, 1994, Venice Young Viewers' prize, 1994, Rolling Vencie award, 1994, Leoncino d'oro award, Venice, 1994, Venice Internat. Cath. Orgn. for Cinema, 1994, Kodak award for Best First Feature award, Venice, 1994, Audience award for Best Film award Sao Paolo Festival, 1994, Jury award for Best Film award Puerto Rico Festival, 1994, Audience award for Best Film Puerto Rico Festival, 1994, Best Dir. award Puerto Rico Festival, 1994, Best First Film ward Puerto Rico Festival, 1994, Best Debut Film award Puerto Rico Festival, 1994, Charlot d'or award Mons Festival, Belgium, 1995, Grand Prix St. Petersburg, 1995, Burgos Festival prize, Spain, 1995, Best Screenplay award Gorizia Festival of Screenplay, Italy, 1995, Best Film award award Film Forum, Bratislava, Slovakia, 1995, UNESCO prize, Panteleria, Italy, 1995, Warsaw Film Fest Audience award, 1995, Cath. Film. Commn. prize, Austria, 1995, David di Donatello Spl. award to a Non-Italian Film award, Italy, 1995, Swedish Film Inst. Golden Bug for Best Foreign Film award, 1995, Oscar Nomination for Best Foreign-Lang. Film, 1995, Indep. Spirit award for Best Foreign-Lang. Film, 1996, Argentinian Critics Assn. Silver Condor for Best Foreign Film, 1997); Dust, 2001; numerous music videos; dir.: The Wire, 2002, Law and Order:SVU, 2003; exhibitions include SCCA Group Show, 2000—01, Mus. Contemporary Art, Macedonia, 1999, Skulpturen Mus., Stockholm, 1999; author: (short stories) Loneliness, 1976, All Day, 1977, Twelve Years Ago, 1998, Wishes, 1999, The Ghost of My Mother, 2000, Marcus' Portrait, 2002, Flight, 2002, My Grandfather, 2002; dir.: Tennessee 1992 (Best Rap Video, MTV, Best Pop/Rock Video, Billboard). Mem.: Dir.'s Guild Am., Pen Ctr. Avocation: basketball.

MANCHIN, JOE, III, secretary of state; m. Gayle Conelly; children: Heather, Joseph IV, Brooke. BS in Bus. and Econs., W.Va. U., 1970. Operator Manchin's Carpet Center, Marion County, W.Va., 1970; elected rep. W.Va. Ho. of Dels., 1982—86, elected. senator, 1986—92; elected Sec. of State State of W.Va., 2001. Past chmn. banking and ins. com. W.Va. State Senate, past vice chair fin. com., past chair rule making rev. Office: Bldg 1 Ste 157-K 1900 Kanawha Blvd E Charleston WV 25305-0770

MANCINELLI-CAHILL, MAGGIE, theater director; married; 1 child. Co. dir. Playwrights Preview Prodns., Manhattan, NY, 1991—95; artistic dir. Capital Repertory Theatre, Albany, NY, 1995—. Creator Urban Express, N.Y.C. Office: Capital Repertory Theatre 111 N Pearl St Albany NY 12207-2208

MANCINI, ERNEST ANTHONY, geologist, educator, researcher; b. Reading, Pa., Feb. 27, 1947; s. Ernest and Marian K. (Filbert) M.; m. Marilyn E. Lee, Dec. 27, 1969; children: Lisa L., Lauren N. BS, Albright Coll., 1969; MS, So. Ill. U., 1972; PhD, Tex. A&M U., 1974. Petroleum exploration geologist Cities Svc. Oil Co., Denver, 1974-76; asst. prof. geology U. Ala., Tuscaloosa, 1976-79, assoc. prof., 1979-84, prof., 1984—. State geologist, oil and gas supr. State Ala., Tuscaloosa, 1982-96; dir. Ea. Gulf Region of the Petroleum Tech. Transfer Coun., 1995—, Ctr. for Sedimentary Basin Studies, U. Ala., 1998—. Contbr. articles to profl. jours. Cushman Found. fellow, Geol. Soc. Am. fellow; recipient Nat. Coun. Citation Albright Coll., 1983, Pratt-Haas Disting. Lectr. Am. Assn. Petroleum Geologists, 1987-88. Mem. Geol. Soc. Am. (past chmn. S.E. sect.), Am. Assn. Petroleum Geologists (A.I. Levorsen petroleum geology Meml. award Gulf Coast Assn., geol. socs. sect. 1980, chair rsch. com. 2001-04, assoc. editor, 2003-04, editor, 2004—, Disting. Educator award 2000), Assn. Am. State Geologists (hon., past pres.), Am. Geol. Inst. (Ian Campbell medal 2004), Nat. Assn. State Univs. and Land-Grant Colls. (past chair, mineral and energy resources sect. mem. bd. natural resources), Soc. Econ. Paleontologists and Mineralogists Gulf Coast sect. (hon., past pres.), Paleontol. Soc. (past pres. southeast sect.), N.Am. Micropaleontology Soc., Ala. Geol. Soc. (past pres.), Gulf Coast Assn. Geol. Scis. (hon., Outstanding Educator award 1998), Sigma Xi (past chpt. pres.), Phi Kappa Phi (past chpt. pres.), Phi Sigma. Presbyterian. Home: 15271 Four Winds Loop Northport AL 35475-3325 Office: U Ala Dept Geol Scis PO Box 870338 Tuscaloosa AL 35487-0338 Business E-Mail: emancini@wgs.geo.ua.edu.

MANCINO, DOUGLAS MICHAEL, lawyer; b. May 8, 1949; s. Paul and Adele (Brazaitis) M.; m. Carol Keith, June 16, 1973. BA, Kent State U., 1971; JD, Ohio State U., 1974. Bar: Ohio 1974, U.S. Tax Ct. 1977, Calif. 1981, D.C. 1981. Assoc. Baker & Hostetler, Cleve., 1974-80; ptnr. Memel & Ellsworth, L.A., 1980-87, McDermott, Will & Emery, L.A., 1987—. Bd. dirs. Health Net of Calif. Inc. Author: Taxation of Hospitals and Health Care Organizations, 2000, (with others) Hospital Survival Guide, 1984, Navigating the Federal Physician Self-Referral Law, 1998; (with F. Hill) Taxation of Exempt Organizations, 2002; co-author quar. tax column Am. Hosp. Assn. publ. Health Law Vigil, (with L. Burns) Joint Ventures Between Hosps. and Physicians, 1987; contbr. articles to profl. jours. Chmn. bd. dirs. The Children's Burn Found.; bd. dirs. Kent State U. Found., Inc. Mem. ABA (tax, bus., real property, probate and trust sects., chair exempt orgns. com. 1995-97, coun. dir. 1999—), Calif. State Bar Assn. (tax, bus. law sects.), Ohio Bar Assn., Calif. State Bar, D.C. Bar Assn., Am. Health Lawyers Assn. (bd. dirs. 1986-95, pres. 1993-94), Calif. Soc. for Healthcare Attys., Bel Air Country Club, The Regency Club, Calif. Yacht Club. Office: McDermott Will & Emery 2049 Century Park E Fl 34 Los Angeles CA 90067-3101 E-mail: dmancino@mwe.com.

MANCINO, JOHN GREGORY, software company executive; b. N.Y.C., Nov. 14, 1946; s. John D. and Carmela A. Mancino. BA, Colgate U., 1968. Chief appraiser Rusciano Appraisers & Cons., N.Y.C., 1968-70; v.p. Pisces Prodns., Boulder, Colo., 1971-73; v.p. ops. Celestial Seasonings, Inc., Boulder, Colo., 1973-84, also dir.; dir. Strategic Info. Group, 1994—; founder, owner DeviceWorks Co., 2002—. Bd. dirs. Computer Connection, Inc., Mr. Software, Inc., Spruce St. Mktg., Inc., Fortune 44 Co., Inc.; pres., bd. dirs. Decision Makers Software, 1984—; chmn. Generation 5 Tech., 1985-89, Preferred Bus. Investments, Ltd., 1986-90; founder, dir. DeviceWorks Co., 2002—. Author: (software) Tattletale, 1991. Office: 214 Mountain Meadows Rd Boulder CO 80302-9256 E-mail: mancino@decismkr.com.

MANCL, DUSTIN BERNARD, elementary school educator, language educator; b. Hastings, Minn., Nov. 26, 1977; s. Bernard Ernie Mancl and Joan Marie Smith - Mancl; life ptnr. Phillip Edward Burns - Mancl, Feb. 12, 1999. BS in Elem. Edn., U. Nev., Las, Vegas, 2001. Cert. ESL Sierra Nev. Coll., 2002. Athletic advisor Young Olympians Inc., Tustin, Calif., 1998—2002; educator Jack Dailey Elem. Sch., Las Vegas, Nev., 2001—. Dir. of coaches Young Olympians Inc., Tustin, Calif., 1999—2002; chair tchrs. Jack Dailey Elem. Sch., Las Vegas, Nev., 2001—02, grade level chair, 2003—. Performer: All Stars Performance One, 1999 (Nat. Championship award Divsn. A), All Stars Performance Two, 2000 (Nat. Championship award Divsn. A), All Stars Performance Three, 2001 (Nat. Championship award Divsn. A), All Stars Performance Four, 2002 (Nat. Championship award Divsn. A). Named to Nat. Team, Nat. Cheerleading Assn., 1996 - 1998. Mem.: NEA, Profl. Learning Communities. Independent. Avocations: music, yoga, writing children's books, feng shui, Czech language and culture. Home: 3020 Spokan Dr Las Vegas NV 89121 Office: Clark County Sch Dist Dailey Elem Sch 2001 East Reno Ave Las Vegas NV 89119 E-mail: dbmancl@interact.ccsd.net.

MANCUSI, ROBERTO FRANCESCO COSTANTINO, vocalist, educator; b. Kenosha, Wis., Aug. 15, 1971; s. Robert Arnold Emory Tapley and Diane Jean Broughton; m. Staci Lyn Peiffer, July 27, 1996; 1 child, Matthew Robert. MusB in Performance, Simpson Coll., Indianola, Iowa, 1994; MusM in Performance, U. Mo., Kansas City, 1998, DMA in Performance, 2000. Dir. music Franksville United Meth. Ch., Franksville, Wis., 1998—99; adj. voice faculty Baker U., Baldwin City, Kans., 2001—. Treas., bd. dirs. Opera Kadopera, Raytown, Mo., 2002—, set designer/builder, 2002. Singer: (opera) Amahl and the Night Visitors, Magic Flute, Cosi fan tutte, Manon, Ariadne auf Naxos. Friends of the Conservatory Music scholar, U. Mo. Conservatory of Music, 2001—02. Mem.: Nat. Assn. Tchrs. of Singing, Lambda Chi Alpha (risk mgr. 1992—93, v.p. 1993—94). Avocations: videophile, magic, walking. Home: 4705 Sycamore Ave Kansas City MO 64129-2179 Personal E-mail: rmancusi1@yahoo.com.

MANCUSO, FRANK G. entertainment and communications company executive; b. Buffalo, July 25, 1933; married Ed., SUNY. Film buyer, ops. supr. Basil Enterprises, 1959-63; joined Paramount Pictures Corp., 1963, booker Buffalo br., 1963-64, sales rep. Buffalo br., 1964-67, br. mgr., 1967-70; v.p., gen. sales mgr. Paramount Pictures Can. Ltd., 1970-72, pres., 1972-76; U.S. we. divsn. mgr. Paramount Pictures Corp., L.A., 1976-77, gen. sales mgr. N.Y.C., 1977, v.p. domestic distbn., 1977-79, exec. v.p. distbn. and mktg., 1979-83, pres. motion picture divsn., 1983-84, chmn., CEO, 1984-91; chmn, CEO Metro-Goldwyn-Mayer, 1993-99. Bd. dirs. Metro-Goldwyn Mayer. Bd. dirs. Will Rogers Meml. Fund, N.Y.-Cornell Med. Ctr., Burke Rehab. Ctr., UCLA Med. Ctr., Mus. of Broadcasting, MGM Motion Picture TV Found. Mem. Acad. Motion Picture Arts and Scis. (bd. dirs.), Motion Picture Assn. (bd. dirs.), Am. Film Inst. (bd. dirs.), Motion Picture Pioneers (bd. dirs.), Variety Clubs Internat. (bd. dirs.). Office: Metro Goldwyn Mayer Inc 2500 Broadway Ste B-201 Santa Monica CA 90404-3065*

MANCUSO, JOSEPH EDWARD, medical psychotherapist; b. Rockford, Ill., Dec. 1, 1955; s. Robert Fredrick and Anne Mancuso. Student, Bradley U., Peoria, Ill., 1974-76; BA in Psychology, Marquette U., 1984, MEd in Ednl. Psychology, 1987. Cert. alcohol and drug abuse counselor III, WCB, ICR; cert. clin. assoc. med. psychotherapist, nat.; diplomate, fellow med. psychotherapist ABMP; cert. ind. clin. social worker, Wis.; cert. profl. counselor, Wis.; cert. trauma responder and trauma specialist ATSS. Child care worker Community Care Svcs. Inc., Milw., 1984; day care dir. Mich. Street Day Care, Milw.; adminstrv. unit clk. Milw. Jewish Nursing Home; day care tchr. St. Mary's Children's Sch., Milw.; psychotherapist Wis. Correctional Svcs., Milw.; coord. alcohol and other drug abuse St. Mary's Psychiat. Hosp., Milw., 1990-92; cons. social worker St. Mary's Med. Hosp., Milw., 1990-91; pvt. practice, 1993-99; emergency rm. social worker Sinai Samaritan Med. Ctr., Milw., 1994-99; intake psychotherapist psychiat. svcs. Behav. Health Intake Ctr.-Sinai Samaritan Med. Ctr., Milw., 1999-2000; childrens psychotherapist Sinai Samaritan Med. Ctr., Milw., 2000—. Presenter in field. Cartoonist, published and shown in galleries throughout Milw. Mem. Am. Psychol. Assn., Wis. Psychol. Assn. (assoc.), Am. Ednl. Rsch. Assn. Avocations: hiking, drawing, painting, birding. Home: 1612 E Hartford Ave Milwaukee WI 53211-3036 Office: Sinai Samaritan Med Ctr Dept Psychiatry 1020 N 12th St Milwaukee WI 53233-1305

MANCUSO, MICHAEL JOHN, ship and submarine company executive; Grad., Villanova U.; MBA, Ea. Coll. Exec. in fin. mgmt. space systems divsn. GE; CFO land systems divsn. Gen. Dynamics, Falls Church, Va., 1993-94, v.p., contr., 1994-97, sr. v.p., CFO, 1997—. Office: Gen Dynamics Corp 3190 Fairview Park Dr Ste 1 Falls Church VA 22042-4523

MANCUSO, VINCE, advertising executive; Chief ifn. officer, sr. v.p. Rubin Postaer & Assocs., Santa Monica, Calif. Office: Rubin Postaer & Assocs 1333 2d St Santa Monica CA 90401

MAND, MARTIN G. financial executive; b. Norfolk, Va., Sept. 26, 1936; s. Meyer J. and Lena (Sutton) M.; m. Shelly Cohen, Aug. 29, 1965; children: Gregory S., Michael E., Brian C. BS in Commerce, U. Va., 1958; MBA, U. Del., 1964. Various fin. staff and mgmt. positions E.I. du Pont de Nemours & Co., Wilmington, Del., 1961-81, v.p. taxes and fin. svcs., 1981-84, v.p., comptr., 1984-88, v.p., treas., 1989-90; sr. v.p., CFO, Nortel Networks, Mississauga, Canada, 1990—93, exec. v.p., CFO, 1993—94; chmn. pres., CEO Mand Assocs., Ltd., Wilmington, 1995—. Bd. dirs. Mizuho Corp Bank U.S.A., N.Y.C., Townsends, Inc., Wilmington, Del., Factory Card and Party Outlet, Naperville, Ill., Christiana Bank & Trust Co., Wilmington; pres. Fin. Execs. Rsch. Found., 1988—90; adv. dir. Global IP Sound, Stockholm, 2001—. Co-author: (book) Partnering for Performance: Unleashing the Power of Fin. in the 21st Century Org., 2000. Lt. USN, 1958-61. Mem. Fin. Execs. Inst., Am. Mgmt. Assn. (chmn. fin. coun.). Office: 618 Berwick Rd Ste 100 Wilmington DE 19803-2204 Office Phone: 302-478-5644. E-mail: mandassociates@comcast.net.

MANDABACH, CARYN, television producer; m. Paul Mandabach; children: Marisa, Jon. Pres. Carsey-Werner Co., Studio City, Calif., 1987—; co-founder Oxygen Media, NYC, 1998—. Prodr.: (TV series) The Cosby Show, Roseanne, A Different World, Grace Under Fire, Cybill, Third Rock from the Sun, That 70's Show. Bd. dirs. The Center Theatre Group, The Curtis Sch., AFI Third Decade C. Recipient Emmy for The Cosby Show, Humanitas award, People's Choice award, Peabody award. Office: Oxygen Media 75 9th Ave New York NY 10011-7006

MANDAL, ASHIS K. cardiothoracic surgeon; b. Burdwan Town, India, Sept. 1, 1931; came to U.S., 1959; s. Mrigendra N. and Sarala Bala Mandal; m. Bina Bhatacharjee, July 14, 1957 (dec. June 1978); 1 child, Aloke; m. Mina R. Mandal, Apr. 24, 1987. MB BChir, Calcutta Nat. Med. Coll., 1957. Civil asst. surgeon Govt. India, Nefa, 1957-59; resident in gen. surgery Howard U., Washington, 1960—63; fellow in cardiovasc. surgery U. Minn., Mpls., 1965-66; resident in cardiothoracic U. Alta., Edmonton, Can., 1966-67, in-charge cardiovasc. rsch. lab., 1967-69; cons. surgeon Ft. St. John (B.C., Can.) Med. Clinic, 1969-73; from asst. prof. surgery to assoc. prof. surgery Drew-UCLA Med. Ctr., L.A., 1973-84, prof. surgery, 1984-98, prof. surgery emeritus, 1999—. Author: Anatomical Basis of Infectious Disease, 1985 (Assam Govt. award 1956), Antimicrobial Therapy in Abdominal Surgery, 1991. Fellow ACS, Royal Coll. Surgeons, Am. Coll. Chest Physicians; mem. Am. Assn. Thoracic Surgeons, Soc. Thoracic Surgeons. Office: King-Drew Med Ctr 12021 Wilmington Ave Los Angeles CA 90059-3019

MANDALAKIS, STRATOS JOHN, director, music educator; b. N.Y.C., Apr. 5, 1962; s. John James and Geneurve Triankafellides Mandalakis; m. Suzanne Marie Miller, Oct. 8, 1989; children: Christopher John, Kathryn Anne. BA, Fordham U., 1984; MA, Maryknoll, 1985. Tchr. music Bergenfield Pub. Schs., NJ, 1986—2002, dist. supr. music, 2002—. Condr. Bergen County Festival Chorus, 2001; condr. choirs Ea. Region Antiochan Orthodox Christian Archdiocese. Contbr. articles to profl. jours. Mem.: Prin. and Suprs. Assn., N.J. Music Educators Assn., Music Educators Nat. Conf. Avocations: reading, walking, cooking, writing. Office Fax: 201-385-9411. E-mail: smardalakis@bergenfield.org.

MANDARICH, DAVID D. real estate corporation executive; b. 1948; With Majestic Savs. and Loan, 1966-67; formerly chief operating officer, exec. v.p. MDC Holdings Inc., pres., co-chief operating officer, from 1986, now pres., chief operating officer. Office: MDC Holdings Richmond Amer Homes 3600 S Yosemite St Ste 900 Denver CO 80237-1867

MANDEL, ADRIENNE ABRAMSON, state legislator; b. Irvington, N.J., Sept. 30, 1936; d. Nathaniel and Florence (Lebovitz) Abramson; m. Emanuel Mandel, 1958; children: Lisa Mandel-Trupp, David. BA, Rutgers U., 1958; MA, George Washington U., 1984. Chairwoman, vice chairwoman Precinct 13-56, 1979-94; parole officer, social svc. case worker N.J. Dept. Inst. & Agencies, 1958-60; survey interviewer U.S. Census Bur., 1973-77; monitoring and evaluation specialist Divsn. Labor Svc., Montgomery County Govt., 1979-81; asst. dir. Sr. Ctr. Divsn. Elder Affairs, Dept. Family Resources, 1981-84; staff asst. Office Chief Adminstr., 1984-85; legis. rep. Office Intergovt. Rels., 1985-94; mem. Md. State Legislature, 1995—, mem. commerce govt. matters com., 1995—2002, mem. health and govt. ops. com., 2003—, dep. majority whip, 2003—. Pres. Women's Caucus, 2002—03; bi-county chair Montgomery County Del., 1999—; health issues chair Nat. Order Women Legislators, 1999—; mem. exec. bd. Nat. Found. Women Legislators, 2004—. Recipient Woman of Valor award B'nai B'rith Women, 1972; named among Md. Top 100 Women, 2002, 04. Mem. Women's Polit. Caucus, Mothers Against Drunk Driving, Md. Govt. Rels. Assn., Montgomery County Ethnic Heritage Festival, LWV, Alpha Psi Omega, Delta Phi Delta.

MANDEL, H(AROLD) GEORGE, pharmacologist, educator; b. Berlin, June 6, 1924; came to U.S., 1937, naturalized, 1944; s. Ernest A. and Else (Crail) M.; m. Marianne Klein, July 25, 1953; children: Marcia Mandel Halgren, Audrey Lynn Todd. BS, Yale U., 1944, PhD, 1949. Lab. instr. in chemistry Yale U., 1942-44, 47-49; research asso. dept. pharmacology George Washington U., 1949-50, asst. research prof., 1950-52, assoc. prof. pharmacology, 1952-58, prof., 1958—, chmn. dept. pharmacology, 1960-96. Advanced Commonwealth Fund fellow Molteno Inst. Cambridge (Eng.) U., 1956; Commonwealth Fund fellow U. Auckland (N.Z.) and U. Med. Scis., Bangkok, Thailand, 1964; Am. Cancer Soc. Eleanor Roosevelt Internat. fellow Chester Beatty Research Inst. London, 1970-71; Am. Cancer Soc. scholar U. Calif., San Francisco, 1978-79; fellow Med. Research Council toxicology unit, Carshalton, Eng., 1986; Burroughs Wellcome Rsch. travel grant, Carshalton, 1988; hon. rsch. fellow dept. biochemistry and molecular biology U. Coll., London, 1993, 96, 97; mem. com. problems drug safety NRC-NAS, 1965-76, mem. com. on toxicology, 1978-82, mem. various panels, 1981-86; mem. cancer chemotherapy com. Internat. Union Against Cancer, 1966-73, fellow, Lyon, France, 1989; mem. external rev. com. Howard U. Cancer Research Center, 1972-74; cons. Bur. Drugs, FDA, 1975-79, EPA, 1978-82; mem. toxicology adv. com. FDA, 1975-78; mem. med. research service merit rev. bd. in alcoholism and drug dependence VA, 1975-78; mem. cancer spl. program adv. com. Nat. Cancer Inst., 1974-78, chmn., 1976-78; mem. Nat. Large Bowel Cancer Project Working Cadre, 1980-84; mem. Kettering award selection com. GM Cancer Rsch. Found., 1979-81; bd. advisors Roswell Park Cancer Inst., Buffalo, 1972-74. Editorial bd.: Jour. Pharmacology and Exptl. Therapeutics, 1960-65, field editor, 1978-94; editorial bd.: Molecular Pharmacology, 1965-69, Rsch. Comm. in Chem. Pathology, Pharmacology, 1972-98, Cancer Drug Delivery, Selective Cancer Therapeutics, 1983-92, Cancer Research, 1974-76, assoc. editor, 1977-81. Served with AUS, 1944-46. Recipient John J. Abel award in pharmacology Eli Lilly and Co., 1958, Disting. Achievement award Washington Acad. Scis., 1958, Golden Apple Teaching award AMA, 1969, 85, 97, Sci. Emeritus award Soc. Biology & Medicine, 1999. Mem. AAAS, Am. Chem. Soc., Am. Soc. Biochemistry and Molecular Biology, Am. Soc. Pharmacology and Exptl. Therapeutics (pres. 1973-74), Am. Assn. Cancer rsch., Assn. Med. Sch. Pharmacology (pres. 1976-78), Nat. Caucus of Basic Biomed. Sci. Chairs (chmn. 1991—), Citizens Pub. Rsch. and Edn. Funding (sec. 1996-99), Cosmos Club (Washington), Sigma Xi, Alpha Omega Alpha. Democrat. Achievements include research, numerous publs. on cancer chemotherapy, mechanism of growth inhibition, antimetabolites, drug disposition, chemical carcinogenesis. Home: Apt 302 4956 Sentinel Dr Bethesda MD 20816-3594 Office: George Washington U Dept Pharmacology 2300 I St NW Washington DC 20037-2336 Office Phone: 202-994-3542. Business E-Mail: phmhgm@gwumc.edu. E-mail: hgmandel@aol.com.

MANDEL, HERBERT MAURICE, civil engineer; b. Port Chester, NY, May 11, 1924; s. Arthur William and Rose (Schmeiser) M.; m. Charlotte Feldman, Aug. 22, 1954; children: Rosanne Mandel Levine, Elliott D., Arthur M. BSCE, Va. Poly. Inst., 1948; M Engring., Yale U., 1949. Registered profl. engr., N.Y., Conn., Fla., Md., Mich., Minn., Ohio, Pa., Va., W.Va. Structural engr. Madigan Hyland Co., LI, NY, 1949—50; mem. Parsons, Brinckerhoff, Quade & Douglas, Inc., 1950—86; v.p. GAI Cons., Inc., Monroeville, Pa., 1986—2004, prin. staff cons., 1993—2004, sr. staff cons., 2004—. Resident engr., Chgo., 1961, Atlanta, 1962, project. mgr., N.Y.C., 1963-70, Honolulu, 1970-74, v.p., 1974, sr. v.p., Pitts., 1977-86; mem. faculty Yale U., 1948-49; adj. faculty Bklyn. Poly. Inst., 1956-64, U. Pitts., 1986; gen. chmn. 6th Internat. Bridge Conf., Pitts., 1989. Prin. works include (prin.-in-charge) Williamstown-Marietta Bridge, W.Va.-Ohio, Dunbar Bridge, W.Va., I-64 Bridge over Big Sandy River, W.Va.-Ky., Davis Creek Bridge, Charleston, W.Va., Tygart R. Bridge, W.Va., Easley Bridge, Bluefield, W.Va., Fayette Sta. Bridge, Fayetteville, W.Va., Mon Valley Expwy., W.Va., King Coal Hwy, W.Va., Romney Bridge, W.Va., (project mgr.) Newport Bridge, Narragansett Bay, R.I., (designer/project engr.) Hackensack River Bridge, N.J., Housatanic River Bridge, Conn., Arthur Kill Vertical Lift R.R. Bridge, S.I., N.Y., 62d St. Bridge, Pitts., Savannah River Cantilever Bridge, Ga., I-84 Bridges, Danbury, Conn., (structural rehab. designer) Avondale Bridge, N.J, Lincoln Bridge, N.J., B&O R.R. Bridge, Vincennes, Ind., Hawk St. Viaduct, Albany, N.Y., Congress Ave. Bridge, Austin, Tex., Ohio St. Bridge, Buffalo, Panhandle Bridge, Pitts.; project dir. design and constrn. Pitts. Light Rail Transit Sys., 1977-84; designer Elizabeth R. Tunnel, Norfolk, Va., 1950. Served to 1st lt. U.S. Army, 1943-46, 50-52, ETO. Fellow ASCE, Soc. Am. Mil. Engrs.; mem. NSPE, Engrs. Soc. Western Pa. (exec. com. Internat. Bridge Conf. 1986—, gen. chmn. 1988-89), Am. Rwy. Engring. and Maintenance of Way Assn. (steel structures specifications com. 1974—), Profl. Engrs. in Pvt. Practice (bd. govs. 1994-96, profl. devel. coun. 1995-97), Pa. Profl. Engrs. in Pvt. Practice (state vice-chmn. 1992-94, chmn. 1994-96), Pa. Soc. Profl. Engrs. (dir. Pitts. chpt. 1995-98), Internat. Assn. Bridge and Structural Engring., Assn. for Bridge Constrn. and Design, Engrs. Club Pitts., Tau Beta Pi, Chi Epsilon, Omicron Delta Kappa, Phi Kappa Phi, Pi Delta Epsilon, Scabbard and Blade. Jewish. Home: 920 Parkview Dr Pittsburgh PA 15243-1116 Office: GAI Cons Inc 570 Beatty Rd Monroeville PA 15146-1334 Office Phone: 412-856-9220. E-mail: h.mandel@gaiconsultants.com.

MANDEL, IRWIN DANIEL, dentist; b. Bklyn., Apr. 9, 1922; s. Samuel A. and Shirley (Blankstein) M.; m. Charlotte Lifschutz, Apr. 1, 1944; children: Carol, Nora, Richard. BS, CCNY, 1942; DDS, Columbia U., 1945; DSc (hon.), U. Medicine and Dentistry N.J., 1981, U. Göteborg, 1984, Columbia U., 1996. Rsch. asst. Dental Sch. Columbia U., 1946-48, mem. faculty Dental Sch., 1946—, prof. dentistry, dir. div. preventive dentistry Dental Sch., 1969-84, dir. Ctr. Clin. Rsch. in Dentistry Dental Sch., 1984-91, assoc. dean rsch., 1991-92; prof. emeritus Dental Sch., 1992—; pvt. practice dentistry, 1946-68; vis. prof. various dental schs.; chmn. oral biology and medicine study sect. Nat. Inst. Dental Rsch., 1974-76. Co-author: The Plaque Diseases, 1972; contbr. over 250 articles to profl. jours., chpts. to books. Active local chpt. Peace Action, Physicians for Social Responsibility. Lt. Dental Corps USNR, 1945-46, 52-54. Recipient Career Scientist award, N.Y.C. Health Rsch. Coun., 1969—72, Leadership award in periodontology, Tufts U. Dental Sch., 1971, Internat. award, U. Conn. Sch. Dental Medicine, 1979, Seymour J. Kreshover NIDR Lectr. award, 1986, Townsend Harris medal, CCNY, 2000. Fellow AAAS, Am. Coll. Dentists; mem. ADA (chmn. coun. dental rsch. 1978-80, Gold medal for excellence in rsch. 1985), Dental Soc. (Henry Spenadel award 1973, Jarvie-Burkhart Internat. award 1990), Am. Assn. Dental Rsch. (pres. 1980), Am. Assn. Pub. Health Dentists (Disting. Svc. award 1991), Fed. Dentair Internat. (W. D. Miller prize 1992), Internat. Assn. Dental Rsch. (Salivary Rsch. award 1994, Disting. Svc. award 2001), N.Y. Acad. Scis., Sigma Xi, Omicron Kappa Upsilon. Home: 60 Pine Dr Cedar Grove NJ 07009-1036 Office: 630 W 168th St New York NY 10032-3702 E-mail: irwindmandel@aol.com.

MANDEL, JACK N. manufacturing executive; b. Austria, July 16, 1911; s. Sam and Rose M.; m. Lilyan, Aug. 14, 1938 (dec.) Student, Fenn Coll., 1930-33. Founder, former pres., chmn. Premier Indsl. Corp., Cleve.; chmn., pres. Manbro Corp.; exec. dir. Parkwood Corp.; gen. ptnr. Courtland Assocs. Former mem. exec. com. NCCJ; former life trustee Wood Hosp.; trustee Fla. Soc. for Blind; life trustee South Broward Jewish Fedn., Cleve. Jewish Welfare Fedn.; former pres., life trustee Montefiore Home for Aged; pres. adv. bd. Barry U.; hon. trustee Hebrew U.; trustee Tel Aviv U. Mus. of the Diaspora; life trustee The Temple, Woodruff Found.; trustee Cleve. Play House. Mem. Beachmont Country Club, Commede Club, Union Club. Office: Parkwood Corp 2829 Euclid Ave Cleveland OH 44115-2413 Office Phone: 216-875-6502.

MANDEL, JACK SHELDON, epidemiologist, educator; b. Nov. 24, 1944; MPH, U. Minn., 1973, PhD, 1981. Assoc. prof. U. Minn., Mpls., 1981-88, prof., 1988-99, head divns. environ. and occupl. health, 1995-99, Mayo chair pub. health, 1996-99; group v.p. Exponent, Menlo Park, Calif., 1999—2002; Rollins prof., chair dept. epidemiology Sch. Pub. Health, Emory U., Atlanta, 2002—. Home: 2810 Payton Rd Atlanta GA 30345 Office Phone: 404-712-2288. E-mail: jsmande@sph.emory.edu.

MANDEL, JOEL EMANUEL, orthopedist; b. BKlyn., Mar. 1, 1930; s. Morris and Minnie Mandel. BA, N.Y. U., 1951; MS, Ga. Inst. Tech., 1952; MD, Chgo. Med. Sch., 1956. Diplomate Am. Bd. Med. Examiners, Am. Bd. Orthop. Surgery, Am. Bd. Profl. Disabled Cons. Intern D.C. Gen. Hosp., 1956—57; resident in gen. surgery VA Hosp., 1957—58; resident in orthopedic surgery D.C. Gen. Hosp., 1958—60, N.Y. U., Bellevue, 1960—61; pres., founding ptnr. The New City (N.Y.) Orthopedic Group, P.C., 1961—85; med. dir. Post-Trauma Med. Svcs., New Windsor, NY, 1985—. Host weekly radio program Medicine Today, 1973—76. Mem. editl. bd. Jour. Disability, 1990—93, Disability, 1995—96. Bd. govs. Rockland County (N.Y.) Health Complex, 1977—88; mem. coord. coun. Rockland County Emergency Med. Svc., 1977—81. Recipient Rockland County Dist. Svc. award, 1973. Fellow: ACS, NY State Soc. Surgeons, Am. Acad. Orthop. Surgeons, Internat. Coll. Surgeons, Am. Acad. Disability Evaluating Physicians (bd. dirs. 1988—93, sec. 1990—93); mem.: Rockland County Med. Soc. (dir. pub. rels. 1967—73, exec. com. 1967—76, peer rev. com. 1973—85, pres. 1974—75, chmn. bd. censors 1975—76), Orange County Med. Soc. (peer rev. com. 1987—, exec. com. 1994—), Ea. Orthop. Assn., NY State Soc. Orthop. Surgeons (bd. dirs. 1976—82). Avocations: sailing, windsurfing, computer science, astronomy. Office: Post-Trauma Med Svc PC 833 Blooming Grove Tpk New Windsor NY 12553 Office Phone: 845-561-2000. E-mail: bonedoc@frontiernet.net.

MANDEL, KARYL LYNN, accountant; b. Chgo., Dec. 14, 1935; d. Isador J. and Eve (Gellar) Karzen; m. Fredric H. Mandel, Sept. 29, 1956; children: David Scott, Douglas Jay, Jennifer Ann. Student, U. Mich., 1954-56, Roosevelt U., 1956-57; AA summa cum laude, Oakton Community Coll., 1979. CPA, Ill; registered investment advisor; lic. life ins. provider. Pres. Excel Transp. Service Co., Elk Grove, Ill., 1958-78; tax mgr. Chunowitz, Teitelbaum & Baerson, CPA's, Northbrook, Ill., 1981-83, tax ptnr., 1984—. Sec-treas. Lednam, Inc., Coffee Break, Inc.; mem. acctg. curriculum adv. bd. Oakton C.C., Des Plaines, Ill., 1987—; pres. Lednam Enterprises, LLC, 2001—. Contbg. author: Ill. CPA's News Jour., Acctg. Today. Recipient State of Israel Solidarity award, 1976. Mem. AICPA, Am. Soc. Women CPA, Women's Am. ORT (pres. Chgo. region 1972-74, v.p. midwest dist. 1975-76, nat. endowment com., nat investment adv. com.), Ill. CPA Soc. (chmn. estate and gift tax com. 1987-89, legis. contact com. 1981-82, pres. North Shore chpt., award for Excellence in Acctg. Edn., Bd. dirs. 1989-91), Chgo. Soc. Women CPA, Chgo. Estate Planning Coun., Nat. Assn. Women Bus. Owners, Lake County Estate Planning, Coun., Greater North Shore Estate Planning Coun. Office: 401 Huehl Rd Northbrook IL 60062-2300 E-mail: KLM@CTBLTD.COM.

MANDEL, LESLIE ANN, investment advisor, business owner, author; b. Washington, July 29, 1945; d. Seymour and Marjorie (Syble) Mandel; m. Arthur Herzog III. BA in Art History, U. Minn., 1967; cert., N.Y. Sch. Interior Design, 1969. Cert. Brailled Libr. Congress. Pres. Leslie Mandel Enterprises, Inc., N.Y.C., 1968—; sr. v.p. Maximum Entertainment Network, L.A. and N.Y.C., 1988-90; pres. Rich List Co., 1968—; pres., CEO Mandel Airplane Funding and Leasing Corp., N.Y.C., Hong Kong, China and Mongolia, 1990—; CEO Mandel-Khan Inc., Ulaanbaatar, Mongolia, 1994—, keep hers, keep his, 2002—. Fin. advisor Osmed, Inc., Mpls., 1986—, Devine Comm./Allen & Co., NY, Del., Utah, N.Mex., NY, N.Y. WUWV, Utah KBER, WKTC-AM-FM, 1984—89, Am. Kefir Corp., N.Y.C., 1983—89, Shore Group (Internat., Guyana), Flight Internat., 1991—; owner The Rich List Co., 150 internat. catalogs, mags. and fundraising lists; joint venture Mongolian Ind. Broadcasting Channel, Ulaanbaatar, 1995; pres., owner Mandel Airplane Funding and Leasing Corp.; rep. Israeli Govt. IAI Satellite, China, Romania, Costa Rica, Mongolia, Amos Satellite Network, China, 1992—; advisor rep. Gt. Wall Corp., Long March Corp., China, 1992—, Chinese Silk, 1993—, Am. Oil Refinery, 1993—; bd. dirs. Coastal Equipment Co., Bristol Airlines; cons. Exclusive Miat Airlines, Mongolia; purchasing agt. People's Republic of China-Aircraft; advisor Aeropostalis, Mexico, 1994—95; photographer; lectr. UN Internat. Direct Mail; advisor Aruba Airlines, Mexicana Airlines; aircraft agt., bd. dirs. Lazorlines Landing Equipment, 1997—; lease Estafada Airlines 757-200-C, 2000—, Chile Airlines 757-200C, 2002; advisor Guyana 2000 Airlines. Photographer: Vogue, 1978, New Earth Times, 1995, Fortune mag.; Braille transcriber: The Prophet (Kalil Gibran), 1967, Getting Ready for Battle (R. Prawe Jhabuala), 1967; exec. prodr. film: Hospital Audiences, 1975 (Cannes award 1976); author: Hungry at the Watering Hole, Gardiners Island, 1636-1990, 1989, Expedition: In the Steps of Ghengis Kahn, 1994; advisor Port Liberté Ptnrs., 1988-94; contbr. articles to profl. jours. Fin. advisor Correctional Assn., Osborn Soc., 1977—; founder, treas. Prisoners Family Transportation and Assistance Fund, N.Y., 1972-77; judge Emmy awards of Acad. TV Arts and Scis., N.Y.C., 1970; bd. dirs. Prisoners Assn., 1990; chmn. U.S.A. com. Violeta B. de Chamarro for Pres. of Nicaragua Campaign. Recipient Inst. for the Creative and Performing Arts fellowship, N.Y.C., 1966, Appreciation cert. Presdl. Inaugural Com., Washington, 1981. Fellow N.Y. Women in Real Estate, Explorers Club (lectr. on Mongolia, fin. com., housing, student, hospitality and Lowell Thomas coms.); mem. Com. on Am. and Internat. Fgn. Affairs, Lawyers Com. on Internat. Human Rels., Bus. Exec. Nat. Security, Venture Capital Breakfast Club, The Coffee Club House, Sigma Delta Tau, Sigma Epsilon Sigma. Democrat. Avocations: painting, writing, fishing, canoeing, horseback riding, breeding cockatiels. Home: 4 E 81st St New York NY 10028-0235 Office: Mandel-Khan Inc PO Box 97 care Boldbaatar Mandel Kahn Ulaanbaatar 210648 Mongolia also: Leslie Mandel Enterprises PO Box 294 Wainscott NY 11975-0294 also: PO Box 29A Wainscott NY 11975-0029 Office Phone: 917-270-6677.

MANDEL, LEWIS RICHARD, retired pharmaceutical executive, consultant; b. Bklyn., Nov. 13, 1936; s. Murray and Belle (Teller) M.; m. Rochelle Holtzman, Mar. 27, 1960; children: Beth, Susan, Stefanie. BS, Columbia U., 1958, PhD, 1962. Registered pharmacist, N.Y., N.J., Pa. Lectr. biochemistry, then asst. prof. pharmacology Columbia U., N.Y.C., 1961-64; rsch. biochemist Merck & Co., Inc., Rahway, N.J., 1964-76, dir. biochemistry, 1976-79, sr. dir. univ. and indsl. rels., 1979-89, exec. dir. indsl. and acad. rels., 1989—, exec. dir. external sci. affairs worldwide, 1993-99, v.p. external sci. affairs worldwide, 1999—2002, emeritus, external rsch. and acad. affairs, 2002—03; cons. to pharm. industry, 2003—. Patentee in field; contbr. articles to profl. publs. Grantee NIH, 1963-64; recipient Wellcome travel award, 1963. Mem. Am. Soc. Pharmacology and Exptl. Therapeutics, Am. Soc. Biochemistry and Molecular Biology.

MANDEL, MARTIN LOUIS, lawyer; b. L.A., May 17, 1944; s. Maurice S. and Florence (Byer) M.; m. Duree Dunn, Oct. 16, 1982; 1 child, Max Andrew. BA, U. So. Calif., 1965, JD, 1968; LLM, George Washington U., 1971. Bar: Calif. 1969, U.S. Dist. Ct. (ctrl. dist.) Calif. 1972, U.S. Ct. Claims 1971, U.S. Tax Ct. 1971, U.S. Supreme Ct. 1972. With office of gen. counsel IRS, Washington, 1968-72; ptnr. Stephens, Jones, LaFever & Smith, L.A., 1972-77, Stephens, Martin & Mandel, 1977-79, Fields, Fehn, Feinstein & Mandel, 1979-83; sr. v.p., gen. counsel Investment Mortgage Internat., Inc., 1983-84; ptnr. Feinstein, Gourley & Mandel, 1984-85, Mandel & Handin, San Francisco, 1985—; gen. counsel L.A. Express Football Club, 1983-85. Instr. corps. U. West L.A., 1973-83. Mem. ABA, L.A. County Bar Assn., L.A. Athletic Club, Phi Delta Phi. Office: 652 Bair Island Rd #210 Redwood City CA 94063 Office Phone: 650-482-2860. E-mail: martin@tmgtalent.com.

MANDEL, MAURICE, II, lawyer, educator, mediator; b. Hollywood, Calif. s. Maurice and Wynne Mandel. BSBA, U. So. Calif., 1971, MEd, 1972; JD, Western State U., 1979. Bar: Calif. 1980, U.S. Dist. Ct. (ctrl. dist.) Calif. 1982, U.S. Ct. Appeals (fed. and 9th cirs.) 1983, U.S. Dist. Ct. (we. dist.) Tenn. 1987, U.S. Dist. Ct. Ariz. 1990, U.S. Dist. Ct. (so. dist.) Calif. 1991, U.S. Supreme Ct. 1991, cert. level I ski instr. PSIA Nat. Acad. 1998, settlement officer, USDC-CDCa. Tchr. Orange County (Calif.) Sch. Dist., 1972-82; pvt. practice law Newport Beach, Calif., 1982—; fed. settlement officer CDCA, 1998—. Instr. Coastline C.C., 1987-95, prof., 1995—, Coastline C.C. Acad. Senate, Coastline C.C. Parlimentarian 1996-99; prof. law Irvine (Calif.) U. Coll. of Law, 1994-98; instr. Orange County Bar Assn. Coll. of Trial Advocacy, 1994—; instr. Orange County Bar Assn. Mandatory Continuing Legal Edn., 1992—, Bear Mountain Calif. Ski Sch., 1996—, Ziet Maros, 1998—; FBA/OCC Mandatory Continuing Legal Edn. provider, 1994—, COURSE Vail Co. Alpine World Cup Finals, 1997, Alpine World Championships, 1999, World Cup, 1999, COURSE St. Anton am Arlberg, Alpine World Championships, 2001, COURSE Ladies' Norams, Snowbasin, Utah, 2001, COURSE XIX Olympic Games, Salt Lake City, 2002, Alpine Ski, COURSE St. Moritz, Switzerland, Alpine World Championships, 2003, Rutch dir. CAL/NEV Reg. Championships, 2004. Counselor Troy Camp, 1969-72; chmn. Legal Edn. for Youth, 1984-86; active Ctr. Dance Alliance, Orange County, 1986-97; JOC racing dir. So. Cal. 1998-2000; mem. Friends Am. Ballet Theatre, Opera Pacific Guild, Opera Pacific Bohemians, Calypso Soc., World Wildlife Found., L.A. County Mus. Art, Newport Beach Art Mus., Met. Mus. Art, Laguna Beach Mus. Art, Smithsonian Instn., Friend of Ballet Pacifica, Friends of Joffrey Ballet; assoc. U.S. Ski Team, 1975—; com. assoc. U.S. Olympics, 1988—; 100th Olympics vols., 1996, XIX Olympics, 2002; F.I.S. vol., 1997—, COURSE Alpine World Cup Finals, Vail, Colo., 1997, Alpine World Championships, 1999, 2001, 03, XIX Olympics, 2002; mem. alumni and scholarship com. Beverly Hills H.S.; Opera Pacific Bohemians, Friends of Ballet Pacifica. Recipient cert. of appreciation U.S. Dist. Ct., L.A., 1985, U.S. Dist. Ct. Mediation award O.C., 2000, Thwarted Thwart award Newport Harbor C. of C., 1989, Tovarich award Kirov Ballet, 1989, 92, Perostroika award Moscow Classical Ballet, 1988-89, 94, Skrisivi Nogi award Bolshoi Ballet, 1990, Marinskii Dance award St. Petersburg, 1993; ABT Romeo & Juliet, 1996, Thwarted Thwart award Newport Harbor, 1996; Ziet Maros award Moscow Classical Ballet, 1998, 99, 2000, 2nd Place award JOC Slalom, 1998, 1st place award JOC Slalom, 2000, 2d place award Big Bear Instrs. Giant Slalom, 2000, 1st place award JOC Concourse, 2000, 14th pl. nat. standing JCNA Slalom, 1999. Mem. ABA, ATLA, Assn. Bus. Trial Lawyers, Fed. Bar Assn., (founding pres. Orange County chpt. 1986, nat. del. 1988-90, founder criminal indigent def. panel 1986, mem. numerous other coms., nat. chpt. activity award 1987, nat. membership award 1987, chpt. svc. award 1989, nat. regional membership chmn. 1990, spl. appointee nat. membership com. 1991), Calif. Bar Assn. (Pro Bono awards 1985-89), Pres.'s Coun. (founder 1996—), Orange County Bar Assn. (legal edn. for youth com. 1982-90, chmn. 1985, fed. practice com., sports com., mandatory fee arbitration com. 1985—, lawyer's referral svc. com. 1984-98, Merit award 1986), Orange County Bar Found. (trustee 1984-87), Women Lawyers of Orange County, U.S. Supreme Ct. Hist. Soc., 9th Jud. Cir. Hist. Soc., Am. Inns of Ct., Calif. Trial Lawyers Assn., Calif. Employee Lawyers Assn., Plaintiff Employee Lawyers Assn., Employees Rights Coun., Bar Leaders Coun. Dist. 8, Amicus Publico, U. So. Calif. Alumni Assn., Mensa, Cougar Club of Am., So. Calif. Cougar Club, San Diego Cougar Club, So. Calif. Jaguar Owners Assn. Clubs: Balboa Yacht. Avocations: skiing, yachting. Home: PO Box 411 Newport Beach CA 92662 Office: Ste 360 881 Dover Dr Newport Beach CA 92663-6929 Office Phone: 949-759-1799. Personal E-mail: mmandelz@aol.com.

MANDEL, MICHAEL, editor; PhD in Economics, Harvard U. Tchr. NYU Stern Sch. Bus.; chief economist Bus. Week. Author: The High Risk Society, 1998, The Coming Internet Depression: Why the High-Tech Boom Will Go Bust, Why the Crash Will be Worse Than You Think, and How to Prosper Afterwards, 2000, The Internet Depression: The Boom, the Bust, and Beyond, 2001, Rational Exuberance: Silencing the Enemies of Growth and Why the Future is Better Than You Think, 2004. Named one of The Top 100 U.S. Business Journalists of the 20th Century; recipient Gerald Loeb award. Office: Business Week 1221 6th Ave New York NY 10020

MANDEL, MORTON, molecular biologist; b. Bklyn., July 6, 1924; s. Barnet and Rose (Kliner) M.; m. Florence H. Goodman, Apr. 1, 1952; children: Robert, Leslie. BCE, CUNY, 1944; MS, Columbia U., 1949, PhD in Physics, 1957. Scientist Bell Telephone Labs., Murray Hill, N.J., 1956-57; asst. prof. physics dept. Stanford (Calif.) U., 1957-61; scientist Gen. Telephone & Telegraph, Mountain View, Calif., 1961-63; rsch. assoc. dept. genetics Stanford U., 1963-64; rsch. fellow Karolinska Inst., Stockholm, Sweden, 1964-66; assoc. prof. sch. of medicine U. Hawaii, Honolulu, 1966-68, prof., 1968—; founder, dir. Hawaii Biotechnology Group, Inc., 1982-95. Cons. Fairchild Semiconductor, Hewlett Packard, Lockheed, Rheem, Palo Alto, Calif., 1957-61. Contbr. articles to profl. jours. Lt. (j.g.) USN, 1944-46. Recipient Am. Cancer Soc. Scholar award Am. Cancer Soc., 1979-80, Eleanor Roosevelt Internat. Cancer fellowship, 1979; named NIH Spl. fellow Karolinska Inst., 1964-66. Fellow Am. Phys. Soc.; mem. Sigma Xi. Achievements include citation classics; optimal conditions for mutagenesis by N-methyl-N-

nitro-N-nitrosoguanidine in E. coli K12; calcium dependent bacteriophage DNA infection. Office: Dept Biochemistry 1960 E West Rd Honolulu HI 96822-2319 Home: 250 Hammond Pond Pkwy Apt 6105 Chestnut Hill MA 02467-1519

MANDEL, RUTH BLUMENSTOCK, politics educator, educational association administrator, researcher; b. Vienna; came to U.S., 1947; d. Michael and Lea (Schmelzer) Blumenstock; m. Barrett John Mandel, June 18, 1961 (div. 1976); 1 child, Maud S.; m. Jeffrey Lucker, Feb. 24, 1991. BA, Bklyn. Coll., 1960; MA, U. Conn., 1962, PhD, 1969. Part-time instr. dept. English U. Conn., 1960-66; lectr. dept. English U. Pitts., 1968-70; asst. prof. dept. English Rider Coll., 1970-71; asst. prof. Eagleton Inst. Politics Rutgers U., 1973-78, assoc. prof., 1978-85, prof., 1985-94, ednl. coord. Ctr. Am. Woman and Politics, Eagleton Inst. Politics, 1971, dir. ednl. programs and adminstrn., 1971-73, dir., 1973-94, bd. govs., prof. politics, 1994—, dir. Eagleton Inst. Politics, 1995—. Organizer Conf. Women in Legis. Leadership, 1985, Conf. Newly Elected Women Legis., 1989; founder Pub. Leadership Edn. Network; designer Nat. Edn. Women's Leadership; TV appearances include CBS Evening News, Nightline, Good Morning Am., Today, Charlie Rose, Nightly Bus. Report; lectr. in field. Author: In the Running: The New Woman Candidate, 1983, The Impact of Women in Public Office: An Overview, 1991; co-editor: The Douglas Series on Women's Lives and the Meaning of Gender; mem. editorial bd. Signs: Jour. Women in Culture and Soc., Women & Politics: Jour. Rsch. and Policy Studies; exec. prodr. (documentary) Not One of the Boys, 1984; contbr. articles to newspapers and mags. including USA Today, Working Woman, Ms. Cons. women in power com. Nat. Commn. on Observance Internat. Women's Yr., 1975; mem. state coordinating com. N.J. Internat. Women's Yr. Conf., 1976, co-chairperson nominating com., 1977; N.J. del. U.S. Nat. Women's Conf., Houston, 1977; mem. Mercer County Commn. Status of Women, 1977-84; appointed by gov. of N.J. Commn. to Study Need and Necessary Fiscal Commitments for Creating Chair Women's Studies at Douglass Coll., 1982, chair com. acad. needs; participant The Women's Dialogue—U.S./U.S.S.R., 1984; mem. program com. Women and Constitution, 1988; organizer Nat. Hispana Leadership Initiative, Ctr. Am. Women and Politics segment, 1988; bd. dirs. Nat. Coun. Rsch. Women, 1985-92, vice-chair, 1989-91, chairperson bd. com. on future, 1988-89; mem. Nat. Commn. Renewal Am. Democracy, 1992-93;appointed by Pres. of U.S. to Holocaust Meml. Coun., 1991; mem. search com. for dir. U.S. Holocaust Meml. Mus., 1992-93, com. collections and acquisitions; appointed by Pres. Clinton vice chairperson U.S. Holocaust Meml. Coun., 1993, 96-01; Mary Louise Smith chair in women and politics Iowa State U., 1997-98. Named one of N.J.'s Most Powerful Women, N.J. Monthly, 1983; recipient Douglass medal Associate Alumnae Douglass Coll., 1989, Barbara Boggs Sigmund award Women's Political Caucus N.J., 1992, Jerseyan of Week award Sunday Star-Ledger, 1992, Woodrow Wilson Pub. Svc. award Gov. N.J. Award Program, 1992, Breaking the Glass Ceiling award Women Execs. in State Govt., 1998, 21st Century Leadership award Nat. Women's Hall of Fame, 1996, Gloria Steinem Woman of Vision award Ms. Fedn. for Women, 1996, Achievement award LWV of N.J., 1996. Office: Rutgers U Eagleton Inst Politics New Brunswick NJ 08901

MANDEL, SHELDON LLOYD, dermatologist, educator; b. Mpls., Dec. 6, 1922; s. Maurice and Stelle R. M.; m. Patricia E., Oct. 15, 1978; 1 child, Melissa A. BA, U. Minn., Mpls., 1943, BS, 1944, BM, MD, U. Minn., Mpls., 1946. Diplomate Am. Bd. Dermatology, 1953. Intern U. Okla., 1946-47; resident Valley Forge (Pa.) Gen. Hosp., 1947—49, VA Hosp., Mpls., 1949—51, VA Hosp. and U. Minn., Mpls., 1949—51; pvt. practice dermatology Mpls., 1951—; prof. clin. dermatology U. Minn., Mpls., 1970—. Contbr. articles to profl. jours. Capt. MC, U.S. Army, 1947-49. Fellow Royal Soc. Medicine (Britain), Am. Acad. Dermatology (life); mem. AMA, Minn. Med. Soc., Noah Worcester Dermatol. Soc. (bd. dirs. 1988-91), Internat. Dermatol. Soc. Address: Downtown Dermatology PA 825 Nicollet Mall Ste 1629 Minneapolis MN 55402-2705

MANDEL, STEPHEN, JR., financier; m. Susan Mandel. Grad., Dartmouth, 1978. Retail analyst Goldman, Sachs & Co., 1985—87, v.p., retail analyst, 1987—90; retail analyst Tiger Mgmt. Corp., 1990—97; CEO Lone Pine Capital, 1998—. Office: Lone Pine Capital LLC 2 Greenwich Plz Greenwich CT 06830-6353*

MANDELBAUM, HAROLD NEIL, accountant; b. Englewood, N.J., Sept. 13, 1967; s. Diane M. (Kaufman) Kubik; m. Shari Patt, Sept. 9, 1995. BA in Econs., Syracuse U., 1990; BS in Acctg., William Paterson Coll., 1993. CPA; CFP; cert. personal fin. specialist; lic. ins. N.Y.; lic. securities. Brokerage Lehman Brothers, N.Y.C., 1990-91; accountant NSCSA Am. Inc., Staten Island, N.Y., 1992; accountant, fin. cons. Joseph A. Salamo, CPA, N.Y.C., 1992-96, Harold N. Mandelbaum CPA, PFS, CFP, N.Y.C., 1996—. Mem. AICPA, N.Y. State Soc. CPA. Office: 555 5th Ave Fl 9 New York NY 10017-2416 Office Phone: 212-949-0500. E-mail: hnmandelbaum@msn.com.

MANDELBROT, BENOIT B. mathematician, scientist, educator; b. Warsaw, Nov. 20, 1924; arrived in U.S., 1958; s. Charles and Belle (Lurie) M.; m. Aliette Kagan, Nov. 5, 1955; children: Laurent, Didier. Diploma, Ecole Polytechnique, Paris, 1947; MS in Aeronautics, Calif. Inst. Tech., 1948; PhD in Math., U. Paris, 1952; DS (hon.), Syracuse U., 1985, Laurentian U., Ont., Can., 1986, Boston U., 1987, SUNY, 1988, U. Bremen, Germany, 1988, U. Guelph, Ont., Can., 1989, Pace U., 1989, U. Dallas, 1992, Union Coll., 1993, U. Buenos Aires, 1993, U. Tel Aviv, 1995, Open U., U.K., 1998, Athens U. Bus. and Fin., 1998, U. St. Andrews, Scotland, 1999, Emory U., 2002; AM (hon.), Yale U., 2000. Postdoctoral mem. and Rockefeller scholar Inst. for Advanced Study, Princeton, NJ, 1953—54; jr. prof. math. U. Geneva, 1955-57, U. Lille and Ecole Polytechnique, Paris, 1957-58; rsch. staff mem. IBM Watson Rsch. Ctr., Yorktown Heights, NY, 1958-74, IBM fellow, 1974-93, IBM fellow emeritus, 1993—; vis. prof. engring. Yale U., New Haven, 1970, prof. math. scis., 1987—99, Sterling prof., 1999—. Vis. prof. econs. Harvard U., 1962-63, applied math., 1963-64, U. Paris, 1966, physiology Einstein Coll. Medicine, 1970, Coll. France, 1973, math., 1979-80, Inst. Hautes Etudes Sci. Bures, 1980, math., 1984-87, Mittag-Leffler Inst., Sweden, 1984, 2001, Max Planck Inst. Math, Bonn, Germany, 1988, Cambridge, 1990, Oxford U., 1990, Imperial Coll., London, 1991; Hitchcock prof. U. Calif., Berkeley, 1992; visitor MIT, 1953, lectr. inst., 1964-; lectr. in field; spkr. and organizer profl. confs. Author: Logique, langage et théorie de l'information, 1957, Les objets fractals: forme, hasard et dimension, 1975, 4th edit., 1995, Fractals: Form, Chance and Dimension, 1977, The Fractal Geometry of Nature, 1982, La Geometria della Natura, 1987, Fractals and Scaling in Finance: Discontinuity, Concentration, Risk, 1997, Fractales, hasard et finance, 1997, Multifractals and 1/f Noise: Wild Self-Affinity in Physics, 1999, Nel mondo dei frattali, 2001, Gaussian Self-Affinity and Fractals: Globality, The Earth, 1/f Noise and R/S, 2002, Fractals and Chaos: The Mandelbrot Set and Beyond, 2004; (with M.L. Frame) Fractals, Graphics and Mathematics Education, 2002, (with R. Hudson) The Misbehavior of Markets: A Fractal View of Risk, Ruin, and Reward, 2004; contbr. articles to profl. jours. Recipient Franklin medal Franklin Inst., 1986, Alexander von Humboldt Preis, 1987, Caltech disting. svc. award, 1988, Moet-Hennessy prize, 1988, Harvey prize, 1989, Nev. prize U. Nev. Sys., 1991, Wolf prize for physics, 1993, Honda prize, 1994, Medal of City of Paris, 1996, John Scott award City of Phila., 1999, L.F. Richardson medal European Geophys. Soc., 2000, Sven Berggren prize, Lund, Sweden, 2002, Japan prize for Sci. and Tech., 2003; Guggenheim fellow, 1968. Fellow AAAS, IEEE (Charles Proteus Steinmetz medal 1988), Am. Acad. Arts and Scis., European Acad. Arts, Scis. and Humanities, Am. Phys. Soc., French Physics Soc. (hon.), Inst. Math. Stats., Econometric Soc., Am. Geophys. Union, Am. Statistic Assn.; mem. NAS U.S.A. (Barnard medal 1985), Am. Philos. Soc., Internat. Statis. Inst. (elected.), Am. Math. Soc., Norwegian Acad. Sci. and Letters (fgn. mem.), Sigma Xi (nat. lectr. 1980-82, Procter prize 2002). Achievements include origination of theory of fractals, anascent interdisciplinary theory of roughness; this theory provides mathematical conjectures including very difficult ones, and also provides practical tools to handle financial data, mountains, clouds, fractures of metals, dynamic attractors, and all other shapes and phenomena in nature or man's works that are equally irregular or broken-up at all scales; the best known fractal is called Mandelbrot set. Office: Yale Univ Math Dept New Haven CT 06520-8283 E-mail: benoit.mandelbrot@yale.edu.

MANDELKER, LAWRENCE ARTHUR, lawyer; b. N.Y.C., Dec. 2, 1943; s. Murray and Sally (Levine) M.; m. Carolyn Anne Bareish, Oct. 4, 1970; children: Daniel H., Benjamin E. BA, Queens Coll., CUNY, 1964; JD, NYU, 1968. Bar: N.Y. 1968, Pa. 1981, U.S. Dist. Ct. (so. and ea. dists.) N.Y. 1973, U.S. Dist. Ct. (ea. dist.) Wis. 1980, (no. dist.) N.Y., 1995, U.S. Ct. Appeals (2d cir.) 1979, U.S. Ct. Appeals (9th cir.) 1989. Law sec. N.Y.C. Civil Ct., 1970-71, N.Y. State Supreme Ct., 1972; mem. Kantor, Davidoff, Wolfe, Mandelker & Kass, P.C.; mem. com. character and fitness 9th Jud. Dist.; counsel N.Y. State Athletic Commn., 1995—2001. Mem. Lewisboro Bd. Assessment Rev., N.Y., 1979—, chmn., 1984—; mem. Lewisboro Bd. Ethics. Former mem. bd. editors: NY Law Jour.; contbr. articles to profl. jours. Served as staff sgt. USAR, 1968-74. Mem. Assn. Bar City N.Y. (mem. coun. on jud. adminstrn., past mem. com. on state cts. superior jurisdiction, civil ct. com., mem. task force on jud. selection, mem. and past chmn. spl. com. on election law, mem. spl. com. on constl. conv.), NYU Law Alumni Assn. (v.p.). Home: 206 Todd Rd Katonah NY 10536-2410 Office: Kantor Davidoff Wolfe Mandelker & Kass PC 51 E 42nd St New York NY 10017-5404 Office Phone: 212-682-8383.

MANDELKER, LESTER, veterinarian; b. Memphis, July 31, 1945; s. Maurice and Alice (Herman) M.; m. Brenda Conger, Oct. 21, 1989; children: Zev and Blakelee (twins). BS, Mich. State U., 1968, DVM, 1969. Diplomate Am. Bd. Vet. Practitioners. Assoc. veterinarian Yarbrough Animal Hosp., Miami, Fla., 1969-71, Gulf Bay Animal Hosp., Clearwater, Fla., 1971-72; owner, dir. Cmty. Vet. Hosp., Largo, Fla., 1972—. Mem. Am. Bd. Vet. Practitioners; mem. adv. bd. Vet. Forum, N.Y.C., 1980—, Vetoquinol USA, Inc., Tampa, Fla., 1996—; computer specialist Network of Animal Health, Chgo., 1995-97; pharmacology cons. Vet. Info. Network; nat. spkr. on pharmacology. Author: Veterinary Practice Tips I, 1980, II, 1985, Pharmaceutical Index, 1994; guest editor Veterinary Clinics of North America, 2004, Nutraceuticals and Other Biological Therapies. Founder, past pres. Class Inc., Clearwater, 1973-80. Mem. AVMA, Am. Animal Hosp. Assn., Pinellas County Vet. Med. Soc. (past pres.). Jewish. Avocations: tennis, cooking, dance, computers. Office: Cmty Vet Hosp 1631 W Bay Dr Largo FL 33770-3001 E-mail: lestervet2@aol.com.

MANDELKERN, LEO, biophysics and chemistry educator; b. N.Y.C., Feb. 23, 1922; s. Israel and Gussie (Krostich) M.; m. Berdie Medvedoff, May, 1946; children: I. Paul, Marshal, David. BA, Cornell U., 1942, PhD, 1949. Postdoctoral rsch. assoc. Cornell U., Ithaca, N.Y., 1949-52; phys. chemist Nat. Bur. Standards, Washington, 1952-62; prof. chemistry and biophysics Fla. State U., Tallahassee, 1962—, R.O. Lawton Disting. prof., 1984—. Vis. prof. U. Miami (Fla.) Med. Sch., 1963, U. Calif. Med. Sch., San Francisco, 1964, Cornell U., 1967; mem. biophysics fellowship com. NIH, 1967-70; mem. study panel crystal growth and morphology NRC, 1960; cons. in field. Author: Crystallization of Polymers, 1964, An Introduction to Macromolecules, 1972, 1983, Crystallization of Polymers, Vol. 1, 2002; contbr. numerous articles to profl. jours. 1st lt. USAAF, 1942-46, PTO. Recipient Meritorious Svc. award U.S. Dept. Commerce, 1957, Arthur S. Fleming award Washington Jaycees, 1958, Mettler award N.Am. Thermal Analysis Soc., Phila., 1984, Disting. Svc. in Advancement of Polymer Sci. award Soc. Polymer Sci., Japan, 1993. Fellow: AAAS, Biophys. Soc., Am. Phys. Soc. (Outstanding Educator of Am. 1973, 1975), Am. Chem. Soc. (Polymer Chemistry award 1975, Fla. award 1984, Rubber divsn. Whitby award 1988, Charles Goodyear medal 1993, Applied Polymer Sci. award 1989, Disting. Svc. in Advancement of Polymer Sci. 1993, Polymer Divsn. P.J. Flory award 1994, Polymer Materials Sci. & Engring. Divsn. Coop. Rsch. award 1995, Herman F. Mark award 2000), Polymer Soc. Japan (sr.; sr.), Cosmos Club Washington, Alpha Epsilon Pi. Home: 1503 Old Ft Dr Tallahassee FL 32301-5637 Office: Fla State U Dept Chemistry Tallahassee FL 32306

MANDELL, GERALD LEE, internist, educator; b. NYC, Aug. 20, 1936; s. Herman and Sylvia (Keller) M.; m. Judith Rensin Mandell, Dec. 22, 1960; children: James, Pamela, Scott. BA, Cornell U., 1958; MD, Cornell U., N.Y.C., 1962. Diplomate Am. Bd. Internal Medicine. Intern, resident NY Hosp. Cornell Med. Ctr., NYC, 1965-67; instr. Med. Coll., Cornell U., NYC, 1968-69; asst. prof. U. Va., Charlottesville, 1969-71, assoc. prof., 1972-75, prof., 1976—, Owen R. Cheatham prof. sci., 1981—, chief infectious diseases, 1970—2002. Editor: Principles and Practice of Infectious Diseases, 1979, 5th edit., 2000. Lt. comdr. USPHS, 1963-65. Recipient Merit award NIH, 1986; named Outstanding Alumnus, Cornell Med. Coll, 2002. Master ACP; fellow AAAS, Infectious Diseases Soc. Am. (pres. 1994, Bristol award 2000), Nat. Inst. Allergy and Infectious Diseases (adv. coun.), Inst. Medicine; mem. Assn. Am. Physicians, Am. Soc. Clin. Investigation, Phi Beta Kappa, Alpha Omega Alpha. Jewish. Avocations: photography, tropical fish, sculling. Office: U VA Health Scis Ctr MR4 Rsch Bldg Rm 2112 PO Box 801341 Charlottesville VA 22908-1341 Office Phone: 434-924-5942. E-mail: gm@virginia.edu.

MANDELL, GORDON KEITH, aerospace engineer; b. N.Y.C., Mar. 6, 1947; s. Bertram Herman and Maria Catherine (O'Hagan) M. BS, MIT, 1969, MS, 1970. Rsch. aerospace engr. MIT, Cambridge, 1970—72; aero. cons. Eagle River, Alaska, 1972—76; designated engring. rep., 1976—82; aerospace engr. FAA, Anchorage, 1982—. Author/editor: Topics in Advanced Model Rocketry, 1973; mng. editor Model Rocketry mag., Cambridge, 1968-72; contbr. articles to profl. jours. NSF fellow, MIT, 1969; scholar Grumman Aerospace Corp., MIT, 1965. Mem. Nat. Assn. Rocketry, Planetary Soc., Nat. Space Soc., Sigma Xi, Sigma Gamma Tau, Tau Beta Pi. Buddhist. Avocations: rural living, model building, home computing. Home: PO Box 671388 Chugiak AK 99567-1388 Office: FAA Aircraft Cert Office ACE-115N 222 W 7th Ave Unit 14 Anchorage AK 99513-7587 Business E-Mail: gkm1441@mtaonline.net.

MANDELL, JAMES, health facility executive, urologist, educator; b. SI, NY, Feb. 20, 1945; s. Gustave and Rose (Zimmerman) M.; m. Valerie Steele, Jan. 20, 1967; children: Joshua Lindstrom, Jeremy Hill, Bethany Shalom. AA, U. Fla., 1965; MD, U. Fla. Coll. Medicine, 1970; MS, Union U., 1999. Am. Bd. Diplomate Urology 1979. Intern U. Fla. Sch. Medicine, Gainesville, 1970-71, resident in surgery, 1971-72; resident in urology U. NC Sch. Medicine, Chapel Hill, 1974-77, fellow in pediatric urology, 1977-78, asst. prof. surgery and pediatrics, 1979-84, assoc. prof., 1984-85; dir. pediatric urology NC Meml. Hosp., Chapel Hill, 1979-85; instr. surgery Harvard U. Med. Sch., Boston, 1978-79, asst. prof. surgery (urology), 1985-90, assoc. prof. surgery, urology, 1990-94, prof. surgery (urology); prof. surgery and pediat., chief divsn. urology, exec. med. dir. Albany Med. Coll., NY, 1994-97, dean, 1996-2000; fellow in surgery (urology) Children's Hosp., Boston, 1978-79, asst. in surgery (urology), 1985-90, sr. assoc. surgery, 1990-94, CEO, pres., 2000—. Contbr. numerous articles to med. jours., chpts. to books. Lt. comdr. M.C., USNR, 1971-74. Fellow ACS, Am. Acad. Pediatrics (exec. com. 1996—); mem. Am. Urol. Assn. (New England sec.), Soc. Pediatric Urology (mem.-at-large exec. com. 1988-92), Soc. Univ. Urologists (pres. 2001-02). Avocations: Financial Investing, fishing, skiing, tennis. Office: Children's Hosp Boston Dept Urology Hunnewell 3 300 Longwood Ave Boston MA 02115-5724 Office Phone: 518-355-2080., 617-355-6000. Office Fax: 617-730-0474. Business E-Mail: james.mandell@childrens.harvard.edu.

MANDELL, MARSHALL, pediatrician, allergist, consultant; b. N.Y.C., Feb. 4, 1922; s. Albert and Beatrice (Roth) M.; m. Thelma Sylvia Cantor, Aug. 1, 1944 (div. 1974); children: Joan Arlene, Steven Marshall, Nori Lyn; m. Blanca Aurora Abrego, June 22, 2001. BA in Zoology, U. Conn., 1943; MD, L.I. Coll. Medicine, 1946. Diplomate Am. Bd. Pediat., Pediat. Allergy, Am. Bd. Allergy and Immunology, Am. Bd. Environ. Medicine. Intern in pediat. Yale U. Med. Sch./New Haven Hosp., 1946—47; jr. resident in pediat. St. Louis Children's Hosp./Washington U. Med. Sch., 1949-50; resident in pediat. Gen. Hosps. #1 and #2, Kansas City, Mo., 1950-51; instr., clin. asst. N.Y. Med. Coll., 1955-58, asst. prof. allergy, 1958-80. Adj. prof. nutrition and allergy U. Bridgeport, Conn., 1976—90; cons. in allergy and bio-ecologic disorders in mental illness Fuller Meml. Sanitarium, South Attleboro, Mass., 1972—76; cons. in cerebral allergy Ctr. Neurol. Rehab., Morton, Pa., 1980—; lectr. in field. Author: 5-Day Allergy Relief System, 1979, Lifetime Arthritis Relief System, 1983, It's Not Your Fault You're Fat Diet, 1983; co-author Brian Injury, 1986, The Unsuspected Brain Allery Connection, 2003; editor: Let's Have Healthy Children, 1981; creator and pub. large print edit. Tom Sawyer; contbr. more than 35 articles to profl. jours. Capt. U.S. Army, 1947-49. Recipient Founders medal demonstrating the role of brain allergy in schizophrenia, Huxley Soc., 2 awards Citizens Commn. Human Rights showing the role of nervous sys. sensitivity to dietary and environ. factors in mental and behavioral disorders. Fellow: Internat. Acad. Nutrition and Preventive Medicine, Acad. Orthomolecular Medicine and Psychiatry (Spl. Commendation for Contbns. to Mental Illness), Am. Acad. Environ. Medicine (Jonathan Forman Gold medal), Am. Coll. Allergy, Asthma and Immunology (mem. com. nervous sys. allery); mem.: Am. Acad. Allergy, Lions (pres. Norwalk club 1956—58), Phi Sigma Delta (pres. 1941—43). Avocations: medical writing, woodcarving, gardening, swimming. Home and Office: 112 Canterbury Ln Laredo TX 78041 Personal E-mail: drmarshallmandell@sbcglobal.net.

MANDELL, MARVIN, retired humanities educator; b. Rochester, N.Y., Jan. 26, 1927; s. Harold and Frieda Sarachan Mandell; m. Betty Reid Mandell, Apr. 15, 1954; children: Christine, Charlotte. BA with honors, U. Rochester, 1950; MA, Columbia U., 1951; PhD, U. Iowa, 1971. H.s. tchr., N.Y.C., 1952—59; prof. English Colo. State Coll. (now No. Colo. U.), Greeley, 1959—61, SUNY, Potsdam, 1964—67, U. Conn., Hartford, 1967—69; prof., chair humanities Curry Coll., Milton, Mass., 1969—93. Contbr. stories and essays to jours.; author: (radio play) Adaptation of Billy Budd; mem. editl. bd. New Politics, 1993—. Served with U.S. Army, 1944—46. Recipient Creative Writing award, Nat. Endowment Arts, 1974—75. Mem.: Phi Beta Kappa. Avocations: skiing, sailing, swimming, hiking. Home: 102 Anawan Ave West Roxbury MA 02132 E-mail: mmandell@curry.edu.

MANDELL, RAYMOND ANDREW, music educator; s. Raymond James and Sophia Mandell; m. Catherine Mandell, June 30, 1991; children: Zachariah James, Jacob Alexander, Rachel Sophia. MusB, Grove City (Pa.) Coll., 1985. Dir. of instrumental and choral music Philipsburg-Osceola (Pa.) Area HS, 1986—89; dir. of instrumental music Clearfield (Pa.) Area HS, 1989—. Choir dir. Nativity of the Virgin Mary Orthodox Ch., Osceola Mills, Pa., 1985—2000, St. Michael Orthodox Ch., Irvona/Madera, Pa., 2001—, St. Mary's Orthodox Ch., Irvona/Madera, 2001—. Nominee Am. Tchr. award, Disney, 2002. Mem.: NEA, Pa. Music Educator's Assn., Music Educators Nat. Conf., Nat. Band Assn. Avocations: gardening, cooking. Office: Clearfield Area High School PO Box 910 Clearfield PA 16830

MANDELSTAM, CHARLES LAWRENCE, lawyer; b. Brookline, Mass., July 6, 1927; s. Felix and Sarah (Odence) M.; m. Gloria Messinger, June 2, 1957; children: Emily F., Peter D. BA, Harvard Coll., 1949; LLB, Yale U., 1952. Bar: Conn. 1952, NY 1953, DC 1953. Mem. staff office gen. counsel Internat. Ladies' Garment Workers Union, NYC, 1952-56; assoc. Kaye, Scholer, Fierman, Hays & Handler, NYC, 1956-60; ptnr. Dornbush Mensch Mandelstam & Schaeffer, LLP, NYC, 1968—2004, McLaughlin & Stern, LLP, NYC, 2004—. Bd. dirs. Domaine de Bonserine, Ampuis, France; counsel North Salem (NY) Open Land Found., 1975—. Comment editor Yale Law Jour., 1951-52; contbr. articles Yale Law Jour., 1951, 52 Bd. dirs. Samuel Rubin Found., 1975—; trustee Rubin Mus. of Art, NYC, 2001—. Mem. Assn. Bar City NY, Phi Beta Kappa. Home: 27 W 86th St New York NY 10024-3615 Office: 260 Madison Ave NW New York NY 10016 Office Phone: 212-448-1100.

MANDELSTAM, STANLEY, physicist; b. Johannesburg, Dec. 12, 1928; came to U.S., 1963; s. Boris and Beatrice (Liknaitzky) M. BSc, U. Witwatersrand, Johannesburg, 1952; BA, Cambridge U., Eng., 1954; PhD, Birmingham U., Eng., 1956. Boese postdoctoral fellow Columbia U., N.Y.C., 1957-58; prof. math. physics U. Birmingham, 1960-63; asst. rsch. physicist U. Calif., Berkeley, 1958-60, prof. physics, 1963-94, prof. emertitus, 1994—. Vis. prof. physics Harvard U., Cambridge, Mass., 1965-66, Univ. de Paris, Paris Sud, 1979-80, 84-85. Editorial bd. The Phys. Rev. jour., 1978-81, 85-88; contbr. articles to profl. jours. Recipient Dirac medal and prize Internat. Ctr. for Theoretical Physics, 1991. Fellow AAAS, Royal Soc. London, Am. Phys. Soc. (Dannie N. Heineman Math. Physics prize 1992). Jewish. Office: U Calif Dept Physics Berkeley CA 94720-0001

MANDELSTAMM, JEROME ROBERT, lawyer; b. St. Louis, Apr. 3, 1932; s. Henry and Estelle (London) M.; m. Carolyn A. White; stepchildren: John M. Gagliardi, Maria A. Amundson, Amy E. Gagliardi. AB, U. Pa., 1954; LL.B., Harvard U., 1957. Bar: Mo. 1957. Since practiced in, St. Louis; ptnr. Greenfield, Davidson, Mandelstamm & Voorhees, 1969—81, Schmitz, Mandelstamm, Hawker & Fischer, 1981—82; pvt. practice St. Louis, 1982—. Bd. dirs. Legal Aid Soc. City and County St. Louis, 1967-75, pres., 1969-70; bd. dirs. Lawyers Reference Service Met. St. Louis, 1976-83, chmn., 1978-83; bd. dirs. Mo. Legal Aid Soc., 1977-82; mem. 22d Jud. Cir. Bar Com., 1983-85, gen. chmn., 1984-85 Mem. St. Louis County Bd. Election Commrs., 1973-77. Served with AUS, 1957. Mem. ABA, Mo. Bar Assn., Am. Arbitration Assn. (panel of arbitrators 1984-2003), Bar Assn. Met. St. Louis (v.p. 1974-75, treas. 1975-76). Home: 7217 Princeton Saint Louis MO 63130-3000 Office: 1010 Market St Ste 1600 Saint Louis MO 63101-2082

MANDERS, KARL LEE, neurosurgeon; b. Rochester, NY, Jan. 21, 1927; s. David Bert and Frances Edna (Cohan) Mendelson; m. Ann Laprell, July 28, 1969; children: Karlanna, Maidena; children by previous marriage; Karl, Kerry, Kristine. Student, Cornell U., 1946; MD, U. Buffalo, 1950. Diplomate Am. Bd. Neurol. Surgery, Am. Bd. Clin. Biofeedback, Am. Bd. Hyperbaric Medicine, Am. Bd. Pain Medicine, Nat. Bd. Med. Examiners. Intern U. Va. Hosp., Charlottesville, 1950-51, resident in neurol. surgery, 1951-52, Henry Ford Hosp., Detroit, 1954-56; pvt. practice Indpls., 1956—. Med. dir. Cmty. Hosp. Rehab. Ctr. for Pain, 1973—92; chief hosp. med. and surg. neurology Cmty. Hosp., 1983, 93; coroner Marion County, Ind., 1977—85, 1992—96. With USN, 1952-54, Korea. Recipient Cert. achievement Dept. Army, 1969, Disting. Physician award Comm. Hosp., 1997. Fellow ACS, Internat. Coll Surgeons, Am. Acad. Neurology; mem. Congress Neurol. Surgery, Internat. Assn. Study of Pain, Am. Assn. Study of Headache, N.Y. Acad. Sci., Am. Coll. Angiology, Am. Soc. Contemporary Medicine and Surgery, Am. Holistic Med. Assn. (co-founder), Undersea Med. Soc., Am. Acad. Forensic Sci., Am. Assn. Biofeedback Clinicians, Soc. Cryosurgery, Pan Pacific Surg. Assn., Biofeedback Soc. Am., Acad. Psychosomatic Medicine, Pan Am. Med. Assn., Internat. Back Pain Soc., North Am. Spine Soc., Am. Soc. Stereotaxic and Functional Neurosurgery, Soc. for Computerized Tomography and Neuroimaging, Ind. Coroners Assn. (pres. 1979), Royal Soc. Medicine, Nat. Assn. Med. Examiners, Am. Pain Soc., Midwest Pain Soc. (pres. 1988), Am. Acad. Pain Medicine, Cen. Neurol. Soc., Interurban Neurosurg. Soc., Internat. Soc. Aquatic Medicine, James A. Gibson Anat. Soc., Am. Bd. Med. Psychotherapists (mem. profl. adv. council), James McClure Surg. Soc., Brendonwood Country Club, Highland Country Club. Home: 5845 High Fall Rd Indianapolis IN 46226-1018 Office Phone: 317-546-6691. Personal E-mail: annlmanders@comcast.net.

MANDERSCHEID, LESTER VINCENT, agricultural economics educator; b. Andrew, Iowa, Oct. 9, 1930; s. Vincent John and Alma (Sprank) M.; m. Dorothy Helen Varnum, Aug. 29, 1953; children: David, Paul, Laura, Jane. BS, Iowa State U., 1951, MS, 1952; PhD, Stanford U., 1961. Grad. asst. Iowa State U., Ames, 1951-52, Stanford (Calif.) U., 1952-56; asst. prof. Mich. State U., East Lansing, 1956-65, assoc. prof., 1965-70, prof., 1970-73, prof., assoc. chmn., 1973-87, prof., chmn., 1987-92, prof., 1992-95, prof. emeritus, 1996—, coord. Grad. Sch., 1993—. Reviewer Tex. A&M Agrl. Econ. Program, College Station, 1989; cons. Consortium Internat. Earth Sci. Info. Network, Ann Arbor, 1990. Co-author: Improving Undergraduate Education, 1967; contbr. articles to jours. in field. Pres. parish coun. St. Thomas, East Lansing, 1984-87; coll. coord. United Way, East Lansing, 1983-84; pres. bd. dirs. Cristo Rey Cmty. Ctr., 1998-2001. Recipient Disting. Faculty award Mich. State U., 1977. Mem. Am. Agrl. Econ. Assn. (pres. 1988-89, bd. dirs. 1982-85, excellence in teaching award 1974), Am. Statis. Assn., Am. Evaluation Assn., Am. Econ. Assn., University Club, Sigma Xi (pres. 1986-87), Phi

Kappa Phi (pres. 1979-80). Roman Catholic. Home: 2372 Burcham Dr East Lansing MI 48823-3885 Office: Mich State U Dept of Agrl Econs Circle Dr East Lansing MI 48824-1039 Office Phone: 517-353-3262. Business E-Mail: manderse@msu.edu.

MANDERSCHEID, RONALD WILLIAM, federal program administrator; b. LaCrosse, Wis., Sept. 28, 1943; s. William Joseph and Norene Elsine (Batteen) M.; m. Frances Elizabeth Fedkiw, Sept. 1, 1973; children: William Derrick, Kristen Elizabeth, Erika Marie. BA maxima cum laude, Loras Coll., 1965; MA, Marquette U., 1967; PhD, U. Md., 1975; Cert., Fed. Exec. Inst., 1986. Rsch. asst. U. Md., College Park, 1970—72; research assoc. NIMH, Adelphi, Md., 1972—75, sr. rsch. sociologist, 1975—80, chief evaluation rsch. sect. Rockville, Md., 1980—81, chief stats. rsch. br., 1981—92; acting dir. divsn. state and cmty. sys. devel. Ctr. for Mental Health Svcs., Rockville, 1992—93, chief survey & analysis, 1992—. Cons. George Washington U., Washington, 1978-83, WHO, 1993—, Pan Am. Health Orgn., 1995—, Columbia U., 1998-2001; mem. Internat. Consortium Mental Health Policy & Rsch., 2000—. Author, editor: Mental Health in the United States, 1987, 90, 92, 94, 96, 98, 2000, 02, 04, editor: System Science and the Future of Health, 1976; prodr.: Making the Numbers Work for You, 1987; contbr. articles to profl. jours. Active West Montgomery Citizens Assn., Potomac, Md., 1983—. With U.S. Army, 1967-69. Decorated Army Commendation medal; recipient Disting. Alumni award, Loras Coll., 1998, Sec. Disting. Svc. award, 1999, 2004, Mental Health Stats. Improvement Program Leadership award, 2001, Irving Blumberg Humanitarian award, Am. Assn. for Psychosocial Rehab., 2002, Saul Feldman Lifetime Achievement award, Am. Coll. Mental Health Adminstrn., 2003. Fellow Washington Acad. Scis. (life, pres. 1987 88), World Acad. Art and Sci., mem. APHA (chair mental health 1997-98, Mental Health Sect. award 2000, Mental Health Chairperson's Disting. Svc. award 2001, Consumer Leadership award 2003), N.Y. Acad. Scis., Am. Sociol. Assn. (chmn. various coms. 1983-91, chmn. com. fed. stds. sociologists 1983-88), Soc. for Gen. Sys. Rsch. (chmn. Washington chpt. 1976—), Ea. Sociol. Soc. (exec. com. 1979 84, chmn. various coms., Peter Gellman award 1984), D.C. Sociol. Soc. (pres. 1992-93), Fed. Exec. Inst. Alumni Assn. (exec. bd. 1997—2004, chair policy issues com. 1995-2000, pres. 2003, pres. found. 2003—, Meritorious Svc. award 1999), Soc. Applied Sociology (Nat. Sociol. Practice award 1995), Cosmos Club, Alpha Kappa Delta (pres. 1972-73), Delta Epsilon Sigma, Phi Kappa Phi. Avocations: coin collecting/numismatics, historical reading. Office: CMHS 5600 Fishers Ln Rm 15C-04 Rockville MD 20852-1750 Office Phone: 301-443-3343. E-mail: rmanders@samhsa.gov.

MANDEVILLE, HUBERT TURNER, JR., oil company executive; b. N.Y.C., Apr. 24, 1974; s. Hubert Turner Mandeville and Judith Knudsen. BBA, So. Meth. U., 1994, JD, 1998. Fin. analyst Amerada Hess Corp., Houston, 1994-95; sr. fin. analyst Santa Fe Energy, Houston, 1995-96; v.p. Mandeville Oil Co., Houston, 1996—; pres. Mandeville Corp., Houston, 1997—, EncrypTech Corp., Miami, 1999—. Cons. Oracle Software, Houston, 1996-97. Mem. Dallas Symphony, Houston Symphony. Mem. Dallas Hall Soc., Houstonian Club, Houston Livestock Show and Rodeo, One Hundred Club, River Oaks Country Club, Petroleum Club, Met. Racquet Club. Republican. Presbyterian. Avocations: financial markets, golf, tennis, skiing, fundraising. Home: 111 N Post Oak Ln Houston TX 77024-7703 Office: Mandeville Oil Corp 2323 N Field St Apt 2500 Dallas TX 75201-1761 also: EncrypTech Corp 1101 Brickell Ave Fl 5 Miami FL 33131-3105 Address: 1111 Brickell Bay Dr Ph 2 Miami FL 33131-2950

MANDIL, I. HARRY, nuclear engineer; b. Istanbul, Turkey, Dec. 11, 1919; s. Harry Robert and Bertha (Presente) M. (parents Am. citizens); m. Beverly Ericson, June 22, 1946; children: Jean Dale, Eric Robert. BS, U. London, 1939; MS, MIT, 1941; grad., Oak Ridge Sch. Reactor Tech., 1950; DSc (hon.), Thiel Coll., Greenville, Pa., 1960. Devel., design process controls for textile mills and chem. plants Norcross Corp., 1941-42, asst. to pres. charge field engring., 1946-49; asst. to tech. dir. naval reactors br. reactor devel. div. AEC, 1950-54, dir. reactor engring. div. Bur. Ships, Navy Dept. and chief reactor engring. br. Naval Reactors, 1954-64; prin. officer, dir. MPR Assos., Inc. (engrs.), Washington, 1964-85, cons., dir. Alexandria, Va., 1985—. Developer nuclear power for propulsion naval vessels, also for Shippingport Atomic Power Ctrl. Sta.; mem., sec. Energy Adv. Bd., Washington, 1990-93; mem. corp. vis. com. for nuclear engring. dept. MIT, 1984-93; mem. sr. tech. rev. group for plutonium, Amarillo, Tex., 1995-99. Author numerous papers in field. Served with USNR, 1942-46. Recipient Naval Letter of Commendation, 1946, Meritorious Civilian Svc. award Navy Dept., 1952, ASME Prime Movers award, 1956, Disting. Civilian Svc. award, 1959. Mem. Nat. Acad. Engring. Home: 150 Moorings Park Dr K302 Naples FL 34105 Office: 320 King St Alexandria VA 22314-3238 Fax: (703) 519-0224. Office Phone: 703-519-0200.

MANDL, ALEX J(OHANN), telecommunications company executive; b. Vienna, Dec. 14, 1943; came to U.S., 1958, naturalized, 1968; s. Otto William and Charlotte J. (Peshek) M.; m. Nancy J. Scott, June 10, 1967; 1 dau., Melanie. BA, Willamette U., 1967; MBA, U. Calif., Berkeley, 1969. With Boise Cascade Corp., 1969-80, dir. internat. fin., asst. treas., then fin. chmn., 1973-80; sr. v.p. fin. and corp. planning Seaboard System R.R. Co., Jacksonville, Fla., 1980-85; sr. v.p. corp. devel. and adminstrn. CSX Corp., Richmond, Va., 1985-86; chmn., CEO CSX Tech., 1986-88, Sea-Land Corp. subs. CSX Corp., Iselin, N.J., 1988-91; exec. v.p. comm. svc. group AT&T, N.Y.C., 1991-96; chmn., CEO Teligent, Vienna, Va., 1996—. Bd. dirs. CSX Comm., CSX Transp., Inc., Richmond Renaissance, Cybernetics and Systems Inc. Trustee Jacksonville Art Mus. Mem. Fin. Execs. Inst., Soc. Internat. Treasurers, Young Pres. Orgn., Bus. Week Corp. Planning 100, Mgmt. Policy Council, Council Planning Execs. (conf. bd.), Fin. Execs. Inst. (com. on corp. fin.). Clubs: River, University, The Bull and Bear. Office: Teligent 460 Herndon Pkwy Ste 100 Herndon VA 20170-5293

MANDL, HERBERT JAY, rabbi; b. Balt., Jan. 9, 1945; s. Sigmund and Ruth (Lefkowitz) M.; m. Barbara Sue Toltzis, Aug. 18, 1968; children: Aron M., Seth S., Debra A., Miriam D. AB, Johns Hopkins U., 1965; MHL, Jewish Theol. Sem., 1967, DDiv, 1994; PhD, U. Montreal, 1981. Ordained rabbi, 1969. Lectr. U. Alta., Edmonton, 1969-71; sr. rabbi Beth Shalom Synagoge, Edmonton, Alta., Can., 1969-71; asst. rabbi Congregation Shaar Hashomayim, Montreal, Que., Can., 1971-77; sr. rabbi Kehilath Israel Synagogue, Kansas City, Mo., 1977—; chaplain Overland Park Police Dept., Kans., 2000—. Adj. prof. U. Mo., Kansas City, 1978-80, Rockhurst Coll., adj. prof., 1989—; chaplain Kansas City Police Dept., 1988—. Bd. dirs. Shalom Geriatric Group, Kansas City, 1985-1990, Jewish Fedn., Kansas City, 1977—; chmn. State Mo. Health Facilities Rev. Commn., Jefferson City, 1980-86; chmn. Kansas State Holocaust Commn., Topeka, 1987—; mem. Kansas City Sister City Commn., 1980—, Kans. Pub. Disclosure Commn., 1991-97. Mem. Rabbinical Assembly (com. Jewish law and standards 1989-94), Internat. Order Police Chaplains, Rabbinical Assn. Kansas City (pres. 1980-81, 94-96), Union for Traditional Judaism (panelist on Jewish law 1985—), B'nai Brith, Rabbinic Cabinet United Jewish Cmtys., Fedn. of North Am. Office: Kebilath Israel Synagogue 10501 Conser St Shawnee Mission KS 66212-2600

MANDLE, EARL ROGER, design school president, former museum executive; b. Hackensack, N.J., May 13, 1941; s. Earl and Phyllis (Key) M.; m. Gayle Wells Jenkins, July 11, 1964; children: Luke Harrison, Julia Barnes. BA cum laude, Williams Coll., 1963; MA, cert. in Museum Training, NYU, 1967, postgrad.; DFA (hon.), U. Toledo, 1983, Kenyon Coll., 1986; PhD, Case Western Reserve U., 2002; DFA (hon.), Brown U., 2003. Intern in drawings Met. Mus. Art, N.Y.C.; intern in sculpture and architecture Victoria and Albert Mus., London, 1966-67; assoc. dir. Mpls. Inst. Arts, 1967-74, Toledo Mus. Art, 1974-76, dir., 1977-88; dep. dir. Nat. Gallery Art, Washington, 1988-93; pres. RISD, Providence, 1993—. Chmn. exec. com. Am. Fedn. Arts, 1987-93; mem. adv. panel New Zealand-U.S. Arts Found., Mus. Mgmt. Inst.; trustee Internat. Exhbns. Found., Sterling & Francine Clark Art Inst., Spanish Found. for Restoration of Toledo (Spain); mem. NEA, Nat. Com. Standards in Arts, 1992-94, steering com. 1993-94; mem. adv. council Nat. Mus. Act, Smithsonian Instn.; mem. adv. com. on mus. mgmt. J. Paul Getty Trust; adv. bd. Charles Hosmer Morse Found., Inc., Wexner Ctr., 1986, search com. dirs., 1988; chmn. U.S. Com. on Restoration of Toledo; cons. Nat. Mus. Western Art, Tokyo, Kerr Found., Oklahoma City; chair cultural adv. council Netherlands-Am. Amity Trust, Inc., Annual Coun. Retreats, 1990, 91, co-chmn. agenda com., 1992, cultural diversity task force, 1993, chair Clinton adminstrn. liaison com., 1993; mem., exec. Ohio Arts Coun.; mem. exec. adv. com. Williams Coll. Mus. Art; mem. arts adv. com. Barnes Found.; com. for the preservation of the U.S. Treasury Bldg., hist. advisor, 1989-93; vis. prof. Robert Sterling Clark Prof. of Art Williams Coll., Williamstown, Mass., 1993; mem. bd. trustees, sec. Art Mus. Assn., 1983, v.p. 1985, pres. 1986; com. mem. Art Against Aids, 1987, The Barnes Found. Conservation, 1992; founding trustee Coun. Mus. and Edn. in the Visual Arts, 1971; exec. com. Intermuseum Conservation Assn., 1977; appted. to Nat. Coun. Arts, Pres. Reagan, 1988, Pres. Bush, 1990-94; mem. search adv. com. U.S. State Dept. Curator, 1992; resource cons. Arts Edn. Partnership Working Group Subcommittee, Nat. Ctr. Arts Edn., 1992 93;bd. mem. Assn. Independent Coll. Art & Design (AICAD), Fraunhofer Gesellschaft; hon. bd. mem. Sterling & Francine Clark Art Inst., Toledo Mus. Art; testimony to the adv. bd. Nat. Mus. African Art, Smithsonian Instn., 1990; adv. session for bd. trustees The Textile Mus., Wash., D.C., 1993. Contbr. to profl. mags. and jours. Chmn., bd. dirs. Health and Edn. Leadership for Providence, 1996-99; trustee Providence Found., 1996, Toledo Arts Commn. 1975-78, Toledo Hosp., 1979, pub. rels. Com., 1979-88; mem. City Film Commn., 1995, Coun. Ambs; bd. dirs. Cranston Print Works, 1994-99; mem. adv. bd. Corp. Design Found., 1995, Alliance of Artists' Cmtys., chmn. com. on trustees, 1997-99; mem. nat. policy bd. Ams. for Arts, 1998; mem. steering com. Nat. Endowment for Arts, 1999; bd. trustees nom. com. Am. Red Cross, Toledo chpt., 1976, chmn. youth com.; founder English Speaking Union, Mpls. chpt., 1974; trustee long range planning com. Maumee Valley Country Day Sch., 1983-84, v.p., chmn. com. on trustees, 1987-88; Mayor's com. planning, City of Perrysburg, Ohio, 1985; mem. Rotary, vice-chmn. internat. svc. com., 1987, chmn. 75th anniversary sculpture com. 1987; design review bd. Toledo 1% for Art, 1978-88; mem. Toledo Bicentennial commn. 1974-76; mem. Toledo's com. of One Hundred, Cultural Task Force, 1987; bd. mem. Toledo's Cmty. And Cultural Arts Ctr., 1983; mem. Toledo Econ. Planning Coun., Cmty. and Cultural Programs Subcommittee, chmn. design com., 1981; mem. Toledo Exec. Forum, 1974-81, Toledo Mayor's Citizen Forum, 1975, Toledo Mayor's Com. on Renaissance Bldg. Redevelopment, 1983, Toledo Modern Art Group, 1974-1981, Toledo Sesquicentennial Commn., 1986-87, Young Pres. Org., Wash. Metro chpt., 1988-91, Greater Providence C. of C., 1994-; mem. task force com. Toledo Pub. Sch. "Partners in Edn.", 1981; coord. and speaker United Way Campaign Toledo, Company Program, 1975-81; mem. Warren/Sherman City Venture Project Mobility/Land Use Design Use com., 1977; mem. corp. bd. Trustcorp, Inc., audit, loan and nom. com., 1981-88. Decorated by the His Majesty Juan Carlos Knight of the Order of Isabel the Cath., Spain, 1985; Andover teaching fellow, 1963-64; Ford Found. fellow, 1966; Nat. Endowment Arts fellow, 1974; recipient Am. Hellenic Educational Progressive award, 1983, Distinguished Citizen for Art award Ohio Art Edn. Assn., 1983, Resolution for Leadership award Ohio Senate, 1983, Governor's award State of Ohio, 1983, Marketer of the Year award Am. Marketing Assn., 1983. Mem. Am. Assn. Mus. (trustee, v.p.), Art Mus. Assn. (pres.), Assn. Art Mus. Dirs., Am. Arts Alliance (trustee, policy com.), Coll. Art Assn. (mem. pres.' adv. bd.), Ohio Found. for Arts, Ohio Art Coun., Am. Assn. 18th Century Studies (treas.), Young Pres. Orgn., R.I. Ind. Higher Edn. Assn., Am. Fedn. Arts (chmn. exec. com., chmn. exhbn. com. 1985-93), R.I. Commodores, Confrerie des Chevaliers du Tastevin, Phi Kappa Phi. (hon. mem.), Providence Art Club, Univ. Club, Tile Club, Century Club (N.Y.C.), The Answer Club, Williams Club (N.Y.C.), Carranor Hunt and Polo Club, Catawba Island Yacht Club, The Toledo Club (mem., trustee 1977-88), Hope Club. Office: RISD Office of President 2 College St Providence RI 02903-2784

MANDLER, GEORGE, psychologist, educator; b. Vienna, June 11, 1924; came to U.S., 1940, naturalized, 1943; s. Richard and Hede (Goldschmied) M.; m. Jean Matter, Jan. 19, 1957; children: Peter Clark, Michael Allen. BA, NYU, 1949; MS, Yale U., 1950, PhD, 1953; post grad., U. Basel, Switzerland, 1947-48. Asst. prof. Harvard U., 1953-57, lectr., 1957-60; prof. psychology U. Calif., San Diego, 1965-94, chmn. dept. psychology, 1965-70, prof. emeritus, 1994—; dir. Ctr. Human Info. Processing, U. Calif., San Diego, 1965-90; prof. U Toronto, Canada. Hon. rsch. fellow Univ. Coll. London., 1977-78, 82-90, vis. prof., 1990—. Author: Mind and Emotion, 1975, (German edit.), 1980, Mind and Body, 1984, (Japanese edit.), 1987, Cognitive Psychology, 1985, Japanese edit., 1991, Human Nature Explored, 1997, Interesting Times, 2001; co-author: (with W. Kessen) The Language of Psychology, (Italian edit.), 1959, (with J.M. Mandler) Thinking: From Association to Gestalt, 1964; contbr. articles and revs. to profl. jours.; editor: Psychol. Rev., 1970-76. Served with U.S. Army, 1943-46. Fellow Ctr. for Advanced Study in Behavioral Scis., 1959-60; vis. fellow Oxford U., Eng., 1971-72, 78; Guggenheim fellow, 1971-72. Fellow AAAS, Am. Acad. Arts and Scis.; mem. AAUP, Am. Assn. Advancement Psychology (1974-82); Psychonomic Soc. (governing bd., chmn. 1983), Am. Psychol. Soc., Am. Psychol. Assn. (pres. div. exptl. psychology 1978-79, pres. div. gen psychology 1982-83, mem. coun. reps. 1978-82, William James prize 1986), Internat. Union Psychol. Scis. (U.S. com. 1985-90), Soc. Exptl. Psychologists, Fedn. Behavioral Psychol. and Cognitive Scis. (pres. 1981). Home: 1406 La Jolla Knoll La Jolla CA 92037-5236 Office: U Calif San Diego Dept Psychology La Jolla CA 92093-0109 also: 3 Perrins Lane London NW3 1QY England E-mail: gmandler@ucsd.edu.

MANDLER, JEAN MATTER, psychologist, educator; b. Oak Park, Ill., Nov. 6, 1929; d. Joseph Allen and May Roberts (Finch) Matter; m. George Mandler, Jan. 19, 1957; children: Peter Clark, Michael Allen. Student, Carleton Coll., 1947-49; BA with highest honors, Swarthmore Coll., 1951; PhD, Harvard U., 1956. Rsch. assoc. lab. social rels. Harvard U., 1957-60; rsch. assoc. dept. psychology U. Toronto, Ont., Can., 1961-65; assoc. rsch. psychologist, lectr. U. Calif. at San Diego, La Jolla, 1965-73, assoc. prof., 1973-77, prof. psychology, 1977-88, prof. cognitive sci., 1988-2000, rsch. prof., 2000—; mem. adv. com. memory and cognitive processes NSF, 1978-81. Hon. rsch. fellow U. Coll., London, 1978-89, vis. prof., 1990—; hon. mem. Med. Rsch. Coun. Cognitive Devel. Unit, 1982-98. Author: (G. Mandler) Thinking: From Association to Gestalt, 1964, Stories, Scripts and Scenes, 1984, The Foundations of Mind: Origins of Conceptual Thought, 2004; assoc. editor Psychol. rev., 1970-76; mem. editl. bd. Child Devel., 1976-89, Discourse Processes, 1977-94, Jour. Exptl. Psychology, 1977-85, Text, 1979-97, Jour. Verbal Learning and Verbal Behavior, 1980-88, Lang. and Cognitive Processes, 1985-, Cognitive Devel., 1990-99, Jour. Cognition and Devel., 1999-; contbr. articles to profl. jours. Pres. San Diego Assn. Gifted Children, 1968-71; v.p. Calif. Parents for Gifted, 1970-71; mem. alumni council Swarthmore Coll., 1975-78. NIMH research grantee, 1968-81; NSF research grantee, 1981-99. Fellow: APA (mem. exec. com. divsn. 3 1983—85), Am. Acad. Arts and Scis.; mem.: Soc. Exptl. Psychologists, Cognitive Devel. Soc., Cognitive Sci. Soc., Psychonomic Soc. (mem. governing bd. 1982—87, chmn. 1985—86), Phi Beta Kappa. Office: U Calif San Diego Dept Cognitive Sci La Jolla CA 92093-0515

MANDLES, MARTINN H. facility services company executive; b. Tacoma, Wash., Nov. 1, 1940; m. Connie Mandles; children: Melanie, Valarie Barsky. BS in Engring., Stanford U., 1964. Pilot U.S. Navy, 1964—68; dir., western corp. opers. Microdot Inc., 1969—72; v.p., mem. mgmt. com. ABM Industries Inc., L.A., 1973—91, exec. v.p., mem. bd. dirs., exec. com., 1992—96, chmn. bd., 1997—. Dir. Nat. Multi-Housing Coun., Washington, 1988—90, Bldg. Owners & Mgrs. Assn. of Greater L.A., 1995—. Founding dir. Century City C. of C., 1971—, chmn. bd., 1994; trustee Jewish Big Brothers & Sisters Assn., 1977—; charter mem. Fraternity of Friends of the L.A. Music Ctr., 1978—; trustee The Hebrew U. of Jerusalem, 1996—, vice chmn., dir. western region Am. Friends, 1996—. Named Century City Citizen of Yr., Century City C. of C., 1986. Mem.: The Regency Club (L.A.), Hillcrest Country Club (L.A.). Office: ABM Industries Corp Office Ste 3160 North Tower 2029 Century Park E Los Angeles CA 90067

MANDRA, YORK T. geology educator; b. N.Y.C. s. Raymond and Irene (Farruggio) M.; m. Highoohi Kechijian, Jan. 26, 1946. BA, U. Calif., Berkeley, 1947, MA in Paleontology, 1949; PhD in Geology, Stanford U., 1958. From instr. to assoc. prof. geology San Francisco State U., 1950-63, prof., 1964—, head geology sect., chmn. dept., 1960-67. Vis. prof. U. Aix-Marseille, France, 1959, Syracuse U., summer 1963, U. Maine, summer 1969, U. Calif., Santa Barbara, summers 1972—2002; rsch. assoc. U. Glasgow, 1959, Calif. Acad. Scis., 1966-88; vis. scientist New Zealand Geol. Survey, fall 1970. Contbr. numerous articles to profl. jours. Pres. David S. Sohigian Found., 1975—. Served with USAAF, 1942-46. Recipient Neil A. Miner Disting. Coll. Teaching award, 1984; Danforth Found. teaching fellow, 1958, NSF fellow, 1959; NSF rsch. grantee, 1967-77. Fellow Geol. Soc. Am. (Sr.), Calif. Acad. Scis., AAAS; mem. Nat. Assn. Geology Tchrs. (pres. Far Western sect. 1953-54, 73-74, Robert Wallace Webb award 1977). Avocations: walking, reading, music. Office: San Francisco State U Dept Geoscis 1600 Holloway Ave Dept Geoscis San Francisco CA 94132-1722 E-mail: ytjmandra@sfsu.edu.

MANDREKAR, MICHELLE NELSON, research scientist; b. St. Paul, Minn. d. Ronald John and Sandra Jeanette Nelson; m. Paraj Vidyadhar Mandrekar, May 23, 1998; 1 child, Alexander Atma. BS, U. of Minn., 1991; MS, U. of Wis., 1997. Rsch. scientist Promega Corp., Madison, Wis., 1997—. Contbr. articles to profl. jours. Recipient R & D 100 award, R & D Mag., 2002. Mem.: Am. Soc. of Plant Biologists. Achievements include patents for Detection of nucleic acid hybrids; Analytical methods and materials for nucleic acid detection; Multiplex method for nucleic acid detection; Exogenous nucleic acid detection; Depolymerization method for nucleic acid detection of amplified nucleic acid target; Detection of nucleic acid hybrids; Nucleic acid detection. Office: Promega Corp 2800 Woods Hollow Rd Madison WI 53711

MANDRELL, BARBARA ANN, singer, entertainer, actress, producer, writer; b. Houston, Dec. 25, 1948; d. Irby Matthew and Mary Ellen (McGill) M.; m. Kenneth Lee Dudney, May 28, 1967; children: Kenneth Matthew, Jaime Nicole, Nathaniel. Grad. high sch. Country music singer and entertainer, 1959—, performed throughout U.S. and in various fgn. countries; mem., Grand Ole Opry, Nashville, 1972—; star TV series Barbara Mandrell and the Mandrell Sisters, 1980-82, Barbara Mandrell: Get to the Heart, 1987; albums include Midnight Oil, Treat Him Right, He Set My Life To Music (Grammy award, Dove award 1983), This Time I Almost Made It, This is Barbara Mandrell, Midnight Angel, Barbara Mandrell's Greatest Hits, Christmas at Our House, 1987, Morning Sun, 1990, Greatest Country Hits, 1990, Standing Room Only, 1993; star TV series Barbara Mandrell and the Mandrell Sisters, 1980-82, TV movie Burning Rage, 1984, TV specials Barbara Mandrell, Something Special, 1985, The Lady is A Champ, (TV) The Wrong Girl, 1999, Stolen from the Heart, 2000; guest star TV series The Commish, Touched By an Angel, Dr. Quinn, Medicine Woman, Baywatch, Diagnosis Murder, (TV series) Sunset Beach, 1997-98, Touched By an Angel, 1994, Love Boat: The Next Wave, 1998, others; author (with George Vecsey): Get To the Heart: My Story, 1990; co-exec. (TV) Get to the Heart: The Barbara Mandrell Story, 1997; discs include No Nonsense, 1990, Key's in the Mailbox, 1991, The Best of Barbara Mandrell, 1992, The Ultimate Barbara Mandrell, 1994, The Barbara Mandrell Collection, 1995, Fooled By a Feeling, 1995. Named Miss Oceanside, Calif., 1965; Named Most Promising Female Singer, Acad. Country and Western Music, 1971; Female Vocalist of Yr., 1978; Female Vocalist of Yr., Music City News Cover Awards, 1979; Female Vocalist of Yr., Country Music Assn., 1979, 81, Entertainer of Yr., 1980, 81, 95; People's Choice awards (9), 1983-87. Mem. Musicians Union, Screen Actors Guild, AFTRA, Country Music Assn. (v.p.) Mem. Order Eastern Star. Home: PO Box 620 Hendersonville TN 37077-0620 Office: Creative Artists Agy 3310 W End Ave Fl 5 Nashville TN 37203-1028

MANDRY, CHRISTINE M. public adminstator; b. Waukegan, Ill., June 16, 1964; d. James and Linda (Lambert) LaPonsie; m. Dennis Robert Mandry; children: Sherri Ann, Casey Lynn, Nicole, Rebekah. BS, Auburn U., 2000, MPA, 2003. Cert.: (legal asst.); victim svcs. officer. Records tech. Adminstrv. Office of Cts., Montgomery, Ala.; restitution coord. Dist. Atty.'s Office, Montgomery, 2000—. Softball coach Millbrook Girls Softball League; vol. VOCAL (Victims of Crime and Leniency). Mem.: Nat. Orgn. Victim Assistance, Am. Soc. for Pub. Adminstrs. Home: 40 Green Ct Deatsville AL 36022 Office: Dist Atty's Office 100 South Lawrence St Montgomery AL 36102 Office Phone: 334-832-2545. Business E-Mail: christinemandry@mc-ala.org. E-mail: cmandry@justice.com.

MANDULA, JEFFREY ELLIS, physicist; b. N.Y.C., July 23, 1941; s. Andrew and Gertrude Phyllis (Entenberg) M.; m. Barbara Blumenstein, June 2, 1963. BA, Columbia U., 1962; MA, Harvard U., 1964, PhD, 1966. Fellow Harvard U., Cambridge, Mass., 1966-67; rsch. fellow Calif. Inst. Tech., Pasadena, 1967-69, asst. prof. theoretical physics, 1970-73; mem. Inst. for Advanced Study, Princeton, N.J., 1969-70; assoc. prof. applied math. MIT, Cambridge, 1973-79; prof. physics Washington U., St. Louis, 1979-87; sr. scientist theoretical physics Dept. Energy, Washington, 1987—. Program dir. for theoretical physics NSF, Washington, 1980-81; sec. Signition Corp., Los Alamos, N.Mex., 1986—; vis. prof. U. Minn., Mpls., 1979, U. Southampton, Eng., 1979; invited prof. U. Louvain, Belgium, 1980; adj. prof. physics Washington U., St. Louis, 1987—. Contbr. over 90 articles to profl. jours. NSF fellow, 1966, Alfred P. Sloan Found. fellow 1973; recipient Cottrel Rsch. award Rsch. Corp., 1984. Mem. AAAS, Am. Phys. Soc., Fedn. Am. Scientists. Home: 500 23d St NW Washington DC 20037-2828 Office: US Dept Energy Office High Energy Physics Washington DC 20585-0001 Business E-Mail: jeffrey.mandula@science.doe.gov.

MANEA, NORMAN, writer, educator; b. Suceava, Bukovina, Romania, July 19, 1936; came to U.S., 1988; s. Marcu and Janeta (Braunstein) M.; m. Josette-Cella Boiangiu, June 28, 1969. MS in Engring., Inst. Constrn., Bucharest, Romania, 1954. Engr., Romania, 1959-74; writer, 1969-86; fellow Deutscher Akademischer Austauschdienst, West Berlin, Germany, 1987; fellow Internat. Acad. Scholarship and the Arts Bard Coll., Annandale On Hudson, N.Y., 1989-92, writer in residence, 1992-96, Francis Flournoy prof. in European studies and culture, 1997—. Author: October, eight o'clock, 1992, On Clowns: The Dictator & the Artist, 1992, Compulsory Happiness, 1993, The Black Envelope, 1995, The Hooligan's Return, 2003; contbr. articles, stories to profl. jours. Recipient MacArthur Found. award, 1992, Nat. Jewish Book award Jewish Book Coun., 1993, Literary Lion award Nat. Pub. Libr., 1993, Nonino Internat. Lit. prize, Italy, 2002; Guggenheim grantee, 1992; Fulbright fellow, 1988. Mem. Am. Pen. Office: Bard Coll Dept Lang and Lit Annandale On Hudson NY 12504

MANEKER, DEANNA MARIE, advertising executive; b. Albany, N.Y., Dec. 13, 1938; d. Marion K. and Florence R. (Krell) Colle; m. Morton Maneker, Sept. 15, 1957 (div. Feb., 1981); children: Meryl C., Amy J., Marion Kenneth. AB, Barnard Coll., 1960. Dir. circulation Westchester Mag., Mamaroneck, N.Y., 1971-73; pub. Change Mag., New Rochelle, N.Y., 1973-78; gen. mgr. Ctr. for Direct Mktg., Westport, Conn., 1978-81; sr. v.p. The Stenrich Group, Glen Allen, Va., 1981-88, exec. v.p., 1988-94; COO Martin Direct (formerly The Stenrich Group), Glen Allen, Va., 1994-96, exec. v.p. database, fulfillment, call ctr. svcs., 1995-97; exec. v.p. Relationship Group The Martin Agy., Richmond, Va., 1997—. Home: 206 Tamarack Rd Richmond VA 23229-7039 Office: The Martin Agency One Shockoe Plz Richmond VA 23219-4132

MANEKER, MORTON M. lawyer; b. N.Y.C., Nov. 14, 1932; s. Arthur and Estelle (Hochberg) M.; m. Roberta S. Wexler, 1985; children: Meryl Colle, Amy Jill, Marion Kenneth. AB, Harvard U., 1954, LL.B., 1957. Bar: N.Y. State 1957. Assoc. Shearman & Sterling, N.Y.C., 1957—62; trial atty. antitrust divsn. Dept. Justice, 1962—63; ptnr. Proskauer Rose LLP, N.Y.C., 1963—94; ret., 1994. Trustee Beth Israel Hosp., N.Y.C., 1977—2001. Mem. Am. Law Inst., N.Y. State Bar Assn., Harmonie Club. Jewish. Home: 30 E 65th St New York NY 10021-7013 E-mail: maneker@aol.com.

MANEKER, ROBERTA S(UE), public relations executive; b. N.Y.C., July 9, 1937; d. Maxwell Roy and Esther (Gerson) Scheff; m. Hannan Wexler, June 4, 1961 (div. 1983); children: Daniel, Joanna; m. Morton M. Maneker, June 1, 1985. BA, Oberlin Coll., 1957. Mng. editor True Love mag., N.Y.C., 1960-62; publicity dir. Capt. Kangaroo, CBS, N.Y.C., 1962-66; syndicated columnist

Oleg Cassini, N.Y.C., 1967-69; freelance writer, N.Y.C., 1967-70; dir. pub. rels. Direct Mktg. Assn., N.Y.C., 1983-85, v.p. pub. rels., 1985-87; v.p. pub. rels. Christie's, N.Y.C., 1987-91, sr. v.p. corp. comm./mktg., 1991—. dir. Lechters, Inc. Ford Found. scholar, 1953-57. Mem. Oberlin Coll. Alumni Assn. (pres. 1989-91), Phi Beta Kappa. Home: 30 E 65th St New York NY 10021-7013 Office: Christie's 20 Rockefeller Plz New York NY 10020-1902

MANELLA, NORA M. federal judge; BA in Italian with high honors, Wellesley Coll., 1972; JD, U. So. Calif., 1975. Bar: Calif. 1976, U.S. Ct. Appeals (5th cir.) 1976, D.C. Ct. Appeals 1978, U.S. Dist. Ct. (ctrl., so., no. and ea. dists.) 1980-81, U.S. Ct. Appeals (9th cir.) 1982. Law clk. to Hon. John Minor Wisdom U.S. Ct. Appeals (5th cir.), New Orleans, 1975-76; legal counsel Subcom. on Constn., Senate Com. on Judiciary, Washington, 1976-78; assoc. O'Melveny & Myers, Washington and L.A., 1978-82; asst. to U.S. Atty. U.S. Dept. Justice, L.A., 1982-90, trial asst. major crimes, 1982-85, dep. chief, criminal complaints, 1986-87, chief criminal appeals, 1988-90; judge L.A. Mcpl. Ct., 1990-92; justice pro tem Calif. Ct. Appeals (2nd dist.), 1992; judge L.A. Superior Ct., 1992-93; U.S. atty. (ctrl. dist.) Calif. U.S. Dept. Justice, L.A., 1994-98; judge U.S. Dist. Ct. (ctrl. dist.) Calif., L.A., 1998—. Instr. U.S. Atty. Gen. Advocacy Inst., 1984-86, Calif. Jud. Coll., 1992-93; mem. Atty. Gen.'s Adv. Com., 1994-95. Mem. editl. bd. State Bar Criminal Law Newsletter, 1991-92. Mem. adv. bd. Monroe H.S. and Govt. Magnet, 1991-94; acad. specialist USAID Delegation, 1993; judge L.A. Times Cmty. Partnership Awards, 1993; bd. councilors Law Sch. U. So. Calif., 1996—. Mem. Am. Law Inst., Calif. Judges Assn., Nat. Assn. Women Judges, Calif. Women Lawyers, Women Lawyers of L.A., Order of the Coif. Office: US Dist Ct 312 N Spring St Los Angeles CA 90012-4701 Office Phone: 213-894-0413. E-mail: Arlene_Chavez@cacd.uscourts.gov.

MANELLI, DONALD DEAN, screenwriter, film producer; b. Burlington, Iowa, Oct. 20, 1936; s. Daniel Anthony and Mignon Marie (Dean) M.; m. Susan Linda Allen, June 16, 1964 (div. Aug. 1973); children: Daniel, Lisa. BA, U. Notre Dame, 1959. Communications specialist Jewel Cos., Melrose Park, Ill., 1959; script writer Coronet Films, Chgo., 1960-62; freelance writer Chgo., 1962-63; creative dir. Fred A. Niles Communications Ctrs., Chgo., 1963-67; sr. writer Wild Kingdom NBC-TV, Chgo., 1967-70; freelance film writer, producer Chgo., 1970-76; pres. Donald Manelli & Assocs., Inc., Chgo. and Paris, 1976—. Screenwriter, prodr. more than 225 documentary films, 1970—, numerous episodes Wild Kingdom, 1967-82 (Emmy award 1969, 70). Recipient numerous awards various orgns. including N.Y. Internat. Film Festival, Houston Internat. Film Festival, Berlin, Paris, Venice Internat. Film Festivals, CINE, 1976—. Mem. Writers Guild Am. Roman Catholic. Avocations: photography, travel, tennis. Office: 1 E Delaware Pl Ste 200 Chicago IL 60611-1449 also: 1 Rue Goethe 75116 Paris France E-mail: dmanelli@earthlink.net. *A simple truth is played out in most lives: what we believe ourselves to be, we are. We may be tested with our own failed efforts and plain bad luck, but our personal vision gives us strength. Success brings satisfaction and the responsibility to help others form and follow their own visions.*

MANERI, REMO R. management consultant; b. Cleve., Aug. 16, 1928; s. Quinto Peter and Lucia (Massenzi) M.; m. Camille Ann Caranna, Aug. 26, 1950; children: Peter, Alisa, Leonard, Celia. BS in Chem. Engring., Case Inst. Tech., 1950; grad., Advanced Mgmt. Program, Harvard U., 1969. Devel. engr. Dow Corning, 1950-53, market researcher, 1956, comml. devel. mgr., 1957-63, chief engr., 1964-66, unit mfg. mgr., 1967-69, dir. tech. service and devel., 1970-72, bus. mgr., v.p., 1973-74, mgr. bus., group v.p., 1975-76; pres. Dow Corning U.S.A., 1977-80; exec. v.p. Dow Corning Corp., 1981-82, also bd. dirs.; chmn. bd. Quantum Composites, 1982-85, pres., chmn. bd., 1985-87, chmn. bd., 1987-89, also bd. dirs.; mgmt. cons., 1989—. Bd. dirs. Comerica Bank-Midland, Duro-Last Roofing, Inc., Quantum Composites, Inc.; cons. in field. Contbr. articles to profl. jours.; patentee in field. Bd. dirs. Midland Hosp. Assn. Served with Signal Corps, U.S. Army, 1954-56. Named Man of Year Adhesives and Sealants Coun., 1988. Mem. AAAS, Chem. Spltys. Mfg. Assn. (dir.), Am. Chem. Soc., Sigma Xi, Tau Beta Pi, Alpha Chi Sigma. Clubs: Midland Country. Roman Catholic. Home and Office: 5808 Siebert St Midland MI 48640-2753

MANES, STEPHEN GABRIEL, concert pianist, educator; b. Bennington, Vt., Apr. 11, 1940; s. Julius H. and Edna E. (Silberstein) M.; m. Frieda Green, July 7, 1963; children: Sonya Ruth, Daniel Ira. BS, Juilliard Sch. Music, 1961, MS, 1963; postgrad. (Fulbright fellow), Acad. Music, Vienna, 1963-64. Vis. instr. music Oberlin Coll. Conservatory, Ohio, 1966-67; asst. prof. Ball State U., Muncie, Ind., 1967-68; prof. music U. Buffalo-SUNY, 1968—, chair, 1989-93, 99—; co-music dir. Sebago-Long Lake Region Chamber Music Festival, North Bridgton, Maine, 1982-85. Concert piano soloist maj. orchs. U.S. and abroad; debuts in Washington, 1962, N.Y.C., 1963, Vienna, Austria, 1964, Berlin, 1975, Amsterdam, 1975, London, 1975, chamber music concerts, radio, TV appearances, four-hand piano recitals with Frieda Manes in U.S., Australia, Can. and P.R.; rec. artist Orion Master Records, 1974—, Spectrum Records, 1986—; mem. Baird Piano Trio, 1986-90, 2000—. Recipient Kosciuszko Chopin prize, 1960, Town Hall award Concert Artists Guild, 1962; finalist Leventritt Internat. Competition, 1962; Harriet Cohen Internat. Beethoven prize, 1964 Mem. Music Tchrs. Nat. Assn., Coll. Music Soc., Am. Fedn. Musicians. Home: 89 High Park Blvd Amherst NY 14226-4210 Office: U Buffalo-SUNY Dept of Music 222 Baird Hall Buffalo NY 14260-4700

MANESS, EDWIN CLINTON, III, highway patrol officer, video coordinator; b. Charlotte, N.C., Feb. 5, 1955; s. Ed Clinton Jr. and Blanche (Jones) M.; m. Diane Mease, July 15, 1981; 1 child, Brooke. Grad. in radio/TV comm., Carolina Sch. Broadcasting, Charlotte, 1974. Sgt., video sect. N.C. Hwy. Patrol, Raleigh, 1981—. Mem. adv. bd. Boy Scouts Am., Morganton, N.C., 1979, Charlotte, 1991. Named Trooper of Yr., Mecklenburg County Rotary Club, Charlotte, 1991, Man of Yr. Morganton Jaycees, 1979; recipient Gov.'s Heroism award, 2000. Mem. Law Enforcement Video Assn. Baptist. Avocation: golf. Home: 7121 Westworth Dr Willow Spring NC 27592-9607 Office: NC State Hwy Patrol 3318 Garner Rd Raleigh NC 27610-5618 Office Phone: 919-662-4440. E-mail: emaness@ncshp.org.

MANESS, ELEANOR PALMER, research analyst; b. Raleigh, N.C., June 24, 1935; d. Oren Alston and Lillian Way Palmer; m. Charles B. Maness, Feb. 1, 1955 (dec. July 1989); children: Reid, Brian, Teresa. BA, Meredith Coll., 1958. Tchr. St. Timoth Sch., Raleigh, 1958—64; rsch. analyst N.C. State U., Raleigh, 1966—99; cons., 1999—. Contbr. articles to sci. jours. Recipient L.M. Ware Rsch. award, Am. Soc. for Hort. Sci., 1974, Excellence in Environment Rsch. award, Fed. Hwy. Adminstrn., 1997. Presbyterian. Avocations: hiking, swimming, gardening, rock hunting, fishing. Home: 2104 Gray Walsh Dr Wilmington NC 28405

MANESS, JOEL H. gas industry executive; BS, Tex. A&M U., 1973. Former pres. Mobil de Venezuela, Caracas, Venezuela; with Mobil, 1973—2000; sr. v.p. refining and supply Sunoco Inc., Phila., 2000—. Office: Sunoco Inc Ten Penn Ctr 1801 Market St Philadelphia PA 19103-1699

MANETTA, RICHARD, chemicals executive; b. 1945; BA, U. Mich.; JD, Wayne State U. Legal advisor Detroit City Coun., 1973—74; chief supervising asst./corp. counsel City of Detroit Law Dept., 1974—78; asst. gen. counsel for automotive safety and product litigation Ford Motor Co., 1989—94, asst. gen. counsel for discovery, 1994—99, assoc. gen. counsel for litigation, 1999—2000, dep. gen. counsel, dir. regulatory compliance, 2000—01; corp. v.p., gen. counsel The Dow Chem. Co., Midland, Mich., 2001—. Spkr. in field. Recipient Pres. award, Nat. Bar Assn., 2001, award, Wolverine Bar Assn., 2001. Fellow: Mich. State Bar Found. (life); mem.: ABA, Mich. Gen. Counsel Assn., Mich. State Bar. Office: The Dow Chem Co 2030 Dow Center Midland MI 48674

MANEY, MICHAEL MASON, lawyer; b. Taihoku, Japan, Aug. 13, 1936; s. Edward Strait and Helen M. M.; m. Suzanne Cochran, Oct. 22, 1960; 1 child, Michele. BA, Yale U., 1956; MA, Fletcher Sch. Law and Diplomacy, Tufts U., 1957; LL.B., U. Pa., 1964. Bar: N.Y. 1966, D.C. 1977. Case officer CIA, 1957-61; law clk. Justice John Harlan, Supreme Ct. U.S., Washington, 1964-65; asso. Sullivan & Cromwell, N.Y.C., 1965-70, ptnr., 1971-77, 81—, mng. ptnr. Washington, 1977-81. Law fellow Salzburg Seminar in Am. Studies, 1967; mem. bd. overseers Fletcher Sch. Law and Diplomacy. Mem. bd. overseers U. Pa. Law Sch. 1st lt. USAF, 1957-61. Mem. ABA, Am. Law Inst., Am. Coll. Trial Lawyers, N.Y. State Bar Assn., Union Club, Down Town Assn., Madison Beach Club, Madison Country Club, Met. Opera Club, New Haven Country Club. Home: 1220 Park Ave New York NY 10128-1733 also: 48 Neptune Ave Madison CT 06443-3210 Office: Sullivan & Cromwell LLP 125 Broad St New York NY 10004-2498 E-mail: maneym@sullcrom.com.

MANFREDI, DAVID PETER, architect; b. Hartford, Conn., Aug. 9, 1951; s. Domenic George and Elizabeth Frances (Ferrando) M. BA, U. Notre Dame, 1973; MA, U. Chgo., 1976; BArch, U. Notre Dame, 1979. Registered architect. V.p. The Architects Collaborative, San Francisco & Cambridge, Mass., 1979-88; prin. Elkus/Manfredi Architects, Boston, 1988—. Prin. works include SONY Gallery, 1992 (Chgo. Interiors Grand Prize 1993), West Roxbury Dist. Courthouse, 1992, Franklin Pierce Law Ctr., 1992. Mem. AIA, Boston Soc. Architects, Phi Beta Kappa. Office: Elkus/Manfredi Architects 530 Atlantic Ave Boston MA 02210-2218

MANGAN, JOHN LEO, retired electrical manufacturing company executive, international trade and trade policy specialist; b. Lakewood, Ohio, May 24, 1920; s. Mark A. and Celia M. Mangan; m. Mildred J. Livingston, June 21, 1946; children: John, Scott. BSME, Carnegie Inst. Tech., 1942. Registered profl. engr., Mass., N.Y. Turbine design engr. Gen. Electric Co., Lynn, Mass., 1946-48, turbine application and sales engr. Fitchburg and Lynn, Mass., Schenectady, St. Louis, 1948-55, mgr. gas turbine indsl. sales Schenectady, 1955-60, mgr. gas turbine product planning, 1960-64, mgr. turbine bus. strategy devel., 1966-86; mgr. turbine indsl. customer requirements Boeing Co., Seattle, 1964-66. Contbr. articles profl. jours., chpts. in books; inventor in field. Mem. com. Boy Scouts Am., 1955-59, 64-66; bd. dirs. United Way Schenectady County, Inc., 1991-96, chmn., 1992-93. 1st lt. U.S. Army, 1942-46. Recipient Profl. and Social Activities award GE, 1977, cert. of merit N.Y. State Assembly, 1995. Fellow ASME (v.p. 1975-79, bd. govs. 1983-87, Gas Turbine citation, Centennial medal 1980, Dedicated Svc. award 1988); mem. Internat. Combustion Engine Coun. (permanent com. 1974-81, v.p. 1977-81), Mohawk Golf Club (Schenectady). Home: 1345 Ruffner Rd Niskayuna NY 12309-2505

MANGAN, TERENCE JOSEPH, federal agency professional, retired protective services official; b. Utica, N.Y., Feb. 17, 1938; BA, St. Mary's Coll., 1961; MA, St. Albert's Coll., 1965; postgrad. in pub. adminstrn., U. So. Calif., 1972-76; Grad., FBI Nat. Acad., N.W. Law Enforcement Exec., 1986. Cert. Wash. State Criminal Justice Tng. Commn., Calif.; cert. Gov.'s Rev. Team Child Abuse Svscs., 1986. With Seaside (Calif.) Police Dept., 1967-72, Lakewood (Calif.) Police Dept., 1972-76, chief, dir. cmty. safety, 1976; chief Bellingham (Wash.) Police Dept., 1976-87, Spokane (Wash.) Police Dept., 1987-98; ret., 1998; mem. FBI Leadership Devel. Inst. FBI Acad., Quantico, Va., 1998—; program mgmt. FBI Nat. Exec. Inst. and Major City Chiefs Program. Past chair Wash. Stae Criminal Justice Tng. Commn., working group counter-terrorism, futures; mem. Mgmt. Adv. Group Organized Crime and Narcotics Enforcement; apptd. to death investigations coun. Spl. Task Force on Child Abuse, Gov.'s Criminal Justice Adv. Bd.; master mentor Waspc's Exec. Leadership Inst., coord. N.W. Law Enforcement Command Coll. Program; mem. Wash. Law Enforcement Exec. Forum, past chair; mem. Wash. State Inst. Cmty. Oriented Policing. Mem. archdiocesan steering com. Ann. Catholic Appeal, 1982; chair fund-raising drives Am. Cancer Soc., Am. Heart Assn., Salvation Army, Easter Seal Soc., Assn. Retarded Citizens; bd. advs. Holy Names Ctr.; exec. bd. Inland Empire coun. Boy Scouts Am.; bd. dirs. Spokane Goodwill Industries, United Way, Whatcom County, Calif. Paul Harris fellow Rotary Internat., 1986; recipient citation U.S. Secret Svc., 1969, Congl. Com. Internal Security, 1971, Svc. award City of Seaside, 1972, Disting. Svc. award City of Lakewood, Wash. Assn. Sheriffs and Police Chiefs, 1978-81, Cmty. Svc. award Wash. Toastmasters Internat., 1980, Pres. award Pacific Luth. U., 1981; named Police Officer of Yr. Nat. Exch. Club, 1979, Lawman of Yr. VFW, 1980, Law Enforcement Officer of Yr. VFW, 1980. Secret Svc. Honor award, 1998, Defender of Freedom award, 1998. Mem. Internat. Assn. Chiefs of Police (com. terrorism), Nat. Coun. Crime and Delinquency, Wash. Assn. Sheriffs and Police Chiefs (life mem.; past pres.), Internat. Peace Artch Law Enforcement Coun., VFW (life). Roman Catholic. Office: FBI Acad L Msu Rm 112 Quantico VA 22135-0001 Office Phone: 703-632-3164. Business E-Mail: tmangon@fbiacademy.edu.

MANGANARO, FRANCIS FERDINAND, naval officer; b. Providence, Feb. 27, 1925; s. Ralph and Ada Susanna (Hobden) M.; m. Carol Anne Slater, Sept. 8, 1948; children: Carol Sue, William Francis, John Thomas, Linda Anne, Mary Kathryn. Student, U. R.I., 1943-44; BS in Elec. Engring, U.S. Naval Acad., 1944-47; Post MD, Naval Engr., MIT, 1956; cert., Advanced Mgmt. Program, Harvard U. Sch. Bus., 1971; cert. pub. utilities exec. program, U. Mich., 1984. Registered profl. engr., Conn. Commd. ensign U.S. Navy, 1947, advanced through grades to rear adm., 1975; served in destroyers Atlantic Fleet, 1947-49; served in submarines Pacific Fleet, 1949-53; repair officer, submarines Pearl Harbor Naval Shipyard, 1956-59; design project officer, submarines Bur Ships, 1959-63; inspection and planning officer Office Supr. of Shipbldg., 1963-68; prodn. officer Portsmouth Naval Shipyard, 1968-72; comdg. officer Puget Sound Naval Shipyard, 1972-76; chmn. navy claims settlement bd. Naval Material Command, 1976-78; vice comdr. Naval Sea Systems Command, 1978-80; ret. (Naval Sea Systems Command), 1980. V.p., dir. GPU Nuclear Corp., 1980-90; cons. Burns & Roe Utility Mgmt. Cons., 1990-94; cons. Raytheon Engrs. & Constructors, Inc., 1994-96. Decorated DSM, Legion of Merit. Mem. Soc. Naval Architects and Marine Engrs., Am. Soc. Naval Engrs., Sigma Xi, Tau Beta Pi, Beta Psi Alpha.

MANGANELLO, JAMES ANGELO, psychologist; b. Cambridge, Mass., Nov. 30, 1944; s. Almando and Carmella (Spera) M.; m. Rosemarie Bombara, Dec. 26, 1965; children: Jason, Jennifer. BA, Eastern Nazarene Coll., 1966; MA, Boston U., 1970; EdM, Suffolk U., 1969; EdD, Boston U., 1977; M in Pub. Health, Harvard U., 1980. Instr. biology N.Y. Christian Acad., Bklyn., 1966-67; minister youth, edn. St. Paul Ch., Somerville, Mass., 1967-69; dir., founder Community Nursery Sch., Somerville, 1967-69; resident dir., instr. Malone Coll., Canton, Ohio, 1969-70; clin., research fellow dept. psychiatry Mass. Gen. Hosp., Boston, 1973-75; psychologist North Shore Counseling Ctr., Beverly, Mass., 1975-79; instr. North Shore Community Coll., Beverly, 1975-78; pres. Health Integration Services, Peabody, Mass., 1978-83; clin. fellow dept. psychiatry Harvard U. Med. Sch., Boston, 1983-84; pres. Dr. Manganello & Assocs., Danvers, Mass., 1983—, The Charis Inst., Lexington, Mass., 1994—; pres., CEO First Lexington Investments, Lexington, Mass. Cons. psychologist Erich Lindemann Mental Health Ctr., Boston, 1971-75, Westwood Lodge, 1973-74. Contbr. articles to profl. jours. Chpt. mem. Rep. Presdl. Task Force, Washington, 1983—; mem. guidance adv. bd., bd. trustees Lexington Christian Acad., Mass., 1977—; mem. pres.'s council Gordon-Conwell Theol. Sem., Hamilton, Mass., 1983—. Mem. AAAS, Am. Orthopsychiat. Assn., Am. Pub. Health Assn., Am. Coll. Health Care Execs., Am. Sci. Affiliation, Soc. for Sci. Study of Religion, MIT Enterprise Forum, Pi Lambda Theta. Avocations: tennis, basketball, music. Home: 2 Crest Cir Lexington MA 02421-7144 Office: 3 Militia Dr Lexington MA 02421-4739

MANGANELLO, TIMOTHY M. auto parts company executive; B of Mech. Engring., U. Mich.; postgrad., Harvard U.; grad., Chrusler Inst. Program. V.p. ops. BorgWarner TorqTransfer Systems, Inc., Muncie, Ind., 1995—99, pres., gen. mgr. Chgo., 1999—2001; v.p. BorgWarner, Inc., 1999—2001, exec. v.p., 2001—02, pres., CEO, 2002—03, pres., 2002—, chmn., CEO, 2003—. Office: BorgWarner Inc 200 S Michigan Ave Chicago IL 60604

MANGANIELLO, LOUIS OTTO JOSEPH, retired neurosurgeon; b. Waterbury, Conn., June 6, 1915; s. Angelo M. and Raimonda (Membrino) M.; m. Carol Graham Pryor, June 11, 1950; children: Carol Helen, Victoria R. AB, Harvard U., 1937; MD, U. Md., 1942; JD, Augusta Law Sch., 1967. Diplomate Am. Bd. Neurol. Surgery. Intern Uuniv. Hosp., Balt., 1942-43, resident in neurol. surgery, 1946-50; pvt. practice medicine specializing in neurosurgery Augusta, Ga., 1951-96; ret., 1996. Mem. staff Univ. Hosp., Doctors Hosp., St. Joseph Hosp., Augusta; mem., past pres. composite state bd. Med. Examiners Ga.; cons. VA Hosp., Augusta; dir. Blue Cross/Blue Shield; assoc. prof. neurosurgery Med. Coll. Ga., 1951-96, ret., 1996. Contbr. articles to profl. jours. Bd. dirs. ARC. Served with USN, 1942-46. Fellow ACS; mem. AMA, Richmond County Med. Soc., Med. Assn. Ga., Am. Assn. Neurol. Surgery, Congress Neurosurgeons, So. Neurosurg. Soc., Southeastern Surg. Congress, Am. Assn. Cancer Rsch., Am. Assn. Med. Colls., Internat. Assn. Lex and Sci., Ga. Neurosurg. Soc. (past pres.), Country Club of Augusta, Pinnacal Club, Rotary. Home: 656 Milledge Rd Augusta GA 30904-4388

MANGANO, MICHAEL F. federal official; AB, Villanova U., 1968; postgrad., U. Md., 1968-69. Dep. inspector gen. Ofice Evaluation & Inspections, 1988-94; prin. dep. inspector gen. HHS, 1994—. Contbr. articles to profl. jours. Recipient Presdl. Meritorious Rank award, 1989, 1995, Myrdal Govt. Svc. award, Am. Evaluation Assn., 1991, Sec.'s award for disting. svc., 1996, 1997, 1999, Presdl. Disting. Rank award, 1999. Office: Office of Inspector Gen 330 Independence Ave SW Washington DC 20201-0003

MANGANO, SALVATORE NICHOLAS, surgeon; b. Cambridge, Mass., 1922; s. Santo and Rose (Costa) M.; m. Anna Barney Stevenson, Apr. 28, 1956; children: Paul Stephen, John Joseph. AB, Harvard U., 1944; MD, Tufts U., 1947. Diplomate Am. Bd. Surgery. Intern Cambridge City Hosp., 1947-48, resident in surgery, 1949-51; resident Carney Hosp., Boston, 1948-49; pvt. practice gen. and colon-rectal surgery, 1953-90; cons. Mass. Dept. Correction, 1990—. Surgeon Lemuel Shattuck, Boston; asst. clin. prof. surgery Tufts U. Sch. Medicine, 1994—. Capt. USAF, 1951-53. Fellow ACS; mem. Am. Soc. Colorectal Surgery, Nat. Bd. Med. Examiners, Mass. Bd. Registration in Medicine (sec. 1984-87), Fedn. State Med. Bds. (cert. of appreciation 1987), Middlesex Dist. Med. Soc. (exec. sec. 1970—). Roman Catholic. Home: 145 Black Bear Dr Unit 2011 Waltham MA 02451-0229 Office: 145 Black Bear Dr #2011 Waltham MA 02451

MANGAPIT, CONRADO, JR., manufacturing executive; b. Cavite, Philippines, Oct. 17, 1946; s. Conrado Lebang Sr. and Amparo Ajuste (Odion) M.; m. Rosalinda Martinez Travis, Dec. 19, 1970; 1 child, Regina. BEE, U. So. Calif., Los Angeles, 1969; MA in Human Resource Mgmt., Pepperdine U., 1978. Commd. ensign USN, 1969, advanced through grades to lt. comdr., resigned, 1979; project engr. Continental Can Co., Houston, 1979-80; from applications engr. to sr. sales exec. Toshiba Houston Internat. Corp., 1980—97, sr. sales exec., 1997-98; sales mgr. Power Conversion Divsn., Liteon, Houston, 1998-99; dir. engring. Factory Automation Sys., College Park, Ga., 1999-2000; product mgr. IMC, Tucson, 2000—01; sales mgr. Magtrol/A.E.A., Tucson, 2001—02; regional mgr. Rosens Power Sys., Tucson, 2002; pres., CEO Nat. Phone Svc., Tucson, 2002—. Advisor Filipino-U.S. Mil. Assn., Guam, 1977-78; co. rep. Japan-Am. Soc., Houston, 1985—, Houston Minority Bus. Coun., 1997—. Recipient Humanitarian Service medal U.S. Dept. Def., 1978; named Outstanding Young Man of Am. U.S. Jaycees, 1980. Mem. IEEE, Am. Mgmt. Assn. Clubs: Mission Bend Homeowners Assn. (Houston), Toastmasters Internat. (Tucson), Bus. Network Internat. (Tucson). Republican. Roman Catholic. Avocations: reading, guitar, electronics, camping, college recruiting for the university of southern california.

MANGELSDORF, THOMAS KELLY, psychiatrist, consultant; b. St. Louis; s. Albert Henry and Hazel (Kelly) M.; m. Helen Louise Kareth, Apr. 12, 1958 (div. Jan. 1986); children: Ellen S., Steven T., Thomas K. Jr., Laura E. BS, U. Notre Dame, 1952; MD, St. Louis U., 1956. Diplomate Am. Bd. Psychiatry and Neurology (examiner 1968, 95), cert. Am. Bd. Profl. Disability Cons.; forensic expert in psychiat. trauma. Cons. in mental health various municipalities and pvt. practice, 1972—. Author and editor computerized system to interpret Minn. Multiphasic Personality Inventory profiles. Served to capt. U.S. Army, 1960-62. Fellow: Am. Psychiat. Assn. Avocation: sailing. Office: 621 S New Ballas Rd Ste 112 A Saint Louis MO 63141-8232

MANGER, WILLIAM MUIR, internist, educator, writer; b. Greenwich, Conn., Aug. 13, 1920; s. Julius and Lilian (Weissinger) M.; m. Lynn Seymour Sheppard, May 30, 1964; children: William Muir, Jr., Lilian Wade (Mrs. Porter Fleming), Stewart Sheppard, Charles Seymour. BS, Yale U., 1944; MD, Columbia U., 1946; PhD, Mayo Found., U. Minn., 1958. Diplomate Nat. Bd. Med. Examiners, Am. Bd. Internal Medicine. Intern Presbyn. Hosp., NYC, 1946-47, resident, 1949-50, asst. physician, 1957—2001; fellow internal medicine Mayo Found., 1950-55; dir. Manger Rsch. Found., 1961-77; clin. asst. attending physician Columbia divsn. Bellevue Hosp., 1964-68; asst. attending physician NYU Bellevue Hosp., 1969-77, assoc. attending physician, 1977-83, attending physician, 1983—; instr. medicine Columbia U. Coll. Physicians and Surgeons, 1957-66, assoc. medicine, 1966-70, lectr., 1981—. Asst. attending physician Presbyn. Hosp., 1966—68; asst. clin. prof. medicine NYU Med. Ctr., 1968—75, assoc. clin. prof. medicine, 1975—83, clin. prof. medicine, 1983—; mem. devel. com. Mayo Clinic, 1981; vice chmn. bd. Manger Hotels, Inc., 1957—73. Co-author: Chemical Quantitation of Epinephrine and Norepinephrine in Plasma, 1959, Pheochromocytoma, 1977, Clinical and Experimental Pheochromocytoma, 1996, 100 Questions and Answers About Hypertension, 2001; author: Catecholamines in Normal and Abnormal Cardiac Function, 1982; editor, co-author: Hormones and Hypertension, 1966; editor: Am. Lecture Series in Endocrinology, 1962-75; guest editor First Irvine H. Page Internat. Hypertension Rsch. Symposium, 1990; contbr. articles to profl. and lay jours. Mem. bd. govs. St. Albans Sch., Washington, 1958-64, 67-73, 83-89, chmn., 1967-69; trustee Found. Rsch. in Medicine and Biology, 1971-77, Buckley Sch., 1975-85, Lycee Francais, NY, 1996-98, Found. for Advancement Internat. Rsch. in Microbiology, 1977-82, Thyroid Found., 1980-85; mem. bd. visitors Boston U. Med. Sch., 1992—; trustee Found. for Depression and Manic Depression, 1978-89, pres., 1980-89; elder Presbyn. Ch., 1968-70, 92-93, trustee, 1962-67, 80-84, deacon, 1959-61; founder Values Initiative Tchg. About Lifestyle program, 2002. Lt. (j.g.) M.C., USNR, 1947-49. Recipient Mayo Found. Alumni award for Meritorious Rsch., 1955, Disting. Alumnus award, 1992. Fellow ACP, Acad. Psychosomatic Medicine, Am. Geriatric Soc., Coun. on Geriatric Cardiology, NY Acad. Medicine (admission com. 1976-78, edn. com. 1979-92) Am. Coll. Cardiology, Am. Coll. Clin. Pharmacology, Royal Soc. Health, Am. Inst. Chemists; Nat. Hypertension Assn. (founder, trustee, chmn. 1977—), AMA, Am. Soc. Internal Medicine, NY State Med. Soc., NY County Med. Soc., Am. Heart Assn. (fellow coun. on circulation and coun. for high blood pressure rsch.), Nat. High Blood Pressure Edn. Program (mem. coord. com.), Inter-Am. Soc. Hypertension, Internat. Soc. Hypertension, Am. Soc. Hypertension (designated hypertension specialist), Am. Thoracic Soc., NY Acad. Sci., AAAS, Am. Physiol. Soc., Am. Chem. Soc., Am. Soc. Pharmacology and Exptl. Therapeutics, Am. Soc. for Clin. Pharmacology and Therapeutics, Clin. Autonomic Rsch. Soc., Am. Autonomic Soc., Med. Strollers, NYC, Endocrine Soc., Pan Am. Med. Assn., Harvey Soc., Soc. Exptl. Biology and Medicine, Rsch. Discussion Group (founding mem., sec.-treas. 1958-80), Am. Fedn. Clin. Rsch. Am. Soc. Nephrology, Royal Soc. Medicine (affiliate), Fellows Assn. Mayo Found. (v.p., pres. 1953), Mayo Alumni Assn. (v.p. 1981-82, exec. com. 1981-89, pres. elect 1982-85, pres. 1985-87), Chatecholamine Club (founder, sec.-treas. 1967-80, pres. 1981-82), Drs. Mayo Soc., Plummer Soc., Albert Gallatin Assocs., The 1941 Soc., New Eng. Soc., SAR (chmn. admissions com. 1959-67, bd. mgrs. 1959-67, 69-70), Soc. Colonial Wars, Soc. of the Cin., Sigma Xi, Nu Sigma Nu, Phi Delta Theta, Explorers, Meadow (L.I., NY), Univ. Club, NY Athletic Club (NYC), Southampton Bathing Club. Achievements include research on the mechanism of salt-induced hypertension, the mechanism whereby potassium lowers blood pressure and prevents stroke, and on pheochromocytoma. Home: 8 E 81st St New York NY 10028-0201 Fax: 212-447-7032. Office Phone: 212-689-0873. Personal E-mail: nathypertension@aol.com.

MANGES, JAMES HORACE, investment banker; b. N.Y.C., Oct. 8, 1927; s. Horace S. and Natalie (Bloch) M.; m. Joan Brownell, Oct., 1969 (div.); m. Mary Seymour, 1974 (div. Oct. 2000); children: Alison, James H. Jr. Grad., Phillips Exeter Acad., 1945; BA, Yale U., 1950; MBA, Harvard U., 1953. With Kuhn, Loeb & Co., N.Y.C., 1954-77, ptnr., 1967-77; mng. dir. Lehman Bros., Kuhn Loeb Inc., N.Y.C., 1977-84, Shearson Lehman, Inc., N.Y.C., 1984-90;

adv. dir. Lehman Bros., N.Y.C., 1990-96. Dir. Baker Industries, 1967—77, Proudfoot PLC, 1996—98; dir., exec. com. Metromedia, Inc., 1970—86. Trustee The Episcopal Sch., 1978-92, St. Bernard's Sch., 1985-2000, Phillips Exeter Acad., 1985-89, mem. trustee coun., 1989-95; mem. Ctr. Strategic and Internat. Studies, Washington. Mem. Bond Club, Yale Club (N.Y.C.), Century Country Club (Purchase, N.Y.), Harvard Club (N.Y.C.). Home: 888 Park Ave New York NY 10021-0235 Office: #2016 45 Rockefeller Plz New York NY 10111-0100

MANGIA, ANGELO JAMES, lawyer; b. Bklyn., Mar. 12, 1954; AB in Govt. cum laude, Georgetown U., 1975; JD, St. John's U., 1978. Bar: N.Y. 1979, U.S. Dist. Ct. (so. and ea. dists.) N.Y. 1979, U.S. Ct. Appeals (2d cir.) 1985. Asst. atty. Town of North Hempstead, N.Y., 1979-81; assoc. Ain, Libert & Weinstein, Garden City, N.Y., 1981; atty. Town of North Hempstead, N.Y., 1982; counsel senate com. on crime State of N.Y., 1983-85, counsel senate com. on banks, 1985-88; chief counsel to majority N.Y. State Senate, 1989-94; mng. dir. Sandler, O'Neill & Ptnrs., L.P., N.Y.C., 1995-2001; pres., CEO Std. Funding Corp., Woodbury, NY, 2001—. Bd. advisors Coll. Mgmt. L.I. (N.Y.) U. Mem. bd. editors N.Y. Law Jour., 1994-96. Recipient Outstanding Work in Field of Criminal Justice Legis. award N.Y. State Bar Assn., 1985, Disting. Svc. award Civil Trial Inst./St. John's Law Sch., 1987, Luther Gulick award for Outstanding Achievement in Pub. Svc. Long Island U., 1992; Toll fellow, 1991. Mem.: Nassau County Bar Assn. Office: 335 Crossways Park Dr Woodbury NY 11797 Office Phone: 516-364-0200 x222. Business E-Mail: amangia@standardfunding.com.

MANGIAPANE, JOSEPH ARTHUR, consulting company executive, applied mechanics consultant; b. N.Y.C., Aug. 1, 1926; s. Michael and Rose D'Amico M.; m. Marcia Balut, Oct. 30, 1954 (div. Apr. 1974); children: Rosemarie, Michael, Diana, Joseph J., Susan. BS, Fordham U., 1950. Stress analyst Republic Aviation, Farmingdale, N.Y., 1951-55; pvt. practice tech. cons., 1955-58; sect. mgr. Aerojet-Gen., Sacramento, 1958-61; project engr. Pratt & Whitney Aircraft, East Hartford, Conn., 1961-71; pvt. practice tech. cons., 1971-79; pres. Joseph A. Mangiapane & Assocs., Inc., Tampa, Fla., 1979-92. Author numerous tech. reports. Served as cpl. USAAF, 1945-47, ETO. Fellow: AIAA (assoc.); mem.: Pine Acres Club (Wethersfield, Conn. chpt.) (pres. 1968—69), Equestrian Order of the Holy Sepulchre of Jerusalem (Southeastern Lieutenancy) (knight 2004). Republican. Roman Catholic. Avocations: reading, photography, genealogical research. Home: 5410 Aragon Ct Tampa FL 33624-4884 E-mail: Jam50ram@aol.com.

MANGION, RICHARD MICHAEL, health care executive; b. Haverhill, Mass., Apr. 26, 1941; s. Michael Anthony and Evelyn (Cote) M.; m. Gail Elizabeth Donne, Apr. 27, 1968; children: Catherine Jean, James Richard, Ian Kyle. BBA, Suffolk U., 1963; MBA, Syracuse U., 1965; MPH, U. Calif., Berkeley, 1972. Asst. adminstr. Nashua (N.H.) Meml. Hosp., 1972-75, assoc. adminstr., 1975-77; pres. and chief exec. officer Harrington Meml. Hosp., Southbridge, Mass., 1977—. Lectr. U. N.H., Durham, 1972-74. Pres. Tri-Community Devel. Corp., Southbridge, 1983-88. Capt. USAF, 1966-70. Fellow Am. Coll. Health Care Execs. (regent Mass. area B 1995-99); mem. Am. Hosp. Assn., Mass. Hosp. Assn., Ctrl. Mass. Hosp. Coun. (pres. 1982-84), Ctrl. Mass. Health Care Found., Tri-Cmty. C. of C. (pres. 1983-84). Clubs: Hosp. Supts. Lodges: Rotary. Democrat. Roman Catholic. Avocations: tennis, swimming, hiking. Home: 50 Old Village Rd Sturbridge MA 01566-1069 Office: Harrington Meml Hosp 100 South St Ste 1 Southbridge MA 01550-4047 Office Phone: 508-765-9771 3451. E-mail: rmangion@harringtonhospital.org.

MANGLANO-OVALLE, INIGO, sculptor; BA in Art with highest honors, BA in L.Am. and Spanish Lit. cum laude, Williams Coll., 1983; MFA in Sculpture, Sch. Art Inst. Chgo., 1989. One-man shows include Mus. Contemporary Art, Chgo., 1993, 1997, Andera Rosen Gallery, N.Y.C., 1996, Contemporary Arts Ctr., Cin., 1997, Inst. Cultural Cabanas Mus., Guadalajara, Mex., 1997, Max Protech Gallery, N.Y.C., 1998, Southeastern Ctr. Arts, Winston-Salem, N.C., 1998, Henry Art Gallery, U. Wash., Seattle, 1999, exhibited in group shows at U. Ill., Chgo., 1992, 1993, U. Wis., Eau Claire, 1992, Sch. Art Inst. Chgo., 1992, Walker Arts Ctr., Mpls., 1992, Randolph St. Gallery, Chgo., 1992, 1996, No. Ill. U. Art Gallery, 1992, Terrain Gallery, San Francisco, 1992, 1998, Mexican Fine Arts Ctr. and Mus., Chgo., 1992, Otis Gallery, L.A., 1993, Berlin Gallery Mus. Modern Art, 1994, Lowe Art Mus., U. Miami, 1996, Mus. Contemporary Art, Chgo., 1996, Ariz. State U. Art Mus., Phoenix, 1998, Christopher Grimes Gallery and Track 16 Gallery, Santa Monica, Calif., 1998, Represented in permanent collections Mus. Contemporary Art, Chgo., also corp. collections, work represented in numerous publs. Recipient spl. projects award, Ill. Arts Coun., 1993; Hutchinson fellow, Williams Coll., 1983—85, fellowship award, Ill. Arts Coun., 1992, Gt. Cities fellow, U. Ill. Coll. Urban Planning, Chgo., 1995, Orion fellow, U. Victoria, B.C., Can., 1995, visual artist fellow, NEA, 1995, internat. artist residency fellow, ArtPace Found., San Antonio, 1997, grantee, Chgo. Dept. Cultural Affairs, 1992, 1993, 1994. Address: care Max Protetch Gallery 511 W 22d St New York NY 10011-1109

MANGLONA, JOHN A. judge; b. Rota, Northern Marianas, June 12, 1959; m. Mona V. Monglona; 2 children. BA in Polit. Econ., U. Calif., Berkeley, 1981; JD, Creighton U., 1984; LLM in Taxation, U. Pacific, 1988. Pvt. practice; assoc. judge Commonwealth Superior Ct., 1998—2000; justice Commonwealth Supreme Ct., 2000—. Designated justice Guam Supreme Ct., 1999—2003. Office: House Justice Guma Hustisia, Imwaal Aweewe PO Box 502179 Saipan MP 96950-2179 Business E-Mail: supreme.court@saipan.com.

MANGLONA, RAMONA V. judge, former state attorney general; b. 1967; BA, U. Calif., 1990; JD, U. N.Mex., 1996. Bar: New Mex. Bar Assn. 1997, No. Mariana Islands Bar Assn. 1997. Asst. atty. gen.; atty. gen. No. Mariana Islands, Saipan, 2002—03; assoc. judge Commonwealth Superior Ct., 2003—.

MANGOLD, ARCHIE WAYNE, II, insurance agent; b. Pekin, Ill., Dec. 8, 1973; s. Archie Wayne, Sr. and Rebecca Ann Mangold. BA in English, U. No. Iowa, 1996. Bean walker Arthur Milikins Farm, Hedrick, Iowa, 1991; tel. sales rep. APAC Customer Svcs., Oskaloosa, Iowa, 1995, tel. sales rep., ins. agt., 1996—2002. Editor: Literary: Mag. Writing, 1990—2000. Home and Office: PO Box 116 117 1/2 1st Ave W #12 Oskaloosa IA 52577 Office Phone: 641-672-2976.

MANGOLD, JOHN FREDERIC, manufacturing company executive, former naval officer; b. La Grange, Ill., Jan. 24, 1927; s. John Frederic and Helvig Victoria (Anderson) M.; m. Margaret Ellen Gore, Oct. 25, 1947; children: John, Andrew, Jennifer. BS, U.S. Naval Acad., 1947; MSEE, U.S. Naval Postgrad. Sch., Monterey, Calif., 1958. Registered profl. engr., Conn. Commd. ensign USN, 1947, advanced through grades to comdr., 1962, comdg. officer nuclear submarine U.S.S. Halibut, 1962—63, comdg. officer nuclear tng. unit, 1963—67, ret., 1967; v.p. mfg. Combustion Engring., Inc., Windsor, Conn., 1972—78, group pres., 1982—86, v.p. utility boilers, 1990—91; pres. Vetco, Inc., Ventura, Calif., 1978—82; cons., 1992; pres. Detrex Corp., Southfield, Mich., 1992—93, ret., 1993. Bd. dirs. Detrex Corp. Mem. IEEE, U.S. C. of C. (energy com. 1984-87). Republican.

MANGOLD, SYLVIA PLIMACK, artist; b. N.Y.C., Sept. 18, 1938; d. Maurice and Ethel (Rein) Plimack; m. Robert Mangold. Student, Cooper Union, 1956-59; BFA, Yale U., 1961. Exhibited one-person shows Daniel Weinberg Gallery, San Francisco, 1974, 75, Fischbach Gallery, N.Y.C., 1974, 76, Fischbach, 1974, 76, Annemarie Verna Gallery, Zurich, 1978, 91, 97, Droll-Kolbert Gallery, N.Y.C., 1978, 80, Young Hoffman Gallery, Chgo., 1980, Ohio State U., Columbus, 1980, Pa. Acad., 1981, Contemporary Arts Mus., Houston, 1981, Madison Art Ctr., (Wis.), 1982, Brooke Alexander, Inc., 1982, 83, 84, 85, 86, 89, 92, 95, Duke Art Mus., N.C., 1982, Rhona Hoffman Gallery, Chgo., 1982, 85, Tex. Gallery, 1986, Fuller Goldeen Gallery, San Francisco, 1987, U. Mich. Ann Arbor, 1992, Minn. Inst. Arts, 1992, Grunwald Ctr. for Graphic Arts, UCLA, 1992, Neuberger Mus. Art, SUNY, Purchase, 1993, Davison Art Ctr., Wesleyan U., Middletown, Conn., 1993, Albright-Knox Art Gallery, Buffalo, 1994, Wadsworth Atheneum, Hartford, Conn., 1994, Blaffer Gallery U. Houston, 1994, Mus. Fine Arts, Boston, 1994, Herbert F. Johnson Museum, 1998, Cornell U., Ithaca, N.Y., 1998, Alexander and Bonin, N.Y., 2000, 2003, group shows at Young Hoffman Gallery, Chgo., 1979, Walker Art Ctr., Mpls., 1979, Droll-Kolbert Gallery, 1979, Denver Art Mus., 1979, U. So. Calif., 1979, Honolulu Acad. Art, 1979, Oakland Mus., (Calif.), 1979, Univ. Art Mus. of U. Tex.-Austin, 1979, Cornell U., Ithaca, N.Y., 1979, The New Museum of Contemporary Art, N.Y.C., 1979, Nat. Museum, Belgrade, Yugoslavia, 1979, Internat. Biennial Ljibljana, Yugoslavia, Phoenix Art Mus., 1979, Art Latitute Gallery, N.Y.C., 1980, Thorpe Intermedia Gallery, Sparkhill, N.Y., 1980, U. Colo. Art Galleries, Boulder, 1980, Nina Freudenheim Gallery, Buffalo, 1980, U.S. Pavillion of Venice Biennial, 1980-81, Indianapolis Museum of Art, 1980, Civici Musei e Gallerie di Storia e Arte, Sala Ajace, Udine, Italy, 1980, Young Hoffman, Chicago, 1980-81, Delahunty, Dallas, 1980, Museum of Modern Art, 1981, Wesleyan U. Art Gallery, 1981, Davison Art Ctr., Middleton, Conn., 1981, Virginia Museum of Fine Arts, Richmond, 1981, Oakland Museum, Calif., 1981, Inst. Contemporary Art of U. Pa., Phila, 1980-81, Yale U. Art Gallery, 1981, San Antonio Mus. Art, 1981, Indpls. Mus. Art, 1981, Tucson Mus. Art, 1981, Pa. Acad., 1981, Mus. Art of Carnegie Inst., Pitts., 1981, Brooke Alexander, Inc., N.Y.C., 1982, Ben Shahn Ctr. Visual Arts, 1982, Castle Gallery, Coll. of New Rochelle, N.Y., 1983, Thomas Segal Gallery, Boston, 1982-83, Siegel Contemporary Art, N.Y., 1983, Freedman Gallery, Albright Coll., Reading, Pa., 1983, Fuller Goldeen, San Francisco, 1983, Yale U. Art Gallery, New Haven, 1983-84, 86, Wilcox Gallery, Swarthmore, Pa., 1984, The Hudson River Mus., Yonkers, N.Y., 1984, Sardonia Art Gallery, Wilkes Coll., Wilkes-Barre, Pa., 1985, Kent State U. Gallery, Ohio, 1985, Brooke Alexander, N.Y., 1985, John C. Stoller Co., Minn., 1985, Knight Gallery, Spirit Sq. Arts Ctr., Charlotte, N.C., 1986, Mus. Art, R.I. Sch. Design, Providence, 1986, Yale U. Gallery, 1986, CUNY, 1986-87, Lorence Monk Gallery, N.Y.C., Vanquard Gallery, Phila., 1986-87, Aldrich Mus., Ridgefield, 1986-87. Flander's Contemporary Art, Mpls., 1987, Annemarie Verna Galerie, Zurich, 1988, U. N.C., 1988, R.I. Sch. Design, 1988, Grace Borgenicht Gallery, N.Y.C., 1988, Fay Gold Gallery, Atlanta, 1988, U. N.C., Greensboro, Three Rivers Arts Festival, Pitts., 1989, Cin. Art Mus., New Orleans Mus. Art, Denver Art Mus., Pa. Acad. Fine Arts, 1989, U. Mich., 1992, Mpls. Inst. Arts, 1992, Grunwald Ctr. Graphic Arts, UCLA, L.A., Neuberger Mus. Art, SUNY Purchase, 1993, Davison Art Ctr., 1993, Montgomery Glasoe Fine Art, Mpls., 1993, Yale U. Art Gallery, New Haven, 1993, Daniel Weinberg Gallery, Santa Monica, Calif., 1993, Museum of Fine Arts, Boston, 1993, Barbara Mathes Gallery, N.Y.C., 1993, Nina Freudenheim Gallery, Buffalo, 1993, Kansas City Gallery of Art, U. Mo., 1994, Midtown Payson, N.Y.C., 1994, Katonah Museum of Art, N.Y., 1994, Rhona Hoffman Gallery, Chgo., 1994, Feigen Inc., Chgo., 1994, Brooke Alexander, N.Y.C., 1994, Elga Wimmer Gallery, N.Y.C., 1995, Aargauer Kunsthaus Aarau, Austria, 1995, The Am. Acad. of Arts and Letters, N.Y.C., 1995, Andre Zarre Gallery, N.Y.C., 1996, Aspen Art Museum, Colo., 1996, The Am. Acad. of Arts and Letters, N.Y.C., 1996, Anne Marie Verna Gallery, Zurich, Switzerland, 1997, Queens Museum of Art, 1997, Aspen Art Museum, 1997, U. Gallery, Fine Arts Ctr., U. Mass., Amherst James Graham & Sons, N.Y.C., 1997, The Museum of Modern Art, 1997, Seattle Art Museum, 1997, State U. N.Y., 1998, N.Y.C. Dowd Fine Arts Gallery, 1998, The Am. Acad. of Fine Arts and Letters, 1998, Karen McCready Fine Art, 1999, Alexander and Bonin, N.Y.C., 1999, Henry Art Gallery, Seattle, 2000, Small Work, Nina Freudenheim Inc., Buffalo and numberous others; exhibited in permanent collections, Albright-Knox Art Gallery, Buffalo, Allen Meml. Art Mus., Oberlin, Ohio, Bklyn. Mus., Dallas Mus. Fine Arts, Detroit Inst. Art, Mus. Fine Arts, Houston, Indpls. Mus. Art, Madison (Wis.) Art Ctr., Milw. Art Mus., Yale U. Art Gallery, Mus. Modern Art, N.Y.C., Mus. Fine Arts, U. Utah, Tampa (Fla.) Mus., Walker Art Mus., Mpls., Whitney Mus. Am. Art, N.Y., Weatherspoon Art Gallery, Greensboro, N.C., Wadsworth Athenaeum, Hartford, U. Mich., Utah Mus. Fine Art, Museum of Fine Arts, Boston, N.Y.C. Public Library, Smith Coll. Museum, Northampton, Mass., Achenbach Found. for Graphic Arts, San Francisco, St. Louis Art Museum, The Tampa Museum, Art Inst. Chgo., Modern Art Mus. Fort Worth Tex., Indpls. Mus. Art, Telfair Mus. Art, Savannah Ga. Achievements include work reviewed in newspapers and mags.

MANGONE, GERARD J. international and maritime law educator; b. N.Y.C., Oct. 10, 1918; s. Gerard Francis and Viola (Schumm) M.; m. Emma Haddad, Apr. 13, 1958; children— Cleopatra, Regina, Flaminia. AB, CCNY, 1938; MA, Harvard, 1947, PhD (Charles Summer prize), 1949. Asst. prof. polit. sci. Wesleyan U., Middletown, Conn., 1948-51; assoc. prof. Swarthmore Coll., 1951-56; prof. polit. sci. and internat. relations Syracuse U., 1956-67; dir. grad. overseas tng. program, exec. officer Maxwell Center Study Overseas Operations, 1958-60; exec. asst. to dean Maxwell Grad. Sch., 1961-64, asso. dean dir. internat. relations program, 1961-67; dean Coll. Liberal Arts, v.p., provost Temple U., Phila., 1967-69; sr. fellow Woodrow Wilson Internat. Ctr., 1970-72; prof. internat. law U. Del., Newark, 1972-74, dir. Ctr. for Study of Marine Policy, 1973-89, H. Rodney Sharp prof. internat. law and orgn., 1975-89, univ. rsch. prof. internat. and maritime law, 1989—, prof. legal studies, 2001—, coord. grad. studies, 1976-79; adj. prof. Maine Maritime Acad., 1992—94. Vis. prof. Trinity Coll., Mt. Holyoke Coll., Yale, Princeton, Johns Hopkins; Tagore law prof. U. Calcutta, 1979; disting. lectr. U. Ind., 1980; vis. scholar U. Western Australia, 1983, 87, Peking U., 1984, Capetown U., 1986, 89, U. Natal, 1989, Hanyano U., 1994, Hong Kong U., 1997; mem. Presdl. Commn. Trust Territory Pacific, 1963; cons. AID, 1965-67, Nat. Commn. Marine Resources and Engring. and State Dept., 1967-73, UN, 1965, U.S. Corps Engrs., 1975; vice chmn. exec. com. Commn. Study Orgn. Peace; exec. dir. Pres.' Commn. on UN, 1970-71; dir. diploma program, shipping and pt. mgmt. Pt. of Singapore, 1990-97. Author: The Idea and Practice of World Government, 1951, A Short History of International Organization, 1954, The Elements of International Law, 2d edit, 1967, Marine Policy for America, 1977, 2d edit., 1989, Law for the World Ocean, 1981, Mangone's Concise Marine Almanac, 2d edit., 1991, United States Admiralty Law, 1997; co-author, editor: The Art of Overseasmanship, 1958, The Overseas Americans, 1960, European Political Systems, 1960, UN Administration of Economic and Social Programs, 1966, Energy Policies of the World, 3 vols, 1976-79, Internat. Straits of the World, 14 vols., 1978-2004; editor: Future of Gas and Oil from Sea, American Strategic Minerals, 1984; editor in chief: Marine Policy Reports, 1981-91, Internat. Jour. Marine and Coastal Law, 1991— . Capt. AUS, 1942-46, maj. res., 1946-54. Mem. Am. Soc. Internat. Law, Internat. Law Assn., Maritime Law Assn., Port of Wilmington Maritime Soc. (bd. dirs. 1980-, chmn. 1989, sec. Alison Soc., 1990-, Francis Alison award 1983), Del. Acad. Sci. (pres. 1993), Cosmos Club (Washington), Harvard Club (N.Y.C.). Home: 201 Unami Trl Newark DE 19711-7508 Office: Univ Del Grad Coll Marine Studi Newark DE 19716 Office Phone: 302-831-8087.

MANGOUNI, NORMAN, publishing executive; b. Detroit, Oct. 19, 1932; s. Nazareth Lazarus and Isabelle (Garabedian) M.; m. Anahid Apelian, May 10, 1964; 1 child, Marie-Isabelle. AB, U. Mich., 1954; MS, Columbia U., 1955; postgrad., U. Mich., 1957-58. Reporter Ann Arbor (Mich.) News, 1957-59; editor Mich. Alumnus, U. Mich., Ann Arbor, 1959-62; sr. editor Coll. Entrance Exam. Bd., N.Y.C., 1962-64; dir. fin. aid U. Miami, Coral Gables, Fla., 1965-66; dir. State U. N.Y. Press, Albany, 1966-78; pres., gen. editor Scholars' Facsimiles & Reprints, Ann Arbor, Mich., 1972—; pres. Caravan Books, Ann Arbor, Mich., 1972—, Acad. Resources Corp., Las Vegas, Nev., 1988—; corr. DuPont-Columbia Survey and Awards, 1976-78; rep. to com. on standards in field of library work, documentation and related pub. practices Am. Nat. Standards Inst., 1974-78. Exec. asst. to majority caucus Mich. State Senate, 1964; dir. summer session Am. Coll. Switzerland, 1979, 81, 82. Co-translator: The Gaucho Martin Fierro, 1974; contbr. articles to profl. jours.; mem. editorial bd. Ararat mag, 1962-66, 77-78. Served to lt. USAF, 1955-57. Mensa, Phi Sigma Kappa, Sigma Delta Chi, Phi Alpha Delta, Kiwanis. Home: PO Box 5934 Carefree AZ 85377 Office Phone: 480-575-9945. E-mail: n.mangouni@att.net.

MANGUAL, JESUS A. army officer; b. San Juan, P.R., Nov. 20, 1949; BA in Econs., Norwich U., 1973; MS in Contracts and Acquisition Mgmt., Fla. Inst. Tech., 1986; grad., Army Command/Gen. Staff Coll., Indsl. Coll. Armed Forces. Commd. 2d lt. U.S. Army, 1973, advanced through grades to col.; comdr. 46th Corps Support Group, Ft. Bragg, N.C., 1995-97; chief supply policy divsn. Army DCSLOG, Pentagon, Washington, 1997-98; exec. officer, mil. asst. to Dep. Asst. Sec. Def., Pentagon, Washington, 1995; dep. for acquisition and readiness U.S. Army Soldier and Biol. Chem. Command, Soldier Sys. Ctr., Natick, Mass., 1998-2000, also installation comdr., 1998-2000; comdr. Def. Supply Ctr. Phila. U.S. Army Def. Logistics Agy., Phila., 2000—02; dir. force projection and distbn. Office Dep. Chief Staff G-4 U.S. Army, Washington, 2002—04. Decorated Legion of Merit with one oak leaf cluster, others; recipient Meritorious Svc. award Nat. IMAGE, Inc., 2002.*

MANGUM, GARTH LEROY, economist, educator; b. Delta, Utah, July 23, 1926; s. James L. and Golda (Elder) M.; m. Marion Poll, Nov. 20, 1953; children: Stephen, David, Mary, Elizabeth. BS, Brigham Young U., 1956; MPA, Harvard U., 1958, PhD, 1960; JD, U. Utah, 1989. Instr. econs. Harvard U., 1960, asso. prof. econs. Brigham Young U., 1960-63; sr. staff analyst Presdl. R.R. Commn., 1961; research dir., subcom. employment and manpower U.S. Senate, 1963-64; exec. dir. President's Com. Manpower, 1964-65; exec. sec. Nat. Com. Tech., Automation and Econ. Progress, 1965-66; research prof. econs. George Washington U., 1967-71; co-dir. George Washington U. (Center Manpower Policy Studies), 1967-69; Max McGraw prof. econs. and mgmt. U. Utah, Salt Lake City, 1969-97, prof. emeritus, 1997—, dir. Inst. Human Resource Mgmt., 1969-90. Lectr. U. Tel Aviv, Israel, 1969, 84, Am. Seminar at Salzburg, 1975, U. South Africa, 1977, Monash U., Australia, 1984; spl. mediator Fed. Mediation and Conciliation Svc., 1962-63; mem. Adv. Coun. Vocat. Edn., 1966-67; vice chmn. Nat. Manpower Policy Task Force, 1966-69, chmn., 1969-71, mem., 1966-76; mem. Nat. Coun. on Employment Policy, 1976—, chmn., 1979-81, sec.- treas., 1990-2002; chmn. Nat. Inst. Career Edn., 1976 81; cons. fed., state and local govts., bus. firms, govts. of, Saudi Arabia, Kuwait, Jordan, Yemen, Bahrain, United Arab Emirates, Indonesia, Yugoslavia, Romania, Uganda, Nigeria, Israel, South Africa, Russia, Korea, China, other countries; cons. AID, ILO, World Bank; also arbitrator. Author: The Operating Engineers: Economic History of a Trade Union, 1964, MDTA, Foundation of Federal Manpower Policy, 1968, The Emergence of Manpower Policy, 1969, Federal Work and Training Program in the 1960's, 1969, Economic Opportunity in the Ghetto, 1970, Human Resources and Labor Markets, 1971, Career Education: What It Is and How To Do It, 1972, A Decade of Manpower Development and Training, 1973, Career Education and the Elementary School Teacher, 1973, Career Education in the Middle/Junior High School, 1973, Manpower Planning for Local Labor Markets, 1974, Career Education for the Academic Classroom, 1975, Employability, Employment and Income, 1976, Career Education in the High School, 1976, Your Child's Career, 1977, The Lingering Crisis of Youth Unemployment, 1978, Coming of Age in the Ghetto, 1978, Job Market Futurity, 1979, The Coal Industry and its Industrial Relations, 1985, Capital and Labor in American Copper, 1992, Labor Struggle in The Post Office, 1992, The Mormons War on Poverty, 1993, Union Resilience in Troubled Times, 1994, Portable Pension Plans for Casual Labor Markets, 1995, Transnational Industrial Marriages, 1996, The Rise, Fall and Replacement of Industry-Wide Bargaining in the Basic Steel Industry, 1996, Programs in Aid of the Poor, 8th edit., 2003, On Being Poor in Utah, 1997, The Public Employment Svc. In a One Stop World, 1998, Poverty Ain't What It Used To Be, 1999, Confronting The Youth Demographic Challenge, 2000, The Persistance of Poverty in the United States, 2003; also articles, monographs.; editor: The Manpower Revolution: Its Policy Consequences, 1965, Automation and Economic Progress, 1966, Metropolitan Impact of Manpower Programs, 1973, The T in CETA, 1981, Of Heart and Mind: Social Policy Essays in Honor of Sar A. Levitan, 1996. With USAAF, 1944-45. Mem. Ch. of Jesus Christ of Latter-day Saints (missionary 1950-53, bishop 1971-78, other positions). Home: 2130 Ridgewood Way Bountiful UT 84010-1632 E-mail: garthmangum@aros.net.

MANGUM, WILLIAM GOODSON, artist; b. Kinston, N.C., Jan. 31, 1924; s. Charles Preston and Margaret Edwards Mangum; m. Ariana Holliday Mangum; children: Ariana, William, Alice, Laura, Grace. BA in Art, U. N.C., 1956, MA in Art History, 1959; postgrad., Notre Dame U.; student, U. Florence, Italy, Art Students League N.Y., 1948-50, Corcoran Sch. Art, Washington, 1946-48. Prof. art emeritus Salem Coll. One-man shows include U. N.C., Chapel Hill, 1957, Western Carolina U., U. Tenn., Winthrop Coll., 1957, N.C. Mus. Art, Va. Mus. Art, 1959, Salem Coll., 1960, Southeastern Ctr. for Creative Art, 1958, Lynn Kottler Galleries, N.Y., 1960, Philip Morris Corp. Hdqs., Richmond, Va., 1962; exhibited in group shows Art Students League of N.Y., Bodley Gallery, N.Y.C., 1963, Springfield (Mass.) Mus. Art, N.C. Mus. Art, Va. Mus. Art, 1959, Isaac Delgado Mus., New Orleans, 1964, High Mus., Atlanta, 1964, Mint Mus., Charlotte, N.C., 1964, Southeastern Ctr. for Creative Art, 1968;; represented in permanent collections N.C. Mus. Art, U. N.C., Chapel Hill, Greensboro, Salem Coll., R.J. Reynolds Industries, Wachovia Bank, various pvt. collections; executed Prometheus monument The Lamp of Learning, Greensboro, 1962, portrait bust of Carl Sandburg, Sandburg Mus., Flat Rock, N.C., 1962; trombonist in concert band and jazz groups. Served with 8th Air Force USAF, Eng., WW II. Recipient awards N.C. Mus. Art, Va. Mus. Art, SECCA, Isaac Delgado Mus., High Mus. Address: 106 Ascot Dr Chapel Hill NC 27517-7991

MANHART, GRANT LEE, music educator; b. Columbus, Ohio, July 6, 1957; s. Harold Eugene and Sharon Lee Manhart; m. Nicole Marie Hiar, Oct. 4, 1996 (dec. Dec. 4, 2000); children: Logan Grant, Chase Lee. MusB, U. of Wis., Madison, WI, 1977—81; MusM - trumpet performance, U. of Cin. - Coll. Conservatory of Music, Cincinnati, OH, 1981—83; MusD - trumpet performance, Ind. U., Bloomington, IN, 1986—94. First Aid CPR ARC, 1987. Trumpet artist Salsa Picante Band, San Juan, PR, 1989—94; factory sales Keystone RV, Elkhart, Ind., 1996—97; head wrangler Cheley Colo. Camps, Estes Park, Colo., 1976—78; assoc. prof. of music No. State U., Aberdeen, SD; trumpet artist Buddy Rich Band, Various, NY, 1984—85, Carol Channing-Rita Moreno show, Various, Elkhart Symphony, Elkhart, Ind., Carmine Cavallero/Herb Jeffires/June Valli Show, Various, Calif., Dreamgirls Broadway Show, New York, NY; leader Jif and the Choosey Mothers Band, Bloomington, Ind.; trumpet artist Columbia Artists Gene Krupa Band, LA, 1991—92, Jimmy Coe Band, Indianapolis, Ind., 1987—94. Composer: (music for band) Various titles for band, jazz ensemble, pep band, (trumpet teaching method) Manhart's Trumpet Method; author: (internet music masterclass) Improving the Trumpet Section, High Notes for Trumpets. Artist in residence Gt. Live Music Productions, Aberdeen, SD, 1998—2003, Elkhart, Ind., 1995—98, Madison, Wis., 1977—81. Recipient 2002 Outstanding Faculty Award, No. State U. Found., 2002, Coclaser Award, U. of Cin. Bands, 1983, Gold Key, Gold Spurs, Cheley Colo. Camps, 1975, Performance Award-Teaching, No. State U., 2001. Mem.: Am. Federations of Musicians Union Local 131 (licentiate; active mem. 1977—2003), Pi Kappa Lambda (licentiate; active mem. 2000—03), Phi Beta Mu (licentiate; mem. 2001—03). Achievements include development of Dr. Manhart's Summer Jazz Workshops; design of Fishing Lure Badger Coppertail; Compositions: Multiple, for jazz ensemble, pep band, marching band; first to Distance Learning: Music Masterclasses in South Dakota; Continuing the teachings of William Adam, combining Gestalt and Zen psychology, principles of Tai Chi and athletic performance in the teaching of trumpet and music in general. Avocations: fishing, lure making, cedar strip canoe building, woodworking, gardening, ice skating, golf. Office: Northern State Univ 1200 S Jay St Aberdeen SD 57401 E-mail: manhartg@northern.edu.

MANHART, MARCIA Y(OCKEY), art museum director; b. Wichita, Kans., Jan. 14, 1943; d. Everett W. and Ruth C. (Correll) Yockey; children: Caroline Manhart Sanderson, Emily Alexandrea Morrison. BA in Art, U. Tulsa, 1965, MA in Ceramics, 1971. Dir. edn. Philbrook Art Ctr., Tulsa, 1972-77, exec. v.p., asst. dir., 1977-83, acting dir., 1983-84; exec. dir. Philbrook Mus. Art (formerly Philbrook Art Ctr.), Tulsa, 1984—, The Judith and Jean Pape Charitable Foun. Instr. Philbrook Art Ctr. Mus. Sch., Tulsa, 1963-72; gallery dir. Alexandre Hogue Gallery, Tulsa U., 1967-69; NEH Challenge Grant panelist, 1991, presenter to AAM Conv., 1991; MAAA Craft Fellowship panelist, 1988, 93, NEA Craft Fellowship panelist, 1990; NEA spl. exhbn. panelist, 1996; curator nat. touring exhibit Nature's Forms/Nature's Forces: The Art of Alexandre Hogue, 1984-85; co-curator internat. exhbn.: The Eloquent Object, 1987-90; curator Sanford and Diane Besser Collection exhbn., 1992. Author essays in field. Vis. com. Smithsonian Instn./Renwick Gallery, Washington, 1986; cultural negotiator Gov. George Nigh's World

Trade Mission (Okla.), China., 1985; com. mem. State Art Coll. of Okla., 1985—; mem. Assocs. of Hillcrest Med. Ctr., 1983-88, exec. com., 1985-88; com. mem. Neighborhood Housing Services, 1985-87; mem. City of Tulsa Arts Commn., 1996-2003; steering com. Harwelden Isnt. for Aesthetic Edn., 1983; com. mem. River Parks Authority, 1976; mem. Jr. League of Tulsa Inc., 1974-78; adv. panel mem. Nat. Craft Planning Project, NEA, Washington, 1978-81; craft adv. panel mem. Okla. Arts and Humanities Council, 1974-76; juror numerous art festivals, competitions, programs; reviewer Inst. Mus. Services, Washington, 1985, 88, 92, 95, 98; auditor Symposium on Language & Scholarship of Modern Crafts, NEA and NEH, Washington, 1981; nominator MacArthur Fellows Program, 1988; panelist Lila Wallace Reader's Digest Internat. Artists Fellowship, 1992, panelist Pew Charitable Trust, 1996. Recipient Harwelden award for Individual Contbrn. in the Arts, 1989, Gov.'s award State of Okla., 1992. Mem. Assn. Am. Mus., Assn. Art Mus. Dirs., Art Mus. Assn. Am., Mountain Plains Assn. Mus., Am. Craft Coun., Okla. Mus. Assn., Tulsa Met. C. of C. (bd. dirs. 1997-99), Rotary, Phi Beta Kappa. Home: 105 S Cherry St Fredericksburg TX 78624 E-mail: mmanhart@austin.rr.com.

MANHEIM, CAMRYN, television and film actress; b. N.J., Mar. 8, 1961; BFA, UC Santa Cruz, 1984; MFA, NYU, 1987. Star (TV series) The Practice, 1997—, appeared in (TV films) Jackie's Back!, 1999, The Loretta Claiborne Story, 2000, (TV miniseries) The 10th Kingdom, 2000; actor: (films) Bonfire of the Vanities, 1990, The Road to Wellville, 1994, Jeffrey, 1995, Eraser, 1996, Romy and Michele's High School Reunion, 1997, David Searching, 1998, Wide Awake, 1998, Mercury Rising, 1998, Happiness, 1998 (Nat. Bd. Rev. award, 1998), Fool's Gold, 1998, Joe the King, 1999, What Planet are You From?, 2000; prodr., performer Kiss My Act, 2000; actor: (films) East of A, 2000, The Laramie Project, 2002, Just Like Mona, 2003; appeared on TV shows Law and Order, Touched By an Angel, New York Undercover, Ally McBeal, Oh Baby, Chicago Hope, Will and Grace, star (one-woman show) Wake Up, I'm Fat, 1995, theater appearances include N.Y. Shakespeare Festival, Lincoln Ctr., Yale Repertory, N.Y. Theatre Workshop, Classic Stage Co., Home for Contemporary Theater. Recipient Obie award, 1995, Emmy award as best supporting actress, 1998, Golden Globe award, 1999, Quality TV for Viewers award, 1999. Office: Creative Artists Agy 9830 Wilshire Blvd Beverly Hills CA 90212

MANI, INDERJEET, computer scientist, educator; married. PhD with distinction, Georgetown U., 1997; BSc, Delhi U., 1976; BSc hons., U. Sussex, 1979; MS, U. Pa., 1980. Mem. tech. staff Tex. Instruments, Dallas, 1984—88, MCC, Austin, Tex., 1988—92; sr. prin. scientist MITRE, McLean, Va., 1992—2003; assoc. prof. Georgetown U., Washington, 2003—. Author: Automatic Summarization, 2001, (magazine) WIND (Short Fiction award, 2003); contbr. articles to profl. jours., chapters to books; editor: Advances in Automatic Summarization, 1999; mem. editl. bd. Computational Linguistics, 2002—04. Achievements include patents for grammar tutoring computer system; research in natural language processing. Office: Linguistics Georgetown U 37th and O Sts Washington DC 20057

MANIATIS, THOMAS PETER, molecular biology educator; b. Denver, May 8, 1943; s. Peter T. and Jane V. (Swearingen) M.; m. Jessie Marion Klyce, Aug. 27, 1968; children: Ethan David, Silas Dana. BA, U. Colo., 1965, MA, 1967; PhD in Molecular Biology, Vanderbilt U., 1971. European molecular biology rsch. fellow Med. Rsch. Coun. Molecular Biology, Cambridge, Eng., 1973-74; NIH fellow Harvard U., Cambridge, Mass., 1971-73, rsch. assoc. in biology, 1974-75, asst. prof., 1975-77, prof. molecular biology, 1981—; sr. staff investigator Cold Spring Harbor Lab., N.Y., 1975-77; assoc. prof. Calif. Inst. Tech., Pasadena, 1977-79, prof., 1979-81; co-founder, advisor Genetics Inst., Boston, 1981—; chmn. dept. biochemistry and molecular biology Harvard U., Cambridge, 1985-88, prof. biochemistry and molecular biology, 1981—, now Thomas H. Lee prof. molecular and cellular biology. Author: Molecular Cloning, 1982; assoc. editor: Cell. jour., 1978—. Recipient award Rita Allen Found., 1978; recipient Eli Lilly research award Am. Soc. Microbiology, 1981; Richard Lounsbery award for biology and medicine U.S. and French Acads. Sci., 1985. Fellow Am. Acad. Scis.; mem. Nat. Acad. Scis. Office: Harvard U Dept Molecular/Cellular Biology 7 Divinity Ave Cambridge MA 02138-2019

MANIKA, JOHN FRANCIS, computer systems educator, computer information systems analyst; b. Phila., Jan. 22, 1922; s. John F. and Mary T. (Johnston) M.; m. Marie Susan Valeo, Feb. 20, 1944; 1 child, Suzanne Manika Frauenhoffer. A in Bus. Adminstrn., U. Pa., 1967, BBA, 1979, postgrad., 1979-85; grad., U.S. Army Mgmt. Sch., 1968. Mgmt. analyst, internat mgmt. cons. VA, 1946-49; mgr. mgmt. engring. dept. Aviation Supply Office, USN, 1949-51, mgr. mgmt. engring. dept. Shipbldg. Activity, 1951-53; dir. mgmt. planning dept. U.S. Army Ordnance Dist., Phila., 1953-59; computer sys. mgr., sys. analyst Def. Logistics Agy., 1959-79; faculty Peirce Coll., Phila., 1967-98, prof. computer info. sys., 1979-98, chmn. computer info. system dept., 1982-89. Adj. instr. Temple U., 1951-56; cons. in field, 2000—. Capt. U.S. Army, 1942-46; lt. col. USAR ret. Fellow Assn. Data Comm. Users (chmn. ednl. com. 1986-86); mem. AAUP, Am. Soc. Profl. Cons., Toastmasters (past pres., founder Mil. Clothiers chpt.), Wharton Club, U. Pa. Faculty Club.

MANILOW, BARRY (BARRY ALAN PINCUS), singer, composer, arranger; b. N.Y.C., June 17, 1946; s. Harold Pincus and Edna M. Student, N.Y. Coll. Music. Former positions include mailroom CBS; film editor WCBS-TV. Dir. music Callback series, Ed. Sullivan's Pilots; dir. music, condr., arranger, producer for Bette Midler, singer and composer; recorded hit songs: Can't Smile Without You, I Write the Songs, At the Copa (Grammy award, best male pop performance, 1979), Mandy, Looks Like We Made It, Let Me Be Your Wings; albums include Barry Manilow I, 1973, Barry Manilow II, 1974, Tryin' to Get the Feeling, 1975, This One's For You, 1976, Live, 1977, Even Now, 1977, One Voice, 1979, Barry, 1980, A Nice Boy Like Me, 1980, If I Should Love Again, 1981, Here Comes the Night, 1982, Oh, Julie!, 1982, 2 A.M. Paradise Cafe, 1984, Manilow, 1985, Swing Street, 1987, Live on Broadway, 1987, Barry Manilow, 1989, Because It's Christmas, 1990, Showstoppers, 1991, Live in Britain, 1993, Singin' with The Big Bands, 1994, Summer of '78, 1996, Manilow Sings Sinatra, 1998, Here at the Mayflower, 2001, A Christmas Gift of Love, 2002, 2 Nights Live, 2004; (video) The Best of Me: The Greatest Hits Tour, 1993; star TV movie Copacabana, 1985, Because It's Christmas: Barry Manilow, 1991; appeared TV specials The Barry Manilow Special (Emmy award, 1977), The Second Barry Manilow Special, also Big Fun on Swing Street, 1988, Barry Manilow: SRO on Broadway, 1989; TV appearances include Murphy Brown, 1993, Ally McBeal, 2001, Will & Grace, 2003, American Idol, 2004; Broadway prodn.: Barry Manilow at the Gershwin, 1989; author Sweet Life: Adventures on the Way to Paradise; recipient Spl. Tony award, 1977, Ruby award After Dark mag. 1976, Photoplay Gold medal award 1976. Office: Arista Records 6 W 57th St New York NY 10019-3999*

MANIMTIM, WINSTON MENDOZA, pediatrician, neonatologist; b. The Philippines, July 11, 1961; arrived in U.S., 1994; s. Florencio and Suprema (Mendoza) Manimtim. BS in Zoology, U. St. Tomas, The Philippines, 1981, MD, 1985. Diplomate Am. Bd. Pediatrics. Pediatric resident Philippine Children's Med. Ctr., 1987-90; registrar neonatology Mercy Hosp. Women, Melbourne, Australia, 1992-94; pediatric resident Albert Einstein Coll. Medicine, Bronx, N.Y., 1995-97; fellow in neonatology U. Md., Balt., 1997—2000, clin. instr. Instr. Neonatal Resucitation Program, Balt.; attending neonatologist Rsch. med. Ctr., 2000-. Capt. Philippine Med. Corps., 1986. Resident scholar Philippine Pediatric Soc., 1987; Internat. fellow Am. Respiratory Care Found., 1991; recipient Alien of Extraordinary Ability in field of medicine. Fellow Am. Acad. Pediat.; mem. AMA, Ea. Soc. Pediatric Rsch. Avocations: reading, russian art. Home: 4949 Wornall Rd #409 Kansas City MO 64112 Office: Rsch Med Ctr 2316 E Myer Blvd Rm 526 Kansas City MO 64132

MANION, DANIEL ANTHONY, federal judge; b. South Bend, Ind., Feb. 1, 1942; s. Clarence E. and Virginia (O'Brien) Manion; m. Ann Murphy Manion, June 29, 1984. AB, U. Notre Dame, 1964; JD, Ind. U., 1973. Bar: Ind., U.S. Dist. Ct. (no. dist.) Ind., U.S. Dist. Ct. (so. dist.) Ind. Dir., indsl. devel. Ind. Dept. Commerce, 1968—73; dep. atty. gen. State of Ind., 1973—74; from assoc. to ptnr. Doran, Manion, Boynton, Kamm & Esmont, South Bend, 1974—86; judge U.S. Ct. Appeals (7th cir.), South Bend, 1986—. Mem. Ind. State Senate, Indpls., 1978—82; dir. St. Joseph Bank & Trust Co., 1979—86. With U.S. Army, 1965—66. Office: US Ct Appeals US Courthouse & Federal Bldg 204 S Main St Rm 301 South Bend IN 46601-2122

MANION, MICHAEL T. finance educator; b. Sterling, Ill., Dec. 6, 1949; s. John James and Catherine Clair (Holzknecht) Manion; children: Cathryn Lennox, Elizabeth Kennedy. BA, U. Notre Dame, 1971; MBA in Mgmt., Northwestern U., 1977; PhD, U. Ill., 1999. V.p. Am. Nat. Bank, Chgo., 1977—81, Continental Bank, Chgo., 1981—85; mgmt. cons. Coopers & Lybrand, Chgo., 1985—90; sr. v.p. First Chgo Bank, 1990—95; prof. U. Wis., Kenosha, 1995—. Cons. in field. Contbr. articles to profl. jours. Lt. USN, 1971—76. Home: PO Box 86 Northbrook IL 60065 Office: Univ of Wis Sch Bus and Tech 900 Wood Road Kenosha WI 53141 Business E-Mail: manion@uwp.edu. E-mail: mikemanion1@aol.com.

MANION, THOMAS A. chancellor; b. Aug. 10, 1934; m. Maureen O'Mara; children: Gregory, Marcy, Andrew, Margaret, Vicki, Tina, Thomas. BBA, St. Bonaventure U., 1959; MBA, Boston Coll., 1962; PhD, Clark U., 1968; D.Pedagogy, Bryant Coll., 1973. Chmn. econs. dept., dean grad. sch., acad. provost v.p. Bryant Coll., Smithfield, R.I.; pres. Coll. Saint Rose, Albany, N.Y., 1973-83, St. Nobert Coll., De Pere, Wis., 1983-2000, chancellor, 2000—. Bd. dirs. Associated Kellogg Bank, Green Bay, Wis. Bd. dirs. Higher Edn. Aids Coun., State of Wis. Mem. NCAA, Nat. Assn. Ind. Colls. and Univs. (mem. commn. on campus concerns), Am. Assn. Higher Edn., Am. Coun. Edn., Nat. Cath. Edn. Assn., Assn. Cath. Colls. and Univs., Coun. Ind. Colls. (bd. dirs.), Wis. Assn. Ind. Colls. and Univs. (pres.), Wis. Found. Ind. Colls., Delta Epsilon, Delta Mu Delta. Office: St Norbert Coll 100 Grant St De Pere WI 54115-2002

MANIRE, JAMES MCDONNELL, lawyer; b. Memphis, Feb. 22, 1918; s. Clarence Herbert and Elizabeth (McDonnell) M.; m. Nathalie Davant Latham, Nov. 21, 1951 (dv. 1979); children: James McDonnell, Michael Latham, Nathalie Manire Willard; m. Nancy Whitman Colbert, Dec. 30, 1995. LL.B., U. Va., 1948. Bar: Tenn. 1948, U.S. Supreme Ct. 1957. Pvt. practice, Memphis, 1948—; city atty., 1968-71; of counsel Williams, McDaniel, Wolfe & Womack, Memphis, 2001—. Editor in chief Va. Law Rev., 1947-48. Served to lt. comdr. USNR, 1941-46. Fellow Am. Coll. Trial Lawyers, Am. Bar Found. (life); mem. Tenn. Bar Assn. (pres. 1966-67), Memphis and Shelby County Bar Assn. (pres. 1963-64, Lawyer's Lawyer award 1995), Tenn. Bar Found. (charter), 6th Circuit Jud. Conf. (life), Raven Soc., Memphis Hunt and Polo Club. Home: 2927 Frances Pl Memphis TN 38111-2401 Office: 5521 Murray Rd Memphis TN 38119-3717

MANIS, MELVIN, psychologist, educator; b. N.Y.C., Feb. 18, 1931; s. Alex and Hanna (Oyle) M.; m. Jean Denby, May 28, 1954; children: Peter Eugene, David Denby. AB in Psychology, Franklin and Marshall Coll., 1951; PhD, U. Ill., 1954. Instr. psychology U. Pitts., 1956-58; rsch. psychologist Ann Arbor VA Med. Ctr., Mich., 1958-89; prof. psychology U. Mich., Ann Arbor, 1966-98, assoc. chmn. dept., 1990-91; ret., 1998. Author: Cognitive Processes, 1966, An Introduction to Cognitive Psychology, 1971; editor Jour. Personality and Social Psychology, 1980-84. Served with USPHS, 1954-56 Mem. APA, Soc. Exptl. Social Psychology, Phi Beta Kappa. Clubs: Racquet (Ann Arbor). Democrat. Jewish. Home: 20 Harvard Pl Ann Arbor MI 48104-1726 Business E-Mail: Melmanis@umich.edu.

MANISCALCO, JOSEPH, artist, educator; b. Tampa, Fla., Feb. 24, 1921; s. Michaelangelo and Rosa (Belluccia) M.; m. Ann Lynn Laurence Cadman, Sept. 24, 1954 (div. June 1962); children: Michael, James, Elizabeth, Robert; m. Barbara Ann Fisher Insley, Jan. 3, 1976. Student, Art Students League of N.Y., 1939-41, 46-49. Portrait artist, 1941—. Lectr. in field; judge exhbns. Represented in permanent collections including Mich. Supreme Ct., U.S. House of Reps., Nat. Archives, Washington. With U.S. Army, 1942-46, ETO and PTO. Recipient Fitch award Mich. Acad. Letters, Arts and Sci., Artistic Excellence and Cmty. Commitment award Wayne County Coun. of the Arts, 1992. Mem. Scarab Club (bd. dirs. 1967—, pres. 1972-73, 80-81, 4 gold medals, 1st prize Silver Medal Show), Prismatic Club of Detroit (pres. 2000), Grosse Point Theatre (scenic artist), Fine Art Soc. of Detroit (chmn. art com. 1975), Adcraft Club of Detroit. Avocations: acting and singing in community theater productions, church choral singing. Home: 41110 Fox Run Rd #108 Novi MI 48377

MANISTER, CRAIG ALAN, artist, educator; b. Bklyn., Sept. 12, 1951; s. Robert and Beatrice Manister. Student, N.Y. Studio Sch. Drawing, Painting and Sculpture; cert. in appraisal studies in fine and decorative arts, NYU, 1989; MFA, CUNY, 1997. Dir. Gallery Coll. S.I., CUNY, 1994—. Bd. dirs. Coun. on the Arts and Humanities for S.I., 1992—98; chair bd. dirs. Art Lab., S.I., 1995—; adj. asst. prof. art history Coll. S.I., 1999—. Exhibitions include Beijing Art Inst., Mei Shu Guan Art Mus., Shanghai, 1987—88, Elizabeth Harris Gallery, N.Y.C., 1993, Nat. Acad. Mus. Design, 1996, Newhouse Ctr. for Contemporary Art, Snug Harbor Cultural Ctr., 1997—98, Nat. Acad. Mus. Design, 1998, Fairleigh Dickinson U., 2001, S.I. Inst. Arts and Scis., 2004. Recipient Profl. Staff Congress-CUNY Rsch. award for painting, Rsch. Found. CUNY, 1996—2004. Home: 149 Highview Ave Staten Island NY 10301-1357 Office: College Staten Island CUNY 2800 Victory Blvd Staten Island NY 10314 Office Phone: 718-982-2553.

MANIVANNAN, DAKSHNAMOORTHY, computer scientist, educator; s. Munusamy and Radhammal Dakshnamoorthy; m. Bala Soulossana Manivannan; children: Suganya, Vasudevan. Ph.D, Ohio State U., Columbus, 1997. Vis. instr. Temple U., Phila., 1997—98; asst. prof. U. Ky., Lexington, 1998—. Referee NSF, Arlington, Va., 1998—. Grantee CAREER Award, NSF, 2000-2004. Mem.: IEEE, Assn. for Computing Machinery. Office: Univ Kentucky 301 Rose Street Rm 231 Lexington KY 40506 Office Phone: 859-257-9234.

MANK, EDWARD WARREN, marketing professional; b. Boothbay Harbor, Maine, Oct. 2, 1962; s. Edward Raymond Jr. and Sandra Gail (Strahan) M. Assoc. in Liberal Arts, C.C. Vt., 1985; cert. ophthalmic technician, Nat. Edn. Ctr., San Francisco, 1992; cert. real estate broker, Am. Sch. Mortgage Banking, Walnut Creek, Calif., 1994. Lic. real estate salesman, Calif.; cert. Am. Bd. Optometry Dispensing. Tng. coord. Burger King Corp., South Burlington, Vt., 1985-87, San Francisco, 1988-89; asst. mgr. Bonanza Family Restaurant, South Burlington, 1987-88; supr. U.S. Census Bur., San Francisco, 1990; sales rep. Viacom Cablevision, San Francisco, 1991; programming researcher NBC, San Francisco, 1992; mktg. cons. Calyx & Corolla, San Francisco, 1993; mktg. rep. Alliance Bancorp, Millbrae, Calif., 1993—. Sustaining mem. Rep. Nat. Com., Washington, 1989—; sponsor Heritage Found., Washington, Cato Inst., Washington. Mem. Acad. Polit. Sci., Coun. Fgn. Rels., World Affairs Coun., Nat. Rifle Assn. (life), Reason Found. Republican. Episcopalian. Home: 3401 E 18th St Apt 3 Oakland CA 94601-3003 Office: Alliance Bancorp 800 El Camino Real Millbrae CA 94030-2010 E-mail: edmank@canada.com.

MANKA, RONALD EUGENE, lawyer; b. Wichita, Kans., Dec. 12, 1944; s. James Ashford and Jane Bunn (Meeks) M.; m. Frances Ann Patterson, Aug. 7, 1965 (dec. Dec. 1985); children: Kimberly Ann, Lora Christine; m. Linda I. Bailey, Mar. 11, 1995. BBA cum laude, U. Kans., 1967; JD cum laude, U. Mich., 1970. Bar: Conn. 1970, Mo. 1974, Kans. 1985, Colo. 2001. Assoc. Day, Barry & Howard, Hartford, Conn., 1970-73, Lathrop & Gage L.C., Kansas City, Mo., 1973-78, mem., 1979-82, 85—; group counsel Butler Mfg. Co., Kansas City, 1982-83, div. gen. mgr., 1983—84. Legal com. Boulder County Cmty. Found., Colo., 2002—. Trustee, clk., elder Village Presbyn. Ch., Prairie Village, Kans.; dir., treas. Lyric Opera of Kansas City, 1995—; pres. Genesis Sch., Kansas City, 1987-89; devel. chmn. Kansas City Friends of Alvin Ailey, 1987-89; chmn. Kansas City Mus., 1988-92, gen. counsel, 1994—; gen. counsel Kansas City C. of C., 1989-2001; pres. Ctr. for Mgmt. Assistance, Kansas City, 1991-93; dir. Colo. Music Festival, 2002-. Mem. ABA, Mo. Bar Assn. (alt. dispute resolution com. 1986-2002), Lawyers Assn. Kansas City, Silicon Prairie Tech. Assn. (bd. dirs. 1990-92), Homestead Country Club (pres. 1984-85). Democrat. Avocations: bicycling, swimming. Home: 875 11th St Boulder CO 80302 Office: Colorado Venture Mgmt 2575 Park Ln #200 Lafayette CO 80026-3200 Fax: 720-931-3001. E-mail: RManka@LathropGage.com.

MANKEL, FRANCIS XAVIER, former principal, priest; b. Knoxville, Tenn., Nov. 8, 1935; s. George Whitehead Sr. and Willia Frances (Duncan) M. BA, St. Ambrose U., 1957; STB, St. Mary's Sem. and U., Balt., 1959, STL, 1961; MEd, Loyola Coll., Balt., 1965. Ordained priest, Roman Cath. Ch., 1961. Assoc. pastor Holy Ghost Ch., Knoxville, 1962-67; prin. Knoxville Cath. High Sch., 1967-79; pastor Sacred Heart Ch., Lawrenceburg, Tenn., 1979-84, St. John Neumann Ch., Knoxville, 1984-87, Sacred Heart Cathedral, Knoxville, 1987-97, Holy Ghost Ch., Knoxville, 1997—. Chancellor Cath. Diocese Knoxville, 1988-96, vicar gen., 1988-98, 99—; supt. Cath. Schs., Diocese of Knoxville, 1989-92. Bd. dirs. Knoxville area chpt. ARC, 1986—; sch. bd. Knoxville Cath. HS, 1967—79, 1984—85, 1987—; com. mem. Sacred Heart Cathedral Sch., Knoxville, 1987—97, St. Joseph Sch., Knoxville, 1997—. Mem. Knoxville Ministerial Assn. Home and Office: 111 Hinton Ave Knoxville TN 37917-6418 Office Phone: 865-522-2205. Personal E-mail: hgchurch@bellsouth.net.

MANKIEWICZ, FRANK F. journalist, writer; b. N.Y.C., May 16, 1924; s. Herman J. and Sara (Aaronson) M.; m. Holly Jolley, 1952 (div.); children: Joshua, Benjamin; m. Patricia O'Brien, 1988. AB, UCLA, 1947; MS, Columbia U., 1948; LL.B., U. Calif.-Berkeley, 1955. Bar: Calif. 1955, D.C. 1985. Engaged in journalism, Washington and Los Angeles, 1948-52; practice law Beverly Hills, 1955-61; dir. Peace Corps, Lima, Peru, 1962-64, Latin Am. regional dir. Washington, 1964-66; press sec. Senator Robert F. Kennedy, 1966-68; syndicated columnist and TV news commentator, 1968-71; nat. polit. dir. Presdl. campaign of Senator George McGovern, 1971-72; columnist Washington Post, 1976-77; pres. Nat. Pub. Radio, 1977-83; vice-chmn. Hill and Knowlton (formerly Gray and Co.), 1983—. Author: Perfectly Clear: Nixon from Whittier to Watergate, 1973, U.S. v. Richard M. Nixon: The Final Crisis, 1974, With Fidel: A Portrait of Castro and Cuba, 1975, Remote Control: Television and the Manipulation of American Life, 1977; contbr. articles to newspapers and mags. Served with inf. AUS, 1943-46 Office: Hill and Knowlton 600 New Hampshire Ave NW Washington DC 20037-2403

MANKIEWICZ, THOMAS FRANK, screenwriter, director, producer; b. L.A., June 1, 1942; s. Joseph Leo and Rosa M. Student, Yale U., 1959-63. Author: (book, Broadway musical) Georgy!, 1970; screenwriter: (teleplay, musical spl.) Movin' with Nancy, 1967, The Sweet Ride, 1968, (teleplay, musical spl.) The Beat of the Brass, 1968, Diamonds Are Forever, 1971, Live and Let Die, 1973, The Man With the Golden Gun, 1974, The Eagle Has Landed, 1976, The Cassandra Crossing, 1977, Ladyhawke, 1985; screenwriter, co-prodr.: Mother, Juggs and Speed, 1976; creative cons.: Superman, 1978, Superman II, 1980; dir. (teleplay, tv pilot) Hart to Hart, 1979-80, (screenplay) Dragnet, 1987, Delirious, 1991, (cable tv series) Tales from the Crypt, 1992, (cable tv movie) Taking the Heat, 1993; exec. prodr. Hot Pursuit, 1985. Bd. dirs. William Holden Wildlife Found., L.A., 1995—. Mem. Greater L.A. Zoo Assn. (bd. trustees 1997—, chmn. 2002--), Motion Picture Acad. Arts and Scis. (bd. govs. 1979-81). Avocations: wildlife conservation, thoroughbred horse racing and breeding.

MANKILLER, WILMA PEARL, tribal leader, retired; b. Stilwell, Okla., Nov. 18, 1945; d. Charley and Clara Irene (Sitton) M.; m. Hector N. Olaya, Nov. 13, 1963 (div. 1975); children: Felicia Marie Olaya, Gina Irene Olaya; m. Charlie Soap, Oct. 13, 1986. Student, Skyline Coll., San Bruno Coll., 1973, San Francisco State Coll., 1973-75; BA in Social Sci., Union Coll., 1977; postgrad., U. Ark., 1979; DHL (hon.), U. New Eng., 1986; PhD in Pub. Svc. (hon.), R.I. Coll., 1989; DHL (hon.), Yale U., 1990; PhD (hon.), Dartmouth Coll., 1991; LLD (hon.), Mills Coll., 1992. Cmty. devel. dir. Cherokee Nation, Tahlequah, Okla., 1977-83, dep. chief, 1983-85, prin. chief, 1985-95; Montgomery fellow Darmouth Coll., 1996. Author: Mankiller: A Chief and Her People, 1993; co-editor: The Readers Companion to the History of Women in the U.S., 1998. Recipient Donna Nigh First Lady award Okla. Commn. for Status of Women, 1985, Am. Leadership award Harvard U., 1986, Elizabeth Blackwell award, 1996, Dorothy Height Lifetime Achievement award, 1997, Presdl. Medal of Freedom, 1998; inducted Okla. Women's Hall of Fame, 1986. Avocations: reading, writing. Home: PO Box 308 Park Hill OK 74451-0308

MANKIN, HENRY JAY, orthopedist, educator, health facility administrator; b. Pitts., Oct. 9, 1928; s. Hyman Isaac and Mary (Simons) M.; m. Carole Jane Pinkney, Aug. 20, 1952; children: Allison Joan, David Philip, Keith Pinkney. BS magna cum laude, U. Pitts., 1952, MD, 1953; MA (hon.), Harvard U., 1973. Diplomate Am. Bd. Orthopaedic Surgery (mem. bd. 1976-82, pres. bd. 1980-81). Intern U. Chgo. Clinics, 1953-54; resident orthopaedics Hosp. for Joint Diseases, N.Y.C., 1957-60; instr. orthopaedics U. Pitts. Sch. Medicine, 1960-62, asst. prof., 1962-64, assoc. prof., 1964-66; dir., prof. orthopaedics Hosp. for Joint Diseases and Mt. Sinai Sch. Medicine, 1966-72; chief orthopaedics Mass. Gen. Hosp., Boston, 1972-96, chief orthopaedic oncology, 1972—. Edith M. Ashley prof. orthopaedics Harvard Med. Sch., 1972—; mem. surgery B study sect. NIH, 1969-73; mem. adv. com. on surg. treatment FDA, 1973-75; corporator Boston Five Cent Savs. Bank, 1982-83; mem. exec. com. Am. Bd. Med. Spltys., 1982-85; adv. council on grad. med. edn., 1986-96; mem. Nat. Arthritis Avd. Bd., 1986-89; mem. human resources and research rev. group A Nat. Inst. Arthritis, Metabolism and Digestive Diseases, 1981-85, chmn., 1983-85. Assoc. editor Arthritis and Rheumatism, 1967-77, Jour. Bone and Joint Surgery, 1967-82; mem. editorial bd. Jour. Orthopedic Research, 1982-85; trustee Jour. Bone and Joint Surgery, 1985-91, chmn. bd., 1988-91; contbr. more than 560 articles to profl., med. jours. Served to lt. comdr. USNR, 1955-57. Fellow ACS, Royal Coll. Surgeons (hon.); mem. Am. Acad. Orthopaedic Surgeons, Acad. Orthopaedic Soc. (pres. 1991-92), Am. Orthopaedic Assn. (pres. 1982-83), Orthopaedic Research Soc. (pres. 1969-70), Musculoskeletal Tumor Soc. (pres. 1991-92), Brit. Orthopaedic Research Soc., Argentine Orthopedic Assn. (hon.), N.Y. Acad. Medicine (chmn. orthopaedic sect. 1971-72), Am. Rheumatism Assn., Soc. Internat. Chirurgerie Orthopaedice et Traumatologia, Hip Soc., Interurban, Forum Orthopaedic clubs, Brit. Orthopaedic Assn. (hon.), Can. Orthopaedic Assn. (hon.), Australian Orthopaedic Assn. (hon.), N.Z. Orthopaedic Assn. (hon.), Japanese Orthopaedic Assn. (hon.), Israel Orthopaedic Assn. (hon.), Thai Orthopaedic Assn (hon.). Office: Mass Gen Hosp 55 Fruit St Boston MA 02114-2696 Business E-Mail: hmankin@partners.org.

MANKIN, ROBERT STEPHEN, financial executive; b. N.Y.C., Mar. 26, 1939; s. Samuel Harry Mankin and Dorothy (Rosenblum) Goldstein; m. Joyce Marie Cabel, June 13, 1971 (div.); children: Seth Howard, Laura Nicole, Gina Danielle; m. Ruth Inwin, July 20, 2002. BA cum laude, Bklyn. Coll., 1961; MBA, Bernard Baruch Coll., 1970; Dr. Profl. Studies with distinction, Pace U., 1982. Mgr. ABC, N.Y.C., 1969-71, Babcock and Wilcox, N.Y.C., 1971-74; v.p. Chase Manhattan Bank, N.Y.C., 1974-84; sr. v.p. 1st Interstate Bank, N.Y.C., 1984-87; mng. dir., co-head fixed income, mem. mgmt. com. Nomura Securities Internat., N.Y.C., 1987-94; mng. dir. Paine Webber, N.Y.C., 1994-95; pres., CEO Lakeside Fin. Svcs., Hoboken, N.J., 1995—; COO Thomson Fin. Electronic Settlements Group, Boston, 1997-98; acting pres. Ocwen Tech. Exch., West Palm Beach, Fla., 1999; CEO Sutton Strategic, LLC, 2001—02. Bd. dirs., sec. Nomura Mortgage Capital Corp., N.Y.C.; bd. dirs., pres., CEO Nomura Asset Capital Corp., N.Y.C., 1988-94; trustee Hudson Inst., 2004—. Contbr. articles to profl. jours. Mem. Planning Forum, Assn. for Computing Machinery, Assn. Computer Programmers and Analysts (chmn. bd. 1971). Home and Office: 155 E 73rd St 6A New York NY 10021

MANKIW, NICHOLAS GREGORY, economics professor, federal agency administrator; b. Trenton, N.J., Feb. 3, 1958; s. Nicholas and Dorothy (Sawchak) M.;m. Deborah Jean Roloff, June 16, 1984. AB, Princeton U., 1980; PhD, MIT, 1984. Staff economist Coun. Econ. Advisers, Washington, 1982-83; instr. MIT, Cambridge, 1984-85; asst. prof. Harvard U., Cambridge, 1985-87, prof. econs., 1987—; chmn., mem. Coun. of Econ. Adv., Washington, 2003—. Research assoc. Nat. Bureau of Economic Research; adviser Fed. Reserve Bank of Boston, Congressional Budget Off.; mem. test devel. comm.

ETS. Author: Macroeconomics, 1992, Principles of Economics, 1998; contbr. articles Am. Economic Review, Jour. of Polit. Economy, Quarterly Jour. of Economics, The NY Times, The Financial Times, The Wall Street Journal, Fortune. Recipient Presidential Young Investigator award NSF, 1986. Office: Harvard U Dept Econs Littauer 223 Cambridge MA 02138 also: Eisenhower Exec Office Bldg 17th St and Pennsylvania Ave NW Rm 94 Washington DC 20502*

MANKOFF, DAVID ABRAHAM, nuclear medicine physician; b. July 10, 1959; BS in Physics summa cum laude, Yale U., 1981; MD, PhD in Bioengring., U. Pa., 1988. Diplomate Am. Bd. Internal Medicine, Am. Bd. Nuclear Medicine. Rsch. scientist UGM Med. Systems, Phila., 1988-89, dir. engring., 1989-90; rsch. assoc. nuclear medicine sect. U. Pa., Phila., 1988-90; resident in internal medicine U. Wash., Seattle, 1990-92, resident in nuclear medicine, 1992-96, asst. prof. radiology, 1996—2001, assoc. prof. radiology, 2001; 0. Office: Divsn Nuc Medicine U Wash Med Ctr Box 356113 1959 NE Pacific St Seattle WA 98195-0001 Office Phone: 206-598-4244. E-mail: dam@u.washington.edu.

MANKOFF, RONALD MORTON, retired lawyer; b. Gettysburg, S.D., Oct. 13, 1931; s. Harry B. and Sarah (Frank) M.; m. Joy Faith Shechtman, Nov. 3, 1959; children: Jeffrey Walker, Douglas Frank. BSL, U. Minn., JD, 1954; LLM in Taxation, NYU, 1959. Bar: Minn. 1954, Tex. 1959. With Leonard, Street & Deinard, Mpls., 1957-58; research analyst Inst. Jud. Adminstrn., N.Y.C., 1958-59; assoc. Lyne, Blanchette, Smith & Shelton, Dallas, 1959-60; ptnr. Durant and Mankoff, Dallas, 1960-85; pres. Brice & Mankoff PC, Dallas, 1985 89, Mankoff, Hill, Held & Metzger, L.L.P., Dallas, 1989-95, chmn./gen. counsel RAC Fin. Group, Inc. (now 1st Plus Fin Group, Inc.), 1994-96. Lectr. law So. Meth. U., 1974-77; speaker in field. Contbr. articles to profl. jours. Chmn. bd. Dallas chpt. Am. Cancer Soc., 1976-77, bd. dirs. Tex. divsn., 1981-94; chmn. Dallas Crusade, 1974-75, bd. dirs., mem. exec. com., 1963-88; mem. Dallas Mcpl. Libr., 1973-75; exec. com. Dallas Citizens Charter Assn., 1971-75; pres. Dallas Arts Found., Inc., 1973-75; mem. exec. com. Nat. Pooled Income Fund, Coun. Jewish Welfare Fedns. and Funds, 1975-77; adv. dir. Dallas Cmty. Chest Trust Fund, 1976-78; chmn. Found. Dallas Jewish Fedn., 1976-77; pres. Temple Emanu-el, Dallas, 1977-79; bd. dirs. Jewish Fedn. Greater Dallas, 1977 79, 99 2002, Dallas Civic Opera, 1981-83, World Union Progressive Judaism, 1981-90; mem. S.W. regional liaison com. IRS, 1980-83; exec. com. Union Am. Hebrew Congregations, 1979-89, trustee, 1979-97, chmn. nat. coll. com., 1983-87, vice chmn. bd. dirs., 1984-88, vice chmn. devel. commn., 1997-99; sec. Dallas Assembly, 1979-84; exec. com. Jewish Cmty. Rels. Coun., 1982-83, Com. for Qualified Judiciary, 1982—; sec. Child Care Partnership, 1984-86, bd. dirs., 1986-88; bd. dirs. Dallas Women's Found., 1985-89, adv. coun., 1989—, chair adv. coun., 1997-99; bd. dirs. Am. Jewish Com., 1982-88, pres. Dallas chpt. 1986-90; bd. dirs. Tex. coun. Girl Scouts U.S., 1982-85, Goodwill Industries of Greater Dallas, 1979-83, Title One Home Improvement Lender's Assn., 1994-96; mem. Mayor's Task Force on Child Care, 1984; bd. govs. Dallas Symphony Assn., 1988-92, 98—; chmn. Temple Emanu El Found., 1988-95; bd. dirs. Dallas Inst. Humanities and Culture, 1998—, Ctr. for Interreligious Understanding, 2001—, Cardio-Pulmonary Rsch. Inst., 2002—, Jane's Due Process, Inc., 2002—, Cmty. Home for Adults Found., 2001—. Lt. (j.g.) USN, 1954-57. Mem. ABA, State Bar Tex., Dallas Bar Assn., Columbian Country Club (bd. dirs. 1967-73), LaJolla Country Club, Crescent Club, Zeta Beta Tau, Delta Sigma Rho. Democrat. Jewish. Home: 22 Lakeside Pk Dallas TX 75225 Address: 8510 El Paseo Grande La Jolla CA 90237 Office Phone: 214-365-0000. E-mail: von@mankoff.com.

MANLEY, AUDREY FORBES, retired academic administrator, pediatrician, military officer; b. Jackson, Miss., Mar. 25, 1934; d. Jesse Lee and Ora Lee (Buckhalter) Forbes; m. Albert Edward Manley, Apr. 3, 1970. AB with honors (tuition scholar), Spelman Coll., Atlanta, 1955; MD (Jesse Smith Noyes Found. scholar), Meharry Med. Coll., 1959; MPH, Johns Hopkins U.-USPHS traineeship, 1987; LHD (hon.), Tougaloo (Miss.) Coll., 1990, Meharry Med. Coll., Nashville, 1991; LLD (hon.), Spelman Coll., 1991, Tskegee U., 1998; DSc (hon.), Coll. New Rochelle, 1998, Morehouse Coll., 2002, U. Del., 2002. Diplomate: Am. Bd. Pediatrics. Intern St. Mary Mercy Hosp., Gary, Ind., 1960; from jr. to chief resident in pediatrics Cook County Children's Hosp., Chgo., 1960—62; NIH fellow neonatology U. Ill. Rsch. and Ednl. Hosp., Chgo., 1963—65; staff pediatrician Chgo. Bd. Health, 1963—66; practice medicine specializing in pediatrics Chgo., 1963—66; assoc. Lawndale Neighborhood Health Ctr. North, 1966—67; asst. med. dir., 1967—69; asst. prof. Chgo. Med. Coll., 1966—67; instr. Pritzker Sch. Medicine, U. Chgo., 1967—69; asst. dir. ambulatory pediatrics, asst. dir. pediatrics Mt. Zion Hosp. and Med. Center, San Francisco, 1969—70; med. cons. Spelman Coll., 1970—71, med. dir. family planning program, chmn. health careers adv. com., 1972—76; med. dir. Grady Meml. Hosp. Family Planning Clinic, 1972—76; with Health Services Adminstrs., Dept. Health and Human Services, 1976—97; commd. officer, advanced though grades to rear adm. USPHS, 1976—97; chief genetic diseases services br. Office Maternal and Child Health, Bur. Community Health Services, Rockville, Md., 1976—81; acting assoc. adminstr. clin. affairs Office of Adminstr. Health Resources and Services Adminstrn., 1981—83, chief med. officer, dep. assoc. adminstr. planning, evaluation and legis., 1983—85; sabbatical leave USPHS Johns Hopkins Sch. Hygiene and Pub. Health, 1986—87; dir. Nat. Health Service Corps.; asst. surgeon gen., 1988; dep. asst. Sec. for Health USPHS/HHS, 1989—93, acting asst. Sec. Health, 1993, dep. asst. Sec. Health/intergovtl. affairs, 1993—94; dep. surgeon gen., acting dep. asst. sec. for minority health USPHS, 1994—95, acting surgeon gen., 1995—97; pres. Spelman Coll., 1997—2002, pres. emerita, 2003—. Mem. U.S. del. UNICEF, 1990-94, Am. Acad. Family Physicians (pub. adv. bd.), Am. Coun. Learned Socs., Am. Med. Assn. Minority Affairs Consortium (sr. advisor), Ctrs. for Disease Control Found. (bd. visitors), Morehouse Sch. Medicine (clin. Prof. Pediats., Pub. Health Lectr.), Rollins Sch. Pub. Health Emory U (Commrs., Adv. Coun., Ga. Leadership Commn. Organ, Tissue, Blood Marrow donation amont African Ams. Author numerous articles, reports in field. Trustee Spelman Coll., 1966-70; The Coll. Fund(UNCF (com. Archives, Hist. Govtl. Affairs Com.), Coun. Fgn. Rels., bd. dirs. coun. Ind. Colls.; bd. dirs. March of Dimes, 1998, Nat. Merit Scholarship Corp., Nat. Minority Mil. Mus. Found. Edl. Adv. Coun., Am. Cancer Soc. Found., CDC Found., Compas Compact, Downtown Atlanta Chpt. Rotary, Atlanta 2000 Adv. Com., adv. bd. Atlanta Regional Health Summit, Commerce Club, Ga. Found. Ind., Food and Drug Adv. Com. Rear adm. USPHS, ret. USPHS. Recipient Meritorious Svc. award USPHS, 1981, Mary McLeod Bethune award Nat Coun. Negro Women, 1979, Dr. John P. McGovern Ann. Lectureship award Am. Sch. Health Assn., Disting. Alumni award Meharry Med. Coll., 1989, Spelman Coll. 108 Founder's Day Convocation, 1989, Disting. Svc. medal USPHS, 1992, Hildrus A. Poindexter award OSG/PHS, 1993, numerous other svc. and achievement awards. Fellow Am. Acad. Pediatrics; mem. Nat. Inst. Medicine of Nat. Acad. Sci., Nat. Med. Assn., APHA, AAUW, AAAS, Spelman Coll. Alumnae Assn., Meharry Alumni Assn., Operation Crossroads Africa Alumni Assn., Atlanta C. of C., Rotary, Delta Sigma Theta (hon.), Phi Beta Kappa. Address: 2807 18th St NW Washington DC 20009 Personal E-mail: amanley009@aol.com.

MANLEY, DAVID THOMAS, employee benefits plan administration executive; b. Youngstown, Ohio, Apr. 13, 1938; s. Harry T. and Margaret M. (Stein) M.; m. Virginia Borcik, Sept., 1961 (div. 1975); children: Kelly A., Scott D., Lynne M., Brian D., Leslie; m. Ruth Ann Osterhage, Dec. 31, 1975; children: David Louis, Mollie O. Student, Youngstown U., 1956-60. Dist. sales mgr. Res. Life, Dallas, 1960-63, Guarantee Res. Life, Hammond, Ind., 1963-64; mgr. brokerage CNA Ins. Group, Chgo., 1964-68; pres. Greater Del. Corp., Dover, 1981-85, Variable Protection Adminstrn., Cleve., 1968—, also bd. dirs.; pres. VPA Ins., Ltd., 1985—, also bd. dirs.; with VPI, Inc. Rep. precinct committeeman, 1966-72, ward leader, 1970-72; mem. Cuyahoga County Rep. Com., 1970-72; mem. Bd. Zoning Appeals, Hinckley, Ohio Twp.; pres. Our Lady of Grace Bd. Fin., 1980-89; bd. trustees Cath. Charities, mem.bd. dirs. Mem. Soc. Profl. Benefit Adminstrs., Mass Market Ins. Inst., Internat. Found. Employee Benefits, Am. Mgmt. Assn., KC. Roman Catholic. Home: 2485 Bethany Ln Hinckley OH 44233-9741 Office: Variable Protection Adminstrs Inc 6902 Pearl Rd Ste 500 Cleveland OH 44130-3625 Office Phone: 440-884-5454.

MANLEY, DOUGLAS HEATH, music educator; b. Cleveland, Tenn., Nov. 12, 1972; s. A. C. and Sarah Margaret Manley. MusB, Carson Newman Coll., 1993; MusM, U. Louisville, 1995; D of Music, Grad. Found. Oxford, 2003; post grad., Cin. Conservatory of Music. Organist St. Paul United Meth. Ch., Cin., 1995—98; faculty Carson-Newman Coll., Knoxville, 1998—2000; organist First Bapt. Ch., 1999—2000; faculty Midwestern Sem., Kansas City, Mo., 2000—01, Tusculum Coll., Knoxville, 2002—, Cleveland State C.C., 2002—. Recipient Austin C. Lovelace award, Hymn Soc., Boston, 1997. Mem.: Organ Hist. Soc., Coll. Music Soc., Am. Musicological Soc., Am. Guild Organists. Democrat. Episcopalian. Home: 2904 Henderson Ave #2 Cleveland TN 37312 Office: Cleveland State C C 3535 Adkisson Dr Cleveland TN 37312 Office Phone: 423-472-7141.

MANLEY, EDWARD HARRY, JR., food products executive; b. Staten Island, NY, Sept. 12, 1941; s. Edward H. and Dorothy I.; m. Judith Manley; children: Deborah Szymchack, Michael E. BS, Cornell U., 1975; MS, Rollins Coll., 1978. Cert. food svc. exec., cert. HACCP mgr., 2003. Joined USN, 1959, commd. ensign, 1970, advanced through grades to lt. comdr., 1979; food svc. dir. Naval Hosp., Annapolis, Md., 1972-73; asst. food svc. dir. Nat. Naval Med. Ctr., Bethesda, Md., 1971-72; food svc. dir. Naval Regional Med. Ctr., Orlando, Fla., 1975-80, ret., 1980; food svc. dir. North Broward Hosp., Pompano Beach, Fla., 1981-89; pres. Creative Food Concepts, Inc.; founder Workaholics Internat. Network, 1999—. Mem. adv. bd. Mid-Fla. Tech. Food Svc. Program, 1978-80, Atlantic Vo-Tech Dietetic Program, 1981-89; chmn. Skills Std. Bd., Hospitality and Tourism. Mem. evaluation team Hennessey award US Air Force, 1982; mem. adv. bd. Broward Community Coll., 1985— Ed Manley Scholarship Fund established, 1984, named Accomplished Health Care Food Svc. Adminstr., 1985; recipient Peter Gust Economou award, 1987. Mem. Internat. Food Svc. Exec. Assn. (pres. Orlando br. 1979-80, pres. South Fla. br. 1983-84, internat. sec., treas. 1986-87, chairman- 1988-1989, named mem. of yr. Orlando br. 1978, mem. of yr. South Fla. br. 1984, Disting. Svc. award 1984, chmn. bd. 1988-89, pres. 1989—, Dignified Order of the Dinner Gong 2001), Cornell Soc. Hotelmen (pres. Ctrl. Fla. chpt. 1976-80), Cornell Hotel Soc. (Las Vegas, treas. 2001—), Fla. Restaurant Assn. (bd. dir. 1980), Am. Soc. Hosp. Food Svc. Adminstr. (sec. South Fla. chpt.), Chaine des Rotisseurs, Cornell of Ctrl. Fla. Club, Naval Tng. Ctr. Officers Club (pres. 1978-80), Pompano Sq. Mall Walkers Club (founder), pres., Internat. Food Svc. Exec. Assn, 1989-present; pres., VIP Food Safety, 2002-pres. Home and Office: 2609 Surfwood Dr Las Vegas NV 89128-1282

MANLEY, FRANK, retired English language educator, writer; b. Scranton, Pa., Nov. 13, 1930; s. Aloysius F. and Kathryn L. (Needham) M.; m. Carolyn Mary Holliday, Mar. 14, 1952; children: Evelyn, Mary. BA, Emory U., 1952, MA, 1953; PhD, Johns Hopkins U., 1959. Instr., then asst. prof. Yale U., New Haven, 1959-64; assoc. prof., then prof. dept. English Emory U., Atlanta, 1964-2000, chmn. dept., 1968-70, Candler prof. English, 1982-2000, dir. creative writing program, 1990-2000, retired, 2000. Editor: The Anniversaries (John Donne), 1963, (with R. Sylvester) De Fructu qui ex Doctrina Percipitur, 1967, All Fools (George Chapman), 1968, A Dialogue of Comfort (St. Thomas More), vol. 12, 1977 and Epistola ad Pomeranum, vol. 7, 1990, Yale edit. More's complete works; author: Resultances, 1980 (Devins award for poetry 1980), Two Masters (co-winner Gt. Am. New Play Contest 9th Ann. Humana Festival New Am. Plays 1985), (with F. Watkins) Some Poems and Some Talk About Poetry, 1985, Within the Ribbons: 9 Stories, 1989, (play) The Trap, 1993, The Cockfighter: a Novel, 1998, Among Prisoners: Stories, 2000, (poems) The Emperors, 2001, True Hope: A Novel, 2002. With U.S. Army, 1953—55. Guggenheim Found. fellow, 1966-67, 78-79; recipient NEH transl. program fellowship, 1981-83, Nat. Endowment Arts Creative Writing Fellowship in Fiction, 1995-97, Disting. Teaching award, 1984, Univ. scholar/tchr. of yr. award, 1989, Disting. Alumnus award The Marist Sch., 1993. Roman Catholic. Home: 401 Adams St Decatur GA 30030-5207 also: Doublehead Gap Rd Ellijay GA 30540 Office: Emory U Dept Theater Studies 212 Rich Bldg Atlanta GA 30322-0001 E-mail: fmanley@emory.edu.

MANLEY, JAMES P. congressional press secretary; b. St. Paul, Minn., Feb. 23, 1961; s. Earl John Manley and Shiela Ruth Mullin. BA in polit. sci., U. of St. Thomas, 1979—83. Asst. press sec. Senate Majority Leasder George Mitchell, 1990—93; press sec. Senator Kennedy, 1993—. Democrat. Roman Catholic. Avocations: jogging, music. Home: 311 South Carolina Ave, Se Washington DC 20003 Office: Office of Senator Kennedy SR-315 Washington DC 20510

MANLEY, JOAN A(DELE) DANIELS, retired publishing executive; b. San Luis Obispo, Calif., Sept. 23, 1932; d. Carl and Della (Weinmann) Daniels; m. Jeremy C. Lanning, Mar. 17, 1956 (div. Sept. 1963); m. Donald H. Manley, Sept. 12, 1964 (div. 1985); m. William G. Houlton, May 31, 1991. BA, U. Calif., Berkeley, 1954; DBA (hon.), U. New Haven, 1974; LLD (hon.), Babson Coll., 1978. Sec. Doubleday & Co., Inc., N.Y.C., 1954-60; sales exec. Time Inc., 1960-66, v.p., 1971-75, group v.p., 1975-84, also bd. dir.; circulation dir. Time-Life Books, 1966-68, dir. sales, 1968-70, pub., 1970-76; chmn. bd. Time-Life Books Inc., 1976-80. Vice chmn. bd. Book-of-the-Month Club, Inc., N.Y.C., until 1984; supervising dir. Time-Life Internat. (Nederland) B.V., Amsterdam, until 1984; bd. dirs. Dreyfus Founders Funds, Sara Lee Corp., R.R Donnelley & Sons. Past trustee Mayo Found., Rochester, Minn., Nat. Repertory Orch., William Benton Found.; former mem. adv. coun. Stanford U. Bus. Sch., Haas Sch. Bus. U. Calif. Named to Direct Mktg. Hall of Fame, 1993; U. Calif.-Berkeley fellow, 1989. Mem. Assn. Am. Pubs. (past chmn.).

MANLEY, JOHN HUGO, computing technology executive, educator; b. Highland Park, Mich., July 9, 1932; s. Hugo Edward and Linda Amelia (Kuure) M.; m. Josephine Theresa Catanzaro, Sept. 3, 1958; children: Lisa Linn, Michele Ann, John David, Marc Darrin. B. Metall. Engring., Cornell U., 1955; MS Indsl. Engring., U. Pitts., 1965, PhD, 1971. Metall. engr. GE, Schenectady, NY, 1955—56; commd. 2d lt. USAF, 1956, advanced through grades to lt. col., 1973, ret., 1976; asst. to dir. Johns Hopkins Applied Physics Lab., Laurel, Md., 1976—80; exec. ITT Corp., Stratford, Conn., 1980—83; v.p. Nastec Corp., Southfield, Mich., 1983—85; dir. emeritus Software Engring. Inst. Carnegie Mellon U., Pitts., 1985—87; pres., chmn. Computing Tech. Transition, Inc., Wilmington, Del., 1983—2004; prof. emeritus mfg. and info. tech. sys. engring., dir. mfg. sys. engring. program U. Pitts., 1987—2002. Tech. adv. bd. Tartan Inc., Pitts.; com. on nat. weather svc. modernization NRC, 1991-94. Editor-in-chief Jour. Systems and Software, 1978-82; contbr. articles to profl. jours. Pres. Point Field Community Assn., Millersville, Md., 1979-80; v.p. Greater Severna Park Coun., Severna Park, Md., 1980. Lt. col. USAF, 1955-76, Vietnam. Decorated Legion of Merit, Bronze Star. Mem. IEEE Computer Soc. (TC exec. bd.), Soc. Mfg. Engrs., Gulf Harbour Golf & Country Club. Republican. Episcopalian.

MANLEY, JOHN PAUL, former Canadian government official; b. Ottawa, Ontario, Canada, Jan. 5, 1950; s. John Joseph and Mildred Charlotte (Scharf) Manley; m. Judith Mary Rae, Apr. 21, 1973; children: Rebecca Jane, David John, Sarah Kathleen. Attended, Carleton U.; Doctorate (hon.), U. Ottawa. Law clerk for Rt. Hon. Bora Laskin Chief Justice Can., 1976-77; chair Ottawa-Carleton Bd. Trade, 1985-86; min. Industry Govt. of Can., 1993-2000, min. Western Econ. Diversification, min. Atlantic Can. Opportunities Agy., 1996; min. for Can. Econ. Devel. for Que. Regions, 1996-2000; min. fgn. affairs, 2000—02; chair cabinet com. on pub. security and anti-terrorism, 2001—; dep. prime minister of Can., 2002—03; min. of fin, 2002—03. Chmn. cabinet com. on pub. security and anti-terrorism Ho. of Commons, Ottawa, Canada, 2001—, min. infrastructure and crown corps., 2002, polit. min. for Ontario and chmn. cabinet com. on econ. union and social union, 2002—. Elected to H. of C. g.e., 1988. Named Time Can. Mag. Newsmaker of the Yr., 2001. Avocation: marathon running. Office: Ho of Commons 1883 Bank St K1A 0A6 Ottawa ON Canada E-mail: manlej@parl.gc.ca.

MANLEY, JUDITH L. director; b. Columbus, Ohio; B in Bus., Ohio State U., 1970; MEd, Xavier U., 1986. Copy writer advt. agy., Columbus, 1970—74; program asst. Ohio State U., Columbus, 1974—. Advisor, counselor dept. Spanish and Portuguese Ohio State U., Columbus, 1991—. Author poems. Area commr. Greater Hilltop Area Commn., Columbus, 1989—; bd. mem. Greater Hilltop Cmty. Devel. Corp., Columbus, 1989—; alumnae Leadership Columbus, Columbus, 1993. Named Vol. of the Month, Children's Hosp., Columbus, 2002; recipient Pres.'s Vol. Svc. award, 2003, Va. Denman Vol. award, 2004. Mem.: ACA. Avocations: writing, photography, music, theater.

MANLEY, ROBERT EDWARD, lawyer, economist; b. Cin., Nov. 24, 1935; s. John M. and Helen Catherine (McCarthy) M.; m. Roberta L. Anzinger, Oct. 21, 1971 (div. 1980); 1 child, Robert Edward. ScB in Econs, Xavier U., 1956; AM in Econ. Theory, U. Cin., 1957; JD, Harvard U., 1960; postgrad., London Sch. Econs. and Polit. Sci., 1960, MIT, 1972. Bar: Ohio 1960, U.S. Supreme Ct. 1970. Pvt. practice law, Cin., 1960—; chmn. Manley Burke, 1977. Taft teaching fellow econs. U. Cin., 1956-57, vis. lectr. community planning law Coll. Design, Architecture and Art, 1967-73, adj. assoc. prof. urban planning Coll. Design, Architecture, Art and Planning, 1972-81, adj. prof., 1981—, adj. prof. law, 1980—. Author: Metropolitan School Desegregation, 1978, (with Robert N. Cook) Management of Land and Environment, 1981, others; chmn. editl. adv. bd. Urban Lawyer, 1986-95. Mem. Hamilton County Pub. Defender Commn., 1976-79; trustee HOPE, Cin., Albert J. Ryan Found.; counsel, co-founder Action Housing for Greater Cin.; mem. Spl. Commn. on Formation U. Cin. Health Maintenance Orgn., Mayor Cin. Spl. Com. on Housing; chmn. Cin. Environ. Adv. Coun., 1975-76; trustee The Americas Fund for Ind. Univs., 1987-2000; trustee Ohio Planning Conf., 1982-91, pres., 1987-89, trustee, 1987-90; sec. Cin. Mounted Patrol Com., 1993—; active Bd. Cin. Downtown Coun., 1991-98. Mem. ABA (coun. sect. local govt. law 1976-80, 81 85, 88 92), Ohio Bar Assn., Cin. Bar Assn., Am. Judicature Soc., Law and Soc. Assn., Nat. Coun. Crime and Delinquency, Harvard U. Law Sch. Assn. Cin. (pres. 1970-71), Am. Econ. Assn., Am. Acad. Polit. and Social Sci., Queen City Club, Explorers Club (N.Y.C.) (trustee, sec. Clark chpt. 1992—), Athenaeum Club (Phila.), S.Am. Explorers (Lima, Peru). Republican. Roman Catholic. Office: Manley Burke 225 W Court St Cincinnati OH 45202-1052 Office Phone: 513-721-5525. E-mail: rmanley@manleyburke.com.

MANLY, MARC EDWARD, lawyer; b. Knoxville, Tenn., Mar. 11, 1952; s. William Donald and Jane (Wilden) M.; m. Colby A. Chapman, July 20, 1974; children: Justin C., Allison C. BA summa cum laude, Amherst Coll., 1974; MA in Econs., JD magna cum laude, U. Mich., 1977. Bar: Ill. 1978, D.C. 1988, U.S. Dist. Ct. (no. dist.) Ill. 1978. Assoc. Sidley & Austin, Chgo., 1978-84, ptnr., 1986—94; with AT&T, 1995—2000; mng. dir., law & govtl. holdings, gen. counsel, sec. Newpower Holdings, Inc., 2000—02; exec. v.p., chief legal officer Cinergy Corp., 2002—. Mem. ABA, Order of Coif, Phi Beta Kappa. Office: Cinergy Corp 139 E 4th St Cincinnati OH 45202

MANLY, SARAH LETITIA, retired state legislator, ophthalmic photographer, angiographer; b. Greenville, S.C., Feb. 1, 1927; d. Victor Harris and Elsie Clippard (Burnett) Gillespie; m. Basil Manly IV, Sept. 11, 1947; children: Sarah Manly Cornish, Basil V, Jean Manly McDowell, Mary Manly Mounce. BS cum laude, Furman U., 1947; postgrad., MIT, 1972; MEd, Clemson U., 1974; postgrad., Cambridge (Eng.) U., 1981. Cert. physics tchr., Pa., S.C.; cert. retinal angiographer. Ward sec. Roper Hosp., Charleston, S.C., 1947; analytical chemist Parker Labs., Charleston, 1948; tchr. sci. Upper Darby (Pa.) Sch. Dist., 1961-63; tchr. physics Sch. Dist. Greenville (S.C.) County, 1963-64, 70-76; ophthalmic photographer Basil Manly IV, MD, Greenville, 1976-96; lectr. physics Clemson (S.C.) U., 1979-81. Cons. MIT, Cambridge, 1972-75, Georgetown U., Washington, 1974-76, NASA, Houston, 1974-76. Editor, cons. physics study guides MIT, 1972-75; editor lab. materials NASA, 1974-76; contbr. articles to profl. jours. Trustee Sch. Dist. Greenville County, 1976-88. Named S.C. Legislator of Yr., S.C. Sch. Bds. Assn., 1991, Hon. Alumnus of Phi Beta Kappa, 1994. Mem. Greenville County Med. Aux. (sec. 1953-54), Delta Kappa Gamma. Democrat. Baptist. Avocations: travel, reading, volunteering. Home: 2 Chanticleer Dr Greenville SC 29605-3106

MANLY, WILLIAM DONALD, metallurgist; b. Malta, Ohio, Jan. 13, 1923; s. Edward James and Thelma (Campbell) M.; m. Jane Wilden, Feb. 9, 1949; children: Hugh, Ann, Marc, David. Student, Antioch Coll., 1941-42; BS, U. Notre Dame, 1947, MS, 1949; postgrad., U. Tenn., 1950-55; PhD in Engring. (hon.), U. N.D., 2000. Metallurgist Oak Ridge Nat. Lab., 1949-60, mgr. gas cooled reactor program, 1960-64; mgr. materials research Union Carbide Corp., N.Y.C., 1964-65; gen. mgr. Union Carbide Corp. (Stellite div.), N.Y.C., 1967-69, v.p. Kokomo, Ind., 1969-70; sr. v.p. Cabot Corp., Boston, 1970-83, exec. v.p., 1983-86; ret., 1986; also dir. chmn. adv. com. for reactor safety AEC, 1964-65. Served with USMC, 1943-46. Recipient Honor award U. Notre Dame, 1974, Nat. Medal of Tech., Nat. Sci. Found., 1993. Fellow Am. Soc. Metals (hon. mem., pres. 1972-73, medal for advanced rsch. 1987), AIME, Am. Nuclear Soc. (Merit award 1966); mem. Nat. Acad. Engring., Nat. Assn. Corrosion Engrs., Metall. Soc., Masons. Presbyterian. Home: 103 Cypress Ln Oak Ridge TN 37830-8772

MANN, AIMEE, singer, songwriter; b. Richmond, Va., Aug. 9, 1960; m. Michael Penn. Vocals, bass 'Til Tuesday, 1983—89; solo artist, 1993—. Singer: (albums) (with 'Til Tuesday) Voices Carry, 1985, Welcome Home, 1986, Everything's Different Now, 1988, (solo) Whatever, 1993, I'm With Stupid, 1995, Bachelor No. 2, 2000, Lost in Space, 2002, (songs) Save Me, 1999 (nom. for Acad. Award for Original Song, 1999). Office: SuperEgo Records 511 Ave of the Americas #197 New York NY 10011*

MANN, ALFRED, pharmaceutical executive; b. Portland, Oreg., 1925; MS in Physics, UCLA; DHL (hon.), U. So. Calif., 2001, Johns Hopkins U., 2001. Chmn., CEO MannKind Corp., Sylmar, Calif.; chmn., co-CEO Advanced Bionics Corp.; chmn. emeritus MiniMed Inc.; founder, chmn. Med. Rsch. Group, Inc.; chmn., CEO Siemens-Pacesetter, Inc. and predecessor Pacesetter Sys., Inc.; pres. Spectrolab, Heliotek. Chmn. bd. trustees Alfred Mann Found., Alfred Mann Inst., U. So. Calif.; U. So. Calif. trustee mem. bd. overseers Keck U. So. Calif. Sch. Medicine; chmn. So. Calif. Biomed. Coun., Second Sight, LLC, Allecure Corp., Quallion, LLC, CTL Immunotherapy, Inc., Pharm. Discovery Co., Inc. Named Man of Yr., WISE Sr. Svcs., 1999, Humanitarian of Yr., House Ear Inst., 1999; named one of 10 Most Influential People on Tch Coast, L.a. Times, 1999; recipient Spirit of Edison award for cmty. svc., Thomas Edison State Coll., 1999, Vision of the Future award, RP Internat., 1999, Reynolds Soc. Achievement award, Harvard Med. Sch., 1999. Fellow: Am. Inst. Med. and Biol. Engring.; mem.: NAE. Office: MannKind Corp 12744 San Fernando Rd Lake View Terrace CA 91342-3728

MANN, BRUCE ALAN, lawyer, bank executive, investment banker; b. Chgo., Nov. 28, 1934; s. David I. and Lillian (Segal) M.; m. Naomi Cooks, Aug. 31, 1980; children: Sally Mann Stull, Jonathan Hugh, Andrew Ross. BBA, U. Wis., 1955, SJD, 1957. Bar: Wis. 1957, N.Y. 1958, Calif. 1961. Assoc. Davis, Polk & Wardwell, N.Y.C., 1957-60, Pillsbury, Madison & Sutro, San Francisco, 1960-66, ptnr., 1967-83; adminstrv. mng. dir. L.F. Rothschild Unterberg Towbin, San Francisco, 1983-87; ptnr. Morrison & Foerster, San Francisco, 1987—; sr. mng. dir. W.R. Hambrecht & Co., San Francisco, 1999—2003. Cons. SEC, 1978; vis. prof. law Georgetown U., 1978; lectr. in field. Author: (with Mattson) California Corporate Practice and Forms, 1999; contbr. articles to profl. jours. Served with USAR, 1957. Mem.: NASD (gov.-at-large 1981—83), ABA (chmn. fed. regulation of securities com. 1981—83, mem. bus. law sect. coun. 1996—99, standing com. on ethics and profl. responsibility 1997—2003, chmn. com. on venture capital 2000—03), Bar Assn. San Francisco (bd. dirs. 1974—75), State Bar Calif., Am. Law Inst., The Family Club. Office: Morrison & Foerster 425 Market St Ste 3100 San Francisco CA 94105-2482 E-mail: bmann@mofo.com.

MANN, CEDRIC ROBERT, retired institute administrator, oceanographer; b. Auckland, N.Z., Feb. 14, 1926; came to Can., 1949; s. Duncan and Winifred Mary (Hood) M.; m. Muriel Frances May, Dec. 19, 1950; 1 child, Robin Carl B.Sc., U. N.Z., Auckland, 1948, M.Sc., 1950; PhD, U. B.C., Vancouver, Can., 1953; D.Eng., N.S. Tech. Coll., Halifax, Can., 1972. Physicist Naval Research Establishment, Halifax, N.S., Can., 1953-61; oceanographer Atlantic Oceanographic Lab., Halifax, N.S., Can., 1961-75, dir., 1975-78; dir. gen. Bedford Inst. Oceanography, Halifax, N.S., Can., 1978-79, Inst. Ocean Scis., Sidney,

B.C., Can., 1979-87. Assoc. prof. Dalhousie U., Halifax, 1961-75; chmn. sci. adv. bd. Intergovtl. Oceanographic Commn., Paris, 1978-81; mem. Can. Climate Planning Bd., Ottawa, 1983-86; chmn. Sea Use Council, Seattle, 1981-86. Contbr. articles to profl. jours. Fellow Royal Soc. Can.; mem. Can. Meteorol. and Oceanographic Soc. (life, recipient J.P. Tully medal in Oceanography, 1994). Anglican. Avocations: golf, gardening. Home: 301-2373 Henry Ave Sidney BC Canada V8L 2B4

MANN, CHARLES ROY, statistician; b. NYC, Mar. 27, 1941; s. Gerard and Gertrude (Krieger) M. BS in Applied Math., Poly. U. N.Y., 1961; MS in Math. Stats., Mich. State U., 1963; PhD in Stats., U. Mo., 1969. Asst. prof. stats. George Washington U., Washington, 1969-73; head stats. divsn. Group Ops., Inc., Washington, 1973-77; pres. Charles R. Mann Assocs., Inc., Washington, 1977—. Cons. in field. Contbr. articles to profl. jours. Bd. dirs. No. Va. C.C., 1978-82. Fellow Am. Statis. Assn., Washington Acad. Scis.; mem. Inst. Math. Stats., Washington Statis. Soc., Profl. Testing Coun. of Met. Washington. Home: 5501 Seminary Rd Unit 2011S Falls Church VA 22041 Office: 1111 14th St NW Ste 800 Washington DC 20005-5666 Office Phone: 202-466-6161. Business E-Mail: crmann@mannassociates.com.

MANN, DAVID, energy and services company executive; b. Drummondville, Que., 1939; m. Lois Dyer Mann; children: Geoffrey, Peter, Gillian. B.Commerce, Dalhousie U., Halifax, N.S., 1961, B.Laws, 1965; M.Laws, U. London, 1966. With Cox Hanson O'Reilly Matheson, Halifax, 1967-96, mng. ptnr., 1974-91; pres., CEO Emera Inc. and Nova Scotia Power Inc., 1996—; also bd. dirs. Bd. dirs., chmn. Emera Fuels, Maritimes & N.E. Pipeline L.P., L.L.C.; chmn. Bangor Hydro-Electric Co.; bd. dirs. Logistec Corp., Can. Coun. Chief Exec., Emera, Inc., Nova Scotia Power, Inc., Can. Electricity Assn., Conf. Bd. of Can., Atlantic Inst. Market Studies. Gov. Olympic Trust of Can.; mem. adv. bd. Dalhousie Sch. Bus.; with Atlantic Salmon Fedn.; bd. dirs., chmn. Found. for Ednl. Exch. between Can. and U.S. (The Can.-U.S. Fulbright Program). Queen's Counsel, 1982. Fellow: Coll. Law Practice Mgmt. Avocations: golf, sailing, skiing, fly fishing, cooking. Office: Emera Inc PO Box 910 Halifax NS Canada B3J 2W5 Fax: (902) 428-6112. E-mail: david.mann@emera.com.

MANN, DAVID SCOTT, lawyer; b. Cin., Ohio, Sept. 25, 1939; s. Henry M. and Helen Faye M.; m. Elizabeth Taliaferro, Oct. 5, 1963; children: Michael, Deborah, Marshall. AB cum laude, Harvard Coll., 1961, LLB magna cum laude, 1968. Bar: Ohio 1968. Assoc. Dinsmore & Shohl, Cin., 1968-74, ptnr., 1974-83, Taliaferro and Mann, Cin., 1983-92; councilman City of Cin., 1974-92, mayor, 1980-82, 91; mem. 103d Congress 1st Ohio dist., Washington, 1993-94; mem. armed svcs. com., mem. jud. com. Washington; of counsel Thompson, Hine and Flory, Cin., 1995-96; pvt. practice Mann & Mann, LLC, Cin., 1997—. Adj. prof. Coll. Law U. Cin., 1995—2002. Editor Harvard Law Rev., 1966-68, notes editor, 1967-68; contbr. articles to profl. jours. Mem., chmn. Cin. Bd. Health, 1972-74. With USN, 1961-65. Mem. Cin. Bar Assn. Democrat. Methodist. Home: 568 Evanswood Pl Cincinnati OH 45220-1527 E-mail: david@mannandmannlaw.com.

MANN, DAVID WILLIAM, minister; b. Elkhart, Ind., Apr. 17, 1947; s. Herbert Richard and Kathryn (Bontrager) M.; m. Brenda Marie Frantz, June 7, 1969; children: Troy, Todd, Erika. BA, Bethel Coll., 1969; MS, Nat. Louis U., 1986. Ordained to ministry Missionary Ch., 1978. Campus life dir. Youth for Christ, Elkhart, 1969-77; denominational youth dir. Missionary Ch., Ft. Wayne, Ind., 1977-81, Christian edn. dir., 1981-88, U.S. dir. missions, 1990—; assoc. dir. World Ptnrs., Ft. Wayne, 1988-90. Dir. Missionary Ch. Vol. Svc., Ft. Wayne, 1983—, World Ptnrs. USA, 1998—. Author: (with others) Youth Leaders Source Book, 1985; contbr. articles to prof. jour. Mgr. Little League, Ft. Wayne, 1981-89, bd. dirs. 1986. Recipient Alumnus of the Year award, Bethel Coll., 2003. Mem. Nat. Assn. Evangelicals, Evangelical Fellowship of Mission Agys. (nat. bd. dirs. 1999—), Denominational Execs. in Christian Edn. (chmn. 1988), Aldersgate Pub. Assn. (bd. dirs. 1985, 87), Nat. Christian Edn. Assn. (exec. com. 1987-89). Avocations: baseball, skiing, fishing, woodworking. Office: Missionary Ch PO Box 9127 Fort Wayne IN 46899-9127 Office Phone: 219-747-2027. E-mail: manndw@aol.com.

MANN, DONALD CAMERON, record company executive; b. Memphis, Jan. 31, 1949; s. Cameron Mann and Jane Snowden (Treadwell) Martin; m. Natacha Luba Plotnikoff, June 1, 1972 (div. Nov. 1998); 1 child, Cameron Alexander; m. Donna Marie Reed, April 17, 1999. BA, Brown U., 1971; MBA, Columbia U., 1978. Assoc. pub. Portfolio Mag., N.Y.C., 1978-80; mktg. dir. Bloom & Gelb, N.Y.C., 1980-82; gen. mgr. Malmo Dir. Advt., Memphis, 1982-88; pres. Fusion Mktg. Group unit Axiom Corps., Memphis, 1988—2002; pres., founder Memphis Records, 2002—. Spkr. Fin. Inst. Mktg. Assn., Chgo., 1988-90, Bank Mktg. Assn., Database Mktg. Conf., 1995, OKRA Mktg. User Conf., Tampa, Fla., 1989-94, Customer Insights Corp. Conf., 1989, Bank Mktg. Assn. Argentina, Buenos Aires, 1994, Strategic Rsch. Inst., N.Y., 1994-95; founder, dir. Advanced Fin. Database Mktg. Sch. Northwestern U., Chgo., 1990-2000. Editor, author: (book) The New Age of Financial Marketing, 1991. Bd. dirs. Concerts Internat., Memphis, 1989, Experience Art Memphis, 2001—; mem. Leadership Memphis, 1993; mem. adv. bd. Case-in-Point, Axciom Corp., 1995-99. Recipient Cert. Merit Direct Mktg. Assn., 1983, Fin. Inst. Mktg. Assn., 1987, ADDY, Am. Assn. Advt. Agys., 1988. Mem. The Univ. Club, The Porsche Club Am., The Dixon Gallery and Gardens, Memphis Brooks Mus. of Art, The Gullwing Owners Group, The Ferrari Club Am., Shelby Am. Automobile Club, Mercedes Benz Club Am. Avocation: automobile restoration. Office: Memphis Records 2258 Young Ave Memphis TN 38104 E-mail: don@memphisrecordsonline.com.

MANN, DONEGAN, lawyer; b. Birmingham, Ala., Mar. 6, 1922; s. Ephriam DeValse and Edna Atkins (Donegan) M.; m. Frances Virginia Hindman, Apr. 6, 1957 (dec. May 1993); m. Frances M. Jenkins, Jan. 7, 1995 (dec. Dec. 1997). Student, Birmingham-So., 1940-41; AB, George Washington U., 1947, JD, 1950. Bar: U.S. Dist. Ct. D.C. 1950, U.S. Ct. Appeals (D.C. cir.) 1950, U.S. Ct. Claims 1957, U.S. Supreme Ct. 1961, U.S. Ct. Appeals (fed. cir.) 1982. Acting bur. counsel Civil Aeronautics Bd., Washington, 1953-55; gen. rates atty. GAO, Washington, 1955-57; spl. rate counsel Gen. Svcs. Administrn., Washington, 1957-60; assoc. Wolf & Case, Washington, 1960-66; sr. atty., office gen. counsel. U.S. Dept. Treasury, Washington, 1966-79; of counsel Shands & Stupar, Washington, 1979-82; pvt. practice Washington, 1984—. Pres. Friends of Historic Great Falls Tavern, Inc., Potomac, Md., 1977-80, bd. dirs., 1980-83. With USN, 1943-46, PTO. Mem. ABA (treas. pub. contracts sect. 1965-66, chmn. awards com. 1975-76, svc. award sr. lawyers' divsn. 1991, counsel sr. lawyers divsn., 1995-97, chmn. guardianship and conservatorship com. 1989-95, sr. lawyers' divsn. task force to reform guardianship laws 1992-94, vice chmn., wills probate and trust com., 1995—, chmn. citizenship com. 1996-97, vice chmn. Law Day and citizenship com. 1997—), FBA, Fed. Energy Bar Assn., D.C. Bar Assn., Montgomery County Hist. Soc. (exec. v.p. 1980-83, bd. dirs. 1984-86). Democrat. Episcopalian. Avocations: fishing, hunting, golf, tennis, gardening. Office: 1000 Connecticut Ave NW Ste 204 Washington DC 20036-5337

MANN, EMILY BETSY, writer, artistic director, theater director; b. Boston, Apr. 12, 1952; d. Arthur and Sylvia (Blut) M.; m. Gary Mailman; 1 child, Nicholas Isaac Bamman. BA, Harvard U., 1974; MFA, U. Minn., 1976; D of Fine Arts (hon.), Princeton U., 2002. Resident dir. Guthrie Theater, Mpls., 1976-79; dir. BAM Theater Co., Bklyn., 1980-81; freelance writer, dir. N.Y.C., 1981-90; artistic dir. McCarter Theater Ctr. for the Performing Arts, Princeton, N.J., 1990—. Author: (plays) Annulla, An Autobiography, Still Life (6 Obie awards 1981, Fringe First award 1985), Execution of Justice (Helen Hayes award, Bay Area Theatre Critics Circle award, HBO/USA award, Playwriting award Women's Com. Dramtists Guild for Dramatizing Issues of Conscience 1986), Greensboro: A Requiem, Having Our Say (L.A. NAACP award for Best Play), Meshugah; co-author: (with Ntozake Shange) (musical) Betsey Brown; (screenplays) Fanny Kelly, The Winnie Mandela Story, Having Our Say (Christopher award, Peabody award), Having Our Say (Peabody award); dir. Hedda Gabbler, A Doll House, Annulla, Still Life (Obie award), Execution of Justice (Guthrie and Broadway), Betsey Brown, The Glass Menagerie, Three Sisters, Cat on a Hot Tin Roof, Twilight: L.A., 1992 (L.A. NAACP award for best dir.), The Perfectionist, The Matchmaker, Safe as Houses, The Mai, Betrayal, Fool for Love, The Cherry Orchard, Because He Can, Romeo and Juliet, All Over, The Tempest, Uncle Vanya (McCarter and Lo Jolla Playjpise); adaptor, dir. Miss Julie, Having Our Say (Tony nomination-direction of a play 1995, Dramatist Guild's Hull Warriner award, L.A. NAACP award), Greensboro, A Requiem, The House of Bernarda Alba, Meshugah, The Cherry Orchard, Because He Can, Romeo and Juliet, Uncle Vanya; translator: Nights and Days (Pierre Laville), 1985; pub. in New Plays U.S.A. 1, New Plays 3, American Plays and the Vietnam War, The Ten Best Plays of 1986, Out Front, Testimony: 4 Plays by Emily Mann, 1997; co-editor: Political Stages, 2002. Recipient BUSH fellowship, 1975-76, Rosamond Gilder award New Drama Forum Assn., 1983, NEA Assocs. grant, 1984, Guggenheim fellowship, 1985, McKnight fellowship, 1985, CAPS award, 1985, NEA Playwrights fellowship, 1986. Mem. Soc. Stage Dirs. and Choreographers, Theatre Comms. Group (v.p.), New Dramatists, PEN, Writers' Guild, Dramatists' Guild (exec. bd. mem.), Phi Beta Kappa.

MANN, FRANK BERT, visual artist, painter; b. Washington, Apr. 22, 1950; s. Frank Bert and Wilda Vendetta Kaufman. BS, High Point Univ., 1972; BA, George Washington Univ., 1978; MFA, Pratt Inst., 1981. Guest lectr. Corcoran Sch. of Art, Washington, 1979, Pa. State U., Reading, 1986-87, Pratt Inst., Bklyn., 1987-88, Parsons Sch. Art & Design, NYC, 1996-97. Exec. dir. Colaborative Projects, Inc., NY, 1987-88, Basicarts Network, NY, 1989-90; vis. artist Coalition for the Homeless Camp, 1997, Children's Friends for Life, NY, 1997, Project for St. Cyrils Ch., NY, 1992. Author: Eye of the Painter, 1997; illustrator (film) Nerves, 1993; author: (Essay) The American Society of Contemporary Artists-The First Eighty-Five Years, 2003; exhibitions include Biennale Internat., Florence, Italy, 2001 (Lorenzo Il Magnifico medal in painting, 2001), Represented in permanent collections Guggenheim Mus., NYC, Mus. Contemp. Art, Nice, France. U.S. rep. Biennale Internazionale, Florence, 1999, 2001. Recipient Mable Sanger Webb award, Ford Found., 1980, Lorenzo le Magnifico medal, Internat. Dell'Anfe Contemporanea, 2001; grantee, N.Y. State Coun. Arts, 1988, N.Y. City Dept. Cultural Affairs, 1989. Mem.: Assn. D'Art Internat., Contemporary Artists' Guild, Am. Soc. Contempoarary Artists, Drawing Soc., Artists Equity (bd. dirs. 2000—03, v.p. 2003—04), Am. for the Arts. Lutheran. Home and Office: 212 E 34th St Apt 3E New York NY 10016-4846 Office Phone: 212-689-9003. E-mail: fmann100@hotmail.com.

MANN, GEORGE STANLEY, real estate and financial services corporation executive; b. Toronto, Ont., Can., Dec. 23, 1932; s. David Philip and Elizabeth (Green) M.; children: Michael, Tracy. Attended, North Toronto Collegiate Sch.; LLD (hon.), U. Windsor. Ptnr. Mann & Martel Co. Ltd., 1959-68, CEO, 1968-70, United Trust Co., 1970-76; pres. Unicorp Canada Corp., Toronto, 1972-76, chmn. bd., 1976-90; dir. Nat. Bank Canada, 1978-91; chmn. bd. Union Gas Ltd., 1986-93; owner co., Toronto. Pres. chmn. bd. Lincorp Holdings, Inc., N.Y.C. Bd. govs. Mt. Sinai Hosp., Toronto. Mem. Oakdale Golf & Country Club (Toronto), High Ridge Country Club (Palm Beach, Fla.), Mar-a-Lago Club (Palm Beach, Fla.), Trump Internat. Golf Club (Palm Beach, Fla.). Avocation: golf. Home: #10 Bellair St Ste 302 Toronto ON Canada M5R 3T8 also: 505 South County Rd Palm Beach FL 33480 Office: 2 St Clair Ave W Ste 1004 Toronto ON Canada

MANN, HENRY DEAN, accountant; b. El Dorado, Ark., Feb. 8, 1943; s. Paul L. and Mary Louise (Capps) M.; m. Rebecca Balch, Aug. 14, 1965; children: Julie Elizabeth, Betsey Sawyer Mann. BSBA, U. Ark., 1965. CPA, Mo., Tex. Staff acct., mgr. Ernst & Whinney, Houston, 1967-76, ptnr., 1976-77; regional personnel ptnr. Ernst & Whinney (now Ernst & Young), St. Louis, 1977-78, mng. ptnr., 1978-88; pres. Mann Industries, Inc., St. Louis, 1988-89; pres., dir. 1st Capital Corp., Ft. Scott, Kans., 1989—, chmn., CEO, dir., 1989—, Citizens Bank, N.A., Fort Scott, Kans., 1989—. CEO, chmn. bd. dirs. Humble (Tex.) Nat. Bank, 1992-98; adv. bd. U. Mo. Sch. Accountancy, Columbia, 1979-82; bd. dirs. Cupples Co. Mfrs., St. Louis. Treas. Jr. Achievement, St. Louis, 1984-98, bd. dirs., 1986-98; treas., bd. dirs. United Way, St. Louis, 1986-92, Art and Edn. Coun., St. Louis, 1986-91; bd. dirs. St. Louis Symphony, 1988-89, Mercy Hosp. Found., Ft. Scott, Kans., 2000—, Bankers Bank of Kans., Wichita, 2000—; bd. dirs. Kammergild Chamber Orch., St. Louis, 1986, pres., 1983-85. Mem. AICPA, Mo. Soc. CPAs, Ft. Scott C. of C. (bd. dirs., pres.2001—), Bellerive Country Club (treas. 1986-87, v.p. 1988-89), Beta Gamma Sigma, Beta Alpha Psi. Presbyterian. Office: Citizens Bank NA 200 S Main St Fort Scott KS 66701-2045

MANN, J. KEITH, retired law educator, arbitrator; b. May 28, 1924; s. William Young and Lillian Myrle (Bailey) M.; m. Virginia McKinnon, July 7, 1950; children: William Christopher, Marilyn Keith, John Kevin, Susan Bailey, Andrew Curry. BS, Ind. U., 1948, LLB, 1949; LLD, Monmouth Coll., 1989. Bar: Ind. 1949, D.C. 1951. Law clk. Justice Wiley Rutledge and Justice Sherman Minton, 1949-50; pvt. practice Washington, 1950; with Wage Stblzn. Bd., 1951; asst. prof. U. Wis., 1952, Stanford (Calif.) U. Law Sch., 1952-54, assoc. prof., 1954-58, prof., 1958-88, prof. emeritus, 1988—, assoc. dean, 1961-85, acting dean, 1976, 81-82, cons. to provost, 1986-87. Vis. prof. U. Chgo., 1953; mem. Sec. of Labor's Adv. Com., 1955-57; mem. Pres.'s Commn. Airlines Controversy, 1961; mem. COLC Aerospace Spl. Panel, 1973-74; chmn., mem. Presdl. Emergency Bds. or Bds. of Inquiry, 1962-63, 67, 71-72; spl. master U.S. vs. Alaska, U.S. Supreme Ct., 1980-97. Editor book rev. and articles Ind. U. Law Jour., 1948-49. Ensign USNR, 1944-46. Sunderland fellow U. Mich., 1959-60; scholar-in-residence Duke U., 1972. Mem. ABA, AAUP, Nat. Acad. Arbitrators, Indsl. Rels. Rsch. Assn., Acad. Law Alumni Fellows Ind. U., Order of Coif, Tau Kappa Epsilon, Phi Delta Phi. Democrat. Presbyterian. Home: 872 Lathrop Dr Stanford CA 94305-1053 Office: Stanford U Sch Law Stanford CA 94305-8610 E-mail: jkmann@leland.stanford.edu.

MANN, JACK MATTHEWSON, bottling company executive; b. Marshall, Tex., Apr. 14, 1932; s. Jack Slater and Mary (Matthewson) M.; m. True Sandlin, Sept. 4, 1954 (div. 1989); children: Jack, Robert, Daniel, Nathaniel. Student, N.Mex. Mil. Inst., 1952; BBA, U. Tex., 1954; MBA, Harvard U., 1960. Credit analyst Republic Nat. Bank, Dallas, 1959; chem. coord. Humble Oil and Refining Co., Baytown, Tex., 1960-61; asst. sales mgr. The Made-Rite Co., Marshall, Tex., 1957-58; asst. gen. mgr. The Made Rite Co., Marshall, Tex., 1961-63, gen. mgr. Longview, Tex., 1963-92, pres., 1972—, owner, chmn., 1982—; v.p. Longview Econ. Devel. Corp., 1994-2000, treas., 1995-96, pres., 1996-97. Bd. dirs. Longview Nat. Bank, Region's Bank; mem. pres.'s adv. coun. Le Tourneau U., 1994—97; mem. devel. coun. U. Tex.-Tyler Longview U. Ctr., 2000—. Exec. com. Rep. Party Tex., 1962-65; mem. Trinity Episcopal Ch., Longview, 1963-, sr. warden, jr. warden, treas.; mem. exec. bd. Episcopal Diocese Tex., Houston, 1974-76; mem. small bus. adv. com. Tex. Dept. Commerce, 1988-91. Mem.: Nat. Dr. Pepper Bottlers Assn. (pres. 1983—85), Tex. Soft Drink Assn. (pres. 1972), Longview C. of C. (dir. 1965—68, 1984—86), Pinecrest Country Club, Longview Summit Club (gov. 1982—94). Avocation: University of Texas athletics. Home: 45 Stonegate Dr Longview TX 75601-3600 Office: The Made Rite Co PO Box 3283 Longview TX 75606-3283

MANN, JAMES L. computer company executive; Degree in bus. adminstrn., Wichita State U. Pres., COO Bradford Nat. Corp., NYC, 1981—83, SunGard Data Sys. Inc., Wayne, Pa., 1983—86, chmn., CEO, 1986—. Past chmn. Info. Tech. Assn. Am. With USAF. Office: Sungard Data Sys Inc 680 E Swedesford Rd Wayne PA 19087

MANN, JAMES ROBERT, former congressman; b. Greenville, S.C., Apr. 27, 1920; s. Alfred Cleo and Nina (Griffin) M.; m. Virginia Thomason Brunson, Jan. 15, 1945; children— James Robert, David Brunson, William Walker, Virginia Brunson. BA, The Citadel, 1941, LL.D. (hon.), 1978; JD, U. S.C., 1947. Bar: S.C. 1947, U.S. Ct. Appeals (4th cir.) 1948, U.S. Supreme Ct. 1970. Practice in, Greenville, 1947—; del. S.C. Ho. of Reps. from, Greenville County, 1949-52; solicitor 13th Jud. Circuit, 1953-63; mem. 91st-95th Congresses 4th Dist. SC. Sec. Greenville County Planning Commn., 1963-67; Trustee Greenville Hosp. System, 1965-68; bd. govs. Greenville Shriners Hosp., 1983-90. Served to lt. col. AUS, 1941-46; col. USAR ret. Mem. Am., S.C., Greenville County bar assns., Am. Judicature Soc., Greater Greenville C. of C. (pres. 1965), V.F.W. (dep. comdr. 1951-52), Am. Legion. Lodges: Mason; Shriners; Kiwanis; Elks; Woodmen of World. Democrat. Baptist. Office: 414 Univ Park Greenville SC 29601

MANN, JENNIFER L. state representative; b. Allentown, Pa., May 17, 1969; BA, Lehigh U., 1991. Office mgr. Instant Access, 1994—95, owner, 1995—98; Dem. com. person Allentown 18th Ward, 2d Dist., 1999—. Bd. mem. Jr. Achievement of Lehigh Valley, 1997—, Allentown Bus. Coun. of Lehigh County C. of C., 1998—; mem. Hamilton Pk. Crime Watch, 1998—; bd. mem. Mayfair Festival of the Arts, 1999—; commr. Pa. Commn. on Crime and Deliquincy, 1999—; dir. Small Bus. Coun. West Pk. Civic Assn. Democrat. Office: 121B E Wing Harrisburg PA 17120-2020 E-mail: jlmann@pahouse.net.

MANN, JOEL FRANKLIN, medical technologist; b. Gadsden, Ala., Jan. 10, 1953; s. Bonnie Frank and Betty Sue Mann; m. Carol Mann, Mar. 10, 1972; 1 child, Eric Gregory. BS, U. Ala., 1973, cert. med. technologist, 1974; postgrad., So. Bapt. Theol. Sem., Louisville, 1976—77. Med. technologist VA Hosp., Birmingham, Ala., 1974—75, Louisville, 1976, Louisville Med. Labs., 1976—77, Medlab/Roche/Labcorp, Birmingham, 1977—, Children's Hosp. of Ala., Birmingham, 1990—; mem. clin. faculty U. Ala., Birmingham, 2000—. Author: (children's book) The Little Man Who Knocked Down Walls, 2003, (novel) Beginnings, 2004. Baptist. Avocation: genealogy. Office: Labcorp/Brookwood Hosp Clin Lab 2010 Brookwood Med Ctr Dr Birmingham AL 35209 Personal E-mail: writingmann@cs.com.

MANN, JOHN MARTIN, minister; b. McKeesport, Pa., Nov. 18, 1946; s. Glenn Grant and Mary Dorothy (Flaherty) M. BA, Clarion State Coll., 1967; MDiv, Duke U., 1970, ThM, 1972; D Ministry, Wittenberg U., 1976. Ordained to ministry Luth. Ch. in Am., 1972. Pastor 1st Luth. Ch., Edinboro, Pa., 1971-82; sr. pastor St. John's Luth. Ch., Erie, Pa., 1982-91. Instr. Edinboro State Coll., 1971-82; adj. prof. religion Thiel Coll. Greenville, Pa., 1980-82, baccalaureate preacher, 1980-84, trustee, 1974-80, 82—; chmn. synod vocations examining com. N.W. Pa.-W.Va. Synod, 1984-88; chmn. intersynodical candidacy com. N.W. Pa.-Allegheny Synods, 1988-90; chmn. ch. vocations examining com. N.W. Pa. Synod, 1990—; chmn. Luth. Coalition of Erie, 1990-91; dean Cond. I, Northwestern Pa. Synod, 1991—, faculty post grad Family Systems Seminars, 2004. Contbr. articles to profl. jours. Bd. dirs. Luth. Home, Erie, 1976-79, 82—, Inter-Ch. Ministries N.W. Pa., 1979-84, South Erie Hillside Cmty. Orgn., 1982—, Holy Trinity Cmty. Ctr., Erie, 1984-88, Nesting Inn, 1988—, Hospice Met. Erie, 1988—; chmn. Erie City Strategy for Luths., 1989—; pastor Trinity Luth. Ch., Canton, Ohio, 1992—; pres. UrbanArk Urban Ministry Coalition; active ELCA N.E. Ohio Synod, ecumenical com., chmn. synod outreach com., 1998—, dean conf., Canton, mission planner, Urban Strategy com.; founding chmn. Interfaith Roundtable of Canton and N.W. Neighborhood Assn.; covenant commr. Youngstown Roman Cath. Diocese, N.E. Ohio Synod. Recipient Outstanding Young Man of Am. award Jaycees, 1982. Mem. Luth. Assn. Larger Chs., Am. Assn. Pastoral Counselors, Luth. Campus Ministry Assn., Interdenominational Ministerial Assn. (sec.), Canton Downtown Pastors Assn., Synod Evangelism Com. Home: 6671 Firestone Ave NE Canton OH 44721-2514 Office: Trinity Luth Ch 415 Tuscarawas St W Canton OH 44702-2017 *In a global environment where fundamentalist religions create division and terrorism, we need a constructive, reappropriation of faith in God.*

MANN, KAREN, consultant, educator; b. Kansas City, Mo., Oct. 9, 1942; d. Charles and Letha (Anderson) M. BA, U. Calif., Santa Barbara, 1964; MPA, Golden Gate U., 1975, PhD, 1994. Cert. lay min. and lay monk Order of Buddhist Contemplatives. Mem., tchr. Sisters of Immaculate Heart, L.A., 1964-68; group counselor San Francisco and Marin County Probation Depts., 1968—70; parole agt. Calif. Dept. Corrections, Sacramento, San Francisco, 1970-86; rschr. and cons. Non-profit Orgnl. Devel., 1986—, Computer Applications for Persons with Disabilities, 1986—. Adj. faculty Grad. Theol. Uion, Berkeley, 1984—; Compuserve Disabilities Forum, 1985-2000; forum adminstr., 1988-2000; mem. faculty Golden Gate U., 1990. Co-author: Prison Overcrowding, 1979, Community Corrections: A Plan for California, 1980. Sec., bd. dirs. Spirit Rock Mediation Ctr., 1989-93; co-founder Network Ctr. for Study of Ministry, San Francisco, 1982; pres. San Francisco Network Ministries, 1980-82; mem. Disabled Children's Computer Resource Group, 1988-90, Spingwater Ctr. for Mediative Inquiry and Retreats, 1986-88; emotional support counselor Marin AIDS Project, 1992-97; bd. dirs. Siskiyou Humane Soc., pres., 2003—. Fellowship of Reconciliation, N.Y., 1970—, Buddhist Peace fellowship, 2000—. Office: 400 Shasta Ave Mount Shasta CA 96067 Office Phone: 530-925-2997. E-mail: blueroof@nctv.com.

MANN, KENNETH HENRY, marine ecologist; b. Dovercourt, Essex, Eng., Aug. 15, 1923; arrived in Can., 1967, naturalized, 1973; s. Harry and Mabel (Ashby) M.; m. Isabella Gilmour Ness, Apr. 18, 1946; children: Ian Malcolm, Sheila Helen, Colin Gilmour. B.Sc., U. London, 1949; PhD, U. Reading, 1953; D.Sc., U. London, 1965. Lectr. zoology, then reader U. Reading, Eng., 1949-64; 64-67; sr. biologist marine ecology lab. Bedford Inst. Oceanography, Dartmouth, Can., 1967-72, dir. marine ecology lab., 1980-87, sr. rsch. scientist, 1987-93, emeritus rsch. scientist, 1993—. Prof., chmn. biology Dalhousie U., Halifax, N.S., Canada, 1972—80, adj. prof. biology, 1980—2002. Author: Leeches: Their Structure, Physiology, Ecology and Embryology, 1961, Ecology of Coastal Waters: A Systems Approach, 1982, Ecology of Coastal Waters: Implications for Management, 2000; co-author: (with J. Lazier) Dynamics of Marine Ecosystems: Biological-Physical Interactions in the Sea, 1991; 2d edit., 1996; (with R.S. Barnes) Fundamentals of Aquatic Ecology, 1991, Korean edit., 2002; editor, contbr.: (with T. Platt and R. Ulanowicz) Mathematical Models in Biological Oceanography, 1981, (with F. Wulff and J.G. Field) Network Analysis in Marine Ecology, 1989, (with A. Payne, K. Brink and R. Hilborn) Benguela Trophic Functioning, 1992; editor Jour. Animal Ecology, 1966-67. Served with Royal Air Force, 1942-46. Fellow Royal Soc. Can.; mem. Am. Soc. Limnology and Oceanography. Home: 23 Woodward Cres Halifax NS Canada B3M 1J6 Office: Bedford Inst Oceanography Box 1006 Dartmouth NS Canada B2Y 4A2 Office Phone: 902-426-3696. Personal E-mail: ken.mann@ns.sympatico.ca.

MANN, KENNETH WALKER, retired minister, psychologist; b. Nyack, N.Y., Aug. 22, 1914; s. Arthur Hungerford and Ethel Livingston (Walker) M. AB, Princeton U., 1937; STB, Gen. Theol. Sem., N.Y.C., 1942; MS, U. Mich., 1950, PhD, 1956. Ordained priest Episcopal Ch., 1942; diplomate Am. Assn. Pastoral Counselors; lic. clin. psychologist, Calif., Conn.; lic. marriage, family and child counselor, Calif. Vicar in Valley Cottage, Pearl River, N.Y., 1941-43; priest in charge Yonkers, N.Y., 1943-45. Dir. youth work and Christian edn. Diocese L.A., 1945-47; curate in Beverly Hills, Calif., 1947-49; counselor Bur. Psychol. Svcs., U. Mich., 1951-52; chaplain, clin. psychologist dept. psychiatry St. Luke's Hosp., N.Y.C., also priest-psychotherapist Cathedral St. John Divine, N.Y.C., psychol. examiner ministerial candidates Diocese N.Y., 1952-58; assoc. chaplain Hosp. Good Samaritan, L.A., 1958-65; exec. pastoral svcs., exec. coun. Episc. Ch. N.Y.C., 1965-70; program officer Acad. Religion and Mental Health, N.Y.C., 1970-72; sr. adviser profl. affairs Inst. Religion and Health, 1972-74; sr. psychol. staff Silver Hill Found., New Canaan, Conn., 1974-84; pres. Rockland County (N.Y.) Mins. Assn., 1942-43; exec. sec. social svc. commn. Diocese N.Y., 1943-45; chmn. div. pastoral svcs. Diocese L.A., 1958-65; field dir. Western region Acad. Religion and Mental Health, 1958-61; assoc. nat. chaplain U.S. Power Squadrons, 1956-57. Author: On Pills and Needles, 1969, Deadline for Survival—A Survey of Moral Issues in Science and Medicine, 1970; contbr. articles to profl. jours. Pres. Adoption Inst. L.A., 1964; mem. edn. com. Calif. Heart Assn., 1962-64; trustee, treas. Acad. Religion and Mental Health, 1954-59, mem. profl. bd., 1960-70; trustee Vis. Nurse Assn. L.A., 1963-65, Children's Home Soc. Calif. in L.A., 1964-65, North Conway Inst., 1966-80. USPHS grantee, 1950-51. Fellow AAAS; mem. APA (chmn. com. rels. between psychology and religion 1956-58), Western Psychol. Assn., Calif. Psychol. Assn., L.A. County Psychol. Assn., N.Y. Acad. Scis., Planetary Soc., Assembly Episc. Hosps. and Chaplains, Upper Nyack Tennis Club, Princeton Club N.Y., Exch. Club Beverly Hills (pres.). Republican. Home: 32 Tallman Ave Nyack NY 10960-1606 *I have strongly held to the principle that the total "health" of mankind cannot be considered apart from the values and aspirations by which people live, and by which they may*

even be prepared to die. Amidst the confusions that exist today over loyalties, traditions, and ideals, many are asking: What is the right way to behave? How should I think? What kind of person am I supposed to be? To help such people in quandary to live responsibly, and still be true to their individuality, is a large task, but it is one that is central to a religious ministry. It has always been my chief concern.

MANN, LAURA ANN, soprano; MusB, Eastman Sch. Music, 1965, MusM, 1972; studied with Herbert Brauer Kammersanger, Berlin, Germany; studied with Edwin McArthur, N.Y.; studied with Edith Land Kammersangerin, Lubeck, Germany; studied with David Garvey, studied with Stefan Scaggiari and Rayburn Wright; Dr.Mus.Arts, U. Md., 1995. Prin., owner vocal studio Vocal Advancement, Fairfax, Va., 1979—. Prof. voice Tex. A&I U., Kingsville, Tex., 1984—85; asst. prof. voice Tex. Tech. U., Lubbock, Tex., 1984—86; vis. prof. voice We. Carolina U., Cullowhee, NC, 1986—88; prof. voice Anne Arundel C.C., Annapolis, Md., 1989—94; adj. prof. voice and opera George Mason U., Fairfax, Va., 1995—2001, dir. opera, 1995—, mem. women's studies faculty, 1998—; presenter in field; lectr. in field; clinician and adjudicator. *Laura A. Mann, Soprano, has sung over 40 opera and operetta roles in multiple productions in both the USA and Europe, where she resided for 10 years. She has appeared at international festivals and as a soloist with many prestigious orchestras both here and abroad such as the Berlin Philharmonic, Rochester and Buffalo Philharmonics, and the Dallas Baroque Ensemble. She is currently touring with a one act, one person opera/monodrama by Natalia Raigorodsky called "The White Cliffs" based on a poem by Alice Dyer Miller, 1940, which continues to receive excellent reviews. Also with In a Woman's Voice, music by women composers sung in the Washington National Cathedral. Dr. Mann also specializes in singing world premiere works of women composers' such as, "The White Cliffs" opera/monodrama for one singer by Naltalia Raigondsky, performed at the Washington National Cathedral, July 9, 2001.* Singer: (CD) The Joy of Christmas, 1996, Operas, (albums) Christ Is Born, Laura Mann In Recital, Songs of Light and Joy, 2002, (CD) Laura Mann in Concert, 1999. Grantee, Prince George's Arts Coun., 1993—96, Va. Commn. Arts, 2000—, Fulbright grant, Martha Rockefeller grant. Mem.: Music Tchrs. Nat. Assn., Internat. Alliance for Women in Music, Opera Am., Nat. Acad. Recording Arts and Scis., South Tex. Assn. Tchrs. Singing, Nat. Assn. Tchrs. Singing, Pi Kappa Lambda. Office: Music Dept George Mason Univ 4400 University Dr Fairfax VA 22030-4422

MANN, LAWRENCE MOSES, lawyer; b. Wilmington, N.C., Jan. 30, 1940; s. Irving Murray and Ada (Frohm) M.; m. Susan Beth Bernstein, Dec. 1, 1961 (div. Nov. 1994); children: Rachel (dec.), Michael, Debra; m. Pat Rosenthal, Mar. 3, 1996. BA, U. N.C., 1962; LLB, Georgetown U., 1966. Bar: D.C. 1967, U.S. Dist. Ct. D.C. 1967, U.S. Ct. Appeals (D.C. and 7th cirs.), 1967, U.S. Ct. Claims, 1970, U.S. Tax Ct. 1970, U.S. Supreme Ct. 1972, U.S. Ct. Appeals (9th, 8th and 4th cirs.) 1975, U.S. Ct. Appeals (10th cir.) 1978, U.S. Ct. Appeals (11th and 5th cirs.) 1981, U.S. Dist. (ea. dist.) Ky. 1983, U.S. Ct. Appeals (3d cir.) 1987, U.S. Ct. Appeals (2d cir.) 1988, U.S. Ct. Appeals (6th cir.) 1990. Spl. asst. to Sen. Vance Hartke, U.S. Senate, Washington, 1964-65; legal asst. post office and civil svc. com. U.S. Ho. of Reps., Washington, 1965-66; counsel Commn. on Polit. Activity of Govt. Pers., Washington, 1967; ptnr. Alper & Mann, Washington, 1968—. Author: What Every Railroad Worker Should Know About Federal Railroad Safety Laws, 1988. Former mem. bd. dirs. Washington Hebrew Congregation. Mem. ABA, ATLA, Acad. Rail Labor Attys., D.C. Bar Assn. Avocations: art, collecting shells. Office: Alper & Mann 1667 K St NW 11th Fl Washington DC 20006 Office Phone: 202-298-9191.

MANN, LYNNE MARIE, executive administrative assistant; b. Columbus, Ohio, Dec. 22, 1964; d. Robert James Greenlee and Lois Etta Mann. AA, Hocking Coll., 1986; BA, DeVry U., 1993. Asst. med. lab. Progenitor, Athens, Ohio, 1992; crew mgr. Marlboro Van Promotions, Columbus; massage therapist San Francisco, Columbus; part-time makeup artist Glamour Shorts, Columbus; adminstrv. asst. Columbus; exec. asst. various cos., San Francisco; coord. humane edn. Americorp, St. Croix, Vt., 2003—. Founder, pres., CEO Madame Diva/LM Manus, Columbus, 2002. Author, editor: Poems & Short Stories of a Fat Woman, 2002. Vista vol. U.S. Govt., 2003—; voting poll officer Athens County Dem. Party, Nelsonville, Ohio, 1988. Recipient 2nd prize cake design, Athens County Fair, 1978, Spanish Costumes award, 1981, 2nd prize future clothing design, Athens County Fair, 1982. Mem.: Nat. Fat Acceptance Assoc., Large and Lovely Club (leader 2002). Avocations: tai-chi, sewing, cooking, swimming, hiking. Mailing: 3016 Estate Orange Grv #6 Christiansted VI 00820-4251

MANN, MARIA, photojournalist, director; Dir. of photography Agence France-Presse for North Am., 1984, internat. editor; dir. of photography Toronto Sun; employed United Press Internat. World Hdqrs. Recipient Joseph Costa Award for Leadership and continuing svc. to photojournalists, NPPA, 2002, Kenneth P. McLaughlin Award, 2002. Mem.: Workshop Bd. of Dir., Nat. Press Photgraphers Assoc. Best of Photojournalism Contest (chairwoman), Latin Am. Photojournalism Workshop (co-organizer), Knight Found., Latin Am. Task Force. Office: Agence France Presse Dir of Photography 747 Third Ave New York NY 10017

MANN, MARION, pathologist, educator; b. Atlanta, Mar. 29, 1920; s. Levi James and Cora (Casey) Mann; m. Ruth Maurine Reagin, Jan. 16, 1943; children: Marion Jr., Judith Walk. BS in Edn., Tuskegee Inst., Ala., 1940; MD, Howard U., 1954; PhD, Georgetown U., 1961; grad., 1965, U.S. Army War Coll., 1970; DSc (hon.), Georgetown U., 1979, U. Mass., 1984, Tuskegee U., 1998; grad., U.S. Army War Coll., 1970. Diplomate Nat. Bd. Med. Examiners, Am. Bd. Pathology. Intern USPHS Hosp., Staten Island, NY, 1954—55; resident Georgetown U. Hosp., 1956—60; practice medicine, specializing in pathology Washington, 1961—; instr. pathology Georgetown U., 1960—61; professorial lectr. Georgetown U. Sch. Medicine, 1970—73; asst. prof. pathology Howard U. Coll. Medicine, 1961—67, assoc. prof., 1967—70, prof., 1970, dean, 1970—79; v.p. rsch. Howard U., 1988—91. Capt. U.S. Army, 1942—50, brig. gen. Res. U.S. Army. Mem.: Nat. Acad. Scis., Inst. Medicine, Sigma Pi Phi, Alpha Omega Alpha. Mem. United Ch. Of Christ. Home: 1453 Whittier Pl NW Washington DC 20012-2845 Office: 520 W St NW Washington DC 20059-0001

MANN, MICHAEL K. producer, director, writer; b. Chgo. Ed., U. Wis., London Film Sch. Dir.: (documentaries) 17 Days Down the Line, 1972; screenwriter, dir. (films) The Keep, 1983, Manhunter, 1986, screenwriter, exec. prodr., dir. Thief, 1981, screenwriter, prodr., dir. The Last of the Mohicans, 1992, Heat, 1995 (Dir., Screenwriter, Prodr. Acad. award nominee), The Insider, 1999, Ali, 2001, screenwriter (TV films) River of Promises, 1977, screenwriter, dir. The Jericho Mile, 1979 (Best Dir. award Dir. Guild Am., Emmy award, 1979), screenwriter Swan Song, 1980, screenwriter, exec. prodr., dir. L.A. Takedown, 1989, screenwriter, exec. prodr. (TV miniseries) Drug Wars: The Camarena Story, 1990 (Emmy award, 1990), screenwriter (TV series) Starsky and Hutch, 1975, Bronk, 1975, screenwriter, exec. prodr. Miami Vice, 1984. Mem.: Dirs. Guild, Writers Guild. Office: c/o CAA 9830 Wilshire Blvd Beverly Hills CA 90212-1804

MANN, MICHAEL MARTIN, electronics company executive; b. N.Y.C., Nov. 28, 1939; s. Herbert and Rosalind (Kaplan) M.; m. Mariel Joy Steinberg, Apr. 25, 1965. BSEE, Calif. Inst. Tech., 1960, MSEE, 1961; PhD in Elec. Engring. and Physics, U. So. Calif., 1969; MBA, UCLA, 1984. Cert. bus. appraiser, profl. cons., mgmt. cons., lic. real estate broker, Calif. Mgr. high power laser programs office Northrop Corp., Hawthorne, Calif., 1969-76; mgr. high energy laser systems lab. Hughes Aircraft Co., El Segundo, Calif., 1976-78, mgr. E-0 control systems labs., 1978-83, asst. to v.p., space & strategic, 1983-84; exec. v.p. Helionetics Inc., Irvine, Calif., 1984-85, pres., chief exec. officer, 1985-86, also bd. dirs.; ptnr. Mann Kavanaugh Chernove, 1986-87; sr. cons. Arthur D. Little, Inc., 1987-88; chmn. bd., pres., CEO, Blue Marble Devel. Group, Inc., 1988—; exec. assoc. Ctr. Internat. Cooperation and Trade, 1989—; sr. assoc. Corp. Fin. Assocs., 1990—; exec. assoc. Reece and Assocs., 1991—; dir. Reece & Assocs., 1991—; mng. dir. Blue Marble Ptnrs. Ltd, 1991—; chmn. bd. dirs., CEO Blue Marble Ptnrs., 1992—; chmn., CEO, En Compass Techs., Inc., Torrance, Calif., 1994-98; chmn. En Compass Knowledge Systems, Inc., 2000—. Mem. Army Sci. Bd., Dept. Army, Washington, 1986-91; chmn. Ballistic Missile Def. Panel, Directed Energy Weapon Panel, Rsch. and New Initiatives Panel; cons. Office of Sec. of Army, Washington, 1986—, Inst. of Def. Analysis, Washington, 1978—, Dept. Energy, 1988—, Nat. Riverside Rsch. Inst., 1990—; bd. dirs. Datum, Inc.,1988—, Fail-Safe Tech., Corp., 1989-90, Safeguard Health Enterprises, Inc., 1988—, Am. Video Communications, Inc., Meck Industries, Inc., 1987-88, Decade Optical Systems, Inc., 1990—, Forum Mil. Application Directed Energy, 1992—, Am. Bus. Consultants, Inc., 1993—; chmn. bd. Mgmt. Tech., Inc. 1991—, Encompass Tech., Inc., 1994-98; bd. dirs., mem. adv. bd. Micro-Frame, Inc., 1988-91; chmn. bd. HLX Laser, Inc., 1984-86; bd. dirs. Cons's. Roundtable, 1992—, Am. Bus. Cons., Inc., 1993—, Country Home Bakers, Inc., 1999—, C.L.E.A.R., Inc., 1999—; chmn. TEC, 1999—; rsch. assoc., mem. extension teaching staff U. So. Calif., L.A., 1964-70; chmn. Ballistic Missile Def. Subgroup, 1989-90, Tactical Directed Energy Weapons Subgroup, 1988-90; chmn., chief exec. officer Mgmt. Tech., Inc., 1991—; dir. Am. Bus. Cons., Inc., 1993—; faculty mem. Asia Pacific Inst., 1998—; faculty Nat. Technol. U., 1997—. Contbg. editor, mem. adv. bd. Calif. High-Tech Funding Jour., 1989-90; contbr. over 50 tech. articles to profl. jours.; patentee in field. Mem. adv. com. to Engring. Sch., Calif. State U., Long Beach, 1985—; chmn. polit. affairs Am. Electronics Assn., Orange County Coun., 1986-87, mem. exec. com., 1986-88; adv. com. several Calif. congressmen, 1985—; mem. dean's coun. UCLA Grad. Sch. Mgmt., 1984-85; bd. dirs. Archimedes Circle U. Soc. Calif., 1983-85, Ctr. for Innovation and Entrepreneurship, 1986-90, Caltech/MIT Venture Forum, 1987-91; chmn. adv. coun. and adj. prof., indsl. and sys. engring. U. So. Calif., 1996 ; mem. bd. examiners Nat. Quality Award, 1998—. Hicks fellow in Indsl. Rels. Calif. Inst. Tech., 1961, Hewlett Packard fellow. Mem. IEEE (sr.), So. Calif. Tech. Execs. Network, Orange County CEO's Network, Orange County CEO's Roundtable, Pres. Roundtable, Nat. Assn. Corp. Dirs., Aerospace-Def. CEO's Roundtable, Am. Def. Preparedness Assn., Security Affairs Support Assn., Acad. Profl. Cons. and Advisors, Internat. Platform Assn., Inst. Mgmt. Cons. (bd. dirs. So. Calif. chpt.), Pres. Assn., Cons. Roundtable, King Harbor Yacht Club. Republican. Avocations: sailing, photography, writing. Home: 4248 Via Alondra Palos Verdes Peninsula CA 90274-1545 Office: Blue Marble Partners 406 Amapola Ave Ste 125 Torrance CA 90501-7238 E-mail: drmmmann@bluemarblecorp.com.

MANN, NANCY LOUISE (NANCY LOUISE ROBBINS), entrepreneur; b. Chillicothe, Ohio, May 6, 1925; d. Everett Chaney and Pauline Elizabeth R.; m. Kenneth Douglas Mann, June 19, 1949 (div. June 1979); children: Bryan Wilkinson, Laura Elizabeth. BA in Math., UCLA, 1948, MA in Math., 1949, PhD in Biostatistics, 1965. Sr. scientist Rocketdyne Divsn. Rockwell Internat., Canoga Park, Calif., 1962-75; tech. staff Rockwell Sci. Ctr., Thousand Oaks, Calif., 1975-78; rsch. prof. UCLA Biomath., L.A., 1978-87; pres., CEO, owner Quality Enhancement Seminars, Inc., L.A., 1982—; pres., CEO Quality and Productivity, Inc., L.A., 1987—. Curriculum adv. UCLA Ext. Dept. of Bus. and Mgmt., L.A., 1991—; mem. com. on Nat. Statistics, Nat. Acad. Scis., Washington, 1978-82; mem adv. bd. to supt. U.S. Naval Posgrad. Sch., Monterey, Calif., 1979-82. Co-author: Methods for Analysis of Reliability and Life Data, 1974; author: Keys to Excellence, 1985, The Story of the Deming Philosophy, 2d edit., 1987, 3d edit., 1989; contbr. articles to profl. jours. Recipient award IEEE Reliability Soc., 1982, ASQC Reliability Divsn., 1986. Fellow Am. Statis. Assn. (v.p. 1982-84); mem. Internat. Statis. Inst. Office: Quality Productivity Inc 10724 Wilshire Blvd # 711 Los Angeles CA 90024-4463

MANN, OSCAR, retired physician, internist, educator; b. Paris, Oct. 13, 1934; arrived in U.S., 1953; s. Aron and Helen (Biegun) Mann; m. Amy S. Mann, July 19, 1964; children: Adriana, Karen. AA with distinction, George Washington U., 1958; MD cum laude, Georgetown U., 1962. Diplomate Am. Bd. Med. Examiners, Am. Bd. Internal Medicine, Am. Bd. Cardiovasc. Disease, cert. advanced achievement in internal medicine. Intern Georgetown U. Med. Ctr., Washington, 1962-63, jr. asst. med. resident, 1963-64, clin. fellow in cardiology with Proctor Harvey program, 1965-66; sr. asst. resident in medicine Georgetown svc. D.C. Gen. Hosp., Washington, 1964-65; clin. prof. medicine Georgetown U. Sch. Medicine, 1985—; nat. chmn. med. alumni fund Georgetown U. Med. Sch., Washington, 1993-95; pvt. practice internal medicine and cardiology, Washington, 1966-99. Mem. med. nursing com. Georgetown U. Med. Ctr., mem. adv. com. CME, mem. tchg. adv. com., opthalmology dept. rev. com., surgery dept. rev. com., faculty com., search com. for a new dean for acad. affairs; appointed coun. to the dean Georgetown U. Sch. Medicine, 1977—; mem. Instnl. Self Study Task Force. Contbr. articles to profl. jours. Nat. chmn. med. alumni fund Georgetown U., 1997—99. Served with U.S. Army, 1953—55, with U.S. Army, 1953—55. Recipient Mead Johnson Postgrad. Scholar ACP, 1964—65, Physicians Recognition award, AMA, 1987—96, Advanced Achievement in Internal Medicine, 1987, John Carroll award, Georgetown U., 1999. Fellow: ACP, Am. Coll. Chest Physicians, Am. Coll. Cardiology; mem.: AMA, Med. Soc. D.C., Am. Heart Assn. (coun. clin. cardiology), Am. Soc. Internal Medicine, Georgetown U. Alumni Assn. (bd. govs. 1993—, chair med. alumni bd. 1995—, nat. chmn. med. alumni fund 1997—99), Cosmos Club, Phi Delta Epsilon, Alpha Omega Alpha. Home: 5137 Yuma St NW Washington DC 20016 E-mail: oscarmann@comcast.net.

MANN, RICHARD ALAN, physician, educator; b. Bklyn., Dec. 18, 1952; s. Daniel Isaac and Claire Ethel (Spiller) M.; m. Judith Fleischer, Aug. 6, 1977; 1 child, David Michael Mann. BS in Math., Union Coll., Schenectady, N.Y., 1973; MS in Biophysics, SUNY, Buffalo, 1975; MD, Albert Einstein Coll. Medicine, The Bronx, N.Y., 1979. Diplomate Am. Bd. Internal Medicine. Intern Grad. Hosp. U. Pa., Phila., 1979-80; resident Temple U. Hosp., Phila., 1980—82; clin. nephrology fellow Hosp. U. Pa., Phila., 1982—83, rsch. fellow, 1983—86; asst. prof. medicine Rutgers U. Med. Sch., New Brunswick, NJ, 1986—93; assoc. prof. medicine, microbiology and molecular genetics; physician Robert Wood Johnson Med. Sch., New Brunswick, 1993—, med. dir. Kidney/Pancreas Transplant Program, 1993—; mem. grad. program in microbiology and molecular genetics Rutgers U., Piscataway, NJ, 1989—. Mem. antiviral drug adv. com. FDA, Rockville, Md., 1993—; spl. study sect. NIH, Bethesda, Md., 1994; NIH Reviewers Res.; State Dept. Task Force, Operation Desert Storm, 1991. Contbr. over 50 articles, chpts. and abstracts to profl. jours. Recipient Young Investigator award Nat. Kidney Found., 1987, Nat. Medal award Kidney and Urology Found. Am., 2004, others.; grantee, NIH, 1988-93, William Lightfoot Schultz Found., 1987-88, UMDNJ Found., 1987-88. Mem. Am. Soc. Nephrology (co-chair basic immunology free comm. session 1989, 90), Am. Fedn. for Clin. Rsch., Am. Heart Assn. (Coun. on the Kidney in Cardiovascular Disease), Nat. Kidney Found., Nephrology Soc. N.J., Am. Assn. for Lab. Animal Sci., Am. Soc. Transplantation, Alpha Omega Alpha (Acad. Excellence and Outstanding Tchg. award 1995). Office: UMDNJ Robert Wood Johnson Med Sch Acad Health Sci Ctr CN-19 New Brunswick NJ 08903 Office Phone: 732-235-7783.

MANN, RICHARD O. public relations consulting company executive; b. NYC, July 1, 1933; s. Otto and Ruth (Buchwald) M.; m. Anne Marie Seidenschwang, Apr. 28, 1956; children: Melinda, Susan, Carolyn. BA in History and Polit. Sci., Hofstra U., 1955. Reporter Newsday, Garden City, N.Y., 1951-56; pub. rels. v.p., cons. Carl Byoir & Assoc., NYC, 1957—76; v.p. corp. affairs Mack Trucks, Inc., Allentown, Pa., 1976-79; v.p. pub. rels. Transway Internat., NYC, 1979—85; pres. Mann Assoc., Danbury, Conn., 1985—. Track and field ofcl., U.S. Internat. meets, including 1984 Olympics, 1970—. Bd. dirs. Vol. Ctr. United Way, Westchester County. 1st lt. U.S. Army, 1956-57. Mem. Met. Golf Writers Assn., Mt. Kisco Country Club. Republican. Presbyterian. Avocations: golf, sports. Home and Office: 63 Woodcrest Ln Danbury CT 06810

MANN, ROBERT CHRISTOPHER, communications educator, television host, producer; b. Bklyn., Mar. 18, 1953; s. Alvin Charles and Marion Theresa (Hensch) M.; m. Virginia Rohan, Apr. 29, 1979 (div. Feb. 1995); 1 child, Christopher Robert. BA, Fordham U., 1975; MA, Montclair State U., 1993. Radio newscaster, sportscaster Sta. WOBM-AM-FM, Toms River, N.J., 1976-77; TV host, prodr. United Artists Cable (now Cablevision), Oakland, N.J., 1977-84; on air host Sta. WNET-TV, N.Y.C., 1983-85; feature reporter Sta. WOR-AM, N.Y.C., 1985; prof. comm., chair dept. Caldwell (N.J.) Coll., 1988—; TV host, prodr. Mann Media Inc., Bergenfield, N.J., 1989—. Mem. faculty coun. Caldwell Coll., 1990—. Host, prodr. (TV show) Healthview From Hackensack U. Med. Ctr., 1989— (Percy award 1990), Healthtalk, 1996—; host (radio program) Healthbeat, 1991— (Percy award 1996). Class father Roy Brown Mid. Sch., Bergenfield, 1994; vol. TV host Am. Cancer Soc., Bergen County, N.J., 1996. Recipient Cable Programming award Cable TV Network N.J., 1996. Mem. AFTRA, Nat. Acad. Cable Programming (CableACE award (3), 1984-85), Soc. Profl. Journalists, AAUP. Avocations: tennis, travel, N.Y. Yankees baseball, comedy, movies. Home: 163 Phelps Ave Bergenfield NJ 07621-1422 Office: Caldwell Coll 9 Ryerson Ave Caldwell NJ 07006-6109 E-mail: profmann@aoo.com.

MANN, ROBERT PAUL, retired lawyer; b. Pitts., July 24, 1929; s. O. Paul and Floy Melinda (Foster) M.; m. Dorothy Neeld, Sept. 4, 1953; children: Robin Duvall Francik, Stewart Neeld Mann. BS, U. Md., College Park, 1951; JD, U. Md., Balt., 1953. Bar: Md. 1954, U.S. Dist. Md. 1965, U.S. Tax Ct. 1976. Pvt. practice, Ruxton, Md., 1956-96; ret., 1996. Trial magistrate, 1957-59. Past pres. Artists Equity, Timonium Rotary, Towson Libr.; active wildlife orgns.; art donor to numerous major mus. Mem. Omicron Delta Kappa, Delta Theta Phi, Sigma Chi. Episcopalian.

MANN, ROBERT WELLESLEY, biomedical engineer, educator; b. Bklyn., Oct. 6, 1924; s. Arthur Wellesley and Helen (Rieger) M.; m. Margaret Ida Florencourt, Sept. 4, 1950; children: Robert Wellesley, Catherine Louise. SB, MIT, 1950, SM, 1951, ScD, 1957 With Bell Tel. Labs., N.Y.C., 1942 43, 46-47, U.S. Army Signal Corps, 1943-46; rsch. engr. MIT, 1951-52, rsch. supr., 1952, mem. faculty, 1953—, prof. mech. engring., 1963-70, Germeshausen prof., 1970-72, prof. engring., 1972-74, Whitaker prof. biomed. engring., 1974-92, Whitaker prof. emeritus, sr. lectr., 1992—, head systems and design divsn., mech. engring. dept., 1957-68, 82-83, founder, dir. engring. projects lab., 1959-62; founder, chmn. steering com. Ctr. Sensory Aids Evaluation and Devel., 1964-86, chmn. divsn. health scis., tech., planning and mgmt., 1972-74, founder, dir. Newman biomechanics and human rehab. lab., 1975-92; dir. bioengring. programs Whitaker Coll. MIT, 1986-89; dir. Harvard-MIT Rehab. Engring. Ctr., 1988-93. Mem exec. com. Divsn. Health Scis. and Tech. Harvard U. MIT, 1972-85; prof., 1979—, mem. Com. on Use of Humans as Exptl. Subjects MIT, 1984-93, co-chair Pub. Svc. Ctr., 1988-92; lectr. engring. Faculty of Medicine, Harvard U., 1973-79; rsch. assoc. in orthop. surgery Children's Hosp. Med. Ctr., 1973—; cons. in engring. sci. Mass. Gen. Hosp., 1969—; cons. in field, 1953—; mem. Nat. Commn. Engring. Edn., 1962-69; com. prosthetics rsch. and devel. NRC, 1963-69; chmn. sensory aids subcom., 1965-68, com. skeletal sys., 1969; mem. com. interplay engring. with biology and medicine NAE, 1969-73; mem. bd. health scis. policy Inst. Medicine, 1973-74, 82-86; mem. com. on nat. needs for rehab. physically handicapped NAS, 1975-76; mem.-at-large confs. com. Engring. Found., 1975-81; chair sensory aids panel scis. merit rev. bd. Rehab., R & D Svc., Dept. Vets. Affairs, 1983-95, 99—, mem. Visual/Hearing Impairment Rehab. Panel, 1999—; mem. Commn. on Life Scis. NRC, 1984-88, Com. on Strategic Tech. for U.S. Army, NRC, 1989-93; NRC Com. on Space Biology and Medicine, 1992-95. Consulting editor: Ency. Sci. and Tech., 1962-67; assoc. editor: IEEE Trans. in Biomed. Engring., 1969-78, ASME Jour. Biomech. Engring., 1976-82; mem. editl. bd. Jour. Visual Impairment and Blindness, 1976-80, SOMA, 1986-92; mem. editl. adv. bd. new liberal arts program Alfred P. Sloan Found., 1986-92; contbr. over 400 articles to profl. jours. Pres., trustee Amanda Caroline Payson Scholarship Fund, 1965—86; trustee Nat. Braille Press, 1982—, pres., 1990—94; trustee Mary Flannery O'Connor Charitable Trust, 2002—; bd. dirs. Carroll Ctr. Blind, 1967—74, pres., 1968—74; mem. corp. Perkins Sch. Blind, 1970—2000, Mt. Auburn Hosp., 1972—2000, mem. bd. overseers, 2000—; mem. Cardinal's adv. com. on social justice Archdiocese of Boston, 1993—96; bd. overseers St. Marguerite D'Youville Found., Youville Lifecare Inc., 1994—98; chmn. Flannery O'Connor-Andalusia Found., Inc., 2002—. Recipient Sloan award for Outstanding Performance, 1957, Talbert Abrams Photogrammetry award, 1962, Assn. Blind of Mass. award, 1969, IR-100 award for Braillemboss, 1972, UCP Goldenson Rsch. for Handicapped award, 1976, New Eng. award, 1979. Fellow Am. Acad. Arts and Scis., Am. Inst. Med. and Biol. Engring., IEEE (mem. editl. bd. Spectrum 1984-86), AAAS, ASME (gold medal 1977, H.R. Lissner award for biomed. engring. 1977); mem. NAS, Inst. Medicine NAS, NAE, Biomed. Engring. Soc. (bd. dirs. 1981-84), Orthop. Rsch. Soc., Rehab. Soc. N.Am., MIT Alumni Assn. (pres. 1983-84, Alumni Fund Bd. 1978-80, bd. dirs. 1980-86, 93-95, corp. joint adv. com. 1983-84, chair nat. selector com. 1985-88, awards com. 1992-94, chmn. 1994, bd. Tech. Rev. 1986-95, chmn. 1993-95), Sigma Xi (nat. lectr. 1979-81), Tau Beta Pi, Pi Tau Sigma, Sigma Xi. Roman Catholic. Achievements include patents on missile power units, founding of computer aided design in 1963, earliest braille translation software and hardware in 1962, cybernetic amputation prosthesis, 1966, in vivo measurements of human cartilage pressures, 1984. Home: 5 Pelham Rd Lexington MA 02421-5707 Office: MIT 77 Massachusetts Ave Rm 3-137 Cambridge MA 02139-4307 Business E-Mail: rwmann@mit.edu.

MANN, SALLY, photographer; b. Lexington, Va., 1951; married; children: Emmett, Jessie, Virginia. Student, Putney Sch., 1966-69, Bennington Coll., 1969-71, Praestegaard Film Sch., Denmark, 1971-72, Aegean Sch. Fine Arts, Greece, 1971-72; BA summa cum laude, Hollins Coll., 1974, MA, 1975. Guest lectr. Honolulu Acad. Arts, 1989, Women Photog. Conf., 1989, Md. Inst. Art, 1989, Bard Coll., 1989, San Francisco Cameraworks, 1990, Photog.-Retrospect/Prospect Conf., 1990, others; instr. Maine Photog. Workshops, 1985-89, Palm Beach Photog. Workshops, 1987-89, Ctr. Photog. Woodstock, 1988, 90, Internat. Ctr. Photog., N.Y., 1989, Image Found., Honolulu, 1989, Okla. Arts Found., 1989, Friends Photog. Workshops, 1990. One-woman shows include Cleve. Ctr. Contemporary Art, 1990, Edwynn Houk Gallery, Chgo., 1990, 92, Tartt Gallery, Washington, 1990, Md. Art Pl., Balt., 1991, Houk Friedman, N.Y., 1992-94, Mus. Contemporary Photog., Chgo., 1993-94, Mus. Modern Art, N.Y., 1991, Milw. Mus. Art, 1991, Whitney Mus. Am. Art, N.Y., 1991, Met. Mus. Art, N.Y., 1991, Frumpkin Adams Gallery, N.Y., 1994, Elizabeth Leach Gallery, Portland, Oreg., 1994, Bard Coll., Mass., 1994, Wellesley Coll., Mass., 1995, Edwynn Houk Gallery, N.Y., 1997, Gagosian Gallery, Calif., 1997; exhibited in group shows Corcoran Gallery Art, Washington, 1977, Va. Mus. Fine Arts, Richmond, 1988, New Orleans Mus. Art, 1990; represented in permanent collections Addison Gallery Am. Art, Andover, Mass., Balt. Mus. Art, Birmingham (Ala.) Mus. Art, Boston Mus. Fine Art, Corcoran Gallery Art, Hirshhorn Mus. and Sculpture Garden, Nat. Mus. Am. Art, Smithsonian Inst., Washington, Met. Mus. Art, N.Y., Mus. Modern Art, N.Y., Whitney Mus. Am. Art, N.Y., San Francisco Mus. Art, Va. Mus. Fine Arts, Richmond, others; author/photographer: (with Ann Beattie) Second Sight: The Photographs of Sally Mann, 1984, (with Reynolds Price) At Twelve: Portraits of Young Women, 1988, Imediate Family, 1992, Still Time, 1994, What Remains, 2003. Fellow Nat. Endowment Arts, 1982, 88, 92, Guggenheim Found., 1987, Southeastern Ctr. Contemporary Arts, 1989, Artists Visual Arts, 1989; named Best Photographer in Am., Time Mag., 2001.*

MANN, SAM HENRY, JR., lawyer; b. St. Petersburg, Fla., Aug. 2, 1925; s. Sam Henry and Vivian (Moore) M.; m. Mary Joan Bishop, Sept. 7, 1948; children: Vivian Louise, Sam Henry III, Wallace Bishop. BA, Yale U., 1948; LLB, Fla. U., 1951, JD, 1967. Bar: Fla. 1951, U.S. Dist. Ct. (mid. and so. dists.) Fla. 1951, U.S. Ct. Appeals (5th cir.) 1955, U.S. Ct. Appeals (11th cir.) 1996, U.S. Supreme Ct. 1971. Ptnr. Greene, Mann, Rowe, Stanton, Mastry & Burton, St. Petersburg, 1951-84, Harris, Barrett, Mann & Dew, St. Petersburg, 1984—. Trustee, v.p. Mus. Fine Arts, St. Petersburg, 1980-94, Eckerd Coll., St. Petersburg, 1976-79, Webb Sch., Bell Buckle, Tenn., 1966-75; bd. dirs. Regional Cmty. Blood Ctr., St. Petersburg, 1966-93, Fla. Blood Svcs., 1993-94, mem. emeritus 1996—; mem. Disting. Alumni Soc. Webb Sch.; mem., chmn. H. Milton Rogers Heart Found.; bd. dirs., pres. Family and Children's Svc., Inc., 1956-61. Lt. (j.g.) USNR, 1943-48. Fellow Am. Coll. Trial Lawyers, Am. Bar Found., Fla. Bar Found.; mem. ABA, Fla. Bar Assn., Fla. Supreme Ct. Hist. Soc., Am. Counsel Assn., Def. Rsch. Inst., Internat. Assn. Def. Counsel, Pinellas County Trial Lawyers Assn., Nat. Assn. Railroad

Trial Counsel, Fla. Def. Lawyers Assn., Assn. Hostp. Attys., Bay Area Vanderbilt, St. Petersburg Bar Assn., Yale and U. Fla. Alumni Assns., Phi Alpha Delta, Delta Kappa Epsilon. Republican. Presbyterian. Avocations: rv travel, boating, gardening, workshop. Home: 531 Brightwaters Blvd NE Saint Petersburg FL 33704-3713 Office: Harris Barrett Mann & Dew 1700 66th St N Ste 403 Saint Petersburg FL 33710

MANN, STEPHEN ASHBY, financial consultant; b. Richmond, Va., Feb. 20, 1947; s. Milton Ashby and Rebecca (George) Mann; m. Patricia Ann Kofron, Aug. 25, 1982; 1 child, Michael Joseph Ashby stepchildren: Christine Ferguson, Tracy Kofron. BS in Gen. Bus., Va. Poly. Inst. and State U., 1970. Cert. sr. advisor, CLU. Supr. mfg. Brown & Williamson Tobacco Corp., Petersburg, Va., 1970—72; pres. Cumberland Woodyard, Va., 1972—79; mgr. Ragland Woodyards, Goochland, Va., 1980—81; advt. mgr., reporter Gazette Newspapers, Goochland, 1982—85; fin. counselor, ins. and fin. planner Peoples Security Ins. Co., Mechanicsville, Va., 1986—98, Monumental Life Ins. Co., Mechanicsville, Va., 1999—2003; v.p. Roberts-Funai Ins. Agy., Richmond, 2003—. Pres. Millquarter Property Owners Assn., Powhatan, Va., 1987. Named to All-Star Honor Roll, Ins. Sales Mag., 1989—90; Life Underwriters Tng. Coun. fellow. Fellow: Life Underwriters Tng. Coun.; mem.: SCV (lt. comdr. Powhatan 1980—82, inspector gen. state divsn 1981, nat. adc 1982—83, comdr.), All Harley Drag Racing Assn. (Racer of Yr. Award 1996, nat. ranked # 4 st. eliminator 1996—97, nat. ranked #2 super sport 1999, ranked #6 in East, 13th Nat. 2002, ranked #1 in East, 7th Nat. 2003), Richmond Assn. Ins. and Fin. Advisors (bd. dirs. 1989—92), Assn. Health Ins. Agts., Soc. Fin. Svc. Profls., Nat. Assn. Ins. and Fin. Advisors (Nat. Quality Award 1986, Nat. Sales Achievement Award 1986, Nat. Health Inst. Award 1986), Sons of South Motorcycle Club, Masons (master 1990, Samis Grotto treas. 1991—93, master 1994, 16th dist. blood coord. 1995—96, chaplain Powhatan Lodge # 295 1995—2004, Scottish Rite, life mem. Royal Arch), Golden Key Soc (com. mem. 1991—96). Republican. Baptist. Avocations: church piano/organ, history, motorcycle racing. Home: 1433 E Overlook Dr Powhatan VA 23139 Office: Roberts & Funai Ins Agy Richmond VA 23236 Office Phone: 804-794-3281.

MANN, SUSAN LOUISE, education educator; b. Detroit, Mich., Nov. 3, 1943; d. John Raymond and Mary Louise Mann; m. G William Skinner, Apr. 26, 1980; 1 child, Alison Jane; m. Thomas M Jones (div.); children: Christopher, Benjamin. BA, U. Mich., 1964; MA, Stanford U., 1966, PhD, 1972. Lectr. U. Chgo., 1976—80; asst. and assoc. prof. U. Calif. at Santa Cruz, 1982—89; prof. U. of Calif. at Davis, 1989—. Author: (book) Local Merchants and the Chinese Bureacracy, 1987, Precious Records: Woman in China's Long Eighteenth Century, 1997 (Joseph Levinson award, 1997); editor: Under Confucian Eyes, 2001. Mem.: Am. Hist. Assn., Assn. for Asian Studies (pres. 1999—2000). Office: Hist Dept U Calif at Davis One Shields Ave Davis CA 95616

MANN, THEODORE R. lawyer; b. Czechoslovakia, Jan. 31, 1928; came to U.S., 1929, naturalized, 1930; s. Aaron and Bertha (Schreiber) M.; m. Rowena Joan Weiss, 1954; children: Julie Ellen, Rachel Beth, Marcus Eliyahu. Pvt. practice, Phila., 1953—; ptnr. Wolf, Block, Schorr, Solis-Cohen; advocate in civil liberties, anti-trust and securities fraud cases. Chmn., pres. Nat. Jewish Cmty. Rels. Adv. Coun., 1976-80; Conf. Pres. Major Am. Jewish Orgns., 1978-80; Nat. Conf. Soviet Jewry, 1981-83; Am. Jewish Congress, 1984-88; founding chmn. Mazon-A Jewish Response to Hunger, 1985-90, Project Nishma, 1988-97; exec. com. chair Israel Policy Forum, 1997-2001; trustee internat. coun. New Israel Fund, 2002-. Fellow Temple U. Alumni. Office: 1650 Arch St Fl 22 Philadelphia PA 19103-2097

MANN, THOMAS EDWARD, political scientist; b. Milw., Sept. 10, 1944; s. Edward Emil and Eleanor (Hoffman) M.; m. Sheilah Rosenhack, June 4, 1976; children: Edward Matthew, Stephanie Rachael. BA, U. Fla., 1966; MA, U. Mich., 1968, PhD, 1977. Staff assoc. Am. Polit. Sci. Assn., Washington, 1970-76, asst. dir., 1977-81, exec. dir., 1981-87; co-dir. congress project Am. Enterprise Inst., Washington, 1979-81; dir. govtl. studies Brookings Instn., 1987-99, W. Averell Harrimann sr. fellow in Am. governance, 1991—. Mem. bd. overseers Nat. Election Study, 1987-94, chmn., 1990-94. Author: Unsafe At Any Margin, 1978; co-author: Vital Statistics on Congress, 1980, 82, 84-85, 87-2002; Renewing Congress, 1992, 93; co-editor: The New Congress, 1981, The American Elections of 1982, 1983, Media Polls in American Politics, 1992, Values and Public Policy, 1994, Elections at Home and Abroad, 1994, Congress, the Press, and the Public, 1994, Intensive Care: How Congress Shapes Health Policy, 1995,Campaign Finance Reform, A Source Book, 1997, The Permanent Campaign and Its Future, 2000, Governance for a New Century: Japanese Challenges, American Experience, 2002, The New Campaign Finance Sourcebook, 2003, Inside the Campaign Finance Battle, 2003; editor: A Question of Balance: The President, The Congress and Foreign Policy, 1990. Mem. Democratic Nat. Com.'s Commn. on Presdl. Nomination and Party Structure, 1975-78; mem. tech. com. Dem. Nat. Com. Commn. on Presdl. Nominations, 1981-82, The Fairness Commn., 1985. U. Mich. NDEA grad. fellow, 1966-69; Am. Polit. Sci. Assn. Congl. fellow, 1969-70 Fellow Am. Acad. Arts and Scis., Nat. Acad. Pub. Adminstrn.; mem. Coun. on Fgn. Rels., Phi Beta Kappa (Frank J. Goodnow award, Charles E. Merriam award). Home: 6508 Goldleaf Dr Bethesda MD 20817-5837 Office: Brookings Instn 1775 Massachusetts Ave NW Washington DC 20036-2103 E-mail: tmann@brookings.edu.

MANN, WESLEY F. editor, writer, reporter; BA, Calif. State U.; MA, Northwestern U.; MBA Program Mgmt. Devel., Harvard Sch. Bus. Editor, co-author Investor's Business Daily, L.A., 1988—. Office: Investors Business Daily 12655 Beatrice St Los Angeles CA 90066-7303

MANN, WILLIAM CRAIG, lawyer; b. Norwalk, Ohio, Nov. 17, 1953; s. Abraham and Shirley (Smith) M. BA, Case Western Res. U., Ohio, 1976; JD, U. Dayton, Ohio, 1979. Bar: Ohio 1979, U.S. Dist. Ct. (no. dist.) Ohio 1979, U.S. Supreme Ct. 1986, U.S. Dist. Ct. (so. dist.) Ohio 1988. Law clk. Ohio Supreme Ct., Ohio, 1985-86; pvt. practice Cleve., 1986-87; assoc. Wolske and Blue, Columbus, Ohio, 1987-97; ptnr. Sunbury, Mann & Young, Columbus, Ohio, 1997-99; of counsel Mitchell, Allen, Catalano & Boda, Columbus, 1997—. Spkr. various orgns. in field, including Ohio Legal Ctr. Inst., Ohio Acad. of Trial Lawyers; mem. Ohio Supreme Ct. commn. on professionalism, 1997-2002 Contbr. articles to profl. jours. Bd. dirs. United Way, Huron County, Ohio, 1983; mem. exec. and cen. coms. Huron County Dem. Com., 1976-79. Mem. Ohio State Bar Assn. (ethics com. 1987—), Columbus Bar Assn., Ohio Acad. Trial Lawyers (pres. 2001—), Franklin County Trial Lawyers Assn. (pres. 2001-2002. Avocations: football, history, economics. Home: 2041 Ramblewood Ave Columbus OH 43235-7340 Office: Mitchell Allen Catalano & Boda 580 S High St Columbus OH 43215 E-mail: Mannlaw99@aol.com.

MANN, WILLIAM JOSEPH, JR., gynecologic oncologist; b. Wilkes Barre, Pa., Apr. 13, 1947; s. William Joseph and Irene Bertha M.; m. Katie Gallagher, Aug. 8, 1980; children: William Joseph Mann III, Kelly Catherine Rena. BA cum laude, Amherst Coll., 1969; MD, Pa. State U., 1973; MBA, Coll. of William and Mary, 1997. Diplomate Am. Bd. Ob-Gyn. Intern, resident M.S. Hershey Med. Ctr., Hershey, Pa., 1973-78, ACOG-Ortho fellow, 1976-77; fellow in gynecol. oncology U. Ala., Birmingham, 1978-80; assoc. prof., dir. gynecol. oncology SUNY, Stony Brook, 1980-91; dir. ob-gyn. residency Riverside Regional Med. Ctr., Newport News, Va., 1991-2001; prof. ob-gyn. Med. Coll. of Va., Richmond, 1993-2001; chmn., dept. ob-gyn. and dir. Jersey Shore Med. Ctr., Neptune, NJ, 2001—. Contbr. numerous articles to profl. jours., chpts. in books, revs. in various publs. Coach Smithtown Kickers soccer league, 1988-89, Rugby Club, SUNY at Stony Brook, 1980-87; vol. fireman Nissequogue Fire Dept., St. James, N.Y., 1988-91, Setauket (N.Y.) Vol. Fire Dept., 1983-88 Recipient Silver Sword award Am. Cancer Soc., 1991. Fellow ACS, Am. Coll. Ob-Gyn.; mem. Soc. Gynecol. Oncologists, Assn. Profs. Ob-Gyn., So. Med. Soc., So. Oncology Assn. (founding), Gyn. Urology Soc., Am. Soc. for Colposcopy and Cervical Pathology, Suffolk County Soc. Ob-Gyns., Internat. Gyn. Cancer Soc., Am. Soc. for Laser Medicine and Surgery, Inc., Newport News Med. Soc., Va. Ob-Gyn. Soc., Am. Soc. for Parenatal and Enteral Nutrition, Mid-Atlantic Gyn. Oncologic Soc. Avocations: rugby, Karate. Office: 1945 State Route 33 Neptune NJ 07753-4859 Office Phone: 732-776-3790. E-mail: wmann@meridianhealth.com.

MANNAN, M. SAM, chemical engineer, educator, consultant; b. Comilla, Bangladesh, Nov. 10, 1954; came to U.S., 1981; s. Abdul and Nargis Ara Mannan; m. Afroza Mannan, Dec. 26, 1982; children: Joya, Rumki. BSChemE, Engring. U., Dhaka, Bangladesh, 1978; MSChemE, U. Okla., 1983, PhDChemE, 1986. Registered profl. engr., Tex., La. Engr. Devel. Bank, Dhaka, 1978; chem. engr. Ministry Mcpls., Agedabia, Libya, 1978-81; grad. rsch. asst. U. Okla., Norman, 1981-86, vis. asst. prof., 1986-89; program dir. RMT, Inc., Austin, Tex., 1990-94, v.p. Ausitn, Tex., 1994-97; assoc. prof., dir. chem. engring. Tex. A&M U., College Station, 1997—. Presenter papers at numerous confs., meetings, and symposia. Author: Guidelines for Safe Process Operations and Maintenance, 1995; contbr. articles to profl. jours. including Oil and Gas Jour., Chem. Engring. Process, and Internat. Jour. Physics. Recipient Quality Recognition award PPG Industries, 1998. Mem. AIChE (IIA com. 1998—, dir. safety and health divsn. 1999—), Am. Soc. Safety Engrs., Sys. Safety Soc. Mem. AIChE (IIA com. 1998—, safety and health divsn. 1999—), Am. Soc. Safety Engrs., Sys. Safety Soc. Avocations: travel, fishing, hunting. Office: Tex A&M U Dept Chem Engring College Station TX 77843-0001

MANNARI, RAJAN KRISHNAMACHARY, biotechnologist, researcher; arrived in U.S., 1998; s. Krishnamachary R. and Vasantha Mannari; m. Lakshmi Prabha R. Monda; 1 child, Shreya Rajan. MTech with distinction, Anna U., Chennai, India, 1991, PhD in Biotech., 1997. Postdoc. scientist Nat. Inst. Sericultural and Entomol. Scis., Tsukuba, Japan, 1998; rsch. scientist U. Tex. M.D. Anderson Cancer Ctr., Houston, 1998—2003. Rschr., cons. Ctr. for Biotech., Anna U., Chennai, 1989—97. Fellow, UT-MD Anderson Cancer Ctr.; sr. rsch. fellow, Coun. of Sci. and Indsl. Rsch., New Delhi, 1993—97, Indo-Swiss Biotech. Collaborative Rsch. Project, 1997—98, GATE Fellow, Govt. of India, 1989—91. Mem.: Am. Assn. for Cancer Rsch. (assoc.), UT-MD Anderson Alumni Assn. (assoc.). Achievements include design of silk protein (heavy chain fragment) extraction technology; four different pilot projects in last three years in leukemia dept. of MD Anderson Cancer Ctr; development of antibodies to cocoon fibroin protein of silk fibres of Bombyx mori; methodology for easy sequencing of DNA clones for CpG containing genes; diagnostic tools for filarial disease; methodologies in silkworm research projects; cDNA probes for fibroin to study gene expression in vivo and in vitro; first to identify and confirm hundreds of genes with CpG islands in tumors with substractive hybridization procedure; construct rDNA expression of GMCSF- and IFN-gamma in industrial projects; correlateDNA methylation pattern in different cancer patient samples; study efficacy of DECITABINE in de/hypo- methylation in leukemic patient samples in clinical trials; establish high degree of accuracy in methylation studies with bisulfite treated patient samples in analysis; research in bacteriostatic property of silk fibres; gene-therapy based on adeno-virus methods; microbial feed for prawn in commercial projects.

MANNE, DEBORAH SUE, dental hygienist, educator, oncological nurse; b. Vincennes, Ind., Nov. 20, 1954; d. Charles Kenneth and Susan Jane (Fox) Thornberry; m. Marshall Stanley Manne, Dec. 21, 1985. AA, Maplewoods C.C., Kansas City, Mo., 1973; BS in Dental Hygiene, U. Mo., 1975; BSN, St. Louis U., 1991, MSN in Oncology Nursing, 1998, PhD in Nursing, 2004. RN, reg. dental hygienist, Mo. Dental hygienist Dr. Marshall S. Manne, St. Louis, 1978—2001, office nurse, 1991—2001; oncology nurse CIRCLE Barnes-Jewish Hosp., St. Louis, 1993—98; staff nurse Radiation Oncology Ctr. Barnes-Jewish Hosp. North, 1997; nurse educator Cancer Family Care, St. Louis, 1998; clin. asst. prof. divsn. dental hygiene Sch. Dentistry U. Mo., Kans. City, 1999—; clin. nurse John Krey Cancer Info. Ctr., St. John's Mercy David C. Pratt Cancer Ctr., St. Louis, 2001—04. Instr. dental hygiene dept. St. Louis C.C., Forest Pk., 1999—2000; clin. instr. So. Ill. U., Carbondale, 2000; coord., cons. Oncology Dental Support Svcs., St. Louis, 1992—; mem. curriculum rev. com. dental hygiene program St. Louis C.C., 1993; mem. adv. bd. ACCESS Dental Hygiene Jour., 1994—2003; editl. bd. Jour. of Dental Hygiene, 2003—; reviewer Oncology Nursing Forum, 2003—; pilot reviewer Clin. Jour. of Oncology Nursing, 2003—. Contbr. articles to profl. jours. Chair Gt. Am. Smokeout, 1992; mem. Breast Cancer task force, 1994—98; bd. dirs, v.p. Am. Cancer Soc., St. Louis, 1992—93; mem. profl. adv. com. Wellness Cmty., St. Louis, 1994—; chmn. Tobacco-Free Mo. Super Coalition, St. Louis, 2000. Recipient Vol. Recognition award, Am. Cancer Soc., 1995, Irene Newman award, 1997, Susan Brockman-Bell Humanitarian award, U. Mo. Kans. City Dental Hygiene Alumni Assn., 2000. Mem. Am. Dental Hygienists Assn. (council on pub. rels., coun. on edn., coun. on rsch., 2004-), Oncology Nursing Soc. (chair oral care focus group, pres.-elect St. Louis chpt. 1998, pres. 1999, editor patient edn. sig newsletter 1999-2000), Mo. Dental Hygienists' Assn. (pres.), Greater St. Louis Hygienists' Assn. (pres.), Sigma Phi Alpha, Sigma Theta Tau. Avocations: walking, raising golden retrievers. Home: 11617 Larkmont Dr Creve Coeur MO 63141-6907

MANNE, HENRY GIRARD, lawyer, educator; b. New Orleans, May 10, 1928; s. Geoffrey and Eva (Shainberg) M.; m. Bobbette Lee Taxer, Aug. 19, 1968; children: Emily Kay, Geoffrey Adam. BA, Vanderbilt U., 1950; JD, U. Chgo., 1952; LL.M., Yale U., 1953, J.S.D., 1966; LLD, U. Seattle, 1987, U. Francisco Marroquin, Guatemala, 1987, George Mason U., 2000. Bar: Ill. 1952, N.Y. 1969. Practice in Chgo., 1953-54; assoc. prof. St. Louis U. Law Sch., 1956-57, 59-62; vis. prof. law U. Wis., Madison, 1957-59; prof. George Washington U. Law Sch., 1962-68; Kenan prof. law and polit. sci. U. Rochester, 1968-74; vis. prof. law Stanford (Calif.) Law Sch., 1971-72; disting. prof. law, dir. Law and Econs. Center, U. Miami Law Sch., 1974-80; prof. law Emory U. Law and Econs. Ctr., Atlanta, 1980-86; dean Law Sch., chmn. Law and Econs. Ctr. George Mason U., 1986-96, univ. prof., 1986-99, dean emeritus, 2000—. Vis. prof. law U. Wis., Madison, 1957-59, Stanford (Calif.) Law Sch., 1971-72, U. Chgo. Law Sch., 2000-02; dir. Econs. Insts. Fed. Judges, 1976-89. Author: Insider Trading and the Stock Market, 1966, (with H. Wallich) The Modern Corporation and Social Responsibility, 1973, (with E. Solomon) Wall Street in Transition, 1974, Med. Malpractice Guidebook: Law and Economics, 1985; editor: (with Roger LeRoy Miller) Gold, Money and the Law, 1975, Auto Safety Regulation: The Cure or the Problem, 1976; editor: Economic Policy and the Regulation of Corporate Securities, 1968, The Economics of Legal Relationships, 1975; editor: (with James Dorn) Econ. Liberties and the Judiciary, 1987. Served to 1st lt. USAF, 1954-56. Recipient Salvatori award Excellence in Acad. Leadership, 1994; named Cultural Laureate of Va., 1992. Adj. scholar CATO Inst.; fellow Am. Law and Econs. Assn. (hon. life), Mont Pelerin Soc., Order of Coif, Phi Beta Kappa. E-mail: Henry@themannes.com.

MANNELLY, PATRICK J. food products executive; With Johnston Coca-Cola Bottling Group, The Coca-Cola Co.; group v.p. Ea. N.Am. group; divsn. gen. mgr. So. Calif. divsn.; chief fin. officer Western N.Am. group; corp. v.p., fin. & adminstrn. Coca-Cola Enterprises, inc., Atlanta, 1998, CFO, 1999—. Office: Coca-Cola Enterprises Inc 2500 Windy Ridge Pkwy SE Atlanta GA 30339-5677

MANNERS, PAMELA JEANNE, secondary school educator; b. Holyoke, Mass., Mar. 20, 1951; d. Francis Edward and Helen Mary (Kurtyka) Herbert; div. 1985; children: Tracy, Kristen. BA, U. So. Miss., 1986, MEd, 1993. Cert. elem. edn. K-3, 4-8, secondary Eng., Social Studies; cert. elem. prin., secondary prin., elem. and secondary adminstrn. Registrar Michel Mid. Sch., Biloxi, Miss., 1987-88, tchr. Eng. and Social Studies, 1988-90, tchr. reading/law related edn., 1990-95; curriculum coord. Biloxi Pub. Schs., 1995-98; adminstrator Fernwood Jr. High Sch., Biloxi Pub. Schs., 1998-2000; dir. ABA Reading Curriculum Program, 1989-95; prin. Michel Jr. H.S., Biloxi Pub. Schs., 2000—04, Biloxi H.S., 2004—. Law-related edn. trainer Miss. Law-Related Edn. Ctr., Jackson, 1990-2002; law-related trainer Ctr. Civic Edn., Calabasas, Calif., 1993; law-related trainer Constitutional Right Found., 1994-2002. Participant program Lawyer in Every Class Miss. Bar Assn., Jackson, 1990-93 On-site target grantee Miss. Bar/Dept. Justice, 1992; A+ Site recognition U.S. Dept. Edn. Mem. Leadership Gulf Coast C. of C. (edn. com. 1996—). Roman Catholic. Office: Biloxi Pub Schs 1845 Richard Dr Biloxi MS 39532 Office Phone: 228-435-6105. Business E-Mail: pamela.manners@biloxischools.net.

MANNES, ELENA SABIN, film and television producer, director; b. N.Y.C., Dec. 3, 1943; d. Leopold Damrosch and Evelyn (Sabin) M. BA, Smith Coll., 1965; MA, Johns Hopkins U., 1967. Rschr. Pub. Broadcast Lab. Nat. Ednl. TV, N.Y.C., 1968-70; writer Sta. WPIX-TV, N.Y.C., 1970-73; assignment editor Sta. ABC-TV, N.Y.C., 1973-76; prodr., writer Sta. WCBS-TV, N.Y.C., 1976-80; prodr. CBS News, N.Y.C., 1980-87, Pub. Affairs TV/Bill Moyers PBS Documentaries, N.Y.C., 1987-90. Ind. documentary dir. and prodr., 1987—. Recipient Emmy award NATAS, 1984, 85, 87, 90, 94, 96, 2002, Peabody award, 1985, Cine Golden Eagle award, 1988, 90, 93, 94, 95, 99, Robert F. Kennedy Journalism award, 1989, DGA awards, 1987, 90. Mem. Writers Guild Am., Dirs. Guild Am., Am. Film Inst. (dir. Workshop for Women). Avocations: tennis, still photography.

MANNHEIMER, ZACHARY R. performing company executive; b. Phila., Sept. 14, 1977; s. Jeffrey Saul Mannheimer and Marsha Susan Queen. BA in Theatre Arts and Philosphy, Muhlenberg Coll., 1999. House mgr. The Royal Ct., London, 1999—2000; Fringe Al Fresco dir. N.Y.C. Internat. Fringe Festival, 2000—02; producing artistic dir. The Subjective Theatre Co., N.Y.C., 2001—; adminstr. N.Y. Children's and Dance Affinity, N.Y.C., 2003. Adj. prof. Wagnor Coll., N.Y.C., 2003. Dir.: (event) Busking Bonanza, 2001—, Off-Off Community Dish, 2002—. Home: 116 Garfield Pl #1 Brooklyn NY 11215

MANNICK, JOHN ANTHONY, surgeon; b. Deadwood, S.D., Mar. 24, 1928; s. Alfred and Catherine Elizabeth (Schuster) M.; m. Alice Virginia Gossard, June 9, 1952; children— Catherine Virginia, Elizabeth Eleanor, Joan Barbara. BA, Harvard U., 1949, MD, 1953. Diplomate: Am. Bd. Surgery (dir. 1971-77). Intern Mass. Gen. Hosp., 1953-54, resident in surgery, 1956-60; instr. in surgery to asst. prof. Med. Coll. Va., 1960-64; asso. prof. to prof. surgery Boston U., 1964-76, chmn. div. surgery, 1973-76; Moseley prof. surgery Harvard U., 1976-94, Moseley Disting. prof. surgery, 1994—; dir. ednl. programs Harvard Med. Internat., 1994-96; chmn. dept. surgery Peter Bent Brigham Hosp. and Brigham and Women's Hosp., Boston, 1976-94. Mem. surgery, anesthesiology and trauma study sect. NIH, 1978-82, mem. medicine study sect., 1967-70; rsch. com. Med. Found., Inc., 1970-76. Author: (with others) Modern Surgery, 1970, Core Textbook of Surgery, 1972, Surgery of Ischemic Limbs, 1972, The Cause and Management of Aneurysms, 1990; mem. editorial bd. AMA Archives of Surgery, 1973-84, Clin. Immunology and Immunopathology, 1972-84, Surgery, 1982-97, Brit. Jour. Surgery, 1982-92, European Jour. Vascular Surgery, 1988-96, Shock, 1997—; mem. editl. bd. Advances in Surgery, 1979—, editor, 1984-86; mem. editl. bd. Jour. Vascular Surgery, 1984-97, assoc. editor, 1990-97; also articles. Served to capt. M.C. USAF, 1954-56. Markle scholar in acad. medicine, 1961-66 Fellow ACS (gov.), Royal Coll. Surgeons (hon., Eng.), Royal Coll. Surgeons (hon., Edinburgh), Vascular Soc. Gt. Britain and Ireland (hon.); mem. Am. Fedn. Clin. Rsch., Am. Assn. Immunologists, Am. Soc. Exptl. Pathology, Soc. Clin. Investigation, Soc. Clin. Surgery, Soc. Univ. Surgeons, Soc. Surg. Chmn. (sec. 1985-87, pres. 1987-88), Am. Surg. Assn. (pres. 1989-90), Internat. Cardio-vascular Soc. (recorder N.Am. chpt., 1973-76, pres. N.Am. chpt. 1991-92, internat. v.p. 1993, Disting. Svc. award 2002), Soc. Vascular Surgery (pres. 1981), N.E. Surg. Soc., New Eng. Soc. Vascular Surgery (pres. 1994-95), Royal Coll. Surgeons (hon., Australasia) So. Surg. Assn., So. Soc. Vascular Surgery (hon.), Surg. Infection Soc., Halstead Soc., Lifeline Found. (pres. 1997-2002), Shock Soc. (Sci. Achievement award 2000), Phi Beta Kappa. Home: 81 Bogle St Weston MA 02493-1056 Office: 75 Francis St Boston MA 02115-6110 Fax: 617-582-6169.

MANNING, BARTON HARLEY, neuroscientist; b. St. John's, Nfld., Can., Apr. 28, 1968; s. Barton Harley and Audrey Yvonne (Hatcher) M. BSc, McGill U., 1991; PhD, Va. Commonwealth U., 1996. Postdoctoral fellow U. Calif., San Francisco, 1996-2000; asst. prof. Ohio State U., 2000; sr. rsch. biologist Merck Rsch. Labs., Merck & Co., Inc., West Point, Pa., 2001—. Contbr. chpt. to book, articles to profl. jours. Centennial fellow Med. Rsch. Coun. Can., 1999; Life Scis. Rsch. Found. fellow, 1999; U.S. NIH fellow, 1999. Mem. AAAS, Soc. for Neurosci., Internat. Assn. Study of Pain, Am. Pain Soc. Avocations: piano, guitar. Office: Merck and Co Inc Merck Rsch Labs WP46-300 770 Sumneytown Pike West Point PA 19486-0004 E-mail: barton_manning@merck.com.

MANNING, BLANCHE M. federal judge; b. 1934; BEd, Chgo. Tchrs. Coll., 1961; JD, John Marshall Law Sch., 1967; MA, Roosevelt Univ., 1972; LLM, Univ. of Va. Law Sch., 1992; DHL (hon.), Chgo. State U., 1998. Asst. states atty. State's Atty.'s Office (Cook County), Ill., 1968-73; supervisory trial atty. U.S. EEOC, Chgo., 1973-77; gen. atty. United Airlines, Chgo., 1977-78; asst. U.S. atty. U.S. Dist. Ct. (no. dist.) Ill., 1978-79; assoc. judge Cir. Ct. of Cook County, 1979-86, circuit judge, 1986-87; appellate court judge Ct. of Review Ill. Appellate Ct., 1987-94; district judge U.S. Dist. Ct. (no. dist.) Ill., Chgo., 1994—. Tchr. A. O. Sexton Elem. Sch. James Wadsworth Elem. Sch., Wendell Phillips H.S. Adult Program, Morgan Park H.S. Summer Sch. Program, South Shore H.S. Summer Sch. Program, Carver H.S. Adult Edn. Program; lectr. Malcolm X C.C., 1970-71; adj. prof. NCBL C.C. of Law, 1978-79, DePaul Univ. Law Sch., 1992—; tchg. team mem. Trial Advocacy Workshop, Harvard Law Sch., U. Chgo. Law Sch., 1991—; chmn. Com. on Recent Devels. in Evidence, Ill. Judicial Conf., 1991; faculty mem. New Judges Seminar, Ill. Judicial Conf.; past faculty mem. Profl. Devel. Seminar for New Assoc. Judges, Cook County Cir. Ct.; past mem. bd. dirs., trained intervenor Lawyers' Assistance Program, Inc.; past mem. adv. coun. Lawyer's Asst. Program, Roosevelt U. Former trustee Sherwood Music Conservatory Bd.; clarinetist Cmty. Concert band Chgo. State U.; saxophonist Jazz ensemble, Chgo. State U. Jazz Band, jazz band Diversity. Mem. Cook County Bar Assn. (second v-p 1974), Nat. Bar Assn., Nat. Judicial Coun., Ill. Judicial Coun. (treas. 1982-85, chmn. 1988, chmn. judiciary com. 1992), Ill. State Bar Assn. (past mem. bd. dirs. Lawyers Assistance Program Inc.), Am. Bar Assn. (fellow 1991), Chgo. Bar Assn. (clarinetist Symphony Orch., saxophonist), John Marshall Law Sch. Alumni Assn. (bd. dirs.), Chgo. State Univ. Alumni Assn. (bd. dirs.). Office: US Dist Ct 2156 US Courthouse 219 S Dearborn St Ste 2050 Chicago IL 60604-1800

MANNING, BRENT V. lawyer; b. Preston, Idaho, Jan. 18, 1950; s. Leon W. and Gwen (Briscoe) M.; m. J. Christine Coffin, Oct. 25, 1969; children: Justin, Britten, John. BA, Idaho State U., 1972; JD, Harvard U., 1975. Bar: Colo. 1975, Utah 1981, U.S. Ct. Appeals (10th cir.) 1978. Assoc. Holme Roberts & Owen, Denver, 1975-80, ptnr., 1980-97, Salt Lake City, 1981-97; founding ptnr. Manning Curtis Bradshaw & Bednar, LLC, Salt Lake City, 1997—. Mem. panel mediators and arbitrators U.S. Dist. Ct. Utah, 1993—; mediation and settlement judge pro tempore 3d Jud. Dist. State of Utah, 1996—; mem. jud. nominating commn. 2d Jud. Dist. Ct. Utah., judge pro tem, 2000—. Trustee Bountiful (Utah) Davis Art Found., 1985-91, Utah Tibetan Resettlement Project. Mem. ABA, Utah Bar Assn. (chmn. continuing legal edn. com. 1988, mem. disciplinary com. 1991-93, chmn. cts. and judges com. 1996-97, chmn. And Justice for All campaign, 2001—), Am. Inns of Ct. (pres. 1997-98, master of bench 1988—), Am. Alpine Club (N.Y.C.) Democrat. Avocations: climbing, mountain biking, backcountry skiing, running. Home: 2079 Maple Grove Way Bountiful UT 84010-1005 Office: Manning Curtis 3d Fl Newhouse Bldg 10 Exchange Pl Salt Lake City UT 84111-2714 E-mail: BManning@mc2b.com.

MANNING, CHARLES W. university chancellor; b. Mar. 18, 1943; s. Charles Manning; m. Sharon Fischer; children: Shannon, Charles, Kelly. BS in Chemistry, McDaniel Coll., 1965; PhD in Analytical Chemistry, U. Md., 1969; postgrad., Johannes Gutenberg U., Mainz, Germany, 1969—70. Sr. staff assoc. Nat. Ctr. Higher Edn. Mgmt. Systems, Boulder, Colo., 1971-74; asst. provost, asst. prof. chemistry U. Mo., Kansas City, 1974-79; assoc. exec. dir. acad. affairs Colo. Commn. Higher Edn., Denver, 1979-81, dep. exec. dir., 1982-88; v.p. acad. affairs U. No. Colo., Greeley, 1981-82; exec. vice chancellor Okla. State Regents for Higher Edn., Oklahoma City, 1988-90; chancellor U. System W.Va., Charleston, 1991-2000, Tenn. Bd. Regents, Nashville, 2000—. Cons.

as v.p. for planning and fin. Fed. U., Ceara, Brazil, 1976-77; presenter in field. Contbr. articles to profl. jours. Capt. U.S. Army, 1970-71. Office: Tenn Bd Regents 1415 Murfreesboro Pike Ste 350 Nashville TN 37217-2829

MANNING, CHRISTOPHER ASHLEY, finance educator, consultant; b. L.A., June 26, 1945; s. Ashley and Vivian LaVerne (Wagner) M.; m. Cathy Ann Nichols, July 30, 1977 (div. Sept. 1993). BS, San Diego State U., 1967; MBA, Northwestern U., 1971; PhD, UCLA, 1983. Corp. loan officer Security Pacific Nat. Bank, L.A., 1971-75; v.p. fin. Solitude Ski Resort, Bravo Ski Corp., Salt Lake City, 1975-78; pres. Sequoia Spa Co., L.A., 1976-79, Manning and Co., L.A., 1971-86, Manning's Little Red Piano Shop, L.A., 1971-86; instr. corp. fin. Pepperdine U., L.A., 1979-83; instr. corp. fin. and real estate Long Beach (Calif.) State U., 1983-86; assoc. prof. fin. Loyola Marymount U., L.A., 1986-92, prof. fin., 1992—. Mng. prin. Denver office Houlihan Valuation Advisors, 1993-94; founder, mng. prin. Manning Advisors. Mem. editl. bd. Jour. of Real Estate Rsch., 1988-90, 91-93, 94-96, 97-99, 2003—; contbr. articles to profl. jours. 1st lt. U.S. Army, 1967—70. Decorated Bronze Star. Mem.: Am. Real Estate Soc. (bd. dirs. 1994—96, 1997—99, v.p./program chair 2000—01, bd. dirs. 2000—, pres.-elect 2001—02, pres. 2002—03), Phi Eta Sigma, Beta Gamma Sigma. Republican. Episcopalian. Home and Office: Manning Advisors 29438 Quailwood Dr Palos Verdes Peninsula CA 90275-4929 Office Phone: 310-541-0353.

MANNING, CLARENCE BOND, lawyer; b. Richmond, Va., Nov. 5, 1945; s. Clarence F. and Hazel M. (Bond) Manning; m. Judy P. Fary, Mar. 25, 1967; children: Kirsten D., Patrick B. BA, Washington and Lee U., 1968; JD, U. Va., 1971. Bar: Ill. 1971. Ptnr. Sidley & Austin, Chgo., 1971—83; atty. BellSouth Corp., Atlanta, 1983—. Served with USCGR, 1967—73. Mem.: ABA, Chgo. Bar Assn. Mem. United Ch. Of Christ. Home: 624 Sycamore St Decatur GA 30030-1958 Office: 675 W Peachtree St NW Atlanta GA 30308-1989

MANNING, DENNIS J. insurance company executive; Ins. agent Guardian Life Ins. Co. Am., Houston, 1983—91, v.p. life mktg., agy. distbn., 1991—2000, COO, 2000—02, pres., 2002—, CEO, 2003—. Office: 7 Hanover Sq New York NY 10004-2616

MANNING, ELI (ELISHA NELSON MANNING), professional football player; b. Jan. 3, 1981; BA in Mktg., U. Miss., 2003. Quaterback N.Y. Giants, East Rutherford, NJ, 2004—. Recipient Maxwell award, 2003, Johnny Unitas Golden Arm award, 2003. Achievements include selected #1 overall NFL Entry Draft, 2004; comes from a prestigious family with brother Peyton and father Archie both great NFL quarterbacks. Office: c/o New York Football Giants Giants Stadium East Rutherford NJ 07073*

MANNING, ERIC, computer science and engineering educator, university dean, researcher; b. Windsor, Ont., Can., Aug. 4, 1940; g. George Gorman and Eleanor Katherine (Koehler) M.; m. Betty Goldring, Sept. 16, 1961; children: David, Paula. BSc, U. Waterloo, Ont., 1961, MSc, 1962; PhD, U. Ill., 1965. Registered profl. engr., B.C. With MIT and Bell Tel. Labs., 1965-68; prof. computer sci. U. Waterloo, 1968-86, founding dir. computer comms. networks group, 1973-82; founding dir. Inst. for Computer Rsch., 1982-86; prof., dean engring. U. Victoria, Canada, 1986-92, prof. computer sci., elec. engring., 1993-2000, New Media Ctr./Nortel Networks Prof. Network Performance, 2000—03; prin. scientist, strategic advisor Sysor R&D Inc., 2003—. New MIC Chief Scientist, Networks Cluster, 2000-03; dir. Natural Sci. and Engring. Rsch. Coun. Can., mem. exec. com., chair strategic grants com., 1982-87; dir. Comm. Rsch. Centre, Govt. of Can., 1995-97, Consortium for Software Engring. Rsch., Ottawa, 1997-99; trustee B.C. Advanced Sys. Found., 1986-93; dir. Sci. Coun. B.C., 1988-91; bd. dirs. Can. Microelectric Corp.; adv. com. on artificial intelligence NRC, 1987-91; internat. rsch. adv. com. Alta. Informatics Ctr. Rsch. Excellence, 2002-; IBM chair computer sci. Keio U., Yokohama, 1992-93; hon. prof. South East U., Nanjing, China. Author: Fault Diagnosis of Digital Systems, 1970; also numerous articles. V.p. Greater Victoria Concert Band, 1995-96; trumpet sect., Sooke Philharm. & 5th Field Arty. Band, Royal Can. Arty. Fellow IEEE, Engring. Inst. Can.; mem. Assn. Computing Machinery (mem. snowbird com. 1999—), Assn. Profl. Engrs. B.C., Soc. for Computer Simulation, Can. Inst. for Advanced Rsch. (adv. com. on artificial intelligence and robotics 1986-90), Can. Assn. for Computer Sci. (pres. 1994-2000), Can. Soc. for Fifth Generation Rsch. (trustee 1987-88), B.C. Microelectronics Soc. (bd. dirs. 1986-87). Avocations: amateur radio, scuba diving, sailing, flying, musical performance. Home: 440 Simcoe St #1431 Victoria BC Canada V8V 1L3 Office: U Victoria Faculty Engring PO Box 3055 Victoria BC Canada V8W 3P6 E-mail: eric.manning@engr.uvic.ca.

MANNING, J. RICHARD, lawyer; b. Seattle, Nov. 2, 1932; BA, Seattle U., 1954; LLB, Gonzaga U., 1960. Bar: Wash. 1960. Pvt. practice, Seattle. Chmn. Seattle adv. coun. Am. Arbitration Assn., 1985—96, Bd. Govs., 1997—2000; Mem. Law Adv. Bd. Gonzaga U., 1988—; pres. Wash. State Bar Assn., 2002—03. Recipient Nat. Outstanding Svc. award, Am. Arbitration Assn., 1988, Wash. Law and Politics Super Lawyer award, Top 100 Lawyers award, 2002. Mem.: ABA, Assn. Trial Lawyers Am., King County Bar Found. (pres. 1991—93), Am. Judicature Soc., King County Bar Assn. (pres. 1995—96). Office: 925 Logan Bldg 500 Union St Seattle WA 98101

MANNING, J. TERRY, company executive; BBA, U. Notre Dame. Audit sr. BDO Seidman, LLP, 1973-78, ptnr., 1978—, nat. dir. strategic planning, 1986-90, nat. dir. human resources, 1989-90, mng. ptnr. Richmond office, 1990-91, internat. svc. coord., vice chmn. fin., exec. officer, 1995—; dir. Henley Healthcare, Inc., Sugar Land, Tex., 1999. Mem. AICPA.

MANNING, JEROME ALAN, retired lawyer; b. Bklyn., Dec. 31, 1929; s. Emanuel J. and Dorothy (Levine) M.; m. Naomi Jacobs, Oct. 31, 1954; children: Joy, Stephen, Susan. BA, NYU, 1950, LLB, 1952; LLM, Yale U., 1953. Bar: N.Y. 1953, Fla. 1977. Assoc. Joseph Trachtman, N.Y.C., 1956-61; ptnr. Stroock & Stroock & Lavan, N.Y.C., 1961-96; prof. NYU Sch. Law, 1956-96. Editor: NYU Law Rev.; author: Estate Planning, 1980, rev. edit., 2004, Estate Planning for Laymen, 1992. Trustee N.Y.U. Sch. Law. Capt. USAF, 1953-56. Home: 1835 Franklin St San Francisco CA 94109-3483 E-mail: jmanning@stroock.com.

MANNING, JOAN ELIZABETH, health association administrator; b. Davenport, Iowa, July 7, 1953; d. George John and Eugenie Joan (Thomas) Stolzc; m. Michael Anthony Manning, July 30, 1977. BA, U. No. Iowa, 1975; MPH, U. Minn., 1990. Traveling collegiate sec. Alpha Delta Pi Nat. Sorority, Atlanta, 1975—76; recreational therapist Americana Healthcare Ctr., Mason City, Iowa, 1976—81; communication coord. Area Agy. on Aging, Mason City, 1981—83; exec. dir. United Way Cerro Gordo County, Mason City, 1983—85, Health Fair of the Midlands, Omaha, 1985—87; dir. health services ARC, Omaha, 1987—90, COO, 1990—95, CEO, Pacific Northwest region, 1995—. Vis. rsch. prof. Niels Bohr Inst., Denmark, 1995-96. Bd. dirs. YMCA of U.S.A., Chgo., 1981-83, Mason City YMCA, 1980-84, Mason City Parks and Recreation Bd., 1983-85, Camp Fire Coun., 1989—. Potters Therapy House, 1989—; mem. spl. adv. bd. Cerro Gordo County Human Svcs. Bd., 1983-85; mem. spl. activities com. Omaha Wellness Coun. of Midlands, 1986-89; chmn. wider opportunity task force Great Plains (Nebr.) Girl Scouts U.S., 1986-89; bd. dirs. Omaha South YMCA, Cath. Charities; mem. Jr. League of Omaha. Mem. U. Minn. Alumnae Assn., Suburban Rotary, Alpha Delta Pi. Republican. Roman Catholic.

MANNING, JOHN WARREN, III, retired surgeon, medical educator; b. Phila., Nov. 24, 1919; s. John Warren Jr. and Edith Margaret (Reagan) M.; m. Muriel Elizabeth Johnson, Oct. 11, 1944; children: John, Melissa, Susan. BS in Chemistry with honors, Ursinus Coll., 1940; MD, U. Pa., 1943; postgrad., 1978. Diplomate Am. Bd. Surgery. Naval intern Pa. Naval Hosp., 1946; resident Saginaw (Mich.) Gen. Hosp., 1947-50; preceptor Dr. H.M. Bishop, 1950-52; pvt. practice Saginaw, 1950—, Sr. staff mem. Saginaw Gen. Hosp., St. Luke's Hosp., Saginaw; past chief of surgery, chmn. tissue com. St. Mary's Hosp., Saginaw; cons. VA Hosp., Saginaw; assoc. clin. prof. surgery Mich. State U., assoc. prof. surgery, 1976-92, prof. emeritus, 1992—; mem. search com. Saginaw Coop. Hosp. Contbr. articles to profl. publs. Lt. USN, 1942-46, PTO. Fellow ACS; mem. AMA, Mich. State Med. Soc., Saginaw Surg. Soc., Soc. Abdominal Surgeons, Am. Coll. Angiology, Soc. Am. Gastrointestinal Endoscopic Surgeons. Office: 4515 Gratiot Rd Saginaw MI 48603-6261 Home: Apt 10 4515 Gratiot Rd Saginaw MI 48603-6238

MANNING, JUDITH HUBERT, state legislator, real estate executive; b. Oct. 24, 1942; children: Hank, Elizabeth. Postgrad., U. Vienna (Austria), 1963-64; BS in Edn., U. Ga., 1964. Tchr. soc. studies Coll. Pk. H.S., Fulton County, Ga., 1966-67, McEachern Middle Sch., Cobb County, Ga., 1967-69; past real estate agent, broker Manning Properties, Marietta, Ga.; co-owner, real estate agent, broker, appraiser property mgmt., leasing, sales and appraisal firm; mem. Ga. House of Reps., Atlanta, 1997—. Mem. Retirement Com., Natural Resources Com., Banks and Banking Com.; active Women Leaders Summit, 1995, 96; mem. edn. task force Am. Legis. Exch. Coun. Del. 7th dist. Rep. Party Convention; past adv. pres. ARC; mem. Atlanta Regional Commn., Cobb Emergency Aid, Cobb Youth Leadership; mem. Girls, Inc., past chair, bd.dirs.; bd. dirs. Jubilee Fine Arts Fesival, OpenGate, Gateway Vis. and Info. Ctr., Dept. Family and Children Svcs.; past bd. dirs. Cobb Symposium, Vol. Atlanta; publicity chair, past bd. dirs. YMCA; vol. Kennestone Hosp.; vol. task force, exec. mem. United Way; 1st pres. Vol. Cobb-Marietta; vice-chmn. Friends of the Park; historian, past bd. dirs. Ptnrs. Fund; participant Women Leaders Summit, 1995-96. W. Wyman Pilcher Jr. Meml. scholar; recipient Leadership Cobb Class of 1984-85, Leadership Ga. Class of 89-90, Disting. Leadership award Nat. Assn. Cmty. Leadership, 1989, Phoenix award Cobb County Bd. Realtors, 1996. Mem. Nat. Assn. Realtors, Cobb-Marietta Jr. League, Hon. Comdrs. Assn., The Walker Sch. Parents Assn., Assn. Metro Atlanta DFCS (co-vice chmn.). Home: 830 Whitlock Ave SW Marietta GA 30064-3034 Office: Legis Office Bldg Rm 607 Atlanta GA 30334

MANNING, KENNETH ALAN, lawyer; b. Buffalo, July 22, 1951; s. Jack Edwin and Dorothea Ann (Ruhland) Manning; children: Michael John, Kathyrn Ann. BS in Engring. Sci., SUNY, Buffalo, 1974, JD, 1977. Bar: N.Y. 1978, U.S. Dist. Ct. (we. dist.) N.Y. 1978, U.S. Dist. Ct. (no. dist.) N.Y. 1980, U.S. Ct. Appeals (2d cir.) 1983, U.S. Ct. Appeals (3d cir.) 1988. Confidential law asst. to assoc. justice Appellate Divsn. 4th Dept., Buffalo, 1977—79; assoc. Phillips, Lytle, Hitchcock, Blaine & Huber, Buffalo, 1979—84; ptnr. Phillips Lytle LLP, Buffalo, 1985—. Vol. Lawyers Project, Erie County, 1985-2002, Criminal Appeals Program, Erie County, 1988-89; mem. Western N.Y. region NCCJ. Woodburn fellow SUNY, Buffalo, 1973-76. Mem. ABA (TIP sect.), N.Y. State Bar Assn. (ins. negligence sect.), Erie County Bar Assn., Gyro Club (pres. 1988), Park Club. Avocations: sports, hunting. Home: 167 Leicester Rd Buffalo NY 14217-2113 Office: Phillips Lytle LLP 3400 HSBC Ctr Buffalo NY 14203-2887

MANNING, KENNETH PAUL, technologies company executive; b. N.Y.C., Jan. 18, 1942; s. John Joseph and Edith Helen (Hoffmann) M.; m. Maureen Lambert, Sept. 12, 1964; children: Kenneth J., John J., Elise, Paul, Carolyn, Jacqueline. BME, Rensselaer Poly. Inst., 1963; postgrad., George Washington U., 1965-66; MBA in Ops. Rsch., Am. U., 1968. With W.R. Grace & Co., N.Y.C., 1973-87, v.p. European consumer divsn., 1975-76, pres. ednl. products divsn., 1976-79, pres. real estate divsn., 1979-81, v.p. corp. tech. group, 1981-83, pres., CEO, Ambrosia Chocolate Co. divsn. Milw., 1983-87; group v.p. Sensient Techs. Corp., Milw., 1987-89, exec. v.p., dir., 1989-92, pres., COO, dir., 1992-96, pres., CEO, dir., 1996—, chmn., CEO, 1997—. Bd. dirs. Firstar Corp., Milw., Badger Meter, Inc., Milw. Vice chmn. Greater Milw. Com.; bd. dirs. Milw. Harbor Commn. Served as lt. USN, 1963-67; rear adm. USNR, ret. Decorated Legion of Merit, Nat. Def. medal, others. Mem. Am. Chem. Soc., Navy League, U.S. Naval Inst., Naval Res. Assn., Milw. Metro Assn. Commerce (bd. dirs.), Union League (N.Y.C.), Milw. Club, Knights of Malta. Republican. Roman Catholic. Home: 5240 N Lake Dr Milwaukee WI 53217-5369 Office: Sensient Techs Corp 777 E Wisconsin Ave Milwaukee WI 53202-5304

MANNING, KEVIN JAMES, academic administrator; b. N.Y.C., Nov. 8, 1944; s. James and Helen (Gurry) M.; m. Sara Garrity; children: Elizabeth Ann, Meagan Garrity, Kevin James. BA in Theatre, Webster U., St. Louis, 1967; MS in Pers., Shippensburg (Pa.) U., 1976; PhD in Ednl. Adminstrn., Ohio State U., 1982; attended, Inst. Ednl. Mgmt., Harvard U., 1989. Adminstr., intr. Webster U., St. Louis, 1967-68; mgmt recruiter L.S. Brady, Inc., St. Louis, 1969; adminstr. Washington U., St. Louis, 1969-71; admissions counselor Elizabethtown (Pa.) Coll., 1972-76, dir. admissions, 1976-80, spl. asst. to pres., 1982-83; rsch. asst. Ohio State U., Columbus, 1980-82; chief staff Gov.'s Commn. Higher Edn., Harrisburg, Pa., 1983-84; v.p. devel. Immaculata (Pa.) Coll., 1984-2000; pres. Villa Julie Coll., Md., 2000—. Workforce adv. panel Commonwealth of Pa. Mem. attractions com. Phila. Econ. Devel. Coalition, 1988—; bd. trustees Peirce Coll., 1998—2001; mem. oversight com. Vision 2030; bd. dirs. Chester County Export Ctr., Exton, Pa., 1990. Mem. Sr. Devel. Officers Phila. (chmn. 1995-96), Great Valley C. of C. (bd. dirs.). Avocations: reading, arts, film, golf. Home: 1907 Billy Barton Cir Reisterstown MD 21136 Office: Villa Julie Coll 1525 Greenspring Valley Rd Stevenson MD 21153-0641

MANNING, LESLIE CARLTON, counselor; b. Chamblee, Ga., Jan. 11, 1952; d. Robert Lee and Ella (Crandall) Carlton; m. Robert Hamer Manning III, Oct. 2, 1971; 1 child, Robert Hamer IV. BA, Francis Marion U., 1977, MS, 1990. Lic. profl. counselor, profl. counselor supr., Master Addiction Counselor Nat. Assn. Alcohol and Drug Counselors, Nat. Cert. Addictions Counselor II Nat. Assn. Alcohol and Drug Counselors. Prevention coord./counselor Dillon (S.C.)/Marion Commn. on Alcohol and Drug Abuse, 1977—79, sch. intervention program coord./counselor, 1979—81, treatment coord./counselor, 1981—83; counselor Dillon Commn. on Alcohol and Drug Abuse, 1984—85; family preservation coord. Tri-County Mental Health, Bennettsville, SC, 1990—92; site mgr./counselor Spring Branch Residential Treatment Ctr., Marion, SC, 1992—94, Dillon Commn. on Alcohol and Drug Abuse, 1994—97; clin. supr. Dillon/Marion Commn. on Alcohol and Drug Abuse, 1997—. Mem. various coms. Recipient Dillon County Young Careerist award, Dillon County Bus. and Profl. Women, 1980. Mem.: S.C. Assn. Alcohol and Drug Counselors (cert. addictions counselor I), Nat. Assn. Alcohol and Drug Counselors. United Methodist. Avocation: reading. Home: 402 W Academy St Latta SC 29565 Office: Marion/Dillon Commn Drug Abuse Marion SC 29571 Office Phone: 843-423-8292.

MANNING, MARTHA MARY, writer, psychologist; b. Chgo., Aug. 18, 1952; d. John Eugene and Mary Louise M.; m. Brian J. Depenbrock, Oct. 20, 1973; 1 child, Keara. BA with high honors, U. Md., College Park, 1974; MA, Cath. Univ. Am., 1978, PhD, 1981. Postdoctoral fellow McLean Hosp./Harvard Med. Sch., Boston, 1981-83; asst. prof. George Mason U., Fairfax, Va., 1983-88; pvt. practice Alexandria, Va., 1994-96. Psychology instr., 1989-93. Author: A Season of Mercy, 1985, Undercurrents: A Life Beneath the Surface, 1995, Chasing Grace, 1996; co-author: Restoring Intimacy: A Patients Guide to Maintaining Relationships During Depression, 1999, All Seasons Pass: Grieving & Miscarriage, 2000; columnist, Salt of the Earth, 1993-96; contbr. to popular mags. including Health, Mirabella, New Woman, Ladies' Home Jour., Glamour, U.S. Cath., N.Y. Times Book Review, Family Therapy Networker, Washington Post. Recipient Merit award Associated Ch. Press, 1994, 96, Best Mag. Column Cath. Press Assn., 1995, Presdl. award for Patient Advocacy, Am. Psychiat. Assn., 1996, Stephen Logan award Nat. Alliance for Mentally Ill. Office: Arielle Eckstut James Levine Comm Inc care FWI 307 7th Ave 1904 New York NY 10001

MANNING, MICHAEL J. lawyer; b. Wichita, Kans., July 18, 1944; BA, U. Kans., 1966; JD, Washburn U., 1969. Bar: Kans. 1969, D.C. 1970. Mem. Fulbright & Jaworski LLP, Washington. Mem. ABA, Fed. Energy Assn., D.C. Bar, Phi Alpha Delta. Office: Fulbright & Jaworski Market Sq 801 Pennsylvania Ave NW Fl 3-5 Washington DC 20004-2623

MANNING, MICHAEL NICHOLAS, actor, singer; b. Cin., Ohio, Apr. 5, 1958; s. Nicholas George and Catherine. BA in psychology, U. Cin., 1999. Regional mktg. and develop. mgr. SCA Wolff Sys., Redmond, Wash., 1986—90; mktg. cons. Manning & Assoc., Dallas, 1990—; news anchor/reporter CBS Westwood One Radio, NYC, 1999—2003, program host prodr., comml. copywriter, scriptwriter, dir. of mktg. and promotions; helicopter traffic reporter WLWT TV5 NBC, Cin.; actor AFTRA, 2003—. Author: (book) No Artificial Flowers During the Mowing Season, 1990; contbg. editor: Airways Mag., 1995—; actor(voice over): (pilot for TV series) When Dreams Come True, 2004,: in numerous commls. Adv. bd. Families for the Rainforest, Carrollton, Tex., 1998—; chmn., pub. rels. Lupus Found of Am. No. Tex. Chpt., Dallas, 1987—93. Recipient vol. svc. award, Talbert Inst., 1980, Nicholson award, Lupus Found. of Am., 1993. Mem.: AFTRA, Pan Am World Airways Hist. Found., Nat. Parkinson's Found.

MANNING, PETER KIRBY, sociologist educator; b. Salem, Oreg., Sept. 27, 1940; s. Kenneth Gilbert and Esther Amelia (Gibbard) M.; m. Victoria Francis Shaughnessy, Sept. 1, 1961 (div. 1981); children— Kerry Patricia, Sean Peter, Merry Kathleen; m. Betsy Cullum-Swan, Aug. 4, 1991 (div. 1997). BA, Willamette U., 1961; MA, Duke U., 1963, PhD, 1966; MA (hon.), Oxford U., Eng., 1983. Instr. sociology Duke U., 1964-65; asst. prof. sociology U. Mo., 1965-66, Mich. State U., East Lansing, 1966-70, assoc. prof. sociology and psychiatry, 1970-74, prof., 1974—; prof. criminal justice, 1993—. Beto chair lectr. Sam Houston State U., 1990; Ameritech lectr. E. Ky. U., 1993; vis. prof. U. Victoria, 1968, MIT, 1982, SUNY, Albany, 1982, U. Mich., 1990—91, York U., Toronto, 1999; vis. sr. scholar Northeastern U. Coll. Criminal Justice, 2001, E.V. and E.M. Brooks chair; cons. Nat. Inst. Law Enforcement and Criminal Justice, U.S. Dept. Justice, Rsch. Triangle Inst., NSF, Nat. Health and Med. Rsch. Coun., Australia, 1980—, Social Sci. Rsch. Coun. Eng., AID, Jamaica, 1991, Sheehy com. Police Pay and Performance, England, 1993. Author: Sociology of Mental Health and Illness, 1975, Police Work, 1977, 2d edit., 1997, The Narcs' Game, 1980, 2d edit., 2003, Semiotics and Fieldwork, 1987, Symbolic Communication, 1988, Organizational Communication, 1992, Private Policing, 1999, Policing Contingencies, 2003, others; also book chpts., articles in profl. jours.; cons. editor series: Principal Themes in Sociology; co-editor Sage Series in Qualitative Methods,Crime, Law and Scoial Change, 204; mem. editl. bd. numerous jours. in social scis. Recipient Bruce Smith Sr. award Acad. Criminal Justice Scis., 1993, O.W. Wilson award, 1997, Charles H. Cooley award Mich. Sociol. Assn., 1994; NDEA fellow, 1962-64, NSF fellow, 1965, fellow Balliol Coll., Oxford U., 1982-83, vis. fellow Wolfson Coll., Oxford U., 1981, 82-83, fellow, 1984-86; Am. Bar Found. rsch. fellow, 1998; Rockefeller resident, Bellagio, Italy, 2000. Mem. Am. Soc. Criminology, Am. Sociol. Assn., Brit. Soc. Criminology, Internat. Sociol. Assn., Midwest Sociol. Soc., Soc. Study Social Problems, Soc. for Study Symbolic Interaction (spl. recognition award 1990, v.p. 1992-93, program chair 1993), Internat. Soc. Semiotics and Law. Office: Northeastern U Coll Criminal Justice Boston MA 02115 E-mail: manningpk@hotmail.com.

MANNING, PEYTON, professional football player; b. Mar. 24, 1976; m. Ashley. Grad., U. Tenn. Quarterback Indpls. Colts, 1998—. Appeared in The Pro Bowl (AFC), 1999, 2000, 02, 03. Named NFL Co-MVP, 2003; recipient Espy Award for Best College Football Player, 1998, Espy Award for Best NFL player, 2004. Achievements include led NFL in completions and passing yards 2000, 2003. Office: Indianapolis Colts PO Box 535000 Indianapolis IN 46253-5000 also: Indianapolis Colts 7001 West 56th Strreet Indianapolis IN 46254*

MANNING, PHYLLIS JANE MEISSNER BRISBY, retired elementary school educator, photographer, writer; b. Omaha, Nebr., Oct. 5, 1931; d. Gustaf Adolphus and Hazel Georgiana (Larkin) Meissner; m. Ivan Lyle Manning, July 2, 1969 (dec.); children: Kent Lee Brisby, Karol Lynne Brisby Saritas. BA, U. Omaha, 1953; MA, U.S. Internat. U., 1973. Cert. Lifetime Elem. Tchr. (K-8) Calif. State Dept. of Edn., 1972, Pupil Pers. K-12 (Lifetime) Calif. State Dept. of Edn., 1975, School Adminstrn. K-12 (Lifetime) Calif. State Dept. of Edn., 1975, Lifetime Secondary Tchr. (7-14) Calif. State Dept. of Edn., 1972. Tchr. of k-8 in rural, one-room schoolhouse Douglas County Pub. Schools, Omaha, 1950—52; elem. classroom tchr. (grades 6-7-8) Omaha Pub. Sch. Dist., 1952—57; classroom tchr. (grades 9-12 + adults) of English, writing, photography Coun. Bluffs Cmty. Sch. Dist., Iowa, 1957—64; classroom tchr. ESL Hopwood H.S., Chalan Kanoa, 1964—66; tchr. trainer U. Hawaii, Oahu and Ponape, 1966—67; curriculum cons. in lang. arts Fed. Project I.M.P.A.C.T., 1967—70; dean, vice-prin., acting prin. Poway Unified Sch. Dist., Calif., 1971—77; asst. supt. activities and info. Internat. Sch. Bangkok, 1977—82; prin. Los Molinos Unified Sch. Dist., Calif., 1982—86, Am. Sch. Milan, 1986—88; supt., prin. Hamilton Union Elem. Sch. Dist., Hamilton City, Calif., 1988—93; free lance writer & photographer Chico, Calif., 1993—. Author: (magazine and newspaper writing) About 40 Articles & Stories, (hist. novel) Kiti on Ice, 2004. Vol. Kirshner Wildlife Found.; cons., test giver Myers-Briggs Personality Type Indicator. Achievements include one of original Iowa City Ten; initiated literacy program, Apple Tree, in deaf education. Personal E-mail: filmafrica40@cs.com.

MANNING, ROBERT HENDRICK, media consultant; b. Soerabaja, Java, Indonesia, Aug. 23, 1941; s. William and Gertrude (Unk) Manning. BS, No. Mich. U., 1974. Lic. master of motor, steam, and sail vessels USCG. Instr. sailing USCG Acad., New London, Conn., 1959-63; dir. audio visual/media svcs. No. Mich. U., Marquette, 1965-93, capt. univ. rsch. vessel, 1977-79, dir. audio visual svcs. emeritus, 1997—; dir. devel. Bresnan Comm. Co., Marquette, 1993-97. Ind. media cons., Marquette, 1969—; comm. cons., 1996—. Host (TV series) Ask the Doctors, Sta. WNMU-TV, 1977—98. Pub. rels. dir. Charter Comm., 2000—02. Mem.: Marquette-Alger County Med. Soc. (hon.; exec. dir. 1975—2000). Avocations: astronomy, navigation, medical history, sailing, amateur radio. Home and Office: PO Box 309 Marquette MI 49855-0309

MANNING, ROBERT JOSEPH, editor; b. Binghamton, N.Y., Dec. 25, 1919; s. Joseph James and Agnes Pauline (Brown) M.; m. Margaret Marinda Raymond, Dec. 28, 1944 (dec. 1984); children: Richard Raymond, Brian Gould, Robert Brown; m. Theresa M. Slomkowski, July 11, 1987. Nieman fellow, Harvard, 1945-46; LittD (hon.), Tufts U., 1966; LHD, St. Lawrence U., 1971. Reporter Binghamton (N.Y.) Press, 1936-41, AP, 1942; State Dept. and White House corr. UPI, 1944-46; chief UN corr. United Press, 1946-49; writer Time mag., 1949-55, sr. editor, 1955-58; chief London bur. Time, Life, Fortune, Sports Illus. mags., 1958-61; Sunday editor N.Y. Herald Tribune, 1961-62; asst. sec. state for pub. affairs Washington, 1962-64; exec. editor Atlantic Monthly, 1964-66, editor-in-chief, 1966-80; v.p. Atlantic Monthly Co., 1966-80; editor-in-chief Boston Pub. Co., 1981-87; pres., editor-in-chief Bobcat Books Inc., Boston, 1987—. Served with AUS, 1942-43. Fellow Kennedy Inst. Politics, Harvard U., 1980. Mem. AAAS, Century Assn. (N.Y.C.), Tavern Club, St. Botolph Club. Home and Office: 1200 Washington St #507 Boston MA 02118 E-mail: bobcat1225@rcn.com.

MANNING, ROBERT THOMAS, physician, educator; b. Wichita, Kans., Oct. 16, 1927; s. Thomas Earl and Mary Francis (Schlegel) M.; m. Jane Bell, July 29, 1949; children: Mary Kay Travers, Phillip Trenton, Susan Ann Shiba. AB, Wichita U., 1950; MD, Kans. U., 1954; DHL, Med. Coll. Hampton Rds., 1991. Diplomate Am. Bd. Internal Medicine. Intern Kansas City (Mo.) Gen. Hosp., 1954-55; resident Kans. U., Kansas City, 1955-58; from asst. prof. to prof. Kans. U. Med. Ctr. Sch. of Medicine, Kansas City, 1958-71, assoc. dean students, 1969-71; dean Eastern Va. Med. Sch., Norfolk, Va., 1971-74, chmn., prof. internal medicine, 1974-77; prof. internal medicine U. Kans. Sch. of Medicine, Wichita, 1977-93; prof. emeritus U. Kans. Sch. Medicine, Wichita, 1993—; assoc. dean, clin. affairs U. Kans. Sch. of Medicine, Wichita, 1985-89; chmn. internal medicine U. Kans. Sch. Medicine, Wichita, 1987—89; pres. Wesley Med. Rsch. Inst., 1986-88. Nat. cons. surgeon gen. USAF, 1973-78. Author: Major's Physical Diagnosis, 9th edit., 1982; contbr. articles to profl. jours. Pres. Kans. Health Ethics, Inc., 1994-96. Served with USAF, 1945-47. Recipient Advanced Achievement award Am. Bd. Internal Medicine, 1987. Fellow ACP (laureate Kans. chpt., bd. govs. Kans. 1984-88); mem. Am. Fedn. Clin. Rsch., Cen. Soc. Clin. Rsch., Am. Assn. Study Liver Disease, Sigma Xi, Alpha Omega Alpha. Presbyterian. Avocations: woodworking, golf. Home: 126 Trail Of The Flowers Georgetown TX 78628-4814

MANNING, SYLVIA, English studies educator; b. Montreal, Que., Can., Dec. 2, 1943; came to U.S., 1967; d. Bruno and Lea Bank; m. Peter J. Manning, Aug. 20, 1967; children— Bruce David, Jason Maurice BA, McGill U., 1963; MA, Yale U., 1964, PhD in English, 1967. Asst. prof. English Calif. State U.-Hayward, 1967-71, assoc. prof., 1971-75, assoc. dean, 1972-75; assoc. prof. U. So. Calif., 1975-94, prof., assoc. dir. Ctr. for Humanities, 1975-77, assoc. dir. Ctr. for Humanities, 1975-77, chmn. freshman writing, 1977-80, chmn. dept. English, 1980-83, vice provost, exec. v.p., 1984-94; prof. English U. Ill., Champaign, 1994—, v.p. for acad. affairs, prof. English, 1994—, interim chancellor Chgo., 1999-2000, chancellor, 2000—. Author: Dickens as Satirist, 1971; Hard Times: An Annotated Bibliography, 1984. Contbr. essays to mags. Woodrow Wilson fellow, 1963-64, 66-67 Mem. MLA, Dickens Soc. Office: U of Ill Office of Chancellor 2833 University Hall 601 S Morgan St Chicago IL 60607-7100

MANNING, WALTER SCOTT, JR., veterinarian; b. Bryan, Tex., Mar. 3, 1945; s. Walter Scott and Eleanor May (Jones) Manning; m. Mary Ann Hurliman, Mar. 11, 0972; children: Adrienne Emily, Walter Scott III. BS, Tex. A&M U., 1967, 76, DVM, 1977, PhD, 1986; MS, East Tex. State Univ., 1972. Mixed practitioner Benton (Ark) Vet. Hosp., 1977-81; vet. clin. assoc. dept. vet. anatomy, Coll. Vet. Medicine Tex. A&M U., College Station, 1981-84; regional animal care specialist USDA Animal and Plant Health Inspection Svc., Regulatory Enforcement Animal Care, Ft. Worth, 1986-89; clin. vet. Alcon Labs., Inc., Ft. Worth, 1989-90, mgr., 1990-94, asst. dir., 1995-98, sr. scientist III, 1998—; enlisted pvt. U.S. Army, 1967, advanced through grades to capt., ret., 2003. Charter orgn. rep. troop 431 Sante Fe Dist. Longhorn Coun., Boy Scouts Am. Decorated Purple Heart. Mem.: SAR, AVMA, Assn. Primate Vets., Tex. br. Lab. Animal Sci., Am. Assn. Lab. Animal Sci., Am. Soc. Lab. Animal Practitioners, Tex. Vet. Med. Assn., Am. Assn. Indsl. Vets., Nat. Eagle Scouts Assn. (past pres. Maj. K. M. Van Zandt bhpt. 1994—96), Phi Eta Sigma, Beta Beta Beta. Presbyterian. Avocations: genealogy, coin collecting/numismatics, photography. Home: 2055 Mary Ann Ln Burleson TX 76028-2229 Office: Alcon Rsch Ltd 6201 South Fwy R3-12 Fort Worth TX 76134-2099 E-mail: scottman@flash.net.

MANNING, WILLIAM FREDERICK, retired wire service photographer; b. Gardner, Mass., Aug. 18, 1920; s. Seth Newton and Jennie May (Bennett) M.; m. Yvonne J.C. Winslow, Feb. 29, 1964; children: Pamela Ann, Jeffrey Newton. AA, Boston U., 1950, BS in Comm., 1952. With AP, Boston, 1951-53; photographer UPI, Boston, 1953-88; ret., 1988. Contbr. photos to books, mags., newspapers throughout the world. Served with USN, 1940-46, PTO. Recipient Look 1st Prize All Sports award, 1958; Pictures of the Yr. award U. Mo., 1964, 74; Nat. Headliners Club award for outstanding syndicate photography, 1974. Mem. Boston Press Photographers Assn., Nat. Headliners Club, Delta Kappa Alpha. Congregationalist. Home: 23 Sunset Dr Beverly MA 01915-2319

MANNING, WILLIAM HENRY, lawyer; b. Dallas, Feb. 5, 1951; BA, Creighton U., 1973; JD, Hamline U., 1978. Bar: Minn. 1978, U.S. Dist. Ct. Minn. 1978, U.S. Ct. Appeals (8th cir.) 1979; cert. civil trial specialist. Spl. asst. atty. gen. Minn. Atty. Gen.'s Office, St. Paul, 1980-83, dir. tort litigation div., 1984-86; ptnr. Robins, Kaplan, Miller & Ciresi, Mpls., 1986—. Office: Robins Kaplan Miller & Ciresi 2800 Lasalle Ave Ste 2800 Minneapolis MN 55402-2015

MANNING, WINTON HOWARD, psychologist, educational administrator; b. St. Louis, Feb. 9, 1930; s. Winton Harry and Jane (Swanson) M.; m. Nancy Mercedes Groves, Aug. 1, 1959; children: Cecelia Groves Tazelaar, Winton H. III. AB with honors, William Jewell Coll., 1951; PhD in Psychology, Washington U., St. Louis, 1959. Instr. psychology William Jewell Coll., Liberty, Mo., 1954-55, asst. prof., acting head dept. psychology, 1955-56; rsch. psychologist Washington U., St. Louis, 1956-58, rsch. assoc., 1958-59; from asst. prof. to prof. psychology Tex. Christian U., Ft. Worth, 1959-65, assoc. dir. univ. honors program, 1962-65; from assoc. dir. rsch. to exec. dir. R & D Coll. Entrance Examination Bd., N.Y.C., 1965-69; from dir. devel. rsch. divsn. to sr. v.p. R & D Ednl. Testing Svc., Princeton, N.J., 1969-83, v.p., 1970-77, sr. v.p. devel. and rsch., 1977-83, sr. scholar, 1983-93; pres. Ednl. Devel. Svc., Princeton, 1993—2000. Vis. fellow Princeton U., 1982-83; cons. Gallup Internat. Inst., 1990—, Applied Ednl. Rsch., 1993-95; cons. Grad. Mgmt. Admissions Coun., 1992-95, Carnegie Found. for the Advancement of Tchg. 1993-95; vis. lectr. Washington U., St. Louis, summer, 1961. Author: The Pursuit of Fairness in Admissions to Higher Education, 1977; Student Manual for Essentials of Psychology, 1960. Contbr. articles on ednl. measurement and psychology of learning to profl. publs. Patentee in field U.S. and Europe. Trustee Assn. for Advancement of Mentally Handicapped, 1975-78, Nat. Chicano Coun. on Higher Edn., 1977-85, N.J. Arts Festival, 1980-85; vice-chmn. Found. for Books to China, 1980-98; chmn. bd. trustees Princeton Day Sch., 1981-93; trustee Princeton Area Found., 1991-94, Our House Found., 1991-92; bd. dirs. The Princeton Singers, 1992-99, Christian Renewal Effort in Emerging Democracies, 1992-94, George H. Gallup Internat. Inst., 1992-98; chmn., trustee Trinity-All Saints' Cemetery, 1993-98; chmn. Affordable Housing Bd. of Princeton Borough, 1987-89; chmn., commr. Princeton Pub. Housing Authority, 1995-99, 2000-03; sr. warden All Saints Episc. Ch., 1987-89; chmn. ins. com. Diocese N.J., 1993-95; coun. mem. Diocese of N.J., 1996-99, 2003—, mem. audit com., 1997-98, mem. standing com., 1998-2002, 03—, mem. fin. com., 2003—; adv. coun. U. Okla. Ctr. for Rsch. on Minority Edn., 1987-92, Ind. Sch. Chmn. Assn., 1987-92; trustee Friends of Princeton Open Space, 1995-98; trustee Russian Ministry Network, 1995-98; cons. Carnegie Found. for Advancement of Tchg., 1987-95; cons. The Coll. Bd., 1988-91; spl. cons. Commn. on Admission to Grad. Mgmt. Edn., 1987-89; chair Princeton Residents Traffic Safety Com., 1994—2002; mem. Princeton Borough Traffic and Transp. Com., 2003—. Recipient Alumni Achievement citation William Jewell Coll., 1970; named Gallup Scholar in Edn., 1995. Fellow Am. Psychol. Soc. (charter), Eastern Psychol. Assn., Psychometric Soc., Nat. Assn. Scholars, Am. Ednl. Rsch. Assn., Nat. Coun. on Measurement in Edn. (mem. com. on legal issues in measurement 1977-79), N.Y. Acad. Scis., Nassau Club, Pendragon Soc., Old Guard of Princeton, Oratory of Good Shepherd, Phi Beta Kappa, Sigma Xi, Order of St. John of Jerusalem (comdr.). Home: 12 Morven Pl Princeton NJ 08540-3024 Office Fax: 609-924-9528. E-mail: win.manning@verizon.net.

MANNINO, EDWARD FRANCIS, lawyer, educator; b. Abington, Pa., Dec. 5, 1941; s. Sante Francis and Martha Anne (Hines) M.; m. Mary Ann Vigilante, July 17, 1965 (div. 1990); m. Antoinette K. O'Connell, June 25, 1993; children: Robert John, Jennifer Elaine. BA with distinction, U. Pa., 1963, LLB magna cum laude, 1966. Bar: Pa. 1967. Law clk. 3d cir. U.S. Ct. Appeals, 1966-67; assoc. Dilworth, Paxson, Kalish & Kauffman, Phila., 1967-71, ptnr., 1972-86, co-chmn. litigation dept., 1980-86, sr. ptnr., 1982-86; sr. prin. Elliott, Mannino & Flaherty, PC, Phila., 1986-90; chmn. Mannino Griffith PC, Phila., 1990-95; sr. ptnr. Wolf, Block, Schorr & Solis-Cohen, Phila., 1995-98; ptnr. Akin, Gump, Strauss, Hauer & Feld LLP, Phila., 1998—. Hearing examiner disciplinary bd. Supreme Ct. Pa., 1986—89, mem. adv. com. on appellate ct. rules, 1989—95; lectr. Temple U. Law Sch., 1968—69, 1971—72; mem. Phila. Mayor's Sci. and Tech. Adv. Com., 1976—79; project mgr. Pa. Environ. Master Plan, 1973; chmn. Pa. Land Use Policy Study Adv. Com., 1973—75; chmn. adv. com., hon. faculty history dept. U. Pa., 1980—85, lectr. Am. history, 2001—. Author: Lender Liability and Banking Litigation, 1989, Business and Commercial Litigation: A Trial Lawyer's Handbook, 1995, The Civil RICO Primer, 1996; mem. editl. bd. Litigation mag., 1985-87, Comm. Lending Litigation News, 1988-2001, Bank Bailout Litigation News, 1989-93, Bus. Torts Reporter, 1988-99, Practical Litigator, 1989—2003, Civil RICO Report, 1991-2001; contbr. articles to profl. jours. Pres. parish coun. Our Mother of Consolation Ch., 1977-79; bd. overseers U. Pa. Sch. Arts and Scis., 1985-89, chmn. recruitment and retention of faculty com.; commonwealth trustee Temple U., 1987-90, audit, bus. and fin. coms. Named one of Nation's Top Litigators Nat. Law Jour., 1990, Pa.'s Top Ten Trial Lawyers, 1999, listed in The Best Lawyers in Am., Am.'s Leading Bus. Lawyers. Fellow Am. Bar Found., ABA (chmn. various coms.), Am. Law Inst., Hist. Soc. U.S. Dist. Ct. Ea. Dist. Pa. (bd. dirs.), Pa. Bar Assn., Phila. Bar Assn. (gov. 1975), Pa. Soc., Order of Coif, Phi Beta Kappa, Phi Beta Kappa Assocs. Democrat. Office: Akin Gump Strauss Hauer Et Al 2005 Market St Fl 22 Philadelphia PA 19103-7014 Office Phone: 215-965-1340. E-mail: emannino@akingump.com.

MANNINO, J. DAVIS, psychologist, educator, author; b. Patchoque, N.Y., Sept. 27, 1949; s. Joseph I. and Adrienne Adele (Davis) M. BA magna cum laude, SUNY, Stony Brook, 1971; MSW summa cum laude, San Francisco State U., 1974; EdD in Counseling and Ednl. Psychology, U. San Francisco, 1989. Lic. psychotherapist, Calif.; lic. clin. social worker, Calif., marriage, family and child counselor. Instr. U. Malaysia, 1974-76; dir. refugee programs City San Francisco, 1979-82; instr. U. San Francisco, 1979-85; pvt. practice specializing in psychology San Francisco, Sonoma Counties, 1979—. Cons. foster care Calif. State Legis., 1980, cmty. rels., San Francisco Police Dept., 1982-87, Hospice Sonoma County, 1990, Sonoma County Mental Health, 1990; forensic task force on AIDS, San Francisco Pub. Health Dept., 1984-85; child abuse investigation supr. City of San Francisco, 1985-88; supr. Reasonable Efforts to Families Unit; project coord. Edna McConnell Clark Found. Family Mediation Demonstration Grant, 1987-88; prof. human sexuality, death and dying, Intro. to Psychology Santa Rosa Jr. Coll., 1990—, chair dept. behavioral scis.; commr. Calif. Bd. Behavioral Sci. Examiners, 1990. Author: Grieving Days, Healing Days, 1997, Sexually Speaking, 1998, Sexual Themes and Variations, The New Millennium, 2000; contbr. articles to profl. jours.; local psychology columnist Art of Caregiving, 1986—. Mem. APA, NASW (diplomate clin. social work), Orthopsychiat. Assn., Am. Assn. Counseling and Devel., Am. Soc. Sex Educators, Counselors and Therapists, Soc. for Sci. Study Sexuality, Calif. Assn. Marriage Family and Child Therapists, Golden Gate Bus. Assn. (ethics com. 1986, Disting. Svc. award, 1985), Am. Assn. Marriage and Family Therapists, Nat. Register Clin. Social Workers, Lions (bd. dirs. San Francisco chpt. 1986). Avocations: running, gym and fitness, writing, gardening. Office: PO Box 2880 Guerneville CA 95446-2880 Office Phone: 707-524-1742. E-mail: psychdavis@aol.com. *Personal philosophy: A life is to be enjoyed not endured. How people get through life is a piece of art not a piece of cake. Everyday is a canvas and our actions brushstrokes, let our brushstrokes be bold each day.*

MANNINO, J(OSEPH) ROBERT, medical educator; b. Altoona, Pa., May 6, 1941; s. Joseph Robert and Helen La Rue (Menza) M.; m. Rosemary Kathleen McGrath, Apr. 8, 1978; 1 child, Angela Christine. BS, Juniata Coll., 1963; MA, East Carolina U., 1965; PhD, Colo. State U., 1974; DO, Kansas City Coll. Osteo. Med., 1971. Diplomate Am. Osteo. Bd. Family Practice. Intern Rocky Mountain Hosp., Denver, 1971-72; physician pvt. practice, Denver, 1972-77; dir. med. edn.nt Kansas City Coll. Osteo. Medicine, 1977-80; prof. family medicine Ohio U. Coll. Osteo. Medicine, Athens, 1981-94, Nova Southeastern U., Coll. Osteo. Medicine, North Miami Beach, Fla., 1994—. Teaching asst. physiology East Carolina U., 1965; coord. rsch. Phila. Coll. Osteo. Medicine, 1966-67; asst. dir. med. edn. Rocky Mountain Hosp., Denver, 1972-73, dir. med. edn., 1975-77, bd. trustees, 1975-77; dir. gen. practice residency Drs. Hosp., Columbus, 1980-94; dir. med. edn. & program dir. family practice residency North Broward Hosp. Dist., Ft. Lauderdale, Fla., 1994-96; clin. assoc. Cleveland Clinic, Ft. Lauderdale, 1996-2000; regional med. dir., Wexfold Health Sources, Ft. Lauderdale, Fla., 2002—; cons. in field. Contbr. articles to profl. jours. Rsch. fellow Colo. State U., 1968-69. Fellow Am. Coll. Osteo. Family Practice, Am. Soc. Colposcopy & Cervical Pathology, Am. Soc. Laser Medicine & Surgery; mem. Am. Osteo. Assn., Am. Coll. Cyrosurgery, N.Y. Acad. Scis., Fla. Soc. Osteo. Medicine, Fla. State Soc. Am. Coll. Osteo. Family Physicians, Broward County Acad. Fla. Soc. Osteo. Medicine, Endocrine Soc., Chi Beta Phi. Republican. Roman Catholic. Avocation: restoring antique cars.

MANNIX, KEVIN LEESE, lawyer, political organization executive; b. Queens, N.Y., Nov. 26, 1949; s. John Warren Sr. and Editta Gorrell M.; m. Susanna Bernadette Chiocca, June 1, 1974; children: Nicholas Chiocca, Gabriel Leese, Emily Kemper. BA, U. Va., 1971, JD, 1974. Bar: Oreg. 1974, U.S. Ct. Appeals (9th cir.) 1976, U.S. Supreme Ct. 1978, Guam 1979. Law clk. to judge Oreg. Ct. Appeals, Salem, 1974-75; asst. atty. gen. Oreg. Dept. Justice, Salem, 1975-77, Govt. of Guam, Agana, 1977-79; judge adminstrv. law Oreg. Workers' Compensation Bd., Salem, 1980-83; assoc. Lindsay, Hart, Neil & Weigler, Portland, Oreg., 1983-86; pres. Kevin L. Mannix Profl. Corp., Salem, 1986—. Chmn. St. Joseph Sch. Bd., Salem, 1981-86; pres. Salem Cath. Schs. Corp., 1985; v.p. Salem Cath. Schs. Found., 1985-88, pres., 1988-90, 91-94, 2000—; pres. bd. dirs. Blanchet Sch., 1995--; vice chair Oreg. Rep. Party, 1998-2000, chair 2003--; state rep., 1989-97, 99-2001; State Senator, 1998-99. Mem. Marion Bar Assn., Rotary (bd. dirs. East Salem 1985-89, pres. 1987-88), KC. Republican. Avocations: photography, scuba diving, travel. Home: 375 18th St NE Salem OR 97301-4307 Office: 2003 State St Salem OR 97301-4349

MANNWEILER, MARY-ELIZABETH, painter; b. Norwood, Ohio, June 23, 1916; d. Wilbur Lawrence Young and Augusta Minnis (Newman) Davis; m. Robert Mays Lang, Sr., May 25, 1940 (dec. July 1981); children: Robert Mays Lang, Jr., Gary Davis Lang, Julianna Elizabeth Lang Crawford; m. Gordon Bannatyne Mannweiler, Apr. 17, 1982(dec. Aug. 2001). Student, Miami U., Oxford, Ohio, 1935-37. Portrait painter; permanent collections; donated (with husband) stained glass window to Congl. Ch., Naugatuck, Conn. Past pres. Athena Club, Freeport, N.Y., Woodbury (Conn.) Women's Club, 1977-78, Watertown (Conn.) Art League; past dir. Waterbury (Conn.) Symphony Orch.; pres. Mannweiler Found., Naugatuck, Conn.; trustee YMCA, Naugatuck; mem. scholarship com. Naugatuck H.S., 2003. Recipient blue ribbons for artwork; Paul Harris fellow Rotary, 2001; music room named in honor of Mr. and Mrs. Mannweiler Conn. Jr. Republic, Litchfield, 1997. Mem. DAR (regent Ruth Floyd Woodhull chpt. 1966-67, pres.). Home: 435 Hillside Ave Naugatuck CT 06770-2727

MANNY, CARTER HUGH, JR., architect, foundation administrator; b. Michigan City, Ind., Nov. 16, 1918; s. Carter Hugh and Ada Gage (Barnes) M.; m. Mary Alice Kellett, Dec. 6, 1942 (dec. Jan. 1994); children: Elizabeth, Carter Hugh III; m. Maya Moran, Dec. 27, 1995. AB magna cum laude, Harvard U., 1941, Indsl. Adminstr., 1942; Taliesin fellow, Scottsdale, Ariz., 1946; BS in Architecture, Ill. Inst. Tech., 1948. With Murphy/Jahn (name formerly Naess & Murphy and C.F. Murphy Assocs.), Chgo., 1948-83, partner, 1957-61; dir. 1st Citizens Bank, Michigan City, Ind., 1970-86; sr. v.p. Murphy/Jahn (name formerly Naess & Murphy and C.F. Murphy Assocs.), 1978-83. Mem. adv. com. on architecture Art Inst. of Chgo., 1982—, oversight com. Ill. Inst. Tech. Sch. of Architecture, Chgo., 1989-94; trustee Graham Found. Advanced Studies in Fine Arts 1956-74, exec. dir., 1972-93, hon. trustee, 1994—. Projects include O'Hare Internat. Airport, Chgo., FBI Hdqrs, Washington, First Nat. Bank Chgo, Chgo. Civic Center, Chgo. Bd. Trade. Fellow AIA (pres. Chgo. chpt. 1973, dir. Ill. council 1972-73), Soc. Archtl. Historians (dir. 1982-85), Chgo. Bldg. Congress (dir. 1978-83); mem. Phi Beta Kappa, Pottawattomie Country Club, Mich. City Yacht Club, Arts Club, Cliff Dwellers Club (Chgo., hon.). Home: 200 Lake Ave Michigan City IN 46360

MANOFF, RICHARD KALMAN, advertising executive, writer, public health service officer, consultant; b. Bklyn., June 24, 1916; s. Kalman and Sarah (Glatman) M.; m. Lucy B. Deutscher, Nov. 27, 1942; children: Robert K., Gregory P. BS, CCNY, 1937, postgrad., 1940. Asst. regional dir. War Manpower Commn., 1942-45; marketing dir. Welch Grape Juice Co., 1949-53; v.p. Kenyon & Eckhardt Advt., N.Y.C., 1953-56; pres., chmn. bd. Richard K. Manoff Inc. Advt., N.Y.C., from 1956; now pres. Manoff Internat. Inc.; spl. adv. mktg. and communications to exec. dir. UNICEF, 1980—. Dir. Thomas J. Lipton, Inc.; adj. prof. dept. health Scis. Sargent Coll. Allied Health Professions, Boston U., 1978—; lectr. pub. health Columbia U. Sch. Medicine, 1982-83; Mem. U.S. del. FAO World Conf., Rome, Italy, 1966; spl. advisor UNICEF and WHO, 1968-78; cons. spl. mission to Food and Agr. Ministry, Govt. India, AID, 1969; Ford Found. offices Pub. Edn. Pub. Broadcasting for children's TV; participant 1st World Conf. on Social Communication for Devel. Mass Communications, Mexico, 1970, 7th Asian Advt. Congress, Delhi, 1970, 3d Western Hemisphere Nutrition Congress, Fla., 1971, Internat. Conf. Nutrition, Nat. Devel. and Planning, Mass. Inst. Tech., 1971, Symposium Eating Patterns and Their Influence on Purchasing Behavior and Nutrition, Nev., 1971, Nutrition Workshop, AID, 1971, 9th Annual Summer Workshop Family Planning, 1971, 4th & 5th Seminar Workshop on Mgmt. and Planning of Population Family Planning Programs, 1971, New Products Symposium, 1971, Communication Seminar series Cornell U., 1971, Exploration The Frontiers of Nutritional Edn. Seminar, 1972, 9th Internat. Congress of Nutrition, Mexico, 1972, East-West Center Comml. Resources Conf. on Family Planning, Hawaii, 1972; Protein adv. group UN Systems Annual Mtg., 1973; mem. panel White House Conf. Food, Nutrition and Health, 1969; mem. Sec.'s Adv. Com. on Population Affairs, Dept. HEW, 1971-76; mem. adv. com. Population Reference Bur., Washington, 1977—, Population Inst., 1980—; mem. Nelson A. Rockefeller's Commn. on Critical Choices for Ams.; cons. HRSA Healthy Start Campaign to reduce infant mortality, 1991; bd. dirs. Population Comm. Internat.; Martin J. Forman Meml. lectr., Washington, 1993. Author: Social Marketing: New Imperative for Public Health, 1985. Bd. dirs. Planned Parenthood World Population, Pathfinder Fund, Boston, 1977-80, United Nutrition Edn. Found., Alexandria, Va., 1978—; mem. com. on internat. nutrition programs NAS-NRC, 1973; founder, mem. Com. for Shakespeare Festival, N.Y.C.; bd. visitors Grad. Sch. and Univ. Ctr., CUNY; mem. adv. bd., cons. to the pres. Henry J. Kaiser Family Found., 1987-91; dir. City Coll. Fund, 1990—. Recipient 5th Ann. Global award for media excellence Population Inst., China, 1985, Townsend Harris medal Alumni Assn. CCNY, 1986. Mem. Am. Assn. Advt. Agys. (gov. 1967—, sec.-treas. 1975—), Population Comms. Internat. (dir. 1992—), Friars Club, Harmonie Club (N.Y.C.), Century Assn. Home: 322 E 57th St New York NY 10022-2949 also: PO Box 1276 14 Donahue Rd Litchfield CT 06759

MANOGUERRA, PAUL ANDREW, curator; b. Daly City, Calif., Nov. 1, 1970; s. Anthony Steven and Margaret Ellen Manoguerra; m. Michelle Darnell, July 10, 1993. BA, U. Notre Dame, 1992; MA, George Washington U., 1994; PhD, Mich. State U., 2002. Curatorial asst. Nat. Firearms Mus., Fairfax, Va., 1992—94; curatorial intern Corcoran Gallery of Art, Washington, 1993—94; dir. of exhibitions/collections Paine Art Ctr. & Gardens, Oshkosh, Wis., 1994—98; tchg. asst., history dept. Mich. State U., East Lansing, 1998—99; adj. prof., humanities Lansing C.C., 1998—2000; grad. asst. Kresge Art Mus., East Lansing, 1999—2000; mus. studies program grad. asst. Mich. State U., East Lansing, 1999—2001; asst. prof., direct encounter with the arts program Western Mich. U., Kalamazoo, 2000—02; vis. instr., history of art Kalamazoo Coll., 2001—02; curator of Am. art Ga. Mus. of Art, Athens, 2002—. Roman Catholic. Office: Ga Mus of Art 90 Carlton St Athens GA 30602 Office Phone: 706-542-0463. E-mail: manoguer@uga.edu.

MANOLIO, TERI A, physician; d. Henry and Mary Jo Manolio. M.D., U. of Md. at Balt., Baltimore, MD, 1976—80; M.H.S., Johns Hopkins Sch. of Pub. Health, Baltimore, MD, 1984—87, Ph.D., 1998—2001. Diplomate Nat. Bd. of Med. Examiners, 1981, Nat. Bd. of Internal Medicine, 1984, License to Practice Medicine Dept. of Health and Mental Hygiene/Md., 1987. Dir., epidemiology and biometry program Nat. Heart, Lung, and Blood Inst., Bethesda, Md., 1994—, med. officer, epidemiology and biometry program, 1987—94. Adj. prof. of preventive medicine and biometrics and clin. prof. of medicine Uniformed Services U. of the Health Sciences, Bethesda, Md., 1987—. Author 105 scientific research presentations, 10 book chapters; contbr. more than 145 sci. rsch. papers to profl. publs. Instr. NIH Tae Kwon Do Club, Bethesda, Md., 1996—2003. Recipient Presdl. Rank Award for Meritorious Svc., Pres., U.S., 2001, Phi Kappa Phi Honor Soc., U. of Md., Coll. Pk., 1974, Phi Beta Kappa Honor Soc., 1976. Fellow: ACP, Am. Heart Assn. Office: National Heart Lung and Blood Institute 6701 Rockledge Drive MSC 7934 Bethesda MD 20892-7934 E-mail: manolio@nih.gov.

MANOLIS, JAMES WILLIAM, lawyer; b. New Castle, Pa., Feb. 19, 1960; s. William and Rose Marie (Moses) M.; m. Rosemary Ritchie, June 24, 1984; children: William James, Nicholas James, Macy Rose. BA, U. Pitts., 1982; JD, U. Dayton, 1986. Bar: Pa. 1986. Assoc. Gamble, Verterano, Mojock, Piccione and Green, New Castle, 1986-91; ptnr. Verterano & Manolis, New Castle, 1991—2004; solicitor City of New Castle, Pa., 1996—2004. Dist. and County reporter, Lawrence County Reporter. Mem. ABA, Pa. Bar Assn., Lawrence County Bar Assn. (treas. 1988—, opinion editor jour. 1988—), Am. Trial Lawyers Assn., Pa. Trial Lawyers Assn. Democrat. Mem. Eastern Orthodox Ch. Home: 301 E Euclid Ave New Castle PA 16105-2622 Office: Verterano & Manolis 2622 Wilmington Rd New Castle PA 16105-1530 Office Phone: 724-652-0300.

MANOOGIAN, RICHARD ALEXANDER, manufacturing executive; b. Long Branch, N.J., July 30, 1936; s. Alex and Marie (Tatian) M.; children: James, Richard, Bridget. BA in Econs, Yale U., 1958. Asst. to pres. Masco Corp., Taylor, Mich., 1958-62, exec. v.p., 1962-68, pres., 1968-85, chmn. bd., CEO, 1985—. Chmn., dir. Mascotech, Inc., Trimas Corp.; dir. First Chgo. NBD Corp., Detroit Renaissance, Am. Bus. Conf. Trustee U. Liggett Sch., State Dept. Fine Arts Comsn., Founder's Soc., Detroit Inst. Arts, Center for Creative Studies; trustee coun. Nat. Gallery Art. Mem. Yale Alumni Assn. Clubs: Grosse Pointe Yacht, Grosse Pointe Hunt, Country Club Detroit, Detroit Athletic. Office: Masco Corp 21001 Van Born Rd Taylor MI 48180-1300

MANOS, CHRISTOPHER LAWRENCE, lawyer, mediator; b. Ft. Bragg, N.C., July 1, 1952; m. B.J. Osmon, June 14, 1974; children: Monica, Kelly. BS, U.S. Mil. Acad., 1974; JD, U. N.D., 1982. Bar: Mont. 1983, U.S. Dist. Ct. (Mont.) 1983, U.S. Ct. Appeals (9th cir.) 1983. Assoc. to ptrn. Moore, O'Connell, Refling & Manos, Bozeman, Mont., 1982-92; ptnr. Biglen & Manos, Big Timber, Mont., 1992—97, Manos law firm; part-time dep. county atty. Sweet Grass county, 1992—98; county atty, 1998—. Trainer for mediators The Settlement Ctr. and Alternative Dispute Resolution Assocs., Bozeman and Palo Alto, Calif., 1990—. Contbr. articles to profl. jours. Bd. dirs. Mont. Pub. TV, Bozeman, 1985-92, Mont. Coun. for Internat. Visitors, Bozeman, 1992; mem. Mont. Stat Bar Dispute Resolution Com., Helena, Mont., 1989—. Capt. U.S. Army, 1974-79. Mem. ABA, State Bar of Mont. (pres. 2001-02), Soc. of Profls. in Dispute Resolution.

MANOS, JOHN, editor-in-chief; Editor-in-chief Consumer's Digest, Chgo., 1987—. Office: Consumer Digest 8001 Lincoln Ave Skokie IL 60077-3695

MANOS, JOHN M. federal judge; b. Cleve., Dec. 8, 1922; m. Viola Manos; 4 children. BS, Case Inst. Tech., 1944; JD, Cleve.-Marshall Coll. Law, 1950. Bar: Ohio 1950. Asst. plant mgr. Lake City Malleable Iron Co., Cleve., 1946-50; atty. Manos & Manos, 1950-63; law dir. City of Bay Village, 1954-56; industries rep. Cleve. Regional Bd. of Rev., 1957-59; judge Ohio Ct. Common Pleas, Cuyahoga County, 1963-69, Ohio Ct. Appeals, Cuyahoga County, 1969-76; sr. judge U.S. Dist. Ct. (no. dist.) Ohio, Cleve., 1976-91, 1991—. With USN, 1942-45. Named Phi Alpha Delta Man of Yr., 1972, Outstanding Alumnus Cleve.- Marshall Law Alumni Assn., 1976. Mem. ABA, Fed. Bar Assn., Ohio State Bar Assn., Nat. Lawyers Club (hon.), Bar Assn. Greater Cleve., Cuyahoga County Bar Assn., Delta Theta Phi (Man of Yr. 1970). Office: US Dist Ct 801 W Superior # 16B Cleveland OH 44113-1841

MANOS, PETE LAZAROS, supermarket executive; b. Washington, Dec. 29, 1936; s. George and Ardemecia (Saranides) M.; m. Barbara Lorraine Isper, July 16, 1960; children— Helene Deborah, Cynthia Denise B. Comml. Sci., Benjamin Franklin U., Washington, 1956, M. Comml. Sci., 1962. C.P.A., Md. Buyer Giant Food Inc., Washington, 1961-63, sr. buyer, 1963-70, mgr., 1970-74, dir., 1974-77, v.p., 1977-81, sr. v.p., 1981-92, pres., 1992-96, chmn., CEO, 1996-99. Pres. Giant Food Fed. Credit Union, Greenbelt, Md., 1980-86. Mem. Prince George's Environ. Trust, Prince George's County, Md., 1969-70; mem. U.S. Selective Svc. bd., Prince George's County, 1974-76; mem. Prince George's Solid Waste Disposal Task Force, 1972-73; chmn. Balt.-Washington Food Industry Friends of Children's Cancer Found., 1988—. With USN, 1956-59. Recipient Disting. Alumni award Ben Franklin U., 1993, George Washington U., 1994, Am. Hellenic Heritage award, 1994. Mem. United Fresh Fruit and Vegetable Assn. (bd. dirs. 1983-86), Product Mktg. Assn. Lodges: Masons. Democrat. Greek Orthodox. Home: 947 Coachway Annapolis MD 21401-6409

MANOS, PETER JOHN, social studies educator, theater director, writer, actor; b. Cleve., Dec. 29, 1960; s. Eli and Katharine Greenman Manos; m. Sandra Kay Manos, Aug. 31, 1986; 1 child, Sean Nicholas Elias. BA in History, McGill U., Montreal, Can., 1983; MA in Social Studies Edn., Lehman Coll., Bronx, N.Y., 1998; post. grad., Ashland Coll., Ohio, 2001, Fresno Pacific U., Calif., 2003—. Cert. tchg. Ohio. Classical music buyer Tower Records, N.Y.C., 1986—97; tchr. history Evander Childs H.S., 1997—98; investigator Cuyahoga County Probate Ct., Cleve., 1998—99; tchr. st. law and govt. John Marshall H.S., 1999—; dir. Brown Theatre Co., 1999—. Pvt. investigator Mansour Gavin, Etc., Cleve., 1980—83; tchg. mentor Cleve. Pub. Schs., 2002—; actor Brown Theatre Co., 1999—, prodr., 1999—; bldg. coord. U.S. Kid's Voting, Cleve., 2002—. Author: (plays) Child's Play, 1987 (Manhattan Punchline award, 1987), Pastoral Symphony, 1990 (Pilgrim award, 1992); adaptor: (plays) The Prisoner of Zenda, 1995. Recipient Best Actor, Montreal Drama Fest, 1983, 2d place, City Shakespeare Competition, 2002, 3d Pl., City Cleve. Mock Trial, 2003; grantee, Paper Mill Playhouse, 1995. Mem.: Dramatists Guild, Actor's Equity Assn., Cleve. Tchrs. Union, Western Res. Hist. Soc., Cleve. Botanical Gardens. Democrat. Avocations: tennis, running, writing, reading, theater. Home: 3667 Avalon Rd Shaker Heights OH 44120 Office: John Marshal HS 3952 W 140 St Cleveland OH 44111 Office Phone: 216-476-4993. E-mail: petermanos216@aol.com.

MANOSEVITZ, MARTIN, psychologist; b. Mpls., June 22, 1938; s. Julius and Ethel (Cohen) M.; m. Carolyn Heather Margulius, Sept. 17, 1959; children— Bradley, Jason. BA, U. Minn., Mpls., 1960, PhD, 1964. Diplomate in clin. psychology, psychoanalysis Am. Bd. Profl. Psychology. Asst. prof. psychology Rutgers U., 1964-67; asst. prof. psychology U. Tex., Austin, 1967-69, assoc. prof., 1969-75, prof., 1975-87; pvt. practice clin. psychology Austin, 1975-99, Aspen, Colo., 1999—. Adj. prof. psychology U. Tex., 1987-93; dir. psychol. svcs. CPC Capital Hosp., Austin, 1987-93, Shoal Creek Hosp., Austin, 1994-99; allied profl. staff Aspen Valley Hosp., 2000—. Trustee Austin-Travis County Mental Health-Mental Retardation Center, 1978-80. Fellow APA (bd. dirs. divsn. psychoanalysis, 1999-2000, membership chmn. 1997-2000, bd. mem. at large 1999-2000, treas. 2003—), Acad. Clin. Psychology, Acad. Psychoanalytic Psychology; mem. Colo. Psychol. Assn., Austin Soc. for Psychoanalytic Psychology (pres. 1994-95), Denver Psychoanalytic Soc. Office: Ste 200 106 S Mill St Aspen CO 81611 Mailing: PO Box 7976 Aspen CO 81612 E-mail: mmanosev@earthlink.net.

MANOUKIAN, ARAM V. gastroenterologist; MD, SUNY, 1984. Diplomate Am. Bd. Internal Medicine and Gastroenterology. Intern Cornell U., Manhasset, NY, 1984—85; resident in internal medicine, 1985—87; fellow in gastroenterology SUNY Sch. Med., Stony Brook, 1987—89; assoc. therapeutic endoscopy/ERCP St. Luke's Digestive Disease Ctr., Racine, Wis., 1991—92; assoc. prof. medicine divsn. gastroenterology and hepatology Robert Wood Johnson U. Med. Sch., New Brunswick, NJ, 1992—, assoc. dir. endoscopy, 1992—. Office: Robert Wood Johnson U Med Group Clinical Acad Bldg 125 Paterson St Ste 5100B New Brunswick NJ 08901-1977

MANOUS, PETER J. lawyer; m. Susan Severtson Manous. BS in pub. adminstrn. & mgmt., Ind. Univ., 1984; law degree, Valparaiso U., 1987. Bar: Ind. State Bar Assn. Pvt. atty., 1994—; coord. Frank O'Bannon's Campaign, 1996—2000; adv. Governor Residence Commn. Bd. dirs. Lake Area United Way; past pres. Millennium Housing Found.; Lake County Welfare to Work Coun.; mem. N.W. Ind. Quality Life Coun.; bd. dirs. Tradewinds; mem. Ind. Dem. Party Deputy Chairmen; regional coord. Evan Bayh U.S. Senate; vol. Kennedy for Pres. Campaign, 1980; mem. St. George Greek Orthodox Ch. Mem.: Am. Bar Assn., Lake County Bar Assn. Democrat. Office: 9111 Broadway Ste GG Merrillville IN 46410

MANOWITZ, PAUL, biochemist, researcher, educator; b. Monticello, NY, Dec. 13, 1940; s. Jacob M. and Rose (Levine) M.; m. Joyce L. Swartz, June 16, 1968; children: Neal J., Lauren H. BA in Chemistry with honors, Cornell U., 1962; PhD in Biochemistry, Brandeis U., 1967. Fellow NYU Sch. Medicine, 1967-70, instr., 1970-72; asst. prof. psychiatry U. Medicine and Dentistry N.J. Robert Wood Johnson Med. Sch., Piscataway, 1972-78, assoc. prof. psychiatry, 1978-96, prof. psychiaty, 1996—. Rsch. cons. VA Med. Ctr., Lyons, N.J., 1987—. Mem. editl. bd. Jour. of Studies on Alcohol, 1993—2003; contbr. articles to profl. jours. Mem. AAAS, Internat. Soc. for Biomed. Rsch. on Alcoholism, Am. Soc. Human Genetics, Am. Soc. Neurochemistry, Soc. Biol. Psychiatry, Rsch. Soc. on Alcoholism. Home: 7 Guernsey Ln East Brunswick NJ 08816-3506 Office: U Medicine and Dentistry NJ Robert Wood Johnson Med Sch 671 Hoes Ln Piscataway NJ 08854-5627 Office Phone: 732-235-4347.

MANROSS, MARY, mayor; m. Larry; 4 children. BS in Polit. Sci. Mayor City of Scottsdale, Ariz., 2000—. Mem. Scottsdale (Ariz.) City Coun., 1992—. Chmn. Scottsdale (Ariz.) Parks and Recreation Commn., Maricopa Assn. Govts. Youth Policy Adv. Com.; bd. dirs. Ariz. Women in Mcpl. Govt.; mem. Planning Commn.; vice chmn. Scottsdale Bond Com.; mem. Sub-com. TPC-Westworld, City Ct., C. of C./Econ. Devel.; mem. Govs. Task Force on Urban Planning, Ariz. Town Hall, Nat. League of Cities Energy, Environment and Nat. Resource Policy Com.; mem. steering com. NLC Transp., Infrastructure and Svcs. Address: 3939 N Drinkwater Blvd Scottsdale AZ 85251-4433 Office: City Hall 3939 N Drinkwater Blvd Scottsdale AZ 85251-4433

MANSELL, DARREL LEE, JR., English educator; b. Canton, Ohio, Apr. 9, 1934; s. Darrel Lee and Virginia (Shepherd) M.; m. Elizabeth Meihack, Jan. 1957 (div. July 1970); 1 child, Benjamin Lloyd; m. Adriana Saviane, July 16, 1983. BA, Oberlin Coll., 1956; student, Oxford U., 1961—62; PhD, Yale U., 1963; MA (hon.), Dartmouth Coll., 1975. Instr. Dartmouth Coll., Hanover, NH, 1962-64, asst. prof., 1964-68, assoc. prof., 1968-74, prof., 1974-99, prof. emeritus, 1999—. Author: The Novels of Jane Austen, 1973; contbr. articles to scholarly jours. Mem. Jane Austen Soc. N.Am. (founding patron), Phi Beta Kappa. Home: 2 Dana Rd Hanover NH 03755-2227 Office: Dartmouth Coll Dept English Hanover NH 03755 E-mail: darrel.mansell@dartmouth.edu.

MANSELL, JOYCE MARILYN, retired special education educator; b. Minot, N.D., Dec. 17, 1934; d. Einar Axel and Gladys Ellen (Wall) Alm; m. Dudley J. Mansell, Oct. 31, 1954; children: Michael, Debra Mansell Richards. BS, U. Houston, 1968; MEd, Sam Houston State U., 1980. Cert. provisional elem. tchr. 1-8, provisional mentally retarded tchr., provisional lang. and/or learning disabilities tchr., profl. elem. tchr. gen. 1-9, reading specialist. From 1st grade tchr. to 3rd grade tchr. Johnson Elem. Sch., 1968-77; spl. edn. tchr. mentally retarded/learning disabled Meml. Parkway Jr. HS, 1982-86, Waller Mid. Sch., 1986-90; spl. edn. tchr. mentally retarded Royal Mid. Sch., Tex., 1990-95, Royal HS, 1995-96; ret., 1996. Tchr. Am. sign lang. for retarded students in pub. schs. Lutheran. Avocations: painting, bridge, reading, fishing, travel, watercolor painting. Home: 2155 Paso Rello Dr Houston TX 77077-5622

MANSELL, KEVIN B. retail executive; Sr. exec. v.p. merchandising and mktg. Kohl's Corp., Menomonee Falls, Wis., pres., also bd. dirs. Office: Kohl's Corp N 56 W 17000 Ridgewood Dr Menomonee Falls WI 53051

MANSELL, L. ALMA, state legislator; b. Midvale, Utah, Jan. 23, 1944; m. Margurite Mansell. Student, U. Utah. Lic. real estate broker. Real estate broker; mem. Utah Senate, Dist. 10, Salt Lake City, 1994—; asst. majority whip Utah Senate, 1999—2000; mem. legis. mgmt. com., state and local affairs com.; co-chair econ. devel. and human resources appropriations; pres. Utah Senate, 2003—. Mem. Salt Lake Bd. Realtors (pres. 1983, Realtor of Yr. 1986), Utah Assn. Realtors (pres. 1990, Realtor of Yr. 1988, Pres.'s award 1992), Nat. Assn. Realtors (v.p. 1992), Sandy Rotary Club (past pres.). Republican. Office: 6995 Union Park Ctr Ste 100 Midvale UT 84047-4135

MANSEN, STEVEN ROBERT, manufacturing executive; b. Chgo., Nov. 26, 1955; s. Robert Lee and Dorothy Nora (Nichols) M.; m. Leesa mansen, May 7, 1988; children: Ambur, Christopher. B in Indsl. Adminstrn., Gen. Motors Inst., 1978. Data processing sys. analyst in traffic Gen. Motors Corp., Oklahoma City, 1979-81, premium freight sys. coord., rate analyst in traffic, 1981-83; sr. mfg. sys. analyst Tech. Oil Tool Co. divsn. Baker Internat., Norman, Okla., 1983-86; v.p. mgmt. infosys. W. Pat Crow Forgings, Inc., 1986-88; material mgr. Aerospace Techs. Inc. divsn. Alco Standard Group, Ft. Worth, 1988-89; mgr. infosys. Wynn-Kiki divsn. Diesel-Kiki (now Zexel Tex., Inc. divsn. Zexel Corp.), Grand Prairie, 1989-98; ind. systems implementation cons., 1998; MIS/material mgr. Spray Booth Sys., Inc., Ft. Worth, 1999—2002; gen. mgr. Customized Computer Svcs. Inc., Arlington, Tex., 2003—. Pres. Emerald Park Neighborhood Assn., 1997—, treas. 2000. Mem. S.W. States ASK Users Group (v.p. 1984-86, pres. 1986, Hewlett Packard liaison 1992), Camus. Home: 2214 Diamond Point Dr Arlington TX 76017-4517 Office: 109 W Randol Mill Arlington TX 76011

MANSFIELD, CARL MAJOR, radiation oncology educator; b. Phila., Dec. 24, 1928; m. Sarah Lynn Flower; children: Joel, Kara. AB in Chemistry, Lincoln U., 1951; postgrad., Temple U., 1952; MD, Howard U., 1956, ScD (hon.), Lincoln U., 1991. Diplomate Am. Bd. Radiology, Am. Bd. Nuclear Medicine. Rotating intern Episcopal Hosp., Phila., 1956-57, resident in radiology, 1957-58, 60, 61-62; resident in radiation therapy and nuclear medicine Thomas Jefferson Med. Coll. Hosp., Phila., 1960-61, NIH fellow in radiation therapy and nuclear medicine, 1962-63, instr. radiology, chief div. nuclear medicine, 1964-65, Chernicoff fellow in pediatric radiation therapy, 1964-66, assoc. in radiology, chief div. nuclear medicine, 1966-67, asst. prof. radiology, chief div. nuclear medicine, 1967-69, assoc. prof. dept. radiation therapy and nuclear medicine, chief sect. of ultrasound, 1970-74, prof., chief div. nuclear medicine and sect. of ultrasound, 1974-76, prof., chmn. dept. radiation therapy and nuclear medicine, 1983-95; assoc. dir. divsn. cancer treatment Nat. Cancer Inst. NIH, Bethesda, Md., 1995-97; prof., chmn. dept radiation oncology U. Md., Balt., 1997—. NIH postdoctoral fellow in radiation therapy Middlesex Hosp. and Med. Sch., London, 1963-64; lectr. in radiology U. Pa. Sch. Medicine, Phila., 1967-73; vis. prof. radiation therapy and nuclear medicine Hahnemann Med. Coll. Hosp., 1971; sabbatical leave Myerestein Inst. Radiotherapy, Middlesex Hosp. and Med. Sch., London, 1972-73; mem. grad. faculty in radiation biophysics U. Kans. Med. Ctr., Kansas City, 1977-83, prof., chmn. dept. radiation therapy, 1976-83; chmn. dept. radiation therapy Menorah Med. Ctr., Kansas City, Mo., 1977-83. Author 2 books, also author or co-author over 129 articles in med. jours. Served with USAF, 1958-60. Fellow Am. Coll. Radiology, Coll. Physicians of Phila., Am. Coll. Nuclear Medicine; mem. AMA, Am. Coll. Radiology, Am. Cancer Soc. (dir.-at-large, nat. bd. dirs. 1981-85, med. and sci. com. 1981-88, profl. edn. com. 1981-88, pres. Phila. divsn. 1989), Am. Radium Soc. (pres. 1988), Radiation Rsch. Program Nat. Cancer Inst. (dir.), Sigma Xi. Office: U Md Med Sys 22 S Greene St Baltimore MD 21201-1544 E-mail: cmansfiel@QIS.net.

MANSFIELD, CHRISTOPHER CHARLES, insurance company legal executive; b. 1950; married. BA, Boston Coll., 1972, JD, 1975. With Liberty Mut. Ins. Co., Boston, 1975—, v.p., 1983, sr. v.p., gen. counsel, 1983—; underwriter Liberty Lloyds of Tex. Ins. Co., 1984-94; v.p., dir. Liberty Ins. Corp., 1985—; v.p. Liberty Mut. Fire Ins. Co., 1985—; v.p., gen. counsel LEXCO Ltd., 1986—; sr. v.p., gen. counsel Liberty Mut. Capital Corp., 1986—. Bd. dirs. Liberty Mut. Ins. Co., Liberty Fin. Cos., Liberty Mut. Bermuda, Liberty Internat., Employers Ins. Wausau, Golden Eagle Ins. Corp., Wausau Gen. Ins. Co., Pine Street Inn; bd. overseers Rand Inst. Civil Justice, 2002--. Office: Liberty Mut Ins Co PO Box 140 175 Berkeley St Boston MA 02117-5066

MANSFIELD, EDWARD PATRICK, JR., advertising executive; b. Warren, Pa., Oct. 29, 1947; s. Edward Patrick and Frieda (Dahler) M.; m. Norma L. Johnson, Apr. 17, 1971. AS in Acctg., Jamestown Bus. Coll., 1967; BS in Mktg. Advt., Myers U., 1970. Promotion mgr., ad dir. The News-Herald, Lake County, Ohio, 1973-77; dir. advt. The Eagle, Butler, Pa., 1977-78; dir. mktg. Baltimore Mag., 1978-79; dir. advt. The Washingtonian, Washington, 1979—. Founder, chmn. Warm-A-Heart Fund, 1988—; bd. dirs. Columbia Lighthouse for the Blind, 1988—, chmn., 1988-93; bd. dirs. The Lighthouse; mem. adv. bd. Ann Arundel County Mental Health. Avocations: amateur radio operator gen. class, sailing. Home: 347 Cottswold Pl Riva MD 21140-1528 Office: Washingtonian Mag 1828 L St NW Ste 200 Washington DC 20036-5169 Office Phone: 202-296-3600. Business E-Mail: emansfield@washingtonian.com.

MANSFIELD, ELAINE SCHULTZ, molecular geneticist, automation specialist; b. Boulder, Colo., Apr. 20, 1954; d. William Varley and Juanita M. (Zingg) M.; m. Gary G. Schultz, Nov. 24, 1983; children: Matthew, Greggory Mark. BA in Molecular Biology, San Jose State U., 1975; MS in Genetics, U. Calif., Berkeley, 1978, PhD in Genetics, 1983. Diplomate Am. Bd. Med. Genetics (fellow), Am. Bd. Clin. Molecular Genetics. Customer cons. IntelliGenetics, Mountain View, Calif., 1983-86; staff scientist Applied Biosys., Foster City, Calif., 1986-93; sr. staff scientist Molecular Dynamics, Sunnyvale, Calif., 1993-98; dir. pharmacogenomics diaDexus, LLC, Santa Clara, Calif., 1998-99; prin. scientist Aclara Bio Sci., Mountain View, 1999—. Lectr. in the field. Author (with others) Mutations in the Human Genome, 1993; contb. to profl. jours.; patentee in field. U. Calif. grantee, Chancellors Patent Fund grantee U. Calif., NIH SBIR grantee, 1995-99. Mem. AAAS, Am. Soc. Human Genetics, Am. Soc. Histocompatibility and Immunogenetics, Women in Sci., Black Masque (pres. 1975). Avocations: skiing, quilting. Office: Aclara Bio Sci 1288 Pair Ave Mountain View CA 94043

MANSFIELD, GORDON HALL, federal agency administrator; BA, Villanova U., 1964; JD, U. Miami, 1973. Commd. U.S. Army, 1964, co. comdr. 101st Airborne Divsn.; lawyer Ocala, Fla.; various positions including assoc. exec. dir. govt. rels. Paralyzed Vets. Am., 1981—89, exec. dir., 1993—2001; asst. sec. fair housing and equal opportunity U.S. Dept. Housing and Urban Devel., 1989—93; asst. sec. congl. and legis. affairs U.S. Dept. Vets. Affairs, Washington, 2001—04, dep. sec., vets. affairs, 2004—. Decorated Bronze Star, Purple Heart (2), Combat Infantryman's badge, Presdl. Unit Citation. Office: US Dept Vets Affairs 810 Vermont Ave NW Rm 1004 Washington DC 20420*

MANSFIELD, JAMES E. marketing professional, consultant; b. Phila., Feb. 15, 1973; s. James E. and Mary T. M.; m. Heather L. Creps, Sept. 9, 2000. BS in Biology, Villanova U., 1994; MBA, U. Chgo., 1999. Mktg. rep. Johnson & Johnson/Janssen Pharms., Titusville, N.J., 1995-96, sales rep. Chgo., 1996-97, hosp. specialist, 1997-98; mgr. Knoll Pharm., Chgo., 1998-99; dir., client mgmt. IMS Health, Chgo., 1999—. Bd. dirs. Am. Cancer Soc., 1996-99. E-mail: jmansfield@us.imshealth.com.

MANSFIELD, KAREN LEE, lawyer; b. Chgo., Mar. 17, 1942; d. Ralph and Hilda (Blum) Mansfield; children: Nicole Rafaela, Lori Michele. BA in Polit. Sci., Roosevelt U., 1963; JD, DePaul U., 1971; student U. Chgo., 1959-60. Bar: Ill. 1972, U.S. Dist. Ct. (no. dist.) Ill. 1972. Legis. intern Ill. State Senate, Springfield, 1966-67; tchr. Chgo. Pub. Schs., 1967-70; atty. CNA Ins., Chgo., 1971-73; law clk. Ill. Apellate Ct., Chgo., 1973-75; sr. trial atty. U.S. Dept. Labor, Chgo., 1975—, mentor Adopt-a-Sch. Program, 1992-95. Contbr. articles to profl. jours. Vol. Big Sister, 1975-81; bd. dirs. Altgeld Nursery Sch., 1963-66, Ill. div. UN Assn., 1966-72, Hull House Jane Addams Ctr., 1977-82, Broadway Children's Ctr., 1986-90, Acorn Family Entertainment, 1993-95; active Oak Park Farmers' Market Commn., 1996-2002; rsch. asst. Citizens for Gov. Otto Kerner, Chgo., 1964; com. mem. Ill. Commn. on Status of Women, Chgo., 1964-70; del. Nat. Conf. on Status of Women, 1968; candidate for del. Ill. Constl. Conv., 1969. Mem. Chgo. Council Lawyers, Women's Bar Assn. Ill., Lawyer Pilots Bar Assn., Fed. Bar Assn. Unitarian. Clubs: Friends of Gamelan (performer), 99's Internat. Orgn. Women Pilots (legis. chmn. Chgo. area chpt. 1983-86, legis. chmn. North Cen. sect. 1986-88, legis. award 1983, 85). Home: 204 S Taylor Ave Oak Park IL 60302-3307 Office: US Dept Labor Office Solicitor 230 S Dearborn St Fl 8 Chicago IL 60604-1505

MANSFIELD, LORRAINE J. lawyer; JD, U. Wyo., 1979. Bar: Wyo. 1979, Nev. 1981, U.S. Ct. Appeals (10th cir.) 1980, U.S. Ct. Appeals (9th cir.) 1983, U.S. Ct. of Claims, 1990, U.S. Supreme Ct. 1985. Law clk. Wyo. Supreme Ct., Laramie, 1980; sole practitioner law Las Vegas, 1981—. Arbitrator 8th Jud. Cir., Las Vegas, 1992—. Contbr. articles to profl. jours. Avocation: sailing. Office: Mansfield Law Office 6655 W Sahara Ave # B 200 Las Vegas NV 89146

MANSI, JOSEPH ANNEILLO, public relations company executive; b. Oct. 8, 1935; s. Joseph C. and Vinnie (Chirico) M.; m. Mary P. Fusco, Aug. 1, 1959; children: Karen M. D'Attore, Jeanine V. Dimenna. BS, NYU, 1957. Newsman Internat. News Service, UPI, 1953-58; mem. pub. relations staff Lawrence Orgn., N.Y.C., 1960-63; acct. supr. Philip Lesly Co., N.Y.C., 1963-67; dir. corp. communications Ward Foods, Inc., N.Y.C., 1967-72; dir. pub. relations Metromedia Inc., N.Y.C., 1973-75; pres. Corp. Relations Network, Inc., N.Y.C., 1975-80; mng. ptnr. KCSA Pub. Rels. Worldwide, N.Y.C., 1980—. Served with AUS, 1958-60. Mem. Pub. Rels. Soc. Am. (accredited). Home: 10 Beatrice Ln Glen Cove NY 11542-1202 Office: KCSA Pub Rels Worldwide 800 2nd Ave New York NY 10017-4709 E-mail: jmansi@kcsa.com.

MANSKE, PAUL ROBERT, orthopedic hand surgeon, educator; b. Ft. Wayne, Ind., Apr. 29, 1938; s. Alfred R. and Elsa E. (Streufert) M.; m. Sandra H. Henricks, Nov. 29, 1975; children: Ethan Paul, Claire Bruch, Louisa Hendricks. BA, Valparaiso U., 1960, DSc (hon.), 1985; MD, Washington U., St. Louis, 1964. Diplomate Am. Bd. Surgery. Intern U. Wash., Seattle, 1964-65, resident in surgery, 1965-66; resident in orthopedic surg. Washington U., St. Louis, 1969-72; hand surgery fellow U. Louisville, 1971; instr. orthopedic surgery Washington U. Med. Sch., St. Louis, 1972-76, asst. prof. orthopedic surgery, 1976-83, prof., 1983—, chmn. dept., 1983-95. Editor-in-chief Jour. Hand Surgery, 1996—, contbr. over 215 articles to profl. jours. Lt. comdr. USN, 1966-69, Vietnam. Fellow AMA, Am. Acad. Orthopaedic Surgery, Am. Orthopaedic Assn.; mem. Am. Soc. Surgery of the Hand, Alpha Omega Alpha. Office: Washington Univ Dept Orthop Surgery 1 Barnes Hospital Plz Saint Louis MO 63110-1036

MANSMANN, PARIS TAYLOR, medical educator; b. Pitts., Feb. 19, 1957; s. Herbert Charles Jr. and Margaret Marshal (Miller) M.; m. Leslie Ann Windstein, July 8, 1978; children: Erin Hart, Paris Corey, Maureen Ellyse. Student, Lafayette Coll., 1975-76; BS in Math., St. Joseph's U., Phila., 1980; MD, Jefferson Med. Coll., 1984. Diplomate Am. Bd. Medicine, Am. Bd. Internal Medicine, Am. Bd. Pediatrics, Am. Bd. Allergy and Immunology. Resident in medicine, pediatrics Geisinger Med. Ctr., Danville, Pa., 1984-88, chief resident, 1987-88; fellow in allergy, immunology Duke U. Med. Ctr., Durham, N.C., 1988-90; asst. prof. medicine and pediat. W.Va. U., Morgantown, 1990-93, asst. prof. medicine, 1990-95, assoc. prof. medicine, 1995-2000; clin. assoc. prof. medicine and pediat. U. New Eng., U. Vt., 2000—. Program coord. medicine, pediat., W.Va. U., Morgantown, 1990-93. Author: (with others) Current Pediatric Therapy, 1994; contbr. articles to profl. jours. Recipient Outstanding Commitment award Vis. Clinicians, 1990. Fellow Am. Acad. Pediatrics, Am. Coll. Allergy and Immunology, ACP, Am. Acad. Allergy and Immunology, European Acad. Allergy and Clin. Immunology, W.Va. Allergy Soc. (pres. 1992—). Republican. Roman Catholic. Avocations: fishing, farming, cross country skiing, soccer. Office: Shearwater Allergy Sch Medicine PO Box 1298 Yarmouth ME 04096 also: 9 Royal River Ctr Yarmouth ME 04096 E-mail: pmansba@aol.com.

MANSOLILLO, CHARLES RONALD, lawyer; b. Mar. 8, 1949; s. Nicholas William and Adeline Ann Marie (Marcello) Mansolillo. BA, St. Michael's Coll., 1971; postgrad., Weston Jesuit Sch. Theology, 1997—99; JD, Suffolk U., 1985. Mem. Ho. Reps. State of R.I., Providence, 1973—75; city councilman City of Providence, 1975—83, chief of staff Mayor's office, 1983—84; legal counsel Dept. Children and Families State of R.I., 1987—88; dir. govs. Office Housing, Energy and Intergovtl. Rels., 1989—90; dir. Govs. Policy Office, 1990—91; dep. city solicitor City of Providence, 1991—92, city solicitor, 1992—2003, city solicitor emeritus, 2003—. Mem. exec. bd. R.I. League Cities and Towns, 1979—84; mem. Providence Home Rule Charter Commn., 1979—80, Narragansett Bay Commn., 1980—83. Bd. dirs. Providence Indsl. Devel. Corp.; trustee Providence Pub. libr., 1979—87; chmn. bd. dirs. Providence Cmty. Action Program, Inc., 1975—84; nominee Rep. Mayor Providence, 1986. Roman Catholic. Home: 6 Rockland Ave Cranston RI 02910

MANSON, ANNE, music director; Grad., Harvard U.; postgrad., King's Coll., London, Royal Coll. Music, Royal Northern Coll. Music; studied with Norman Del Mar, James Lockhart. Music dir. Kansas City (Mo.) Symphony, 1998—. Condr. Mecklenburgh Opera, 1991, Endymion Ensemble, 1992-93, London Mozart Players, 1993-94, BBC Scottish Symphony and Iceland Symphony Orch., 1994-95, Northern Sinfonia, Resedentie Orch. in The Hague, Ensemble Inter Contemporain, Paris, 1996-97, Bournemouth Symphony Orch., Royal Scottish Nat. Orch., 1997-98. Dir. operas The Emperor of Atlantis, Die Weisse Rose, Manekiny, Hansel and Gretel, Marriage of Figaro, Cosi fan Tutte, The Magic Flute, Il Combattimento, Echoes, Royal Opera House, Don Pasquale, Don Giovanni, English Touring Opera, House of the Dead, Salzburg Festival, Lohengrin, Blood Wedding, 1992-93, Petrified, The Place Theatre, London, 1992, Brundibar, Queen Elizabeth Hall, London, 1993, Craig's Progress, 1994, Boris Godunov, Vienna State Opera, 1994, Vanessa, 1994-95, Rise and Fall of the City of Mahagonny, Netherlands Touring Opera, 1996, Dangerous Liaisons, Washington Opera, 1997, Voices, Berlin Biennale, 1997-98. Marshall scholar Royal Coll. Music; Conducting fellow Royal Northern Coll. Music. Office: Kansas City Symphony 1020 Central St Ste 300 Kansas City MO 64105-1663

MANSON, HAROLD CRAIG, federal agency administrator; b. Mo. Grad., USAF ACad.; JD, U. of the Pacific. Asst. sec. Fish, Wildlife and Parks U.S. Dept. Interior, Washington, 2002—. Faculty McGeorge Sch. Law, 1992—. With USAF, with Air Nat. Guard. Office: US Dept Interior Fish Wildlife and Parks 1849 C St NW Washington DC 20240

MANSON, JOANN ELISABETH, endocrinologist; b. Cleve., Apr. 14, 1953; d. S. Stanford and Therese (Palay) M.; m. Christopher N. Ames, June 12, 1979; children: Jennifer, Jeffrey, Joshua Simon. AB magna cum laude, Harvard U., 1975; MD, Case Western Res. U., 1979; MPH, Harvard Sch. Pub. Health, 1984, DPH, 1987. Bd. cert. internal medicine; bd. cert. in subspecialty of endocrinology and metabolism. Intern and resident internal medicine NEDH, Harvard Med. Sch., Boston, 1979-82; fellowship in endocrinology U. Hosp. Boston, Mass., 1982-84; rsch fellow in medicine Brigham and Women's Hosp., Boston, 1984-87, Andrew W. Mellon Found. fellow, 1987-89; dir. endocrinology, co-dir. women's health Brigham and Women's Hosp., Divsn. Preventive Medicine, Boston, 1993—; chief Divsn. Preventive Medicine Brigham and Women's Hosp., Boston, 1999—; staff physician, consulting endocrinologist Harvard Vanguard Med. Assocs., Peabody, Mass., 1986—; prof. medicine Harvard Med. Sch., Boston, 1999—; Elizabeth Brigham prof. women's health, 2003—. Mem. editl. bd. Am. Jour. Preventive Medicine, 1992—, Jour. Women's Health, 1996—; author textbooks and monographs; contbr. more than 400 articles to profl. jours. Vol. physician Lynn (Mass.) Shelter for the Homeless, 1989-93; med. adv. bd. Harvard Health Letter, Boston, 1992—, Greater Boston (Mass.) Diabetes Soc., 1993—, Harvard Women's Health Watch, Boston, 1993—; vol. Am. Heart Assn., 1992—. Named Hero in Women's Health, Am. Health for Women Mag., 1997, one of Top 10 Champions of Women's Health, Ladies Home Jour., 2000, one of Top Docs for Women. Boston mag., 2001; recipient Connors award for outstanding leadership in women's health, 1999-, Woman in Sci. award, Am. Med. Women's Assoc., 2003, Henry I. Bowditch award for excellence in pub. health Mass. Med. Soc., 2002. Fellow ACP, ACE; mem. AMA, Am. Med. Women's Assn., Am. Heart Assn., Women's Health Initiative (mem. steering com.), Alpha Omega Alpha. Avocations: playing with my children, reading, hiking, music, travel. Home: 14 Washington St Beverly MA 01915-5820 Office: Brigham and Women's Hosp 900 Commonwealth Ave E Fl 3 Boston MA 02215-1204 Office Phone: 617-278-0871. Business E-Mail: jmanson@rics.bwh.harvard.edu.

MANSON, JOSEPH LLOYD, III, lawyer; b. Richmond, Va., May 5, 1949; s. Joseph Lloyd Jr. and Nan Smith (Copley) M.; children: Martha Stuart, Joseph Scott, Rachel Smith. BS, U. Va., 1970; JD, Emory U., 1974. Assoc. Verner, Liipfert, Bernhard & McPherson, Washington, 1974—80; ptnr. Verner, Liipfert, Bernhard, McPherson & Hand, 1981—2002, co-chmn. exec. com., 1998—2001; ptnr. Piper, Rudnick, 2002—. Pres., CEO, bd. dirs. Barrow Grocery Co., DBM Group. Founder Alexandria Youth Sports Found., 1993; bd. govs. St. Stephens and St. Agnes Sch., Emory U. Law Sch. Coun.; bd. dirs. Mesa Air Group; trustee St. Stephens and St. Agnes Sch. Found. 2d lt. U.S. Army, 1973. Mem. ABA (ry. and airline labor law com., co-chmn. mgmt. 1993-94), D.C. Bar Assn. Republican. Episcopalian. Avocations: music, tennis, theater, movies. Office: Piper Rudnick 1200 Nineteenth St NW Washington DC 20036-2412

MANSON, LEWIS AUMAN, energy research executive; b. Cleve., July 12, 1918; s. Lewis Frederick and Ina Josephine (Auman) M.; m. Alva Anne London, Sept. 3, 1960 (div. 1982); children: Anita, Howard; m. Shirley Anne Traeger, Jan. 27, 1982; children: Lewis, Jean, Phillip, Edward. Student, Gen. Motors Tech. U., 1943-44, Purdue U., 1942-43, Rice U., 1950-54. Cons. numerous oil, gas, and mining cos., 1951-57; cons. The Space Agy., Washington, 1958-59, Douglas Aircraft, El Segundo, Calif., 1964; dir. Copper Range Mines, Wyo., 1965; dir. explorations, cons. Nico Internat., S.A. de C.V., Mex., 1968-71; builder Spring, Tex., 1971-74; dir., conductor explorations Minerals of the Sun, S.A. de C.V., Honduras, 1975; dir. Asheville Petroleum Corp., Ill., 1976; conductor explorations Neozoic Minerals & Petroleum, Ltd., Colo., N.Mex., Tex., 1976-77; conductor explorations, dir. Primal Energy Rsch. Found., Houston, 1982—. Pres. Transzoic Orebody Locators, Ltd., Vancouver, B.C., Pleiades Petroleum Corp., Lexington, Tenn. and Houston; pres., dir. Neozoic Geophys. Survey, Ltd., 1999; lectr. grade schs., high schs., Kiwanis, and Rotary, 1962—. Author: The Discovery of the Primal Energy Transverter, 1966, Birth of the Moon, 1978, Origins of Solar Flares and Keys to Predicting Them, 1978, Automatic Recording of Deep Space (interplanetary) Gravity, 1978, Arriving Ionospheric High Energy (Solar Generated), 1978, Out of the Grey Mist, 1992, Life's Continuum, 1992, The Real Origin of Stellar Energy, 1993, The Great Mystery, 1994, Why the Earth Quakes, 2003; patentee in field. Scoutmaster Boy Scouts Am., Houston, 1956-63; cubmaster Cub Scouts, Pasadena, Calif., 1962. With Ind. NG, 1942-43. Republican. Achievements include developed and placed in service new equipment, The Affinity System, that indicates petroleum or gas from the surface to any depth and defines if commercial quality. Office: Primal Energy Rsch Found 31 Rush Haven Dr The Woodlands TX 77381-3227 also: Neozoic Geophysical Survey Ltd 31 Rush Haven Dr The Woodlands TX 77381 Office Phone: 281-419-0446. E-mail: smans6@aol.com.

MANSON, PAUL NELLIS, plastic surgeon; b. Kansas City, Mo., Dec. 28, 1943; s. Nellis Emanuel and Alice Winifred (Olson) M.; m. Kathryn Garland, 1968; children: Ted, Jenner. BA in Chemistry, Northwestern U., 1965, MD, 1968. Prof., chmn. plastic surgery Johns Hopkins Sch. Medicine, Balt., 1990—. Maj. U.S. Army, 1970-73. Republican. Presbyterian. Office: 8152 F McElderry Wins 601 N Caroline St Baltimore MD 21287-0006 Office Phone: 410-955-9469.

MANSOUR, GEORGE P. Spanish language and literature educator; b. Huntington, W.Va., Sept. 4, 1939; s. Elia and Marie (Yazbek) M.; m. Mary Ann Rogers, Dec. 27, 1961; children: Alicia, Philip. AB, Marshall U., 1961; MA, Mich. State U., 1963, PhD, 1965. Assoc. prof. Mich. State U., East Lansing, 1968-77, prof., 1977—, chmn. dept. Romance and Classical langs., 1982—. Cons. Mich. Dept. Edn., Lansing, 1984-85. Contbr. articles to profl. jours., including Hispania, Revista de estudias, hispanicos, also chpts. to books. Mem. Am. Assn. Tchrs. Spanish and Portuguese (v.p. 1969-71), Mich. Fgn. Lang. Assn. (pres. 1982-84). Democrat. Mem. Eastern Orthodox Ch. Avocations: pysanky, golf. Home: 1303 Lucerne Dr Dewitt MI 48820-9528 Office: Mich State U Dept Romance & Classical Langs East Lansing MI 48824

MANSOUR, KAMAL A. cardiothoracic surgeon; b. Nov. 25, 1929; m. Sylvia Cleopatra Sideros, June 19, 1956; 1 child, Sylvia Frederica. M.B., B.Ch., Ein Shams U., Cairo, Egypt, 1954. Diplomate Am. Bd. Surgery, Am. Bd. Thoracic Surgery; lic. physician, Ga. Intern Tanta (Egypt) Gen. Hosp., 1954-55; surgeon Bapt. Hosp., Ajlun, Jordan, 1956-60, Gaza, Egypt, 1961-62; asst. resident in surgery Ch. Home & Hosp., Balt., 1962-63; asst. and chief resident in surgery Ga. Bapt. Hosp., Atlanta, 1963-66; asst. and chief resident cardio thoracic surgery Emory U. Hosp., Atlanta, 1966-68; pvt. practice specializing in cardiothoracic surgery Atlanta, 1968—. Active staff Emory U. Hosp., Grady Meml. Hosp., Crawford W. Long Hosp., Henrietta Egleston Children's Hosp., VA Hosp., Piedmont Hosp.; instr. surgery Emory U. Sch. Medicine, 1968-71, asst. prof. surgery, 1971-76, assoc. prof. surgery, 1976-87, prof. cardiothoracic surgery, 1987—. Contbr. numerous articles to profl. jours. Fellow ACS, Am. Coll. Cardiology, Am. Coll. Chest Physicians, Am. Coll. Angiology, Southeastern Surg. Congress; mem. Council on Critical Care, Am. Assn. Thoracic Surgery, Am. Heart Assn., Soc. Thoracic Surgeons, So. Thoracic Surg. Assn. Internat. Coll. Surgeons (vice regent Ga.), Am. Thoracic Soc., Ga. Surg. Soc., AMA, Med. Assn. Ga., Med. Assn. Atlanta, N. Am. Soc. Pacing and Electrophysiology, Internat. Soc. for Diseases of the Esophagus, Gen. Thoracic Surg. Club. Home: 823 Lullwater Rd NE Atlanta GA 30307-1239 Office: The Emory Clinic 1365 Clifton Rd NE Atlanta GA 30322-1013 Office Phone: 404-778-3554. E-mail: kamal_mansour@emoryhealthcare.org.

MANSOUR, TAG ELDIN, pharmacologist, educator; b. Belkas, Egypt, Nov. 6, 1924; came to U.S., 1951, naturalized, 1956; s. Elsayed and Rokaya (Elzayat) M.; m. Joan Adela MacKinnon, Aug. 6, 1955; children— Suzanne, Jeanne, Dean. DVM, Cairo U., 1946; PhD, U. Birmingham, Eng., 1949, DSc, 1974. Lectr. U. Cairo, 1950-51; Fulbright instr. physiology Howard U., Washington, 1951-52; sr. instr. pharmacology Case Western Res. U., 1952-54; asst. prof., assoc. prof. pharmacology La. State U. Med. Sch., New Orleans, 1954-61; assoc. prof., prof. molecular pharmacology Stanford U. Sch. Medicine, 1961—, chmn. dept. pharmacology, 1977-91, Donald E. Baxter prof., 1977-98, prof. emeritus, 1999—. Cons. USPHS, WHO, Nat. Acad. Scis.; Mem. adv. bd. Med. Sch., Kuwait U.; Heath Clarke lectr. London Sch. Hygiene and Tropical Medicine, 1981 Author: Chemotherapeutic Targets in Parasites, 2002; contrbr. sci. articles to profl. jours. Commonwealth Fund fellow, 1965; Macy Found. scholar NIMR, London, 1982. Fellow AAAS; mem. Am. Soc. Pharmacology and Exptl. Therapeutics, Am. Soc. Biol. Chemists, Am. Heart Assn., Sierra Club, Stanford Faculty Club. Office: Stanford Sch Medicine Dept Molecular Pharm CCSR 269 Campus Dr Stanford CA 94305-5174 Office Phone: 650-723-5957.

MANSOURI, LOTFOLLAH (LOTFI MANSOURI), retired performing company executive; b. Tehran, June 15, 1929; arrived in Can., 1976; s. Hassan and Mehri (Jalili) M.; m. Marjorie Anne Thompson, Sept. 18, 1954; 1 child, Shireen Melinda. AB, UCLA, 1953. Asst. prof. UCLA, 1957-60; resident stage dir. Zurich Opera, 1960-65; chief stage dir. Geneva Opera, 1965-75; gen. dir. Can. Opera Co., Toronto, Ont., 1976-88, San Francisco (Calif.) Opera, 1988—2001, gen. dir. emeritus, 2001—; dramatic coach Music Acad. West, Santa Barbara, Calif., 1959; dir. dramatics Zurich Internat. Opera Studio, 1961-65, Centre Lyrique, Geneva, 1967-72; artistic adviser Tehran Opera, 1973-75; opera adviser Nat. Arts Centre, Ottawa, Ont., 1977; v.p. Opera America, 1979—. Operatic cons. dir. Yes, Giorgio, MGM, 1981; dir. opera sequence for film Moonstruck (Norman Jewison), 1987; stage dir. Fla. Grand Opera Mus. Acad. of West. Guest dir. opera cos. including Met. Opera, San Francisco Opera (70 prodns.), N.Y.C. Opera, Lyric Opera of Chgo., L.A. Opera, guest dir. opera cos. San Diego Opera, guest dir. opera cos. including Teatro Colon, Buenos Aires, Utah Opera, Canadian Opera Co. (30 new prodns.), Houston Grand Opera, La Scala, Covent Garden, Verona Opera, Kirov Opera, Australian Opera, Vienna Staatsoper, Vienna Volksoper, Salzburg Festival, Amsterdam Opera, Holland Festival, Nice (France) Opera, Festival D'Orange, France, Verona Arena Festival; co-author: An Operatic Life, 1982. Decorated chevalier Order Arts and Letters (France), 1992. Mem. Am. Guild Mus. Artists, Can. Actors Equity Assn. Achievements include initiating above-stage projection of subtitles as a simultaneous translation of opera, 1983. Address: Columbia Artists Mngmt Crittenden Divsn 165 W 57th St New York NY 10019-2201 Office Phone: 415-387-9167. E-mail: lotfimansouri@hotmail.com.

MANTEL, ALLAN DAVID, lawyer; b. N.Y.C., June 27, 1951; s. Bernard and Ruth (Weichman) M.; m. Janet Mantel, June 17, 1985; children: Bernard, Elizabeth. BA, NYU, 1973; JD, SUNY, Buffalo, 1976. Bar: N.Y. 1977, U.S. Dist. Ct. (so. and ea. dists.) N.Y. 1977. Assoc. Rosenthal & Herman P.C., N.Y.C., 1977-82; ptnr. Rosenthal, Herman & Mantel, N.Y.C., 1983-94, Hofheimer, Gartlir & Gross, LLP, N.Y.C., 1995-98, Stein Riso Mantel LLP, N.Y.C., 1999—. Fellow Am. Acad. Matrimonial Lawyers (bd. mgrs. 1998-2000, N.Y. chpt. treas. 2001—); mem. ABA (family law sect.), N.Y. State Bar Assn. (equitable distbn. com.), Assn. Bar City N.Y. (matrimonial law com. 1985-88), N.Y. County Lawyers Assn. (matrimonial law and comml. law). Jewish. Office: Stein Riso Mantel LLP 405 Lexington Ave New York NY 10174-0002 E-mail: allan.mantel@steinrisomantel.com.

MANTEL, SAMUEL JOSEPH, JR., management educator, consultant; b. Indpls., Nov. 17, 1921; s. Samuel Joseph and Beatrice Smith (Talmas) M.; m. Dorothy Jean Friedland, June 28, 1950; children— Michael Lee, Samuel Joseph, III, Margaret Irene, Elizabeth Baer. AB, Harvard U., 1948, MPA, 1950, PhD, 1952. Asst. prof. social sci. Ga. Inst. Tech., 1953-56; asst. prof., then assoc. prof. econs., dir. Econs.-in-Action program, Case Western Res. U., 1956-69; prof. mgmt. and quantitative analysis U. Cin., 1969-89, prof. emeritus quantitative analysis and ops. mgmt., 1989—, Joseph S. Stern prof. mgmt., 1973—89, prof. emeritus, 1989, exec. dir. Grad. Ctr. for Mgmt. of Advanced Tech. and Innovation, 1987—89, emeritus, 1989. Mgmt. cons., condr. mgmt. seminars. Author: Cases in Managerial Decisions, 1964, Project Management: A Managerial Perspective, 1985, 2d edit., 2004, Operations Management for Pharmacists: Strategy and Tactics, 1992, Project Management in Practice 5th edit., 2003, Core Concepts of Project Management, 2001; mem. editl. bd. Technovation; contbr. chapters to books, articles to profl. jours. Vice pres. Jewish Fedn. Cin., 1978-80; past pres., life mem. Cin. Hillel Found., Cleve. Hillel Found.; historian Rockdale Temple, 1969-77; mem. mgmt. and adminstrn. com. Anti-Defamation League, B'nai B'rith, 1976; trustee Jewish Hosp., Cin., 1975-84, Sarah Marvin Found. for Performing Arts, 1990—; mem. mgmt. adv. com. Cin. Police Dept., 1991-92. Maj. USMCR, 1942-46, 51-53. Decorated D.F.C. with 3 oak leaf clusters, Air medal with 11 oak leaf clusters; Econs.-in-Action fellow, 1955; fellow Inst. Policy Rsch., 1980; named Prof. of Year, Delta Sigma Pi, 1974. Mem. IEEE, Project Mgmt. Inst., Iota Epsilon, Beta Gamma Sigma. Home: 608 Flagstaff Dr Cincinnati OH 45215-2525 Business E-Mail: mantelsj@email.uc.edu.

MANTELL, MURRAY I. engineering educator; b. N.Y.C., Sept. 6, 1917; s. John and Anna Mantell; m. Rose T. Plansky, Apr. 29, 1944; children: Melodie, Andrea, Tobi, John. B in Mech. Engring., U. Fla., 1940; MS in Civil Engring., So. Calif. U., L.A., 1945; PhD, U. Tex., 1952. Registered profl. engr., Fla. Pres. Mantell Constrn. Co., Miami, Fla., 1940—41, 1946; consulting engr. R. Belsham, Miami, Fla., 1941; naval arch. Charleston (S.C.) Navy Yard, 1941—43, Terminal Island Naval Shipyard, Long Beach, Calif., 1943—45; prof., dept. chmn. emeritus U. Miami, Coral Gables, Fla., 1946—. Chmn. Parks Planning Com., Miami Beach, Fla., 1950; vis. prof. U. Sheffield, England, 1965—66; mem. Fire Prevention and Safety Bd., Dade County, Fla., 1968; chmn. Adv. Panel on Planning and Zoning, Coral Gables, 1970. Author: Ethics & Professionalism in Engineering, 1964, Strength of Materials, 1968, Handbook for Living, 1992; co-author: Orientation in Engineering, 1955, Structural Analysis, 1962, Engineering Properties and Construction Applications of Phosphogypsum, 1990. State sport chmn. Amateur Athletic Union, Fla., 1949; pres. Tigertail Civic Assn., Coconut Grove, Fla., 1960—62; v.p. Pine Ridge Civic Assn., Miami, 1966. Named Engr. of Yr., Fla. Engring. Soc., 1961; recipient Commendation for Engring. Achievement, Brit. Admiralty, 1942. Fellow: NSPE (life; chpt. v.p.), ASCE (life; chpt. pres.), Am. Soc. for Engring. Edn. (life; sect. pres., award for excellence in tchg. Western Electric Fund 1969). Avocations: stamp and coin collecting, sports, agriculture. Home: 9015 SW 78 Ct Miami FL 33156 Office: Dept Civil Engring Univ Miami Coral Gables FL 33124

MANTELL, SUZANNE RUTH, editor; b. West Orange, N.J., Nov. 26, 1944; d. Milton A. and Florence B. M.; m. Peter Gray Friedman, 1985; 1 child, Erica Mantell Friedman Student, U. Chgo., 1962; B.F.A., Pratt Inst., 1967. Formerly assoc. editor Harper's mag., N.Y.C., exec. editor, 1977-80; editor Harper's Bookletter, 1974-77, Learning Mag., 1980-81, Family Learning Mag., 1983-84; reader Book of the Month Club, 1985-87, 91-99; editor Travel Bookstore Catalogue, Banana Republic, 1985-87; assoc. editor The N.Y. Observer, N.Y.C., 1987-91; acting Book News editor Pubs. Weekly, 1992-93, contbg. editor, 1993—. Also lectr. mag. writing Stanford U., U. Calif. at Santa Cruz. Consulting editor Spelman Coll. Messenger, 1994-98; columnist L.A. Times Book Review, 1998-99; arts editor New Times L.A., 1999-2001; author Art of the State: Vermont, 1998. Mem. PEN, PEN West USA, Nat. Book Critics Circle. Home: 101 Warwick Pl South Pasadena CA 91030-4062

MANTELLA, TINO J. former medical association administrator; m. Deb Mantella; children: Cara, Dana, Brock. MS, Temple U.; postgrad., Columbia U. Inst. Non-Profit Mgmt. Pres. and CEO Arthritis Found., 2001—03; consultant Georgia Center for Nonprofits, 2003—. Office: Georgia Ctr for Nonprofits 50 Hurt Plaza SE Ste 845 Atlanta GA 30303*

MANTELLO, JOSEPH, theater director; b. Rockford, Ill., Dec. 27, 1962; Studied acting, N.C. Sch. Arts, 1984; studied directing, Cir. Repertory Co. Co-founder Edge Theater, N.Y.C., 1984. Dir.: (plays) Imagining Brad, 1989, Nebraska, 1991, Coq au Vin, 1991, Babylon Gardens, 1991, Three Hotels, 1993, Fat Men in Skirts, 1994, Blue Window, 1996, The Santaland Diaries, 1996, God's Heart, 1997, Schmucks, 1998, Lillian, 1998, Corpus Christi, 1998, Bash, 1999, The Mineola Twins, 1999—2000, The Vagina Monologues, 1999—2003, Another American: Asking & Telling, 1999, Assassins, 2001, A Man of No Importance, 2002; (Broadway plays) What's Wrong with the Picture?, 1994, Love! Valour! Compassion!, 1994—97 (Obie award), Proposals, 1997, Design for Living, 2001, Take Me Out, 2002 (Lucille Lortel award for outstanding dir., 2003, Drama Desk award nom. for outstanding dir. of a play, 2003, Tony award best dir. of a play, 2003), Frankie and Johnny in the Clair de Lune, 2002, Wicked, 2003—04 (Tony nom. best dir. of a musical, 2004, Drama Desk award best book of a musical, 2004), Assassins, 2004— (Tony award best dir. of a musical, 2004); actor: Angels in America, 1994 (Drama Desk award for best featured actor in a play, 1994). Recipient Outer Critics Cir. award, Helen Hayes award, Clarence Derwent award, Joe A. Callaway award. Office: Creative Artists Agy 9830 Wilshire Blvd Beverly Hills CA 90212*

MANTEY, ELMER MARTIN, food company executive; b. Malone, Tex., July 20, 1926; s. Edward G. and Margaret H. Mantey; m. Donna May Scritsmier, Dec. 27, 1948; children: Patricia Mantey Rooks, Carol Mantey Callis, Cynthia Mantey Stockdale. BS in Chemistry with honors, Bradley U., 1949. Chemist, plant mgr. Am. Petrochem. Co., Mpls., 1949-63, v.p. ops., 1963-66; v.p. Polychem. Group Whittaker Corp., L.A., 1966-69, pres. textile divsn., 1969-71; CEO, pres., chmn. bd. dirs. Flavorite Labs. Inc., Memphis, 1971-89; chmn. emeritus. Bd. dirs. A.M. Todd Co., dir. emeritus; bd. dirs. The Dupps Co.; chmn. emeritus Chrichton Coll. Trustee John Brown U., 1991-2000. Served with USN, 1944-46. Mem. Rotary (Memphis), Crescent Club. Home: 6925 Sugar Maple Cv Memphis TN 38119-5619 Office: PO Box 1315 Memphis TN 38101-1315

MANTHEI, RICHARD DALE, retired lawyer, health care company executive; b. Olivia, Minn., Dec. 23, 1935; s. Alvin R. and Sidonia (Klatt) M.; m. Karen J. Peterson, Sept. 6, 1959 (dec. Mar. 1985); children: Steven, Jana, Kari, John, Rebecca; m. Lynn E. Graham, Aug. 9, 1986. BS in Pharmacy (Rexall award 1960), S.D. State U., 1960; JD, U. Minn., 1967. Bar: Ind. 1967, Ill. 1970, D.C. 1987, U.S. Supreme Ct. 1987. Sales rep. Eli Lilly & Co., Indpls., 1962-64, atty., 1967-70; atty., then asst. corp. sec., dir. regulatory affairs Am. Hosp. Supply Corp., Evanston, Ill., 1970-79, corp. sec., dep. gen. counsel, 1979-85; assoc. gen. counsel Baxter Travenol Labs., Deerfield, Ill., 1986-87; ptnr. Burditt, Bowles & Radzius, Washington, 1987-90, McKenna & Cuneo, Washington, 1990-96; sr. v.p. regulatory scis. C.R. Bard, Inc., Murray Hill, N.J., 1996-2000. Author articles in field.; Editorial adv. staff: Med. Devices and Diagnostic Industry, 1979. Mem. bd. edn. Libertyville H.S., 1984-87; mem. governing bd. Spl. Edn. Dist. of Lake County, Ill., 1985-87; trustee N.J. Ctr. for Visual Arts. With AUS, 1954-56. Mem. ABA, Health Industry Mfrs. Assn. (chmn. law sect. 1976), Health Industry Assn. (chmn. legal com. 1973), Am. Soc. Corp. Secs. (corp. practices com. 1983-88, group pres. 1985-86, Chgo. regional group 1986-87), Ill. Bar Assn., Ind. Bar Assn., D.C. Bar Assn., Univ. Club (Evanston, Ill., bd. dirs. 1984-86). Home: 11608 Stonewall Jackson Dr Spotsylvania VA 22553

MANTILLA, GONZALO, JR., pediatrician; b. Quito, Ecuador, Nov. 2, 1943; came to U.S., 1965; s. Gonzalo M. Mantilla and Victoria Cabeza de Vaca; m. Marthalicia Calisto; children: Martita, Sebastian, Gigi, Victoria. MD, U. Ctrl., Quito, 1971; postgrad., U. Fla., 1971-76. Diplomate Am. Bd. Pediatrics, sub-bd. neonatal-perinatal medicine. Asst. prof. U. Fla., Gainesville, 1976-93; v.p. Met. Hosp., Quito, 1985-90; dean USFQ Med. Sch., Quito, 1993—; pvt. practice. Clin. prof. pediats. U. South Fla.; adj. prof. Internat. Health, George Washington U., Washington, 1997—. Editor: Salud Infantil, 1987. Advisor Health Ministry, Ecuador, 1985-93. Fellow Am. Acad. Pediatrics. Home and Office: 17 Davis Blvd Ste 200 Tampa FL 33606-3438

MANTIONE, MERYL E. director, education educator; b. Chgo., Apr. 30, 1952; d. Arthur A. and Meryl E. Biggane. BS, Elmhurst Coll., Elmhurst, IL., 1974; BM, U. Wis., 1981; M.Mus., U. Colo., 1984, DMA, 1989. Asst. prof. Mont. State U., Bozeman, Mont., 1987—90, U. Okla., Norman, Okla., 1990—94, assoc. prof., 1994—99, asst. dir., 1997—2002, prof., 1999—2002; prof., dir. Ohio U., Athens, Ohio, 2002—. Okla. Dist. Gov. Nat. Assn. Teachers of Singing, Norman, Okla., 1999—2002. Singer: (Operas) Inter Mountain Opera Co., Cimarron Circuit Opera Co., Opera Okla., oratorio soloist, performer recitals. Recipient Outstanding Faculty, Coll. of Fine Arts, U. Okla., 1993. Mem.: Coll. Music Soc., Nat. Assoc. Teachers of Singing. Achievements include Selected as Nat. Assoc. of Teachers of Singing intern program, 1992. Home: 199 Louise Ln Athens OH 45701-3416 Office: Ohio U Sch of Music Athens OH 45701 Office Phone: 740-593-4244. Business E-Mail: mantione@ohio.edu.

MANTLE, PETER JOHN, aerospace executive, consultant; b. London, Apr. 29, 1935; came to U.S., 1960; s. George Henry and Winifred Mantle; m. Lisa Margaret Taylor, June 26, 1965 (div. July 1979); children: Tracy Lynn Gage, Christopher James; m. Kathleen Anne Kinney, Dec. 27, 1987. MSc in Aero, Cranfield Tech., Bedford, Eng., 1958; MSc in Math. magna cum laude, Laval U., 1960; AeE, CalTech, 1964. Program mgr. Bell Aerospace, New Orleans, 1965-73; pres. Mantle Engring., Rosslyn, Va., 1976-78; dir. tech. assessment U.S. Navy, Pentagon, Washington, 1978-84; dir. surveillance programs Lockheed Martin, Sunnyvale, Calif., 1984-87, dir. European bus., 1987-97; cons. Mantle & Assocs., Vashon Island, Wash., 2000—. Chmn. NATO indsl. adv. group on missile def., Brussels, 1990-2000. Author: Tech Summary of Air Cushion Craft, 1975, Air Cushion Craft Development, 1980; designer fastest U.S. Navy ship, 1972; patentee advanced marine vehicles. Recipient Nat. Cert. prize Insn. Mech. Engrs., London, 1955, Superior Civilian Svc. award Sec. of Navy, 1984. Mem. Masons, Scottish and York Rites. Avocations: sculpture, art, photography, skiing. Home: 7703 SW 259th St Vashon WA 98070-8540 E-mail: mantlep@ix.netcom.com.

MANTLE, RAYMOND ALLAN, lawyer; b. Painesville, Ohio, Oct. 15, 1937; s. Junius Dow and Ada Louise (Stinchcomb) M.; m. Judith Ann LaGrange, Nov. 26, 1967; children: Amanda Lee, Rachel Ann, Leah Amy. BSBA summa cum laude, BA summa cum laude, Kent State U., 1961; LLB cum laude, NYU, 1964. Bar: N.Y. 1964, N.J. 1976, U.S. Supreme Ct. Asst. counsel Gov. Nelson A. Rockefeller, N.Y., 1964-65; assoc. Paul Weiss Rifkind Wharton & Garrison, 1967-69; mem. Varet & Fink P.C. (formerly Milgrim Thomajan & Lee, P.C.), N.Y.C., 1969-95; ptnr. Piper & Marbury L.L.P., N.Y.C., 1995-98; mem. Reitler Brown LLC (formerly Brock Silverstein, LLC), 1998—2003, counsel, 2004—. Lectr. in computer law field. Contbr. author: Doing Business in China and Intellectual Property China, 1990—. Capt. U.S. Army, 1965-67. Mem.: N.J. Bar Assn., N.Y. State Bar Assn. (co-chmn. ann. meeting seminar on intellectual property 2000—03, chair intellectual property sect. internat. com., exec. com. intellectual property sect.). Republican. Methodist. Office: Reitler Brown LLC 800 3rd Ave Fl 21 New York NY 10022-7604 also: 1050 Riverside Ave Jacksonville FL 32204 E-mail: rmantle@reitlerbrown.com.

MANTON, EDWIN ALFRED GRENVILLE, insurance company executive; b. Earls Colne, Essex, Eng., Jan. 22, 1909; came to U.S., 1933; s. John Horace and Emily Clara (Denton) M.; m. Florence V. Brewer, Feb. 1, 1936; 1 child, Diana H. Manton Morton. Student, London (Eng.) U., 1925-27, N.Y. Ins. Soc., 1933-35; DHL (hon.), Coll. of Ins., 1994. With B.W. Noble Ltd., Paris, 1927-33; casualty underwriter Am. Internat. Underwriters Corp., N.Y.C., 1933-37, sec., 1937-38, v.p., 1938-42, pres., 1942-69, chmn., 1969-75. Sr. advisor Am. Internat. Group, Inc.; hon. dir. C.V. Starr & Co., Inc. Trustee St. Luke's-Roosevelt Hosp., N.Y.C. Mem. Salmagundi Club, Mendelssohn Glee Club, Williams Club, St. George's Soc., Downtown Assn. Episcopalian. Office: Am Internat Group Inc 70 Pine St New York NY 10270-0002

MANTON, THOMAS JOSEPH, former congressman; b. N.Y.C., Nov. 3, 1932; m. Diane Schley; children: Cathy, Tom, John, Jeanne. BBA, St. John's U., 1958, LLB, 1962. Mem. N.Y.C. Police Dept., 1955-60; mktg. rep. IBM, 1960-64; practice law, 1964-84; mem. 99th-105th Congresses from 9th (now 7th) N.Y. Dist., Washington, 1984-98; former mem. commerce com.; mem. Manton, Sweeney, Gallo, Reich & Bolz, N.Y.C., 1999—. Mem. N.Y.C. Council, 1970-84; chmn. exec. com. Queens County Dem. Orgn., 1986—. Served with USMC, 1951-53. Democrat. Address: Ste 626 95-25 Queens Blvd Rego Park NY 11374

MANTON, WILLIAM INWOOD, geologist, educator; b. Durban, Natal, South Africa, Feb. 8, 1937; arrived in U.S., 1964; s. Geoffrey Charles Manton and Constance Irene Melsens; m. Renee Southernwood Manton, Dec. 9, 1982; m. Janet Rae Humphrey, Sept. 1, 1968 (div. May 15, 1982); children: Gabrielle Marcelline, Iris Irene, Piers Kingsley, Geoffrey Leonard. BSc with honors, U. of the Witwatersrand, Johannesburg, South Africa, 1959, MSc, 1962, PhD, 1964. Prof. U. Tex. Dallas, Richardson, 1964—. Recipient Best paper award, Soc. Toxicology, 1997. Episcopalian. Achievements include research in applied techniques of geochemistry to toxicology and showed that most of lead in blood is derived from stores in bone. Demonstrated that blood lead rises in pregnancy due to bone resorption; made fundamental observations pertaining to lead poisoning from gunshot wounds, acquisition of lead by young children and role of lead in amyotrophic lateral sclerosis. Avocations: antique furniture, classical languages. Home: 300 Ridgewood Richardson TX 75080-1912 Office: Univ Tex Dallas PO Box 830688 Richardson TX 75083-0688 Personal E-mail: inwood@attbi.com. E-mail: manton@utdallas.edu.

MANTON, WILLIAM JEFFREY, operating engineer, fleet consultant; b. Oak Park, Ill., Sept. 29, 1959; s. Herman Charles Manton and June Gertrude Kasman; m. Joanne Marie Maciejewski ((div. Oct. 1987); children: Jessica Lynn, Jeffrey William; m. Kimberly Ann May, Sept. 3, 1988; children: Charles James (dec.), Amanda Nicole and Courtney Elizabeth (twins). Grad. high sch., Hillside, Ill., 1977. Svc. mgr. Warnimont's Farm Supply, Bloomingdale, Ill., 1983-88; fleet mgr. Crane & Steel Inc., Addison, Ill., 1988—. Trustee, Village of Hanover Park, Ill., 1996—, vice chmn. Devel. Commn., 1994-96. Mem. Internat. Union Operating Engrs., Knights of Columbus. Republican. Roman Catholic. Avocations: sporting clays, trap shooting. Home: 1819 Seneca Dr Hanover Park IL 60133-6751 Office: 2121 W Lake St Hanover Park IL 60133-4301 Office Phone: 630-627-6830. E-mail: williammanton@msn.com., w.manton@hanoverparkillinois.org.

MANTONI, PHILIP JOSEPH, principal; b. Springfield, Mass., Dec. 3, 1944; s. Adelino Philip and Mary (Barberis) M.; m. Susan Beth Hartley Mantoni, Aug. 4, 1973; 1 child, Christian Philip. BSE in Elem. Edn., North Adams (Mass.) State Coll., 1969; MEd in Edn., Springfield Coll., 1979; C.A.G.S. in Adminstrn., Westfield (Mass.) State Coll., 1988. Tchr. Washington Sch., Springfield, 1969-77, Ecology Ctr. of Springfield, 1977-89; asst. prin. New North Cmty. Sch., Springfield, 1989-90; prin. A.G. Zanetti Elem. Sch., Springfield, 1990-95, Alice B. Beal Sch., Springfield, 1995—. Exec. bd. South End Cmty. Ctr., 1992—; mem. chmn., exec. bd., bldg. rep. Springfield Fedn. Tchrs. Mem. Springfield Citywide Sch. Centered Decision Making Team, 1993-99; chmn. Springfield Park Commn., 1982-91; mem. Forest Park Zool. Soc. Edn. and Curriculum Com., 1981-89; mem. Olmstead grants Com. for Forest Park, 1986-88; mem. Springfield Schs. Sci. Curriculum Com., 1978-83; mem. Springfield Mcpl. Planning Bd., 1983-91. Mem.: Springfield Elem. Prins. Assn. (treas. 1992—93, sec. 1993—94, v.p. 1994—95). Home: 41 Texel Dr Springfield MA 01108-2637 Office: Alice B Beal Sch 285 Tiffany St Springfield MA 01108-3333 Office Phone: 413-739-0161. E-mail: pjmsiri@aol.com.

MANTONYA, JOHN BUTCHER, lawyer; b. Columbus, Ohio, May 26, 1922; s. Elroy Letts and Blanche (Butcher) M.; m. Mary E. Reynolds, June 14, 1947 (dec. 1987); children: Elizabeth Claire, Mary Kay, Lee Ann; m. Carole L. Lugar, Sept. 28, 1989. AB cum laude, Washington and Jefferson Coll., 1943; postgrad., U. Mich. Law Sch., 1946-47; JD, Ohio State U., 1949. Bar: Ohio 1949. Assoc. A.S. Mitchell (Atty.), Newark, Ohio, 1949-50, C.D. Lindrooth, Newark, 1950-57; partner firm Lindrooth & Mantonya, Newark, 1957-74, firm John B. Mantonya, 1974-81, John B. Mantonya, L.P.A., 1981—. Mem. North Fork Local Bd. Edn., 1962-69; adv. com. Salvation Army, Licking County, 1965—, Mayor of, Utica, Ohio, 1953-59. Served with AUS, 1943-45. Mem. ABA, Ohio Bar Assn., Licking County Bar Assn. (pres. 1967), Phi Delta Phi, Beta Theta Pi. Home: 11055 Reynolds Rd Utica OH 43080-9549 Office: 3 N 3rd St Newark OH 43055-5506

MANTOVANI, JOHN F. pediatric neurologist; b. St. Louis, Jan. 17, 1949; s. John F. and Marinelle Mantovani; children: John R. and Ann Marie. BA cum laude, U. Evansville, 1971; MD, U. Mo., 1974. Diplomate Am. Bd. Pediat., Am. Bd. Psychiatry and Neurology in child neurology and in neurodevel. disabilities. Resident pediatrics, neurology, fellow child neurology Washington U.-St. Louis Childrens Hosp., 1974-79; practitioner adult and child neurology Dean Clinic, Madison, Wis., 1979-84; dir. child neurology, vice chmn. dept. pediatrics St. John's Mercy Med. Ctr., St. Louis, 1984—. Clin. asst. prof. neurology U. Wis., Madison, 1980-84; instr. clin. pediatrics and neurology Washington U., 1985-95, asst. prof., 1995-99, assoc. prof., 1999—. Mem. editl. bd., vice chmn. Dev. Med. and Child Neurology; Contbr. articles to profl. jours. Fellow Am. Acad. Pediatrics; mem. AMA, Am. Acad. Cerebral Palsy and Devel. Medicine (bd. dirs. 1994-2003, v.p. 1997-98, pres.-elect 1999, pres. 2000), Am. Acad. Neurology, Child Neurology Soc., Alpha Omega Alpha. Office: 621 S New Ballas Rd Ste 5009 Saint Louis MO 63141-8232

MANTSCH, HENRY HORST, chemistry educator; b. Mediasch, Transylvania, Romania, July 30, 1935; emigrated to Can., 1968; s. Heinrich Johann and Olga Augusta (Gondosch) M.; m. Amy Emilia Kory, Nov. 2, 1959; children: Monica, Marietta. BSc, U. Cluj, Transylvania, 1958, PhD, 1964. Rsch. scientist Romanian Acad. Sci., Cluj, 1958-65, Tech. U. Munich, Germany, 1966-68; with NRC, Ottawa, Can., 1968-72; prof. biochemistry U. Cluj, 1973-74, Liebig U., Giessen, Germany, 1975-76; head molecular spectroscopy NRC, Ottawa, 1977—; mem. Can. Rsch. Coun., Ottawa, 1977-91, Winnipeg, Can., 1992—. Adj. prof. Carleton U., Ottawa, 1978-90, U. Ottawa, 1990-92, U. Manitoba, Winnipeg, 1992—. Contbr. articles to profl. jours.; patentee in field. Recipient medal Ministry of Edn., Bucharest, 1972, Humboldt Found. medal Bonn, 1980, Herzberg award, 1984, Marcus Marci medal, 1998; Chem. Inst. Can. fellow, 1979, Royal Soc. Can. fellow, 1982. Mem. Am. Biophys. Soc., Soc. Applied Spectroscopy, Chem. Inst. Can. (chmn. biol. chem. divsn. 1980-81), Can. Spectroscopy Soc. (nat. exec. com. 1981-90), Can. Biophys. Soc. (sec. 1999—). Home: 2222 W Taylor Blvd R3P 2J5 Winnipeg MB Canada R3P 2J5 Office: NRC Can 435 Ellice Ave Winnipeg MB Canada R3B 1Y6 E-mail: henry.mantsch@nrc.ca.

MANTZ, ARLAN W. physics educator; b. Slatington, Pa., July 25, 1940; s. Harold H. and Irene A. (Herber) M.; m. Barbara Dae Mantz, Dec. 28, 1963; 1 child, Yves Andre. BA, Catawba Coll., 1962; MSc, Ohio State U., 1966, PhD, 1969. Sr. scientist Air Force Avionics Lab., Ohio, 1966-73; postdoctoral fellow Labo Aime Cotton, Orsay, France, 1973-74; sr. scientist Digilab, Inc., Cambridge, Mass., 1974-76; engring. mgr. Laser Analytics Inc., Bedford, Mass., 1976-79, pres., gen. mgr., 1979-89; assoc. prof. Franklin and Marshall Coll., Lancaster, Pa., 1990-95; Oakes Ames prof. physics Conn. Coll., New London, 1995—. Editl. adv. bd. Spectrochemica Acta, 1990, revs. editor, 1995. Mem. AAAS, Optical Soc. of Am., Am. Chem. Soc., Am. Phys. Soc., N.Y. Acad. Sci. Avocation: sailing. Home: 145 Wamphassuc Rd Stonington CT 06378-2816

MANUEL, CHARLIE FUQUA, JR., professional baseball manager; children: Charles Jr., Julie. Outfielder Minn. Twins, 1963-74; with Bklyn. Dodgers, 1974-75, Yakult Swallows and Kintetsu Buffaloes, Japan, 1976-81; scout Minn. Twins, 1982; mgr. class A Wisconsin Rapids, 1983; various coaching and mgr. positions, 1983-99; mgr. Cleve. Indians, 1999—. Inducted Salem-Roanoke Baseball Hall of Fame, 1995. Office: Cleve Indians 2401 Ontario St Cleveland OH 44115-4003

MANUEL, JERRY, former professional sports team manager; b. Hahira, Ga., Dec. 23, 1953; m. Renette Caldwell; children: Angela, Jerry, Anthony, Natalie. Switch-hitting infielder Detroit Tigers, 1972, Class A Lakeland, Class AAA Toledo, 1973, Class AAA Evansville, 1974-75, Detroit Tigers, 1975-76, Montreal, Can., 1980-81, San Diego, 1982, Class AAA Iowa, 1983, Class AAA Denver, 1984; scout White Sox, 1985; player, coach Indpls. orgn., 1986, infield instr., 1987; minor-league fielding coord. Expos orgn., 1988-89; mgr. Class AAA Indpls. Montreal Expos Sys., 1991; coach maj. league baseball Montreal Expos, 1991-96; mgr. Chgo. White Sox, 1997—2003. Bench coach Fla. Marlins, 1997. Named So. League Mgr. of Yr., 1992.

MANUEL, RALPH NIXON, retired private school executive; b. Frederick, Md., Apr. 21, 1936; s. Ralph Walter and Frances Rebecca (Nixon) M.; m. Sarah Jane Warner, July 22, 1960; children: Mark, David, Stephen, Bradley. AB, Dartmouth Coll., 1958; M.Ed., Boston U., 1967; PhD, U. Ill., 1971. Assoc. dean Dartmouth Coll., Hanover, N.H., 1971-72, dean of freshmen, 1972-75, dean, 1975-82; pres. Culver (Ind.) Acad. and Culver Edn. Found., 1982-99. Bd. dirs. Ind. Sch. Cen. States, 1986-99, chair, 1993-95. Mem. Assn. Mil. Colls. and Schs. of U.S. (pres., bd. dirs.), Nat. Assn. Ind. Schs. (bd. dirs. 1995-99).

MANUEL, SANDRA LORRAINE, minister; b. Lakewood, NJ, July 29, 1951; d. Samuel Blackstone and Curtis Burnett; m. Alexander Manuel, July 12, 1967 (dec. Feb. 27, 1995); children: Darnell, Tasha, Alexia;. Diploma in nursing, Charles Gregory Sch. Nursing, 1985; B in Religious Edn., United Bible Coll., 1991. RN NJ; cert. student group adviser Kean U., 00. HIV and AIDS instr. NJ Dept. Criminal Justice, Police Tng. Commn., NJ; med. supr. NJ Tng. Sch. for Boys, Jameburg; head nurse, group advisor Kean U., Union, NJ; pastor Mission of Faith Ministry, Neptune, NJ. Pres. Euphrates Project, Neptune, NJ; developer workshop on non-violence Tchg. Non-Violence: Begin in Infancy, 1996. Organizer: first gospel program for cable TV in Monmouth County. Active Neighborhood Leadership Initiative Cmty. Found. of NJ, Morristown, 2002. Recipient plaque, Harde Hank Cable, 1984, Letter of Accomodation, NJ Tng. Sch., 1990. Mem.: Nat. Coun. Netro Women. Avocation: bird watching. Home: PO Box 653 Neptune NJ 07753

MANUELIAN, LUCY DER, art historian, educator, architecture educator; b. Arlington, Mass. AB in English lit., Radcliffe Coll.; MA in Art History, Boston U., 1975, PhD in Art History, 1980. Head tchg. fellow Boston U., 1975-76; vis. lectr. Framingham State Coll., 1979-80; archivist Armenian Archtl. Archives Project, 1979-84; holder Lectureship in Armenian Art and Architecture Tufts U., Harvard U., McGill U., Boston U., Boston Coll., U. Mass., 1984—89; Arthur H. Dadian and Ara Oztemel Prof. Armenian Art and Architecture Tufts U., Medford, 1989—. Mus. cons. Dartmouth Coll.; lectr. Poly Inst., U. Erevan, USSR, U. Aarhus, Denmark, Courtauld Inst., England, McGill U., U. Mich., U. Pa., Harvard U., Brown U., U. Chgo., Columbia U., Northeastern U., UCLA, Dartmouth Coll., Wellesley Coll., Mt. Holyoke Coll., Queens Coll., Rutgers U., London Sch. Econs.; Libr. Congress lectr. Met. Mus. N.Y., cultural and cmty. orgns. U.S. and abroad; author, narrator 4 TV documentaries on Armenian art. Author: Armenian Architecture, 4 vols., 1981—88, Dictionary of Middle Ages, 1982—89, Dictionary of Art, The Gregorian Collection-Armenian Rugs, 1983, Weavers, Merchants and Kings: The Inscribed Rugs of Armenia, 1984; contbr. chapters to books, articles to profl. jours. Fellow to USSR, 1977-78, fellow Bunting Inst., Radcliffe Coll., 1971-73; Samuel H. Kress grantee Boston U., 1975, 78, Rsch. grantee Nat. Assn. for Armenian Studies and Rsch. to USSR, 1972, 78; sr. scholar grantee Am. Coun. Learned Socs./Soviet Acad. Scis., 1983; recipient Jack H. Kolligian award Nat. Assn. Armenian Studies and Rsch., 1981, Boyan award Armenian Students Assn., Woman of Achievement award Armenian Internat. Women's Assn., 1994, Kohar award Armenian Rugs Soc., named to Boston U. Acad. Disting. Alumni, 1986, Armenian of Yr., Masons, 1990. Mem. Armenian Acad. Sci. (cons. Art Inst. symposium 1990—), Nat. Assn. Armenian Studies and Rsch. (adv. bd. 1991—), Soc. Armenian Studies, Aga Khan Program Islamic Architecture (affiliate), Middle East Studies Assn., Coll. Art Assn., Medieval Acad. Accademia Tiberina Rome (assoc.), Assn. Internat. Etudes Armeniennes, Nat. Assn. Armenian Studies & Rsch. (hon. life), Phi Beta Kappa (hon. Radcliffe Coll.). Achievements include research in archaeological ground penetrating radar technology. Avocations: music, piano, tennis, the restoration of Medieval Armenian churches. Office Phone: 617-484-0668. Business E-Mail: lucy.manuelian@tufts.edu.

MANUELL, LYNN MARIE, booking agent, singer, actress; b. Grand Rapids, Mich., Apr. 17, 1961; d. Richard James and Barbara Ann (Reeves) M. AA, Prairie State Coll., Chicago Heights, Ill., 1983; BA with honors, Columbia Coll., Chgo., 1985; postgrad., Am. Acad. Dramatic Arts, N.Y.C., 1985-86, Wavendon Allmusic Plan, U.K., 1987-89; MA, Hunter Coll., 2002. Singer, actress Ill. Theatre Ctr., Park Forest, 1975-83; pub. rels. photographer Columbia Coll., Chgo., 1983-84, Connie Zonka and Assocs., Chgo., 1984; promotional sales agt. Cliff Steward & Assocs., N.Y.C., 1985; mgr. Raymond Annlisa Promotional, N.Y.C., 1985; office coord., agt. Nat. Shakespeare Co., N.Y.C., 1985-86; singer Whaler/Madison Towers, N.Y.C., 1986; spl. events coord. Cultural Coun. Found., N.Y.C., 1986-89; exec. asst./booking NAMCO Booking, N.Y.C., 1990-91; assoc. in booking devel. Shofer/Gold/Lamero Ltd., N.Y.C., 1991—. Coord. Minority Arts Mgmt., N.Y.C., 1987; events coord. Soho Booking, N.Y.C., 1987; assoc. Gatchell & Neufeld Ltd., N.Y.C., 1990; exec. dir. Tour de Force Internat., Inc., 1992, AIS Prodns. assoc. and co. mgr., 1994; internat. sales assoc. Bresner Mgmt., Inc., 1996; co. mgr. Donald Byrd Dance Found., 1999, (broadway show) Grease!, 2000—, Smokey Joe's Cafe, 2001; founder Internat. Prodn. Mgmt. Author: (poetry) Unicorns and Golden Traces, 1981, Standing Tall--the journals, emails, and creative writings since 9/11, 2001; prodr. Unity Variety Show; contbr. articles to profl. jours.; performer in Remember Me from Holy Redeemer High at Don't Tell Mama's, N.Y.C.; recorded CD: Return to Love, 1999; in over 150 theatrical prodns.; performs for Am. Theatre Wing is lyricist on music recorded and performed by singers of note. Friend, Community Literacy Rsch. Project, N.Y.C., 1986-87; polit. worker NOW, Chgo., 1978-80. Mem. Nat. Orgn. Female Execs., Theatre Devel. Fund, Am. Friends of Royal Shakespeare Co., Dickens Fellowship of N.Y. Avocations: photography, poetry, antiques, reading, cabaret theatre. Home and Office: 12 Dongan Pl Apt 201 New York NY 10040-1592 E-mail: lynninoz302@hotmail.com.

MANUS, NANCY MANNING, writer; b. Jesup, Ga., Jan. 13, 1945; d. Charlie Dalton and Zellie Adell (Flowers) Manning; children: Andrew Ceaphus, Kevin Charles, Thomas Lindsey. AB in Journalism, U. Ga., 1967. Ga. state merit sys. cert. caseworker, 1968, level II, 1969, eligibility supr., 1970. Case worker I Wayne County Dept. Family and Children Svcs., Jesup, 1968-69; case worker II Coffee County Dept. Family and Children Svcs., Douglas, Ga., 1969-70, eligibility supr., 1970-73; freelance writer Odum, Ga., 1975-80; dir. med. social svcs. Wayne Meml. Hosp., Jesup, 1981-98. Com. mem. Edn./Cons. Social Work Found. of Ga. Hosp. Assn., 1982-98. Vol. hosp. blood drive coord. Red Cross Low Country Chpt., Hinesville, Ga., 1982-87; mem. Adv. Coun. Health and Edn., Wayne County, Ga., 1985-98; assisted living cons. in cmty., 1992—. Recipient Recognition for Svc. award Red Cross Low Country Chpt., Hinesville, 1985. Mem. Ga. Soc. Social Workers in Health Care of Ga. Hosp. Assn. (dist. chmn. S.E. dist. 1996-97, sec. 1996-97, Com. Achievement award 1996, cert. appreciation service, 1997-98). Avocations: do-it-yourself building projects, gardening, exploring nature, dance, reading.

MANVILLE, STEWART ROEBLING, archivist; b. White Plains, NY, Jan. 15, 1927; s. Leo and Margaret (Roebling) Manville; m. Ella V. Grainger, Jan. 19, 1972 (dec.). Student, U. Wyo., 1944-46; BS, Columbia U., 1962. Various office positions, N.Y.C., 1947-51, 56-58; asst. stage dir. several European opera houses, 1951-55; editor Jas. T. White & Co., N.Y.C., 1959-63; archivist, curator Percy Grainger Library, White Plains, 1963—. Author: The Manville/Manvel Families in America; contbr. articles to mags. and newspapers. Mem.: SAR, Archivists Round Table Met. NY, N.Y. Archivists Orgn., St. Nicholas Soc. N.Y., Westchester Trails Assn. (pres. 2001—), Brit. Music Soc., Société des Antiquaires de Picardie, Victorian Soc. Am. (past. dir. N.Y. chpt.), Nat. Trust Hist. Preservation. Mem. Soc. Of Friends. Office: 7 Cromwell Pl White Plains NY 10601-5005

MANWELL, JOHN PARKER, II, lawyer; b. Syracuse, NY, May 28, 1931; s. Reginald Dickinson and Elizabeth (Moore) Manwell; m. Bonnie Lee Clem, May 11, 1963; children: Constance, Claire, John Parker. BA, Oberlin Coll., 1953; LLB, Harvard U., 1956. Bar: NY 1956, DC 1960, Md. 1979. Mem. firm Kirkland & Ellis, Washington, 1960—83, ptnr., 1965—83, Wiley, Rein & Fielding, Washington, 1983—. Contbr. articles to profl. jours. Served to 1st lt. USAF, 1956—60. Mem.: ABA (chmn. com. legis. recommendations sect. taxation 1973—75), DC Bar Assn. Address: 1776 K St NW Washington DC 20006-2304

MANZ, CALVIN KIM, technology sector entrepreneur; b. Regina, Can., May 31, 1953; married, July 5, 1980. CEO, pres. Horizon, Inc., Calgary, Alta., Can., 1978-82, Interalia, Inc., Calgary, 1982-87, Manz Devels. Inc., Calgary, 1985—; dir. Telebackup Sys. Inc., Calgary, 1997-99; CEO, pres. Odyssey Fin. Inc., Calgary, 1997—; dir. Internat. Properties Group Ltd., Calgary, 1997—; chmn. J-Commerce, Calgary, 1999—; dir., founder LAUNCHworks Inc., Calgary, 1999—. Founder, dir. MCK Comm., Inc., Boston; bd. dirs. Scyther Corp., Investorplus.com. Avocation: golf. Office: Manz Devels Inc Site 30 Box 1 RR # 12 Calgary AB Canada T3E 6W3 Fax: 403-242-3670.

MANZ, CHARLES C. management educator; Nirenberg prof. bus. leadership U. Mass., Amherst, 1997—. Author: The Art of Self-Leadership: Strategies for Personal Effectiveness in Your Life and Work, 1983, Mastering Self-Leadership: Empowering Yourself for Personal Excellence, 1992, 3d edit., 2004, The Power of Failure: 27 Ways to Turn Life's Setbacks Into Success, 2002, Emotional Discipline: The Power to Choose How You Feel, 2003, Temporary Sanity: Instant Self-Leadership Strategies for Turbulent Times, 2004; co-author: Superleadership, 1990, Business Without Bosses: How Self-Managing Teams are Building High-Performance Companies, 1993, Company of Heroes: Unleashing the Power of Self-Leadership, 1996, For Team Members Only, 1997, The Leadership Wisdom of Jesus: Practical Lessons for Today, 1998, Teamwork and Group Dynamics, 1999, The Wisdom of Solomon at Work: Ancient Virtues for Living and Leading Today, 2001, The New Super Leadership: Leading Others to Lead Themselves, 2001, Fit to Lead: The Proven 8-Week Solution for Shaping Up Your Body, Your Mind and Your Carrer, 2004. Office: U Mass Sch of Mgmt Amherst MA 01003

MANZ, JOHANNES JAKOB, Swiss diplomat; b. Zurich, Switzerland, Dec. 15, 1938; s. Jakob J. and Margaret (Ruegg) M.; m. Marie-Antoinette Kunz, May 26, 1966; children: Alexander Cyril, Isabel Carmela. Student, Oreg. State U., 1958-59; LLD, U. Zurich, 1969. Sec. Mission of Switzerland, N.Y.C., 1971-75; counselor Swiss Embassy, Vienna, 1975-81; min., dep. head mission Mission of Switzerland, Geneva, 1981-84; amb., chief protocol Swiss Confedn., Bern, 1984-88; amb., dir. adminstrn. and pers. Swiss Dept. for Fgn. Affairs, Bern, 1988-91; under sec. gen., spl. rep. to sec. gen. for Western Sahara, UN, N.Y.C., 1990-91; amb., head of mission, permanent observer to UN, Mission of Switzerland, N.Y.C., 1992-97; amb. to Japan, Swiss Embassy, Tokyo, 1997—2002. Contbg. author: Manual of Swiss Foreign Policy, 1991. Pres. Platform for Young Citizens, Zollikon, Switzerland, 1967-68. Mem. Delta Upsilon (hon. Oreg. State U. chpt.). Avocations: cross country skiing, golf, swimming, classical music.

MANZI, JIM P. computer software company executive; b. N.Y.C., Dec. 22, 1951; s. Walter Edward and Ann (Smirka) M.; m. Glenda Baugh, May 20, 1978 BA, Colgate U., 1973; MALD., Fletcher Sch., Tufts U., 1979. Editorial asst. Nat. Rev. Mag., N.Y.C., 1973-74; news reporter Gannet Newspapers, Port Chester, N.Y., 1974-77; cons. McKinsey & Co., Los Angeles, Boston and N.Y.C., 1979-83, v.p. mktg. and sales Lotus Devel. Corp., Cambridge, Mass., 1983-84, pres., 1984-86, 89-1996, CEO, 1986-1996; pres., CEO Industry Net, 1996. Recipient In-Depth Reporting award AP, N.Y., 1976, 77, Investigative Reporting award N.Y. State Pubs. Assn., 1976, 77 Office: Industry Net 5 Cambridge Ctr Ste 8 Cambridge MA 02142-1493

MANZO, EDWARD DAVID, patent lawyer; b. N.Y.C., Nov. 23, 1950; s. Edward Joseph and Elvira Helen (Melone) M.; m. Fern Rita Siegel, Oct. 30, 1978 (div. 1984); 1 child, Justin Edward; m. Margaret Ruth Johnson, Oct. 11, 1985; children: Hunter Roy, Kira Nicole. BS in Physics, Poly. Inst. Bklyn., 1972; JD cum laude, SUNY, Buffalo, 1975. Bar: N.Y. 1976, Ill. 1979, U.S. Patent and Trademark Office 1976, U.S. Ct. Appeals (fed. cir.) 1982, U.S. Supreme Ct. 1982. Assoc. Darby & Darby, P.C., N.Y.C., 1975-77; group patent counsel Schlumberger Ltd., N.Y.C., 1977-79; ptnr. Cook, Wetzel & Egan, Chgo., 1979-85, 88-90, Jenner & Block, 1985-88; sr. ptnr. Cook McFarron & Manzo, Ltd., Chgo., 1990-99; sr. ptnr., exec. v.p., treas., CFO Cook, Alex, McFarron, Manzo, Cummings & Mehler, Ltd., Chgo., 1999—. Instr. DePaul U., Chgo., 1989-91, 2002-03; mem. adv. bd. DePaul Law Sch., 2002—. Author (with others): Intellectual Property Law in Illinois, 1988; contbr. articles to profl. jours. Bd. dirs. Concertante di Chgo., 1997-; grantor Edward Manzo Patent Law scholarship DePaul Law Sch., 2001-03, mem. adv. bd., 2002-. Jaeckle Fleishman grantee, 1973. Mem. Am. Intellectual Property Law Assn., Intellectual Property Law Assn. Chgo. (chmn. litigation com. 2002-03), Stradivari Soc., Sicilian Am. Cultural Assn. (treas. 1996-98, v.p. 1998-99, pres. 2000-02). Avocations: classical music, tennis, bridge. Office: Cook Alex McFarron Manzo Cummings & Mehler Ltd 200 W Adams St Ste 2850 Chicago IL 60606-5206 E-mail: emanzo@cammcm.com.

MANZULLO, DONALD A, congressman, lawyer; b. Rockford, Ill., Mar. 27, 1944; s. Frank A. Sr. and Catherine M.; m. Freda Teslik; children: Neil, Noel, Katie. BA in Polit. Sci./Internat. Rels., American U., 1967; JD, Marquette U. Law Sch., 1971. Atty., 1970—; mem. U.S. Congress from 16th Ill. Dist., 1993—. Mem. House Com. on Internat. Rels., subcom. internat. econ. policy and trade, subcom. on Asia and the Pacific, House Com. on small bus., chmn. on subcom. on tax, fin. and exports, Banking Com. and its capital markets, securities and govt.-sponsored enterprises subcom. Mem. No. Ill. Alliance for Arts, Friends of Severson Dells, Citizens Against Govt. Waste, Rep. Nat. Com. Recipient George Washington honor medal for excellence in pub. comm. Freedoms Found., Valley Forge, Pa., 1991. Mem. ABA, Ill. Bar Assn., Ogle County Bar Assn. (pres. 1971, 73), Nat. Legal Found., Acad. Polit. Sci., Ill. Press Assn., Ill. C. of C., Oregon City C. of C., Nat. Land Inst., Nat. Fedn. Ind. Bus., Ogle County Hist. Soc., Aircraft Owners and Pilots Assn., Ogle County Pilots Assn., Ill. Farm Bur., Ogle County Farm Bur. Republican. Office: US Ho of Reps 2220 Rayburn House Office Bldg Washington DC 20515-1316

MAO, HO-KWANG, geophysicist, educator; b. Shanghai, June 18, 1941; came to U.S., 1964; s. Sen and Tak-chun (Hu) M.; m. Agnes Liu, Feb. 10, 1968; children: Cynthia, Linda, Wendy. BS, Nat. Taiwan U., Taepei, 1963; MS, U. Rochester, 1966, PhD, 1968. Rsch. asst., teaching asst. U. Rochester, N.Y., 1964-67, rsch. assoc., 1967-68; postdoctoral fellow Geophys. Lab., Carnegie Instn., Washington, 1968-70, rsch. assoc., 1970-72, geophysicist, 1972—. Recipient Bridgman Gold medal Internat. Assn. for Advancement of High Pressure Sci. and Tech., 1989. Fellow Am. Geophys. Union, Am. Phys. Soc., Mineral Soc. Am. (award 1979); mem. AAAS, NAS (Arthur L. Day prize and lectureship 1990), Academia Sinica, Sigma Xi. Home: 11322 Edenderry Dr Fairfax VA 22030-5441 Office: Carnegie Inst Geophysics Lab 5251 Broad Branch Rd NW Washington DC 20015-1305

MAO, JEREMY J, orthodontist, educator; m. Susan Fu, Oct. 19, 1963. PhD, U.Alta., Edmonton, Can., 1992. American Board of Orthodontists Am. Bd. of Orthodontists, 1992. Asst. prof. U. Pitts., Pa., 1996—99; assoc. prof. U. of Ill. at Chgo., Chicago, Ill., 1999—. Cons. NIH, Bethesda, Md., 1999—. Editor: (Jour.) Tissue Engr. and Regenerative Medicine (Multiple NIH awards, 2003); author: (Jour. article) Tissue engineered cranial sutures (Whitaker Biomedical Engring. Rsch. Award, 2002). Recipient Tissue Engring. Webwatch, Tissue Engring. Soc. Internat., 2003; grantee Rsch. Award (total $1.9M), NIH, 1999, Biomedical Engring. Rsch. Grant, Whitaker Found., 2002, Rsch. Award (total $3.2M), NIH, 2003, Biotech. Grants, U. of Ill., 2003. Mem.: Orthopaedic Rsch. Soc., Biomedical Engring. Soc. (Outstanding Rschr. 2003). Achievements include invention of tissue engineered tissues and organs; patents for Microprocessor controlled devices; research in tissue engineered tendons and ligaments; development of tissue engineering articular joints. Office: Univ Illinois Chicago Rm 237 Tissue Engineering Chicago IL 60612 E-mail: jmao2@uic.edu.

MAPEL, WILLIAM MARLEN RAINES, retired banking executive; b. Maryville, Mo., Sept. 17, 1931; s. William and Evelyn (Raines) M.; m. Gail Manchee, June 21, 1958; children: Daniel B., Susan L., Stephen W. BA, Yale U., 1953. Indsl. relations asst. Union Carbide Corp., N.Y.C., 1953-57; with Citibank (N.A.), N.Y.C., 1957-88, asst. cashier, 1959-62, asst. v.p., 1962-64, v.p., 1964-69, sr. v.p., 1969-88. Bd. dirs. Churchill Capital Ptnrs., Atlantic Salmon Fedn., Que.-Labrador Found. Mem. U.S. Srs. Golf Assn., Woodway Country Club, Anglers Club, Pine Valley Golf Club, Wolf's Head, Miramichi Salmon Assn., Delta Kappa Epsilon. Home: 18 Stephanie Ln Darien CT 06820-2723

MAPES, GLYNN DEMPSEY, newspaper editor; b. N.Y.C., July 15, 1939; s. John George and Dorothy (Glynn) M.; m. Elizabeth Adlum, Apr. 13, 1963; children— Timothy Glynn, Susannah Glynn. BA, Williams Coll., 1961. Reporter Wall St. Jour., San Francisco, 1965-67, bur. chief Phila., 1967-70, fgn. editor N.Y.C., 1970-71, bur. chief, 1971-75, Page One editor, 1975-88, Reports editor, 1988-89, bur. chief London, 1989-93, money and investing editor N.Y.C., 1993-99, asst. mgn. editor, 1999—. Served to lt. (j.g.) USN, 1961-65. Mem.: Bronx Opera Chorus, London Concert Choir Club, Collegiate Chorale Club. Democrat. Home: 37 W 12th St Apt 2H New York NY 10011-8503 Office: Wall St Jour 200 Liberty St New York NY 10281-1003 E-mail: gmapes@pipeline.com.

MAPES, JEFFREY ROBERT, journalist; b. San Francisco, Nov. 21, 1954; s. James Robert and Phyllis June (Bloemker) M.; m. Karen Jane Minkel, Aug. 20, 1978; children: Katharine, James. BA, San Jose State U., 1976. Reporter Napa (Calif.) Register, 1976-79; Washington corr. Scripps League Newspapers, 1979-83; reporter The Oregonian, Portland, 1984-87, chief polit. reporter, 1987—. Office: The Oregonian 1320 SW Broadway Portland OR 97201-3499

MAPES, WILLIAM RODGERS, JR., lawyer; b. Cleve., Nov. 29, 1952; s. William R. and Marian (Atkins) M.; m. Patricia Soochan, Sept. 3, 1984. BS in Bus. Adminstrn., Miami U., Oxford, Ohio, 1974; JD, Am. U., 1977. Bar: D.C. 1978, U.S. Ct. Appeals (D.C. cir.) 1979, U.S. Ct. Appeals (fed. cir.) 1980, U.S. Ct. Appeals (5th cir.) 1981, U.S. Supreme Ct. 1982, U.S. Ct. Appeals (3d cir.) 1985, U.S. Ct. Appeals (4th cir.) 1987, U.S. Ct. Appeals (6th cir.) 1988. Ptnr. Ross, Marsh & Foster, Washington, 1984—2000, Duane Morris, Washington,

2000—. Bd. dirs. Holy Land Christian Ecumenical Found. Mem. ABA (editor nat. resources sect. newsletter 1984-89), Fed. Energy Bar Assn. Avocations: boating, tennis, bicycling. Home: 11430 Hollowstone Drive Rockville MD 20852 Office: Duane Morris 1667 K St NW #700 Washington DC 20006-1608 Office Phone: 202-776-7895. Business E-Mail: wrmapes@duanemorris.com.

MAPLE, MARILYN JEAN, educational media coordinator; b. Turtle Creek, Pa., Jan. 16, 1931; d. Harry Chester and Agnes (Dobbie) Kelley; 1 child, Sandra Maple. BA, U. Fla., 1972, MA, 1975, PhD, 1985. Journalist various newspaper including Mountain Eagle, Jasper, Ala., Boise (Idaho) Statesman, Daytona Beach (Fla.) Jour., Lorain (Ohio) Jour.; account exec. Frederides & Co., N.Y.C.; prodr. hist. films Fla. State Mus., Gainesville, 1967-69; writer, dir., prodr. med. and sci. films and TV prodns. for 6 medically related colls. U. Fla., Gainesville, 1969—. Pres. Media Modes, Inc., Gainesville. Author: On the Wings of a Butterfly; columnist Health Care Edn. mag.; contbr. Fla. Hist. Quar. Recipient Blakslee award, 1969, spl. award, 1979; Monsour lectr., 1979. Mem. Health Edn. Media Assn. (bd. dirs., awards 1977, 79), Phi Delta Kappa, Kappa Tau Alpha. Home: 1927 NW 7th Ln Gainesville FL 32603-1103 Office: U Fla PO Box 16J Gainesville FL 32602-0016 E-mail: mmaple@atlantic.net.

MAPLES, JIMMIE KAY, mechanical engineer; b. Berryville, Ark., Jan. 11, 1940; s. William Floyd and Edith (Bowman) M.; m. Beverly Florence Hadden, June 12, 1965 (div. Dec. 1968); children: Myrtle Venita, Beverly Sue; m. Sharon Gay Jennings Stewart (div. June 1974). BSME, U. Ark., 1962; MSRP, S.W. Mo. State U., 1991. Registered profl. engr., Mo., Ala., Ga., W.Va., Ark. Assoc. engr. Lockheed Aircraft Service Co., Ontario, Calif., 1962-63; design engr. McDonnell Aircraft Co., St. Louis, 1965-68; bookkeeper, salesman, co-owner Glen Isle Shoes, Springfield, Mo., 1969-72; mech. engr. Warren and Goodin, Inc., Springfield, 1972-77; engr. systems and equipment Piper Aircraft Corp., Lakeland, Fla., 1977-81; sr. facility engr. Zenith Electronics Corp., Springfield, 1981-88; with Boone Internat. Corrugated Svcs., Inc., Waco, Tex., 1988-89; cons., author Maples Enterprizes, Springfield, 1989—; v.p. Corrugated Mech. Svcs. Inc., Nixa, Mo., 1990-95, Heartland Electronics Corp., 1995-97; engr. Godwin & Assocs., 1997—; treas. Mohawk Quality Remodeling Inc., 2000—. Mem. Boone County Hist., Harrison, Ark., Carroll County Hist. and Geol., Berryville, Ozark Geol., Springfield, The Air Force Hist. Found., White River Valley Hist. Soc. Served with U.S. Army, 1963-65. Mem. Air Force Assn., Am. Aviation Hist. Soc., Nat. Rifle Assn., Nat. Geog. Soc., The Rich Family Assn., The Maples Family News, U. Ark. Alumni Assn., Frontiersmen Camping Fraternity (Royal Rangers Daniel Boone chpt.), Am. Soc. Programmetric and remote Sensing. Democrat. Mem. Assembly of God. Avocations: stamp collecting/philately, genealogy, computers. Home: 2545 W Swallow St Springfield MO 65810-3623 Office: Maples Enterprizes 2545 W Swallow St Springfield MO 65810-3623 also: Godwin & Assocs 1200 E Woodhurst Bldg P Springfield MO 65804 E-mail: godwinae@aol.com., jkmtree@aol.com.

MAPLESDEN, CAROL HARPER, marital and family therapist, music educator; b. Phila., Aug. 27, 1947; d. Emmitt Dewain and Helen Esther (Davison) Harper; m. James Paul Maplesden, May 27, 1967; children: Andrew James, Elizabeth Elvira. BA, Holy Family Coll., Phila., 1979; MA, La Salle U., Phila., 1984. Cert. counselor Nat. Bd. Cert. Counselors, lic. profl. counselor of mental health Del., Pa. Child, youth and family therapist People Acting To Help (PATH), Phila., 1983-86, Benjamin Rush Cmty. Mental Health, Phila., 1987-88; clin. dir. N.E. Treatment, Phila., 1988-89; outpatient supr. Interact Com. Mental Health, Phila., 1989; program supr. Cath. Charities Christopher House, Trenton, N.J., 1989-90; dir. Carden Family Inst., Phila., 1984—, instr. keyboard, organist, vocal performer, vocal choir and handbell choir dir. Carden music div., 1993—. Seminar lectr. in Phila. area. Author: (piano course and audio tape) Young Beginnings Piano Course, Part I, 1993. Mem.: NRC (hon. bus. chmn. 2004), ACA, Internat. Assn. Marriage and Family Counselors, Daughters Am. Colonists, Daughters Union Vets. Civil War (Pa. state pres. 2001—02). Republican. Methodist. Avocations: history studies, genealogy, crafts.

MAPOTHER, DILLON EDWARD, physicist, academic administrator; b. Louisville, Aug. 22, 1921; s. Dillon Edward and Edith (Rubel) M.; m. Elizabeth Beck, June 29, 1946; children: Ellen, Susan, Anne. BS in Mech. Engring, U. Louisville, 1943; D.Sc. in Physics, Carnegie-Mellon U., 1949. Engr. Westinghouse Rsch. Labs., East Pittsburgh, Pa., 1943-46; instr. Carnegie Inst. Tech., Pitts., 1946; mem. faculty U. Ill., Urbana, 1949-94, prof. physics, 1959-94, dir. acad. computing services, 1971-76, assoc. vice chancellor for rsch., 1976-94, acting dean grad. coll., vice chancellor research, 1977-78, assoc. dean grad. coll., 1979-94, assoc. vice chancellor rsch. emeritus, 1995—, assoc. dean emertus grad. coll., prof. emeritus physics, 1995—. Cons. in field. DuPont fellow, 1947-49; Alfred P. Sloan fellow, 1958-61; Guggenheim fellow, 1960-61 Fellow Am. Phys. Soc.; mem. AAAS, Assn. Univ. Tech. Mgrs., Am. Assn. Physics Tchrs., Sigma Xi. Achievements include research on ionic mobility in alkali halides, thermodynamic properties of superconductors, calorimetric study of critical points, administration of university research, commercialization of academic research technology. Home: 1013 Ross Dr Champaign IL 61821-6631 Office: U Ill Physics Dept Loomis Lab 1110 W Green St Urbana IL 61801-9013 Business E-Mail: mapother@uiuc.edu.

MAPOTHER, TOM CRUISE See CRUISE, TOM

MAPP, ALF JOHNSON, JR., writer, historian, educator; b. Portsmouth, Va., Feb. 17; s. Alf Johnson and Lorraine (Carney) M.; m. Hartley Lockhart, Mar. 28, 1953; 1 son, Alf Johnson III; m. Ramona Hartley Hamby, Aug. 1, 1971. AA, Coll. William and Mary, 1945, AB summa cum laude, 1961. Editorial writer Portsmouth Star, 1945-46, assoc. editor, 1946-48, editorial chief, 1948-54; news editor, editorial writer Virginian-Pilot, Norfolk, 1954-58; free-lance writer, 1958—; lectr. Old Dominion U., 1961-62, instr., 1962-67, asst. prof. English and history, 1967-73, asso prof. English, journalism, creative writing, history, 1973-79, prof., 1979-82, eminent prof., 1982-89, eminent scholar, 1989-92, eminent scholar emeritus, 1992—, Louis I. Jaffe prof. English, 1990-92; Louis I. Jaffe prof. emeritus, 1992—. Radio commentator WSAP, Portsmouth, Va., 1947-48; profl. lectr., 1984—; frequent analyst or guest on radio and TV including individual stas. and Universal Studio and BBC radio networks, CBS-TV, 1985—, C-SPAN, 1998—, PBS, 2001, NPR, 2001, CNN, 2001—; mem. Nat. Jefferson-Hemings Scholars commn., 2001-2002. Host TV series Jamestown to Yorktown, 1975-77; author: The Virginia Experiment, 1975, 3d edit., 1987, Frock Coats and Epaulets, 1963, 5th edit., 1996, America Creates Its Own Literature, 1965, Just One Man, 1968, The Golden Dragon: Alfred the Great and His Times, 1974, 4th edit., 1990, Thomas Jefferson: A Strange Case of Mistaken Identity, 1987, 3d edit., 1989 (Book-of-Month Club feature selection 1987), Thomas Jefferson: Passionate Pilgrim, 1991, 3d edit., 1993 (Book-of-Month Club feature selection 1991), (novel) Bed of Honor, 1995, 2d edit., 2000, Three Golden Ages: Discovering the Creative Secrets of Renaissance Florence, Elizabethan England, and America's Founding, 1998, Faiths of our Fathers: What America's Founders Really Believed, 2003; co-author: Chesapeake Bay in the Revolution, 1981, Portsmouth: A Pictorial History, 1989, Constitutionalism: Founding and Future, 1989, Constitutionalism and Human Rights, 1991, Great American Presidents, 1995; mem. editl. bd. Jamestown Found., 1967—; author lyrics for symphonic composition, world debut with Va. Symphony, 1998; author nationally distributed AP editl., 1998; contbr. to N.Y. Times, Wall St. Jour., other newspapers and mags. Mem. Portsmouth-Norfolk County Savs. Bond Com, 1948-51, Va. Com. on Libr. Devel., 1949-50; mem. publs. com. 350th Anniversary of Rep. Govt. in the Western World, 1966-69, War of Independence Comm., 1967-83; chmn. Portsmouth Revolutionary Bicentennial Com., 1968-81; chmn. awards jury Baruch award United Daus. Confederacy-Columbia U., 1976, mem., 1980; chmn. Portsmouth Mus. and Fine Arts Commn., 1983-85, Southeastern Va. Anglo-Am. Friendship Day, 1976, Bicentennial Commemoration of Cornwallis' Embarkation for Yorktown, 1981, World Premiere of Mary Rose Marine Archeol. Exhibit, 1985; mem. grant rev. com. Va. Commn. for the Arts, 1986-87; bd. dirs. Portsmouth Pub. Libr., 1948-58, v.p., 1954-56; bd. dirs. Va. Symphony, 1986-87, trustee, 1987—; mem. taxes and mandates com. City of Portsmouth, 1982-86; mem. adv. com. City Mgr. of Norfolk, 1988-94; bd. dirs. Portsmouth Area Cmty. Chest, 1948-52, Va. YMCA Youth and Govt. Found., 1950-52; mem. All-Am. cities com. for award-winning city Nat. League Municipalities, 1976; bd. advisors Ctr. Study Interactive Learning, Pasadena, Calif., 1993—; mem. steering com. Old Dominion U. Friends of the Libr., 1994-2002, dir., 1995-2002; trustee Coun. for Am.'s First Freedom, 1994-98; chair ad hoc com. Joint Portmouth-Suffolk Libr., 1999—; dir. Va. R.R. Mus., 2000--. Named Portsmouth Young Man of Year, 1951; recipient honor medal Freedoms Found., 1951, Disting. Rsch. award Old Dominion U., 1987, Great Citizen award Hampton Roads 8 Cities, 1987, Notable Citizen award Portsmouth, Va., 1987; English award Old Dominion Coll., 1961; Troubadour, Great Tchrs. award, 1969; Outstanding Am. Educator award, 1972, 74; Nat. Bicentennial medal Am. Revolution Bicentennial Adminstrsn., 1976; medal Comité Francais du Bicentenaire de l'Independence des Etats-Unis, France, 1976; (with Ramona Mapp) Nat. Family Svc. award Family Found. Am., 1980; Laureate award Commonwealth of Va., 1981; Disting. Alumnus award Old Dominion U., 1982; Liberty Bell award Portsmouth Bar Assn., 1985; Old Dominion U. Triennial Phi Kappa Phi Scholar award, 1986, 91; History medal Daus. Am. Revolution; Portsmouth Downtown Merchants award, 1984, 85, Nat. Founders and Patriots award, 1995; Old Dominion U. Outstanding Achievement award, 1995; Gladstone Hill Friend of the Arts award (with Ramona H. Mapp), 1995, Richard Hakluyt award for Am. history, 1996; named to Order of the Crown of Charlemagne, 1993. Mem. Am. Hist. Assn., Va. Hist. Soc., Portsmouth Hist. Soc. (historiographer 1975-82, v.p. 1982-84, pres. 1985), Norfolk Hist. Soc. (dir. 1965-72), No. Neck Hist. Soc., Hist. Socs. Eastern Va. (dir. 1971—), SAR, Am. Assn. U. Profs., Authors Guild, Va. Library Assn. (legislative com. 1950-51), Poetry Soc. Va. (pres. 1974-75, adv. com. 1976—), Va. Writers Club, Assn. Preservation of Va. Antiquities, Order of Cape Henry (dir. 1970—, nat. pres. 1975-76), Jamestowne Soc. (chief historian 1975-77, internat. sec. state 1978-79), English Speaking Union (dir. 1976-77), Modern Lang. Assn., Order of First Families Va. 1607-1624 (councillor 1996-99), Nat. Historians Circle, Phi Theta Kappa, Delta Phi Omega (chpt. pres. 1961), Phi Kappa Phi. Baptist. Home: Willow Oaks 2901 Tanbark Ln Portsmouth VA 23703-4828

MAPP, EDWARD CHARLES, speech educator; b. N.Y.C., Aug. 17, 1929; s. Edward Cameron and Estelle Viola (Sampson) Mapp; children: Andrew, Elmer, Everett. BA, CCNY, 1953; MS, Columbia U., 1956; PhD, NYU, 1970. Tchr. Bd. Edn., N.Y.C., 1957-64; dir. librs. N.Y.C. Tech. Coll. CUNY, 1964-77, dean of faculty Borough of Manhattan CC N.Y.C., 1977-81, prof. speech and communication, 1983-92, prof. emeritus, 1994—; vice chancellor City Colls. Chgo., 1982-83. Commr. N.Y.C. Commn. Human Rights, 1987—94, vice chair, 1992—94; treas. univ. faculty senate CUNY, 1974—77; model, 1994—. Compiler Books for Occupational Education Programs, 1971; author: (book) Blacks in American Films: Today and Yesterday, 1972; editor: Puerto Rican Perspectives, 1974; compiler Directory of Blacks in Performing Arts, 1978; columnist: Movie/TV Mktg., 1979—91; compiler Directory of Blacks in Performing Arts, 2d edit., 1990; co-author: (book) A Separate Cinema, 1992; author: African-Americans and the Oscar, 2003. Mem. Bklyn. Borough Pres. Adv. Panel, 1981—84; mem. exec. com. Com. Pub. Higher Edn., N.Y.C., 1978—81; bd. dirs. UN Assn. N.Y., 1975—78; trustee N.Y. Met. Ref. and Rsch. Agy., 1980—82. Named to Black Collectors Hall of Fame, 1992; recipient Founders Day award, NYU, 1970, award, Acad. Motion Picture Arts and Scis., 1996. Mem.: Theatre Libr. Assn., Black Filmmakers Found., Audelco, Friends Thirteen (bd. dirs. 2000—, 1st vice chmn. 2003—), Archons Colophon (convenor 1985—86). Democrat.

MAPP, RHONDA, professional basketball player; b. Oct. 13, 1969; Ctr.-forward Charlotte Sting, 1997—. Named Kodak and Street & Smith All-Am., 1992, Street & Smith All-Am., 1990; named to, ACC All-Tournament Team, 1989, 1991, First-Team All-ACC, 1991, 1992. Office: Charlotte Sting 3308 Oak Lake Blvd # B Charlotte NC 28208-7707

MAQUET, JACQUES JEROME PIERRE, anthropologist, writer; b. Brussels, Aug. 4, 1919; came to U.S., 1967, naturalized, 1974; s. Jerome and Jeanne (Lemoine) M.; m. Emma de Longrée, June 17, 1946; children: Bernard, Denis; m. Gisèle Cambresier, Nov. 13, 1970. JD, U. Louvain, Belgium, 1946, D.Phil., 1948; student, Harvard, 1946-48; PhD, U. London, Eng., 1952; Dr. ès-lettres, Sorbonne, France, 1973. Field anthropologist Inst. Sci. Research in Central Africa, 1949-51; head Inst. Sci. Research in Central Africa (Social Scis. Center), 1951-57; prof. State U. of Congo, Elisabethville, 1957-60; research dir. Ecole pratique des Hautes Etudes, U. Paris, 1961-68; prof. anthropology Case Western Res. U., 1968-71; prof. UCLA, 1971-91, chmn. dept. anthropology, 1978-83, prof. emeritus anthropology, 1991—. Vis. prof. Northwestern U., 1956, Harvard, 1964, U. Montreal, 1965, U. Pitts., 1967; extraordinary prof. U. Brussels, 1963-68 Author: The Sociology of Knowledge, 1951, Aide-mémoire d'ethnologie africaine, 1954, Ruanda, 1957, (with others) Elections en Société féodale, 1957, The Premise of Inequality in Ruanda, 1961, Power and Society in Africa, 1971, Civilizations of Black Africa, 1972, Africanity, The Cultural Unity of Black Africa, 1972, Introduction to Aesthetic Anthropology, 1979, The Aesthetic Experience, 1986, L'Anthropologue et l'esthétique, 1993, La Experiencia Estética, 1999; co-editor: (with others) Dictionary of Black African Civilization, 1974. Recipient Waxweiler award Royal Acad. Belgium, 1961; First World Festival of Negro Arts award Dakar, 1966 Mem. Am. Anthrop. Assn., Internat. Assn. Buddhist Studies, Pali Text Soc., AAUP, Fedn. Am. Scientists. Address: UCLA Dept Anthropology Los Angeles CA 90095-0001 E-mail: jmaquet@ucla.edu.

MARA, JOHN LAWRENCE, retired veterinarian, consultant; b. Whitesboro, N.Y., May 17, 1924; s. William Edward and Olive Pearl (Brakefield) M.; m. Kathleen Keefe, 1946 (div. 1958); children: William, Michael, Daniel, Patrick; m. Patricia Louise Paulk, 1970 (div. 1994); children: Jennifer Lee, Kennon. DVM, Cornell U., 1951. Diplomate Am. Coll. Vet. Nutrition. Intern N.Y. State Coll. Vet. Medicine, Cornell U., Ithaca, 1951-52; assoc. veterinarian L.W. Goodman Animal Hosp., Manhasset, N.Y., 1952-55; owner, pres. Mara Animal Hosp., Huntington, N.Y., 1955-79; profl. rep. Hills Pet Products, Topeka, Kans., 1979-80, mgr. profl. rels., 1980-81, dir. profl. affairs, 1981-88, dir. vet. affairs, 1988-94, sr. fellow profl. and acad. affairs, 1994-97, sr. fellow global vet. bus. devel., 1997-2000; ret., 2000. V.p. Huntington United Fund; chmn. Huntington Taxpayers Party, 1968-78, Ch. in the Garden, Garden City, N.Y., 1975-77, trustee, 1975-77; trustee, v.p. vet. divsn. Morris Animal Found.; bd. dirs. Topeka Symphony; mem. dean's coun. Kans. State U. Coll. Vet. Medicine. Sgt. U.S. Army, 1943-45, ETO. Recipient Disting. Svc. award We. Vet. Conf., 1988; named hon. alumnus Coll. Vet. Medicine, Wash. State U.; Jack L. Deans scholarship named in his honor Sch. Vet. Medicine U. Pa. Mem. AVMA (Pres.'s award, Jack L. Mara vet. technician program), L.I. Vet. Medicine Assn., N.Y. State Vet. Medicine Assn. (Outstanding Svc. award 2001), Am. Animal Hosp. Assn. (disting. life, Outstanding Svc. award 1996-97), Kans. Vet. Medicine Assn., Am. Coll. Vet. Nutrition (hon. diplomate), Greater Topeka Area C. of C. (legis. com.). Republican. Baptist. Avocations: gardening, swimming, reading. Home: 5500 SW 7th St Topeka KS 66606-2332 E-mail: jmara@kscable.com.

MARA, TIMOTHY GERALD, lawyer; b. Cin., July 30, 1949; s. Thomas James and Rose Marie (Sansone) M. B in Community Planning, U. Cin., 1972; JD, No. Ky. U., 1978. Bar: Ohio 1978, U.S. Dist. Ct. Cin. 1979, U.S. Ct. Appeals (6th cir.) 1983. Regional planner Ohio-Ky.-Ind. Regional Coun. of Govts., Cin., 1972-77; spl. asst. U.S. Rep. Thomas A. Luken, Cin., 1977-78; pvt. practice Cin., 1979—. Trustee Green Twp., Hamilton County, Ohio, 1982-86. Mem. Ohio State Bar Assn., Cin. Bar Assn., Hamilton County Dem. Steering Com. Avocations: nature walks, biking. Office: 1500 Chiquita Ctr 250 E 5th St Cincinnati OH 45202-4119

MARA, VINCENT JOSEPH, college president; b. Worcester, Mass., Sept. 19, 1930; s. Edward Stephan and Mary Stephanie (Kavanaugh) M.; m. Clare Owens, Feb. 15, 1958; children: John, Kevin, Maryellen, Thomas, Clare. BS in Edn., Worcester State Coll.; EdM, U. Conn.; PhD; LLD (hon.), Framingham State Coll., 1995; LHD, Fitchburg State Coll., 1995. From asst. prof. to assoc. prof. Framingham (Mass.) State Coll., 1960-63, dir. admissions, 1963-69, acad. dean, 1969-76; acting pres. Salem (Mass.) State Coll., 1974-75; pres. Fitchburg (Mass.) State Coll., 1976-95, prof. emeritus, 1995—, pres. emeritus, 1995—. Corporator Fitchburg Savs. Bank, 1976-85; mem. Montachusett Region Pvt. Industry Coun., 1983—; dir. Safety Fund Nat. Bank. Contbr. articles to profl. jours. Trustee Notre Dame Prep. Sch., Fitchburg, 1985-86, Worcester Pub. Libr., 1967-70, pres. bd. trustees, 1970; bd. dirs Fitchburg Civic Ctr., 1977-80, Cushing Acad., 1978-80, North Ctrl. Mass. Mental Health Assn., 1979-81, United Way, 1981-87, Montachusett Region Pvt. Industry Coun., 1983-93, Thayer Symphony Orch., 1987-90, pres., 1994-95; active Mass. Commn. Edn. Telecomm., 1983-90, Fitchburg Bd. Health, 1982-93, Fitchburg Sch. Com., 1998-2002. With U.S. Army, 1953-55. Named Outstanding Young Man of Yr. Worcester C. of C., 1960; recipient Disting. Citizen award City of Fitchburg, 1989. Mem. NEA, Am. Conf. Acad. Deans, Am. Assn. State Colls. and Univs., N.Am. C. of C. (bd. dirs. 1984-91), Fitchburg C. of C. (bd. dirs. 1977-83), Fay Club, Phi Delta Kappa, Kappa Delta Pi. Democrat. Roman Catholic. Home: 242 Pearl Hill Rd Fitchburg MA 01420-2019 Office: Fitchburg State Coll 160 Pearl St Fitchburg MA 01420-2631 E-mail: vmara@fsc.edu.

MARA, WELLINGTON T. (DUKE MARA), professional football team executive; b. NYC, Aug. 14, 1916; m. Ann Mumm, 1954; children: John Kevin, Susan Ann, Timothy Christopher, Stephen Vincent, Francis Xavier, Shelia Marie, Kathleen Mary, Ann Marie, Meghan Ann; children: Maureen Elizabeth, Colleen Elizabeth. Graduated, Fordham U., 1937. Ballboy, training camp to on-the-field operations to scouting and general orgn. NY Giants, pres., co-chief exec. officer. Chmn. exec. com. NFL Mgmt. Coun., 1971—77; pres. Nat. Football Conf., 1984; mem. Hall of Fame Com., Competition Com.; mem. exec. com. Mgmt. Coun. Lt. comdr. USN, World War II. Elected to Pro Football Hall of Fame, 1997. Achievements include being the labor arm of the NFL, and it was under his leadership that the league achieved five years of labor peace from 1977 to 1982. Office: NY Giants Giants Stadium East Rutherford NJ 07073 also: Nat Football League 410 Park Ave New York NY 10022-4407*

MARABLE, ROBERT BLANE, secondary school educator, agricultural studies educator; b. Athens, Ga., Jan. 7, 1959; s. Robert S. and Judy M.; m. Judy ANdrews Marable, July 20, 1985; 1 child, Mary Ashley Marable. BSA, U. Ga., 1981, MEd, 1982, EDS, 1985. Agr. edn. instr. Winder-Barrow High Sch., Winder, Ga., 1981-82, Greene-Taliaferro Comp. High Sch., Greensboro, Ga., 1982-89, Morgan County High Sch., Madison, Ga., 1989-98, Area Forestry Inst. Ga. Dept. Edn., 1998—. Named Young Agr. Tchr. of Yr., Ga., 1985, Tchr. of Yr. Morgan County Sch. System, 1992, Nat. Conservation Tchr. of Yr. Soil Conservation Svc., 1992, Youth Conservation Group of Yr., Ga. Wildlife Fedn., 1992. Mem. Ga. Vocat. Assn., Nat. Vocat. Assn., Ga. Vocat. Agr. Tchr's. Assn., Nat. Vocat. Agr. Tchr's Assn., profl. Assn. Ga. Educators Assn., Ga. Conservancy, Ga. Wildlife Fedn. Home: 1041 Buckeye Pointe Athens GA 30606-7617 Office: U Ga Four Towers Ga Dept Edn Athens GA 30602

MARABLE, SIMEON-DAVID, artist; b. Phila., May 10, 1948; s. Daniel Berry and Marsima (Maddela) M.; m. Pamela Joyce Sorenson, June 1, 1969; children: Simeon-David dePaul, Daniel-Dale Christopher (dec.), Jason-Andrew Bartley, Jo Anna Lee, Benjamin Arthur Kurtis. BA in Art and English, Lea Coll., Minn., 1970; postgrad., Tyler Sch. Art, Phila. Art tchr. 7-8th grade Pennsbury Sch. Sys., Pa., 1970—88; Art tchr. 9-10th grade Charles H. Boehm H.S., Pennsbury, 1988—, Medill Bair H.S., Pennsbury, 1990—; Art tchr. 9-12th grade Pennsbury H.S. W, 2002—. Tchr. Neshaminy Adult Edn., 1972-82; resident artist Middletown Hist. Assn., 1976, Three Arches Corp., 1975, also treas.; founder, creator Rivulet Art 2000. Permanent collections include Albert Lea (Minn.) Libr., chapel Ft. Dix, N.J., pencil/charcoal Am. Eagle superimposed over outline Levittown, Pa., James A. Michener Mus., 2003; portraits of Mr. Mike Schmidt, Mr. Lee Elia; creator Phila. City of Champs logo, 50th anniversary logo Fairless Hills, Pa. 1951-2001 Celebration; creator children's ednl. programs Falls Twp. 300th Pa. statehood; artwork represented in Middletown Twp. calendar, 1992, Falls Twp. calendar, 1992; creator Olde Phila. Ednl. Program and Pa. Statehood Program, Nat. Rep. Conv., Phila., 2000; creator scale model homes exhibit Pa. Hist. Mus., 2002; author, creator Levittown Pennsylvania, 1952-2002 A Garden Community, 2002; sketch presented to Gov. of Pa. 2002. Vol. Rep. Nat. Conv., Phila., 2000; mgr. Boys Soccer League, Boys Little League, Middletown Twp.; sr. Babe Ruth coach, mgr. Langhorne Athletic Assn., 1988-89; sr. coach Babe Ruth League, 1989; J.V. baseball coach, 1989; mem. Presdl. Task Force; elected to Nat. Trust for Hist. Preservation, 1995; involved with ednl. program Honoring the 200th Anniversary U.S. Constn. Commemorative Olde Phila. Constn. Atty.; curator Levittown Exhibit, Pa.; pres. Levittown Internationally Known Communities Inc., 2003—. Served with USAR, 1970. Named Artist of Yr., Albert Lea Lions Club, 1970. Mem. Buck County Art Educators (pres. 1973-74), Levittown Artists Assn., Nat. Soc. Arts and Lit., Internat. Platform Assn. Roman Catholic. Achievements include development of Levitt Mobile that houses memorabilia and photog. of the 1950's in Buck's Co., Pa. Home: 18 Spindletree Rd Levittown PA 19056-2215 Office: 600 S Olds Blvd Fairless Hills PA 19030-2441 Office Phone: 215-945-4558. Personal E-mail: amx_12345@hotmail.com.

MARACEK, LEIGH, association administrator; s. Rickie Tsceekasatana. Grad., Women's Health Leadership Inst., 1999. Cmty. outreach coord. Project Safe, Athens, Ga.; dir. devel. and program dir. Oakland Relationship Abuse Prevention, Calif.; exec. dir. Physicians for a Violence-Free Soc., San Francisco. Author: (book) The Educator's Guide and Appendix to the Oakland RAP Curriculum. Scholar scholar, Cmty. Devel. Inst. Profl. Devel. for Cons. Program. Avocation: art. Office: Physicians for a Violence-Free Society 160 14th St San Francisco CA 94103

MARADIAGA KIEFFER-AANONSEN, NORA LUDMILA, language educator; b. La Ceiba, Honduras, Dec. 18, 1957; arrived in U.S., 1980; d. Carlos Maradiaga and Ana Ludmila Kieffer-Maradiaga; m. Richard Alfred Aanonsen, June 8, 2002. AA, El Camino C.C., Torrance, Calif., 1989; BA in Global Politics, Spanish Lit., Calif. State U., Dominguez Hills, 1993, MA, 1995; postgrad., Calif. Coast U., Santa Ana, 1999. Bilingual tchr. asst. LA Unified Sch. Dist., 1981—90, bilingual spl. edn. trainee, 1990—94; bilingual spanish educator Compton (Calif.) Sch. Dist., 1994—2000; Spanish educator Compton Coll., 1997—, Spanish prof. upward bound math. and sci. program, 2002—. Spanish translator Compton Coll., 1999—2001, student campus climate surveys, 1997, 98, 2000. Mem.: Calif. Tchr. Assn., Calif. Bilingual Edn., El Camino Coll. Student Assn., Dominguez Hills U. Student Assn., Alpha Phi. Democrat-Npl. Roman Catholic. Avocations: reading, acting, jogging, travel, martial arts. Home: 15327 Mansel Ave Lawndale CA 90260 Office: Compton C C 1111 E Artesia Blvd Compton CA 90221 E-mail: noraludmila1@aol.com.

MARADUDIN, ALEXEI A. physics educator; b. San Francisco, Dec. 14, 1931; BS, Stanford U., 1953, MS, 1954; PhD in Physics, Bristol U., 1957. Rsch. assoc. physics U. Md., College Park, 1956-57, rsch. asst. prof., 1957-58; asst. rsch. prof. Inst. Fluid Dynamics & Applied Math., 1958-60; physicist Westinghouse Rsch. Labs., Churchill Borough, Pa., 1960-65; cons. semiconductor br. U.S. Naval Rsch. Lab., Washington, 1958-60, Los Alamos (N.Mex.) Sci. Lab., 1965-67, 83-89, Gen. Atomic Divsn. Gen. Dynamics Corp., 1965-71; prof. physics U. Calif., Irvine, 1965—, chmn. dept., 1968-71. Recipient Alexander von Humboldt U.S. Sr. Scientist award, 1980-81. Fellow Am. Phys. Soc., Optical Soc. Am., AAAS, Inst. Physics (U.K.); mem. Phi Beta Kappa, Tau Beta Pi, Sigma Xi. Office: U Calif Irvine Dept Physics & Astronomy Frederick Reines Hl # 2180 Irvine CA 92697-0001 Office Phone: 949-824-5943. E-mail: aamaradu@uci.edu.

MARAFIOTI, KAYALYN A. lawyer; b. Rochester, N.Y., 1954; AB cum laude, Harvard U., 1976; JD, NYU, 1979. Bar: N.Y. 1980. Ptnr. Skadden, Arps, Slate, Meagher & Flom, N.Y.C. Note and comment editor NYU Jour. Internat. Law and Politics, 1978-79. Office: Skadden Arps Slate Meagher & Flom 4 Times Sq Fl 24 New York NY 10036-6595

MARAMAN, KATHERINE ANN, judge; b. Los Alamos, N.Mex., Aug. 13, 1951; d. William Joseph and Katherine Ann (Thorpe) Maraman. BA, Colorado Coll., 1973; JD, U. N.Mex., 1976. Bar: N.Mex. 1976, Guam 1978, Trust Territory Pacific Islands, Commonwealth of No. Mariana Islands, U.S. Ct.

Appeals (9th cir.), U.S. Supreme Ct. Draftsperson N.Mex. Legis. Coun. Svc., Santa Fe, 1976—77; atty. Brooks & Klitzkie, P.C., Agana, 1977—84; pvt. practice Agana, 1985—88; counsel Office of Gov., Agana, 1988—94; judge Superior Ct., Agana, 1994—. Mem. asst. legis. counsel Guam Legis., Agana, 1977—80, mem. minority counsel, 1981—87; bd. dirs. Pub. Defender Svc. Corp., Agana, 1988—94. Trustee Guam Ter. Law Libr., 1994—; counsel Rep. Party, Agana, 1981—94; deacon First Presbyn. Reformed Ch., Agana; bd. dirs. Guam Rehab. and Workshop, Inc., Tumon, 1983—95. Mem.: Mem. Guam Bar Assn. Office: Superior Ct Guam 120 W Obrien Dr Hagatna GU 96910-5174

MARAMOROSCH, KARL, virologist, educator; b. Vienna, Jan. 16, 1915; came to U.S., 1947, naturalized, 1952; s. Jacob and Stefanie Olga (Schlesinger) M.; m. Irene Ludwinowska, Nov. 15, 1938; 1 dau., Lydia Ann. MS magna cum laude in Entomology, Agrl. U., Warsaw, Poland, 1938; student, Poly. U. Bucharest, Rumania, 1944-46; fellow, Bklyn. Bot. Garden, 1947-48; PhD (predoctoral fellow Am. Cancer Soc. 1948-49), Columbia, 1949. Civilian internee in, Rumania, 1939-46; asst., then assoc. Rockefeller U., N.Y.C., 1949-61; sr. entomologist Boyce Thompson Inst., Yonkers, N.Y., 1961-74, program dir. virology and insect physiology, 1962-74; prof. microbiology Waksman Inst., Rutgers U., New Brunswick, N.J., 1974-85; prof. entomology Cook Coll., Rutgers U., New Brunswick, 1985—, Robert L. Starkey prof., 1983—; vis. prof. agr. U. Wageningen, Netherlands, 1953, Cornell U., 1957, Rutgers U., 1967-68, Fordham U., 1973, Hokkaido U., Sapporo, Japan, 1980, Justus Liebig U., Giessen, Ger., 1983. Mendel lectr. St. Peters Coll., Jersey City, 1963; virologist FAO to Philippines, 1960; Disting. Vis. prof. Fudan U., Shanghai, 1982; cons. FAO-UN, World-wide survey, 1963; chmn. U.S.-Japan Coop. Seminar, 1965, 74, 85; mem. panel food and fiber Nat. Acad. Scis., 1966; cons. rice virus diseases AID-IRRI, Hyderabad, India, 1971; cons. UNDP, Bangalore, India, 1978-79; virologist FAO/UNDP, Sri Lanka, 1981, 82, 83, Mauritius, 1985; AIBS lectr., 1970-72, Found. Microbiology Nat. lectr., 1972-73, Fulbright Disting. prof., Yugoslavia, 1972, 78; mem. tropical medicine and parasitology study sect. NIH, 1972-76; chmn. 1st 3d Internat. Confs. Comparative Virology, 1969, 73, 76. Author: Comparative Symptomatology of Coconut Diseases of Unknown Etiology, 1964; editor: Biological Transmission of Disease Agents, 1962, Insect Viruses, 1968, Viruses, Vectors and Vegetation, 1969, Comparative Virology, 1971, Mycoplasma Diseases, 1973, Viruses, Evolution and Cancer, 1974, Invertebrate Immunity, 1975, Legume Diseases in the Tropics, 1975, Invertebrate Tissue Culture: Research Applications, 1976, Invertebrate Tissue Culture: Applications in Medicine, Biology and Agriculture, 1976, Aphids as Virus Vectors, 1977, Insect and Plant Viruses: An Atlas, 1977, Viruses and Environment, 1978, Practical Tissue Culture Applications, 1979, Leafhopper Vectors and Plant Disease Agents, 1979, Vectors of Plant Pathogens, 1980, Invertebrate Systems in Vitro, 1980, Vectors of Disease Agents, 1981, Mycoplasma Diseases of Trees and Shrubs, 1981, Mycoplasma and Allied Pathogens of Plants, Animals and Human Beings, 1981, Plant Diseases and Vectors: Ecology and Epidemiology, 1981, Invertebrate Cell Culture Applications, 1982, Pathogens, Vectors and Plant Diseases: Approaches to Control, 1982, Subviral Pathogens of Plants and Animals, 1985, Viral Insecticides for Biological Control, 1985, Biotechnology Advances in Insect Pathology and Cell Culture, 1987, Mycoplasma Diseases of Crops, 1988, Invertebrate and Fish Tissue Culture, 1988, Biotechnology for Biological Control of Pests and Vectors, 1991, Viroids and Satellites: Molecular Parasites at the Frontier of Life, 1991, Plant Diseases of Uncertain Etiology, 1992, Insect Cell Biotechnology, 1994, Arthropod Cell Culture Systems, 1994, Forest Trees and Palms: Diseases and Control, 1996, Invertebrate Cell Culture: Novel Directions and Biotechnology Applications, 1997, Invertebrate Cell Culture: Looking Toward the XXI Century, 1997, Biotechnology and Plant Protection in Forestry Sci., 1998, Maintenance of Human, Animal, and Plant Pathogen Vectors, 1999; Methods in Virology, 1964—, Advances in Virus Research, 1972—, Archives of Virology, 1973-78, Intervirology, 1973-77, Advances in Cell Culture, 1979—; editor in chief Jour. N.Y. Entomol. Soc, 1972-84; assoc. editor: Virology, 1964-68, 75-79. Recipient Sr. Rsch., Lalor Found., 1957, Nat. Ciba-Geigy awad in agr., 1976, Wolf prize in agr., 1980, Jurzykowski prize in biology, 1980, Disting. Svc. award, Am. Inst. Biol. Scis., 1983, Lifetime Achievement award, Soc. In Vitro Biology, 2001. Fellow AAAS (hon., Campbell award 1958), Entomol. Soc. Am., Am. Phytopath. Soc., N.Y. Acad. Scis. (A. Cressy Morrison prize natural sci. 1951, chmn. div. microbiology 1956-60, rec. sec. 1960-61, v.p. 1962-63), Nat. Acad. Scis. India (hon.); mem. Harvey Soc., Growth Soc., Phytopath. Soc., Indian, Japan, Can. phytopath. socs., Leopoldina Acad., Internat. Com. Virus Nomenclature, Electron Microscopy Soc., Am. Soc. Microbiology (Waksman award 1978), Soc. In Vitro Biology (Tissue Culture Assn., pres. N.E. br. 1978-81, pres. history br. 1988-90, Disting. Lifetime Achievement award 2001), Soc. Invertebrate Pathology (founder's lectr., Adelaide 1990, Founder's honoree Sapporo 1998), Internat. Assn. Medicinal Forest Plants (pres. 1989—), Sigma Xi (pres. Rugers chpt. 1978, Khailshanker Durlabhji award Jaipur 1993). Home: 17 Black Birch Ln Scarsdale NY 10583-7456 Office: Rutgers U Dept Entomology New Brunswick NJ 08901 Office Phone: 732-932-9329. E-mail: maramorosch@aesop.rutgers.edu.

MARAN, STEPHEN PAUL, astronomer; b. Bklyn., Dec. 25, 1938; s. Alexander P. and Clara F. (Schoenfeld) M.; m. Sally Ann Scott, Feb. 14, 1971; children: Michael Scott, Enid Rebecca, Elissa Jean. BS, Bklyn. Coll., 1959; MA, U. Mich., 1961, PhD, 1964. Astronomer Kitt Peak Nat. Obs., Tucson, 1964-69; project scientist for orbiting solar observatories NASA-Goddard Space Flight Center, Greenbelt, Md., 1969-75; head advanced systems and ground observations br. NASA-Goddard Space Flight Ctr., 1970-77, mgr. Operation Kohoutek, 1973-74, sr. staff scientist Lab. for Astronomy and Solar Physics, 1977-95; asst. dir. Space Scis. for Info. and Outreach, 1995—. Cons. Westinghouse Rsch. Labs., 1966; vis. lectr. U. Md., College Park, 1969-70; sr. lectr. UCLA, 1976; press officer Am. Astron. Soc., 1985—; A. Dixon Johnson lectr. in sci. comm., Pa. State U., 1990; vis. scholar Univ. Ctr. Ga., 1997; lectr. on astronomy cruises and eclipse tours. Author: (with John C. Brandt) New Horizons in Astronomy, 1972, 2d edit., 1979, Arabic edit., 1979, (with Jacqueline Mitton) Gems of Hubble-Superb Images from the Hubble Telescope, 1996, Astronomy for Dummies, 1999, German edit. 2000, French edit. 2001; editor: Physics of Nonthermal Radio Sources, 1964, The Gum Nebula and Related Problems, 1971, Possible Relations Between Solar Activity and Meteorological Phenomena, 1975, New Astronomy and Space Science Reader, 1977, A Meeting with the Universe, 1981, Astrophysics of Brown Dwarfs, 1986, The Astronomy and Astrophysics Encyclopedia, 1991; assoc. editor: Earth, Extraterrestrial Scis, 1969-79; editor: Astrophys. Letters, 1974-77, assoc. editor, 1977-85; contbg. editor Air & Space/Smithsonian, 1990—; mem. editl. adv. bd. Astronomy Mag., 1997—, Astronomy and Geophysics, 1997—; contbr. articles on astronomy, space to popular mags. Named Disting. Visitor Boston U., 1970; recipient Group Achievement awards NASA, 1969, 74, Exceptional Achievement medal, 1991, Klumpke-Roberts award Astron. Soc. of Pacific, 1999. Fellow AAAS; mem. Internat. Astron. Union (editor daily newspaper 1988, Minor Planet 9768 named Stephenmaran in honor 2000), Am. Astron. Soc. (Harlow Shapley vis. lectr. 1981—), press. officer 1985—), Royal Astron. Soc., Am. Phys. Soc., Am. Geophys. Union. Office: Code 600 Nasa Goddard Space Flight Ctr Greenbelt MD 20771-0001 Business E-Mail: maran@aas.org.

MARANDA, GUY, retired oral maxillofacial surgeon, Canadian health facility executive, educator; b. Paris, Sept. 9, 1936; arrived in Canada, 1937; s. Emilien and Lucille (Fortin) M.; married; children: Lucille, Jean, Isabelle. BA, U. Ottawa, Ont., Can., 1957; DDs, U. Montreal, Can., 1962; cert. oral surgeon, U. Pa., 1965. Pvt. practice, Quebec, 1965-70; mem. faculty U. Laval, Ste. Foy, Que., Can., 1970—, asst. prof., 1987-94, prof., 1995—; ret., 2001. Bd. dirs. Ordre Dentistes du Québec; pres. Quebec Assn. Oral Surgeons, 1979-80; cons. Quebec Health Bd., Assurance Auto Quebec, various law firms. Mem. Royal coll. Dentists Can. (diplomate, pres. 1991), Internat. Assn. Oral Surgeons, Can. Assn. Oral Surgeons, Can. Dental Assn. Ordre Dentistes Que. (chmn. found.). Roman Catholic. Home: 6031 Route De Fossambault Fossambault Sur Le Lac QC Canada G0A-3M0

MARANELL, DEBRA JEAN, human resources specialist, quality assurance professional, insurance agent; d. Richard Jesse and Darlene Mae Maranell; 1 child from previous marriage, Jaclynne Marie. Student, Augustana Coll., 1973—75, Buena Vista Coll., 1983. Lic. ins. agt. Iowa. Tel. sales rep. APAC Customer Svcs., Spencer, Iowa, 1998—2002, ins. agt., 1999—2002, trainer, 2001—02; ins. agt. Top Grade Inc., Spencer, 2003—, trainer, 2003—04, quality assurance mgr., 2003—, human resource mgr., 2004—. Mem.: U.S. Jr. C. of C. (10th degree Jaycee). Democrat. Roman Catholic. Avocations: writing, crocheting, graphic design. Office: Top Grade Inc 1900 N Grand Ave Ste E-1 Spencer IA 51301 Office Phone: 712-580-2200. Office Fax: 712-580-2206. Personal E-mail: djac@ncn.net.

MARANO, ANTHONY JOSEPH, cardiologist; b. White Plains, N.Y., Apr. 14, 1934; s. Anthony Joseph and Mary Antoinette (Perrotta) M.; m. Mary Regina Marbach, Aug. 23, 1958; children— Thomas, Kathryn, Michele. B.A., Williams Coll., 1956; M.D., Cornell Med. Coll., 1960. Diplomate Am. Bd. Internal Medicine, Am. Bd. Cardiovascular Disease. Intern Bellevue Hosp., N.Y.C., 1960-61; resident St. Luke's Hosp., N.Y.C., 1961-63; NIH fellow in cardiology Mt. Sinai Hosp., N.Y.C., 1963-64, research assoc., 1964-75; clin. assoc. in medicine Coll. Physicians and Surgeons, N.Y.C., 1970-86; pres. med. staff White Plains Hosp., 1984-86, chief cardiology, 1985-91, chief cardiology emeritus, 1991—, bd. dirs., 1983-88; cons. in cardiology Burke Rehab. Ctr.; med. dir., founder Paramedic Ambulance, White Plains, 1976-82. Contbr. articles to med. jours. Trustee Pace U., N.Y.C., 1975—, Home Savs. Bank, White Plains, 1973-90; bd. dirs. YMCA, White Plains, 1978-82; team physician White Plains High Sch., 1967—; cons. physician Dept. Pub. Safety, White Plains, 1968—; cons. physician City of White Plains Sch. System, 1994—; bd. dirs. Westchester County Sports Hall of Fame, 1993—; alumni trustee Tyng Found., Williams Coll., 1994—. Tyng scholar Williams Coll., 1952-59; recipient Outstanding Achievement award Emergency Med. Services Council, 1982; named to White Plains High Sch. Hall of Fame, 1998. Fellow ACP, Am. Coll. Cardiology; mem. AMA, Am. Coll. Sports Medicine, Am. Heart Assn., N.Y. State Heart Assn. (bd. dirs. 1982-85), Westchester Heart Assn. (v.p. 1983-86, pres. 1987-90), Phi Beta Kappa. Clubs: University (White Plains) (pres. 1970-71); Westchester Country (Harrison, N.Y.). Avocations: tennis, skiing, gardening. Home: 46 Eagle Ct White Plains NY 10605-5116 Office: 15 North Broadway White Plains NY 10605 Office Phone: 914-948-8838.

MARANO, RICHARD MICHAEL, judge; b. Waterbury, Conn., June 22, 1960; s. Albert Nicholas and Angeline Domenica (Viotti) M.; m. Eileen N. Barry. BA, Fairfield U., 1982; JD, Seton Hall U., 1985. Bar: Conn. 1985, US Dist. Ct. Conn. 1985, US Tax Ct. 1986, US Supreme Ct. 1990, US Ct. Appeals (2d cir.) 1991; cert. criminal trial advocate. Assoc. Moynahan, Ruskin, Mascolo & Mariani, Waterbury, 1985-87; ptnr. Marano & Diamond, Waterbury, 1987—2001, Marano Law Offices, 2001—04; superior ct. judge, 2004—. Bd. of examiners Nat. Bd. Trial Advocacy, 1999—. Author: History of the Order Sons of Italy of Waterbury, Connecticut, 1995, Connecticut Criminal Legal Forms, 1999, Vote Your Conscience: The Last Campaign of George McGovern, 2003; co-author: Growing Up Italian and American in Waterbury, 1997; co-editor: Counsel for the Defense, 1991-93, editor, 1993-98; contbr. law articles to Conn. Bar Jour. Bd. dirs. Italian-Am. Dem. Club, Waterbury, 1988-2004, Ctrl. Naugatuck Valley HELP, 1992—, Anderson Boys Club, 1989-2002, pres. 1996-98, Waterbury Housing Police Fund, 1992-94, Waterbury Crime Stoppers Inc., 1994-97; pres. Conn. Young Dems., 1981-82; state coord. McGovern for US Presdl. campaign, 1983-84; campaign mgr. Orman for Congress, 1984; active Oxford Dem. Town Com., 2002-2004; commr. Waterbury Pub. Assistance, 1986-88, Waterbury Fire Bd., 1996-98; justice of the peace, Waterbury, 1989-99; gen. counsel Waterbury Dem. Town Com., 1990-96; trustee Our Lady of Lourdes Ch., 1993—; alderman City of Waterbury, 1988-90. Mem. ABA, ATLA, KC, Conn. Bar Assn., Nat. Assn. Criminal Def. Lawyers (life), Conn. Criminal Def. Lawyers Assn. (pres.-elect 1997-98, pres. 1998-99), Conn. Italian-Am. Bar Assn. (pres. 1993-95), Conn. Trial Lawyers Assn., Waterbury Bar Assn. (bd. dirs. 1993-2002, pres. 1996-98), New Haven County Bar Assn., Nat. Italian-Am. Bar Assn. (Conn. delegate 1993—), Sons of Italy (pres. lodge #66 1994-96), Unico Club (pres. Waterbury chpt. 1997-99), Cath. Lawyers Guild, Conn. Acad. Cert. Trial Lawyers, Nat. Eagle Scout Assn. (life), Elks, Alpha Mu Gamma, Pi Sigma Alpha. Roman Catholic. Home: 24 Lake Dr Oxford CT 06478-1172 E-mail: richardmarano@aol.com.

MARANO, THOMAS J. marketing professional; V.p. Coca-Cola, USA; pres., COO mktg. support svcs. AHL Svcs., Inc., Atlanta, 1999—. Office: AHL Svcs Inc 3353 Peachtree Rd NE Ste 1120 Atlanta GA 30326-1053

MARANS, J. EUGENE, lawyer; b. Butte, Mont., May 26, 1940; s. Edward and Florence M.; m. Anne Marie Borger, Sept. 3, 1978; children: Julia C., John E. AB, Harvard U., 1962, LLB, 1965. Bar: N.Y. 1966, D.C. 1971. Law clk. to Judge John M. Wisdom U.S. Ct. Appeals (5th cir.), New Orleans, 1965-66; assoc. Cleary, Gottlieb, Steen & Hamilton, N.Y.C., 1966-70, Paris, 1970-71, Washington, 1971-74, ptnr., 1975-90, 93-00, of counsel, 2001—, ptnr. Hong Kong, 1990-93. Mem. N.Y. State adv. com. U.S. Commn. Civil Rights, 1969-70; mem. nat. eval. com. on simplified method of determining eligibility in pub. assistance HEW, 1969-70; sec., counsel Bipartisan Com. on Absentee Voting, 1973— Contbr. articles to legal jours. Bd. dirs. New Leadership Fund, chmn. 1977-79; mem. Sabre Found., pres. 1990; trustee Internat. Inst. Rural Reconstrn., vice chair, 2001—. Mem. Assn. Ams. Resident Overseas, Ripon Soc. (nat. governing bd. 1962-2001, chmn. 1969-70), Coun. on Fgn. Rels., ABA, D.C. Bar (chmn. internat. sect. 1978-79), Assn. of Bar of City of N.Y., Am. Soc. Internat. Law, Union Internat. des Avocats, Washington Fgn. Law Soc. (pres. 1985-86), Am. Law Inst. Office: 2000 Pennsylvania Ave NW Washington DC 20006-1812 E-mail: emarans@cgsh.com.

MARASHIO, PAUL WILLIAM, humanities educator; b. Woburn, Mass., May 30, 1941; s. Peter and Catherine (Danizio) M.; m. Nancy Feeney, June 24, 1967. BEd, Keene State Coll., 1963; MA, U. N.H., 1968; cert. advanced studies, Wesleyan U., 1977. Tchr., Somersworth, N.H., 1963-66; history dept. head Salem, N.H., 1966-69; supr. instrn. and curriculum, 1969-71; prin. Woodbury Sch., Salem, 1971-77; curriculum coord. Salem Sch. Dist., 1977-83, educator, 1983-86; prof. humanities N.H. Cmty. Tech. Coll., Claremont, 1986—. Mem. N.H. Excellence in Edn. Commn., 1983-84. Editor: Myth in U.S. Culture; editor Pedagogy Jour.; contbr. articles to profl. jours. Pres. Salem Hist. Soc., 1977-80; mem. Salem Com. on Environ. Issues, 1977, Old Town Hall Restoration Com., Salem Mus. Com.; rschr. N.H. Bicentenial Celebration U.S. Constn., 1985. Recipient award N.H. Coun. Better Schs., 1974, Tchrs. Who Inspire award Lawrence Eagle Tribune, 1983; Ariz. State U. fellow, 1968; scholar U.S. Constn. Bicentenial, 1986—. Mem. Am. Hist. Assn., Orgn. Am. Historians, Coll. Humanities Assn., Nat. Assn. for Humanities Edn., Sunapee Yacht Club, Phi Delta Kappa. Roman Catholic. Address: PO Box 2211 Mount Sunapee NH 03255-2211

MARATOS-FLIER, ELEFTHERIA, medical educator, physician; b. N.Y.C., Dec. 15, 1951; d. Costas and Anna (Domenikos) Maratos; m. Jeffrey Scott Flier, Dec. 7, 1975; children: Sarah, Lydia. BS, NYU, 1972; MD, Mt. Sinai Sch. Medicine, N.Y.C., 1976. Intern and resident George Washington U. Hosp., Washington, 1976-78; resident Beth Israel Hosp., Boston, 1978-79; rsch. fellow Harvard Sch. Pub. Health, Boston, 1980-81; fellow Joslin Diabetes Ctr., Boston, 1981-82; instr. Brigham & Women's Hosp., Harvard Med. Sch., Boston, 1982-87, asst. prof., 1987—. Contbr. articles to Sci., Jour. Cell Biology, Jour. Virology, Jour. Clin. Investigation. Mary K. Iacocca Rsch. fellow, 1981. Mem. Am. Soc. Virology, Am. Microbiol. Assn., Am. Diabetes Assn., Phi Beta Kappa. Office: Joslin Diabetes Ctr One Joslin Pl Boston MA 02215 also: Brigham & Womens Hosp 75 Francis St Boston MA 02115-6110

MARAYNES, ALLAN LAWRENCE, filmmaker, television producer; b. N.Y.C., Apr. 26, 1950; s. Harry and Dorothy (Kaufman) Maraynes; m. Bitsy Healy, Oct. 14, 1978; children: Sean, Megan, Matthew. BA, Queens Coll., 1972; MA, Loyola U., L.A., 1974. Assoc. prodr. CBS News, N.Y.C., 1976-77, prodr. 60 Minutes, 1974-88, writer, dir. 60 Minutes, 1976-88; pres. No. Films, N.Y.C., 1988-90; exec. prodr. "SST" program ABC, N.Y.C., 1989; prodr. 20/20 ABC News, N.Y.C., 1990-93, sr. investigative prodr. 20/20, 1994-96; sr. investigative prodr. Dateline NBC, N.Y.C., 1996—. Lectr. New Sch., N.Y.C., 1979, Columbia U., N.Y.C. Author: (plays) A Straight Line to the Market Place, 1975, (screenplays) Smithereens, 1999. Recipient Emmy award, NATAS, 1981, 1985, 1988, 1989, 1991, 1993, 1995, 1997, 1998, 2002, George Foster Peabody award, 1989, 2000, Edward R. Murrow award, 1997, 1998, 2000, Investigative Reporters and Editors award, 1997, 2000—01, DuPont Columbia Journalism award, 2000, George Polk award, 2000, Overseas Press Club award, 2002. Mem.: NATAS, Writers Guild Am. Office: NBC 30 Rockefeller Plz Fl 2 New York NY 10112-0036 E-mail: ALLAN.MARAYNES@NBC.COM.

MARAZITA, MARY LOUISE, genetics researcher; b. Cheboygan, Mich., June 13, 1954; m. Richard T. McCoy, 1984; 5 children. BS, Mich. State U., 1976; PhD in Genetics, U. N.C., 1980. Fellow U. So. Calif., 1980-82; statistician, instr. UCLA, 1982-86; asst. prof. human genetics Med. Coll. Va., 1986-93; dir. Cleft Palate-craniofacial Ctr. U. Pitts., 1993-00, head divsn. oral biology, 1999—, asst. dean for rsch. Sch. Dental Medicine, 2000-2001, assoc. dean rsch., 2001—. Instr. biomath. U. Calif., 1984-86; asst. prof. dentistry Med. Coll. Va., 1992-93; assoc. prof. human genetics and oral maxillofacial surgery U. Pitts., 1993-97, prof. human genetics and oral and maxillofacial surgery, 1997—. Fellow Am. Coll. Med. Genetics, Am. Cleft Palate Assn., Am. Soc. Human Genetics, Internat. Genetic Epidemiol. Soc., Internat. Assn. Dental Rsch. Achievements include research in genetics of cleft lip, cleft palate and other craniofacial anomalies, including statistical genetic analysis and gene mapping studies. Office: U Pitts Divsn Oral Biology/Genetics Ste 500 Cellomics Bldg/100 Technology Dr Pittsburgh PA 15219

MARBLE, DUANE FRANCIS, geography educator, researcher; b. Seattle, Dec. 10, 1931; s. Francis Augustus and Beulah Belle (Simmons) M.; m. Jacquelynne Hardester, Aug. 18, 1957; children: Kimberley Eileen Beauclair, Douglas Craig. BA, U. Wash., 1953, MA, 1956, PhD, 1959. Asst. prof. real estate U. Oreg., Eugene, 1959; asst. prof. regional sci. U. Pa., Phila., 1960-63; from assoc. prof. geography to prof. geography Northwestern U., Evanston, Ill., 1963-73, assoc. dir. Transp. Ctr., 1966-73; prof. geography and computer sci. SUNY at Buffalo, Amherst, NY, 1973-87; prof. geography and natural resources Ohio State U., Columbus, 1987-98, prof. emeritus, 1998—. Chmn. com. on geog. data sensing and processing Internat. Geog. Union, 1980-88; bd. dirs. Castlereagh Enterprises, Phoenix; founder Internat. Symposium Spatial Data Handling; cons. on geog. info. systems to U.S. Bur. Census, UN, also pvt. orgns. Editor: Intro Readings in GIS, 1990, Taylor & Francis, 1990-95; author computer program (best software award Assn. Am. Geogs. 1990); mem. editl. bd. Annals of Assn. Am. Geography, 2000—. Recipient Legend in Leadership award, Environ. Sys. Rsch. Inst., 1997. Mem.: AAAS, Assn. Am. Geographers (honors 1993). Home: 2226 Primrose Ln Florence OR 97439-7627

MARBURGER, DARLA A. federal agency administrator; d. Maynard and Dawn Marburger. BS in agr. Journalism, Tex. A&M U.; MS in agr. econ., Tex. A&M. Dep. asst. sec. US Dept. Edn., Off. Elem. Sec. Edn. Policy, Wash., 2002—; sr. policy analyst Tex. Senate Edn. Com., Tex.; Congl. adv., agr. nat. resources issues Tex. Leg., Tex., 1994. Vol. tchr. ESL. Office: US Dept Edn Policy Dept FOB-6 Rm 3W305 400 Maryland Ave SW Washington DC 20202 E-mail: darla.marburger@ed.gov.

MARBURGER, JOHN HARMEN, III, federal agency administrator; b. S.I., N.Y., Feb. 8, 1941; s. John H., Jr. and Virginia A. (Smith) M.; m. Carol Preston Godfrey, June 12, 1965; children: John Harmen, Alexander Godfrey. BA in Physics magna cum laude, Princeton U., 1962; PhD in Applied Physics (NASA trainee), Stanford U., 1967; LHD (hon.), Hofstra U., 2000; DS (hon.), Stony Brook U., 2002, Moscow State U., 2002. Physicist Goddard Space Flight Center, NASA, 1962—63; asst. prof. physics and elec. engring. U. So. Calif., Los Angeles, 1966—69, assoc. prof., 1969—75, prof., 1975—80, chmn. physics dept., 1972—75, interim dean Coll. Letters, Arts and Scis., 1976—77, dean Coll. Letters, Arts and Scis., 1977—80; pres. SUNY, Stony Brook, 1980—94, prof. physics and elec. engring., 1994—98; pres. Brookhaven Sci. Assoc., 1998—2001; dir. Brookhaven Nat. Labs, 1998—2001, Off. Sci. & Tech. Policy, Washington, 2001—. Cons. laser fusion program Lawrence Livermore Labs., 1972-76; chmn. N.Y. State fact finding panel on Shoreham Nuclear Power Facility, 1983; chmn. bd. trustees Universities Rsch. Assn., 1988-94; co-chair NASULGC Bd. on Oceans and Atmosphere, 1992-93; bd. dirs. N.Y. State Edn. and Rsch. Network, Inc., 1986-98; bd. dirs., chair L.I. Rsch. Inst., 1989-95; bd. dirs. L.I. High Tech. Incubator Corp., 1992-98, chair 1994-98. Contbr. articles to tech. publs. Bd. dirs. Mus. at Stony Brook, 1980-92, 94-98, L.I. Assn., Inc., 1983-93, 98—, Action Com. for L.I., 1980-83, L.I. Forum for Tech., Inc., 1980—, Rsch. Found. SUNY, 1990—; bd. trustees Princeton U., 1985-89; chmn. N.Y. State Energy Office Rev. Commn., 1980-81, Suffolk County (N.Y.) Task Force on Priorities in Fin., 1980-81; campaign chmn. United Way of L.I., 1991-92. Recipient Shuichi Kusaka Meml. Prize Princeton U., 1962 Fellow AAAS, APS; mem. Assn. of Colls. and Univs. State of N.Y. (pres. 1988-90), Coleman Chamber Music Assn. (bd. dirs. 1969-80). Office: OSTP Eisenhower Exec Office Bldg 17th and Pennsylvania Ave NW Washington DC 20502

MARBURY, RITCHEY MCGUIRE, III, engineering executive, surveyor; b. Albany, Ga., May 18, 1938; s. Ritchey McGuire and Shirley Kathryn (VanHouten) M.; m. Fonda Gayle Starnes, June 16, 1962; children: Mary Kathryn, Ritchey McGuire IV. BCE, Ga. Tech. Inst., 1960, M in City Planning, 1966. Registered profl. engr., Ga., Fla., Idaho, Ala.; land surveyor, Ga. V.p. Marbury Engring. Co., Albany, Ga., 1965-78, pres., chmn. bd., 1981—; pres. Marbury, Ritter, Scott & Turner, Inc., Albany, 1970-78, 81-92, Marbury Assocs., Inc., 1991—, Idaho Boise Mission of Latter-day Saints Ch., 1978-81. Presenter seminars on total quality mgmt. to nat. convs. of Am. Cons. Engrs. Coun., Design Constrn. Quality Inst., Sml. Firm Coalition of Cons. Engrs., Assn. for Project Mgrs. Exec. bd. Boy Scouts Am., Southwest Ga., 1982—. Served to 1st lt. U.S. Army, 1963-65. Mem. NSPE (South Ga. chpt. pres. 1993-95), Am. Cons. Engrs. Coun., Surveying and Mapping Soc. of Ga. (bd. dirs. 1966-78), Ga. Planning Assn., Home Builders Assn. (bd. dirs. 1985-86), Rotary. Mem. Lds Ch. Avocations: fishing, writing, music, computer, golf. Home: 1824 Green Valley Dr Albany GA 31707-3116 Office: 2334 Lake Park Dr Albany GA 31707-3132 Office Phone: 229-435-6133. E-mail: mec@marbury.com., marbury3@marbury.com. *Always be a role model of Christlike behavior and do those things that make a significant differenc for good. Do what's right simply because it's the right thing to do. The greatest results come through kindness.*

MARBURY, STEPHON, professional basketball player; b. Feb. 20, 1977; children: Stephanie, Xaviera. Student, Ga. Tech., 1996. Guard Minn. Timberwolves, 1996—98; guard, forward N.J. Nets, 1998—2001; guard Phoenix Suns, 2002—04, N.Y. Knicks, 2004—. Mem. U.S. Olympic Basketball Team, Athens, 2004. Hosts The Stephon Marbury Basketball Classic. Named National High School Player of the Year (Abraham Lincoln H.S.) by Parade Magazine, 1995; named to 1996-97 NBA All-Rookie First Team, NBA All-Star game, 2001, 2003. Office: c/o NY Knickerbockers 2 Pennsylvania Plz New York NY 10121*

MARBURY, VIRGINIA LOMAX, insurance and investment executive; b. Ruston, La., June 25, 1918; d. Dallas Daniel and Della (Southern) Lomax; m. William A. Marbury Jr., Sept. 5, 1943; children: Rebekah, Caroline. BA, La. Tech. U., 1936, LLD (hon.), 1987; MusB, La. State U., 1938. Exec. v.p. Marbury Corp., Ruston, La., 1944—; sec.-treas. Bankers Life La., Ruston, 1959—. 1st v.p., membership chmn. Lincoln Parish Mus. and Hist. Soc., Ruston, La., 1992—. Recipient Tower Medallion award La. Tech. U., 1991. Mem. Shreveport Symphony Soc. Republican. Episcopalian. Office: Marbury Corp 601 N Trenton St Ruston LA 71270-3840

MARBUT, ROBERT GORDON, communications, electronic security and broadcast executive, investor; b. Athens, Ga., Apr. 11, 1935; s. Robert Smith and Laura Gordon (Powers) M.; m. Margo Susan Spitz, Sept. 24, 1989; children: Robert Gordon, Laura Dodd, Michael Powers, Marcy Lizbeth. B Indsl. Engring., Ga. Inst. Tech., 1957; MBA with distinction, Harvard U., 1963. Registered profl. engr., Calif. Engr. Esso Standard Oil Co., Baton Rouge, 1957; corp. dir. engring. and plans Copley Press, La Jolla, Calif., 1963-70; v.p. Harte-Hanks Newspapers, Inc., San Antonio, 1970-71; pres.,

CEO Harte-Hanks Comm., Inc., San Antonio, 1971-91, also dir., 1971-91, vice chmn. bd. dirs., 1991; founder, chmn., CEO Argyle Comm., Inc, San Antonio, 1992—; founder, CEO, dir. Argyle TV Holding, Inc., San Antonio, 1993-95; co-founder, chmn., CEO Argyle TV, Inc., San Antonio, 1994-97; chmn., co-CEO Hearst-Argyle TV, Inc., N.Y.C., 1997-2000, chmn., 2001—02; co-mng. ptnr. Argyle Global, LP, 2001—; founder, chmn., CEO SectecGLOBAL, Inc., 2002—. Dir. AP, 1979—88, vice chmn., 1987—88; chmn. Newspaper Advt. Bur., 1988—90, exec. com. dir., 1974—89, 1982—90; bd. dirs. Valero Energy Corp., Tupperware, Inc., Hearst-Argyle TV, Inc., Bus. Execs. Nat. Security; mem. adv. bd. U. Ga. Henry W. Grady Sch. Journalism, 1975—83, Ga. Tech., 1978—81, 1998—; founding mem. Am. Bus. Conf., 1981—89; mem. U. Tex. Centennial commn., 1981—83; pres. adv. coun. U. Tex. Coll. Comm., 1982—83; bd. dirs. Up With People, 1983—2001, exec. com., 1984—2001; instr. Armstrong Coll., 1951, Calif. State U., L.A., 1964, Woodbury Coll., 1964. Author: (with Healy, Henderson and others) Creative Collective Bargaining, 1965. Coordinating chmn. San Antonio Target 90 commn., 1983-84; campaign chmn. United Way, San Antonio, 1985, chmn. bd. trustees 1988-89; vice chmn. Tex. select com. on Tax Equity, 1987-89; mem select com. Tex. Revenues, 1991-92; mem. Tex. World Trade Coun., 1986-87. Capt. USAF, 1958-61. Salzburg Inst. Am. Studies sr. fellow, 1997—; recipient Isaiah Thomas award Rochester Inst. Tech., 1980, EXCEL award in comm., 1987, People of Vision award, 1991; selected to Acad. Disting. Engring. Alumni Ga. Tech., 1995. Mem. Am. Newspaper Publs. Assn. (chmn. task group on future, chmn. telecomm. com. 1974-81, bd. dirs. 1976-84, chmn. future task group), So. Newspaper Pubs. Assn. (pres. 1979-80, dir. 1975-81, treas. 1977), Am. Newspaper Pubs. Assn. Found. (trustee 1976-79), Tex. Daily Newspaper Assn. (pres. 1979, Tex. Newspaper Leader of Yr., 1981), N.Y. Met. Club, Doubles, San Antonio Country Club, Argyle Club, Greater San Antonio C. of C., Delta Tau Delta (Alumni Achievement award 2000), Omicron Delta Kappa, Phi Eta Sigma. Office: Hearst-Argyle Television Inc 200 Concord Plaza Dr Ste 700 San Antonio TX 78216-6941

MARCALI, JEAN GREGORY, retired chemist; b. Jermyn, Pa., May 29, 1926; d. John Robert and Anna Marie Gregory; m. Kalman Marcali, Oct. 6, 1956; children: Coleman, Frederick. Student, U. Pa., 1948—52, U. Del., 1971—72. Microanalyst E.I. du Pont de Nemours & Co., Deepwater, NJ, 1943-60, tech. info. analyst, organic chems. dept., 1960-64, tech. info. analyst info. systems dept. Wilmington, Del., 1964-67, sr. adviser tech. info., 1967-70, supr. tech. info., 1970-82, 85-89, supr. adminstrv. svcs. Ctrl. Rsch. Dept., 1982-85, cons., 1989-92, ret., 1992. Sec. Alfred I. Dupont Elem. PTA, 1971, pres. 1972; pres. PTA Brandywine Sch. Dist., 1973; mem. Wilmington Dist. Rep. Com., 1976—. Mem. Am. Chem. Soc. (treas. divsn. chem. info. 1976-81, chmn.-elect 1981, chmn. 1982, 83, divsn. councilor 1983-90), Am. Chem. Soc. (com. on chem. abstracts svc. 1983-85, 87-93, mem. joint bd. coun. com. on chem. abstracts svc. 1994-96, 98, 99, 2000, Del. sec. chem. lit. topical group, chmn. 1979-80, chem. vets. chmn.-elect 1999), Order Ea. Star, Du Pont Country Club. Lutheran. Home: 312 Waycross Rd Wilmington DE 19803-2950

MARCATANTE, JOHN JOSEPH, educational administrator; b. N.Y.C., Mar. 3, 1930; s. Joseph and Matilda Clara (Grasso) M. Student, NYU, 1948-50; AB, Bklyn. Coll., 1955; MS in Edn., Hunter Coll., 1958. English tchr. secondary schs., N.Y.C., 1955-72; asst. prin. Astoria Intermediate Sch., N.Y.C., 1967—. Instr. Hunter Coll., 1963; lectr. in edn. Grad. Sch., Queens Coll., N.Y.C., 1965-67. Cons., Anglo-Am. Seminar on Teaching English, Dartmouth Coll., 1966, Anglo-Am. Seminar on Teaching the Disadvantaged, West Midlands Coll., Great Britain, 1968. Author: Identification and Image Stories, 1964, American Folklore and Legends, 1967, (with others) Macmillan Gateway English Series, 1969, Tales from World Epics, 1990; also numerous articles in profl. jours., poetry; editor: Fourteenth Yearbook N.Y. Society for Experimental Study for Education, 1970. Mem. Nat. Coun. Tchrs. English, N.Y.C. Tchrs. English, Coun. Supervisory Assns., Cath. Tchrs. Assn., Columbia Assn. N.Y.C., Poetry Soc. Am. Home: 52 Daffodil Ln Wantagh NY 11793-1802

MARCDANTE, KAREN JEAN, medical educator; b. Milw., Sept. 15, 1955; d. Willard Karl and Beth Elaine (Maule) Kohn; m. Mark Wendelberger, Aug. 5, 1978 (div. Sept. 1985); m. Anthony Marcdante, Oct. 17, 1998. Student, Marquette U., 1973-76; MD, Med. Coll. Wis., 1980. Diplomate Am. Bd. Pediat. Resident in pediat. Med. Coll. Wis. affiliated hosps., Milw., 1980-83; instr. pediat. Med. Coll. Wis., Milw., 1983-85, asst. prof. pediat., 1987-94, assoc. prof. pediat., 1994-2000, prof. pediat., 2000—, assoc. dean curriculum, 1997—2003, vice-chair edn. dept. pediat., 1994—; fellow in pediatric critical care U. Calif., San Francisco, 1985-87; vice chief staff Children's Hosp. Wis., Milw., 1995-97. Dir. Respiratory Care Svcs., 1992-98, Transport Program, 1998—; chief dept. pediat. Children's Hosp. Wis., 1991-95, dept. critical care 1993-95, mem. numerous coms., including care mgmt. steering com., 1994-98, critical care com., 1991—, pres.-elect, 2003--. Contbr. numerous articles to profl. jours. Recipient New Investigator award Assn. Am. Med. Colls., 1992, Cert. Leadership award YWCA and Marquette Electronics Found., 1992; grantee Dept. HHS, 1996—. Mem. Am. Acad. Pediat. (pub. rels. chair Wis. chpt. 1988-91, sec.-treas. 1990-95, v.p. 1995-96, chair careers and opportunities 1996-2001), Soc. Critical Care Medicine (chair task force on quality improvement pediat. 1994-96, quality indicator devel. work group 1997-98, Presdl. citation 1996, 97), Coun. on Med. Student Edn. in Pediat. (co-chair task force on tchg. methods 1991-96, nominating com. 1993-95, exec. com. 1996-99, sec.-treas. 1997—). E-mail: kwendel@mail.mcw.edu.

MARCEAU, JUDITH MARIE, retired elementary school educator, small business owner; b. Gardner, Mass., Aug. 10, 1946; d. George Joseph and Bernice Victoria (Johnson) Babineau; m. James Victor Krymowski, Aug. 20, 1976 (div. Mar. 1985); children: Kathryn Victoria, Kenneth James; m. Glenn Francis Marceau, Aug. 30, 1989. Grad., Sch. Worcester Art Mus., 1967; BFA, Clark U., 1971. Tchr. elem. art Quabbin Regional Pub. Schs., Barre, Mass., 1967-70, Gardner (Mass.) Pub. Schs., 1970—2003, ret., 2003; propr. Babineau's Corner Antiques Shop, Hubbardston, 2003—. Author, editor: Fascinating Facts of Gardner, 1977, 2d edit., 1999, Hubbardston as Seen Through the Eyes of its Children, 1987; author numerous poems. Active Hubbarston Hist. Commn.; vol. Hubbarston Recycling Initiative; bd. dirs. Gardner Edn. Assn., 1975-86; bd. dirs. Youth Advocacy and Counseling Ctr., Gardner, 1979-82. Recipient Citation of Outstanding Edn. City of Gardner, 1994, 2000, Cert. of Commendation, Mayor of City of Gardner. Mem. Mass. Tchrs. Assn., Nat. Tchrs. Assn. Avocations: writing history, poetry, antiques, watercolor painting, sketching. Home: 221 Gardner Rd Hubbardston MA 01452-1655 Office: Babineau's Corner Antiques 221 Gardner Rd Hubbardston MA 01452 Office Phone: 978-632-2840.

MARCEAU, YVONNE, ballroom dancer, educator; b. Chgo., July 13, 1950; BFA, U. Utah, 1972; AA, Imperial Soc. Ballroom Dance. Ballet dancer Ballet West; ptnr. with Pierre Dulaine, 1976; founder, artistic dir. Am. Ballroom Theatre, N.Y.C., 1984-93; educator dance divsn. Julliard Sch., N.Y.C., 1993—. Guest tchr. Sch. Am. Ballet, N.Y.C.; tchr. ballroom dancing Juilliard Sch. Appearances include The Smithsonian Inst., JFK Ctr. for Performing Arts, N.Y. State Theater, N.Y.C., Sadlers Wells, London, (Broadway and London show) Grand Hotel, 1989-92, toured with Pierre Dulaine and Am. Ballroom Theatre worldwide. Recipient Recipient Brit. Theatrical Arts Championships 4 times, Spl. Astaire award, Dance Educator awards, Outstanding Achievement in Dance award Nat. Coun. Dance Am., 1992, Dance Mag. award, 1993.

MARCELLA, JOSEPH, information system administrator; BS in Biochemistry, Temple U., 1970. Computer operator/sys. programmer, asst. mgr. King Kullen Grocery Co./Gen. Fire & Casualty, L.I., 1971-72; asst. v.p., electronic banking Bank of Am., Las Vegas, 1972-83; sr. v.p., dir. info. svcs. Primerit Bank of Nev., Las Vegas, 1983-96; dir. info. technologies City of Las Vegas, 1997—. Bd. dirs., past pres. Bank Adminstrn. Inst.; past pres., v.p. Nev. Clearing House Assn.; bd. dirs. Western Payments Alliance; mem. Rules Com. Nat. Automated Clearning House, Task Force to Build Acad. Advanced Tech., Focus Sch. Partnership program. Mem. South Nev. Entities Tech. Alliance (bd. dirs.). Office: City Las Vegas Dept Info Techs City Hall 5th Fl 400 Stewart Ave Las Vegas NV 89101-2927

MARCELLO, FRANK F. lawyer, educator, writer; b. Chgo., Aug. 11, 1961; s. Fred Anthony and Antoinette Marie (Colombo) M. BS, DePaul U., 1983; MBA, Dominican U., 1996; JD, The John Marshall Law Sch., 1986. Exec. legal coord. Office of Cook County Pub. Defender, Chgo., 1985-87, asst. dep. chief, 1987-89; v.p. exec. counsel Connaught Corp., Chgo., 1989-93; v.p. sr. counsel Internat. Cons. Group, Chgo., 1993-96; prof. law Northwestern Bus. Coll., Chgo., 1996—, Dominican U., River Forest, Ill., 1996—. Active Joint Civic Com. Italian Ams., Chgo. Mem. ABA, AAUP, Justinian Soc., Nat. Italian Am. Bar Assn., Sons of Italy Found., Assn. Cath. Colls. and Univs. Office: Northwestern 7725 S Harlem Ave Bridgeview IL 60455 E-mail: ffm@abanet.org.

MARCELYNAS, RICHARD CHADWICK, management consultant; b. New London, Conn., Aug. 21, 1937; s. Anthony F. and Elizabeth A. (Chadwick) M.; m. Betty A. Forray, July 1, 1961; children: Michael R., Thomas R. BA in Bus. Adminstrn., U. Wash., 1961; postgrad. Seattle U., 1971-72. Mgmt. trainee, installation foreman Pacific Bell, Fullerton, Calif., 1964-65; cost acct. Scott Paper Co., Everett, Wash., 1965-68; asst. v.p. pers. and adminstrn. Nat. Pub. Svc. Ins. Co., Seattle, 1968-77; pers. ops. mgr. Olympia Brewing Co., 1977-78; mgr. indsl. rels. Heath Tecna Precision Structures Inc., Kent, Wash., 1978-85; mgmt. cons., recruiter Pilon Mgmt. Co., Seattle, 1985-90; pers. adminstr. Peninsula Group Olympia, Wash., 1990-94; pres. Chadwick & Assocs., Olympia, 1994-2000; info. tech. recruiter Red Rover Solutions, Bellevue, Wash., 2000-01; career cons. Hay and Assocs., Bellevue, 2002—. Served to maj. USMCR, 1961-77. Decorated commendations for bravery and tech. expertise, 1962-64; recipient Seattle chpt. Pacific N.W. Personnel Mgrs. Assn. Bd. Dirs. award, 1975. Mem. Pacific N.W. Personnel Mgrs. Assn. (past pres. Tacoma chpt.), Human Resources Consultants Network. Office: 623 Sherman St SW Olympia WA 98502-5454

MARCH, JACQUELINE FRONT, retired chemist; b. Wheeling, W.Va., 1914; m. A.W. March (dec.); children: Wayne Front, Gail March Cohen. BS, Case Western Res. U., 1937, MA, 1939; postgrad., U. Chgo.; PhD, U. Pitts., 1945. Clin. chemist U. Chgo.; rsch. analyst Koppers Co.; info. scientist Union Carbide Corp., Carnegie-Mellon U., Pitts.; propr. March Med. Rsch. Lab. etiology of diabetes, Dayton, Ohio; ret. Guest scientist Kettering Found., Yellow Springs, Ohio; Dayton Found. fellow Miami Valley Hosp. Rsch. Inst.; chemistry faculty U. Dayton, computer/chem. info. scientist Rsch. Inst. U. Dayton; on-base prin. investigator Air Force Info. Ctr. Wright-Patterson AFB, 1969-79; chem. info. specialist Nat. Inst. Occupl. Safety and Health, Cin., 1979-90; propr. JFM Cons., Ft. Myers, Fla., 1990-93; ret., 1993; designer info. sys., spkr. in field. Contbr. articles to profl. jours. Active Retired and Sr. Vol. Program Lee County Sch. Dist., 1992-93, Lee County Hosp. Med. Libr., Rutenberg County Libr. Recipient Letter of Commendation, Girl Scouts U.S., 1931, Cert. of Recognition, U. Dayton, 1950, Outstanding Profl. Achievement award Affiliated Engring. and Sci. Found. of Dayton, 1978, others; Wyeth Gastrointestinal fellow Med. rsch. U. Chgo., 1940-42. Mem. AAUP (exec. bd. 1978-79), Am. Soc. Info. Sci. (treas. South Ohio 1973-75), Am. Chem. Soc. (emeritus, Fla. chpt., pres. Dayton 1977), Dayton Engring. Soc. (hon.), Soc. Advancement Materials and Process Engring. (Fla. chpt., pres. Midwest chpt. 1977-78), 60 Dayton Affiliated Tech. Socs. (Outstanding Scientist and Engr. award 1978), Alumni Assn. of Carnegie-Mellon U. (hon.), Sigma Xi (emeritus Fla. chpt., pres. Cin. fed. environ. chpt. 1986-87).

MARCH, JAMES GARDNER, social scientist, educator; b. Cleve., Jan. 15, 1928; s. James Herbert and Mildred (MacCorkle) M.; m. Jayne Mary Dohr, Sept. 23, 1947; children: Kathryn Sue, Gary Clifton, James Christopher, Roderic Gunn. BA, U. Wis., 1949; MA, Yale U., 1950, PhD, 1953, Copenhagen Sch. Econs., 1978, Swedish Sch. Econs., 1979, U. Wis., Milw., 1980, U. Bergen, 1980, Uppsala U., 1987, Helsinki Sch. Econs., 1991, Göteborg U., 1998, U. Poitiers, 2001, Budapest U. Econs., 2003. From asst. prof. to prof. Carnegie Inst. Tech., 1953-64; prof., dean Sch. Social Scis. U. Calif., Irvine, 1964-70; prof. mgmt., higher edn., polit. sci. and sociology Stanford (Calif.) U., 1970-95, prof. emeritus, 1995—. Cons. in field; mem. Nat. Council Ednl. Research, 1975-78, Nat. Sci. Bd., 1968-74; mem. sociol.-social psychology panel NSF, 1964-66; social sci. tng. com. NIMH, 1967-68; mem. math. social sci. com. Social Sci. Research Council, 1958-60; mem. Assembly Behavioral and Social Sci., NRC, 1973-79, chmn. com. on aging, 1977-82, chmn. com. on math., sci., tech. edn., 1984-86 Author: (with H.A. Simon) Organizations, 1958, 2nd edit., 1993, (with R.M. Cyert) A Behavioral Theory of the Firm, 1963, 2nd edit., 1992, Handbook of Organizations, 1965; (with B.R. Gelbaum) Mathematics for the Social and Behavioral Sciences, 1969; (with M.D. Cohen) Leadership and Ambiguity, 1974, 2nd edit., 1986, Academic Notes, 1974; (with C.E. Lave) An Introduction to Models in the Social Sciences, 1975; (with J.P. Olsen) Ambiguity and Choice in Organizations, 1976, Aged Wisconsin, 1977, Autonomy as a Factor in Group Organization, 1980, Pleasures of the Process, 1980, Slow Learner, 1985; (with R. Weissinger-Baylon) Ambiguity and Command, 1986, Decisions and Organizations, 1988; (with J.P. Olsen) Rediscovering Institutions, 1989, Minor Memos, 1990, A Primer on Decision Making, 1994, Fornuft og Forandring, 1995; (with J.P. Olsen) Democratic Governance, 1995; The Pursuit of Organizational Intelligence, 1999, (with M. Schulz and X. Zhou) The Dynamics of Rules, 2000, Late Harvest, 2000; (with M. Augier) The Economics of Choice, Change and Organization, 2002, (with M. Augier), Models of a Man, 2004; contbr. articles to profl. jours. Fellow Ctr. Advanced Study in Behavioral Scis., 1955-56, 73-74; recipient Wilbur Lucius Cross medal Yale U., 1968, Viipuri prize, Finland, 2004; decorated knight 1st class Royal Norwegian Order of Merit, comdr. Order of Lion of Finland. Mem. NAS, APA, Nat. Acad. Edn., Accademia Italiana di Economia Aziendale, Royal Swedish Acad. Scis., Norwegian Acad. of Sci. and Letters, Am. Acad. Arts and Scis., Am. Econ. Assn., Am. Polit. Sci. Assn. (v.p. 1983-84, John Gaus award 1997, Wildavsky award 2004), Am. Sociol. Assn., Acad. Mgmt. (Disting. Scholar award 1999), Russell Sage Found. (trustee 1985-94, chmn. 1990-93), Finnish Soc. Scis. and Letters, Citigroup Behavioral Scis. Rsch. Coun. (chmn. 1994-2000), Am. Philos. Soc., Phi Beta Kappa, Sigma Xi. Home: 501 Portola Rd Box 8136 Portola Valley CA 94028 Office: Stanford U 71 Cubberley Stanford CA 94305-3096 Office Phone: 650-723-9890. Business E-Mail: march@stanford.edu.

MARCH, KATHLEEN PATRICIA, judge; b. May 18, 1949; married; 2 children. BA, Colo. Coll., 1971; JD, Yale U., 1974. Bar: N.Y. 1975, Calif. 1978. Law clk. to hon. judge Thomas J. Griesa U.S. Dist. Ct. (so. dist.) N.Y., 1974-75; assoc. Cahill, Gordon & Reindel, N.Y.C., 1975-77; asst. U.S. atty. criminal div. Office of U.S. Atty. Cen. Dist. Calif., L.A., 1978-82; assoc. Adams, Duque & Hazeltine, L.A., 1982-85; ptnr. Demetriou, Del Guercio & Lovejoy, L.A., 1985-88; judge U.S. Bankruptcy Ct. Cen. Dist. Calif., L.A., Calif., 1988—. Bd. editors Yale U. Law Jour. Mem.: ABA, Fin. Lawyers Assn., L.A. Bankruptcy Forum (bd. dirs.), Nat. Assn. Women Judges, Women Lawyers Assn., L.A. County Bar Assn., Fed. Bar Assn., Phi Beta Kappa. Avocations: horseback riding, scuba diving, photography. Office: Roybal Fed Ct Bldg 255 E Temple St Ste 1460 Los Angeles CA 90012-3332

MARCH, KEVIN P. electronics executive; BS Economics, U. Pittsburgh, 1983, MBA, 1984. Various positions including dir. fin., contr. semicondr. units Tex. Instruments, Dallas, 1984—97, v.p., fin. planning mgr. global ops., 1997—2002, contr., 2002—03, sr. v.p., CFO, 2003—. Mem. Fin. Exec. Internat., Conf. Bd.'s Coun. Fin. Exec. Office: Texas Instruments MS 3905 7839 Churchill Way Dallas TX 75266-0199

MARCH, LIONEL JOHN, architecture educator, researcher; b. Hove, Sussex, Eng., Jan. 26, 1934; came to U.S., 1984; s. Leonard James and Rosina Amelia March; m. Maureen Mary Francis; children: Candida, Ben Oliver, Ben, Talitha, Anna, Sarah. BA with honours, Cambridge (Eng.) U., 1959, Dip Arch, 1961, MA, 1962, ScD, 1978. Lectr. Cambridge U. Sch. Architecture, 1968-76; prof. U. Waterloo (Ont., Can.) Faculty Engring., 1974-76, Open U. Faculty Tech., Milton Keynes, Eng., 1976-81; rector, v.p. Royal Coll. Art, London, 1981-84; prof. Grad. Sch. Architecture and Urban and Design, UCLA, 1984-94, prof. emeritus Sch. Architecture and Arts, 1994—2003. Dir. Ctr. for Land Use and Built Form Studies, Cambridge, 1969-73; chmn. Applied Rsch. Lbd., Cambridge, 1969-73; gov. Imperial Coll. Sci. and Tech., London, 1981-84. Author: The Geometry of Environment, 1971, Architectonics of Humanism, 1998, Schindler and How Houses, 1999; editor, author: Urban Space and Structures, 1972, The Architecture of Form, 1976, R.M. Schindler, 1995; gen. editor: Cambridge Architectural and Urban Studies, 12 vols., 1970-89; founding editor Planning and Design, 1974—. Sub-lt. Royal Navy, 1953-55. Commonwealth Fund Harkness fellow Joint Ctr. for Urban Studies, Harvard U. and MIT, 1962-64. Fellow Inst. Math. and Its Applications, Royal Soc. Arts, Royal Coll. Art. Avocations: restoration, gardening, family. Home: Spring Cottage 20 High St Stretham Ely Cambridgeshire CB6-3JQ England E-mail: lmarch@ucla.edu.

MARCH, MICHAEL F. propulsion systems analyst, consultant; b. Detroit, Mar. 3, 1962; s. Stanley and Dorothy M. AAS in Archtl. Design, Macomb C.C., Warren, Mich., 1983; BS in Mech. Engring., Lawrence Technol. U., 1986; ME, U. Fla., 1994. Sr. analytical engr. United Techs. Corp.-Pratt & Whitney, West Palm Beach, Fla., 1986-93; pvt. practice propulsion analysis cons. Tullahoma, Tenn., 1994—. Mem. ASME.

MARCHAK, MAUREEN PATRICIA, anthropology and sociology educator; b. Lethbridge, Alta., Can., June 22, 1936; d. Adrian Ebenezer and Wilhelmina Rankin (Hamilton) Russell; m. William Marchak, Dec. 31, 1956; children: Geordon Eric, Lauren Craig. BA, U.B.C., Vancouver, Can., 1958, PhD, 1970. Asst. prof. U. B.C., Vancouver, 1972-75, assoc. prof., 1975-80, prof., 1980—, head dept. anthropology and sociology, 1987-90, dean faculty arts, 1990-96, disting. scholar in residence Peter Wall Inst., 2000—, prof., dean emerita of arts, 2001—; sr. rsch. fellow Ctr. Internat. Rels. Liu Inst. for Study of Global Issues, 2002—. Author: Ideological Perspectives on Canada, 1975, 2d edit., 1981, 3d edit., 1988, In Whose Interests, 1979, Green Gold, 1983 (John Porter award 1985), The Integrated Circus, The New Right and The Restructuring of Global Markets, 1991, Logging the Globe, 1995, Falldown, Forest Policy in British Columbia, 1999, Racism, Sexism and the University, the Political Science Affair at UBC, 1996, God's Assassins. State Terrorism in Argentina in the 1970's, 1999 (Wallace J. Ferguson prize, Hon. Mention), Reigns of Terror, 2003; author, co-editor: Uncommon Property, 1987; mem. editl. bd. Can. Rev. Sociology and Anthropology, Montreal, Que., 1971-74, Studies in Polit. Economy, Ottawa, Ont., Can., 1980-87, Current Sociology, 1980-86, Can. Jour. Sociology, 1986-90, B.C. Studies, 1988-90, 2000—. Bd. dirs., chair ethics com. Univ. Hosp., 1992-93, Cedar Lodge Trust Soc., 1989-92; mem. adv. coun. Ecotrust, 1991-93, bd. dirs., 1993-97, Eco-trust Can., 1995-99; chmn. bd. dirs. B.C. Bldgs. Corp., 1992-95; mem. B.C. Forest Appeals Commn., 1992-2002; bd. govs. U. B.C., 1999-2001; bd. dirs. Pub. Svc. Employees for Environ. Ethics, 2002--; mem. sector study steering com. Can. Coun. Profl. Fish Harvesters, 2002-. Named Woman of Distinction, YWCA, 1999. Fellow Royal Soc. Can. (v.p. Acad. II 1994-98, pres. Acad. II 1998-2000); mem. Can. Sociology and Anthropology Assn. (pres. 1979-80, other offices), Internat. Sociol. Assn., Can. Polit. Sci. Assn., Assn. for Can. Studies, Forest History Soc. (mem. exec. com. 1991-92). Avocations: hiking, swimming, travel, listening to music. Home: 4455 W 1st Ave Vancouver BC Canada V6R 4H9 Office: Univ BC - Ctr Internat Rels Inst for Study of Global Issues 6476 NW Marine Dr Vancouver BC Canada V6T 1Z2 Business E-Mail: pmarchak@interchange.ubc.ca.

MARCHAN, MARISSA L. social worker; b. Muntinlupa, Philippines, Sept. 6, 1960; arrived in U.S., 1976; d. Vedasto A. Layola Sr. and Mailde V. Layola; m. Leon P. Marchan Jr.; children: Lesley-Anne, Matt-Derek. Bookkeeper Dave Morken Sailmakers, Honolulu, 0979—80; fund raising sec. Hawaii Heart Assn., Honolulu, 1980—81; data entry Hawaiian Fin., Honolulu, 1981—83; accts. payable Paul, Hastings, Janofsky, L.A., 1983—90; acctg. clk. Powerine Oil Co., Santa Fe Springs, Calif.; family support specialist DA Family Support Divsn., Las Vegas, 1996—. Author: A Marriage Made in Heaven and Hell, 2003. Avocations: sewing, interior decorating.

MARCHAND, MICHAEL J. military officer; b. Rice, Minn. BA, St. John's U., Collegeville, Minn., 1970. Commd. Judge Advocate Gen.'s Corps, U.S. Army, 1974, asst. staff judge advocate, 1974—77, US Army Forces Command, Ft. McPherson, Ga., 1977—79; instr., sr. instr. contract law Judge Advocate Gen.'s Sch., Charlottesville, Va., 1980—83; dep. staff judge advocate U.S. Army Transp. Ctr. and Ft. Eustis, Ft. Eustis, Va., 1983—85; plans officer Office of the Judge Advocate Gen., Washington, 1986—88; staff judge advocate 6th Inf. Divsn. (Light) Alaska, 1988—91, U.S. Army Garrison, Ft. Polk, La., 1991—93; chief adminstrv. law divsn. Office of Judge Advocate Gen., Washington, 1994—95, exec. to Judge Advocate Gen., 1995—97, asst. judge advocate gen. for civil law and litigation, 1997—98; comdr. U.S. Army Svcs. Agy., 1998—2001; chief judge U.S. Army Ct. Criminal Appeals, 1998—2001; asst. judge advocate gen. Judge Advocate Gen. Corps, 2001—. Decorated Legion of Merit, Meritorious Svc. medal with 3 oak leaf clusters, Army Commendation medal with one oak leaf cluster, Army Achievement medal with one oak leaf cluster, Nat. Def. Svc. medal with one svc. star. Office: Office of Judge Advocate General US Army Pentagon Washington DC 20310-1500

MARCHAND, RUSSELL DAVID, II, retired protective services official; b. Lafayette, Ind., May 14, 1950; s. Russell David and Mable May (Gean) M.; m. Sandra Green, June 12, 1951 (div. Nov. 1986); 1 child, Russell David III; m. Carol Bella Flashenburg, May 31, 1987 (div. Feb., 1996); m. Dorian L. Jones, Feb. 28, 2000. AA in Fire Sci., Clark County Community Coll., Las Vegas, Nev., 1979. Cert. fire service instr., supr. instr. Firefighter North Las Vegas Fire Dept., 1973-78, engr., 1978-82, capt., 1982-95, divsn. chief, officer-in-charge bldg. and constrn., 1990-2000, ret., 2000. Pres. Local 1607 Internat. Assn. Fire Fighters, Las Vegas, 1980— (v.p. 1976-80); instr. N. Las Vegas Fire Dept., 1986. Chmn. N. Las Vegas Firefighters Polit. Action Com., 1980—, Muscular Dystrophy Assn., 1980-83, 85. Sgt. USMC, 1968-72, South Vietnam. Named Fireman of Yr., Optimist Club, 1981, Lions Club Nev., 1989, Profl. Ins. Agts. of Am.; received citation of merit Muscular Dystrophy Assn., 1982, commendation City of N. Las Vegas, 1980, 83, 85. Mem. Fed. Firefighters Nev. (received commendation 1982), Internat. Assn. Fire Fighters (local 1607 pres. emeritus 1990). Avocations: sailing, computers. Office: 2626 E Carey Ave North Las Vegas NV 89030-6215

MARCHAND, WAYNE, architectural firm executive; BArch, La. State U., 1976. Sr. project designer FKP Arch., 1985—. Mem.: Nat. Coun. Archtl. Registration Bds., Am. Coll. Healthcare Archs. (founding mem.). Avocation: woodworking. Office: 8 Greenway Plz Ste 300 Houston TX 77046-0899

MARCHANT, DAVID BRIAN, music educator; b. Tifton, Ga., Apr. 25, 1976; s. Billy Eugene and Sandra Kay Marchant. MusB, Brewton-Parker Coll., Mt. Vernon, Ga., 1994—98; MusM Edn., Valdosta State U., Ga., 1999—2000; Edn. Specialist in Ednl. Adminstrn. and Supervision, Albany State U., Ga., 2002—03. Cert. Music Edn. Ga., 1998, Educational Leadership Ga., 2003, Early and Middle Childhood/Music Nat. Bd. for Profl. Tchg. Standards, 2002. Gen. music tchr. Holley Elem. Sch., Sylvester, Ga., 1998—; interim ch. music dir. Brighton Rd. Bapt. Ch., Tifton, Ga., 2002—03; pvt. voice and piano instr. Abraham Baldwin Agrl. Coll., Tifton, 2002—; ch. music dir. Coll. Hill Bapt. Ch., Mt. Vernon, 1996—98; ch. pianist Alston Bapt. Ch., Ga., 1995—96; summer youth worker TyTy Bapt. Ch., Ga., 1997—97, New River Bapt. Ch., Tifton, 1996—96. Praise band mem. First Bapt. Ch., Tifton, 1999—, children's choir worker, 1998—99, Tifton, 2003—. Recipient Superintendent's Spotlight Award, Worth County Bd. of Edn., 2001, 2002; grantee Local Tech. Grant, Worth County Sch. Sys., 1998. Mem.: Ga. Assn. of Educators, Ga. Music Educators Assn., Rho Lambda Chi (academic advisor 1997—98). Southern Baptist. Avocations: singing, weightlifting, landscaping.

MARCHANT, JOANN REVICZKY, English language educator, actress; b. Putnam, Conn., May 22, 1964; d. James and Joan Alicia (Gronus) Reviczky; m. Jonathan Edward Marchant, June 24, 1995; 1 child, Zoltán. BFA, U. Conn., 1985, MA, 1991; MEd, Plymouth (N.H.) State Coll., 1995; grad., Creative Sch. Cosmetology, Manchester, Conn., 1989. Cert. tchr., English, N.H. Rsch. asst. U. Conn., Storrs, 1990-91, lectr., 1990-91; educator N.H. Coll., Laconia, 1992-95; educator English and drama Coe-Brown Northwood (N.H.) Acad., 1995-97; actress Players' Ring, Portsmouth and Alton, N.H., 1997—; educator Hesser Coll., Portsmouth, 1997—, Franklin Pierce Coll., Concord, N.H.,

1997—. Owner Theatre for Life, Sanborton, 1996-02; tchr. spl. edn., English, and drama Brentwood Sch., Merrimack, 1999-2002; model East Coast Focus, Concord, N.H., 1997—; stage mgr. premier Tom Dulack's Ah! Bright Wings, Storrs, Conn., extra in film Meet Joe Black; lectr. Plymouth State Coll., 1997-99; bd. dirs. Plymouth Writer's Group, spl. edn tchr. Belmont (NH) H.S., 2002—. Vol.l campaign worker Nancy Wyman, Conn., Christopher Dodd, Conn., Michael Helfgott, Conn.; vol. Habitat for Humanity, N.H., 1995. Mem. Nat. Coun. Tchrs. English, New Eng. Theatre Conf., N.H. Coun. English Tchrs., Friends of the Bard, Phi Delta Kappa. Democrat. E-mail: j3revmar@metrocast.net.

MARCHASE, RICHARD BANFIELD, cell biologist, educator; b. Sayre, Pa., Mar. 12, 1948; s. Nicholas and Vivian H. (Banfield) M.; m. Susan Elizabeth Darrow, Apr. 14, 1979; children: Nicholas Darrow, Allison Elizabeth. BS in Engring., Cornell U., 1970; PhD in Biophysics, Johns Hopkins U., 1976; postgrad., Duke U., 1978. Muscular Dystrophy Assn. postdoctoral fellow divsn. neurology Duke U. Med. Ctr., 1976-77, USPHS postdoctoral fellow dept. anatomy, 1977-78, asst. prof. anatomy, 1978-86; assoc. prof. cell biology U. Ala.-Birmingham, 1986—90, prof., 1990—, chmn., 1992—2000, sr. assoc. dean biomed. rsch., 2000—, v.p. rsch. Contbr. chpts. to books, articles to profl. jours. Recipient Hamilton Watch award Cornell U., 1970, award Juvenile Diabetes Found., 1995; Grad. fellow NSF, 1970-73, Danforth Found. grad. fellow, 1973-76; Nanaline H. Duke scholar, 1982-85; grantee USPHS, NSF, Presdl. Young Investingator grant, 1982-87. Mem. AAAS, Am. Soc. Cell Biology, Am. Soc. Zoology, Assn. of Anatomy, Cell Biology, and Neurobiology Chairpersons (pres. 1995-96), Am. Assn. Anatomists, Nat. Caucus of Basic Biomed. Sci. Chairs, Coun. Acad. Socs. (rep.), Am. Assn. Med. Colls. (rep.), Fed. Am. Soc. Exptl. Biology (bd. dirs. 2000— v.p. elect sci. policy, 2004), Group on Rsch. Advancement and Devel. (steering com.), Sigma Xi. Home: 2117 Magnolia Way Birmingham AL 35243-2024 Office: U Ala Dept Cell Biology Birmingham AL 35294-0001 Office Phone: 205-934-1294. Business E-Mail: marchase@uab.edu.

MARCHESE, MICHAEL JAMES, JR., radiation oncologist; b. N.Y.C., Mar. 9, 1955; s. Michael James Sr. and Mabel Gladys (Rosero) M.; m. Kathryn Allen, Aug. 7, 1982 (div. May 1993); 1 child, Michael James III; m. Kathleen Spahr, Oct. 18, 1997; 1 child, Melissa June. BA magna cum laude, NYU, 1976; MD, Baylor Coll. Medicine, 1979. Diplomate Am. Bd. Radiology. Intern Monmouth Med. Ctr., Hahnemann Med. Coll., Long Branch, N.J., Phila., 1979-80; resident and chief resident radiation therapy Presbyn. Hosp., Columbia U. Coll. Physicians and Surgeons, N.Y.C., 1980-83, asst. attending physician radiation oncology, 1983-87; resident brachytherapy svc. Meml. Sloan Kettering Cancer Ctr., Cornell U. Med. Coll., N.Y.C., 1982; asst. clin. prof. radiation oncology Columbia U. Coll. Physicians & Surgeons, N.Y.C., 1983-84, asst. prof. radiation oncology, 1984-87; attending staff radiology/radiation oncology Cmty. Med. Ctr., Toms River, N.J., 1987-96, Kimball Med. Ctr., Lakewood, N.J., 1994—, Med. Ctr. Ocean County, Brick, N.J., 1996—; dir. Ocean Radiation Therapy Ctr., Toms River, N.J., 1997—. Investigator Nat. Cancer Inst., 1983-87, investigator radiation therapy oncology group, 1983-87, 95—, physician surveyor, 1983-85, investigator cancer and leukemia group B, 1986-87, investigator Ea. Coop. Oncology Group, 1995—; physician surveyor practice accreditation program Am. Coll. Radiology, 1986-87; Cancer liason Am. Coll. Surgeons, Kimball Med. Ctr., 2001-04. Author: (with others) Radiation Therapy of Gynecological Cancers, 1987, Frontiers of Radiation Therapy and Oncology, vol. 22, 1988; contbr. articles to profl. jours. Bd. dirs. Am. Cancer Soc., Ocean County, N.J., 1993—, v.p., 1993-94, pres., 1994-98, chief med. officer, 2000-01. Recipient Resident/Fellow award Am. Radium Soc., Travel award European Soc. Therapeutic Radiology and Oncology, Clin. Oncology Career Devel. award Am. Cancer Soc., Physician of the Year, Amer. Canc. Soc., 1998; fellow Am. Coll. Radiation Oncology. Fellow Am. Coll. Radiation Oncology; mem. Am. Soc. Therapeutic Radiology and Oncology, Am. Soc. Clin. Oncology, Acad. Medicine N.J., Radiation Rsch. Soc., N.Y. Acad. Sci., Ocean County Med. Soc. (bd. trustees 1997—), Med. Soc. N.J. (del. 2000—). Roman Catholic. Home: 44 Lake Shore Dr Red Bank NJ 07701-5840 Office: Ocean Radiation Therapy Ctr 19 Mule Rd Toms River NJ 08755-5029 Office Phone: 732-914-0420.

MARCHESE, RICHARD B. manufacturing executive; V.p. fin., CFO Ga. Gulf Corp., Atlanta, 1993—. Office: Georgia Gulf Corp PO Box 105197 400 Perimeter Center Terr Ste 595 Atlanta GA 30346

MARCHESE, RONALD THOMAS, ancient history and archaeology educator; b. Fresno, Calif., Mar. 17, 1947; s. John Anthony and Julie Rita (Ferrarese) M.; m. Marcia Lynn Schneider, Apr. 6, 1974 (div. Apr. 1980); 1 child, Stephanie Jo; m. K. Werdin, 1988; children: Alexander Joseph, Kayla Marie. BA summa cum laude, Calif. State U., Fresno, 1970; MA, N.Y.U., 1972, PhD with distinction, 1976; postgrad., Columbia U., 1972-73. Asst. prof. Va. Poly. Inst., Blacksburg, 1976-77; asst. to assoc. prof. ancient history and archaeology U. Minn., Duluth, 1977-87, prof., 1987—. Rsch. assoc. dept. classics NYU, 1972—74; evaluator grant proposals NEH, NSF; excavator numerous sites in Israel, Turkey, and Greece; lectr. in field. Author, editor 7 books; author articles on nomadic material culture and religious textiles. Recipient Fulbright-Hays Sr. Research fellowship, Turkey, 1984-85, 91-92, The Am. Council Learned Socs. fellowship, 1977-78, NDEA Title VI Fgn. Languages fellowship, 1972-75, Spl. Commendation for Excellence award Phi Alpha Theta, 1979; grantee NEH, 1978, 80, nat. Geographic Soc., 1974, Andrew Mellon Found., NSF, Ford Found., 1971-72, U. Minn., others. Mem. NEH, Nat. Assn. Scholars, Coun. for Internat. Exchange, Am. Coun. Learned Socs., Fulbright Alumni Assn., Phi Alpha Theta, Sigma Xi, Alpha Phi Omega. Roman Catholic. Avocations: tennis, golf, dressage. Home: 5789 220th St N Forest Lake MN 55025-9677 Business E-Mail: rmarches@ubc.umn.edu.

MARCHESI, VINCENT T. biochemist, educator; b. N.Y.C., Sept. 4, 1935; married, 1959; three children. BA, Yale U., 1957, MD, 1963; PhD in Pathology, Oxford (Eng.) U., Eng., 1961. Intern, resident in pathology Wash. U., Bethesda, Md., 1963-65; rsch. assoc. cell biology Rockefeller U., New Haven, 1965-66; staff assoc. Nat. Cancer Inst., 1966-68; chief sect. chem. pathology Nat. Inst. Arthritis, Metabolism & Digestive Disorders, 1968-77; prof. pathology Sch. Medicine Yale U., New Haven, Conn., 1972-73, prof. pathology and cell biology Sch. Medicine, 1973-77, Anthony N. Brady prof. pathology Sch. Medicine, 1977—. Dir. Boyer Ctr. Molecular Medicine Yale U., New Haven, 1989—; cons. Miles Pharm., West Haven, Conn., 1982—. Bd. dirs. Am. Cyanamid, N.J., 1992-94. Lt. comdr. USPHS, 1966-72. Mem. Inst. Medicine-NAS, Histochem. Soc., N.Y. Acad. Sci., Am. Soc. Cell Biology. Avocations: tennis, history. Office: Yale U Sch Medicine Brady Meml Lab New Haven CT 06520 also: Boyer Ctr Molecular Medicine 295 Congress Ave Rm 109 New Haven CT 06519-1418

MARCHI, JON, former investment brokerage executive, cattle rancher, exporter, venture capitalist; b. Aug. 6, 1946; s. John Robert and Joan Trimble (Toole) M.; m. Mary Stewart Sale, Aug. 12, 1972 (div. 1999); children: Aphia Jessica, Jon Jacob. Student, Claremont Men's Coll., 1964-65; BS, U. Mont., 1968, MS, 1972. Sec., treas. Marchi, Marchi & Marchi, Inc., Morris, Ill., 1968-69; account exec. D. A. Davidson & Co., Billings, Mont., 1972-75, asst. v.p., office mgr., 1976-77, v.p. mktg. and adminstrn. Great Falls, Mont., 1977—. Sec., dir., v.p. fin. svcs. and exec. devel. D. A. Davidson Realty Corp., Great Falls, 1978-85, chmn. rsch. com., 1980; bd. dirs. Ligocyte Corp., Bozeman, Mont., Big Sky Airlines, Billings, chmn. bd. dirs., 1995; bd. dirs. Implemax Equipment Co., Inc., Bozeman, Energy Overthrust Found., Mansfield Found., Mont. Beverages, Mont. Venture Capital Network, Direct Advantage, Inc., Hamilton, Mont., Mont. Naturals Internat., Inc., Eclipse Techs., Inc., Mont. Small Bus. Investment Corp., Phillips Environ. Corp., Bozeman, Mont.; chmn., dir. Devel. Corp. Mont., Helena, 1995; cattle rancher, Polson, Mont., 1986—; dir. Mont. Econ. Devel. Action Group, 2001-; guest lectr. London Sch. Econs., London, 2004. Chmn. Mont. Gov.'s Subcom. for Venture Capital Devel., Mont. Cmty. Fin. Corp., Helena; chmn. investment com. State of Mont. Sci. and Tech. Alliance, 1985—; chmn. seed capital com. State of Mont., bd. dirs. job svc. com.; mem. Mont. Peoples Action; sec.-treas. Valley View Assn., 1987—; trustee sch. dist. # 35, Polson, Mont., 1990—, chmn., 1991—; bd. dirs. Mont. Entrepreneurship Ctr., Missoula, Mont., 1990—; pres., dir. sec.-treas. Mont. Pvt. Capital Network, Bozeman, Mont., 1990—, pres., 1992—; chmn., dir. Mont. Naturals Internat., Inc., 1991; dir. Mont. State Rural Devel. Coun., 1992, Mont. SBA Adv. Coun., 1992; dir. Ctr. Econ. Renewal and Tech. Transfer Mont. State U., Bozeman, 1994—; del. to White House Conf. on Small Bus., Washington, 1994-95; chmn. Glacier Venture Fund, Helena, Mont., 1996—; mem. investment adv. com. DCC Growth Fund, Washington, 1998—. With U.S. Army, 1969-71; dir. Mont. State U., Billings, Coll. of Bus. Bd., 1995-, Mont. Econ. Devel. Action Group, 2001-; mem. Gov.'s Com. Tax Restructuring, 2002-, Gov.'s Task Force on Access to Capital, 2002-; regional dir. Mus. of Rockies, Bozeman, Mont. Named Amb. of Yr., State of Mont., 2003, Alumni of Yr., U. Mont. Sch. Bus., 2004; named to Mont. Acad. Disting. Entrepreneurs, U. Mont., 2003. Mem. Nat. Cattlemen's Assn. (fgn. trade com.), Am. Wagyu Assn. (bd. dirs. 2000—, 1st v.p.), Can. Wagyu Assn., Polson C. of C. (bd. dirs.), Valley View Assn. (bd. dirs.), Mont. Cattle Feeders Assn., Mont. Angus Assn., Western Mont. Angus Assn., Am. Angus Assn., Western Mont. Stockgrowers Assn., Securities Industry Assn., Mont. Stock Growers Assn., Mont. Ambassadors (dir. 1995, pres. 2001—), Polson C. of C. (dir.), Leadership Great Falls Club, Ski Club, Mont. Club, Helena Wilderness Riders Club, Rotary. Episcopalian. Office: Marchi Angus Ranches 7783 Valley View Rd Polson MT 59860-9302

MARCHI, LORRAINE JUNE, social services administrator; b. June 5, 1923; d. Leopold and Josephine Lillian (Trieber) Heiman; m. Gene Marchi, Apr. 10, 1943 (div. 1973); children: Gene, Jeffrey, Debra, Beth; m. Robert L. Fastie, Oct. 21, 1973. Student, Stanford U., 1941—42, U. Calif., Berkeley, 1942—43; LHD (hon.), SUNY, 2002. Founder Coun. Aid Visually Handicapped Children, San Francisco, 1954-57; pres. Aid Visually Handicapped, San Francisco, 1957-59; founder, CEO Nat. Assn. Visually Handicapped, N.Y.C. and San Francisco, 1972—. Sec. Calif. Conf. Exceptional and Rehab. Needs, San Francisco, 1955—66; chmn. bd. dirs. Langley Porter Neuropsychiatric Inst., San Francisco, 1966—73. Named Woman of the Yr., San Francisco sect. Nat. Coun. Jewish Women, 1957; named one of Ten Disting. Women, San Francisco Examiner Bay Area, 1959; recipient Spl. Svc. award, Los Angeles County Soc. Ophthalmology, 1971, award for visual awareness, N.Y. Acad. Optometry, 1997, Honor award, Am. Acad. Ophthalmology and Otolaryngology, 1971, Lifetime Achievement award, Nat. Assn. Visually Handicapped, 1989, cert. of appreciation, Lions Club Internat., 1998, Ira G. Ross Innovative Award by Elizabeth Pierce Olmsted, MD, Ctr. for the Visually Impaired/ Buffalo, New York, 2002, Dist. Svc. award, APHA, 2004. Home: 305 E 24th St New York NY 10010-4011 Office Phone: 212-889-3141. Business E-Mail: staff@navh.org.

MARCHI, SERGIO SISTO, Canadian government official; b. Buenos Aires, May 12, 1956; s. Ottavio and Luisa (D'Agostinis) M.; m. Laureen Storozuk, Oct. 1, 1983. BA with honors, York U., Toronto, 1979. Alderman City of North York, 1982-84; M.P. for York West dist. Ho. of Commons, Ottawa, 1984-99, min. citizenship and immigration, 1993-96; min. of environment, 1996-97; min. internat. trade Govt. Canada, 1997-99; Canadian amb. of UN and WTO Permanent Missions of Can. to Office of UN, Geneva, 2000—; chmn. WTO Coun. for Trade in Svcs., 2000—01; chair working party on accession of Ukraine WTO, 2000—; mem. policy adv. commn. WIPO, 2000—; chair gen. coun. WTO, 2002—03. Mem. cabinet coms. on treasury bd., social policy and program review. Mem. Cabinet Com. on Treas. bd., Social Policy and Program Review; vice chmn. North York Planning Bd., Toronto, 1982-84, Standing Com. on Transport, Ottawa, 1990-93; chmn. Nat. Liberal Caucus, Ottawa, 1990-93. Liberal Party Can. Office: Perm Mission Amb of Can #5 Ave de L'Ariana Geneva 1202 Switzerland E-mail: sergio.marchi@dfait-maeci.gc.ca.

MARCHILENA, FRANK S. engineering company executive; b. Pitts., Dec. 1945; Bachelor's, Duquesne U., 1967; Master's, Northeastern U., 1969. With Raytheon, 1967—, various program mgmt. positions, mgr. patriot internat. programs; mgr. Raytheon Electronic Sys. Labs.; asst. gen. mgr. Raytheon Electronic Sys.; exec. v.p. and gen. mgr. tng. and svcs. Raytheon Sys. Co., exec. v.p. and gen. mgr. command, control and comm. sys.; sr. v.p. and pres. C3I Raytheon Co., exec. v.p. and pres. command, control, comm., and info. sys., exec. v.p., head discontinued ops., 2002—. Mem. Def. Sci. Bd. Trustee Merrimack Coll. Office: Raytheon Co 141 Spring St Lexington MA 02421

MARCHUK, DOUGLAS ALAN, medical educator; b. Cleve., July 17, 1956; BS in Biology cum laude, U. Dayton, 1978; MS in Microbiology, U. Conn., 1980; PhD in Molecualr Genetics and Cell Biol., U. Chgo., 1985. Postdoctoral U. Mich. Med. Sch., Ann Arbor, 1987-91, asst. rsch. scientist, 1991-93; asst. prof. genetics Duke U. Med. Ctr., Durham, N.C., 1993—; co-dir. Duke Comprehensive Cancer Ctr., Durham, N.C. Vis. asst. prof. biology Hope Coll., Holland, Mich., 1985-87; lectr. in field. Mem. editorial bd. jour. Genome Rsch., 1993—; ad hoc reviewer jours.; contbr. chpts. to books and numerous articles to profl. jours. Mem. med. adv. bd. Hereditary Hemorrhagic Telengietasis Found., 1992—. Baxter Found. scholar, 1983—; grantee NIH, 1992—, Share Found., 1992-93, Am. Heart Assn., 1995—, Sandoz Pharms. Corp., 1995, Baxter Found., 1993—. Mem. Alpha Sigma Tau. Office: Duke U Med Ctr CARL Bldg MS 3175 Rsch Dr Rm 277 Durham NC 27715-3175

MARCIANO, MAURICE, apparel executive; CEO Guess?, L.A. Office: Guess Inc 1444 S Alameda St Los Angeles CA 90021-2433

MARCIC, DOROTHY ANNE, education educator; b. Milw., Mar. 5, 1949; d. Oswald Raymond and Leona Geraldine (Stordock) Marcic; m. Samandar M. Hai (dec.); children: Roxanne Hai, Solange Hai, Elizabeth Hai; m. Richard L. Daft, Dec. 19, 1995. BA, U. Wis., 1972; MEd, U. Mass., 1974; MPH, U. Pitts., 1975; EdD, U. Mass., 1975. Assoc. prof. Ariz. State U., Tempe, 1975—79; prof. St. Bonaventure U., Olean, NY, 1979—84, U. Wis., La Crosse, 1984—89, Metro State U., St. Paul, 1989—92; dir. grad. program human resource devel. Vanderbilt U., Nashville, 1997—2001; afj. prof. Owen Grad. Sch. Mgmt., Vanderbilt U., 2001—. Pres., dir sys. DM Systems, various, 1988—; dir. Dr. Dorothy Productions, Nashville. Author: Respect: Women & Popular Music, 2002, Managing With The Wisdom of Love, 1997, Understanding Management, 1997. Bd. mem. Baha'i Publ. Trust, Wilmette, Ill., 1977—79, Baha'i nat. Tchg. Com., Evanston, Ill., 2001—03. Nominee Athena award, Nashville, 2004; named Woman of Yr., YWCA LaCrosse, Wis., 1988, Dist. Educator, Org. Bch. Tchg. Soc., 2003; recipient Fulbright Scholarship award, 1992—95. Mem.: Am. Pub. Health Assn., Acad. of Mgmt., Org. Bch. Tchg. Soc. Avocations: walking, skiing, video editing. Home: 165 Charleston Pk Nashville TN 37205 Office: Dr Dorothy Productions 1008 19th Ave S Nashville TN 37205 Office Phone: 615-321-0354. Office Fax: 615-292-9819. E-mail: dorothy@marcic.com.

MARCIL, WILLIAM CHRIST, SR., publisher, broadcast executive; b. Rolette, N.D., Mar. 9, 1936; s. Max L. and Ida (Fuerst) M.; m. Jane Black, Oct. 15, 1960; children: Debora Jane, William Christ Jr. BSBA, U. N.D., 1958. Br. mgr. Community Credit Co., Mpls., 1959-61; with Forum Comms. Co., Fargo, N.D., 1961—, pres., pub., CEO, 1969—. Pres. Forum Comm. Found.; past bd. dirs. North Ctrl. region Boy Scouts Am. With U.S. Army, 1958-59. Mem. Inland Newspaper Press Assn., N.D. Press Assn., Am. Newspaper Pubs. Assn. (past dir., chmn.), Fargo Morehead C. of C., N.D. State C. of C. (past pres.), U.S. C. of C. (past chmn.), Sigma Delta Chi, Lambda Chi Alpha. Lodges: Masons, Shriners, Elks. Republican. Office: Forum Comm Co 101 5th St N Fargo ND 58102-4826 Home: 1618 S 8th St Fargo ND 58103

MARCIN, PETER R. lawyer, real estate broker; b. Balt., Md., Aug. 4, 1972; m. Megan E. Walsh, Aug. 12, 2000; 1 child, Christopher Andrew. BS in Architecture, U. Va., Charlottesville, 1994; JD, Cath. U., Washington, 1997. Bar: Md. 1998, DC 1999; lic. comml. real estate broker Md., 2001, DC, 2001, Va., 2001. Atty. Huddles and Jones, Columbia, Md., 1998—2000; gen. counsel Capitol CREAG, LLC, Washington, 2001—. Named Fourth highest producing Comml. Real Estate Broker Va., Greater Wash. Comml. Assn. of Realtors, 2002; named to Multi Million Dollar Leasing Club, 2002. Mem.: AIA (assoc.), Nat. Contract Mgmt. Assn., Va. Assn. of Realtors, Nat. Assn. of Realtors, Greater Wash. Comml. Assn. of Realtors, Internat. Facility Manager's Assn. Roman Catholic. Avocations: golf, fishing, travel. Office: Capitol CREAG LLC Ste 700 1300 Penn Ave NW Washington DC 20004 Office Phone: 202-204-3010. Office Fax: 202-204-3091. E-mail: peter.marcin@capitolcreag.com.

MARCIN, ROBERT H. automotive executive; BBA, SUNY, 1971; MBA, Calif. State U., 1973. With Ford Aerospace, San Jose, Calif., 1973—89; exec. v.p., dir., external & employee affairs First Nationwide Fin. Corp., 1989—93; dir., compensation planning office Ford Motor Co., 1993—95, dir., internat. labor affairs, 1995—98, exec. dir., labor affairs, 1998—2000; sr. v.p., human resources Visteon Corp., Dearborn, Mich., 2000—03, sr. v.p., corp. relations, 2003—. Office: Visteon Corp 1700 Rotunda Dr Dearborn MI 48120

MARCINEK, MARGARET ANN, nursing educator; b. Uniontown, Pa., Sept. 29, 1948; d. Joseph Hugh and Evelyn (Bailey) Boyle; m. Bernard Francis Marcinek, Aug. 11, 1973; 1 child, Cara Ann. RN, Uniontown Hosp., 1969; BSN, Pa. State U., 1970; MSN, U. Md., 1973; EdD, W.Va. U., 1983. Staff nurse Presbyn. U. Pitts., 1970-71; instr. nursing W.Va. U., Morgantown, 1973-77, asst. prof., 1977-80, assoc. prof., 1980-83, Calif. U. Pa., 1983-87, prof., 1987—, dept. chmn., 1985—. Program evaluator Commn. on Collegiate Nursing Edn., Nat. League for Nursing Accrediting Commn.; mem. adv. coun. In Home Health, Inc.; mem. adv. coun. Albert Gallatin VNA. Contbg. author: Critical Care Nursing; contbr. articles to profl. jours. Mem.: ANA, Commn. on Collegiate Nursing Edn. (site evaluator), Oncology Nursing Soc., Sigma Theta Tau. Office Phone: 724-938-4130. E-mail: marcinek@cup.edu.

MARCKS, RONALD HENRY, lawyer, abrasives and diversified products manufacturing company executive; b. New Haven, Dec. 4, 1931; s. Henry John and Mildred Josephine (Perinchief) M.; A.B., Dartmouth Coll., 1952; LL.B., Harvard U., 1960; m. Barbara Ann Wye, Aug. 17, 1968. Bar: Mass. 1960. Assoc., then ptnr. Goodwin, Procter & Hoar, Boston, 1960-74; chief legal counsel Norton Co., Worcester, Mass., 1974 79, v.p., gen. counsel, sec., 1979—. Served with USNR, 1952-56. Mem. Phi Beta Kappa. Author: (under pseudonym Jens O. Parsson) Dying of Money: Lessons of the Great German and American Inflations, 1974.

MARCOCCIA, LOUIS GARY, accountant, university administrator; b. Syracuse, NY, Nov. 6, 1946; s. George A. and Rose J. (Misita) M.; m. Susan Evelyn Miller, June 21, 1974; 1 child: Rachel Kathryn. BS, Syracuse U., 1968, MS, 1969; EdD, U. Pa., 2003. CPA, N.Y. Acct. Price Waterhouse & Co., Syracuse, N.Y., 1969-75; dir. internal audit Syracuse U., 1975-76, comptroller, 1976-82, v.p., comptroller, 1982-95, sr. v.p. bus., and fin., 1985-95, sr. v.p. bus., fin. and adminstrv. svcs., 1995—. Bd. dirs. Syracuse Bd. Chase Manhattan Bank, Syracuse Divsn., 1985-2001, Lincoln Life and Annuity Co. N.Y., Univ. Hill Corp., Upstate Med. Univ. Found.; pres. Syracuse U. Hotel and Conf. Ctr., LLC; spkr. Harvard U. Inst. Ednl. Mgmt., 1984-88, 90-91. Pres. parish coun. St. Michael's Ch., Syracuse, 1985-88; pres. Syracuse U. Theatre Corp., 1987—; bd. dirs. Friends of Burnet Park Zoo, 1987-93, Syracuse U. Press., 1982—, Syracuse Sports Corp., 1990-91. Mem. AICPA, N.Y. Soc. CPA, Nat. Assn. Accts., Fin. Execs. Inst., Inst. Internal Auditors. Clubs: Drumlins (pres. 1976—); Century. Republican. Roman Catholic. Avocations: sports, tennis. Home: Hedge Ln Cazenovia NY 13035 Office: Syracuse U Off of VP Bus Fin Adminstrv Svc Skytop Rd Syracuse NY 13244-0001 E-mail: lmarcocc@syr.edu.

MARCOGLIESE, RICHARD J. energy executive; BSChemE, NYU. Various operational and tech. supervisory positions Exxon; v.p., gen. mgr. Benicia; sr. v.p. strategic planning Valero, San Antonio, 2001—02, sr. v.p. refining ops., 2002—. Office: Valero Corp Hdqrs 1 Valero Pl San Antonio TX 78212-3186

MARCONI, DOMINIC ANTHONY, retired bishop; b. Newark, Mar. 13, 1927; s. Sabato Joseph and Antoinette (Ricciardi) M. BA, Seton Hall U., 1949; postgrad., Immaculat Conception Sem., Mahwah, N.J., 1952; S.T.L., Catholic U., Washington, 1953. Ordained priest Roman Cath. Ch., 1953; asso. pastor St. Anthony's Ch., Union City, N.J., 1953-66; asso. dir. family life apostolate Archdiocese of Newark, 1966-70, dir., 1970-75; co-dir. div. for services to elderly Associated Cath. Charities, 1975-76; aux. and regional bishop Union County, Newark, 1976—2002; ret., 2002. Mem.: K.C. Roman Catholic. Address: 71 Washington Ave Chatham NJ 07928-2014 Office Phone: 973-635-8777. E-mail: dmarc@worldnet.att.net.

MARCOPOULOS, GEORGE JOHN, history educator; b. Salem, Mass., June 30, 1931; s. John George and Urania Christou (Moustakis) M. BA, Bowdoin Coll., 1953; MA, Harvard U., 1955, PhD, 1966. Instr. Tufts U., Medford, Mass., 1961-66, asst. prof., 1966-71, assoc. prof., 1971-92, prof., 1992—. Contbr. articles to profl. jours. and Am. Ann. yearbooks. Bd. dirs. Gerondelis Found., Inc., Lynn, Mass., 1987—, treas., 1994—. Recipient Mellon Faculty Devel. grant Tufts U., 1983. Mem. AAUP, Am. Assn. Advancement Slavic Studies, Am. Hist. Assn., New Eng. Hist. Assn., Modern Greek Studies Assn., Phi Beta Kappa. Greek Orthodox. Avocations: music, films, reading, performing arts, excursions. Office: Tufts U Dept History East Hall Medford MA 02155 Business E-Mail: george.marcopoulos@tufts.edu.

MARCOSSON, THOMAS I. service company executive; b. N.Y.C., Jan. 31, 1936; s. Mark and Mollie (Schreiber) M.; m. Carla F. Hunt, May 15, 1988; children: Mark, Susan, Samuel, Jill. Student, Union Coll., Schenectady, 1953-55; BS, NYU, 1959. CPA, N.Y. Mgr. Touche Ross & Co., N.Y.C., 1959-63; v.p. fin., dir. Superior Surg. Mfg. Co., Inc., Huntington, N.Y., 1964-66; div. pres., gen. mgr. OEI div., Vernitron Corp., Great Neck, N.Y., 1967-71; controller Allied Maintenance Corp., N.Y.C., 1972-75, v.p. fin., 1975-82; chief fin. officer Remco Maintenance Corp., N.Y.C., 1982-84, exec. v.p., chief operating officer, 1984-88; pres. MBW Advt. Network Inc., N.Y.C., 1988-89; founder, pres. Dunmarc Assocs., Inc., N.Y.C., 1989—; pres., dir. Square Arch Realty Corp., N.Y.C., 1986—2004. Exec. v.p. Greater Talent Network, Inc., 1991—; co-founder, dir. Village Alliance Bus. Improvement Dist., 1993-2004. Office: 437 5th Ave 7th Fl New York NY 10016 Personal E-mail: tmarcosson@nyc.rr.com.

MARCOTTE, BRIAN, transportation executive; BAS in Civil Engring., U. Toronto, Ont., 1971; Diploma in Local Govt. Adminstrn., U. Alta., 1985; Cert., U. Va., 1994. With Ont. Ministry of Transp., North Bay, Toronto, 1971-74, Regional Municipality of York, Newmarket, Ont., 1974-81, Alberta Transp., Edmonton, Canada, 1981—. Office: Alberta Transp Policy & Planning Divsn Asst Dep Min 4999 98 Ave 3rd Flr Edmonton AB Canada T6B 2X3 Fax: 780-427-1066. Office Phone: 780-415-1386. Business E-Mail: brian.marcotte@gov.ab.ca.

MARCOTTE, MICHAEL STEVEN, municipal administrator; b. New Orleans, Jan. 17, 1951; s. Steven Stephen and Gloria Catherine (DeValcourt) Marcotte; m. Mary Jane Kilgore, May 28, 1972; children: Matthew David, Margaret Katherine. BA, M of Environ. Engring., Rice U., 1973. Cert. profl engr, DC, Tex, Colo. Engr., sr. engr., mgr. Turner, Collie & Braden, Inc., Houston, 1973—82; chief maintenance engr. water divsn. City of Houston, 1982—83, mng. engr. water divsn., 1984—85, asst. to the dir. pub. works dept., 1985—87, exec. asst. to the dir. pub. works dept., 1987—88, acting dir. dept. planning and devel., 1988—89; dir. Dallas Water Utilities, 1989—95; dir. econ. devel. City of Dallas, 1995—97; chief engr. D.C. Water & Sewer Authority, 1997—. Fellow: ASCE; mem.: Am Acad Environ Engrs (trustee), Tex Water Conservation Asn (bd dirs), Metropolitan Washington Coun Govts, Water Environ Fedn, Am Water Works Asn (trustee Research Found), Water Resources Coun. Presbyterian. Avocation: high school and college sports official. Home: 900 N Stafford St Apt 2522 Arlington VA 22203-4138 Office: DC Water Sewer Authority 5000 Overlook Ave SW Washington DC 20032-5212 Business E-Mail: mmarcotte@dcwasa.com.

MARCOTTE, PAUL HENRY, state representative; b. LaCrosse, Wis., Jan. 26, 1928; m. Kathleen Marcotte; 4 children. BA, St. John's Univ., 1951. State Rep. House of Rep., Dist. 60, 1994—; exec. v.p. Ohio Valley AFM Inc., 1984—95, Convenient Food Mart, Inc., 1975—84; dir. comms. IGA Internat. Hdqs., 1969—75; v.p. Gateway Foods, Inc., 1958—69. Chair Boone County

Rep. Party, 1993—94; mem. Capital Projects & Bond Oversight Licensing and Occupations; Vice chair State Gov.; mem. transportation. T/4, CAC USAR. caucuses: Am. Legis. Exch. Coun.(ALEC); mem. Nat. Homeland Sec. working Group, 2002-present; chair, Trade & Transp. Task Force, 2001-present. Republican. Roman Catholic. Office: Capitol Capitol Annex, Rm 413E Frankfort KY 40601 also: Dist 10674 Palestine Dr Union KY 41091

MARCOTTE, PAUL JOHN, neurosurgeon, educator; b. Ottawa, Ont., Can., Oct. 15, 1958; (parents Can. and Am. citizens); s. Paul John and Elinor Ann (Simeone) M. BSc, U. Ottawa, 1980, MD, 1984. Intern Ottawa Civic Hosp., 1984-85; resident U. Ottawa, 1985-90, asst. prof., 1990-92; fellow in spinal surgery Barrow Neurol. Inst., Phoenix, 1991-92; assoc. prof. U. Pa., Phila., 1993—. Contbr. articles to profl. jours., chpts. to books. Fellow: ACS, Royal Coll. Physicians and Surgeons (Can.); mem.: Can. Congress Neurol. Surgeons, Am. Assn. Neurol. Surgeons, Congress Neurol. Surgeons. Roman Catholic. Avocations: hockey, model railroading, automobiles. Office: Hosp U Pa 3400 Spruce St Philadelphia PA 19104-4206

MARCOULLIS, ERATO KOZAKOU, ambassador; b. Limassol, Cyprus, Aug. 3, 1949; m. George Marcoullis; 1 child, Panos. Degree in law, U. Athens, Greece, 1972; degree in pub. law and polit. scis., Dept. Pub. Law and Polit. Scis., 1975; PhD Social Scis., U. Helsinki, Finland, 1979. Practice law, 1973—74; advisor Permanent Mission of Cyprus UN, 1980—83, attaché Permanent Mission of Cyprus, 1983—88; consulate gen. Cyprus, 1982—83; amb. extraordinary and plenipotentiary with concurrent accreditation to Finland, Lithuania, Latvia, Sweden, Iceland, Norway, Denmark, and Estonia, 1996—98; mem. 1st polit. divsn. Cyprus question Ministry Fgn. Affairs, 1989—93, dir. office of permanent sec., 1993—96, amb. extraordinary and plenipotentiary to U.S. with concurrent accreditation to Can., Brazil, Guyana, Jamaica, 1998—. Office: Embassy of Cyprus 2211 R St NW Washington DC 20008

MARCOUX, CARL HENRY, former insurance executive, writer, historian; b. San Francisco, Jan. 6, 1927; s. Henry Roderick and Margaret (Carlin) M.; m. Ana Virginia Penate-Melara, Nov. 11, 1967; children: Eric Henry, Grant Reynold. BA, Stanford U., 1950; MBA, Golden Gate U., San Francisco, 1958; MA in Latin Am. History, U. Calif., Irvine, 1988; PhD in Latin Am. History, U. Calif., Riverside, 1994. Gen. mgr. Nat. Union Ins. Co., Pitts., 1953-68; exec. v.p. Transam. Ins. Co., 1968-85. Author: (novels) Sailing West, 2001. Served with U.S. Mcht. Marine, 1944-46; USAF, 1951-53. Mem. Stanford Alumni Assn. Republican. Home: 1967 Port Cardigan Pl Newport Beach CA 92660-5347

MARCOUX, JULIA A. midwife; b. St. Helens, Eng., Aug. 7, 1928; d. Robert Patrick and Margaret Mary Theresa (White) Ashall; m. Albert Marcoux, Apr. 23, 1955; children: Stephen, Ann Marie, Richard, Michael, Maureen, Patrick, Margaret, Julie. Diploma, Withington Hosp., Manchester, England, 1950; grad., Cowley Hill Hosp., St. Helens, England, 1952; BS in Pub. Adminstrn., St. Joseph's Coll. RN, Conn.; lic. midwife, Conn. Nurse, labor, delivery rm. and nursery Day Kimbal Hosp., Putnam, Conn.; sch. nurse Marianapolis Prep. Sch., Thompson, Conn.; occupational nurse U.S. Post Office, Hartford, Conn.; pvt. duty and gerontology nurse Conn. Cons. in field. Contbr. articles to profl. jours. Named Internat. Cath. Family of Yr., 1982.

MARCOVITZ, LEONARD EDWARD, retail executive; b. Bismarck, N.D., Sept. 6, 1934; s. Jacob and Frieda Marcovitz. Asst. mgr. Greengard's Clothing, Mandan, N.D., 1955-58; mgr. K-G Men's Stores, Inc., Bismarck, 1958-61, Billings, Mont., 1961-69, v.p. store ops., 1969-73; pres. Leonard's Men's Stores, Yakima, Wash. and Billings, Mont., 1973-77; chief exec. officer K-G Retail div. Chromalloy Am. Corp., Englewood, Colo., 1977-81; pres. DeMarcos Men's Clothing, Casper, Wyo., 1982—, Idaho Falls, Idaho, 1984—, Billings, Mont., 1986-96, Twin Falls, Idaho, 1996—, Ft. Collins, Colo., 1999—, Boise, Idaho, 2000, DeMarcos, Men's Clothing, Boise Town Square, 2002. Mem. Menswear Retailers Am. (past dir.), Order of Demolay (Degree of Chevalier 1952, Internat. Master Councilor 1953, Demolay Dad 1959), Elks. Home: PO Box 95124 Las Vegas NV 89193-5124

MARCUCCIO, PHYLLIS ROSE, retired association executive, editor; b. Hackensack, N.J., Aug. 25, 1933; d. Filippo and Rose (Henry) Marcuccio. AB, Bucknell U., 1955; MA, George Washington U., 1976. Trainee Time, Inc., 1956—57; art prodn. for mags. of Med. Econs., Inc., 1958—60; mem. staff Nat. Sci. Tchrs. Assn., Washington, 1961—99; assoc. editor Sci. and Children, 1963, editor, 1964—93, dir. divsn. elem. edn., 1974—78, dir. divsn. program devel. and continuing edn., 1978—83, pub., 1993—99; dir. publs. Nat. Sci. Tchrs. Assn., 1983—99, assoc. exec. dir., 1990—99; pub. Dragonfly, 1996—99. Lectr., cons. in field. Author (photographer, illustrator numerous articles); co-author: Investigation in Ecology, 1972; editor: Science Fun, 1977, Science Fun, 2d edit., 1994; Selected Readings for Students of English as a Second Language, 1966; compiler: Opportunities for Summer Studies in Elementary Science, 1968, Opportunities for Summer Studies in Elementary Science, 2d edit., 1969, pub.: Sci. and Children, 1993—99, Dragonfly Mag., 1997—99. Apptd. commr. Rockville (Md.) Housing Authority, 1981—91, chairperson, 1984—86; bd. dirs. Nat. Sci. Resource Ctr., NAS, 1986—96, Hands on Sci. Outreach, Inc., 1991—2001; pres. East Rockville Civic Assn., 2000—. Recipient Citizenship medal, DAR, 1951, Golden Lamp award, Edpress, 1998. Mem.: AAAS, NSTA (life), Pocono Environ. Edn. Ctr. (bd. dirs. 1989—98), Sci. Tchg. Assn. N.Y. (Outstanding Svc. to Sci. Edn. award 1987), Ednl. Press Assn. Am. (regional dir. 1969—71, sec. 1979—, Disting. Achievement award 1969, 1971—74, 1976, 1977, Eleanor Fishburn award 1978, Disting. Achievement award 1980, 1988, 1993, 1995), The Washington Forum, Washington edn. Press Assn. (treas. 1966—67, pres. 1975—76), Ohio Coun. Elem. Sch. Sci. (life), Nat. Assn. Industry Edn. Coop. (bd. dirs. 1980—86), Nat. Press Club (Silver Owl), Am. Nature Study Soc., Coun. Elem. Sci. Internat. (Internat. award for outstanding contbns. sci. edn. 1971, 1972, 1986, 1994), Kiwanis Internat., Sigma Delta Chi, Phi Delta Kappa, Phi Delta gamma, Theta Alpha Phi. Home: 406 S Horners Ln Rockville MD 20850-1556 E-mail: marcu@erols.com.

MARCUM, DEANNA BOWLING, library administrator; b. Salem, Ind., Aug. 5, 1946; d. Anderson and Ruby (Mobley) Bowling; m. Thomas P. Marcum, June 13, 1974; 1 child, Ursula. BA, U. Ill., 1967; MA, So. Ill. U., 1969; MLS, U. Ky., 1971; PhD, U. Md., 1991. Tchr. Deland-Weldon (Ill.) High Sch., 1967-68; instr. English U. Ky., Lexington, 1969-70, cataloging librarian, 1970-73, asst. to dir., 1973-74; asst. dir. pub. svcs. Joint U. Librs., Nashville, 1974-77; mgmt. tng. specialist Assn. Rsch. Librs., Washington, 1977-80; sr. cons. Info. Systems Cons., Inc., Washington, 1980-81; v.p. Coun. on Libr. Resources, Washington, 1981-89; dean Sch. Libr. and Info. Sch. Cath. U., Washington, 1989-92; dir. pub. svcs. and collections mgmt. Libr. of Congress, Washington, 1993-95, assoc. libr., 2003—; pres. Coun. on Libr. Resources and Info., Washington, 1995—2003. Adv. bd. So. Edn. Found., Atlanta, 1986-91; chmn. grants com. Coun. on Libr. resources, Washington, 1990-94. Author: Good Books in a Country Home, 1993, Development of Digital Libaries, An American Perspective, 2001; co-author: (with Richard Boss) The Library Catalog, 1980, On-Line Acquisitions Systems, 1981; contbr. articles to profl. jours. Pres., Commn. on Preservation and Access, 1995—. Mem. ALA, Am. Studies Assn., Orgn. Am. Historians, Am. Antiquarian Soc. (adv. bd. 1989—), Beta Phi Mu, Phi Kappa Phi. Home: 3315 Wake Dr Kensington MD 20895-3218 Office: Coun on Libr and Info Resources Ste 500 1755 Massachusetts Ave NW Washington DC 20036-2124 E-mail: dmarcum@loc.gov.

MARCUM, JOSEPH LARUE, insurance company executive; b. Hamilton, Ohio, July 2, 1923; s. Glen F. and Helen A. (Stout) M.; m. Sarah Jane Sloneker, Mar. 7, 1944; children: Catharine Ann Marcum Lowe, Joseph Timothy (dec.), Mary Christina Marcum Manchester, Sarah Jennifer Marcum Shuffield, Stephen Sloneker. BA, Antioch Coll., 1947; MBA in Fin, Miami U., 1965. With Ohio Casualty Ins. Co. and affiliates, 1947—, now chmn. bd., also bd. dirs. Capt., inf. U.S. Army. Mem. Soc. CPCU, Queen City Club, Bankers Club, Princeton Club N.Y., Little Harbor club, Walloon Lake Country Club, Mill Reef Club. Presbyterian. Office: Ohio Casualty Corp 136 N 3rd St Hamilton OH 45011-2726 Home: 1278 Stephanie Dr Hamilton OH 45013-1290

MARCUM, JOSEPH SUSONG, education educator; b. Middlesboro, Ky., July 10, 1952; s. Clyde and Wilma Jean Marcum. BA, Ea. Ky. U., 1975; MA, U. Tenn., 1982. Hist. prof. Southeast Cmty. Coll., Middlesboro, Ky. Bd. mem. Bell County Hist. Soc. Mem.: Ky. Hist. Soc., Org. of Am. Historians, Am. Hist. Assn. Avocations: reading, walking. Office: Southeast Cmty Coll 1300 Chichester Ave Middlesboro KY 40965

MARCUM, WALTER PHILLIP, manufacturing executive; b. Bemidji, Minn., Mar. 1, 1944; s. John Phillip and Johnnye Evelyn (Edmiston) M.; m. Barbara Lynn Maloof, Apr. 17, 1976. BBA, Tex. Tech. U., 1967. Rschr. Collins Securities, Denver, 1968-70, Hanifin Imfoff, Denver, 1970-71; cons. Marcum-Spillane, Denver, 1971-76; with MGF Oil Corp., Midland, Tex., 1976-87, sr. v.p., 1978, exec. v.p., 1979-83, pres., CEO, 1983-87; sr. v.p. corp. fin. Boettcher & Co., Denver, 1987-90; pres., CEO Marcum Natural Gas Svcs., Inc., Denver, 1991-99, Metretek Techs., Denver, 2000—. Dir. Key Energy Group, New Hope, Pa., Contour Energy, Inc., Houston. Dir. Colo. Endowment Humanities, Denver. Republican. Presbyterian. Home: 342 Monroe St Denver CO 80206-4445 Office: 303 East 17th Ave Ste 660 Denver CO 80203

MARCUS, BERNARD, lawyer, consultant; b. Wilkes-Barre, Pa., Mar. 10, 1924; m. Frances Frank; children: Kate, Aaron, Charles, Mary. Student, U. Pa., 1941-43, Carnegie-Mellon U., 1943-44; LL.B., Harvard U., 1948; postgrad., Loyola U. of South, New Orleans, 1958. Bar: D.C. 1949, La. 1958. Atty. legis. reference service Library of Congress, 1949-50; acting counsel small bus. com. Ho. of Reps., 1950; atty. NLRB, Washington, Cin., Buffalo and New Orleans, 1950-57; assoc. Deutsch, Kerrigan & Stiles, New Orleans, 1957-58, ptnr., 1958-95, mng. ptnr., 1985-89, emeritus ptnr., 1995—2004; of counsel Lehmann, Norman & Marcus, New Orleans, 2004—. Cons. Dept. State, 1965-69; labor arbitrator Am. Arbitration Assn., Fed. Mediation and Conciliation Svc., NASD, Arbitration Forum, USDA, U.S. Dept. Def., U.S. Dept. Transp., U.S. Dept. Justice, U.S. Dept. Labor, U.S. Dept. Interior, U.S. Dept. Treasury, U.S. Dept. Agrl., City of Oklahoma City, City of Fort Worth, Computer Sci. Raytheon, City of Houston, Houston Met. Transit Authority, Sanyo Mfg. Co., TU Elec., Internat. Paper Co., Inland Paper, ADM Corp., PPG Industries, Ga. Pacific Corp., Westvaco, Hertz, Schering Plough, Chevron, Bryan Foods, SBC Corp., Verizon, GTE, GAF, Citgo, Conoco Phillips Petroleum Co., others. Author: Congress and the Monopoly Problem, 1950; contbr. to casebooks. Pres. New Orleans Jewish Community Center, 1973-75; mem. Nat. Jewish Welfare Bd., 1974-83; bd. dirs. New Orleans Jewish Welfare Bd., Jewish Family and Children's Service, New Orleans, Communal Hebrew Sch.; v.p. New Orleans Home for Jewish Aged, 1978-80, Florence Heller Rsch. Found. Served U.S Army, 1943-46. Mem. ABA, Fed. Bar Assn., La. Bar Assn., New Orleans Bar Assn. (exec. com. 1971-74), D.C. Bar Assn. Home: 630 Burdette St New Orleans LA 70118-3937 Office: Texaco Bldg Ste 2050 400 Poydras St New Orleans LA 70130 Office Phone: 504-680-6045. E-mail: bmarcus@lnmlaw.com.

MARCUS, BERNARD, retired retail executive; b. 1929; married. BS, Rutgers U., 1954. V.p. Vornado Inc., 1952-68; pres. Odell Inc., 1968-70; v.p. Daylin Inc., 1970-73; with Handy Dan Home Improvement, L.A., 1972-78; co-founder (ex. chmn. and CEO) Home Depot Inc., Atlanta, 1978—2002, ret., 2002. Chmn. The Marcus Found. Inc.; chmn., founder The Marcus Inst.; founder Ga. Aquarium. Office: The Marcus Found 2455 Paces Ferry Rd SE Atlanta GA 30339-4024

MARCUS, CLAUDE, advertising executive; b. Paris, Aug. 28, 1924; s. Jacques and Louise (Bleustein) M.; m. Claudine Pohl, May 27, 1948; children: Michele, Pierre, Anne-Marie, Isabelle. Diploma in Econs., U. Paris, 1947; Lic., Paris Law Sch., 1947. Sec. gen. Publicis, Paris, 1948-55, dir. comml. to dir. gen. adjoint, 1961, dir. gen., 1962-68; mng. dir. Publicis Conseil, Paris, 1968-83; pres. Publicis Internat., Paris, 1984-88; vice-chmn. Publicis Comm., Paris, 1988—96. Decorated chevalier de la Legion d'Honneur. Mem. Bur. Verification de la Publicite (vice-chmn.), Racing Club (France). Home: 12 Rue Felicien David 75016 Paris France Office: Publicis 133 Champs Elysees 75008 Paris France E-mail: claudius6@wanadoo.fr.

MARCUS, DEVRA JOY COHEN, internist; b. Bronx, N.Y., Sept. 5, 1940; d. Benjamin and Gertrude (Siegel) Cohen; m. Robert A. Marcus, Apr. 1963 (div. 1974); children: Rachel, Adam; m. Michael J. Horowitz, Mar. 2, 1975; 1 child, Naomi. BA, Brandeis U., 1961; MD, Stanford U., 1966. Diplomate Am. Bd. Internal Medicine. Intern Stanford U., 1966-67, resident in internal medicine, 1967-68; gen. internist D.C. Dept. Pub. Health, 1968-69, Cardozo Neighborhood Health Ctr., Washington, 1969-73; med. dir. East of the River Health Assn., Washington, 1973-75; fellow in infectious disease Washington Hosp. Ctr., 1975-77; gen. internist Police and Fire Clinic, Washington, 1977-78; pvt. practice Washington, 1977—; assoc. clin. prof. medicine George Washington U. Med Ctr., Washington, 1978—; gen. internist World Bank, Washington, 1978-81; ptnr. Traveller's Med. Svc. D.C., 1980-82; gen. internist Community of Good Hope Med. Clinic, Washington, 1984-85; assoc. clin. prof. medicine Georgetown U. Med. Ctr., Washington, 1987—. Preceptor Georgetown U. Hosp., 1986—; med. missions to Honduras, 2001, Romania, 2002, Dominican Rep., 2004. Contbr. articles to profl. jours. Exec. com. Woodley Park Citizen's Assn., 1979-80; chair mayor's adv. com. on prevention, 1982-83; bd. dirs. Exodus Youth Svcs., 1987-89. Named Best Physicians of Washington, Washingtonian Mag., 1999. Fellow: ACP; mem.: AMA (Physicians Recognition award 1981, 1984, 1987, 1990, 1993, 1996, 1999, 2002), Physicians for Human Rights (asylum applications), Med. Soc. D.C. (founder com. on women 1983, pres. com. on women 1985—87, med. ethics and judiciary com. 1987—91, judiciary coun. 1992—96, credentials com., communicable disease com.). Home: 1205 Crest Ln Mc Lean VA 22101-1837 Office: 1145 19th St NW Ste 510 Washington DC 20036-

MARCUS, DONALD HOWARD, advertising executive; b. Cleve., May 16, 1916; s. Joseph and Sarah (Schmitman) Marcus; m. Helen Olen Weiss, Feb. 12, 1959; children: Laurel Kathy Heifetz, Carol Susan, James Randall(dec.), Jonathan Anthony. BA, Cleve. State U., 1996. Mem. publicity dept. Warner Bros. Pictures, Cleve., 1935-37; mem. advt. dept. RKO Pictures, Cleve., 1937-40; mem. sales dept. Monogram Pictures, Cleve., 1940-42; pres. Marcus Advt. Inc., Cleve., 1946-85, chmn., 1986-2000; chmn. emeritus Marcus Thomas, 2001—. Vice-chmn. comm. divsn. Jewish Welfare Fund Appeal Cleve., 1964—70, chmn., 1971—72; trustee Cleve. Jewish News, 1974—96, v.p., 1983—85; mem. Ohio Dem. Exec. Com., 1969—70, del. nat. conv., 1968; trustee Jewish Cmty. Fedn., 1973—74, No. Ohio regional office Anti-Defamation League of B'nai B'rith, 1986—, Jewish Cmty. Ctr., 1988—90; bd. dirs. Cuyahoga County unit Am. Cancer Soc., 1979—, Cleve. State U. Devel. Found., 1987—. Recipient Disting. Alumnus award, Cleve. State U., 2001. Mem.: NATAS (Silver Cir. award 1994), Cleve. Advt. Club (elected to Hall of Fame), Mensa, Cleve. Growth Assn., Beechmont Country Club (past pres.), Union Club Cleve., Ohio Commodores. Jewish. Office: Marcus Thomas 25700 Science Park Dr Cleveland OH 44122-7319 Home: 26600 George Zeiger Dr Apt 410 Cleveland OH 44122-7541

MARCUS, EDWARD, economist, educator; b. Bklyn., Apr. 29, 1918; s. Herman and Rose (Marayna) M.; m. Mildred Rendl, Aug. 10, 1956. BS, Harvard, 1939, MBA, 1941; student, King's Coll., Cambridge (Eng.) U., 1946-47; PhD, Princeton, 1950. Economist Fed. Res. Bd., 1950-52; prof. econs. Bklyn. Coll., 1952-81, chmn. dept., 1966-79. Cons. Nat. Acad. Scis., 1959, UN Conf. Trade and Devel., 1966; dir. Syracuse U. Maxwell Sch. Nigerian Project, 1961; participant Internat. Econometrics Assn., Amsterdam, Holland, 1968 Author: Canada and the International Business Cycle, 1927-1938, 1954, (with Mildred Rendl Marcus) Investment and Development Possibilities in Tropical Africa, 1960, International Trade and Finance, 1965, Monetary and Banking Theory, 1965, Economic Progress and the Developing World, 1971, Economics, 1978. Served with AUS, 1941-42, to comdr. USCGR, 1942-46. Grantee Merrill Found., 1953 Mem. AAUP, Am. Econ. Assn., Canadian Econ. Assn., N.Y. Met. Econ. Assn. (pres. 1966-67), Am. Fin Assn., Royal Econ. Soc., Econ. Soc. South Africa, New Canaan Hist. Soc. (treas. 1983—), Phi Beta Kappa.

MARCUS, ERIC PETER, lawyer; b. Newark, Aug. 31, 1950; s. John J. and Alice M. (Zeldin) M.; m. Terry R. Toll, Oct. 9, 1983. BA, Brown U., 1972; JD, Stanford U., 1976. Bar: N.Y. 1977, N.J. 1977. Assoc. Kaye, Scholer, Fierman, Hays & Handler LLP, N.Y.C., 1976-84, ptnr., 1985—. Contbr. articles to profl. jours. Mem. Phi Beta Kappa. Office: Kaye Scholer LLP 425 Park Ave New York NY 10022-3506

MARCUS, ERIC ROBERT, psychiatrist; b. NYC, Feb. 16, 1944; s. Victor and Pearl (Maddow) M.; m. Eslee Samberg, Nov. 24, 1985; children: Max, Pia. AB, Columbia U., 1965; MD, U. Wis., 1969. Diplomate Am. Bd. Psychiatry and Neurology. Intern NYU Med. Ctr. Bellevue Hosp., 1969-70; resident Columbia Presbyn. Med. Ctr.-NY State Psychiat. Inst., 1972-75; dir. St. Marks Free Clinic, NYC, 1971-75; from co-dir. to dir. neuropsychiat//diagnostic treatment unit Columbia-Presbyn. Med. Ctr., NYC, 1975-84; dir. med. student edn. in psychiatry Columbia U. Coll. Physicians and Surgeons, NYC, 1981—; supervising-tng. analyst Columbia U. Ctr. for Psychoanalytic Tng.-Rsch., NYC, 1994—; clin. prof. psychiatry and social medicine Columbia U. Coll. Physicians and Surgeons, NYC, 1995—. Bd. govs. student health Columbia U., 1986-2003. Author: Psychosis and Near Psychosis, 1992, 2d edit., 2003; mem. editl. bd.: The Psychoanalytic Study of Society, 1989—94, Jour. Clin. Psychoanalysis, 1998—2002; co-editor: Psychiatry, 1998; contbr. articles to profl. jours. Recipient Weber Rsch. award Columbia U. Psychoanalytic Ctr., 1991, O'Connor Tchg. award, 1995, Columbia U. Presdl. award for Outstanding Tchg., 1999. Fellow: NY Acad. Medicine, Am. Coll. Psychoanalysts, Am. Psychiat. Assn. (pres. NY County Dist. 2002—03, Roeske award 1991); mem.: Assn. Psychoanalytic Medicine (pres. 1999—2001), Am. Psychoanalytic Assn. (chmn. com. on univ. and med. edn. 1999—, mem. editl. bd. Jour. 2000—03, Sabshin award 2003). Avocations: classical music, photography, swimming, reading. Office: Columbia U Dept Psychiatry 1051 Riverside Dr New York NY 10032-1013 Office Phone: 212-427-0543.

MARCUS, FRANK ISADORE, cardiologist, educator; b. Haverstraw, N.Y., Mar. 23, 1928; s. Samuel and Edith (Sattler) M.; m. Janet Geller, June 30, 1957; children: Ann, Steve, Lynn. BA, Columbia U., 1948; MS, Tufts U., 1951; MD cum laude, Boston U., 1953. Diplomate Am. Bd. Internal Medicine, subspecialty cardiovascular diseases. Intern Peter Bent Brigham Hosp., Boston, 1953-54, asst. resident, 1956-57, research fellow in cardiology, 1957-58; clin. fellow in cardiology Georgetown U. Hosp., 1958-59, chief med. resident, 1959-60; chief of cardiology Georgetown U. Med. Service, D.C. Gen. Hosp., Washington, 1960-68; instr. medicine Georgetown U. Sch. Medicine, 1960-63, asst. prof., 1963-68, assoc. prof., 1968; prof. medicine, chief cardiology sect. U. Ariz. Coll. Medicine, Tucson, 1969-82, disting. prof. internal medicine (cardiology), 1982-99, emeritus prof., 1999—, dir. electrophysiology, 1982—2001; prin. investigator multidisciplinary study of right ventricular dysplasia, 2001—. Cons. cardiology VA Hosp., Tucson, 1969, USAF Regional Hosp., Davis-Monthan AFB, Tucson, 1969; mem. panel drug efficacy study, panel on cardiovascular drugs Nat. Acad. Scis.-NRC, 1967-68; chmn. undergrad. cardiovascular tng. grant com. HEW-NIH, 1970; dir. Arrhythmia Svcs., 1996-2001. Editor: Modern Concepts of Cardiovascular Disease, 1982—84; mem. editl. bd. Circulation, 1976—81, Current Problems in Cardiology, 1976—80, Cardiovascular Drugs and Therapy, 1986—, New Trends in Arrythmias, 1984—, Jour. Am. Coll. Cardiology, 1984—87, 1996—2000, Am. Jour. Cardiology, 1984—, Jour. Cardiovasc. Drugs and Therapy, 1994—, Pacing and Clin. Electrophysiology, 1995—, Annals of Noninvasive Electrocardiology, 1996—, Cardiology, 2000—; contbr. articles to profl. jours. Chmn. Washington Heart Assn. High Sch. Heart Program, 1966-68. Served to capt. USAF, 1954-56. Recipient Career Devel. award NIH, 1965, Student AMA Golden Apple award Georgetown U. Sch. Medicine, 1968, Disting. Alumni award Boston U. Sch. Medicine, 2003; Mass. Heart Assn. fellow, 1957-58; John and Mary Markle scholar, 1960-65; grantee NHLBI, 2001—. Fellow Coun. on Clin. Cardiology Am. Heart Assn., ACP (Ariz. laureate award 1987), Am. Coll. Cardiology (bd. govs. Ariz. 1984-87, asst. sec. 1987-89, trustee); mem. Assn. Univ. Cardiologists, Inc. (v.p. 1989-90, pres. 1990-91), Ariz. Heart Assn. (dir. 1970, v.p. 1972-73, chmn. rsch. com. 1970-72), So. Ariz. Heart Assn. (dir. 1969), N.Am. Soc. for Pacing and Electrophysiology, Alpha Omega Alpha. Home: 4949 E Glenn St Tucson AZ 85712-1212 Office: U Ariz Univ Med Ctr 1501 N Campbell Ave Tucson AZ 85724-0001 Office Phone: 502-626-6358.

MARCUS, GREIL GERSTLEY, critic; b. San Francisco, June 19, 1945; s. Gerald Dodd and Eleanore (Hyman) M.; m. Jenelle Bernstein, June 26, 1966; children: Emily Rose, Cecily Helen. BA, U. Calif., Berkeley, 1967, MA, 1968. Record editor Rolling Stone mag., San Francisco and N.Y.C., 1969-70, book columnist, 1975-80, Calif. Mag., L.A., 1982-83, 88-90; pop music columnist Music Mag., Tokyo, 1978-94, New West mag., L.A., 1978-82, Artforum mag., N.Y.C., 1983—87, 1991—98, Village Voice newspaper, N.Y.C., 1986—91, Interview Mag., N.Y.C., 1992—; dir. Falter newspaper, Vienna, 1997-98; cultural columnist N.Y. Times, 1998, Esquire mag., 1998-99; music columnist Salon.com, 1999—2003, City Pages, 2003—04. Seminar presenter U. Calif., Berkeley, 2000, Princeton U., 2000, 02. Author: Mystery Train: Images of America in Rock 'n Roll Music, 1975, U.S. rev., 1982, 90, 97 (Brit., German, Greek, Dutch, Japanese, Italian and French edits.), Real Life Rock (Japanese), 1984, Lipstick Traces: A Secret History of the 20th Century, 1989 (Brit., Italian, Spanish, German, French and Turkish edits.), Dead Elvis: A Chronicle of a Cultural Obsession, 1991 (Brit., French, Japanese and German edits., rev. 1999), Ranters and Crowd Pleasers: Punk in Pop Music, 1977-92, 93, In The Fascist Bathroom: Writings on Punk, 1999 (Brit., German and US edits.), The Dustbin of History (Brit. and German edits.), 1995, Invisible Republic: Bob Dylan's Basement Tapes, 1997 (Brit., Italian, German, Dutch and French edits.), Double Trouble: Bill Clinton and Elvis Presley in a Land of No Alternatives, 2000, rev. edit., 2001 (Brit. edit.), The Old, Weird America: The World of Bob Dylan's Basement Tapes, 2001, The Manchurian Candidate (Brit. edit.), 2002; editor: Stranded, 1979, rev. 1996, Psychotic Reactions and Carburetor Dung (Lester Bangs), 1987, (with Sean Wilentz) The Rose and the Briar: Death, Love and Liberty in The American Ballad, 2004; contbr. criticism to publs. including Creem, Express-Times, New Mus. Express, Another Room, RAW, Rock and Roll Confidential, Threepenny Rev., Representations, Common Knowledge, La Nouvelle Revue Francaise; curator Whitney Mus. Arm. Art, N.Y., 1998.

MARCUS, GWEN ELLEN, sculptor; b. NYC; d. David Oscar and Doris (Sherman) M. BS, NYU, 1977. One-woman shows include Galeries Lafayette Trump Tower, NYC, 1994, exhibited in group shows at Catharine Lorillard Wolfe Art Club Inc., 2002, Wobun Abbey, Bedfordshire, Eng., 2002, Sudeley Castle, Gloucestershire, Eng., 2002, Stoneleigh Abbey, Warwickshire, Eng., 2002, Castle Howard, Yorkshire, Eng., 2002, Chi Mej Mus., Taiwan, 2002—03, Ind. U., 2003, Gallery North, Setacket, NY, 2003, others. Recipient Elliot Liskin Meml. awawrd, Salmagundo Photography & Sculpture Exhbn., N.Y., 1993, Excellence award, 1994, BBI award, 1995, Excellence award, Knickerbocker Artists, Washington, 1993, cert. Merit, Nat. Acad. Design Mus., N.Y., 1996, Elliot Liskin award, 2001, Coun. Am. Artists Soc. award, 1998, Michael Gressel Meml. award, 2001. Fellow Nat. Sculpture Soc.(Tallix Foundry Prize 69th annual exhibition, 2002); mem. Allied Artists Am. (Philip Eisenberg award 1990, Lindsey Morris Meml. award 1994, Gold Medal 1996, Josephine Beardsley Sander Meml. award 1999, 2001, Elliot Liskin Meml. award 2002), Catharine Lorillard Wofe Art Club (Medal of Honor 1993, Harriet W. Frishmuth Meml. award 1994, Anna Hyatt Huntington Bronze Medal 1995, CLWAC Centennial award 1996, Paul Manship Meml. award 2003-), Pen and Brush Club (sculpture soc., Solo Show award 1995, Leonard J. Meiselman Meml. award 1997, Charlotte Dunwiddie Meml. award 2001, Josephine B,. Sandor mem. award, 2002), Am. Medallic Sculpture Assn., Nat. Assn. Women Artists Inc., Hudson Valley Art Assn., Inc. (Agop Agopoff award 1998, Gold Medal honor 2000), Am. Artist Profl. League Inc. (Medal of Honor 1994, 96, President's award 1995, Granville Carter Meml. award 1998, Frank C. Wright Meml. award 1999, Am. Artists Fund award), Nat. Sculpture Soc.

(Gloria Medal 1990), Medallic Sculpture Assn. (bd. dirs.), Audubon Artists (Gold medal 1998, Renee and Chaim Mem. award, 2002). Avocations: travel, theater, music, dance, vol. work. Home and Office: 401 E 80th St Apt 19E New York NY 10021-0651 E-mail: marcustudio@aol.com.

MARCUS, HARRIS LEON, materials science educator; b. Ellenville, N.Y., July 5, 1931; s. David and Bertha (Messite) M.; m. Leona Gorker, Aug. 29, 1962; children: Leland, M'Risa. BS, Purdue U., 1963; PhD, Northwestern U., 1966. Registered profl. engr., Tex. Tech. staff Tex. Instruments, Dallas, 1966-68, Rockwell Sci. Ctr., 1968-70, group leader, 1971-75; prof. mech. engring. U. Tex., Austin, 1975-79, Harry L. Kent Jr. prof. mech. engring., 1979-90, Cullen Found. prof., 1980-95, dir. ctr. for Materials Sci. and Engring., dir. program, 1979-95; prof. materials sci. and engring., dir. Inst. for Material Sci., U. Conn., 1995—. Cons. numerous orgns. Contbr. numerous articles to profl. publs. Recipient U. Tex. faculty U. Tex. Engring. Found., 1983; Krengel lectr. Technion, Israel, 1983; Alumni Merit medal Northwestern U., 1988, Disting. Purdue Univ. Engring. Alumnus award, 1994. Fellow Am. Soc. Metals; mem. ACS, AIME (bd. dirs. Metall. Soc. 1976-78, 84-86), Materials Rsch. Soc., Conn. Acad. Sci. and Engring. Achievements include 22 patents. Home: 78 Ellise Rd Storrs Mansfield CT 06268-1424 Office: Inst Materials Scis 97 N Eagleville Rd Unit U-3136 Storrs Mansfield CT 06269-3136 E-mail: hmarcus@mail.ims.uconn.edu.

MARCUS, JOHN, wholesale distribution executive; b. N.Y.C., Oct. 18, 1941; s. Sam and Margaret (McCoy) M.; m. Helen S. Bondurant, Aug. 14, 1965; children: Lisa Marie, Lynn Michelle. AA, Wentworth Mil. Acad., Lexington, Mo., 1961. Buyer Foley Bros. Dept. Stores, Houston, 1963-65; owner JOMARC, Houston, 1965-66; sales mgr. Firestone Tire & Rubber Co., Houston, 1966-67; distbn. mgr. Matthews Book Co., St. Louis, 1967-69, office mgr., 1969, gen. mgr., 1970, v.p. ops., 1971, pres., 1972, chmn., CEO, 1974—. Pres., CEO McCoy Collegiate Svcs., St. Louis, 1969—, NACSCORP Inc., Oberlin, Ohio, 1983, Coll. Stores Rsch. and Edn. Found., 1984-85, chmn., CEO Founders Bookstore Svcs.; CEO Coll. Bookstores of Am., St. Louis, 1986—. Contbr. articles to publs. Bd. dirs. YMCA, Wentworth Mil. Acad. Mem. Nat. Assn. Coll. Stores (pres. 1981-82), The Employee Stock Ownership Plans Assn. Office: Matthews Book Co 11559 Rock Island Ct Maryland Heights MO 63043-3596

MARCUS, JOSEPH, child psychiatrist; b. Cleve., Feb. 27, 1928; s. William and Sarah (Marcus) Schwartz; m. Cilla Furmanovitz, Oct. 3, 1951; children: Oren, Alon. B.Sc., Western Res. U., 1963; MD, Hebrew U., 1958. Intern Tel Hashomer Govt. Hosp., Israel, 1956-57; resident in psychiatry and child psychiatry Ministry of Health, Govt. of Israel, 1958-61; acting head dept. child psychiatry Ness Ziona Rehab. Ctr., 1961-62; sr. psychiatrist Lasker dept. child psychiatry Hadassah U. Hosp., 1962-64; research asso. Israel Inst. Applied Social Research, 1966-69; practice medicine specializing in psychiatry Jerusalem, 1966-72; assoc. dir. devel. neuropsychiatry Jerusalem Infant and Child Devel. Ctr., 1969-70; dept. head Eytanim Hosp., 1970-72; cons. child psychiatrist for Jerusalem Ministry of Health, 1970-72; dir. dept. child psychiatry and devel. Jerusalem Mental Health Ctr., 1972-75; prof. child psychiatry, dir. unit for research in child psychiatry and devel. U. Chgo., 1975-85, prof. emeritus, co-dir. unit for research in child psychiatry and devel., 1986—; vis. research psychiatrist UCLA Dept. Psychiatry, 1987—. Chief editor: Early Child Devel. and Care, 1972-76; mem. editorial bd.: Israel Annals of Psychiatry and Related Disciplines, 1965-70, Internat. Yearbook of Child Psychiatry and Allied Professions, 1968-74; contbr. articles to med. jours. Mem. Am. Acad. Child Psychiatry (com. on research, com. on psychiat. aspects of infancy), Soc. Research in Child Devel., Internat. Assn. Child Psychiatry and Allied Professions (asst. gen. sec. 1966-74), European Union Paedopsychiatry (hon.), World, Israel psychiat. assns., Internat. Coll. Psychosomatic Medicine, Israel Center Psychobiology. Home: 910 Chelham Way Santa Barbara CA 93108-1049

MARCUS, KENNETH HEARNE, historian, educator; b. NYC, Jan. 21, 1961; s. Rudolph Arthur and Laura Hearne M.; m. Christine Ersig-Marcus, Dec. 23, 1997; 1 child: David Christopher. BA, U. Calif., Berkeley, 1984; MBA, Ecole Superieure de Commerce, Paris, 1987; PhD, Cambridge U., Eng., 1992. Lectr. Boston Coll., 1992; tutor Harvard U., Cambridge, Mass., 1992-93, rsch. asst., 1992-93; lectr. Calif. State Polytech. U., Pomona, 1994-2001, Woodbury U., Burbank, Calif., 1995-99; vis. asst. prof. U. La Verne, 2001—02, asst. prof., 2002—04, dir. Internat. Studies Inst., 2002, assoc. prof., 2004—. Author: The Politics of Power: Elites of an Early Modern State in Germany, 2000, Musical Metropolis: Los Angeles and the Creation of a Music Culture, 1880-1940, 2004; composer, musician: (CD) Some American Music, 1999, Colorado Boulevard, 2000. Scholar Am. Friends of Cambridge U., 1989, fellowship Inst. for European History, Mainz, Germany, 1995, Huntington Libr., 2001, 2002. Mem. Clare Coll. Assn., Am. Hist. Assn., Am. Musicol. Soc. Avocations: music, skiing, tennis, gardening. Home: 1111 Blanche St Apt 110 Pasadena CA 91106-3018 Office: U La Verne Dept History and Polit Sci 1950 Third St La Verne CA 91750 Office Phone: 909-593-3511 x 4283. E-mail: marcusk@ulv.edu.

MARCUS, LEE EVAN, small business owner, consultant, accountant; b. Cleve., 1953; s. Morton and Bluma Marcus. BA in English, Amherst Coll., 1975. CPA, Fla. Audit staff acct. Arthur Andersen, Tampa, 1976-78; tax mgr. Price Waterhouse, Miami, Fla., 1978-83; controller Williams Island Assocs., Ltd., North Miami Beach, Fla., 1983-84; corp. contr. Suncoast Land Devel. Co., Inc., and Affiliates, Stuart, Fla., 1984-85; fin. officer, contr. Haydn Cutler Cos., Ft. Worth, 1985-89; pres. Global Solutions Co., Plantation, Fla., 1989-2000, Positive Changes Broward, Inc., Plantation, Fla., 2000—. Office Phone: 954-942-1120. Personal E-mail: LeeMcpa@aol.com.

MARCUS, LINDA SUSAN, dermatologist; b. Bklyn. d. Nathaniel and Eugenia (Portnay) Marcus; m. Ronald Carlin, July 5, 1976; children: Robert Adam, Neal Marc. BS, Adelphi U., Garden City, N.J., 1970; MD, Downstate Med. Sch., Bklyn., 1975. Diplomate Am. Bd. Dermatology. Intern Long Island (N.Y.) Jewish Med. Ctr., 1975-76; resident in dermatology Columbia-St. Luke's, N.Y.C., 1976-77, Boston U.-Tufts U., 1977-79; pvt. practice Wyckoff, N.J., 1980—. Dir. dermatology Valley Hosp. Ridgewood. Contbr. articles to profl. jours. Mem. Am. Acad. Dermatology (chair pamphlet com.), Am. Soc. Dermatol. Surgeons, Internat. Soc. Dermatol. Surgeons, N.J. Dermatol. Soc. (program dir.), N.J. North Dermatol. Soc. (co-chair). Avocations: swimming, ice skating. Office: 271 Godwin Ave Wyckoff NJ 07481-2057 Office Phone: 201-891-4373. Personal E-mail: sexyderm@earthlink.net.

MARCUS, MARIA LENHOFF, lawyer, law educator; b. Vienna, June 23, 1933; came to U.S., 1938, naturalized, 1944; d. Arthur and Clara (Gruber) Lenhoff; m. Norman Marcus, Dec. 23, 1956; children: Valerie, Nicole, Eric. BA, Oberlin Coll., 1954; JD, Yale Law Sch., 1957. Bar: N.Y. 1961, U.S. Dist. Ct. (so. and ea. dists.) N.Y. 1962, U.S. Ct. Appeals (2d cir.) 1962, U.S. Supreme Ct. 1964. Assoc. counsel NAACP, N.Y.C., 1961-67; asst. atty. gen. N.Y. State, N.Y.C., 1967-78; chief litigation bur. Atty. Gen. N.Y. State, 1976-78; adj. assoc. prof. NYU Law Sch., 1976-78; assoc. prof. Fordham U. Law Sch., N.Y.C., 1978-86, prof., 1986—, Joseph M. McLaughlin prof., 1997—. Arbitrator Nat. Assn. Securities Dealers; chair subcom. interrogatories U.S. Dist. Ct. (so. dist.) N.Y., 1983-85. Contbr. articles to profl. jours. Named Tchr. of Yr., Fordham Law School Students, 2001. Fellow N.Y. Bar Found.; mem. Assn. Bar City of N.Y. (v.p. 1995-96, long range planning com. 1996-2000, exec. com. 1976-80, com. audit 1988-95, labor com. 1981-84, judiciary com. 1975-76, chmn. civil rights com. 1972-75), N.Y. State Bar Assn. (exec. com. 1979-81, ho. dels. 1978-81, com. constitution and by-laws 1984-93), N.Y. Women's Bar Assn. (Pres.'s award 1999). Office: Fordham U Law Sch 140 W 62nd St New York NY 10023-7485

MARCUS, MARVIN, mathematician, educator; b. Albuquerque, July 31, 1927; s. David Clarence and Esther (Rosenthal) M.; m. Arlen Ingrid Sahlman, Sept. 14, 1951; children: Jeffrey Thomas, Karen Melissa; m. Rebecca Elizabeth Michael, Oct. 12, 1965. BA, U. Calif. at Berkeley, 1950, PhD, 1953. Instr., then asst. prof. U. B.C., 1954-56, asso. prof., 1957-62; postdoctoral research fellow Nat. Bur. Standards, Washington, 1956-57; prof. U. Calif. at Santa Barbara, 1962—; dir. Inst. for Interdisciplinary Applications of Algebra and Combinatorics, 1973-79, chmn. dept. math., 1963-68, dean research devel., 1978, assoc. vice-chancellor research and acad. devel., 1979-86. Vis. distinguished prof. U. Islamabad, West Pakistan, 1970; Cons. Bur. Naval Ordnance, Pasadena, Calif. Author books and articles in field.; Editor: Linear and Multilinear Algebra. Served with USN, 1945-46. Mem. Am. Math. Soc., Math. Assn. Am., Soc. Indsl. and Applied Math., Assn. for Computing Machinery, Sigma Xi, Pi Mu Epsilon. Home: 2937 Kenmore Pl Santa Barbara CA 93105-2223

MARCUS, PAUL, law educator; b. N.Y.C., Dec. 8, 1946; s. Edward and Lillian (Rubin) M.; m. Rebecca Nimmer, Dec. 22, 1968; children: Emily, Beth, Daniel. AB, UCLA, 1968, JD, 1971. Bar: Calif. 1971, U.S. Dist. Ct. (cen. dist.) Calif. 1972, U.S. Ct. Appeals (D.C. cir.) 1972, U.S. Ct. Appeals (7th cir.) 1976. Law clk. U.S. Ct. Appeals (D.C. cir.), 1971-72; assoc. Loeb & Loeb, L.A., 1972-74; prof. law U. Ill., Urbana, 1974-83; dean Coll. Law U. Ariz., Tucson, 1983-88, prof., 1988-92; Haynes prof. law Coll. William and Mary, Williamsburg, Va., 1992—, interim dean, 1993-94, 97-98. Reporter, cons. Fed. Jud. Ctr. Commn., Nat. Com.on the Right to Counsel. Author: The Entrapment Defense, 1989, 3d edit., 2003, The Prosecution and Defense of Criminal Conspiracy, 1978, 5th edit., 2002, Gilbert Law Summary, 1982, 8th edit., 2004, Criminal Law: Cases and Materials, 1982, 5th edit., 2003, Criminal Procedure in Practice, 2001, 2d edit., 2003. Office: Coll William & Mary Law Sch PO Box 8795 Williamsburg VA 23187-8795 Office Phone: 757-221-3900. E-mail: pxmarc@wm.edu.

MARCUS, PHILIP IRVING, virology educator, researcher; b. Springfield, Mass., June 3, 1927; s. Julius and Marley Amelia (Speir) M.; m. Angela Joan Francis, Dec. 4, 1953; children: Craig F., Wendy L., Valerie L. BS, U. So. Calif., 1950; MS, U. Chgo., 1953; PhD, U. Colo., 1957. Asst. prof. biophysics U. Colo. Sch. Medicine, Denver, 1957-60; asso. prof. microbiology Albert Einstein Coll. Medicine, Bronx, N.Y., 1961-66, prof., 1967-69; prof. microbiology U. Conn., Storrs, 1969-75, head dept., 1969-75, prof. virology, 1969—, dir. Biotech. Ctr., 1990-95, 2002—, Bd. of Trustees Disting. prof., 2003—. Dir. Nat. Cancer Inst. Program Project, 1973-83; cons. NIH, NSF; mem. sci. adv. coun. Damon Runyon-Walter Winchell Cancer Fund, 1970-74, Am. Cancer Soc., 1986-88, Am. Found. for AIDS Rsch., 1990—. Editor Jour. Cellular Physiology, 1969-96; editor in chief Jour. Interferon Rsch., 1984-95, Jour. Interferon & Cytokine Rsch., 1995—2002, sr. cons. editor, 2003—; contbr. numerous articles to profl. jours.; patentee in field. Served with USAAC, 1945-47. Recipient USPHS rsch. career devel. award, 1960-70, excellence in rsch. award U. Conn. Alumni Assn., 1987; NIH grantee, 1960-94, NSF, USDA grantee. Mem. AAAS, Am. Soc. Microbiology, Am. Soc. Cell Biology, Am. Soc. Virology, Brit. Soc. Microbiology, Internat. Soc. Interferon and Cytokine Research, Soc. In Vitro Biology, Harvey Soc., Conn. Acad. Sci. and Engring. Home: 24 Thompson Rd Storrs Mansfield CT 06268-1806 Office: U Conn Dept Molec & Cell Biol U-3044 Storrs Mansfield CT 06269 Office Phone: 860-486-4254.

MARCUS, RICHARD ANDREW, accountant, mayor; b. N.Y.C., Apr. 14, 1954; s. Richard Andrew and Joan Rose Mary Marcus; m. Janet Marcus, May 6, 1978; children: Richard A. III, John Patrick. BBA in Acctg., Iona Coll., 1976. Pub. acct. Alexander Grant & Co., N.Y.C., 1975-79; audit supr. Polygram Corp., N.Y.C., 1979-82; mgr. internal audit MGM/UA Entertainment, Culver City, Calif., 1982-84, dir. internal audit, 1984-86, Turner Entertainment, Culver City, 1986-88; contr. Consolidated Film Industries, Hollywood, 1989-97; pres. Marcus Acctg. Svcs., Culver City, 1997—; city councilman Culver City, 1996-99, mayor, 1999-2000. Bd. dirs. Am. Heart Assn., Culver City, 1997—, Culver City Pks. and Svc. Found., 1995—; civil svc. commr. City of Culver City, 1994-96; patron Culver City Edn. Found., 1994—; asst. den leader Pack 18 Boy Scouts Am., Culver City, 1994—, asst. scoutmaster Boy Scouts Am. Troop 113, 1998—; mem. Culver City PTA, 1993—, Culver City Sister Cities Com., 1994—. Mem. Culver City C. of C., Culver City Homeowners Assn., Elks, YMCA Century Plus Club. Democrat. Avocations: music, gardening, camping, military history, writing. Home: 5426 Diller Ave Culver City CA 90230-5331

MARCUS, RICHARD LEON, lawyer, educator; b. San Francisco, Jan. 28, 1948; s. Irving Harry and Elizabeth (McEvoy) M.; m. Andrea June Saltzman, Apr. 26, 1981; 1 child, Ruth. BA, Pomona Coll., 1969; JD, U. Calif., Berkeley, 1972. Bar: Calif. 1973, U.S. Dist. Ct. (no. dist.) Calif. 1976, U.S. Dist. Ct. (cen. dist.) Calif. 1978, U.S. Ct. Appeals (9th cir.) 1981. Law clk. to judge Calif. Supreme Ct., San Francisco, 1972; assoc. Boalt Hall U. Calif., 1973-74; law clk. to judge U.S. Dist. Ct. Calif., San Francisco, 1974-75; from assoc. to ptnr. Dinkelspiel, Pelavin, Steefel & Levitt, San Francisco, 1976-81; assoc. prof. law U. Ill., Champaign, 1981-84, prof. law, 1984-89, U. Calif. Hastings Sch. Law, San Francisco, 1989-97, disting. prof. law, 1997-99, Horace O. Coil '57 prof., 1999—. Vis. prof. law U. Mich., 1986-87, U. Calif., Hastings, 1988; assoc. reporter Fed. Cts. Study Com., 1989-90; reporter com. civil motions Ill. Jud. Conf., Chgo., 1984, com. on evidence, 1985; cons. Nat. Commn. on Judicial Discipline and Removal, 1992-93; reporter Civil Justice Ref. Act Adv. Group No. Dist. of Calif., 1992-99, chair local rules adv. com. No. Dist. Calif., 1994-99; spl. reporter advisory commn. on the civil rules, jud. conf. of the U.S., 1996—; mem. 9th Cir. local rules and internal operating procedures com., 1996-2002, 9th Cir. task force on self-represented lit., 2002—. Author: Complex Litigation, 1985, 4th edit., 2004, Civil Procedure: A Modern Approach, 1989, 3d edit., 2000, Federal Practice and Procedure, vols. 8, 8A, and 12, 2d edit., 1994, 1997; rsch. editor U. Calif. Law Rev., 1971-72; contbr. articles to profl. jorus. Mem. ABA, Am. Law Inst., Am. Assn. Law Schs. (chmn. sect. civil procedure 1988,chmn. complex litigation com. 1991), Order of the Coif. Democrat. Home: 70 Domingo Ave Berkeley CA 94705-2436 Office: U Calif Coll Law 200 Mcallister St San Francisco CA 94102-4707 Office Phone: 415-565-4829.

MARCUS, RICHARD SARGON, research scientist; AB, U. Pa., 1954, BSEE, 1955; MSEE, MIT, 1957, EE, 1958. Rsch. fellow MIT Rsch. Lab. for Electronics, 1955-58; prin. rsch. scientist MIT Lab. for Info. and Decision Systems, 1958-62, 67—; sr. systems engr. Itek Corp., 1962-67. Editl. bd. Info. Processing and Mgmt., Jour. of Intelligent Info. Systems; reviewer other jours. Mem. Am. Soc. for Info. Sci. (Best article of Yr. to Jour.), Assn. for Computing Machinery, Assn. for Computational Linguistics. Achievements include research on modeling of indexing and retrieval processes for bibliographic and textual databases and the application of those models in the development of expert search assistance systems. E-mial. Office: MIT LIDS 77 Mass Ave Rm 35-421 Cambridge MA 02139-4307 E-mail: rmarcus@mit.edu.

MARCUS, ROBERT, aluminum company executive; b. Arlington, Mass., Feb. 24, 1925; s. Hymen David and Etta (Arbetter) M.; m. Emily Patricia Ulrich, 1988; children: Lawrence Brian, Janie Sue, Clifford Scott, Emily. AB, Harvard U., 1947; MBA, U. Mich., 1949; MEd, Tufts U., 1950. Market analyst Govt. Commodity Exch., N.Y.C., 1952-54; market rsch. analyst Gen. Electric Co., 1954-55; corp. market analyst Amax Inc., N.Y.C., 1955-62, staff market mgr. aluminum group, 1962-65, pres. internat. aluminum div., 1965-70, v.p., 1970-71; exec. v.p. Amax Pacific Corp., San Mateo, Calif., 1971-72; exec. v.p., dir. Alumax Inc., San Mateo, 1973-82, pres., chief exec. officer, dir., 1982-86; ptnr. Am. Indsl. Ptnrs., San Francisco, 1987-92; dir. Saybrook Inst., 1992-99. Dir. Domtar, Montreal, 1984-90, Kaiser Aluminum Corp., 1990-99. Trustee Mex. Mus., 1988-93, 97-98, World Affairs Coun., 1975-90. Ensign USN, 1943-46. Mem. Japan Soc. (bd. dirs.), Harvard Club (N.Y.C.). Home: 2700 Scott St San Francisco CA 94123-4637

MARCUS, ROBERT BRUCE, lawyer; b. N.Y.C., June 19, 1942; s. Henry Edward and Fannie S. (Siegler) M.; children: Peter J., Gabrielle Beth; m. Jeanie Elizabeth Neyer, Dec. 14, 1984. Bar: N.Y. 1967, N.Y. Dist. Ct. (so., ea. and no. dists.) N.Y. 1968, U.S. Supreme Ct. 1980. Assoc. Shatzkin & Cooper, P.C., N.Y.C., 1967-69, Jay Wallman, P.C., N.Y.C., 1969-72, Klotz & Gould, P.C., N.Y.C., 1972-75; sr. assoc. Weiss, Molod, Berkowitz & Godosky, P.C., N.Y.C., 1975-79, Richard Frank, P.C., N.Y.C., 1979-82; ptnr. Wallman & Wechsler, P.C., N.Y.C., 1982-84, Metnick & Bernstein, P.C., N.Y.C., 1984-88, Metnick, Marcus & Schuchman, P.C., N.Y.C., 1988-89; pres. Robert B. Marcus, P.C., N.Y.C., 1989—; counsel to Kelner and Kelner Esq., N.Y.C., 1989-97; ptnr. Marcus and Yodowitz, LLP, New City, N.Y., 1998—. Bd. advisors Art Hazzards Inst., N.Y.C., 1981—; chmn., founder Willow Tree Civic Assn., Ramapo, N.Y., 1977-81; bd. dirs. Rockland Family Shelter. Mem. ABA, Assn. Trial Lawyers Am., N.Y. State Trial Lawyers Assn., Assn. Trial Lawyers of City of N.Y. Home: 203 Strawtown Rd New City NY 10956-6815 Fax: (845) 638-6303. E-mail: boblawpc@tco.com.

MARCUS, RUDOLPH ARTHUR, chemist, educator; b. Montreal, July 21, 1923; arrived in U.S., 1949, naturalized, 1958; s. Myer and Esther (Cohen) Marcus; m. Laura Hearne, Aug. 27, 1949 (dec. Jan. 2003); children: Alan Rudolph, Kenneth Hearne, Raymond Arthur. BS in Chemistry, McGill U., 1943, PhD in Chemistry, 1946, DSc (hon.), 1988, U. Chgo., 1983, Poly. U., 1986, U. Göteborg, Sweden, 1987, U. N.B., Can., 1993, Queens U., 1993, U. Oxford, Eng., 1995, Yokohama Nat. U., Japan, 1996, U. N.C., 1996, U. Ill., 1997, Technion-Israel Inst. Tech., 1998, Polytechnic U. Valencia, 1999, Northwestern U., 2000, U. Waterloo, Can., 2002. Rsch. staff RDX Project, Montreal, 1944—46; rsch. assoc. NRC of Can., Ottawa, 1946—49, U. N.C., 1949—51; asst. prof. Poly. Inst. Bklyn., 1951—54, assoc. prof., 1954—58, prof., 1958—64, acting head, div. phys. chem., 1961—62; prof. U. Ill., Urbana, 1964—78, head, div. phys. chem., 1967—68; Arthur Amos Noyes prof. chem. Calif. Inst. Tech., Pasadena, 1978—; vis. prof. theoretical chem. U. Oxford, 1975—76; Baker lectr. Cornell U., Ithaca, NY, 1991; Linnett vis. prof. chemistry Cambridge (Eng.) U., 1996; hon. prof. Fudan U., Shanghai, 1994—; hon prof. Inst. Chem. Chinese Acad. Scis., Beijing, 1995—; hon. fellow Univ. Coll., Oxford, 1995—; hon. prof. Tianjin U., China, 2002, China Ocean U., China, 2002. Professorial fellow Univ. Coll., Oxford, 1975—76; mem. Courant Inst. Math. Scis., NYU, 1960—61; trustee Gordon Rsch. confs., 1966—69, assoc. mem. Ctr. Advanced Studies, U. Ill., Urbana, 1968—69; chmn. bd. dirs. Gordon Rsch. confs., 1968—69, mem. coun., 1965—68; mem. rev. panel Argonne Nat. Lab., 1966—72, chmn., 1967—68; mem. rev. panel Brookhaven Nat. Lab., 1971—74; mem. rev. com.Radiation Lab., U. Notre Dame Radiation Lab., U. Notre Dame, 1975—80; mem. panel on atmospheric chemistry climatic impact com. NAS-NRC, 1975—78, mem. com. kinetics of chem. reactions, 1973—77, chmn., 1975—77, mem. com. chem. scis., 1977—79; lectr. in field, 1982; mem. com. to survey opportunities in chem. scis., 1982—86; mem. math. panel Internat. Benchmarking of U.S. Rsch. Fields, 1996—97; mem. panel on accountability of federally funded rsch. Com. on Sci., Engring. and Pub. Policy, 2000—01; adv. com. for chemistry NSF, 1977—80; external adv. bd. NAS Ctr. Photoinduced Charge Transfer, 1990—; mem. presdl. chairs com., Chile, 1994—96; advisor, Ctr. for Molecular Scis. Chinese Acad. Scis. and State Key Lab. for Structural Chemistry of Unstable and Stable Species, Beijing, 1995—; co-hon. pres. 29th Internat. Chemistry Olympiad, 1997; hon. visitor Nat. Sci. Coun., China, 1999. Former mem. editl. bd. Jour. Chem. Physics, Ann. Rev. Phys. Chemistry, Jour. Phys. Chemistry, Accounts Chem. Rsch., Internat. Jour. Chem. Kinetics Molecular Physics, Theoretica Chimica Acta, Chem. Physics Letters, Faraday Trans., Jour. Chem. Soc., editl. bd. Laser Chemistry, 1982—, Advances in Chem. Physics, 1984—, World Sci. Pub., 1987—, Internat. Revs. in Phys. Chemistry, 1988—, Progress in Physics, Chemistry and Mechanics (China), 1989—, Perkins Transactions 2, Jour. Chem. Soc., 1992—, Chem. Physics Rsch. (India), 1992—, Trends in Chem. Physics Rsch. (India), 1992—, hon. editor Internat. Jour. Quantum Chemistry, 1996—. Named Hon. Citizen, City of Winnipeg, 1994, Treasure of L.A., Ctrl. City Assn., 1995; recipient Anne Molson prize in chem., McGill U., 1943, Sr. U.S. Scientist award, Alexander von Humboldt-Stiftung, 1976, Electrochem. Soc. Lecture award, 1979, 1996, Robinson medal, Faraday divsn. Royal Soc. Chemistry, 1982, Centenary medal, 1988, Chandler medal, Columbia U., 1983, Wolf prize in Chem., 1985, Nat. medal of Sci., 1989, Evans award, Ohio State U., 1990, Nobel prize in Chem., 1992, Hirshfelder prize in Theoretical Chemistry, U. Wis., 1993, Golden Plate award, Am. Acad. Achievement, 1993, Lavoisier medal, French Chem. Soc., 1994, Oesper award, U. Cin., 1997, Key to City of Taipei, Taiwan, 1999, William Jost lectr. and medal, Deutsche Bunsenges and Acad. Sci., Göttingen, 1999; fellow Alfred P. Sloan, 1960—61, NSF sr. postdoctoral, 1960—61; scholar sr. Fulbright-Hays, 1972. Fellow: AAAS, Royal Soc. Can. (hon.), Internat. Acad. Quantum Molecular Sci. (hon.), Chinese Acad. Scis. (hon.), Internat. Soc. for Theoretical Chem. Physics (hon.), Royal Soc. Chemistry (hon.), Royal Soc. (London) (hon.), Internat. Soc. Electrochemistry (hon.), Am. Acad. Arts and Scis. (hon.; exec. com. western sect., co-chmn. 1981—84, rsch. and planning com. 1989—91); mem.: NAS (hon.), Am. Chem. Soc. (past divsn. chmn., mem. exec. com., mem. adv. bd. petroleum rsch. fund, Irving Langmuir award in chem. physics 1978, Peter Debye award in physic. chemistry 1988, Willard Gibbs medal Chgo. sect. 1988, S.C. Lind Lecture, East Tenn. sect. 1988, Theodore William Richards medal Northwestern sect. 1990, Edgar Fahs Smith award Phila. sect. 1991, Ira Remsen Meml. award Md. sect. 1991, Pauling medal Portland, Oreg., and Puget Sound sect. 1991, Auburn-Kosolapoff award 1996, Theoretical Chemistry award 1997, Top 75 Chem. & Engring. News award 1998), Am. Phys. Soc., European Acad. Scis. (hon.), Korean Chem. Soc. (hon.), Am. Philos. Soc. (hon.), Alpha Chi Sigma. Achievements include development of the Marcus Theory of electron transfer reactions in chemical systems and RRKM theory of unimolecular reactions. Home: 331 S Hill Ave Pasadena CA 91106-3405 Office Phone: 626-395-6566. Business E-Mail: ram@caltech.edu.

MARCUS, RUTH BARCAN, philosopher, educator, writer, lecturer; b. N.Y.C. d. Samuel and Rose (Post) Barcan; divorced; children: James Spencer, Peter Webb, Katherine Hollister, Elizabeth Post. BA, NYU, 1941; MA, Yale U., 1942, PhD, 1946; DLH (hon.), U. Ill., 1995. Rsch. assoc. in anthropology Inst. for Human Relations, Yale U., New Haven, Conn., 1945-47; AAUW fellow U. Chgo., 1947-48; vis. prof. (intermittently) Northwestern U., 1950-57, Guggenheim fellow, 1953-54; asst. prof., assoc. prof. Roosevelt U., Chgo., 1957-63; NSF fellow, 1963-64; prof. philosophy U. Ill. at Chgo., 1963-70, head philosophy dept., 1963-69; fellow U. Ill. Center for Advanced Study, 1968-69; prof. philosophy Northwestern U., 1970-73; Reuben Post Halleck prof. philosophy Yale U., 1973-93; sr. rsch. scholar, 1994—. Fellow Ctr. Advanced Study in Behavioral Sci., Stanford, Calif., 1979; vis. fellow Inst. Advanced Study, U. Edinburgh, 1983, Wolfson Coll., Oxford U., 1985, 86; vis. fellow Clare Hall, Cambridge U., 1988, lifetime mem. coll. room, 1989—; past or present mem. adv. coms. Princeton U., MIT, Calif. Inst. Tech., Cornell U. Humanities Ctr., Columbia U., UCLA, Ohio State U., U. Calif. Santa Barbara, Carnegie Mellon, Brown U., U. Va., U. Tex., others; disting. vis. prof. U. Calif., Irvine, 1995—. Author: Modalities, 1993; editor: The Logical Enterprise, 1975, Logic Methodology and Philosophy of Science VII, 1986; mem. editorial bd. Past or Present Metaphilosophy, Monist, Philos. Studies, Signs, Jour. Symbolic Logic, The Philosophers Annual; editor, contbr. to profl. jours. and books. Recipient Machette prize for contbn. to profession; Medal, College de France, 1986, Wilbur Cross medal Yale U., 2000; Mellon sr. fellow Nat. Humanities Ctr., 1992-93; vis. disting. prof. U. Calif., Irvine, 1994, 96, 97, 98, 99; fellow Conn. Acad. Arts & Scis. Fellow Am. Acad. Arts and Scis.; mem. Coun. on Philos. Studies (pres. 1988-90), Assn. for Symbolic Logic (past exec. coun., exec. com. 1973-83, v.p. 1980-82, coun. 1980-85, pres. 1982-84), Am. Philos. Assn. (past sec., treas., nat. bd. dirs. 1977-83, pres. ctrl. divsn. 1975-78, chmn. nat. bd. officers 1977-85), Philosophy of Sci. Assn., Inst. Internat. Philosophie (past exec. com., v.p. 1983-86, pres. 1990-93, hon. pres. 1994—), Fedn. Internat. Philosophy (exec. com., steering com. 1985-99), Elizabethan Club (v.p. 1989, pres. 1989-90), Phi Beta Kappa. Office: Yale U Dept Philosophy PO Box 208306 New Haven CT 06520-8306 E-mail: ruth.marcus@yale.edu.

MARCUS, SHELDON, adult education educator; b. N.Y.C., Aug. 4, 1937; s. Manny and Sarah (Lande) M.; m. Phyllis Knight; children: Beth, Jonathan, Evan. BA, CCNY, 1959, MS, 1960; EdD, Yeshiva U., 1970. Tchr. N.Y.C. Pub. Schs., 1959-68; lectr. social sci. CUNY, 1965-68; mem. faculty Fordham U., N.Y.C., 1968-70, chmn. divsn. urban edn., 1970-76, assoc. dean grad. edn. Tarrytown campus, 1976-93, prof., 1993—. Mem. exec. bd. tchr. corps program U.S. Office Edn., 1974-82; trustee Doctoral Assn. N.Y., 1973-82; co-dir. Fordham Inst. for Rsch. on Supervision and Tchg., 1992-94, Fordham U./N.Y.C. Supts. Network, 1995—. Author or co-author: Conflicts in Urban Education, 1970; Urban Education: Crisis or Opportunity?, 1972; Father Coughlin: The Tumultuous Life of the Priest of the Little Flower, 1973, (nominated for Pulitzer Prize); The Urban In-Service Education Experience, 1977; Administrative Decision Making in Schools: A Case Study Approach to Strategic Planning, 1986, Strategic Planning: A Case Study Approach to

Administrative Decision Making. Case Teaching Notes, 1987; contbr. articles to profl. jours. Recipient Scanlon award for contbns. to edn., 1992, Adminstr. of Yr. award Phi Delta Kappa, 1993. Mem. Am. Ednl. Rsch. Assn. (proposal reviewer 1992-97). Home: 36 Pocantico River Rd Pleasantville NY 10570-3510 Office: Fordham U Sch Educ Tarrytown NY 10591 Office Phone: 718-817-5677. Business E-Mail: marcus@fordham.edu.

MARCUS, STANLEY, federal judge; b. NYC, 1946; BA, CUNY, 1967; JD, Harvard U., 1971. Law clerk Hon. John Bartels, US Dist. Ct. (ea. dist.), NY; assoc. Botein, Hays, Sklar & Herzberg, NYC, 1974-75; asst. atty. U.S. Dist. Ct. (ea. dist.)NY, 1975-78; spl. atty., dep. chief U.S. organized crime sect. Detroit Strike Force, 1978-79, chief U.S. organized crime sect., 1980-82; US atty. So. Dist. of Fla., Miami, 1982-85; judge US Dist. Ct. (so. dist.) Fla., Miami, 1985-97, US Ct. Appeals (11th cir.), 1997—. Mem. Fed. Bar Assn., Fla. Bar Assn, NY Bar Assn. Mem. U.S. Army, 1968—74. Office: US Ct of Appeals 11th Cir 99 NE 4th St Rm 1262 Miami FL 33132-2185

MARCUS, STEPHEN CECIL, former printing company executive; b. Phila., Mar. 8, 1932; s. Jerome Milton and Helen Gertrude (Jacobs) M.; m. Seena Hymowitz, Nov. 2, 1958; children: Nancy Joy, Julie Bea; m. Lois Simon, Oct. 7, 1984 (div. Nov. 2002). BS, Drexel U., 1957. Jr. ptnr. Liess-Marcus Co., Inc., Phila., 1957-59; v.p. sales Mid-City Press, Inc., Phila., 1959-70; pres., CEO, founder Mars Graphic Svcs., Inc., Westville, NJ, 1970-86, chmn., 1986-97; prin., chmn. Emerging Growth Equities, King of Prussia, Pa., 1999—. Mem. Phila. Mgmt. Negotiating Com.; mem. Phila. br. Jr. Execs./Graphic Arts; bd. dirs. Covenant Ptnrs., Phila., Rodale Press Inst., 1990—, First Pa. Bancorp, Phila., First Penn Bank, IZ Co., San Diego, Harte Hanks, Inc.; mem. adv. bd. First Virtual Co. Holding Co., San Diego. Active Am. Cancer Soc., Phila. Big Bros.; trustee Friends Ctrl. Sch., 1977—80; trustee, co-founder Beth Tovin Synagogue, Phila., 1972—; bd. dirs. Ea. Penitentiary Prison, 1999—, Philly Pops Orch., Phila., Maritime Mus., 2002—. With U.S. Army, 1953—55. Recipient Ann. award Exch. Club NJ, 1981, Big Bros. Am. award Am. Cancer Soc. Mem. Am. Arbitration Assn. (various awards), Nat. Direct Mail Mktg. Assn., Graphic Arts Tech. Found., South Jersey Graphic Arts Assn., Graphic Arts Assn. Del. Valley (bd. dirs. 1988), Poor Richard Club (Phila.), Tau Kappa Epsilon. Republican. Jewish. Home: 915 Exeter Crst Villanova PA 19085-2001 Office: Emerging Growth Ewuities 1150 1st Ave King Of Prussia PA 19406 Office Phone: 610-783-4760. E-mail: stephenmarcus@egequities.com.

MARCUS, STEPHEN HOWARD, hospitality and entertainment company executive; b. Mpls., May 31, 1935; s. Ben D. and Celia Marcus; m. Joan Glasspiegel, Nov. 3, 1962; children: Greg, David, Andrew. BBA, U. Wis., Madison, 1957; LL.B., U. Mich., 1960. Bar: Wis. 1960. V.p. Pfister Hotel Corp., Milw., 1963-69, exec. v.p., 1969-75; pres. Marcus Hotel Corp., Milw., 1975-91; chmn., COO Marcus Corp., Milw., 1980—, COO, dir., 1988; exec. v.p. Marc Plaza Corp., Milw.; v.p. Wis. Big Boy Corp., Milw., Marcus Theatres Corp., Milw.; dir. Med. Coll. Wis., Milw., 1986—; chmn., CEO Marcus Corp., Milw. Dir. Preferred Hotels Assn., 1972—, chmn. bd., 1979; dir. Bank One N.A. Pres. Milw. Conv. and Visitors Bur., 1970-71, bd. dirs., mem. exec. com., 1968—; chmn. Wis. Gov.'s Adv. Council on Tourism, 1976-81; bd. dirs. Multiple Sclerosis Soc. Milw., 1965-67, Milw. Jewish Fedn., 1968-76, Milw. Jewish Chronicle, 1973-76, Children's Hosp. Found., Inc., Competitive Wis.; asso. chmn. bus. div. United Fund Campaign, Milw., 1971; co-chmn. spl. gifts com. United Performing Arts Fund, Milw., 1972-74, bd. dirs., 1973-81, chmn. maj. gifts, 1982, co-chmn., 1983—; bd. dirs. Friends of Art, Milw., 1973-74; pres. Summerfest, 1975; bd. dirs. MECCA, Milw., 1975-82, mem. exec. com., 1977; bd. dirs. Jr. Achievement, Milw., 1976—; trustee Mt. Sinai Med. Center, 1977—, Nat. Symphony Orchestra, 1985; bd. govs. Jewish Community Campus; co-chmn. Ann. Freedom Fund Dinner, NAACP, 1980-81; chmn. Icebreaker Festival, 1989. Served with U.S. Army, 1960-61. Recipient Ben Nickoll award Milw. Jewish Fedn., 1969, Headliner award Milw. Press Club, 1986, Humanitarian award NCCJ, 1988, Lamplighter award Greater Milw. Conv. and Visitors Bur., 1991. Mem. Am. Hotel and Motel Assn. (dir. 1976-79, exec. com. 1978-79), Greater Milw. Hotel and Motel Assn. (pres. 1967-68), Wis. Innkeepers Assn. (pres. 1972-73), Variety Club, Milw. Assn. Commerce (bd. dirs. 1982-85), Downtown Assn., Young Pres.'s Orgn., Wis. Assn. Mfrs. and Commerce (dir. 1978-82), Greater Milw. Com. (dir. 1981) Office: The Marcus Corp 100 E Wisconsin Ave Ste 1900 Milwaukee WI 53202-1900

MARCUS, STEPHEN HOWARD, lawyer; b. N.Y.C., June 30, 1945; s. Jacob and Mildren (Cohen) M.; m. Carol Sylvia Beatrice, June 11, 1967; children: Joshua David, Rebecca Lynn, Daniel Benjamin. BME, MIT, 1967; JD, Harvard U., 1970. Bar: Calif. 1971, U.S. Dist. Ct. (cen. dist.) Calif. 1971, U.S. Dist. Ct. (so. dist.) Calif. 1974, U.S. Dist. Ct. (so. dist.) Calif. 1975, U.S. Ct. Appeals (9th cir.) 1980. Assoc. Mitchell, Silberberg & Knupp, L.A., 1971-72, Greenberg, Bernhard, Weis & Karma, L.A., 1972-76; ptnr. Greenberg, Bernhard, Weiss & Rosin, L.A., 1976-85; assoc. Frandzel & Share, L.A., 1985-87, ptnr., 1987-97, Gittler & Bradford, L.A., 1997—; dir. Cerriton Valley Bancorp., 2001—02. Judge pro tem L.A. Mcpl. Ct., 1976-83. Editor Harvard Law Rev., 1970. Dir. legal com. Temple B'Nai Hayim, 1999-2003, bd. dirs., 1999-2003. Mem. Los Angeles County Bar Assn. (client rels. com. arbitrator 1982—, vice chair, 1996—), Century City Bar Assn. (bd. govs. 1984-90), MIT Club So. Calif. (pres. 1978-79, bd. govs. 1979—), Sigma Xi, Tau Beta Pi. Democrat. Jewish. Avocations: senior soccer, square dancing. Office: Gittler & Bradford 10537 Santa Monica Blvd 3d Fl Los Angeles CA 90025-1793 E-mail: csmarcus@aol.com., smarcus@gblaw.net.

MARCUS, STEVEN IRL, electrical engineering educator; b. St. Louis, Apr. 2, 1949; s. Herbert A. and Peggy L. (Polishuk) M.; m. Jeanne M. Wilde, June 4, 1978; children: Jeremy A., Tobin L. BA, Rice U., 1971; SM, MIT, 1972, PhD, 1975. Research engr. The Analytic Scis. Corp., Reading, Mass., 1973; asst. prof. U. Tex., Austin, 1975-80, assoc. prof., 1980-84, prof., 1984-91, assoc. chmn., dept. elec. and computer engring., 1984-89, L.B. Meaders prof. engring., 1987-91; prof. elec. and computer engring. U. Md., College Park, 1991—, acting chair dept., 2000-01, chair, 2001—, dir. Inst. for Sys. Rsch., 1991-96, acting chair, 2000-01. Cons. Tracor Inc., Austin, 1977, 90, ALPHATECH Inc., Arlington, 1999—. Assoc. editor Math. of Control Signals and Systems, 1987—, Jour. on Discrete Event Dynamic Systems, 1990, Acta Applicandae Mathematicae, 1983—. NSF fellow, 1971-74; Werner W. Dornberger Centennial Teaching fellowship in engring., U. Tex., Austin, 1982-84. Fellow IEEE (prize paper awards com. 1985-88, field awards com. 1989-90, assoc. editor Transactions Info. Theory 1990-92), IEEE Control Systems Soc. (bd. govs. 1985-90, chmn. conf. on decision and control program com. 1983, chmn. working group on stochastic control and estimation 1984-87, assoc. editor Transactions Automatic Control 1980-81); mem. Am. Math. Soc., Soc. Indsl. and Applied Math. (corr. editor Jour. Control and Optimization 1990—, editor-in-chief, 2000—), Acta Applicandae Math., 1983—, Eta Kappa Nu, Tau Beta Pi. Home: 9516 Thornhill Rd Silver Spring MD 20901-4836 Office: U Md Inst for Systems Rsch 2227 Ave Williams Bldg 115 College Park MD 20742-0001

MARCUS, WILLIAM MICHAEL, rubber and vinyl products manufacturing company executive; b. Boston, Jan. 31, 1938; s. Richard and Diana (Litch) M.; m. Cynthia Steinman, Dec. 9, 1962; children: Melanie, Daniel, Richard. BS in Bus. Adminstrn., Babson Inst., 1959. With Am. Biltrite Inc., Wellesley Hills, Mass., 1960—, exec. v.p., treas., 1983—, also dir. Bd. dirs. Congoleum Corp. Served with U.S. Army, 1960-61. Office: Am Biltrite Inc 57 River St Wellesley Hills MA 02481-2013

MARCUSA, FRED HAYE, lawyer; b. Paterson, N.J., Jan. 31, 1946; s. Harry and Alice Marcusa; m. Andrea Disario, June 28, 1986; children; Michael, Daniel. AB, Dartmouth Coll., 1967; JD, U. Pa., 1970. Bar: N.Y. 1971. Assoc. Davis, Polk & Wardwell, N.Y.C., 1970-79; v.p., gen. counsel The Coca-Cola Bottling Co. of N.Y., Inc., N.Y.C., 1979-81; ptnr. Kaye Scholer LLP, N.Y.C., 1981—. Office: Kaye Scholer LLP 425 Park Ave New York NY 10022-3506 E-mail: fmarcusa@kayescholer.com.

MARCUSE, ADRIAN GREGORY, academic administrator; b. N.Y.C., Mar. 25, 1922; s. Maxwell Frederick and Mildred Ann (Hitter) M.; m. Janet Constance Radlo, Oct. 28, 1945 (dec. Mar. 22, 1980); children: Nancy Ruth Marcuse Marshall, Sally Ann Marcuse Crawford, Elizabeth Susan Marcuse; m. Betty Jane Lieberman Rossman, Jan. 11, 1985; 1 stepchild, Amy Beth Rossman Schurtz. BS, MIT, 1942, MS, 1946; LLD (hon.), Lab Inst. Merchandising, 1992. Registered profl. engr. N.Y., Fla. Rsch. assoc. MIT, Cambridge, Mass., 1945-46; rsch. scientist United Aircraft Co., E. Hartford, Conn., 1946-47; application engr. Westinghouse Electric Corp., Boston, N.Y.C., 1947-60; consulting engr. pvt. practice, N.Y.C., 1955-62; v.p. mktg. and sales Corrosion Control Corp., N.Y.C., 1960-62; sales and merchandising mgr. B. Altman & Co., N.Y.C., 1962; v.p., COO Lab. Inst. of Merchandising, N.Y.C., 1962-72, pres., CEO, 1972—2002, pres. emeritus, counsel to pres., 2002—. Pres. LIM Fashion Edn. Found., N.Y.C., 1978—; chmn. Assn. Regionally Accredited Prvt. Colls. and Univs., Washington, 1990-93. Charter commr. City of Glen Cove, N.Y., 1964, chmn. bd. engrs., 1964-68, mem. planning bd., 1980-87; past treas. Community Concert Assn., Glen Cove; past trustee and budget chmn. North Country Reform Temple, Glen Cove; past mem. YMCA Fund-Raising Coun., Glen Cove. 1st lt. USAAF, 1942-45, PTO. Mem.: N.Y. State Counselors Assn., Assn. Proprietary Colls., Am. Coun. on Edn., Am. Assn. Higher Edn., Sigma Beta Delta, Sigma Xi. Republican. Avocations: sailing, bicycling, travel, theater. Office: Lab Inst of Merchandising 12 E 53rd St Fl 2 New York NY 10022-5268 Home (Winter): 356 Golfview Rd #306 North Palm Beach FL 33408 E-mail: amarcuse@limcollege.edu.

MARCUSE, DIETRICH, retired physicist; b. Koenigsberg, East Prussia, Germany, Feb. 27, 1929; came to U.S., 1957; s. Richard and Gertrud (Solty) M.; m. Haide Schwarz, Jan. 13, 1959; children: Christina, Mikel. Diplom Physiker, Freie Universität, Berlin, 1954; Doktor Ingenieur, Karlsruhe Universität, 1962. Mem. tech. staff Siemens and Halske, Berlin, 1954-57, AT&T Bell Labs., Holmdel, N.J., 1957-94, dist. mem. tech. staff, 1982-94; ret., 1994. Vis. rsch. prof. U. Md., Balt. County, 1995-99. Author: Principles of Quantum-Electronics, 2d edit., 1980, Light Transmission Optics, 2d edit., 1982, Theory of Dielectric Optical Wave-guides, 1972, 2nd edit.,1991, Principles of Optical Fiber Measurements, 1981; also over 200 articles. Fellow IEEE (Quantum Electronics award 1981), Optical Soc. Am. (Max Born award 1989). E-mail: dietermarcuse@aol.com.

MARCUSS, ROSEMARY DALY, economist; b. Stamford, Conn., Aug. 27, 1945; d. Eugene Lawrence and Margaret Mary (Murphy) Daly; B.A. in Econs. cum laude, Newton (Mass.) Coll., 1967; M.S., U. Md., 1973, Ph.D., 1979; m. Stanley J. Marcuss, July 6, 1968; children— Elena Daly, Aidan Stanley. Jr. staff economist President's Council of Econ. Advisers, 1968-70; economist, asst. to pres. Am. Fedn. State, County and Mcpl. Employees, Washington, 1973; economist, mgmt. cons. Data Resources, Inc., Washington, 1974-78; dep. asst. dir. tax analysis Congressional Budget Office, Washington, 1980-83, asst. dir. tax analysis, 1983-98; dep. dir. Bur. Econ. Analysis, Washington, 1998—. NSF fellow, 1970-73. Mem. Am. Econ. Assn., Nat. Tax Assn., Tax Inst. Am., So. Econ. Assn., Soc. Govt. Economists, Nat. Economists Club, Nat. Assn. Business Economists (v.p. 2003-), Washington Women Economists. Home: 4616 29th Pl NW Washington DC 20008-2105 Office: Congressional Budget Office 2nd & D Sts SW Washington DC 20515-0001

MARCUSS, STANLEY JOSEPH, lawyer; b. Hartford, Conn., Jan. 24, 1942; s. Stanley Joseph and Anne Sutton (Leone) M.; m. Rosemary Daly, July 6, 1968; children: Elena Daly, Aidan Stanley. BA, Trinity Coll., 1963, Cambridge U., 1965, MA, 1968; JD, Harvard U., 1968. Bar: D.C., N.Y., Conn., U.S. Supreme Ct. Staff atty. office of gen. counsel HUD, Washington, 1968; atty. firm Hogan and Hartson, Washington, 1968-73; counsel to internat. fin. subcom. U.S. Senate Com. on Banking, Housing and Urban Affairs, 1973-77; dep. asst. sec. for trade regulation Dept. Commerce, Washington, 1977-78, sr. dep. asst. sec. for industry and trade, 1978-79, acting asst. sec. for industry and trade, 1979-80, acting asst. sec. for trade regulation, 1980; mem. firm Milbank, Tweed, Hadley & McCloy, Washington, 1980-93, Bryan Cave, 1993—. Former adj. prof. Am. U. Law Sch. Author: Effective Washington Representation, 1983; mem. bd. overseers U. Calif. Berkeley Law Jour.; contbr. articles to profl. jours. Former trustee Trinity Coll., Hartford. Marshall scholar. Mem. ABA, D.C. Bar (former chmn., steering com. internat. law div.), Phi Beta Kappa. Home: 4616 29th Pl NW Washington DC 20008-2105

MARCUVITZ, NATHAN, electrophysics educator; b. Bklyn., Dec. 29, 1913; s. Samuel and Rebecca (Feiner) M.; m. Muriel Spanier, June 30, 1946; children— Andrew, Karen. B.E.E., Poly. Inst. Bklyn., 1935, M.E.E., 1941, D.E.E., 1947; Laurea Honoris Causa, Politecnico Di Torino, 1993; D in Engring. (hon.), Polytechnic U., 2000. Engr. RCA Labs., 1936-40; research asso. Radiation Lab., Mass. Inst. Tech., 1941-46; asst. prof. elec. engring. Poly. Inst. Bklyn., 1946-49, asso. prof., 1949-51, prof., 1951-65; dir. Poly. Inst. Bklyn. (Microwave Research Inst.), 1957-61; v.p. research, acting dean Poly. Inst. Bklyn. (Grad. Center), 1961-63, prof. electrophysics, 1961-66, dean research, dean, 1964-65; asst. dir. def. research and engring. Dept. Def., Washington, 1963-64; prof. applied physics N.Y.U., 1966-73; prof. electrophysics Poly. Inst. N.Y., 1973—, prof. emeritus, 1978—. Vis. prof. Harvard U., spring 1971 Author: Waveguide Handbook, Vol. 10, 1951, (with L. Felsen) Radiation and Scattering of Waves, 1973; also numerous articles. Recipient Microwave Career award IEEE Microwave Theory and Techniques Soc., 1985. Fellow IEEE (Heinrich Hertz medal 1989); mem. Nat. Acad. Engring., Am. Phys. Soc., Sigma Xi, Tau Beta Pi, Eta Kappa Nu. Home: Apt 1403 7225 Pelican Bay Blvd Naples FL 34108-5524 E-mail: marc@rama.poly.edu.

MARCY, ALVIN NEWELL, contractor; b. Southbridge, Mass., Sept. 28, 1935; s. Herman Alvin and Pauline Grace Marcy; m. Laura Erma Ripley, June 14, 1958; children: Laura Lee, Steve, Grace, James. BA, Wheaton Coll., 1958; BD, Gordon Divinity Sch., Wenham, Mass., 1961. Active Fairfax County Taxpayers Assn.; active govtl. orgns. Mem. John Birch Soc. Avocations: long distance running, reading, writing.

MARCY, CHARLES FREDERICK, food company executive; b. Buffalo, Aug. 25, 1950; s. Charles and Mary Jane (Frederick) M.; m. Helen Jean Shank, May 6, 1972 (div. Dec. 1986); children: Michelle Catherine, Adam Charles; m. Cynthia Louise Shockey, June 17, 1989; 1 child, Brooke Allison. BA, Washington and Jefferson Coll., Washington, Pa., 1972; MBA, Harvard U., 1974. Various mktg. and strategic planning positions Gen. Foods Corp., White Plains, N.Y., 1974-84; v.p. mktg. Sara Lee Bakery, Deerfield, Ill., 1984-86; v.p., gen. mgr. Wolferman's Inc. divsn. of Sara Lee Corp., Lenexa, Kans., 1987-89; v.p. strategy and mktg. Kraft Gen. Foods Frozen Products, Glenview, Ill., 1989-90; pres. Kraft Gen. Foods Nat. Dairy Products Corp., Phila., 1991-92, Golden Grain Co., Pleasanton, Calif., 1993-95; pres., CEO Sealright Packaging Co., Inc., DeSoto, Kans., 1995-98; prin. Marcy & Ptnrs. Strategy Cons., Leawood, Kans., 1999; pres., COO Horizon Organic Dairy, Longmont, Colo., 1999, pres., CEO, 2000. Bd. dirs. Phila. Police Athletic League, 1991-92, Boys and Girls Club of Kansas City, Mo., 1987-90, Lake Forest (Ill.) Symphony, 1984-87. Office: Horizon Organic Dairy 6311 Horizon Ln Longmont CO 80503-7176

MARCY, RAYMOND, staffing and consulting company executive; BS, MBA, U. Deyton. Chient svc. rep. Manpower, Inc., Dayton, Ohio, from 1972, mem. mgmt. team, head corp. sales ctr. and nat. accounts; sr. v.p. Adia Svcs., Inc., pres., CEO NurseFinders, Inc. health care subs.; pres. Interim Svcs. Inc., Fort Lauderdale, Fla., 1989—, CEO, 1991—, chmn., 1997—. Human resource issues expert. Office: Interim Svcs Inc 2050 Spectrum Blvd Fort Lauderdale FL 33309-3008

MARCY, WILLIAM L. physician, consultant; b. Memphis, Mar. 28, 1952; s. Jewel Doris Marcy; children: Leigh Michele, William L. III, Kelly Christian, Forrest Kingsley, Simon Cutler. BS with honors, Rhodes Coll., 1974; MD, U. Tenn., 1978. Diplomate Am. Bd. Family Practice, 1981. Med. resident family medicine U. Tenn., 1978—81; pvt. practice Tupelo, Miss., 1981—; med. dir. Mantachie (Miss.) Rural Health Care, Inc., 2002—; med. dir., cons. Children's Advocacy Ctr. of N.E. Miss., Mantachie, 2002—. Former chmn. Stop The Hurt! Conf. Planning Com., Tupelo, Miss., 1990—, mem., 1990—. Mem., chair Rep. Exec. Com. Lee County, Tupelo, Miss., 1988—. Mem.: Miss. State Med. Assn., Am. Med. Assn. (conv. del. 1984—, N/A N/A). Republican. Avocations: history, musician percussion, hunting, debate. Office: Mantachie Rural Health Care Inc 5500 Hwy. 363 Mantachie MS 38855

MARDEN, BRICE, artist; b. Bronxville, N.Y., Oct. 15, 1938; s. Nicholas Brice and Kathryn (Fox) M.; m. Pauline Thalia Baez, 1960 (div. 1964); 1 son, Nicholas Brice; m. Helen Regina Harrington, Nov. 7, 1968; 2 daus., Maya Mirabelle Zahara, Melia Io Bricia. Student, Fla. So. Coll., 1957-58; BFA, Boston U., 1961; MFA, Yale U., 1963. Pres. Plane Image, Inc. Exhibited in one man shows including Wilcox Gallery, Swarthmore, Pa., 1964, Bykert Gallery, N.Y.C., 1966, 68-70, 72-74, Galerie Yvon Lambert, Paris, 1969, 73, Galleria Francoise Lambert, Milan, Italy, 1970, 73, Konrad Fischer, Dusseldorf, Fed. Republic of Germany, 1971-73, 75, 80, Gian Enzo Sperone, Turin, Italy, 1971, 77, Locksley-Shea Gallery, Mpls., 1972, 74, Jack Glenn Gallery, Corona del Mar, Calif., 1973, Cirrus Gallery, Los Angeles, 1974, Sable-Castelli Gallery, Toronto, Can., 1974, Contemporary Arts Mus., Houston, 1974, Loretto Hilton Gallery, St. Louis, 1974, Ft. Worth (Tex.) Art Mus., 1974, Mpls. Inst. Arts, 1975, D'Allesandro/Ferranti, Rome, 1975, Solomon R. Guggenheim Mus., N.Y.C., 1975, Sperone Westwater Fischer, N.Y.C., 1976, Max Protech Gallery, Washington, 1977, Bell Gallery, Providence, 1977, Jean and Karen Bernier, Athens, 1977, Pace Gallery, N.Y.C., 1978, 80, 82, 84, Kunstraum, Munich, 1979, Inst. für Moderne Kunst, Nurnberg, Fed. Republic of Germany, 1979, Ink, Zurich, 1980, Stedelijk Mus., Amsterdam, 1981, Daniel Weinberg Gallery, Los Angeles, 1984, Mary Boone Gallery, N.Y.C., 1987, Mary Boone/Michael Werner Gallery, N.Y.C., 1988, 89, Gallery Montenay, Paris, 1988, Anthony d'Offay Gallery, London, 1988, Van Straaten Gallery, Chgo., 1989, Galerie Michael Werner, Cologne, 1990, Kunsthalle im Kulturhaus Palazzo, Baselland, Switzerland, 1991, Gagosian Gallery, N.Y., 1993, Mus. Fine Arts, Boston, 1993, Matthew Marks Gallery, N.Y., 1993, 95, 96, 98, Dia Ctr. for the Arts, N.Y., 1993, Walker Art Ctr., Mpls., 1993, Menil Collection, Houston, 1993, Mus. Nat. Ctr. de Arte, Madrid, 1993, Kunstmus., Bonn, Germany, 1993, Tate Gallery, London, 1993, Mus. d'Art Moderne de la Ville de Paris, 1993, Balt. Mus. Art, 1993, Curwen Gallery, London, 1993, Kunstmus. Basel, 1995, Mus. fur Gegenwartskunst, 1995, Mus. Fridericianum, Kassel, 1995, Kunsthalle, Bern, 1995, Vienna Secession, 1995, Stedelijk, Amsterdam, 1995, St. Louis Art Mus., 1995, Pace Gallery, N.Y., 1996, Thomas Ammann Fine Art AG, Zurich, Switzerland, 1997, Staatliche Graphisch Sammlung, Munchen, 1998, Kunstmus., Winterthur, Switzerland, 1998, Wexner Art Ctr., Ohio, 1999, Fogg Art Mus., Cambridge, Mass., 1999, Dallas Mus. Art, 1999; represented in group shows including Lyman Allen Mus., New London, Conn., 1960, Leo Castelli Gallery, N.Y.C., 1966, Park Place Gallery, N.Y.C., 1966, Ithaca (N.Y.) Coll. Mus. Art, 1967, Krannert Art Mus., Champaign, Ill., 1967, Bykert Gallery, 1967-68, 70-71, 74, Inst. Contemporary Art, Phila., 1967, U. Omaha, 1967, Mus. Fine Arts, Houston, 1967, Clemson U. Sch. Architecture, 1968, Vassar Coll. Art Gallery, Poughkeepsie, N.Y., 1969, Stadtische Kunsthalle, Dusseldorf, 1969, Ft. Worth Art Mus., 1969, 74, Carmen Lamanna Gallery, Toronto, 1969, Whitney Mus. Am. Art, N.Y.C., 1969, 71, 73, 77, 83, Locksley-Shea Gallery, 1970, Albright-Knox Gallery, Buffalo, 1970, Found. Maeght, St. Paul-de-Vence, France, 1970, Utah Mus. Fine Arts, Salt Lake City, 1970, Minn. Mus. Art, St. Paul, 1971, Henry Gallery, Seattle, 1972-73, Ariz. State U., Tempe, 1972, Ga. Mus. Art, Athens, 1972, Mus. Contemporary Art, Chgo., 1972, 86, Indpls. Mus. Art, 1972, Walker Art Ctr., Mpls., 1972, Univ. Art Mus., Berkeley, Calif., 1972, Art Inst. Chgo., 1972, Mus. Friderichianum and Neue Galerie, Kassel, Fed. Republic of Germany, 1972, Galerie Yvon Lambert, 1972, Yale U. Art Gallery, New Haven, 1973, Genthofte Kunstvenner and Genthofte Kommune, Denmark, 1973, Stadtisches Mus., Monchengladbach, Fed. Republic of Germany, 1973, I.C.C., Antwerp, Belgium, 1973, Centro Communitario di Brera, Milan, 1973, Royal Coll. Art, London, 1973, Parcheggio di Villa Borghese, Rome, 1974, Kathonah (N.Y.) Gallery, 1974, Nat. Gallery of Victoria, Australia, 1974, Art Gallery of New South Wales, Australia, 1974, Art Gallery of South Australia, Akelaide, 1974, West Australian Art Gallery, Perth, 1974, City of Auckland (Australia) Art Gallery, 1974, Westfalischer Kunstverein, Munster, Fed. Republicof Germany, 1974, Scottish Arts Council, Edinburgh, 1974, Mus. Modern Art, N.Y.C., 1974, 76, Rice Mus. and Sewall Gallery, 1975, Rijksmuseum Kroller-Muller, Otterlo, Holland, 1975, Basel (Switzerland) Kunstmuseum, 1975, Kunstahlle, Zurich, 1976, Staatliche Kunsthalle, Baden-Baden, Fed. Republic of Germany, 1976, Graphische Sammlung Albertina, Vienna, 1976, Sidney Janis Gallery, N.Y.C., 1977, Wildenstein and Co., London, 1980, Bklyn. Mus., 1980, Mus. Contemporary Art, Los Angeles, 1983, Hayden Gallery, Cambridge, Mass., 1983, Pratt Inst. Gallery, N.Y.C., 1983, Gallery Maeght Lelong, N.Y.C., 1983, The Renaissance Soc., Chgo., 1984, Blum Helman Warehouse, N.Y.C., 1984, Daniel Weinberg Gallery, Los Angeles, 1985, Guggenheim Mus., N.Y.C., 1985, Condeso Lawler Gallery, N.Y.C., 1985, Mary Boone Gallery, 1985, Carnegie Inst., Pitts., 1985, Ft. Lauderdale (Fla.) Mus. Art, 1986, P.S. 1, L.I. City, 1986, Charles Cowles Gallery, N.Y.C., 1986, Musee d'Art Moderne, Paris, 1986, Los Angeles County Mus., 1986, Gemeentemuseum, The Hague, The Netherlands, 1986, Ludwig Mus., Kolm, Fed. Republic of Germany, 1986, Galerie Nachst St. Stephan, Vienna, 1986, CAPC Musee d'Art Contemporain de Bordeaux, France, 1986, Anthony d'Offay Gallery, London, 1987, The SAra Hilden Art Mus., Tampere, Finland, 1988, Carnegie Mus. Art, Pitts., 1988, Musee d'art contemporain, Lyon, 1988, Hirschl and Adler Modern, New York, 1989, Whitney Mus. Am. Art, N.Y., 1989, Albright Knox Art Gallery, Buffalo, Ctr. for the Fine Arts, Miami, Fla., Milwaukee Art Mus., Wis., Yale U. Art Gallery, New Haven, Conn., 1989, The Albertina, Vienna, 1990, Musee du Louvre, Paris, 1990, The Mus. of Modern Art, New York, 1992, Margo Leavin Gallery, L.A., 1992, The Balt. Mus. Art, 1992, Kassel, Germany, 1992, The Aldrich Mus., Ridgefield, Conn., 1993, Luhring Augusting, N.Y., 1994, Nat. Gallery, Washington, 1994, The Art Inst. Chgo., 1995, Nat. Mus. Modern Art, Tokyo, 1995, Whitney Mus. Am. Art, N.Y., 1995, Musee national d'art modern, Centre Georges Pompidou, 1995, Mus. Contemporary Art, Chgo., 1996, La Biennale di Venizia, Venice, Italy, 1997, Mitchell-innes & Nash, N.Y., 1998, Hirshhorn Mus. and Sculpture Garden, Washington, Miami (Fla.) Art Mus., 1999-2000, Carnegie Mus. Art, Pitts., 2000, Serpentine Gallery, London, 2000, Kunst Mus., Luzern, Switzerland, 2000, Instituto Nazionale Per La Gradica, Rome, 2001, Archivio di Stato, Torino, Italy, 2002, Landesmuseum fur Kunst und Kulturgeschichte, Munster, Germany, 2002, Boston U. Gallery, 2002, Matthew Marks Gallery, N.Y.C., 2002, Daros Collection, Zurich, Switzerland, 2003. Office: 131 Varick St Rm 1003 New York NY 10013-1417

MARDEN, JACK MORTIMER, lawyer; b. N.Y.C., Jan. 29, 1933; BA in Polit. Sci., NYU, Washington Sq. Coll., 1953; JD, NYU, 1956; LLM equivalent, Judge Advocate Gen.'s Sch. U.S. Army, Charlottesville, Va., 1964. U.S. Dist. Ct. (so. dist.) W.Va., U.S. Dist. Ct. (so., ea. dist.) N.Y., (Bar: N.Y. 1956, W.Va. 1986, Pa. 1994-, U.S. Ct. Mil. Appeals, U.S. Army Ct. Mil. Review, U.S. Ct. Appeals (4th cir.), U.S. Supreme Ct., 1964; cert. U.S. Army mil. judge, appellate judge, NASD arbitrator, U.S. arbitration and mediation svc. mediator, nat. arbitration forum arbitrator. Commd. 1st lt. U.S. Army, 1957; advanced through grades to col. 1st U.S. Army, 1977; asst. staff judge adv. Hdqrs. U.S. Army Inf. Ctr., Ft. Benning, Ga., 1958-59, U.S. Army, Carribbean, Ft. Amador, C.Z., 1959-63; project officer plans div., plans and publs. dept. Judge Adv. Gen.'s Sch., Charlottesville, 1964, chief plans div., 1964-65; post judge adv. U.S. Army Intelligence Command, Ft. Holabird, Md., 1965, command staff judge adv., 1965-68; corps. judge adv. XXIV Corps, Phu Bai, Republic Vietnam, 1968-69, asst. staff judge adv., comdr.-in-chief Pacific, 1969-71, dep. staff judge adv., comdr.-in-chief Pacific, 1971-72; dep. staff judge adv. 1st U.S. Army, Ft. Meade, Md., 1972-74, staff judge adv., 1974-78, supervisory cir. judge Ft. Dix, NJ, 1978-81; legal advisor AF South (NATO), Naples, Italy, 1981-82; supervisory cir. judge U.S. Army, Mannheim, Fed. Republic Germany, 1982-84, sr. appellate judge, ct. mil. rev. Falls Church, Va., 1984-86, ret., 1986; bar counsel The W.Va. State Bar, Charleston, 1986-89; counsel W.Va. Workers Compensation Fund, Charleston, 1989—91; adminstrv. law judge W.Va. Worker's Compensation, 1991—94; pvt. practice, 1994—; assoc. dir. litig. strategies group (formerly med.-legal strategies group) Med. Horizons Unltd., San Antonio, 1996—; assoc. (part time) Mayerson Law Offices, 1999. Instr. bus. law Chaminade Coll., Honolulu, 1971-72, Howard Community Coll., Columbia, Md., 1972-78; nat. judge adv. Nat. Sojourners, 1973-78, nat. pres., 1985-86; tchr. 6th dept. labor adminstrv. law judge conf., nat. assn. adminstrv. law judge conf., 2000, various other courses on legal issues, mil. law, and legal ethics. Contbr. articles to profl.

jours. including Sojourner Mag., Ten Year Report, The New Age, 1971, 20 Mil. Law Rev. 139. Past pres. Ner Torah Congregation, Columbia; mem. Sr. Adult Activities Ctr. Indian Valley, 1997-. Decorated Legion of Merit with Oak Leaf Cluster, Meritorious Svc. medal with Oak Leaf Cluster, Army Commendation medal with Oak Leaf Cluster, Good Conduct medal, Nat. Def. Svc. medal, Vietnam Svc. medal with 4 Battle Stars, Republic of Vietnam Campaign medal, Republic of Vietnam Cross of Galantry with Palm, Meritorious Unit Commendation, Overseas Svc. Ribbon, Army Svc. Ribbon. Mem. ABA (past tchr. presdl. showcase meeting 2000), Ret. Officers Assn. W.Va., Pa. Bar Assn., Mont. County Bar Assn., Souderton Borough, Zoning Bd. (chmn.), Assn. Conflict Resolution, Nat. Sojourner's (past nat. pres. 1985-86, past pres. Panama chpt. #35, Charleston, Va. #440, Saigon, #409, Valley Forge, #444, past mem., chmn. com. 33, past nat. trustee, past chmn.), Heroes of '76 (past nat. comdr. 1995-96), Ret. Officer's Assn. (Willow Grove chpt., past pres Mountaineer chpt. 1988 90), Congreg. Tifcres B'nai Israel, Jewish War Vets. U.S. (Post 98), Valley of Charleston (so. jurisdiction), A.F. & A.M., Ft. Benning Lodge, Shiloh Lodge, Scottish Rite. Office: 347 Madison Ave Souderton PA 18964-1863 Office Phone: 215-721-4530.

MARDEN, KENNETH ALLEN, advertising executive; b. Dec. 12, 1928; s. Allen H. and Doris (Littlefield) M.; m. Julia Lee Black, June 11, 1949; children: Priscilla Anne, Emily Gage. BA, U. Maine, 1950. Hosp. salesman Johnson & Johnson, New Brunswick, N.J., 1959-61, product dir. hosp divsn., 1962-68, advt. and pub. rels. mgr. hosp. divsn., 1969-71, group product dir., patient care divsn., 1972-74, advt. dir. patient care divsn., 1974-78; v.p. E.J. Axelrod, Inc., N.Y.C., 1978-80; v.p. account mgmt. Vicom/FCB, Phila., 1980-87; pres. Am. Kennel Club, N.Y., 1987-90. Cons. on dog legislation, 1990—, also bd. dirs.; pres. Crossing Creek Comm., 1991—, bd. dirs. The Dog Mus., 1995—. 1st lt. U.S. Army, 1951-53; capt. Md. N.G., 1956-59. Mem. Dog Writers Assn. Am., German Shorthaired Pointer Am. Club (del. 1976—, v.p. 1985-96), Eastern German Shorthaired Pointer Club (pres. 1972-74, 94-98), Jersey Rag Racers (pres. 1994-96), Kennel Club Phila. (bd. dirs.), Katahdin German Shorthaired Pointer Club of Greater Portland, Nat. Animal Interest Alliance (bd. dirs. 1994—), Nat. Breed Clubs Alliance (v.p. 1996-2000). Republican. Episcopalian. Home: 183 E River Rd Whitefield ME 04353 Office: Crossing Creek Communications 183 E River Rd Whitefield ME 04353

MARDER, JOHN G. real estate investor, marketing consultant, corporate director, bison rancher; b. N.Y.C., Dec. 27, 1926; s. Joseph T. and Rhea Marder; m. Barbara Sand, 1956 (div. 1971); children: Jonathan A., Susan Zelouf, Jane Martin; m. Joan Kron, 1971. Student, Cornell U., 1944-45; BS in Bus., Columbia U., 1950. Merchandising exec. Macy's, N.Y.C., 1951-56; exec. v.p. Grey Advt. Inc., N.Y.C., 1956-86; real estate investor-developer Miami Beach, Anguilla B.W.I., 1986—2004; ptnr. buffalo ranch and mktg. enterprise Belle-Air Farms, Thompson, Pa., 1999—. Bd. dirs. several profit, not-for-profit and ednl. corps. Served as radio officer U.S. Maritime Service, U.S. Army Transport Service, 1945-46; 2d Lt. Q.M.C. U.S. Army, 1951-53. Home: 205 E 63rd St New York NY 10021-7425 also: 18 Hedges Banks Dr East Hampton NY 11937-3505 E-mail: jgm@buffalobelle.com.

MARDER, MICHAEL ZACHARY, dentist, researcher, educator; b. NYC, Aug. 30, 1938; s. Jospeh Theodore and Rhea (Greenspun) M.; (widowed); children: Sherri Ellen, Robert Whitney. Student, Tufts U., 1959; DDS, Columbia U., 1963. Diplomate: Am. Bd. Oral Medicine. Practice dentistry, NYC, 1963-66, 68—; asst. Sch. Dental and Oral Surgery, Columbia U., NYC, 1963-66, instr., 1968, asst. clin. prof., 1968-72, assoc. clin. prof., 1972-76, NYC clin. prof. dentistry, 1976—, rschr., 1963—; dir. oral medicine, 1972-84; dir. clin. cancer tng., 1993—; attending dental surgeon Presbyn. Hosp., 1972-76; assoc. attending dentist, 1976-82; attending dentist, 1982—; cons. Good Samaritan Hosp., Suffern, NY. Lectr. field. Author 2 textbooks in dental medicine; contbr. chpts. to med. and dental textbooks, articles to profl. jours. Served to capt. US Army, 1966-68. Recipient Cert. Achievement US Army, 1968. Fellow NY Acad. Dentistry; mem. ADA, Internat. Assn. Dental Rsch., Am. Acad. Oral Medicine, Frist Dist. Dental Soc. NY, Omicron Kappa Upsilon, Sigma Xi. Office: 119 W 57th St New York NY 10019-2303 Office Phone: 212-265-8291.

MARDER, SETH RICHARD, science educator, small business owner; b. Brooklyn, N.Y., June 25, 1961; PhD, U. Wis., Madison, 1985. Mem. beckman inst. Caltech, Pasadena, Calif., 1990—98; prof. chemistry U. Ariz., Tucson, 1998—2003; prof. chemistry Ga. Inst. Tech., Atlanta, 2003—. Dir. ctr. organic electronics and photonics Ga. Inst. Technolog, Atlanta, 2003—. Fellow: AAAS, Optical Sci. of Am. Achievements include patents for Hold 10 US patents. Office: Ga Inst Tech 770 State St Atlanta GA 30332 Personal E-mail: seth.marder@chem.stry.gatech.edu. Business E-Mail: seth.marder@chem.stry.gatech.edu.

MARDER, TOD A. art historian, educator; PhD, Columbia U. Prof. Rutgers U., New Brunswick, N.J., chmn. dept. art history, 1999—. Author: Bernini's Scala Regia at the Vatican Palace, 1997, Bernini and the Art of Architecture, 1998; editor-in-chief Jour. Soc. Archtl. Historians, 1987-90; contbr. articles to profl. jours. Fellow Am. Acad. in Rome. Office: Dept Art History Rutgers U Voorhees Hall 71 Hamilton St New Brunswick NJ 08903

MARDER, WILLIAM DAVID, health economist; b. Phila., Apr. 5, 1947; s. Nathan and Sylvia (Roseman) M.; m. Donna Rhae, Jan. 22, 1975; children: Jessica E., Andrew N., Julia A. AB, U. Chgo., 1968, AM, 1972, PhD, 1990. Tchr. jr. high sch. Phila. Pub. Schs., 1970-71; asst. prof. Roosevelt U., Chgo., 1975-80; economist AMA, Chgo., 1980-82, sr. economist, 1982-84, dept. dir., 1985-89; dir. health labor mkt. rsch. Abt Assocs. Inc., Cambridge, Mass., 1990-92, area mgr., 1993-94, mng. v.p., 1994-95; v.p., gen. mgr. Medstat Cambridge Mfg., Mass., 1995—2002, sr. v.p., 2002—. Author: Organizational Medical Practice, 1985, Physician Supply and Utilization by Specialty, 1988; contbr. articles to profl. jours. Traineeship NIMH, 1971-75. Mem. APHA (chmn. economists com. 1990-91), Internat. Health Econs. Assn., Am. Econ. Assn., Ill. Econ. Assn. (pres. 1986-87). Office: Medstat 125 Cambridgepark Dr Cambridge MA 02140-2329 E-mail: bill.marder@medstat.com.

MARDEROSIAN, ARMENA PEARL, music educator; b. Providence, Jan. 1, 1949; d. Diran Martin and Vanouhi (Kazanjian) Mardirossian; m. Ronald Grigor Suny, Aug. 14, 1971; children: Grikor Martiros Suni(dec.), Sevan Siranoush Suni, Anoush Tamar Suni. BA, Oberlin Coll., 1970. Substitute tchr. French Pennsbury Pub. Schs., Fairless Hills, Pa., 1970—71; tchr. and tchr. trainer Suzuki piano Suzuki Assn. Am., Oberlin, Ohio, 1972—80, Watertown, Mass., 1980—81, tchr. trainer Suzuki piano Ann Arbor, Mich., 1981—, Palo Alto, Calif., 2001—02; pianist, dir. The Suni Project: Music Preservation, 1992—. Composer (children's) songs. Mem.: Suzuki Assn. Ams., Ann Arbor Area Piano Tchrs. Guild, Mich. Music Tchrs. Assn., Piano Basic Found., Am. Nat. Hygiene Soc., Nat. Health Assn., Music Tchrs. Nat. Assn.

MARDIAN, DANIEL, construction company director; b. Pasadena, Calif., Apr. 10, 1917; s. Samuel and Akabe (Lekerian) M.; m. Katherine Evkhanian, Jan. 30, 1942; children: Daniel Jr., Tom, John, Paul, Scott. Student, Pasadena City Coll., 1937; diploma, U.S. Army Engring. Sch., Ft. Belvoir, Va., 1944, U.S. Army Command and Gen. Staff Coll., 1961. Commd. U.S. Army, 1942, advances through grades to lt. col., 1962, ret., 1970; ptnr. Mardian Constrn. Co., Phoenix, 1945-47, exec. v.p., 1947-66, pres., 1966-78, also bd. dirs. Past chmn., mem. Nat. Joint Apprenticeship/Tng. commn. Oper. Engrs., Washington, 1975-78; mem. adv. bd. constrn. programs Ariz. State U., Tempe, 1957—, mem. adv. bd. Coll. Engring., 1957—; mem. adv. bd. constrn. program No. Ariz. U., Flagstaff; bd. dirs. Citibank, Phoenix, 1962-87. Pres. Am. Coun. Constrn. Edn., Monroe, La., 1991-93; past pres., bd. dirs. Fiesta Bowl, Tempe, 1986-92; gen. campaign chmn. United Way, Phoenix, 1967; pres. Met. Phoenix C. of C., 1967-68. Capt. C.E., U.S. Army, 1942-46, PTO, 1970—. Recipient Hall of Fame award Ariz. State U., 1990, medallion of merit, 1984, Excellence in Constrn. award Am. Subcontractors Assn., 1988, Hall of Fame award Nat. Football Found., 1987, Brotherhood award Ariz. chpt. NCCJ, 1981, Fellow award Am. Inst. Constructors, 1996. Mem. Associated Gen. Contractors Am. (life bd. dirs., chmn. yr. award 1970, mem. workforce devel. com., trustee, chmn. laborers tng. com., 1969—), Sun Angel Found. (chmn. 1989-91), Ariz. Acad., Phoenix Country Club (bd. dirs., pres. 1985-86), Phoenix Kiwanis Club (past dir.). Republican. Mem. United Ch. Christ. Avocations: golf, fishing. Office: Perini Building Co 360 E Coronado Rd Phoenix AZ 85004-1524 Home: 1630 W Glendale Ave Apt 24 Phoenix AZ 85021-8982

MARDILOVICH, IVAN P, education educator, researcher; b. Stolbtsy, Belarus, Sept. 21, 1952; s. Peter L and Elena I (Zvytsevich) Mardilovich; m. Galina A Semyonov, Apr. 23, 1977; children: Anastasia I, Katerina I. MSc, Belarus State U., 1970—75; PhD in phys. chemistry, Russian U. of Peoples' Friendship, 1975—82. Sr. rsch. scientist NAS of Belarus, Minsk, Belarus, 1985—99; rsch. asst. prof. Worcester Poly. Inst., Worcester, Mass., 1999—. Sci. sec. of the divsn. of chem. and earth sciences NAS of Belarus, Minsk, Belarus, 1998—99. Sec.- gen. Internat. Fedn. of Chem. Societies, Minsk, Belarus, 1993—2000. Recipient Bronze medal, USSR Exhbn. of the Nat. Economy Achievements, 1985. Achievements include developed and characterized unique Pd and Pd-alloy membranes on porous supports for high temperature hydrogen separation and for a variety of hydrogen-related processes. Office: Worcester Polytechnic Institute 100 Institute Rd Worcester MA 01609 E-mail: ivanpm@wpi.edu.

MARDIN, ARIF, music industry executive, musician; b. Istanbul, Turkey, Mar. 15, 1932; Grad., Istanbul U.; postgrad., D (hon.), Berklee Coll. Music. V.p. Atlantic Records, 1969, sr. v.p. Prodr.: The Young Rascals, Dusty Springfield, Aretha Franklin, Roberta Flack, Donny Hathaway, Hall & Oats, John Prine, Willie Nelson, The Average White Band, The Bee Gees, Phil Collins, Bette Midler, Judy Collins, Carly Simon, Laura Nyro, Dionne Warwick, Culture Club, Howard Jones, George Benson, Melissa Manchester, Chaka Khan. Named to NARAS Hall of Fame, 1990; recipient Man of Yr. award, Assembly Turkish Am. Assns., 1990, Shofar of Peace award, Sephardic Hebrew Acad., 1992, Best Musical Show Album Grammy award, 1996; Quincy Jones scholar, 1958. Office: Atlantic Records 1290 Avenue Of The Americas New York NY 10104-0184

MARDINKHA, KHNANIA, IV, church administrator; Catholic patriarch Apostolic Catholic Assyrian Ch. of the E. Mem. Apostolic Cath. Assyrian Ch. Office: Apostolic/Cath Assyrian Ch 3d Ave # 32 Tehran 14 Iran also: Apostolic & Cath Assyrian Ch East 7201 N Ashland Blvd Chicago IL 60626-2503

MARDIS, ELIZABETH WILLIAMS, occupational health nurse; b. Colbert County, Ala., July 31, 1953; d. Bobby Joe and Nell Elizabeth (Cochran) Williams; m. Danny Richard Mardis, Dec. 18, 1976; children: Paige, Patrick. Diploma nursing, Sanford U., 1973; BS in Nursing, U. North Ala., 2004. Cert. occupl. health nurse; cert. occupl. hearing conservationist. Occupl. health mgr. Huntsville Hosp., Ala., Goodyear Dunlop Tire Corp., Huntsville, Ala.; occupl. health nurse Delphi Automotive Systems, Athens, Ala.; dir. case mgmt. Parkway Med. Ctr., Decatur, Ala., emergency rm. supr.; asst. dir. nursing svcs. Lawrence County Hosp., Moulton, Ala.; patient cdn. and infection control nurse Humana Hosp., Russelville, Ala. Instr. prepared childbirth. Mem. Am. Assn. Occupl. Health Nurses. Home: 2006 Cotaco Valley Trl SE Decatur AL 35603-5145

MARDIS, HAL KENNEDY, urological surgeon, educator, researcher; b. Lincoln, Nebr., Apr. 4, 1934; s. Harold Corson and Marie (Swaim) M.; m. Janet Reimers Schenken, June 22, 1956; children: Michael Corson, Anne Lucille, Jeanne Marie. BS, U. Nebr., Lincoln, 1955; MD, U. Nebr., Omaha, 1958. Diplomate Am. Bd. Urology. Intern Nebr. Meth. Hosp., Omaha, 1958-59, med. dir. The Stone Ctr., 1966—; resident in urology Charity Hosp. La., New Orleans, 1959-62, chief resident in urology, 1962-63; pvt. practice Omaha, 1965—; instr., asst. prof. La. State U. Sch. Medicine, New Orleans, 1963-65; asst. prof., assoc. prof. surgery U. Nebr. Med. Ctr., 1965-85, prof., 1985—. Investigator North Cen. Cancer Treatment Group, Rochester, Minn., 1988—, Technomed Internat., Inc., Danvers, Mass., 1988—; cons. Boston Sci. Corp., Watertown, Mass., 1988—. Assoc. editor Jour. Stone Disease; contbr. articles to Jour. AMA, So. Med. Jour., Jour. Urology, Urology, Urol. Clinics N.Am., Seminars in Interventional Radiology. Sec., pres. Omaha Symphony Assn., 1973-76; advisor United Arts Omaha, 1983-88. Recipient Outstanding Contbn. award dept. surgery U. Nebr. Med. Ctr., 1990. Fellow ACS; mem. AMa (del. med. staff sect. 1983-86), Am. Urol. Assn. (pres. South Cen. chpt. 1990-91, 1st prize 1976, best clin. exhibit award 1977, Gold Cane achievement award 2001), Am. Lithotripsy Soc. (pres. 1989-90), Alpha Omega Alpha (pres. 1991-92). Republican. Achievements include development of guidewire techniques for angiography and endourology, thermoplastic internal ureteral stent; description of benefits of hydrophilic polymers for endourologic devices. Office: The Urology Ctr 111 S 90th St Omaha NE 68114-3907 Office Phone: 402-397-9800. Business E-Mail: hkmardis@urologycenterpc.net.

MARDUEL, ALIX, venture capitalist; Ptnr. Sofinnova Ventures, 1990—97; med. residency Paris; postdoctoral fellowship U. Calif., San Francisco, Stanford U.; mng. dir. Alta Partners, San Francisco, 1997—. Office: Alta Partners One Embarcadero Ctr Ste 4050 San Francisco CA 94111

MARDY, MICHAEL JOHN, food products executive; BA in History, Princeton U., 1970; MBA, Rutgers U., 1976. CFO Keystone Foods Corp., Bala Cynwyd, Pa.; with PriceWaterhouse Coopers, 1976—80; sr. v.p. Nabisco, 1980—96; exec. v.p., CFO Keystone Foods Corp., 1996—2001. Mem.: FEI, AICPA. Office: Keystone Foods Corp 801 City Ave Ste 800 Bala Cynwyd PA 19004 E-mail: michael.mardy@keystonefoods.com., mmardy@aol.com.

MARE, OLINDO FRANCO, professional football player; b. Hollywood, Fla., June 6, 1973; m. Sandy. Student, MacMurray Coll., Valencia C.C., Orlando, Fla., Syracuse U. Kicker Miami Dolphins, 1996—. Active Cystic Fibrosis Found., Habitat for Humanity. Named to Pro Bowl, 1999; named first-team All-Pro, AP, USA Today, The Sporting News, Football Digest, Pro Football Weekly, Coll. and Pro Football Newsweekly, 1999, NFL Alumni Assn. Spl. Teams Player of Yr., 1999. Office: Miami Dolphins Tng Facility 7500 SW 30th St Davie FL 33314

MAREADY, WILLIAM FRANK, lawyer; b. Mullins, S.C., Sept. 13, 1932; s. Jesse Frank and Vera (Sellers) M.; m. Brenda McCanless, Nov. 3, 1979. AB, U. N.C., 1955, JD with honors, 1958. Bar: N.C. 1958, U.S. Dist. Ct. N.C. 1960, U.S. Ct. Appeals (4th cir.) 1962, U.S. Supreme Ct. 1968. Assoc. Mudge, Stern, Baldwin & Todd, N.Y.C., 1958-60, Hudson, Ferrell, Carter, Petree & Stockton, Winston-Salem, N.C., 1960-65; ptnr. Petree, Stockton & Robinson, Winston-Salem, 1965-92, Robinson, Maready, Lawing & Comerford, 1992-97, Maready, Comerford & Britt, 1997-99; prin. Law Offices of William F. Maready, 1999—. N.C. chmn. Winston-Salem/Forsyth County Bd. Edn., 1968-70, chmn., bd. dirs. and mem. exec. com., N.C. State Port Authority, 1984-97. With Green Berets, U.S. Army, 1952-54. Recipient Disting. Svc. award N.C. Sch. Bds. Assn., Freedom award John Locke Soc., 2000. Fellow Am. Coll. Trial Lawyers, Am. Bar Found.; mem. ABA (chmn. standing com. on aero. law 1979-82, chmn. forum com. on air and space law 1982-86), N.C. Bar Assn. (chmn. litigation sect. 1981-82, adminstrn. of justice com. 1981-82), Nat. Parent Tchr. Assn. (life), Forsyth Country Club, Rotary (Winston-Salem), Order of Coif, Phi Delta Phi, Phi Beta Kappa. Republican. Methodist. Office: 1076 W 4th St Ste 100 Winston Salem NC 27101-2411 Office Phone: 336-722-1027. E-mail: billmaready@mareadylaw.com.

MARECEK, JEANNE, psychologist, educator; b. Berwyn, Ill., May 28, 1946; d. Frank J. and Josephine (Serio) M. BS, Loyola U., Chgo., 1968; MS, Yale U., 1971, PhD, 1973. From asst. prof. to prof. psychology Swarthmore (Pa.) Coll., 1972—, chmn. dept., 1986-91, 94-95, 98—, head women's studies program, 1996—. Fulbright sr. lectr., Sri Lanka, 1988. Co-author: Making a Difference: Psychology and the Construction of Gender; contbr. numerous articles to profl. jours. and chpts. to books. Bd. dirs. Women in Transition, Phila., 1980-86; vice patron Nest, Hendala, Sri Lanka, 1995—; bd. dirs. Women's Therapy Ctr., Phila., 1996—. Fellow Swedish Collegium for Advanced Study in Social Scis., 1997; various fed. research grants. Mem. APA, Ea. Psychol. Assn., Assn. for Asian Studies, Am. Inst. Sri Lanka Studies (sec. 1995—). Office: Swarthmore Coll Dept Psychology 500 College Ave Ste 2 Swarthmore PA 19081-1306

MARECI, THOMAS HAROLD, biophysicist, educator; b. Orlando, Fla., Sept. 14, 1949; s. Joseph Dominic Mareci and Virginia Lee Fisher; m. Debra Ann Neill, Apr. 1, 1978; children: Joseph Robert, Kathryn Sarah. BS in Physics, U. of Fla., 1972, MS in Physics, 1979; PhD in physical chemistry, U. of Oxford, Eng., 1982. Asst. prof. radiology U. of Fla., Gainesville, 1982—87, assoc. prof, biochemistry and molecular biology, 1987—, senator, 2002—. Dir. Ctr. for Structural Biology U. of Fla., 1993—; cons. NIH, Bethesda, Md., 1983—2002, NSF, Arlington, Va., 1993—94; lectr. numerous sci. meetings. Contbr. numerous articles to profl. jours. Mem. com. on ministry Uniterian Universalist Fellowship, Gainesville, 2001—, youth advisor, 1998—2002. NIH grantee, 1984—97, 2000—, Whitaker Found. grantee, 1989—92, Am. Paralysis Assn. grantee, 1990—91, Nat. Spinal Cord Injury Assn. grantee, 1995—96, U.S. Dept. Def. grantee, 2000—03, NIH grantee, 2001—. Mem.: Soc. for Neurosci., AAAS, Internat. Soc. for Magnetic Resonance in Medicine. Achievements include patents for Method for making an NMR coil; development of molecular structure determination methods using nuclear magnetic resonance spectroscopy; methods of imaging biological structure using magnetic resonance; methods of measuring tissue biochemistry using magnetic resonance spectroscopy; invented implantable magnetic resonance receivers to detect images and spectra from spinal cords in living organisms. Avocations: backpacking, travel. Office: University of Florida Box 100245 Gainesville FL 32610 0245

MAREK, JOYCELYN, publishing executive; m. Andrew Marek; children: Allison, Matthew. BBA, U. Houston, 1978; postgrad., Northwestern U., 1996, Hearst Mgmt. Inst., 1997-98. Rsch. analyst Houston Chronicle, 1978, chief analyst, 1978-84, asst. rsch. mgr., 1984-85, rsch. mgr., 1985-88, display advt. dir., 1988-90, mktg. dir., 1990-95, v.p. mktg. and electronic products, 1995—. Bd. dirs., exec. com. Sheltering Arms; mem. mktg. com. Houston Symphony; former bd. dirs. Houston Advt. Fedn. Mem. Am. Mktg. Assn. (edn./intern chair, past pres. Houston chpt.), Newspaper Assn. Am. (former chair market devel. and promotion coun.). Avocations: tennis, reading, golf. Office: Houston Chronicle PO Box 4260 Houston TX 77210-4260

MARELLA, PHILIP DANIEL, broadcasting company executive; b. Italy, Sept. 9, 1929; came to U.S., 1930; s. T. Joseph and Julia (Santolina) M.; m. Lucinda Minor, Dec. 30, 1955; children: Philip Daniel, Laura Ann, William Scott. BS, Calif. State U., 1955; MS, Syracuse U., 1956. Account exec. WGR-TV, Buffalo, 1956-57; account exec., sales mgr. WIIC-TV, Pitts., 1957-66; gen. mgr. WCHS-TV, Charleston, W.Va., 1966-68; v.p. radio and television Rollins, Inc., Atlanta, 1968-70; pres. WAVY-TV, Inc., Tidewater, Va., 1970—; v.p. ops. Lin Broadcasting, Inc., N.Y.C.; also dir.; pres., owner WMGC-TV, Binghamton, N.Y., 1978-86; CEO, pres. Pinnacle Comm., Inc., 1987—. CEO Pinnacle Broadcasting Co., 1987; owner radio stas. WFXC-FM, WDUR, WFXK, Raleigh, N.C., WRNS-AM-FM, WANG-FM, WMSQ-AM, WERO-FM, WCPQ, WDLX-AM, Coastal, N.C., WKOO-FM, WKJA-FM, Jacksonville, N.C., WYAV-FM, WRNN-FM, WMYB-FM, WYAK-FM, Myrtle Beach, S.C., KLLL-AM-FM, KONE-FM, KMMX-FM, Lubbock, Tex., WYNG-FM, Evansville, Ind., WSOY-AM-FM, WDZQ-FM, WDZ-AM, WCZQ-FM, Decatur, Ill., WPXX-FM, Danville, Va.; bd. dirs. Radio Advt. Bur., N.C. Assn. Broadcasters. Bd. dirs. Salvation Army, 1966-68; bd. dirs., v.p. United Fund; bd. dirs. Portsmouth chpt. ARC, Tidewater Regional Health and Planning Commn.; bd. dirs., v.p. Binghamton Symphony. Served with USMC, 1948-49, 50-52. Mem. Nat. Assn. Broadcasters (v.p., radio advt. bd. dirs.), Va. Assn. Broadcasters, N.C. Assn. Broadcasters (bd. dirs.), Nat. Adv. Bur. (bd. dirs.), Variety Club Pitts., Radio and TV Club, Portsmouth C. of C. (pres.-elect), Norfolk C. of C., Newport News C. of C., Cavalier Golf and Yacht Club (Virginia Beach, Va.), N.Y. Athletic Club, Binghamton Country Club, Boca Raton Club and Resort. Home: 2073 Cheshire Rd Binghamton NY 13903-3199 Address: 2924 S Ocean Blvd # A4 Boca Raton FL 33432

MARELLO, MATT, artist; b. Reading, Pa., Aug. 17, 1960; s. Matthew and Joan Marello; m. Ellen Prochnik, May 29, 1997; 1 child, Alexandra Elizabeth. BFA, U. of the Arts, Phila., 1993. One-man shows include Il Ponte Contemporanea, Rome, 1999, 2004, Cin. Contemporary Art Ctr., 1999, Bill Maynes Gallery, NYC, 2001, Contemporary Arts Ctr., Vilnius, Lithuania, 2001, Pierogi, Bklyn., 2002, Shoshanawayne Gallery, Santa Monica, Calif., 2002. Fellow, NY Found. for the Arts, 2002, John Simon Guggenheim Found., 2004. Home: 615 E Eleventh St New York NY 10009 Personal E-mail: marello@mindspring.com.

MARENDT, CANDACE L. state legislator; Student, Ind. U. Mem. Ind. State Ho. of Reps. Dist. 94, mem. commerce and econ. devel. com., mem. judiciary and pub. safety com., vice-chmn. families, children and human affairs com. Mem. MIBOR, Circle City Child Care Assn., N.W. Roundtable, Pike, Wayne, Washington and Eagle Creek GOP Clubs. also: Electronics Divsn 302 W Washington St Rm 204 Indianapolis IN 46204

MARENGI, JOSEPH ALEXANDER, computer company executive; b. Lynn, Mass., June 9, 1953; s. Joseph and Anna Maria (Fatello) Marengi. B.S. in Pub. Adminstrn., U. Mass., 1977; M.S. in Systems Mgmt., U. So. Calif., 1983; grad. Naval War Coll., 1986. Ops. Mfg. systems analyst Gen. Electric, Lynn, Mass., 1972-74, supr., 1974-77; mgr. ops. systems Westinghouse, Sunnyvale, Calif., 1981-84; systems sales exec. Stanley Vidmar, Sunnyvale, Calif., 1984; dir. channels, Excelan Inc.; joined Novell Inc. as v.p. Eastern region, 1989, v.p. channel sales, v.p. worldwide sales, 1992-93, sr. v.p. worldwide sales, 1993-94, exec. v.p. worldwide sales, 1994-96, pres., COO, 1996-97; sr. v.p. relationship group, Dell Inc. Round Rock, Tex., 1997, sr. v.p. Americas, 1997-; Served to lt. comdr., USCG and USCGR, 1978-81, tng. officer, San Francisco, 1981-86, exec. officer, 1986. Mem. Corp. Adv. Bd., Marshall Sch. Bus. U. So. Calif. Mem. Soc. Mfg. Engrs., Res. Officers Assn., Tech. Communications Assn., Nat. Greyhound Assn. Roman Catholic. Home: PO Box 161042 Austin TX 78716-1042 Office: Dell Inc One Dell Way Round Rock TX 78682*

MARENTETTE, ELIJAH CHANDLER, health services executive; b. Bklyn., Dec. 28, 1970; s. David Booth and Darthea Chandler Marentette. BA, MA, Boston U., 1993. Asst. v.p. corr. lending Graystone Mortage Corp., Boston, 1993—95; v.p. client devel. Concentra, Inc., Dallas, 1995—. Bd. trustees Windsor Pl. Condominium, Boston, 2000—01. Mem.: U. Club of Boston, Omicron Delta Epsilon. Achievements include design of medical office software. Avocations: yachting, skiing, squash, international travel. Home: 3912 Amherst Ave University Park TX 75225 Office: Concentra Inc 4100 McEwen Dallas TX 75244 Home Fax: 214-361-0879; Office Fax: 972-980-3164. E-mail: elijah.marentette.1993@alum.bu.edu.

MARESCA, ROBERT A. broadcasting and advertising executive; CFO Metromedia Co., East Rutherford, N.J., sr. v.p. fin. Office: Metromedia Co One Meadowlands Plaza East Rutherford NJ 07073

MARES-GUIA, MARCOS LUIZ, biochemist, consultant; b. Santa Barbara, Brazil, June 3, 1935; came to U.S., 1994; s. Jose Maria and Judith (Coelho) M-G.; m. Henriqueta Martins, May 22, 1959; children: Frederico, Christiana, Juliana, Luciana, Tatiana, Fabiana. MD, Fed. U. Minas Gerais, Belo Horizonte, Brazil, 1958; PhD, Tulane U., 1964. Prof. Biochemistry Fed. U. Minas Gerais, Belo Horizonte, 1958-93; emeritus prof., 2000—; v.p. rsch. Biobras S.A., Belo Horizonte, 1971-93; pres. Biomm, Inc., Miami, Fla., 1993—. Cons. Diabetes Rsch. Inst., U. Miami, 1994—; bd. dirs. Biobras S.A., 1994—. Patentee in field. Recipient Order of Scientific Merit Ministry of Sci., Brasilia, 1992. Mem. Am. Chem. Soc., N.Y. Acad. Scis., Brazilian Acad. Scis. Achievements: founder of Biobras S.A., 1971; co-founder Pythagoras Ednl. Sys. in Brazil, 1966; founder of Biomm, Inc., 1993; work on active ctr. chemistry of proteolytic enzymes. Office: Biomm Inc 14775 SW 132nd Pl Miami FL 33186-7685 Home: 20355 NE 34TH CT Apt 327 Aventura FL 33180-3311 E-mail: maresguia@aol.com.

MARESH, RICHARD JOSEPH, mathematics professor; b. Mitchell, SD, Feb. 18, 1947; m. Joan M. Keller, June 20, 1970; 1 child, Karin Maresh Silva. BS, St. Louis U., 1965—69; MA, U. Calif., Irvine, 1969—71; MS, U. Evansville, Ind., 1984—85. Assoc. prof. math., dept. chair Viterbo U., La Crosse, Wis., 1980—. Sch. bd. mem. Holmen Pub. Schs., Wis., 1988—91. Mem.: Nat. Coun. Tchrs. of Math., Math. Assn. Am. Home: 213 Third Ave E Holmen WI 54636 Office: Viterbo U 900 Viterbo Way La Crosse WI 54601 Personal E-mail: rjmaresh@charter.net. Business E-Mail: rjmaresh@viterbo.edu.

MARGALIT, SHLOMO, educator; b. Tiberias, Israel, Apr. 30, 1914; s. Nehemiah and Bath-Sheva (Kuperman) M.; m. Dina Rivlin, Feb. 8, 1938; children: Nehemiah, Yael Margalit Moses. DHL (hon.), Gratz Coll., 1985. Ordained rabbi, 1933. Rabbi Kefar Vitkin, Israel, 1934; religion instr. Haifa, Israel, 1937; assoc. rabbi Congregation Rodeph Shalom, Atlantic City, 1955; prof. Hebrew, Bible and rabbinics Gratz Coll., Phila., 1959-85. Author: Agartal, 1996; contbr. articles to profl. jours. With Israel Def. Forces. Mem. Am. Assn. of Jewish Edn., Nat. Coun. of Jewish Edn., Hebrew Tchrs. and Prins. of Am. (chtp. past pres.), Histadruth Ivrith of Am., Master Har-Zion Lodge-Jerusalem. Avocations: poetry, singing. Address: PO Box 203 Stevenson MD 21153

MARGALITH, HELEN MARGARET, retired librarian; b. N.Y.C., Nov. 19, 1914; d. Louis and Caroline (Stern) Fleischer; m. Aaron Margalith, Jan. 26, 1947 (dec.); children: Carol Lenore, Joan Louise. BA, Hunter Coll., 1936, MA, 1944; MLS, Columbia U., 1958. Editl. corr. Book of the Month Club, 1936-47; rschr. libr. N.Y.C. Bd. Edn., 1955-80; prof. pibr. Touro Coll., N.Y.C., 1980-90; mentor in libr. Empire State Coll., SUNY, 1991—. Cons. in field. Fellow Royal Soc. Medicine (libr. com., gerontology com., history of medicine com.); mem. Ch. and Synagogue Libr. Assn. (book reviewer), Internat. Honor Soc. Women in Edn., Delta Kappa Gamma. Democrat. Avocations: reading, travel, research. Home: 205 W End Ave Apt 25S New York NY 10023-4804

MARGEN, SHELDON, public health educator; b. Chgo., May 19, 1919; s. Paul and Sarah M.; m. Jeanne Carmel Sholtz, Mar. 16, 1943; children: Claude, Paul, Peter, David. BA, UCLA, 1938, MA, 1939; MD, U. Calif., San Francisco, 1943. Diplomate Am. Bd. Internal Medicine. Assoc. prof. U. Calif., Berkeley, 1963-68, prof. public health and nutrition, 1968-89, prof. emeritus, 1989—. Cons., mem. adv. coms. NIH, WHO,; bd. dirs. Omnicare. Cin. Editor-in-chief U. Calif. Wellness Letter; author and editor 10 books on Nutrition and/or Pub. Health. Bd. dirs. Calif. Wellness Found., Woodland Hills, 1991-96. Capt. M.C., U.S. Army, 1943-48, ETO. Grantee NIH, State of Calif., Ford Found., numerous others. Fellow Am. Inst. Nutrition and many other profl. orgns. in fields of nutrition and pub. health. Office: U Calif Sch Pub Health Berkeley CA 94720-0001 E-mail: shellym@velink4.berkeley.edu.

MARGER, EDWIN, lawyer; b. N.Y.C., Mar. 18, 1928; s. William and Fannie (Cohen) M.; m. Kaye Sanderson, Oct. 1, 1951; children: Shari Ann, Diane Elaine, Sandy Ben; m. L. Suzanne Smyth, July 5, 1968; 1 child, George Phinney; m. Mary Susan Hamel, May 6, 1987; 1 child, Charleston Faye. BA, U. Miami, 1951, JD, 1953. Bar: Fla. 1953, Ga. 1971, D.C. 1978. Pvt. practice, Miami Beach, Fla., 1953-67, Atlanta, 1971—. Gen. counsel Physicians Nat. Risk Retention Group, 1988-91, Physicians Reliance Assn., 1988-91, Physicians Nat. Legal Def. Corp., 1988-91; spl. asst. atty. gen. Fla., 1960-61; atty., agt. Republic of Haiti, 1962-67, City of Port-au-Prince for Transp. and Housing, 1962, Dominican Republic for Trade and Industry, 1964-65; of counsel Richard Burns, Miami, 1967—. Contbr. articles to profl. jours. Tchr. Nat. Inst. Trial Advocacy; mem. Miami Beach Social Svc. Commn., 1957; chmn. Fulton County Aviation Adv. Com., 1980—; chmn. Pickens County Airport Adv. Com., 2004; trustee Forensic Scis. Found., 1984-88, v.p., 1986-88; lt. col., a.d.c. Gov. Ga., 1971-74, 80-84; col., a.d.c. Gov. La., 1977-87; Khan Bahador and mem. exiled King of Afghanistan Privy Coun., 1980—. With USAAF, 1946-47. Fellow Am. Acad. Forensic Scis. (chmn. jurisprudence sect. 1977-78, sec. 1976-77, bd. dirs. 1978-79, exec. com. 1983-86); mem. ATLA, ABA, Fla. Bar Assn. (aerospace com. 1971-83, bd. govs. 1983-87, 90-94, exec. com. 1993-94), State Bar Ga. (chmn. sect. environ. law 1974-75, aviation law sect. 1978, bd. govs. 1999—, stds. of the profession com.), Ga. Trial Lawyers Assn., Nat. Assn. Criminal Def. Lawyers, Ga. Assn. Criminal Def. Lawyers, Am. Judicature Soc., Am. Arbitration Assn. (commn. panel 1978), Inter-Am. Bar Assn. (sr.), World Assn. Lawyers (founding), Lawyer-Pilots Bar Assn. (founding, v.p. 1959-62), VFW, Rotary, Lions, Advocates Club, Lawyers Club Atlanta. Office: 44 N Main St Jasper GA 30143-1501 Office Phone: 706-692-3060.

MARGERISON, RICHARD WAYNE, diversified industrial company executive; b. Phila., Nov. 5, 1948; s. Kenneth Hilton and Edythe Margerison; m. Leah Blythe Margerison, July 18, 1970; children: Andrew Kenneth, Ashley Creed. BA in Econs., U. N.C., 1970; MBA with distinction, Harvard U., 1977. Mgr. So. Bell Telephone Co., Greensboro, N.C., 1972-75; mgr. sub. liaison Atlas Powder Co. subs. Tyler Corp., Dallas, 1978-79, dir. mktg. svcs., 1979-80; exec. v.p. Micro-Term, Inc., St. Louis, 1980-83, pres., chief exec. officer, 1983-85; mgr. acquisitions Tyler Corp., Dallas, 1977-78, v.p., 1985-88, sr. v.p., 1988-89, exec. v.p., 1989-94, pres., COO, 1994-97, also bd. dirs.; CEO Sammons Distbn., Inc., Dallas, 1997—2001, Legacy Assocs. Investments, 2001—. Mem. Northway Christian Ch., Dallas, 1985--; coach Youth Soccer, Dallas, 1987—; advisor YMCA Indian Princess and Indian Guides, 1987-89; adult leader Boy Scouts Am., 1988-93; active Dallas United Way, 1990. Love fellow Harvard Grad. Sch. Bus., 1975-77. Mem. Harvard Bus. Sch. Club of Dallas, Lakewood Country Club, Order of Old Well, Phi Beta Kappa. Avocations: golf, youth soccer, running. Home: 3115 Stanford Ave Dallas TX 75225-7702

MARGESON, THEODORE EARL, judge; b. New Glasgow, N.S., Can., Aug. 15, 1938; children: Theodore Jason, Mark Andrew Earl. BA, Mt. Allison U., Sackville, N.B., Can., 1959, BEd, 1960; LLB, Dalhousie U., Halifax, N.S., 1965. Barrister, solicitor, notary pub. Tchr. Shelburne (N.S.) H.S., 1960-61, New Glasgow H.S., 1961-62; barrister, solicitor New Glasgow and Toronto, Ont., 1965-90; judge Tax Ct. of Can., Ottawa, 1990—. Bd. dirs. N.S. Legal Aid. Recipient Confedn. medal Govt. of Can., 1992; Jubilee medal, 2003. Mem. Can. Judges Conf., N.S. Barrister's Soc. (mem. of coun.), Continuing Legal Edn. Soc. (dir.). Avocations: golf, hockey, squash. Office: Tax Ct of Can 200 Kent St 3d Fl Ottawa ON Canada K1A OM1

MARGETON, STEPHEN GEORGE, law librarian; b. Elizabeth, N.J., Mar. 22, 1945; s. Louis George and Josephine A. (Bednarik) M.; m. Margaret Mary Salter, May 14, 1977; children: Catherine Ann, Elizabeth Ann. AB, Mt. St. Mary's Coll., 1967; JD, George Washington U., 1970; MSLS, Cath. U., 1973. Reference librarian Am.-Brit. law div. Library of Congress, Washington, 1968-72; law libr. Steptoe & Johnson, Washington, 1972-85; librarian Supreme Ct. of U.S., Washington, 1985-88; dir. Judge Kathryn J. DuFour Law Libr. The Cath. Univ. Am., 1988—. Instr. George Mason Law Sch., Arlington, Va., 1977-80. Mem. Am. Assn. Law Libraries, Internat. Assn. Law Libraries., Am. Soc. Internat. Law. Office: Cath U Am Judge Kathryn J DuFour Law Libr 3600 John Mccormack Rd NE Washington DC 20064-0001

MARGIOTTA, JOSEPH M. printing company executive; b. Staten Island, N.Y., Aug. 14, 1973; s. Sam and Vickie Margiotta. Student, Union County Coll., N.J., 2001—. Pres. Paragon Forms and Paper Co., N.Y.C., 1992—. Author poetry. Home: 1541 Cooper Rd Scotch Plains NJ 07076-2521

MARGITIĆ, MILORAD R. language educator, researcher; b. Kragujevac, Serbia, June 6, 1934; arrived in USA, 1963; s. Radomir B. and Olga J. Margitić; m. Susan E. Kent, Oct. 5, 1969; children: Alexandra Margitic, Tatiana Margitic. MA Candidatus Degree, Univ. of Leiden, Leiden, the Netherlands, 1963; PhD French, Wayne State Univ., Detroit, Mich., 1971. Tchg. asst., instr., asst. prof. (French) Wayne State Univ., Detroit, 1963—72; asst. prof. (French) Univ. of Chgo., Chgo., 1972—78; asst. prof., assoc. prof., prof. (French) Wake Forest Univ., Winston-Salem, NC, 1978. Author: (book) Essai sur la mythologie du Cid, 1976, La Suivante, comédie, de Pierre Corneille, édition critique, 1978, La Galerie du Palais, ou l'amie rivale, comédie, de Pierre Corneille, édition critique, 1981, Corneille comique: Nine Studies of Pierre Corneille's Comedy with an Intro. and a Bibliography., 1982, Actes de Wake Forest/ procs. of the NASSCFL 19th Ann. Conf., 1987, Le Cid, tragi-comédie, de Pierre Corneille, édition critique, 1989, Cornelian Power Games: Variations on a Theme in Pierre Corneille's Theater from "Mélite" to "Polyeucte", 2002. Recipient Scholarship (full stipend), Universitair Asyl Fonds/ Holland, 1960—63, Outside evaluator in tenure and promotion cases, UCLA, Vassar Coll., U. Ga., Loyola U.; grantee Publ. Subsidy Grant, Univ. of Chgo., 1975. Democrat. Serbian Orthodox. Achievements include played the accordion professionally from 1950-1959 and semi-professionally from 1959-1972. Avocation: play accordion as a hobby. Home: 5660 Angel Oaks Dr Winston Salem NC 27105 Office: Wake Forest Univ Dept of Romance Lang PO Box 7566 Winston Salem NC 27109

MARGO, KATHERINE LANE, family physician, educator; b. Buffalo, June 3, 1952; d. Warren Wilson and Virginia (Penney) Lane; m. Geoffrey Myles Margo, Apr. 20, 1980; 1 child, Benjamin stepchildren: Jenny, Judy. BA, Swarthmore Coll., 1974; MD, SUNY Health Sci. Ctr., Syracuse, 1978. Resident physician St. Joseph's Hosp., Syracuse, 1979-82; attending physician Health Svcs. Assn., Syracuse, 1982-90, asst. med. dir. for quality assurance, 1985-90; asst. prof. family medicine SUNY-HSC at Syracuse, 1990-94; mem. residency faculty Harrisburg (Pa.) Hosp., 1994-2000; med. dir. Harrisburg Kline Family Practice Ctr., 1996-2000; assoc. residency dir. Harrisburg Family Practice Residency, 1997-2000; predoctoral dir. Dept. Family Practice Cmty. Medicine U. Pa., 2000—, asst. prof., assoc. dir. family practice residency, 2000—. Clin. assoc. prof. Allegheny Med. Sch., 1997—2000. Contbr. articles to profl. jours. Bd. trustees Pt. Choice, Syracuse, 1993—94; chair med. com. Planned Parenthood, Syracuse, 1984—94; bd. dirs. Planned Parenthood Susquehanna Valley, 1996—2000; active Friends of Chamber Music, Syracuse, 1985—94; keyboard player Old World folk Band. Recipient Excuplary Tchg. award, Pa. Acad. of Family Practice, 2003. Mem.: Am. Acad. Family Practitioners (v.p. Syracuse chpt.), Soc. Tchrs. of Family Medicine (chair group on predoctoral edn. 2003—04). Home: 426 Carpenter Ln Philadelphia PA 19119-3040 Office Phone: 215-662-8777. E-mail: margok@uphs.upenn.edu.

MARGOLIASH, EMANUEL, biochemist, educator; b. Cairo, Feb. 10, 1920; s. Wolf and Bertha (Kotler) M.; m. Sima Beshkin, Aug. 22, 1944; children: Reuben, Daniel. BA, Am. U., Beirut, 1940, MA, 1942, MD, 1945. Rsch. fellow, lectr., acting head cancer rsch. labs. Hebrew U., Jerusalem, 1945-58; rsch. fellow Molteno Inst. Cambridge (Eng.) U., 1951-53; Dazian fellow Nobel Inst., 1958; rsch. assoc. U. Utah, Salt Lake City, 1958-60, McGill U., Montreal, Que., Can., 1960-62; rsch. fellow Abbott Labs., North Chicago, Ill., 1962-69, sr. rsch. fellow, 1969-71, head protein sect., 1962-71; prof. biochemistry and molecular biology Northwestern U., Evanston, Ill., 1971-90, prof. chemistry, 1985-90, Owen L. Coon prof. molecular biology, 1988-90, Owen L. Coon prof. molecular biology emeritus, 1990—; prof. biol. scis. U. Ill., Chgo., 1989—, coord. lab. for molecular biology, 1990-93. Mem. com. on cytochrome nomenclature Internat. Union Biochemistry, 1962-75; mem. adv. com. Plant Research Lab., Mich. State U./AEC, 1967-72; co-chmn. Gordon Research Conf. on Proteins, 1967 Editl. bd. Jour. Biol. Chemistry, 1966-72, Biochem. Genetics, 1966-80, Jour. Molecular Evolution, 1971-82, Biochemistry and Molecular Biology Internat., 1981-99, Jour. Protein Chemistry, 1982-86, Chemtracts, Biochem. Molecular Biology, 1990-99; contbr. over 280 articles and revs. to sci. jours. Rudi Lemberg fellow Australian Acad. Sci., 1981; Guggenheim fellow, 1983 Fellow Am. Acad. Arts and Scis., Am. Acad. Microbiology, Am. Inst. Chemists; mem. Nat. Acad. Scis., Biochem. Soc. (Keilin Meml. lectr. 1970), Harvey Soc. (lectr. 1970-71), Am. Soc. Biochem. Molecular Biology (publs. com. 1973-76), Am. Chem. Soc., Am. Soc. Microbiology, Can. Biochem. Soc., Soc. Devel. Biology, Biophys. Soc. (exec. com. U.S. bioenergetics group 1980-83), N.Y. Acad. Sci., Ill. Acad. Sci., Am. Soc. Naturalists, Sigma Xi (nat. lectr. 1972-73, 74-77). Home: 353 Madison Ave Glencoe IL 60022-1809 Office: Biochemistry Molecular & Cell Biology Hogan Hall 2-100 Northwestern U Evanston IL 60208-3500

MARGOLIN, ABRAHAM EUGENE, lawyer, director; b. St. Joseph, Mo., Oct. 16, 1907; s. Jacob and Rebecca (Cohn) M.; m. Florence Solow, Feb. 1, 1931 (dec. Feb. 1998); children: Robert J., Judith (Mrs. Goodman), James S. BA, Dartmouth Coll.; LLB, Mich. U., Ann Arbor, JD, 1929. Pvt. practice, Kans. City. Bd. mem. Tension Envelope Corp., UMB Mortgage Co.; pres. ctrl. governing bd. Children's Mercy Hosp., 1972-76, life mem.; dir. life Truman Med. Ctr., Menorah Med. Ctr.; mem. bd. govs. City Trust Kansas City, Rsch. Mental Health Found.; dir., v.p. Jewish Fedn. Greater Kanas City. Bd. govs. Hebrew Acad. Kans. City; gov. Am. Royal Assn.; pres. coun., fellow Brandeis U.; trustee B'nai B'rith Found.; mem. adv. bd. Anti-Defamation League; mem. nat. exec. coun. Am. Jewish Com., Am. Joint Distbn. Com. Named Disting. Law Alumnus, Washington U.; recipient Man of Yr. award Congregations Beth Shalom. Mem. ABA, ATLA, Am. Judicature Soc., Fed. Bar Assn., Mo. Bar Assn., Met. Kans. City Bar Assn., U.S. Supreme Ct. Hist. Soc., Heritage Found., Cato Inst., World Jewish Congress, Am. Jewish Congress, Kans. City Club, Oakwood Golf and Country Club, Nat. Lawyers Club, Order of Coif, Delta Sigma Rho. Office: 2345 Grand Blvd Ste 2500 Kansas City MO 64108-2603 Home: # E206 5500 W 123rd St Shawnee Msn KS 66209-3193

MARGOLIN, CARL M. psychotherapist; b. N.Y.C., Jan. 23, 1939; s. Samuel and Henrietta (Kressel) M.; B.A., CUNY, 1961; M.S.W., Columbia U., 1965; postgrad. Nat. Psychol. Assn. for Psychoanalysis, 1968-70; m. Susie Echols Watts, Feb. 10, 1964; children— Christopher, Andrew; m. Paula Jean Beatty, March 26, 1993. Sr. psychiat. social worker W.J.C.S., White Plains, N.Y., 1964-76; psychotherapist Whitehill Counseling Service, Yorktown Hights, N.Y., 1973-76; pvt. practice psychotherapy, 1976—; tng. supr. Yeshiva U., 1972-76. Mem. exec. com. No. Westchester Mental Health Council, 1973-79, chmn. planning com., 1975-79. Cert. social worker, N.Y. State. Mem. Nat. Assn. Social Workers (diplomate), Acad. Cert. Social Workers, Soc. Clin. Social Work Psychotherapists (bd. cert. diplomate in clin. social work). Office: 19 Long Ridge Rd Bedford NY 10506-1529

MARGOLIN, HAROLD, metallurgical educator; b. Hartford, Conn., July 12, 1922; s. Aaron David and Sonia (Krupnikoff) M.; m. Elaine Marjorie Rose, July 4, 1946; children: Shelley, Deborah, Amy. B in Engring., Yale U., 1943; M in Engring., Yale Univ., 1947, DEng, 1950. Rsch. assoc./scientist divsn. rsch. NYU, N.Y.C., 1949-56, assoc. prof. metall. engring., 1956-62, prof., 1962-73; prof. phys. metallurgy Poly. U. N.Y., Bklyn., 1973-93, disting. rsch. prof., 1993—2003. Theodore W. Krengel vis. prof. Technion, Haifa, Israel, 1983; cons. in field. Co-author books; contbr. articles to profl. pubs.; patentee in field. With USNR, 1944-46. Fellow Am. Soc. Metals (edn. award N.Y. chpt. 1967); mem. Metall. Soc. (honoree symposium in his name San Francisco 1994), ASM Internat., TMS. Democrat. Jewish. Home: 81 Stony Run New Rochelle NY 10804-3415 E-mail: hmemxox@aol.com. *Achievement, work, and refusal to accept defeat are intimately intertwined.*

MARGOLIN, JEAN SPIELBERG, artist; b. N.Y.C., Oct. 12, 1926; d. Jack and Ida (Grossman) Spielberg and Bess Liebowitz Spielberg (stepmother); m. Paul Margolin, May 19, 1946 (dec. Mar. 1989). Student, Ind. U., 1951-55, Skowhegan Sch. Painting/Sculp., 1954. Tchr. painting and drawing Ind. U., Bloomington, 1954-55; curator group show Pace U. Gallery, N.Y.C., 1984. Paintings exhibited John Herron Art Mus., Indpls., 1952-55, J.B. Speed Art Mus., Louisville, 1953, Cin. Mus. Art, 1955, L.A. County Mus. Art, 1956, A.C.A. Gallery, N.Y.C., 1959-60, Pa. Acad. Fine Arts, Phila., 1962, Heckscher Mus., Huntington, N.Y., 1964, Skowhegan Benefit Exbhn., Nat. Arts Club, N.Y.C., 1974, Arthouse, Storrs, Conn., 1979, Landmark Gallery, N.Y.C., 1980-82, Pace U. Gallery, N.Y.C., 1980, 84, The Artists Choice Mus., Alex Rosenberg Gallery, N.Y.C., 1983; paintings exhibited by appointment only, N.Y.C., 1985—. Recipient 1st prize purchase award for painting Skowhegan Sch. Painting and Sculpture, 1954, scholar, 1954. Home: 4 Washington Square Vlg Apt 12S New York NY 10012-1908

MARGOLIN, LEON, physician; BA with high honors, BSc with high honors, Bar-Ilan Univ., Israel, 1994; MD, Hebrew Univ Hadassah Med. Sch., 2002; PhD, Hebrew Univ. Hadassah Med. Sch., 2002. Internship Staten Island Univ. Hosp., 2002; physician AECOM, Bronx, NY, 2003—. *Dr. Margolin has published more than 25 high quality publications which had a significant impact on medical science. He received multiple awards including the second place award in NY State research competition, Certificate of Merit of the American College of Physicians, and many others. Recently, he patented a unique device for headache relief that received the Kaye Innovation Awards.* Contbr. scientific papers. Recipient Kaye Prize, 1999, Pratt Found. award, 2001; scholar Sholarship of Dean of Students, Bar-Ilan Univ., 1991—94, Scholarship for MD/PhD program, Hadassah Med. Sch.-Hebrew Univ., 1994—99. Jewish. Achievements include proficiency in Hebrew, English and Russian; patents for mask for headache relief. Avocations: reading, travel. Home: 3450 Wayne Ave Apt 10A Bronx NY 10467

MARGOLIN, ROBERT JEREMY, lawyer; b. Kansas City, Mo., Mar. 21, 1935; s. Abraham Eugene and Florence Margolin; m. Dorothy Ann Macy, Sept. 20, 1959; children: Kathryn R. Margolin Richter, Charles D. AB, Dartmouth Coll., 1957; JD, LLB, U. Mich., 1960. Bar: Mo., U.S. Ct. Appeals (8th cir.). Ptnr. Margolin and Kirwan, Kansas City, 1960—. Bd. dirs. Kansas City Kings, Feld Leasing. Asst. editor Mich. Law Rev. Bd. dirs. Menorah Med. Ctr., Kansas City, Kansas City Philharm. Assn.; mem. exec. com. Jewish Vocat. Svc., Kansas City. Mem. ABA, Nat. Basketball Assn. (bd. govs.), Mo. Bar Assn., Kansas City Bar Assn. Avocations: golf, skiing. Home: 1628 River Ridge Williamsburg VA 23185-7546 E-mail: bobj757@aol.com.

MARGOLIN, SOLOMON BEGELFOR, pharmacologist, consultant; b. Phila., May 16, 1920; s. Nathan and Fannie (Begelfor) M.; m. Gerda Levy, Jan. 17, 1947 (div. Feb. 1985); children: David, Bernard, Daniel; m. Nancy A. Cox, Apr. 30, 1987. BSc, Rutgers U., 1941, MSc, 1943, PhD, 1945. Asst. Rutgers U., New Brunswick, N.J., 1943-45; rsch. biologist Silmo Chem. Co., Vineland, N.J., 1947-48; rsch. pharmacologist Schering Corp., Bloomfield, N.J., 1948-52, dir. pharmacology dept., 1952-54; chief pharmacologist Maltbie Labs., Belleville, N.J., 1954-56, Wallace Labs, Carter-Wallace, Inc., Cranbury, N.J., 1956-60, dir. pharmacology dept., 1960-64, v.p. biol. rsch., 1964-68; pres. AMR Biol. Rsch., Inc., Princeton, N.J., 1968-78; from prof., chmn. pharmacology dept. to emeritus prof. St. George's (Grenada) U. Sch. Medicine, 1978—; pres. MARNAC, Inc., Dallas, 1990—. Author: Harper's Handbook Therapeutic Pharmacology, 1981; author: (with others) Physiological Pharmacology, 1963, World Review, Nutrition and Dietetics, 1980; contbr. more than 100 articles to profl. jours. Mem. AAAS, Endocrino Soc., Am. Chem. Soc., Soc. Exptl. Biology and Medicine, Am. Soc. Pharmacology and Exptl. Therapeutics, N.Y. Acad. Scis., Drug Information Assn. Achievements include over 40 U.S., European, and Japanese patents for prevention and treatment of fibrotic lesions, multiple sclerosis and other neurodegenerative disorders; research in anti-histamines anti-cholinergics, endorphins, sedative-hypnotics, tranquilizers, muscle relaxants, glucocorticoids, cardiovascular agents, anti-inflammatory drugs, anti-fibrotic agents, multiple sclerosis agents. Home: 6723 Desco Dr Dallas TX 75225-2704 E-mail: marnacinc@aol.com.

MARGOLIS, BERNARD ALLEN, library administrator; b. Greenwich, Conn., Oct. 2, 1948; s. Sidney S. and Rose (Birkenfeld) M.; m. Amanda Batey, Nov. 2, 1973. BA in Polit. Sci., U. Denver, 1970, MLS, 1973; Doctorate (hon.), Wentworth Inst. Tech., 1999. Cert. libr., Mich. Libr. asst. Denver Pub. Libr., 1970-72; br. head Virginia Village Libr., Denver Pub. Libr., 1972-73; dep. dir. Monroe County Libr. Sys., Mich., 1973-75; dir. Raisin Valley Libr. Sys., Monroe, 1976-88, Pikes Peak Libr. Dist., Colorado Springs, Colo., 1988-97; pres. Colo. Ctr. for Books, 1989-92, Colo. Ctr. for the Book, 1993-97, Boston Pub. Libr., 1997—. Cons. in libr. pub. rels., 1976—; founding trustee United Colo. Investment Trust, 1993-95; chmn. Colo. Gov.'s Conf. on Libr. and Info. Svcs., 1990; lectr. Western Mich. U., Kalamazoo, 1978-81; appraiser rare books, Monroe, Colorado Springs, 1970—. Contbr. articles to profl. jours.; mem. editl. bd. Bottom Line Mag. Fin. Mgmt. for Librs., 1986—. Bd. dirs. Mass. Ctr. for the Book, Back Bay Assn., Monroe Sr. Citizens Ctr., 1976-80, Monroe Fine Arts Coun., 1978-81, Am. the Beautiful Centennial Celebration, Inc., 1993, Libr. Consortium, 1993-97, Downtown Colorado Springs, Inc., 1994-97, Friends of Copley Sq., Care & Share, Inc., sec., 1994-95, vice chmn., 1995, chmn., 1995-97; chmn. Blue Cross-Blue Shield Consumer Coun., Detroit, 1984-88; adv. bd. Access Colo. Libr. and Info. Network, 1991-97, Mercy Meml. Hosp., Monroe, 1984-86, 5th Congl. Art Competition Com., 1992-97; Dem. candidate for Mich. Senate, 1986; allocations com. Pikes Peak United Way, 1988-91, chmn., 1990-91, bd. dirs., 1990-91, 94-97; chmn. Great Pikes Peak Cowboy Poetry Gathering, 1990-92, 94-96; del. White House Conf. on Libr. and Info. Scis.; mem. El Paso County, Colo. Retirement Bd., 1995-97, sec., 1996-97; fellow Boston Found., 1998—; overseer Hancock Shaker Village, Pittsfield, Mass., 1999—; leadership mgmt. com. Assn. Rsch. Librs., 2003—. Recipient Mayoral Cert. Commendation award Denver, 1972, 73; named Mich. Libr. of Yr., 1985, Colo. Libr. of Yr., 1990, commendation John F. Kennedy Ctr. for Performing Arts, 1993, Frank Waters award Pikes Peak Writer's Conf., 1996. Mem.: ALA (cons. ann. swap and shop 1979—84, governing coun. 1982—, endowment trustee 1989—93, chmn. resolutions com. 1991—92, sr. endowment trustee 1993—2001, John Cotton Dana award 1977, 1991, Libr. Awareness Idea Search award Washington 1982), Pub. Libr. Assn., Libr. Adminstrv. Mgmt. Assn., Colo. Libr. Assn. (legis.com., Intellectual Freedom award 1993), Internat. Fedn. Libr. Assns. and Instns., New Eng. Libr. Assn., Mass. Libr. Assn. Democrat. Jewish. Office: Boston Pub Libr Copley Sq 700 Boylston St Boston MA 02116 E-mail: bmargolis@bpl.org.

MARGOLIS, BETTE SHULA, writer, educator; d. Daniel and Evelyn Margolis; children: Laurie Khan, Lisa Daugherty, Marcus Stern. BA in English and Journalism, Bklyn. Coll., 1972; MA in Art, NYU, 1974. Mktg. dir., art dir. Flexitoys, Berkeley, Calif., 1989—91, Harbor House Coffee Co., Novato, Calif., 1991—94; publisher, editor, dir. mktg. Bette's Books, Highlands Ranch, Colo., 1995—; dir. New Perspectives Workshop, Washingtonn, DC, 2000—; producer, writer, pres. Shakti Prodns., Colo., 2003—. Vis. lectr. DuCret Sch. of the Arts, Plainfield, NJ, The Dominican Coll., San Rafael, Calif., Contra Costa Coll., San Pablo, Calif., The Learning Annex, San Francisco, The Art League of Houston, Lee Coll., Baytown, Tex., First Class, Washington, Southwest Coll., Houston, U. Houston, Victoria, Front Range CC, Westminster, Colo., The Chatauqua, Boulder, Colo., Naropa U., Boulder, Colo. Author: A Heart Full of Love, 1999, Alive and Well: Into the New Millennium with Edgar Cayce's Health Care Wisdom, 2003; author: (illustrator) Saints' Craftbook, 1984, Salsa, 1998, Angora Kidd, 2003; illustrator Frogs, 1972, It's Great to Pray, 1973, Sister Death, 1974, I Can Hear the Cowbells Ring, 1994; prodr.: Women in the Arts, 1992; comml. advt. art & tech. illustrator Am. Mus. of Natural History, N.Y.C., 1971, freelance writer, illustrator Better Homes & Gardens, 1977, freelance writer Body Smart Mag., 1199, Venture Inward Mag., 2001, 2003. Mem.: Poetry Soc. Colo. Avocations: golf, biking. Office: 8301 S Pebble Creek Way Suite 102 Highlands Ranch CO 80126 Office Phone: 303-713-9805.

MARGOLIS, DANIEL HERBERT, lawyer; b. Feb. 11, 1926; s. Morris Abraham and Miriam M.; m. Anabel Tendler, Dec. 23, 1951 (dec.); children: Peter, Beth, Laura, James; m. Sidney Millman Moore, Feb. 5, 1983. BA, Johns Hopkins U., 1948; LLB, Harvard U., 1951. Bar: DC 1951, U.S. Supreme Ct. 1959. Atty. adv. Office Price Stblzn., Washington, 1951-52; trial atty. Antitrust divsn. Dept. Justice, Washington, 1952-56; sr. ptnr. Bergson, Borkland, Margolis & Adler, Washington, 1962—86, McGuire, Woods, Battle & Boothe, Washington, 1986-89, Patton, Boggs LLP, Washington, 1989—2001; sr. counsel DC Office of Corp. Counsel, 2001—03; prin. Law Offices of Daniel H. Margolis, 2003—. With USN, 1945—46. Fellow: ABA. Avocations: sailing, skiing, cooking.

MARGOLIS, DAVID I(SRAEL), industrial manufacturing executive; b. NYC, Jan. 24, 1930; s. Benjamin and Celia (Kosofsky) M.; m. Barbara Schneider, Sept. 7, 1958; children: Brian, Robert, Peter, Nancy. BA, CCNY, 1950, MBA, 1952; postgrad., NYU, 1952-55. Asst. treas. Raytheon Co., 1956-59; treas. IT&T, N.Y.C., 1959-62; with Coltec Industries Inc., N.Y.C., 1962-95, pres., 1968-91, CEO, 1984-95, chmn. bd. dirs., 1985-95; chmn. exec. com., 1995-99. Mem. bd. trustees Presbyn. Hosp. City N.Y.; bd. overseers NYU Stern Sch. Bus. Mem.: Coun. Fgn. Rels. Office: 147 E 48th St New York NY 10017-1223

MARGOLIS, DAVID LESLIE, government agency administrator; b. 1949; s. Milton and Sylvia Margolis; m. Cynthia Margolis; children: Rachel, Lara, Leslie, Aaron. BA, Dickinson Coll., 1971; MA, U. Toronto, 1973. Budget analyst Pa. Gov.'s Office of Budget, Harrisburg, 1974—79; dir. bur. fiscal mgmt. Pa. Dept. of Environ. Resources, Harrisburg, 1979—84; chief budget officer Pa. Dept. of Transp., Harrisburg, 1984—87, dir., bur. of fiscal mgmt., 1987—98, project leader, strategic planning, 1999—2001, dir. bur. fiscal mgmt., 2001—. Comptr. State Hwy. and Bridge Authority, Harrisburg, 1989—92; mem. strategic mgmt. com. Transp. Rsch. Bd., Washington, 2002—. Contbr. articles to profl. jours. Dir. sch. bd. Camp Hill Sch. Dist., Pa., 2002—; coach Youth Sports Associations, Camp Hill, 1984—98; tchr. and prin. Temple Beth Shalom, Mechanicsburg, 1985—92. Mem.: ASPA. Avocations: jogging, reading, listening to music, gardening. Office: PA Dept of Transp PO Box 3351 Harrisburg PA 17105-3351

MARGOLIS, DORIS MAY ROSENBERG, editor, writer; b. Washington, May 10, 1936; d. Samuel Jacob and Eva (Mendelsohn) Rosenberg; m. Lawrence S. Margolis, Jan. 30, 1960; children: Mary Aleta, Paul Oliver. BA, George Wash. U., 1958. Founder, v.p., CEO Editorial Assocs., Washington, 1963-82, founder, pres., CEO, 1982— . Founder, pub., exec. editor Margolis Health Report, 1999—; bd. govs. Nat. Press Club, 1991-94; mem. adv. bd. Washington Journalism Conf., 1991-96; judge Biomedical Writing awards Am. Med. Writers Assn.-Mid-Atlantic, 1987-91, Blue Pencil Writing awards Nat. Assn. Govt. Contractors, 1992, 94, Rose Kushner Breast Cancer Writing award Am. Med. Writers Assn., 1992, Nat. Essay competition Pres.'s Com. on Employment of the Handicapped, Nat. Worker of Yr. competition Goodwill Industries of Am., Nat. Essay Competition Hospitalized Vets. Assn., others. Author: This Is Goodwill, 1968; editor-in-chief Jour. Rehab., 1960-67, (newsletters) Nat. Assn. Sheltered Workshops and Homebound Programs News, 1964-68, Jewish Occupational Coun. News, 1968-70, Aspen Update, 1976-80; contbg. editor (newspapers) Pediatric News, 1968-69, Ob-Gyn News, 1968-69, Internal Medicine News, 1968-69; columnist Jour. Rehab., 1960-67, Washington Jewish Week, 1968-73, Sports Medicine Monthly, 1984-85, Gazette Newspapers, 1999-2000; radio news corr. Physicians Radio News Network, 1969, 1976; contbr. articles to profl. jours.; editor: Concrete Facts Magazine, 1960, Rehabilitation of the Mentally Ill, 1961, Rehabilitation International, 1962, Rehabilitation of the Mentally Retarded, 1962, To Aid the Disabled, 1963, The Stroke Spectrum: Prevention, Treatment, and Rehabilitation, 1963, Workshops at the Crossroads, 1961, Sheltered Workshops. The Road Ahead, 1965, Sheltered Workshops, 1965, The Coronary Spectrum: Prevention, Treatment, and Rehabilitation, 1966, Medical Rehabilitation Model Delivery Systems, 1978; asst. editor NEA News, 1958-59. Singer, dancer Montgomery Light Opera Co., 1970's, Washington Civic Opera, 1978-84; singer, dancer, actress Hexagon Players, 1970-72; bd. dirs. Jewish Social Svcs. Agy., 1970-72; bd. govs. Am. Newspaper Women's Club, 1982-84, Woman's Nat. Dem. Club, 1983-88; exec. com. bd. dirs. People-to-People Com. on Disability, 1992-2000, vice-chmn., 1995-2000; pres. Inner Wheel Club of Washington, 1993-94. Recipient Ellen Woodhull scholastic scholarship George Washington U., 1957, Disting. Alumni Achievement award George Washington U., 1978, Nat. Press Club Vivian award, 1997, 99; personal commendations Pres. John F. Kennedy, 1963, Pres. Lyndon B. Johnson, 1966; Paul Harris fellow Rotary Internat., 1996. Fellow Am. Med. Writers Assn. (bd. dirs. 1989-94, nominating com. 1990-91, chair pub. rels., advt. and mktg. sect. 1989-90, pres. Mid-Atlantic chpt. 1990-91, exec. com. bd. dirs. 1993-94); mem. Nat. Assn. Sci. Writers, Rotary Club Wash. (bd. dirs. 1999-2001, 2002-, v.p., pres. elect 2003-2004, pres. 2004-), Cosmos Club, Alpha Epsilon Phi Alumni Assn. (pres. 1959-60), Mortar Bd. (treas. 1957-58), Phi Delta Epsilon (v.p. 1957-58), Psi Chi, Alpha Theta Nu. Office: Editorial Assocs Nat Press Bldg Washington DC 20045

MARGOLIS, EMANUEL, lawyer, educator; b. Bklyn., Mar. 18, 1926; s. Abraham and Esther (Levin) M.; m. Edith Cushing; m. Estelle Thompson, Mar. 1, 1959; children: Elizabeth Margolis-Pineo, Catherine, Abby Margolis Newman, Joshua, Sarah. BA, U. N.C., 1947; MA, Harvard U., 1948, PhD, 1951; JD, Yale U., 1956. Bar: Conn. 1957, U.S. Dist. Ct. Conn. 1958, U.S. Supreme Ct. 1969. Instr. dept. govt. U. Conn., 1951-53; assoc. Silberberg & Silverstein, Ansonia, Conn., 1956-60, Wofsey Rosen Kweskin & Kuriansky, Stamford, Conn., 1960-66, ptnr., 1966-96, of counsel, 1996—. Arbitrator State of Conn., 1984-85; adj. prof. Quinnipiac U. Sch. Law, 1986—. Sr. editor Conn. Bar Jour., 1971-80, 83—, editor-in-chief, 1980-83; contbr. to profl. jours. Mem. nat. bd. ACLU, 1975-79; mem. Westport (Conn.) Planning and Zoning Commn., 1971-75; chmn. Conn. CLU, 1988-95, legal advisor, 1995—; exec. com. Yale Law Sch., 2000—. With U.S. Army, 1944-46. Decorated Purple Heart; recipient First Award for Disting. Svc. to Conn. Bar, Conn. Law Tribune, 1987. Fellow Conn. Bar Found. (James W. Cooper fellow 1996); mem. ABA, Conn. Bar Assn. (chmn. human rights sect. 1970-73), Nat. Assn. Criminal Def. Lawyers, Am. Arbitration Assn. (arbitrator 1998—, trial referee 1985—). Office: 600 Summer St Stamford CT 06901-1490 Home: 72 Myrtle Ave Westport CT 06880-3512 Office Phone: 203-327-2300. E-mail: emesq@optonline.net.

MARGOLIS, GERALD JOSEPH, psychiatrist, psychoanalyst; b. Bronx, N.Y., May 7, 1935; s. Max and Sophie (Siegel) M.; m. June Edelman Greenspan, July 13, 1976; children: David J., Peter S., Steven J. AB, U. Rochester, 1957; MD, U. Chgo., 1960; postgrad., Inst. Phila. Assn. Psychoa., 1972. Diplomate in psychiatry Am. Bd. Psychiatry and Neurology. Intern to resident in psychiatry Upstate Med. Ctr. SUNY, Syracuse, 1960-64, instr. psychiatry, 1966-67; from instr. to clin. prof. psychiatry Med. Sch. U. Pa., Phila., 1967—. Practice medicine specializing in psychiatry and psychoanalysis, Cherry Hill, NJ; tng. and supervising analyst Inst. of the Psychoanalytic Ctr. Phila. Contbr. articles to profl. jours. Served with M.C., USAF, 1964-66. Mem.: AMA, Med. Socl N.J., Camden County Med. Soc., Psychoanalytic Ctr. Phila. (tng. and supervising analyst), Am. Psychiat. Assn., Am. Psychoanalytic Assn. (cert.), B'nai B'rith, Phi Beta Kappa. Office: One Mall Dr Ste 930 Cherry Hill NJ 08002-2194 Office Phone: 856-667-1055.

MARGOLIS, GWEN, county commissioner; 4 children. Grad., Temple U. Mem. Fla. Ho. of Reps., 1974-79, Fla. Senate, 1980, chair fin., tax and claims com., chmn. appropriations com., senate pres., 1990-92; mem. dist. 4 Metro-Dade County Commn., Fla., 1994—, chairperson, commr. dist. 4. Bd. dirs. Holocaust Documentation Ctr. Fla. Internat. U.; chmn. Coconut Grove Playhouse, chmn., 1997—. Recipient Econ. Devel. award Fla. C. of C., 1992, Legislator of Yr. award Fla. C. of C., 1992, Good Govt. award Dade League of Cities, 1992, Fla. Motion Picture and TV award, 1992, Glass Ceiling award Fla. Fedn. Bus. and Profl. Women, 1992. Office: Office County Commr 111 NW 1st St Fl 2 Miami FL 33128-1902

MARGOLIS, HAROLD STEPHEN, epidemiologist; b. Tucson, Ariz., Feb. 22, 1946; s. Maurice H. and Helen (Letz) M.; m. Susan Helen Quinn, July 3, 1971; children: Ellis, Leah, Amber. BS, U. Ariz., 1968, MD, 1972. Diplomate Am. Bd. Med. Examiners. Resident in pediatrics U. Colo. Health Scis. Ctr., Denver, 1972-75; med. epidemiologist Ctrs. for Disease Control, Anchorage, 1975-79, Phoenix, Ariz., 1981-83, dep. chief hepatitis br. Atlanta, 1983-87; chief hepatitis br., 1995—; chief Ctrs. for Disease Control, Atlanta, 1987-94; rsch. fellow Nat. Jewish Hosp., Denver, 1979-81. Dir. WHO Collaborative Ctr. for Rsch. and Reference in Viral Hepatitis, Atlanta, 1987—; cons. WHO, 1988, 89, Agy. for Internat. Devel.; guest advisor Inst. Medicine, 1989, 92. Editor: Viral Hepatitis and Liver Disease, 1991; contbr. articles to profl. jours. Capt. USPHS, 1975—. Fellow Am. Acad. Pediats., Infectious Disease Soc. Am.; mem. Alpha Omega Alpha, Sigma Xi. Achievements include development of strategies to prevent viral hepatitis through immunization; research in characterization of hepatitis A viruses and molecular pathogenesis of viral hepatitis.

MARGOLIS, JAY M. clothing executive; b. N.Y.C., Feb. 11, 1949; s. Mac and Sarah Margolis; m. Donna Brenda Polsky, June 12, 1972; children: Jared Michael, Stacey Allyse. BA, Queens Coll., N.Y.C., 1971. Asst. mdse. mgr. Manhattan Shirt Co., N.Y.C., 1972-74; mdse. mgr. Arrow Shirt Co., N.Y.C., 1974-78; pres. Yves St. Laurent-Biderman Inc., N.Y.C., 1978-81, Ron Chereskin div. Cluett Peabody, N.Y.C., 1981-83, Claiborne Mens-Liz Claiborne Inc., N.Y.C., 1983-86; group pres., exec. v.p. corp. Liz Claiborne Inc., N.Y.C., 1986-88, vice chmn., 1988—92; pres., vice chmn. Tommy Hilfiger, 1992—95; chmn., CEO Esprit de Corp., 1995—99, E7th.com, 1999—2001; pres. splty. bus. group Reebok Internat. Ltd., 2001—. Mem. bd. Fathers Day/Mothers Day Coun. Mem. City Athletic Club. Avocations: skiing, swimming, tennis, environmental studies. Office: President & COO Reebok International 67 Wyman Rd Abington MA 02351*

MARGOLIS, JEFFREY ROBERT, financial services executive; b. Englewood, N.J., July 2, 1957; s. Frederick Paul and Florence (Goldner) M.; m. Nancy Dee Epstein, Oct. 28, 1984; 1 child, Lisa. BA, Cornell U., 1979, MBA, 1980. CPA, N.Y.; chartered fin. analyst. Acct. Arthur Young & Co., N.Y.C., 1980-83; COO Continental Asset Mgmt., N.Y.C., 1983-94; mng. dir. Morgan Stanley Dean Witter Investment Mgmt., 1994—. Media contbr., interviewee and critic for fin. community; speaker in field. Editor, contbr. various publs. Mem. AICPA, Assn. for Investment Mgmt. and Rsch., N.Y. Soc. CPAs, Ins. Investment Strategy Group (founder, chmn.). Home: 85 Barberry Ln Roslyn Heights NY 11577-1501 Office: Morgan Stanley Dean Witter Investment Mgmt 5th Fl 1221 Avenue Of The Americas Fl 5 New York NY 10020-1001

MARGOLIS, JULIUS, economist, educator; b. N.Y.C., Sept. 26, 1920; s. Sam and Fannie (Weiner) M.; m. Doris Lubetsky, Oct. 30, 1942; children—Jane S., Carl W. BSS., City Coll. N.Y., 1941; Ph.M. in Econs, U. Wis., 1943; M.P.A. in Econs, Harvard, 1947, PhD, 1949. Instr. econs. Tufts Coll., 1947-48; asst. prof. econs. and planning U. Chgo., 1948-51; asst. prof. econs. Stanford, 1951-54; prof. bus adminstrn. U. Calif. at Berkeley, 1954-64; prof. econs. and engring. econ. systems Stanford, 1964-69; prof., dir. Fels Center of Govt., U. Pa., 1969-76; prof. econs. U. Calif. at Irvine, 1976—. Dir. Ctr. on Global Peace and Conflict Studies, 1985—; cons. to govt. and industry, 1958— Author: (with others) The Public Economy of Urban Communities, 1965, The Northern California's Water Industry, 1966, Public Economics, 1969, Public Expenditure and Policy Analysis, 1984; also articles. Served with AUS, 1943-46. Mem. Am. Econ. Assn., Royal Econ. Soc. Home: 45 Whitman Ct Irvine CA 92612-4059 Office: U Calif Dept Econ Irvine CA 92697-0001 Office Phone: 949-854-3911. E-mail: jmargoli@uci.edu.

MARGOLIS, LAWRENCE STANLEY, federal judge; b. Phila., Mar. 13, 1935; m. Doris May Rosenberg, Jan. 30, 1960; children: Mary Aleta, Paul Oliver. BSME, Drexel U., 1957; JD, George Washington U., 1961. Bar: D.C. 1963. Patent examiner U. S. Patent Office, Washington, 1957-62; patent counsel Naval Ordnance Lab., White Oak, Md., 1962-63; asst. corp. counsel D.C., 1963-66; atty. criminal div., spl. asst. U.S. atty. Dept. of Justice, Washington, 1966-68; asst. U.S. atty. for D.C., 1968-71; U.S. magistrate judge U.S. Dist. Ct., Washington, 1971-82; judge U.S. Ct. Fed. Claims, Washington, 1982—; chmn. task force on discovery reform U.S. Claims Ct., Washington, chmn. alt. dispute resolution. Chmn. Space and Bldg. com., chmn. Ct. Security Com., mem. faculty Fed. Jud. Ctr. Editor-in-chief The Young Lawyer, 1965-66, D.C. Bar Jour., 1967-73; bd. editors The Dist. Lawyer, 1978-82. Trustee Drexel U., 1983-89; bd. govs. George Washington U. Alumni Assn., 1978-85, 93-96 Recipient Contbn. award D.C. Jaycees, 1966, Svc. award Boy Scouts Am., 1970, Alumni Svc. award George Washington U., 1976, Disting. Alumni Achievement award George Washington U., 1985, Disting. Alumni Achievement award Drexel U., 1988, Drexel 100 award, 1992, Alternative Dispute Resolution award Ctr. for Pub. Resources, 1988, Alternative Dispute Resolution Svc. award Ct. of Fed. Claims, 1996, Alumni Recognition award George Washington U., 1996. Fellow Inst. Jud. Adminstrn., Am. Bar Found.; mem. ABA (chmn. jud. adminstrn. divsn., Disting. Svc. award 1981), ABA Nat. Conf. Spl. Ct. Judges (chmn., Disting. Svc. award 1978), D.C. Jud. Conf., Bar Assn. D.C. (bd. dirs. 1970-72, jour. editor-in-chief, Chmn. of Yr. award, Contbn. award young lawyers sect. 1983), Fed. Bar Assn., George Washington U. Nat. Law Assn. (pres. D.C. chpt. 1974-76, nat. pres. 1983-84), Univ. Club., Rotary (bd. dirs. Washington 1984-90, pres. 1988-89, dist. gov. 1991-92, Rotarian of Yr. 1984, Rotary Internat. Rep. to the World Bank and Orgn. of Am. States, 1998-99, pres. Rotary Found. 1999-2000), Charles Fahy Am. Inn of Ct. (Nat. Program award, 1997), Phila. Cen. High Sch. Alumni (bd. mgrs. 2001—). Office: US Ct Fed Claims 717 Madison Pl NW Ste 703 Washington DC 20005 Business E-Mail: lawrence_margolis@ao.uscourts.gov.

MARGOLIS, PHILIP MARCUS, psychiatrist, educator; b. Lima, Ohio, July 7, 1925; s. Harry Sterling and Clara (Brunner) M.; m. Nancy Nupuf, July 26, 1959; children: Cynthia, Marc, David, Laurence. BA magna cum laude, U. Minn., 1945, MD, 1948. Diplomate Am. Bd. Psychiatry and Neurology, 1966 (examiner 1973—1999, 2003-), recert. com., 1998-2004. Intern Milw. County Hosp., 1948-49; resident VA Hosp. and U. Minn., 1949-52, Mass. Gen. Hosp. and Harvard U., Boston, 1952-54; instr. U. Minn., Milw., 1953-55; asst. prof. dept. psychiatry Med. Sch., U. Chgo., 1955-60, assoc. prof., 1960-66; prof. psychiatry Med. Sch. U. Mich., 1966—, prof. cmty. mental health, 1968—; prof. psychiatry emeritus L.S.A., 1997—, instr., 1977-97; chief psychiat. inpatient service U. Chgo. Hosps. and Clinics, 1956-66; dir. Civil Forensic Tng. Program, 1997—. Cons. Forensic Psychiat. Ctr., State of Mich., 1972—, coord. med. student edn. program, 1975-78, dir., 1978-82; cons. Turner Geriatric Clin., 1978-86, cons. Breast Cancer Clinic, 1988, Powertrain subs. Gen. Motors, 1984—, Dept. Mental Health, U.S. Dept. Justice; assoc. chief clin. affairs U. Mich. Hosps., 1981-85, chair legis. govt. com., 1996—, chmn. ethics com.; bd. dirs., mem. profl. rev. com. PSRO Area VII, 1982-86, PROM, 2003—; mem. Mich. State Bd. Medicine, 1986-94, chmn. 1992-94, senate adv. com. Univ. Affairs., 1986-89; bd. dirs. Fedn. of State Med. Bds., 1994-98, spl. com. on profl. conduct and ethics, 1998—, Mich. del., 1988-96, FLEX Com. Nat. Bd. Med. Examiners, 1988-98; mem. civil liberties bd. U. Mich., 1995-2004, chmn., 1996-2002, mem. gen counsel adv. com., 2002—; dir. Civil Forensic Tng. Program, 1997—. Author: Guide for Mental Health Workers, 1970, Patient Power: The Development of a Therapeutic Community in a General Hospital, 1974; also articles.; cons. editor: Community Mental Health jour, 1967— . Recipient Commonwealth Fund fellow award, 1964, Career Svc. award, 1992, Resident Appreciation award, 1991. Fellow: Am. Coll. Psychiatrists (chmn. bylaws com. 1997—), Am. Psychiat. Assn. (life; chmn. membership com. 1979—83, cons. ethics com. 1983—86, trustee 1985—88, sec. 1989—91, chmn. ethics appeals bd. 1989—, cons. steering com. on practical guidelines 1991—, budget com. 1991—, mem. assembly 1992, coun. med. edn. and career devel. 1993—, pres. Lifers 1994—, recertification com. 1998—, mem. pub. funding com. 2001—, assembly rep. 2003—, newsletter editor 2003—, cons. mem. com. 2004—, mem. audit com. 2004—, annual Lifers award 1999); mem.: Am. Acad. Psychiatry and Law (com. on psychoanalytic edn. 1995—, edn. com. 1998, treas. midwest chpt. 1998—2000, pres. 2001—02, forensic tng. com. 2000—), Am. Acad. Psychoanalysis, Mich. State Med. Soc. (bioethics com. 1989—, com. on med. licensure and discipline 1995—, mental health liaison com. 1995—, legis. and regulations com. 1995—, liaison com. Gen. Motors 1998—, chair 2000—, chair com. on med. licensure and discipline 2000—), Mich. Psychiat. Soc. (pres. 1980—81, chmn. ethics com. 1983—86, resolutions officer student rights responsibilities 1996—, chmn. legislation and govt. com. 1996—, v.p. 2000—, Career Achievement award 2000), Washtenaw County Med. Soc. (exec. coun. 1982—, chmn. ethics com. 1983—87, pres. 1987—88, editl. bd. 1995—, chair legis. commn. 1999—). Home: 228 Riverview Dr Ann Arbor MI 48104-1846 Office: 2101 Commonwealth Blvd Ste B Ann Arbor MI 48105-0722 Office Phone: 734-647-8762. Business E-Mail: margolis@umich.edu.

MARGOLIS, SHERRY, newscaster; m. Jeff Zaslow, 1987; children: Jordan, Alexandra, Eden. BA in English, SUNY, Buffalo. Anchor and reporter WKBW-TV, Buffalo; reporter WJBK-TV, Detroit, 1984—, anchor "In the News", co-anchor 5am and noon news. Named Best Newscast in Mich., AP, 1990; recipient Best News Anchor Emmys, NATAS, 1993, 1999, Emmy Reporting, 2002. Office: WJBK-TV FOX 2 PO Box 2000 Southfield MI 48037-2000

MARGOLIS, THOMAS IRA, vitreoretinal ophthalmologist; b. Uniontown, Pa., May 11, 1962; s. Herbert and Barbara M.; m. Robin Deborah Small, Mar. 12, 1989; children: Rebecca, Joshua, Jennifer. BA summa cum laude, U. Pa., 1984; MD magna cum laude, Harvard U., 1989. Cert. Am. Bd. Ophthalmology. Intern Cedars Sinai Med. Ctr., L.A., 1989-90; resident Wills Eye Hosp., Phila., 1990-93; fellowship (vitreoretinal) Tufts U.-New Eng. Eye Ctr., Boston, 1993-95. Instr. ophthalmology Tufts U. Med. Sch., Boston, 1993-96; hosp. staff Atlantic City Med. Ctr., Shore Meml. Hosp., Somers Point, N.J. Contbr. sci. articles to profl. jours. and chpt. to book. Recipient Benjamin Franklin scholar U. Pa., 1980-84, Laurence B. Ellis scholar Harvard Med. Sch., 1987; named one of "Top Docs", NJ Monthly, 2003, Phila. Mag., 2004. Mem. AMA, Am. Acad. Ophthalmology, N.J. Acad. Ophthalmology, N.J. Med. Soc., Atlantic County Med. Soc., Wills Eye Hosp. Soc., N.J. Retina Soc., Am. Soc. Retina Specialists, Phi Beta Kappa. Jewish. Avocations: running, skiing, golf, tennis, travel. Office: Retinal and Ophthalmic Cons PC 1500 Tilton Rd Northfield NJ 08225-1827 also: Bldg 3A 1138 E Chestnut Ave Ste 3A Vineland NJ 08360-5053 Office: Ste 102 211 S Main St Cape May Court House NJ 08210 Office Phone: 609-646-5200. E-mail: vitrector@aol.com.

MARGOLIUS, HARRY STEPHEN, pharmacologist, physician; b. Albany, N.Y., Jan. 29, 1938; s. Irving Robert and Betty (Zweig) M.; m. Francine Rockwood, May 22, 1964; children: Elizabeth Anne, Craig Matthew. BS, Union U., 1959, PhD, 1963; MD, U. Cin., 1968. Diplomate Nat. Bd. Med. Examiners, 1969, chmn. pharmacology test com., 1990-94. Intern, resident Harvard Med. Svc. Boston City Hosp., 1968-70, pharmcology rsch. assoc., 1970-72; sr. clin. investigator NHLBI NIH, Bethesda, 1972-74, assoc. prof. pharmacology, asst. prof. medicine Med. U. S.C., Charleston, 1974-77, prof. pharmacology, assoc. prof. medicine, 1977-80, prof. pharmacology, prof. medicine, 1980—, chmn. pharmacology, 1989—. Cons. NIH, FDA, VA, NSF, Washington, Bethesda, 1975—; mem. editorial bd. Am. Heart Assn., Dallas, 1980—. Editor: Kinins IV, 1986, Renal Function, Hypertension and Kallikrein-Kinin System, 1988; contbr. numerous articles to profl. jours. Commdr. USPHS, 1967-74. Recipient S.C. Gov.'s award for sci. S.C. Acad. Scis., 1988, Frey-Werle Commemorative medal for biomed. rsch., 1997; Burroughs-Wellcome scholar, 1976; vis. scholar U. Cambridge, Eng., 1980-81; sr. fellow Fitzwilliam Coll., 1996; NIH grantee, 1975—; named Theodore Cooper Meml. Lectr., 1995. Fellow Coun. for High Blood Pressure Rsch., Am. Heart Assn.; mem. Am. Soc. for Pharmacology and Exptl. Therapeutics, Am. Soc. for Clin. Investigation and 10 additional med., sci. socs. Jewish. Achievements include studies of the role of kallikreins and kinins in human and animal forms of hypertension; discovery of abnormalities which signify roles in causing high blood pressure. Office: Medical Univ SC Coll Medicine 171 Ashley Ave Charleston SC 29425-0001

MARGON, BRUCE HENRY, astrophysicist, educator; b. N.Y.C., Jan. 7, 1948; s. Leon and Maxine E. (Margon) Siegelbaum; 1 dau., Pamela. AB, Columbia U., 1968; MA, U. Calif.-Berkeley, 1971, Ph.d., 1973. Asst. rsch. astronomer U. Calif.-Berkeley, 1973-76; assoc. prof. astronomy UCLA, 1976-80; prof. astronomy U. Wash., Seattle, 1980—2001, chmn., 1981-87, 90-95, sci. dir. Sloan Digital Sky Survey, 1998-99; assoc. dir. Space Telescope Sci. Inst., Balt., 2001—. Bd. govs. Astrophys. Rsch. Consortium, Inc., Seattle; chmn. bd. dirs. AURA, Inc., Washington; co-investigator Hubble space telescope NASA, Washington, 1977—. NATO postdoctoral fellow, 1973-74; Sloan Found. research fellow, 1979-83 Fellow AAAS, Am. Phys. Soc.; mem. Internat. Astron. Union, Am. Astron. Soc. (Pierce Prize 1981), Royal Astron. Soc. Office: Space Telescope Sci Inst 3700 San Martin Dr Baltimore MD 21218 Business E-Mail: margon@stsci.edu.

MARGULIES, JAMES HOWARD, editorial cartoonist; b. Bklyn., Oct. 8, 1951; s. Henry Norman and Miriam Margulies; m. Martha Anne Golub, May 21, 1978; children: Elana, David. BFA, Carnegie-Mellon U., 1973. Editorial cartoonist Jour. Newspapers, Springfield, Va., 1980-84, Houston Post, 1984-90, The Record, Hackensack, N.J., 1990—. Syndicated cartoonist various newspapers, 1985—. Author: My Husband Is Not a Wimp, 1988, Hitting Below the Beltway, 1998; contbr. columns to profl. jours.; cartoons featured on TV programs. Mem. leadership com. Jewish Community Ctr., Houston, 1987, 88. Recipient Best Cartoon award Population Inst., 1985, Global Media award, 1985, 2d Place Editl. award Pavillion of Humor, 1985, Judges award World Hunger Media awards, 1986, Katie award Press Club of Dallas, 1989, Best Black and White Illustration in Advt. and Graphic Arts Addy award Houston Advt. Fedn., 1990, John Peter Zenger award N.Y. State Bar Assn., 1992, Nat. Headliner award for editl. cartoons Press Club of Atlantic City, 1996, 1st prize Fischetti Editl. Cartoon Competition, Columbia Coll., Chgo., 1996, Deadline Club award for editl. cartoons N.Y. chpt. Soc. Profl. Journalists, 1998, 1st pl. for editl. cartoons Garden State Assn. of Black Journalists, 1999-2003, 3d Pl. Nat. Headliner awards for Editl. Cartoons. Press Club of Atlantic City, 2003, 04; named One of Texans Who Made the Eighties Winter, Ultra mag., 1990. Mem. Assn. Am. Editl. Cartoonists. Avocation: running. Office: The Record 150 River St Hackensack NJ 07601-7155 Office Phone: 201-646-4468. E-mail: jimmarg@aol.com.

MARGULIES, JULIANNA, actress; b. Spring Valley, NY, June 8, 1966; BA, Sarah Lawrence Coll., 1989. Actress (film) Out for Justice, 1991, Traveller, 1997, Paradise Road, 1997, A Price Above Rubies, 1997, The Newton Boys, 1998, What's Cooking, 2000, Ten Unknowns, 2001 (Lucille Lortel Award for outstanding featured actress, 2001), The Man From Elysian Fields, 2001, Ghost Ship, 2002, Evelyn, 2002, (voice) Dinosaur, 2000, (TV) Murder, She Wrote, Law and Order, Homicide, Philly Heat, ER, 1994-2000 (Emmy award for supporting actress Drama, 1995, Golden Globe award winner, 1998, SAG award winner 1997, 98, 99), The Mists of Avalon, 2001, Jennifer, 2001, Hitler: The Rise of Evil, 2003 (theater) The Substance of Fire, At Home, Fefu and Her Friends, Living Expenses, Dan Drift, and Book of Names, The Vagina Monologues, 2000. Office: c/o William Morris Agency 151 S El Camino Dr Beverly Hills CA 90212

MARGULIES, LEE, newspaper editor; Television editor Los Angeles Times, Calif., 1976—. Office: Los Angeles Times Times Mirror Sq Los Angeles CA 90053

MARGULIES, MARTIN B. lawyer, educator; b. N.Y.C., Oct. 6, 1940; s. Max N. and Mae (Cohen) M.; m. Beth Ellen Zeldes, July 26, 1981; children: Max Zeldes, Adam Zeldes. AB, Columbia Coll., 1961; LLB, Harvard U., 1964; LLM, NYU, 1966. Bar: N.D. 1968, N.Y. 1974, Mass. 1977, Conn. 1988, U.S. Dist. Ct. Mass. 1977, U.S. Ct. Appeals (2d cir.) 1984, U.S. Supreme Ct. 1995. Asst. prof. law U. N.D., Grand Forks, 1966-69; editor-in-chief Columbia Coll. Today, Columbia U., N.Y.C., 1969-71; assoc. editor Parade Mag., N.Y.C., 1971-72; assoc. prof. law Western New Eng. Law Sch., Springfield, Mass., 1973-76; Bernard Hersher prof. law U. Bridgeport, Conn., 1977-92; prof. law Quinnipiac U., 1992—, Neil H. Cogan Pub. Svc. prof. law, 1997-99. Author: The Early Life of Sean O'Casey, 1970; contbr. articles to profl. jours. Cooperating atty. Conn. Civil Liberties Union, Hartford, 1979—, bd. dirs., 1982-94; bd. dirs. Conn. Attys. for Progressive Legislature, New Haven, 1982: bd. dirs. ACLU, 1987-94, mem. free speech-assn. and poverty constl. rights com., 1988-94; chmn. bd. dirs. Fairfield County Civil Liberties Union, 1982-87, Hampden County Civil Liberties Union, 1976-78; bd. dirs. Civil Liberties Union Mass., Boston, 1975-78, Greater Springfield Urban League, 1976-78, Conn. Civil Liberties Union, 1982-94, ACLU, 1987-94, Ctr. for First Amendment Rights, Inc., 1993—. Recipient Media award N.Y. State Bar Assn., 1972, Gavel award ABA, 1973, Outstanding Tchr. award U. Bridgeport Law Sch., 1986, 87. Mem. Mass. Bar Assn., N.Y. State Bar Assn. Jewish. Home: 79 High Rock Rd Sandy Hook CT 06482-1623 Office: Quinnipiac Univ Sch Law 275 Mt Carmel Ave Hamden CT 06518-1947 Office Phone: 203-582-3252. E-mail: mmargulies023@earthlink.net.

MARGULIS, ALEXANDER RAFAILO, physician, educator; b. Belgrade, Yugoslavia, Mar. 21, 1921; arrived in U.S., 1946; s. Rafailo and Olga (Weiss-Belic) Margulis; m. Hedvig Hricak, Feb. 26, 1983; 1 child, Peter Hricak. Student, U. Belgrade, 1939—41; MD, Harvard U., 1950; hon. doctorates, Aix-Marseille U. Sch. Medicine, 1980, Med. Coll. Wis., 1986, Cath. U. Louvain, 1986, Karolinska Inst., Stockholm, 1986, U. Munich, 1987, U. Toulouse, 1987, U. Montpellier, 1993; student, U. Belgrade, 1945—46. Diplomate Am. Bd. Radiology. Intern Henry Ford Hosp., Detroit, 1950—51; resident in radiology U. Mich. Hosps., 1951—53; jr. clin. instr. U. Mich., 1953—54; instr., then asst. prof. U. Minn., 1954—59; asst. prof. sch. medicine Washington U., St. Louis, 1959—60, assoc. prof. to prof., 1960—63; prof. radiology, chmn. dept. U. Calif., San Francisco, 1963—89, dir. magnetic resonance Sci. Ctr., assoc. chancellor spl. projects, 1989—93, spl. cons. to vice chancellor, 1993—2000; clin. prof. radiology Cornell U. Weill Med. Coll.,

N.Y.C., 2000—; radiologist N.Y.-Presbyn. Med. Ctr., 2000—. Radiologist in chief U. Calif. Hosps., 1963—89; cons. VA Hosp., Letterman Gen. Hosp., San Francisco, U.S. Naval Hosp., Oakland, Calif.; cons. in radiology Office Surgeon Gen., 1967—71. Author (with others): Roentgen Diagnosis of Abdominal Tumors in Childhood, 1957; editor: Modern Alimentary Tract Radiology; co-editor: Alimentary Tract Roentgenology; editl. bd. Calif. Medicine, 1964—74, Radiology, 1975—93, assoc. editor Investigative Radiology, 1980—89; editor: Opinion in Radiology, 1988—91; author: Be in Charge: A Leadership Manual, 2002. Capt. U.S. Army, 1957—59. Recipient Cannon medal, Radiol. Soc. N.Am., 1977, Gold medal, Am. Roentgen Ray Soc., 1988, J.P. Allyn medal, P. Roberts Rsch. Inst., 1989, Gold medal, Am. Coll. Radiology, 1999, UCSF medal, 2000. Fellow: Royal Coll. Surgeons (hon.), Royal Coll. Radiologists (hon.); mem.: AMA (cons. drugs 1961—), Royal Coll. Radiologists of Thailand, Polish Soc. Radiology, Thai Coll. Radiology, Chinese Radiol. Soc., Russian Radiol. Soc., Royal Coll. Surgeons Ireland, French Radiol. Soc., Swiss Radiol. Soc., Italian Radiol. Soc., Russian Acad. Scis. (fgn.), Serbian Acad. Scis. (fgn.), Soc. Magnetic Resonance in Medicine (pres. 1983), Calif. Acad. Medicine (pres. 1978), San Francisco Radiol. Soc. (pres. 1973—74), Radiol. Soc. N.Am. (Gold medal 1983), Soc. Chmn. Acad. Radiology Depts. (pres. 1968—69), Am. Gastroenterology Assn., Assn. Univ. Radiologists (pres. 1966—67, chmn. adv. com. acad. radiology 1971, pres. 1971), Roentgen Ray Soc., NAS-Inst. Medicine, Japan Radiol. Soc. (hon.), German Radiol. Soc. (hon.), Rocky Mountain Radiol. Soc. (hon.). Office: NY Presbyn Hosp Rm N-09 Box 141 525 E 68th St New York NY 10021-4870

MARGULIS, GREGORY A. mathematics educator, researcher; b. Moscow, Feb. 24, 1946; came to U.S., 1991; s. Alexander Y. Margulis and Tsilya M. Osherenko; m. Raisa T. Kristal, Aug. 30, 1972; 1 child, Boris. Diploma, Moscow U., 1967, PhD, 1970; DSc, Belorrussian Acad. Scis., Minsk, 1983. Rschr. Inst. Problems in Info. Transmission, Soviet Acad. Scis., Moscow, 1970-91; prof. math. Yale U., New Haven, 1991—. Mem. sci. adv. coun. Math. Scis. Rsch. Inst., Berkeley, Calif., 1993-97; mem. sci. adv. bd. Clay Math. Inst., Cambridge, Mass., 2003—. Author: Discrete Subgroups of Semisimple Lie Groups, 1991; mem. editl. bd. math. jours. Recipient prize for young mathematicians Moscow Math. Soc., 1968, Fields medal Internat. Math. Union, 1978, Humboldt Found. prize, 1995, Lobachevski prize Russian Acad. Scis., 1996. Mem. AAAS (fgn. hon.), NAS. Avocations: chess, jogging, swimming. Home: 20 Vista Ter New Haven CT 06515-2402 Office: Yale U Dept Math 10 Hillhouse Ave Dept Math New Haven CT 06511-6814

MARGULIS, HEIDI, managed health care company executive; Licensure analyst Humana, Inc., 1985—95, v.p. govt. affairs, 1995—2000, sr. v.p. govt. affairs, 2000—. Mem. fed. adv. com. to streamline regulations to ensure quality health care svcs., 2002; mem. com. on Medicare edn. HFCA. Mem.: Women's Polit. Forum (bd. dirs.), Bus. and Profl. Women (pres. 1978—79), Bus. Roundtable, Health Care Leadership Coun., Am. Assn. Health Plans (policy, legis., advocacy and strategic planning coms.). Office: Humana Inc 500 W Main St Louisville KY 40202

MARGULIS, LYNN (LYNN ALEXANDER), evolutionist, educator; b. Chgo., Mar. 5, 1938; d. Morris and Leone Alexander; m. Carl Sagan, June 16, 1957; children: Dorion Sagan, Jeremy Sagan; m. Thomas N. Margulis, Jan. 18, 1967; children: Zachary Margulis-Ohnuma, Jennifer Margulis di Properzio. AB, U. Chgo., 1957; A.M., U. Wis., 1960; PhD, U. Calif., Berkeley, 1965. Mem. faculty Boston U., 1966—68, asst. prof. biology, 1967—71, assoc. prof., 1971—77, prof., 1977—88, Univ. prof., 1986—88; Disting. Univ. prof. U. Mass., Amherst, 1988—. Sherman Fairchild Disting. scholar Calif. Inst. Tech., 1976—77; vis. prof. dept. microbiology U. Autónoma de Barcelona, Spain, 1986, Spain, 88; Disting. univ. prof. U. Mass. Author: Origin of Eukaryotic Cells, 1970, Symbiosis in Cell Evolution, 1981, Early Life, 1982, 2d edit., 2002, Symbiosis in Cell Evolution, 2d edit., 1993, Microcosmos Videos, 1999, Luminous Fish: Tales of Science and Love, 2003; editor (with Mitchell Rambler and René Fester): Global Ecology, 1989; editor: (with others) Handbook of Protoctista, 1990; editor: Looking at Microbes, An Introduction to the Microbiology Laboratory for Students, Symbiotic Planet. A New Look at Evolution, 1997; co-editor (with René Fester): Symbiosis as a Source of Evolutionary Innovation: Speciation and Morphogenesis, 1991; co-editor: Concepts of Symbiogenesis: A Historical and Critical Study of the Research of Russian Botanists, 1992, Environmental Evolution: Effects of the Origin and Evolution of Life on Planet Earth, 1992, Environmental Evolution: Effects of the Origin and Evolution of Life on Planet Earth, 2d edit., 2000, Glossary of Protoctista, 1993; co-editor: (with Dorion Sagan) What Is Sex?, 1998; co-editor: Slanted Truths: Essays on Gaia, Evolution and Symbiosis, 1997, What is Life?, 1995, Diversity of Life: The Illustrated Guide to the Five Kingdoms, 2d edit., 1999; co-author: Five Kingdoms, 1982, 3d edit., 1998, Microcosmos, 1986; co-author: (with Dorion Sagan) Origins of Sex, 1986; co-author: Garden of Microbial Delights, 1988, 2d edit., 1998, Biospheres From Earth To Space, 1988, Mystery Dance: On the Evolution of Human Sexuality, 1991, What Happens to Trash and Garbage: An Introduction to the Carbon Cycle, 1993, Living Sands: Mapping Time and Space with Forams, 2000, Early Life, 2d edit., 2002, Acquiring Genomes: A Theory of the Origins of Species, 2002; contbr. chapters to books, articles to profl. jours. Recipient Nat. Medal Sci., 1999, Humboldt Prize, 2002, Commonwealth of Mass. award; Guggenheim fellow, 1979. Fellow: AAAS; mem.: NAS, Soc. Evolutionary Protistology (co-founder). Office: U Mass Geosci Dept 611 No Pleasant St Amherst MA 01003-9297 Office Phone: 413-545-3244. Business E-Mail: celeste@geo.umass.edu. *We must, as E. M. Forster admonished, "only connect" and lower our population's growth rate. The sciences, the quest for knowledge about the universe and life are intrinsically unified. Like all other species ever to have lived on Earth, ours too will be replaced. The quality of that demise depends directly on preservation of habitat of our planetmates, and our own population growth rates.*

MARIANI, CHRISTOPHER LEONARD, veterinarian, educator; b. North York, Ont., Can., Jan. 7, 1971; s. Brian Joseph and Sharon Ann Mariani. BSc, DVM, U. Guelph, Ont., Can., 1996. Diplomate Am. Coll. of Vet. Internal Medicine, 2001. Intern Mich. Vet. Specialists, Southfield, 1996—97; assoc. vet. Beverly Hills Vet. Assocs., Mich., 1997—98; resident in neurology/neurosurgery Coll. Vet. Medicine, U. Fla., Gainesville, 1998—2001, grad. asst. dept. neuroscience, 2001—, vis. asst. prof. neurology/neurosurgery, 2003. Author: (veterinary textbook) Neurology for the Small Animal Practioner; contbr. articles to profl. jours. Mem.: AVMA (assoc.), Vet. Emergency and Critical Care Soc. (assoc.), Am. Coll. of Vet. Internal Medicine (assoc.), OTS Profl. Vet. Frat. (life; pres. Delta chpt. 1995—96). Avocations: soccer, hiking, literature. Office: U Florida Dept Neuroscience PO Box 100244 Gainesville FL 32611 Business E-Mail: marianic@mail.vetmed.ufl.edu.

MARIANI, DAVID FRANK, retired artist; b. Buffalo, Jan. 19, 1942; s. Guido James and Mable Lucretiam (Pantano) M.; children: Mack David, Todd James. Asst. art dir. Gelia and Wells Advt., Snyder, N.Y., 1967-72; art dir. Rich Advt., Buffalo, 1972-74, Mainspring Advt., Buffalo, 1974-76; freelance illustrator N.Y., 1976-86; sr. artist rsch. and devel. Fisher-Price, East Aurora, N.Y., 1986-88, sr. project artist, 1988-93, illustrator, art dir., product stylist, 1993—. Instr. visual comm. SUNY, Buffalo, 1974-78, lectr. casual comm., 1999; with edtl. dept. Courier-Express, Buffalo, 1982. Com. chmn. Elma (N.Y.) Wheat and Barley Festival, 1991. With USAF, 1960-64. Recipient 1st place Addy award Am. Advt. Fedn., 1973. Mem. Graphic Artist Guild Western N.Y. (pres., co-founder 1981-82), Art Dirs. Club Buffalo (best of show, 1978). Republican. Roman Catholic. Avocations: bagpipe music, rodeo clowning. Home and Studio: 6551 E Quaker St SteA2 Orchard Park NY 14127

MARIANI, EVELYN JULIA, music educator; b. Montevideo, Uruguay, Aug. 13, 1936; d. Daniel Juan Weiss and María Luisa Riffel; 1 child, Gisela Kristine Hanson. MusB, Andrews U., 1969; MusM, Mich. State U., 1971, PhD in Musicology, 1988; courses, Ariz. State U., 1981. Nat. cert. tchr. music and piano. Tchr. Maplewood Acad., Hutchison/Minn., 1971—77, Ga.-Cumberland, Calhoun, 1977—78, Thunderbird Acad., Scottsdale, Ariz., 1978—81; prof. music Montemorelos U., Mexico, 1981—89; tchr. Monterey Bay, La Selva Beach, Calif., 1989—2003, Walla Walla C.C., Wash., 2003—04. Advisor Inst. Nat. Anthropology, Mexico City, 1998—2003. Author: Samuel Martí: Vida y Obra, 2001. Mem.: Nat. Music Tchrs. Assn., Monterey Bay Acad. (Tchr. of Yr. 1997). Home: 26 SW 13th St College Place WA 99324

MARIANI, MARITA C. secondary school educator; b. Springfield, Mass., Apr. 26, 1953; d. Alberto C. and Mary C. Mariani. BA, Elms Coll., 1975; M Natural Sci., Worcester Poly. Inst., 1986. Cert. biology and chemistry edn. Sci. tchr. Cathedral H.S., Springfield, 1975—. Named Celebrated Tchr., C. of C., Springfield, 2002. Mem.: Nat. Sci. Tchrs. Assn., Am. Chem. Soc., Nat. Assn. Biology Tchrs. Office: Cathedral High Sch 260 Surrey Rd Springfield MA 01118 E-mail: mmariani@cathedralhigh.org.

MARIANI, MICHAEL MATTHEW, lawyer; b. West Pittston, Pa., Sept. 25, 1950; s. Stephen Francis and Tulia Felicia (DelCorso) M.; m. Patricia Mary Leptak, June 26, 1976; children: Kathryn Elizabeth, Michael Joseph. BS with honors, Wilkes Coll., 1972; JD, St. John's U., Jamaica, N.Y., 1975; LLM, NYU, 1980. Bar: N.Y. 1976, U.S. Dist. Ct. (so. and ea. dists.) N.Y. 1976, U.S. Tax Ct. 1980. Law sec. to presiding judge Surrogate's Ct., New City, N.Y., 1976-80; assoc. Law offices of Edward S. Schlesinger P.C., N.Y.C., 1981-97; sr. v.p., trust counsel Fiduciary Trust Co. Internat., N.Y.C., 1997—. Co-author: New York Probate, 1986, supplements 1987-2004; contbr. articles to profl. jours. Trustee Cath. Charities, Diocese of Bklyn., 1981—, treas., 1985—87, v.p., 1987—89, pres., 1989—91; bd. dirs. Mercy Home for Children, Bklyn., 1989—97, mem. adv. bd., 1997—; mem. profl. adv. bd. Calvary Hosp., 2002—. Recipient Benemerenti medal Pope John Paul II, 1997. Mem. ABA (real property, probate and trust law sects.), N.Y. State Bar Assn. (trusts and estates sects.), Assn. Bar City N.Y. (com. on estate and gift taxation). Democrat. Home: 53-32 215th St Bayside NY 11364-1835 Office: 600 Fifth Ave New York NY 10020-2302 Office Phone: 212-632-3255. E-mail: mmaria@ftci.com.

MARIANO, RAYMOND V. former mayor; b. Worcester, Mass., Sept. 23, 1950; m. Antonia Kouvaros; children: Gina Marie, Raymond, Anthony. BA in Sociology, Worcester State Coll., 1974; MPA, Clark U., 1982. Co-founder Mariano & Wright, 1984; mayor City of Worcester, 1993—2001; exec. dir. Worcester Housing Authority, 2003—. Mem. Worcester Sch. Com., 1975-81; mem City Coun., 1981—, vice chmn., 1985-87; chmn. Pub. Works and Rules Com.

MARIANO, ROBERT A. retail executive; Pres., CEO Dominick's Finer Foods, 1996—98; commr. Ill. Gaming Bd., 2001—02; chmn., CEO, pres. Roundy's Inc., 2002—. Office: Roundys-Kee Trans PO Box 473 Milwaukee WI 53201-0473

MARICLE, ROBYN LUANN (FORD), band director, choir director; b. Waco, Tex., Dec. 29, 1959; d. Robert Charles and Peggy Lou (Brown) Ford; m. Dale Louis Maricle; children: Alan Louis, Aaron Lee. AA, McLennan C.C., 1981; MusB Edn., Baylor U., 1984. Cert. all-level music. Asst. dir. of music First United Meth. Ch., Waco, Tex., 1977—95, music sec., 1982—84; music tchr. Waco I.S.D. (Mountainview Elem.), Waco, Tex., 1984—85, Waco I.S.D. (Parkdale Elem.), Waco, Tex., 1990—99; dir. music Florence United Meth. Ch., Florence, Tex., 1995—98; choral dir. middle sch. and h.s. Lorena I.S.D., Tex., 1999—. Cub scout/boy scout leader Pack 308/Troop 308, Waco, 1991—2001; chmn. worship com. Mooreville United Meth. Ch., 2000—02, leader children's time, 1999—2002; asst. leader for youth Mooreville United Methodist Ch., 2000—02; youth Sunday sch. tchr. Mooreville United Meth. Ch., 2001—. Recipient Harry Hosier award, Ctrl. Tex. Conf. of the United Meth. Ch., 2000. Mem.: Ctrl. Tex. Conf. Music Edn., Music Educators Nat. Conf., Tex. Music Educator Assn. Methodist. Avocations: outdoors, crafts. Home: 1029 FM 1239 Eddy TX 76524-2442 Office: Lorena ISD PO Box 97 Lorena TX 76655 Business E-Mail: RobynMaricle@lorena-isd.net.

MARICQ, HILDEGARD RAND, physician, researcher; b. Rakvere, Estonia, Apr. 23, 1925; came to U.S., 1954; d. August and Elvine Rosalie (Vunderlich) Rand; m. John George Maricq, Oct. 9, 1948; children: Michel Matti, Andres Villu, Peter Toivo. Candidate in natural and med. sci., Free U., Brussels, 1946-49, MD, 1953; post-doctoral fellow, Columbia U., 1965-67. Clin. investigator VA Hosp., Lyons, N.J., 1963-65, dir. Schizophrenic Research Sect., 1970-73; fellow biological sci. in relation to mental health Columbia U., NYC, 1965—67, rsch. assoc. Coll. Physicians and Surgeons N.Y.C., 1973-75; assoc. prof. research medicine Med. U. S.C., Charleston, 1975-81, prof. research medicine, 1981—97, prof. emeritus, 1997—. Contbr. articles to sci. jours. Mem. Am. Physiol. Soc., Am. Rheumatism Assn., Microcirculatory Soc., Soc. Biol. Psychiatry. Office: Med U SC Div Rheumatology 171 Ashley Ave Charleston SC 29425-0001

MARIENTHAL, GEORGE, telecommunications company executive; b. Kansas City, Mo., Nov. 15, 1938; s. George and Sadie (James) M.; children: Shawn Ann Capon, Patrick James, Shannon Lee Van Winter. BS, U.S. Naval Acad., 1962; MS, Stanford U., 1963; MBA, Am. U., 1974. Sr. rsch. assoc. Logistics Mgmt. Inst., Washington, 1967-71; dir. regional ops. EPA, 1971-75, dir. water policy, 1984-85; dep. asst. sec. def. Dept. Def., Washington, 1975-81; v.p. Survival Tech., Inc., Bethesda, Md., 1981-84; dep. asst. sec. agr. Dept. Agr., Washington, 1985-86; dep. adv. programs Titan Systems, Inc., 1986-87; mgr. mktg. Computer Scis. Corp., Falls Church, Va., 1987-89; dir. MCI Comm Corp., McLean, Va., 1989—. Bd. dirs. Home Security Title Ins. Co. Served with USAF, 1962-67. Mem.: Internat. Telephone Pioneers Assn., Armed Forces Comms. and Electronics Assn., Masons. Republican. Episcopalian. Home: 2157 Sandcastle Ct Annapolis MD 21403-5505 Personal E-mail: george.marienthal@mci.com.

MARIER, ROBERT L. dean, hospital administrator; b. Mar. 29, 1943; m. Joanne Cain Marier; 2 children. AB, Boston Coll., 1965; MD, Yale U., 1969; MHA, Tulane U., 1990. Diplomate Am. Bd. Internal Medicine and Infectious Diseases. Intern in internal medicine Mass. Gen. Hosp., Boston, 1969-70, asst. resident in medicine, 1970-71; epidemic intelligence svc. officer Nat. Ctr. Disease Control USPHS, Atlanta, 1971-73; clin. rsch. fellow in inflammatory disease Yale U., New Haven, 1973-75, asst. prof. medicine, 1975-78; assoc. prof. medicine La. State U., New Orleans, 1978-83, acting head sect. infectious disease, 1982-83, dir. intro. to clin. medicine, 1982-85, dir. residency program, 1982-86, prof. medicine, 1983—, dir. office infection control, 1982—91; med. dir. Med. Ctr. La., 1982—92; chmn. Dept. Pub. Health La. State U. Sch. Medicine, New Orleans, 1993—95, dean, 1995—2002; acting dean La. State U. Sch. Pub. Health, New Orleans, 2003—; CEO La. Pub. Hosp. Sys., 1997—99. Vis. physician Yale-New Haven Hosp., 1975-78. Fellow ACP, Infectious Disease Soc. Am.; mem. AMA, La. State Med. Soc., Orleans Parish Med. Soc., Alpha Omega Alpha. Office: La State U Health Scis Ctr Sch Pub Health 1600 Canal St New Orleans LA 70112-2825

MARIL, DAVID C. editor; b. Balt., Apr. 2, 1950; s. Herman and Esta Cook Maril. BA in English, Clark U., 1972. Sports editor News Recorder, Worcester, Mass., 1972-75, Milford (Mass.) Daily News, 1975-2000; news copy editor, Sunday columnist Brockton (Mass.) Enterprise, 2000—. V.p. Herman Maril Paintings, Balt., 1995—; sports editor AP Assn. Editor, writer Baseball Odyssey supplements, 1977-98 (award UPI 1988); columnist Off the Field, 1999. Bd. dirs. Highwood Condo Assn., Franklin, Mass., 1995—; mem. cable adv. com. Town of Franklin, 1988-91; mem. art adv. bd. Univ. Coll. of Univ. Md., 2001—. Recipient sports column awards UPI, 1986, 87, New Eng. Newspaper Assn., Boston, 1999, Cmty. Newspapers, Needham, Mass., 1999. Mem. Baseball Writers Assn. (Hall of Fame voter), Soc. Baseball Rsch., Boston Baseball Writers (bd. dirs.). Avocations: reading, cinema history, baseball history. Home: 37 Highwood Dr Franklin MA 02038

MARILLEY, SUZANNE MARIE, political scientist, educator; b. Watertown, N.Y., Aug. 18, 1954; d. James Maurice Marilley and Catherine Fay Durkan; m. Robert Peter Burke, July 25, 1987; 1 child, Cecilia. AB, Smith Coll., 1976; MA, Harvard U., 1981, PhD, 1985. Asst. prof. dept. govt. & internat. studies U. Notre Dame, Ind., 1986—95; asst. prof. dept. history & polit. Sci. Capital U., Columbus, Ohio, 1995—2001, assoc. prof. dept. polit. sci., 2001—. Mem.: LWV. Home: 917 Pleasant Ridge Bexley OH 43209 Office: Dept Polit Sci 2199 E Main St Rm 335 Columbus OH 43209

MARIMOW, WILLIAM KALMON, editor; b. Phila., Aug. 4, 1947; s. Jay and Helen Alma (Gitnig) M.; m. Diane K. Macomb, Oct. 18, 1969; children: Ann Esther, Scott Macomb. BA, Trinity Coll., Conn., 1969. Asst. editor Comml. Car Jour., Chilton Co., Bala Cynwyd, Pa., 1969-70; asst. to econ. columnist Phila. Bull., 1970-72; staff writer Phila. Inquirer, 1972—, city hall bur. chief, 1979-81, editor Main Line Neighbors, 1986-87, N.J. editor, 1987-89, city editor, 1989-91; city editor, asst. to pub. Phila. Inquirer and Daily News, 1991-93; met. editor Balt. Sun, 1993, assoc. mng. editor, 1993-95, mng. editor, 1995-2000, editor, sr. v.p., 2000—04; mng. editor Nat. Pub. Radio, Washington, 2004—. Instr. urban studies U. Pa., 1979; instr. English Rutgers U., Camden, NJ, 1981; nominating jury Pulitzer Prize, 1991—92, 1996—97, 2002—03; bd. fellows Trinity Coll., 1998—2000; mem. adv. bd. Knight Ctr. for Specialized Journalism at U. Md., 1999—2000; bd. visitors U. Md. Sch. Journalism, 2000—; mem. nat. adv. bd. Poynter Inst., 2004—. Recipient 1st pl. award for team reporting Phila. Press Assn., 1977, 1st pl. award for deadline reporting AP Mng. Editors of Pa., 1977, Pub. Svc. awards, 1978, 85, Nat. Pub. Svc. award Sigma Delta Chi, 1978, 1st pl. award for best news story Sigma Delta Chi Phila., 1977, 2nd pl. award for deadline reporting, 1980, Pub. Svc. awards, 1978, 85, Pub. Svc. awards Sigma Delta Chi N.J., 1978, Pulitzer prize for disting. pub. svc., 1978, Pulitzer prize for investigative reporting, 1985, Silver Gavel award ABA, 1978, 82, Roy W. Howard Pub. Svc. award Scripps-Howard Found., 1978, Robert F. Kennedy Journalism award, 1978, 2nd pl. award for investigative reporting Keystone Press Assn., 1978, 85, 1st pl. award for best news story, 1982, Media Achievement award Phila. Bar Assn., 1982, William Schnader award Pa. Bar Assn., 1982, Nat. Headliners award, 1985, Trinity Coll. Alumni Achievement award, 1984; Nieman fellow Harvard U., 1982-83. Mem. Am. Soc. Newspaper Editors, Pen and Pencil Club, Investigative Reporters and Editors, Inc. Office: Nat Pub Radio 635 Mass Ave NW Washington DC 20001 Office Phone: 202-513-2220. E-mail: bmarimow@npr.org.

MARIN, CYNTHIA MYERS (CHERYL MARIN), systems engineer; b. Rocky Mount, Va., July 17, 1958; d. Edward Douglas and Ethel Beatrice (Cassidy) Myers. AAS in Avionics Tech., C.C. Air Force, 1982, AAS in Electronics Engring., 1987; BSEE, Ariz. State U., 1987; MS in Indsl. Engring., U. Ctrl. Fla., 1998. Cert. program mgr., acquisition mgr., electronics engr., space comm. engr., network contr. Avionics specialist USAF, Luke AFB, Ariz., 1976-78, avionics technician, analyst Eglin AFB, Fla., 1978-81, instr. leadership, mgmt. Zaragoza AFB, Spain, 1981-84, office tng. program Tempe, Lackland AFB, Ariz., Tex, 1984-88, engr. space comms. Vandenberg AFB, Calif., 1988-90, sys. engr., network contr. Cape Canaveral, Fla., 1990-92; mgr. ITTFSC, Cocoa Beach, Fla., 1992-93; mgr. integrated product LORAL, Rockledge, Fla., 1993-95; mgr. engring. Lockheed Martin, Rockledge, 1996-99, program mgr., sys. engr. Gaithersburg, Md., 1999—. Mem. AFCEA (past dir., pres., life), Air Force Assn. (life), Tau Beta Pi, Eta Kappa Nu. Avocation: space science. Home: 45639 Paddington Sta Ter Sterling VA 20166 Office: Lockheed Martin 182 700 N Frederick Ave Gaithersburg MD 20879 E-mail: cynthia.c.marin@lmco.com.

MARIN, DEBORAH B. psychiatrist, educator; b. Cleve., Oct. 9, 1957; d. Emanuel and Klara Blumenthal; m. Michael Marin; children: Lea, Max. BA, Wellesley Coll., 1979; MD, Mt. Sinai Med. Sch., 1984. Resident Mt. Sinai Med. Ctr., NYC, 1984—88; fellowship Cornell U., 1988—92; vice chair, prof. psychiatry Mt. Sinai Med. Ctr., NYC, 1992—, exec. v.p. for strategic devel., chief med. officer, 2004—; dean clin. rsch. Mt. Sinai Med. Sch., NYC, 2003—. Office: Mt Sinai Med Ctr 1425 Madison Ave New York NY 10029 E-mail: deborah.marin@mssm.edu.

MARIN, MICHAEL, vascular surgeon; b. June 7, 1956; BS, SUNY, Stony Brook, 1978; MD, Mt. Sinai Sch. Medicine, 1984. Bd. cert. surgery 1992. Intern in surgery Columbia-Presbyn. Med. Ctr., NYC, 1984—85, resident in surgery, 1985—89, chief resident surgery, 1989—90; fellow in transplant surgery Coll. Physicians and Surgeons, Columbia U., NYC, 1987—88; fellow in vascular surgery Montefiore Med. Ctr., NYC, 1990—92, attending physician surgery, 1992—96, Albert Einstein Coll. Medicine, NYC, 1992—96, asst. prof. surgery, 1992—96, assoc. prof. surgery, 1996—; attending physician surgery Bronx Municipal Hosp. Ctr., NYC, 1992—96, N. Cent. Bronx Hosp., NYC, 1992—96, Mt. Sinai Med. Ctr., NYC, 1996—, assoc. prof. surgery, 1996—, prof. vascular surgery, 1999—, prof. surgery, 1999—. Office: Mt Sinai Med Ctr Divsn Vascular Surgery 14th Fl 5 E 98th St New York NY 10029-6501 Office Phone: 212-241-7646.

MARIN, MINDY, casting agent, entrepreneur, film producer, writer; Casting agt. TV divsn. Paramount Pictures, 1978, asst.; casting agt. own projects, mem. staff, mgr. talent, casting Warner Bros.; self employed, 1989—; established prodn. co. Bluewater Ranch Entertainment, Bluewater Ranch Books, Santa Monica, Calif. Casting agt. films, CarolCo/IndiePro (with Steve Martin) L.A. Story, CarolCo/Tri-Star (with Sylvester Stallone) Cliffhanger, Paramount Pictures (with Harrison Ford) Clear and Present Danger, Columbia Pictures (with Sandra Bullock) The Net, HBO (with Demi Moore, Sissy Spacek, and Cher) If These Walls Could Talk, Paramount Pictures/Douglas-Reuther Prodns. (with John Travolta and Nicolas Cage) Face Off, Paramount Pictures/Mace Neufeld Prodns. (with John Travolta) The General's Daughter, New Line Cinema/New Redemption/Industry Entertainment/Tribe (with Robert De Niro) Fifteen Minutes, MGM/Lionrock Prodns. (with Nicolas Cage) Windtalkers, Paramount Pictures/Mace Neufeld Prodns. (with Ben Affleck and Morgan Freeman) The Sum of All Fears, DreamWorks/Warner Bros. (with Guy Pearce and Jeremy Irons) The Time Machine; author: The Secret to Tender Pie; assoc. prodr. MGM (own feature film starring James Spader, Jeff Daniels, etc.) 2 Days in the Valley, I-5 Films, Fox's Searchlight (with Tilda Swinton, Goran Visnjic) The Deep End, 2001. Office: Casting Artists Inc 1433 6th St Santa Monica CA 90401

MARIN, ROSARIO, former federal agency administrator; b. Mexico City, Mex., Aug. 4, 1958; m. Alex Marin; children: Eric, Carmen, Alvaro. BS bus. adminstrn., Calif. State U., L.A., 1983, LLD (hon.), 2002; grad., Harvard U., 1998. With City Nat. Bank, Beverly Hills, 1981—86; chief legis. affairs Calif. Dept. Devel. Svcs., 1992—93; chair Calif. State Coun. Developmental Disabilities, 1994—96; asst. dep. dir. Calif. State Dept. Social Svcs., 1996—97; dep. dir. Gov.'s Office Cmty. Rels., L.A., 1997—98; mayor City of Huntington Park, Calif., 1999—2000; 41st U.S. treas. U. S. Dept. Treasury, Washington, 2001—03. Recipient Rose Fitzgerald Kennedy award, U.N., 1995, Excellence in Pub. Svc. award, Latino Perspective Conf., 2000, Alumna of the Year, Calif. State U., 2002.*

MARINACCIO, CHARLES LINDBERGH, lawyer, consultant; b. Stratford, Conn., Dec. 10, 1933; BA, U. Conn., 1957; JD with honors, George Washington U., 1962. Bar: Conn. 1962, D.C. 1982. Trial lawyer U.S. Dept. Justice, Washington, 1963-69; advisor supervisory and regulation div. Fed. Res. Bd., Washington, 1969-73; dir., exec. sec. law enforcement assistance adminstrn. U.S. Dept. Justice, Washington, 1973-75; gen. counsel banking housing and urban affairs com. U.S. Senate, Washington, 1975-84; commr. SEC, Washington, 1984-85; ptnr. Kelley, Drye & Warren, Washington, 1985-94; ind. cons. Washington, 1995—. Apptd. by Pres. Clinton to bd. dirs. Securities Investor Protection Corp. Home and Office: 4911 Massachusetts Ave NW Washington DC 20016-4310

MARINAKIS, MARKOS K. water transportation executive; b. Kardamyla, Chios, Greece, July 17, 1945; came to U.S., 1971; s. Konstantinos and Maria M. Grad., Tech. Sch., 1963, Ministry Greek Merchant Marine, 1969; postgrad., World Trade Bus. Sch., 1972. Firefighting, life-saving lic. Joined as apprentice officer, able bodied seaman Merchant Marine, 1963, advanced through grades to second officer, 1964; joined Greek Navy, 1968, discharged, 1970, signal man, comdr. on motor vessel Niki, 1968-70; chief officer Motor Vessel Antigone, 1970-71; shipbroker Heath-Rosenthal Chartering Corp., Freeport, N.Y., 1972-73; responsible for cargo ops. dry cargo ships, tankers

U.S.A. Steamship Agy., N.Y., N.J., 1973-77; owner, dir., CEO M.K.M. Chartering, Inc., 1977—; pres., CEO Marinakis Chartering Inc., N.Y.C. Mem. Panama Canal Commn.; del. Dem. Nat. Convention, N.Y.C., 1992; active cmty. svc. Office: Marinakis Chartering Inc Ste 1810 39 Broadway Rm 1810 New York NY 10006-3003

MARINCOLA, ELIZABETH MARK, scientific society executive; b. New Haven, Conn., Aug. 31, 1959; d. James B.D. and Jean M. (Rambar) Mark; m. Francesco M. Marincola, Jan. 1, 1982; children: James Paul, Paula Rambar, Rachel Angela. AB, Stanford U., 1981, MBA, 1986. Dir. devel. Stanford (Calif.) U. Hosp., 1987-90; dep. dir. policy rsch. analysis NIMH, Rockville, Md., 1990-91; exec. dir. The Am. Soc. Cell Biology, Bethesda, Md., 1991—. Mem. cell biology com. of visitors NSF, 2001; com. for divsn. on earth and life studies Nat. Acad. Sci., 2001—; mem. PubMed Ctrl. Nat. adv. com. Nat. Libr. of Medicine Nat. Inst. Health, 2000-03; 20th Annual Fae Golden Kass lectr. Harvard Med. Sch., 1999; mem. adv. bd. Krasnow Inst. for Advanced Study, George Mason U., 2002—; elected first citizen mem. Am. Soc. Cell Biology, 2003. Home: 10110 Chapel Rd Potomac MD 20854-4143 Address: Amer Society for Cell Biology 8120 Woodmont Ave Suite 750 Bethesda MD 20814-2762 E-mail: emarincola@ascb.org.

MARINCOLA, JOHN, classics educator; b. Phila., Dec. 14, 1954; Student, Swarthmore Coll., 1972-74; BA magna cum laude, U. Pa., 1979; PhD, Brown U., 1985. Instr. Coll. Holy Cross, Worcester, Mass., 1984-85, asst. prof., 1985-86; vis. asst. prof. Union Coll., Schenectady, N.Y., 1986-88, asst. prof., 1989-93, assoc. prof., 1994-97; exec. dir. Am. Philol. Assn., 1997-99; assoc. prof. classics NYU, N.Y.C., 1999—2003, Fla. State U., Tallahassee, 2003—. Vis. rschr. Inst. Alte Geschichte U. Munich, Germany, 1989—90; Astor vis. lectr. Oxford U., 2002. Author: Authority and Tradition in Ancient Historiography, 1997, Herodotus: The Histories, 1996, Greek Historians, 2001; (with M.A. Flower) Herodotus: Book IX, 2002; contr. Histos. A New Jour. of Ancient Historiography, 1996—; reviewer, contbr. articles to profl. jours. William A. Michaelides fellow in Greek studies, 1983, jr. fellow Ctr. Hellenic Studies-Harvard U., Washington, 1999-2000; faculty scholar Brown U., 1983-84; grantee Deutscher Akademischer Austauschdienst, 1990. Mem. Internat. Plutarch Soc., Cambridge Philol. Soc., Classical Assn. (Eng.), Classical Assn. Atlantic States, Columbia U. Classical Civilization Sem., Women's Classical Caucus, Assn. Ancient Historians. Home: 817 Ingleside Ave Tallahassee FL 32303 Office: Dept Classics Fla State U Tallahassee FL 32306 Office Phone: 850-644-0300. Fax: 850-644-4073. E-mail: john.marincola@fsu.edu.

MARINE, CLYDE LOCKWOOD, agricultural business consultant; b. Knoxville, Tenn., Dec. 25, 1936; s. Harry H. and Idelle (Larue) M.; m. Eleanor Harb, Aug. 9, 1958; children: Cathleen, Sharon. BS in Agr., U. Tenn., 1958; MS in Agrl. Econs., U. Ill., 1959; PhD in Agrl. Econs., Mich. State U., 1963. Sr. market analyst Pet Milk Co., St. Louis, 1963-64; mgr. market planning agr. chems. div. Mobile Chem. Co., Richmond, Va., 1964-67; mgr. ingredient purchasing Central Soya Co., Ft. Wayne, Ind., 1970-73, corp. economist, 1967-70, v.p. ingredient purchasing, 1973-75, sr. v.p., 1975-90; pres. Marine Assocs., Ft. Wayne, 1991—; bd. dirs. SCAN, 1992—. Mem. agrl. policy adv. com. U.S.D.A. Bd. dirs. Ft. Wayne Fine Arts Found., 1976-79, Ft. Wayne Pub. Transp. Corp., 1975-83, Libr. Found.; commr. Metro Human Rels. Commn.; v.p. Ft. Wayne Philharm., 1974-76. Served with U.S. Army, 1959-60. Mem. Nat. Soybean Processors Assn. (chmn.), U.S. C. of C., Am. Agrl. Econs. Assn., Am. Feed Mfrs. Assn. (chmn. purchasing coun.). Clubs: Ft. Wayne Country. Episcopalian. Office: Marine Assocs 4646 W Jefferson Blvd Fort Wayne IN 46804-6842 Office Phone: 260-436-4180. E-mail: lmarine@attglobal.net.

MARINE, MICHAEL R. healthcare company executive; b. Mar. 12, 1954; BS in Econs. and Pub. Policy, Cornell U., 1976; MPH in Hosp. Adminstrn., Tulane U., 1979. CPA, Md. Asst. dir. reimbursement Georgetown U., Washington, 1988-90; divsn. mgr. Columbia/HCA, Ft. Lauderdale, Fla., 1995-97; CFO Pharmacy Svcs. Group, Ft. Lauderdale, 1999—. Seminar leader Bus. Network, Nashville, 1995—; nat. seminar instr. Optimizing Medicare Reimbursement, 1995—. Home: 16792 Royal Poinciana Dr Fort Lauderdale FL 33326-1541 E-mail: mmarine@rxmail.com.

MARINE, SUSAN SONCHIK, analytical chemist, educator; b. Maple Heights, Ohio, Mar. 10, 1954; d. Stephen Robert and Gloria Ann (Hach) Sonchik; m. Michael David Marine; 1 child, Matthew Robert Marine. BS in Chemistry magna cum laude, John Carroll U., 1975; MS in Analytical Chemistry, Case Western Res. U., 1978, PhD in Phys. Chemistry, 1980. Asst. chemist Horizons Research Inc., Beachwood, Ohio, 1974-75; chemist specialist Standard Oil of Ohio, Warrensville Heights, Ohio, 1975-79; organic chemistry br. mgr. Versar, Inc., Springfield, Va., 1980-83; mgr. gas chromatography program IBM Instruments Inc., Danbury, Conn., 1983-87, radiation safety officer, 1985-87; expert witness, cons. Martin, Craig, Chester & Sonnenschein, Chgo., 1981-83; adv. engr. in advanced lithography IBM Corp., Essex Junction, Vt., 1987-95; vis. assoc. prof. chemistry Centre Coll., Danville, Ky., 1995-98; asst. prof. chemistry and biochemistry, coord. tech. program Miami U., Middletown, Ohio, 1998—2004; spl. term appointment energy sys. divsn. Argonne Nat. Lab., Ill., 2003—; assoc. prof. chemistry and biochemistry, coord. tech. program Miami U., Middletown, Ohio, 2004—. Vis. asst. prof. chemistry and math. Heritage Coll., 1991—92; spkr. in field. Author: African Walking Safari, 1985; editl. adv. bd. Jour. Chromatographic Sci., 1977-93, guest editor, 1987. Mem. Danbury Conservation Commn., 1986-87, tchr. and tutor chemistry, 1985-89, 91-92, 94; troop leader Lake Erie coun. Girl Scouts U.S.A., 1971-80, Southwestern Conn., 1983-87; leader explorer post Cleve. coun. Boy Scouts Am., 1977-78; managerial advisor Jr. Achievement, Warrensville Heights, Ohio, 1977-78; judge State or Regional Sci. Fair, 1977, 80, 89-91, 99, 2000, Odyssey of the Mind, 1994; asst. leader Internat. Folk Dancers, Newtown, Conn., 1985-87; tchr. religion, 1981-84, 87-90, 93-94; mem. sch. bd. John XXIII Elem. Sch., 2004—. Recipient Overall Best Paper award Eastern Analytical Symposium, 1984, First Gas Chromatograph award IBM Instruments Inc., 1985, contbn. award (tech. paper) 10th Internat. Congress of Essential Oils, Flavors, Fragrances, Washington, 1986. Mem. ASTM (exec. com. E-19 1985-2000, chmn. subcom. 1986-2000, vice chmn. arrangements 1994-98), Am. Chem. Soc. (chmn. membership com. Green Mountain sect. 1988-89, chair elect 1989-90, chmn. 1990-91, local coord. Nat. Chemistry Week 1991, 93-98, 2002-04, Phoenix award 1994, 97), Iota Sigma Pi (pres. N.E. Ohio chpt. 1978-79, mem.-at-large fin. mgr. 1993-97, nat. v.p. 1996-99, nat. pres. 1999-2002, immediate past pres. 2002-), No. Vt. Canoe Cruisers (treas. 1990-92), Green Mountain Steppers (sec. 1993-95), Centre Coll. Outdoors Club (faculty liaison 1996-98), Miami U. Middletown Chemistry Club (faculty liaison 2003-04), Phi Theta Kappa (faculty advisor Miami U. Middletown 2004—). Roman Catholic. Avocations: camping, dance, travel. Home: 4667 Sebald Dr Franklin OH 45005-5328 Office: Miami U Middletown 4200 E University Blvd Middletown OH 45042-3458 Business E-Mail: mariness@muohio.edu.

MARINEAU, PHILIP ALBERT, apparel executive; b. Chgo., Oct. 4, 1946; s. Philip Albert and Bernice (Collins) Marineau; m. Susan Anne Graf, June 28, 1969. AB in History, Georgetown U., 1968; MBA, Northwestern U., 1970. Coordinator sales research The Quaker Oats Co., Chgo., 1972-73, mktg. asst., 1973-74, asst. brand mgr., then brand mgr., 1974-78, product group mgr., 1978-80, dir., then v.p. product mgmt., 1980-85, pres. grocery specialties div., 1985-87, exec. v.p. grocery specialties and market devel., 1987-88, exec. v.p. internat. grocery products, 1988, exec. v.p., U.S. grocery products, 1989-93, pres., COO, 1993-96; pres. & CEO Dean Foods Co., 1996, Pepsi-Cola N. America, 1997-99, Levi Strauss & Co., San Francisco, 1999—. Bd. dirs. Travelers and Immigrant Aid, Chgo., 1987; bd. mem. Georgetown Univ.; trustee . Northlight Theatre, Evanston, Ill., 1985. Mem.: Am. Mktg. Assn. (Steuart Hendersen Britt award 1987), Westmoreland Country Club (Wilmette, Ill.). Office: Levi Strauss & Co 1155 Battery St San Francisco CA 94111*

MARINELLI, JANICE, broadcast executive; b. N.Y., 1958; m. Thomas Mazza; 3 children. BS in comm., St. John's U., N.Y. Rsch. analyst TeleRep; sr. rschr. Lorimar TV, Katz TV Group; acct. exec. Buena Vista TV, 1985, dir. sales western divsn., exec. v.p., 1996—99, pres., 1999—. Office: Buena Vista TV 500 S Buena Vista St Burbank CA 91521

MARINELLI, JOSEPH MARCELLO, aerospace advisor; b. Phila., Aug. 15, 1948; s. William Marinelli and Lillian (Nicolena) Navarro. Grad. high sch., Phila. Aerospace advisor Rissler Sci. Orgn., Phila., 1982 . Mem. Air Force Assn. (life), U.S. Naval Inst. (life), Navy League (life), Am. Def. Preparedness Orgn. (life), World Future Soc. (life), Tailhook Assn. (life), Assn. Am. Politics (life), Assn. Naval Aviation (life), Cruiser Olympia Assn. Inc. (life), F-4 Phantom 2 Soc. (life), Am. Aviation Hist. Soc. (life), Nat. Space Soc., Planetary Soc., Nat. Air and Space Soc. Democrat. Roman Catholic. Home: 2141 S 21st St Philadelphia PA 19145-3502

MARINER, WILLIAM MARTIN, chiropractor; b. Balt., Jan. 2, 1949; s. William Joseph and Ellen (Dexter) M. AA, Phoenix Coll., 1976; BS in Biology, D Chiropractic summa cum laude, L.A. Coll. of Chiropractic, 1980; DD (hon.), Universal Life Ch., Modesto, Calif., 1986. Health food restaurant mgr. Golden Temple of Conscious Cookery, Tempe, Ariz., 1974-75; health food store mgr. Guru's Grainery, Phoenix, 1975; physical therapist A.R.E. Clinic, Phoenix, 1975-76; research dir., founder G.R.D. Healing Arts Ctr., Phoenix, 1974-77; aminstrv. asst., acad. dean L.A. Coll. Chiropractic, Whittier, Calif., 1977-80; faculty Calif. Acupuncture Coll., L.A., 1978-80; ednl. cons. Avanti Inst., San Francisco, 1985-91; found, dir., head clinician Pacific Healing Arts Ctr., Del Mar, Calif., 1980-93, Mt. Shasta, Calif., 1993—. Ednl. cons. John Panama Cons., San Francisco, 1991-99. Patentee in field. Co-dir. "We Care We Share" Charitable Orgn., San Diego, 1985-86. Named Outstanding Sr., L.A. Coll. Chiropractic, 1980. Mem. Calif. Chiropractic Assn., Am. Chiropractic Assn., Internat. Coll. Applied Kinesiology, Holistic Dental Assn., Brit. Homopathic Assn. Avocations: yoga, meditation, personal growth, natural healing methods, cooking. Office: Pacific Healing Arts Ctr PO Box 192 Mount Shasta CA 96067-0192 Office Phone: 530-926-6448. Personal E-mail: wmariner@jps.net.

MARINESCU, DAN CRISTIAN, computer sciences educator, consultant; b. Craiova, Dolj, Romania, Mar. 4, 1942; s. Nicolae and Aurelia Marinescu; m. Gabriela Magdalena Sezon; 1 child, Andrei. PhD in EECS, Polytechnic Inst., Bucharest, Romania, 1972—75. Prof. computer sci. Purdue U., West Lafayette, Ind., 1984—2001, U. Ctrl. Florida, Orlando, 2001—02; sr. rschr. GSI, Darmstadt, Fla., Germany, 1980—84, Inst. Atomic Physics, Bucharest, Romania, 1965—79; assoc. prof. Polytechnic Inst., Bucharest, Romania, 1970—79. Vis. prof. INRIA Rocquencourt, Paris, 2000—00, Paris, 1999—99, IBM Rsch., Yorktown Heights, NY, 1985—85, Intel Supercomputer Sys., Portland, 1992—92. Author: Internet-Based Workflow Management, 2002; contbr. articles to profl. jours., 1987. Recipient Grand Challenge, National Science Foundation, 1995-2002, Virtual Lab for Computational Biology, Nat. Sci. Found., 2001—, Workflow Management, 2001—, 3D Reconstruction of Viruses, 2000—. Greek Orthodox. Avocations: skiing, photography, travel. Home: 14449 Dover Forest Dr Orlando FL 32828 Office: Computer Sci Dept UCF 4000 Central Florida Blvd Orlando FL 32816

MARINETTI, GUIDO V. biochemistry educator; b. Rochester, N.Y., June 26, 1918; s. Michael and Nancy (Lippa) M.; m. Antoinette Francione, Sept. 19, 1942; children: Timothy D., Hope L. BS, U. Rochester, 1950, PhD, 1953. Research biochemist Western Regional Lab., Albany, Calif., 1953-54; instr. U. Rochester, N.Y., 1954-57, asst. prof., 1957-60, assoc. prof., 1960-66, prof. sch. medicine and dentistry, 1966—97; prof. emeritus dept biochemistry and biophysics, 1997—. Cons. Eastman Kodak, 1978, Rochester Gas & Electric, 1979 Author: Disorders of Lipid Metabolism, 1990; editor: Lipid Chromatographic Analysis, 3 vols., 1969, 2nd edit., 1976; contbr. 160 pub. articles in sci. jours. Served with USAAF, 1942-46. Recipient Nat. Infantile Paralysis award, 1952; recipient Glycerine Research award, 1957; NSF grantee, 1953; recipient Lederle Med. Faculty award, 1955, 56 Mem. Am. Soc. Biol. Chemists, Am. Chem. Soc., AAAS, Sigma Xi, Phi Beta Kappa Achievements include research in membrane structure and function, biochemistry of phospholipids, phosphatidylinositiol metabolism in isolated synaptomsomes.

MARING, MARY MUEHLEN, state supreme court justice; b. Devils Lake, N.D., July 27, 1951; d. Joseph Edward and Charlotte Rose (Schorr) Muehlen; m. David Scott Maring, Aug. 30, 1975; children: Christopher David, Andrew Joseph. BA in Polit. Sci. summa cum laude, Moorhead State U., 1972; JD, U. N.D., 1975. Bar: Minn., N.D. Law clk. Hon. Bruce Stone, Mpls, 1975-76; assoc. Stefanson, Landberg & Alm, Ltd., Moorhead, Minn., 1976-82, Ohnstad, Twichell, Breitling, Rosenvold, Wanner, Nelson, Neugebauer & Maring, P.C., West Fargo, N.D., 1982-88, Lee Hagan Law Office, Fargo, 1988-91; pvt. practice Maring Law Office, Fargo, 1991-96; justice N.D. State Supreme Ct., Bismarck, ND, 1996—. Women's bd. mem. 1st Nat. Bank, Fargo, 1977-82; career day speaker Moorhead Rotarians, 1980-83. Contbr. note to legal rev.; note editor N.D. Law Rev., 1975. Mem. ABA (del. ann. conv. young lawyers sect. 1981-82, bd. govs. 1982-83), Minn. Women Lawyers, N.D. State Bar Assn. (bd. govs. 1991-93), Clay County Bar Assn. (v.p. 1983-84), N.D. Trial Lawyers Assn. (pres. 1992-93), Internat. Soc. of Barristers, Nat. Assn. of Women Judges (dist. 10 dir. 2001-03). Roman Catholic. Office: ND Supreme Ct 600 E Boulevard Ave Dept 180 Bismarck ND 58505-0530

MARINI, ANN MARIE, medical researcher, educator; b. Stamford, Conn., May 27, 1949; d. Alfred Francis and Theresa Maryann Marini; m. Robert Henry Lipsky, Sept. 6, 1990; 1 child, Sarah. BA, Erskine Coll., 1971; PhD, Georgetown U., 1978, MD, 1980. Diplomate Am. Bd. Internal Medicine, Am. Bd. Psychiatry and Neurology. Med. resident U. Mass., Worcester, 1980-83; neurology resident Albert Einstein Coll. Medicine, Bronx, N.Y., 1983-86; post-doctoral fellow NIH, Bethesda, Md., 1986-93; staff neurologist Dept. Vet. Affairs, Washington, 1993-94; asst. prof. Uniformed Svcs. U. Health Scis., Bethesda, 1994-2001, assoc. prof., 2001—. Mem. Am. Acad. Neurology (tech. and therapeutics subcom. 1994-99), Soc. for Neurosci., Sigma Xi. Office: Uniformed Svcs U Health Scis 4301 Jones Bridge Rd Bethesda MD 20814-4712 Office Phone: 301-295-9686. E-mail: amarini@usuhs.mil.

MARINI, ROBERT CHARLES, environmental engineering executive; b. Quincy, Mass., Sept. 29, 1931; s. Larry and Millie (Cirillo) M.; m. Myrna Lydia Pellegrini, June 26, 1955 (dec. June 1994); children: Debra, Robert Charles, Larry; m. B. Anne Jones, May 27, 1995. BSCE with honors, Northeastern U., 1954, hon. dr., 1997; SMSE, Harvard U., 1955, postgrad. Advanced Mgmt. Program, 1985. Registered profl. engr., Mass., N.Y., Calif., Mich., Va. Jr. engr. Camp Dresser & McKee Inc., Boston, 1955-56, project engr., 1958-64, assoc., 1964-67, ptnr., sr. v.p., 1967-77, pres. environ. engring. div., 1977-82, exec. v.p., 1982-84, pres., 1984-90, CEO, 1989-98, chmn. bd. dirs., 1998—99, vice chmn. bd. dirs., 1999-2001, chmn. emeritus, 2001—. Mem. civil engring. adv. com. Worcester (Mass.) Poly. Inst., 1985-90, U. Mass., 1986-90, U. Tex., Austin, 1989-91, chmn., 1991-92, mem. engring. found. adv. coun., 1991-98; trustee South Shore Savs. Bank, 1990—. Contbr. articles to profl. jours. Dir. nat. coun. Northeastern U., Boston, 1983—, mem. corp. bd., 1983—, bd. overseers, 1985-89, trustee, 1989—; chmn. Leadership Phase Century II Fund, 1989-91, chmn. devel. com., 1991-98, vice chmn. bd. trustees, 1997—; bd. dirs. Mass. Bus. Round Table, 1991-99, vice chmn., 1995-97, chmn., 1997-99. Recipient Disting. Eagle Scout award Boy Scouts Am., 1986, Mass. Patriots award Old Colony Coun., 1998, W. Erwin Story award, 1991, Outstanding Civil Engring. Alumni award Northeastern U., 1992, Outstanding Alumni award, 1993; named Man of Yr., Don Orione, 1999. Fellow ASCE (hon., Opal award 2003), NAE, Boston Soc. Civil Engrs. (hon.); mem. Am. Pub. Works Assn. (Man of Yr. award New Eng. chpt. 1981), Am. Water Works Assn., Mass. Soc. Profl. Engrs. (Young Engr. of Yr. award 1966), Am. Acad. Environ. Engrs. (diplomate, trustee at large 1989-92, v.p. 1992-93, pres.-elect 1993-94, pres. 1994-95, Stanley E. Kappe award 1992), Water Environment Fedn. (hon., N.E. chpt., Founders award 1999), Internat. Assn. Water Pollution Rsch. and Control, Engring. Soc. New Eng. (New Eng. award 1994), Greater Boston C. of C. (bd. dirs. 1997-99), Water Environ. Rsch. Found. (bd. dirs. 1998-2001), Tau Beta Pi, Phi Kappa Phi. Roman Catholic. Home: 1 Nevin Rd Weymouth MA 02190-1610 Office: Camp Dresser & McKee Inc 50 Hampshire St Cambridge MA 02139

MARINIS, THOMAS PAUL, JR., lawyer; b. Jacksonville, Tex., May 31, 1943; s. Thomas Paul and Betty Sue (Garner) M.; m. Lucinda Cruse, June 25, 1969; children: Courtney, Kathryn, Megan. BA, Yale U., 1965; LLB, U. Tex., 1968. Bar: Tex. 1968. Assoc. Vinson & Elkins, Houston, 1969-76, ptnr., 1977—. Bd. dirs. Phoenix House of Tex., Inc., Covenant House Tex. Fellow Tex. Bar Found.; mem. ABA (sec. taxation sect. 1986-87), Houston Country Club, Houston Ctr. Club, Coronado Club. E-mail: tmarinis@velaw.com.

MARINO, DAN, JR., retired professional football player, sports broadcaster; b. Pitts., Sept. 15, 1961; BA in Comm., U. Pitts., 1983. Profl. football player Miami Dolphins, NFL, 1983—99; ret.; co-host Inside the NFL, HBO, 2000—, NFL Today, CBS, 2002—. Film appearance: Ace Ventura: Pet Detective, 1994. Named All-Am. team quarterback, The Sporting News, 1981, Rookie of Yr., 1983, NFL All-Pro team, 1984—86, MVP, Nat. Football League, 1984—85; named to Pro Bowl Team, 1983—87, 1991—92. Achievements include having the NFL career record for most games (12) with 400 or more yards passing; NFL records for most seasons (6) with 4,000 or more yards passing, most seasons (9) with 3,000 or more yards passing, 1984-92; most consecutive games (4) with four or more touchdown passes, 1984; NFL record for lowest percentage (2.03) of passes interecepted by a rookie, 1983; NFL record for most games (17) with four or more touchdown passes, 1984. Office: 1100 Avenue of the Americas New York NY 10036

MARINO, DONALD C. lawyer; b. Mar. 22, 1939; s. Charles and Vera Marino; m. Vinnie A. Carcione, Nov. 6, 1965; 1 child, Justin Michael. BA polit. sci., St. Joseph's U., 1960; JD, Temple U., 1963. Bar: Pa. 1964, US Supreme Ct. 1969. Mem. staff Dist. Atty.'s Office, Phila., 1964—70; counsel Manchel, Lundy & Lessin, Phila., 1970—; spl. counsel Redevelop. Authority Phila., Phila., 1974—77, mem. hearing com. Disciplinary Bd. Supreme Ct. Pa., Pa., 1978—80; chmn., 1980—81; trustee Pop Warner Little Scholars; spl. counsel Phila. Parking Authority, 1980. Served U.S. Army, 1963—64, served USAR, 1964—69. Fellow Am. Bd. Criminal Lawyers. Mem.: Italian-Am. Press, Phila. Trial Lawyers Assn., Pa. Bar Assn., Justinian Soc., Pa. Trial Lawyers Assn., Nat. Assn. Criminal Def. Lawyers, Assn. Trial Lawyers Am., ABA, Fraternal Order of Police, Radio and TV Assn., St. Joseph's Coll. Law Alumni Assn., Temple U. Downtown Club, Temple U. Law Alumni Assn., St. Thomas More Soc., Police Athletic League, Temple U. Assoc., Sons of Italy, Temple U. Varsity Club. Home: 225 S 4th St Apt 306 Philadelphia PA 19106-3817 Office: 8th Floor Robinson Bui Philadelphia PA 19102

MARINO, EUGENE LOUIS, publishing company executive; b. N.Y.C., Jan. 7, 1929; s. Salvatore A. and Florence M. (Casabona) M.; m. Patricia Ryan, Mar. 11, 1948; children: Jeanette, Anthony, John, Eugene III. Student, Columbia U., 1945-48. Credit mgr. Sears, Roebuck Inc., L.I., N.Y., 1951-60; gen. credit mgr. Davison-Paxon div. R.H. Macy, Inc., Atlanta, 1960-63, Grand-Way div. Grand Union Co., N.Y.C., 1963-66; v.p., gen. credit mgr. Consumer Products div. Singer Co., N.Y.C., 1966-75, Grolier, Inc., Danbury, Conn., 1975-90; ret. Officer, v.p., gen. credit mgr., dir. numerous subsidiaries. Recipient Quarter Century cert. Internat. Consumer Credit Assn., 1981. Mem. Mchts. Rsch. Coun., Internat. Consumer Credit Assn., Nat. Assn. Credit Mgmt., Alpha Sigma Phi. Home: 4858 Tivoli Ct Sarasota FL 34235-3653 E-mail: elmarino@comcast.net.

MARINO, IGNAZIO ROBERTO, transplant surgeon, educator, researcher; b. Genoa, Italy, Mar. 10, 1955; s. Pietro Rosario and Valeria (Mazzanti) M.; m. Rossana Parisen-Toldin, Sept. 15, 1990; 1 child, Stefania Valeria. Maturità-Classica, Coll. of Merode, Rome, 1973; MD, Cath. U., Rome, 1979. Diplomate Nat. Bd. Gen. Surgery, Nat. Bd. Vascular Surgery. Intern, then resident Gemelli U. Hosp., Rome, 1979-84; temp. asst. dept. surgery Cath. U., Rome, 1981, asst. prof. surgery, 1983-92; asst. prof. surgery Transplantation Inst. U. Pitts., 1991-95, assoc. prof. surgery Transplantation Inst./, 1995-99; prof. surgery postgrad. Sch. Microsurgery, Exptl. Surgery U. Milan, 1994—; prof. surgery Sch. Medicine U. Perugia, 1994—; attending surgeon U. Pitts. Med. Ctr., Pitts., 1991—2002; assoc. dir. transplant divsn. VA Med. Ctr., Pitts., 1992—2002; attending surgeon Children's Hosp. Pitts., 1993—; prof. surgery Transplantation Inst., U. Pitts., 1999—2002, Thomas Jefferson Med. Coll., Phila., 2002—; dir. divsn. liver transplantation and hepatobiliary surgery Thomas Jefferson U. Hosp., Phila., 2004—. Mem. surg. team 1st and 2d baboon to human liver transplants U. Pitts. Med. Ctr., 1992-93, dir. European med. divsn., 1995-2002; sci. journalist Agenzia Nazionale Stampa Associata, 1992—; nat. ad hoc donations com. United Network for Organ Sharing, 1995—; cons. Nat. Transplant Com. Italy, 1999—; regional com. Organ Procurement Orgn. for Sicily, 1999—; mem. Nat. Tech. Commn. for Informative Campaign on Organ Donation of Italy, 1999—, Nat. Ctr. for Transplantation of Italy, 2000—. Author: New Technique to Avoid the Revascularization Syndrome in Liver Transplantation, 1985 (Ann. prize Italian Soc. Surgery, 86), New Technique in Liver Transplantation, 1996 (De Angelis award, 86); mem. editl. bd.: Clin. Transplantation, Leadership Medica, Transplantation, Jour. Investigative Surgery; contbr. more than 562 sci. articles to profl. jours. Grantee Italian Nat. Coun. Rsch., 1979, 86-93, Gastroenterology Soc., 1988; recipient award Inst. Nazionale Previdenza Dirigenti Aziende Industriali, 1982. Mem. ACS, Am. Soc. Transplantation Surgeons, Am. Soc. Transplant Physicians, Italian Soc. Surgery, Transplantation Soc. (grant 1988), European Soc. for Organ Transplantation, Soc. Surgeons Under 40 (ann. prize 1986), Cell Transplant Soc. (founding mem.), Acad. Surg. Rsch., Soc. Critical Care Medicine, Internat. Liver Transplantation Soc., Italian Order Journalists, Assn. Italian Corrs. in N.Am. (assoc.), Xenotransplantation Club (founding mem.), Internat. Coll. Surgeons, Assn. for Acad. Surgery, Nat. Assn. VA Physicians, Univ. Physician Practice Assn., Xenotransplantation Assn., Am. Assn. for the Study of Liver Diseases. Avocations: reading (history books), sailing, scuba diving, yoga, Annibale (pet cat). Home: Corso Italia 29 Rome 00198 Italy Office: Thomas Jefferson U Ste 605 Coll Bldg 1025 Walnut St Philadelphia PA 19107-5083 Office Phone: 215-955-4845. Business E-Mail: ignazio.marino@jefferson.edu.

MARINO, MICHAEL FRANK, III, lawyer; b. Little Falls, N.Y., Feb. 19, 1948; s. Michael Frank and Betty (Roberts) M.; m. Catherine Viladesau, Aug. 31, 1970 (div. Nov. 1996); m. Ann Buttfield Feb. 15, 1997; children: Michael John, Lisa Kathryn, Matthew Christopher. BS, Cornell U., 1971; JD, Syracuse U., 1974; LLM, Georgetown U., 1982. Bar: D.C. 1975, U.S. Dist. Ct. D.C. 1975, U.S. Ct. Mil. Appeals 1975, N.Y. 1976, U.S. Dist. Ct. (ea. and we. dists.) Va. 1977, U.S. Dist. Ct. Md. 1980, U.S. Ct. Appeals (4th cir.) 1982, Va. 1982, U.S. Ct. Appeals (9th cir.) 1994. Civilian employee head rels. br. Office of the Judge Adv. of the Navy, Washington, 1975-76; spl. asst. to the gen. counsel Office of Sec. of Navy, Washington, 1977; asst. gen. counsel labor and employment Office of the Gen. Counsel of the Navy, Washington, 1978; assoc. Pierson, Ball & Dowd, Washington, 1978-81; ptnr. Boothe, Prichard & Dudley, Fairfax and Mc Lean, Va., 1981-87, McGuire, Woods, Battle & Boothe, Mc Lean, 1987-89, Reed, Smith, Shaw & McClay, N.Y.C., 1989-2000, Hunton & Williams, McLean, Va., 2000—. Labor group head, Washington, Va.; mng. ptnr. McLean Office. Author: Virginia Employer's Guide to Labor Law, 1982; co-author: New York Employer's Guide, 1989, 1992—2001, Florida Labor and Emloyment Law, 2001, Labor Employment Law in Pennsylvania, 1994. Mem. planning com. SMU Multi State labor Law Conf., Dallas; chmn. Arlington (Va.) Chamber Employee Rels. Com.; bd. dirs. Arlington Chamber; mem. Va. Chamber Mgmt. Rels. Com. Richmond, 1980—; bd. dirs. Dan Marino Found. Capt. USMC, 1971-78. Mem.: ABA (labor law com. 1974—), Fairfax Bar Assn. (Pro Bono award 2000), N.Y. Bar Assn. (labor law com. 1974—), Va. Bar Assn. (labor law com. 1974—, sec.-treas. labor law sect. 1995, vice chair 1996—97), D.C. Bar Assn. (labor law com. 1974—). Roman Catholic. Avocations: exercise, boating. Office: Hunton & Williams 1751 Pinnacle Dr Ste 1700 Mc Lean VA 22102-3836 E-mail: mmarino@hunton.com.

MARINO, MIGUEL ANGEL, engineering educator; b. Cienfuegos, Cuba, Nov. 10, 1940; s. Ramon and Julia Marino; m. Irma Padovani, July 27, 1968; 1 child, Raquel Christina. AA, Andrew Coll., 1959; BS, N.Mex. Inst. Mining and Tech., 1962, MS, 1965; PhD, UCLA, 1972. Cert. profl. hydrologist, Am. Inst. Hydrology. Asst. geohydrologist N.Mex. State Engrs. Office, Santa Fe, 1964; asst. hydrologist Ill. State Water Survey, Champaign, 1965-69; from asst. prof. to assoc. prof. U. Calif., Davis, 1972—80, prof., 1980-99, dir. hydrology program, 1996-98, prof. above-scale, 1999—2003, disting. prof., 2003—. Author: Groundwater and Seepage, 1982, Regional Management of Water Resources, 2001, Integrated Water Resources Management, 2001, (monograph) Subsurface Flow and Contamination, 1987; contbr. articles to

profl. jours. Pres./elect Am. Inst. of Hydrology, 2003—05; v.p. Internat. Commn. Water Resources Sys.; bd. dirs. Univs. Coun. Water Resources. Recipient Warren A. Hall medal, Univs. Coun. Water Resources. Fellow: Am. Geophys. Union, Am. Water Resources Assn. (hon.); mem.: ASCE (hon. Outstanding Jour. Paper awards 1986, 1990, Julian Hinds award 1996, Richard R. Torrens award 1986), Internat. Assn. Hydrol. Scis. (Best Paper award), Am. Inst. Hydrology (pres.-elect), Am. Water Resources Assn., N.Y. Acad. Scis., Sigma Xi, Tau Beta Pi. Home: 813 Harrier Pl Davis CA 95616-0173 Office: Univ Calif 139 Veihmeyer Hall Davis CA 95616 Office Phone: 530-752-0684.

MARINO, NANCY A. marketing professional; b. N.Y.C., Aug. 11; d. Thomas and Ruth Firriolo; m. J. Richard Marino. BA in Mktg., Hunter Coll., 1971. Exec. v.p. AMC, N.Y.C., 1990—97; pres., CEO Frederick Atkins, N.Y.C., 1997—99; pres. Linmark, N.Y.C., 1999—2002, SVP Brond Devel. Worldwide Sourcing, 2002—. Bd. dirs. USA-ITA, N.Y.C., Cotton Inc., N.Y.C.; mem. steering com. Fashion Group Internat., N.Y.C., 1999—. Mem. found. bd. Fashion Inst. Tech., N.Y.C., 1999—. Mem.: Retail Mktg. Soc. (bd. dirs. 1998—). Office: 3333 Beverly Dr Hoffman Estates IL 60179 Business E-Mail: nancymarino@earthlink.net.

MARINO, NATALIE MARIE, artist; b. Elizabeth, NJ, July 4, 1951; d. John T. and Stefana (Sarullo) Marino; m. Anthony Paul D'Alessio, Aug. 28, 1968 (div. 1998); 1 child, Stephanie Elsbeth; m. Brian James Blackmore, Mar. 27, 1998; children: Jonathan Brian, Ronnie Marin, Stefana. BA, NYU, 1969; postgrad., New Sch., N.Y.C., 1969-72; cert., N.J. Ctr. Visual Arts, 1977. One-woman shows include Exxon Corp., Linden, NJ, 1985, Florence Gallery, Dallas, 1985, Rosalyn Sailors, Phila., 1993, ART Insights, NY, Marino Galleries, Millburn, NJ, 1994, 96, YMCA Patterson, NJ, 2004; exhibited in group shows at NJ State Mus., 1979, Bergen Cmty. Mus., Paramus, NJ, 1980, Nat. Art Club, NYC, 1981, Lincoln Ctr., NYC, 1983, Cork Art Gallery, NYC, 1983, Phila. Port of History Mus., 1984, others; represented in permanent collections including Rosalyn Sailor Gallery and Mus. Fine Art, Margate, NJ, Phila., Tom Weiner's Art Insights, NYC, Marino Galleries, Inc., Millburn; editor, designer: Once Upon a Star, 2003; illustrator (book) A Place in the Sky, Andrew's Dragon; author: (screenplay) The Successor, 1989; illustrator: Art Lovers Cookbook, 1975, A Place in the Sky, 2003, Tappi Shuffle and Her Shiny Black Tap Shoes, 2003, Andrews Dragon, 2004, Once Upon a Star, 2004; host cablecast series Art Forum; prodr., dir. video and TV programs. Vol. cons. N.J. Ctr. for Visual Arts, Summit, 1989; trustee TV 36, Communities on Cable, Summit, 1989; judge for sr. citizen art shows, Newark, 1989. Recipient Bee Co. award Pastel Soc. Am., 1981, European Banner of Arts, Accademia d'Europa, 1984, award-artists grant Union County Divsn. of Art and Cultural Affairs; N.J. state Coun. for Arts grantee Union County Cultural Commn., 1985-86, Ludwig Vogelstein Found. grantee, 1989. Fellow Artists Equity, Women's Caucus for Art, Riker Hill Art Park (exec. com.); mem. N.J. Ctr. Visual Art (award 1979). Home: PO Box 225 Springfield NJ 07081-0225

MARINO, PAUL MICHAEL, science education educator; b. Hazleton, Pa., Nov. 1, 1945; m. Joan M. Marino, June 12, 1976; children: Kristen, Jeffrey, Jonathan. MEd in Biology, Pa. State U., 1971, MEd in Earth Sci., 1973, PhD, 1976. Lic. tchr., Pa., N.J., N.Y., Mass. Assoc. prof. Del. Valley Coll., Doylestown, Pa., 1992—. Mem. ASCD, Phi Delta Kappa. Office: Del Valley Coll 700 E Butler Ave Doylestown PA 18901-2607

MARINO, THOMAS A. lawyer; AA, Williamsport Area C.C., 1983; BA, Lycoming Coll.; JD, Dickinson U. Assoc. McNemey, Page, Vanderlin & Hall, Williamsport, Pa., 1988—96; dist. atty. Lycoming County, Pa., 1996—2002; U.S. atty. Mid. Dist. Pa., 2002—. Office: PO Box 309 Scranton PA 18501

MARINO, WILLIAM FRANCIS, telecommunications industry executive, consultant; b. Phila., Dec. 28, 1948; s. William F. and Edith Ellen (Dougherty) M.; m. Mary Ellen Klems, Sept. 29, 1979; children: Kiersten Leigh, Meghan Lyn. Student, Ohio State U., 1967; BS in Fin. and Acctg., Widener U., 1970. Sr. acctg., fin. positions U.S. Steel Corp., Pitts., 1970-83; v.p. U.S. Steel Credit Corp., Pitts., 1983-85; dir. fin. programs CIS Corp., Syracuse, N.Y., 1985, v.p. instl. sales, 1986; pres. CIS Credit Corp., Syracuse, N.Y., 1987, v.p. fin., 1988; v.p., chmn. reorganization com. Continental Info. Systems Corp., Syracuse, N.Y., 1989; v.p. fin., CFO ITEC Corp., Lake Bluff, Ill., 1990-91, pres., CEO, 1991—, Global Telecom Svcs. Corp., 2000—. Advisor, cons. Chong & Assocs., N.Y.C., 1989. Advisor Hiawatha coun. Boy Scouts Am., Syracuse, 1987; dir. Cystic Fibrosis Found., Syracuse, 1987-88. Recipient Century award Boy Scouts Am., Syracuse, 1988. Mem. Am. Assn. Equipment Lessors, Am. Mgmt. Assn., Fin. Execs. Inst., Aircraft, Owners & Pilots Assn. Republican. Avocations: flying, cross country skiing. Home: 8763 Muirfield Dr Naples FL 34109-4352 Office: Global Telecom Svcs Corp 8763 Muirfield Dr Naples FL 34109-4352

MARINO, WILLIAM J. insurance executive; Various positions Prudential Ins. Co. Am., 1968-91, Horizon Blue Cross & Blue Shield of N.J., Inc., Newark, 1991-94; pres., CEO Horizon Blue Cross & Blue Shield of NJ Inc, Newark, 1994—. Mem. exec. com. Blue Cross/Blue Shield Assn. (BCBSA), chair Inter-Plan Operating Com. and Emerging Issues of BCBSA, bd. dirs. of Health Insurance Assn. of America, Nat. Inst. for Health Care Mgmt. Trustee, chmn. United Way of Essex and West Hudson, N.J., campaign chmn., 1993-94; chmn., bd. dirs., mem. exec. com. Regional Bus. Partnership; trustee N.J. Network Found., St. Peter's Coll., Newark Mus.; bd. pres. advisors Fairleigh Dickinson U.; mem. chief justice com. on efficiency N.J. Jud. Sys.; past trustee Kessler Inst. for Rehab., Inc. Mem. N.J. State C. of C., past chmn. bd. dirs., exec. com. Blue Cross/Blue Shield Assn. (BCBSA), Inter-Plan Operating Com., mem. Emerging Issues Com. of BCBSA, bd. dirs. Health Insurance Assn. of Amer., Nat. Inst. for Health Care Mgmt. Office: Horizon Blue Cross/Blue Shield NJ Inc 3 Penn Plz E Newark NJ 07105-2245*

MARIO, ERNEST, pharmaceutical company executive; b. Clifton, N.J., June 12, 1938; s. Jerry and Edith (Meijer) M.; m. Mildred Martha Daume, Dec. 10, 1961; children: Christopher Bradley, Gregory Gerald, Jeremy Konrad. BS in Pharmacy, Rutgers U., 1961; MS in Phys. Scis., U. RI., 1963, PhD in Phys. Scis., 1965. Registered pharmacist, R.I., N.Y. Vice pres. mfg. Smith Kline Corp., Phila., 1975-77; v.p. mfg. ops. U.S. Pharm. Co. (divsn. E. R. Squibb), New Brunswick, NJ, 1977-79; v.p., gen. mgr. chem. div. E. R. Squibb, Princeton, NJ, 1979-81; pres. chem. and engring. div., sr. v.p. Squibb Corp., Princeton, 1981-84, v.p., 1984-86; pres., COO Glaxo Inc., 1986-88, chmn., CEO, 1988, chmn., 1989-91; CEO Glaxo Holdings plc, 1989-93, dep. chmn., 1991-93; co-chmn., CEO, Alza Corp., Palo Alto, Calif., 1993-97, chmn., ceo, 1997—. Grad. asst., instr. U. R.I., Kingston, 1961-66; research fellow Inst. Neurol. Diseases, Bethesda, Md., 1963-65. Contbr. articles to profl. jours. Trustee Duke U., Rockefeller U., U. R.I. Found.; mem. pres.'s coun. U. R.I.; chmn. Am. Found. for Pharm. Edn.; bd. dirs. Nat. Found. Infectious Diseases, Pharm. Product Devel., Catalytica Energy Sys., Inc., Cor Therapeutics, SonoSite, Inc., Orchid Bioscis. Office: 25 Haslet Ave Princeton NJ 08540

MARION, ANN, school psychologist, educator; b. Mobile, Ala., Apr. 30, 1936; d. Edmund Charles and Lela Marie (Franklin) Guidroz; m. Donald Orrin Marion, June 25, 1965; children: Janet Marie, Kathryn Elizabeth. BA, Millsaps Coll., Jackson, Miss., 1963; MEd, U. So. Miss., Hattiesburg, 1972. Cert. tchr., cert. sch. psychologist, Miss. Classrm. tchr. Natchez-Adams Sch. Dist., Natchez, Miss., 1963-72, tchr. Title III ESEA, 1967-69, psychometrist, 1969-72, sch. psychologist, 1977-94; ret. Past pres. Mental Health Assn., Adams County Assn. for Child Protection; mem. Gov.'s Criminal Justice Task Force, 1991; bd. dirs. Natchez Child Protection Assn.; mem. craft com. Natchez Career and Tech. Ctr. Mem. Pilgrimage Garden Club, Nat. Rep. Assn., Phi Delta Kappa. Avocations: reading, study groups, bridge, collecting antiques, dollhouses. Home: 105 Mansfield Dr Natchez MS 39120-4930 E-mail: agmarion@netscape.net.

MARION, JOHN MARTIN, information technology educator; b. Fitchburg, Mass., Jan. 11, 1947; s. Don Louis and Violet Pearl Marion; m. Joann Elizabeth Trzcinski, Aug. 8, 1970; children: Benjamin Andrew, Jessica Noelle. BS in Edn., Fitchburg State Coll., 1969, MEd, 1971; postgrad., Pepperdine U. Tchr. Groton (Mass.) Dunstable Regional Schs., 1969-84; computer tchr. Littleton (Mass.) Pub. Schs., 1985-86; computer coord. K-12th grades Newburyport (Mass.) Pub. Schs., 1986-90; assoc. dean Acad. Computing Endicott Coll., Beverly, Mass., 1990—98; dir. tech. Reading (Mass.) Pub. Schs., 1998-00; media tech. specialist Dracut Pub. Schs., Mass., 2000—03; tech. edn. specialist Jefferson County (Colo.) Pub. Sch., 2003—. Instr. Merrimack Edn. Ctr., Chelmsford, Mass., 1980-90; trainer, cons. Logo Computer Sys., Inc., N.Y.C., 1984-90; tchr. trainer Lego-Decta, Lego Sys., Inc., Enfield, Conn., 1987-90; mem. adv. bd. Claris Software Co.; bd. dirs. Mass. Computer Using Educator, 1989-90. Bd. dirs. Reading Cmty. TV, Inc., 1998-99. Fulbright scholar tchr. exch., Southampton, Eng., 1973-74. Mem. Internat. Soc. Tech. in Edn., Phi Delta Kappa. Office: Jeffco Schs 9201 W Columbine Dr Littleton CO 80128 Home: 29191 Shadow Mountain Dr Conifer CO 80433-8612 Personal E-mail: jmarion@aol.com.

MARION, MARJORIE ANNE, English language educator, education consultant; b. Winterset, Iowa, May 6, 1935; d. Virgil Arthur and Marilyn Ruth (Sandy) Hammon; m. Robert H. Marion, Dec. 20, 1964; 1 child, Kathryn Ruth. BA, Colo. Coll., 1958; MA, Purdue U., 1969; postgrad., Inst. Mgmt. Lifelong Edn. Harvard U., 1981. Chairperson English dept. Lincoln-Way H.S., New Lenox, Ill., 1964-68; dir. pub. rels. U. St. Francis, Joliet, Ill., 1966-70, chairperson English dept., 1971-75, chairperson divsn. humanities and fine arts, 1975-79, coord. instrnl. devel., 1979-80, dir. continuing edn., 1980-84, acting v.p. acad. affairs, 1984-85, dean of faculty, 1985-89, assoc. prof. English, 1989-97, dir. Freshman Core Program, 1993-95; dir. Writing Ctr. Joliet, Ill., 1996; prof. emeritus U. St. Francis, Joliet, Ill., 1997—. Cons. to presdl. search U. St. Francis, 2001—02; mem. vis. team North Ctrl. Assn., Joliet and Lockport, Ill., 1975—79; lectr. at ednl. workshops and instns.; condr. writing workshops for adults returning to coll., 1995—; TV and radio appearances regarding lifelong edn., Chgo., St. Louis, Albuquerque, Phoenix, 1982—85; lectr. writing workshops. Author: A Guide to Writing for the Faint at Heart, 1996; author monograph; drama critic Joliet Herald News, 1970-82. Recipient Pres.'s award Coll. St. Francis, 1975. Mem. Am. Assn. Higher Edn., Nat. Coun. Tchrs. of English, Nat. Acad. Advising Assn. Roman Catholic. E-mail: rhmarion@msn.com.

MARION, SHAWN, professional basketball player; b. Waukegan, IL, May 7, 1978; Student, Vincennes U., Ind., UNLV. Player Phoenix Suns, 1999—. Mem. Team USA, Goodwill Games, Brisbane, Australia, 2001, Team USA, World Championships, Indpls., 2002, US Olympic Basketball Team, Athens, Greece, 2004. Named to All-Rookie second team, 2000, NBA All-Star Game, 2003. Achievements include Won Gold medal with team USA, Goodwill Games, 2001. Office: c/o Phoenix Suns 201 E Jefferson St Phoenix AZ 85004

MARIOTTI, STEVE J. entrepreneur, finance educator; b. Ann Arbor, Mich, Aug. 14, 1953; s. John and Nancy Gilbert (Mason) M. BBA, U. Mich., 1975, MBA, 1977; PhD in Bus. and Entrepreneurship (hon.), Johnson & Wales U., 1990. Fin. analyst Ford Motor Co., Dearborn, Mich., 1977-79; pres., founder Mason Import/Export, NYC, 1979-82; spl. edn. tchr. NYC Pub. Sch., 1982-88; pres. Nat. Found. for Tchg. Entrepreneurship, 1988—. Author: Homeboys: Diary of an Inner-City Teacher, 1990; co-author: (with Tony Towle) Entrepreneurship How to Start and Operate a Small Business, 1995, (with Debra DeSalvo and Tony Towle) The Young Entrepreneurs Guide to Starting and Running a Business, 1996; contbr. articles to profl. jour. Recipient Leavey award for Outstanding Achievement in the Field of Free Enterprise Edn., 1985, Best Bus. Tchr. of Year. Nat. Fedn. Ind. Bus., 1988, Entrepreneur of Yr. award NY State in Supporter of Enterpreneurship Inc. mag., 1992, Appel award Price Inst. for Entrepreneurial Studies, 1994. Home: 125 W 12th St New York NY 10011-8269 Office: 120 Wall St Fl 29 New York NY 10005-4001 E-mail: stevem@nfte.com.

MARIS, CHARLES ROBERT, surgeon, otolaryngologist; b. Champaign, Ill., Nov. 24, 1948; s. Harold Franklin and Marjorie Ellen Maris; m. Karen Lynne Richardson, Dec. 27, 1970; children: Katherine, Emily, Charles Jr. BS, Eastern Ill. U., 1971; MD, U. Ill., 1975. Diplomate Am. Bd. Surgery, Am. Bd. Otolaryngology. Resident in otolaryngology U. Nebr. Med. Ctr., Omaha, 1982; chief of surgery Sarah Bush Lincoln Health Ctr., Mattoon, Ill., 1984-85, chmn. exec. com., 1985, 89, 94, chief of staff, 1986, 90, 95; bd. dirs. Carle Found., Urbana, Ill., 1998—. Bd. dirs. 1st Mid-Ill. Bank & Trust. Mem. Charleston Cmty. Unit Dist. #1 Sch. Bd., 1984-88; v.p. fin., pres.-elect Lincoln Trails coun. Boy Scouts Am., pres., 2001-03. Col. USAR, 1990-91, Desert Storm. Named one of Outstanding Young Men in Am., 1985. Fellow ACS, Am. Acad. Otolaryngology-Head and Neck Surgery. Methodist. Office: 200 Lerna Rd S Mattoon IL 61938-9388

MARIS, STEPHEN S. lawyer, educator; b. Dallas, Dec. 19, 1949; children: Shane, Kara. BS, Stephen F. Austin State, 1971; JD, So. Meth. U., 1975. Bar: U.S. Dist. Ct. (no. dist.) Tex. 1975, U.S. Dist. Ct. (ea. dist.) Tex. 1986, U.S. Dist. Ct. (so. dist.) Tex. 1992, U.S. Ct. Appeals (5th cir.) 1980, U.S. Ct. Appeals (11th cir.) 1981, U.S. Supreme Ct. Tex. 1975. Assoc. Passman & Jones, Dallas, 1975-80, ptnr., 1980-87, Fulbright & Jaworski, Dallas, 1987-97, Jenkens & Gilchrist, Dallas, 1997—. Prof. So. Ill. U., 1979-80, So. Meth. U., Dallas, 1980—; mem. faculty Nat. Inst. Trial Advocacy, 1980—. Editor: Southwest Law Journal, 1973-75. Mem. ABA, State Bar Tex., Dallas Bar Assn., Barristers, Order Coif, Phi Delta Phi. Office: Jenkens & Gilchrist 1445 Ross Ave Ste 3200 Dallas TX 75202-2785 E-mail: smaris@jenkens.com.

MARITZ, PHILIP F. (FLIP MARITZ), hotel executive; Grad., Stanford U. Co-founder Maritz, Wolff & Co.; chmn. bd. dirs. Rosewood Hotels & Resorts. Bd. dirs. St. Louis chpt. Salvation Army; bd. dirs. Laumeier Sculpture Pk., Forum for Contemporary Art. Office: Rosewood Corp Office 500 Crescent Ct Ste 300 Dallas TX 75201

MARITZ, W. STEPHEN, marketing professional, service executive; b. St. Louis; BS, Princeton U., 1980. With Maritz Inc., Fenton, Mo., 1983—, dir. sales, 1993—95, vice chmn. bd., 1994—, sr. v.p., 1995—97, pres., COO, 1997—98, CEO, pres., 1998—2001, chmn., CEO, 2001—. Office: Maritz 1375 N Highway Dr Fenton MO 63099

MARIUCCI, ANNE L. real estate development company executive; BA in Accounting/Finance, U. Ariz. In corp. fin. KPMG Peat Marwick, Am. Continental Corp.; v.p. corp. planning & devel. Del Webb Corp., 1982-86, pres, CEO Del Webb Investment Properties, 1986-87, sr. v.p., 1988—.

MARIUCCI, STEVE, professional football coach, former college coach; b. Iron Mountain, Mich., Nov. 4, 1955; m. Gayle Mariucci; 4 children. Football coach No. Mich. U., 1978-79, Calif. State U., Fullerton, 1980-82; asst. head coach U. Louisville, 1983-84; receivers coach Orlando Renegades U.S. Football League, 1985; quality control coach L.A. Rams, 1985; receivers/spl. teams coach U. So. Calif., L.A., 1986, wide receivers/spl. teams coach, 1987-89, quarterbacks coach, offensive coord., 1990-91; quarterbacks coach Green Bay (Wis.) Packers, 1992-95; head coach Golden Bears U. Calif., 1996-98; head coach San Francisco 49ers, 1996—2003, Detroit Lions, 2003—. Office: Detroit Lions Inc 222 Republican Dr Allen Park MI 48101

MARIYA, DEBORAH LUETHJE, minister; b. Long Beach, Calif., Feb. 26, 1953; d. Betty and Keith Luethje; m. Sam John Tangredi, May 21, 1994. BA, Augustana Coll., 1977; MDiv, Garrett-Evangelical Theol. Sem., 1984; D in Ministry, Wesley Theol. Sem., 2003. Ordained United Meth. Ch., 1983. Assoc. pastor Wesley United Meth. Ch., Muscatine, Iowa, 1982—83; pastor Danbury United Meth. Ch. and Oto United Ch. of Christ, Iowa, 1984—86, Dawson-Cooper-Greenbrier United Meth. Chs., Iowa, 1986—90; commd. lt. j.g. USN, 1988, advanced through grades to lt. comdr.; comd. chaplain USS Cape Cod, San Diego, 1990—93; hosp. chaplain, Protestant chapel pastor Nat. Naval Med. Ctr., Bethesda, Md., 1993—95; Protestant chaplain USNS Comfort, Balt., 1993—95; squadron chaplain Amphibious Squadron Five, San Diego, 1995—96; supr. chaplain Command Chaplains Assistance Team, Comdr. Naval Surface Force, U.S. Pacific Fleet, San Diego, 1996—98; comd. chaplain, chapel pastor Naval Security Sta., Washington, 1998—2000; ret. USN, 2000; pastor Chicamuxen (Md.) United Meth. Ch., 2001—; with Joint Mil. Attaché Sch., 2004—. Chaplain CAP, U.S. Air Force, Forest Glen, Md., 1994—. Author: Holy Places: Sacred Sites in Washington, DC and the Surrounding Region. County election ofcl. Bd. Elections, Arlington, Va., 2001—03; elder Iowa ann. conf. United Meth. Ch., 1986; deacon Iowa annual conf., 1983. Decorated Navy and Marine Corps Commendation Medal (five awards) Sec. of the Navy, Armed Forces Expeditionary Medal Sec. of Def., South West Asia Svc. Medal-three awards, Kuwait Liberation Medal Govt. of Saudi Arabia, Kuwaiti Freedom Medal Govt. of Kuwait, Navy and Marine Corps Achievement Medal Sec. of the Navy, Nat. Def. Medal Sec. of Def. Mem.: Balt.-Washington Ann. Conf. of United Meth. Ch., Navy Mut. Aid Assn. (resident dir. 1994—99), Mil. Chaplains Assn., Navy League, Women in Mil. Svc. for Am. Meml. Methodist. Avocation: adventure collector. Home: 2332 Butte Pl Waldorf MD 20603 Office: Chicamuxen United Meth Ch PO Box 2338 La Plata MD 20646 Home: USDAO Athens PSC 108 Box 21 Apo 09842 Personal E-mail: debmariya@aol.com.

MARJANCZYK, JOSEPH ANICETUS, priest; b. Elizabeth, N.J., Apr. 17, 1921; s. Joseph John and Catherine Frances (Cwik) M. BA, Seton Hall U., 1941; MDiv, Darlington Sem., 1975. Ordained priest Roman Cath. Ch., 1945; named monsignor, 1979. Asst. pastor St. Valentine's Ch., Bloomfield, N.J., 1945-72; pastor St. Adalbert's Ch., Elizabeth, 1972-83, Our Lady of Mt. Carmel Ch., Bayonne, N.J., 1983-96; named protonotary apostolic, 1988; vicar episcopal South Hudson Vicariate, 1991—96; prof. Polish Master Sch. Fgn. Langs., Seton Hall U., 1948-60; pastor emeritus Our Lady of Mt. Carmel Ch., Bayonne, 1996—. Chmn. pers. bd. Archdiocese of Newark, 1972-74, mem. pastoral coun., 1972-83, archdiocesan trustee 1975-86; chmn. adminstrv. com., mem. exec. bd. Archdiocesan Pastoral Coun., 1972-84; dean Union County East Deanery, 1975-83; Polish Apostolate rep. Nat. Conf. Cath. Bishops Com. on Migration, 1989-96, chmn. Polish adv. bd. to conf. office for pastoral care of migrants and refugees, 1989-96. Chmn. bd. dirs. Polish Cultural Found., 1974-90, 92-97, 98-2000; trustee Seton Hall U., 1978-96, Immaculate Conception Sem., South Orange, N.J., 1979-86; commr. bd. edn. City of Elizabeth, 1979-83; nat. chaplain Polish Army Vets. Assn. Am., 1980-98; founder, pres. emeritus N.J. chpt. John Paul II Found., 1986-2000; chmn. exec. bd. Polish chapel renovation and rededication Nat. Shrine of Immaculate Conception, Washington, 1986-89. Decorated Gold Order of Merit (Republic of Poland), 1988; recipient Polish Apostolate Pride of Polonia award, 1996; named Canon of Cathedral chpt. Archdiocese Warsaw, Poland, 1995. Mem. Archdiocesan Polish Clergy Soc. (hon. pres. 1979—), Polish Am. Priests Assn. (exec. com. 1991-99), Polish Am. Congress, Polish Am. Hist. Assn., N.J. Hist. Soc., Polish Am. Numis. Assn., Polonians Club, KC. Home: PO Box 456 Point Pleasant NJ 08742-0456

MARK, DANIEL BENJAMIN, cardiologist; b. Boston, Aug. 1, 1953; s. Vernon H. and Alexandra M.; m. M. Lee Cheney. BA, Hampshire Coll., 1974; MD, Tufts U., 1978; MPH, Harvard Sch. of Pub. Health, 1979. Intern U. Va. Hosp., Charlottesville, 1979-80, resident, 1980-82; fellow Duke U. Med. Ctr., Durham, N.C., 1982-85, assoc. in medicine, 1985-86, asst. prof. of medicine, 1987-92, assoc. prof. of medicine, 1993-98, prof. of medicine, 1998—, dir. Outcomes Rsch. and Assessment Group, 1994—. Editor: Am. Heart Jour., 1996—; author: (book) Acute Coronary Care; contbr. articles to numerous profl. jours. and publs. Recipient Rsch. Excellence award Assn. of Pharmacoecons. and Outcomes Rsch., 1997. Fellow: ACP, AHA (rsch. com. 2002—), Am. Soc. Clin. Investigation, Am. Coll. Cardiology (guideline com. AHCPR-NIH Unstable Angina Guideline 1994, database R&D com. 1998—2001, Coronary Stent Consensus Guidelines 2001—02, Exercise Testing Guidelines 2002); mem.: European Soc. Cardiology, Assn. Am. Physicians, Assn. Health Svcs. Rsch., Soc. for Med. Decision Making. Office: Duke Clin Rsch Inst 2400 Pratt Ave Rm 311 Durham NC 27705-3976 E-mail: daniel.mark@duke.edu.

MARK, EDNA BROWN, health facility administrator, writer; b. Burlington, N.C., Aug. 18, 1950; d. Berkeley Herbert and Willie Elizabeth (Long) Brown; m. Bernard Mark, June 3, 1994; children from previous marriage: Daryl Nathaniel Leath, Walter Preston Leath Jr. BS, Kennedy-Western U., Cheyenne, Wyo. Mgr. Hutzel Profl. Bldg., Detroit, 1976—78, U. N.C. Health Care, Chapel Hill, 1978—; author Publish Am., 2004—. Co-chmn. CBA task force U. N.C. Health Care. Author: Sweeping Through the City, 2004, poetry, composer songs. Mem.: N.C. Writer's Network (Chapel Hill chpt.). Baptist. Avocations: philosophy, dance, children's, homeless, diversity advocacy. Home: 35 Lakeside Ave Burlington NC 27217

MARK, HANS MICHAEL, physicist, government official; b. Mannheim, Germany, June 17, 1929; arrived in U.S., 1940, naturalized, 1945; s. Herman Francis and Maria (Schramek) M.; m. Marion G. Thorpe, Jan. 28, 1951; children: Jane H., Rufus J. AB in Physics, U. Calif., Berkeley, 1951; PhD, MIT, 1954; ScD (hon.), Fla. Inst. Tech., 1978; DEng (hon.), Poly. U. NY, 1982, Milw. Sch. Engring., 1991; LHD (hon.), St. Edward's U., 1993. Rsch. assoc. MIT, Cambridge, 1954-55, asst. prof., 1958-60; rsch. physicist Lawrence Radiation Lab. U. Calif., Livermore, 1955-58, 60-69, exptl. physics divsn. leader, 1960-64, assoc. prof. nuc. engring. Berkeley, 1960-66, prof., 1966-69, chmn. dept. nuc. engring., 1964-69, lectr. dept. applied sci. Davis, 1969-73; cons. prof. engring. Stanford (Calif.) U., 1973-84; dir. NASA-Ames Rsch. Ctr., 1969-77; undersec., dir. Nat. Reconnaissance Office USAF, Washington, 1977-79, sec., 1979-81; dep. adminstr. NASA, Washington, 1981-84; chancellor U. Tex. Sys., Austin, 1984-92; prof. aerospace engring. and engring. mechanics U. Tex., Austin, 1988—; dir. defense rsch. and engring. Dept. Def., Washington, 1998-2001. Mem. Pres.'s Adv. Group Sci. and Tech., 1975-76; bd. dirs. Astronautics Corp. Am.; trustee Poly. U., 1984—. Author: (with N.T. Olson) Experiments in Modern Physics, 1966; (with E. Teller and J.S. Foster, Jr.) Power and Security, 1976; (with A. Levine) The Management of Research Institutions, 1983, The Space Station-A Personal Journey, 1987, (with Victor G. Szebehely) Adventures in Celestial Mechanics, 1998; also numerous articles; editor: (with S. Fernbach) Properties of Matter Under Unusual Conditions, 1969; (with Lowell Wood) Energy in Physics, War and Peace, 1988. Recipient Disting. Svc. medal NASA, 1972, 77, medal for exceptional engring. achievement, 1984, Exceptional Civilian Svc. award USAF, 1979, Disting. Pub. Svc. medal, Dept. Def., 1981, 2001, Sec.'s Gold medal Dept. Energy, 2001. Fellow AIAA (hon., Von Karman lectr. astronautics 1992), Am. Phys. Soc.; mem. NAE, Am. Nuc. Soc., Am. Geophys. Union, Coun. Fgn. Rels., Cosmos Club. Achievements include research on nuclear energy levels, nuclear reactions, applications, nuclear energy for practical purposes, atomic flourescence yields, measurement X-rays above atmosphere, spacecraft and experimental aircraft design. Office: U Tex Dept Aerospace Engring/Engr Austin TX 78712 Office Phone: 512-471-5077. Business E-Mail: hmark@mail.utexas.edu.

MARK, HON FONG LOUIE, cytogeneticist, researcher; m. Roger Mark; children: Yvonne, Roger Jr., Seamus. PhD, Brown U. Diplomate Am. Bd. Med. Genetics. Postdoctoral fellow in med. genetics R.I. Hosp., Providence, asst., assoc. dir. cytogenetics, fellow molecular biology, dir. cytogenetics, 1990-99, clin. cytogeneticist Cancer & Leukemia Group B, 1990-99; pres., CEO KRAM Corp., 1994—; dir. cytogenetics dept. Presbyn. Lab. Svcs., Charlotte, NC. Instr. pathology Brown U., Providence, asst. prof. pathology; clin. prof. Brown Med. Sch., 1998—; assoc. mem. Maine Toxicology Inst., 1993—; chair grants rev. com. mem., prenatal diagnosis com., chair cancer genetics com., steering com.; grant reviewer NIH, U.S. Army Breast Cancer Rsch. Program, U.S. Army Prostate Cancer Rsch. Program; reviewer numerous other panels. Author: Medical Cytogenetics, 2000; mem. editl. rev. bd. Applied Cytogenetics, Pathobiology, Exptl. and Molecular Pathology, Cancer Genetics and Cytogenetics; contbr. 180 articles to profl. jours. Recipient award Time Mag. Essay Writing Contest, Balfour award, Award R.I. Found.; NSF rsch. grantee Brown U., co-grantee Dept. Energy; Florence Seibert postdoctoral fellow AAUW Ednl. Found.; North Providence Citizens scholar, Fruithill Jr. Women's Club scholar; others. Fellow Am. Coll. Med. Genetics; mem. AAAS, Am. Soc. Human Genetics, Assn. Genetic Technologists, Sigma Xi.

MARK, JAMES B. D. surgeon, educator; b. Nashville, June 26, 1929; s. Julius and Margaret (Baer) M.; m. Jean Rambar, Feb. 5, 1957; children: Jonathan, Michael, Margaret, Elizabeth, Katherine. BA, Vanderbilt U., 1950, MD, 1953. Intern, resident in gen. and thoracic surgery Yale-New Haven Hosp., 1953-60; instr. to asst. prof. surgery Yale U., 1960-65; assoc. prof. surgery Stanford U., 1965-69, prof., 1969-97, prof. emeritus, 1997—, Johnson

and Johnson prof. surgery, 1978—97, head div. thoracic surgery, 1972-97, assoc. dean clin. affairs, 1988-92; chief staff Stanford U. Hosp., 1988-92. Governing bd. Health Systems Agy., Santa Clara County, 1978-80; sr. Fulbright-Hays fellow, vis. prof. surgery U. Dar es Salaam, Tanzania, 1972-73 Mem. editl. bd.: Jour. Thoracic and Cardiovasc. Surgery, 1986-94, World Jour. Surgery, 1995-2003, The Pharos, 2002-; contbr. numerous articles to sci. jours. Bd. dirs. Stanford U. Hosp., 1992-94. With USPHS, 1955-57. Fellow ACS (pres. No. Calif. chpt. 1980-81), Am. Coll. Chest Physicians (pres. 1994-95); mem. Am. Assn. Thoracic Surgery, Am. Surg. Assn., Western Surg. Assn., Pacific Coast Surg. Assn., Halsted Soc. (pres. 1984), Western Thoracic Surg. Assn. (pres. 1992-93), Calif. Acad. Medicine (pres. 1978), Santa Clara County Med. Soc. (pres. 1976-77), Internat. Surg. Soc. Home: 921 Casanueva Pl Stanford CA 94305-1001 Office: Stanford U Med Ctr CVRB Stanford CA 94305 Office Phone: 650-723-6649. E-mail: jbdm@stanford.edu.

MARK, JONATHAN GREENFIELD, political scientist, educator, writer; b. N.Y.C., Dec. 22, 1948; s. Sidney Carl and Patricia (Greenfield) Mark. BA, U. Tex., Austin, 1971; MA, U. Pa., 1976; PhD, U. Okla., 1981; grad., Indsl. Coll. Armed Forces, 1987. Vice-pres. Stas. KAKC-KBEZ, Tulsa, 1976-80; instr. polit. sci. Tulsa Jr. Coll., 1981-84; admissions liaison officer USAF Acad., 1981—. Vis. lectr. mass comm., 1977; vis. lectr. polit. sci. U. Tulsa, 1977, Air Command and Staff Coll., Montgomery, Ala., 1988; adj. faculty Nat. Def. U., Washington, 1986—2001; mem. DC Congl. Adv. Com. svc. acad. appointments, 1989—; res. asst. to dep. asst. res. affairs Sec. of USAF, Washington, 1989—91; res. asst. Office Asst. Sec. of Def. Res. Affairs, Washington, 1991—2001; sr. assoc. Orion Sci. Sys., Washington, 2002—. Contbr. articles and photography to newspapers including L.A. Herald Examiner, Dallas Morning News, Kansas City Star, Balt. Sun, others. Served to capt. USAF, 1971—75, col. USAFR, 1975—2001. Mem.. Washington Ind. Writers, USAF Assn., Res. Officers Assn.

MARK, JONATHAN I. lawyer; b. N.Y.C., Oct. 18, 1947; s. Sandor and Ruth (Weiss) M.; m. B. Kathleen Munguia, May 25, 1986; children: Ramona G., Sandor A. AB, Dartmouth Coll., 1969, JD, Columbia U., 1974. Bar: N.Y., Calif., U.S. Dist. Ct. (so. and ea. dists.) N.Y., U.S. Ct. Appeals (2d cir.). Law clk. to presiding justice U.S. Dist. Ct. (so. dist.) N.Y., N.Y.C., 1974-75; assoc. Cahill Gordon & Reindel, N.Y.C., 1975-82, ptnr., 1982—. Office: Cahill Gordon & Reindel LLP 80 Pine St Fl 17 New York NY 10005-1790 Office Phone: 212 701-3100. Personal E-mail: jmark58@aol.com.

MARK, JUDI, actress, choreographer; b. Chgo., Mar. 20; d. Leonard and Dorothy March. BS in Edn., So. Ill. U.; postgrad., San Diego State U., U.S. Internat. U. Performing Arts. Dancer U.S. Internat. Dance Theatre, Balboa Park Theatre, San Diego. Founder, choreographer Judi Mark & Co.; dance instr. P.S. 190, N.Y.C., 1986—; elem. schs., tchr. Dade County Schs., 1970-74. Appeared in (stage prodns.) West Side Story, The Rose Tattoo, The Rainmaker, Time and Involvement, (films) Deathtrap, 1982, Turk 182!, 1985, Private Resorts, 1986, (TV) Miami Vice. Mem. AFTRA. Jewish. Avocation: travel.

MARK, LAURENCE MAURICE, film producer; b. N.Y.C., Nov. 22; s. James Mark and Marion Lorraine (Huebner) Green. BA, Wesleyan U., 1971; MA, NYU, 1973. Exec. dir., publicity Paramount Pictures, N.Y.C., 1978-80, v.p., West Coast mktg. L.A., 1980-82, v.p., prodn., 1982-84; exec. v.p., prodn. Twentieth Century Fox, L.A., 1984-86; pres. Laurence Mark Prodns., L.A., 1986—. Exec. prodr.: (films) Black Widow, 1987, My Stepmother is an Alien, 1988, Working Girl, 1988, Mr. Destiny, 1990, Sister Act 2: Back in the Habit, 1993, As Good As It Gets, 1997, (TV) Sweet Bird of Youth, 1989, Oliver Twist, 1997, The Last Laugh, 2000, These Old Broads, 2001; prodr.: (films) Cookie, 1989, True Colors, 1991, One Good Cop, 1991, The Adventures of Huck Finn, 1993, Cutthroat Island, 1995, Tom and Huck, 1995, Jerry Maguire, 1996, Romy and Michele's High School Reunion, 1997, Deep Rising, 1998, The Object of My Affection, 1998, Simon Birch, 1998, Anywhere But Here, 1999, Bicentennial Man, 1999, Hanging Up, 2000, Center Stage, 2000, Finding Forrester, 2000, Glitter, 2001, Riding In Cars With Boys, 2001, I, Robot, 2004; prodr. (theatre) Brooklyn Laundry, 1991, (Broadway) Big, 1996. Mem. Acad. Motion Pictures Arts and Scis. Office: Columbia Pictures Sony Studios 10202 Washington Blvd Culver City CA 90232-3119 Home: 12437 Mulholland Dr Beverly Hills CA 90210-1336

MARK, MELVIN, consulting mechanical engineer, educator; b. St. Paul, Nov. 15, 1922; s. Isadore William and Fannye (Abrahamson) M.; m. Elizabeth J. Wyner, Sept. 9, 1951; children: Jonathan S., David W., Peter B. B.M.E., U. Minn., 1943, MS, 1946; Sc.D. (Teaching, Research fellow), Harvard, 1950. Registered profl. engr., Mass., Minn. Instr. N.D. State U., 1943-44, U. Minn., 1945-47; project mgr. Gen. Electric Co., Lynn., Mass., 1950-52; mgr. Raytheon Co., Wayland, Mass., 1952-56; cons. engr., 1956—; prof. Lowell Technol. Inst., 1957-59, dean faculty, 1959-62; prof. mech. engring. Northeastern U., Boston, 1963-84, dean engring., 1968-79, provost, sr. v.p. for acad. affairs, 1979-84. Vis. lectr. Mass. Inst. Tech., 1955, Brandeis U., 1958; vis. prof. U. Mass., 1984-86; mem. Mass. Bd. Registration of Profl. Engrs. and Land Surveyors, 1990-2001. Author: Thermodynamics: An Auto-Instructional Text, 1967, Concepts of Thermodynamics, 1975, Thermodynamics: Principles and Applications, 1979, Engineering Thermodynamics, 1985; contbr. articles to profl. jours.; patentee in field. Served with USAAF, 1944-45. Recipient prize Lincoln Arc Welding Found., 1947 Hon. fellow ASME (fellow 1948-50); mem. Am. Soc. Engring. Edn., Sigma Xi, Tau Beta Pi, Pi Tau Sigma, Phi Kappa Phi Home: 17 Larch Rd Waban MA 02468-1413 Office: 93 Union St Ste 400 Newton Center MA 02459-2241 E-mail: mel@cartesianinc.com.

MARK, MICHAEL DAVID, lawyer; b. Bklyn., Sept. 16, 1944; s. Irving and Mildred Mark; children: Dana Lynne, Stephanie Lauren. BA, Rutgers U., 1966; JD, U. Tenn., 1969. Bar: Tenn. 1969, N.J. 1970, U.S. Dist. Ct. N.J. 1970, U.S. Supreme Ct. 1973; cert. civil trial atty., N.J. Supreme Ct. 1992. House counsel Liberty Mut. Ins. Co., East Orange, N.J., 1969-71; assoc. Skoloff & Wolfe, Newark, 1971-73; pvt. practice, Union, N.J., 1973—. Past assoc. bd. dirs. United Jersey Bank, Union; Police Benevolent Assn. lawyer City of Linden, N.J., 1980—, Clark Twp., Clark, N.J., 1986; mem. Union-Essex County Early Settlement Panels, Elizabeth and Newark. Mem. Am. Acad. Matrimonial Lawyers (bd. mgrs. 1982—), N.J. Bar Assn., Union County Bar Assn., Union Lawyers Club (past pub. defender). Republican. Avocation: private pilot. Office: 2444 Morris Ave Union NJ 07083-5711

MARK, MICHAEL LAURENCE, retired music educator; b. Schenectady, N.Y., Dec. 1, 1936; s. David and Ruth (Garbowitz) M.; m. Lois Nitekman, Jan. 28, 1942; children: Michelle, Diana. BM, The Cath. U. of Am., 1958, DMA, 1969; MA, George Washington U., 1960; M in Music Edn., U. Mich., 1962. Tchr. Prince George's County, Md. Pub. Schs., 1958-60, 61-66; assoc. prof. music Morgan State U., Balt., 1966-70; supr. music Auburn (N.Y.) Enlarged Sch. Dist., 1970-72; dir. music Elmira (N.Y.) Enlarged Sch. Dist., 1972-73; assoc. prof., sch. music Cath. U. Am., Washington, 1973-81; dean grad. sch., prof. music Towson (Md.) U., 1981-95, prof. music, 1995-98, prof. emeritus, 1998; pres. Spectrum Assocs., Inc. Mem editl. com. five jours. in field. Author: Contemporary Music Education, 1978, 3rd rev. edit., 1996, Source Readings in Music Education History, 1982, 2d edit., 2002; co-author: A History of American Music Education, 1992. Mem. Music Educators Nat. Conf. (numerous coms., Music Educators Hall of Fame), Coll. Music Soc., Md. Music Educators Assn. (pres. 1999-2003). Avocations: travel, woodworking. E-mail: mimark@comcast.net.

MARK, PETER, director, conductor; b. N.Y.C., Oct. 31, 1940; s. Irving and Edna M.; m. Thea Musgrave, Oct. 2, 1971. BA (Woodrow Wilson fellow), Columbia U., 1961; MS, Juilliard Sch. Music, 1963. Prof. music and dramatic art U. Calif., Santa Barbara, 1965-94. Fellow Creative Arts Inst., U. Calif., 1968-69, 71-72; guest condr. Wolf Trap Orch., 1979, N.Y.C. Opera, 1981, L.A. Opera Theater, 1981, Royal Opera House, London, 1982, Hong Kong Philharm. Orch., 1984, Jerusalem Symphony Orch., 1988, Tulsa Opera, 1988, Compania Nacional de Opera, Mexico City, 1989, 92, N.Y. Pops, Carnegie Hall, 1991. Concert violist U.S., S.Am., Europe, 1961-67; artistic dir., condr. Va. Opera, Norfolk, 1975—, art dir., 1978—; condr.: Am. premier of Mary, Queen of Scots (Musgrave), 1978; World premier of A Christmas Carol (Musgrave), 1979, of Harriet, the Woman Called Moses (Musgrave), 1985, of Simon Bolivar (Musgrave), 1984, Porgy and Bess, Buenos Aires, Mexico City and São Paulo, 1992, Orlando Opera co., 1993, Richmond Symphony, 1993, Salome, 1994, Krakow Opera, 1995, Pacific Opera Victoria (Can.), 1996, Cleve. Opera, 1996, Festival Pucciniano-Torre del Lago, Italy, 1996, The Flying Dutchman, 1996, Orfeo et Euridice, 1999, Rodelinda, 2000, Elektra, 2002, Die Walkure, 2002, Andrea Chenier, 2003, Fidelio, 2004. Recipient Elias Lifchey viola award Juilliard Sch. Music, 1963; named hon. citizen of Norfolk (Va.) Mem. Musicians Union, Phi Beta Kappa. Office: Va Opera PO Box 2580 Norfolk VA 23501-2580 E-mail: pmark@vaopera.com.

MARK, REBECCA P. environmental services administrator; BA in Psychology, MA in Internat. Mgmt., Baylor U.; MBA with distinction, Harvard U. From mem. staff to v. chmn. Enron, Houston, 1982—, v. chmn.; chmn., CEO, bd. dirs. Azurix Corp., Houston, 1999—. Office: Azurix Corp 333 Clay St Ste 1000 Houston TX 77002-4000 Fax: 713-345-5290.

MARK, REUBEN, consumer products company executive; b. Jersey City, N.J., Jan. 21, 1939; s. Edward and Libbie (Berman) M.; m. Arlene Slobzian, Jan. 10, 1964; children: Lisa, Peter, Stephen. AB, Middlebury Coll., 1960; MBA, Harvard U., 1963. With Colgate-Palmolive Co., N.Y.C., 1963—, pres., gen. mgr., 1972-73, 1973-74, v.p., gen. mgr. Far East div., 1974-75, v.p., gen. mgr. household products div., 1975-79, group v.p. domestic ops., 1979-81, exec. v.p., 1981-83, chief operating officer, 1983-84, pres., 1983-86, CEO, 1984—, chmn. bd., 1986—. Lectr. Sch. Bus. Adminstrn., U. Conn., 1977 Served with U.S. Army, 1961. Mem. Soap and Detergent Assn. (bd. dirs.), Grocery Mfrs. Am. (dir.), Nat. Exec. Service Corp. Office: Colgate-Palmolive Co 300 Park Ave Fl 8 New York NY 10022-7499*

MARK, RICHARD KUSHAKOW, internist; b. N.Y.C., Feb. 11, 1951; s. Eugene and Gertrude (Kushakow) M.; m. Harriet Bass, Sept. 17, 1989; children: Sabrina, Ari, Etan. BS, Hofstra U., 1972; MD, U. Autonomous Guadalajara, 1976, SUNY, Bklyn., 1977 Diplomate Am. Bd. Internal Medicine. Resident in medicine Maimonides Med. Ctr., Bklyn., 1977-82; clin. instr. medicine Downstate Med. Ctr., Bklyn., 1982-90, asst. prof. medicine, 1990-93; prof. clin. medicine CUNY, 1993—; pvt. practice internal medicine Bklyn., 1982—. Dept. attending emergency Cabrini Med. Ctr., N.Y.C., 1982-84; med. cons. The Lighthouse. Author: Consumer's Guide to Preventive Medicine, 1996. Mem. N.Y.C. Coalition for the Homeless, 1986—, The Children's Fund., N.Y.C., 1990—. Recipient Cmty. Svc. award Borough of Bklyn., 1986, Physicians Recognition award AMA, 1993-97, Preceptorship award ACP, 1996, Tchr. of Yr. Maimonides Clin. Tchg. award CUNY, 1995, 96, 97, 98, 99, 2001, recipient Tchr. of Yr. award, 1982, 83, Citizen of Yr. awrd C.O.C.I.G, 2002. Fellow ACP; mem. Acad. Medicine, Inter-Am. Coll. Medicine, King's County Med. Soc. Democrat. Jewish. Avocations: sailing, photography, skiing. Office: 8023 19th Ave Brooklyn NY 11214-1753

MARK, WAYNE MICHAEL, technical education marketing professional; b. Rochester, N.Y., June 26, 1952; s. Henry S. and Mary (Bucci) M.; m. Peggy Halling, Apr. 1, 1971 (div. Apr. 1987); children: Crystal, Jonathan; m. Janet Louise Richards, Dec. 18, 1987 (div. Aug. 1996); children: Michael, Christopher, Joshua; m. Candace F. Crosnoe, Apr. 18, 1998. Grad. high sch., Rochester. Cert. automotive technician. Mgr. NAPA Auto Parts, Hollywood, Fla., 1970-73, Canandaigua, N.Y., 1973-78, gen. mgr., 1978-80; sales rep. Echlin, Inc., Branford, Conn., 1980-83, tech. tng. specialist, 1983-88, dir. advanced tech. edn., 1988-93, mgr. spl. tng. svcs., 1994-96; mgr. Tech. Tng. Mktg. Svcs., 1996-99; auto group sales mgr. Sierra Internat., Inc., 1999—. Cons. Genuine Parts Co., Atlanta, 1991—, T.H. Pickens Tech. Ctr., Aurora, Colo., 1992-96, Automotive Svc. Excellence, Hampton, Va., 1992—, Internat. Platform Assn., 1994—. Editor, dir, advisor: (video prodn.) Automotive Servicing, 1990, 92, Soc. of Automotive Engineers, 1995—; contbr. editorials to profl. publ. Roman Catholic. Avocations: model railroading, camping, auto restoration, gardening. Office: Sierra Internat Inc 1 Sierra Pl Litchfield IL 62056-3029

MARKARD, MARLENE MARIA, lawyer; b. N.Y.C., Sept. 29, 1971; d. Hildegarde Maria (Von Stehr) Markard; m. Adam Edward Hirshfield, May 6, 2000. Music cert., Mannes Coll. Music, 1989; internat. baccalaureate, UN Internat. Sch., 1989; BA cum laude, Columbia U., 1992; JD, Cardozo Sch. Law, 1998. Bar: N.Y. 1999. Corp. lawyer Camhy Karlinsky & Stein LLP, N.Y.C., 1998—2000, McDermott Will & Emery, N.Y.C., 2000, Greenberg Traurig LLP, N.Y.C., 2000—; lic. real estate broker. Dir. Choices Theatre Project, N.Y.C., 2001—. Author various children's books. Bd. mgrs. Belaire Condominium, N.Y.C., 2002—; mentor Barnard Coll., N.Y.C., 2002—. Mem.: ABA, N.Y. State Bar Assn., Bar Assn. of City of N.Y. Office: Greenberg Traurig LLP 200 Park Ave New York NY 10166 Home: 524 E 72nd St #26E New York NY 10021

MARKEE, DAVID JAMES, university official, education educator; b. Madison, Wis., Oct. 26, 1942; s. Richard L. and Cathrine Ann (Whalen) M.; m. Lou Ann Markee, Aug. 14, 1965; children: Jeffrey, Gregory. BS in English and Geography, U. Wis., Platteville, 1964, MEd in Counseling and Guidance, 1968; PhD in Counseling Psychology, U. Mo., 1974. Tchr. English, Platteville High Sch., 1964-67; asst. dir. residence halls U. Wis., 1967-69; asst. dir. student life U. Mo., Columbia, 1970-71, assoc. dir., 1971-72, dir., 1972-75; prof. edn. U. Wis., Whitewater, 1973-80, asst. chancellor student affairs, 1975-80; prof., v.p. for student svcs. No. Ariz. U., Flagstaff, 1980-94; v.p. instl. advancement, 1994-96; chancellor U. Wis., Platteville, 1996—. Contbr. articles to profl. jours. Pres., bd. dirs. Cath. Social Svcs., Flagstaff, 1983—; bd. dirs. Citizens Against Drug Abuse, Flagstaff, 1987-89, Flagstaff Arboretum, 1988—; chmn. Flagstaff Beautification Commn., 1988-93; co-chair Flagstaff United Way. Recipient Person of Yr. award U. Wis.-Whitewater Student Govt., 1975, Chief Manueleto award Navajo Nation, 1990. Mem. Nat. Assn. Student Pers. Adminstrs. (bd. dirs. 1989-90), Ariz. Assn. Student Pers. Adminstrs. (pres. 1986-87), Kiwanis (Outstanding Mem. award Flagstaff 1983-85), Kappaa Delta Pi. Democrat. Office: U Wis One Univ Plz Platteville WI 53818 E-mail: markee@uwplatt.edu.

MARKEE, KATHERINE MADIGAN, librarian, educator; b. Cleve., Feb. 24, 1931; d. Arthur Alexis and Margaret Elizabeth (Madigan) M. AB, Trinity Coll., Washington, 1953; MA, Columbia U., 1962; MLS, Case Western Res. U., 1968. Employment mgr., br. store tng. supr. The May Co., Cleve., 1965-67; assoc. prof. libr. sci., data bases libr. Purdue U. Libr., West Lafayette, Ind., 1968—, libr. spl. collections, 1996—. Contbr. articles to profl. jours. Mem. ALA, AAUP, Spl. Librs. Assn., Ind. Online Users Group, Sigma Xi (Rsch. Support award 1986). Avocations: photography, sailing, gardening. Office: Purdue U Libr 504 W State St West Lafayette IN 47907-2058 E-mail: kmarkee@purdue.edu.

MARKEE, RICHARD L. retail executive; Degree in Econs., U. Wis. Buyer Famous-Barr May Co.; v.p., divisional mdse. mgr. Target Stores Dayton Hudson Corp.; from v.p., gen. mdse. mgr. Kids "R" Us Divsn. to vice chmn. Toys "R" Us, Inc., Wayne, NJ, 1990—2003, vice chmn., 2003—, pres. U.S. Toy Stores, 2003—. Chmn. bd. Kids in Distressed Situations, Inc., bd. dir. Office: Toys R Us Inc 1 Geoffrey Way Wayne NJ 07470-2030

MARKEL, HOWARD, medical educator; b. Detroit, Apr. 23, 1960; s. Samuel and Bernice Markel; m. Marcia Deborah Gordin, Sept. 20, 1987 (dec. Oct. 1988); m. Kate Gelya Levin, Aug. 17, 1997. AB in English Lit. summa cum laude, U. Mich., 1982, MD cum laude, 1986; PhD in History of Sci., Medicine & Tech., Johns Hopkins U., 1994. Intern, resident Johns Hopkins Hosp. & Sch. Medicine, Balt., 1986-89; asst. prof. pediatrics, communicable diseases U. Mich., Ann Arbor, 1993-98, assoc. prof. pediatrics, communicable diseases, 1998—2002, George E. Wantz prof. history medicine, 2000—, prof. pediat. and communicable diseases, prof. history, 2002—, prof. pub. health, psychiatry, 2004—. Dir. Ctr. for History of Medicine, U. Mich., 1996—. Author: The H.L. Mencken Baby Book, 1990, The Portable Pediatrician, 1992, The Portable Pediatrician, 2nd edit., 2000, The Practical Pediatrician, 1996 (Child Mag. Book of Yr., 1997), Quarantine! East European Jewish Immigrants and the New York City, 1997 (Viseltear prize APHA, 2003), When Germs Travel, 2004. Recipient Nat. Rsch. Svc. award, NIH, 1991, James A. Shannon Dirs. award, 1996, Burroughs Wellcome Fund 40th Ann. History Medicine award, 1996; fellow Clin., Adolescent Medicine & Gen. Pediat. Johns Hopkins Hosp. & Sch. Medicine, 1989—91, History Medicine, 1991—93; scholar Robert Wood Johnson Found., 1996—2000. Fellow: Am. Acad. Pediat.; mem.: Am. Pediat. Soc., Soc. Pediat. Rsch., Am. Assn. History Medicine (exec. coun. 1994—97), Am. Hist. Assn. Democrat. Jewish. Office: U Mich Ctr for History of Medicine 100 Simpson Meml Inst 102 Observatory Ann Arbor MI 48109-0725 Office Phone: 734-647-6914.

MARKEN, WILLIAM RILEY, magazine editor; b. San Jose, Calif., Sept. 2, 1942; s. Harry L. and Emma Catherine (Kraus) M.; m. Marilyn Tonascia, Aug. 30, 1964; children— Catherine, Elizabeth, Michael, Paul Student, Occidental Coll., 1960-62; BA, U. Calif., Berkeley, 1964. Editor-in-chief Sunset Mag., Menlo Park, Calif., 1981-96, eHow.com, 1999-2001, Garden Design Mag., 2001—. Bd. dirs. Calif. Tomorrow, 1979-83; pres. League to Save Lake Tahoe, 1994-97. Avocations: tennis, skiing, basketball.

MARKER, CARL W. diversified financial services company executive; BS in Computer Sci., U. Oreg. Fin. sys. analyst, Mercedes-Benz, Gen. Motors; pres. IMS Capital Mgmt., Portland, Oreg., CIO. Bd. dir. Clackamas County Libr. Found. Mem.: Portland (Oreg.) Soc. Fin. Analysts. Office: IMS Capital Management 8995 SE Otty Rd Portland OR 97266*

MARKER, MARC LINTHACUM, lawyer, investor, entrepreneur; b. Los Angeles, July 19, 1941; s. Clifford Harry and Voris (Linthacum) M.; m. Sandra Vocom, Aug. 29, 1965; children: Victor, Gwendolyn. BA in Econs. and Geography, U. Calif.-Riverside, 1964; JD, U. So. Calif., 1967. Asst. v.p., asst. sec. Security Pacific Nat. Bank, L.A., 1970-73; sr. v.p., chief counsel, sec. Security Pacific Leasing Corp., San Francisco, 1973-92; pres. Security Pacific Leasing Svcs. Corp., San Francisco, 1977-85, dir., 1977-92. Bd. dirs., sec. Voris, Inc., 1973-86; bd. dirs. Refiners Petroleum Corp., 1977-81, Security Pacific Leasing Singapore Ltd., 1983-85, Security Pacific Leasing Can. Ltd., 1989-92; lectr. in field. Served to comdr., USCGR. Mem. ABA, D.C. Bar Assn; Club: Army and Navy. Republican. Lutheran.

MARKERT, CYNTHIA ALLIN, artist; b. Oak Ridge, Tenn., Apr. 7, 1954; d. George Wilbur and Barbara Anderson Allin. BFA in Fine Arts, U. Tenn., 1977. Exhibitions include So. Living Mag. Dream Ho., Atlanta, Bennett Gallery, Alexis Georges, New Orleans, Circa Gallery, Setting the Stage Artspace, Alexandria, Va., DC Space, Washington, Veni Vidi Vici, Zenith Gallery, Fla. Design Mag., Susan Key Gallery, Knoxville, Tenn., Vetrum Gallery, Asheville, NC, Michael B. Tusing Gallery, Staunton, Va., Impeccable Art, Winston Salem, NC, Kress Emporium, Asheville, Hanson Gallery, Knoxville, Studio E Gallery, Jupiter, Fla., Raiford Gallery, Roswell, Ga., C.J. Varnum Gallery, Palm Beach, Fla., archives, Nat. Mus. Women in the Arts, Washington, commns. include, Stanford U. Dept. Lively Arts, No. Ky. U. Dept. Dance, U. Tenn. Dept. Theatre, Pandora's Books, Knoxville, Tenn. Festival Ballet, Tressa'a Jazz Club, Asheville. Office: Markert Du Jour PO box 724 Knoxville TN 37901 Office Phone: 865-523-8696.

MARKERT, MARY LOUISE, pediatrics educator; MD, Duke U., 1982. Dir. Duke General Clinical Research Center Duke U., Durham, NC, 1982, resident, 1982-84, assoc. prof. pediatrics, 1984—, asst. prof immunology; chmn. American Board of Allergy & Immunology, 1998—. Office: Duke U DUMC Box 3010 368 Jones Bldg Durham NC 27710*

MARKESBERY, WILLIAM R. neurology and pathology educator, physician; b. Florence, Ky., Sept. 30, 1932; s. William M. and Sarah E. (Tanner) M.; m. Barbara A. Abram, Sept. 5, 1958; children— Susanne Hartley, Catherine Kendall, Elizabeth Allison BA, U. Ky., 1960; MD with distinction, U. Ky. Med. Coll., 1964. Diplomate Am. Bd. Neurology and Psychiatry Diplomate Am. Bd. Pathology. Intern U. Hosp., Lexington, KY, 1964-65; resident neurology Presbyn. Hosp., N.Y.C., 1965-67; fellow neuropathology Coll. Physicians and Surgeons, Columbia U., N.Y.C., 1967—; asst. prof. pathology, neurology U. Rochester, N.Y., 1969-72; assoc. prof. pathology, neurology U. Ky., Lexington, 1972-77, prof. neurology, pathology, anatomy, 1977—, dir. Ctr. on Aging, 1979—, prof. neurology, pathology, dir., 1977—. Mem. pathology study sect. NIH, Washington, 1982-85, nat. adv. coun. NIH, 1990-94; chmn. Med. Sci. Adv. Bd., Chgo., 1989-94, Nat. Alzheimer's Assn., Chgo., 1985-86, adv. panel on dementia U.S. Congress of Tech., Washington, 1985-86; dir. Alzheimer's Disease Research Ctr., 1985—, Alzheimer's Diseases Program Project Grant, 1984—. Mem. editorial bd. Jour. Neuropathology and Exptl. Neurology, 1983-86, 89—, Neurobiology of Aging, 1986—, Ann. Neurology, 1990—; contbr. numerous articles to profl. jours. With U.S. Army, 1954-56 Recipient Disting. Achievement award Ky. Research Found., Lexington, 1978; named U. Ky. Disting. Alumni prof., 1985, Disting. Research prof., U. Ky., 1977, Disting. Alumni U. Ky. Coll. Medicine, 1993; inductee U. Ky. Disting Alumni, 1989; prin. investigator NIH, Washington, 1977—. Mem. Am. Acad. Neurology, Am. Assn. Neuropathologists (exec. com. 1984-86, pres1991—), Soc. Neurosci., Am. Neurol. Assn., Alpha Omega Alpha. Home: 1555 Tates Creek Rd Lexington KY 40502-2229 Office: U Ky Coll Med Dept Neurology & Pathology 800 Rose St Lexington KY 40536-0001

MARKEY, EDWARD JOHN, congressman; b. Malden, Mass., July 11, 1946; s. John E. and Christine M. (Courtney) M. BA, Boston Coll., 1968, JD, 1972. Bar: Mass. Mem. Mass. Ho. of Reps., 1973-76, U.S. Congress from 7th Mass. dist., 1975—, New Eng. Congl. Caucus, N.E.-Midwest Econ. Advancement Coalition, Dem. Study Group; mem. energy and commerce com. Mem. editorial staff: Boston Coll. Law Rev. Served with USAR, 1968-73. Mem. Mass. Bar Assn. (Mass. Legislator of Year 1975) Clubs: K.C. Democrat. Home: 7 Townsend St Malden MA 02148-6322 Office: US Ho of Reps 2108 Rayburn House Office Bldg Washington DC 20515-0001

MARKEY, HOWARD THOMAS, retired law educator, former federal judge; b. Chgo., Nov. 10, 1920; s. Thomas Joseph and Vera Marie (Dryden) M.; m. Elizabeth Catherine Pelletier, Mar. 17, 1942; children: Jeffrey, Christopher, Thomas (dec.), Jennifer Catherine. JD cum laude, Loyola U., Chgo., 1949; M. Patent Law, John Marshall Law Sch., 1950; LL.D. (hon.), N.Y. Law Sch., 1977, Western State U. 1982, Dickinson Sch. Law, 1982; DSc (hon.), Worcester Poly. Inst., 1982; LL.D. (hon.), Loyola U., Chgo., 1983. Bar: Ill. 1950. Practiced law, Chgo., 1950-72; ptnr. Parker & Carter, 1949-50, then Parker, Markey & Plyer, 1952-72; chief judge U.S. Ct. Customs and Patent Appeals, 1972-82, U.S. Ct. Appeals (fed. cir.), Washington, 1982-91; dean John Marshall Law Sch., Chgo., 1991—. Lectr. on jets, rockets, missiles and space, 1946-50, on U.S. Constn., 1950—; instr. patent law Loyola U., 1970-71. Bd. advisers Loyola U. Sch. Law, 1978— . Served to lt. col. USAAF, 1941-46; to lt. col. USAF, 1950-52; pioneer jet test pilot 1944-46; maj. gen. Res. Decorated Legion of Merit, D.F.C., Soldier's medal, Air medal, Bronze Star (U.S.); Mil. Merit Ulchi medal (Korea); Recipient George Washington Honor medal Freedoms Found., 1964. Fellow Am. Bar Found.; mem. ABA, Fed. Bar Assn., Am. Judicature Soc., Am. Legion (post comdr.), Air Force Assn. (pres. 1960-61, chmn. 1961-62). Republican. Roman Catholic. Office: John Marshall Law Sch 315 S Plymouth Ct Chicago IL 60604-3968

MARKEY, JAMES KEVIN, lawyer; b. Springfield, Ill., July 15, 1956; s. James Owen and Marjorie Jean (Desmeus) M.; m. Allison Markey; children: Lauren, Katherine. BBA with highest honors, U. Notre Dame, 1977; JD cum laude, U. Mich., 1980; MBA, U. Chgo., 1987; LLM in Taxation, DePaul U., 1993. CPA Ill.; bar: Ill. 1980. Assoc. Chapman & Cutler, Chgo., 1980-81; atty. Quaker Oats Co., Chgo., 1981-84; corp. counsel Baxter Healthcare Corp., Deerfield, Ill., 1984-90; v.p. law and other positions Motorola, Inc., Schaumburg, Ill., 1990-2000; v.p., chief counsel-securities and internat. Kellogg Co., Battle Creek, Mich., 2000—. Mem. ABA, Beta Alpha Psi, Beta Gamma Sigma. Avocations: racquetball, running, bridge. Home: 3541 Sandhill Ln Portage MI 49024 Office: 1 Kellogg Sq Battle Creek MI 49017-3534 E-mail: jim.markey@kellogg.com.

MARKEY, MARGARET M. state legislator; m. Charles J. Markey. BS, The Berkeley Sch. Acct. exec. Projects In Knowledge; asst. dir. econ. devel. Queens Borough; dir. Tourism Borough of Queens; assemblywoman N.Y. State, 1998—. Mem. Cmty. Bd. 2, Cmty. Bd. 5, Maspeth Chpt. Kiwanis. Mem.: Daughters of Erin (founder), Am.-Irish Legislators Soc. of N.Y. (treas.). Democrat.

MARKEY, RANDOLPH DAVID, marketing professional; s. Robert Guy and Carol Sogg Markey; m. Molly Clare Sindelar; children: Max, Isabel. MBA, Weatherhead Sch. At Case Western Res. U. Nat. sales mgr. Matrix Essentials, Inc., Cleve., 1990—94; dir., mktg. Bristol-Myers Squibb, 1994—2000; mng. dir. Parkland Group, 2000—03; prin. Capital Acceleration Ptnrs., 2003—. Bd. dirs. Sogg Found., Corp. Bd., OEM Labeling, Inc., LaVar Holdings, Inc.; chmn. bd. dirs. Geotrac, Inc. Contbr. chapters to books. Mem.: Social Venture Ptnrs., Assn. for Corp. Growth, Turnaround Mgmt. Assn.

MARKEY, ROBERT GUY, lawyer; b. Cleveland, Ohio, Feb. 25, 1939; s. Nate and Rhoda (Gross) Markey; m. Nanci Louise Brooks, Aug. 25, 1990; children: Robert Guy, Randolph. AB, Brown U., 1961; JD, Case Western Res., 1964. Bar: Ohio 1964. Ptnr. Baker & Hostetler, Cleve., 1983—. Office: Baker & Hostetler 3200 National City Ctr 1900 E 9th St Ste 3200 Cleveland OH 44114-3475

MARKEY, WILLIAM ALAN, healthcare administrator, consultant; b. Cleve., Dec. 29, 1927; s. Oscar Bennett and Claire (Feldman) M.; m. Irene Nelson, Oct. 31, 1954; children: Janet Ellen Markey-Hisakawa, Suzanne Katherine Markey-Johnson. Student, Case Inst. Tech., 1945—48; BA, U. Mich., 1950; MS, Yale U., 1954. Resident in hosp. adminstrn. Beth Israel Hosp., Boston, 1953-54; asst. dir. Montefiore Hosp., Pitts., 1954-56; asst. adminstr. City of Hope Med. Ctr., Duarte, Calif., 1956-57, adminstrv. dir., 1957-66; assoc. dir. cancer hosp. project, instr. pub. health U. So. Calif. Sch. Medicine, 1966-67, asst. clin. prof. pub. health and cmty. medicine, 1968-70, asst. prof., 1970-75, dep. dir. regional med. programs, 1967-71; adminstr. Health Care Agy., County of San Diego, 1971-74, health svcs. cons., 1974-75; dir. Maricopa County Dept. Health Svcs., Phoenix, 1975-79, cons., 1979-80; adminstr. Sonoma Valley Hosp., Calif., 1980—83. Lectr. pub. health Sch. Pub. Health, UCLA, 1969-74; lectr. cmty. medicine Sch. Medicine, U. Calif., San Diego, 1973-75; cons. LA County Dept. Hosps., 1966-71, cons. Hosp./Health Svcs., 1983—; CEO Chinese Hosp., San Francisco, 1985-86, 90-91; adj. instr. Golden Gate U., 1992-96. Mem. bd. edn. Duarte Unified Sch. Dist., 1967-72, pres., 1970-72; bd. dirs. Hosp. Coun. So. Calif., 1963-67, sec., 1966-67, Duarte Pub. Libr. Assn., 1965-72, Duarte-Bradbury chpt. Am. Field Svc., 1965-72, Duarte-Bradbury Cmty. Chest, 1961-68, Ctrl. Ariz. Health Svcs. Agy., 1975-80, Vis. Nurse Assn. The Redwoods, Santa Rosa, Calif., 1985-86, Sonoma Greens Homeowners Assn., 1990-95, 2002-, Sonoma City Opera, 1987, 93, United Way, Sonoma, 1996—; com. chmn. Sonoma County Bd. Realtors, 1990-92; active Sonoma County Multiple Listing Svc., 1987—; mem. Sonoma County Human Svcs. Commn., 2003-. With AUS, 1950-52. Fellow Am. Coll. Health Care Execs. (life); mem. Am. Hosp. Assn. (life), APHA, Royal Soc. Health, Calif. Hosp. Assn. (trustee 1966-69, dir. 1966-69), Internat. Fedn. Hosps., Hosp. Coun. No. Calif. (dir. 1981-83), Kiwanis, Rotary (past pres. Duarte). Home: 866 Princeton Dr Sonoma CA 95476-4186 Office: PO Box F Sonoma CA 95476-0370 Office Phone: 707-996-2212.

MARKEY, WINSTON ROSCOE, aeronautical engineering educator; b. Buffalo, Sept. 20, 1929; s. Roscoe Irvin and Catherine L. (Higgins) M.; m. Phoebe Anne Sproule, Sept. 10, 1955; children: Karl Richard, Katherine Ilse, Kristina Anne. BS, MIT, 1951, Sc.D., 1956. Engr. MIT, 1951-57, asst. prof., 1957-62, assoc. prof., 1962-66, prof., 1966—, undergrad. officer, 1988-2000, dir. Measurement Systems Lab., 1961-89. Chief scientist USAF, 1964-65, mem. sci. adv. bd., 1966-69 Author: (with J. Hovorka) The Mechanics of Inertial Position and Heading Indication, 1961; Assoc. editor: AIAA Jour, 1963-66. Recipient Exceptional Civilian Service award USAF, 1965 Mem. Sigma Xi, Tau Beta Pi, Gamma Alpha Rho. Home: 11 Edgewood Rd Lexington MA 02420-3501 Office: MIT Bldg 33-208 Cambridge MA 02139 Office Phone: 617-253-2923. Personal E-mail: wrmarkey@earthlink.net.

MARKEZICH, RON, information technology executive; BA in Mgmt. Info. Sys., U. Notre Dame. With electronics and high tech. group Accenture (formerly Andersen Consulting); joined Microsoft, 1998; gen. mgr. fin. and adminstrn. info. tech. Microsoft Info. Tech., gen. mgr. info. tech. client svcs., gen. mgr. global tech. svcs.; CIO Microsoft Corp., Redmond, Wash., 2004—. Office: Microsoft Corp 1 Microsoft Way Redmond WA 98052-8300*

MARKGRAF, J(OHN) HODGE, chemist, educator; b. Cin., Mar. 16, 1930; s. Carl A. and Elizabeth (Hodge) M.; m. Nancy Hart, Apr. 4, 1957; children: Carrie G., Sarah T. AB, Williams Coll., 1952; M.Sc., Yale U., 1954, PhD, 1957; postgrad., U. Munich, W. Ger., 1956-57. Research chemist Procter & Gamble Co., Cin., 1958-59; asst. prof. chemistry Williams Coll., Williamstown, Mass., 1959-65, assoc. prof., 1965-69, prof., 1969-98, Ebenezer Fitch prof. chemistry, 1977-85, 94-98, prof. emeritus, 1998—, provost, 1980-83, v.p. for alumni relations and devel., 1985-94, coll. marshal, 1995-98. Vis. prof. U. Calif., Berkeley, 1964—65, 1968—69, 1976—77, Duke U., 1983—84, 2001, U. Houston, 1999, Williams Coll., 2002—04. Contbr. articles to profl. jours.; patentee in field. NSF sci. faculty fellow, 1964-65; NSF grantee, 1961-63, Am. Chem. Soc.-Petroleum Rsch. Fund grantee, 1965-68, 70-72, 93-95, Merck & Co. grantee, 1967, Rsch. Corp. grantee, 1963, 75, 90-92, Pfizer Inc. grantee, 1996, 97, 98, Camille and Henry Dreyfus Found. grantee, 2000-01, 04—. Mem.: Am. Chem. Soc., Phi Beta Kappa, Sigma Xi. Home: 104 Forest Rd Williamstown MA 01267-2029 Office: Williams College Dept Chemistry Williamstown MA 01267-2692 E-mail: j.hodge.markgraf@williams.edu.

MARKHAM, CHARLES BUCHANAN, retired lawyer; b. Durham, N.C., Sept. 15, 1926; s. Charles Blackwell and Sadie Helen (Hackney) M. AB, Duke U., 1945; postgrad., U. N.C., 1945-46; LL.B., George Washington U., 1951. Bar: D.C. 1951, N.Y. 1961, N.C. 1980, U.S. Ct. Appeals (2d cir.) 1962, U.S. Ct. Appeals (D.C. cir.) 1955, U.S. Supreme Ct. 1964. Reporter Durham Sun, 1945; asst. state editor, editorial writer Charlotte (N.C.) News, 1947-48; dir. publicity and rsch. Young Dem. Clubs Am., Washington, 1948-49, exec. sec., 1949-50; polit. analyst Dem. Senatorial Campaign Com., Washington, 1950-51; spl. atty. IRS, Washington and N.Y.C., 1952-60; assoc. Battle, Fowler, Stokes and Kheel, N.Y.C., 1960-65; dir. rsch. U.S. Equal Employment Opportunity Commn., Washington, 1965-68; dep. asst. sec. U.S. Dept. HUD, Washington, 1969-72; asst. dean Rutgers U. Law Sch., Newark, 1974-76; assoc. prof. law N.C. Central U., Durham, 1976-81, prof. law, 1981-83; mayor City of Durham, 1981-85; ptnr. Markham and Wickham, Durham, 1984-86. Trustee Hist. Preservation Soc. Durham, 1982-86; bd. dirs. Stagville Ctr., 1984-86; mem. Gov.'s Crime Commn., Raleigh, 1985; dep. commr. N.C. Indsl. Commn., Raleigh, 1986-93. Editor: Jobs, Men and Machines: The Problems of Automation, 1964 Mem. Carolina Club, Phi Beta Kappa, Omicron Delta Kappa, Phi Delta Phi, Phi Delta Theta. Republican. Episcopalian. Home: 204 N Dillard St Durham NC 27701-3404

MARKHAM, CHARLES HENRY, neurologist; b. Pasadena, Calif., Dec. 24, 1923; s. Fred Smith and Maziebelle Valeta (Glover) M.; m. Kathleen Tiernan, Sept. 29, 1945 (div. 1971); children: Charles H., Arthur Tiernan, Daphne, James Daniel; m. Lisa Wells Overly, July 10, 1971; children: John Wells, Sara Brennan. Student, Colo. Sch. Mines, 1941-43; AB, Stanford U., 1947, MD, 1951. Intern, med. asst. resident Lane Hosp., San Francisco, 1950-52; fellow in neurology Children's Med. Ctr., Boston, 1952-53; asst. resident Boston City Hosp., 1953-54, chief resident, 1954-55; asst. prof. neurology UCLA Sch. Medicine, 1958-65, assoc. prof., 1965-70, assoc. prof. neurology, 1970-71, prof. neurology, 1971-94, prof. emeritus, 1994—; rsch. prof. dept. psychology U. Calif., Santa Barbara, 1995—. Sci. dir. Dystonia Med. Rsch. Found., Chgo., 1985-94, mem. bd. trustees, 1994—; sci. dir. Hereditary Disease Found., L.A., 1979-81; mem. adv. bd. Am. Parkinson Disease Assn., N.Y.C., 1976-83; attending physician UCLA Sch. Medicine, 1957—, cons. in neurology St. John's Hosp., Santa Monica, Calif., 1960-94. Contbr. articles to profl. jours.; author numerous books and abstracts. Trustee Westlake Sch. for Girls, L.A., 1965-74, St. Matthews Parish Sch., L.A., 1985-87; bd. dirs. Jubilee Christian Acad., 1996-99, Wildling Mus., 1997—, Las Positas Park Found., 1998-2000. With U.S. Army, 1943-45, ETO. Grantee NIH, NASA. Mem. Am. Acad. Neurology, AAAS, Am. Bd. Psychiatry and Neurology, Am. Epilepsy Soc., Am. Neurol. Assn., Am. Pain Soc., Am. Soc. for Gravitational and Space Biology, Bárány Soc. (Hallpike-Nylen prize 1990), Internat. Brain Rsch. Orgn., Internat. League Against Epilepsy, L.A. Soc. Neurology and Psychiatry, N.Y. Acad. Scis., Soc. for Neurosci., Western Inst. on Epilepsy, Rsch. Soc. for Parkinson Disease and Movement Disorders (pres. 1984-2000). Republican. Achievements include research in L-dopa and medical and surgical therapy for Parkinson's disease, dystonia, brain stem mechanisms for vestibular and quick and slow eye movements, long-term exposure to microgravity, space motion sickness.

MARKHAM, CLAIRE AGNES (M. CLARE MARKHAM), retired chemistry educator, consultant; b. New Haven, Aug. 12, 1919; d. James J. and Agnes V. (Manning) M. BA, St. Joseph Coll., West Hartford, Conn., 1940, DHL (hon.), 1989; PhD, Cath. U. Am., 1952. Joined Sisters of Mercy, Roman Cath. Ch., 1940. Tchr. chemistry and math. Sacred Heart H.S., Waterbury, Conn., 1945-49; mem. faculty chemistry St. Joseph Coll., 1952-97, cons. instl. advancement, 1996—, prof. emeritus in chemistry, 1997—. Dept. chair St. Joseph Coll., 1959-70, dean Grad. Sch., 1979-87, asst. to pres. acad. affairs, 1987-95; dir. numerous tchr. insts., 1959-89; mem. vis. faculty Calvin's Lab., NSF, U. Calif., Berkeley, 1967-68. dir. CT Talent Prog., 2002-03. Contbr. articles to profl. jours.; editor sci. series McGraw Hill, 1956-60. Undersec. for Energy, Office of Policy and Mgmt., State of Conn., Hartford, 1977—79; mem. adv. com. Permanent Commn. Status of Women, Hartford, 1995—; mem. adv. coun. Dept. Higher Edn., State of Conn., Hartford, 1970—80; energy advisor Nat. Gov.'s Assn., 1977—79; bd. dirs. Conn. Energy Co-op, 2000—03. Recipient Equity award AAUW, 1992, Sci. Advocacy award, CSTA, 2002, award for outstanding sci. adv. Conn. Sci. Tchrs. Assn., 2002; Faculty fellow NSF, Trondheim, Norway, 1967, Travel grantee, cons., Madras, India, 1974-77. Fellow Conn. Acad. for Edn.; mem. AAAS, Am. Chem. Soc. (councilor 1968-88, chair Conn. Valley sect. 1955-67, 20 Yr. award 1988), Conn. Acad. Sci. and Engring. (founding mem., chair tech. bd. 1994-98), Sigma Xi (sect. chair 1993-95). Democrat. Avocations: photography, music, literature. Home: 1678 Asylum Ave West Hartford CT 06117-2791 Office: St Joseph Coll West Hartford CT 06117 Office Phone: 860-231-6730.

MARKHAM, FRED WILLIAM, JR., medical educator; s. Fred William Markham, Sr. and Muriel Barnes Markham; m. Anne L. duBreuil; children: Elizabeth Anne, Sarah Francis, Meredith Marie. MD, Dartmouth Med. Sch., 1976. Diplomate Pa. Clin. asst. prof. of family medicine Jefferson Med. Coll., Phila., 1992—99, clin. assoc. prof. of family medicine, 1999—. Asst. dir. physician shortage area program Jefferson Med. Coll., Phila., 1996—. Contbr. articles to profl. jours. Personal E-mail: fred.markham@mail.tju.edu.

MARKHAM, IAN STEPHEN, theology studies educator, dean; b. Crediton, England, Sept. 19, 1962; arrived in U.S., 2001; s. Stephen Keith Markham and Beryl Evelyn Walker; m. Lesley Patricia Dunn, July 4, 1987; 1 child, Luke Stephen Austin. BTh, Kings Coll., London, Eng., 1985; MLitt, Cambridge univ., Cambridge, Eng., 1990; PhD ethics, Exeter Devon, Exeter, Eng., 1994. Lectr. in theology Univ. Exeter, Devon, England, 1989—96; prof. of theology and pub. life Liverpool Hope Univ., Liverpool, England, 1996—2001; dean of the seminary, prof. of theology and ethics Hartford Seminary, Conn., 2001—. Coun. mem. and dir. Advertising Standards Authority, London, 1993—99. Author: Plurality and Christian Ethics, 1994, Truth and the Reality of God, 1999; editor: September 11: Religious Perspectives on the causes and Consequences, 2002, Theology of Engagement, 2003. Mem.: Am. Acad. of Religion. Office: Hartford Seminary 77 Sherman St Hartford CT 06105 Office Phone: 860-509-9536.

MARKHAM, J. DAVID, educator, writer, historical consultant; b. Austin, Tex., Dec. 26, 1945; s. James Walter and Myrtle (Sturges) M.; m. Barbara Ann Munson, May 14, 1983. BS, U. Iowa, 1971; MA, U. No. Iowa, 1972; postgrad., So. Ill. U., 1972-74, U. Wis., 1981-82; MEd, Ariz. State U., 1991; postgrad., Fla. State U., 1996—97, Oxford (Eng.) U., 1996. Instr. sociology U. Wis., Fond du Lac/Stevens Point, 1974-76; dir. Vietnam edn. grants Wis. Dept. Vet. Affairs, Madison, 1979-83; coordinator internat. edn. AFSCME, Phoenix, 1983-84; vets. svc. officer Ariz. Vets. Service Commn., Phoenix, 1984-86; asst. to dir. Commn. on Ariz. Environ., Phoenix, 1986-88; div. supr. Ariz. Dept. Liquor Lics. and Control, Phoenix, 1988-89; world history and English tchr. Tolleson Union H.S. Dist., 1990-92; world history tchr. Lake Worth H.S., Palm Beach, Fla., 1992-2000; history tchr. Tumwater H.S., 2000—01, Centralia H.S., 2001—02, Orting HS, 2002—. Instr. sociology and polit. sci., Maricopa C.C. Dist., Phoenix, 1985-91; instr. Palm Beach C.C., 1993-95; pres. Olympia (Wash.) World Affairs Coun. Author: Napoleon's Road to Glory: Triumphs, Defeats and Immortality, 2003, Imperial Glory: The Bulletins of Napoleon's Grande Armée, 2003, Encyclopedia of Leadership, 2004; co-author: Napoleon: The Final Verdict, 1996; contbr. articles to profl. jours.; contbr.: Ency. of Leadership, 2004. Bd. dirs. World Affairs Coun. Ariz., 1987-90; v.p. Ariz. Com. for Bicentennial of the French Revolution, 1988-89; exec. v.p. Napoleonic Alliance, 1996-2003, pres. 2003-; pres. Olympia World Affairs Coun., 2003—. With U.S. Army, 1968-69, Vietnam. Decorated Bronze Star; recipient medal of Landtag of Badden-Württemberg, Germany, 1987, Spl. Svc. award Alliance Francaise of Phoenix, 1992, Marengo medal Province of Alessandria, Italy, 1997, medal City of Ajaccio, Corsica, France, 1997. Fellow Internat. Napoleonic Soc. (exec. v.p. and editor-in-chief 1995—, Legion of Merit 1996); mem. Napoleonic Alliance (exec. v.p. 1992—, editor conf. procs., editor bull., Pres. medal 1998), Inst. on Napoleon and the French Revolution, Western Soc. for French History, Am. Byron Soc., Sierra Club, Population Connection, Alpha Kappa Delta, Phi Kappa Phi, Phi Alpha Theta. Democrat. Avocations: collecting Napoleonic items, writing history, outdoor activities, travel, music. Home: 1841 52nd Way SE Olympia WA 98501-8000 E-mail: imperialglory@comcast.net.

MARKHAM, JOHN THOMAS, social worker, educator; b. Fitchburg, Mass., Jan. 14, 1952; s. John and Marion Markham; m. Catherine M. Marashio, Aug. 26, 1978; 1 child, Colleen. Assoc., Mt. Wachusett C.C., Gardner, Mass., 1975; BASW, Anna Maria Coll., 1981; MSW, Boston Coll., 1985. Clin. social worker Lunenburg (Mass.) Family Therapy Assn., 1981—97, Lipton Cmty. Health Ctr., Fitchburg, Mass., 1989—, Bedrosian Assocs., Leominster, Mass., 1998—; mem. faculty, educator Mt. Wachusett C.C., Gardner, Mass., 1988—. Office: Bedrosian Assocs 1205 Central St Leominster MD

MARKHAM, REED B. education educator, consultant; b. Alhambra, Calif., Feb. 14, 1957; s. John F. and Reeda (Bjarason) M. BA, MA, Brigham Young U., 1982; BS, Regents Coll., 1981, MA, 1982; MPA, U. So. Calif., 1983; MA, UCLA, 1989; PhD, Columbia Pacific U., 1991. Mem. faculty Brigham Young U., Provo, Utah, 1984, Calif. State U., Fullerton and Long Beach, 1984, Northridge, 1985, El Camino Coll., Torrance, Calif., 1986, Orange Coast Coll., Costa Mesa, Calif., 1986, Pasadena (Calif.) Coll., 1986, Fullerton (Calif.) Community Coll., 1986; instr., mem. pub. rels. com. Chaffey (Calif.) Coll., 1986-87; prof., CARES dir. Calif. State Poly. U., Pomona, 1987-98; adj. prof. Calif. State U., L.A., 1992-93, dir. Ctr. for Student Retention, 1995—; prof. East L.A. Coll., 1996-98, Salt Lake C.C., 1998—; adj. prof. Fla. C.C.-Jacksonville, 2004. Rsch. asst. to pres. Ctr. for the Study of Cmty. Coll., 1985; mem. faculty Riverside (Calif.) Coll., 1989-90, Rio Hondo (Calif.) Coll., 1989-90, English Lang. Inst., 1994, Calif. Poly Summer Bridge, 1989-95, East L.A. Coll.; adj. prof. Citrus Coll., 1998—; speechwriter U.S. Supreme Ct., Washington, 1980; cons. gifted children program Johns Hopkins U./Scripps Coll., Claremont, Calif., 1987-88; mem. faculty PACE Program East L.A., 1995-96; faculty East L.A. Coll., 1996-97; adj. prof. U. So. Calif., 1998—; prof. Salt Lake C. C., 1998-99; mem. Pres.'s Coalition for Am. Reads Challenge, 1999; mem. Olympic News Svc. 2002, 2001-. Author: Power Speechwriting, 1983, Power Speaking, 1990, Public Opinion, 1990, Advances in Public Speaking, 1991, Leadership 2000: Success Skills for University Students, 1995, Excellence in Public Speaking, 1997; co-author: Student Retention: Success Models in Higher Education, 1996, Upward Bound Program Grant Proposal, 1996, Making Marriage Magnificent, 1998; editor Trojan in Govt., U. So. Calif., 1983; editl. bd. mem. Edn. Digest, Speaker and Gavel, Innovative Higher End., Pub. Rels. Rev., Nat. Forensic Jour., The Forensic Educator, Clearinghouse for the Contemporary Educator, Hispanic Am. Family Mag.; writer N.Y. times, Christian Sci. Monitor; ednl. columnist San Bernardino (Calif.) Sun., 1992-98. VOICE, 2000-01; contbg. editor Great Lives, 2002, American Lives, 2004. Pres. bd. trustees Regents Coll., 1986; appointed to Pres.'s Coalition for Am. Reads Challenge; mem. Olympic News Svc., 2001—; mem. Coun. Study of Cmty. Colls., 2002—; torchrearer Olympic Winter Games, 2002; unit commr. Boy Scouts of Am., 2002— Mem. Am. Comm. Assn., Doctorate Assn. N.Y. Scholars, Nat. Assn. Pvt. Nontraditional Colls. (accrediting com. 1989—), Pub. Rels. Soc. Am. (dir.-at-large inland empire 1992-93, faculty advisor), Ctr. Study Cmty. Colls. Mem. Lds Ch. Office: Salt Lake CC Comm Dept PO Box 30808 Salt Lake City UT 84130-0808 Office Phone: 801-957-4183. E-mail: rljmar11@aol.com., markhare@slcc.edu.

MARKHAM, SANFORD MAX, obstetrician-gynecologist, educator; b. Pittsburg, Kans., 1934; BS, U. Kans., 1956, MD, 1960. Intern Ind. Med. Ctr., Indpls., 1960-61; resident ob-gyn. Cornell Med. Ctr., N.Y.C., 1963-67; fellow reproductive endocrinology Johns Hopkins Hosp., Balt., 1986-88; prof. ob-gyn. U. Iowa. Hosps. and Clinics, Iowa City. Mem. ACS, AMA, Am. Coll. Ob-Gyn., Am. Soc. for Reproductive Medicine. Office: U Iowa Hosps and Clinics Dept Ob-Gyn 200 Hawkins Dr Iowa City IA 52242-1009 Office Phone: 319-356-2638. Business E-Mail: sanford-markham@uiowa.edu.

MARKIDES, KYRIAKOS SOCRATES, gerontology educator; b. Nicosia, Cyprus, Mar. 21, 1948; arrived in U.S., 1968; s. Socrates and Persoulla Markides; m. Evelyn A. Stanton, Dec. 18, 1971; 1 child, Michael. BA, Bowling Green State U., 1972; MA, La. State U., 1973, PhD, 1976. Asst. prof. U. Tex. Health Sci. Ctr., San Antonio, 1976—82, assoc. prof., 1982—87; prof. U. Tex. Med. Br., Galveston, 1987—, Annie and John Gnitzinger Endowed prof., 1999—. Author (with others): Older Mexican Americans, 1983, Aging and Ethnicity, 1987, Retirement in Industrialized Societies, 1987, Aging and Health, 1989, Aging, Stress and Health, 1989, Minorities, Aging and Health, 1997; mem. editl. bd. The Gerontologist Jour., 1980—, founding editor Jour. of Aging and Health, 1989—. Grantee Rsch. grantee, Nat. Inst. Aging, 1980—, Hogg Found., 1984—, Rockefeller Found. Fellow: Am. Coll. Epidemiology, Gerontol. Soc. Am.; mem.: APHA, Population Assn. Am., Am. Sociol. Assn. Office: Univ Tex Med Branch Galveston TX 77550 Office Phone: 409-772-2551.

MARKIN, DAVID ROBERT, motor company executive; b. N.Y.C., Feb. 16, 1931; s. Morris and Bessie (Markham) M.; children: Sara, John, Christopher, Meredith. BS, Bradley U., 1953. Foreman Checker Motors Corp., Kalamazoo, 1955-57, factory mgr., 1957-62, v.p. sales, 1962-70, pres., 1970—, dir. Bd. dirs. Jackpot Inc. Trustee Kalamazoo Coll. Served to 1st lt. USAF, 1953-55. Mem. Alpha Epsilon Pi Clubs: Standard (Chgo.); Park (Kalamazoo). Home: 2121 Winchell Ave Kalamazoo MI 49008-2205 Office: Checker Motors Corp 2016 N Pitcher St Kalamazoo MI 49007-1894

MARKIN, KAREN MARY, research scientist, journalist; b. Hartford, Conn., Jan. 20, 1957; d. Walter Anthony Markin, Katherine Irene Markin; m. Benjamin Adams Cray, June 6, 1987; 1 child, Colleen Cray. BA, Clark U., 1979; MA, Ohio State U., 1986; PhD, U. N.C., 1993. Reporter The Day, New London, Conn., 1975—85; dir. rsch. devel. U. R.I., Kingston, RI, 1999—. Head law divsn. Assn. for Edn. in Journalism and Mass Comm., Columbia, SC, 2004—; dir. Ctr. for Humanities U. R.I., Kingston, 2001; proposal reviewer NSF, Arlington, 1999—2004, U.S. Dept. Edn., Washington, 1998—2001. Author: (govt. publ.): Ballot Access, volumes 2-4, 1995. V.p. program AAUW, Middletown, RI, 1997—99, pres. Westerly, RI; program panelist AAUW Ednl. Found., 2002—. Mem.: Soc. Rsch. Adminstrs., Nat. Coun. Univ. Rsch. Adminstrs., Internat. Comm. Assn. Office: Univ Rhode Island Rsch Office 70 Lower College Rd Kingston RI 02881

MARKIN, KARL EDWARD, obstetrician/gynecologist; b. Rochester, N.Y., 1929; MD, SUNY Syracuse, 1955. Diplomate Am. Bd. Ob-Gyn. Intern, resident pathology Ea. Maine Gen. Hosp., Bangor, 1955-56; resident ob-gyn St. Mary's Hosp., Rochester, N.Y., 1958-61; ob-gyn Selah, Wash., 1961—; lectr. medex program U. Wash. Med. Sch., 2002—. Fellow Am. Coll. Ob-Gyn, Am. Fertility Soc.; mem. YCMS, Ducks Unltd., Pheasants Forever, Mule Deer Found., Safari Club Internat. (pres. ctrl. Wash. chpt., chmn. Amazon Project). Home: 181 Reitmeier Ln Selah WA 98942-8713 Office Phone: 509-697-3913.

MARKING, T(HEODORE) JOSEPH, JR., transportation and urban planner; b. June 28, 1945; s. Theodore Joseph and Alvena Cecilia (Thieman) M.; m. Kathy K. Hagerman, Nov. 25, 1969. BA, So. Ill. U., 1967, M City and Regional Planning, 1972. Intelligence rsch. specialist Def. Intelligence Agy., Washington, 1967-68; planner I St. Louis City Plan Commn., 1970; transp. planner Alan M. Voorhees & Assocs., St. Louis, 1970-74, sr. transp. planner, 1974-78, assoc., 1978; sr. transp. planner Booker Assocs, Inc., St. Louis, 1978-80, chief traffic and transp. sect., 1980-85; mgr. transit planning East-West Gateway Coord. Coun., St. Louis, 1985-88; mgr. planning dept. Harland Bartholomew & Assocs., St. Louis, 1988-91; sr. transp. planner Burns & Mcdonnell Engring. Co., St. Louis, 1992-95, PB Booker Assoc. Inc., St. Louis, 1996-98, Parsons Brinckerhoff, St. Louis, 1998—2002; sr. project mgr. Econ. Devel. Resources, St. Louis, 2002—04; geospatial analyst Nat. Geospatial-Intelligence Agy., St. Louis, 2004—. Planner-in-charge, Mo.; guest lectr. St. Louis C.C. Dist., Webster U., St. Louis U. Mem. am. Inst. Cert. Planners (charter), Am. Planning Assn. (charter, treas. transp. planning divsn., past pres., pres., sec., bd. dirs. St. Louis sect.), Inst. Transp. Engrs., Traffic Engrs. Assn. Met. St. Louis (past pres.), Transp. Rsch. Bd. Office: 3200 S 2d St Saint Louis MO 63118 Personal E-mail: tjtransit@aol.com.

MARKISON, BRIAN, pharmaceutical executive; Pres. Bristol-Myers Squibb's Oncology, Virology and Oncology Therapeutics; COO King Pharm., Briston, Tenn., 2004, acting pres. & CEO, 2004—. Office: King Pharmaceuticals Inc 501 Fifth St Bristol TN 37620

MARKKULA, A.C., JR., entrepreneur, computer company executive; Co-founder, former pres., chief exec. officer Apple Computer Inc., now chmn. bd. dirs.; founder, vice chmn. Echelon, Los Gatos, Calif.; with ACM Investments, Woodside. Office: ACM Investments PO Box 620170 Woodside CA 94062-0170

MARKLAND, FRANCIS SWABY, JR., biochemist, educator; b. Phila., Jan. 15, 1936; s. Francis Swaby Sr. and Willie Lawrence (Averritt) M.; m. Barbara Blake, Jun. 27, 1959 - April 5, 1996; children: Cathleen Blake, Francis Swaby IV. BS, Pa. State U., 1957; PhD, Johns Hopkins U., 1964. Postdoctoral fellow UCLA, 1964-66, asst. prof. biochemistry, 1966-73; vis. asst. prof. U. So. Calif., Los Angeles, 1973-74, assoc. prof., 1974-83, prof., 1983—, acting chmn. dept. biochemistry, 1986-88, vice-chmn., 1988-92. Cons. Clin. Lab. Med. Group, LA, 1977-88, Cortech, Inc., Denver, 1983-88, Maret Corp., Wayne, Pa., 1996-2000; founder Pivotal BioScis., Inc., 2003-; mem. biochem., endocrinology study sect. NIH, 1986-90, mem FLAIR prog., rev. NIH NCI, 2002-2003. Contbg. editor: Toxicon, Jour. Natural Toxins; contbr. articles to profl. jours.:. Mem. Angeles Choral, L.A. Capt. USNR, 1957-59, ret. Recipient NIH rsch. career devel. award USPHS, NIH, 1968-73; rsch. grantee Nat. Cancer Inst., 1979-86, 91-93, Nat. Heart Lung and Blood Inst., 1984-88, 95-2002, State of Calif. Breast Cancer Rsch. Program, 1995-2002, State Calif. Cancer Rsch. Program, 2000-03, U.S. Army Prostate Cancer Rsch. Program, 2004—, Komen Found., 2004—; fellow study sec. reviewer Western region Am. Heart Assn., 2003— . Mem. AAAS, Am. Soc. Biochem. and Molecular Biology, Am. Chem. Soc., Internat. Soc. on Toxinology, Internat. Soc. on Thrombosis and Haemostasis (subcom. exogenous hemostatic factors, chair 1994-96, co-chair 1999-2003), Am. Assn. Cancer Rsch., Am. Soc. Hematology, Sigma Xi, Alpha Zeta. Avocations: singing, skiing, aerobics, golf. Office: U So Calif Keck Sch Medicine Cancer Rsch Lab Rm 106 1303 N Mission Rd Los Angeles CA 90033-1020 Office Phone: 323-224-7981. E-mail: markland@usc.edu.

MARKLE, CHERI VIRGINIA CUMMINS, nurse; b. N.Y.C., Nov. 22, 1936; d. Brainard Lyle and Mildred (Schwab) Cummins; m. John Markle, Aug. 26, 1961 (dec. 1962); 1 child, Kellianne. RN, Ind. State U. and Union Hosp., 1959; BS in Rehab. Edn., Wright State U., 1975; BSN, Capital U., 1987; postgrad. in nursing adminstrn., Wright State U., 1987-89; MS, Calif. Coll. Health Sci. Administration, 1994; postgrad., Columbia Pacific U., 1996-2000. Cert. clin. hypnotherapist Nat. Guild Hypnotherapists. Coordinator Dayton (Ohio) Children's Psychiat. Hosp., 1962-75; dir. nursing Stillwater Health Ctr., Dayton, 1975-76; rehab. cons. Fairborn, Ohio, 1976-91, N.Y.C.; sr. supr. VA, Dayton, 1977-85, nurse coord. alcohol rehab., 1985-86; DON Odd Fellows, Springfield, Ohio, 1987-88, Miami Christel Manor, Miamisburg, Ohio, 1988-99; DON, rehab. cons. NMS Tng. Sys., Dayton, 1989-91. Psychiat. nurse VA Med. Ctr., N.Y. Rehab., 1991, mem. com. women vets., 1991-93; advisor Calif. Coll. Health Sci. Newspaper columnist Golden Times, Clark County. Bd. dirs. Temple Universal Judaism, 1992, 97; mem. Town and Village Synagogue, 1999—. 1st lt. USAF, 1959-61. Mem. ANA (cert. adminstrn. 1983, cert. gerontology 1984), AAUW, Nurse Mgrs. Assembly, Gerontol. Nurse Assembly, Rehab. Soc., Nat. Guild Hypnotherapists, Internat. Assn. Counselors and Therapists, Nat. Coun. Jewish Women, Jewish War Vets. (sr. vice comdr. Post 1), Wright State U. Alumni Assn., Am. Legion (life), Hadassah, Women's City Club N.Y., Gilbert and Sullivan Soc., Internat. Consortium Parse Scholars, Alpha Sigma Alpha, Sigma Theta Tau. Democrat. Jewish. Avocations: cats, reading, music, needlecrafts, swimming, grandchildren. E-mail: cherimarklern@yahoo.com.

MARKLE, JOHN, JR., lawyer; b. Allentown, Pa., July 20, 1931; s. John Markle II and Pauline (Powers) Mulligan; m. Mary B. McLean, Apr. 19, 1952 (div. Apr. 1990); children: Ellen, John III, Patricia, Stephen, Mary; m. Kathryn E. Wheeler, July 14, 1990. Grad., The Hill Sch., Pottstown, Pa., 1949; BA, Yale U., 1953; LLB, Harvard Law Sch., 1958. Bar: Pa. 1959, U.S. Dist. Ct. (ea. dist.) Pa. 1959, U.S. Supreme Ct. 1980, U.S. Ct. Appeals (3d cir.) 1973. Assoc. Drinker Biddle & Reath, Phila., 1958-64, ptnr., 1964-97, counsel, 1997-2000. Chmn. Pa. Labor Rels. Bd., 1996—; bd. dirs. Main Line Health. Contbg. editor: The Developing Labor Law, 1976—. Bd. dirs. Paoli (Pa.) Meml. Hosp. Found., 1982—, chmn., 1995—2000; bd. dirs. The Hill Sch., Pottstown, Pa., 1970—, chmn., 1985—93. Lt. col. USMC, 1950—73. Named Most Outstanding Young Rep. (Pa.), 1966. Mem. ABA, Pa. Bar Assn., Am. Arbitration Assn., Coll. Labor and Employment Lawyers, Yale Club (Phila.), Merion Golf Club, Ekwanok Country Club. Republican. Avocations: golf, photography. Home: 205 Cambridge Chase Exton PA 19341-3137 Office: Drinker Biddle & Reath 1000 Westlakes Dr Ste 300 Berwyn PA 19312-2409 E-mail: jackmarkle@prodigy.net., marklej@dbr.com.

MARKLE, SANDRA, publishing company executive; 7th grade sci. tchr., Ohio; pres. CompuQuest, Inc., Bartlett, Ill. Office: CompuQuest Inc 366 S Main St Bartlett IL 60103-4423

MARKMAN, JON, business journalist; Grad., Duke U., Columbia U. Grad. Sch. Journalism. Editor, investments columnist, investigative reporter LA Times, 1984—97; mng. editor, columnist MSN Money, 1997—2002; co-portfolio mgr. Helios Equity Fund, LLC; sr. investment strategist Pinnacle Investment Advisors, LLC; editor, founder StockTactics Advisor, 2002—. Author: Swing Trading, Online Investing. Recipient award, Soc. Profl. Journalists, 2001, Gerald Loeb award for disting. fin. journalism, 2002. Office: Pinnacle Investment Advisors 206 S Fourth Ave Ann Arbor MI 48104 Office Phone: 734-662-1746. Office Fax: 734-662-5299.

MARKMAN, RONALD, artist, educator; b. Bronx, N.Y., May 29, 1931; s. Julius and Mildred (Berkowitz) M.; m. Barbara Miller, Sept. 12, 1959; 1 dau., Ericka Elizabeth. B.F.A., Yale U., 1957, M.F.A., 1959. Instr. Art Inst. Chgo., 1960-64; prof. fine arts Ind. U., 1964—. Color cons. Hallmark Card Co., 1959-60 One-man shows Kanegis Gallery, 1959, Reed Coll., 1966, Terry Dintenfass Gallery, 1965, 66, 68, 70, 76, 79, 82, 85, The Gallery, Bloomington, Ind., 1972, 79, Indpls. Mus., 1974, Tyler Sch. Art, Phila., 1976, Franklin Coll., 1980, Dart Gallery, Chgo., 1981, Patrick King Gallery, Indpls., 1983, 86, John Heron Gallery, Indpls., 1985, New Harmony Gallery, 1985; two-man show Dintenfass Gallery, 1984; group shows include Kanegis Gallery, Boston, 1958, 60, 61, Boston Arts Festival, 1959, 60, Mus. Modern Art, 1959, 66, Whitney Mus., N.Y.C., 1960, Art Inst. Chgo., 1964, Gallery 99, Miami, Fla., 1966, Ball State Coll., 1966, Butler Inst., 1967, Indpls. Mus., 1968, 69, 72, 74, Phoenix Gallery, N.Y.C., 1970, Harvard U., 1974, Skidmore Coll., 1975, Am. Acad. Arts and Letters, 1977, 89, Tuthill-Gimprich Gallery, N.Y.C., 1980, Patrick King Gallery, 1988, numerous others; represented in permanent collections Met. Mus. Art, Mus. Modern Art, Art Inst. Chgo., Library of Congress, Cin. Art Mus., Bklyn. Mus., Ark. Art Center, others; commns. include 5 murals Riley Children's Hosp., Indpls., 1986; installation Evanston (Ill.) Art Ctr., 1989, 2-part installation Ortho Child Care Ctr., Raritan, N.J., 1991; illustrator Acid and Basics-A Guide to Acid-Base Physiology, 1992. Served with U.S. Army, 1952-54. Recipient Ind. Arts Commn. award, 1990, 93; Fulbright grantee, Italy, 1962, grantee Ctr. for New TV, Chgo., 1992; Lilly Endowment fellow, 1989, honorable mention, Ohio Film Festival, 1995. Home and Office: 1623 Saint Margarets Rd Annapolis MD 21401-5540 Office: Ind U Dept Fine Arts Bloomington IN 47401

MARKMAN, SHERMAN, investment banker, venture capitalist, financial consultant; b. Denver, Aug. 21, 1920; s. Abe and Julia (Rosen) M.; m. Paula Elaine Henderson; children: S. Michael, Joan, Lori. Student, So. Meth. U., 1962-64. V.p. Lester's Inc., Oklahoma City, 1940-59; exec. v.p. Besco Enterprises, San Francisco, 1960-61; sr. v.p. Zale Corp., Dallas, 1962-69; pres. CAC Fin. Group, Dallas, 1965; pres., CEO Zale Leased Jewelry divsn., 1965-69; CEO Designcraft Industries, N.Y.C., 1969-75, Tex. Internat. Export Co., Dallas, 1975—. Fin. advisor Vocat. Video, Huntington, N.Y., Consol. Transplant Network, Metairie, La., Thera-Test Diagnostic Labs., Chgo., Kemper Mil. Acad., Boonville, Mo., Soft-Trac Info. Systems, Jasper, Ala.; fin. project analyst, AFL-CIO; client referal arrangement The Dai-Ichi Kangyo Bank, Ltd.; former cons. Homecare Mgmt., Ronkonkoma, N.Y., Credicorp, Chgo., The Windy City Group, Chgo.; charter mem. N.Y. Ins. Exch.; guest lectr. fin. risk confs., 1982—, spkr. Am. Real Estate Investment Conf., London, 1986; pres., CEO The Markman Fin. Orgn., Dallas, 1975—. Contbr. articles to profl. jours. Vol. social worker Presbyn. Hosp., Dallas; mem. Dallas Coun. World Affairs, 1962—; active NCCJ. With USMCR, 1942-45, PTO. Mem. Press Club, City Club (Dallas), India Temple Club (Oklahoma City), L.A. Athletic Club, Columbian Golf and Country Club, Young Men's Philanthropic League (N.Y.C.). Address: 3013 W Country Hill Dr Tucson AZ 85742 E-mail: shermanmarkman@aol.com.

MARKMAN, STEPHEN J. state supreme court justice; b. Detroit, June 4, 1949; s. Julius and Pauline Markman; m. Mary Kathleen Sites, Aug. 25, 1974; children: James, Charles. BA, Duke U., 1971; JD, U. Cin., 1974. Legis. asst. to Rep. Edward Hutchinson, Mich., 1975, Rep. Tom Hagedorn, Minn., 1976—78; chief counsel, staff dir. subcom. on constn. Senate Com. on Judiciary, 1978—85, dep. chief counsel, 1983; asst. atty. gen. Office Legal Policy, Dept. Justice, Washington, 1985-89; U.S. atty. U.S. Dept. Justice, Detroit, 1989-93; mem. Miller, Canfield, Paddock & Stone, Detroit, 1993—95; judge Mich. Ct. Appeals, 1995—99; justice Mich. Supreme Ct., Lansing, Mich., 1999—. Office: Mich Supreme Ct Hall of Justice 925 W Ottawa St Fl 6 Lansing MI 48915

MARKO, ANDREW PAUL, school system administrator; b. Kingston, Pa., Aug. 16, 1936; s. Andrew Paul and Anna (Stragis) M.; m. Janet Thimm, Aug. 10, 1988; 1 child, Danielle. BA, Kings Coll., Wilkes-Barre, Pa., 1962; MA, Scranton U., 1968, prin.'s cert., 1971; postgrad., Oxford (Eng.) U., 1988, Lehigh U., 1991, Widener U., 1991—. Cert. tchr., secondary prin., supt.'s letter of eligibility, Pa. Elem. tchr. Dundalk Elem. Sch., Balt., 1963-64; English tchr. Kingston (Pa.) High Sch., 1964-66, Wyoming Valley West High Sch., Plymouth, Pa., 1966-90, vice prin., 1980, 89; secondary curriculum adminstr. Wyoming Valley West Sch. Dist., Kingston, 1990, dir. instrnl. svcs. and pupil svcs., 1991-95, apptd. supt., 1995—. Wrestling coach Kingston High Sch., 1964-69; jr.-sr. class advisor Wyoming Valley West High Sch., Plymouth, 1968-88, newspaper advisor, 1970-90, literary mag. advisor, 1970-90, publs. bus. mgr., 1988-90. Councilman Kingston Borough Coun., 1969-77; pres. Holy Name Soc.; ward capt. Heart Fund and March of Dimes; bd. dirs. Childrens Svc. Ctr. United Way, Diversity Bd. Coll. Misricordia, Dallas, Pa.; exec. dir. Northeastern Health Trust Pa.; mem. adv. bd. Blue Cross/Blue Shield; chmn. Sch. to Work, bd. dirs. libr. bd. Leham campus Pa. State U.; exec. dir. Northeast Pa. Sch. Dist. Health Trust, 2001-04. With USN, 1954-57. Fellow Ednl. Policy and Leadership Pa.; mem. ASCD, Pa. Assn. Student Assistance Profls., Pa. Assn. for Supervision and Curriculum Devel., Pa. Assn. Pupil Svcs. Adminstrs., Nat. Assn. Pupil Svcs. Adminstrs., Pa. Staff Devel. Coun., Nat. Mid. Sch. Assn., Ptnrs. for Quality Learning, VFW, Am. Legion, KC. Democrat. Roman Catholic. Avocations: sports, gardening, building, reading. Home: 6 Halowich Rd Harveys Lake PA 18618-9629 Office: Wyoming Valley West Sch Dist 450 N Maple Ave Kingston PA 18704-3683 Office Phone: 570-718-0433. E-mail: amarko@liu18.org.

MARKO, MARLENE, psychiatrist; b. N.Y.C., July 3, 1945; m. Loren R. Skeist; children: Marc, David, Sarah. BA, Sarah Lawrence Coll., 1967; MD, Mt. Sinai Sch. Medicine, 1972. Diplomate Am. Bd. Psychiatry. Intern Lenox Hill Hosp., 1973; resident Mt. Sinai Hosp., 1976; clin. instr. Mt. Sinai Sch. Medicine.

MARKOE, ARNOLD MICHAEL, radiation oncologist; b. NYC, Apr. 15, 1942; s. Joseph Markoe and Claire (Hershkowitz) Markoe Berger; m. Tana Kates, Sept. 3, 1967; 1 child, Zaharah. BA, Adelphi U., 1963; MS, U. Rochester, 1966; ScD, U. Pitts., 1972; MD, Hahnemann U., 1977. Diplomate, Am. Bd. Radiology (Therapeutic Radiology). Rsch. assoc. Albert Einstein Coll. Medicine, Bronx, N.Y., 1966-69; USPHS postdoctoral fellow Allegheny Gen. Hosp., Pitts., 1972 73; Am. Cancer Soc. spl. postdoctoral fellow Hahnemann Med. Coll., Phila., 1975-77; from sr. instr. to assoc. prof. radiation oncology Hahnemann U., Phila., 1977-89; staff physician Jackson Meml. Hosp., Miami, Fla., 1990—; mem. Sylvester Comprehensive Cancer Ctr., Miami, 1990—; assoc. prof. radiation oncology U. Miami, 1989-92, prof., 1992—, interim chmn. radiation oncology Sch. Medicine, 1994-96; chmn., 1996—; staff physician U. Miami Hosp. & Clinics, 1990—, VA Hosp., Miami, 1996—, JFK Med. Ctr., Atlantis, Fla., 1997—2004. Cons. Anna Bates Leach Hosp. of Bascom-Palmer Eye Inst., 1990—, Cancergrams Info. Ventures, Inc., Phila., 1989-92; spl. site vis. radiation oncology Accreditation Coun. for Grad. Med. Edn., 1986—; adv. bd. radiation therapy tech. tng. program Gwynedd-Mercy Coll., Gwynedd Valley, Pa., 1988-89, Miami Dade C.C./Jackson Meml. Hosp. Consortium, 1989—, med. advisor, 1995—; adv. panel Radiation Oncology Self-Assessment Program, 1992-97, Pro Bono Expert Witness Program, State of Fla., Dept. Health and Human Svcs., 1997—. Mem. editl. bd. Am. Jour. Clin. Oncology, 1991-2003, Radiation Oncology Investigations, 1992-97; reviewer Cancer, 1994—, Jour. Neuro-Oncology, 1994—; ad hoc reviewer Internat. Jour. Radiation Oncology Biol. Physics, 1996—, Am. Jour. Neuroradiology, 2003—; contbr. articles to profl. jours. Bd. dirs. Jewish Leadership Inst.; exec. bd. Young Israel of Miami Beach, 1997-2002. Grantee, Soc. Nuclear Medicine, 1976; named One of Best Drs. in Am., 1996-. Mem Am. Radium Soc., Am. Soc. Clin. Oncology, Am. Coll. Radiology, Am. Coll. Radiation Oncology, Am. Soc. Therapeutic Radiation Oncology, So. Med. Soc., Fla. Med. Soc., Dade County Med. Soc., Fla. Soc. Clin. Oncology, Alpha Omega Alpha, Beta Beta Beta. Avocations: reading, music, fishing. Office Phone: 305-243-4319.

MARKOE, FRANK, JR., lawyer, business and hospital executive; b. Balt., Sept. 5, 1923; s. Frank and Margaret (Smith) M.; m. Margaret McCormack (div.); children: Andrée Markoe Caldwell, Ritchie Harrison Markoe Scribner. AB, Washington and Lee U., 1947; LLB, U. Md., 1950. Bar: Md. 1950. Pntr. Karl F. Steinmann, Balt., 1948-50, 50-53, Cable & McDaniel, Balt., 1954-55; gen. counsel, dir. Emerson Drug Co., Balt., 1955-56, adminstrv. v.p., 1957-58; v.p., sec., dir., gen. counsel Warner-Lambert Pharm. Co., 1958-67, exec. com., sr. v.p., dir., gen. counsel, sec., 1967-69, exec. asst. chmn. bd., 1970-71, sr. v.p., 1971-73; exec. v.p. Warner-Lambert Co., Morris Plains, N.J., 1973-77, vice chmn. bd., 1977-81; vice chmn. adv. bd. N.Y. Hosp.-Cornell Med. Ctr., 1987—, also chmn. major gifts com. Capital Campaign; hon. holder Alfred E. Driscoll chair Fairleigh Dickinson U. Bd. dirs. N.J. Coll. Medicine and Dentistry, Bd. Internat. Broadcasting, Radio Free Europe/Radio Liberty, Kips Bay Boys; bd. dirs., exec. com., pres. N.J. Ballet. With USAAF, 1942-45, PTO. Mem. U.S. C. of C., Proprietary Assn. (chmn., bd. dir., exec. com.), Pharm. Mfrs. Assn. (bd. dir., exec. com.), N.J. State C. of C. (bd. dir.), Phi Beta Kappa. Home and Office: 201 Grenville Rd Hobe Sound FL 33455-2414 also: Cleft Rd Mill Neck NY 11765

MARKOFF, GARY DAVID, investment executive; b. Brookline, Mass., July 29, 1956; s. Leon Fred and Marylyn Sue (Goldstein) M.; m. Cicely Beston Butler, Sept. 23, 2000; 1 child, Aiden Tenyson Markoff. BA in Econs., Trinity Coll., Hartford, Conn., 1978. From acct. exec. to v.p. E.F. Hutton & Co. Inc., Chestnut Hill, Mass., 1978-88; first v.p. investments Salomon Smith Barney, Boston, 1988-99, corp. client group dir., 1999-2000, sr. v.p., 2001—. Founding mem. Intuition Network Bus. Cons. Group, 1994. Co-author: Intuition at Work: An Anthology, 1996. Fundraiser Hunger Project, 1985—; active Spl. Olympics, 1988; founding mem. fin. profls. unit B'nai B'rith, 1988; class agent class of 1978 Trinity Coll., 1993—. Named one of Best Stockbrokers in Am., Money mag., 1987. Mem. Boston Jaycees, World Runners Club. Clubs: World Runners (San Francisco). Avocations: marathons (goodwill games, moscow, 1986), triathlons, tennis, skiing, windsurfing. Home: Jamaica Pond Estates 100 Pond St Apt 7 Boston MA 02130-2759 Office: Smith Barney Inc 28 State St Fl 26 Boston MA 02109-1775

MARKOFF, STEVEN C. finance company executive; CEO, pres., founder A. Mark Fin., Santa Monica, Calif., 1965—. Office: A Mark Financial 100 Wilshire Blvd Fl 3 Santa Monica CA 90401

MARKOPOLOS, HARRY M. investment professional; b. Erie, Pa., Oct. 22, 1956; s. Louis Harry and Georgia Ann (Pappas) M. BABA, Loyola Coll., Balt., 1981; MS in Fin., Boston Coll., 1997. Chartered Fin. Analyst. Dist. mgr. ATFC Fin. Corp., Towson, Md., 1981—87; trader Makefield Securities Corp., Washington Crossing, Pa., 1987—88; asst. portfolio mgr. Darien Capital Mgmt., Greenwich, Conn., 1988—91; portfolio mgr. Rampart Investment Mgmt., Boston, 1991, chief investment officer, 2002—; v.p. edn. Boston Security Analysts Soc., 2000—02, pres., 2002—03. Bd. dirs. Boston Security Analysts, QWAFAFEW, Boston, Boston GARP; derivatives instr. Boston Security Analysts. Maj. U.S. Army Res., 1978-95. Decorated US Army Achievement medal, Nat. Def. Svc. medal. Mem. Internat. Assn. Fin. Engrs., Am. Fin. Assn., Fin. Mgmt. Assn., Assn. for Investment Mgmt. and Rsch., Boston Security Analysts Soc. (v.p. edn. 2000-02, pres. 2002-03), U.S. Army Command and Gen. Staff Coll. Alumni (life mem.). Avocations: trout fishing, hunting. Office: Rampart Investment Mgmt 1 International Pl Boston MA 02110-2602 Office Phone: 617-342-6914.

MARKOS, CHRIS, retired real estate company executive; b. Cleve., Nov. 25, 1926; s. George and Bessie (Papathatou) Markos; m. Alice Zaharopoulos, Dec. 11, 1949 (dec.); children: Marilyn Martin, Irene Matthews, Betsy Feierabend; m. Marilyn Gardanier, Nov. 8, 2002; children: Kathleen Mitchel, Patricia Hickle. BA, Case Western Reserve, Cleve., 1960; LLB, LaSalle U., Chgo., 1964. Cert. gen. real estate appraiser, Ohio. Pres. Brooklyn Realty Co., Cleve., 1953—63; vice-pres. Herbert Laronge Inc., Cleve., 1963-76; v.p. Calabrese, Racek and Markos Inc., Cleve., 1976-83, Herbert Laronge Inc., Cleve., 1983-87, pres., 1987-88; v.p. Cragin Lang, Inc., Cleve., 1989-91; sr. cons. Grubb & Ellis, Cleve., 1991-93; sr. v.p. Realty One Appraisal Divsn., Independence, Ohio, 1993-98. Pres. Alcrimar Inc., 1989-98. Co-author: Ohio Supplement to Modern Real Estate Practice, 5th-7th edits.; cons. editor, co-author: Modern Real Estate Practice in Ohio, 1st-3rd edits. Bd. dirs. David N. Meyers Coll., Cleve., 1984-97. With U.S. Army, 1945-46. Mem. Am. Soc. Appraisers (sr., pres. 1973, state dir. 1976), Cleve. Bd. Realtors (hon. life mem., pres. 1974, Realtor of Yr. award 1976). Republican. Greek Orthodox. Home: Corinthian Condominium 936 Intracoastal Dr Apt 6-H Fort Lauderdale FL 33304 E-mail: alcrimar@webtv.net. *Everyone's life has a beginning and an ending. It is what happens between these two points that makes up the essence of a person.*

MARKOVCHICK, VINCENT J. surgeon; b. Hazleton, Pa., 1944; MD, Temple U., 1970. Intern Presbyn. Med. Ctr., Denver, 1970-71; resident emergency medicine U. Chgo. Hosps.-Clinics, 1974-76; mem. staff Denver Gen. Hosp.; assoc. prof. U.Colo. Health Sci. Ctr.; pres. Am. Bd. Emer. Med., East Lansing; dir. emergency med. Denver Health Med. Center, Denver, 2000—. Mem. Am. Coll. Emergency Physicians, Colo. Med. Soc., STEM. Office: Denver Gen Hosp Emergency Medicine Dept 777 Bannock St Denver CO 80204-4507 also: Amer Bd Emerg Med 3000 Coolidge Rd East Lansing MI 48823-6319

MARKOVICH, PATRICIA HELEN, economist; b. Oakland, Calif. MS in Econs., U. Calif., Berkeley; postgrad., Stanford U. Cert. emergency mgmt. planner. Pub. rels. Pettler Advt., Inc.; pvt. practice polit. and econs. cons.; aide to majority whip Oreg. Ho. of Reps.; lectr., instr. various Calif. instns., Chemeketa (Oreg.) Coll., Portland (Oreg.) State U.; commr. City of Oakland (Calif.), 1970-74. Chairperson, bd. dirs. Cable Sta. KCOM; econ. and emergency mgmt. cons. Mem. Piedmont (Calif.) Gen. Plan Commn. NSF grant Oreg. Grad. Rsch. Ctr., Lilly Found. grant. Mem.: Nat. Coordinating Coun. Emergency Mgmt., Mensa.

MARKOVITS, ANDREI STEVEN, political science educator; b. Timisoara, Romania, Oct. 6, 1948; came to U.S., 1960, naturalized, 1971; s. Ludwig and Ida (Ritter) M. BA, Columbia U., 1969, MBA, 1971, MA, 1973, MPhil, 1974, PhD, 1976. Mem. faculty NYU, 1974, John Jay Coll. Criminal Justice, CUNY, 1974, Columbia U., 1975; rsch. assoc. Inst. Advanced Studies, Vienna, Austria, 1973-74, Wirtschafts und Sozialwissenschaftliches Inst., German Trade U. Fedn., Düsseldorf, Germany, 1979, Internat. Inst. Comparative Social Rsch., Sci. Ctr. Berlin, 1980; asst. prof. govt. Wesleyan U., Middletown, Conn., 1977-83; assoc. prof. polit. sci. Boston U., 1983-92; prof., chair dept. politics U. Calif., Santa Cruz, 1992-99; prof. dept. Germanic langs. and lit. U. Mich., Ann Arbor, Mich., 1999—2003, Karl W. Deutsch Collegiate prof. comparative politics and German studies, 2003—; Fulbright prof. U. Innsbruck, Austria, 1996. Vis. prof. Tel Aviv U., 1986, Osnabruck U., 1987, Bochum U., 1991; vis. prof. com. degrees social studies Harvard U., 2002—03; sr. rsch. assoc. Ctrl. European Studies Harvard U., 1975—99; adj. prof. polit. sci. and sociology U. Mich., 1999—. Author, editor books and papers in field; TV and radio commentator. Univ. Pres.'s fellow Columbia U., 1969, B'nai B'rith Found. fellow, 1976-77, Kalmus Found. fellow, 1976-77, Ford Found. fellow, 1979, Hans Boeckler Found. fellow, 1982 Inst. for Advanced Study Berlin fellow, 1998-99; N.Y. State scholar Columbia U., 1969. Mem. N.Y. Acad. Scis., Am. Polit. Sci. Assn., Internat. Polit. Sci. Assn., AAUP. Home: 718 Onondaga St Ann Arbor MI 48104-2611 Office: Univ Mich 3110 Modern Lang Bldg 812 E Washington St Ann Arbor MI 48109-1275 Office Phone: 734-764-8018., 734-764-6313. Personal E-mail: andreimarkovits@cs.com. Business E-Mail: andymark@umich.edu.

MARKOVSKY, BARRY NEIL, sociology educator; b. Framingham, Mass., Apr. 3, 1956; s. Louis Joseph and Freida Judith Markovsky; m. Rose Marcia Garfinkle, July 15, 1987; 1 child, Tess. BA, U. Mass., 1978; PhD, Stanford U., 1983. NIMH postdoctoral fellow Stanford (Calif.) U., 1983; asst. prof. sociology U. Iowa, Iowa City, 1983-88, assoc. prof. sociology, 1988-94, prof. sociology, 1994-2001; prof., chair sociology U. S.C., Columbia, 2001—. Dir. Ctr. Study of Group Processes, U. Iowa, 1992-2001; grant rev. panelist, NSF, 1988—, sociology program dir., NSF, Arlington, Va., 1997-99. Editor (ann. vol.) Advances in Group Processes, 1987-97; contbr. over 60 articles to profl. jours., including Am. Sociol. Rev. NSF fellow, 1990. Mem. Am. Sociol. Assn., Internat. Network Social Network Analysis, Skeptics Soc., ACLU (bd. mem. Iowa chpt. 1997-2001), Phi Beta Kappa. Democrat. Avocations: guitar, coffee roasting, cooking. Office: Univ SC Sloan Hall Columbia SC 29208 E-mail: barry@sc.edu.

MARKOWICZ, ELAINE C. writer; b. Phila., Apr. 10, 1951; d. Benjamin Joseph and Marie Castellano; m. James Michael Markowicz, Nov. 16, 1974; children: David, Jimmy, Andrew, Eric. Student, Art Inst., Phila., 1996-97. Sec. Colonial Pann, Phila., 1972-78. Author: Tender Temptation, 1978, Secret of Evergreen, 2000. Avocations: drawing children's series, painting, Karate, violin.

MARKOWITZ, DEBORAH LYNN, state government official; b. Tarrytown, N.Y., Sept. 14, 1961; d. Gerald Harvey and Sandra Lee (Schulner) M.; m. Paul William Markowitz, June 19, 1988; children: Aviva Lee, Sandra Rose, Ari David. BA with honors, U. Vt., 1982; JD magna cum laude, Georgetown U., 1987. Bar: Vt. 1988, U.S. Dist. Ct. Vt. 1989. Assoc. Covington & Burling, Washington, summer 1986; jud. law clk. Justice Peck-Vt. Supreme Ct., Montpelier, 1987-88; assoc. Langrack, Sperry & Wool, Burlington, Vt., 1988-90; dir. Law Ctr. Vt. League of Cities and Towns, Montpelier, Vt., 1990—97; devel. cons. Vt. Law Sch., South Royalton, 1997—; sec. of state State of Vt., 2000—. Adj. faculty Vt. Law Sch., South Royalton, 1992; examiner Vt. Bd. Bar Examiners, Montpelier, 1994-98. Contbr. articles to profl. jours. Bd. dirs. Ctrl. Vt. Cmty. Action Agy., Vt. Hist. Soc.; trustee Woodbury Coll. Mem. ABA (state and local govt. sect.), Vt. Bar Assn. (mcpl. com.), Internat. Mcpl. Lawyers Assn. (chair pers. sect. 1993—), Nat. Assn. Secs. of State, Nat. Mus. of Women in the Arts (bd. dirs. Vt. chpt.), Order of Coif. Democrat. Avocations: cross country skiing, singing, sketching, gardening. Office: Sec of State Redstone Bldg 26 Terrace Street, PO Box 9 Montpelier VT 05609-0001

MARKOWITZ, GERALD E. historian, educator; b. N.Y.C., July 12, 1944; s. Irving and Esther Wittes Markowitz; m. Andrea Ades, Nov. 25, 1994; children: William, Tobias, Elena Kennedy, Isa Vasquez, Anton Vasquez. BA, Earlham Coll., Richmond, Ind., 1965; PhD, U. of Wis., 1971. Disting. prof. history John Jay Coll., CUNY, N.Y.C., 1970—, Grad. Ctr., CUNY, N.Y.C., 1990—; adj. prof. sociomed. sci. Mailman Sch. of Pub. Health, Columbia U., N.Y.C., 2002—. Mem., bd. of dirs. Am. Social History Project, N.Y.C., 2002—. Author (with David Rosner): (book) Deceit and Denial: The Deadly Politics of Industrial Pollution, Deadly Dust: Silicosis and the Politics of Industrial Disease in Twentieth Century America (Outstanding Academic Book of 1991 by Choice, 1991); author: (with Marlene Park) Democratic Vistas: Post Offices and Public Art in the New Deal; editor (with David Rosner): Slaves of the Depression: Workers Letters About Life on the Job, Dying for Work: Workers' Safety and Health in Twentieth Century America; contbr. articles to profl. jours. Recipient Arthur Viseltear Award for Outstanding Contribns. to the History of Pub. Health, Med. Care Sect., APHA, 2000; grantee Power and Pollution: The Politics of Indsl. Disease, NSF, 2001—02, Interpretative Rsch. grantee, NEH, 1992—94, 1987—89, History of Occupl. Safety and Health grantee, Milbank Meml. Fund, 1985—86, The Un-Natural History of Pub. Health grantee, Robert Wood Johnson Investigator Awards in Health Policy Rsch., 2002—. Mem.: Am. Soc. for Environ. History, Orgn. of Am. History, Am. Hist. Assn. Office: John Jay College 899 Tenth Ave New York NY 10019 Office Phone: 212-237-8458. E-mail: gmarkowitz@jjay.cuny.edu.

MARKOWITZ, HARRY MAX, finance and economics educator; b. Chicago, Ill., Aug. 24, 1927; s. Morris and Mildred (Gruber) M.; m. Barbara Gay. PhB, U. Chgo., 1947, MA, 1950, PhD, 1954. With research staff Rand Corp., Santa Monica, Calif., 1952-60, 61-63; chmn. bd., tech. dir. Consol. Analysis Ctrs., Inc., Santa Monica, 1963-68; prof. UCLA, Westwood, 1968-69; pres. Arbitrage Mgmt. Co., N.Y.C., 1969-72; pvt. practice cons. N.Y.C., 1972-74; prof. Wharton Sch Bus., U. Pa., 1972—74; with research staff T.J. Watson Research Ctr. IBM, Yorktown Hills, NY, 1974-83; prof. Rutgers U., 1980—82; Marvin Speiser Disting. Prof. of Fin. and Econs. Baruch Coll. CUNY, N.Y.C., 1982-93; dir. rsch. Daiwa Securities Trust Co, Jersey City, N.J., 1990-2000; prin., owner Harry Markowitz Co., 1993—; rsch. prof. dept. econs. U. Calif. San Diego. V.p. Inst. Mgmt. Sci., 1960-62. adv. bd. Jour. Investment Mgmt. Author: Portfolio Selection: Efficient Diversification of Investments, 1959, Mean-Variance Analysis in Portfolio Choice, 1987; co-author: SIMSCRIPT Simulation Programming Language, 1963; co-editor: Process Analysis of Economic Capabilities, 1963. Recipient John von Neumann Theory prize Ops. Rsch. Soc. Am. and Inst. Mgmt. Sci., 1989, Nobel Prize in Econs., 1990. Fellow Econometric Soc., Am. Acad. Arts and Scis., Am. Fin. Assn. Office: Ste 245 1010 Turquoise St San Diego CA 92109*

MARKS, ANDREW H. lawyer; b. N.Y.C., May 5, 1951; s. Theodore and Rosalie Ruth (Goldman) M.; m. Susan G. Esserman, Aug. 3, 1975; children: Stephen Matthew, Clifford Michael, Michael David. AB, Harvard U., 1973; JD, U. Mich., 1976. Bar: Fla. 1976, D.C., 1977, Md. 1984, U.S. Ct. Appeals (D.C. cir.). Law clerk for Hon. Charles R. Richey U.S. Dist. Ct. D.C., Washington, 1976-78; exec. asst. to personal rep. of Pres. to Middle East Peace negotiations, Washington, 1979-81; assoc. Shea & Gardner, Washington, 1978-79, 81-84, ptnr., 1984-86, Crowell & Moring L.L.P., Washington, 1986—. Mem. D.C. Bar (pres. 1998-99, bd. govs. 1989-95, chmn. task force civility in the profession 1993-96), Harvard Club Washington (pres. 1994-96). Office: Crowell & Moring LLP 1001 Pennsylvania Ave NW Fl 10 Washington DC 20004-2505

MARKS, ANNIE, playwright, writer; b. Louisville, Feb. 14, 1966; d. Charles Robert Marks and Virginia McCoy; m. Cal W. Austin, II, Jan. 15, 1994. BA in Philosophy and English, Wake Forest U., Winston-Salem, N.C., 1988; MA in English, Ind. U., Bloomington, 1991; post grad., N.Y. U., N.Y.C., 2001—. Investigator U.S. Office of Fed. Investigations, Augusta, Ga., 1988—89, U.S. OPM Office of Fed. Investigations, Bloomington, Ind., 1989—91; ops mgr./acct/ exec. Mid-Atlantic Securities, Raleigh, NC, 1992—94; editor-in-chief Computer Digest, Raleigh, 1994—97; artistic dir. Stage Write! Devel. Theatre, Raleigh, 1998—2001; self-employed writer Raleigh, NC, 1997—2001, N.Y.C., 2001—. Author: (plays) Best It's Ever Looked, 2002, Cocktales, 2003, Computer Digest; contbr. articles to periodicals. Moderator Pullen Arts Ctr. Stage and Screen Writers Group, Raleigh, 1997—2002. Finalist Nat. Tournament 9-Ball Team, Am. Pool Assn., 2000. Mem.: Phi Beta Kappa. Democrat.

MARKS, BERNARD BAILIN, lawyer, director; b. Sioux City, Iowa, Sept. 6, 1917; s. Meyer A. and Beulah (Bailin) M.; m. Betty L. Marks; 1 child, Susan E. BA, Harvard U., 1939, JD, 1942. Bar: Iowa 1942. With firm Shull, Marshall & Marks, Sioux City, 1946-85, ptnr., 1949-85, Marks & Madsen, Sioux City, 1985-97, of counsel, 1998-99, ret., 2000, sec., asst. treas., dir., 1962-81; sec., dir. KTIV-TV Co., Sioux City, 1965-74; bd. dirs. First Nat. Bank, Firstar Bank, Sioux City, 1963-91; with Flavorland Industries, Inc. Bd. dirs. Iowa Heart Assn., 1960, Woodbury County chpt., 1958-64, pres., 1962-64; bd. dirs. Sioux City Art Center, 1952-54, Sioux City United Fund, 1965-71, Sioux City Community Appeals Bd., 1965-68; trustee Briar Cliff Coll., Sioux City, 1968-74. Served with USAAF, 1942-46. Fellow Iowa Bar Assn. Found.; mem. ABA, Iowa Bar Assn., Woodbury County Bar Assn. (pres. 1958), Am. Coll. Trust and Estate Counsel, Sioux City C. of C. (bd. dirs. 1964-67, treas. 1965-66), Sioux City Lawyers Club (pres. 1951), Sioux City Country Club (bd. dirs. 1963-64).

MARKS, BRUCE, performing company executive, choreographer; b. N.Y.C., Jan. 23, 1937; s. Albert and Helen (Kosersky) M.; m. Toni Pihl Petersen, Jan. 27, 1966 (dec. May 1985); children: Erik Antony, Adam Christopher, Kenneth Rikard. Student, Brandeis U., 1954—55, Juilliard Sch., 1955—56; DFA, D, Northeastern U., 1997. Prof. U. Utah, 1981, 84-86; artistic dir. Boston Ballet Co., 1985-97, artistic dir. emeritus, 1998—. Mem. dance adv. panel Nat. Endowment for Arts, 1979, chmn. internat. selection com., 1979, chmn. dance adv. panel, 1981, mem. nat. adv. bd. on arts and edn., 1989; bd. dirs., mem. exec. com., Dance/USA 1989, 92—, chmn., 1990-92, chmn. govt. affairs, 1992—; mem. U.S.-USSR Commn. on Dance and Theatre Studies, Am. Coun. Learned Socs./IREX; mem. jury Internat. Moscow Internat. Ballet Competition, 1989; mem. arts in edn. adv. coun. Harvard U., 1997; chmn. 3d Japan Internat. Ballet and Modern Dance competition, 1999; jury mem. Prague Internat. Ballet Competition, 2001; artistic advisor Ft. Worth/Dallas Ballet, 2000-01. Prin. dancer Met. Opera, 1956-61, Am. Ballet Theatre, 1961-72, Royal Swedish Ballet, 1963, Festival Ballet, London, 1965, Royal Danish Ballet, 1971-76; artistic dir. Ballet West, Salt Lake City, 1976-85; choreographer Eliot Feld Ballet Co., 1970, Royal Danish Ballet, 1971-76, Netherlands Dance Theatre, 1974, Ballet West, 1976-85; artistic fellow Aspen Inst. for Humanistic Studies, 1979—. Bd. dirs. Am. Arts Alliance, 1983-85, Am. Coun. for Arts, 1985—; bd. dirs. Dance U.S.A., 1988-94, chmn., 1990-92; chmn. U.S.A. Internat. Ballet Competition, Jackson, Micc., 1990—, vice chair jury Helsinki, Finland, 1991, judge Helsinki Ballet Competition 1995; mem. nat. adv. bd. on arts and edn. NEA, 1989-91; mem. internat. jury 1st and 2d Japan Internat. Ballet Competition, Nagoya, Japan, 1993, 96, Am. jury for Prix de Lausanne, 1994, 98; mem. Brandeis Creative Arts Awards Commn., 1993, chmn. Brandeis Creative Arts Awards Dance, 1994; chair Grants to Dance Cos. panel NEA, 1993, overview panel, 1994; chmn. 3d Japan Internat. Ballet Competition, Nagoya, 1999; artistic advisor Ft. Worth/Dallas Ballet, 2000-2001. Recipient Disting. Svc. award for artistic prodn. Nat. Govs. Assn., 1994, Capezio award Balletmakers, Inc., 1995, Dance Mag. award, 1997, Honors award Dance/USA, 1998, Proscenium award, Boston, 2001.

MARKS, CHARLES, architect; b. Bklyn., May 19, 1938; s. Louis and Nettie Marks; m. Margery Green; children: Melissa Gabrielle, Joshua Wolf. BFA, Carnegie Mellon U., 1960; BArch, Columbia U., 1967, MArch, 1968. Registered N.Y., Conn., NCARB. Architect, long-range planner Am. Airlines, N.Y.C., 1969-79; prin. Graves Marks Assocs., 1979-86, Charles Marks Assocs., Greenwich, Conn., 1986—. Chmn. airlines planning com. San Francisco Airport, 1976-80; mem. planning com. Cin. Airport, 1972-78, Pan Am. Flight Ctr., JFK Airport, Engrng. Ctr., JFK Airport; mem. U.S. Dept. Commerce, U.S.-Haiti Bus. Devel. Coun., 1998-2000. Projects include Republic of Haiti New Passenger Terminal and Office, Tech. Ctr. Ctrl. Bank Haiti, Port-au-Prince, numerous banks and office bldgs. With U.S. Army, 1961-63. Mem. AIA, Nat Coun. Archtl. Registration Bds. Address: 111 Mason St Greenwich CT 06830-6605 Fax: 203-661-7920.

MARKS, CHARLES, surgeon, educator; b. Kiev, Ukraine, Jan. 28, 1922; came to U.S., 1963; s. Abe and Sonia (Beck) M.; m. Joyce Wernick, Dec. 11, 1949; children: Malcolm, Peter, Ian, Anthony. MD, U. Cape Town, South Africa, 1945; MS, Marquette U., 1966; PhD, Tulane U., 1973. Intern and surg. resident Groote Schuur Hosp., Cape Town, 1946-49; surg. resident Royal Coll. Surgeons Affiliated Hosps., London, 1950-53; cons. surgeon Salisbury (Rhodesia) Gen. Hosp., 1953-63; assoc. prof. surgery Marquette U. Med. Sch., Milw., 1963-67; dir. dept. surgery Mt. Sinai Hosp., Cleve., 1967-71; assoc. clin. prof. surgery Case Western Res. U. Sch. Medicine, Cleve., 1967-71; prof. surgery La. State U. Sch. Medicine, New Orleans, 1971-88; sr. attending surgeon Charity, VA, Touro and Hotel Dieu Hosps., New Orleans, 1971—88; med. exec. dir. Fla. Dept. Corrections, Charlotte, Fla., 1994-97. Cons. cardiothoracic surgeon Ministry of Health, Govt. Zimbabwe, Harare, 1989-94; Hunterian prof. Royal Coll. Surgeons, 1956. Mem. bd. govs. Drs. Hosp. Sarasota, 1997-2004, chmn. bd. govs., 2001—; mem. inner senatorial com. Rep. Party, Washington, 1997—. Recipient Schlieder Rsch. award, 1975. Fellow ACS, Royal Coll. Physicians Edinburgh, Am. Coll. Cardiology; mem. Internat. Cardiovasc. Soc., Am. Transplantation Soc., New Orleans Surg. Soc. (pres.). Republican. Avocations: tennis, golf, travel. Home: # 1517 988 Blvd of the Arts Sarasota FL 34236

MARKS, CHARLES DENNERY, insurance consultant; b. New Orleans, Nov. 22, 1935; s. Sidney Leroy Marks and Melanie Dennery; m. Gillian E. Otter, Sept. 1, 1963; children: Elizabeth Dennery, Richard Dennery. BA, Yale U., 1957. CLU; ChFC; accredited estate planner; cert. long term care, sr. advisor. With Charles Dennery, Inc., 1959-63; sales rep. Prudential Ins. Co., New Orleans, 1964-97. Past bd. dirs. Boys Club Greater New Orleans, Big Bros. Greater New Orleans, United Way; past pres. Goodwill Rehab. Ctr.; vice-chmn. Jr. Achievement; active Temple Sinai Synagogue; bd. dirs. Am. Coll., 2000-2003, exec. com., 2001-2003; bd. dirs. Am. Coll. Found., 2001—. 1st lt. U.S. Army, 1957-59. Recipient award Volunteer Activist, 1983. Mem.: Nat. Assn. Ins. and Fin. Advisors (vice chmn. fin. com. 1993—99, mem. audit com. 2003—, pres. Greater New Orleans chpt. 1983, Man of Yr. 1981), Million Dollar Round Table (exec. com. 1990—94, pres. 1993, Top of the Table 1986—89), New Orleans Estate Planning Coun. (pres. 1986—87), La. Assn. Ins. and Fin. Advisors (pres. 1986—87, Advisor of Yr. 1985, Advisor or Yr. 1987, Advisor of Yr. 2002), Soc. Fin. Svc. Profls. (pres. New Orleans chpt. 1984—85), Life and Health Found. for Edn. (life; chmn. 1996—98). Republican. Home: 1525 Eleonore St New Orleans LA 70115-4242 Office Phone: 504-586-8741. E-mail: cdmdrt@msn.com.

MARKS, DAVID HUNTER, civil engineering educator; b. White Plains, N.Y., Feb. 22, 1939; s. Sidney M. and Jean (Berger) M.; div.; 1 child, Joanna; m. Lilian Kemp, Dec. 17, 1998. BCE, Cornell U., 1962, MS in Environ. Engrng., 1964; PhD, Johns Hopkins U., 1969. Registered profl. engr., N.Y., Mass.; registered hydrologist, Am. Inst. Hydrology. Sr. sanitary engr. USPHS, Phila., 1964-66; asst. prof. civil engrng. MIT, Cambridge, Mass., 1969-72, assoc. prof., 1972-75, prof., 1975—, head dept., 1985-92, dir. program in environ. edn. and rsch., 1991-2000, James Mason Crafts prof., 1992-2000, Goulder Family prof., 2001—; coord. Alliance for Global Sustainability, 1996—; dir. Ctr. Environ. Initiatives, 1997-2001, Lab. for Energy and the Environment, 2001—. Office: Mit 1 Amherst St Rm E40-455 Cambridge MA 02139-4307

MARKS, EDWARD G. lawyer; b. Cin., Jan. 11, 1941; s. Grauman and Louise (Dreyfoos) Marks; m. Anita Louise Stith, Aug. 7, 1965; children: Alison L., Amy R. Bar: Ohio 1967, U.S. Dist. Ct. (so. dist.) Ohio 1967, U.S. Ct. Appeals (6th cir.) 1967, U.S. Supreme Ct. 1970. Ptnr. Marks, Goldsmith & Weiner, Cin., 1967—78, Marks, Weiner & Marks, Cin., 1978—. Adj. prof. broadcast law U. Cin., 1970—78. Sec. Cin. Music Hall Assn., 1974—, Wyo. Youth Svcs. Bur., 1981—83; pres. Cin. Civic Club, 1974; trustee Corbett Found., 1973—79, Rockdale Temple, 1974—77. Fellow: ABA, Ohio State Bar Found. (exec. com. 1978—81, chmn. commn. jud. candidates 1986), Am. Bar Found.; mem.: Cin. Bar Assn. (award of merit 1974). Office: 105 E 4th St Ste 700 Cincinnati OH 45202

MARKS, ESTHER L. metals company executive; b. Canton, Ohio, Oct. 3, 1927; d. Jacob and Ella (Wisman) Rosky; m. Irwin Alfred Marks, June 29, 1947; children: Jules, Howard, Marilyn. Student, Ohio State U., 1945-46, Youngstown State U., 1946-47. V.p. Steel City Iron & Metal, Inc., Youngstown, Ohio. Pres. Jr. Hadassah, Youngstown, 1943-45, Pioneer Women, Youngstown, 1951, Anshe Emeth Sisterhood, Youngstown, Broadway Theatre League, Youngstown, 1958, B'nai B'rith Women, Youngstown, 1962, Dist. 2 B'nai B'rith Women, Cleve., 1969-70, Jewish Cmty. Ctr., Youngstown, Youngstown Area Jewish Fedn., 1988-90; v.p. United Way, Youngstown, 1991, chmn., 1996; grad. Leadership Youngstown, 1991; bd. Akiva Acad. Commn. for Jewish Edn., Temple El Emeth, Stambaugh Auditorium. Named Guardian of the Menorah B'nai B'rith, Youngstown, 1978; recipient B'nai B'rith Girls Alumda award, Washington, 1989, Woman of Valor award Jewish Fedn., 1996. Mem. LMV, YWCA, Ohio Hist. Soc. Democrat. Jewish. Avocations: knitting, organizational work. Home: 1295 Virginia Trl Youngstown OH 44505-1637 Office: 703 Wilson Ave Youngstown OH 44506-1445

MARKS, HERBERT EDWARD, lawyer; b. Dayton, Ohio, Nov. 3, 1935; s. I.M. and Sarah S. M.; m. Marcia Frager; children: Jennifer L., Susan E. AB with high distinction, U. Mich., 1957; JD, Yale U., 1960; postgrad., George Washington U. Law Sch., 1965-67. Bar: Ohio 1960, D.C. 1964, U.S. Supreme Ct. 1965. Law clk. to chief judge U.S. Ct. Claims, 1964-65; assoc. Wilkinson, Cragun & Barker, Washington, 1965-69, ptnr., 1969-82, Squire, Sanders & Dempsey, Washington, 1982—2003, sr. counsel, 2004—. Assoc. gen. counsel Presdl. Inaugural Coms., 1969, 73, 81; chmn. U.S. State Dept. Adv. Panel on Internat. Telecom. Law, 1987—91; mem. adv. com. on internat. comm. and info. policy U.S. State Dept., 1988—91, 2002—; mem. U.S. del. ITU European Telecom. Devel. Conf., 1991, ITU Plenipotentiary Conf., 1998, ITU Coun., 2000, 04; mem. ITU Sec. Gen.'s Expert Group, 1999—2002; vice chair working group ITU, Italy; dir. Nat. Vets. Legal Svcs. Program, 2003—. Contbr. articles to legal jours. Served to capt. JAG USAF, 1960-64. Mem. ABA (chair sci. and tech. sect. 1990-91, chmn. communications div. 1986-88), D.C. Bar Assn., Computer Law Assn. (pres. 1975-77, bd. dirs. 1972-85, adv. bd. 1985—), Fed. Communications Bar Assn., Cosmos Club, Kenwood Golf & Country Club, Phi Beta Kappa. Office: Squire Sanders & Dempsey 1201 Pennsylvania Ave NW PO Box 407 Washington DC 20044-0407 also: 5317 Cardinal Ct Bethesda MD 20816-2908

MARKS, JAMES GARFIELD, JR., dermatologist; b. Trenton, N.J., May 19, 1945; s. James Garfield and Lavinia May (Ellis) M.; m. Joyce Lynne Turner, Aug. 9, 1969; 1 child, Shannon. BA, Wilkes Coll., 1967; MD, Temple U., 1971. Intern Geisinger Med. Ctr., Danville, Pa., 1971-72; resident Wilford Hall USAF Med. Ctr., San Antonio, 1975-78; clin. instr. dermatology U. Tex. Health Sci. Ctr., San Antonio, 1978-80; staff dermatologist Pa. State U. Coll. Medicine, Hershey, 1980—, asst. prof., 1980-85, assoc. prof., 1985-91, prof. dermatology, 1991—; chair dept. dermatology Hershey Med. Ctr. Team leader Cosmic Ingredient Rev. Expert Panel. Author: Atlas of Differential Diagnosis in Dermatology, 1998, Principles of Dermatology, 2000, Handbook of Contact Dermatitis, 2000, Contact and Occupational Dermatology, 2002, Principles and Practice of Dermatology, 1990, 2d edit., 1996, Occupational Skin Diseases, 1999, Conn's Current Therapy, 1988, 2d edit., 1989; author: (with others) Principles of Clinical Diagnosis, 1992, Dermatology, 2003; contbr. articles to profl. jours. Bd. dirs. Braun Sta. East Cmty., 1976. Maj. USAF, 1972-80. Decorated Meritorious Svc. Commendation meadl; Am. Acad. Dermatology Exch. fellow, 1984; recipient Roerig Pharms. Challenges in Dermatology Ednl. award, 1982. Mem. Am. Acad. Dermatology, Am. Contact Dermatitis Soc. (v.p. 1993, pres. 2001), N.Am. Contact Dermatitis Group, Pa. Acad. Dermatology, Phila. Dermatology Soc., European Soc. Contact Dermatitis, Soc. Investigative Dermatology, Assn. Mil. Dermatologists, Dermatology Found., Agromedicine Consortium, Lions (v.p. 1982, pres. 1983). Office: Hershey Med Ctr 500 University Dr # 850 Hershey PA 17033-2360 Office Phone: 717-531-8307. E-mail: jmarks@psu.edu.

MARKS, JAMES S. public health service administrator; b. May 13, 1948; AB cum laude, Williams Coll., 1969; MD, SUNY, Buffalo, 1973; MPH, Yale U., 1980. Diplomate Am. Bd. Pediatrics. Intern in pediat. U. Calif., San Francisco, 1973-74, resident in pediat., 1974-75, chief resident pediatric outpatient dept., 1975-76; resident in preventive medicine Ctrs. for Disease Control, Atlanta, 1977-78; fellow Robert Wood Johnson Clin. Scholars Program Yale U., New Haven, Conn., 1978-80; resident in preventive medicine Ctrs. for Disease Control, Atlanta, 1981-82, chief epidemiology and rsch. br., nutrition divsn., 1982-84, asst. dir. preventive medicine residency program, 1985-87, dir. divsn. reproductive health, 1987, coord. for chronic disease control activities, 1987-88, acting dir. divsn. diabetes transl., 1988-89, acting dir. divsn. chronic disease control, 1990-91, dir. divsn. reproductive health, 1992-95, dir. Nat. Ctr. Chronic Disease Prevention/Health Promotion, 1995—; adj. assoc. prof. Emory U. Sch. Pub. Health, Atlanta, 1990—. Asst. surgeon general, 1996—; editor Chronic Disease Notes and Reports, 1989-92; clinic physician Planned Parenthood of San Francisco Teen Clinic, San Francisco, 1975-76; cons. physician Ohio Dept. Health Bur. Preventive Medicine, 1978-79; cons. PAHO Consultative Group on Perinatal Care, Washington, 1982, WHO Malaysia Ministry of Health, 1982, 83, WHO Maternal and Child Health Unit Geneva, 1983, World Bank China Program Third Health Project, 1988, 1991, World Bank Poland, Health Promotion/Chronic Disease Prevention, 1992, World Bank China, Seventh Health Project, 1993. Contbr. articles to profl. jours, chpts. to books. Exec. sec. Diabetes Tech. Adv. com., 1989-92; liaison mem. Nat. Diabetes Adv. Bd., 1988-89; mem. Diabetes Mellitus Interagy. Coording. com., 1988-89; mem. subcom. adult edn., Am. Cancer Soc., 1987-92; staff White House Task Force on Infant Mortality, 1989; presenter in field. Epidemic Intelligence Svc. Officer USPHS Field Svcs. Divsn., 1976-78. Recipient Alexander D. Langmuir award, 1978, CDC Group award, 1984, Commendation Medal USPHS, 1984, and many other awards and citations. Fellow Am. Coll. Epidemiology; mem. APHA (active in com. work), Am. Epidemiol. Soc., Soc. Epidemiol. Rsch., Am. Acad. Pediat. (com. pediatric rsch. 1994-95), Internat. Epidemiol. Assn., Physicians for Social Responsibility, Soc. on Med. Decision Making, Epidemic Intelligence Svc. Alumni Assn., Sigma Xi. Home: 3158 Kings Arms Ct NE Atlanta GA 30345-2153 Office: Ctrs for Disease Control 4770 Buford Hwy NE Mail Stop K40 Atlanta GA 30341-3717*

MARKS, JOHN HENRY, Near Eastern studies educator; b. Denver, Aug. 6, 1923; s. Ira and Clara E. (Dralle) M.; m. E. Aminta Willis, July 21, 1951; children: Peter A., Fleur A., John B. BA, U. Denver, 1946; BD (O.T. fellow), Princeton Theol. Sem., 1949; ThD, U. Basel, (Switzerland), 1953. Instr. Princeton Theol. Sem., 1953-54, Princeton U., 1954-55, asst. prof. to assoc. prof. Near Eastern studies, 1955-61, prof., 1979-93. Dir. Am. Schs. Oriental Research, Jerusalem, 1966-67; pres. Am. Ctr. Oriental Research, Amman, Jordan, 1969-79; trustee Am. Schs. Oriental Research, Phila, 1971-86; Acting dean Princeton U. Chapel, 1980 Author: Der Textkritische Wert des Psalterium Hieronymi iuxta Hebraeos, 1956, Visions of One World, Legacy of Alexander, 1985; also translator. Pres. Sch. Bd. Princeton, 1969-71; mem. Planning-Zoning Bds. Princeton, 1964-66. Served with U.S. Army, 1943-45. Democrat. Presbyterian. Home: 107 Moore St Princeton NJ 08540-3308 Office: Princeton U 110 Jones Hl Princeton NJ 08544-0001

MARKS, JONATHAN BOWLES, mediator, arbitrator; b. Dec. 17, 1943; s. Herbert Simon Marks and Rebecca (Bowles) Marks Hawkins; m. Nandita Wagle, Dec. 18, 1971; children: Joshua Benegal, Natasha. BA cum laude, Harvard U., 1966, JD cum laude, 1972. Asst. U.S. Atty., Washington, 1973-76; assoc. Munger, Tolles & Rickershauser, L.A., 1976-78, ptnr., 1979; counsel, assoc. dir. planning and evaluation Peace Corps, Washington, 1979-80; gen. counsel Internat. Devel. Coop. Agy., Washington, 1980-81; dispute resolution cons. Washington, 1981-82; pres. EnDispute, Inc., Washington, 1982-94; vice chmn. Jams-EnDispute, Washington, 1994-99; prin. MarksADR, LLC, Washington, 1999—. Home: 4410 Chalfont Pl Bethesda MD 20816-1804 Office: 1120 G Street NW Suite 410 Washington DC 20005

MARKS, LAWRENCE EDWARD, psychologist, educator; b. N.Y.C., Dec. 28, 1941; s. Milton and Anne (Parnes) M.; m. Joya Ellen Cazes, Dec. 24, 1963; children: Liza, Laura. AB, Hunter Coll., N.Y.C., 1962; PhD, Harvard U., Cambridge, Mass., 1965; PhD honoris causa, Stockholm U., 1994. Rsch.-assoc. prof. Yale U., New Haven, 1966-84; asst.-assoc. fellow John B. Pierce Lab., New Haven, 1966-84; prof. epidemiology and psychology Yale U., New Haven, 1984—; fellow John B. Pierce Lab., New Haven, 1984—, dir., 1999—. Author: Sensory Processes: The New Psychophysics, 1974, The Unity of the Senses, 1978. Named to Hall of Fame, Hunter Coll., N.Y.C., 1985; recipient Jacob Javits award NIH, Washington, 1987. Fellow AAAS, Am. Psychol. Assn., Am. Psychol. Soc., N.Y. Acad. Sci. Democrat. Jewish. Achievements include elucidation of common principles underlying sensory processes in various sense modalities; development of validational scheme for quantifying magnitudes of sensory experience; indication of role of cross-modal (synesthetic) perception in relation to language and literature. Home: 48 Maplevale Dr Woodbridge CT 06525-1118 Office: John B Pierce Lab 290 Congress Ave New Haven CT 06519-1403 Office Phone: 203-562-9901. Business E-Mail: marks@jbpierce.org.

MARKS, LEONARD, JR., retired corporate financial executive; b. N.Y.C., May 22, 1921; s. Leonard M. and Laura (Colegrove) Rose; m. Antonia Saldaña Riley, July 19, 1986; children from previous marriage: Linda, Patricia Anne, Peter K. AB in Econs., Drew U., 1942; MBA, Harvard U., 1948, DBA, 1961. Asst. prof. bus. adminstrn. Harvard U., 1949-55; prof. fin. Stanford U., 1955-64; asst. sec. USAF, Washington, 1964-68; v.p. corp. devel. Times Mirror Co., Los Angeles, 1968-69; sr. v.p. Wells Fargo Bank, San Francisco, 1969-72; exec. v.p. Castle & Cooke Inc., San Francisco, 1972-85; gen. ptnr. Marks-Hoffman Assocs., Venture Capital, 1985-92; sr. adviser Corp. Asset Advisors, 2002—. Co-author: Case Problems in Commercial Bank Management, 1962; contbg.: Credit Management Handbook, 1958. Capt. AUS, 1942-46, ret. brig. gen. USAFR. E-mail: proftmarks@aol.com.

MARKS, LEONARD HAROLD, lawyer; b. Pitts., Mar. 5, 1916; s. Samuel and Ida (Levine) M.; m. Dorothy Ames, June 3, 1948; children: Stephen Ames, Robert Evan. BA, U. Pitts., 1935, LL.B., 1938. Bar: Pa. 1938, D.C. 1946. Asst. prof. law U. Pitts. Law Sch., 1938-42; prof. law Nat. U., 1943-55; asst. to gen. counsel FCC, 1942-46, ops. counsel, 1986—; ptnr. Cohn & Marks, Washington, 1946-65, 69-86. Chmn. exec. com. Nat. Savs. and Trust Co., 1977-85; chmn. Internat. Conf. on Comm. Satellites, 1968-69; Am. del. Internat. Broadcasting Confs., 1948-69; pres. Internat. Rescue Com., 1973-79, Honor Am. Com., 1977-86; chmn. U.S. Adv. Commn. on Internat. Ednl. and Cultural Affairs, 1973-78; chmn. Fgn. Policy Assn., 1981-87, exec. com., 1987-96; head U.S. del. Internat. Telecom. Union, 1983, 87; chmn. U.S. del. to London Info. Forum, Commn. on Security and Cooperation in Europe, 1989. Mem. ABA (ho. of dels. 1962-64), Fed. Comm. Bar Assn. (pres. 1959-60), Bar Assn. D.C., Acad. Diplmacy (chmn. exec. com. 2000—), World Affairs Council Washington (chmn.), Cosmos Club, Metropolitan Club (v.p., gov.), Federal City Club, Broadcasters Club (pres. 1957-59), Alfalfa Club (Washington), Order of Coif, Phi Beta Kappa, Omicron Delta Kappa, Sigma Delta Chi. Clubs: Cosmos, Metropolitan, Federal City, Broadcasters, (pres. 1957-59), Alfalfa (Washington). Home: 2700 Calvert St NW Washington DC 20008-2621 Office: 1920 N St NW Washington DC 20036-1601

MARKS, LILLIAN SHAPIRO, secretarial studies educator, author; b. Bklyn., Mar. 16, 1907; d. Hayman and Celia (Merowitz) Shapiro; m. Joseph Marks, Feb. 21, 1932; children: Daniel, Sheila Blake, Jonathan. BS, NYU, 1928. High sch. tchr., N.Y.C., 1929-30; tchr. Evalina de Rothschild Sch., Jerusalem, 1930-31; social worker United Jewish Aid Bklyn., 1931-32; tchr. Richmond Hill High Sch., 1932-40, Andrew Jackson High Sch., Cambria Heights, N.Y., 1940-71; mem. faculty New Sch. Social Rsch., N.Y.C., 1977-87; staff Vassar Summer Inst., 1946. Vol. tchr. English Israel schs., 1987—2000. Am. editor: Teeline, A System of Fast Writing, 1970; author: College Teeline, 1977, College Teeline Self Taught, 1988, Touch Typing Made Simple, 1985; contbr. articles to profl. lit. jours. Mem. Am. Fedn. Tchrs. Democrat. Home and Office: 300 E46 St 17J New York NY 10017

MARKS, MARILYN, trailer company executive; b. 1952; BS, U. Tenn., 1975. Acct. Ernst & Ernst, Chattanooga, 1975-76; with Deloitte, Haskins & Sells, Chattanooga, 1976-79; v.p. corp. planning The Dorsey Corp., Chattanooga, 1979-87; pres., chmn. of bd., CEO Dorsey Trailers, Atlanta, 1987-97, chmn. bd., 1997—. Office: Dorsey Trailers Inc 3850 W Main St Ste 806 Dothan AL 36305-1006

MARKS, MARTHA ALFORD, writer; b. Oxford, Miss., July 27, 1946; d. Truman and Margaret Alford; m. Bernard L. Marks, Jan. 27, 1968. BA, Centenary Coll., 1968; MA, Northwestern U., 1972, PhD, 1978. Tchr. Notre Dame High Sch. for Boys, Niles, Ill., 1969-74; teaching asst. Northwestern U., Evanston, Ill., 1974-78, lectr., lang. coord., 1978-83; asst. prof. Kalamazoo (Mich.) Coll., 1983-85; writer Riverwoods, Ill., 1985—. Cons. WGBH Edn. Found., Boston, 1988-91, Am. Coun. on the Tchg. of Fgn. Langs., 1981-92, Ednl. Testing Svcs., 1988-90, Peace Corps., 1993. Co-author: Destinos: An Introduction to Spanish, 1991, 96, Al corriente, 1989, 93, 97, Que tal?, 1986, 90; author: (workbook) Al corriente, 1989, 93; contbr. articles to profl. jours. Mem. Lake County (Ill.) Bd., Forest Preserve Commn., 1992-2002, Lake County Conservation Alliance; vice chmn. Friends of Ryerson Conservation Area Bd.; co-founder, pres. REP Am., Reps. for Environ. Protection.

MARKS, MELVIN I. physician, educator, hospital administrator, consultant; b. Montreal, July 30, 1940; came to U.S., 1979; s. Irving and Kate Marks; div. March 1999; children: Suzanne, Jennifer, Daniel. BSc, McGill U., 1961, MD CM, 1965; Cert. in Exec. Mgmt., UCLA, 1990. Diplomate Am. Bd. Pediat., Am. Bd. Pediat. Infectious Disease. Intern Montreal Gen. Hosp., 1965-66; resident in pediat. Montreal Children's Hosp., 1966-68; fellow in pediat. infectious diseases U. Colo. Med. Ctr., 1968-70; asst. prof. McGill U., Montreal, 1970-75, assoc. prof., 1975-79; prof. U. Okla., Oklahoma City, 1979-86; prof., vice-chmn. dept. U. Calif., Irvine, 1986—; clin. prof. U. So. Calif., 1997-99. Author: Pediatric Infectious Disease for the Practitioner, 1985; editor: Cystic Fibrosis, 1996. Bd. dirs. StarBright Found., L.A., 1995—. Office: Miller Childrens Hosp 2801 Atlantic Ave Long Beach CA 90806-1737 Office Phone: 562-933-8001. E-mail: mmarks@memorialcare.org.

MARKS, MELVIN PAUL, entomologist, consultant; s. Paul and Ruth Jean Marks; m. Frances McClenny, Nov. 14, 1945; children: Lacey Elizabeth Joy, Emily Albright. BS, Purdue U., 1971. Cert. Entomologist Entomol. Soc. Am., 2004, Master Gardener Clemson U., 2002. Vet. food inspector U.S. Army, 1967—70; entomologist Naval Facilities Engrng. Command, North Charleston, SC, 1971—81, mgr. applied biology program, 1981—2001; specialist pest mgmt. J. M. Waller, Assocs., Inc., Burke, Va., 2002—. Master gardener

Clemson County Ext. Svc., Moncks Corner, SC, 2002—04. Decorated Army Commendation Medal. Home: 126 Fairbury Dr Goose Creek SC 29445 Home Fax: 843-824-2633. Personal E-mail: mpmarks@comcast.net.

MARKS, MERTON ELEAZER, lawyer, international arbitrator, mediator, consultant; b. Chgo., Oct. 16, 1932; s. Alfred Tobias and Helene Fannie (Rosner) M.; m. Radee Maiden Feiler, May 20, 1966; children: Sheldon, Elise Marks Vazelakis, Alan, Elaine Marks Ianchiou. BS, Northwestern U., 1954, JD, 1956. Bar: Ill. 1956, U.S. Ct. Mil. Appeals 1957, Ariz. 1958, U.S. Dist. Ct. Ariz. 1960, U.S. Ct. Appeals (9th cir.) 1962, U.S. Supreme Ct. 1970; cert. arbitrator U.S. Dist. Ct. Ariz. Assoc. Moser, Compere & Emerson, Chgo., 1956-57; ptnr. Morgan, Marks & Rogers, Tucson, 1960-62; asst. atty. gen. State of Ariz., Phoenix, 1962-64, counsel indsl. commn., 1964-65; from assoc. to ptnr. Shimmel, Hill, Bishop & Greunder, Phoenix, 1965-74; ptnr. Lewis & Roca, Phoenix, 1974—2001; prin. Merton E. Marks, PC, 2001—. Lectr. on arbitration and mediation, product liability and ins. subjects; Judge Pro Tempore Ariz. Ct. Appeals, 1994; legal columnist Exec. Golfer mag.; comml. panelist, large complex case panelist, reinsurance panelist Am. Arbitration Assn.; CPR Inst. Dispute Resolution Inter-Insurer Arb. Panel; spl. master Ariz. Superior Ct., 2001—; U.S. and internat. alternative dispute resolution cons. Contbr. articles to profl. jours. Past trustee Ariz. Opera Co., past chmn. endowment commn.; past mem. U.S. Olympic Com. for Ariz. Capt. JAGC, USAR, 1957-64. Fellow Chartered Inst. Arbitrators (London); mem. ABA (trial, tort and ins. practice sect., chmn. spl. com. on fed. asbestos legis. 1987-89, chmn. workers compensation and employers liability law com. 1983-84, dispute resolution sect., bus. law sect., internat. law and practice sect.), Am. Bd. Trial Advs., Am. Coll. Legal Medicine, Internat. Bar Assn. (sect. on bus. law, product liability, advt., unfair competition and consumer affairs com., internat. litig. com., ins. com., arbitration and alt. dispute resolution com.), State Bar Ariz. (chmn. workers compensation sect. 1969-73), Fedn. Def. and Corp. Counsel (chmn. pharm. litig. sect. 1989-91, chmn. workers compensation sect. 1977-79, v.p. 1978-79, 81, bd. dirs. 1981-89, mem. products liability sect., mem. reinsurance sect., vice chmn. alternative dispute resolution sect.), Internat. Assn. Def. Counsel, Ariz. Assn. Def. Counsel (pres. 1976-77), Maricopa County Bar Assn., Pima County Bar Assn., Def. Rsch. Inst. (drug and device com., chmn. workers compensation com. 1977-78), Assn. Internat. de Droit des Assurances (cert. arbitrator), Reinsurance and Ins. Arbitration Soc., Union Internat. des Avocats, London Ct. of Internat. Arbitration., Nat. Assn. Securities Dealers Dispute Resolution (bd. arbitrators), Internat. C. of C. Office: Scottsdale Exec Office Pk 8655 E Via De Ventura Ste G200 Scottsdale AZ 85258-3321 also: 850 N Kolb Rd Tucson AZ 85710-1333 Office Phone: 480-346-1055.

MARKS, MICHAEL, association administrator; BS in Speech Comms./Edn., MS in Pub. Rels., U. So. Miss. Tchr. Perry County Schs., Lumberton Schs.; debate/drama coach Hattiesburg (Miss.) H.S., to 1997; pres. Miss. Assn. Educators, 1997—. State chair Miss. Forensic League, 1996-97. Recipient Miss. Tchr. of Yr. award, 1998, Milken Nat. Educator award, 1996, Disney/McDonald's Outstanding Tchr. of Performing Arts award, 1996. Office: Miss Assn Educators 775 N State St Jackson MS 39202-3086

MARKS, MICHAEL E. electronics company executive; BA, MA, Oberlin Coll.; MBA, Harvard U. Formerly pres., CEO Metcal Inc.; chmn. bd. dirs. Flextronics, 1993—2003, CEO, 1994—. Office: Flextronics 2090 Fortune Dr San Jose CA 95131-1823*

MARKS, PAUL ALAN, oncologist, cell biologist, educator; b. N.Y.C., Aug. 16, 1926; s. Robert R. and Sarah (Bohorad) Marks; m. Joan Harriet Rosen, Nov. 28, 1953; children: Andrew Robert, Elizabeth Susan Marks Ostrer, Matthew Stuart. AB with gen. honors, Columbia U., 1945, MD, 1949, DSc (hon.), 2000; D in Biol. Sci. (hon.), U. Urbino, Italy, 1982; PhD (hon.), Hebrew U., Jerusalem, Israel, 1987, U. Tel Aviv, 1992; DSc (hon.), Ben Gurion U., Beer Sheva, Israel, 2003. From fellow to prof. Coll. Physicians and Surgeons Columbia U., N.Y., 1952—67, prof. medicine Coll. Physicians and Surgeons, 1967—82, dean faculty of medicine, v.p. med. affairs Coll. Physicians and Surgeons, 1970—73, dir. Comprehensive Cancer Ctr. Coll. Physicians and Surgeons, 1972—80, v.p. health scis. Coll. Physicians and Surgeons, 1973—80; prof. cell biology and genetics Coll. Medicine Cornell U., N.Y.C., 1980—, prof. medicine Grad. Sch. Med. Scis., 1983—; pres., CEO Meml. Sloan-Kettering Cancer Ctr., N.Y.C., 1980—99, pres. emeritus, 2000—. Instr. Sch. Medicine George Washington U., 1954—55; cons. VA Hosp., N.Y.C., 1962—66; attending physician Presbyn. Hosp., N.Y.C., 1967—82, Meml. Hosp. for Cancer and Allied Diseases, 1980—; prin. investigator, Devel. Cell Biology Sloan-Kettering Inst. for Cancer Rsch., 1980—; adj. prof. Rockefeller U., 1980—; vis. physician Rockefeller U. Hosp., 1980—; hon. staff N.Y. Hosp., 1981—; bd. sci. counselors divsn. cancer treatment Nat. Cancer Inst., 1980—83, mem. steering com. Frederick Cancer Rsch. Facility, 1982—86; chmn. program adv. com. Robert Wood Johnson Found., 1983—89; mem. adv. com. on NIH to Sec. HHS, 1989—90, 1993—98; external adv. com. Intramural Rsch. Program Rev. NIH; mem. gov. com. NYPRHA, 1996; mem. tech. adv. group UN Assn. U.S.; mem. coun. biol. scis. Pritzker Sch. Medicine U. Chgo., 1977—88; William Dameshek vis. prof. hematology Mt. Sinai Med. Ctr., 1985; nat. vis. com. CUNY Med. Sch., 1986—89; trustee Feinberg Grad. Sch. Weizmann Inst. Sci., Rehovot, Israel, 1986—; vis. prof. Coll. de France, 1988; Alpha Omega Alpha vis. prof. N.Y. Med. Coll., 1990; Mario A. Baldini vis. prof. Med. Sch. Harvard U., 1991; mem. sci. adv. bd. City Hope Nat. Med. Ctr., Duarte, Calif., 1987—92, Raymond and Beverly Sackler Found., Inc., 1989, Ikonysis, 2004—, PTC Biotech., Inc., 2002—; v.p. Jefferson Cancer Inst., Phila., 1989; mem. Found. Biomed. Rsch., 1989—; sci. adv. com. Imperial Cancer Rsch. Fund, 1994—2003; pres., CEO Meml. Sloan-Kettering Cancer Ctr., 1980—99; sr. adv. Lazard Freres, 2000—; co-founder, sec. and vice chmn. Aton Pharma, Tarrytown, NY, 2001—04; mem. internat. adv. coun. Singapore Econ. Devel. Bd., 2000—03; dir. Biostratum, NC; lectr. in field. Author: 11 books; mem. editl. bd.: Blood, 1964—76, editor-in-chief:, 1978—82, mem. editl. bd.: Jour. Clin Investigation, 1970—71, editor-in-chief:, mem. editl. bd.: Cancer Treatment Revs., 1981—, Japanese Jour. Cancer Rsch., 1985—, Molecular Reprodn. and Devel., 1988—, Cancer Preventions, 1989, Sci., 1990, Current Opinion Oncologic Endocrine and Metabolic Drugs, 1998, expert analyst: Chemistry and Molecular Biology edit. of Chemtracts, 1990—92, mem. adv. bd.: Internat. Jour. Hematology, 1992, Stem Cells, bd. contbg. editors: Blood Cells, Molecules and Diseases, 1994, Comité des Sages, 1994; contbr. over 400 articles to profl. jours. Trustee St. Luke's Hosp., 1970—80, Roosevelt Hosp., 1970—80, Presbyn. Hosp., 1972—80, Metpath Inst. Med. Edn., 1977—79, Hadassah Med. Ctr., Jerusalem, 1996; mem. jury Albert Lasker Awards, 1974—82; bd. dirs. Revson Found., 1976—91, Am. Found. for Basic Rsch. Israel, Israel Acad. Scis., 1991; mem. tech. bd. Milbank Meml. Fund, 1978—85; bd. govs. Friends of Sheba Med. Ctr., Tel Hashomer; mem. commn. sci. and tech. Mayor, N.Y.C., 1984—87; mem. commn. Shoreham Nuc. Plant Gov., N.Y.C., 1983; mem. task force biomed. rsch. and tech. Mayor, N.Y.C., 1999. Recipient Stevens Triennial prize, 1960, award, Swiss-Am. Found., 1965, Centenary medal, Inst. Pasteur, 1987, Found. for Promotion of Cancer Rsch. medal (Japan), 1984, Disting. Svc. medal, Robert Wood Johnson Found., 1989, Outstanding Achievement award in hematopoiesis, U. Innsbruck, 1991, Pres.'s Nat. Medal Sci., 1991, Japan Found. for Cancer Rsch. award, 1995, Lifetime Achievement award, Greater N.Y. Hosp. Assn., 1997, Am. Italian Cancer Found., 1999, Humanitarian award, Breast Cancer Rsch. Found., 2000, Disting. Lifetime Achievement award, Healthcare Chaplaincy, NY, 2001, John Stearns award for lifetime achievement, NY Acad. Medicine, 2002, Annie Blount Storrs Humanitarian award, Calvary Hosp., NY, 2002; fellow Commonwealth Fund fellow, Pasteur Inst., 1961—62; Ayrey fellow, 1985. Master: ACP, Coll. Physicians and Surgeons (Gold medal 1994); fellow: AAAS, Pasteur Inst. Paris (Commonwealth Fund fellow 1961—62), Am. Acad. Arts and Scis., Royal Soc. Medicine; mem.: NAS (chmn. Acad. Forum Adv. Com. 1980—81, chmn. sect. med. genetics, hematology and oncology 1980—83, coun. 1984—87, del. biol. warfare com. Internat. Security and Arms Control 1986—89, bd. dirs. 2002), N.Y. Acad. Sci. (bd. dirs. 2004), European Acad. Scis., UN Assn. U.S.A. (tech. adv. group), Weizmann Inst. Sci. (bd. govs. 1976—, gov. emeritus, Israel), Third World Acad. Scis. (advisor), Soc. Study Devel. and Growth, Japan Soc. Hematology (Disting. lectr. 1989, Disting. lectr. 1989), Soc. Devel. Biology, Internat. Soc. Devel. Biologists, Harvey Soc. (pres. 1973—74), Assn. Am. Physicians, Am. Soc. Hematology (pres.-elect 1983, pres. 1984, chmn. adv. bd. 1985), Soc. Cell Biology, Assn. Am. Cancer Insts. (bd. dirs. 1983—88), Am. Assn. Cancer Rsch., Am. Soc. Human Genetics (past mem. program com.), Am. Soc. Biol. Chemists, Italian Assn. Cell Biology and Differentiation (hon.), Chinese Anti-Cancer Assn. (hon.), Japanese Cancer Assn. (hon.), Am. Soc. Clin. Investigation (pres. 1972—73), Am. Fedn. Clin. Rsch. (past councillor Ea. dist.), Red Cell Club (past chmn.), Inst. Medicine (coun. 1973—76, chmn. com. study resources clin. investigation with NAS 1988), Univ. Club, Century Assn., Soc. Interurban Clin. Club, Econ. Club, Alpha Omega Alpha. Office: Meml Sloan-Kettering Cancer Ctr 1275 York Ave New York NY 10021-6094 Office Phone: 212-639-6568. Business E-Mail: PaulA_Marks@mskcc.org.

MARKS, RAY, education educator, researcher; d. Hyman and Hassia Harber, m. Philip Marks, Dec. 31, 1972. EdD, Columbia U., Teachers Coll., 1997—2001. Physical therapist, England; lectr. rehab. med. U. Alberta, U. Toronto; co-instr. behavioral med. U. So. Conn.; adj. prof. health ed. Columbia Univ. Teachers Coll.; rsch. assoc. Nat. Ctr. Health Edn., NY. Dir. Osteoarthritis Res. Ctr., Toronto, Canada. Contbr. scientific papers Jour. of Theoretical Biology (Andrew Stewart Rsch. Prize, 1992), Aging Rsch. Reviews, Clin. Rheum., Arthritis Care and Rsch.; editor: (scientific works) related to Osteoarthritis. Sec. to pres. Soc. for Pub. Health Edn., N.Y.C., 2002—. Grantee Province of Alta. Fellowship, 1990, Dewey Scholarship, Columbia U., Teachers Coll., 1999, 2000, Arthritis Found. Dissertation Grant, Arthritis Found., N.Y. Chpt., 1999-2000. Mem.: Nat. Soc. Pub. Health Edn. (assoc.; ethics co-chair 2002—03, SOPHE/CDC Fellowship Award 2000). Achievements include research in Discoveries on neuromuscular basis of osteoarthritis. Avocation: reading. Home: 60 Charnwood Pl Ontario Thornhill Canada L3T 5H3 Office: Osteoarthritis Rsch Ctr Box 1153 Adelaide Postal Sta Toronto ON Canada M5C 2K5 Office Phone: 905-889-2725. Office Fax: 905-889-2046. E-mail: rm251@columbia.edu.

MARKS, STEPHEN J. neurologist, educator; b. Bklyn., Aug. 30, 1953; s. Ansel R. Marks and Frances L. Carpenter; m. Cindy G. Marks, Mar. 27, 1994; children: Jordan, Avery. BA, Colgate U., 1979. Diplomate Am. Bd. Neurology & Psychiatry. Intern Lenox Hill Hosp., NYC; resident Mt. Sinai Hosp., NYC; assoc. prof. N.Y. Med. Coll., Valhalla, 1987—. Team neurologist N.Y. Jets, Hempstead, 1986. Co-author: (chapter) Principle & Practice of Emergency Medicine, 1992, (book), 1997. Fellow: Am. Heart Assn. (mem. stroke coun.); mem.: Soc. Neuroscience, Nat. Stroke Assn., Am. Acad. Neurology. Avocations: skiing, windsurfing. Office: Dept Neurology Munger Pavilion, NYMC Valhalla NY 10595

MARKS, SUSAN COLLIN, foundation administrator; MA in internat. relations, U. Kent, Canterbury, 1987; BA in social anthropology, U. Cape Town, 1969. Exec. v.p. Search Common Ground, Washington; journalist, filmaker freelance, 1970-85. Exec. bed. Western Cape Peace Com.; chair Regional Police Cmty. Relations Com., Regional Transportation Com. Editor: Track Two jour., 1992. Recipient Peace fellowship, U.S. Inst. Peace, Washington, D.C., 1994. Mem. Women in Internat. Security (exec. bd.) Office: Search Common Ground 1601 Connecticut Ave NW Ste 200 Washington DC 20009-1035 Fax: 202-232-6718. E-mail: search@sfcg.org.

MARKS, THEODORE LEE, lawyer; b. N.Y.C., Oct. 18, 1935; s. Irving Edward and Isabel (Goodman) M.; m. Benita Cooper, July 13, 1958; children: Eric, Robert, Jennifer BS, NYU, 1956, LL.B., 1958. Bar: N.Y. 1959, U.S. Dist. Ct. (so. dist.) N.Y. 1963, U.S. Supreme Ct. 1964, U.S. Ct. Appeals (2d cir.) 1975, U.S. Dist. Ct. (ea. dist.) N.Y. 1978. Assoc. Silver, Bernstein, Seawell & Kaplan, N.Y.C., 1959-65; sole practice N.Y.C., 1965-70; ptnr. Lee, Cash & Marks, N.Y.C., 1970-76, Vogel, Marks & Rosenberg, N.Y.C., 1976-79, Bromberg, Gloger, Lifschultz & Marks, N.Y.C., 1979-85, Epstein Becker Borsody & Green, P.C., N.Y.C., 1985-86, Gelberg & Abrams, 1986-87, Morrison Cohen Singer & Weinstein, 1987—. Speaker at meetings of profl. assns. Contbr. articles to profl. jours. Served with Army N.G., 1958-61. Mem. N.Y. State Bar Assn. (mem. real property, banking, corp. and bus. law sects.), N.Y. County Lawyers Assn., Fed. Bar Coun., T&M. Office: Morrison Cohen Singer & Weinstein LLP 750 Lexington Ave New York NY 10022-1200

MARKULIS, HENRYK JOHN, career military officer; b. Columbia, S.C., July 10, 1945; s. Henryk F. Markulis and Judith E. (Taylor) Kassman; children: Mark C., Melinda L. BA, U. Buffalo, 1968; MA, Ctrl. Mich. U., 1977. Commd. USAF, 1969; advanced through ranks to col.; aircraft cmdr. 53d Weather Recon Squadron, 1970-74; gunship aircraft cmdr. 16th Spl. Ops. Squadron Korat RTAB, Thailand, 1974-75; cmdr. 437th Field Maintenance Squadron Sect. Charleston AFB, S.C., 1975-78; exercise and contingency support 1701st Mobility Support Shaw AFB, S.C., 1978-82; air staff action officer Joint Chiefs of Staff Pentagon, 1982-84; chief internat. programs Singapre, Malaysia & Brunei, 1984-93; dep. cmdr., chief staff Iceland Def. Force NATO, 1993-95, ret., 1995; pres., CEO Internat. Security and Mktg. Cons., 1996—. Cons. Nissan Motor Acceptance Corp., 1996—, Infiniti Fin. Svcs., 1996—. Mem. Am. Legion, VFW, Mil. Officers Assn. Am., Aircraft Owners and Pilots Assn., Army Navy Country Club, Order of Daedalians, Kiwanis, KC (4th degree). Avocation: golf. Office: 52 Union St Hamburg NY 14075 Home: 56 Union St Hamburg NY 14075-4910 Office Phone: 716-646-1589. E-mail: colonelm@adelphia.net.

MARKULY, MARK STEVEN, religious studies educator; b. St. Louis, Mo., Oct. 15, 1954; s. Lazarus Nicholas and Dorothy Mary Markuly; m. Teresa Mary Nuessle, Dec. 4, 1992; children: Sandra Erin Spaunhorst, Stacie Elizabeth. PhD, St. Louis U., St. Louis, MO, 1993—2001; MA, Aquinas Inst. of Theology, St. Louis, MO, 1986—89; BJ, Sch. of Journalism, U. of Mo. - Columbia, Columbia, MO, 1974—76. Diocesan dir. of religious cdn. Cath. Diocese of Belleville, Belleville, Ill., 1993—2002; dir. of cath. campus ministry So. Ill. U. at Edwardsville, Edwardsville, Ill., 1989—93; dir. of mktg. and rsch. Chrismark Corp., St. Louis, Mo., 1985—89; news editor The Monitor Pub. Co., Perryville, Mo. Cons. Nat. Cath. Ednl. Assn., Washington, 2001—01; assoc. rschr. Ctr. for Applied Rsch. in the Apostolate (CARA), Georgetown U., Washington, 1999—2003; cons. William Sadlier Co., New York, NY, 2003—03, Concordia Pub. Co., St. Louis, 1995—99. Author (production consultant): (tolerance educ., harcourt publishing) Enduring Faith; author: (production director) (win the prize) Ed. materials combining religious ed. and sports tng., Concordia Pub. Co. Mem. St. Louis U. Ednl. Leadership Asst. Superintendent's Coun., St. Louis, 1998—2000; mem. rep. coun. Nat. Conf. of Catechetical Leadership, Washington, 1995—98, 1995—98; chair dept. of religious edn. Cath. Conf. of Ill., Springfield, Ill., 1995—2001. Mem.: Nat. Conf. of Catechetical Leadership (workshop presenter), Nat. Cath. Ednl. Assn. (apptd. to adv. com. for religious edn. surveys 2002), Am. Ednl. Rsch. Assn. (AERA). Independent. Catholic. Achievements include research in affective dimension of religious education; Explored the connection between religion and U.S. culture, particularly in the area of popular psychological conceptualizations of the human person, sports, and business. Office: Loyola Univ New Orleans 6363 St Charles Ave Box 67 New Orleans LA 70118 E-mail: mmarkuly@loyno.edu.

MARKUS, ALLAN LEWIS, lawyer; b. Newark, Nov. 8, 1948; s. Seymour Bernard and Pearl (Weiss) Markus; m. Debra J. Ross, Jan. 6, 1973; children: Dara, Lindsey. BA, Monmouth Coll., 1970; JD, Western New Eng. Sch. Law, 1975. Bar: NJ 1976, US Dist. Ct. NJ 1976, US Supreme Ct. 1985. Assoc. Miller & Platt, Paterson, NJ, 1976—78; sr. ptnr. Markus & Cohen, Parsippany, NJ, 1978—. Asst. atty. pub. defender Essex County, Newark, 1978—81, Morris County, Morristown, NJ, 1979—82; mcpl. prosecutor Twp. of Parsippany Troy-Hills, NJ, 1980—82. Leader organizing rent control Tenants Assn., Parsippany-Troy Hills, 1977—80; Committeeman Committeeman Parsippany-Troy Hills (NJ) Dem. Com., 1977—80; mayoral campaign treas., 1979—80. Recipient Bancroft-Whitney award, Lawyers Coop. Pub. Co., 1974—75. Mem.: Morris County Bar Assn., NJ Bar Assn., Zeta Beta Tau. Republican. Jewish. Home: 6 Normandy Rd Pine Brook NJ 07058-9750 Office: Markus & Cohen 322 Rt 46 Suite 210 Parsippany NJ 07054 Office Phone: 973-227-5553.

MARKUS, KENT RICHARD, lawyer; b. Cleve., Feb. 1, 1959; s. Richard and Carol (Slater) M.; m. Susan Mary Gilles, Apr. 15, 1987; 1 child Robinson Reno. BS, Northwestern U., 1981; JD with honors, Harvard U., 1984. Bar: Ohio 1984, U.S. Dist. Ct. (no. dist.) Ohio 1984, U.S. Dist. Ct. (so. dist.) Ohio 1996, U.S. Ct. Appeals (6th cir.) 1986. Jud. clk. to Hon. Alvin I. Krenzler U.S. Dist. Ct. (no. dist.) Ohio, Cleve., 1984-86; litigation assoc. Gold, Rotatori, Schwartz & Gibbons, Cleve., 1986-89; transition dir. Ohio Atty. Gen. Office, Columbus, Ohio, 1990-91, first asst. atty. gen., chief of staff, 1991-93; counsel to dep. atty. gen. U.S. Dept. Justice, Washington, 1994, dep. assoc. atty. gen., 1994-95, acting asst. atty. gen. legis affairs, 1995, counselor to atty. gen, 1996-98, dep. chief of staff, 1997-98; prof., dir. Nat. Ctr. for Adoption Law & Policy, Capital U. Law Sch., 1998—. Adj. prof. law Cleveland-Marshall Coll. Law, 1987-88. Co-editor: Trial Handbook for Ohio Lawyers, 2nd edit., 1988; contbn. editor for law Webster's New World Dictionary, 4th edit., 1999. Past bd. dirs., past legis. chair Handgun Control Fedn. of Ohio, 1984-93; adv. coun. Northwestern U. Sch. Speech, 1985—; spl. projects dir. Celeste for Gov. Com., Cleve., 1986; campaign mgr. Lee Fisher for Atty. Gen., Cleve. and Columbus, 1989-90; bd. dirs., former trustee, life mem. Cleve. NAACP, 1986-87, chief of staff Dem. Nat. Com., Washington, 1993-94; at-large mem. bd. dirs. SEARCH, Inc., 2000-; bd. dirs. Ohio Legal Assistance Found. 2002-; chair Ctr. Ohio Neighborhood Safety Working Group, 2003-. Named Rising Star of Dem. Party, Campaigns and Elections mag., 1991. Mem. ABA, Ohio State Bar Assn. (former chair young lawyers divsn.), Columbus Bar Assn. Home: 5636 Indian Hill Rd Dublin OH 43017-8209 Office: Capital Univ Law Sch 303 E Broad St Columbus OH 43215-3201 E-mail: kmarkus@law.capital.edu.

MARKUS, LAWRENCE, retired mathematics educator; b. Hibbing, Minn., Oct. 13, 1922; s. Benjamin and Ruby (Friedman) M.; m. Lois Shoemaker, Dec. 9, 1950; children: Sylvia, Andrew. BS, U. Chgo., 1942, MS, 1946; PhD, Harvard U., 1951. Instr. meteorology U. Chgo., 1942-44; rsch. meteorologist Atomic Project, Hanford, 1944; instr. math. Harvard U., 1951-52; instr. Yale U., 1952-55; lectr. Princeton U., 1955-57; asst. prof. U. Minn., Mpls., 1957-58, assoc. prof., 1958-60, prof. math., 1960-93, assoc. chmn. dept. math., 1961-63, dir. control scis., 1964-73, Regents' prof. math., 1980-93, Regents' prof. emeritus, 1993—, dir. Control Sci. and Dynamical Sys. Ctr., 1980-89. Leverhulme prof. control theory, dir. control theory ctr. U. Warwick, Eng., 1970-73, Nuffield prof. math., 1970-85, hon. prof., 1985—; regional conf. lectr. NSF, 1969; vis. prof. Yale U., Columbia U., U. Calif., U. Warsaw, 1980, Tech. Inst. Zurich, 1983, Peking U. (China), 1983; dir. conf. Internat. Ctr. Math., Trieste, 1974; lectr. Internat. Math. Congress, 1974, Iranian Math. Soc., 1975, Brit. Math. Soc., 1976, Japan Soc. for Promotion Sci., 1976, Royal Instn., London, 1982, U. Beer Sheva, Israel, 1983; vis. prof. U. Tokyo, 1976, Tech. U., Denmark, 1979; mem. panel Internat. Congress Mathematicians, Helsinki, 1978; sr. vis. fellow Sci. Rsch. Coun., Imperial Coll., London, 1978; mem. UNESCO sci. adv. com. Control Symposium, U. Strasbourg, France, 1980; IEEE Plenary lectr., Orlando, Fla., 1982; Sci. and Engring. Rsch. Coun. vis. prof. U. Warwick, Eng., 1982-90; Neustadt Meml. lectr. U. So. Calif., 1985, prin. lectr. symposium U. Minn., 1988, dir. NSF workshop, 1989, prin. lectr. symposium in honor of his 75th birthday, 1997; Tate lectr. U. Cin., 1998; chmn. Conf. Markus-80, 2002; mem. adv. bd. Office Naval Rsch., Air Force Office Sci. Rsch. Author: Flat Lorentz Manifolds, 1959, Flows on Homogeneous Spaces, 1963, Foundations of Optimal Control Theory, 1967, rev. edit., 1985, Lectures on Differentiable Dynamics, 1971, rev. edit., 1980, Generic Hamiltonian Dynamical Systems, 1974, Distributed Parameter Control Systems, 1991, Boundary Value Problems and Symplectic Algebra, 1998, Multi-Interval Linear Ordinary Boundary Value Problems and Complex Symplectic Algebra, 2001, Elliptic Partial Differential Operators and Symplectic Algebra, 2003, Infinite Dimensional Computer Symplectic Spaces, 2004; editor Internat. Jour. Nonlinear Mechanics, 1965-73, Jour. Control, 1963-67; mem. editl. bd. Proc. Georgian Acad. Sci. Math., 1993—; contbr. articles to profl. jours. Lt. (j.g.) USNR, 1944-46. Recipient Rsch. prize Internat. Conf. Nonlinear Oscillations, Ukrainian Acad. Sci., Kiev, 1969, Festschrift volume, 1993; Fulbright fellow Paris, 1950; Guggenheim fellow Lausanne, Switzerland, 1963. Fellow Royal Soc. of Edinburgh (hon.); mem. Am. Math. Soc. (past mem. nat. coun.), Am. Geophys. Soc., Soc. Indsl. and Applied Math. (past nat. lectr.), Phi Beta Kappa, Sigma Xi. Office: 109 Vincent Hall 206 Church St S Minneapolis MN 55455 E-mail: markus@math.umn.edu.

MARKUS, MAURA, bank executive; BA summa cum laude, Boston (Mass.) Coll.; MBA, Harvard U. Joined Citibank, N.Y.C., 1987, pres. North Am. Retail Distbr. Group, 2000—. Office: CBNA One Court Sq 49th Fl Long Island City NY 11120

MARKUS, RICHARD M. judge, mediator; b. Evanston, Ill., Apr. 16, 1930; s. Benjamin and Ruby M.; m. Carol Joanne Slater, July 26, 1952; children: Linda, Scott, Kent. BS magna cum laude, Northwestern U., 1951; JD cum laude, Harvard U., 1954. Bar: D.C. 1954, Ohio 1956, Fla. 1994. Appellate atty., civil div. Dept. Justice, Washington, 1954-56; ptnr. civil litigation law firms Cleve., 1956-76, 89-98; judge Cuyahoga County (Ohio) Common Pleas Ct., 1976-80, Ohio Ct. Appeals, 1981-88. Instr. M.I.T., 1952-54; adj. prof. Case Western Res. U. Law Sch., 1972-78, 84-87, Cleve. State U. Law Sch., 1960-80, prof. 1999-2000; prof. Harvard Law Sch., 1980-81; mem. Nat. Commn. on Med. Malpractice, 1971-73; chmn. Nat. Inst. Trial Advocacy, 1978-81, trustee 1971—. Author: Trial Handbook for Ohio Lawyers, all edits., 1971—, Ohio Evidence Rules with Commentary, 1999; contbr. articles to profl. jours.; editor Harvard U. Law Rev, 1952-54. Republican nominee Justice of Ohio Supreme Ct., 1978; bd. dirs. Luth. Metro Ministry, 1988—, Fairview Luth. Hosp., 1985—. Mem. Ohio State Bar Assn. (pres. 1991-92), Cuyahoga County Bar Assn., Greater Cleve. Bar Assn. (trustee 1967-70, 85-90), Assn. Trial Lawyers Am. (nat. pres. 1970-71), Ohio Acad. Trial Lawyers (pres. 1965-66), Phi Beta Kappa, Pi Mu Epsilon, Delta Sigma Rho, Phi Alpha Delta. Home and Office: Pvt Judicial Svcs Inc 3903 N Valley Dr Cleveland OH 44126-1716 Office Phone: 440-356-2728. E mail: judgemarkus1@cs.com.

MARKUS, ROBERT MICHAEL, retired journalist; b. Chgo., Jan. 30, 1934; s. David White and Anna (Tonkonogy) M.; m. Leslie Winnifred Ator, Aug. 25, 1962; children— Catherine Mary, Patricia Anne, Michael Hughes. B.J., U. Mo., 1955. Gen. assignment reporter Moline (Ill.) Dispatch, 1955-59; successively copy editor, sports columnist, feature writer, baseball writer, coll. sports writer, hockey writer Chgo. Tribune, 1959-96, ret., 1996. Mem. Northbrook (Ill.) Caucus, 1967. Served with U.S. Army, 1956-58. Recipient Nat. Headliner award as best columnist, 1973; named Ill. Sports Writer of Year, 1970, 71, 72 Mem. Football Writers Assn. Am., Baseball Writers Assn. Am., Am. Auto Racing Writers and Broadcasters Assn. Home: 3000 Holiday Dr #1102 Fort Lauderdale FL 33316

MARKUSON, RICHARD K. former pharmaceutical association executive; Mem. adv. com. on pharmacy practice Nat. Assn. Bds. Pharmacy, pres.; exec. dir. Idaho State Bd. Pharmacy; adj. prof. pharmacy law Idaho State U.; chmn. Nat. Assn. Bds. Pharmacy, 2002—04. Mem.: Idaho State Pharm. Assn., Idaho Soc. Health Sys. Profls. (life). Office: 280 N 8th St Ste 204 Boise ID 83702*

MARKWELL, DICK R(OBERT), retired chemist; b. Muskogee, Okla., Feb. 20, 1925; s. Alex J. and May (Albright) M.; m. Virginia Ann Gass, Aug. 28, 1949 (dec. Nov. 2002); children: Steven R., Scot L., Eric R., Cheryl F.; m. Marjorie H. Melville, Feb. 20, 2003. BS, Wichita State U., 1948, MS, 1950; PhD, U. Wis., 1956. Commd. 2d lt. U.S. Army, 1951, ret. lt. col., 1967; with Office Chief Rsch. and Devel.; assoc. prof. chemistry San Antonio Coll., 1967-74; chemist Corpus Christi Dept. Health, 1975-77; supr. chemistry sect. lab. div. San Antonio Met. Health Dist., 1977-87. With USMC, 1942-45. Mem. Am. Chem. Soc. Home: 7887 Broadway Unit 501 San Antonio TX 78209-2537

MARLAND, ALKIS JOSEPH, leasing company executive, computer scientist, educator, financial planner; b. Athens, Greece, Mar. 8, 1943; arrived in U.S., 1961, naturalized, 1974; s. Basil and Maria (Pervanides) Mouradoglou; m. Anita Louise Malone, Dec. 19, 1970 (dec. Mar. 27, 2003); children: Andrea Weber, Alyssa. BS, Southwestern U., 1963; MA, U. Tex., Austin, 1967; MS in Engring. Adminstrn., So. Meth. U., 1971. CLU; cert. data processing, enrolled

agt., fund specialist, ChFC, CFP, accredited tax advisor, accredited tax preparer. With Sun Co., Richardson, Tex., 1968-71, Phila., 1971-76; mgr. planning and acquisitions Sun Info. Svcs. subs. Sun Co., Dallas, 1976-78; v.p. Helios Capital Corp. subs. Sun Co., Radnor, Pa., 1978-83; pres. ALKAN Leasing Corp., Wayne, Pa., 1983—, also bd. dirs. Prof. dept. computer scis. and bus. adminstrn. Ea. Coll., St. Davids, Pa., 1985—87; prof. math. Villanova (Pa.) U., 1987—89. Contr. Christian Counseling and Ednl. Found., 2003—; bd. dirs. Radnor Twp. Sch. Dist., 1987—91, Delaware County Intermediate Unit, 1988—91. Mem.: IEEE, Assn. Investment Mgmt. and Rsch., Phila. Union League, World Affairs Coun. Phila., Fgn. Policy Rsch. Inst., Phila. Fin. Assn. (mem. award 1988, sec. 1989—92, bd. dirs. 1989—92), Fin. Planning Assn. (treas. 2000—01, bd. dirs. Phila. Tri-State Area 2000—, pres. elect 2002, pres. 2003, chmn. 2004), Fin. Analysts Phila., Nat. Assn. Pub. Accts., Nat. Assn. Tax Practitioners, Nat. Assn. Enrolled Agts., Inst. Cert. Fin. Planners (bd. dirs. Phila. Tri-State Area 1993—99, v.p. membership 1994—95, treas. 1995—99), Am. Assn. Equipment Lessors, Fin. Svc. Profls., Data Processing Mgmt. Assn., Assn. Computing Machinery, Main Line C. of C., Masons, Rotary (pres. 1989—90, asst. gov. 1990—92, pres. 1993—94, treas. dist. 7450 2002—, Wayne). Republican. Home: 736 Brooke Rd Wayne PA 19087-4709 Office: PO Box 8301 Radnor PA 19087-8301 Office Phone: 610-293-1059. E-mail: almarland@aol.com., marlandatalkan@aol.com.

MARLAR, DONALD FLOYD, lawyer; b. Little Rock, Jan. 15, 1944; s. Floyd Howard and Ruth May (Lawson) M.; m. Janet Jeanne Clark, Mar. 29, 1963; children: Jennifer Clark, Christopher Decker. BA, Ark. State U., 1966; JD, U. Tulsa, 1969; Masters in Taxation, George Washington U., 1972. Bar: Okla. 1969. Ptnr. Pray, Walker, Jackman, Williamson & Marlar, Tulsa, Okla., 1973-96, pres., 1996—. Chmn. Okla. Bar Tax Section, 1979-80. Dir. Tulsa Ballet Theatre, 1987—, pres., 1991-92; gen. coun., v.p. Gilcrease Mus., Tulsa, 1989—, pres., 2000-01, chmn. bd. dirs., 2001—; trustee Grace and Franklin Bernsen Found., Tulsa, 1992—. Capt. U.S. Army, 1969-73. Mem. Am. Bar Assn., Tulsa Bar Assn., The Summit Club (bd. govs. 1986-92, pres. 1992). Home: 3517 E 70th Pl Tulsa OK 74136-2647 Office: Pray Walker Jackman Williamson & Marlar 900 Oneok Plz 100 W 5th St Tulsa OK 74103 E-mail: DFM@fraywalker.com.

MARLAR, JANET CUMMINGS, retired public relations officer; b. Burnsville, Miss., Dec. 22, 1942; d. James E. and Juanita (Hale) Cummings; m. David C. Linton, May 21, 1961 (div. 1984); 1 child, Jeffory Mark; m. Thomas Gilbert Cupples, Mar. 5, 1984 (div. 1990); m. Fredrick Marlar, Nov. 19, 1994. Student, N.E. Miss. Jr. Coll., 1960—61, Memphis State U., 1975—76, Sheffield Tech. Ctr., Memphis, 1984—85. Property owner, Burnsville, 1974—, Glen, Miss., 1994—2003. Mem. bus. adv. com. Sheffield Tech. Ctr., 1997—; docent Curlee House, Corinth, Miss., 1989—; exec. bd. Internat. Heritage Commn., Memphis, 1987-92; pub. rels. officer Internat. Heritage Ethnic Festival, Memphis. Co-editor: Internat. Heritage Bull./Newsletter; contbr. articles to Tishomingo County Newspaper. Vol. Memphis Brooks Mus. Art, 1980—; mem. exec. co., pub. info. officer Bldg. Bridges for A Better Memphis, 1985—; pres. Eagle Watch Assn.; founder Janet C. Cupples Citizenship awards, Memphis City Inter-City Sch., 1975, Founded Citizenship award, 1975, Memphis City Schs.; founder, chair women's com. on crime City of Memphis, 1985—, chair Heritage-City of Memphis, chair internat. heritage program, 1987, 88—, Ethnic Outreach Neighborfest, 1988—; hon. mem. city coun., 1987; donor, exec. com. Women of Achievement, Inc., Memphis, 1986; mem. spkrs. bus. United Way of Greater Memphis, Friends of Shelby County Libr., 1986—, YMCA; chair ethnic outreach com. Neighborfest, Memphis, 1987, chairperson exec. com., 1988; amb. Memphis Internat. Heritage Commn., 1988; youth mentor Memphis Youth Leadership Devel. Inst.; internat. coord. Neighborfest '88; chairperson Internat. Heritage City of Memphis, 1987; mem. cmty. coun. Memphis City Schs., Memphis Cablevision Edn. Task Force; apptd. col. aide de camp to Gov. Ned McWherter of Tenn., 1988; apptd. hon. mem. Tenn. State Senator Steve Cohen's staff, 1989; sec. safety com. St. Francis Hosp., 1992, sec. Burnsville H.S. com., 1960; participant Vol. Miss. Food Network Distbn. for Disabled Persons, 1996; active Dem. Nat. Com., 1994—; founder Inter City Sch. Citizenship award, 1986; founder Burnsville Sch. Accelerated Reader awards, 2000, Libr. award, Citizenship Essay award, 2001—, founder book donation program, Mr. Jim Cummings Citizenship essay awards, 2000; sec., pub. rels. officer Burnsville H.S. 1960 Exec. Com., 1994-2004; chair Burnsville High 1960 Book Donation Com., 2000-04. Recipient 11 certs. of recognition Memphis City Coun., 1986-89, Outstanding Svc. to Pub. Edn. award 1986, merit award City of Memphis, 1987, Royal award HRH Prince Kevin, 1996; named Outstanding Female Participant, Neighborhood, Inc., 1987; honored by Pres. George Bush as Outstanding Vol., 1989; featured as one of top 1000 Vols. in Mid-South, 1989; Svc. award Cummings Sch., 1993; apptd. Hon. Memphis City Councilwoman, 1995-96; recognized by Gen. Colin Powell, 1997; Burnsville Libr. Project commended by First Lady, Laura Bush, 2002; recipient Outstanding Svc. award Memphis City Schs., 2002, 03. Mem. NAFE, NOW (2d v.p. Memphis chpt. 1987, del. nat. conf. 1987, 2d v.p.), Network Profl. Women's Orgn., NCCJ, Rep. Career Women, Memphis Peace and Justice Ctr., Women's Polit. Caucus Tenn., Nat. Children's Cancer Soc. (friend 1995-96). Methodist. Avocations: community service, writing, teaching.

MARLAR, JOHN THOMAS, environmental engineer; b. Jackson, Ala., Sept. 24, 1939; s. John Thomas and Ada Jean (Hamilton) M.; m. Maryjo Borges, June 22, 1963 (div. 1979); children: John Thomas III, Jeannine Marie, Jennifer Joanne; m. Joyce A. Moon, Aug. 12, 1988 (dec. June 1997); children: Regina Etheridge, Preston E. Moon. Student, Miss. So. Coll., 1957-58; BCE, Auburn U., 1963; MS, Ga. Inst. Tech., 1968. Coop. student U.S. Amry C.E., Mobile, Ala., 1958-63; staff engr. Fed. Water Pollution Control Adminstrn., Atlanta, 1967-68, Alameda, Calif., 1968-69; superfisory san. engr. Fed. Water Quality Adminstrn., San Francisco, 1969-71; chief tech. assessment unit U.S. EPA, Atlanta, 1971-73, chief tech. support br., 1973-76, chief water quality planning br., 1976-81, chief facilities performance br., 1981-91, chief environ. compliance br., 1991-97, ret., 1997, sr. tech. authority internat program-Ukraine, 1996-97; prin. J.T. Marlar, Inc., 1997—; sr. environ. employee EPA, 1998—. With USPHS, 1963-66. Recipient Bronze medal EPA, 1973, 86, 94, 97, Silver medal, 1985, Gold medal, 1988; Alcoa scholar, 1962-63. Mem. Water Pollution Control Fedn., Sigma Xi, Chi Epsilon, Phi Kappa Phi. Home: 85 Sims Rd Winder GA 30680-3594 Office: EPA Sci and Ecol Support Divsn 980 College Station Rd Athens GA 30605-2720 E-mail: budbyepa@alltel.net.

MARLAS, JAMES CONSTANTINE, holding company executive; b. Chgo., Aug. 22, 1937; s. Constantine J. and Helen (Cotsirilos) M.; m. Kendra S. Graham, 1968 (div. 1971); m. Glenn Close, 1984 (div. 1987); m. Marie Nugent-Head, 1993. AB cum laude, Harvard U., 1959; MA in Jurisprudence, Oxford (Eng.) U., 1961; JD, U. Chgo., 1963. Bar: Ill. 1963, N.Y. 1966. Assoc. firm Baker & McKenzie, London and N.Y.C., 1963-66; exec. v.p. South East Commodity Corp., N.Y.C., 1967-68; chmn. bd. Union Capital Corp., N.Y.C., 1968—; vice chmn. bd. Mickelberry's Food Products Co., N.Y.C., 1970-71; pres., dir. Mickelberry Comm. Corp., N.Y.C., 1972—, chief exec. officer, 1973—; chmn. bd. Mickleberry Commn. Corp., 1984—; chmn. bd., CEO Newcourt Industries, Inc., 1976—. Chmn. bd. dirs. Bowmar Instrument Corp., chmn. exec. com., 1983-92. Co-editor: Univ. Chgo. Law Rev, 1962-63; Contbr. articles to profl. jours. Bd. dirs. N.Y.C. Opera, Commanderie de Bordeaux, Brasenose Coll. Charitable Found. Mem. Am. Fgn. Law Assn., Young Pres.'s Orgn. Clubs: Boodle's (London); RKnickerbocker (N.Y.C.), Racquet and Tennis (N.Y.C.). Office: Mickelberry Comm Corp 405 Park Ave New York NY 10022-4405

MARLATT, MICHAEL JAMES, lawyer; b. L.A., Jan. 15, 1957; s. James Raymond and Norma Jean (Greenfield) M.; m. Donna Marie Healey, Apr. 13, 1985. BA, U. So. Calif., Calif. Poly., Pomona, 1981; JD, Pepperdine U., 1984. Bar: Calif. 1984, U.S. Dist. Ct. (ctrl. dist.) Calif. 1985, U.S. Supreme Ct. 1990. Project liaison U. So. Calif., Sch. Medicine, L.A., 1975-78; documentation rschr. NASA-Jet Propulsion Lab., Pasadena, Calif., 1978-81; ptnr. Thompson & Colegate, Riverside, Calif., 1984—. Bd. dirs. Assn. So. Calif. Def. Counsel, L.A., U. Calif., Riverside; lectr. Calif. Trial Lawyers Assn., 1991-94, Princeton U., 1993, U. Amsterdam Law Sch., 1994, Loma Linda (Calif.) U. Sch. Medicine, 1991-94, 99, 2001-03, Boston Coll. Law Sch., 1997, U. London, 1998; chair Am. Legal Sys. Internat. Law Program Civil Litigation U. of Calif., 1997; lectr., spkr. to ins. cos. on health care, 1988—; radio commentator Stas. KCKC, KCAL, KMEN and KPRO. Pres. U. Calif., Riverside, 1996—99, mem. steering com.NCAA/ Big West Athletic Assn., 2003; v.p. Mission Inn Found., 1996—98, pres., 1999—2001; mem. bioethics com. Riverside Cmty. Hosp., 1999—2002; bd. dirs. Humane Soc.; bd. visitors Calif. Bapt. U., 2003—; Mem. ctr. com. Calif. Rep. Party, Sacramento, 1990—93; bd. dirs. U. Calif., Riverside, Mission Inn Found., Riverside County Regional Med. Ctr., ARC, 2002—; bd. regents La Salle Cath. Pasadena, 2002—; bd. visitors Calif. Bapt. U., 2003—. Mem. Am. Bd. Trial Advocates, So. Calif. Assn. Hosp. Risk Mgrs. (bylaws com. 1996-99), Victoria Country Club, Lincoln Club Riverside County, Phi Alpha Delta. Roman Catholic. Avocations: rare book collecting, collegiate athletics, travel. Office: Thompson & Colegate PO Box 1299 3610 14th St Riverside CA 92501-3843 Office Phone: 909-682-5550. Business E-Mail: mmarlatt@tclaw.net.

MARLAY, ROBERT CHARLES, physicist, engineer; b. Seaside, Oreg., Dec. 19, 1946; s. Myron George Jr. and Margaret Alice (Bump) M.; m. Nancy Evelyn Tate, Oct. 18, 1980; children: Jennifer Lynn, Sarah Elizabeth. BS in Engring., Duke U., 1969; MS, M City Planning, MIT, 1971, PhD, 1983. Profl. engr., D.C. Engr. Office of Policy U.S. Dept. Energy, Washington, 1977-83, engr. office of energy conservation, 1983-85, scientist office of energy rsch., 1985-89, dir. office of energy strategy devel., 1989-90, dir. office of program rev. & analysis, office of policy, 1990-92, dir. office tech. policy, 1992-93, dir. office sci. policy, 1993—. Contbr., editor (govt. publ.) Nat. Energy Strategy, 1991. Lt. Civil Engring. Corps, USNR, 1971-74, rear admiral, 1997—. Mem. AAAS, Internat. Assn. for Energy Econs., Sigma Xi. Episcopalian. Achievements include development of quantitative methods for characterizing structural change in industrial economies; development of a national energy strategy; use of technology assessments to guide federal funding priorities for energy research and development. Office: US Dept Energy 1000 Independence Ave SW Washington DC 20585-0001 Address: USN 1510 Gilbert St Norfolk VA 23511-2701 also: Naval Facility Engring Command 1322 Patterson Ave SE Ste 1000 Washington DC 20374-5065

MARLEAU, DIANE, Canadian government official; b. Kirkland Lake, Ont., Can., June 21, 1943; d. Jean-Paul and Yvonne (Desjardins) LeBel; m. Paul C. Marleau, Aug. 3, 1963; children: Brigitte, Donald, Stéphane. Student, U. Ottawa, Ont., 1960-63; BA in Econs., Laurentian U., Sudbury, Ont., 1976. With Donald Jean Acctg. Svcs., Sudbury, 1971-75; receiver mgr. Thorne Riddell, Sudbury, 1975-76; treas. No. Regional Residential Treatment Program for Women, Sudbury, 1976-80, Com. for the Industry and Labour Adjustment Program, Sudbury, 1983; mem. transition team Ont. Premier's Office, Toronto, 1985; firm adminstr. Collins Barrow-Maheu Noiseux, Sudbury, 1985-88; M.P. from Sudbury House of Commons, Ottawa, 1988—; min. of health for Can., 1993-96; min. of public works Canada, 1996-97; min. for internat. cooperation, min. responsible for La Francophonie, 1997-99; vice chair Fgn. Affairs Com., 2002—. Councilor Regional Municipality of Sudbury, 1980-85, chair fin. com., 1981; alderman City of Sudbury, 1980-85; mem. No. Devel. Coun., Sudbury, 1986-88; vice chair Nat. Liberal Standing Com. on Policy, 1989; chair Ont. Liberal Caucus, 1990; apptd. nat. exec. Liberal Party Can., 1990, assoc. critic Govt. Ops., 1990, Dep. Opposition Whip, 1991, assoc. critic Fin., 1992; vice chair standing com. fin., 1992. Chmn. fund-raising Canadian Cancer Soc., Sudbury, 1987-88; co-chmn. Laurentian Hosp. Cancer Care Svcs. fund-raising campaign, Sudbury, 1988; chair bd. govs. Cambrian Coll., 1987-88, bd. govs., 1983-88; mem. Sudbury and Dist. Health Unit Bd., 1981-82; mem. fin. com., bd. dirs. Laurentian Hosp., 1981-85; chair Can. Games for the Physically Disabled, 1983; apptd. Ont. Adv. Coun. Women's Issues, 1984. Recipient Paul Harris award, 1996. Mem. Sudbury Bus. and Profl. Women Club. Liberal Party Can. Avocations: playing piano, gardening, cooking. Office: House of Commons Parliament Bldgs Ottawa ON Canada K1A 0A6 also: 36 Elgin St Sudbury ON Canada P3C 5B4

MARLEN, JAMES S. chemical, plastics and building materials manufacturing company executive; b. Santiago, Chile, Mar. 14, 1941; came to U.S., 1961; m. Carolyn S. Shields, Jan. 23, 1965; children: James, Andrew, John. B.S. chem engring., U. Ala., 1965; MBA, U. Akron, 1971. With GenCorp., Akron, Ohio, 1965-93, engring., mktg. and gen. mgmt. positions domestic and internat. ops., 1977—80; group pres. fabricated plastics GTR Coated Fabrics Co., 1980-87; pres. consumer and indsl. sects. GenCorp Polymer Products, Akron, Ohio, 1988—; v.p. and officer GenCorp, Akron, 1988-93; pres., CEO Ameron Internat. Corp., Pasadena, Calif., 1993—. Bd. dirs., Ameron, Inc., chmn. bd. dirs., pres. and CEO, 1995—; dir. A. Schulman, Inc., Tamco Steel, Parsons Corp.; gen. and hon. chmn. Nat. Inventors Hall of Fame Induction, 1993. Bd. dirs. YMCA Met. L.A., The Employers Group of Calif., Town Hall of L.A., gov.; mem. the Beavers; dir. L.A. Sports Coun.; mem. bd. visitors Anderson Sch. Bus., UCLA, 1999-2001. Mem. Chem. Mfrs. Assn. (past pres.), Assocs. Caltech, Calif. C. of C., L.A. C. of C. (dir.), Portage Country Club (Akron, Ohio), Calif. Club (L.A.), Annandale Golf Club (Pasadena), L.A. Country Club, Valley Hunt Club (Pasadena), Soc. Fellows of Huntington Libr. (L.A.), Birnam Wood Golf Club (Santa Barbara, Calif.). Office: Ameron Internat Corp 245 S Los Robles Ave Pasadena CA 91101-2820

MARLER, CHARLES HERBERT, journalism educator, historian, consultant; b. Garfield, Ark., Apr. 13, 1933; s. William Owen and Velma Valentine (Poe) M.; m. Peggy Lucille Gambill, Dec. 30, 1954; children: David Owen, Todd Alan, Scott Ladd. BA, Abilene Christian U., 1955, MA, 1968; PhD, U. Mo., 1974. Publicity asst. Abilene (Tex.) Christian U., 1955-56, sports info. dir., 1958-63, assoc. dir. devel., 1963-64, dir. info. and pubs., 1964-71, prof. journalism, 1974—2003, chmn. dept. journalism and mass comm., 1987-98, prof. emeritus journalism and sr. faculty, 2003—; rsch. asst. U. Mo., Columbia, 1973-74. Editor: Horizons, 1963-71, Lone Star Christmas, 1989, No Ordinary University, 1998; cons. Parenting Today, Christian Woman, Gospel Advocate, IdeaShop, Christian Chronicle; mem. editl. bd. Am. Journalism, Southwestern Mass Comm. Jour.; contbr. articles to profl. jours. Elder Univ. Ch. Christ, Abilene, 1977—; trustee Christian Village of Abilene, 1981-2000, Members of Chs. of Christ for Scouting, Abilene, 1985—, nat. chmn., 1989-91; mem. coun. bd. Boy Scouts Am., Abilene, 1981-2001. With U.S. Army, 1956-57, Germany. Frank Luther Mott Hist. Rsch. fellow U. Mo., Columbia, 1972-74, Cullen Fund grantee, 1982-84, 85-87; recipient Improvement award Time/Life Alumni Mag., 1966, Journalism Excellence award 20th Century Christian Mag., 1968, Clinton H. Denman Freedom of Info. Writing award U. Mo., 1974, Scoutmaster's key Boy Scouts Am., 1981, Dist. Merit award, 1982, Keith Ware award U.S. Army Journalism Competition, 1985, Tchr. of Yr. Trustees award, 1987, Silver Beaver award Boy Scouts Am., 1988, Christian Journalism award The Christian Chronicle, 1993; named Advisor of Yr., Tex. Intercollegiate Press Assn., 1982, Faithful Servant, Chs. Christ for Scouting, 1990, Faculty Senate award, 2000, Coll. Arts and Scis. Career Achievement award, 2000, Charlie Marler scholarship, Southwestern Journalism Congress, 2001; named to Tex. Intercoll. Press Assn. Hall of Fame, 2003, Pioneer award, 2003, S.W. Edn. Coun. for Edn. in Jour. and Mass Commn. Mem. Am. Journalism Historian Assn. (bd. dirs. 1985-88, chmn. pub. com. 1983-87, 95-96, chmn. election and site com. 1987-90), Nat. Conf. Editorial Writers, S.W. Edn. Coun. for Edn. in Journalism and Mass Comm. (pres. 1988-89), SW Journalism Congress (pres 1987-88, 1997-98, 1998-99, 99-2000), Texas Intercollegiate Press Assn. Advs. (pres. 1987-89), Soc. Newspaper Design, Soc. Profl. Journalists (dep. dir. journalism edn. 1988-90, mem. nat. journalism edn. com. 1988-90), Assn. for Edn. in Journalism and Mass Comm. and Religion and Media Interest Group (chair 1999-2000). Avocations: geneaology, newspaper coffee mug collecting, travel, research, camping. Home: 818 Radford Dr Abilene TX 79601-4613 Office: Dept Journalism and Mass Comm ACU Box 27892 Abilene Christian U Abilene TX 79699-7892 E-mail: charlie.marler@jmc.acu.edu.

MARLER, HELEN, writer, actress; b. Alexandria, Va., Oct. 24, 1945; d. Howard Bradley Marler and Ruth Winnifred Austin; m. Patrick John O'Donnell, 1970 (div. 1999); children: Christopher, Rebecca, Jared, Jonathan, Kathryn. Student, Columbia Union Coll. Radio announcer; profl. rschr. for pub. opinion and product devel.; actor, writer; officer mgr. 2 cos. Cons. for organizing individuals and cos.; history cons. for film Grey Stone Inc., Calif.; history and cast cons. for TV show Turner Films; cons. Fed. Hill Found.; founder, dir. Anti-ERA; genealogist; history cons. for congressman and bdwy. producers. Author: 1860 Census of Johnston County, 1850 Census of Johnston County, Romance Stories of Fredericksburg; actor: film for BBC and PBS; ghostwriter: books and articles. Pres. Living History Co. Fredericksburg; past dir. Family History Libr. Fredericksburg VA Stake of the Ch. of Jesus Christ of Latter-day Saints. Mem. Ch. Of Jesus Christ Of Latter-Day Saints. Address: Ste C7 904 Princess Anne St Fredericksburg VA 22401-5800

MARLER, JOAN, writer, educator; b. Chico, Calif., June 6, 1947; d. William Thomas Marler and Grace Elizabeth Paddock; m. Dan Dimitrov Smith, Jan. 1, 1975; 1 child, Sorrel Smith. BA in Dance, Mills Coll., Oakland, CA, 1969; MA in Archaeomythology, Sonoma State U., 1998. Instr. folk and ethnic dance Santa Rosa (Calif.) Jr. Coll., 1975—; prof. archaeomythology Calif. Inst. Integral Studies, San Francisco, 1996—. Radio prodr. KPFA, Berkeley, 1982—96; vis. prof. art history Sonoma State U., Rohnert Park, 1998; adj. faculty New Coll. Calif., San Francisco, 1998—2001; founder, dir. Inst. Archaeomythology. Editor: From the Realm of the Ancestors: An Anthology in Honor of Marija Gimbutas, 1997; author: (article in anthology) Treasures: Studies in Honor of Ivan Marazov, 1998, In Le radici prime dellÆEuropa: Gli intrecci genetici, linguistici, storici, 2002, In Women in Transition: Voices, 2001, Il Mito e il Cueto della grande Dea, 2003, Die Diskriminierung der Matriarchatsforschung, 2003, Notable American Women, 2003; editor: (jour.) ReVision Jour., (by Marija Gimbutas) Civilization of the Goddess, 1991. Founding mem. Monastery Project. Grantee, Calif. Inst. Integral Studies, 2000. Mem.: Anthrop. Assn. Am. (assoc.). Office: Institute of Archaeomythology 1645 Furlong Road Sebastopol CA 95472 Personal E-mail: jmarler@sonic.net. E-mail: jmarler@archaeomythology.org.

MARLETT, CHARLES D. air transportation executive; b. Corry, Pa. BA in Econ. and Math., U. Pitts., 1976, JD, 1979; MBA, U. Pa., 1984. Bar: Pa., Tex. Atty. MacDonald Illig Jones & Britton, Erie, Pa., Drinker Biddle & Reath, Phila.; atty., legal dept. AMR Corp., 1984—88, corp. sec., 1988—. Mem.: Pa. Bar Assn., Tex. Bar Assn. Office: AMR Corp 4333 Amon Carter Blvd Fort Worth TX 76155

MARLETT, JUDITH ANN, nutritional sciences educator, researcher; b. Toledo; BS, Miami U., Oxford, Ohio, 1965; PhD, U. Minn., 1972; postgrad., Harvard U., 1973-74. Registered dietitian. Therapeutic and metabolic unit dietitian VA Hosp., Mpls., 1966-67; spl. instr. in nutrition Simmons Coll., Boston, 1973-74; asst. prof. U. Wis., Madison, 1975-80, assoc. prof. dept. nutritional scis., 1981-84, prof. dept. nutritional scis., 1984—. Cons. U.S. AID, Leyte, Philippines, 1983; acting dir. dietetic program dept. Nutritional Scis. U. Wis., 1977-78, dir., 1985-89; cons. grain, drug and food cos., 1985—, adv. bd. U. Ariz. Clin. Cancer Ctr., 1987-95; sci. bd. advisors Am. Health Found., 1988—; reviewer NIH, 1982—. Mem. editl. bd. Jour. Sci. of Food and Agrl., 1989—, Jour. Food Composition and Analysis, 1994-2000, Jour. of Nutrition, 2002—; contbr. articles to profl. jours. Mem. AAAS, NIH (Diabetes amd Digestive and Kidney Disease spl. grant rev. com. 1992-96), Am. Soc. Nutritional Scis., Am. Dietetic Assn., Am. Soc. Clin. Nutrition. Achievements include research and international speaker on human nutrition and disease, dietary fiber and gastrointestinal function. Office: U Wis Dept Nutritional Sci 1415 Linden Dr Madison WI 53706-1527 Office Phone: 608-262-2895. Business E-Mail: jmarlett@nutrisci.wisc.edu.

MARLETTA, MICHAEL A. biochemistry educator, researcher, protein chemist; b. Rochester, N.Y., Feb. 12, 1951; m. Margaret Gutowski, 1991. BA, SUNY, 1973; PhD in Pharm. Chemistry, U. Calif., 1978. Fellow MIT, Cambridge, 1978-80, from asst. prof. to assoc. prof. toxicology, 1980-87; assoc. prof. med. chemistry U. Mich., Ann Arbor, 1987-91, assoc. prof. biol. chemistry, 1989-91, John G. Searle prof. med. chemistry, prof. biol. chemistry, 1991—2001; prof., dept. of chem. and biology U. Calif. at Berkeley, 2001—; prof., dept. of cellular and molecular pharmacology U. Calif. at San Franciso, 2001—. Investigator Howard Hughes Med. Inst., 1997. John D. and Catherine T. MacArthur fellow, 1995. Mem. AAAS, Am. Soc. Biochem. and Molecular Biology, Am. Chem. Soc. Achievements include research in protein/structure function with a particular interest in enzyme reaction mechanisms and molecular mechanisms of signal transduction, study of nitric oxide synthase, guanylate cyclase and related enzymes in this signaling system. Office: U Calif at Berkeley Dept Chemistry 211 Lewis Hall 1460 Berkeley CA 94720-1460

MARLEY, BRIAN THOMAS, accountant; b. Asheboro, N.C., Apr. 29, 1957; s. Edison Earl and Irma Patricia (Krewson) M.; m. Mary Anna Jackson; 1 child, Brian Thomas Jr. BS, U. N.C., 1980. CPA, N.C. Staff acct. KMG Main Hurdman, Charlotte, N.C., 1980-83; sr. acct. Peat Marwick Main and Co., Charlotte, 1983-86, audit mgr., 1986—. Mem. acctg. adv. com. Cen. Piedmont Community Coll., Charlotte, 1986—; merit badge counselor Boy Scouts Am., Charlotte, 1985—; mem. membership com. Charlotte Uptown YMCA, 1988—. Mem. Am. Inst. CPA's, N.C. Assn. CPA's, Constrn. Fin. Mgmt. Assn. (bd. dirs. Charlotte chpt. 1987—). Office: Peat Marwick Main and Co 1800 First Union Plz Charlotte NC 28282

MARLEY, JAMES EARL, former manufacturing company executive; b. Marietta, Pa., Mar. 18, 1935; s. Earl W. () and Elsie H. (Fahringer) Marley; m. Kathleen Y. Robinson, Nov. 22, 1974; children: Kathy L., Robert B., Kimberly J., Lora B. BS in Aero. Engring., Pa. State, 1957; MS in Mech. Engring., Drexel U., 1963, PhD, 1995. Group dir. automachine AMP Inc., Harrisburg, Pa., 1969-70, v.p. automachine group, 1970-79, v.p. mfg. resources, 1979-80, v.p. mfg., 1980-81, corp. v.p. mfg., 1981-83, corp. v.p. ops., 1983-86, pres., 1986—, COO, 1990—, chmn. bd., 1993-98, also bd. dirs. Inventor and patentee in field. Mem.: Mem. IEEE, Am. Soc. Mech. Engrs., Am. Mgmt. Assn., Mfg. Council of the Machinery and Allied Products Inst., Harrisburg C. of C., Meritor Automotive. Clubs: Harrisburg Country (Pa.) (bd. dirs., bd. govs. 1983). Republican. Office: AMP Inc PO Box 3608 470 Friendship Rd Harrisburg PA 17111-1203

MARLIN, ARTHUR EDWARD, pediatric neurosurgeon, educator; b. Boston, Jan. 28, 1947; s. Herman and Eva Marlin; m. Bebby Marlin; children: Sarah Jane, Tamara Eve, Evan Seth. BSc with distinction, McGill U., 1968, MD, 1972; MHA, Trinity Sch. Health Care Admn., 1999. Diplomate Am. Bd. Neurol. Surgery; lic. surgeon, N.Y., Tex. Surg. intern U. Minn. Hosps., 1972-73; resident NYU Med. Ctr., 1973-78; clin. instr. neurosurgery NYU Sch. Medicine, 1978; asst. prof. surgery/neurosurgery, asst. prof. pediatrics U. Tex. Health Sci. Ctr., San Antonio, 1978-80, clin. asst. prof. surgery/neurosurgery, 1980-84, clin. asst. prof. pediatrics, 1980-82, clin. assoc. prof. pediatrics, 1982-91, clin. assoc. prof. orthopedics, 1985-91, clin. prof. pediatrics, 1991—2001; CEO Meth. Womens and Childrens Hosp., 1998, Meth. Childrens Hosp. of So. Tex., 1998—2003. Chief sect. pediatric neurosurgery Santa Rosa Childrens Hosp., San Antonio, 1984-97; mem. adv. bd. South Tex. Organ Bank, 1987-90; mem. tech. adv. com. to gen. program Crippled Children's Svcs., Tex. Dept. Health, Austin, 1983-84; mem. Childrens Hosps. and Related Instns. Tex. Author: Handbook of Pediatric Neurology and Neurosurgery, 1993; editor: Concepts in Pediatric Neurosurgery, Vol. VII, 1987, Vol. VIII, 1988, Vol. IX, 1989, Vol. X, 1990, Vol. XI, 1991, Shortcuts, 1989-91; mem. editl. bd. Clin. Neurosurgery, 1981, 82, 83; ann. meeting editor Jour. Pediatric Neurosurgery, 1992-2002, mem. editl. bd., 1992-2002; prodr. movies Brain Retraction Pressure Monitoring, 1983, The Use of Surgical Isolation Bubble, 1986; contbr. articles to profl. jours. Fellow ACS, Am. Acad. Pediatrics; mem. AMA, Bexar County Med. Soc., Tex. Med. Assn., Internat. Soc. Pediatric Neurosurgery, San Antonio Pediatric Soc., Am. Soc. Pediatric Neurosurgery (chmn. edn. com. 1986-91), Tex. Pediatric Soc., Am. Assn. Neurol. Surgeons (chmn. pediatric sect. 1993-95), Am. Acad. Pediatrics (neurosurgery sect.). Office: 4499 Medical Dr Ste 397 San Antonio TX 78229-3713 Office Phone: 210-615-1218. E-mail: aem@pediatric-neurosurgery.com.

MARLIN, JOHN TEPPER, economist, writer, consultant; b. Washington, Mar. 1, 1942; s. Ervin Ross and Hilda (van Stockum) M.; m. Alice Rose Tepper, Sept. 25, 1971; children: John Joseph Tepper (Jay), Caroline Alice Tepper. AB cum laude, Harvard U., 1962; MA, Oxford U., 1969; PhD in

Econs., George Washington U., 1968. Fin. economist Fed. Res. Bd., 1964-66, SBA, Washington, 1966-67, FDIC, Washington, 1967-69; asst. prof. Baruch Coll., CUNY, 1969-73; founder, pres. Coun. Mcpl. Performance, N.Y.C., 1973-88; pres. JTM Reports, Inc., N.Y.C., 1989-92; first social auditor Ben and Jerry's Homemade, 1989; dir. Conversion Info. Ctr., Coun. Econ. Priorities, 1991-92; chmn., bd. advisors CIC, CEP, 1992-95, advisor internat. security program, 1995—2001. Cons. J.M. Kaplan Fund, 1991-92; chief economist Office Comptr., City of N.Y., 1992-94, 97—, sr. policy advisor, 1994-97; adj. prof. fin. Pace U. Lubin Sch. Bus., N.Y.C., 2000—; adj. prof. markets, ethics and law NYU Stern Sch. Bus., N.Y.C., 2002--. Author: The Wealth of Cities, 1974, Cities of Opportunity, 1988, Catalogue of Healthy Food, 1990, The Livable Cities Almanac, 1992, Take up the Song, 1998 (prod. in Rochester's Geva Theatre, 1988, video produced, 2000); co-author: Let's Go Guide to Europe, 1961, Book of American City Rankings, 1983, Contracting Municipal Services, 1984, Book of World City Rankings, 1986, Soviet Conversion, 1991, Building a Peace Economy, 1992, NYC's Sports Economy, 1996, N.Y.C.'s Software/Information Technology Industry, 1999, The Impact of the September 11 WTC Attack on NYC's Economy and City Revenues, 2001, One Year Later: The Fiscal Impact of 9/11 on New York City, 2002; founding editor: Jour. Fin. Edn., 1972—73; editor: Nat. Civic Rev., 1987—88, Privatization Report, 1986—88, Econ. Notes, 1992—94, 1997—; contbr. to N.Y. State Ency., 2003. Donor-advisor E.R. Marlin Fund, N.Y. Cmty. Trust, 1994—; elder, chmn. budget and fin. com. Springs Cmty. Presbyn. Ch., 2000—. Mem. Am. Econ. Assn. (life), Fin. Mgmt. Assn. (life), Economists Allied Arms Reduction (treas., mem. exec. com. 1994—), Harvard Club (N.Y.C.), Devon Yacht Club (bd. govs. 2003—), Trinity (Oxford) Soc. U.S.A. (pres. 1969-94), Oxford U. Soc. (trustee, exec. com. 1999-2002), Brit. Schs. and Univs. Found. (treas. 2002—), Oxford U. Alumni Assn. N.Y. (sec. 1994-99), Oxford Cambridge Dinner Com. (N.Y.C., pres. 1992—), Money Marketeers NYU, N.Y. Assoc. Bus. Economists (v.p. 2000-02, pres. 2002-03). Home: 360 W 22nd St New York NY 10011-2600 Office: City of New York Office Comptr 1 Centre St Rm 621 New York NY 10007-1602 Office Phone: 212-669-2939. E-mail: jmarlin@comptroller.nyc.gov., jtmarlin@post.harvard.edu., TepperMarlin@aol.com.

MARLIN, RICHARD, lawyer; b. N.Y.C., June 1, 1933; s. Edward and Lillian (Milstein) M.; m. Merrel Pincus, June 12, 1955 (div. 1972); children: John F., Elizabeth; m. Jenesta Rutherford, July 29, 1974 (div. 1981); m. Caroline Mary Hirsch Magnus, Nov. 1, 1981. BA magna cum laude, Yale U., 1955, LLB, 1958; LLM, NYU, 1964. Bar: N.Y. 1959, Fla. 1978. Law clk. to presiding justice U.S. Dist. Ct. Conn., New Haven, 1958-59; assoc. Cleary, Gottlieb, Steen & Hamilton, N.Y.C., 1959-62, Wien Lane & Klein, N.Y.C., 1962-64; ptnr. Mnuchin Moss & Marlin, N.Y.C., 1964-66, Marshall, Bratter, Greene, Allison & Tucker, N.Y.C., 1966-79; sr. ptnr. Kramer, Levin, Naftalis & Frankel LLP, N.Y.C., 1979—. Bd. dirs. FAB Industries, Inc., N.Y.C. Bd. editors Yale Law Jour. Mem. ABA, Assn. Bar City N.Y., N.Y. County Lawyers' Assn. (corp. law com., chmn. subcom.), Glen Oaks Club (Old Westbury, N.Y.) (bd. govs. 1979-85, 92-94), Phi Beta Kappa. Office: Kramer Levin Naftalis & Frankel LLP 919 3rd Ave New York NY 10022-3902

MARLIN, STERLING, race car driver; b. Columbia, Tenn., June 30, 1957; Profl. driver NASCAR, 1976—. Named winner, Daytona 500, 1994, 1995, Tran South 400, 1995, Die Hard 500, 1995, Winston Select, 1996, Pepsi 500, 1996. Office: Team SABCO 114 Meadow Hill Cir Mooresville NC 28117-8089

MARLING, KARAL ANN, art history and social sciences educator, curator; b. Rochester, N.Y., Nov. 5, 1943; d. Raymond J. and Marjorie (Karal) M. PhD, Bryn Mawr Coll., 1971. Prof. art history and Am. studies U. Minn., Mpls., 1977—. Author: Federal Art in Cleveland, 1933-1943: An Exhibition, 1974, Wall-to-Wall America: America: A Cultural History of Post-Office Murals in the Great Depression, 1982, 2d edit., 2001, The Colossus of the Roads: Myth and Symbol Along the American Highway, 1984, 2d edit., 2000, Tom Benton and His Drawings: A Biographical Essay and a Collection of His Sketches, Studies and Mural Cartoons, 1985, Frederick C. Knight (1898-1797), 1987, George Washington Slept Here: Colonial Revivals and American Culture, 1876-1986, 1988, Looking Back: A Perspective on the 1913 Inaugural Exhibition, 1988, Blue Ribbon: A Social and Pictorial History of the Minnesota State Fair, 1990; author: (with John Wetenhall) Iwo Jima: Monuments, Memories, and the American Hero, 1991; author: Edward Hopper, 1992, As Seen on T.V.: The Visual Culture of Everyday Life in the 1950's, 1994, Graceland: Going Home with Elvis, 1995; editor (with Jessica H. Foy): The Arts and the American Home, 1890-1930, 1994; editor: Norman Rockwell, 1997, Designing the Disney Theme Parks: The Architecture of Reassurance, 1997, Merry Christmas! Celebrating America's Greatest Holiday, 2000, Looking North, 2003, Debutante, 2004, Old Glory Unfurled, 2004; contbr. essays to catalogs. Recipient Minn. Humanities Commn. award 1986, Minn. Book award History, 1994, Robert C. Smith award Decorative Arts Soc., 1994, Internat. Assn. of Art Critics award, 1998. Office: 1920 S 1st St Ste 1301 Minneapolis MN 55454-1190 Office Phone: 612-339-6172. E-mail: kmarling@mn.rr.com.

MARLON, ANTHONY M. healthcare company executive, cardiologist; Intern, resident, cardiology fellow Stanford (Calif.) U., 1967-72; chief cardiology U. Med. Ctr. So. Nev., 1972-85; pvt. practice cardiology, from 1972; founder, chmn. bd., CEO Sierra Health Svcs., Inc., Las Vegas, Nev. Office: Sierra Health Svcs Inc 2724 N Tenaya Way Las Vegas NV 89128

MARLOW, AUDREY SWANSON, artist, designer; b. N.Y.C.; d. Sven and Rita (Porter) Swanson; student (scholarships) Art Students League, 1950-55; spl. courses SUNY (Stony Brook), L'Alliance Française m. Roy Marlow, Nov. 30, 1968. With Cohn-Hall-Marx Textile Studio, 1961-65, R.S. Assocs. Textile Studio, 1965-73; freelance designer, illustrator Prince Matchabelli, Lester Harrison Agy., J. Walter Thompson Agy., 1957-78; portrait and fine artist, Wading River, N.Y., 1973—; instr. Phoenix Sch. Design (N.Y.C.); illustrator children's books: Breads of Many Lands and 4H Club Bakes Bread, 1966, Anna Smith Strong and the Setauket Spy Ring, 1991, Timothy and the Acrobat, 1992; exhibits include: Nat. Arts Club, NAD, Parish Art Mus., South Hampton, N.Y., Guild Hall, East Hampton, N.Y., Portraits Inc., Lincoln Ctr., Chung-Cheng Art Gallery, St. John's U., Mystic (Conn.) Art Assn., Harbour Gallery, St. Thomas, V.I., Palais Rameau, Lisle, France, 1988, Sumner Mus., Washington, 1992, East End Arts & Humanities Coun., L.I., N.Y., 1996; one-person shows: Salmagundi Club, 1982, Rockefeller Gallery, N.Y.C., 1992; portrait commns. include: Millicent Fenwick, Harrison J. Goldin, Thomas R. Bayles, Mons. John Fagan, others. Trustee, Middle Island Public Library, 1972-76. Recipient John W. Alexander medal, 1976, award Council on Arts, 1978, award of excellence Cork Gallery, Lincoln Center, 1982; Grumbacher Bronze medal, 1983; Grumbacher Silver medal 1986; Best in Show award N.Y. Arts Council, 1986, Suburban Art League, 1993, Excellence award Town of Oyster Bay, 1995, Brookhaven Arts & Humanities Coun., 1996. Mem. Pastel Soc. Am. (award 1977, 80, 90), Am. Artists Profl. League (2 1st prize awards), Hudson Valley Art Assn. (award), Knickerbocker Artists (2 awards), Catharine Lorillard Wolfe Art Club (award 1982), Salmagundi Club (5 awards), Nat. League Am. Pen Women (Gold award, Gold medal of Honor, Best in Show 1990). Works represented at NYU, Longwood Pub. Libr., Sr. Citizen's Complex, Newark, St. Theresa of the Child Jesus Convent, Wading River Congl. Ch., L.I., pvt. collections. Home: 147 N Side Rd Wading River NY 11792-1112

MARLOW, EDWARD A. former army officer; b. Cleve., Nov. 22, 1946; m. Gari Ann Dill, Sept. 20, 1975. AA, Long Beach City Coll., 1971; cert., Officer Candidate Sch., Ft. Benning, 1974, Basic Infantry Officer Course, 1976; student, Am. Law Inst., N.Y., 1979-80; cert., Advance Armor Officer Course, Ft. Knox, 1982, U.S. Army Command and Gen. Staff Coll., 1986; BS in Bus. Mgmt. and Polit. Sci., SUNY, 1987; MPA, U. So. Calif., 1990; cert., Advance Intelligence Officer Course, Ft. Huachuca, 1991. Registered investment adv. with SEC, 1978-90. Commd. 2d lt. inf. U.S. Army, 1974, advanced through grades to maj., 1988; chief real property br. Mil. Dept., Sacramento, 1968—; pres. and dir. TEAM Mgmt. Corp., 1978—2003; pres. Western Res. Corp., Goldfield, Nev., 2000—, also bd. dirs.; CEO Team Internat. LLC, Sacramento, 2004—. Del. Korean Svc. Vets. Revisit Program, Seoul, Republic of Korea, 1975. Mng. sr. ptnr. Caribbean Basin Latin Am. Devel. Orgn., Sacramento, 1988-98; trustee Hosp. Relief Fund Caribbean, Inc., Washington, 1989-92; mem. Caribbean Pvt. Sector Disaster Coord. subcom. White House Internat. Disaster Adv. Com., 1991-92; sr. ptnr. Caribbean Basin Latin Am. Devel. Orgn. Endowment Group, Sacramento, 1992 ; chair bd. trustees CABALADO Relief Fund, Inc., 1993-99; provided disaster assistance and med. equipment to Glendon Hosp., Plymouth, Montserrat, West Indies, 1994-95. Mem. DAV (life), Am. Assn. Retired Persons, Park and Recreation Com. Found. (steering com. 2004—). Avocations: sailing, fishing.

MARLOW, IAN MICHAEL, real estate company executive; b. Bklyn., Jan. 18, 1975; s. David Zachary and Ann Marlow. BSChemE, Rensselaer Poly. Inst., 1996. Environ. engr. Dept. Def., N.Y., 1993-96; nuc. engr. Dept. Energy, N.Y., 1996-97; v.p., dir. info. scis. Homestead Ins. Co., Florham Park, NJ, 1997-99; v.p., chief engring. and mktg. officer Signet Star Re, Florham Park, 1999—2002; exec. v.p., COO, CIO The Gale Co. LLC, Florham Park, 2002. Mem. Datawarehousing Inst., Phi Lambda Phi (Nat. Engring. award). Avocations: sailing, automobiles, travel. Home: 11 Champion Blvd Livingston NJ 07039-8240

MARLOW, PATRICIA BAIR BOND, realtor; b. Altoona, Pa., Dec. 3, 1932; d. John Lesley and Gladys Marie Bair; m. Neal Nelson Jensen Bond, Aug. 7, 1953 (dec. July 1963); children: John Scott Bond, Lisa Suzanne Moody, Lesley Ann Stephen; m. Laurin Purcell Marlow, Apr. 4, 1967. Student, Mary Washington Coll., 1950-52. Realtor Everitt/Luby, Dallas, 1971-80; with Merrill Lynch, Dallas, 1980-89; realtor Adleta & Poston, Dallas, 1989—. Contbr. poetry to anthologies. Recipient Diamond Summit. Mem. Dallas Mus. Art, Dallas Arboretum, Les Femmes du Monde, Dallas Mus. Art League, Tex. Kidney Found. Avocation: watercolor painting. Home: 4531 Nashwood Ln Dallas TX 75244-7520 E-mail: patti@pattimarlow.com.

MARLOW, SHELLEY F. writer; b. Malden, Mass., Feb. 25, 1959; d. Robert E. and Beatrice Marlow; life ptnr. Martha R. Keith. BFA, Mass. Coll. Art and Design, 1986; MFA, Calif. Inst. of Arts, 1986—88. Asst. dir. Estate of Charmion Von Wiegand, N.Y.C., 2000—02; freelance writer, articles/reviews/interviews Shout Mag., Zingmagazine, Gurl.com, Wburg-.com, Girlfriends Mag., New Observations Mag., Sandbox Arts Mag., Publishers Weekly., N.Y.C., 1997—2003. Awards juror Scholastic Writing Awards, N.Y.C., 2002, Mass. Coll. Art, Boston, 2003. Author: (book) Two Augusts in a Row in a Row, Swann in Love Again in the Lesbian Arabian Nights; author: (lyricist) (short musical) (un) Knot Turandot; solo exhibition, Eels Chopped and Cooked (reviewed by Greg Masters for Cover Mag., 1992); author: (articles, interviews and reviews) for Zingmagazine, Gurl.com, Wburg.com, Sandbox Mag., New Observations Mag., Publishers Weekly, others; exhibitions include The La Fontaine Fables Exhbn., Ctr. for Advanced Art and Culture, Aix en Provence, France, Jacob Lawrence Gallery, U. Wash., Perogi Gallery Libr., exhibitions include numerous others. Donation of artworks and services Sandbox Arts Orgn., The Coalition for the Homeless, 4 Walls Benefit, etc., N.Y.C., 1994—2001. Recipient Blue Ribbon, Gold Medal, Scholastic Art Awards, 1970—71; Ahmanson Award ($4000 not necessary to include?), Calif. Inst. of the Arts, 1987, residency, Macdowell Colony, N.H., 1992, residency Montescaglioso, Matera Region, Italy, Oreste (Italian art Group), 1999. Mem.: Amnesty Internat. Jewish. Avocations: bicycling, reading, singing, travel, cooking. Home: 110 Bedford Ave Brooklyn NY 11211 Personal E-mail: sfmarlow@mindspring.com.

MARLOWE, CHRIS SEAN, safety engineer; b. Newark, Dec. 2, 1950; s. Thomas John and Elaine Marie (Kall) M.; m. Mary Haddad, July 1, 1972; children: Charles, Danelle, Jon, Fred, Karen, Leila. BA in Chemistry, Rutgers U., 1976; M Environ. Engring., N.J. Inst. Tech., 1984. Cert. indsl. hygienist, hazardous materials mgr., qualified environ. profl. Indsl. hygienist OSHA, U.S. Labor Dept., Newark, 1977-82; chemist Jacobs Engring., Edison, N.J., 1984-85; mgr. safety and health Envirespone, Inc., Livingston, NJ, 1985; health and safety mgr. Camp Dresser & McKee, Edison, N.J., 1987—. Author: Safety Now Action Levels for Hazardous Waste Operations. Exxon NJDEP fellow in environ. engring., 1982-84. Mem. Am. Chem. Soc. (past chair divsn. chem. health and safety), Am. Indsl. Hygiene Assn. (past chair hazardous waste com., Drum Buster award 1996). Democrat. Unitarian Universalist. Avocations: computers, peace activism. Home: 42 Highlander Dr Scotch Plains NJ 07076-2424 Office: Camp Dresser & McKee Inc Raritan Plz I 42 Highlander Dr Scotch Plains NJ 07076 E-mail: chrismarlowe@comcast.net., Marlowecs@cdm.com.

MARLOWE, WILLIE, artist, fine arts educator; b. Whiteville, N.C., Jan. 17, 1943; d. John David and Tessie Ernestine (McLawhorn) M.; m. Thomas Blakeslee Speight, July 11, 1980. Student, Pa. Acad. Fine Arts, Phila., 1964; BS, East Carolina U., 1965; MFA, U. Idaho, 1969; postgrad., Peace Coll., 1993. Instr. dept. art Skidmore Coll., Saratoga Springs, NY, 1970-74, mentor univ. without walls, 1972-74; instr. dept. art Columbia-Greene C.C., Hudson, NY, 1973-74; instr. Empire State Coll. SUNY, Albany, 1974; prof. Dept. Visual Arts Sage Coll., Albany, 1977—; chmn. The Sage Colls., Albany, 1979-81. Co-founder, tchr. Saratoga Arts Workshop, Saratoga Springs, N.Y., 1970-74; watercolor tchr. abroad Sage Colls., Scotland, Ireland, 2001; tchr. Somerville Coll., Oxford U., Eng., 1992; vis. artist U. Ga. studies abroad program, Cortona, Italy, 1989; vis. artist, Wexford Arts Ctr., Ireland, 1998, artist-in-residence for Ptnrs. of the Americas, Barbados, W.I., 1986, The Millay Colony for the Arts, Austerlitz, N.Y., 1999; artist selection com. Albany Ctr. Gallery, 1998; lectr. in field. One-woman shows include The Mint Mus. Art, Charlotte, N.C., 1971, Schenectady Mus., N.Y., 1975, Marist Coll., Poughkeepsie, N.Y., 1976, Stockton State Coll., Pomono, N.J., 1977, The Greenville Mus. Art, N.C., 1982, 97, Ann Grey Gallery The Casino, Saratoga Springs, N.Y., 1985, The Barrett Art Gallery Utica Coll. Syracuse U., N.Y., 1986, The Atrium Gen. Electric Corp. R&D Ctr., Schenectady, 1988, The Forum Gallery, Gütersloh, Germany, 1992, Albany Ctr. Gallery, 1992, 97, McHenry County Coll., Crystal Lake, Ill., The Main St. Gallery, Dobbs Ferry, 1995, The Wexford Arts Ctr., Ireland, 1998, The Saratoga Arts Ctr., Saratoga Springs, N.Y., 2000, Rathbone Gallery, Albany, 2001, Fondo del Sol Gallery and Visual Arts Ctr., Washington, 2002, Barrett Arts Ctr., Poughkeepsie, N.Y., 2002, Gallery C, Raleigh, 2003, others; exhibited in group shows at Art Ctr. for the Capital Region, Troy, N.Y., 2002, Reprize Internat. Invitational Show, Wexford Arts Ctr., Wexford, Ireland, 2002, Martinez Gallery, Troy, NY, 2002, Artemisia Gallery, Chgo., 2000, 03, Nexus Gallery, N.Y.C., 1997-99, The Gang Gallery, N.Y.C., Eng. & Co., London, 1993, Steinbaum-Krauss Gallery, N.Y.C., 1990, Stux Gallery, Boston, 1987, Nat. Mus. Women Arts, Washington, 1987, Westbeth Gallery, N.Y.C., 1994, Clocktower, N.Y.C., 1986, The Rice Gallery The Albany Inst. History & Art, 1986, Deborah Davis Fine Arts, Hudson, 2003, 04, Firlefanz Gallery, Albany, 2004, Gallery 100, Saratoga Springs, 2004, U. West Eng., Bristol, Eng., 2004, Nat. Coll. Art and Design, Dublin, Ireland, 2004, Neptune Gallery, Bethesda, Md., others; represented in pvt. collections; represented in permanent collections Legis. Offices Empire State Plz., Albany, First Albany Corp., The Md. Dept. Econ. & Cmty. Devel., Balt., Quad Graphics, Boston, SUNY Albany, N.C. Nat. Bank, Charlotte, The Greenville Mus. Art, East Carolina U., Greenville, N.C., Boston Pub. Libr., The Budapest Gallery, Russell Sage Coll., Troy, N.Y., The Mint Mus. Art, Charlotte, N.C., Four Winds Ctr., Saratoga Springs, The Univ. Mus. SUNY Albany, Bullard and McLeod & Assocs., Inc., Albany, N.Y., Rocky Mount Art Ctr., N.C.; co-curator and curator for mail art shows. Recipient Purchase award in painting Hudson Mohawk Regional Am., SUNY Albany, 1977, 95, 97, honorable mention in watercolor The Oswego Art Guild, N.Y., 1986, medal Internat. Art Competition Metro Arts, Inc., Scarsdale, N.Y., 1986, honorable mention in painting Third Ann. Nat. C.C. Miniature Painting Show, Lexington, 1987, Sywer award, 1995, and numerous others; N.Y. State Coun. on the Arts grantee Barrett Art Gallery Syracuse U., 1986, grantee Artists' Space, 1988, Spl. Opportunity grant N.Y. Found. Arts. Mem. Nat. Assn. Women Artists, Albany Inst. History and Art, Fulton St. Gallery, Albany Ctr. Gallery, Woman's Caucus For Art. Avocations: painting, visual poetry, mail art.

MARMADUKE, JOHN H. retail executive; b. Amarillo, Tex., May 6, 1947; m. Martha Ann Harter, July 29, 1975; children: Margaret, Owen, Samuel. Student, Amarillo Coll., 1965-67; BBA in Fin., U. Tex., Austin, 1969. Advt. mgr., salesman Western Merchandisers, Inc., Amarillo, 1969-73, pres., dir., chief exec. officer, 1982-94; v.p. Hastings Books & Records, Inc., Amarillo, 1973-76, pres., dir., chief exec. officer, 1976—. Bd. dirs. Video Software Dealers Assn.; pres. Gift of Music Found., 1982—84. Past bd. dirs. Amarillo Art Ctr.; bd. dirs. Ctr. for Non-Profit Mgmt., Amarillo, 1988—, Amarillo Area Found., 1989; chmn. Don & Sybil Harrington Cancer Ctr., Amarillo, 1988-91. Recipient spl. merit award, Internat. Music Industry Conf., Berlin, 1982, Golden Nail award, Amarillo, 1987; named Vol. of Yr., Panhandle chpt. Tex. Multiple Sclerosis assn., 1988. Mem. Nat. Assn. Recording Merchandisers (pres. 1981-82), Video Software Dealers Assn. (bd. dirs.). Republican. Roman Catholic. Avocations: skiing, fly fishing, cooking, travel, racquetball. Office: Hastings Entertainment Inc 3601 Plains Blvd Amarillo TX 79102

MARMANN, SIGRID, software development company executive; b. Voelklingen, Saarland, Germany, Feb. 8, 1938; s. Leo and Karoline Anna (Weidenhof) M. Postgrad., Norwood Coll., London, 1962; BS in Acctg., Ind. & Handelskammer, Saarbruecken, Fed. Republic Germany, 1956; postgrad., Golden Gate U., 1970-85; BA in Mgmt., St. Mary's Coll., Moraga, Calif., 1984. Controller M.O.M., Paris, 1965-69; bookkeeper Chrissa Imports, Brisbane, Calif., 1970-78; acctg. mgr. Highcity Internat., San Anselmo, Calif., 1978-80; acctg. mgr., system analyst Kukje Korean Trading Co., Rutherford, N.J., 1980-81; asst. treas. Am. Mercantile Co., Brisbane, 1981-84; controller Provident Credit Union, Burlingame, Calif., 1984; owner Datatech EDI Systems, San Rafael, Calif., 1984—, pres., chief owner, 1989—; pres. Telepay Express, Inc., 1989. Founder No. Calif. Electronic Data Interchange Users Group, San Francisco, 1990. Mem. ANSI ASC X12 Electronic Data Interchange (fin. subcom. Alexandria, Va. chpt., nominee Membership award 1990) Great Plains Software (qualified installer), Computer Assocs. Internat. (installer). Avocations: travel, skiing, swimming, sailing, fishing, baking. Home: 8900 Silk Bonnet Ct Las Vegas NV 89143-5412

MARMARELIS, VASILIS ZISSIS, engineering educator, writer, consultant; b. Mytilini, Greece, Nov. 16, 1949; came to U.S., 1972; s. Zissis P. and Elpis V. (Galinos) M.; m. Melissa Emily Orme, Mar. 12, 1989; children: Zissis Eugene and Myrl Galinos. Diploma in elec. and mech. engring., Nat. Tech. U. of Athens, Greece, 1972; MS in Info. Sci., Calif. Inst. Tech., 1973, PhD in Engring. Sci., 1976. Rsch. fellow Calif. Inst. Tech., Pasadena, 1976-78; asst. prof. U. So. Calif., L.A., 1978-83, assoc. prof., 1983-88, prof., 1988—, also dir. biomed. simulations resource, 1985—, chmn. dept. biomed. engring., 1990-96; pres. Multispec Corp., L.A., 1986-2000. Author: Analysis of Physiological Systems, 1978, translated in Russian 1981, translated in Chinese 1990; Advanced Methods of Physiological Systems Modeling, vol. I, 1987, vol. II, 1989, vol. III, 1994, Nonlinear Dynamic Modeling of Physiological Systems, 2004; contbr. numerous articles to profl. jours. Fellow IEEE, Am. Inst. for Med. and Biol. Engring.; mem. N.Y. Acad. Scis., Biomed. Engring. Soc., Neural Networks Soc. Office: U So Calif Ohe 500 Los Angeles CA 90089-0001

MARMAS, JAMES GUST, retired business educator, retired college dean; b. Virginia, Minn., July 11, 1929; s. Gust George and Angela (Fatili) M.; m. Ruth Phyllis Leinonen, May 23, 1952; children— James Matthew, Lynn Marie, Brenda Kay. BS, St. Cloud (Minn.) State Coll., 1951; MA, U. Minn., 1956; Ed.D., Stanford, 1961. Tchr. bus. Littlefork (Minn.) High Sch., 1951-53, Lake City (Minn.) High Sch., 1953-55, Austin (Minn.) High Sch., 1955-59; asst. prof. bus. edn. Los Angeles State Coll., 1961-62; chmn. dept. bus. edn., dir. Ctr. Econ. Edn. St. Cloud State U., 1962-66, dean Coll. of Bus., 1966-87. Bd. dirs. Ins. and Savs. and Loan Contbr. articles to profl. jours. Bd. dirs., mem. exec. com. Minn. Council Econ. Edn.; bd. dirs. St. Cloud (Minn.) Econ. Devel. Ptnrship., chmn. research and planning com. (sec., bd. dirs.). Mem. Nat. Bus. Edn. Assn., Minn. Bus. Edn. Assn., N. Central Bus. Edn. Assn. (2d v.p.), Midwest Bus. Adminstrn. Assn., St. Cloud C. of C., Phi Delta Kappa, Delta Pi Epsilon (nat. research com.), Beta Gamma Sigma. Clubs: Rotary (pres. St. Cloud, Paul Harris Fellow). Home: 26194 County Road 4 Nisswa MN 56468-2185

MARMER, ELLEN LUCILLE, pediatric cardiologist, mayor; b. Bronx, N.Y., June 29, 1939; d. Benjamin and Diane (Goldstein) M.; m. Harold O. Shapiro, June 5, 1960; children: Cheri, Brenda. BS in Chemistry, U. Ala., 1960; MD, U. Ala., Birmingham, 1964. Cert. Nat. Bd. Med. Examiners; diplomate Am. Bd. Sports Medicine, Bd. Pediat., Bd. Qualified and Eligible Pediatric Cardiology, Bd. cert. sports medicine. Intern Upstate Med. Ctr., Syracuse, NY, 1964-65, resident, 1965-66; fellow in pediatric cardiology Columbia Presbyn. Med. Ctr.-Babies Hosp., N.Y.C., 1967-69; pvt. practice Hartford, Vernon, Conn., 1969—. Examining pediatrician child devel. program Columbia Presbyn. Med. Ctr.-Babies Hosp., N.Y.C., 1967, instr. pediat., 1967-69; dir. pediatric cardiology clinic St. Francis Hosp., Hartford, 1970-80; asst. state med. examiner, Tolland County, Conn., 1974-79; sports physician Rockville (Conn.) High Sch., 1976—; advisor Cardiac Rehab. com., Rockville, 1984-90; mem. bd. examiners Am. Bd. Sports Medicine, 1991—, chmn. credentials com., 1991-93. Mem. Vernon Town Coun., 1985-89; bd. dirs. Child Guidance Clinic, Manchester, Conn., 1970—; life mem. Tolland County chpt. Hadassah, v.p., 1969-70, pres., 1970-72, bd. dirs., 1973-74; mem. B'nai Israel Congregation and Sisterhood, Vernon, 1969—, chmn. youth commn., 1970-72; mayor Town of Vernon, 2003--. Recipient Outstanding Svc. award Indian Valley YMCA, 1985. Fellow Am. Acad. Pediat., Am. Coll. Cardiology, Am. Coll. Sports Medicine; mem. Conn. Med. Soc., Am. Heart Assn. (mem. coun. cardiovasc. disease in young 1969—, chmn. elect New Eng. regional heart com. 1990-91, mem. Heritage affiliate 1998—), Conn. Heart Assn. (bd. dirs. 1974-75, 83-84, pres. 1986-88), Heart Assn. Greater Hartford (bd. dirs. 1970-89, mem. exec. com. 1972-73, 79-84, pres. 1982-84), Tolland County Med. Assn. (sec. 1971-72), Vis. Nurse and Cmty. Care Tolland County, LWV (state program chairperson Vernon chpt. 1971-73). Democrat. Jewish. Avocation: sports. Office: 520 Hartford Tpke Vernon Rockville CT 06066 Office Phone: 860-870-9366.

MARMER, NANCY, editor; b. N.Y.C., Nov. 19, 1932; d. Carl and Frances Marmer; m. Gerald Jay Goldberg, Jan. 23, 1954; 1 child, Robert. BA magna cum laude, Queens Coll., 1954; postgrad., U. Minn., 1954-57, UCLA, 1968-71. L.A. corr. Art Internat., 1965-67; West Coast editor Artforum, 1976-77; sr. editor Art in America, N.Y.C., 1979-81, exec. editor, 1981-83, book rev. editor, 1983-97, mng. editor, 1983-97, editor-at-large, 1997-98, contbg. editor, 1998—. Lectr. Mellon seminar R.I. Sch. Design, 1983; lectr. art criticism Visual Arts dept. U. Calif., San Diego, 1978; faculty expository writing Dept. English, U. Minn., 1954-57. Author: The Modern Critical Spectrum, 1962; contbr. numerous articles to profl. jours.; art critic/reviewer for Art in America, Art Internat., Artforum, L.A. Times. Recipient Samuel Kress Found. Award in Art History; Nat. endowment for the Arts fellow in art criticism. Mem. Phi Beta Kappa. E-mail: 102424.711@compuserve.com.

MARMER, WILLIAM N. chemist, researcher; b. Phila., Pa., July 19, 1943; s. George Marmer and Sylvia Tischler; m. Benne S. Finkelstein, Oct. 20, 1973; children: David A., Rachel M. BA, U. Pa., 1961—65; PhD, Temple U., 1965—70. Rsch. leader, fats, oils & animal coproducts rsch. unit USDA, ARS, ERRC, Wyndmoor, Pa., 1987—. Mem.: Am. Leather Chemists Assn. (councilor 2002—), Am. Oil Chemists' Soc., Am. Chem. Soc. (chair, cell divsn. 2000). Office: USDA Agr Res Serv ERRC 600 E Mermaid Ln Wyndmoor PA 19038 E-mail: wmarmer@errc.ars.usda.gov.

MARMET, GOTTLIEB JOHN, lawyer; b. Chgo., Mar. 24, 1946; s. Gottlieb John and Margaret Ann (Saylor) M.; m. Jane Marie Borkowski, Sept. 12, 1970; children: Gottlieb John, Philip Stanley, Thomas Jacob. BS with distinction in Acctg., San Diego State U., 1967; JD, Northwestern U., 1970. Bar: Ill. 1970, U.S. Dist. Ct. (no. dist.) Ill. 1970, U.S. Tax Ct. 1981; CPA, Calif., Ill., Minn. Tax acct. Touche Ross & Co., Chgo., 1970-75; assoc. atty. Howington, Elworth, Osswald & Hough, Chgo., 1975-79; tax mgr. Peat, Marwick, Mitchell & Co., Mpls., 1979-81; assoc. Shefsky, Saitlin & Froelich, Ltd., Chgo., 1981-83; prin. G. John Marmet, Glenview, Ill., 1983—. Lectr. corp. law William Rainey Harper Coll., Arlington Heights, Ill., 1984; instr. Ill. Soc. CPAs, 1976, 77, Minn. Soc. CPAs, 1980. Author: Farm Corporations and Their Income Tax Treatment, 1970, 74; contbr. articles to jours., pubs. Active Northeast Ill. Coun. Boy Scouts Am., 1984—, dist. chmn. Skokie Valley, 1988,

mem. exec. bd., 1989-91, 99—; bd. dirs. North Shore Sr. Ctr., 1995-99. Recipient Hon. Mention Chgo. Bar Assn. Art Show, 1972, Boy Scouts Am. Dist. award of merit, 1990, Silver Beaver award, 1997. Mem. AICPA, ABA, Ill. Bar Assn., Chgo. Bar Assn., Rotary (Service Above Self award 1986, 96, bd. dirs. 1988-90, v.p. 1990-91, pres. 1991-92, 2004—), Beta Gamma Sigma, Beta Alpha Psi, Phi Alpha Delta. Office: 950 Milwaukee Ave Ste 318 Glenview IL 60025-3779 Office Phone: 847-298-9428. E-mail: gmarmet@aol.com.

MARMOR, MICHAEL FRANKLIN, ophthalmologist, educator; b. N.Y.C., Aug. 10, 1941; s. Judd and Katherine (Stern) M.; m. C. Jane Breeden, Dec. 20, 1968; children: Andrea K., David J. AB, Harvard U., 1962, MD, 1966. Diplomate Am. Bd. Ophthalmology. Med. intern UCLA Med. Ctr., 1967; fellow neurophysiology NIMH, 1967-70; resident in ophthalmology Mass. Eye and Ear Infirmary, Boston, 1970-73; asst. prof. ophthalmology U. Calif. Sch. Medicine, San Francisco, 1973-74; asst. prof. surgery (ophthalmology) Stanford (Calif.) U. Sch. Medicine, 1974-80, assoc. prof., 1980-86, prof., 1986—, head. div. ophthalmology, 1984-88, chmn. dept., 1988-92, dir. Basic Sci. Course Ophthalmology, 1993—. Faculty mem. program in human biology Stanford U., 1982—; chief ophthalmology sect. VA Med. Ctr., Palo Alto, Calif., 1974-84; mem. sci. adv. bd. No. Calif. Soc. to Prevent Blindness, 1984-92, Calif. Med. Assn., 1984-92, Nat. Retinitis Pigmentosa Found., 1985-95. Author: The Eye of the Artist, 1997, Degas Through his own Eyes, 2002; editor: The Retinal Pigment Epithelium, 1975, The Effects of Aging and Environment on Vision, 1991, The Retinal Pigment Epithelium: Function and Disease, 1998; editor-in-chief Doc. Ophthalmologica, 1995-99; history editor: Survey of Ophthalmology; editl. bd. Healthline; contbr. more than 250 articles to sci. jours., 50 chpts. to books. Mem. affirmative action com. Stanford U. Sch. Medicine, 1984-92. Sr. asst. surgeon USPHS, 1967-70. Recipient Svc. award Nat. Retinitis Pigmentosa Found., Balt., 1981, Rsch. award Alcon Rsch. Found., Houston, 1989; rsch. grantee Nat. Eye. Inst., Bethesda, Md., 1974-94. Fellow Am. Acad. Ophthalmology (bd. councillors 1982-85, pub. health com. 1990-93, rep. to NAS com. on vision 1991-93, mus. com. 2004—, Honor award 1984, Sr. Honor award 1996), Cogan Ophthalmology Hist. Soc. (pres. 2003—); mem. Internat. Soc. Clin. Electrophysiology of Vision (v.p. 1990-98, dir. stds.), Assn. Rsch. in Vision and Ophthalmology, Internat. Soc. for Eye Rsch., Macula Soc., Retina Soc. Democrat. Avocations: tennis, cycling, chamber music (clarinet), art, medical history. Office: Stanford U Sch Medcine Dept Ophthalmology Stanford CA 94305-5308

MARMOR, THEODORE RICHARD, political science and public management educator; b. Bklyn., Feb. 24, 1939; s. James and Mira Bernice (Karpf) M.; m. Jan Schmidt, Oct. 20, 1961; children— Laura Carleton, Sarah Rogers BA, Harvard U., 1960, PhD, 1966; postgrad., Wadham Coll., Oxford U., Eng., 1961-62. Asst. and assoc. prof. polit. sci. U. Wis.-Madison, 1967-69; assoc. prof. pub. affairs U. Minn.-Mpls., 1970-73; prof. U. Chgo., 1973-79; prof. polit. sci. Yale U., New Haven, 1979—, chmn. Ctr. Health Studies, 1979-85, [009b]prof. pub. mgmt. Sch. Orgn. and Mgmt., 1983—. Vis. fellow Russell Sage Found., 1987-88; cons., lectr. in field. Author: The Politics of Medicare, 1973, Political Analysis and American Medical Care, 1983, Understanding Health Care Reform, 1994; co-author: Health Care Policy, 1982, America's Misunderstood Welfare State, 1992; editor: Poverty Policy, 1971, National Health Insurance, 1980, Social Security: Beyond the Rhetoric of Crisis, 1988, Why Some People Are Healthy and Others Not, 1994, Jour. Health Politics Policy and Law, 1980-84; contbr. articles to profl. jours. Mem. Council on Fgn. Relations, N.Y.C., 1979-80, Pres.' Commn. on 1980s, 1980; social policy adviser Walter Mondale Presdl. Campaign, 1984. Can. Inst. Advanced Rsch. fellow, 1987—; fellow Adlai Stevenson Inst., J.F.K. Inst. Politics. Fellow Inst. Medicine, Nat. Acad. Social Ins.; mem. U.S. Squash Racquets Assn. (bd. dirs. 1983—), Century Assn. (N.Y.C.), United Oxford and Cambridge Club (London), Lawn Club. Democrat. Jewish. Home: 139 Armory St Hamden CT 06517-4005 Office: Yale Univ Sch of Mgmt 135 Prospect St New Haven CT 06511-3729

MARNELL, ANTHONY AUSTIN, II, architect; b. Riverside, Calif., Mar. 30, 1949; s. Anthony Austin and Ida Marie (Comforti) M.; m. Sandra Jean Graf, June 24, 1972 (div.); children: Anthony, Alisa. BArch, U. So. Calif., 1972. Architect, draftsman firms in Calif. and Nev., 1969-72; project coordinator Zuni Constrn. Co., Las Vegas, Nev., 1973-74; office mgr., architect Corrao Constrn. Co., Inc., Las Vegas, Nev., 1973-74, 1974-82; chmn. bd. Marnell Corrao Assocs., Las Vegas, Nev., 1976—; pres. Marinelli Internat., Inc., Las Vegas, Nev., 1978—, A.A. Marnell II, Architect, Las Vegas, Nev., 1978—, 1980—, Air Continental Jet Charter, Inc., Las Vegas, Nev., 1980-99; CEO Maxwell Corrao Assocs., Las Vegas, 1999—. Mem. ethics com. Nev. Bd. Architects, 1974; chmn. bd. Rio Hotel & Casino, Inc., 1986—, Focus 2000, Inc., 1989—. Prin. works include Mirage, Rio, Maxim Hotel, Treasure Island, Boulder Station, Sundance Hotel, Sam's Town, Excalibur; additions to Caesar's Palace, Desert Inn, Sands, Stardust, California, Frontier and Dunes Hotels (all Las Vegas), Caesar's, Atlantic City, others. Mem. Founders Bd. U. Nev., Las Vegas. Mem. Nat. Council Archtl. Registration Bds., Post Tensioning Inst. YPO (Nev. chmn. 1990). Roman Catholic. Office: Marnell Corrao Assoc Inc 4495 Polaris Ave Las Vegas NV 89103-4119 also: Rio Hotel & Casino Inc 3700 W Flamingo Rd Las Vegas NV 89103-4046

MARNEY, SAMUEL ROWE, JR., immunologist, educator; b. Bristol, Va., Feb. 15, 1934; m. Elizabeth Ann Bingham, Oct. 1, 1966; children: Samuel Rowe III, Annis Morison. BA in Chemistry, U. Va., 1955, MD, 1960. Diplomate Am. Bd. Internal Medicine, Am. Bd. Allergy and Immunology; cert. in Diagnostic Lab. Immunology, 1988. Staff physician VA Hosp., Nashville, 1968—69, clin. assoc., 1969—71, clin. investigator, 1971—74, staff physician, infectious disease and allergy cons., 1974—; asst. prof. medicine Med. Ctr. Vanderbilt U., Nashville, 1971—76, assoc. prof., 1976—, dir. allergy and immunology, 1974—. Vis. investigator Scripps Clinic and Rsch. Found., La Jolla, Calif., 1973-74. Capt. USAF, 1962—64, Korea. Fellow ACP, Am. Acad. Allergy and Immunology, Am. Coll. Allergy and Immunology; mem. Southeastern Allergy Assn. (pres. 1986-87, Hal M. Davison Meml. award, 1981, 99), Tenn. Soc. Allergy and Immunology. Home: 4340 Sneed Rd Nashville TN 37215-3242 Office: Vanderbilt U Med Ctr Allergy & Immunology 2611 W End Ave Nashville TN 37203-6013 Office Phone: 615-936-2727. Business E-Mail: samuel.marney@vanderbilt.edu.

MAROLDA, ANTHONY JOSEPH, management consulting company executive; b. Winthrop, Mass., Sept. 7, 1939; s. Daniel Arthur and Rose Marie (Pagliarulo) M.; m. Maria Theresa Rizzo, Oct. 10, 1970; children: Matthew, Ria. BS in Physics, Northeastern U., 1962; MS in Physics, Northeaster U., 1968; MBA, Harvard U., 1970. Rsch. physicist High Voltage Engring. Corp., Burlington, Mass., 1962-65; sr. scientist E.G. & G. Inc., Wellsley, Mass., 1965-68; v.p. Arthur D. Little, Inc., Cambridge, Mass., 1970-85; pres. The Winbridge Group, Inc., Cambridge, Mass., 1985—. Bd. advs. Daetwyler N.Am., Burlington, N.J., Altdorf, Switzerland, 1995-96; bd. dirs. Stratbridge, Inc., Cambridge, Mass. Inventor Apparatus High Density Plasma, 1965; co-author: Business Problem Solving, 1980, Modern Marketing, 1986, Regional Resiliance and Defense Conversion, 1997. Adv. Waterbury-Leningrad. Intersport, Waterbury, Conn., 1988-92; mem. comty. action program Harvard Bus. Sch. Alumni Orgn., 1997--. Recipient Hayden Meml. Scholarship, Northeastern U., 1957. Mem. Harvard Club, Harvard Bus. Sch. Alumni Assn. Republican. Roman Catholic. Avocations: hiking, sailing, tennis. Office: The Winbridge Group 33 Adams Hill Rd Gloucester MA 01930-1303 E-mail: amarolda@winbridgegroup.com.

MARON, ARTHUR, pediatrician, medical administrator; b. Asbury Park, N.J., Apr. 15, 1933; s. Isidore Chaim and Sadie (Raskin) M.; m. Lynn Sunshine Maron, Aug. 5, 1956 (dec. Aug. 1994); children: Stuart Glenn, Andrea Kim, Scott Michael; m. Ruth Fuerth, Dec. 17, 1995. BS in Biology, Rutgers U., 1954; MD, Union U., 1958; MPA in Health Care, Seton Hall U., 1994. Diplomate Am. Bd. Pediat. Rotating intern USPHS Hosp., Norfolk, Va., 1958-59; pediat. resident Babies Hosp., Newark, 1961-63; pvt. practice specializing in pediat. West Orange, NJ, 1963-94; dir. med. edn. St. Barnabas Med. Ctr., Livingston, NJ, 1988—2001; assoc. dean for acad. affairs Mount Sinai Sch. of Medicine, 1997—2001; exec. dean Saba U. Sch. Medicine, 2001—. Pres. med. staff St. Barnabas Med. Ctr., Livingston, 1991-93; med. dir. Found. Health Plan, Short Hills, N.J., 1989-91; bd. dirs. Alliance Ind. Acad. Med. Ctrs.; v.p. for med. edn. Saint Barnabas Health Care Sys., 1997-2001. Mem. bd. health West Orange Twp., 1970-90, Roseland Bd., 1996—; chmn. physicians divsn. United Jewish Appeal, 1994-97; chmn. med. arts divsn. State of Israel Bonds, 1998—. Recipient Maimonides award State of Israel Bonds, 1992. Fellow Am. Acad. Pediat. (bd. dirs., chmn. 1982-88, Presdl. award 1989); mem. AMA, (residency rev. com. for pediat. 1989-96, chmn. 1994-96, nat. residency matching program, bd. dirs. 1996—), Am. Hosp. Assn. (com. on med. edn. 1996—), Assn. for Hosp. Med. Edn. of N.J. (pres.). Jewish. Avocation: travel. Office Phone: 973-464-4590. E-mail: artmaron@aol.com.

MARONDE, ROBERT FRANCIS, internist, clinical pharmacologist, educator; b. Monterey Park, Calif., Jan. 13, 1920; s. John August and Emma Florence (Palmer) M.; m. Yolanda Cerda, Apr. 15, 1970; children: Robert George, Donna F. Maronde Varnau, James Augustus, Craig DeWald. BA, U. So. Calif., 1941, MD, 1944. Diplomate: Am. Bd. Internal Medicine. Intern L.A. County-U. So. Calif. Med. Ctr., 1943-44, resident, 1944-45, 47-48; asst. prof. physiology U. So. Calif., L.A., 1948-49, asst. clin. prof. medicine, 1949-60, assoc. clin. prof. medicine, 1960-65, assoc. prof. medicine and pharmacology, 1965-67, prof. medicine and pharmacology, 1968-90, emeritus, 1990—, prof. emeritus, 1990—; spl. asst. v.p. for health affairs, 1990—. Cons. FDA, 1973, Medco Containment Co. Inc., 1991-97, State of Calif. Dept. Health Svcs., 1993; mem. adv. panel State of Calif., 1997—. Served to lt. (j.g.) USNR, 1945-47. Fellow ACP; mem. Am. Soc. Clin. Pharmacology and Therapeutics, Alpha Omega Alpha. Home: 785 Ridgecrest St Monterey Park CA 91754-3759 Office: 2025 Zonal Ave Los Angeles CA 90089-0110 *Scientific integrity, objectivity, concern for the quality of life and adherence to the ethics of Nuremberg are ingredients for the evaluation of therapy for human illness. This is the ultimate objective of the practice of medicine.*

MARONEY, JANE P. former state legislator, consultant; b. Boston, July 29, 1923; d. John Henry and Mary (Boland) Perkins; m. John Walker Maroney, July 7, 1956; children: Jane Maroney El Dahr, John Walker Jr. Student, Radcliffe Coll., 1940—41, Katharine Gibbs Sch., 1941—42; LHD (hon.), Golden Beacom Coll., 1995. Elected ofcl. Del. Gen. Assembly, Dover, 1978-98; former project mgr. Milbank Meml. Fund, N.Y.C. Del. Family Law Commn., 1990—99, Health and Human Devel. Com., 1984—99; moderator, panelist Pub. Policy Conf., annually; past mem. Jr. League Wilmington (Del.); vice chair Creative Grandparenting, Inc., 1999—; pres. Lincoln Club of Del., 2002—03; trustee Christiana Care Health Sys., 2000—; mem. bd. Health and Nursing Scis. U. Del., 1998—; bd. dirs. YWCA, New Castle County, Family and Workplace Connection, Coord. Coun. Children with Disabilities, chmn., 1990—91; mem. adv. bd. Rockwood Mus., Del. Hospice, Girl Scouts Del., Del. Internat. Yr. of Family, March of Dimes, Coalition for Literacy, Inst. Human Behavior; bd. dirs. Afghanistan-Del. Cmtys. Together, 2001—, St. Michaels Sch. and Nursery, 2000—. Named 1 of 10 Best Rep. Legislators of Yr., Pres. Reagan, 1985; named to, Women's Hall of Fame, Del., 1996, Outstanding Legislator of Yr., Easters Seals of Del., 1998; recipient Outstanding Svc. to Children award, Acad. Pediat., Disting. Svc. award, Del. Bar Assn., Alfred R. Shands Disting. Svc. award, 1992, Order of Merit award, U. Del., 1993, J. Donaldson Brown Disting. Svcs. award, Children and Family Svcs. Del. to Dr. & Rep. Maroney, 1992, Nathan Davis award, AMA, 1996, Order of the First State award, Gov. of Del., 1998, Advocacy and Leadership in Children's Issues award, Epilepsy Found. Del., 2000, Outstanding Lifetime Contbn. award, Health Edn. Network Del., 2001, Cmty. Builder award, Nat. Conf. for Cmty. and Justice, 2001, Woman Pioneer award, Boy Scouts Am., 2001, Liberty Bell award, Del. State Bar Assn. Law Day, 2003, Carrie Chapman Catt award, Wilmington LWV, 2004. Roman Catholic. Avocation: travel. Fax: 302-478-2677.

MARONEY, THOMAS JOSEPH, lawyer; b. Nassau County, N.Y., Sept. 27, 1955; s. George Edward and Elaine (Murphy) M.; m. Michelle Carol Entin, Nov. 15, 1997; 1 child, Susan Isabella. BA, Siena Coll., 1977; JD, St. John's U., 1980. Bar: N.Y. 1982, U.S. Ct. Appeals (fed. dist.) 1981. Shareholder, founding ptnr. Hawkins, Feretic, Daly, Maroney & Hayes, P.C., N.Y.C., 1990—. Mem. com. on character and fitness Appellate Divsn., N.Y. State, 1998. Mem. N.Y. State Bar Assn., N.Y. County Lawyers Assn., N.Y. Trial Lawyers, Def. Assn. N.Y. Office: Hawkins Feretic Daly Maroney & Hayes PC 60 John St New York NY 10038-3714

MARONEY, THOMAS P. lawyer, political party executive; AB, Marshall U.; JD, Am. U. Pvt. practice, Charleston, WV. Chmn. W.Va. State Dem. Party, 1996—.

MARONEY-DAVOREN, DANETTE EDNA, pharmacist, writer, publishing executive; b. Bklyn., Aug. 21, 1976; d. Robert Edward Maroney and Aida Maria Rivera; m. Robert Levar Davoren; 1 child, Rahsaun Thomas Davoren. Grad., Bklyn. Comprehensive Night H.S., 1996. Asst. tchr. Reach and Grow Day Care and Prep. Sch., Queens Village, NY, 1994—2002; author Envisage Pub., Queens Village, NY, 2000—03; pharmacy specialist Prison Health Svcs., East Elmhurst, NY, 2003—. Pub. Envisage Pub., Queens Village, NY, 2003—. Author: Completely Satisfied. Advisor Take Time to Reach and Grow Youth Orgn., Queens, NY, 2001—03. Right To Life Party. Baptist. Avocations: travel, writing, reading, arts and crafts. Office: Envisage Pub PO Box 557 Queens Village NY 11428 E-mail: envisagepub1@aol.com.

MARONI, DONNA FAROLINO, biologist, researcher; b. Buffalo, Feb. 27, 1938; d. Enrico Victor and Eleanor (Redlinska) Farolino; m. Gustavo Primo Maroni, Dec. 16, 1974. BS, U. Wis., 1960, PhD, 1969. Project assoc. U. Wis., Madison, 1960-63, 68-74; Alexander von Humboldt fellow Inst. Genetics U. Cologne, Fed. Republic Germany, 1974-75; Hargitt fellow Duke U., Durham, N.C., 1975-76, rsch. assoc., 1976-83, rsch. assoc. prof., 1983-87; sr. program specialist N.C. Biotech. Ctr., Research Triangle Park, 1987-88, dir. sci. programs div., 1988-92, v.p. for sci. programs, 1992-94, ret., 1995. Mem. adv. com. MICROMED at Bowman Gray Sch. Medicine, Winston-Salem, NC, 1988—94; mem. sci. adv. bd. NC Biosci. Fund, LLC, 1998—99, Minority Sci. Improvement Alliance for Instrn. and Rsch. in Biotech, Ala. A&M U., Normal, 1990—91. Contbr. over 20 articles and revs. to profl. jours. Grantee NSF, 1977-79, NIH, 1979-82, 79-83, 82-87. Mem. Genetics Soc. Am., N.C. Acad. Sci., Inc. (bd. dirs. 1983-86), Sigma Xi (mem. exec. com. Duke U. chpt. 1989-90). Achievements include research in electron microscopy, evolution of chromosomes, chromosome structure, evolution of mitosis, and mitosis and fungal phylogeny.

MARONI, KEVIN JACQUES, venture capitalist; b. Detroit, Oct. 4, 1962; s. Jacques Robert and Marilyn Emma (Paterson) M. BA, U. Mich., 1984; MBA, Harvard Bus. Sch., 1990. Account exec. Young & Rubicam, N.Y.C., 1984-88; investor Harvard Mgmt. Co., Boston, 1990-92; fin. dir. Time Warner, Boston, 1992-94; gen. ptnr. Spectrum Equity Investors, Boston, 1994—. Bd. dirs. Homebase Acquisition LLC., Dominion 700 LLC. Treasurer, bd. dirs. Park Sch., Brookline, Mass.; trustee John F. Kennedy Library Found., Boston; bd. mem. Nat. Geographic Holdings, Washington. Mem. Pouts Neck Country Club. Democrat. Presbyterian. Avocations: history, tennis, politics. Office: Spectrum Equity Investors 123 High St Boston MA 02110-2447 also: Spectrum Equity Investors One International Place Boston MA 02110 Office Phone: 617-464-4600. Office Fax: 617-464-4601.*

MAROONE, MICHAEL E. car and truck sales executive; b. 1962; CEO Maroone Car & Truck Sales, Pembroke Pines, Fla.; COO, pres. Auto Nation, Ft. Lauderdale, Fla. Bd. dirs. Intercontinental Bank; chmn. South Fla. Internat. Auto Show, 1995. Bd. dirs. Dan Marino Found., Boys and Girls Club of Broward County, Children Cancer Caring Ctr., Police Athletic League. Named Humanitarian of Yr. Transflorida Bank, Forbes mag. Top 500 Cos., 1994. Mem. South Fla. Auto Truck Dealers Assn. (pres. 1994), South Fla. Chevrolet Dealers Mktg. Assn. (pres. 1994), Fla. Automotive Dealers Assn. (bd. dirs.). Office: Auto Nation PO Box 029030 Fort Lauderdale FL 33302-9030

MAROT, LOLA, retired accountant; b. Providence, Oct. 6, 1939; d. Frank and Iola (Lombardi) Ansuini; m. Joseph Marot (div. 1973); 1 child, David Joseph BA with distinction, U. R.I., 1973; postgrad., Bryant Coll. Bookkeeper Diamond Paper Box Co., Providence, 1958-69; export sales adminstr. Brite Industries, Providence, 1973-77; property svcs. asst. Met. Property and Liability Ins. Co., Warwick, R.I., 1977-79, buyer, 1979-83, sr. buyer, 1983-86, supr. printing adminstrn., 1986-87, expense control adminstr., 1987-88; acct. Dept. Adminstrn. State of R.I., Divsn. Ctrl. Svcs., 1992-99; ret., 1999. Mem. Univ. Soc. Providence (pres. 1978)

MAROTTA, JOSEPH THOMAS, medical educator; b. Niagara Falls, N.Y., May 28, 1926; emigrated to Can., 1930; s. Alfred and Mary (Montemuro) M.; m. Margaret Hughes, Aug. 31, 1953; children: Maureen, Patricia, Margaret, Fred, Thomas, Jo Anne, Michael, Martha, John, Virginia. MD, U. Toronto, 1949. Trainee in internal medicine U. Toronto, 1949-52; trainee in neurology Presbyn. Hosp., N.Y.C., 1952-55, U. London, Eng., 1955-56; mem. faculty U. Toronto, 1956—, prof. medicine, 1969—; former assoc. dean clin. affairs U. Toronto (Faculty of Medicine), 1981-89; hon. prof. of neurology U. Western Ontario, 1990—. Fellow Royal Coll. Physicians (Can.); mem. Alpha Omega Alpha, Phi Chi. Home and Office: 46 Carnforth Rd London ON Canada N6G 4P6 Office Phone: 519-642-4698.

MARPILLERO, SANDRO, architectural firm executive; MS in Architecture and Bldg. Design, Columbia U.; DArch, U. Venice. Pvt. practice, Venice, Italy; prin. Marpillero Pollak Arch., 2002. Contbr. articles to profl. jours. Recipient Merit award, Am. Soc. Landscape Archs., 2002. Office: Marpillero Pollak Arch 132 Duane St # 1 New York NY 10013

MARPLE, DOROTHY JANE, retired church executive; b. Abington, Pa., Nov. 24, 1926; d. John Stanley and Jennie (Stetler) M. AB, Ursinus Coll., 1948; MA, Syracuse U., 1950; Ed.D., Columbia U. Tchrs. Coll., 1969; L.H.D., Thiel Coll., 1965, Gettysburg Coll., 1979, Ursinus Coll., 1981; D. Humanitarian Services, Newberry Coll., 1977; DD, Trinity Luth. Sem., 1987. Counselor, asst., office dean undergrad. women Women's Coll., Duke, 1950-53; dean women, fgn. student adv. Thiel Coll., 1953-61; asst. social dir. Whittier Hall, Columbia Tchrs. Coll., 1961-62; exec. dir. Luth. Ch. Women, Luth. Ch. Am., Phila., 1962-75; asst. to bishop Luth. Ch. Am., 1975-85; coord. Transition Office Evang. Luth. Ch. Am., 1986-87; asst. gen. sec. ops. Nat. Coun. Chs. of Christ in U.S., N.Y.C., 1987-89. Coordinator Luth. Ch. in Am. commn. on function and structure, 1970-72 Home: 8018 Anderson St Philadelphia PA 19118-2936

MARPLE, GARY ANDRE, management consultant; b. Mt. Pleasant, Iowa, Feb. 22, 1937; s. Kenneth Lowry and Truma Janice (Cook) M.; m. Ellen I. Metcalf, May 29, 1971 (div. 1981); m. Meredith Ann Rutter, July 23, 1988; children: Brian Edward, Stephen Lowry. BS, Drake U., 1959; MBA, Mich. State U., 1962, DBA, 1963. Postdoctoral fellow mgmt. MIT, 1963; cons. Arthur D. Little Inc., Cambridge, Mass., 1963-82; pres. Commonwealth Strategies, Inc., Acton, Mass., 1982—, Oceanus Holding, Ltd., S.W., Harbor, Maine, 1985—, Answer Pharm. Corp., Norwood, Mass., 1997-99, 2001. Exec.-in-residence Ctr. Entrepreneurial Leadership, Ewing Marion Kauffman Found., Kansas City, Mo., 1996—99; pres., CEO Lessac Techs., Inc., White Plains, NY, 2002. Editor, author: Grocery Manufacturing in the U.S., 1968; contbr. to Conquering Government Regulation, 1982. Trustee Nat. Arts & Learning Collaborative, Natick, Mass., Linden Hill Sch., Northfield, Mass. Mem. Arthur D. Little Alumni Assn. (bd. dirs., past pres. Lexington, Mass. 1992—), Am. Bonanza Soc., Minuteman Bearded Collie Club (bd. dirs., past pres. 1996—), Bearded Collie Club Am. (treas. 2000-02). E-mail: gary@cwstrategies.com.

MARPLE, THOMAS FRANKLIN, columnist, reporter; b. Winchester, Va., June 24, 1956; s. Thomas Franklin Marple Jr. and Mary Ellen Marple. BS in Mgmt., Shenandoah U., 1980. Reporter The Journal, Martinsburg, W.Va., 1997—2001; writer Mid-Atlantic Thoroughbred, Timonium, Md., 2001—, Horsemen's Jour., Austin, Tex., 2000—, Md. Jockey Club and Preakness Media Rels., 2002—. With U.S. Army, 1980—82. Named Best Sports Columnist, W.Va. Press Assn., 2001. Mem.: W.Va. Sports Writers Assn., W.Va. Breeders Assn. (publicity dir. 2001—). Avocations: fishing, bicycling, weightlifting, basketball, gardening. Home: 1801 Sam Mason Rd Bunker Hill WV 25413

MARQUARDT, CHRISTEL ELISABETH, judge; b. Chgo., Aug. 26, 1935; d. Herman Albert and Christine Marie (Geringer) Trolenberg; children: Eric, Philip, Andrew, Joel. BS in Edn., Mo. Western Coll., 1970; JD with honors, Washburn U., 1974. Bar: Kans. 1974, Mo. 1992, U.S. Dist. Ct. Kans. 1974, U.S. Dist. Ct. (we. dist.) Mo. 1992. Tchr. St. John's Ch., Tigerton, Wis., 1955-56; pers. asst. Columbia Records, L.A., 1958-59; ptnr. Cosgrove, Webb & Oman, Topeka, 1974-86, Palmer & Marquardt, Topeka, 1986-91, Levy and Craig P.C., Overland Park, Kans., 1991-94; sr. ptnr. Marquardt and Assocs., L.L.C., Fairway, Kans., 1994-95; judge Kans. Ct. Appeals, 1995—. Mem. atty. bd. discipline Kans. Supreme Ct., 1984—86; mem. Kans. Sentencing Commn. Mem. editorial adv. bd. Kans. Lawyers Weekly, 1992-96; contbr. articles to legal jours. Bd. dirs. Topeka Symphony, 1983-92, 95-2002, Arts and Humanities Assn. Johnson County, 1992-95, Brown Found., 1988-90; hearing examiner Human Rels. Com., Topeka, 1974-76; local advisor Boy Scouts Am., 1973-74; bd. dirs., mem. nominating com. YWCA, Topeka, 1979-81; bd. govs. Washburn U. Law Sch., 1987-2002, v.p., 1996-98, pres., 1998-2000, disting. alumni, 2004; mem. dist. bd. adjudication Mo. Synod Luth. Ch., Kans., 1982-88. Named Woman of Yr., Mayor, City of Topeka, 1982; Obee scholar Washburn U., 1972-74; recipient Jennie Mitchell Kellogg Atty. of Achievement award, 1999, Phil Lewis medal of Distinction, 2000, Atty. of Achievement award Kans. Women Attys. Assn., Disting. Svc. award Washburn U. Law Sch., 2002; named Disting. Alumni, Washburn U. Fellow: Kans. Bar Found. (trustee 1987—89), Am. Bar Found.; mem.: ABA (specialization com. 1987—93, mem. ho. dels. 1988—, chmn. 1989—93, lawyer referral com. 1993—95, state del. 1995—99, bar svcs. and activities 1995—99, bd. govs., program and planning com. 1999—2002, bd. govs. 1999—2002, ctrl. and ea. European law initiative 2001—02, del-at-large ho. of dels. 2002—, African law coun. 2002—, scope & correlation com. 2003—), Law and Organizational Econ. Ctr. (bd. dirs. 2000—02), Am. Bus. Women's Assn. (lectr., corr. sec. 1983—84, pres. career chpt. 1986—87, named one of Top 10 Bus. Women of Yr. 1985), Topeka Bar Assn., Kans. Trial Lawyers Assn. (bd. govs. 1982—86, lectr.), Kans. Bar Assn. (sec., treas. 1981—85, bd. dirs. 1983—, v.p. 1985—86, pres. 1987—88). Home: 3408 SW Alameda Dr Topeka KS 66614-5108 Office: 301 SW 10th Ave Topeka KS 66612-1502 E-mail: marquardt@kscourts.org.

MARQUARDT, STEVE ROBERT, library director; b. St. Paul, Sept. 7, 1943; s. Robert Thomas and Dorothy Jean (Kane) M.; m. Judy G. Brown, Aug. 4, 1968; 1 child, Sarah. BA in History, Macalester Coll., 1966; MA in History, U. Minn., 1970, MLS, 1973, PhD in History, 1978. History instr. Macalester Coll., St. Paul, 1968-69; cataloger N.Mex. State U. Libr., Las Cruces, 1973-75; acting univ. archivist, acting dir. Rio Grande Hist. Collections N. Mex. State U. Libr., Las Cruces, 1973-74; acquisitions librarian Western Ill. U. Libr., Macomb, 1976-77, head cataloger, Online Computer Libr. Ctr. coord., 1977-79; asst. dir. resources & tech. svcs. Ohio U. Libr., Athens, 1979-81; dir. librs. U. Wis., Eau Claire, 1981-89; dir. univ. librs. No. Ill. U., DeKalb, 1989-90; dir. librs. U. Wis., Eau Claire, 1990-96; dean of librs. S.D. State U., Brookings, 1996—. Editor Jour. Rio Grande History, 1974; contbg. editor: Library Issues, 1994-2003; contbr. articles to profl. jours. Coord. Amnesty Internat. Adoption Group 275, Eau Claire, 1985-88; pres. Chippewa Valley Free-net, 1994-96. Mem. ALA, Assn. Coll. and Rsch. Librs. (chmn. performance measures in acad. librs. com. 1985-89). Lutheran. Avocations: tennis, bicycling. Office: SD State U Briggs Libr PO Box 2115 Brookings SD 57007-1098 E-mail: steve_marquardt@sdstate.edu.

MARQUESS, LAWRENCE WADE, lawyer; b. Bloomington, Ind., Mar. 2, 1950; s. Earl Lawrence and Mary Louise (Coberly) M.; m. Barbara Ann Bailey, June 17, 1978; children: Alexander Lawrence, Michael Wade. BSEE, Purdue U., 1973; JD, W.Va. U., 1977. Bar: W.Va. 1977, Tex. 1977, U.S. Dist.

Ct. (so. dist.) W.Va. 1977, U.S. Dist. Ct. (no. dist.) Tex. 1977, Colo. 1980, U.S. Dist. Ct. Colo. 1980, U.S. Ct. Appeals (10th cir.) 1980, U.S. Supreme Ct. 1984, U.S. Dist. Ct. (no. dist.) Ohio 1988, U.S. Ct. Appeals (DC cir.) 1997, U.S. Dist. Ct. Nebr. 1999. Assoc. Johnson, Bromberg, Leeds & Riggs, Dallas, 1977-79, Bradley, Campbell & Carney, Golden, Colo., 1979-82, ptnr., 1983-84, Stettner, Miller & Cohn P.C., 1984-87, Nelson & Harding, Denver, 1987-88, Heron, Burchette, Ruckert & Rothwell, 1989-90, Harding & Ogborn, 1990-94, Otten, Johnson, Robinson, Neff & Ragonetti, Denver, 1994-2001, Littler Mendelson, P.C., Denver, 2001—, mng. shareholder, 2001—. Mem. faculty Am. Law Inst. - ABA Advanced Labor and Employment Law Course, 1986, 87. Mem.: ACLU, ABA (labor, antitrust and litig. sects.), Coll. Labor and Employment Lawyers, 1st Jud. Dist. Bar Assn., Denver Bar Assn., Colo. Bar Assn. (co-chmn. labor law com. 1989—92), Nat. Rlwy. Hist. Soc., Sierra Club. Democrat. Methodist. Home: 11883 W 27th Dr Lakewood CO 80215-7000 Office: Littler Mendelson PC 1200 17th St Ste 2850 Denver CO 80202 Business E-Mail: lmarquess@littler.com.

MARQUEZ, ALFREDO C. federal judge; b. 1922; m. Linda Nowobilsky. BS, U. Ariz., 1948, JD, 1950. Bar: Ariz. Practice law Mesch Marquez & Rothschild, 1957-80; asst. atty. gen. State of Ariz., 1951-52; asst. county atty. Pima County, Ariz., 1953-54; adminstrv. asst. to Congressman Stewart Udall, 1955; judge U.S. Dist. Ct. Ariz., Tucson, 1980-91, sr. judge, 1991—. Served with USN, 1942-45 Office: US Dist Ct US Courthouse Rm 327 405 W Congress Ste 6180 Tucson AZ 85701-5060

MARQUEZ, JENNIFER TRACHSEL, health facility administrator; d. Wayne Herbert and Margaret Eloise Trachsel; m. Efrain Marquez, Aug. 22, 2002; 1 child, Efrain Trachsel Jr. BS, Calif. Poly. Pomona, 1992. Cert. fundraising exec. Dir. pub. rels. Angeles Girl Scout Coun., L.A., 1994—95; dir. devel. HealthView, Inc., San Pedro, Calif., 1995—. Bd. dirs. YWCA, San Pedro, 2000—02. Mem.: Assn. Fundraising Profls., Toastmasters (assoc.).

MARQUEZ, JOAQUIN ALFREDO, lawyer; b. Humacao, PR, Aug. 1, 1942; s. Joaquin and Emelina (Tudela) M.; m. Jocelyn Christiansen, Mar. 27, 1967; children: Joaquin A. Jr., Julian A. BS in Econ., U. Pa., Wharton, 1964; LLB, U. P.R., 1967; LLM in Taxation, Georgetown U., 1974. Bar: P.R. 1967, U.S. Dist. Ct. P.R. 1968, U.S. Ct. Appeals (1st cir.) 1968, D.C. 1972, U.S. Dist. Ct. D.C. 1972. Assoc. Goldman, Antonetti & Subira, San Juan, PR, 1967-68; adminstrv. asst. to resident commr. from P.R. Washington, 1971-72, 77-78; sr. atty.-advisor AID U.S. Dept. State, Washington, 1973-76; dir. PR Fed. Affairs Adminstrn., Washington, 1978-81; ptnr. Hopkins & Sutter, Washington, 1981-94, Drinker, Biddle & Reath, LLP, Washington, 1994—. Mem. P.R. Export Promotions Coun., San Juan, 1979-81; staff dir. So. Govs.' Assn., Washington, 1980-81. Capt. U.S. Army, 1968-70, Vietnam. Decorated Bronze Star. Mem. ABA, P.R. Bar Assn., D.C. Bar Assn. Republican. Roman Catholic. Avocations: sailing, reading. Office: Drinker Biddle & Reath LLP 1500 K St NW Ste 1100 Washington DC 20005-1209

MARQUEZ-MAGAÑA, LETICIA MARIA, biology professor; b. Sacramento, Aug. 15, 1963; d. Jesús José and Guadalupe María Márquez; married; children: Joaquín, Elías. BS,MS in Biol. Scis., Stanford U., 1986; PhD in Biochemistry, U. Calif., Berkeley, 1991. Postdoctoral fellow Stanford (Calif.) U., 1991-94; assoc. prof. biology San Francisco State U., 1994—, microbial geneticist, 1994—. Contbr. articles to profl. jours., including Jour. Bacteriology and Jour. Biol. Chemistry. Motivational spkr. to minority students, No. Calif., 1994—; mem. task force Hispanic-Serving Inst. Hispanic Assn. Colls. and Univs.; mentor to UC San Fransico Tchg. postdoctoral fellows, 2002—. Named Hispanic Powerhitter, Hispanic Engr. mag., 2003; named one of 100 Most Influential Hispanics, Hispanic Bus. mag., 1998. Mem.: AAAS (Mentor award 2001), Soc. Advancement of Chicanos and Native Americans in Sci. (e-mentor for K-12 educators 2001—, bd. dirs. 1989—91), Am. Soc. Microbiology. Office: San Francisco State U Dept Biology 1600 Holloway Ave San Francisco CA 94132

MARQUIS, HARRIET HILL, social worker; b. Rocky Mount, N.C., Sept. 4, 1938; d. Robert Foster and Anne Ruth (Daughtry) Hill; m. James Ralph Marquis, Apr. 23, 1967; children: Margaret Anne, Karen Lee. BA in English, Meredith Coll., 1960; MA in English, Seton Hall U., 1971; PhD in English, Drew U., 1984; MSW, NYU, 1987; cert., N.Y. Sch. Psychoanalytic Psychotherapy, 1991, Inst. Study Psychotherapy & Psychoanalysis N.J., 1998. Tchr. English S.C. Pub. Schs., 1960-62, Peace Corps, Sierra Leone, West Africa, 1963-65; adj. prof. English Farleigh Dickinson U., Madison, 1983-85; psychotherapist Child Guidance & Family Svc. Ctr., Orange, N.J., 1987; staff clinician Esther Dutton Counseling Ctr., Morristown, N.J., 1987-90; psychotherapist Ctr. Evaluation & Psychotherapy, Morristown, N.J., 1990-93; pvt. practice Madison, N.J., 1990-98, Brevard, N.C., 1998—. Mem. Internat. Conf. Advancement of Pvt. Practice Clin. Social Work; speaker in field. Fellow N.C. Soc. Clin. Social Workers; mem. NASW (bd. cert. diplomate in social work), Nat. Fedn. of Socs. for Clin. Social Work (nat. membership com. psychoanalysis in clin. social work). Democrat. Methodist. Avocations: reading, walking, writing, travel. E-mail: harrieth@brinet.com.

MARR, CARMEL CARRINGTON, retired lawyer, retired state official; b. Bklyn., June 23, 1921; d. William Preston and Gertrude Clementine (Lewis) Carrington; m. Warren Marr II, Apr. 11, 1948; children: Charles Carrington, Warren Quincy III. BA, Hunter Coll., 1945; JD, Columbia U., 1948. Bar: N.Y. 1948, U.S. Dist. Ct. (ea. dist.) N.Y. 1950, U.S. Dist. Ct. (so. dist.) N.Y. 1951. Clk. Dyer & Stevens, N.Y.C., 1948-49; pvt. practice N.Y.C., 1949-53; adviser legal affairs U.S. mission to UN, N.Y.C., 1953-67; sr. legal officer Office Legal Affairs UN Secretariat, 1967-68; mem. N.Y. State Human Rights Appeal Bd., 1968-71, N.Y. State Pub. Svc. Commn., 1971-86; cons. Gas. Rsch. Inst., 1987-91. Lectr. N.Y. Police Acad., 1963-67. Contbr. articles to profl. jours. Mem. N.Y. Gov.'s Com. Edn. and Employment of Women, 1963-64; mem. Nat. Gen. Svcs. Pub. Adv. Council, 1969-71; mem., former chmn. adv. coun. Gas. Rsch. Inst.; mem. chmn. tech. pipeline safety standards com. Dept. Transp., 1979-85; former mem. task force Fed. Energy Regulatory Commn. and EPA to examine PCBs in gas supply system; past chmn. gas com. Nat. Assn. Regulatory Utility Commrs.; past pres. Great Lakes Conf. Pub. Utilities Commrs., mem. exec. com.; mem. UN Devel. Corp., 1969-72; bd. dirs. Amistad Rsch. Ctr., New Orleans, 1970—, chmn. bd. dirs., 1981-94; bd. dirs. Bklyn. Soc. Prevention Cruelty to Children, Nat. Arts Stblzn. Fund, 1984-93, hon. bd. mem., 1998, Prospect Park Alliance, 1987-98; bd. visitors N.Y. State Sch. Girls, Hudson, 1964-71; mem. exec. bd. Plays for Living, N.Y.C., 1968-75; pres. bd. dirs. Billie Holiday Theatre, 1972-80; mem. nat. adv. coun. Hampshire Coll.; pres.'s coun. Tulane U., 1988-95. Mem. Phi Beta Kappa, Alpha Chi Alpha, Alpha Kappa Alpha. Republican. Episcopalian.

MARR, CHRISTOPHER P. real estate company executive; V.p. fin. reporting, contr. Storage USA, 1994—97, sr. v.p. fin. and acctg., 1997—98, sr. v.p., CFO, 1998—2002, Brandywine Realty Trust, Plymouth Meeting, Pa., 2002—. Office: Brandywine Realty Trust Ste 500 401 Plymouth Rd Plymouth Meeting PA 19462*

MARR, DANIEL G. food products executive; Divsn. v.p., N. Tex. Coca-Cola Enterprises, 1988—92, divsn. v.p., gen. mgr., E. Tex., 1992—96, v.p., mktg., 1996—2000, sr. v.p., chief customer officer, 2000—03, pres., N.Am. sales, 2003—. Office: Coca-Cola Enterprises 2500 Windy Ridge Pkwy Atlanta GA 30339

MARR, DAVID E. lawyer; BA, Colby Coll.; MA, Wesleyan U.; JD with honors, U. Conn. Bar: Conn. 1970, Mass. 1974, U.S. Dist. Ct. Conn. 1971, U.S. Dist. Ct. Mass. 1975, U.S. Ct. Appeals (2d cir.) 1971, U.S. Supreme Ct. 1974, U.S. Tax Ct. 1992. Assoc. Day, Berry & Howard, Hartford, Conn., 1970-73; counsel Honeywell Info. Sys., Inc., Waltham, Mass., 1973-75; pvt. practice Boston, 1975—79, Natick, Mass., 1980—. Editor-in-Chief Law Review, 1970. Author: Employment Law in Connecticut; opinion editor Mass. Lawyers Weekly, 1976-86. Rep. Regional Vocat. Sch.; chmn. Hist. Dist. Com.; bd. dirs. Hist. Soc. and Mus. Mem.: ATLA, Mass. Bar Assn. Office: 199 Union St Natick MA 01760-4759 Office Phone: 508-655-5522. E-mail: marrlaw@yahoo.com.

MARR, JAMES JOSEPH, venture capitalist; b. Hamilton, Ohio, Oct. 21, 1938; s. J. Joseph and Mildred Adele Marr; m. Martha Eleanor Marr, June 29, 1963; children: Kathleen, Joseph, John, Kerry, James. BS, Xavier U., 1959; MD, Johns Hopkins U., 1964; MS, St. Louis U., 1968. Diplomate Am. Bd. Internal Medicine, Am. Bd. Infectious Diseases. Intern Johns Hopkins Hosp., Balt., 1964-65; resident Barnes Hosp., Washington U., St. Louis, 1969-70; postdoctoral fellow in microbiology St. Louis U., 1967-69; asst. prof. medicine and microbiology Washington U., St. Louis, 1970-75, assoc. prof., 1975-76; prof. medicine and microbiology St. Louis U., 1976-82; prof. medicine and biochemistry U. Colo., Denver, 1982-89; sr. v.p. drug discovery Monsanto/Searle, Skokie, Ill., 1989-93; v.p. R&D Ribozyme Pharms., Boulder, Colo., 1993-96; CEO Immunologic Pharm. Corp., Waltham, Mass., 1996-99; gen. ptnr. Pacific Rim Ventures, Inc., 2000—. Bd. dirs. Sequitur, Inc., Immunologic Pharms., Primal, Inc. Contbr. articles to profl. jours.; patentee in field. Bd. trustees Estes Park (Colo.) Med. Ctr., 1994-96; bd. dirs. Estes Park Med. Ctr. Found., Larimer County Dept. Health; advisor Cub Scouts/Boy Scouts Am., St. Louis, 1975-82; advisor, lectr. schs., St. Louis, Denver, 1976-89; physician Free Med. Clinic, St. Louis, 1970-80; advisor Jefferson County Sch. Dist., 1986-89. Capt. U.S. Army Spl. Forces, 1966-68. Fellow ACP, Am. Acad. Microbiology, Infectious Diseases Soc. of Am., Am. Assn. of Physicians; mem. Am. Soc. Clin. Investigation, Am. Coll. Physician Execs., Phi Beta Kappa, Alpha Omega Alpha, Sigma Xi. Avocations: scuba diving, climbing, skiing, martial arts (2 black belts), poetry. Home and Office: 180 Centennial Dr Estes Park CO 80517-6901

MARR, PHEBE ANN, retired historian, educator; b. Mt. Vernon, N.Y., Sept. 21, 1931; d. John Joseph and Lillian Victoria (Henningsen) Marr. BA, Barnard Coll., 1953; PhD, Harvard U., 1967. Rsch. assoc. ARAMCO, Dhahran, Saudi Arabia, 1960-62; dir. mid. east program Fgn. Svc. Inst., 1963-66; asst. prof. Stanislaus State Coll., Turlock, Calif., 1970-71, assoc. prof., 1971-74; assoc. prof. history U. Tenn., Knoxville, 1974-85, chmn. Asian studies program, 1977-79. Cons. ARAMCO, 1979-83. Author: The Modern History of Iraq, 1985, 2d edit., 2003; co-editor: Riding the Tiger: Middle East Challenge After the Cold War, 1993; contbr. articles to profl. jours. Bd. dirs. Mid. East Policy Coun., 2004. Rsch. fellow Mid. East Ctr., Harvard U., Cambridge, Mass., 1968-70, sr. fellow Nat. Def. U., Washington, 1985-97, Woodrow Wilson Ctr. fellow, 1998-99, Coun. on Fgn. Rels., U.S. Inst. Peace fellow, 2004-. Mem. Mid. East Inst., Mid. East Studies Assn. Home: 2902 18th St NW Washington DC 20009-2954 Office Phone: 202-462-3580. E-mail: marrphebe@aol.com.

MARR, ROBERT BRUCE, physicist, researcher; b. Quincy, Mass., Mar. 25, 1932; s. Ralph George and Ethel (Beals) M.; m. Nancy Rosa Parkes, June 12, 1954; children: Richard, Jonathan, Rebecca. BS, MIT, 1953; MA, Harvard U., 1955, PhD, 1959. Research asso. Brookhaven Nat. Lab., Upton, N.Y., 1959-61, asso. physicist, 1961-64, physicist, 1964-68, sr. physicist, 1968-95, assoc. chmn. applied math. dept., 1974-75, 83-88, chmn., 1975-78; ret., 1995. Adj. assoc. prof. Columbia U., 1969; lectr. SUNY at Stony Brook, 1969-70, vis. prof. dept. computer sci., 1979; guest mathematician U. Colo., 1970; vis. mathematician Lawrence Berkeley Lab., 1978; cons. NSF, NIH, 1969— Contbr. articles to profl. jours. Served with U.S. Army, 1958-59. NSF grantee, 1974 Mem. Soc. for Magnetic Resonance in Medicine (trustee 1982-87, sec.-treas. 1984-86, treas. 1986-87). Home: 368 Private Rd Patchogue NY 11772-5827

MARRA, ANTHONY TULLIO, audio visual specialist; b. Newark, N.J., June 26, 1947; s. John and Christine (Sapparito) M.; m. Erica Jane Curci, Nov. 25, 1987; children: Becky Michelle George, Antonio Tullio, Becky Lynn George, Crystal Marra, Heather Leigh Marra, Megan Marra. Advisor Govt. Liason for Edni. Insts., Washington, 1978-91; media specialist, advisor Washington & Lee U., Lexington, Va., 1978-91; media specialist Longwood Coll., Farmville, Va., 1978-91, Hollins Coll., Salem, Va., 1978-91, Lynchburg (Va.) Coll., 1978-91, Randolph Macon Women's Coll., Lynchburg, Va., 1978-91; dir. audio-visual Sweet Briar (Va.) Coll., 1978-91; media cons. Africa Global Perspectives, 1994—; pres., owner Audio/Visual Advisors, 1997—; agt. bus. comms. sys. divsn. Lucent Techs./Bell Labs, 1997—. Acoustic expert rsch. and devel. NASA Langley Field, Hampton, Va., 1971-78; quality engr. Tyco-M/A-Com; ESD/MSD coord. Lynchburg facilities M/A-Com. Author: (books) Poetry in LIfe To Be in Death I Am, 1972, The Holy Quran-The Hereafter, 1989; inventor: overhead copy stand for ch.-sch. system, 1991, marking device for NASA Test Flights, 1972; designer TV studio and control room, 1994. Bd. dirs. S.W. Va. Free Clinic. With USMC, 1964-68, Vietnam. Recipient cert. appreciation NASA fors rsch. 1976, 78. Avocations: photgraphy, videography, working with bldg. computers, cmty. work. Home: PO Box 575 Madison Heights VA 24572-0575 Office: 3421 Plymouth Pl Lynchburg VA 24503-1300

MARRA, THOMAS M, investment company executive; Grad., St. Bonaventure U. Assoc. actuary Hartford Fin. Svcs. Group, 1980, v.p., dir. of individual annuities, 1990—94, head, individual life and annuities divsn., 1994—98, exec. v.p., 1996—2000, sr. v.p., 1994—96, dir. investment products divsn., 1998—2000, exec. v.p., 2000—, COO, Hartford Life, 2000—, pres., Hartford Life, 2002—. Mem., office of the chmn. Hartford Fin. Svcs. Group, 2000—; past chmn. Nat. Assn. of variable annuities. Mem. Bushnell Ctr. for the Performing Arts. Fellow: Soc. of Actuaries; mem.: Am. Acad. of Actuaries. Office: Hartford Financial Services Group Hartford Plaza 690 Asylum Ave Hartford CT 06115

MARRACK, ALEXANDER CASE, lawyer; b. Honolulu, May 12, 1933; BA cum laude, Amherst Coll., 1955; LLB cum laude, Harvard U., 1958. Bar: Hawaii 1958. Ptnr. Reinwald, O'Connor and Marrack, Honolulu. Mem.: ABA, Hawaii State Bar Assn. Home: 512 Portlock Rd Honolulu HI 96825-2022 Office: Reinwald O'Connor Marrack Hoskins & Playdon 733 Bishop St Honolulu HI 96813-4022

MARRAM, ELLEN R. investment company executive; BS, Wellesley Coll., 1968; MBA, Harvard U., 1970. CEO, pres. Nabisco Biscuit Co., 1987—88, pres. grocery divsn., 1987-93; pres. Tropicana Beverage Group The Seagram Co. Ltd., Bradenton, Fla., 1993-97, pres. and CEO Tropicana Products and Tropicana Beverage Group, 1997-98; pres., CEO EfDex, Stamford, Conn., 1999; mng. dir. N. Castle Partners, 2000—. Bd. dirs. Ford Motor Co., N.Y. Times Co., Eli Lilly and Co., The Conf. Bd., Advt. Coun. Bd. dirs. N.Y. Presbyn. Hosp., Lincoln Ctr. Theater, Families and Work Inst., Assocs. of Harvard Bus. Sch. Office: N Castle Partners 138 E Putnam Ave Greenwich CT 06830*

MARRERO, VICTOR, lawyer, judge; b. Santurce, P.R., Sept. 1, 1941; s. Ezequiel Marrero and Josefina (Sanabria) Santos M.; m. Veronica M. White, Dec. 1987. BA, NYU, 1964; LLB, Yale U., 1968; postgrad. (Fulbright scholar), U. Sheffield, Eng., 1966-67. Bar: N.Y. 1982. Exec. dir. N.Y.C. Dept. City Planning, 1973-74; spl. counsel to comptroller City of N.Y., 1974-75; 1st asst. counsel to gov. State of N.Y., Albany, 1975-76; chmn. N.Y.C. City Planning Commn., 1976-77; commr. N.Y. State Divsn. Housing and Cmty. Renewal, N.Y.C., 1977-79; under-sec. HUD, Washington, 1979-81; ptnr. Tufo & Zuccotti, N.Y.C., 1982-85, Brown & Wood, N.Y.C., 1986-93; amb., U.S. rep. UN Econ. and Social Coun., N.Y.C., 1993-97; amb., permanent U.S. rep. OAS, Dept. State, Washington, 1998-99; judge U.S. Dist. Ct., N.Y.C., 1999—. Vis. lectr. Yale U. Law Sch., New Haven, 1986, Columbia U. Law Sch., 1991-93. Trustee N.Y. Pub. Libr., 1989—, SUNY, Albany, 1985-93, Cooper Union, 1989-93, Consolidated Edison Co., 1988-93; bd. dirs. P.R. Legal Def. and Edn. Fund., N.Y.C., 1972-86, N.Y. Telephone Co., 1987-93; chmn. N.Y. State Chief Judge's Com. to Improve Availability of Legal Svcs., 1988-90. Mem. ABA (Pro Bono Publico award 1993), N.Y. State Bar Assn. (Root/Stimson Pub. Svc. award 1992), Assn. Bar City N.Y. (mem. com. modern cts. 1980-93, exec. com. 1986-89, judiciary com. 1991-92, v.p. 1992-93). Office: US Dist Court of NY 40 Centre St New York NY 10007-1502

MARRETT, CORA B. science educator; b. Richmond, Va., June 15, 1942; d. Horace Sterling and Clora Ann (Boswell) Bagley; m. Louis Everard Marrett, Dec. 24, 1968. BA, Va. Union U., 1963; MS, U. Wis., 1965, PhD, 1968. Asst. prof. U. N.C., Chapel Hill, 1968-69; from asst. to assoc. prof. Western Mich. U., Kalamazoo, 1969-73; from assoc. prof. to full prof. U. Wis., Madison, 1973-97; asst. dir. NSF, Arlington, Va., 1992-96; provost, vice chancellor for acad. affairs U. Mass., Amherst, 1997—2001; sr. v.p. for acad. affairs U. Wis. System, 2001—. Mem. sci. adv. panel U.S. Army, Washington, 1976-77; mem. Naval Rsch. Adv. Com., Washington, 1978-81, Pres. Commn. on the Accident at Three Mile Island, 1979; bd. govs. Argonne (Ill.) Nat. Lab., 1983-90, 96-99. Editor: Research in Race and Ethnic Relations, 1988, Gender and Classroom Interaction, 1990. Resident fellow NAS, 1973-74; fellow Ctr. for Advanced Study in Behavioral Scis., 1976-77. Mem. AAAS, ASA, Phi Kappa Phi. Avocations: reading, travel, film appreciation. Home: 7517 Farmington Way Madison WI 53717 Office: Office of Acad Affairs U of Wisconsin Syatem 1620 Van Hive Hall Madison WI 53706 E-mail: cmarrett@uwsa.edu.

MARRETT, MICHAEL MCFARLENE, chaplain; b. Greenwich Town, Surrey, Jamaica, Oct. 7, 1935; s. Kenneth Louis and Ivy Lynmae (McFarlane) M.; m. Margery Eva Mugford, Jan. 29, 1984. Cert. gen. ordination, Oxford (Eng.) U., 1961; cert. edn. in English lang., London U., 1967; MDiv, Gen. Theol. Sem., 1969, STM, 1970, N.Y. Theol. Sem., 1972; postgrad., Princeton Theol. Sem., 1972-73, Columbia U., 1973-75; BA, Fordham U., 1974; postgrad., The Coll. of Preachers, 1979, Yale U., 1979-81; PhD, NYU, 1980; MS, So. Conn. State U., 1982. Lic. pastoral counselor, Md.; cert. profl. mental health clergy, chaplain and fellow of Coll. Chaplains; nat. cert. bereavement facilitator Am. Acad. Bereavement; diplomate Am. Psychotherapy Assn. Staff chaplain St. Elizabeths Hosp., Washington, 1986-99; ret., 1999. Author: The Lambeth Conferences and Women Priests, 1981. Appointed commissary Diocese of Akoko, West Africa, 1984, appointed hon. canon St. Stephens Cathedral, 1987. Mem. Assn. Clin. Pastoral Edn. (clin.), Am. Assn. Christian Counselors, Am. Assn. Family Counselors. Home: PO Box 48232 1902 C St NE Washington DC 20002-6714

MARRIÉ, WILLIAM, dancer; b. Montreal, Quebec, Can. Student, L'École Supérieur de Danse du Quebec. Mem. Nat. Ballet Can., Toronto, Canada, 1990—97, first soloist, 1997—. Guest artist Metropolitan Opera House, Am. Ballet Theatre, New York, 2000. Dancer (ballets) The Taming of the Shrew, Onegin, Swan Lake, Romeo and Juliet, Giselle, Rite of Spring, Soldiers' Mass, Cruel World, Herman Schmerman pas de deux, Petruchio The Taming of the Shrew, Am. Ballet Theatre, N.Y., 2000. Office: Walter Carsen Ctr Nat Ballet Can 470 Queens Quay West Toronto ON Canada M5V 3K4

MARRINGA, JACQUES LOUIS, manufacturing executive; b. Rotterdam, The Netherlands, Aug. 8, 1928; arrived in U.S., 1965; s. Jakob and Christine Antoinette (Vandervalk) Marringa; divorced; children: Jack, Bob, Katy. Student, Erasmus U., Rotterdam, 1946—49, D in Econ., 1954; grad., Advanced Mgmt. Program Harvard U., 1984. Rsch. asst. Chem. Projects, N.Y.C., 1955; product mgr. Philips, N.V., Eindhoven, The Netherlands, 1956—61; product line mgr. ITT, Brussels and N.Y.C., 1961—70; v.p. Elco Corp., Willow Grove, Pa., 1970—72, Crouse-Hinds, Syracuse, NY, 1972—77; group v.p. Sta-Rite Industries, Milw., 1977—94; pres. Marringa Internat. Corp., 1994—. Bd. dirs. Marlo Inc., Racine, Wis. Mem.: Rotary (Milw.), Milw. Country Club. Home: 2520 W Dean Rd Milwaukee WI 53217-2019

MARRINGTON, BERNARD HARVEY, retired automotive company executive; b. Vancouver, B.C., Can., Nov. 9, 1928; s. Fredrick George and Constance Marie (Hall) M.; m. Patricia Grace Hall, Sept. 3, 1953 (dec.); children: Jodie Lynn, Stacey Lee. Student, U. Pitts., 1982, Bethany Coll., W.Va., 1983; BS in Mktg. Mgmt., Pacific Western U., 1955. V.p., sales mgr. W & L of La Mesa, Calif., 1960-66, pres., gen. mgr., 1966-68, terr. mgr., 1968-77; regional mgr. PPG Industries, Inc., L.A., 1977-88, regional mgr. profit ctr., 1988-91. Cons. L.A. Unified Sch. Dist., 1972, South Coast Air Quality Mgmt. Dist., El Monte, Calif., 1987-91; adv. com. So. Calif. Regional Occupational Ctr., Torrance, 1978-91; mem. Ford Arbitration bd. U. Wis., 1997-99. Contbr. articles to profl. jours. Sustaining sponsor Ronald Reagan Presdl. Found., Simi, 1987—; sustaining mem. Rep. Nat. Com., L.A., 1985-92, Rep. Presdl. Legion of Merit, 1986-99; del. Rep. Platform Planning com., L.A., 1992; charter mem. Nat. Tax Limitation Com., Washington, 1988, Jarvis Gann Taxpayers Assn., L.A., 1978-2004; sponsor Reagan Presdl. Libr., 1986; mem. Ford Arbitration Bd., U. Wis., 1997-99; mem. Daimler Chrysler Arbitration bd. U. Wis., 1999-2000. Recipient Award for Outstanding Community Support, So. Calif. Regional Occupational Ctr., 1986. Episcopalian. Avocations: rose gardening, citrus culture, golf, sailing, classical music.

MARRIOTT, JOHN WILLARD, JR., lodging and senior living executive; b. Washington, Mar. 25, 1932; s. John Willard and Alice (Sheets) M.; m. Donna Garff, June 29, 1955; children: Deborah, Stephen Garff, John Willard, David Sheets. BS in Banking and Fin., U. Utah, 1954. V.p. Marriott Hot Shoppes Inc., 1959-64, exec. v.p., bd. dirs., 1964; pres. Marriott Corp., 1964—, CEO, 1972—; chmn. bd. Marriott Internat., Inc. (formerly Marriott Corp.), 1985—. Bd. dirs. GM, U.S.-Russia Bus. Coun., Host Marriott Svcs. Corp., Naval Acad. Endowment Trust. Trustee Nat. Geog. Soc.; mem. nat. adv. bd. Boy Scouts Am.; mem. Bus. Coun., Bus. Roundtable.; exec. com. World Travel and Tourism Coun. Lt. USNR, 1954-56. Recipient Bus. Leader of Yr. award, Georgetown U. Sch. Bus. Adminstrn., 1984, Svc. Above Self award, Rotary Club at JFK Internat. Airport, 1985, Am. Mgr. of Yr. award, Nat. Mgmt. Assn., 1985, Golden Chain award, Nation's Restaurant News, 1985, Hall of Fame award, Consumer Digest Mag., 1985, Citizen of Yr. award, Boy Scouts of Am., 1986, Restaurant Bus. Leadership award, Restaurant Bus. Mag., 1986, Gold Plate award, Am. Acad. Achievement, 1986, Hall of Fame, Am. Hotel and Motel Assn., 1986, Hall of Fame award, Culinary Inst. of Am., 1987, Hospitality Exec. of Yr. award, Pa. State U., 1987, Bronze winner in Fin. World's Chief Exec. Officers award, 1988, Silver Plate award Lodging Hospitality Mag., 1988, Chief Exec. Officer of Yr. Chief Exec. Officer Mag., 1988, Signature award CA chpt. Nat. Multiple Scelerosis, 1988, Excellence Cmty. award Suburban Hosp., 1993, Silver Plate award Internat. Foodsvc. Mfrs. Assn., 1993, Good Scout award Boy Scouts Am. Greater N.Y. Coun., 1990, Trendsetter award Foodsvc. Cons. Soc., 1989 Mem. Conf. Bd., U.S. C. of C., Bald Peak C.C. (N.J.), Avenel Golf Club, Sigma Chi. Mem. LDS Ch. Clubs: Burning Tree (Washington), Met. (Washington). Office: Marriott Intl Inc 1 Marriott Dr Washington DC 20058-0001*

MARRIOTT, MARCIA ANN, business and economics educator, health facility administrator; b. Rochester, N.Y., Mar. 21, 1947; d. Coyne and Alice (Schleper) M.; children: Brian, Jonathan. AA, Monroe C.C., Rochester, 1967, BS, SUNY, Brockport, 1970, MA, 1975; PhD, S.W. U. La., 1985. Program adminstr. N.Y. Dept. of Labor, N.Y.C., 1970-75; employment mgr. Rochester Gen. Hosp., 1975-77, salary adminstr., 1982-98, compensation mgr., 1996—; corp. dir. wage and salary dept. Gannett Newspapers, Rochester, 1977-80; compensation and benefits adminstr. Sybron Corp., Rochester, 1980-82; compensation mgr. Rochester Gen. Hosp., 1996—; dir. compensation Via Health, Rochester, 1995-98; pres. Compensation Link, 1997—; prof. Grad. Sch. Bus. Rochester Inst. Tech., 1998—2003, SUNY, Brockport, 1998—2003. Instr. N.Y. State Sch. Indsl. Rels., Cornell U., N.Y.C., 1976-79; assoc. prof. Rochester Inst. Tech., 1978—, Monroe C.C., 1981—, dir. career adv. coun., 1989—; assoc. prof. SUNY, Brockport; assoc. prof. Nazareth Coll., 1998; dir. Rochester Presbyn. Home, 1987-91, 96—, v.p. bd. dirs., 1997-98, pres. bd. dirs., 1998—; dir. area hosp. coun. Kidney Svc. Ctrs., Rochester, 1988-91; cons. in field. Author: (pamphlets) Guideline for Writing Job Descriptions, 1983, (manual) Career Planning Manual, 1985, (booklet) Guideline for Writing Criteria-Based Job Descriptions, 1988, Skill-based Job Descriptions: A Quality Approach, 1994, Redesigning the Performance Appraisal Process, 1996. Campaign mgr. Carter Campaign Commn., Rochester, 1975; mem. coun. Messiah Luth. Ch., Rochester, 1991-94. Davenport-Hatch Found. grantee, 1973, Wegman Found. grantee, 1975. Mem. Am. Compensation Assn., Single Adopted Parents Group (pres. 1988-93). Avocations: tennis, hiking, reading, swimming, skiing. Office: Rochester Gen Hosp 1425 Portland Ave Rochester NY 14621-3095

MARRIOTT, RICHARD EDWIN, hotel and contract services executive; b. Washington, Jan. 9, 1939; s. John Willard and Alice Taylor (Sheets) M.; m. Nancy Peery, Mar. 20, 1962; children: Julie Ann, Sandra, Karen, Mary Alice. BS, U. Utah, 1963; MBA, Harvard U., 1965. With Marriott Corp., Washing-

ton, 1965—, group v.p. restaurant ops., 1976-78, corp. group v.p. restaurant and theme park ops., 1979-84, exec. v.p., 1984, vice chmn., 1986—, also bd. dirs. Chmn. bd. dirs. Media Corp., 1973—; bd. dirs. Riggs Nat. Bank of Washington. Mem. Nat. Commn. Against Drunk Driving; trustee Boys Clubs Am., Dole Found. for Employemnt of Persons with Disabilities. Mem. Nat. Restaurant Assn., Sigma Chi. Mem. Lds Ch. Office: Marriott Corp Marriott Dr Dept 97701 Washington DC 20058-0001

MARRIS, ROY O. agriculturist, consultant; b. Bogata, Tex., Oct. 6, 1922; s. Dick and Clara E. Marris; m. Myrle A. Marris, May 7, 1927; children: Dicky O., Donna, Dwight. MS, Sam Houston State U., 1951. Cert. real estate appraiser, Tex. Tech., 1953, Tex. A & M, 1966. Technician soil conservation USDA, Palestine, Tex., 1953—64; supr. Farmers Home Adminstrn., USDA, Nacogdoches, Tex., 1964—65, Ft. Worth, 1965—72; advisor to young farmers and ranchers Bogata, Tex., 1972—. Mem. Civil Def. Orgn., Ft. Worth, 1965—72; former membership chmn. Farm Bur. Tex.; former county chmn. Dem. Primary, Red River, Tex., former election judge; deacon First Bapt. Ch., 1954—. With U.S. Army, 1942—45. Mem.: Agr. Workers. Democrat. Baptist. Achievements include research in program on animal breeding to determine the sex of animal at breeding time. Avocations: raising and training spotted horses, cow dogs. Home: Rt 2 Box 361 Bogata TX 75417 Office Phone: 903-632-5324.

MARRO, ANTHONY JAMES, newspaper editor; b. Middlebury, Vt., Feb. 10, 1942; s. Francis James and Esther Martha (Butterfield) M.; m. Jacqueline Helen Cleary, June 5, 1965; 1 child, Alexandria. BA in History, U. Vt., 1965; MS in Journalism, Columbia U., 1968. Reporter Rutland (Vt.) Herald, 1964-67, Newsday, L.I., N.Y., 1968-74, chief Washington bur., 1979-81, mng. editor, 1981-86, exec. editor, 1986-87, editor, 1987—; reporter Newsweek, Washington, 1974-76, N.Y. Times, Washington, 1976-79. Co-recipient Pulitzer prizes for Pub. Service Reporting, 1970, 74. Office: Newsday 235 Pinelawn Rd Melville NY 11747-4250

MARRON, DARLENE LORRAINE, real estate company executive; b. Auburn, N.Y., July 20, 1946; d. William Chester and Elizabeth Barbara (Gervaise) Kulakowski; m. Edward W. Marron Jr., Apr. 28, 1973. BS cum laude, Rider U., 1968; MBA, NYU, 1970. Lic. securities broker. Dir. mktg. Am. Airlines, N.Y.C., 1970-79; asst. v.p. Merrill Lynch, N.Y.C., 1979-83; v.p. Kidder, Peabody & Co., N.Y.C., 1983-86; prin. Marron Bros. Realty Corp., Upper Saddle River, N.J., 1990—; prin. real estate fin. svcs. firm Hendrickson Advisors, LLC, 2000—. Avocations: pianist, flutist, skiing, fly fishing. Home: 9 Normandy Ct Ho Ho Kus NJ 07423-1217 Office: Marron Cos 118 State Rt 17 Upper Saddle River NJ 07458

MARRON, DONALD BAIRD, investment banker; b. Goshen, N.Y., July 21, 1934; m. Catherine D. Calligar. Student, Baruch Sch. Bus., 1949-51, 55-57. Investment analyst N.Y. Trust Co., N.Y.C., 1951-56, Lionel D. Edie Co., N.Y.C., 1956-58; mgr. research dept. George O'Neill & Co., 1958-59; pres. D.B. Marron & Co. Inc., N.Y.C., 1959-65, Mitchell Hutchins & Co. Inc. (merger with D.B. Marron & Co. Inc. 1965), N.Y.C., 1965-69, pres., chief exec. officer, 1969-77; pres. PaineWebber Inc. (merger with Mitchell Hutchins & Co. Inc. 1977), N.Y.C., 1977-88, CEO, 1980—, chmn. bd., 1981—, also bd. dirs.; co-founder, former chmn. Data Resources, Inc.; chmn., CEO, founder Lightyear Capital, LLC, N.Y.C., NY. Former dir. N.Y. Stock Exchange; bd. mem. Fannie Mae Bank, Shinsei Bank; chmn. of bd. mgrs Lightyear Portfolio Co., Collegiate Funding Svcs.; former gov., vice chmn. Securities Industry assn., Soc. of Nat. Assn. Securities Dealers; chmn. Ctr. for Study of Presidency; mem. Coun. Foreign Rels; trustee Ctr. Strategic & Internat. Studies; chmn. Vice chmn. bd. trustees Mus. of Modern Art; bd. overseers and mgrs. Meml. Sloan-Kettering; trustee for cultural resources N.Y.C., trustee Dana Found.; bd. dirs. N.Y.C. Partnership; mem. Govs.'s Sch. and Bus. Alliance Task Force, N.Y.; former mem. pres.'s com. on The Arts and The Humanities, Inc. also: Mus Modern Art 11 W 53rd St New York NY 10019-5401 Office: Lightyear Capital LLC 51 W 52nd St 23rd Fl New York NY 10019 Office Phone: 212-882-5800. E-mail: dbmarron@lycap.com.

MARRON, RICHARD C. hotel executive, state representative; b. Albany, N.Y., Feb. 17, 1938; m. Mildred T. Noce; 3 children. BA, U. Vt., 1959; student in Law, NYU; student, SUNY. Prin., owner Town & Country Resort, Stowe; rep. Vt. State Ho. Reps., 1997—. Mem. Stowe (Vt.) Selectboard; pres. Stowe (Vt.) Performing Arts, dir. emeritus; trustee Vt. State Colls.; dir. Vt. chpt. Am. Red Cross; N.Y. state commn. Lake Placid Olympic Games, 1980. Major USAR, ret. USAR. Mem.: Nat. Guard Assn., Stowe (Vt.) Area Assn., Stowe (Vt.) Rotary Club (pres. 1998—99). Republican. Roman Catholic. Home: 788 Tamarack Rd Stowe VT 05672

MARROQUIN-MERINO, VICTOR MIGUEL, lawyer; b. Lima, Peru, Feb. 10, 1962; s. Victor S. and Maria Isabel (Merino) M.; m. Marisa Jenny Torres, May 2, 1987; 1 child, Victor Andres. AB, Univ. Miami, 1989, JD, 1992; LLM, Harvard Law Sch., 1993. Staff mem. legal dept. Internat. Monetary Fund, Washington, 1993-94; sr. assoc. Baker & McKenzie, Chgo., 1994—. Contbr. articles to profl. jours. Recipient Disting. Svc. award Chgo. Vol. Legal Svcs. Found., 1994, Merit award Legal Clinic for the Disabled, 1996; named Internat. Lawyer of Yr. Univ. Miami, 1994. Avocations: writing, reading, foreign travel, tennis. Office: Baker & McKenzie One Prudential Plaza Chicago IL 60601

MARROU, CHRIS RENÉ, television newscaster; b. San Antonio, Nov. 12, 1947; s. André Noel and Annette (Deason) M.; m. Kathleen Mary O'Connor, Aug. 17, 1974; children: Mirage Marie and Molly O'Connor (twins). Student, Princeton U., 1964-67. News editor, anchor KRLD Radio, Dallas, 197-73; news anchor KENS-TV, San Antonio, 1973-80, news anchor, mng. editor, 1981—; news anchor WBZ-TV, Boston, 1980-81. Bd. dirs. Alliance Media Group; co-owner Ties.com. Contbr. weekly column San Antonio Light, 1986-93. Recipient award Tex. AP Broadcasters, 1976, 77, 87, Most Respected Local TV News Anchor award TV-Radio Age Mag., 1985, My Turn, Newsweek mag., 1996. Office: KENS-TV 5400 Fredericksburg Rd San Antonio TX 78229-3597

MARRS, JAMES F., JR., (JIM MARRS), author, journalist, educator; b. Ft. Worth, Dec. 5, 1943; s. James Marrs; m. Carol Ann Worcester, May 25, 1968; children: Cathryn Nova Ayn, Jayme Alistar. BA in Journalism, U. North Tex., 1966; postgrad., Tex. Tech. Coll., 1967-68. Editor/owner Magpie Mag., 1963-64; sports/news writer, cartoonist Denton (Tex.) Record Chronicle, 1965-66; reporter, copy editor, cartoonist and photographer Lubbock (Tex.) Avalanche-Jour., 1967-68; news and feature writer, cartoonist, photographer Lubbock Sentinel, 1968; reporter, feature writer, photographer, cartoonist Ft. Worth Star-Telegram, 1968-80; prodr. "Texas Roundup" Sammons Cable TV, Ft. Worth, 1982-83; scriptwriter Spindletop Prodns., Dallas, 1982-83; pub. rels. cons. The Mktg. Group, Dallas, 1982-83; pubr., co-owner The Springtown (Tex.) Current, 1983-84; comm. dir. Continental State Bank, Springtown, 1985-95. Editl. page editor Campus Chat, North Tex. State U., 1965-66; part-time copywriter, pub. rels. dir., cartoonist Jerre R. Todd & Assocs., 1972-74, dir. spl. projects, account exec., pub. rels. dir., 1980-81; editor/pub. and co-owner Cowtown Trails, Ft. Worth, 1983-84; faculty Office Continuing Edn. U. Tex., Arlington, 1976—; comm. dir. N.E. HealthCare Ctr., Hurst, Tex., 1985-86. Author: Crossfire: The Plot That Killed Kennedy, 1989, Alien Agenda, 1997, Rule by Secrecy, 2000, Psi Spies, 2001, The War on Freedom, 2003, Inside Job, 2004; scriptwriter, dir. video: Fake, 1991, The Many Faces of Lee Harvey Oswald, 1992, Aurora, The Secret of Redgate, 2004; contbr. articles to profl. jours. Prodr. Tex. Gridiron Show, Ft. Worth, 1978-79, dir., 1980; chmn. pub. info. subcom. Ft. Worth Mayor's Com. on Employment of Handicapped, 1979-82; co-chmn. Springtown Centennial Com., 1984; workshop tchr. Operation CLASP, Neighborhood Adv. Coun., Community Devel. Block Grant, City of Ft. Worth, 1984; community rels. cons. All Church Home for Children, Ft. Worth, 1984-95. With USAR, 1969-70. Recipient White Helmet award Ft. Worth Fire dept., 1969, 71, Assoc. Press writing awards, 1969-76, Nat. Writing award Aviation/Aerospace Writers Assn., 1972, Human Rights Leadership award Freedom Mag., 1993; named Arts and Entertainment Newsmaker of the Yr., Tex. Gridiron Club, Soc. Profl. Journalists, 1991. Mem. Tex. Mil. Hist. Soc., Springtown Optimist Club, Delta Sigma Phi, Sigma Delta Chi. Libertarian. Methodist. Avocation: civil war reenactor. Home and Office: Wise Comms PO Box 189 Springtown TX 76082-0189 Office Phone: 940-433-2916. Business E-Mail: jmarrs@ntws.net.

MARS, FORREST E., JR., candy company executive; s. Forrest Mars Sr. Grad., Yale U., 1953. Chmn. bd. dirs., former CEO Mars Inc., Mc Lean, Va. Office: Mars Inc 6885 Elm St Mc Lean VA 22101-3810

MARS, JACQUELINE BADGER, food products executive; m. David Badger, 1961 (div.); 3 children; m. Harold Vogel, 1986 (div.). Degree in anthropology, Bryn Mawr Coll., 1961. Co-owner Mars, Inc., McLean, Va., 1973—, corp. v.p., 1990—. Trustee Bryn Mawr Coll. Office: Mars Inc 6885 Elm St Mc Lean VA 22101*

MARS, JOHN EUGENE, protective services official, artist; b. Rochester, N.Y., Apr. 4, 1953; s. John Francis Mars and Matilda Salvi. AA in Bus. Adminstrn., SUNY, Alfred, 1973. Firefighter City of Rochester, 1979—. Freelance stained glass artist, 1979—; tchr. stainglass Rochester Sch., 1997, Sch. Holy Childhhod, Rochester, 1998. Recipient Vol. of Yr., Family Svc. Rochester, 1993, Vol. of Month, Ford Motor Co., 1993. Avocations: art, music. Home: 37 Wilmington St Rochester NY 14620

MARS, JOHN FRANKLIN, candy company executive; b. 1935; m. Adrienne Mars. Student, Yale U., 1957. Chmn. Kal Kan Foods Inc.; co-pres. Mars Inc., 1973—, CEO, 2000—. Office: Mars Inc 6885 Elm St Mc Lean VA 22101

MARS, TOM, lawyer; BA criminology, Ark. State Univ., 1980; law degree, Univ. of Ark. Sch. of Law, Fayetteville, NC, 1985. Pvt. practice Little Rock's Rose Law Firm, Little Rock, Springdale, Kutak Rock LLP, Fayetteville, Nebr., 2001; dir. Ark. State Police, Ark.; gen. coun. Wal-Mart, Bentonville, Ark., 2002—. Mars, while working at his law office of Kutak Rock LLP, used to represent clients who sued companies was hire by Wal-Mart in 2002 as its litigation chief. Office: Wal-Mart 702 SW 8th St Bentonville AR 72712

MARSALIS, BRANFORD, musician; b. Breaux Bridge, LA, Aug. 26, 1960; s. Ellis Marsalis. Student, So. U., 1978, Berklee Coll. Music, 1979-81. Mem. Art Blakey big band, 1980, Art Blakey's Jazz Messengers, 1981, Wynton Marsalis Quintet, 1982—85; ind. saxophonist, 1983—; bandleader The Tonight Show, L.A., 1992-95. Rec. Artist: (with Wynton Marsalis) Wynton Marsalis, 1981, Think of One, 1983, Hot House Flowers, 1984, Black Codes (From the Underground), 1985, Popular Songs...The Best of Wynton, 2001, (with Dizzy Gillespie) New Faces, 1984, Closer to the Source, 1984, (with Miles Davis) Decoy, 1984, (with Andy Jaffe) Manhattan Projects, 1984, (with Kevin Eubanks) Opening Nights, 1985, (with Carole King) City Streets, 1989, (with Art Blakey) Concord Jazz Heritage Series, 1979, Live at Montreux and Northsea, 1980, Keystone 3, 1982, Art Blakey (Timeless), 2001, (with Harry Connick Jr.) We Are in Love, 1990, Songs I Heard, 2001, (with James Taylor) New Moon Shine, 1991, Hourglass, 1997, New Moon Shine/Never Die Young..., 2000, (with Bela Fleck) Tales From the Acoustic Planet, 1994, Ten From Little Worlds, 2003, Little Worlds, 2003, (with Sting) Dream of the Blue Turtles, 1985, Bring on the Night, 1986, Nothing Like the Sun, 1987, The Soul Cages, 1991, Mercury Falling, 1996, Strange Fruit, 1997, Brand New Day, 1999, and appeared on many other recordings; (solo albums) Romances for Saxophone, 1986, Royal Garden Blues, 1986, Renaissance, 1986, Random Abstract, 1987, Tio Jeepy, 1988, Crazy People Music, 1990, The Beautiful Ones Are Not Yet Born, 1991, Bloomington, 1991, I Heard You Twice the First Time, 1992, Dark Keys, 1996, Requiem, 1999, Contemporary Jazz, 2000, Creation, 2001, Footsteps of Our Fathers, 2002, Romare Beardon Revealed (Live), 2003, Steep Anthology, 2004; appears on:(Guru) Jazzmatazz, 1995; composer various pieces including No Backstage Pass, Solstice, Waiting for Rain, (video) David and Goliath, 1993, (film) Bring on the Night, 1985, Throw Momma From The Train, 1987, School Daze, 1988, Mo' Better Blues, 1990, The Music Tells You, 1992, Mr. and Mrs. Loving, 1996, Eve's Bayou, 1997, Men in Black soundtrack, 1997, and others (TV movie) To My Daughter with Love, 1994. Winner Down Beat magazine's readers' poll, best soprano sax player, 1991-92; Grammy award, Best Pop Instrumental 1994 for "Barcelona Mona" with Bruce Hornsby. Office: Columbia Records 550 Madison Ave New York NY 10022-3211*

MARSALIS, WYNTON, musician; b. New Orleans, Oct. 18, 1961; s. Ellis and Dolores Marsalis. Studied with John Longo; student, New Orleans Ctr. for Performing Arts, Berkshire Music Ctr., Juilliard Sch. Music, 1979-81. Trumpet soloist with New Orleans Philharm. Orch., 1975, recitalist with New Orleans Ctr. for Creative Arts, 1979, played with various New Orleans and N.Y.C. orchs, with Art Blakey's Jazz Messengers, 1980—81, Herbie Hancock's V.S.O.P. quartet, formed own group, 1981, albums Fathers and Sons, 1982, Hummel/Haydn/L. Mozart Trumpet Concertos, 1983 (Grammy award, 1983), Wynton Marsalis (Best Jazz Record, Downbeat readers' poll, 1982), Think of One, 1983 (Grammy award), Handel, purcell, Torelli, Fasch, Moler, Trumpet Concertos, 1983, Hot House Flowers, 1984, Black Codes from the Underground, 1985 (2 Grammy awards), J Mood, 1986, Carnaval, Marsalis Standard Time, Vol. 1, 1987 (Grammy award), Majesty of the Blues, 1989, Standard Time, Vol. 3, 1990, Intimacy Calling Standard Time, Soul Gestures in Southern Blue, Vols. 1, 2, 3, 1991, Blue Interlude, 1992, Citi Movement, 1993, In This House, On This Morning, 1994, Wynton Marsalis, 1995, (with others) The All-American Hero, Live at Bubba's, In Gabriel's Garden, Sound of Jazz, All American Hero, 1996, Blood on the Fields, Jump Start and Jazz, Crescent City Xmas Card, 1997, Standard Time, Vol. 5: The Midnight Blues, One by One, Gold Collection, 1998. Named Jazz Musician of Yr., Downbeat readers' poll, 1982, 1984—86, 1989, Best Trumpet Player, Downbeat critics' poll, 1984, Acoustic Jazz Group of Yr., 1984, Best Trumpet Player, Downbeat readers' poll, 1985; recipient Grammy award for best solo jazz instrumental, 1983—85, Grammy award for best solo classical performance with orch., 1984—85, Grammy award for best jazz instrumental performance with group, 1985, 1987, musician of the Year, Down Beat Readers, 1992, Pulitzer prize for music, 1997, Algur H. Meadows award, Southern Meth. Univ., 1997.

MARSCHKE, SEAN M. police commander, emergency management director; s. Gregory G. and Catherine A. Marschke; m. Laurel L. Lischka, Oct. 22, 1994; 1 child, Caylyn C. AS in Police Sci., Waukesha County Tech. Coll., Pewaukee, Wis., 1991; BS in Criminal Justice Adminstrn., Mt. Senario Coll., Ladysmith, Wis., 2000; grad., Northwestern U. Sch. Police Staff and Command, 2001, FBI Law Enforcement Exec. Devel. Seminar, Wis., 2003. Cert. Unified Tactical Instr. Wis. Dept. Justice. Law enforcement ranger Wis. Dept. Natural Resources, Eagle, 1991—92; police officer Village of Merton, Wis., 1991—97; police comdr. Village of Sturtevant (Wis.) Police Dept., 1992—; emergency mgmt. dir. Village of Sturtevant, 1998—. Tng. and mgmt. cons. Fall River (Wis.) Police Dept., 1996—; tng. cons. Randolph (Wis.) Police Dept., 1996—, Fox Lake (Wis.) Police Dept., 1996—, Rio (Wis.) Police Dept., 1996—, Cambria (Wis.) Police Dept., Cambria, Wis., 1996—2003. Campaign mgr. Racine County (Wis.) Dems., 1999—2003. Named Law Enforcement Officer of Yr., VFW Post # 9929, 1994; recipient Traffic Safety Enforcement award, Wis. Dept. Transp., 1996, Commendation, Office of Dir. of Pub. Safety, Village of Sturtevant, 1999, John Edgar Hoover Meml. award, Am. Police Hall of Fame, 2001, Commendation, Office of Dir. of Pub. Safety, Village of Sturtevant, 2001, 2002, Office of Dir. Pub. Safety, Village of Sturtevant, 2003. Mem.: NRA (life; police firearms instr. 1992—), Soc. Police Futurists, Nat. Law Enforcement Trainers Assn., FBI Law Enforcement Exec. Devel. Assn. (assoc.), Internat. Assn. Chiefs of Police (assoc.), Loyal Order of Moose (assoc.). Roman Catholic. Avocations: camping, hunting, shooting, boating. Office: Village of Sturtevant 2801 89th St Sturtevant WI 53177 Office Phone: 262-886-7229. E-mail: sgtsmm@yahoo.com.

MARSDEN, BRIAN GEOFFREY, astronomer; b. Cambridge, Eng., Aug. 5, 1937; came to U.S., 1959; s. Thomas and Eileen (West) M.; m. Nancy Lou Zissell, Dec. 26, 1964; children: Cynthia Louise, Jonathan Brian. BA, Oxford U., U.K., 1959, MA, 1963; PhD, Yale U., 1965. Rsch. asst. Yale U., New Haven, 1959-65; lectr. astronomy Harvard U., Cambridge, Mass., 1966-83; astronomer Smithsonian Astrophys. Obs., Cambridge, 1965—; assoc. dir. planetary scis. Harvard-Smithsonian Ctr. for Astrophysics, Cambridge, 1987—2002. Dir. Ctrl. Bur. Astron. Telegrams, 1968-2000, Minor Planet Ctr. Internat. Astron. Union, 1978—. Editor: The Earth-Moon System, 1966, The Motion, Evolution of Orbits and Origin of Comets, 1972, Catalogue of Orbits of Unnumbered Minor Planets, 1996, Catalogue of Cometary Orbits, 2003. Recipient Merlin medal Brit. Astron. Assn., 1965, Goodacre medal, 1979; Van Biesbroeck award U. Ariz., 1989, Camus-Waitz prize Societé astronomique de France, 1993, Dirk Brouwer award Am. Astron. Soc., 1995, Lacchini prize Unione Astrofili Italiani, 2001. Fellow Royal Astron. Soc.; mem. Am. Astron. Soc. (chmn. div. on dynamical astronomy 1976-78), Internat. Astron. Union (pres. commn. 1976-79, 2000-03), Astron. Soc. Pacific, Sigma Xi. Office: Harvard-Smithsonian Ctr Astrophysics 60 Garden St Cambridge MA 02138-1516 Business E-Mail: bmarsden@cfa.harvard.edu.

MARSDEN, GEORGE, writer; b. Feb. 25, 1939; BA in History, Haverford Coll., 1959; BD, Westminster Theol. Sem., 1963; MA, Yale U., 1961, PhD in Am. Studies, 1965. Asst. in instrn. Yale U., 1964—65, instr., asst. and assoc. prof., 1965—74; prof. dept. history Calvin Coll., 1974—86, dir. MA in Christian Studies Program, 1980—83; prof. history of Christianity in Am. Duke U., The Divinity Sch., 1986—92; Francis A. McAnaney prof. history U. Notre Dame, Ind., 1992—. Vis. prof. ch. history Trinity Evang. Div. Sch., Deerfield, Ill., 1976—77; vis. prof. history U. Calif., Berkeley, Calif., 1986, Berkeley, 90. Author: The Evangelical Mind and the New School Presbyterian Experience, 1970, Fundamentalism and American Culture: The Shaping of Twentieth-Century Evangelicalism, 1980, Reforming Fundamentalism: Fuller Seminary and the New Evangelicalism, 1987, Religion and American Culture, 1990, Understanding Fundamentalism and Evangelicalism, 1991, The Soul of the American University, 1994, The Outrageous Idea of Christian Scholarship, 1997, Jonathan Edwards: A Life, 2003; assoc. editor: social scis. Christian Scholar's Rev., 1970—77; editor: (mem. sr. editl. bd.) The Reformed Jour., 1980—90. Fellow, Calvin Ctr. for Christian Scholarship, 1979—80, John Simon Guggenheim Meml. Found.; grantee, J. Howard Pew Freedom Trust, 1988—92; Younger Humanists fellow, NEH, 1971—72, Calvin Rsch. fellow, 1982—83. Mem.: Am. Soc. Ch. History (coun. mem. 1983—86, pres. 1992), Inst. for the Study of Am. Evangelicals (mem. adv. coun. 1989—). Office: Univ Notre Dame 321 Decio Faculty Hall Notre Dame IN 46556 E-mail: marsden.1@nd.edu.

MARSDEN, HERCI IVANA, classical ballet artistic director; b. Omis-Split, Croatia, Dec. 2, 1937; d. Ante and Magda (Smith) Munitic; m. Myles Marsden, Aug. 10, 1957 (div. 1976); children: Ana, Richard, Mark.; m. Dujko Radovnikovic, Aug. 27, 1977; 1 child, Dujko. Student, Internat. Ballet Sch., 1955. Mem. corps de ballet Nat. Theatre, Split, 1954-58; founder Braecrest Sch. Ballet, Lincoln, R.I., 1958—, State Ballet of R.I., Lincoln, 1960—, artistic dir., 1976—. Artistic dir. U. R.I. Classical Ballet, Kingston, 1966—, lectr., 1966—. Office: Brae Crest School of Ballet 52 Sherman Ave Lincoln RI 02865-3809 Office Phone: 401-334-2560. Business E-Mail: hmarsden@stateballet.com.

MARSDEN, JAMES (JAMES PAUL MARSDEN), actor; b. Stillwater, Okla., Sept. 18, 1973; m. Lisa Linde Marsden, July 2000; 1 child, Jack. Student, Okla. State U. Actor: (films) No Dessert Dad, Til You Mow the Lawn, 1994, Public Enemies, 1996, Campfire Tales, 1997, Disturbing Behavior, 1998, Gossip, 2000, X-Men, 2000, Sugar & Spice, 2001, Zoolander, 2001, Interstate 60, 2002, X2, 2003, The 24th Day, 2004, The Notebook, 2004; (TV films) In the Line of Duty: Ambush in Waco, 1993, Search and Resume, 1994, 919 Fifth Avenue, 1995, Gone in a Heartbeat, 1996, One the Edge of Innocence, 1997, Bella Mafia, 1997; (TV series) Boogies Diner, 1994, Second Noah, 1996—97, Ally McBeal, 2001—02. Office: BWR Pub Rels 9100 Wilshire Blvd Sixth Fl W Tower Beverly Hills CA 90212*

MARSDEN, LAWRENCE ALBERT, retired textile company executive; b. Mpls., May 28, 1919; s. Lawrence N. and Carrie Elizabeth (Ross) M.; m. Millicent Irene Snyder, Mar. 24, 1941; children: Millicent Carrie, Andrea Leigh, Lawrence Stewart, John Daniel. BS in Law, U. Minn., 1941; LL.B., George Washington U., 1946. Bar: D.C. 1946. Ptnr. Onion, Marsden & New, Washington, 1947-48; pres. Marsden-Slate, Inc., High Point, N.C., 1949-68; v.p. Guilford Mills, Inc., Greensboro, N.C., 1968-72, sr. v.p., 1973-84. Chmn. Marcor, Inc., High Point, 1980—; ptnr. SPM Investments; pres. Fabrilux Products, Inc., High Point, 1995-96. Author: Attack Transport, 1946, Gemini Ship, 2002. Served to lt. comdr. USN, 1941-46, PTO. Mem.: Aircraft Owners and Pilots Assn., Am. Assn. Textile Chemists and Colorists, Sportsman Pilots Assn. (past pres.), Isla del Sol Yacht and Country Club (St. Petersburg, Fla.), Willow Creek Golf Club (High Point), Quiet Birdmen, Rolls Royce Owner's Club, High Point Country Club, Phi Delta Theta, Phi Delta Phi. Republican. Home: 1706 Maryfield Ct High Point NC 27260-2684

MARSEE, SUSANNE IRENE, mezzo-soprano; b. San Diego, Nov. 26, 1941; d. Warren Jefferson and Irene Rose (Wills) Dowell; m. Mark J. Weinstein, May, 1987; 1 child, Zachary. Student, Santa Monica City Coll., 1961; BA in History, UCLA, 1964. Mem. voice faculty Am. Mus. and Dramatic Acad., N.Y.C., 1994-97, Pitts. Civic Light Opera Acad., 1997—, Duquesne U., 1998-2000; artist's lectr. Carnegie Mellon U., 2000—. Assoc. prof. La State U. Appeared with numerous U.S. opera cos., 1970—, including N.Y.C. Opera, San Francisco Opera, Boston Opera, Houston Grand Opera; appeared with fgn. cos., festivals, Mexico City Bellas Artes, 1973, 78, Canary Islands Co., 1976, Opera Metropolitana, Caracas, Venezuela, 1977, Spoleto (Italy) Festival, 1977, Aix en Provence Festival, France, 1977, Calgary, Alta., Can., 1986; recorded Tales of Hoffmann, ABC/Dunhill Records; TV appearances include Live from Lincoln Center, Turk in Italy, Cenerentola, 1989, Live from Wolftrap Roberto Devereux, 1975, Rigoletto, 1988, A Little Night Music, 1990, Marriage of Figaro, 1991, (PBS TV) Rachel, La Cubana; recs. and CDs Anna Bolena with Ramey, Scotto, Roberto Devereux with Beverly Sills, Roberto Devereux with Monserat Caballé Carreras, Tales of Hoffmann with Beverly Sills, Rigoletto with Quilico and Carreras; videotape Roberto Devereux with Beverly Sills. Recipient 2d place award Met. Opera Regional Auditions, 1968, San Francisco Opera Regional Auditions 1968; named winner Liederkranz Club Contest, 1970; Gladys Turk Found. grantee, 1968-69; Corbett Found. grantee, 1969-73; Martha Baird Rockefeller grantee, 1969-70, 71-72 Mem. AFTRA, Am. Guild Mus. Artists (past bd. dirs.), Nat. Assn. Tchrs. of Singing (past bd. dirs. for N.Y.). Democrat.

MARSELIS-MOORE, JADEH, emergency room nurse, alcohol/drug abuse nurse; b. La., Aug. 13, 1960; s. Willie and Mildred (Marselis) M. Diploma lic. practical nurse, Hinds Jr. Coll., Vicksburg, Miss., 1980; AAS, Utica (Miss.) Jr. Coll., Utica, Miss., 1982; ADN, N.Mex. State U., 1984; BSN, City U., L.A., 1993; MS, Am. Inst. of Holistic Theology, 1999; grad., Brodsky Sch. Real Estate, 2001; PhD, Madison U., 2001. Lic. realtor. Charge nurse, relief adminstrv. supr. Miss. State Hosp., Whitfield, 1980-81; RN, relief charge nurse Med. Unit Meml. Gen. Hosp., Las Cruces, N.Mex., 1982-88; dir. med./surg. unit Physicians & Surgeons Hosp., Atlanta, 1988-89; asst. head nurse drug addictions/behavior South Fulton Med. Ctr., East Point, Ga., 1989-93, charge nurse Emergency dept., 1993-2000; adminstr. supr. Desert Gardens Clin. Care Campus, Tucson, 1999—; RN in emergency dept. Eldorado Hosp., Tuscon, 1999—. Recipient The Samaritan award, Libr. Svc. award. Mem. Emergency Nurses Assn., Tucson Assn. Realtors, Multiple Listing Svc. E-mail: Jadehmmoore@hotmail.com.

MARSELLA, ANTHONY JOSEPH, psychologist, educator; b. Cleve., Sept. 12, 1940; m. Joy Anne Marsella, June 22, 1963; children: Laura Joy, Gianna Malia. BA in Psychology with honors, Baldwin-Wallace Coll., 1962; PhD in Clin. Psychology, Pa. State U., 1968; PhD (hon.), U. Copenhagen, D (hon.), 1999. Lic. psychologist, Hawaii. Intern Worcester (Mass.) State Hosp., 1966-67; Fulbright rsch. scholar Alteneo de Manila U., Quezon City, The Philippines, 1967-68; postdoctoral rsch. scholar NIMH Culture-Mental Health Program, East-West Ctr., Honolulu, 1968-69; prof. psychology, dir. clin. studies program U. Hawaii, Honolulu, 1969—, dir. disaster and humanitarian assistance program, 2001—. Dir. WHO Psychiat. Rsch. Ctr., Honolulu; cons. Inst. Stress Rsch. of Karolinska Inst., Stockholm, Divsn. Mental Health, WHO, Geneva; v.p. acad. affairs U. Hawaii, 1985-89; vis. prof. Melbourne U., Monash U., Korea U., King George Med. Coll., India, Shanghai Psychiat.

Inst., Ateneo de Manila U., Johns Hopkins U., Balt.; lectr. in field Author 10 books and over 150 articles to profl. jours. and chpts. to books; assoc. editor: Encylopedia of Psychology; jour. reviewer. Recipient Medal of Highest Honor, Soka U., Tokyo, 1995. Fellow APA (Internat. Advancement of Psychology award 1997); mem. Hawaii Psychol. Assn., Amnesty Internat., Psi Chi, Omicron Delta Kappa, Sigma Xi. Home: 8925 Nesbit Lakes Dr Alpharetta GA 30022-4039

MARSH, BENJAMIN FRANKLIN, lawyer; b. Toledo, Apr. 30, 1927; s. Lester Randall and Alice (Smith) M.; m. Martha Kirkpatrick, July 12, 1952; children: Samuel, Elizabeth. BA, Ohio Wesleyan U., 1950; JD, George Washington U., 1954. Bar: Ohio 1955. Pvt. practice law, Toledo, 1955-88; assoc., ptnr. Doyle, Lewis & Warner, Toledo, 1955-71; ptnr. Ritter, Boesel, Robinson & Marsh, Toledo, 1971-88; mem. Marsh & McAdams, Maumee, 1988-98; personnel officer AEC, 1950-54; asst. atty. gen. State of Ohio, 1969-71; asst. solicitor City of Maumee, 1959-63, solicitor, 1963-92; ptnr. Marsh McAdams, 1999—. Mem. U.S. Fgn. Claims Settlement Commn., Washington, 1990-94; counsel N.W. Ohio Mayors and Mgrs. Assn., 1990-2000; regional bd. rev. Indsl. Commn. Ohio, Toledo, 1993-94; mem. Ohio Dental Bd., 1995-2000; trustee Corp. for Effective Govt., 1998-2003; mem. Ohio Elections Commn., 2001—, chmn. 2003-04 U.S. rep. with rank spl. amb. to 10th Anniversary Independence of Botswana, 1976; past pres. Toledo and Lucas County Tb Soc.; co-chmn. citizens for metro pks.; past mem. Judges Com. Notaries Pub.; formerly mem. Lucas County Bd. Elections; former chmn. bldg. commn. Riverside Hosp., Toledo; past trustee Com. on Rels. with Toledo, Spain; past chmn. bd. trustee Med. Coll., Ohio; past pres. Coglin Meml. Inst.; chmn. Lucas County Rep. Exec. Com., 1973-74; precinct committeeman, Maumee, 1959-73; legal counsel, bd. dirs. Nat. Coun. Rep. Workshops, 1960-65, pres. Rep. Workshops, Ohio, 1960-64; alt. del. Rep. Nat. Conv., 1964; candidate 9th dist. U.S. Ho. of Reps., 1968; adminstrv. asst. to Rep. state chmn. Ray C. Bliss, 1954; chmn. Lucas County Bush for Pres., 1980; co-chmn. Reagan-Bush Com. for Northwestern Ohio, 1980, vice chmn. fin. com. Bush-Quayle, 1992; co-chmn. Ohio steering com. Bush for Pres., mem. nat. steering com., 1988; del. Rep. Nat. Conv., 1988; past bd. dirs. Ohio Tb and Respiratory Disease Assn.; apptd. Ohio chmn. UN Day, 1980, 81, 82; adminstrv. asst. Legis. Svc. Commn., Columbus, 1954-55; mem. Lucas County Charter Commn., Toledo, 1959-60; vice-chmn. U.S. Nat. Commn. for UNESCO, mem. legal com., del. 17th gen. conf., Paris, 1972, U.S. observer meeting of nat. commns., Africa, 1974, Addis Ababa, Ethiopia; past mem. industry functional adv. com. on standards trade policy matters; mem. nat. def. exec. res. Dept. Commerce; active Am. Bicentennial Presdl. Inauguration, Diplomatic Adv. Com. With USNR, 1945-46. Named Outstanding Young Man of Toledo, 1962. Mem. ABA, Maumee C. of C. (past pres.), UN Assn., Ohio State Bar Assn., Toledo Bar Assn., Ohio Mpcl. League (past pres.), Am. Legion, Lucas County Maumee Valley Hist. Soc. (past pres.), Internat. Inst. Toledo, Ohio Mcpl. Attys. Assn. (past pres.), Orgn. Security and Cooperation in Europe (registration supr., adjudicator, elections supr. in Bosnia), West Lake Erie Hist. Soc., Ohio Hist. Soc., Canal Soc. Ohio, Toledo Mus. Art, Ohio Wesleyan U. Alumni Assn. (past pres.), Ohio State Bar Found., Toledo Bar Found., Rotary, Toledo Country Club, Capitol Club (Columbus), Torch Club Toledo, Navy League, Omicron Delta Kappa, Delta Sigma Rho, Theta Alpha Phi, Phi Delta Phi. Presbyterian. Home: 124 W Harrison St Maumee OH 43537-2119 Office: 204 W Wayne St Maumee OH 43537-2125 Office Phone: 419-893-4880. E-mail: bmarsh124@aol.com.

MARSH, BRIAN RICHARD, management executive, playwright, educator, clergyman; b. Montague, Mass., Nov. 7, 1948; s. Walter Raymond and Elizabeth Hazel (McClary) M.; m. Ljuba Greene, July 25, 1977; children: Alexandra Whitney, Colin Webster. BA, U. Mass., 1970; MA, Bowling Green U., 1971; MDiv, The Gen. Theol. Sem., 1996; DMin, Laud Hall. Pres. Profl. Tng. Inc., Springfield, Mass., 1982—, Almadan Inc., Belchertown, 1984—95; prodr. The Hampshire Shakespeare Co., 1989—94; dir. theatre Pioneer Valley Performance Arts, 1997—; pres. Spiritstage, 1998—; rector St. George Anglican Ch., 1998—2000, Ch. of Good Shepherd, 2000—. Clergy del. Nat. Synod, 1999, 2002, standing com., 2003—. Playwright: This Particular Place, 1988, Play for 21 Voices, 1988, The Church-250 Years, 1987, The Search for Emily, 1988, The Letter from Hope, 1989, The Passenger Pigeon, 1991, Home to Hawley, 1991, Julian (The Moment is a Mask), 1993, Lear Solo, 1993, Fellowship of the Mystery, 1994, The Christmas Copier, 1995, Foul Play: The Paper City Caper, 2002, Double Play: The Paper City Caper, 2003. Pres. Carriage Towne Players, 1980—84. Mem. Founders of Hartford (Councillor 1988-90), Colonial Wars, Soc. St. George. Anglican. Home: 21 Sherwood Dr Belchertown MA 01007-9541 E-mail: spiritstage@yahoo.com.

MARSH, BRUCE DAVID, geologist, educator; b. Munising, Mich., Jan. 4, 1947; s. William Roland and Audrey Jane (Steinhoff) M.; m. Judith Anne Congdon, Jan. 24, 1970; children: Hannah Eyre, William Noah. BS, Mich. State U., 1969; MS, U. Ariz., 1971; PhD, U. Calif.-Berkeley, 1974. Geologist, geophysicist Anaconda Co., Tucson, 1969-71; asst. prof. dept. earth/planet sci. Johns Hopkins U., Balt., 1974-78, assoc. prof., 1978-81, prof., 1981—. Chmn., 1989-93; vis. prof. Calif. Inst. Tech., Pasadena, 1985, U. Maine, 1992-93; co-chmn. Gordon Rsch. Conf. on Inorganic Geochemistry, Holderness, N.H., 1983-84; advisor NASA, Washington, 1975-84, NSF, Washington, 1978-90, NRC, 1985-91; Hallimond lectr. Mineral. Soc. Great Britain and Ireland, 1995. Assoc. editor Geology, 1981-83, Jour. Volcanology and Geothermal Rsch., 1978—, Jour. Petrology, 1986—; editor Jour. Volcanology and Geothermal Rsch., 1985—. Fellow Geol. Soc. Am. (assoc. editor Bulletin 1986-92), Royal Astron. Soc., Mineral. Soc. Am., Am. Geophys. Union (sec. sect. on volcanology, geochemistry and petrology 1984-86, pres. elect 1988-90, pres. 1990-92, Bowen award 1993, Daly lecture 2000); mem. Model A Ford Club Am. Office: Johns Hopkins U Dept Earth-Planetary Scis 322 Olin Hall Baltimore MD 21218 E-mail: bmarsh@jhu.edu.

MARSH, CAROLE, author, photographer, publisher; b. Marietta, Ga., Mar. 22, 1946; CEO, Gallopade Internat., Peachtree City, Ga. Author more than 10,000 books and software including: (children's ednl. series) CArole Marsh State Books, Our Black Heritage Series, Smart Sex Stuff for Kids 7-17, Quantum Leap Books, The Naked Gourmet, Lifewrite and Propub Books, History Mystery Books, Lost Colony Collection; author curriculum materials based on state standards for all 50 state and Can. Recipient Top Honors, Nat. C. of C.; named Communicator of Yr., Assn. Bus. Communicators. Office: Gallopade Publishing Group 665 Hwy 74 S Peachtree City GA 30269

MARSH, CARYL AMSTERDAM, museum exhibitions curator, psychologist, advisor; b. N.Y.C., Mar. 9, 1923; d. Louis and Kitty (Weitz) Amsterdam; m. Michael Marsh, Sept. 3, 1942 (dec. 1993); children: Susan E., Anna L. BA, Bklyn. Coll., 1942; MA, Columbia U., 1946; PhD, George Washington U., 1978. Lic. psychologist, D.C. Asst. cultural attache Am. Embassy, Paris, 1946-48; psychologist D.C. Recreation Dept., 1957-69; spl. asst. Smithsonian Instn., Washington, 1966-73; curator exhbns. Nat. Archives, Washington, 1978-85, sr. exhbns. specialist, 1985-86; dir. traveling psychology exhbn. Am. Psychol. Assn., 1986-93, sr. advisor, 1993-95; chair humanities seminars in sci. mus. Assn. Sci. Tech. Ctrs., 1994—. Rsch. fellow exptl. gallery Smithsonian Instn., 1992; rsch. cons. Nat. Zoo, 1981-92, Smithsonian Folk Life Festival, Nat. Mus. Am. History, 1977-78; organizer Discovery Room Nat. Mus. Natural History, 1969-73; cons. Meyer Found., 1964-66; advisor Lemelson Ctr. for Study of Invention and Innovation, Nat. Mus. Am. History, 1999-2000. Editor: Exhibition: The American Image, 1979. Organizer Anacostia Neighborhood Mus., Washington, 1967, bd. dirs., 1974—, v.p. 1993—; sec. D.C. Commn. on Arts and Humanities, 1969-72; pres. Pre-Sch. Parents Coun., Washington, 1956-57; adv. bd. Youth Alive, 1997-99. Fellow Nat. Mus. Am. Art, 1975-77; vis. scholar Nat. Mus. Am. Art, 1978—; grad. fellow CUNY, 1945-46; scholar George Washington U.; noted for Disting. Contbn. to Pub. Understanding of Psychology, APA, 1993. Mem. AAAS, APA (Outstanding Svc. award 1992, Disting. Contbn. to Pub. Understanding of Psychology award 1993), D.C. Psychol. Assn., Am. Assn. Mus., Mus. Edn. Roundtable (bd. dirs. 1983-87). Home and Office: 10450 Lottsford Rd # 3011 Mitchellville MD 20721-2734

MARSH, DONALD JAY, medical school dean, medical educator; b. N.Y.C., Aug. 5, 1934; m. Wendy G. Clough; 2 children. AB, U. Calif., Berkeley, 1955; MD, U. Calif., San Francisco, 1958. Intern in medicine UCLA Hosp., 1958-59; postdoctoral fellow dept. physiology NYU, 1959-60, instr. dept. physiology, 1960-61, asst. prof. physiology and biophysics, 1963-67, assoc. prof. physiology and biophysics, 1967-71; prof. biomed. engring. U. So. Calif., 1971-92, prof., chmn. dept. physiology and biophysics, 1978-92, prof. medicine, 1982-92, rsch. prof. physiology and biophysics, 1992—; prof. physiology Brown U., Providence, 1992—, dean medicine and biol. scis., 1992—, Frank L. Day prof. biology, 1995—. Mem. engring. in medicine and biology tng. com. NIH, 1973, cardiovascular renal study sect., 1983-86, ad hoc mem. med. lab. scis. rev. com., 1976, inst. gen. med. scis. adv. com., 1982; ad hoc reviewer NSF; mem. rsch. com. Am. Heart Assn., 1979-82, rev. coms. for grants-in-aid, pub. affairs com., 1986-88; cons. com. interdisciplinary rsch. Nat. Rsch. Coun.- Inst. of Medicine, 1989; mem. med. schs. sect. task force AMA, 1994—; lectr. in field. Mem. editorial bd. Annals of Biomed. Engring., 1972-74, mng. editor, 1974-78; mem. editorial bd. Am. Jour. Physiology and Jour. of Applied Physiology, 1972-76, Am. Jour. Physiology: Regulatory, Integrative and Comparative Physiology, 1977-79, Am. Jour. Physiology: Renal, Fluid and Electrolyte Physiology, 1977-82, 88-94, Am. Jour. Physiology: Modelling Methodology Forum, 1984-91; guest reviewer Biophys. Jour., Circulation Rsch., Jour. Clin. Investigation, Jour Theoretical Biology, Kidney Internat., Sci., Pfluegers Archiv European Jour. Physiology; contbr. articles to profl. jours., chpts. to books. Named Career Scientist, Health Rsch. Coun. N.Y., 1964-71; Spl. fellow NIH, 1970-71; NIH grantee, 1963—. Fellow AAAS; mem. Assn. Am. Med. Colls. (coun. of deans), Am. Soc. Nephrology, Am. Physiol. Soc. (com. on coms. 1980-83, chmn. renal sect. 1982-83, long range planning com. 1990-93), Biophys. Soc., Microvascular Soc., Soc. Gen. Physiologists, Soc. Math. Biology (nominating com. 1983, publs. com. 1984-85, bd. dirs. 1986-88), Alpha Omega Alpha. Home: 148 Pratt St Providence RI 02906-1411 Office: Brown U Sch Medicine PO Box G-a1 Providence RI 02912-0001

MARSH, DONALD LOUIS, investment banker; b. Pitts., Pa., July 3, 1946; s. Donald Louis and Aileen Margaret (Klebe) M.; m. Joan Sylvia Waldron, Sept. 10, 1971; children: Nicholas Waldron, Collier Robinson. BS in Engring., Princeton U., 1968; MBA, Harvard U., 1973. With Capital Markets Group Chem. Bank, N.Y.C., 1968—, asst. sec. petroleum and minerals div., 1973-77, v.p., dist. head, 1977-78, v.p., dist. head energy and minerals div., 1978-81, worldwide energy dir., 1981-82, sr. v.p., 1982-84, mng. dir., 1984-86; with Ind. Oil and Gas Investments, Clinton, N.J., 1986—. Chmn. 98 Main St. Inc., N.J., 1984; pres. Leigh St. Galleries, Clinton, N.J., 1981— Mem. Ind. Petroleum Assn. Am., Princeton U. Rowing Assn. (pres. 1971-75) Methodist. Avocations: wildlife conservation, gardening. Home: Route 2 Stonemill Rd Annandale NJ 08801 Office: Commonwealth Industries Inc 500 W Jefferson St Ste 1900 Louisville KY 40202-1900

MARSH, DONALD REPPERT, holding company executive; b. Beaver Falls, Pa., Apr. 7, 1930; s. Donald Excell and Ruth Isabelle (Reppert) M.; m. Josephine Newell Roberts (div. Dec. 1980); children: Duncan Roberts, Tobin Clark, Kevin Reppert; m. Takako Satoh, Feb. 13, 1981. BA in Econs., U. Mich., 1955. V.p. Morgan Guaranty Trust Co., N.Y.C., 1957-76, New Eng. Mchts. Nat. Bank, Boston, 1976-77; sr. v.p. Rainier Nat. Bank, Seattle, 1977-84; v.p. internat. Burlington No., Inc., Seattle, 1984-89; pres. Burlington No. Internat. Services, Inc., Seattle, 1985-89; sr. adv. Pacific N.W. Advisors, Seattle, 1992—; adj. prof. Seattle U., 1993—2001; lectr. U. Wash., 2001—. Mem. Wash. Export Council, Seattle, 1979-86, Keizai Doyukai, Japan, 1987-91; bd. dirs., treas. Wash. Council Internat. Trade, Seattle, 1978-86; chair bd. dirs. Wash. Coun. Econ. Edn., 2000-2003. Contbr. articles on internat. fin. and trade to profl. jours. D. dirs. YMCA, Seattle, 1978-80; trustee Blakemore Found.; bd. dirs. World Affairs Coun., 1990-94, Am.-Japan Soc. Served as cpl. U.S. Army, 1951-53. Mem. Bankers' Assn. Fgn. Trade (bd. dirs., exec. com. 1979-83), Japan Am. Soc. (bd. dirs.), Seattle C. of C. (chmn. internat. trade com. 1982-85), Olympic Club(Seattle); Internat. House (Tokyo). Avocations: skiing, backpacking, sailing, travel. Home and Office: 8170 Grand Ave Bainbridge Island WA 98110-2947 E-mail: DonaldMarshNova@aol.com.

MARSH, ELLA JEAN, pediatrician; b. Chgo., Dec. 16, 1941; d. Charles and Eleanor (Canfield) M. BA, St. Mary of Woods (Ind.) Coll., 1963; DO, Chgo. Coll. Osteo. Medicine, 1971. Diplomate Am. Coll. Osteo. Pediatricians (chmn. evaluating com. 1981-89), Nat. Osteo. Bds. Intern Doctor's Hosp., Columbus, Ohio, 1971-72; resident in pediatrics Chgo. Coll. Osteo. Medicine, 1972-74, asst. prof., 1974-78, assoc. prof. pediatrics, 1978-82; assoc. prof. W.Va. Coll. Osteo. Medicine, 1975-86; clin. assoc. prof. pediatrics South Eastern Osteo. Sch. Medicine, 1984-96, chmn. pediatric and newborn nursery, 1982-94; assoc. dir. med. edn. Orlando (Fla.) Gen. Hosp., 1985-88. Mem. staff Arnold Palmer Children's Hosp., Fla. Hosp., Health Ctr.; pediatric cons. Nat. Bd. Osteo. Examiners; lectr., cons. in field. Alumni bd. dirs. St. Mary of Woods Coll., 1992-95, Ctrl. Fla. Primary Care, 1994-97. Donald Bucknar Moore scholar, 1963. Fellow Am. Coll. Osteo. Pediatricians (v.p. 1986, pres. 1988), Am. Acad. Pediat.; mem. AMA, Am. Osteo. Assn., Fla. Osteo. Assn., Fla. Med. Soc., Orange County Med. Soc., Cen. Fla. Pediatric Soc., Chgo. Coll. Osteo. Medicine Alumni Assn., Am. Coll. Osteo. Pediatricians, Am. Acad. Pediatricians, Irish Am. Pediatric Soc., Am. Acad. Osteopathy. Roman Catholic. Home: 8210 Imber St Orlando FL 32825-8233 Personal E-mail: emarsh16@aol.com.

MARSH, G. THOMAS, aerospace transportation executive; BSEE, U. N.Mex.; MBA, U. Colo.; postgrad. Sloan Sch. Mgmt., MIT. With Lockheed Martin Corp., 1969—, v.p. ops. for def. space and comm., v.p. and dep. Astronautics' civil space and comm. co., v.p. tech. ops. for Astronautics, pres. Manned Space Systems, pres. Spl. Programs for Lockheed Martin Space and Strategic Missiles, exec. v.p. Lockheed Martin Missiles and Space, pres. Lockheed Martin Astronautics Ops., pres., gen. mgr. Lockheed Martin Space and Strategic Missiles, exec. v.p. Lockheed Martin Space Systems Co., and officer of the Corp., 2003—. Extensively active in campaigns United Way and U.S. Savs. Bonds; bd. trustees Denver Mus. Nature and Sci.; bd. dirs. Denver Area Coun. Boy Scouts Am., Denver Metro C. of C., Alliance for Choice in Edn., Mountain States Employers Coun., Inc., Jr. Achievement, Rocky Mountain, Inc. Served USN. Recipient pub. svc. award, NASA, 1977. Mem.: IEEE, AIAA (sr.). Office: Lockheed Martin Corp 6801 Rockledge Dr Bethesda MD 20817-1877

MARSH, GARY MARTIN, environmental biostatistician, epidemiologist, educator; b. Wheeling, W.Va., Jan. 27, 1952; s. Floyd Martin and Alma Elizabeth (Custer) M.; m. Valerie A. Marsh, Aug. 28, 1991; children: Brian, Eric, Gregory, Anastasia. BS, U. Pitts., 1973, MS, 1974, PhD in Biostatistics, 1977. From asst. prof. to prof. U. Pitts. Grad. Sch. Pub. Health, 1978—. Asst. dir. Ctr. Environ. Epidemiology, Pitts., 1983-92. Fellow Am. Coll. Epidemiology; mem. Am. Statis. Assn., Internat. Soc. Environ. Epidemiology, Soc. Occupl. Environ. Health, Soc. Epidemiol. Rsch., Brit. Occupl. Health Soc. Avocations: Karate, performance driving, classical music. Office: U Pitts 130 Desoto St Pittsburgh PA 15213-2535 Office Phone: 412-624-3032. Business E-Mail: gmarsh@pitt.edu.

MARSH, GARY W. interior designer; b. Independence, Mo., Jan. 5, 1948; s. James Albert and Dorothy Jean (Adams) M. BS, Cen. Mo. State U., 1970. Designer/apprentice Sermon-Anderson Inc., Independence, 1967-70; designer Savage Furniture Co., Independence, 1970-71, J.C. Penney Corp., Kansas City, Mo., 1971-76; owner, designer Marsh-LeFevbre & Assocs., Kansas City, 1980—2002; pres., CEO Sermon-Anderson Inc., 2002—. Mem. Am. Soc. Interior Designers (bd. dirs. 1982-90, chmn. home yr. com. 1986-90, presdl. citation 1987, chair hist. preservation 1983—, pres.-elect Mo./West Kans. chpt. 1993), Nat. Trust Conf., Design Excellence Awards (bd. dirs. 1986, dir. 1982), Nat. Trust Hist. Preservation, Hist. Kansas City Found. Episcopalian. Avocations: theater, opera, travel, reading, woodworking. Office: Sermon-Anderson Inc 10815 Winner Rd Independence MO 64052 Personal E-mail: sermon-anderson@sbcglobal.net.

MARSH, HAROLD MICHAEL, anesthesiologist; b. Sydney, Australia, Mar. 7, 1939; came to U.S., 1974; m. Elizabeth Eleanor. BSc in Medicine, U. Sydney, 1956, MBBS, 1963. Intern Royal Prince Alfred Hosp., Sydney, Australia, 1964, resident, 1965-68, Mayo Grad. Sch. Medicine, Rochester, Minn., 1969-71; clin. assoc. dept. anesthesiology Toronto Western Hosp., 1971; dir. dept. intensive care Royal Prince Alfred Hosp., 1972-74; instr. anesthesiology Mayo Med. Sch., Rochester, 1975-76, asst. prof. anesthesiology, 1976-83; assoc. prof. anesthesiology Mayo Grad. Sch., Rochester, Minn., 1981-89, prof. anesthesiology, 1989; chmn. dept. anesthesiology Henry Ford Hosp., Detroit, 1989-98; prof. chmn. dept. anesthesiology Wayne State U., 1998—; spec.-in-chief anesthesiology Detroit Med. Ctr., 1998—. Part-time lectr., tutor faculty medicine U. Sydney, 1972-74; cons. anesthesiology Mayo Clinic, 1974-89, med. dir. surg. and respiratory intensive care units, 1977-81, dir. critical care svcs., 1981-83, 87-89, assoc. dir. critical care svcs., 1984-87, chmn. divsn. intensive care & respiratory therapy, 1985-89; vis. prof. dept. anesthesia U. Pa., 1976, Nat. Naval Med. Sch., 1981, Northwestern U., 1982, 89, Royal Prince Alfred Hosp., 1983, Sir Charles Gairdner Hosp., 1984, U. Md., 1987, Sloan-Kettering Inst., 1990, Rush-Presbyn.-St. Luke's Med. Ctr., Chgo., 1991, U. Hosp., London, Ont., 1993; invited lectr. dept. anesthetics IV Pan Am. Congress of Diseases of Chest, Caracas, Venezuela, 1987, Uniformed Svcs. U. Health Scis. Med. Sch., Bethesda, Md., 1987, Walter Reed Amry Med. Ctr., 1987, Naval Hosp., 1987, Bethesda, World Congress Intensive Care, Kyoto, Japan, 1989, Uddevalla (Sweden) Hosp., 1993, Karolinska Hosp., Stockholm, Sweden, 1993, Nat. Inst. Cardiology, Mexico City, Mexico, 1993; presenter in field. Contbr. chpts. to books and articles to profl. jours. With Australian Mil., 1958-61. Faculty of Anaesthetists, Royal Australasian Coll. Surgeons fellow, 1968. Fellow Am. Coll. Chest Physicians; mem. AAAS, Am. Bd. Anesthesiology, Am. Coll. Anesthesiologists, Wayne County Med. Soc. (pres. 2002). Achievements include research on general anesthesia and the lung, acute lung injury, metabolism, epidemiology in critical care. Office: Detroit Med Ctr DRH/UHC Dept Anesthesiolog 4201 Saint Antoine St Detroit MI 48201-2153

MARSH, JOAN KNIGHT, educational film, video and computer software company executive, publisher children's books; b. Apr. 8, 1934; d. E. Lyle and Ruth (Hopkins) Knight; m. Alan Reid Marsh, Sept. 27, 1958; children: Alan Reid, Clayton Knight. BA, Tex. Tech U., 1956. Owner, pres. MarshMedia, Kansas City, Mo., 1969—. Mem. ctrl. governing bd. Children's Mercy Hosp., 1996—; mem. coun. Family Study Ctr., U. Mo., Kansas City, 1983-89, Children's Relief Assn. Mercy Hosp., Kansas City, 1984—, pres., 1989-91; chmn., hon. co-chmn. Rose Brooks Ctr. Cabaret, 1995, 2000; pres. Friends of Children's Mercy Hosp., 1996-98; chmn. The Jewel Ball, 1997, Great Ball of China II, 1999, Genevieve Byrne Spkr. Series ARC Kansas City chpt., 2004. Mem. Jr. League (sustaining chmn. 1982-84, Cmty. Svc. award 1999), Gamma Phi Beta. Republican. Presbyterian. Avocations: egyptology, filmology.

MARSH, JOSEPH FRANKLIN, JR., emeritus college president, educational consultant; b. Charleston, W.Va., Feb. 24, 1925; s. Joseph Franklin and Florence (Keller) M. Student, Concord Coll., 1941-42, W.Va. U., 1942-43; AB, Dartmouth Coll., 1947; student, Nat. Inst. Pub. Affairs, Washington, 1947-48; M.P.A., Harvard U., 1949; LL.D., Davis and Elkins Coll., 1968; L.H.D., Alderson-Broaddus Coll., 1982. Cons. Hoover Commn., Washington, 1948; instr. in gt. issues Dartmouth, 1952—54, instr. econs., 1953—55, asst. prof., 1955—59; pres. Concord Coll., Athens, W.Va., 1959—73, pres. emeritus, 1985—; ednl. cons., 1973—74; pres. Waynesburg (Pa.) Coll., 1974—83, pres. emeritus, 1983—; v.p. The Armand Hammer United World Coll. of the Am. West, Montezuma, N.Mex., 1984—85; pres. Marsh Edn Cons., Athens, W.Va., 1985—. Dir. One Valley Bank of Mercer County, 1987-98, hon. dir., 1998-2000. Contbr. articles to profl. jours. Mem. State Dept. Ednl. Mission to U.A.R., 1964, Mercer County (W.Va.) Planning Commn., 1964-74, 83-94, hon., 1994—; vice chmn. W.Va. Com. for Constl. Amendments, 1966; mem. regional coun. Internat. Edn. Study Mission to Europe, 1970; bd. dirs. Am. Assn. State Colls. and Univs., 1972-73, Regional Coun. for Internat. Edn., 1973, Hospice Care Mercer County, W.Va., 1987-91, Faculty Merit Found. W.Va., 1990—, Greater Mercer County Charitable Found., Inc., W.Va., 1998-02, exec. com. 2001-02, chmn., pres., 1998-2001; bd. dirs. Charitable Found. of the Virginians, Inc., 2002—, Pa. Assn. Colls. and Univs., 1974-83, exec. com., 1980-82; bd. dirs. Pa. Commn. for Ind. Colls. and Univs., 1974-83, sec.-treas., 1976-77, vice chmn., 1977-80, chmn., 1980-82; trustee Found. Ind. Colls. Pa., 1974-83, mem. exec. com., 1979-82; bd. visitors Midway Coll., Ky., 1979-93; adv. com. Pa. State Coun. Higher Edn., 1980-82; trustee Concord Coll. Found., 1986, bd. dirs., 1987—; active Town of Athens Planning Commn., 1986-94, pres. commn. 1987-94; bd. trustees, Princeton (W.Va.) Cmty. Hosp. Found., 1989-98, vice chmn., 1989-97; Gov's. appointee to bd. dirs. State Coll. System W.Va., 1989-96, chmn. adminstrv. com., 1990-91, vice chmn. of bd., 1991-95, chmn., 1995-96; gov.'s appointee to the W.Va. Parkways, Econ. Devel. and Tourism Authority, 1998—, asst. sec., 2001-02, sec., 2002-03, vice chmn., 2003-; gov.'s appointee Edn. Commn. of the States, 1998-2002. Served as gunnery officer USNR, 1943-46. Named Outstanding Young Man, W.Va. Jr. C. of C., 1960; recipient Alumnus of Yr. award Concord Coll., 1973, Golden Alumnus award, 1992, Outstanding Alumnus award for Career Achievement, 1996; Outstanding Citizen award Athens Woman's Club, 1992, Total Community Involvement Award, Town of Athens, WV, 2001; Rotary fellow Oxford (Eng.) U., 1950-52. Mem. AAUP, Am. Assn. Univ. Adminstrs., Am. Econ. Assn., Royal Inst. Pub. Adminstrn., Oxford Union Debating Soc. (life), Oxford Soc. (life), Pa. Soc., Duquesne Club (Pitts.), Univ. Club (Bluefield), Masons, Rotary (dist. gov. 1992-93), The Guild of Carillonneurs N.Am. (hon.), Phi Beta Kappa, Phi Tau, Phi Delta Pi, Phi Sigma Kappa, Alpha Kappa Psi (hon.). Methodist. Home: 106 First Ave Athens WV 24712 Office: PO Box 734 Athens WV 24712-0734

MARSH, KEVIN B. energy executive; b. Atlanta; married; 2 children. CPA. Group mgr. tech. acctg. S.C. Electric & Gas Co., 1984—89, v.p., contr., CFO, 1996—, former v.p. corp. planning; former v.p. fin., treas., contr. SCANA Corp., Columbia, SC, CFO, 1996—, sr. v.p., 1998—. Past bd. dirs. Palmetto Place Children's Emergency Shelter; bd. dirs. Bus. Devel. Corp. of S.C. Mem.: AICPA. Methodist. Office: SCANA Corp 1426 Main St Columbia SC 29218

MARSH, MALCOLM F. federal judge; b. Portland, Oreg., Sept. 24, 1928; m. Shari Marsh. BS, U. Oreg., 1952, LLB, 1954, JD, 1971. Bar: Oreg. 1954, U.S. Dist. Ct. Oreg. 1955, U.S. Ct. Appeals (9th cir.) 1968. Ptnr. Clark & Marsh, Lindauer & McClinton (and predecessors), Salem, Oreg., 1954-87; judge U.S. Dist. Ct. Oreg., Portland, 1987—98, sr. judge, 1998—. With U.S. Army, 1946-47. Fellow Am. Coll. Trial Lawyers; mem. ABA, Oreg. Bar Assn. Office: US Dist Ct 1507 US Courthouse 1000 SW 3d Ave Portland OR 97204

MARSH, MALCOLM ROY, JR., electronics engineer; b. Bedford, Va., Oct. 12, 1932; s. Malcolm Roy and Mildred (Overstreet) M.; BEE, U. Va., 1956; children: Lauranne Ashton, James Overstreet. Elec. engr. Sperry Piedmont, Inc., Charlottesville, Va., 1957-58, Martin Orlando Co., Orlando, Fla., 1958-60; electronic engring. cons., Orlando, 1960—. Served with U.S. Army, 1958. Mem. IEEE. Methodist. Home and Office: 2609 Tradewinds Trail Orlando FL 32805-5840

MARSH, MARTHA, hospital administrator; BS, U. Rochester; MPH, MBA, Columbia U. Pres. and CEO Matthew Thornton Health Plan, Dartmouth-Hitchcock Med. Ctr., 1986—94; sr. v.p., profl. svcs. and managed care and v.p. managed care U. Pa. Health Sys., 1994—98; COO U. Calif.-Davis Health Care Sys., 1999—2002; dir., Hosp. and Clinics U. Calif.-Davis Medical Ctr., 1999—2002; pres. and CEO Stanford (Conn.) Hosp. and Clinics, 2002—. Apptd. by Pres. Bush Nat. Infrastructure Adv. Coun., 2003; bd. dirs. Calif. Healthcare Assoc., Integrated Healthcare Assoc., Blue Cross of Calif. Hosp. Relations Com. Office: Stanford Hosp 300 Pasteur Dr Ste H3200 Stanford CA 94305*

MARSH, MELISSA, newscaster; m. Jim Harmston. BA in Comm., Campbell U. Cert. aerobics instr. AFAA. Intern WECT, Fayetteville, NC; gen. assignment reporter WTVD, Fayetteville, NC, 1998—99; asst. prodr. NBC 17,

Raleigh, NC, 1999—2000, Tech Watch reporter, 2000—01, gen. assignment reporter, 2001—. Instr. aerobics Gold's Gym, Cary and Raleigh. Avocations: travel, snorkeling, scuba diving, reading, exercising. Office: NBC 17 Studios 1205 Front St Raleigh NC 27609

MARSH, MERRILYN DELANO, sculptor, painter; b. Larchmont, N.Y., Dec. 26, 1923; d. Merrill Potter and Hazel (Holmes) Delano; m. George Estabrook Marsh, Sept. 18, 1954; children: Merrill Delano, George Estabrook Jr., Robert Houston. Diploma, Sch. of Mus. of Fine Arts, Boston, 1946, cert., 1947; postgrad., Acad. Grande Chaumière, Paris, 1947-48. Art tchr. Choate Sch., Brookline, Mass., 1948, 49, Brookline Cmty. Ctr., 1948, 49; pvt. art tchr. Newton, Mass., 1948-49; comml. sculptor for display and mfg. cos., 1948-55; sculpture tchr. De Cordova Mus., Lincoln, Mass., 1950-54. Juror for numerous art exhbns., New Eng. area, 1954-55, 72-74. One-woman show at Copley Soc. of Boston, 1996; commd. 7 reliefs for Sch. for Environ., Levine Sci. Ctr., Duke U., Durham, N.C., 1994, bronze statue for cloister garden St. Andrew's Episcopal Ch., Wellesley, Mass., 1995, bronze portrait reliefs for Houston and Sargent Athletic awards Tufts U., Medford, Mass., 1997, 2 bronze reliefs, Ellis Oval Athletic Field Tufts U., 2001, bronze portrait relief of Clarence P. "Pop" Houston, Houston Hall, Tufts U., 1965, bronze portrait relief for Rocco J. Carzo Cage, Cousens Gymnasium, Tufts U., 2002, others. Mrs. David Hunt Sculpture scholar Mus. Fine Arts, 1947; recipient Katherine Thayer Hobson award Pen and Brush Soc., 1991, Best in Show award Juliani Gallery, 1991, Pres.'s Cup award for golf Wellesley (Mass.) Country Club, 1998. 2d Pl. award Wellesley Soc. Artists, 2003. Mem. Copley Soc. Boston (Copley master, Maria Maravigna award 1988, 1st prize in sculpture and large works 1994, other awards, 1983, 89), New Eng. Sculptors Assn. (bd. dirs. 1986, award 1988), Wellesley Soc. Artists (awards 1985, 87, 89, 91-92, 95, 2001-02, 2d pl. award 2003, bd. dirs. 1970, 88—, Hon. Mention award 2003), Cambridge Art Assn. (Jack Schultz award, 2000, other awards 1993-94). Republican. Episcopalian.

MARSH, MICHAEL LAWRENCE, track and field athlete; b. Hawthorne, Calif., Aug. 4, 1967; Grad., UCLA, 1989. Olympic runner, Barcelona, Spain, 1992. Recipient 200m Track and Field Gold medal, Olympics, Barcelona, 1992, 1st USA outdoor 200m, 1993, 1st USA outdoor 100m, 1995. Office: US Track and Field 1 Rca Dome Ste 140 Indianapolis IN 46225-1023

MARSH, MICHELE, former newscaster; married; 1 child. Anchor/reporter WABI-TV, Bangor, Maine, KSAT-TV, San Antonio, WCBS, 1979-96; co-anchor WNBC/News Channel 4 at 6 p.m., N.Y.C., 1996—2003. Recipient Emmy awards for Best Broadcast (3). Office: WNBC-TV 30 Rockefeller Plz New York NY 10112-0002

MARSH, MILES L. paper company executive; b. 1947; With various divsns. Dart & Kraft Inc., Gen. Foods USA; chmn., CEO Pet Inc., St. Louis, until 1995; pres., CEO Ft. James Corp., Richmond, 1995—, chmn. bd., 1996—, chmn., CEO Deerfield, Ill. Office: Fort James Corp 1919 S Broadway Green Bay WI 54304-4905

MARSH, RICHARD H. utilities company executive; BA, Kent State U.; MA in Clinical Psychology, MBA, U. Akron. CFA. Joined Ohio Edison, 1980, various financial positions, 1980—91; treasurer Ohio Edison (merged with Centerior Energy to form FirstEnergy), 1991—97; v.p. finance FirstEnergy Corp., Akron, Ohio, 1997, v.p., CFO, 1998—2001, sr. v.p., CFO, 2001—. Mem. advancement coun. Coll. Bus. Admin. U. Akron, v.p. alumni coun.; chair We. Reserve Girl Scout Coun.; trustee FirstEnergy Found., H.M. Life Opportunity Services; mem. advisory com. for Master of Sci. in Fin. Engring. prog. Kent State U. Office: First Energy Corp 76 Simain St Akron OH 44308-1890*

MARSH, ROBERT BUFORD, chemical engineer, consultant; b. Chgo., Nov. 16, 1946; s. Ivar Buford and Blanche Julien (Morrisette) M.; m. Claudia Ann Werner, Feb. 14, 1970; children: Julie Ann, Kristy Louise. BSChemE, Mich. Tech. U., 1968. Registered profl. engr., Mass. Engr. 1 design engr. Chevron Rsch., Richmond, Calif., 1968-70, tech. svc. engr., 1970-73; lustrex supr. Monsanto, Long Beach, Calif., 1973-78, mfg. supr. Everett, Mass., 1978-83, environ. engr., 1984-85, mfg. tech. specialist, 1986-91, worldwide plasticizer tech. expert engring. specialist Everett, Indian Orchard, Mass., 1992-93; pres. Marsh Engr., Inc., Andover, Mass., 1992—. Environ. instr., U. Mass., 1994; cons. Mass. Dept. Environ. Protection, Lowell, 1993-94; cons. EPA Rsch. grant, 1994, Shawsheen Environ. Action, 1995-96; compliance coord., bd. dirs. Shawsheen Watershed Assn., 1999—; compliance coord. Am. Chestnut Found., 2003—; spkr. in field. Adv., co. Leady Jr. Achievement, Long Beach, 1975-77; vol. Andover Sch. System, 1983-84, Chicopee River Watershed Assn., Springfield, Mass., 1993; compliance contact, Shawsheen River Watershed Assn., 1998-2003; election com. State Senator O'Brien com., 1994-97, State Senator Tucker, 1998-2004, Sierra Club; mem. Andover Citizen Environ. Com. Independent. Methodist. Achievements include rsch. in ammonia-Hydrogen Sulfide Equilibrium in the 10-50% range. Home: 8 Mulberry Cir Andover MA 01810-3231 Office: Marsh Engring Inc 8 Mulberry St Andover MA 01810-0804 Office Phone: 978-684-5040. E-mail: robertmarsh@worldnet.att.net.

MARSH, ROBERT HARRY, chemical company executive; b. Camden, N.J., Sept. 6, 1946; s. Harry Louis and Margaret Charlotte (Starke) M. BA, BS in Mech. Engring., Rutgers U., 1969; MBA in Mgmt. and Fin., Temple U., 1980. Registered profl. engr., N.J., Pa., Del. From mech. engr. to mech. specialist and project engr. Rohm & Haas Engring., Bristol, Pa., 1967—76; from staff engr. to sr. engring. specialist Hercules, Inc., Wilmington, Del., 1976-80, sr. fin. analyst for corp. strategic planning, 1980-81, sr. bus. analyst bus. group, 1982-83; mgr. bus. analysis Himont, Inc., 1983-86, dir. strategy and planning, 1986-88, dir. bus. mgmt., 1988-91, mng. dir. China, 1991-95, dir. strategy, 1991-95; founder R.H. Marsh & Assoc. Internat. Mgmt., 1995—; pres., prin., CEO, chmn. bd. dirs. Internat. Bus. and Mktg. Mgmt., 1996—. Founder, bd. dirs. various cos., 1995—. Contbr. articles to profl. jours. Active Haddonfield (N.J.) Civic Affairs, Bethlehem (Pa.) Civic Affairs, Wesley Meth. Ch., Bethlehem, Pa., 2001—. Mem.: NSPE, ASME (vice chmn. awards com. 1980, membership chmn. 1982, nat. power com. 1977—84), Engrs. Club Phila., Pyramid Club Phila., Beta Gamma Sigma. Home: 225 Flagstone Dr Bethlehem PA 18017

MARSH, ROBERT MORTIMER, sociologist, educator; b. Everett, Mass., Jan. 22, 1931; s. Henry Warren and Ruth (Dunbar) M.; children: Eleanor L., Christopher S.H., Diana E. Student, Boston U., 1948-50; AB, U. Chgo., 1952; MA, Columbia, 1953, PhD, 1959. Fellow Ford Found., Japan, Taiwan, Hong Kong, 1956-58; instr. sociology U. Mich., 1958-61; asst. prof. sociology Cornell U., 1961-65; asso. prof. Duke, 1965-67; mem. faculty Brown U., 1967—, prof. sociology, 1968—, chmn. dept., 1971-75. Manpower personnel and tng. rsch. prof. U.S. Naval Acad., Annapolis, 1987-88; vis. prof. Nat. Tsing Hua U., Taiwan, 1991. Author: The Mandarins: The Circulation of Elites in China, 1961, Comparative Sociology: A Codification of Cross-Societal Analysis, 1967; (with H. Mannari) Modernization and the Japanese Factory, 1976, Organizational Change in Japanese Factories, 1988, The Great Transformation: Social Change in Taipei, Taiwan Since the 1960s, 1996; also articles; assoc. editor Adminstrv. Sci. Quar., 1963-67, Jour. Comparative Family Studies, 1970-74; co-editor: (with J. Michael Armer) Comparative Sociological Research in the 1960s and 1970s. East Asian Inst. summer fellow Chinese Columbia, 1955; Ford Found. and Guggenheim Found. fellow Japan, 1969-70; Japan Soc. Promotion Sci. fellow, 1976, 83; Chiang Ching Kuo Found. and Nat. Sci. Coun. fellow (Taiwan, Republic of China). 1991-93. Mem. Am. Sociol. Assn., Ea. Sociol. Assn., Assn. Asian Studies, Internat. Studies Assn. (exec. com. comparative interdisciplinary studies sect. 1971-76), Japan Human Rels. Assn. (councilor 1970—). Office: Dept Sociology Brown Univ Providence RI 02912-0001 E-mail: robert_marsh@brown.edu.

MARSH, SUE ANN, special education educator; b. Marshall, Tex., Dec. 5, 1949; d. Orman and Della Florence (Floyd) M. BS in Edn., Stephen F. Austin State U., Nacogdoches, Tex., 1971, MEd, 1975. Cert. elem. tchr., reading tchr., spl. edn. in mental retardation, Tex. Tchr. Title 45 Dickinson (Tex.) Ind. Sch. Dist., 1971, tchr. Title I, 1971-72; tchr. trainable mentally retarded Conroe (Tex.) Ind. Sch. Dist., 1972-85, tchr. Option III, 1985—. Coach, asst. coach Vol. Spl. Olympics, Conroe, 1973—, advt. chmn for golf tournament, 1989-90. Editor: Almost Reader Series. Leader for mentally retarded boys and girls Boy Scouts Am., Conroe, 1990—; chmn. Crockett Cougars Year Book Advertisement 50th Anniversary Edit. Named Crockett Intermediate Tchr. of Yr., 1992; recipient Sam Houston Disting. Scouting award of merit, 1993, Sam Houston Disting. Scouting award of Merit, 1996; co-recipient State Centennial Farm award, Career Ladder, 1984-93. Mem. Assn. Tex. Profl. Educators (bldg. rep. 1983—), Classroom Tchrs. Assn. (bldg. rep. 1975-78), Floyd Family Assn. (sec.-treas. Plantersville, Tex.), River Plantation Lions (camp chmn. 1990-94, chmn. attendance 1990-91, bd. dirs. 1990-96, 3rd v.p. 1992-93, 2nd v.p. 1993-94, v.p. 1994-95, pres. 1995-96, treas. 1996). Democrat. Baptist. Avocations: travel, needlecrafts, plays, concerts. Office: Wash Intermediate Sch 507 Avenue K Conroe TX 77301-3881

MARSHAK, ALAN HOWARD, electrical engineer, educator; b. Miami Beach, Fla., Mar. 21, 1938; s. Jerome and Yetta (Feiner) M.; children: Jerry Brian; m. Joan Grode Milner, May 25, 1997. BScEE, U. Miami, 1960; MS, La. State U., 1962; PhD, U. Ariz., 1969. Asst. prof. elec. engring. La. State U., Baton Rouge, 1969-73, assoc. prof., 1973-78, prof., 1978—2002, chmn. dept. elec. and computer engring., 1983—2002, prof. emeritus, 2002—. Vis. prof. Electron Device Rsch. Ctr., U. Fla., Gainesville, 1979-80; tech. reviewer NSF, 1976—, panelist, 1993-96; panelist NRC, 1993, 2001; mem. Southeastern Ctr. Elec. Engring. Edn., 1984-2002, life mem., 2002—, chmn., CEO, 1992-2001, trustee, 1994—; spkr. profl. confs. Tech. referee various jours. including Solid-State Electronics, Jour. Applied Physics; editor: Device and Process Modeling, IEEE Trans. Electron Devices, 1991-2001; author: (with D. J. Hamilton and F. A. Lindholm) Principles and Applications of Semiconductor Device Modeling, 1971, Basic Experiments in Electronics: A Laboratory Manual, 1978, also 56 tech. papers. NSF grad. trainee, 1967-69; grantee, 1970, 73, 75, 78; named F.H. Coughlin/CLECO prof. of elec. engring., 1993. Fellow IEEE (life); mem. Electron Devices Soc., Sigma Xi, Eta Kappa Nu. Home: 113 Clipper Cove Lafayette LA 70508-7023

MARSHAK, ARTHUR, artist, sculptor; s. Isadore and Lillian Marshak; m. Theodora Armstead, Nov. 19, 1990; children: Jennifer Suzanne Gerson, Beth Rachel Armstead children: Jay Stuart, Laurie Susan Shelansky. Studied, Venice Sch. Art, Venice, Calif., 1968—69, Sun Casting Foundry, Long Beach, Calif., 1969—70, South Fla. Art Inst., Ft. Lauderdale, Fla., 1977—78, Fla. Atlantic U., Boca Raton, Fla., 1980—81, Atlantic Tech. Vocat., Coconut Creek, Fla., 1980—81. Sculptor (bronze sculpture limited editions) Birth, 1977, Timeless, 1977, With These Hands, 1979, Dawn 2K, 1985, La Harpe, 1991. Decorated Am. Theatre Medal and Victory Medal USN. Mem.: Boca Mus. Profl. Artist Guild. Avocations: growing orchids, birdwatching, travel. Home: 4960 Swans Ln Coconut Creek FL 33073 Office: Marshak Sculpture Studio 4960 Swans Ln Coconut Creek FL 33073 Office Phone: 954-725-3381. Personal E-mail: msculpture@aol.com.

MARSHAK, HARRY, plastic surgeon; b. L.A., Oct. 1, 1961; s. Herbert and Pearl (Engelson) M. BS, U. Calif., Riverside, 1981; MD, UCLA, 1984. Diplomate Am. Bd. Surgery, Am. Bd. Plastic Surgery. Pvt. practice, Beverly Hills, Calif., 1991—. Fellow ACS (hon.), Internat. Coll. Surgeons; mem. Am. Soc. Plastic and Reconstructive Surgeons, Calif. Soc. Plastic Surgery, Am. Soc. for Aesthetic Plastic Surgery. Republican. Avocation: sports. Office: 120 S Spalding Dr Ste 300 Beverly Hills CA 90212-1841 Office Phone: 310-657-7600. E-mail: drharrymarshak@aol.com.

MARSHAK, ROBERT REUBEN, former university dean, medical educator, veterinarian; b. N.Y.C., Feb. 23, 1923; s. David and Edith (Youselovsky) Marshak; m. Ruth Emilie Lyons, Dec. 4, 1948 (div. 1983); children: William Lyons, John Ball, Richard Best; m. Margo Post Marshall, June 25, 1983. Student, U. Wis., 1940—41; DVM, Cornell U., 1945, U. Bern, 1968; MA (hon.), U. Pa., 1971. Diplomate Am. Coll. Vet. Internal Medicine (charter). Practice vet. medicine, Springfield, Vt., 1945—56; prof., chmn. dept. medicine Sch. Vet. Medicine, U. Pa., Phila., 1956—58; prof. medicine Grad. Sch. Medicine, 1957—64; chmn. dept. clin. studies Sch. Vet. Medicine, 1958—73; dir. Bovine Leukemia Research Center, 1965—73; dean Sch. Vet. Medicine, 1973—87; co-dir. Center on Interactions Animals and Soc., 1975—79, also mem. grad. group com. in comparative med. scis.; prof. medicine, chief sect. epidemiology and pub. health Sch. Vet. Medicine U. Pa., 1990—93, prof. medicine emeritus, 1993—. Mem. adv. bd. Pa. Dept. Agr., 1973—87; chmn. Gov.'s STudy Group on Horse Racing Industry in Pa., 1979; mem. del. to evaluate vet. med. and rsch. Chinese Ministry Agr.; mem. adv. com. Stround Water Rsch. Ctr., 1992—; mem. adv. coun. Coll. Vet. Medicine, Cornell U., 1993—; mem. animal use and care com. Calif. Inst. Tech., 2003—. Sr. co-editor: Advances in Veterinary Science and Comparative Medicine; contbr. numerous articles to sci. jours. Mem. sci. adv. bd. Sch. Vet. Medicine The Hebrew U., Jerusalem, 1984—, mem. rev. com., 1997—; chmn. external com. Sch. Vet. Medicine Tuskegee U.; trustee Upland Country Day Sch., 1988—91; mem. animal adv. com. City of Phila., 1989—93; mem. Pres.'s Rev. Com. Korest Sch. Vet. Medicine Hebrew U. Jerusalem, 1997—98; bd. dirs. Humane Soc. U.S., 1978—82, Bide-a-wee Home Assn., 1980—85. With U.S. Army, 1943—44. Recipient Disting. Vet. award, Pa. Vet. Med. Assn., 1984, Barnraiser award, Pa. Farmers Assn., 1987. Fellow: Phila. Coll. Physicians; mem.: AAAS, NAS Inst. Medicine (sr.), Pa. Livestock Assn. (dir.), Pa. Vet. Med. Assn., Am. Vet. Med. Assn., Am. Assn. Cancer Rsch., John Morgan Soc. (pres. 1967—68), Phila. Zool. Soc. (bd. dirs. 1986—87), James A. Baker Inst. for Animal Health (mem. adv. coun. 1977—), Phila. Soc. for Promoting Agr., Westminster Kennel Club, Phi Zeta, Sigma Xi. E-mail: rmarshak@ucaltech.edu.

MARSHALL, ALAN GEORGE, chemistry and biochemistry educator; b. Bluffton, Ohio, May 26, 1944; s. Herbert Boyer Marshall Jr. and Cecile (Mogil) Rosser; m. Marilyn Gard, June 13, 1965; children: Gwendolyn Scott, Brian George. BA in Chemistry with honors, Northwestern U., 1965; PhD in Phys. Chemistry, Stanford U., 1970. Instr. II U. B.C., Vancouver, Can., 1969-71, asst. prof., 1971-76, assoc. prof., 1976-80; prof. chemistry and biochemistry, dir. Chem. Instrument Ctr. Ohio State U., Columbus, 1980—93; prof. chemistry and biochemistry Fla. State U., Tallahassee, 1993—, disting. rsch. prof., 1999, Kasha prof., 2000—. Dir. Ion Cyclotron Resonance Program Nat. High Magnetic Field Lab., 1993—. Author: Biophysical Chemistry, 1978, Fourier Transforms in NMR, Optical and Mass Spectroscopy, 1990; editor: Nat. High Magnetic Field Lab. ICR/ION Trap newsletter, 1986—92, Rapid Comm. on Mass Spectrometry, 1988—; mem. editl. adv. bd.: Analytical Chemistry, 1990—92, mem. editl. bd.: Internat. Jour. Mass Ion Procs., 1987—, Jour. Am. Soc. Mass Spectrometry, 1989—97; mem. editl. bd. (jour.) Jour. Am. Soc. Mass Spectrometry, 1999—2002; mem. editl. bd.: Mass Spectrometry Rev., 1994—, Jour. Magnetic Resonance, 1996—2000, Chemometrics and Intelligent Lab. Systems, 1986—89, Ency. of Mass Spectrometry, 2000—, mem. internat. editl adv. bd.: ACS Ency. of Chem. Instrumentation, 1992—95; contbr. more than 370 articles to profl. jours. Recipient Disting. Scholar award, Ohio State U., 1988, award in analytical chemistry, Ea. Analytical Symposium, 1991, Maurice F. Hasler award, Spectroscopy Soc. Pitts., 1997, Two-Yr. Creativity award, NSF, 1997, gold medal, N.Y. Soc. Applied Spectroscopy, 1998, Pitts. Spectroscopy award, Spectroscopy Soc. Pitts., 2002; grad. fellow, NSF, 1965—69, Alfred P. Sloan rsch. fellow, 1976. Fellow: AAAS, Am. Phys. Soc.; mem.: Am. Soc. Mass Spectroscopy (bd. dirs. 1991—93, 2003—, Disting. Contbn. award 1999), Am. Chem. Soc. (Akron Sect. award 1988, award in chem. instrumentation 1990, Frank H. Field and Joe L. Franklin award in mass spectrometry 1995, award in analytical chemistry 2002, Fla. sect. award 2003—, Herty Medal Georgia Sect. 2003), Soc. Applied Spectroscopy (hon.; chmn. local sect. 1990—93), Internat. Mass Spectrum Soc. (Thomson medal 2000). Office: Fla State Univ Nat High Magnetic Field Lab 1800 E Paul Dirac Dr Tallahassee FL 32310-4005

MARSHALL, ALLEN WRIGHT, III, communications executive, financial consultant; b. Griffin, Ga., Dec. 4, 1941; s. Allen Wright and Evelyn Louise (Halliburton) Marshall; m. Monica Hodgins McKellar; 1 child, Allen Wright IV. BA in Journalism, U. Ga., 1964; diploma, Elkins Inst. Radio, Atlanta, 1964; postgrad., Ga. State U., 1968, MBA, 1988; cert., Coll. Fin. Planning, Denver, 1991. 1st class radio telephone lic. FCC; cert. fin. planner. Pres. Sta. WKEU-AM-FM, Griffin, 1954-86; co-founder, v.p. Griffin Cable TV, 1971-74; co-founder, pres. Custom Svcs. Inc. (now Marshall Plans Inc.), Griffin, 1974—; co-founder, v.p. Cobbwells Marshall Inc., Griffin, 1982-87, Page One, Griffin, 1983-87; co-founder, pres. Toolware Inc., Griffin, 1993-97; co-founder, sec./treas. Magnolia Broadcasting Inc., laGrange, Ga., 1993-95; founder, mng. mem. Spalding Speculators LLC, Griffin, 1995—. Bd. dirs. Wachovia Bank, Griffin, Face Internat. Corp., Norfolk, Va.; spkr. in field. Author radio progrms, editorials (Ga. AP award 1969-84); also articles. Bd. dirs. Goals for Griffin and Spalding Counties INc., 1981-92, pres. 1991; mem. adv. com. Griffin Vocat.-Tech. Sch., 1982-87; bd. dirs. Jr. Achievement, Griffin, 1977-87; chmn. Griffin-Spalding Indsl. Authority, 1984; mem. Gov.'s Adv. Com. on Area Planning and Devel. Commns., 1971-72; bd. dirs. McIntosh Trail Area Planning and Devel. Commn., Ga., 1971-73; founding trustee, vice chair, treas. St. George's Episc. Sch., 1995-2001; treas., trustee Nat. Episc. Radio/TV Found., 1986-93. Sgt. U.S. Army, 1966-68. Named Man of Yr., Exch. Club of Griffin, 1984. Mem. Ga. Assn. Broadcasters 9bd. dirs. 1970-74, Radio Sta. of Yr. 1977), Griffin Area C. of C. (bd. dirs. 1980, chmn. indsl. com. 1980, 81), C.C. (charter mem. 1966), Rotary (pres. 1976-77). Avocations: photography, landscape design, archtl. renovation. Home and Office: 1800 Maple Dr Griffin GA 30224-7405

MARSHALL, ALTON GARWOOD, real estate counselor; b. Flint, Mich., Sept. 19, 1921; s. William Robert and Lela Christine (Brabon) M.; m. Mary Lee Golden, June 22, 1945 (div. July 1971); children: William A., Stephen B., Bruce S., Mary Ann Marshall Trebian, John L.; m. Sarah Elizabeth DeLand, Sept. 4, 1971; 1 child, Sarah Graham. BA, Hillsdale Coll., 1942; MS, Syracuse U., 1948, LLD (hon.), 1974; D Pub. Service & Bus. Adminstrn. (hon.), Hillsdale Coll., 1980. Sec. utility regulations pub. svc. commn. N.Y. State, Albany, 1953-61, dep. dir. div. budget, 1961-65, exec. officer, then sec. to gov., Office of Gov., 1965-70; pres., bd. dirs. Rockefeller Ctr., N.Y.C., 1971-81; pres. A.G. Marshall Assocs., N.Y.C., 1981—; chmn., pres., chief exec. officer Lincoln Savs. Bank, N.Y.C., 1984-88, chmn., chief exec. officer, 1988-91, also bd. dirs. Mem. exec. com. Nat. Realty Com., Washington, 1970-99; bd. dirs. N.Y. State Electric & Gas Corp., 1971-98; ind. gen. ptnr. Equitable Capital Ptnrs. and Equitable Capital Ptnrs. Retirement Fund, 1989-99; trustee Hudson River Trust, 1991-97. Mem. exec. com., steering com. Assn. for a Better N.Y., 1971—; mem. exec., landmarks and polit. action coms. Real Estate Bd. N.Y.; chmn. Nat. Assn. on Drug Abuse Problems, 1990-92. Sr. fellow The Nelson A. Rockefeller Inst. Govt., 1991-94. Mem. Am. Soc. Real Estate Counselors. Office: Alton G Marshall Assocs Inc 136 E 79th St New York NY 10021-0328 Office Phone: 212-407-2514.

MARSHALL, BARRY JAMES, gastroenterologist; b. Kalgoorlie, Western Australia, Australia, Sept. 30, 1951; came to U.S., 1986; s. Robert William and Marjory Jean (Donald) M.; m. Adrienne Joyce Feldman, Dec. 27, 1972; children: Luke, Bronwyn, Caroline, Jessica. MBBS, U. Western Australia, Perth, 1974, postgrad., 1986. Intern Sir Charles Gairdner Hosp., Western Australia, 1975-76, resident, 1976-77, med. registrar, 1977-78, Royal Perth Hosp., Western Australia, 1979-82, Fremantle Hosp., Western Australia, 1983-84, microbiology register, 1984; research scientist Royal Perth Hosp., Western Australia, 1985-86; research fellow U. Va. Sch. Med., Charlottesville, 1986-87, asst. prof. medicine, 1988-99; dir. pharm. Tri-Med., Charlottesville, Va., 1990-1998. Cons. Procter and Gamble Co., Cin., 1984—, Delta West Perth, 1985—; bd. dirs. JARM Pty. Ltd., Perth, 1987—. Inventor Clotest (rapid urease test), 1985, Carbon-14 Urea Breath Test, 1985; co-discoverer Helicobacter Pylori bacilli in stomach of patients with gastritis and peptic ulcers, 1984; first person to culture Helicobacter Pylori bacilli. Named one of Outstanding West Australians, Perth Jaycees, 1985; research grantee Australian Nat. Health and Med. Research Council, 1985-86; recipient Albert Lasker Clinical Medical Rsch. award Albert and Mary Lasker Foundation, 1995, Gairdner Found. Internat. award, 1996, Keio Med. Sci. prize, 2002. Fellow Royal Australian Coll. Physicians, Am. Coll. Gastroenterolgy; mem. Australian Med. Assn., Australian Gastroent. Soc. Avocations: computer hardware and software, photography, skin diving, american cuisine.

MARSHALL, BENJAMIN VAUGHAN, literature and language professor; s. Benjamin Orange and Frances Catherine Marshall. BA, Kean U., 1973; MFA, U. Mass., 1978. Instr. of creative writing Yarmouk U., Irbid, Jordan, 1980—82; instr. Kuwait U., 1982—84; assoc. prof. Middlesex Coll., Edison, NJ, 1986—. Author: (plays) Boom Box, 1987, Henry's Bridge, 1997, Snow, 1999. Fellow, Nat. Endowment Humanities, 1991; grantee, N.J. Coun. on Arts, 1987, 1992, 2003, Geraldine R. Dodge Found., 1999, 2002. Mem.: Phi Kappa Phi. Avocations: piano, photography.

MARSHALL, BRIAN LAURENCE, trade association executive; b. Kingston-on-Thames, Eng., Apr. 6, 1941; arrived in US, 1949; s. John and Marguerite Elizabeth (Sandele) Marshall. BA in European History, U. N.C., 1963; MS in Internat. Mgmt., Am. Grad. Sch. Internat. Mgmt., Glendale, Ariz., 1973. Commd. 2d lt. USAF, 1964, advanced through grades to capt., 1972; instr. Armed Forces Air Intelligence Tng. Ctr., Denver, 1965-68; intelligence analyst Task Force Alpha, Nakhon Phanom, Thailand, 1968-69; intelligence systems analyst Hdqs. Tactical Air Command, Langley AFB, Va., 1969-72, resigned, 1972; sr. analyst Computer Scis. Corp., Falls Church, Va., 1974-87; dir. U.S. membership and pubs. U.S.-Mexico C. of C., Washington, 1987-91; v.p. pub. affairs, bd. dirs. N.Am. Free Trade Assn., Washington, 1991-96; v.p. N.Am. Trade and Investment Group, Washington, 1991-97, also bd. dirs. Contract team leader strategic planning studies and analyses U.S. Dept. Def., Joint Chiefs Staff, Washington, 1976—82; regional oper. supr. elections in Bosnia Orgn. Security and Coop. in Europe (OSCE), 1997, election supr., Bosnia and Kosovo, 1997—98, Bosnia and Kosovo, 2000; internat. trade cons., 1998—. Contbr. articles to booklets and newsletters. Bd. dirs. Columbia Plz. Tenants Assn., Washington, 1981—84; vol. Pres. Ford Com., Washington, 1976. Mem.: VFW, Washington Mgmt. and Bus. Assn. (vice chmn. 1981—83, treas. 1987—91), Thunderbird Alumni Assn. (pres. Washington chpt. 1980—87), Fgn. Policy Assn. (group leader discussion program), World Affairs Coun., Assn. Former Intelligence Officers, Has House Harriers. Republican. Avocations: jogging, tennis, travel, discussion groups, reading. Home: 5304 Albemarle St Bethesda MD 20816-1827 Office: US Mex C of C 1300 Pennsylvania Ave NW Washington DC 20004 Office Phone: 202-312-1520., 202-312-1526. Personal E-mail: brnmarsh@hotmail.com.

MARSHALL, CAROLYN ANN M. church official; b. Springfield, Ill., July 18, 1935; d. Hayward Thomas and Isabelle Bernice (Hayer) McMurray; m. John Alan Marshall, July 14, 1956 (dec. Sept. 1990); children: Margaret Marshall Bushman, Cynthia Marshall Kyrouac, Clinton, Carol Bentler. Student, De Pauw U., 1952-54; BSBA, Drake U., 1956; D of Pub. Svc. (hon.), De Pauw U., 1983; LHD (hon.), U. Indpls., 1990. Corp. sec. Marshall Studios, Inc., Veedersburg, Ind., 1956-89, exec. cons., 1989-93; sec. Gen. Conf., lay leader South Ind. conf. United Meth. Ch., Veedersburg, Ind., 1988-96; exec. dir. Lucille Raines Residence, Inc., Indianapolis, 1996—. Carolyn M. Marshall chair in women studies Bennett Coll., Greensboro, N.C., 1988; fin. cons. Lucille Raines Residence, Inpls., 1977-95. Pres. Fountain Ctrl. Band Boosters, Veedersburg, 1975-77; del. Gen. Conf., United Meth. Ch., 1980, 84, 88, 92, 96, 2000, pres. women's divsn. gen. bd. global ministries, 1984-88; bd. dirs. Franklin (Ind.) United Meth. Ch. Mem. United Meth. Ch. Home: 204 N Newlin St Veedersburg IN 47987-1358 Office: Lucille Raines Residence Inc 947 N Pennsylvania St Indianapolis IN 46204-1070 E-mail: cmarshall@sprintmail.com.

MARSHALL, CHARLES, communications company executive; b. Vandalia, Ill., Apr. 21, 1929; s. William Forman and Ruth (Corson) M.; m. Millicent Bruner, Jan. 2, 1953; children: Ruth Ann, Marcia Marshall Rinek, William Forman, Charles Tedrick. BS in Agr, U. Ill., 1951. With Ill. Bell Telephone Co., 1953-59, 61-64, 65-70, 71-72, 77-81, pres., chief exec. officer, 1977-81; with AT&T, 1959-61, 64-65, 70-71, 76-77, 81-89; chmn., chief exec. officer Am. Bell, Morristown, N.J., 1983-84, AT&T Info. Systems, 1984-85; vice chmn. AT&T, N.Y.C., 1985-89. Bd. dirs. Moorings Park, Naples; trustee U. Ill.

Found.; vice-chmn. Naples Philharm. Soc. for the Arts. Served to 1st lt. USAF, 1951-53. Mem.: Chgo. Club, Club of Pelican Bay, Comml. Club Chgo., Econ. Club Chgo. Avocations: fishing, golf, reading. Home: 6001 Pelican Bay Blvd Ph B Naples FL 34108-8168

MARSHALL, CHARLES NOBLE, rail transportation executive; b. Phila., Feb. 18, 1942; s. Donnell and Cornelia Lansdale (Brooke) M.; m. Ann Shaw Donovan, Jan. 12, 1971; children— Elizabeth, Caroline, Cornelia, Edward BS in Engring., Princeton U., 1963; JD, U. Mich., 1967. Bar: Md. 1967, D.C. 1975, Pa. 1978. Atty. Balt. & Ohio R.R., Balt. and Cleve., 1967-73; gen. atty. So. Ry., Washington, 1973-78; gen. counsel commerce Conrail, Phila., 1978-83, v.p. mktg., 1983-85, sr. v.p. mktg. and sales, 1985-89, sr. v.p. devel., 1989-95; pres., COO Genesee & Wyoming Inc., 1997—. Bd. dirs. Phila. Reg. Port Authority, Rails to Trails Conservancy, Pa. Hort. Soc.

MARSHALL, CHRISTOPHER L. research scientist, chemist; b. Rochester, N.Y., Dec. 31, 1952; s. Lyle L. and Kay L. Marshall; m. Susan B. Bolda, June 16, 1979; children: Dianne F., Lisa K. BA, SUNY, Potsdam, 1975; MS, Mich. State, East Lansing, 1977, PhD, 1980. Rsch. chemist Amoco Oil Co., Naperville, Ill., 1980—92, Argonne Nat. Lab., Ill., 1993—. Mem.: N.Am. Catalysis Soc., Am. Chem. Soc. Achievements include patents in field. Office: Argonne Nat Lab 9700 South Cass Ave Argonne IL 60439-4837 Office Phone: 630-252-4310. E-mail: clmarshall@anl.gov.

MARSHALL, CODY, bishop; Bishop Ch. of God in Christ, No. Ill. Mem. Ch. Of God In Christ. Office: Freedom Temple Church of God in Christ 6028 S Champlain Ave Chicago IL 60637-2512

MARSHALL, LORD COLIN (LORD MARSHALL OF KNIGHTSBRIDGE), airline executive; b. Edgware, Middlesex, Eng., Nov. 16, 1933; s. Edward Leslie and Florence Mary Marshall; m. Janet Winifred Cracknell, May 10, 1958; 1 child. Student, U. Coll. Sch., Hampstead, Eng., 1946-51. From cadet purser to dep. purser Orient Steam Navigation Co., 1951-58; mgmt. trainee Hertz Corp., Chgo. and Toronto, Ont., Can., 1958-59; gen. mgr. Hertz Corp., Mexico City, 1959-60, asst. to pres. N.Y.C., 1960, gen. mgr. U.K. divsn. London, 1961-62, gen. mgr. U.K. The Netherlands and Belgium divsn., 1962-64; regional mgr., v.p. Avis Co., London, 1964-66, gen. mgr. Europe and Middle East divsn., 1966-69, v.p. gen. mgr. internat. divsn., 1969-71, exec. v.p., chief operating officer, 1971-75, pres., chief operating officer, 1975-76, pres., chief exec. officer, 1976-79; exec. v.p., sector exec. Norton Simon Inc., N.Y.C., 1979-81; dir. dep. chief exec. Sears Holdings Plc, London, 1981-83; CEO Brit. Airways, London, 1983-95, apptd. dep. chmn. bd. dirs., 1989-93, exec. chmn. bd. dirs., 1993-95, chmn. bd. dirs., 1996—, Invensys Plc, London, 1999—. Bd. dirs. Brit. Airways, HSBC Holdings, Brit. Telecomm.; chair internat. adv. bd. Brit. Am. Bus. Coun., 1994—. Awarded Knight Bachelor, Her Majesty the Queen, 1987. Mem. Queens Club, All Eng. LTC. Clubs: Queens. Avocations: tennis, cross country skiing. Office: British Airways Plc Waterside PO Box 365 Harmondsworth UB7 OGB England Fax: 020 7495 4845.

MARSHALL, CONRAD JOSEPH, entrepreneur; b. Detroit, Dec. 23, 1934; s. Edward Louis Fedak and Maria Magdalena Berzsenyi; m. Dorothy Genieve Karnafil, Dec. 1, 1956 (div. 1963); children: Conrad Joseph Jr., Kevin Conrad, Lisa Marie; m. Beryle Elizabeth Callahan, June 15, 1965 (div. 1972); children: Brent Jasmer, Farah Elizabeth. Diploma, Naval Air Tech. Tng. Ctr., Norman, Okla., 1952; student, Wayne State U., 1956-59; Diploma, L.A. Police Acad., 1961. Dir. mktg. Gulf Devel., Torrance, Calif., 1980-83; sales mgr. Baldwin Piano Co., Santa Monica, Calif., 1977-80; dir. mktg., v.p. Western Hose, Inc., L.A., 1971-76; city letter carrier U.S. Post Office, L.A., 1969-71; writer freelance L.A., 1966—; police officer L.A. Police Dept., 1961-66; asst. sales mgr. Wesson Oil Co., Detroit, 1958-60; agt. Life Ins. Co. of Va., Wayne, Mich., 1956-58; pres. Am. Vision Mktg., L.A., 1990—, Con-Mar Prodns., L.A., 1983—; sr. v.p. Pacific Acquisition Group, 1992—, Invest. Admin. HealthCom., Int., 1993—; pres. Midway TV Co., 1994—. Tech. advisor Lion's Gate Films, Westwood, Calif., 1970-74, Medicine Wheel Prodns., Hollywood, Calif., 1965-75; mng. gen. ptnr. Encino Wireless #1, 1994—; CEO Midway TV Inc., 1995; v.p. nat. bus. affairs MMA Internat., 1997; v.p. mktg. Kidkritter, Inc., 1998; sr. prodn. exec. Alpine Pictures Inc., 1999. Author: (series) "Dial Hot Line", 1967, (screenplay) "Heads Across the Border", 1968, "The Fool Card", 1970, "Probable Cause", 1972; author, sr. prodn. exec. (screenplay) The Home, 2003; co-author: The Fedak File, 1995; albums include Song Shark, 1992, Conrad Marshall Quintet, 1991. Campaign vol. Dem. Ctrl. Com., L.A., 1976, Rep. Ctrl. Com., 1994. Mem. Screen Actors Guild, Internat. Platform Assn. Avocations: poetry, song writing, club singing, philosophy, theology. Office: Con Mar Prodns 2026 Holly Hill Ter Hollywood CA 90068-3812 Home: Apt 4 1958 Sams Loop Bend OR 97701-6089

MARSHALL, CONSUELO BLAND, federal judge; b. Knoxville, Tenn., Sept. 28, 1936; d. Clyde Theodore and Annie (Brown) Arnold; m. George Edward Marshall, Aug. 30, 1959; children: Michael Edward, Laurie Ann. AA, L.A. City Coll., 1956; BA, Howard U., 1958, LLB, 1961. Bar: Calif. 1962. Dep. atty., City of L.A., 1962-67; assoc. Cochran & Atkins, L.A., 1968-70; commr. L.A. Superior Ct., 1971-76; judge Inglewood Mcpl. Ct., 1976-77, L.A. Superior Ct., 1977-80, U.S. Dist. Ct. Central Dist. Calif., L.A., 1980—. Lectr. U.S. Information Agy. in Yugoslavia, Greece and Italy, 1984, in Nigera and Ghana, 1991, in Ghana, 1992. Contbr. articles to profl. jours.; notes editor Law Jour. Howard U. Mem. adv. bd. Richstone Child Abuse Center. Recipient Judicial Excellence award Criminal Cts. Bar Assn., 1992, Ernestine Stalhut award; named Criminal Ct. Judge of Yr., U.S. Dist. Ct., 1997; inducted into Langston Hall of Fame, 2000; rsch. fellow Howard U. Law Sch., 1959-60. Mem. State Bar Calif., Century City Bar Assn., Calif. Women Lawyers Assn., Calif. Assn. Black Lawyers, Calif. Judges Assn., Black Women Lawyers Assn., Los Angeles County Bar Assn., Nat. Assn. Women Judges, NAACP, Urban League, Beta Phi Sigma. Office: US Dist Ct 312 N Spring St Los Angeles CA 90012-4701

MARSHALL, DALE ROGERS, academic administrator, political scientist, educator; b. Mar. 22, 1937; m. Donald J. Marshall; children: Jessica, Cynthia, Clayton. BA in Govt., Cornell U., 1959; MA in Polit. Sci., U. Calif., Berkeley, 1960; PhD in Polit. Sci. with distinction, UCLA, 1969. Lectr. in polit. sci. UCLA, 1969-70, U. Calif., Berkeley, 1970-72, from asst. prof. to prof. Davis, 1972-86, faculty asst. to vice chancellor acad. affairs, 1980-82, assoc. dean Coll. Letters and Scis., 1983-86; acting pres. Wellesley (Mass.) Coll., 1987-88, dean of coll., prof. polit. sci., 1986-92; pres. Wheaton (Mass.) Coll., 1992—. Mem. exec. bd. Calif. Assembly Fellowship Program, 1980-86; bd. trustees, bd. overseers Newton-Wellesley Hosp., 1989-93; bd. trustees Cornell U., Ithaca, N.Y., 1983-93, chair Cornell Fund, co-chair Coll. Arts and Scis. Capital Campaign, 1990-93; bd. trustees New Eng. Zenith Fund, New Eng. Mut. Life Ins. Co., 1995—; bd. dirs. Am. Student Assistance Guarantor, Am. Student Assistance Corp, 1994-2001. Author: (with John C. Bollens) Guide to Participation: Field Work, Role Playing Cases and Other Forms, 1973, (with Rufus P. Roger Montgomery) Housing Policy for the 80's, 1980, (with Rufus P. Browning and David H. Tabb) Protest is Not Enough: The Struggle of Blacks and Hispanics for Equality in Urban Politics, 1984 (APSA Ralph J. Bunche award for best book on ethnic rels. 1985, Gladys Kammerer award for best book in Am. policy 1985); editor: Urban Policy Making, 1979, (with David K. Leonard) Institutions of Rural Development for the Poor: Decentralization and Organizatonal Linkages, 1982, (with Rufus P. Browning and David H. Tabb, co-editor), Racial Politics in American Cities, 1990, 3d edit., 2003; mem. edit. bd. Am. Polit. Sci. Rev., 1972-76, Pub. Adminstrn. Rev., 1985-86; contbr. articles to profl. jours. Woodrow Wilson fellow, 1959-60, Calif. Regents fellow, 1966-67, 67-68; NSF grantee, 1976-78, 79-80; recipient Disting. Teaching award Significant Contbn. to Status of Women citation Chancellor's Com. on Status of Women at U. Calif. at Davis, 1978. Mem. Am. Polit. Sci. Assn. (mem. exec. coun. 1974-76, v.p. 1985-86, mem. nominating com. 1988-90), Western Polit. Sci. Assn. (mem. exec. coun. 1973-75, pres. 1984-85), Nat. Acad. Pub. Adminstrn., Nat. Assn. Ind. Colls. and Univs. (bd. dirs.), Assn. Ind. Colls. and Univs. Mass. (exec. com.), Mortar Bd., Phi Beta Kappa, Phi Kappa Phi. Office: Wheaton Coll Office of Pres Norton MA 02766 E-mail: dmarshal@wheatonma.edu.

MARSHALL, DAVID D. electric utilities executive; Pres., CEO DQE, Inc., Corapolis, Pa., 1997—, chmn., 1999—. Office: DQE Inc 411 7th Ave Pittsburgh PA 15219-1919

MARSHALL, DAVID DOUGLAS, science educator; b. Cleve., Ohio, Mar. 10, 1948; s. William and Virginia Ann Marshall; m. Linda Lou Nickum, May 7, 1949; children: Amy Colleen Nickum, David Andrew Doran-Marshall. BA, Baldwin-Wallace Coll., Berea, Ohio, 1970; MA, Cleve. State U., 1972; PhD, U. of Ill., Urbana, 1976. Rsch. psychologist U. of Wis., Stevens Point, 1976—78; prof. of math. and computer sci. Tex. Woman's U., Denton, 1978—. Software engr., courseware author and cons. Micro Power & Light Co., Dallas, 1979—83; conf. presenter in field. Contbr. articles to sci. publs.; mem. editl. bd.: Jour. of Theory Constrn. and Testing, 1999—. Candidate for sch. bd., Denton, Tex., 1980. Mem.: Math. Assn. of Am., Am. Statis. Assn. Avocations: cooking, aviation, reading (philosophy, history, mathematics, cosmology, physiology, physics), carpentry. Office: Tex Woman's U PO Box 425886 TWU Station Denton TX 76204-5886 Office Phone: 940-898-2175. Personal E-mail: dmarshall@twu.edu. E-mail: dmarshall@mail.twu.edu.

MARSHALL, DONALD GLENN, English language and literature educator; b. Long Beach, Calif., Sept. 9, 1943; s. Albert Louis and Margaret Corinne (Morrison) M.; m. Kathleen Bonann, June 21, 1975; children: Stephanie Deborah, Zachary Louis AB summa cum laude, Harvard U., 1965; MPhil, Yale U., 1969, PhD, 1971. Asst. prof. English UCLA, 1969-75; from assoc. prof. to prof. English U. Iowa, Iowa City, 1975-90; honors dir. U. Iowa Coll Liberal Arts, 1981 85; prof. English dept. U. Ill., Chgo., 1990—2003, head dept., 1990—2000; prof. Great Books Pepperdine U., Malibu, Calif., 2003—. Editor: Philosophy as Literature/Literature as Philosophy, 1986; compiler: Contemporary Critical Theory: A Selective Bibliography, 1993; translator: (with Joel Weinsheimer) Truth and Method by Hans-Georg Gadamer, 1989; contbr. articles and revs. to profl. jours. Recipient Bell prize Harvard U., 1965, Webster prize Yale U., 1967; NEH Younger Humanist fellow, 1973-74; grantee UCLA, U. Iowa Mem.: MLA, Ill. Humanities Coun. (bd. dirs. 1994—2000, Chgo. Humanities Festival 1997—2003), Modern Poetry Assn. (pres. 1998—2000), Conf. Christianity and Lit. (bd. dirs. 2000—03). Democrat. Roman Catholic. Office: Pepperdine U Divsn Humanities and Tchr Edn 24255 Pacific Coast Hwy Malibu CA 90263 Office Phone: 310-506-7654. Business E-Mail: Donald.Marshall@pepperdine.edu.

MARSHALL, DONALD THOMAS, retired medical technician, theology studies educator; b. Omaha, June 9, 1955; s. William A. and Alma J. Marshall; m. Beverly Ann Everett, Sept. 22, 1990. Cert. in med. tech., Pikes Peak Inst. Med. Tech., 1977; EMT, Pikes Peak CC, Colorado Springs, 1979; PhD in Religion, D in Metaphysics, Universal Life Ch., 1995. Registered med. technologist, cert. clin. lab. technologist; ordained minister Universal Life Ch., 1983. X-ray and med. lab. technician St. Joseph Hosp. Plains, Cheyenne Wells, Colo., 1977—79; med. lab. technician Conejos County Hosp., La Jara, Colo., 1979—84; med. technologist Nat. Health Lab., Englewood, Colo., 1984—91; med. technologist, tech. cons., quality assurance officer Cmty. Health Svcs. Denver Health, 1996—2001, med. technologist, 1996-2001; ret., 2001; pvt. tchr. Religious Philosophy/Metaphysics in classes, workshops, seminars. Cons. in field. EMT, fireman La Jara Vol. Fire Dept., 1979—84. Recipient Meritorious Svc. citation, La Jara Vol. Fire Dept., 1983. Mem.: Am. Med. Technologists, Am. Assn. Bio-Analysts, Colo. Irish Pipeband (drum maj. 2002—03), ScottishRite, YorkRite, Shriners (pipeband, drummer 1999—2003, drum maj. 2000—01), Masons (worshipful master 1994). Republican.

MARSHALL, DOUGLAS WILLIAM, medical administrator, educator; b. Indpls., July 1, 1943; s. William Pryor and Virginia (Guthrie) M.; m. Heidi Christina Amenda, May 30, 1985; 1 child, W. Parker. BA, Denison U., 1965; AM, U. Mich., 1967, PhD, 1976. Western field mgr. U. Mich. Alumni Assn., San Francisco, 1967-69; assoc. curator W.L. Clements Libr. Am. History U. Mich., Ann Arbor, 1970-82; project dir. Campbell-Ewald Co., Warren, Mich., 1982-83; sr. account exec. N.W. Ayer, Inc., Detroit, 1984; mgr. strategic planning GM, Detroit, 1985-91; program mgr. GM Internat., Detroit, 1991-96; CEO Onkoservices, Detroit, 1996-97; v.p. new bus. devel. Innovative Solution in Healthcare, Detroit, 1997-99; prin. Blitz and Assoc. LLC, 2000—. Adj. assoc. prof. radiation oncology Sch. Medicine, Wayne State U., Detroit, 1996-2000; coord. program in history of discovery U. Mich., Ann Arbor, 1973-81. Co-author: (with H.H. Peckham) Campaigns of the American Revolution: An Atlas Manuscript Maps, 1976; exec. editor Terrae Incognitae: Annals of the Soc. for the History of Discoveries, 1975-82; editor: Research Catalog of Maps of America to 1860, 4 vols., 1972; writer, narrator: (ednl. TV series) Maps: Horizons to Knowledge, 1981. Dir. Gt. Lakes region Am. Cancer Soc. Found., 1996—; mem. dean's adv. bd. Rackham Grad. Sch., U. Mich., 1999—; mem. S.E. Mich. strategic planning bd. United Found., Detroit, 1982-83; trustee City of Grosse Pointe Found., 2004—. Rsch. fellow Nat. Geog. Soc., 1977; recipient Bicentennial award Bicentennial Commn., State of Mich., 1974; Fulbright lectr. U.S. Fulbright Commn., Helsinki U., 1980-81; William Andrews Clark postdoctoral fellow UCLA, 1979. Mem. Mich. Map Soc. (pres. 1984-85), Soc. for the History of Discoveries (coun. 1979-81), Bohemian Club Calif. Episcopalian. Home: 545 University Pl Grosse Pointe MI 48230-1639 also: 7090 Windemere PO Box 152 Harbor Springs MI 49740 Office: 21 Kercheval Ave Ste 270 Grosse Pointe MI 48236 Office Phone: 313-966-8734. E-mail: marshall@karmanos.org.

MARSHALL, ELAINE FOLK, state official; b. Lineboro, Md., Nov. 18, 1945; d. Donald and Pauline Folk; m. Sol Marshall; 3 stepchildren. BS in Textiles and Clothing, U. Md., 1968; JD, Campbell U., 1981. Bar: N.C., U.S. Dist. Ct. (ea. and mid. dists.), U.S. Ct. Appeals (4th cir.), U.S. Supreme Ct. Owner retail bus., 1968-79; assoc. Bain Law Firm, Lillington, N.C., 1981-84; ptnr. Bain & Marshall, Lillington, 1985-92, Marshall & Marshall, Lillington, 1993-96; sec.of state State of N.C., 1997—. Legal advisor Bus. and Profl. Women, N.C., 1982-90; mem. 15th dist. N.C. Senate, 1993-94, N.C. Planning Commn., 1993-94, N.C. Cts. Commn., 1993-94. Bd. dirs. Harnett County United Way, 1987-97, N.C. 4-H Devel. Fund, Inc., 1990—, N.C. Rural Econ. Devel. Fund, 1993-95, N.C. Bd. Econ. Devel., 1993-94, 97—, N.C. Ctr. Pub. Policy Rsch., 1994—, N.C. Justice Acad. Found., 1994—; mem. Divine St. United Meth. Ch.; founding chmn., hon. chmn. Harnett HelpNet Children, 1992—; trustee Meredith Coll., 1997—. Recipient N.C. Friends Ext. award, 1992. Fellow N.C. Inst. Polit. Leadership (bd. dirs. 1996—); mem. Women's Forum N.C. Democrat. Office: Office Sec State 300 N Salisbury St Raleigh NC 27603-5925 Mailing: PO Box 29622 Raleigh NC 27626-0622

MARSHALL, ELLEN RUTH, lawyer; b. N.Y.C., Apr. 23, 1949; d. Louis and Faith (Gladstone) M. AB, Yale U., 1971; JD, Harvard U., 1974. Bar: Calif. 1975, D.C. 1981, N.Y. 1989. Assoc. McKenna & Fitting, LA, 1975-80; ptnr. McKenna, Conner & Cuneo, LA and Orange County, Calif., 1980-88, Morrison & Foerster, LLP, Orange County, 1988—2003, Manatt, Phelps & Phillips LLP, Orange County, 2003—. Mem. ABA (bus. law sect., mem. savs. inst. com., mem. asset securitization com., tax sect., mem. employee benefits com.), Orange County Bar Assn., Center Club (Costa Mesa, Calif.), Yale Club (N.Y.C.). Office: Manatt Phelps & Phillips LLP 695 Town Ctr Dr Costa Mesa CA 92626

MARSHALL, FRANCIS JOSEPH, aerospace engineer; b. N.Y.C., Sept. 5, 1923; s. Francis Joseph and Mary Gertrude (Leary) M.; m. Joan Eager, June 14, 1952; children— Peter, Colin, Stephen, Dana. BS in Mech. Engring, CCNY, 1948; MS, Rensselaer Poly. Inst., 1950; Dr. Eng. Sci., N.Y. U., 1955. Engr. Western Union Co., N.Y.C., 1948, Gen. Electric Co., Schenectady, 1948-50; engr. Wright-Aero Corp., Woodridge, N.J., 1950-52; group leader Lab. for Applied Scis., U. Chgo., 1955-60; instr. Ill. Inst. Tech., 1957-59; prof. Sch. Aeros. and Astronautics, Purdue U., West Lafayette, Ind., 1960—. Engr. U.S. Naval Underseas Warfare Center, Pasadena, Calif., 1966-68; faculty fellow NASA-Langley, 1969-70; vis. prof. Inst. Tech. Mara-Midwest Univs. Consortium for Internat. Activities, Malayasia, 1989. Contbr. articles to profl. jours. Served with U.S. Army, 1943-46. Decorated Combat Inf. badge.; NASA research grantee, 1970-76; Fulbright scholar, Turkey, 1988-89. Asso. fellow AIAA; mem. Am. Soc. Engring. Edn., AAUP. Home: 120 Leslie Ave West Lafayette IN 47906-2410 Office: Sch Aeros and Astronautics Purdue U West Lafayette IN 47907

MARSHALL, FRAY FRANCIS, urology educator; b. N.Y.C., Aug. 27, 1944; s. Victor Fray and Barbara (Walsh) M.; m. Lindsay Wheatley, Oct. 6, 1975; children: Wheatley, Brooks. BA, U. Va., 1965, MD, 1969. Diplomate Am. Bd. Urology. Asst. prof. Urology Johns Hopkins Hosp., Balt., 1975-79, assoc. prof. Urology, 1979-86, prof. Urology, 1986—, dir. adult Urology, 1990—. Editor (books) Urologic Complication, 1990, Textbook of Operative Urology, 1996. Office: Johns Hopkins Hosp Dept Urology Marburg 150 601 N Wolfe St Baltimore MD 21287-0004

MARSHALL, GAILEN DAUGHERTY, JR., physician, scientist, educator; b. Houston, Sept. 9, 1950; s. Gailen D. and Evelyn C. (Gresham) M.; m. Elizabeth M. Marek, Nov. 5, 1978; children: Sarah Elizabeth, Jonathan David, Rebecca Marie. BS, U. Houston, 1972; MS, Tex. A&M U., 1973, PhD, U. Tex., 1979, MD, 1984. Rsch. sci. U. Tex., Galveston, 1981-84; rsch. fellow U. Iowa, Iowa City, 1985-86; lab. dir. Biotherapeutics Inc., Memphis, 1986-88; chief med. resident Bapt. Meml. Hosp., Memphis, 1988-89; assoc. dir. Rsch. for Health Inc., Houston, 1989-90; dir. divsn. allergy and immunology U. Tex., Houston, 1990—2004, clin. asst. prof. medicine, 1990-91, asst. prof. medicine, 1991—98, assoc. prof. medicine and pathology, 1998—2003, prof., 2003—04; vice chair medicine, dir. divsn. clin. immunology and allergy U. Miss. Med. Ctr., Jackson, Miss., 2004—. Mem. sci. adv. com. Carrington Labs., Dallas, 1992-94; mem. Merck Rhinitis Adv. Bd., 2002—, Genentech/Novartis Adv. Bd., 2003—. Mem. editl. bd. Molecular Biotherapy, 1992-93, Cancer Biotherapy, 1994-96, Allergy Procs., 1994—2003, Annals Allergy, Asthma and Immunology, 1995-99, Jour. Interferon Cytokin Rsch., 1999—, Clin. Immunology, 2001—, Jour. Clin. Immunology, 2002—, Cellular Molecular Allergy, 2003—; contbr. articles to profl. jours. Judge Greater Houston Sci. Fair, 1992—. Fellow ACP, Am. Coll. Allergy and Immunology, Am. Acad. Allergy-Immunology (chair com.); mem. Tex. Allergy-Immunology Soc. (chair com., bd. dirs. 1999-2002), Greater Houston Allergy Soc. Republican. Baptists. Avocations: classical music, fishing. Office: U Miss Med Ctr 2500 N State St Jackson MS 39216 E-mail: gmarshall@medicine.umsmed.edu.

MARSHALL, GEORGE DWIRE, retired supermarket chain executive; b. Washington, Feb. 7, 1940; s. Joseph Paull and Jane Schouler (Dwire) M.; m. Sharon Ruth Carter, Nov. 17, 1968; children: Sarah Dwire, Benjamin Carter. BA, Amherst Coll., 1962; JD, U. Calif., Berkeley, 1965. Bar: Calif. 1966. Atty., then sr. atty. legal div. Safeway Inc., Pleasanton, Calif., 1970-79, v.p., mgr. labor rels. divsn., 1979-97. Employer trustee UFCW Internat. Union-Industry Pension Fund, 1980—. Served to lt. USNR, 1966-70, Korea, Vietnam. Mem. State Bar Calif., Psi Upsilon, Phi Delta Phi. Republican. Presbyterian.

MARSHALL, GERALD FRANCIS, optical engineer, consultant, physicist; b. Seven Kings, Feb. 26, 1929; BSc in Physics, London U., 1952. Physicist Morganite Internat., London, 1954—59; sr. rsch. devel. engr. Ferranti Ltd., Edinburgh, Scotland, 1959—67; project mgr. Diffraction Limited Inc., Bedford, Mass., 1967—69; dir. engring. Medical Lasers, Inc., Burlington, Mass., 1969—71; staff cons. Speedring Systems, Troy, Mich., 1971—76; dir. optical engring. Energy Conversion Devices, Inc., Troy, Mich., 1976—87; sr. tech. staff specialist Kaiser Electronics, San Jose, Calif., 1987—89; cons. in optics design and engring., 1989—. Editor, contbg. author: Laser Beam Scanning, 1985, Optical Scanning, 1991, Handbook of Optical and Laser Scanning, 2004. Fellow: Inst. Physics, SPIE - Internat. Soc. Optical Engring. (bd. dirs. 1991—93), Optical Soc. Am. Achievements include patents in field. Office: 410 Dusenbury St Niles MI 49120-1468

MARSHALL, GERALD LEE, mathematician, educator; b. Franklin County, Nc, June 27, 1947; s. George Eugene Marshall and Roberta Odell Perry; m. Judy Faye Beck, Nov. 24, 1991; 1 child, Kera Beck; m. Karen Louise Gebhart, June 19, 1971 (div.); children: Katharine Elizabeth, Katrina Marie. BS in Chem. Engring., N.C. State U., 1969; ThM in Christian Theology, Luther Rice Sem., Jacksonville, Fla., 1975; MS in Libr. Sci., Fla. State U., 1977; MDiv in New Testament Greek, Luther Rice Sem., Jacksonville, Fla., 1976, DMin Theol. Libr., 1979; AA, C.C. Chgo., Wiesbaden, Germany, 1985; MA in Math., U. Ala., Huntsville, 1997; PhD in Math. Edn., Ill. State U., 2000. Ordained Christian min. So. Bapt. Conv., 1985. Pastor Aschaffenburg Bapt. Ch., Aschaffenburg, Germany, 1985—87; adj. lectr. C.C. Chgo., Wiesbaden, Germany, 1984—87; min. edn. Hillsboro Heights Bapt. Ch., Huntsville, Ala., 1987—89; environ. svcs. supr. Huntsville Hosp. Sys., Huntsville, Ala., 1989—98; adj. instr. Calhoun C.C., Decatur, Ala., 1989—98, Heartland C.C., Bloomington, Ill., 1998—2000; head, math. dept. Tri-County Tech. Coll., Pendleton, SC, 2001—. V.p. Tri-County Tech. Edn. Assn., Pendleton, SC, 2002—04; master presenter Nat. Inst. for Staff and Orgnl. Devel., Austin, Tex., 2002; presenter S.C. Tech. Edn. Assn., Myrtle Beach, SC, 2002—02. Contbr. articles to profl. jours. Capt. USAF, 1969—72, U.S. and Thailand. Grantee NSF, 2000—02, Sustainable Univs. Initiatives, 2002. Mem.: S.C. Math. Assn. Two-Yr. Colls. (pres. 2004—), S.C. Coun. Tchrs. of Math., Assn. Math. Tchr. Educators, Am. Math. Assn. Two-Year Colls., Nat. Coun. Tchrs. of Math., Math. Assn. of Am. Southern Baptist. Avocations: grandparenting, travel, mathematics history. Home: 2701 Bellview Rd Anderson SC 29621 Office: Tri-County Tech Coll P O Box 587 Pendleton SC 29670 Office Phone: 864-646-1368. E-mail: gmarshal@tctc.edu.

MARSHALL, GRAYSON WILLIAM, JR., biomaterials scientist, health sciences educator; b. Balt., Feb. 12, 1943; s. Grayson William and Muriel Marie Marshall; m. Sally Jean Rimkus, July 4, 1970; children: Grayson W. III, Jonathan Charles. BS in Metall. Engring., Va. Poly. Inst., 1965; PhD in Materials Sci., Northwestern U., 1972, DDS, 1986; MPH, U. Calif., Berkeley, 1992. Rsch. assoc., design and devel. ctr. Northwestern U., Evanston, Ill., 1972-73, NIH fellow, 1973, instr. Dental and Med. Schs. Chgo., 1973-74, asst. prof. Dental Sch., 1974-78, assoc. prof. Dental Sch. and Grad. Sch., 1978-87; prof. preventive and restorative dental scis. U. Calif., San Francisco, 1987—, chief biomaterials sect., 1988-92, chmn. biomaterials and bioengring. divsn., 1992—. Chmn. oral and craniaofacial scis. program U of Calif., San Francisco, 2002—; guest scientist Lawrence Livermore Nat. Lab., 1989—, Lawrence Berkeley Nat. Lab., 1989—; cons. oral biology and medicine study sect. NIH, 1988-92; dir. Clin. Rsch. Unit, 1992-96, Dentist-Sci. Award Program, 1996—, Integrated DDS-PhD Program, 1996—, Comprehensive Oral Health Rsch. Tng. Program, 2001—. Contbr. articles to profl. jours. Recipient Spl. Dental Rsch. award Nat. Inst. Dental Rsch., 1975; vis. fellow U. Melbourne, Australia, 1981. Fellow: AAAS, Acad. Dental Materials (exec. sec. 1983—85, chmn. credentials 1984—91, bd. dirs. 1985—93, mem. editl. bd. Scanning Microscopy 1987—93, sec. 1988—91, pres. 1991—93, Cells and Materials 1992—2000, sect. editor 1993—2000, Jour. Oral Rehab. 1994—, Dent Mater 1998—, Am. Jour. Dentistry 2004—), Am. Coll. Dentists, Internat. Coll. Dentists; mem.: AIME, APHA, ADA (assoc. editor Jour. ADA 2002—), U.S. Power Squadrons, U.S. Naval Inst., Calif. Pub. Health Assn.-North, Calif. Acad. Scis., N.Y. Acad. Scis., Am. Assn. Dental Rsch. (bd. dirs. 1996—98, San Francisco coun. 1997—), Microscopy Soc. Am., Am. Soc. Metals, Am. Coll. Sports Medicine, Internat. Assn. Dental Rsch. (Chgo. sect. officer 1978—80, dental materials coun. 1990—96, pres. 1998—99), Soc. Biomaterials, Am. Dental Edn. Assn. (sect. officer 1981—83), Omicron Kappa Upsilon, Sigma Gamma Epsilon, Sigma Xi, Alpha Sigma Mu. Office: U Calif Dept Preventive and Restorative Dental Scis San Francisco CA 94143-0001 Office Phone: 415-476-9119. Business E-Mail: graymar@itsa.ucsf.edu, gwmarshall@lbl.gov.

MARSHALL, GREGORY K. food service executive; m. LaNese Marshall; 4 children. Bachelor's Degree, Colo. Coll.; MBA, U. Denver. V.p. mktg. Nobel/Sysco Food Svcs. Co., Denver; sr. v.p. Sysco Corp., Houston, 1993—, CEO Sygma Network Inc., 1993—. Office: Sysco Corp 1390 Enclave Pkwy Houston TX 77077-2099

MARSHALL, HEMAN ALEXANDER, III, lawyer; b. Roanoke, Va., Feb. 15, 1950; s. Heman Alexander Jr. and Jeanne (Martin) M.; children: Alexander Tevis, Claiborne Henebry, Courtney Littlepaige; m. Judith Skaff, July 6, 1996. BA, U. Va., 1972, JD, 1975. Bar: Va. Assoc. Woods, Rogers, Muse, Walker & Thornton, Roanoke, Va., 1975-80, ptnr., 1981-85, Woods, Rogers & Hazlegrove, P.L.C., Roanoke, Va., 1985-93, prin., 1994—, pres., 1995—2001, chmn., 1997—2002. Contbr. articles to profl. jours. Bd. dirs. Binaba Found., 2003—, Nat. Conf. Cmty. and Justice, Roanoke, 2000—04, Art Mus. Western Va., 2000—04. Fellow Va. Law Found., Am. Bar Found.; mem. ABA, Va. State Bar (chmn. health law sect. 1988-89, antitrust law sect. 1989-90), Va. Bar Assn. (chmn. health law sect. 1991-92, bd. govs. 2000-04, chmn. law practice mgmt. divsn. 2002-04), Roanoke Bar Assn., Am. Health Lawyers Assn. Home: 6629 Cotton Hill Rd Roanoke VA 24018-6915 Office: Woods Rogers & Hazlegrove PLC 10 S Jefferson St Ste 1400 Roanoke VA 24011-1331 Office Phone: 540-983-7600. Business E-Mail: marshall@woodsrogers.com.

MARSHALL, HOWARD LOWEN, musicologist, retired music educator; b. Nokesville, Va., July 21, 1931; s. Howard Hampton and Florence Annie (Nash) Marshall; m. Doris Mae Rosencranz, July 14, 1962. B in Music Edn., Shenandoah U., 1952; MusM, U. Cin., 1958; PhD, U. Rochester, 1968. Asst. prof. music Lake Forest (Ill.) Coll., 1966-73; Charles B. Thompson prof. music Mercer U., Macon, Ga., 1974—98, Charles B. Thompson emeritus prof. music, 1998—, chmn. dept. music, 1974-97. Author: The Four-Voice Motets of Thomas Crecquillon, Symbolism in Schubert's Winterreise in Studies in Romanticism, The Motets of Georg Prenner. Lt. comdr. USNR. Mem.: Am. Musicological Soc., Phi Kappa Lambda, Phi Mu Alpha. Avocation: photography. Home: 7 W Harbor Pond Rd West Boothbay Harbor ME 04575

MARSHALL, J. STEPHEN, lawyer; b. Grand Rapids, Mich., Mar. 19, 1948; s. Harry D. and Judy (Corrigan) M.; m. Pamela K. Bergmans, June 17, 1972; children: Sarah Aubrey, Heather Elizabeth. BBA, U. Mich., 1970; JD, Ind. U., Indpls., 1975. Bar: Mich. 1975, U.S. Dist. Ct. (we. dist.) Mich. 1975. Assoc. Norris & Keyser, Grand Rapids, 1975-80; pvt. practice Grand Rapids, 1980—. Dir. Med. Pers. Pool, Grand Rapids, 1980-96. Vol. Big Brothers/Big Sisters, 2000—; trustee Westminster Presbyn. Ch., Grand Rapids, 1989—92, 1994—97, U. Mich. Club of Grand Rapids Scholarship Fund, 1986—. Recipient Disting. Svc. award, U. Mich. Alumni Assn., 1999. Mem. Grand Rapids Bar Assn., U. Mich. Alumni Assn. (dir. 1989-92, 94—, accolade 1994), U. Mich. Club of Grand Rapids (pres., v.p., sec., dir. Grand Rapids chpt. 1975—). Home: 2634 Beechwood Dr SE Grand Rapids MI 49506-4207 Office: 40 Pearl St NW Grand Rapids MI 49503-3028

MARSHALL, JAMES ANDREW, civil engineer, real estate developer; b. Chgo., May 27, 1932; s. William Emmet and Margaret (Fitzgerald) Marshall. BSCE, Ill. Inst. Tech., 1955, MS in City and Regional Planning, 1960. Registered profl. engr., Ill. Civil engr. Hoyer-Schlesinger-Turner, Chgo., 1973-76, Harza Engrs., Chgo., 1990-91. Mem. Ill. and Mich. Canal Nat. Hist. Corridor, Lockport, Ill., 1993—. With U.S. Army, 1953—57. Mem.: Owasippe Staff Assn. Boy Scouts Am., Chgo. Area Orienteering Club, Chgo. Lit. Club, Caxton Club Chgo., Adventurers Club Chgo. Democrat. Achievements include discovery of mathematical knowledge of prehistoric Native Americans. Avocation: surveying and mapping indian mounds and earthworks. Home and Office: 1828 S Roselle Rd Roselle IL 60172-5016

MARSHALL, JAMES CREEL, congressman; b. Ithaca, N.Y., Mar. 31, 1948; s. Robert Creel and Mary Elizabeth (Pie) M.; m. Camille Hope, Mar. 17, 1976; children: Elizabeth, Robert Creel III. AB, Princeton Univ., 1972; JD, Boston Univ., 1977. Bar: Ga. 1977. Mayor City of Macon, 1995—99; mem. U.S. Ho. Reps. from 3rd Ga. dist., 2003—. Contbr. articles to profl. jours. Pres. Macon Heritage Assn., 1989-90, Leadership Macon, 1988-90; commn. Macon Housing Authority, 1989-95; mem. bd. govs. State Bar Ga., 1995—, mem. adv. bd. U.S. Conf. of Mayors, 1997—; co-chair econ. devel. Nat. Conf. of Dem. Mayors, 1996—, chair criminal justice com. Ga. Mcpl. Assn., 1997—. With U.S. Army, 1968-70, Vietnam. Mem. Macon Bar Assn. (pres. 1992-93), Palaver Club of Macon, League of Women Voters. Democrat. Roman Catholic. Avocations: reading, sports, hunting, piddling. Office: 502 Cannon Ho Office Bldg Washington DC 20515-1003

MARSHALL, JANE PRETZER, newspaper editor; b. Chase County, Kans. married; 2 children. BS in Home Econs. and Journalism, Kans. State U., 1967; student, Tex. A&M, U. Mo., Tex. Christian U., Brite Divinity Sch. Asst. editor dept. agr. info. Tex. Agrl. Ext. Sta. Tex. A&M U., College Station, 1967-70; staff writer Gazette-Telegraph, Colorado Springs, Colo., 1970-72; editor corporate publ. Colorado Interstate, Colorado Springs, 1972-75; co-editor The Pampa (Tex.) News, 1975-78; exec. features editor Ft. Worth Star-Telegram, 1978-84; features editor Denver Post, 1984-88, Houston Chronicle, 1988—. Author: (children's book) Going for the Gold: Hakeem Olajuwon, 1996. Recipient 1st place for feature writing Tex. AP Mng. Editors Assn., 1978. Mem. Am. Assn. Sunday and Features Editors (bd. dirs., founding chairperson Features First), Women's Fund Health Edn. and Rsch. (bd. dirs.), Journalism and Women Symposium (1st pres.). Office: Houston Chronicle 801 Texas St Houston TX 77002-2996

MARSHALL, JEAN MCELROY, physiologist; b. Chambersburg, Pa., Dec. 31, 1922; d. Frank Lester and Florence (McElroy) M. AB, Wilson Coll., 1944; MA, Mt. Holyoke Coll., 1946; PhD, U. Rochester, 1951. Instr. Johns Hopkins U. Med. Sch., Balt., 1951-56, asst. prof., 1956-60; research postdoctoral fellow Oxford (Eng.) U., 1954-55; asst. prof. Harvard U. Med. Sch., Boston, 1960-66; asso. prof. physiology Brown U., Providence, 1966-69, prof., 1969-88, prof. emerita, 1988, E. Brintzenhof Prof. Med. Sci., 1987—; rsch. prof. medicine R.I. Hosp., 1988—2000; rsch. cons. C.V. Rsch. Inst. Boston Med. Ctr., 2000—04. Mem. physiology study sect. NIH, 1967-71, mem. tng. com. engring. in biology and medicine, 1971-74, mem. tng. com. lab. medicine, 1976-77; physiol. test com. Nat. Bd. Med. Examiners, 1972-76, neurobiology adv. com., 1977-80 Editor: The Initiation of Labor, 1964; mem. editorial bd. Jour. Pharmacology and Exptl. Therapeutics, 1963-69, Am. Jour. Physiology, 1969-73, Circulation Research, 1973-81; contbr. articles to profl. jours. Mem. Am. Physiol. Soc., Am. Pharmacol. Soc., N.Y. Acad. Scis., Soc. Reproductive Biology, Soc. Gen. Physiologists, Phi Beta Kappa, Sigma Xi. Home: 14 Aberdeen Rd Weston MA 02493-1733

MARSHALL, JEFFREY SCOTT, mechanical engineer, educator; b. Cin., Feb. 10, 1961; s. James C. and Norma E. (Everett) M.; m. Marilyn Jane Patterson, July 16, 1983; children: Judith K., Eric G., Emily J., Paul E. BS summa cum laude, UCLA, 1983, MS, 1984; PhD, U. Calif., Berkeley, 1987. Asst. rsch. engr. U. Calif., Berkeley, 1988; engr. Creare, Inc., Hanover, N.H., 1988-89; from asst. to assoc. prof. dept. ocean engring. Fla. Atlantic U., 1989-93; from assoc. prof. to prof. dept. mech. engring. U. Iowa, Iowa City, 1993—2001, prof., chair dept. mech. and indsl. engring., 2001—. Assoc. editor Jour. Fluids Engring.; contbr. articles to profl. jours.; textbook author. Recipient Young Investigator award, 1992-95. Mem. ASME (assoc. editor jour. Fluids Engring. 2001-03, Henry Hess award 1992), Am. Phys. Soc., Tau Beta Pi. Achievements include research in fluid mechanics, three-dimensional vortex dynamics and vortex-structure interaction and thin film flows. Office: U Iowa Dept Mech & Indsl Engring Iowa City IA 52242 Business E-Mail: jeffrey-marshall@uiowa.edu.

MARSHALL, JO TAYLOR, social worker; b. N.Y.C. BA, Sarah Lawrence Coll., 1957; MSW, Columbia U., 1959. Cert. social worker, N.Y.; clin. diplomate. Caseworker Youth Cons. Svcs., 1960-62; program cons. Social Work Recruiting Ctr., 1962-63; casework supr. Louise Wise Svcs., 1963-68; faculty field instr. sch. social work Columbia U., N.Y.C., 1968-70; coord. social work vol. and student tng. programs St. Lukes/Roosevelt Hosp. Ctr., 1970-75; asst. dir. fieldwork, faculty lectr. in health care Columbia U., N.Y.C., 1975-78; dir. social work and psychiat. emergency svcs. Morristown Meml. Hosp., 1978—95; social worker pvt. practice, 1995—2002; ret., 2002. Adj. prof. Columbia U.; adv. bd., faculty Nat. Discharge Planning Inst. SUNY, Buffalo; prin. speaker, cons. Hosp. Assn. Pa., 1983, Mid-Atlantic Health Congress, 1985, VA, East Orange, N.J., 1986, Hosp. Assn. Tenn., 1987; adv. com. Rutgers GGrad. Sch. Social Work; mem. multidisciplinary state rev. com. for discharge planning standards in N.J. Contbr. articles to profl. jours.; produced and cons. on numerous film and TV prodns. Dir. of Yr. N.J. Hosp. Social Work, 1989-90. The New Welcome Ter. at Columbia grad. sch. of social work is being named in her honor. Mem.: NASW, Soc. Hosp. Social Wk. Dirs. (exec. bd., pres. N.J. chpt. 1988—89, chmn. nat. media task force, Hosp. Social Wk Dir. of Yr.). Address: 1230 Hillsboro Mile Hillsboro Beach FL 33062-1344 also: PO Box 40 Far Hills NJ 07931-0040 Office Phone: 908-879-4999. Personal E-mail: jomase@msn.com.

MARSHALL, JOAN See HELPERN, JOAN

MARSHALL, JOHN, federal agency administrator; b. Omaha; B, M, U. Va. Apptd. Gov. Va.'s Commn. Govt. Reform; fin. mgmt. analyst Pres.'s Office Mgmt. and Budget; deputy adminstr. mgmt. Agrl. Stabilization and Conservation; CEO Fed. Crop. Ins. Corp.; sr. advisor to chmn. Senate Com. Govt. Affairs, 1995—97; prin. IBM Bus. Innovations Svcs., Bethesda, Md., 1997—2001; asst. adminstr. USAID, Washington, 2001—. Contbr. articles to profl. jours. Office: USAID RRB 1300 Pennsylvania Ave NW Washington DC 20523

MARSHALL, JOHN CROOK, internal medicine educator, researcher; b. Blackburn, Lancashire, Eng., Feb. 28, 1941; came to US, 1976; s. Albert Acey and Marion Miller (Crook) M.; m. Marilyn Dallas Parry, Sept. 20, 1969; children: Samantha Jane, Susannah Crook. BS, Victoria U., Manchester, Eng., 1962, MB, ChB, 1965, MD, 1973. Diplomate Am. Bd. Internal Medicine, Am. Bd. Endocrinology and Metabolism. Intern Manchester Royal Infirmary, 1965-66; resident Brompton Hosp., Nat. Heart Hosp., Nat Hosp. Queen Sq., London, 1966-69, Hammersmith Hosp., London, 1966-69, rsch. fellow, 1969-72; lectr. U. Birmingham, Eng., 1972-76; assoc. prof. internal medicine U. Mich., Ann Arbor, 1976-79, prof., 1979-91, chief endocrinology and metabolism, 1987-91; prof. U. Va., Charlottesville, 1991—, dir. Ctr. for Rsch. in Reprod., 1996—. Sci. counselor NIH, Bethesda, Md., 1983-84. Editor Endocrinology Jour., 1979-84, Endocrinology Text, 1990—; contbr. articles to profl. jour. Grantee NIH, 1977-2008. Fellow ACP, Royal Coll. Physicians, Royal Soc. Medicine; mem. Ctrl. Soc. for Clin. Rsch. (coun. 1983—), Assn. Am. Physicians, Am. Soc. for Clin. Investigation, Am. Clin. and Climatological Soc. Anglican. Avocations: vintage racing cars, golf. Office: U Va Sch Medicine Dept Internal Medicine Charlottesville VA 22908-0001 E-mail: jcm9h@virginia.edu.

MARSHALL, JOHN DAVID, lawyer; b. Chgo., May 19, 1940; s. John Howard and Sophie (Brezenk) M.; m. Marcia A. Podlasinski, Aug. 26, 1961; children: Jacquelyn, David, Jason, Patricia, Brian, Denise, Michael, Catherine. BS in Acctg., U. Ill., 1961; JD, Ill. Inst. Tech., 1965. Bar: Ill. 1965, U.S. Tax Ct. 1968, U.S. Dist. Ct. (no. dist.) Ill. 1971; CPA, Ill. Ptnr. Mayer, Brown & Platt, Chgo., 1961—. Bd. dirs. Levinson Ctr. for Handicapped Children, Chgo., 1970-75. Fellow Am. Coll. Probate Counsel; mem. Ill. Bar Assn., Chgo. Bar Assn. (agribus. com. 1978—, trust law com. 1969-95, probate practice com. 1969—, com. on coms. 1983-00, vice chmn. 1988-89, chmn. 1989-90, legis. com. of probate practice com. 1983—, chmn. and vice chmn. legis. com. of probate practice com. 1983-84, rules and forms com., 1996—, chmn. exec. com. probate practice com. 1982-83, vice chmn. exec. com. 1981-82, sec. exec. com. 1980-81, div. chmn. 78-79, div. vice chmn. 1977-78, div. sec. 1976-77, Appreciation award 1982-83), Chgo. Estate Planning Council. Clubs: Union League (Chgo.). Roman Catholic. Office: Mayer Brown & Platt 190 S La Salle St Ste 3100 Chicago IL 60603-3441 Home: 429 N Willow Wood Dr Palatine IL 60074-3831

MARSHALL, JOHN DAVID, retired librarian, author; b. McKenzie, Tenn., Sept. 7, 1928; s. Max Cole and Emma (Walpole) M. BA, Bethel Coll., McKenzie, 1950; MA in Libr. Sci., Fla. State U., 1951, postgrad., 1951-52, Oxford (Eng.) U., summer 1989. Grad. asst. Sch. Libr. Sci. Fla. State U., 1951-52; ref. libr. Clemson (S.C.) U. Libr., 1952-55; head ref. dept. Auburn (Ala.) U. Libr., 1955-57; head acquisitions divsn. U. Ga. Libr., Athens, 1957-67; libr., assoc. prof. Mid. Tenn. State U., Murfreesboro, 1967-76, univ. bibliographer, assoc. prof., 1976-80, prof., 1980-93, prof. emeritus, 1994—; Mary Ball Holmes lectr. Bethel Coll., 1999. Book rev. staff Libr. Jour., 1953-64. Contbg. editor So. Observer, 1953-66; gen. editor Contributions to Library Literature series, 1963-78; book rev. editor Jour. Libr. History, 1966-76, Southeastern Librarian, 1979-82; author: Books in Your Life, 1959, Louis Shores: A Bibliography, 1964, A Fable of Tomorrow's Library, 1965, Louis Shores, Author-Librarian: A Bibliography, 1979, One Librarian's Credo, 1986, Lizzie Borden and the Library Connection, 1990, Churchill's Fulton Speech, 1994, Books are STILL Basic, 1994, And Now Buzz Off: Wit and Wisdom of Sir Winston S. Churchill, 2000; co-editor: Books-Libraries-Librarians, 1955; editor: Of, By, and For Librarians (1st series), 1960, An American Library History Reader, 1961, In Pursuit of Library History, 1961, Mark Hopkins' Log and Other Essays by Louis Shores, 1965, Approaches to Library History, 1966, The Library in the University, 1967, Of, By, and For Librarians: Second Series, 1974, Southern Books Competition at Twenty-Five: A Silver Anniversary Tribute, 1980, Books are Basic: The Essential Lawrence Clark Powell, 1985. Bd. govs. Friends of Linebaugh Pub. Libr., Murfreesboro, Tenn., 1994-2002, pres., 1984, treas., 1996; mem. Murfreesboro City Libr. Bd., 1985-93, treas., 1990-93; mem. Highland Rim Reg. Libr. Bd., 1989-95, treas., 1993-95, Rutherford County Libr. Br., 1989-95; bd. govs. Winston Churchill Meml. Libr., 1989—. Recipient Disting. Alumni award Sch. Libr. and Info. Sci., Fla. State U., 1989, Alumni Achievement award Bethel Coll., 1989, Disting. Alumni Svc. award, 1992; Churchill fellow Westminster Coll., 1982. Mem. ALA (membership com. 1953-55, libr. history round table 1956—, sec. 1969-72), Assn. Coll. and Rsch. Librs. (pubs. com. 1957-62), Southeastern Libr. Assn. (hon. life, chmn. awards com. 1986-88, Outstanding Author Award com. 1990-92, 96-2002, Mary Utopia Rothrock award 1994), Tenn. Libr. Assn. (chmn. intellectual freedom com. 1968-70, 84-85, mem. Tenn. History Book Award com. 1985-2003, chmn. 1985-86, Frances Neel Cheney award 1984, Honor award 1992), Internat. Churchill Soc., Phi Kappa Phi, Beta Phi Mu. Avocations: reading, writing/editing, collecting Churchilliana. Home: PO Box 2506 Murfreesboro TN 37133-2506

MARSHALL, JOHN ELBERT, III, foundation executive; b. Providence, July 2, 1942; s. John Elbert Jr. and Millicent Edna (Paige) M.; m. Diana M. Healy, Aug. 16, 1968; children: Nelson John, Priscilla Anne. BA, Brown U., 1964. Advt. mgr. U.N. Alloy Steel Corp., Boston, 1968-70; devel. officer Brown U., Providence, 1970—72, assoc. dir. devel., 1972—75; exec. dir. R.I. Found., Providence, 1975—79; v.p. Kresge Found., Troy, Mich., 1979-82, exec. v.p., 1982-87, pres., 1987—, trustee, 1991—, CEO, 1993—. Former chmn. Mich. Cmty. Found. Youth Project. Bd. dirs. United Way Cmty. Svcs., Detroit Symphony Orch. Hall, Greater Downtown Partnership, New Detroit, City Year Detroit, Detroit 300 Conservancy Endowment, East Riverfront Conservatory; former bd. dirs. Mich. Campus Compact, Mich. Nonprofit Forum, Coun. Mich. Founds., Detroit Cmty. Devel. Funders Collaborative; former bd. dirs., vice chmn. Family Svc. Detroit and Wayne County; past pres. Bloomfield Village Assn.; former trustee Coun. on Founds., Washington; mem. com. CFSEM Greenways Initiative, Nonprofit Facilities Ctr., Henry Ford Health Sys. Sch.-Based Initiative. Office: Kresge Found PO Box 3151 Troy MI 48007-3151

MARSHALL, JOHN HARRIS, JR., geologist, oil company executive; b. Dallas, Mar. 12, 1924; s. John Harris and Jessie Elizabeth (Mosley) M.; m. Betty Eugenia Zarecor, Aug. 9, 1947 (dec. 2003); children: John Harris III, George Z., Jacqueline Anne. BA in Geology, U. Mo., 1949, MA in Geology, 1950; LHD, Garrett Evangelical Theolgical, 1996. Registered geologist Calif., Wyo., Ky., Tex. Geologist Magnolia Oil Co., Jackson, Miss., 1950-59; assoc. geologist Magnolia/Mobil Oil, Okla. City, Okla., 1959-63; from dist. and divsn. geologist to chief geologist worldwide Mobil Oil Corp., various, 1963-81, gen. mgr. exploration for Western Hemisphere N.Y.C., 1981-82; chief geologist Ambrex, 1982—84; prin., owner Marshall Energetics, Inc., Dallas, 1982—. Dir. exploration Anschutz, 1985-91; pres. Summit Oil and Gas Worldwide, 1993-99, Madera Prodn. Co., 1992—; adv. bd. Salvation Army, Manhattan, 1980-82; trustee The Sci. Place, Dallas, 1995-2002, pres. adv. coun. U. Mo. Geology devel. bd. U. Mo., past pres., 1982-, pres. Coll. Arts and Sci. devel. program, 1996—, mem. devel. coun., 1996-2000, arts and scis. strategic devel. bd., 2000—; councilman, City of Warr Acres (Okla.), 1962-63; active United Meth. Ch., 1951—, Boy Scouts Am., 1960-68; trustee Found. of Evangelism, United Meth. Ch., 1984-, chair, 1988-96. With U.S. Army, 1943—46. Decorated 3 Battle Stars U.S. Army; recipient Curator's medal, U. Mo., 1949, Disting. Alumni Svc. award, 1996, Arts and Sci. award, The Mosaic Soc., U. Mo., 2000, Faculty-Alumni award, U. Mo., 2001, Hon. Life Mem., Geology Devel. Bd., U. Mo., 2004. Mem. Am. Assn. Petroleum Geologists (Pub. Svc. award 2000), Am. Geol. Inst., Am. Geol. Soc. (Dallas, Alaska, Oklahoma City; L.A. Basin pres. 1969-70), Rocky Mountain Assn. Geologists, N.Y. Acad. Sci., Pacific Petroleum Geologists, Am. Sci. Affiliation, Assn. Christian Geologists, United Meth. Gen. Bd. of Discipleship (nat. hispanic evangelization com., 2003-), Meth. Men Club, Denver Pinnacle Club, Sigma Xi. Democrat. Office: 9526 Moss Haven Dr Dallas TX 75231-2608 Office Phone: 214-220-4300.

MARSHALL, JOHN PATRICK, lawyer; b. Bklyn., July 3, 1950; s. Harry W. and Mary Margaret (Kelly) M.; m. Cheryl J. Garvey, Aug. 10, 1975; children: Kelly Blake, Logan Brooke. BA, Rutgers U., 1972; JD cum laude, N.Y. Law Sch., 1976. Bar: N.Y. 1977, N.J. 1977, U.S. Dist. Ct. N.J. 1977, U.S. Dist. Ct. (so. and ea. dists.) N.Y. 1978, U.S. Ct. Appeals (3rd cir.) 1982, U.S. Dist Ct. (no. dist.) N.Y. 1991. Assoc. Kelley Drye & Warren, N.Y.C., 1976-84, ptnr., 1985-98; pres., CEO Metro Ventures, Inc., Short Hills, NJ, 1997—. Pres., CEO Metro Ventures, Inc. Mem. editl. bd. N.Y. Law Sch. Law Rev., 1975-76, staff mem., 1974-75; contbr. articles to profl. jours. Jud. screening com. N.Y. Dem. Com., N.Y. New Dem. Coalition, 1988; exec. v.p. Humanitarian Found. for Nicaragua; sec. Respect for Law Found., 1996; active So. Dist. N.Y. Mediation Panel, 1994—, Coun. on Jud. Adminstrn., 1996-98. Fellow Am. Bar Found.; mem. ABA, N.Y. County Lawyers' Assn. (sec. 1984-87, mem. com. on Supreme Ct. 1984-94, mem. legal edn., admission to bar and lawyer placement com. 1983-93), Am. Arbitration Assn. (mem. nat. panel arbitrators N.Y. and N.J. regions 1991—, mem. corp. counsel com. 1993-98), Assn. of Bar of City of N.Y. (sec. judiciary com. 1989-92, mem. com. on arbitration 1994-96, sec. coun. on judical adminstrn. 1996-98). Home and Office: 50 Highland Ave Short Hills NJ 07078-2812 E-mail: marshall.highland@prodigy.net.

MARSHALL, JOHN PAUL, broadcast engineer; came to U.S., 1967. Degree, U. Grenoble, France, 1963; student, U. Munich, 1964-65, San Francisco State, 1969-71, John O'Connell Tech. Inst., 1973-74. Cert. Novell adminstr., cert. broadcast technologist, A+ computer svc. technician Microsoft Cert. Profl.; cert. Networkplus Tech., Microsoft Cert. Profl., Microsoft Cert. Sys. Engr. Mem. faculty law and econ. scis. U. Grenoble, 1963-64; mem. Expo '67 staff City of Montreal, Que., Can., 1967; filmmaker Cinemalab, San Francisco, 1970; engr. film and TV Able Studios, San Francisco, 1971-73; radio and TV engr. Sta. KALW-FM (Nat. Pub. Radio), San Francisco, 1973-74; broadcast engr. Sta. KRON-TV (NBC), San Francisco, 1974-91; intern Centre d'Informatique et de Maintenance Automatisme, 1993; founder Marshall U.S.A., San Francisco, 1994; freelance broadcast engr. KPIX-TV (CBS), KGO-Radio (ABC), KSFO-Radio (ABC), KPST-TV, San Francisco, 1995—2001; adminstr. Thomson Prometric, San Francisco, 2003—. Freelance audio visual tech. advisor, San Francisco area, 1975—, lectr. radio, TV, motion pictures, 1975—, cons. customized electronic effects; tech. advisor, assoc. Broadkast Skills Bank. Translator tech. pubs. and manuals, 1975—. Mus. dir., participant in theater prodns., 1950-59; active Boy Scouts Am. Govt. of France scholar, 1960-63. Mem. Rolls Royce Owners Club Found. (life), Internet Soc., Soc. Broadcast Engrs. (cert. broadcast networking technologist), Elec. Tech. Assn. Avocations: classical pianist, polyglot, world traveler. Personal E-mail: johnpaul@ispwest.com. *Personal philosophy: (French proverb) Aide toi, le ciel t'aidera--Use your own resources and you will always receive a helping hand from heaven.*

MARSHALL, JOHN TREUTLEN, lawyer, educator; b. Macon, Ga., Nov. 1, 1934; s. Hubert and Gladys (Lucas) M.; m. Katrine White, May 1, 1959; children: Allison, Rebecca, Paul, Mary Anne. BA, Vanderbilt U., 1956; LLB, Yale U., 1962. Bar: Ga. 1962, U.S. Dist. Ct. (no., mid. and so. dists.) Ga. 1962, U.S. Ct. Appeals (5th cir.) 1962, U.S. Supreme Ct. 1978, U.S. Ct. Appeals (11th cir.) 1982. Ptnr. Powell, Goldstein, Frazer & Murphy, Atlanta, 1962—. Chmn. bd. visitors Ga. State U. Law Sch.; chmn. No. Dist. Ga. Bar Coun., 1989; chmn. Ga. State Commn. on Continuing Lawyer Competency, 1991-93, Ga. State Commn. on Stds. of Profession, 1996—; bd. dirs. Ga. Eye Bank, Inc., Atlanta Bar Found. Bd. editors: Yale Law Jour. Bd. dirs. Atlanta Legal Aid, 1972-73; trustee Ga. Inst. Continuing Legal Edn., 1983-90; chmn. adv. bd. Atlanta Vol. Lawyers Found. Recipient S. Phillip Heiner award Atlanta Vol. Lawyers Assn., 1992, A. Gus cleveland award Ga. Commn. on Continuing Edn., Tradition of Excellence award State Bar Ga., 1995. Fellow Am. Coll. Trial Lawyers (state chmn. 1985-86), Am. Acad. Appellate Lawyers, Am. Bar Found. (bd. dirs.), Ga. Bar Found.; mem. ABA (ho. of dels. 1976-86, Harrison Tweed award 1986), Am. Arbitration Assn., State Bar Ga. (chmn. stds. profession com.), Atlanta Bar Found. (bd. dirs.), Atlanta Bar Assn. (pres. 1974-75, Charles E. Watkins Jr. award 1988, Leadership award 1996), Ga. Inst. Trial Advocacy (chmn. 1982-83), Lawyers Club. Office: Powell Goldstein Frazer & Murphy 191 Peachtree St NE Fl 16 Atlanta GA 30303-1740

MARSHALL, JONATHAN, charitable foundation administrator, journalist; b. N.Y.C., Jan. 20, 1924; s. James and Lenore (Guinzburg) M.; m. Maxine Besser, Apr. 6, 1955; children: Lucinda, Laura, Robert Louis, Jonathan Herbert. BA in Econs., U. Colo., 1946; postgrad., U. N.C., 1947—49; MS in Journalism, U. Oreg., 1962; LHD (hon.), Ariz. State U., 1994. Program assoc. Planning Dept., West Chester County, NY, 1949—52; editor, pub. Arts mag., N.Y.C., 1953-58, Scottsdale (Ariz.) Daily Progress, 1963-87; program assoc. Ford Found., N.Y.C., 1958-59; pres. New Hope Found., N.Y.C., 1985-98, Marshall Fund Ariz., Scottsdale, 1987—. Pulitzer prize juror, 1983, 84; Ruhl fellow lectr. U. Oreg., 1986, Allen lectr., 91. Former mem. editl. bd. Amicus Jour.; contbr. articles to various publs., including Masthead, ASNE Bull., Quill, Amicus Jour. Chmn. Oreg. Vols. for Stevenson, 1960, Ariz. Grandparents Day, 1972, 73; bd. dirs. Ariz. Theatre Co., Phoenix Art Mus., Nat. Com. for Effective Congress; former mem. bd. dirs. Am. Jewish Com., Camelback Hosp., Phoenix Urban League, Phoenix Symphony Assn. Recipient Nat. Phys. Fitness Leadership award U.S. Jaycees, 1973, Ariz. Newspapers' Master Editor-Pub. award, 1978, Disting. Svc. award Ariz. Press Club, 1988, Ariz. Philanthropist award Nat. Soc. Fundraising Execs., 1997, Ariz. State U. Coll. Liberal Arts, 1988, Pub. Interest award Ariz. Ctr. for Law in Pub. Interest, 1998, John W. Creasman award for excellence Ariz. State U., 1999, Martin Luther King, Jr. Diversity Champion award, 2001; named Ariz. Civil Libertarian of Yr., 1996; inducted into Ariz. Newspapers Hall of Fame, 1996; named to U. Oreg. Journalism Sch. Hall of Achievement, 2001. Mem. Nat. Conf. Editl. Writers, Am. Soc. Newspapers Editors (past mem. editl. bd. Bull.), Soc. Profl. Journalists (1st Amendment award 1979). Democrat. Jewish. Office: Marshall Fund Ariz 3295 N Drinkwater Blvd Scottsdale AZ 85251

MARSHALL, KATHLEEN, choreographer, theater director, theater producer; Mem. exec. bd. Soc. Stage Dirs. and Choreographers. Asst. choreographer (Broadway plays) Kiss of the Spider Woman, 1993—95, She Loves Me, 1993—94, Damn Yankees, 1994—95, choreographer Swinging on a Star, 1996, Victor/Victoria, 1995—97, 1776, 1997—98, Ring Round the Moon, 1999, Kiss Me, Kate, 1999—2001 (Tony nom. best choreography, 2001, Laurence Olivier nom. best choreography, 2002), Seussical, 2000—01, Follies, 2001, Little Shop of Horrors, 2003; dir.: (Broadway plays) Wonderful Town, 2003 (Tony nom. best dir. musical, 2004, Drama Desk award best choreography, 2004); choreographer (Broadway plays) Wonderful Town, 2003 (Tony award best choreography, 2004), (TV films) The Music Man, 2003. Office: Al Hirschfeld Theatre 302 W 45th St New York NY 10036

MARSHALL, KATHRYN SUE, lawyer; b. Decatur, Ill., Sept. 12, 1942; d. Edward Elda and Frances M. (Minor) Lahniers; m. Robert S. Marshall, Sept. 5, 1964 (div. Apr. 1984); m. Robert J. Arndt, June 25, 1988 (dec. 1999); children: Stephen Edward, Christine Elizabeth Arndt. BA, Lake Forest Coll., 1964; JD, John Marshall Law Sch., Chgo., 1976. Intern U.S. Atty.'s Office, Chgo., 1974-76; mng. ptnr. Marshall and Marshall Ltd., Waukegan, Ill., 1976-84; pvt. practice Waukegan, 1984-93, Preemptive Solutions, Wash.

Contbr. articles to profl. jours. Bd. dirs., v.p. Lake Forest (Ill.) Fine Arts Ensemble; bd. dirs. Island Hosp. Health Found.; mem. steering com. Equal Justice Coalition; cert. jud. Dem. candidate Lake County, Ill.; bd. dirs. Camerata Soc., Lake Forest. Fellow: ABA (gov. 1993—96), Coll. Law Practice Mgmt., Ill. Bar Assn.; mem.: Navy League (life). Avocations: boating, reading, travel.

MARSHALL, LINDA MURPHY, linguist, government official; b. St. Louis, Aug. 6, 1950; d. Samuel Baldwin and Barbara Anne (Chivvis) Murphy; m. Joseph A. Kelley, Aug. 31, 1974 (div. Sept. 1987); children: Alex, Mia; m. William Peyton Marshall, July 8, 1989. BA, U. Denver, 1972; MA, St. Louis U., 1974, PhD, 1978; postgrad., Washington U., 1981-85, Georgetown U., 1997-98. Translator Aerospace Ctr., Def. Mapping Agy., St. Louis, 1978-81; multi-linguist U.S. Fed. Govt., Washington, 1985—. Cons. Sotho Newspaper Reader, Reference Grammar and Lexicon, 1998. Contbr. articles to profl. jours.; co-author: Xhosa Newspaper Reader and Lexicon, 2002. Mem. Phi Beta Kappa. Episcopalian. Avocations: classical piano, poetry, travel, foreign languages. Home: 10391 Green Mountain Cir Columbia MD 21044-2455

MARSHALL, MARGARET HILARY, state supreme court chief justice; b. Newcastle, Natal, South Africa, Sept. 1, 1944; came to U.S., 1968; d. Bernard Charles and Hilary A.D. (Anderton) M; m. Samuel Shapiro, Dec. 14, 1968 (div. Apr. 1982); m. Anthony Lewis, Sept. 23, 1984. BA, Witwatersrand U., Johannesburg, 1966; MEd, Harvard U., 1969; JD, Yale U., 1976; LHD (hon.), Regis Coll., 1993. Bar: Mass. 1977, U.S. Dist. Ct. Mass., U.S. Dist. Ct. N.H., U.S. Dist. Ct. D.C., U.S. Dist. Ct. (ea. dist.) Mich., U.S. Tax Ct., U.S. Ct. Appeals (1st, 11th and D.C. cirs.), U.S. Supreme Ct. Assoc. Csaplar & Bok, Boston, 1976-83, ptnr., 1983-89, Choate, Hall & Stewart, Boston, 1989-92; v.p., gen. counsel Harvard U., Cambridge, Mass., 1992-96; justice Supreme Jud. Ct. Commonwealth Mass., 1996-99, chief justice, 1999—. Mem. jud. nominating coun., 1987-90, 92; chairperson ct. rules subcom. Alternative Dispute Resolution Working Group, 1985-87; mem. fed. appts. commn., 1993; mem. adv. com. Supreme Judicial Ct., 1989-92, mem. gender equality com., 1989-94, mem. civil justice adv. group U.S. Dist. Ct. Mass., 1991-93; spl. counsel Jud. Conduct Commn., 1988-92; trustee Mass. Continuing Legal Edn., Inc., 1990-92. Trustee Regis Coll., 1993-95; bd. dirs. Internat. Design Conf., Aspen, 1986-92, Boston Mcpl. Res. Bur., 1990-94, Supreme Judicial Ct. Hist. Soc., 1990-94, sec., 1990-94. Fellow Am. Bar Found. (Mass. state chair); mem. Boston Bar Assn. (treas. 1988-89, v.p. 1989-90, pres.-elect 1990-91, pres. 1991-92), Internat. Women's Forum, Mass. Women's Forum, Boston Club, Phi Beta Kappa (hon.). Office: 1 Beacon St 3rd Floor Boston MA 02108

MARSHALL, MARK F. lawyer; b. 1954; BS, U. S.D., 1977, JD, 1981. Bar: S.D. 1981, U.S. Dist. Ct. S.D. 1981, U.S. Ct. Appeals (8th cir.) 1981, U.S. Supreme Ct. 1984. Law clk. hon. Fred J. Nichol, 1981-83; ptnr. Bangs, McCullen, Butler, Foye & Simmons, Rapid City, SD, 1983-96; of counsel Johnson, Heidepriem, Miner, Marlow & Janklow, Sioux Falls, SD, 1996—2000; magistrate judge U.S. Dist. Ct. S.D., Sioux Falls, 1996-2000; ptnr. Davenport Law Firm, Sioux Falls, 2000—. Office: 206 W 14th St Sioux Falls SD 57105

MARSHALL, MARTIN VIVAN, business administration educator, business consultant; b. Kansas City, July 22, 1922; s. Vivan Dean and Marie (Church) M.; m. Rosanne Borden, Sept. 5, 1951 (dec. Feb. 8, 1986); children: Martin Dean, Michael Borden, Neil McNair; m. Hildegard Meyer, June 24, 1988. AB, U. Mo., 1943; MBA, Harvard U., 1947, D.C.S., 1953. Instr. mktg. and advt. U. Kans., 1947-48; mem. faculty Harvard U., 1948—, Henry R. Byers prof. bus. adminstrn., 1960—, chmn. mktg. area faculty, 1962-66, chmn. Smaller Co. Mgmt. Program, 1981-84, chmn. Owner/Pres. Mgmt. Program, 1985-94, mem. faculty Inst. Ednl. Mgmt., 1981-90, endowed chair, Martin Marshall prof. bus. adminstrn., 1999. Cons. U.S. and internat. bus., 1950—; dir. ann. seminar mktg. and advt. Am. Advt. Fedn., 1958-78; vis. prof. mktg. IMEDE Mgmt. Inst., Lausanne, 1965-66; sr. prof., ednl. dir. Internat. Mktg. Inst., 1967-71; vis. prof. Indian Inst. Mgmt., Agra, 1968, IPADE, Mexico City, 1969, U. Melbourne, Australia, 1977, 79; bd. dirs. Western Stone & Metal.; lectr. Templeton Coll., Oxford, summer 1998. Author: Automatic Merchandising, 1954, (with N.H. Borden) Advertising Management, 1960, Notes on Marketing, 1983, 88, 90, 92, 93. Bd. dirs. Youth Svcs. Internat., Inc., 1994-97, Moclean Co., 1998-99. Served to lt. (s.g.) USNR, 1943-46. Home: 130 Mount Auburn St Apt 309 Cambridge MA 02138-5779 Office: Harvard U Cumnock Hall Boston MA 02163

MARSHALL, MARY JONES, civic worker; b. Billings, Mont.; d. Leroy Nathaniel and Janet (Currie) Dailey; m. Harvey Bradley Jones, Nov. 15, 1952 (dec. 1989); children: Dailey, Janet Currie, Ellis Bradley; m. Boyd T. Marshall, June 27, 1990. Student, Carleton Coll., 1943-44, U. Mont., 1944-46, UCLA, 1959. Owner Mary Jones Interiors. Founder, treas. Jr. Art Coun., LA County Mus., 1953-55, v.p., 1955-56; mem. costume coun. Pasadena (Calif.) Philharm.; co-founder Art Rental Gallery, 1953, chmn. art and architecture tour, 1955; founding mem., sec. Art Alliance, Pasadena Art Mus., 1955-56; benefit chmn. Pasadena Girls Club, 1959, bd. dirs., 1958-60; chmn. LA Tennis Patron's Assn. Benefit, 1965; sustaining Jr. League Pasadena; mem. docent coun. LA County Mus.; mem. costume coun. LA County Mus. Art, program chmn. 20th Century Greatest Designers; mem. blue ribbon com. LA Music Ctr.; benefit chmn. Venice com. Internat. Fund for Monuments, 1971; bd. dirs. Art Ctr. 100, Pasadena, 1988—; pres. The Pres.'s LA Children's Bur., 1989; co-chmn. benefit Harvard Coll. Scholarship Fund, 1974, steering com. benefit, 1987, Otis Art Inst., 1975, 90th Anniversary of Children's Bur. of LA, 1994; mem. Harvard-Radcliffe scholarship dinner com., 1985; mem. adv. bd. Estelle Doheny Eye Found., 1976, chmn. benefit, 1980; adv. bd. Loyola U. Sch. Fine Arts, LA, Art Ctr. Sch. Design, Pasadena, 1987—; patron chmn. Benefit Achievement Rewards for Coll. Scientists, 1988; chmn. com. Sch. Am. Ballet Benefit, 1988, NYC; bd. dirs. Founders Music Ctr., LA, 1977-81; mem. nat. adv. coun. Sch. Am. Ballet, NYC, nat. co-chmn. gala, 1980; adv. coun. on fine arts Loyola-Marymount U.; mem. LA Olympic Com., 1984, The Colleagues; founding mem. Mus. Contemporary Art, 1986; chmn. The Pres.'s Benefit LA Children's Bur., 1990; exec. com. LA Alive for LA Music Ctr., 1992; mem. exec. com. Children's Bur. of LA Found., 1992; chmn. award dinner Phoenix House, 1994, 96; bd. dirs. Andrews Sch. Gerontology, U. So. Calif., 1996—, Leakey Found., 1996—; bd. regents Children's Hosp. LA, 1996—. Mem. Am. Parkinson Disease Assn. (steering com. 1991), Valley Hunt Club (Pasadena), Calif. Club (LA), Kappa Alpha Theta. Home: 10375 Wilshire Blvd Ste 8B Los Angeles CA 90024-4712

MARSHALL, MICHAEL BORDEN, marketing executive; b. Boston, Mar. 16, 1957; s. Martin Vivan and Rosanne (Borden) M.; m. Susan Diane (Parks), June 15, 1991; children: Samantha Rosanne, Brenton Alexander. BA, Oberlin Coll., 1979; MBA, Harvard U., 1983. Analyst Benton and Bowles, Inc., N.Y.C., 1977—80; mktg. mgr. Thor Metal Works, Ltd., Syracuse, NY, 1980—81; asst. mgr. Am. Express Co., N.Y.C., 1982; sr. analyst Bank of Boston Corp., 1983—85; cons. John Hancock Mut. Life Ins. Co., Boston, 1985—89; corp. v.p. N.Y. Life Ins. Co., N.Y.C., 1989—. Cons. assoc., Bank Mktg. Assn., Boston, 1983-89, N.Y., 1991—; advisor bus. analysis, Arthur D. Little, Inc., Cambridge, Mass., 1985-93. Contbr. articles to profl. journals. Adv. bd. Youth Enrichment Svc. Boston, 1984-90; treas. St. James Episcopal Ch., North Salem, N.Y., 1996-99. Recipient Jerome Davis Award Oberlin Coll., 1979, Copeland Sect. Award Harvard Bus. Sch., 1982, Corp. Spl. Award John Hancock Exec. Com., 1986. Mem. Am. Mktg. Assn. (sr. v.p. 1984-93), Mktg. Sci. Inst. (bd. dir. 1985-89), Life Ins. Mktg. and Rsch. Assn. (devel. bd. 1991-98, market rsch. com. 1995—, chmn. 2002-03, market rsch. conf. com. 2004-), Coun. on Fin. Competition (adv. bd. 1991—, market rsch. conf. com. 2004—), Soc. Ins. Strategists (founding mem.), Fin. Industry Rsch. Study Team (founding mem.), Am. Coun. on Life Ins. (rsch. advisor 1994-2003), N.Y. Mktg. Coun., Harvard Club. Office: NY Life Ins Co 51 Madison Ave New York NY 10010-1603 Business E-Mail: mmarshal@newyorklife.com.

MARSHALL, MONTY GLENN, political research scientist, consultant; b. Anamosa, Iowa, Feb. 5, 1952; s. Glenn Nelson and Jacqueline Anne M.; m. Beth Julia Rose Elzinga, Aug. 15, 1987 (div. May 1994); 1 child, Gabrielle Elzinga-Marshall; m. Donna Faye Ramsey, Mar. 20, 1999; 2 children, Nathan and Anais. BA, U. Colo., 1983-87; MA, U. Md., 1990; PhD, U. Iowa, 1996. Vis. asst. prof. U. S.Fla., Tampa, 1994-97; integrated network societal conflict rsch. program mgr. U. Md. Ctr. Internat. Devel. and Conflict Mgmt., College Park, 1998—. Dir. Ctr. Systemic Peace, Severn, Md., 1997—; sr. cons. State Failure Task Force, Washington, 1998—; mem. adv. bd. Minorities at Risk Project, College Park, 1998—; dir., mem. adv. bd. Polity IV Project, College Park, 1999—. Author: Third World War: System, Process, and Conflict Dynamics, 1999, Peace and Conflict 2001, 03: A Global Survey of Armed Conflicts, Self-Determination Movements, and Democracy; contbg. author: Minorities at Risk, 1993, Federalism Against Ethnicity?, 1997, Wars in the Midst of Peace, 1997, Peoples versus States, 2000, From Reaction to Conflict Prevention: Opportunities for the UN System, 2002. Fellow, U. Iowa, 1990-93. Mem. Internat. Studies Assn., Am. Polit. Sci. Assn., Peace Sci. Soc. Avocations: biking, hiking, squash, stained glass, travel. Home: 7939 Heather Mist Dr Severn MD 21144 Office: CIDCM U Md Tydings Hall College Park MD 20742 Fax: 301-314-9256. E-mail: CSPmgm@aol.com., mmarshall@cidcm.umd.edu.

MARSHALL, NATALIE JUNEMANN, economics professor; b. Milw., June 13, 1929; d. Harold E. and Myrtle (Findlay) Junemann; m. Howard D. Marshall, Aug. 7, 1954 (dec. 1972); children: Frederick S., Alison B.; m. Phillip Shatz, May 27, 1988. AB, Vassar Coll., 1951; MA, Columbia U., 1952, PhD, 1963, JD, 1994. Instr. Vassar Coll., Poughkeepsie, N.Y., 1952-54, 59, 59-60, 63, dean studies, prof. econs., 1973-75, v.p. for student affairs, 1975-80, v.p. for adminstrn. and student services and prof. econs., 1980-91, prof. econs., 1991-94; teaching fellow Wesleyan U., Middletown, Conn., 1955-56; from asst. prof. to prof. SUNY, New Paltz, 1964-73; prof. econs. Vassar Coll., Poughkeepsie, N.Y., 1973-94; of counsel Donoghue, Thomas, Auslander & Drohan, Hopewell Junction, N.Y., 1997—. Editor: (with Howard Marshall) The History of Economic Thought, 1968; Keynes, Updated or Outdated, 1970; author: (with Howard Marshall) Collective Bargaining, 1971. Trustee St. Francis Hosp., 1979-88, Area Fund Dutchess County, 1981-87, Coll. New Rochelle, 1994-2000, Hudson Valley Philharm., 1985-92, pres., 1989-91. Mem. AAUP, Am. Assn. Higher Edn., Am. Econ. Assn., AAUW (v.p. N.Y. State div. 1964-66), Poughkeepsie Vassar Club (pres. 1965-67). Home: 157 Skidmore Rd Pleasant Valley NY 12569-5001 E-mail: Natalie_Marshall@vh.net.

MARSHALL, PENNY (C. MARSHALL), director, actress; b. N.Y.C., Oct. 15, 1943; d. Anthony W. and Marjorie Irene (Ward) M.; m. Michael Henry (div.); 1 child, Tracy Lee; m. Robert Reiner, Apr. 10, 1971 (div. 1979). Student, U. N.Mex., 1961-64. Appeared on numerous television shows, including The Odd Couple, 1972-74, Friends and Lovers (co-star), 1974, Let's Switch, 1974, Wives (pilot), 1975, Chico and the Man, 1975, Mary Tyler Moore, 1975, Heaven Help Us, 1975, Saturday Night Live, 1975-77, Happy Days, 1975, Battle of Network Stars (ABC special), 1976, Barry Manilow special, 1976, The Tonight Show, 1976-77, Dinah, 1976-77, Mike Douglas Show, 1975-77, Merv Griffin Show, 1976-77, Blansky's Beauties, 1977, Network Battle of the Sexes, 1977, Laverne and Shirley (co-star), 1976-83; TV films More Than Friends, 1978, Love Thy Neighbor, 1984, Challenge of a Lifetime, 1985, The Odd Couple: Together Again, 1993; guest appearances include Mary Tyler Moore, 1975, Happy Days, 1975, Chico and the Man, 1975, Mork & Mindy, 1978, Bosom Buddies, 1982, Taxi, 1983, The Simpsons (voice), 1990, Frasier, 2004, I'm With Her, 2004; appeared in motion pictures How Sweet It Is, 1967, The Savage Seven, 1968, The Grasshopper, 1970, 1941, 1979, Movers and Shakers, 1985, She's Having a Baby, 1988, The Hard Way, 1991, Hocus Pocus, 1993, Get Shorty, 1995; dir. films: Jumpin' Jack Flash, 1986, Big, 1988, Awakenings, 1990, A League of Their Own, 1992, Renaissance Man, 1994, The Preacher's Wife, 1996, The Time Tunnel: The Movie, 1999, Special Delivery, 1999, Riding in Cars with Boys, 2001, appeared in TV movie Jackie's Back, 1999; prodr. TV series A League of Their Own, 1993 (also dir. pilot), Dynasties, 2003; prodr. films Getting Away With Murder, 1995, With Friends Like These, 1998, Risk, 2003 Office: c/o William Morris Agy 151 El Camino Dr Beverly Hills CA 90212

MARSHALL, PHYLLIS ELLINWOOD, health facility administrator, consultant; b. Kansas City, Mo., Dec. 20, 1929; d. Herbert Dwight and Mildred (Gillham) Ellinwood; m. John D. Reich, July 1, 1950 (div. 1964); children: Martha Reich Millican, Michael David, Donald Martin; m. C. Randolph Marshall, Nov. 27, 1969. BA, Washington U., St. Louis, 1951, MSW, 1969. Adult program dir. St. Louis YWCA, 1964-67; alcoholism caseworker Malcolm Bliss Mental Health Crt., St. Louis, 1968; exec. dir. Cobb County YWCA, Ga., 1969-72; dir. Coastal Area Cmty. Mental Health Ctr., Brunswick, Ga., 1973-77; dir. mental health svcs. Ga. Dept. Human Resources, Atlanta, 1977-84; exec. dir. Integrated Mental Health, Inc., Rochester, N.Y., 1984-92, No. Va. Mental Health Inst., Falls Church, Va., 1992-95; mgr. MHMRSA Reorgn., Alexandria, Va., 1995-96; state health reform dir. Nat. Mental Health Assn., Alexandria, Va., 1997; project mgr. nat. women's health info. ctr. Soza & Co., Ltd., Fairfax, Va., 1998-99; ret. Bd. dirs. Anne Arundel Co. Md. Mental Health Agy., 1996—; cons. NIMH, Washington, 1979-84, So. Regional Ednl. Bd., Atlanta, 1979-84, N.Y. State Office Mental Health, Albany, 1980-84, State of Ill. Dept. Mental Health, 1988, WHO, 1989, Ont., Can., 1990-91, The Netherlands, 1991-93, 97, Sch. Medicine U. Md., 1997-98, ind. behavioral health cons., P.E.M. cons., 1996—; with mental health programs in Ohio, Mich., Ariz., Md., S.C., N.Y., Pa.; co-chair Metro Atlanta Deinstitutionalization Task Force, 1983-85; bd. dirs. Children Have All Rights, Legal, Ednl. and Emotional, Menninger Found. project, Atlanta, 1983-84; chmn. Monroe County Adv. Com. on Women's Issues, 1991-92; steering com. Mental Health Liaison Group, Com. on Health Care Reform, Washington, 1994-99; program devel. Young Women's Sailing Womenship, Inc., 2000-2003. Contbg. author: Perspectives in Mental Health Svcs., 1998, New Frontiers in Mental Health, 1989; contbr. articles to profl. pubs. Bd. dirs., pres. Ga. Human Resources Credit Union, Atlanta, 1982-84; bd. dirs. Annapolis Chorale, 2001-02; with program devel. for young womens sailing Womanship Sailing Sch., 2000—, Womanship Sailing Sch., Annapolis, Md.; mem. Ann Arundel, Md., Commn. for Women, 2003—. Recipient Boss of Yr. award Brunswick Jaycees, 1977, Good Friend award Brunswick Mental Health Assn., 1977, Cmty. Mental Health award Atlanta U., 1980, Outstanding Achievement award Am. Soc. for Pub. Adminstrn., 1990. Mem. AAUW (chpt. pres. 1978), Assn. Mental Health Adminstrs. (chair health policy com. 1995-96), Assn. Behavioral Healthcare Mgmt. (newsletter columnist 1996-99), Ga. Assn. Cmty. Mental Health Ctrs. (pres. 1975-77), Rochester Women's Network (bd. dirs., treas. 1990-92), Anne Arundel Commn. Women, New Annapolitans (pres. 2000-01, bd. dir. Annapolis Chorale, 2001-). Avocations: sailing, music, tennis, golf. E-mail: pemcon@att.net.

MARSHALL, RAYMOND CHARLES, lawyer; b. Aquadilla, Puerto Rico, July 23, 1953; m. Piper Kent-Marshall; 1 child, Kyle. BA summa cum laude, Coll. Idaho, 1975; JD, Harvard U., 1978. Bar: Calif. 1978, D.C. 1989. Ptnr. Bingham McCutchen, San Francisco. Chmn. Calif. Supreme Ct. Adv. Multi-Jurisdictional Practice. Co-author: Environmental Crimes, 1992; contbr. chpt. to manual; contbr. articles to profl. jours. Bd. dirs. Nat. Multiple Sclerosis Soc. Northern Calif. chpt., 1992—; adv. bd. United Negro Coll. Fund Northern Bay Area Chpt., 1992—; bd. trustees Alta Bates Found., 1994—; mem. San Francisco leadership bd. Am. Red Cross Bay Area; adv. coun. mem. San Francisco Sports Coun. Recipient San Francisco Neighborhood Legal Assistance Found. award, 1989, Earl Warren Legal Svcs. award NAACP Legal Def. & Ednl. Found., 1990, Unity award Minority Bar Coalition, 1992, Cmty. Svc. award Wiley Manuel Law Found., 1994, Disting. Jesuit award Anti-Defemation League, 2001. Mem. ABA (mem. bar caucus exec. com. 1992-94, vice-chmn. natural resources & energy litigation com. 1989-93, environmental crimes com. 1990-92, nominating com. conf. of minority ptnrs. in maj. corp. law firms 1991, commn. on women in the profession 1994-95, co-chmn. environmental crimes subcom. of white collar crime com. 1994-95), Nat. Bar Assn., Calif. State Bar (bd. govs. 1995—, pres. 1998-99), Charles Houston Bar Assn. Avocations: travel, recreational sports. Office: Bingham McCutchen Three Embarcadero Ctr San Francisco CA 94111

MARSHALL, RICHARD TREEGER, lawyer; b. NYC, May 17, 1925; s. Edward and Sydney (Treeger) M.; m. Dorothy M. Goodman, June 4, 1950; children: Abigail Ruth Marshall Bergerson, Daniel Brooks; m. 2d Sylvia J. Kelley, June 10, 1979. BS, Cornell U., 1948; JD, Yale U., 1951. Bar: Tex. 1952, U.S. Ct. Appeals (5th cir.) 1966, U.S. Ct. Appeals (10th cir.) 1980, U.S. Supreme Ct. 1959; lic. Tex. Dept. Ins. Pvt. practice, El Paso, Tex., 1952-59, 61-79; assoc. Fryer & Milstead, El Paso, 1952; sr. ptnr. Marshall & Wendorf, El Paso, 1959-61, Marshall & Volk, El Paso, 1979-81; sr. atty. Richard T. Marshall & Assocs., PC, El Paso, 1981-85; sr. ptnr. Marshall, Thomas & Winters, El Paso, 1985-87; sr. atty. Marshall & Winters, 1987-88, Marshall, Sherrod & Winters, 1988-90; pvt. practice El Paso, 1990—. Instr. polit. sci. U. Tex., El Paso, 1961-62; instr. ins. law C.L.U. tng. course Am. Coll.; officer, dir. Advance Funding, Inc., El Paso. Editor El Paso Trial Lawyers Rev., 1973-80; contbr. articles to profl. jours. Mem. ABA, ATLA (sec. personal injury law sect. 1967-68, nat. sec. 1969-70, sec.-treas. environ. law sect. 1970-71, vice chmn. family law litigation sec. 1971-72), El Paso Bar Assn., El Paso Trial Lawyers Assn. (pres. 1965-66), Roscoe Pound-Am. Trial Lawyers Found. (commn. on profl. responsibility 1979-82), Nat. Acad. Elder Law Attys., Soc. Cert. Sr. Advisors, Nat. Assn. Charitable Estate Counselors. Office: 5959 Gateway Blvd W El Paso TX 79925-3331 Office Phone: 915-779-6627. E-mail: marshall@texseniorlaw.com.

MARSHALL, ROBERT, film director, television director, theater director, choreographer; b. Madison, Wis., Oct. 17, 1960; Student, Carnegie-Mellon U., 1982. Broadway dancer, N.Y.C. Dir.: (plays) Chicago, 1992; co-choreographer (Broadway plays) Kiss of the Spider Woman, 1993; choreographer (Broadway plays) Damn Yankees (revival), 1994, Victor/Victoria, 1995, A Funny Thing Happened On the Way to the Forum (revival), 1996; overseer dance sequences (TV films) Mrs. Santa Claus (CBS), 1996; choreographer (TV films) Rogers and Hammerstein's Cinderella (ABC), 1997, (films) The Cradle Will Rock, 1998; dir.(with Sam Mendes): (Broadway plays) Cabaret (revival), 1998 (Dora Mavor Moore award),: (TV films) Annie, 1999 (Emmy award, Am. Choreography award), (uncredited): (Broadway plays) Suessical, 2000,: (films) Chicago, 2002 (Nat. Bd. Rev. award, Dirs. Guild of Am. award, nominated for Oscar award). Office: c/o Paul Martino ICM 40 W 57th St New York NY 10019

MARSHALL, ROBERT CHARLES, computer company executive; b. Berwyn, Ill., June 19, 1931; s. Joseph H. and Rose M.; m. Sarane Virruso, Aug. 1, 1954; children— Joseph, Lisa, Jim. BSE.E., Heald Engrng. Coll., 1956; MBA, Pepperdine U., 1976. Engr. Lawrence Radiation Lab., Livermore, Calif., 1956-64; systems engr. Electronics Assos., Palo Alto, Calif., 1964-69; v.p. mfg. Diablo Systems, Hayward, Calif., 1969-75; with Tandem Computers, Inc., Cupertino, Calif., 1975—, sr. v.p., chief operating officer, dir., 1979-96; pres., CEO Info Gear, 1996-97; gen. ptnr. Selby Venture Ptnrs., 1998—. Served with U.S. Army, 1952-54. E-mail: Bob@selbyventures.com.

MARSHALL, ROBERT HERMAN, economics professor; b. Harrisburg, Pa., Dec. 6, 1929; s. Mathias and Mary (Bubich) M.; m. Billie Marie Sullivan, May 31, 1958; children: Mellisa Frances, Howard Hylton, Robert Charles. AB magna cum laude, Franklin and Marshall Coll., 1951; MA, Ohio State U., 1952, PhD, 1957. Teaching asst. Ohio State U., 1952-57; mem. faculty, then prof. econs. U. Ariz., Tucson, 1957-95, prof. emeritus, 1995; dir. Internat. Bus. Studies Project, 1969-71. Research observer Sci.-Industry Program, Hughes Aircraft Co., Tucson, summer 1959 Author: Commercial Banking in Arizona: Structure and Performance Since World War II, 1966, (with others) The Monetary Process, 2d edit, 1980. Bd. dirs. Com. for Econ. Opportunity, Tucson, 1968-69. Faculty fellow Pacific Coast Banking Sch., summer 1974 Mem. Am. Econ. Assn., Phi Beta Kappa, Beta Gamma Sigma, Pi Gamma Mu, Phi Kappa Phi, Delta Sigma Pi. Democrat. Roman Catholic. Home: 6700 N Abington Rd Tucson AZ 85743-9795

MARSHALL, ROBERT LEWIS, musicologist, educator; b. N.Y.C., Oct. 12, 1939; s. Saul and Pearl (Shapiro) M.; m. Traute Maass, Sept. 9, 1966; children— Eric, Brenda. AB, Columbia U., 1960; M.F.A., Princeton U., 1962, PhD, 1968; postgrad., U. Hamburg, W. Ger., 1965. Instr. dept. music U. Chgo., 1966-68, asst. prof., 1968-71, assoc. prof., chmn. dept., 1972-78, prof., 1978-83, Brandeis U., 1983-2000, chmn. dept., 1985-93, incumbent endowed chair Louis, Frances and Jeffrey Sachar prof. music, 1986-2000; emeritus, 2000—. Vis. assoc. prof. Princeton U., 1971-72; endowed prof. Univ. Ala., 1994; mem. rev. bd. rsch. materials program NEH, 1982, rev. bd. edits., 1991. Author: The Compositional Process of J.S. Bach, 2 vols., 1972, The Music of Johann Sebastian Bach: The Sources; The Style; The Significance, 1989, Mozart Speaks: Views on Music, Musicians and the World, 1991, Dennis Brain on Record: A Comprehensive Discography of His Solo, Chamber, and Orchestral Recordings, 1996; editor New Bach Edit., Eighteenth Century Keyboard Music, 1994, 2d edit., 2003; contbr. articles to musical jours. in U.S., Gt. Brit., Germany. Mem. music adv. bd. Ill. Arts Council, 1977-79. Recipient Deems Taylor award ASCAP, 1990; NEH fellow, 1978-79; Hon. Harold Spivacke consultantship Library of Congress. Mem. Am. Musicol. Soc. (bd. dirs. 1974-75, v.p. 1985-86, editl. bd. jour. 1975-80, rev. editor 1986-89, chmn. publs. com. 1991-94, Otto Kinkeldey prize 1974, hon. 2003), New Bach Soc. (chmn. Am. chpt. 1977-80), Phi Beta Kappa. Home: 100 Chestnut St Newton MA 02465-2538 E-mail: rmarshall@brandeis.edu.

MARSHALL, ROBERT WAYNE, human services administrator; b. Pecos, Tex., May 10, 1970; s. Don and Judy Marshall; m. Shannon L Marshall, Dec. 11, 1993; children: Katelyn Elizabeth, Kyleigh Grace. MEd, Hardin-Simmons U., Abilene, Tex., 1992—94; BA, McMurry U., Abilene, Tex., 1988—92. Lic. profl. counselor Tex. State Bd. of Counselor Licensing, child care adminstr. Tex. Dept. of Protective and Regulatory Services. Campus adminstr. Cal Farley's Girlstown, U.S.A., Whiteface, Tex., 2001—, asst. adminstr., 1999—2001; mgr., mental health services MHMR Services for the Concho Valley, San Angelo, Tex., 1995—99. County chmn. Rep. Party of Tex., Morton, 2001. Mem.: Tex. Alliance of Child and Family Services. Nazarene. Avocations: Sunday school teacher, outdoor activities. Home: Girlstown Whiteface TX 79379 Office Phone: 806-229-6361. Business E-Mail: robertmarshall@calfarley.org.

MARSHALL, ROBERT WILLIAM, lawyer, rancher; b. L.A., Apr. 12, 1933; s. Kenneth L and Helen (Putnam) M.; m. Nanette Hollenbeck, June 10, 1965; children: Thomas, Victoria, Rebecca, Kathleen. AB in Pre Law, Stanford U., 1955, JD, 1957. Bar: Calif. 1958, Nev. 1958, U.S. Dist. Ct. (so. dist.) Calif. 1958, U.S. Dist. Ct. Nev. 1958. Assoc. Vargas & Bartlett, Reno, Nev., 1958-64, ptnr., 1964-85, sr. ptnr., 1985-94; chmn. of bd. Marshall, Hill, Cassas & de Lipkau, 1994—. Owner Intermountain Cattle Co.; founder Intermountain Pipeline Ltd. Advisor Explorer Boy Scouts Am., Reno, 1971-76, 87-89, scoutmaster Troop 444 Boy Scouts Am., Reno, 1981-85; state chmn. Nev. Young Reps., 1962-64. Mem. ABA, Nat. Cattlemen's Assn., Calif. Bar Assn., Nev. Bar Assn., Washoe County Bar Assn., No. Nev. Large Power Users (organizer), So. Nev. Large Power Users (organizer), Nev. Cattlemen's Assn., Reno Stanford Club (pres. Reno chpt. 1974). Republican. Office: Marshall Hill Cassas & deLipkau 333 Holcomb Ave Ste 300 Reno NV 89502-1665

MARSHALL, RON, retail executive; BS with honors, Wright State U. V.p., CFO Barnes & Noble Bookstores; sr. v.p., CFO Dart Group Corp., Md., 1991-94; exec. v.p., CFO, Pathmark Stores, N.J., 1994-98; pres., CEO, Nash Finch Co., Mpls., 1998—. Mem. Food Mktg. Inst. (bd. dirs.). Office: Nash Finch Co 7600 France Ave S Ste 200 Minneapolis MN 55435-5920

MARSHALL, ROSEMARY, state representative; married; 3 children. Cert. in pub. policy disputes, MIT-Harvard U.; student, U. Colo., Colo. State U. State rep. State of Colo., 2002—, mem. fin. com., mem. judiciary com. Mem.: NAACP, Colo. Bus. Women Prof. Assn. Democrat. Address: 3451 E 26th Ave Denver CO 80203 Office: State Capitol #271 200 E Colfax Ave Denver CO 80203 E-mail: rosemary.marshall.house@state.co.us.

MARSHALL, RUSSELL FRANK, consulting company executive; b. Fort Madison, Iowa, Sept. 10, 1941; s. William Frank and Dorothy Eleanor (Mikels) M.; m. Mary Jean Bailey, June 19, 1966; children: William Russell, Robert Scott (dec.), Gregory Howard. AB, Monmouth Coll., 1963; MS, U. Ill., 1965, PhD, 1971. Rsch. engr. Materials Rsch. Lab, Urbana, Ill., 1970-75; mgr. acad. computing Drake U., Des Moines, 1975-80; v.p. GMI Ltd., Des Moines, 1980-83; sr. v.p., treas. Communication Devel. Co., West Des Moines,

1983-96; pres. Marshall Assocs., West Des Moines, Iowa, 1996—; dir. info. svcs. Grand View Coll., Des Moines, 1996—. Contbr. articles to profl. jours. Active Boy Scouts Am., 1982—; mem. Des Moines Cmty. Theatre. Grantee AEC, 1964-71. Mem. Assn. Computing Machinery, Am. Phys. Soc., Assn. Info. Tech. Mgrs., Des Moines Symphony Assn. Presbyterian. Avocations: music, reading. Home: 1625 19th St West Des Moines IA 50265-1622 Business E-Mail: RMarshall@gvc.edu.

MARSHALL, SHEILA HERMES, lawyer; b. N.Y.C., Jan. 17, 1934; d. Paul Milton and Julia Angela (Meagher) Hermes; m. James Josiah Marshall, Sept. 30, 1967; 1 child, James J.H. BA, St. John's U., N.Y.C., 1959; JD, NYU, 1963. Bar: N.Y. 1964, U.S. Ct. Appeals (2d, 3d, 5th and D.C. cirs.), U.S. Supreme Ct. 1970. Assoc. LeBoeuf, Lamb, Greene & MacRae, N.Y.C., 1963-72, ptnr., 1973—95, of counsel, 1996—. Specialist in field. Mem. ABA, N.Y. State Bar Assn., Assn. of Bar of City of N.Y. Republican. Home: 325 E 72nd St New York NY 10021 Office: LeBoeuf Lamb Greene & MacRae 125 W 55th St New York NY 10019-5369 Office Phone: 212-424-8000.

MARSHALL, SHERRIE, newspaper editor; Metro editor Star Tribune, Mpls., to 1998, editor news content, 1995—, dep. managing editor, 1999—. Office: Star Tribune 425 Portland Ave Minneapolis MN 55488-0002

MARSHALL, SIRI SWENSON, lawyer; BA, Harvard U., 1970; JD, Yale U., 1974. Bar: N.Y. 1975. Assoc. Debevoise & Plimpton, 1974-79; atty., sr. atty., asst. gen. counsel Avon Products, Inc., N.Y.C., 1979-85, v.p. legal affairs, 1985-89, sr. v.p., gen. counsel, 1990-94, Gen. Mills, Inc., Mpls., 1994-99, sr. v.p. corp. affairs, gen. counsel, sec., 1999—. Bd. dirs. Am. Arbitration Assn. Trustee Mpls. Inst. Arts. Office: Gen Mills Inc Number One Gen Mills Blvd Minneapolis MN 55426

MARSHALL, SUSANNE T. government agency administrator; Student, U. Maryland Branch Campus, Munich, American U. Legislative asst., 1981—82; Republican staff asst. House Govt Operations Comm., 1983—85; Republican staff Comm. on Governmental Affairs, 1985—2002; chmn. Merit Systems Protection Bd., 2002—. Office: US Merit Systems Protection Bd 1615 M Street NW Washington DC 20419

MARSHALL, TOM, publishing executive; b. Shreveport, La., 1954; With Lousiana Life; pub. Alaska mag., 1987—89; gen. mgr. Cooking Light, 1991—98; v.p. mktg. So. Living, 1998—2003; v.p., pub. Sunset, N.Y.C., 2003—. Recipient Gen. Excellence Nat. Mag. award, 1983. Office: Sunset Time and Life Bldg 20th Fl 1271 Avenue of the Americas New York NY 10020

MARSHALL, VINCENT DE PAUL, industrial microbiologist, researcher; b. Washington, Apr. 5, 1943; s. Vincent de Paul Sr. and Mary Frances (Bach) M.; m. Sylvia Ann Kieffer, Nov. 15, 1986; children from previous marriage: Vincent de Paul III, Amy. BS, Northeastern State Coll., Tahlequah, Okla., 1965; MS, U. Okla. Health Sci. Ctr., Oklahoma City, 1967, PhD, 1970. Rsch. assoc. U. Ill., Urbana, 1970, postdoctoral fellow, 1971-73; rsch. scientist The Upjohn Co., Kalamazoo, Mich., 1973-74, rsch. head, 1975, sr. rsch. scientist, 1976-91, sr. scientist, 1991-2000; cons., 2000—. Mem. editl. bd. Jour. of Antibiotics, 1990-2001, Jour. Indsl. Microbiology, 1989-2001, Devels. in Indsl. Microbiology, 1990; contbr. numerous articles to profl. jours., chpts. to books; patentee in field. Served with U.S. Army Nat. Guard, 1960-65. NIH predoctoral fellow, 1967-70; NIH postdoctoral fellow, 1971-73. Fellow Am. Acad. Microbiology; mem. Soc. for Indsl. Microbiology (membership com. 1988-90, co-chair edn. com. 1989-93, local sects. com. 1991-96, chair nominating com. 1993-94, mem. nominating com. 1999-2000, co-chair program com. 1993-94, dir. 1994-96, pres. So. Great Lakes sect. 1992-95), Am. Soc. Microbiology, Am. Soc. Biochemistry and Molecular Biology, Internat. Soc. for Antimicrobial Activity of Non-Antibiotics (sci. adv. bd.), Sigma Xi. Republican. Lutheran. Home and Office: 203 Paisley Ct Kalamazoo MI 49006-4359 Office Phone: 269-349-3795. E-mail: vince3795@aol.com.

MARSHALL, WAYNE KEITH, anesthesiology educator; b. Richmond, Va., Feb. 9, 1948; s. Chester Truman and Lois Ann (Tiller) M.; m. Dale Claire Reynolds, June 18, 1977; children: Meredith Reynolds, Catherine Truman, Whitney Wood. BS in Biology, Va. Poly. Inst. and State U., 1970; MD, Va. Commonwealth U., 1974. Diplomate Am. Bd. Anesthesiology, Nat. Bd. Med. Examiners; bd. cert. in pain mgmt. Surg. intern U. Cin., 1974-75, resident in surgery, 1975-77; resident in anesthesiology U. Va. Coll. Medicine, Charlottesville, 1977-79, rsch. fellow, 1979-80; asst. prof. anesthesia Pa. State U. Coll. Medicine, Hershey, 1980-86, assoc. prof., 1986-95, assoc. clin. dir. oper. rm., 1982-95, dir. pain mgmt. svc., 1984-95, chief divsn. pain mgmt., 1992-95; prof., chmn. dept. anesthesiology Med. Coll. Va., Richmond, 1995-99; med. dir. operating rms. MCV Hosp., 1995-99; prof. anesthesiology Coll. Medicine Pa. State U., Hershey, 1999—. Moderator nat. meetings. Mem. editorial bd. Am. Jour. Anesthesiology, 1987-99, Jour. Neurosurg. Anesthesiology, 1988—; contbr. articles and abstracts to med. jours. Recipient Antarctic Svc. medal NSF, 1980. Mem. AMA, Soc. Neurosurg. Anesthesia and Critical Care (sec.-treas. 1985-87, v.p. 1987-88, pres. 1989-90, bd. dirs. 1985-91), Assn. Univ. Anesthetists, Am. Soc. Anesthesiologists (del. ASA ho. of dels. 1990-92), Internat. Anesthesia Rsch. Soc., Pa. Soc. Anesthesiology. Republican. Baptist. Office: Dept Anesthesiology Penn St Univ Coll Med PO Box H-187 Hershey PA 17033-2360 E-mail: wkmarshall@psu.edu.

MARSHALL, WILLIAM, III, think-tank executive; b. Norfolk, Va., 1952; m. Katryn S. Nicolai; children: Olivia, William. BA in English and History, U. Va., 1975. Reporter Richmond Times-Dispatch; various positions on Capitol Hill and electoral politics; policy dir. Dem. Leadership Coun., 1985-89; pres. Progressive Found., 1989—; pres., founder Progressive Policy Inst., Washington, 1989—. Sr. editor 1984 House Dem. Caucus policy, Renewing America's Promise; participant in drafting nat. legis., including a demonstration project for vol. nat. svc. Nat. Cmty. Svc. Act of 1990; press sec., spokesman, speechwriter for 1984 U.S. Senate campaign of current N.C. Gov. Jim Hunt; speechwriter, policy analyst for late U.S. Rep. Gillis Long of La., chmn. of House Dem. Caucus; spokesman, speechwriter 1982 U.S. Senate campaign of former Va. Lt. Gov. Dick Davis. Co-editor: Mandate for Change, 1992; contbr. articles to profl. jours. Office: Progressive Policy Inst 600 Pennsylvania Ave SE Ste 400 Washington DC 20003-4350

MARSHALL, WILLIAM EDWARD, historical association executive; b. St. Paul, Apr. 19, 1925; s. William Edward and Louise (White) M.; m. Ruth Marie Winner, Sept. 3, 1947 (div.); children: Michael Scott, Terry Lee, Sharon; m. Loretta E. Slota, Nov. 6, 1976; children: Marc William, Matthew Ryan. BA, U. Mont., 1950; BFA, Wittenberg U., 1951; postgrad., Ohio State U., 1951-52. Owner, operator Public Library Public Relations Service, 1952-55, Specialized Press, 1952-60; graphic and exhibits designer Ohio Hist. Soc., 1952-60, State Historic Soc. Colo., Denver, 1960-61, dep. exec. dir., 1961-63, exec. dir., 1963-79; cons. to hist. agys., author, 1979—. Founding mem. Little Kingdom Hist. Found.; condr. historic interpretation seminars and workshops. Author historic TV and film prodns., books, fiction and non-fiction in nat. publs.; editor: Humboldt Historian, 1990-91, CEO MediFacts, 1992—; illustrator, photographer books and periodicals; contbr. articles to profl. jours. Bd. dirs. Rocky Mountain Center on Environment, 1967-72, Trinidad Mus. Soc., 1986-89; chmn. Colo. Humanities Program Com., 1971, 75. With USMCR, 1943-45. Mem. Am. Assn. Museums (exec. com. 1973-74, mus. accreditation evaluator), Am. Assn. State and Local History (mem. council 1966-72, awards com. 1966-80, com. on fed. programs in history), Orgn. Am. Historians (hist. sites com. 1974-75) Presbyterian. Home: Moonstone Heights 719 Driver Rd Trinidad CA 95570-9722 E-mail: marshall@marshallgallery.com.

MARSHALL-BEASLEY, ELIZABETH, landscape architect; b. Wilton, Conn., Mar. 14, 1959; d. Hamilton West Marshall, Jr. and Mary Barno Marshall; m. James W. Beasley, Jr., Nov. 28, 1986. BA, Princeton U., 1981; M in Landscape Arch., Fla. Internat. U., 1998. Policy analyst N.J. Legislature, 1981; field devel. dir. The Rouse Co., 1984; devel. mgr. Disney Devel. Co., Orlando, Fla., 1988; devel. dir. Norton Mus. Art, West Palm Beach, Fla., 1995; state orgn. dir. Jeb Bush for Gov., Tallahassee, 1996; project mgr., apprentice Morgan Wheelock Inc., West Palm Beach, 1999—2001; cons. Elizabeth Marshall-Beasley, West Palm Beach, 2001—02; pres. Elizabeth Marshall-Beasley, MLA, West Palm Beach, 2003—. Pres. coun. Nat. Pub. Radio, Washington, 2001—; gov. apptd. Bd. Landscape Arch., Tallahassee, 2002—; bd. dirs. Habitat for Humanity, West Palm Beach, New Horizon Svc. Dogs, Orlando. Recipient, ADDY, 1987, Comml. Project of 1989, Architecture Record, 1989; Fairchild Tropical Gardens: Off Site Collection Grad. scholar, 1997. Mem.: Am. Soc. Landscape Arch. (cert.), Sigma Alpha Lambda, Phi Kappa Phi. Episcopalian. Avocations: travel, theater. Office: Ste 1500 505 S Flagler Dr West Palm Beach FL 33401 E-mail: em-b@landplandesign.com.

MARSHALL-CHAPMAN, PAULA, food products executive; d. Paul Marshall. BS in Bus., Okla. City U., 1983, PhD in commercial sci., 1993. CEO Bama Companies, Tulsa, Okla., 1984—. Adv. bd. Fed. Reserve Bank, Kans. City; bd. dirs. Am. Fidelity Corp., Bank of Oklahoma, Helmerich and Payne. Pres. Okla. Quality Found. Bd.; trustee Tulsa Community Found.; mem. Ronald McDonald Advisory Bd.; chmn. Salvation Army Advisory Bd.; bd. mem. U. Tulsa. Named Advocate of the Year, Domestic Violence Intervention Services, 2000; named to Bus. Hall of Fame, Okla. Dept. of Commerce, 1998, Hall of Fame, Sales and Mktg. Executives Internat. Academy of Achievements, 1999; recipient Entrepreneur of Yr. award, Ernst & Young LLP, 1997, Pinnacle award, Sales and Mktg. Executives Internat. Academy of Achievements, 1999, Outstanding Philanthropist award, 2001, Amigo of the Year, Tulsa Hispanic C. of C., 2001. Mem.: Women's Foodservice Forum (bd. mem), Tulsa C. of C. (past chair). Office: Bama Companies 2745 E 11th St Tulsa OK 74104*

MARSHALL-DANIELS, MERYL, communications executive, mediator; b. L.A., Oct. 16, 1949; d. Jack and Nita Corinblit; m. Raymond Daniels, Aug. 19, 2000. BA, UCLA, 1971; JD, Loyola Marymount U., L.A., 1974. Bar: Calif. 1974. Dep. pub. defender County of L.A., 1975—77; sole practice L.A., 1977—78; ptnr. Markman and Marshall, L.A., 1978—79; sr. atty. NBC, Burbank, Calif., 1979—80, dir. programs, talent contracts bus. affairs, 1980, asst. gen. atty. N.Y.C., 1980—82, v.p., compliance and practices Burbank, 1982; v.p. program affairs Group W Prodns., 1987—89, sr. v.p. future images, 1989—91, TV prodr., Meryl Marshall Prodns., 1991—93; pres. Mediation Ptnrs. and Two Oceans Entertainment Group, 1991—. Chmn., Nat. Women's Polit. Caucus, Westside, Calif., 1978-80; mem. Calif. Dem. Ctrl. Com., 1978-79; mem. Hollywood Women's Polit. Com., 1988; bd. mem. George Foster Peabody Awards. Mem.: Women in Film, Acad. TV Arts and Scis. (treas. 1985, treas. 1993—97, bd. govs. 1989—2001, pres. 1997—99, chmn. bd., CEO 1999—2001). Democrat. Jewish. Office: Mediation Ptnrs Two Oceans and Entertainment Group 2017 Lemoyne St Los Angeles CA 90026 Office Phone: 323-669-0824.

MARSHANSKY, VLADIMIR NIKOLAEVICH, medical educator, biochemist, cell biologist; arrived in US, 1998; s. Nikolay Ivanovich and Avrora Sergeivna (Sorokina) Marshansky; 1 child, Serguei Vladimirovich. MSc in Med. Biophysics, Bio-Med. Faculty of Russian State Med. U., Russia, 1980; PhD in Biochemistry, Biol. Faculty Moscow State U., Russia, 1984. Cert. physician-biophysicist Russian State Med. U., 1980. Prof. and dir. dept. biochemistry of faculty of sci. Javeriana U., Bogota, Colombia, 1989—92; rsch. asst. prof. dept. medicine U. Montreal, Canada, 1993—98; asst. prof. medicine dept. medicine Harvard Med. Sch., Boston, 2003—. Contbr. chapters to books, articles to profl. jours. Mem.: Am. Soc. for Biochemistry and Molecular Biology, Proteomic Soc., Can. Soc. of Biochemistry and Molecular Biology, The Am. Physiol. Soc., Am. Soc. for Cell Biology, The Salt and Water Club. Office: Prog in Member Biology and Renal Unit Mass Gen Hosp Harvard Med Sch Dept Med 149 13th Street CNY-8 Ste #8203 Boston MA 02129-2020 E-mail: vladimir_marshansky@hms.harvard.edu.

MARSTON, EDGAR JEAN, III, lawyer; b. Houston, July 5, 1939; s. Edgar Jr. and Jean (White) M.; m. Graeme Meyers, June 21, 1961; children: Christopher Graham, Jonathan Andrew. BA, Brown U., 1961; JD, U. Tex., 1964. Bar: Tex. 1964. Law clk. to presiding justice Supreme Ct. Tex., Austin, 1964-65; assoc. Baker & Botts, Houston, 1965-71; ptnr. Bracewell & Patterson, L.L.P., Houston, 1971-89, 96—, of counsel, 1990-96; exec. v.p., gen. counsel Southdown, Inc., Houston, 1987-95, also bd. dirs. Mem. ABA, Tex. Bar Assn., Tex. Bar Found., Houston Bar Assn., Houston Country Club, Coronado Club. Episcopalian. Avocations: hunting, fishing, stamp collecting/philately, reading. Office: Bracewell & Patterson LLP 711 Louisiana St Ste 2900 Houston TX 77002-2781 Office Phone: 713-221-1315. E-mail: edgar.marston@bracepatt.com.

MARSTON, MICHAEL, urban economist, asset management executive; b. Dec. 4, 1936; s. Lester Woodbury and Josephine (Janovic) Marston; m. Alexandra Lynn Geyer, Apr. 30, 1966; children: John, Elizabeh. BA, U. Calif., Berkeley, 1959; postgrad., London Sch. Econs., 1961—63. Cert. rev. appraiser Nat. Assn. Rev. Appraisers and Mortgage Underwriters, 1984. V.p. Larry Smith & Co., San Francisco, 1969—72, exec. v.p. urban econ. divsn., 1969—72; chmn. bd. Keyser Marston Assocs., Inc., San Francisco, 1973—87; gen. ptnr. The Sequoia Partnership, 1979—91; pres. Marston Vineyard and Winery, 1982—, Marston Assocs., Inc., 1982—. Pres. The Ctr. Individual and Instnl. Renewal, 1996—. Contbr. articles to profl. jours. Mem. spkr. bus. Am. Embassy, London, 1961—63; mem. Gov.'s Issue Analysis Com. and Spkr. Bur., 1966; v.p., bd. dirs. Dem. Forum, 1968—72; chmn. San Francisco Waterfront Com., 1969—86; v.p. People for Open Space, 1972—87, mem. exec. com., 1972—87; chmn. fin. com. San Francisco Planning and Urban Rsch. Assn., 1976—87, bd. dirs., 1976—87, mem. exec. com., 1976—87, treas., 1976—87; bd. trustees Cathedral Sch. Boys, 1981—82, Marin Country Day Sch., 1984—90; pres. Presidio Heights Assn. Neighbors, 1983—84; mem. Napa Valley Vintners, 1986—, mem. gov. affairs com.; v.p. St. Luke's Sch., 1986—91; chmn. Presidio Com., 1991—; v.p., trustee Youth for Svc. Served to lt. USNR. Mem.: Napa Valley Vintners, World Congress Land Policy, Urban Land Inst., Pacific Union Club, Bohemian Club, Order of Golden Bear, Chevalier du Tastevin, Lambda Alpha. Home: 3375 Jackson St San Francisco CA 94118-2018 *Personal philosophy: Success is what you do with what you have not what others think or what is in vogue.*

MARSTON, ROBERT ANDREW, public relations executive; b. Astoria, N.Y., Aug. 6, 1937; s. Frank and Lena (DiDomenico) M.; m. Maryann Doherty, Sept. 23, 1990; children: Robert Brendan, Bradford Scott. BA, Hofstra U., 1959. Sr. v.p. Rowland Co., N.Y.C., 1959-68, Rogers & Cowen, Inc., N.Y.C., 1968-70; founder, chmn., CEO Robert Marston And Assocs., Inc., N.Y.C., 1970—. Contbr. articles and photographs to profl. jours. and popular mags. Mem. Pub. Rels. Soc. Am. (counselors sect.), Doubles Club, Southampton Bath & Tennis Club, Sky Club. Roman Catholic. Home: 570 Park Ave New York NY 10021-7370 also: 130 Captains Neck Ln Southampton NY 11968-4561 Office: 485 Madison Ave New York NY 10022-5803

MARSTON-SCOTT, MARY VESTA, nurse, educator; b. St. Stephen, N.B., Can., Apr. 5, 1924; d. George Frank and Betsey Mildred (Babb) M.; m. John Paul Scott, June 30, 1979. BA, U. Maine, 1946; M.N., Yale U., 1951; M.P.H., Harvard U., 1957; MA, Boston U., 1964, PhD, 1969. Research asst. Roscoe B. Jackson Meml. Lab., Bar Harbor, Maine, 1946-48; nurse, 1952-54; instr. Yale U. Sch. Nursing, 1955-56; nurse cons. Div. Nursing, Washington, 1957-62; asso. prof. Frances Payne Bolton Sch. Nursing, Case-Western Res. U., Cleve., 1969-74; prof. grad. program community health nursing Boston U., 1974-86; assoc. prof. Coll. Nursing U. Ill., Chgo., 1986-94, assoc. prof. emerita, 1994—. Cons. in field. Contbr. articles to profl. jours. Served with USPHS, 1957-62. Fellow Am. Acad. Nursing; mem. Am. Psychol. Assn., Am. Public Health Assn., Am. Nurses Assn., Sigma Theta Tau. Home: Dirigo Pines 2 Hawthorn Ct Orono ME 04473

MARTEL, JOHN SHELDON, lawyer, writer; b. Stockton, Calif., Jan. 1, 1931; s. Henry T. and Alice L. M.; m. Bonnie Martel; children: John Sheldon, Melissa Ann. BS, U. Calif.-Berkeley, 1956, JD, 1959. Bar: Calif. 1959. Dep. dist. atty., Alameda County, 1960-61; assoc. trial atty. firm Bronson, Bronson & McKinnon, San Francisco, 1961-64; ptnr. firm Farella, Braun & Martel, San Francisco, 1964—. Lectr., mem. adv. bd. Hastings Ctr. for Trial and Appellate Adv., 1983—. Author: (novels) Partners, 1988, Conflicts of Interest, 1994, The Alternate, 1999, Billy Strobe, 2001; author, editor legal publs.; composer-writer popular songs; profl. musician. Pilot USAF, 1951-54. Winner Am. Song Festival awards, 1978-80, 82, 85, 87. Fellow Am. Coll. Trial Lawyers (state chmn. 1985-87, bd. regents 1993-98); mem. ABA (litigation, antitrust, tort and ins. sects.), Calif. Bar Assn., San Francisco Bar Assn. (former chair litigation sect.), Am. Bd. Trial Advocates (bd. dirs. 1991-93), Am. Fedn. Musicians, Phi Delta Phi, Kappa Sigma. Office: Farella Braun & Martel 235 Montgomery St Ste 3100 San Francisco CA 94104-2902 Office Phone: 415-954-4422. E-mail: jmartel@fbm.com.

MARTEL, LISA, food service executive; Student, Regis Coll.; grad., Johnson and Wales Coll. Culinary Arts, 1986. Line cook then banquet chef The Bay Tower Room; chef Rebecca's, Boston, 150 Wooster St. and Remi, N.Y.C., The Sherry Netherlands Hotel, N.Y.C., 224 Boston St., Boston, 1990; chef, owner On the Park, Boston. Office: 55 Greenough St #2 Brookline MA 02445-6152

MARTELET, FRANCOIS R. pharmaceutical executive; b. Dijon, France, Feb. 17, 1960; m. Marie Santiard, July 9, 1991; children: Marie-Alix, Alexandre, Astrid-Marie. degree in Bus., MD, Dijon U. Product mgr. F. Hoffman-La Roche, Stockholm, 1992—94, group product mgr., 1994—95, internat. product mgr. Basel, Switzerland, 1996—96; head regional bus. unit Eli Lilly Corp., London, 1996—99; bus. unit head benelux Schering-Plough, Brussels, 1999—2000; v.p. pharma oncology Novartis Pharma, E. Hanover, NJ, 2001—03, regional head, Cen. and Ea. Europe, Mid. East, Africa, 2003—. Maj. French Army Res., 1992—2001. Home: Egglsee 8A 85560 Ebersberg Germany Office: Novartis Pharm Corp AG CH-4002 Basel Switzerland Office Phone: +49 61 6962107. Personal E-mail: francoismartelet@hotmail.com. Business E-Mail: francois.martelet@pharma.novartis.com.

MARTELL, KEITH, bank executive; Chmn. First Nations Bank Can., Saskatoon. Avocation: scuba diving. Office: First Nations Bank Can 224 4th Ave S Saskatoon SK S7K 5M5 Canada

MARTELL, THOMAS STEWART, accountant; b. Boston, Oct. 1, 1955; s. Stewart Dunham martell and Virginia Angelina (Zammito) Martell. AS in Bus. Admin., Northeastern U., BS, BA in acctg., 1998. Accountant Robert Half Accountemps, Boston, 2000—. Musician: (songs) (copywrited) Flowers For Darness, Tell Me Why, Its Just Impossible. Democrat. Roman Catholic. Avocations: piano, guitar, art, running, wrist watch collection. Home: 21078 SW Honeysuckle St Dunnellon FL 34431

MARTEN, GORDON CORNELIUS, research agronomist, educator, federal agency administrator; b. Wittenberg, Wis., Sept. 14, 1935; s. Clarence George and Cora Levina (Verpoorten) M.; m. Lynette Joy Hanson, Sept. 9, 1961; 1 dau., Kimberly Joy. BS, U. Wis., 1957; MS, U. Minn., 1959, PhD, 1961; postgrad., Purdue U., 1962. Rsch. agronomist U.S. Dept. Agr., U. Minn., St. Paul, 1961-72, supervisory rsch. agronomist, rsch. leader, 1972-89; adj. prof. agronomy U. Minn., St. Paul, 1971-96; assoc. dir. USDA-Agr. Rsch. Svc., Beltsville, Md., 1989-96; prof. emeritus U. Minn., St. Paul, 1996—. Mem. governing body and U.S. rep. to OECD Biol. Resource Mgmt. Program, Paris, 1990-96; adminstrv. coun. USDA Sustainable Agrl. Rsch. and Edn. Program, 1993-95. Assoc. editor: Crop Sci., 1972-74; sr. editor USDA Handbook Near Infrared Reflectance Spectroscopy: Analysis of Forage Quality, 1985, rev. edit., 1989; mem. edit. bd. Sci. of Food and Agriculture, 1985-90; contbr. numerous articles to profl. jours. NSF grad. fellow, 1959-61; recipient Merit award Am. Forage and Grassland Coun., 1976, Outstanding Svc. award, 1981, Civil Servant of Yr. award Twin Cities, Minn., 1976, Cert. of Merits, USDA Agrl. Rsch. Svc., Northrup King Faculty Outstanding Performance award U. Minn., 1986, Superior Svc. award USDA, 1987; named to Hall of Fame, Wausau Wis. Sch. Dist., 1998. Fellow: Crop Sci. Soc. Am. (bd. dirs. 1975—77), Am. Soc. Agronomy; mem.: Agronomic Sci. Found. (trustee 1984—89), Coun. Agr. Sci. and Tech. (bd. dirs. 1985—90), Am. Forage and Grassland Coun. (bd. dirs. 1977—80), North Suburban St. Paul Golden K Kiwanis (bd. dirs. 1998—2001), Biol. Club, Sigma Xi, Phi Kappa Phi, Delta Theta Sigma, Alpha Zeta, Gamma Sigma Delta (Adminstrn. award of merit Nat. Capital Area 1994). Lutheran. Home: 1312 Willow Cir Roseville MN 55113-3235

MARTEN, JAMES ALAN, historian, educator; b. Madison, S.D., Sept. 10, 1956; s. Roy Carl and Mary Lou Marten; m. Linda Carol Gist, Dec. 30, 1977; children: Lauren Ruth, Eli James. BS, S.D. State U., 1978; MA, U. of S.D., 1981; PhD, U. of Tex., 1986. English tchr. Woodbine (Iowa) HS, 1978—80; prof. of history Marquette U., Milw., 1986—. Dir. children in urban Am. project Marquette U., Milw., 1999—; Fulbright lectr. N.E. Normal U., Changchun, Jilin Province, China, 1999. Author: The Children's Civil War (Outstanding Academic Book award Choice Mag., 1999, Alpha Sigma Nu SJ Nat. Book award for history, 1999), Texas Divided: Loyalty and Dissent in the Lone Star State, 1856-1874, 1990; editor: Children and War: A Historical Anthology, 2001; author: Civil War America: Voices from the Homefront., 2003; editor: Am. Childhoods, 2003—, Milw. (Wis.) History Mag., 2003—. Grantee, Bradley Inst. for Democracy and Pub. Values, 1994, 1998, Edn. Devel. grant, NEH, 2000—03. Mem.: Milw. County Hist. Soc. (bd. dir. 1999—), Soc. for the History of Children and Youth (sec. 2000, treas. 2000), So. Hist. Assn. (membership com. 1999—2000), Soc. of Civil War Historians (mem. adv. bd. 1999), Orgn. of Am. Historians. Unitarian. Avocations: reading, travel, basketball. Office: History Department Marquette University P O Box 1881 Milwaukee WI 53201-1881

MARTENS, ERWIN W. risk management consultant; M, U. N.D. Profl. hockey player, Germany; with Coopers & Lybrand, 1985; founder Analytic Info. Mgmt., Inc., Toronto; global market risk mgmt., dep. head global risk mgmt. group Credit Suisse Group; sr. v.p. Lehman Bros.; exec. v.p. risk mgmt. TIAA-CREF, N.Y.C., 2003—. Mem. U. N.D. Alumni Bd. Named Buy Side Risk Mgr. of Yr., Risk Mgmt. Mag., 2000. Office: TIAA-CREF 730 3d Ave New York NY 10017

MARTENS, HARVEY ARTHUR, retired government worker, academic administrator; b. Bancroft, S.D., Mar. 19, 1928; s. Henry Martens and Anna Naeve; m. Barbara Colwell, Oct. 7, 1956 (div. Jan. 0, 1979); children: Craig Colwell, Eric Harvey, Douglas Henry. BS in Polit. Sci., S.D. State U., 1951; MPA, Maxwell Sch., Syracuse U., N.Y., 1952, PhD, 1973. Asst. to dir. Navy Adminstrv. Office, Washington, 1952—58; head, mgmt. devel. staff Navy Mgmt. Office, Washington, 1958—62; mgmt. analyst U.S. Dept. of Agr., Washington, 1962—64; dir. spl. projects ASPA, Washington, 1964—65; dir. pub. adminstrn. programs, lectr. in pub. adminstrn. Maxwell Sch., Syracuse U., NY, 1965—73; project dir. Nat. Acad. of Pub. Adminstrn., Washington, 1970—71; dir. rsch. & planning, prof. pub. adminstrn. U. of Nebr., Omaha, 1973—77; dir. grants, prof. pub. adminstrn. Drake U., Des Moines, 1978—86; dir. grants Des Moines U., 1986—93. Editor: Navy Mgmt. Rev., 1960—62, ASPA News, 1962—64; author: (study report) The Orgn. and Adminstrn. of Federally Funded Cmty. Mental Health Ctrs. Pres. Ea. Nebr. Nutrition for Elderly, Omaha, 1974—77, Neighborhood Housing Svcs. of Des Moines, 1985—89; chpt. pres. AARP, West Des Moines, Iowa; adv. com. of Polk County sr. svcs. Area Agy. on Aging, Des Moines, 1996—2003; mem. Older Iowans Legislature, Des Moines, 1998—2003; north am. adv. com. Internat. Coun. of Unitarian and Universalists, Prague, Czech Republic, 1999—2003; moderator. summer patio ch. First Unitarian Ch., Des Moines, 1985—2000. Lt. col. USAR, 1951—88, cpl. U.S. Army, 1953—55. Decorated Nat. Def. Svc. medal U.S. Army, Meritorious Svc. medal 103d Corps Command; Scholarship, Syracuse U., 1951—52, Hixson Fellow, Kiwanis Internat., 1997. Mem.: Coun. Fgn. Rels. (Omaha), Am. Humanist Assn. (life), Torch Club Internat. (club pres. 1999—2000), Kiwanis Internat., Mason, Scottish Rite, Shriner. Liberal. Unitarian Universalist. Avocations: travel, genealogy. Home: 2935 Rutland Ave Des Moines IA 50311-3916 Personal E-mail: hmartens4@mchsi.com.

MARTENS, LESLIE VERNON, dentistry educator, consultant; b. Peoria, Ill., Oct. 15, 1938; s. Vernon Christ and Lydia Rachel (Weisenburger) M.; m. Judith A., June 15, 1961 (div. Nov. 1988); children: Michael J., Philip S., Eric W., Pamela A. Student, Bradley U., Peoria, Ill., 1956—59; DDS, Loyola U. Chgo., 1963; MPH, U. Minn., Mpls., 1969. Dental officer, maj. U.S. Army Dental Corps., Tex., 1963-68; asst. prof., assoc. dir. Grad. Program in Dental Pub. Health, U. Minn., 1969-72; assoc. prof. Schs. of Dentistry and Pub. Health, Mpls., 1972—82, prof., 1982—; prof., chair dept. preventive scis. Sch. Dentistry U. Minn., Mpls., 1982—2001. Cons. to 21 dental schs. and 40 other health related agys. and orgns., 1972—. Author 89 manuscripts and rsch. abstracts in numerous jours.; patentee in field. Chmn. Red Cross Vol. Program, U.S. Army, 1963-67; merit badge counselor Boy Scouts Am., Anoka, Minn., 1972-89. Maj. U.S. Army, 1963-68, Germany. Grantee, U. Minn., 1970—; recipient commanding gen. citation U.S. Army, Fort Campbell, Ky., 1968, 84. Mem. ADA, Am. Assn. for Dental Rsch., Internat. Assn. for Dental Rsch., Am. Assn. Dental Schs., Omicron Kappa Upsilon, Delta Omega. Achievements include patents in field. Avocation: thoroughbred racing. Office: Sch Dentistry U Minn 515 Delaware SE Minneapolis MN 55455 E-mail: marte001@tc.mn.edu.

MARTENSEN, BARBARA, electronics executive; BS in Math., U. Ariz. With Motorola Semiconductor Products, 1978—99; global info. officer Avnet, Inc., Phoenix, 1999—2001, corp. v.p., sr. v.p. integrated bus. solutions, 2001—. Office: Avnet Inc 2211 S 47th St Phoenix AZ 85034

MARTENS REBOLLEDO, ERNESTO, secretary of energy for Mexico; b. Tlilapan, Veracruz, Mex., Jan. 28, 1933. Chem. engring., Technol. Inst. Superior Studies, Monterrey, Mex.; postgrad., Technol. Inst. of Karlsruhe, Germany, Harvard Business School. Various positions to gen. mgr. Union Carbide; various positions to CEO VITRO, 1977—93; dir. gen. CINTRA; sec. of energy Govt. of Mexico, 2000—; chmn. PEMEX, 2000—. Bd. dir. Transportes Mexicanos Maritimos. Office: Avenida Insurgentes Sur Num 552-30 PISO Colonia Roma Sur 06769 Mexico*

MARTI, GERARDO, sociologist, educator, minister; s. Rafael Gerardo and Caridad Marti; m. Laura Elaine Petrovich; 3 children. BA in Orgnl. Comm. and Sociology, Pepperdine U., 1987; MA in Sociology, U. So. Calif., L.A., 1990, PhD in Sociology, 2002. Market analyst and project mgr. Pacific Telesis, San Francisco, 1986; rsch. asst. Pepperdine U., Malibu, Calif., 1986—87; ch. planting cons. Calvary Ch. Santa Ana, Calif., 1990—92, overseas missions pastor and leadership team, 1992—94; vis. prof. sociology U. Calif., Irvine, 1992; pastor for new ministry devel. and congl. elder Evang. Free Ch. Orange, Calif., 1994—95; adj. prof. sociology Biola U., La Mirada, Calif., 1995—97; pastoral staff and core leadership team Mosaic, L.A., 1996—; ch. planting pastor and dir. on exec. bd. Anaheim Hills (Calif.) Cmty. Ch., 1996; adj. prof. global studies and sociology Azusa (Calif.) Pacific U., 1997—2004; adj. prof. Calif. State Univ., Long Beach, 2003—04; adj. prof. sociology Pepperdine Univ., 2003—04; asst. prof. sociology Davidson Coll., 2004—. Lectr. and cons. in field. Author: A Mosaic of Believers: Diversity and Religions Innovation in a Multi Ethnic Church, 2004. Recipient Key to the City of Ensenada, Mex., Civic Govt. of Ensenada represented by Mayor Daniel Quintero and Pres. of D.I.F. Georgina Quintero, 2000, Award of Merit for Svc. to the Poor, 2001; Dean's scholar, Pepperdine U., 1983—87, A.A.R.P. Outstanding Student Scholar, U. So. Calif., 1991, Pre-Doctoral fellow, Andrus Gerontology Ctr., U. So. Calif., 1989—91. Mem.: Gerontol. Soc. Am., Am. Sociol. Assn., Pacific Sociol. Assn., Soc. for the Sci. Study Religion. Evangelical. Avocations: travel, reading, gaming.

MARTI, VIRGIL, artist; b. St. Louis, 1962; BFA, Washington U., 1984; MFA, Temple U., 1990; student, Skowhegan Sch., 1990. Paley Gallery, Moore Coll. Art and Design, Phila., 1992, one-man shows include Samuel S. Fleisher Art Meml., 1994, White Columns, N.Y., 1996, Thread Waxing Space, 1998, exhibited in group shows at Cmty. Edn. Ctr., Phila., 1992, Larry Becker Cmty. Edn. Ctr., 1992, Inst. Contemporary Art, Boston, 1993, Vox Populi, Phila., 1994, Caren Golden Fine Art, N.Y., 1994, Ea. State Penitentiary, Phila., 1995, 88 Room, Boston, 1995, Nexus, Phila., 1996, Beavery Coll. Art Gallery, Glenside, Pa., 1996, The Fabric Workshop and Mus., Phila., 1997, exhibited in group shows, Columbus, 1997, exhibited in group shows, Mus. Am. Art of Pa. Acad. Fine Arts, Phila., 1998, Represented in permanent collections Art Resources Transfer, Inc., N.Y., The Fabric Workshop and Mus., Phila., Phila. Mus. Art, Victoria and Albert Mus., London. Recipient Louis Comfort Tiffany Found. award, 1997; Art Matters fellow, 1995, Pew Fellow in the Arts, 1995, Pa. Coun. Arts fellow, 1997.

MARTIA, DOMINIC FRANCIS, academic administrator; b. Canton, Ohio, May 9, 1935; s. Joseph James and Anita (Cimadevilla) Martia; m. Roberta Christine Abel, Feb. 13, 1954; children: Laura Ann, Paul Abel. BA, Roosevelt U., 1962; MA, U. Chgo., 1963; PhD, Loyola U., Chgo., 1972. Assoc. prof. English Roosevelt U., Chgo., 1972—93, asst. to pres., 1972—76, dean grad. divsn., 1976—79, v.p. student svcs., 1979—93, prof. English and humanities, 1993—2000, prof. emeritus, 2000—. Author: Getting Verse, 1985, Present, Tense, Direct Light, 2002, numerous poems; contbr. articles to profl. jours. Scholarship com. Stone Found., Chgo., 1981—2000. With U.S. Army, 1954—56. Fellow, Woodrow Wilson Found., 1962. Mem.: Nat. Assn. Scholars. Avocation: writing. Home: 5318 Huntingwood Ct Sarasota FL 34235

MARTIKAINEN, A(UNE) HELEN, retired health education specialist; b. Harrison, Maine, May 11, 1916; d. Sylvester and Emma (Heikkinen) M. AB, Bates Coll., 1939, DSc (hon.), 1957; MPH, Yale U., 1941; DSc, Harvard U., 1964, Smith Coll., 1969. Health edn. sec. Hartford (Conn.) Tb and Pub. Health Assn., 1941-42; cons. USPHS, 1942—49; chief health edn. WHO, Geneva, 1949—74; chair internat. affairs AAUW-NC, 1986—94, rep. to NC Coalition on Aging, 2001—, bd. dirs., 2001—; mem. NC Health Adv. Bd. for Aging, 2001—. Hon. trustee Bridgton Acad., North Bridgton, Maine; mem. NC Women's Forum, 1984—; bd. dirs. NC Ctr. of Laws Affecting Women, Inc.; bd. dirs. West Triangle chpt. UNA-USA; chair residents health and social svcs. com., residents coun., residents com. for cmty. rels. Carol Woods. Recipient Delta Omega award Yale U., Nat. Adminstrv. award Am. Acad. Phys. Edn., Key award Bates Coll., Internat. Svc. award, France, 1953, Prentiss medal, 1956, Spl. medal, cert. for internat. health edn. svc. Nat. Acad. Medicine for France, 1959, Profl. award Soc. Pub. Health Educators, 1963, Benjamin Elijah Mays award Bates Coll. Alumni Assn., 1989, Legacy of Leadership honoree Pines of Carolina coun. Girl Scouts U.S., 2002; named to Bridgeton Acad. Hall of Fame, Maine, 2003. Fellow APHA (chmn. health edn. sect., Excellence award 1969); mem. AAUW, LWV, Women's Internat. League for Peace and Freedom, U.S. Soc. Pub. Health Educators, Internat. Union Health Edn. (Parisot medal, tech. adviser), Acad. Phys. Edn. (assoc.), NC Coun. Women's Orgns. (mem. coun. assembly 1988-92, Women of Distinction award 1989), Phi Beta Kappa. Home: 3113 Carol Woods 750 Weaver Dairy Rd Chapel Hill NC 27514-1443 Personal E-mail: ahm3113@hotmail.com.

MARTIN, ACE, music educator; s. Norman Leonard and Francis Maxine Martin; 1 child, Matthew. AA, Fla. Jr. Colleg, 1974; MusB in Edn., Flroida State U., 1976; MusM in Trumpet Performance, Fla. State U., 1978. Cert. Trumpet Performance Fla. State U., 1976, tchr. Fla. Dept. of Edn., 1976. Asst. prof. music Austin Peay State U., Clarksville, Tenn., 1979—80; band dir. Landon Jr. H.S., Jacksonville, Fla., 1981—84; instr. high brass Ga. State U., Statesboro, 1982—83; instr. trumpet, dir. trumpet ensemble Valdosta State U., 1983—83; chmn. instrumental music Douglas Anderson Sch. Arts, Jacksonville, 1984—. Utility trumpet Jacksonville Symphony Orch., 1978—88; assitant condr. St. Johns River City Band, 1988—98, youth band dir., 1991—98, prin. trumpet, 1985—; adj. instr. trumpet. dir. trumpet ensemble dir. Valdosta State U., 1978—79. Musician (producer/soloist): (albums) Worship in the Key of Brass. Orch. mem. First Bapt. Ch., Jacksonville, 1978. Recipient Best Arts Sch. Big Band, Downbeat Mag., 2001. Mem.: Internat. Assn. Jazz Educators, Internat. Trumpet Guild, Music Educators Nat. Conf., Fla. Music Educators, Fla. Band Masters Assn., Phi Beta Chi, Phi Mu Alpha, Kappa Kappa Psi, Pi Kappa Lambda.

MARTIN, AGNES, artist; b. Maklin, Sask., Can., 1912; arrived in U.S., 1932, naturalized, 1950; Student, Western Wash. State Coll., 1935-38; BS, Columbia U., 1942, MFA, 1952. One-woman shows include Betty Parsons Gallery, N.Y.C., 1958, 1959, 1961, Robert Elkon Gallery, 1961, 1963, 1972, 1976, Nicolas Wilder Gallery, L.A., 1963—66, 1967, Visual Arts Ctr., N.Y.C., 1971, Kunstraum, Munich, 1973, Pace Gallery, N.Y.C., 1975, 1976, 1977, 1978, 1979, 1980—81, 1981, 1983, 1984, 1985, 1986, 1989, 1991, 1992, 1994, 1995, Mayor Gallery, London, 1978, 1984, Galerie Rudlof Zwirner, Cologne, Fed. Republic Germany, 1978, Harcus/Krakow Gallery, Boston, 1978, Margo Leavin Gallery, L.A., 1979, 1985, Mus. N.Mex., Santa Fe, 1979, 1998, Richard Gray Gallery, Chgo., 1981, Garry Anderson Gallery, Sydney, 1986, Waddington Galleries Ltd., London, 1986, Stedelijk Mus., Amsterdam, 1991, Whitney Mus. Am. Art, N.Y.C., 1992, 2000, Wildenstein Gallery, Tokyo, 1993, Serpentine Gallery, London, 1993, Galerie Michael Werner, Cologne, 1994, Pace Wildenstein, N.Y.C., 1995, 1996, 1997, 1998, 2000, 2001, Santa Fe Mus. Fine Arts, 1994, Galerie Daniel Blau, Munich, 1996, Harwood Mus., Taos, N.Mex., 1997, 2002, Galeria 56, Budapest, 1998, Royal Botanic Garden, Edinburgh, Scotland, 1999, Anthony d'Offay Gallery, London, 2001, Menil Collection, Houston, 2002, exhibited in group shows at Carnegie Inst., Pitts., 1961, Whitney Mus. Am. Art, 1962, 1966, 1967, 1974, 1977, 1992, Tooth Gallery, London, 1962, Gallery Modern Art, Washington, 1963, Wadsworth Atheneum, Hartford, Conn., 1963, Solomon R. Guggenheim Mus., N.Y.C., 1965, 1966, 1976, Mead Corp., 1965—67, Mus. Modern Art, N.Y.C., 1967, 1976, 1985, Inst. Contemporary Art, Phila., 1967, Detroit Inst. Art, 1967, Corcoran Gallery Art, Washington, 1967, 1981, Finch Mus., N.Y., 1968, Phila. Mus. Art, 1968, Zurich Art Mus., Switzerland, 1969, Ill. bell Telephone Co., Chgo., 1970, Mus. Contemporary Art, 1971, Inst. Contemporary Art, U. Pa., Phila., 1972, Randolph-Macon Coll., N.C., 1972, Kassel, Fed. Republic Germany, 1972, Stedelijk Mus., Amsterdam, 1975, U. Mass, Amherst, 1976, Venice Biennale, 1976, 1980, Cleve. Mus. Art, 1978, Albright-Knox Gallery, Buffalo, 1978, Inst. Contemporary Art, Boston, 1979, ROSC Internat. Art Exhbn., Dublin, Ireland, 1980, Marilyn Pearl Gallery, N.Y.C., 1983, Kemper Gallery, Kansas City Art Inst., 1985, Am. Acad. and Inst. Arts and Letters, N.Y.C., 1985, Charles Cowles Gallery, 1986, Moody Gallery Art U. Ala., Birmingham, 1986, Butler Inst. Am. Art, 1986, Art Gallery Western Australia, Perth, 1986, Mus. Contemporary Art, L.A., 1986, Mus. Fine Arts, Boston, 1989, Represented in permanent collections Mus. Modern Art, N.Y.C., Albright-Knox Gallery, Aldrich Mus., Ridgefield, Conn., Art Gallery Ont., Can., Australian Nat. Gallery, Canberra, Grey Art Gallery and Study Ctr., N.Y.C., Solomn R. Guggenheim Mus., High Mus. Art, Atlanta, Hirshhorn Mus. and Sculpture Garden, Washington, Israel Mus., Jerusalem, La Jolla (Calif.) Mus. Contemporary Art, L.A. County Mus. Art, Mus. Art R.I. Sch. Design, Providence, Mus. Modern Art, Neuegalerie der Stadt, Aachen, Fed. Republic Germany, Norton Simon Mus. Art, Pasadena, Calif., Stedelijk Mus., Amsterdam, Mus. Modern Art, Paris, Tate Gallery, London, Wadsworth Atheneum, Walker Art Ctr., Mpls., Whitney Mus Am. Art, Worcester (mass.) Art Mus., Yale U. Art Gallery, New Haven, Conn.; subject of various articles. Office: 414 Placitas Rd # 37 Taos NM 87571-2513

MARTIN, ALAN JOSEPH, lawyer; b. Berwyn, Ill., Dec. 9, 1959; s. Daniel George and Lillie (Chalupa) M.; m. Dawne Michelle Martin, June 24, 1989; children: Rebecca Marie, Melissa Nicole, Sarah Anne, reid Anthony. BA summa cum laude, U. Ill., 1982; JD, U. Va., 1985. Bar: Ill. 1985, U.S. Dist. Ct. (no. dist.) Ill., 1985, U.S. Ct. Appeals (7th cir.) 1997, U.S. Ct. Appeals (3d cir.) 1999. Analyst office politico-mil. analysis, bur. intelligence and rsch. Dept. State, Washington, 1981; assoc. Isham, Lincoln & Beale, Chgo., 1985-87, Mayer, Brown & Platt, Chgo., 1987—, ptnr., 1993. Mng. and exec. editor Jour. Law and Politics, 1984-85. Counselor terminally ill Mercy Hosp. Hospice, Urbana, Ill., 1980-82; pro bono lawyer, 1985—. Merriam scholar, 1980-82, James, 1982. Mem. ABA, Phi Beta Kappa, Phi Delta Phi. Avocations: racquetball, running, chess. Home: 1500 White Eagle Dr Naperville IL 60564-9761 Office: Mayer Brown & Platt 190 S La Salle St Ste 3100 Chicago IL 60603-3441

MARTIN, ALBERT CHARLES, manufacturing executive, lawyer; b. San Lucido, Italy, Sept. 20, 1928; s. Joseph and Carmela M.; m. Jean Perrin, Aug. 22, 1953 (dec.); children: Lynne, Ken; m. Frances Doughty, June, 1996. BS, Mich. State U., 1952; MS, U. Mich., 1953; JD, Detroit Coll. Law, 1962. Bar: Mich. 1962. Corp. counsel, sec. Udylite Corp., Detroit, 1963-68; corp. counsel Hooker Chem. Corp., N.Y.C., 1968-70, Grow Chem. Co., N.Y.C., 1970-71; group v.p. Leeds & Northrup Internat., North Wales, Pa., 1971-79, pres., 1979—. Served with U.S. Army, 1946-48. Mem. Mich. Bar Assn. E-mail: franal8@aol.com.

MARTIN, ALICE HOWZE, prosecutor; b. Memphis, Apr. 25, 1956; BSN, Vanderbilt U., 1978; JD, U. Miss., 1981. Bar: Tenn. 1981, Miss. 1981, Ala. 1989. Asst. U.S. atty. U.S. Attys. Office, Memphis, 1983-89; ptnr. Harris Harris & Martin, Florence, Ala., 1992—94; dist. mcpl. judge City of Florence, Ala., 1993—97; judge Cir. Ct. State of Ala., 1997—99; U.S. Atty. No. Dist. Ala., 2001—. Avocations: travel, skeet shooting.

MARTIN, ALLEN, retired lawyer; b. Manchester, Conn., Aug. 12, 1937; s. Richard and Ruth Palmer (Smith) M.; m. Bonnie Reid, Sept. 8, 1979; children: Elizabeth Palmer, Samuel Bates. BA, Williams Coll., 1960, Oxford U., 1962; LLB, Harvard U., 1965. Ptnr. Downs, Rachlin and Martin, Burlington, Vt., 1971—2002. Chmn. bd. dirs. Wicor Ams., 1991—; bd. dirs., chmn. compensation com. IDX Systems Corp.; bd. dirs., chmn. fin. com. Union Mut. Ins. Co., New Eng. Guaranty Ins. Co.; mem. Vt. Jud. Responsibility Bd., vice-chmn., 1978-80; trustee Vt. Law Sch., 2000-04. Chmn. Vt. Bd. Edn., 1978-83; chmn. Vt. Rep. Party, 1991-95; mem. Rep. Nat. Com., 1991-95, 97-99. Mem. ABA, Am. Law Inst. (life), Vt. Bar Assn. Republican. Home: PO Box B Six Chimneys Orford NH 03777 Office Phone: 603-640-6100. E-mail: amartin@valley.net.

MARTIN, ANDREA LOUISE, actress, comedienne, writer; b. Portland, Maine, Jan. 15, 1947; Grad., Emerson Coll. Appearances include (plays) Hard Shell, 1980 (off-Broadway debut), Sorrows of Stephen, 1980, What's a Nice Country Like You Doing in a State Like This?, 1974, She Loves Me, My Favorite Year, 1993 (Tony award, Featured Actress in a Musical), (films) Cannibal Girls, 1973, Black Christmas, 1974, Wholly Moses!, 1980, Soup for One, 1982, Club Paradise, 1986, Innerspace, 1987, Martha Ruth and Eddie, 1988, Worth Winning, 1989, Boris and Natasha, 1989, Rude Awakening, 1989, Too Much Sun, 1991, Stepping Out, 1991, All I Want for Christmas, 1991, (voice) The Itsy Bitsy Spider, 1992, Striking Distance, 1993, Bogus, 1996, (voice) Anastasia, 1997, Wag the Dog, 1997, The Rugrats Movie (voice), 1998, Bartok the Magnificent, 1999 (TV) Second City TV, 1977-81, That Thing on ABC, 1978, Torn Between Two Lovers, 1979, The Robert Klein Show, 1981, Kate and Allie, 1982, The Comedy Zone, 1984, Late Night Film Festival, 1985, Second City Twenty-Fifth Anniversary, 1985, Martin Short Concert for the North Americas, 1985, The Smothers Brothers Comedy Hour, 1988, Poison, 1988, The Martin Short Show, 1994, Earthworm Jim, 1995, Life...and Stuff, 1997, Damon, 1998, others; (TV movie) Charles Dickens' David Copperfield, 1993, Gypsy, 1993, In Search of Dr. Seuss, 1994, Harrison Bergeron, 1995; TV host Women of the Night II, 1988, Second City Fifteen Anniversary Special, 1988, Andrea Martin: Together Again, 1989; actress/writer: TV series SCTV Network 90, 1981-83 (2 Emmy awards 1982, 83), TV pilot From Cleveland, 1980; also The Completely Mental Misadventures of Ed Grimley, 1988-90 (voice of Mrs. Freebus).

MARTIN, ANDREW AYERS, lawyer, physician, educator; b. Toccoa, Ga., Aug. 18, 1958; s. Wallace Ford and Dorothy LaTranquil (Ayers) M.; children: William Ayers, Malorie Ayers. BA, Emory U., Atlanta, 1980, MD, 1984; JD, Duke U., 1988. Bar: Calif. 1989, La. 1990, D.C. 1991; diplomate Am. Bd. Pathology, Nat. Bd. Med. Examiners; lic. physician, La., Miss., Ark. Intern in pediatrics Emory U./Grady Meml. Hosp., Atlanta, 1984; intern Tulane U./Charity Hosp., New Orleans, 1989-90, resident in anatomic and clin. pathology, 1990-94; surg. pathology fellow Baylor Coll. Medicine, Houston, 1994-95; law clk. Ogletree, Deakins, Smoak, Stewart, Greenville, S.C., summer 1986, Thelen Marrin Johnson Bridges, L.A., summer 1987, Duke Hosp. Risk Mgmt., 1987-88; assoc. Haight Brown Bonesteel, Santa Monica, Calif., 1988; pvt. practice L.A., 1989; physician/atty. Tulane Med. Ctr./Charity Hosp., New Orleans, 1989-94, Baylor Coll. Medicine/Tex. Med. Ctr., Houston, 1994-95; lab. dir. King's Daus. Hosp., Greenville, Miss., 1995—; asst. clin. prof. pathology Tulane U.; lab. dir., owner Vicksburg Pathology Lab., Bolivar Med. Ctr., Cleveland, Miss.; staff pathologist Delta Regional Ctr., Greenville, Miss., N.W. Miss. Regional Medical Ctr., Clarksdale, Miss., No. Sunflower County Hosp., Ruteville, Miss., Tallahatchie County Hosp., Charleston, Miss. Sr. ptnr. Mid-South Pathology Assocs.; med. dir. of labs. Vicksburg Pathology Lab., N.W. Miss. Regional Med. Ctr., Bolivar Med. Ctr., Delta Regional Med. Ctr., North Sunflower County Hosp., 1997—, Tallahatchie (Miss.) County Hosp., N.W. Miss. Regional Med. Ctr., Clarksdale, Lab Corp., Southaven, Miss., Tallahatchie County Hosp.; adj. faculty Moorhead U.; bd. dirs. Martin Bldrs., Inc., Toccoa; mem. AIDS Legis. Task Force for La.; case cons. Office of Tech. Assessment, Washington; tech. cons. and autopsy extra Oliver Stone's "JFK"; adj. clin. faculty Moorhead Coll. Contbr. articles to profl. jours.; author: Reflections on Rusted Chrome (book of poetry). Fellow Coll. Am. Pathologists, Coll. Legal Medicine, La. State Med. Soc. (del. meeting 1992-93). Home: 935 Lakehall Rd Lake Village AR 71653-6096 also: 4104 Alabama Ave Kenner LA 70065-5603 also: 3850 Old Highway 27 Vicksburg MS 39180-8829 Office: Mid-South Pathology Assocs PO Box 5880 Greenville MS 38704-5880

MARTIN, ANN, newscaster; b. Portland, Oreg. married; 1 child. BA in comm., U. Wash. Anchor, reporter KABC-TV, Los Angeles, 1980—94; anchor KCBS 2, Los Angeles, 1994—, anchor, CBS 2 News at 4 and 6pm, 1997—. Guest host Good Morning America. Mem. Nat. Charity League. Recipient Golden Mike Award for Best 30 min. newscast, 1993. Office: CBS 2 News 6121 Sunset Blvd Los Angeles CA 90028

MARTIN, ANN BODENHAMER, minister, writer; d. Richard Clinton and Vera von Hein Bodenhamer, Jewel Little Bodenhamer (Stepmother); children: Richard Clinton Elliott, Mark Andrew Elliott. BA, PhD, Univ of Ar, Southwestern Univ, Ark., Fla. and USVI. Lic. FCC First Class, FCC, 1965. Sr. min. Unity of Palm Springs, Calif., 1987—. Home: Post Office Box 1508 Palm Springs CA 92263-1508 Office: Unity of Palm Springs 815 South Camino Real Palm Springs CA 92264

MARTIN, ANNE LOUISE, music educator; b. Bethesda, Md., May 21, 1956; d. Gordon Morehouse and Frances Fetter Martin; m. David Jones, Aug. 14, 1985; 1 child, Jessica Caitlin Jones. MusB, New Sch. Music, 1979; MusM, Yale Sch. Music, 1983; AS in Nursing, Santa Fe C.C., 1994. RN N.Mex Bd. Nursing, 1994. Violist PR Symphony, San Juan, 1983—85; dir. strings NW Coll., Powell, Wyo., 1985—89; condr. Santa Fe Youth Symphony, 1995—2001, Taos Cmty. Orch. and Chorus, Taos, 1989—2001; staff nurse St. Vincent Hosp., Santa Fe, 1994—96; asst. prin. violist Santa Fe Symphony, 1989—2001; dir. orch. & strings Modesto Jr. Coll., Calif., 2001—. Musician: (recording) Eclectic Acoustic (NW Coll. Faculty grantee, 1986), Puerto Rican Composers Series, (albums) Taos Chamber Music Series. Vol. ct. accompanist Women Organzied Against Rape, Phila.; faculty sponsor Amnesty Internat., Powell, Wyo., 1986—89. Grantee, Wyo. Arts Coun., 1987—88. Mem.: Am. Fedn. Musicians (union steward 1989—91), Am. String Teachers Assn. (sec. treas. 1986—89), Kappa Kappa Psi. Democrat. Unitarian. Avocations: Karate, swimming, gardening, bicycling. Office: Modesto Junior College 435 College Avenue Modesto CA 95350 E-mail: martinan@yosemite.cc.ca.us.

MARTIN, ARTHUR MEAD, lawyer; b. Cleveland Heights, Ohio, Mar. 29, 1942; s. Bernard P. and Winifred (Mead) M. AB, Princeton U., 1963; LLB, Harvard U., 1966. Bar: Ill. 1966, U.S. Dist. Ct. (no. dist. Ill.) 1969, U.S. Ct. Appeals (7th cir.) 1970, U.S. Supreme Ct. 1980, U.S. Ct. Appeals (fed. cir.) 2000. Instr. law U. Wis., Madison, 1966-68; assoc. Jenner & Block, Chgo., 1968-74, ptnr., 1975—2003. Co-trustee Dille Family Trust, 1982—. Author: Historical and Practice Notes to the Illinois Civil Practice Act and Illinois Supreme Court Rules, 1968-88. Trustee 4th Presbyn. Ch., Chgo., 1996-99, sec. 1997-99, exec. com. 1997-99; bd. dirs. Stop Colon/Rectal Cancer Found., 1998—. Mem. ABA, Am. Law Inst., Ill. Bar Assn., Chgo. Bar Assn. (bd. editors 1972-86), Ill. State Hist. Soc. (adv. bd. 1998-99, bd. dirs. 1999—, exec. com. 1999—, fin. com. 1999—, treas. 2002—), Ill. Centennial Bus. Com., Lake Mich. Fedn. (bd. dirs. 1993-2002, 03—, exec. com. 1994-2002, treas. 1994-99, 2001-02, sec. 1999-2001), Law Club Chgo., Legal Club Chgo. Office: Jenner & Block 1 IBM Plz Fl 4400 Chicago IL 60611-7603 E-mail: amartin@jenner.com.

MARTIN, BECKY ROGERS, state representative, realtor; b. Mullins, S.C., July 7, 1950; d. Phillip V. and Inez M. Rogers; m. Johnny Wayne Martin, July 11, 1969; children: Jayne Marie, Mollie Katherine. A, Columbia Jr. Coll., 1969. Realtor; state rep. dist. 8 S.C. Legis., 1997—, mem. edn. and pub. works com., 2d vice-chmn. ops. and mgmt. com. Mem. Center Rock Fire Dept. Bd.; county chmn. United Way; mem. March of Dimes, Clemson Parents Coun., Anderson & Oconee Legis. Del., Women's Caucus, Appalachian Regional Coun. Govts.; pacesetter Stennis Ctr. So. Women Pub. Svc., 1998—2000; mem. Women's Rep. Caucus; 1st vice chair Freshman Caucus. Mem.: SCSEA (state mem. chmn., chpt. pres.), Nat. Found. Women Legislators (state dir. 1998), Women's Profl. Orgn. Women in Govt., Assn. Realtors, S.C. Pub. Health Assn., State Employee's Assn., Women's Golfing Assn., Rotary. Republican. Office: State Capitol 326B Blatt Bldg Columbia SC 29211 Home: 1103 Hunters Trail Anderson SC 29625 E-mail: BRM@scstatehouse.net.

MARTIN, BENJAMIN GAUFMAN, ophthalmologist; b. Louisville, Aug. 18, 1937; s. Benjamin and Catherine L. Martin; m. Caroline Sue Martin, May 25, 1975; children: Benjamin, Lori, Tamara, Farrell, Steven, David. BME, U. Louisville, 1954, M. Engring., 1973; MD, U. So. Calif., 1964. Design engr. Philco/Ford, Palo Alto, Calif., 1957-60; rsch. engr. N.Am./Rockwell, Inglewood, Calif., 1961-63; intern Wright-Patterson Med. Ctr., Dayton, Ohio, 1964-65; ophthalmology resident Wilford Hall Med. Ctr., San Antonio, 1968-71; commd. USAF, 1963, advanced through grades to col., ret., 1980; CEO Cape Coral (Fla.) Eye Ctr., 1980—. With USN, 1954-57. Decorated Legion of Merit, DFC, Bronze Star, Air medal. Mem.: DFC Soc., Daedalions, Elks, Shriners, Masons. Republican. Lutheran. Office: Cape Coral Eye Ctr 4120 Del Prado Blvd S Cape Coral FL 33904-7165 Office Phone: 239-542-2020.

MARTIN, BETTY J. speech, language pathologist; b. East St. Louis, Ill., Nov. 2, 1950; d. Nathaniel and Minnie Mae (Long) Gause; m. Leander Martin, Jr.; children: Leander III, Lavell, Kenneth. BS, So. Ill. Univ., 1978, MS, 1980; postgrad., So. Ill. U. Cert. speech-lang. pathologist, Ill., Mo., early intervention specialist, LD tchr.; lic., Ill. Bd. sec. State C.C., East St. Louis, 1970-75; speech-lang. pathologist East St. Louis Sch. Dist. 189, 1980—. Site coord. Educom, St. Peter's, Mo., 1993. Tutor Project Love, East St. Louis, 1990; tchr. Vacation Bible Sch., East St. Louis, 1994, 95; sec. Steward BBd. #2, East St. Louis, 1994-96; staff mentor, cooperating clinician for student tchrs. in speech pathology. Mem. Am. Speech Hearing Lang. Assn. (cert.), Ill. Speech Hearing Assn., So. Ill. Speech Hearing Assn., Alliance for Mentally Ill, Natl. Alliance for Mentally Ill. Methodist. Home: 520 Green Haven Dr Swansea IL 62226-1801 Office: Mandela Elem Sch East Saint Louis IL 62201

MARTIN, BEVERLY, federal judge; b. Macon, Ga. BA, Stetson U., Deland, Fla., 1976; JD, U. Ga., 1981. Bar: Ga. 1981. Assoc. Martin, Snow, Grant & Napier, Macon, Ga., 1981-84; trial and appellate ct. litigator, sr. asst. atty. gen. and dir. bus. and profl. regulation divsn. Office of Atty. Gen. State of Ga., Macon, 1984-94; asst. U.S. atty. mid. dist. Ga. Macon, 1994-98; U.S. atty. mid. dist. Ga. U.S. Dept. Justice, Macon, 1998-2000; dist. judge U.S. Dist. Ct. for No. Dist. Ga., Atlanta, 2000—. Mem. Ga. Bar Assn., Macon Bar Assn., Am. Judicature Soc., Ga. Assn. Women Lawyers, Lawyers Club of Atlanta. Office: US Dist Ct for No Dist Ga 2388 US Courthouse 75 Spring St SW Atlanta GA 30303

MARTIN, BOB, airport executive; V.p., asst. sec. Memphis-Shelby County Airport Authority; v.p. ops. Memphis Internat. Airport. Office: Memphis Internat Airport Memphis-Shelby County Airport Authority 2491 Winchester Rd Memphis TN 38116-3851

MARTIN, BOE WILLIS, lawyer; b. Texarkana, Ark, Oct. 6, 1940; s. E.H. and Dorothy Annette (Willis) M.; m. Carol J. Edwards, June 12, 1965; children: Stephanie Diane, Scott Andrew. BA, Tex. A&M U., 1962; LLB, U. Tex., 1964; LLM, George Washington U., 1970. Bar: (Tex.) 1964. Law clk. Tex. Supreme Ct., 1966-67; assoc. Snakard, Brown & Gambill, Ft. Worth, 1967-69, assoc., ptnr., 1971-72; asst. counsel US Senate Labor and Pub. Welfare Com., 1969; legal asst. U.S. Senator Ralph W. Yarborough, 1969-71; assoc., ptnr. Stalcup & Johnson, Dallas, 1972-77; assoc. ptnr. Coke & Coke, Dallas, 1977-80; ptnr., shareholder Johnson & Gibbs, Dallas, 1981—95, Bell, Nunnally & Martin, Dallas, 1996—. Vis. prof. law So. Meth. U. Sch. Law, 1972-73, 75, 88-89, 95, 99-2000, 2002-2004, U. Tex. Sch. Law, 1977, 79. Contbr. articles to profl. jours. Staff Carter-Mondale Campaign, 1976, 80; cons. to v.p. of US, 1977-80; cons. Mondale for Pres. Campaign, 1983-84, Dukakis for Pres. Campaign, 1988; dep. coord. of visit of Pres. Mikhail Gorbachev to State of Minn., 1990. Capt. US Army, 1964-69. Mem. ABA, Tex. Bar Assn., Dallas Bar Assn. Democrat. Methodist. Home: 4055 Sweetwater Dr College Station TX 77845-964 Office: Bell & Nunnally & Martin 3232 Mckinney Ave Ste 1400 Dallas TX 75204-2426 E-mail: boem@bellnunnally.com.

MARTIN, BOSTON FAUST, neurosurgeon; b. Tampa, fla., June 1, 1927; s. Boston Francis and Cantherina Heidi Martin; m. Roselle Bayot, May 26, 1988; children: Sandrine, Nathalie, Samantha, Arielle. BS, Howard U., 1949; BMS, U. Fribourg, Switzerland, 1954; MD, U. Geneva, 1958. Diplomate Am. Bd. Neurological and Orthopedic Surgeons, Am. Bd. Minimally Invasive Spinal Surgery. Intern in gen. surgery Danbury (Conn.) Hosp., 1959-60; resident in gen. surgery Stamford (Conn.) Hosp.-Yale U. Affiliate, 1960-61; resident in neurology Met. Hosp., N.Y.C., 1961-62; resident in neurosurgery NYU Bellevue Med. Ctr., N.Y.C., 1962-65; chief resident in neurosurgery NYU Med. Ctr., N.Y.C., 1965-66, fellow in neurosurgery, 1966-67; interim chief neurol. surgery sect. Sch. Medicine and Univ. Hosp., U. P.R., San Juan, 1969-70, asst. prof. neurosurgery, 1969-75; clin. instr. in neurol. surgery NYU, 1966-67; clin. instr. in rehab. medicine U. Medicine and Dentistry N.J./N.J. Med. Sch., Newark, 1978-86, clin. instr. surgery, 1996—; attending neurosurgeon Hosp. Ctr. at Orange, N.J., 1976—, Meadowlands Hosp. Med. Ctr., Secaucus, N.J., 1981—, chief neurol. surgery, 1998—; attending neurosurgeon Christ Hosp., Jersey City, 1987—. Pvt. practice, West Orange, 1976—; attending neurosurgeon Doctors Hosp., Santuce, 1970-75, Matilde Brenes Hosp., Bayamon, P.R., 1970-75, San Jorge Hosp., Santice, P.R., 1970-75, Tchrs. Hosp., Haty Rey, P.R., 1971-75, Auxilio Muto Hosp., Hato Rey, 1971-75, Presbyn. Hosp., Santuce, 1972-75; asst. attending neurosurgeon Knud-Hansen Meml. Hosp., St. Thomas, V.I., 1967-69, U. P.R. Univ. Hosp., 1969-75; attending neurosurgeon East Orange Gen. Hosp., 1976-86, chief neurol. surgery, 1990-2000; chief spinal cord injury svc. VA Med. Ctr., East Orange, 1975-84; active attending neurosurgeon Newark Beth Israel Med. Ctr., 1998—; presenter in field. Co-author: the Conus Medullaris: Physiological Anatomy and Clinical Considerations. 1987; contbr. articles to profl. jours. Lt. col., flight surgeon USAF, 1984-90. Recipient Cert. of Merit Lions Club Internat., 1969, Disting. citation DAV, 1977, spl. trophy for disting. svc. DAV, 1979. Mem. ACS, AAUP, Internat. Coll. Surgeons, Acad. Medicine N.J., Congress Neurol. Surgeons (mem. internat. com. 1974, socio-econ. com. 1974-76, med. legal subcom. 1978-84), Societe de Neuro-Cirurgie De Langue Francaise, N.J. Neurosurg. Soc., Assn. Mil. Surgeons U.S., Am. Acad. Neurol. and Orthopedic Surgeons, Air Force Assn., Orange Mountain Med. Soc., Alpha Phi Alpha. Home: 9 Maple Ave West Orange NJ 07052-2407 Office: 81 Northfield Ave West Orange NJ 07052-5338

MARTIN, BOYCE FICKLEN, JR., federal judge; b. Boston, Oct. 23, 1935; s. Boyce Ficklen and Helen Artt Martin; m. Mavin Hamilton Brown, July 8, 1961; children: Mary V.H., Julia H.C., Boyce Ficklen III, Robert C.G. II. AB, Davidson Coll., 1957; JD, U. Va., 1963. Bar: Ky. 1963. Law clk. to Hon. Shackelford Miller, Jr. U.S. Ct. Appeals 6th Cir., Cin., 1963—64; asst. U.S. atty. Western Dist. Ky., Louisville, 1964; instructor Louisville Law school, 1965—67; U.S. atty. Western Dist. Ky., 1965; pvt. practice Louisville, 1966—74; 1st asst. Office of the County Attorney, Jefferson County, 1970—74; judge Jefferson Circuit Ct., Louisville, 1974—76; chief judge Ct. Appeals Ky., Louisville, 1976—79; judge U.S. Ct. Appeals 6th Cir., Cin. and Louisville, 1979—96, chief judge, 1996—2003. Jud. coun. U.S. Ct. Appeals (6th cir.), 1979—96, chmn., 1996—; mem. Jud. Conf. of U.S., 1996—, exec. com., 1998—. Trustee Isaac W. Bernheim Found., Louisville, 1981—97, chmn., 1982—95; trustee Blackacre Found., Inc., Louiville, 1983—94, chmn., 1986—94; trustee Hanover (Ind.) Coll., 1982—, vice-chmn., 1992—97, chmn., 1998—; exec. bd. Old Ky. Home coun. Boy Scouts of Am., 1968—72; pres. Louisville Zool. Commn., 1971—74; vestry mem. St. Francis in the Fields Episcopal Ch., Harrods Creek, Ky., 1979—83; bd. vis. Davidson (N.C.) Coll., 1980—86, trustee, 1994—98. Capt. JAGC U.S. Army, 1958—66. Fellow: Am. Bar Found.; mem.: ABA (com. effective appellate advocacy Conf. Appellate Judges), Louisville Bar Assn., Ky. Bar Assn., Fed Bar Assn., Am. Judicature Soc., Inst. Jud. Adminstrn. Office: US Ct Appeals 209 US Courthouse 601 W Broadway Louisville KY 40202-2227

MARTIN, BRIAN, Olympic athlete; b. Palo Alto, Calif., Jan. 19, 1974; Student, Denver U. Luge racer with 2 man team, back driver, 1988—; mem. U.S. 1st Olympic Team; named to devel. team, 1989. Named winner, World Cup Races (4), 1997—98, All-Japan Championships, Nagano; recipient Bronze medal Luge Men's Doubles, Nagano Olympics, Japan, 1998, World Cup, 1998, Silver medal, Bell Atlantic Nat. champion, 1998, Bronze medal, World Championship, 2000, Silver medal, Luge Challenge Cup, 2000. Address: US Luge Association 35 Church St Lake Placid NY 12946-1805

MARTIN, BRUCE JAMES, newspaper editor; b. Pontiac, Mich., Sept. 2, 1956; s. James Patrick and Patricia Ann (Taylor) M.; m. Elizabeth Hartley Nutting, July 30, 1988. BJ, U. Mo., 1982. Reporter Spinal Col. Newsweekly, Union Lake, Mich., 1982; sports editor Northville (Mich.) Record/Novi News, 1982-85; news editor Novi News, Northville, 1984-85; copy editor Kalamazoo Gazette, 1985-89, Ann Arbor (Mich.) News, 1989-91, homes editor, 1991, arts and entertainment editor, 1991—. Recipient 1st Place in Sports Writing in Circulation Category, Mich. Press Assn., 1993. Avocations: songwriting, playing piano and guitar. Office: Ann Arbor News 340 E Huron St Ann Arbor MI 48104-1900

MARTIN, BURCHARD SAMUEL, lawyer; b. Vineland, N.J., Sept. 3, 1961; s. Burchard Viliger and Elizabeth Marie (DelRossi) M.; m. Paula Ann Mikutovicz, June 13, 1987; children: Caroline Mary Elizabeth, Burchard W.J. BA in Polit. Sci., Villanova U., 1983, JD, 1986. Bar: N.J. 1986, Pa. 1986, U.S. Dist. Ct. (ea. dist.) Pa. 1986, U.S. Dist. Ct. N.J. 1986, U.S. Ct. Appeals (3d cir.) 1986, U.S. Supreme Ct. 1990. Assoc. Tomar, Seliger, Simonoff, Adourian & O'Brien, P.C., Haddonfield, N.J., 1986-87, Martin, Crawshaw & Mayfield, P.A., Westmont, N.J., 1987-91; ptnr. Martin, Gunn & Martin, P.A., Westmont, N.J., 1991—. Instr. bus. law Burlington County Coll., adj. instr. Mem. Internat. Assn. Def. Counsel, Am. Arbitration Assn. (arbitrator), N.J. Bar Assn. (product liability and toxic/tort com. 1990), Camden County Bar Assn. (comml. and environ. law com.), Burlington County Bar Assn., Justinian Soc. Roman Catholic. Avocations: golf, travel, coaching basketball. Home: 5 Winston Ct Medford NJ 08055-8200 Office: Martin Gunn Martin PA PO Box 358 216 Haddon Ave Ste 420 Westmont NJ 08108-2812

MARTIN, BURCHARD V. lawyer; b. Millville, N.J., May 9, 1933; s. William J. and Helen (Mullane) M.; m. Elizabeth Del Rossi, June 11, 1955; children: Doris, Burchard S., William J., Thomas O. BS in Econs., Villanova (Pa.) U., 1954, LLB, 1958. Bar: N.J. 1960, U.S. Dist. Ct. N.J. 1960, U.S. Ct. Appeals (3d cir.), U.S. Supreme Ct. 1976. Assoc. Carroll, Taylor & Bischoff, Camden, N.J., 1960-63; ptnr. Taylor, Bischoff, Neutze & Williams, Camden, 1963-70, Taylor, Bischoff, Williams & Martin, Camden, 1970-72, Martin, Crawshaw & Mayfield, Haddonfield-Westmont, N.J., 1972-91, Martin, Gunn & Martin, Westmont, 1991—. Bd. cons. Villanova Law Sch., 1983—. Recipient Trial Bar award, Trial Attys. of N.J., 1987. Fellow Am. Coll. Trial Lawyers (state chmn. 1982-83); mem. ABA, N.J. Bar Assn., Camden County Bar Assn. (bd. dirs., Peter J. Devine award 1981). Avocation: golf. Office: Martin Gunn & Martin PA 216 Haddon Ave Apt 420 Collingswood NJ 08108-2812

MARTIN, CAROL JACQUELYN, artist, educator; b. Ft. Worth, Tex., Oct. 6, 1943; d. John Warren and Dorothy Lorene (Coffman) Edwards; m. Boe Willis Martin, Oct. 6, 1940; children: Stephanie Diane, Scott Andrew. BA summa cum laude, U. N. Tex., 1965; MA, U. Tex., El Paso, 1967. Tchr. Edgemere Elem. Sch., El Paso, Tex., 1965—66, Fulmore Jr. H.S., Austin, Tex., 1966-67, Monnig Jr. H.S., Ft. Worth, 1967-68, Paschal H.S., Ft. Worth, 1968-69; instr. Tarrant County Jr. Coll., Ft. Worth, 1968-69, 71-72; press sec. U.S. Sen. Gaylord Nelson, Washington, 1969-71; instr. Eastfield CC, Dallas, 1981, Richland CC Dist., 1982; instr. Meml. Student Ctr. UPlus Tex. A&M U., 2002—03. Artist Vt. Studio Ctr., 1998. Editor The Avesta Mag., 1964-65; exhibited in group shows at City of Richardson's Cottonwood Park, 1970-86, Students of Ann Cushing Gantz, 1973-85, Art About Town, 1979, 80, shows by Tarrant County and Dallas County art assns. Mem. Nat. Mus. Women in Arts; mem. Friends Assn. of the Brazos Valley Symphony Orch., Brenham Fine Arts League, Brazos Valley Symphony Orch., Friends of Meml. Student Ctr.-Opera and Performing Arts Soc., The Woman's Club. Mem. Internat. Platform Assn., Mortar Bd., Lone Star Art Guild, Brazos Valley Art League, The Friends Assn. Symphony Orch., Brazos Valley Symphony Soc., The Women's Club, Nat. Women in Arts, Alpha Chi, Sigma Tau Delta, Kappa Delta Pi, Delta Gamma. Democrat. Methodist. Avocations: travel, photography, skiing, painting. Address: 4055 Sweetwater Dr College Station TX 77845-9650

MARTIN, CAROLINE JUNE, state senator; b. Brownsville, Tex., Feb. 28, 1952; d. W.J. Funkhouser and Lucille Cherry; married. Owner jewelry store; mem. Okla. State Senate, 1994—. Mem. Agr. and Rural Devel., Appropriations, Edn., Sunset Rev., Tourism and Recreation, Transp. coms. Okla. State Senate. Promoted Chisholm Trail Commn. for Econ. Devel. through Tourism; mem. Eagle Forum of Okla., Christian Coalition; active Ray of Hope Ch., Comanche, Okla.; lobied for locally controlled edn., right-to-life and econ. devel. issues. Republican. Office: State Capitol Bldg 2300 N Lincoln Blvd Rm 529B Oklahoma City OK 73105-4805

MARTIN, CAROLYN A. (BIDDY MARTIN), provost; BA in English, Coll. of William and Mary, 1973; PhD in German Lit., U. Wis., 1985. Mem. faculty Cornell U., Ithaca, NY, 1983—, sr. assoc. dean Coll. Arts and Scis., 1977—2000, univ. provost, 2000—. Grad. field rep. for German studies Cornell U., 1991—96, grad. field rep., co-founder lesbian and gay studies, 1992—96, assoc. dir. program women's studies, 1993—94, chair dept. German studies, 1994—97. Author: numerous books; contbr. articles to profl. jours.; mem. edtl. bd.: Studies in Gender and Sexuality, New German Critique, Gay and Lesbian Quar., Diacritics, Signs, Women in German. Mem.: Phi Beta Kappa. Office: Office of the Provost Cornell U Ithaca NY 14853

MARTIN, CHESTER Y. sculptor, painter; b. Chattanooga, Nov. 2, 1934; s. Woodfin Ballenger and Mabel Willett (Young) M.; m. Patricia Ann Parnell, Aug. 15, 1963; 1 child, Sharon Elizabeth (Mrs. Christopher Pruitt). Student, U. Chattanooga, 1952-55, 60-61, Internat. Medallic Workshop-Pa. State U., 1984. Freelance artist, Chattanooga, 1967-86; sculptor, engraver U.S. Mint, Phila., 1986-92. One-man shows include Hunter Mus. Art, Chattanooga, 1979; group shows: Kottler Galleries, N.Y.C., 1966; Internat. Exposition Contemporary Medals, Italy, 1983, Sweden, 1985, Finland, 1990; U.S. Dept. State, 1984, Nat. Sculpture Soc., N.Y.C., 1984, 85, 99, Cast Iron Gallery, N.Y.C., 1992, Internat. Exhbn. of Contemporary Medals, Brit. Mus., London, 1992, Hungarian Nat. Gallery, Budapest, 1994, Neuchatel, 1996, Nat. Sculpture Soc., N.Y.C., 1999, Weimar, 2000, Paris Mint, 2002, Lisbon, 2004, numerous others; permanent collections: British Mus., London; Smithsonian Instn.; Food and Agrl. Orgn., Rome; Am. Numismatic Soc., N.Y.C.; Julius Wile Sons and Co., N.Y.C.; Brookgreen Gardens, S.C., U.S. Mint, Phila.; major comms.: World Food Day Medal, UN, 1984, others; other major works: History of Chattanooga Mural, 1974; theme painting of Br. Colonial Ft. Loudon, 1975; Centennial Mural for Chattem Inc., Chattanooga, 1980; sculptured Congl. Bicentennial Silver Dollar, 1989, Eisenhower Centennial Dollar reverse, Mt. Rushmore Dollar obverse, 1991; designer Andrew Wyeth Congl. medal, 1989, George H.W. Bush Presdl. medal reverse; designer Yosemite Nat. Park Centennial Congressional Medal, 1991, Gen. Colin L. Powell Congressional Medal, 1992, White House Bicentennial Dollar reverse, 1992; designer mural Chattanooga Met. Airport, 1999. Served with USAF, 1956-60. Recipient numerous art awards, most recent being Purchase award Benedictine Art Competition, 1975, Medallic Sculpture award Am. Numismatic Assn., 1993. Mem. Fedn. Internationale de la Medaille (Am. del.), Am. Medallic Sculpture Assn. (v.p. 1987). Methodist. Avocation: modern languages. Mailing: 4110 Sunbury Ave Chattanooga TN 37411-5232 Office Phone: 423-698-3561.

MARTIN, CHRIS, vocalist; b. Devon, England, Mar. 2, 1977; m. Gwenyth Paltrow, 2003; 1 child, Apple Blythe Alison. Student in Ancient World Studies, U. Coll. London. Sign painter; vocalist, pianist, rhythm guitarist Coldplay, 1998—. Singer: (albums) Parachutes, 2000 (Grammy award: Best Alternative Music Album, 2001), A Rush of Blood to the Head, 2002 (Grammy awards: Best Alternative Music Album, 2002, Best Rock Performance By A Duo Or Group With Vocal for song "In My Place", 2002, Record Of The Yr. for song "Clocks", 2003), Live 2003, 2003. Office: Capital Records 1750 North Vine St 10th Fl Hollywood CA 90028*

MARTIN, CLARENCE EUGENE, III, lawyer; b. Martinsburg, W.Va., Mar. 24, 1946; s. Clarence Eugene Jr. and Catherine Dubois (Silver) M.; m. Judith Anne Gray; 2 children: McKenna Gray Martin, Morgan Elizabeth Martin. AB in English, U. Ariz., 1968; JD, Cath. U., Washington, 1974. Bar: W. Va. 1974, D.C. 1974, Md. 1987, Pa., 1992, U.S. Dist. Ct. D.C. 1975, U.S. Ct. Appeals (D.C. cir.) 1975, U.S. Dist. Ct. (no. dist.) W.Va. 1976, U.S. Dist. Ct. (so. dist.) W.Va., U.S. Dist. Ct. Md. 1986, U.S. Ct. Appeals (4th cir.) 1976, U.S. Supreme Ct. 1979, U.S. Dist. Ct. (no. and ea. dists.) Pa. 1984, U.S. Ct. Appeals (3d cir.) 1984. Asst. couonsel U.S. Ho. Reps., Washington, 1974-75; trial atty. U.S. Dept. Justice, 1975-76; assoc. Martin & Seibert, L.C., Martinsburg, 1976-79, ptnr., 1979—. Bd. dirs. Mchts. & Farmers Bank, Martinsburg, W.Va. Legal Svcs. Plan. Author: (seminar) Impeachment of Witnesses, 1984; co-author ABA publ. Emerging Problems Under the Federal Rules of Evidence, 2d edit., Bad Faith Litigation, The Ethics of Surveillance. Mem. W.Va. Ho. Dels., Charleston, 1976-82; trustee Nat. Parks and Conservation Assn., Washington, 1980-85; bd. govs. Def. Trial Counsel W.Va., 1984-92; commr. Interstate Commn. Potomac River Basin, 1980-86, U.S. Commn. on Agrl. Workers, 1988-94; bd. advs. Shepherd Coll., 1989-93, 95-99, chmn. 1990-93, 95-97; mem. bd. visitors Cath. U. Sch. Law; mem. W.Va. Coun. Cmty. and Econ. Devel.; chmn. W.Va. Devel. Found., W.Va. Devel. Corp.; pres. Discover the Real W.Va. Found.; mem. Greater Ea. Panhandle Ch. Com., 1988—, chmn. 1988—; chmn. St. Joseph's Parish Coun., 1997-99; pres. Washington-Balt. chpt. Patrons of the Arts in the Vatican Mus.; bd. dirs. Region IX Planning and Devel. Coun., Holy Family Hosp. Found.; mem. Berkeley County Devel. Authority. Recipient Am. Jurisprudence Scholastic Achievement award, 1972, Assn. Govt. Employees award, 1980. Fellow W.Va. Bar Found.; mem. ABA, W.Va. Bar Assn. (pres. 1990-91), W.Va. State Bar, D.C. Bar Assn., Berkeley County Bar Assn. (pres. 1984), Nat. Assn. R.R. Trial Counsel, Am. Legis. Exch. Coun., Am. Judicature Soc., Def. Rsch. Inst., D.C. Bar Assn., Md. Bar Assn., Pa. Bar Assn., Am. Bd. Trial Advocates (bd. dirs. 1986-94), Internat. Assn. Def. Counsel, Def. Trial Counsel of W.Va. (founding mem., bd. dirs. 1984-92), Md. Def. Trial Counsel, W.Va. Law Inst., Berkeley County Roundhouse Authority (chmn. 1999—), W.Va. C. of C. (bd. dirs.), John Carroll Soc., KC, Univ. Club, Order of Malta (bd. dirs. 2003-). Home: Pendleton House 6393 Arden Nollville Rd Martinsburg WV 25401-8866 Office: Martin & Seibert LC PO Box 1286 Martinsburg WV 25402-1286 Office Phone: 304-262-3213. E-mail: cemartin@martinandseibert.com.

MARTIN, CLAUDE RAYMOND, JR., marketing consultant, educator; b. Harrisburg, May 11, 1932; s. Claude R. and Marie Teresa (Stapf) M.; m. Marie Frances Culkin, Nov. 16, 1957; children: Elizabeth Ann, David Jude, Nancy Marie, William Jude, Patrick Jude, Cecelia Marie. BS, U. Scranton, 1954, M.B.A, 1963; PhD, Columbia U., 1969. Newsman Sta. WILK-TV, Wilkes-Barre, Pa., 1953-55; news dir. Sta. WNEP-TV, Scranton, Pa., 1955-60; dir. systems Blue Cross & Blue Shield Ins., Wilkes-Barre, 1960-63; lectr. mktg. St. Francis Coll., Bklyn., 1964, U. Mich., Ann Arbor, 1965-68, asst. prof., 1968-73, asso. prof., 1973-77, prof., 1977-80, Isadore and Leon Winkelman prof. retail mktg., 1980—92, chmn. mktg. dept., 1986-90, prof. retail mktg. Isadore and Loen Winkerman, 1992—. Bd. dirs. Perry Drug Stores, cons. mktg., 1983-89; spl. cons. on rsch. changes in U.S. currency Fed. Res. Sys., 1978—; pub. mem. Nat. Advt. Rev. Bd., 1989-94. Contbr. articles to profl. jours. Trustee U. Scranton, 1996—. Served with USNR, 1955-57. Mem. Acad. Mktg. Sci., Am. Mktg. Assn., S.W. Mktg. Assn., Bank Mktg. Assn., Assn. Consumer Rsch., Am. Collegiate Retailing Assn., Am. Acad. Advt. (Disting. Fellow). Roman Catholic. Home: 1116 Aberdeen Dr Ann Arbor MI 48104-2812 Office Phone: 734-764-1391. Personal E-mail: claudemartinjr@hotmail.com.

MARTIN, CLYDE VERNE, psychiatrist; b. Coffeyville, Kans., Apr. 7, 1933; s. Howard Verne and Elfrieda Louise (Moehn) Martin; m. Barbara Jean McNeilly, June 24, 1956; children: Kent Clyde, Kristin Claire, Kerry Constance, Kyle Curtis. Student, Coffeyville Coll., 1951—52; AB, U. Kans., 1955, MD, 1958; MA, Webster Coll., St. Louis, 1977; JD, Thomas Jefferson Coll. Law, L.A., 1985. Diplomate Am. Bd. Psychiatry and Neurology. Intern Lewis Gale Hosp., Roanoke, Va., 1958—59; resident in psychiatry U. Kans. Med. Ctr., Kansas City, 1959—62, Fresno br. U. Calif.-San Francisco, 1978; staff psychiatrist Neurol. Hosp., Kansas City, 1962; practice medicine specializing in psychiatry Kansas City, Mo., 1964—84; founder, med. dir., pres. bd. dirs. Mid-Continent Psychiat. Hosp., Olathe, Kans., 1972—84; adj. prof. psychology Baker U., Baldwin City, Kans., 1969—84; staff psychiatrist Atascadero State Hosp., Calif., 1984—85; clin. prof. psychiatry U. Calif., San Francisco, 1985—; chief psychiatrist Calif. Med. Facility, Vacaville, 1985—87. Pres., editor Corrective and Social Psychiatry, Olathe, 1970—84, Atascadero, 1984—85, Fairfield, Calif., 1985—97; cons. psychiatrist Brit. Health Svc. Plymouth (Eng.) Trust, 1999—2001. Contbr. articles to profl. jours. Bd. dirs. Meth. Youthville, Newton, Kans., 1965—75, Spofford Home, Kansas City, 1974—78; del. Kans. East Conf. Meth. Ch., 1972—80, bd. global ministries, 1974—80. Served to capt. USAF, 1962—64, ret. col. USAF. Scholar Oxford Law and Soc., 1993. Fellow: Am. Orthopsychiat. Assn., World Assn. Social Psychiatry, Royal Soc. Health (London), Am. Assn. Mental Health Profls. in Corrections, Am. Psychiat. Assn.; mem.: AMA, Assn. Mental Health Adminstrs. (cert.), Am. Assn. Sex Educators, Counselors and Therapists (cert.), Assn. for Advancement Psychotherapy, St. James Club (London), Capitol Hill Club (Washington), Marines Meml. Club (San Francisco), Pi Kappa Alpha, Phi Beta Pi. Office: PO Box 3365 Fairfield CA 94533-0587 Office Phone: 707-688-3790. Business E-Mail: cvkcmartin@msn.com.

MARTIN, CRAIG LEE, engineering company executive; b. Dodge City, Kans., Nov. 23, 1949; s. Ray N. and Nadia C. Martin; m. Diane E. Hensley, Mar. 19, 1977. BSCE, U. Kans., 1971; MBA, U. Denver, 1982. Project mgr. Martin K. Eby Constrn. Co., Wichita, Kans., 1972-83; exec. v.p., COO CRSS Constructors, Inc., Denver, 1983-89; exec. v.p. CRSS Comml. Group, Houston, 1989-90; sr. v.p. CRSS Capital, Houston, 1990-92, CRSS Inc., Houston, 1992-94; pres. CRSS Architects, Inc., Houston, 1992-94; sr. v.p. ops. Jacobs Engring. Group Inc., 1994-95; pres. Jacobs Constructors, Inc., 1994-95; sr. v.p. gen. sales and mktg. Jacobs Engring. Group, Inc., 1995-2000, exec. v.p. global sales, 2000—02, pres., 2002—. Adv. bd. Constrn. Bus. Rev., 1993—. Bd. govs. Woodbury U. Sch. Bus. Mem. ASCE. Avocations: golf, clay shooting. Home: 930 S El Molino Ave Pasadena CA 91106-4414 Office: Jacobs Engring Group Inc 1111 S Arroyo Pkwy Pasadena CA 91105-3254 Office Phone: 626-578-6813. Business E-Mail: craig.martin@jacobs.com.

MARTIN, CURTIS, professional football player; b. Pitts., Pa, May 1, 1973; Student, U. Pitts. Running back New Eng. Patriots, Foxboro, Mass., 1995—98, N.Y. Jets, 1998—. Named to Pro Bowl, 1995, 1996, 1998, 2001. Office: care NY Jets 1000 Fulton Ave Hempstead NY 11550-1030

MARTIN, DALLAS REA, lawyer; b. Kansas City, Kans., Aug. 3, 1954; s. H. Thayne and Frances Colleen (Hay) M.; m. Lianne Marie Taylor, June 2, 1979; 1 child, Elise Taylor. BA in Philosophy with honors and distinction, U. Kans., Lawrence, 1976, JD, 1979. Bar: Kans. 1979, U.S. Dist. Ct. Kans., 1979, U.S. Ct. Appeals (10th cir.) 1979, Colo. 1985, U.S. Dist. Ct. Colo. 1985. Pvt. practice, Olathe, Kans., 1979-81; contracts counsel Midwest Rsch. Inst., Kansas City, Mo., 1981-84; counsel and contracts mgr. Precision Visuals, Inc., Boulder, Colo., 1984-90; mgr. tech. transfer Nat. Renewable Energy Lab., Golden, Colo., 1990-94; dir. intellectual property, tech. transfer office U.S. West Advt. Tech., Inc., Boulder, 1994-97; sr. counsel intellectual property First Data Corp., Englewood, Colo., 1997-2000; v.p., gen. counsel, sec. Switch-Point Networks, Inc., Englewood, 2001—. Contbr. articles to profl. jours. Bd. dirs. Blue Knights, Inc., Denver, 1997—. Mem. ABA (intellectual property sect. 1991—), Tech. Transfer Soc. (bd. dirs. 1996-98), Licensing Execs. Soc. (co-chair Denver chpt. 2001—). Office: SwitchPoint Networks Inc 4582 S Ulster St Denver CO 80237 Home: 4991 Sanford Cir W Cherry Hills Village CO 80110-5128 E-mail: drmartin@switchpointnetworks.com.

MARTIN, DANIEL C. surgeon, gynecologist, educator; b. St. Louis, Apr. 7, 1946; s. Dan Allen and Ruth Keel (Fields) M.; m. Glenn Ann Blakemore, July 7, 1970; children: Josh, Adam. BS in Physics, Emory U., 1968, MD, 1972. Diplomate Am. Bd. Ob-Gyn. Rsch. asst. physics and radiology Emory U., Atlanta, 1968-69; intern, resident, fellow, instr. The Johns Hopkins Med. Instns., Balt., 1972-77; from asst. prof. to clin. asst. prof. U. Tenn., Memphis, 1977-90, clin. assoc. prof., 1990—; surgeon Reproductive Surgery, P.C., Memphis, 1977—. Gynecologist, reproductive surgeon Bapt. Meml. Hosp., 1977—; Axel Munthe presenter, Naples, Italy, 1992; guest spkr. 15th Annual Japanese Endometrosis Symposium, Osaka, 1994; dir. gynecologic laser and endoscopy workshops, 1982-93. Editor: (textbooks) Lasers in Endoscopy, 1990, Laparoscopic Appearance of Endometriosis, 1990, Manual of Endoscopy, 1990, Atlas of Endometriosis, 1993, Endoscopic Management of Gynecologic Disease, 1996. Basketball coach Grace St. Luke's Ch., Memphis, 1992-95. Picker Found. fellow Emory U., 1969; Tex. Assn. Ob-Gyn. hon. fellow, 1989; recipient Bridges trophy for athletics Emory U., 1968, Codman surg. award, 1982, 83, Video award Am. Fertility Soc., 1992, Physician Recognition awrd Endometriosis Assn., 1995; named one of Best Drs. Am. Woodward and White Inc., 1992, 94, 96, 98, 00,02, 04, Hon. mem. Australian Gynecol. Endoscopy Soc., 1993. Mem. ACOG (sect. chair jr. fellows Md.), Tenn. Med. Assn., Memphis and Shelby County Med. Soc. (comm. com.), Am. Nat. Std. Inst. (subcom. on laser safety in med. facility), Am. Assn. Gynecol. Laparoscopists (pres. 1990-91, Videoendoscopy award 1993), Gynecologic Surgery Soc. (pres. 1994-96, chmn. bd. 1996-98), Australian Gynecol. Endoscopy Soc. (hon.), Argentinian Ob-Gyn. Soc. (hon.). Office: Martin Ctr for Women's Health and Fertility PC 6215 Humphreys Blvd Ste 450 Memphis TN 38120 Office Phone: 901-751-0300. E-mail: DrDanMartin@aol.com.

MARTIN, DANIEL FRANCIS, small business owner; b. Kansas City, Mo., Feb. 26, 1949; s. Clyde Edwin and Mirium Eve (Zimmerman) Martin; m. Rita Kaye Hurst, Mar. 1, 1951; children: Bridgett Ann (Martin) Coe, Kevin Douglas. BS in Edn., Huntington Coll., Ind., 1972. Owner Martin's Automotive, Kendallville, Ind., 1970—85; v.p. All States Auction Co., 1973—75; owner Martin Distbn., 1990—2002, On Stage Promotions, 1982—92, Martin Mfg., 1985—. V.p. Rollin Oldies Antique Car Club, Kendallville, Ind., 1980—83. Coach little league basketball Cole Ctr. YMCA, Kendallville, Ind., 1991, 1993. Recipient Am. Heritage award, Bay Car Show, Mich., 2003, numerous classic and antique car show awards. Democrat. Methodist. Avocations: collecting old cars, writing, collectibles. Home: 424 Garden St Kendallville IN 46755

MARTIN, DANIEL RICHARD, pharmaceutical company executive; b. Lima, Peru, June 9, 1937; s. James Marion and Clemmy Caroline (Valencia) M.; m. Barbara Artemis Cyrus, June 23, 1962; children: Daniel Richard Jr., John Alexander, Christopher Andrew. BA, Cornell U., 1958; MS, Columbia U., N.Y.C., 1959. Area sales supr. Schering Corp., Bloomfield, N.J., 1960-64; assoc. McKinsey & Co., N.Y.C., 1964-69; treas. Harper & Row, Pubs., N.Y.C., 1969-72; mng. dir. Merck & Co., Rahway, N.J., 1972-77; group v.p. Bell & Howell Co., Chgo., 1977-80; pres. Howland Martin Corp., N.Y.C., 1980-85; pres. Sterling Europe, Middle East, Africa Sterling Drug, Inc., N.Y.C., 1986-89; pres., CEO, also bd. dirs. E-Z-EM, Inc., Westbury, N.Y., 1990-97; pres., also bd. dirs. Milestone Scientific, Inc., Livingston, N.J., 1998-99. Adj. prof. mgmt. Pace U., N.Y.C., 1996—. Co-chmn. Accion Internat., Cambridge,

Mass., 1988-98; trustee Bangor (Maine) Theol. Sem., 1991-2000; dir. Americas Found.; bd. dirs., fin. com. White Plains (N.Y.) Hosp. Decorated Order of Merit (Ecuador). Mem. Coun. on Fgn. Rels., Americas Soc., Cornell Club (N.Y.C.). Independent. Congregationalist. Home: 31 Rochambeau Dr Hartsdale NY 10530-3017 E-mail: drm1937@aol.com.

MARTIN, DARRYL JAMES, audio-visual specialist; b. St. Albans, N.Y., Sept. 4, 1950; s. Sydney and Helen Martin; m. Theresa McCarthy, July 29, 1978 (div. 1986); children: Jamielynn, Kristina Marie. Student in bus. adminstrn., Nassau C.C., 1971-73; assoc. in fire sci., Fire Svc. Acad., 1971-78; paramedic tng. in advanced cardiac care, St. Francis Hosp., Roslyn, N.Y., 1973-77; BA in Audio Visual Tech., N.Y. Inst. Tech., 1975; M in Computer Sci. and Tech., U. Berkeley, 1999. Audio-visual coord. Farmingdale (N.Y.) Pub. Schs., 1971-79; dir. audio-visual svcs. Bethpage (N.Y.) Pub. Schs., 1979—. Audio visual coord. evening classes C.W. Post Coll., L.I.U., Green Vale, N.Y., 1982-85, lead call ctr. ops. Cablevision L.I., 1996—. Author: Security Procedures for An Educational Institution, 19981, Poems of the Heart, 1990, Class of 68, 1991, Suffer In Silence, 1999. Engine capt. Bethpage Fire Dept., 1972-82. With U.S. Army, 1968-71. Mem. Nat. Assn. Ednl. Radio, N.Y. State Ednl. Comm. Assn., Nat. Audio Visual Assn. Home: 36 Acme Ave Bethpage NY 11714-4610 Office: Bethpage Pub Schs Adminstrn Bldg Cherry Ave Bethpage NY 11714

MARTIN, DAVID ALAN, law educator; b. Indpls., July 23, 1948; s. C. Wendell and Elizabeth Bowman (Meeker) M.; m. Cynthia Jo Lorman, June 13, 1970; children: Amy Lynn, Jeffrey David. BA, DePauw U., 1970; JD, Yale U., 1975. Bar: D.C. Law clk. to Hon. J. Skelly Wright U.S. Ct. Appeals (D.C. cir.), 1975-76; law clk. to Hon. Lewis F. Powell U.S. Supreme Ct., Washington, 1976-77; assoc. Rogovin, Stern & Huge, Washington, 1977-78; spl. asst. bur. human rights and humanitarian affairs U.S. State Dept., Washington, 1978-80; from asst. prof. to assoc. prof. U. Va. Sch. Law, Charlottesville, 1980-86, prof., 1986-91, Henry L. & Grace Doherty prof. law, 1991—2003, F. Palmer Weber Rsch. prof. civil liberties and human rights, 1992—95, 2000—03, Warner-Booker disting. prof. internat. law, 2003—, Class of 1963 rsch. prof., 2004—. Cons. Adminstrv. Conf. U.S., Washington, 1988-89, 91-92, U.S. Dept. Justice, 1993-95, U.S. Dept. of State, 2003-04; gen. counsel U.S. Immigration and Naturalization Svc., 1995-98. Author: Immigration: Process and Policy, 1985, 5th edit., 2003, Asylum Case Law Sourcebook, 1994, 4th edit., 2003, The Endless Quest: Helping America's Farm Workers, 1994; editor: The New Asylum Seekers, 1988, Immigration Admissions, 1998, Immigration Controls, 1998, Rights and Duties of Dual Nationals: Evolution and Prospects, 2002; mem. bd. editors Am. Jour. Internat. Law, 2004—; contbr. articles to profl. jours. Nat. governing bd. Common Cause, Washington, 1972-75; elder Westminster Presbyn. Ch., Charlottesville, 1982-84, 89-92; bd. dirs. Internat. Rescue Com., 2000—; bd. editors Am. Jour. Internat. Law, 2004-. German Marshall Fund Rsch. fellow, Geneva, 1984-85. Mem. Am. Soc. Internat. Law (v.p. 2003—, Book award 1986), Internat. Law Assn. Democrat. Office: U Va Sch Law 580 Massie Rd Charlottesville VA 22903-1738 Office Phone: 434-924-3144.

MARTIN, DAVID EDWARD, health sciences educator; b. Green Bay, Wis., Oct. 1, 1939; s. Edward Henry and Lillie (Luckman) M. BS, U. Wis., 1961, MS, 1963, PhD, 1970. Ford Found. research trainee Wis. Regional Primate Ctr., Madison, 1967-70; asst. prof. health scis. Ga. State U., Atlanta, 1970-74, assoc. prof., 1974-80, prof., 1980-91, regents prof., 1992-00, regents prof. emeritus, 2000—. Affiliate scientist Yerkes Primate Rsch. Ctr., Emory U., Atlanta, 1970-98; U.S. rep. to Internat. Olympic Acad., 1978; sports medicine rsch. assoc. U.S. Olympic Com., 1981-84; chmn. sports scis. U.S.A. Track and Field; mem. coaching staff U.S. teams to world championships in distance running, Rome, 1982, Gateshead, Eng., 1983, Budapest, Hungary, 1994, Vilamoura, Portugal, 2000, head coach, Paris, 1980, Madrid, 1984, Hiroshima, Japan, 1985, Warsaw, Poland, 1987, Antwerp, Belgium, 1991; mem. Olympic med. support group Atlanta Olympic Games. Author: Laboratory Experiments in Human Physiology, 4th edit., 1980, The Marathon Footrace, 1979, La Corsa Di Maratona, 1982, The High Jump Book, 1982, The High Jump Book, 2d edit., 1987, Respiratory Anatomy and Physiology, 1987, Training Distance Runners, 1991, Training Distance Runners, 2d edit., 1997, Training Distance Runners, German edit., 1992, Training Distance Runners, Spanish edit., 1995, Training Distance Runners, Japanese edit., 2001, The Olympic Marathon, 2000. Trustee Ga. Found. for Athletic Excellence. Recipient fed. and univ. grants for physiol. research; named Disting. prof. Ga. State U., 1975, 81, 85 Fellow Am. Coll. Sports Medicine; mem. Internat. Soc. Olympic Historians, Am. Physiol. Soc., Atlanta Track Club. Home: 510 Coventry Rd Apt 13A Decatur GA 30030-5038 Office: Ga State U Dept Cardiopul Care Atlanta GA 30303 Office Phone: 404-651-1499. Business E-Mail: drdave@gsu.edu.

MARTIN, DAVID GEORGE, historian, Latin educator, author; b. Midland, Mich., Feb. 8, 1949; s. Robert A. Martin and Viola B. Weaver; 1 child, Peter Joseph Martin. BA, U. Mich., 1971; MA, Princeton (N.J.) U., 1973, PhD, 1975. Latin instr. The Peddie Sch., Hightstown, N.J., 1975—. Editor Longstreet House, Hightstown, N.J., Combined Publs., Conshohocken, Pa. Author: Gettysburg, July 1, 1995 (award 1997), Jackson's Valley Campaign, 1988; co-author: Regimental Strengths at Gettysburg, 1982; author, editor 20 books on civil war. Recipient Good Citizenship award N.J. Dept. Sons of Union Vets. of the Civil War, 1984, 96. Fellow Company of Mil. Historians; mem. SAR, N.J. Civil War Heritage Assn. (2d v.p. 1998—), Friends of Monmouth Battlefield (bd. trustees 1996—), Sons of the Unions Vets. of the Civil War (comdr. N.J. dept. 1993-95), Sons of Vets. Res. (capt. 1990-92). Office: The Peddie Sch South Main St Hightstown NJ 08520

MARTIN, DAVID HUBERT, internist, epidemiologist, educator; b. Detroit, Mar. 24, 1943; s. Hubert Cillis and Mable Anita (Stewart) M.; m. Jane Ellen Schlichtemeier, Nov. 22, 1970; children: Jennifer, Jason. BA with distinction, U. Kans., 1965; MD cum laude, Harvard Coll., 1969. Diplomate Nat. Bd. Med. Examiners, Am. Bd. Internal Medicine, Infectious Disease Subspecialty Bd. Am. Bd. Internal Medicine. Intern Bronx (N.Y.) Mcpl. Hosp. Ctr., 1969-70; staff assoc. Nat. Inst. Allergy and Infectious Diseases, Mid. Am. Rsch. Unit, NIH, Panama Canal Zone, 1970-73; med. resident U. Wash. Affiliated Hosps., 1973-75; sr. fellow in infectious diseases U. Wash., 1976-78; chief resident in medicine USPHS Hosp., Seattle, 1975-76, staff internal medicine clinic, 1975, attending physician internal medicine, 1976-78, staff dept. internal medicine New Orleans, 1979-81; staff Hotel Dieu Hosp., New Orleans, 1982-94; clin. asst. prof. medicine La. State U. Med. Sch., New Orleans, 1979-81, asst. prof. medicine divsn. infectious diseases, 1981-82, assoc. prof. medicine divsn. infectious diseases, 1982-88, assoc. prof. microbiology, 1986-88, prof. internal medicine and microbiology, 1988, asst. chief sect. infectious diseases, 1988-89, chief sect. infectious diseases, 1990—, Harry E. Dascomb M.D. prof. of medicine, 1990—. Instr. dept. medicine U. Wash. Sch. Medicine, Seattle, 1975-78, acting asst. prof. medicine, 1978-79; chmn. infection control com., chmn. instnl. rev. bd. human rsch. com., chmn. antibiotic utilization com., sec. rsch. and editl. com., sec. animal welfare com. USPHS Hosp., New Orleans, 1979-81, dep. chief clin. rsch. dept., 1979-81, chmn. credentials com., 1980-81; mem. infection control com. Hotel Dieu Hosp., New Orleans, 1983-84, chmn. pharmacy and therapeutics com., 1988-94, mem. infection control com., 1990-94; vis. physician Charity Hosp. (now Med. Ctr. of La. at New Orleans), New Orleans, 1982—, chmn. antibiotics com., 1982—, dir. infection control program, 1993—, chmn. infection control com., 1993—, vice chmn. pharmacy and therapeutics com., 1995—; chmn. comprehensive medicine head search com. La. State U. Med. Sch., 1989-90, dept. medicine faculty promotion com., 1988—, AIDS policy com., 1992; adv. bd. La. State Labs., 1993—, State La. Pub. Health Lab. Adv. Com., 1994—, U.S. Pub. Health Region 6 Infertility Prevention Adv. Com., 1995—; mem. nat. STD treatment guidelines com. Ctrs. Disease Control, 1993, 98. nat. Chlamydia and gonorrheadiagnosis guidelines com., 1997—; dir. La. STD/HIV rsch. ctr., 2001-04, Gulf South STI/TM Collaborative Rsch. Ctr., 2004—. Peer reviewer various jours. including Sexually Transmitted Diseases, The Jour. of Infectious Diseases, The Am. Jour. of the Med. Scis., Archives of Internal Medicine, Clin. Infectious Diseases, New Eng. Jour. Medicine, Annals Internal Medicine, Jour. AMA; contbr. chpts. to books and articles to profl. jours. Dir. La. STD/HIV Rsch. Ctr., 2002—. With USPHS, 1970-82. Achievements include established the first chlamydia laboratory in the Gulf South. Fellow ACP (La. chpt. program chmn. 1994-95), Infectious Diseases Soc. Am.; mem. Internat. Soc. for Sexually Transmitted Disease Rsch. (bd. dirs. 1991-99, chmn. 1995 meeting organizing com., pres. 1993-95, sec.-treas. 1999—), Am. Fedn. for Clin. Rsch., Am. Sexually Transmitted Diseases Assn. (v.p. 1992-94, pres. 1994-96), Am. Soc. for Microbiology, European Soc. for Clin. Microbiology and Infectious Diseases, So. Soc. for Clin. Investigation, La./Miss. Infectious Diseases Soc. (bd. dirs., sci. program chmn. 1993, pres. 1997-99), Phi Beta Kappa. Achievements include research in the effect of sexually transmitted microorganisms on pregnancy outcome, antibiotic treatment of sexually transmitted diseases and in particular C. trachomatis, epidemiology of C. trachomatis in normal populations, chancroid and other genital ulcer diseases. Office: La State U Med Sch 1542 Tulane Ave New Orleans LA 70112-2825

MARTIN, DAVID O'BRIEN, congressman; b. St. Lawrence County, N.Y., Apr. 26, 1944; s. Edson Albert and Anne (O'Brien) M.; children: Victoria, Kelly, Julia. BBA, U. Notre Dame, 1966; JD, Albany Law Sch., 1973. Mem. N.Y. State Assembly from 112th Dist., 1977-80; mem. 97th-102nd Congresses from 26th N.Y. dist., 1981—. Served to capt. USMC, 1966-70, Vietnam. Mem. ABA, N.Y. State Bar Assn., Am. Legion. Clubs: Elks. Republican. Roman Catholic. Office: US Ho of Reps Cannon House Office Bldg Rm 442 Washington DC 20515-0001

MARTIN, DAVID S. retired secondary school educator, administrator; b. N.Y.C., May 14, 1941; s. Perry Johnson and Polly Edith (Shedlov) M.; m. Florence E. Martin, Jan. 14, 1989; children: Drew Michael, Amy Davida. BA, Adelphi Coll., 1962, MA, 1966; profl. cert., Hofstra U., 1969. Cert. secondary tchr., sch. dist. adminstr., N.Y. Adj. assoc. prof. Pace U., White Plains, N.Y., 1978-92; tchr., computer coord. Jericho (N.Y.) Pub. Schs., 1962-99. Author: Teachers Manual for Introduction to Pascal; co-author: How To Prepare for SAT II: Physics, 6th edit.; also author other books; contbr. articles to profl. jours. Fulbright-Hays grantee, 1967-68; recipient Grand award L.I. Sci. Congress, 1958, Disting Achievement award Electronic Learning, 1983, Outstanding Accomplishment award RITEC, 1984. Mem.: IEEE (sr.), N.Y. State United Tchrs., Assn. Computing Machinery, Am. Assn. Physics Tchrs., Jericho Retirees Assn., Flambeau, Sigma Pi Sigma, Phi Delta Kappa, Omicron Delta Kappa. Home: 16 Elm Pl Sea Cliff NY 11579-1634

MARTIN, DAVID STANDISH, education educator; b. New Bedford, Mass., Aug. 24, 1937; s. Theodore Tripp and Elinor Louise (Raymond) M.; m. Susan Katherine Orowan, June 30, 1962. BA, Yale U., 1959; MEd, Harvard U., 1961, CAS, 1968; PhD, Boston Coll., 1971. Cert. tchr., prin. Tchr. Newton (Mass.) Pub. Schs., 1961-68, asst. prin., 1969-70; teaching asst. Boston Coll., Chestnut Hill, Mass., 1968-69; curriculum dir. Beverly (Mass.) Pub. Schs., 1970-73; prin. Mill Valley (Calif.) Pub. Schs., 1973-75, curriculum dir., 1975-80; chmn. dept. edn. Dominican Coll., San Rafael, Calif., 1978-80; coordinator undergrad. tchr. edn. Gallaudet U., Washington, 1980-85, dean sch. edn. and human svcs., 1985-95, prof. edn., 1995—2001, prof., dean emeritus, 2002—. Cons. Curriculum Devel. Assocs., Washington, 1975-2001; mem. bd. examiners Nat. Coun. Accreditation Tchr. Education; bd. dirs. USA-SINO Tchr. Education Consortium, Western Pa. Sch. for the Deaf; Fulbright fellow U. Witwatersrand, South Africa, 2003; vis. rsch. prof. Open U., London. Author: Case Studies in Curriculum, 1989; editor: Cognition, Education and Deafness, 1985, Advances in Cognition Education and Deafness, 1991; contbr. articles to profl. jours. Grantee Dept. Edn., 1970, 85, Knight Found., 1995-2001, Ford Found., 1998-2001. Mem. D.C. Assn. Colls. Tchr. Edn. (pres. 1989-92), Assn. for Supervision and Curricum Devel., Nat. Coun. for Social Studies, Am. Ednl. Rsch. Assn., Am. Assn. Colls. for Tchr. Edn. (bd. dirs.), Coun. for Exceptional Children, Phi Delta Kappa, Kappa Delta Pi (chair publ.), Ednl. Consulting Schs. and Univs. (prof., dean emeritus 2002-). Democrat. Unitarian Universalist. Avocations: genealogy, sailing, classical organ, astronomy. Home and Office: 10 Colonial Farm Cir Marstons Mills MA 02648 Office Phone: 508-420-0224.

MARTIN, DAVID WARREN, management consultant; b. West Grove, Pa., Apr. 21, 1941; s. Raymond Conard and Katharine (McLimans) M.; m. Hope Wingate, Aug. 17, 1963; children: Jennifer W., Jonathan W. BA, Lincoln U., 1964; MSA, G. Washington U., 1974; grad., USAF Air War Coll., 1974; postgrad., U. Va., 1984. Tchr. of English Mt. Pleasant H.S., Wilmington, Del., 1963-66; commd. 2d lt. USAF, 1966, advanced through grades to col., 1988; ret. USAFR, 1993; pers. mgr. S.E. Nat. Bank of Pa., Malvern, 1976-81; regional pers. officer U.S. Nuclear Regulatory Commn., King of Prussia, Pa., 1981-83; sr. dir. human resources Amtrak, Washington, 1985-97; CEO, pres. HRA Svcs., Inc., Chadds Ford, Pa., 1998—. Bd. trustees Upland Sch., Kennett Sq., Pa., 1987-93, chmn. strategic planning, fin., pers. coms. Home: 582 Coatesville Rd West Grove PA 19390-9232 Office: HRA Svcs PO Box 818 Chadds Ford PA 19317-0628 E-mail: dave@hraservices.com.

MARTIN, DAVID WILLIAM, JR., biomedical research company executive, educator; b. West Palm Beach, Fla., Jan. 15, 1941; s. David W. Sr. and Joanna (Law) M.; m. Kathleen McKinnon, Aug. 22, 1964; children: David McKinnon, Gillian Hope. Student, MIT, 1958-60; MD, Duke U., 1964. Intern in internal medicine Duke U. Med. Ctr., Durham, N.C., 1964-65, asst. resident dept. medicine, 1965-66; rsch. assoc. lab. molecular biology, Nat. Inst. Arthritis and Metabolic Diseases NIH, Bethesda, Md., 1966-69; instr. dept. medicine, dept. biochemistry and biophysics U. Calif., San Francisco, 1969-70, asst. prof. medicine, chief med. genetics service, lectr. dept. biochemistry and biophysics, 1970-75, assoc. prof. medicine in residence and biochemistry in residence, chief med. genetics service, 1975-79, prof. medicine in residence and biochemistry in residence, chief med. genetics service, 1979-82; sr. v.p. R&D Genentech, Inc., South San Francisco, Calif., 1983-89; exec. v.p. R & D, Du Pont Merck Pharm. Co., Wilmington, Del., 1991-93; sr. v.p. Chiron Corp., Emeryville, Calif., 1993—97; pres. Chiron Therapeutics, Emeryville, 1993—97; pres., CEO EOS Biotechnology, Inc., San Francisco, 1997—2003; chmn., CEO GangaGen Inc., 2003—04. Sci. adv. bd. Alliance for Lupus Rsch.; bd. dirs. Varian Med. Systems Inc., Palo Alto, Calif., 1994-, Cubist Pharmaceuticals Inc., BayBio; trustee, U. Pa. Med. Ctr., 1991-93; mem. bd. overseers U. Pa. Sch. Med., Phila., 1991-93; mem. adv. bd. Ctr. Health Sci. U. Calif. Irvine, 1991; investigator Howard Hughes Med. Inst., 1974-82, dir. med. scientist tng. program, 1978-82, mem. adv. com. biotech. rsch. and program, 1986-89; mem. recombinant DNA adv. com. NIH, 1981-85. Editor Harper's Rev. Biochemistry, 18th-20th edits., 1980-85, Sci. Yr., World Book Ency., 1981-86, Jour. Biol. Chemistry, 1983-87; contbr. numerous articles to profl. jours. Adv. coun. R & D Coun. Cystic Fibrosis Found., 1983-88; bd. overseers Duke U. Comprehensive Cancer Ctr., 1985-88. Sr. surgeon, USPHS. Named Disting. Alumnus of Duke U. Sch. Medicine, 1985. Mem. Am. Fedn. Clin. Research, Am. Soc. Biol. Chemists, Am. Soc. Clin. Investigation, Assn. Am. Physicians, Western Assn. Physicians, Alpha Omega Alpha. Office: BayBio 651 Gateway Blvd Ste 1145 San Francisco CA 94080

MARTIN, DEAN FREDERICK, chemist, educator; b. Woodburn, Iowa, Apr. 6, 1933; s. Herman A. and Frances M. (Rausis) M.; m. Barbara Bursa, Dec. 22, 1956; children: Diane, Bruce, John, Paul, Brian, Eric. BA, Grinnell Coll., 1955; PhD, Pa. State U., 1958. NSF postdoctoral fellow Univ. Coll., London, 1958—59; instr. inorganic chemistry U. Ill., Champaign-Urbana, 1959—61, asst. prof., 1961—64; assoc. prof. chemistry U. South Fla., Tampa, 1964—69, prof., 1969—, Disting. Svc. prof. chemistry, 1992—. Vis. prof. physiology and pharmacology Duke, 1970-71 Author: (with Barbara B. Martin) Coordination Compounds, 1964, (with Therald Moeller) Laboratory Chemistry, 1965, Marine Chemistry, 2 vols, 1968, 70; editor (with George M. Padilla) Marine Pharmacognosy, 1973; editor Fla. Scientist, 1984—. Recipient Alumni award Grinnell Coll., 1971; USPHS rsch. career award, 1969-74; named Disting. Svc. prof., 1992—. Fellow AAAS; mem. Am. Chem. Soc., Royal Soc. Chemistry (London), Aquatic Plant Mgmt. Soc., Alpha Chi Sigma, Phi Beta Kappa, Sigma Xi. Roman Catholic. Avocation: woodworking. Home: 3402 Valencia Rd Tampa FL 33618-3950 Office: U South Fla Dept Chem 4202 E Fowler Ave Tampa FL 33620-5205 Office Phone: 813-974-2374.

MARTIN, DENISE BELISLE, magazine editor; b. West Springfield, Mass., Sept. 15, 1940; d. Paul E. and Grace A. (St Onge) Belisle; m. Roger H. Martin, Jr., Aug. 18, 1962 (div.); 1 dau., Sara B. BA magna cum laude, Smith Coll., 1961; MA, Radcliffe Coll., 1962; postgrad., U. Minn., 1968-70. Vol. Peace Corps., Colombia, 1966-68; prodn. mgr. Soho Weekly News, N.Y.C., 1976-77, assoc. editor, 1977-78, mng. editor, 1978, arts editor, 1979; assoc. editor Portfolio, N.Y.C., 1979-80, exec. editor, 1980-84; sr. editor The American Lawyer, 1984-85, editor, 1985-86, exec. editor, 1986—, Money. Mem. Phi Beta Kappa Home: 35 Bond St New York NY 10012-2426 Office: Money Time & Life Bldg Rockefeller Ctr New York NY 10020

MARTIN, DONALD JAMES, marketing professional; b. Brantford, Ont., Can., May 2, 1928; s. Norman Wilfred and Leeta Maude (Woodley) M.; m. Annette Roselyn Mills, Aug. 25, 1952; children: Paul Stuart, Cheryl Anne. PhB, Northwestern U., 1964; postgrad., U. Chgo., 1965-66. Account rep. J. Walter Thompson, Toronto, Can., 1951-56, supr. mgmt. Sao Paulo, Brazil, 1956-60, v.p. Chgo., 1960-66; dir. corp. rels. Kraft, Inc., N.Y.C., Chgo., 1966-73; v.p. external affairs Scott Paper, Phila., 1973-76; v.p. com. Conrail, Phila., 1976-79; pres. Rennoc Corp., Vineland, N.J., 1979-84, Martin Broadcasting Inc., Vineland, 1979-84; v.p. internat. paper real estate Hilton Head Island, S.C., 1979-84; pres. Marcom Inc., S.C., 1989—; talk show host Sta. WIIII-TV, 1992—. Instr. internat. mktg. Northwestern U., Evanston, Ill., 1964-66; prof. broadcast mgmt. Mercer (N.J.) Coll., 1980-83; dir. Broadcast Pioneers Am. Mgr. Hilton Head Concert Orch., 1985-89; exec. prodr. summer festival Hilton Head Eastman Sch. Music, 1986-89; bd. dirs. Hilton Head Dance Theater, 1986, 87, Cultural Coun. Hilton Head Island, 1987-90; mem. cmty. adv. bd. Hilton Head Med. Ctr. Clinics, 1995—; actor Hilton Head Playhouse. Recipient Svc. Appreciation award Sunshine Found., 1979, Outstanding Media award United Way, 1998. Mem. Rotary (Svc. Above Self award 1992-93), S. C. Yacht Club. Avocations: tennis, sailing, acting. Office: WIIII-TV Courtyard Building Ste 103 Hilton Head Island SC 29928-4637

MARTIN, DONNA LEE, retired publishing company executive; b. Detroit, Aug. 7, 1935; d. David M. Paul and Lillian (Paul); m. Rex Martin, June 5, 1956; children: Justin, Andrew. BA, Rice U., 1957. Mng. editor trade dept. Appleton-Century-Crofts Co., N.Y.C., 1961-62; dir. publs. Lycoming Coll., Williamsport, Pa., 1966-68; editor Univ. Press of Kans., Lawrence, 1971-74; mng. editor Andrews McMeel Publ., Kansas City, Mo., 1974-80, v.p., editorial dir., 1980-95, v.p., editor-at-large, 1995-98; v.p. Universal Press Syndicate, Kansas City, 1980-98. Lectr. U. Mo., Kansas City, Johnson County Cmty. Coll., Kans.; free-lance writer, editor; cons. Kansas City Star Books. Author: (adaptation) Charles Dickens' A Christmas Carol: Adapted for Theatre; contbr. articles to profl. jours. Named Disting. Alumna Rice U., 1990. Mem. Ctrl. Exchange (Kansas City), The Groucho Club (London), Phi Beta Kappa. Home: 6810 W 66th Ter Shawnee Mission KS 66202-4147 E-mail: DLPMartin@msn.com.

MARTIN, DOUGLAS KENTON, state agency administrator; s. Lonnie Douglas Martin and Ida Elwina Bryan; married, Oct. 21, 1970; m. Christina Marner, Feb. 6, 1965 (dec. June 3, 1968); children: Christopher Wyman, Kevin Wyman, Jeffery Wyman, Allison Wyman, Alicia, Thatcher. BA, Ariz. State U., 1964; BS, U. Ariz., 1969. Cert. Mine Safety Profl. Internat. Soc. of Mine Safety Profl., 1997. Bus. mgr. Valentine Enterprises, Tucson, 1966—68; project engr. Cmty. Sci. Tech., San Diego, 1968—69, Kitchell Contractors, Phoenix, 1970—72; US adminstr. Various Can. Co., Vancouver, Canada, 1972—86; owner, engr. D.K. Martin & Assoc., Phoenix, 1972—; elected Ariz. state mine insp. State of Ariz., Ariz., 1989—. Pres. Ariz. Energy Assn., Phoenix, 1972—82; commn. mem. Ariz. Emergency & Mil. Affairs, Phoenix, 1989—; co-chairman Ariz. Mex. Commn., Phoenix, 1989—; vice chmn. World Affairs Coun., Scottsdale, Ariz., 1990. Dir.: (conference) Nat. Safety Council, Mining Sec. (Chairman's Achievement, 1995). Dir. Ariz. Mine Emergency Assn., Ariz. Safety Edn. grant, U.S. Dept. Labor, 1989-2006. Mem.: Internat. Soc. of Mine Safety Profl. (life; bd. mem./treas. 1997, Disting. Svc.). Conservative. Achievements include research in successful placering. Avocation: thoroughbred breeding. Office: Ariz State Mine Inspector Capitol Tower #403 1700 W Washington Phoenix AZ 85007 Office Phone: 602-542-5971. Office Fax: 602-542-5335. Personal E-mail: asmi11@mindspring.com. E-mail: dmartin@mi.state.az.us.

MARTIN, EARIN MILLER, grant administrator, program director, educator, trainer; b. Austin, Tex., July 6, 1952; d. Alse Edward Jr. and Wilma Nell (Maufrais) Ethridge; m. Paul Chapman Goggan, Jan. 11, 1975 (div. Nov. 1982); m. Bobby Lee Martin, May 24, 1986. BA, S.W. Tex. State U., 1974; MA, U. Tex., 1987, EdD, 1996. Cert. English and sociology tchr., Tex. Tchr. aide, tchr. English Irving (Tex.) Ind. Sch. Dist., 1976-78; tchr. English Frenship Ind. Sch. Dist., Wolfforth, Tex., 1978-79; staff asst. Farm Credit Banks Tex., Austin, 1982-85, tng. specialist, 1985-87; fiscal program specialist II Tex. Edn. Agy., Austin, 1987-90, ednl. program dir., 1990, dir. programs II, 1990-98, assoc. sr. dir., 1998-99, sr. dir., 1999—. Strategic planning com. Tex. Edn. Agy., 1994—, bus. reingineering task force, 1995—, coord. funding adv. com., 1997—; chairperson Title VI Nat. Steering Com., 1996-98, 2000—; mem. state electronic grant tech. assistance workgroup, 2001—; legis. com. chair Title VI Nat. Steering Com. Recipient fellowship Alexander Caswell Ellis, 1986-87. Mem. ASCD, Phi Kappa Phi, Kappa Delta Pi, Phi Delta Kappa. Methodist. Avocations: water sports, gardening, reading, writing. Home: 5301 Waterbrook Dr Austin TX 78723-4042

MARTIN, EDWARD BRIAN, electrical engineer; b. Lawrence, Kans., Feb. 9, 1936; s. Edward Brian and Dorothy Irene (Dowers) M.; m. Sharon Anne Zimmerman, Dec. 21, 1955; children: Terry Brian, Ricky Lynn, Mindy Anne, Timothy Alan. BSEE, U. Kans., 1958; MSEE, St. Louis U., 1969. Registered profl. engr., Mo. Program mgr. McDonnell Douglas, St. Louis, 1980-85, mgr. avionics, 1985-86, dir. engring., 1986-88, dir. electronics, 1988-89, sr. dir. tech. processes, 1989-91, sr. dir. avionics tech., 1991-92, dir. advanced missile systems, 1992-95, dir. advanced weapon systems, 1995-97; dir. advanced tactical missiles The Boeing Co., 1997—2000. Pres./chmn. bd. dirs. Martin Internat., Ltd. Contbr. numerous articles to profl. jours. Pres. PTA, St. Louis, 1972; founder Martin Family Found. Mem. AIAA. Avocations: running, mountain climbing, writing. Home and Office: 5335 Lancelot Dr Saint Charles MO 63304-5742

MARTIN, EDWARD CURTIS, JR., landscape architect, educator; b. Albany, Ga., Aug. 21, 1928; s. Edward Curtis and Mildred Lee (Tyler) M.; m. Roberta Inman Parker, Mar. 18, 1967; children: Edward Curtis III, Andrew Parker. BFA, U. Ga., 1950, M of Landscape Architecture, 1969. Landscape arch. Norman C. Butts Landscape Contractor, Atlanta, 1950, M.T. Brooks Office of Landscape Architecture, Birmingham, Ala., 1950-56; Univ. landscape arch., horticulturist Miss. State U., 1956-70, prof. landscape architecture, 1970-92, Disting. prof., 1988, prof. emeritus, 1993—, part-time prof., 1992—93; originator, chmn., lectr. Miss. Landscape Design Symposium, 1957—. Guest lectr. U. San Luis Potosi, Mex., 1990, U. Mexico, Mex. City, 1991, La. State U., 1990, 91, 92, 94, 96, Biendenharn Found., Monroe, La., 1991, Longue Vue Found., New Orleans, 1991, So. Garden Symposium. 1993, 2001, St. Francisville, La., 1993, 2001, Southern Regional Meeting Garden Writers Assn. Am., Memphis, 1993, Rotary Internat. Dist. Conf., Memphis, 1993, Deep S. Regional Conf. Nat. Coun. State Garden Clubs, Lafayette, La., 1993, Nat. Capital Area Garden Coun., U. Md., 1996, Memphis Hort. Soc., 2001; guest instr. Nat. Landscape Design Study Courses Nat. Coun. State Garden Clubs, Inc., US, Mex., 1960—, Guatemala first study course, 1995, 96; originator, lectr. Garden Design Workshops, Miss. State U., 1988-2001; host Flower and Garden Tour of British Isles, Southland Travel Svcs., 1985, Flower and Garden Tour of Europe, 1981, 82; host, lectr. Hampton Ct. Palace Flower Show and English Gardens Tour, 1996, 98, 2003, Ireland and Scotland Gardens Tour, 1997, 99, 2001, Italian Gardens Tour, 1998, 2000, 02, 04, French Gardens Tour, 1999, 2000, 2001, So. Germany Tour, 2000, Austria Gardens Tour, 2000; host, lectr. Gardens of Spain and Portugal Tour, 2001, host, lectr. Portugal, No. Spain Gardens Tour, 2003, host, lectr. Southwest France Gardens Tour, 2003, Gardens of Belgium and Holland, 2002, Floraide, 2002, Gardens of Denmark and Sweden Tour, 2004; So. hist. gardens lectr., tour host Elderhostel Conf., Miss. U. for Women, 1997, 98, 99, 2000; photographic landscape arch. rsch. study: Europe, 1958, 66, 74, 85, S.Am., 1960, Israel, 1993, 95, Greece, Turkey, 1998; vis. prof. La. State U., 1990-93, vis. landscape architecture prof., 1994, 97; instr. landscape design Bot. Gardens, Huntsville, Ala., 1996; host, lectr. hist. southern gardens on Miss.

River, New Orleans to Vicksburg, Delta Queen Steamboat, 1994, Am. Queen Steamboat, 1999, 2000, New Orleans to St. Francisville, La., The Garden Clubs of Miss., Inc., Miss. Queen Steamboat, 1996, Memphis to New Orleans, 1997, 98; host Chelsea Flower Show and English Gardens Tour, 1994, Nat. Coun. State Garden Clubs, 1994, Fla. Wild Flower Conf. Fla. Fedn. Garden Clubs, Inc., 1994; instr. ecology tour Copper Canyon, Mex., 1994; spkr. Miss. Urban Foresters, Miss. Arboriculturist Ann. Conv., Vicksburg, 1999, Ga. Nursery Men's Ann. Winter Landscaping Seminar, Athens, 1999, Crosby Arboretum, Picayune, Miss., 1999, Hist. Preservation Regional Conf. Am. Soc. Landscape Archs., Natchez, Miss., 1999, Urban Landscape Design Pascagula, Miss., 1999, Hist. Preservation City Starkville, Miss., 2000, 44th Ann. Conv. Constrn. Specifications Inst., Atlanta, 2000; lectr. 65th Colonial Williamsburg Garden Symposium, 2001, McCall Lecture Series, Montreat (NC) Coll., 2002; guide, lectr. hist. preservation tour Black Mountain, NC, 2002, 03, part time gardens tour guide for the hist. Biltmore Estate, Asheville, NC. on state Edn. TV Network for same; lectr., NC Arboretum, Asheville, NC; 2003, lectr. Nat. Garden Club 74th Ann. Convention, Biloxi, Miss., 2003, N.C. Landscape Design Study Course, Greensboro, 2004; Miss. Gulf Coast Landscape Design Tour for Landscaping Design Cons. of Nat. Garden Club, Biloxi, 2003, Cons., Nat. Garden Club Conv., Biloxi, Miss.; keynote spkr. 40th Anninversary Miss. State U. Dept. Landscape Architecture, 2004; spkr. Montrea & Cmty. Group, 2003. Author: Landscape Plants in Design, A Photographic Guide, 1983; co-author: Home Landscapes, Planting Design and Management, 1994; invited to participate in Attingham Summer Program in Hist. Preservation (English country houses and gardens) Eng., 1985; author/photographer of 80-captioned slide series, one on Home Landscapes, another on Urban Landscape Design for use by Nat. Coun. State Garden Clubs, Inc., 1994. Mem. Miss. State Bd. Landscape Archs. for Profl. Registration, 1973-74; mem. Starkville (Miss.) Park and Recreation Bd., 1973-79; mem. civic beautification com. Black Mountain, N.C., 2002—; bd. visitors Warren Wilson Coll., Asheville, NC, 2002—. Recipient Silver Seal award Nat. Coun. State Garden Clubs 1969, honoree 1995; recipient Landscape Heritage award Fraser Found. Calif. 1986, Helent S. Hull Lit. award, 1996; Paul Harris fellow Rotary Internat., 1998; reception area (lobby) of Miss. State U. Dept. Landscape Architecture donated in his honor by Garden Clubs Miss. Inc., 2003. Fellow Am. Soc. Landscape Archs. (chmn. edn. com. 1960-61, pres. Miss. sect. S.W. chpt. 1975, chmn. S.W. chpt. ann. awards com. 1976, trustee Miss. chpt. 1977-81); mem. Nat. Trust for Hist. Preservation, So. Garden History Soc., Nat. Coun. State Garden Clubs (chmn. landscape design 1993-97), Garden Clubs Miss. (bd. dirs. 1958—, Silver Trophy 1961, Spl. Silver award 1980, Gold trophy 1993). Presbyterian. Home: 464 Chapel Rd Black Mountain NC 28711-2640 Office: Dept Landscape Architecture Box 9725 Mississippi State MS 39762-9725

MARTIN, ELLIOT EDWARDS, theatrical producer; b. Denver, Feb. 25, 1924; m. Marjorie Cuesta, Oct. 7, 1949; children: Richard, Linda Lisa. Student, U. Denver, 1943-46. Actor, singer, stage mgr., assoc. producer Theatre Guild, N.Y.C. and London, 1947-53; prodn. stage mgr. 20 Broadway plays and musicals, 1953-61; theatrical producer Never Too Late, Nobody Loves an Albatross, N.Y.C., 1962-66; theatre producer London, 1963; mng. dir. Center Theatre Group, Music Ctr., Los Angeles, 1966-71; producer Elliot Martin Prodns., N.Y.C., 1972—. Mem. exec. bd. Nat. Theatre of the Deaf, Chester, Conn., 1981-, Westport-Weston Arts Council, 1976- Prodns. on Broadway include: Dinner at Eight, 1966, More Stately Mansions, 1967, Abelard and Heloise, 1971, Emperor Henry IV, 1973, A Moon for the Misbegotten, 1973 (spl. Tony award), When You Comin' Back, Red Rider, 1974 (Outer Critics award), Of Mice and Men, 1975, Touch of the Poet, 1976, Dirty Linen and New Found Land, 1977, Caesar and Cleopatra, 1977, Kingfisher, 1979, Clothes for a Summer Hotel, 1980, Kingdoms, 1981, American Buffalo, 1981, Angels Fall, 1983, Glengarry Glen Ross, 1984 (Pulitzer prize), Woza Albert, 1984, American Buffalo, 1984, Harrigan 'n' Hart, 1985, Arsenic and Old Lace (Broadway and nat. tour), 1986-87, Joe Turner's Come and Gone (7 Tony nominations, N.Y. Drama Critic's award best play), 1988, Steel Magnolias (nat. tour), 1989, The Circle, 1989-90, Shadowlands, 1990-91, Breaking Legs, 1991-92, She Loves Me (9 Tony noms.), 1993-94, Death of a Salesman, 1995-96, A Moon For the Misbegotten, 2000, Down the Gaden Paths, 2001, I'm Not Rappaport, 2002. Mem. bd. assocs. U. Bridgeport, 1978-83. Recipient Tony award for most innovative revival, 1977-78, Larry Tajiri award for outstanding contbn. to arts Denver Post, 1970, Congl. commendation, 1970, Profl. Achievement award U. Denver, 1987. Mem. Platform Speakers Am., League N.Y. Theatres and Prodrs. (gov.), Am. Friends of Theatre (pres.), Players Club, N.Y. Athletic Club (N.Y.C.). Republican. Office: Elliot Martin Prodns 152 W 58th St New York NY 10019-2139 Office Phone: 212-245-4176.

MARTIN, FRED, artist, college administrator; b. San Francisco, June 13, 1927; s. Ernest Thomas and Leona (Richey) M.; m. Genevieve Catherine Fisette, Jan. 29, 1950 (dec.); children: T. Demian, Fredericka C., Anthony J.; m. Stephanie Zuperko Dudek, 1992. BA, U. Calif., Berkeley, 1949, MA, 1954; postgrad., Calif. Sch. Fine Arts, 1949—50. Registrar Oakland (Calif.) Art Mus., 1955-58; dir. exhbn. San Francisco Art Inst., 1958-65, 1965-75, dean acad. affairs, 1983-92, dean acad. affairs emeritus; represented by Paul Sunderholm Gallery, San Francisco. Exhibited one man shows, Zoe Dusanne Gallery, Seattle, 1952, M.H. deYoung Meml. Mus., San Francisco, 1954, 64, Oakland Mus. Calif., 1958, 2003, San Francisco Mus. Modern Art, 1958, 73, Dilexi Gallery, San Francisco, 1961, Minami Gallery, Tokyo, 1963, Royal Marks Gallery, NYC, 1965-70, Hansen Fuller Gallery, San Francisco, 1974, 75, 76, Quay Gallery, San Francisco, 1979, 81, 84, Natsoulas Gallery, Davis, Calif., 1991, Belcher Studios Gallery, San Francisco, 1994, Frederick Spratt Gallery, San Jose, 1996, Ebert Gallery, San Francisco, 1997, 98, 99, 2001, 2003, Art and Consciousness Gallery/John F. Kennedy U., Berkeley, 1997, Shasta Coll., 1998, Han Art Contemporaire, Montreal, 1999; represented in permanent collections, Mus. Modern Art, NYC, San Francisco Mus. Modern Art, Oakland Art Mus., Whitney Mus., Fogg Mus.; author: Beulah Land, 1966, Log of the Sun Ship, 1969, Liber Studiorum, 1973, A Travel Book, 1976, From an Antique Land, 1979; Bay area corr.: Art Internat., 1967-69, 75-76; contbg. editor Art Week, 1976-93. Recipient prizes Oakland Art Mus., 1951, 58, prizes San Francisco Mus. Art, 1957, 58, prizes Richmond (Calif.) Art Ctr., 1962, prizes Nat. Found. for Arts, 1970. Home: 232 Monte Vista Ave Oakland CA 94611-4922 Office: San Francisco Art Inst 800 Chestnut St San Francisco CA 94133-2206 E-mail: Fred_T_Martin@attglobal.net.

MARTIN, FREDDIE ANTHONY, agronomist, educator; b. Raceland, La., Nov. 17, 1945; s. of Abraham and Flossie Margarette (Foret) M.; m. Rose Ann Hill, Aug. 23, 1969; children: Samson, Jonathan, Robert. BS, Francis T. Nicholls State Coll, Thibodaux, La., 1966; MS, Cornell U., 1968, PhD, 1970. Asst. prof. plant pathology dept. La. State U., Baton Rouge, 1971-76, assoc. prof., 1976-80, prof., 1980, prof. agronomy dept., 1980—, head Sugar Sta./Audubon Sugar, 1988-97, head dept. agronomy, 1997—. Editor Am. Soc. Sugar Cane Technologists jour., 1980-94; author profl. manuscripts, jours. Recipient Rsch. Excellence Award, La. Agricultural Experimental Sta., 1984, Tipton Team award, 2000, Svc. Award, St. James Sugar Growers, 1989. Mem. Internat. Soc. Sugarcane Technologists (biology commr. 1995—), Am. Soc. Agronomy, Crop Sci. Soc. Am., Am. Soc. Sugarcane Tech., Gamma Sigma Delta. Office: La State U Agronomy Dept Baton Rouge LA 70803-0001

MARTIN, FREDERICK KANE, portfolio manager, investor; b. Elkhart, Ind., Oct. 29, 1946; s. William Frederick and Mary Amalia (Kohlhaas) M.; m. Margery Hickey, Dec. 20, 1969; children: Peter, Thomas, William. BA, Dartmouth Coll., 1968, MBA, 1969. CFA. Analyst, portfolio mgr. Northwestern Nat. Bank, 1973-78; sr. portfolio mgr., mng. dir. Mitchell Hutchins Asset Mgmt., Mpls., 1978-97; founder, sr. portfolio mgr. Disciplined Growth Investors, Mpls., 1997—. Lt. USN, 1969-73, Vietnam. Mem. Two Cities Soc. Security Analysis, Mpls. Club. Avocations: flight instructor, soccer coaching. Office: Disciplined Growth Investor 900 2d Ave S Minneapolis MN 55402

MARTIN, FREDERICK NOEL, audiology educator; b. N.Y.C., July 24, 1931; s. Philip and Mildred Ruth (Austin) M.; m. Mary Catherine Robinson, Apr. 4, 1954; children: David C., Leslie Anne. BA, Bklyn. Coll., 1957, MA, 1958; PhD, CUNY, 1968. Audiologist, Lenox Hill Hosp., N.Y.C., 1957-58; Audiologist Ark. Sch. for the Deaf, Little Rock, 1958-60; dir. audiology Bailey Ear Clinic, Little Rock, 1960-66; mem. faculty Bklyn. Coll., 1966-68, U. Tex., Austin, 1968—, endowed prof. audiology, 1982—. Author: Introduction to Audiology, 1975, 8th edit., 2003, interactive CD ROM, 2003, Pediatric Audiology, 1978, Medical Audiology, 1981, Basic Audiometry, 1986; editor: Remediation of Communication Disorders, Vol. 10, 1978, Hearing Disorders in Children, 1986, Effective Counseling in Audiology, 1994, Hearing Care for Children, 1996, Exercises in Audiometry, 1998; contbr. numerous articles to profl. jours. Served with USAF, 1951-55. Fellow Am. Speech-Language Hearing Assn., Am. Acad. Audiology; mem. Tex. Speech-Lang.-Hearing Assn., Am. Auditory Soc., Tex. Acad. Audiology. Home: 8613 Silver Ridge Dr Austin TX 78759-8144 Office: U Tex Austin TX 78712

MARTIN, G. STEVEN, biochemist, educator; b. Oxford, Eng., July 19, 1943; came to U.S., 1968; s. Kurt and Hanna M.; m. Gail R., June 30, 1969; 1 child, Nicholas. BA, Queens' Coll., Cambridge, Eng., 1964; MA, PhD, U. Cambridge, 1968. Staff Imperial Cancer Rsch. Fund, London, 1971-75; from asst. prof. zoology to prof. molecular & cell biology U. Calif., Berkeley, 1975—, Richard and Rhoda Goldman disting. prof., 2002—. NIH grantee, 1975—. Fellow Royal Soc. Avocations: hiking, bicycling, reading. Home: 818 Spruce St Berkeley CA 94707-2043 E-mail: smartin@socrates.berkeley.edu.

MARTIN, GARY J. retired business executive, mayor; b. Des Moines, Feb. 8, 1937; s. William Carl Martin and Mary Louise Sweeney; m. Carolyn J. Karau, July 28, 1956; children: Victoria, Cheryl, Dennis. BBA, Marquette U., 1972. CPA Wis., 1973. Mfr. GM, Milw., 1957-68, engring. mgr., 1968—73; CFO Miller Brewing Co., 1974—76, dir. corp. planning, 1977—78; pres. Better Brands of N.Y., N.Y.C., 1978—79; exec. v.p. Seven Up Co., St. Louis, 1979-85; v.p. mktg. Schenley Industries, Dallas, 1985-86; cons. Martin & Assocs., 1986—89; mayor Osage Beach, Mo., 1992-95; ret., 1995. Bd. dirs. Family Hosp., Milw., 1976-78; mem. lay bd. St. Mary Health Ctr., St. Louis, 1980-85. With USN, 1954-57. Avocations: computers, boating, golf, travel. Home: 2349 Fairskies Dr Spring Hill FL 34606-7257 E-mail: gama@tampabay.rr.com.

MARTIN, GARY JOSEPH, medical educator; b. Chgo., Mar. 12, 1952; m. Helen Gartner; children: Daniel T., David G. BA in Psychology, U. Ill., 1974, MD, 1978. Diplomate Am. Bd. Internal Medicine, Am. Bd. Cardiovascular Disease, Nat. Bd. Med. Examiners; lic. physician, Ill. Intern, resident internal medicine Northwestern U. Med. Sch., Chgo., 1978-81, instr. medicine, 1981-82, asst. prof. medicine, 1984-90, assoc. prof., 1990-96, prof., 1996—, divsn. chief, divsn. gen. internal medicine, 1988-2001, assoc. chmn. dept. medicine, 1998-2000, vice chmn. dept. medicine, 2001—; cardiology fellow Loyola U. Med. Ctr., 1982-84; attending physician Northwestern Meml. Hosp./Northwestern Med. Faculty Found., Chgo., 1984—; chief med. resident, attending physician Northwestern Meml. Hosp., Chgo., 1981-82; dir. primary care clerkship Nat. Ctr. for Advanced Med. Edn., 1984—. Chmn. outpatient utilization rev. and quality assurance com., 1985-93; chmn. Northwestern Meml. Hosp./Lakeside VA Rsch. Com., 1988-91; dir. tng. gen. internal medicine residency program, 1985-95; bd. dirs. com. Northwestern Med. Faculty Found., 1993—; cons. health care divsn. Ernst & Young, 1991—; peer reviewer Faculty Devel. Rev. Com. Panel 1, 1994. Contbr. articles to profl. jours. Fellow Buehler Ctr. on Aging. Fellow Am. Coll. Cardiology; mem. ACP, Soc. Gen. Internal Medicine, Am. Heart Assn. Office: Northwestern U Med Sch Divsn Gen Internal Medicine 675 N Saint Clair St Ste 18-200 Chicago IL 60611-5929

MARTIN, GARY WAYNE, lawyer; b. Cin., Feb. 14, 1946; s. Elmer DeForrest and Nellie May (Hughes) M.; m. Debra Lynn Goldsmith, June 25, 1982; children: Christopher, Jeremy, Joie, Casey. BA, Wilmington Coll., 1967; JD, U. Cin., 1974. Bar: Fla. 1974. Bd. dirs. Fowler White Gillen Boggs Villareal & Banker, Tampa, Fla., 1974—. Lt. USNR, 1967-71. Mem. Harbour Island Athletic Club. Republican. Presbyterian. Avocation: tennis. Office: Fowler White Gillen Boggs Villareal & Banker 501 E Kennedy Blvd Ste 1600 Tampa FL 33602-5240 Office Phone: 813-222-1183. E-mail: gmartin@fowlerwhite.com.

MARTIN, GEORGE (GEORGE WHITNEY MARTIN), writer; b. N.Y.C., Jan. 25, 1926; s. George Whitney and Agnes Wharton (Hutchinson) M. BA, Harvard U., 1948; student, Trinity Coll., Cambridge (Eng.) U., 1950; LL.B., U. Va., 1953. Bar: N.Y. 1955. With firm Emmet, Marvin & Martin, N.Y.C., 1955-59; engaged in writing, 1959—. Author: The Opera Companion, A Guide for the Casual Operagoer, 1961, 5th edit., 1999, The Battle of the Frogs and Mice, An Homeric Fable, 1962, 2d edit., 1987, Verdi, His Music, Life and Times, 1963, 4th edit., 2001, The Red Shirt and The Cross of Savoy, The Story of Italy's Risorgimento, 1748-1871, 1969, Causes and Conflicts, The Centennial History of the Association of the Bar of the City of New York, 1870-1970, 1970, 2d edit., 1997, Madam Secretary: Frances Perkins, 1976, The Damrosch Dynasty, America's First Family of Music, 1983, Aspects of Verdi, 1988, 2nd edit., 1993, Verdi at the Golden Gate, San Francisco in the Golden Years, 1993, Twentieth Century Opera, A Guide, 1999; contbr. articles to profl. jours., mags. Home: 53 Crosslands Dr Kennett Square PA 19348-2010

MARTIN, GEORGE FRANCIS, lawyer; b. Yuba City, Calif., July 7, 1944; s. John Severd and Albina Marie M.; m. Linda Louise D'Aoust, Mar. 17, 1968; children: Brandon, Bry. BA in Govt., Calif. State U., Sacramento, 1968; JD, U. Calif., Davis, 1971. Bar: Calif. Adminstr. asst. Assemblyman E. Richard Barnes, Sacramento, 1967-68; with Borton, Petrini & Conron, Bakersfield, Calif., 1971—, mng. gen. ptnr., 1977—; dean Calif. Pacific Sch. Law, Bakersfield, 1993-95. Holdings numerous ventures, partnerships; lectr. in field; founder, owner theatrical bus. Mgmt. by Martin, Inc., Shower of Stars, Frantic Records, 1962-67. Editor-in-chief Verdict Jour. of Law, 1984-85, Calif. Def. Mag.; newspaper reporter Appeal Democrat, Marysville, Calif., 1959-62. Former vice chmn. Kern County Rep. Ctrl. Com.; past pres. So. Calif. Def. Counsel; past chmn. Ctrl. Calif. Heart Inst.; bd. dirs. Calif. State U. at Bakersfield Found., chair, 1998; bd. dirs. Calif. Coun. Partnerships, Kern Econ. Devel. Corp; mem. adv. bd. Automobile Club So. Calif.; chmn. adv. bd. Witkin Legal Inst. Mem. Greater Bakersfield C. of C. (bd. dirs., past pres.). Office: Borton Petrini & Conron 1600 Truxtun Ave Bakersfield CA 93301-5111

MARTIN, GEORGE J., JR., lawyer; b. Port Chester, N.Y., June 7, 1942; s. George J. and Eileen Ann (Buckley) M.; m. Joanne L. Frost, Aug. 21, 1965 (div. May 1986); children: Amy Anne, Ryan Frost; m. Anna Marie Cipriati, June 21, 1986; children: Marissa McCreay, Jill McCreay. BA, Georgetown U., 1964, JD, 1967. Bar: N.Y. 1969; conseil juridique, France, 1977-82. From assoc. to ptnr. Mudge Rose Guthrie Alexander & Ferdon, N.Y.C., 1967-95; ptnr. Coudert Bros., N.Y.C., 1995—. Mem. French Heritage Soc. (gen. counsel, dir.). Roman Catholic. Home: 163 Congress St Brooklyn NY 11201-6103 Office: Coudert Bros 1114 Ave of The Americas New York NY 10036-7710 E-mail: george0607@nyc.rr.com., marting@coudert.com.

MARTIN, GEORGE M. pathologist, gerontologist, educator; b. NYC, June 30, 1927; s. Barnett J. and Estelle (Weiss) M.; m. Julaine Ruth Miller, Dec. 2, 1952; children: Peter C., Kelsey C., Thomas M., Andrew C. BS, U. Wash., 1949, MD, 1953. Diplomate Am. Bd. Pathology, Am. Bd. Med. Genetics. Intern Montreal Gen. Hosp., Canada, 1953-54; resident, instr. U. Chgo., 1954-57; instr., prof. U. Wash., Seattle, 1957—. Vis. scientist Dept. Genetics Albert Einstein Coll., NYC, 1964, Rockefeller U., 1998-99; chmn. Gordon Confs. Molecular Pathology, Biology of Aging, 1974-79; chmn., nat. res. Plan on Aging Nat. Inst. on Aging, Bethesda, Md., 1985-89; dir. Alzheimer's Disease Rsch. Ctr. U. Wash., 1985—, assoc. dir., 1999—. Editor Werner's Syndrome and Human Aging, 1985, Molecular Aspects of Aging, 1995; contbr. articles in field to profl jours. Active Fedn. Am. Scientists. With USN, 1945-46. Recipient Allied Signal award in Aging, 1991, Rsch. medal Am. Aging Assn., 1992, Kleemeier award, 1994, Paul Glenn award for aging rsch., 1998; named Disting. Alumnus, U. Wash. Sch. Medicine, 1987; USPHS rsch. fellow dept. genetics, Glasgow U., 1961-62; Eleanor Roosevelt Inst. Cancer Rsch. fellow Inst. de Biologie, Physiologie, Chimie, Paris, 1968-69; Josiah Macy faculty scholar Sir William Din Sch. Pathology, Oxford (Eng.) U., 1978-79, Humboldt Disting. scientist dept. genetics U. Wurzburg, Germany, 1991. Fellow: AAAS, Tissue Culture Assn. (pres. 1986—88), Gerontol. Soc. Am. (chmn. Biol. Sci. 1979, pres. 2003, Brookdale award 1981, Lifetime Acheivement award for rsch. in alzheimer's disease World Alzheimer's Congress 2000); mem.: Am. Fedn. Aging Rsch. (pres. 1999—2001, sci. dir. 2003—), Am. Soc. Investigative Pathology, Am. Soc. Human Genetics, Am. Assn. Univ. Pathologists (emeritus), Inst. Medicine. Democrat. Avocations: travel, jazz, reading. Home: 2223 E Howe St Seattle WA 98112-2931 Office: U Wash Sch Medicine Dept Pathology Rm K543 Seattle WA 98195 Office Phone: 206-543-5088. E-mail: gmmartin@u.washington.edu.

MARTIN, GREGORY KEITH, lawyer, mayor; b. Conway, SC, Nov. 7, 1956; s. George Henry Martin and Julia Ann (Johnson) M. Land. BS in Fin. Mgmt., Clemson U., 1979; JD, U. S.C., 1983. Bar: S.C. 1983. Intern U.S. Senate, 1980; law clk. to presiding judge 15th Jud. Cir. Ct., Conway, 1983; assoc. Johnson & Martin, Conway, 1983-88, ptnr., 1988-93, Martin & Smith, Conway, 1993-98; mayor City of Conway, 1995—; pvt. practice, Conway, 1998—. Mem. Conway Planning Commn., 1986-89, chmn., 1989; bd. dirs. Conway-Main St. U.S.A., 1986-90, chmn., 1988; mem. Conway Bd. Appeals, 1987-89, Horry County Bd. Archtl. Rev., 1987-90; mem. Conway City Coun., 1991-94; pres., Horry County Hist. Soc., 1988, 90, mayor pro tem, 1994; mem. adv. bd. Pee Dee Heritage Ctr., 1988-2003. Mem. ABA, S.C. Bar Assn., Horry County Bar Assn., Sigma Nu, Phi Delta Phi. Methodist. Avocations: tennis, coin collecting/numismatics. Home: 706 Elm St Conway SC 29526-4373 Office: PO Box 736 Conway SC 29528-0736

MARTIN, GUY, lawyer; b. Los Angeles, Jan. 22, 1911; s. I.G. and Mary Pearl (Howe) M.; m. Edith Kingdon Gould, Oct. 12, 1946; children— Guy III, Jason Gould, Christopher Kingdon, Edith Maria Theodosia Burr. AB, Occidental Coll., 1931; BA (1st class hons.), Oxford U., 1934, MA, 1944; LL.B., Yale, 1937. Bar: N.Y. 1938, D.C. 1947. Practiced with Donovan, Leisure, Newton & Lumbard, N.Y.C., 1938-41; gen. counsel All Am. Aviation, Inc., 1942, Am. Mexican Claims Commn., U.S. Dept. State, 1945-47; ptnr. Martin, Whitfield, Smith & Bebchick (and predecessors), Washington, 1952-80; counsel Martin and Smith (and predecessors), 1981-86; pres., vice chmn. bd., dep. chief exec. officer Internat. Bank, 1981-86; with Law Office of Saltzstein & Martin, 1988-99. Served with USN; sea duty 1942-45. Mem. ABA, Assn. of Bar of City of N.Y., Bar Assn. D.C, Phi Beta Kappa, Sigma Alpha Epsilon. Clubs: Yale, Brook, Knickerbocker (N.Y.C.); Metropolitan, City Tavern (Washington). Episcopalian. Home: 3300 O St NW Washington DC 20007-2813

MARTIN, HAROLD CLARK, humanities educator; b. Raymond, Pa., Jan. 12, 1917; s. Henry Floyd and Anna May (Clark) M.; m. Elma Hicks, Dec. 21, 1939; children— Thomas, Joel, Ann, Rebecca. AB, Hartwick Coll., Oneonta, N.Y., 1937, LL.D. (hon.), 1965; AM, U. Mich., 1941; PhD, Harvard, 1954; student, U. Wis., 1936, Columbia, 1941; LHD (hon.), Elmira Coll., 1967, Siena Coll., 1968, Concord Coll., 1968; DHL (hon.), Trinity Coll., Conn., 1970; Litt.D. (hon.), Skidmore Coll., 1974; LHD (hon.), Coll. St. Rose, 1974, Union Coll., 1975. High sch. tchr. English and French langs., Adams, N.Y., 1937-39; high sch. tchr. English Goshen, N.Y., 1939-44; prin. high sch., 1944-49; mem. faculty Harvard U., 1951-65, dir. gen. edn., 1951-63, lectr. comparative lit., 1954-65; chancellor Union U.; also pres. Union Coll., Schenectady, 1965-74; pres. Am. Acad., Rome, Italy, 1974-76; Margaret Bundy Scott prof. Williams Coll., 1977; Charles A. Dana prof. humanities Trinity Coll., Conn., 1977-82, prof. emeritus, 1982—, sr. lectr. humanities, 1982—. Author: Logic and Rhetoric of Exposition, 1958, Spanning Three Centuries, 1984, Outlasting Marble and Brass, 1986; editor: Inquiry and Expression (with Richard Ohmann), 1958, Style in Prose Fiction, 1959, Pearson Diary, 2 vols., 2001. Chmn. Mass. Com. Fulbright Awards, 1955-65, Coll. Bd. Com. English, 1959-64; Trustee Hartwick Coll., Siena Coll., Franklin Coll., Switzerland, Wenner-Gren Found. With USNR, 1945-46. Home: 70 Matthew Dr Brunswick ME 04011-3275

MARTIN, HAROLD G. engineering consultant; b. Scotland, Pa. s. Abram Earl and Eula Mae Martin; m. Christina Shipley Martin, June 5, 1948; children: Susan (dec.), Judith Krieger, Bruce. BSCE, Pa. State U., 1944. Stress analyst, chief structures Fairchild Republic Co., Hagerstown, Md., 1967-70, mgr. tech. engring., 1970-71, chief problem analysis and corrective action, 1977-81, chief quality engring., 1981, project engr. F14, FAA airworthiness coord., 1981-84; engring. cons., FAA designated engring. rep. Waynesboro, Pa., 1984—. Mem. sch. bd. Waynesboro Area Sch. Bd., 1978-84. Staff sgt. U.S. Army, 1944-46. Mem.: Mid Atlantic Air Mus., Am. Aviation Hist. Soc., Soc. of Automotive Engineers. Avocations: auto restoration, travel, writing, boating, fishing. Home and Office: 833 Anthony Ave Waynesboro PA 17268

MARTIN, HARRY CORPENING, lawyer, retired state supreme court justice; b. Lenoir, N.C., Jan. 13, 1920; s. Hal C. and Johnsie Harshaw (Nelson) M.; m. Nancy Robiou Dallam, Apr. 16, 1955; children: John, Matthew, Mary. AB, U. N.C., 1942; LLB, Harvard U., 1948; LLM, U. Va., 1982. Bar: N.C. 1948. Pvt. practice, Asheville, N.C., 1948-62; judge N.C. Superior Ct., Asheville, 1962-78, N.C. Ct. Appeals, Raleigh, 1978-82; justice N.C. Supreme Ct., 1982-92; ptnr. Martin & Martin, Attys., Hillsborough, N.C., 1992—. Adj. prof. U. N.C. Law Sch., 1983-92, Duke U., 1990-91, Dan K. Moore disting. vis. prof., U. N.C. Law Sch., 1992-94; sr. conf. atty. U.S. Ct. Appeals for 4th Cir., 1994-99; chief justice Supreme Ct. ea. bd. of Cherokee Indians, 2000—. With U.S. Army, 1942-45, South Pacific. Mem. U.S. Supreme Ct. Hist. Soc., N.C. Supreme Ct. Hist. Soc. (pres.). Democrat. Episcopalian. Home: 1 Hilltop Rd Asheville NC 28803-3017 Office: Cherokee Supreme Ct PO Box 455 Cherokee NC 28719 Office Phone: 828-497-1077. E-mail: judgemartin@bellsouth.net.

MARTIN, HARRY S., III, law educator, law librarian; AB in History, Harvard U., 1965; JD, U. Minn., 1968; MLS, U. Pitts., 1971. Libr., prof. Harvard Law Sch., Cambridge, Mass., 1981—2002, Henry N. Ess II libr., prof., 2002—. Contbr. articles to profl. jours. Office: Harvard Law Sch Areeda 511 1563 Massachusetts Ave Cambridge MA 02138 Business E-Mail: martin@law.harvard.edu.

MARTIN, HELEN ELIZABETH, educational consultant; b. West Chester, Pa., Feb. 19, 1945; d. Thomas Edwin and Elizabeth Temple (Walker) M. BA, The King's Coll., N.Y.C., 1967; MEd, West Chester U., 1970; postgrad., Goethe Inst., Freiberg, Fed. Republic Germany, 1979, Oxford (Eng.) U., 1979. Nat. bd. cert. tchr. adolescent/young adult sci., 2000. Tchr. math. and sci. Unionville (Pa.) H.S., 1967-99; ret., 1999; ednl. cons. Adj. prof. West Chester U., 1989—; mem. Carnegie Forum on Edn. and the Economy. Mem. Pa. Rep. State Com., 1982-90, Rep. Com. of Chester County, 1984-94. Named Alumna of Yr., The King's Coll., 1987; recipient State Presdl. award, 1989, Frank G. Brewer Civil Air Patrol Meml. Aerospace award, 1989, Outstanding Achievement award U.S. Dept. Commerce, 1993; Bus. Week/Challenger Seven fellow, 1991. Fellow Am. Sci. Affiliation; mem. AAAS, Nat. Bd. Profl. Tchg. Stds. (founding dir., 1987-94), Satellite Educators Assn. (pres. 1990-2000), Nat. Sci. Tchrs. Assn., Nat. Coun. Tchrs. Math., Nat. Sci. Tchrs. Assn. (internat. lectr. 1987), Assn. for Sci. Edn. in U.K. (internat. lectr. 1987). Home: PO Box 605 Unionville PA 19375-0605 E-mail: SatTeacher@aol.com.

MARTIN, HELEN SCHATKOWSKI, music educator, television producer; b. Phila., Apr. 15, 1940; d. Edwin Oscar Schatkowski and Helen Emma Schumann; children: Scott Thomas, Michelle Linda. BA, U. Calif., San Diego, 1987; scholarship student, Eastman Sch. Music, 1958—68; student, Ind. Univ. Sch. Music; Student, of Josef Gingold. Instr. Ctr. for Young Musicians, London, 1979—83, Moravian Coll., Bethlehem, Pa., 1987—91; artist in residence Mt. Pocono H.S., Mt. Pocono, Pa., 2000—02; instr. Fretless Studio, Easton, Pa., 2000—; founder, dir. Mt. Jefferson Inst. for Music and the Arts, Easton, Pa., 2003—. Author: (instl. video) Violin For Musicians; prodr.: (instl. video) Violin For Musicians (Finalist, NY Festivals, 2000); author: (plays) Secret Life of Antonio Vivaldi; performer; author: (violin method for adults) Forever Fretless; prodr.: (TV series) Music a la Mode; musician: (TV series) Music a la Mode. Recipient Chamber Music Award of Merit, Nat. Fedn. of Music Clubs, 2002. Mem.: Music Tchrs. Nat. Assn. Achievements include development of forever fretless string method; (violin method) combines the

musical found. of Dr. Edwin Gordon with the actions (physical technique) of Paul Rolland and Marla Mutschler; it emphasises the language aspects of music, blending essential musical literacy and the skills of playing by ear. Office Phone: 610-704-8461.

MARTIN, HENRY ALAN, public defender; b. Nashville, Sept. 5, 1949; s. James Alvin and Mary Elizabeth (Long) M.; m. Gloria B. Ballard, May 9, 1975; children: Nathan Daniel, Anna Elizabeth. BA, Vanderbilt U., 1971, JD, 1974. Bar: Tenn. 1975, U.S. Dist. Ct. (mid. dist.) Tenn. 1975, U.S. Ct. Appeals (6th cir.) 1976, U.S. Supreme Ct. 1979. Pvt. practice, Nashville, 1975-76; ptnr. Haile & Martin, P.A., Nashville, 1976-82; assoc. firm Barrett & Ray, P.C., Nashville, 1982-85; fed. pub. defender U.S. Dist. Ct. (mid. dist.) Tenn., Nashville, 1985—. Mem. adv. com. on rules criminal procedure U.S. Judicial Conf., 1994-99. CO-author, co-editor trial manual, Tools for the Ultimate Trial, 1985, 2d edit., 1988, contbr. articles to profl. jours. Del., Witness for Peace, Managua, Nicaragua, 1987. Mem. ABA (coun. criminal justice sect. 1993-96), NACDL, Assn. Fed. Defenders (pres. 1995-98), Nashville Bar Assn., Napier Looby Bar Assn., Tenn. Assn. Criminal Def. Lawyers (bd. dirs. 1978-94, pres. 1984-85, Pres.'s award 1984). Democrat. Avocations: jogging, swimming. Home: 3802 Whitland Ave Nashville TN 37205-2432 Office: Fed Pub Defender 810 Broadway Ste 200 Nashville TN 37203-3861 Office Phone: 615-736-5047. Business E-Mail: henry_martin@fd.org.

MARTIN, HENRY JOHN, music educator, composer; b. New Haven, Conn., Feb. 20, 1950; s. Henry John and Mary Gine Martin; life ptnr. Barbara Fiorella. MusB, Oberlin (Ohio) Conservatory, 1973; AB, Oberlin Coll., 1973; MusM, U. Mich., 1975; PhD, Princeton U., 1980. Lectr. Princeton U., 1978—81, 1987; dir. music theory/composition New Sch. Jazz Program, N.Y.C., 1986—98; assoc. prof. music Rutgers U., Newark, 1998—2002, prof. music, 2002—. Composer: (composition for piano) Preludes and Fugues, 1990—2000, (composition for violin and orchestra) Shadows of the Moon, 1992, (composition for trio) Trio in C# Minor, 2002; author: (textbook) Jazz: The First 100 Years, (monographs) Charlie Parker & Thematic Improvisation, Enjoying Jazz; co-editor: Ann. Rev. Jazz Studies, 1995—. Fellow Ligura Study Ctr., Bogliasco Found., 1999; winner, Barlow Internat. Composition Competition, 1998. Mem.: Soc. for Music Theory (co-founder, chair jazz spl. interest group 1995—). Home: 11 Riverside Dr Apt 3JW New York NY 10023-2506 Office: Rutgers U Visual/Performing Arts Bradley Hall Newark NJ 07102 E-mail: martinh@andromeda.rutgers.edu.

MARTIN, HERBERT WOODWARD, English educator, poet; b. Birmingham, Ala., Oct. 4, 1933; s. David Nathaniel and Willie Mae (Woodward) M.; m. Elizabeth Susan McAfee Altman, Dec. 13, 1952; children: Sarah Elizabeth Altman, Julia Johanna Martin. BA in English, U. Toledo, 1964; MLitt in Drama, Middlebury (Vt.) Coll., 1972; DA in Poetry, Carnegie Mellon U., 1979; LHD (hon.), Urbana (Ohio) U., 1998; LHD (hon.), U. Dayton, 2002. From instr. to asst. prof. English Aquinas Coll., Grand Rapids, Mich., 1967-70; from asst. prof. to assoc. prof. U. Dayton, Ohio, 1970-98. Disting. vis. prof. Ctrl. Mich. U., Mt. Pleasant, 1972; advisor Ohio Arts Coun., Columbus, 1980; cons. Ohio Humanities Coun., Columbus, 1996. Author: (poems) N.Y. The Nine Million, 1968, The Shit-Storm Poems, 1972, The Persistence of the Flesh, 1976, The Forms of Silence, 1980, Galileo's Suns, 1999, In His Own Voice: The Uncollected Works of Paul Laurence Dunbar, 2002, Selected Poems of Paul Laurence Dunbar, 2004, The Log of the Vigilante, 2000; librettist (with Joseph Fennimore) Six Songs, 1989, (with Philip Magnuson) Seven Songs, 1992, (with Adolphus Hailstork) Common Ground, 1995, (with Philip Magnuson) It Pays to Advertise, 1996, Magnificat, 2000, Voices: A Requiem, 1998, Crispus Attucks, A Cantata with Adolphus Hailstork, 2004. Paul Laurence Dunbar laureate City of Dayton, 1996; Paul Laurence Dunbar writer-in-residence Dunbar Ho., Dayton, 1996. Recipient Opus award Culture Works, 1996, Richard Bjornson Humanities award Ohio Humanities Coun., 1996, Paul Laurence Dunbar Humanities award Inner-W. Priority Bd., 1996, Gov.'s award Ohio Arts Coun., 2002, Mark Twain award Soc. for Study of Midwestern Lit., 2002; named 10 Top African Males City of Dayton, 1996; named Outstanding Alumnus in Humanities, U. Toledo, 2003; Fulbright scholar Janus Pannonius U., 1990-91. Avocations: singing, acting, giving public readings of poetry. Home: 5193 Chapin St Dayton OH 45429-1905 Office: U Dayton Dept English 300 College Park Ave Dayton OH 45469-1502 E-mail: Herbert.Martin@notes.udayton.edu.

MARTIN, IONIS B. artist, educator; b. Chicago, Ill., 1936; d. Francis Wright and Hattie Robinson Bracy; m. Allyn Aubrey Martin; 1 child, Allyn Bracy Fletcher. MFA, PRATT I NSTITUTE, Brooklyn,Ny, 1987; MED, U. Of Hartford, West Hartford,Ct, 1968; BS, Fisk U., Nashville,Tn, 1957. Lectr./and adj. prof. Ctrl. Ct State U., New Britain, Conn., 1985; art tchr. h.s. Bloomfield Bd. of Educatiion, Bloomfield, Conn., 1971—2001; art tchr. weaver h.s. Hartford Bd. of Edn., Hartford, Conn., 1961—67, art tchr. Arsenal elem sch., 1961—61; tchr. CT Child Welfare Assn, New Haven, 1959—61; Y-teen associate dir. YWCA of Greater Hartford, Hartford, Conn., 1957—59. Co founder, sec. treas., v.p. Artist collective bd. of Dir, Hartford, Conn., 1972—; corporator U. of Hartford bd. of Dir., West Hartford, Conn., 2001; trustee Wadsworth Atheneam Mus. of art, Hartford, Conn., 1978—97. Author: (book) A Curriculum Sampler, (almanac entry) Gale Researchers' African American. Co-trustee Ella Burr McManus Trust, Hartford, Conn., 1985; am. bd. of dir. Ancient Burial Ground, Hartford, Conn., 1998; dir. Huntington Ho. Mus., Windsor, Conn., 2001. Recipient Fellowship, DuBois Inst., Harvard U., 1994, Grant Through Young Black Eyes, CT Commn. on the Arts, Hartford,CT. Mem.: The Links Greater Hartford Chpt. (assoc.; sec. pres.), Art Works Gallery (assoc.; pres. 1984—86), Delta Signa Theta. Home: 1234 Prospect Avenue Hartford CT 06105 Personal E-mail: dr.a.martin@snet.net.

MARTIN, J. LANDIS, manufacturing company executive, lawyer; b. Grand Island, Nebr., Nov. 5, 1945; s. John Charles and Lucile (Cooley) M.; m. Sharon Penn Smith, Sept. 23, 1978; children: Mary Frances, Sarah Landis, Emily Penn. BS in Bus. Adminstrn., Northwestern U., 1968, JD cum laude, 1973. Bar: Ill. 1974, D.C. 1978, Colo. 1982. Assoc. Kirkland & Ellis, Chgo., 1973-77, ptnr. Washington, 1978-81, mng. ptnr. Denver, 1981-87, firm com. mem., Chgo., 1983-87; chmn., bd. dirs. Titanium Metals Corp., 1987—, CEO, 1995—, pres.; pres., CEO NL Industries Inc., Houston, 1987—, also bd. dirs.; chmn., CEO Baroid Corp., Houston, 1987-94; chmn. bd., pres., CEO Tremont Corp., 1990—, also bd. dirs. Dir. Halliburton Co., Dallas, Aimco. Editor-in-chief: Exchange Act Guide to SEC Rule 144, 1973; articles editor Northwestern U. Law Rev., 1972-73. Pres Ctrl. City Opera House Assn., Denver, 1986-88, chmn. 1987-96; pres. Ctrl. City Opera House Endowment Fund, 1995—; vis. com. Northwestern U. Sch. Law, 1987—; mem. exec. com. Houston Grand Opera, 1991—, sr. v.p. devel. 1992-93, pres. 1993-95, chmn. 1995-97; bd. trustees Denver Art Mus., 1994—, Graland Country Day Sch., 1992-97. With U.S. Army, 1969-71. Mem. Colo. Bar Assn., D.C. Bar Assn. Clubs: Chevy Chase (Md.), John Evans (Evanston, Ill.), Denver, Denver Country, Castle Pines Golf. Office: Titanium Metals Corp 1999 Broadway Ste 4300 Denver CO 80202-5743

MARTIN, JACK, physician; b. Northport, Ala., Aug. 11, 1927; s. Marvin Oscar and Glenavis (Rice) M.; m. Ann Inman, Apr. 7, 1957; children: Sarah, Richard, Charles Randall, Robert. BS, U. Ala., 1949; MD, Vanderbilt U., 1953. Intern Charity Hosp., New Orleans, 1953-54; resident in adult and child psychiatry Cin. Gen. Hosp., 1954-58; dir. child psychiatry U. Tex. Health Scis. Ctr., Dallas, 1958-67, clin. prof. child psychiatry, 1967—; med. dir. Shady Brook Rsch. Ctr., Richardson, Tex., 1963-81; physician pvt. practice, Dallas, 1981—. With USNR, 1945-47. Independent. Episcopalian. Avocations: bridge, golf. Office: 3636 Dickason Ave Dallas TX 75219-4911 Office Phone: 214-528-3095. Personal E-mail: jam4757@aol.com.

MARTIN, JACK, federal agency administrator; m. Bettye Martin; children: Randy, Ingrid. BS, MBA, Wayne State U.; postgrad., U. Minn. CPA. With Gen. Motors Corp., Detroit; various mgmt. positions Control Data; cons. acct. Touche Ross & Co. (now Deloitte and Touche); mng. dir., CEO, founder Jack Martin and Co. P.C., CPAs, 1975—; chmn., acting CEO Home Fed. Savings Bank, Detroit, 1995—; chmn. provider reimbursement rev. bd. U.S. Dept. Health and Human Svcs., 1991—94; CFO Dept. Edn., Washington, 2001—. Chmn. of bd. Health Alliance Plan; mem. investment com. Mercy Health Sys. (now Trinity Health); chair Mich. adv. com. U.S. Civil Rights Commn.; v.p. Merrill Palmer Inst. Wayne State U. Treas. Alzheimer's Assn. Mem.: AICPA (mem. practice stds. subcom.), Det. Athletic Club (bd. dirs.). Office: Dept Edn Office CFO 400 Maryland Ave SW Washington DC 20202-4110

MARTIN, JACQUELINE BRIGGS, author juvenile prose; b. Maine; m. Rich Martin; children: Sarah, Justin. Author: Bizzy Bones and Moosemouse, 1986, Bizzy Bones and the Lost Quilt, 1988, Bizzy Bones and Uncle Ezra, 1984, Button, Bucket, Sky, 1998, The Finest Horse in Town, 1992, Grandmother Bryant's Pocket, 1996 (Lupine award 1996), The Green Truck Garden Giveaway: A Neighborhood Story and Almanac, 1997, Good Times on Grandfather Mountain, 1992, Higgins Bend Song and Dance, 1997, Snowflake Bentley, 1998 (Caldecott Award 1999, Lupine Award 1998), Washing the Willow Tree Loon, 1995, The Lamp, The Ice and The Boat Called Fish, 2001, The Water Gift and the Pig of the Pig (Lupine award 2003), 2003, On Sand Island, 2003. Office: Houghton Mifflin Co Juvenile Dept Boston MA 02116

MARTIN, JACQUES, professional hockey coach; b. St. Pascal, Ont., Can., Oct. 1, 1952; Coach St. Louis Blues, 1986-88; asst. coach Chgo. Blackhawks, 1988-96; head coach Ottawa Senators, 1996—2004, Fla. Panters, 2004—. Named NHL Coach of the Year, 1999. Office: c/o Florida Panthers 1 Panther Pkwy Miami FL 33323

MARTIN, JAMES CHARLES, physician; b. Coleman, Tex., 1948; MD, U. Tex., San Antonio, 1973. Resident Bexar County Hosp., San Antonio, 1973-76; clin. prof. U. Tex. Health Sci. Ctr.; physician pvt. practice, 1976-96; dir. residency program Santa Rosa Family Practice, 1996—. Mem. Am. Acad. Family Physicians (pres. 2002-03), Am. Bd. Family Practice (pres. 1997-98), Tex. Med. Assn. Office: Ste 4703 333 N Santa Rosa San Antonio TX 78207-3108 E-mail: james.martin@christushealth.org.

MARTIN, JAMES DOUGLAS, neurologist; b. Cullman, Ala., Dec. 10, 1926; s. Charles L. and Sylvia J. (Johnson) M.; m. Elizabeth Mason, June 22, 1956; children: James, Julia, Ann. BA, Vanderbilt U., 1949, MD, 1959. Diplomate Am. Bd. Psychiatry and Neurology. Med. intern U. Va., Charlottesville, Va., 1959-60, neurology resident, 1960-63; fellow in neuropathology Harvard Med. Sch., Boston, 1963-65; asst. prof. neurology W. Va. U., Morgantown, 1965-70, assoc. prof., 1970-72, prof., 1972—. Fellow Am. Acad. Neurology. Office: W Va Univ Dept Neurology PO Box 9180 Morgantown WV 26506-9180

MARTIN, JAMES FREDERICK, media consultant; b. Sebring, Fla., June 29, 1944; s. George William and Elizabeth (Knudson) Martin; m. Hope Hamilton McCulloch, May 31, 1969; children: Faith Hamilton, Aimee Leavenworth. BFA in Visual Comm., Syracuse U., 1967; MA in Non-Verbal Communication, Mich. State U., 1968. Film producer Foote, Cone & Belding, Chgo., 1968-73, sr. producer, v.p., 1973-77, exec. producer, 1977-80, dir. broadcast prodn., 1980—83, dir. advt. services, 1983-84, sr. v.p. global broadcast prodn., 1984—2002; broadcast prodn. cons. Jim Martin, Glenview, Ill., 2003—. Home and Office: 1115 Normandy Ln Glenview IL 60025 3211 E-mail: jamesfm@earthlink.net.

MARTIN, JAMES GRUBBS, medical executive, former governor; b. Savannah, Ga., Dec. 11, 1935; s. Arthur Morrison and Mary Julia (Grubbs) M.; m. Dorothy Ann McAulay, June 1, 1957; children: James Grubbs, Emily Wood, Arthur Benson. BS, Davidson Coll., 1957; PhD, Princeton U., 1960. Assoc. prof. chemistry Davidson (N.C.) Coll., 1960-72; mem. 93d to 98th Congresses from N.C., 1973-85; gov. State of N.C., 1985-92; v.p. Carolinas HealthCare System, Charlotte, N.C., 1993—. Mem. Mecklenburg (NC) Bd. County Commrs., 1966-72, chmn., 1967-68, 70-71; pres. NC Assn. County Commrs., 1970-71; tuba player Charlotte Symphony, 1961-66; bd. dirs. Family Dollar Stores, Inc., Duke Energy Co., aaiPharma, Inc., Palomar Med. Technologies, Inc. Chmn. Global TransPark Found., 1993—; trustee Davidson Coll., 1998—; trustee Union Theol. Sem., Va., 2002-. Danforth fellow, 1957—60. Mem. Beta Theta Pi (v.p., trustee 1966-69, pres. 1975-78), Masons (33 deg.), Shriners. Presbyterian. Office: Carolinas Med Ctr PO Box 32861 Charlotte NC 28232-2861 E-mail: jgmartin@carolinas.org.

MARTIN, JAMES HANLEY, deputy state attorney general; b. N.Y.C., Dec. 22, 1960; s. James Patrick and Josephine Anne (Hanley) M. AB, Georgetown U., 1983; JD, Fordham U., 1986. Bar: N.J. 1986, U.S. Dist. Ct. N.J. 1986, N.Y. 1987, D.C. 1988, U.S. Dist. Ct. (so. and ea. dists.) N.Y. 1991, U.S. Ct. Appeals (D.C. and 3d cirs.) 1991, U.S. Supreme Ct. 1991. Dep. atty. gen. State of N.J., Newark, 1987—. Mem. ABA, Am. Judicature Soc., Bergen County Bar Assn., N.J. State Bar Assn., D.C. Bar, Assn. Bar of City of N.Y. Roman Catholic. Office: State of NJ Divsn Law PO Box 45029 124 Halsey St Newark NJ 07101

MARTIN, JAMES INGRAM, education educator; b. Homestead, Pa., Oct. 12, 1954; s. Roger Eugene and Joyce Hauck Martin; m. Linda Irene Fields, Aug. 16, 1980; 1 child, James Ingram Jr. BA, Duke U., 1976; MA, East Carolina U., 1981; PhD, Emory U., 1990. Social studies tchr. and coach James Kenan H.S., Warsaw, NC, 1986—91; asst. prof. hist. Campbell U., Buies Creek, NC, 1991—95, assoc. prof. hist., 1995—, chair, govt., hist. and justice dept., 2003—. Asst. scoutmaster, cubmaster Boy Scouts of Am., Cape Fear Dist., 1991—. Mem.: Southern Jewish Hist. Soc., N.C. Assn. of Historians. Office: Dept of Govt Hist and Justice Campbell Univ Buies Creek NC 27506

MARTIN, JAMES JOHN, JR., retired consulting research firm executive, systems analyst; b. Paterson, NJ, Feb. 3, 1936; s. James John and Lillian (Lea) M.; m. Lydia Elizabeth Bent, June 11, 1954; children: David, Peter, Laura, Daniel, Lucas. BA, U. Wis.-Madison, 1955; postgrad., Div. Sch., Harvard U., 1955-57; MS, Navy Postgrad. Sch., 1963; PhD, MIT, 1965. Commd. ensign USN, 1957, advanced through grades to comdr., 1971, ret., 1977; sector v.p. Sci. Applications Internat. Corp., La Jolla, Calif., 1977-95. Author: Bayesian Decision Problems and Markov Chains, 1967; editor: On Not Confusing Ourselves, 1991; author articles on nat. security. Bd. dirs. Mil. Conflict Inst., 1986-92. Decorated Legion of Merit; recipient Superior Svc. medal Dept. Def. Mem. Internat. Inst. Strategic Studies, Ops. Research Soc. Am., Mil. Ops. Research Soc. (bd. dirs. 1974-77) Democrat. Avocation: cooking. Home: 6603 Aranda Ave La Jolla CA 92037-6216

MARTIN, JAMES KAY, government official; b. Montreal, Que., Sept. 20, 1948; s. Douglas and Margaret Martin; m. Emma Lim Abrenica, Sept. 12, 1986. B of Math., U. Waterloo, Ont., 1970; PhD, U. Toronto, 1974. Sr. analyst Health & Welfare, Ottawa, 1974-79; asst. dir. transfer payments Social Devel. Ministry, Ottawa, 1980-84; exec. dir. planning Dept. Agr., Ottawa, 1984-90; exec dir. regulatory affairs Treasury bd. Can., Ottawa, 1990-96; dir. gen. Internal Audit and Risk Mgmt. Human Resources Can., Ottawa, 1997—2004; dir. gen. audit and evaluation Human Resources and Skills Devel., Ottawa, 2004—. Chmn. regulatory mgmt. group OECD, Paris, 1995-97. Contbr. articles to profl. jours. Chmn. grad. students union U. Toronto, 1973, mem. bd. govs., 1974. Fellow Nat. Rsch. Coun., 1970, Ont. Inst. for Edn., 1971, Can. Coun., 1972, 73. Mem. Ottawa Humane Soc. Roman Catholic. Avocations: running, canoeing, skiing, swimming. E-mail: james.martin@hrsdc-rhdcc.gc.ca.

MARTIN, JAMES KIRBY, historian, educator; b. Akron, Ohio, May 26, 1943; s. Paul Elmo and Dorothy Marie (Garrett) M.; m. Karen Wierwille, Aug. 7, 1965; children: Darcy Elizabeth, Sarah Marie, Joelle Kathryn Garrett. BA summa cum laude, Hiram Coll., 1965; MA, U. Wis., 1967, PhD, 1969. Asst. prof. history Rutgers U., New Brunswick, N.J., 1969-73, assoc. prof., 1973-79, prof., 1979-80, asst. provost, 1972-74, v.p. acad. affairs, 1977-79; vis. prof. Rutgers Ctr. of Alcohol Studies, 1978-88; prof. history U. Houston, 1980-97, disting. univ. prof., 1997—, chmn. dept., 1980-83; vis. prof. history Rice U., Houston, 1992. Chmn. bd. sponsors Papers of Thomas Edison Project, 1977-80; founding ptnr. PastQuest Rsch. Svcs., 1999. Author: Men in Rebellion, 1973, In the Course of Human Events, 1979, (with M.E. Lender) A Respectable Army: The Military Origins of the Republic, 1982 (contemporary mil. reading list), Drinking in America: A History, 1982, rev. edit. 1987, (with others) America and Its Peoples, 1989, 5th edit. 2004, concise edit. 1995, Benedict Arnold: Revolutionary Hero, 1997 (Homer D. Babbidge, Jr. award), audio edit., 2001; editor: Interpreting Colonial America, 1973, 2d edit. 1978, The Human Dimensions of Nation Making, 1976, (with K. Stubaus) The American Revolution, Whose Revolution?, 1977, 81, (with M.E. Lender) Citizen-Soldier: The Revolutionary War Journal of Joseph Bloomfield, 1982 (R.P. McCormick prize), Ordinary Courage: The Revolutionary War Adventures of Joseph Plumb Martin, 1993, 2d edit., 1999; mem. editl. bd. Papers of William Livingston Project, 1973-80, Houston Rev., 1981-2003, N.J. History, 1986—, Conversations with the Past Series, 1993-95; gen. editor Am. Social Experience Series, 1983-2002. Recipient N.J. Soc. of the Cin. prize for Disting. Achievement in Am. History, 1995, Hiram Coll. Alumni Achievement award, 1996. Mem. Tex. Assn. for Advancement History (bd. dirs. 1981-93, v.p. 1986-90), Inst. for Internat. Bus. Analysis (adv. coun. 1982-86), Am. Hist. Assn. (Beveridge-Dunning prize com. 1990-93), Orgn. Am. Historians, So. Hist. Assn., Soc. Historians Early Am. Republic (adv. coun. 1985-88), Soc. for Mil. History, Phi Beta Kappa, Phi Kappa Phi, Pi Gamma Mu, Omicron Delta Kappa, Phi Alpha Theta. Office: U Houston Dept History 524 Arnold Hall Houston TX 77204-3003

MARTIN, JAMES LARENCE, dentist, educator; b. Dubuque, Iowa, Sept. 3, 1940; s. James Larence and Ada Virginia (Boone) M.; m. Willie Mae Walker, Jan. 23, 1941; children: Linda Gail, James Larence III, John Lance. BS, Loras Coll., Dubuque, 1959, LittD, 1982; MS, Tenn. State U., 1960; DDS, Meharry Med. Coll., 1966; MPH, U. Mich., 1975. Dental dir. children and youth Meharry Med. Coll., Nashville, 1967-72, acting dir. children and youth program, 1972-73, dir. primary dental svcs., 1973-75, coord. dental component Ctr. for Health Care Rsch., 1975 77, prof., 1981—; owner Martin Dental, Nashville, 1980—. Dental cons. Medically Dedicated, Washington, 1992—; pres. faculty senate Meharry Med. Coll., 1989-93, mem. pres.'s exec. mgmt. team, 1989-93, dir. divsn. dental public health 1999—, chmn. dept. dental pub. health, 1999—. Contbr. articles to profl. jours., chpts. to books. Bd. regents Loras Coll., 1997—. Recipient Meritorious Svc. award Acad. Oral Medicine, 1977. Mem. ADA, Am. Pub. Health Assn. (med. com.), Am. Assn. Pub. Health Dentistry, Nat. Assn. Cmty. Health Ctrs., Am. Acad. Goil Foil Operators, Soc. of the Upper 10th, Nashville Area C. of C., Beta Kappa Chi, Phi Sigma. Avocations: reading, swimming, photography. Home: 3515 Geneva Cir Nashville TN 37209-2524 Office: 908 34th Ave N Nashville TN 37209-2502 E-mail: jmartin@mmc.edu., jmarti3817@aol.com.

MARTIN, JAMES ROBERT, identification company executive; b. Indpls., Mar. 31, 1943; s. Walter and Helen (Snider) M.; m. Jan. 24, 1970 (div. Dec. 1990); children: Julia, Justin; m. Tamara Hicks, Dec. 21, 1991; stepchildren: Hunter Hoskins, Laura Hoskins. BA, DePauw U., 1965; MBA, Ind. U., 1967. Bus. analyst TRW, Inc., Redondo Beach, Calif., 1967-70; fin. analyst Internat. Industries, Beverly Hills, Calif., 1970; v.p. fin., treas. A & E Plastik Pak Co., Inc., Industry, Calif., 1970-75; pres. Plasti-Line, Inc., Knoxville, Tenn., 1975-92, chmn., CEO, 1992—. Bd. dirs. 1st Am. Corp., Nashville, Signal Thread Co., Chattanooga, Tenn. Bd. dirs. Knoxville Symphony Soc., 1976, Knoxville United Way, 1986, Knoxville Mus. Art; bd. dirs., chmn. fin. com. Thompson Cancer Survival Ctr., Knoxville, 1985. Mem. Chief Execs. Orgn., Club LeConte (bd. dirs.), East Tenn. Automobile Club (bd. dirs.), St. Francis Yacht Club, Cherokee Country Club. Aspen Mountain Club. Republican. Episcopalian. Home: 1029 Scenic Dr Knoxville TN 37919 Office: ImagePoint PO Box 59043 Knoxville TN 37950-9043

MARTIN, JAMES VICTOR, JR., foreign service officer, writer; b. Tokyo, Nov. 15, 1916; (parents Am. citizens); s. James Victor Sr. and Esther Belle (Ludwig) M.; m. Elizabeth Shaler Smith, June 28, 1941; children: Sarah Martin Brown, Susan P. Martin, David Ludwig Martin. BA, DePauw U., 1938; MA, Tufts U., 1939, PhD, 1948; postgrad. in Japanese lang., Harvard U., 1941—42, Yale U., 1948—49; student, Nat. War Coll., 1961—62. Vice consul U.S. Consulate Gen., Bombay, 1946-48; polit. officer, head transl. sect. Office of Polit. Adviser, Tokyo, 1949-50; econ. officer U.S. Consulate Gen., Kobe-Osaka, Japan, 1951-53; prin. officer U.S. Consulate, Fukuoka, Japan, 1953-56; officer-in-charge Japanese Affairs U.S. Dept. State, Washington, 1956-58, personnel planning staff, 1958-61; chief polit. sect. U.S. Embassy, Rangoon, Burma, 1962-64; U.S. polit. adviser Office of U.S. High Commn. to the Ryukyu Islands, Okinawa, 1964-67; polit. counselor U.S. Embassy, Canberra, Australia, 1968-70; country dir. for Australia, N.Z. and Pacific Islands, U.S. Dept. State, Washington, 1970-73. Lectr. Far East internat. rels. Am. U., Washington, summer 1961; occasional lectr. U.S. Asian policy U. Md. Extension, Okinawa, 1965-67; cons. Pacific Islands, U.S. Dept. of Interior, Washington, 1973-74. Contbr. articles to profl. jours. Trustee Japan-Am. Soc. Washington, Inc., 1982-89; bd. dirs. Com. for Community Democracies-U.S.A., Washington, 1983-92, v.p., 1986-87; sec., treas. Com. for Community of Democracies (D.C.), Washington, 1985-88. Lt. USN, 1941-46, PTO. Mem. Assn. for Asian Studies, Mid-Atlantic Region Chpt. Assn. for Asian Studies (treas. 1972-76), Diplomatic and Consular Officers Ret. Methodist. Avocations: painting, woodblock printing, photography.

MARTIN, JAY GRIFFITH, lawyer; b. Washington, Oct. 13, 1951; s. Drexel Reese and Joyce (Towne) M.; 1 child, Trevor. BBA, So. Meth. U., 1973, MPA, JD, So. Meth. U., 1976. Bar: Tex., D.C., U.S. Ct. Appeals (5th cir.), U.S. Dist. Ct. (so. dist.) Tex., U.S. Dist. Ct. D.C., U.S. Supreme Ct. Counsel Pennzoil Co., Houston, 1976-78, sr. counsel, 1978-81; divsn. counsel The Superior Oil Co., Houston, 1981-85; sr. counsel Mobil Natural Gas, Houston, 1985-87, gen. counsel, 1987-91; asst. gen. counsel Mobil Oil Corp., Fairfax, Va., 1991-96; ptnr. Andrews & Kurth LLP, Washington, 1996-2000, Phelps Dunbar LLP, Houston, 2000—01, Winstead Sechrest & Minick, Houston, 2001—04; v.p., chief compliance officer, sr. deputy Gen. Coun. Baller Hughes, Inc., Houston, 2004—. Mem. sr. adv. bd. Bus. Laws Inc., Chesterland, Ohio, 1997—; mem. adv. bd. Inst. Transnat. Arbitration, Southwestern Legal Found., 1996—, Oil and Gas sec. of Inst. Am. and Internat. Law. Author: (books) Environmental Management Systems, 1998, Dispute Resolution for Oil and Gas Practitioners, 2000, Environmental Dispute Resolution, 2002; contbr. articles; mem. adv. bd.: jour. Natural Gas Contracts, 1991—; contbr. articles to profl. jours. Chmn. fundraising com. So. Meth. U., Washington, 1996—97, mem. dean's adv. coun. Sch. Law, 1995—; trustee Rocky Mountain Mineral Law Found., 2003—. Named Tex. Super Atty., Tex. Monthly Mag.; named one of World's Outstanding Energy Lawyers, Euromoney, 1997, 1999, 2001, 2003. Fellow: State Bar Coll. of Tex., Tex. Bar Found., State Bar Tex. (life; adv. bd. 1985—, chmn. corp. counsel sect. 1990—91, mem. corp counsel sect. adv. bd. 2003—04, mem. coun. for oil, gas and resources sect. 2003 , coun. oil and gas sect. 2003—, dir. Tex. C-Bar); mem.: Instit. Am. and Internat. Law (adv. bd. 2004), Fed. Bar Assn. (chmn. 1986—87, bd. dirs. 1990—92, antitrust sect. 1991—98, chmn. internat. energy com. 1997—), Delta Theta Phi, Rocky Mountain Law Inst. (trustee 1991—), Am. Soc. Internat. Law, Assn. Internat. Petroleum Negotiators, Houston Bar Assn., ABA (litig. sect. rep. on ABA coord. com. on energy law 1991—97, sect. pub. utility law 1991—, chmn. natural resources, energy and environ law internat. energy com. 1996—98, exec. coun., budget chmn. sect. on environment, energy and law 1996—, liaison to Fed. Energy Bar Assn. 1997—, ad hoc mem. of com. 1997—, sr. liaison oversight responsibility for all energy and resource coms. 1998—, vice chmn. sect. on environment, energy and resources' natural gas and), Energy Bar Assn. (chmn. antitrust sect. 1986—87, chmn. internat. energy com. 1998—99, chmn. internat. com.), Internat. Bar Assn. (sect. energy and natural resources 1994—), D.C. Bar Assn. (internat.sect.), Tex. Bar Assn. (dir. Tex.). Avocations: history, current events and politics, tennis, golf, jogging. Home: 3133 Buffalo Speedway Apt 7207 Houston TX 77098-1828 Office: Winstead Sechrest & Minick 910 Travis St Ste 2400 Houston TX 77002 E-mail: jmartin@winstead.com.

MARTIN, JAY HERBERT, psychoanalyst, English and political science educator; b. Newark, Oct. 30, 1935; s. Sylvester K. and Ada M. (Smith) M.; m. Helen Bernadette Saldini, June 9, 1956; children: Helen E., Laura A., Jay Herbert. AB with honors, Columbia U., 1956; MA, Ohio State U., 1957, PhD, 1960; PhD in Psychoanalysis, So. Calif. Psychoanalytic Inst., 1983. Instr. English Pa. State U., 1957-58; instr., then asst. to assoc. prof. English and Am. Studies Yale U., New Haven, 1960-68; prof. English and comparative culture U. Calif., Irvine, 1968-79; asst. prof. psychiatry and human behavior, clin. supr. residency program Calif. Coll. Medicine Calif. Coll. Medicine U.

Calif.-Irvine, 1978—96; Leo S. Bing prof. English and Am. lit. U. So. Calif., L.A., 1979-96, dir. undergrad. program in Am. studies, 1968-69, dir. program in comparative culture, 1969-71, dir. edn. abroad program, 1971-75; prof. govt., Edward S. Gould prof. humanities Claremont McKenna Coll., 1996—; dir. civilization program Claremont (Calif.) McKenna Coll., 1996—2000, acting dir. Gould Ctr. for Humanistic Studies, 1998-2000, prof., English, grad. sch., 2004—. Instr. psychoanalysis So. Calif. Psychoanalytic Inst., 1984-96; Bicentennial prof. Am. lit. and culture Moscow State U., USSR, 1976, Dai Ho Chun (Wisdom) chair Prof. U. Hawaii, 2000-01; vis. Parmenter lectr. Children's Hosp., San Francisco, 1989, Ann. William Faulkner Lecture, 1991, Herman Serota Found. lecture, 1992; cons. to pub. houses; lectr. USSR, Poland, Norway, France, Costa Rica, Germany, Brazil, Can., U. London, Hebrew U., Jerusalem, Seoul, Rep. Korea, China, Peru, Durham, Eng., Helsinki, Mex.; dir. NEH summer sems., 1976, 77; mem. evaluation com. dept. pvt. post-secondary edn. State of Calif., 1986; cons. numerous univs., pubs., NEA, NEA, J.S. Guggenheim Found., Calif. Coun. for Humanities and Pub. Policy, U.S. Congress Com. on Edn. and Labor; faculty assoc. Coun. Internat. Exch. of Scholars; frequent speaker profl. orgns. and sems., univs., confs., hosps. Author: (criticism and biography) Conrad Aiken: A Life of His Art, 1962, Harvests of Change: American Literature 1865-1914, 1967, Nathanael West: The Art of His Life, 1970 (U. Calif. Friends Libr. award), Robert Lowell, 1970, Always Merry and Bright. The Life of Henry Miller, 1978, (U. Calif. Friends of Libr. award, Phi Kappa Phi Best Faculty Publ. prize U. So. Calif., transl. in French, Japanese and German), (fiction) Winter Dreams: An American in Moscow, 1979, Who Am I This Time, Uncovering the Fictive Personality, 1988 (trans. Portuguese), Burlington No. Found. award 1989); Swallowing Tigers Whole, 1996, A Corresponding Leap of Love: Henry Miller, 1996, Henry Miller's Dream Song, 1996, Journey to Heavenly Mountain, 2002 (ForeWord mag. Book of Yr. prize), The Education of John Dewey, 2003; author one hour radio drama, William Faulkner. Sound Portraits of Twentieth-Century Humanists, starring Tennessee Williams, Glenn Close, Colleen Dewhurst, Nat. Pub. Radio, 1980; author one-act docudrama Trial Days in Coyocoan, Antioch Rev., 2001; author sects. 24 books including most recently American Writing Today, vol. I, 1982, The Haunted Dusk: American Supernatural Fiction, 1820-1902, 1983, Frontiers of Infant Psychiatry, vol.II, 1986, Centenary Essays on Huckleberry Finn, 1985, Robert Lowell: Essays on the Poetry, 1987, William Faulkner: The Best from American Literature, 1989, The Homosexualities: Reality, Fantasy and the Arts, 1991, Life Guidance Through Literature, 1992, Biography and Source Studies, 1995, William Faulkner and Psychology, 1995, Psychotherapy East and West, 1996, Readings on Huckleberry Finn, 1999, John Fante: A Critical Gathering, 2000, Uncollected Works By...Paul Laurence Dunbar, 2000, American Literature of the Civil War, 2004, Blackwell Companion to Modernist Literature and Culture, 2004; contbr. numerous articles and revs. to profl. jours., bulls., L.A. Times Book Rev., Partisan Rev., N.Y. Times Book Rev., Internat. Rev. Psycho-Analysis, Am. Lit., London Times Lit. Supplement, Psychoanalytic Quarterly, Jour. Applied Psychoanalysis; editor: Winfield Townley Scott (Yale series recorded poets), 1962, Twentieth Century Interpretations of the Waste Land: A Collection of Critical Essays, 1968, Twentieth Century Views of Nathanael West, 1972, A Singer in the Dawn: Reinterpretations of Paul Laurence Dunbar (with intro.), 1975, Economic Depression and American Humor (with intro.), 1986; mem. editl. bd. Am. Lit., 1978-81, Humanities in Society, 1979-1983; editor-in-chief Psychoanalytic Edn., 1984-89; editor Humanitas/Communitas, 1998-2000; appearances on TV and radio including Connie Martinson Talks Books, Barbara Brunner Nightline, Sonya Live in L.A., Oprah Winfrey Show, C-SPAN, 1988-89. Pres. Friends of Irvine Pub. Libr., 1974-75; mem. Com. for Freud Mus. Recipient Fritz Schmidl Meml. prize for rsch. applied psychoanalysis Seattle Assn. Psychoanalysis, 1982, Marie H. Briehl prize for child psychoanalysis, 1982, Franz Alexander prize in psychoanalysis, 1984, Disting. Writers award Antioch Rev., 2004; Morse rsch. fellow, 1963-64, Am. Philos. Soc. fellow, 1966, J.S. Guggenheim fellow, 1966-67, Rockefeller Found.humanities sr. fellow, 1975-76, Rsch. Clin. fellow So. Calif. Psychoanalytic Soc. 1977-81, Rockefeller fellow, Bellagio, Italy, 1983, NEH sr. fellow, 1983-84; Durfee Found. fellow to China, 2004; fellow Bogliasco Found. Liguria Ctr. for Arts and Humanities, 2004. Mem. So. Calif. Am. Studies Assn. (pres. 1969-71), Am. Studies Assn. (exec. bd. 1969-71, del. to MLA Assembly 1974, chmn. Ralph Gabriel prize com. 1975-77), MLA (chmn. prize com. Jay B. Hubbell Silver medal in Am. lit. 1978-84), Nat. Assn. Arts and Letters (prize com. 1987-88), Nat. Humanities Faculty (advisor to Valhalla High Sch., El Cajon, Calif. 1979-81), Nat. Am. Studies Faculty, Internat. Psychoanalytic Assn., Internat. Assn. Empirical Aesthetics, Internat. Assn. U. Profs. English, Internat. Karen Horney Soc., Newport Psychoanalytical Inst., Phi Beta Kappa. Home: 748 Via Santo Tomas Claremont CA 91711-1569 Office Phone: 909-398-0193. Business E-Mail: jmartin@mckenna.edu.

MARTIN, JEANETTE ST. CLAIR, adult education educator; b. Jackson, Mich., Sept. 25, 1947; d. George Washington and Doris Janette (Robins) St. Clair; m. Stevens John Martin Jr., July 17, 1976; 1 child, Andrea Lynne. BA in Bus. Edn., Mich. State U., 1970; MBA in Mktg., U. Chgo., 1974; EdD in Curriculum and Instrn., U. Memphis, 1991. Product availability coord. Quaker Oats Co., Chgo., 1971-74; market analyst and inventory mgr. Robert Bosch Corp., Broadview, Ill., 1974-76; materials sys. analyst Zenith Corp., Chgo., 1976-77; purchasing rsch. analyst Baxter, Deerfield, Ill., 1977-78; owner Carriage Gallery, Memphis, 1981-85; instr. Shelby State Coll., Memphis, 1986-90; instr., tchg. asst. U. Memphis, 1986-91; asst. prof. U. Miss., University, 1991-98, assoc. prof., 1999—. Cons. Sharp Corp., Memphis, 1989-90, Benchcraft, Blue Mountain, Miss., 1995, IPR, 1997—. Author: (with L. Chaney) Intercultural Business Communication, 1995, 3d edit., 2004. Mem. Assn. Bus. Comm. (assoc. editor 1990-2002), Internat. Acad. Intercultural Rels. Republican. Episcopalian. Avocations: golf, swimming. Office: U Miss Sch Bus Adminstrn University MS 38677 Office Phone: 662-915-5454. E-mail: jmartin@bus.olemiss.edu.

MARTIN, JERRY HAROLD, bank examiner; b. Richwood, W.Va., Apr. 28, 1945; s. Weaver Eugene and Hazel Lee (Adkins) M.; m. Phyllis Lowe, Apr. 26, 1967 (div. 1980); m. Deborah Ann Perry, June 6, 1983 (div. 1994); children: Marlene, Renee; m. Mamie E. Scott, Mar. 1, 1994. BA in Econs., U. Charleston (W.Va.), 1967; Cert. Banking, La. State U., Baton Rouge, 1980. Asst. examiner Comptroller of the Currency, Charleston, 1969-74, bank examiner, 1974-77, examiner-in-charge, 1977-84, field mgr., 1984-97; banker Wesbanco Bank, Charleston, 1998—; sr. fin. instn. examiner W.Va. Banking Divsn., 1998—. With U.S. Army, 1967-69. Recipient Cert. of Appreciation, Comptroller of Currency, 1986. Methodist. Avocations: jogging, coin collecting/numismatics. Home: PO Box 3934 Charleston WV 25339-3934

MARTIN, JERRY LEE, organization executive, educator; b. Turkey, Tex., Oct. 16, 1941; m. Abigail L. Rosenthal, 1998. Student, San Diego State Coll., 1961; BA in Polit. Sci., U. Calif., Riverside, 1963; MA in Philosophy and Polit. Sci., U. Chgo., 1966; PhD in Philosophy, Northwestern U., 1970; DHL (hon.), Thomas Moore Coll. Liberal Arts, 2003. Asst. prof. U. Colo., Boulder, 1967-74, chmn. dept. philosophy, 1979-81, assoc. prof., 1974-84, adjunct prof., 1984—; rsch. analyst House Rep. Rsch. Com., 1982-87; legis. asst. Congressman Hank Brown, 1982-87; dir. divisn. edn. programs NEH, Washington, 1987-88, asst. chmn. studies and evaluation, 1988-89, asst. chmn. programs and policy, 1989-95, acting chmn., 1993. Adj. prof. Georgetown U., 1993-95; adj. scholar Am. Enterprise Inst., 1993—; dir. Ctr. Study Values and Social Policy, U. Colo., Boulder, 1981-82; founding mem. organized rsch. program State of Colo., 1981-82; mem. exec. com. faculty adv. coun. Colo. Commn. Higher Edn., 1980-82; pres. Am. Coun. Trustees and Alumni, 1995—; spkr. in field, frequent guest on radio and TV. Contbr. articles to profl. jours. Mem. Gov.'s Blue Ribbon Commn. on Higher Edn., 1998—2000. Andrew W. Mellon Found. Congl. fellow, 1992-93. Mem. AAUP (state pres. 1977-79), Am. Philos. Assn., Soc. Historians Early Am. Republic, Am. Polit. Sci. Assn., Soc. Social, Polit. and Legal Philosophy. Avocations: tennis, baseball, hist. tours. Home: 145 C Selner Ln Doylestown PA 18901 Office: Am Coun Trustees and Alumni 1726 M Street NW # 800 Washington DC 20036

MARTIN, JOANNE, social sciences educator; b. Salem, Mass., Sept. 25, 1946; d. Richard Drake and Nathalie (Ashton) M.; m. Beaumont A. Sheil, July 9, 1977; 1 child, Beaumont Martin Sheil. BA, Smith Coll., 1968; PhD in Social Psychology, Harvard U., 1977; PhD in Econs. and Bus. Adminstrn. (hon.), Copenhagen Bus. Sch., 2001; PhD (hon.), Vrije U., Amsterdam. Assoc. cons. McBer & Co. (formerly Behavior Sci. Ctr. of Sterling Inst.), 1968-70, dir. govt. mktg., 1970-72; asst. prof. orgnl. behavior and sociology Grad. Sch. Bus., Stanford (Calif.) U., 1977-80; assoc. prof. grad. sch. bus. Stanford U., 1980-91, prof. grad. sch. bus., 1991—, dir. doctoral programs, grad. sch. bus., 1991-95, Fred H. Merrill prof. orgn. behavior and sociology, 1996—. Sec. adv. bd. Stanford U., 1995—96, vice chair adv. bd., 1996—97; vis. scholar Australian Grad. Sch. Mgmt. U. N.S.W., 1989—90, Copenhagen Bus. Sch., 1998, 2004; vis. scholar dept. psychology Sydney (Australia) U., 1989—90; Ruffin fellow bus. ethics Darden Grad. Sch. Bus. Adminstrn. U. Va., 1990; mem. bd. advisors iMahal, 1990—; mem. audit com. and compensation chair C.P.P., Inc., 1993—2003; mem. internat. adv. bd. Internat. Ctr. for Rsch. in Orgnl. Discourse, Strategy and Change; Bus. Sch. rep. Stanford U., 1995—. Mem. editl. bd. Adminstrv. Sci. Qtrly., 1984—88, Jour. Social Issues, 1981—83, Acad. Mgmt. Jour., 1984—85, Social Justice Rsch., 1985—90, Jour. Mgmt. Inquiry, 1991—, Orgn., 1994—, Jour. Mgmt. Studies, 1996—2004, Gender, Work and Organization, 1998—, Orgn. Studies, 2003—, Scandinavian Jour. Mgmt., 2003—, consulting editor Internat. Jour. Mgmt. Reviews, 1998—; co-author: five books; contbr. over 60 articles to profl. jours. and edited books. Recipient Centennial medal for contbns. to soc. Harvard U. Grad. Sch. Arts and Scis., 2002; Lena Lake Forrest Rsch. fellowship Bus. and Profl. Women's Found., 1978, James and Doris McNamara Faculty fellowship Grad. Sch. of Bus., Stanford U., 1990-91. Fellow: APA, Am. Psychol. Soc., Acad. Mgmt. (rep.-at-large 1983—85, divsn. program chair 1985—87, divsn. chair 1987—89, nat. bd. govs. 1992—95, we. divsn. Promising Young Scholar award 1982, Nat. Disting. Educator award 2000, We. Divsn. Sr. Scholar award 2003); mem.: Nat. Assn. Corp. Dirs. (adv. bd. 2000—04). Office: Stanford U Grad Sch Bus Littlefield Ctr 353 Stanford CA 94305

MARTIN, JOHN C. medical products executive; b. 1952; PhD in Organic Chemistry, U. Chgo. With Syntex Corp., 1978-84; dir. antiviral che3mistry Bristol-Myers Squibb, 1984-90; v.p. R&D Gilead Scis., Inc., Foster City, Calif., 1990-95, COO, 1995-96, pres., CEO, dir., 1996—. Mem. Internat. Soc. for Antiviral Rsch. (pres.). Office: Gilead Scis Inc 333 Lakeside Dr Foster City CA 94404-1146 Fax: 650-573-4800.

MARTIN, JOHN CHARLES, judge; b. Durham, N.C., Nov. 9, 1943; s. Chester Barton and Mary Blackwell (Pridgen) M.; m. Margaret Rand; children: Lauren Blackwell, Sarah Conant, Mary Susan; step-children: Louise Short, Carl (Trip) Short. BA, Wake Forest U., 1965, JD, 1967; postgrad., Nat. Judicial Coll., Reno, 1979; cert. justice execs. program, U. N.C. Bar: N.C. 1967, U.S. Dist. Ct. (mid. dist.) N.C. 1967, U.S. Dist. Ct. (ea. dist.) N.C. 1972, U.S. Dist. Ct. (we. dist.) N.C. 1975, U.S. Ct. Appeals (4th cir.) 1976, U.S. Supreme Ct. 2002. Assoc. Haywood, Denny & Miller, Durham, N.C., 1969-72, ptnr., 1973-77; resident judge Superior Ct. 14th Jud. Dist. N.C., Durham, 1977-84; judge N.C. Ct. Appeals, Raleigh, 1985—88, 1993—2004, chief judge, 2004—; ptnr. Maxwell & Hutson, P.A., Durham, 1988-92; arbitrator U.S. Dist. Ct. (mid. dist.) N.C., 1988-92. Study com. rules of evidence and comparative negligence N.C. Legis. Research Commn., 1980; mem. N.C. Pattern Jury Instrn. drafting com., 1978-84, N.C. Trial Judge's Bench Book Drafting Com., 1984-87, N.C. News Media-Adminstrn. of Justice Coun., 1987, state/fed. Jud. Coun. N.C., 1985-87, chmn., 1987; bd. visitors Wake Forest U. Sch. Law, 1986—; mem. alumni coun. Wake Forest U., 1993-96, 2001—; mem. N.C. State Jud. Edn. Study Com., 2000—; chmn. N.C. Jud. Stds. Commn., 2001—. Mem. Durham City Coun., 1975—77, chair pub. works com.; panel of arbitrators Duke U. Pvt. Adjudication Ctr., 1988—92; mem. N.C. Judicial Coun.; mem. parent adv. bd. Chatham Hall Sch., 2003—. With Mil. Police Corps USAR, 1967—69. Recipient Disting. Svc. award Durham Jaycees, 1976. Mem. ABA, Appellate Judges Conf., Coun. of Chief Judges, N.C. Bar Assn. (chmn. adminstrn. of justice study com. 1990-92, bench, bar and law sch. com. 1987-91, jud. campaign oversight com. 1990, Lit. Sect. Coun. 1991-94, conv. planning com. 1995—, adminstrn. justice task force 1996-98, appellate rules study com. 1999-2001, strategic planning/emerging trends com. 2002-04, endowment com. 2004—, v.p. 1997-98), Durham County Bar Assn. (bd. dirs. 1991-92), Wake County Bar Assn., 10th Jud. Dist. Bar Assn., N.C. Jud. Conf. (v.p. 1999-2000), Hope Valley Country Club, Appalachian State U. Parents Assn. (bd. dirs. 1997-2001), Phi Delta Phi. Democrat. Methodist. Office: PO Box 888 Raleigh NC 27602-0888 Office Phone: 919-733-4293. E-mail: mnj@coa.state.nc.us.

MARTIN, JOHN DRISCOLL, school administrator; b. Chgo., July 28, 1954; s. Walter Roy and Constance Kathleen (Driscoll) M.; children: Patrick, Kelsey; m. Caroline J. Martin, Mar. 28, 1996. BA, Augustana Coll., 1976; MA, Northwestern U., 1982. Cert. tchr., Ill. Tchr. J.D. Darnall High Sch., Geneseo, Ill., 1976-77, St. Viator High Sch., Arlington Heights, Ill., 1977-79, Hoffman Estates (Ill.) High Sch., 1979-88, athletic dir., 1988-90, Adlai E. Stevenson High Sch., Lincolnshire, Ill., 1990—. Adv. com. Ill. High Sch. Assn., Bloomington, 1989-92; master tchr. Gov.'s Master Tchr. Program, 1984—. Mem. AAHPERD, Ill. Assn. Health, Phys. Edn., Recreation and Dance, Nat. Athletic Adminstrs. Assn., Ill. Athletic Dirs. Assn. (conf. chair 1995, cert. athletic adminstr.). Avocations: golf, reading. Office: 1 Stevenson Dr Lincolnshire IL 60069-2824 E-mail: jmartin@district125.k12.il.us.

MARTIN, J(OHN) EDWARD, architectural engineer; b. L.A., Oct. 23, 1916; s. Albert C. and Carolyn Elizabeth (Borchard) M.; m. Elizabeth Jane Hines, May 27, 1944; children: Nicolas Edward, Peter Hines, Sara Jane McKinley Reynolds, Christopher Carey, Elizabeth Margaret Ferguson. Student, U. So. Calif., 1934-36; BS in Archtl. Engring., U. Ill., 1939. Registered profl. engr., Calif., Ill. Structural engr. Albert C. Martin & Assocs., L.A., 1939-42, ptnr., 1945-75, mng. ptnr., 1975-86. Founding mem. bd. trustees Thomas Aquinas Coll., Santa Paula, Calif., 1971-98, emeritus, 1998. Lt. CEC, USNR, 1942-45. Fellow ASCE; mem. Structural Engrs. Assn. Calif., Cons. Engrs. Assn. Calif., Jonathan Club (bd. dirs. 1978-81), Calif. Club, Ranchero Visitadores, Valley Hunt Club, Flintridge Riding Club, West Hills Hunt Club (Master of Fox Hounds 1975-88), Saddle & Sirloin Club, Heritage Found., Traditional Mass Soc. (founder), Pacific Legal Found. (charter). Republican. Roman Catholic. Avocation: horsemanship. E-mail: bzmartin@pacbellnet. Office: AC Martin Ptnrs 444 S Flower St Los Angeles CA 90017-3475 Home: 1763 Royal Oaks Dr Apt C3 Bradbury CA 91010-1981 Fax: 626-440-0889.

MARTIN, JOHN HUGH, lawyer, retired; b. Los Angeles, Apr. 19, 1918; s. John Hume and Carrie Suzanne (Hatcher) M.; m. Jean Morrison Park, Sept. 17, 1945; 1 dau., Suzanne L. BS, Monmouth Coll., 1939; JD, U. Chgo., 1942. Bar: Ill. 1943, Calif. 1962. Practice law, Chgo., 1943-52; sec., gen. counsel Am. Community Builders, Park Forest, Ill., 1952-54; dep. counsel Bur. Aero., Dept. Navy, Washington, 1954-57; with Lockheed Aircraft Corp., Burbank, Calif., 1957-79, European counsel, 1960-61, div. counsel, 1961-71, asst. sec., chief counsel, 1971-77, corp. adv., 1977-79; pvt. practice law, 1980-94; retired, 1994. Mem. Am., Fed., Internat., Los Angeles County bar assns., Phi Alpha Delta. Clubs: Legal (Chgo.);. Democrat. Episcopalian. Home: 538 E Alder St Walla Walla WA 99362-2014

MARTIN, JOHN JOSEPH, journalist; b. N.Y.C., Dec. 3, 1938; s. John and Marie Agnes (Jacobsen) M.; children from previous marriage: Sophie Suzanne, Claire Catherine; m. Katherine Fitzhugh, Feb. 14, 1987. BA in Journalism, San Diego State U., 1995. Copy editor, reporter San Diego Union, 1958-62; copy editor Augusta (Ga.) Chronicle, 1963, N.Y. Times Internat. Edit., Paris, 1964-65; editorial asst. Temple Fielding Publs., Mallorca, Spain, 1965-66; reporter, producer Sta. KCRA-TV News, Sacramento, 1966-75; corr. ABC-TV News, 1975—2002. Adj. prof. Columbia U. Grad. Sch. of Journalism, 2002—. Editor, pub. Aztec Tennis Reporter, 1999—; contbg. writer Tennisone.com, 2000-02. Served with U.S. Army, 1962-64. Recipient Nat. Headliner awards, 1980, 89, Emmy award, 1993, George Polk award, 1994, DuPont-Columbia U. Gold baton, 1994, Nat. Assn. Black Journalists award, 2002, Peabody award, 2002. Mem. AFTRA, U.S. Tennis Assn., Coffee House Club N.Y.C., Nat. Press Club, Overseas Press Club, U.S. Tennis Writers Assn. Office Phone: 212-854-1957.

MARTIN, JOHN L. airport executive; Dir. San Francisco Airport, 1999—. Office: San Francisco Airport Commn PO Box 8097 San Francisco CA 94128-8097

MARTIN, JOHN LEWIS, state legislator; b. Eagle Lake, Maine, June 5, 1941; s. Frank and Edwidge (Raymond) M. BA in History and Govt., U. Maine, 1963, postgrad., 1963-64. Tchr. Am. govt. and history Ft. Kent (Maine) Community High Sch., 1966-72; instr. U. Maine, Ft. Kent, 1972-89, asst. prof., 1989—; mem. from Eagle Lake and St. Francis dist. Maine Ho. of Reps., 1964-94, minority fl. leader, 1970-74, speaker of ho., 1975-94, chmn. com. on energy & natural resources, 1994-95, mem. from dist. 151, 1998-2000. Mem. Maine Senate, Dist. 1, 2000—; chmn. Com. Natural Resources, 1999-2000; adj. lectr.; mem. intergovtl. rels. com. Nat. Legis. Conf., 1970-74; chmn. Maine Land Use Regulation Commn., 1972-73, Maine Bur. Human Rels., 1972, State Legis. Leaders Found., 1979-83; mem. exec. bd. Nat. Conf. State Legislatures, chmn. state-fed. assembly, 1985-86, chair task force on reapportionment, 1987-88, vice chmn. budget, fiscal and rules com., 1986-87, v.p., 1988-89, pres.-elect, 1989-90, pres., 1990-91, immediate past pres., 1991-92; mem. exec. com. New Eng. Caucus of State Legislatures, 1978-95, chmn., 1982; mem. regional exec. com. Nat. Dem. State Legis. Leaders Assn., 1991-95, chmn., 1987-89; bd. dirs. Found. for State Legislatures, 1988-94; mem. exec. com. Dem. Nat. Com., 1991-94. Trustee Eagle Lake Water and Sewer Dist., 1966—, No. Maine Gen. Hosp., Eagle Lake, Ea. Maine Health Care, 1991-92; mem. rural health steering com. Nat. Acad. for State Health Policy; advisor White House Task Force on Health Care Reform; dir. intergovtl. affairs Nat. Health Care Campaign, 1994; trustee Maine Med. Ctr., Ft. Kent. Mem. New Eng. Polit. Sci. Assn. Democrat. Home: PO Box 250 Eagle Lake ME 04739-0250 Office: Maine Senate State House Augusta ME 04333-0003 Office Phone: 207-834-7568.

MARTIN, JOHN RANDOLPH, judge; b. Lexington, Ky., May 26, 1948; s. Harry and Geraldine (Gray) M.; m. Jacqueline Lauren Snyder, Apr. 24, 1976; 1 child, Lauren Elizabeth. BA, U. Okla., 1973, MA, 1976, JD, 1980. Bar: Okla. 1981, U.S. Ct. Mil. Appeals 1981, U.S. Dist. Ct. (we. dist.) Okla. 1982, S.C. 1983, U.S. Ct. Appeals (10th cir.) 1983, U.S. Dist. Ct. S.C. 1984, U.S. Ct. Appeals (4th cir.) 1984, U.S. Supreme Ct. 1995. Assoc. Finkel, Georgaklis et al, Columbia, S.C., 1984-86; ptnr. Mumford, Wishart & Martin, North Myrtle Beach, S.C., 1986-87, Gertz, Kastanes, Moore & Martin, North Myrtle Beach, S.C., 1987-91; with Office of Hearings and Appeals, Social Security Adminstrn., Houston, 1991—. Lt. col. U.S. Army, 1967-70, Vietnam, with Res. 1975-78, 84-97, Desert Storm, JAGC, 1981-84. Mem. NRA, Masons, Shriners, Elks, Phi Delta Phi, Pi Kappa Alpha. Republican. Episcopalian. Avocations: singing, shooting. Office: Office of Hearing and Appeals 1927 Thurmond Mall Blvd Ste 200 Columbia SC 29201-2375

MARTIN, JOHN SHERWOOD, JR., federal judge; b. Bklyn., May 31, 1935; BA, Manhattan Coll., 1957; LLB, Columbia U., 1961. Bar: N.Y. 1961, U.S. Dist. Ct. (so. dist.) N.Y. 1963, U.S. Supreme Ct. 1966, U.S. Ct. Appeals (2d cir.) 1983. Law clk. to Hon. Leonard P. Moore U.S. Ct. Appeals (2d cir.), 1961-62; asst. U.S. atty. U.S. Dist. Ct. (so. dist.) N.Y., 1962-66; ptnr. Johnson, Hekker & Martin, Nyack, N.Y., 1966-67; asst. to solicitor gen., 1967-69; sole practitioner, 1969-72; ptnr. Martin, Obermaier & Morvillo, 1972-79, Schulte, Roth & Zabel, 1979-80; U.S. atty. U.S. Dist. Ct. for So. Dist. N.Y., N.Y.C., 1980-83; ptnr. Schulte, Roth & Zabel, 1983-90; judge U.S. Dist. Ct. for So. Dist. N.Y., N.Y.C., 1990—. Cons. Nat. Commn. Law Enforcement and the Adminstrn. of Criminal Justice, 1966-67; counsel to commn. to investigate disturbances Columbia U., 1968. Fellow Am. Coll. Trial Lawyers; mem. Assn. Bar City N.Y. Office: US Dist Ct So Dist NY 500 Pearl St New York NY 10007-1316

MARTIN, JOHN THOMAS, physician, author, educator; b. Cleve., June 8, 1924; s. Clarence Henry and Clara May (Feeney) M.; m. Marion Elizabeth George, Feb. 18, 1946; children: Thomas R., David B., Richard G., Janet E., Patricia L., Robert W. MD, U. Cin., 1948. Commd. 1st lt. USAF, 1949, advanced through grades to maj., 1953; resident in anesthesiology Lackland AFB Hosp., San Antonio, 1953-55; asst. chief USAF Sch. Anesthesiology, Lackland AFB, 1955-57; attending anesthesiologist Baylor U. Hosp., Dallas, 1957-58; cons. dept. anesthesiology Mayo Clinic, Rochester, Minn., 1958-72, head Meth sect. anesthesiology, 1966-72; assoc. clin. prof. anesthesiology, 1968-72; chmn. dept. anesthesiology Ochsner Med. Ctr., New Orleans, 1972-74; clin. assoc. prof. anesthesiology Tulane U. Sch. Medicine, New Orleans, 1972-74; prof. anesthesiology Med. Coll. Ohio, Toledo, 1974-90, chmn. dept. anesthesiology, 1980-89, emeritus prof. anesthesiology, 1990—. Editor, author: Positioning Patients Anesthesia/Surgery, 1978, 2d edit., 1987, 3d edit., 1997; editor ASA Handbook of Hosp. Facilities for Anesthesia, 1972, 2d edit., 1974; contbr. articles to profl. jours. Chmn. conductor selection com. Rochester Symphony Orch., 1963-66; pres. Rochester Civic Music, 1965. Mem. Internat. Anesthesia Rsch. Soc. (chmn. 1979-81, trustee 1965-90), Minn. Soc. Anesthesiologists (pres. 1966-67), Ohio Soc. Anesthesiologists (pres. 1988-89), Am. Med. Writers Assn. (pres. Minn. chpt. 1970-71), Assoc. Physicians Med. Coll. Ohio (bd. dirs. 1974-89), Am. Soc. Anesthesiology, Sigma Xi, Alpha Omega Alpha, Sigma Chi, Phi Chi. Republican. Avocations: medical writing, computers, music, fishing. Office: Med Coll of Ohio PO Box 10008 Toledo OH 43699-0008 Home: 4306 Todd Dr Sylvania OH 43560-3297

MARTIN, JOHN WILLIAM, JR., retired lawyer, automotive industry executive; b. Evergreen Park, Ill., Sept. 1, 1936; s. John William and Frances (Hayes) M.; m. Joanne Cross, July 2, 1966; children: Amanda Hayes, Bartholomew McGuire. AB in History, DePaul U., 1958, JD, 1961. Bar: Ill. 1961, D.C. 1962, N.Y. 1964, Mich. 1970. Antitrust trial atty. Dept. Justice, Washington, 1961-62; assoc. Donovan, Leisure, Newton & Irvine, N.Y.C., 1962-70; sr. atty. Ford Motor Co., Dearborn, Mich., 1970-72, assoc. counsel, 1972-74, counsel, 1974-76, asst. gen. counsel, 1976-77, assoc. gen. counsel, 1977-89, v.p., gen. counsel, 1989-99; ret., 1999. Contbr. articles to profl. jours. Trustee DePaul U., 1998—; bd. dirs. Ctr. Social Gerontology, Inc., Nat. Women's Law Ctr., Friends of Legal Svcs. Corp. Mem.: Am. Law Inst., Assn. Gen. Counsel, Little Traverse Yacht Club. Republican. Roman Catholic. Personal E-mail: jwmartinjrsail@netscape.net.

MARTIN, JOHNNY BENJAMIN, accountant; b. Gainesville, Ga., June 9, 1947; s. John Daniel and Helen Amanda (Meeks) M.; m. Mary Sue West, June 8, 1969; 1 child, Tammy Michelle. BBA, U. Ga., Athens, 1969, MA, 1971. CPA, Ga. Tchr. high sch. Hall County Sch. Systems, Gainesville, 1969-70; instr. acctg. Austin Peay State U., Clarksville, Tenn., 1972-76; instr. bus. Gainesville Jr. Coll., 1976-77; contr. Home Fed. Savs. and Loan, Gainesville, 1977-83; ptnr. Kendrick & Jessup, CPA's, Gainesville, 1983-92; pvt. practice, Gainesville, 1992—. Mem. AICPA, Ga. Soc. CPAs, Civitan (bd. dirs., treas. 1981-82, treas. 1986-87), Phi Kappa Phi, Beta Gamma Sigma. Democrat. Baptist. Home: 3751 Robinson Dr Oakwood GA 30566-3408 E-mail: JohnnyBMartin@netzero.com.

MARTIN, JOSÉ GINORIS, education administrator; b. Feb. 4, 1941; married; two children. BS in Nuclear Engring. with honors, Miss. State U., 1964; MS in Nuclear Engring., U. Wis., 1966, PhD in Engring., 1970; MDP, Harvard U., 1997. Mem. faculty U. Mass., Lowell, 1975—96, grad. coord. for energy engring., 1984-90; chmn. chem. and nuclear engring. dept. Coll. of Engring., U. Mass., Lowell, 1990-96; dean Coll. Sci., Math and Tech. U. Tex., Brownsville, 1996—2000, provost and v.p. acad. affairs, 2000—, Houston Found. faculty chmn. sci. Bd. dirs. Enersol, Inc., Tech Prep of the Rio Grande Valley, Inc., Valley Regional Hosp.; Fulbright prof. Curso de Postgraduacão em Ecologia, U. Federale do Rio Crande do Sul, Porto Alegre, Brazil, 1995; vis. prof. Ariz. State U. Coll. of Architecture, 1983, U. Mex., 1976-77, I.M.E., Rio de Janeiro, 1973; dir. Mass. Photovoltaic Ctr., 1987-96; cons. Corp. for Energy Devel. of Andalucia, 1992-96, Corp. for the 1992 Universal Exposion in Seville, Spain, 1982-88; prin. gov.'s task force on energy Commonwealth of Mass., 1994. Contbr. numerous articles to profl. jours. Mem.: Sigma Xi. E-mail: jmartin@utbl.utb.edu.

MARTIN, JOSEPH BOYD, dean, neurologist, educator; b. Bassano, Alta., Can., Oct. 20, 1938; s. Joseph Bruce and Ruth Elizabeth (Ramer) Martin; m. Rachel Ann Wenger, June 18, 1960; children: Bradley, Melanie, Douglas, Neil. BSc, Eastern Mennonite Coll., Harrisonburg, Va., 1959; MD, U. Alta., 1962; PhD, U. Rochester, N.Y., 1971; MA (hon.), Harvard U., 1978; ScD (hon.), McGill U., 1994, U. Rochester, 1996, U. Wis., 1997, U. Alta., 1998. Resident in internal medicine Univ. Hosp., Edmonton, 1962—64; resident in neurology

Case-Western Res. U. Hosps., 1964—67; rsch. fellow U. Rochester, NY, 1967—70; mem. faculty McGill U. Faculty Medicine, Montreal, Canada, 1970—78; prof. medicine and neurology, neurologist-in-chief Montreal Neurol. Inst., 1976—78; chmn. dept. neurology Mass. Gen. Hosp., Boston, also Dorn prof. neurology Harvard U. Med. Sch., 1978—89; dean Sch. Medicine U. Calif., San Francisco, 1989—93; chancellor U. Calif., San Francisco, 1993—97; dean faculty medicine Harvard U., Boston, 1997—. Mem. med. adv. bd. Gairdner Found., Toronto, 1978—83, Toronto, 1997—; adv. coun. neurol. disorders program Nat. Inst. Neurol., Communicative Disorders and Stroke, 1979—82. Co-author: Clinical Neuroendocrinology, 1977, The Hypothalamus, 1978, Clinical Neuroendocrinology: A Pathophysiological Approach, 1979, Neurosecretion and Brain Peptides: Implications for Brain Functions and Neurological Disease, 1981, Brain Peptides, 1983; editor: Harrison's Principles of Internal Medicine, 1980—99, Molecular Neurology, 1998—. Recipient Moshier Meml. gold medal, U. Alta. Faculty Medicine, 1962, John W. Scott gold med. award, 1962, Abraham Flexner award, AAMC, 1999; scholar, Med. Rsch. Coun. Can., 1970—75. Mem.: NAS, Inst. of Medicine, Am. Acad. Arts and Scis., Assn. Am. Physicians, Soc. Neurosci., Royal Coll. Phys. and Surg. Can., Am. Physiol. Soc. (Bowditch lectr. 1978), Am. Neurol. Assn. (pres. 1990). Office: Dean Faculty Medicine Harvard U 25 Shattuck St Boston MA 02115-6027

MARTIN, JOSEPH CHEKEL, not-for-profit developer; b. Cleve., Apr. 21, 1944; s. Eugene Chekel and Fern Simenson; m. Nancy Costa, May 27, 2001; children: Courtney A. Langdon, Christian A. Chekel. Degree in bus. mgmt., Bemidji State U., 1965. Chmn. Text N Tone, London, Eng., and Dover, Del., 1994—; founder The Talking Page Literacy Org., Newport Beach, Calif., 1997—. Mgmr. Dayton Hudson Retail Corp., Mpls., 1966—77, Carter, Hawley, Hales Retail Stores, L.A., 1977—80; pres. M. Chekel and Assocs. Retail Cons., London, N.Y., and L.A., 1980—89; mng. ptnr. Am. on Sale Retail Stores, London, 1989—94. Author: English Linguistics Program, with SONO audio. State chmn. Keep Am. Beautiful, Tulsa, 1974—75; v.p. Tulsa Jaycees, 1973—77; retail chmn. Tulsa United Way, 1975—77. Achievements include Books and SONO Audios copyrights. Office: The Talking Page Literacy Orgn Registered Offices: 1738 Tradewinds Lane Newport Beach CA 92660 Office Phone: 949-650-8101. E-mail: talkingpage@hotmail.com.

MARTIN, J(OSEPH) PATRICK, lawyer, judge; b. Detroit, Apr. 19, 1938; s. Joseph A. and Kathleen G. (Rich) Martin; m. Denise Taylor, June 27, 1964; children: Timothy J., Julie D. AB magna cum laude, U. Notre Dame, 1960; JD with distinction, U. Mich., 1963; postgrad., London Sch. Econs., 1964. Bar: Mich. 1963, U.S. Dist. Ct. (ea. dist.) Mich. 1963, U.S. Ct. Appeals (6th cir.) 1967, U.S. Supreme Ct. 1979, U.S. Dist. Ct. (we. dist.) Mich. 1981, U.S. Ct. Fed. Claims 1999. Spl. asst. to gen. counsel Ford Motor Co., Dearborn, Mich., 1962; assoc. Dykema, Wheat, Spencer et al, Detroit, 1963-66; from assoc. to ptnr. Poole Littell Sutherland, Detroit, 1966-76; sr. atty., ptnr., shareholder Butzel Long, Detroit and Birmingham, Mich., 1976-94; sr. atty., shareholder Vlcko, Lane, Payne & Broder PC, Bingham Farms, Mich., 1994-96; sr. atty. Gourwitz and Barr PC, Southfield, Mich., 1996-99; pvt. practice, 2000—; adminstrv. law judge State of Mich., 2002—. Arbitrator Am. Arbitration Assn., Southfield, Mich., 1968—; bd. arbitrators, Nat. Assn. Security Dealers, 1988—, N.Y. Stock Exch., 1991—; adj. prof. remedies and alternative dispute resolution U. Detroit Law Sch., 1989—, Wayne State U. Law Sch., 1996—, Cooley Law Sch., 2001—; state ct. adminstrv. office approved mediator all Mich. cts. under new ADR rules; case evaluator, mediator, discovery master Oak County Cir. Ct., Pontiac, Mich., 1985—; mediator Lex Mundi, Coll. Mediators, 1992—; case evaluator, mediator Mediation Tribunal Assn. Wayne County Cir. Ct., 1992—, Oakland County Dist. Cts., 1998—, Wayne County Dist. Cts., 1998—; moderator Mich. State Ct. Appeals, 1995—. Author, editor: Laches-Oak County Bar Assn. Legal Jour., 1984, 1992, 1996, Real Property Rev., 1989—90, Mich. Law Weekly, 1990, ADR Newsletter, 2000. Scholar, Cook Found., Ford Found., London, 1963—64. Mem.: ABA, Oakland County Bar Found., Mich. State Bar Found., Oakland County Bar Assn. (chair fed. ct. com., chair Mich. dist. ct. com., mem. ADR com., bd. dirs.), State Bar Mich. (chair alternative dispute sect.). Roman Catholic. Avocations: gardening, golf, walking. Home and Office: 1663 Hoit Tower Dr Bloomfield Hills MI 48302-2630 Office Phone: 248-932-8694. Home Fax: 248-932-0368. Personal E-mail: jpatrickmartin@aol.com.

MARTIN, JOSEPH ROBERT, corporate financial executive; b. Phila., Dec. 9, 1947; s. Robert and Elva Ruth (Griffen) M.; m. Catherine Marie Kelly, Sept. 5, 1970; children: Joseph Robert Jr., Jennifer H., Patrick F., Kathleen K., Mariah E. BS, Embry Riddle U., 1974; MBA, U. Maine, 1976. Sr. corp. fin. analyst Keyes Fibre Co., Waterville, Maine, 1976—80; mgr. fin. analysis and planning Schlumberger, Fairchild, South Portland, Maine, 1980—83; divsn. contr. Schlumberger, Factron, Clifton Park, NY, 1983—84; corp. contr. VTC, Inc., Bloomington, Minn., 1984—87, v.p. fin., CFO, 1987—88, sr. v.p., CFO, 1989—90; dir. fin. Nat. Semiconductor, South Portland, Maine, 1990—91; v.p. fin. std. products group Nat. Semicondr., Santa Clara, Calif., 1991—95; v.p. fin. worldwide ops. Nat. Semiconductor, Santa Clara, Calif., 1995—96; exec. v.p., CFO, vice chmn. bd. dirs. Fairchild Semiconductor, South Portland, Maine, 1996—2003, vice chmn. bd. dirs., sr. exec. v.p., 2003—. Bd. visitors U. So. Maine, 1998—2001; pres.'s bd. advisors Embry-Riddle Aero. U., 2000—; bd. dirs. Brooks Automation LLC, Chelmsford, Mass., Synqor, Inc., Hudston, Mass., Chippac, Inc., Santa Clara, Calif. Served to capt. U.S. Army, 1967-72, Vietnam. Decorated D.F.C., Purple Heart, Bronze Star medal, Air medal, Vietnamese Cross of Gallantry. Home: 17 Stornoway Rd Cumberland Foreside ME 04110 Office: Fairchild Semicondr Corp 82 Running Hill Rd South Portland ME 04106 E-mail: joseph.martin@fairchildsemi.com.

MARTIN, JOSEPH VINSON, neuroscientist, educator; b. Boston, Sept. 17, 1952; s. James Cullen and Mary Louise (Echols) M.; m. Jean Ann Rusteberg, Apr. 27, 1989; 1 child, Lara Jean. BA, Northwestern U., Evanston, Ill., 1973; PhD, U. So. Calif., 1987. Rsch. asst. L.A. Harbor Commn., 1978—79; chemist NIMH, Bethesda, Md., 1982—87; postdoctoral rsch. assoc. SUNY, Stony Brook, 1987—88, rsch. instr.; asst. prof. Biology Dept., Rutgers U., Camden, NJ, 1989—95, assoc. prof., 1995—. Proposal reviewer NSF; manuscript reviewer European Jour. Pharmacology, Pharmacology Biochemistry and Behavior, Sleep; lectr. in field. Contbr. articles to profl. jours. Recipient Nat. Merit Letter of Commendation, 1969, NSF Undergrad. Summer Rsch. fellowship, 1972, NIMH Predoctoral Rsch. fellowship, 1977-78, Rutgers U. Acad. Svc. Increment award, 1991, 93, 98, NSF Rsch. grantee, 1994-97, 98-2001, 02—. Mem. AAAS, Assn. Profl. Sleep Socs., Internat. Brain Rsch. Orgn., N.J. Acad. Sci., N.Y. Acad. Scis., Sleep Rsch. Soc., Soc. for Neuroscience. Office: Rutgers U Biology Dept 315 Penn St Medford NJ 08055 E-mail: jomartin@camden.rutgers.edu.

MARTIN, JOYCE E. education educator; d. John Henry and Mary Elizabeth (Ellis) Koppelmann; m. Robert E. Martin, Aug. 28, 1971; children: Edward Lee, Bobbi Lynn Fessler. Masters, Webster U., St. Louis. Secondary Education Teaching Mo. Dept. of Edn., 1985, Special Needs Mo. Dept. of Ed. Instrnl. asst. math. East Ctrl. Coll., Union, Mo., 1978—85, faculty, 1985—, math. divsn. chair, 1997—2001. Editor (co-author): (book) Elementary Algebra; book reviewer Addison Wesley & McGraw Hill. Mem. Order of the Ea. Star, Sullivan, Mo. Grantee Grant funding advanced tech. use in cmty. svc., East Ctrl. Coll. Found., 1996. Mem.: Midwest Region Assn. for Devel. Edn., AMATYC (registration coord. 1991—93, Appreciation award 1994), Mo. Math. Assn. for Two Yr. Coll. (pres., president-elect, dir.), Phi Theta Kappa (hon.; advisor 1996, Horizon award 1997). Office: East Ctrl Coll 1964 Prairie Dell Rd Union MO 63084 Office Phone: 636-583-5193. Home Fax: 636-583-1897; Office Fax: 636-583-1897. Personal E-mail: martin@fidnet.com. E-mail: martinje@eastcentral.edu.

MARTIN, JUDITH SYLVIA, journalist; b. Washington, Sept. 13, 1938; d. Jacob and Helen (Aronson) Perlman; m. Robert Martin, Jan. 30, 1960; children: Nicholas Ivor, Jacobina Helen. BA, Wellesley Coll., 1959; DHL (hon.), York Coll., 1985, Adelphi U., 1991. Reporter-critic, columnist Washington Post, 1960—83; syndicated columnist United Feature Syndicate, N.Y.C., 1978—; columnist Microsoft, 1996—. Critic-at-large Vanity Fair, 1983-84. Author: The Name on the White House Floor, 1972, Miss Manners' Guide to Excruciatingly Correct Behavior, 1982, Gilbert, 1982, Miss Manners' Guide to Rearing Perfect Children, 1984, Common Courtesy, 1985, Style and Substance, 1986, Miss Manners' Guide for the Turn-of-the-Millennium, 1989, Miss Manners on (Painfully Proper) Weddings, 1996, Miss Manners Rescues Civilization, 1996, Miss Manners' Basic Training: Communications, 1997, Miss Manners' Basic Training: Eating, 1997, Miss Manners' Basic Training: The Right Thing to Say, 1998, Miss Manners' Guide to Domestic Tranquility, 1999, Star-Spangled Manners, 2002. Bd. dirs. Washington Concert Opera, Friends of Scuola San Rocco. Mem. Cosmos Club, Literary Soc. Office: United Feature Syndicate 200 Madison Ave Fl 4 New York NY 10016-3911

MARTIN, JULIE, women's healthcare company executive; BA in Liberal Arts and Scis., MS in Exercise Physiology, San Diego State U. Propr. 2 cos., 1983-90; gen. mgr. Dale Fitzmorris, 1990-92; dir. health promotion Ctr. for Women's Medicine, 1993-96; co-CEO, As We Change, LLC, 1995-98; v.p. catalog ops. Women First HealthCare, Inc., San Diego, 1998—. Fax: 619-509-1353.

MARTIN, JULIE A. retired insurance company executive; BS, Tex. Tech. U.; MS in Fgn. Svc., MBA in Fin., George Washington U. Dir. investment missions program Overseas Pvt. Investment Corp., investment ins. officer, regional mgr. ins. dept., mng. dir. L.Am. and Caribbean ins. dept., mng. dir. policy and underwriting, chief underwriter polit. risk ins. dept., dep. v.p. ins., v.p. ins., 1997—. Office: Overseas Pvt Investment Corp 1100 New York Ave NW Washington DC 20527-0001

MARTIN, JUNE JOHNSON CALDWELL, journalist; b. Toledo, Oct. 06; d. John Franklin and Eunice Imogene (Fish) Johnson; m. Erskine Caldwell, Dec. 21, 1942 (div. Dec. 1955); 1 child, Jay Erskine; m. Keith Martin, May 5, 1966. AA, Phoenix Jr. Coll., 1941; BA, U. Ariz., 1943, 59; postgrad., Ariz. State U., 1939, 40. Freelance writer, 1944—; columnist Ariz. Daily Star, Tucson, 1956-59, 70-94, book reviewer, 1970-94, co-founder Ann. Book and Author Event; editor Ariz. Alumnus mag., Tucson, 1959-70; ind. book reviewer, audio tape columnist Tucson, 1994—; coord. S.W. Books of Yr. sponsored by Tucson Pima Pub. Libr., Ariz., 2000—. Panelist, co-producer TV news show Tucson Press Club, 1954-55, pres., 1958. Contbg. author: Rocky Mountain Cities, 1949; contbr. articles to World Book Ency., and various mags. Mem. Tucson CD Com., 1961; vol. campaigns of Samuel Goddard, U.S. Rep. Morris Udall, U.S. amb. and Ariz. gov. Raul. Castro. Recipient award Nat. Headliners Club, 1959, Ariz. Press Club award, 1957-59, 96, Am. Alumni Coun., 1966, 70. Mem. Nat. Book Critics Circle, Ariz. Press Women, Jr. League of Tucson, Tucson Urban League, PEN U.S.A. West, Planned Parenthood So. Ariz., Tucson Press, Pi Beta Phi. Democrat. Methodist. Home: Desert Foothills Sta PO Box 65388 Tucson AZ 85728-5388

MARTIN, KAREN SIEBENTHAL, community health nurse; b. Bloomington, Ill., Sept. 15, 1942; d. Arthur A. and Evelyn R. (Ehresman) Siebenthal; m. Stanley A. Martin, Mar. 31, 1963; children: Steven, Kathleen, Kelly. Diploma, Meth. Hosp. Sch. Nursing, 1963; BSN, U. Iowa Coll. Nursing, 1969; MS in Nursing, U. Nebr. Coll. Nursing, 1977. Staff nurse, dir. nursing Champaign (Ill.)-Urbana Pub. Health, 1966-67, 69-73; dir. rsch. Vis. Nurse Assn. Omaha, 1978—93. Prin. investigator Nat. Ctr. for Nursing Rsch., 1989—93; health care cons., 1993—; adj. prof. Midland Luth. Coll. Divsn. Nursing, Fremont, Nebr., 1994—; vis. prof. Japan and Taiwan, 1998, U.K., 2000—01, Ireland, 2001; workshops and cons. Europe, 1992—93, Canada, 1997, New Zealand, 2000, Austria, 02, Slovenia, 02, Wales, 03, Canada, 03; co-chair Omaha Sys. Internat. Conf., St. Paul, 2001, Milw., 03; spkr. in field; bank of nurse experts Internat. Coun. Nurses, 2002. Author: 4 books, 1 translated into Japanese; editor: Home Health Focus, 1994—2000; mem. editl. adv. bd.: Pub. Health Nursing, 1990—, mem. editl. bd.: Outcomes Mgmt. for Nursing, 1997—2003, Home Care Provider, 1996—2001, bd. of review: Nursing Outlook, 1990—; contbr. articles to Australian, Japanese and Dutch profl. jours. Recipient Alumnus of Yr. award Meth. Med. Ctr. of Cen. Ill. Sch. Nursing, Peoria, Ill., 1995. Mem.: Am. Acad. Nursing (expert panel on electronic networks 1995—97, expert panel on informatics 2002—), APHA, ANA (Congress of Nursing Practice 1994—98, dist. bd. dirs. 1999—2001), Am. Med. Informatics Assn., Internat. Coun. Nurses (internat. classification of nursing practice adv. com. 1994—), Midwest Nursing Rsch. Soc., N.Am. Nursing Diagnosis Assn., Sigma Theta Tau.

MARTIN, KATE ABBOTT, lawyer; b. Pasadena, Calif., Mar. 11, 1952; BA, Pomona Coll., 1973; JD, U. Va., 1977. Bar: D.C. 1978, U.S. Ct. Appeals (D.C. cir.) 1979, U.S. Supreme Ct. 1989. Assoc. Nussbaum, Owen & Webster, Washington, 1977-83, ptnr., 1983-88; dir. Nat. Security Litigation Project ACLU, Washington, 1988-92, dir. Ctr. for Nat. Security Studies, 1992—. Office: Gelman Libr 2130 H St NW Ste 701 Washington DC 20037-2521 also: Dir Ctr for Natl Sec Studies ACLU 122 Maryland Ave NE Washington DC 20002*

MARTIN, KATHLEEN, medical center administrator; BS, RN, U. Bridgeport, 1964; MS, N.Y. Med. Coll., 1966; JD, Tulane U., 1991. RN, La, Conn., N.Y.; cert. nurse-midwife; bar: La. 1991. Instr. U. Mass. Sch. of Health Scis., Amherst, Mass., 1975-77, La. State U. Sch. of Nursing, New Orleans, 1978-79; nurse practitioner Planned Parenthood of La., 1986-88; pvt. practice in nurse-midwife New Orleans, 1978-80, 83-91; assoc. atty. Thompson & Lavender, New Orleans, 1991-95; nurse-midwife, coord. maternity svcs. Saint Thomas Health Svc., Inc., 1995-96; dir. WomanCare Midwife Ctr., Columbia Lakeland Med. Ctr., 1996—. Mem. Am. Coll. of Nurse-Midwives (treas., pres. 1996-98), La. Nurse Practitioners Assn., Nurse-Midwives Svc. Dirs. Network, La. Hosp. Assn. Office: Am Coll of Nurse-Midwives 818 Connecticut Ave NW Ste 900 Washington DC 20006-2702

MARTIN, KATHLEEN L. military officer, hospital administrator; BSN, Boston U., 1973; MS in Nursing Adminstrn., U. San Diego, 1992. Commd. ensign USN, 1973; advanced through grades to rear admiral Nat. Naval Med. Ctr.; staff nurse, then charge nurse in pediats. Naval Hosp., Camp Lejeune, NC, 1973—76, charge nurse pediat. ward Jacksonville, Fla., 1979—82; med. programs officer Navy Recruiting Dist., Phila., 1976—79; divsn. officer mil. medicine, credentials coord., risk mgr., quality assurance coord. Naval Med. Clinic, Pearl Harbor, Hawaii, 1982—86; head amb. med. nursing dept. Naval Hosp., San Diego, 1986—90; dir. nursing svcs. Naval Med. Clinic, Port Hueneme, Calif., 1992—93, commdg. officer, 1993—95, Naval Hosp., Charleston, SC, 1995—98, med. inspector gen., 1998—99; 19th dir. Navy Nurse Corps, 1998—99; comdr. Nat. Naval Med. Ctr., Bethesda, Md., 1999—. Decorated Legion of Merit (3), Def. Meritorious Svc. medal, Meritorious Svc. medal, Navy Commendation medal. Mem.: Assn. Mil. Surgeons of the U.S., Am. Acad. Amb. Care Nursing, Am. Coll. Healthcare Execs., Sigma Theta Tau. Office: National Naval Med Ctr 8901 Wisconsin Ave Bethesda MD 20889-5600

MARTIN, KATHRYN A. academic administrator; Dean Sch. Fine and Performing Arts Wayne State U., Detroit; chancellor U Minn, Duluth, 1995—. Office: University of Minnesota-Duluth Office of the Chancellor Admin Bldng 10 University Dr Duluth MN 55812-2496

MARTIN, KELLI ALYSE, editor; b. Mich., Aug. 10, 1972; d. Albert Andrews and Maggie Davis Martin. BA in Psychology, Williams Coll., 1996. Bookseller Borders Books, Dearborn, Mich., 1996; art coord. Simon and Schuster, NYC, 1996—97, pub. asst., 1997—98; editl asst. HarperCollins Pub., NYC, 1998—. Bd. dirs. Frederick Douglas Creative Arts Ctr., 2001—, workshop leader, 2003—. Office: HarperCollins Pub 10 East 53rd St New York NY 10022

MARTIN, KELLIE (NOELLE), actress; b. Riverside, Calif., Oct. 16, 1975; Movie and motion picture actress. Actress T.V. series Life Goes On, 1989, (voice) Taz-Mania, 1992, Christy, 1994-1995, Crisis Ctr., 1997, ER, 1998-2000, Fiona, 2002, others; movies and TV movies include Jumpin' Jack Flash, 1986, Secret Witness, 1988, Troop Beverly Hills, 1989, Matinee, 1993, If Someone Had Known, 1995, Her Last Chance, 1996, On The Edge of Innocence, 1997, About Sarah, 1999, All You Need, 2001, Malibus Most Wanted, 2003, Open House, 2003; voice characterization A Goofy Movie, 1995, also T.V. guest appearances. Office: c/o The Gersh Agy 232 N Canon Dr Beverly Hills CA 90210-5302

MARTIN, KENNETH J. pharmaceutical executive; BA magna cum laude, Hofstra U. cert. CPA. Audit mgr. Arthur Andersen LLP; pres. Am. Home Foods, 1995-97, Robins Healthcare, 1997; sr. v.p., CFO Wyeth-Ayerst Pharmaceuticals, Am. Home Products. Office: American Home Products 5 Giralda Farms Madison NJ 07940

MARTIN, KENYON, professional basketball player; b. Saginaw, Mich., Dec. 30, 1977; BA in Criminal Justice, U. Cin. Player N.J. Nets, 2000—04, Denver Nuggets, 2004—. Player U.S. Nat. Sr. Team, 2003. Named Nat. Player of Yr., AP, 2000; named to NBA All-Rookie First Team, 2001, NBA All-Star Game, 2004. Office: c/o Denver Nuggets 1000 Chopper Cir Denver CO 80204*

MARTIN, KEVIN DOUGLAS, surgeon; b. Kansas City, Mo., Oct. 26, 1955; BA, MS, Northwestern U., 1978; MD, Vanderbilt U., 1982. Diplomate Am. Bd. Surgery. Resident in surgery Vanderbilt Med. Ctr., Nashville, 1982-84, Baystate Med. Ctr., Springfield, 1984-87; fellow in vascular surgery U. Cin., 1987—89; mem. staff Good Samaritan Hosp., Cin., St. Elizabeth, Edgewood, Ky., St. Luke's Hosp., Ft. Thomas, Ky. Mem. ACS, Internat. Soc. for Endovascular Surgery, Peripheral Vascular Surgery Soc., Midwest Vascular Surgery Soc., Ky. Med. Soc., Ohio State Med. Assn., Soc. for Vascular Surgery. Office: Ste 394 20 Medical Village Dr Edgewood KY 41017

MARTIN, KEVIN J. federal agency administrator; m. J. Catherine Martin. BA, U. N.C., Chapel Hill; M Pub. Policy, Duke U.; JD, Harvard U. Bar: Fla., D.C. Ud. clk. Judge William M. Hoeveler U.S. Dist. Ct., Miami; assoc. Wileu, Rein & Fielding, Washington; with Office Ind. Counsel; advisor commr. Harold Furchtgott-Roth FCC; deputy gen. counsel Bush Campaign; with transition team Bush-Cheney; commr. FCC, 2001. Mem.: D.C. Bar Assn., Fla. Bar Assn., Fed. Comm. Bar Assn. Republican. Office: FCC 445 12th St SW Washington DC 20554

MARTIN, KEVIN JOHN, nephrologist, educator; b. Dublin, Jan. 18, 1948; came to U.S., 1973; s. John Martin and Maura Martin; m. Grania E. O'Connor, Nov. 16, 1972; children: Alan, John, Ciara, Audrey. MB BCh, Univ. Coll. Dublin, 1971. Diplomate Am. Bd. Internal Medicine, Am. Bd. Nephrology. Intern St. Vincent's Hosp., Dublin, 1971-72, resident, 1972-73, Barnes Hosp., St. Louis, 1973-74, fellow, 1974-77; asst. prof. Washington U., St. Louis, 1977-84, assoc. prof., 1984-89; prof., dir. div. nephrology St. Louis U., 1989—. Contbr. numerous articles to med. jours. Office: Saint Louis Univ Med Ctr 3635 Vista Ave Saint Louis MO 63110-2539

MARTIN, LARRY A(NTHONY), state legislator, textile company executive; b. June 20, 1957; s. Edgar M. and Lois B. Martin; m. Susan Lynn Evatt, June 25, 1983; children: Caroline Elizabeth, Larry Anthony Jr., Anna Leigh. Student, Tri-County Tech. Coll. With Alice Mfg. Co., Pickens, S.C.; mem. S.C. Ho. of Reps., Columbia, 1979-92, S.C. Senate, Columbia, 1993—. Mem. banking and ins. com., corrections and penology com., gen. com., judiciary com., rules com.; mem. adv. bd. Pickens 1st Nat. Bank, 1987-90 Former mem. bd. S.C. Appalachian Coun. Govts.; past chmn. Liaison Com. on Small Bus.; moderator, Sunday sch. tchr. Pickens 1st Bapt. Ch.; former chmn. bd. S.C. 4-H Found.; pres. Pickens County United Way, 1983; mem. Econ. Devel. Commn., So. Legis. Conf.; mem. adv. bd. Rocky Bottom Camp of Blind; mem. bd. Partnership and Career Edn.; chmn. S.C. Gov.'s Sch.-to-Work Coun., 1997. Mem. Lions. Republican. Office: 510 Gressette Bldg Columbia SC 29202

MARTIN, LAURABELLE, real estate and farm land owner and manager; b. Jackson County, Minn., Nov. 3, 1915; d. Eugene Wellington and Mary Christina (Hansen) M. BS, Mankato State U., 1968. Tchr. rural schs., Renville County, Minn., 1936-41, 45-50, Wabasso (Minn.) Pub. Sch., 1963-81; pres. Renville Farms and Feed Lots, 1982-86. Author: Hist. Biography of Joseph Renville, 1996; poet: Nat. Libr. Poetry (Silver Cup award, 2003). Pres. Wabasso (Minn.) Edn. Assn., 1974-75, publicity chmn., 1968-74; sec. and publicity agt. Hist. Renville Preservation Com., 1978-86; publicity chmn., sec. Town and Country Boosters, Renville, 1982-83. Recipient Outstanding Achievement in Poetry Award, Internat. Soc. Poets. Mem. Genealogy Soc. Renville County, Am. Legion Aux. Democrat. Lutheran. Avocations: antique furniture, travel, sewing, poetry. Home and Office: 334 NW 1201st Rd Holden MO 64040-9378

MARTIN, LAWRENCE M. lawyer; b. N.Y.C., Aug. 23, 1950; BA, Yale U., 1973, JD, 1981; MA, U. Chgo., 1978. Bar: N.Y. 1982, U.S. Dist. Ct. (so. and ea. dist.) N.Y. 1982, U.S. Ct. Appeals (2d. cir.) 1985. Assoc. Debevoise & Plimpton, N.Y.C., 1981—87, Shereff Friedman Hoffman & Goodman, N.Y.C., 1987—90; asst. chief, affirmative litigation divsn. N.Y.C. Law Dept., 1990—97, spl. ins. counsel, 1997—, chief disaster planning and ins., 2004—. Mem. Assn. of the Bar of the City of N.Y. (ins. com. 1995-98). Office: New York City Law Dept 100 Church St New York NY 10007-2601 E-mail: lmartin@law.nyc.gov.

MARTIN, LEISA ANN, social sciences educator; BS in Psychology, Fla. State U., 1992; MS in Indsl. and Orgnl. Psychology, Fla. Internat. U., 1999; PhD in Instrnl. Leadership and Acad. Curriculum Social Studies, U. Okla., 2003. Asst. dir. bilingual edn. grant The U. of Okla., 2000—; edn. mentor Americorps, Norman, Okla., 2002—; tchr. 8th grade Am. history Longfellow Mid. Sch., Norman, 2003; asst. prof. Fla. State U., Tallahassee, 2004—. Adj. asst. prof. U. Okla., Norman. Contbr. articles to profl. jours. Publicity com. Nat. Coun. for the Social Studies, Washington, 2002—02; judge Okla. History Day State Contest, 2000—02, SE H.S. History Day Contest, 2001—02; mem. The U. of Okla. Grad. Student Adv. Coun., 2000—02. The U. of Okla. Rsch. and Creative Activity Grant award, The U. of Okla., 1999, Lew Wentz Grad. and Law scholarship, 2001—02, A. E. Clark Meml. scholarship, 2001, The U. of Okla. Coll. of Edn. Grad. scholarship, The U. of Okla. Coll. of Edn., 2002. Mem.: Okla. Coun. for the Social Studies, Okla. Assn. of Tchr. Educators, Nat. Coun. for the Social Studies, Assn. of Tchr. Educators. Home: 2305 Killearn Ctr Blvd Apt 2A Tallahassee FL 32309

MARTIN, LELAND MORRIS (PAPPY MARTIN), history educator; b. Patrick Springs, Va., Aug. 8, 1930; s. Rufus Wesley and Mary Hilda (Biggs) M.; m. Mildred Greer, May 12, 1956; children: Lee Ann Martin Powell, Mitzi Jo. AB, Berea Coll., 1953; MS, U. Tenn., 1954; grad., Air War Coll., Maxwelll AFB, Ala., 1978; MA in History, U Tex. Pan-Am., 1993; cert. machinist, Tex. State Tech. Coll., 1997, AAS in Machining Technology-Tool and Die Making, 1999. Enlisted USAF, 1954, advanced through grades to col., 1977; comdr. RAF, Greenham Common, Welford, 1974-76; comdt., comdr. Mil. Airlift Command Noncommisioned Officers Acad., McGuire AFB, N.J., 1976-79; vice comdr., comdr. RAF Mildenhall and RAF Chicksands, Eng., 1979-83; chief of staff 21st Air Force, McGuire AFB, 1983-84; pres. Air Force Phys. Evaluation Bd., Randolph AFB, N.J., 1984-86; ret., 1986; dep. exec. dir. Confederate Air Force, Harlingen, Tex., 1986-88; exec. dir. Am. Airpower Heritage Found., Harlingen, 1986-88; tchg. asst., lectr. in history U. Tex. Pan Am., Edinburg, 1989-93; adj. prof. history Tex. State Tech. Coll., Harlingen, 1994—2001. Co-chair (with Sir Douglas Bader) 1976 Internat. Air Tatoo at RAF Greenham Common; chair Air Fete 80 and 81, RAF Mildenhall, Eng. Co-editor: History of Military Assistance Command, Vietnam, 1970. Decorated Legion of Merit with two oak leaf clusters, Bronze Star; Cross of Gallantry (Vietnam); recipient Amb.'s award Ct. St. James, London, 1974, 83. Mem. Air Force Assn., Am. Watchmakers Inst., Nat. Assn. Watch and Clock Collectors, Brit. Officers Club Phila. (hon.), Rotary (gov. internat. dist. 5930 1995-96), Phi Alpha Theta, Phi Kappa Phi. Republican. Presbyterian. Avocations: clock repairs, photography, golf, fishing. Home: 3001 Emerald Lake Dr Harlingen TX 78550-8621

MARTIN, LEONARDO S.J. retired urologist, surgeon; b. Macati, Rizal, The Philippines, Nov. 26, 1926; came to U.S., 1953; s. Nemesio Martin and Felicidad San Juan; m. Helen Mary Dougherty, May 24, 1958; children: Leonard, John and David (twins), Mark, Regina Mary Martin Dawson, Daniel. AA, U. The Philippines, 1947; MD, U. Santo Tomas, Manila, The Philippines, 1952. Diplomate Am. Bd. Urology; cert. physician and surgeon, Calif. Resident in urology Phila. Gen. Hosp., 1954-57; fellow in urology Mass. Gen. Hosp., Boston, 1957-59; urologist Manila Specialists Med. Ctr., 1959-63; instr. urology U. Santo Tomas, 1959-63; assoc. cancer urologist Roswell Pk. Meml. Hosp., Buffalo, 1963-65; urologist Sunnyvale (Calif.) Med. Ctr., 1965-94; mem. clin. tchg. staff Stanford (Calif.) Med. Ctr., 1965-94; cons. urology Los Altos, 1994—. Commr., med. expert Calif. Med. Bd. Licensure, Sacramento, 1987-2000. Contbr. articles to profl. jours. Bd. dirs. Flint Cultural Ctr., Cupertino, Calif., 1970-80; past adv. bd. Santa Clara County unit Boys and Girls Club Am. Named one of 10 Outstanding Young Men, Jaycees, The Philippines, 1960, Disting. Men of Medicine, U. The Philippines Coll. Medicine, 1960. Fellow ACS (cert. merit 1964); mem. AMA (cert. Inc. merit 1964), Am. Urol. Assn. (AUA, Inc. cert. merit 1964), Am. Assn. Clin. Urologists, Philippine-Am. Urol. Soc. (founding pres. 1972), U. Santo Tomas Med. Alumni Assn. in Am. (pres. 1996-97, Most Outstanding Alumnus of Yr. 2000, Most Outstanding Golden Jubilarian of Yr., 2002). Republican. Roman Catholic. Avocations: painting, piano and organ, stained glass, tennis, golf. Home and Office: 1931 Deodara Dr Los Altos CA 94024-7055

MARTIN, L(ESLIE) JOHN, retired journalism educator and dean; b. Budapest, Hungary, Jan. 5, 1921; came to U.S., 1948; s. Joseph and Elizabeth Caroline Martin; m. Lois Ann Henze, Mar. 22, 1951; children: Keith Douglas, Brian John. BA, Am. U., Cairo, 1947; postgrad., U. Oreg., 1948-49; MA, U. Minn., 1951, PhD, 1955. Corr., reporter, editor various newspapers, London, Paris, others, 1941-47; asst. prof. comm. U. Nebr., Lincoln, 1954-57; copy editor, night editor Detroit Free Press, 1957-58; prof. comm. U. Fla., Gainesville, 1958-61; divsn. chief, overseas rsch. dir. USIA, Washington, 1961-69; prof. internat. and cross-cultural comm., rsch. methods in mass communication, public opinion and propaganda U. Md., College Park, 1969-89, prof. emeritus, 1989—, dir. grad. studies, 1974-79, 82-89, dean Coll. Journalism, 1975, 79-80, assoc. dean, 1988-89, dir. PhD program in pub. comm., 1983-85, faculty ombuds officer, 1999—2002. Author: International Propaganda: Its Legal and Diplomatic Control, 1958, rev. edits., 1969, 1994; editor (with A. Chaudhary): Comparative Mass Media Systems, 1983, Arabic edit., 1991, Malaysian edit., 1997; editor: (with R. Hiebert) Current Issues in International Communication, 1990; editor: 3 other books; contbr. chapters to books, 3 encys., numerous articles to profl. jours. and confs. procs. Recipient Disting. Svc. to Internat. Comm. award, Assn. Edn. in Journalism and Mass Comm., Washington, 1989, Nat. Disting. Svc. award for rsch. about journalism Sigma Delta Chi, 1959. Mem. Kappa Tau Alpha. Avocations: reading, writing, travel, walking, computers. Home: 5313 Iroquois Rd Bethesda MD 20816-3104 Office: U Md Office Of Pres College Park MD 20742-0001 E-mail: ljmartin@wam.umd.edu.

MARTIN, LINDA GAYE, demographer, economist; b. Paris, Ark., Dec. 17, 1947; d. Leslie Paul and Margie La Verne (Thomas) Martin. BA in Math., Harvard U., 1970; MPA, Princeton U., 1972, PhD in Econs., 1978; DHL (hon.), Marlboro Coll., 2002. Dir. mgmt. info. sr. ctrs. bur. purchased social svcs. for adults City of N.Y., 1972—74; rsch. assoc., rsch. dir. U.S. Ho. of Reps. Select Com. on Population, Washington, 1977—79; rsch. assoc. East-West Population Inst., Honolulu, 1979—89, asst. dir., 1982—84; asst. prof. econs. U. Hawaii, Honolulu, 1979—81, assoc. prof., 1981—89, prof., 1989; dir. com. on population Nat. Acad. Scis., Washington, 1989—93; dir. domestic rsch. divsn., v.p. RAND, Santa Monica, Calif., 1993—95, v.p. for rsch. devel., 1995—99; pres. Population Coun., N.Y.C., 1999—. Mem. neurosci. behavior and sociology of aging rev. com. Nat. Inst. on Aging, Bethesda, 1991—95; chair panel on aging in developing countries NAS, Washington, 1987, mem. com. on population, 1993—99, mem. panel on internat. aging data, 1999—2001; mem. peer rev. oversight group NIH, 1998—. Editor: The ASEAN Success Story, 1987; co-editor: Demographic Change in Sub-Saharan Africa, 1993, The Demography of Aging, 1994, Racial and Ethnic Differences in the Health of Older Americans, 1997; author: (monograph) The Graying of Japan, 1989; contbr. articles to profl. jours. Mem. adv. coun. Woodrow Wilson Sch. Pub. and Internat. Affairs, Princeton U., NJ, 2000—. Recipient Fulbright Faculty Rsch. award, Coun. for Internat. Exch. of Scholars, 1988. Mem.: AAAS (adv. coun. 2003—), Population Assn. Am. (bd. dirs. 1991—93), Internat. Union for Sci. Study Population, Gerontol. Soc. Am. Democrat. Office: Population Council 1 Dag Hammarskjold Plz New York NY 10017-2220

MARTIN, LISA ANN, literary agent, writer; b. L.A., Feb. 10, 1952; d. Gerald Earl Kravitz and Ann (Bodenhamer) Martin; children: Jade Lian, Lily Ayna. BS in Psychology, Calif. State U., Northridge. Freelance writer, Palm Springs, Calif., 1997—; mktg. mgr. NAMM, Calif., Ontario, 2000—03; owner, lit. agt. Martin-McLean Lit. Assocs., Palm Springs, Calif., 2002—. Journalist The Desert Sun Gannet, Palm Springs, 1999—2002. Contbr. articles to publs. Mentor, tutor Salvation Army, Cathedral City, Calif., 1997—2000; vol. animal rights and edn. ASPCA, Thousand Palms, Calif., 1997—2003; active Ann. Pet Blessing Unity Ch., Palm Springs, Calif., 1997—2002. Mem.: Families with Children from China. Avocations: children's advocacy, public speaking, tutoring, reading, writing. Office: Martin-McLean Lit Assocs 1602 S Cerritos Dr Ste D Palm Springs CA 92264 E-mail: martinmcleanlit@aol.com.

MARTIN, LOREN WINSTON, allergist; b. Albertsville, Ala., Apr. 20, 1938; s. Loren d. and Byrda G. (Crotwell) M.; m. Vivian Elizabeth Sanger Martin, Dec. 29, 1960; children: Lori Ann, Karen Lynn, James Winston. BA in Chemistry, Duke U., 1959; MD, U. Tenn., 1962. Lic. physician, Ariz. Rotating internship Fitzsimons Army Hosp., Denver, 1963; med. residency Honolulu, 1964-67; med. officer U.S. Army, 1962-70; fellowship allergy U. Colo., Denver, 1970-71; pvt. practice Tucson, 1971—. Decorated Bronze Star. Fellow Am. Acad. Allergy & Immunology, Am. Coll. Allergy & Immunology; mem. Pima County Med. Soc. Republican. Office: 1661 N Swan Rd Ste 300 Tucson AZ 85712-4053 Office Phone: 520-795-1185.

MARTIN, LOUIS FRANK, surgery and healthcare outcomes analyst; b. Troy, N.Y., Nov. 7, 1951; s. Eugene Lavern and Lois Jane (Perkins) Martin; m. Deborah Lynn Tjarnberg, Mar. 12, 1977; children: Jesse Tjarnberg, James Casey, Tyler Gene. BA, Brown U., 1973, MD, 1976; MS in Health Adminstrn., U. Louisville, 1993. Diplomate Am. Bd. Surgery, Am. Bd. Med. Mgmt. Resident in gen. surgery U. Wash. Affiliated Hosps., Seattle, 1977-78, U. Louisville, 1978-83, rsch. fellow trauma rsch. and health care ednl. adminstrn., 1980-82; asst. prof. surgery Pa. State U., Hershey, 1983-88, asst. prof. physiology, 1986-88, assoc. prof. surgery and cellular and molecular physiology, 1988-92; prof. surgery La. State U., New Orleans, 1992—, prof. preventative medicine and pub. health, 1994—; prof. neurosci., 1995—; med. dir. St. Charles Weight Mgmt. Ctr. La. State U., New Orleans, 1995—. Vis. scientist INSERM, Poste Orange, France, 1990-91; cons. TENET Health Care Corp. Med. Affairs Dept., 1995—, Ethicon Endo-Surgery, Inc., 2000—. Mem. editl. bd., Shock, 1994-97, Obesity Surgery, 1997—, Jour. Surgical Outcomes, 1997-99; author med. books; contbr. articles to newspapers and profl. jours. Recipient Loyal Davis Traveling Surg. scholar ACS, 1990, Clin. Investigator award NIH, 1985-90; named to Guide to America's Top Surgeons Gen. Surgery So. Region, Consumer's Rsch. Coun., 2004. Mem.: ACS, Shape Up Am., New Orleans Surg. Soc. (pres. 1999), Soc. Univ. Surgeons, Soc. Internat. Chirurgie, Collegium Internat. Chirurgiae Digestivae, Assn. for Acad. Surgery (councilman 1988—90), Am. Physiol. Soc., Am. Coll. Critical Care Medicine, Am. Soc. Bariatric Surgery (program chmn. 1997, 1998, mem. exec. coun. 1997—2000). Home: 3005 Palm Vista Dr Kenner LA 70065-1560 Office: La State U Dept Surgery 1542 Tulane Ave New Orleans LA 70112-2825 Office Phone: 504-899-5511.

MARTIN, LUCY Z. public relations executive; b. Alton, Ill., July 8, 1941; d. Fred and Lucille J. M. BA, Northwestern U., 1963. Adminstrv. asst., copywriter Batz-Hodgson-Neuwoehner, Inc., St. Louis, 1963-64; news reporter, Midwest fashion editor Fairchild Publs., St. Louis, 1964-66; account exec. Milici Advt. Agy., Honolulu, 1967; publs. dir. Barnes Med. Ctr., St. Louis, 1968-69; comms. cons. Fleishman-Hillard, St. Louis, 1970-74; comms. cons., CEO, pres. Lucy Z. Martin & Assocs., Portland, Oreg., 1974—. Spkr. Marylhurst Coll., 1991, 92, 93, Concordia Coll., 1992, Women Entrepreneurs of Oreg., 1992, Oreg. Assn. Hosps. and Health Sys. Trustees, 1992, Healthcare Assn. Hawaii, Honolulu, 1993, USBancorp for Not-for-Profits, 1993, Multnomah County Ret. Srs. Vol. Program, 1993, Healthcare Fin. Mgmt. Assn., N.W., 1993, Healthcare Comms. Oreg., 1994, Area Health Edn. Ctrs., OHSU/statewide, 1994, Columbia River chpt. Pub. Rels. Soc. Am., 1994, 96; spkr., workshop conducter Healthcare Assn. Hawaii, 1993, USBancorp Not-for-Profit, 1993, Healthcare Communicators Oreg., 1994, Pathways to Career Transition, 1995, among others; bd. dirs. Ctrs. Airway Sci., Oregon Coll. Arts & Crafts, 1989-95, Good Samaritan Hosp. Assn., 1991-94, Am. Mktg. Assn., Oreg. chap., 1992-93, Inst. Managerial and Profl. Women, 1992-94, YMCA Public Policy com., 1993-95, Jr. League Cmty. adv. bd., 1994—, Bus. Social Responsibility Steering com., 1996—, Ctrs. for Airway Sci. Bd., 1996—; spkr. in field. Featured in Entrepreneurial Woman mag.; contbr. articles to profl. jours. Chmn. women's adv. com. Reed Coll., Portland, 1977-79; mem. Oreg. Commn. for Women, 1984-87; bd. dirs. Ronald McDonald House Oreg., 1986, Oreg. Sch. Arts and Crafts, 1989—, Northwestern U. Alumni Coun., 1992—; bd. dirs. Good Samaritan Hosp. Assocs., 1991-94, chair 1993-94; mem. pub. policy com. YMCA, 1993-95; mem. adv. bd. Jr. League, 1994—; mem. steering com. Bus. for Social Responsiblity, 1996—; bd. dirs. Ctrs. for Airway Sci., 1996—. Recipient MacEachern Citation Acad. Hosp. Pub. Relations, 1978, Rosey awards Portland Advt. Fedn., 1979, Achievement award Soc. Tech. Comms., 1982, Disting. Tech. Comm. award, 1982, Exceptional Achievement award Coun. for Advancement and Support Edn., 1983, Monsoon award Internat. Graphics, Inc., 1984, William Marsh Achievement award PRSA, 1998; named Woman of Achievement Daily Jour. Commerce, 1980. Mem. Pub. Rels. Soc. Am. (pres. Columbia River chpt. 1984, chmn. bd. 1980-84, Oreg. del. 1984-86, jud. panel N. Pacific dist 1985-86, exec. bd. health care sect. 1986-87, mem. Counselors Acad., Spotlight awards 1985, 86, 87, 88, nat. exec. com. 1987-91; William Marsh Achievement award 1998), Portland Pub. Rels. Roundtable (chmn. 1985, bd. dirs. 1983-85), Assn. Western Hosps. (editl. adv. bd. 1984-85), Best of West awards 1978, 80, 83, 87), Oreg. Hosp. Pub. Rels. Orgn. (pres. 1981, chmn. bd. 1982, bd. dirs. 1992-93), Acad. Health Service Mktg., Am. Hosp. Assn., Am. Mktg. Assn. (Oreg. chpt. bd. dirs. 1992-93), Am. Soc. Hosp. Mktg. & Pub. Rels., Healthcare Communicators Oreg. (conf. keynote speaker 1994), Internat. Assn. Bus. Communicators (18 awards 1981-87), Oreg. Assn. Hosps. (keynote speaker for trustee, 1991, speaker, 1993, bd. dirs. 1992-93), Oreg. Press Women, Nat. and Oreg. Soc. Healthcare Planning and Mktg., Women in Comms. (Matrix award 1977), Bus. for Social Responsibility (steering com. 1996—), Inst. for Managerial and Profl. Women (bd. dirs. 1992-94). Office: 1881 SW Edgewood Rd Portland OR 97201-2235 Fax: 503-227-1569. E-mail: lucyz@lzma.com.

MARTIN, LYNN MORLEY, former secretary of labor; b. Evanston, Ill., Dec. 26, 1939; d. Lawrence William and Helen Catherine (Hall) Morley; children from a previous marriage: Julia Catherine, Caroline; m. Harry D. Leinenweber, Jan. 1987; stepchildren: Jane, John, Stephen, Justin, Thomas Leinenweber. BA, U. Ill., 1960. Former tchr. pub. schs.; mem. Ill. Ho. of Reps., 1977-79, Ill. Senate, 1979-81, 97th-101st Congresses from 16th Ill. Dist., 1981-91; sec. Dept. of Labor, Washington, 1991-93; prof. Harvard Univ., 1993—. Co-chmn. Bush-Quayle Presdl. campaign, 1988. Named one of Outstanding Young Women in Am., U.S. Jaycees; named Rep. Woman of the Yr., 1989; named a Mother of the Yr., Nat. Mother's Day Com., 1992; 1st woman elected to leadership post in House of Reps., 1982. Mem. AAUW, Jr. League, Phi Beta Kappa (hon. doctorate). Republican. Office: Harvard Univ Cambridge MA 02138

MARTIN, MALCOLM A. health facility administrator; b. Washington, Aug. 3, 1938; AA, George Washington U., 1958; MD, Yale U., 1962. Intern Strong Meml. Hosp., Rochester, NY, 1962—63, resident, 1963—64; commd. surgeon USPHS, Rockville, Md., 1964—71; rsch. assoc. and surgeon Lab. Biology Viruses Nat. Inst. Arthritis and Infectious Diseases NIH, Bethesda, Md., 1964—69, acting head biophysical and biochemical sect. and med. officer Lab. Biology Viruses Nat. Inst. Arthritis and Infectious Diseases, 1969—71, head physical biochemistry sect. and med. officer Lab. Biology Viruses Nat. Inst. Arthritis and Infectious Diseases, 1971—78, head DNA recombinant rsch. unit office sci dir. Nat. Inst. Arthritis and Infectious Disease, 1978—81, chief Lab. Molecular Microbiology Nat. Inst. Arthritis and Infectious Disease, 1981—, sr. exec. svc. and chief Lab. Molecular Microbiology Nat. Inst. Arthritis and Infectious Disease, 1984—; collaborator, vis. investigator Carnegie Inst. Washington, 1965—67. Adj. assoc. prof. dept. parasitology and lab. practice U. N.C., Chapel Hill, 1981—87; mem. AIDS vaccine com. USPHS, 1986—; mem. com. on biols. WHO, 1986—98; mem. fellowship selection com. Lucille P. Markey Charitable Trust, 1985—97; mem. fellowship rev. com. Life Scis. Rsch. Found., 1983—85; mem. sci. rev. bd. Howard Hughes Med. Inst., 1989—97; mem. sci. adv. com. New Eng. Regional Primate Ctr. Med. Sch. Harvard U., 1990—; mem. fellowship selection com. Aaron Diamond Found., 1991—98; mem. sr. biomedical rsch. scientist policy bd. Norman P. Salzman Found., 1998—, mem. meml. award in virology selection com., 1999—. Mem. editl. bd. Jour. Virology, 1976—80, 1983—, Jour. Biol. Chemistry, 1977—81, Virology, 1996—. Mem. adv. com. on cell and devel. biology Am. Cancer Soc., 1983—85. Recipient Bazeley award, Australian Soc. Microbiology, 1995, Meritorious Rank award, SES, 1997. Mem.: NAS, Am. Acad. Microbiology, Phi Beta Kappa. Office: Lab Molecular Microbiology Nat Inst Allergy and Infectious Diseases 4 Center Dr MSC 0460 Bldg 4 Rm 315 Bethesda MD 20892-0460

MARTIN, MALCOLM ELLIOT, lawyer; b. Buffalo, Dec. 11, 1935; s. Carl Edward and Pearl Maude (Elliot) M.; m. Judith Hill Harley, June 27, 1964; children: Jennifer, Elizabeth, Christina, Katherine. AB, U. Mich., Ann Arbor, 1958, JD, 1962. Bar: NY 1963, US Ct. Appeals (2d cir.) 1966, US Supreme Ct. 1967. Assoc. Chadbourne Parke Whiteside & Wolff (now Chadbourne & Parke LLP), NYC, 1962-73, ptnr., 1974—. Dir., sec. Carl and Dorothy Bennett Found., Inc.; sec., counsel Copper Devel. Assn., Inc. With US Army, 1958-60. Mem. ABA, NY State Bar Assn., Assn. Bar City NY, St. Andrew's Soc. NY, Met. Opera Guild, Oratamin Club (Blauvelt, NY), Nyack Boat Club, Rockefeller Ctr. Club, Copper Club (NYC). Home: 74 S Highland Ave Nyack NY 10960-3609 Office: Chadbourne & Parke LLP 30 Rockefeller Plz Fl 31 New York NY 10112-0129 Office Phone: 212-408-1040. E-mail: mmartin@chadbourne.com.

MARTIN, MARCELLA EDRIC, retired community health nurse; b. Rosedale, Miss., Jan. 25, 1930; d. Amos and Alma Allen; m. Reuben Clifton Martin, Jan. 25, 1969; children: Brunetta, Jacqueline, Cornell, Constance. Student, Marygrove Coll., Detroit, 1971; ADN, Highland Park Sch. Nursing, Mich., 1979; ThB, Cmty. Bible Coll., Detroit, 1968. Lic. LPN. LPN VA Hosp., Ann Arbor, Mich., Crittendon Hosp., Detroit, Vis. Nurses Assn., Detroit. Instr. Charles H. Mason Bible Sch., Detroit, 1991—95; mem. C.O.G.I.C. Bus. owners Assn., 1982—. Author: (book) Women Who Struggle, 2001; prodr.: (plays) And Didn't Those Knees Bow, 2004. Founder Prime of Life Adult Foster Care Home, 1979, Somebody's Got To Care Min., 2003; mem. Nat. Campaign Tolerance-The Wall of Tolerance, 2003; missionary over women Chs. of God in Christ, 1986—2002; vol. Redford Geriatric Home, Mich., 1999—. Named to Wall of Tolerance, New Civil Rights Meml. Ctr., Montgomery, Ala., 2003; recipient Spirit of Detroit award, City of Detroit, 1978, 2000, 2002, Disting. Citizen of Detroit award, 1980, Testimonial Resolution award, 1985. Mem.: Detroit Writers Guild. Democrat. Pentecostal Ch. Avocations: reading, writing. Home: 25332 Shiawassee Cir Apt 106 Southfield MI 48034

MARTIN, MARCI, writer, former advertising specialist; b. Corsicana, Tex., Oct. 20, 1927; d. Roy Rhoston McNutt and Maggie Mae Price; m. Harold Durward Martin, May 31, 1947 (dec. Dec. 15, 1998); children: Jennifer Ann Martin Svihus, Gary(dec.). Student, North Tex. State U., 1945—46, So. Meth. U., 1946, Miracosta Coll., 1990—91. Bus. rep. Southwestern Bell, Dallas, 1946—55; advt. rep. Christian Sci. Monitor, San Diego, 1982—89. Author: Go To Hell and Make a U-Turn, 1996, rev. edit., 2000, Secrets and Lies, 2000, License To Steal, 2001, (short stories, essays, articles) The Muse on My Shoulder, 2001; co-editor: A Way With Murder, An Anthology by Arizona Mystery Writers, 2004. Vol. prison chaplain, San Diego, 1989—95. Recipient 1st pl. for poetry, Nat. U., 1991, 3d pl. for essay, Writer's Jour., 2d pl. and hon. mention, Ann. Showcase Writers Club, 1994, Tangled Webs 2d pl., Jim Woods prize, 2002. Mem.: Sisters in Crime, Ariz. Mystery Writers (coord./pres. 1998—), Soc. Southwestern Authors (mentor 1998—), Mystery Writers Am. Avocation: golf. Home: 3011 W Sawmill Spring Trail Tucson AZ 85742

MARTIN, MARGARET ANNE See STEELE, ANITA

MARTIN, MARILYN JOAN, library director; b. Golden Meadow, La., Jan. 17, 1940; d. Marion Francis Mobley and Audrey Virna (Goza) Sapaugh; m. James Reginald Martin, Dec. 16, 1958; children: James Michael, Linda Jill Michaels. BA in History, U. Wash., 1975, MLS, 1976; MA in Pub. History, U. Ark., 1992; PhD in Libr. Sci., Tex. Woman's U., 1993. Cataloger, reference libr. St. Martin's Coll., Lacey, Wash., 1976-78; asst. reference libr. Pacific Luth. U., Tacoma, 1978-85; serials libr. Henderson State U., Arkadelphia, Ark., 1985-86, collection devel. libr., 1987-88, dir. learning resources, 1989-95; dean libr. svcs. Rowan U., Glassboro, 1995—. Contbr. articles to profl. jours. Bd. dirs. N.J. Acad. Libr. Network; mem. exec. com. Tri-state Coll. Libr. Mem. ALA (rsch. com. 1993—, stds. com. 1994—), Assn. Coll. and Rsch. Librs. Republican. Avocations: walking, reading, collecting names. Office: Library Rowan U Glassboro NJ 08028-1701

MARTIN, MARILYN MANN, retired library media specialist; b. Greencastle, Ind., July 14, 1939; d. Emil Albert and Edith Costa Mann; m. Max Lee Martin; children: Michael Lee, Melanie Sue Martin Boesen. BS, Ind. State U., 1960, MS, 1970, 88. Tchr. Latin, sch. libr. Danville H.S., Ind., 1960; libr., media specialist Greencastle H.S., Ind., 1971—2002, ret., 2002. Mem. tech. connections com. Greencastle H.S., 1997-98; mem. exec. bd. Stone Hills Libr. Svcs., Bloomington, Ind., 1990-96. Mem.: NEA, ASCD, Greencastle Classroom Tchrs. (scholarship chmn. 1985—2002), Assn. Ind. Media Educators (dist. advocacy chmn. 1998), Ind. Coop. Libr. Svcs., Ind. Libr. Found., Ind. Ret. Tchrs. Assn., Phi Kappa Phi. Avocations: gardening, reading, volunteering.

MARTIN, MARK, race car driver; b. Batesville, Ark., Jan. 9, 1959; m. Arlene Martin; children: Heather, Rachel, Stacy, Matthew Clyde. Profl. race car driver, 1978—; driver Winston Cup, 1981—. Named winner, ASA Championship, 1978, 1979, 1980, 1986, AC Delco 500, 1989, Pontiac 500, 1989, Pontiac Excitement 400, 1990, Tyson/Holly Farms 400, 1990, Hardee's 500, 1991, Hanes 500, 1992, Mello Yello 500, 1992, Bud 500, 1993, Montain Dew So. 500, 1993, Slick 50 500, 1993, The But at the Glen, 1993, 1994, 1995, Hooters 500, 1994, Winston 500, 1995—97, Tyson 400, 1995, VAW-GM 500, 1995, Savemart 300, 1997, MENA 400, 1997, Las Vegas 400, 1998, Tex. 500, 1998, Calif. 500, 1998, Miller Lite 400, 1997, Goody's Headache Powder 500, 1998, VAW-GM Quality 500, 1998, MBNA Gold 400, 1998, 1999, Dura-Lube/Big KMart 400, 1999, IROC Championship, 1999, Goody's Body Pain 500, 2000. Office: Roush Racing 122 Knob Hill Rd Mooresville NC 28117-6847 also: care NASCAR 1801 W Internat Speedway Bd Daytona Beach FL 32114

MARTIN, MARK D. state supreme court justice; b. Apr. 29, 1963; s. M. Dean and Ann M. BS summa cum laude, Western Carolina U., 1985; JD (hon.), U. N.C., 1988; grad., ~~Nat. Jud.~~ Coll., 1993; LLM, U. Va., 1998; attended, U. Dayton, Ohio, 1981. Bar: N.C., U.S. Dist. Ct. (ea. and mid. dists.); N.C. U.S. Ct. Appeals (4th cir.); U.S. Supreme Ct. Law clk. to Hon. Clyde H. Hamilton U.S. Dist. Ct., Columbia, SC, 1988-90; pvt. practice McNair Law Firm, Raleigh, NC, 1990-91; legal counsel to gov. Office of Gov., Raleigh, NC, 1991-92; superior ct. judge Jud. Dist. 3A, Greenville, NC, 1992-94; judge N.C. Ct. Appeals, 1994-99; assoc. justice N.C. Supreme Ct., 1999—. Mem. N.C. Dept. Correction Master Plan Adv. Com., 1992; mem. N.C. Coun. for Women, 1992; legis. and law reform com. Conf. Superior Ct. Judges, 1993-94; co-chair legis liason com. N.C. Jud. Conf., 1995-97; sec. N.C. Jud. Conf., 1997-99; adj. prof. law U. N.C., Chapel Hill; adj. faculty N.C. Ctrl. U. Sch. Law; chair Commn. on Future of N.C. Bus. Ct., 2003-. Editor-in-chief: Jour Internat. Law and Comml. Regulation. Office coord., United Way Ann. Combined Campaign, 1991, 92. Recipient, Order of Long Leaf Pine, 1992, Disting. Alumnus award We. Carolina U., 1995, Svc. Award City of Raleigh Cmty. Svc. Dept.; Lloyd C. Balfour Fellow, N.C. Inst. Polit. Leadership Fellow, 1992, Coun. of State Govt. Toll Fellow, 2001. Mem., ABA (jud. adminstrv. divsn., coalition for justice com., mem. commn. on state ct. funding, John Marshall award, mem. rev. com., mem. nominating com., appellate judges conf.); N.C. Bar Assn. (minorities in profession com. 1995-2001, multidisciplinary practice task force 1999-01, v.p. 2000-01, strategic planning emerging trends com. 2001-, litigation sect. coun. 2000-03, mem. program com. 2004 Brown v. Bd. Edn. 50th anniversary); N.C. Assn. Black Lawyers, Assn. N.C. Women Attorneys, Wake County Bar Assn. (bd. dirs., C.L.E. presenter, 2003-); UNC Law Davis Soc.; Mortar Board, Carolina Law Alumni Assn. (bd. dirs.), Internat. Hon. Soc., Alpha Lambda Delta, Phi Kappa Phi, Pi Gamma Mu, Omicron Delta Epsilon, Phi Alpha Delta, Delta Sigma Phi (scholar 1986), Beta Gamma Sigma (hon.). Office: North Carolina Supreme Court PO Box 2170 Raleigh NC 27602

MARTIN, MARY, secondary school educator; b. Detroit, May 17, 1954; d. Enos and Sara (Evans) M. AS, Highland Park C.C., 1975; BA, Wayne State U., 1975, MA in Teaching, 1981; postgrad., So. Calif. Sch. Ministry, Detroit, 1992—. Dietary aide Allan Dee Nursing Home, Detroit, 1972, Harper Hosp., Detroit, 1973, 74, nurse aide, 1974-75, respiratory technician, 1975-80, Dr.'s Hosp., Detroit, 1980; head cook, supr. Focus Hope, Detroit, 1981; substitute tchr. Detroit Bd. Edn., 1984-90, tchr. adult edn., 1990-93, tchr., 1993—. Interim advisor student coun. Wayne State U., Detroit, 1985. Sunday sch. teaching trainer People's Missionary Bapt. Ch., Detroit, 1986, del., 1984-87, mem. All Aid, 1984-87, mem. choir, 1984, usher, 1984; precinct del. 13th Congl. Dist., 1986-88, 90-92, model, 1985. Recipient Spirit of Detroit award Detroit City Coun., 1993, Spl. Congl. cert. Hon. Barbara Rose Collins, 1994, Proclamation, Wayne County Commr. George Cushingberry, 1994. Mem. Nat. Sociol. Honor Soc. Democrat. Avocations: reading, shopping, movies, golf, driving.

MARTIN, MARY ANNE, art gallery owner; b. Hoboken, N.J., Apr. 26, 1943; d. Thomas Philipp and Ruth (Kelley) Martin; m. Henry S. Berman, June 9, 1963 (div. 1976); 1 child, Julia Coyote. Student, Smith Coll., 1961—63; BA, Barnard Coll., 1965. Head dept. painting Sotheby Parke Bernet, N.Y.C., 1971-78; founder Latin Am. dept. Sotheby's, N.Y.C., 1977, sr. v.p., 1978-82; pres. Mary Anne Martin, Fine Art, N.Y.C., 1982—. Mem.: Art Dealers Assn. Am. (sr. v.p.). Avocations: art collecting, scuba diving. Office: Mary Anne Martin Fine Art 23 E 73rd St New York NY 10021-3522 E-mail: mamartin@mamfa.com.

MARTIN, MARY ELLEN, state legislator, human development specialist; b. Southfield, Mich. m. George Martin; 3 children. Student, Mercy Coll. Nursing; BS, Daniel Webster Coll., 1988. Human devel. specialist; mem. from dist. 34 N.H. State Ho. of Reps., mem. resources com., mem. recreation and devel. com. Home: 5 Lone Star Dr Nashua NH 03062-3411 Office: NH Ho of Reps State Capitol Concord NH 03301

MARTIN, MELISSA CAROL, radiological physicist; b. Muskogee, Okla., Feb. 7, 1951; d. Carl Leroy and Helen Shirley (Hicks) Paden; m. Donald Ray Martin, Feb. 14, 1970; 1 child, Christina Gail. BS, Okla. State U., 1971; MS, UCLA, 1975. Cert. radiol. physicist Am. Bd. Radiology, radiation oncology Am. Bd. Med. Physics. Asst. radiation physicist Hosp. of The Good Samaritan, L.A., 1975-80; radiol. physicist Meml. Med. Ctr., Long Beach, Calif., 1980-83, St. Joseph Hosp., Orange, Calif., 1983-92, Therapy Physics, Inc., Bellflower, Calif., 1993—. Cons. in field. Editor: (book) Current Regulatory Issues in Medical Physics, 1992. Fund raising campaign divsn. mgr. YMCA, Torrance, Calif., 1988-92; dir. AWANA Youth Club-Guards Group, Manhattan Beach, Calif., 1984—. Named Dir. of Symposium, Am. Coll. Med. Physics, 1992. Fellow Am. Coll. Med. Physics (chancellor western region 1992-95, treas. 2004-), Am. Assn. Physicists in Medicine (profl. coun. 1990-95, treas.

1998-2003, bd. dirs. 1994-2003), Am. Coll. Radiology (econs. com. 1992-95, govt. rels. com. 1998—, coucilor at large 2001-, commn. on med. physics 2002-); mem. Calif. Med. Physics Soc. (treas. 1991-98), Am. Soc. for Therapeutic Radiology and Oncology, Health Physics Soc. (pres. So. Calif. chpt. 1992-93), Am. Brachytherapy Soc. Baptist. Avocation: christian youth group dir. Home: 507 Susana Ave Redondo Beach CA 90277-3953 Office: Therapy Physics Inc 9156 Rose St Bellflower CA 90706-6420 Office Phone: 562-804-0611. E-mail: melissamartin@compuserve.com.

MARTIN, MICHAEL TOWNSEND, racing horse stable executive, sports marketing executive; b. NYC, Nov. 21, 1941; s. Townsend Bradley and Irene (Redmond) M.; m. Jennifer Johnston, Nov. 7, 1964 (div. Jan. 1977); children: Ryan Bradley, Christopher Townsend; m. Jean Kathleen Meyer, Mar. 1, 1980 Grad., The Choate Sch., 1960; student, Rutgers U., 1961-62. Asst. gen mgr N.Y. Jets Football Club, N.Y.C., 1968-74; v.p. NAMANCO Prodns., N.Y.C., 1975-76; v.p., gen. mgr. Cosmos Soccer Club, N.Y.C., 1976-77; exec. asst. Warner Communications, N.Y.C., 1978-84; owner, operator Martin Racing Stable, N.Y.C., 1983—; pres. Sports Mark, Inc., N.Y.C., 1990—2003. Bd. dirs. Mote Marine Lab., Sarasota, Fla., Morris Animal Found., Coun. of Visitors, Woods Hole Marine Biol. Lab., Nat. Lighthouse Ctr. and Mus., Lemur Conservation Found., Ringling Sch. Art and Design; program com. WNET Channel 13; bd. advisors The Pennington Sch., Dir.'s Cir., Scripps Instn. Oceanography. Mem. Athletics Congress (life, cert. official 1984—), U.S. Tennis Assn. (life), Internat. Oceanographic Found. (Miami life mem.), Fla. Thoroughbred Breeders Assn., Quogue Field Club, The Union Club. Republican. Episcopalian. Avocation: collecting inuit (eskimo) art. Home: 131 E 69th St Apt 11A New York NY 10021-5158 Office: 575 Madison Ave Ste 1006 New York NY 10022-2511 Personal E-mail: mmartl1237@aol.com.

MARTIN, MIKE W. philosophy educator; s. Theodore R. and Ruth Martin; m. Shannon Snow, Aug. 1, 1968; children: Sonia Renée, Nicole Marie. BS, U. Utah, 1969, MA, 1972; PhD, U. Calif., Irvine, 1977. Instr. dept. philosophy Chapman U., Orange, Calif., 1976-78, asst. prof., 1978-82, assoc. prof., 1982-86, prof., 1986—. NEH sponsor Nat. Project Philosophy and Engring. Ethics, 1978-80. Co-author: Ethics in Engineering, 1996, Introduction to Engineering Ethics, 2000, Physical Therapy Ethics, 2003; author: Self-Deception and Morality, 1986, Virtuous Giving, 1994, Love's Virtues, 1996, Meaningful Work, 2000; Meaningful Work: Rethinking Professional Ethics, 2000; editor: Self-Deception and Self-Understanding, 1985; contbr. articles to profl. jours. Recipient Graves award Pomona (Calif.) Coll., 1983, Matchette Found. award U. Calif., Irvine, 1976; Coll. Tchrs. fellow NEH, 1981-82. Mem. Am. Philos. Assn., Soc. Bus. Ethics, Soc. Study Profl. Ethics, Phi Beta Kappa, Phi Kappa Phi. Democrat. Office: Dept Philosophy Chapman U 1 University Dr Orange CA 92866-1005

MARTIN, MYRON GREGORY, foundation administrator; b. Houston, Jan. 14, 1958; s. Monty Gene and Vera Mae (Saurage) M. MusB, U. North Tex., 1980; MBA, Golden Gate U., 1989. Various sales and mktg. positions Baldwin Piano Co., N.Y.C., 1980-1990, dir. concert and artists, 1990-95; exec. dir. Liberace Found., Las Vegas, Nev., 1995-98; dir. U. Las Vegas, 1998—. Mem. adv. bd. Thelonious Monk Inst., Washington, D.C., 1994-95; bd. dirs. Cystic Fibrosis Found., Chgo., 1990, Liberace Found., 1993-95, Museums and Attractions, Las Vegas, 1996—. Recipient Special award Cystic Fibrosis Found., 1990. Mem. Nev. Mus. Assn. (bd. dirs. 1997—). Avocations: tennis, judging scholarship pageants for miss america organization. Home: 3996 Placita Del Rico Las Vegas NV 89120-2629 Office: U Las Vegas Performing Art Ctr 4505 S Maryland Pkwy Las Vegas NV 89154-9900

MARTIN, NANICE S. software company executive; Editor, writer numerous publs., including Tiger Beat, Seventeen; dir. software devel. Mattel, dir. online content; pres. PlanetGirl.com., Los Angeles. Author 4 books; prodr. CD-ROM Barbie Fashion Designer, also entertainment CD-ROMs. Office: PlanetGirl-com 1964 Westwood Blvd Ste 425 Los Angeles CA 90025-4651 Fax: 310-446-1405. E-mail: christiana@planetgirl.com.

MARTIN, NOEL, graphic design consultant, educator; b. Syracuse, Ohio, Apr. 19, 1922; s. Harry Ross and Lula (Van Meter) M.; m. Coletta Ruchty, Aug. 29, 1942; children— Dana, Reid Cert. in Fine Arts, Art Acad. Cin., Doctorate (hon.), 1994. Designer Cin. Art Mus., 1947-93, asst. to dir., 1947-55; freelance designer for various ednl., cultural and indsl. orgns., 1947—; instr. Art Acad. Cin., 1951-57, artist-in-residence, 1993—. Design cons. Champion Internat., 1959-82, Xomox Corp., 1961—, Federated Dept. Stores, 1962-83, Hebrew Union Coll., 1969—; designer-in-residence U. Cin., 1968-71, adj. prof., 1968-73; mem. adv. bd. Carnegie-Mellon U., R.I. Sch. Design, Cin. Symphony Orch., Am. Inst. Graphic Arts; lectr. Smithsonian Instn., Libr. of Congress, Am. Inst. Graphic Arts, Aspen Design Conf., various additional schs. and orgns. nationally. One man shows include Contemporary Arts Ctr., Cin., 1954, 71, Addison Gallery Am. Art, 1955, R.I. Sch. Design, 1955, Soc. Typographic Arts, Chgo., 1956, White Mus. of Cornell U., 1956, Cooper & Beatty, Toronto, Ont., Can., 1958, Am. Inst. Graphic Arts, 1958, Ind. U., 1958, Ohio State U., 1971; exhibited in group shows at Mus. Modern Art, N.Y.C., Library of Congress, Musee d'Art Moderne, Paris, Grafiska Inst., Stockholm, Carpenter Ctr., Cambridge, Gutenberg Mus., Mainz, U.S. info. exhbns. In Europe, South America and USSR; represented in permanent collections Mus. Modern Art, Stedelijk Mus., Amsterdam, Cin. Art Mus., Boston Mus. Fine Arts, Cin. Hist. Soc., Library of Congress; contbr. to various publs. Served to sgt. U.S. Air Force, 1942-45 Recipient Art Directors medal, Phila., 1957, Sachs award, Cin., 1973, Lifetime Achievement award Cin. Art Dirs., 1989. Office Phone: 513-731-1287.

MARTIN, PATRICIA, dean, nursing educator; BSN, U. Cin.; MS, Wright State U.; PhD, Case Western Res. U. Dir. nursing rsch., interim dean, assoc. prof. Wright State U. Contbr. articles to profl. jours. Office: Wright State U 168 University Hall Dayton OH 45435-0001

MARTIN, PATRICIA CARMELLA, counselor, entrepreneur; b. Wilmington, Del., Sept. 11, 1958; d. Emily Coston; children: Janel L. Martin-Brown, Alfred V.D. Rogers, Jr. BS cum laude, Springfield Coll., 2002. Entrepreneur Chandelier, Wilmington, Del., 1994—; counselor, coord. Wilmington Hosp., 1999—. V.p. PBS Corp., Wilmington, 2001—02; spiritual intercessory prayer JABA, Wilmington, 1990—. Author poetry. Recipient Unsurpassed Excellent Gold award, Christiana Care, 2001—03. Mem.: YWCA, Cooking Club, Nat. Tree Orgn. Home: PO Box 26018 Wilmington DE 19899

MARTIN, PATRICK J. technology company executive; b. 1941; BS in math., Iona Coll.; MS in Elec. Engring., Doctorate in Elec. Engring., George Washington U.; grad. exec. edn. program, Harvard U. With US Dept. Agriculture; exec. Xerox Corp., pres. N.Am. solutions group; chmn., pres., CEO StorageTek, Louisville, Colo., 2000—. Past mem. bd. dirs. US C. of C., US/China Bus. Coun.; bd. trustees George Washington U.; adv. bd. com. George Washington U. Sch. Engring.; adv. com. Ohio State U. Fisher Sch. Bus. Recipient Jonas Bronck award, Bronx Hist. Soc., 2001, Ellis Island Medal Honor, 2003. Office: Storage Tech 1 Storage Tek Dr Louisville CO 80028

MARTIN, PAUL, Prime Minister of Canada; b. Windsor, Ont., Can., Aug. 28, 1938; s. Paul Joseph and Eleanor (Adams) M.; m. Sheila Ann Cowan, Sept. 11, 1965; children: Paul William, Robert James, David Patrick. BA in Philosophy and History, U. Toronto, Can., 1962, LLB, 1965. Bar: Ont. 1966. Exec. asst. to pres. Power Corp. Can. Ltd., 1966-69, v.p., 1969-71; v.p. spl. projects Consol.-Bathurst Ltd., 1971-73; v.p. planning and devel. Power Corp., Can., 1973-74; pres. Can. S.S. Lines Ltd., Montreal, 1974-80, chief exec. officer, 1976-80; pres., chief exec. officer CSL Group Inc., 1980-88; M.P. Ho. of Commons, 1988—; min. for fed. office of regional devel. Can. Govt., 1993-95; min. of fin. Dept. of Fin. Can., 1993—2002; leader Liberal Party Can., 2003—; prime minister Canada, 2003—. Co-chair Nat. Platform Com. of Liberal Party of Can. Author: Making History: The Politics of Achievement; co-author (with Chaviva Hosek): Creating Opportunity: The Liberal Plan for Canada. Former mem. C.D. Howe Inst. Policy Analysis Com., Birt, N.Am. Com., Ctr. Rsch. Action on Race Rels.; former bd. dirs. Can. Coun. Christians and Jews; founding dir. emeritus North-South Inst., Can., Coun. Native Bus.; bd. govs. Concordia U., coun., v.p., past mem. bd. advisors; inaugural chair G-20, 1999. Liberal. Avocations: sports, reading. Office: Office of the Prime Minister Langevin Block 80 Wellington St Ottawa ON Canada K1A 0A2

MARTIN, PAUL CECIL, physicist, researcher; b. Bklyn., Jan. 31, 1931; s. Harry and Helen (Salzberger) M.; m. Ann Wallace Bradley, Aug. 7, 1957; children: Peter, Stephanie Glennon, Daniel. AB, Harvard U., 1952, PhD, 1954. Mem. faculty Harvard U., Cambridge, Mass., 1957—, prof. physics, 1964-82, J. H. VanVleck prof. pure and applied physics, 1982—, chmn. dept. physics, 1972-75, dean divsn. engring. and applied scis., 1977-98, assoc. dean Faculty Arts and Scis., 1981-98, dean rsch. and info. tech., 1998—. Vis. prof. Ecole Normale Superieure, Paris, 1963, 66, U. Paris, Orsay, 1971; mem. materials rsch. adv. coun. NSF, 1986-89; bd. dirs. Mass. Tech. Pk. Corp., 1990—, exec. com., 1992—. Bd. editors: Jour. Math Physics, 1965-68, Annals of Physics, 1968-82, Jour. Statis. Physics, 1975-80, Proc. Nat. Acad. Scis., 2000—. Bd. dirs. Assoc. Univs. for Rsch. in Astronomy, 1979-85; bd. dirs. Assoc. Univs., Inc., 1981—, exec. com., 1986-90, 92-94, chmn. bd. dirs., 1996-2000. NSF postdoctoral fellow, 1955; Sloan Found. fellow, 1959-62; Guggenheim fellow, 1966, 71 Fellow: AAAS (chair physics sect. 1986), Am. Phys. Soc. (councillor-at-large 1982—84, panel on pub. affairs 1983—86, chmn. nominating com. 1994), Am. Acad. Arts and Scis., NAS. Office: Harvard U Dept Physics Cambridge MA 02138 E-mail: martin@harvard.edu.

MARTIN, PAUL EDWARD, retired insurance company executive; b. Santa Claus, Ind., Sept. 10, 1914; s. James F. and Anna (Singer) M.; m. Pauline Peva, Dec. 22, 1939 (dec. Feb. 1982); 1 child, Peter McDowell; m. Ann Parker, Oct. 14, 1983. BA, Hanover Coll., 1936. With actuarial dept. State Life Ins. Co., Indpls., 1936-42; asst. actuary Ohio Nat. Life Ins. Co., Cin., 1946-48, asso. actuary, 1948-49, actuary, 1949-55, actuarial v.p., 1955-56, adminstrv. v.p., 1956-67, sr. v.p. ins. adminstrn., 1967-71, pres., 1971-72, chmn. bd., chief exec. officer, 1972-79, also dir. Trustee Hanover (Ind.) Coll. Served to maj. F.A. AUS, 1942-46, PTO. Fellow Soc. Actuaries, Acad. Actuaries; mem. Comml. Club, Skyline Club, Masons, Shriners, Gamma Sigma Pi, Beta Theta Pi. Presbyterian.

MARTIN, PAUL EDWARD, lawyer; b. Atchison, Kans., Feb. 5, 1928; s. Harres C. and Thelma F. (Wilson) M.; m. Betty Lou Crawford, Aug. 28, 1954; children: Cherry G., Paul A., Marylou. BBA, Baylor U., 1955, LLB, 1956; LLM, Harvard U., 1957. Bar: Tex. 1956, Pa. 1958. Assoc. Ballard, Spahr, Andrews & Ingersoll, Phila., 1957-58; ptnr. Fulbright & Jaworski, Houston, 1959-77; shareholder Chamberlain, Hrdlicka, White, Williams & Martin, 1977—; instr. in estate planning U. Houston. Exec. com. Met. Houston March of Dimes, 1980-82; chmn. deacons West Meml. Bapt. Ch., 1979-80; trustee Baylor U., 1970-89, Meml. Hosp. Sys., 1975—, Fgn. Mission Bd., So. Bapt. Conv.; pres. Baylor U. Devel. Coun., 1973-74. Lt. comdr. USN, 1947-53. Fellow Am. Coll. Trust and Estate Coun.; mem. ABA (sect. real property, probate and trust law and sect. taxation), State Bar Tex., Houston Bar Assn., Houston Estate and Fin. Forum (pres. 1965-66), Houston Bus. and Estate Planning Coun., Houston Club, Phi Delta Phi. Republican. Co-author: How to Live and Die with Texas Probate. Home: 126 Lakeside Dr Montgomery TX 77356 Office: Chamberlin Hrdlicka Et Al 1200 Smith St Ste 1400 Houston TX 77002-4401 Fax: (713) 658-2553. E-mail: paul.martin@chamberlainlaw.com.

MARTIN, PAUL ROSS, editor; b. Lancaster, Pa., May 14, 1932; s. Paul Rupp and Amanda (Minnich) M.; m. Julia Ibbotson, June 5, 1954 (div. Apr. 1979); children: Monica Martin Goble, Julia, Paul Jr., Barbara, Drew, Eric. BA, Dartmouth Coll., 1954. Reporter, wire editor Lancaster New Era, Lancaster Newspapers Inc., 1954-60; copyreader, makeup man Wall St. Jour. divsn. Dow Jones & Co., N.Y.C., 1960-63, copy editor nat. news, 1963-69, editor bus. and fin. column, 1969-72, nat. copydesk chief, 1972-75, page one sr. spl. writer, 1975-90, asst. to mng. editor, 1990-93, asst. mng. editor, 1993—2002. Editor: The Possible Dream, 1978, Retirement Without Fear, 1981, Wall Street Journal Style Book, 1981, 4th edit., 1995, The Wall Street Journal Guide to Business Style and Usage, 2002; co-author, editor: American Dynasties Today, 1983. Bd. dirs. Cmty. Bd. 1, S.I., N.Y., 1976-80. Mem. N.Y. Fin. Writers Assn. (past officer). Avocations: basketball, tennis, travel. Office: Wall St Jour 200 Liberty St New York NY 10281-1003 E-mail: paul.martin-sr@wsj.com.

MARTIN, PETER GERARD, marketing infosystems specialist, consultant, secondary school educator; b. Weymouth, Mass., May 2, 1952; s. John Augustine and Jean Anita (Murphy) M.; m. Elizabeth Anne Collins, Aug. 24, 1974; children: Derek Grant, Erin Jean. BA, Nasson Coll., 1974; MS, U. R.I., 1979; postgrad., Boston Coll., U. So. Maine, 1977, 79; MA, Columbia Pacific U., 1991; PhD, U. Heriseau, 2000. Computer programmer Baybank Data Services, Waltham, Mass., 1975-76; mathematician Factory Mut. Engring., Norwood, Mass., 1976-78; tchr. Kennebunk (Maine) High Sch., 1978-79; v.p. strategic planning The Foxboro (Mass.) Co., 1979-84, systems cons., 1984-85, mgr. system product planning, 1986-88, v.p. market strategies and comm., 1996-99, v.p. corp. mktg., 1999—; v.p. mktg. Intec Controls Corp., 1993-94; v.p. Automation Rsch. Corp., 1996. Instr. Dean Jr. Coll., Franklin, Mass. 1980-96; tech. cons. Balance Inc., Wiscassett, Maine, 1985-89. Author: Dynamic Performance Management: A Path to World Class Manufacturing, 1992, Bottom-Line Automation, 2001; contbr. articles to profl. jours. Pres. East Woonsocket Sch. Parent Council, R.I., 1983-85; mem. Parents Involvement Com., Woonsocket, 1985; Cub Scout den leader, Woonsocket, 1985-86; instr. religious edn. Our Lady of Lourdes Ch. Mem. Soc. Mfg. Engrs., Mfrs. Automation Protocol Users Group, Inst. Soc. of Am. Roman Catholic. Avocations: camping, tennis, boating. Office: The Foxboro Co Bristol Park 351-2C Bristol Park Foxboro MA 02035 E-mail: pmartin@foxboro.com.

MARTIN, PETER ROBERT, psychiatrist, pharmacologist; b. Budapest, Hungary, Sept. 6, 1949; came to U.S.,1980; s. Nicholas M. and Eva (Horvat) M.; m. Barbara Bradford, Dec. 23, 1985; 1 child, Alexander Bradford. BSc with honors, McGill U., Montreal, Que., Can., 1971, MD, CM, 1975; MSc, U. Toronto, Ont., Can., 1978. Diplomate Am. Bd. Psychiatry and Neurology, Psychiatry, Addiction Psychiatry. Resident in internal medicine U. Toronto, Can., 1975-76, resident in psychiatry, 1978-80; fellow clin. pharmacology Addiction Rsch. Found., Toronto, 1976-78; chief sect. clin. sci. Nat. Inst. on Alcohol Abuse & Alcoholism, Bethesda, 1983-86; assoc. prof. Vanderbilt U. Sch. Medicine, Nashville, 1986-92, prof., 1992—, dir. divsn. addiction medicine, 1986—, dir. addiction ctr., 1994—; dir. Vanderbilt Inst. for Coffee Studies, 1999—. Vis. scientist Lab. of Clin. Sci., NIMH, Bethesda, Md., 1980-83; investigator John F. Kennedy Ctr. for Rsch. on Human Devel., Nashville, 1993—. Fellow Royal Coll. Physicians (Can.), Am. Psychiatric Assn.; mem. AAAS, Am. Soc. Clin. Pharmacology and Therapeutics, Am. Acad. Addiction Psychiatry, Rsch. Soc. on Alcoholism, Internat. Soc. Biomed. Rsch. in Alcoholism. Office: Psychiatric Hosp at Vanderbilt Ste 3068 1601 23rd Ave South Nashville TN 37232-8650 Office Phone: 615-322-3527. E-mail: peter.martin@vanderbilt.edu.

MARTIN, PETER WILLIAM, lawyer, educator; b. Cin., Apr. 11, 1939; s. Wilfred Samuel and Elizabeth (Myers) M.; m. Ann Wadsworth, Nov. 28, 1964; children: Leah, Elliot, Isaac. BA, Cornell U., 1961; JD, Harvard U., 1964. Bar: Ohio 1964. Atty. AF Gen. Counsel's Office, 1964-67; asso. prof. law U. Minn., 1967-71; vis. asso. prof. law Cornell U., 1971-72, prof. law, 1972—, dean, 1980-88, Edward Cornell prof. law, 1989-92, Jane Foster prof. law, 1992—; co-dir. Legal Info. Inst., 1992—2003; pres. Ctr. for Computer Assisted Legal Instrn., 1986-88. Cons. Adminstrv. Conf. U.S., 1977-79; reporter Am. Bar Assn. Task Force on Lawyer Competency and the Role of the Law Schs. Author: The Ill-Housed, 1971, (with others) Social Welfare and the Individual, 1971, Cases and Materials on Property, 1974, 3d edit., 1992, Social Security Law, 2003, Basic Legal Citation, 2002, Social Security Plus, 1994, Introduction to Copyright, 2003; editor Jour. Legal Edn., 1985. Chmn. Ithaca Bd. Zoning Appeals, 1974-79. Served to capt. USAF, 1964-67. Mem. ABA (task force on law schs. and legal profession 1990-92), Am. Bar Found. (vis. com.), Assn. Law Schs. (chmn. law and computers sect. 1987-88, 93-94). Office: Cornell U Law Sch Myron Taylor Hall Ithaca NY 14853 E-mail: martin@lii.law.cornell.edu.

MARTIN, PHILLIP DWIGHT, bank consulting company executive, mayor; b. Nevada, Mo., Jan. 4, 1943; s. E. Dwight and Berniece E. (Leedy) M. BS, U. Mo., 1964, MBA, 1965, cert. math. and bus. edn., 1966. Tchr. Warsaw (Mo.) Pub. Schs., 1966—68; investment analyst Bus. Men's Assurance Co. Am., Kansas City, Mo., 1968—70; exec. v.p. Farmer's Bank Walker, Mo., 1970—71; banking cons. Howard J. Blender Co., Dallas, 1971—84; chmn. Profit Motivators Internat., Inc., Boulder, Colo., 1984—2002; mayor City of Walker, 1986—2000, 2002—; math. tchr. El Dorado Springs, Mo., 2002—. Bd. dirs. Nev. Regional Med. Ctr., 2004—. Mem. Walker R-4 Alumni Assn. (co-founder, life mem. scholarship com., pres. 1994-96). Home: 214 E Marvin Ave Walker MO 64790-0069 E-mail: pdm19@centurytel.net.

MARTIN, PHILLIP HAMMOND, lawyer; b. Tucson, Jan. 4, 1940; s. William P. and Harriet (Hammond) M.; m. Sandra S. Chandler, June 17, 1961 (div. Mar. 1989); children: Lisa, Craig, Wade, Ryan; m. Erika Zetty, May 9, 1990. BA, U. Minn., 1961, JD, 1964. Bar: Minn. 1964, U.S. Tax Ct. 1967, U.S. Dist. Ct. Minn. 1968, U.S. Ct. Appeals (8th cir.) 1973, U.S. Supreme Ct. 1981, U.S. Claims Ct. 1983, U.S. Ct. Appeals (fed. cir.) 1988, U.S. Ct. Appeals (7th cir.) 1989. Assoc. Dorsey & Whitney, Mpls., 1964-69, ptnr., 1970—. Home: 487 Portland Ave Saint Paul MN 55102-2216 Office: Dorsey & Whitney LLP Ste 1500 50 S 6th St Minneapolis MN 55402-1498 Office Phone: 612-340-2845. Business E-Mail: martin.phil@dorsey.com.

MARTIN, PRESTON, financial services consultant; b. L.A., Dec. 5, 1923; s. Oscar and Gaynell (Horn) M.; 1 child, Pier Preston. BS in Fin., U. So. Calif., 1947, MBA, 1948; PhD in Monetary Econs., U. Ind., 1952. Prof. fin. Grad. Sch. Bus. Adminstrn. U. So. Calif., 1950-60; prin. in housebldg. firm, 1952-56; with mortgage fin. and consumer fin. instns., 1954-57; commr. savs. and loan State of Calif., 1967-69; chmn. Fed. Home Loan Bank Bd., Washington, 1969-72; founder, CEO PMI Mortgage Ins. Co., 1972-80; chmn., CEO Seraco Group subs. Sears, Roebuck & Co., 1980-81, also bd. dirs. parent co.; chmn., CEO WestFed Holdings Inc., L.A., 1986-92, SoCal Holdings, Inc., L.A., 1987-93, H.F. Holdings, Inc., San Francisco, 1986, Honolulu Fed. Bank, Honolulu. Vice-chmn. Fed. Res. Bd., Washington, 1982-86; founder Fed. Home Loan Mortgage Corp., 1970—; prof. bus. econ. and fin. Inst. Per Lo Studio Orgn. Aziendale, Italy. Author: Principles and Practices of Real Estate, 1959; co-author: The Complete Idiot's Guide to the Federal Reserve, 2003. Mem. President's Commn. on Housing, 1980-81; prin. Coun. Excellence in Govt., Washington. Recipient House and Home award, 1969; award Engring. News Record, 1971; Turntable award Nat. Assn. Home Builders, 1973; Housing Hall of Fame award, Nat. Assn. Home Builders, 2001. Mem. Lambda Chi Alpha. Presbyterian. Office Phone: 415-283-3224.

MARTIN, QUINN WILLIAM, lawyer; b. Fond du Lac, Wis., 1948; s. Quinn W. and Marcia E. Martin; m. Jane E.; children: Quinn W., William J. BSME, Purdue U., 1969; postgrad., U. Santa Clara, 1969-70; JD, U. Mich., 1973. Bar: Wis. 1973, U.S. Dist. Ct. (ea. dist.) Wis. 1973, U.S. Ct. Appeals (7th cir.) 1973. Sales support mgr. Hewlett-Packard, Palo Alto, Calif., 1969-70; assoc. Quarles & Brady, Milw., 1973-80, ptnr., 1980—. Bd. dirs. Associated Bank Milw., U-Line Corp., Gen. Timber and Land, Inc., Fond du Lac. Chmn. Gov. McCallum Trans Com., Wis., U. Mich. Law Sch. Fund; bd. dirs. Milw. Zool. Soc., Found. for Wildlife Conservation. Mem. ABA, Wis. Bar Assn., Milw. Club, Ozaukee Country Club, Chaine des Rottiseurs, Delta Upsilon (sec.), Milw. Club, Rotary. Office: Quarles & Brady 411 E Wisconsin Ave Ste 2550 Milwaukee WI 53202-4497

MARTIN, R. BRAD, retail executive; Chmn., ceo Proffitts, Inc. (now Saks Inc.), Memphis. Office: Saks Inc 750 Lakeshore Pkwy Birmingham AL 35211-4400

MARTIN, R KEITH, business and information systems educator, consultant; b. Seattle, Sept. 5, 1933; s. Jerome Milton and Winifred (Gifford) M.; m. Carolyn Joanne Carosella, June 15, 1957; children: Jefferson, Sean, Jennifer, Katherine. AB, Whitman Coll., 1955; MBA with high honors, CCNY, 1965; PhD, U. Wash., 1973. Registered, lic. profl. engr.; cert. data processing, cert. systems profl., cert. computer profl. Div. mgr. Campus Merchandising Bur., Inc., N.Y.C., 1955-56; sales rep. IBM, Seattle, 1956, Svc. Bur. Corp. subs. IBM, N.Y.C., 1957-58; specialist mgmt. adv. svcs. Price Waterhouse & Co., N.Y.C., 1959-65, Seattle, 1965-66, mgr., 1966-67; dir. mgmt. systems dept. U. Wash., 1967-71, lectr. dept. acctg. Sch. Bus. Adminstrn., 1971-73; asst. prof. dept. accountancy Baruch Coll., CUNY, 1973-76, assoc. prof., 1977-79; prof. acctg. Fairfield U., 1979-84, prof. acctg. and info. systems, 1984-94, assoc. dean Sch. Bus., 1980-82, dean, 1982-93, acting dean grad. Sch. of Communications, 1988-90, prof. info. systems, 1994-2001, prof. info. systems and ops. mgmt., 2001—, dept. chmn., 1999—2002, holder Stephen and Camille Schramm chair in bus., 2000—. V.p. Eastalco Systems, 1971-72; faculty fin. div. Am. Mgmt. Assn., 1963-64; part-time lectr. Bellevue Community Coll., 1967-69, Shoreline Community Coll., 1968-72, Seattle U., 1971-72 Co-author: Management Control of Electronic Data Processing, 1965; author: Management Information Systems in Higher Education: Case Studies at Three Universities, 1973, Effective Business Communications, 1976, 79, 91, Systems Development and Computer Concepts, 1977; assoc. editor: Industry Guides for Accountants and Auditors, 2 vols., 1980; mem. editorial rev. bd. Dickenson Pub. Co., 1974-75, Prentice-Hall, Inc., 1977-78, 87-88, 90-91, Reston Pub. Co., 1977-78, Jour. Acctg. Edn., 1981-83; featured roles (Amateur Comedy Club prodns.) Guys and Dolls, Our Town, The Fantastics, The Night of the Iguana, The Rainmaker, My Fair Lady; stage mgr. Some Assembly Required, Arcadia, Murder by the Book; house mgr. The Real Thing, The Tempest (play com., 2004-, chair, 2004); program dir., summer program at Heslier (Rotterdam) 2000, 2001, Nat. Univ. Galway, 2003; author numerous monographs; contbr. numerous articles to profl. jours. Mem. Mendelssohn Choir of Conn., Amateur Comedy Club, Westchester Chordsmen. Recipient cert. of appreciation Am. Mgmt. Assn., 1966, cert. of merit for disting. service to Mgmt. Scis., 1969, for disting. service to info. systems profession, 1973; Merit award Assn. Systems Mgmt., 1971, Achievement award, 1972, Internat. award World Assn. for Case Method Rsch. and Application, 1996, 2002; cert. for service City of Seattle, 1973; named Outstanding Young Man Am., 1970, One of 300 Outstanding Alumni, Whitman Coll., 1979; Kellogg fellow, 1971-72, Price Waterhouse faculty fellow, 1976. Mem. Am. Inst. Indsl. Engrs. (dir. Seattle chpt. 1967-70, chmn. regional conf. 1969), World Assn. for Case Method Rsch. and Application (adv. bd. 1996-99, exec. bd. dirs. 1999—, vice-chair internat. case stds. setting com. 2001—), Acad. for Creative Tchg. (exec. bd. 1998—), Inst. Mgmt. Accts. (assoc. dir. N.Y. chpt. 1963-64, 75-85 Seattle chpt. 1967-70), Assn. Systems Mgmt. (sec. 1968-69, v.p. 1969-70, pres. Pacific N.W. chpt. 1970-71), Data Processing Mgmt. Assn., Assn. Computing Machinery, Soc. Cert. Data Processors, NSPE, N.Y. Soc. Profl. Engrs., Soc. Mgmt. Info. Systems, AAUP, Am. Acctg. Assn., Phi Delta Theta (province pres. 1986-87), Beta Gamma Sigma, Mu Gamma Tau, Phi Delta Kappa, Beta Alpha Psi. Clubs: Bronxville Field. Home: 338 Collins Ave Mount Vernon NY 10552-1602 E-mail: rkmartin@mail.fairfield.edu., rkmartin6221@msn.com.

MARTIN, RALPH DRURY, lawyer, columnist; b. Pittsburg, Kans., Mar. 4, 1947; s. Kent Wills and Kathleen (Drury) M.; m. Ruchirawan Meemeskul, Oct. 28, 1982; 1 child, Chanida Kathleen. BA, Tulane U., 1969; JD, Washington U., 1972. Bar: La. 1972, D.C. 1981, Calif. 1992, U.S. Dist. Ct. (mid. dist.) La. 1985, U.S. Dist. Ct. D.C. 1991, U.S. Ct. Appeals (9th cir.) 1979, U.S. Ct. Appeals (D.C. cir.) 1991, U.S. Supreme Ct. 1976. Law clk. to Hon. Frederick J.R. Heebe U.S. Dist. Ct., Ea. Dist. La., New Orleans, 1972-74; spl. asst. to U.S. atty. U.S. Dept. Justice, Washington, 1974-75, trial atty. civil rights div., 1975-80; dep. asst. legal advisor U.S. Dept. State, Washington, 1980-82; sr. prosecutor pub. integrity sect. U.S. Dept. Justice, Washington, 1982-90; spl. counsel U.S. Dept. State, Washington, 1990-91; ptnr. Storch & Brenner, Washington, 1991-2000, Dilworth Paxson PLLC, Washington, 2001—02; sr. counsel Nat. Assn. Securities Dealers, 2002—. Adj. prof. Washington Coll. Law, The Am. Univ., 1991-92; chmn. Lawyers Com. Effective Assistance of Counsel, 1995—. Comments editor Washington U. Law Quarterly, 1971-72 (honors scholar award 1971). Bd. dirs. Thomas and Bertie T. Smith Arts Found., 1996—, James Madison Project, 1999—. Mem. ABA, Am. Soc. Internat. Law, Nat. Assn. Criminal Def. Lawyers, Univ. Club,

D.C. Assn. Criminal Def. Lawyers (v.p. 1995-97), Order of Coif, Stan Musial Soc., E.B. Williams Inn of Ct. (master). Office: Dilworth Paxson PLLC 1200 19th St NW Washington DC 20036 E-mail: khaki@verizon.net.

MARTIN, RANDI CHRISTINE, psychology educator; b. Salem, Oreg., May 24, 1949; d. Harold Raymond and Maxine Constance (Torgeson) M.; m. Lawrence P. Chan, Aug. 30, 1974. BA, U. Oreg., 1971; MA, Johns Hopkins U., 1977, PhD, 1979. Lectr. U. Calif., Santa Cruz, 1979-80; assoc. rsch. scientist Johns Hopkins U., Balt., 1980-82; asst. prof. Rice U., Houston, 1982-87, assoc. prof., 1987-93, prof., 1993—, chair psychology dept., 2002—. Assoc. editor Psychonomic Bulletin & Rev., Austin, Tex., 1995—; editl. bd. mem. Cognitive Neuropsychology, London, 1994—, Jour. Neurolinguistics, Cambridge, Eng., 1994—; contbr. articles to profl. jours. Recipient Claude Pepper award NIH Deafness and Comm. Disorders Inst., 1995—. Fellow APA; mem. Psychonomic Soc. (sec./treas. 1993-95, bd. dirs. 1997—), Acad. Aphasia (program com. 1990-93). Achievements include research in short term memory deficits in brain damaged patients. Office: Rice U Dept Psychology 6100 Main St Houston TX 77005-1892

MARTIN, RAYMOND BRUCE, plumbing equipment manufacturing company executive; b. NYC, Oct. 23, 1934; s. Raymond M. and Margaret (Lennon) M.; m. Suzanne Ruth Longpre, Sept. 3, 1960; 1 son, Christopher Haines. AB, Villanova U., 1956. With Corning (NY) Glass Works, 1956-68, nat. plumbing sales mgr., 1966-68; v.p. mktg. Briggs Mfg. Co., Warren, Mich., 1968-69, v.p., gen. mgr. plumbing fixture div., 1969-72; pres., CEO, chmn. bd. Water Control Internat. Inc., Troy, Mich., 1972-91; pres., CEO W/C Technology Corp., 1991—2002; chmn. Intertech. Corp., 2003—; mem. plumbing harmonization Fed. N.Am. Free Trade Delegation, 1992; ret., 2002. Served with AUS, 1957-58. Mem. Am. Soc. Plumbing Engrs., Plumbing Mfrs. Inst. (chmn. HUD Task Group 1981-82, chmn. comm. com. 1983-86, chmn. fed. water conservation com. 1988-90, chmn. flushing devices com. 1999—, chmn. info. tech. com. 2002—), Am. Soc. Sanitary Engrs. (chmn. std. com. pressurized flushing devices 2004), ASME (panel 19, chmn. definitions task group 1993-94, chmn. water closet hydraulic performance task group 1993-94, chmn. flushing devices com. 2000-02). Republican. Roman Catholic. Office: 2820-228 W Maple Rd Troy MI 48084 Business E-Mail: rbmartin@intertechcorp.us.

MARTIN, REX, manufacturing executive; Chmn, pres., CEO Nibco, Elkhart, Ind. Office: NIBCO Inc 1516 Middleburry St PO Box 1167 Elkhart IN 46515-1167

MARTIN, RICHARD H. principal; b. Washington, Pa., Feb. 25, 1956; s. Henderson E. and Margaret Roxena Martin; m. Lori Confer Martin, Nov. 6, 1982. BS in Edn., Calif. State Coll., 1978, MA in Comms., 1980; EdD in Edn. Adminstrn., W.Va. U., 1991. Cert. tchr., supr., prin., supt. schs. Asst. to dean Calif. State Coll., 1978-80; tchr. Turkeyfoot Sch. Dist., Confluence, Pa., 1980-81, Somerset (Pa.) Sch. Dist., 1981-82, Frazier Sch. Dist., Perryopols, Pa., 1982-85, dept. chair, 1985-90, prin., 1990-96, Mt. Lebanon Sch. Dist., Pitts., 1996-99, Bethlehem Ctr. High Sch., 1999—. Cons. W.Va. Dept. of Edn., Charleston, 1990—, Intermediate Unit #1, Calif., 1982-90; mem. safety coun. Mt. Lebanon Sch. Dist., Pitts., 1997—; trainer in IDEA Allegheny Intermediate Unit, Pitts., 1998—; adj. asst. prof. W.Va. U., 1991—. Contbr. articles to profl. jours. Recipient Cmty. Svc. award Perrypolis Heritage Soc., 1991. Mem. NASSP/PASSP, AASA, ASCD, CEFPI, Mt. Lebanon Found., Masons (floor officer 1985—), Monessen Commandary Knights Templar (floor officer 1985—), Shriners, Uniontown Masons, Phi Delta Kappa. Avocations: fly fishing, hunting, good cigars. Home: 225 Nobles Rd Brownsville PA 15417-9283 E-mail: lmartin@mail.mlynk.com.

MARTIN, RICHARD J. food wholesale executive; Exec. v.p., CFO Rykoff-Sexton, Wilkes-Barre, Pa.; sr. v.p. fin. & adminstrn., CFO Cert. Grocers Calif., 1998-2000; CFO, exec. v.p. fin. & adminstrn. Unified Western Grocers, Inc., Commerce, Calif., 2000—. Office: Unified Western Grocers Inc 5200 Sheila St City Of Commerce CA 90040

MARTIN, RICHARD JAY, medical educator; b. Detroit, May 16, 1946; s. Peter Aaron and Tillie Jean (Munch) M.; m. Helene Iris Horowitz, Dec. 23, 1967; children: Elizabeth Hope, David Evan. BS, U. Mich., 1967, MD, 1971. Diplomate Am. Bd. Internal Medicine and Pulmonary Disease. Intern, Ariz., 1971-72; resident Tulane U., New Orleans, 1974-76; pulmonary fellow, 1976-78; asst. prof. medicine U. Okla., Okla. City, 1978-80, U. Colo., Denver, 1980-85, assoc. prof., 1985-92, prof., 1992—. Dir. Cardiorespiratory Sleep Rsch., Nat. Jewish Med. and Rsch. Ctr., Denver, 1980-89, staff physician, 1980-, head divsn. pulmonary medicine, 1993-, vice chair dept. medicine, 1997-, acting chair, dept. medicine, 2004-. Author: Cardiorespiratory Disorders During Sleep, 1984, 2d edit., 1990, (with others) Current Therapy in Internal Medicine, 1984, Clinical Pharmacology and Therapeutics in Nursing, 1985, Interdisciplinary Rehabilitation of Multiple Sclerosis and Neuromuscular Disorders, 1984, Drugs for the Respiratory System, 1985, Current Therapy in Pulmonary Medicine, 1985, Abnormalities of Respiration During Sleep, 1986, Mitchell's Synopis of Pulmonary Medicine, 1987, Pulmonary Grand Rounds, 1990, Asthma and Rhinitis, 1994, The High Risk Patient: Management of the Critically Ill, 1995, Manual of Asthma Management, 1995, 2000, Severe Asthma: Pathogenesis and Clinical Management, 1995, Curret Pulmonology, 1995, Pulmonary and Respiratory Therapy Secrets, 1996, (book chpts.) Lung Biology in Health and Disease, 1995, 3d edit., 2000, Allergy, 1997, Asthma, 1997, Emergency Asthma, 1999, Difficult Asthma, 1999, Asthma and Rhinitis, 1999, Imaging of Diffuse Lung Disease, 2000, Manual of Asthma Management, 2000, Severe Asthma, 2001, Asthma Critical Debates, 2002, Inhaled Steroids in Asthma, 2002, The Merck Manual, 2002, Current Review of Asthma, 2003; editor: Nocturnal Asthma: Mechanisms and Interventions, 1993, Cardiothoracic Interrelationships in Clinical Practice, 1997; author, editor: Nocturnal Asthma: Mechanisms and Treatment, 1993, Combination Therapy for Asthma and Chronic Obstructive Pulmonary Disease, 2000; mem. editl. bd. Chronobiology Internat., 1997—, Am. Jour. Respiratory and Critical Care Medicine, 1994-98, Bronchial Asthma: Index and Review, 1996-97; assoc. editor: Clinical Care for Asthma, 1995-97; contbr. articles to profl. jours. Pres. Congregation Rodef Shalom, Denver, 1984-85; regional v.p. United Synagogues of Am., Denver, 1988-89. Pulmonary fellow Am. Lung Assn., 1977-79, James F. Hammarsten Outstanding fellow U. Okla. Health Scis. Ctr., 1978; grantee Am. Lung Assn., VA, U. Okla. Lung Assn., NIH, Parker B. Francis Found.; recipient Best Paper in Internal Medicine award Okla. Soc. Interna. Medicine, 1977-78, U. Okla. Gastroenterology sect, 1977, Amb. award Nat. Jewish Med. and Rsch. Ctr., 2002; named Disting. Lectr. Royal Coll. Physicians and Surgeons Can., 1998, Cardio-Pulmonary Congress, Argentina, 1998, Assn. Argentina Allergy and Immunology, 2001. Mem. ACP, Am. Thoracic Soc., Am. Fedn. for Clin. Rsch., Am. Coll. Chest Physicians (Disting. scholar in respiratory health 2003—), Colo. Trudeau Soc., Western Soc. Clin. Investigation. Avocations: biking, golf, Karate. Office: Nat Jewish Med Rsch Ctr 1400 Jackson St Denver CO 80206-2761 Office Phone: 303-398-1847. Business E-Mail: martinr@njc.org.

MARTIN, RICHARD KELLEY, lawyer; b. Tulsa, June 30, 1952; s. Richard Loye and Maxine (Kelley) M.; m. Reba Lawson, June 12, 1993; children from previous marriage: R. Kyle, Andrew J. BA, Westminster Coll., 1974; JD, So. Meth. U., 1977. Bar: Tex. 1977, U.S. Tax Ct. 1979. Ptnr. Akin, Gump, Strauss, Hauer & Feld, LLP, Dallas, 1977-95, Haynes and Boone LLP, Dallas, 1995—. Bd. dirs. Goodwill Industries, Dallas, 1986-2000, v.p., 1986-91; bd. dirs. Greater Dallas Youth Orchs., 1987-90; bd. dirs., v.p., pres. Big Bros. and Sisters Met. Dallas, 1988-91; bd. dirs. Tejas coun. Girl Scouts U.S., 1997-2001, Salvation Army, Dallas, 2003--. Mem. Tex. Bar Assn., Salesmanship Club Dallas. Republican. Methodist. Office: Haynes and Boone LLP 2505 N Plano Rd Ste 4000 Richardson TX 75082-4101 E-mail: rick.martin@haynesboone.com.

MARTIN, RICHARD L. retired insurance executive; b. Franklin, N.J., Feb. 2, 1932; s. Richard Lewis and Elizabeth (Roe) M.; m. Susan Mazuy, June 20, 1970; children: David Cory, Scott Mazuy; m. Victoria Lee Morton, May 30, 1998; 1 stepchild, Robert M. Ferguson. BEd, U. Miami, 1958; MA, Columbia U., 1963. Chartered Property Casualty Underwriter. Educator Franklin (N.J.) Sch. Dist., 1958-60; mng. dir. Sparta (N.J.) Sch. Dist., 1960-66; adminstr. Orange (N.J.) Sch. System, 1966-71; chief exec. officer Montague (N.J.) Sch. Dist., 1971-72, Stanhope (N.J.) Sch. System, 1972-73; v.p. Selective Ins. Group, Branchville, N.J., 1973-87; pres., chief exec. officer Med. Malpractice Ins. Assn., N.Y.C., 1987-98; ret., 1998. Chmn. N.J. Anti-Car Theft Com., Trenton, 1980-87; treas. N.J. Ins. News Svc., Newark, 1982-87; chmn. AIA-N.J. State Conf., Trenton, 1983-87. Contbr. several articles to mags. With USMC, 1952-54. Mem. CPCU, Am. Mgmt. Assn., Soc. Ins. Research, Soc. for Corp. Planning, City Midday, Newton Country, Branchville Rotary, Sons of Am. Revolution, Mayflower Soc. Presbyterian. Avocations: golf, hunting. Home: Two Plains Rd Augusta NJ 07822

MARTIN, ROBERT BRUCE, chemistry professor; b. Chgo., Apr. 29, 1929; s. Robert Frank and Helen (Woelffer) M.; m. Frances May Young, June 7, 1953. BS, Northwestern U., 1950; PhD, U. Rochester, 1953. Asst. prof. chemistry Am. U., Beirut, Lebanon, 1953-56; research fellow Calif. Inst. Tech., 1956-57, Harvard U., 1957-59; asst. prof. chemistry U. Va., Charlottesville, 1959-61, assoc. prof., 1961-65, prof., 1965—, chmn. dept., 1968-71. Spl. fellow Oxford U., 1961-62; Program dir. Molecular Biology Sect., NSF, 1965-66 Author: Introduction to Biophysical Chemistry, 1964. Fellow AAAS; mem. Am. Chem. Soc. Office: Univ Va Dept Chemistry Charlottesville VA 22901

MARTIN, ROBERT D. former hospital executive; m. Theresa Martin. PhD in econ. & fin., Southern Mehodist U.; MA in econ. & fin., Southern Methodist U.; graduate, U. North Tex. Sr. v.p., fin. and admin. Scottsdale Meml. Health Sys., 1989—95; chief adminstrv. officer, treas. Mayo Clinic, Scottsdale, Ariz.; exec. dir., Clinical Care Assocs. U. Pa. Health Sys., 1997—99, COO, CFO, 1999—2001, interim CEO, 2000—01, CEO, 2001—03.*

MARTIN, ROBERT DAVID, judge, educator; b. Iowa City, Oct. 7, 1944; s. Murray and G'Ann (Holmgren) M.; m. Ruth A. Haberman, Aug. 21, 1966; children: Jacob, Matthew, David. AB, Cornell Coll., Mt. Vernon, Iowa, 1966; JD, U. Chgo., 1969. Bar: Wis. 1969, U.S. Dist. Ct. (we. dist.) Wis. 1969, U.S. Dist. Ct. (ea. dist.) Wis. 1974, U.S. Supreme Ct. 1973. Assoc. Ross & Stevens, S.C., Madison, Wis., 1969-72, ptnr., 1973-78; chief judge U.S. Bankruptcy Ct. We. Dist. Wis., 1978—. Instr. gen. practice course U. Wis. Law Sch., 1974, 76, 77, 80, lectr. debtor/creditor course, 1981-82, 83, 85, 87, 2001, farm credit seminar, 1985, advanced bankruptcy problems, 1989, 91, 96; co-chmn. faculty Am. Law Inst.-ABA Fin. and Bus. Planning for Agr., Stanford U., 1979; faculty mem. Fed. Jud. Ctr. Schs. for New Bankruptcy Judges, 1985-96; chmn. Ann. Continuing Legal Edn. Wis. Debtor Creditor Conf., 1981—. Author: Bankruptcy: Annotated Forms, 1989; co-author: Secured Transactions Handbook for Wisconsin Lawyers and Lenders, Bankruptcy-Text Statutes Rules and Forms, 1992, Ginsberg and Martin on Bankruptcy, 4th edit., 1996. Chmn., bd. dirs., mem. exec. com. Luth. Social Svc. Wis. and Upper Mich.; bd. dirs., mem. exec. com. Turnaround Mgmt. Assn., 1997—2002. Mem. Wis. State Bar, Am. Coll. Bankruptcy, Nat. Conf. Bankruptcy Judges (bd. govs. 1989-91, sec. 1993-94, v.p. 1994-95, pres. 1995-96), Nat. Bankruptcy Conf. Office: 120 N Henry Rm 340 PO Box 548 Madison WI 53701-0548

MARTIN, ROBERT EDWARD, architect; b. Dodge City, Kans., Mar. 17, 1928; s. Emry and Alice Jane (Boyce) M.; m. Billie Jo Lange, Aug. 16, 1952 (div. Feb. 1970); m. Kathryn M. Arvanitis, June 26, 1971; children: Lynn, Amy, Blaine. Student, McPherson Coll., 1946-48; BArch, U. Cin., 1954. Registered architect, Ohio. Architect Samborn, Steketee, Otis & Evans, Inc., Toledo, 1956-58; prin. Schauder & Martin, Toledo, 1958-72, The Collaborative, Inc., Toledo, 1972-93. Mem. Bd. Examiners Archs., Ohio, 1985-95, pres., 1989-94; bd. examiners Nat. Coun. Archtl. Registration Bds., 1986-95, edn. com., 1992; chmn. site design divsn. Archtl. Registration Exam., 1989, 90, 91; mem. Nat. Coun. Archtl. Registration Bds. Grading, 1987-94; chmn. study of Toledo Fire & Rescue Dept., Corp. for Effective Govt., 1994. Artist numerous paintings. Mem. Toledo Planning Commn., 1971-74, Toledo Zoning Appeals Bd., 1973, Toledo Bd. Bldg. Stds., 1967-84, Citizens Fire Adv. Commn., 1974-80, Citizens Urban Area Adv. Commn., 1962, Toledo Area Coun. Govts., 1977-80, Com. of 100, Toledo, 1987-89, Spectrum Friends Fine Arts, Inc., Toledo; chmn. bd. Toledo Area Govtl. Rsch. Assn., 1981-90; chmn. Corp. for Effective Govt., Study of Toledo Fire and Rescue Dept., 1994; chmn. Cystic Fibrosis, Toledo. 1985. Served to capt. USAF, 1954-56. Recipient numerous watercolor awards. Fellow AIA (pres. Toledo chpt. 1966, Arch. of Yr. 1993), Archs. Soc. Ohio (pres. 1975), Ohio Watercolor Soc. (trustee 1999—), N.W. Ohio Watercolor Soc., Toledo Fedn. Art Socs. (pres. 1989, 90), Spectrum, Tile Club (v.p.), Toledo Artists Club, Sylvania Country Club, Rotary, Masons, Shriners, Jesters. Mem. Ch. of Brethren. Avocation: painting. Home: 5119 Regency Dr Toledo OH 43615-2946 Office: 1700 N Reynolds Rd Toledo OH 43615-3628 Office Phone: 419-531-5753.

MARTIN, ROBERT LESLIE, physician; b. Abilene, Tex., Oct. 28, 1934; s. Leslie Resa and Garnet Iva (Brown) M.; m. Henrietta Montgomery, 1956; children: Randal, Christopher. BA, U. Kans., 1956, MD, 1960. Diplomate in clin. pathology Am. Bd. Pathology; diplomate Nat. Bd. Med. Examiners; lic. physician, Calif., Fla. Intern U. Kans., 1960-61, resident and fellow in pathology, 1964-67; asst. prof. pathology Case We. Res. U., Cleve., 1967-78; dir. clin. labs. Univ. Hosps. of Cleve., 1972-76; assoc. prof. pathology U. South Fla., Tampa, 1978-82; chief clin. pathology James A. Haley Vets. Hosp., Tampa, 1978-82; project mgr. Scott Sci. & Tech., Albequerque, N.Mex., 1982-83; physician advisor Profl. Found. for Health Care Inc., Tampa, 1984-89; primary care physician Tampa, Fla., 1986-98; med. rev. officer MBA Meditest, Bartow, Fla., 1995—. Contbr. articles to profl. jours. Fellow Coll. Am. Pathologists; Alpha Omega Alpha, Phi Gamma Delta. Republican. Episcopalian. Home: 15840 Sanctuary Dr Tampa FL 33647-1075 E-mail: rlmartinmd@aol.com.

MARTIN, ROBERT SIDNEY, federal agency administrator; b. Houston, Aug. 13, 1949; s. Sidney A. and Elizabeth Ann Martin. BA, Rice U., 1971; MLS, U. N. Tex., 1979; PhD, U. N.C., 1988. Libr. assoc. U. Tex., Austin, 1972-76; debt claims adjustor US Gen. Acctg. Office, Washington, 1977; libr. U. Tex., Arlington, 1977-80; instr. Sch. Libr. and Info. Sci. U. Wis., Madison, 1984; assoc. dean Librs. La. State U., Baton Rouge, 1985-95; dir., libr. Tex. State Libr. and Archives Commn., Austin, 1995—99; prof., interim dir. Sch. Library and Info. Studies, Texas Women's U., 2001; dir. Inst. of Museum and Library Services, Washington, 2001—. Co-author: Countours of Discovery, 1982, Maps of Texas and the Southwest, 1513-1900, 1984 (Kate Broock Bates award 1985); editor: Scholarly Communication in an Electronic Environment: Issues for Research, 1993, Carnegie Denied: Communities Rejecting Carnegie Library Construction Grants, 1993; mem. editl. bd. Am. Archivist, 1994-01, Libr. Quar., 1995-01. Mem. ALA (councilor 1998-01), Nat. Assn. Govt. Archivists and Records Adminstrs. (mem. exec. bd. 1996—), Tex. Map Soc. (v.p. 1996-00), Book Club Tex. (v.p. 1996-00). Avocations: hiking, photography, music. Office: Inst of Museum and Library Serv 1100 Pennsylvania Ave NW Washington DC 20506 E-mail: rmartin@imls.gov.*

MARTIN, ROBERT WILLIAM, corporate director; b. Toronto, Ont., Can., June 7, 1936; s. William George and Evelyn Irene (Phillips) M.; m. Patricia Lorraine Norris, June 27, 1959; children: Stephen Gregory, Robert Scott, Adrienne Christine Teron. BASc., U. Toronto, 1958. Pres., CEO, Consumers Gas, Toronto, 1973—92. Bd. dirs. Enbridge Inc., Aon Reed Stenhouse, HSBC Bank Can., Allied Properties Income Trust. Hon. gov. York U.; trustee York U. Found., Atlas Cold Storage Income Trust; past chmn. Toronto Symphony Orch. Recipient Meritorious Svc. award, U. Toronto, 1983, Arbor award, U. Ontario, Queen's Jubilee medal, 125 Yrs. Confederators medal, Govt. of Can., 1992. Mem.: Assn. Profl. Engrs. Ont., Toronto Club, Mad River Golf Club. Home: 118 Farnham Ave Toronto ON Canada M4V 1H4 Office Phone: 416-869-7088.

MARTIN, ROBERT WILLIAM, econometrician; b. Elizabeth, N.J., Nov. 14, 1961; s. Edward Robert Martin and Vivienne Angela Schaul. BA in English, U. N.C., 1984, BA in Econs., 1985; MA in Econs., Clemson U., 1989. Rsch. asst. dept. econs. Clemson (S.C.) U., 1988-89, lectr., policy analyst Ctr. Policy Studies, 1989-90; econometrician, exec. mgr. Bd. Econ. Advisors, Columbia, S.C., 1990—. Cons. Clemson U., 1990; adj. instr. Midlands Tech. Coll., Columbia; adj. faculty mem. of the yr. Sch. of Social & Behavioral Sciences, 1997; mem. S.C. budget and control bd. Grad. Leadership Acad., 2003. Contbr. articles to profl. jours. Mem. Am. Econ. Assn., Nat. Assn. Bus. Economists (Carolinas chpt. regional v.p. and sec.), Omicron Delta Epsilon, Sigma Tau Delta. Avocations: golf, running. Home: 933 Paces Run Ct Columbia SC 29223-7951 Office: Bd Econ Advisors Rembert Dennis Buildin Ste 446 Columbia SC 29201

MARTIN, ROBLEE BOETTCHER, retired cement manufacturing executive; b. St. Louis, Apr. 21, 1922; s. Henry W. and Esther (Boettcher) M.; m. Lillian Seegraves, July 15, 1940; children: Mary Katherine, Bruce Daniel, Amy Lee. BS in Chem. Engring., Columbia U., 1943, MS in Chem. Engring., 1947; D.Sc. in Bus. Adminstrn. (hon.), Cleary Coll., 1962. Prodn. supr. Monsanto Chem. Co., St. Louis, 1946-49; dir. research and devel. Miss. Lime Co., Ste. Genevieve, Mo., 1949-59; pres. Dundee Cement Co., Mich., 1959-69; v.p. Fruehauf Corp.; gen. mgr. (Fruehauf Bldgs. div.), Detroit, 1969-72; pres. Presidents Assn. div. Am. Mgmt. Assn., N.Y.C., 1972-74; pres. insulation div. Keene Corp., Princeton, N.J., 1974-76; chmn., chief exec. officer Keystone Cement Co., Bath, Pa., 1976-89, Giant Cement Co., Harleyville, S.C., 1985-89; sr. v.p., dir. Giant Group Ltd., Beverly Hills, Calif., 1985-89. Served to lt. (j.g.) USNR, 1944-46, PTO. Mem.: Phi Lambda Upsilon, Tau Beta Pi, Sigma Xi. Baptist. Home: 2151 Palermo Pl Charleston SC 29406-9231

MARTIN, RODNEY O., JR., insurance company executive; b. Portland; BSBA, Alfred U., 1974. Various mgmt. positions including pres. Conn. Mut. Ins. Svcs., 1975—95; pres., CEO Am. Gen. Life Ins. Co., NY, 1995—97, chmn., CEO, 1997—2000; sr. vice chmn. AIG Am. Gen. Co., 2000—01; pres., CEO AIG Am. Gen. Corp., 2001—; exec. v.p. Am. Internat. Group Inc., N.Y.C., 2002—. Office: Am Internat Group Inc 70 Pine St New York NY 10270

MARTIN, ROGER BOND, landscape architect, department chairman; b. Virginia, Minn., Nov. 23, 1936; s. Thomas George and Audrey (Bond) M.; m. Janis Ann Kloss, Aug. 11, 1962; children: Thomas, Stephen, Jonathan. BS with high distinction, U. Minn., 1958; M. Landscape Arch., Harvard U., 1961. Asst. prof. U. Calif.-Berkeley, 1964-66; from assoc. prof. to prof. emeritus U. Minn., Mpls., 1966—99, prof. emeritus, 1999—; owner Roger Martin & Assoc., site planners and landscape architects, Mpls., 1966-68, 99—; prin. InterDesign, Inc., Mpls., 1968-84, Martin & Pitz Assocs., Inc., 1984-98; vis. prof. U. Melbourne, 1979-80. Vis. prof. coll. architecture U. Minn., 2000—03. Prin. works include Minn. Zool. Gardens, 1978 (merit award Am. Soc. Landscape Archs., 1978), Mpls. Pkwy. Restorations, 1972—87 (merit award, 1978, Minn. Classic award Am. Soc. Landscape Archs., 1994), South St. Paul Ctrl. Sq., 1978 (merit award, 1978), Festival Park, Chisholm, Minn., 1986 (merit award, 1986), Miss. Wildlife Refuge Visual Image assessment (merit award, 1989), Nicollet Island Park, Hennepin Avenue Master Plan, 1995 (merit award, 1995). Recipient Fredrick Mann award for svc. to edn. U. Minn., 1990, Disting. Educator award Sigma Lambda Alpha, 1990, Bradford Williams medals for outstanding articles in landscape Architecture mag., 1968, 69, Minn. chpt. Lob Pine award for outstanding svc. to Landscape architecture, 1988, Mpls. Com. on Urban Environ. award for design of Whittier Park, 1997; fellow Am. Acad. in Rome, 1962-64. Fellow Am. Soc. Landscape Archs. (pres. Minn. chpt. 1970-72, trustee 1980-84, nat. pres. 1987, chmn.-elect coun. fellows 1991, chmn. 1992-94, past chmn. 1994-96, Pub. Svc. award 1985, Minn. chpt. Classic award 1994); mem. Nat. Coun. Instrs. Landscape Architecture (pres. 1973-74), Can. Soc. Landscape Archs. (hon.);jury, 911 Pentagon Mem.,2003; Minn. WWII Mem. 2003 Home and Office: 2912 45th Ave S Minneapolis MN 55406-1829 Business E-Mail: marti009@tc.umn.edu.

MARTIN, ROGER JOHN, computer scientist; b. Ft. Atkinson, Iowa, Sept. 11, 1947; s. Raymond Charles and Linda R. (Kuennen) M.; m. Jane Degnan, Nov. 21, 1970; children: John, Kathryn, Susan, Jacquelyn. BS in Computer Sci., Iowa State U., 1969, MS in Computer Sci., 1971. Computer specialist Naval Ship R & D Ctr., Bethesda, Md., 1971-76; supervisory sys. analyst Exec. Office of Pres., Washington, 1976-82; computer scientist, mgr. software engring. group Inst. Computer Scis. and Tech., Nat. Inst. Stds. and Tech., Washington, 1982-92, chief sys. and software tech. divsn., 1993-95, mgr. software methods, 1995-96; mgr. stds. strategy. Sun Microsys., Palo Alto, Calif., 1996—2002; dir. stds. AOL-TW, Dulles, Va., 2002—. Program co-chmn. Conf. on Software Maintenance, 1985, gen. mgr., 1987; gen. chmn. Computer Stds. Comf., 1988. Soccer coach Montgomery Country Recreation Dept., Rockville, Md., 1979-83; treas., del. Mill Creek Towne Elem. Sch. PTA, Rockville, 1981-84, pres., 1986-87; Magruder clustr PTA coord., 1984-856; leader Cub Scouts Am., Rockville, 1983-84, asst. troop scoutmaster, 1984-92. Recipient award for tech. excellence Interagy. Com. on Info. Resources Mgmt., 1989, Fed. Computer Week 100 award, 1992, cert. of recognition Nat. Bur. Stds., 1983, bronze medal Dept. Commerce, 1984, silver medal, 1989, Hans Karlsson award IEEE, 1995, Standards Medallion, 1992. Mem. Assn. for Computing Machinery, IEEE Computer Soc. (chmn. working group on test methods for POSIX 1986-93, tech. com. on conformance testing 1989-94, mem. tech. com. on operating sys. project mgmt. com. 1991-93, cert. of recognition 1987, Meritorious Svc. award 1991, Stds. medal 1992). Home: 1102 Round Pebble Ln Reston VA 20194-1002 Office: AOL 44900 Prentice Dr Sterling VA 20166 E-mail: rjmartin99@aol.com.

MARTIN, RON, newspaper editor-in-chief; Editor Atlanta Journal-Constitution, Ga., 1989—. Office: Atlanta Jour-Constn 72 Marietta St PO Box 4689 Atlanta GA 30302-4689

MARTIN, RUSSELL, historian, educator; b. McKees Rocks, Pa., Apr. 26, 1963; s. Marion Sylvester and Elizabeth (Zarycki) Martin; children: Alexandra Zarycki, Peter Wargo. BA, U. PItts., 1986; AM, Harvard U., 1989, PhD, 1996. Tchg. fellow, asst. Harvard U., Cambridge, Mass., 1990—96; assoc. prof. history Westminster Coll., New Wilmington, Pa., 1996—, Henderson lectr., 2001. Contbr. articles to profl. jours. McCandlin scholar, Westminster Coll., 2003—04. Mem.: Early Slavic Studies Assn., Assn. for History of Early Christianity (v.p., pres. elect 2003—), Am. Hist. Assn. Office: Westminster Coll Market St New Wilmington PA 16172 Office Phone: 724-946-6254. Fax: 724-946-7256. Business E-Mail: martinre@westminster.ledu.

MARTIN, SARAH, medical researcher; b. Framingham, Mass., Dec. 10, 1965; d. Coleman and Selma Levin; m. Maurice Martin. Student, Coll. of the Holy Cross, Worcester, Mass., 1984—86; AB, Brown U., 1989; MS, U. N.Mex., 1994; PhD, U. S.C., 1999. Cmty. health educator Pawtucket Heart Health Program, Pawtucket, RI, 1988—91; wellness coord. A.T. Cross Pen Co., Lincoln, 1991—92; rsch. asst. U. N.Mex., Albuquerque, 1993—96; rsch. assoc. U. S.C., Columbia, 1997—2000; asst. prof. Morehead State U., Ky., 2002—03; health scientist CDC, Atlanta, 2001—. Evaluation cons. Nike, Inc., Beaverton, Oreg., 2002—; wellness cons. Gruner & Jahr Pub., N.Y.C., 2002—; evaluator Take Aim Media, Silver Springs, Md., 2000—01. Author: Tents, Trailers and Tribulations, 2004, Physical Activity Evaluation Handbook, 2002; creator (evaluation methodology) PEANUT, 2004, editl. bd. ISHIB, Atlanta, 2002—. Exec. mem.-at-large Ky. Cardiovascular Coalition, Lexington, 2002—03; bd. dirs. S.C. Coalition for Promoting Phys. Activity, Columbis, 2000. Fellow CDC fellow, Oak Ridge Inst., 1998; grantee Planning grantee, U.S. Dept. Edn., Rsch. grantee, AAHPERD; scholar Gertrude Cox scholar, Am. Statis. Assn., 1997. Fellow: AAHPERD; mem.: APHA, Am. Coll. Sports Medicine. Avocations: running, hiking.

MARTIN, SHANE PATRICK, education educator, consultant; b. LA, Aug. 7, 1958; s. Robert Curtis and Lucille Catherine (Koch) M. BA in History, Loyola Marymount U., 1980; MDiv, Jesuit Sch. Theology, Berkeley, Calif., 1991, ThM, 1992; PhD, U. So. Calif., 1995. Clear secondary tchg. credential, Calif. Mem. faculty Bellarmine Coll. Prep. Sch., San Jose, Calif., 1984, 85-88, dir. campus ministry, 1987-88; grad. tchg. asst. Jesuit Sch. Theology, 1990-92; lectr. Loyola Marymount U., L.A., 1994-95, assoc. prof. edn., 1995—, coord. secondary edn., 2000—02, acting coord. bilingual and multicultural edn.

programs, 1999-2000, assoc. dean edn. LA, 2002—04, acting dean edn., 2004—. Adj. prof. U. San Francisco, 1996—; cons., sr. assoc. Karadenes & Assocs., L.A., 1998—; sr. rsch. cons. Imoyase Group, Inc., 2001--. Author: Cultural Diversity in Catholic Schools, 1996. Treas., sec., v.p. Assn. Jesuit Colls. and Univs. Edn. Coun., 2003—; trustee Loyola H.S., L.A., 1997—98; bd. mem. Greendot Pub. Charter Schs., 2000—; bd. dirs., chmn. com. Coun. on Anthropology and Edn., 1998—2004. Grantee, Loyola Marymount U., 1996, 1998—99, 2001—04. Mem. Am. Anthrop. Assn., Am. Ednl. Rsch. Assn., Am. Assn. for Colls. Tchr. Edn., Assn. Tchr. Educators, Nat. Assn. for Multicultural Edn., Nat. Cath. Edn. Assn. (McGivney Meml. Fund grantee 1993). Avocations: travel, cultural events, music, technology, mentoring. Office: Loyola Marymount U Sch Edn 1 LMU Dr UH Ste 2612 Los Angeles CA 90045-2659 Office Phone: 310-338-7301. Business E-Mail: smartin@lmu.edu.

MARTIN, SHARON D. automotive executive; b. El Paso, Oct. 16, 1955; d. Edgar George and Doirs Delane Shockley; m. Steven Andrew Martin, Aug. 30, 1984; children: John Anthony, Alicia Izetta, Thomas Wesley, Joshua Joel. Student, Greenville Tech., S.C., 1977—78, student, 1999, Greenville Art Mus., 1989—91. Clk. Sky City, Greenville; curator Greenville Zoo, 1976—81; photographer PCA, Matthews, NC, 1982—84; delivery, grower Happy Plants, Easley, SC, 1984—85; with Cryovac, Simpsonville, SC, 1985—90; owner Cosmic Amuesment Inc, Mauldin, SC, 1990—2001, Apostle Auto Finders, Mauldin, 2002—. Author: Sisters Forever, 2001. Mem.: Circle of Friends (leader 1994—2001), Carolina Ladies Investment Club (sec. 2002—03). Democrat. Avocations: painting, fishing, hiking, writing. Home: 606 Brooks Rd Mauldin SC 29662 Office: Apostle Auto Finders 101 Sunset Dr Mauldin SC 29662

MARTIN, SHERLONDA S. personnel director; d. Robert Glen and Shirley (Borders) Harris; m. Jeffery F. Martin, July 25, 1992; children: Brett, LaJohnda, Jaya, Chandler. BBA, U. Ga., 1991. Sales rep. Merck Human Health, NJ, 1991—93; field coord. Innovex, Parsippany, NJ, 1995—96, dist. mgr., 1996—2000, Novartis Pharm., East Hanover, NJ, 2000—03, assoc. dir. regional tng., 2003—. Women in leadership Novartis Pharm., 2000—. Author: Stepping Into Parenthood (A Practical and Spiritual Guide to Taking The Step Out of Stepparenting). Chair Lionshead Homeowners Assoc. Hospitality Com., Lithonia, Ga., 2000—, asst. dir. marriage ministry World Chargers Ch. Internat., Coll. Pk., Ga., 1994—. Mem.: Nat. Assn. Profl. Pharm. Reps., Delta Sigma Theta (mem. of yr. 1990). Office: Novartis Pharm 500 Colonial Ctr Pkwy Ste 550 Marietta GA 30067 Office Phone: 770-322-6006.

MARTIN, STANLEY ALLEN, lawyer; b. Logansport, Ind., Apr. 9, 1955; s. Richard James and Helen Elizabeth M.; m. Kellie Lea McCabe, Aug. 14, 1988. BS, MIT, 1977; JD, Boston Coll., 1984. Bar: Mass. 1985, U.S. Dist. Ct. Mass. 1985, U.S. Ct. Appeals (1st cir.) 1985, N.H. 1986, U.S. Dist. Ct. N.H. 1987. Prin. Stan Martin, Designer/Builder, Andover, Mass., 1977-84; assoc. Gadsby & Hannah LLP, Boston, 1984-91, ptnr., 1992—2001, Holland & Knight LLP, Boston, 2001—. Lectr. Northeastern U., Boston, 1989—95, MIT, 2000—01. Author: Mechanic's Liens, Performance and Payment Bonds under Massachusetts Law, 1989, 7th rev. edit., 1996; co-author: Architect-Engineer Liability Under Massachusetts Law, 1985, 5th rev. edit., 1990; contbg. author ann. Aspen Construction Law Update, 1995—; contbr. articles to profl. jours. Bd. dirs. Andover Com./A Better Chance-ABC, 1981—84, Associated Gen. Contractors of Mass., 1999—2001, Boston Archtl. Ctr., 2000—, Edgewood Retirement Cmty., 2001—. Mem. ABA (pub. contract sect., chair region I 1990-96), Am. Arbitration Assn. Constrn. Industry Panel, Mass. Bar Assn. (chair pub. law sect. 1993-94), Internat. Bar Assn., N.H. Bar Assn. Home: 7 Pendant Ct Andover MA 01810-6305 Office: Holland & Knight LLP 10 St James Ave Boston MA 02116 E-mail: stan.martin@hklaw.com.

MARTIN, STANLEY DONALD, publishing executive, editor; b. Hamilton, Bermuda, Jan. 1, 1942; s. John Hewitt Mitchell and Dorothy Emily Martin; life ptnr. Lillian Guardino; children: Danamarie, Torilyn Martin Dunn, Mary K. children: Grant Shelton Kilbourne, Thayne Mitchell. BA In Jouralism, Idaho State U., 1964; MBA, MS in Journalism, U. Utah, 1970. Commercial Pilot NW Aviation, 1978. Editor & pub. Straus Newspapers, Inc., Monroe, NY, 1986—; v.p. mktg. News Voice Newspapers, Inc., Highland Park, Ill., 1985—86. Pres. & pub. Hammell Newspapers of Fla., Clewiston, Fla., 1982—85. Contbg. editor: (newspapers) Various Publications (Over 150 awards in pub. industry). Mem. Rotary Internat., Warwick, NY, 1982—2003. Capt. U.S. Army Signal Corps, 1965—68, Germany. Mem.: N.Y. Press Assn. (assoc.). Avocations: travel, aviation. Office: Straus Newspapers Inc 45 Gilbert St Ext Monroe NY 10950

MARTIN, STEPHEN CLARKE, lawyer, mediator, arbitrator; b. N.Y.C., Nov. 14, 1942; s. Walter Henry and Clare Hix Martin; m. Mary Porter Johns, Dec. 21, 1968; children: Meredith Page, Alice Phinizy. BSME, Princeton U., 1964; JD, NYU, 1974. Bar: N.Y. 1975, D.C. 1975, Va. 1978, U.S. Dist. Ct. Va. 1980, U.S. Supreme Ct. 1986. Math. and physics tchr. Thessaloniki (Greece) Internat. H.S., 1964-65; clk. to Sr. Judge Luther W. Youngdahl, motions clk. U.S. Ct. Appeals (D.C. cir.), 1974-75; atty. Bur. Competition FTC, 1975-77; acting dir. Office Competition U.S. Dept. Energy, Washington, 1977-78; founding ptnr. Martin & Nicks, Amherst, Va., 1980-88; ptnr. Pendleton, Martin, Henderson and Garrett, Amherst, 1989-95; pvt. practice Amherst, 1996—. Gen. and family mediator, 1996—; co-commr. accts. Amherst County, 1996—; former substitute judge, commr. in chancery, spl. justice 24th Jud. Dist. Assoc. editor Rev. Law and Social Change, NYU. Treas., counsel Amherst/Nelson Christmas in April; counsel Habitat for Humanity of Amherst County, Va., Peace Through Edn., Bedford, Va., ReSource Coalition, Lynchburg; former bd. dirs. Sweet Briar Coll. Friends of Libr.; bd. dirs. Amherst County Pub. Schs. Edn. Found., former pres., bd. dirs. Amherst/Nelson Alliance for Arts; former bd. dirs. Lime Kiln Theatre, Lexington, Va., Winton Country Club, Amherst, Amherst County Bur.; former mem. exec. com. Blue Ridge Group Sierra Club; former mem. Amherst County Litter Commn. Mem. Va. State Bar (criminal law sect.), Va. Coll. Criminal Def. Attys., Ctrl. Va. Plaintiff Atty. Assn. (treas.), Amherst/Nelson Bar Assn. (past pres.), pub. rels/edn. com.), Va. Mediation Network, Lynchburg Bar Assn. (past pres. exec. bd., past mem. jud. nomination com., family law sect.). Office: 220 South Main ST PO Box 910 Amherst VA 24521-0910 Office Phone: 434-946-5510. E-mail: stormyscm@aol.com.

MARTIN, STEPHEN DAVID, lawyer; b. Paducah, Ky., May 14, 1947; s. Guy Francis and Hazel (Davis) M.; m. Deborah Sue Brown, Aug. 2, 1974; 1 child, Gary C. BA, Rutgers U., 1969; JD, Capital U., 1973. Bar: Ohio 1974, U.S. Dist. Ct. (so. and no. dists.) Ohio 1977, U.S. Supreme Ct. 1978, U.S. Ct. Appeals (6th cir.) 1982, U.S. Tax Ct. 1991, U.S. Dist. Ct. Ariz. 1992, U.S. Ct. Appeals (9th cir.) 1993. Pers. supr. Janitrol div. Andro Corp., Columbus, Ohio, 1969-72; labor rels. mgr. Celanese Plastics, Hilliard, Ohio, 1972-74; atty. govt. rels. Ohio Edn. Assn., Columbus, 1974-76; prin. Manos, Martin, Pergram & Dietz Co., LPA, Columbus, Delaware, Ohio, 1976—. Adv. bd. dirs. First Merit Bank of Columbus. Committeeman Delaware County Democratic Party, Delaware, Ohio, 1988; trustee Main Street Delaware, Inc., Cmty. Found. Del. County, Marron Palace Theatre Assn., Inc. Fellow Columbus Bar Found.; mem. Ohio Coun. Sch. Bd. Attys., Nat. Coun. Sch. Bd. Attys., Ohio State Bar Assn., Columbus Bar Assn., Delaware County Bar Assn., Worthington C. of C., Delaware C. of C., Ohio State U. Pres.'s Club, Rotary. Office: Manos Martin Pergram & Dietz Co LPA 50 N Sandusky St Delaware OH 43015-1926

MARTIN, STEPHEN F. chemist, educator, researcher; BS, U. N.Mex., 1968; PhD, Princeton U., 1972. Alexander von Humboldt stipendiat Inst. fur Organische Chemie U. Munich, 1972-73; NIH postdoctoral fellow MIT, 1973-74; M. June and J. Virgil Waggoner Regents Chair in chemistry U. Tex., Austin. Recipient Rsch. Career Devel. award NIH, 1980-85, Arthur C. Cope Scholar award Am. Chem. Soc., 1996, Alexander von Humboldt Sr. Scientist award, 1995-97. Office: U Tex Dept Chemistry and Biochemistry Austin TX 78712 E-mail: sfmartin@mail.utexas.edu.

MARTIN, STEVE, comedian, actor; b. Waco, Tex., 1945; s. Glenn and Mary Lee Martin; m. Victoria Tennant, Nov. 20, 1986 (div. 1994). Student, Long Beach State Coll., UCLA. Exec. prodr. TV show Domestic Life, 1984. TV writer for Smothers Bros. (co-winner Emmy award 1969), Sonny and Cher, Pat Paulsen, Ray Stevens, Dick Van Dyke, John Denver, Glen Campbell; nightclub comedian; guest and host appearances NBC's Saturday Night Live, Tonight Show; appeared on Carol Burnett Show; starred in TV spls. Steve Martin: A Wild and Crazy Guy, 1978, Comedy is Not Pretty, 1980, Steve Martin's Best Show Ever, 1981; rec. comedy albums Let's Get Small, 1977 (Grammy award 1977), A Wild and Crazy Guy, 1978 (Grammy award 1978), Comedy is Not Pretty, 1979, The Steve Martin Brothers, 1982; actor, screenwriter (films) The Absent Minded Waiter, 1977 (Academy award nomination best short film 1977), The Jerk, 1979, Pennies From Heaven, 1981, Dead Men Don't Wear Plaid, 1982, The Man With Two Brains, 1983, All of Me, 1984 (Nat. Soc. Film Critics award best actor 1984, New York Film Critics' Circle award best actor 1984), Three Amigos, 1986, Roxanne, 1987, (Nat. Soc. Film Critics award best actor 1988, Los Angeles Film Critics' award best actor 1988), L.A. Story, 1991; actor (films) Sergeant Pepper's Lonely Hearts Club Band, 1978, The Muppet Movie, 1979, The Kids Are Alright, 1979, The Lonely Guy, 1984, Little Shop of Horrors, 1986, Planes, Trains and Automobiles, 1987, Dirty Rotten Scoundrels, 1988, Parenthood, 1989, My Blue Heaven, 1990, Father of the Bride, 1991, Grand Canyon, 1991, Housesitter, 1992, Leap of Faith, 1993, Mixed Nuts, 1994, Twist of Fate, 1994, Sgt. Bilko, 1995, The Spanish Prisoner, 1998, Bowfinger, 1999, Joe Gould's Secret, 2000, Novocaine, 2001, Bringing Down the House, 2003; (theatre) Waiting For Godot, 1988; (television) And the Band Played On, 1993, Rutles 2: Can't Buy Me Lunch, 2002; screenwriter (films) Easy Money, 1983, Bowfinger, 1999; author: Cruel Shoes, 1977, Pure Drivel, 1998, playwright Picasso at the Lapin Agile, 1993. Recipient Georgie award Am. Guild Variety Artists 1977, 78; Grammy award 1978. Office: PO Box 929 Beverly Hills CA 90213

MARTIN, SUSAN KATHERINE, librarian; b. Cambridge, Eng., Nov. 14, 1942; came to U.S., 1950, naturalized, 1961; d. Egon and Jolan (Schonfeld) Orowan; m. David S. Martin, June 30, 1962. BA with honors, Tufts U., 1963; MS, Simmons Coll., 1965; PhD, U. Calif., Berkeley, 1983. Intern libr. Harvard U., Cambridge, Mass., 1963-65, systems libr., 1965-73; head systems office gen. libr. U. Calif., Berkeley, 1973-79; dir. Milton S. Eisenhower Libr. Johns Hopkins U., Balt., 1979-88, exec. dir. Nat. Commn. on Libraries and Info. Sci., 1988-90; univ. libr. Georgetown U., Washington, 1990-2001, tchr., cons., 2001—; pres. SKM Assocs. Inc., 2001—; cons. dir. Marstons Mills Pub. Libr., 2003—. Mem. libr. com. Princeton (N.J.) U., 1987—95; mem. vis. com. Harvard U. Libr., 1987—93, 1994—2000; bd. overseers for univ. libr. Tufts U., 1986—2001, Tufts U. Sch. Arts and Scis., 2001—; cons. various librs. and info. cos., 1975—; mem. libr. adv. com. Hong Kong U. Sci. Tech., 1988—95; mem. acad. libr. adv. group U. Md. Sch. Librs. and Info. Scis., 1994—96; mem. adv. bd. ERIC, 1990—92; mem. Chadwyck-Healey N.Am. Adv. Com. on Lit. Online, 1997—99; vice chair, chair Chesapeake Info. and Rsch. Libr. Alliance, 1996—98; cons. libr. devel. & fundraising, 1998—; spkr. in field; mem. bd. trustees Marstons Mills Pub. Libr., 2002—03; bd. mem. adv. coun. Georgetown U. Libr., 2001—03. Author: Library Networks: Libraries in Partnership, 1986—87; editor: Jour. Libr. Automation, 1972—77; co-editor: Portal: Libraries and the Academy, 2000—; mem. editl. bd.: Advanced Tech./Librs., 1973—93, Jour. Libr. Adminstrn., 1986—2000, Libr. Hi-Tech., 1989—93, Jour. Acad. Librarianship, 1994—99; contbr. articles to profl. jours. Trustee Phila. Area Libr. Network, 1980—81; bd. dirs. Universal Serials and Book Exch., 1981—82, v.p., 1983, pres., 1984; trustee Capital Consortium, 1992—95; mem. bd. Potomac Internet, 1995—96; pres., trustee Marstons Mills Pub. Libr., 2002—03. Named Samuel Lazerow disting. lectr., Drexel U., 1984, L.I. U., 2002; recipient Simmons Coll. Disting. Alumni award, 1977; Coun. on Libr. Resources fellow, 1973. Mem.: ALA (coun. 1988—92, structure revision TF 1995—97, chair task force on external accrediting body 1999—2002), Assn. Coll. and Rsch. Librs. (pres. 1994—95, vis. program officer for scholarly com. 2002—03), Coalition for Networked Info. (leader working group 1990—92), Assn. Jesuit Colls. and Univ. Librs. (chair 1997—98), Libr. of Congress (optical disk pilot project adv. com. 1985—89), Assn. Rsch. Librs. (info. policy com. 1995—97, stats. com. 1998—2000), Libr. and Info. Tech. Assn. (pres. 1978—79), Rsch. Librs. Group (exec. com. 1985—87, gov.), Internat. Fedn. Libr. Assns. Commn. on Access to Info. and Freedom of Expression, Cranberry Shores Chorus (publicity coord. 2002—, v.p., Cranberry Shores Chorus 2003—), Sweet Adelines Internat., Cosmos Club (libr. com. 1986—96), Phi Beta Kappa (chair Georgetown U. chpt. 2000—01). Home and Office: 10 Colonial Farm Cir Marstons Mills MA 02648 Business E-Mail: martin@skmassociates.net.

MARTIN, SUSAN TAYLOR, newspaper editor; b. N.Y.C., Aug. 3, 1949; d. Lewis Randolph and Carolyn Emmons (Douthat) Taylor; m. James Addison Martin Jr., Nov. 15, 1975; 1 child, Steven Randolph. BA in Polit. Sci., Duke U., 1971. Reporter Ft. Myers (Fla.) News Press, 1972-75, Tampa (Fla.) Tribune, 1975-77, Associated Press, Detroit, 1977-78; bur. chief Detroit News, 1978-81; asst. city editor Orlando (Fla.) Sentinel, 1981-82; exec. bus. editor St. Petersburg (Fla.) Times, 1982-86, city editor, 1986-87, nat. corr., 1987-91, asst. mng. editor, 1991-93, dep. mng. editor, 1993-97, chief fgn. corr., 1997—. Trustee Poynter Fund, St. Petersburg, 1992—. Recipient Non-Deadline Reporting award Soc. Profl. Journalists, 1990, Investigative Reporting award, 1991, Feature, Depth Reporting award Fla. Soc. Newspaper Editors, 1990, Depth Reporting award, 1991. Mem. Suncoast Figure Skating Club. Democrat. Episcopalian. Avocations: figure skating, travel, antiques, reading. Home: 1312 51st Ave NE Saint Petersburg FL 33703-3209 Office: St Petersburg Times 490 1st Ave S Saint Petersburg FL 33701-4204

MARTIN, TERRELL OWEN, retired university administrator; b. Florence, Ala., Mar. 25, 1937; s. Terrell Owen and Ruth Alice (Nowell) Martin. MS in Student Pers., Ind. U., 1964, D in Recreation, 1972. Dir. student activities Franklin Coll., Ind., 1964—66; acad. adv. U. Akron, Ohio, 1966—68, counselor, 1972—74; resident counselor Ind. U., Bloomington, 1968—72, dir. spl. programs and orgns., 1974—83; dean student devel. Tex. A&M, Kingsville, 1983—87; dir. acad. counseling and advising So. Ill. U., Edwardsville, 1987—2003. Lt. U.S. Army, 1960. Mem.: ACD, Order of Omega, Nat. Recreation and Park Assn., Nat. Assn. Student Pers. Adminstrs., Nat. Assn. Campus Activities, Am. Coll. Pers. Assn., Phi Delta Kappa. Democrat. Methodist. Avocations: travel, swimming, reading. Home: 901 Pine Cone Trail Anderson SC 29621

MARTIN, THEODORE KRINN, former university administrator; b. Blue Mountain, Miss., Jan. 2, 1915; s. Thomas Theodore and Ivy (Manning) M.; m. Lorene Garrison, Sept. 6, 1947; children: Glenn Krinn, Mary Ann, Janet Kay. AB, Georgetown (Ky.) Coll., 1935; MA, La. State U., 1941; PhD, George Peabody Coll., 1949. Tchr. Consol. Sch., Dumas, Miss., 1935-36; prin. Mississippi Heights Acad., 1936-39; tchr. Murphy High Sch., Mobile, Ala., 1940-41; registrar Miss. State U., 1949-53, registrar, adminstrv. asst. to pres., 1953-56, dean Sch. Edn., 1956-61, exec. asst. to pres., 1961-66, v.p., 1966-85, dir. Summer Sch., 1956-70, ret., 1985. Served as capt. AUS, 1941-46. T.K. Martin Ctr. for Tech. and Disability on Miss. State U. Campus named in his honor. Mem. Masons, Kappa Alpha, Phi Kappa Phi, Omicron Delta Kappa, Kappa Delta Pi, Phi Delta Kappa. Home: 1151 East Dr Starkville MS 39759-9491

MARTIN, THOMAS LYLE, JR., academic administrator; b. Memphis, Sept. 26, 1921; s. Thomas Lyle and Malvina (Rucks) M.; m. Helene Hartley, June 12, 1943 (dec. Sept. 1983); children: Michele Marie, Thomas Lyle; m. Mildred L. Moore, June 5, 1984. B.E.E., Rensselaer Poly. Inst., 1942, M.E.E., 1948, D.Eng., 1967; PhD, Stanford U., 1951. Prof. elec. engring. U. N.Mex., 1948-53; prof. engring. U. Ariz., 1953-63, dean engring., 1958-63, U. Fla., Gainesville, 1963-66, So. Meth. U., Dallas, 1966-74; pres. Ill. Inst. Tech., Chgo., 1974-87, pres. emeritus. Capt. Signal Corps AUS, 1943-46. Mem. ASEE Hall of Fame. Fellow IEEE; mem. Nat. Acad. Engring. Achievements include being one of the founders of Dallas-Ft. Worth Internat. Airport. Home and Office: PO Box 167845 Irving TX 75016-7845

MARTIN, THOMAS R. medical educator, medical association administrator; b. Cincinnati, Ohio, Oct. 27, 1947; MD, U. Pa., 1973; BA in Chemistry, Macalester Coll., St. Paul, 1969. Asst. prof. medicine U. Wash., Seattle, 1982-85, assoc. prof. medicine, 1985—, v. chair dept. medicine, dir., Pulmonary Rsch. Training Prog., 1990—; chief medicine svc. VA Pugent Sound Health Care Sys., Seattle. Pres. Am. Thoracic Soc., 2002—. Office: Seattle VA Med Ctr 1660 S Columbian Way Seattle WA 98108-1532

MARTIN, TONY, humanities educator; b. Port of Spain, Trinidad, Feb. 21, 1942; arrived in U.S., 1969; s. Claude G. and Vida Beryl M. BSc in econ. with honors, U. Hull, England, 1968; MA, Mich. State U., 1970, PhD, 1973. Barrister-at-law Honorable Soc. Gray's Inn, London, 1965; asst. prof. of history, African-Afro Am. studies U. Mich., Flint, 1971-73; assoc. prof. history and Africana studies Wellesley (Mass.) Coll., 1973—75, assoc. prof. Africana studies, 1975—79, prof. Africana studies, 1979—. Vis. prof. history U. Minn., 1975, The Colo. Coll., Colo. Springs, 1985-86; vis. prof. African-Am. Studies, Brown U., Providence, R.I., 1991, Brandeis U., Waltham, Mass., 1974, 81; hon. rsch. fellow U. of West Indies, Trinidad, 1986-87; lectr. DuBois-Padmore-Nkrumah, Ghana, 1990; cons. founds.; expert witness Congl. Hearings, 1987; guest lectr. numerous univs., U.S., Can., Caribbean, Australia, Africa, Eng.; featured spkr. Conf. of Intellectuals of Africa and its Diaspora, Dakar, Sengaal, 2004. Author: Race First, 1976, Literary Garveyism, 1983, The Pan-African Connection, 1983, The Jewish Onslaught, 1993; reviewer articles for profl. jours.; contbr. articles to profl. jours., encys., and other ref. books; contbr. editor profl. jours. Pres. Union of West Indian Students in Gt. Britain and No. Ireland, 1966—68. Recipient Rsch. award Am. Philos. Soc., Phila., 1990, Cmty. award Emancipation Support Com. Mem. Assn. of Caribbean Historians, African Heritage Studies Assn., Assn. for the Study of Classical African Civilizations (John Henrik Clarke Living Legacy award). Office: Wellesley Coll Africana Studies Dept Wellesley MA 02481 Office Phone: 781-283-2564. Business E-Mail: amartin@wellesley.edu.

MARTIN, TONY DERRICK, professional football player; b. Miami, Fla., Sept. 5, 1965; Student, Bishop Coll., Mesa State U. Wide receiver Miami Dolphins, 1990-93, San Diego Chargers, 1994-98; wide reciever Miami Dolphins, 1999—2000. Named to Pro Bowl, 1996. Office: Miami Dolphins 7500 SW 30th St Davie FL 33314-1020

MARTIN, VIVIAN, soprano; b. Detroit, May 09; d. George W. and Lillie (Champion) M.; m. Clement A. McDowell. Student, Detroit Conservatory Music; BS in Edn., Wayne State U.; studied with, Nadia Boulanger, Germaine Martinelli, France, Samuel Margolis, N.Y.C., Paul Daubner, Munich, Elsa Verena, Berlin, Celeste Cole, Detroit. Educator Bd. of Edn., Detroit, N.Y.C. Vocal coach and tchr. private, 1996—. Soloist with Robert DeCormier Singers, Munich Philharm., Neurnberg Symphongy and Philharm. Chorus, 1970, Gävleborgs Symfoniorkester, Gavle, Sweden, 1978, Symphony Radio Concert, Paris, 1978, Warsaw Symphony Orch.; operatic debut as Leonora in La Forza del Destino, 1971; appeared in Antigone and Carmina Burana with Munich Philharm. Orch. and Chorus, Das ewige Evangelium with Nürnberg Symphony Orch. and Philharm. Chorus, L'Africaine in Ghent, Belgium, Oberon in Wexford (Ireland) Opera Festival, 1972, Bess from Porgy and Bess, Bratislava, 1979, Il Travatore, Constantza, 1980; performed with Royal Opera Ghent, Stadt Opera Essen, Badische Opera Karlsruhe, Stadt Opera Bonn, Mainz Opera, Royal Opera Lisbon, Portugal, Stadtheatre Bremen; TV broadcasts include BBC, BRT Belgium, Bratislava (Czechoslovakia) Philharm. Orch. and Opera, Bavarian Radio; rec. artist RCA, Command Records, Concord Records, Halo Records; tour India, Iran, Afghanistan, U.S. State Dept., 1976; toured with Gävleborgs Symphony Orch., Sweden, 1981-84; appeared in opera concert on radio and TV, Bucharest, 1979; sang Leonora in Il Travatore in opera festival, Constantza, Rumania, 1979; concerts in Belgrade, Tivoli Gardens, Copenhagen, Zagreb, Yugoslavia, 1979; opera concert tour of Sweden with Gävle Symphony Orch., 1979; soloist Belgium TV Flanders Expo, Gent, Belgium, 1990, concert tour Czechoslovakia, 1991, performed New Opera House, Maastricht, Holland with Limburgs Symphony Orchestra, 1992, Concert Koor, 1992, Olavshallen, Trondheim, Norway with Trondheim Symfoniorkester and Trondheim Kammerkor, 1993, concert tours U.S.A., 1994-96, soprano soloist Gershwin Gala Porgy and Bess, 1989-96, (with Philharm. Orch.)concerts and performances in U.S.A. and abroad. World of Gershwin, 1998; concert tours Belgium, Germany, (with St. Petersburg (Russia) Phil. Orch.) Shostakovich, 1998, (with Russian Nat. Symphony Orch.), Moscow, 1998; solo recitals festival St. Petersburg, 1998, Moscow, 1998. Recipient Jean Paul Alaux award Conservatoire de Fontianbleau, 18 singing scholarships and awards. Mem. AFTRA, Am. Guild Mus. Artists, Actors Equity Assn., New Initiatives for the Arts, Wayne State U. Alumni Assn., Alpha Kappa Alpha. Office: Dr Gosta Schwarck Intl Ltd 18 Groennegade 1st Fl DK-1007 Copenhagen K Denmark

MARTIN, VIVIAN BONITA, journalist, educator; b. Mar. 29, 1956; d. Rutrell and Ruth Vivian (Robinson) Martin. MA in Am. Studies, Vt. Coll., 1997; PhD in Interdisciplinary Studies, Media and Culture, The Union Inst., 2004. Reporter Hartford Courant, Conn., 1978—86, Op-ed columnist, 1997—2003; freelance writer, 1987—; asst. prof. Dept. English Ctrl. Conn. State U., New Britain, 1999—. Reporter Conn. Law Tribune, 1989—90; mem. part-time faculty Ctrl. Conn. State U., 1996—99. Author: Astrocycles, 1990; contbr. articles to profl. jours. Recipient Best Op-ed Column award, Conn. Soc. Profl. Journalists. Mem.: Nat. Assn. Black Journalists, Am. Sociol. Assn., Assn. for Edn. in Journalism and Mass Comm. Office: Central Conn State Univ 1615 Stanley Rd New Britain CT 06050 Office Phone: 860-832-2776. E-mail: martinv@ccsu.edu.

MARTIN, WALTER, retired lawyer; b. Crookston, Minn., Nov. 7, 1912; s. Frederick and Rosalie (Mertz) M.; m. Catherine Mary Severin, May 1, 1942 (dec. May 1979); children: Frederick H., Jacqueline K., Patricia, Priscilla, Walter Jr., John E. BA, Albion Coll., 1937; JD, U. Mich., 1939. Bar: Mich. 1939, U.S. Dist. Ct. (fed. dist.) 1939, U.S. Ct. Appeals (6th cir.) 1947, U.S. Supreme Ct. 1958. Ptnr. Martin & Martin, Saginaw, Mich., 1939-94; ret., 1994. Fellow Mich. Bar Assn., Saginaw County Bar Assn. (pres. 1958). Lutheran. Avocations: hunting, fishing. Office: 803 Court St Saginaw MI 48602-4223

MARTIN, WILFRED WESLEY FINNY, psychologist, property owner and manager; b. Rock Lake, N.D., Dec. 3, 1917; s. William Isaac and Anna Liisa (Hendrickson-Juntunen) M.; m. Stella Helland, Sept. 25, 1943; children: Sydney Wayne, William Allan. BA, Jamestown Coll., 1940; army specialized tng. program, Hamilton Coll., 1944; MS, EdD, U. So. Calif., 1956. Highsch. prin., coach pub. sch., Nekoma, ND, 1940—42; contact rep., psychologist VA, L.A., 1946—49, psychologist, chief rehab., 1972—77; guidance dir. Moorhead (Minn.) Pub. Schs., 1951—53; instr. Concordia Coll., Moorhead, 1952—53; from intern to resident Fargo VA Hosp., ND, 1953—58; psychologist VA, Fargo, 1953—58; assoc. Sci. Rsch. Assoc./IBM, Boulder, Colo., 1958—65, regional dir. L.A., 1966—72; owner, mgr. Martin Investments, Huntington Beach, Calif., 1977—. Adjutant U. Miss., Oxford, 1942; trustee Wilfred W. and Stella Martin Trust, Huntington Beach, 1991. Author: Veterans Administration Work Simplification, 1948, 57. Charter mem. Rep. Presdl. Task Force, 1980; adv. sr. ptnrs. bd. dirs. U. Calif. Med. Sch., Irvine, 1990; donor Dr. and Mrs. W.W. Martin Endowment, Jamestown Coll., N.D., 1985; mem. Assocs. of James Ford Bell Libr., U. Minn., Pres.'s Cir. Finlandia U. With U.S. Army, 1942-45. Mem. Am. Psychol. Assn., Cardinal & Gold U. So. Calif., Jamestown Coll. Heritage Circle (charter, Pres.'s Cir.), Suomi Coll. Second Century Soc., Elks. Republican. Lutheran. Avocations: reading, Finnish heritage, swimming, sports, card playing. Home: PO Box 5445 Huntington Beach CA 92615-5445 *The dominant force in my life is described by the Finnish word SISU, which means perseverence, determination, competitiveness, and tenacity toward goal-oriented achievements. Due to SISU, faith, and hard work I enjoy an active successful life.*

MARTIN, WILLARD GORDON, JR., lawyer; b. Boston, Dec. 12, 1937; children: Yves, Sylvie, Melissa, Helen, Abigail, Galya. AB, Bates Coll., 1959; LLB, Harvard U., 1962; LLM, Boston U., 1984. Bar: N.H. 1962, U.S. Dist. Ct. N.H. 1962. Ptnr. Martin, Lord & Osman, P.A., Laconia, N.H., 1962—. City solicitor, Laconia, 1963-66; Belknap County atty., N.H., 1967-68; rep. to gen.

ct., N.H., 1969-70; mem. N.H. Jud. Coun., 1971-75; N.H. bar examiner, 1972—; Spl. justice Laconia Dist. Ct., 1973—; judge N.H. family divsn., 1998—; mem. com. on character and fitness N.H. Supreme Ct., 1975—. Mem. Am. Judicature Soc. (bd. dirs. 1980-84), N.H. Bar Assn. (bd. govs. 1980-82), Belknap County Bar Assn., Phi Beta Kappa. Office: 1 Mill Plz Laconia NH 03246-3438

MARTIN, WILLIAM ALLEN, sociology educator; b. Galveston, Tex. s. James F. and Myra F. Martin; m. Debra J. Taylor; children: Zachary, Michelle. BA, So. Meth. U., 1970; MA, Tex. Christian U., 1971; PhD, U. Tex., 1976. Rsch. assoc. II U. Tex., Austin, 1970-74, part-time instr., 1974-75; instr. Ark. State U., State University, 1975-77; asst., assoc. prof. U. Tex. at Tyler, 1977-89, prof., 1989—. Faculty adv. coun. U. Tex. Sys., 1994-99; pres. faculty senate U. Tex. at Tyler, 1994-98; rsch. cons. Nat. Pk. Svc., 1984; mem. spl. com. AAUP, 1998-99. Author: (book) Race & Ethnic Relations, 1999, The Urban Community, 2004; contbr. articles to profl. jours. Mem. Phys. Environment Com. Tex. Coun. of Govts., 1995—. Recipient Tex. Higher Edn. Coordinating Bd. fellowship, 1992. Mem. Am. Sociol. Assn., Population Assn. Am., Assn. Am. Geographers, Southwestern Sociol. Assn. (v.p.), Tex. Assn. Coll. Tchrs. (pres. 1999-2001). Office: U Tex 3900 University Blvd Tyler TX 75799-0001 E-mail: Amartin@mail.uttyl.edu.

MARTIN, WILLIAM C. sociology educator, writer; b. San Antonio, Dec. 31, 1937; s. Lowell Curtis and Joe Bailey (Brite) M.; m. Patricia Dale Summerlin, Dec. 31, 1957; children: Rex Martin, Jeff Martin, Elisabeth Dale Martin Thomas. BA, Abilene Christian U., 1958, MA, 1960; BD, Harvard Divinity Sch., 1963; PhD, Harvard U., 1969. Instr. history Dana Hall Sch., Wellesley, Mass., 1965-68; instr. sociology Rice U., Houston, 1968-69, asst. prof. sociology, 1969-73, assoc. prof. sociology, 1973-79, prof. sociology, 1979—, Chavanne prof. religion and pub. policy, 1996—, master Sid W. Richardson Coll., 1976-81, chair dept. sociology, 1983—86, 1989—94, 2003—04. Cons. films and TV documentaries; speaker in field. Author: These Were God's People, 1966, Christians in Conflict, 1972, A Prophet With Honor: Billy Graham Story, 1991 (Christianity Today's Critic's Choice award 1992), My Prostate and Me: Dealing With Prostate Cancer, 1994, With God on our Side: The Rise of the Religious Right in America, 1996; contbg. editor Tex. Monthly (Nat. Headliner award 1982); contbr. numerous articles to profl. jours. and pop mags.; numerous radio and TV appearances. Dir. House of the Carpenter, Inc., inner-city youth program, Boston, 1963-66, pres. and bd. dirs. non-profit housing corp.; bd. dirs. Fellowship Racial and Econ. Equality, 1970-71; mem. exec. com. Houston Coun. Human Rels. Recipient Nicholas Salgo Outstanding Tchr. award Rice U., 1971, 93, Brown Coll. award for Teaching in the Humanities Rice U., 1974, 76, George R. Brown Award for Superior Teaching, alumni Rice U., 1974, 76, 77, 84, for Excellence in Teaching, 1975, 82, Life Honor award, 1985, Sr. scholar James A. Baker III Inst. Pub. Policy; grantee Am. Coun. Learned Socs. and Am. Philos. Soc., 1974. Mem. Am. Sociol. Assn., Soc. Scientific Study Religion, Religious Rsch. Assn., Tex. Inst. Letters (J. Frank Dobie/Paisano fellowship 1980). Democrat. Protestant. Avocation: bicycling. Home: 2929 Buffalo Speedway 312 Houston TX 77098 Office: Rice U Dept Sociology MS 28 6100 Main St Houston TX 77005-1892 Office Phone: 713-348-3481. Business E-Mail: wcm@rice.edu.

MARTIN, WILLIAM COLLIER, hospital administrator; b. Atlanta, Aug. 16, 1926; s. William Henry and Lillian (Collier) M.; m. Alice Elizabeth Nickle, Jan. 12, 1952 (dec.); children: Mary Anne, Patricia Jean, William Collier, Nancy Lee; m. Carol J. Sullivan, July 25, 1998. BS, U. Ga., 1950; diploma, Charlotte Meml. Hosp., 1952; postgrad., U. Okla., 1969. Operating room technician Athens (Ga.) Gen. Hosp., 1949-50; hosp. adminstrn. intern/resident Charlotte (NC) Meml. Hosp., 1950-52; hosp. adminstr. Rockmart-Aragon Hosp., Rockmart, Ga., 1952-54; asst. hosp. adminstr. St. Agnes Hosp., Raleigh, NC, 1954-56; hosp. adminstr. Florence-Darlington Tb. Sanitorium, Florence, SC, 1956-58; commd. 1st lt., MSC US Army, 1959; advanced through grades to lt. col.; adj. US Army Hosp., 1959; comdg. officer med. co. US Army Hosp., 1959-61; comdg. officer US Army Med. Svc. Detachment, 1961-64; exec. officer 5th Evacuation Hosp. Ft. Bragg, NC, 1964; comdg. officer, 1964-65; adj. personnel officer 55th Med. Group, 1965-66, Qui Nhon, Vietnam, 1966-67; comdg. officer 47th Gen. Hosp., Fitzsimons Gen. Hosp. Denver, 1967-68; exec. officer Evans Health Care Facility Ft. Buckner, Japan, 1968-69; dir. security plans and ops. U.S. Army Med. Ctr., Camp Kue, Japan, 1969-71; med. ops. officer VII Corps Moehringen, Germany, 1971-73; chief tng., exercise and readiness US Army Med. Command Heidelberg, Germany, 1973-74; dir. security plans and tng. Fitzsimons Army Med. Ctr., 1974-77; ret., 1977—. Guest lectr. healthcare adminstrn. US Army Med. Command in Europe, 1973-74; exec. dir. Thoms Rehab. Hosp., Asheville, NC, 1977-78; pres./chair Escambia County Pub. Health Trust, 1978-86; founder Hospice of Northwest Fla. and Exec. Dir., 1979-86. Mem. Pres.'s Com. on Employment of the Handicapped, 1978; sec. United Meth. Bd. Pastoral Care and Counseling, 1988-90; mem., v.p., bd. ministries Pensacola Dist. United Meth. Ch., Inc., 1988-98; dir. lay speaking, bd. laity, coun. on ministries Pensacola Dist. United Meth. Ch., Inc., 1988-98; dir. lay speaking, bd. laity Ala.-West Fla. Conf. United Meth. Ch., 1988-97; mem. Health and Human Svcs. task force citizens goals for Pensacola, 1981-86; vice chmn. adminstrv. bd. Pine Forest United Meth. Ch., Pensacola, 1979-86; mem. fin. com., 1979-86; dir. lay speaking Pensacola Dist. United Meth. Ch., 1985-88; bd. dirs. Hispanic Ministries, Inc., 1986-93, Meth. Homes for the Aging, Inc., 1990—. Served with USN, 1944-46. Decorated Legion of Merit, Bronze Star, Meritorious Svc. medal (3); Vietnam Royal Cross of Gallantry with bronze palm; cert. lay speaker United Meth. Ch. Fellow Am. Acad. Med. Adminstrs.; mem. Am. soc. Tng. and Devel. (dir. 1977-78), Ret. Officers Assn., Assn. US Army (dir. Denver-Centennial chpt. 1974-77, Greater Gulf Coast chpt. 1979-86), US Power Squadrons, Ret. Officers Assn. (bd. dirs. Bob Sikes chpt. 1996-2000, bd. dirs. Escarosa chpt. 1985-99, pres. ESCAROSA chpt. 1989-90), VFW, Masons, Phi Delta Theta. Democrat.

MARTIN, WILLIAM EDWIN, lawyer, business executive; b. Bowling Green, Ky., Oct. 16, 1943; s. John Edwin and Bess Carolyn (Matherly) M.; children: Anne Whitson, William Whitson; m. Jean Clinton Nelson, Aug. 1, 1981. BA, Vanderbilt U., 1965, JD, 1968. Bar: Tenn. 1968. Ptnr. Waller Lansden Dortch & Davis, Nashville, 1968-75; sr. ptnr. Harwell Martin & Stegall, Nashville, 1975-93; dep. asst. sec. for internat. affairs U.S. Dept. Commerce-NOAA, Washington, 1993-98; chmn. Will Martin Co., 1998—; sr. v.p. Pvt. Bus. Inc., Brentwood, Tenn., 1999; vice chmn. Tecniflex, Inc., Nashville, 2000—01; chmn. Imagic Corp., Nashville, 2000—01. Sr. fellow World Wildlife Fund, 1999—; bd. dirs. Marine Stewardship Coun., London, Board Mem. Inc., Brentwood. Contbr. articles to newspapers and law revs. Dir. polar programs Wilderness Soc., Washington, 1990—92. Democrat. Episcopalian. Avocations: mountain climbing, photography, running, tennis, biking. Office: 9020 Overlook Blvd Brentwood TN 37027

MARTIN, WILLIAM FRANCIS, JR., lawyer; b. Lowell, Mass., Sept. 13, 1961; s. William F. and Patricia A. Martin; m. Martha Doherty, Oct. 23, 1988; children: William F. III, Daniel J., Jacqueline E. BA in English, Coll. of Holy Cross, Worcester, Mass., 1983; JD, Boston Coll., 1986. Bar: Mass. 1986, N.H. 1991. Law clk. to Hon. Joseph R. Nolan Mass. Supreme Jud. Ct., Boston, 1986-87; assoc. Hale and Dorr, Boston and Manchester, 1987-93; ptnr. Eno, Boulay, Martin Donahue, LLP (and predecessor firm), Lowell, 1994—. Bd. dirs. Lowell Parks and Conservation Trust, Lowell, 1991—; mem. Lowell Conservation Commn., 1993-94, chmn., 1994-99. Articles editor Boston Coll. Law Review, 1985-86. Mem. Lowell City Coun., 2000—; bd. dirs. D'Youville Sr. Care, 1997—. Mem. Omicron Delta Epsilon, Order of the Coif. Home: 173 Clark Rd Lowell MA 01852 Office: Eno Boulay Martin & Donahue LLP 21 George St Lowell MA 01852 Office Phone: 978-452-8902. E-mail: b.martin@ebmdattorneys.com.

MARTIN, WILLIAM JOSEPH, II, dean, educator; m. Joyce Martin; 2 children. MD, U. Minn. Resident in internal medicine Mayo Grad. Sch. Medicine, Rochester, Minn., fellow in pulmonary medicine; faculty and med. staff Mayo Clinic, Rochester, Minn., 1981—88; Floyd and Reba Smith prof. respiratory disease Ind. U. Sch. Medicine, 1988—2002, exec. assoc. dean clin. affairs, dir. divsn. pulmonary, allergy, critical care and occupl. medicine, 1988—2000; Christian R. Holmes prof., dean Coll. Medicine U. Cin., 2002—, acting sr. v.p., 2002—03. Pres. and CEO Ind. U. Med. Group; health policy fellow U.S. Sen. for Sen. Labor and Human Resources Com., 1995—96; funded prin. investigator Nat. Heart, Lung and Blood Inst. Mem.: Am. Thoracic Soc. (pres. 2000—01), Assn. Pulmonary and Critical Care Medicine Program Dirs. (past pres.), Am. Lung Assn. Ind. (past pres.). Office: Coll Medicine 231 Albert Sabin Way Cincinnati OH 45267*

MARTIN, WILLIAM RAYMOND, retired financial manager; b. Phila., Oct. 16, 1939; s. Clyde Davis and Mary Anna (Coates) M.; m. Michaela Roberta Smink, Sept. 8, 1962 (div. 1969, dec. 2002); 1 child, James; m. Margaret Scouten, Oct. 16, 1970 (div. 1983); children: Mary Frances, Susanna; m. Joan Friedman Kennedy, Jan. 29, 1988 (div. 1999). BSME, Lehigh U., 1960; MBA, U. Pa., 1973. Mem. engring. staff Pa. R.R., 1960-65; asst. gen. mgr. Excelsior Truck Leasing, Phila., 1965-71; sr. analyst Assn. Am. R.R.s, Washington, 1973-76, mgr. engring. econ., 1976-78; mgr. fin. analysis So. Ry., Washington, 1978-83; dir. fin. planning Norfolk (Va.) So. Corp., 1984-92, asst. v.p. fin., 1992-95. Contbr. articles to profl. jours. Bd. dirs. Williams Sch., Norfolk, 1988—96, pres., 1992—96; bd. dirs. Va. Stage Co., Norfolk, 1995—2001, Feldman Chamber Music Soc., 2001—, Norfolk Chamber Consort, 1998—, treas., 2001—. Mem. ASME, Soc. Automotive Engrs. Home: 2725 River Rd Virginia Beach VA 23454-1210

MARTIN, WILLIAM ROYALL, JR., retired association executive; b. Raleigh, N.C., Sept. 3, 1926; s. William Royall and Edith Ruth (Crocker) M.; m. Betty Anne Rader, June 14, 1952; children: Sallie Rader Martin Busby, Amy Kemp Martin Lewis. AB, U. N.C., 1948, MBA, 1964; BS, N.C. State U., 1952. Chemist Stamford (Conn.) rsch. labs. Am. Cyanamid Co., 1952—54; chemist Dan River Mills, Danville, Va., 1954—56, Union Carbide Corp., South Charleston, W.Va., 1956—59; rsch. assoc. Sch. Textiles N.C. State U., 1959—63; tech. dir. Am. Assn. Textile Chemists and Colorists, Research Triangle Park, NC, 1963—73, exec. dir., 1974—96. Adj. asst. prof. Coll. Textiles, N.C. State U., 1966-88, adj. assoc. prof., 1989-97; del. Internat. Orgn. Standardization, Pan Am. Standards Commn. With USNR, 1944-46. Fellow Am. Inst. Chemists, Soc. Dyers and Colourists, Textile Inst.; mem. Am. Chem. Soc., Coun. Engring. and Sci. Soc. Execs. (past pres. 1992-93), Fiber Soc., Am. Assn. Textile Chemists and Colorists, Masons, Rotary, Phi Kappa Phi, Phi Gamma Delta. Methodist. Home and Office: 224 Briarcliff Ln Cary NC 27511-3901 E-mail: wrbrm@aol.com.

MARTIN, WILLIAM RUSSELL, nuclear engineering educator; b. Flint, Mich., June 2, 1945; s. Carl Marcus and Audrey Winifred (Rosene) M.; m. Patricia Ann Williams, Aug. 13, 1967; children: Amy Leigh, Jonathn William. BSE. in Engring. Physics, U. Mich., 1967; MS in Physics, U. Wis., 1968; MSE. in Nuclear Engring., U. Mich., 1975, PhD in Nuclear Engring., 1976. Prin. physicist Combustion Engring., Inc., Windsor, Conn., 1976-77; asst. prof. nuclear engring. U. Mich., Ann Arbor, 1977-81, assoc. prof. nuclear engring., 1981-88, prof. nuclear engring., 1988—, dir. lab. for sci. computation, 1986—2001, chmn. nuclear engring., 1990-94, assoc. dean for acad. affairs Coll. Engring., 1994-99, dir. Ctr. for Advanced Computing, 2002—. Cons. Lawrence Livermore Nat. Lab., Livermore, Calif., 1982—, Los Alamos (N.Mex.) Nat. Lab., 1980-89, 2001—, IBM, Inc., Kingston, N.Y., 1984, Rockwell Internat., Pitts., 1985. Author: Transport Theory, 1979; author tech. and conf. papers. Recipient Glenn Murphy award Am. Soc. for Engring. Edn., 1993; Disting. scholar U. Mich. Coll. Engring., 1967; vis. fellow Royal Soc., London, 1989. Fellow Am. Nuclear Soc.; mem. Am. Phys. Soc., Soc. for Indsl. and Applied Math., IEEE. Avocations: running, reading, skiing, sailing. Home: 420 Huntington Dr Ann Arbor MI 48104 Office: U Mich Dept Nuclear Engring Ann Arbor MI 48109 Business E-Mail: wrm@umich.edu.

MARTINBOROUGH, SAMUEL NEIL, music educator, conductor, musician; s. Gordon Ornsley and Waveney Vivina Martinborough. AA, Caribbean Union Coll., Trinidad, West Indies, 1986; MusB in Edn., Atlantic Union Coll., 1991; MA in Theatre Edn., Emerson Coll., 2000. Elem. educator Antigua SDA Sch., St Johns, Antigua and Barbuda, 1987—88; music educator South Lancaster Acad. and Browning Elem. Schs., 1991—96, Brookwood Sch., Manchester - by- the- Sea, Mass., 1996—2000; theatre educator Boston Arts Acad., 2001—02, music educator, 2002—. Choir dir. Indian Hill Arts, Inc, Littleton, Mass., 1997—2002, Sharing a New Song, Inc., Newton, Mass., 2001—03; gospel choir dir. Framingham State Coll., 1999—2002, Gordon Coll., Wenham, 1998—2002; dir. handbell choir Pilgrim Ch., Southborough, Mass., 1994—2000; vocalist New Eng. Spiritual Ensemble, Boston, 2000—04. Actor: Baby!, Annie, Guys & Dolls, King and I, How Bush Got Kerryed Away; author: Where in The World is Belle Voce de Cantar von Destrucken, Oh Black and Unknown Bards, Where in the World is Belle Noce de Cantor Von Destruchen, 2001—02, Oh Black and Unknown Bards, 2002—04. Recipient Silver medal, Mass. Instrumental and Choral Condr.'s Assn. Choral Competition, 1995, 1996, Gold medal, 1996, Silver and Bronze medals, 2004. Mem.: Handel and Haydn Soc. (vocalist Outreach Quartette 2000—), Boston Musician's Assn., Ctr. Black Music Rsch., Internat. Fedn. Choral Music, Am. Choral Dirs. Assn. (life). Avocations: roller-blading, reading, music. Home: 35A Fort Ave Roxbury MA 02119 Business E-Mail: exordiumma@aol.com.

MARTIN-BOWEN, LINDSEY, freelance writer; b. Kansas City, Kans., Aug. 4, 1959; d. Lawrence Richard and V. Marie Pickett; m. Frederick E. Nicholson (div.); l child, Aaron Frederick; m. Edwin L. Martin (div.); l child, Ki Elise; m. Michael L. Bowen (div.). BA in English Lit., U. Mo., Kansas City, 1972, MA in English and Creative Writing, l988, postgrad., 1991-94; JD, U. Mo. Kansas City Sch. Law, Kansas City, 2000. Bar: Mo. 2001. Tech. editor Office Hearings and Appeals, U.S. Dept. Interior, Washington, 1976-77; reporter, photographer Louisville Times, 1982-83; reporter, features editor Sun Newspapers, Overland Park, Kans., 1983-84; assoc. editor Modern Jeweler, Overland Park and N.Y.C., 1984-85; writer Coll. Blvd. News, Overland Park, 1985-89, KC View, Kansas City, Mo., 1988-89; editor Number One, Kansas City, Mo., 1986-88, cons., 1988-89; copywriter Sta KXEO/KWWR Radio, Mexico, Mo., 1989; editorial asst. New Letters, 1985—; features writer, columnist The Squire, Prairie Village, Kans., 1990-95. Instr. lit., fiction writing, intro. to journalism, reporting, English, cultural studies, tech. writing, acad. writing and lit. U. Mo., Kansas City, 1986-88, 97-, Johnson County C.C., 1988-95; fiction writer, 2002-; instr. world lit., writing Rockhurst U., 2002-03; tchr. English and fiction Longview C.C., 1988-95, 97-98, 2004—; instr. writing and mass comm. Webster U., 1990; instr. world lit., Am. lit., women in lit., creative writing Penn Valley C.C., 1993-97, faculty sponsor The Penn; owner, writer Paladin Freelance Writing Svc., Kansas City, 1988—; prodn. editor Nat. Paralegal Reporter, 1992-95, editor 1994-97, also columnist; staff writer, columnist NPR, 1992—; writing contest judge New Letters, 1987; judge poetry contest BkMk Press, U. Mo., Kansas City, 1998—. Author: (novel) The Dark Horse Waits in Boulder, 1985, (poetry) Waiting for the Wake-Up Call, 1990, Second Touch, 1990, (fiction) Cicada Grove and Other Stories, 1992, (novel) Harvest, 2002, (novel) Denvie USA, 2003; contbr. poems, book revs., features, cartoon artwork, and photographs to numerous pubs. including New Letters, Lip Service, Contemporary Lit. Criticism, UMKC Law Rev., River King Poetry Supplement, Thorny Locust, The Same, Coal City Rev., I-70 Rev., Black Bear Rev., The Kans. City Star; lead actress prodns. Coach House Players, 1969-70; extra HBO film Truman, 1995; staff mem., contbr. UMKC Law Rev., 1997-99. Campaigner McGovern for Pres. Campaign, Kansas City, 197l-72. Regents scholar, 1967; GAF fellow, 1986. Mem. U. Mo.-Kansas City Alumni Assn. (media com. 1983-84), Phi Kappa Phi. Roman Catholic. Avocations: acrylic and oil painting, downhill skiing, music, Greek cooking, paralegal work. Office: U Mo Kansas City English Dept Cockefair Hall Rm 111 5100 Rockhill Rd Kansas City MO 64110-2481 Home: 1129 SE 7th St Lees Summit MO 64063-6442

MARTINDALE, CARLA JOY, retired librarian; b. Ladysmith, Wis., Sept. 9, 1947; d. Howard Walter and Audrey Elizabeth (Stanton) Martindale. BA, Mt. Senario Coll., 1970; MLIS, U. South Fla., 1990. Libr. Blackhawk Schs., South Wayne, Ind., 1975-79, Osceola County Libr., Kissimee, Fla., 1989-90, Fla. Tech. Coll., Orlando, 1991-92, Orlando Coll. South, 1993-98; ret., 1998; libr. U. of Ctrl. Fla., 2003—. Vis. prof. distance learning libr. St. Leo (Fla.) U., 1999—2002; chair libr. 21st curriculum Phillips Coll., Orlando, 1995, acad. com., 1993—98, accreditation steering com., 1996. Named libr. in her honor, Orlando Coll. South, 1995. Mem.: ALA, Fla. Libr. Assn. Avocations: reading, pets, stock investing. Home: 10 Chapel Lake Cir Quitman AR 72131 E-mail: carlajoy52@yahoo.com.

MARTINDALE, COLIN EUGENE, psychology educator, author; b. Ft. Morgan, Colo., Mar. 21, 1943; s. Roy Woodrow and Martha Martindale; m. Mee Lee Goh, May 15, 1993. BA summa cum laude, U. Colo., 1964; PhD, Harvard U., 1970. From asst. prof. to prof. dept. psychology U. Maine, Orono, 1970—. Author: Romantic Progression: The Psychology of Literary History, 1975, Cognition and Consciousness, 1981, The Clockwork Muse: The Predictability of Artistic Change, 1990, Cognitive Psychology: A Neural-Network Approach, 1991; editor sci. jours., 1982—. Recipient 1st prize 9th Ann. Creative Talent Awards program Am. Insts. for Rsch., 1970, Socio-psychol. prize AAAS, 1984. Fellow APA; mem. Assn. for Computers and the Humanities, Internat. Assn. Empirical Aesthetics, Assn. for Lit. and Linguistic Computers, Phi Beta Kappa. Republican. Home: 89 3rd St Bangor ME 04401-6104 Office: Dept Psychology Univ Maine Orono ME 04469-0001 E-mail: rpy393@maine.edu.

MARTINEAU, LYNN, retail executive; Pres. western divsn. Home Depot, Atlanta. Office: Home Depot Inc 2455 Paces Ferry Rd SE Atlanta GA 30339-4024

MARTINEAU, ROBERT JOHN, law educator; b. May 18, 1934; s. Francis Joseph and Gertrude (Schauer) M.; m. Constance Ann Zimmerman, Dec. 21, 1957; children: Robert John, Renee, Anne, Jeanne. BS, Coll. Holy Cross, 1956; JD, U. Chgo., 1959. Bar: Md. 1960, U.S. Supreme Ct. 1964, Iowa 1969, Mo. 1974, Wis. 1974. Law clk. to chief judge Md. Ct. Appeals, 1959-60; pvt. practice Md., 1960-68; asst. atty. gen., 1964-65; assoc. prof. U. Iowa, 1968-71; prof., 1971-72; cir. exec. U.S. Ct. Appeals (8th cir.), Mo., 1972-74; exec. officer Wis. Supreme Ct., 1974-78; prof. U. Dayton (Ohio), 1978-80; assoc. dean U. Cin., 1980-82; prof. law, 1980-88; disting. rsch. prof., 1988-93; emeritus, 1994—. Acting dean, 1985-86; spl. prof. alw U. Birmingham, Eng., 1987; cons. Fed. Jud. Ctr., 1978, Nat. Ctr. State Cts., 1978-79, 87, UN Devel. Program, Bhutan, 1999. Author: Wisconsin Appellate Practice, 1978, Judicial Reform in Wisconsin, in Court Reform in Seven States, 1980, Modern Appellate Practice-Federal and State Civil Appeals, 1983, Fundamentals of Modern Appellate Advocacy, 1985, Cases and Materials on Appellate Practice and Procedure, 1987, Appellate Justice in England and the United States: A Comparative Analysis, 1990, Drafting Legislation and Rules in Plain English, 1991. Sec. Md. Constnl. Conv. 1967-68; reporter Wis. Supreme Ct. Com. on Discipline of Attys., 1975-77, Wis. Jud. Coun. Com. Appelate Practice and Procedure, 1976-78. Mem. Assn. Am. Law Schs. (mem. Ho. of Reps. 1981-86), ABA (appellate judges conf. com. on appellate skills tng. 1984-85, co-chair, appellate judges conf. com. on appellate practice 1984-86, mem. Ohio Supreme Ct. adv. com. on rules 1988-91), Md. bar Assn. (v.p. 1967), Am. Jud. Soc. (bd. dirs. 1966-68). Democrat. Roman Catholic. Office: U Cin Coll Law Cincinnati OH 45221-0001 Office Phone: 941-488-0455. Personal E-mail: r.j.martineau@verizon.net. E-mail: r.j.maritneau@netzero.net.

MARTINEN, JOHN A. travel company executive; b. Sault Ste Marie, Mich., June 26, 1938; s. John Albert and Ina Helia (Jarvi) M. BS with highest honors, Mich. State U., 1960; JD, NYU, 1963. With Grace Line, N.Y.C., 1963-69; cons. Empresa Turistica Internat., Galapagos Cruises, Quito, Ecuador, 1969-70; regional mgr. Globus & Cosmos (Group Voyagers Inc.), N.Y.C., 1970-73, v.p., 1974-76, exec. v.p., 1977-78, pres., CEO, 1979-92, Littleton, Colo., 1993-98, chmn., 1998; pres., CEO Vista Travel Ventures, Inc., Denver, 1999—2001; pres. Trafalgar Tours, Long Island City, NY, 2002; prin. Safe Passage Internat., Lakewood, Colo., 2003—. Participant Root-Tilden Program, NYU Law Sch., 1960—63. Mem. U.S. Tour Operators Assn. (bd. dirs. 1993-99, treas. 1996-97, sec. 1998-99), Am. Soc. Travel Agts., Lotus, Sky and Wings Club (N.Y.), Columbine Country Club, Denver Athletic Club. Democrat. Home: 915 W End Ave Apt 7 A New York NY 10025 Office: Safe Passage Internat 3609 S Wadsworth Blvd Ste 565 Lakewood CO 80235 Office Phone: 800-777-7665. E-mail: JohnMartinen@TravelStrategies.net.

MARTINETTI, RONALD ANTHONY, lawyer; b. N.Y.C., Aug. 13, 1945; s. Alfred Nathan and Frances Ann (Battipaglia) M.; m. Ky Le Du, June, 2002. Student, The Hotchkiss Sch., 1963, U. Chgo., 1981-82; JD, U. So. Calif., 1982. Bar: Calif. 1982; U.S. Dist. Ct. (cen. and no. dists.) Calif. 1982, U.S. Dist. Ct. Ariz., 1992; U.S. Ct. Appeals (9th cir.) 1982. Ptnr. Kazanjian & Martinetti, Glendale, Calif., 1986—. Co-founder Am. Legends Website, 1995, Am. Legends Pub., 1996. Author: James Dean Story, 1995, Nine Easy Ways to Strengthen Your Bad Faith Care in Discovery, 1991; co-author: Rights of Owners of Lost, Stolen or Destroyed Instruments Under UCC Section3-804: Can They Be Holders in Due Course, 1993; contbr. to Wall St. Jour., Washington Post, The Harvard Conservative, Newsday, Balt. Sun, The New Leader, Columbia U. Forum, 1968-76; pub. James Dean Scrapbook, 1996. Vol. arbitrator L.A. Sup. Ct., 1987—; judge pro tem L.A. Superior Ct., 1994—. Mem. Calif. Bar Assn. Office: Kazanjian & Martinetti 520 E Wilson Ave Glendale CA 91206-4374 Fax: 818-241-2193. Office Phone: 818-241-1011. E-mail: amlegends@aol.com.

MARTINEZ, ADOLFO ROBERTO, secondary school educator; b. Laredo, Tex., June 7, 1937; s. Luis Felipe and Ofelia Resendez Martinez; m. Irma Hernandez; children: Mayra Ofelia, Mariela Odette. AA, Laredo C.C., 1959; BS, Tex. A&M, 1961; MEd, U. Tex., 1995. Cert. tchr. Tex. Edn. Agy., 1961. Tchr. McAllen ISD, McAllen, Tex., 1961—62, Jim Hogg ISD, Hebbronville, 1962—65, United ISD, Laredo, 1966—67, 1967—72, 1972—73, Roma ISD, 1978—. Adj. instr. South Tex. C.C., Rio Grande City, 2000—. With U.S. Army, 1955—58. Mem.: Math. Assn. Am. (corr.). Independent. Roman Catholic. Avocation: reading. Home: PO Box 117 Roma TX 78584 Office: Roma Independent School District PO Box 187 Roma TX 78584 Personal E-mail: adolfomar2000@yahoo.com.

MARTINEZ, ADRIANA, political organization worker, photographer; Student, U. Nev., Las Vegas; BA, Brooks Inst. Photography. Photography instr. C.C. So. Nev.; wedding photographer So. Nev. News Bur.; chair Nev. State Dem. Party, Las Vegas, 2003—. Mem.: PTA. Office: 1325 Vegas Valley Dr Ste C Las Vegas NV 89109-6219

MARTINEZ, ALEX J. state supreme court justice; b. Denver, Apr. 1, 1951; m. Kathy Carter; children: Julia, Maggie. Diploma, Phillips Exeter Acad., N.H., 1969; student, Reed Coll., 1969-72; BA, U. Colo., 1973, JD, 1976. Bar: Colo. 1976. Dep. state pub. defender, Pueblo and Denver, 1976-83; county ct. judge Pueblo, 1983-88; dist. ct. judge, 1988-97; justice Colo. Supreme Ct., Denver, 1997—. Supreme Ct. liaison Colo. Criminal Rules Com., Colo. Criminal Jury Instns.; chmn. Pub. Access Com., Jud. Edn. Com.; bd. dirs. Servicios de la Raza. Chmn. Pueblo adv. bd. Packard Found., 1993-96; chmn. site-based governing coun. Pueblo Sch. Arts and Scis., 1994-95; mem. site-based governing coun. Roncalli Mid. Sch., 1993-94; bd. dirs. Colo. U. Law Alumni. Mem. Colo. Bar Assn. (regional v.p. 1995-96), Colo. Hispanic Bar Assn., Pueblo Bar Assn. (mem. exec. coun. 1994-96), Pueblo Hispanic Bar Assn. Office: Colo Supreme Ct 2 E 14th Ave Denver CO 80203-2115 E-mail: AJMarti@aol.com.

MARTINEZ, ALMA R. actress, theater director, educator; b. Monclova, Coahuila, Mex. Student, U. Guadalajara-Artes Plasticas, Mex., 1972-73, Ibero-Am. U., 1976, UNAM, Mexico City, 1976-77; BA in Theatre, Whittier Coll., 1984; MFA in Acting, U. So. Calif., 1995; postgrad., Stanford U., 1994—; student, Jerzy Grotowski Para Theatre, Berkeley, Calif., 1977, Lee Strasberg Theatre Inst., Hollywood, Calif., 1982, Royal Acad. Dramatic Arts, London, Eng., 1987, Mnouchkine/Theatre du Soleil, Paris, 1993. Asst. prof. theatre arts U. Calif., Santa Cruz, 2001—. Appeared in plays including In the Summer House, Lincoln Ctr., N.Y.C., Greencard, Joyce Theatre, N.Y.C., Zoot Suit, Mark Taper Forum, L.A., Bocon, Mark Taper Forum, L.A., Macbeth, Oreg. Shakespeare Festival, The Skin of Our Teeth, Oreg. Shakespeare Festival, Hello Dolly, Long Beach Civic Light Opera, A Christmas Carol, South Coast Repertory, House of Blue Leaves, Pasadena Playhouse, Sundance

Inst., Sundance, Utah, Fuente Ovejuna, Berkeley Repertory Theatre, Burning Patience, San Diego Repertory Theatre, Marriage of Figaro, Ariz. Theatre Co., Sons of Don Juan, Asolo Theatre, Fla., Wait Until Dark, Pa. Stage Co., La Carpa de los Rasquachis, Teatro Campesino; TV appearances include Gen. Hosp., Twilight Zone, Sequin, Corridos (Peabody award), Tough Love, Dress Gray, The Boys, In a Child's Name, The Gambler Returns, Quiet Killer, The New Adam 12 (series regular), 500 Nations, Nash Bridges (guest star); film appearances include Ballad of a Soldier, Jacaranda, The Novice, Trial by Terror, Dollie Dearest, Maria's Story, For A Loves One, Soldado Razo, Shattered Image, Zoot Suit, Barbarosa, Born in East L.A., Under Fire, among others; dir. (plays) Bed of Stone, 1996, La Gran Carpa de los Rasquachis, 1997, Heroes & Saints, 2001. Active Assistance with Alcohol and Sobriety Uniting Latinas, United L.Am. Youth, Med. Aid for El Salvador, Save the Children, the Christian Children's Fund; vol. and charity work in refugee camps in Ethiopia, India, Thailand, Sri Lanka, and The Philippines; bd. dirs. Mexican Mus., El Teatro Compresing. Recipient Cert. of Appreciation El Teatro Campesino, 1978, Recognition award Barrio Sta., 1980, Alumni Hall of Fame, El Rancho H.S., 1982, Outstanding Hispanic Alumni award Whittier Coll., 1984; co-recipient with Anthony Quinn and Edward James Olmos Hispanic Entertainer of Yr., The Equitable Co., 1987; Escobedo fellow Stanford U., 1996, Dorothy Danforth Compton Rsch. fellow, 1996. Mem. NATAS, AFTRA, SAG (John Dales scholar 1995-96, 98), TCG, Modern Lang. Assn., Assn. for Theatre in Higher Edn., Nat. Theatre Conf., Nat. Assn. Chicas and Chicano Studies, Actors Equity Assn. Address: JE Talent 323 Geary St #302 San Francisco CA 94102 Office: Univ Calif J-14 Theatre Arts Ctr Santa Cruz CA 95064 Office Phone: 831-459-4948. E mail: almamar@ucsc.edu.

MARTINEZ, ARTHUR C. retail company executive; b. N.Y.C., Sept. 25, 1939; s. Arthur F. and Agnes (Caulfield) M.; m. Elizabeth Rusch, July 30, 1966; children: Lauren, Gregory. BSME, Polytech. U., 1960; MBA, Harvard U., 1965; JD (hon.), U. Notre Dame, 1997. Dir. planning Internat. Paper Co., N.Y.C., 1967-69; asst. to pres. Talley Industries, Mesa, Ariz., 1969-70; dir. fin. RCA Corp., N.Y.C., 1970-73, v.p., 1973-80; sr. v.p., CFO Saks Fifth Ave., N.Y.C., 1980-84, exec. v.p., 1984-87, vice chmn., dir., 1990-92; sr. v.p. and group chief exec. Batus Inc., Louisville, 1987-90; vice chmn., dir. Saks Fifth Ave., 1990-92; chmn., CEO Sears Merchandise Group, Chgo., 1992-95, Sears, Roebuck and Co., 1995—2000. Bd. dirs. Sears, Roebuck and Co., Ameritech, Martha Stewart Living Omnimedia, Inc., PepsiCo, Inc.; dep. chmn. Fed. Res. Bank, Chgo.; former chmn. Nat. Minority Supplier Devel. Coun., Inc. Bd. dirs. Defenders of Wildlife, 1992—, Nat. Urban League; chmn. bd. trustees Polytech. U., 1990—; trustee Art Inst., Orch. Assn. Chgo. Symphony Orch.; bd. dirs. Northestern Meml. Hosp., Chgo. 1st lt. U.S. Army, 1961-63. Named CEO of Yr., Fin. World Mag., 1996; recipient T.C. and Elizabeth Clarke medallion Sch. of Bus., Coll. William and Mary, 1997, Olin Sch. of Bus. Excellence in Bus. award, Washington U., St. Louis, 1997. Mem. Nat. Retail Fedn. (chmn. bd. dirs.). Avocations: tennis, golf, gardening. Office: Sears Roebuck and Co 3333 Beverly Rd Hoffman Estates IL 60179

MARTINEZ, CARLOS, insurance adjuster, company manager; b. Havana, Cuba, Apr. 15, 1940; came to U.S., 1960; s. Serafin and Micaela (Contreras-Cutie) M.; m. Laurel Louise Hancock, Sept. 24, 1970; children: Carl Edward, Emily Louise. BS, Edison Inst., Havana, 1958; postgrad. studies in civil engring., U. Havana, 1959-60; AA, Miami-Dade C.C., Miami, Fla., 1968; BA, Fla. Atlantic U., 1971. Lic. ins. adjuster, Fla. Student rsch. asst. Fla. Atlantic U., Boca Raton, 1968-70; collection supr. Burdine's Dept. Stores, Miami, Fla., 1970-72; ins. adjuster Crawford and Co., Miami, 1972-75, All Risks Mgmt. Svcs., Miami, 1977, Allstate Ins. Co., Miami, 1975-77, Globe Adjustment Co., North Miami, 1977-86, Ins. Servicing & Adjusting Co., Miami, 1986-89; br. mgr. Crittenden Adjustment Co., Hollywood, Fla., 1989—. Mem. Young Ams. for Freedom, Boca Raton, Fla. 1968-71, Young Reps., Boca Raton, 1968-71. PO USN, 1960-61. Mem. S. Fla. Claims Assn. (assoc. mem.), Edison Inst. Alumni Assn., Fla. Atlantic U. Alumni Assn. Roman Catholic. Avocations: swimming, bicycle riding, history, sociology, insurance, law, gymnastics. Home: 3030 SW 123rd Ct Miami FL 33175-2250 Office: Crittenden Adjustment Co 1414 NW 107th Ave Ste 202 Hollywood FL

MARTINEZ, CARMEN M. ambassador; b. Pensacola, Fla., July 1950; married; 1 child. MA in Medieval History, MS in Nat. Security and Strategic Resources. Various positions U.S. Fgn. Svc., Sao Paulo, Brazil, 1981; chief of the consular sect. Quito, Ecuador, 1989—93; prin. officer U.S. consulate, Barranquilla, Colombia, 1993—94; dep. chief of mission US Dept. State, Maputo, Mozambique, 1997—99; prin. officer U.S. consulate, Sao Paolo, Brazil, 1999—2000; charge d'affaires to Burma US Dept. State, Rangoon, 2002—. Office: DOS Amb 4250 Rangoon Pl Washington DC 20521

MARTINEZ, DAVID R. electrical engineer, science educator; BSEE, N.Mex. State U., 1976; MS in Elec. Engring., MIT, 1979; EE in Elec. Engring., MIT/Woods Hole Oceanographic Instn., 1979; MBA, So. Meth. U., 1986. Prin. rsch. engr. Atlantic Richfield Co., 1979—88; group leader, assoc. divsn. head MIT Lincoln Lab., Lexington, Mass., 1988—. Mem. Army Sci. Bd. Recipient Spl. Achievement award, ARCO. Mem.: IEEE, Assn. for Computing Machinery. Achievements include patents for in field. Office: Lincoln Lab MIT 244 Wood St Lexington MA 02420-9108

MARTINEZ, DONNA F. federal judge; BA, U. Conn., 1973, MSW, 1975, JD, 1978. Bar: Conn. 1979. Corp. counsel City of Hartford, Conn., 1979-80; asst. U.S. atty. Office U.S. Atty., Hartford and New Haven, 1980-94; chief organized crime drug enforcement task force Dist. of Conn., New Haven, 1989-94; magistrate judge U.S. Magistrate Ct., Hartford, 1994—. Instr. trial practice Yale U. Law Sch., New Haven, 1996-2001. Mem. Conn. Bar Assn., Fed. Bar Assn., Hispanic Bar Assn., Fed. Magistrate Judges Assn., Am. Inns of Ct. (past. v.p., past pres.), Am. Leadership Forum (bd. dirs.). Office: US Magistrate Ct 450 Main St Rm 262 Hartford CT 06103-3002 Office Phone: 860-240-3605.

MARTINEZ, EDGAR, retired professional baseball player; b. N.Y.C., Jan. 2, 1963; Student, American Coll., Puerto Rico. Baseball player Seattle Mariners, 1982—2004. Named. to Am. League All-Star Team, 1992, 95, 96, 97, 2000, 2001, 2003 Achievements include Am. League Batting Champion, 1992, 95, led in Runs (121), 1995.

MARTINEZ, EURI ANTHONY, music educator, small business owner; b. Tuy, Batangas, Philippines, Nov. 6, 1966; s. Galicano Paradero and Minda Tolentino Martinez; m. Maria Carolina Nuguid, Apr. 18, 1998; children: Erica Lourdes, Christian Anthony. MusB, North Pk. U., 1990. Prin., owner Martinez Music Studio, Carpentersville, Ill., 2002—. Adjudicator Sam & Rose Licata Meml., Chgo., 1995—, Granquist Music Competition, Geneva, 1997—. Choir dir. Filipino-Am. of the N.W. Suburbs, St. Mary Ch., Huntley, Ill.; organist, pianist St Gregory The Gt. Parish, Chgo., 1996—2000. Named to Filipino-American Hall Of Fame In Music, Via Times and The Chgo. Philippine Report TV, 1997; recipient Excellence In Music Instrn. award, Am. Music World, 1993. Mem.: Ill. Music Assn. (adjudicator 1996—, mem. scholarship bd. 1997—, sec. 1998—), Steinway Soc. Chgo., Northshore Music Tchrs. Assn., Ill. State Music Tchrs. Assn., Music Tchrs. Nat. Assn. Roman Cath. Avocations: travel, gardening, physical fitness. Office: American Music World 7727 N Milwaukee Avenue Niles IL 60743 Office Phone: 312-760-8795.

MARTINEZ, FERNANDO V. civil engineer; b. Blewett, Tex., July 2, 1927; s. Catarino G. and Refugia V. M.; m. Dora Garza, Sept. 27, 1953; children: Fernando G., Karen Martinez Solano, Edward A. BS in Civil Engring, Tex A&M U., 1951. Registered profl. engr., Tex. Field engr. Farnsworth & Chambers Co, Houston, Tex., 1953-54; design engr. Link Belt Co., Houston, 1954, Anderson Clayton & Co., Houston, 1954-59; project engr. Olin Mathieson Chem. Corp., Pasadena, Tex., 1959-80; project mgr. Mobil Oil Corp., Pasadena, 1980—. 1st lt. U.S. Army, 1951-53, Korea. Republican. Roman Catholic. Home: 710 Skylark Rd Pasadena TX 77502-4560 Office: Mobil Oil Corp 2001 Jackson Rd Pasadena TX 77501

MARTINEZ, GARY STEVEN, actor; b. San Francisco, May 1, 1951; s. Bellarmine Joseph Martinez and Lila Marie Monkhouse. One-yr. cert., Royal Acad. Dramatic Arts, London, 1970; BA, Loyola-Marymount U., L.A., 1972; MFA, U. Minn., Mpls., 1974. Exec. acct. mgr. The Negotiating Edge, Saratoga, Calif., 2001—; voice actor Webtone Prodns., Los Gatos, 2002; actor Sacramento Theatre Co., 2000, TheatreWorks, Palo Alto, 2002, San Jose Stage Co., 2003, Delta King Theatre, Sacramento, 2003, Willows Theatre, Concord, 2004. Devel. cons. Flamenco Soc. of San Jose, 2001; mem. governing bd. Acad. TV Arts and Scis., San Francisco, 2001. Author: (plays) The Power Payoff, 1982, Dracul/Vampyre, 1983, Everyman on the Streets, 2000. Recipient acting award, Bank of Am., 1968, Alexander J. Cody, 1968; fellow, Bush-McKnight Found./Minn., 1972; performance fellowship, Mich. State, 1977. Mem.: AFTRA, Actor's Equity Assn. Avocations: dialects, guitar, blues harmonica, occult.

MARTINEZ, GUSTAVE See SOLOMONS, GUS JR.

MARTINEZ, HERMINIA S. economist, banker; b. Havana, Cuba; came to U.S., 1960, naturalized, 1972; d. Carlos and Amelia (Santana) Martinez Sanchez; m. Mario Aguilar, 1982; children: Mario Aguilar, Carlos Aguilar. BA in Econs. cum laude, Am. U., 1965; MS in Fgn. Svc. (Univ. fellow); MS in Econs., Georgetown U., 1967, PhD in Econs., 1969; postgrad., Nat. U. Mex. Instr. econs. George Mason Coll., U. Va., Fairfax, 1967-68; researcher World Bank, 1967-69, indsl. economist, devel. econs. dept., 1969-71; economist World Bank Latin Am. (Ctrl. Am., Mex., Venezuala, Equador, Panama and Dominican Republic, Washington, 1971-79, sr. loan officer for Middle East and North Africa World Bank, 1977-81, sr. loan officer for Western Africa region, 1981-84, sr. economist Africa Region, 1988-91, prin. ops. officer pvt. sector fin. group Africa region, 1992-96, lead specialist, sub-regional mgr., 1996-2000; pvt. practice fin., econ. devel., 2000—. Contbg. author: The Economic Growth of Colombia: Problems and Prospects, 1973, Central American Financial Integration, 1975. Mid Career fellow Princeton U., 1988-89. Mem. Am. Econ. Assn., Soc. Internat. Devel., Brookings Inst. Latin Am. Study Group. Roman Catholic. Home: 5145 Yuma St NW Washington DC 20016-4336 Office: World Bank 1818 H St NW Washington DC 20433-0001

MARTINEZ, IRIS, state senator; b. Chgo. 1 child. Grad., Northeastern U., U. Ill., Chgo. Mem. Ill. State Senate, Springfield, 2003—, mem. appropriations II com., health and human svcs. com. and sbucom. on health care, vice chhair com. on ins. and pensions, mem. subcom. on mandates. Liaison to Hispanic Ministry. Committeewoman Ill. Dem. State Com.; mem. Dem. Nat. Com. Democrat. Catholic. Office: Capitol M-106 Capitol Bldg Springfield IL 62706 also: District 3024 N Pulaski Rd Chicago IL 60641 also: Home office 3912 W Byron St #2W Chicago IL 60618

MARTINEZ, JEAN, newscaster; BA in journalism, U. Mo., 1985. Morning anchor, reporter WXII, Winston-Salem, NC, 1985—86; anchor, reporter KGBT, CBS affiliate, Harlingen, Tex., 1986—88; morning anchor KSAT, ABC affiliate, San Antonio, 1988, KCNC, CBS affiliate, Denver, 1988—95; anchor, reporter KTTV Fox 11, Los Angeles, 1995—. Host News for Kids, 1993—95. Office: KTTV Fox 11 1999 S Bundy Dr Los Angeles CA 90025-5235

MARTINEZ, JOE LOUIS, JR., neurobiologist, educator; b. Albuquerque, Aug. 1, 1944; s. Joe Louis and Maria Elena (Werner) M.; m. Janice Susanna Hepner, Sept. 17, 1967 (div. Oct. 1987); children: Adan, Adria, Aric; m. Kimberly Smith, Dec. 2, 1990; 1 child, Ariel. BA, U. San Diego, 1966; MS, N.Mex. Highlands U., 1968; PhD, U. Del., 1971. From asst. to assoc. prof. Calif. State U., San Bernardino, 1971-75; assoc. researcher U. Calif., Irvine, 1975-82, prof. Berkeley, 1982-94; prof. neurobiology, dir. Cajal Neurosci. Inst. U. Tex., San Antonio, 1994-2001, assoc. vice provost for rsch., 2001—. Mem.: Rsch. Inst. NIDA (bd. sci. counselors 1999—2003), AAAS (lifetime mentor award 1994), Am. Coll. Neuropsycopharmacology, Assn. Neurosi. Depts. and Programs (Edn. award 2003). Office: U Tex 6900 N Loop 1604 W San Antonio TX 78249-1130 E-mail: jmartinez@utsa.edu.

MARTINEZ, JOSEMARIA ESPINO, computer services administrator; b. Manila, Philippines, Nov. 10, 1963; came to U.S., 1974; s. Rogelio Alaras and Rosita (Espino) M.; m. Kamala Lynn Hendricks, July 27, 1991; 1 child, Christian Sinclair Garrison Martinez. Student, U. Ill., Chgo., 1980-81; BA, DePaul U., Chgo., 1993; postgrad., Northwestern U., 1999—. Data processing mgr. Nationwide Credit & Collection, Chgo., 1982-84; project leader/analyst Met. Chgo. Coun., 1984-86; systems dir. Fifield Cos., Ltd., Chgo., 1986-90; dir. MIS Thorek Hosp. and Med. Ctr., Chgo., 1991-93; MIS dir. Chgo. Zool. Soc. and Brookfield Zoo, 1993-97; prin. Whittman-Hart, Chgo., 1997—. Contbr. articles to mags. and profl. jours. Mem. Assn. for Systems Mgmt., Common Users Group. Republican. Presbyterian. Avocations: tennis, racquetball, golf. Home: 4312 Camelot Cir Naperville IL 60564-3189 Office: Whittman-Hart #3500 311 S Wacker Dr Ste 3500 Chicago IL 60606-6621

MARTINEZ, JUDY PERRY, lawyer; b. New Orleans, La., Aug. 15, 1957; BS, La. State U., 1979; JD cum laude, Tulane U., 1982. Bar: La. 1982. Atty., chair Simon, Peragine, Smith & Redfearn, LLP, New Orleans, 1982—. Mem. Elmo B. Hunter Ctr. for Jud. Excellence, 1994—97; chairperson New Orleans Pro Bono Project, 1989. Fellow: Am. Bar Found., La. Bar Found. (life); mem.: ABA (commn. on women in the profession 1991—94, spl. advisor standing com. on fed. jud. 1994—95, bd. govs. 1996—99, exec. com. 1998—99, del.-at-large 1999—, gen. mem. sect. on litigation ABA Ho. of Dels. 2000—, nominating com. 1993—96, chair young lawyers divsn. 1990—91, chair commn. on domestic violence 1999—2001, young lawyers divsn. liaison to sect. litigation 1991—93, mem. exec. coun. young lawyers divsn. 1986—96, divsn. del. 1991—96), Am. Judicature Soc., Assn. for Women Attys., La. State Bar Assn. (chairperson minority involvement com. 1984—87, long range planning com. 1987—92, chairperson professionalism and quality of life com. 1992—93, chairperson post-conviction representation com. 1997—99), New Orleans Bar Assn. (chairperson young lawyers sect. 1986—87). Office: Simon Peragine Smith & Redfearn LLP 30th Fl Energy Ctr 1100 Poydras St New Orleans LA 70163-3000

MARTINEZ, KATHRYN MARIE, music educator; b. St. Paul, Dec. 20, 1957; d. Lloyd Gerald and Patricia Anne Schleusner; m. Michael David Martinez, Feb. 27, 1982 (div. Aug. 22, 1994); children: Kristin Marie, Kelly Anne. BA in Elem. Edn., Coll. St. Catherine, St. Paul, 1979. Tchr. grade 2 South Pk. Consol. Sch., Mpls., 1979—80, St. Peters Sch., North St. Paul, Minn., 1980—81; tchr. pre-sch. St. Marks Ch., Independence, Mo., 1985—86; ind. piano tchr. Independence, Mo., 1985, Geneva, Ill., 1986, St. Paul, 1987—. Mem. pageant comm. Vadnais Heights Heritage Days, Minn., 1994, pageant co-dir., 1995—96. Recipient Miss Little Can., Little Can. Jaycees / Roseville, Minn., 1977, 1st Runner-up Miss Minn., Austin, Minn., 1978. Mem.: St. Paul Piano Tchr. Assoc. (3rd V.P. 2002—), Minn. Music Tchr. Assoc. (mem. 1991—), Ea. Suburban Fed. Music Club (co-chair 2002—04, pres. 2002—04). Catholic. Avocations: gardening, playing piano, travel, rubber stamping. Home and Office: 4309 Greenhaven Court Vadnais Heights MN 55127

MARTINEZ, LORI ANNE BRUBAKER, mathematician, educator; b. Breman, Ind., Sept. 19, 1969; d. Paul Kenneth Brubaker Sr. and Barbara Ann (Wehrle) Brubaker; m. Fernando Naranjo Martinez Jr., May 31, 1997; children: Magdalena Anne, Carolina Rose, Annamarie Kate, Fernando Brubaker III. AA, Art Instrn. Schs., Mpls., 1993; BS in Secondary Edn., Ind. U. N.W., 1992. Cert. nurses asst. Ind.; secondary tchr. Ind., Tex. Nurse's asst. Chesterton Health Care Ctr., Ind., 1989—90; daycare provider Boys and Girls Club, Valparaiso, Ind., 1990—92; tchr. math. MacArthur H.S., Houston, 1993—99, MacArthur 9th Grade Sch., Houston, 1999—. Substitute tchr. Duneland Sch. Sys., Chesterton, 1992—93; owner Quixtar Indep. Bus., 2001—. Life mem. Girl Scouts Am., 1977—. Mem.: Nat. Coun. Tchrs. Math. Avocations: art, writing, genealogy, crocheting, collecting Donald Ducks and rampant unicorns. Home: 21423 Tophill Dr Spring TX 77388 Office: MacArthur 9th Grade Sch 12111 Gloger Houston TX 77039 Office Phone: 281-985-7400. E-mail: brumar97@quixnet.net.

MARTINEZ, LUIS OSVALDO, radiologist, educator; b. Havana, Cuba, Nov. 27, 1927; came to U.S., 1962, naturalized, 1967; s. Osvaldo and Felicita (Farinas) M.; children Maria Elena, Luis Osvaldo, Alberto Luis; m. Nydia M. Ceballos. MD, U. Havana, 1954. Cert. in diagnostic radiology. Intern Calixto Garcia Hosp., Havana, 1954-55; resident in radiology Jackson Meml. Hosp., Miami, Fla., 1963-65, fellow in cardiovascular radiology, 1965-67; instr. radiology U. Miami, 1965-68, asst. prof., 1968, clin. asst. prof., 1968-70, assoc. prof., 1970-76, prof., 1976-91, clin. prof., 1991-94; chief radiol. svcs. VA Med. Ctr., 1991—. Assoc. dir. dept. radiology Mt. Sinai Med. Ctr., Miami Beach, Fla., 1969-91, chief divsn. diagnostic radiology, 1970-91, dir. residency program in diagnostic radiology, emeritus mem. med. staff, 1991; dir. Spanish Radiology Seminar. Reviewer Am. Jour. Radiology, Radium Therapy and Nuclear Medicine, 1978; contbr. articles to profl. jours. Former pres. League Against Cancer. Recipient Gold medal Interam. Coll. Radiology, 1975, Antoine Bèclere medal Internat. Congress Radiology, 1989, Carlos J. Finlay Gold medal Cuban Med. Convb., 1990, Honors Achievement award, Cert. of Merit Mallinckrodt Pharms., 1972-74; Luis O. Martinez M.D. Lecture named in his honor, Interam. Coll. Radiology, Mem. AMA (Physician's Recognition award 1971, 74-83), AAUP, Radiol. Soc. France (hon. 1991), Internat. Soc. Lymphology, Interam. Coll. Radiology (pres.), Internat. Coll. Surgeons, Internat. Coll. Angiology, Internat. Soc. Radiology, Cuban Med. Assn. in Exile, Am. Coll. Chest Physicians (assoc.), Radiol. Soc. N. Am., Am. Coll. Radiology, Am. Roentgen Ray Soc., Am. Assn. Fgn. Med. Grads., Am. Profl. Practice Assn., Am. Thoracic Soc., Pan Am. Med. Assn., Am. Assn. Univ. Radiologists, Brit. Inst. Radiology, Am. Heart Assn. (mem. council cardiovascular radiology), Faculty Radiologists, Soc. Gastrointestinal Radiologists, Am. Geriatrics Soc., Am. Coll. Angiology, Royal Coll. Radiologists, Am. Soc. Therapeutic Radiologists, Assn. Hosp. Med. Edn., Cuban Radiology Soc. in exile (founder, pres.), Cuban chpt. Inter Am. Coll. Radiology (founder, pres.), Am. Coll. Med. Imaging, Interasma, So. Med. Assn., N.Y. Acad. Scis., Fla. Thoracis Soc., Fla. Radiol. Soc., Dade County Med. Assn., Greater Miami Radiol. Soc., cuban Radiol. Soc. (sec.), Can. Assn. Radiologists, Soc. Thoracic Radiologists (founding mem.), Emeritus mem. Am. Coll. Angiology, 1989, Emeritus mem. Am. Heart Assn., 1992; hon. mem. numerous med. socs. of Mex., Cen. and S. Am. Roman Catholic. Office: 1201 NW 16th St Miami FL 33125-1624

MARTINEZ, MARIA, computer software company executive; BA in elec. engring., U. PR; MA in computer engring, Ohio State U. Various mgmt. and engring. positions AT&T Bell Labs.; v.p., gen. mgr. Internet Connectivity Solutions Divsn. Motorola Inc.; CEO Embrace Network, Inc.; corp. v.p. comm. and mobile solutions unit Microsoft Corp. Named an Elite Woman, Hispanic mag., 2004; recipient several process and quality awards. Achievements include led Motorola's launching of first CDMA comml. sys. in world; played a leadership role in Bell Lab's devel. of UNIX sys. for symmetrics multiprocessing and high availability; patents for devel. and disk storage sys; launched first software platform and developed customer base for Embrace Networks, Inc; first female Hispanic named v.p. at Microsoft. Office: Microsoft Corp One Microsoft Way Redmond WA 98052-6399 Office Phone: 425-882-8080. Office Fax: 425-706-7329.

MARTINEZ, MATTHEW GILBERT, former congressman; b. Walsenburg, Colo., Feb. 14, 1929; children: Matthew, Diane, Susan, Michael, Carol Ann. Cert of competence, Los Angeles Trade Tech. Sch., 1959. Small businessman and bldg. contractor; mem. 97th-106th Congresses from 31st Calif. dist., 1982-2001; mem. edn. and labor com., fgn. affairs com. Mem. Monterey Park Planning Commn., 1971-74; mayor City of Monterey Park, 1974-75; mem. Monterey Park City Council, 1974-80, Calif. State Assembly, 1980-82; bd. dirs. San Gabriel Valley YMCA. Served with USMC, 1947-50. Mem. Congl. Hispanic Caucus, Hispanic Am. Democrats, Nat. Assn. Latino Elected and Apptd. Ofcls., Communications Workers Am., VFW, Am. Legion, Latin Bus. Assn., Monterey Park C. of C., Navy League (dir.) Lodges: Rotary. Democrat.

MARTINEZ, MELQUIADES R. (MEL MARTINEZ), former secretary of housing and urban development; b. Sagua La Grande, Cuba, Oct. 23, 1946; came to U.S., 1962; naturalized, 1971; s. Melquiades C. and Gladys V. (Ruiz) M.; m. Kathryn Tindal, June 13, 1970; children: Lauren Elizabeth, John Melquiades, Andrew Tindal. BA, Fla. State U., 1969, JD, 1973. Bar: Fla. 1973, U.S. Dist. Ct. (mid. dist.) Fla. 1973, U.S. Supreme Ct. 1979, U.S. Dist. Ct. (so. dist.) Fla. 1986; cert. Nat. Bd. Trial Advocacy. Civil trial atty. Fla. Ptnr., Martinez, Dalton, Dellecker and Wilson, Orlando, Fla., 1973-85, Martinez, Dalton, Dellecker, Wilson and King, 1985-98; chmn. Orange County, 1998-2001; sec. U.S. Dept. Housing & Urban Devel., Washington, 2001—03. Bd. dirs. Cath. Social Svcs. Orlando, 1978-86; founder, chmn. Mayor's Hispanic Adv. Com., Orlando, 1981-82; chmn. bd. commrs. Olando Housing Authority, 1983-86; commr. Orlando Utilities Commn., 1992-97, pres. 1995-97; chmn. Orange County, 1998. Mem. Fla. Bar (bd. govs. young lawyers sect. 1980-81), Acad. Fla. Trial Lawyers (dir. 1981-85, treas. 1986-87, pres. 1988-89), 9th Jud. Cir. (jud. nomination commn. 1986). Republican. Roman Catholic.

MARTINEZ, MIGUEL ACEVEDO, urologist, consultant, lecturer; b. Chihuahua, Mex., Aug. 18, 1953; came to U.S., 1956; s. Miguel Nuñez and Velia (Acevedo) M. AB, Stanford U., 1976; MD, Yale U., 1983. Diplomate Am. Bd. Urology. Intern U. S.C. Med. Ctr., 1983-84; resident in urology White Meml. Med. Ctr., L.A., 1984-89, urologist, 1989—. Cons., lectr. physician asst. program U. So. Calif., L.A., 1990—, clin. instr.; patient edn. cons. ICI Pharm., Del., 1991—, Zeneca's Speaker Forum; patient edn. and med. cons., lectr. Abbott Labs., 1991—; mem. edn.cons. several radio/TV stas., 1991—; mem. subcom. for diseases on kidney and transplantation NIH, Washington, 1991; mem. nat. Hispanic adv. bd. Pfizer Pharms., Inc., 1998—; mem. adv. bd. Glaxo Smith Kline, 2002—; cons. spkrs. bur. Pfizer, Bayer/ESK. Author: Intercellular Pathways, 1981. Polit. cons. Xavier Becerra, U.S. Congress, 1992, Martin Gallegos, Gil Cedillo, Calif. State Assembly, 1993, others; bd. dirs. Latino Ctr. for Prevention and Action in Health, Orange County, calif.; bd. govs., sec., rep. Zeneca Urology Econ. Summit, Washington, 1993; mem. Pfizer Nat. Hispanic Adv. Bd. Named one of Outstanding Young Men of Am., 1981; Nat. Hispanic Med. Assn. Pub. Policy fellow, 2000-01. Mem. AMA, Nat. Hispanic Med. Assn. (public policy fellow), Am. Urological Assn., Calif. Med. Assn. (polit. action com. bd. dirs. 1997—, del.), L.A. Med. Assn. (polit. action com. 1992—), L.A. County Med. Assn., Yale Alumni Assn., Stanford Alumni Assn., L.A. Athletic Club. Office: White Meml Med Ctr Rm 500 1701 Cesar Chavez Ave Los Angeles CA 90033 2438 Office Phone: 323-261-0108.

MARTINEZ, NATALIE, newscaster; b. Buffalo; Degree, SUNY, Buffalo. Anchor, reporter, prodr. at upstate N.Y. radio and TV stations; reporter and weekend anchor WXAA-TV, Albany, NY, primary anchor; co-anchor weekend morning news and reporter WMAQ-TV, Chgo., 2001—. Mem.: Nat. League Female Execs., Nat. Assn. of Hispanic Journalists, One Voice. Office: WMAQ-TV NBC Tower 454 N Columbus Dr Chicago IL 60611-5555 Office Phone: 312-836-5830.

MARTINEZ, PEDRO JAIME, professional baseball player; b. Manoquayabo, Dominican Republic, July 25, 1971; With L.A. Dodgers, 1992—93; pitcher Montreal Expos, 1994—97, Boston Red Sox, 1998—. Named Minor League Player of Yr., Sporting News, 1991, Nat. League Earned Runs Average (ERA) Leader, 1997, Am. League Earned Runs Average (ERA) Leader, 1999—2003, Am. League Wins Leader, 1999, Am. League Strikeouts Leader, 1999, 2000, 2002, All-Star MVP, 1999; named to Nat. League All-Star Team, 1996—97, Am. League All-Star Team, 1998—2000, 2002; recipient Nat. League Cy Young award, 1997, Am. League Cy Young award, 1999, 2000. Office: Boston Red Sox 4 Yawkey Way Boston MA 02215-3496*

MARTINEZ, RICARDO, research and development company executive; m. Robin Rosser. MD, La. State U. Sch. Medicine, 1980. Intern Lafayette (La.) Charity Hosp., 1980-81; resident Charity Hosp., New Orleans, 1983-85; vis. fellow accident rsch. unit Ctr. Automotive Engring./U. Birmingham, U.K., 1989; adminstr. Nat. Hwy. Traffic Safety Adminstrn, Washington, 1994—99; sr. v.p. health affairs Healtheon Web MD Corp., Atlanta, 1999—2000; pres., CEO Safety Intelligence Sys., Atlanta, 2000—. Clin. prof. emergency medi-

cine Emory U. Sch. Medicine, Atlanta, assoc. dir. Ctr. for Injury Control. Home: 1254 Spring Creek Way Decatur GA 30033-2643 Office: Safety Intelligence Systems 790 Atlantic Drive S 0355 Atlanta GA 30332

MARTINEZ, RICHARD C. state senator; Magistrate judge; Dem. senator dist. 5 N.Mex. State Senate. Mem. judiciary com. N.Mex. State Senate, vice chair conservation com. Home: Box 934 Espanola NM 87532 Office: NMex State Senate State Capitol Mail Rm Dept Santa Fe NM 87503 E-mail: senate@state.nm.us.

MARTINEZ, ROSE MARIE, health science association administrator; PhD, Johns Hopkins Sch. Hygiene and Pub. Health. Former asst. dir. health fin. and policy U.S. Gen. Acctg. Office; sr. health rschr. Mathematica Policy Rsch.; dir. IOM Bd. Health Promotion and Disease Prevention, 1999—. Office: Inst of Med 500 Fifth St NW Washington DC 20001*

MARTINEZ, TERESITA, playwright, educator; b. San Juan, Oct. 3, 1965; d. Gabriel Martinez and Muneca Geigel; life ptnr. Barbara Vlahides. BA in Drama, U. P.R., 1986; MA in Ednl. Theatre, NYU, 1988. Actor, tchr. Creative Arts Team, NYU, N.Y.C., 1989—91; adj. prof. CUNY, 1991—. Author (actor): (drama) Mi ultima noche con Ruben Blades/For mi Chichi; author: Borinquen Vive en el Barrio, Agria.Tierra.Dulce, La Partida y El Regreso. Vol. God's Love We Deliver, N.Y.C., 1993—2003. Mem.: Hispanic Orgn. Latin Actors (bd. dirs. 1993—), Dramatists Guild Am. (assoc.).

MARTINEZ, TINO, professional baseball player; b. Tampa, Fla., Dec. 7, 1967; Baseball player Seattle Mariners, 1988-95, N.Y. Yankees, 1996—2002, St. Louis Cardinals, 2002—03, Tampa Bay Devil Rays, 2003—. Mem. U.S. Olympic baseball team, 1988. Named 1st baseman Sporting News Coll. All-Am. team, 1988, Pacific Coast MVP, 1991; part of World Series winning N.Y. Yankees, 1998; most wins of alltime 127 regular season wins. Achievements include member 1996 World Series Champions. Office: Tampa Bay Devil Rays Tropicana Field 1 Tropicana Dr Saint Petersburg FL 33705

MARTINEZ, VERA, academic administrator; b. San Bernardino, Calif., Nov. 12, 1939; d. Daniel Galvan and Adela (Machado) M.; 1 child, Stephanie Ann Murguia-Hammond. BA in Spanish, Calif. State U., 1962; MA in Sociology, U. Calif., Riverside, 1971, PhD in Ednl. Adminstrn., 1979. Spl. asst. to chancellor UCLA, 1979-81, dir., 1981-84; asst. dean Santa Monica (Calif.) College, 1984-85, dean, 1985-86, spl. assignment to pres., 1987-88, adminstrv. dean, 1990-92, 94-95, acting provost, 1992-94; pres. Fullerton (Calif.) Coll., 1995-98; vice chair instrnl. svcs. for dist. Fullerton, 1998-99; cons., 1999—. Presdl. appointee Nat. Institution Edn., Washington, 1971-75. Harvard fellow 1994. Mem. Cmty. Coll. League Calif., Calif. Assn. Cmty. Colls., Calif. Comm. Colls. (cons. chancellor's office 1992, bd. Latina Leadership 1988—), Nat. Network Hispanic Women (bd. dirs. 1980—). Home: 1041 Madison Pl Laguna Beach CA 92651-2805

MARTINEZ, YOLANDA R. social services administrator; b. Feb. 11, 1936; d. Eduardo R. and Consuelo (Rincon) Martinez; m. William Edward Hawkins, Mar. 27, 1963 (dec. May 11, 1996); children: Ricardo, Eduardo, William T. AA, San Bernardino Valley Coll., 1959; BA, U. Wash., 1974. Tchr. pub. schs., Calif., 1958—59; parole adviser, project dir., counselor Active Mexicanos, Seattle, 1972—76; instr. Everett (Wash.) C.C., 1975—76; rschr., translator Wash. State Coun. Crime and Delinquency, Seattle, 1977; program asst., minority affairs Seattle Ctrl. C.C.; cons. to cmty. offenders programs, 1977—81; sr. cmty. svc. rep. Seattle Dept. Human Resources, 1981—, ret., 2003. Cons. in field. Author: Usted y La Ley, 1977. Translator ARC Lang. Bank, 1975—; chmn. Region 10 Chicago Task Force on Drug Abuse, 1977—79; mem. Seattle Cable Citizens Adv. Bd., 1988—90; v.p. Concilio for Spanish Speaking; state dir., mem. nat. exec. bd. League United L.Am. Citizens, 1980—82; chmn. Hispanic adv. bd. Seattle Cmty. Coll. Dist. 6, 1981—83; chmn. Seattle/Mazatlan Sister City Assn., 1981—83; v.p. Neighborhoods U.S.A., 1987—92, 1995—, bd. dirs., 1986, United Way of King County; dist. adv. com. group health Northgate Clinic; del. White House Conf. on Families, L.A., 1980; bd. dirs. N.W. Kidney Ctr. Regional Coun., 2002; bd. mem. Northgate Chamber, 2002; Dem. precinct committeeman, 1968, 1970, 1988—2002; vol. worker various local and state polit. campaigns. Named One of 100 Women Role Models for Pub. Schs., State Office Pub. Instrn., Lake City Citizen of Yr., 2000; recipient Gov.'s citation, 1974, award for committment to higher edn., Seattle C.C. Dist., 1983, One of 10 Unsung Heroes in Seattle, Radical Women, 1983, Cmty. Svc. award, Am. G.I. Forum, 1984, Golden Maple Leaf award, Maple Leaf Cmty. Coun., 1991, Commn. award, Seattle Commn. on Children and Youth, 1991, 1993, assoc. mem., Eastern Washington U. Found., Seattle Works award, Cmty. Ambassador, 2001, Seattle Works Award, 2002. Mem.: Northgate C. of C. (founding mem.), Rotary. Home: 12018 17th Ave NE Seattle WA 98125-5116 E-mail: ymart@earthlink.net.

MARTINEZ-CARBONELL, KARELIA, not-for-profit fundraiser; b. Havana, Cuba, Jan. 6, 1962; arrived in U.S., 1968, naturalized; d. Francisco and Amada Martinez; m. Marino E. Carbonell, May 29, 1983; 1 child, Brenden Marino Carbonell. BA, Fla. Internat. U., Miami, 1994, MBA, 1997; DPA, Nova Southeastern U., Fort Lauderdale, Fla., 2002. Dir. devel. Carrollton Sch. of the Sacred Heart, Coconut Grove, Fla., 1998—. Bd. dirs. St. Philip's Episcopal Sch., Coral Gables, Fla., 1995—. Contbr. articles to profl. jours. Mem. Jr. League of Miami, Coral Gables, Fla., 1995—2002; adv. com. Blue Ribbon Ethics Commn., Miami, Fla., 2000—02. Mem.: Ocean Reef Club, Riviera Country Club (arts com. 1992—2002), Pi Alpha Alpha. Republican. Roman Catholic. Avocations: reading, travel, research, writing. Office: Carrollton School of the Sacred Heart 3747 Main Highway Coconut Grove FL 33133 E-mail: kcarbonell@carrollton.org.

MARTINEZ FALLON, ALMA URANIA, mechanical engineer; b. Constanza, Dominican Republic, Dec. 1, 1958; m. Stephen J. Brady. BSME, Old Dominion U., 1987. Engr. submarine design Newport News Shipbuilding, 1988-92, sr. engr. comml. design, 1992-95, engrng. supr. aircraft carrier design, 1995-96, process mgr. process innovation, 1996—. Mem. ASME (mem. bd. on minorities and women 1996—), Soc. Women Engrs. (chmn. multi-cultural com. 1994-96, Disting. New Engr. 1997). Home: 2687 Heywood Ln Hayes VA 23072-4427

MARTINEZ-MALDONADO, MANUEL, medical service administrator, internist, nephrologist; b. Yauco, PR, Aug. 25, 1937; s. Manuel and Josefa Maldonado (Josefa Maldonado) Martinez; m. Nivia Elena Rivera, Dec. 18, 1959; children: Manuel, David, Ricardo, Pablo. BS, U. PR, 1957; MD, Temple U., 1961. Diplomate Am. Bd. Internal Medicine, Am. Bd. Nephrology. Intern St. Charles Hosp., Toledo, 1961—62; resident VA Hosp., San Juan, PR, 1962—65, chief resident, 1964—65; instr. U. Tex. Southwestern Med. Sch., Dallas, 1967—68; from asst. prof. to prof. medicine, dir. renal sect. Baylor Coll. Medicine, Houston, 1968—73; prof. medicine U. PR Sch. Medicine, 1973—90, prof. physiology, 1974—90; prof. medicine U. Caribbean, Bayamon, PR, 1980—90; chief med. svcs. VA Hosp., San Juan, 1973—90, dir. renal metabolic lab., 1973—90; prof., vice chmn. dept. medicine Emory U. Sch. Medicine, 1990—98; chief med. svcs. and clin. affairs Atlanta VA Med. Ctr., 1990—98; v.p. for rsch., prof. medicine Oreg. Health Scis. U., Portland, 1998—99, v.p. rsch., 1999—2000; pres., dean Ponce (PR) Sch. Medicine, 2000—. Assoc. mem. nephrology com. Am. Bd. Internal Medicine, 1982—86; nat. adv. bd. gen. medicine B study sect. Nat. Inst. Arthritis, Metabolism and Digestive Diseases NIH; bd. sci. counselors, sci. advisors com. Nat. Heart, Lung and Blood Inst., NIH. Author: La Voz Sostenida, 1984, Palm Beach Blues, 1986, Por Amor al Arte, 1989, Hotel Maria, 1989, Isla Verde, 1999, Novela de Medioidia, 2003; film critic: El Reportero, 1983—86, El Mundo, 1987—90, editor/co-editor: in field, mem. editl. bd.: U. P.R. Press; editor: Am. Jour. of Med. Scis., 1994—98, Am. Jour. Kidney Disease, 1997—2002; contbr. over 200 articles to profl. jours. Com. mem. 500th Anniversary of Discovery Am., PR, 1987—92; pres. bd. trustees Inst. Puerto Rican Culture and Performing Arts Ctr.; trustee Corp. for Musical Arts, Inst. Puerto Rican Lit.; chair culture and recreation panel P.R. 2025; health com. Popular Dem. Com., PR, 1982—84; bd. dirs. All for P.R., Inc. Named one of Outstanding Young Men, P.R. C. of C., 1976; recipient Lederle Internat. award, 1966—67, Macy Faculty Scholar award, 1979—80, Grand Mobil prize medicine, Mobil Oil Corp., 1981, Disting. Alumnus award, Temple Med. Sch., 1988, Presdl. award, Nat. Kidney Found., 1988, Donald W. Seldin award, 1994, Disting. Physician award, P.R. Hosps. Assn., 1988, Orden del Cafetal award, Municipality of Yauco, 1989, Abelardo Díaz Alfaro award, Medicine & Humanites, 2002. Fellow: AAAS, ACP, Am. Heart Assn. (hypertension rsch. coun.), Coun. for High Blood Pressure Rsch.; mem.: Nat. Kidney Found. (chmn. pub. policy com. 1992—94), Consortium Southeastern Hypertension Ctrs. (bd. dirs.), Assn. Am. Physicians, Inter-Am. Soc. Hypertension Assn. (bd. govs., chmn. 8th Sci. Congress 1989, U.S. Pharmacopeial Conv. Cardio Renal Drugs com. 1990—96), Am. Acad. Arts and Scis. (hon.), L.Am. Soc. Nephrology (v.p. 1987—91, pres.-elect 1991—94, pres. 1994—96, Miatello award 1999), Am. Soc. for Clin. Investigation, So. Soc. Clin. Investigation (sec.-treas. 1983—85, pres. 1985—86, Founders medal 1990, Pub. Svc. medal, Donald W. Seldin award), Am. Soc. Nephrology (legis. liaison com., chmn. audit com. 1988), Inst. Medicine of NAS (com. on human rights 1987—92), Alpha Omega Alpha. Achievements include research in kidney physiology and pathophysiology, treatment of clinical disturbances of blood composition, clinical use of diuretics, mechanisms of the devel. of hypertension. Office Phone: 787-844-3710. Personal E-mail: martinem_pms@hotmail.com. Business E-Mail: mmartinez@psm.edu.

MARTINEZ-MUNOZ, HECTOR, lawyer; b. San Juan, PR, Dec. 14, 1924; s. Oscar Martinez-Mercado and Soledad Munoz-Deucheth; m. Lily Jimenez, July 29, 1950; children: Hector, Marisol, Maria Emilia, Carlos Fernando. BS in Bus. Adminstrn., Va. Poly. Inst., 1947; LLB, U. P.R., 1951. Bar: P.R. 1951, U.S. Dist. Ct. P.R. 1951, U.S. Ct. Appeals (1st cir.) 1952. Assoc. Cordova & Gonzalez, 1951—59; ptnr. Martinez-Munoz, Agrait & Otero, 1960—70; assoc. justice P.R. Supreme Ct., San Juan, 1970—73; ptnr. Blanco-Lugo, Martinez-Munoz, Moran & Lavastida, San Juan, 1974—76, Brown, Newsom & Cordova, San Juan, 1976—. Mem. P.R. Bd. Bar Examiners, 1962—63, chmn., 1970—73; chmn. jud. reform com. Jud. Conf., 1973; mem. Adv. Com. to Gov. P.R. on Jud. Appointments, 1977—82; chmn. Jud. Nominating Com. for U.S. Dist. Ct. for Dist. P.R., 1979. Mem. coun. higher edn. U. P.R., 1979. Served with U.S. Army, 1946. Fellow: Am. Bar Found., Am. Coll. Trial Lawyers (state chmn. 1981—); mem.: Asociacion Fraternal de Amigos. Roman Catholic. Office: PO Box 3464 San Juan PR 00902-3464

MARTINEZ-PONS, MANUEL, psychologist, educator; b. Dominican Republic, Apr. 19, 1940; arrived in US, 1954; s. Manuel and Alsacia (Gorsd) Martinez. AA, U. State of N.Y., 1973, BS, 1975; BGS, U. Nebr., Omaha, 1973, MS, 1975; PhD, U. Nebr., Lincoln, 1977; MPh, CUNY, 1985, PhD, 1988. Lic. pilot. Rsch. assoc. CUNY, 1982-85, instr. computer programing, 1985-86, assoc. prof. Sch. Edn., Bklyn. Coll., 1986—2004, prof. Sch. Edn., Bklyn. Coll., 2004—. Adj. instr. U. Nebr., Lincoln, 1975—77, Omaha, 1978; adj. instr. City Coll. CUNY, 1980—81, adj. asst. prof. Medgar Evers Coll., 1985, adj. asst. prof. Queens Coll., 86. Author (with others): (book) Student Perceptions in the Classroom: Causes and Consequences, 1992; author: Research in the Social Sciences and Education: Principles and Process, 1997, Statistics in Modern Research: Applications in the Social Sciences and Education, 1999, The Psychology of Teaching and Learning: A Three-Step Guide, 2001, Le tranfert effectiv comme un processus d'auto-regulation, 2002, Continuum Guide to Successful Teaching in Higher Education, 2003; cons. editor: Jour. Exptl. Edn., 1997—; contbr. articles to profl. jours. Recipient numerous grants. Mem.: Am. Psychol. Soc., Am. Ednl. Rsch. Assn., Am. Mensa. Home: 453 Beach 138th St Rockaway Park NY 11694-1341 Office: Brooklyn Coll Sch of Edn Brooklyn NY 11210 Office Phone: 718-951-5068. Personal E-mail: mpons@msn.com.

MARTINEZ-SOLIS, LUIS FERNANDO, journalist, writer, historian; b. Medellin, Antioquia, Colombia, Apr. 29, 1946; arrived in U.S., 1999; s. Edelberto A. Martínez-Márquez and Myriam C. Solís-Escobar; m. Alicia Ester Posada; children: Isabel Kristina, Ludoviko Ernesto, Enver Kamilo. BA in Journalism, Antioquia U., Medellin, 1987; Tchg. Cert., Nat. Learn Svc. SENA, Apartado, Colombia, 1996; Historian and Academic (hon.), Antioquia History Acad., Medellin, 1998. Speech writer CORVIDE, Medellin, 1992—99; human develoment SENA, Apartado, 1996—99; Spanish composition Cooperativ U., Turbo, Colombia, 1997—98; comm. theory Apya Yala U., Apartado, 1997—98; columnist, editor El Periodiko, St. Louis, 1999—. Journalist Comunal Action, Medellin, 1970—85, Patriot Union, Medellin, 1985—99. Author: (27 books) Geopolitics and Comunications, 1998; editor: (newspaper) EL PERIODIKO, 2001. Recipient Gold Medal, SEDUCA, 1987, Heroic Journalism award, SIP, 1989, Ariza Flower flower, COMFENALCO, 1998. Mem.: Universala Esperanto Asocio (rotterdam 1970—). Avocations: walking, athletics. Office: El Periodiko 2nd Fl 3337 Texas Ave Saint Louis MO 63118 Business E-Mail: elperiodiko@cs.com.

MARTING, MICHAEL G. lawyer; b. Cleve., Nov. 5, 1948; BA summa cum laude, Yale U., 1971, JD, 1974. Bar: Ohio 1974. Assoc. Jones, Day, Reavis & Pogue, Cleve., 1974-83, ptnr., 1984—. Mem.: Chagrin Valley Hunt Club, Tavern Club (treas., sec., trustee local chpt. 1985—88), Cleve. Racquet Club, Union Club. Avocations: fly fishing, bird shooting, big game hunting, squash. Office: Jones Day Reavis & Pogue N Point 901 Lakeside Ave E Cleveland OH 44114-1190

MARTINI, PERRY JAMES, educational consultant; b. Warren, Ohio, Apr. 20, 1948; s. Perry Enio and Angeline Martini; m. Jean Marie Gaby, Mar. 24, 1952; children: Yolanda Joan, Ellen Raffaela, Stephen Ray Collins, Bernadette Mitchell. BS, US Naval Acad., 1971; MA in Strategic Studies, Navy War Coll., 1989; MEd, Marymount U., 1994; MS, Salve Regina Coll., 1989; EdD, George Wash. U., 2000. Commd. ensign USN, 1971, advanced through grades to capt., ret., 1998; asst. sec. higher edn. Md. Higher Edn. Commn., Annapolis, Md., 1998—2000; assoc. dir. class giving US Naval Acad. Found., 2000—03; dir. exec. leadership programs Acad. Leadership, King of Prussia, Pa., 2003—. Leadership cons. Acad. Leadership, King of Prussia, 2003—; adj. prof. Regent U., Alexandria, Va., 2001. Author: Inspiring Leadership: Character and Ethics Matter. Named to Ohio Football Hall Fame, Trumbull Hall Fame, 1990. Mem.: U.S. Naval Acad. Alumni Assn. (life; pres., trustee 1980—). Conservative. Avocations: travel, golf, reading, speaking. Home: 853 Holly Drive South Annapolis MD 21401 Office: Academy Leadership 10120 Valley Forge Circle King Of Prussia PA 19406 Office Phone: 610-783-0630. Personal E-mail: pjmartini@comcast.net. E-mail: pmartini@academyleadership.com.

MARTINI, RICHARD K. theatrical producer; b. Bergenfield, N.J., Mar. 11, 1952; s. John F. and June L. (Fenton) M.; m. Susan C. Weaving, Aug. 1, 1981. BA, St. Francis Coll., Loretto, Pa., 1974; MEd, U. S.C., 1975. V.p. Am. Theatre Prodns., N.Y.C., 1975-81; pres. Edgewood Orgn., N.Y.C., 1981-86; pres., owner KL Mgmt., N.Y.C., 1986—; owner, operator Martini Entertainment, Inc., N.Y.C., 1991—. Home: 201 E 37th St New York NY 10016-3159 Office: Martini Entertainment Co 1501 Broadway Ste 1401 New York NY 10036-5601

MARTINI, ROBERT EDWARD, wholesale pharmaceutical and medical supplies company executive; b. Hackensack, N.J., 1932; BS, Ohio State U., 1954. With Bergen Brunswig Corp., Orange, Calif., 1956-92, v.p., 1962-69, exec. v.p., 1969-81, pres., 1981-92, CEO, 1990-97, chmn., 1992—. Chmn. exec. com. Bergen Brunswig Corp. Capt. USAF, 1954.

MARTINI, WILLIAM J. former congressman, state commissioner, judge; b. Passaic, N.J. m. Gloria Martini; children: William Jr., Marissa. Degree, Villanova U., 1968; JD, Rutgers U., 1972. Elected mem. City Coun. of Clifton, N.J., Passaic County Bd. Chosen Freeholders, U.S. House of Reps., 1994-96; ptnr. Sills Cummis Radin Tischman Epstein & Gross PA, Newark; commr. Port Authority of N.Y. and N.J.; judge U.S. Dist Ct. N.J. Pres. Nicholas Martini Found.; trustee United Way of Passaic County, Ctr. Italian Am. Culture, Passaic Valley Coun. Boys Scouts of Am., Hackensack U. Med. Ctr., Freedom House. Republican. Office: US Dist Ct Newark NJ 07102

MARTIN-LIAMAZARES, CARLOS, academic administrator; b. Madrid, Mar. 20, 1970; arrived in U.S.A., 1998; s. Antonio Martin-Rodriguez and Margarita liamazares-Palazon. MA in Gen. Psychology, U. Madrid; student, Northeastern Ill. U., 2002—. Youth program coord. Social Psychology and Methodology Dept. U. Madrid, 1993—95; cons. Ednl. and Social Rsch. Inst., Madrid, 1996—98; clk. ADECCO, Chgo., 1999—2000; ednl. advisor Lulac Nat. Ednl. Svc. Ctr., Chgo., 2000—02; multicultural specialist Truman Coll., Chgo., 2002—. Leader Boy Scouts, Madrid, 1989—93. Avocation: music. Home: 2326 1/2 N Spaulding 2A Chicago IL 60647

MARTINO, CHERYL DERBY, insurance company secretary; b. Paterson, N.J., Jan. 19, 1946; d. Elles Mayo and Sarah Emma (Steele) D.; m. Leonard D. Martino, Nov. 4, 1995. BA, Elmira Coll., 1967; MBA, NYU, 1982. Tchr. Ramsey (N.J.) High Sch., 1967-70; contbns. analyst Met. Life Ins. Co., N.Y.C., 1970-83, fin. writer investments dept., 1983-93, asst. sec., 1994—. Bd. trustees United Meth. Ch. of Waldwick, N.J., v.p., 1989-91, pres., 1992-93, fin. sec., 2000—. Fellow Life Mgmt. Inst. (bd. dirs. Greater N.Y. chpt. 1984-91, pres. 1986, edn. coun. 1990-93), Life Mgmt. Inst. Edn. Coun. (nat. adminstrv. com. chmn. 1990-92, mktg. subcom. 1985-93), Nat. Orchestral Assn. (bd. dirs. 1990-92); mem. Elmira Coll. Alumni Club N.J. (exec. bd. 1982-87); mem. alumni bd. dirs. Elmira Coll.,1992—. Methodist. Office: Met Life 1 Madison Ave New York NY 10010-3603

MARTINO, DONALD JAMES, composer, clarinetist, educator; b. Plainfield, N.J., May 16, 1931; s. James Edward and Alma Ida (Renz) M.; m. Mari Rice, Sept. 5, 1953 (div. June 1968); 1 child, Anna Maria; m. Lora Harvey, June 5, 1969; 1 child, Christopher James. BMus, Syracuse U., 1952; MFA, Princeton U., 1954; MA (hon.), Harvard U., 1983. Instr. music Princeton U., 1957-59; asst. prof. theory music Yale U., 1959-66, assoc. prof., 1966-69; chmn. dept. composition New Eng. Conservatory Music, Boston, 1969-80; Irving Fine prof. music Brandeis U., 1980-82; prof. music Harvard U., 1983—, Walter Bigelow Rosen prof. music, 1989-93; Walter Bigelow Rosen prof. emeritus, 1993—. Tchr. composition and theory Yale Summer Sch. of Music and Art, 1960-63; tchr. composition Berkshire Music Ctr., summers, 1965-67, 69; composer in residence Berkshire Music Ctr., 1973, Composers' Conf., Johnson, Vt., summer 1979, May in Miami, 1994, Festival Internat. Musica de Morelia, Mex., 1996, Composers' Conf., Wellesley, Mass., 1997, Ernest Block Music Festival Composers Conf., Newport, Oreg., summer 1998; vis. lectr. Harvard U., 1971; Maurice Abravanel vis. disting. composer U. Utah, 1994, Mary Duke Biddle disting. composer Duke U., 1995; master artist-in-residence Atlantic Ctr. for the Arts, 1997; BMI composer in residence Vanderbilt U., 1998. Composer: Separate Songs, 1951; for high voice and piano, Sonata for Clarinet and Piano, 1951, Piano Quartet, 1951, With Little Children In Mind, 1951, String Quartet No. 2, 1951, The Bad Child's Book of Beasts, 1952, Suite of Variations on Medieval Melodies cello sonata, 1952; String Quartet No. 3, 1953, sonata for Violin and Piano, A Set for Clarinet, 1954, Quodlibets for Flute, 1954, Three Dances for Viola and Piano, 1954, String Trio, 1954, Three Songs, 1955, Portraits; a secular cantata for chorus, soloists and orch., 1955, Sette Canoni Enigmatici, 1956, Contemplations for Orch. (commd. by Paderewski Fund), 1956, 24 Tin Pan Alley Tunes, 1956, Quartet for Clarinet and Strings, 1957, After Lennie, Canon Ball, Cathy, Three Way, Late In The Day (performed by Core Ensemble with Martio clarinet soloist, Boston and on tour 2991-97), Mac Fugal, Lover Come Bach, 1957, Piano Fantasy, 1958, Trio for violin, clarinet and piano, 1959, Cinque Frammenti, 1961, Two Rilke Songs, 1961, Fantasy-Variations for violin, 1962, Concerto for Wind Quintet (commd. by Fromm Found. and Berkshire Music Center), 1964, Parisonatina Al'Dodecafonia; for cello solo, 1964, Concerto for Piano and Orch. (commd. by New Haven Symphony), 1965, B, a, b, b, it, t; for clarinet, 1966, Strata; for bass clarinet, 1966, Mosaic for grand orch. (commd. for Chgo. Symphony by U. Chgo.), 1967, Pianississimo; sonata for piano, 1970, Seven Pious Pieces, 1971, Concerto for Violoncello and Orch., 1972, Augenmusik, 1972, Notturno, 1973 (Naumburg Chamber Music award commn., Pulitzer prize in music 1974), Paradiso Choruses for Chorus, Soloists, Orch. and Tape, 1974 (Paderewski Fund commn., Classical Critics citation Record World mag. 1976), Ritorno for Orch. (Plainfield Symphony Bicentennial commn.), 1975, Triple Concerto for Clarinet, Bass Clarinet and Contrabass Clarinet with Chamber Ensemble (N.Y. State Council on Arts and Andrew W. Mellon Found. commn.), 1977, Impromptu for Roger; piano solo, 1977, Quodlibets II (Am. Music Ctr. commn.); flute solo, 1980, Fantasies and Impromptus, piano solo (Koussevitzky Found. commn.), 1981, Divertisements for Youth Orch. (Groton, Mass. Arts Ctr. Commn.), 1981, Suite in Old Form, piano solo, 1982, String Quartet (Elizabeth Sprague Coolidge Commn., winner 1st prize Kennedy Ctr. Friedheim Awards 1985), 1983, Canzone e Tarantella, clarinet and cello, 1984, The White Island, for chorus and chamber orc. (Boston Symphony Centennial Commn.), 1985, Concerto for Alto Saxophone and Chamber Orch. (Nat. Endowment Consortium commn.), 1987, From the Other Side, Divertimento for Flute, Cello, Percussion and Piano (commd. by Flederman New Music Ensemble for the Australian Bicentennial, 1988), 12 Preludes (commd. Meet the Composer-Readers Digest), 1990, 15, 5, '92 AB for Carinet solo, 1992, Three Sad Songs, 1993, Viola and Piano (Elizabeth Sprague Coolidge commn.), Concerto for Violin and Orchestra (Nat. Endowment Commn.), 1997, Variazioni sopra un soggetto cavato, cl. solo, 1998, Serenata Concertante (Koussevitzky Found. Com.), 1999, Piccolo Studio, Alto Saxaphone solo, 1999, Romanza, Violin solo, 1999, Sonata for Violin Solo (Naumburg commn.), 2002, Trio for Cello Clarinet & Piano (NY New Music Ensemble Commn.), 2003, Soliloquy for Vibraphone (Michael Parola Commn.), 2003, Trio for Cello, Viraphone and Piano (Core Ensemble Commn.), 2003, Concertino for Clarinet and orch., 2003, String Quartet No. 5, 2004, Sonata No. 2 for Violin and piano, 2004, numerous others; contbr. articles to profl. jours. Recipient BMI Student Composer awards, 1952-53; Bonsall fellow, 1953-54; Kosciuszko scholar, 1953-54; Nat. Fedn. Music Clubs award, 1953; Kate Neal Kinley fellow U. Ill., 1954-55; Fulbright grantee Florence, Italy, 1954-56; Pacifica Found. award, 1961; Creative Arts citation Brandeis U., 1963; Morse Acad. fellow, 1965; Nat. Inst. Arts and Letters grantee, 1967; Guggenheim fellow, 1967-68, 73-74, 82-83; Nat. Endowment on Arts grantee, 1973, 76, 79, 89, Mass. Council on Arts grantee, 1973, 79, 89; recipient Pulitzer prize in music, 1974, Kennedy Ctr. Friedheim Awards 1st prize, 1985, Mark M. Horblit award Boston Symphony Orch., 1987, Paul Revere award for mus. autography Music Publ. Assn., 1990-92. Mem. AAAS, AAAL, Coll. Music Soc., Am. Composers Alliance, Broadcast Music Inc., Am. Music Ctr., Internat. Soc. Contemporary Music (a founder New Haven chpt. 1964, dir. U.S. sect. 1961-64), Am. Soc. U. Composers (founding mem., exec. com. 1965-66, trustee 1965—), Internat. Clarinet Soc. Office: Harvard U Dept Music Cambridge MA 02138 E-mail: dantinfo@dantalian.com.

MARTINO, DONNA FRANCES, newspaper sales administrator; BA, Coll. Mt. St. Vincent, 1969; MA, Columbia U., 1972. Cert. early childhood tchr., N.Y., N.J. Acct. mgr. Contra Costa Times, Walnut Creek, Calif., 1980-83; nat. acct. mgr. San Francisco Chronicle/Examiner, 1983-85; retail acct. exec. The N.Y. Times, N.Y.C., 1986—96, nat. acct. mgr., 1994-96; nat. sales mgr. pharms. advt. Newspaper Nat. Network, N.Y.C., 1996—2000; dir. pharm. Valassis Commn., 2000—02; cons., bd. mem. bus. mgr. Media Women, Inc., 2003—. Mem. Columbia U. Alumni Club Bergen/Passaic Counties (bd. dir., pres. 1998-2000). Avocations: sailing, rock climbing, antiques, art.

MARTINO, FRANK DOMINIC, union executive; b. Albany, N.Y., Apr. 9, 1919; s. Benedetto and Rosina (Esposita) M.; m. Phyllis E. Higgins, June 15, 1963; children— Michael M., Lisa R. Student, Rutgers U., Cornell U., Oxford U. Timekeeper N.Y.C. R.R., 1937-41; chem. operator Sterling Drug Co., 1946-56; internat. rep. Internat. Chem. Workers Union, Akron, Ohio, 1956-70, internat. v.p., 1970-72, sec.-treas., 1972-75; internat. pres. Internat. Chem. Workers Union Coun./United Food Comml. Workers/UFCW, 1975—; Washington rep., dir. Internat. Chem. Workers Union Coun./USCW, 1962-70. Served with USAF, 1941-45. Democrat. Roman Catholic. Office: Internat Chem Workers Union Coun/UFCW 1655 W Market St Akron OH 44313-7004

MARTINO, JOSEPH F. bishop; b. Phila., May 1, 1946; Student, St. Charles Borromeo Sem., Overbrook, Pa., Gregorian U. Rome. Ordained priest Roman Cath. Ch. 1970. Titular bishop Diocese of Cellae, 1996—; bishop Diocese of Phila., 1996—2003, Diocese of Scranton, Pa., 2003—.

MARTINO, JOSEPH PAUL, research scientist, researcher; b. Warren, Ohio, July 16, 1931; s. Joseph and Anna Elizabeth (Kubina) M.; m. Mary Lou Bouquot, May 18, 1957 (dec. Jan. 1988); children: Theresa, Anthony, Michael; m. Nancy McCoy, Dec. 28, 2000. AB, Miami U., Ohio, 1953; MS, Purdue U., 1955; PhD, Ohio State U., 1961. Commd. 2d lt. USAF, 1953, advanced through grades to col., 1973, project engr. armament lab., 1955-58, mathematician Office Sci. Rsch. Washington, 1961-62, staff scientist Avionics Lab. Wright-Patterson AFB, 1972-73, dir. engring. standardization Def. Electronics Supply Ctr. Dayton, Ohio, 1973-75, ret., 1975; sr. scientist, rsch. inst. U. Dayton, 1975-93. Author: Technological Forecasting for Decisionmaking, 1972, rev. edit., 1983, 3d edit., 1992, A Fighting Chance-The Moral Use of Nuclear Weapons, 1988, Science Funding: Politics and Porkbarrel, 1992, Research and Development Project Selection, 1995, (novel) The Justice Cooperative, 2004; assoc. editor: Tech. Forecasting and Social Change Jour., 1968—. Fellow IEEE, AAAS, AIAA (assoc.); mem. Inst. for Ops. Rsch. and Mgmt. Sci., Am. Soc. Engring. Mgmt., Engrs. Club of Dayton. Roman Catholic. Office Phone: 937-492-4729. E-mail: j.p.martino@iee.org.

MARTINO, MICHAEL CHARLES, entertainer, musician, actor; b. Phila., Sept. 10, 1950; s. Salvatore Joseph and Marie Angela (Langone) M. Grad. high sch., Upper Darby, Pa. Spokesperson/rep. Petosa Accordion Co., Seattle, 1979—; featured TV entertainer Mike Martino Show, Delaware County, Pa., 1987-89; accordion tchr. Drexel Hill, Pa., 1989—; featured artist Am. Accordion Soc. Conv., King of Prussia, Pa., 2003; actor TV series Hack, Channel 3, 2003. Entertainer, host, prodr. St. Jude's Children's Hosp. Marathon, King of Prussia, Pa., 1973; opening act comedian Morty Gunty, 1973, Pat Cooper, Phila., 1981; guest artist, entertainer Internat. Platform Assn. Conv., Washington, 1979, Am. Accordion Musicological Soc. Festival and symposium, King of Prussia, 2003; nite club performer Glen Mills, Pa., 1989; actor TV comml s., Elkton, Md., 1979, Halloween Spl. KYW-TV, Phila., 1986, TV show Hack, 2003; performed radio contest jingle Sta. KISS 100 radio, Media, Pa., 1992; featured soloist Am. Accordian Festival, King of Prussia, Pa., 2003. Author: (movie) Forever Fiftys, 1990; composer, dir., prodr., actor: (video) Forever Fiftys; composer: (movie) That First September; creator, performer Suspended Triple Bellows Shake Technique for the Accordion, 1994; composer (ballad) Through the Music, Through the Words I Sing, 1995, Through the Music Through the Words I sing, 1998; actor: (movie) Jesus' Son, 1999, (TV show) Hack, 2003; guest performer Accordion Conv., King of Prussia, 2003. Recipient citation U.S. Ho. Reps., 1989, Proclamation Mike Martino Day Mayor Ward, Del. County, 1988, Danny Thomas Hon. award St. Jude's Hosp., Del. County, 1973, Mayor's Svc. award Upper Darby, Pa., 1994. Roman Catholic. Avocations: antique cars, dogs. Home: 2530 Stoneybrook Ln Drexel Hill PA 19026-1610 Office Phone: 610-789-5753.

MARTINO, PETER DOMINIC, financial software company executive, real estate developer, real estate broker, federal agency administrator, consultant; b. N.Y.C., Sept. 21, 1963; s. Rocco Leonard and Barbara Italia (D'Iorio) Martino; m. Manelle Victoria Nunez, July 31, 2004; 1 child, Elizabeth Marie. BS, U.S. Naval Acad., 1985; postgrad., Georgetown U., 2004—. Cert. cash mgr.; cert. Treasury profl. Commd. ensign USN, 1985, advanced through grades to lt., 1989, resigned, 1990; with USNR, 1990-99; from v.p. mktg. to exec. v.p., COO XRT, Inc., Wayne, Pa., 1990-93, pres., 1993-98, CEO, 1996-98; pres., CEO XRT-CERG Am., Inc., 1998-2000; exec. v.p. XRT-CERG S.A., Paris, 1998-2000; pres., CEO, chmn., founder CharitEx, Inc., N.Y.C., 2000—01; real estate broker Corcoran Group, N.Y.C., 2001—03; real estate developer, 2001—03; COO dept. homeland security Infrastructure Protection, U.S. Govt. Sr. Exec. Svc., Washington, 2003—04; pres., CEO, founder The Develop. Coun., LLC, Washington, 2004—. Founder, dir. XRT Europe, Ltd., 1994-98; founder, dir., pres Four Star Software, Inc., Wayne, 1994-98; bd. dirs. Nat. Kidney Found. Delaware Valley; founder internet e-commerce bus. for charitable giving. Mem. Phoenixville Borough Coun., 1993—94; Rep. committeeman, 1995—97; mem. coun. Nat. Italian Am. Found., 2003; bd. dir. Nat. Kidney Found. Delaware Valley, 1997—2001, Martino Found., 1998—2003, World Affairs Coun. Phila., 1999—2001; adv. bd. Pres.'s Cir. Naval Acad. Found, 2002—03. Mem. Treasury Mgmt. Assn., Naval Acad. Alumni Assn., Naval Acad. Athletic Assn., Naval Acad. Sailing Squadron, Nat. Italian Am. Found. (coun. mem.), N.Y. Athletic Club, Pyramid Club (Phila.), Avalon Yacht Club, Army-Navy Club. Roman Catholic. Avocations: sailing, boating, real estate, fine wine, architecture. Home: 168 W Lake Dr Annapolis MD 21403 Office: The Development Coun LLC 128 Lubrano Dr Ste 200 Annapolis MD 21401 Personal E-mail: pmartino@igi.net. Business E-Mail: peter.martino@dhs.gov.

MARTINO, ROBERT SALVATORE, orthopedic surgeon; b. Clarksburg, W.Va., May 31, 1931; s. Leonard L. and Sarafina (Foglia) M.; m. Lenora Cappellanti, May 22, 1954; children: Robert S. Jr., Leslie F. Reckziegal. AB, W.Va. U., 1953, postgrad., 1955-56, BS in Medicine, 1958; MD, Northwestern U., 1960. Diplomate Am. Bd. Orthop. Surgery; lic. Ill., Calif., Ind. Intern Chgo. Wesley, 1960-61; resident dept. orthopaedic surgery Northwestern U., 1961-65, Chgo. Wesley Meml., 1961-62, Am. Legion Hosp. for Crippled Children, 1962-63, Cook County Hosp., Chgo., 1964, 64-65; orthopaedic surgeon Gary, Ind., 1965-67; orthopaedic surgeon Merrillville, Ind., 1967—. Fellow Nat. Found. Infantile Paralysis, 1956, Office of Vocat. Rehab., Hand Surgery, 1965; chief of staff St. Mary Med. Ctr., 1976, chief of surgery, 1974-85; chief of staff Gary Treatment Ctr./Ind. Crippled Children's Svcs., 1974-84; adj. asst. prof. anatomy Ind. U., 1978, clin. asst. prof. orthop. surgery, 1980, emeritus asst. prof. anatomy and cell biology Ind. U., 2003, emeritus clin. asst. prof. orthop. surgery, 2003; mem. Zoning Bd., 1989-90. Chmn. Planning Bd. Town of Dune Acres, 1992-96; bd. dirs. United Steel Workers Union Health Plan, 1994—, St. Mary's Med. Ctr., Hobart, Ind.; com. on Health Care Reform. Capt. U.S. Army, 1953-56. Fellow ACS (emeritus), Am. Acad. Orthop. Surgery (emeritus); mem. AMA, Ind. Med. Soc., Ill. Med. Soc., Chgo. Med. Soc., Ill. Orthop. Soc., Ind. Orthop. Soc., Mid-Am. Orthop. Assn., Tri-State Orthop. Soc., Clin. Orthop. Soc. Home: 22 Oak Dr Dune Acres IN 46304-1016 Office Phone: 219-887-9506. Personal E-mail: indorth@aol.com.

MARTINO, SILVANA, osteopath, medical oncologist; b. Guardia Piemontese, Italy, Sept. 7, 1948; came to U.S., 1958; d. Antonio and Elena (Iannuzzi) M. BS in Psychology, Wayne State U., 1970; DO, Mich. State U., 1973. Bd. cert. internal medicine and med. oncology. Intern Detroit Osteo. Hosp., 1973-74; resident in internal medicine Botsford Hosp., Farmington, Mich., 1974-77; fellow in oncology Wayne State U. Sch. Medicine, Detroit, 1977-79, asst. prof. med., 1979-88, assoc. prof., 1988-93; med. dir. Westlake Comprehensive Breast Ctr., Westlake Village, Calif., 1993-97, Breast Ctr., Van Nuys, Calif., 1997-99; med. oncologist John Wayne Cancer Inst., Santa Monica, Calif., 1999—. Full-time staff Harper-Grace Hosps., Detroit, 1979-93, coord. oncology housestaff 1979-83; univ. affiliate, sect. of oncology, dept. medicine, Hutzel Hosp., Detroit, 1979-93; clin. advisor breast cancer prognostic study Mich. Cancer Found., Detroit, 1981-86; univ. affiliate dept. medicine Detroit Receiving Hosp., 1983-93; adj. faculty dept. medicine Wayne State U. 1989-92; mem. oncology drug adv. com. FDA, 2002-2006; spkr. in field. Co-author: Diet & Cancer: Markers, Prevention and Treatment, 1994; contbr. articles to profl. jours., chpt. to book. Bd. dirs. Wellness Cmty., Conjeo Valley/Ventura, Calif., 1995-99; bd. dirs. ACS Greater Conjeo Valley Unit, Thousand Oaks, Calif., 1994-99. Fellow Am. Coll. Osteo. Internists; mem. AAAS, Am. Osteo. Assn., Am. Soc. Clin. Oncology, Internat. Assn. Breast Cancer Rsch., Am. Soc. of Preventive Oncology, Am. Assn. for Cancer Rsch., Inc., Southwest Oncology Group (chair breast com. 1992-2000, co-chair cancer control rsch. com. 87-92, oncology adv. com. 2002—), Oncology Drug Adv. Com. for FDA, 2002-06. Office Phone: 310-582-7900. E-mail: martinos@jwci.org.

MARTINS, HEITOR MIRANDA, foreign language educator; b. Belo Horizonte, Brazil, July 22, 1933; came to U.S., 1960; s. Joaquim Pedro and Emilia (Miranda) M.; m. Teresomja Alves Pereira, Nov. 1, 1958 (div. 1977); children— Luzia Pereira, Emilia Pereira; m. Marlene Andrade, Jan. 11, 1984 AB, U. Federal de Minas Gerais, 1959; PhD, U. Federal de Minas Gerais, 1962. Instr. U. N.M., Albuquerque, 1960-62; asst. prof. Tulane U., New Orleans, 1962-66, assoc. prof., 1966-68; prof. dept. Spanish and Portuguese Ind. U., Bloomington, 1968—, chmn. dept., 1972-76. Vis. prof. U. Tex., Austin, 1963, Stanford U. 1968 Author: poetry Sirgo nos Cabelos, 1961; essay Manuel de Galhegos, 1964; essays Oswald de Andrade e Outros, 1973; critical anthology Neoclassicismo, 1982; Essays Do Barroco a Guimarães Rosa, 1983; editor: essays Luso-Brazilian Literary Studies. Social Sci. Research Council grantee, 1965; Fulbright-Hays Commn. grantee, 1966; Ford Found. grantee, 1970, 71 Mem. MLA, Renaissance Soc. Am., Am. Comparative Lit. Assn., Am. Assn. for 18th Century Studies. Home: 1316 S Nancy St Bloomington IN 47401-6050 Office: Indiana U Dept Spanish and Portuguese Bloomington IN 47405 E-mail: martins@indiana.edu.

MARTINS, NELSON, physics educator; b. Santos, Brazil, Oct. 18, 1930; s. Aniceto and Angelica Martins; m. Maria Lucia, Jan. 8, 1959 (div. Sept. 1983); children: Flavia, Paulo. BS in Physics, Mackenzie U., São Paulo, Brazil, 1958; D in Physics, Pontifica U., Campinas, Brazil, 1977. Cert. physicist. Dir. engring. Mackenzie U., 1971-73, dir. Exact Sci., 1983-90; gen. dir. Ednl. Found., Barretos, Brazil, 1973-76; chief physics dep. Engring. Sch., Araraquara, Brazil, 1991; chief physics dept. U. Santo Amaro, São Paulo, 1990-92; dir. CCET Ctr. Exact Scis. and Tech., São Paulo, 1992-95. Author: (with others) Electriciy and Magnetism, 1973, Dimensional Analysis, 1980, Dynamics, 1982. Mem. Am. Assn. Physics Tchrs., Brazil Soc. Physics. Office: Sorocaba Engring Sch Rod Sen Jose Ermirio Moraes Sorocaba 18001970 Brazil

MARTINS, PETER, ballet master, choreographer, dancer; b. Copenhagen, Oct. 27, 1946; arrived in U.S., 1967, naturalized, 1970; m. Lisa LaCour (div.); 1 child, Nilas; m. Darci Kistler. Pupil of Vera Volkova and Stanley Williams with Royal Danish Ballet. With N.Y.C. Ballet, 1967—, tchr., 1975, ballet master, 1981-83, co-ballet master-in-chief, 1983 89; ballet master-in-chief, 1989—. Tchr. Sch. Am. Ballet, 1975; artistic advisor Pa. Ballet, 1982—. Choreographer Broadway musicals Dream of the Twins, 1982, On Your Toes, 1982, Song and Dance, 1985, Calcium Light Night, 1977, Tricolore-Pas de Basque sect., 1978, Rossini Pas de Deaux, 1978, ice ballet Tango-Tango, 1978, Dido and Aeneas, 1979, Sonate di Scarlatti, 1979, Eight Easy Pieces, 1980, Lille Suite, 1980, Suite from Histoire du Soldat, 1981, Capricio Italien, 1981, The Magic Flute, 1981, Symphony No. 1, 1981, Delibes Divertissement, 1982, Piano-Rag-Music, 1982, Concerto for Two Solo Pianos, 1982, Waltzes, 1983, Rossini Quartets, 1983, Tango, 1983, A Schubertiad, 1984, Mozart Violin Concerto, 1984, Poulenc Sonata, 1985, La Sylphide, 1985, Valse Triste, 1985, Eight More, 1985, We Are the World, 1985, Eight Miniatures, 1985, Ecstatic Orange, Tanzspiel, 1988, Jazz, 1993, Symphonic Dances, 1994, Barber Violin Concerto, 1994, Mozart Piano Concerto No. 17, 1994, X-Ray, 1995; author (autobiography): Far From Denmark, 1982. Named Knight of Order of Danneborg, Denmark, 1983; recipient Dance Mag. award, 1977, Golden Apple award, Cue, 1977, Merit award, Phila. Art Alliance, 1985, Liberty award, N.Y.C., 1986, H.C. Andersen Ballet prize, Royal Danish Theatre, 1988. Office: NY State Theater NYC Ballet 20 Lincoln Center Plz New York NY 10023-6913*

MARTINSON, CONSTANCE FRYE, television personality, television producer; b. Boston, Apr. 11, 1932; d. Edward and Rosalind Helen (Sperber) Frye; m. Leslie Herbert Martinson, Sept. 24, 1955; 1 child, Julianna Martinson Carner. BA in English Lit., Wellesley Coll., 1953. Dir. pub. rels. Coro Found., LA, 1974-79; prodr., host KHJ Dimensions, LA, 1979-81, Connie Martinson Talks Books, LA, 1981—. Instr. dept. humanities UCLA, 1981—, bd. dirs. Friends of English; moderator, instr. U. Judaism; celebrity advisor Book Fair-Music Ctr., LA, 1986; advisor, moderator LA Times Festival Books, 1996; TV rep. LA Pub. Libr. LA Cityview, Sta. WNYE-TV. Author: Dramatization of Wellesley After Images, 1974; book editor, columnist: Calif. Press Bur. Syndicate, 1986—, columnist: Beverly Hills Courier, 1997—. Pres. Mayor's Adv. Coun. Volunteerism, LA, 1981—82; chmn. cmty. affairs dept. Town Hall of Calif., LA, 1981—85; bd. dirs. legal def. fund NAACP, LA, 1981—84. Mem.: Nat. Book Critics Assn., PEN, Am. Film Inst., Women in Cable, Jewish TV Network (bd. dirs. 1985—87), Mulholland Tennis Club, Wellesley Coll. Club (pres. 1979—81). Democrat. Jewish. Avocations: tennis, theater, reading. Home and Office: 2288 Coldwater Canyon Dr Beverly Hills CA 90210-1756 E-mail: talksbooks@lycos.com.

MARTINSON, IDA MARIE, nursing educator, physiologist, medical/surgical nurse; b. Mentor, Minn., Nov. 8, 1936; d. Oscar and Marvel (Nelson) Sather; m. Paul Varo Martinson, Mar. 31, 1962; children: Anna Marie, Peter. Diploma, St. Luke's Hosp. Sch. Nursing, 1957; BS, U. Minn., 1960, M.N.A., 1962; PhD, U. Ill., Chgo., 1972. Instr. Coll. St. Scholastica and St. Luke's Sch. Nursing, 1957—58, Thornton Jr. Coll., 1967—69; lab. asst. U. Ill. at Med. Ctr., 1970—72; lectr. dept. physiology U. Minn., St. Paul, 1972—82, asst. prof. Sch. Nursing, 1972—74, assoc. prof. rsch., 1974—77, prof., dir. rsch., 1977—82; prof. dept. family health care U. Calif., San Francisco, 1982—2003, chmn. dept., 1982—90. Vis. rsch. prof. Nat. Taiwan U., Def. Med. Ctr., 1981; vis. prof. nursing Sun Yat-Sen U. Med. Scis., Guang Zhou, China, Ewha Women's U., Seoul, Republic of Korea, Frances Payne Bolton Sch. Nursing, Case Western Res. U., Cleve., 1994—96; chair, prof. dept. health scis. Hong Kong Poly. U., 1996—2000. Author: Mathematics for the Health Science Student, 1977; editor: Home Care for the Dying Child, 1976, Women in Stress, 1979, Women in Health and Illness, 1986, The Child and Family Facing Life Threatening Illness, 1987, Family Nursing, 1989, Home Health Care Nursing, 1989, Home Health Care Nursing, 2d edit., 2002; contbr. chapters to books, articles to profl. jours. Active Am. Cancer Soc. Recipient Book of Yr. award, Am. Jour. Nursing, 1977, 1980, 1987, 1990, Humanitarian award for pediat. nursing, 1993; fellow, Fulbright Found., 1991. Mem.: ANA, Inst. Medicine, Am. Acad. Nursing, Coun. Nurse Rschrs., Sigma Theta Tau, Sigma Xi. Lutheran. Address: 12149 E Movil Lake Rd NE Bemidji MN 56601 *The challenge of quality health care to all of society and the critical role nursing has to play in order to achieve this goal has motivated me throughout my professional life. The richness of talent in this country spurs me on.*

MARTINSON, RITA R. state legislator; b. Gloster, Miss., Sept. 11, 1937; d. D.M. and Beulah (LeDoux) Randall; m. William K. Martinson Sr., Aug. 2, 1958; children: Ginny Martinson Vampran, Karen Martinson McKie, W.K. Jr., Allen. BA in Polit. Sci., Millsaps Coll., 1991. Mem. Miss. Ho. of Reps., 1992—. Mem. Madison County Rep. Exec. Com., 1988-91; active Madison Arboretum, 1992—. Mem. Madison County C. of C. (Outstanding Citizen 1992), City of Madison C. of C., Madison County Rep. Women's Club, Ridgeland/Northpark Lions Club (past v.p. 1990-91), Ofcl. Miss. Women's Club (pres.), Rep. Elected Ofcls. Club (sec.). Roman Catholic. Avocations: flying, reading, gardening, photography. Home: 1472 Highway 51 Madison MS 39110-9095 Office: Miss State Ho of Reps PO Box 1018 Jackson MS 39215-1018

MARTINSSON, PER-GUNNAR JOHAN, mathematician, mechanical engineer; b. Goteborg, Sweden, Aug. 17, 1972;, US, 1996; s. Thomas and Inger Margareta Martinsson. MSc, Chalmers U. Tech., Goteborg, 1995, M in Math., 1998; PhD, U. Tex., 2002. Rsch. assoc. U. SC., Columbia, SC, 1996—97; gibbs instr. Yale U., New Haven, 2002—. Contbr. articles to profl. jours. Cipher analyst Swedish M.I., 1991—98, Lovon, Stockholm, Sweden. Recipient John Ericsson medal, Chalmers U. Tech., 1996; fellow, U. Tex., 1998—2001, Dissertation award, Sweden-America Found., 2001, Yale U., 2002—; scholar Swedish Physics Olympics Third Pl., Swedish Dept. Edn., 1991, Adlerbertska scholar, Chalmers U. Tech., 1995. Mem.: US Assn. Computational Mechanics, Soc. Indsl. Applied Math. Avocations: freediving, travel, music, cooking, spearfishing. Home: 412 Whitney Ave Apt 2 New Haven CT 06511 Office: Yale University Dept Math 10 Hillhouse Ave New Haven CT 06511 Personal E-mail: pgmartinsson@yahoo.com.

MARTINUZZI, LEO SERGIO, JR., banker; b. Newton, Mass., Aug. 1, 1928; s. Leo Sergio and Jessica (Stewart) M.; m. Helen Renfrew Gibson, Oct. 26, 1957; children: John James, Georgiana Gibson, Samuel Stewart. BA, Harvard U., 1950; B.Litt., Oxford U., 1952. With Chase Manhattan Bank, N.Y.C., 1956-81, asst. treas., 1960, asst. v.p. Japanese brs., 1961-64, v.p. Japanese brs., 1964-68, marketing exec. internat. staff, 1968-72, sr. v.p., 1971-81; corporate devel. officer Chase Manhattan Corp., 1972-75, group exec. info. services, 1975-81; chmn. Chase Econometric Assocs. Inc., 1975-80; sr. v.p. strategic planning Squibb Corp., 1981-87, cons., 1988-91. Chmn. Strategic Dimensions, Inc., 1990—; adj. prof. econs. Edison C.C., 1993-97. Lt. (j.g.) USNR, 1952-56. Home: 336 Galleon Dr Naples FL 34102-7638

MARTIROSYAN, KAREN, research scientist; b. Yerevan, Armenia, Aug. 3, 1962; arrived in U.S., 2001; s. Sergey and Margarita Martirosyan; m. Ivetta Martirosyan, June 26, 1961; children: Margarita, Alice. Doctoral, U. of Armenia, Yerevan, Armenia, 1991. Dept. head Sci. and Indsl. Ctr. of SHS, Yerevan, Armenia, 1993—97; prin. investigator Inst. of Phys. Chemistry, Moscow, 1997—2001; rschr. U. of Houston, Houston, 2001—. Author: (handbook) Powder metallurgy on the Third Millennium Eve, 2000; (discovery) Electromagnetic phenomenon during the rapid high-temperature chem. reactions, New environmentally appropriate synthesis of magnetic materials. Reviewer Powder Mettallurgy Com. of Armenia, Yerevan, Armenia, 1992—2001. Mem.: Powder Metallurgy Com. of Armenia, NY Acad. of Sci., Sigma-Xi. Home: 1420 Richmond 3043 Houston TX 77006 Office: University of Houston 4800 Calhoun Bld1 RmS222 Houston TX 77204 Office Phone: 713-743-4336. Business E-Mail: kmartirossian@uh.edu.

MARTIS, LEO, healthcare researcher; b. Pangala, Karnatka, India, June 3, 1945; s. Gregory and Apolina Martis; m. Jacintha B. Castelino, June 10, 1975; children: Sameeth, Nikhil. MS, U. Wash., 1970, PhD, 1973; MBA, Northwestern U., 1980. Diplomate Am. Bd. Toxicology. Postdoctoral fellow dept. neurosci. U. Wash., Seattle, 1973-74; mgr., dir., v.p. Baxter Healthcare, Deerfield, Ill, 1974—. Guest lectr. U. Ill., Chgo., 1985—. Contbr. over 200 articles and abstracts to sci. jours.; inventor in field. Pres. India Cath. Assn. Am., Chgo., 1992-93. Mem. Am. Soc. Nephrology, Fedn. Am. Socs. Exptl. Biology, Am. Soc. Pharmacology and Exptl. Therapeutics, Am. Soc. Toxicology, Am. Chem. Soc. Avocations: tennis, golf, running. Home: 5524 Old Wood Ln Long Grove IL 60047-8215 Office: Baxter Healthcare 1620 Waukegan Rd Waukegan IL 60085-6730 E-mail: martisl@baxter.com.

MARTLAND, T(HOMAS) R(ODOLPHE), philosophy educator; b. Port Chester, N.Y., May 29, 1926; s. Thomas Rodolphe and Anne Elizabeth (Newbury) M.; m. Agatha Murphy, Apr. 3, 1952; children: David Allen, Luke Thomas. BS magna cum laude, Fordham U., 1951; MA, Columbia U., 1955, PhD, 1959. Asst. prof. Lafayette Coll., Easton, Pa., 1959-65; assoc. prof. So. Ill. U., Carbondale, 1965-66; assoc. prof. philosophy U. Albany, N.Y., 1966-84, prof., 1984-97, rsch. prof., 1997—, dir. religious studies program, 1980-87, dir. philosophy grad studies program, 1988-91. Disting. Jeannette K. Watson vis. prof. of religion, Syracuse U., 1987; dir. Master of Arts in Liberal Studies Program, 1995-97. Author: Religion as Art: An Interpretation, 1982; The Metaphysics of William James and John Dewey, 1969; mem. editl. bd. Jour. Comparative Lit. and Aesthetics, 1982-91; guest editor Annals of Scholarship, 1982; contbr. articles to profl. jours., essays to profl. publs. Served to lt. (s.g.) USN, 1944-47, 51-53. Faculty Exch. Guest scholar, 1976-77, rsch. fellow, 1967, 68, 71, 87; Jones Fund award Lafayette Coll., 1962-63, Signum Laudis award for excellence in tchg. and rsch., 1986. Mem. Am. Philos. Assn., Am. Soc. Aesthetics (steering com. 1985-88), Internat. Assn. Philosophy and Lit. (exec. com. 1976-81). Office: Dept Philosophy Coll Arts and Sci U Albany Albany NY 12222-0001 E-mail: t.martland@albany.edu.

MARTO, PAUL JAMES, retired mechanical engineering educator, consultant, researcher; b. Flushing, N.Y., Aug. 15, 1938; s. Peter Joseph and Natalie Janet (Verrinoldi) M.; m. Mary Virginia Indence, June 10, 1961; children: Terese V. Marto Sanders, Paul J. Jr., Wayne T., Laura C., Marto Mahoney. BS, U. Notre Dame, 1960; SM, MIT, 1962, ScD, 1965. Asst. prof. Naval Postgrad. Sch., Monterey, Calif., 1965-69, assoc. prof., 1969-77, prof., 1977-85, disting. prof., 1985-96, chmn. dept. mech. engring., 1978-86, dean rsch., 1990-96, disting. prof. emeritus, 1996—. Cons. Modine Mfg. Co., Racine, Wis., 1986—. Editor: Power Condenser Heat, 1981; regional editor N.Am. Jour. of Enhanced Heat Transfer, 1993-98; editor-in-chief Internat. Jour. Transport Phenomena, 1997-2002, founding editor; contbr. articles to profl. jours. Bd. trustees Naval Postgrad. Sch. Found., Inc., 1997—. Lt. USN, 1965-67. Lt. USN, 1965—67. Recipient Rear Adm. John J. Schieffelin award Naval Postgrad. Sch., 1976, Alexander von Humboldt U.S. Sr. Scientist award Humboldt Stiftung, Fed. Republic Germany, 1989-90, Disting. Civilian Svc. award Sec. of Navy, 1996. Fellow ASME (assoc. tech. editor Jour. of Heat Transfer 1984-90); mem. Am. Soc. Naval Engrs., Am. Soc. for Engring. Edn., Sigma Xi. Avocations: walking, tennis, music. Office: Naval Postgrad Sch Dept Mechanical Engring Code ME MX Monterey CA 93943

MARTOCCI, LEWIS NICHOLAS, III, writer; b. Forrigga, Italy, July 10, 1960; s. Lewis Nicholas Martocci, Jr. and Maria Laub. AA in World History, Naval Base Coll., Sassabo, Japan, 1988; AA in Crimilogy, Allentown Bus. Sch., Ctr. Valley, Pa. With USMC, 1978—97. Author: (poetry books) From Within, 2001, Doodles of the Mind, 2002. Recipient Pres.'s Award for Lit. Excellence, Nat. Authors Registry, 2000. Mem.: Grange. Republican. Presbyterian. Avocations: reading, fishing, music, book collecting, antique collecting. Home and Office: 722 W Pennsylvania Ave Pen Argyl PA 18072 Office Phone: 610-657-0110. E-mail: max1887@nni.com.

MARTON, EVA, opera singer; b. Budapest, Hungary, June 18, 1943; m. Zoltan Marton; children: Zoltan, Diana. Student, Liszt Acad., Budapest. Debut Budapest State Opera, 1968-72; performed with Frankfurt Opera, 1972-77, Hambrug State Opera, 1977-80, Maggio Musicale Fiorentino, Vienna State Opera, La Scala Milan, Met. Opera, N.Y., Lyric Opera, Chgo., Grand Opera, Houston, San Francisco Opera, Convent Garden, London, Teatro Liceo, Barcelona, Munich State Opera, Berlin, Paris, Sydney, Teatro Colon Buenos Aires, Bayreuth Festival, Salzburg Festival, Area of Verona, others; roles include Manon Lescaut, Tosca, Turandot, Aida Elisabetta in Don Carlo, Leonora in Forza del destino and in Il Trovatore, Fedora, Maddalena in A Chenier, Wally, Gioconda, Leonore in Fidelio, Salome, Ariadne, Helene in Agyptische Helene, Chrysothemis and Electra in Electra, Empress/Wife in Die Frau ohne Schatten, Vensu and Elisabeth in Tannhäuser, Elsa and Ortrud in Lohengrin, Sieglinde and Brüunnhilde in the Ring, Isolde, others; rec. include Turandot, Tosca, La Fanciulla del West, A Chenier, Fedora, La Gioconda, Violanta, Tiefland, La Wally, Semirama, Bluebeards Castle, Mefistofele, Electra, Salome, Die Walkuere, Siegfrid, Götterdämmerung, Gurrelider, Forza del destino, Puccini Arias, Wagner arias, Songs by Bartok and Liszt, others. Address: 31 Ave Princesse Grace Monte Carlo 98 Monaco also: Theateragentur Dr Hilbert Maximilian St 22 80539 Munchen Germany E-mail: mez_floria1974@compuserve.com.

MARTONE, FREDERICK J. judge; b. Fall River, Mass., Nov. 8, 1943; BS, Coll. Holy Cross, 1965; JD, U. Notre Dame, 1972; LLM, Harvard U., 1975. Bar: Mass. 1972, Ariz. 1974, U.S. Dist. Ct. Mass. 1973, U.S. Dist. Ct. Ariz. 1974, U.S. Ct. Appeals (1st cir.) 1973, U.S. Ct. Appeals (9th cir.) 1974, U.S. Supreme Ct. 1977. Law clk. to Hon. Edward F. Hennessey Mass. Supreme Judicial Ct., 1972-73; pvt. practice Phoenix, 1973-85; assoc. presiding judge Superior Ct. Ariz., Maricopa County, judge, 1985-92; justice Supreme Ct. Ariz., Phoenix, 1992—2002; U.S. dist. judge Dist. of Ariz., 2002—. Editor notes and comments Notre Dame Law Rev., 1970-72; contbr. articles to profl. jours. Capt. USAF, 1965-69. Mem. ABA, Fed. Judges Assn., Maricopa County Bar Assn., Am. Judicature Soc., State Bar Ariz., Horace Rumpole Inn of Ct. Office: US Dist Ct Sandra Day O'Conner US Courthouse 401 W Washington St Spc 62 Ste 526 Phoenix AZ 85003-2158 E-mail: Frederick_Martone@azd.uscourts.gov.

MARTONE, MICHAEL, writer; b. Fort Wayne, Ind., Aug. 22, 1955; s. Anthony S. and Patty A. M.; m. Theresa O. Pappas, Apr. 3, 1984; children: Samuel Martone, Nick Pappas. AB, Ind. U., 1977; MA, Johns Hopkins U., 1979. Prof. English dept Iowa State U., Ames, 1980-87, Harvard, Cambridge, Mass., 1987-90, Syracuse (N.Y.) U., 1990-95, U. Ala., Tuscaloosa, 1995—. Author: Alive and Dead in Indiana, 1984, Safety Patrol, 1987, Fort Wayne is Seventh on Hitler's List, 1989, Pensees The Thoughts of Dan Quayle, 1990, Seeing Eye, 1995, Sex Life of the Fantastic Four, 1998, The Flatness and Other Landscapes, 2000, The Blue Guide to Indiana, 2001; editor: A Place of Sense, 1984, Townships, 1988, The Scribners Anthology of Contemporary

Short Fiction, 2000, Trying Fiction, 2001, Extreme Fiction, 2003. NEA fellow, Washington, 1984, 88, AWP Creative Nonfiction award, 1998. Home: 29 Country Club Hls Tuscaloosa AL 35401-1300 Office: U Ala Dept English PO Box 870244 Tuscaloosa AL 35487 E-mail: martone@english.as.ua.edu.

MARTONE, PATRICIA ANN, lawyer; b. Bklyn., Apr. 28, 1947; d. David Andrew and Rita Mary (Dullmeyer) Martone. BA in Chemistry, NYU, 1968, JD, 1973; MA in Phys. Chemistry, Johns Hopkins U., 1969. Bar: N.Y. 1974, U.S. Dist. Ct. (so. and ea. dists.) N.Y. 1975, U.S. Ct. Appeals (2d cir.) 1975, U.S. Ct. Appeals (1st cir.) 1981, U.S. Patent and Trademark Office 1983, U.S. Ct. Appeals (fed. cir.) 1984, U.S. Supreme Ct. 1984, U.S. Dist. Ct. (ea. dist.) Mich. 1985, U.S. Dist. Ct. (no. dist.) Calif. 1995. Tech. rep. computer timesharing On-Line Sys., Inc., N.Y.C., 1969-70; assoc. Kelley Drye & Warren, N.Y.C., 1973-77, Fish & Neave, N.Y.C., 1977-82, ptnr., 1983—. Adj. prof. NYU Sch. Law, 1990—; mem. adv. coun. Engelberg Ctr. Innovation Law & Policy, 1996—; participating atty. Cmty. Law Offices, N.Y.C., 1974—78; atty. Pro Bono Panel U.S. Dist. Ct. (so. dist.) N.Y., 1982—84; lectr. Practising Law Inst., N.Y.C., 1995—, Aspen Law & Bus., 1990—95, Franklin Pierce Law Sch., 1992—97, Lic. Exec. Soc.; chair, bd. dirs. N.Y. Lawyers for the Pub. Interest, 1996—98, vice chair, 1998—2000, 2002—, Legal Svcs., N.Y.C., 1991—95. Mng. editor NYU Law Sch. Rev. Law and Social Change, 1972-73; contbr. articles to profl. jours. Recipient Founder's Day award NYU Sch. Law, 1973; NSF grad. trainee Johns Hopkins U., 1968-69; NYU scholar, 1964-68. Mem. ABA, Assn. Bar City N.Y. (mem. environ. law com. 1978-83, trademarks, unfair competition com. 1983-86), Fed. Bar Coun., Fed. Cir. Bar Assn., Copyright Soc., Am. Chem. Soc., Licensing Execs. Soc., N.Y. Intellectual Property Law Assn., Univ. Club. Office: Fish & Neave Fl 49 1251 Ave of the Americas New York NY 10020-1105 Office Phone: 212-596-9021. E-mail: pmartone@fishneave.com.

MARTONOSI, ANTHONY NICHOLAS, biochemistry educator, researcher; b. Szeged, Hungary, Nov. 7, 1928; came to U.S., 1957; s. Antal and Anna (Zsoter) M.; m. Mary Alice Gouvea, May 2, 1959; children: Mary Anne, Anthony, Margaret, Susan. MD, U. Med. Sch., Szeged, 1953. Asst. prof. dept. physiology Med. Sch., Szeged, 1955-57; rsch. fellow Mass. Gen. Hosp., Boston, 1957-59; rsch. assoc. Retina Found., Boston, 1959-62, asst. dir. dept. muscle rsch., 1962-65; assoc. prof. biochemistry St. Louis U. Sch. Medicine, 1965-69, prof., 1969-79; prof. biochemistry SUNY Health Sci. Ctr., Syracuse, 1979-98. Albert Szent-Gyorgyi prof. U. Med. Sch., Szeged, Hungary, 1994; adj. prof. Kwangju Inst. f Sci. and Tech., Korea, 1995—; vis. scientist dept. biochemistry U. Birmingham, Eng., 1963-64. Author: The Development of Sarcoplasmic Reticulum, 2000; editor: The Enzymes of Biological Membranes, Vols. 1-4, 1976, 2d edit., 1985; Membranes and Transport, Vols. 1-2, 1982; contbr. over 180 articles to sci. publs.; mem. editl. bd. Biochimica et Biophysica Acta, 1988-96. Recipient Established Investigator award Am. Heart Assn., 1961-66; rsch. grantee USPHS, NIH, 1959-89, NSF, 1963-96, Muscular Dystrophy Assn., 1975-89. Mem. Am. Soc. Biochemists and Molecular Biologists. Roman Catholic. Home: 110 Stanwood Ln Manlius NY 13104-1412 Personal E-mail: gouveama@aol.com.

MARTONYI, CSABA LASZLO, ophthalmic photographer, imager; b. Budapest, Hungary, Mar. 23, 1941; came to U.S., 1951; s. Louis Péter and Magda (Gyürky) M.; m. Elnajean Beyst, Sept. 4, 1976; 1 child, Erika Lyn. Cert. retinal angiographer. Chief photographer U. Mich. Photog. Svcs., Ann Arbor, 1967-71; dir. ophthalmic photography, dept. ophthalmology U. Mich., Ann Arbor, 1971-75, instr. dept. ophthalmic photography, 1975-80, asst. prof., 1980-83, assoc. prof., 1983-2000, assoc. prof. emeritus, 2000—. First author: Clinical Slit-Lamp Biomicroscopy and Photo Slit-Lamp Biomicrography, 1985; author, artist exhibit of eye images Landscapes of the Eye, 1993; author sci. exhibits. With U.S. Naval Air Res., 1965-67. Recipient Disting. Tchg. award Joint Commn. on Allied Health Pers. in Ophthalmology, 1997. Fellow Ophthalmic Photographers Soc. (parliamentarian 1988—, chair hon. life membership com. 1991—, fellowship com., pres. 1978-80, chair bd. certification 1978-84, chmn. editl. com. 1987-89, awards including top award for outstanding contbns. to ophthalmic photography), Am. Acad. Ophthalmology (assoc., Honor award 1984, Sr. Honor award 2001). Avocations: guitar (classical-traditional), woodsculpting, fine art photography, tennis. Home: 1261 Laurel View Dr Ann Arbor MI 48105-9765 E-mail: martonyi@comcast.net.

MARTORANA, BARBARA JOAN, secondary school educator; b. N.Y.C., Oct. 18, 1942; d. Samuel and Joan Renee (Costello) M. BA, St. John's U., Jamaica, N.Y., 1970; MS in English Edn., St. John's U., 1972; advanced cert. computers in edn., L.I. U., 1988, profl. diploma in edn. adminstrn., 1990. Cert. sch. dist. adminstr., sch. adminstr. and supr., tchr. English grades 7-12, NY, Ed.D, Lit. Studies, Hofstra U., Hempstead, NY, 2003. Exec. sec. Am. Petroleum Inst., N.Y.C., 1960-65; exec. asst. to v.p. Goldring, Inc., 1965-67; exec. asst. Rsch. Inst. for Cath. Edn., 1967-69; English tchr. St. Martin of Tours Sch., Amityville, 1970-77, Oceanside Jr. HS, 1977-78, Freeport HS, 1979—. Rec. sec. Freeport (N.Y.) Tchr. Ctr. Policy Bd., 1986-89; co-chair Middle States Steering Com., Freeport, 1988-90; chair Freeport H.S. Shared Decision Team, 1992-93; adv. bd. L.I. Writing Project, Garden City, N.Y., 1993—, co-leader Summer Insts.; adj. prof. literacy studies dept. Hofstra U., N.Y., 1999—. Co-author: (textbooks) Writing Competency Practice, 1980, Writing Competency Practice-Revised and Expanded, 1989. With Seaford (NY) Rep. Club, 1975—. Mem. Nat. Coun. Tchrs. English (conf. on English edn.), N.Y. State English Coun., L.I. Writing Project. Avocations: reading, writing, travel. Office: Freeport HS 50 S Brookside Ave Freeport NY 11520-3144 Office Phone: 516-867-5300. E-mail: engteech@aol.com.

MARTORELL, CLAUDIA, infectious diseases physician; b. San Juan, Puerto Rico, May 25, 1972; d. Edgar and Maria (Berrios) Martorell. BS in Gen. Sci., U. P.R., 1994, MD magna cum laude, 1998; MPH, Harvard U. Diplomate in internal medicine and infectious diseases Am. Bd. Internal Medicine. Trainee in internal medicine Baystate Med. Ctr. Tufts U., Springfield, Mass., 1998—2001, fellow in infectious diseases, 2001—02; rsch. fellow in social medicine, Commonwealth Fund/Harvard U. Fellowship in Minority Pub. Health Harvard Med. Sch., 2003—04. Coord. Mass. Legis. Oversight Hearings on Health Disparities, 2004. Vol. HIV Awareness and Support Group Mochilas Salvavidas, 1997—98, Primary Health Care Clinics for Medically Underserved People., Lares, PR, 1996, Primary Health Care Clinics for the Underserved and Geriatric Population, Loiza, PR, 1993, Jarabacoba, Dominican Republic, 1993. Recipient Bristol Myers Squibb scholarship, 1997, NHMA resident leadership program, 2000, AMA Found. Leadership award, 2004. Mem.: ACP, AMA (governing coun. rep. Minority Affairs Consortium 2004—), Mass. Med. Soc., Mass. Infectious Diseases Soc., Nat. Hispanic Med. Assn., Infectious Diseases Soc. Am., Alpha Omega Alpha. Avocations: Tae Kwan Do (black belt), piano, sports. Home: 275 Upper Virginia Ave West Springfield MA 01089 Office Phone: 617-534-2646.

MARTORI, JOSEPH PETER, lawyer; b. NYC, Aug. 19, 1941; s. Joseph and Teresa Susan (Fezza) M. BS summa cum laude, NYU, 1964, MBA, 1968; JD cum laude, U. Notre Dame, 1967. Bar: DC 1968, U.S. Dist. Ct. DC 1968, U.S. Dist. Ct. Ariz. 1968, U.S. Ct. Appeals (9th cir.) 1969, U.S. Supreme Ct. 1977. Assoc. Sullivan & Cromwell, NYC, 1967-68, Snell & Wilmer, Phoenix, 1968-69; pres. Goldmar Inc., Phoenix, 1969-71; ptnr. Martori, Meyer, Hendricks & Victor, P.A., Phoenix, 1971-85, Brown & Bain, P.A., Phoenix, 1985-94, chmn. corp. banking & real estate dept., 1994—; chmn. bd. ILX Resorts, Inc., Phoenix. Chmn. ILX Inc., Varsity Clubs Am. Inc. Author: Street Fights, 1987; also articles. Trustee Boys' Clubs Met. Phoenix, 1974-99; consul for Govt. of Italy, State of Ariz., 1987-97. Mem. ABA, State Bar Ariz., Maricopa County Bar Assn., Lawyers Com.for Civil Rights Under Law (trustee 1976—), Phoenix Country Club, Plaza Club (founding bd. govs. 1979-90). Republican. Roman Catholic. Office: ILX Resorts Inc 2111 E Highland Ave Ste 210 Phoenix AZ 85016-4786 Office Phone: 602-957-2777. E-mail: jmartori@ILXresorts.com.

MARTUCCI, VINCENT JAMES, composer, pianist; b. Medford, Mass., Oct. 21, 1954; s. Vincent James Sr. and Grace Alice (Giorgio) M.; m. Elizabeth Nicoll Lawrence, Sept. 20, 1981; children: Katharine Amalia, James Lawrence. Student, Berklee Coll. Music, Boston, 1974—75; BA in Music, Colby Coll., 1977; studied with Hal Galper, NYC, 1978—80; studied with Dave Holland, Woodstock, NY, 1982—84; MusM, SUNY, Purchase, 2001. Lectr. music Alfred (NY) U., 1978-80; registrar, instr. Creative Music Studio, Woodstock, 1980-82; owner, composer, performer Vinnie Martucci Prodns., West Hurley, NY, 1987—; prof. jazz studies SUNY, New Paltz, 1991—. Performer, composer, 1977—; free-lance composer, prodr. recs. and TV, 1986—; cons. synthesis and audio technique, 1985—; mem. U.S. Embassy tour concert series, Bogota, Colombia, 1991; participant conf. Internat. Assn. Jazz Educators, Boston, 1994; instr. music theory and piano Ashokan Fiddle & Dance, 1996—. Composer, performer, corporate spl. events The Dolphins, N.Am., S.Am., Europe, Can., including Newport Jazz at Saratoga, North Sea Jazz Festival, JVC Jazz Festival at Nice, France, The Hague, Holland, Jazz Mecca Festival, Holland, Pori Jazz Festival, Finland, Levercusen Jazz Festival Germany, Brubeck Family Project Tours, and many others, 1987—; performed with Hubert Laws, Nick Brignola, Livingston Taylor, Rory Block, Don Mclean; arranger radio concert series Karl Berger Composer, 1985; co-author, arranger Adventures of Comander Crumbcake - TV series, 1987; composer: (rec.) Malayan Breeze, 1991, network theme redesign package lifetime med. TV, 1988; travel channel, 1990, CNN-Daily Menus, 1991; composer, performer, arranger underscore CBS's As the World Turns, 1993—, NBC's Another World, 1993—, Guiding Light; co-composer: (rec.) Old World/New World, 1991, Ain't I a Woman, 1992; author instrnl. tape series Arranging and Recording Electronic Instruments, 1987—; co-prodr., performer, engr. music for theatrical prodns. McCarter Theatre (1 Tony award), Princeton, Asolo Theatre, Sarasota, Fla.; co-prodr., music for theatre prodn. Having Our Say, 1995—; performer, music dir. numerous live TV and radio performances; music dir. for Eileen Fulton star of As the World Turns, 1990-, music dir. Laurel Massé, 1997-; author: (book series) Introduction to Jazz Keyboards, Introduction to Blues Keyboards, Introduction to Rock Keyboards, 1997. Recipient 2d pl. jazz composition Billboard Mag., 1988. Mem. ASCAP, AFTRA, Am. Fedn. Musicians. Avocations: photography, bicycling, swimming. Home and Office: Vinnie Martucci Prodn 29 Pleasant Ridge Dr West Hurley NY 12491-5441 E-mail: tuch.tune@aol.com.

MARTUZA, ROBERT L. neurosurgeon; b. Wilkes-Barre, Pa., July 1, 1948; BA, Bucknell U., Lewisburg, Pa., 1969; MD, Harvard U., 1973. Diplomate Am. Bd. Neurol. Surgery. Instr. surgery Harvard Med. Sch., Boston, 1980-81, asst. prof., 1981-86, assoc. prof., 1986-91; prof., chmn. dept neurosurgery Georgetown U., Washington, 1991-2000; Higgins prof. neurosurgery Harvard Med. Sch., Boston, 2000—; chief neurosurgery Mass. Gen. Hosp., Boston, 2000—. Dir. Georgetown Brain Tumor Ctr., Washington, 1993-2000, Mass. Gen. Hosp. Neurofibromatosis Clinic, Boston, 1990-91; chair Decade of the Brain Task Force, Chgo., 1994—. Contbr. articles to profl. jours. Recipient Von Recklinghanson award Nat. NF Found., N.Y.C., 1989. Mem. Am. Acad. Neurol. Surgeons, Soc. Neurol. Surgery (Grass award), Am. Assn. Neurol. Surgeons, Congress Neurol. Surgeons. Achievements include development of genetically engineered viruses for brain tumor therapy; first development of replication-competent viral vectors for tumor therapy. Office: Mass Gen Hosp White 502 Boston MA 02127-1109

MARTY, ALVIN LEONARD, economist, educator; b. N.Y.C., Jan. 29, 1927; s. Harry and Pearl (Bailin) M. Student, Cambridge (Eng.) U., 1947-50; PhD, U. Calif., Berkeley, 1955; AB, UCLA, 1947. Mem. faculty Northwestern U., Evanston, Ill., 1955-60; prof. econs. CUNY, N.Y.C., 1960—, prof. econs. and fin. Ctr. for Study of Bus. and Govt., Baruch Coll., 1960—. Vis. prof. U. Chgo., 1962, U. Hawaii, 1973, Columbia U., 1974, City U. of London, 1987-88, U. N.S.W., Australia, 2002; vis. scholar Fed. Res. Bank of St. Louis, 1993; Simon rsch. prof. Manchester (Eng.) U., 1975-76. Mem. editorial bd. Am. Econ. Assn.; contbr. articles to profl. jours. Ehrman student Cambridge U., 1947-50; Ford Found. fellow, 1956-57. Home: 545 W End Ave New York NY 10024-2713 Office: Baruch Coll Ctr for Study of Bus & Govt 17 Lexington Ave New York NY 10010-5518

MARTY, MARTIN EMIL, religion educator, editor; b. West Point, Nebr., Feb. 5, 1928; s. Emil A. and Anne Louise (Wuerdemann) Marty; m. Elsa Schumacher Marty, 1952 (dec. 1981); children: Frances, Joel, John, Peter, James, Micah, Ursula; m. Harriet Lindemann Marty, 1982. MDiv, Concordia Sem., 1952; STM, Luth. Sch. Theology, Chgo., 1954; PhD in Am. Religious and Intellectual History, U. Chgo., 1956; LittD (hon.), Thiel Coll., 1964; LHD (hon.), W.Va. Wesleyan Coll., 1967, Marian Coll., 1967, Providence Coll., 1967; DD (hon.), Muhlenberg Coll., 1967; LittD (hon.), Thomas More Coll., 1968; DD (hon.), Bethany Sem., 1969; LLD (hon.), Keuka Coll., 1972; LHD (hon.), Willamette U., 1974; DD (hon.), Wabash Coll., 1977; LLD (hon.), U. So. Calif., 1977, Valparaiso U., 1978; LHD (hon.), St. Olaf Coll., 1978, De Paul U., 1979; DD (hon.), Christ Sem.-Seminex, 1979, Capital U., 1980; LHD (hon.), Colo. Coll., 1980; DD (hon.), Maryville Coll., 1980, North Park Coll. Sem., 1982; LittD (hon.), Wittenberg U., 1983; LHD, Rosary Coll., 1984, Rockford Coll., 1984; DD (hon.), Va. Theol. Sem., 1984; LHD (hon.), Hamilton Coll., 1985, Loyola U., 1986; LLD (hon.), U. Notre Dame, 1987; LHD (hon.), Roanoke Coll., 1987, Mercer U., 1987, Ill. Wesleyan Coll., 1987, Roosevelt U., 1988, Aquinas Coll., 1988; LittD (hon.), Franklin Coll., 1988, U. Nebr., 1993; LHD (hon.), No. Mich. U., 1989, Muskingum Coll., Coe Coll., Lehigh U., 1989, Hebrew Union Coll. and Governors State U., 1990, Whittier Coll., 1991, Calif. Luth. U., 1993; DD (hon.), St. Xavier Coll. and Colgate U., 1990, Mt. Union Coll., 1991, Tex. Luth. Coll., 1991, Aurora U., 1991, Baker U., 1992; LHD (hon.), Luth. U., 1993, Calif. Luth. U., 1993, Midland Luth. Coll., 1995; DD, Hope Coll., 1993, Northwestern Coll., 1993; LHD (hon.), George Fox Coll., 1994, Drake U., 1994, Centre Coll., 1994, Fontbonne Coll., 1996; DD, Yale U., 1995; LHD (hon.), Otterbein Coll., 1996; ThD (hon.), Lycoming Coll., 1997; LHD, Dana Coll., 1998; LittD (hon.), Alma Coll., 1998, Concordia U. Portland, 1998, Niagara U., 1998; LHD (hon.), Kalamazoo Coll., 1999, William Jewell Coll., 1999; LittD, LittD, Lynchburg Coll., 2003; DD (hon.), Trinity Coll., 2001, Wake Forest U., 2003; DHum (hon.), Westminster Choir Coll., 2001; LHD (hon.), U. Scranton, 2001; DD (hon.), Wake Forest U., 2003; LHD (hon.), Ea. Mennonite U., 2003. Ordained to ministry Luth. Ch., 1952. Pastor, Washington, 1950—51; asst. pastor River Forest, Ill., 1952—56; pastor Elk Grove Village, Ill., 1956—63; prof. history of modern Christianity Div. Sch. U. Chgo., 1963—, Fairfax M. Cone Disting. Svc. prof., 1978—98, prof. emeritus, 1998—; assoc. editor Christian Century mag., Chgo., 1956—85, sr. editor, 1985—98; co-editor Ch. History mag., 1963—97. Pres. Park Ridge (Ill.) Ctr., 1989—, sr. scholar-in-residence, 1989—; pres. Am. Inst. for Study of Health, Faith and Ethics, 1985—89; dir. The Pub. Religion Project, 1996—99; interim pres. St. Olaf Coll., 2000—01. Author: A Short History of Christianity, 1959, The New Shape of American Religion, 1959, The Improper Opinion, 1961, The Infidel, 1961, Baptism, 1962, The Hidden Discipline, 1963, Second Chance for American Protestants, 1963, Church Unity and Church Mission, 1964, Varieties of Unbelief, 1964, The Search for a Usable Future, 1969, The Modern Schism, 1969, Righteous Empire, 1970, Protestantism, 1972, You Are Promise, 1973, The Fire We Can Light, 1973, The Pro and Con Book of Religious America, 1975, A Nation of Behavers, 1976, Religion, Awakening and Revolution, 1978, Friendship, 1980, By Way of Response, 1981, The Public Church, 1981, A Cry of Absence, 1983, Health and Medicine in the Lutheran Tradition, 1983, Pilgrims in Their Own Land, 1984, Protestantism in the United States, 1985, Modern American Religion, The Irony of it All, Vol. 1, 1986, An Invitation to American Catholic History, 1986, Religion and Republic, 1987, Modern American Religion: The Noise of Conflict, Vol. 2, 1991; author: (with R. Scott Appleby) The Glory and the Power, 1992; editor (with Jerald C. Brauer): The Unrelieved Paradox: Studies in the Theology of Franz Bibfeldt, 1994; editor: (with Micah Marty) Places Along the Way, 1994; editor: Our Hope for Years to Come, 1995, Modern American Religion, Under God, Indivisible, Vol. 3, 1996, The One and the Many, 1997, The Promise of Winter, 1997, When True Simplicity is Gained, 1998, Politics, Religion, and the Common Good, 2000, Education, Religion, and the Common Good, 2001; editor: (jours.) Context, 1969—; editor: Second Opinion; sr. editor: The Christian Century, 1956—98; contbr. articles to religious publs. Chmn. bd. regents St. Olaf Coll., 1996—2001, sr. regents, 2002—; dir. The Pub. Religion Project, 1996—2000. Recipient Nat. Medal Humanities, 1997, Alumni medal, U. Chgo., 1998. Fellow: Soc. Am. Historians, Am. Acad. Arts and Scis. (dir. fundamentalism project 1988—94); mem.: Am. Antiquarian Soc., Am. Acad. Religion (pres. 1987—88), Am. Cath. Hist. Assn. (pres. 1981), Am. Soc. Ch. History (pres. 1971), Am. Philos. Soc. Lutheran. Office: 239 Scottswood Rd Riverside IL 60546-2223 E-mail: memarty@aol.com.

MARTYL, (MRS. ALEXANDER LANGSDORF JR.), artist; b. St. Louis, Mar. 16, 1917; d. Martin and Aimee (Goldstone) Schweig; m. Alexander Langsdorf, Jr., Dec. 31, 1941; children: Suzanne, Alexandra. AB, Washington U., St. Louis, 1938. Instr. art dept. U. Chgo.; artist in residence Tamarind Inst., U. N.Mex., Albuquerque, 1974 Solo shows include, Calif. Palace of Legion of Honor, 1956, Chgo. Art Inst., 1949, 76, Feingarten Galleries, N.Y.C., Beverly Hills and Chgo., 1961, 62, 63, St. Louis, 1962, Feingarten Gallery, N.Y.C., 1963, L.A., 1964, Kovler Gallery, Chgo., 1967, Washington U., St. Louis, 1967, U. Chgo. Oriental Inst. Mus., 1970, Deson&Zaks Gallery, 1973, Fairweather-Hardin Gallery, 1977, 81, 83, Ill. State Mus., 1978, Fermilab, 1985, 91, Bklyn. Mus., 1986, Oriental Inst. Mus., 1987, Gibbes Art Mus., Charleston, S.C., 1988, Fairweather-Hardin Gallery, 1988, Tokyo Internat. Art Expo, 1990, State of Ill. Art Gallery, Chgo., 1990, Expo Navy Pier, Chgo., 1993, Printworks Gallery Ltd., Chgo., 1995, 97, 99, 2002, 04, Navy Pier, Chgo., 2003, 04, Oriental Inst. Mus., Chgo., Martyl: Nature/Artifice Ft. Wayne Mus. Art, 2000; represented in permanent collections, Met. Mus. Art, Chgo. Art Inst., Pa. Acad. Fine Arts, Ill. State Mus., Bklyn. Mus., DuSable Mus., Chgo., Los Angeles County Mus., Whitney Mus. Am. Art, Davenport (Iowa) Municipal Mus., St. Louis Art Mus., Washington U., U. Ariz., Arnot Gallery, Elmira, N.Y., Greenville (S.C.) Mus., Nat. Coll. Fine Arts, Hirshhorn Mus. and Sculpture Gallery, Rockford (Ill.) Mus. Recipient 1st prize City Art Mus., St. Louis, 1943, 44; Armstrong prize Chgo. Art Inst., 1947; William H. Bartels award, 1953; Frank Logan medal and prize, 1950; Walt Disney purchase award Los Angeles Museum; purchase prize Portrait of America competition, Colo. Springs Fine Arts Center, 1961; honor award for mural AIA, 1962, Outstanding Achievement award in the Arts YWCA, 1986; named Artist of Year Am. Fedn. Arts, 1958 Mem. Chgo. Network, Arts Club (Chgo.). Unitarian Universalist. *To be an artist means devoting a lifetime to an intensely difficult activity— one that requires concentration and skill. I've spent my time learning the power of color, line, shape and meaning. I like to think that I have opened out experiences people cannot reveal by themselves.*

MARTZ, CLYDE OLLEN, lawyer, educator; b. Lincoln, Nebr., Aug. 14, 1920; s. Clyde O. and Elizabeth Mary (Anderson) M.; m. Ann Spieker, May 29, 1947; children: Robert Graham, Nancy. AB, U. Nebr., 1941; LLB, Harvard U., 1947. Bar: Colo. 1948, U.S. Ct. Appeals (D.C. cir.) 1968, U.S. Supreme Ct. 1969. Prof. U. Colo., Boulder, 1947-58, 60-62; jud. adminstr. State of Colo., Denver, 1959-60; ptnr. Davis, Graham & Stubbs, Denver, 1962-67, 69-80, 81-87, of counsel, 1988—; asst. atty. gen. U.S. Dept. Justice, Washington, 1967-69; solicitor U.S Dept. Interior, Washington, 1980-81; exec. dir. dept. natural resources State of Colo., 1987. Adj. prof. U. Denver, 1961-79, U. Colo., Boulder, 1988-96; cons. Pres. Materials Policy Commn., 1951; mem. Colo. Adv. Bd. Bur. Land Mgmt., 1967-69; bd. dirs., adv. bd. Natural Resources Law Ctr., 1982-2003. Author: Cases and Materials on Natural Resources Law, 1951, Water for Mushrooming Populations, 1954; co-author: American Law of Property, 1953, Water and Water Rights, 1963; editor, co-author: American Law of Mining, 1960. Co-chmn. Jud. Reorganization Commn., 1961-63; elder Presbyn. Ch., Boulder; pres. Rocky Mountain Mineral Law Found., 1961-62, others. Comdr. USN, 1942-58, PTO, with Res. Decorated Silver Star, Bronze Star, Letter of Commendation, Disting. Svc. award; honored by creation of Clyde O. Martz Natural Resources Scholarship Fund, 2002. Mem. ABA (chmn. natural resources sect. 1985-86), Fed. Bar Assn., Am. Health Lawyers Assn., Colo. Bar Assn. (chmn. water sect. 1957, chmn. mineral sect. 1961, award of merit 1962), Nat. Mining Assn. (Disting. Svc. award 1997), Order of Coif, Phi Beta Kappa. Democrat. Avocations: horticulture, woodworking, mountain climbing, skiing. Home: 970 Aurora Ave Apt 205F Boulder CO 80302-7299 Office: Davis Graham & Stubbs PO Box 185 Denver CO 80201-0185

MARTZ, JUDY HELEN, governor; b. Big Timber, Mont., July 28, 1943; m. Harry Martz, June 23, 1965; children: Justin, Stacey. Owner, operator Martz Disposal Svc., Butte, Mont., 1971—; skater U.S. World Speed Skating Team, Japan, 1963, U.S. Olympic Team, Innsbruck, Austria, 1964; exec. dir. U.S. High Altitude Speed Skating Ctr., Butte, Mont., 1985-89; field rep. Senator Conrad Burns, 1989—95; lt. gov. State of Mont., 1997-2001, gov., 2001—. Coach Mont. Amateur Speed Skating Assn.; bd. dirs. Youth Hockey Assn.; pres. adv. bd. U.S. Internat. Speed Skating Assn. Bd dirs. St. James Cmty. Hosp., Legion Oasis HUD Housing Project. Named Miss Rodeo Mont., 1963; inducted Butte Sports Hall of Fame, 1987. Republican. Office: Office of the Gov Capitol Bldg PO Box 0801 Helena MT 59620

MARTZ, LAWRENCE STANNARD, retired periodical editor; b. Bklyn., Apr. 2, 1933; s. Lawrence Stannard Martz and Jean Lee Bailey; m. Anne-Sophie Uldall, May 28, 1955; children: Geoffrey Stannard, Jenny-Anne Horst-Martz. AB, Dartmouth Coll., 1954; postgrad., U. Edinburgh, 1955. Reporter The Pontiac (Mich.) Press, 1955-56, The Detroit News, 1956-59; copy editor The Wall St. Jour., N.Y.C., 1959-60; bus. writer/editor to asst mng. editor, editor internat. editions Newsweek Mag., N.Y.C., 1961-93, contbg. editor, 1993-99; editor World Press Rev. Mag., 1993-99. Co-author: Ministry of Greed, 1988; author: Making Schools Better, 1992. Recipient J.C. Penney-Mo. award for bus. writing, U. Mo. Sch. of Journalism, 1969, Silver Gavel award ABA, 1990, Media award N.Y. State Bar Assn., 1986. Mem.: Overseas Press Club of Am. (bd. govs. 1994—, pres. 2000—02). E-mail: larrymartz@aol.com.

MARTZ, MIKE, professional football coach; b. Sioux Falls, S.D., May 13, 1951; BS summa cum laude, Fresno State. Asst. coach Los Angeles Rams, 1992—99, Washington Redskins, 1997-98; offensive coord. St. Louis Rams, 1999—2000, head coach, 2000—. Office: Saint Louis One Rams Way Saint Louis MO 63045

MARTZEN, PHILIP D. physicist, software developer; b. Dinuba, Calif., Oct. 23, 1948; s. Dave and Vivian M.; m. Eloise Thompson, Jan. 29, 1972 (div. May 1988); Children: Natashya, Kinarii; m. Cynthia Stapp Landriz, July 1, 1995 (div. May 1997). BS, U. Calif., Santa Barbara, 1973, PhD, 1979. Staff mem. Geodynamics Corp., Santa Barbara, Calif., 1979-95; cons. Frontier Tech. Inc., Santa Barbara, Calif., 1996; cons. speech tech. lab. Panasonic, Santa Barbara, 1997; engring. splst. Aerospace Corp., El Segundo, Calif., 1997—, mem. physics patent com., 1999—. Contbr. to profl. jours. V.p. REACTS, Santa Barbara, 1995-96; mem. Sci. and Engring. Coun. Santa Barbara, 1995—. Republican. Episcopalian. Avocations: golf, rock climbing, sailing, hiking. Home: 4166 San Martin Way Santa Barbara CA 93110-1429

MARUCA, RITA, real estate company executive, real estate broker; b. Italy, Sept. 15, 1957; came to the U.S., 1974; d. Italo Talarico and Rosa Rotundo; m. Luigi Maruca, Oct. 27, 1973; children: Concetta, Italo, Anthony. Ed. in Italy. Mgr. FNY, Jackson Heights, N.Y., 1988-90, Era Vision, Corona, N.Y., 1990-91; salesperson Century 21 Sam & Raj, Corona, 1991-95, Era Today, Floral Park, N.Y., 1995-97; broker, owner Parkview Realty LLC, Corona, 1997—. Mem. Lions Internat. Office: Parkview Realty LLC 50-07 108th St Corona NY 11368

MARUMOTO, WILLIAM HIDEO, management consultant; b. L.A., Dec. 16, 1934; s. Harry Y. and Midori Mary (Koyama) M.; m. Jean Masako Morishige, June 14, 1959; children: Wendy H. Vlahos, Todd M., Lani M. Moore, J. Tamiko Smith. BA, Whittier Coll., 1957; postgrad., U. Oreg., 1957-58. Dir. alumni rels. Whittier (Calif.) Coll., 1958-65; assoc. dir. alumni and devel. UCLA, 1965-68; v.p. planning and devel. Calif. Inst. of the Arts, L.A., 1968-69; sr. cons. Peat, Marwick & Mitchell, L.A., 1969; asst. to sec. HEW, Washington, 1969; spl. asst. Pres. of U.S., Washington, 1970-73; pres. The Interface Group Ltd., Washington, 1973-89; chmn. The Interface Group Ltd./Boyden, Washington, 1989-92, mng. dir. ptnr., 1992-2000, chmn., CEO, 2000—. Lectr. on career strategy, planning and diversity, 1973—; mem. White House Pers. Task Force, 1981-88, White House Conf. on Small Bus., 1986. Trustee Whittier Coll., 1978-2002, Japanese Am. Nat. Mus., 1989—, Mex.

Am. Legal Def. and Ednl. Fund, 1989-93, Wolf Trap Found. for Performing Arts, 1995-2001, Coun. for Advancement and Support Edn., 1980-84; chmn. Nat. Japanese Am. Meml. Found., 1994-97, chmn., 1995-97; chmn. Leadership Edn. for Asian Pacifics, Inc., 1994-97; bd. dirs. Congl. Asian Am. Caucus Inst., 1997—, chmn. 2001—, Nat. Asian Pacific Ctr. on Aging, 1999—; mem. assocs. coun. George Washington U. Sch. Bus. and Pub. Mgmt., 1997—. Recipient Stanley Suyat Meml. Leadership award Asian Am. Govt. Exec. Network, 2002; named one of Am.'s Top 150 Exec. Recruiters, Harper & Rowe Pubs., 1992, 94, One of 500 Most Influential Asian Americans, Ave. Avenue Mag., 1996, Most Influential Asian Am. in Washington, Asian Week, 1997. Mem. Assn. Exec. Search Cons. (bd. dirs. 1994-97), U.S. Nat. Assn. Corp. and Profl. Recruiters, Congl. Country Club. Republican. Methodist. Home: 8808 Brook Rd Mc Lean VA 22102-1509 Office: The Interface Group Ltd 1054 31st St NW Ste 270 Washington DC 20037 E-mail: intrfacegrp@aol.com.

MARÚN, GIOCONDA, Spanish language educator; b. San Juan, Argentina, Nov. 21, 1942; arrived in US, 1973; d. Simón and Josefina Victoria Marún. MA in Spanish Am. Lit., St. John's U., 1974; PhD, Nat. U. Buenos Aires, 1979. Chair modern langs. and lits. dept. Fordham U., Bronx, N.Y., 1993-96, prof. Spanish, 1995—. Mem. Ctr. d'Etudes des Lit. et des Civilisations du Rio de la Plata, U. Sorbonne; pres. 6th Internat. Congress, Fordham U., 1998; presenter in field. Author: Origenes del Costumbrismo etico-social Addison y Steele: antecedentes del articulo costumbrista espanol y argentino, 1983, El modernismo argentino incógnito en La Ondina del Plata y Revista literaria (1875-1880), 1993; editor: Olimpio Pitango de Monalia, 1994, Eduardo L. Holmberg Cuarenta y tres años de obras manuscritas e inéditas (1872-1915) Sociedad y cultura de /2 Argentina moderna, 2002; contbr. articles to profl. jours. Recipient award, NEH, 1982, OAS, 1992. Mem.: Am. Assn. Tchrs. of Spanish and Portuguese (co-chair Biennial N.E. meeting 1986—88, editl. bd. 2001—), Internat. Assn. Iberoam. Lit. (editl. bd. 1992—96), Columbia U. L.Am. Seminar (assoc.). Home: 4-B 470 Halstead Ave Harrison NY 10528 Office: Fordham U Modern Langs Dept 441 E Fordham Rd Bronx NY 10458 E-mail: marun@fordham.edu.

MARUOKA, JO ANN ELIZABETH, retired information systems manager; b. Monrovia, Calif., Jan. 1, 1945; d. John Constantine and Pearl (Macovei) Gotsinas; m. Lester Hideo Maruoka, Nov. 8, 1973 (div. Aug. 1992); stepchildren: Les Scott Kaleohano, Lee Stuart Keola. BA with honors, UCLA, 1966; MBA, U. Hawaii, 1971. Office mgr. and asst. R. Wenkam, Photographer, Honolulu, 1966-69; computer mgmt. intern and sys. analyst Army Computer Sys. Command, Honolulu, 1969-78; reservations mgr. Hale Koa Hotel, Honolulu, 1978-79; equal employment opportunity specialist U.S. Army Pacific Hdqs., Honolulu, 1979-80, computer specialist, 1980-87, supervisory info. sys. mgr., chief info. tech. plans and programs, 1987-2001; ret., 2001. Bd. dirs. High Performance Computing and Comm. Coun., Tiverton, R.I.; pacific v.p. Fedn. Govt. Info. Processing Couns., Washington, 1992-95. Mem. Nat. and Hawaii Women's Polit. Caucus, Honolulu, 1987—; pres. Fed. Women's Coun. Hawaii, Honolulu, 1976-77, advisor, 1977—; sec. Hawaii LWV, 2003—. Recipient Svc. award Fed. Women's Coun. Hawaii, 1986, EEO Excellence award Sec. of Army, 1989, Pacific Fed. Mgr. award Honolulu-Pacific Fed. Exec. Bd., 1990, Info. Resources Mgmt. award Interagy. Com. on Info. Resources Mgmt., 1991, Lead Dog Leadership award Fedn. Govt. Info. Processing Couns., 1993; named One of Fed. 100 (Execs.) of Yr., Fed. Computer Week, 1996. Mem. NAFE, Nat. Women's Polit. Caucus, AAUW, LWV, Armed Forces Comm.-Electronics Assn. (Hawaii chpt., Internat. award for Info. Resources Mgmt. Excellence 1992), Assn. U.S. Army (Pacific Fed. Mgr. award 1990), Federally Employed Women (advisor Aloha and Rainbow chpts. 1977—), Army Signal Corps Regtl. Assn. (Bronze Order of Mercury 1997, Silver Order of Mercury, 2001), Hawaii Intergovt. Info. Processing Coun. (pres. 1988-89, svc. award 1989), Hawaii LWV (sec.), Beta Gamma Sigma. Avocations: travel, reading, tai chi, support of performing arts. E-mail: maruokaj@hawaii.rr.com.

MARUPUDI, SAMBASIVA RAO, surgeon, educator; b. Chintalapudi, India, July 1, 1952; came to U.S., 1976; s. Venkateswarlu and Nagendramma (Gaddipati) M.; m. Usha Nandipati, Mar. 25, 1976; children: Neena, Neelima. MB, BS, Guntur (India) Med. Coll., 1974. Diplomate Am. Bd. Surgery, Am. Bd. Colon and Rectal Surgery. Rotating internship St. Clare's Hosp., Schenectady, NY, 1976-77; resident in gen. surgery St. Agnes Hosp., Balt., 1977-78, Franklin Sq. Hosp., Balt., 1978-82; fellow in colon and rectal surgery U. Tex. Health Scis. Ctr., Houston, 1982-83; pvt. practice Amarillo, Tex., 1983—. Clin. asst. prof. dept. surgery Tex. Tech. U. Health Scis. Ctr., Amarillo, 1984—. Fellow ACS, Am. Soc. Colon and Rectal Surgeons, Internat. Coll. Surgeons; mem. AMA, Tex. Med. Assn., Potter-Randall County Med. Soc. (past pres.), Tex. Soc. Colon and Rectal Surgeons (past pres.). Republican. Hindu. Office: 800 Quail Creek Dr # 103 Amarillo TX 79124-1609 Office Phone: 806-358-7911. Personal E-mail: smarupudi@aol.com., drmarupudi@hotmail.com.

MARUYAMA, MAGOROH, business educator, researcher, consultant; b. Tokyo, Apr. 2, 1929; came to U.S., 1950; s. Shinsaku and Toyoko (Takashima) M.; m. Pierrette Duriez, Apr. 1966 (div. 1974); 1 child, Yukon; m. Kuniko Sakakibara, July 23, 1976; 1 child, Yuki. BA in Math., U. Calif., Berkeley, 1951; postgrad., U. Munich, U. Heidelberg, Fed. Republic of Germany, 1954-55, U. Copenhagen, 1955-57; PhD, U. Lund, Sweden, 1959. Asst. prof. human devel. U. Calif., Berkeley, 1960-62; rsch. assoc. psychology Stanford U., Calif., 1962-64; assoc. prof. psychology San Francisco State U., 1965-70; prof. computer sci. Antioch Coll., 1971-72; prof. systems sci. Portland (Oreg.) State U., 1973-76; vis. prof. anthropology and architecture U. Ill., Urbana, 1976-77; vis. prof. anthropology U. Uppsala, Sweden, 1982; vis. prof. mgmt. UCLA, 1983, Nat. U., Singapore, 1983-84; vis. prof. bus. administrn. U. Hawaii, Honolulu, 1984-86; prof. internat. bus. Aoyama Gakuin U., Tokyo, 1987-96, Aomori (Japan) Koritsu Daigaku, 1996—. Vis. prof. U. Oreg., U. Montpellier, France, 1986; cons. U.S. Dept. Commerce 1971, Can. Fed. Ministry Urban Affairs, 1974, NASA, 1975, Monsanto Chems., 1980, Volvo, Sweden, 1982, Fed. Motors of Indonesia, 1984, Technopolises Japan, 1984, MITI of Japan, 1985, Fujitsu, Japan, 1985, Hakuhodo, Japan, 1985, Gadelius, Sweden, 1988, Michelin, France, 1989, NEC, Japan, 1989-90, C. Itoh, Japan, 1990, OECD, France, 1990, Ministry of Rsch. and Tech., France, 1992. Author: The Second Cybernetics, 1963, Mindscapes and Science Theories, 1980, Mindscapes in Management, 1994, Heterogram Analysis, 1999, Interactive Heterogeneity, 2003. Sgt. USMC, 1952-54. Grantee NSF, NIMH, 1965-76. Fellow AAAS, APA; mem. Sigma Xi, Pi Mu Epsilon, Acad. Mgmt., Internat. Sociological Assn. Avocations: garden design, african and asian folkore, architecture. Fax: 858-452-3826. Office Phone: 858-452-3826.

MARVEL, L. PAIGE, judge; b. Easton, Md., Dec. 6, 1949; d. E. Warner Marvel and Louise Harrington Harrison; m. Robert H. Dyer, Jr., Aug. 9, 1975; children: Alex W. Dyer, Kelly E. Dyer. BA magna cum laude, Notre Dame Coll., 1971; JD with honors, U. Md., 1974. Bar: Md. 1974, U.S. Dist. Ct. Md. 1974, U.S. Tax Ct. 1975, U.S. Ct. Appeals (4th cir.) 1977, U.S. Supreme Ct. 1980, U.S. Ct. Claims 1981, D.C. 1985. Assoc. Garbis & Schwait, P.A., Balt., 1974-76, shareholder, 1976-85, Garbis, Marvel & Junghans, P.A., Balt., 1985-86; mem. Melnicove, Kaufman, Weiner, Smouse & Garbis, P.A., Balt., 1986-88; ptnr. Venable, Baetjer and Howard LLP, Balt., 1988-98; judge U.S. Tax Ct., Washington, 1998—. Mem. U. Md. Law Sch. Bd. Vis., 1995—2001; mem. adv. com. U.S. Dist. Ct. Md., 1991—93; mem. Commr.'s Rev. Panel on IRS Integrity, 1989—91. Co-editor procedure dept. Jour. Taxation, 1989-98; contbr. chpts. to books, articles to profl. jours. Active Women's Law Ctr., 1974-85, Md. Dept. Econ. and Cmty. Devel. Adv. Com., 1978-80; trustee Loyola-Notre Dame Libr., Inc., 1996-2003. Recipient Recognition award Balt. Is Best Program, 1981; named One of Md.'s Top 100 Women, The Daily Record, 1998; recipient MSBA Taxation section's Tax Excellence award, 2002. Fellow Am. Bar Found., Md. Bar Found., Am. Coll. Tax Counsel (regent 1995-98); mem. ABA (sect. taxation coun. dir. 1989-92, vice-chair com. ops. 1993-95, Disting. Svc. award, Jules Ritholz award 2004), Am. Law Inst. (advisor restatement of law third, law governing lawyers), Md. Bar Assn. (chmn. taxation sect. 1982-83, bd. dirs. 1988-90, 96-98, Disting. Svc. award), Balt. Bar Assn. (at-large exec. coun.), Am. Tax Policy Inst. (trustee 1997-98), Serjeant's Inn, Rule Day Club. Avocations: golf, music, travel. Home: 7109 Sheffield Rd Baltimore MD 21212-1628 Office: US Tax Ct 400 2d St NW Washington DC 20217-0001 Office Phone: 202-606-8871.

MARVEL, THOMAS STAHL, architect; b. Newburgh, N.Y., Mar. 15, 1935; s. Gordon Simis and Madelyn Emigh (Jova) M.; m. Lucilla Wellington Fuller, Apr. 19, 1958; children— Deacon Simis, Jonathan Jova, Thomas Stahl AB, Dartmouth Coll., 1956; MArch, Harvard U., 1962. Registered architect, N.C., P.R., Mass., N.Y. Designer Synergetics, Inc., Raleigh, N.C., 1958; designer IBEC Housing, N.Y.C., 1959; ptnr., architect Torres-Beauchamp-Marvel, San Juan, P.R., 1960-85, Marvel-Flores-Cobian, San Juan, P.R., 1985-97; ptnr. Thomas S. Marvel Architects, San Juan, P.R., 1997—. Prof. Sch. Architecture, U. P.R., Rio Piedras, 1967-89. Author: Antonin Nechodoma, Architect, 1994; co-author: Parish Churches of Puerto Rico, 1984. Works include Am. Embassy, Guatemala, 1973, U.S. Courthouse and Fed. Office Bldg., V.I., 1976, City Hall, Bayamon, P.R., 1978, Mcpl. Baseball Stadium, Bayamon, 1975, Am. Embassy, Costa Rica, 1986. Bd. dirs. St. John's Sch., San Juan, 1976-93. Recipient 1st award for regional coll. design U. P.R., Utuado, 1983; Harvard Grad. Sch. Design Julia Amory Appleton travelling fellow, 1962, Henry Klumb prize, 1991. Fellow AIA (bd. dirs. 1993-96, Design award for Fla. Caribbean region 1981, 84-85, 90-91); mem. P.R. Coll. Architects, Acad. Arts and Scis. Clubs: Harvard (N.Y.C.). Roman Catholic. Home: 450 Calle Del Valle San Juan PR 00915-3315 Office: Thomas S Marvel Architects 161 Calle San Jorge Santurce San Juan PR 00911-2018 Office Phone: 787-289-9494. E-mail: tsmarvel@marvelarch.com.

MARVICK, ELIZABETH WIRTH, retired political scientist; b. Chgo., Oct. 4, 1925; BA, MA, U. of Chgo.; PhD, Columbia U., 1968. Lectr. in polit./social sci. CUNY, 1947—51; lectr. in polit. sci. UCLA, 1974—90. Author: The Young Richelieu, A Psychoanalytic Approach to Leadership, 1983, Louis XIII, the Making of a King, 1986. Rsch. grantee, tchg. fellow, Am. Coun. Learned Socs., Fulbright Commn., 1974, 1975, 1976. Mem.: Internat. Polit. Sci. Assn. (rsch. com. chair 1978—91), Western Soc. French History (coun.), Internat. Soc. Polit. Psychology (coun.). Avocation: tennis.

MARVIN, CATHERINE A. financial consultant; b. Asheville, N.C., Aug. 16, 1966; d. Robert L Morrison and Anne C. Veitch, Thomas H Veitch (Stepfather), Kay Morrison (Stepmother). BBA, S.W. Tex. State U., 1988. Cert. Series 7, 63, 65. Asst. v.p./trust officer Bank of Am., Dallas, 1994—99; fin. cons. Salomon Smith Barney, San Antonio, 1999—2002. Mem. Bexar County Young Republicans, San Antonio, 2001—02. Mem.: Southwest Tex. State U. Alumnae Assn., Humane Soc. U.S., Zeta Tau Alpha Alumnae Assn. (coord. collegiate/alumnae rels. 2000—02). Baptist. Avocations: travel, reading, cooking. Office: Smith Barney 300 Convent St 28th Fl San Antonio TX 78205 Business E-Mail: catherine.a.marvin@rssmb.com.

MARVIN, CHARLES ARTHUR, law educator; b. July 14, 1942; s. Burton Wright and Margaret Fiske (Medlar) Marvin; m. Elizabeth Maureen Woodrow, July 4, 1970 (div. July 1987); 1 child, Kristin; m. Elizabeth Dale Wilson, Mar. 20, 1999; 1 child, Colin. BA, U. Kans., 1964; postgrad., U. Toulouse, France, 1964-65; JD, U. Chgo., 1968, M of Comparative Law, 1970. Bar: Ill. 1969. Legal intern EEC, Brussels, 1970; lectr. law U. Kent, Canterbury, England, 1970-71; asst. prof. law Laval U., Quebec City, Canada, 1971-73; legal adv. Constnl., internat. and adminstrv. law sect. Can. Dept. Justice, Ottawa, 1973-76, dir. Adminstrv. Law Reform Project, 1983-85; assoc. prof. law U. Man., Winnipeg, Canada, 1976-77; dir. adminstrv. law project Law Reform Commn., Ottawa, 1977-80; prof. law Villanova (Pa.) U., 1980-83, Ga. State U., 1985—, assoc. dean, 1987-89. Legal advisor on adminstrv. code revision Govt. of Kazakhstan, 1993; law faculty devel. adviser, Bulgaria, 93; dir. internat. human rights law summer program Regent U. Sch. Law., 1998; USIS lectr., Ivory Coast, Iceland, 98; Fulbright prof. Riga Grad. Sch. Law, Latvia, 2000—03. Scholar, U. Chgo., 1965—68; Fulbright scholar, U. Toulouse, 1964—65, Summerfield scholar, U. Kans., 1961—64, Ford Found. Comparative Law fellow, 1968—70. Mem.: ABA, Can. Coun. Internat. Law, Can. Bar Assn., Internat. Law Assn., Internat. Bar Assn., Am. Fgn. Law Assn., Am. Soc. Internat. Law, Chgo. Bar Assn., Ill. Bar Assn., Phi Beta Kappa, Phi Delta Phi, Phi Beta Delta, Omicron Delta Kappa. Office: Ga State U Coll Law PO Box 4037 Atlanta GA 30302-4037 Office Phone: 404-651-2436. Business E-Mail: cmarvin@gsu.edu.

MARVIN, CHARLES RODNEY, JR., lawyer; b. Elizabeth, N.J., Feb. 26, 1953; s. Charles Rodney and Doris Marie (Richards) Marvin; m. Carol Ann Welteroth, Aug. 30, 1975 (dec.); children: Kathryn, Kristin, Cynthia, Gregory; m. Nancy Agnes Ruggiero, Mar. 24, 2001; 1 stepchild, Susanna Myirski. BA in Econs., Mich. State U., 1975; JD, Boston U., 1978; LLM in Mil. Law, Judge Advocate Gen. Sch., 1987; LLM in Govt. Contracts, George Washington U., 1995. Bar: N.J. 1982, U.S. Dist. Ct. N.J. 1982, U.S. Ct. Mil. Appeals 1982, U.S. Ct. Appeals (fed. cir.) 1994, D.C. 1996, U.S. Ct. Fed. Claims 1996. Commd. 2nd lt. U.S. Army, 1975, advanced through grades to major, 1994, nuclear missile officer, 1979-82, mil. prosecutor Fort Sill, Okla., 1983-86; sr. def. counsel U.S. Army Trial Def. Svc., Ft. Polk, La., 1987-89; trial counsel, chief protest br. U.S. Army Contract Appeals Divsn., Arlington, Va., 1990-94; ptnr. Venable, Baetjer, Howard & Civiletti, Washington, 1994—. Mem. ABA (vice-chair, bid protest com., pub. contract law sect. 1992-93), FBA, Bd. Contract Appeals Bar Assn. (bd. govs. 1993-96), Fed. Cir. Bar Assn., John Carroll Soc., Nat. Contract Mgmt. Assn., Bishop McNamara High School (bd. dirs.), Forestville, MD. Roman Catholic. Avocations: musical composing, adult education, golf. Office: 575 7th St Washington DC 20004-1601

MARVIN, D. JANE, consumer products company executive; B in Econs., U. Sussex, Eng.; MBA, U. Mich. V.p. human resources Ameritech, Gen. Bus. Svcs., 1997—99; exec. v.p. human resources Covad Com. Group, Inc., 1999—2001, AT&T Wireless Svcs., Inc., Redmond, Wash., 2001—. Office: AT&T Wireless Svcs Inc NE Bldg 1 7277 164th Ave Redmond WA 98052

MARVIN, DAVID EDWARD SHREVE, lawyer; b. Jan. 6, 1950; s. George Charles Marvin and Shirley Mae (Martin) Schaible; m. Mary Anne Kennedy, Sept. 16, 1972; 1 child, John. BS cum laude, Mich. State U., 1972; JD cum laude, Wayne State U., 1976. Bar: Mich. 1976, U.S. Dist. Ct. (ea. dist.) Mich. 1976, U.S. Dist. Ct. (we. dist.) Mich. 1978, U.S. Ct. Appeals (7th cir.) 1977, U.S. Ct. Appeals (6th cir.) 1979, U.S. Supreme Ct. 1979, U.S. Ct. Appeals (D.C. cir.) 1982, D.C. 1982. Asst. mgr. Alta Supply Co., Lansing, 1972-73; rsch. asst. Wayne State U., Detroit, fall 1975; jud. intern U.S. Dist. Ct., Detroit, summer 1975, shareholder Fraser Trebilcock Davis & Dunlap, P.C., Lansing, 1976—, chair Govt. Law dept., 1992—, v.p., 1997—, also bd. dirs. Pres. Red Rock Prodns., Inc., 1990-94; exec. dir. Inst. CLE, 1989; mem. qualifications rev. com. U.S. Dist. Ct. (we. dist.) Mich., 2001—. Exec. editor Wayne Law Rev., 1975-76; contbr. articles to law jours. Commr. Mich. Solar Resource Adv. Panel, Lansing, 1978-81, Mich. Commn. Profl. and Occupl. Licensure, 1981-83; chmn. Ingham County Energy Commn., Mason, Mich., 1978-80 (state bar rep. assembly 1985-88); dir., corp. sec. Friends Mich. Hist. Ctr., Inc., 1988-92; treas. Lansing Lawyer Referral Svc., 1981; state del. Nat. Solar Congress, Washington, 1978; hearing officer City of East Lansing, 1985; Tri-County Coun. of Bar Leaders (chmn. 1986); bd. dirs. East Lansing Edn. Found., 1990-92, Impression Five Sci. Mus., 1991-97; regional fin. chmn. Abraham for U.S. Senate, 1993-94, Abraham Senate 2000, 1995-2000; mem. transition team, Gov. Engler, 2000—03, Atty. Gen. Cox, 2002-03; exec. bd. chief Okemos coun. Boy Scouts Am., 1996—, pres., 2001-03. Recipient Disting. Vol. award Tri-County Voluntary Action Ctr., 1990, Gov.'s Minuteman award, 1990, John W. Cummiskey award State Bar Mich., 1990, George Washington Honor medal Freedoms Found., 1990; named Outstandin Young Man Am., 1984, The Outstanding Young Lawyer in Mich., 1985-86, Small Bus. Adv. Yr., C. of C., 1991, Silver Beaver award Boy Scouts Am., 2003; Wm. D. Traitel scholar, 1975. Fellow ABA, Am. Bar Found., Mich. State Bar Found. (life); mem. ABA, State Bar Mich. (com. chmn., sect. coun. 1982—, state chmn. 1988-89), Mich. Soc. Assoc. Execs., Ingham County Bar Assn. (pres. 1985-86), Pro Bono Lawyers Svc. (pres. 1982-83), Lansing Regional C. of C. (v.p. 1987), Mich. Audubon Soc. (bd. dirs. 1991-93), Mich. State Univ. Alumni Assn. (nat. bd. dirs. 1992—), State Capital Law Firm Group (nat. bd. dirs. 1989—, chmn. com. Can. 1990-93, chair pub. utility, energy and comm. sect. 1994—, nat. sec. 1996-97, vice-chmn. 1997-98, chmn. 1998-99), Downtown Coaches Club (bd. dirs., pres. 1987), Nat. Resource Ctr. on State Laws and Regulations (nat. bd. dirs. 1993-99, chmn. 1998-99), Mich. State U. Pres.'s Club, Rotary (bd. dirs. 1995-97, pres. 2004—, Paul Harris fellow), Phi Alpha Delta, Phi Eta Sigma, Theta Delta Chi (pres. 1972). Republican. Home: 1959 Groton Way East Lansing MI 48823-1347 Office: Fraser Trebilcock Davis & Dunlap PC Michigan Nat Towers Fl 10 124 West Allegran Street Lansing MI 48933 Office Phone: 517-482-5800.

MARWEDEL, WARREN JOHN, lawyer; b. Chgo., July 3, 1944; s. August Frank and Eleanor (Wolgamot) M.; m. Marilyn Baran, Apr. 12, 1975. BS in Marine Engring., U.S. Merchant Marine Acad., 1966; JD, Loyola U., Chgo., 1972. Bar: Ill. 1972, U.S. Dist. Ct. (no. dist.) Ill. 1972, U.S. Supreme Ct. 1974. With U.S. Merchant Marines, 1966-70. Mem. ABA (Ho. of Dels. 1989-96), Ill. Bar Assn., Chgo. Bar Assn., Maritime Law Assn.(2d v.p.), Propeller Club (Chgo. pres. 1982). Avocations: boating, reading, history. Office: Marwedel Minichello & Reeb PC 10 S Riverside Plz Ste 720 Chicago IL 60606-3708 Office Phone: 312-902-1200. Personal E-mail: wjmmmandr@aol.com.

MARX, ANNE (MRS. FREDERICK E. MARX), poet; b. Germany; came to U.S., 1936, naturalized, 1938; d. Jacob and Susan (Weinberg) Loewenstein; m. Frederick E. Marx, Feb. 12, 1937; children: Thomas J., Stephen L. Student, U. Heidelberg, U. Berlin. Mem. staffs N.Y.C. Writers Conf., 1965, Iona Coll., 1964, 65, 70, Wagner Coll., 1965, Poetry Workshop, Fairleigh Dickinson U., 1962, 63, 64, Poetry Soc. Am. Workshop, 1970-71, 78-79; Bronxville Adult Sch. Lecture Series, 1972; bd. dir. poetry series Donnell Library Ctr. (N.Y. Pub. Library), 1970-74; poetry day chmn. Westchester County, 1959—; Poetry Day Workshop, Ark., 1966, 70, Ark. Writers Conf., 1971, South and West Conf., Ark., 1972; vis. poet So. U., 1979; tchr., poetry readings, Jakarta, Indonesia, summer 1979; poetry workshop leader Scarsdale Cultural Ctr., 1981-82; conv. speaker Nat. Fedn. State Poetry Socs., 1974, 81, 82; condr. symposium Immigrant Voices, Pa. State U., 1986; judge Chapbook Award Nat. Federation of Poetry Socs., 1994, 1996-97; judge various nat. poetry contests; ongoing project: Selected Poems from Half a Century, 1997—. Poet over 1500 poems pub. in nat. mags., anthologies, lit. jours. and newspapers; author: Ein Buechlein, 1935, Into the Wind of Waking, 1960, The Second Voice, 1963, By Grace of Pain, 1966, By Way of People, 1970, A Time to Mend; selected poems, 1973; A Conversation with Anne Marx; 2 hour talking book for blind, 1974; Hear of Israel and Other Poems, 1975, 40 Love Poems for 40 Years, 1977, Face Lifts for All Seasons, 1980, 45 Love Poems for 45 Years, 1982, Holocaust: Hurts to Healings, 1984, German edit. Wunden und Narben, 1986; A Further Semester, 1985, Love in Late Season (New Poems by Anne Marx), 1993, Selected and New Poems, 2003, Full Circle, 2004; co-editor: Pegasus in the Seventies, 1973; contbr. to American Women Poets Discuss Their Craft, 1983, The Courage to Grow Old, 1989, A Collection of Essays by Ballantine Books, 1989; nat. editor poetry recs., Lamont Library at Harvard, stas. WFAS, WRNW, WEVD, WRVR, Voice of Am., The Pen Woman, 1986-88, Christian Sci. Monitor Anthology of Poems, 1989, Canadian Anthology, 1991, Irish Anthology, 1991, M. Rukeyser Anthology, 1999. Recipient Am. Weave Chapbook award 1960, Nat. Sonnet 1959, 67, 81, award World Order Narrative Poets, 1981-85 1959, 67, prizes Nat. Fedn. Women's Clubs 1959, 60, Nat. Fedn. State Poetry Socs. 1962, 65, 66, 73, 80-83, South and West Publn. award 1965, Greenwood prize Eng. 1966, 2d Ann. Viola Hayes Parsons award 1977, award Delbrook Center Advanced Studies 1978, 1st prize Nat. Essay Competition, 1990, N.Y. State Outstanding Writer award, 1991; named Poet of the Year N.Y. Poetry Forum, 1981; winner Chapbook competition Crossroads Press, 1984, Ann. Writer's Digest award, 1983-90; recipient N.Y. State 1st prize for Poetry, 1995. Mem. Poetry Soc. Am. (life, exec. bd. 1965-70, v.p. 1971-72, 2 fellowships, Cecil Hemley Meml. award 1974), Poetry Soc. Gt. Britain, Nat. League Am. Pen Women (pres. Westchester county br. 1962-64, North Atlantic regional chmn. 1964-66, nat. letters bd. 1972-74, biennial poetry workshop leader, nat. poetry editor 1974-78, N.Y. State lit. chmn. 1979-80, N.Y. State pres. 1982-84, 2d nat. v.p. 1984-86, nat. editor Pen Woman mag. 1986-88, contbg. editor 1990—, Biennial Book award 1976, Biennial awards (4), 1982, (2), 1984, Writer of Yr. 1991, N.Y. State Poetry award 1996, 1st prize Biennial Conv. 1998, established Anne Marx Sestina award 1998, Helen Sutton Booth Spl. Biennial award 2002), Acad. Am. Poets, Poet Soc. Pa., Composers, Authors and Artists Am., Inc. (poetry editor mag. 1973-78), Poets and Writers, Inc., N.Y. Poetry Forum (life). Achievements include being subject of story "An American by Choice, A Poet's Credo" pub. in The PEN Woman mag., Nov. 1988, The Courage to Grow Old, 1989, N.Y. Times interview "Finding Poetry in All of Life's Events," 1993; collected works N.Y. Pub. Libr.: Anne Marx Archives, 1992, early German material added to collection, 1994, Juvenile Diaries, 2000. *To be undeterred is the key to any achievement that is important to our lives. Undeterred by detractors asserting that one's goal is impossible to reach. Undeterred by blame or praise. Undeterred by demands of custom and fashion. Undeterred by all but the most essential bonds of family and friends. Undeterred even by the knowledge that there will be no greatness at the end of the long climb - only the satisfaction that we have tried to bring out the best that is in us, that we have added to our years that special ingredient we needed most to add zest to existence.*

MARX, ANTHONY W. academic administrator; b. NYC, Feb. 28, 1959; s. Peter and Marion E. (Mankin) M.; m. Karen Barkey, Sept. 7, 1993; children: Joshua, Anna-Claire. Student, Wesleyan U., Middletown, Conn., 1977-79; BA, Yale U., 1981; MPA, Princeton U., 1986, MA, 1987, PhD, 1990. Adminstrv. aide to the pres. U. Pa., Phila., 1981-84; cons. SACHED Trust, Johannesburg, 1984, 86; vis. scholar Community Agy. for Social Enquiry, Johannesburg, 1988, 90; prof. polit. sci. Columbia U., N.Y.C., 1990—2003; pres. Amherst (Mass.) Coll., 2003—. Rsch. asst. Ctr. for Ednl. Rsch. and Devel., Santiago, Chile, 1985; cons. UNDP, N.Y.C., 1991; vis. scholar Ctr. for Afro-Asian Studies, Rio de Janeiro, Brazil, 1993. Author: Lessons of Struggle, 1992, Making Race and Nation: A Comparison of the United States, South Africa and Brazil, 1998 (Ralph J. Bunche award Am. Polit. Sci. Assn., 1999, Barrington Moore prize Am. Sociol. Assn., 2000), Faith in Nation: Exclusionary Origins of Nationalism, 2003; contbr. articles to profl. jours. Trustee, treas. Fund for Edn. in South Africa, N.Y.C., 1991—94. Grantee J. D. and C.T. MacArthur Found., Chgo., 1989-90, Social Sci. Rsch. Coun., N.Y.C., 1992-93, U.S. Inst. Peace, Washington, 1992-93; named fellow H.F. Guggenheim Found., N.Y.C., 1994.; John Simon Guggenheim fellow, 1997. Office: Amherst Coll PO Box 5000 Amherst MA 01002-5000

MARX, DAVID EARL, chemistry professor, consultant; b. Nazareth, Pa., July 25, 1960; s. William John and Shirley Ackerman Marx; m. Patricia Ellen Wood, Feb. 17, 1996. BS, East Stroudsburg U., 1982; PhD, SUNY, Vestal, 1987. Assoc. prof. chemsitry U. Scranton, Pa., 1987—, chair dept. chemistry, 1998. Sci. cons. Sauquoit Industries, Inc., Scranton, Pa., 1992—98, Argentum Med. Corp., Chgo., 2000—, Cocciardi and Assocs, Inc., Mechanicsburg, Pa.; faculty sponsor U. Scranton, Pa., 1994. Deacon candidate Roman Cath. Ch., Scranton, Pa., 2001—04. ILI grant, NSF, 1992-1994, Ben Franklin Challenge grant, Commonwealth of Pa., 1999-2000, 2000-2001, CHE grant, NSF, 2001-2003. Mem.: Am. Chem. Soc., Sigma Xi, Phi Lamda Upsilon. Republican. Roman Catholic. Achievements include patents pending for Electroless Plating of fibers and fabrics with the aid of ultrasound. Home: 605 Timber Ln Clarks Summit PA 18411 Office: Univ Scranton Linden and Monroe Sts Scranton PA 18510 Business E-Mail: marxd1@scranton.edu.

MARX, GARY DEAN, international education consultant, association executive, futurist; b. Manchester, South Dakota, Nov. 28, 1938; s. Harvey Fredrick and Lucille (Stemple) M.; m. Judy Rae (Marx), June 18, 1961; children: John Fredrick, Daniel Winston. BA, U. S.D., 1960. CAE, ASPR, APR. Newscaster, announcer, dir. KSOO radio and TV sta., Sioux Falls, SD, 1958-61; newscaster, announcer WOW radio and TV sta., Omaha, 1961-71; dir. comms. Westside Cmty. Schs., Omaha, 1971-77; exec. dir. comms. Jefferson County Pub. Schs., Denver, 1977-79; sr. assoc. exec. Am. Assn. Sch. Adminstrs., Arlington, Va., 1979-96, exec. dir. Leadership for Learning Found., 1996-98; pres. Ctr. for Pub. Outreach, Inc., Vienna, Va., 1998—. Sr. rsch. fellow Health, Energy and Productivity in Sch. project, Bethesda, Md., 2000-02; pub. rels. cons. Nat. Sch. Pub. Rels. Assn., Rockville, Md., 1972—; v.p., owner Sta. KOAK Radio, Red Oak, Iowa, 1977-82; v.p. Comms. Devel. Inc., Denver, 1974-76; chief evaluator CIVITAS Internat. Exch. Program,

Calabasas, Calif., 2000—; cons., spkr. in field. Author: Radio...Your Publics are Listening, 1976; Radio...Get the Message, 1977; Excellence in Our Schools...Making it Happen, 1984; Public Rels. for Administrators, 1984, 88; Working with the News Media, 1993; Preparing Students for the 21st Century, 1996, 99; The Future of Cmty., 1999; Preparing Schools and School Systems for the 21st Century, 1999; Ten Trends ... Educating Children for a Profoundly Different Future, 2000; contbg. articles to profl. jour.; Internat. speaker, lectr. Founder, chmn. Keystone Cmty. Task Force, Omaha, 1970-77; mem. Omaha Parks and Recreation Bd., City of Omaha, 1975-77; mem. urban growth policy bd., 1976; mem. nat. edn. adv. com. for restoration Statue of Liberty-Ellis Island Found., N.Y.C., 1984-86; mem. exec. com. edn. Commn. on Bicentennial of the U.S. Constitution, Washington, 1986-92; bd. dir. Campaign for New Priorities, Washington, 1992-93; bd. dir., founder Coalition for America's Children, Washington, 1992-98; mem. steering com. Libr. of Congress, Ctr. for the Book, Washington, 1992-99; mem. design arts program steering com. NEA, Washington, 1993-94; mem. grants selection com. Alliance for Arts Edn., John F. Kennedy Ctr. for the Performing Arts, Washington, 1993-96; mem. steering com., judge Disney Salute to the Am. Tchr., Burbank, Calif., 1993-97; mem. steering com., Emmy awards judge NATAS, N.Y.C., 1995-97; mem. adv. bd. NBC The More You Know campaign, N.Y.C., 1992-98; mem. nat. adv. bd. PBS, 1990-98; mem. steering com., Goals 2000 Arts Edn. Partnership NEA, Washington, 1993-98; mem. selection com. Nat. Tchr. of Yr. Program, Washington, 1979-99; judge USA Today All USA Acad. Team, Arlington, Va., 1995-2000, Nat. History Day, 2002-; internat. cons., spkr., Ctr. for Civic Edn., Calabasas, Calif., 1996—, USIA, U.S. Dept. State, Washington, 1996—; mem. internat. steering com., Civitas Internat., Brussels, Belgium, 1996—; selection com. Fulbright Scholars, 1998—. Recipient Radio Advertising Bureau Commercial award, 1967. Mem. Nat. Sch. Pub. Rels. Assn. (numerous offices and bd. 1971—, accredited, Pres.'s award 1999), Pub. Rels. Soc. Am. (accredited), Am. Soc. Assn. Exec. (cert.), Edn. Writers Assn. (bd. dir. 1979—), Am. Assn. Sch. Adminstrs. (Disting. Svc. award 2000), World Future Soc. (profl. mem.). Avocations: folk art, travel, reading, writing, photography. Office: Ctr for Pub Outreach 1831 Toyon Way Vienna VA 22182-3355 Office Phone: 703-938-8725. E-mail: gmarxcpo@aol.com.

MARX, GARY T. sociologist, writer; b. Hanford, Calif., Oct. 1, 1938; BA, UCLA, 1960; MA, U. Calif., Berkeley, 1962, PhD, 1966. Rsch. assoc. U. Calif., Berkeley, 1965-67, lectr. dept. sociology, 1966-67; rsch. assoc. Harvard-MIT Joint Ctr. for Urban Studies, 1967-73; asst. prof., lectr. dept. social rels. Harvard U., 1967-73; sr. rsch. assoc. Ctr. for Criminal Justice Harvard Law Sch., 1973-75; assoc. prof. MIT, 1973-79, prof., 1979-94, emeritus prof. dept. urban studies and planning, 1994; prof. U. Colo., Boulder, 1992-98, chair dept. sociology, 1992-96; vis. scholar U. Wash., 1999—. Vis. prof. U. Calif., San Diego, 1977-78, SUNY, Albany, 1980, Cath. U., Louvain, and Louvain La Neuve, Belgium, Tech. U., Vienna, Austria, 1993, Nankai U., China, 1995, U. Calif. Irvine, 2000, Berkeley, 2001, Northwestern U., 2001; A.D. Carlson disting. vis. prof. in social scis. W.Va. U., 2003; mem. exec. com. Am. Sociol. Assn., 1973-76; mem. adv. bd. Office of Tech. Assessment, 1985-87, NAS, 1989-91, Electronic Privacy Info. Ctr., 1992—; presenter testimony U.S. Congress, 1981, 91, 97; mem. Nat. Rsch. Coun. Panel, 1989-91, 2002-04. Author: Protest and Prejudice, 1967, rev. edit., 1969, Japanese edit., 1971, Undercover: Police Surveillance in America, 1988, Chinese edit., 1995; co-author: (with others) Inquiries in Sociology, 1972, (with N. Goodman) Society Today, rev. edit., 3d. edit., 1978, 4th edit., 1982, (with Doug McAdam) Collective Behavior and Collective Behavior Process, 1993; contbr. numerous articles to profl. jours.; editor: (book) Muckracking Sociology: Research as Social Criticism, 1972, (jours.) Social Problems, 1969-75, Am. Sociol. Rev., 1972-75, Ann. Rev. Sociology, 1978-84, 97-98, Jour. Conflict Resolution, 1984-91, Qualitative Sociology, Justice Quar., 1990-93, Sociol. Forum, 1991-96, Criminology, 1991-93; co-editor: (books) (with others) Confrontation: Psychology and Problems of Today, 1970, (with N. Goodman) Sociology: Classic and Popular Approaches, 1980, (with C. Fijnaut) Undercover: Police Surveillance in Comparative Perspective, 1995, (with J. Alexander and C. Williams) Self, Social Structure, and Beliefs, 2004; mem. editl. bd. The Info. Soc., 1995—, The Am. Sociologist, 1997—, Policing and Society, 1997—, Ethics and Info. Tech., 1998—. Recipient Disting. Scholarship award Am. Sociol. Assn., 1990, named Jensen lectr., 1989; Outstanding Book award Acad. Criminal Justice Scis., 1990, Bruce Smith Lifetime Achievement award, 1999; Silver Gavel award ABA, 1991; Guggenheim fellow, 1970-71, rsch. fellow Ctr. for Advanced Study in the Behavioral Scis., 1987-88, 96-97, fellow Woodrow Wilson Internat. Ctr. for Scholars, Washington, 1997-98; rsch. grantee NSF, 1973-75, 85-86, 91-95, 20th Century Fund, 1982-87, Austauschdienst, Whiting Found., Deutscher Akademischer, 1991; resident scholar Rockefeller Study and Conf. Ctr., Belagio, Italy, 1990, Stice Meml. lectr. in social scis. U. Wash., 1992, Appel Disting. lectr. in law and tech., Denver U., 1994; Chancellor's Disting. fellow U. Calif., 2000.

MARX, HERBERT LEWIS, JR., arbitrator; b. Feb. 1, 1922; AB, Dartmouth Coll., 1943; MBA, NYU, 1955. With Office of Strategic Svcs., Washington, London, Paris, 1943-45; assoc. editor Scholastic Mags., N.Y.C., 1945-51; with Gen. Cable Corp., 1951-75, v.p. indsl. rels.; pvt. practice arbitrator, mediator N.Y.C., 1975—. V.p. Nat. Acad. Arbitrators, 2004—. Home and Office: 20 Waterside Plz Apt 23J New York NY 10010-2688 Office Phone: 212-686-1553. E-mail: waterside20@aol.com.

MARX, JEFF, composer, lyricist; Attended, BMI Lehman Engel Musical Theater Workshop, 1999. Composer children's musicals Theatreworks/USA; composer various songs The Disney Channel. Composer, lyricist (with Robert Lopez) (Broadway plays) Avenue Q, 2003 (Lucille Lortel award for best musical, 2003, Tony award best original score, 2004), (plays) Kermit, Prince of Denmark (Ed Kleban award). Office: John Golden Theatre 252 W 45th St New York NY 10010

MARX, KENNETH R. music educator; b. Evergreen Park, Ill., May 10, 1957; s. Robert P. and Katherine B. Marx; m. Darrelyn M. Brawders, Apr. 2, 1991. MusB, DePaul U., Chgo., 1979; MusM Edn., Vandercook Coll. Music, Chgo., 1982. Cert. tchr. Type 10 Music and Type 03 Classroom Ill. State Bd. Edn., 1979. Dir. instrumental music edn. Lemont (Ill.)-Bromberek Sch. Dist. 113A, 1979—. Mem. alumni bd. DePaul U. Sch. Music, Chgo., 1997—99; instrumental music adjudicator, clinician Ill. Grade Sch. Music Assn., Ill. Music Assn. Author: Rehearsal Techniques for Young Bands. Dir. Lemont Band Boosters, 1979—2003; pres. Beau Ridge Homeowner's Assn., Park Ridge, Ill., 1995—99; cons. S.E. DuPage Ednl. Conf., Lemont. Recipient Excellence in Edn. award, Ill. State Bd. Edn., 1991, Chicagoland Outstanding Educator award, Quinlan & Fabish Music, 1996. Mem.: ASBDA, Nat. Band Assn., Music Educators Nat. Conf. (assoc.), Ill. Music Educators Assn. (assoc.), Phi Beta Mu. Home: 1219 Beau Dr Park Ridge IL 60068 Office: Old Quarry Middle School 16100 W 127th St Lemont IL 60439 Personal E-mail: kdmarx@comcast.net. E-mail: kenmarx@lemontschools.com.

MARX, MARJORIE MCCULLOUGH, service organization executive; b. Cin., July 12, 1923; d. Robert Stedman and Mildred (Rogers) McCullough; m. Homer E. Lunken, Apr. 15, 1944 (dec. 1970); children: Karen (dec. 1948), Kathryn Lunken Summers, Margo Lunken Yesner; m. William McLeod Ittmann, Mar. 17, 1972 (dec. 1982); m. Harold Hiatt, Apr. 14, 1984 (dec. 1999); m. Graham E. Marx, Jan. 4, 2003 (dec. 2003). Student, U. Cin., 1941—43, DFA (hon.), 2003. Active Girl Scouts U.S., 1962—, chmn. conv. com., 1972, del. world convs., 1969, 72, 75, 78, 81, 84, 87, 93, chmn. pub. relations com., 1963-66, mem. nat. exec. com., 1963-75, mem. nat. bd., 1962—, 4th v.p., 1966-69, 1st v.p., 1969-72, nat. pres., 1972-75, chmn. nat. adv. council, 1975-82, mem. birthplace adv. com., 1980-97. Vice chmn. world conf., Orleans, France, 1981; world com. World Assn. Girl Guides and Girl Scouts, 1978-87, vice chmn., 1984-87. Regional dir. Assn. Jr. Leagues Am., 1958—60, nat. pres., 1960—62; mem. br. Nat. Assembly for Social Policy and Devel., 1968—71; mem. exec. com. Coun. Nat. Orgns. for Children and Youth, 1960—62, 1968—72; mem. br. Jr. League Cin., 1944—58, Nat. Tng. Labs., 1963—66; mem. policy com. Ctr. Vol. Soc., 1971—72; mem. Ohio Citizens Coun., 1956—58; bd. dirs. U. Cin. Coll. of Nursing, 2001—; mem. bd. advisors U. Cin. Coll. Nursing, 2000—; mem. Bd. Fine Arts Ford, 2002—; bd. dirs. 7th Presbyn. Ch., 1967—74, 1985—, ruling elder, 1976—78, 1995—, chmn. bd. trustees, 1992—94; sr. warden St. Martin's in the Field, Biddeford Pool, Maine; bd. dirs. United Way Am., 1962—67, sec., 1965—66, v.p., 1966—67, 1989—; bd. dirs. Coll. Prep. Sch., Cin., 1962—69, pres., 1964—69; bd. dirs. Cin. Speech and Hearing Ctr., 1955—66, v.p., 1958—62, pres., 1963—66, trustee emeritus, 1966—; mem. bd. Children's Theatre, Cin., 1948—58, pres., 1948—50; bd. dirs. Cmty. Health and Welfare Coun. Cin., 1957—63, Hamilton County (Ohio) Rsch. Found., 1963—65, Cancer Family Care, Cin., 1971—72, Boys Clubs Greater Cin., Marjorie P. Lee Home for the Aged, Ctrl. Psychiat. Clinic, Music Hall Assn., Cin. Symphony Orch., Beechwood Home for Incurables, 1975—87, St. Margaret Hall, 1991—, Cin. Civic Garden Ctr., 1992—95, Greater Cin. Found., 1979—87, Ctrl. Clinic, 2000—, YWCA, 1998—, Fine Arts Fund, 2002—. Recipient Mary Herriman award, 2000. Mem. Olave Baden-Powell Soc. (v.p. 1991-93, pres. 1993-97), World Found. for Girl Guides and Girl Scouts (v.p. 1989—), Garden Club Am. (vice chmn. founder's fund 1991-92), Am. Psychiat. Assn. Aux. (bd. dirs., rec. sec. 1991-92). Home: 2353 Bedford Ave Cincinnati OH 45208-2656

MARX, MICHAEL WILLIAM, language educator, writer; b. Phila., Nov. 1, 1951; s. Elmer Edward and Katharine Scott Marx; children: Tristan, Ashlynn. Student, Loyola U.; BA in Polit. Sci., Hobart Coll., 1973; MFA in Film Making, NYU, 1976; MA in English, Ind. State U., 2001. Freelance writer, Calif., 1976-90; owner, head chef Freelandville Novelist Cafe, Ind., 1990—95; pub. Marx & Marx Writers & Pubs., 1998—; instr. English lang. and lit. Ind. State U., Terre Haute, 1999—; instr. Lakeland Coll., Danville, Ill., 2000—01, Ivy Tech State Coll., Terra Haute & Greenfield, Ind., 2000—01, Mira Costa Coll., Oceanside, Calif., 2001—03, Southwestern Coll., Chula Vista, Calif., 2001—02, San Diego City Coll., 2001—, Palomar Coll., San Marcos, Calif., 2001—03, Miramar Coll., San Diego, 2001—03, Cuyumaca Coll., El Cajon, Calif., 2001—03, Inter-Am. Coll., National City, Calif., 2001—03, San Diego State U., 2002—, Nat. U., 2003—, Art Inst. Calif., San Diego, 2004—, Webster U., 2004—, Chapman U., 2004—. Part-time tchr. Vincennes U., Ind., 1991—93, Ind. Bus. Coll., 1995. Author: (book) A War Ends, 1977, A War Ends, 2d edit., 1985 (Artisan award Acad. Fine Arts and Friends), Eric Greenfield: Middle American, 1987, Justus: A Utopia, 1999; columnist: North Knox Leader, 1997—98, Knox County Daily News, Wabash Weekly News, 1991—92; movie reviewer. Home: PO Box 472 Del Mar CA 92014-0472 E-mail: michael@michaelmarx.com.

MARX, NICKI DIANE, sculptor, painter; b. L.A., Oct. 3, 1943; d. Donald F. and Ruth H. (Ungar) M. Student, U. Calif., Riverside, 1965, U. Calif., Santa Cruz, 1973. Represented by Nicki Marx Studio, Taos, N.Mex., Fred Kline Gallery, Santa Fe, N.Mex. One-woman shows include Palm Springs Desert Mus., 1977, Julie Artisans Gallery, N.Y.C., 1975, Phoenix Art Mus., 1975, Weston Gallery, Carmel, Calif, 1981, Kirk de Gooyer Gallery, L.A., 1982, Rocklands Gallery, Monterey, Calif., 1983, Fetish Gallery, Taos, 1988, Fenix Gallery, Taos, 1991, Earthworks, 1993, Lamberts, 1994, Stables Gallery, Taos, 1995, Fred Kline, 1995, Sun Cities Mus. Art, Ariz., 1996, Harwood Mus. Art, Taos, 1999, others; group exhbns. include E.P. Smith Gallery, Santa Cruz, 1994, Lumina Gallery, Taos, 1994, Cafe Gallery, Albuquerque, 1991, Bareiss Gallery, Taos, 1990, Ctr. for Contemporary Art, Santa Fe, 1989, Jordan Gallery, Taos, N.Mex., 1988, 89, Stables Art Gallery, Taos, 1988, 94, Albuquerque State Fair Grounds, 1986, San Francisco Mus. Modern Art, 1977, 78, The Elements Gallery, Greenwich, Conn., 1977, Pacific Design Ctr., L.A., 1976, Lester Gallery, Inverness, Calif., 1976, numerous others; work included in sixteen invitational shows; represented in pub. collections IBM, Milford, Conn., N.Y.C., San Jose, Calif., Bank of Am., San Francisco, The Continental Group, Inc., Stamford, Conn., Cedars-Sinai Hosp., L.A., Farm Bur. Fedn., Sacramento, Calif., Sherman Fairchild Sci. Ctr., Stanford, Calif., Palm Springs (Calif.) Desert Mus., Univ. Mus., Ariz. State U. at Tempe, Mills Coll. Art Gallery, Berkeley, Calif.; exhibited in pvt. collections of Estate of Eugene Klein, Estate of Louise Nevelson, Estate of Georgia O'Keeffe, Fritz Scholder, Ray Graham, Bunny Horowitz, Sue and Otto Meyer, Burt Sugarman, Craig Moody, Paul Pletka, others; subject of numerous articles in jours. and mags. MacDowell Colony fellow, 1975; recipient Adolph and Esther Gottleib Found. grant, 1985. Studio: PO Box 1135 Ranchos De Taos NM 87557-1135 Office Phone: 505-758-4892.

MARX, PAUL LOUIS, economist; b. Washington, May 3, 1953; s. Walter John and Phyllis Durand (Peterson) M.; m. Patricia Garrett, May 20, 1974. BS in Fin., U. Md., 1980; MBA in Internat. Fin., George Washington U., 1983; MS in Strategy and Policy, U.S. Naval War Coll., 1989. Statis. asst. Bur. Econ. Analysis, Washington, 1977-80; economist Maritime Adminstrn., Washington, 1980-90; sr. economist Fed. Transit Adminstrn., Washington, 1990—. Policy com. Intelligent Transp. Sys., Washington, 1996-97. Author: Innovative Financing Techniques, 1998. Chmn. transp. group City of College Park (Md.) Vision 2000, 1994-97. Mem. Nat. Railway Hist. Soc., Wooden Canoe Heritage Assn., Potomac Appalachian Trail Club (trail supr.). Avocations: canoe restoration, hiking, genealogy, writing fiction. Office: Fed Transit Adminstrn TBP-10 400 7th St SW Washington DC 20590-0001 Home: 9904 Edgehill Ln Silver Spring MD 20901-2518

MARX, RICHARD, vocalist, musician; b. Chgo., Sept. 16, 1963; Songwriter, prodr., musician, singer; founder Signal 21 Records, 1999—. Musician: (albums) Richard Marx, 1987 (nominee Grammy award Best Male Rock Vocal Performance, 1988), Repeat Offender, 1989 (triple platinum album, nominee Grammy award Best Male Pop Vocal Performance, 1989), Rush Street, 1991, Paid Vacation, 1994 (platinum album), Flesh & Bone, 1997, Greatest Hits, 1997, Days in Avalon, 2000, The Best of Richard Marx, 2000, Ballads, 2003, My Own Best Enemy, 2004; appeared on: Dance with My Father, by Luther Vandross, 2003 (Grammy award Song of Yr., 2003).*

MARX, THOMAS GEORGE, economist; b. Trenton, NJ, Oct. 25, 1943; s. George Thomas and Ann (Szymanski) Marx; m. Arlene May Varga, Aug. 23, 1969; children: Melissa Ann, Thomas Jeffrey, Jeffrey Alan. BS summa cum laude, Rider Coll., 1969; PhD, U. Pa., 1973. Fin. analyst Am. Cyanamid Co., Trenton, 1968; economist FTC, Washington, 1973; econ. cons. Foster Assocs. Inc., Washington, 1974-77; sr. economist GM, Detroit, 1977-79, mgr. indsl. econs., 1980-81, dir. econs. policy studies, 1981-83, dir. corp. strategic planning group, 1984-86, gen. dir. market analysis and forecasting, 1986-88, gen. dir. econ. analysis, 1988-90, gen. dir. issues mgmt. on industry govt. rels. staff, 1990-96, dir. econ. issues and analysis corp. affairs staff, 1996-97, dir. global climate issue, 1997—. Mem. faculty Temple U., Phila., 1972—73, U. Pa., Phila., 1972—73; adj. prof. Wayne State U., 1981—89, U. Detroit, 1988—. Assoc. editor: Bus. Econs., 1980—98, mem. editl. bd.: Akron Jour. Bus. and Econs., 1981—90; contbr. articles to profl. jours. With USAF, 1961—65. Mem.: Assn. Pub. Policy Analysts, Planning Forum, Western Econ. Assn., So. Econ. Assn., Econ. Soc. Mich., Detroit Area Bus. Economists (v.p.), Nat. Assn. Bus. Economists, Am. Econ. Assn., Nat. Econs. Club, Beta Gamma Sigma, Pi Gamma Mu. Roman Catholic. Home: 3312 Bloomfield Park Dr West Bloomfield MI 48323-3514 Office: GM Corp MC 482-C27-C22 PO Box 300 300 Renaissance Ctr Detroit MI 48265-3000 Office Phone: 313-665-2961. Business E-Mail: tom.marx@gm.com.

MARYANSKI, FRED, academic administrator; BA in Math., Providence Coll.; MA in Computer Sci., Stevens Inst. Tech.; PhD in Computer Sci., U. Conn. Faculty U. Conn., Storrs, 1983—, provost, 1999—. With Digital Equipment Corp., 1986—89. Office: U Conn Office of the Provost Gulley Hall Storrs Campus 352 Mansfield Rd U-86 Storrs Mansfield CT 06269-2086*

MARZIO, PETER CORT, museum director; b. Governor's Island, N.Y., May 8, 1943; s. Francis and Katherine (Mastroberte) M.; m. Frances Ann Parker, July 2, 1979; children: Sara Lon, Steven Arnold. BA (Neva Miller scholar), Juniata Coll., Huntingdon, Pa., 1965; MA, U. Chgo., 1966, PhD (univ. fellow, Smithsonian Instn. fellow), 1969. Rsch. asst. to dir., then historian Nat. Mus. History and Tech., Smithsonian Instn., 1969-73, assoc. curator prints, 1977-78, chmn. dept. cultural history, 1978; dir., CEO Corcoran Gallery Art, Washington, 1978-82; dir. Mus. Fine Arts, Houston, 1982—. Instr. Roosevelt U., Chgo., 1966-68. Author: Rube Goldberg: His Life and Works, 1973, The Art Crusade, 1976, The Democratic Art: An Introduction to the History of Chromolithography in America, 1979; editor: A Nation of Nations, 1976. Wallace Found. Sr. Fulbright fellow Italy, 1973-74. Mem. Cosmos Club (Washington), Coronado Club (Houston). Home: 101 Westcott St Houston TX 77007-7044 Office: Mus Fine Arts 1001 Bissonet St PO Box 6826 Houston TX 77265-6826 Office Phone: 713-639-7300. E-mail: pmarzio@mfah.org.

MARZKE, RONALD OSCAR, physics and astronomy educator; b. Chapel Hill, N.C., Dec. 11, 1966; s. Robert Franklin and Mary (Walpole) M.; m. Heidi May Waterfield, July 20, 1997; 1 child, Cassandra. BS in Physics, Ariz. State U., 1987; AM in Astronomy, Harvard U., 1988, PhD in Astronomy, 1994. Rsch. assoc. Nat. Rsch. Coun. Can., Victoria, B.C., 1994-97; Hubble fellow Obs. Carnegie Instn. Washington, Pasadena, Calif., 1997-2000; asst. prof. physics and astronomy San Francisco State U., 2000—. Contbr. articles to sci. jours., including Astrophys. Jour., Astronom. Jour., Astronomy and Astrophysics, publs. of Astron. Soc. Pacific. Rsch. grantee NSF, 1999, major rsch. instrumentation grantee, 1999. Mem. Am. Astron. Soc., Astron. Soc. Pacific. Avocations: outdoor activities, wilderness preservation. Office: San Francisco Stat U Dept Physics and Astronomy 1600 Holloway Ave San Francisco CA 94132

MARZLUFF, WILLIAM FRANK, medical educator; b. Washington, May 7, 1945; BA in Chemistry magna cum laude, Harvard Coll., 1967; PhD in Biochemistry, Duke U., 1971; postdoctoral study, Johns Hopkins U., 1971-74. From asst. prof. to prof. chemistry Fla. State U., Tallahassee, 1974-84, prof. chemistry, 1984-91; prof., dir. program molecular biology, biotech. U. N.C., Chapel Hill, 1991—, exec. assoc. dean for rsch., 1997—. Cons. physiology course Marine Biol. Lab., Woods Hole, Mass., 1976; instr. sci. summer and math. camp Fla. State U., 1985, dir. program molecular biophysics, 1986-91; acting chmn. dept. biochem. and biophysics, U. N.C., 1994-97; mem. rsch. com. Fla. Divsn. Am. Cancer Soc., 1977-91, chmn. summer rsch. fellowship subcom., 1979-83, 90-91; mem. site visit team NIH, 1980-88, ad hoc mem. molecular cytology study sect., 1982-85, ad hoc mem. molecular biology study sect., 1982-83, 86, 88, 89, mem. molecular biology study sect., 1989-91, chmn. molecular biology study sect., 1991-93; mem. cell biology panel NSF, 1987-89, mem. rev. panel biological ctrs., 1987-90; lectr. in field. Co-editor: Histone Genes: Organization and Expression, 1984; mem. editl. bd. Gene Expression; contbr. over 100 articles to profl. pubs. Marine Biol. Lab. fellow, 1975, NIH fellow; recipient Career Devel. award USPHS, 1975-80, tchg. award Program Med. Scis., 1978. Office: Univ NC 132 Mol Bio Biotech Res Lab CB # 3280 Coker Hall Chapel Hill NC 27599-3280

MARZOL, ADOLFO, mortgage company executive; BS in Bus. Adminstrn., M in Fin., U. Fla. Sr. v.p. interest rate risk Chase Manhattan Mortgage Corp., 1991—93, exec. v.p., CFO, 1993—96; sr. v.p. capital markets Fannie Mae, 1996, sr. v.p. single family bus. mgmt., 1996—98, exec. v.p., chief credit officer, 1998—2002, exec. v.p. fin. and credit, 2002—. Office: Fannie Mae 3900 Wisconsin Ave NW Washington DC 20016-2892

MARZORATI, GERALD, editor; BA, Villanova U., 1975. Editor SoHo (N.Y.) News, Harper's Mag., NY, New Yorker Mag., 1994—98; editl. dir. N.Y. Times Mag., N.Y.C., 1998—2003, editor, 2003—. Author: A Painter of Darkness: Leon Golub and Our Times, 1990 (PEN/Martha Albrand award). Office: The New York Times 229 W 43rd St New York NY 10036-3959

MARZULLI, JOHN ANTHONY, JR., lawyer; b. Orange, NJ, Jan. 3, 1953; s. John Anthony Sr. and Ruth Eileen (Dyer) M.; m. Penelope Bennett, Dec. 13, 1986; children: Emily Mooers, John A. III, Peter Bennett. BA magna cum laude, Middlebury Coll., 1975; JD, NYU, 1978. Bar: NJ 1978, NY 1979. Law clk. to chief judge US Dist. Ct., NJ, 1978-80; assoc. atty. Shearman & Sterling, NYC, 1980-87, pntr., 1988—. Contbg. author: Corporate Restructuring, 1990, European Corporate Finance Law, 1990. Mem. ABA, NY State Bar Assn., Bar Assoc. City of NY, NJ Bar Assn., Order of Coif, Phi Beta Kappa. Office: Shearman & Sterling 599 Lexington Ave New York NY 10022-6030 E-mail: jmarzulli@shearman.com.

MASA, GEORGE JOHN, retired bank executive; b. Chgo., Apr. 29, 1947; s. George John Sr. and Barbara Ann (Kos) M.; m. Judy Ann Martin, Apr. 24, 1971; children: Kimberly Janine, Kristin Marie. BS in Commerce, De Paul U., 1969; cert. banking, Rutgers U., 1979; cert. mgmt., Pa. State U., 1987. Field bank examiner FDIC, Chgo., 1969-77, rev. examiner, 1977-82, asst. regional dir. Dallas, 1982-85, asst. dir. policy Washington, 1985-86, asst. dir. ops., 1986-89, regional dir. Chgo., 1989-91, San Francisco, 1991—2002; ret., 2002. With USAR, 1970-76. Personal E-mail: gjm@aol.com.

MASAKOWSKI, YVONNE ROSE, psychologist, researcher; d. Joseph L. and Cecilia Centak; m. Daniel Masakowski, Dec. 26, 1964; children: Daniel, Jennifer. BA in Psychology, Rutgers U., 1982; MA in Psychology, U. Conn., 1991; MPhil, CUNY, 1994, PhD, 1996; diploma in foreign policy, nat. security, MIT, 2004. Rsch. psychologist Naval Submarine Med. Rsch. Ctr., Groton, Conn., 1987—91, Naval Undersea Warfare Ctr., Newport, RI, 1997—2000, advanced concepts human factors psychologist, 1997—2003; assoc. dir. human factors Office Naval Rsch., London, 2000—02; CNO strategic studies sci. adv. US Navy War Coll., Newport, 2003—04. Contbr. articles to profl. jours. Religious edn. tchr. St. Lawrence Ch., Kellingworth, Conn., 1982—91. Decorated Cross of Merit Czech Republic; named fellow, World Innovation Found., 2002; recipient Merit medal, French Def. Dept., 2000—01, medal, Dept. Air Force, Poland, 2001, 2 medals for scientific achiev., Min. of Def., France, 2000—01, Scientific Achiev. medal, Air Force Poland, 2001. Mem.: Human Factors & Ergonomics Assn., European Human Factors & Ergonomics, Human Factors & Ergonomics. Avocations: opera, art. E-mail: masakowy@nwc.navy.mil.

MASCARA, FRANK R. former congressman; b. Belle Vernon, Pa., Jan. 19, 1930; married; 4 children. BS, Calif. U. Pa., 1972. Pub. acct., 1956-75; contr. Washington County, 1974-80; chmn. Wash. Bd. County Commrs., 1980-94; mem. U.S. Congress from 20th Pa. dist., 1995—2003; mem. fin. svcs. com., transp. and infrastructure com. U.S. Army, 1946—47. Democrat.

MASCAVAGE, JOSEPH PETER, training executive; b. Allentown, Pa., July 7, 1956; s. John Joseph and Florence M.; m. Jo Ellen Huhnke, Aug. 8, 1981; children: Lauren Christine, Gregory Joseph. BS in Environ. Resource Mgmt., Pa. State U., 1978. Tech. sales rep. Am. Cyanamid Co., Los Angeles, 1978-82, supr. utilites application Azusa, Calif., 1982-83, asst. to mktg. mgr. Wayne, N.J., 1983, dist. sales mgr. Houston, 1984-86, mgr. sales tng. Wayne and Charlotte, N.C., 1986-91, mgr. comml. tng. Charlotte, 1991-93; exec. Cytec Industries, Charlotte, 1993-94, mgr. of tng. and employee devel., 1994-96, mgr. corp. edn., 1996-98, mgr. edn. and employee devel., 1999—; mgr. Cytec U On-line Corp. Univ., 2002—. Author: Cytec Sales Manual, 1993. Office: Cytec Industries PO Box 32787 Charlotte NC 28232-2787 E-mail: joe.mascavage@cytec.com.

MASCETTA, JOSEPH ANTHONY, principal; b. Canonsburg, Pa., Sept. 2, 1931; s. Joseph Alphonso and Amalia (Ciavarra) M.; m. Jean Verrone, June 18, 1960; children: Lisa Marie, Linda Jo, Lori Jean. BS, U. Pitts., 1954; MS, U. Pa., 1963; cert. advanced study, Harvard U., 1970. Cert. tchr. math., phys. scis., adminstr. secondary sch., Pa. Tchr. chemistry Canonsburg High Sch., 1956-59, Mt. Lebanon High Sch., Pitts., 1959-75, chair sci. dept., 1967-75; coord. secondary curriculum Mt. Lebanon Sch. Dist., Pitts., 1975-81; prin. Mt. Lebanon Sr. High Sch., Pitts., 1981-91; ret., 1991; ednl. cons., 1991—. Vis. team Mid. States Assn. Colls. and Schs., Phila., 1967-78, chair vis. teams, 1981-96, Pa. state adv. com., 1988-91; sch. bd. and edn. commn. St. Patrick Sch., Canonsburg, 1972-85, 95-2002; tchr. undergrad. and grad. courses Duquesne U., Pitts., 1975-81; regional dir. Pa. Jr. Acad. Sci., Pitts., 1976-82; ednl. cons. Pitts. area schs., 1992—; quality edn. com. Pitts. Diocese, 1995-97. Author: Modern Chemistry Review, 1968, Chemistry the Easy Way, 1989, rev. edit., 2003, Barron's SAT II, Chemistry, 1994, rev. edit., 2003; contbg. author: (ency.) Barron's Student Concise Ency., 1988, rev. 1994, Barron's New Student's Concise Ency., 1993, Perry Como Commemorative Booklet, 1998. Recipient Outstanding Tchr. award Spectroscopy Soc., 1973; grantee NSF, 1961, 62-63, 63, 67, 69-70, 73; sci. fellow GE, 1959. Mem. ASCD, Nat. Assn. Secondary Sch. Prins. (cert. recognition 1991), Pa. Assn. Curriculum & Supervision (exec. bd. dirs. 1985-87, regional pres. 1987), Western Pa. Assn.

Curriculum & Supervision (v.p. 1983-85, pres. 1985-87, exec. bd. dirs. 1989-2001), Greater Canonsburg Heritage Soc., Italian-Am. Heritage and Cultural Soc. Washington County (chair scholarship com. 1992—), Phi Delta Kappa. Roman Catholic. Avocations: painting, writing. Home: 451 McClelland Rd Canonsburg PA 15317-2258 E-mail: jmascett@bellatlantic.net.

MASCHERONI, ELEANOR EARLE, marketing communications executive; b. Boston, June 6, 1955; d. Ralph II and Eleanor Forbes (Owens) Earle; m. Mark Mascheroni, May 30, 1981; children: Olivia Forbes, Isabella Starbuck, Rex Owens. AB, Brown U., 1977. Dept. adminstr. Sotheby Parke Bernet, N.Y.C., 1978-79; asst. dir. devel. Inst. Architecture and Urban Studies, N.Y.C., 1979-81; assoc. in pub. rels. Prudential Securities Inc., N.Y.C., 1981-84, asst. v.p., 1984-86, assoc. v.p., 1986-87, v.p., mgr., 1987—89, 1st v.p., dir. corp. commns., 1989—91; v.p. corp. comms. Zurich Scudder Investments, Inc., N.Y.C., 1991-95, prin., sr. v.p., dir. corp. comms., 1996-99, mng. dir., 1999—2001; CMO Ogilvy & Mather, 2001—. N.Y. Alumnae bd. govs. St. Timothy's Sch., Stevenson, Md., 1994—; trustee Hartley House, 2000—. Avocations: running, photography. Office Phone: 212-237-7239. Business E-Mail: eleanor.mascheroni@ogilvy.com.

MASCI, JOSEPH RICHARD, medical educator, physician; b. New Brunswick, N.J., Nov. 27, 1950; s. Joseph Nicholas and Delfina (Musa) M.; m. Elizabeth Bass, May 21, 1993; 1 child, Jonathan Samuel. BA, Cornell U., 1972; MD, NYU, 1976. Diplomate Am. Bd. Internal Medicine, Am. Bd. Infectious Diseases. Instr. medicine Boston U. Sch. Medicine, 1979—80, Mt. Sinai Sch. Medicine, NYC, 1982—84, asst. prof. clin. medicine, 1984—88, asst. prof. medicine, 1988—90, assoc. prof. medicine, 1990—2003, prof. medicine, 2003—, chief infectious diseases, 1999—2002; assoc. dir. medicine Elmhurst (NY) Hosp. Ctr., 1987—2002, dir. medicine, 2002—. Peer reviewer NIH, 1994—. Author: Primary and Ambulatory Care of the HIV-Infected Adult, 1992, Outpatient Management of HIV-Infection, 2d edit., 1996, 3d edit., 2001. Recipient Dr Linda Laubenstien award for Excellence in AIDS Care, 2002. Fellow Am. Coll. Chest Physicians; mem. ACP, Am. Soc. Microbiology, Assn. Program Dirs. Internal Medicine, Assn. Profs. of Medicine. Office: Elmhurst Hosp Ctr 79-01 Broadway Elmhurst NY 11373-1329

MASCIA, MARK JOSEPH, language educator; b. N.Y.C., May 12, 1970; s. Joseph Serafino and Ritva (Halinen) Mascia; m. Tara Marie Ulrich, June 19, 1999. BA summa cum laude, U. Pa., Phila., 1992; MA, Columbia U., 1993, MPhil, 1996, PhD, 1998. Asst. prof. Spanish Ohio Dominican Coll., Columbus, 1998—99, Sacred Heart U., Fairfield, Conn., 1999—. Contbr. articles to profl. jours. Mem.: MLA, Soc. Renaissance and Baroque Hispanic Poetry, Am. Assn. Tchrs. Spanish and Portuguese, Phi Beta Kappa. Avocation: stamp collecting/philately. Office: Sacred Heart U 5151 Park Ave Fairfield CT 06825 Business E-Mail: masciam@sacredheart.edu.

MASCOLA, RICHARD F. former medical association administrator; Degree in prosthodontics, N.Y.U. Coll. Dentistry, 1962. Pres. ADA, 2001—02. Recipient Albert L. Borish Award, 2001.

MASDEU, JOSE CRUZ, neurologist, medical school administrator; b. Madrid, Sept. 15, 1946; arrived in U.S., 1972; s. Jose and Maria Luisa Masdeu. MD, U. Madrid, 1969. Diplomate Am. Bd. Psychiatry and Neurology. Resident in neurology Chgo. Med. Sch., 1972-75; fellow in neuropathology Peter Bent Brigham Hosp., 1976-77; sect. chief neurology Hines (Ill.) VA Hosp., 1978-82; asst. prof. neurology Loyola, 1978-82; head, neurology sect. North Ctrl. Bronx (N.Y.) Hosp., 1982-87; assoc. attending staff Montefiore Med. Ctr., Bronx, 1982-87; assoc. prof. neurology Einstein, 1982-87; dir. neurology St. Vincent's Hosp./Med. Ctr., N.Y.C., 1987—; attending staff, clin. prof. neurology Bellevue Hosp./NYU Med. Ctr., N.Y.C., 1987—; prof., chmn. neurology dept. N.Y. Med. Coll./West County Med. Ctr., Valhalla, 1991—. Author (with C. Gonzalez, C.B. Grossman): Head and Spine Imaging, 1985; author: (with P. Brazis, J. Biller) Localization in Neurology, 4 edits., 1985—2001; author: (with L. Sudarsky, L. Wolfson) Gait Disturbances of Aging, 1997; contbr. Named Outstanding New Citizen of Yr., Chgo. Citizenship Coun., 1977, Among Best Neurologists in N.Y., N.Y. Mag., 1991, 1996, Among 22 Best Neurologists in U.S., Am. Health Mag., 1996. Mem.: World Fedn. Neurology (chmn. neuroimaging rsch. group 1997—), Am. Soc. Neuroimaging (pres. 1994—96), Am. Acad. Neurology (chmn. neuroimaging sect. 1996—, chmn. subcom. practice com. 1990—, bd. dirs.). Roman Catholic. Avocation: Avocations: tennis, golf. Address: Neurology CUN Avda Pio XII 31008 Pamplona Spain

MASEAR, CLAUDE, music educator, musician; b. Bklyn., Mar. 16, 1964; s. Clyde Benjamin and Elizabeth Demetriades Masear. MusB cum laude, Bklyn. (N.Y.) Coll., 1988, MusM, 1991—91; cert. in Sch. Adminstrn. and Supr., Bklyn. (N.Y.) Coll., 1993; EdD, Columbia U., 1999; diploma in Ednl. Adminstrn., Coll. New Rochelle, 2001. Cert. music tchr. N.Y., 1992, sch. adminstr./Supervisor N.Y., 1998. Music educator Intermediate Sch. N.Y. City Schs., Hollis, NY, 1988—90, music educator Intermediate Sch Bklyn., 1990—91; music educator Lawrence (N.Y.) Pub. Schs., 1992, Hicksville (N.Y.) Pub. Schs., 1992—93, 1994—95, Huntington (N.Y.) Pub. Schs., 1993—94, 1995—. Asst. dir. Salute To Music Program NY. State Schs., Bklyn., 1990—93; concert master Spirit Improvisation Ensemble Columbia U., N.Y., 1995—; lectr. music edn. Bklyn. (N.Y.) Coll., Bklyn., 1996; presenter, balanced Mind Conf. L.I. U. C.W. Post Coll., 2001. Author: The Development And Field Test Of A Model For Evaluating Elementary String Programs, 1999; composer: (songs) Funky Town (Gold award N.Y. State Maj. Orgn. Festival, 1997), Rock Around The Clock (Silver award N.Y. State Maj. Orgn. Festival, 2000); musician Bouree For Solo Violin; conducted: Queens Borowide Concert, 1999. Coach 68 Precint Police Athletic League Youth Coun., Bklyn., 1981—93. Scholar, Teachers Coll., Columbia U., 1994. Mem.: N.Y. State Sch. Music Assn. (assoc.), Kappa Delta Pi (assoc.). Greek Orthodox. Achievements include development of standards for string instruction grades3-12; design of program evaluation models for public school music programs. Avocations: exercise, music, travel, cooking, languages. Home: 404 South 13 Th Street Bottom Lindenhurst NY 11757 Office: Huntington Public Schools Woodhul Road Huntington NY 11743 Office Phone: 631-673-2030. Personal E-mail: clmaedd@aol.com.

MASEFIELD, OLIVER LESLIE PETER, aerospace transportation executive, aerospace engineer; b. London, June 10, 1948; BSc in Aereo. Engring., Loughborough U. of Tech., Loughborough, Leics, Eng., 1972; PhD in Aerodynamics, Loughborough U. of Tech., 1991. Chartered engr., Royal Aero. Soc., UK, 1978. Future projects engr. Hawker Siddeley Aviation, Kingston, England, 1972—73; v.p. R & D Pilatus Aircraft Ltd, 6370 Stans, Switzerland, 1973—99; v.p. eclipse engring. Williams Internat., Walled Lake, Mich., 2000—01; v.p. engring. Eclipse Aviation Corp, Albuquerque, 2000—. Study group mem. Joint Aviation Authority, 1991—99; bd. mem., dir. Dynamic Test Centre, Biel, Bern, Switzerland, 1997—99; adv. bd. Mech. Engring., U. N.Mex., Albuquerque, 2002—. Internat. editor (periodical) Jour. of Aircraft. Fellow: Royal Aero. Soc.; mem.: AIAA, Internat. Coun. of Aero. Scis. (program com. mem. 1990—), Internat. Coun. of Aero. Scis. (coun. mem. 1986—99), Swiss Soc. of Aero. Scis. (coun. mem. 1986—99). Achievements include led team which developed Pilatus PC-7, PC-9, PC-12 and PC-7 Mk II aircraft; led Pilatus team in partnership with Beech Aircraft, which obtained contract for JPATS trainer aircraft for USAF & USN; led team which first introduced Friction Stir Welding production in aviation; led team whic developed revolutionary Eclipse 500 personal jet aircraft. Avocations: reading, snowboarding, squash, windsurfing, wine tasting. Home: 819 El Alhambra Cir NW Albuquerque NM 87107 Office: Eclipse Aviation Corp 2503 Clark Carr Loop SE Albuquerque NM 87106 E-mail: oliver.masefield@eclipseaviation.com.

MASEK, BEVERLY, state representative; b. Anvik, Alaska, Sept. 30, 1963; m. Jan Masek; 1 child, Michael. Asst. mgr. Stuckagain Heights Lodge; bookkeeper Chena Hot Springs; operator Masek Racing Kennels; owner, operator Rustic Wilderness Lodge; spokesperson Alyeska Pipeline, Charter North, Payless Drug Stores; mem. Alaska Ho. of Reps., 1994—. Commr. Alaska Native Commn., Alaska Hist. Commn.; mem. state adv. com. U.S. Civil Rights Commn.; spkr. child abuse prevention program, goal setting and achievement program. Mem. Alaska Outdoor Coun., Hugh O'Brien Youth Found. Mem.: NRA, Alaska Boating Assn. Republican. Avocations: dog mushing, hiking, fishing. Office: Rm 403 State Capitol Juneau AK 99801-1182 Address: 600 E Railroad Ave Ste 1 Wasilla AK 99654

MASELLI, JOHN ANTHONY, food products company executive; b. N.Y.C., Feb. 18, 1928; s. Anthony and Livia M.; m. Brigitta Degenkolb, Dec. 26, 1948; children: Elisa, John A. Jr. BS in Chemistry, CCNY, 1947; MS in Chemistry, Fordham U., 1949, PhD in Chemistry, 1952. Dir. research and devel. Standard Brands, Stamford, Conn., 1952-64; mgr. product devel. M&M/Mars, Hackettstown, N.J., 1964-67; pres. OZ Food Corp., Chgo., 1967-79; v.p. tech. Nabisco Brands, East Hanover, N.J., 1979-85; v.p. corp. research and devel. RJR Nabisco, Winston-Salem, N.C., 1985-87; sr. v.p. tech. Planters LifeSavers Co., Winston-Salem, 1987-91, cons., 1991—. Bd. dirs. Cultor Food Scis. (Finland), N.C. Biotech. Ctr., Sci-Works, Winston Salem, Winston Salem Symphony. Patentee in field. Bd. dirs. Chgo. Boy's Club, 1975-79, YMCA, Wilton, Conn, 1980-84. Mem. AAAS, ACS, Inst. Food Tech., Am. Soc. Bakery Engrs., Indsl. Biotechnology Assn., Indsl. Research Inst. Republican. Avocations: sailing, photography, music. Home: 529 Knob View Pl Winston Salem NC 27104-5107

MASERITZ, GUY B. lawyer; b. Balt., June 5, 1937; m. Sally Jane Sugar, Mar. 30, 1961; children: Marjorie Ellen, Michael Louis. BA, Johns Hopkins U., 1959, MA in Econs., 1961; LLB, U. Md., 1966. Bar: Md. 1966, D.C. 1968, U.S. Supreme Ct. 1975, U.S. Dist. Ct. Md. 1979. Atty. SEC, Washington, 1966-70; asst. gen. counsel securities Am. Life Ins. Assn., Washington, 1971-74; atty. eval. sect., chief legis. unit antitrust divsn. U.S. Dept. Justice, Washington, 1974-78, spl. asst. U.S. atty. Alexandria, Va., 1978; pvt. practice Columbia, Md., 1978—. Author: U.S. Department of Justice Antitrust Report on Property-Liability Insurance Industry, 1977; contbr. articles to profl. jours. Mem. Howard County (Md.) Charter Revision Commn., 1979; bd. dirs. Howard County YMCA, 1997-99, disting. bd. mem. 1999. With USAR, 1960-66. Mem. Md. Bar Assn., D.C. Bar Assn., Howard County Bar Assn., Greater Howard County C. of C. (dir., gen. counsel 1981-84). Office: Hobbits Glen 5040 Rushlight Path Columbia MD 21044-1295 E-mail: consult@maseritzlaw.com.

MASERU, NOBLE A.W. city health department administrator; b. Detroit; BS, Wayne State U.; MPH, Emory U. Sch. Medicine; PhD in Health Policy, Atlanta U. Founding dir., master of pub. health program Morehouse Sch. Medicine, Atlanta; health policy scientist Morehouse Coll., Pub. Health Scis. Inst.; v.p., cmty. health Greater Detroit Area Health Coun. Inc., 1998—2000; dir. and health officer Detroit Dept. Health and Wellness Promotion, 2003—. Office: Detroit Health Dept Herman Kiefer Health Complex 1151 Taylore Detroit MI 48202 Office Phone: 313-876-4300. Business E-Mail: manerun@health.ci.detroit.mi.us.

MASEY, JACK, exhibition designer; b. N.Y.C., June 10, 1924; s. Max and Anna Masey; m. Mary Lou Leach, Dec. 27, 1959. Student, Cooper Union, 1941-43; BFA, Yale U., 1950. Pres. MetaForm Inc., N.Y.C., 1979—; co. project mgr. for design of La. Pavilion, World Expo., New Orleans, 1984, Statue of Liberty Exhibit, N.Y.C., 1986; project mgr. for design Johnstown (Pa.) Flood Mus., 1988, Ellis Island Immigration Mus., N.Y.C., 1990; co. project mgr. for design of Nat. D-Day Mus., New Orleans, 1994, designer D-Day Invasion, Pacific Exhbn., 2000; co. project mgr. for design of Harry S. Truman Mus., Independence, Mo., 2001. Lectr. Sch. Art and Arch., Yale U., 1968—69; design cons. State Hermitage Mus., St. Petersburg, Russia, 1998; project mgr. for design of Am. air power since WWII exhbn. The Mighty Eighth Air Force Mus., Savannah, Ga., 2001. Cartoonist Esquire mag, 1946; exhibits officer, USIS, New Delhi, 1951-55; designer U.S. Pavilion, Kabul Internat. Fair, 1956; dir. design Am. Nat. Exhbn., Moscow, 1959, chief, East-West exhibits br. USIA, Washington, 1960-67; chief design U.S. Pavilion, Montreal (Que., Can.) World's Fair, 1967, dep. commr. gen. for planning and design Osaka (Japan) World Expn., 1970; dir. design Am. Revolution Bicentennial Commn., Washington, 1971-73; dir. design and exhbns. Am. Revolution Bicentennial Adminstrn., 1974-77, design dir. Internat. Communication Agy., Washington, 1977—; designer: Medicine-U.S.A. exhbn. for, USSR exchange program, 1962, Tech.-Books exhbns., 1963; co-designer Vis. Complex, UN, UN Found., N.Y.C. Served with AUS, 1943-45, ETO. Recipient Meritorious Service award USIA, 1959, Superior Service award, 1964, Superior Honor award, 1967, 75; award of excellence Fed. Design Council, 1975; Outstanding Achievement award, 1979; award of excellence Soc. Fed. Artists and Designers, 1971; Gold medal Art Dirs. Club, 1965; cert. of excellence Am. Inst. Graphic Arts, 1964; two Fed. Design Achievement awards for Contributions to Excellence in Design, U.S. Govt., 1984, Presdl. awards for Statue of Liberty Exhibit, 1986, for Ellis Island Immigration Mus., 1990. Home: 131 E 66th St Apt 3A New York NY 10021-6129 Office: 15 E 26th St New York NY 10010-1505 Office Phone: 212-532-8580.

MASH, DONALD J. college president; b. Oct. 12, 1942; children: Maria, Christina, Donnie (dec.). BS in Edn., Ind. U. Pa., 1960; MA in Geography, U. Pitts., 1966; PhD, Ohio State U., 1974. Teaching fellow U. Pitts., 1964-65; instr. geography U. Pitts.-Bradford, 1965-68; dean for student svcs. Ohio Dominican Coll., 1968-75; v.p. for student affairs George Mason U., Fairfax, Va., 1975-85, exec. v.p. adminstrn., 1985-88; pres. Wayne (Nebr.) State Coll., 1988-98; chancellor U. Wis.-Eau Claire, 1998—. Office: Univ of Wisconsin-Eau Claire Office of Chancellor PO Box 4004 Eau Claire WI 54702-4004

MASH, SAMUEL DAVID, dean; b. Corsicana, Tex., Jan. 22, 1957; s. Virgil Lee and Linda Rose Mash; m. Colleen Faye Carroll, May 22, 1979; children: Jonathan Andrew children: Brian David, Aaron Joseph. B.S., So. Meth. U., Dallas, Tex., 1975—79; Th.M., Dallas Theol. Sem., Dallas, Tex., 1980—84; M.S., U. of North Tex., Denton, Tex., 1986—87. Head libr. The Stony Brook Sch., NY, 1987—91; dir. of academic info. services Columbia Internat. U., SC, 1991—2001, dean of info. resources and services, 2001—04. Vice-chair, libr. adminstrn. sect. SC. Libr. Assn., Columbia, SC, 1994—95, chair, libr. adminstrn. sect., 1995—96; sec., stats. subcommittee, extended libr. services sect. Assn. of Coll. and Rsch. Libraries, 1995—96. Author: articles in various publications. Mem.: ALA. Avocations: wilderness backpacking, classical music. Office: Columbia International University 7435 Monticello Road Columbia SC 29230 Office Phone: 803-754-4100 3202. E-mail: dmash@ciu.edu.

MASHBERG, ARTHUR, medical educator; b. Nov. 1925; m. Edna Mashberg; children: Marc, Debra. AB in Biology and Chemistry cum laude, Bklyn. Coll., 1945; DDS, NYU, 1949; postgrad., U. Pitts., 1958-59. Diplomate Am. Bd. Oral and Maxillofacial Surgery. Resident in oral & maxillofacial (OMF) surgery VA Hosp., Pitts., 1958-61; chief OMF surgery sect. VA Med. Ctr., East Orange, NJ, 1961-90; clin. prof. to prof. to prof. emeritus of surgery U. Medicine and Dentistry, N.J. Med. Sch., 1977—; clin. assoc. prof. to clin. prof. to vis. prof. OMF surgery U. Medicine and Dentistry, N.J. Dental Sch., 1961—90; clin. assoc. prof. to clin. prof. OMF surgery Fairleigh Dickinson U., NJ, 1976—89. Attending, dept. oral surgery and anesthesiology Martland Hosp., 1969—75; cons. staff St. Joseph's Hosp. and Med. Ctr., Paterson, NJ, 1978—; dep. dir. Cancer Ctr., Va. Med. Ctr., E. Orange, NJ, 1988—90; cons. Vets. Affairs Med. Ctr., 1990—99, Rsch. Epidemiol. of Head & Neck Cancer; scientist US-Italy Cancer exch.; lectr. in head and neck oncology numerous Univ. and orgn. Contbr. articles to profl. jours., chpts. to books, monographs, abstracts. Capt. U.S. Army, 1951—52, Korea. Grantee VA, 1967-72, 71-73, 72-77, NIH, NIDR, 1973-80, NIH, 1980-82, Nat. Cancer Inst., 1981-84, Smokeless Tobacco Rsch. Inst., 1995. Fellow Am. Coll. Dentists; mem. ADA, Acad. Medicine of NJ, Am. Cancer Soc. (profl. edn. com. 1983, med. com. 1993-94, Cancer Achievement award), Am. Soc. OMF Surgery, Am. Coll. OMF Surgeons, Nat. Assn. V.A. Dentists (pres.), Cancer Inst. NJ (edn. com. 1976-77), NJ Soc. Oral Surgeons, Oncology Soc. NJ, Soc. of Head and Neck Surgeons, NY Head and Neck Soc., Soc. of Educators in OMF Surgery. Achievements include patents for in field of cancer detection; identification of erythroplasia as the earlies visual sign of squamous cancer; establishment of alcohol as a primary risk factor in oral and pharyngeal cancer. Home: PO Box 334 Wellfleet MA 02667-0334 E-mail: aartmash@comcast.net.

MASHBURN, DONALD EUGENE, education educator; b. Johnson City, Tenn., June 10, 1944; s. Harvey and Martha (McNeese) M.; m. Mary Juanita McKee, May 30, 1970; 1 child, Donna Sue. BS, East Tenn. State U., 1965, MS, 1971. Tchr. Cocke County High Sch., Newport, Tenn., 1965-66, John S. Battle High Sch., Bristol, Va., 1966-94, Wallace Mid. Sch., Bristol, 1994-97; tech. support tchr. Meadowview (Va.) Elem. Sch., 1997-98, Rhea Valley Elem. Sch., Damascus, Va., 1997-98, Valley Inst. Elem. Sch., Bristol, Va., 1997-98, Watanga Elem. Sch., Abingdon, Va., 1997-98; with Info. Sys. and Media Prodn., Abingdon, 1998-99; tchr. Washington Coll. Acad., Limestone, Tenn., 2001; substitute tchr. Washington County (Tenn.) Schs., 2002—. Adj. faculty N.E. State Tech. C.C., Blountville, Tenn., 1984—99. Mem. Ruritan (sec. Conklin club 1986-91, 98, 2001-03, pres. 1985, 92, 99, 2000, Davy Crockett dist. treas. 1993, zone gov. 2003-04, lt. gov. 2004). Republican. Methodist. Avocations: computers, farming. Home and Office: 195 Mashburn Rd Telford TN 37690-3132

MASHBURN, JOSEPH L. architecture educator; BArch, U. Houston; MArch, Tex. A&M U. Registered arch. Vis. fellow U. Western Australia Sch. Arch. and Fine Arts; arch. dept. head Curtin U. Tech., Perth, Australia; prof. arch. Va. Poly. Inst.; with Tex. A&M U.; prof. arch. U. Houston, Gerald D. Hines Coll. Arch., dean, 1998—. Named to Arch. Hall of Fame, U. Houston, 1996; recipient Outstanding Alumni award, Tex. A&M U. Coll. Arch., 2002. Mem.: AIA. Office: Univ Houston Gerald D Hines Coll Arch 4800 Calhoun Rd Houston TX 77204*

MASHECK, JOSEPH DANIEL, art critic, educator; b. NYC, Jan. 19, 1942; s. Joseph Anthony and Dorothy Anna (Cahill) M. AB, Columbia U., 1963, MA, 1965, PhD, 1973; MLitt, U. Dublin, 2001. Editorial researcher Bollingen Found.-Princeton U. Press, 1967-69; lectr. liberal studies Maidstone Coll. Art, Kent, Eng., 1968-69; preceptor in art history Columbia U., 1970-71; instr. art history Barnard Coll., 1971-73, asst. prof., 1973-82; lectr. visual and environ. studies Harvard U., Cambridge, Mass., 1983-86; assoc. prof. art history Hofstra U., Hempstead, N.Y., 1987-94, prof., 1994—. Coord. grad. program in humanities Hofstra Mus., Hempstead, 1991—99, curatorial cons., 1991. Author: Historical Present: Essays of the 1970s, 1984, Smart Art (Point 1), 1984, Modernites: Art-Matters in the Present, 1993, Building-Art: Modern Architecture Under Cultural Construction, 1993, C's Aesthetics: Philosophy in the Painting, 2004; editor: Marcel Duchamp in Perspective 1975, reprint, 2002, Van Gogh 100, 1996, A.W. Dow's Composition, 1997; editor-in-chief Artforum mag., 1977-79. Bd. dirs. Crosby St. Project, N.Y., 1995-96; mem. adv. bd. Annals of Scholarship, 1998—. Samuel H. Kress Found. fellow, 1968-69, Nat. Endowment Arts fellow, 1972-73, 75-76, Guggenheim fellow, 1977-78; grantee Malevich Soc., 2003; Hon. Armiger, Coll. Arms, London Fellow Royal Soc. Arts, Soc. Antiquaries of Scotland; mem. AAUP, Coll. Art Assn., Internat. Assn. Art Critics, United Arts Club (Dublin). Roman Catholic. Democrat. Office: Hofstra U Dept Fine Arts and Art History Calkins Hall Hempstead NY 11549

MASHIN, JACQUELINE ANN COOK, medical sciences administrator, nursing administrator; b. Chgo., May 11, 1941; d. William Hermann and Ann (Smidt) Cook; m. Fredric John Mashin, June 7, 1970; children: Joseph Glenn, Alison Robin. BS, U. Md., 1984; BSN, Cath. U. Am., Washington, 1993. Cert. realtor. Adminstrv. asst. CIA, Washington, 1963-66; asst. to mng. dir. Aerospace Edn. Found., Washington, 1966-74; exec. asst. to asst exec. dir. Air Force Assn., Washington, 1974-79; v.p., ptnrship. owner Discount Linen Store, Silver Spring, Md., 1979-81; asst. regional polit. dir. Office of Pres.-elect, Washington, 1980-81; confidential asst. to dir. Office of Personnel Mgmt. (US), Washington, 1981-83; spl. asst. to dep. dir. Office of Mgmt. and Budget, Washington, 1983-86; dir. internat. communications and spl. asst. to commr. Dept. of the Interior, Washington, 1986-89, cons., 1989-93; with Washington Hosp. Ctr., 1993—. Chmn., vol. coord. Mo. County Rep. Party, 1999; chmn. Bayclub, Mo. County Fedn. Rep. Women, 1999, 2000; mem. bd. rev. Dept. Health and Mental Hygiene Md. State Senate, Annapolis, Md., 2003—. Pres. Layhill Civic Assn., Silver Spring, Md., 1980; state chmn. Md.'s Reagan Youth Delegation, Annapolis, Md., 1980; state treas., office mgr. Reagan-Bush State Hdqrs. of Md., Silver Spring, 1980; mem. Women's Com. Nat. Symphony Orch.; pres. Rock Creek Women's Rep. Club, 1998, Montgomery County Rep. Party, 1999, Montgomery County Fedn. Rep. Women, 1999—; steering com. Wheaton Redevel. Program, 2001—; gov.'s adv. bd. Md. Bd. Health and Mental Hygiene. Mem.: Air Force Assn. (life), U.S. Capital Hist. Soc., Am. League Lobbyists, Aux. Salvation Army (life), Indian Springs Country Club. Republican. Avocations: golf, horseback riding, collecting wine glasses, hibel plates, lithos and laliqe crystal. Home and Office: 2429 White Horse Ln Silver Spring MD 20906-2243 Office Phone: 301-502-3913. E-mail: Jaguar041@aol.com.

MASHKEVICH, STEFAN VLADIMIROVICH, physicist, researcher, computer scientist; b. Kiev, USSR, Aug. 15, 1971; s. Vladimir Stefanovich Mashkevich and Lyudmila Petrovna Godenko; m. Veronica Petrovna Kaninska, Sept. 15, 1995; 1 child, David Stefan. MS, Kiev State U., 1990; PhD in Physics and Math., Joint Inst. for Nuc. Rsch., Dubna, Russia, 1993. Jr. rschr. Inst. Theoretical Physics, Kiev, 1993—95, rschr., 1995—98; systems analyst Optimark Technologies, Jersey City, 1998—2000; sr. specialist Merrill Lynch, N.Y.C., 2000—02; sci. software developer Schrödinger, Inc., 2002—. Vis. scientist Inst. de Physique Nucléaire, Orsay, France, 1995, Ctr. for Advanced Study, Oslo, 1995-96; vis. scholar U. Wash., Seattle, 1996. Contbr. articles to profl. jours. Linkage grantee NATO, 1993-94; fellow Ctr. Nat. Rsch. Sci., Paris, 1995, Norwegian Acad. Sci. and Letters, Oslo, 1995-96. Avocations: poetry, chess, soccer, history. Home: 1712 Madison Pl Brooklyn NY 11229-2628 E-mail: mash@mashke.org.

MASHNIK, STEPAN G. physicist; b. Brinzeni, Moldova, June 1, 1952;, naturalized, U.S., 2004; s. George I. and Natalia G. Mashnik; m. Nadejda I. Sukhlova; children: Polina, Daria. BS, Kishinev State U., 1973; MS, Moscow State U., 1974; PhD, Joint Inst. Nuc. Rsch., Dubna, Russia, 1981; sr. rsch. diploma, Presidium Acad. Sci. USSR, Moscow, 1989. Jr. rsch. scientist Joint Inst. Nuc. Rsch., Dubna, Russia, 1975—82, sr. rsch. scientist, 1991—97; sr./jr. rschr. Acad. Sci. Moldova, Kishinev, 1982—91, leading rsch. scientist, 1991—; long term vis. staff mem. Los Alamos (N.Mex) Nat. Lab., 1997—2001, staff mem., 2001—. Country coord. XXVIII Int. Conf. High Energy Physics, Hamburg, 1996—97; the Plenipotentiary of the Republic of Moldova Joint Inst. Nuc. Rsch., Dubna, 1992—94, mem. internat. sci. coun., 1992—95; mem. intermediate energy data group NEA/OECD, Paris, 1994—, liaison officer between Paris, France and JINR, Dubna, 1996—97; vis. rschr. Oak Ridge (Tenn.) Nat. Lab., 1995—96, CEA, Centre d'Etudes de Bruyers-le-Chatel, France, 1996. Contbr. articles to profl. jours., 1983. Recipient Several Joint Inst. for Nuc. Rsch. and Dubna County awards, For Excellent Work, 1975—82, Inst. of Applied Physics, Acad. of Sci. of Moldova award, For Investigations in Theoretical Physics, 1983, Several Awards from Am. Biog. Inst. (USA) and Internat. Biographycal Centre, Cambridge, Eng., Internat. Order of Merit, Internat. Diploma of Honor, Nobel Price Award by the UCC, 2000—02, Moldova Award for Young Scientists; NASA Grant, Propagation Model for Cosmic Ray Species in the Galaxy, 2002—, CRDF Grant, Devel. of a Universal Intranuclear Cascade Type Model for Heavy Ion and Nucleon Induced Reactions at Intermediate Energies, 2001—. Mem.: Phys. Soc. of the Republic of Moldova, Internat. Nuc. Soc., Am. Nuc. Soc., Am. Phys. Soc. Avocations: swimming, travel, skiing, jogging. Office Phone: 505-667-9946. Office Fax: 505-667-1931. Personal E-mail: mashniks@qwest.net. Business E-Mail: mashnik@lanl.gov.

MASI, DALE A. research company executive, social work educator; b. N.Y.C. d. Alphonse E. and Vera Avella; children: Eric, Renee, Robin. BS, Coll. Mt. St. Vincent; MSW, U. Ill.; D Social Work, Cath. U. Lectr. Sch. Social Svcs., Ipswitch, Eng., 1970-72; project dir. occupational substance abuse program, asso. prof. Boston Coll. Grad. Sch. Social Work, 1972-79; dir. Office Employee Counseling Svc., Dept. Health/Human Svcs., Washington, 1979-84; pres. Masi Research Cons., Inc., 1984—; prof. U. Md. Grad. Sch. Social Work, 1980—; adj. prof. U. Md. Coll. Bus. and Mgmt., 1980—. Mem. IBM Mental Health Adv. Bd., 1990-95; cons. IBM, Toyota, Mobil Chm., The Washington Post, U.S. Ho. Reps., U.S. Postal Svc., White House, WHO, Bechtel Corp., other orgns. in pub. and pvt. sector; bd. advisors Nat. Security Inst., Wayside

Youth and Family Support Network; USIA Ampart lectr. on alcohol, drugs and AIDS in the workplace; chair CMHS Jooint Industry Alliance, 2002—. Author: Human Services in Industry, Organizing for Women, Designing Employee Assistance Programs, Drug Free Workplace, AIDS Issues in the Workplace: A Response Model for Human Resource Management, The AMA Handbook for Developing Employee Assistance and Counseling Programs, Evaluating Your Employee Assistance and Managed Behavioral Care Program, Internat. Employee Assistance Anthology, Productivity Lost: Alcohol and Drugs in the Workplace; co-author: Shrink to Fit: Answers to Your Questions About Therapy; also over 40 articles. Named Disting. Scholar, Nat. Acad. Practice, 2001—; named to Employee Assistance Program Hall of Fame; recipient award, Employee Assistance Program Digest; fellow Fulbright fellow, 1969—70, 1994, AAUW postdoctoral fellow, NIMH, 1962—64; Fulbright Sr. Specialist Canidate, 2002. Mem. AAUW, NASW (Internat. Rhoda G. Sarnat award 1993), Acad. Cert. Social Workers, Employee Assistance Profls. Assn. (nat. individual achievement award 1983), Fulbright Assn. (nat. bd.). Democrat. Roman Catholic. Office: 2549 Virginia Ave NW Washington DC 20037-1903 Office Phone: 202-223-2399. E-mail: masirsrch@aol.com.

MASI, JANE VIRGINIA, marketing and sales consultant; b. June 6, 1947; d. Vincent Joseph and Virginia Marie (Beddow) Masi; m. Charles Walter Friedman, Feb. 14, 1976 (div. Sept. 1998). BA in Comms. and Psychology, Mercy Coll., N.Y., 1969; MA, New Sch. Social Rsch., 1979, postgrad., 1994. Asst. sales mgr. Chevron Chem., N.Y.C., 1969-71; writer, 1973-75; ptnr. Masi-D'Angelo Constrn. and Devel. Assocs., N.Y.C., 1979-83; pres., founder Beddow Mills Inc., N.Y.C., 1982-85, Beddow Mfg. Inc., N.Y.C., 1983-85; co-pres. TRS Mktg. Inc., N.Y.C., 1985—. Founder Energy Works, 1985, Did You Know, 1989, Range Burgers, 1989, Terramor, 1989, In the Pink!, 1991, The Profl. Salon, 1991, Terramor Foods, 1991, Terramor Catering, 2003; founder, dir. TRS Inc. Profl. Suite, 1986-2002; pub. The Planetary Gazette, 2002. Author 38 novellas. N.Y. Regents scholar, 1965-69. Mem. Soc. Ethical Treatment of Animals. Avocations: woodworking, carpentry, advocating animal rights, design psychology. Office: TRS Mktg Inc 44 E 32nd St Fl 11 New York NY 10016-5508 Office Phone: 212-685-2848. E-mail: terramor@earthlink.net.

MASI, ROBIN, artist, writer, educator; b. Palo Alto, Calif., July 29, 1960; d. Joseph Louis and Dale (Avella) M.; 1 child, Benjamin Westmont. BFA, Tufts U., 1983; MFA, Acad. of Art Coll., San Francisco, 1994. Adj. faculty fine arts Regis Coll., Weston, Mass., 1994-95, Endicott Coll., Beverly, Mass., 1995-96. Vis. faculty Sch. Mus. Fine Arts, 1996—. Author: Shrink-to-Fit: Answers to Your Questions About Therapy, 1998; exhibited in Boston, N.Y., Washington, San Francisco, 1980—; author (screenplay) Searching for Judith, 1997. Dir. The Women's Artist Database Project, 1992; co-founder The Varo Registry of Women Artists, 1995—; moderator Feminist Art History and Women Artist Listserves, 1996—. Democrat. Roman Catholic. E-mail: rmasi@ziplink.net.

MASIE, ELLIOTT, training executive; b. NYC, May 13, 1950; s. Harry H. and Dorothy (Gordon) M. BA, SUNY, 1972. Cons. Irish Ministry Health, Dublin, 1972-73; project evaluator NY State Dept. Edn., NY, 1973-76; dir. Nat. Student Leadership Ctr., Raquette Lake, NY, 1977—; pres. Masie Ctr., 1991—. Cons. Disney, CIA, 1990-91, Dow Chem., NASA, Panama C.Z., Bank of Am., Nat. Assn. Secondary Sch. Prins., Washington, 1985; rsch. fellow Picturetel Corp., 1996; mem. Oracle Adv. Edn. Bd., 1996; pres. Ziff Daus Inst., 1992-94; founder On-Line Learning Coun.; mem. White House Commn. on Tng. Opportunities, Nat. Govs. Assn.'s Commn. on Learning. Author: Computers and Student Activities, 1984, The Computer Training Handbook, 1995, Learning in the Digital Age, others; host Microsoft TV. Mem. Assn. Computer Tng. and Support (pres., dir. 1989—, founder 1989—), Nat. Tng. & Computer Projects (bd. dir., pres. Tools for Tng. 1985—);bd. of trustees, Skidmore Coll.; Bd. of Found., Empire State Coll.; Bd. of Dir., Operation Respect Found. Jewish. Avocation: technology. Office: Masie Ctr PO Box 397 Saratoga Springs NY 12866-0397

MASIELLO, ANTHONY M. (TONY MASIELLO), mayor; b. Buffalo, N.Y., 1947; s. Dan and Bridget M.; married; 1 child, Kimberly; m. Kathleen McCue; children: Kimberly, Ariel, Madeline Rose. BS, Canisius Coll.; LHD (hon.), Medaille Coll., Buffalo. Mem. North Dist. Buffalo Common Coun., 1971, councilman-at-large, 1976, coun. majority leader; mem. NY State Senate, 1980; mayor City of Buffalo, 1994—. Chair Democratic Conf. Office: Office of the Mayor 201 City Hall 65 Niagara Sq Buffalo NY 14202-3331

MASIELLO, ROCCO JOSEPH, airlines and aerospace manufacturing executive; b. N.Y.C., Jan. 9, 1922; s. Joseph and Armanda (Mansueti) M.; m. Rita Elizabeth Amoruso, Feb. 11, 1945; children: Richard, Robin, Janet. Student, CCNY, 1946-48, Hofstra U., 1951-54. Registered profl. engr., Maine. With Pan. Am. World Airways, N.Y.C., 1950-59; v.p. maintenance and engrng. U.S. Air Group, Pitts., 1959-72, Am. Airlines, Tulsa, 1973-82, sr. v.p. ops. Dallas, 1982-86; founder, exec. v.p. USAfrica Airways, 1990-94, also bd. dirs; founder The Reston Group; aerospace cons., prin. R.J. Masiello and Assoc. Mem. Soc. Aerospace Engr., Royal Aero. Soc. Roman Catholic. Office Phone: 207-594-5223. E-mail: rjmasiello@aol.com.

MASILELA, CALVIN ONIAS, land use planner, educator; b. Bulawayo, Zimbabwe, Oct. 27, 1955; s. Stephen Masilela and Martha Ndiweni; m. Sibonisiwe Ntini; children: Zwelihle, Ayanda. BA in Urban Planning, Westminster U., London, 1980; postgrad. diploma, U. Westminster, London, 1981; M in Urban and Regl. Planning, Va. Tech. U., 1983, PhD, 1989. Vis. prof. Indiana U. Pa., 1989—90, asst. prof., 1990—93, W.Va. U., 1993—99, assoc. prof., 1999—2001, dir. Ronald E. McNair scholars program, 1999—2001. Assoc. prof. Ind. U. of Pa., Indiana, 2001—. Bd. dirs. Mon Valley Green Space Coalition, Morgantown, 2000-01. Recipient Outstanding Educator in Conservation Monongahela Soil Conservation Dist., 1999, Cheikh Anta Diop award Ctr. for Black Culture and Rsch., 1995, Urban Indicators award Univ. Consortium for Geographic Info. Sci. U.S. HUD, 2001; named Eberly Coll. Arts and Scis. Outstanding Tchr., 2000. Mem. Am. Planning Assn., Assn. Am. Geographers, Coun. Ednl. Opportunity, Mid-Eastern Assn. Ednl. Opportunity Pers., W.Va. Assn. Ednl. Opportunity Pers. Office: Dept Geography and Regional Planning Indiana U of Pa Indiana PA 15705 Home: 215 College Lodge Rd Indiana PA 15701 E-mail: cmasilel@iup.edu.

MASIN, MICHAEL TERRY, lawyer; came to U.S., 1954; BA, Dartmouth U., 1966; JD, UCLA, 1969. Bar: Calif. 1969, D.C. 1970. Assoc. O'Melveny & Myers, L.A., 1969-76, ptnr. Washington, 1976-91, mng. ptnr. N.Y.C., 1991-93; vice chair, pres. GTE, Irving, Tex., 1993—2000; vice chmn., pres. Verizon Comms., N.Y.C., 2000—02; vice chmn., COO Citigroup, N.Y.C., 2002—. Trustee Carnegie Hall, W.M. Keck Found.; mem. dean's coun. UCLA Sch. Law Mem. Coun. on Fgn. Rels., The Brook. Republican. Methodist. Office: O'Melveny & Meyers 7 Times Sq 30th Fl New York NY 10036 E-mail: mmasin@omm.com.

MASINO, FRANK A. radiologist; b. Newark, 1951; MD, Albert Einstein Coll. Medicine, 1978. Bd. cert. therapeutic radiology. Intern Med. Coll. Va., Richmond, 1978; resident in radium therapy Yale-New Haven Hosp., 1979—82; radiation oncologist Stamford (Conn.) Hosp., 1982—. Office: Stamford Hosp 34 Shelburne Rd Stamford CT 06902-3628*

MASINTER, EDGAR MARTIN, investment banker; b. Huntington, W.Va., Jan. 2, 1931; s. Ralph Leon and Gazella (Schlossberg) M.; m. Margery Flocks, July 8, 1962; children: Robert Andrew, Catherine Diane Hildenbrand. BA, Princeton U., 1952; LLB, Harvard U., 1955. Bar: D.C. 1955, N.Y. 1958. Assoc. Simpson Thacher & Bartlett, N.Y.C., 1957-65, ptnr., 1966-95, The Bridgeford Group, Ltd., N.Y.C., 1996-97; ltd. ptnr. The Beacon Group, LP, 1998—; exec. dir., mem. The Beacon Group Capital Svcs., LLC, N.Y.C., 1997—, The Beacon Coun., N.Y.C., 1997—, The Beacon Group Capital Svcs., LLC, N.Y.C., 1997—. Spl. advisor Nassau Capital. Trustee Grand Teton Music Festival; pres. bd. regents The Mercersburg (Pa.) Acad.; mem. ethics com. Whitney Mus. Am. Art. With U.S. Army, 1955-57. Office: The Beacon Group 399 Park Ave Unit 17 New York NY 10022-4600

MASKALL, MARTHA JOSEPHINE, web site designer, publishing executive, health consultant; b. Kearny, N.J., Mar. 30, 1945; d. Charles Edgar and Mathilda (Comba) M. BA in Biology, Stanford U., 1966; MA, Duke U., 1969. Cert. data processor, 1979. Data base adminstr. Armco Steel, Ashland, Ky., 1972-74; project mgr. Rand Info. Systems, San Francisco, 1974-78; sales rep. Datacom ADR, San Francisco, 1980-81; systems engr. Four-Phase Systems, Sacramento, 1981-83; exec. recruiter, 1983—90; owner Attitude Works Pub., Fair Oaks, Calif., 1990—. Health cons., 1994—. Author: The Attitude Treasury: 101 Inspiring Quotations, 1990, The Athena Treasury: 101 Inspiring Quotations by Women, 1993. NDEA fellow, 1966-68. Mem. Sierra Club, Toastmasters (Disting. Toastmaster award 1989). Democrat. Home: 8456 Hidden Valley Cir Fair Oaks CA 95628-6121 Office: Attitude Works Publishing 8456 Hidden Valley Cir Fair Oaks CA 95628-6121 Office Phone: 916-967-2472. E-mail: mmaskall@pacbell.net.

MASKET, EDWARD SEYMOUR, television executive; b. N.Y.C., Mar. 3, 1923; s. Isadore and Jennie (Bernstein) M.; m. Frances Ellen Rees, June 11, 1958 (div.); children: Joel Daniel, Johanna Rees Bettaeib, Kate Isobel Smiley. BS, CCNY, 1942; LLB, JD, Harvard U., 1949. Bar: N.Y. 1949. Atty., dir. bus. affairs, v.p. bus. affairs ABC, 1951-68; v.p. to exec. v.p. Columbia Pictures TV, Burbank, Calif., 1968-81; sr. v.p. adminstrn. Universal TV, 1982-86, exec. v.p. adminstrn., 1986-90, MCA TV Group, 1990-93; TV cons., 1994—. Served as 2d lt. AUS, 1942-46, PTO. Mem. Motion Picture Pioneers, Phi Beta Kappa. Avocations: tennis, golf. E-mail: telemogul@aol.com.

MASKET, SAMUEL, medical association administrator; b. N.Y.C., 1943; MD, N.Y. Med. Coll., 1968. Diplomate Am. Bd. Ophthalmology. Intern Bronx Mcpl. Hosp.-Einstein, N.Y.C., 1968—69; resident Metro Hosp. Ctr.-N.Y. Med., 1969—73; fellow Columbia-Presbyn. Med. Ctr., N.Y.C.; asst. clin. prof. ophthalmology UCLA; mem. staff West Hills Hosp., Canoga Park, Calif.; chmn. Am. Bd. Ophthalmology, Bala Cynwyd, Pa.; clinical prof. Jules Stein Eye Inst., Los Angeles, Calif. Fellow: Am. Acad. Ophthalmology; mem.: PAAO, ASCRS, AMA. Office: Am Bd Ophthalmology 111 Presidential Blvd Ste 241 Bala Cynwyd PA 19004-1012 also: 7230 Med Ctr Dr Ste 204 Canoga Park CA 91307 Office: Jules Stein Eye Inst 100 Stein Plaza UCLA Los Angeles CA 90095

MASKIN, ERIC STARK, economics professor; b. N.Y.C., Dec. 12, 1950; m. Gayle Sawtelle; children: Joseph, Charlotte. AB in Maths., Harvard U., 1972, AM in Applied maths., 1974, PhD in Applied Maths., 1976. Rsch. fellow Jesus Coll. Cambridge (Eng.) U., 1976-77; asst. prof. econs. MIT, Cambridge, Mass., 1977-80, assoc. prof. econs., 1980-81, prof. econs., 1981-84, Harvard U., Cambridge, 1985—2000; prof. social sci. Inst. for Advanced Study, Princeton, NJ, 2000—. Am. editor: Rev. of Econ. Studies, 1977-82; assoc. editor: Social Choice and Welfare, 1983—, Games and Econ. Behavior, 1988—; editor Quar. Jour. of Econs., 1984-90, Jour. Risk and Uncertainty, 1987-94; editor: Econs. Letters, 1992—. Churchill Coll. fellow, 1980-81; Guggenheim fellow, 1980-81, Sloan fellow, 1983-85, St. John's Coll. fellow, 1987-88. Fellow Econometric Soc., Am. Acad. Arts and Sci., Brit. Acad. (corr.); mem. Am. Econ. Assn. Office: Inst for Advanced Study Einstein Drive Princeton NJ 08540

MASLACH, CHRISTINA, psychology educator; b. San Francisco, Jan. 21, 1946; d. George James and Doris Ann (Cuneo) M.; m. Philip George Zimbardo, Aug. 10, 1972; children: Zara, Tanya. BA, Harvard-Radcliffe Coll., 1967; PhD, Stanford U., 1971. Prof. psychology U. Calif.-Berkeley, 1971—, vice provost for undergrad. edn., 2001—. Author: Burnout: The Cost of Caring, 1982; co-author: Influencing Attitudes and Changing Behavior, 1977, Maslach Burnout Inventory (rsch. scale), 1981, 2d edit., 1986, 3d edit., 1996, Experiencing Social Psychology, 1979, 4th edit., 2001, Professional Burnout, 1993, The Truth About Burnout, 1997, Preventing Burnout and Building Engagement, 2000. Recipient Disting. Teaching award, 1987, Best Paper award Jour. Orgnl. Behavior, 1994, Prof. of Yr. award Carnegie/CASE, 1997. Fellow AAAS, APA, Am. Psychol. Soc., Soc. Clin. and Exptl. Hypnosis (Henry Guze rsch. award 1980), We. Psychol. Assn. (pres. 1989); mem. Soc. Exptl. Social Psychology. Democrat. Office: U Calif Office of Chancellor 200 California Hall # 1500 Berkeley CA 94720-1500 Office Phone: 510-642-9594. E-mail: maslach@socrates.berkeley.edu.

MASLACH, GEORGE JAMES, former university official; b. San Francisco, May 4, 1920; s. Michael J. and Anna (Pszczolkowska) M.; m. Doris Anne Cuneo, Mar. 12, 1943; children: Christina, James, Steven. AA, San Francisco Jr. Coll., 1939; BS, U. Calif., 1942. Staff mem. radiation lab. Mass. Inst. Tech., 1942-45, Gen. Precision Labs., 1945-49; research engr. Inst. Engrng. Research, 1949-52, asst. dir., 1956-58; assoc. prof. U. Calif., Berkeley, 1952-58, prof., 1959-72, dean Coll. Engrng., 1963-72, provost profl. schools and colls., 1972-81, vice-chancellor research and acad. services, 1981-83; internat. cons. edn. and econ. devel., 1982—. Adv. aeros. research and devel. NATO, 1960-78, U.S. Naval Acad. Rev. Bd., 1966-75, Dept. Commerce Tech. Adv. Bd., 1964-69, Ford Found. and Am. Soc. Engrng. Edn., 1966-78 Mem. ASME, AAAS, Sigma Xi. Home: 265 Panoramic Way Berkeley CA 94704-1831

MASLANKA, SANDRA KAREN, social worker, educator, educational consultant; d. Eugene Francis and Adella Cook; m. William Vincent Maslanka, Nov. 4, 1972; children: William Vincent, Jason Anthony, Craig Allan, Angela Sandra, Chaze Robert. AS in Pedology, C.C. Allegheny County, Pitts., 1991; BA in Psychology, Point State Pk., 1993; MSW, U. Pitts., 1995. Lic. social worker Pa., 1995. Educator various agys., Pitts., 1995—, social worker, 1995—2003. Cons. Skm Consultants, Pitts., 2002—. Author: (manual) A Comprehensive Grief Workshop, 2002. Mem.: NASW (assoc.). Office Phone: 724-625-6225. Personal E-mail: skm@nauticom.net.

MASLANSKY, CAROL JEANNE, toxicologist; b. N.Y.C., Mar. 3, 1949; d. Paul Jeremiah and Jeanne Marie (Filiatrault) Lane; m. Steven Paul Maslansky, May 28, 1973. BA, SUNY, 1971; PhD, N.Y. Med. Coll., 1983. Diplomate Am. Bd. Toxicology; cert. gen. toxicology. Asst. entomologist N.Y. State Dept. Health, White Plains, 1973-74; sr. biologist Am. Health Found., Valhalla, N.Y., 1974-76; rsch. fellow N.Y. Med. Coll., Valhalla, 1977-83, Albert Einstein Coll. Medicine, Bronx, N.Y., 1983; copr. toxicologist Texaco, Inc., Beacon, N.Y., 1984-85; prin. GeoEnviron. Cons., Inc., White Plains, N.Y., 1982-97, Maslansky GeoEnviron. Inc., Prescott, Ariz., 1997—. Lectr. in entomology Westchester County Parks and Preserves, 1973-96, lectr. toxicology and hazardous materials, 1985—. Author: Air Monitoring Instrumentation, 1993, Health and Safety at Hazardous Waste Sites, 1997, (with others) Training for Hazardous Materials Team Members, 1991 (manual, video) The Poison Control Response to Chemical Emergencies, 1993. Mem. Harrison (N.Y.) Vol. Ambulance Corps., 1986-91, Westchester County (N.Y.) Hazardous Materials Response Team, 1987-96. Monsanto Fund Fellowship in Toxicology, 1988-90; grad. fellowship N.Y. Med. Coll., 1977-83. Mem. AAAS, Nat. Environ. Health Assn., N.Y. Acad. Sci., Am. Soc. Toxicology, Am. Indsl. Hygiene Assn., Environ. Mutagen Soc. Achievements include participation in development of genetic toxicity assays to identify potential carcinogens; rsch. on air monitoring instrumentation at hazardous materials sites, health and safety for hazardous waste site workers, environmental and chemical toxicology, genetic toxicology.

MASLIAH, ELIEZER, neuroscientist, educator; MD, Nat. Autonomous U. Mexico City, 1983. Resident in gen. pathology Nat. Inst. Nutrition, Mexico City, 1983—84; resident in oncologic pathology Nat. Inst. Cancerology, Mexico City, 1984—85; resident in pediat. pathology Nat. Inst. Pediats., Mexico City, 1985—86; postdoctoral fellow pathology of neurodegenerative diseases U. Calif.-San Diego, La Jolla, Calif., 1988—90, asst. rsch. neuroscientist depts. neurosci. and pathology, 1990—91, from asst. prof. to assoc. prof. depts. neurosci. and pathology, 1991—96, prof. dept. neurosci. and pathology, 1997—, dir. autopsy svc. dept. pathology, 1995—. Contbr. articles to profl. jours. Recipient Weil award, Am. Assn. Neuropathologists, 1989, Alzheimer Assn./George F. Berlinger Faculty Scholar award, 1990. Office: U Calif-San Diego Med Ctr-Hillcrest 200 W Arbor Dr San Diego CA 92103

MASLOW, AARON D. lawyer; b. Bklyn., Dec. 19, 1956; s. Morris J. and Rosalind H. Maslow; m. Lori S. Fajnsod, Dec. 13, 1987; children: Rachel Francine, Sam Irvin, Bernard Jay. BA, Touro Coll., 1977; JD, Yeshiva U., 1980. Bar: N.Y. 1981, U.S. Ct. Appeals (2nd cir.) 1984, U.S. Supreme Ct. 1985. Pvt. law practice, Bklyn., 1981—. Adminstrv. law judge N.Y.C. Taxi & Limousine Commn., 1983—87, 1992—98, atty., 1987—88; legal counsel N.Y.C. Bd. Elections, 1988—92; adminstrv. law judge N.Y.C. Parking Violations Bur., 1989—99; small claims arbitrator N.Y.C. Civil Ct., Bklyn., 1992—98; no-fault ins. arbitrator Am. Arbitration Assn., N.Y.C., 2002—. Contbr. articles to profl. jours. Candidate State Assembly, Bklyn., 1996, Justice of State Supreme Ct., Bklyn., 1997, 2002; active Kings County Dem. County Com., Bklyn., 1976—94, Kings County Rep. County Com., Bklyn., 1995—, 2d vice-chmn., 2001—; v.p. Cong. Bnai Israel of Sheepshead Bay, Bklyn., 1990—91. Recipient Leadership award, Kings County Rep. Party, 2002. Mem.: Bklyn. Bar Assn., Nat. History Soc. Can., Citizens Union, United Zembrover Soc. (life; sec.-treas. 2001—03). Jewish. Avocations: travel, videography, history, philately. Home: 1761 Stuart St Brooklyn NY 11229

MASLOW, JEFFREY R. not-for-profit fundraiser; s. Bernard and Marlene Dell Maslow. Grad. h.s., Dallas. Vol. Beth David Communal Svc., Bklyn., 1979—; vol. CMHC bd. Maimonides Med. Ctr., Bklyn., 1987—, fin. chmn. CMHC bd., 1995—; vol. Guardians of the Sick, Bklyn. Sec. Kehilas Jakob Sulitza Congregation, 1980—; asst. Gabbai svcs. Congregation Agudath Avreichim, 1982—94; office asst. Office of Assemblyman Dov Hikind. Founder neighborhood girls' Sabbath afternoon meetings. Recipient Congregation Agudath Avreichim award, 1983, Boro Park Cmty. Coun. award, 1987, Svc. award, Maimonides Med. Ctr., 2001. Home: 1707 60th St Brooklyn NY 11204-2208

MASON, AIMEE HUNNICUTT ROMBERGER, retired philosophy and humanities educator; b. Atlanta, Nov. 3, 1918; d. Edwin William and Aimee Greenleaf (Hunnicutt) Romberger; m. Samuel Venable Mason, Aug. 16, 1941 (dec. 1988); children: Olivia Elizabeth (Mrs. Mason Butcher), Christopher Leeds. BA, Conn. Coll., 1940; postgrad., Emory U., 1946-48; MA, U. Fla., 1979, PhD, 1980; MA, Stetson U., 1968. Model, coll. shop Saks Fifth Ave., N.Y.C., 1939; jr. exec. merchandising G. Fox & Co., Hartford, Conn., 1940-41; air traffic contr. CAA, Atlanta, 1942; ptnr. Coronado Concrete Products, New Smyrna Beach, Fla., 1953-81; adj. faculty Valencia Jr. Coll., Orlando, Fla., 1969; instr. philosophy and Humanities Seminole C.C., Sanford, Fla., 1969. Area cons. ARC, 1947-50; del. Nat. Red Cross, Washington, 1949; founding mem. St. Joseph Hosp. Aux., Atlanta, 1950-53; v.p., treas. Nw Smyrna Beach PTA, 1955-60; bd. dirs. Atlanta Symphony Orch., Fla. Symphony Orch., 1954-59; mem Code Enforcement Bd., Edgewater, Fla., 1992-94. Lt. USCGR, 1943-46. Recipient award in graphics Nat. Assn. Women Artists, 1939, 41. Mem. AAUP, AAUW (founding mem. New Smyrna Beach, exec. bd. 1984-85, chmn. scholarship com. 1984-87, coll./univ. liaison 1987-91, citizens code enforcement bd. Edgewater 1992-94), DAV, Am. Philos. Assn., Fla. Philos. Assn. (exec. coun. 1978-79), Collegium Phenomenologicum, Soc. Existencial and Phenomenological Philosophy, Soc. Phenomenology in Human Scis., Merleau-Ponty Circle, Fla. Assn. Cmty. Colls., Univ. Club Winter Park. Home: B216/218 1620 Mayflower Court Winter Park FL 32792

MASON, ANDREW, film producer; b. Australia; Founder City Prodns., Sydney, Australia; co-founder, with Alex Proyas Mystery Clock Cinema; documentary and comml. film editor. Exec. prodr.: (films) Dark City, 1997, The Matrix Reloaded, 2003, Scooby-Doo, 2002, The Queen of the Damned, 2002, Kangaroo Jack, 2002; prodr.: Swimming Upstream, 2002; visual effects supr.: The Crow, 1993; Playing Beattie Bow; One Night Stand; Burke and Wills; Navigator; The Time Guardian. Judge Phobos Fiction Contest. Office: c/o New Line Cinema 10877 Wilshire Blvd Los Angeles CA 90024

MASON, BARBARA FOUNTAIN, minister; d. Johnnie Lee and Eddie Fountain; m. William Lawrence Mason, June 12, 1956; children: Johnnie Ann Crawford, Lawrencina Mason Oramalu. AA, Calvary Bible Coll., Kansas City, Mo., 1977; BS in Local Ch. Edn., Calvary Bapt. Bible Coll., Grandview, Mo., 1980; MA Ednl. Adminstrn., U.Mo., Kansas City, 1984; M in Religious Studies, Ctrl. Bapt. Theol. Sem., 1990; degree in spl. edn., Augsburg Coll., 2003. Pastor Little Flock Cmty. of Faith, Mpls., 1994—; tchr. Mpls. Pub. Schs., 1999—2003. Dir. Christian edn. Met. Missionary Bapt. Ch., Kans. City, Mo., 1977—90; asst. pastor Zion Bapt. Ch., Mpls., 1990—92; dir.. ecumenical ptnrs. Greater Mpls. Coun. of Churches, 1993—94, dir., social policy, 1993—94. Bd. dirs. Salvation Army, Mpls., 1993—94, Battered Women's Orgn., Mpls., 1995—97; mem. Mayor's Coun. on Interfaith & Racial Partnerships, Mpls., 1996—98; bd. dirs. Exodus Cmty. Devel., Mpls., 2000—01; mem. Ministerial Alliance, Mpls., 1991—94; bd. dirs. Greater Mpls. Coun. of Churches, Mpls., 1992—93. Named Role Model for Youth, Bd. of Christian Edn., Met. Bapt. Ch., 1990; recipient Regional Workshop Facilitator award, Nat. Bapt. Pub. Bd., 1988; scholar Multicultural Educators' Program, Mpls. Pub. Schs., 2001—03. Mem.: LWV (bd. dirs. 1999—2001), Spl. Needs' Assn. Dfl. Baptist. Achievements include designed summer camp; development of a Christian pre-school; designed a teacher training class; designed a Bible Institute for lay leaders; development of a prayer ministry; outreach ministry; designed curriculum for character development; designed self-esteem program for juveniles; Founding Pastor of Little Flock Community of Faith. Home: 8712 Bass Creek Ave Minneapolis MN 55428 Office: Little Flock Comty Faith Ch 128 W 33rd Street Minneapolis MN 55408

MASON, BOBBIE ANN, novelist, short story writer; b. Mayfield, Ky., May 1, 1940; d. Wilburn A. and Christianna (Lee) M.; m. Roger B. Rawlings, Apr. 12, 1969. BA, U. Ky., 1962; MA, SUNY, Binghamton, 1966; PhD, U. Conn., 1972. Asst. prof. English Mansfield (Pa.) State Coll., 1972-79. Writer-in-residence, U. Ky., Lexington, 2001—. Author: Nabokov's Garden, 1974, The Girl Sleuth: A Feminist Guide to the Bobbsey Twins, Nancy Drew and Their Sisters, 1975, 2d edit., 1995, Shiloh and Other Stories, 1982 (Ernest Hemingway award, Nat. Book Critics Circle award nominee, Am. Book award nominee, PEN Faulkner award nominee), 2d edit., 2001, In Country, 1985, Spence + Lila, 1988, 2d edit., 1998, Love Life, 1989, Feather Crowns, 1993 (Nat. Book Critic's Circle award nominee, So. Book award), Midnight Magic, 1998, Clear Springs, 1999 (Pulitzer prize finalist), Zigzagging Down a Wild Trail, 2001 (So. Book award), Elvis Presley, 2003 (Ky. Literary award); contbr. regularly to the New Yorker, 1980—; contbr. fiction to The Atlantic, Redbook, Paris Rev., Mother Jones, Harpers, N.Am. Rev., Va. Quar. Rev., Story, Ploughshares, So. Rev., Crazyhorse, DoubleTake; contbr. works Best American Short Stories, 1981, 83, The Pushcart Prize, Best of the Small Presses, 1983, 86, 97. Recipient O. Henry Anthology awards, 1986, 88, Hillsdale prize, 1999; grantee Pa. Arts Coun., 1983, 89, Nat. Endowment Arts, 1983, Am. Acad. and Inst. Arts and Letters, 1984; Guggenheim fellow, 1984. Mem.: PEN, Author's Guild, Fellowship of So. Writers. Office: Internat Creative Mgmt care Amanda Urban Agt 40 W 57th St New York NY 10019-4001

MASON, CHARLES ELLIS, III, magazine editor; b. Boston, Oct. 31, 1938; s. Charles Ellis, Jr. and Ada Brooks (Trafford) M. BA, Yale U., 1960. Loan officer State St. Bank, Boston, 1963-68; asso. editor Sail mag., Boston, 1968-74, exec. editor, 1974—. Author: (with Buddy Melges) Sailing Smart, 1983; editor: Best of Sail Trim, 1976, Best of SAIL Navigation, 1981. Mem. exec. com. Sierra Club Greater Boston Group, 1992-. Served with USNR, 1960-62. Home: 16 Joy St Boston MA 02114-4140 Office: Sail Publs 98 N Washington St Boston MA 02110 E-mail: charles.mason@primedia.com.

MASON, CHERYL WHITE, lawyer; b. Champaign, Ill., Jan. 16, 1952; d. John Russell and Lucille (Birden) White; m. Robert L. Mason, Oct. 9, 1972; children: Robert L. II and Daniel G. BA, Purdue U., 1972; JD, U. Chgo., 1976. Bar: Calif. 1977. Assoc. O'Melveny & Myers LLP, L.A., 1976-81, 84-86, ptnr., 1987—; exec. dir. Public Counsel, L.A., 1981-84. Bd. dirs. Pub. Policy Inst. Calif. Chmn. State Bar, Legal Svcs. Trust Fund, 1987; trustee L.A. County Bar, 1985-88; bd. dirs. Challengers Boys and Girls Club, L.A., 1990—, Western Ctr. Law and Poverty, L.A., 1991-94; bd. dirs. James Irvine Found. Mem. ABA (co-chair environ. litigation commn. 1992-94, lawyer rep.

9th cir. jud. conf. 1993-94), Calif. Women Lawyers, L.A. County Bar Assn., Women Lawyers L.A., Black Women Lawyers L.A., Langston Bar Assn. Democrat. Office: O Melveny & Myers LLP 400 S Hope St Los Angeles CA 90071

MASON, CHIP, retired automotive executive; CFO Gulf States Toyota Inc., Houston, until 1998; ret., 1998. Office: Gulf States Toyota Inc PO Box 40306 Houston TX 77240-0306

MASON, CHRISTINE CHAPMAN, psychotherapist; b. El Paso, Tex., Sept. 17, 1948; d. Wilson A. and Mary (McGovern) Chapman; m. Gary R. Mason, Nov. 3, 1973; children: Ryan, Alison, Amanda, Sean. BA in Journalism, Tex. Tech. U., 1970; certificate, Am. U., 1973; MA, Marymount U., 1995, George Washington U., 1997, MA, 1998; PsyD, So. Calif. U., 2003. Cert. Paralegal 1985, Counselor, lic. Profl. Counselor. Flight attendant supr. Eastern Airlines, Washington, 1971—84; pres. Stratford Properties, Charles County, Md., 1980—; psychotherapist Charles County Mental Health Ctr., Loplata, Md., 1993—98, Eva Turner Elem. Sch., Waldorf, Md., 1999—. Dir. rehab. svc. Edgemeade, Waldorf, Md., 1999—2000; emergency psychiat. clinician St. Mary's Hosp., Leonardtown, Md., 1998—; psychotherapist Calvert Psychiat. Assn., Leonardtown, 1998—. Bd. dir. On Our Own of Charles County, Waldorf, Md., 1998—2000, Charles County Mental Health Authority, Waldorf, 1993—96. Mem.: Md. Assn. Counseling-Devel., Am. Counselors Assn. Republican. Roman Catholic. Home: 13535 Waverly Point Road Newburg MD 20664-2821

MASON, DAVID JAMES, English language educator; b. Bellingham, Wash., Dec. 11, 1954; s. James Cameron Mason and Evelyn Mae (Peterson) Brueggeman; m. Jonna Heinrich, Apr. 1, 1978 (div. 1986); m. Anne Harriet Lennox, Oct. 16, 1988; 1 stepchild, Darcy. BA, Colo. Coll., 1978; MA, U. Rochester, 1985, PhD, 1989; LHD (hon.), The Colo. Coll., 1996. Screenwriter Trans World Internat., L.A., 1981-82; poetry fellow Wesleyan Writers Conf., Middletown, Conn., summer 1985; vis. instr. Colo. Coll., Colorado Springs, 1983, 87, vis. prof., 1986, 87, 88; instr. U. Rochester, N.Y., 1989—; asst. prof. English Moorhead (Minn.) State U., 1989-93, assoc. prof., 1993—98; assoc. prof. dept. English Colo. Coll., 1998—. Author: Blackened Peaches, 1989, Small Elegies, 1990, The Buried Houses, 1991, The Country I Remember, 1996, The Poetry of Life and the Life of Poetry, 2000, Arrivals, 2004; editor: Rebel Angels: 25 Poets of The New Formalism, 1986, Western Wind, 2000, Twentieth Century American Poetry, 2004, Twentieth Century American Poetics, 2004; author numerous poems; contbr. articles to profl. jours. Recipient Nicholas Roerich poetry prize, 1991, Alice Fay Di Castagnola award, 1994; Raymond Ball fellow U. Rochester, 1988; Fulbright fellow, Greece, 1996-97. Mem. Wystan Hugh Auden Soc., Phi Beta Kappa, Phi Kappa Phi. Avocations: skiing, hiking, reading. Home: 1131 Paradise Valley Dr Woodland Park CO 80863-8502 Office Phone: 719-389-6502. Business E-Mail: dmason@coloradocollege.edu.

MASON, DEAN TOWLE, cardiologist; b. Berkeley, Calif., Sept. 20, 1932; s. Ira Jenckes and Florence Mabel (Towle) M.; m. Maureen O'Brien, June 22, 1957; children: Kathleen, Alison. BA in Chemistry, Duke U., 1954, MD, 1958. Diplomate Am. Bd. Internal Medicine, Am. Bd. Cardiovasc. Diseases, Nat. Bd. Med. Examiners. Intern, then resident in medicine Johns Hopkins Hosp., 1958-61; clin. assoc. cardiology br., sr. asst. surgeon USPHS, Nat. Heart Inst., NIH, 1961-63, asst. sect. dir. cardiovascular diagnosis, attending physician, sr. investigator cardiology br., 1963-68; prof. medicine, prof. physiology, chief cardiovascular medicine U. Calif. Med. Sch., Davis-Sacramento Med. Center, 1968-82; dir. cardiac ctr. Cedars Med. Ctr., Miami, Fla., 1982-83; physician-in chief Western Heart Inst., San Francisco, 1983—2000; chmn. dept. cardiovascular medicine St. Mary's Med. Ctr., San Francisco, 1986-99, hon. med. staff, 2000—. Co-chmn. cardiovascular-renal drugs U.S. Pharmacopeia Com. Revision, 1970—75; mem. life scis. com. NASA; med. rsch. rev. bd. VA, NIH; prof. medicine (hon.) Peking Med. U., China, 1987; vis. prof. numerous univs.; cons. in field. Editor-in-chief Am. Heart Jour., 1980—96; contbr. chapters to books, articles. Recipient rsch. award, Am. Therapeutic Soc., 1965, Theodore and Susan B. Cummings Humanitarian award, Dept. State-Am. Coll. Cardiology, 1972, 1973, 1975, 1978, Skylab Achievement award, NASA, 1974, U. Calif. Faculty Rsch. award, 1978, Symbol of Excellence, Tex. Heart Inst., 1979, Disting. Alumnus award, Duke U. Sch. Medicine, 1979, award of Honor, Wisdom Soc., 1997, Medal of Honor, Winston Churchill Soc., 1998, Armand Hammer Creative Genius award, 1998, Dwight D. Eisenhower Admirable Am. of Achievement award, 1998, Eternal Jesus Christ award, 1998, Blessed Lord's Prayer award, 1998, Dean Towle Mason Eminent Physician of Wisdom award, 1998, Dean Towle Mason, M.D. Medal of Wisdom award, 2001, Cardiologist of the Century Wisdom award, 2001, Albert Schweitzer world Humanitarian of Wisdom award, 2002, Jonas Salk award for med. rsch., 2003, Albert Einstein Sci. Rsch. award, 2003, John Wayne Pioneer of Am. award, 2003, Ernest Hemingway award for maj. contbns. to med. lit., 2003, Will Durant Philosopher-Physician award, 2004, Paul Dudley White award for disting. svc. in cardiovasc. medicine, 2004. Master Am. Coll. Cardiology (pres. 1977-78); fellow ACP, Am. Heart Assn., Am. Coll. Chest Physicians, Royal Soc. Medicine; mem. Am. Soc. Clin. Investigation, Am. Physiol. Soc., Am. Soc. Pharmacology and Exptl. Therapeutics (Exptl. Therapeutics award 1973), Am. Fedn. Clin. Research, N.Y. Acad. Scis., Am. Assn. U. Cardiologists, Am. Soc. Clin. Pharmacology and Therapeutics, We. Assn. Physicians, AAUP, We. Soc. Clin. Rsch. (past pres.), El Macero Country Club, Phi Beta Kappa, Alpha Omega Alpha. Republican. Methodist. Home: 44725 Country Club Dr El Macero CA 95618-1047 Office: Western Heart Inst St Marys Med Ctr 450 Stanyan St San Francisco CA 94117-1079 Office Phone: 415-750-5598.

MASON, DERRICK, professional football player; b. Detroit, Mich., Jan. 17, 1974; m. Marci Mason; children: Bailee My-Lin, Derrick Jr. Postgrad in comm., Mich. State Univ. Wide receiver Tenn. Titans, 1997—. Named to NFL Pro-Bowl, 2000, 2003. Achievements include the ninth player in NFL history to record consecutive seasons with more than 2,000 all-purpose yards; set NFL record for all-purpose yards (2,690), 2000. Office: Tn Titans Baptist Sports Park 460 Great Cr Rd Nashville TN 37228

MASON, EDWARD EATON, surgeon; b. Boise, Idaho, Oct. 16, 1920; s. Edward Files and Dora Bell (Eaton) M.; m. Dordana Fairman, June 18, 1944; children— Daniel Edward, Rose Mary, Richard Eaton, Charles Henry. BA, U. Iowa, 1943, MD, 1945; PhD in Surgery, U. Minn., 1953. Intern, resident in surgery Univ. Hosps., Mpls., 1945-52; asst. prof. surgery U. Iowa, 1953-55, asso. prof., 1956-60, prof., 1961-91, prof. emeritus, 1991—, chmn. gen. surgery, 1978-91. Cons. VA Hosp.; trainee Nat. Cancer Inst., 1949-52 Author: Computer Applications in Medicine, 1964, Fluid, Electrolyte and Nutrient Therapy in Surgery, 1974, Surgical Treatment of Obesity, 1981; developer gastric bypass and gastroplasty for treatment of obesity; contbr. articles profl. jours. Served to lt. (j.g.) USNR, 1945-47. Fellow ACS; mem. AMA, Am. Surg. Assn., Western Surg. Assn., Soc. Univ. Surgeons, Internat. Soc. Surgery, Ctrl. Surg. Assn., Soc. Surgery Alimentary Tract, Am. Thyroid Assn., Am. Soc. Bariatric Surgery, Sigma Xi, Alpha Omega Alpha. Republican. Presbyterian. Home: 5 Melrose Cir Iowa City IA 52246-2013 Office: Univ Hosp Dept Surgery Iowa City IA 52242 *Continuity of interest and planning weaves the daily decisions into a whole cloth that does more than cover one's imperfections.*

MASON, EILEEN B. federal administrator; b. Bklyn., 1943; m. Arthur Mason; children: Elizabeth, Laura. BA, Cornell U.; MPA, Am. U. Tchr. math. and reading Hephzibah High Sch., Ga.; editor Little Brown, Boston; music adv. panelist Md. State Arts Coun.; v.p. grants Arts and Humanities Coun., Montgomery County, Md.; mgr. and adminstr. U.S. NRC, FERC; sr. dep. chmn. NEA, Washington, 2001—, acting chmn., 2002—03. Performer: (violinist) Cornell U. Symphony, MIT Symphony, Augusta Symphony, Am. U. Symphony Orchestra. Mem.: Phi Alpha Alpha. Office: NEA 1100 Pennsylvania Ave NW Washington DC 20506

MASON, ELI, accountant; b. N.Y.C., Nov. 16, 1920; BBA, Baruch Coll., 1940; LhD (hon.), CUNY, 1978. CPA, N.Y. Acct. RCA, N.Y.C., 1940-41, Klein, Hinds & Fink, N.Y.C., 1941-43; controller Hydrawmatic Machine Corp., N.Y.C., 1943-46; mng. ptnr. Mason & Co., N.Y.C., 1946—. Contbr. articles to profl. jours. Bd. dirs., chmn. Baruch Coll., N.Y.C., 1982-85. Recipient Townsend Harris medal CUNY, 1975, Beta Gamma Sigma medal, N.Y.C., 1989. Mem. N.Y. State Soc. CPAs (pres. 1972-73, Disting. Svc. award 1983), N.Y. State Bd. Pub. Accountancy (chmn. 1972-82), AICPA (v.p. 1968-69), Nat. Conf. CPA Practitioners (chmn. 1985-86). Office: #2400 1212 Avenue of the Americas New York NY 10036-1602*

MASON, ELLSWORTH GOODWIN, librarian; b. Waterbury, Conn., Aug. 25, 1917; s. Frederick William and Kathryn Loretta (Watkins) M.; m. Rose Ellen Maloy, May 13, 1951 (div. Oct. 1961); children: Kay Iris Morice, Joyce Iris Lande; m. Joan Lou Shinew, Aug. 16, 1964; 1 son, Sean David. BA, Yale U., 1938, MA, 1942, PhD, 1948; LHD, Hofstra U., 1973; Diploma, Inst. Children's Lit., 1996. Cert. Christian Writer's Guild, 1997. Reference asst. Yale Library, 1938-42; export license officer Bd. Econ. Warfare, 1942-43; instr. English Williams Coll., 1948-50; instr. humanities div. Marlboro (Vt.) Coll., 1951-52; serials libr. U. Wyo. Libr., 1952-54; reference libr. Colo. Coll. Libr., Colorado Springs, 1954-58; lectr., libr. Colo. Coll., 1958-63; prof., dir. libr. svcs. Hofstra U., Hempstead, N.Y., 1963-72; prof., dir. U. Colo. Librs., Boulder, 1972-76; freelance writer children's lit., 1995—. Adj. prof. U. Ill., Urbana, 1968; pres. Mason Assocs., Ltd., 1977—; rsch. assoc. U. Calif.-Berkeley, 1965; vis. lectr. Northwestern U., 1961, Colo. Coll., 1965, Syracuse U., 1965-68, Elmira Coll., 1966, Columbia U., 1966-68, U. Ill., 1972, Lincoln U., 1969, U. B.C. (Can.), 1969, U. Toronto, 1970, U. Tulsa, 1971, 76, Rutgers U., 1971, Colgate U., 1972, Simmons Coll., 1972, U. Oreg., 1973, Hofstra U., 1974, U. N.C., 1976, U. Ala., 1976, Ball State U., 1977, U. Lethbrige, Can., 1977, U. Ariz., 1981, Ariz. State U., 1981, Victoria U., New Zealand, 1983, U. Canterbury, New Zealand, 1983, U. Nev. Las Vegas, 1992, Remember Pearl Harbor Assn., 1993, 94; libr. cons., 1958—, libr. value engr., 1992—. Editor: (with Stanislaus Joyce) The Early Joyce, 1955, Xerox U.M. edit., 1964, Norwood: Norwod Editions, 1977, Philadelphia: R.West, 1978, (with Richard Ellmann) The Critical Writings of James Joyce, 1959, 2d edit., 1989, Critical Commentary on A Portrait of the Artist as a Young Man, 1966; translator: Recollections of James Joyce (S. Joyce), 1950, Essais de J. Joyce, 1966, Escritos Criticos de James Joyce, (Portuguese edit.), 1967, (Spanish edit.), 1973, 75, James Joyce's Ulysses and Vico's Cycle, 1973, Kritische Schriften v. James Joyce, 1975, Mason on Library Buildings, 1980, (with Walter and Jean Shine) A MacDonald Potpourri, 1988, The University of Colorado Library and Its Makers, 1876-1972, 1994; contbr. Contemporary Authors, 1988—; editor: Colorado College Studies, 1959-62; editor and compiler: Focus on Robert Graves, 1972-88; adv. editor: Focus on Robert Graves and His Contemporaries, 1988—; editor: The Booklover's Bounty, 1977-82; mem. editl. bd. Serial Slants, 1957-59, The Serials Librarian, 1977-98, Choice, 1962-65, Coll. and Rsch. Librs., 1969-72. Mem. exec. bd. U. Ky. Libr. Assocs., 1991-94; exec. bd. Concerned Christians in Ky., 1993-98. Served with USNR, 1943-46. Recipient Harry Bailly spkr.'s award Assn. Colls. of Midwest, 1975; fellow Coun. on Libr. Resources, 1969-70; grantee Am. Coun. Learned Socs., Edn. Facilities Labs., Hofstra U., U. Colo.; named Ky. Col., 1993. Mem. ALA (councillor-at-large 1961-65), Colo. Libr. Assn. (pres. so. dist. 1960-61), Bibliog. Soc. Am., Libr. Assn. (London), N.Z. Libr. Assn., Pvt. Librs. Assn., Alcuin Soc. Vancouver, Conf. Editors Learned Jours., N.Z. Royal Forest and Bird Protection Soc., Colo. Book Collectors (founder, pres. 1975-86), Inst. Vico Studies, James Joyce Found. (chmn. sect. on translation from Joyce, 2d Internat. James Joyce Symposium, Dublin 1969), Nat. Assn. Scholars, Am. Christian Writers, Black America's PAC, Caxton Club, Archons of Colophon, Ghost Town Club, Alpha Sigma Lambda, Sigma Kappa Alpha (pres. 1969-70). Home: 736 Providence Rd Lexington KY 40502-2267 also: 39 Discovery Dr Whitby New Zealand

MASON, FRANK HENRY, III, automobile company executive, leasing company executive; b. Paris, Tenn., Nov. 16, 1936; s. Frank H. and Dorothy (Carter) M.; children: Robert C., William C. B of Elec. Engring., Vanderbilt U., 1958; MS in Indsl. Mgmt., MIT, 1965. With Ford Motor Co., 1965-71; asst. controller Ford Brazil, Sao Paulo, 1971-74; mgr. overseas fin. dept. Ford Motor Co., Dearborn, Mich., 1974-76, asst. controller engine divsn., 1976-78, mgr. facilities and mgmt. svcs., 1978-81; controller Ford Motor Credit Co., Dearborn, Mich., 1981-87; dir. fin. Ford Fin. Svcs. Group, Dearborn, Mich., 1987-89; exec. v.p., chief fin. officer U.S. Leasing, Internat., San Francisco, 1989-92; retired, 1992. Lt. USN, 1958-63.

MASON, GEORGE HENRY, business educator; b. Chgo., Sept. 11, 1929; s. Robert De Main and Dorothy Wills (Belden) M.; m. Constance Eleanor Wolcott, May 14, 1960. AB, Kenyon Coll., 1955; MBA, Cornell U., 1957; MF, Duke U., 1983. CFA. Investment officer Travelers Ins. Co., Hartford, Conn., 1957-88; exec.-in-residence U. Hartford, West Hartford, 1989—98, dir. Bus. Applications Ctr., 1998—2001. Vis. prof. Jagiellonian U., Cracow, Poland, 1996, Yang-En U., Quanzhou, Fujian, China, 1997. Co-author: Timberland Investments, 1992. Investment adv. coun. State of Conn., 1999—2003; tutor Literacy Vol. Greater Hartford, 2004—. Mem.: Hartford Soc. Fin. Analysts, Assn. Investment Mgmt. and Rsch., Dataw Island Club, Mill Reef Club, Country Club of Farmington. Republican. Avocations: skiing, golf, writing.

MASON, GREG, publishing executive; MBA, U. S.F. Pub. PC Computing (now Smart Bus.), San Francisco; exec. v.p. sales CNET Networks, Inc., 2000—. Office: CNET Networks Inc 235 Second St San Francisco CA 94105

MASON, GREGG CLAUDE, orthopedic surgeon, researcher; b. Schenectady, N.Y., July 28, 1958; s. George and Maureen (Murphy) M.; m. Dina Marie Sokolowski, June 16, 1990. BS in Chemistry magna cum laude, Allegheny Coll., 1980; MD, U. Pitts., 1984. Diplomate Am. Bd. Orthop. Surgery, Nat. Bd. Med. Examiners. Gen. surgery intern U. Colo./U. Colo. Med. Ctrs., Denver, 1984-85; orthopaedic rsch. fellow U. Pitts., 1985-86, resident in orthopaedic surgery, 1986-89; orthopedic surgeon U.S. Naval Hosp., Okinawa, Japan, 1989-92; pvt. practice, Erie, 1992—. Active staff St. Vincent Med. Ctr., St. Vincent Surgery Ctr., Hamot Med. Ctr., Union City Meml. Hosp.; lectr. in field. Contbr. articles to profl. jours. Comdr. M.C. USNR, 1980—. Recipient Outstanding Student Rsch. award U. Pitt. Sch. Medicine, 1984, Harold Henderson Sankey Orthop. award, 1984; rsch. grantee Competitive Med. Rsch. Fund., Presbyn.-Univ. Hosp. of Pitts., 1986-87, U. Pitts. Rsch. Devel. Fund, 1986-87. Disting. Alden scholar 1977, 78, 79, 80, Sandra Doane Turk scholar, 1979, Armed Svcs. Health Professions scholar, 1981-84. Fellow ACS, Internat. Coll. Surgeons, Mil. Soc. Orthop. Surgeons, Am. Acad. Orthop. Surgeons (tchg. seal 1993); mem. AMA, Pa. Orthop. Soc. (Best Rsch. Paper 1987, 88), Erie Orthop. Soc., U. Pitts. Med. Ctr. Orthop. Alumni., Am. Orthop. Soc. of Sports Medicine (Cabaud award 1988), Ea. Orthop. Assn. (Founders award 1988), Phi Beta Kappa. Office: Orthopaedic Surgeons Inc 204 W 26th St Erie PA 16508-1898

MASON, GREGORY WESLEY, JR., secondary school educator, educator; b. Chgo., Jan. 21, 1963; s. Gregory Wesley and Diana (Burton) M.; m. LaTanya Yvonne Brown, June 8, 1991; children: Gregory Arthur, Timothy Michael. BS, Ill. State U., 1986; MEd, U. Ill., Chgo., 1996. Cert. secondary tchr., gen. adminstr., Ill. Instr. City Coll. Chgo., 1986-89; instr. project alert Roosevelt U., Chgo., 1989-91, counselor project upward bound, 1991-93; tchr. math. Bowen High Sch., Chgo., 1993-95, chmn. profl. planning adv. com., 1994-95; tchr. math. Whitney M. Young Magnet H.S., Chgo., 1995-2000, chmn. dept. math., 1997-2000; adminstr. Chgo. Pub. Schs., 2000—. Instr. Ill. Math. and Sci. Acad., Aurora, summers 1993-96; lectr. Coll. Edn., Loyola U., Chgo., 1999-2001; tchr. coord. Golden Apple Found., 2000-01; mem. nat. adv. bd. Schs. and Scholars Program, Woodrow Wilson Nat. Fellowship Found. Mem. pres.'s coun. edn. com. Mus. Sci. and Industry; mem. Ill. Robotic Competition Adv. Bd. Named Outstanding Young Men of Am., 1985. Mem. ASCD, Nat. Coun. Tchrs. Math., Ill. Coun. Tchrs. Math., Ill. Coun. for Coll. Attendance (bd. dirs. 1993-97), Nat. Assn. Secondary Sch. Prins., Benjamin Banneker Assn., Masons, Phi Delta Kappa. Avocations: swimming, chess, reading, stock trading, computers. Home: 2729 W 84th St Chicago IL 60652-3909 Office: Chgo Pub Schs 1326 W 14th Pl Chicago IL 60608 E-mail: gmason@csc.cps.k12.il.us.

MASON, HERBERT WARREN, JR., religion and history educator, author; b. Wilmington, Del., Apr. 20, 1932; s. Herbert Warren and Mildred Jane (Noyes) M.; m. Jeanine Young, June 25, 1982; children from previous marriage: Cathleen, Paul, Sarah. AB, Harvard U., 1955, AM, 1965, PhD, 1969. English tchr. Am. Sch. Paris, 1959-60; asst. prof. St. Joseph's Coll., Gorham, Maine, 1960-62; vis. lectr. Simmons Coll., Boston, 1962-63; vis. lectr. in Islamic Hist. Tufts U., Medford, Mass., 1965-66; teaching fellow in English Harvard U., Cambridge, Mass., 1962-66, teaching fellow in Islamic Hist., 1966-67; translator Bollingen Found., N.Y.C., 1968-72; prof. History and Religion Boston U., 1972-2000, William Goodwin Aurelio prof. history and religious thought, 2000—. U.K. cons. editor Banipal. Author: Reflections on the Middle East Crisis, 1970, Two Statesmen of Medieval Islam, 1971, Gilgamesh, 1971, 2d edit., 2003, The Death of al-Hallaj, 1979, Moments in Passage, 1979, (novel) Summer Light, 1980; translator: La Passion d'al-Hallaj, 4 vols., Bollingen Series (Louis Massignon), 1983, abridged 1 vol., 1994, A Legend of Alexander, 1986, Memoir of a Friend: Louis Massignon, 1988, Testimonies and Reflections, 1989, al-Hallaj, 1995, Haythu Taltaqi al Anhar (novel in Arabic "Where the Rivers Meet"), 1999, English edit., 2003, (poems) Disappearances, 1999; co-editor: Humaniora Islamica; cons. editor Banipal, London; contbr. articles, essays, revs., fiction and poetry to popular fiction mags. Sec. Inter-racial Riverside Assn., Cambridge, Mass., 1965-67; trustee Bd. Charity of Edward Hopkins, Boston Athenaeum. Fellow Soc. for Values in Higher Edn.; mem. PEN (bd. dirs. Delos chpt.), Medieval Acad. Am., Am. Oriental Soc., Am. Acad. Religion, Mark Twain Soc., Inst. Internat. des Recherches Louis Massignon in Paris (dir. edn., v.p.), Am. Acad. Poetry, Japan Poetry Mus. (Iwate-Ken). Home: 4 Seaview Lane Newbury MA 01951 Office: Boston U 745 Commonwealth Ave Boston MA 02215 1401 Business E-Mail: masonh@bu.edu.

MASON, J. MURPHY, theater director; d. Robert Victor and Marguerite Anne Murphy; m. Daniel C. Mason, Oct. 7, 2001. BS, Emerson Coll., Boston, 1987—91; postgrad., U. Va., 2002—. Affiliated artist New Georges, N.Y.C., 1998—; mem. Ensemble Studio Theatre - Theatre Lab, N.Y.C., 1999; artistic assoc. Rattlestick Theatre, N.Y.C., 2000—01; participant Shared Experience, London, 2000; mem. Director's Forum at the Women's Project, N.Y.C., 2001—02; presenter in field. Dir. (theatre) Private Lives; dir.: (theatre) The House of Bernarda Alba, The Virtuous Burglar, The Night of the Iguana, Something Made Up, Tasha Walks, A Girl's Guide to the Divine Comedy (workshop), Fate, Loose Knit, A Woman Alone, Heartbreak House (workshop), Harold and Herman met on a Fall Afternoon, The Role of Della, She Tells Her Daughter, Modern Love, Traps, Zodiac, Serpentarium, Orchis, Nada, Bits of String, Cultivation; asst. dir. (theatre) The Piano Lesson, Ascendancy, Fishes, As You Like It, Fool for Love, The Stonewater Rapture; actor: (plays) Footfalls, The Role of Della, All in the Timing, Cyrano de Bergerac, The Cousins, A Kind of Alaska, Who Killed Martha Mitchell?, The Liveliest Afternoon of the Year, A Way With Words, The Bitter Tears of Petra von Kant; (TV films) Blown Away, Healthy Start Public Service Announcement, Straight Up, No Olive, The Script. Devel. assoc. José Limón Dance Found., 1994—95; bd. dirs. Brookline Cmty. Theatre, 1992—94. Recipient Meritorious Achievement award, Kennedy Ctr. Am. Coll. Theater Festival, 2004; fellow, U. Va. Drama Dept., 2002—. Mem.: Soc. Stage Directors and Choreographers (assoc.). Democrat. Avocations: travel, glassblowing, photography, writing, knitting. Personal E-mail: citymurf@aol.com.

MASON, J. WILLIAM L. lawyer; b. Kittery, Maine, Apr. 14, 1940; s. Murray Lawrence and Dolores Elizabeth (Laird) M.; m. Mary Elizabeth Jordan; children: Joseph Patrick, Catherine Shannon, Brendan Michael. BA, U. N.H., 1973, MBA, 1979; JD, New Eng. Sch. Law, 1987. Molder Portsmouth (N.H.) Naval Shipyard, 1958-71, with labor rels., 1973-91; rehab. technician State of N.H., Concord, 1971-73; pvt. practice Portsmouth, 1991—. Staff sgt. N.H. Air Nat. Guard, 1974-81. Mem. ABA, Am. Trial Lawyers Assn., N.H. Bar Assn. Congregationalist. Avocation: coins. Home: 27 Old Concord Tpke Lee NH 03824-6729 Office: 5 Greenleaf Woods Dr Ste 301 Portsmouth NH 03801-5442 Office Phone: 603-427-0313.

MASON, JAMES OSTERMANN, public health administrator; b. Salt Lake City, June 19, 1930; s. Ambrose Stanton and Neoma (Thorup) Mason; m. Lydia Maria Smith, Dec. 29, 1952; children: James, Susan, Bruce, Ralph, Samuel, Sara, Benjamin. BA, U. Utah, 1954, MD, 1958; MPH, Harvard U., 1963, DPH, 1967. Diplomate Am. Bd. Preventive Medicine. Intern Johns Hopkins Hosp., Balt., 1958—59; resident in internal medicine Peter Bent Brigham Hosp.-Harvard Med. Service, Boston, 1961—62; chief infectious diseases Latter-day Saints Hosp., Salt Lake City, 1968—69; commr. Health Services Corp., Ch. of Jesus Christ of Latter-day Saints, 1970—76; dep. dir. health Utah Div. Health, 1976—78, exec. dir., 1979—83; chief epidemic intelligence service Ctr. Disease Control, Atlanta, 1959, chief hepatitis surveillance unit epidemiology br., 1960, chief surveillance sect. epidemiology br., 1961, dep. dir. bur. labs., 1964—68, dep. dir. of Ctr., 1969—70; dir. Ctrs. for Disease Control, Atlanta; adminstr. Agy. for Toxic Substances and Disease Registry, 1983—89; acting asst. sec. health HHS, Washington, 1985, asst. sec. for health, acting surgeon gen., 1989—90, asst. sec. for health, 1990—93; asst. prof. dept. medicine and preventive medicine U. Utah, Salt Lake City, 1968—69, assoc. prof., chmn. div. community medicine, dept. family and community medicine, 1978—79; v.p. planning, devel., prof. preventive medicine and biometrics Uniformed Svcs. U. Health Scis., 1993—94; 2nd quorum of Seventy LDS Ch., 1994—. Physician, cons. to med. svcs. Salt Lake VA Hosp., 1977—83; clin. prof. dept. family and cmty. medicine U. Utah Coll. Medicine, 1979—83, clin. prof. dept. pathology, 1980—83; clin. prof. cmty. health Emory U. Sch. Medicine, 1984—86; chmn. joint residency com. in preventive medicine and pub. health Utah Coll. Medicine, 1975—80; mem. Utah Cancer Registry Rsch. Adv. Com., 1976—83; mem. adv. com. Utah Ctr. Health Stats., 1977—79; chmn. bd. Hosp. Coop. Utah, 1977—79; chmn. exec. com. Utah Health Planning and Resource Devel. Adv. Group, 1977—79; chmn. Utah Gov.'s Adv. Com. for Comprehensive Health Planning, 1975—77; mem. recombinant DNA adv. com. NIH, 1979—83; mem. Gov.'s Nuclear Waste Repository Task Force, 1980—83, chmn., 1980—82; bd. dirs. Utah Health Cost Mgmt. Found., 1980—83; mem. adv. com. for programs and policies CDC, 1980; mem. com. on future of local health depts. Inst. Medicine, 1980—82; mem. exec. com., chmn. tech. adv. com. Thrasher Rsch. Found., 1980—89; mem. Robert Wood Johnson Found. Program for Hosp. Initiatives in Long-Term Care, 1982—84; mem. sci. and tech. adv. com. UNDP-World Bank-WHO Spl. Programme for Rsch. and Tng. in Tropical Diseases, 1984—89; mem. Utah Resource for Genetic and Epidemiologic Rsch., 1982—85, chmn. bd., 1982—83; U.S. rep. WHO Exec. Bd., 1990—93. Author (with H.L. Bodily and E.L. Updyke): Diagnostic Procedures for Bacterial, Mycotic and Parasitic Infections, 1970; author: (with M.H. Maxwell, K.H. Bousfield and D.A. Ostler) Funding Water Quality Control in Utah, Procs. for Lincoln Inst., 1982; contbr. articles to profl. jours. Mem. nat. scouting com. Boy Scouts Am., 1974—78. Recipient Roche award, U. Utah, 1957, Wintrobe award, 1958, Disting. Alumni award, 1973, Adminstr. of Yr. award, Brigham U., 1980, spl. award for outstanding pub. svc., Am. Soc. Pub. Adminstrn., 1984, Disting. Svc. medal, USPHS, 1988, Legacy of Life award, LDS Hosp. Deseret Found., 1992, Gorgas Medal and Scroll, 1993. Mem.: APHA (task force for credentialing of lab. pers. 1976—78, program devel. bd. 1979—81), AMA, Utah Pub. Health Assn. (pres. 1980—82, Beatty award 1979), Utah Acad. Preventive Medicine (pres. 1982—83), Utah State Med. Assn. (trustee 1979—83), Inst. Medicine of NAS, Rotary, Delta Omega, Alpha Omega Alpha, Phi Kappa Phi, Alpha Epsilon Delta, Sigma Xi. Mem. Lds Ch. Office: LDS 47 E South Temple Salt Lake City UT 84150-9701

MASON, JOHN LATIMER, engineering executive; b. Los Angeles, Nov. 8, 1923; s. Zene Upham and Edna Ella (Watkins) M.; m. Frances Howe Draeger, Sept. 1, 1950 (dec. June 1951); m. Mary Josephine Schulte, Nov. 26, 1954; children: Andrew, Peter, Mary Anne, John Edward. BS in Meteorology, U. Chgo., 1944; BS in Applied Chemistry, Calif. Inst. Tech., 1947, MS in Chem. Engring., 1948, PhD, 1950. Registered profl. engr., Calif. Engr. AiResearch Mfg. Co., Los Angeles, 1950-60; dir. engring. AiResearch Mfg. Co. div. Garrett Corp., Los Angeles, 1960-72; v.p. engring. Garrett Corp., Los Angeles, 1972-87; v.p. engring. and tech. Allied-Signal Aerospace Co., Los Angeles, 1987-88, cons., 1989-96; chmn. tech. adv. com. Indsl. Turbines Internat., Inc., Los Angeles, 1972-81, bd. dirs., 1980-88; adj. prof. engring. Calif. State U.,

Long Beach, 1992-96. Mem. tech. adv. bd. Tex. Ctr. for Superconductivity, U. Houston, 1989-02; chair Calif. Coun. Sci. and Tech. Panel on Transp. R&D Ctr., 1993-94; bd. dirs. Planetary Sci. Inst., 1995—, sec., 1998—; cons. Capstone Turbine Corp., 1994-98; mem. tech. adv. bd. Ceryx Inc., 1998-2001; mem. workshop com. Transp. Rsch. Bd., 1998.; cons. Cleaire, Inc., 2001—, Applied Rsch. and Tech., 2001—; ptnr., Applied Rsch. and Tech., 2001-. Patentee in field. Chmn. energy and environment com. FISITA Coun., 1990-94. 1st lt. USAAF, 1943-45, PTO. Fellow AIAA (assoc.). Soc. Automotive Engrs. (bd. dirs. 1984-87, 90-93, pres.-elect 1989-90, pres. 1990-91), Performance Rev. Inst. (chmn. 1990-91, bd. dirs. 1992-93); mem. AAAS, NRC of NAS (com. on alternative energy R&D strategies 1989-90), Office Sci. and Tech. Policy (Nat. Critical Techs. panel 1992-93), Inst. Medicine of NAS (com. on health effects of indoor allergens 1992-93), Nat. Acad. Engring., U.S. Advanced Ceramics Assn. (chmn. tech. com., bd. dirs. 1985-88), Am. Chem. Soc., Am. Ceramic Soc., Caltech Assocs., Sigma Xi (assoc.). Office Phone: 310-573-9821. Personal E-mail: JL-Mason@cox.net.

MASON, JOHN OLIVER, freelance journalist, poet, community activist; b. Kingston, Pa., Aug. 1, 1957; s. Oliver B. and Dorothy Mae (Hunter) Mason. BA, Temple U., 1984. Editl. writer Temple News, Phila., 1983-85; writer Phila. Tribune, 1989-95, Irish Edition, Phila., 1990-95, Northeast Breeze, Rockledge, Pa., 1993—, Germantown Courier, Phila., 1996—, Phila. Sunday Sun, 1996—, Chestnut Hill Local, 2000—. Sec. Concerned Citizens of Delaware Valley, 1990; rec. sec. A. Philip Randolph Inst., Phila., 2001; mem. Jewish Labor Com., Phila., 1985. Mem. Meridian Writers Collective. Avocations: stamp collecting/philately, reading, cultural activities. Office Phone: 215-843-0193. E-mail: jomason57@verizon.net.

MASON, JOSEPH See BUSHINSKY, JAY

MASON, JUDITH ANN, freelance writer; b. Newark, Dec. 27, 1945; d. Richard Algie and Mary Ann (Beneck) M. Diploma in legal sci., Spencerian Bus. Coll., 1965; BA, Northeastern Ill. U., 1984. Legal sec. Harney B. Stover, Atty., Milw., 1967-69, Robert P. O'Meara, Atty., Waukegan, Ill., 1969-70; sec. to pres. First Midwest Bank, Waukegan, 1970-72, asst. cashier, 1972-76; legal sec. Eugene M. Snarski, Atty., Waukegan, 1976-81; adminstrv. aide Lake County Forest Preserve Dist., Libertyville, Ill., 1981-89; freelance writer Tucson, 1989—; legal sec., asst. Jeffrey H. Greenberg, Atty.; office mgr. Greenberg & Assocs., Tucson, 1989-96; legal asst. Leonard, Felker, Altfeld, Greenberg & Battaile, 1997—; exec. adminstr. JHG Devel. Co. LLC, 1995—, 1998—. Travel rep. Antioch (Ill.) Travel Agy., 1980-89, Advance Travel Agy., Zion, Ill., 1980-89; pub. speaker for various orgns., Lake County, Ill., 1984-89. Author: Why I Remember Yesterday, 1979, Haggadah (play), 1982; editor poetry column: Bank Man Magazine, 1972-75; contbg. article writer Compendum Mag. Tchr. Confraternity Christian Doctrine St. Patrick's Ch., Wadsworth, Ill., 1980-85; lector, eucharistic min. Prince of Peace Ch., Lake Villa, Ill., 1980-89; hospice vol. St. Therese Hosp., Waukegan, 1984; speech writer Grace Mary Stern lt. gubernatorial campaign, Lake County, 1984; voter registrar County of Lake Ill., 1986-89; cons. pub. rels. Lake County Cir. Ct. Judge campaign, 1988, Presdl. Campaign Paul Simon; co-chmn., organizer Women's Exhibit, Evergreen Air Show, 1993. Recipient Brian F. Shehanhan Creative Writing award Am. Inst. Banking, 1972, 1st Place pub. speaking, 1974. Mem. AAUW (pub. rels. chair 1986, pres. Chain O'Lakes br. 1988-89, Ill. Pub. Info. award 1987, pub. rels. chair Tucson br. 1991-92), NAFE, Northeastern Ill. U. Alumni Assn., Soc. Southwestern Authors, Pi Rho Zeta (pres. 1964-65). Democrat. Roman Catholic. Office: PO Box 191 Tucson AZ 85702-0191

MASON, LINDA, physical education educator, softball and basketball coach; b. Indpls., Jan. 29, 1946; d. Harrison Linn and Hazel Marie (Bledsoe) Crouch; divorced; children: Cassandra, Andrew. BS, Ind. U., 1968, MS, 1977. Cert. phys. edn. tchr., K-12, Ind. Tchr. phys. edn. Woodview Jr. H.S., Indpls., 1968-71; tchr. phys. edn., coach Ind. U.-Purdue U. of Indpls., 1972-76; basketball coach Butler U., Indpls., 1976-84; head softball coach, asst. basketball coach Westfield Washington High Sch., Westfield, Ind., 1985; tchr. phys. edn., basketball coach Orchard Park Elementary Sch., Carmel, Ind., 1985—; elem. physical edn. tchr. Carmel-Clay Schs., Carmel, 1985—; asst. varsity coach softball Carmel H.S., 1993-95, head varsity softball coach, 1996-99. Head coach Ind. Girls' H.S. All-Stars Basketball Team, Indpls., 1980. Named Coach of Yr. Dist. 4, Nat. Collegiate Athletic Assn., 1983, Coach of Yr. for softball ICGSA, 1997, coach ICGSA Girls All Stars, 1998. Mem. Delta Psi Kappa. E-mail: lmason@ccs.k12.in.us., peteacharl@indy.rr.com.

MASON, LOIS E. (J. DAY MASON), painter, poet, actress, educator; b. Boston, May 4, 1919; d. Harold Monroe and Orpah Cecil (Smith) Scheibe; m. Lucien Bunce Day, June 21, 1941 (div. 1954); children: Felicity, Christopher, Sarah; m. Frederick Dike Mason, Apr. 27, 1964 (dec.); children: Frederick Dike III, Victoria, Johanna. Student, U. Leiden, Netherlands, 1939; BA, Oberlin (Ohio) U., 1940; postgrad., Cranbrook Acad. Art, Bloomfield Hills, Mich., 1941. Set-up and tchr. art dept. Pingree Sch., Hamilton Mass.; TV, lectr. creative arts and writing, Mass. and Conn., 1949-58. Actress appearing in Alien Corn, Twelfth Night, Crucible, George Washington Slept Here, Philadelphia Story, Auntie Mame, Skin of our Teeth, Spoon River, Anything Goes, Call Me Madame, Seven Keys to Baldpate, Other People's Money, Quilters, Golden Pond, Cat on a Hot Tin Roof, Little Foxes, Lettice and Lovage, Close Ties, Grace and Glorie, others; set designer, decorator Auntie Mame, See How They Run, Tea House of the August Moon, Spoon River, Archie and Mehitable; author: Speaking to Strangers, 1987-88; one-woman shows include New Britain (Conn.) Mus., Am. Ballet, N.Y., Green Mountain Gallery, N.Y.C., Essex (Mass.) Inst., Marblehead Arts, Quadrom, Mast Cove, 6 Deering, Miles Hosp., Atty. Gen.'s Office, Kennebec Valley Art Assn., Chocolate Ch. Art Ctr., Maine Gallery, Kristina's, Oliver's, Islesboro Historic Soc., West Island Gallery, Bath, Maine. Ch. ladies com. Hamilton Hall, Salem, Mass., 1975—78; set designer Cmty. Theater, Swampscott, Mass., 1973—78. Recipient C. Law/Watkins fellowship Phillips Gallery, Mus., Washington, 1944-46. Mem. Nat. Assn. Women Painters, Conn. Acad., Silvermine, Maine Gallery, Kennebec Valley Arts, Chocolate Ch. Art Ctr., Marblehead Arts, Conn. Acad., Maine Writers and Publs. Avocations: cooking, sailing, gardening.

MASON, LORETTA ANN, accountant assistant; b. Albertville, Ala., Dec. 14, 1959; d. Robert Dewayne Hudgins and Tassie Marie Strong; div.; 1 child, Shannon David. Student, Calhoun C.C., Decatur, Ala., 2001—. Asst. acct. NAFECO, Decatur, Ala. Author: (book of poetry) Yesterday's Memories, 1997; contbr. poems to anthologies. Mem. Internat. Soc. Poets (disting. mem.), So. Poetry Assn., Eastern Star. Republican. Avocations: horseback riding, reading, writing. Home: 3345 Pigeon Roost Rd Pulaski TN 38478 Office: NAFECO 1515 W Moulton Decatur AL 35601 E-mail: rettaann@mindspring.com.

MASON, MARILYN GELL, library administrator, writer, consultant; b. Chickasha, Okla., Aug. 23, 1944; d. Emmett D. and Dorothy (O'Bar) Killebrew; m. Carl L. Gell, Dec. 29 1965 (div. Oct. 1978); 1 son, Charles E.; m. Robert M. Mason, July 17, 1981. BA, U. Dallas, 1966; M.L.S., N. Tex. State U., Denton, 1968; M.P.A., Harvard U., 1978. Libr. N.J. State Libr., Trenton, 1968-69; head dept. Arlington County Pub. Libr., Va., 1969-73; chief libr. program Metro Washington Coun. Govts., 1973-77; dir. White House Conf. on Librs. and Info. Svcs., Washington, 1979-80; exec. v.p. Metrics Rsch. Corp., Atlanta, 1981-82; dir. Atlanta-Fulton Pub. Libr., Atlanta, 1982-86, Cleve. Pub. Libr., 1986-99; writer, cons., 1999—. Trustee Online Computer Library Ctr., 1984-97; Evalene Parsons Jackson lectr. div. librarianship Emory U., 1981; commr. Nat. Commn. Libr. Info. Svcs., 2001-02. Author: The Federal Role in Library and Information Services, 1983, Strategic Management for Today's Libraries, 1999; editor: Survey of Library Automation in the Washington Area, 1977; project dir.: book Information for the 1980's, 1980. Bd. visitors Sch. Info. Studies, Syracuse U., 1981-85, Sch. of Libr. and Info. Sci., U. Tenn.-Knoxville, 1983-85; trustee Coun. on Libr. Resources, Washington, 1992-2000. Recipient Disting. Alumna award N. Tex. State U., 1979, Herbert and Virginia White award, ALA, 1999; inducted into Ohio Libr. Coun. Hall of Fame, 1999. Mem. ALA (mem. council 1986—90), Am. Assn. Info. Sci., Ohio Library Assn., D.C. Library Assn. (pres. 1976-77) Home and Office: 811 Live Oak Plantation Rd Tallahassee FL 32312-2412 Personal E-mail: marilyngmason@earthlink.net. Business E-Mail: mgmason@oclc.org.

MASON, MARSHA, actress, theater director, writer; b. St. Louis; d. James and Jacqueline M.; m. Gary Campbell, 1965 (div.); m. Neil Simon, Oct. 25, 1973 (div.). Grad., Webster (Mo.) Coll. Performances include cast broadway and nat. tour Cactus Flower, 1968; other stage appearances include The Deer Park, 1967, The Indian Wants the Bronx, 1968, Happy Birthday, Wanda June, 1970, Private Lives, 1971, You Can't Take It With You, 1972, Cyrano de Bergerac, 1972, A Doll's House, 1972, The Crucible, 1972, The Good Doctor, 1973, King Richard III, 1974, The Heiress, 1975, Mary Stuart, 1982, Amazing Grace, 1995, Night of the Iguana, 1996; one-woman show off-Broadway, The Big Love, Perry St. Theatre, 1988, Lake No Bottom, Second Stage, 1990, Escape From Happiness, With Naked Angels, 1994, Amazing Grace, 1998, House, 1998, (London) Prisoner of Second Avenue, 1999; film appearances include Blume in Love, 1973, Cinderella Liberty, 1973 (recipient Golden Globe award 1974, Acad. award nominee), Audrey Rose, 1977, The Goodbye Girl, 1977 (recipient Golden Globe award 1978, Acad. award nominee), The Cheap Detective, 1978, Promises in the Dark, 1979, Chapter Two, 1979 (Acad. award nominee), Only When I Laugh, 1981 (Acad. award nominee), Max Dugan Returns, 1982, Heartbreak Ridge, 1986, Stella, 1988, Drop Dead Fred, 1990, I Love Trouble, 1994, Nick of Time, 1995, Two Days in the Valley, 1996; TV appearances include PBS series Cyrano de Bergerac, 1974, The Good Doctor, 1978, Lois Gibbs and the Love Canal, 1981, Surviving, 1985, Trapped in Silence, 1986, The Clinic, 1987, Dinner at Eight, 1989, The Image, 1990, Broken Trust, 1994, series Sibs, 1991, Dead Aviators, 1999; dir. (plays) Juno's Swans, 1987, Heaven Can Wait; dir. ABC Afternoon Spl. Little Miss Perfect, 1988; Frasier, 1997(Emmy Nom.), Me & My Shadows: The Judy Garland Story, 2001, author: Journey: A Personal Odyssey (Simon & Schuster), 2000. E-mail: douhlem@newmexico.com.

MASON, MARSHALL W. theater director, educator; b. Amarillo, Tex., Feb. 24, 1940; s. Marvin Marshall and Lorine (Chrisman) M. BS in Speech, Northwestern U., 1961. Prof. Ariz. State U., 1994-2005; chief drama critic New Times, Phoenix, 1994-96. Founder, artistic dir. Circle Repertory Co., 1969-87, guest artistic dir., Ctr. Theater Group, 1988; dir. Broadway prodns. Redwood Curtain, 1993, The Seagull, 1992, Solitary Confinement, 1992, Burn This, 1987, As Is, 1985 (Drama Desk award, Tony nomination), Passion, 1983, Angels Fall, 1983 (Tony nomination), Fifth of July, 1981 (Tony nomination), Talley's Folly, 1980, (Pulitzer Prize, N.Y. Drama Critics Circle award, Tony nomination), Murder at the Howard Johnsons, 1979, Gemini, 1977, Knock Knock, 1976 (Tony nomination); Off-Broadway prodns. Book of Days, 2002, Sympathetic Magic, 1997, Robbers, 1997, Cakewalk, 1996, A Poster of the Cosmos/The Moonshot Tape, 1994, The Destiny of Me, 1992, Sunshine, 1989, Talley and Son, 1985, Childe Byron, 1980, Hamlet, 1979, Serenading Louie, 1976 (Obie award), Knock Knock, 1976 (Obie award), The Mound Builders, 1975 (Obie award), Battle of Angeles, 1974 (Obie award), The Sea Horse, 1974, The Hot L Baltimore, 1973 (Obie award); dir. numerous prodns. including Who's Afraid of Virginia Woolf?, Tokyo, 1985, Talley's Folly, 1982, London, Home Free! and The Madness of Lady Bright, 1968, London, Nat. Tour Sleuth, 1988, L.A. Summer and Smoke, 1988, Whisper in the Mind, 1990, King Lear, 1998, The Elephant Man, London, 1998, Long Day's Journey into Night, 1998, Riga, 1999, Los Alamos, 1999, Ginger, 2000; transl. Pirandello's Enrico IV, 2001, Ghosts, 2001, Private Lives, 2002, The Drawer Boy, 2003, The Cherry Orchard, 2004, The Cripple of Inishman, 2004, The Member of the Wedding, 2005; dir. numerous TV prodns. including Picnic, 1986, Kennedy's Children, 1982, The Fifth of July, 1983. Recipient Vernon Rice award, 1975, Drama Desk award, 1977, Margo Jones award, 1977, Outer Critics Circle award, 1978, Theatre World award, 1979, Shubert's Vaughan award, 1980, Obie award for Sustained Achievement, 1983, Inge Festival award for lifetime achievement, 1990, Last Frontier award, 1994, award Ariz. Press Club, 1995, Erwin Piscator award, 1996, Millennium Mr. Abbott award, 1999, Creative Achievement award Ariz. State U., 2001. Mem. Soc. Stage Dirs. and Choreographers (pres. 1983-85), Dirs. Guild Am., Actors Equity Assn., Coll. Fellow of Am. Theater. Address: 165 Christopher St 5I New York NY 10014 E-mail: mwm@asu.edu.

MASON, NANCY TOLMAN, retired state agency director; b. Buxton, Maine, Mar. 14, 1933; d. Ansel Robert and Kate Douglas (Libby) M. Grad., Bryant Coll., Providence, R.I., 1952; BA, U. Mass., Boston, 1977; postgrad., Inst. Governmental Services, Boston, 1985, The Auditor's Inst., 1988. Asst. to chief justice Mass. Superior Ct., Boston, 1964-68; cmty. liaison Action for Boston Cmty. Devel., Boston, 1968-73; mgmt. cons. East Boston Cmty. Devel. Assn., Boston, 1973-78; asst. dir. Mass. Office of Deafness, Boston, 1978-86; dir. of contracts Mass. Rehab. Commn., Boston, 1986-98; ret., 1998. Cons. Jos. A Ryan Assocs., Boston and Orleans, Mass., 1981-86, Radio Sta. WFCC, Chatham, Mass., 1987-91. Author: Bromley-Heath Security Patrols, 1974, Reorganization of East Boston Community Development Corporation, 1976, How to Start Your Own Small Business, 1981. Bd. dirs. Deaf-Blind Contact Ctr., Boston, 1988-91; vol. Am. Cancer Soc., Winchester, Mass., 1986-93, Tax Equity Alliance Mass., 1994; treas. Sunset Bay Condo Assn., 1998-99, bd. dirs. 1998-2001, Highland Cemetery Assn., 2002-. Recipient Good Citizen award DAR, 1950, Community Svc. award Northeastern U., 1986, Gov.'s citation for outstanding performance, 1993; named to Outstanding Young Women of Am., 1965. Mem. NOW, NAFE, Mass. State Assn. Deaf, Mass. Rehab. Commn. Statewide Cen. Office Dirs. (chair 1995-98, MRC procurement mgmt. team 1997-98, co-chair Take Your Daughters to Work Day 1998-99). Democrat. Episcopalian. Avocations: reading, music, bridge, swimming, sign language. Address: 5 Elmwood Dr Saco ME 04072-2103

MASON, RAYMOND ADAMS, brokerage company executive; b. Lynchburg, Va., Sept. 28, 1936; s. Raymond Watsi and Marion (Adams) M.; married; children: Paige Adams, Pamela Ann, Carter Meade, Morgan Rand. BA in Econs., Coll. William and Mary, 1959. Rep. Mason & Lee Inc., Richmond, Va., 1960-62; founder, pres. Mason & Co. Inc., Newport News, Va., 1962-70; pres. Legg, Mason & Co., Inc., Washington, 1970-73, Legg, Mason Wood Walker, Inc., Balt., 1978—, chmn. bd. dirs.; pres., chmn., chief exec. officer Legg Mason, Inc., 1981—. Chmn. regional firms com. N.Y. Stock Exchange, 1978-81; bd. dirs. Legg Mason Value Trust, Howard Weil Fin., Western Asset Mgmt. Trustee emeritus Endowment Assn., Coll. William and Mary; bd. dirs. emeritus William and Mary Sch. Bus. Adminstrn. Sponsors, Inc.; former trustee Balt. Mus. Art; former bd. dirs. Nat. Aquarium, Balt.; bd. dirs., exec. com., chair fin. com. Johns Hopkins Hosp.; mem. exec. com., chair endowment funds, fin. com. Johns Hopkins U.; former chmn. bd. sponsors Sch. Bus. & Mgmt. Loyola Coll., Balt., 1980-88; bd. dirs. Greater Balt. Com., 1982—, chmn., 1987-89; chmn. United Way Ctrl. Md. Mem. Nat. Assn. Securities Dealers (bd. govs. 1971-75, chmn. bd. govs. 1974-75), Securities Industry Assn. (bd. dirs. 1982—, chmn. 1985-86, bd. govs. 1984-88, chmn. bd. govs. 1987). Clubs: Ctr., Md., Balt. Country, L'Hirondelle, Caves Valley, New Orleans Country Club. Home: 1832 Circle Rd Baltimore MD 21204-6415 Office: Legg Mason Inc Legg Mason Tower 111 S Calvert St Ste 1900 Baltimore MD 21202-6189

MASON, RAYMOND E., JR., distributing company executive; b. Columbus, Ohio, Mar. 20, 1920; s. Raymond E. and Lula Estella (Potter) Mason; m. Margaret E. Edwards, Feb. 6, 1942; children: Raymond E. III, Michael D., Bruce R. BS, Ohio State U., 1941; grad., U.S. Command and Gen. Staff, 1962, U.S. Army War Coll., 1965; D of Bus. Sci. (hon.), Ohio State U., 2001. Ops. mgr. Suburban Motor Freight, Columbus, 1946-47; pres., gen. mgr. CFL Lines, Columbus, 1947-48; pres., chmn. Columbus Truck & Equipment Co., 1949—. Pres., chmn. REM Realty, Columbus, 1962—, Bode-Finn Co., Cin., 1966—99; chmn. Ford Bros. Inc., Ironton, Ohio, 1975—79; mem. distbr. adv. coun. Mack Trucks; mng. dir. J. D. Ranch, Myakka City, Fla. Active Boy Scouts Am.; former trustee Freedoms Found. Valley Forge, Ohio Hist. Found.; vice-chmn. New Coll. Found.; dir. Mote Marine Lab. Ohio State U. Found.; chmn. bd. trustees emeritus Franklin U. With U.S. Army, 1941—45, maj. gen. USAR. Decorated Bronze Star medal with V for Valor, Legion of Merit, Silver Star; named State of Ohio Vet. Hall of Fame, 1997, Buckeye Boys State Hall of Fame, 1999, Ohio State U. ROTC Hall of Fame, Jr. Achievement Ctrl. Ohio Bus. Hall of Fame, 2000; recipient Pres. Unit citation, Truck Dealer of the Yr. award, Time mag., 1972, Good Scout award, Ctrl. Ohio Coun. Boy Scouts Am., Silver Beaver award, Boy Scouts Am., Silver Antelope award, Disting. Citizen of Yr. award, Centennial medal, Ohio State U., Pacesetters award, Coll. Bus. ISU, 1996, Virginia Steckler Internat. Svc. award, ARC, 1998, Lifetime Achievement award, Ohio State U., 1999, Harrison Sayre award, 2001, Philanthropist of the Yr., Columbus Found., 2001; Baden-Powell fellow, World Scout Found. Mem.: Ohio Truck Assn., Am. Truck Dealers, Ohio State U. Alumni Assn., Armor Assn., Army War Coll. Alumni Assn., U.S. Army Arty. Assn., Queen City Club, Columbus Club, Rotary (past dist. gov., Man of Yr., Paul Harris fellow), Masons. Office: Columbus Truck Equipment Co PO Box 83250 Columbus OH 43203-0250 Home: 85 Sugar Mill Dr Osprey FL 34229-9067

MASON, RICHARD J. lawyer; b. Syracuse, N.Y., June 16, 1951; BA with high honors, U. Ill., 1973; MBA, U. Chgo., 1980; JD, U. Notre Dame, 1977. Bar: Ill. 1977. Ptnr., mem. exec. com. Ross & Hardies, Chgo., 1995—. Adj. prof. law Kent Coll. Law, Inst. Tech., Chgo., 1984—. Bd. dirs. Ill. Farm Legal Assistance Found., 1985-88. Mem. ABA (chmn. bus. bankruptcy subcom. on use and disposition of property under the bankruptcy code 1989—), Am. Bankruptcy Inst., Ill. State Bar Assn. (mem. banking and bankruptcy law sect. coun. 1986-88), Chgo. Bar Assn. (mem. bankrupcty and reorgn. com. 1978—), Comml. Law League. Office: Ross & Hardies 150 N Michigan Ave Ste 2500 Chicago IL 60601-7567

MASON, ROBERT MCSPADDEN, technology management educator, consultant; b. Sweetwater, Tenn., Jan. 16, 1941; s. Paul Rankin and Ruby May (McSpadden) M.; m. Betty Ann Durrence (div. 1980); children: Michael Dean, Donald Robert; m. Marilyn Killebrew Gell, July 17, 1981. SB, MIT, 1963, SM, 1965; PhD, Ga. Inst. Tech., 1973. Tech. staff mem. Sandia Labs., Livermore, Calif., 1965-68; rsch. scientist Ga. Inst. Tech., Atlanta, 1971-75, sr. rsch. scientist, 1975; prin. Metrics, Inc., Atlanta, 1975-80; pres. Metrics Rsch. Corp., Atlanta, 1980-86, Cleve., 1986-98, Tallahassee, 1998—; adj. prof. Weatherhead Sch. Mgmt. Case Western U., 1987-88, vis. prof., 1988-91, prof. for practice of tech. mgmt., 1991-98; dir. Ctr. Mgmt. Sci. and Tech., 1988-96; Sprint prof. mgmt. and prof. mgmt. info. sys. Coll. Bus. Fla. State U., Tallahassee, 1998—, chair mgmt. info. sys., 1998—2002. Co-author: Library Micro Consumer, 1986; co-editor: Information Services: Economics, Management, and Technology, 1981, Management of Technology V: Technology Management in a Changing World, 1996; co-author: The Impact of Office Automation on Clerical Employment, 1985-2000, 1985; Am. editor Technovation, 1994—; contbr. article series "Mason on Micros" to Libr. Jour., 1983-86, articles to various profl. publs. Mem. Internat. Assn. for Tech. Mgmt. (newsletter editor 1992-93, program chair internat. conf., 1996, pres. 1996-98, mem. exec. com. 1998—). Republican. Presbyterian. Avocations: flying, skiing, sailing, scuba diving, photography. Home: 811 Live Oak Plantation Rd Tallahassee FL 32312-2412 Office: Fla State U MIS Dept Coll of Bus Tallahassee FL 32306-1110 Office Phone: 850-644-4713. E-mail: rmmason@alum.mit.edu.

MASON, RODNEY, performing arts educator; b. Phila. Dancer Urban Colors, Portland, Oreg. Instr. hip-hop dance U. Arts Phila. Recipient Bessie Ward award, 2002. Office: Univ Arts Phila 320 S Broad St Philadelphia PA 19102

MASON, SALLY KAY FROST, biology professor, provost, dean; b. N.Y.C., May 29, 1950; d. Michael and Alberta Viparina; m. John S. Frost, Aug. 1975 (div. Feb. 1982); m. Kenneth Andrew Mason, Mar. 17, 1990. BA in Zoology, U. Ky., 1972; MS in Cell/Devel. Biology, Purdue U., 1974; PhD in Cell/Devel. Biology, U. Ariz., 1978. Rsch. assoc. Ind. U., Bloomington, 1978-80; asst. prof. biology U. Kans., Lawrence, 1981-86, assoc. prof. biology, 1986-91, prof. biology, 1991-2001, chair dept. physiology and cell biology, 1986-89, assoc. dean scis., 1990-95, dean arts and scis., 1995-2001; provost, prof. biology Purdue U., West Lafayette, Ind., 2001—. Mem. Ind. Proteomics Consortium; mem. adv. bd. NSF, 2003—; mem. exec. com. Nat. Assn. State U. and Land Grant Colls., 2002—. Mem. editl. bd. Pigment Cell Rsch., 1988-99; contbr. chpts. to books and articles to profl. jours. Dissertation fellow AAUW, 1977-78, Kemper Tchg. fellow U. Kans., Lawrence, 1997; grantee NSF, NIH, Washington, 1981-98; Wesley Found. grantee Welsey Health Found., Wichita, Kans., 1991-93. Mem. Internat. Fedn. Pigment Cell Scis. (coun. mem. 1997-2000), Pan Am. Soc. for Pigment Cell Rsch. (coun. mem. 1988-98, pres. 1996-98), Coun. Colls. Arts and Scis. (bd. mem. 1997-99, pres. elect 1999-2000, pres. 2000-2001). Avocations: travel, reading, writing. Office: Purdue U Office of Provost Hovde Hall West Lafayette IN 47905

MASON, SCOTT MACGREGOR, entrepreneur, inventor, consultant; b. NYC, Feb. 11, 1923; s. Gregory Mason and Mary Louise Turner; m. Mildred Davidson, Mar. 13, 1949 (div. 1970); children: Alan Gregory, Phoebe Louise, Caleb; m. Virginia Frances Perkins, May 5, 1970 (dec. 1990). AB, Princeton U., 1943; MS, NYU, 1947. Control chemist Firestone Tire & Rubber Co., Akron, Ohio, 1943-44; R & D chemist Am. Cyanamid Co. Rsch. Labs., Stamford, Conn., 1948-52; mgr. stearate dept. Warwick Chem. div. Sun Chem. Corp., Wood River Junction, R.I., 1952-58; cons., Stonington, Conn., 1958-59; instr. Williams Meml. Inst., New London, Conn., 1959-63; NSF fellow Brown U., Providence, 1963-64; tchr. Moses Brown Sch., Providence, 1964-70; owner, mgr. Innoventures, Wakefield, R.I., 1970—. Cons. Greene Plastics Corp., Canonchet, R.I., 1972-80, Dorette Inc., Pawtucket, R.I., 1982-83. Trustee Pine Point Sch., Stonington, 1956-62, pres. bd., 1959-61. With AUS, 1944-46, ETO. Named Tchr. of Week, Sta. WICE, Providence, 1967; summer rsch. fellow NSF, U. R.I., 1960. Mem. AAAS, N.Y. Acad. Scis. Achievements include patents in field. Avocations: tennis, fishing, snorkeling, photography, music. Office: Innoventures PO Box 369 Wakefield RI 02880-0369

MASON, STEPHEN OLIN, academic administrator; b. Fresno, Calif., July 11, 1952; s. Olin James and Mary Edna (Moyer) Mason. BA, Bridgewater (Va.) Coll., 1974; MEd, James Madison U., 1979; PhD, Loyola U., Chgo., 1991. Asst. to the dir. student ctr. Bridgewater Coll., 1974-76; guidance counselor Woodlawn Elem. Sch., Sebring, Fla., 1976-77; asst. dean for student devel. Bridgewater Coll., 1977-81; dir. student life Roger Williams Coll., Bristol, R.I., 1981-83; assoc. dean for residential svcs. Dickinson Coll., Carlisle, Pa., 1983-84; v.p., dean student affairs Westmar Coll., LeMars, Iowa, 1984; rsch. assoc. to pres. Elmhurst (Ill.) Coll., 1986-87; v.p. student affairs Felician Coll., Chgo., 1987-88; dean students Huntingdon Coll., Montgomery, Ala., 1988-90; dir. devel. McPherson (Kans.) Coll., 1990-94, v.p. fin. svcs., 1994-97; exec. dir. Assn. of Brethren Caregivers, Elgin, Ill., 1997—2003; v.p. coll. adv. Manchester Coll., No. Manchester, Ind., 2004—. Participant ARC Blood Drive, 1978—79; mem. allocations com. United Way, Carlisle, 1984; adv. bd. mem. LeMars chpt. Siouxland Coun. for Alcoholism and Drug Abuse, 1984; site coord. for coat drive Mental Health Greater Chgo., 1985; dir.-at-large Alumni Bd. Bridgewater Coll., 1987—93; v.p. McPherson Habitat for Humanity, 1993, 1994, bd. dirs., 1993—96, pres., 1994; bd. dirs. McPherson Mus. and Arts Found., 1992—94, Assn. Brethren Caregivers, 1993—97, Assn. Anabaptist Risk Mgmt., 2000—03; governing coun., mem. adv. Bethany Hosp., 2001—02. Mem.: Brethren Benefit Trust (bd. dirs. 2002—). Avocation: Avocations: calligraphy, community theatre, barbershop singing, spelunking. Home: 106 S Merkle St North Manchester IN 46962 Office Phone: 260-982-5212. Business E-Mail: somason@manchester.edu.

MASON, THEODORE W. lawyer; b. June 17, 1943; AB, Yale U., 1965; JD, U. Pa., 1972. Bar: Pa. 1972, Fla. 1987. Shareholder Greenberg Traurig, Phila., 1997—2001. Treas., bd. dirs. Nat. Adoption Ctr., Adoption Ctr. Del. Valley, The Hill Top Preparatory Sch. Mem. Nat. Assn. Bond Lawyers (steering com. workshop, enforcement com.). Office: Greenberg Traurig LLP 2700 Two Commerce Sq 2001 Market St Philadelphia PA 19103 Fax: 215-988-7801. E-mail: masont@gtlaw.com.

MASON, THOMAS ALBERT, lawyer; b. Cleve., May 4, 1936; s. Victor Lewis and Frances (Speidel) M.; m. Elisabeth Gun Sward, Sept. 25, 1965; children: Thomas Lewis, Robert Albert. AB, Kenyon Coll., 1958; LLB, Case-Western Res. U., 1961. Bar: Ohio 1961. Assoc. Thompson, Hine and Flory, Cleve., 1965-73, ptnr., 1973—. Trustee Cleve. YMCA, 1975-94. Capt.

USMCR, 1962-65. Mem. Am. Coll. Real Estate Lawyers, Am. Land Title Assn. (lender's counsel group), Mortgage Bankers Assn. of Met. Cleve., Ohio Bar Assn., Cleve. Bar Assn., The Country Club. Republican. Episcopalian. Avocations: tennis, golf. Home: 23375 Duffield Rd Cleveland OH 44122-3101 Office: Thompson Hine LLP 3900 Key Ctr 127 Public Sq Cleveland OH 44114-1291 Office Phone: 216-566-5519. E-mail: tom.mason@thompsonhine.com.

MASON, THOMAS ALEXANDER, historian, educator, author; b. Port Huron, Mich., Oct. 29, 1944; s. Frank Hallgren and Charlotte (Hamilton) M.; m. Christine Huguette Guyonneau, Aug. 11, 1984; 1 child, Charlotte Guyonneau. BA in History with highest honors, Kenyon Coll., 1966; MA, U. Va., 1970, PhD, 1975. Asst. prof. history Pembroke (N.C.) State U., 1976-79; assoc. editor Papers of James Madison, U. Va., 1979-86, acting editor, 1986-87; dir. publs. Ind. Hist. Soc., 1987—2001, v.p. publs., 2001—02; v.p. Ind. Hist. Soc. Press, 2002—. Author: Serving God and Mammon: William Juxon, 1582-1663, 1985; exec. editor: Traces of Indiana and Midwestern History, 1989—; editor: Documentary Editing, 1989-93, Mag. of Albermarle County History, 1984-86; co-editor: Papers of James Madison, congl. series, vols. 14-16, 1983-89, presdl. series, vol. 1, 1984; project dir.: Papers of Lew Wallace, 1992—; mem. editl. bd. Jour. of the Early Republic, 1991-95, Ency. of Indpls., 1990-94, Documentary Editing, 2002—; contbr. articles to encys. and scholarly jours. Served with USMC, 1966-68. Mem. Am. Assn. for State and Local History, Am. Hist. Assn., N.Am. Conf. on Brit. Studies, So. Hist. Assn., Assn. Documentary Editing (councillor-at-large 1999-2002, dir. publs. 1995-98, Disting. Svc. award 1993), Hist. Soc. of the Episcopal Ch. (sec. 1995—, bd. dirs. 1993—), English-Speaking Union U.S. (chmn. region VI 1996-2002, bd. dirs. 1995-2002, pres. Indpls. br. 1989-96, Lily Dabney scholar 1972, Merit award 2002), Raven Soc., Rotary (Indpls., bd. dirs. 1998-2000), Colonnade Club (Charlottesville), Royal Commonwealth Soc. (London), Omicron Delta Kappa (faculty sec. Va. Cir. 1984-86), Alpha Delta Phi. Episcopalian. Home: PO Box 20331 Indianapolis IN 46220-0331 Office: Ind Hist Soc 450 W Ohio St Indianapolis IN 46202-3269 E-mail: tmason@indianahistory.org.

MASON, THOMAS OLIVER, materials science and engineering educator, researcher; b. Cleve., Oct. 14, 1952; s. Alden Oliver and Wilma Ruth Mason; m. Karen Elaine Bickel, June 1, 1952; children: James Ian, Charlotte Ann. BS in Ceramic Sci., Pa. State U., 1974; PhD in Materials Sci. & Engring., MIT, 1977. Assoc. prof. Northwestern Univ. Materials Sci. & Eng., Evanston, Ill., 1983—89, prof., 1989—. Nato postdoctoral fellow U. of Hannover, Germany, 1977—78; asst. prof. Northwestern Univ. Materials Sci. & Eng., Evanston, Ill., 1978—83, asst. chmn., 1987—92. Cited rschr. Am. Soc. for Info. Rsch. Founding elder Evanston (Ill.) Bible Fellowship, 1987—2002. Recipient Academician, Acad. of Ceramics, 1999. Fellow: Am. Ceramic Soc. (v.p. 1995—96, Richard M. Fulrath Pacific award 1994, Schwartzwalder Profl. Achieveement in Ceramic Engring. award 1991); mem.: Nat. Inst. of Ceramic Engrs., Materials Rsch. Soc., Ceramic Ednl. Coun. (pres. 1992—93). Avocations: amateur radio, classical music collector, poetry, fishing. Office: Northwestern Univ Materials Sci and Engring 2220 Campus Dr Evanston IL 60201 E-mail: t-mason@northwestern.edu.

MASON, THOMAS R. utilities executive; Pres., CEO CalEnergy Operating Svcs., Inc., 1995—99; sr. v.p. Calpine Corp., 1999, exec. v.p., 1999—. Office: Calpine 50 W San Fernando St 5th Fl San Jose CA 95113

MASON, WILLIAM, general director of opera company; b. Chgo. m. Diana Davis; 2 children. MusB, Roosevelt U. Asst. to co-artistic dir. Pino Donati, 1962—66; asst. stage mgr. Lyric Opera Chgo., 1968—70; asst. to Felix Popper N.Y.C Opera, 1971; prod. stage mgr. Cin. Opera, 1972; stage mgr., asst. in musical preparation Light Opera of Manhattan, 1972; prod. mgr., asst. dir. Ohio-based Corbett Found., 1973; prod. dir. Lyric Opera Chgo., 1974—78, gen. dir., 1997—; artistic adminstr. San Francisco Opera, 1979—80. Mem. Lyric Children's Chorus, 1954—56. Office: Lyric Opera Chgo 20 N Wacker Dr Chicago IL 60606-2806

MASON, WILLIAM A(LVIN), psychologist, educator, researcher; b. Mountain View, Calif., Mar. 28, 1926; s. Alvin Frank and Ruth Sabina (Erwin) M.; m. Virginia Joan Carmichael, June 27, 1948; children: Todd, Paula, Nicole, Hunter. BA, Stanford U., 1950, MS, 1952, PhD, 1954. Asst. prof. U. Wis.-Madison, 1954-59; research assoc. Yerkes Labs. Primate Biology, Orange Park, Fla., 1959-63; head dept. behavioral sci. Delta Primate Research Ctr., Tulane U., Covington, La., 1963-71; prof. psychology, research psychologist U. Calif., Davis, 1971-91, leader behavioral biology unit Calif. Primate Rsch. Ctr., 1972-96, prof. emeritus, 1991. Bd. dirs. Jane Goodall Inst., 1978-92, Karisoke Rsch. Ctr., 1980-86. Mem. Editorial bd. Animal Learning and Behavior, 1973-76, Internat. Jour. Devel. Psychobiology, 1980-91, Internat. Jour. Primatology, 1980-90; contbr. numerous articles to profl. jours., chpts. to books. With USMC, 1944-46. USPHS spl. fellow, 1963-64. Fellow AAAS, APA (pres. divsn. 6 1982, disting. sci. contbn. award 1995), Am. Psychol. Soc., Animal Behavior Soc.; mem. Internat. Primatological Soc. (pres. 1976-80, 81-84), Am. Soc. Primatologists (pres. 1988-90, disting. primatologist award), Internat. Soc. Devel. Psychobiology (pres. 1971-72, Best Paper of Yr. award 1976), Sigma Xi. Home: 2809 Anza Ave Davis CA 95616-0257 Office: U Calif Regl Primate Rsch Ctr 1 Shields Ave Davis CA 95616 Business E-Mail: wamason@ucdavis.edu.

MASON, WILLIAM CORDELL, III, hospital administrator; b. Montgomery, Ala., June 7, 1938; s. William C. and Sibyl (Evans) M.; m. Mona Holloway, Jan. 5, 1957 (div. June 1992); children: Michael C., Rebecca Mason Malone, Stephen E., Holly M.; m. Juliette Baldwin Woodruff, Apr. 17, 1993 BS, U. La., 1961; M. Hospital and Health Care, Trinity U., 1971. Hosp. rep. Eaton Labs., Norwich, N.Y., 1962-66; fgn. service officer U.S. Dept. State, Manila and Saigon, 1966-69; chief exec. officer Bapt. Hosp. of East Africa, Mbeya, Tanzania, 1971-74, Bapt. Hosp., Bangalore, India, 1974-78; chief operating officer Bapt. Med. Ctr., Jacksonville, Fla., 1978-84, vice chmn., CEO, 1984-95; vice chmn. bd. dirs., CEO Bapt./St. Vincent's Health Sys. Inc., Jacksonville, Fla., 1995-98, CEO, chmn. bd., 1998, chmn. bd. dirs., 1998—. Prof. health adminstrn. U. No. Fla.; cons. So. Bapt. Fgn. Mission Bd., Richmond, Va., 1980-85; bd. dirs. Bank Am., SunHealth Corp., sec. exec. com., 1990-94. Contbr. articles to profl. jours. Chmn. deacons Hendricks Ave. Bapt. Ch., Jacksonville, 1984-85, Calvary Bapt. Ch., Bangalore, 1976-77; treas. Karnataka State Bapt. Conv., Bangalore, 1975-77; trustee Jacksonville Symphony Orch.; bd. dirs. U. No. Fla.Assn. Vol. Hosps., 1986, Med. Assistance Program Internat., 1986-87, United Way, 1990; chmn. Greater Jacksonville Area Hosp. Coun., 1985, Mayor's Health Econ. Devel. Coun., 1986-87, Greater Jacksonville U.S. Savs. Bond Campaign, 1987; mem. adv. coun. Jacksonville U. Sch. Bus., 1986-88; chmn. area devel. coun. So. Bapt. Fgn. Mission Bd., 1987-91 Fellow Am. Coll. Hosp. Execs.; mem. Am. Hosp. Assn., Fla. Hosp. Assn. (trustee 1982, 83-85, 86), Fla. Hosp. Assn. (chmn. 1992-93, trustee 1994—), Healthcare Exec. Study Soc., Jacksonville C. of C. (vice chmn. exec. com. 1988-89, chmn. health econ. devel. 1992-95, chmn. cornerstone econ. devel. initiative), Epping Forest Yacht Club (bd. govs. 1990—), Beta Sigma Gamma, Rotary. Avocations: golf, boating, reading. Home: 947 Greenridge Rd Jacksonville FL 32207-5203 Office: Ste 902 1325 San Marco Blvd Jacksonville FL 32207-8571

MASON, WILLIAM VANHORN, dermatologist; b. Pitts., Jan. 8, 1930; AB, Harvard U., 1951; MD, Baylor Coll. Medicine, Houston, 1961. Diplomate Am. Bd. Dermatology. Pvt. practice, Albuquerque, 1979—; clin. assoc. prof. dermatology U. N.Mex. Sch. Medicine, Albuquerque, 1986—. Lt. (j.g.) USN, 1951-54. Mem. Phi Beta Kappa, Alpha Omega Alpha. Office: 200 Oak St NE Albuquerque NM 87106-4740

MASONI, PATRICIA M. writer; d. Maurice H Bouton and Dorothy M Hogan; m. Viltorio G Masoni, Apr. 11, 1958; children: Stefania, Gabriella, Gianmarco. BSc, U. of Utah, 1956. Author: (novels) Steeple, 2001. Avocation: jewelry design. Home: 6431 Dahlonega Bethesda MD 20816 E-mail: triciabouton@aol.com.

MASOTTI, LOUIS HENRY, real estate educator, consultant; b. N.Y.C., May 16, 1934; s. Henry and Angela Catherine (Turi) Masotti; m. Iris Patricia Leonard, Aug. 28, 1958 (div. 1981); children: Laura Lynn, Andrea Anne; m. Ann Randel Humm, Mar. 5, 1988. AB, Princeton U., 1956; MA, Northwestern U., 1961, PhD, 1964. Fellow Nat. Ctr. Edn. in Politics, 1962; asst. prof. polit. sci. Case Western Res. U., Cleve., 1963-67, assoc. prof., 1967-69, dir. Civil Violence Rsch. Ctr., 1968-69; sr. Fulbright lectr. Johns Hopkins U. Ctr. Advanced Internat. Studies, Bologna, Italy, 1969-70; assoc. prof. Northwestern U., Evanston, Ill., 1970-72, prof. polit. sci. and urban affairs, 1972-83, dir. Ctr. Urban Affairs, 1971-80, dir. Program in Pub. and Not-for-Profit Mgmt., Kellogg Sch. Mgmt., 1979-80, prof. mgmt. and urban devel. Kellogg Sch. Mgmt., 1983-94, dir. Real Estate Research Ctr. Kellogg Sch. Mgmt., 1986-88. Cons. to numerous publs, govt. agys., real estate firms, and corps.; vis. assoc. prof. U. Wash., 1969; exec. dir. Mayor Jane Byrne Transition Com., Chgo., 1979; vis. prof. Stanford Sch. Bus., 1989—92, UCLA Sch. Mgmt., 1989—92; prof., dir. real estate mgmt. program U. Calif. Grad. Sch. Mgmt., Irvine, 1992—98; bd. dirs. Mfd. Home Cmtys., Inc., Facilities Mgmt. Internat., S. Calif. Physicans Ins. Co. Author: (book) Educaiton and Politics in Suburbia, 1967, Shootout in Cleveland, 1969, A Time to Burn?, 1969, Suburbia in Transition, 1973, The New Urban Politics, 1976, The City in Comparative Perspective, 1976; co-editor: Metropolis in Crisis, 1968, Metropolis in Crisis, 2d edit., 1971, Riots and Rebellion, 1968, The Urbanization of the Suburbs, 1973, After Daley: Chicago Politics in Transition, 1981, Downtown Development, 1985, Downtown Development, 2d edit., 1987; editor: Edn. and Urban Soc., 1968—71, Urban Affairs Quar., 1973—80; sec. editor: Econ. Devel. Quar., 1986—92, vice chmn. bd.: Ill. Issues Jour., 1986—92, BOMA Office Mag., 1990—95. Mem. Cleveland Heights Bd. Edn., 1967—69; devel. coord. high tech. State of Ill. - City of Chgo., 1982—83; Rsch. dir. Carl Stokes for Mayor Cleve., 1967; advisor to various congl., gubernatorial and mayoral campaigns Ohio; cons. urban devel. issues corps. developers, govt agys. and news media. Lt. USNR, 1956—59. Recipient Disting. Svc. award, Cleve. Jaycees, 1967; fellow, Homer Hoyt Inst. Advanced Real Estate Studies; grantee Rsch., numerous fed. and found., 1963—2000. Mem.: Internat. Econ. Devel. Coun., Nat. Assn. Indsl. Office Properties, Internat. Devel. Rsch. Coun., Internat. Assn. Corp. Real Estate Execs., Nat. Trust Hist. Preservation, Habitat, Urban Land Inst., Lambda Alpha Internat. Address: Unit 300 4344 Promenade Way Marina Del Rey CA 90292-6291 E-mail: lmasotti@dc.rr.com.

MASOUREDIS, SERAFEIM PANAGIOTIS, pathologist, educator; b. Detroit, Nov. 14, 1922; s. Panagiotis and Lemonia Masouredis; m. Marion Helen Mykytew, Oct. 1943; children: Claudia, Linus. AB, U. Mich., 1944, MD, 1948; PhD in Med. Physics, U. Calif., Berkeley, 1952. Diplomate Am. Bd. Pathology. Intern U. Calif. Svc./San Francisco Gen. Hosp., 1952-53, asst. resident in medicine, 1954-55; fellow Clinic Hematology/Donner Lab./Univ. Calif., Berkeley, 1953-54; asst. prof., then assoc. prof. pathology U. Pitts. Med. Sch., 1955-59; asst. dir. Cen. Blood Bank Pitts., 1955-59; assoc. prof. preventive medicine U. Calif., San Francisco, 1959-62, assoc. prof. medicine, 1962-67, assoc. prof. clin. pathology, 1966-67; prof. medicine Marquette U., Milw., 1967-69; exec. dir. Milw. Blood Ctr., 1967-69; prof. pathology U. Calif., San Diego, 1969-90, prof. emeritus, 1990—. Cons. WHO, Geneva, 1965-67; bd. dirs. Am. Assn. Blood Banks, Washington,1 981-83. Assoc. editor Jour. Transfusion, Washington, 1981-90; contbr. sci. articles and rsch. papers to various publs. Emily Cooley Meml. lectr. Am. Assn. Blood Banks, 1973, recipient Karl Landsteiner Meml. award, 1979. Mem. Am. Assn. Immunologists, Am. Soc. Clin. Investigation, Am. Soc. Hematology, Brit. Soc. Immunology, Am. Assn. Cancer Rsch., Internat. Soc. Blood Transfusion, Western Assn. Physicians. Avocations: woodworking, travel. Office: U Calif San Diego Dept Pathology Sch Medicine La Jolla CA 92093-0612

MASRI, MERLE SID, biochemist, consultant; b. Jerusalem, Palestine, Sept. 12, 1927; came to U.S., 1947; s. Said Rajab and Fatima M.; m. Maryjean Loretta Anderson, June 28, 1952 (div. 1974); children: Kristin Corinne, Allan Eric, Wendy Joan, Heather Anderson. BA in Physiology, U. Calif., Berkeley, 1950; PhD in Mammalian Physiology and Biochemistry, U. Calif. Berkeley, 1953. Rsch. asst. Dept. Physiology, Univ. Calif., Berkeley, 1950-53; predoctoral fellow Baxter Labs., Berkeley, 1952-53; rsch. assoc. hematology Med. Rsch. Inst., Michael Reese Hosp., Chgo., 1954-56; sr. rsch. biochemist Agrl. Rsch. Svc., USDA, Berkeley, 1956-87; supervisory rsch. scientist Agrl. Rsch. Svc., USDA, N.D. State U. Sta., Fargo, N.D., 1987-89; pvt. practice as cons. Emeryville, Calif., 1989—. Lectr. numerous confs. Contbr. articles to profl. jours. and books. Recipient Spl. Svc. and Merit awards USDA, 1966, 76, 77, Superior Svc. award USDA, 1977. Mem. AAAS, Am. Chem. Soc., Am. Oil Chemists Soc., Am. Assn. Cereal Chemists, N.Y. Acad. Scis., Inst. Food Technologists, Commonwealth Club Calif., Internat. Platform Assn., World Affairs Coun. of No. Calif., Sigma Xi. Achievements include patents for detoxification of aflatoxins in agricultural crops and aflatoxin contaminated milk, improved dyeability of cotton fabrics and reduced dye and electrolyte discharge in plant effluent, new closed-circuit raw wool scouring technology to conserve water and energy and control pollution, synthesis and use of polymers and modification of biopolymers for wastewater treatment, and for encapsulation, enzyme immobilization, toxic heavy metals removal and textile finishing treatment, non-polluting new technology for scouring raw wool in a closed circuit with water recycling and re-use and waste effluent control; studied chlorination of water in food processing operations and water re-use and recycle and the generation of mutagens and means of improving disinfection efficiency and reducing mutagen formation, pharmacology, metabolism, and toxicology of natural and synthetic compounds, cereal and baking technology and wheat and durum quality, carbohydrate chemistry, fermentation and enology, confectionery, and ceramic chemistry; discovered new methods and reagents for protein and amino acid residue modification and analysis, new mammalian metabolic pathways; developed other non-polluting textile finishing treatments (shrink, wrinkle, insect and fire resistance). Home: 9 Commodore Dr Emeryville CA 94608-1652

MASRY, EDWARD L. lawyer; b. Patterson, N.J., July 29, 1932; m. Jacqueline Wilson; children: Louanne, Louis, Nichole; m. Joette Levinson, 1992; children: Chris, Tim. Student, Valley Jr. Coll., 1950—52, U. Calif., Santa Barbara, UCLA, U. So. Calif.; JD, Loyola U., L.A., 1960. Bar: Calif. 1961, U.S. Dist. Ct. Calif. 1961, U.S. Ct. Appeals (9th cir.) 1961, U.S. Supreme Ct. 1961. Pvt. practice, L.A., 1961—75, San Fernando Valley, Calif., 1975—82; ptnr. Masry & Vititoe, San Fernando Valley, 1982—97, Westlake Village, Calif., 1997—. Pres., CEO Save World Air, Inc.; mem. adv. bd. Boys & Girls Club, Conejo, Calif., Las Virgenes, Calif.; mem. Thousand Oaks City Coun., Calif., 2000; mayor pro tem City of Thousand Oaks, mayor, 2003—. With U.S. Army, 1952—54, Korea. Recipient U.S. Congl. award Outstanding Lawyer of the Yr., 1982, 1988, 1990, cert. of appreciation, Las Virgenes Unified Sch. Dist., 2002, cert. spl. congl. recognition, Def. Ctr. Commitment Environment Justice, 2002, Environ. Hero award, 2002, award, Nat. Jewish Fund, 2002, Santa Monica Mountains Recreational Area, Calif. Dept. Pks. and Recreation Angeles Dist., Mountains Restoration Trust, others. Mem.: ATLA, ABA, Consumer Attys. Assn. L.A., Los Angeles County Bar Assn., Ventura County Bar Assn., Consumer Attys. Calif., Trial Lawyers Pub. Justice (Acad. Justice award 2001), Phi Alpha Delta (justice, L.A. alumni justice). Office: Masry and Vititoe 5707 Corsa Ave Westlake Village CA 91362 Office Phone: 818-991-8900. E-mail: masry@masryvithoe.com.

MASS, MICHAEL DON, state legislator; b. McAlester, Okla., Oct. 29, 1951; s. Fred Jr. and Lois M.; m. Suzanne Kline; children: Elena, Angie, Micah, Lucas. Student, Grayson C.C., Sherman, Tex., Ea. Okla. State Coll. Mem. Ho. of Reps., 1991—. Dist. mgr. Pittsburg County Conservation Dist.; chair Okla. Dem. Party. Mem. McAlester C. of C. (exec. dir.), Latimer and Pittsburg County Cattlemen's Assn., Hartshorne C. of C. (v.p.). Democrat. Office: State Capitol Bldg Rm 335 2300 N Lincoln Blvd Oklahoma City OK 73105

MASSA, CONRAD HARRY, religious studies educator; b. Bklyn., Oct. 27, 1927; s. Harry Frederick and Josephine W. (Lepold) M.; m. Anna W. Rossi, Aug. 19, 1951; children: Stephen Mark, Barbara Ann. AB with honors, Columbia U., 1951; M.Div., Princeton Theol. Sem., 1954, PhD, 1960; HHD, Lafayette Coll., 1987. Ordained to ministry Presbyn. Ch., 1954. Pastor Elmwood Presbyn. Ch., East Orange, N.J., 1954-57; asst. prof. homiletics Princeton Theol. Sem., 1957-61; sr. pastor Old First Ch., Newark, 1961-66, Third Presbyn. Ch., Rochester, N.Y., 1966-78; dean acad. affairs Princeton Theol. Sem., 1978-94, dean emeritus, 1994—, Charlotte W. Newcombe prof., 1978-95, Charlotte W. Newcombe prof. emeritus, 1995—. 1st moderator Synod of the Northeast, United Presbyn. Ch.; vis. prof. St. Bernard's Roman Cath. Sem., Rochester, 1968-70; keynote speaker 11th ann. conf. Inst. Theology, Yonsei U., Seoul, Republic of Korea, 1991. Author articles and book revs. Trustee Lafayette Coll., Easton, Pa., 1982-93. Served with U.S. Army, 1946-47. Mem. Acad. Homiletics, Am. Acad. Religion, Internat. John Bunyan Soc. Home: 9583 SW 90th St Ocala FL 34481-7495 *I have learned to try to understand all events and persons in terms of their relationships to other things, persons and events. While it is sometimes fruitful to isolate a particular and study it in its solitude, nothing and no one really exists in such isolation. This has become a guiding principle in my continued research and growth in those areas of greatest interest - religion, education and society.*

MASSA, RICHARD WAYNE, retired communications educator; b. Carona, Kans., May 2, 1932; s. Columbo and Ella (Whitehead) M.; m. Mary Lou Marshall, May 29, 1960 (div. 1969); m. Teresa Rose Ramirez, Mar. 19, 1971; children: Tod, Daphne, Sara. B in Journalism, U. Mo., 1954, MA, 1955; postgrad., U. Ark., 1964-65. Instr. U. Mo., Columbia, 1955, Miss. State Coll. for Women, Columbus, 1957-58; from instr. to assoc.prof. comm. Okla. Coll. for Women/Okla. Coll. Liberal Arts, Chickasha, 1958-69; assoc. prof. Mo. So. State Coll., Joplin, 1972-87, prof., 1987-99, head dept. comm., 1980-99, dir. Inst. Internat. Studies, 1996-99, acting head dept. lang. and lit., 1979-80; ret., 1999. V.p. Interpersonal Comm. Consultants, Oklahoma City, 1969-72. Co-author: Principal Ideas of Medieval and Renaissance Man, 1967, Contemporary Man in World Society, 1969; co-editor: Classical Readings for Contemporary Man, 1967, Inquisitive Man; His Quest for Truth, 1970. With U.S. Army, 1955-57. Recipient Gov.'s award for Excellence in Tchg., Mo. Dept. Higher Edn., Jefferson City, 1996. Home: 25399 Demott Dr Joplin MO 64801-6309 Personal E-mail: massa727@aol.com.

MASSA, SALVATORE PETER, psychologist; b. Queens, N.Y., Aug. 5, 1955; s. Joseph and Marie Massa; m. Patricia Louise Kathryn Kelley, Mar. 12, 1979; children: Kathryn Kelley, Kristopher Kelley, KayLynn Kelley, Patrick Kelley, Grace Kellley, Frank Kelley. BA in Psychology, CUNY, 1975; MA, St. John's U., 1978, profl. diploma, 1979, PhD, 1985. Lic. psychologist, N.Y.; cert. sch. psychologist, N.Y.; nat. cert. sch. psychologist. Intern psychologist Sagamore Children's Psychiat. Hosp., Melville, N.Y., 1978-79; habilitation supr. Suffolk Child Devel. Ctr., Smithtown, N.Y., 1979; staff psychologist Cumberland Mental Health Ctr., Bklyn., 1979-81; asst. program dir., dir. clin. svcs. Rhinebeck (N.Y.) Country Sch., 1981-87; cons. psychologist Brookwood Ctr., 1985-86, Anderson Sch., 1987-89, Renssalaer Columbia Greene BOCES, 1987—97. Sch. psychologist Red Hook Ctrl. Sch. Dist.; cons. psychologist Rhinebeck Ctrl. Sch. Dist., 1986-90; cons. Columbia County Advocacy and Resource Ctr., Rehab. Programs, Inc., 1989; adj. prof. Marist Coll., Poughkeepsie, N.Y., 1994—. Co-author study on relaxation tng. in residential treatment; contbr. papers to profl. confs., chairman of the Bd. Trustee J.A. Coleman Cath. H.S.; head football coach YMCA Winter League, 1979-81; asst. football coach Rhinebeck Country Sch., 1982; coach Germantown Little League, Germantown Winter Basketball League, Saugerties Babe Ruth; treas. Red Hood Soccer Club, 1999—. Recipient pub. svc. award for vol. work Middletown State Hosp., 1975, spl. recognition Internat. Coun. Psychology, 1981. Mem. NASP, Soc. Personality Assessment. Democrat. Roman Catholic. E-mail: SJU@rhcsd.dcboces.org.

MASSACHI, DALYA FAITH, writer, consultant; b. Rochester, N.Y., Dec. 8, 1969; d. Ben Massachi and Rose Marlene Diamond. BA in Internat. Studies, U. N.C., 1992; MA in Internat. Affairs, Ohio U., 1997. Pvt. practice writing and comm. cons., Oakland, Calif., 1993—; exec. dir. Bay Area Internat. Devel. Orgns., Oakland, 2000—, also bd. dirs.; writing trainer, 2002—. Co-editor: (book) Women's Voices on FIRE, 2000, Uncovering the Right on Campus, 1994; co-prodr.: (video) BAIDO: Joining the Global Village, 2002; author: (opinion column) Columbus Dispatch; prodr.: (radio program) En La Casa: Domestic Violence in Latin America, 1999, Women's Voices from Around the World, 1996; author (newsletter): Nonprofit Writing Tips O' the Month, 2003—. Scholar, Ohio U., 1995—97. Mem.: NAFE, Nat. Writers' Union, Young Nonprofit Profls. Network. Green Party. Avocations: hiking, writing, cooking, travel. Office: Ste 205 678 Thirteenth St Oakland CA 94612 Personal E-mail: dalya@dfmassachi.net. E-mail: dalya@dfmassachi.net.

MASSAD, JORDAN ELIAS, mathematician; b. Tulsa, Okla., May 20, 1976; s. Joseph James and Darlene Ann Elizabeth Massad. BS, Worcester Poly. Inst., 1998; MS, N.C. State U., 2001, PhD, 2003. Html developer Worcester Poly. Inst., Mass., 1997—98; rsch. scientist Boeing Co., Bellevue, Wash., 1999—2000, Sandia Nat. Labs., Albuquerque, 2001—; rsch. fellow/asst. N.C. State U., Raleigh, NC, 1998—2003. Contbr. articles to profl. jours. Eucharitic min. and lector Cath. Campus Ministry, Worcester, Mass., 1994—98, Raleigh, NC, 1998—2003. Mem.: Soc. Physics Students, Soc. Photo-Optical Instrumentation Engineers (assoc.), Triangle Lebanese Assn., Nat. Apostolate of Maronites, So. Fedn. Syrian Lebanese Am. Clubs, Tau Beta Pi (life), Pi Mu Epsilon (life). Maronite Catholic. E-mail: kroll@alum.wpi.edu.

MASSAD, STEPHEN ALBERT, lawyer; b. Wewoka, Okla., Dec. 20, 1950; s. Alexander Hamilton and Delores Jean (Razook) Massad; children: Caroline, Sarah, Margaret. AB, Princeton U., 1972; JD, Harvard U., 1975. Bar: Tex. 1975. Assoc. Baker Botts L.L.P., Houston, 1975-82, ptnr., 1983—. Office: Baker Botts LLP 3000 One Shell Plz 910 Louisiana St Houston TX 77002 E-mail: stephen.massad@bakerbotts.com.

MASSAD, SUSAN MOORE, internist; b. NYC, 1938; MD, U. Calif., San Francisco, 1962. Bd. cert. internal medicine 1973. Intern Bellevue Hosp. Ctr., NYC, 1962—63, resident in medicine, 1963—64; resident San Francisco VA Hosp., 1967—68; fellow in ambulatory medicine U. Calif., San Francisco Med. Ctr., 1969—70; internist, clinical prof., dir. ambulatory internal medicine LI Coll. Hosp. Office: Long Island Coll Hosp SUNY Bklyn Health Sci Ctr New York NY 10014 Business E-Mail: smassad@aol.com.

MASSAGUE, JOAN, science educator; PhD in Biochemistry, U. Barcelona, Spain. Postdoctoral fellow Brown U.; prof. biochemistry U. Mass. Med. Sch.; prof. cell biology Cornell U. Grad. Sch. Med. Scis., N.Y.C.; sci. investigator Meml.-Sloan Kettering Cancer Ctr., N.Y.C. Mem. cell biology program Meml. Sloan-Kettering Cancer Ctr. Mem.: NAS, Am. Acad. Microbiology, Am. Acad. Arts and Scis. Office: Meml Sloan-Kettering Ctr 1275 York Ave New York NY 10021

MASSALSKI, THADDEUS BRONISLAW, materials scientist, educator; b. Warsaw, June 29, 1926; came to U.S., 1959; s. Piotr and Stanislawa (Andrukaniec) M.; m. Sheila Joan Harris, Sept. 19, 1953; children: Irena, Peter, Christopher. B.Sc., Birmingham (Eng.) U., 1952, PhD, 1954, D.Sc., 1964; fellow, Inst. Study Metals, U. Chgo., 1954-56; D.Sc. (h.c.), Warsaw (Poland) U., 1973. Lectr. Birmingham U., 1956-59; head. metal physics dir. Mellon Inst., Pitts., 1959-75, 1961—69; prof. metal physics and materials sci. Carnegie-Mellon U., 1968—. Vis. prof. U. Buenos Aires, 1962, Calif. Inst. Tech., 1962, Stanford, 1963, U. Calif., 1964, 66, Inst. Physics, Bariloche Argentina, 1966, 70, Harvard, 1969; exchange prof. Krakow (Poland) U., 1968; vis. scientist Nat. Bur. Standards, 1980-81; NAVSEA prof. Naval Postgrad. Sch., Monterey, Calif; chmn. bd. govs. Acta Metallurgica, Inc., 1992—96. Co-author: Structure of Metals, 3d edit, 1966, Advanced Physical Metallurgy, 1965; co-editor Progress in Materials Science, 1969—, Metall. Transactions, 1991—; editor-in-chief ASM/NIST Phase Diagram Program, 1980-2000; author papers and articles on alloy theory, crystallography, metal physics, meteorites. Guggenheim fellow Oxford U., 1965-66; recipient Alexander von Humboldt prize, 1991, Sendzimir prize Polish Inst. Arts and Scis. in Am., 1998. Fellow Am. Soc. Metals (gold medal 1993), Am. Phys. Soc., The Metals Soc. (gold medal 1995), Brit. Inst. Materials (hon.), Brit. Inst. Physics, AIME (Hume-Rotherly prize 1989); mem. Polish Acad. Sci. (fgn.), German Acad. Sci. (fgn.), Phys. Soc., Associazione Italiana di Metallurgia (Losana gold medal). Home: 900 Field Club Rd Pittsburgh PA 15238-2127 Office: Carnegie Mellon U 3303 Wean Hall Pittsburgh PA 15213

MASSARO, DONALD JOHN, medical educator, medical researcher; b. N.Y.C., Aug. 7, 1932; s. Angelo G. and Filomena Massaro; m. Gloria De Carlo Massaro, June 15, 1957; children: Julia Marie, Paul Anthony. BA, Hofstra Coll., 1953; MD, Georgetown U., 1957. Asst. prof. medicine Georgetown U., Washington, 1965—67, Cohen prof., 1990—; assoc. prof. medicine Duke U., Durham, NC, 1967—68, George Washington U., Washington, 1969—72, prof. medicine, 1972—76; Sertel prof. U. Miami, Fla., 1976—90. Mem. Nat. Heart Lung and Blood Inst. adv. coun. NIH, Bethesda, Md., 1988—92. Editor: Lung Cell Biology, 1989, Oxygen, Gene Expression, Cellular Function, 1998; respiration editor: Ann. Rev. Physiol., 1994—98; editor: Am. Jour. Physiol., 1988—92. Vice chmn. Gordon Rsch. Conf., Maine, 1976, chmn., 1978; adv. coun. Parker B. Francis Found., Kans., 1990—94. Named The Joseph H. Bates vis. prof., U. Ark., 1999; recipient The Stony-Wold Lecture, Cornell U., 1990, Sci. Accomplishment award, Am. Thoracic Soc., 1997. Mem.: Am. Physiol. Soc. (chair respiration section), Am. Soc. Clin. Investigation, Assn. Am. Physicians. Achievements include discovery of all trans-retinoic acid abrogates features of pulmonary emphysema in rats. Avocation: walking. Office: Georgetown U Sch Medicine 3900 Reservoir Rd NW Washington DC 20007-1481

MASSARO, LINDA P. science foundation executive; BS in Physics and Math., U. Richmond; MSA in Mgmt. Engring, George Washington U.; postgrad., Nat. Def. U., Fed. Exec. Inst. Structural engr. Naval Ship Rsch. and Devel. Ctr.; tech. info. specialist, phys. sci. adminstr., mgmt. analyst Naval Material Command; dep. br. chief USMC Hdqrs.; dep. adminstr. for mgmt. USDA, 1987-94, acting agy. adminstr., 1992-93; dep. asst. sec. for personnel U.S. State Dept., 1994-96; dir. Office Info. and Resource Mgmt. NSF, 1996—, also chief info. officer. Recipient Presidential Meritorious Rank award. Mem. Exec. Women in Govt., Orgn. Prof. Employees at Agr. (past pres.), Mgmt. Coun. at Agr. (past chmn.), Sr. Execs. Assn. (bd. dirs., co-founder fgn. affairs agy. chpt.).

MASSARO, MIKE, advertising executive; COO, exec. v.p. Goldberg, Moser & O'Neill, San Francisco, Calif., 1988—. Office: 600 Battery St San Francisco CA 94111-1802

MASSARO, TONI MARIE, dean, law educator; BS, Northwestern U., 1977; JD, Coll. William and Mary, 1980. With Vedder, Price, Kaufman and Kammholz; tchr. law Washington and Lee U., U. Fla.; former prof. law U. Ariz., Tucson, dean, Milton O. Riepe chair constl. law, 1999—. Vis. prof. law Stanford U., U. N.C., Johann Goethe U., Frankfurt, West Germany. Author: Constitutional Literacy: A Core Curriculum for a Multi-Cultural Nation; contbr. numerous articles to law revs. Office: U Ariz Coll Law Bldg 204a PO Box 210176 Tucson AZ 85721-0176 Fax: 520-621-9140. E-mail: massaro@nt.law.arizona.edu.

MASSARSKI, LEONID, physicist; b. Leningrad, Russia, Mar. 29, 1949; s. Ilija and Maria Massarski; m. Ekaterina Girovich, Dec. 18, 1951; children: Marina, Igor-David. MS, St. Petersburg State Tech. U., Russia, 1966—72, PhD, 1978—81, DSc, 1989—92. Head of dept. Ctrl. Radiology Rsch. Inst., St. Petersburg, Russia, 1972—96; sr. med. physicist Millennium Diversified Med., Inc., Sierra Vista, Ariz., 2000—02; med. physicist NY Oncology Hematology Associates, Rexford, NY, 2002—04; chief med. physicist Maine Gen. Med. Ctr., Waterville, 2004—. Author: (reference book) Tissues and organs dose equivalents in man from x-ray examinations., (book) A topographically and anatomically unified phantom model for organ dose determination in radiation hygiene, The assessment of population doses from x-ray examinations in USSR in 1970-1980. Mem. expert bd. Internat. Anti-Nuc. Movement Nev.-Semipalatinsk, St. Petersburg, Russia, 1992—96. Mem.: NY Acad. Sciences, Can. Orgn. Med. Physicists, Am. Assn. Physicists in Medicine. Achievements include patents for Irradiation device; Compound lead shield for irradiation fields shaping along small animal; Second collimator system for correcting narrow photon beam deviation while rotation (narrow photon beams for radiosurgery); Method for assessment of organism reactions using non-uniform body irradiation; Phantom for brachytherapy in gynecology; Method for molding of laboratory animal body phantom; Chamber and units for gamma-irradiation. Home: 63 Sherwood Lane Vassalboro ME 04989 Office: Maine Gen Med Ctr 149 North St Waterville ME 04901 Personal E-mail: leonidmas@msn.com. E-mail: leonid.massarski@mainegeneral.org.

MASSAUA, JOHN ROGER, retail executive; b. N.Y.C., Aug. 7, 1947; s. George John and Dorothy Regina (Coyle) M.; m. Janice Grace Vroom, Mar. 29, 1970; children: Matthew, Andrew, Meghan. BS, Fordham U., 1969; MBA, Fairleigh Dickinson U., 1973. Cert. fasttrack instr., sr. bus. coun. NEPD, 2001. Mem. staff Supermarkets Gen., Woodbridge, N.J., 1964-73; dist. mgr. Courtesy Drug Stores, Port Washington, N.Y., 1973-75; exec. v.p. Motts Shop Rite Supermarkets, East Hartford, Conn., 1975-80; sr. v.p. Imperial Distbrs., Auburn, Mass., 1980-86; group v.p. ops. Staples Inc., Newton, Mass., 1986-89; pres. Window Rama, Deer Park, N.Y., 1989-91; exec. v.p. ALP Freddy's Ltd., Rochester, N.Y., 1991-93; v.p. mdse, and mktg. Nature Food Ctrs., Wilmington, Mass., 1994; sr. v.p. purchasing and merchandising McKesson Corp.: Millbrook Distbn. Svcs., Leicester, Mass., 1994-99; bus. mgmt. assistance counselor Coastal Enterprises Inc./Maine Small Bus. Devel. Ctr., Fairfield, Maine, 1999-2001; state dir. Maine Small Bus. Devel. Ctr. U. So. Maine Sch. of Bus., Portland, 2001—. Adj. faculty U. So. Maine, 2000—; grad. Leadership Me., 2003; bd. dirs. Maine Small Bus. Alliance, 2004—; bd. adv. U. Maine Office Rsch., 2004—. Troop com. chmn. Boy Scouts Am., Northborough, Mass., 1979-89; pres. Minnaseroke Community Assn., 1991; bd. dirs. China Village Libr.; mem. Leadership Maine, 2003. Recipient Sales and Mktg. Achievement award Sales and Mktg. Mag., 1978; Price-Babson fellow, 2000, Paul Harris fellow, 2000. Mem.: GMDC (bd. dirs. 1996—99), Soc. Econ. Devel. (coun. of Maine), Am. Mgmt. Assn. Roman Catholic. Avocations: sailing, hiking, photography. Home: PO Box 6427 China Village ME 04926-0427 Office: Maine SBCD U So Maine Sch of Bus PO Box 9300 96 Falmouth St Portland ME 04104 Office Phone: 207-780-4857. Business E-Mail: jrmassaua@maine.edu.

MASSE, WILLIAM BRUCE, archaeologist; b. San Diego, July 10, 1948; s. Gerald John Masse and Viola Hope Bumgarner; m. Judith Lee Peters, Sept. 12, 1971; 1 child, Jeffrey Alan. BA in Anthropology, Stanford U., 1971; MA in Anthropology, U. Ariz., 1977; PhD in Anthropology, So. Ill. U., 1990. Archeologist Nat. Park Svc., Tucson, 1977-79, Ariz. State Mus., Tucson, 1985-86; field archaeologist State Historic Preservation Office, Honolulu, 1988-89; pacific area archaeologist Dept. of Navy, Pearl Harbor, Hawaii, 1990-94; archaeologist Dept. Air Force, Luke Air Force Base, Ariz., 1995-98, Los Alamos (N.Mex.) Nat. Lab., 1999—. Editor: The Protohistoric Period in the North American Southwest, 1981; contbr.: Chaco and Hohokam: Prehistoric Regional Systems in the North American Southwest, 1991, Natural Catastrophes During Bronze Age Civilizations: Archaeological, Geological, Astronomical, and Cultural Perspectives, 1998; editor (spl. issue) Jour. S.W., 1996; contbr. articles to profl. jours. Mem.: AAAS, Soc. Am. Archaeology (repatriation com. 1998—2001), Am. Anthrop. Assn., Sigma Xi. Office: Los Alamos Nat Lab RRES-ECO Ecology Group Mail Stop M887 Los Alamos NM 87545 Fax: (505)667-0731. E-mail: wbmasse@lanl.gov.

MASSENGALE, HOPE VEGA, music educator; d. Hipolito Garza and Hope (Guterriez) Vega; children: Zack, Annette, Kenneth. AA, San Antonio Coll., 1980; BA, U. Tex., San Antonio, 2003. Libr. asst. Dept. Def., Crete, Greece; substitute tchr. Dept. Def. Dependent Schs., Rota, Spain, Northside Ind. Sch. Dist., San Antonio; pvt. music instr. San Antonio; piano Vivace Music Acad., San Antonio. Participant Chopin Internat. Piaho Workshop, Czech Republic. Mem.: Tex. Music Educators Assn., San Antonio Music Tchrs. Assn., Golden Key Nat. Honor Soc. Avocations: dance, tennis, piano. Office: Vivace Music Acad 4770 Research Dr San Antonio TX 78249

MASSENGALE, MARTIN ANDREW, agronomist, university president; b. Monticello, Ky., Oct. 25, 1933; s. Elbert G. and Orpha (Conn) M.; m. Ruth Audrey Klingelhofer, July 11, 1959; children: Alan Ross, Jennifer Lynn. BS, Western Ky. U., 1952; MS, U. Wis., 1954, PhD, 1956; LHD (hon.), Nebr. Wesleyan U., 1987; DS (hon.), Senshu U., Tokyo, 1995. Cert. profl. agronomist, profl. crop scientist. Research asst. agronomy U. Wis., 1952-56; asst. prof., asst. agronomist U. Ariz., 1958-62, assoc. prof., assoc. agronomist, 1962-65, prof., agronomist, 1965-76, head dept., 1966-74, assoc. dean Coll. Agr. assoc. dir. Ariz. Agr. Expt. Sta., 1974-76; vice chancellor for agr. and natural resources U. Nebr., 1976-81; chancellor U. Nebr.-Lincoln, 1981-91, interim pres., 1989-91; pres. U. Nebr., 1991-94, pres. emeritus, 1994, found. disting. prof. and dir., 1994—. Chmn. pure seed adv. com. Ariz. Agrl. Expt. Sta.; past chmn. bd., pres. Mid-Am. Internat. Agrl. Consortium; coord. com. environ. quality EPA-Dept. Agrl. Land Grand U.; past chmn. bd. dirs. Am. Registry Cert. Profls. in Agronomy, Crops and Soils; bd. dirs. Ctr. for Human Nutrition; bd. dirs., trustee U. Nebr. Found.; chair bd. dirs. Agronomic Sci. Found., chmn. selection com; dir. devel. Secretariat, Filippo Maseri Florio World Prize for Disting. Rsch. in Agr.; exec. com. U. Nebr. Tech. Park, LLC; bd. dirs. Lincoln Ins. Group., Woodmen Accident & Life Co., LIG, Inc., Am. First, LLC; mem. adv. bd. Nat. Agrl. Rsch., Ext., Edn. and Econs., 1998—, chair secs. nat. adv. bd., mem. exec. com.; mem. nat. adv. bd. Trees Am., 1998—. Chmn. NCAA Pres.'s Commn., 1988-91; distbn. revenue com., standing com. on appointments North Ctrl. Assn. Commn. on Insts. Higher Edn., 1991; trustee Nebr. Hist. Soc. Found.; bd. dirs. Nebr. Hist. Soc.; bd. govs. Nebr. Sci. and Math. Initiative; mem. Knight Found. Commn. on Intercollegiate Athletics; bd. dirs. Great Plains Funds, IBP; hon. life trustee Nebr. Coun. on Econ. Edn.; hon. lifetime trustee Nebr. Coun. on Econ. Edn. With U.S. Army, 1956-58. Named Midlands Man of Yr., 1982, to We. Ky. U. Hall of Disting. Alumni, 1992, DeKalb Crop Sci. Disting. Career award, 1996, Outstanding Educator Am., 1970, Wayne County H.S., Monticello, Ky., Charter Hall of Fame, 2002; recipient faculty recognition award Tucson Trade Bur., 1971, Ak-Sar-Ben Agrl. Achievement award, 1986, Agrl. Builders Nebr. award, 1986, Walter K. Beggs award, 1986, Vol. of Yr. award for disting. svc. Nebr. Coun. on Econ. Edn., IANR Team Initiation award, Agri award Triumph of Agr. Expn., 1999, Exemplary Svc. to Agr. award Nebr. AgRels. Coun., 2000, Friend of LEAD award Nat. LEAD Alumni Assn., 2001, Outstanding Pres. award All-Am. Football Found., 2001; hon. state farmer degrees Ky., Ariz., Nebr. Future Farmers Am. Assns. Fellow AAAS (sect. chmn.), Crop Sci. Soc. Am. (past dir., pres. 1972-73, past assoc. editor, pres. western soc., disting. career award 1996), Am. Soc. Agronomy (past dir., vis. scientist program, past assoc. editor Agronomy Jour., Disting. Svc. award 1984); mem. Am. Grassland Coun., Ariz. Crop Improvement Assn. (bd. dirs.), Am. Soc. Plant Physiology, Nat. Assn. Colls. and Tchrs. Agr., Soil and Water Conservation Soc. Am., Ariz. Acad. Sci., Nebr. Acad. Sci., Agrl. Coun. Am. (bd. dirs., issues com.), Coun. Agrl. Sci. and Tech. (bd. dirs. budget and fin. 1979-82, 94—, treas., exec. com. 1997—), Nat. Assn. State Colls. and Land Grant Univs. (chmn. com. on info. tech. 1987-94, exec. com. 1990-92, bd. dirs. 1992-94), Edn. Engring. Professions (mem. commn.), Coll. Football Assn. (chmn., bd. dirs. 1986-88), Am. Assn. State Coll. and Univs. (task force instl. resource allocation), Assn. Am. Univs. Rsch. Librs. (steering com. 1992-94), Nebr. Crop Improvement Assn. (disting. svc. award), Grazing Lands Forum (pres.), Nebr. C. of C. and Industry, Nebr. Diplomats Inc. (hon. diplomate), Nebr. Vet. Med. Assn. (hon.), Sigma Xi, Phi Kappa Phi, Gamma Sigma Delta (Award of Merit), Alpha Zeta, Phi Sigma, Gamma Alpha, Alpha Gamma Rho (Bros. of the Century award), Phi Beta Delta, Golden Key Nat. Honor Soc., Innocents Soc. Office: U Nebr 220 Kiehn Hall Lincoln NE 68583-0953 Office Phone: 402-472-4101. E-mail: mmassengale1@unl.edu.

MASSENGILL, MATTHEW H. retail company executive; BE, Purdue U., 1983. Product engr. Western Digital Corp., Irvine, Calif., 1985-94, v.p. mktg. personal storage divsn., 1994-97, sr. v.p., gen. mgr. enterprise storage group, 1997-99, co-chief operating officer, 1999—. Office: Western Digital Corp 20511 Lake Forest Dr Lake Forest CA 92630-7741

MASSEY, ANDREW JOHN, conductor, composer; b. Nottingham, Eng., May 1, 1946; came to U.S., 1978; s. Henry Louis Johnson and Margaret (Park) M.; m. Sabra Ann Todd, May 29, 1982; children: Colin Sebastian, Robin Elizabeth. BA, Oxford U., 1968, MA, 1981, Nottingham U., 1969. Asst. condr. The Cleve. Orch., 1978-80; assoc. condr. New Orleans Symphony, 1980-86, San Francisco Symphony, 1985-88; music dir. Fresno (Calif.) Philharmonic, 1986-93, R.I. Philharmonic, Providence, 1986-91, Toledo Symphony Orch., 1991—2000, also condr. Vis. scholar Brown U., Providence, 1986-91; music dir. Oreg. Mozart Players, 1998—. Composer incidental music (stage prodns.) Murder in the Cathedral, 1968, King Lear, 1971, A Midsummer Night's Dream, 1972. Avocations: trees, computers, astrology, philosophy of karl popper. Office: c/o John Gingrich Management Inc PO Box 1515 New York NY 10023 also: Oregon Mozart Players PO Box 11474 Eugene OR 97440

MASSEY, BEN F., JR., medical association administrator; b. Zebulon, N.C. m. Darlene Sekerak; children: Lara, Nic, James. BS in Phys. Therapy, U. N.C., 1976. Staff phys. therapist Rex Hosp., Raleigh; phys. therapy mgr. Good Hope Hosp., Hand and Orthop. Rehab. Assocs., Raleigh Cmty. Hosp.; exec. dir. N.C. Bd. Phys. Therapy Examiners, Durham. Lectr. in field. Recipient Charles P. Schuch award for excellence in phys. therapy adminstrn., U. N.C., Margaret L. Moore Disting. Alumni award, Outstanding Svc. award, Fedn. of State Bds. of Phys. Therapy. Mem.: Am. Phys. Therapy Assn. (pres., bd. dirs., Spl. Recognition award, Pres.'s award, Olive Wortman Svc. award, Lucy Blair Svc. award). Office: North Carolina Bd Phys Therapy Examiners 18 W Colony Pl Ste 140 Durham NC 27705

MASSEY, CHARLES KNOX, JR., advertising agency executive; b. Durham, N.C., Jan. 16, 1936; s. Charles Knox and Louise (Southerl) M.; m. Mary Ann Keith, Aug. 27, 1960; children: Elizabeth, Knox, Louise. BS in Bus. Adminstrn, U. N.C., 1959. Vice pres. C. Knox Massey & Assoc., Inc., advt. agy., Durham, N.C., 1959-64; account exec. Tucker Wayne & Co., advt. agy., Atlanta, 1964-78, pres., 1978-88, Tucker Wayne/Luckie & Co., Atlanta, 1988-95; chmn., CEO West Wayne, Inc., Atlanta, 1996—2000. Trustee The Lovett Sch., Atlanta, Inst. for the Arts and Scis., U. N.C., Chapel Hill. Mem. Piedmont Driving Club (pres. 1990-92), Coral Beach and Tennis Club (Bermuda), Highlands (N.C.) Country Club, Univ. Club (N.Y.C.), N.Y. Yacht Club. Episcopalian. Home: 67 Brighton Rd NE Atlanta GA 30309-1518 Office: PO Box 77388 Atlanta GA 30357

MASSEY, DONALD E. automotive executive; CEO Don Massey Cadillac. Office: Don Massey Cadillac Inc 40475 Ann Arbor Rd E Plymouth MI 48170-4576

MASSEY, EDWIN R. college president; m. Jo Massey; 3 children. BS, Millsaps Coll.; MS in Marine Biology, PhD in Zoology, U. Southern Miss. Biology prof. Indian River Cmty. Coll., pres., 1988—. Bd. dirs. First Union Nat. Bank. Campaign co-chair United Way, Indian River county, 1995-96, campaign chair, 1991-93, pres. United Way of St. Lucie county, 1992-93; chmn. bd. dirs. Lawnwood Regional Med.; hon. co-chair Capital Campaign for Hospice; mem. St. Lucie County Econ. Devel. Coun.; chmn. high skill/high wage com. Region 20 JEP Bd.; co-chmn. program length and articulation com. SB 1688 Task Force; mem. legislative and high edn. articulation com. Coun. of Pres.; bd. dirs. Quad-County Tech. Prep/Sch.-to-Work Leadership; mem. Treasure Coast Educators' Coalition, Am. Coun. on Edn.'s Com. on Sci. and Math, State Articulation Coordinating com., State Correctional Acad. Adv. Bd.; chmn. Fla.'s statewide com. on accountability and effectiveness; chmn. stds./outcomes task force Divsn. of Cmty. Colls., chmn. performance based budgeting task force; chmn. trustee tng. com. SBCC; mem. adv. coun. Nat. World Class Acad.; mem. Commrs. Workforce Devel. Task Force; pres. Treasure Coast Lit. Soc.; adv. bd. mem. Ctr. for the Arts; active Martin County Bus. Devel. Bd., United Way Indian River County's Leadership Team, Pres. Coun. Steering Com., Jobs and Edn. Partnership Region 20 Bd.; mem. legis. com. Coun. Pres. Recipient Pres. award for Excellence Fla. Assn. of C.C., 1995; inducted Milsaps Coll. Sports Hall of Fame, 1994, St. Lucie County Sports Hall of Fame, 1996. Mem. Nat. Alliance Two-Yr. Coll. Athletic Adminstrs. (bd. dirs.), Fla. Assn. Colls. and Univs., Fla. Assn. C.C., Fla. C.C. Activities Assn. (past pres.), Fla. C.C. Athletic Assn. (past pres. exec. com.), Commn. on Colls. of the So. Assn. of Colls. and Schs., Am. Assn. of C.C., Southern Assn. of Cmty., Jr. and Tech. Colls. (pres. bd. dirs.), Fla. Coun. of C.C. Pres. (past chmn.), Indian River County Coun. 100, Ft. Pierce Breakfast club, Econ. Coun. Martin County, St. Lucie County C. of C. (bd. dirs., mem. higher edn. task force com.), Ft. Pierce Rotary Club. Office: Indian River CC 3209 Virginia Ave Fort Pierce FL 34981-5541

MASSEY, HENRY P., JR., lawyer; b. Montclair, N.J., Sept. 2, 1939; AB, Cornell U., 1961, JD with distinction, 1968. Bar: Calif. 1969. Ptnr. Wilson Sonsini Goodrich & Rosati, Palo Alto, Calif., 1982—. Bd. editors Cornell Law Rev., 1967-68. Mem. ABA (sects. on corp., banking and bus. law, taxation law), State Bar Calif. (mem. corps. com. bus. law sect. 1979-82), Order of Coif, Phi Kappa Phi. Office: Wilson Sonsini Goodrich & Rosati 650 Page Mill Rd Palo Alto CA 94304-1050

MASSEY, HOWARD CLAYLAND, writer; b. Coolidge, Ga., Oct. 21, 1925; s. Paul Lester and Ruby Dell Massey; m. Hilda Dodson Schroer, June 17, 1966; 1 child, Sondra Gayle Siegel; m. Edna Ann Weller (div.); 1 child, Richard Clayton. M in Plumbing and Heating, Lindsey Hopkins Tech. Edn. Ctr., Miami, 1958. Owner Ctr. Plumbing & Heating Corp., Miami-Dade, 1958—73; plans examiner Met. Bldg. & Zoning Dept., Miami-Dade, 1974—88; author Craftsman Book Co., Hollywood, Fla., 1978—85, Vero Beach, Fla., 1986—. Designer plumbing isometrics State of Fla. Lic. Bd., 1982—84; creator exam. questions Constrn. Industry Lic. Bd., Fla., 1983—85. Author: (tech. book) Plumber's Handbook, 1978, Basic Plumbing With Illustrations, 1980, Estimating Plumbing Costs, 1982, Plumber's Exam Preparation Guide, 1985, Planning Drain, Waste & Vent Systems, 1990, International Plumbing & Fuel Gas Codes, 2003. Seaman 3d class USN, 1943—45. Mem.: Gideons Internat., Authors Guild. Republican. Home and Office: 1240 Fifth St Vero Beach FL 32962

MASSEY, JAMES EARL, clergyman, educator; b. Ferndale, Mich., Jan. 4, 1930; s. George Wilson and Elizabeth (Shelton) M.; m. Gwendolyn Inez Kilpatrick, Aug. 4, 1951. Student, U. Detroit, 1949-50, 55-57; BTh, BRE, Detroit Bible Coll., 1961; AM, Oberlin Grad Sch. Theology, 1964; postgrad., U. Mich., 1967-69; DD, Asbury Theol. Sem., 1972, Ashland Theol. Sem., 1991, Huntington Coll., 1994; HumD, Tuskegee U., 1995; DD, Warner Pacific Coll., 1995; LittD, Anderson U., 1995; DD, Wash. and Jefferson Coll., 1997, North Park Theol. Sem., 1999. Ordained to ministry Ch. of God, 1951. Assoc. min. Ch. of God, Detroit, 1951-53; sr. pastor Met. Ch. of God, Detroit, 1954-76, pastor-at-large, 1976; spkr. Christian Brotherhood Hour, 1977-82; prin. Jamaica Sch. Theology, Kingston, 1963-66; campus min. Anderson Coll., Ind., 1969-77, asst. prof. religious studies, 1969-75, assoc. prof., 1975-80, prof. N.T. and homiletics, 1981-84; dean of chapel and univ., prof. religion and society Tuskegee U., Ala., 1984-89; dean, prof. preaching and bibl. studies Anderson Sch. Theology, 1989-95, dean emeritus, prof. at large, 1995—; dean emeritus Tuskagee U. Chapel, 1998—. Chmn. Comm. on Higher Edn. in the Ch. of God, 1968-71; vice chmn. bd. publs. Ch. of God, 1968-78; dir. Warner Press, Inc.; rsch. scholar Christianity Today Inst. Author: When Thou Prayest, 1960, The Worshipping Church, 1961, Raymond S. Jackson, A Portrait, 1967, The Soul Under Seige, 1970, The Church of God and the Negro, 1971, The Hidden Disciplines, 1972, The Responsible Pulpit, 1973, Temples of the Spirit, 1974, The Sermon in Perspective, 1976, Concerning Christian Unity, 1979; gen. editor: Christian Brotherhood Hour Study Bible, 1979, Designing the Sermon, 1980; co-editor: Interpreting God's Word for Today, 1982; editor: Educating for Service, 1984, The Spiritual Disciplines, 1985, The Bridge Between, 1988, Preaching From Hebrews, 1992, The Burdensome Joy of Preaching, 1996, Sundays at The Tuskegee Chapel, 1999, Aspects of My Pilgrimage: An Autobiography, 2002, Remembering William L. Dawson, 2004; mem. editl. bd. The Christian Scholar's Rev. Leadership mag.; mem. editl. bd., contbg. editor Vol I New Interpreter's Bible, 1990—; contbg. editor Preaching mag.; sr. editor Christianity Today mag. Mem. Corp. Inter-Vrsity Christian Fellowship; bd. dirs. World Vision. Served with AUS, 1951-53. Mem. Nat. Assn. Coll. and Univ. Chaplains, Nat. Com. Black Churchmen, Nat. Negro Evang. Assn. (bd. dirs. 1969-86). Office: 367 Beverly Rd Greensboro AL 36744-6034

MASSEY, JEANNE KELLY, music festival producer; b. Charleston, SC, Oct. 30, 1938; d. Lawrence Lees and Margaret Augusta (Montgomery) Kelly; m. William Massey III, June 25, 1960 (div. 1994); children: Kelly Massey-Carlier, John Gant Massey. BA, Duke U., 1960; advanced libr. cert., William and Mary Coll., 1976. Founding libr. Jamestown Acad., Williamsburg, Va., 1974-77; pres. Va. State Ballet, Newport News, Va., 1978-82; founder, pres. Arts Resale of Williamsburg, Va., 1978-88; pres., gen. mgr. Mid-Atlantic Chamber Orch., Washington, 1985-98; exec. prodr. Benedictinus 2000 Internat. Order of Benedictines, 1997—2000; prodr. Annual World Bank Mozart Festival, 1991—. Commr. Va. Commn. for the Arts, Richmond, 1979-84; nat. exec. com. Children of Am. Revolution, Washington, 1973-76; dir., pres. The Wyo. Condominium, Washington, 1988-91; mem. Arts Adv. Bd., Williamsburg, 1979-81. Recipient Platinum Violin award Festival Williamsburg, 1984. Mem. DAR (pres. 1970-76), Jamestowne Soc., Jane Austen Soc. of N.Am., Phi Beta Kappa, Kappa Delta Pi, Sigma Delta Pi. Republican. Presbyterian. Avocations: walking, reading, concerts, museums, theater. Office: JKM Inc PO Box 21439 Washington DC 20009-0939 Fax: 202-483-9320. E-mail: jkminc@infionline.net.

MASSEY, KATHLEEN MARIE OATES, lawyer; b. Chgo., Dec. 2, 1955; d. William Robert Jr. and Ethelyn Rose (Calhoun) Oates. Student, U. Claremont-Ferrand, France, 1976-77; BA cum laude, Kalamazoo Coll., 1978; JD, U. Wis., 1981. Bar: Wis. 1981, Minn. 1981, U.S. Dist. Ct. Minn. 1981, U.S. Dist. Ct. (ea. dist.) Wis. 1983. With Larkin, Hoffman, Daily & Lindgren Ltd., Mpls., 1981-87; ptnr. Habush, Habush & Davis, Milw., 1987-90; asst. gen. counsel A.O. Smith Corp., Milw., 1992-97; sr. litigation counsel Motorola Inc., Schaumburg, Ill., 1997—. Mem. ABA, Minn. Bar Assn., Wis. Bar Assn., Phi Beta Kappa, Alpha Lambda Delta, Phi Eta Sigma.

MASSEY, LEWIS, finance company executive; b. Gainesville, Ga. s. Abit and Kayanne M.; m. Amy Massey; children: Chandler, Cameryn. BBA in Finance, U. Ga. Mem. campaign staff Ct. Appeals Judge Robert Benham; mgr. reelection campaign Gov. Joe Frank Harris; dir. election campaigns various first time candidates apptd. by Gov. Joe Frank Harris; spl. asst. Gov. Joe Frank Harris; campaign mgr. Pierre Howard for Lt. Gov.; chief of staff Lt. Gov. Pierre Howard; v.p. Bank South Securities Corp.; sec. of state. State of Ga., 1996-98; pres., CEO Directo Inc., Norcross, 1999-2000, vice chmn., 2000—. Elder Peachtree Presbyn. Ch.; mem. bd. dirs. Am. Cancer Soc., Eagle Ranch Home For Boys. Recipient Blue Key Alumnus of the Yr. award U. Ga., Outstanding Young Alumnus Bus. Sch. U. Ga. Office: Directo Inc 3091 Governors Lake Dr Ste 300 Norcross GA 30071-1133

MASSEY, MARVIN S., JR., grocery retail executive; CFO Brookshire Grocery, Tyler, Tex., 2000—. Office: Brookshire Grocery PO Box 1411 Tyler TX 75710 Office Fax: (903) 534-2240.

MASSEY, RAYMOND DAVID, lawyer; b. Goldsboro, N.C., Oct. 13, 1946; s. Raymond L. and Dorris L. (Grant) Massey; m. Barbara A. Warner, Aug. 16, 1967; children: Suzanne, Christine. BA, Wofford Coll., Spartanburg, S.C., 1968; JD, U. S.C., 1971; LLM in Taxation, Emory U., 1985. Bar: S.C. 1971, U.S. Dist. Ct. S.C. 1971, cert.: S.C. Supreme Ct. (specialist estate planning and probate law). Assoc. Perrin, Perrin & Mann, Spartanburg, Spartanburg, 1971—74; trust officer Bankers Trust of S.C., Columbia, SC, 1974—78; shareholder Brown, Massey, Evans, McLeod & Haynsworth, PA, Greenville, SC, 1978—. Pres. Greenville Estate Planning Coun., 1982; chair Cmty. Found. of Greater Greenville, 2001—02; dir. Greenville Hosp. Sys. Found., 2002—. Fellow: Am. Coll. Trust and Estate Counsel; mem.: S.C. Bar Assn. (chmn. probate, estate planning and trust sect. 1983), Greenville Bar Assn. (pres. tax sect. 1980—81), Poinsett Club, Greenville Country Club. Presbyterian. Office: PO Box 2464 Greenville SC 29602-2464 Office Phone: 864-271-7424.

MASSEY, RAYMOND LEE, lawyer; b. Macon, Ga., Sept. 25, 1948; s. Ford B. and Juanita (Sapp) M.; m. Lynn Ann Thielmeier, Aug. 23, 1967; children: Daniel, Caroline. BA, U. Mo., St. Louis, 1971; JD, U. Louisville, 1974. Bar: Mo. 1974, Ill. 1976, U.S. Dist. Ct. (ea. and we. dists.) Mo. 1974, U.S. Dist. Ct.

(so. dist.) Ill. 1976. Assoc. Thompson & Mitchell, St. Louis, 1974-79; ptnr. Thompson & Mitchell (now Thompson & Coburn), St. Louis, 1979—. Mem. Maritime Law Assn. of U.S. (bd. dirs., chmn. ocean and river towing). Home: 3 Wild Rose Dr Saint Louis MO 63124-1465 Office: Thompson Coburn US Bank Ste 3400 Saint Louis MO 63101-1643

MASSEY, RICHARD WALTER, JR., retired investment counselor; b. Birmingham, Ala., May 19, 1917; s. Richard Walter and Elizabeth (Spencer) M.; m. Ann Hinkle, Sept. 4, 1959; children— Richard Walter, Dale Elizabeth. BS, U. Va., 1939; MA, Birmingham-So. Coll., 1954; PhD, Vanderbilt U., 1960. Owner, mgr. Massey Bus. Coll., Birmingham, Ala., 1946—56; asst. to chancellor Vanderbilt U., 1959—60; chmn. dept. econs. Birmingham-So. Coll., 1960—66; investment trust officer 1st Nat. Bank of Birmingham, 1966—67; prof. econs. U. Ala., Tuscaloosa, 1967—68; v.p., dir. investment rsch. Sterne, Agee & Leach, Inc., Birmingham, 1968—75; pres. Richard W. Massey & Co., Inc., Investment Counsel, Birmingham, 1975—2001; ret., 2001. Served to maj. U.S. Army, 1941-46. Mem. Country Club of Birmingham. Home: 1304 Kingsway Ln Birmingham AL 35243-2174 E-mail: rmassey1@netzero.net.

MASSEY, ROBERT JOHN, telecommunications executive; b. Montclair, N.J., July 12, 1945; s. William A. and Elizabeth (Grissing) M.; m. Sue A. Lavallee, July 26, 1968; children: Mary Beth, Michelle, Megan. BA, Holy Cross Coll., Worcester, Mass., 1967; MBA, Syracuse U., 1969. Mktg. rep. IBM, Washington, 1969-70, Boston, 1971-73; mktg. rep Control Data Corp., Greenwich, Conn., 1974-75, mktg. mgr., N.Y.C., 1975-76; area mgr. CompuServe Inc., Eastern area, 1976 78, v.p. sales, Stamford, Conn., 1979-83, exec. v.p. bus. svcs., Columbus, Ohio, 1984-86, exec. v.p. software products, 1987-90, exec. v.p. network svcs., 1990, pres., until 1997; exec. v.p. bus. devel. Calltech Comm., Columbus, 1997-98; pres. Massey & Assocs., 1997-99; chmn. Calltech Comm. LLC, Columbus, 1999—. Bd. dirs. CompuServe. Coach Dublin (Ohio) Youth Athletics, 1978-85; parents coun. St. Mary's Coll., Notre Dame, Ind., 1988—. Mem. Dublin C. of C., Ohio State Fastbreakers, Holy Cross Alumni Assn., Syracuse U. Bus. Alumni Assn., Country Club of Muirfield Village (golf. com.). Avocations: golf, tennis. Office: Calltech Comm LLC 4335 Equity Dr Columbus OH 43228-3842

MASSEY, ROBERT UNRUH, internist, educator, dean; b. Detroit, Feb. 23, 1922; s. Emil Laverne and Esther Elisabeth (Unruh) M.; m. June Charlene Collins, May 28, 1943; children: Robert Scott, Janet Charlene. Student, Oberlin Coll., 1939-42, U. Mich. Med. Sch., 1942-43; MD, Wayne State U., 1946. Intern, resident in internal medicine Henry Ford Hosp., Detroit, 1946-50; assoc. Lovelace Clinic, Albuquerque, 1950-68, chmn. dept. medicine, 1958-68, bd. govs., 1957-68; dir. med. edn. Lovelace Found. for Med. Edn. and Research, 1960-68; clin. assoc. U. N.Mex. Sch. Medicine, 1961-68; prof. medicine U. Conn. Sch. Medicine, Farmington, 1968-92, prof. emeritus, 1992—, assoc. dean for grad edn., 1968-71, dean Sch. Medicine, 1971-84, currently prof. emeritus dept. community medicine and health care, acting univ. v.p. for health affairs, 1975-76. Chief staff Newington (Conn.) VA Hosp., 1968-71; trustee Am. Assn. Med. Clinics, 1966-68; exec. com., regional adv. group Conn. Regional Med. Program, 1971-76; trustee, v.p. Capitol Area Health Consortium, 1974-78, pres., 1980-81. Editor-in-chief Conn. Medicine, 1986-99; editor Jour. of the History of Medicine and Allied Scis., 1987-91. Bd. dirs. Health Planning Coun., Inc., 1974-76; bd. dirs. Hartford Inst. for Criminal and Social Justice, 1976-80, Conn. Easter Seal Soc., 1977-85, Hospice Inst. Edn., Tng. and Rsch., 1979-81. With AUS, 1955-57; maj. Res. Fellow ACP; mem. Am. Group Practice Assn. (accreditation commn. 1968-78), Assn. Am. Med. Colls., Am. Assn. History of Medicine, Hartford County Med. Assn., AMA, Conn., Hartford med. socs., Am. Osler Soc., Beaumont Med. Club, Soc. Med. Adminstrs., Twilight Club (Hartford), Acorn Club, Sigma Xi, Alpha Omega Alpha. Roman Catholic.

MASSEY, STEPHEN CHARLES, rare books and manuscripts appraiser, auctioneer; b. London, May 9, 1946; s. Charles Dudley and Sheila Florence (Browne) M.; divorced; 1 child, Sarah Louise. Grad. high sch., U.K. Cataloguer books and manuscripts Christie's, London, 1964-75, sr. dir. rare books and manuscripts dept. N.Y.C., 1975-96, sr. internat. cons., 1997-99. Fellow Pierpont Morgan Libr.; mem. The Grolier Club, The Old Book Table. Avocations: cinema, reading, running, music, forestry.

MASSEY, THOMAS BENJAMIN, retired educator; b. Charlotte, N.C., Sept. 5, 1926; s. William Everard and Sarah (Corley) M.; m. Bylee Hunnicutt Massey, July 10, 1968; children: Pamela Ann, Caroline Forest. AB, Duke U., 1948; MS, N.C. State U., 1953; PhD, Cambridge U., 1968. Assoc. dean students Ga. Inst. Tech., Atlanta, 1950-58; lectr. U. Md. Univ. Coll., 1960-66, asst. dir. London, 1966-69, dir. Toyko, 1969-71, dir. Heidelberg (Fed. Republic of Germany), 1971-76, vice chancellor, 1976-78, chancellor, 1978-88, pres., 1988-98, pres. emeritus, 1998—. Served with USN, 1943-46. Mem. APA, Univ. Continuing Edn. Assn., Am. Assn. Higher Edn., Internat. Confs. on Improving Learning and Tchg. at the Univ. (chair 1975—). Personal E-mail: benmo9056@aol.com.

MASSEY, VINCENT, biochemist, educator; b. Berkeley, NSW, Australia, Nov. 28, 1926; s. Walter and Mary Ann (Mark) M.; m. Margot Grunewald, Mar. 4, 1950; children: Charlotte, Andrew, Rachel. BSc with honors, U. Sydney, Australia, 1947; PhD, U. Cambridge, Eng., 1953; DSc (hon.), U. Tokushima, 1994. Mem. research staff Henry Ford Hosp., Detroit, 1955-57; lectr. to sr. lectr. U. Sheffield, 1957-63; prof. Med. Sch. U. Mich., Ann Arbor, 1963-95, J. Lawrence Oncley Disting. U. prof., 1995—. Permanent guest prof. U. Konstanz, 1975—; mem. fellowship rev. panel NIH, 1965-69, mem. biochemistry study sect., 1972-76, chmn. 1974-76; mem. biochemistry and biophysics rev. panel NSF, 1980-84. Contbg. author numerous books.; co-editor Flavins and Flavoproteins, 1982, 96; contbr. numerous articles, chiefly on oxidative enzymology, to profl. jours. Recipient Alexander von Humboldt U.S. Sr. Scientist award, 1973-74, 86; Imperial Chem. Industries Research fellow, 1953-55. Fellow Royal Soc. London; mem. NAS, Biochem. Soc., Am. Soc. Biochemistry and Molecular Biology (membership com. 1970, nominating com. 1978-80, chmn. 1979-80, chmn. program com. 1992-93), Am. Chem. Soc. (exec. bd. divsn. biol. chemistry 1975-77). Home: 2536 Bedford Rd Ann Arbor MI 48104-4008 Office: U Mich Med Sch Dept Biol Chemistry Ann Arbor MI 48109 E-mail: massey@umich.edu.

MASSEY, WALTER EUGENE, physicist, science foundation administrator; b. Hattiesburg, Miss., Apr. 5, 1938; s. Almor and Essie (Nelson) M.; m. Shirley Streeter, Oct. 25, 1969; children: Keith Anthony, Eric Eugene. BS, Morehouse Coll., 1958; MA, PhD, Washington U., St. Louis, 1966. Physicist Argonne (Ill.) Nat. Lab., 1966-68; asst. prof. physics U. Ill., Urbana, 1968-70; assoc. prof. Brown U., Providence, 1970-75, prof., dean of Coll., 1975-79; prof. physics U. Chgo., 1979-93; dir. Argonne Nat. Lab., 1979-84; v.p. for rsch. and for Argonne Nat. Lab. U. Chgo., 1984-91; dir. NSF, Washington, 1991-93; sr. v.p. acad. affairs U. Calif. System, 1993-95; pres. Morehouse Coll., Atlanta, 1995—. Cons. NAS, 1973-76; mem. NSB, 1978-84; chair Sec. Energy Adv. Bd., 1997-99; bd. dirs. Mellon Found, Bank Am. Corp., McDonald's Corp., BP Amoco; mem. Gates Millennium Scholars Adv. Coun.; mem. coun. visitors Marine Biol. Lab. Contbr. articles on sci. edn. in secondary schs. and in theory of quantum fluids to profl. jours. Bd. fellows Brown U., 1980-90, Mus. Sci. and Industry, Chgo., 1980-89, Ill. Math. and Sci. Acad., 1985-88; bd. dirs. Urban League R.I., 1973-75; mem. Salzburg seminar, 1997—, Atlanta Symphony Orch., 1996—, Woodruf Art Ctr., 1995—, Atlanta Com. Pub. Edn., 1996—, Bd. Project GRAD; chair Atlanta Com. for Pub. Edn., 1996—; trustee U. Chgo. Recipient over 25 hon. degrees; NAS fellow, 1961, NDEA fellow, 1959-60, AAAS fellow, 1962. Mem. AAAS (bd. dirs. 1981-85, pres.-elect 1987-88, pres. 1988-89, chmn. 1989-90), Am. Phys. Soc. (councillor-at-large 1980-83, v.p. 1990), Smithsonian Inst. (bd. regents), Sigma Xi. Office: Morehouse Coll 830 Westview Dr SW Atlanta GA 30314-3773

MASSEY, WILLIAM S. mathematician, educator; b. Granville, Ill., Aug. 23, 1920; s. Robert R. and Alma (Schumacher) M.; m. Ethel Heap, Mar. 14, 1953; children— Eleanor, Alexander, Joan. Student, Bradley U., 1937-39; BS, U. Chgo., 1941, MS, 1942; PhD, Princeton, 1948. Mem. research dept. Princeton, 1948-50; from asst. prof. to prof. Brown U., 1950-60; prof. math. Yale, 1960—, Erastus L. Deforest prof. math, 1964-82, Eugene Higgins prof. math., 1983-91, Eugene Higgins prof. math. emeritus, 1991—, chmn. dept. math., 1968-71. Author: Algebraic Topology: An Introduction, 1967, Homology and Cohomology Theory, 1978, Singular Homology Theory, 1980, A Basic Course in Algebraic Topology, 1991; mem. editorial staff math. jours. Served as officer USNR, 1942-46. Fellow Am. Acad. Arts and Scis.; mem. Am. Math. Soc. Achievements include research in algebraic topology, differential topology, homotopy theory, fibre bundles. Home: 200 Leeder Hill Drive Hamden CT 06517-2729 Office: Yale U Math Dept PO Box 208283 New Haven CT 06520-8283

MASSEY, WILLIAM WALTER, JR., sales executive; b. Lawrenceburg, Tenn., Sept. 21, 1928; s. William Walter and Bess Ann (Brian) M.; m. Virginia Claire Smith, Aug. 16, 1952; children: William Walter III, Laura Ann, Lynn Smith, Lisa Claire. BBA, U. Miami, Fla., 1949; BFA, U. Fla., 1969. Co-owner Massey Motors, Inc., Jacksonville, Fla., 1950—; v.p., dir. Atlantic Discount Co. Inc., Jacksonville, 1954-64; pres. Owners Surety Corp., Jacksonville, 1959—, General Svcs. Corp., Jacksonville, 1960-69, Owners Guaranty Life, Phoenix, 1960-64, Securities Guaranty Life, Phoenix, 1961-64, Fla. Properties, Inc., Jacksonville, 1961-66, Chi-Cha, Inc., Jacksonville, 1965-70, Univ. Square Properties, Jacksonville, 1969-80. V.p., bd. dir. Southside Country Day School, Jacksonville, 1963-68; bd. dirs. Southside Atlantic Bank, Jacksonville, 1965-93. Exhibited in group shows at Internat., N.Y., 1970, Ball State U., 1972. Lt. USAF, 1950-1952. Mem. Ponte Vedra Club, River Club, Epping Forest Club, Deerwood Club, Sigma Chi. Methodist. Avocations: music, painting, writing. Fax: (904) 642-8815. E-mail: billmasseyii@prodigy.net.

MASSICK, JAMES WILLIAM, heavy equipment manufacturing company executive; b. Jan. 19, 1932; s. Peter James and Annetta Jean (Dormaier) M.; m. Joyce Allair Puckey, Apr. 7, 1973; children: Scott, Christopher (dec.), Kit, Timothy, Nina, Sally, John, Jill. BS, U. Wash., 1954; MBA, UCLA, 1966. Constrn. engr. Kaiser Engrs., Oakland, Calif., 1957—58; constrn. mgr. The Boeing Co., Seattle, 1959—62; project mgr. Ralph M. Parsons Co., L.A., 1962—65; engring. mgr. Weyerhauser Co., Tacoma, 1965-68; ops. mgr. Western Gear Corp., Everett, Wash., 1968-70; pres. Truckweld Corp. and subs., Seattle, 1970—. Dir. Truckweld Corp., Truckweld Utilities, Inc., Puget Sound Lease Co., Pacific N.W. Utility & Supply Co.; dir. emeritus Pacific Air Lines, Air West, Hughes Air West, The Budd Corp., Borg Warner Acceptance Corp. Patentee in field. Assoc. chmn. UN Concert and Dinner, Washington, 1975-92; active Nat. UN Day Com., N.Y.C., 1977-95; mem. Young Pres.'s Orgn. Rear adm. USNR, 1950, 54-57. Decorated Navy Cross, Silver Star, Legion of Merit, Purple Heart. Mem. ASCE, Soc. Am. Mil. Engrs., Seattle C. of C., Mcpl. League, Chosen Few, Overlake Golf and Country Club, The Harbor Club, The Lakes Club, Theta Delta Chi. Episcopalian. Home: 2131 NW Pacific Yew Pl Issaquah WA 98027-8462

MASSIE, ANNE ADAMS ROBERTSON, artist; b. Lynchburg, Va., May 30, 1931; d. Douglas Alexander and Annie Scott (Harris) Robertson; m. William McKinnon Massie, Apr. 30, 1960; children: Anne Harris Massie-Apperson, William McKinnon, Jr. Grad., St. Mary's Coll., Raleigh, NC, 1950; BA in English, Randolph Macon Woman's Coll., 1952. Tchr. English E.C. Glass H.S., Lynchburg, 1955-60. Juror Am. Watercolor Soc. Ann. Exhbn., 1998, Ctrl. Va. Watercolor Guild, 1996. Represented in permanent collections at Hotel de Ville, Rueil-Malmaison, France, L'Association des Amis de la Grande Vigne, Dinan, France, Randolph Macon Woman's Coll., Lynchburg Coll., Va. Episcopal Sch., Va. Sch. of Arts, Va. State Bar Assn., Richmond, St. John's Episcopal Ch. Bd. dirs. Lynchburg Hist. Found., 1968-81, 91-95, pres., 1978-81; bd. dirs. Lynchburg Fine Arts Ctr., 1992-98, Point of Honor Mus., 1988-99, collections com., 1970-, chmn. 1989-99; bd. dirs. Amazement Sq. Children's Mus., 1996-2004; trustee Va. Episcopal Sch., Lynchburg, 1983-89, Va. Ctr. for Creative Arts, 1999—; mem. Friends of Rivermont, 2000-, pres. 2000-02. Mem. Am. Watercolor Soc. (signature, Dolphin fellow 1993, Gold medal of Honor 1993), Nat. Watercolor Soc. (signature, Artist's Mag. award), Nat. League Am. Pen Women (pres. 1987, Best in Show 1994), Knickerbocker Artists (signature, Silver medal Watercolor 1993), Watercolor USA Honor Soc., Watercolor West (signature), Catharine Lorillard Wolfe Art Club (signature, medal of honor for water media, 2003), Allied Artists Am., Inc. (signature), Southern Watercolor Soc. (signature), Pa. Watercolor Soc. (artist mem., Best in Show 1992, 97, chmn. exhbns. 1986, pres. 1995-96), Nat. Arts Club (exhibiting artist mem.), Artists' Fellowship, Colonial Dames Am. (chmn. 1987-90), Hillside Garden Club (pres. 1974-76), Jr. League (editor 1953-72), Lynchburg Art Club (bd. dirs. 1995-96, chmn. 1981-4), Antiquarian Club. Episcopalian. Avocations: book club, gardening, tennis. Home: 3204 Rivermont Ave Lynchburg VA 24503-2028

MASSIE, CLIFFORD MICHAEL, music company executive; b. Bklyn., May 11, 1957; s. Michael and Jennifer Massie. BA cum laude with honors, Brandeis U., 1979. Pres. The Hit House, Levittown, NY, 1987—, Shoot No Blanks Music Publishing, Bethpage, NY, 1987—. Producer/remixer Teena Marie, Gloria Gaynor, David Hasselhoff, Evelyn Champagne King, Promoter Jay-Z, Ja Rule, DMX, Ludacris, Ashanti, Janet Jackson, Mariah Carey, Aaliyah, Snoop Dogg, Brian McKnight. Recipient Songwriter 1st Place Billboard Mag. contest, 1988. Mem.: NMPA, NARAS, ASCAP. Achievements include numerous Gold and Platinum singles/albums. Home: 3700 Mallard Rd Levittown NY 11756 Office: The Hit House 3700 Mallard Rd Levittown NY 11756 also: Shoot No Blanks Music Pub PO Box 102 Bethpage NY 11714 Office Phone: 516-735-3452. Fax: 516-735-3329. E-mail: cliffmassie@optonline.net.

MASSIE, MAUREEN TERESA, elementary school educator; b. St. Louis, Apr. 13, 1953; d. James H. and Teresa B. Moran; m. Jim Massie, Feb. 3, 1973; 1 child, Kate. BA in Child Study, Webster Coll., 1977, MAT, 1990. Cert. tchr. K-8, Mo. 1st grade tchr. No. St. Francis County Sch. Dist., Bonne Terre, Mo., 1977-87; 4th grade tchr. Lindbergh Sch. Dist., St. Louis, 1987-89; instr. tchg. methods Ctrl. Meth. Coll. at Mineral Area Coll., Park Hills, Mo., 1991-2001, Farmington (Mo.) Sch. Dist., 1989—, Mineral Area Coll., 2001—; tchr. kindergarten, 1st, 2d, 3d, 5th grades Farmington Sch. Dist., 1998-2001, tchr. gifted edn., 2001—. Asst. youth group leader Teenage Ministry, 1993-2000; resource com. co-chair Habitat for Humanity of St. Francois County, Farmington, Mo., 1997—; bd. dirs. Farmington Soccer Adv. Bd., 1991-93; vol. tchr. Project Head Start, Farmington, 1975-76. Project Aiding Children's Edn. State Incentive grant State of Mo., 1991, Truman Learning Ctrs. Group State Incentive grant, 1994, Learn and Svc. State grant, 1998-2000, How and Why of Sci. grant, 2000, Read to be Ready grant, 2000. Mem. Mo. Nat. Edn. Assn. Home: 770 Market St # 116 Farmington MO 63640-1951 Office: Washington Franklin Elem Sch 104 Murphy St Farmington MO 63640-1370 Business E-Mail: mmassie@farmington.k12.mo.us.

MASSIE, ROBERT JOSEPH, publishing company executive; b. N.Y.C., Mar. 19, 1949; BA, Yale U., 1970; MBA, JD, Columbia U., 1974; diploma, U. d'Aix en Provence, France, 1969. Bar: D.C. 1974. Assoc. Covington & Burling, Washington, 1975-79; mgmt. cons. McKinsey & Co., N.Y.C., 1979-82; v.p. Harlequin Enterprises, Toronto, Ont., Can., 1982-90; pres., CEO Gale Rsch., Inc., Detroit, 1990-92; dir. Chem. Abstracts Svc., Columbus, Ohio, 1992—. Chmn. bd. dirs. Harlequin Mondadori, Milan, Italy, 1985-88; bd. dirs. Harlequin Hachette, Paris, Cora Verlag, Hamburg, Fed. Republic Germany, Mills & Boon, Sydney, Australia. Contbr. articles to law jours. Bd. dirs. Mindleaders.com. Harlan Fiske Stone scholar, 1974. Office: Am Chem Soc Chem Abstracts Svcs PO Box 3012 Columbus OH 43210-0012

MASSIER, PAUL FERDINAND, mechanical engineer; b. Pocatello, Idaho, July 22, 1923; s. John and Kathryn (Arki) M.; m. Miriam Parks, May 1, 1948 (dec. Aug. 1975); children: Marilyn Massier Schwegler, Paulette Massier Holden; m. Dorothy Hedlund Wright, Sept. 12, 1978. *Grandfather Ferdinand Massier pioneered the Baptist missionary movement in Bukovina and Galicia (Austria) during the late 1800's and early 1900's. Father John Massier, a cabinet maker, immigrated to the U.S. from Bukovina in 1903 and in 1951 was elected "Deacon for Life" by the First Baptist Church in Pocatello, Idaho. Mother Katie Arki immigrated from Croatia-Slavonia in 1906 and was an excellent cook and gardener. Daughter Marilyn, a flutist, was awarded "Musician of the Year" at Arcadia, California High School, where daughter Paulette, a violinist, was Concert Mistress of the orchestra. Both toured Europe with the American Youth Symphony Orchestra.* Cert. engring., U. Idaho (so. br.), 1943; BSME, U. Colo., 1948; MSME, MIT, 1949. Engr. Pan-Am. Refining Corp., Texas City, Tex., 1948; design engr. Maytag Co., Newton, Iowa, 1949-50; research engr. Boeing Co., Seattle, 1951-55; sr. research engr., supr. and dep. sect. mgr. Jet Propulsion Lab. Calif. Inst. Tech., Pasadena, 1955-84, task mgr., 1984-88, mem. tech. staff, 1989-94. *More than 40 years of engineering research and supervision led to: concepts and analysis of "far out" rocket propulsion systems such as antimatter, laser, nuclear, and metastable states; evaluation of rocket-engine fuel and oxidizer cooling capabilities including the upper limit of nucleate boiling for numerous liquid propellants such as hydrazine, nitrogen tetroxide, oxygen, alcohol, and many others; experimental determination of fluid mechanics and heat transfer phenomena for high-temperature compressible swirling flows in axisymmetric ducts and convergent-divergent nozzles; identification and evaluation of explanted heart valve prostheses; development of gas turbines for use as engines in trucks and boats and as air compressors.* Contbr. articles to profl. jours. Moderator Arcadia Congl. Ch., 1996-98; mem. Arcadia High Sch. Music Club, 1966-71. With U.S. Army, 1943-46. Recipient Apollo Achievement award NASA, 1969, Basic Noise Rsch. award NASA, 1980, Life Mem. Svc. award Calif. PTA, 1970, Layman of Yr. award Arcadia Congl. Ch., 1971, Mil. Unit Citation award, 1946. Fellow AIAA (assoc., Sustained Svc. award 1980-81); mem. N.Y. Acad. Scis., Planetary Soc., Order of the Engr., Bukovina Soc. of the Ams., Sigma Xi, Tau Beta Pi, Pi Tau Sigma, Sigma Tau. Congregationalist. Achievements include 50% reduction of cooling requirements for rocket engines, experimental evaluation of heat transfer from thermally ionized gases at temperatures up to 13,000 degrees; experimental determination of starting characteristics, shock-wave structures, heat transfer and pressure distributions in supersonic diffusers led to the development of criteria for their design and their use as a means of simulating altitude conditions at ground level for static testing of rocket engines; experimental/analytical determination of the relationships of large-scale turbulent structures, density and temperature fluctuations, inverted velocity profiles, internally generated pure tones, twin jet shielding, and aircraft flight on noise emitted from aircraft supersonic jets; understanding of the formation of cenospheres during the combustion of heavy oils by analysis of electron microscope photo images of droplets and stages of formed globules and cenospheres gathered on slides during combustion experiments. Home: 764 Lava Falls Dr Las Vegas NV 89110 E-mail: dortzekefrompoky@earthlink.net.

MASSING, VIRGINIA REEVES, surgical nurse and administrator; b. Thomaston, Ga., Jan. 15, 1934; d. Joel Farley and Virginia Broughton (Hardy) Reeves; m. Ralph Richard Massing, Oct. 25, 1957 (dec. Mar. 1987); children: Thomas Hardy, Tony Douglas. Diploma in Nursing, Piedmond Sch. Nursing, Atlanta, 1955. CRNA, RN, Ga. Cert. RN anesthetist AA's of Rome, Ga., 1970-72, 76-85; dir. surgery Redmond Regional Med. Ctr., Rome, 1972-76, 85-96. Mem. Assn. of Operating Rm. Nurses, Am. Assn. Nurse Adminstrs., Am. Assn. Nurse Anesthetists. Republican. Methodist. Home: 17 Windrush Dr NW Rome GA 30165-4501

MASSLER, HOWARD ARNOLD, lawyer; b. Newark, July 22, 1946; s. Abraham I. and Sylvia (Botwin) M.; children: Justin Scott, Jeremy Ross, Jano Tsirka. BA, U. Pa., 1969; JD, Rutgers U., 1973; LLM in Taxation, NYU, 1977. Bar: N.J. 1974, U.S. Dist. Ct. N.J. 1974, D.C. 1975, U.S. Ct. Appeals (D.C. cir.) 1975, N.Y. 1977, U.S. Dist. Ct. (we. dist.) N.Y. 1977, U.S. Tax Ct. 1977. Counsel house banking, currency and housing com., chmn. sub-com. U.S. Ho. Reps., Washington, 1974-76; tax atty. Lipsitz, Green, Fahringer, Roll, Schuller & James, N.Y.C. and Buffalo, 1977-79; pvt. practice Mountainside, N.J., 1979-89; pres. Bestway Products Inc., A.A. Records Inc., Servor Corp., 1979-85; pres., chief exec. officer, chmn. bd. Bestway Group Inc., Dover, Del., 1985-91; gen. ptnr. 26/27 Law Drive Assocs., 1988—; ptnr. Shonageri, Pearce & Massler, Hackensack, N.J., 1989-90, Mott, Pearce, Williams & Lee, Hackensack and Washington, 1990-91, Pearce & Massler, Hackensack, N.J., 1991-97. Prodn. staff asst. DECCA House Ltd., London, 1968; chief exec. officer Basura Pub., Inc. (affiliated with BMI), 1974-80; arbitrator U.S. Dist. Ct. N.J., 1985—; adj. prof. law Seton Hall U., Newark, N.J., 1988-89, N.J. Inst. for Continuing Legal Edn., 1986; lectr. N.J. Inst. for Continuing Legal Edn., 1986—; assoc. dir. United Jersey Bank/Franklin State Bank, 1987—; del. adv. com. on indsl. trade and econ. devel. U.S./China Joint Sessions, Beijing, People's Republic of China, 1988. Author: QDROs (Tax and Drafting Considerations), 1986, 2nd. ed., 1987; contbr. West's Legal Forms, Vol. 7., 2d edit., 1987, 3d edit., Domestic Relations with Tax Analysis, Contemporary Matrimonial Law Issues: A Guide to Divorce Economics and Practice; tax author: Matthew Bender, NYCP-Matrimonial Actions and Equitable Distribution Actions, 1988; tax author, tax editor: Matthew Bender, Alimony, Child Support & Counsel Fees-Award, Modification and Enforcement, 1988, 2d edit., 1989, 3d edit., 1991, Matthew Bender, Valuation & Distribution of Marital Property, 1988, 89, 91, 92, 94, 95; contbg. author: How to Make Legal Fees Tax Deductible, 1988, Closely Held Corporations, Forms and Checklists, Buy-Sell Agreement Forms with Tax Analysis, 1988, The Encyclopedia of Matrimonial Practice, 1991, 4th edit., 1995; author: New York Practice Guide: Negligence, Tax Law of Compensation for Sickness and Injury, 2d edit., 1992; contbg. editor Pensions and Ins. Problems, 1984—, Taxation, 1984—, Fair$hare, 1984—, Law & Bus., Inc., 1984—; staff contbr., N.J. Law Jour., 1986—; contbr. articles to law revs. and profl. jours. Bd. dirs., legal counsel western N.Y. chpt. Nat. Handicapped Sports and Recreation Assn., 1977-79; counsel Union County, N.J., 1984-85; candidate Springfield (N.J.) Twp. Commn., 1986. Mem. ABA, N.J. Bar Assn. (vice chmn. taxation comm. family law section 1987—), N.Y. Bar Assn. (taxation com., subcom. on criminal and civil penalties), D.C. Bar Assn., Erie County Bar Assn. (sec. taxation com. 1977-79, continuing edn. lectr. taxation 1977—), Essex County Bar Assn. (tax com. 1981—), Union County Bar Assn. (chmn. tax com. 1984—) Republican. Avocation: Sports Car Club Am. formula Ford racing. Home: 508 Main St PO Box 399 Boonton NJ 07005-0399 Office: 508 Main St Boonton NJ 07005-1716 E-mail: hmassler@aol.com.

MASSMAN, RICHARD ALLAN, lawyer; b. Beaumont, Tex., Aug. 19, 1943; s. Irwin Massman and Sylvia (Schmidt) Schwartz; m. Barbara Elaine Kessler; children: Jason Todd, Karen Faye. BS cum laude, U. Pa., 1965; JD cum laude, Harvard U., 1968. Bar: Tex. 1968; cert. in taxation, Tex. Bd. Legal Specialization. Assoc. Coke & Coke, Dallas, 1968-70, Johnson & Wortley, P.C. (formerly Johnson & Gibbs, P.C.), Dallas, 1970-71, ptnr., 1971-88, shareholder, 1988-94; of counsel Johnson & Wortley P.C., Dallas, 1994-95; sr. v.p., gen. counsel Hunt Consolidated, Inc., Dallas, 1994—. Lectr. So. Meth. U., Dallas, 1973. Bd. dirs. Martin Luther King Jr. Cmty. Ctr., Dallas, 1979-81, Jewish Fedn. Greater Dallas, 1980-83, 89—, The Dallas Opera, 1999—, Retina Found. of the S.W., 2004—; mem. exec. com. Dallas regional bd. Anti-Defamation League, 1979—, chmn., 1990-92; chmn. Dallas Civil Svc. Bd., 1983; trustee Greenhill Sch., Dallas, 1985-92, vice chmn., 1990-92. Recipient Jurisprudence award Anti-Defamation League, 2000. Mem. Am. Coll. Tax Coun., Tex. State Bar (chmn., sec. taxation 1983-84), Dallas Bar Assn. (chmn., sec. taxation 1978), Dallas Petroleum Club, Columbian Club. Office: Hunt Consolidated Inc Fountain Pl 20th Fl 1445 Ross at Field Dallas TX 75202-2785

MASSOF, ROBERT WILLIAM, neuroscientist, educator; b. Minn., Jan. 2, 1948; m. Patricia Massof; children: Eric, Allison. BA, Hamline U., 1970; PhD, Ind. U., 1975. Postdoctoral fellow in ophthalmology Johns Hopkins U. Sch. Medicine, Balt., 1975-76, instr. ophthalmology, 1976-78, from asst. prof. to assoc. prof., 1978-91, prof. ophthalmology, 1991—, prof. neurosci., 1994—, prof. computer sci., 1994—, mem. staff applied physics lab., 2000—. Lectr. in field. Mem. editl. bd. Clin. Vision Scis., N.Y.C., 1986-94, Eye Care Technology/Computers in Eye Care, Folsom, Calif., 1992-96; patentee in field (5); contbr. articles to profl. jours. Recipient Manpower award, 1989, Tech. Transfer award NASA, 1993, Popular Mechanics Design and Engring. award, 1994, EyeCare Tech. Lifetime Achievement award, 1995, Richard E. Hoover Svc. award, 1995, Humanitarian award Lions, 2000, Disting. Svc. in Vision award Am. Pub. Health Assn., William Feinbloom award Am. Acad. of Optometry, 2000, Alfred W. Bressler prize Jewish Guild for the Blind, 2004. Fellow Optical Soc. Am. (chmn. edn. coun. 1993-95, bd. dirs. 1993-95), Am.

Acad. Optometry; mem. Assn. for Edn. and Rehab. of the Visually Impaired, Soc. for Info. Display, Am. Congress Rehab. Medicine, Assn. Rsch. in Vision and Ophthalmology. Office: Johns Hopkins Univ Lions Vision Ctr 550 N Broadway Fl 6 Baltimore MD 21205-2020 Office Phone: 410-502-6246. E-mail: rmassf@hons.med.jhu.edu.

MASSON, GERALD M. computer science educator; BSEE, Ill. Inst. Tech.; MSEE, PhD, Northwestern U. Staff AT&T; faculty U. Pitts., Carnegie-Mellon U.; prof. computer sci. Johns Hopkins U., Balt., 1986—, dir. Info. Security Inst., 2001—. Tech. advisor Compunetix, Inc., Monroeville, Pa. Contbr. over 100 articles to scientific publs. Fellow IEEE. Office: Johns Hopkins U Info Security Inst Wyman Pk Bldg 406 3400 N Charles St Baltimore MD 21218-2608

MASSON, ROBERT HENRY, paper company executive; b. Boston, June 27, 1935; s. Robert Louis and Henrietta Hill (Worrell) M.; m. Virginia Lee Morton, Dec. 28, 1957; children: Linda Anne, Kenneth Morton, Robert Louis, II. BA in Econs. cum laude, Amherst Coll., 1957; MBA, Harvard U., 1964. Fin. staff Ford Motor Co., Dearborn, Mich., 1964-68, mktg. services div. controller, 1968-70; pres. Knutson Constrn. Co., Mpls., 1970-72; v.p. fin., treas. Ellerbe, Inc., Bloomington, Minn., 1972-77; fin. dir. CirTech, Inc., Mpls., 1973-77; v.p. fin. transp. div. PepsiCo., Inc., Tulsa, 1977, corp. v.p., treas. Purchase, N.Y., 1978-80; v.p., treas. Combustion Engring., Inc., Stamford, Conn., 1981-86, v.p. fin. and venture devel., 1986-87, v.p. venture fin. and internat. ops., 1988-90; v.p., CFO Parsons & Whittemore, Inc., Rye Brook, N.Y., 1990—. Mem. adv. bd. Fleet Bank, 1988—. Author: (with others) The Management of Racial Integration in Business, 1964. Pres. North Georgetown Homeowner's Assn., Birmingham, Mich., 1968-70, U.S. Presdl. Advance Man, 1972-76; trustee, chmn. fin. com. Naval Aviation Mus. Found., 1987—; trustee Hebron Acad., 1993-97; elder Presbyn. Ch. of Old Greenwich, 1992—. Served to lt. USN, 1957-62; lt. comdr. Res. Mem. Am. Forest and Paper Assn. (fin. com. 1991—), Fin. Execs. Inst. (com. on corp. fin. 1981—), Fairchester Treas. Group (pres. 1986), Lucas Point Homeowner's Assn. (pres. 1986-87), Theta Delta Chi. Clubs: Wayzata Yacht (dir.-treas. 1973-77), Riverside Yacht (asst. treas. 1985-87). Office: Parsons & Whittemore Inc 4 International Dr Ste 5 Rye Brook NY 10573-1064

MASSURA, EDWARD ANTHONY, accountant; b. Chgo., July 1, 1938; s. Edward Matthew and Wilma C. (Kussy) M.; m. Carol A. Barber, June 23, 1962; children: Edward J., Beth Ann, John B. BS, St. Joseph's Coll., Rensselaer, Ind., 1960; JD, DePaul U., 1963. Bar. Ill. 1963; CPA, Mich., Ill., others. Tax acct. Arthur Andersen LLP, Chgo., 1963-98, ptnr., 1973-98, dir. tax div. Detroit, 1974-84; dep., co-dir. internat. tax Arthur Andersen & Co., Detroit, 1983-84, ptnr.-in-charge internat. trade customs practice, 1983-88. Co-author: West's Legal Forms, 2d. edit., 1984; contbr. numerous articles to bus. jours. Bd. dirs. Arts Found. of Mich., Detroit, 1982-95, treas., 1982-93; bd. dirs. Ctr. for Internat. Bus. Edn. and Rsch., Wayne State U.; bd. trustees St. Joseph's Coll., Rensselaer, Ind. Mem. AICPA, Internat. Fiscal Assn. (v.p. Eastern Gt. Lakes region), Assn. for Corp. Growth, Mich. Assn. CPAs, Mich. Dist. Export Coun. (chmn. 1985-92), Detroit Internat. Tax Group (founder,co-moderator), Licensing Exec. Soc., World Trade Club of Detroit, Bus. Assn. Mexico and Mich, Inc., Orchard Lake Country Club, Butterfield Country Club, Lely Golf & Country Club.

MASSURA, EILEEN KATHLEEN, family therapist; b. Chgo., July 25, 1925; d. John William and Loretta (Feil) Stratemeier; m. Edmund Karamanski, July 24, 1948 (dec.); children: John, Kathleen; m. Alfred Massura, Aug. 30, 1963; children: Michael, Kathryn, Mark. BS in Nursing, DePaul U., 1963; MS in Nursing, St. Xavier Coll., 1971. RN; cert. family therapist. Dir. nurses Franklin Blvd. Hosp., Chgo., 1958-62; adminstr. Mich. Ave Hosp., Chgo., 1962-64; instr. St. Xavier Coll., Chgo., 1972-74, Joliet (Ill.) Jr. Coll., 1972-81; family therapist Oak Lawn (Ill.) Family Svc., 1978-88; prof. nursing Govs. State U., University Park, Ill., 1981-89; family therapist McCarthy & Assocs., Oak Lawn, 1982-93, Massura & Assocs., Oak Lawn, 1994-99, Chgo., 1999—. Preceptor to grads. St. Xavier Coll., 1980-90, Govs. State U., 1980-89; co-leader Clin. Study Med./Surg. Nursing, Moscow, 1984; presenter Am. Nursing Rev., Ala., Fla., Va., Pa., Tex., Md., 1985-86. Leader Campfire Girls, Oak Lawn, 1964—74; co-leader Orient/Am. Med./Surg. Nursing, 1987; mem. Marist Women's Bd., Chgo., 1978—82, Bro. Rice Women's Bd., Chgo., 1969—72; chmn. evangelization commn. Holy Name Cathedral, Chgo., 2000—04; mem. Luth. Family Svc. Bd. Day Care for Srs., 1988—89; PPC Holy Name Cathedral, 2004. Grantee HEW, 1969-71; named Disting. Nurse Alumnae, St. Xavier Coll., 1985; named Nursing Prof. of Yr., Govs. State U., 1983. Mem. Am. Nurses Assn. (nominating com. 1982-87), Ill. Nurses Assn. (program com. 1980-84), Am. Assn. Marital and Family Therapists, Cath. Order Foresters, Sigma Theta Tau (v.p. 1971-75). Roman Catholic. Avocations: crewel, needlepoint, watercolor, travel. Office: 30 E Huron St Apt 4306 Chicago IL 60611-4714 E-mail: EKM@lopener.net.

MASSY, WILLIAM FRANCIS, education educator, consultant; b. Milw., Mar. 26, 1934; s. Willard Francis and Ardys Dorothy (Digman) M.; m. Sally Vaughn Miller, July 21, 1984; children by previous marriage: Willard Francis, Elizabeth BS, Yale U., 1956; SM, MIT, 1958, PhD in Indsl. Econs., 1960. Asst. prof. indsl. mgmt. MIT, Cambridge, 1960-62; from asst. prof. to prof. edn. and bus. adminstrn. Stanford U., Calif., 1962-96, assoc. dean Grad. Sch. Bus., 1971, vice provost for rsch., 1971-77, v.p. for bus. and fin., 1977-88, v.p. fin., 1988-91, prof. emeritus, 1996—; prof. edn., dir. Stanford Inst. Higher Edn. Rsch., Calif., 1988-96; sr. v.p. P.R. Taylor Assocs., 1995-99; sr. rschr. Nat. Ctr. for Postsecondary Imrprovement, 1996—2002; pres. The Jackson Hole Higher Edn. Group, Inc., 1996—. Bd. dirs. Diebold, Inc., chmn. audit com., 2003-; mem. univ. grants com. Hong Kong, 1990-2003; mem. coun. Yale U., 1980-95; mgmt. cons. Stanford Mgmt. Co., 1991-93. Author: Stochastic Models of Buying Behavior, 1970, Marketing Management, 1972, Market Segmentation, 1972, Planning Models for Colleges and Universities, 1981, Endowment, 1991, Resource Allocation in Higher Education, 1996, Honoring The Trust, 2003; mem. editl. bd. Jour. Mktg. Rsch., 1964-70, Harcourt, Brace Jovanovich, 1965-71; contbr. articles to profl. jours. Bd. dirs. Palo Alto-Stanford chpt. United Way, 1978-80, Stanford U. Hosp., 1980-91, MAC, Inc., 1969-84, EDUCOM, 1983-86. Ford Found. faculty rsch. fellow, 1966-67 Mem. Am. Mktg. Assn. (bd. dirs. 1971-73, v.p. edn. 1976-77), Inst. Mgmt. Scis. Office: The Jackson Hole Higher Edn Group Inc PO Box 9849 Jackson WY 83002-9849

MAST, BERNADETTE MIHALIC, lawyer; BS, Ohio State U., 1982; JD magna cum laude, Case Western Res. U., 1988. CPA; bar: Ohio 1988; cert. prodn. and inventory mgr., systems profl. 1985. With Jones Day, Cleve., 1988—, ptnr., 2000—. Mem.: Cleve. Bar Assn. (real estate sect.), Ohio State Bar Assn. Office: Jones Day North Point 901 Lakeside Ave Cleveland OH 44114-1190

MAST, KANDE WHITE, artist; b. St. Louis, Mar. 10, 1950; d. Elliott Maxwell and Mary (Barritt) W. Student, U. Mo., 1968-70, Longview C.C., Kansas City, Mo., 1970-71. Portrait painter, free-lance artist, Albany, N.Y., 1973-74, Kansas City, 1974—; dir., tchr. Studio Kande, Sch. Fine Arts, Kansas City, 1983-86; founder, exec. dir. Art Ctr. Kansas City, 1986-90; behavioral foster parent, 1989—; master foster parent, 1992—. Mem. psychiat. diversion team, mental health rev. team Jackson County Divsn. Family Svcs., 1992-95. Portrait painter and free-lance artist. Pres., bd. dirs. Advocates for Children, Inc., 1996—; vol. Ozanam Home for Boys, Kansas City, 1987—, mem. adv. bd., 1991—; mem. Cmty. Response Team, Jackson County, Divsn. Family Svcs. Named Therapeutic Foster Parent of Yr., 1992. Mem.: Code Pink: Women for Peace, Nat. Mus. of Women in Arts (charter). Home and Office: 10243 Cedarbrooke Ln Kansas City MO 64131-4209

MAST, RICK, race car driver; b. Rockbridge Baths, Va., Mar. 4, 1957; m. Sharon Mast; children: Ricky, Katie, Sarah. Degree in bus. adminstrn., Blue Ridge C.C. Racecar driver Richard Jackson, 1991—97, Butch Mock Motorsports, 1997—98, Carl Yarborough, 1999, Larry Hedrick, 2000, A.J. Foyt, 2000, Hal Hicks, 2001, Jack Birmingham, 2001, Junie Donlavey, 2002—. Recipient 2d pl., ACDelco 500, 1994. Office: Donlavey Racing 5011 Old Midlothain Pike Richmond VA 23224-1119

MAST, STEWART DALE, retired airport manager; b. Kalamazoo, May 10, 1924; s. Virgil S. and S. Louise (Rippey) M.; m. Judy Jo Bolton; children: Peter S., Frances Ann Mast Adams; m. May 20, 1979. Student, U. Mich., 1942-43; grad., Spartan Sch. Aerospace, Tulsa, 1946, Argubright Bus. Coll., Battle Creek, Mich., 1947. Mgr. Mcpl. Airport, Battle Creek, 1948-60; airport dir. Mitchell Field, Milw., 1961-66; mgr. Tampa (Fla.) Internat. Airport, 1966-89; ret., 1989. Pres. Mich. Assn. Airport Mgrs., 1958. Past mem. aviation coun. Milw. C. of C., Hillsborough County C. of C., Tampa; past mem. bd. rev. Boy Scouts Am., Milw.; bd. dirs. Sun'n Fun Aviation Found., Inc., Lakeland, Fla., 1992—, Sun'n Fun Fly-in, Inc., Lakeland, Fla., 1994—. 1st lt. USAAF, 1943-45. Recipient Cmty. Leadership award Greater Tampa C. of C., 1979. Mem. Am. Assn. Airport Execs. (past bd. dirs., Pres.'s award 1979), Fla. Assn. Airport Mgrs. Avocations: aviation philately, photography.

MASTERN, DEAN SCOTT, personal growth and development consultant; b. Warren, Ohio, Aug. 26, 1961; s. Kenneth Richard and Joyce Eileen Mastern; m. Sheree Diane Grier, Aug. 21, 1987; children: Aaron Keith, Rachel Colleen. PhD in Psychology, PhD in Quantum Biophysics, SW Acad. of Mental Health, 1987; DD (hon.), World Christianship Ministries, 1987. Cons. DSM Consulting, Tyler, Tex., 1987—. Author: Theory of Quantum Biophysics, 1987. Mem.: Am. Assn. of Religious Counselors (life). Republican. Avocations: flying, sailing, sports cars, motorcycles. Office: DSM Consulting PO Box 133012 Tyler TX 75713 E-mail: dsmphd@yahoo.com.

MASTERS, ARLENE ELIZABETH, singer; b. Freeport, Ill., Oct. 6, 1960; d. Elmer and Mary (Green) Masters; m. Douglas Dewayne Burck (div.); 1 child, Douglas. Singer classic rock and blues; with The Blues Transit Band, A. Masters Publishing. Home: 2680 S Tissaw Road Cornville AZ 86325 Mailing: PO Box 2832 Cottonwood AZ 86326

MASTERS, BETTIE SUE SILER, biochemist, educator; b. Lexington, Va., June 13, 1937; d. Wendell Hamilton and Mildred Virginia (Cromer) Siler; m. Robert Sherman Masters, Aug. 6, 1960; children: Diane Elizabeth, Deborah Ann. BS in Chemistry, Roanoke Coll., 1959, D.Sc. (hon.), 1983; PhD in Biochemistry, Duke U., 1963. Postdoctoral fellow Duke U., 1963-66, advanced research fellow, 1966-68, assoc. on faculty, 1967-68; mem. faculty U. Tex. Health Sci. Ctr. (Southwestern Med. Sch.), Dallas, 1968-82, assoc. prof. biochemistry, 1972-76, prof., 1976-82, research prof. surgery, dir. biochem. burn research, 1979-82; prof. biochemistry, chmn. dept. Med. Coll. Wis., Milw., 1982-90; Robert A. Welch prof. chemistry, dept. biochemistry U. Tex. Health Sci. Ctr., San Antonio, 1990—. Mem. pharmacology-toxicology rsch. rev. com. Nat. Inst. Gen. Med. Scis., NIH, 1975-79; mem. bd. sci. counselors Nat. Inst. Environ. Health Scis., 1982-86, chmn., 1984-86; mem. adv. com. on biochemistry and endocrinology Am. Cancer Soc., 1989-92, chmn., 1991-92, mem. coun. for extramural grants, 1998—; mem. phys. biochemistry study sect. NIH, 1989-90; vis. scientist Japan Soc. for Promotion Sci., 1978. Mem. editl. bd. Jour. Biol. Chemistry, 1976-81, 96-2001, Archives Biochemistry and Biophysics, 1991-94, Drug Metabolism and Disposition, 1993-, Nitric Oxide, Biology and Chemistry, 1996-, Internat. Union Biochemistry and Molecular Biology Life, 1999-; contbr. chpts. to books and articles, revs. and abstracts to profl. publs. Mem. coun. extramural grants Am. Cancer Soc., 1998-2000. Recipient Merit award Nat. Heart, Lung and Blood Inst., 1988-97, grantee, 1970—; recipient Excellence in Sci. award Fedn. Am. Socs. for Exptl. Biology, 1992; postdoctoral fellow Am. Cancer Soc., 1963-65, advanced rsch. fellow Am. Heart Assn., 1966-68, established investigator, 1968-73; rsch. grantee NIH, 1970—, Nat. Heart Lung Blood Inst., 1970—, Nat. Inst. Gen. Med. Scis., 1980—, Robert A. Welch Found., 1971-82, 90—; elected to Inst. Medicine of NAS, 1996. Fellow AAAS; mem. NIH (adv. com. to the dir. 2000—), Am. Soc. Biochemistry and Molecular Biology (nominating com. 1983, coun. 1985-86, awards com. 1992-96, fin. com. 1993-98, publs. com. 1994-97, pres.-elect 2001, pres. 2002-), Am. Soc. Pharmacology and Exptl. Therapeutics (exec. com. drug metabolism divsn. 1979-81, chmn. exec. com. 1993-94, bd. publs. trustees 1982-87, Bernard B. Brodie award 2000), Am. Chem. Soc., Assn. Am. Med. Colls. (adv. bd. biomed. rsch. 1995-98), Fedn. Am. Socs. for Exptl. Biology (bd. dirs. 1998—, v.p. 2001-2002), Internat. Union Biochemistry and Molecular Biology (nominating com. 1994-97, chair U.S. nat.com. 1997—), Sigma Xi, Alpha Omega Alpha. Office: U Tex Health Sci Ctr Dept Biochemistry 7703 Floyd Curl Dr MSC 7760 San Antonio TX 78229-3900 E-mail: masters@uthscsa.edu.

MASTERS, CLAUDE BIVIN, lawyer; b. Cleburne, Tex., July 25, 1930; s. Claude Pinkney and Ola Mae (Rollins) M.; m. Jenita Whites, June 1, 1949 (div.); children: C. Thomas, Cl Danette Masters McClanahan, Teresa Masters Lebeck; m. Cynthia McCormack, Nov. 4, 1983. BS, U. Houston, 1953, JD, 1969, LLM, 1985. Bar: Tex. 1969, U.S. Dist. Ct. (so. dist.) Tex. 1972, U.S. Dist. Ct. (we. dist.) Tex. 1972, U.S. Ct. Appeals (5th cir.) 1971, U.S. Ct. Appeals (11th cir.) 1983, U.S. Supreme Ct. 1978. Ptnr. Martin & Masters, Houston, 1971-73; v.p., gen. counsel Summit Ins. Co. N.Y., N.Y.C., 1973-75; sr. atty. Ashland Oil Co., Ky., 1975-78; v.p. Houston Oil and Minerals Co., 1978-84; assoc. Dunnam & Strong, Houston, 1984-85; risk mgmt. cons. Masters & Assocs., Houston, 1975—. Bd. dirs. Alford & Assocs., Houston; adj. prof. law U. Houston, 1984—. Dir.-gen. Tex. Safety Assn., Austin, 1959. Served with U.S. Army, 1946-47. Named Outstanding Speaker, Southwest Ins. Info. Svc., Dallas, 1961-62. Fellow Tex. Bar Found. (life), Houston Bar Found (life); mem. Jaycees (bd. dirs. Tulsa 1962; named Outstanding Mem. Tex. 1960), Phi Delta Phi. Republican. Mem. Ch. of Christ. Home: 314 College Ave Cleburne TX 76033 Office: 5444 Westheimer Rd Ste 1775 Houston TX 77056-5325 E-mail: claudemasters@charter.net.

MASTERS, EDWARD E. association executive, former foreign service officer; b. Columbus, Ohio, June 21, 1924; s. George Henry and Ethel Verena (Shaw) M.; m. Allene Mary Roche, Apr. 2, 1956; children: Julie Allene, Edward Ralston. Student, Denison U., 1942—43; BA with distinction, George Washington U., 1948; MA, Fletcher Sch. Law and Diplomacy, 1949; grad., Nat. War Coll., 1964. Joined U.S. Fgn. Svc., 1950; intelligence rsch. analyst Near East Dept. State, 1949-50; resident officer Heidelberg, Germany, 1950-52; polit. officer embassy Karachi, Pakistan, 1952-54; Hindustani lang. and area tng. U. Pa., 1954-55; consul, polit. officer Madras, India, 1955-58; intelligence rsch. specialist South Asia Dept. State, 1958-60, chief Indonesia-Malaya br. Office Rsch. Asia, 1960-61, officer-in-charge Thailand affairs Office Rsch. Asia, 1961-63; counselor for polit. affairs Am. embassy, Djakarta, 1964-68; country dir. for Indonesia Dept. State, 1968-70; dir. Office East Asian Regional Affairs, 1970-71; minister Am. embassy, Bangkok, 1971-75; amb. to Bangladesh, 1976—77, 1977—81; adj. prof. diplomacy Fletcher Sch. Law and Diplomacy, 1981-82; sr. v.p. Natomas Co., 1982-84; pres. Nat. Planning Assn., 1985-92, Edward Masters & Assocs., Washington, 1992—, U.S.-Indonesia Soc., 1994-2000, chmn., 2000—. Adj. prof. Sch. Advanced Internat. Studies, 2000—02. Mem. Am. Fgn. Svc. Assn., Cosmos Club, Phi Beta Kappa, Omicron Delta Kappa, Pi Gamma Mu, Delta Phi Epsilon. Home: 4101 Cathedral Ave NW Apt 1001 Washington DC 20016-7500 Personal E-mail: mastersdc@att.net.

MASTERS, ELAINE, educator, writer; b. Kansas City, Mo, Oct. 6, 1932; d. David Shepherd and Stella Frances (Ragan) M.; m. Donald Ramon Masters, Apr. 27, 1951; children: David, Vicki, Jennifer, Kevin. BS in Edn. with honors, U. Mo., Kansas City, 1968. Cert. tchr., Mo., Va. Tchr. grade 4 Am. Sch., Manila, 1956-57; tchr. grade 5 Escuela Gloria Felix, Caracas, Venezuela, 1960-62; tchr. grade 6 Okinawa Christian Sch., Urasoe, 1968-70; tchr. grade 5 Flint Hill Elem. Sch., Vienna, Va., 1970-73; tchr. Bible Inst. Hawaii, Honolulu, 1991-92; dir. Christian edn. St. Thomas United Meth. Ch., Manassas, Va., 1983-84; tchr. children's ministries Salvation Army, Kaneohe, Hawaii, 1991-94; owner Edon Industries, Quixtar, 1999—. Evangelist, Hong Kong, Malaysia, Nigeria, Thailand, Russia; seminar leader on Bible and Christian living, Hong Kong, Malaysia, Nigeria, Thailand; advisor Pentecostal Assemblies of Tribes, Chiang Mai, Thailand, 1991—; lectr. Christian Writers Workshop, 1993—; workshop leader, soc. of Childrens Book Writers and Illustrators, Honolulu, 2003; writer ednl. measurement, Harcourt Brace, 1998—; workshop leader Conf. on Lit. and Hawaiis Children, 1998—. Author: Ali and the Ghost Tiger, 1967, Teach Us To Pray, 1970, Day Camp and Day Care Handbook, 1989, The Thief in Chinatown, 1998, Footloose the Mongoose and the Jumping Flea, 1999, Malia's Happy Birthday, 2000, Malia and Baby Brother, 2000, Where's Malia's Mama?, 2000, Where's Kimo's Daddy?, 2000, Yumi and Her Best-Forever Friend, 2000, Footloose the Mongoose and His Wonderful Ohana, 2001, Kalani and the Night Marchers, 2001, Momi, A Hawaiian Mermaid in the Land of Delight, 2001, Lullaby Moon, 2002 (Ka Palapala Po'okela Pub.'s award for best children's book fiction and non-fiction pub. in Hawaii, 2002), The Royal Waker-Upper, 2003; contbr. articles to mags. and newspapers; inventor cricket transposer tool for musicians. Mem. spkr. bur. Alzheimer's Assn., Honolulu, 1991-97; mem. steering com. Children's Lit., Hawaii. Mem. Women's Aglow Fellowship Internat., Soc. Children's Book Writers and Illustrators (regional advisor State of Hawaii 1996-98). Avocations: travel, Hawaiian culture, Thai and hill tribes culture, foreign languages. Home: 2355 Ala Wai Blvd Apt 502 Honolulu HI 96815-3404

MASTERS, JOELLEN M. humanities educator; d. Hilary Thomas and Polly Jo Masters; m. Mohammad Nezam-Mafi, July 13, 2001. AB, Mount Holyoke Coll., 1978; MA, Boston U., 1988, PhD, 1996. Asst. prof. humanities Boston U. Coll. Gen. Studies. Office: Boston Univ Coll Gen Studies 87 Commonwealth Ave Boston MA 02215

MASTERS, JOHN CHRISTOPHER, psychologist, educator, writer; b. Terre Haute, Ind., Oct. 25, 1941; s. Robert William and Lillian Virginia (Decker) M.; m. Mary Jayne Capps, June 6, 1970; children— Blair Christopher, Kyle Alexander. AB, Harvard Coll., 1963; PhD, Stanford U., 1967. Asst. prof. Ariz. State U., Tempe, 1968-69; from asst. prof. to prof. U. Minn., Mpls., 1969-79; assoc. dir. Inst. Child Devel., 1974-79; Luce prof. pub. policy and the family, prof. psychology Vanderbilt U., Nashville, 1979-87, interim chair dept. psychology, 1986-88; pres. Profl. Mgmt. Group, Inc., 1991—; dir. Master Ventures, 1989—, Master Travel, 1989—. Assoc. editor: Child Development, 1973-76, Behavior Therapy: Techniques and Empirical Findings, 1974, 79, 88; editor: Psychol. Bull., 1987-89. Home: 4923 Old Oakleaf Dr Sarasota FL 34233-3947 Office Phone: 800-767-6162.

MASTERS, JON JOSEPH, corporate governance consultant, management consultant; b. N.Y.C., June 20, 1937; s. Arthur Edward and Esther (Shady) M.; m. Rosemary Dunaway Cox, June 16, 1962; children: Brooke Alison, Blake Edward. BA, Princeton U., 1958; JD, Harvard U., 1964. Bar: N.Y. 1965, U.S. Dist. Ct. (so. dist.) N.Y. 1965, U.S. Ct. Appeals (2d cir.) 1965. Cons. asst. to under sec. Dept. Army, 1961; mem. policy planning staff asst. sec. for internat. security affairs Dept. Def., 1962; mem. Pres. Johnson's Spl. Polit. Research Staff, Washington, 1964; assoc. Shearman & Sterling, N.Y.C., 1965-68, 69; mem. staff Bedford-Stuyvesant D & S Corp., Bklyn., 1968-69; v.p., sec., gen. counsel, dir. Baker, Weeks & Co., Inc., N.Y.C., 1969-76; ptnr. Christy & Viener, N.Y.C., 1976-96; Vice-chmn. Robb, Peck, McCooey Specialist Corp., N.Y.C., 1996—98; prin. Lear, Yavitz & Assocs., N.Y.C., 1996-2001, mng. prin., 1998—2001; prin. Mercer Delta Cons., N.Y.C., 2001—02; chmn. Masters Governance Cons., LLC, N.Y.C., 2002—. SEC adv. com. broker-dealer compliance, 1972-74; legal advisor NACD Blue Ribbon Commn. on CEO and Dir. Performance Evaluation, 1994; chmn. bd. Clear and Present Prodns., 1992-93; dir. Harris & Harris Group, Inc., 1992-98. Mem. implementation com. Econ. Devel. Task Force of N.Y. Urban Coalition, 1968; mem. bd. Internat. Social Service, Am. Br., Inc., 1978-83, pres., 1979-83; bd. dirs. The Arts Connection, 1979-85; mem. steering com. N.Y. Lawyers Alliance for Nuclear Arms Control, 1983-96. Served with USN, 1958-61. Mem. ABA, Assn. Bar City N.Y. (com. mcpl. affairs 1977-80), N.Y. State Bar Assn. Office: 350 E 82 St New York NY 10028 E-mail: mastersjj@aol.com.

MASTERS, LEE, broadcast executive; married; 2 children. Student, Temple U. Various positions including programmer, sta. mgr., owner radio stas.; exec. v.p., gen. mgr. MTV, 1986—89; pres., CEO E! Entertainment TV, 1990—98; founder, pres., CEO Liberty Digital, 1999—2002; mem. bd. of dir. LodgeNet Entertainment Corp., 2002—. Conf. co-chair CTAM '96. Mem.: Nat. Cable TV Assn. (pub. affairs com., co-chair state and local govt. com., Vanguard award for programmers 1995). Office: LodgeNet Entertainment Corp 3900 W Innovation St Sioux Falls SD 57107

MASTERS, ORLAN VINCENT WADE, gynecologist; b. Corona, Calif., Feb. 29, 1920; s. Francis Wakeman and Grace Elizabeth (Wade) M.; m. Marilyn Jean Miss, June 19, 1949 (div. Sept. 1972); children: Michael Vincent Wade, Martin Wakeman, Susan Lynne, Matthew Christian; m. Judy Jay Alves, Aug. 26, 1975. BA, Stanford U., 1949, MD, 1953. Diplomate Am. Bd. Ob-Gyn. Intern L.A. County Gen. Hosp., 1952-53; resident in gen. practice Kern Gen. Hosp., Bakersfield, Calif., 1953-54; resident in ob-gyn. Akron (Ohio) City Hosp., 1954-58; chief res. ob-gyn. Akron City Hosp., 1957-58; resident in ob-gyn. Chgo. Lying-In-Hosp., U. Chgo., 1956; mem. cons. staff St. Mary's Hosp., Ga., 1973—; mem. courtesy staff Athens (Ga.) Regional Med. Ctr., 1973—; asst. clin. prof. ob-gyn. Med. Coll. Ga., Augusta, 1973—99; dir. Women's Clinic U. Ga. Health Svc., Athens, 1975-96. Reproductive health cons. Clarke County Health Dept., Athens, 1973—. Bd. dirs. Friends of Ga. State Art Mus., Athens, 1994; dir. Colposcopic clinic, N.E. Ga. Health Dist., Ga., 1996—; active Athens Clarke Heritage Found. Fellow ACOG, ACS; mem. AMA, Am. Soc. for Colposcopy and Cervical Pathology. Office: Clarke County Health Dept 345 N Harris St Athens GA 30601-2411

MASTERS, ROBERT EDWARD LEE, psychotherapist, neural researcher, human potential educator, philosopher; b. Jan. 4, 1927; s. Robert and Katherine (Leeper) Masters; m. Jean Houston, May 8, 1965. BA in Philosophy, U. Mo., 1951; PhD in Clin. Psychology, Humanistic Psychology Inst., 1974. Dir. Libr. of Sex Rsch., N.Y.C., 1962-66, Sensory Imagery Program, 1965-68; dir. rsch. Found. for Mind Rsch., N.Y.C. and Ashland, Oreg., 1965—. Dir. Zarathustra Project, Pomona, 1980—99; co-dir. Human Capacities Tng. Program, Ramapo, NJ, 1982—99; pvt. practice psychotherapy, neural re-edn., aging and geropsychology programs; prin. tchr. Hypnotherapist Tng., Pomona, 1982—99; pres. Human Capacities Corp., Ashland, 1982—. Author: Eros and Evil, 1962, Forbidden Sexual Behavior and Morality, 1964; co-author (with J. Houston): Varieties of Psychedelic Experience, 1966, Psychedelic Art, 1968; author: Mind Games, 1972, Listening to the Body, 1978, Psychophysical Method Exercises, vols. I-VI, 1983, The Goddess Sekhmet, 1987, The Masters Technique, 1987, Neurospeak, 1994, The Way to Awaken, 1997, Swimming Where Madmen Drown, 2002; contbr. articles to sci. publs., poetry, fiction and essays to profl. jours., lit. and art criticism and book revs.; author: Sekhmet-Images and Entrances, 2003. With USN, 1945—46, PTO. Grantee, Erickson Found., 1966, Kleiner Found., 1968, Babcock Found., 1970, Doris Duke Found., 1972. Fellow: Am. Acad. Clin. Sexologists (founder); mem.: AAAS, APA, N.Y. Acad. Scis., Am. Psychotherapy Assn. (diplomate), Assn. Humanistic Psychology, Am. Assn. Sex Educators, Counselors and Therapists, Am. Bd. Sexology (clin. supr.). Office: Found Mind Rsch PMB 501 2305 Ashland St Ste C Ashland OR 97520-3777

MASTERS, ROGER DAVIS, government and neurotoxicology educator; b. Boston, June 8, 1933; s. Maurice and S. Grace (Davis) M.; m. Judith Ann Rubin, June 6, 1956 (div. 1984); children— Seth J., William A., Katherine R.; m. Susanne R. Putnam, Aug. 25, 1984 BA, Harvard U., 1955; MA, U. Chgo., 1958, PhD, 1961; MA (hon.), Dartmouth Coll., 1974. Instr. dept. polit. sci. Yale U., 1961-62, asst. prof., 1962-67; assoc. prof. dept. govt. Dartmouth Coll., Hanover, N.H., 1967-73, prof., 1973-98, John Sloan Dickey Third Century prof., 1980-85, chmn. dept., 1986-89, Nelson A. Rockefeller prof., 1991-98, prof. emeritus, 1998—, rsch. prof., 1999—. Cultural attache Am. Embassy, Paris, 1969-71; chmn. France-Am. Commn. Ednl. and Cultural Exch., 1969-71; vis. lectr. Yale U. Law Sch., 1988-89, Vt. Law Sch., 1993-94; sect. editor Social Sci., Info., 1971—; chmn. exec. com. Gruter Inst. Law and Behavioral Rsch., 1995-98; pres. Found. for Neurosci. and Soc., 1998—. *Since formal retirement, Roger D. Masters continued teaching (until last Spring) and research (pursued with great intensity). Over the last 30 years, his primary focus shifted from political philosophy to using contemporary biology to understanding human social behavior. He is deeply indebted to Mike Coplan, a chemical engineer who questioned the effects of treating public water supplies with either hydrofluosilic acid or sodium silicofluoride.*

Equally important is his debt to Lionel Tiger and Mike McGuire, with whom he's collaborated in consulting projects using the perspective of evolutionary biology to illuminate long range problems in several policy areas. His career may now contribute to public policies in areas as diverse as health and relations with foreign societies. Author; The Nation Is Burdened, 1967, The Political Philosophy of Rousseau, 1968, The Nature of Politics, 1989, Beyond Relativism, 1993, Machiavelli, Leonardo, and the Science of Power, 1996, Fortune is a River, 1998; editor: Rousseau's Discourses, 1964, Rousseau's Social Contract, 1978; co-editor: Ostracism: A Social and Biological Phenomenon, 1986, Collected Writings of J.J. Rousseau, 1990—, Primate Politics, 1991, The Sense of Justice, 1992, The Neurotransmitter Revolution, 1994; editor Gruter Inst. Reader in Biology, Law, and Human Social Behavior, 1992. Served with AUS, 1955-57. Fulbright fellow Inst. d'Etudes Politiques, Paris, 1958-59, joint Yale U.-Social Sci. Rsch. Coun. fellow, 1964-65, Guggenheim fellow, 1967-68, Hastings Ctr. for Ethics and Life Scis. fellow, 1973-78. Mem. AAAS, Am. Polit. Sci. Assn., Assn. Polit. and Life Sci. (coun.), Am. Soc. for Legal and Polit. Philosophy, Internat. Soc. Human Ethology, Human Behavior Evolution Soc. Office: Dartmouth Coll Dept Govt Silsby Hall HB6108 Hanover NH 03755 Home: Valley Terrace Apt 214 2820 Christian St White River Junction VT 05001 Business E-Mail: roger.d.masters@dartmouth.edu.

MASTERSON, CARLIN See GLYNN, CARLIN

MASTERSON, CHESTER W. otolaryngologist, state representative; b. Ortman County, Miss., Feb. 26, 1933; m. Martha Masterson; 4 children. MD, U. Tenn., 1960. Resident U. Tulane Med. Ctr., New Orleans, 1962—65; otolaryngologist Army Med. Corps., 1953—56, Pvt. Practice, 1956—77; lobbyist Eye Physicians, Miss. Med. Assn.; rep. Ho. of Reps., Jackson, Miss., 1999—. Mem. County Affairs, Ins., Judiciary B, Pub. Health and Welfare coms. Miss. Ho. Reps., Jackson, 1999—. Mem.: NRA, Jaycees, Miss. Right to Life, Rotary Club (past pres. Vicksburg chpt.). Republican. Office: Dist Office 1845 Hwy 27 Vicksburg MS 39180 E-mail: cmasterson@mail.house.state.ms.us.

MASTERSON, ELLEN HORNBERGER, accountant; b. Ft. Smith, Ark., Feb. 19, 1951; d. Evans Zacharias and Nancy Cravens (Eads) H.; m. Conrad J. Masterson, Jr., Sept. 26, 1987. BA, Emory U., 1973; MBA, So. Meth. U., 1978. CPA, Mass. Staff acct. Coopers & Lybrand, Boston, 1973, gen. practice ptnr. Dallas, 1985—97; CFO Am. Gen. Corp., Houston, 1997—99; ptnr. PricewaterhouseCoopers, N.Y.C., 1999—. Instr. Sch. Mgmt. and Adminstrv. Scis., U. Tex., Dallas, 1980-81. Bd. dirs. Shakespeare Festival Dallas, 1983-86, Leadership Dallas, 1985-86, USA Film Festival, 1986-88, Dental Health Program, Inc., 1986-88; mem. Jr. League, The 500, Inc.; workshop leader, vol. Cmty. Bd. Inst.; cons. Ctr. for Non Profit Mgmt. Mem. AICPA, Mass. Soc. CPAs, Tex. CPAs, So. Meth. U. MBA Alumni Assn., Kappa Kappa Gamma, Alpha Iota Delta, Beta Gamma Sigma. Presbyterian. Office: PricewaterhouseCoopers 1301 Ave of Americas New York NY 10019

MASTERSON, JAMES FRANCIS, psychiatrist; b. Phila., Mar. 25, 1926; s. James Francis and Evangeline (O'Boyle) M.; m. Patricia Cooke, Jan. 28, 1950; children: James F., Richard K., Nancy. BS, U. Notre Dame, 1947; MD, Jefferson Med. Sch., Phila., 1951. Diplomate Am. Bd. Psychiatry, Am. Bd. Neurology. Intern Phila. Gen. Hosp., 1951-52; resident in psychiatry Payne Whitney Clinic, N.Y. Hosp., N.Y.C., 1952-55, chief resident, 1955-56, dir. adolescent OPD, 1956-66, head adolescent program, 1968-75, asst. attending psychiatrist, 1956-60, assoc. attending psychiatrist, 1960-70, attending psychiatrist, 1970—, dir. The Symptomatic Adolescent Research Project, 1957-67; dir. Masterson Group, P.C. for Study and Treatment Personality Disorders, N.Y.C., 1977—. Author: Psychotherapy of the Borderline Adolescent, Psychotherapy of the Borderline Adult, Countertransference, Narcissistic Personality Disorder, The Real Self, The Psychiatric Dilemma of Adolescence, The Test of Time: From Borderline Adolescent to Functioning Adult; contbr. articles to profl. jours. Fellow Am. Psychiat. Assn., Am. Coll. Psychoanalysts; mem. AMA, Am. Coll. Psychoanalysis, N.Y. Soc. Adolescent Psychiatry (founder, past pres.), N.Y. County Med. Soc. Office: 60 Sutton Pl S New York NY 10022-4168 Office Phone: 212-751-4992. E-mail: mastersnin@aol.com.

MASTERSON, JOHN PATRICK, retired English language educator; b. Chgo., Mar. 15, 1925; s. Michael Joseph and Delia Frances (Dolan) M.; m. Jean Frances Wegrzyn, Aug. 18, 1956; children: Mary Beth, Michael, Maureen, Laura. BA, St. Mary of the Lake, 1947; MA, De Paul U., 1952; PhD, U. Ill., 1961. Chmn. English dept. De Paul U., Chgo., 1964-67, head humanities div., 1967-70, prof. English, 1970, dean Coll. Liberal Arts and Scis., 1970-76, prof. mgmt., 1976-80, 82-87, prof. emeritus, 1988—, dean Grad. Sch., 1980-82. Cons. in field. Recipient award Shell Oil Co., 1968, Via Sapientiae award De Paul U., 1987; fellow adminstrn. program Am. Coun. Edn. Roman Catholic. Home: 1922 Belleview Ave Westchester IL 60154-4345 E-mail: mastersonjj@aol.com.

MASTERSON, KENNETH RHODES, lawyer; b. Kennett, M.O., Feb. 22, 1944; s. H. Byron and Mary (Rhodes) M.; children— Michael K., Elizabeth Megel, Grace Megel BA, Westminster Coll., 1966; JD, Vanderbilt U., 1970. Bar: Mo. 1970, Tenn. 1976. Ptnr. Thomason, Crawford & Hendrix, Memphis, 1976-79; v.p. legal Fed. Express Corp., Memphis, 1980-81, sr. v.p., gen. counsel, 1981-93, sr. v.p., gen. counsel and sec., 1993-96, exec. v.p., gen. counsel and sec., 1996-98, FedEx Corp., Memphis, 1998—. Mem. ABA, Mo. Bar Assn., Am. Corp. Counsel Assn. Home: 8679 Classic Dr Memphis TN 38125-8824 Office: FedEx Corp 942 S Shady Grove Rd Memphis TN 38120-4117 Fax: 901-818-7590.*

MASTERSON, KLEBER SANLIN, JR., physicist; b. San Diego, Sept. 26, 1932; s. Kleber Sandlin and Charlotte Elizabeth (Parker) M.; m. Sara Ann Cooper, Dec. 21, 1957; children: Thomas Marshall, John Cooper. BS in Engring., U.S. Naval Acad., 1954; MS in Physics, USN Postgrad. Sch., 1960; PhD in Physics, U. Calif., San Diego, 1963; postgrad. Advanced Mgmt. Program, Harvard Bus. Sch., 1981-82. Commd. ensign USN, 1954, advanced through grades to rear adm., 1979; comdg. officer USS Preble, Pearl Harbor, Hawaii, 1969-71; mgr. antiship missile def. project USN, Washington, 1974-77, exec. asst. to sec. of Navy, 1977-79, asst. dep. comdr. Naval Sea Systems Command, 1979-81, chief Studies, Analyses and Gaming Agy., 1981-82, ret., 1982; prin. Booz, Allen and Hamilton, Inc., Arlington, Va., 1982-87, v.p. and ptnr., 1987-92; sr. v.p. Sci. Applications Internat. Corp., 1992 94; pres. The Riverside Group, Ltd., 1994—. Bd. control U.S. Naval Inst., Annapolis, Md., 1971-82; bd. dirs. Mil. Ops. Rsch. Soc., 1984-90, pres., 1988-89; mem. divsn. rev. com. TSA divsn. Los Alamos Nat. Lab., 1996-2001, chmn. 1998-2001. Editor: Book of Navy Songs, 1954; contbr. articles on plasma and theoretical nuclear physics, computer science, radars, ops. rsch. to profl. publs. Active Historic Alexandria Resources Commn., 1998—, vice-chmn. 2001-02, chmn., 2002-04. Mem. Am. Phys. Soc., U.S. Naval Acad. Alumni Assn. (pres. Washington chpt. 1989-90), U.S. Naval Acad. Found. (trustee 1991—), Soc. of the Cin. (chmn. edn. com. 1997-2001, asst. sec. gen. 2001-2004, editor Cin. Fourteen 2001-04, treas. gen. 2004-), Mass. Soc. of the Cin. (v.p. 1999-2001, pres. 2001-04), Sigma Xi. Achievements include development of NELIAC computer program and strategic simulation methodology. Home and Office: The Riverside Group Ltd 101 Pommander Walk Alexandria VA 22314-3844 Office Phone: 703-548-6183. E-mail: skidmasterson@cs.com.

MASTERSON, MARY STUART, actress; b. N.Y.C., June 28, 1966; d. Peter and Carlin Glynn Masterson. Theatre appearances include Alice in Wonderland, 1982, Been Taken, 1985, The Lucky Spot, 1987, Lily Dale, 1987, Three Sisters, 1991; TV movies include Love Lives On, 1985, City in Fear, 1980, Lily Dale, 1996, On the 2nd Day of Christmas, 1997; films: The Stepford Wives, 1975, Heaven Help Us, 1984, At Close Range, 1985, My Little Girl, 1986, Gardens of Stone, 1987, Some Kind of Wonderful, 1987, Mr. North, 1988, Chances Are, 1989, Immediate Family, 1989, Funny About Love, 1990, Married To It, 1990, Fried Green Tomatoes, 1991, Benny and Joon, 1993, Bad Girls, 1994, Radioland Murders, 1994, Heaven's Prisoners, 1996, Bed of Roses, 1996, Digging to China, 1997, Dogtown, 1997, The Postman, 1997, The Florentine, 1998, The Book of Stars, 1999, Black and Blue, 1999, The Book of Stars, 2000, Leo, 2002, West of Here, 2002; dir., writer for Showtime 2000; TV guest appearances include Amazing Stories, 1985, Inside the Actors Studio, 1994. Office: Creative Artists Agency 9830 Wilshire Blvd Beverly Hills CA 90212-1825

MASTERSON, PETER, actor, director; b. Houston, June 1, 1934; s. Carlos Bee and Josephine Yeager (Smith) M.; m. Carlin Glynn, Dec. 29, 1960; children: Carlin Alexandra, Mary Stuart, Peter Carlos. BA in History, Rice U., 1957. Appeared in Broadway plays Marathon '33, 1963, Blues for Mr. Charlies, 1964; title role in Trial of Lee Harvey Oswald, 1967; appeared in The Great White Hope, 1968, That Championship Season, 1974, The Poison Tree, 1975, (films) The Exorcist, 1972, Man on a Swing, 1973, The Stepford Wives, 1974; playwright The Best Little Whorehouse in Texas, 1978; dir. Broadway prodns. The Best Little Whorehouse in Texas, 1978 (Drama Desk award for Best Dir. of Musical 1978); co-dir., co-writer The Best Little Whorehouse Goes Public, 1994; dir. off-Broadway prodns. The Cover of Life, 1994, The Young Man from Atlanta (Pulitzer prize 1995); screenwriter The Best Little Whorehouse in Texas, 1980; prodr. (TV film) City in Fear, 1980; dir. films The Trip to Bountiful, 1985, Blood Red, 1986, Full Moon in Blue Water, 1987, Night Game, 1988, Convicts, 1989, Arctic Blue, 1993, Lily Dale, 1996, The Only Thrill, 1997, Mermaid, 1999, Lost Junction, 2001. Mem. AFTRA, SAG, Actors Equity Assn., Soc. Stage Dirs. and Choreographers, Writers Guild Am., Actors Studio, Dirs. Guild Am., Seawanhaka Club, Corinthian Yacht Club, Tex. Corinthian Yacht Club.

MASTERSON, WILLIAM A. retired judge; b. N.Y.C., June 25, 1931; s. John Patrick and Helen Audrey (O'Hara) M.; m. Julie Dohrmann Cosgrove, children: Mark, Mary, Timothy, Barbara. BA, UCLA, 1953, JD, 1958. Bar: Calif. 1959, U.S. Supreme Ct. 1965. Assoc. Sheppard, Mullin, Richter & Hampton, L.A., 1952-62, pntr., 1962-79; ptnr. Rogers & Wells, 1979-83, Skadden, Arps, Slate, Meagher & Flom, 1983-87; judge L.A. Superior Ct., 1987-92; justice Ct. Appeals, 1993-2000; ret., 2000. Author, editor: Civil Trial Practice: Strategies and Techniques, 1986. With inf. U.S. Army, 1953-55. Fellow Am. Coll. Trial Lawyers; mem. Order of Coif. Office: PO Box 190 Mendocino CA 95460

MASTHAY, MARK BUELL, chemist, educator, research scientist; b. La Jolla, Calif., Oct. 28, 1955; s. Maurice Buell and Mary Rose Masthay; m. Jean Ritchart Ritchart, Aug. 13, 1981; children: Tyler Maurice, Tara Briana, Thomas Mark, Timothy James, Theodore Joseph, Thaddeus John. BA, U. Calif., San Diego, 1978; MS, U. Calif., Riverside, 1984; PhD, Carnegie-Mellon U., 1988. Asst. prof. chemistry Drake U., Des Moines, 1988—95, Murray (Ky.) State U., 1996—; vis. prof. chemistry N.Mex Highlands U., Las Vegas, N.Mex., 1995—96. Contbr. articles to profl. jours. Sunday sch. tchr. Evang. Covenant Ch., Des Moines, 1993—95; mem. staff Campus Crusade for Christ, Orlando, Fla., 1978—82. Recipient Student Travel award, Am. Soc. Photobiology, 1987; grantee, NIH, 1996—2000; Grad. Student Rsch. fellow, IBM, 1985—87. Mem.: Ky. Acad. Scis. (assoc.). Republican. Achievements include research in characterization of laser-induced color changes in model visual pigments related to diseases of the retina; development of theoretical model to explain electron correlation in excited states of alternant hydrocarbons; theoretical model which explains rapid color change in animals. Avocations: guitar, travel. Home: 1718 Melrose Ct Murray KY 42071 Office: Murray State U Dept Chemisty 456 Blackburn Science Building Murray KY 42071-3346 Personal E-mail: mark.masthay@murraystate.edu. E-mail: mark.masthay@murraystate.edu.

MASTOR, HELEN, career planning administrator, educator; m. Arthur A. Mastor; children: Eric, Elena. BA, UCLA; MA, Calif. State Northridge, L.A., 1986; PhD, Calif. Coast U., 1993. Pvt. composer/tchr., L.A.; sch. psychologist L.A. Unified Sch. Dist.; counselor Sedona (Ariz.) Red Rock H.S.; student svcs. counselor Yavapai Coll. Sedona Ctr. Mem.: Ariz. Assn. Women in C.C. Avocations: composing music, digital media. Home: 73 El Camino Real Sedona AZ 86336

MASTRIAN, JAMES P. retail executive; BS in Pharmacy, U. Pitts., 1965. With People's, 1965; pres. Gray Drug Fair; sr. v.p. mktg. and merchandising Sherwin Williams Paint Stores; exec. v.p. mktg. Revco Drugstores; sr. v.p. Officemax; exec. v.p. category mgmt. Rite Aid, Camp Hill, Pa., 1998-99, exec. v.p. mktg., 1999—. Office: Rite Aid Corp 30 Hunter Ln Camp Hill PA 17011-2410

MASTRO, DANNY FRANK, protective services official; b. Pacoima, Calif., Nov. 26, 1951; s. Joseph and Rosemary Mastro; m. Valerie Mastro, Dec. 4, 1998; 1 stepchild, Andrew Herbert; 1 child from previous marriage, Nicole 1 stepchild from previous marriage, Ray. AA in Adminstr. Justice, Mission Coll., 1975. Cert.: L.A. Police Acad. 1976, Month-long police officers standards on tng. (supr.). Rookie L.A. Police Dept., 1976—77; probationary officer W. Valley Divsn., San Fernando, Calif., 1977—78; officer-jail divsn. Downtown L.A., 1978; officer-spl. problems unit Devonshire Divsn., San Fernando, Calif., 1978—85; tng. officer W. L.A. Divsn., 1985—86; sr. lead officer Foothill Divsn., San Fernando Valley, Calif., 1986—91; sgt. Pacific Divsn., W. L.A., 1989—91; officer in charge W. Valley Gang unit, San Fernando Valley, Calif., 1991—94, asst. watch comdr., 1994—98, Devonshire Divsn., San Fernando Valley, Calif., 1998—2002; security profl. Advanced-Tech Security Svc., Inc., N. Hollywood, Calif., 2003—. Adv. bd. adminstr. justice L.A. Mission Coll., Sylmac, Calif., 2003—. Featured (documentaries) Save Our Streets, L.A. Police Dept., spokesman (news media); prodr.: (documentaries) Neighborhood Watch (recognition from L.A. Police Dept, offl. from Mex., Guatemala, El Salvador, 1992), (Anti-Drug Billboard Campaign) Kings & Raiders. Mem. Cmty. Network Leaders, Granada Hills, 2003—; supported-,vol. Head Start Pre-Schoolers; fundraiser Spl. Olympics, L.A., 1995—97; coord. food drive donated to Regional Food Bank. E3 USN, 1970—71, Viet Nam. Recipient Humanitarian of the Yr., Police Protectors Assn., 1993, Cert. of Spl. Congl. Recognition, Congressman Brad Sherman, 1997, Valley Cmty. Legal Found. Law Enforcement award, Councilwoman Laura Chick, 1997, Recognition: County L.A. Outstand Svc., Councilman Zev Yarolavsky, 1997, Police Officer of the Yr., Woodland Hills post 826 Am. Legion Dept., 1992, Law Enforcement Torch Run for Spl. Olympics award, Tri-Valley-UCLA Games, 1998, Fighting Hunger Giving Hope award, 1998, Commendation, awarded by Gov. George Deukmejian, 1989, awarded by Gov. Pete Wilson, 1988, awarded by Councilman Joel Wachs, 1989. Republican. Christian. Studio: Sony Pictures Entertainment 1202 W Wash Blvd Culver City CA 90232 Home Fax: 805-579-0714. Personal E-mail: sgtdawson50@msn.com.

MASTROGIANNIS, DIMITRIOS S. obstetrician/gynecologist, perinatologist; b. Athens, Greece, June 17, 1958; s. Stamatios and Potitsa-Nota M.; m. Marianna Kapsali, Oct. 24, 1986; children: Stamatios-George, Alexander-John, Dimitrios Nicholas. MD, U. Patras, 1983, PhD, 1989. Diplomate Am. Bd. Obstetrics and Gynecology, Maternal and Fetal Medicine. Resident ob/gyn, 1985-89; fellowship in maternal/fetal medicine, 1989-91; dir. perinatal rsch. unit Temple U., Phila., 1991-94; assoc. dir. obstetrics Winthrop U. Hosp., Mineola, N.Y., 1994-95; dir. maternal fetal medicine Good Samaritan Hosp., West Islip, N.Y., 1996—; clin. prof. obgyn. Coll. Osteopathic Medicine Univ. N.Y. Coll., 1999—. Asst. prof. ob/gyn, Temple U., 1991-94; developer, mem. Am. Inst. Ultrasound in Medicine. Contbr. articles to profl. jours. Recipient award So. Med. Assn., 1990. Fellow Am. Coll. Ob/Gyn.; mem. AMA, Am. Assn. Gynecol. Laparoscopists, Soc. Perinatal Obstetricians. Home: 42 Talisman Dr Dix Hills NY 11746-5323

MASTROIANNI, LUIGI, JR., physician, educator; b. New Haven, Nov. 8, 1925; s. Marion (Dallas) Mastroianni; m. Elaine Catherine Pierson, Nov. 4, 1957; children: John James, Anna Catherine, Robert Luigi. AB, Yale U., 1946; MD, Boston U., 1950, DSc (hon.), 1973; MA (hon.), U. Pa., 1970. Diplomate Am. Bd. Ob-Gyn. and Reproductive Endocrinology and Infertility. Intern, then resident ob.-gyn. Met. Hosp. N.Y., 1950—54; fellow rsch. Harvard Med. Sch. and Free Hosp. for Women, Boston, 1954—55; instr. dept. ob-gyn. Yale U. Sch. Medicine, New Haven, 1955—56; asst. prof. ob.-gyn. dept. Yale U., New Haven, 1956—61; prof. U. Calif., L.A., 1961—65; chief ob-gyn Harbor Gen. Hosp., L.A., 1961—65; William Goodell prof. ob.-gyn., chmn. dept. U. Pa. Sch. of Medicine, Phila., 1965—87, William Goodell prof. ob.-gyn. dept., dir. human reproduction div., 1987—96. Contbr. articles to profl. jours. Recipient Squibb prize, Pacific Coast Fertility Soc., 1965, Christian R. and Mary Lindback award, 1969, Gold medal, Barren Found., 1977, King Faisal prize in medicine, 1989, Pub. Recognition award, Assn. Profls. of Gynecology and Obstetrics, 1990, Disting. Svc. award, Soc. Study Reprodn., 1992, Rector's medal, U. Chile, 1993, Axel Munthe award, 1996, Resolve Svc. award, 1997, medal, Coll. Physicians of Phila., 1998. Mem.: Soc. for Study of Reprodn. (Disting. Svc. award 1992), Endocrine Soc., Soc. for Exptl. Biology and Medicine, Soc. Gynecology Investigation (Disting. Scientist award 2004), Inst. of Medicine of NAS, Am. Physiol. Soc., Am. Soc. for Reproductive Medicine, Am. Gynecol. Club, Am. Gynecol. and Obstet. Soc., ACOG, ACS, Chilean Soc. Ob-Gyn. (hon.), Uruguan Soc. Sterility and Fertility (hon.), Israel Soc. Ob Gyn. (hon.), Soc. Espanola de Fertilidad (hon.), Peruvian Fertility Soc. (hon.), Argentina Fertility Soc. (hon.), Italian Soc. Ob-Gyns. (hon.), Brazilian Fertility Soc. (hon.), Assn. Profs. Ob-Gyn. (hon.), N.C. Gynecol. Soc. (hon.), Tex. Assn. Ob-Gyns. (hon.), Ctrl. Assn. Ob-Gyns. (hon.), Pacific Coast Fertility Soc. (hon.), Alpha Omega Alpha, Sigma Xi. Home: 561 Ferndale Ln Haverford PA 19041-1614 Office: Pa Fertility Care 3701 Market Sq Fl 8 Philadelphia PA 19104-5509

MASTROIANNI, THOMAS OWEN, musician, music educator; b. Pitts., Sept. 1, 1934; s. Lawrence Andrew and Julie Agnes Mastroianni; m. MaryAnn Prosser, Jan. 25, 1964; children: Mary Lauren, Michael, Elizabeth. BS, Juilliard Sch., 1957, MS, 1958; MusD, Ind. U., 1969. Chmn. piano, chmn. applied music Tex. Tech U., Lubbock, 1961—72; prof., dean Sch. Music Cath. U. Am., Washington, 1972—81, prof., chmn. piano, 1981—2000, prof. emeritus, 2000—; co-founder, mem. faculty Amalfi Coast (Italy) Music Festival, 1995—. Found. dir. Washington Internat. Competition, 2001—. Contbr. articles to profl. publs.;, musician numerous piano recitals. Choir dir. various chs., Pitts., N.Y., Washington, 1948—73. With U.S. Army, 1958—60. Recipient medal, Hungarian Liszt Soc., 1992. Mem.: World Pedagogy Conf. (wellness com. 2001—03), Nat. Assn. Schs. Music (grad. commr. 1975—81), Interam. Friends of Music (treas. 1980—), Music Tchrs.' Nat. Assn., Am. Liszt Soc. (exec. sec. 1974—99, pres. 1999—). Roman Catholic. Avocations: tennis, museums, concerts.

MASTROMARINO, JOHN, diversified financial services company executive; Grad., St. Michael's Coll. Commd. Nat. Bank Examiner U.S. Treasury Dept., 1983. Chief risk officer Bank of Boston Corp.; exec. v.p. for risk mgmt. FleetBoston Fin. Corp., Boston, 1999—2002; sr. v.p., chief risk officer John Hancock Fin. Svcs., Inc., Boston, 2003—. Office: John Hancock Fin Svcs Inc John Hancock Pl PO Box 111 Boston MA 02117

MASUCCI, NICHOLAS J. engineering company executive; With The Louis Berger Group, 1975—, leader, environ. ops., 1984—94; pres. VMS, Inc., Richmond, Va., 1995—2002; CEO, pres. The Louis Berger Group, East Orange, NJ, 2002—. Recipient INC 500 award, INC Mag., 2000. Office: Louis Berger Group 100 Halsted St East Orange NJ 07018

MASUI, YOSHIO, zoology educator; b. Kyoto, Oct. 6, 1931; arrived in Can., 1969; s. Fusa and Toyo Masui; m. Yuriko Masui, May 9, 1959; children: Sayuri, Hitoshi. BSc, Kyoto U., 1953, MSc, 1955, PhD, 1961; DSc (hon.), U. Toronto, 1999. Asst. prof. Konan U., Kobe, Japan, 1965; rsch. staff biologist Yale U., New Haven, 1966-69, lectr., 1969; assoc. prof. U. Toronto, Ont., 1969-78, prof., 1978-97, prof. emeritus, 1997—, Konan U., 1999—. Recipient Manning award Manning Found., Calgary, Alta., 1991, Gairdner Internat. award Gairdner Found., Toronto, 1992, Albert Lasker Basic Med. Rsch. award, Lasker Found., 1998; named Officer, Order of Canada, 2003. Fellow Royal Soc. London. Achievements include discovery of Maturation Promoting Factor (MPF) and Cytostatic Factor (CSF) and their roles in cell divison control. Office: U Toronto Dept Zoology 25 Harbord St Toronto ON Canada M5S 3G5 E-mail: masui@zoo.utoronto.ca.

MASULLO, ALFREDO SALVATORE, dermatologist; b. Weehawken, N.J., June 27, 1949; s. Gustavo and Natalina (Caridi) Masullo; m. Linda Bonura, 1983. BA, Rutgers U., 1971; MD, U. Medicine and Dentistry N.J., Newark, 1975. Diplomate Am. Bd. Dermatology. Intern in internal medicine U. Medicine and Dentistry N.J., 1975-76, resident, 1976-77; resident in dermatology St. Lukes, Roosevelt and Columbia-Presbyn. Med. Ctr., N.Y.C., 1977-80; pvt. practice, Hackensack, N.J., 1980—. Attending physician Hackensack Univ. Med. Ctr., 1980—, Holy Name Hosp., Teaneck, N.J., 1980—. Fellow Am. Acad. Dermatology; mem. AMA. Office: 120 Prospect Ave Hackensack NJ 07601-2256 Office Phone: 201-488-0707.

MASUNOV, ARTEM, theoretical chemist, researcher; b. Moscow, July 12, 1966; s. Eduard Sergeevich Masunov and Alla Stepanovna Masunova; life ptnr. Nadya Kobko, Oct. 27, 2002. Diploma, M.V.Lomonosov Moscow State U., 1983—88; PhD, CUNY, New York, 1994—2000. Jr. rschr. chemistry dept., Moscow State U., Moscow, 1988—92, rschr., 1992—94; adj. lectr. Hunter Coll., New York, 1994—2000; postdoctoral fellow City Coll., New York, 2000—02; postdoctoral rsch. assoc. Los Alamos Nat. Lab., N.Mex., 2002—. Grantee Travel Grant, Internat. Union Crystallography, 1992, Juniour Rsch. Grant, Internat. Sci. Found./Soros Found., 1992, Am. Crystallographic Assn., 1994; scholar Scool on Exptl. Electron Density, Argentina, International Union Crystallography, 1995. Mem.: Am. Chem. Soc. (travel grant 1997). Home: 799 6th Sr #10 Los Alamos NM 87544 Office: Los Alamos National Laboratory Mail Stop B268 Los Alamos NM 87545 Personal E-mail: amasunov@yahoo.com. E-mail: artem.masunov@lanl.gov.

MASUR, HENRY, internist; b. N.Y.C., Mar. 8, 1946; s. Jack and Barbara (Forsch) M.; m. Grace Steinacker, Jan. 14, 1979; children: Carrie, Jack, Julia. AB, Dartmouth Coll., 1968; MD, Cornell U., 1972. Diplomate Am. Bd. Internal Medicine, Am. Bd. Infectious Diseases. Intern, resident N.Y. Hosp., 1972-74; resident Johns Hopkins Hosp., Balt., 1974-75; asst. prof. Cornell Med. Coll., N.Y.C., 1978-82; asst. chief critical care medicine NIH, Bethesda, Md., 1982-83, dep. chief critical care medicine, 1983-89, chief critical care medicine, 1989—. Clin. prof. George Washington U. Med. Sch., Washington. Mem. Am. Soc. Clin. Investigation, Assn. Am. Physicians. Office: NIH Rm 7D43 9000 Rockville Pike Bethesda MD 20892-1662 Business E-Mail: hmasur@nih.gov.

MASUR, KURT, conductor; b. Brieg, Silesia, Germany, July 18, 1927; Grad., Nat. Music Schule, Breslau, Germany, 1944, Leipzig Conservatory, 1946-48; hon. degree, U. Mich., Cleve. Inst. Music, Leipzig U., Westminster Choir Coll., Hamilton Coll. Repetiteur and conductor Halle Nat. Theatre, 1948-51; conductor Erfurt City Theatre, 1951-53, Leipzig City Theatre, 1953-55, Dresden Philharm., 1955-58; gen. music dir. Mecklenburg Staatstheater, 1958-60; mus. dir. Komische Oper Berlin, 1960-64; chief conductor Dresden Philharm., 1967-72; conductor Leipzig Gewandhaus Orch., 1970-96; mus. dir. New York Philharmonic, N.Y.C., 1991—2002; conductor London Philharm. Orch., 1989-92, 2000—; music dir. Orchestre National de France, Paris, 2002—; music dir. emeritus Philharmonic Soc. of NY, 2002—. Prof. Leipzig Acad. Music, 1975—; hon. guest condr. Israel Philharm. Orch., 1992. Mailing: The London Philharmonic Orchestra 89 Albert Embankment London SE1 7TP England

MASUREL, JEAN-LOUIS ANTOINE NICOLAS, investment company executive; b. Cannes, France, Sept. 18, 1940; s. Antoine and Anne-Marie (Gallant) M.; children: Anne-Sophie, Aude. Grad., Ecoles des Hautes Etudes Commerciales, 1962; MBA, Harvard U., 1964. With Morgan Guaranty Trust Co., N.Y.C., 1964-80, v.p., gen. mgr. Paris, 1975-78, sr. v.p., 1978-80; sr. exec. v.p. Banque de Paribas, 1980-82, dep. pres., 1982-83; mng. dir. Moët-Hennessy, 1983-87, Moët-Hennessy-Louis Vuitton, 1987-89; pres. Arcos Investissement S.A., 1989—, Hediard S.A., 1991-95, Sogetel, Monaco, 2002—. Bd. dirs. Peugot S.A., Soc. des Bains de Mer (SBM) Monaco, Banque du Gothard Monaco, Oudart S.A., Gondrand. Bd. govs. Am. Hosp., Paris; hon. chmn., dir. Harvard Bus. Sch. Club France. Address: Domaine de Trians F-83136 Neoules France also: 10A rue de la Paix F 75002 Paris France

MASYS, DANIEL RICHARD, medical school director; b. Columbus, Ohio, Mar. 6, 1949; s. Paul John and Jane Marie (Mollenauer) M.; m. Linda Suzanne Bross, June 2, 1974; 1 child, Christopher. AB in Biochemistry, Princeton U., 1971; MD, Ohio State U., 1974. Diplomate Am. Bd. Internal Medicine. Staff hematologist, oncologist U.S. Naval Hosp., San Diego, 1980-84; chief ICRDB br. NIH, Bethesda, Md., 1984-86; dir. Lister Hill Nat. Ctr. Nat. Libr. Medicine, Bethesda, Md., 1986-94; dir. biomed. informatics, prof. Sch. Medicine U. Calif., San Diego, 1994—. Assoc. editor Acad. Medicine jour., 1988-91. Mem. high performance computing White House Office of Sci., Washington, 1991-94; rep. Fed. Networking Coun., Washington, 1991-94. Capt. USPHS, 1984-94. Fellow: ACP, Am. Coll. Med. Informatics (exec. com. 1989—92); mem.: Nat. Acad. Scis., Inst. Medicine, Am. Med. Informatics Assn. (bd. dirs. 1992—95, assoc. editor jour. 1993—, Pres.'s award 1992), Alpha Omega Alpha. Office: U Calif San Diego Sch Medicine Basic Sci 9500 Gilman Dr La Jolla CA 92093-0602

MATA, DAVID JOSEPH, physician; b. Houston, Feb. 3, 1956; s. José and Josephine M.; children: Daniel José, Timothy John. BA in Biology, Point Loma Coll., 1978; postgrad., Calif. State U., L.A., 1978-80; MD, U. Minn., 1987. Diplomate Am. Bd. Family Practice, Nat. Bd. Med. Examiners. Resident in family medicine San Bernardino (Calif.) County Med. Ctr., 1987-90; med. dir. Salud Med. Ctr., Woodburn, Oreg., 1990-96; pvt. practice Hemet, Calif., 1996—; med. dir. Birth Choice Med. Ctr. Adj. asst. prof. Oreg. Health Scis. U. Sch. Medicine, Portland, 1991—96; active staff mem. Salem Hosp., Oreg., 1992—96, Silverton Hosp., Oreg., 1992—96, Hemet Valley Med. Ctr., 1997—; vice-chair Family Medicine, 2000—02; cons., steering com. mem. Am. Lung Assn., Salem, 1992—94; med. dir. Ramona Manor Convalescent Hosp., 2002—. Expert witness to U.S. Congress, Oreg. Supreme Ct., 1992; counselor East L.A. Task Force, 1979-80; chaplain Boy Scouts Am., Hemet, 1998—; adv. com. San Jacinto Head Start, 1998—; vol. physician 20th World Jamboree Boy Scouts Am., Thailand, 2002-03. Geriatric Medicine fellow U. Minn., 1985, Med. Student Rsch. tng. grantee NIH, 1985, scholar Nat. Hispanic Scholarship Found, 1987; named one of 10 Outstanding Young Ams., U.S. Jr. C. of C., 1993, Outstanding Young Person of World, 1993; recipient Golden Aztec award Oreg. Human Devel. Corp., 1993, Citation of Merit award Oreg./Pacific Dist. Ch. of Nazarene, 1993, Mentorship award Dept. Family Medicine Oreg. Health Scis. U., 1993, Disting. svc. award Ch. of the Nazarene, Woodburn, Oreg., 1996; named Family Doctor of the Yr., Oreg., 1995; recipient Congl. Tribute, U.S. Ho. of Reps., 1994. Fellow Am. Acad. Family Physicians; mem. Nazarene Health Care Fellowship, Am. Acad. Family Physicians, Northwest Regional Primary Care Assn. (clinicians com. 1990-93), Riverside County Med. Assn., Calif. Med. Assn. Democrat. Mem. Ch. Of The Nazarene. Avocations: drawing, camping, family activities, church activities, public speaking. Office: Bldg B, Ste A 255 N Gilbert St Hemet CA 92543-4066

MATA, ELIZABETH ADAMS, language educator, land investor; b. Raleigh, NC, Jan. 11, 1946; d. John Quincy Adams and Beulah Honeycutt; m. Juan Mata, June 21, 1968; children: Laura, Juan, Daniel. Student, Sweet Briar Coll., Paris, 1966-67; BA in French, Randolph-Macon Women's Coll., 1968; tchr. cert. in French and Spanish, N.C. State U., 1981; postgrad., U. Salamanca, Spain, 1983-86; MA in Spanish, NYU, 1986; cert. mentor tchr., N.C. State U., 1989; postgrad., Fordham U., 1994, U. N.C., 1995. Lic. real estate agt., N.C., 1991; cert. ESL tchr., 1999; Nat. Bd. cert. in Spanish, 2003. Tchr. ESL, Am. Inst., Madrid, 1968-69; tchr. English, Ay J Garriques, Madrid, 1968-74, pvt. classes, Madrid, 1975-78; tchr. French, Wake County Sch., Cary, NC, 1982—2003, tchr. Spanish, Apex, NC, 1982—; instr. ESL Wake Tech. Coll., Raleigh, NC, 1999—2003; Fulbright tchr. U. del Mar del Plata, Argentina, 2001—. Cons. ETS, 1999—2004. Named Tchr. of Yr., Apex HS, 1992-93. Mem. Am. Assn. Tchr. Spanish and Portuguese, Univ. Coun. on Edn., Alpha Kappa Delta (Beta Omicron chpt. hist. 1996-98, v.p. 1998-2000). Democrat. Avocations: sculpting, reading, gourmet cooking, restoring antiques, writing. Home: 643 Kings Fork Rd Cary NC 27511-5711

MATA, JOSEFINA, health education coordinator; b. Juarez, Mex., Mar. 28, 1968; came to U.S., 1979; d. Angel and Irma Ulloa; m. Jesus Antonio Mata, Aug. 29, 1989; 1 child, Lizbeth Mata. BS, N.Mex. State U., 1991, MS, 1994, MPH, 1999; MBA, U. Phoenix, 2002. News translator Sta. RZOL Radio, El Paso, 1984-86; receptionist aid San Jacinto Sch., El Paso, Tex., 1985-86; nutritionist La Fe Clinic, El Paso, summer 1990; gang prevention and intervention counselor Families and Youth Inc., Las Cruces, N.Mex., 1992-93; health educator Adolescent Family Life, Las Cruces, 1993-95; health edn. and quality inspection coord. Ben Archer Health Ctr., Truth or Consequences, N.Mex., 1995-98; health edn. coord. La Clinica Familia, Las Cruces, 1998—. Mem. adv. bds. Corp. Extend in Svc., Las Cruces, 1993, Health Sci. Dept. N.Mex. State U., Las Cruces, 1995-98, Sierra County Adv. Sch., 1995-98, Am. Cancer Soc., Sierra County, N.Mex., 1995-98. Mem. cmty. involvement Kellog Found. N.Mex. state U., 1997; mem. Nat. Faculty Comenzando Bien March of Dimes Initiative. Grantee N.Mex. Dept. Health, 1994, 98, N.Mex. Teen Pregnancy Coalition peer edn. program, 1996-98; recipient Marathon Participation award Leukemia Soc. Am., 1996. Mem. MPH Assn., Am. Pub. Health Assn., USA Track & Field Assn., Mesilla Valley Track Club, Tobacco Free Coalition. Roman Catholic. Avocation: road racing.

MATALIN, MARY, political consultant; b. Chgo., Aug. 19, 1953; d. Steven and Eileen Matalin; m. Artie Arnold (div.); m. James Carville, Nov. 25, 1993; 2 children. Grad., Western Ill. Univ.; student, Hofstra Univ. With the Rep. Nat. Com., since the early 80's; polit. dir. George Bush's 1992 re-election campaign; co-host CNBC talk show, Equal Time, 1993—96; host The Mary Matalin Show; asst. to the Pres. and Counselor to the V.P., 2001—. Author (with James Carville): All's Fair: Love, War and Running for President, 1992; author: Letters to My Daughters, 2004; contbr. articles various periodicals. Office: The Office of Mary Matalin 424 S Wash St Lower Level Alexandria VA 22314 Office Phone: 703-739-6006. E-mail: mary@matalin.info.

MATALON, NORMA, travel and public relations executive; b. N.Y.C., Jan. 20, 1949; d. Albert and Suzanne Matalon. BA, Skidmore Coll., 1970. Cert. market mgmt., fin. mgmt. Am. Mgmt. Assn., computer automation. Cons., regional sales mgr. Revlon, N.Y.C., 1970-76; dir. sales, mktg. Diane Von Furstenberg Inc., N.Y.C., 1976-78; pres. Norma Matalon Cosmetic Cons., N.Y.C., 1978—, Norma Matalon Internat. Ltd., N.Y.C., 1982—. Cons. to overseas cosmetic and fragrance cos., 1986—. Patentee in field. Com. mem., April in Paris Charities, 1976—, Project Hope, 1986—, United World Coll. Schs., 1983—, Northwood Inst., 1978—, Internat. Debutante Found. Charities, 1976—, Princess Grace Found. for Arts U.S., 1984—, Am. Cancer Soc., 1976—, raffle chmn., 1985, 86, 87. Recipient Outstanding Performance award Revlon, N.Y.C., 1972. Mem. Foreign Policy Assn., N.Y.C. (Nat. Adv. Bd. 1985—), The Fragrance Found., Am. Mgmt. Assn., The Foragers of Am., Newport Preservation Soc., Royal Oak Found., Royal Acad. Art, Royal Acad. Music, Met. Mus. Art, Mus. Modern Art, Whitney Mus. Clubs: The Lansdowne (London), The American (London); Cosmopolitan (N.Y.C.), St. Anthony (N.Y.C.), New Eng. (N.Y.C.), Regency Whist (N.Y.C.), The Tuxedo of N.Y., Annabel's (London). Unitarian Universalist. Avocations: travel, vol. fundraising, foreign languages. Home: 445 E 77th St New York NY 10021-2318

MATAN, LILLIAN KATHLEEN, secondary school educator, consultant, interior designer; b. Boston, Aug. 18, 1937; d. George Francis and Lillian May (Herbert) Archambault; m. Joseph A. Matan, Aug. 6, 1960; children: Maria, Meg, Tony, Elizabeth, Joan, Molly. BS, Seton Hall Coll., 1960; MA, San Francisco State U., 1984; EdD, U. San Francisco, 1999. Tchr. St. Jane de Chantal, Bethesda, Md., 1956-60; tchr. home econs. Surrottsville (Md.) H.S., 1960-61; tchr., head home econs. dept. Bruswick (Md.) H.S., 1972-73; designer Dudley Kelley and Assocs., San Francisco, Calif., 1976-84; designer (prin.) K. Matan Antiques and Interiors, Ross, Calif., 1985-87; designer Charles Lester Assocs., San Francisco, 1987-88; dean of students St. Rose Acad., San Francisco, 1988-90; dir., asst. devel. The Branson Sch., Ross, Calif., 1990-92; prin. St. Anselm Sch., San Anselmo, Calif., 1993-94; adminstrv. head Ring Mt. Day Sch., Tiburon, Calif., 1995-96; sabbatical, 1997-98. Ednl. cons. Head Start, Frederick County, Md., 1972-73. Pres. Cath. Charities, Marin County, Calif.; mem. Ecumenical Assn. for Housing, Marin County. Mem. KM (dame), Am. Soc. of Interior Designers, Am. Assn. Family and Consumer Scis., Serra Club, Phi Delta Kappa. Democrat. Home: PO Box 1140 Ross CA 94957-1140 E-mail: lmatan6561@aol.com.

MATANKY, JAMES E. real estate developer; b. Chgo., Sept. 23, 1960; s. Eugene and Gertrude M. BS, U. Ill., 1982, JD, 1985; LLM, Cambridge U., 1991. Bar: Ill. Lawyer Epton, Mullin & Druth, Chgo., 1985-86, Much, Shelist, Freed et al, Chgo., 1986-90, Curschman, Schubel & Weiss, Hamburg, Germany, 1990; pres. Matanky Realty Group, Chgo., 1991—. Bd. dirs. Chgo. Assn. Neighborhood Devel. Corp., Mus. Contemporary Art-Chgo. Renaissance Soc. U. Chgo., West Humboldt Park Devel. Coun.; pres. Am. Friends of Hebrew U. of Jerusalem; mem. ctrl. bd. JCCs Chgo.; mentor retail devel. City of Chgo. Recipient Chgo. Neighborhood Devel. award, 2000. Avocations: rowing, piano, archeology. Office: Matanky Realty Group 1332 N Halsted St Chicago IL 60622-2624

MATARASSO, ALAN, plastic and reconstructive surgeon; b. NYC, Oct. 19, 1953; s. Daniel and Ethel (Hakim) M. BA magna cum laude, Boston U., 1975; MD, U. Miami, Miami, Fla., 1979. Diplomate Nat. Bd. Med. Examiners, 1980, Am. Bd. Plastic Surgery, 1986. Intern in dept. of gen. surgery Albert Einstein Coll. Med., Montefiore Med. Ctr., Bronx, NY, 1979-80, resident in dept. gen. surgery, 1980—83, chief resident dept. gen. surgery, 1982—83, resident and chief resident dept. of plastic surgery, 1983—85; fellow aesthetic surgery Manhattan Eye, Ear and Throat Hosp., NYU Med. Ctr., NYC, 1985, asst. attending surgeon, 1985—. Surgeon St. Luke's/Roosevelt Hosp. Ctr., 1986—; attending surgeon NY Eye and Ear Infirmary, 1986—, Beth Israel North Hosp. NY, 1988-; asst. attending surgeon, Lenox Hill Hosp., 2000-; assoc. clin. prof. plastic surgery Albert Einstein Coll. Medicine, 1996-; expert cons., State NY, Dept. Health, Office of Profl. Med. Conduct. Contbr. chpt. Encyclopedia of Flpas, Mastery in Plastic Surgery; instrnl. course vol. Plastic Surgery Ednl. Found.; editor Clinics in Plastic Surgery,; sr. sci. editor Aesthetic Surgery Jour.; numerous profl. presentations; contbr. 100 articles to profl. jours. Bd. dirs. Sephardic Home For The Aged, Bklyn.; NE reg. coord., Ultrasonic Assisted Lipoplasty Reg. Workshops, 1996-98. Recipient Physicians Recognition award AMA, 1994; named one of Best Drs. in Am. Am. Health Mag., 1996, Best Doctors in NY, NY Mag., 1996, 98, 99, Castle-Connolly Guide to the Best Drs., NY Metro Area. Fellow ACS, NY Acad. Medicine, Internat. Coll. Surgeons (USA) in Plastic Surgery; mem. Am. Assn. Plastic Surgeons (chair videotape com., 1996-99, symposium com., 1997-99, mem. teaching course subcom., 1996-, vice chair, 1998-99, program com., 1996-, Strategic Planning com., 1999-, travelling prof., 1999-2001, edu. commn., 1999-2000, time and place com., 2000-, chair, corp. sponsorship com., 2000-, rep. to products/svcs. workshop, 2000, parliamentarian, 2001-2002); mem. Am. Soc. Aesthetic Plastic Surgery, Fla. Soc. Plastic and Reconstructive Surgeons, Internat. Soc. Aesthetic Plastic Surgeons (pub. edu. com., 2000), Lipoplasty Endowment for Plastic Surgery, Assn. for Academic Surgeons, Northeastern Soc. Plastic Surgeons (chmn., aesthetic symposium, 1998-99, bd. dirs.), NY Reg. Soc. of Plastic and Reconstructive Surgery, Soc. for Acad. Surgeons, Royal Soc. Medicine, England Oversee Fellow, Am. Cleft Palate Assn., Pan Am. Med. Soc. (mem., sect. on Plastic and Reconstructive Surgery), Pan Pacific Surgical Assn., NY County Med. Soc. (Young Physician's Com., 1992-94, peer review com. I & II, 1993-, grievance com., 1993-, media com., 1993-), Med. Soc. State NY (social discipline com., 1994-, state legis. com., 1994-96), NY Reg. Soc. Plastic Surgeons, (exec. com. 1988-, sci. com. med. program chair, 1988-), NY State Soc. Surgeons, Rhinoplasty Soc., Soc. of Laparoendoscopic Surgeons, So. Med. Assn., AMA, Am. Soc. Plastic Surgeons (Young Plastic Surgeons, 1987-89, Plastic Surgery Product Assessment Commn., 1991-92, CPT/ICD 9 Coding Workshop, 1991-96, Ad Hoc Com. 1992, mktg. com, 2000), Plastic Surgery Edu. Found. (Computerized Exam, 1989, EF Teleplast, 1992-95, vis. scholar, 1993-94, Edu. Assessment, 1992, Internat. Symposia, 1993, chair, Resource Book Subcom. of Resident Information Com., 1995-98, rep. on Domsestic Clin. Symposia, 1997-, In-service Examination Com., Aesthetic and Breast Subcom., 2000, Device and Technique Assessment Com., 2000, Domestic Clin. Symposia Com., 2000), Aesthetic Surgery Edu. and Rsch. Found. (charter mem.), Skin Cancer Found. (med. adv. com., 1986-), Cancers and Careers.org (adv. bd. 2000). Office: 1009 Park Ave New York NY 10028-0936 Fax: 212-628-5000. E-mail: matarasso@aol.com.*

MATARAZZO, HARRIS STARR, lawyer; b. Portland, Oreg., July 24, 1957; s. Joseph Dominic and Ruth Wood (Gadbois) M.; m. Judith Grace Hudson, Jan. 2, 1988. AB in Polit. Sci., Brown U., 1979; JD, Northwestern Sch. Law, Portland, 1983. Bar: Oreg. 1986, U.S. Dist. Ct. Oreg. 1986, U.S. Ct. Appeals (9th cir.) 1986, U.S. Supreme Ct. 1992. With Aitchison, Imperati, Paull, Barnett and Sherwood, Portland, 1986; assoc. Parks & Bauer, Salem, Oreg., 1987-88; pvt. practice Portland, 1988—. Sprk. Mental Health and the Law conf. Med. Ednl. Svcs., Inc., 1995, 96. Contbr. to Criminal Law Handbook, 1994, 98, 2003. Mem. Hist. Preservation League Oreg., Portland, 1984—, Oreg. State Pub. Interest Rsch. Group, Portland, 1985—, The Old Ch. Soc., Portland, 1986; bd. dirs. Bosco Milligan Found., Rape Survivors Inc., 1994, Lincoln H.S. Alumni Assn., 1995—, Morrison Ctr., 1996-2001, Network Housing, Inc., Oreg. Advocacy Ctr., 1998, 2000—, Italian Businessmen's Club, InAct, Inc., Rosemont Treatment Ctr. and Sch., 1998-99, Friends of Simon Benson House, 1998-2002, Parents Anonymous, 2001-02; mem. vestry Trinity Episcopal Ch., 1992-95, 2001-04; mem. Oreg. Advocacy Ctr. Mental Health Adv. Coun., 1996-2000; mem. planned giving com. Multnomah County Libr., 1997—. Mem. ABA, Fed. Bar Assn., Oreg. State Bar Assn., Oreg. Criminal Def. Lawyers Assn. (spkr. State of Mind. conf. 1990, Property Crimes conf. 1999), Multnomah County Bar Assn. Office: Bank Am Fin Ctr 121 SW Morrison St Ste 1020 Portland OR 97204-3140

MATARAZZO, JAMES M. dean, educator; b. Stoneham, Mass., Jan. 4, 1941; s. Angelo M. and Anna M. Matarazzo; m. Alice M. Keohane, Sept. 3, 1966; children: James Jr., Susan E. BA in History and Edn., Boston Coll., 1963; MS in Libr. Sci., Simmons Coll., 1965; MA in Polit. Sci., Boston Coll., 1972; PhD in Libr. and Info. Sci., U. of Pitts., 1979. Asst. sci. libr. MIT, Cambridge, 1965—67, document libr., 1967—68, serials libr., socument libr. and head of tech. reports, 1968—69; instr. Simmons Coll. Grad. Sch. of Libr. and Info. Sci., Boston, 1969—70, asst. prof., 1970—73, assoc. prof. and assoc. dean, 1974—80, prof. and assoc. dean, 1980—88, prof., 1980—2002; sr. assoc. cons. Temple Baker & Sloane, 1980—87; vis. prof. Tex. Women's U., Tex., 1983, U. of Wash., Wash., 1985, U. of Ariz., 1987—89; vis. scholar Ernst & Young Ctr. for Info. Tech. and Strategy, 1988—90; vis. prof. U. of N.C., Chapel Hill, 1991; dean Simmons Coll. Grad. Sch. of Libr. and Info. Sci., Boston, 1994—2002. Author: (book) Corporate Library Excellence, 1990, The Value of Corporate Libraries, 1995; editor: Knowledge and Special Librarians, 1999; contbr. chapters to books, articles to profl. jour. including Pub. Libr. Jour., Jour. Acad. Librarianship. Chair Winthrop Pub. Libr. Bd. Trustees; edn. com. Boston Pub. Libr.; v.p., sec. H.W. Wilson Found., N.Y.C.; past pres. Winthrop Band Parents Assn.; peer rev. Sr. Fulbright Specialist Program. Recipient H.W. Wilson award, Beta Phi Mu, Internat. Libr. Sci. Honor Soc., 1991; Fellowship, Marion and Jasper Whiting Found., 1976—77. Master: Alise (past pres.); mem.: Spl. Libr. Assn. (bd. dirs., Chmn.'s award 1986, President's award 1988, Profl. award 1990, Cert. Excellence 1990), Coun. ALA. Republican. Roman Catholic. Office: Simmons Coll GSLIS 300 The Fenway Boston MA 02115

MATARAZZO, JOSEPH DOMINIC, psychologist, educator; b. Caiazzo, Italy, Nov. 12, 1925; (parents Am. citizens); s. Nicholas and Adeline (Mastroianni) M.; m. Ruth Wood Gadbois, Mar. 26, 1949; children: Harris, Elizabeth, Sara. Student, Columbia U., 1944; BA, Brown U., 1946; MS, Northwestern U., 1950, PhD, 1952. Fellow in med. psychology Washington U. Sch. Medicine, 1950-51; instr. Washington U., 1951-53, asst. prof., 1953-55; rsch. assoc. Harvard Med. Sch., assoc. psychologist Mass. Gen. Hosp., 1955-57; prof., head med. psychol. dept. Oreg. Health Scis. U., Portland, 1957-96, prof. behavioral neurosci., 1996—. Mem. behavioral medicine study sect. NIH; mem. nat. mental health adv. coun. NIMH; mem. bd. regents Uniformed Svcs. U. Health Scis., 1974-80. Author: Wechsler's Measurement and Appraisal of Adult Intelligence, 5th edit., 1972, (with A.N. Wiens) The Interview: Research on its Anatomy and Structure, 1972, (with Harper and Wiens) Nonverbal Communication, 1978; editor: Behavioral Health: A Handbook of Health Enhancement and Disease Prevention, 1984; editorial bd.: Jour. Clin. Psychology, 1962-96; cons. editor: Contemporary Psychology, 1962-70, 80-93, Intelligence: An Interdisciplinary Jour, 1976-90, Jour. Behavioral Medicine, 1977—, Profl. Psychology, 1978-94, Jour. Cons. and Clin. Psychology, 1978-85; editor: Psychology series Aldine Pub. Co, 1964-74; psychology editor: Williams & Wilkins Co, 1974-77; contbr. articles to psychol. jours. With USNR, 1943-47; capt. Res. Recipient Hofheimer prize Am. Psychiat. Assn., 1962 Fellow AAAS, APA (pres. 1989-90), Am. Psychiat. Assn. (divsn. health psychology 1978-89, mem. coun. reps. 1982-91, bd. dirs. 1986-90, Ann. Disting. Profl. Contbn. award 1991, Annual Gold Medal for Life Achievement in the Application of Psychology 2001); mem. Western Psychol. Assn. (pres. 1986-97), Am. Assn. State Psychology Bds. (pres. 1963-64), Nat. Assn. Mental Health (bd. dirs.), Oreg. Mental Health Assn. (bd. dirs., pres. 1962-63), Internat. Coun. Psychologists (bd. dirs. 1972-74, pres. 1976-77), Am. Psychol. Found. (pres. 1994-2000). Home: 1934 SW Vista Ave Portland OR 97201-2455 Office: Oreg Health Scis U Sch Medicine 3181 SW Sam Jackson Park Rd Portland OR 97201-3011 Fax: 503-494-5972. Office Phone: 503-494-8644. Business E-Mail: matarazz@ohsu.edu.

MATARAZZO, PATRICIA ANN, media specialist; b. Oceanside, NY, Apr. 14, 1958; d. Rosario Frank and Carmella Theresa Pulitano; m. Michael A. Matarazzo, Sept. 24, 1989; 1 child, LeeAnna Constance; 1 child, Michael Francis Piscetelli. A in sci. dental hygiene, SUNY, Farmingdale, 1976—78; BA in elem. edn., SUNY, Old Westbury, 1991—93; MA in libr. and info. sci., LI U., Old Brookville, 1995—98; MA in computers and edn., LI U., Old Brookville, New York, 2001—03; SDA, SAS, Coll. New Rochelle, 1999—2001. Cert. Elem. Edn. N-6 NY, 1993, Sch. and Pub. Libr. NY, 2000. Libr. media specialist Westbury Union Free Sch. Dist., NY, 1996—. Nassau sch. libr. adv. coun. Nassau Sch. Libr. Sys., Massapequa, NY, 2000—. Author: (poetry) Milla Granson. Lector St. Brigids Ch., Westbury, NY, 1985—2003; planning bd. mem. Inc. Village Westbury, NY, 1994—98; girl scout leader Nassau County Girl Scout Assn., Garden City, NY, 2000—03. Recipient Golden Apple award, Mar. Dimes, 2000, NY State Tchr. Yr., NY State English Lang. Arts Coun., 2000, Intercounty Tchr. Ctr. Recognition award, 2004, LI Lang. Arts Coun. Tchr. award, 2000. Mem.: ALA, Sch. Libr. Media Assn., Order Sons of Italy Am. (assoc.; trustee 1992—95), Phi Beta Mu (assoc.). Catholic. Avocations: running, bicycling, travel, reading, volunteering. Home: 46 Lenox Ave Westbury NY 11590 Office: Westbury Union Free Pub Schs 2 Hitchcock La Old Westbury NY Personal E-mail: runer414@aol.com.

MATARAZZO, RUTH GADBOIS, psychologist, educator; b. New London, Conn., Nov. 9, 1926; d. John Stuart and Elizabeth (Wood) Gadbois; m. Joseph D. Matarazzo, Mar. 26, 1949; children: Harris, Elizabeth, Sara. AB, Brown U., 1948; MA, Washington U., St. Louis, 1952, PhD, 1955. Diplomate in clin. psychology and clin. neuropsychology Am. Bd. Examiners Profl. Psychology. Rsch. fellow pediat. Washington U. Med. Sch., 1954-55; rsch. fellow psychology Harvard U. Med. Sch., 1955-57; asst. prof. med. psychology Oreg. Health Scis. U., Portland, 1957-63, assoc. prof., 1963-68, prof., 1968—, prof. emeritus, 1997—. Woman liaison officer Assn. Am. Med. Coll.s, 1979—90; cons. Tillamook Job Corps, Oreg. Bd. Med. Examiners, Social Security Adminstrn., Portland Ctr. Hearing and Speech. Author (E. Greif): (book) Behavioral Approaches to Rehabilitation: Coping with Change, 1982; contbr. chapters to books, articles to profl. jours. Bd. dirs. Portland Opera Assn., Morrison Guidance Ctr. Fellow: Oreg. Psychol. Assn. (past pres.), Am. Psychol. Assn. (mem. policy and planning bd., mem. edn. and tng. bd., vice-chair accreditation bd., chair accreditation task force, accreditation bd.); mem.: AAAS, Portland Psychol. Assn. (past pres.), We. Psychol. Assn. (bd. dirs.), Sigma Xi. Home: 1934 SW Vista Ave Portland OR 97201-2455

MATARÉ, HERBERT F. physicist, consultant; b. Aachen, Germany, Sept. 22, 1912; came to U.S., 1953; s. Josef P. and Paula (Broicher) M.; m. Ursula Krenzien, Dec. 1939; children: Felicitas, Vitus; m. Elise Walbert, Dec. 1983; 1 child, Victor B. BS in Physics, Chemistry and Math., Aachen U. Geneva, 1933; MS in Tech. Physics, U. Aachen, 1939; PhD in Electronics, Tech. U. Berlin, 1942; PhD in Solid State Physics summa cum laude, Ecole Normale Supérieure, Paris, 1950. Asst. prof. physics & electronics Tech. U. Aachen, 1945—46; head of microwave receiver lab. Telefunken, A.G., Berlin, 1939—45; mgr. semicondr. lab. Westinghouse, Paris, 1946-52; founder, pres. Intermetall Corp., Düsseldorf, Fed. Republic Germany, 1952-56; head semicondr. R & D, corp. rsch. labs. Gen. Telephone & Electronics Co., N.Y.C., 1956-59; dir. rsch. semicondr. dept. Tekade, Nürnberg, Fed. Republic Germany, 1959-61; head quantum physics dept. rsch. labs. Bendix Corp., Southfield, Mich., 1961—63; tech. dir., acting mgr. hybrid microelectronics rsch. labs. Lear Siegler, Santa Monica, Calif., 1963-64; asst. chief engr. advance electronics dept. Douglas Aircraft Co., Santa Monica, 1964-66; tech. dir. McDonnell Douglas Missile Divsn., 1965—69; sci. advisor to solid state electronics group Autonetics (Rockwell Internat.), Anaheim, Calif., 1966-69; pres. Internat. Solid State Electronics Cons., L.A., 1973—. Prof. electronics U. Buenos Aires, 1953-54; vis. prof. UCLA, 1968-69, Calif. State U., Fullerton, 1969-70; dir. Compound Crystals Ltd., London, 1989—; cons. UN Indsl. Devel. Orgn.; presenter India Inst. Tech., New Delhi and Bombay, 1978. Author: Receiver Sensitivity in the UHF, 1951, Defect Electronics in Semiconductors, 1971, Conscientious Evolution, 1978, Energy, Facts and Future, 1989, (with P. Faber) Renewable Energies, 1993, Bioethics: The Ethics of Evolution and Genetic Interference, 1999; patentee of about 60 patents including first European transistor (1948), first vacuum growth of silicon crystals with levitation, growth of bicrystals, first low temperature transistor with bicrystals, optical heterodyning with bicrystals, first crystal TV transmission link, first color TV transmission over fiber with LEDs and bicrystals, liquid phase epitaxy for LEDs and batch process for III-V-solar cells; contbr. over 100 articles to profl. jours. Fellow IEEE (life); mem. AAAS, IEEE Nuclear Plasma Scis. Soc., IEEE Power Engring. Soc., Inst. for Advancement of Man (hon.), Am. Phys. Soc. (solid state div.), Electrochem. Soc., Am. Vacuum Soc. (thin film div.), Materials Rsch. Soc., N.Y. Acad. Scis. (emeritus). Avocations: astrophysics, biology, classical music, piano. Personal E-mail: hf.matare@verizon.net. Business E-Mail: hf.matare@gmx.de.

MATARIC', MAJA, engineering educator; PhD, MIT, Cambridge. Asst. prof. Brandeis U., Waltham, Mass., 1995—97, U. So. Calif., LA, 1997—2001, assoc. prof., 2001—. Founding dir. Ctr. for Robotics and Embedded Sys., LA, 2002; co-director USC Robotics Lab, LA, 2002—. Named one of TR 100 Young Investigators, MIT Tech. Rev., 1999; recipient NSF Career award, NSF, 1996-2001, Early Career award, IEEE Robotics and Automation Soc., 2000, Young Investigator award, USC Sch. of Engring., 2000. Mem.: ISAB, AAAI (exec. com.), IEEE.

MATAS, MYRA DOROTHEA, interior architect, designer, consultant; b. San Francisco, Mar. 21, 1938; d. Arthur Joseph and Marjorie Dorothy (Johnson) Anderson; m. Michael Richard Matas Jr., Mar. 15, 1958; children: Michael Richard III, Kenneth Scott. Cert. interior design, Canada Coll.; cert. interior design, Calif. Owner, operator Miguel's Antiques Co., Millbrae, Calif., 1969-70, Miguel's Antiques & Interiors Co., Burlingame, Calif., 1979-79, Country Elegance Antiques and Interiors Co., Menlo Park, Calif., 1979-84, La France Boutique Co., 1979-84; owner, operator, interior designer, archtl. designer Myra D. Matas Interior Design, San Francisco, 1984-2000, Lafayette, La., 1994—; pres. LaFrance Imports, Inc., 1982-92; pres., gen. contractor Artisans 3 Inc., Burlingame, 1988-92; gen. contractor Matas Constr., Millbrae, 1993-98; instr. interior design dept. Canada Coll. Contbr. articles in field to profl. jours. Mem. Calif. Coun. Interior or Design. Office: 1616 Hwy 31 Arnaudville LA 70512 also: 324 rue Jefferson Lafayette LA 70501 E-mail: robinplantation@earthlink.net.

MATASA, CLAUDE GEORGE, researcher, science administrator, educator; b. Romania, Apr. 1, 1930; s. George D. and Marguerite A. (Aurand) M.; m. Eugenia Tonca (div.); m. Netty Matasa. Chem. Engr., Polytechnic U., Bucharest, Romania, 1949-54, Polytechnic U., Timisoara, Romania, 1965-70; D in Tech. Sci., Polytechnic U., Vienna, Austria, 1970-72; D in Chem. Engring. (hon.), Ecologic U., Bucharest, 1994. Rsch. engr., sr. rsch. engr., head rsch. and devel. Chem. Combine of Craiova and the Synthetic FibersWorks of Savinesti, 1954-70; cons. Chem. Construction Corp., Corpus Christi, Tex., 1970-73; rsch. scientist Unitek Corp., Monrovia, Calif., 1973-76; chief rsch.

chem. dept. Consol. Aluminum Corp. Sci. Ctr., St. Louis, 1977-79; chief rsch. Imperial Coatings Corp., New Orleans, 1979-82; pres. Ortho-Cycle Co., 1982—; prof. Univ., Bucharest, Romania, 1990, U. Ill., Chgo., 1995—, Nova Southeastern U., Fla., 1998 . Cons., referee Am. Journal of Orthodontics and Dentofacial Orthopedics, Chgo., 1986—; lectr. M. Richter Courses for the Austrian, German, and Swiss orthodontists, U. Innsbruck, Austria, 1990; guest lectr., rsch. cons. David B. Kriser Dental Ctr., NYU, 1991; internat. cons. Journal of Orthopedics-Orthodontics and Pediatric Dentistry, Caracas, Venezuela, 1995; vis. prof. U. Pa., Phila., 1996-97; hon. vis. prof. Valahia U., Targovista, Romania. Co-author: L'industrie moderne des produits azotes, 1968, Basic Nitrogen Compounds, 1973; editor: The Orthodontic Materials Insider, 1987—; contbr. over 100 articles to profl. jours. Mem. AAAS, Am. Chem. Soc., Am. Soc. for Materials, Romanian-Am. Acad., Romanian Acad. Sci., Acad. Medicine of Romania (hon.). Home: 1507 Hollywood Blvd Hollywood FL 33020-5239 Office: Ortho-Cycle Co 2026 Scott St Hollywood FL 33020-2417

MATASAR, ANN B. former dean, business and political science educator; b. N.Y.C., June 27, 1940; d. Harry and Tillie (Simon) Bergman; m. Robert Matasar, June 9, 1962; children— Seth Gideon, Toby Rachel AB, Vassar Coll., 1962; MA, Columbia U., 1964, PhD, 1968; M of Mgmt. in Fin., Northwestern U., 1977. Assoc. prof. Mundelein Coll., Chgo., 1965-78; prof., dir. Ctr. for Bus. and Econ. Elmhurst Coll., Elmhurst, Ill., 1978-84; dean Roosevelt U., Chgo., 1984-92; prof. Internat. Bus. and Fin. Walter E. Heller Coll. Bus. Adminstrn. Roosevelt U., 1992—. Dir. Corp. Responsibility Group, Chgo., 1978-84; chmn. long range planning Ill. Bar Assn., 1982-83; mem. edn. com. Ill. Commn. on the Status of Women, 1978-81 Author: Corporate PACS and Federal Campaign Financing Laws: Use or Abuse of Power?, 1986; (with others) Research Guide to Women's Studies, 1974, (with others) The Impact of Geographic Deregulation on the American Banking Industry, 2002; contbr. articles to profl. jours. Dem. candidate 1st legis. dist. Ill. State Senate, no. suburbs Chgo., 1972; mem. Dem. exec. com. New Trier Twp., Ill., 1972-76; rsch. dir., acad. advisor Congressman Abner Mikva, Ill., 1974-76; bd. dirs. Ctr. Ethics and Corp. Policy, 1985-90. Named Chgo. Woman of Achievement, Mayor of Chgo., 1978. Fellow AAUW (trustee ednl. found. 1992-97, v.p. fin. 1993-97); mem. Am. Polit. Sci. Assn., Midwest Bus. Adminstrn. Assn., Acad. Mgmt., Women's Caucus for Polit. Sci. (pres. 1980-81), John Howard Assn. (bd. dirs. 1986-90), Am. Assembly of Coll. Schs. of Bus. (bd. dirs. 1989-92, chair com. on diversity in mgmt. edn. 1991-92), North Ctrl. Assn. (commr. 1994-97), Beta Gamma Sigma. Democrat. Jewish. Avocations: jogging, biking, tennis, opera, crosswords. Office: Roosevelt U Coll Bus Adminstrn Dept Fin 430 S Michigan Ave Chicago IL 60605-1394 Office Phone: 312-281-3283. E-mail: amatasar@roosevelt.edu.

MATASEJE, VERONICA JULIA, sales executive; b. St. Ann's, Ontario, Can., Apr. 5, 1949; came to U.S., 1985; d. John and Anna Veronica M. Grad. H.S., Smithville, Can. Clk. typist, typesetter Crown Life Ins. Co., Toronto, 1966-70; typesetter Toronto Life/Calendar Mag., 1970-71; typesetter, exec. sec. Cerebrus Prodns. Ltd., Toronto, 1971-74; pres. Veron Prodns. Ltd., Toronto, 1975-81, Acclaim Records Inc., Toronto, 1981-88; pvt. health care provider Las Vegas, 1989-94; retail sales mgr. Top Cats, Las Vegas, 1994-00; pres. Abracadabra Music Corp., 2000—. Campaign vol. Dist. Atty., Las Vegas, 1994; vol. pilot Angel Planes, Las Vegas, 1989. Avocations: gardening, interior design, showing cats, travel, music. Home: 4326 Caliente St Las Vegas NV 89119-5801 Office: Top Cats PO Box 61173 Las Vegas NV 89160-1173 E-mail: vm@abracadabramusic.com.

MATAYOSHI, CORALIE CHUN, lawyer, bar association executive; b. Honolulu, June 2, 1956; d. Peter J. and Daisy (Look) Chun; m. Ronald F. Matayoshi, Aug. 8, 1981; children: Scot, Kelly, Alana. BA, U. Calif., Berkeley, 1978; JD, U. Calif., San Francisco, 1981. Bar: Hawaii 1981, U.S. Dist. Ct. Hawaii 1981. Trial atty. U.S. Dept. Justice Antitrust, Washington, 1981-84; assoc. Chun, Kerr, & Dodd, Honolulu, 1984-86; exec. dir. Hawaii Inst. of CLE, Honolulu, 1987-90, Hawaii State Bar Assn., Honolulu, 1990—. Arbitrator Ct. Annexed Arbitration Program, Honolulu, 1992—; adv. bd. Channel 2 TV Action Line, Honolulu, 1993-96. Contbr. chapters to books. Bd. dirs. Neighborhood Justice Ctr., 1994-97, mediator, 1997—.

MATCHETT, ANDREW JAMES, mathematics professor; b. Chgo., Jan. 30, 1950; s. Gerald James and Margaret Ellen (Stump) M.; m. Nancy Valentine Stasack, Aug. 7, 1976; children: Gerald Albert, Philip Joseph, Melanie Jeanne. BS, U. Chgo., 1971; PhD, U. Ill., 1976. Grad. teaching asst. U. Ill., Urbana, 1971-76; asst. prof. Tex. A&M U., College Station, 1976-82, U. Wis., La Crosse, 1982-86, assoc. prof., 1986—; grad. teaching asst. U. Ill., Urbana, 1971-76. Dir. Consortium for Core Math. Curriculum, Wis., 1987-88. Contbr. articles to profl. jours. Chmn. troop 18 com. Boy Scouts Am., La Crosse, 1990, charter rep. troop 18, 1992-94, scoutmaster, 1994-97, mem. com., 1997—. Mem.: AAAS, Math. Assn. Am. (sec.-treas. Wis. sect. 1989—, adminstr. 1999—), Am. Math. Soc. Unitarian Universalist. Achievements include development of a theory of class group homomorphisms. Home: 327 24th St N La Crosse WI 54601-3850 Office: U Wis Dept Math 1725 State St La Crosse WI 54601 Business E-Mail: matchett.andr@uwlax.edu.

MATCHETT, WILLIAM H(ENRY), English literature educator; b. Chgo., Mar. 5, 1923; s. James Chapman and Lucy H. (Jipson) M.; m. Judith Wright, June 11, 1949; children: David H., Katherine C., Stephen C. BA with highest honors, Swarthmore Coll., 1949; MA, Harvard U., 1950, PhD, 1957. Teaching fellow Harvard U., Cambridge, Mass., 1953-54; instr. English lit. U. Wash., Seattle, 1954-56, asst. prof., 1956-61, assoc. prof., 1961-66, prof., 1966-82, prof. emeritus, 1982—. Author: Water Ouzel, 1955, The Phoenix and the Turtle, 1965, Fireweed, 1980, Shakespeare and Forgiveness, 2002; numerous poems and articles; co-author: Poetry: From Statement to Meaning, 1965; editor: Modern Lang. Quar., Seattle, 1964-82. Mem. Soc. Friends. Home: 1017 Minor Ave Apt 702 Seattle WA 98104-1303

MATE, CHARLES MATHEW, physicist; b. Hamilton, Ont., Can., Dec. 12, 1959; BSc, U. Calif., Berkeley, 1981, PhD in Physics, 1986. Scientist IBM Almaden Rsch. Ctr., San Jose, Calif., 1986—2002, Hitachi San Jose Rsch. Ctr., San Jose, 2003—. Recipient MRS Meda award, Materials Rsch. Soc., 2001. Fellow: Am. Phys. Soc. (life); mem.: Am. Chem. Soc. (continuing chmn. on tribology 1996). Achievements include research in understanding friction and lubrication at the atomic scale. Office: Hitachi San Jose Rsch Ctr 650 Harry Rd San Jose CA 95120 E-mail: mathew.mate@hgst.com.

MATEJKA, ROBERT, chemicals executive; BBA in Acctg., Cleve. (Ohio) State U. V.p. fin. Rockwell Automation Co.; v.p. RPM Internat., Medina, Calif., 2000—, controller, 2000—, CFO, 2001—. Office: RPM International 2628 Pearl Rd Medina OH 44258*

MATEJUK, AGATA, immunologist; b. Jelenia Gora, Poland, May 13, 1967; d. Anna and Stanislaw Matejuk; 1 child, Szymon. Master in Sci., Med. Acad., Wroclaw - Poland, 1986—91; PhD, Inst. of Immunology and Exptl. Therapy, 1994—97. Rsch. instr. in neurology Oreg. Health & Sci. U., 2001—, asst. prof., 2003—. Contbr. articles to profl. jours. Recipient Dale McFarlin Travel award, Nat. Multiple Sclerosis Soc., 2001, 2002; Advanced Postdoctoral Fellowship award, 2000—. Mem.: Polish Soc. of Cytometry (assoc.), Polish Soc. of Oncology (assoc.), Am. Assn. Immunologists (assoc.). Achievements include research in multiple sclerosis. Office: Neuroimmunology Res Portland VAMC 3710 SW US Veterans Hosp Rd Portland OR 97201 Business E-Mail: matejuka@ohsu.edu.

MATELES, RICHARD ISAAC, biotechnologist; b. NYC, Sept. 11, 1935; s. Simon and Jean (Phillips) M.; m. Roslyn C. Fish, Sept. 2, 1956; children: Naomi, Susan, Sarah. BS, MIT, 1956, MS, 1957, DSc, 1959. USPHS fellow Laboratorium voor Microbiologie, Technische Hogeschool, Delft, The Netherlands, 1959-60; mem. faculty MIT, 1960-70, assoc. prof. biochem. engring., 1965-68; dir. fermentation unit Jerusalem, 1968-77; prof. applied microbiology Hebrew U., Hadassah Med. Sch., Jerusalem, 1968-80; vis. prof. dept. chem. engring. U. Pa., Phila., 1978-79; asst. dir. rsch. Stauffer Chem. Co., Westport, Conn., 1980, dir. rsch., 1980-81, v.p. rsch., 1981-88; sr. v.p. applied scis. IIT Rsch. Inst., Chgo., 1988-90; proprietor Candida Corp., Chgo., 1990—. Editor: Jour. Chem. Tech. and Biotech., 1972—; editor: (N.Am. edit.) Biotech., 2001—; editor: Penicillin: A Paradigm for Biotechnology, 1998, Directory of Toll Fermentation and Cell Culture Facilities, 2003; contbr. articles to profl. jours. Mem. Conn. Acad. Sci. Engring., 1981—; mem. vis. com., dept. applied biol. sci. MIT, 1980-88; mem. exec. com. Coun. on Chem. Rsch., 1981-85. Fellow Am. Inst. Med. and Biol. Engring.; mem. AICE, AAAS, SAR, Am. Chem. Soc., Am. Soc. Microbiology, Coun. on Agrl. Sci. and Tech., Soc. for Gen. Microbiology U.K., Inst. Food Technologists, Soc. Chem. Ind. (U.K.) Union League, Sigma Xi. Home: 150 W Eugenie St Apt 46 Chicago IL 60614-5843 Office: Candida Corp Ste 1310 220 S State St Chicago IL 60604 Office Phone: 312-431-1601. Personal E-mail: rmateles@candida.com.

MATEMA, ZSUN-NEE KIMBALL (ANNETTE K. MILLER), social sciences educator; b. Washington, Jan. 11, 1944; d. Emmett Robinson Miller and Annette Kimball Brooks; m. John Fitzgerald Payne, Aug. 31, 1963 (div.); children: Kellie Jon, Jaanai Kimball, Myya Machel, Robin Annette. BA, U. D.C., 1982; MMsc, U. Metaphysics. Cert. in clin. hypnosis Am. Hypnosis Tng. Acad.; lic. practitioner of religious sci. Ch. of Religious Sci.; ordained metaphysical min.; cert. in cmty. mediation Fed. Mediation Svcs.; cert. tchr. social studies. Artistic dir. Annette's Theatre of Dance, Inc., Washington, 1968-78; prodr., writer Nat. Broadcast Corp., Washington, 1971-74; ednl. counseling cons. Something Better/A.K. Millers & Assocs., Silver Spring, Md., 1979-86; dir. cmty. edn. Am. Digestive Disease Soc., Bethesda, Md., 1986-88; cmty. outreach/arena stage multicult. audience devel. assoc. Washington, 1989-92; founding dir. Intercultural Edn. Exch., Washington, 1991—; prof. behavioral scis. Washington Saturday Coll., 1997—; founder, pres. Brannum Robinson Hist. Soc., Inc., 2001—; tchr. social studies Nicholas Orem Middle Sch. Native Am. storyteller The Painted Gourd: Red & Black Voices, Washington, 1991—; hist. interpreter Mt. Vernon; colonial and Civil War reenactor D.C. Ladies Contraband Relief Soc., Washington, 1991—; cmty. policing trainer Met. Police Dept., Washington, 1993-97; nat. dir. All Nations Drum, Washington, 1996; pub. rels. coord. The Walk to Can., Silver Spring, Md., 1996; underground railroad historian Nat. Pk. Svc., Washington, 1996—; cmty. mediator Montgomery County Md., 1996—; nat. adv. bd. Trail of Dreams Walk from North to South, Washington, 1999; founder, pres. Washington, Curtis-Lee Enslaved Remembrance Soc., 2003. Contbg. poet: Gurus and Griots, 1986; prodr., writer (cable) Prejudice Picks on Children, 1988, Scripts, 1989, (radio drama) Underground Railroad Traveling Radio Show, 1998; playwright Tales from Tin Cup Alley, 1991; host, prodr. (radio) The Talking Feather, 2000—, Vital Signs, 2003—. Pub. programs chair Afro-Asian Rels. Coun., Washington, 1989-96; past vice chair Com. for Ethnic Affairs, Silver Spring, 1990-96; mem. AFRIASIA founding dir. Cultural Alliance Greater Washington, 1991-94; cmty. mediator Human Rights Commn., Rockville, Md., 1994—; adv. bd. mem. NAACP, Silver Spring, 1996-98, com. mem. multicultural group, 1996-98; Native Am. adv. rep. Montgomery County Sch. Bd., 1996-97; tng. devel. com. mem. Nat. Area Crisis Response Team, Washington, 1997-99. Grantee Nat. Endowment for the Arts, Washington, 1974-76, Hawaii Arts in the Sch., Inc., Owau, Hawaii, 1994. Mem. Zeta Phi Beta. Avocations: colonial reenactment, creative wall art, travel. E-mail: ZSunRise3@aol.com.

MATERA, FRANCES LORINE, elementary school educator; b. Eustis, Nebr., June 28, 1926; d. Frank Daniel and Marie Mathilda (Hess) Daiss; m. Daniel Matera, Dec. 27, 1973. Luth. tchrs. diploma, Concordia U., Seward, Nebr., 1947, BS in Edn., 1956; MEd, U. Oreg., 1963. Elementary tchr. Our Savior's Luth. Ch., Colorado Springs, Colo., 1954-57; tchr. 5th grade Monterey (Calif.) Pub. Schs., 1957-59; tchr. 1st grade Roseburg (Oreg.) Schs., 1959-60; tchr. several schs. Palm Springs (Calif.) Unified Sch. Dist., 1960—93; tchr. 3rd grade Vista del Monte Sch., Palm Springs, Calif., 1973-93; ret., 1993. Named Tchr. of the Yr., Palm Springs Unified Schs. Mem. Kappa Kappa Iota (chpt. and state pres.). E-mail: Franmatera7@aol.com.

MATERA, RICHARD ERNEST, retired minister; b. Hartford, Conn., July 13, 1925; s. Charles Carlo and Philomena Antoinette Cecile (Liberatore) M.; m. Lynn B. Matera; children: Thomas Charles, Nancy Jean Matera Dye. Student, Trinity Coll., Hartford, 1943, Biarritz Am. U., France, 1945; BA magna cum laude, Colgate U., 1949; MDiv, Andover Newton Theol. Sch., 1953; DD, Calif. Christian U., 1981. Ordained to ministry Bapt. Ch., 1952. Dir. youth work Quincy Point (Mass.) Congl. Ch., 1949-50; pastor, dir. vacation ch. sch. Panton and Addison (Vt.) chs., 1950; min. Thompson (Conn.) Hill Ch., 1950-51, Waldo Congl. Ch., Brockton, Mass., 1951-54, Cen. Congl. Ch., Orange, Mass., 1954-59; sr. min. 1st Congl. United Ch. of Christ, Berea, Ohio, 1959-71, St. Paul Community Ch., Homewood, Ill., 1971-76; interim min. United Ch. Christ, Chgo., 1978-99; min. Immanuel United Ch. of Christ, Bensenville, Ill., 1999—. Pres. Millers River Coun. Chs., 1957-58; mem. dept. ch. world responsibility Mass. Coun. Chs., 1957-59; chmn. internat. affairs com. of state social action com. United Ch. of Christ, 1962-63, del. Gen. Synod, Chgo., mem. peace priority task force Western Res. Assn., 1967-70, mem. commn. on ch. and ministry Ohio conf., 1968-71, chmn. dept. ch. and community Western Res. Assn. Coun., Cleve., 1969-70, peace and internat. rels. com., 1973; mem. ad hoc com. on Vietnam Greater Cleve. Coun. of Chs. of Christ, 1966-68; probation officer DuPage County Probation Dept., Wheaton, Ill., 1985-86; interim min. Chgo. area, 1978—, Sauk Village United Ch. of Christ, 1978-80, Steger 1st Congregation, 1981-83, Forest Park, 1986-88, River Grove Grace, 1989-91, Mont Clare Congregation, 1990-92, St. Nicolai, Chgo., 1992-96. Contbr. poetry to anthologies including Tears of Fire, 1994, A Break in the Clouds, 1994. Participant Civil Rights March, Selma, Ala., 1965; capt. Cleve. United Fund, 1961-63, Colgate Fund Dr., 1963; trustee Cleve. Union, 1961-63, Berea United Fund, 1963-69; mem. Berea Coun. on Human Rels., 1965-71, U.S. com. Christian Peace Conf., Prague, Czechoslovakia, 1967—, Nat. Arbor Day Found.; del. Action Conf. on Nat. Priorities, Washington, 1969; bd. dirs., mem. ecumenical mission com. Community Renewal Soc., Chgo., 1972-76; bd. dirs. Respond Now, Chicago Heights, Ill., 1972-78; mem. Pres.'s Coun., Chgo. Theol. Sem., 1973-81; pres. Mended Hearts Inc., Downers Grove, Ill., 1989-90. With U.S. Army Med. Corps., 1943-46, ETO. Austen Colgate scholar, 1946-49; recipient Harvard Book prize, 1942; name inscribed on The Wall of Liberty, Battle of Normandy Found., France, 1994. Fellow Profl. Assn. Clergy, Acad. Parish Clergy; mem. Living Bank Internat. (organ donor mem.), Smithsonian Instn., Audubon Soc., Internat. Fellowship of Reconciliation, Internat. Soc. Poets, Nat. Libr.Poetry, Steinway Soc. Chgo., Planetary Soc., Jacques Cousteau Soc., Antique Automobile Club, Hupmobile Club, Cadillac Club, Phi Beta Kappa, Beta Theta Pi. Democrat. Achievements include private interview with Prof. Albert Einstein in 1954. Avocations: drawing, poetry, astronomy, piano, working out at health club. Home and Office: 551 Sudbury St Marlborough MA 01752-1656 *From world philosophers, I have gleaned this: While borders stand, we are in prehistory. When all borders are gone, human history will begin.-Yevtushenko A person only has the right to do that which he agrees should become universal law.-Kant Do to others as you want them to do to you.-Hebrew tchg. The human race is now capable of and ready for the above.*

MATERIA, KATHLEEN PATRICIA AYLING, nurse; b. Jersey City, Nov. 7, 1954; d. Donald Anthony and Muriel Cecilia (Joyce) Ayling; m. Francis Peter Materia, June 5, 1983; children: Christopher Michael, Donna Nicole. *Kathleen Materia's son, Christopher Michael, graduated Assumption School in Wood-Ridge, N.J. in June 2002. He received the President's Award for Academic Excellence, State Science Award Scholarship, Math League Certificate of Merit for Superior Achievement, and an award for being the only student to receive High Honors for all four semesters. Christopher received scholarships for all four high schools that he applied to. He is also a Student Ambassador with the People to People Student Ambassador Program and has traveled with the team to Europe (England, Ireland, Wales) in July 2001. Christopher is now attending the Bergen County Academy for Medical Science Technology (class of 2006).* BSN, Fairleigh Dickinson U., 1976. RN, N.J. Critical care nurse Palisades Gen. Hosp., North Bergen, N.J., 1976-87; grad. nurse, 1976-77; nurse critical care unit North Hudson Hosp., Weehawken, NJ, 1977-78. Mem. Alpha Sigma Tau. Democrat. Avocations: bowling, dance.

MATERNA, JOSEPH ANTHONY, lawyer; b. Passaic, N.J., June 13, 1947; s. Anthony E. and Peggy Ann Materna; m. Dolores Corio, Dec. 14, 1975; children: Jodi, Jennifer, Janine. BA, Columbia U., 1969, JD, 1973. Bar: N.Y. 1975, Fla. 1977, U.S. Dist. Ct. (ea. and so. dists.) N.Y. 1977, U.S. Supreme Ct. 1977, U.S. Tax Ct. 1978, U.S. Ct. of Claims 1978. Trusts and estates atty. Chadbourne Parke Whiteside & Wolff, N.Y.C., 1973-76, Dreyer & Traub, N.Y.C., 1976-80, Finley Kumble Wagner Heine Underberg & Casey, N.Y.C., 1980-85; ptnr., head trusts and estates dept. Newman Tannenbaum Helpern Syracuse & Hirschtritt, N.Y.C., 1985-90, Shapiro Beilly Rosenberg Aronowitz Levy & Fox LLP, N.Y.C., 1990—2004, Solomon, Pearl, Blum, Heymann & Stich, LLP, N.Y.C., 2004—. Lectr. in field; expert witness in trusts and estate field ct. litigations, N.Y., 1999—. Contbr. articles to profl. jours. Chmn. planned giving com., mem. bd. govs. Arthritis Found. N.Y. Chpt., N.Y.C., 1980 ; mem. bd. trustees, corp. treas. Cath. Interracial Coun., N.Y.C., 1992—; mem. bequests and planned gifts com. Cath. Archdiocese of N.Y., N.Y.C., 1988—; corp. sec. Arthritis Found. N.Y. chpt., N.Y.C., 1997—, mem. budget and fin. com., 2001—; mem. Meml. Sloan-Kettering Nat. Trusts and Estates Assocs. Recipient Planned Giving award Arthritis Found.-N.Y. Chpt., N.Y.C., 1994, Discovery Alliance award Arthritis Found.-N.Y. Chpt., N.Y.C., 1995; named Accredited Estate Planner, Nat. Assn. Estate Planners, Marietta, Ga., 1995. Mem. ABA, Fla. Bar (trusts and estate com.), N.Y. State Bar Assn. (com. on estates and trusts, com. on surrogate's ct.), Bar Assn. of the City of N.Y. (com. on surrogate's ct.), N.Y.C. Estate Planning Coun. (lectr., author), N.Y. County Lawyers Assn. (mem. com. on trusts and estates 1979—, com. on profl. ethics, com. on taxation 2000—, com. on surrogate's ct.), Queen County Bar Assn. (mem. com. trusts and estates 1990—, mem. com. on taxation, mem. com. on profl. ethics, com. on surrogate's ct.), Am. Judges Assn. (civil ct. arbitrator N.Y.C.), Am. Arbitration Assn. (panel of arbitrators), N.Y. State Trial Lawyers Assn., Richmond County Bar Assn. (com. on surrogates ct., com. on estate taxation), Columbia Coll. Alumni Assn. of Columbia U. (class pres. 1969—), Columbia Law Sch. Assn., S.I. Richmondtown Hist. Soc., Archdiocese N.Y., Regina Coeli Legacy Soc. Republican. Roman Catholic. Avocations: music, history, theater, lecturing, European travel. Home: 155 Johanna Ln Staten Island NY 10309-3604 Office: Solomon Pearl Blum Heymann & Stich LLP 40 Wall Street 35th Fl New York NY 10005

MATERNA, THOMAS WALTER, ophthalmologist; b. Passaic, N.J., Oct. 24, 1944; s. Anthony and Ann (Popowich) M.; m. Johnn Pauline Aronsen, Aug. 18, 1973; children: Richard C., Barbara L. BA, Coll. Holy Cross, Worcester, Mass., 1966; MD, SUNY, N.Y.C., 1971; MBA, Rutgers U., Newark, 1990. Diplomate Am. Bd. Ophthalmology. Intern N.Y. Hosp.-Cornell U. Med. Ctr., N.Y.C., 1971-72; resident N.Y. Eye and Ear Infirmary, N.Y.C., 1975-78; pvt. practice ophthalmology San Francisco, 1986; ophthalmologist N.J. Eye Physicians & Surgeons, Newark. V.p. mktg. Biomark Internat., Lviv, Ukraine, Dezomark, Lviv, 2002—; bd. dirs. Charles Erb Assocs. Fin. Group, Florham Park, N.J. Com. mem. N.J. Sch. for the Arts, Montclair, 1991—. Lt. USN, 1972-74, comdr. USNR, 1974—. Fellow ACS, Am. Acad. Ophthalmology; mem. Rotary, Army-Navy Club. Democrat. Roman Catholic. Avocations: coin collecting/numismatics, rare document collecting, tennis, art history. Home: 87 Lorraine Ave Montclair NJ 07043-2304 Office: NJ Eye Physicians and Surgeons 20 Ferry St Newark NJ 07105-1420

MATERSON, RICHARD STEPHEN, physician, educator; b. Phila., Feb. 11, 1941; s. Alfred Lawrence and June Eileen (Slakoff) M.; m. Rosa Maria Navarro, Aug. 22, 1964; children: Lisa Gail, Lawrence Mark. MD, U. Miami, Coral Gables, Fla., 1965. Diplomate Am. Bd. Phys. Medicine and Rehab. Intern Walter Reed Gen. Hosp., Washington, 1965; resident Letterman Gen. Hosp., San Francisco, 1966—68; chief phys. medicine and rehab. Tripler Gen. Hosp., Honolulu, 1968—72; asst. prof. phys. medicine and rehab. Ohio State U., Columbus, 1972—76; assoc. clin. prof. phys. medicine and rehab. Baylor Coll. Medicine, Houston, 1976—93, prof., 1997—; pres. Materson MD, PA, Houston, 1976—; sr. v.p. for med. affairs, med. dir. Nat. Rehab. Hosp., Washington, 1990—97; prof. neurology George Washington U. Med. Ctr., Washington, 1994—97; med. v.p. Meml. Healthcare Sys., Houston, 1997—; prof. phys. medicine and rehab. U. Tex. Health Sci. Ctr., Houston, 1997—; fellow Kaiser Inst., 1999, 2001; chief med. officer Meml. Hermann Continuing Care Corp., 2000—02; v.p. med. devel. Hermann Healthcare Sys., 2002—. Med. dir. Dept. Phys. Medicine and Rehab., Meml. Hosp. SE, Houston, 1978-90, Ctr. for Sports Medicine and Rehab., 1987-90, Electromyography Lab., 1978-90; faculty Kaiser Inst., 2000—; bd. dirs. Inst. for Religion and Health, Tex. Med. Ctr., 2002—. Co-author: Physical Medicine and Rehabilitation, 1977, 2d rev. edit., 1980, The Practice of Rehabilitation Medicine, 1982; co-editor: Management of Persons with Stroke, 1993; co-editor, author: The Non Surgical Management of Acute Low Back Pain, 1997, Pain Management, 1998; contbg. author: Practice of Medicine, 1978. Trustee Meml. Hosp. System, Houston, 1986-90, Nat. Rehab. Hosp., Washington, 1990-96; host family Experiment in Internat. Living, 1985, 86, 87. Served to maj. U.S. Army, 1965—72. Fellow Am. Acad. Phys. Medicine and Rehab. (pres. 1986-87, Distng. Pub. Svc. award, 1992, Walter J. Zeiter lectr., 1994), Am. Assn. Electrodiagnostic Medicine; mem. AMA (del. 1978-93), Phys. Medicine and Rehab. Edn. and Rsch. Found. (founder, pres. 1982-90, bd. dirs. 1983-2001), Houston Acad. Phys. Medicine and Rehab. (pres. 1979-80), Am. Acad. Pain Mgmt. (chmn. bd. advisors 1989-90, mem. bd. advisors 1990—), Bd. Inst. for Religion and Health, Tex. Med. Ctr., 2002—, Internat. Wine and Food Soc., Knights of Vine (master comdr. 1982—), Confrerie des Chevaliers du Tastevin, Chaine des Rotisseurs. Jewish.

MATES, ROBERT EDWARD, mechanical engineering educator; b. Buffalo, May 19, 1935; s. Cyril S. and Ruth Elizabeth Mates; m. Gail Paxson, June 4, 1960; children: Robert E., Elisabeth, Steven. BS, U. Rochester, 1957; MS, Cornell U., 1959, PhD, 1963. Instr. Cornell U., Ithaca, N.Y., 1958-61; asst. prof. SUNY, Buffalo, 1962-65, assoc. prof., 1965-69, chmn. mech. and aero. engring., 1967-70, 79-82, prof. mech. engring., 1969-97, dir. Ctr. Biomed. Engring., 1989-96, prof. emeritus, 1997—. Editor various symposium proceedings; contbr. articles to profl. jours. NIH spl. rsch. fellow, 1970-71, 78-79, H.R. Lissner award Am. Soc of Mechanical Engineers, 1995. Fellow ASME (chmn. winter ann. meeting com. 1989-93, mem.-at-large bd. comm. 1988-93, v.p. bd. comm. 1994-98), Am. Inst. for Med. and Biol. Engring. (founding, chmn. acad. coun. 1996-97); mem. AAUP, Biomed. Engring. Soc. (bd. dirs. 1991-94, chmn. awards com. 1991-92, mem. pub. bd. 1992-94), Am. Soc. Engring. Edn.

MATES, SUSAN ONTHANK, physician, medical educator, writer, violinist; b. Oakland, Calif., Aug. 8, 1950; d. Benson and Lois (Onthank) M.; m. Joseph Harold Friedman, Dec. 10, 1978; children: Rebecca, Deborah, William. Student, Juilliard Sch. Music, 1967-69; BA magna cum laude with distinction, Yale Coll., 1972; MD, Albert Einstein Coll. Medicine, 1976. Cert. Am. Bd. Internal Medicine, Nat. Bd. Med. Examiners. Intern Boston City Hosp., 1976-77; fellow in gen. medicine Coll. of Physicians and Surgeons-Columbia U., N.Y.C., 1977-78; resident/fellow in infectious diseases Montefiore Hosp., Bronx, 1978-82; asst. prof. medicine Brown U., Providence, 1982-85, asst. prof. biochemistry, 1985-86, clin. assoc. prof. medicine, 1993-98; staff mem., former dir. R.I. State Tb Clinic, R.I. Dept. Health, Providence, 1986-96, cons. Tb program, 1987-96. Judge short story contest Providence Jour., 1994, 98; mem. jury R.I. Coun. Arts Fellowship; contbg. editor Pushcart Prize, Pushcart Press, 1995, 96, 97, 98, 99. Author: (fiction) The Good Doctor, 1994 (John Simmons Short Fiction Award, U. Iowa Press, 1994); contbr. sci. articles to profl. jours., stories to revs. and jours. and anthologies. Recipient Recognition award for young scholars AAUW, 1985, Clin. Investigator award NIH, 1984, R.I. Found. award, 1983; McDowell Colony fellow, 1995, Yaddo fellow, 1996; Symposium scholar in lit. and medicine for 21st Century, Brown U., 1997. Mem. Am. Med. Women's Assn., Poets and Writers, Alpha Omega Alpha.

MATESKY, NANCY LEE, music educator; b. West Point, Mo., Nov. 30, 1941; d. Enoch Ivy and Layla Nixon Miller; m. Michael Paul Matesky, Aug. 10, 1973; children: Angela Lynn, Michael Paul II. BS in Edn., U Ark., 1963, MS in Edn., 1971. Piano tchr. self employed, Tex.,Ark.,Wash., 1960—90; music tchr. Rogers Ark. Sch., 1963—64, Fayetteville (Ark.) Sch., 1964—65, Springdale (Ark.) Sch., 1965—70; instr. U Ark., Fayetteville, 1971—72; asst. prof. West Tex. State U, Canyon, 1972—75; prof. Shoreline Cmty. Coll., Seattle, 1976—. Founder, first pres. Ark. Elem. Music Educators Assn.,

1965—67. Performer: Shoreline C.C., 1981—98, Seattle Art Mus., 2000, 2002, Matesky-Swisher Two Piano Duo. Named one of Outstanding Young Women in Am., 1968; recipient Outstanding Young Educator award, Jaycees, 1967. Mem.: Music Educators Nat. Conf., Music Tchr. Nat. Assn. (assoc.), Seattle Ladies Musical Club, Sigma Alpha Iota (Nat. Coll. Leadership award 1963, Nat. Alumnae Leadership award 2001). United Meth. Home: 23004 35th Ave S E Bothell WA 98021-8913 Office: Shoreline Cmty Coll 16101 Greenwood Ave N Seattle WA 98133 Office Phone: 206-546-4618.

MATHAY, JOHN PRESTON, elementary school educator; b. Youngstown, Ohio, Jan. 27, 1942; s. Howard Ellsworth and Mary Clara (Siple) M.; m. Sandra Elizabeth Rhoades, June 9, 1973 (div. Jan. 1986); children: Elizabeth Anne, Sarah Susannah; m. Judith Anne Matthy, June 19, 1988; 1 child, Andrew Micah. BA in History, Va. Mil. Inst., Lexington, 1964; Cert. Teaching, Cleve. State U., 1972; postgrad., Mich. State U., 1964-65; MEd, Westminster Coll., New Wilmington, 1986. Cert. asst. supt., elem. tchr., elem. prin., high sch. prin. Cabinet maker Artisian Cabinet, Orwig Cabinets, Cleve. and Howland, Ohio, 1970-72; tchr. Urban Community Sch., Cleve., 1972-73, Pymatuning Valley Schs., Andover, Ohio, 1973—. Cross country coach, 7th and 8th grade track coach, Andover, Ohio, 1973—2004; F. and I. engraving, 2005—. Bd. mem. Badger Sch. Bd., Kinsman, Ohio; trustee Kinsman Libr.; trustee, elder Kinsman Presbyn. Ch. Capt. U.S. Army Res., 1966-69. Martha Holden Jennings Found. scholar, Cleve., 1976. Mem. ASCD, Pymatuning Valley Edn. Assn. (pres. 1975-76, 91-92, 94-95), Ohio Edn. Assn., Am. Legion, Rotary (pres. 1991-92, sec. 1992-93, treas. 1995-98, Paul Harris fellow), Masons (jr. deacon 1984-85, 32d deg., York Rite commandery), Ashtabula County Antique Engine Club, Phi Delta Kappa. Republican. Presbyterian. Avocations: sailing, skating, amateur radio, french and indian war reenacting, fishing, reading. Office: Pymatuning Valley Schs W Main St Andover OH 44003 Home: PO Box 418 Kinsman OH 44428-0228 E-mail: jamath@suite224.net.

MATHELIER, AMEDEE C. obstetrician-gynecologist; b. Gonaives, Haiti, 1934; MD, Sch. Medicine State U., Haiti, 1958. Intern Jewish Hosp., Bklyn., 1962-63; resident in ob.-gyn. Balt. City Hosp., 1963-66, fellow, 1968-70. Pvt. practice. Lt. col. U.S. Army Med. Corps. Mem. AMA, Am. Coll. Ob.-Gyn., CGS, ISMS.

MATHENY, ADAM PENCE, JR., child psychologist, educator, consultant, researcher; b. Stanford, Ky., Sept. 6, 1932; s. Adam Pence and Dorotha (Steele) Matheny; m. Ute I. Debus, July 10, 1962 (div.); m. Mary P. Tolbert, June 24, 1967 (div.); children: Laura Steele, Jason Gaverick. BS, Columbia U., 1958; PhD, Vanderbilt U., 1962. Sr. human factors engr. Martin Aerospace divsn., Balt., 1962—63; instr. Johns Hopkins U. Med. Sch., Balt., 1963—65; staff fellow Nat. Inst. Child Health and Human Devel., 1965—67; from asst. prof. to prof. pediat. U. Louisville Med. Sch., 1967—75; assoc. dir. to dir. Louisville Twin Study, 1986—. Mem. rev. panel NIH, 1991—95. Co-author: Genetics and Counseling in Medical Practice, 1969; contbr. articles to profl. jours. Served with USN, 1951—55. Fellow: APA, Am. Psychol. Soc., Am. Assn. Applied and Preventive Psychology, Internat. Soc. Twin Studies; mem.: AAAS, Internat. Soc. Infant Study, Internat. Soc. Behavior Devel., Behavior Genetics Assn., Soc. Rsch. Child Devel., Sigma Xi, Phi Beta Kappa. Office Phone: 502-852-1090. Business E-Mail: apmathoi@louisville.edu.

MATHENY, CHARLES WOODBURN, JR., former army officer, civil engineer, city official; b. Sarasota, Fla., Aug. 7, 1914; s. Charles Woodburn Sr. and Virginia (Yates) M.; m. Jeanne Felkel, July 12, 1942; children: Virginia Ann, Nancy Caroline, Charles Woodburn III. BSCE, U. Fla., 1936; grad., Army Command Gen. Staff Coll., 1944. Lic. comml. pilot, cert. civil engr., surveyor Ga. San. engr. Ga. State Dept. Health, 1937-39; civil engr. Fla. East Coast Rlwy., 1939-41; commd. 2d lt. F.A., USAR through ROTC U. Fla., 1936; 1st lt. F.A., USAR, 1939; vol. active army svc. F.A., US Army, 1941; commissioned 2d lt. F.A., US Army (Regular Army), 1942; advanced through grades to col. F.A., USAR, 1955; comdr. 351st Field Arty. Bn., 1944-45; commr. 33rd Field Arty. Bn., 1st Infantry Divsn., 1946; arty. staff officer 33rd Field Arty. Bn., 1st Inf. Divsn., 1947; gen. staff G-3 Plans Dept. Army, 1948-51; qualified Air Force liaison pilot, 1951; qualified Army aviator airplanes and helicopters, 1952; aviation officer 25th Infantry Divsn., Korea, 1952-53; sr. Army aviation advisor Korean Army, 1953; first dir. combat devel. dept. first dep. comdt. Army Aviation Sch., Ft. Sill, Okla., 1954-55; dep. dir. rsch., dep. dir. dept. tactics U.S. Army Field Arty. and Missile Sch., Ft. Sill, 1955—57; aviation officer 7th U.S. Army, Germany, 1957-58; Munich sub area comdr. So. Area Command, Europe, 1958-59; qualified sr. army aviator, 1959; dep. chief of staff for info. So. Area Command, 1960; Mich. sector comdr. VI Army Corps., 1961-62, ret., 1962; asst. dir. Tampa (Fla.) Dept. Pub. Works, 1963-81, ret., 1981. During World War II, Germany Commd., 351st field arty. Bn. in combat and occupation, 1945, also 33d field arty. bn., 1st Inf. Divsn., in occupation, 1946. Initiator and originator of tactical use of helicopters in Army, 1949, Army warrant officer helicopter aviator program and organization of first five Army Transp. Helicopter Co. and establishment of a new U.S. Army pers. policy making U.S. Army helicopter pilots warrant officers instead of officers, 1950; 1st to envision army combat units and airphibious army divisions equipped with high performance helicopter mobility capable of land, sea or air warfare operations at 200 mph, 1950; initiated and prepared directive signed by Army chief of staff, Gen. J. Lawton Collins ordering first feasibility tests of Army super-mobile inf. and arty. units equipped with helicopter mobility, 1951; pilot 1st combat observation mission in army helicopter, Korea, 1952; organizer, comdr., helicopter pilot 1st Army combat ops. using helicopter mobility to support inf. and engr. front line combat units 25th Inf. Divsn., Korea, 1952 proving feasibility of Army helicopter mobility on the battlefield; 1st to advocate, rsch., prepare orgn. plans and design of super-mobile Army combat units equipped with armed and unarmed helicopter mobility, with model designs of helicopters armed with missiles, rockets, etc. to equip proposed combat units, 1955-56; development O/R Comanche, RAH-66 reconnaissance helicopter; U.S. Army first to exploit and develop helicopter mobility due to Matheny's devotion to its early begining; pilot 100 combat observation missions, Korea, 1952-53; author 1st state legis. to establish profl. sch. civil engring. filed in Fla. Legis. by Sen. Julian Lane, 1974; mem. U.S. Army's Strategic Planning Com., 1950-51. Contbr. articles to profl. jours., popular mags. Troop com. Boy Scouts Am., 1965-73; active various cmty. and ch. activities; patron Tampa Art Mus., 1965-83, Tampa Cmty. Concert Series, 1979-82; bd. dirs. Tampa YMCA, 1967-71, Fla. Easter Seal Soc., 1978, Easter Seal Soc. Hillsborough County, 1971-84, hon. bd. dirs., 1984-95, treas., 1973-76, pres., 1977. Decorated Bronze Star with oak leaf cluster, Air medal with three oak leaf clusters; recipient of the Eagle Scout award, 1928; Letterman football U.F., 1933, 35; named to U. Fla. Student Hall of Fame, 1936. Mem. ASCE (pres. West Coast br., dir. Fla. sect. 1973, Engr. of Yr. award West Coast br. Fla. sect. 1979, life mem. 1980), Am. Soc. Profl. Engrs., Fla. Engring. Soc., Am. Pub. Works Assn. (pres. West Coast br. Fla. chpt. 1972, exec. com. Fla. chpt. 1972-77, v.p. 1977, pres. 1978), Ret. Officers Assn., Army Aviation Assn., SAR, Fla. Blue Key, Alpha Tau Omega, Sigma Tau. Episcopalian. Achievements include research in tactical use of helicopter aerial vehicles. Home: 3501 Bayshore Blvd Apt 1402 Tampa FL 33629-8901

MATHENY, KENNETH L. oil industry executive; b. Akron, Ohio; B in Acctg., U. Akron; MBA, Bowling Green State U. Dir. corp. fin. Marathon Oil Corp., Houston, 1988—89, dir. human resources, 1989—94, v.p. human resources and environment, 1994—97; v.p. contr. USX Corp., Pitts., 1997—2000, v.p. investor rels., 2000—02; v.p. investor rels. and pub. affairs Marathon Oil Corp., 2002—. Mem.: Petroleum Investor Rels. Assn., Nat. Investor Rels. Inst., Am. Inst. CPAs. Office: Marathon Oil Corp Corp Headquarters 5555 San Felipe Rd Houston TX 77056-2723

MATHENY, RUTH ANN, editor; b. Fargo, N.D., Jan. 17, 1918; d. Jasper Gordon and Mary Elizabeth (Carey) Wheelock; m. Charles Edward Matheny, Oct. 24, 1960. BE, Mankato State Coll., 1938; MA, U. Minn., 1955; postgrad., Universidad Autonoma de Guadalajara, Mex., summer 1956, Georgetown U., summer, 1960. Tchr., U.S. and S.Am., 1938-61; assoc. editor Charles E. Merrill Pub. Co., Columbus, Ohio, 1963-66; tchr. Confraternity Christian Doctrine, Washington Court House, Ohio, 1969-70; assoc. editor Jr. Cath. Messenger, Dayton, Ohio, 1966-68; editor Witness Intermediate, Dayton, 1968-70; editor in chief, assoc. pub. Today's Cath. Tchr., Dayton, 1970—2002, editor-in-chief emeritus, 2002—; editor in chief Catechist, Dayton, 1976-89, Ednl. Dealer, Dayton, 1976-80; v.p. Peter Li, Inc., Dayton, 1980—. Editl. collaborator: Dimensions of Personality series, 1969—; co-author: At Ease in the Classroom; author: Why a Catholic School?, Scripture Stories for Today: Why Religious Education?; freelance writer, 1943— Bd. dirs. Friends Ormond Beach Library. Mem.: 3d Order St. Francis (eucharistic min. 1990—), Nat. Coun. Cath. Women. Home: 26 Reynolds Ave Ormond Beach FL 32174-7043 Office: Peter Li Ednl Group 2621 Dryden Rd Ste 300 Dayton OH 45439 E-mail: chilermat@aol.com. *In a world that is constantly changing, a strong religious faith is a dependable compass through which we are able to stay on a positive, forward course.*

MATHER, ANN, film company executive; b. Stockport, Cheshire, Eng., Apr. 10, 1960; came to U.S., 1993; d. Robert Joseph and Theresa (Westhead) M. Grad., Cambridge U., Eng., 1981. CPA. Sr. Peat Marwick, London, 1981-84; sr. fin. analyst Paramount Pictures, London, 1984-85, European contr. Amsterdam, 1985-87, mgr. strategic planning N.Y.C., 1987-88; pres. art import/export Santa Fe Galleries, London/Santa Fe/San Diego, 1988-89; dir. fin. Polo Ralph Lauren Europe, Paris, 1989-91; European contr. life ins. div. AIG, Paris, 1991-92; dir. fin. and adminstrn. Europe internat. film distbn. div. The Walt Disney Co., Paris, 1992-93, v.p. fin. and adminstrn. Buena Vista Internat. Theatrical Divsn. Burbank, Calif., 1993-97, sr. v.p. fin. and adminstrn. Buena Vista Internat. Theatrical Divsn., 1998-99; exec. v.p., CFO Village Roadshow Pictures, 1999, Pixar Animation Studios, 1999—2004. Contbr. Descanso Gardens, La Canada, Calif., 1996. Recipient award for land values paper Royal Soc. Chartered Surveyors, 1981. Mem. Women in Film, Fin. Execs. Inst. (chmn. profl. devel. com.), Brit. Acad. Film and TV Arts. Avocations: skiing, horseback riding, travel, literature, film. Office: Pixar Animation Studios 1200 Park Ave Emeryville CA 94608

MATHER, ELIZABETH VIVIAN, healthcare executive; b. Richmond, Ind., Sept. 19, 1941; d. Willie Samuel and Lillie Mae (Harper) Fuqua; m. Roland Donald Mather, Dec. 26, 1966. BS, Maryville (Tenn.) Coll., 1963; postgrad., Columbia U., 1965-66. Tchr. Richmond Cmty. Schs., 1963-67, Indpls. Pub. Schs., 1967-68; systems analyst Ind. Blue Cross Blue Shield, Indpls., 1968-71, Ind. Nat. Bank, Indpls., 1971; med. cons. Ind. State Dept. Pub. Welfare, Indpls., 1971-78, cons. supr., 1978-86; systems analyst Ky. Blue Cross Blue Shield, Louisville, 1988-89; contracts specialist Humana Corp., Louisville, 1989—. Active Rep. Cen. Com. Montgomery County, Crawfordsville, 1976-86, Centenary Meth. Ch., adminstrv. bd., 1990. Mem. DAR (treas. 1963-66, sec. 1978-86). Avocation: designing and sewing clothes. Home: 6106 Partridge Pl Floyds Knobs IN 47119-9427 Office: 500 W Main St Fl 6 Louisville KY 40202-2946 Business E-Mail: emather@humana.com.

MATHER, GEORGE ROSS, clergy member; b. Trenton, N.J., June 1, 1930; s. Samuel Wooley and Henrietta Elizabeth (Deardorff) M.; m. Doris Christine Anderson, June 28, 1958; children: Catherine Anne Mather-Grimes, Geoffrey Thomas. BA, Princeton U., 1952; MDiv, Princeton Theol. Sem., 1955; DD, Hanover Coll., 1986. Ordained to Ministry, 1955. Asst. pastor Abington (Pa.) Presbyn., 1955-58; pastor 1st Presbyn. Ch. Ewing, Trenton, 1958-71; sr. pastor 1st Presbyn. Ch. Ft. Wayne, Ind., 1971-86; interim pastor 3d Presbyn. Ch. Ft. Wayne, Ind., 1987-95. Author: Frontier Faith: The Story of the Pioneer Congregations, 1992, The Best of Fort Wayne, vol. 1, 2000, vol. 2, 2001; co-editor: On the Heritage Trail, 1994; contbr. articles to profl. jours. Pres. Allen County Libr. Trustees, Ft. Wayne, Allen County Libr. Found., Ft. Wayne, Clergy United for Action, Ft. Wayne; trustee Hanover (Ind.) Coll.; chmn. Bicentennial Religious Heritage Commn., 1994; bd. dirs. Smock Found., 1971-85. Mem. Ind. Religious History Assn. (bd. dirs.), Allen County Ft. Wayne Hist. Soc. (bd. dirs.), The Quest Club (pres.). Avocations: tennis, travel, hiking, canoeing. Home: 6726 Quail Ridge Ln Fort Wayne IN 46804-2874

MATHER, JOHN CROMWELL, astrophysicist; b. Roanoke, Va., Aug. 7, 1946; s. Robert Eugene and Martha Belle (Cromwell) Mather; m. Jane Anne Hauser, Nov. 22, 1980. BA, Swarthmore (Pa.) Coll., 1968; PhD, U. Calif., Berkeley, 1974; DSc (hon.), Swarthmore Coll., 1994. NAS/NRC rsch. assoc. NASA/Goddard Inst. for Space Studies, N.Y.C., 1974-76; lectr. in astronomy Columbia U., N.Y.C., 1975-76; astrophysicist NASA/Goddard Space Flight Ctr., Greenbelt, Md., 1976—, head infrared astrophysics br., 1988-89, 90-93, sr. scientist, 1989-90, 93—, study scientist Cosmic Background Explorer Satellite, 1976-82, project scientist COBE, 1982—, prin. investigator FIRAS on COBE, 1976—. Chmn. external adv. bd. Ctr. for Astrophys. Rsch. in the Antarctic, U. Chgo., 1992—95; mem. lunar astrophysics mgmt. ops. working group NASA Hdqrs., Washington, 1992; study scientist Next Generation Space Telescope, 1995—2002; mem. NRC Bd. Physics and Astronomy, 1998—2001; sr. project scientist James Webb Space Telescope, 2002—. Author: The Very First Light with John Boslough, 1996; contbr. articles to profl. jours. Named to Hall of Fame, Newton (NJ) H.S. Hall of Fame, 2003; recipient Nat. Space Achievement award, Rotary, 1991, Laurels award, Aviation Week and Space Tech., 1992, Space Sci. award, AIAA, 1993, John Scott award, City of Phila., 1995, Mark. Aaronson Meml. prize, 1998, Franklin medal in Physics, 1999, Presdl. Rank award, NASA, 2003. Fellow: AAAS (Rumford prize 1996), Am. Phys. Soc.; mem.: Nat. Acad. Scis., Internat. Astron. Union, Am. Astron. Soc. (councilor 1998—2001, Dannie Heineman prize astrophysics 1993), Sigma Xi. Democrat. Unitarian Universalist. Achievements include proposed Cosmic Background Explorer Satellite, led team to successful launch in 1989; measured spectrum of cosmic microwave background radiation to unprecedented accuracy. Office: NASA/Goddard Space Flight Code 685 Greenbelt MD 20771-0001

MATHER, MILDRED EUNICE, retired archivist; b. Washington, Iowa, July 25, 1922; d. Hollis John and Delpha Irene (Cummings) Whiting; m. Stewart Elbert Mather, Aug. 7, 1955; children: Julie Marie, Thomas Stewart-(dec.). Cert., Burlington and Des Moines, 1941, 1947, Stenotype Inst., 1948. Typist Burlington Willow-Weave, 1941-42, Burlington Basket Co., 1942; clk. typist U.S. Dept. War, Washington, 1942-43; supr. internat. conf. U.S. Dept. State, Washington, 1949-52; bookkeeper Iowa Wesleyan Coll., Mt. Pleasant, 1952-55; clk. typist Herbert Hoover Presdl. Libr., West Branch, Iowa, 1964-69, archives technician, 1964-72, archivist, libr., 1972-92, ret., 1992. With WAC U.S. Army, 1943—46. Mem.: Order Ea. Star (worthy matron). Republican. Home: 1794 Garfield Ave West Branch IA 52358-9403

MATHER, RICHARD BURROUGHS, retired Chinese language and literature educator; b. Baoding, Hebei, China, Nov. 11, 1913; s. William Arnot and Grace (Burroughs) M.; m. Virginia Marjorie Temple, June 3, 1939; 1 dau., Elizabeth Temple. BA, Princeton U., 1935; B.Th., Princeton Theol. Sem., 1939; PhD in Oriental Langs, U. Calif., Berkeley, 1949. Ordained to ministry United Presbyterian Ch. U.S., 1939; pastor Belle Haven (Va.) Presbyterian Ch., 1939-41; asst. prof. Chinese U. Minn., Mpls., 1949-57, assoc. prof., 1957-64, prof., 1964-84. Mem. Am. Council Learned Socs. Com. on Study of Chinese Civilization, 1979-81 Author: Shih-shuo hsin-yu, A New Account of Tales of the World, 1976, rev. edit., 2002, The Poet Shen Yueh (441-513), the Reticent Marquis, 1988, The Age of Eternal Brilliance: Three Poets of the Yung-ming Era, 2003; contbr. articles on medieval Chinese lit. and religion. Guggenheim fellow, 1956-57; Fulbright Hays grantee, 1956-57, 63-64; Am. Council Learned Socs. grantee, 1963-64 Mem. Am. Oriental Soc. (pres. 1980-81), Assn. Asian Studies. Democrat. Home: 2091 Dudley Ave Saint Paul MN 55108-1415

MATHER, ROGER FREDERICK, music educator, writer; b. London, May 27, 1917; came to U.S., 1938; s. Richard and Marie Louise (Schultze) M.; m. Dorothea Meinen, Sept. 11, 1943 (div. Sept. 1971); children: Arielle Diane, Christopher Richard; m. Betty Louise Bang, Aug. 3, 1973. BA with honors, Cambridge U., 1938; MSc, MIT, 1940; MA in Metallurgy, U. Cambridge, 1941. Registered profl. engr., Ohio, Mich., Pa. Rsch. metallurgist Inland Steel Co., East Chicago, Ind., 1940-42; chief metallurgist Willys-Overland Motors, Toledo, 1942-46, Kaiser-Frazer Corp., Willow Run, Mich., 1946-50; project mgr. U.S. Steel Corp., Pitts., 1950-61; dir. rsch. engring. Mine Safety Appliances Co., Pitts., 1961-62; rsch. staff Du Pont Co., Wilmington, Del., 1962-63; chief nuclear power tech. br. NASA, Cleve., 1963-73; adj. prof. music U. Iowa, Iowa City, 1973-96. Instr. pub. speaking and stage fright U. Iowa, 1983-85, Kirkwood C.C., Iowa City, 1983-85; cons. Miyazawa Flutes, U.S.A., Coralville, Iowa, 1985-90; lectr. U. Toledo; Mich. state examiner Registration of Profl. Engrs.; condr. numerous workshops, clinics, classes, and flute recitals regionally, nationally, Europe and Asia. Author: The Art of Playing the Flute, 1980, Vol. 2, 1981, Vol. 3, 1988; contbr. chpts. to several woodwind anthologies; pub., exec. editor The Romney Press, 1980—; contbr. poems to numerous poetry anthologies in US, Eng., numerous articles to sci. and music jours. Mem. Internat. Soc. Poets (Hall of Fame, 1998, Poet of Merit, 2002), Nat. Flute Assn. (life, coms.), The Pa. Assn., Mensa. Episcopalian. Avocations: semi-professional photography, high fidelity sound reproduction contributions, alternative medicine. Home: 715 George St Iowa City IA 52240 E-mail: bangmather@aol.com.

MATHER, RUTH ELSIE, writer; b. Waverly, Wash., Feb. 14, 1934; d. James Orrin and Leona Ezthelda (Mather) Tallman; m. Mike Nicholas Dakis, Apr. 20, 1958 (div. Nov. 1971); children: Cynthia Michelle, Martin Nicholas; m. Fred Junior Morgan, Nov. 20, 1971. BA with highest honors, Brigham Young U., 1961, MA, 1965; postgrad., U. Miss., 1977-78. Cert. secondary tchr., Idaho, cert. elem. tchr. and secondary tchr. grades 7-14, Calif. English tchr. Iglesia Jesucristo Rama Roma, Mexico City, 1955-56, Lemhi County Schs., Leadore, Idaho, 1962-66; English instr. Yonsei U., Seoul, Republic of Korea, 1973-74, U. Md. Far East Divsn., Seoul, 1975-77, Boise (Idaho) State U., 1978-79, Coll. of the Redwoods, Eureka, Calif., 1980-81; writer hist. video scripts History West Pub. Co., Oklahoma City, 1990—; screenwriter Frontier Images, Canyon Country, Calif., 1994—. Cons. on hist. video for PBS, A La Carte, San Francisco, 1994-95; guest expert on Secrets of the Gold Rush-PBS, 1995; cons. Western Mont. Coll. Schmittroth collection of electronically printed Western history books, Dillon, 1997—. Author: Hanging the Sheriff: A Biography of Henry Plummer, 1987, John David Borthwick: Artist of the Gold Rush, 1989, Gold Camp Desperadoes: Study of Crime & Punishment on Frontier, 1990, Vigilante Victims, 1991, Scandal of the West: Domestic Violence on the Frontier, 1998, The Bannack Gallows, 1998, The Cottonwood Murders: Unsolved, 1999; contbr. short stories, book revs., articles to encys. and profl. jours. Local campaign dir. Dem. Party, Arcata, Calif., 1969-70. Mem. Nat. Outlaw and Lawman Assn., Western Outlaw and Lawman Assn., Virginia City Preservation Alliance, People for the Ethical Treatment of Animals, Nat. Anti-Vivisection Soc., Physicians' Com. for Responsible Medicine. Avocations: reading, hiking. Office: History West Pub Co PO Box 23133 Oklahoma City OK 73123-2133

MATHER, STEPHANIE JUNE, lawyer; b. Kansas City, Mo., Dec. 5, 1952; d. Edward Wayne and H. June (Kunkel) M.; m. Miles Christopher Zimmerman, Sept. 23, 1988. BA magna cum laude, Okla. City U., 1975, JD with honors, 1980. Lawyer Pierce, Couch, Hendrickson, Johnston & Baysinger, Okla. City, Okla., 1980-88, Manchester, Hiltgen & Healy, P.C., Okla. City, 1989-90; sr. staff counsel Nat. Am. Ins. Co., Chandler, Okla., 1990-98; atty. Ctr. for Edn. Law, Oklahoma City, 1998—. Asst. v.p. Lagere & Walkingstick Ins. Agy., Inc., Chandler, Okla., 1993-98. Co-chair Lincoln County Dem. Party, 1991-92, 95-97; v.p. Lincoln County Dem. Women, 1992-95, pres., 1995-97; bd. dirs. Lincoln County Partnership for Children, 1994—, Gateway to Prevention and Recovery, 1996-97. Mem. Okla. Bar Assn. (editor, bd. editors, 1992-99), Lincoln County Bar Assn. (mem. libr. bd. 1990—), Nat. Sch. Bds. Assn. (coun. of sch. attys. 1998—), Okla. State Sch. Bds. Assn. (coun. of sch. attys. 1998—, bd. dirs. 2002--), Lincoln County Profl. Women, Alpha Phi (treas. Ctrl. Okla. Alumnae 1997-99). Democrat. Avocations: reading, genealogy, ranching, cooking. Home: PO Box 246 Chandler OK 74834-0246 Office: 900 N Broadway Ave #300 Oklahoma City OK 73102-5828 E-mail: smather@cfel.com.

MATHERLEE, THOMAS RAY, health care consultant; b. Dayton, Ohio, Sept. 18, 1934; s. Dennis R. and Eleanor E. Matherlee; children: Michael, Jennifer, Craig, Brent, Brian. BSBA, Findlay Coll., 1958; MBA, U. Chgo., 1960. Adminstrv. resident Shannon Hosp., San Angelo, Tex., 1959-60; asst. administr. Richland Meml. Hosp., Olney, Ill., 1960-61; adminstrv. asst., then adminstr. Forsyth Meml. Hosp., Winston-Salem, N.C., 1961-68; exec. dir. Gaston County (N.C.) Hosp., 1968-70, Gaston Meml. Hosp., Inc., Gastonia, 1970-80, pres., 1981-85; sr. v.p. Vols. Hosps. of Am., Inc., Washington, 1986-87, exec. v.p. Irving, Tex., 1987-90; pres. AMA Svcs., Inc., 1990-94; sr. v.p. The Hunter Group, 1994-97; pres. Matherlee Assoc., Banner Elk, N.C., 1997—. Cons. Sch. Pastoral Care N.C. Bapt. Hosp., Winston-Salem, 1967-68; mem. sub-area adv. coun. Health Systems Agy., 1975-80; adj. faculty Sch. Cmty. and Allied Health U. Ala.-Birmingham, 1980-85; bd. dirs. Joint Commn. on Accreditation of Healthcare Orgns., 1986-90, treas., audit and fin. com. chmn., mem. exec. com. Contbr. articles on hosp. adminstrn. to profl. jours. Dir. Olney, Ill. CD, 1960-61; mem. fin. com. Piedmont coun. Boy Scouts Am., 1970; mem. adv. bd. Gastonia Wesleyan Youth Chorus, 1972; mem. joint com. nursing edn. N.C. State Bd. Edn. and Bd. Higher Edn., 1969-71; mem. adminstrv. bd. First United Meth. Ch., Gastonia, 1972-74; bd. dirs. Gaston County Heart Assn., 1968-70, Forsyth County Cancer Soc., 1964-65; trustee N.C. Hosp. Edn. and Rsch. Found., 1966-71, pres. 1970-71; trustee N.C. Blue Cross and Blue Shield, Inc., 1971-77, Southeastern Hosp. Conf., 1971-72, 73-81; mem. edn. com. 1978—, mem. program com., 1975-76. Named Boss of Yr., Nat. Secs. Assn., 1970-71. Fellow Am. Coll. Healthcare Execs.; mem. MGMA, N.C. Hosp. Assn. (life, trustee 1966-72, pres. 1970-71, chmn. coun. govt. liaison 1978-81, Disting. Svc. award 1985), N.C. League Nursing, Am. Hosp. Assn. (ho. of dels. 1973-78, 83-85), spkr. Ho. of dels. 1985, trustee 1975-78, 83-85, chmn. bd. trustees 1984), Gastonia C. of C. (health affairs com. 1969-72), Kiwanis.

MATHERN, DEB, state legislator; 2 children., N.D. State Coll. of Sc.; grad. Credit Union mgmt., U. Wis. Mem. N.D. Senate from 45th dist., Bismark, 1999—. Bd. dirs. N. D. Credit Union League, 1999—. Recipient Profl. of the Year, 1997. Mem. Fargo C. of C., NDCUL and affiliates. Office: Dist 45 3228 2nd St N Fargo ND 58102-1109 E-mail: dmathern@state.nd.us.

MATHERS, ALLEN STANLEY, judge, arbitrator, consultant; b. Elmhurst, N.Y., Jan. 20, 1949; s. William Albert and Agnes (Przeniczny) M.; m. Mary Elizabeth Breslin, Oct. 1, 1977; children: Matthew Allen, Sarah Anne, Amanda Mary. BA, St. Francis Coll., 1970; JD, St. John's U., Jamaica, N.Y., 1973. Bar: N.Y. 1974, Conn. 1989, U.S. Dist. Ct. (so. and ea. dists.) N.Y. 1974, U.S. Ct. Appeals (2d cir.) 1974, U.S. Supreme Ct. 1983, U.S. Ct. Mil. Appeals 1986. Assoc. Israelson & Streit, N.Y.C., 1973-80; dir. legal svcs. fund, local 74 Svc. Employees Internat. Union, AFL-CIO, Long Island City, N.Y., 1982—. Village justice Village of Garden City, N.Y., 1997—. Mayor, Village of Garden City; bd. dirs, Arthritis Found. Col., JAG, N.Y. Guard. Mem. ABA, N.Y. State Bar Assn. (spl. com. prepaid legal svcs.), Nassau County Bar Assn., Am. Arbitration Assn., Atlantic Beach Club, Cherry Valley Club, Equestrian Order Knights of Holy Sepulchre. Roman Catholic. Home: 30 Kensington Rd Garden City NY 11530-4241 Office: Service Employees Internat Union Local 74 24-09 38th Ave Long Island City NY 11101-3512

MATHERS, BRADLEY L. music educator; b. Maryville, Mo., Nov. 24, 1947; s. Doyle L. and Bonnie L. Mathers; m. D. Annette Vance, July 29, 2000; children: Becky, Mike, Jessica, Brock, Brice, Clay, Jennelle. B in Music Edn., Kans. U., 1970; MS in Edn., N.W. Mo. State U., 1982. Music instr. Unified Sch. Dist. 806, Wathena, Kans., 1970—71, Fairfax (Mo.) R-III, 1971—76, West Nodaway R-I, Burlington Junction, Mo., 1976—92, Horace Mann Lab. Sch., Maryville, Mo., 1992—99, Tarkio (Mo.) R-I, 1999—. Mem.: Mosha Shrine Temple, St. Joe Mo. Scottish Rite, AF&AM Masonic Lodge (past master 1997—98). Avocations: music, antiques. Home: 901 Main Tarkio MO 64491 Office: Midwest Trophies PO Box 75 123 W Main Burlington Junction MO 64428

MATHERS, MARGARET, reference librarian, archivist; b. Ada, Okla., Feb. 16, 1929; d. Robert Lee and Josiephine Margaret (Reed) Erwin; m. Coleman F. Moss, Sept. 1956 (div. 1966); children: Carol Lee Gibson-Taylor, Marilyn Frances; m. Boyd Leroy Mathers, Apr. 10, 1967 (div. 1987). BS in Music, Tex. U., 1950. Svc. rep. Gen. Tel. Co., Santa Monica, Calif., 1955-58; tchr. pvt. sch. Santa Monica, 1958-60; computer program and data analyst System Devel. Corp., Santa Monica, 1961-66; computer programmer Inst. Def. Analyses,

Arlington, Va., 1966-70; typist, transcriber Edgewater, Md., 1971-80; sec. People Assisting the Homeless, 1992-94; proofreader, copy editor Farmington Daily Times, 1993-99, mem. editl. bd., libr., office mgr., 1999—. Pres. San Juan Coun. Cmty. Agys., 1986-87, treas., 1987-89, sec., 1989-90; cons. in field. Dir. San Juan Cath. Charities, Farmington, N.Mex., 1984-93, asst. dir., 1993-96, sec. bd. dirs., 1997-2000; chmn. county Libertarian Party N.Mex., San Juan County, 1985-99, sec. ctrl. com., 1988-92, mem. ctrl. com., 1988—; mem. selection com. Habitat for Humanity, 1990; mem. San Juan County Task Force on Housing, 1991, Task Force on Transp., 1991; mem. social justice com. Sacred Heart, Farmington, 1992; mem. adv. bd. San Juan County DNA Legal Aid, 1992, sec., 1993; sec. Cmty. Network Coun., 1992-94, treas., 1994—; treas. Neighborhood Watch, 1998—; minister Secular Franciscan Order, 1997-2001. Roman Catholic. Avocations: puzzles, politics, philosophy. Office: The Daily Times PO Box 450 Farmington NM 87499-0450

MATHERS, MARSHALL See EMINEM

MATHERS, WILLIAM HARRIS, lawyer; b. Newport, RI, Aug. 27, 1914; s. Howard and Margaret I. (Harris) M.; m. Myra T. Martin, Jan. 17, 1942; children: William Martin, Michael Harris, John Grinnell, Myra Tutt, Ursula Fraser. AB, Dartmouth Coll., 1935; JD, Yale U., 1938. Bar: NY 1940. With Milbank, Tweed & Hope, 1938-48; mem. Milbank, Tweed, Hope & Hadley, 1948-57; v.p., sec., dir. Yale & Towne Mfg. Co., Stamford, Conn., 1957-60; ptnr. Chadbourne & Parke, 1960-75, counsel, 1983—; exec. v.p., gen. counsel, sec., dir. United Brands Co., 1975-82. Mayor, trustee Village of Cove Neck, N.Y., 1950 82; trustee Barnard Coll., 1958-69. Served as pvt. to maj. U.S. Army, 1942-46. Mem. ABA, N.Y. State Bar Assn., Nassau County Bar Assn., Assn. of Bar of City of N.Y., New Eng. Soc. in City of N.Y., Casque and Gauntlet, Corbey Court, Piping Rock Club, Seminole Golf Club, N.Y. Yacht Club, Cold Spring Harbor Beach Club, Phi Beta Kappa, Psi Upsilon. Home: 1460 King George Farm Rd Sutton VT 05867 Office: 30 Rockefeller Plz New York NY 10112-0127

MATHES, EDWARD CONRAD, architect; b. New Orleans, Mar. 10, 1943; s. Earl L. and Margaret (Gash) M.; m. Anne M. Ergenbright, Mar. 1, 1964 (div. June 2000); children: Margaret Elizabeth Hughes, Anne Catherine Aboud. BArch, U. Southwestern La., 1968. Registered arch., La., Miss., Fla., Tex., Ala., Ga., Tenn., Ky., N.C., S.C., W.Va., Conn. Tchr. U. Southwestern La., Lafayette, 1968-69; asst. to mng. arch. Rogers, Taliaferro, Kostritsky & Lamb, Balt., 1969; pres. Mathes, Bergman & Assocs., Inc., New Orleans, 1969-82, The Mathes Group, New Orleans, 1982—2000; chmn. MathesBrierre Architects, 2001—. Chmn. Orleans Svc. Ctr., ARC, 1993-94; bd. dirs. City Park Improvement Assn., 1996—, pres. Recipient Am. Sch. and Univ. award, 1983, 1985, Partnership award, ARC, 1998, CEO's award, S.E. La. chpt. ARC, People's Choice award for music., comms., theatre complex, Loyola New Orleans, 1989, People's Choice award for Univ. Libr., 2000, Cert. Recognition Design Excellence, Nat. Orgn. Minority Architects, 2002. Mem.: AIA (pres. New Orleans chpt. 1989, Inst. scholar 1968—69, Honor award New Orleans Chpt. 1982, 1989, 2000, Honor award La. 1982, 1986, 2001), Constrn. Industry Assn. (pres. 1984—85, Honor award 1993), City Energy Club, Metairie Country Club, Pickwick Club, Rotary (pres. New Orleans 1985—86). Republican. Presbyterian. Avocations: tennis, travel. Home: # 4 Park Island Dr New Orleans LA 70122 Office: MathesBrierre Architects 201 Saint Charles Ave Fl 41 New Orleans LA 70170-4100 Office Phone: 504-586-9303. E-mail: emathes@mathesbrierre.com.

MATHES, STEPHEN JOHN, plastic and reconstructive surgeon, educator; b. New Orleans, Aug. 17, 1943; s. John Ernest and Norma (Deutsch) M.; children: David, Brian, Edward. BS, La. State U., 1964; MD, La. State U., New Orleans, 1968. Diplomate Am. Bd. Surgery, Am. Bd. Plastic Surgery (dir. 1993—). Asst. prof. surgery Wash. U., St. Louis, 1977-78; assoc. prof. U. Calif., San Francisco, 1978-84, prof. surgery, 1984, prof. surgery, anatomy and cell biology, 1984-85, also bd. dirs. craniofacial anomalies; head plastic surgery sect. U. Mich., Ann Arbor, 1984-85, prof. surgery, 1984-85; prof. surgery, head plastic and reconstructive surgery div. U. Calif., San Francisco, 1985—, prof. growth and devel. Sch. Dentistry, 1985—. Pres. residency rev. com. Accreditation Coun. Grad. Med. Edn., 2004—. Author: (textbook) Clinical Applications for Muscle and Musculocutaneous Flaps, 1983 (Best Med. Book award Physician's category, Am. Med. Writer's Assn., 1983), Clinical Atlas of Muscle and Musculocutaneous Flaps, 1979, Plastic Surgery Principles and Practice, 1990, Reconstructive Surgery, 1996; contbr. articles to profl. jours. including Am. Soc. Plastic Surgery, Am. Soc. Aesthetic Plastic Surgery, 1981. Recipient 1st prize plastic surgery scholarship contest Plastic Surgery Edn. Found., 1981, 83, 84, 86, 93, 99, Spl. Achievement award Am. Soc. Plastic Surgery, 1980, Best Sci. Paper, Am. Soc. Aesthetic Plastic Surgery, 1981; grantee NIH, 1982-85, 86-90. Fellow ACS (chmn. adv. coun. on plastic and maxillofacial surgery 1999—, gov. at large); mem. Am. Assn. Plastic Surgery (sec. 2004—, Clinician of Yr. award 2001), Plastic Surgery Rsch. Coun. (pres. 1988), Am. Soc. Surgery of Hand, Soc. Univ. Surgeons, Assn. Acad. Chairmen in Plastic Surgery (pres. 2001), Plastic Surgery Ednl. Found. (bd. dirs. 1994-2000, v.p. 2001, pres. 2003-04). Republican. Episcopalian. Avocations: gardening, tennis. Home: 2730 Broderick St San Francisco CA 94123 Office: 350 Parnassus St Ste 509 San Francisco CA 94117-0001 Office Phone: 415-353-2410. Business E-Mail: mathess@surgery.ucsf.edu. E-mail: sjmathes@pacbell.net.

MATHESON, ALAN ADAMS, law educator; b. Cedar City, Utah, Feb. 2, 1932; s. Scott Milne and Adele (Adams) M.; m. Milicent Holbrook, Aug. 15, 1960; children: Alan, David Scott, John Robert. BA, U. Utah, 1953, MS, 1957, JD, 1959; postgrad., Columbia U. Bar: Utah 1960, Ariz. 1975. Asst. to pres. Utah State U., 1961-67; mem. faculty Ariz. State U., Tempe, 1967—, prof. law, 1970—, dean, 1978-84, 89, 97-98. Bd. dirs. Ariz. Found. for Legal Svcs. and Edn. Pres. Tri-City Mental Health Citizens Bd., 1973-74. With AUS, 1953-55. Mem. ABA, Utah Bar Assn., Ariz. Bar Assn., Maricopa County Bar Assn., Phi Beta Kappa, Order of Coif. Democrat. Mem. Lds Ch. Home: 720 E Geneva Dr Tempe AZ 85282-3737 Office: Ariz State U Coll Law Tempe AZ 85287

MATHESON, ANN, librarian, writer; b. Lochalsh, Wester Ross, Scotland, July 5, 1940; d. Alexander and Catherine (MacRae) M.; m. T. Russell Walker, Nov. 24, 1973. MA, U. St. Andrews, 1962; Diploma in Scottish Studies, U. Edinburgh, 1968, MLitt, 1970, PhD, 1979; Order of the Brit. Empire, 1998; DLitt, St. And, 1999. Asst. keeper Nat. Libr. Scotland, Edinburgh, 1975 83, keeper, 1983-2000; sec. gen. coun. U. Edinburgh, 2001—. Sec. gen. sec. Ligue des Bibliothèques Européennes de Recherche, 1994-2000; chair lit. com. Scottish Arts Coun., 1997-2003; chair Consortium of European Rsch. Librs., 2000—, NEWSPLAN 2000, 1999—; specialist adviser Scottish Arts Coun., 2003—. Author: (with Mary Ferguson) The Scottish Gaelic Union Catalogue, vol. I, 1984, Theories of Rhetoric in the 18th-century Scottish Sermon, 1995; editor: (with Patrick Cadell) For the Encouragement of Learning, 1989; editor Transactions of the Edinburgh Bibliographical Society, 1973-83; contbr. articles and revs. to profl. jours. Decorated Order Brit. Empire. Mem.: Scottish Libr. Assn. (hon.), Ligue des Bibliothèques Européennes de Recherche (hon.). Home: Yewbank 52 Liberton Brae Edinburgh EH16 6AF Scotland E-mail: a.matheson@tinyworld.co.uk.

MATHESON, JIM, congressman; b. Salt Lake City, 1960; m. Amy; 1 child: Will. BA in govt., Harvard U.; MBA, UCLA. Worked in energy indus., 12 yrs.; founder The Matheson Group, 1998; congressman Utah, 2nd dist., 2000—; mem. fin. svcs. com. Mem. Congressional coms. House Budget, Transportation and Infrastructure, Sci.; subcom. Transportation and Infrastructure, Highways and Transit, Aviation, Energy; liaison with Rep. for freshman class. Mem. Salt Lake Public Utilities bd., Scott M. Matheson Leadership Forum. Democrat. Office: 410 Cannon House Office bldg Washington DC 20515

MATHESON, LINDA, retired social worker; b. Martna, Estonia, Mar. 29, 1918; came to U.S., 1962, naturalized, 1969; d. Endrek and Leena Endrekson; m. Charles McLaren Matheson, Feb. 5, 1955. Diploma, Inst. Social Scis., Tallinn, Estonia, 1944; MS, Columbia U., 1966, D in Social Work, 1974. Diplomate clin. social work. Social work officer UN Rehab. and Resettlement Assn., Germany, 1946-48; social worker Victorian Mental Hygiene, Australia, 1955-62; rsch. assoc., social work project dir. Arthritis Midway House, N.Y.C., 1966-68; rsch. Columbia Presbyn. Med. Ctr., N.Y.C., 1971-75; field instr. Columbia U. Sch. Social Work, 1977-79, Columbia Presbyn. Med. Ctr., NYU Sch. Social Work, 1989-90; ret., 1992. Family Found. fellow, 1966, 89-90; grantee NIMH, 1969-72. Mem. Nat. Assn. Social Workers, Nat. Wildlife Fedn., Ctr. for Study of Presidency, Internat. Platform Assn., United Leaders, BATUN, Baltic-Am. Freedom League, Smithsonian Assn., English Spkg. Union, Alliance Francaise, Columbia U. Alumni Assn., Met. Mus. N.Y. Lutheran. Home: 30-95 29th St Astoria NY 11102-2735

MATHESON, NINA W. medical researcher; Prof., dir. William H. Welch Med. Libr., Balt., 1985—94; prof. emeritus, Welch Med. Libr., Health Divsn. Adminstrn. Johns Hopkins U., Balt., 1994—. Named Disting. prof. nursing, Vanderbilt Sch. Nursing, 1976—82. Office: Johns Hopkins Univ c/o Barbara Todd 720 Rutland Ave Baltimore MD 21205-2109

MATHEU, FEDERICO MANUEL, university chancellor; b. Humacao, P.R., Mar. 17, 1941; s. Federico Matheu-Baez and Matilde Delgado-Vazquez; m. Myrna Delgado-Miranda, May 30, 1963; children: Federico Antonio, Rosa Myrna, Alfredo Javier, David Reinaldo. BS in Chem. Engring, U. P.R., 1962; PhD in Phys. Chemistry, U. Pitts., 1971. Chem. engr. Commonwealth Oil Refining Co., 1962-63; mem. adminstrv. staff and faculty U. P.R., 1963-78, dir. Humacao Coll., 1976-78; chancellor San German campus Inter Am. U. P.R., 1978-91; exec. dir., gen. coun. on edn. Commonwealth of P.R., Hato Rey, 1991-96; chancellor U. Metropolitana-Ana G. Méndez U. System, 1996—. Cons. in field. Author papers, reports in field. Named Disting. Educator P.R. Jaycees, 1974 Mem. Colegio de Quimicos P.R., Am. Chem. Soc., Sci. Tchrs. Assn. P.R. (pres. 1975-76), P.R. Acad. Arts and Scis., Phi Delta Kappa, Phi Tau Sigma. Home: Parque de Villa Caperra No 17 Zuania St Guaynabo PR 00966 Office: UMET PO Box 21150 San Juan PR 00928-1150

MATHEW, JAMES, cardiologist; b. Nariyapuram, Kerala, India, Oct. 15, 1954; came to U.S., 1982; s. T. G. and Mariamma Mathew; 1 child, Shanti. BSc, U. Kerala, 1975; MBBS, Med. Coll. Trivandrum, Kerala, 1980. Diplomate Am. Bd. Internal Medicine, Am. Bd. of Internal Medicine Cardiovascular Diseases. Resident in internal medicine Cook County Hosp., Chgo., 1989, fellowship in cardiology, chmn. divsn. adult cardiology, 1990-97, program dir. fellowship in cardiovasc. disease, 1990-97; pres. LaSalle Cardiology Inc., Galesburg, Ill., 1997—2001; dir. cardiology Galesburg (Ill.) Cottage Hosp., 1998—; clin. assoc. prof. U. Iowa Coll. of Medicine, Iowa City, 2000—. Contbr. articles to med. jours. Fellow Am. Coll. Cardiology, Am. Coll. Chest Physicians, Am. Coll. Angiology, Am. Heart Assn. Office: Galesburg Cottage Hosp 695 N Kellogg St Galesburg IL 61401-3726

MATHEWS, B. J. secondary school educator; b. Navasota, Tex., Nov. 27, 1948; s. Roy Lee Mathews and Clarissa Fuller-Mathews. BS, Jarvis Christian Coll., 1972; diploma in art, Stratford Career Inst., 2003; student, Art Ctr., Waco, TSTI, Southwest Sch. Art, San Antonio, TX, McLennan Community Coll., Waco. Cert. tchr., Tex., in specialized art, Art Instruction Sch., Minn. Tchr. Rochester (N.Y.) City Sch. Dist., 1972-75, Mexia (Tex.) Ind. Sch. Dist., 1977-92, Dallas Ind. Sch. Dist., 1992-93; prison tchr. Windham Sch. Dist., Hondo, Tex., 1993—2001; tchr. GED program Juvenile Detention Residential Ctr., Hondo, 1994-97. Publ. (songs) Ride the Tide, 1997, Desire Afire, 1998. Mem.: Broadcast Music Inc. Avocations: reading, writing, portrait painting, composing music, calligraphic lettering. Home: PO Box 971 Mexia TX 76667 Office: Texas Youth Commission 116 Burleson Rd Mart TX 76664

MATHEWS, BARBARA EDITH, gynecologist; b. Oct. 5, 1946; d. Joseph Chesley and Pearl (Cieri) Mathews. AB, U. Calif., 1969; MD, Tufts U., 1972. Diplomate Am. Bd. Ob-Gyn. Intern Cottage Hosp., Santa Barbara, Calif., 1972-73, Santa Barbara Gen. Hosp., 1972-73; resident in ob-gyn Beth Israel Hosp., Boston, 1973-77; clin. fellow in ob-gyn Harvard U., Boston, 1973-76, instr., 1976-77; gynecologist Sansum Med. Clin., Santa Barbara, 1977-98; sr. scientist Sansum Med. Rsch. Inst., 1998—; med. dir., gynecologist Women's Health Svcs., Santa Barbara, 1998—. Faculty mem. ann. postgrad. course Harvard Med. Sch.; bd. dirs. Sansum Med. Clinic, 1989-96, vice chmn. bd: dirs., 1994-96; dir. ann. postgrad course UCLA Med. Sch. Bd. dirs. Meml. Rehab. Found., Santa Barbara, Channel City Club, Santa Barbara, Music Acad. of the West, Santa Barbara, St. Francis Med. Ctr., Santa Barbara; mem. citizen's contg. edn. adv. coun. Santa Barbara C.C.; moderator Santa Ba rbara Cottage Hosp. Cmty. Health Forum. Author: (with L. Burke) Colposcopy in Clinical Practice, 1977; contbg. author Manual of Ambulatory Surgery, 1982. Fellow ACOG, ACS; mem. AMA, Am. Soc. Colposcopy and Cervical Pathology (dir. 1982-84), Harvard U. Alumni Assn., Tri-counties Obstet. and Gynecol. Soc. (pres. 1981-82), Birnam Wood Golf Club (Santa Barbara), Phi Beta Kappa. Home: 2105 Anacapa St Santa Barbara CA 93105-3503 Office: 2235 De La Vina St Santa Barbara CA 93105-3815 Office Fax: 805-687-0012.

MATHEWS, BERNICE MARTIN, state legislator, small business owner; b. Jackson, Miss., Nov. 12, 1933; children: Arnold II, Anthony, Aileen, Barbara, Ruben, Clive, Allen (dec.). BSN, MEd, U. Nev. Small bus. owner; mem. Nev. Senate, Dist. 1 Washoe, Carson City, 1994—; mem. fin. com., human resources and facilities com. Nev. Senate, mem. legis. affairs and ops. com. City councilwoman, Reno; mem. Regional EMS Coun., 1974-85; past chair Reno Civil Svc. Commn., 1979-89; active Ch. Youth Dept., 1981-87, United Way Distbn. Com., 1992—, Nev. Women's Fund Adv. Bd., 1992—; bd. dirs. Trukee Meadows Boys and Girls Club, 1987—. Mem. Nev. Nurses Assn., Commn. for Women. Democrat. also: Nev State Legis Bldg 401 S Carson St Rm 208 Carson City NV 89701-4747 Office: PO Box 7176 Reno NV 89510-7176 Fax: 706-687-8206; 702-673-2086. E-mail: bmathews@sen.state.nv.us.

MATHEWS, CHRISTOPHER KING, biochemist, educator; b. N.Y.C., 1937; s. Frank Pelletreau and Alison Barstow (Murphy) M.; m. Catherine Anne Zitcer, June 19, 1960; children: Lawrence Stuart, Anne Catherine. BA in Chemistry, Reed Coll., 1958; PhD in Biochemistry (USPHS fellow), U. Wash., 1962. USPHS postdoctoral fellow in biochemistry U. Pa., 1962-63; asst. prof. biology Yale U., 1964-67; asso. prof. biochemistry U. Ariz. Coll. Medicine, 1967-73, prof. biochemistry, 1973-77; prof., chmn. dept. biochemistry and biophysics Oreg. State U., 1978—2002, Disting. prof., 1991, emeritus, 2002—. Mem. virology study sect. NIH, 1977-79, mem. microbial chemistry study sect., 1979-81; Tage Erlander guest prof. Swedish Nat. Sci. Rsch. Coun., 1994-95. Author: Bacteriophage Biochemistry, 1971, Bacteriophage T4, 1983; co-author: (with K.E. Van Holde) Biochemistry, 1990, 96, 2000; contbr. numerous articles on nucleotide and nucleic acid metabolism, biochemistry of virus replication, and regulation of cellular metabolism to profl. jours.; editl. bd. Jour. Virology, 1970-80, Archives Biochemistry and Biophysics, 1973-80, Jour. Biol. Chemistry, 1994—, Biochem. Molecular Biology Edn., 2000—. Am. Cancer soc. scholar grantee, 1973-74; USPHS research grantee, 1964-2002; Am. Heart Assn. grantee, 1968-78; NSF research grantee, 1980-82, 83-86, 90—; Eleanor Roosevelt Internat. Cancer fellow, 1984-85; recipient Discovery award Med. Research Found. Oreg., 1986, Disting. prof. award Oreg. State U. Alumni Assn., 1988. Mem. AAAS, AAUP, Am. Soc. Biochemistry and Molecular Biology, Am. Soc. Microbiology, Am. Chem. Soc., Am. Soc. Cell Biology, various environ. and pub. interest assns. Home: 3336 SW Willamette Ave Corvallis OR 97333-1507 Office: Dept Biochemistry and Biophysics Oreg State U Corvallis OR 97331-7305 Office Phone: 541-737-1865. Business E-Mail: mathewsc@orid.orst.edu.

MATHEWS, DAVID, foundation executive; b. Grove Hill, Ala., Dec. 6, 1935; s. Forrest Lee and Doris (Pearson) M.; m. Mary Chapman, Jan. 24, 1960; children: Lee Ann Mathews Hester, Lucy Mathews Heegaard. AB, U. Ala., 1958; PhD, Columbia U., 1965; LL.D., U. Ala., 1969, Mercer U., 1976; L.H.D., William and Mary Coll., 1976, Med. U. S.C., 1976, Samford U., 1978, Transylvania U., 1978, Stillman Coll., 1980, Miami U., 1982; H.H.D., Birmingham-So. Coll., 1976, Wash. U., St. Louis, 1984; L.H.D., Ctr. Coll., 1985; L.L.D., Ohio Wesleyan U., 1987, Lynchburg Coll., 1987; L.H.D., U. New Eng., 1988, Hofstra U., 1999; L.L.D., Aquinas Coll. Exec. v.p. U. Ala., 1968-69, pres., 1969-80, prof. history, 1977-81; pres., chief exec. officer Charles F. Kettering Found., Dayton, Ohio, 1981—. Sec. HEW, Washington, 1975-77; dir. Birmingham br. Fed. Res. Bank of Atlanta, 1970-72, chmn., 1973-75; mem. council SRI Internat., 1978-85; chmn. Council Public Policy Edn., 1980— Contbr. articles to profl. jours. Trustee Judson Coll., 1968-75, Am. Univs. Field Staff, 1969-80; bd. dirs. Birmingham Festival of Arts Assn., Inc., 1969-75; mem. Nat. Programming Council for Public TV, 1970-73, So. Regional Edn. Bd., 1969-75, Ala. Council on Humanities, 1973-75; vice chmn. Commn. on Future of South, 1974; mem. So. Growth Policies Bd., 1974-75; mem. nat. adv. council Am. Revolution Bicentennial Adminstrn., 1975; mem. Ala. State Oil and Gas Bd., 1975, 77-79; bd. dirs. Acad. Ednl. Devel., 1975—, Ind. Sector, 1982-88,; chmn. Pres.'s Com. on Mental Retardation, 1975-77; chmn. income security com. aging com. Health Ins. Com. of Domestic Council, 1975-77; bd. govs. nat. ARC, 1975-77; bd. govs., bd. visitors Washington Coll., 1982-86, trustee John F. Kennedy Center for Performing Arts, 1975-77, Woodrow Wilson Internat. Center for Scholars, 1975-77; fed. trustee Fed. City Council, 1975-77; bd. dirs. A Presdl. Classroom for Young Americans, Inc., 1975-76; trustee Tchrs. Coll., Columbia U., 1977—85, Nat. Found. March of Dimes, 1977-83, Coun. om Learning, 1977-84, Miles Coll., 1978—; mem. nat. adv. bd. Nat. Inst. on Mgmt. Lifelong Edn., 1979-84; mem. Ala. 2000, 1980—; spl. adviser Aspen Inst., 1980-84; mem. bd. trustees Gerald R. Ford Found., 1988—, bd. visitors Mershon Ctr. Ohio State U., 1988-91; bd. dirs. Nat. Civic League, 1996—. Served with U.S. Army, 1959-60. Recipient Nicholas Murray Butler medal Columbia U., 1976, Ala. Adminstr. of Year award Am. Assn. Univ. Adminstrs., 1976, Educator of Year award Ala. Conf. Black Mayors, 1977, Brotherhood award NCCJ, 1979 Mem. Newcomen Soc. Am., Phi Beta Kappa, Phi Alpha Theta, Omicron Delta Kappa, Delta Theta Phi. Home: 6050 Mad River Rd Dayton OH 45459-1508 Office: Charles F Kettering Found 200 Commons Rd Dayton OH 45459-2788 E-mail: jenkyn@kettering.org.

MATHEWS, E. ANNE JONES, library educator and administrator, consultant; b. Phila; d. Edmond Fulton and Anne Ruth (Reichner) Jones; m. Frank Samuel Mathews, June 16, 1951; children: Lisa Anne Mathews-Bingham, David Morgan, Lynne Elizabeth Bietenhader-Mathews, Alison Fulton Sawyer. AB, Wheaton Coll., 1949; MA, U. Denver, 1965, PhD, 1977. Field staff Intervarsity Christian Fellowship, Chgo., 1949-51; interviewer supr. Colo. Market Rsch. Svcs., Denver, 1952-64; reference libr. Oreg. State U., Corvallis, 1965-67; program dir. Ctrl. Colo. Libr. Sys., Denver, 1969-70; inst. dir. U.S. Office of Edn., Inst. Grant, 1979; dir. pub. rels., prof. Grad. Sch. Librarianship and Info. Mgmt. U. Denver, 1970-76, prof., dir. continuing edn., 1977-80; dir. office libr. programs, office edn. rsch., improvement US Dept. Edn., Washington, 1986-91; dir. Nat. Libr. Edn., Washington, 1992-94; cons. Acad. Ednl. Devel., Washington, 1994—; cons. mil. installation vol. edn. rev. Am. Coun. on Edn., 1990—; from asst. prof. to prof., 1977—85. Mem. adv. com. Golden H.S., 1973—77; faculty assoc. Danforth Found., 1974—84; mem. secondary sch. curriculum com. Jefferson County Pub. Schs., Colo., 1976—78; vis. lectr. Simmons Coll. Sch. L.S., Boston, 1977; mem. book and libr. adv. com. USIA, 1981—91; spkr. in field; cons. USIA, 1984—85; del. Internat. Fedn. Libr. Assns., 1984—93; mem. adv. coun. White House Conf. on Librs. and Info. Svcs., 1991; cons. Walden U., Mpls., 2001. Author, editor 6 books; contbr. articles to profl. jours., numerous chpts. to books. Mem. rural librs. and humanities program Colo. planning and resource bd. NEH, 1982—83; bd. mgrs. Friends Found. of Denver Pub. Libr., 1976—82; pres. Faculty Women's Club, Colo. Sch. Mines, 1963—64; bd. dirs. Jefferson County Libr. Found., 1996—, v.p., 1997—2000. Mem.: ALA (visionary leaders com. 1987—89, mem. coun. 1979—83, com. on accreditation 1984—85, orientation com. 1974—77, 1983—84, pub. rels. com.), English Speaking Union, Assn. Libr. and Info. Sci. Edn. (comm. com. 1978—80, program com. 1977—78), Colo. Libr. Assn. (pres. 1974, bd. dirs. 1973—75, continuing edn. com. 1976—80), Mountain Plains Libr. Assn. (profl. devel. com. 1979—80, pub. rels. and publs. com. 1973—75, continuing edn. com. 1973—76), Am. Soc. Info. Sci. (chmn. pub. rels. 1971), Naples Philharm. League, Pelican Bay Women's League Fla., Mountain Rep. Women's Club (v.p. 1997—2000), Mt. Vernon (Colo.) Country Club, Cosmos Club (Washington). Avocations: travel, reading, museum and gallery activities, volunteer work. Home (Summer): 492 Mount Evans Rd Golden CO 80401-9626 E-mail: afmathews2@earthlink.net.

MATHEWS, FRED LEROY, librarian; b. New Kensington, Pa., Apr. 20, 1938; s. Lyman and Mabel M.; m. Carolyn Zorn, Dec. 2, 1988; 1 child, Eric. Student, U. Md., European Div., 1968-69; AA, Weber State Coll., Ogden, Utah, 1981, B Gen. Studies, 1983; MSLS, Clarion U. Pa., 1985. Enlisted man USAF, 1957, advanced through grades to master sgt., 1977; coord. subscriber svcs. 1920th Communications Group, Washington, 1970-73; noncommd. officer-in-charge phys. therapy USAF, Bitburg, Fed. Republic Germany, 1976-79, supt. phys. medicine Carswell AFB, Tex., 1979-80; ret., 1980; asst. systems libr. Maxwell AFB, Montgomery, Ala., 1985-86; refrence libr. Hdqrs. Tng. and Doctrine Command Libr., Ft. Monroe, Va., 1986-89; trainer, asst. systems libr. Hdqrs. Tng. and Doctrine Command Libr. and Info. Network, Ft. Monroe, 1989-91; systems adminstr. Strategic Def. Command Libr., Huntsville, Ala., 1991-97; command libr. U.S. Army Space & Strategic Def. Command, Huntsville, 1997—; ret. Recipient U.S. Army Achievement medal Hdqrs. Tng. and Doctrine Command, 1990. Mem. ALA, Assn. U.S. Army, Air Force Sgts. Assn., Beta Phi Mu. Avocations: running, reading, bodybuilding. Office: US Army Strategic Def Command Libr PO Box 1500 Huntsville AL 35807-3801

MATHEWS, JACK SHERMAN, foundation administrator, retired insurance company executive; b. Jacksonville, Ill., Aug. 28, 1924; s. Franklin Roosevelt and Helen Adeline Mathews; m. Elizabeth Caldwell Mathews, Jan. 17, 1943; children: Constance Lee Paige, John Harlan. BA, Ill. Coll., 1948; grad. Sch. Ins., Purdue U., 1988. Ins. agt. Equitable Life of NY, Jacksonville, 1948—55; agy. v.p. Ctrl. Nat. Life, Jacksonville, 1955—68; gen. agt. Franklin Life, Springfield, Ill., 1969—84; dir. tng. John Deere, 1984—90; ins. broker, 1990—95; exec. dir. Jacksonville Pub. Schs. Found., 1995—. Pres. Jacksonville C. of C., 1951—52; consistery Valley of Springfield; alderman City of Jacksonville, 1953—61, bd. police and fire com., 1981—88. With Air Corps U.S. Army, 1943—44. Mem.: Elks, Shriners, Masons. Republican. Presbyterian. Avocations: reading, golf, travel. Home: 404 Westwinds Dr Jacksonville IL 62650 Office: Jacksonville Pub Schs Found 516 Jordan Jacksonville IL 62650 E-mail: jmathews@jax117.morgan.k12.il.us.

MATHEWS, JACK WAYNE, journalist, film critic; b. L.A., Dec. 2, 1939; s. Walter Edwin and Dorothy Helen (Friley) M.; m. Lucinda Lucille Herbert, Nov. 5, 1971; children: Darren Brady, Shelby Kay. BA, San Jose (Calif.) State Coll., 1965; MS, UCLA, 1966. Reporter Riverside (Calif.) Press, 1967-69; mktg. exec. Riverside Raceway, 1969-75; columnist, editor Rochester (N.Y.) Democrat & Chronicle, 1975-78; columnist, film critic Detroit Free Press, 1978-82, USA Today, L.A., 1982-85; columnist L.A. Times, 1985-89, film editor, 1989-91; film critic Newsday, L.I., 1991-99; film critic, movie editor N.Y. Daily News, 1999—. Co-host Cinema, PBS, 1995-98; juror Montreal World Film Festival, 1993. Author: The Battle of Brazil, 1987. Democrat. Office: 450 W 33rd St New York NY 10001-2681 Office Phone: 212-210-6344. Business E-Mail: jmathews@edit.nydailynews.com.

MATHEWS, JESSICA TUCHMAN, executive, foreign policy expert; b. N.Y.C., July 4, 1946; d. Lester Reginald and Barbara (Wertheim) Tuchman; m. Colin D. Mathews, Feb. 25, 1978 (divorced); children: Oliver Max Tuchman, Jordan Henry Morgenthau. AB magna cum laude, Radcliffe Coll., 1967; PhD, Calif. Inst. Tech., 1973. Congrl. sci. fellow AAAS, 1973-74; profl. staff mem. Energy and Environment subcom. House Com. on Interior and Insular Affairs, Washington, 1974-75; dir. issues and rsch. Udall Presdl. campaign, 1975-76; dir. Office of Global Issues NSC staff, Washington, 1977-79; mem. editorial bd. The Washington Post, 1980-82; v.p., dir. rsch. The World Resources Inst., Washington, 1982-92; dep. to undersec. for global affairs U.S. Dept. State, Washington, 1993; sr. fellow Coun. on Fgn. Rels., Washington, 1993-97; columnist Washington Post, 1991-97; pres. Carnegie Endowment Internat. Peace, Washington, 1997—. Mem. numerous adv. panels Office Tech. Assessment, NAS, AAAS, EPA; adv. com. Air Products Corp., 1995—99; bd. dirs. Somalogic Inc. Trustee Rockefeller Found., Century Found., Nuc. Threat Initiative; mem. Coun. Fgn. Rels.; bd. dirs. Joyce Found., Chgo., 1984—91, Inter-Am. Dialogue, 1991—2000, Surface Transp. Policy Project,

1991—2003, Radcliffe Coll., 1992—96, Carnegie Endowment for Internat. Peace, Washington, 1992—, Rockefeller Bros. Fund, N.Y.C., NY, 1992—96, Brookings Instn., Washington, 1995—2001. Mem.: Inst. Internat. Econs. (adv. com.), Fedn. Am. Scientists (bd. dirs. 1985—87, 1988—92), Trilateral Commn. Democrat. Jewish. Office: Carnegie Endowment Internat Peace 1779 Massachusetts Ave NW Washington DC 20036-2109

MATHEWS, JOAN HELENE, pediatrician; b. Manchester, N.H., Feb. 3, 1940; d. John Barnaby and Helen A. Wlodkoski; m. Ernest Stephen Mathews, June 1, 1965; 3 children. BS, U. N.H., 1961; MD, Columbia U., 1965. Diplomate Am. Bd. Pediatrics. Med. intern Roosevelt Hosp., N.Y.C., 1965-66; pediatric resident Babies Hosp. Columbia Presbyn. Med. Ctr., N.Y.C., 1966-68, pediatric endocrine fellow Babies Hosp., 1968-70; instr. clin. pediat. Columbia U. Coll. Physicians and Surgeons, N.Y.C., 1973-77; asst. prof. pediat. Cornell U. Med. Coll., N.Y.C., 1977-81; clin. instr. pediat. Harvard Med. Sch., Boston, 1985—2003, clin. asst. prof. pediat., 2003—; clin. assoc. children's svc. Mass. Gen. Hosp., Boston, 1985—. Fellow: Am. Acad. Pediat.; mem.: Phi Beta Kappa. Office: 777 Concord Ave Cambridge MA 02138-1053 Fax: 617-876-5713. Office Phone: 617-876-6800.

MATHEWS, LAURIE A. state agency administrator; m. Andrew Holecek. BS in Environ. Biology, U. Colo., Boulder, 1974; M in Environ. Engring., Stanford U., 1976. Staff mem. U.S. Senate; water cons. DeLew Cather & Co.; asst. dir. Dept. Natural Resources; acting dir. Gov. Roy Romer's Policy Office; dir. State Colo., divsn. State Parks and Outdoor Recreation, Denver, 1991—. Bd. dirs. Nat. Assn. State Park Dirs. Bd. vols. Outdoor Colo. Office: State Colo Divsn State Parks & Outdoor Rec 1313 Sherman St Ste 618 Denver CO 80203-2240 Fax: 303-866-3206.

MATHEWS, LINDA MCVEIGH, newspaper editor; b. Redlands, Calif., Mar. 14, 1946; d. Glenard Ralph and Edith Lorene (Humphrey) McVeigh; m. Thomas Jay Mathews, June 15, 1967; children: Joseph, Peter, Katherine. BA, Radcliffe Coll., 1967; JD, Harvard U., 1972. Gen. assignment reporter L.A. Times, 1967-69, Supreme Ct. corr., 1972-76, corr., 1977-79, China corr., 1979-80, editor op-ed page, 1980-81, dep. nat. editor, 1981-84, dep. fgn. editor, 1985-88, editl. writer, 1988-89, editor L.A. Times Mag., 1989-92; corr. Wall Street Jour., Hong Kong, 1976-77; sr. prodr. ABC News, N.Y.C., 1992-93; nat. editor N.Y. Times, N.Y.C., 1993-96; editor USA Today, McLean, Va., 1997—. Lectr.; freelance writer. Author (with others): Journey into China, 1982, One Billion: A China Chronicle, 1983. Mem. Women's Legal Def. Fund, 1972-76; co-founder, pres. Hong Kong Montessori Sch., 1977-79; bd. dirs. Ctr. for Childhood. Mem. Fgn. Corrs. Club Hong Kong. Office: USA Today 7950 Jones Branch Dr Mc Lean VA 22108 Personal E-mail: LiMathews@aol.com. Business E-Mail: lmathews@usatoday.com.

MATHEWS, LOUISE ROBISON, real estate broker, writer, historian; b. Tecumseh, Okla., Sept. 22, 1917; d. Clarence and Irene (Buzzard) Robison; m. William F. Mathews (dec.); 1 child, William F. Student, East Ctrl. State Coll., 1935, 38, Okla. Bapt. U., 1936-37, BA in Mass Comm., Oklahoma City U., 1981. Law sec. firm Robison-McKinnis, Shawnee, Okla., 1932-36; with Greene's Women's Splty. Shop, Shawnee, 1944-47; v.p. Streets Women's and Children's Splty. Shops, Oklahoma City, 1947-79; broker Assoc. Stewart-Van Cleef Realtors, 1979-86; chmn. Oklahoma City Fashion Week, 1973-75. Contbr. articles to profl. jours. Pres. Oklahoma County Coun. for Mentally Retarded Children, 1953-55, 1969-71: parent-observer White House Conf. Mental Retardation, 1963; chmn. Gov.'s Task Force Mental Retardation; mem. Okla. Mental Health Planning Com., 1963-65; mem. Kirkpatrick Colleagues; chmn., hon. curator First Ladies Okla. Gown Collection. Mem. Okla. Retail Mchts. Assn. (bd. dir. 1971-85), Oklahoma City Regional Fashion Group (bd. dirs., pres. 1969-70), Nat. Assn. Realtors, Okla. State Hist. Soc. (life), Okla. Assn. Mentally Retarded (past pres.), Nat. Assn. for Mentally Retarded Citizens (bd. dirs. 1958-60), Better Bus. Bur., DAR. Democrat. Presbyterian. Home: 14901 N Pennsylvania Ave Oklahoma City OK 73134-6069

MATHEWS, MAX V. acoustical engineer, educator; Dir. Acoustical and Behavior Rsch. Ctr. Bell Labs., 1962-85; sci. advisor Inst. de Recherche et Coordination Acoustique/Musique, Paris; prof. music Stanford (Calif.) U. Recipient Silver medal in musical acoustics Acoustical Soc. Am., Chevalier dans l'order des Arts et Lettres, Republique Francaise. Mem. NAE. Achievements include research in sound and music synthesis with digital computers and with the application of computers to areas in which man-machine interactions are critical, computer methods for speech processing, studies of human speech production, studies of auditory masking, and the invention of techniques for computer drawing of typography, the effect of resonances on sound quality; development of a program (Music V) for the direct digital synthesis of sounds and a program (Groove) for the computer control of a sound synthesizer. Office: Stanford U Knoll Rm 218 Mail Code 8180 Stanford CA 94305-8180 Fax: 650-723-8468. E-mail: mvm@ccrma.stanford.edu.

MATHEWS, MICH, computer company executive; Grad., U. Brighton, England. With Gen. Motors; pub. relations cons., U.K div. Microsoft Corp., head corp. pub. rels. group, 1993, v.p. corp. comms., 1993—, mem., bus. leadership team, 1999—. Office: Microsoft Corp Comms one Microsoft Way Redmond WA 98052-6399

MATHEWS, MICHAEL STONE, investment banker; b. Ohio, Oct. 23, 1940; s. Robert Green and Dallas Victoria (Stone) M.; m. Cecilia Aall, May 13, 1967; children: Brandon, Mark, Alexander. AB, Princeton U., 1962; JD, U. Mich., 1965. Bar: N.Y. 1966. Assoc. White & Case, N.Y.C., 1965—69; v.p. Smith Barney Harris Upham & Co., N.Y.C., 1969—77; sr. v.p. Scandinavian Securities Corp., N.Y.C., 1977—79, DNC Am. Banking Corp., N.Y.C., 1979—89; pres. DNC Capital Corp., 1986—89; ptnr. Bradford Assocs., 1989—92; mng. dir. Westgate Capital Co., 1993—. Bd. dirs. Apptix ASA, TTS Marine ASA, Missota Paper Co. Home: 193 Elm Rd Princeton NJ 08540-2520 Office: 115 E 69th St New York NY 10021

MATHEWS, NORMAN, playwright, composer; b. Rockford, Ill., Sept. 12, 1942; s. Matthew and Mary Cancelose. BA, Hunter Coll., N.Y.C., 1976; MA, NYU, 1978. News editor Dance Mag., N.Y.C., 1963—66; dancer, singer, actor Broadway shows, movies N.Y.C., 1966—70; pianist, piano tchr., 1978—85; mng. editor Sylvia Porter's Personal Fin. Mag., N.Y.C., 1985—87; editl. dir. Merrill Lynch, N.Y.C., 1987—89; composer, playwright N.Y.C., 1990—. Composer: (song cycle) Songs of the Poet, 1994, (musical revue) Somebody Write Me a Song, 2002; composer, playwright: musical You Might As Well Live (based on the life and works of Dorothy Parker), 1999, Lost Empires (based on novel by J. B. Priestley), 2004. Recipient Playwriting grant, Vogelstein Found., Maine, 1999. Mem.: ASCAP, Dramatists Guild, Am. Music Ctr. Avocation: cooking. Home: 667 W 161st St Apt 3H New York NY 10032

MATHEWS, SHARON WALKER, artistic director, secondary school educator; b. Shreveport, La., Feb. 1, 1947; d. Arthur Delmar and Nona (Frye) Walker; m. John William (Bill) Mathews, Aug. 14, 1971; children: Rebecca, Elizabeth, Anna. BS, La. State U., 1969, MS, 1971. Dance grad. asst. La. State U., Baton Rouge, 1969-71, choreographer, 1975-76; 6th grade tchr. East Baton Rouge Parish, 1971-72, health phys. edn. tchr., 1972-74; dance instr. Magnet High Sch., Baton Rouge, 1975—; artistic dir. Baton Rouge Ballet Theatre, 1975—; dance dir. Dancers' Workshop, Baton Rouge, 1971—; choreographer Baton Rouge Opera, 1989-94, Univ. H.S. Musical Theatre, 1998—; choreographer Baton Rouge Gilbert and Sullivan Soc. summer musical La. State U., 2000, 2001; choreographer Baton Rouge Little Theater, 2000, 2002. Author: East Baton Rouge Parish Dance Curriculum. Mem. La. Supts. Task Force for the Arts in Edn., 1999-2001; mem. La. Content Standards Com. for Dance, 2001; mem. East Baton Rouge Parish Curriculum Com. for Dance, 1997; mem. La. Arts Content Standards Com., 2002—; mem. La. Arts Consortium, 2000—; mem. La. Arts Content Revision Com., 2002-03. Named Dance Educator of Yr., La. Alliance for Health, Physical Edn., Recreation and Dance, 1986-87; recipient Mayor-Pres.'s award for Excellence in the Arts, 1999, Stream award S.W. Regional Ballet Assn. for artistic excellence, 1991, Mayor Pres.'s award for excellence in the arts, 1999; inducted into the Univ. H.S. Hall of Distinction, 2003, Baton Rouge Magnet H.S. Hall of Fame, 2003. Mem. Southwestern Regional Ballet Assn. (bd. dirs. 1981—, treas., exec. bd. dirs. 1989-92), La. Assn. for Health, Phys. Edn., Recreation and Dance (dance chairperson 1995). Republican. Baptist. Office: Baton Rouge Ballet Theater 11017 Perkins Rd Baton Rouge LA 70884

MATHEWS, SYLVIA MARY, foundation administrator; b. Hinton, W.Va., June 23, 1965; d. William Peter and Cleo P. M. AB, Harvard Coll., 1987; BA, Oxford U., 1990. Assoc. McKinsey & Co., N.Y.C., 1990-92; dep. dir. econ. policy Clinton/Gore '92, Little Rock, 1992; staff dir. Nat. Econ. Coun., Washington, 1993-94; chief of staff to Sec. Robert Rubin U.S. Dept. Treasury, Washington, 1995-96; dep. chief of staff to Pres. The White House, Washington, 1997-98; dep. dir. Office of Mgmt. & Budget, Washington, 1998—2001; COO, exec. dir., The Bill and Melinda Gates Found., Seattle, 2001—. Rhodes scholar, 1987. Mem. Coun. Fgn. Rels.; bd. dirs. MetLife, Inc., 2004-. Democrat. Office: The Bill & Melinda Gates Found PO Box 23350 Seattle WA 98102

MATHEWS, WALTER MICHAEL, educational consultant; b. Phila., Nov. 13, 1942; s. Walter John and Helen Linda Mathews; m. Mary Florence Richardson, June 13, 1964; children: Lisa, Walter John. BA, La Salle U., 1964; MEd, Temple U., 1967; PhD, U. Wis., 1971. Prof. U. Miss., Oxford, 1971-81; prof., adminstr. Hofstra U., Hempstead, N.Y., 1981-84, L.I. U., Brookville, N.Y., 1984-88, dean acad. affairs, 1988-98, internat. liaison, 1998—. Home: 27 Midway Ave Locust Valley NY 11560-2008 Office: Evaluation Assocs Inc 27 Midway Ave Locust Valley NY 11560-2008 E-mail: evalascs@optonline.net.

MATHEWSON, CHRISTOPHER COLVILLE, engineering geologist, educator; b. Plainfield, NJ, Aug. 12, 1941; s. George Anderson and Elsa Rae (Shrimpton) M.; m. Janet Marie Olmsted, Nov. 2, 1968; children: Heather Alexis, Glenn George Anderson. BSCE, Case Inst. Tech., 1963; MS in Geol. Engring., U. Ariz., 1965, PhD in Geol. Engring., 1971. Registered profl. engr., Tex., Ariz.; cert. geologist Tex., Oreg., Alaska. Officer, lt. Nat. Ocean Survey, 1965-71; prof. Tex. A&M U., College Station, 1981—. Cons., speaker in field. Author: Engineering Geology, 1981 (C.P. Holdredge award); contbr. articles to profl. publs. Chmn. College Station Planning and Zoning Commn., 1973—81; trustee Geol. Soc. Am. Found., 2001—03. Fellow Geol. Soc. Am. (chmn. engring. geology divsn. 1986-87, Meritorious Svc. award 1991); mem. Assn. Engring. Geologists (editor bull. 1981-88, pres. 1988-89, C.P. Holdredge award 1981, F.T. Johnston Svc. award 1995, exec. dir. 1998-2002), Am. Geol. Inst. (pres. 1991-92), Nat. Coal Coun., Internat. Assn. Engring. Geologists (chmn. U.S. nat. com. 1995-98). Office: Tex A&M U Dept Geology And Geophysics College Station TX 77843-3115 E-mail: mathewson@geo.tamu.edu. *Commitment and dedication to the mission will lead to its successful completion regardless of the odds.*

MATHEWSON, DORIS MAY, retired medical/surgical nurse; b. Providence; d. Hugh Edward and Nellie May (Smith) Massey; m. Donald Walter Mathewson, May 25, 1946; 1 child, Susan Elaine. Diploma, R.I. Hosp. Sch. Nursing, 1944; BS in Nurse-Tchr. Edn., R.I. Coll., 1974; MS in Health Svcs. Adminstrs., Salve Regina Coll., 1986. From staff nurse to head nurse R.I. Hosp., Providence, 1961-67, coord., supr., 1967-69, nurse leader orthops., 1969-71, nurse leader med., 1971-81, asst. dir. nursing, 1981-86; primary nurse, chmn. edn. Hospice Care R.I., Providence, 1986-91; parish nurse Beneficent Congl. Ch., Providence, 1992—2002; ret. Mem. health and human svcs. tack force R.I. Conf. U.C.C., Providence, 1990—98; mem. Interfaith Counseling Ctr. Bd., Providence, 1991—; bd. dirs. Lucy Ayres Found. Del. Religious Adminstrs. Exch. U.S.-USSR, Moscow, 1991; mem. adv. bd. Cranston (R.I.) Adult Sr. Svcs., 1989—95; v.p., bd. dirs. Beneficent Congl. Ch., 1990—96, pres., 1996—98; mem. R.I. State Coun. Chs.; bd. dirs. Lucy Ayres Found., Providence. Mem.: ANA, R.I. State Nurses Assn. (mem. govt. affairs com.), Salve Regina Coll. Alumni, R.I. Hosp. Nurses Alumni Assn. (bd. dirs. 1987—), R.I. Coll. Alumni, West Cranston Garden Club (pres. 1994—96). Avocations: travel, gardening, cooking. Home: 44 Forsythia Ln Cranston RI 02921-2315

MATHEWSON, GEORGE ATTERBURY, retired lawyer; b. Paterson, N.J., Mar. 31, 1935; s. Joseph B. and Christina A. (Atterbury) M.; m. Ann Elizabeth, July 31, 1975' 1 child, James Lemuel. AB cum laude, Amherst Coll., 1957; LLB, Cornell U., 1960; LLM, U. Mich., 1961. Bar: N.Y. 1963. Atty office spl. legal assts., trial atty. FTC, Washington, 1963-65; regional atty. N.Y. State Dept. Environ. Conservation, Liverpool, 1972-73; pvt. practice Syracuse, 1967—72, 1973—2002; of counsel Banac and Mathewson, Manlius, NY, 2002—04; ret., 2004. Adj. instr. bus. law Onondaga Community Coll., Syracuse, 1979-84. Bd. dirs. South Side Businessmen, 1971-72, 88-91, v.p., 1992, pres. 1993; elder Onondaga Hill Presbyn. Ch., 1979, 82-85; dir. Manilus C. of C., 1995, v.p., 1997; bd. trustees Steuben County Hist. Soc., 2002—; bd. dirs. Yates County Arts Ctr., 2003—, sec., 2004. Mem. ABA, Fed. Bar Assn., N.Y. State Bar Assn. (former mem. state and county bar assn. coms.), Kiwanis (bd. dirs. Onondaga club 1988-89, v.p. 1989, pres. 1989-91). Patentee safety device for disabled airplanes.

MATHEWSON, HUGH SPALDING, anesthesiologist, educator; b. Washington, Sept. 20, 1921; s. Walter Eldridge and Jennie Lind (Jones) M.; m. Dorothy Ann Gordon, 1943 (div. 1952); 1 child, Jane Mathewson Holcombe; m. Hazel M. Jones, 1953 (div. 1978); children: Geoffrey K., Brian E., Catherine E. Brock, Jennifer A. Jehle; m. Judith Ann Mahoney, 1979 (div. 1990). Student, Washburn U., 1938-39; AB, U. Kans., 1942, MD, 1944. Intern Wesley Hosp., Wichita, Kans., 1944-45; resident anesthesiology U. Kans. Med. Ctr., Kansas City, 1946-48; pvt. practice specializing in anesthesiology Kansas City, Mo., 1948-69; chief anesthesiologist St. Luke's Hosp., Kansas City, 1953-69; med. dir., sect. respiratory therapy U. Kans. Med. Ctr., 1969-92, assoc. prof., 1969-75, prof., 1975-92, prof. anesthesiology emeritus, respiratory care edn., 1992—; examiner schs. respiratory therapy, 1975-95; oral examiner Nat. Bd. Respiratory Therapy; mem. Coun. Nurse Anesthesia Practice, 1974-78; prof. phys. therapy edn., 1993-98. Author: Structural Forms of Anesthetic Compounds, 1961, Respiratory Therapy in Critical Care, 1976, Pharmacology for Respiratory Therapists, 1977; contbr. articles to profl. publs.; mem. editl. bd. Anesthesia Staff News, 1975-84, Respiratory Care, 1980-90, cons. editor, 1980—, editor-in-chief Respiratory Mgmt., 1989-92. Pres. Overland Park Civic Band, 1997, Overland Park Orch., 1998-2001; trustee Kansas City Mus., Kansas City Conservatory of Music, 1993—. Served to lt. comdr. USNR, 1956. Recipient Bird Lit. prize Am. Assn. Respiratory Therapists, 1976, Spl. Recognition award Am. Assn. Nurse Anesthetists, 1997. Mem. Mo. Soc. Anesthesiologists (pres. 1963), Kans. Soc. Anesthesiologists (pres. 1974-77), Kans. Med. Soc. (council), Phi Beta Kappa, Sigma Xi, Lambda Beta (hon.) Office: Kans Med Ctr 39th And Rainbow Blvd Kansas City KS 66160-0001 Office Phone: 913-588-7287. Business E-Mail: hmathews@kumc.edu.

MATHEWSON, JOHN JACOB, emergency and family practice physician; b. Greenville, Ill., Sept. 20, 1924; s. Henry Adolph and Grace Elizabeth (Kimbro) M.; m. Patricia Lou Hendrix, Aug. 31, 1946; children: John Jeffry, Craig Thomas, Susan Patricia. AB, Greenville Coll., 1948; BS, U. Ill., Chgo., 1950, MD, 1952. Bd. cert. Am. Bd. Emergency Medicine, Am. Bd. Family Practice, added qualifications in geriatrics; cert. wound care mgmt., 2002. Physician Pana (Ill.) Med. Group, 1954-71; emergency physician St. Johns Hosp., Springfield, Ill., 1971-74; assoc. prof. emergency medicine Tex. Tech. U. Sch. Medicine, Lubbock, 1974-78; dir., chair emergency dept. Lakeland (Fla.) Regional Med. Ctr., 1978-82; physician Flatonia (Tex.) Med. Clinic, 1982-84; emergency physician Watson Clinic, Lakeland, 1984-95; emergency and family physician Mult Hosp. and Fayette-Lavaca Family Med. Ctr., Lakeland and Shiner, Tex., 1995—. Bd. med. advisors Spectrum Emergency Med. Care, St. Louis, 1979-82; med. advisor Polk County Emergency Med. Svc., Lakeland, 1979—; tchr., organizer 1st course in emergency medicine Tex. Tech. U. Sch. Medicine, 1976; clin. asst. prof. U. So. Fla., Tampa, 1985—. Contbr. articles to med. jours. Mem. sch. bd., Pana, 1965. Col. U.S. Army, 1943-84. Mem. Polk County Med. Soc. (pres. 1993, del. 1992-95, trustee 1993-95), Fla. Coll. Emergency Physicians (bd. dirs. 1985-91), Christian County Med. Soc. (past pres. 1961-62).

MATHEWSON, MARK STUART, lawyer, editor; b. Pana, Ill., Mar. 6, 1955; s. Raymond Glenn and Frances (King) M.; m. Barbara Jean Siegert, Oct. 30, 1980; children: Margie, Molly. BA, U. Wis., Madison, 1978; JD, U. Ill., 1984; MA, U. Iowa, 1985. Bar: Ill. 1985. Reporter Ill. Times, Springfield, 1985; asst. prof. Culver Stockton Coll., Canton, Mo., 1986—87; pvt. practice Pana, Ill., 1987—2000; mng. editor Ill. Bar Jour., Ill. State Bar Assn., Springfield, dir. legal pub., 2000—. Home: RR 1 Box 2 Athens IL 62613-9787 Office: Ill State Bar Assn Ill Bar Journal Ill Bar Ctr Springfield IL 62701

MATHIA, MARY LOYOLA, parochial school educator, nun; b. Hempstead, N.Y., Sept. 14, 1921; d. Paul John and Laura Marie (Linck) Mathia. BA, Coll. Mt. St. Joseph, 1953; M in Pastoral Studies, Loyola U.-Chgo., 1980. Joined Sisters of Charity of Cin., Roman Cath. Ch., 1941. Tchr. various schs. Ohio and Mich., 1943-62, St. John Bapt. Sch., Chillum, Md., 1962-63; social studies tchr. and dept. chmn. Holy Name High Sch., Cleve., 1963-69; ednl. cons. Diocese of Cleve., 1970-78; dir. edn. St. Benedict Ch., Crystal River, Fla., 1979-86; founding prin. Cen. Cath. Sch. of Citrus County, Lecanto, Fla., 1985-90, v.p. devel. and pub. rels., 1990-91; parish cons. and dir. adult edn., St. Scholastica, 1986—. Recipient Mother Seton award, 1998, St. Jude medal Award for Svc. to St. Scholastic Ch., presented by Rev. Robert Lynch, Bishop of the Diocese of St. Petersburg, 2002, St. Jude award, Dick Ribble/Bert Miller award, Interfaith Coun. on Citrus County, 2004. Republican. Office: St Scholastica Ch 4301 W Homosassa Trl Lecanto FL 34461-9106 *Society today is crying out for stability and a purpose for life. Only a God-centered education can fill the void created by the noise of external forces and the deadening of creative ideas stemming from a computer, media*saturated environment. As ministers of the Gospel our "quiet whispers" must penetrate the minds of a weary people, inspire them and bring them safely to the harbor of salvation in Christ Jesus Our Lord.*

MATHIAS, ALICE IRENE, business management consultant; b. N.Y.C., Mar. 2, 1949; d. Murray and Charlotte (Kottle) M. BS in Math., Western New Eng. Coll., 1972. Programmer Carnation Co., L.A., 1973-78; programmer/analyst Cedars-Sinai Med. Ctr., L.A., 1978-79, Union Bank, L.A., 1979-81; group leader Kaiser Found. Health Plan, Pasadena, Calif., 1981-98; sr. cons. KPMG LLP, L.A., 1998—99; prin. Info. Tech. Mgmt., L.A., 1999—. Mem. NAFE, Am. Mgmt. Assn., L.A. County Mus. Art (sponsor), Smithsonian Inst., KCET Pub. TV, Choice In Dying, U.S. Holocaust Meml. Mus. (charter mem.), Caithness Collectors Club, Statue of Liberty Ellis Island Found. Home: 2031 Dracena Drive Apt 320 Los Angeles CA 90027 Office: Info Tech Mgmt 2031 Dracena Dr Ste 320 Los Angeles CA 90027

MATHIAS, BETTY JANE, communications and community affairs consultant, writer, editor, lecturer; b. Oct. 22, 1923; d. Royal F. and Dollie B. (Bowman) M.; 1 child, Dena. Student, Merritt Bus. Sch., 1941—42, San Francisco State U., 1941—42. Asst. publicity dir. Oakland (Calif.) Area War Chest and Comty. Chest, 1943-46; pub. rels. Am. Legion, Oakland, 1946-47; asst. to pub. rels. dir. Cen. Bank of Oakland, 1947-49; pub. rels. dir. East Bay chpt. Nat. Safety Coun., 1949-51; propr., mgr. Mathias Pub. Rels. Agy., Oakland, 1951-60; publicity dir. U.S. Nat. Figure Skating Championships, Berkeley, Calif., 1957; gen. assignment reporter, teen news editor Daily Rev., Hayward, Calif., 1960-62; freelance pub. rels. and writing Oakland, 1962-66, 67-69; dir. corp. comms. Systech Fin. Corp., Walnut Creek, Calif., 1969-71; v.p. corp. comms. Consol. Capital cos., Oakland, 1972-79, v.p. comty. affairs Emeryville, Calif., 1981-84, v.p. spl. projects, 1984-85; v.p., dir. Consol. Capital Realty Svcs., Inc., Oakland, 1973-77, Centennial Adv. Corp., Oakland, 1976-77; comms. cons., 1979—. Cons. Mountainair Realty, Cameron Park, Calif., 1986-87; pub. rels. coord. Tuolumne County Visitors Bur., 1989-90; lectr. in field. Editor: East Bay Mag., 1966-67, TIA Traveler, 1969, Concepts, 1979-83; editor, writer souvenir program: Little House on the Prairie Reunion, 1998. Bd. dirs. Oakland YWCA, 1944-45, ARC, Oakland, So. Alameda County chpt., 1967-69, Family Ctr., Children's Hosp. Med. Ctr. No. Calif., 1982-85, March of Dimes, 1983-85, Equestrian Ctr. of Walnut Creek, Calif., 1983-84, also sec.; mem. Women's Ambulance and Transport Corps of Calif., Oakland, 1942-46; active USO and Shrine Hospitality Ctrs., Oakland, USO-Travelers Aid Soc., Oakland, 1942-46; publicist Oakland Area War Bond Com., 1943-46; adult and publs. adv. Internat. Order of the Rainbow for Girls, 1953-78; comms. arts adv. com. Ohlone (Calif.) Coll., 1979-85, chmn., 1982-84; mem. adv. bd. dept. mass comms. Calif. State U.-Hayward, 1985; pres. San Francisco Bay Area chpt. Nat. Reyes Syndrome Found., 1981-86; vol. staff Columbia Actors' Repertory, Columbia, Calif., 1986-87, 89; mem. exec. bd., editor newsletter Tuolumne County Dem. Club, 1987; publicity chmn. 4th of July celebration Tuolumne County C. of C., 1988; vol. children's dept. Tuolumne County Pub. Libr., 1993-97; vol. Ann. Comty. Christmas Eve Dinner, Sonora, Calif., 1988-96; mem. adv. com. Ride Away Ctr. for Therapeutic Riding for the Handicapped, 1995-96, vol. Hold Your Horses Therapeutic Riding Acad., 1997; vol. Tuolumne County Visitors Bur. and Film Commn., 1996-99. Recipient Grand Cross of Color award Internat. Order of Rainbow for Girls, 1955. Mem. Order Ea. Star (life, worthy matron 1952, publicity chmn. Calif. state 1955), East Bay Women's Press Club (pres. 1960, 84). Home: 20575 Gopher Dr Sonora CA 95370-9034

MATHIAS, CORDULA, art dealer; b. Constance, Baden, W. Germany, Feb. 18, 1955; came to U.S., 1979; d. Gotthold Bernhard and Mathilde (Eisele) M. BA, U. Constance, Germany, 1979; MA, Columbia U., 1981. Rsch. assoc. Soc. for Renewal of Christian Art, N.Y.C., 1982-83; dept. mgr. Logos Corp., Mt. Arlington, N.J., 1983-87; dir. of ops. John Szoke Graphics, N.Y.C., 1987-88; exhbn. curator Pace U., N.Y.C., 1988-89; pres. Mathias Fine Art, Trevett, Maine, 1990—. Exhbn. sponsor Maine Coast Artists, Rockport, 1997-2001; exhbn. co-curator The I of the Eye, Ctr. for Maine Contemporary Art, Rockport, 2002. Fulbright scholar, 1979-80. Mem. Boothbay Harbor C. of C. Avocation: chamber music. Office: Mathias Fine Art West Side Rd Trevett ME 04571

MATHIAS, EDWARD JOSEPH, merchant banker; b. Camden, NJ, Nov. 11, 1941; s. Edward Joseph and Zelma (Pollack) M.; m. Ann Robyn Rafferty, Aug. 3, 1968; 1 child, Ellen Susannah; life ptnr.: Dale Lenzner. BA, U. Pa., 1964; MBA, Harvard U., 1971. Mng. dir. T. Rowe Price Assocs., Inc., Balt., 1971-93, Carlyle Group Merchant Bank, Washington, 1994—. Spl. ltd. ptnr. Trident Capital, dir. Aether Sys. Trustee U. Pa. Lt. USN, 1964—69. Mem. Coun. Fgn. Rels., Harvard Club, Univ. Club (N.Y.C.), Columbia Country Club (Chevy Chase, Md.), Robert Trent Jones Golf Club (Manassas, Va.), Coral Beach Club (Bermuda), Carnegie Abbey (Portsmouth, R.I.), The Brook (N.Y.C.), Ctr. Club (Balt.), Met. Club (Wash. DC), Georgetown Club (Wash. DC), Talbot Country Club (Easton, Md.). Republican. Home: 2804 Q St NW Washington DC 20004 Office: The Carlyle Group 1001 Pennsylvania Ave NW Washington DC 20004-2505

MATHIAS, JOSEPH MARSHALL, lawyer, judge; b. Frankfort, Ky., Jan. 23, 1914; s. Harry L. and Catherine Snead (Marshall) M.; children: Mark Wellington, Marcia Ann Mathias Wilson, Marilyn Roberta. AB, U. Md., 1935; JD, Southeastern U., 1942. Bar: Md. 1942, U.S. Supreme Ct. 1949, U.S. Dist. Ct. Md. 1963. Ptnr. Moorman and Mathias, 1946-50, Jones, Mathias and O'Brien and predecessor firms, 1950-65; judge Md. Tax Ct., 1959-65; assoc. judge Circuit Ct. of Montgomery County (Md.), 1965-80; chief judge 6th Jud. Circuit of Md., 1980-81; spl. assignments, 1981-83; spl. counsel Beckett, Cromwell & Myers, P.A., 1983-88; of counsel Frank, Bernstein, Conaway and Goldman, 1988-92. Past dir. Nat. Bank Md., Bank So. Md.; former mem. adv. bd. Citizens Bank and Trust Co. Chmn. Bd. Property Rev., Montgomery, Md., 1992—. Served with USN, 1942-46. Recipient cert. of disting. citizenship Gov. of Md., 1981. Mem. ABA, Md. State Bar Assn., Md. Bar Found., Montgomery County Bar Assn., Am. Judicature Soc. Democrat. Roman Catholic. Home: 10011 Summit Ave Kensington MD 20895-3835 E-mail: rwmjmm@erols.com.

MATHIAS, LESLIE MICHAEL, electronic manufacturing company executive; b. Bombay, Dec. 17, 1935; arrived in US, 1957; s. Paschal Lawrence and Dulcine M.; m. Vivian Mae Doolittle, Dec. 16, 1962. BSc, U. Bombay, 1957; BS, San Jose (Calif.) State U., 1961. Elec. engr. Indian Standard Metal, Bombay, 1957; sales engr. Bleisch Engring. and Tool, Mt. View, Calif., 1958-60; gen. mgr. Meadows Terminal Bds., Cupertino, Calif., 1961-63;

prodn. mgr. Sharidon Corp., Menlo Park, Calif., 1963-67, Videx Corp., Sunnyvale, Calif., 1967-68, Data Tech. Corp., Mt. View, 1968-69; pres. L.G.M. Mfg., Inc., Mt. View, 1969-83; pvt. practice plating cons. Los Altos, Calif., 1983-87; materials mgr. Excel Cirs., Santa Clara, Calif., 1987-91, 93-98, acct. mgr., 1991-93, materials mgr., 1993-98, internat. materials mgr., 2000—03; buyer Planned Parenthood, San Jose, Calif., 1998-2000; acct. mgr. Streamline Circuits, Santa Clara, Calif., 2003—04. Social chmn. Internat. Students, San Jose, 1958-59. Mem. Nat. Fedn. Ind. Bus., Calif. Cirs. Assn., Better Bus. Bur., Purchasing Assn., U.S. C. of C. Roman Catholic. Avocations: electronics, reading, med. jours. Home: 20664 Mapletree Pl Cupertino CA 95014-0449 Office Phone: 408-727-1418.

MATHIAS, MARGARET GROSSMAN, manufacturing company executive, leasing company executive; b. Detroit; d. D. Ray and Lila May (Skinner) Grossman; children: Deborah, Robert, Lesley, Jennifer, Mary. BA, Mt. Holyoke Coll.; cert., Am. Acad. Art. Artist and co-mgr. Mary Chase Marionettes, NYC; exec. v.p. Star Five Corp., Elkhart, Ind., 1975-88, pres., treas., chmn. bd., 1985-90; sec., chmn. bd. L & J Press Corp., Elkhart, 1985-91, also chmn. bd. dirs.; chmn., pres., CEO Magland Co., Elkhart, 1986—, Magco Inc., Elkhart, 1986—; pres., chmn., CEO Tech Products, Inc., Elkhart, 1992—. Mem. fin. com. United Fund, Elkhart; mem. parents adv. bd. Furman U., Greenville, SC, 1978-83, mem. art adv. bd. Mt. Holyoke Coll., South Hadley, Mass., 1982—; pres. Tri Kappa Svc. Orgn., Elkhart, 1965-66; trustee Stanley Clark Sch., South Bend, Ind., 1977-87; bd. dirs. Bridgework Theatre, Goshen, Ind., also Balt., 1996—; mem. adv. bd. Ruthmere 1910 House Mus. designated one of Am.'s castles, 1999—; instr., spkr. etiquette Montessori Schs., Elkhart, 1998—; vol. Dept. Edn., 2003, Art Inst. Chgo., 2003; weekly vol. dept. edn. Art Inst. Chgo. Recipient Lawson Top Sculpture Purchase award Midwest Mus. Am. Art, 1990. Mem. Elkhart C. of C., Elcona Country Club (Elkhart), Woman's Athletic Club (Chgo.), Thursday Club (Elkhart, pres. 1976). Republican. Avocations: sculpting, travel, skiing. Home: 1077 Greenleaf Blvd Apt 101 Elkhart IN 46514-3562 Office: 429 S Main St Elkhart IN 46516-3210

MATHIAS, MELVIN MERLE, nutrition scientist; b. Columbia City, Ind., Feb. 22, 1939; s. Burrell R. and Mary L. (Wilfong) M.; m. Evelyn J. Clayson, July 20, 1963 (div. Feb. 1989); children: Michael M., Beth Ann, David L.; m. Patricia J. Stedman, June 5, 2000. BS, Purdue U., 1961; MS, Cornell U., 1964, PhD, 1966. Asst. prof. to assoc. prof. dept. food sci. and nutrition Colo. State U., Ft. Collins, 1968-81, prof., 1981-88, Fla. State U., Tallahassee, 1989; program leader Coop. State Rsch. Edn. and Ext. Svc., USDA, Washington, 1990—2003; ret., 2004. Contbr. 80 articles to profl. jours. Capt. U.S. Army, 1967-68. Grantee NIH, 1968-91, USDA, 1968-88. Mem. AAAS, Am. Soc. Nutrition Sci., Am. Oil Chemists, Am. Dietetic Assn. Methodist. Home: 203 S Yoakum Pkwy Apt 1412 Alexandria VA 22304-3737

MATHIAS, MERVIN A. retired surgeon; b. Phila., 1917; MD, Temple U., 1942. Diplomate Am. Bd. Surgery. Intern Jewish Hosp., Phila., 1942-43, resident in pathology, 1946-47; resident in surgery West Jersey Hosp., Camden, N.J., 1948-50; surgeon in pvt. practice, to 1982. Mem. Am. Occupl. Medicine Assn., Internat. Med. Assn.

MATHIAS, REUBEN VICTOR (VIC MATHIAS), chamber of commerce executive, real estate investor; b. Copperas Cove, Tex., Mar. 5, 1926; s. Alvin E. and Ella L. (Teinert) M.; m. Helen I. Thoresen, Jan. 28, 1950; children: Mona, Mark, Matt. BBA, U. Tex., 1950. Cert. Chamber Exec. Dist. mgr. W.A. Shaeffer Pen Co., Youngstown, Ohio, 1950-51; mgr. Cen-Tex Fair, Temple, Tex., 1951-52; dir. info. Tex. Assn. Soil Conservation Suprs., Temple, 1952-53; mgr. membership dept. Austin (Tex.) C. of C., 1953-56, chief exec. officer, 1956-82; dir. corp. devel. Hardin Corp., Austin, 1983-86; real estate and investments, 1987-92; pres. Tex. Travel Industry Assn., Austin, 1992-96. V.p. Austin Tours, Inc.; sec. Longhorn Caverns, Inc.; chmn. bd., instr. Inst. for Orgn. Mgmt., U. Houston; mgmt. cons. not-for-profit orgns., 1997-2003. Contbr. monthly editorial Thoughts While Thinking to Austin Mag., 1961-82. Pres. Austin USO Council, 1958-59; v.p. Beautify Tex. Council, 1975-77; founding pres. Discover Tex. Assn., 1969-71; chmn. Central Tex. Blood Donor Fund, 1979. Served with U.S. Army, 1944-46. Mem. Am. C. of C. Execs., Tex. C. of C. Execs. (pres. 1965), Rotary (pres. Austin 1985-86). Lutheran. Home: 3100 Mistywood Cir Austin TX 78746-7861 *You can find happiness only by giving it to others. Much of my life has been devoted to community building through voluntary action. The fact that my career has allowed me to stay in one community has made it possible for me to make and carry out long-term plans, both for the community and personally.*

MATHIAS, SIDNEY H. state representative; b. Chgo., Nov. 9, 1946; m. Rita Mathias; children: Elliot, Scott. Grad., Roosevelt U., DePaul U. Atty.; mem. Ill. Ho. of Reps., 1999—. Mayor, Buffalo Grove, Ill. Republican. Jewish. Office: 200-1N Stratton Office Bldg Springfield IL 62706 Address: 4256 N Arlington Heights Rd Arlington Heights IL 60004

MATHIES, ALLEN WRAY, JR., former pediatrician, hospital administrator; b. Colorado Springs, Colo., Sept. 23, 1930; s. Allen W. and Esther S. (Norton) M.; m. Lewise Austin, Aug. 23, 1956; children: William A., John N. BA, Colo. Coll., 1952; MS, Columbia U., 1956, PhD., 1958; MD, U. Vt., 1961. Rsch. assoc. U. Vt., Burlington, 1957-61; intern L.A. County Hosp., 1961-62; resident in pediatrics L.A. Gen. Hosp., 1962-64; asst. prof. pediatrics U. So. Calif., L.A., 1964-68, assoc. prof., 1968-71, prof., 1971—, assoc. dean, 1969-74, interim dean, 1974-75, dean, 1975-85, head physician Communicable Disease Svc., 1964-75; pres., CEO Huntington Meml. Hosp., Pasadena, Calif., 1985-94, So. Calif. Healthcare Sys., Pasadena, 1992-95, pres. emeritus, 1995—. Bd. dirs. Pacific Mut. Contbr. articles to med. jours. Bd. dirs. Occidental Coll. With U.S. Army, 1953-55. Mem. Am. Acad. Pediatrics, Infectious Disease Soc. Am., Am. Pediatric Soc., Soc. Pediatric Rsch. Republican. Episcopalian. Home: 314 Arroyo Dr South Pasadena CA 91030-1623 Office: Huntington Meml Hosp PO Box 7013 Pasadena CA 91109-7013

MATHIESON, GARRETT ALFRED, insurance brokerage executive; b. Bronxville, N.Y., June 12, 1952; s. William Frederick and Susan (Prager) M.; m. Doris King, June 21, 1980; children: Christine, William. BA, Hobart Coll., 1974; MBA, N.Y. U., 1980. Account rep. Marsh & McLennan, N.Y.C., 1974-77; sr. broker Frank B. Hall & Co., N.Y.C., 1977-78; risk mgmt. cons. Marsh & McLennan, N.Y.C., 1978-80, cons. mgr.-asst. v.p., 1980-82, v.p., mgr. world consulting svcs., 1982-85; mng. cons. Towers Perrin Forster & Crosby, N.Y.C., 1985-86; sr. v.p. Jardine Ins. Brokers, N.Y.C., 1986-90; exec. v.p. Rollins Burdick Hunter, N.Y.C., 1990-92; chmn., CEO, Rollins Hudig Hall Pa., Phila., 1992-94; vice chmn. Aon Risk Svcs., 1994—99; pres., CEO Willis Risk Solutions, N.Y.C., 1999—. Seminar mgr. World Trade Inst., 1982-84. Contbr. articles to profl. jour. Mem.: N.Y. Choral Soc., Kiawah Island Club, Shenorock Shore Club, Siwanoy Country Club. Presbyterian. Avocations: vocal music, theater, golf, tennis.

MATHIEU, GEORGES VICTOR ADOLPHE, artist; b. Boulogne, France, Jan. 27, 1921; s. Adolphe Mathieu d'Escaudoeuvres and Madeleine Dupre d'Ausque. Ed., Facultés de droit et des lettres, Lille, France. Tchr. English; mgr. pub. rels. U.S. Lines. Exhbns. include Paris, 1950, N.Y.C., 1952, Japan, 1957, Scandinavia, 1958, Eng., Spain, Italy, Switzerland, Fed. Republic Germany, Austria and S.Am., 1959, Middle East, 1961-62, Can., 1963, Musée Municipal d'Art Moderne, Paris, 1963, Galerie Charpentier, Paris, 1965, Musée Nat. d'Art Moderne, Paris, 1967, Musée de la Manufacture Nat. des Gobelins, 1969, Antibes, 1976, Ostend, 1977, Grand Palais, Paris, 1978, Wildenstien Gallery, N.Y.C., Dominion Gallery, Montreal, Que., Can., 1979, Musée de la Poste, Paris, 1980, Palais des Papes, Avignon, 1985, Galerie Sapone, Nice, 1987, Galerie Protée, Paris, 1988, Abbaye de Chateautoux, France, 1990, Musée de Boulogne Sur Mer, St. Germain en Laye, 1994, Refectoize des Jacobins, Toulouse, 1995, Jeu De Paume, 2002, Liege (Belguim), 2003, Milano (Italia), 2003; prin. works include Hommage à la Mort, 1950, Hommage au Marechal de Turenne, 1952, Les Capetiens Partout, 1954, La Victoire de Denain, 1963, Hommage à Jean Cocteau, 1963, Paris, Capitale des Arts, 1965, Hommages aux Freres Boisseree, 1967, Hommages à Condillac, 1968, La prise de Berg op Zoom, 1969, Election de Charles Quint, 1971, Matta-Salums, 1978, La Liberation de Paris, 1980, La liberation d'Orleans par Jeanne d'Arc, 1982, Le Massacre des 269, 1985, Paradis des Orages, 1988, Les enfants de Bogota, 1989, Rumeurs de Paradis, 1991; designed gardens and bldgs. for B.C. transformer factory, Fontenay-le-comte, 1966, 16 posters for Air France; tapestries; 18 medals for Paris Mint, 1971, new 10 F coin, 1974; creater Tachism; author: Audela du Tachisme; Le privilege d'Etre; De la Revolté à Rénaissance; La Réponse de l'Abstraction lyrique; L'Abstraction Prophetique, Les Massacre de la Sensibilité, Desormais, Seul en Face de Dieu, Mathieu: 50 Years of Creation; represented in 90 museums and pub. collections. Mem. Acad. Fine Arts.

MATHIEU, HENRI-PIERRE, physician; b. Oran, Algeria, May 6, 1954; s. Guy Mathieu and Paule Perez; m. Nicole Carne, Nov. 3, 1978; children: Jean-Baptiste, Marie, Suzanne. MD, Montpellier, France, 1982. Resident Montpellier Hosps., Perpignan (France) Hosps.; asst. product mgr. Lab. Servier, Paris, 1982-83; mgr. Sante-Info, S.A.R.L., 1987-95; pvt. practice Paris, 1984-96; mgr. Info. Tech. Works, LLC, Wilmington, Del., 1998—. Adminstrv. mgr. Coll. de Hautes Etudes en Medicine Generale des hauts de Jeine, Paris, 1988-92; v.p. FMC 92, Paris, 1984-91. Contbr. articles to profl. publs. Mem. N.Y. Acad. of Sci. Office: Info Tech Works LLC 3422 Old Capitol Trl Wilmington DE 19808-6124

MATHIEU, MICHELE SUZANNE, grant writer, computer scientist, consultant; b. Chgo., Mar. 24, 1950; d. Joseph Edward Mathieu and Mary Ellen Fisher; m. Robert Steven Harris, May 1, 1988 (dec. Sept. 2000); life ptnr. Kathryn Ruth Huff, Aug. 16, 2002. BS in Mktg., Regents Coll., Albany, NY, 1998; cert. web site design, Columbia Coll., Chgo., 2000; cert. in Perl and CGI Scripting, San Diego C.C., 2003. Microsoft cert. profl. Broadcast coord. Grey-North Advt., Chgo., 1967-71; head drama dept. Patricia Stevens Coll., Chgo., 1972; instr. beginning acting Ted Liss Sch. Performing Arts, Chgo., 1973-75; project coord. grants and contracts Am. Dietetic Assn., Chgo., 1974-81, adminstr. govt. affairs, 1981-86, mgr. licensure comm., 1986-90, adminstr. nutrition svcs. payment systems, 1990-94, team leader, health care fin. team, 1994-97, dir. health care fin. team, 1998—2000, dir. mem. web, 2000—01, dir. applications devel., 2001—02; technician Networks Plus Tech. Group, San Diego, 2003—04; pc imaging technician Knowledge Info. Solutions, San Diego, 2004; dir. grants and contracts Virtual Reality Med. Ctr., San Diego, 2004—. Grant proposal cons. various performance arts, Chgo., 1978-2000; med. reporter, writer various internat. clients, 1994-; PC cons., Chgo., 1994-2002, San Diego, 2002—. Editor Legis. Newsletter, 1981-86; contbg. editor Nutrition Forum, 1986, Courier, 1987—2002; contbr. articles to profl. jours., mags., newspapers. Website project mgr. DigitalEve, Chgo., 2001. Ill. Arts Coun. grantee, 1981. Mem. Am. Soc. Assn. Execs. (Excellence in Govt. award 1989), WebSanDiego. Avocations: reading, fitness walking.

MATHILE, CLAYTON LEE, pet food company executive; b. Portage, Ohio, Jan. 11, 1941; s. Wilbert and Helen (Good) M.; m. Mary Ann Maas, July 7, 1962; children: Cathy, Tim, Mike, Tina, Jennie. BA, Ohio No. U., 1962, DBA (hon.), 1991; postgrad., Bowling Green State U., 1964. Acct. GM, Napoleon, Ohio, 1962-63, Campbell Soup Co., Napoleon, 1963-65, buyer, 1965-67, purchasing agt., 1967-70; gen. mgr. The Iams Co., Dayton, Ohio, 1970-75, v.p., 1975-80, chief exec. officer, 1980-90, chmn., 1990-99, also dir.; ret., 1999. Mem. Pet Food Inst.; bd. dirs. Midwest Group, Cin., Bush Bros. Co., Knoxville, Tenn., The Iams Co., 1999—. Author: A Business Owner's Perspective on Outside Boards. Trustee Chaminade-Julienne High Sch., Dayton, 1987—, U. Dayton; mem. adv. bd. coll. bus. Ohio No. U., Ada, 1987—, also trustee. Named Best of Best Ctr. for Values Rsch., Houston, 1987. Mem. Am. Mgmt. Assn., Am. Agt. Assn. Roman Catholic. Avocations: travel, swimming, golf. Office: The Iams Company PO Box 13615 Dayton OH 45413-0615

MATHIS, DAVID B. insurance company executive; b. Atlanta; BA, Lake Forest Coll., 1960. Leadership roles Kemper Corp., Long Grove, Ill., 1960—92, chmn., 1992—96, also bd. dirs.; chmn., pres., CEO, Kemper Ins. Cos., Long Grove, 1996—97. Office: Kemper Ins Cos 1 Kemper Dr Long Grove IL 60049-0001 E-mail: DMathis@Kemperinsurance.com.

MATHIS, DIANE, cell biologist, educator; BSc in Biology, Wake Forest U., 1971; MSc in Cell Biology, U. Rochester, 1976, PhD in Cell Biology, 1978. Postdoctoral fellow Lab. Génétique Moléculaire des Eucaryotes, Strasbourg, France, 1977—81; postdoctoral fellow Dept. Med. Microbiology Stanford (Calif.) U. Med. Ctr., 1981—83; sr. investigator Dept. Immunology Inst. Génétique et de Biologie Moléculaire et Cellulaire, Strasbourg, 1983—99; sr. investigator immunology and immunogenetics Joslin Diabetes Ctr. Harvard Med. Sch., Boston, 1999—, prof. medicine, 1999—. Vis. prof. Walter and Elisa Hall Inst., Melbourne, 1997—98; mem. adv. bd. Deutsches Rheuma-Forschungszentrum, Berlin, 1997—, Max Planck Inst. Immunology, Freiburg, Germany, 1997—, Walter and Eliza Hall Inst., Melbourne, 1998—, Peptimmune, 2000—, Inst. Pasteur, Paris, 2001—, Jackson Lab., Bar Harbor, Maine, 2001—, Riken Inst., Yokohama, Japan, 2001—, NIH Study Sect., 2001—. Mem. editl. bd.: European Jour. Immunology, 1988—2001, EMBO Jour., 1992—95, 1999—, Internat. Immunology, 1992—96, Immunology Today, 1992—2000, Sci., 1993—, Cell, 1994—; translator: Current Biology, 1994—2001; Jour. Exptl. Medicine, 1996—, Immunity, 1997—, Diabetes, 1999—, Modern Rheumatism, 2000—, EMBO Reports, 2000—, Current Sci. Faculty of 1000, 2001—; contbr. over 120 articles to profl. jours. Fellow, Damon Runyon-Walter Winchell Cancer Fund, 1977—81, Leukemia Soc. Am., 1981—83. Office: Joslin Diabetes Center One Joslin Place Boston MA 02215

MATHIS, F. JOHN, economist, educator; b. Rockford, Ill., Dec. 9, 1941; s. F. John and Jean K. (Vorwald) M.; children: John K., Laura K. BA, U. Calif., Riverside, 1962; MA, U. Iowa, 1964, PhD in Econs., 1966. Asst. prof. U. Ill., Chgo., 1964-66; assoc. prof. SUNY, Brockport, 1966-68; internat. economist Chase Manhattan Bank, N.Y.C., 1968-70; chief internat. economist Continental Bank of Chgo., 1970-83; sr. fin. analyst World Bank, Washington, 1983-85; sr. portfolio mgr. Internat. Fin. Corp., Washington, 1986-88; prof. internat. fin. Thunderbird-Am. Grad. Sch. Internat. Mgmt. & Banking, Phoenix, 1988—2000. Exec. dir. Thunderbird Internat. Trade and Fin. Ctr.; mng. dir. Thunderbird Ctr. Bus. Skills Devel., 2002; dir. faculty Thunderbird Am. Grad. Sch. Internat. Mgmt. Editor: Offshore Lending by U.S. Commercial Banks, 1985, First Steps in Treasury Management, 1991, Financial Management, 2003. Republican. Office: Thunderbird Am Grad Sch Internat Mgmt 15249 N 59th Ave Glendale AZ 85306 3236 Office Phone: 602-978-7168. Business E-mail: mathisj@t-bird.edu.

MATHIS, JACK DAVID, advertising executive, consultant; b. La Porte, Ind., Nov. 27, 1931; s. George Anthony and Bernice (Bennethum) Mathis; m. Phyllis Dene Hoffman, Dec. 24, 1971; children: Kane Cameron, Jana Dene. Student, U. Mo., 1950-52; BS, Fla. State U., 1955. With Benton & Bowles, Inc., 1955-56; owner Jack Mathis Advt., 1956—. Cons. in field. Author: Valley of the Cliffhangers, 1975, Republic Confidential: Vol. 2-The Players, 1992, Valley of the Cliffhangers Supplement, 1995, Republic Confidential: Vol. 1-The Studio, 1999; cons. (films) That's Action, 1977, Great Movie Stunts: Raiders of the Lost Ark, 1981, The Making of Raiders of The Lost Ark, 1981, An American Legend: The Lone Ranger, 1981, Heroes and Sidekicks: Indiana Jones and the Temple of Doom, 1984, The Republic Pictures Story, 1991, The Making of The Quiet Man, 1992, Roy Rogers: King of the Cowboys, 1992, Cliffhangers! Adventures from the Thrill Factory, 1993, The Making of Sands of Iwo Jima, 1993, Gene Autry: Melody of the West, 1994, Happy Trails: America Honors Roy Rogers and Dale Evans, 2001, Modern Marvels: Models, 2002, When Cowboys Were King, 2003. Mem. U.S. Olympic Basketball Com. Named to, Ill. Basketball Hall of Fame; recipient citation, Mktg. Rsch. Coun. N.Y. Mem.: Alpha Delta Sigma. Office: PO Box 3580 Barrington IL 60011-3580 Office Phone: 847-426-3003.

MATHIS, JAMES FORREST, retired petroleum company executive; b. Dallas, Sept. 28, 1925; s. Forrest and Martha (Godbold) M.; m. Frances Ellisor, Sept. 4, 1948; children: Alan Forrest (dec.), Lisa Lynn Lambeth. BSChE, Tex. A&M U., 1946; MS, U. Wis., 1951, PhD, 1953. Rsch. engr. Humble Oil & Refining Co., Baytown, Tex., 1946-49, 53-61, mgr. R & D, 1961-63, mgr. Splty. products planning, 1963-65; v.p. Exxon Rsch. & Engring. Co., Linden, N.J., 1966-68; sr. v.p., dir. Imperial Oil Ltd., Toronto, Ont., Can., 1968-71; v.p. tech. Exxon Chem. Co., Florham Pk., N.J., 1971-80; v.p. sci. and tech. Exxon Corp., N.Y.C., 1980-84; ret., 1984. Cons. Arthur D. Little, 1985-92, ChemShare Corp., 1989-92; chmn. N.J. Commn. Sci and Tech., 1988-96; dir. Laser Recording Systems, Inc., 1989-93, N L Industries, 1985-86, Hanlin Corp., 1989-99, Beaver Lake Realty Co., 1995-98. Bd. dirs. Chem. Industry Inst. Toxicology, 1975-83, treas., 1977-80, chmn., 1980-83; bd. dirs. Tex. Inst. for Advancement of Chem. Tech., 2001-; trustee Wis. Alumni Rsch. Found., 1984-, pres., 1993-97; bd. chem. sci. and tech. of Nat. Rsch. Coun., 1987-89, chem. weapon stockpile demilitarization commn., 1998-2001. Served with AC, USNR, 1944-45. Recipient Disting. Alumni award Coll. Engring. Tex. A&M U., 1982, Disting. Svc. citation Coll. Engring. U. Wis., 1969. Fellow Am. Inst. Chem. Engrs. (interim exec. dir., sec. 1987-88, Robert L. Jacks award in Mgmt. 1985, Van Antwerpen award for Svc. to Inst. 1989); mem. AAAS, NAE, Am. Chem. Soc. (Earle B. Barnes award for Chem. Rsch. Mgmt. 1984), Sigma Xi, Phi Lambda Upsilon, Tau Beta Pi. Presbyterian. Achievements include 2 patents in field. Home: 2714 S Southern Oaks Dr Houston TX 77068-2600 Personal E-mail: jfmathis@aol.com.

MATHIS, JOHN PRENTISS, lawyer; b. New Orleans, Feb. 10, 1944; s. Robert Prentess and Lena (Horton) M.; m. Karen Elizabeth McHugh, May 31, 1966; children: Lisa Lynne Mathis Kirkpatrick, Andrew P. BA magna cum laude, So. Meth. U., 1966; JD cum laude, Harvard U., 1969. Bar: Calif. 1970, D.C. 1975, U.S. Ct. Appeals (D.C. cir.) 1972, U.S. Ct. Appeals (5th cir.) 1975, U.S. Ct. Appeals (3d cir.) 1980, U.S. Supreme Ct. 1982. Assoc. Latham & Watkins, L.A., 1969-71; spl. asst. to gen. counsel FPC, Washington, 1971-72; gen. counsel Calif. Pub. Utilities Commn., San Francisco, 1972-74; assoc. Baker & Botts, Washington, 1974-76, ptnr., 1976-92, Hogan & Hartson, Washington, 1992—2000; v.p., assoc. gen. counsel regulatory affairs Edison Mission Energy, Washington, 2000—. Mem. ABA (litig. sect., chmn. energy litig. com. 1985-89, divsn. dir. 1989-90, chmn. legis. com. 1990-94, rep. to coord. group energy law 1992-97), Fed. Energy Bar Assn., Harvard U. Law Sch. Assn. D.C. (past pres.), Congl. Country Club, Met. Club (Washington), Talbot Country Club (Easton, Md.). Republican. Episcopalian. Office: Edison Mission Energy 555 12th St NW Ste 640 Washington DC 20004

MATHIS, LAURELLE SHEEDY, academic administrator, volunteer; b. Southampton, N.Y., Aug. 29, 1948; d. Edmund Sheedy and Tatiana (Widrin) Brooks; m: Robert Trimble Mathis, 1979, (dec., 2002); children: Liliana Sheedy, Bronwyn Trimble, Kane Timberlake. BA, Stephens Coll., Columbia, Mo., 1970; MBA, Harvard U., 1977. Spl. asst. Congressman Ed Foreman, Washington, 1970; staff asst. Senator James L. Buckley, Washington, 1971-72; staff asst. to Pres. of U.S. Washington, 1973-75; v.p. Blyth Eastman Paine Webber, N.Y.C., 1977-81, Merrill Lynch Capital Markets, N.Y.C., 1981-83; pres. Harris Energy Corp., Greenwich, Conn., 1988-91; CFO Diocese of Mt. Kilimanjaro, Arusha, Tanzania, 1991-93; v.p. TechnoServe, Norwalk, Conn., 1994-96, TMP Exec. Resourcing, N.Y.C., 1997—2001; dir. fin. and adminstrn. Nat. Presbyn. Sch., Washington, 2002—. Bd. curators Stephens Coll., 1981-83; bd. dirs. Putnam Indian Field Sch., Greenwich, 1986-91, chmn. auction, 1987; chmn. Christ Ch. Antiques Show, 1987, 88, 89; bd. dirs. Episcopal Ch., Women of Christ Ch. Recipient Alumni Achievement award Stephens Coll., 1980. Republican. Episcopalian. Home: 3512 Preston Ct Chevy Chase MD 20815

MATHIS, LUSTER DOYLE, college administrator, political scientist; b. Gainesville, Ga., May 5, 1936; s. Luster and Fay Selena (Wingo) M.; m. Rheba Burch, June 5, 1958; children— Douglas James, Deborah Jane. AB, Berry Coll., 1958; MA, U. Ga., 1958, PhD (Univ. Alumni Found. fellow), 1966. Asst. prof. polit. sci. Brenau Coll., Gainesville, 1960-61; asso. prof. Calif. Baptist Coll., 1961-62, Belmont Coll., Nashville, 1962-64; asso. prof., head dept. polit. sci. W.Ga. Coll., Carrollton, 1965-68, prof., 1969-75, head dept., 1969-71, chmn. div. grad. studies, 1970-73; assoc. dean, 1972-75; research asso., asst. editor Papers of Thomas Jefferson Princeton U., 1968-69; v.p., dean of coll. Berry Coll., Mt. Berry, Ga., 1975-93, v.p. acad. affairs, 1993-99, provost, 1999-2000, coll. historian, prof. govt., 2000—03. Cons. Citizens Com. on Ga. Gen. Assembly. Co-author: Courts as Political Instruments, 1970. Mem. Ga. Democratic Charter Commn., 1974-75; mem. consumer adv. com. Floyd Med. Center, 1978-80. Nat. Hist. Pubs. Commn. fellow, 1968-69 Mem. Am. Assn. Higher Edn., Am. Conf. Acad. Deans, Ga. Polit. Sci. Assn. (pres. 1968-69). Democrat. Baptist. Office: 200 Salt Air Dr Unit 136 Saint Simons Island GA 31522 E-mail: dmathis@berry.edu.

MATHIS, SAMANTHA, actress; b. N.Y.C., May 12, 1970; d. Bibi Besch. Actress: (films) Forbidden Sun, 1989, Pump Up the Volume, 1990, This is My Life, 1992, FernGully: The Last Rainforest (voice), 1992, Super Mario Bros., 1993, The Music of Chance, 1993, The Thing Called Love, 1993, Little Women, 1994, Jack and Sarah, 1995, How to Make an American Quilt, 1995, The American President, 1995, Broken Arrow, 1996, Museum of Love, 1996, Sweet Jane, 1998, Waiting for Woody, 1998, Freak City, 1999, The Simian Line, 2000, American Psycho, 2000, Attraction, 2000, The Punisher, 2004; (TV movies) Aaron's Way: The Harvest, 1988, Cold Sassy Tree, 1989, American Nuclear, 1989, Extreme Close-Up, 1990, 83 Hours 'Til Dawn, 1990, To My Daughter, 1990, Harsh Realm, 1999, Mermaid, 2000, Collected Stories, 2002; (TV series) Knightwatch, 1988-89, Aaron's Way, 1988, Harsh Realm, 1999, First Years, 2001; (TV miniseries) The Mists of Avalon, 2001. Office: Creative Artists Agy care Rick Kurtzman 9830 Wilshire Blvd Beverly Hills CA 90212-1804

MATHIS, SHARON BELL, retired writer, librarian, curator; b. Atlantic City, Feb. 26, 1937; d. John Willie and Alice Mary (Frazier) Bell; m. Leroy F. Mathis, July 11, 1957 (div. Jan. 1979); children: Sherie, Stacy, Stephanie. BA, Morgan State Coll., 1958; M.L.S., Catholic U. Am., 1975. Interviewer Children's Hosp. D.C., Washington, 1958-59; tchr. Holy Redeemer Elem. Sch., Washington, 1959-65, Charles Hart Jr. H.S., Washington, 1965-72; spl. edn. tchr. Stuart Jr. H.S., Washington, 1972-74; libr. Benning Elem.Sch., Washington, 1975-76, Friendship Ednl. Ctr. (now Patricia R. Harris Ednl. Ctr.), 1976-95, ret., 1995. Writer-in-charge children's lit. div. D.C. Black Writers Workshop; writer-in-residence Howard U., 1972-73 Author: Brooklyn Story, 1970, Sidewalk Story, 1971 (Council on Interracial Books for Children award 1970), Teacup Full of Roses, 1972 (Outstanding Book of Yr. award New York Times 1972), Ray Charles, 1973 (Coretta Scott King award 1974), Listen for the Fig Tree, 1974, The Hundred Penny Box, 1975 (Boston Globe-Horn Book Honor book 1975, Newbery Honor Book 1976), Cartwheels, 1977, Red Dog Blue Fly: Football Poems, 1991 (Children's Book of Yr. award Bank St. Coll. 1992), Red Dog Blue Fly: An American Bookseller (Pick of the List 1995), Running Girl: The Diary of Ebonee Rose, 1997, Ray Charles, 2001. Mem. bd. advisers lawyers com. D.C. Commn. on Arts, 1972. Nominated Books for Brotherhood list NCCJ, 1970; recipient D.C. Assn. Sch. Librs. award 1976, Arts and Humanities award Archdiocese of Washington Black Secretariat, 1978; Weekly Reader Book Club fellow Bread Loaf Writers Conf., 1970, MacDowell Colony fellow, 1978. Roman Catholic. *My success is due to the glorious African blood which flows throughout my body—and to the dignity, intelligence, strength, pride, efforts, and faith of my very creative parents and all people who have helped me.*

MATHIS, TERANCE, professional football player; b. Detroit, June 7, 1967; Student, U. N.Mex. Wide receiver, kick returner N.Y. Jets, 1990—93, Atlanta Falcons, 1994—2001; wide receiver Pittsburgh Steelers, 2002—. Named to Sporting News Coll. All-Am. 1st team, 1989, Pro Bowl, 1994. Office: Pittsburgh Steelers 100 Art Rooney Ave Pittsburgh PA 15212

MATHIS, VIRGINIA, federal judge; Apptd. magistrate judge U.S. Dist. Ct. Ariz., 1996. Office: 5025 US Courthouse 230 N 1st Ave Phoenix AZ 85025-0230

MATHISEN, DOUGLAS J. thoracic surgeon; b. Spring Valley, Ill., 1948; MD, U. Ill. Diplomate Am. Bd. Thoracic Surgery, Am. Bd. Surgery. Thoracic surgeon Mass. Gen. Hosp., Boston, 1995—; assist. prof. thoracic surgery

Harvard U. Med. Sch., 1989—99, Hermes C. Grillo prof. thoracic surgery, 1999—; chief general thoracic surgery Mass. Gen. Hosp. Fellow Am. Coll. Surgeons; mem. AMA, ACCPA, Am. Assn. Thoracic Surgery, Soc. Thoracic Surgery (bd. mem.), Cardiothoracic Surgery Network, Thoracic Surgery Directors Assn. (pres.), Thoracic Surgery Found. for Rsch. & Edn., Am. Bd. of Thoracic Surgery (bd. dirs.), Soc. of Thoracic Surgeons (treas.). Office: Mass Gen Hosp Thoracic Surgery Blake 1570 55 Fruit St Boston MA 02114

MATHISEN, HAROLD CLIFFORD, foundation administrator; b. East Orange, NJ, Apr. 1, 1924; s. Harold and Ottilie Christine (Nordland) Mathisen; m. Dora Elizabeth Bachtel, Sept. 14, 1946; children: Margaret Bennett, Harold, Elizabeth Mathisen Andersen, Barbara Ramsland. AB, Princeton U., 1943; MBA, Harvard U., 1948. Asst. to contr. Kaiser Frazer Corp., Willow Run, Mich., 1948—52; investment analyst Smith Barney & Co., NYC, 1952—61; pres. Alliance Found., NYC, 1961—. Treas. AGF Mgmt. Co., NYC, 1969—85; portfolio mgr. Legg Mason Wood Walker, Inc., NYC, 1967—78, NYC, 1982—. Pres. Alliance Growth Fund, NYC, 1968—78; trustee, pres. McAuley Water St. Mission, NYC, 1967—99; asst. treas., investment mgr. Christian and Missionary Alliance, Nyack, 1978—80; asst. treas. NY Internat. Bible Soc., NYC, 1980—82. Lt. USNR, 1944—46. Mem.: Inst. Chartered Fin. Analysts, NY Soc. Securities Analysts, Sigma Xi, Phi Beta Kappa. Home: 36 Runnymede Rd Chatham NJ 07928-1374 Office: One Chase Manhattan Plaza New York NY 10005

MATHISEN, HOWARD, psychologist, minister; b. Bklyn., June 3, 1938; s. Olaf and Hjordis K. (Skjaerum) M.; m. Kathleen Ann Poce, Sept. 20, 1980 (dec. Oct. 1987); children: Randi Sue, Lisa Jane; m. Carolynn Anne Burroughs, Aug. 22, 1992. BA, Taylor U., 1960; MDiv, Phila. Theol. Sem., 1963; postgrad., Luth. Theol. Sem., 1964—65; MA in Religion, Concordia Sem., 1967; postgrad., Rutgers U., 1975, Assumption Coll., 1971—76; DMin in Psychology, Andover Newton Theol. Sch., 1976. Lic. psychologist, Mass., marriage and family therapist, Mass.; cert. diplomate of sex therapy Am. Assn. Sex Educators, Counselors and Therapists; diplomate in marital and sex therapy Am. Bd. Family Psychology; diplomate Am. Bd. Sexology. Pastor Christ Meml. Ch., Phila., 1962-66, Zion Luth. Ch., Webster, Mass., 1967-73; dir. Human Svcs. Ctr. Hubbard Regional Hosp., Webster, 1973-81; pvt. practice psychology Boylston, Mass., 1976-81; co-dir. Counseling Affiliates, Worcester, Mass., 1981-97; dir. pastoral counseling Boston Road Clinic, Worcester, 1997—2001; dir. credentialing svcs. Capstan, Worcester, 1998-99; asst. pastor Concordia Luth. Ch., Worcester, 1976-98; dir. min. asst. program New Eng. Synod, Luth. Ch., 1991—; psychologist Prescott Health Care, 2002—. Adj. instr. psychology Nichols Coll., Dudley, Mass., 1981, Assumption Coll., Worcester, 1983-86. Dean ctrl. Mass. conf. New Eng. Synod, Luth. Ch., 1988-90; bd. dirs. Luth. Svc. Assn. New Eng., 1973-87, vice chmn., 1983-85, chmn., 1985-87; bd. dirs. Luth. Home of Worcester, 1987-92, chmn., 1987-89; chmn. bldg. com. Luth. Nursing Home, Worcester, 1977-79; chmn. Family Svcs. Com., 1981-83; mem. Mass. Adv. Com. Continuing Edn. for Nursing, 1979-81; bd. dirs. Family Planning Svcs. Ctrl. Mass., 1975-81; mem. tech. adv. subcom. substance abuse Ctrl. Mass. Health Sys. Agy., 1979-80. Fellow Acad. Family Psychology, Am. Acad. Clin. Sexologists; mem. APA, Am. Assn. Marriage and Family Therapy, Mass. Psychol. Assn., Mass. Assn. Marriage and Family Therapy, Acad. Managed Care Providers. Home: 6 Camelot Cir Dudley MA 01571-6110 Office: 130 Elm St Worcester MA 01609 E-mail: mathisen@charter.net.

MATHISEN-REID, RHODA SHARON, international communications consultant; b. Portland, Oreg., June 25, 1942; d. Daniel and Mildred Elizabeth Annette (Peterson) Hager; m. James Albert Mathisen, July 17, 1964 (div. 1977); m. James Albert Mathisen, July 17, 164 (div. 1977); m. James A. Reid Sr., Jan. 1, 1991. BA in Edn., Music, Bible Coll., Mich., 1964. Cmty. rels. officer Gary-Wheaton Bank, Wheaton, Ill., 1971-75; br. mgr. Stiver Temporary Personnel, Chgo., 1975-79; v.p. sales Exec. Technique, Chgo., 1980-83; prin. Mathisen Assocs., Clarendon Hill., Ill., 1983—. Presenter seminars; featured speaker Women in Mgmt. Oak Brook Chpt., 1988.; cons. Haggai Inst., Atlanta; adv. mem. Nat. Bd. Success Group, 1986. Newsletter editor/publisher: 90th Divsn. Assn. (WWII Vets) 2001—. Mem. Downers Grove Twp. Precinct # 87 Rep. Com., 1998—; pres. chancel choir Christ Ch. Oak Brook, 1985—87; bd. dirs. Career Devel. Inst., Oak Brook, 1992—99, chair operational fin. com., 1997—98; bd. dirs. Crossroads Ministry Internat., 2000—; chmn. 1st Profl. Women's Seminar, 1995; judge Mrs. Ill., USI Pageant, 1994; exec. sec., treas. 90th Divsn. Assn., 2001—. Recipient Denby Steel award, 90th Divsn. Assn., 2001. Mem. Bus. and Profl. Women (charter mem., Woodfield chpt.), Execs. Club Oak Brook, Assn. Commerce and Industry (named Ambassador of Month N.W. suuburban chpt. 1979), Oak Brook Assn. Commerce and Industry (membership com.), Women Entrepreneurs of DuPage County (membership chmn., featured speaker Ja 1988), Art. Inst., Willowbrook/Burr Ridge C. of C., 90th Divsn. Assn. (asst. sec., treas., 2001 Denby Steel award, editor newsletter), US Army WWII Vets. Orgn. (newsletter editor 2001-). Office: Mathisen Assocs 17 Lake Shore Dr Willowbrook IL 60527-2221

MATHISON, IAN WILLIAM, chemistry professor, dean, consultant; b. Liverpool, Eng., Apr. 17, 1938; came to U.S., 1963; s. William and Grace (Almond) M.; m. Mary Ann Gordon, July 20, 1968; children: Mark W., Lisa A. B. Pharm., U. London, 1960, PhD, 1963, D. Sci., 1976. Lic. pharmacist, Gt. Britain. Research assoc. U. Tenn. Ctr. for Health Scis., Memphis, 1963-65, asst. prof., 1965-68, assoc. prof., 1968-72, prof., 1972-76; medicinal chemistry prof. Ferris State U., Big Rapids, Mich., 1977—, dean, prof., 1977—. External examiner U. Sci., Malaysia, 1978-79; mem. Mich. dept. Mental Health Pharmacy Facilities Rev. Panel, Lansing, 1978-90, Quality Assurance Commn., 1979-90; cons. WHO, 1999; mem. adv. com. McKesson Medication Mgmt., 2002—; deans adv. com. Rite Aid, 2000—; cons. in field. Mem. editorial bd.: Jour. Pharm. Sci., 1981-86; contbr. articles to profl. jours.; sr. inventor, patentee in field. Marion Labs. awardee, 1965-74; NSF grantee, 1968-72; Beecham Co. grantee, 1974-79 Fellow Royal Inst. Chemistry, Royal Soc. Chemistry; mem. Am. Pharm. Soc., Am. Chem. Soc., Am. Assn. Coll. Pharmacy (bd. dirs. 1988-90), Nat. Assn. Retail Druggists (edn. adv. com. 1989-94), Royal Pharm. Soc. Gt. Britain, Nat. Assn. Chain Drug Stores (ednl. adv. com. 1993-2002). Home: 820 Osborn Cir Big Rapids MI 49307-2536 Office: Ferris State U 220 Ferris Dr Big Rapids MI 49307-2295

MATHISON, THEODORE E. retired air transportation executive; Exec. dir. Md. Aviation Adminstrn., Balt., retired, 1999. Office: MD Aviation Admin PO Box 8766 Baltimore MD 21240-0766

MATHOG, ROBERT HENRY, otolaryngologist, educator; b. New Haven, Apr. 13, 1939; s. William and Tiby (Gans) M.; m. Deena Jane Rabinowitz, June 14, 1964; children: Tiby, Heather, Lauren, Jason. AB, Dartmouth Coll., 1960; MD, NYU, 1964. Diplomate Am. Bd. Facial Plastic and Reconstructive Surgery. Intern Duke Hosp., Durham, N.C., 1964-65, resident surgery, 1965-66, resident otolaryngology, 1966-69; practice medicine, specializing in otolaryngology Mpls., 1971-77, Detroit, 1977—; chief of otolaryngology Hennepin County Med. Center, Mpls., 1972-77; asst. prof. U. Minn., 1971-74, asso. prof., 1974-77; prof., chmn. dept. otolaryngology Wayne State U. Sch. Medicine, 1977—. Chief otolaryngology Hennepin County Hosp., Mpls., 1972-77, Harper-Grace Hosps., Detroit, 1977—, Detroit Receiving Hosp., 1977-92; cons. staff VA Hosp., Allen Park, Minn., 1977—, Children's Hosp., Detroit, 1977—, Hutzel Hosp., Detroit, 1966, St. Joseph Mercy Hosp., Oakland, Mich., 2001; mem. adv. coun. Nat. Inst. Deaf and Other Communicable Disorders NIH, 1992-96; chief otolaryngology, head and neck surgery June Hosp., 1994-95. Author: Otolaryngology Clinics of North America, 1976, Textbook of Maxillofacial Trauma, 1983; editor in chief Videomed. Edn. Systems, 1972-75; editor: Atlas of Craniofacial Trauma, 1992; contbr. articles to med. jours. Bd. dirs. Bexer County Hearing Soc., 1969-71; adv. coun. WIDCB, 1993. Maj. USAF, 1969-71; chmn. Lens Hearing Ctr. of S.E. Mich. Recipient Valentine Mott medal for proficiency in anatomy, 1961, Recognition award Wayne State Bd. Govs. Faculty, 1993; Deafness Rsch. Found. grantee, 1979-81, NIH grantee, 1986, 92, 96, Lawrence M. Weiner Alumni award Wayne State U. Sch. Med., 1999. Fellow ACS, Am. Acad. Otolaryngology, Head and Neck Surgery (Cert. award 1976, Cert. of Appreciation 1978), Am. Soc. Head and Neck Surgery, Triological Soc. (v.p. 1995-96, mtg. guest of honor 2002), Am. Otol. Soc., Am. Acad. Facial Plastic and Reconstructive Surgery (v.p. 1980), Am. Neurotology Soc.; mem. AMA, Am. Laryngol. Soc. (coun. 1994—), Am. Laryngol. Assn., Mich. Med. Soc., Am. Head and Neck Soc., Soc. Univ. Otolaryngologists (pres. 1995), Assn. Acad. Depts. Otolaryngology, Assn. Rsch. Otolaryngology (pres. 1981). Home: 27115 Wellington Rd Franklin MI 48025-1329 Office: 43494 Woodward Ste 210 Bloomfield Hills MI 48312 Also: Wayne State U Sch Med 540 E Canfield St Detroit MI 48201-1928

MATHON, LAUREN R. judge; b. L.A., Oct. 23, 1949; d. Benjamin D. and Sylvia M.; m. Marvin S. Maslin, Sept. 2, 1990. BA, U. Calif., Berkeley, 1971; JD, Lewis & Clark Law Sch., 1974; MA, U. Southern Calif., 1980. Bar: Calif. 1975, D.C. 1997. Dep. dist. atty. Dist. Atty's. Office, L.A. County, 1976-85; trial atty. Dept. Justice, Immigration & Naturalization Svc., El Centro, Calif., 1986; immigration judge Dept. Justice, Exec. Office Immigration Review, L.A., 1987-94; mem. Dept. Justice, Bd. Immigration Appeals, Falls Church, Va., 1995—. Avocation: yoga. Office: Bd Immigration Appeals 5107 Leesburg Pike Ste 2400 Falls Church VA 22041-3234

MATHRE, LAWRENCE GERHARD, minister, federal agency administrator; b. Vancouver, B.C., Can., Mar. 24, 1925; s. Lawrence Alfred and Nellie Josephine (Thompson) M.; m. Blanche Kathleen Brudevold, Sept. 2, 1951; children: James Lawrence, Jerome Keigh, John Mark, Joel David. BA, St. Olaf Coll., 1948; MDiv., Luther Sem., 1952; MA, Phillips U., 1962. Ordained to ministry Evang. Luth. Ch. in Am., 1952. Pastor First Luth. Ch., Fargo, N.D., 1952-54, Bethlehem Luth. Ch., Buffalo Center, Iowa, 1952-57; founder, pastor Prince of Peace Luth. Ch., Oklahoma City, 1957-63; chaplain fed. prison system U.S. Dept. Justice, Okla., Wash., Ill. and Calif., 1963-73, chaplain dir. Western and N.C. regions, 1973-83; pastor Hope Luth Ch., San Mateo, Calif., 1984-87, Zion Luth. Ch., Stockton, Calif., 1987-91; ret., 1991. Assoc. prof. Pacific Luth. U., Parkland, Wash., 1970-72; chaplain St. Joseph's Regional Med. Ctr. Nat. chaplain Fed. Prison Retirees Assn., 1999—. With AUS, 1943—45, ETO. Decorated Bronze Star. Mem. Am. Protestant Correctional Chaplains Assn. (nat. pres. 1974), Am. Correctional Chaplains Assn. (nat. pres. 1977), Assn. Clin. Pastoral Edn. (regional chmn. 1979-83, v.p. 1977-79, treas. 1984-89), Winnebago Itasc Travelers (chaplain), Lions (chaplain San Mateo club 1985-87). Republican. Home: 78469 Indigo Dr La Quinta CA 92253-6838 *It is not nearly as important what happens to you as it is what you do about what happens to you. A life lived for oneself is empty; a life lived with and for others is full. You truly find yourself when you are well related—to God and to others.*

MATHY, PAMELA ANN, lawyer; b. Green Bay, Wis., Jan. 11, 1952; d. Bernard George and Inez Claire Mathy. AB, Marquette U., Milw., 1973; MA, U. Tex., 1976; JD, U. Wis., 1978; LLM, Georgetown U., Washington, 1982. Bar: Wis. 1978, D.C. 1979, U.S. Dist. Ct. (no. dist.) Ill. 1979, U.S. Ct. Appeals (7th cir.) 1978, Ill. 1979, U.S. Dist. Ct. (we. dist.) Tex. 1983, U.S. Ct. Appeals (5th cir.) 1984, Tex. 1985. Law clk. Chief Judge Walter Cummings, U.S. Ct. Appeals, 7th Cir., Chgo., 1978-80; pvt. practice law Washington, 1980-81; sr. staff atty. U.S. Ct. Appeals (7th cir.), Chgo., 1981-83; asst. U.S. Atty. U.S. Dist. Ct. (we. dist.) Tex., San Antonio, 1983—, 1st asst. criminal divsn., 1996—98; U.S. magistrate judge U.S. Dist. Ct., San Antonio, 1998—. Contbr. articles to profl. jours. Named Prosecutor of Yr., Tex. Narcotics Officers Assn., 1989; recipient Outstanding Arson Prosecution award Tex. Adv. Coun. on Arson, 1991, Dir.'s award U.S. Dept. Justice, 1994. Mem. ABA, Wis. Bar Assn., Tex. Bar Assn., San Antonio Bar Assn., Fed. Bar Assn., Bexar County Women's Bar Assn. Office: US Dist Ct 655 E Durango Blvd San Antonio TX 78206

MATHY, ROBIN MICHELLE, writer; b. Portsmouth, Va., July 21, 1957; BS in sociology, Ariz. State U., 1985; MA, Ind. U., Bloomington, 1989; MSW, U. Minn., 2003; M in Internat. Rels., U. Cambridge, 2004; MSc, U. Oxford, 2004. Author: Male Homosexuality in Four Societies: Brazil, Guatemala, the Philippines, and the United States (Best Book in Print, NY Times Rev. of Books, 2002); contbr. articles to profl. jours., chapters to books; editor: Lesbian and Bisexual Women's Mental Health, 2004. Pres. GLBT&Q Suicide Prevention Coalition, Washington, 2003. Office: U Minn 51 E River Rd Minneapolis MN 55455

MATIA, PAUL RAMON, federal judge; b. Cleve., Oct. 2, 1937; s. Leo Clemens and Irene Elizabeth (Linkert) M.; m. Nancy Arch Van Meter, Jan. 2, 1993. BA, Case Western Res. U., 1959; JD, Harvard U., 1962. Bar: Ohio 1962, U.S. Dist. Ct. (no. dist.) Ohio 1969. Law clk. Common Pleas Ct. of Cuyahoga County, Cleve., 1963-66, judge, 1985-91; asst. atty. gen. State of Ohio, Cleve., 1966-69, adminstrv. ast. to atty. gen. Columbus, 1969-70; senator Ohio State Senate, Columbus, 1971-75, 79-83; ptnr. Hadley, Matia, Mills & MacLean Co., L.P.A., Cleve., 1975-84; judge U.S. Dist. Ct. (no. dist.) Ohio, 1991-99, chief dist. judge, 1999—; mem. 6th Cir. Jud. Coun., 1999—. Candidate Lt. Gov. Rep. Primary, 1982, Ohio Supreme Ct., 1988. Named Outstanding Legislator, Ohio Assn. for Retarded Citizens, 1974, Watchdog of Ohio Treasury, United Conservatives of Ohio, 1979; recipient Heritage award Polonia Found., 1988. Mem. Fed. Bar Assn., Club at Key Ctr. Avocations: skiing, gardening, travel. Office: US Dist Ct 801 W Superior Ave Cleveland OH 44113-1834

MATIJEVIC, EGON, chemistry professor; b. Otocac, Croatia, Apr. 27, 1922; came to U.S., 1957; s. Grgur and Stefica (Spiegel) M.; m. Bozica Biscan, Feb. 27, 1947. Diploma in Chem. Engring., U. Zagreb, 1944, PhD in Chemistry, 1948, D Habilitation in Phys. Chemistry, 1952; DSc (hon.), Lehigh U., 1977, M. Curie-Sklodowska U., Lublin, Poland, 1990, Clarkson U., 1992, Zagreb U., Croatia, 1998, Nat. U. San Martin, Buenos Aires, 2003, U. Ljubljana, Slovenia, 2003. Instr. chemistry U. Zagreb, 1944-47, sr. instr. phys. chemistry, 1949-52, privat dozent in colloid chemistry, 1952-54, dozent in phys. and colloid chemistry, 1955-56, on leave, 1956-59; rsch. assoc. Inst. Cinematography, Zagreb, 1948; rsch. fellow dept. colloid sci. U. Cambridge, England, 1956-57; vis. prof. Clarkson Coll. Tech., Potsdam, NY, 1957-59, assoc. prof. chemistry Postdam, NY, 1960-62; prof. Clarkson U., Postdam, NY, 1962-86, disting. univ. prof., 1986-99, LaMer prof. colloid and surface sci., 2000—; assoc. dir. Inst. Colloid and Surface Sci. Clarkson Coll. Tech., 1966-68, dir. inst., 1968-81, chmn. dept. chemistry, 1981-87. Vis. prof. Japan Soc. for Promotion Sci., 1973, U. Melbourne, Australia, 1976, Sci. U. Tokyo, 1979, 84, fgn. guest Inst. Colloid and Interface Sci., 82; vis. scientist U. Leningrad, Russia, 1977; advisor IAEA, Buenos Aires, 1978, Buenos Aires, 80; lectr. in field. Author: (with M. Kesler) General and Inorganic Chemistry for Senior High Schools, 11 edits., including Croatian, Macedonian, Hungarian, Italian, 1943-63; translator: Einfuhrung in die Stochiometrie (Nylen and Wigern), 1948; editor: (with Alter J. Weber) Adsorption from Aqueous Solution, 1968, Surface and Colloid Science, vols. 1-17, 1969-2002; contbr. numerous articles to profl. publs. Recipient Gold medal, Am. Electroplaters Soc., 1976, guest of honor 56th and 63d Colloid and Surface Sci. Symposia, Blacksburg, Va., 1982, Seattle, 1989, Boston, 2002, Egon Matijevic chair endowed in his name, Clarkson U., 1992. Mem. Am. Chem. Soc. (councilor divsn. colloid and surface chemistry 1982-87, chmn. 1969-70, Kendall award 1972, Langmuir Disting. Lectureship award 1985, Ralph K. Iler award 1993), Kolloid Gesellschaft (hon. life, Thomas Graham award 1985), Internat. Assn. Colloid Interface Sci. (pres. 1985-87), Chem. Soc. Japan, Inst. Colloid and Interface Sci. of U. of Tokyo (hon.), Phalanx Soc., Croatian Acad. Scis. and Arts (fgn.), Am. Ceramic Soc. (hon.), Materials Rsch. Soc. Japan (hon.), Acad. Ceramics (Italy), Croatian Chem. Soc. (hon., Bozo Tezak medal 1991), Sigma Xi (Clarkson Coll. Tech. chpt. award 1972, nat. lectr. 1987-89). Roman Catholic. Office: Ctr Advanced Materials Proc Clarkson U Dept Chem Potsdam NY 13699-5814 Business E-Mail: matiegon@clarkson.edu.

MATJASKO, M. JANE, anesthesiologist, educator; b. Harrison Twp., Pa., 1942; MD, Med. Coll. Pa., 1968. Diplomate Am. Bd. Anesthesiology. Resident in anesthesiology Md. Hosp., Balt., 1968-72; prof., chmn. anesthesiology U. Md., Balt., 1990—. Bd. dirs. Am. Bd. Anesthesiology. Mem. Am. Soc. Anesthesiologists, Assn. Univ. Anesthesiologists. Office: U Md Hosp Dept Anesthesiology 22 S Greene St Baltimore MD 21201-1544

MATJIAS, CHRISTIAN, music educator, musician; b. L.A., June 9, 1963; BA, U. of So. Calif., L.A., 1988; MusM, U. of So. Calif., 1993. Instr. of music Interlochen Arts Acad., Mich., 1991—98; prof. of dance and music U. of Mich., Ann Arbor, 1998—. Edtl. dir. The George Balanchine Trust, N.Y.C., 2000—. Composer: (audio recording) Standing Alone, Suites for Dance, Works for Cello and Piano, (dance music) Statues in Motion, Interlude, Catch, Hold, Save. Mem.: Broadcast Music Inc., Am. Guild Organists, Internat. Coun. Kinetogrphy Laban, Soc. of Dance History Scholars. Avocations: record collecting, book collecting, road travel. Home: 12 W Eden Ct Ann Arbor MI 48108 Office: University of Michigan 1310 N University Ct Ann Arbor MI 48109-2217 Personal E-mail: matjiasc@umich.edu.

MATKOWSKY, BERNARD JUDAH, applied mathematician, educator; b. N.Y.C., Aug. 19, 1939; s. Morris N. and Ethel H. M.; m. Florence Knobel, Apr. 11, 1965; children: David, Daniel, Devorah. BS, CCNY, 1960; M.E.E., NYU, 1961, MS, 1963, PhD, 1966. Fellow Courant Inst. Math. Scis., NYU, 1961-66; mem. faculty dept. math. Rensselaer Poly. Inst., 1966-77; John Evans prof. applied math., mech. engring. & math. Northwestern U., Evanston, Ill., 1977—, chmn. engring. sci. and applied math. dept., 1993-99. Vis. prof. Tel Aviv U., 1972-73; vis. scientist Weizmann Inst. Sci., Israel, summer 1976, summer 1980, Tel Aviv U., summer 1980; cons. Argonne Nat. Lab., Sandia Labs., Lawrence Livermore Nat. Lab., Exxon Research and Engring. Co. Editor Wave Motion—An Internat. Jour., 1979-99, Applied Math. Letters, 1987—, SIAM Jour. Applied Math., 1976-95, European Jour. Applied Math., 1990-96, Random and Computational Dynamics, 1991-97, Internat. Jour. SHS, 1992—, Jour. Materials Synthesis and Processing, 1992-2002; mem. editl. adv. bd. Springer Verlag Applied Math. Scis. Series; contbr. chpts. to books, articles to profl. jours. Fulbright grantee, 1972-73; Guggenheim fellow, 1982-83 Fellow: AAAS, Am. Acad. Mechs.; mem.: Soc. Natural Philosophy, Com. Concerned Scientists, Conf. Bd. Math. Scis. (coun., com. human rights math. scientists), Am. Assn. Combustion Synthesis, Am. Phys. Soc., Combustion Inst., Am. Math. Soc., Soc. Indsl. and Applied Math., Eta Kappa Nu, Sigma Xi. Home: 3704 Davis St Skokie IL 60076-1745 Office: Northwestern U Technological Institute Evanston IL 60208-0001 Office Phone: 847-491-5396. Business E-Mail: b-matkowsky@northwestern.edu.

MATLACK, MARIA THERESA, elementary school educator; d. Bernadette Rose and Vernon Finkle; m. Randall Gerard Matlack, Aug. 9, 1960; children: Timothy Andrew, Peter Michael. BA, La Salle U., 1982; MEd, Coll. N.J., 1988. Cert. reading specialist N.J., 1988, tchr. handicapped N.J., Pa., 1982. Resource program tchr. F.L. Walther Sch., Lumberton, NJ, 1982—93, Lumberton (N.J.) Mid. Sch., 1993—. Seminar presenter/spkr. Pracrtical Seminars for Teachers, Sewell, NJ, 2000—02; adj. prof. La Salle U., Philadelphia, Pa., 2000—00; presenter Lumberton Bd. Edn., 1998—2001, Ednl. Resource Ctr., Sewell, NJ, 1989—89; mentor Lumberton Mid. Sch., 2002—03; online instr. U. Phoenix, 2003—. Author: (teacher resource book) Using My Louisiana Sky in the Classroom; contbr. textbook. Choir mem. All Saints Ch., Burlington, NJ, 1993—2003, coord. renew program, 1998—2001; regent Burlington County Region of Trenton Diocesan PTA, Trenton, NJ, 2003—, treas., 1997—99, Trenton Diocesan PTA, NJ, 1999—2003; pres. All Saints Sch. PTA, Burlington, 1994—96; rec. sec. All Saints Sch. Adv. Coun., Burlington, 1995—2003. Recipient Sch. Leader award, N.J. Sch. Bds. Assn., 1998. Mem.: Internat. Reading Assn., West Jersey Reading Coun. Home: 318 Elm Ave Burlington NJ 08016-2505 Personal E-mail: mmatlack@comcast.net.

MATLAGA, BRIAN RICHARD, physician; b. Summit, N.J., Nov. 15, 1972; s. Richard and Danise Matlaga; m. Leigh Elmore, Aug. 4, 2001. BA, Dartmouth Coll., N.H., 1995; MD, MPH, Tulane U., New Orleans, 1999. Lic. Physician N.C., 1999. Physician Wake Forest U. Sch. of Medicine, Winston-Salem, NC, 1999—. Author articles in numerous sci. jours. Mem.: Am. Urol. Assn. Office: Wake Forest U Sch of Medicine Med Ctr Blvd Winston Salem NC 27157

MATLICK, ELDON R. music educator; b. Ft. Wayne, Ind., July 27, 1951; s. Roy Harrison and Loretta (Rinearson) Matlick; m. Pamela Ann Shepherd, June 20, 1974; 1 child, Jeremy. BME, Ea. Ky. U., 1973; MusM in Performance, Ind. U., 1980, D of Music in Brass Pedagogy, 1997. Dir. Bands Crittenden County Pub. Schs., Marion, Ky., 1973—78; prof. Horn Murray State U., Ky., 1980—83, U. Okla., Norman, 1983—. Assoc. prin. horn Owensboro Symphony, Ky., 1974—83, Evansville Philharm., Ind., 1982—83; prin. horn Okla. City Philharm., 1989—. Contbr. articles to profl. jours. Pres. Okla. City Philharm., 1992; clinician Conn. Selmer Musical Instruments. Mem.: Am. Fedn. Musicians, Internat. Horn Soc. (state rep. 1985—). Office: Univ Okla Sch Music 500 W Boyd Norman OK 73019

MATLIN, MARLEE, actress; b. Morton Grove, Ill., Aug. 24, 1965; m. Kevin Grandalski, Aug. 29, 1993; 3 children Attended William Rainey Harper Coll. Appeared in films Children of a Lesser God, 1986 (Acad. award for best actress, Golden Globe award), Walker, 1987, Linguini Incident, 1990, The Player, 1992, Hear No Evil, 1993, It's My Party, 1996, When Justice Fails, 1998, Freak City, 1999; TV films: Bridge to Silence, 1989, Against Her Will: The Carrie Buck Story, 1994, When Justice Fails, 1997, Dead Silence, 1997, Where the Truth Lies, 1999; TV series: Reasonable Doubts, 1991-93; guest star: Picket Fences, 1993, 94-96 (Emmy nomination, Guest Actress-Drama Series, 1994), Seinfeld, 1993 (Emmy nomination Guest Actress-Comedy Series, 1994), The Larry Sanders Show, 1992, Spin City, 1996, ER, 1999, Judging Amy, 1999, The West Wing, 2000—; author: Deaf Child Crossing, 2002 Office: care ICM 8942 Wilshire Blvd Beverly Hills CA 90211-1934

MATLINS, STUART M. management consultant, publisher; b. N.Y.C., July 25, 1940; s. Louis Karl and Lillian (Keit) M. m. Andrea Cines, June 20, 1960 (div.); children: Seth, Andrew; m. Antoinette Leonard, Oct. 9, 1977. Student, London Sch. Econs., 1958-59; BS, U. Wis., 1960; AM, Princeton U., 1962, postgrad., 1962-63. Internat. economist Bur. Internat. Commerce, U.S. Dept. Commerce, Washington, 1963-66; cons. Booz Allen & Hamilton, Inc., N.Y.C., 1966-67, asst. to pres. internat./adminstrv. dir., 1967-70, v.p. internat. ops., 1970-71, v.p./mng. officer, instl. and pub. mgmt. div., 1971-74; pres., mgmt. cons. Stuart Matlins Assocs., Inc., Woodstock, Vt., 1974—. Chmn. bd. dirs. LongHill Ptnrs., Inc.; publisher Gemstone Press, Jewish Lights Pub., SkyLight Paths Pub. Bd. dirs. Health Edn. Found., Woodstock (Vt.) Area Jewish Cmty.; chmn. emeritus bd. overseers N.Y. Sch., Hebrew Union Coll.-Jewish Inst. Religion; bd. govs. Hebrew Union Coll.; trustee South Woodstock Fire Protection Assn., Inc., Mertens House, Woodstock, Vt.; elected auditor Town of Woodstock; mem. adv. bd. Abraham Geiger Coll., Germany; dir. Jewish Book Coun. Woodrow Wilson fellow, 1960-61, Herbert O. Peet fellow, 1961-62, Phillip A. Rollins fellow, 1962-63. Mem. Princeton Club. Office: LongHill Ptnrs Inc PO Box 237 Woodstock VT 05091-0237 also: Sunset Farm Offices Rt 4 Woodstock VT 05091

MATLOCK, JACK FOUST, JR., diplomat; b. Greensboro, N.C., Oct. 1, 1929; s. Jack Foust and Nellie (McSwain) M.; m. Rebecca Burrum, Sept. 2, 1949; children: James, Hugh, Nell, David, Joseph. AB summa cum laude, Duke U., 1950; MA, Columbia U., 1952; cert., Russian Inst., 1952; LLD (hon.), Greensboro Coll., 1989, Albright Coll., 1992, Conn. Coll., 1993; LLD (hon.), Latvian Acad. Scis., 2002. Instr. Dartmouth, 1953-56; fgn. service officer Dept. State, 1956-91; assigned Washington, 1956-58, Am. Embassy, Vienna, 1958-60; Am. consul. gen. Munich, 1960-61; assigned Am. Embassy, Moscow, 1961-63, Accra, Ghana, 1963-66, Am. Consulate, Zanzibar, 1967-69, Am. Embassy, Dar es Salaam, Tanzania, 1969-70, Sr. Seminar in Fgn. Policy, Dept. State, 1970-71; country dir. for USSR State Dept., 1971-74; minister-counselor, dep. chief mission Am. Embassy, Moscow, 1974-78; diplomat-in-residence Vanderbilt U., Nashville, 1978-79; dep. dir. Fgn. Service Inst., Washington, 1979-80; chargé d'affaires ad interim Am. Embassy, Moscow, 1981; ambassador to Czechoslovakia, 1981-83; spl. asst. to pres., sr. dir. European and Soviet Affairs Nat. Security Council, 1983-87; U.S. ambassador to the Soviet Union, Moscow, 1987-91; sr. rsch. fellow Columbia U., N.Y.C., 1991-93, Kathryn and Shelby Collum Davis prof. Practice Internat. Diplomacy, 1993-96; George F. Kennan prof. Inst. for Advanced Study, Princeton, N.J., 1996-2001; John L. Weinberg/Goldman Sachs and Co. vis. prof. pub. and internat. affairs Princeton U., 2001—02. Author: Autopsy on an Empire: The American Ambassador's Account of the Collapse of the Soviet Union, 1995,

Reagan and Gorbachev: How the Cold War Ended, 2004; compiler, editor: Index to J.V. Stalin's Works, 2d edit., 1971. Mem. Am. Acad. Diplomacy, Coun. on Fgn. Rels., Century Assn. N.Y., Am. Philos. Soc. Home: 940 Princeton Kingston Rd Princeton NJ 08540-4128 also: 32 Wagoner Hill Rd Fayetteville TN 37334 Office Phone: 609-252-1953. Personal E-mail: jfmatlo@attglobal.net.

MATLOCK, JOHN HUDSON, science administrator, materials engineer; b. San Angelo, Tex., Nov. 23, 1944; s. Lee Hudson Jr. and Harriett (Kidder) M.; m. Kathe Lynne Reep, Sept. 3, 1966; children: Michelle, Joseph. B in Engring. Sci., U. Tex., 1967, MSME, 1969, PhD in Material Sci. and Engring., 1970; MBA, So. Ill. U., Edwardsville, 1976. Registered profl. engr., Mo., Wash., Oreg. Sr. rsch. engr. Monsanto Co., St. Peters, Mo., 1970-72, rsch. specialist, 1972-74, supt. tech. svcs., 1974-79; sr. staff engr. Mostek Corp., Carrollton, Tex., 1979-80, mgr. material tech. group, 1980-83; v.p. tech. SEH Am., Inc., Vancouver, Wash., 1983-90, exec. v.p., 1990-96, Komatsu Silicon Am., Hillsboro, Oreg., 1996, pres., CEO, 1997—; global officer Komatsu, Ltd., 1999—2003; dir. Komatsu Electronic Metals, Ltd., 1999—. Mem. vis. com. Engring. Coll., U. Wash., Seattle, 1985-94, mem. indsl. adv. bd. Material Sci. and Engring., 1988-2000; mem. engring. adv. bd. Wash. State U., Pullman, 1984-96, adj. lectr., 1985; adj. prof. mech. engring., mem. grad. faculty Oreg. State U., Corvallis, 1985-90; adj. asst. prof. physics So. Ill. U., Edwardsville, 1973-76. Contbr. approximately 40 articles on silicon crystal growing and the effect of silicon properties on electronic device performance to profl. and trade jours. Mem. bd. trustees 1st Ch. of God, Vancouver, 1988-91, tchr. adult ch. sch., 1986-91, 2001-02; mem. sch. bd. Kingsway Christian Sch., Vancouver, 1990-91, elder Sunrise Ch., Hillsboro, 2004-. Mem. Electrochem. Soc., Metall. Soc., AIME, Am. Soc. for Materials, Soc., Tau Beta Pi, Pi Tau Sigma, Phi Kappa Phi, Beta Gamma Sigma. Home: 787 NE Rogahn St Hillsboro OR 97124-1652 Office Phone: 503-640-7000. E-mail: jmatlock@komsil.com.

MATLOCK, KENT, advertising executive, public relations executive; BS, Morehouse Coll. Chmn., CEO Matlock & Assocs. Inc., 1984—. Office: Matlock Adv & Pub Rels Peachtree Pointe 1545 Peachtree St NE Ste 300 Atlanta GA 30309-2492

MATLON, DAVID MICHAEL, insurance agent, treasurer; b. Mpls., Minn., Nov. 10, 1961; s. Joseph John and Mary Jean Matlon; m. Lori Ann Marquardt, Sept. 21, 1985; children: Jacob Michael, Charles David, Luke Steven. BS in Bus. Adminstrn., Winona State U., Minn., 1985. CPCU 1995. Field rep. Western Nat. Ins., Edina, Minn., 1991—. Treas. Bloomington Fire Dept. Relief Assn., Bloomington, Minn., 1996—. Fire fighter Bloomington Fire Dept., Minn., 1988—. Home: 9625 4th Ave S Bloomington MN 55420-4422 Office: Bloomington Fire Dept Relief 10 West 95th St Bloomington MN 55420-4422 Home Fax: 952-884-7678; Office Fax: 952-884-7678. Personal E-mail: dave.matlon@worldnet.att.net. E-mail: dave.matlon@worldnet.att.net.

MATLPREWITT, LOIS TUDOR, lawyer; b. Madison County, Ky., Feb. 19, 1939; d. Humphrey Hill Jr. and Mary Elizabeth (Noland) Tudor; m. Gerry L. Calvert Sr., Sept. 25, 1960 (div. Apr. 1981); children: Catherine Deloach, Gerry L. II, Stephanie Calvert. Grad., Good Samaritan Hosp., 1960; BSN, U. Ky., 1966, JD, 1980. Bar: Ky. 1981. Assoc. Greenbaum Doll & McDonald, Lexington, Ky., 1981-85; atty. pvt. practice primarily family law and workers compensation, Lexington, Ky., 1985—. Bd. trustees Lexington United Meth. Ch., 1982-84, adminstrv. bd., 1991-93; pres. PTA Beaumont Jr. High Sch., Lexington, 1982-83. Methodist. Office: 125 Church St Lexington KY 40507-1102 Office Phone: 859-252-5678.

MATOS, CRUZ ALFONSO, environmental consultant; b. N.Y.C., Mar. 6, 1929; s. José and Gertrudes (Manzanares) M.; m. Aurelia Santos, Dec. 13, 1963; children: Miguel, Veronica, Monica, Angélica. B in Engring. Sci., Oxford U., 1957, M in Engring. Sci., 1958; DSc (hon.), U. Met., P.R., 1995. Pres., CEO Fischer & Porter de P.R., 1964-69; asst. sec. dept. pub. works Govt. of P.R., 1969-70, exec. dir. Environ. Quality Bd., 1970-73, sec. dept. natural resources, 1973-75, cabinet mem., 1970-75; UN chief tech., dir. Inst. Marine Affairs, Trinidad and Tobago, 1975-79; UN Devel. Program regional rep. Trinidad and Tobago, Barbados, Surinam and Dutch West Indies, 1978-80; UN chief tech. adviser South Pacific, dir. Com. for Coordination of Offshore Prospecting in the South Pacific, Suva, Fiji, 1980-89; ret. Advisor to pres. P.R. Senate for natural resources, the environ. and energy, 1993-97; advisor to exec. dir. UN Environ. Program for L.Am. and Caribbean, 1994-98; mem. various adv. panels and overseas mission U.S. NAS; mem. U.S. Nat. Commn. on Environment, Consejo Consultive Recursos Naturales y Ambientales (apptd. Gov. P.R.), Com. Sobre Política Publica Energetíca P.R., Consejo Asesor Sobre Energia. Contbr. articles to sci. jours. and mags. Bd. dirs. Caribbean Environment and Devel. Inst. With U.S. Army, 1952-54. Recipient Boriquen Conservation award, 1971. Office: PO Box 7627-HC77 Playa Cerro Gordo Vega Alta PR 00692

MATROS, RICHARD K. insurance company executive; b. Queens, N.Y. m. Adrienne Matros; children: Carly, Chelsea, Alex. BA in Psychology, Alfred U.; MA in Gerontology, U. S.C. Facility adminstr. Extended Care Inc., Catered Living Inc.; regional adminstr., v.p. We. Ops. Beverly Enterprises Inc.; exec. v.p. ops. Care Enterprises, 1988—91, pres., COO, 1988—91, 1991—94, pres., CEO, 1994; pres., COO Regency Health Svcs. Inc., 1994—95, pres., CEO, 1995—97, Bright Now! Dental, 1998—2000; chmn., CEO Sun Healthcare Group, 2001—. Office: Sun Healthcare Group 101 Sun Ave NE Albuquerque NM 87109*

MATSA, LOULA ZACHAROULA, social services administrator, educator; b. Piraeus, Greece, Apr. 16, 1935; came to U.S., 1952, naturalized 1962; d. Eleftherios Georgiou and Ourania E. (Fraguiskopoulou) Papoulias; m. Ilco S. Matsa, Nov. 27, 1953; 1 child, Aristotle Ricky. Student, Pierce Coll., Athens, 1948-52; BA, Rockford Coll., 1953; MA, U. Chgo., 1955. Diplomate clin. social worker; bd. cert. clin. social workers, N.Y. cert. social orkers, pub. employees fedn. Marital counselor Family Soc., Cambridge, Mass., 1955-56; chief unit II social svc. Queen's (N.Y.) Children's Psychiat. Ctr., 1961-74; dir. social svcs., supr.-coord. family care program Hudson River Psychiat. Ctr., Poughkeepsie, N.Y., 1974-91; supr. social work Harlem Valley Psychiat. Ctr., Wingdale, N.Y., 1991-93, Hudson River Psychiat. Ctr., 1993—. Field instr. Adelphi, Albany and Fordham univs., 1969—. Contbr. articles to profl. jours.; instrumental in state policy changes in treatment and court representation of emotionally disturbed and mentally ill. Fulbright Exch. student, 1952-53; Talcott scholar, 1953-55. Mem. NASW, Internat. Platform Assn., Internat. Coun. on Social Welfare, Acad. Cert. Social Workers, Assn. Cert. Social Workers, Pierce Coll. Alumni Assn. Democrat. Greek Orthodox. Home: 81-11 45th Ave Elmhurst NY 11373-3553

MATSCHULLAT, ROBERT W. chemicals executive; married. BA, MBA, Stanford U. CFO The Seagram Co. Ltd., 1995—99, vice chmn., 1995—2000, ret., 2000; head worldwide investment banking Morgan Stanley & Co. Inc., 2000—04; non-exec. chmn. Clorox Co., Oakland, Calif., 2004—. Bd. dir. The Clorox Co., The Walt Disney Co., McKesson Inc. Bd. dir. The Riverview Sch., East Sandwich, Mass. Mem.: Duke U. Parent's Assn. (nat. co-chmn.). Office: Clorox Co 1221 Broadway Oakland CA 94612-1888

MATSEN, FREDERICK ALBERT, III, orthopedic educator; b. Austin, Tex., Feb. 5, 1944; s. Frederick Albert II and Cecilia (Kirkegaard) M.; m. Anne Lovell, Dec. 24, 1966; children: Susanna Lovell, Frederick A. IV, Laura Jane Megan. BA, U. Tex., Austin, 1964; MD, Baylor U., 1968. Intern Johns Hopkins U., Balt., 1971; resident in orthopaedics U. Wash., Seattle, 1971-74, acting instr. orthopaedics, 1974, asst. prof. orthopaedics, 1975-79, assoc. prof. orthopaedics, 1979-82, prof., 1982-85, 86—, adjunct prof. Ctr. Bioengring., 1985—, dir. residency program orthopaedics, 1978-81, vice chmn. dept. orthopaedics, 1982-85, acting chmn. dept. orthopaedics, 1983-84, prof., chmn. dept. orthopaedics, 1981—. Mem. Orthopaedic Residency Rev. Com., Chgo., 1981-86. Author: Compartmental Syndromes, 1980; editor: The Shoulder, 1990; contbr. articles to profl. jours., chpts. to textbooks; assoc. editor Clin. Orthopaedics, Jour. Orthopaedic Rsch., 1981—. Lt. comdr. USPHS, 1969-71. Recipient Traveling fellowship Am. Orthopaedic Assn., 1983, Nicholas Andry award Assn. Bone and Joint Surgery, 1979, Henry Meyerding Essay award Am. Fracture Assn., 1974. Mem. Am. Shoulder and Elbow Surgeons (founding, pres. 1991—), Am. Acad. Orthopaedic Surgeons (bd. dirs. 1984-85), Orthopaedic Rsch. Soc., Western Orthopaedic Assn., Phi Beta Kappa. Office: U Wash Dept Orthopaedics RK 10 1959 NE Pacific St Seattle WA 98195-0001

MATSEN, JOHN MARTIN, academic administrator, pathologist; b. Salt Lake City, Feb. 7, 1933; s. John M. and Bessie (Jackson) M.; m. Joneen Johnson, June 6, 1959; children: Marilee, Sharon, Coleen, Sally, John H., Martin K., Maureen, Catherine, Carl, Jeri. BA, Brigham Young U., 1958; MD, UCLA, 1963. Diplomate Am. Bd. Pediatrics, Am. Bd. Pathology, Spl. Competence in Med. Microbiology. Intern UCLA, 1963-65; resident Los Angeles County Harbor/UCLA Med. Ctr., Torrance, Calif., 1965-66; USPHS fellow U. Minn., Mpls., 1966-68, asst. prof., 1968-70, assoc. prof., 1971-74, prof., 1974, U. Utah, Salt Lake City, 1974—, assoc. dean, 1979-81, chmn. dept. pathology, 1981-93, univ. sr. v.p. health scis., dean Sch. Medicine, 1993-98. Pres. Associated Regional and Univ. Pathologists, Inc., Salt Lake City, 1983-93, chmn. bd. dirs., 1993-99. Author over 200 publs. in field. Recipient Sonnenwirth Meml. award Am. Soc. Microbiology, 1993. Mem. Acad. Clin. Lab. Physicians and Scientists (pres. 1978-79), Assn. Pathology Chmn. (pres. 1990-92). Mem. Lds Ch.

MATSEOANE, CAROL, social worker; b. N.Y.C., July 10, 1944; d. Joseph Daniel Taylor and Nannie Lee Winborne; m. Stephen Matseoane, Jan. 21, 1968; children: Dara, Joyce, Karen. BA, Hunter Coll., 1966, MSW, 1970; PhD, Walden U., 1992. Cert. social worker, N.Y. Social worker Spl. Svcs. for Children Protective Svcs., N.Y.C.; psychotherapist counselor O. Quentin Hyder MD, N.Y.C.; social work supr. JHMCB Ctr. for Nursing and Rehab./Long Term Home Care Prog., Bklyn.; clin. dir. Lamb's Counseling Ctr., New Hope Counseling Ctr. Recipient Apple Polisher award, Women's Inner Circle of Achievement award. Mem.: NAFE, NASW, Am. Bd. Med. Psychotherapists (life). Home: 15900 Riverside Dr W Apt 7D New York NY 10032-1011

MATSKO, ANDREY B. research scientist; b. Kiev, Ukraine, June 28, 1971; m. Nelli A. Matsko, Nov. 16, 2002. PhD, Moscow State U., 1988—96. Postdoctoral rsch. assoc. Tex. A&M U., College Station, 1997—2001; sr. mem. tech. staff Jet Propulsion Lab Caltech, Pasadena, Calif., 2001—. Vis. scientist Max Plank Inst. Quantenoptick, 1998, 2000. Mem.: Optical Soc. Am. Office: Jet Propulsion Lab MS 298-100 4800 Oak Grove Dr Pasadena CA 91101

MATSON, PAMELA ANNE, environmental scientist, science educator; b. Eau Claire, Wis., Aug. 3, 1953; BS, U. Wis., 1975; MS, Ind. U., 1980; PhD, Oreg. State U., 1983. Prof. U. Calif., Berkeley, 1993—97, Stanford U., Calif., 1997—. Fellow MacArthur fellow, 1995. Fellow: Am. Acad. Arts & Scis.; mem.: Nat. Acad. Sci. Achievements include research in in interactions between the biosphere and the atmosphere; pioneer into the role of land-use changes on atmospheric change, analyzing the effects of greenhouse gas emissions resulting from tropical deforestization; in the effects of intensive agriculture on the atmosphere, especially the effects of tropical agriculture and cattle ranching; development of ways in which agricultural productivity can be expanded without causing off-site environmental consequences. Office: Stanford U Sch Earth Scis Stanford CA 94305-2210

MATSON, ROBERT EDWARD, public management educator, leadership consultant; b. Chauncey, Ohio, Dec. 2, 1930; s. William I. and Mary Royal (Rivers) M.; m. Mary Athearn, June 27, 1954; children— Laurie, Jeanne, Scott BS, Ohio U., 1956, M.Ed., 1957; Ed.D., Ind. U., 1961. Dean men Carroll Coll., Wis., 1961-65; v.p. student affairs Kent State U, Ohio, 1965-70; pres. Ricker Coll., 1970-74; sr. prof. Fed. Exec. Inst., Charlottesville, Va., 1974-80, acad. dean, 1980-82, dir., 1982-87, sr. prof., dir. emeritus, 1987-89; prof., dir. leadership edn. program Ctr. Pub. Svc., U. Va., Charlottesville, 1989—, dir. Inst. Govt., 1994-96. Served to 1st. lt. U.S. Army, 1953-55; Korea Recipient Sweeney Acad. award Internat. City and County Mgrs. Assn., 1993. Fellow Nat. Acad. Pub. Adminstrn. Methodist. Office: U Va Ctr for Pub Svc 918 Emmet St N Charlottesville VA 22903-4829

MATSON, WESLEY JENNINGS, educational administrator; b. Svea, Minn., June 25, 1924; s. James and Ettie (Mattson) Matson; m. Doris Cragg. BS with distinction, U. Minn., 1948; MA, U. Calif., Berkeley, 1954; EdD, Columbia U., 1960. High sch. tchr. Santa Barbara County Pub. Schs., Santa Maria, Calif., 1948-50; instr. U. Calif., Berkeley, 1950-54, Columbia U., N.Y.C., 1954-55; lectr. Fordham U., N.Y.C., 1955-56; asst. prof. U. Md., College Park, 1956-59; prof., asst. dean U. Wis., Milw., 1959-72; dean, prof. Winona (Minn.) State U., 1972-88, emeritus, 1989—. Vis. prof. U. P.R., Rio Peidras, We. Wash. U., Bellingham, San Diego State U., U. Minn., Mpls., U. Hawaii; adj. faculty St. Olaf Coll., Northfield, Minn.; cons. U.S. Dept. Edn., Washington, Ill. State U.; bd. regents Wis. Dept. Pub. Instrn.; examiner Nat. Coun. Accreditation Tchr. Edn. North Ctrl. assn., Chgo. Contbr. Exec. com. Minn. Alliance of Arts, Mpls.; mem. Minn. com. Certification Stds., St. Paul; cons. ARC; bd. dirs. Ft. Snelling Meml. Chapel Found.; apptd. by Minn. Supreme Ct. to Minn. Bd. CLE. Capt. USAF. Decorated Bronze Star; recipient Disting. Svc. award, Wis. Assn. Tchr. Edn., 1972. Mem.: NEA (life), VFW, Minn. edn. Assn., Assn. Higher Edn., Nat. Assn. Tchr. Educators (exec. com.), Minn. Assn. Colls. for Tchr. Edn. (pres. 1983—85, Hon. life Award of Merit), U. Minn. Alumni Soc. (Outstanding Educator award 1984), Am. Legion, Minn. Hist. Soc., Rotary Club, Alpha Sigma Phi, Kappa Delta Pi, Phi Delta Kappa. Home: 6615 Lake Shore Dr S Minneapolis MN 55423-2218

MATSUDA, FUJIO, retired academic administrator; b. Honolulu, Oct. 18, 1924; s. Yoshio and Shimo (Iwasaki) M.; m. Amy M. Saiki, June 11, 1949; children: Bailey Koki, Thomas Junji, Sherry Noriko, Joan Yuuko, Ann Mitsuyo, Richard Hideo. BSCE, Rose Poly. Inst., 1949; DSc, MIT, 1952; DEng (hon.), Rose Hulman Inst. Tech., 1975. Rsch. engr. MIT, 1952-54; rsch. asst. prof. engring. U. Ill., Urbana, 1954-55; from asst. prof. engring. to prof. engring. U. Hawaii, Honolulu, 1955-66, chmn. dept. civil engring., 1962—63, v.p. bus. affairs, 1973-74, pres., 1974-84, exec. dir. Rsch. Corp., 1984-94; pres. Japan-Am. Inst. Mgmt. Sci., Honolulu, 1994-96. Dir. Hawaii Dept. Transp., Honolulu, 1963-73; v.p. Park & Yee, Ltd., Honolulu, 1956-58; pres. SMS & Assocs., Inc., 1960-63; pvt. practice structural engring., 1958-60; bd. dirs. C. Brewer & Co., Ltd., Buyco, Ltd., First Hawaiian Bank, BancWest Corp., Inc., Rehab. Hosp. of Pacific; chmn. bd. dirs. Pacific Internat. Ctr. High Tech. Rsch. With U.S. Army, 1943—45. Recipient Honor Alumnus award Rose Poly. Inst., 1971, Disting. Svc. award Airport Ops. Coun. Internat., 1973, Disting. Alumnus award U. Hawaii, 1974, 91; named Hawaii Engr. of Yr., 1972. Mem. NAE, NSPE, ASCE (Parcel-Sverdrup Engring. Mgmt. award 1986), Social Sci. Assn., Japan-Am. Soc. Honolulu (trustee 1976-84, adv. coun. 1984—), Japan-Hawaii Econ. Coun., Sigma Xi, Tau Beta Pi. E-mail: fmatsuda@hawaii.rr.com.

MATSUDA, TAKAYOSHI, surgeon, educator, biomedical researcher; b. Tonan, Japan, 1937; came to U.S., 1965; MD, Keio Gijuku U., Tokyo, 1963. Diplomate Am. Bd. Surgery. Rotating intern Cook County Hosp., Chgo., 1965-66, resident in surgery, 1966-71, dir. burn ctr., 1975-93; asst. prof. surgery Kyorin U., Tokyo, 1971-75; asst. prof. U. Ill., Chgo., 1977—; pres. TM & Assocs., Oak Park, Ill., 1994—; CEO, Matsuda Clean Energy Co., Oak Park, 2001—. Cons. alternative medicine, cons. leadership devel., fin. freedom; investigator renewable energy; spkr. in field. Editl. bd. Jour. Burn Care Rehab., 1987-93; contbr. articles to profl. publ., chpt. to books. Recipient Jerry and Thelma Stergios award for Excellence in Basic Rsch., U. Ill. at Chgo., 1979, The Superior Pub. Serv. award, County of Cook, State of Ill., 1993. Fellow ACS; mem. Internat. Soc. Surgery, Internat. Soc. Burn Injuries, Am. Burn Assn., Am. Assn. Surgery Trauma, Soc. Critical Care Medicine, Chgo. Surg. Soc. Achievements include research in and devel. of a novel approach for the production of electricity without pollution; established the first human skin bank in the State of Illinois at the Burn unit of Cook County Hospital, 1977. Office: TM & Assocs Alternative Medicine Cons 103 Bishop Quarter Ln Oak Park IL 60302-2672 Office Phone: 708-386-2522. Personal E-mail: takimatsuda@hotmail.com.

MATSUHISA, NOBUYUKI, chef, restaurant owner; b. Japan; Chef, owner Matsuhisa, Beverly Hills, 1987—, Aspen, Colo., 1997—, Nobu, N.Y.C., 1994—, London, 1997—, Tokyo, 1998—, Malibu, Calif., 1999—, Nobu Next Door, N.Y.C., 1998—, Ubon, L.A., 1999—. Named one of Am.'s 10 Best New Chefs, Food & Wine Mag., 1989, So. Calif.'s Rising Stars, L.A. Times Mag., 1998. Office: Nobu 105 Hudson St New York NY 10013-2331

MATSUI, CONNIE L. pharmaceutical executive; b. Piedmont, Calif. m. William Beckman; 2 children. BA, Stanford U., MBA, 1977. Various positions Wells Fargo Bank, 1977—91; sr. dir., planning and resource devel. IDEC Pharm., 1992—94, v.p., planning and resource devel., 1994—2000, sr. v.p., planning and resource devel., 2000—03; exec. v.p. corp. strategy and communication Biogen Idec Inc., 2003—. Nat. pres. Girl Scouts Am., 1999—2002. Office: Biogen Inc 14 Cambridge Ctr Cambridge MA 02142*

MATSUI, DOROTHY NOBUKO, elementary school educator; b. Honolulu, Jan. 9, 1954; d. Katsura and Tamiko (Sakai) M. Student, U. Hawaii, Honolulu, 1972-76, postgrad., 1982; BEd, U. Alaska, Anchorage, 1979, MEd in Spl. Edn., 1986. Clerical asst. U. Hawaii Manoa Disbursing Office, Anchorage, 1974-76; passenger service agt. Japan Air Lines, Anchorage, 1980; bilingual tutor Anchorage Sch. Dist., 1980, elem. sch. tchr., 1980—. Facilitator for juvenile justice courses Anchorage Sch. Dist., Anchorage Police Dept., Alaska Pacific U., 1992-93; mem. adv. bd. Anchorage Law-Related Edn. Advancement Project. Vol. Providence Hosp., Anchorage, 1986, Humana Hosp., Anchorage, 1984, Spl. Olympics, Anchorage, 1981, Municipality Anchorage, 1978, Easter Seal Soc. Hawaii, 1975. Mem. NAFE, NEA, Alaska Edn. Assn., Smithsonian Nat. Assoc. Program, Nat. Space Soc., Smithsonian Air and Space Assn., World Aerospace Edn. Orgn., Internat. Platform Assn., Nat. Trust for Hist. Preservation, Nat. Audubon Soc., Planetary Soc., Cousteau Soc., Alaska Coun. for the Social Studies, Alaska Coun. Tchrs. Math., World Inst. Achievment, U.S. Olympic Soc., Women's Inner Circle Achievement, U. Alaska Alumni Assn., World Wildlife Fund, Japanese-Am. Nat. Mus., Alpha Delta Kappa (treas. Alpha chpt. 1988-92, corr. sec. 1993-96, sgt. at arms 1996-98). Avocations: reading, sports, learning. Office: Anchorage Sch Dist 7001 Cranberry St Anchorage AK 99502-7145

MATSUI, ROBERT TAKEO, congressman; b. Sacramento, Sept. 17, 1941; s. Yasuji and Alice (Nagata) M.; m. Doris Kazue Okada, Sept. 17, 1966; 1 child, Brian Robert. AB in Polit. Sci, U. Calif., Berkeley, 1963; JD, U. Calif., San Francisco, 1966. Bar: Calif. 1967. Practiced law, Sacramento, 1967-78; mem. Sacramento City Coun., 1971-78, vice mayor, 1977; mem. 96th-108th Congresses from 5th Calif. dist., 1979—; mem. ranking minority, ways and means, s.s. subcom.; dep. chair Dem. Nat. Com., 1995—; bd. regents Smithsonian Inst., Washington, 2000—. Chmn. profl. bus. forum Dem. Congl. Campaign Com.; mem. fin. coun. Dem. Nat. Com.; mem. adv. coun. on fiscal policy Am. Enterprise Inst. Chmn. Profl. Bus. Forum of the Dem. Congl. Co. and Com.; congl. liaison Nat. Fin. Council, Dem. Nat. Com.; mem. Am. Enterprise Inst. Adv. Council on Fiscal Policy. Named Young Man of Yr. Jr. C. of C., 1973; recipient Disting. Service award, 1973 Mem. Sacramento Japanese Am. Citizens League (pres. 1969), Sacramento Met. C. of C. (dir. 1976) Clubs: 20-30 (Sacramento) (pres. 1972), Rotary (Sacramento). Democrat. Office: US Ho Reps 2310 Rayburn Hob Washington DC 20515-0505

MATSUKAGE, FAY MARIKO, lawyer; b. Honolulu, Sept. 1, 1955; d. Daniel Ryuzo and Nobuko M. BA summa cum laude, Colo. Coll., 1976; JD, U. Denver, 1979. Bar: Colo. 1980. Assoc. firm McKie and Assocs., Denver, 1980-81, Olsen & Guardi, Denver, 1981-83; ptnr. Olsen & Matsukage, Denver, 1984-86; pvt. practice, Denver, 1986—97, officer, shareholder Dill Dill Carr Stonbraker and Hutchings, Denver, 1997-. Mem. ABA, Denver Bar Assn., Colo. Bar Assn., Phi Beta Kappa. Office: Ste 300 455 Sherman St Denver CO 80203-4404 Office Phone: 303-777-3737.

MATSUMOTO, GEORGE, architect; b. San Francisco, July 16, 1922; s. Manroku F. and Ise (Nakagawa) M.; m. Kimi Nao, Dec. 15, 1951; children— Mari-Jane, Kiyo-Ann, Kei-Ellen, Kenneth Manroku, Miye-Eileen. Student, U. Calif. at Berkeley, 1938-42; B.Arch., Washington U., 1944; M.Arch., Cranbrook Acad. Art, 1945. Designer Heathers Garden Devel. Co., Calif., 1941-42; designer with George F. Keck, Chgo., 1943-44; sr. designer, planner Saarinen & Swanson, Birmingham, Mich., 1945-46; sr. designer Skidmore, Owings & Merrill, Chgo., 1948; partner Runnells, Clark, Waugh, Matsumoto, Kansas City, Mo., 1946-47; practice architecture Okla., 1948, 1948—61, San Francisco, 1962—92; pres. George Matsumoto and Assocs., San Francisco, 1992-93; ret., 1993. Instr. U. Okla., 1947-48; prof. N.C. State Coll., 1948-61, U. Calif. at Berkeley, 1961-67 Important works include libraries, office bldgs., schs., recreation ctrs., chs., govt. bldgs., pvt. residences, med. research labs. and offices. Bd. dirs. Young Audiences, Oakland Mus. Assn., Oakland Arts Coun., Friends of Oakland Park and Recreation, East Bay Agy. for Children. Recipient over 50 archtl. awards and prizes. Fellow AIA (dir. chpt.), Internat. Inst. Arts and Letters; mem. Mich. Soc. Architects, Assn. Coll. Sch. Architecture, Raleigh Council Architects, San Francisco Planning and Urban Renewal Assn., Nat. Council Archtl. Registration Bds., Calif. Assn. Architects, Bldg. Research Inst., Japanese-Am. Citizens League. Home: 1170 Glencourt Dr Oakland CA 94611-1405 E-mail: georkimi@aol.com.

MATSUMURA, VERA YOSHI, pianist; b. Oakland, Calif. d. Naojiro and Aguri Tanaka; m. Jiro Matsumura, Aug. 8, 1942; 1 son, Kenneth N. BA in Piano Pedagogy, Coll. Holy Names, Oakland, 1938; pvt. studies with F. Moss, M. Shapiro, L. Kreutzer, P. Jarrett. Mem. staff, pianist Radio Sta. KROW, Oakland, 1938-39. Numerous concert performances in Far East (Japan, Thailand), 1940—; numerous tchg. appointments, 1940—; dir. Internat. Music Coun., Berkeley, Calif., 1969—. Named to Hall of Fame, Piano Guild, 1968. Mem. Nat. Music Tchrs. Nat. Assn., Music Tchrs. Assn. Calif., Internat. Platform Assn., Alpha Phi Mu. Methodist. Home: 2 Claremont Cres Berkeley CA 94705-2324

MATSUNAGA, MATTHEW MASAO, state legislator, lawyer, accountant; b. Honolulu, Nov. 22, 1958; s. Spark Masayuki and Helene (Tokunaga) M.; m. Loretta Ann Sheehan, Apr. 20, 1986, children, Hannah, Sarah. BS, Bucknell U., 1980; JD, Georgetown U., 1985. Bar: Hawaii 1985, U.S. Ct. Appeals (9th cir.); CPA, Hawaii. Assoc. Carlsmith, Ball, Wichman, Murray & Case, Honolulu, 1985—; CPA Price Waterhouse, 1980-82; mem. Hawaii Senate, Dist. 9, Honolulu, 1992—. Bd. dirs. Moiliili Community Ctr., Honolulu, 1987—. Mem. ABA, Hawaii Bar Assn., Am. Judicature Soc., Hawaii Soc. CPAs. Office: Carlsmith Ball Wichman Murray & Case PO Box 656 Honolulu HI 96809-0656 Address: Hawaii State Capitol 415 S Beretania St Rm 226 Honolulu HI 96813-2407

MATSUNAKA, STANLEY T. former state legislator; b. Akron, Colo., Nov. 12, 1953; m. Kathleen Matsunaka; three children. BS, Colo. State U., 1975; JD, U. San Diego. Atty.; mem. Colo. Senate, Dist. 15, Denver, 1994—2002. Cubmaster, den leader Boy Scouts Pack 190; active Namaqua Sch. Accountability Com. Mem. ABA, Colo. Bar Assn. (former sect. young lawyers sect.), Larimer County Bar Assn. (former sec.), Loveland Sertoma Club (pres.). Democrat. Presbyterian. E-mail: stanseante@aol.com.

MATSUSHIMA, AKIRA PAUL, international company executive; b. Tokyo, July 7, 1937; arrived in U.S., 1970; s. Hiromasa and Tomiko (Watanabe) M.; m. Kathleen Sue Rowland, Aug. 18, 1968; children: John Hikaru, Kenn Emi, Amy Kathryn. BS, Waseda U., Tokyo, 1961, MS in Mech. Engring., 1964; M in Mgmt., Northwestern U., 1981. Registered profl. engr., Calif. Asst. R & D mgr. NOK Corp. (Nippon Oil Seal Industry), Tokyo, 1961—85, mgr. rsch. planning, 1968-70; dir. engring. NOK-USA, Inc., LA, 1970-72, v.p., 1973-74, exec. v.p. Chgo., 1975-83, sec., 1979-82, dir., 1971-85; dep. gen. mgr. engring. divsn. NOK Corp., Tokyo, 1983-85; with Chgo. Rawhide Mfg. Co. (SKF), Elgin, Ill., 1985—98, sr. v.p., 1995-98; pres. Matsushima Mgmt., Palatine, Ill., 1999—. Bd. dirs. K.K. Arai Seisakusho, Tokyo, Hi-Tech Arai, Inc., Madurai, India, Koyo-Chgo. Rawhide Co., Ltd., Osaka, Japan, v.p., 1986-99; chmn. K.C. Engring., Ltd., Yokohama, Japan, 1989-95, pres., 1991-95; treas. PLACO Co., Ltd., Saitama, Japan, 2000-02; Japanese govt. del. to Internat. Standardization Orgn., 1973-78; del. Motor Equipment Mfr. Assn./Japan Auto Mfr.

Assn. Conf., 1990, 92, 94; exec. dir. U.S. ops. Yaguchi Seisakusho Co. Ltd., 1999-; bd. dirs., pres., sec., treas. ARAI Ams. Inc., Virginia Beach, Va., 2001-; v.p., bd. dirs. Nihon Clin Co., Inc., Virginia Beach, 2002-; comisario PT Arai Rubber Seal Indonesia, Jakarta, 2002-. Contbr. articles to tech. jours.; patentee sealing device; holder numerous Japanese patents in field. Fund dirve chair western divsn. Jr. Achievement, Chgo., 1988—89, mem. governing bd., 1990—98, United Way of Elgin, 1988—96, v.p. planning, 1991—92; pres. Oak Crest Residence, Elgin, 1993—95; commr. to gen. assembly Presby. Ch. U.S.A., 2001. Mem. Soc. Automotive Engrs. (adv. bd. seals com., chmn. various subcoms., Cert. Appreciation 1986), NSPE, Internat. House of Japan. Presbyterian. Office: Matsushima Mgmt 1332 Shire Cir Inverness IL 60067-4727 Office Phone: 847-705-9130. E-mail: apmatsu@aol.com.

MATSUSHIMA, TERESA TAKAKI, school nurse practitioner; b. Chgo., Apr. 7, 1953; d. George Hideo Takaki and Lilly Yuriko Kaneko; m. Robert J. Matsushima, Aug. 26, 1978; children: Ann Misa, Paul Isamu. BA, U. Calif., LA, 1977; AA, LA Harbor Coll., 1977; BS, U. Calif., San Francisco, 1983, MS, 1985. RN 1977, cert. Women's Health Care Nurse Practitioner, Harbor-UCLA Women's Health Care Nurse Practitioner Program, 1979, Lamaze Childbirth Educator, U. Calif., 1980, Pub. Health Nurse, 1983, Nurse Practitioner, Nat. Cert. Corp., 1986, Sch. Nurse, Calif. State U., 1999. Nurse practitioner Clinic for Women, Inc., LA, 1977—80, Kaiser Permanente, Richmond, Calif., 1980—85, South Bay Free Clinic, Gardena, Calif., 1986—89, El Camino Jr. Coll., Torrance, Calif., 1989—98; instr. LA Harbor Coll., Harbor City, Calif., 1998—99; sch. nurse Lawndale Elem. Sch. Dist., Lawndale, Calif., 1999—; faculty undergrad. nursing Calif. State. Dominguez U., Larson, Calif., 2002—. Author: Asian Women's Health Research Project, 1980. Youth choir leader Gardena Valley Baptist Ch., Gardena, Calif., 1990—97. Mem.: Calif. Tchrs. Assn., Calif. State Nurses Orgn. Avocations: astronomy, crocheting, guitar, travel, films. Office: Lawndale Sch Dist 4535 W 153rd Pl Lawndale CA 90260

MATSUURA, JOHN HENRY, surgeon; b. Mpls., June 25, 1958; MD, U. Hawaii, 1987. Diplomate Am. Bd. Surgery, Am. Bd. Vascular Surgery. Intern Wright State U. Sch. Medicine, 1987-88, resident in gen. surgery, 1988-92; surgeon 93d Med. Group, Castle AFB, Calif., 1992-94; fellow in vascular surgery Med. Coll. Va., 1994—; pvt. practice. Asst. prof. surgery Med. Coll. Ga., Emory U. Address: 315 Boulevard NE Ste 412 Atlanta GA 30312-1264

MATSUURA, KENNETH RAY, counselor, articulation officer; b. Urbana, Ill., July 17, 1954; s. George Shigeo and Sally Sueko (Kawasaki) M.; m. Peggy Ai Iwata, May 27, 1995; 1 child, Claire Miya Sara. BA, U. Calif., Santa Barbara, 1976; MA, UCLA, 1978, PhD, 1996. Career counselor Calif. State U. Dominguez Hills, Carson, 1984-85; grad. recruitment coord. U. Calif., Irvine, 1985-90; counselor/articulation officer Cerritos Coll., Norwalk, Calif., 1990—. Mem. accreditation teams Western Assn. Schs. and Colls., L.A., 1994, Alameda, 1999, mem. accreditation task force Project Renewal; chair South Coast Higher Edn. Coun.; co-chair region 8 articulation officers and transfer ctre. dirs.; program reviewer Am. Coll. Pers. Assn. Ann. conf., Washington, 1988; presenter to confs. UCLA grad. advancement program fellow, 1977-78. Avocations: singing, music. Home: 1066 Rocton Dr Pasadena CA 91107-5917 Office: Cerritos Coll 11110 Alondra Blvd Norwalk CA 90650-6298 Office Phone: 562-860-2451 2141. Business E-Mail: kpmatsu@attglobal.net.

MATT, SUSAN J. historian, educator; b. Chgo., Feb. 9, 1967; d. Joseph and Barbara Jipson Matt; m. Luke O. Fernandez, Sept. 26, 1995. BA, U. Chgo., 1989; M, Cornell U., 1992, PhD, 1996. Assoc. prof. Weber State U., Ogden, Utah, 1999—. Vis. asst. prof. Clark U., Ogden, Utah, 1996—97. Author: Keeping Up with the Joneses: Envy in American Consumer Society, 1890-1930; contbr. articles to profl. jours. Exec. com. Sierra Club, Ogden, Utah, 2000—04; lobbyist Colo. Pub. Interest Rsch. Group, Denver, 1998—99; campaign staff Adlai Stevenson for Gov., Chgo., 1986—86; pres. U. Chgo. Student Body, 1988—89. Fellow, Andrew Mellon Found., 1992, 1995—96; grantee, Murray Ctr., Radcliffe Coll., 1993, Hartman Ctr., Duke U., 2000; scholar, U. Chgo., 1985—89. Mem.: Am. Hist. Assn., Orgn. Am. Historians. Avocation: running. Office: History Department Weber State Universi 1205 University Circle Ogden UT 84408-1205 Office Phone: 801-626-7325. Personal E-mail: smatt@weber.edu.

MATTA, JAIME L, research scientist, educator; b. Fajardo, P.R., Sept. 7, 1955; s. Antonio Matta and Ana Murias; m. Gladys Matta, Nov. 26, 1985. PhD, DSc, UCLA, 1988. Prof. Ponce (P.R.) Sch. Medicine, 2002—, chair dept. pharmacology and toxicology, 1999—2004. Mem. editl. bd.: jour. Biol. Trace Element Rsch. Vol. Self-Realization Fellowship, L.A., 1987—2004. Pres. Postdoctoral fellow, U. Calif., 1988. Mem.: Soc. Toxicology, Am. Assn. for Cancer Rsch. (phila., Faculty Scholar award in cancer rsch. 2004). Achievements include research in in early cancer detection and prevention in Puerto Rico and the U.S. mainland. Office: Ponce School of Medicine Ana D Perez Marchand St Ind Reparada Ponce PR 00731 Office Phone: 787-259-7025. Business E-Mail: jmatta@psm.edu.

MATTA, WILLIAM B. language educator; b. Grand Forks, N.D., Sept. 27, 1951; s. William C. and Dorothy R. Matta; m. Victoria Fonseca, Jan. 15, 1982; m. Yvonne D. Formella, June 30, 1973 (div. Oct. 17, 1977); children: Camille M., William M., Vanessa C., Lorraine V. BA, Bemidji State Coll., 1973, U. N.D., 1983, MA, 1985; PhD, U. Tex., 1992. Tenured assoc. prof. English U. Guam, Mangilao, 1993—99, acting assoc. dean, Coll. Arts & Scis., 1997—98; asst. prof. English No. State U., Aberdeen, SD, 1999—. Admissions liaison officer U.S. Air Force Acad., Colorado Springs, 1984—. Contbr. articles to profl. jours. Youth hockey coord. & asst. coach Aberdeen Hockey Assn., SD, 2002—03. Col. USAR, 2001—04. Grantee, State of S.D., 2001, LOFTI, 2002. Dfl. Lutheran. Avocations: gardening, fishing, wild fruit gathering, hunting. Home: 1323 S 3rd St Aberdeen SD 57401 Office: Northern State U 1200 S Jay St Aberdeen SD 57401 E-mail: matta@northern.edu.

MATTAR, LAWRENCE JOSEPH, lawyer; b. Buffalo, Apr. 17, 1934; s. Joseph and Anne (Abraham) M.; m. Elaine Kolbe, Aug. 1, 1959; children: Lorraine, Brenda, Anne, Deborah. Grad., Canisius Coll., 1956; JD, SUNY, Buffalo, 1959. Bar: N.Y. 1959, Fla. 1977, U.S. Supreme Ct. 1972. Sole practice, Buffalo, 1959-62; sr. ptnr. Mattar & D'Agostino and predecessors, Buffalo, 1962—. Asst. to county ct. judge, 1961-66; counsel N.Y. State Senate Pub. Utilties Com., 1969-71. Bd. dirs. Better Bus. Bur. Western N.Y.; mem. exec. com. pres.'s coun. Canisius Coll.; mem. ho. of dels. United Way of Buffalo and Erie County; mem. Nat. Maronite Bishops' Adv. Coun., U.s. Congl. Adv. Bd.; Selective Svc. Bd., Western N.Y. Rep.Presdl. Task Force; del. Rep. Jud. Conv. 8th Dist., 1985. Decorated Knight of St. Charbiel, highest honor available to a Maronite Cath.; recipient award for outstanding svc. Buffalo Eye Bank, 1962, Leadership award Lions Club Buffalo, 1963, Citizen's award Erie C.C., 1982, Nat. Tree of Life award Bd. dirs. Jewish Nat. Fund Am., 1987. Mem. Erie County Bar Assn., Erie County Trial Lawyers Assn., N.Y. State Bar Assn., Fla. Bar Assn., N.Y. State Trial Lawyers Assn., Buffalo C. of C., NFL Players Alumni Assn. (assoc.), Di Gamma (life), Rotary Club (sec. 1978-79, dir. 1978-80, trustee, sec., mem. exec. com. Buffalo Rotary Found.), Buffalo Club (Buffalo), Transit Valley Country Club (East Amherst, N.Y.). Roman Catholic. Avocations: golf, skiing. Home: 386 Woodbridge Ave Buffalo NY 14214-1530 Office: Mattar & D'Agostino LLP 17 Court St Ste 600 Buffalo NY 14202-3294 Office Phone: 716-856-4022.

MATTAR, PHILIP, writer; b. Haifa, Palestine, Jan. 21, 1944; came to U.S. 1961; m. Evelyn Ann Keith, June 20, 1971; 1 child, Christina. MPhil, Columbia U., 1977, PhD, 1981. Exec. dir. Inst. for Palestine Studies, Washington, 1984-2001; assoc. editor Jour. Palestine Studies, Washington, 1985-2001; fellow Woodrow Wilson Ctr., 2001—02; sr. fellow U.S. Inst. Peace, 2002—03; guest scholar U.S. Inst. of Peace, 2003—. Adj. lectr. history Yale U., 1981; adj. prof. history Georgetown U., 1990, 91, 94. Author: Mufti of Jerusalem, 1988, 2d edit., 1991; co-editor: Encyclopedia of the Modern Middle East, 1996; editor: Encyclopedia of the Palentinians, 2000; contbr. articles to profl. jours., including Fgn. Policy, Middle East Jour., Middle Ea. Studies. Mem. adv. com. Human Rights Watch/Middle East. Vis. scholar Columbia U., 1984; Fulbright-Hays Rsch. fellow, 1978. Mem. Middle East Studies Assn., Middle East Inst. Avocations: jogging, chess, reading, travel. E-mail: pjmattar@aol.com.

MATTAS, RICHARD FRANK, nuclear energy industry executive; b. Chgo., Sept. 14, 1947; s. Charles Joseph and Lillian (Sebek) M.; m. Loretta Ann Urbaczewski, June 27, 1970. BA, Yale U., 1969; MS, U. Ill., 1971, PhD, 1974. Lab. asst. U. Ill., Champaign, 1969-74; post-doctoral appointee Argonne (Ill.) Nat. Lab., 1974-75, metallurgist, 1975-81, prin. investigator, 1981-85, mgr. fusion blanket tech., 1985-89, assoc. dir. fusion power, 1989-99, sr. scientist, 1999, dir. fusion power, 1999—2001. Task leaderr liquid metals tech. Internat. Energy Agy., Vienna, 1993--; chmn. tech. program Internat. Symposium on Fusion Nuclear Tech., L.A., 1995, tech. program com., 2002; nat. coord. Advanced Limiter-Divertor Program, 1998—. Contbr. articles to sci. and profl. jours. Bd. dirs. Galena (Ill.) Territory Assn., 1997—, v.p., 2001—. Recipient Cert. of Appreciation U.S. DOE, 1988, 90. Mem. Am. Soc. for Metals, Fusion Power Assocs, Driftless Area Ptnrship. Natural Resource Conservation Orgn. (vice chmn. 1997-2002, chmn. 2002—), Sierra Club. Avocations: photography, painting, bird watching. Home: 1585 Stonebridge Trl Wheaton IL 60187-7112 Office: Argonne Nat Lab 9700 Cass Ave Argonne IL 60439-4803 E-mail: mattas@anl.gov.

MATTAUCH, ROBERT JOSEPH, electrical engineering educator; b. Rochester, Pa., May 30, 1940; s. Henry Paul and Anna Marie (Mlinarcik) M.; m. Frances Sabo, Dec. 29, 1962; children: Lori Ann, Thomas J. BS, Carnegie Inst. Tech., Pitts., 1962; MEE, N.C. State U., Raleigh, 1963, PhD, 1967. Asst. prof. elec. engring. U. Va., Charlottesville, 1966-70, assoc. prof. elec. engring., 1970-76, prof. elec. engring., 1976-83, Wilson prof. elec. engring., 1983-86, Standard Oil Co. prof. sci. and tech., 1986-89, chmn. dept. elect. engring., 1987-95, BP Am. prof. sci. and tech., 1989-95; Commonwealth prof., founding chair dept. elec. engring. Va. Commonwealth U., Richmond, 1995-99, dean of engring., Commonwealth prof., 1999—. Cons. The Rochester Corp., Culpeper, Va., 1983-88, Milltech Corp., Deerfield, Mass., 1985. Patentee: infrared detector; solid state switching capacitor; thin wire pointing method, whiskerless Schottky diode, controlled in-situ etch back growth technique. Bd. dirs. U. Va. Patent Found., 1989-95, Greater Richmond Technology Coun., 2001—, Va. Bioscis. Devel. Ctr., 2000—, Richmond Symphony Orch., 2003-. Recipient Excellence in Instruction of Engring. Students award Western Electric, 1980. Fellow IEEE (Centennial medal 1984); mem. Eta Kappa Nu (recipient Oustanding Prof. in Elec. Engring. 1975), Sigma Xi, Tau Beta Pi, Sigma Pi Sigma. Office: Va Commonwealth U Office of the Dean PO Box 843068 Richmond VA 23284-3068 E-mail: rjmattau@vcu.edu.

MATTEO, MARTHA R. biochemist; b. N.Y.C., Mar. 11, 1942; m. Charles C. Matteo, Apr. 17, 1971; children: Evan Daniel, Benjamin Charles. BA in Biology, U. Rochester, 1962; PhD in Biochemistry, Brandeis U., 1967. From asst. prof. to assoc. prof. biology U. Mass., Boston, 1968—75; project leader to group leader Corp. Res. Inst. Union Carbide Corp., Tarrytown, NY, 1975—80; sr. prin. scientist Boehringer Ingelheim Pharm., Ridgefield, Conn., 1980—88; project leader bldg. constrn. Boehringer Ingelheim Pharmaceuticals, Inc., Ridgefield, Conn., 1988—93, analyst tech. assessment, 1988—94, assoc. dir. tech. assessment, 1994—97, dir. tech. assessement, 1997—2001, dir. knowledge mgmt. and R&D planning, 2001—. Fellow: N.Y. Acad. Sci. (former gov.-at-large, chair biochem. sect., chair biochem. pharmacology discussion group). Office: Boehringer Ingelheim Pharm Inc 900 Ridgebury Rd Box 368 Ridgefield CT 06877

MATTER, HARRY H. retired wholesale business executive, reflexologist; b. Lykens, PA, May 23, 1914; s. Homer Calvin and Edith Ellen (Seesoltz) Matter; m. Rita M. De Nicholas Matter, July 24, 1949; children: Robert, Tina. Grad., Air War Coll., Maxwell AFB, Maxwell, AL, 1972. Cert. Am. Reflexology Bd., Internat. Inst. of Reflexology, St. Petersburg, FL, 1992, ARCB, PRA. Salesman Baums Sporting Goods, Sunbury, Pa., 1941—48, vice pres. and treas., 1948—64; sales mgr. Coughlanath Mart, Pottstown, Pa., 1965—78; vice pres. Penna Reflexology Assn., Phila., 1984—99; performer, vocals & guitar Western Music Assn. Festival, Tucson, 1991—99; entertainer Am. Fedn. of Musicians, Pocono Mts., 1965—99. Dir. treas., Baums Sporting Goods, Inc., 1948-60, vice pres., Baums Sporting Goods, Inc., 1958-64, sales mgr., Coughlan Athletic Mart, Pottstown, PA, 1965-78, vice pres. (ret.) Penna Reflexology Assn., Phila., PA, 1980-99. Artist, prodr. The Am. Cowboy Legend (cassette, 1981, compact disc, 1991), The Old Rugged Cross (cassette, 1992), Great COuntry Songs (cassette, 1994). Performs, Selinsgrove Ctr. Home for Mentally Challenged, Selinsgrove, PA, 1986-99. Named to Country Music Hall of Fame, Colo. Country Music. Found., 1985; recipient Nat. Commanders Citation, Civil Air Patrol, USAF, 1973, Top Songwriter, Wyo. Country Music Assn., 1981, Meritorious award, Civil Air Patrol, Pa. Wing, 1983, Exceptional Svc. award, Civil Air Patrol, USAF, Pa. Wing, 1984, Pioneer award, Colo. Country Music. Found., 1985—92, Lifetime Achievement Songwriters award, 2001, Artist Trailblazer Kingeagle award, Nashville, Tenn., 2001, Internat. Star award, Lifetime Achievement Songwriters Divsn., London, 2001, King Earle award, Airplay Internat., Nashville, 2001, Artist Trailblazer award, 2001. Mem. BPO Elks Lodge, Loyal Order of Moose, (vice pres.), Penna Reflexology Assn., 1990-99, Country Music Assn., Western Music Assn. (performer), 1991-99, Officer's Club, Indiantown Gap Mil. Res. Republican. Lutheran. Avocations: walking, music, photography, gardening. Home: 29 Helen St Shamokin Dam PA 17876

MATTERN, DOUGLAS JAMES, think-tank executive; b. Creede, Colo., May 19, 1933; s. John A. and Ethel (Franklin) Mattern; m. Noemi E. Del Cippo, May 4, 1963. Student, San Jose State U., 1956-58. Reliability engr. Intersil, Sunnyvale, Calif., 1973-80; sr. engr. Data Gen. Corp., Sunnyvale, 1981-87; staff engr. Apple Computer, Cupertino, Calif., 1987-97; sr. engr. Trimble Navigation, Sunnyvale, 1998-2000. Sec. Gen. World Citizens Assembly, San Francisco, 1975—86; dir. World Citizens Diplomats, Palo Alto, Calif., 1988—90; pres. Assn. World Citizens, San Francisco, 1989—; CEO World Citizens Found., San Francisco, 1979—; chmn. World Citizens Assembly, San Francisco, 1995, Taipei, Taiwan, 2001. Author: Resolution to End the Arms Race, 1982; editor: World Citizen Newsmag., 1973—; contbr. Bd. dirs. San Francisco chpt. UN Assn.; bd. dirs. War/Peace Found. With USN, 1951—55. Recipient Albert Einstein Peace award, Internat. World Educators for World Peace, 2001. Home: 2671 South Ct Palo Alto CA 94306-2462 Office: 55 New Montgomery St Ste 224 San Francisco CA 94105-3421 Office Phone: 415-541-9610. E-mail: worldcit@best.com.

MATTERN, JOANNE, writer, educator; b. Nyack, NY, Mar. 5, 1963; d. Robert Frederick and Genevieve Porri Gise; m. James Jude Mattern, June 16, 1990; children: Christina Xinwei, Leanne Pengjing. BA in English, Hartwick Coll., 1985. Asst. editor Morrow Jr. Books, NYC, 1985—88; sr. editor, writer Troll Comms., Mahwah, NJ, 1988—95; freelance writer, 1995—. Author: (series) Wildlife of North America, 1998, Compete Like a Champion: Gymnastics, 1999, Barbie First-Grade Workbooks, 1999, Fisher-Price Little People Toddler Sticker Workbooks, 2000, Explorers, 2000—01, Working Together, 2001, Animal Geography, 2001, Safety First, 2000, Learning About Cats, 2000—01, Native Peoples, 2001, (children's books) Brer Rabbit in the Briar Patch, 1997, I Can't Believe My Eyes! Extraordinary Photos or Ordinary Things, 1997, Smart Thinking! Clever Ways Animals Make Their Lives Easier, 1997, Telling Time with Goofy, 1997, The Story of Molly Pitcher, 1999, The Trojan Horse, 1999, Big and Small, Homes for All: The Story of Bird Nests, 1999, From Flowers to Honey: The Story of Beekeeping, 1999, Mountain Climb, 1999, A Visit to the Past, 1999, Tower of Stone: The Story of a Castle, 1999, Claws and Wings and Other Neat Things, 2000, Power Rangers Power-Up Skills Learning Pads, 2000, Wishbone Adventures: Curse of Gold, 2000, Teletubbies Fun with Favorite Things Giant Coloring Activity Book, 2000, Animals Animals, 2001, People in the News: Tom Cruise, 2001, Nature's Greatest Hits, 2001, Reading Progress Indicators, 1998, Texas Assessment of Academic Skills, 2000, Reading Workbook, 2001, many others. Mem.: Soc. Children's Book Writers and Illustrators. Roman Catholic. Avocations: choral music, needlecrafts, church activities, reading, travel.

MATTERS, CLYDE BURNS, former college president; b. Fargo, N.D., Nov. 10, 1924; s. Lester H. and Pearl Lila (Burns) M.; m. Anna R. Skeels, Mar. 24, 1948; children— Cynthia (Mrs. Charles V. Carroll), Richard B. BS, Whitworth Coll., Spokane, Wash., 1950, M.Ed., 1951; PhD, U. Wash., 1960; L.H.D. (hon.), Hastings Coll., 1985. Tchr. Spokane Pub. Schs., 1950-51; prof. Whitworth Coll., 1950-57, 70-72; research assoc. U. Wash., 1957-60; asst. supt. schs. King County, Wash., 1960-63; program adviser Ford Found., West Africa, 1963-70; pres. Hastings (Nebr.) Coll., 1972-85. Pres. Nebr. Ind. Coll. Found.; mem. nexus com. Presbyn. Coll. Union; pres. Assn. Ind. Colls. and Univs. Nebr. Resident camp dir. Spokane YMCA, 1952-57, bd. dirs., 1970-72; bd. dirs. United Good Neighbors, Spokane County, 1969-70; trustee Synod of Alaska N.W. Found., 1995-99. With AUS, 1943-46. Decorated Bronze Star Mem. Assn. Ind. Colls. and Univs. (pres. Nebr. 1979-80), Phi Delta Kappa. Presbyterian (elder). Lodge: Kiwanis. Home: 4415 E 51st Ln # 3 Spokane WA 99223-7888

MATTES, MARTIN ANTHONY, lawyer; b. San Francisco, June 18, 1946; s. Hans Adam and Marion Jane (Burge) M.; m. Catherine Elvira Garzio, May 26, 1984; children: Nicholas Anthony, Daniel Joseph, Thomas George. BA, Stanford U., 1968; postgrad., U. Chgo., 1968-69, U. Bonn, Germany, 1971; JD, U. Calif., Berkeley, 1974. Bar: Calif. 1974, U.S. Ct. Appeals (D.C., 5th and 9th cirs.) 1978, U.S. Dist. Ct. (no. dist.) Calif. 1979, U.S. Dist. Ct. (ea. dist.) Calif. 1991. Asst. legal officer Internat. Union Conservation of Nature and Natural Resources, Bonn, 1974-76; staff counsel Calif. Pub. Utilities Commn., San Francisco, 1976-79, legal advisor to pres., 1979-82, adminstrv. law judge, 1983, asst. chief adminstrv. law judge, 1983-86; ptnr. Graham & James, San Francisco, 1986-98, Nossaman Guthner Knox and Elliott, LLP, San Francisco, 1998—. Adv. group. Calif. Senate Subcom. on Pub. Utilities Commn. Procedural Reform, 1994. Mng. editor Ecology Law Quar., 1973-74; contbr. articles to profl. jours. Mem. Conf. Calif. Pub. Utility Counsel (treas. 1988-90, v.p. 1990-91, pres. 1991-92), Internat. Coun. Environ. Law, San Francisco Bar Assn., Fed. Comms. Bar Assn., Power Assn. No. Calif. Office: Nossaman Guthner Knox Elliott LLP 50 California St Fl 34 San Francisco CA 94111-4624 Office Phone: 415-398-3600. Business E-Mail: mmattes@nossaman.com.

MATTESON, CAROL J. academic administrator; BS in Health Edn., Slippery Rock U. of Pa.; MS in Psychomotor Learning, U. Oreg.; PhD in Bus. Adminstrn., U. Pitts. Faculty Sturt Coll. of Edn., Slippery Rock U., U. Maine, Augusta, Rowan U., NJ; asst. to pres. Slippery Rock U. of Pa.; dean coll. of bus. Bloomsburg U., Pa., provost and v.p. academic affairs, 1992—95; exec. v.p. and provost Rowan U., NJ, 1995—2000; pres. Mt. Ida Coll., Newton, Mass., 2000—. Office: Mt Ida Coll 777 Dedham St Newton MA 02459

MATTESON, CLARICE CHRIS, artist, educator; b. Winnipeg, Man., Can., Sept. 2, 1918; came to U.S., 1922; d. Sergis and Nina (Balter) Alberts; m. D.C. Matteson, 1956 (dec. 1976); children: Kemmer, Gretchen. BA, Met. State U., 1976; MA in Liberal Studies, Hamline U., 1986; PhD in Humanities, LaSalle U., 1995. Mem. Orson Welles' staff, Hollywood, Calif., 1945-46; owner Hilde-Gardes Co., L.A., 1952—56; instr. art North Hennepin C.C., Brooklyn Park, Minn., 1975-81; instr. continuing edn. for women U. Minn., 1980. Prodr., host TV program Accent on Art, St. Paul, 1979—; instr. art Lakewood C.C., 1979, U. Minn., Bloomington (Minn.) Sch. Dist., 1980-2004, Mpls. Sch. Dist., St. Paul Sch. Dist., 1981-2002, 03-04; guest artist Montserrat Gallery, Soho, N.Y.C., 1999; appeared as guest artist WCCO-TV, 1998; spkr. on TV, Nat. Am. Pen Women Spirituality and Creativity in Art, 2003. (one-woman shows) Decathlon Club, 1998, State Capital Rotunda, 1986, Lindbergh Home, 1988, Hamline U., 2002, exhibited (group shows) Mpls. Inst. Art, 1994—98, Art in Bloom, 1999—2002, St. Paul, 2000, Landmark Ctr., Hamline U., St. Paul, 2002, U. Minn. Womens Club, 2002, U. Minn. Womens Club Art Show, 2003, Fairmount Hotel, 2002; Exhibited in group shows at Art in Bloom, 1999—2003; (represented by) Gov. Ventura's Ofcl. Residence and now by Gov. Jim Pawlenty, 2003—04, Montserrat Art Gallery, N.Y.C., Gallery 416, Mpls., Jean Stephen Art Gallery, 1999—2002, Premier Gallery, 2001—02, (corr.) Schaumburg (III) Newspapers, 1962—68; prodr.: (TV series, host) Kids Art, 1995—, (series program) Internat. Cafe Internet Arts, 1996—; patentee plastic products; prodr.: Men Aware TV, 2001—02, Punt, Pass, or Pie TV, 2001—02; composer: I Want You Near; Exhibited in group shows at Women's Club, 2002—03, exhibited in group shows, Gov. Ventura's and Gov. Tim Pawlenty's, 2001—05; composer: You Make a Difference, God is in my Heart, Art Works Art is Everywhere. Active Minn. Orch. (WAMSO), Mpls., 1972—, vol. Recipient award for creative leadership Minn. Assn. for Continuing Adult Edn., 1977, Gold Cup award Bloomington Cable, 1989, Gov.'s Letter of Commendation, 1994; named Outstanding Grad. for past 25 yrs. Met. State U., 1997, Disting. Alumna John Marshall H.S., L.A., 2002, Outstanding Nominee of Grad. Students Met. State U., 2002; Park Cable TV grantee, 1982, Minn. Humanities Commn. grantee, 1985. Qem. ASCAP (award 1997-2003, award for popular music, 2003-04), AAUW (dir. arts com. 1989-90, bd. dirs. 1990-92), Am. Pen Women (Minn. chpt. 1994—, v.p. 1998), Internat. Biog. Assn. (dep. dir. Cambridge, Eng. 2001, participate art and comm. congress, 2001), Am. Composers Forum, Minn. Artists Assn., Minn. Territorial Pioneers (bd. dirs. 1995—, v.p. 1997-99, 1st v.p. 1999-2003, elected Minnesotan of Yr., 1999-2002, elected 1st v.p. 2003-04), Internat. Alliance for Women in Music, St. Paul Neighborhood Network (elected bd. dirs. TV station SPNN, 2002-04), N.Y. Neighborhood Network, Internat. Platform Speakers (award 1998), Mpls. Telecom. Network, Metro Cable Network, Adelphi Cable, Duluth-Superior Cable, NDT, Eagan. Avocations: tennis, dance, writing children's books, composing liturgical music. Home and Office: 2119 Sargent Ave Saint Paul MN 55105-1126

MATTESON, KARLA J. health science association administrator; BS in Chemistry, Beloit (Wis.) Coll., 1969; MS in Chemistry, Marquette U., 1976; PhD, Med. Coll. Wis., 1981. Postdoctoral fellow Baylor Coll. Medicine, Houston, 1981—83; former asst. dir. U. Tenn Devel. and Genetic Ctr., Knoxville; assoc. prof. med. genetics and pathology U. Tenn., Knoxville, 1986—, dir. biochem. and molecular genetics lab., 1986—; bd. dirs. Am. Bd. Med. Genetics, 1998—2001, exec. dir., 2001—. Fellow: Am. Coll. Med. Genetics; mem.: AAAS, Soc. for Inborn Metabolic Disorders. Office: U Tenn Grad Sch Medicine 1924 Alcoa Hwy Knoxville TN 37920-6999 also: Am Bd Med Genetics 9650 Rockville Pike Bethesda MD 20814-3998

MATTESON, WILLIAM BLEECKER, lawyer; b. N.Y.C., Oct. 20, 1928; s. Leonard Jerome and Mary Jo (Harwell) M.; m. Marilee Brill, Aug. 26, 1950; children: Lynn, Sandra, Holly. BA, Yale U., 1950; JD, Harvard U., 1953. Bar: N.Y. 1954. Clk. to judge Augustus N. Hand U.S. Ct. Appeals, 1953-54; clk. to U.S. Supreme Ct. Justice Harold H. Burton, 1954-55; assoc. firm Debevoise & Plimpton (and predecessors), N.Y.C., 1955-61, ptnr., 1961—98, Debevoise & Plimpton (European office), Paris, 1973-78; presiding ptnr. Debevoise & Plimpton, 1988-93. Lectr. Columbia U. Law Sch., 1972-73, 78-80. Trustee Peddie Sch., Hightstown, N.J., 1968-73, Kalamazoo Coll., 1972-77, Miss Porter's Sch., Farmington, Conn., 1977-83, N.Y. Inst. Spl. Edn., 1981—, Salk Inst., La Jolla, Calif., 1993-96, vice-chair, 1994-96, Statue of Liberty Ellis Island Found., 1996—, Hartford Found., 1996—; active USA Bus. and Industry Adv. Com. to the Orgn. for Econ. Coop. and Devel., Paris, 1986-2000; chmn. Worldwide Bus. and Industry Adv. Com., 1994-96; vice chmn. U.S. Coun. for Internat. Bus., 1990-2000, hon. trustee. Mem. ABA, FBA, Internat. Bar Assn., N.Y. State Bar Assn., Assn. of Bar of City of N.Y. (chmn. securities regulation com. 1968-71), Harvard U. Law Sch. Assn. N.Y.C. (trustee 1968-73), Coun. Fgn. Rels., Union Club, Sky Club, Sankaty Head Club, John's Island Redstick, and Windsor Clubs, N.Y. Yacht Club. Office: Debevoise & Plimpton 919 3d Ave 47th Fl New York NY 10022 E-mail: wbmatteson@debevoise.com.

MATTESSICH, RICHARD VICTOR (ALVARUS), business administration researcher; b. Trieste, Venezia-Julia, Italy, Aug. 9, 1922; s. Victor and Gertrude M.; m. Hermine Auguste Mattessich, Apr. 12, 1952. Mech. engr., Engring. Coll., Vienna, Austria, 1940; Diplomkaufmann, Hochschule für Welthandel, Vienna, 1944; Dr.rer.pol., Hochschule für Welthandel, 1945; Accademico Ordinario, Accademia Italiana di Economia Aziendale, Bologna, 1980—; D honoris causa, U. Complutense, Madrid, 1998. Rsch. fellow Austrian Inst. Econ. Rsch., Vienna, 1945-47; instr. Rosenberg Coll., St.

Gallen, 1947-52; dep. head Mt. Allison U., Sackville, Canada, 1953-59; assoc. prof. U. Calif., Berkeley, 1958-67; prof. econs. Ruhr U., Bochum, Germany, 1966-67; prof. indsl. adminstrn. U. Tech., Vienna, 1976-78; prof. bus. adminstrn. U. B.C., Vancouver, Canada, 1967-87, prof. emeritus, 1988—, Arthur Andersen & Co. Disting. chair, 1980-87. Vis. prof. Free U., Berlin, 1965, U. Social Scis., St. Gallen, Switzerland, 1965-66, U. Canterbury, 1970, Austrian Acad. Mgmt., 1971, 73, City Univ. Hong Kong, 1992, Chuo U., Tokyo, 1992; hon. prof. Centro Univ. Francesco de Vitoria, Madrid; mem. bd. nominations Acctg. Hall of Fame, Columbus, Ohio, 1978-87; bd. govs. Sch. Chartered Accountancy, Vancouver, 1981-82; bd. dirs. Can. Cert. Gen. Accts. Rsch. Found., 1984-90, internat. adv. bd., 1993—. Author: Accounting and Analytical Methods, 1964, in German, 1970, in Japanese, 1972, in Spanish, 2002, Simulation of the Firm Through a Budget Computer Program, 1964, Instrumental Reasoning and Systems Methodology, 1978, Critique of Accounting, 1995, Foundational Research in Accounting: Professional Memoirs and Beyond, 1995, The Beginnings of Accounting and Accounting Thought, 2000; editor: Modern Accounting Research History, Survey and Guide, 1984, 89, 92, Accounting Research in the 1980s and Its Future Influence, 1991, French transl., 1993, others, mem. editl. bd. Theory and Decision Libr., Jour. Bus. Adminstrn., Economia Azlendale, Praxiology, Acctg., Bus. and Fin. History. Sec.-treas. Internat. House, U. B.C., 1969-70. Served to lt. Orgn. Todt., 1944-45. Recipient Lit. award AICPA, 1972, Haim Falk award Can. Acad. Acctg. Assn., 1991, highest rsch. award Acad. Accounting Historians, 2003, Hourglass award; Ford Found. fellow, 1961-62; Disting. Erskine fellow U. Canterbury, 1970; Killam sr. fellow U. B.C., 1971-72; nominated Nobel Meml. prize in Econs., 2002. Fellow Accademia Italiana di Economia Aziendale (accademico ordinario 1980—); mem. Am. Acctg. Assn. (lit. award 1972), Schmalenbach Gesellschaft, Verb. d. Hochschullehrer für Betriebswirtschaft (exec. adv. coun. 1976-78), Inst. Chartered Accts. of B.C. (bd. of govs. 1981-82), Austrian Acad. Scis. (corr.), Acad. Acctg. Historians (life). Achievements include pioneering analytical methods in accounting and the computerized spreadsheet. Office: U BC Sauder Sch Bus Vancouver BC Canada V6T 1Z2 *Cautious optimism is the best long run strategy.*

MATTEUCCI, DOMINICK VINCENT, real estate developer; b. Oct. 19, 1924; s. Vincent Joseph and Anna Marie (Zoda) M.; m. Emma Irene DeGuia, Mar. 2, 1968; children: Felisa Anna, Vincent Eriberto. BS, Coll. of William and Mary, 1948, MIT, 1950. Registered profl. engr., Calif.; lic. gen. bldg. contractor, real estate broker. Owner Matteucci Constrn. Co., Newport Beach, Calif.; pres. Nat. Investment Brokerage Co., Newport Beach. Home: 2104 Felipe Newport Beach CA 92660-4040 Office: PO Box 10474 Newport Beach CA 92658-0474

MATTEUCCI, SHERRY SCHEEL, former prosecutor; b. Columbus, Mont., Aug. 17, 1947; d. Gerald F. and Shirley Scheel; m. William L. Matteucci, Dec. 26, 1969 (div. June 1976); children: Cory, Cody. Student, Kinman Bus. U., 1965-66, Mont. State U., 1967-69, Gonzaga U., 1971-72; BS, Eastern Wash. State U., 1973; JD, U. Mont., 1979. Bar: Mont., U.S. Dist. Ct. Mont., U.S. Ct. Appeals (9th cir.), U.S. Supreme Ct. Mont. Spl. asst. Commr. Higher Edn., 1974-76; assoc. Crowley, Haughey, Hanson, Toole & Dietrich, Billings, Mont., 1979-83, ptnr., 1984-93; U.S. atty. Dist. of Mont., Billings, 1993—2001. Bd. visitors U. Mont. Law Sch., 1988—. Mem. editorial bd. U. Mont. Law Rev., 1977-78, contbg. editor, 1978-79. Bd. dirs. Big Bros. & Sisters, Billings, 1982-85, City/County Library Bd., Billings, 1983-93, Billings Community Cable Corp., 1986, chmn., 1987; vice chmn., bd. dirs. Parmley Billings Library Found. Named one of Outstanding Young Women in Am., 1983. Mem. ABA, State Bar Mont. (chmn. jud. polling com. 1985-87, chmn. women's law sect. 1985-86, trustee, sec., treas. 1988—), Yellowstone County Bar Assn. (dir. 1984-87, pres.-elect 1986-87, pres. 1987-88), Billings C. of C. (leadership com. 1986, legis. affairs com. 1984). Democrat. Mem. Unitarian Ch.

MATTHAU, CHARLES MARCUS, film director; b. N.Y.C., Dec. 10, 1965; s. Walter and Carol M. BA, U. So. Calif., 1986. Pres. The Matthau Co., L.A., 1987—. Bd. govs. Cedar Sinai Med. Ctr., L.A. Dir. motion picture Doin' Time on Planet Earth, 1990 (Saturn award Coun. Film Orgns., Silver Scroll award Acad. Sci. Fiction); dir., prodr. TV show Mrs. Lambert Remembers Love, 1993 (Golden Angel award Best TV Spl. 1993, Golden Medal award Best Drama Prodn. 1993, Grand award The Houston Internat. Film Festival); dir., prodr. motion picture The Grass Harp, 1996 (recipient Best Dir. Family Film awards 1996); dir. The Marriage Fool, 1998; dir. over 50 feature shorts. Nat. spokesperson Am. Lung Assn., L.A., 1989—; active Action on Smoking and Health, Washington, 1986—. Recipient Cine award, Coun. Non-Theatrical Events, Washington, 1985, Golden Seal award, London Amateur Film Festival, 1986, Platinum Circle award Am. Film Inst. Mem. Dirs. Guild Am.

MATTHEI, EDWARD HODGE, architect; b. Chgo., Dec. 21, 1927; s. Henry Reinhard and Myra Beth (Hodge) M.; m. Mary Nina Hoffmann, June 30, 1951; children: Edward Hodge, Suzanne Marie, Christie Ann, Laura Jean, John William. BS in Archtl. Engring, U. Ill., 1951. Registered arch. 17 states, including Ariz., Fla., Ill., Mich., N.Y., Wis., Calif.; cert. NCARB. Dir. health facilities planning and constrn. Child & Smith (architects and engrs.), Chgo., 1951-60; sr. v.p. health facilities planning Perkins & Will, Chgo., 1960-74; ptnr. firm Matthei & Colin Assoc., Chgo., 1974-96; planning and archtl. design cons. Chgo., 1996—. Com. chmn. Am. Nat. Standards Inst., 1983-89; lectr. 1st Internat. Conf. on Rehab. of Handicapped, Beijing, 1986, Design USA, Novosibirsk and Moscow, USSR, 1990. Editor: Inland Architect, 1956-58; prin. works health facilities projects, med. ctr. master plans including Akron (Ohio) Gen. Hosp., Heritage Hosp., Taylor, Mich., Rose Meml., Denver, Silver Cross Hosp., Joliet, Ill., Shands Tchg. Hosp. & Med. Sch., U. Fla., Gainesville, Mercy Hosp., Davenport, Iowa, Westlake Cmty. Hosp., Chgo., Highland Park (Ill.) Hosp., Ctrl. DuPage Hosp., Winfield, Ill., Nebr. Meth. Hosp., Omaha, Rockford (Ill.) Meml. Hosp., U. Ala. Med. Ctr., Birmingham, U. Calif. Sch. Medicine, Irvine, Kent Hall, U. Chgo., Holy Cross Hosp., Md., West Mich. Cancer Ctr. Second v.p. Nat. Easter Seal Soc., 1978; mem. bd. dirs. St. Scholastica H.S., Chgo., 1973-83, 86-96; mem. Welfare Coun. Greater Met. Chgo., 1965-72; chair profl. adv. coun. Nat. Easter Seal Soc., 1988-89. With AUS, 1946-47. Recipient Leon Chatelain award for barrier-free environ. Nat. Easter Seals Soc., 1979, Disting. Svc. award, 1990, 99, Meritorious Svc. award Am. Nat. Standards Inst., 1987, Speedy award Paralyzed Vets. Am., 1993. Fellow AIA (Disting. Svc. award Chgo. chpt. 1988); mem. Am. Hosp. Assn., Am. Assn. Hosp. Planning, Internat. Hosp. Fedn., Nat. Center Barrier Free Environ. (dir.), Builders Assn. Chgo., Chgo. Assn. Commerce and Industry. Home: 1437 W Glenlake Ave Chicago IL 60660-1801 Office: Matthei & Colin Assocs 332 S Michigan Ave Chicago IL 60604-4434

MATTHEW, LYN, sales executive, consultant, marketing professional, consultant; b. Long Beach, Calif., Dec. 15, 1936; d. Harold G. and Beatrice (Hunt) Matthew; m. Wayne Thomas Castleberry, Aug. 12, 1961 (div. Jan. 1976); children: Melanie Castleberry, Cheryl Castleberry, Nicole Castleberry, Matthew Castleberry. BS, U. Calif., Davis, 1958; MA, Ariz. State U., 1979. Cert. hotel sales exec., meeting profl., hospitality mktg. exec., hospitality mgmt. exec. Pres. Davlyn Cons. Found., Scottsdale, Ariz., 1979-82; cons., vis. prof. Art Bus., Scottsdale, 1982—; pres., dir. sales and mktg. Embassy Stes., Scottsdale, 1987-98; pres. Matthew Enterprises, Inc., Scottsdale, 1998—. Vis. prof. Maricopa CC, Phoenix, 1979—, Ariz. State U., Tempe, 1980—83; cons. Women's Caucus Art, Phoenix, 1983—88; coun. adminstr. Lynn Andrews Prodns., 2001—. Author: (book) The Business Aspects of Art, Book I, 1979, Book II, 1989, Marketing Strategies for the Creative Artist, 1985, Moxibustion Manual, 1999. Bd. dirs. Rossom Ho. and Heritage Sq. Found., Phoenix, 1987—88; trustee Hotel Sales and Mktg. Assn. Internat. Found., 1988—90, chmn., 1991—93, mem. exec. com., 1993—95. Recipient Cmty. Bldg. award, 2000. Mem.: Am. Orgn. Bodywork Therapies Asia (pres., state dir. 1999—2003), Ariz. Acad. Performing Arts (v.p. bd. dirs. 1987—88, pres. 1988—89), Soc. Govt. Meeting Planners (charter bd. dirs. 1987, nat. conf. co-chair 1993—94, Sam Gilmer award 1992), Meeting Planners Internat. (v.p. Ariz. Sunbelt chpt. 1989—91, pres. 1991—92, CMP cert. trainer 1995—, Supplier of the Yr. award 1988), Cert. Hospitality Mktg. Execs. (profl. designation tng. chair 1995), Hotels Sales and Mktg. Assn. Internat. (bd. dirs. 1985—90, pres. Great Phoenix chpt. 1988—89, regional dir. 1989—90, mktg. exec. 1998—), Ariz. Vocat. Edn. Assn. (sec. 1978—80), Ariz. Women's Caucus Art (pres. 1980—82, hon. advisor 1986—87), Nat. Women's Caucus Art (v.p. 1981—83), Women in Higher Edn., Ariz. Visionary Artists (treas. 1987—88), Women Image Now (Achievement and Contbn. in Visual Arts award 1983), Coun. Whistling Elk (worldwide coun. adminstr. 2001—). Office Phone: 928-699-7070.

MATTHEW, NEIL EDWARD, artist, educator; b. Anderson, Ind., Jan. 19, 1925; s. Mark Neil and Mary Bertha (Clifford) Matthew; m. Jeannette Morrow, Dec. 22, 1963 (dec. Aug. 30, 2000). BA in Edn., Ariz. State U., 1949; MFA, Ind. U., 1955; postgrad., U. Iowa, 1957-58, State Acad. of Fine Arts, Stuttgart, Germany, 1959-60. Tchr., art Covington (Ind.) Jr. HS, 1949-50, Clay HS, South Bend, Ind., 1955-57; instr. art Ind. U., Kokomo, 1960-64, from instr. to asst. prof. art. Indpls., 1964-71; from asst. to assoc. prof. Herron Sch. Art/Ind. U. Purdue U., Indpls., 1971-87, assoc. prof. emeritus, 1987—. Art exhibit judge Kokomo Art Assn., 1970; rschr. salary studies AAUP, Ind. U. Purdue U., others. One-man shows include Lieber's Gallery, Indpls., 1962, 1968, Purdue U. Gallery, 1962, Ind. U. Med. Ctr., Indpls., 1966, Ind. U., Kokomo, 1967, Ind. U. Purdue U. at Indpls., 1996, 1998, Lyman-Snodgrass Gallery, Indpls., 1984, others, exhibited in group shows at Libr. Congress, 1956, 1958, 1959, Purdue U., 1966, 1969, Ind. Arts Competition, 1988, others, Represented in permanent collections U. Ariz. Mus. Art, Tucson, Ctr. Creative Photography, Archives, Ind. U. - Purdue U., Indpls., Indpls. Mus. Art, Ind. U. Art Mus., Bloomington, Ind., Ind. State Mus., Indpls., Ind.; copper plate included in edn'l. show U. Ariz. Mus. Art, 2000, Ctr. Creative Photography, 2003. With U.S. Army, 1950—52. Scholar, U. Iowa, 1957—58; Fulbright grantee, Stuttgart, 1959—60. Mem.: Coll. Art Assn., Fulbright Assn., Ctr. Creative Photography, Soc. Ind. Pioneers. Republican. Presbyterian. Avocations: travel, reading, history, fiction. Home: 5233 North Via Sempreverde Tucson AZ 85750-5967

MATTHEWS, ALLAN FREEMAN, geologist; b. Wakefield, Mass., May 27, 1916; s. Ralph Freeman Matthews and Mary (Morrill) Hill; m. Shirley Jean Spencer, Dec. 23, 1937 (div. Oct. 1955, dec. 1989); children: David Allan, Kim; m. Mary Cerantonio Thomas, Feb. 24, 1956, (div. Jan. 5, 1962); m. Doris Olive Haignere, June 26, 1962 (Dec. 2003). BA, Carleton Coll., 1937; MS, Antioch Coll., 1939; postgrad., Johns Hopkins U., 1939-40. Tech. editor Ceramic Industry Jour., Chgo., 1940-41; editor, sect. chief U.S. Bur. of Mines, Washington, 1941-51; asst. dir., staff Pres.'s Materials Policy Commn., Washington, 1951-52; materials cons. Nat. Security Resources Bd., Washington, 1952-53; ops. analyst Johns Hopkins Ops. Rsch. Office, Chevy Chase, Md., 1953-54; program officer U.S. Agy. for Internat. Devel., Washington, 1954-75; editor, pub. Developing Country Courier, McLean, Va., 1978-85. Del. UN Global Modeling Conf., Paris, 1982; initiated citizens transnat. constl. conv., The Hague, Netherlands, 1998; chmn. constn. action group Alliance for Democracy, Waltham, Mass., 1997-99; minerals cons. Global 2000 Project, 1978-80; cons. and presenter in field. Author: Sovereigns Peacefully Take Charge, 1997; editor: Minerals Yearbook, 1947-50; contbr. articles to profl. jours. and chpts. to books. Dir. Streit Council for a Union of Democracies, Washington, 1957—; core planner 20/20 Vision, Washington, 1991-97; a founder The Reston Forum, 1990-92; pres. Waterford Sq. Condominium Assn., Reston, 1992; apptd. adv. bd. Phila. Two Orgn. Direct Democracy, 2001, Signatory of Natl. Initiative for Democracy, 2002. Lt. (j.g.) USN, 1944-46. Recipient Meritorious award U.S. Agy. for Internat. Devel., 1955, Commendation for Devel. Analysis, 1957; named Fellow in Geology, 1937-39. Mem. AAAS, ACLU, Democratic Socialists Am., Natural Resources Def. Coun., U N Assn., World Federalist Movement, Unitarian Universalist Assn., Fed. Am. Scientists, Phila. Two Direct Democracy, Soc. for Internat. Devel. (proposer continental fed. unions at N.Am. regional conf. 2000), Ctr. Def. Info, Initiative and Referendum Inst., Tikkum Cmty. Green Party. Achievements include evaluation of mineral resources adequacy and advancement of transnational constitutions. Home: Apt 624 900 N Taylor St Arlington VA 22203-1863 Personal E-mail: afmatthews@earthlink.net.

MATTHEWS, BARBARA, state legislator; b. Nov. 26, 1939; m. Barry Matthews; 2 children. AA, Chabot Coll. Mgr. Calif. govt. affairs Albertson's; mem. Tracy (Calif.) Planning Commn., Tracy City Coun., 1991—2000; mem., dist. 17 Calif. State Assembly, 2000—. Mem. Tracy Econ. Devel. Com., Tracy "Main Street City" Com.; chair Agriculture Com.; mem. Arts, Entertainment, Sports, Tourism, and Internet Media Com., Higher Edn. Com., Water, Parks and Wildlife Com., Vets. Affairs Com., San Joaquin Waste Mgmt. Task Force. Mem. Delta Protection Commn.; bd. dirs. Tracy's Arts Leadership Alliance. Mem.: Soroptimist Internat. (Tracy-Daybreak). Democrat. Mailing: PO Box 942849 Rm 5155 Sacramento CA 95814 Office: 31 E Channel St St 306 Stockton CA 95202 also: 806 W 18th St Merced CA 95340

MATTHEWS, BARBARA CARIDAD, lawyer; d. Frederick Lawrence and Caridad Ofelia Matthews; m. Andrew Michael Danas, Nov. 6, 1999; 1 child, Lydia Marguerite Danas. B.Sc.F.S., Georgetown U., 1986; JD, LLM, Duke U., 1991. Bar: N.Y. 1992. Assoc. banking advisor Inst. Internat. Fin., Washington, 1992—94, banking advisor, regulatory counsel, 1996—2003; assoc. Morrison & Foerster, Washington, 1994—96; sr. coun., Fin. Svc. Com. House of Rep., 2003. Mem. editl. bd. Jour. Derivatives Use, Trading and Regulation, 1997—2003; contbr. articles to profl. jours., chapters to books. Pres. Friends Assisting the Nat. Symphony, Washington, 1998—99; bd. dirs. Young Audiences, Washington, 2000—04; mem. exec. com. women's leadership group Boys & Girls Clubs Greater Washington, 2000. Fellow internat. law, Ford Found., 1991—92. Mem.: ABA, N.Y. State Bar Assn., Internat. Assn. Fin. Engrs., Pi Sigma Alpha, Alpha Sigma Nu. Avocations: photography, tennis, travel. Office: US Ho of Reps Rayburn House Office Bldg Rm 2129 Washington DC 20515 Business E-Mail: barbara.matthews@mail.house.gov.

MATTHEWS, BRENDA J. human resources specialist; b. Hot Springs, Ark., Apr. 5, 1950; d. Earl Black and Mizella Roberts; m. Leonard Matthews, Nov. 22, 1979 (div. Jan. 1988); 1 child, Ebony. BA, U. Md., 1983; MA, Webster U., 1986. Sec. Dept. Vets. Affairs, Columbia, SC, 1984—87, pers. specialist Biloxi, Miss., 1987—88, Battle Creek, Mich., 1988—91, asst. pers. officer Salem, Va., 1991—96, assoc. chief human resources, 1996—2002, supr. human resources New Orleans, 2002—. Cons. ARC, Roanoke, Va., 2001—. Bd. dirs. ARC, Roanoke, 1995—2001, mem. exec. com., 1995—2001, chmn. vol. com., 2000—; mem. Kellogg Cmty. Leadership Acad., 1989. With U.S. Army, 1976—80. Recipient Chpt. Chmn.'s award, ARC, Roanoke, 2001. Mem.: Va. Soc. Human Resources Adminstrs. Avocations: reading, music, volunteer work, golf. Office: Dept Vets Affairs Med Ctr 1601 Perdido St New Orleans LA 70130

MATTHEWS, BRIAN W. molecular biology educator; b. Mount Barker, Australia, May 25, 1938; came to U.S., 1967; s. Lionel A. and Ethlinda L. (Harris) M.; m. Helen F. Denley, Sept. 7, 1963; children: Susan, Kristine. BS, U. Adelaide, Australia, 1959, BS with honors, 1960, PhD, 1964, DSc, 1986. Mem. staff Med. Rsch. Coun., Cambridge, Eng., 1963-66; vis. assoc. NIH, Bethesda, Md., 1967-69; prof. molecular biology U. Oreg., Eugene, 1969—, chmn. dept. physics, 1985-86, dir. Inst. Molecular Biology, 1980-83, 90-92; Drummond lectr. U. Calgary (Can.), 1995. Advisor NSF, Washington, 1975-77; investigator Howard Hughes Med. Inst., 1989—; mem. U.S. Nat. Commn. for Crystallography, Washington, 1980-86, 88-90. Rsch. fellow Alfred P. Sloan Found., 1971, Guggenheim fellow, 1977; recipient Career Devel. award NIH, 1973, Faculty Excellence award Oreg. Bd. Edn., 1984, Discovery award Med. Rsch. Found. Oreg., 1987, Reed Coll. Vollum award, 1994, Stein and Moore award Protein Soc., 2000. Mem. NAS, AAAS, Crystallographic Assn., Am. Chem. Soc., Protein Soc. (pres. 1995-97), Biophysical Soc. (nat. lectr. 2001). Office: U Oreg HHMI Inst Molecular Biology Eugene OR 97403 Office Phone: 541-346-2572. E-mail: brian@uoxray.uoregon.edu.

MATTHEWS, BRUCE RANKIN, former professional football player; b. Arcadia, Calif., Aug. 8, 1961; BS in Indsl. Engring., U. So. Calif., 1983. Center, guard Houston Oilers, 1983-96, Tenn. Oilers (formerly Houston Oilers), 1996-97; offensive guard Tennessee Titans, 1997—2002. Named NFL All-Pro Team Guard by Sporting News, 1988-90, 92, Leader, 1993. Played in Pro Bowl, 1988-93.

MATTHEWS, CHARLES LEROY, JR., director; b. Sterling, Ill., Sept. 30, 1959; s. Charles Leroy and Barbara Elaine Matthews; m. Margaret Dawn Fuller, Sept. 9, 1978; children: Aaron Isaac, Kalem Seth. Commd. ensign USN, 1976, master acoustic analyst, 1976—94; pvt. practice Virginia Beach, Va., 1994—95; job developer Lites Supported Employment, Bolivar, Mo., 1996; employment counselor City of Springfield, Mo., 1996—99; youth dir. Ozarks Area Cmty. Action Corp., Springfield, Mo., 1999—. Chmn. Rep. Party, Dallas County, Mo., 1999—. Grantee, Mo. Dept. Edn., 2001—02. Mem.: Nat. Assn. Workforce Devel. Profl., Mo. Assn. Workforce Devel. (bd. dirs. 2003, membership chmn. 1998—). Republican. Avocations: gardening, basketball. Office: Ozarks Area Cmty Action Corp 215 S Barnes Springfield MO 65802

MATTHEWS, CHARLES SEDWICK, petroleum engineering consultant, research advisor; b. Houston, Mar. 27, 1920; s. Charles James and Zadoc Coleman (Sedwick) M.; m. Miriam Loraine Ormerod, June 2, 1945; children— Joan Gail, Wendy Loraine BSChemE, Rice U., 1941, MSChemE, 1943, PhD in Chemistry, 1944. Registered profl. engr., Tex. Engr. Shell Devel. Co., San Francisco, 1944-48, rsch. engr. Houston, 1948-56, dir. rsch., 1967-72; chief reservoir engr. Shell Oil Co., Houston, 1965, mgr. engring., 1972-73, sr. petroleum engring. cons., 1973-89. Engring. adv. com. Rice U., Houston, 1973-77; cons. Dept. Energy, Washington, 1974-78, adv. com., 1975-79; spl. asst. Nat. Petroleum Council, Washington, 1981-83; reserves com. Am. Petroleum Inst. Author: Pressure Buildup and Flow Tests in Wells, 1967; contbr. articles to profl. jours.; patentee in field. Chmn. Tex. Engrs. for Conservation, Houston, 1973 Recipient Disting. Alumnus award Rice U., 1994. Mem. NAE, Soc. Petroleum Engrs. (hon. mem., Lester Uren award 1975, disting. author, disting. lectr. 1968, Disting. lectr. emeritus 1986), Phi Beta Kappa, Sigma Xi, Tau Beta Pi, Phi Lambda Upsilon. Clubs: Houston, Meyerland (treas. 1982-85). Republican. Methodist. Avocations: swimming, fishing. Home: 5307 S Braeswood Blvd Houston TX 77096-4149

MATTHEWS, CHARLES W., JR., oil industry executive; b. Houston, Tex., Feb. 27, 1945; BA, U. Tex., 1967; JD, U. Houston, 1970. Bar: Tex. 1970, Tenn. 1980, admitted to: U.S. Dist. Ct., So. Dist. Tex. 1975, U.S. Supreme Ct., U.S. Ct. Appeals, Dist. Columbia Circuit, U.S. Ct. Appeals, Fifth and Eleventh Circuits 1981. Trial atty. law dept. Exxon Corp., 1971-78, region atty. southeastern and southern region mktg. offices, 1978-81, assoc. gen. atty. litigation sect., gen. counsel & dir. Petroleum Casualty Co. and Exxon Risk Mgmt. Svcs., 1981-92; from assoc. gen. counsel law dept. to gen. counsel law dept. Exxon U.S.A., 1992; v.p., gen. counsel Exxon Mobil Corp., 1995—. Instr. State Bar Tex. Profl. Develop. Program, Litigating the Oil and Gas Case, 1988; adv. dir. U. Houston Law Found., mem. bd. trustees. Author: Recent Developments in Liability for Oil and Gas Operations, 1987. Nat. trustee Southwest Region Boys and Girls Club Am.; bd. trustees Nat. Judicial Coll., 1996—2002; chair U. Tex. Chancellor's Coun., 2002; mem. bd. overseers Rand Inst. Civil Justice; co-chair Campaign for Equal Access for Legal Svcs. N. Tex.; mem. develop. bd. U. Tex. Recipient Alumnus of the Yr., Univ. of Houston, 2000. Fellow: Tex. Bar Found.; mem.: Chancellor's Coun. of the U of Tex. (chmn.), Chief Legal Officers Roundtable, Am. Inns Ct. Found. (trustee, mem. leadership coun.), Nat. Ctr. State Courts (co-chair gen. council com. 2002—), Defense Rsch. Inst., State Bar Tex. (vice chmn. adminstrn. justice com. 1988, corp. counsel liaison to litigation section 1988—89), Ctr. Am. and Internat. Law (chmn. exec. com. 2002—, trustee), Internat. Assn. Def. Counsel Found. (chmn. corp. counsel com. 1991, v.p. 1993—95, bd. dirs.), Assn. Gen. Counsel, Dallas Bar Assn., Dallas Bar Found. (fellow, v.p., gen. counsel), Houston Bar Assn. (bd. dirs. 1994—95, fellow), Order Barons, ABA (public trustee 1996—97, fellow, mem. com. corp. gen. counsel). Office: Exxon Mobil Corp Law Dept 5959 Las Colinas Blvd Irving TX 75039-2298

MATTHEWS, CLARK J(IO), II, retail executive, lawyer, retired; b. Arkansas City, Kans., Oct. 1, 1936; s. Clark J. and Betty Elizabeth (Stewart) M.; children: Patricia Eleanor, Pamela Elaine, Catherine Joy. BA, So. Meth. U., 1959, JD, 1961. Bar: Tex. 1961. Trial atty. Ft. Worth Regional Office, SEC, 1961-63; law clk. to chief U.S. dist. judge No. Dist. Tex., Dallas, 1963-65; atty. Southland Corp., Dallas, 1965-73, v.p., gen. counsel, 1973-79, exec. v.p., chief fin. officer, 1979-83, sr. exec. v.p., chief fin. officer, 1983-87, exec. v.p., chief fin. officer, 1987-91, pres., chief exec. officer, 1991-2000; retired, 2000. Bd. dirs. 7-Eleven, Inc. Mem. ABA, Tex., Dallas, Bar Assns., Am. Judicature Soc., Alpha Tau Omega, Pi Alpha Delta. Clubs: DeMolay. Methodist. Home: 7005 Stefani Dr Dallas TX 75225-1747 Office: 7-Eleven Inc 2711 N Haskell Ave Ste 41N Dallas TX 75204-2946

MATTHEWS, CRAIG GERARD, energy company executive; b. Bklyn., Mar. 8, 1943; m. Carol O. Olsen, Sept. 10, 1971; children: Kenneth C., Bradford P., Melinda M. BCE, Rutgers U., 1965; MS in Indsl. Mgmt., Polytech. Inst. Bklyn., 1971. Vice chmn., COO, KeySpan Corp. (formerly Bklyn. Union Gas Co.), 1965—2002, ret., 2002; pres., CEO, NUI Corp., 2004—. Bd. dirs. Amerada Hess Corp.; mem. adv. bd. SI Bancorp, Republic Fin. Bd. dirs. Bklyn. Philharm., Poly. Univ., Salvation Army. Republican. Presbyterian. Home: 132 Canterbury Way Basking Ridge NJ 07920 Office Phone: 908-719-4290.

MATTHEWS, DAVE, singer, musician; b. Johannesburg, Jan. 9, 1967; s. John and Val Matthews; m. Jennifer Ashley Harper, 2000; 2 children. Vocalist, guitarist Dave Matthews Band, 1991—; founder ATO Records, 2000—. Bd. dirs. Farm Aid, 2001—. Musician: (albums) Remember Two Things, 1993, Under the Table and Dreaming, 1994, Crash, 1996 (Grammy award Best Rock Performance by A Duo Or Group, 1996), Live at Red Rocks, 9-15-95, 1997, Before These Crowded Streets, 1998, Live at Luther College, 1999, Listener Supported, 1999, Live in Chicago 12-19-98, 2001, Everyday, 2001, Live at Folsom Field, Boulder Colorado, 2002, Busted Stuff, 2002, Central Park Concert, 2003, The Gorge, 2004, (solo albums) Some Devil, 2003 (Grammy award Best Male Rock Vocal Performance, 2003). Office: ATO Records 157 Chambers St New York NY 10007*

MATTHEWS, DAVID, clergyman; b. Indianola, Miss., Jan. 29, 1920; s. Albert and Bertha (Henderson) M.; m. Lillian Pearl Banks, Aug. 28, 1951; 1 dau., Denise. AB, Morehouse Coll., Atlanta, 1950; student, Atlanta U., 1950, Memphis Theol. Sem., 1965, Delta State U., Cleveland, Miss., 1969, 71, 72; D.D. (hon.), Natchez (Miss.) Jr. Coll., 1973, Morris Booker Meml. Coll., 1988. Ordained minister Nat. Baptist Conv. U.S.A., 1946; pastor chs. in Miss., 1951—, Bell Grove Baptist Ch., Indianola, 1951—, Strangers Home, Greenwood, 1958—. Tchr., chmn. dept. social sci. Gentry H.S., Indianola, 1958-83; moderator Sunflower Bapt. Assn., 1957—; v.p. Gen. Bapt. Conv. Miss., 1958—, former lectr., conv. congress religious edn.; v.p. Nat. Bapt. Conv. U.S.A., 1971-94; del. to Nat. Coun. Chs., 1960, supr. oratorial contest, 1976; pres. Gen. Missionary Bapt. State Conv. Miss., 1974-98. Mem. Sunflower County Anti-Poverty Bd., 1965-71, Indianola Bi-Racial Com., 1965—; mem. Gov.'s Advisory Com.; col. on staff Gov. Finch, 1976-80; mem. budget com. Indianola United Fund, 1971—; chmn. bd. Indianola FHA, 1971—; trustee Natchez Jr. Coll.; mem. Miss. Gov.'s Research and Devel. Council, 1984—; apptd. mem. So. Govs. Ecumenical Coun. Infant Mortality, 1987. Served with U.S. Army, 1942-45, PTO. Recipient citation Morehouse Coll., 1950, citation Miss. Valley State Coll., 1956, J.H. Jackson Preaching award Midwestern Baptist Laymen Fellowship, 1974, Gov.'s Merit award, 1975, Human Svc. award Miss. Valley State U., 2004. Mem. NEA, Miss., Indianola Tchrs. Assns., Am. Bible Soc. (adv. coun. 1991-2000, student reform theol. sem. centennial edn. 1990—). Democrat. Baptist. Home: PO Box 627 Indianola MS 38751-0627 Fax: 662-887-9078. *I have learned not to seek honors and success but to become so involved in worthwhile works that I lose myself and by such actions success and honors have come.*

MATTHEWS, DAVID FORT, career officer; b. Lancaster, N.H., Sept. 25, 1944; s. Clinton Fort and Mabel Sawin (Oaks) M.; m. Eva Mae Horton, Nov. 10, 1990. BA, Vanderbilt U., 1966; MA, Mid. Tenn. U., 1973. Cert. acquisition mgr. Rsch. and devel. officer U.S. Army Rsch. Inst., Washington, 1974-77; exec. officer 194th Maintenence Battalion-Camp Humphreys, Korea, 1978-79; career program mgr. U.S. Army Mil. Pers. Ctr., Washington, 1979-82; logistics staff officer Dep. Chief of Staff Logistics, Washington, 1982-83; team chief Chief of Staff Army Study Group, Washington, 1983-85; logistics div. chief Multiple Launch Rocket System Project Office, Huntsville, Ala., 1985-88;

comdr. Ordnance Program Div., Riyadh, Saudi Arabia, 1988-90; project mgr. Army Tactical Missile System, Huntsville, 1990-94; sr. lectr. weapon systems acquisition Naval Postgrad. Sch., Monterey, Calif., 1994—. Decorated Legion of Merit, Bronze Star; recipient award as project mgr. of yr. Sec. of Army, 1991. Mem. Nat. Def. Indsl. Assn., Assn. U.S. Army. Avocations: spectator sports, water-skiing, reading, scuba diving. Home: 83 High Meadow Ln Carmel CA 93923 Office: Naval Postgrad Sch Monterey CA 93943 Office Phone: 831-656-2360. E-mail: DMatthews@nps.navy.mil.

MATTHEWS, DOUGLAS EUGENE, lawyer, educator, consultant; b. Highland Park, Mich., July 28, 1953; s. Max and Mary Elizabeth (Crane) Matthews. BA with high distinction, Judson Coll., Elgin, Ill., 1982; JD cum laude, U. Wis., 1985, MS in Legal Instns., 1988; LLM, Harvard U., 1991. Bar: Fla. 1986, Ill. 1987, D.C. 1989. Assoc. Gunster, Yoakley, Criser & Stewart, West Palm Beach, Fla., 1986, Zukowski, Rogers, Flood & McArdle, Crystal Lake, Fla., 1987; asst. pub. defender McHenry County, Woodstock, Ill., 1988—89; law lectr. No. Ill. U., De Kalb, 1990; asst. prof. St. Thomas U. Sch. Law, Miami, Fla., 1991—94, assoc. prof., 1994—96, adj. prof. law, 1996—2002; co-founder, v.p. The Grifo Group, Inc., Miami, Fla., 1997—. Past v.p., bd. dirs. Youth Svc. Bur., Woodstock. Mem.: Ind. Computer Cons. Assn., Dade County Bar assn., Ill. Bar Assn., Fla. Bar Assn., Harvard Club Miami. Democrat. Unitarian Universalist. Avocations: gardening, historic preservation. Office: 686 NE 74th St Miami FL 33138-5114 E-mail: matthews@post.harvard.edu.

MATTHEWS, DREXEL GENE, quality control executive; b. Vanzant, Ky., Feb. 1, 1952; s. Marcus Ivan and Lillia Mae (Lake) M.; m. Roberta June Eby, Oct. 16, 1971; children: Tracie Marie, Marcia Nichole. Student, Brescia Coll., Owensboro, Ky., 1976-79, Morehead State U., 1969-71. Cert. ISO lead auditor. With Nat. Aluminum Divsn., Nat. Steel Corp., Hawesville, Ky., 1971-78, customer svc. mgr., 1977-78; quality control. mgr. Hunter Douglas Bldg. Products divsn., Roxboro, N.C., 1979-81; process engrng. mgr., mgr. quality control and specification engrng. Mepco-Electra Co., Roxboro, N.C., 1981-84; quality assurance sr., mng. engr. Sumitomo Electric Co., Rsch. Triangle Park, N.C., 1984-87; quality assurance supplier, quality engrng. resource Consolidated Diesel Co. (divsn. Cummins Engine Co.), Whitakers, N.C., 1987-95; quality assurance mgr. Fuel Systems Bus., Whitakers, N.C., 1987-94; mgr. quality devel. and improvement Consol. Diesel Co., Whitakers, N.C., 1994-95; mgr. bus. analysis and audit Cummins Engine Co., Columbus, Ind., 1995—, mgr. bus. process audits fin. dept., 1995-97, mgr. quality info. sys., 1997—. Mem. ASM, SAE (diesel standards com. 1993-95), Am. Soc. Quality Control (sr. mem.; guest speaker 1987, 91), Am. Statis. Assn., Am. Nat. Standards Inst. (fiber optics com. 1986-90). Republican. Baptist. Home: 614 N National Rd Columbus IN 47201-7851 E-mail: drexel.matthews@cummins.com.

MATTHEWS, EDWARD E. insurance company executive; b. 1931; AB, Princeton U., 1953; MBA, Harvard U., 1957. With Morgan Stanley & Co., 1957-73; exec. v.p. fin., vice chmn. bd. dirs. Am. Internat. Group, Inc., N.Y.C., from 1973, now vice chmn. fin., also bd. dirs. Vice chmn. Investment Internat. Fin. Svcs. With U.S. Army, 1953-55. Office: Am Internat Group Inc 70 Pine St New York NY 10270-0002

MATTHEWS, ERIC JODDY, film director; s. Matthew Gaddson and Levernna Ann Matthews. BFA, U. of Mich., 1993. Creative dir. Axentis Inc, Warrensville, Ohio, 2000—; dir./prodr. Madwerkz Studios, Euclid, Ohio, 1998—. Dir.: (feature film) 3 Penny Pawn; prodr.: (documentary) Freeze Defrost. Diary of Midwest Hip Hop (Best Documentary - Doubletake Film Festival, 2002); envirnomental design, Cleveland Browns PSL Monument; dir.: (3d animation 3 minute open) Sherwin Williams New Product 2000 Open, (feature film) Rundown; novel, Chicken Soup for the College Soul. Mentor Tremont Mentoring, Cleve/, 1990—99. Mem.: Midwest Filmmakers Alliance (pres. 2000—01), Siggraph, AIGA, Cleve. Advt. Assn., Midwest Maya User Group, Detroit Filmmakers Coalition, Music Video Producers Assn., Am. Ind. Comml. Producers. Avocations: painting, weightlifting, writing. Office: Madwerkz Studios 38 Lexington Sq Euclid OH 44143 E-mail: ematthews@madwerkz.com.

MATTHEWS, GAIL THUNBERG, marketing executive; b. Hartford, Conn., July 29, 1938; d. Harold Einar and Mildred (Wentland) Thunberg; m. Glenn Holbrook Matthews, Aug. 9, 1959; children: Scott Holbrook, Brett Holbrook. Student, Boston U., 1958-59. Hostess show, copywriter Sta. WJDA, Boston, 1956-58; fashion coord. Jordan Marsh, Boston, 1958-59, Miller & Rhoades, Richmond, Va., 1959-60, Sage Allen, Hartford, 1960-61; columnist Boston Globe, 1962-63, Hartford Times, 1961-63; freelance writer, contbr. articles to New Englander mag. Christian Sci. Monitor, Yankee, 1961-65; v.p., treas. Coll. Mktg. Group, Inc.(CMGi), Winchester, Mass., 1968-86. Corporator Reading Savings Bank; mem. adv. coun. Baybank Middlesex; coord. Harrods London, New London, 1992, Brit. Isles Festival for Scotland-England, Wales, No. Ireland by Brit. Dept. Trade and Industry for New London, 1994—. Author: Hors'd'oeuvre Cooking, 1966, Gourmet Cooking, 1966, Birthday Fortune Book, 1967, (children's series) The Adventures of a Shih Tzu, The Good Luck Puppy, 1980; co-host TV show Kearsarge Valley Magazine. Choral dir. Barrows Sch., Reading; pres. local PTA; chmn. Heart Fund, Reading; founder, chmn. Reading chpt. Am. Cancer Soc., Love Lights a Tree chpt. New London Am. Cancer Soc.; pres. Kimpton Brook Gardens Restorations; coord. London, Eng.-New London, N.H. Twinning, 1992, anniversary oldest theatre N.H., 1993; founder smart baby program New London Hosp. Birth Ctr., 1999; founder Nurses Appreciation Fund, Lahey Clinic, Burlington, Mass., 2001, N.H. Women Who Make A Difference for Well Child Clin., 2000. Recipient Svc. to Youth award Reader's Digest, 1962, CAP award, 1965, Spl. award Am. Cancer Soc., 1981-82, Citizenship award Reading Tchrs. Assn, 1980; named Citizen of Yr., New London Am. Cancer Soc., 1983-84. Mem.: Boston Atheneum, Women Who Make a Difference (founder), Dartmouth Coll. Women's Assn. (bd. dirs., founder mammography fund for women in need 2000), Antiquarian Soc., Rose Hill Equestrian Club. Avocation: raising Norweigan Fjord horses.

MATTHEWS, GEORGE ROBERT, retired radiologist; b. Paoli, Pa., 1915; BA, Ursinus Coll., 1936; MD, Temple U., 1940. Diplomate Am. Bd. Radiology. Intern Reading Hosp., West Reading, Pa., 1940-41, resident in radiology, 1948-51, assoc. in radiology, 1951-69, chief, dept. dir., 1969-80, emeritus mem. staff, 1980—. Mem. AMA, Am. Coll. Radiology.

MATTHEWS, GILBERT ELLIOTT, investment banker; b. Brookline, Mass., Apr. 24, 1930; s. Martin W. and Charlotte (Cohen) M.; m. Anne Lisbeth Barnett, Apr. 20, 1958 (div. 1975); children: Lisa Joan, Diana Kory (dec. 1995); m. Elaine Rita Siegal Pulitzer, Jan. 2, 1978 (div. 1999); 1 child, Jennifer Rachel. AB, Harvard U., 1951; MBA, Columbia U., 1953. Chartered fin. analyst. Dept. mgr. Bloomingdale's, N.Y.C., 1953, 56-60; security analyst Merrill Lynch, N.Y.C., 1960; investment banker Bear, Stearns & Co., N.Y.C., 1960-95, gen. ptnr., 1979-85; mng. dir. Bear, Stearns & Co. Inc., 1985-86, sr. mng. dir., 1986-95, Sutter Securities Inc., San Francisco, 1995—, chmn. bd. dirs., 1997—. Served as lt. (j.g.) USN, 1953-56. Mem. N.Y. Soc. Security Analysts. Democrat. Jewish. Office: Sutter Securities Inc 555 California St Ste 3330 San Francisco CA 94104 Business E-Mail: gil@suttersf.com.

MATTHEWS, JAY ARLON, JR., publisher, editor; b. Apr. 13, 1918; s. Jay Arlon and Mary (Long) M.; m. May Clark McLemore, Jan. 16, 1944; children: Jay Arlon III, Emily Cochrane, Sally McLemore. BLS summa cum laude, St. Edward's U., 1994. Asst. dir. personnel Adj. Gen.'s Dept., Tex., 1947-53, dept. adj., 1957-65, mil. support plans officer, 1965-69, chief emergency operations, 1965-71. Past Dir. Civil Def., Austin; mem. adv. bd. Confed. Research Center, Hill Jr. Coll.; mil. historian 65th Legislature, Tex., 1977-78. Pub. Presidial Press, Mil. History Press; editor: Mil. History of Tex. and S.W. Quar., 1961-88; editor emeritus Mil. Hist. of the West, 1989. Served with AGC, Tex. N.G., 1946—, brig. gen. ret., 1973. Named to Tex. Nat. Guard Hall of Honor, 1990. Fellow Co. Mil. Historians (gov. 1981-84); mem. Austin (state v.p. 1951-52), U.S. Jaycees (chmn. nat. security com. 1952-53), N.G. Assn. Tex. (minute man award 1964), N.G. Assn. U.S. (chmn. publicity 81st Gen. Conf.), Instituto Internationale de Historia Militar (hon. life), Mil. Order World Wars (comdr. Austin chpt. 1980). Club: Exchange (pres. Austin chpt. 1982-83). Episcopalian. Home and Office: 4847 W Lawther Dr #211 Dallas TX 75214-1853 E-mail: jmattsri@aol.com.

MATTHEWS, JOSEPH VIRGIL, pianist, music educator; b. Taneyville, Mo., June 13, 1941; s. Roy Elza and Violet Myrtle (Redfern) Matthews. MusB in piano, Univ. Mo., Columbia, Mo., 1963, MA, 1965; Mus D, Ind. Univ., Bloomington, Ind., 1977. Piano tchr. Christian Coll. Prep Dept., Columbia, Mo., 1962—63; tchg. asst.-piano Univ. Mo., Columbia, Mo., 1963—64, Ind. Univ., Bloomington, Ind., 1964—65, 1969—72; asst. prof. Coll. of the Sch. of the Ozarks, Point Lookout, Mo., 1965—69; prof. music Chapman Univ., Orange, Calif., 1972—. Musician: (recitals) as soloist, accompanist, duo-pianist and soloist with orch., 1963—. Recipient Graves award in Humanities, Am. Coun. of Learned Soc., 1981, Valerie Scudder Disting. Tchng. award, Chapman Univ., 1989. Mem.: Music Tchr. Nat. Assn., Calif. Assn. of Profl. Music Tchr., Music Tchr. Assn. of Calif. (state co-chair, solo-concerto). Achievements include my students have won local, nat. and internat. prizes in piano competitions. Avocation: collecting movie memorabilia. Home: 5721-2 E Stillwater Ave Orange CA 92869 Office: Chapman Univ One Univ Dr Orange CA 92866

MATTHEWS, KATHLEEN SHIVE, biochemistry educator; b. Austin, Tex., Aug. 30, 1945; d. William and Gwyn Shive; m. Randall Matthews. BS in Chemistry, U. Tex., 1966; PhD in Biochemistry, U. Calif., Berkeley, 1970. Post doctoral fellow Stanford (Calif.) U., 1970-72; mem. faculty Rice U., Houston, 1972—, chair dept., 1987-95, Wiess prof., 1989-96, Stewart Meml. chair, 1996—, dean natural scis., 1998—. Mem. BBCB study sect. NIH, Bethesda, Md., 1980-84, 86-88, BRSG adv. com., 1992-94; mem. adv. com. on rsch. programs Tex. Higher Edn. Coord. Bd., Austin, 1987-92; mem. undergrad. edn. initiative rev. panel Howard Hughes Rsch. Inst., Bethesda, 1991, mem. rsch. resources rev. panel, 1995, mem. predoctoral fellowships rev. panel, 2001, trustee S.W. Rsch. Inst., 2003—, Steering Com. Vinson & Elkins Women's Initiative Adv. Bd., 2001—. Mem. editl. bd. Jour. Biol. Chemistry, 1988-93, assoc. editor, 1994-99; contbr. 140 reviewed papers. Fellow AAAS; mem. Am. Soc. Biochemistry and Molecular Biology (nominating com. 1993-94, 96-97, fin. com. 2001-2002), Protein Soc., Biophys. Soc. (pub. affairs com. 2002—), Am. Chem. Soc., Phi Beta Kappa. Office: Rice Univ PO Box 1892 6100 Main St MS102 Houston TX 77005-1892 E-mail: ksm@rice.edu.

MATTHEWS, L. WHITE, III, railroad executive; b. Ashland, Ky., Oct. 5, 1945; s. L. White and Virginia Carolyn (Chandler) M.; m. Mary Jane Hanser, Dec. 30, 1972; children: Courtney Chandler, Brian Whittlesey. BS in Econs, Hampden-Sydney Coll., 1967; MBA in Fin. and Gen. Mgmt, U. Va., 1970. Corp. fin. Chem. Bank, N.Y.C., 1970-72, asst. sec., 1972-74, asst. v.p., 1974-75, v.p., 1976-77; treas. Mo. Pacific Corp., St. Louis, 1977-82; v.p. fin. Mo. Pacific R.R. Co. subs. Mo. Pacific Corp., St. Louis, 1979-82; v.p., treas. Union Pacific Corp. and Union Pacific R.R. Co., N.Y.C., 1982-87; sr. v.p. fin. Union Pacific Corp., Bethlehem, Pa., 1987-92, exec. v.p. fin., 1992-98; exec. v.p., CFO Ecolab Inc., 1999—. Bd. dirs. Union Pacific Corp., 1995, 98, Ecolab Inc., Lexent Inc., Nortrax Inc., 2000—.

MATTHEWS, LARRYL KENT, mechanical engineering educator; b. Lubbock, Tex., Sept. 18, 1951; s. Morrison Arliss and Juanita Ruby (Parr) M.; m. Marie Elizabeth Twist, May 15, 1972. MS, N.Mex. State U., 1975; PhD, Purdue U., 1982. Test engr. Sandia Nat. Labs., Albuquerque, 1976-81; rsch. dir., educator N.Mex. State U., Las Cruces, 1982—, assoc. dean for rsch., 1989-99; dean coll. engrng., prof. mech. engrng. U. Maine, Orono, 2000—. Cons. Sandia Nat. Labs., 1985-89, ISOTEC, Santa Fe, N.Mex., 1986-88; bd. dirs. Waste-Mgmt. Edn. Rsch. Consortium, Las Cruces, 1990-99; chmn. Maine Space Grant Consortium Bd., 2000—; bd. dirs. Pulp and Paper Found., 2000—. Author: (with Gabe Garcia) Laser and Eye Safety in the Laboratory, 1994; contbr. articles to Jour. Solar Energy, Internat. Jour. Exptl. Heat Transfer, ASME Jour. Solar Engrng., Internat. Jour. Heat and Mass Transfer, Intech mag., Jour. Quantitative Specifications and Radiol. Transfer. Mem. AAAS, ASME, Am. Astron. Soc., Soc. de Ingenieros (founder), Pi Tau Sigma. Democrat. Methodist. Achievements include develoment of multiple-head radiometer for large pool-fire environments, of CSMP (Circum Solar Measurement Package) for contentrating solar applications, and the LODS (Laser Optical Displacements System) for measuring large and small 2-D structural displacements. Office: U Maine Coll Engrng Barrows Hall 101 Orono ME 04473

MATTHEWS, LEONARD SARVER, advertising and marketing executive; b. Glendean, Ky., Jan. 6, 1922; s. Clell and Zetta Price (Sarver) M.; m. Dorothy Lucille Fessler; children: Nancy, James, Douglas. BS summa cum laude, Northwestern U., 1948. With Leo Burnett Co., Inc., Chgo., 1948-75, v.p., dir., 1958-59, exec. v.p. charge mktg. services, 1959-61, exec. v.p. client svc., 1961-69, pres., 1970-75; asst. sec. commerce for domestic and internat. bus., 1976; pres., exec. com., dir. Young and Rubicam, 1977-78; pres. Am. Assn. Advt. Agys., 1979-89; co-founder Matthews & Johnston, Stamford, Conn., 1989-92; chmn. Next Century Media, 1992—99. Mem. adv. bd. Scripps Capital, San Diego. Ensign USCGR, 1942-46. Named to Advt. Hall of Fame, 1999. Mem. Advt. Coun. (life bd. dirs.), Sky Club (N.Y.C.), Pine Valley Golf Club (N.J.), Rancho Santa Fe Golf (Calif.), Georgetown Club (Washington), Delta Sigma Pi, Beta Gamma Sigma. Republican. Lutheran. Office: PO Box 2629 Rancho Santa Fe CA 92067-2629

MATTHEWS, MANYALIBO JOSEPH, physicist, researcher; b. Berkeley, Calif., Mar. 14, 1970; s. Kwame Mugodo and Elizabeth Rodriguez. BS, U. Calif., Davis, 1993; PhD in Physics, MIT, 1998. Part-time rsch. asst. Lawrence Berkeley Labs., 1988-91; cons. Lawrence Livermore (Calif.) Nat. Lab., 1994-95; mem. tech. staff Bell Labs., Lucent Technologies, Murray Hill, N.J., 1998—. Tech. cons., Bronx, N.Y., 1998-99; inventor in field. Chmn. Nat. Conf. of Black Physics Students, Cambridge, 1997; physics instr. Interphase Program, Cambridge, 1995; student mentor, advisor U. Calif., Davis, 1990-92. Grad. fellow NSF, 1993; Ronald E. McNair scholar U. Maine, 1992. Mem. Am. Phys. Soc., Materials Rsch. Soc., Alpha Phi Alpha (pres. U. Calif. 1991-93, advisor MIT 1996-98, Exceptional Svc. 1998). Avocations: saxophone, cooking, running, travel. Office: Bell Labs Lucent Technologies 600 Mountain Ave # 1a361 New Providence NJ 07974-2008

MATTHEWS, MELONY KERRY, opera singer, actress; b. Greenwood, SC, Nov. 20, 1961; d. Robert Montgomery Matthews and Vernell (Mazyck) Starks. BA, Spelman Coll., 1986; postgrad., Columbia U., 1988. Cert. tchr. State of N.Y., lic. tchr. K-6. Ance dir. for mentally challenged YM-YWHA, N.Y.C., 1987—90; dir. dance magnet sch. Pub. Sch. # 75 and # 166, N.Y.C., 1988—89; prin. ballerina Hudson Repertory Dance Theatre, Jersey City, 1987—91; dance dir. Jazz Mobile, Inc., N.Y.C., 1990—91; opera singer Met. Opera, N.Y.C., 1992, San Diego Opera, 2001—. Organizer, performer coord., prison tours, 1998—2000; founder, dir. Rift Valley Opera Soc. Recipient McAllister award, Ind. Opera, Indpls., 1992. Mem.: AFTRA, SAG, Nat. Assn. Negro Musicians, Inc., Actors' Equity Assn., Am. Guild Musical ARtists. Democrat. Baptist. Home: 4159 Somerset Dr # 1 Los Angeles CA 90008 Office Phone: 323-291-1619. E-mail: raamen3@juno.com.

MATTHEWS, MILDRED SHAPLEY, scientific editor, freelance writer; b. Pasadena, Calif., Feb. 15, 1915; d. Harlow and Martha (Betz) Shapley; m. Ralph Vernon Matthews, Sept. 25, 1937; children: June Lorrain, Bruce Shapley, Melvin Lloyd, Martha Alys. AB, U. Mich., 1936. Rsch. asst. Calif. Inst. Tech., Pasadena, 1950-61; bilingual editor, rsch. asst. Astron. Obs. Merate-Milan and Trieste, Italy, 1960-70; rsch. asst. Lunar-Planetary Lab., editor space sci. series U. Ariz., Tucson, 1970-96; retired, 1996. Contbr. articles to Sky and Telescope, Astronomia. Recipient Masursky Meritorious Svc. award div. planetary sci. Am. Astron. Soc., 1993. Avocations: classical music concerts, especially opera, travel. Home: 1600 Milvia St Berkeley CA 94709-2012

MATTHEWS, NORMAN STUART, department store executive; b. Boston, Jan. 13, 1933; s. Martin W. and Charlotte (Cohen) M.; m. Joanne Banks, June 11, 1956; children: Gary S., Jeffrey B., Patricia A. BA, Princeton U.; MBA, Harvard U. Ptnr. Beacon Mktg. and Advt. Assocs., N.Y.C., 1956-71; sr. v.p. Broyhill Furniture Co., Lenoir, N.C., 1971-73, E.J. Korvettes, N.Y.C., 1973-78; chmn., chief exec. officer Gold Circle Stores, Columbus, Ohio, 1978-82; vice chmn. Federated Dept. Stores, Cin., from 1982, pres., chief oper. officer, 1987-88, retail cons., 1988—. Dir. Progressive Corp., Cleve., Sunoco, Phila., Finlay Fine Jewelry, N.Y.C., Galyan's Trading Co., Indpls., Toys 'R' Us, Wayne, NJ, Henry Schein, Inc., Melville, NY. Office: 650 Madison Ave New York NY 10022-1029

MATTHEWS, PAUL AARON, lawyer; b. Memphis, May 7, 1952; s. Joseph Curtis and Sarah Rebecca (Barret) M.; m. Roberta Bartow, July 29, 1978; children: Sarah Pierrepont, Elizabeth Barret. AB, Duke U., 1974; JD, Vanderbilt U., 1977. Bar: Tenn. 1977, U.S. Dist. Ct. (we. dist.) Tenn. 1977, U.S. Dist. Ct. (ea. dist.) Mich. 1987, U.S. Dist. Ct. (ea. dist.) Tenn. 1991, U.S. Ct. Appeals (6th cir.) 1991, U.S. Dist. Ct. (ea. and we. dists.) Ark. 1995, U.S. Dist. Ct. (mid. dist.) Tenn. 1998, U.S. Dist. Ct. (no. and so. dists.) Miss. 2000, U.S. Supreme Ct. 1998; cert. in bus. bankruptcy law and consumer bankruptcy law, Am. Bd. Certification and Tenn. Comm. on Cont. Legal Edn. and Specialization. Assoc. Armstrong Allen, PLLC, Memphis, 1977-82, mem., 1982—. Chief justice Vanderbilt Law Sch. Moot Ct. Bd., Nashville, 1976-77. Co-author: Passport to Tennessee History, 1996; contbg. editor: Martindale-Hubbell Tenn. Law Digest, 1994—99; contbr. articles to profl. publs. Com. chmn. Memphis-in-May Internat. Festival, 1977-79, Tenn. Hist. Commn., 1987-97; bd. dirs. Davies Manor Assn., Brunswick, Tenn., 1994-99, pres. 1996-97; mem. Leadership Memphis Class of 1987, alumni adv. coun., 2000—; trustee Tenn. Hist. Commn. Found., 1998—, Shelby County Hist. Commn., 1997—, vice-chmn. 1999, chmn., 2000-01; commr. Tenn. Wars Commn., 1994-97; vestry Episcopal Ch. of the Holy Communion, 1995-98; trustee St. Mary's Episcopal Sch., 2001—. Recipient Newman award Memphis Heritage, Inc., 1992. Fellow, Tenn. Bar Found.; mem. ABA, SAR (Isaac Shelby chpt.), Am. Bankruptcy Inst., Tenn. Bar Assn., Memphis Bar Assn. (publs. coun. 1990-98, bd. dirs. 1999-2001, jud. practice and procedures com. 2000-02, vice chmn. professionalism com. 2003, chmn. 2004), Memphis and Shelby County Mental Health Assn. (pres. 1984-85), Duke U. Alumni Assn. (pres. Memphis chpt. 1986-88), Descendants of Early Settlers of Shelby County (v.p. 1999-2003, pres. 2004—), Sigma Alpha Epsilon. Episcopalian. Home: 4271 Heatherwood Ln Memphis TN 38117-2302

MATTHEWS, PHILIP RICHARD, lawyer; b. San Francisco, Aug. 27, 1952; s. Richard Thomas and Marjorie Hilda (Dean) M.; m. Dana Lynn Meier, Aug. 8, 1981; children: Lauren Alison, Lyndsey Ann. BA in Polit. Sci., George Washington U., 1974; JD, U. Calif.-San Francisco, 1977. Bar: Calif. 1978, U.S. Ct. Appeals (9th cir.) 1978, U.S. Dist. Ct. (no. and so. dists.) Calif. 1978, U.S. Dist. Ct. (ea. dist.) Calif. 1980. Assoc. Dinkelspiel, Pelavin, San Francisco, 1978—80, Hancock, Rothert & Bunshoft, San Francisco, 1980—85, ptnr., 1985—, mgmt. com. mem., 1989—94, 1996—99, 2004—, mng. ptnr., 1992—94, 1997—99, chairperson, 2004—. Mem. ABA, State Bar Assn. of Calif., Bar Assn. of San Francisco, Commonwealth Club. Democrat. Episcopalian. Avocations: sports, outdoors, genealogy, travel, hiking. Office: Hancock Rothert & Bunshoft Ste 300 4 Embarcadero Ctr San Francisco CA 94111-4168 Office Phone: 415-981-5550.

MATTHEWS, RIKI, retired language educator; b. Colorado Springs, Colo., Dec. 19, 1953; d. Claude and Ruth Matthews. MA in English, U. of Colo., Denver, 1988; student PH.D. in Curriculum Devel. and Instruction, Denver University, 2004—. Dir. Continuum Modern Dance Co., Denver, 1979—83; English prof. Met. State Coll., Denver, 1983—2001; editor Aigis Publications, Littleton, Colo., 1990—96; tchg. at-risk youth Humanex Acad., Lakewood, Colo., 1997—2003, ret., 2003—. Tutor Pvt., Denver, 1983—2004; editor Freelance, Denver, 1986—2004. Choreographer (modern dance performances); author: (poetry) The Bulemic (best poem of the yr., 1992); proofreading/editor (nonfiction) Since Predator Came (nominated for best nonfiction Colo. book of the yr., 1993); contbr. articles to profl. jours. Buddy for at-risk youth Rainbow Alley, Denver, Colo. Avocations: dance, writing, theater.

MATTHEWS, RONDRA J. publishing executive; d. Nedra Plummer; m. Keith Matthews. BS in Behavioral Sci., High Point U.; MBA, Rollins Coll. Various mgmt. positions Orlando (Fla.) Sentinel Comms., 1980—99, v.p., gen. mgr., 1999—2000; pres., pub., CEO Daily Press, Newport News, Va., 2000—. Office: Daily Press 7505 Warwick Blvd PO Box 746 Newport News VA 23607

MATTHEWS, STEVE ALLEN, lawyer; b. Columbia, S.C., Oct. 11, 1955; s. Philip Garland and Vernecia Neely (Wilson) M.; m. Caroline Elizabeth FitzSimons, Sept. 26, 1987; children: Philip Garland II, Nathalie FitzSimons, Caroline Salley. BA in History, U. S.C., 1977; JD, Yale U., 1980. Bar: S.C. 1980, D.C. 1982. Assoc. Boyd, Knowlton, Tate & Finlay, Columbia, 1980—81, Dewey, Ballantine, Bushby, Palmer & Wood, Washington, 1981—85; spl. counsel to asst. atty. gen. Civil Rights Divsn. U.S. Dept. Justice, Washington, 1985—86, dep. asst. atty. gen. for jud. selection, Office of Legal Policy, 1986—88; exec. asst. to U.S. Atty. Gen., 1988; mem. Haynsworth Sinkler Boyd, PA, Columbia, 1988—, mng. ptnr., 2001—. Sec. Landmark Legal Found. Mem. Federalist Soc., Nat. Assn. Bond Lawyers (bd. dirs. 1995-96), Am. Coll. Bond Counsel (bd. dirs. 1995-99), Collegiate Network, Inc. (chmn. bd. dirs.), Am. Intellectual Property Lawyers Assn., Cultural Coun. Richland and Lexington Counties, Phila. Soc., St. Andrews Soc. Columbia. Office: Haynsworth Sinkler Boyd PA 1201 Main St Fl 22 Columbia SC 29201-3226 Office Phone: 803-779-3080. E-mail: smatthews@hsblawfirm.com.

MATTHEWS, SIR STUART, aviation industry executive; b. London, May 5, 1936; came to U.S., 1974; s. Bernard De Lides and Daisy Vera (Woodcock) M.; m. Kathleen Hilary Adams, Jan. 12, 1974; children: Anthony, Caroline, Joanna. Student, Hatfield Coll. Advanced Tedh., 1958. Apprentice de Havilland Aircraft Ltd., Hatfield, 1952-53; aircraft project design engr. Hawker Siddeley Aviation Ltd., Hatfield, 1953-64; with mktg. dept. Brit. Aircraft Co., Bristol, 1964-67; gen. mgr. planning Brit. Caledonian Airways, London, 1967-74; v.p. N.Am. divsn. Fokker-VFW Internat., Washington, 1974-80; pres., CEO Fokker Aircraft USA, Alexandria, Va., 1980-93, chmn., 1993-94, Aircraft Fin. and Trade, Alexandria, 1984-94; pres., CEO Flight Safety Found., Alexandria, 1994—. Chmn. Flight Safety Found.; mem. adv. bd. Am. Security Bank. Fellow Royal Aero. Soc. (chartered engr.), Inst. Transp. (charter);mem. AIAA, Commuter Airlines Assn. Am. (chmn. assoc. mem. group 1979-80), Royal Order of Orange Nassau (The Netherlands) (knight), NEtherlands/Am. C. of C. (bd. dirs.), Alexandria C. of C. (bd. dirs.), Aero Club, Nat. Aviation Club (Washington), Royal Air Force Club (London), Wings (N.Y.C., mem. bd. govs.), Lions (pres. Engleside, Va. 1977-78), Rotary Internat., Mt. Vernon Yacht Club (commodore). Home: 9439 Mt Vernon Cir Alexandria VA 22309-3221 Office: Flight Safety Found 601 Madison St Alexandria VA 22314-1756

MATTHEWS, THOMAS J. game company executive; BS in Fin., U. So. Calif., 1986. From pres. to pres., CEO, COO Global Gaming Distributors Inc. (now Internat. Game Tech.), Reno; pres. Internat. Game Tech., 2003—, CEO, 2003—, COO, 2003—, bd. dirs. Office: International Game Technology 9295 Prototype Dr Reno NV 89521*

MATTHEWS, THOMAS M. utilities company executive; m. Sherry Matthews; children: Stephanie, Leslie. BSCE, Tex. A&M U., 1965; postgrad., U. Okla., Stanford U., Columbia U. Various engrng., mgmt. and exec. positions Exxon; exec. v.p. Tenneco Gas; pres. Tenn. Gas Pipeline Co., Texaco Refining and Mktg., Inc., Dynegy, Houston; sr. exec. v.p. Avista Corp., Spokane, 1998—, chmn. bd. dirs. Bd. dirs. Wash. CEO Roundtable; mem. adv. coun., mem. vision 2020 com. Tex. A&M U. Office: Avista Corp 1411 E Mission Ave Spokane WA 99202-2600

MATTHEWS, THOMAS MICHAEL, former energy company executive; b. Luling, Tex., May 20, 1943; s. Chester Raymond and Mary Lucille (Stutts) Matthews; m. Sherry Dianne Klein, May 25, 1968; children: Stephanie Dianne, Leslie Michelle. BSCE, Tex. A & M U., 1965; postgrad., U. Okla., 1967, UCLA, 1975, Stanford U., 1988, Columbia U., 1993. Staff engr. Exxon Co. USA, Houston, New Orleans, 1965—69, project engr. L.A., 1974—76, div. engr. Houston, 1969—74, engring. mgr. Anchorage, 1976—78; v.p. Exxon Gas, Houston, 1978—81, Tenn. Gas/Tenneco, Houston, 1981—86, pres., 1986—89; v.p., gen. mgr. Texaco USA, Houston, 1989—; pres. Texaco Gas, 1990—93; pres., CEO Texaco Refining & Mktg., Inc.; v.p. Texaco, Inc.; pres. NGC Corp., 1996—98; chmn., CEO & pres. Avista Corp., Wash. Power Co., Spokane, 1998—2001; mem. bd. dir. Global Water Tech. Inc., Denver, 2002—. Dir. Offshore Tech. Ctr.; adv. coun. Tex. A and M U., 1987—89; bd. dirs. Inroads, Inc. Contbr. articles to profl. jours.; inventor in field. Pres., chmn. Ponderosa Forest Cmty. Coun., Houston, 1980—85; mem. PTO, Scenic Pk. Sch., Anchorage, 1976—78. Mem.: Gas Rsch. Inst., Natural Gas Supply Assn., Am. Petroleum Inst., Soc. Ga. Assn., NSPE (bd. dirs.), Northgate Forest Country Club, Petroleum Club, Soc. Petroleum Club. Republican. Lutheran. Avocations: skiing, golf, reading, running, singing. Office: 433 Park Pointe DR STE 250 Golden CO 80401-7602

MATTHEWS, W. THOMAS, investment banker; Grad., McPherson Coll. With Merrill Lynch; producing mgr. N.J. brs. Smith Barney divsn. Citigroup, 1975—87; mnr. N.Y.C. br. then regional dir. Chesapeake Bay and the Atlantic regions Smith Smith Barney divsn. Citigroup, 1989—94; dir. nat. sales Citigroup, 1994—2002, pres., CEO Global Pvt. Client Divsn., 2002—. With USMC. Mem.: Securities Industry Assn. (bd. dirs. 2002—). Office: Citigroup Global Pvt Client Divsn 390 Greenwich St New York NY 10013*

MATTHEWS, WARREN WAYNE, state supreme court justice; b. Santa Cruz, Calif., Apr. 5, 1939; s. Warren Wayne and Ruth Ann (Maginnis) M.; m. Donna Stearns, Aug. 17, 1963; children: Holly Maginnis, Meredith Sample. BA, Stanford U., 1961; LL.B., Harvard U., 1964. Bar: Alaska 1965. Assoc. firm Burr, Boney & Pease, Anchorage, 1964-69, Matthews & Dunn, Matthews, Dunn and Baily, Anchorage, 1969-77; assoc. justice Alaska Supreme Ct., Anchorage, 1977—, justice, chief justice. Bd. dirs. Alaska Legal Services Corp., 1969-70. Mem. Alaska Bar Assn. (bd. govs. 1974-77), ABA, Anchorage Bar Assn.

MATTHEWS, WILLIAM, health products executive; PhD in Cell Biology, Southwestern Med. Sch., Dallas. Scientist in stem cell biology Genentech Inc., 1992—97; co-founder, pres. Deltagen, Inc., Menlo Park, Calif., 1997—, CEO, 1998—. Fellow postdoctoral fellow, Harvard Med. Sch., Princeton U. Office: Deltagen 700 Bay Rd Redwood City CA 94063-2469

MATTHEWS, WILLIAM DOTY, lawyer, consumer products manufacturing company executive; b. Oneida, N.Y., Aug. 25, 1934; s. William L. and Marjorie L. (Doty) M.; m. Ann M. Morse, Aug. 4, 1956; children: Judith Anne, Thomas John. AB, Union Coll., 1956; LLB, Cornell U., 1960. Bar: N.Y. 1960, D.C. 1962. Atty. divsn. corp. fin. SEC, Washington, 1960-62; assoc. Whitlock, Markey & Tait, Washington, 1962-69; gen. counsel Oneida (N.Y.) Ltd., 1973—86, from v.p. to exec. v.p., 1977-86, also dir., chmn., CEO, 1986-2000. Chmn., bd. dirs. Oneida Fin. Corp., Conmed Corp.; trustee, chmn. Oneida Savs. Bank. Alderman City of Oneida, 1972-79; mem. Madison County Bd. Suprs., 1984-86. Presbyterian. Home: 621 Patio Circle Dr Oneida NY 13421-1820

MATTHEWS, ZAKEE, psychiatrist, educator; Prof. psychiatry sch. medicine Stanford U., Palo Alto, Calif. Recipient Presdl. Scholar award Am. Acad. Child and Adolescent Psychiatry, 1993. Office: Stanford U Sch Med PBS Bldg C108c 401 Quarry Rd Palo Alto CA 94304-1419

MATTHIAS, GEORGE FRANK, retired educator; b. Aug. 22, 1934; s. George and Marguerite (Blanchard) M.; m. Mary Jo Avery, Aug. 18, 1956; children: Todd Avery, Tara Lynn. BS, SUNY, Cortland, 1957; MS, Syracuse U., 1962; MA, Conn. Wesleyan U., 1970. Tchr. secondary earth sci. Belleville (N.Y.) Acad., 1957-58, Croton-Harmon H.S., Croton-on-Hudson, N.Y., 1961-89; tchr., prin. Raquette Lake (N.Y.) Elem. Sch., 1958-61; ret., 1989. Mem. N.Y. State Earth Sci. Syllabus Revision Writing Commn., 1967-70, 89-91; coord. Bur. of Sci. Edn., N.Y. State Dept. Edn., 1971-72; instr. Finger Lakes Inst., Alfred U., 1970; guest staff Coll. of St. Rose, summers 1984-85, 88-90; freelance cons. earth science edn.; item writer Nat. Testing Service, Nat. Assessment for Ednl. Progress, 1984; cons. in field. Author: (with Berey, Higham, Knabel, Maust) Observation and Interpretation in Earth Science, 1972; (with Daley and Higham) Earth Science: A Study of a Changing Planet, 1986; (with Deacon) Plate Tectonics, 1980; developer: (with Snyder) Individualized Earth Science Program, 1975-89; (with Snyderetal) Prentice-Hall General Science Series, 1986, NYS Student Performance Examination (Ed. Assessment), 1994; contbr. articles to profl. jours. NSF grant, 1963, 67-70; Merit fellow Shell, 1971. Mem. Nat. Assn. Geology Tchrs., Nat. Assn. Rsch. in Sci. Tchg., Sci. Tchrs. Assn. N.Y. State, N.Y. State United Tchrs., Am. Fedn. Tchrs. Home and Office: 143 Dutch St Montrose NY 10548-1505 Fax: 914-734-1725. E-mail: gfmjmatt@mymailstation.com.

MATTHIAS, JOHN EDWARD, English literature educator; b. Columbus, Ohio, Sept. 5, 1941; s. John Marshall and Lois (Kirkpatrick) M.; m. Diana Clare Jocelyn, Dec. 27, 1967; children— Cynouai, Laura. BA, Ohio State U., 1963; MA, Stanford U., 1966; postgrad., U. London, 1967. Asst. prof. dept. English U. Notre Dame, Ind., 1966-73, assoc. prof., 1973-80, prof., 1980—. Vis. fellow Clare Hall, Cambridge U., 1966-77, assoc., 1977—; vis. prof. dept. English, Skidmore Coll., Saratoga Springs, N.Y., 1975, U. Chgo., 1980. Author: Bucyrus, 1971, Turns, 1975, Crossing, 1979, Five American Poets, 1980, Introducing David Jones, 1980, Contemporary Swedish Poetry, 1980, Bathory and Lermontov, 1980, Northern Summer, New and Selected Poems, 1984, The Battle of Kosovo, 1987, David Jones: Man and Poet: A Gathering of Ways, 1991, Reading Old Friends, 1991, Swimming at Midnight, 1995, Beltane at Aphelion, 1995, Pages: New Poems and Cuttings, 2000, Working Progress, 2002, Three-Toed Gull: Selected Poems of Jesper Svenbro, 2003, New Selected Poems, 2004. Recipient Columbia U. Transl. award, 1978, Swedish Inst. award, 1981, Poetry award Soc. Midland Authors, 1984, Ingram Merrill Found. award, 1984, 90; Woodrow Wilson fellow, 1963, Lily Endowment fellow, 1993; Fulbright grantee, 1966. Mem. AAUP, PEN, Poets and Writers, Poetry Soc. Am. (George Bogin Meml. award 1990). Office: U Notre Dame Dept English Notre Dame IN 46556

MATTHIES, FREDERICK JOHN, civil and environmental engineer; b. Omaha, Oct. 4, 1925; s. Fred. J. and Charlotte Leota (Metz) M.; m. Carol Mae Dean, Sept. 14, 1947; children: John Frederick, Jane Carolyn Matthies Goding BSCE, Cornell U., 1947; postgrad., U. Nebr., 1952-53. Diplomate Am. Acad. Environ. Engrs.; registered profl. engr., Nebr. Civil engr. Henningson, Durham & Richardson, Omaha, 1947-50, 52-54; sr. v.p. devel. Leo A. Daly Co., Omaha, 1954-90; cons. engr., 1990—. Lectr. in field; mem. dist. export coun. U.S. Dept. Commerce, 1981-83. Contbr. articles to profl. jours. Mem. Douglas County Rep. Cen. Com., Nebr., 1968-72; bd. regents Augustana Coll., Sioux Falls., S.D., 1976-89; bd. dirs. Orange County Luth. Hosp. Assn., Anaheim, Calif., 1961-62, Nebr. Humanities Coun., 1988-94, Omaha-Shizuoka City (Japan) Sister City Orgn.; trustee Luth. Med. Ctr., Omaha, 1978-82; mem. adv. bd. Marine Mil. Acad., Harlingen, Tex. 1st lt. USMCR, 1943-46, 50-52, Korea. Fellow ASCE, Instn. Civil Engrs. (London, Euro Engr. European Econ. Commn.); mem. NSPE, Am. Water Works Assn. (life), Air Force Assn., Am. Legion, VFW. Home: 950 Southridge Greens Blvd # 15 Fort Collins CO 80525-6726

MATTHIESEN, LANCE, publishing executive; m. Tracey R. Griffin, Oct. 23, 1993; children: Logan E., Cole T. BA, Bates Coll., 1985; MBA, Stanford U., 1992. Cert. Goethe Inst., Germany, 1990. Advt. sales account exec. The Wash. Post, Washington, 1992—96, mgr. new presses transition, 1996—98; sr. dir. industry mktg. Nat. Cable Telecom. Assn., Washington, 1998—99; dir. sales Cyveillance, Arlington, Va., 1999—2000; v.p. sales and mktg. Overture, Rockville, Md., 2001—03; v.p. advt. Congl. Quar., Washington, 2003—. Bd. dirs. Bright Beginnings, Washington, 1995—2001; alumni coun. Bates Coll., Lewiston, Maine, 2000—04. Scholar, Bates Coll., 1981—85, Stanford U., 1990—92. Avocations: basketball, travel, golf, triathlons. Office: Congressional Quar 1255 22nd St NW Washington DC 20037 Office Phone: 202-419-8447. Office Fax: 201-419-8743. Personal E-mail: lance.matthiesen@verizon.net. E-mail: lmatthiesen@cq.com.

MATTHIESEN, ROBERT L. education educator, farmer, rancher; b. Ponca City, Okla., Feb. 20, 1947; s. Rex Andrew and Nellie Pearl Matthiesen; m. Freda Joanne Wilkins, Dec. 12, 1976; children: Peter Andrew, Chance Lee, Trenton Jack. BS in Agr., Okla. State U., 1970, MSc in Agr., 1972; PhD in Agr., Champaign/Urbana U., 1976. Rsch. asst., agronomy dept. Okla. State U., 1970—72; teaching asst./rsch. asst. U. of Ill., Champaign/Urbana, 1972—76; asst. prof. agr. Northwestern Okla. State U., 1976—78, tchr. Billings Pub. Schools, 1978—91; farmer Billings, Okla., 1991—93; instr. biology/agr. No. Okla. Coll., Tonkawa, 1993—2004. Reviewer/programs Kay County Soil Conservation Svc., Newkirk, 1994—2003; rsch./salt fork river No. Okla. Coll., 1995—2004. Inventor (invention) Farm Jour. ($100.00 award, 1993) Chmn. bd. Union Cemetery Assoc., Billings, 1995—2004; chmn. Noble County Democrats, Okla., 1998—2004. Mem.: Okla. Wheat Growers Assn., Am. Assn. U. Professors (sec. 1999—2003), Nat. Sci. Teachers Assn., Lions Club (pres. 1992). Democrat. Baptist. Achievements include invention of tool to simplify on/off switch for ammonia tool applicator for farm use. Avocation: farm rsch. and testing. Home: 5801 Acre Billings OK 74630

MATTHIESSEN, ROBERT E. business executive, Pres., CEO Intest Corp., Cherry Hill, N.J. Office: Intest Corp 7 Esterbrook Ln Cherry Hill NJ 08003-4003

MATTICE, HARRY SANDLIN, JR., prosecutor; b. Chattanooga, Mar. 10, 1954; s. Harry Sandlin Sr. and Kathryn (McCoy) M.; m. Janet Lynn LeVan, Jan 4, 1975; children: Harry Sandlin III, Bryan Christopher, Kevin LeVan. BS, U. Tenn., Chattanooga, 1976; JD, U. Tenn., 1981. Bar: Tenn. 1981, U.S. Dist. Ct. (ea. dist.) Tenn. 1981, U.S. Ct. Appeals (6th cir.) 1984, U.S. Tax Ct. 1984, U.S. Claims Ct. 1984, U.S. Dist. Ct. (we. dist.) Tenn. 1989. Staff acct. Deloitte, Haskins & Sells, Chattanooga, 1976-78; from assoc. to ptnr. Miller & Martin, Chattanooga, 1981—2000; shareholder Baker, Donelson, Bearman & Caldwell, Chattanooga, 2000—01; U.S. atty. ea. dist. U.S. Dept. of Justice, Tenn., 2001—. Pres. Chattanooga Tax Practitioners; sr. counsel U.S. Senate Com. on Govtl. Affairs, Spl. Investigation, 1997. Asst. to pres. Chattanooga Goodwill Industries, 1988—; chmn. Hamilton County Rep. Party, 1993-95. Mem. Order of Coif, Signal Mountain Golf and Country Club, Phi Kappa Phi. Episcopalian. Home: 609 Marr Dr Signal Mountain TN 37377-2280 Office: US Atty 1110 Market St Ste 301 Chattanooga TN 37402

MATTICE, HOWARD LEROY, retired education educator; b. Roxbury, N.Y., Sept. 23, 1935; s. Charles Pierce and Loretta Jane (Ellis) M.; m. Elaine Grace Potts, Feb. 4, 1956 (dec. Jan. 2002); children: Kevin, Stephen. BA, King's Coll., 1960; MA, L.I. U., 1965, NYU, 1969; cert., CUNY, 1972; EdD, NYU, 1978. Cert. tchr. N.Y., clin. educators trainer, Fla. Dept. Edn. Social studies tchr. N.Y.C. Bd. Edn., 1961-90, mid. and jr. H.S. asst. prin., 1970-72, 73-75; assoc. prof. edn. and history Clearwater (Fla.) Christian Coll., 1990-92, chmn. divsn. of edn., prof. edn. and history, 1992-99, ret., 1999; prof. of edn. and history Clearwater Christian Coll., 2002—; social studies curriculum writer Accelerated Christian Edn., 2003. Adj. lectr. history S.I. C.C., CUNY, 1969-75; curriculum writer N.Y.C. Bd. Edn., 1985, Accelerated Christian Edn., Largo, Fla., 2003—; program reviewer Fla. Dept. Edn., Tallahassee, 1994—; item writer GED Testing Svc., Washington, 1988-92; mem. So. Assn. Colls. and Schs. Accreditation Team H.S., 1995—. Chmn. bd. New Dorp Christian Acad., S.I., 1973-90; chmn. bd. deacons New Dorp. Bapt. Ch., S.I., 1981-90. Mem. ASCD, Assn. Tchr. Educators, Nat. Coun. Social Studies, So. Assn. Colls. and Schs. (h.s. accreditation review team 1995—). Avocations: reading, travel, gardening. Office Phone: 727-726-1153.

MATTIE, JEANNE MARIE, public relations and communications consultant; b. Sendai, Japan, Aug. 4, 1950; came to U.S., 1952; d. John D. and Edna H. M.; m. Donald J. Patrican, June 14, 1986; 1 child, Julian M. Patrican. BA, U. Del., 1970. Co-founder Cyrk, Inc., Gloucester, Mass., 1975-80; pres. Mattie Assocs., Inc., Boston and Franklin Lakes, N.J., 1980—. Office: Mattie Assocs Inc 707 Horseshoe Trl Franklin Lakes NJ 07417-1532 Fax: 201-848-7892. E-mail: jmmattie@aol.com.

MATTILA, MARY JO KALSEM, elementary and art educator; b. Canton, Ill., Oct. 26, 1944; d. Joseph Nelson and Bernice Nora (Milbauer) Kalsem; m. John Peter Mattila, Jan. 27, 1968. BS in Art, U. Wis., 1966; student, Ohio State U., 1972, Drake U., 1981; MS in Ednl. Adminstrn., Iowa State U., 1988. Cert. tchr., prin., supr., adminstr., art tchr., secondary tchr., Iowa. Tchr. 2d grade McHenry (Ill.) Pub. Schs., 1966-67, Wisconsin Hts. Schs., Black Earth, Wis., 1967-69; substitute tchr. Columbus (Ohio) City Schs., 1969-70; elem. art tchr. Southwestern City Schs., Columbus, 1972-73; adminstrv. intern Ames, Iowa, 1984-86; lead tchr. at Roosevelt Sch. Ames Cmty. Schs., 1986-87, art vertical curriculum chair, 1983-89, art educator, elem. and spl. edn., 1973—2003. Author articles. Fundraiser Altrusa, Ames, 1992—; mem. human rels. commn. City of Ames, prevention policy bd. youth and shelter svcs. Recipient Very Spl. Svc. award for Disting. Svc. in Very Spl. Arts, Gov. of Iowa, 1984. Mem.: LWV, Ctrl. Iowa Orchid Soc., Questers, Am. Orchid Soc. Avocations: collecting old stoneware jugs, growing orchids, reading. Home: 2822 Duff Ave Ames IA 50010-4710 Office: Ames Cmty Schs 120 S Kellogg Ave Ames IA 50010-6719

MATTINGLY, J. VIRGIL, JR., federal lawyer; b. Leonardtown, Md., Oct. 18, 1944; BBA in Acctg., JD, George Washington U. Sr. atty. Fed. Res. Bd., Washington, 1974-79, asst. gen. counsel, 1979-81, assoc. gen. counsel, 1981-85, dep. gen. counsel, 1985-89, gen. counsel, 1989—. With JAGC, U.S. Army, 1970-74. Office: Fed Res Bd Bd Govs 20th & C Sts NW Washington DC 20551-0001

MATTINGLY, JAMES EDWARD, finance educator, writer; b. Monett, Mo., July 16, 1962; s. Jerry Lee and Janet Florence Mattingly; m. Michelle Lynn Organ, Oct. 29, 1994; children: Hannah Michelle, Luke Jameson. BSBA, Avila Coll., Kansas City, Mo., 1988; MBA, S.W. Mo. State U., 1994; PhD, U. of Mo., 2003. Prof. bus. U. No. Iowa, Cedar Falls. Fellow Preparing Future Faculty fellow, U. of Mo., 2001—02, Rsch. fellow, 2002, U. of No. Iowa, 2003—04; scholar Ponder scholar, U. of Mo., 1999—2003, Grad. Profl. Coun. scholar, 2001. Mem.: Soc. for the Advancement of Socio-Econs., Internat. Assn. for Bus. and Soc., Acad. of Mgmt., Beta Gamma Sigma (life). Liberal. Catholic. Avocations: writing, gardening, art.

MATTINGLY, MACK FRANCIS, former ambassador, former senator, entrepreneur; b. Anderson, Ind., Jan. 7, 1931; m. Carolyn Longcamp, 1957 (dec.); children: Jane, Anne; m. Leslie Ann Davisson, 1998. BS, Ind. U., 1957. Acct. supr. IND, Arvin, Ind., 1957-59; mktg. mgr. IBM, Ga., 1959-79; owner, pres. M's Inc., Ga., 1975-80; U.S. senator from Ga., 1981-87; asst. sec. gen. def. support NATO, Brussels, 1987-90; amb. to Seychelles Dept. State, 1992-93. Spkr./author econ., def., fgn. policy, entrepreneur, 1993—; mem. U.S. Senate Com. Appropriations, chmn. legis. and mil. constrn. subcoms.; mem. energy and water devel., agt. rural devel., treasury, postal svc. and gen. govt., mil. constrn. legis. subcoms., U.S. Senate com. Banking, Housing and Urban Affairs, chmn. rural housing, econ. policy subcoms.; mem. select com. ethics, 1981-83, joint econ. com., 1983-87; chmn. Rep. Com. on Coms., mem. Rep. Senate Leadership, 1985-87, Holocaust Commn.; U.S. del. GATT, Geneva, 1982; bd. dirs. CompuCredit Corp.; hon. co-chmn. GMACC, Hemisphere, Inc. Author 40 U.S. Sen. Bills, Amendments and Resolutions. Sgt.-at-Arms, Rep. Nat. Convs., del. Georgian Rep. Party Convs., 1964-90; chmn. 8th Dist. Goldwater for Pres., 1964, Ga. 8th Congl. Dist., Cand. U.S. Congress, 8th Dist., 1966; mem. Ga. Rep. Ctrl. Com.; mem. Ga. Exec. Com., vice chmn., 1968-75, chmn., 1975-77; elected 1st Rep. U.S. Senator from Ga. since 1871, 1980; bd. dirs. NOVECON., Cumberland Preservation Soc., Inst. for Global Econ. Growth, Ga. Portts Authority; hon. bd. dirs. M.L. King Jr. Fed. Holiday Commn., Brunswick Golden Isles C. of C. Staff sgt. USAF, 1951-55. Recipient S.E. Father of Yr. award 1984, Ga. Wildlife Fed. Conservationist of Yr. award 1985, Selective Svc. System Dist. Svc. Gold medal 1985, Watchdog of Treasury award 1981-86, Nat. Taxpayers Union Taxpayers Best Friend award 1981-86, NFIB's Guardian of Small Bus. award 1981-86, Am. Security Coun. award 1981-86, Sec. Def. medal for Outstanding Pub. Svc. 1988. Mem. Am. Legion. Episcopalian.

MATTIS, LOUIS PRICE, pharmaceutical and consumer products company executive; b. Balt., Dec. 12, 1941; s. Louis Wadsworth and Sara Helene (Myers) M.; children: Louis Wadsworth, Deborah Cook Collier. AB in Internat. Affairs, Lafayette Coll., Easton, Pa., 1962; MBA, Tulane U., 1964. V.p., gen. mgr. Warner Lambert Co., Manila, 1971-74, regional dir. Hong Kong, 1974-76, region pres. Sydney, Australia, 1976-79; exec. v.p. Americas-Far East Richardson-Vicks, Inc., 1979-81, pres. Americas-Far East, 1981-84, exec. v.p., 1985-87; group v.p. Sterling Winthrop Inc., N.Y.C., 1987-88, chmn., pres., CEO, 1988-94; dir. Salomon Bros. Fund, 1992—. Mem. Shek-o Golf Club, Turnberry Golf Club, Roaring Fork Club, Snowmass Club. Avocations: skiing, golf, woodworking. Home: 146 Oak Ridge Rd Snowmass Village CO 81615 Office: PO Box 6535 Snowmass Village CO 81615-6535

MATTISON, DONALD ROGER, gynecologist, toxicologist, educator, medical association administrator, public health service officer; b. Mpls., Apr. 28, 1944; s. Milford Zachary and Elizabeth Ruth (Davey) M.; m. Margaret Rose Libby, Jan. 28, 1967; children: Jon, Amy. BA cum laude in Chemistry and Math., Augsburg Coll., Mpls., 1966, MS in Chemistry, MIT, 1968; MD, Columbia U., 1973. Resident in ob-gyn Presbyn. Hosp., N.Y.C., 1973-75, 77-78; commd. officer, rsch. assoc. USPHS, 1975, advanced through grades to comdr., 1984; rsch. assoc. Nat. Inst. Child Health and Human Devel., NIH, Bethesda, Md., 1975-77, med. officer, 1978-84; assoc. prof. ob-gyn. U. Ark., Little Rock, 1984-87; prof. U. Pitts., 1987-90, assoc. prof. toxicology, 1984-88, prof., 1988-90, dean Grad. Sch. Pub. Health, prof., 1990-99; med. dir. March of Dimes, 1998—2002; sr. advisor to dirs. NICHD and CRMC, 2002—. Contbr. articles, astracts, letters and editls. to profl. publs. Recipient Am. Chem. Soc. medal Minn. sect. Am. Chem. Soc., 1966, Assn. Am. Publs. award, 1983. Fellow AAAS; mem. APHA, Inst. of Medicine NAS, Soc. Risk Analysis (editl. bd. jour. 1988—), Pitts. chpt. Soc. Risk Analysis, Am. Assn. Cancer Rsch., N.Y. Acad. Sci., Am. Coll. Toxicology, Am. Fertility Soc., Soc. Gynecologic Investigation, Soc. Toxicology. Avocations: photography, computer sciences, fly fishing, cross country skiing. Office: NICHD/NIH 6100 Executive Blvd MSC 7510 Bethesda MD 20892 E-mail: mattisod@mail.nih.gov.

MATTLI, WALTER, political scientist, educator; b. Luzern, Switzerland; Lic., U. Geneva, 1986; PhD, U. Chgo., 1994. Asst. prof. Columbia U., N.Y.C., 1995—2001, assoc. prof., 2001—. Recipient J.P. Morgan Internat. prize, Am. Acad. Berlin, 2003. Mem.: Am. Polit. Sci. Assn. (Helen Dwight Reid award 1995). Office: Oxford U St Johns Coll OX1 3JP Oxford England

MATTOLI, AGOSTINO MARRON, international business projects advisor; b. Rome, Feb. 23, 1938; s. Giorgio Mattoli and Doris Virginia Marron; m. Patrizia Chiavarelli Costa, June 11, 1966; children: Maurizio, Michele, Giorgio, Alessio, Agostino. BA in Arts and Sci., Rutgers U., 1962. Internat. advisor to pres. Fisvina, Rome, 1991-95; cons. Armemise Harva Found. Sci. Rsch. in Medicine, 1995—96; advisor, asst. to chmn. Armemise-Harvard Found. for Rsch. in Medicine, 1996—99; bd. dirs. Orders of the Royal House of Savoy, 2000—. Dir. bus. rels. Africa Ctr./Oil and Mineral Explorations, Rome and London, 1970—78. Editor, founder (journal) Cambridge Transcontinental, 1957 (Spl. Fgn. Student award, 1958). Cons. internat. ops. Red Cross, Rome, 1996-2001. Named a knight, officer, Savoy Order SS Maurizio & Lazzaro, senator, Sacro Romano Impero; recipient award for hunting achievements, Safari Club Internat., 1968—2000. Mem.: Gruppo Savoia, Royal Circolo Canottieri Tevere Remo (life socio sr. 1954), Sons of Am. Revolution, Inst. of The Holy Roman Empire. Roman Catholic. Avocations: travel, sailing, yachting, big game hunting. E-mail: trailmas@unete.cl.

MATTOO, AUTAR K. biochemist; b. Prithvi N. and Soomawati Mattoo; children: Kanchan Autar, Amrita. BSc, J & K U., Kashmir, India, 1963; MSc, Maharaja Sayajirao U. of Baroda, Vadodara, India, 1965, PhD, 1969. Lectr. Maharaja Sayajirao U. of Baroda, 1969—79; postdoctoral rsch. fellow U. Adelaide, Australia, 1975—76; vis. scientist USDA, Beltsville, Md., 1976—77, joint rsch. assoc., 1980—84, plant physiologist, 1984—88, rsch. leader, 1988—; DAAD scholar Weizmann Inst. of Sci., Israel, 1979—80. Cons. biochemist Biotech Rsch. Labs., Rockville, Md., 1981—82; adj. prof. U. Md., Catonsville, 1986—93, spl. mem. grad. faculty, College Park, 1996—98. Editor: (book) The Plant Hormone Ethylene. Editor newsletter Kashmiri Overseas Assn., Rockville, Md., 1982—86. Named Scientist of the Yr., Beltsville Agrl. Rsch. Ctr., 1998; recipient Svc. to U.S. award, Israel BARD TAC, 2002. Achievements include research in regulation of ethylene biosynthesis and fruit ripening; molecular aspects of chloroplast function with particular emphasis on the photosystem II reaction center proteins; first to novel concept of regulation of protein dynamics by light using a protein critical to photosynthesis. He showed that the D1 photosystem II protein is photo-regulated; complete metabolic life history of this key component of photosynthesis and demonstrated its reversible, photo-regulated posttranslational covalent attachment of phosphate; regulatory interaction and metabolic linkage between biosynthesis of polyamines and ethylene in higher plants.

MATTOON, JAMES RICHARD, biology professor; b. Loveland, Colo., Dec. 9, 1930; s. Arthur Maxwell and Margaret (Scilley) M.; m. Martha Jean McKissick, June 16, 1953; children: Thomas Edward, Jean Ellen. BS in Chemistry, U. Ill., 1953; MS in Biochemistry, U. Wis., 1954, PhD in Biochemistry, 1957. From instr. to asst. prof. chemistry U. Nebr., Lincoln, 1957-62; rsch. assoc. physiol. chemistry Johns Hopkins U. Sch. Medicine, Balt., 1962-64, from asst. to assoc. prof. physiol. chemistry, 1964-79; prof. biology U. Colo., Colorado Springs, 1979—, dir. Biotech Ctr., 1988—. Vis. prof. biochemistry Fed. U. Rio de Janeiro, 1975-77; vis. rsch. prof. Autonomous U. Mex., Mexico City, summer 1971, 74, San Marcos U., Lima, Peru, 1974, faculty of medicine U. Buenos Aires, summer 1980, 84, 93; organizing chmn. Rocky Mountain Microbrewing Symposium, Colorado Springs, 1995—. Contbr. rsch. articles to profl. jours. Fellow in chem. tchg. and rsch. Nat. Acad. Sci., U.S. and Brazil, 1975-77. Mem. Am. Chem. Soc., Am. Soc. for Biochemistry and Molecular Biology, Am. Soc. Brewing Chemists, Genetics Soc. of Am., Nat. Acad. Exact Phys. and Natural Scis. of Argentina (corr. mem.), Sigma Xi. Achievements include patent for enhancing production of hemoproteins. Home: 1090 Garlock Ln Colorado Springs CO 80918-3134 Office: Biotech Ctr 1420 Austin Bluffs Pkwy Colorado Springs CO 80918-3733 Office Phone: 719-262-3231. E-mail: jmattoon@corb.net., jmattoon@mail.uccs.edu.

MATTOON, PETER MILLS, lawyer; b. Bryn Mawr, Pa., Oct. 22, 1931; s. Harold Gleason and Marguerite Jeanette (Mills) M.; m. Mary Joan Henley, June 27, 1953; children: Pamela M. Zisselman, R. Stephen, Peter H., Philip P. AB, Dartmouth Coll., 1953; LLB, Harvard U., 1959; LLD (hon.), Widener U., 2001. Bar: Pa. 1960. Assoc. Ballard Spahr Andrews & Ingersoll, Phila., 1959-67; ptnr. Ballard Spahr Andrews & Ingersoll, LLP, Phila., 1967—2001, sr. counsel, 2002—. Emeritus trustee Episcopal Acad., Merion, Pa., 1970—, past chmn.; trustee, v.p. Widener Meml. Found., Lafayette Hill, Pa., 1972—; trustee, vice-chmn. Thomas Jefferson U., Phila., 1989—; overseer Widener U. Law Sch., Wilmington, 1979—. Lt. USN, 1953-56. Office: Ballard Spahr Andrews & Ingersoll LLP 1735 Market St Fl 51 Philadelphia PA 19103-7599

MATTOS, WILLIAM HAROLD, trade association executive, newspaper publisher; b. Calif., July 4, 1952; s. Irma A. Mattos; m. Susan Elizabeth Coelho, Nov. 11, 1978; children: Antoinette, Natalie. BS in Journalism, Calif. Polytech. State U., 1974; MS, U. Wis., 1975. Pres., pub. Mattos Newspapers, Inc., Newman, Calif., 1976—; pres. Calif. Poultry Fedn., Modesto, Calif., 1991—. Dir. Stanislaus County Fair Bd., Turlock, Calif., 1993, Agrl. Network, Sacramento, Calif., 1994—. Bd. regents Stanislaus State U., Turlock, 1999; bd. govs. Doctor's Hosp., Modesto, Calif., 2001; area 9 coord. Gov. George W. Bush for Pres., Modesto, 2000; dir. Stanislaus County Fair, Turlock, Calif.,

1994; campaign cabinet United Way of Stanislaus County, Modesto, 1999; bd. supr. Stanislaus County Bd. Suprs., 1990-91. Recipient John Silveira Meml. Svc. award Newman C. of C., 1990; named Outstanding Young Man of Am. Calif. Jaycees, 1986, Grand Marshall Newman Fall Festival, 1990, Disting. Citizen of Yr. Summer League Bseball, 1980; Paul Harris fellow Newman Rotary Club. Mem. Newman Rotary Club (Paul Harris fellow 1985), Phi Kappa Phi. Avocations: walking, swimming, travel, speaking. Office: Calif Poultry Fedn 3117A McHenry Ave Modesto CA 95350

MATTOX, DOUGLAS E. otolaryngologist; MD, Yale U., 1969—73. Cert. MD Am Bd. Otolaryngology. Chair, dept. of otolaryngology Emory U. Sch. of Medicine, Atlanta, Ga., 1993—2003. Office: Emory University School of Medicine 1365 Clifton Rd A 2328 Atlanta GA 30322

MATTOX, ETHEL ODESSA, writer; b. Houston, July 9, 1950; d. Gordy Mattox and Effie Olden Jones; m. Curtis Bernard West, Feb. 23, 1980; children: Earnest James, Roger Keith. At, Jarvis Christian Coll., Hawkins, Tex., 1968—70. Prodn. worker, comm. Motorola, Inc., Phoenix, 1971—85; prodn. worker Compaq Computer, Houston, 1988—89; casual US Post Office, Houston, 1986. Participant leadership workshop Motorola, Inc., Phoenix, 1977, participant S-D comm. workshop, 78; entrepreneur of home remedy products. Author: (poetry) Inspirational, 2000; inspirational spkr., 2002—03; performer: Bible Prayer Band, 2002—03, author poetry listed in various publs. Asst. mgr. customer svc. Tamina Cmty. Ctr., 2003. Democrat. Avocations: music, reading, writing, sewing, cooking. Home: #811 9393 Tidwell Houston TX 77078

MATTOX, ROBERT F. architectural firm executive; BArch, Rice U.; MBA, U. Mich. COO Payette Assocs. Inc., Boston, 1997—. Author: Financial Management for Architects; co-author: Success Strategies for Design Professionals. Fellow: AIA. Office: Payette Assocs Inc 285 Summer St Boston MA 02210-1522*

MATTRAN, DONALD ALBERT, management consultant, educator; b. Chgo., July 8, 1934; s. George Charles and Lucille Alice (Boule) M.; m. Betty Elena Flores, July 18, 1953 (div. Mar. 1988); children: Donald, Julie, Kimberly, Guy, Christy; m. Rose Lynn Castellano, May, 1988. B.Mus., U. Mich., 1957, M.Mus., 1960. Tchr. Van Buren Schs., Belleville, Mich., 1957-61; asst. prof. U. N.H., Durham, 1961-65, Boston U., 1965-66; assoc. prof. Hartt Sch. Music, West Hartford, Conn., 1966-82, dean, 1971-80; dir. Syracuse U. Sch. Music, N.Y., 1982-83; dean Sch. Fine and Performing Arts Montclair State Coll, Upper Montclair, N.J., 1983-87; pres. Sales Consultants of Sarasota (Fla.) Inc., 1987—. Cons. Music div. Kaman Corp., Bloomfield, Conn.; cons., evaluator Nat. Assn. Schs. of Music and Joint Commn. Theater and Dance Accreditation; guest condr. Hartford Symphony Orch., Hartt Opera Theatre, All-State Festivals, 1976-83, Soc. New Music, Syracuse, N.J. Sch. Arts Orch., 1985-87. Co-author: (with Mary Rasmussen) A Teacher's Guide to the Literature of Woodwind Instruments, 1966; condr.: rec. Concerto for Cello and Jazz Band, 1972. Chmn. adv. com. Prodigy Inc., Syracuse, 1982-86; trustee Conn. Opera Assn., 1977-80; bd. advs. Watkinson Sch. Creative Arts Program, Hartford, 1977-80; mem. humanities adv. com. N.J. Dept. Higher Edn., 1984—; mem. multi-disciplinary panel N.J. State Council on Arts, 1985-87; mem. adv. com. on auditions Met. Opera Nat. Council, 1984-87; mem. adv. com. Frank and Lydia Bergen Found., 1986-87. Mem. Nat. Assn. Schs. Music (exec. bd., sec. 1978-81). Home: Apt 204 888 Boulevard Of The Arts Sarasota FL 34236-4827 Office: 1343 Main St Ste 600 Sarasota FL 34236-5630 Office Phone: 941-365-5151.

MATTRICK, DON A. interactive entertainment software company executive; Founder, chmn. Distinctive Software Inc. (acquired by Electronic Arts in 1991), 1982—91; sr. v.p. N.Am. Studios, exec. v.p., gen. mgr. EA Canada, v.p. Electronic Arts, 1991—96, exec. v.p. N.Am. Studios, 1996—97, pres. Worldwide Studios, 1997—. Office: Electronic Arts 209 Redwood Shores Pkwy Redwood City CA 94065*

MATTSON, CAROL LINNETTE, social services administrator; b. Frederic, Wis., Oct. 3, 1946; d. Clarence Waldemar and Lucille Anna Mathilda (Bengtson) Hedlund; m. Wesley Harlan Mattson, June 24, 1967; 1 child, Aaron Ray. BS, U. Wis., Menomonie, 1968. Home econs. tchr. Luck (Wis.) High Sch., 1968-72; clk. Daniels Twp., Siren, Wis., 1973-75; family living instr. Wis. Indianhead Tech. Inst., New Richmond, 1974-77; aging program dir. Polk County, Balsam Lake, Wis., 1977—. Treas., bd. dirs. Polk County Transp. for the Disabled and Elderly, Inc., Balsam Lake, 1978—; mem. com. Long Term Support Com., Balsam Lake, 1985—. Mem. Wis. Assn. Nutrition Dirs., Wis. Assn. Aging Unit Dirs. Lutheran. Avocations: reading, needlecraft. Office: Polk County Aging Programs 300 Polk County Plz Ste 20 Balsam Lake WI 54810-9096

MATTSON, CLARENCE RUSSELL, safety engineer; b. Norwood, Mass., Nov. 3, 1924; s. Clarence R. and Jane P. (Dawson) M.; m. Constance W. Towne, June 7, 1953; children: Jennifer Lynn, Sue Ann. AA in Transp., Northeastern U., 1953, BBA, 1956. Cert. safety profl.; registered profl. engr., Calif. Ins. industry safety engr., 1953-62; mgr. accident prevention Dravo Corp., Pitts., 1962-72; corp. mgr. safety and environ. affairs Perini Corp., Framingham, Mass., 1972-84; dir. safety and tng. The Marr Co., South Boston, Mass., 1984; mng. dir. Long Beach-L.A. rail project Transit Ins. Adminstrs.-L.A. County Transp. Commn., 1984-86; v.p. tech. svcs. Fred S. James & Co., Short Hills, N.J., 1987-89; pres. Athena Assocs. Ltd., Safety Mgmt. Cons., Sunset Beach, N.C., 1990—. Deacon Scituate (Mass.) Congl. Ch. Recipient Disting. Svc. award Nat. Safety Coun., 1988. Mem. Am. Soc. Safety Engrs., Nat. Safety Coun. (hon. life, past gen. chmn. constrn. exec. com., disting. svc. award 1988), Assn. Gen. Contractors Am. (past chmn. safety and health com., safety engrs. adv. com.), Nat. Constructors Assn., Vets. of Safety, Mass. Safety Coun. (bd. dirs.), Mass. Constrn. Safety Congress (bd. dirs.), Elks. Republican. Home and Office: 655 Kings Ct Sunset Beach NC 28468-5326

MATTSON, HAROLD FRAZYER, JR., mathematics professor; b. Ann Arbor, Mich., Dec. 7, 1930; s. Harold Frazyer and Jane (Reynolds) M.; m. Jeanette Asare, Oct. 2, 1966; children: David Frazyer, Jennifer. AB magna cum laude, Oberlin Coll., 1951; PhD, MIT, 1955; Docteur Honoris Causa, U. Paul Sabatier, Toulouse, France, 1992. Mathematician AF Cambridge Rsch. Ctr., Bedford, Mass., 1955-60; mathematician Applied Rsch. Lab. GTE Sylvania, Waltham, Mass., 1960-69, mathematician Needham, Mass., 1969-71; owner Frazyer Rsch. Co., Syracuse, N.Y., 1971—; prof. Syracuse U., 1971-94, rsch. prof., 1994—. Mem. conf. bd. Applied Algebra and Error-Correcting Codes Symposia, 1986—91, 1997; sci. dir. Applied Algebra and Error-Correcting Codes 7, Toulouse, 1989; sci. co-chair Applied Algebra and Error-Correcting Codes 9, New Orleans, 1991, Applied Algebra and Error-Correcting Codes 12, Toulouse, 1997; cons. in field of discrete math. Author: Discrete Mathematics, 1993; mem. editl. bd. Applicable Algebra in Engring., Comm. and Computing, 1990—, Jour. Discrete Math. Scis. and Cryptography, 1998—, others; contbr. articles to profl. jours. Founding pres. S.E. Univ. Neighborhood Assn., Syracuse, 1973. Fellow IEEE; mem. Am. Math. Soc., Math. Assn. Am. Office Phone: 315-443-3046. Business E-Mail: hmattson@syr.edu.

MATTSON, JAMES STEWART, lawyer, environmental scientist, educator; b. Providence, July 22, 1945; s. Irving Carl and Virginia (Lutey) M.; m. Carol Sandry, Aug. 15, 1964 (div. 1979); children: James, Birgitta; m. Rana A. Fine, Jan. 5, 1983. BS in Chemistry, U. Mich., 1966, MS, 1969, PhD, 1970; JD, George Washington U., 1979. Bar: D.C. 1979, Fla. 1983, U.S. Dist. Ct. D.C. 1979, U.S. Dist. Ct. (so. dist.) Fla. 1984, U.S. Ct. Appeals (D.C. cir.) 1979, U.S. Ct. Claims 1985, U.S. Supreme Ct. 1985, U.S. Ct. Appeals (11th cir.) 1985, U.S. Ct. Appeals (5th cir.) 1987, U.S. Ct. Appeals (fed. cir.) 1990. Staff scientist Gulf Gen. Atomic Co., San Diego, 1970-71; dir. R & D Ouachita Industries, Inc., Monroe, La., 1971-72; asst. prof. chem. oceanography Rosenstiel Sch. Marine & Atmospheric Sci., U. Miami, Fla., 1972-76; phys. scientist NOAA, Washington, 1976-78; mem. profl. staff & congl. liaison Nat. Adv. Commn. on Oceans and Atmosphere, 1978-80; ptnr. Mattson & Pave, Washington, Miami, Key Largo, 1980-86, Mattson & Tobin, Key Largo, 1987-2000; founder/CEO Great House of Wine, Inc, Ft. Lauderdale, Fla. and Napa, Calif., 1997—2003; sole practitioner Key Largo, Fla., 2000—. Adj. prof. law U. Miami, 1983-93; cons. Alaska Dept. Environ. Conservation, 1981-91. Author: (with H.B. Mark) Activated Carbon: Surface Chemistry and Adsorption from Solution, 1971; editor (with others): Computers in Chemistry and Instrumentation, 8 vols., 1972-76; The Argo Merchant Oil Spill: A Preliminary Scientific Report, 1977, (with H.B. Mark) Water Quality Measurement: Modern Analytical Techniques, 1981; contbr. articles to profl. jours. Candidate dist. 120 Fla. Ho. of Reps., 1994. Fellow Fed. Water Pollution Control Adminstrn., 1967-68; recipient Spl. Achievement award U.S. Dept. Commerce, 1976-77; Regents Alumni scholar U. Mich., 1963. Mem. ABA, Am. Chem. Soc. (chmn. Symposium on Oil Spill Indentification 1971), Order of Coif. Address: PO Box 586 Key Largo FL 33037-0586 Office Phone: 305-451-3951. Personal E-mail: mattsonj@bellsouth.net.

MATTSON, JOY LOUISE, oncological nurse; b. Moline, Ill., Feb. 1, 1956; d. Norman O. and Jeannette (Squier) M.; m. Duncan F. Crannell, Sept. 9, 1988. BA magna cum laude, Bates Coll., 1977; MTS, Harvard U., 1982; BSN magna cum laude, Rutgers U., Newark, 1988; MLS, Rutgers U., 1993. RN, N.J. Staff nurse oncology Muhlenberg Reg. Med. Ctr., Plainfield, N.J., 1987-88; staff nurse St. Lawrence Rehab. Ctr., Lawrenceville, N.J., 1988-89; clin. rsch. asst. G.H. Besselaar Assocs., Princeton, N.J., 1990-91; med. writer Convatec, Skillman, N.J., 1991-92, G.H. Besselaar Assocs., Princeton, N.J., 1992-94; sr. clin. safety assoc. Pfizer Inc., N.Y.C., 1994-99, sr. project mgr., antibiotics, 1999-2000, mgr. regulatory submissions, 2000—. Mem. Phi Beta Kappa. Home: 653 Ravine Rd Plainfield NJ 07062-2037

MATTSON, MARLIN ROY ALBIN, health facility administrator, psychiatry educator; b. Bellingham, Wash., Apr. 25, 1939; s. Conrad Roy and Ruth Viola (Thompson) M. BA, U. Wash., 1961, MD, 1965. Diplomate Am. Bd. Psychiatry and Neurology. Intern and resident in medicine Cornell U. program at Bellevue and Meml. Hosps., N.Y.C., 1965-67; resident in psychiatry Payne Whitney Clin. The N.Y. Hosp., N.Y.C., 1969-72, chief resident in psychiatry, 1972-73, asst. med. dir., 1973-89, assoc. med. dir., 1989-99; asst. med. dir. quality assurance Westchester Divsn. N.Y. Hosp., White Plains, 1979-89, assoc. med. dir. quality assurance, 1989-93, head quality assurance program dept. psychiatry N.Y.C., 1979-94; assoc. med. dir. for quality mgmt. Dept. Psychiatry N.Y. Presbyn. Hosp., Payne Whitney Clinic and Westchester divsn., 1999—2001, assoc. vice chmn. quality mgmt., 2002—03, assoc. vice chmn. compliance, 2003—. Asst. prof. psychiatry Cornell U. Med. Coll., N.Y.C., 1973-79, assoc. prof. clin. psychiatry, 1979—, sec. gen. faculty coun., 1999-2001, vice chmn. gen. faculty coun., 2001-03, chmn. gen. faculty coun., 2003—; bd. visitors Manhattan Psychiat. Ctr., 1991—; bd. dirs. N.Y. County Health Svcs. Rev. Orgn., N.Y.C., 1983-95; mem. stds. com. URAC/Am. Accreditation Health Care Commn., 1996-2000, bd. dirs., 2000—. Editor Manual of Psychiat. Quality Assurance, 1992; contbr. numerous articles to profl. jours. Capt. U.S. Army Med. Corp., 1967-69, Korea. Fellow Am. Psychiat. Assn. (disting., mem. nat. com. on quality assurance 1988-95, chmn. 1992-95, mem. com. champus peer rev. program 1984-86, sec. N.Y. County dist. br. 1987-91, pres.-elect 1991-92, pres. 1992-93, co-pres. 1995-96, assembly rep. 1996-2003, cons. or mem. nat. com. on stds. and survey procedures 1996—), N.Y. Acad. Medicine (com. pub. health 1984-92, sect. on psychiatry 1993-94, chmn. 1994-95); mem. N.Y. State Psychiat. Assn. (chmn. peer rev. com. 1982-95, mem. com. econ. affairs 1995—), N.Y. County Med. Soc. (bd. dirs. 2002—), Republican. Episcopalian. Avocations: piano, european travel, theater, swedish-american organizations. Home: 501 E 87th St Apt 4J New York NY 10128-7609 Office: NY Presbyterian Hosp Payne Whitney Psychiat Clinic 525 E 68th St New York NY 10021-4885 Office Phone: 212-746-3775. E-mail: mmattson@med.cornell.edu.

MATTSON, STEPHEN JOSEPH, lawyer; b. Abilene, Tex., Oct. 11, 1943; s. Joseph Martin and Dorothy Irene (Doyle) M.; m. Lynn Louise Mitchell, Mar. 13, 1965; children: Eric, Laura. BA (hon.), U. Ill., 1965, JD (hon.), 1970. Bar: Ill., 1970, U.S. Dist. Ct. (no. dist.) Ill. 1970. Assoc. Mayer, Brown, Rowe & Maw, Chgo., 1970—77, ptnr., 1978—. Mem. ABA, Ill. State Bar Assn., Chgo. Bar Assn., Order of Coif. Office: Mayer Brown Rowe & Maw 190 S La Salle St Ste 3100 Chicago IL 60603-3441

MATTSSON, AKE, psychiatrist, physician; b. Stockholm, May 30, 1929; came to U.S., 1956, naturalized, 1964; s. Erik H. and Thyra (Bergtsson) M.; m. Margareta Fürst, Jan. 5, 1953; children: Erik, Peter, Nicholas; m. Judith Whitley Powell, Nov. 25, 2000. MB, Karolinska Inst., Stockholm, 1950, MD, 1955. Intern Vanderbilt U. Med. Sch., Nashville, 1955-56; resident in pediat. and child psychiatry Karolinska Hosp., Stockholm, 1958-60; fellow in child devel. Case Western Res. U. Med. Sch., 1957-58, resident in psychiatry and child psychiatry, 1960-64, asst. prof. psychiatry, 1964-70; prof. psychiatry and pediat. U. Va. Med. Sch., 1970-77, U. Pitts Med. Sch., 1977-78; prof. psychiatry and pediat., dir. divsn. child and adolescent psychiatry NYU Med. Sch., 1978-85, rsch. prof. psychiatry, 1985—; prof. psychiatry U. Va. Med. Sch., 1985-91; prof. psychiatry and pediat., dir. divsn. child and adolescent psychiatry Med. Sch., East Carolina U., Greenville, NC, 1991-97; med. dir. divsn. mental health V.I. Dept. Health, St. Thomas, 1997—2003; med. dir. First Home Care, Washington, 2003—. Clin. prof. psychiatry Med. Sch. George Washington U., 2004—; sr. attending psychiatrist Riverside Hosp., Washington, 2004—. Contbr. numerous articles to med. jours. Served with Swedish Navy, 1948-59. Fulbright-Hays grantee, 1975. Mem. Am. Psychiat. Assn., Am. Psychoanalytical Assn., N.Y. Psychiat. Soc., Am. Acad. Child Adolescent Psychiatry, N.Y. Acad. Scis., Soc. Biol. Psychiatry, Am. Acad. Psychiatry and the Law. Office: 700 New Hampshire Ave NW Apt 1409 Washington DC 20037

MATULICH, SERGE, accounting educator, author; b. Split, Croatia, June 8, 1933; came to U.S., 1946; s. Daniel M. and Josephine (Schuster) Raseta; m. Margarete Manderscheid, Dec. 7, 1957; children: Alexander Matulich, Erika Matulich. BS in Acctg. with honors, Calif. State U., Sacramento, 1964; PhD in Bus., U. Calif., Berkeley, 1971. CPA, Fla.; cert. cost analyst. Grad. asst. U. Calif., Davis, 1964-65; asst. prof. Calif. State U., Hayward, 1966-67; assoc. in acctg. U. Calif., Berkeley, 1968-71, vis. asst. prof., 1974-75; asst. prof. Sch. Bus. Ind. U., 1971-76; assoc. prof. acctg. Sch. Bus. Tex. Christian U., 1976-84; vis. prof. U. North Tex., spring 1983; prof. Crummer Grad. Sch. Bus. Rollins Coll., Winter Park, Fla., 1984—2001, prof. emeritus, 2002—. Bd. dirs. Marconi Med. Ctr., Inc., Sacramento, 1967-71, Bazeghi Corp., Oakland, Calif., 1968-71, Crescent Gen. Corp., 1969-71 (also v.p.), Fin. Floorplans, Inc., Ft. Worth, 1980-2003, Way To Go, Inc., Orlando, Fla., 1988-2000, Unicorn Rsch. Corp., Orlando, 1989—, Global Ptnrs. Corp., Orlando, 1994-2000 (also sec.). Author number of fin. acctg., mgmt. acct., cost acctg. textbooks, study guides; contbr. many articles to profl. jours. With U.S. Army, 1956-58. Recipient U. Pitts. BEFEE grant, 1993, 94, Ernst & Ernst Acctg. Achievement award, 1967, EMBA Outstanding Prof. award Class of 1986, 88, Delta Sigma Pi Scholarship key, 1964; Fulbright fellowship, 1999; Fulbright Alumni Initiatives Awards program grant, 2000-02. Mem. AICPA, Am. Acctg. Assn., World Future Soc., Fulbright Assn. (founding mem., treas. mid-Fla. chpt. 2002--), Beta Alpha Psi, Beta Gamma Sigma. Avocations: classical music, travel. Home: 4621 N Landmark Dr Orlando FL 32817-1235 Office: Crummer Grad Sch Bus Rollins Coll 1000 Holt Ave Winter Park FL 32789-4499 E-mail: serge@rollins.edu., serge@unicorn.us.com.

MATUNE, FRANK JOSEPH, lawyer; b. Youngstown, Ohio, Jan. 11, 1948; s. Walter John and Eve (Skiljo) M.; m. Doreen Mary Dolan, June 1, 1974; children: Molly Catherine, John Walter, Kelly Dolan. BA, Ill. Benedictine Coll., 1970; JD, Thomas M. Cooley Law Sch., Lansing, Mich., 1979; LLM, Georgetown U., 1980. Bar: Pa. 1979, Ohio, 1998, U.S. Dist. Ct. (western dist.) Pa. 1982, U.S. Tax Ct. 1980. Tax clk. Bd. Tax Appeals State Mich. Dept. Revenue, Lansing, 1978-79; ptnr. Routman, Moore, Goldstone & Valentino, Sharon, Pa., 1981-98, Nadler, Nadler & Burdman Co., LPA, Youngstown, Ohio, 1998—. Author: Pennsylvania Tax Service, 1987, Federal Tax Service, 1988. Mem. ABA, Ohio Ba Assn., Pa. Bar Assn., Mercer County Bar Assn. (treas. 1983-86). Republican. Roman Catholic. Avocations: sports, classical music. Home: 798 Lillian Dr Hermitage PA 16148-1571 Office: Nadler Nadler & Burdman Co 20 Federal Plz W Ste 600 Youngstown OH 44503-1424

MATURO, J. MICHAEL, real estate company executive, corporate financial executive; Grad. in acctg. and fin., Seton Hall U. CPA. Sr. mgr. E&Y Kenneth Leventhal Real Estate Group (formerly Kenneth Leventhal & Co.); exec. v.p., CFO, corp. treas., chmn. invesmtent com. Reckson Assocs. Realty Corp., Melville, NY, 1995—. Mem.: Nat. Assn. Real Estate Investment Trusts (mem. acctg. com.). Office: Reckson Assocs Realty Corp 225 Broadhollow Rd Melville NY 11747-4833*

MATUS, WAYNE CHARLES, lawyer; b. NYC, Mar. 10, 1950; s. Eli and Alma (Platt) M.; children: Marshall Scott, Scott Adam. BA, Johns Hopkins U., 1972; JD, NYU, 1975. Law clk. Superior Ct. D.C., 1975-76; assoc. Marshall, Bratter, Greene, Allison and Tucker, N.Y.C., 1976-79, Christy & Viener, N.Y.C., 1979-83, ptnr., 1984—98, Salans Hertzfeld Heilbronn Christy & Viener, NYC, 1999—2001, Leboeuf Lamb Greene & MacRae, NYC, 2001—04, Mayer, Brown, Rowe & Maw LLP, NYC, 2004—. Faculty ABA-Am. Law Inst., 1988; neutral mediator comml. divsn. 1st jud. dist. Supreme Ct. State of NY Unified Ct. Sys., 1997—. Assoc. editor Nanotechnology Law and Bus. Jour., mem. editl. bd. ABA Model Jury Instructions for Trademarks, Trade Dress and Copyright; contbg. editor: Commercial Corporate Strategies for Drafting and Negotiating. Mem. Assn. Bar City of N.Y. (com. on computer law 1985-88, chmn. com. on state cts., subcom. on motion practice 1982-84, com. product liability 1994-97), N.Y. State Bar Assn. (com. on class actions and complex civil litigation comml. fed. litigation sect. 1990-99, com. on Internet and litigation 2000—2002, lectr.), N.Y. Litigators Club (steering com. 1985—), Johns Hopkins U. Alumni Assn. (bd. dirs. met. N.Y. chpt., v.p. 1988—2002, nat. alumni counsel 1996—2002, pres. 2002—). Office: Mayer Brown Rowe & Maw 1675 Broadway New York NY 10019

MATUSCHKA, PAUL R. pharmacist; b. Riverside, Calif., Apr. 25, 1953; s. Ernest P. and Verla L. Matuschka; m. Jaime L. Olson, Feb. 16, 1974; children: Jordan P., Cole A. PharmD, U. Nebr., 1980; student in med. tech. and prepharmacy, U. Nebr., Kearney. Cert. Diabetes educator Am. Assn. Diabetes Educators, 1989. Staff pharmacist, instr. U. Nebr. Med. Ctr. Hosp. and Coll. Pharmacy, Omaha, 1980—81; staff/clin. pharmacist Jewish Hosp., Louisville, 1981—92; clin. pharmacy specialist VA Med. Ctr., Louisville, 1992—. Composer: (song) Middle Man; contbr. chapters to books, articles to profl. jours. Republican. Avocations: travel, horticulture. Office: VA Med Ctr 800 Zorn Ave #119 Louisville KY 40206-1499 Office Phone: 502-287-4025. Personal E-mail: paul.matuschka@med.va.gov. E-mail: paul.matuschka@med.va.gov.

MATUS-MENDOZA, MARIADELALUZ, language educator, sociologist; b. Mexico City, Apr. 10, 1961; arrived in U.S., 1991; d. MariadelaPaz Matus-Mendoza; m. Geoffrey Fitch, Sept. 3, 1993. BA in English Lit. and Applied Lang., Mex. Autonoman U., Mexico City, 1984; MA, Temple U., 1993, PhD, 1999. Tchr. Mex. Autonoman U., 1984—91; tchg. asst. Temple U., Phila., 1991—94, adj. instr., 1994—95, LuSulle U., Phila., 1995—98, U. Pa., Phila., 1996—99; asst. prof. Spanish U. Ctrl. Fla., Orlando, 1999—2001, Drexel U., Phila., 2001—. Cons. ETS, Princeton, NJ, 2001—. Mem.: MLA, Am. Assn. Tchrs. of Spanish and Portugese, Nat. Assn. Hispanic and Latino Studies. Roman Catholic. Office: Drexel Univ 229 N 33rd St Philadelphia PA 19104

MATUSOW, NAOMI C. state legislator; b. Nashville, Oct. 31, 1938; m. Gene R. Matusow; children: Gary, Jason. BA cum laude, Vanderbilt U., 1960; MA in Counseling and Guidance, NYU, 1966; JD, Pace U., 1979. Bar: N.Y. 1981. Editl. asst. Golden Press, 1960-62; tchr. math. N.Y.C. Pub. Schs., 1962-65, guidance counselor, 1965-67; pvt. practice as lawyer Armonk, 1981-92, White Plains, 1981-92; mem. N.Y. State Assembly, 1992—, chair librs. and edn. tech. com., mem. assembly coms., econ. devel. environ. conservation, local govt., transp., consumer affairs, tourism, arts, sports devel., spkrs. steering com. Chmn. Women's Bus. Devel. subcom.; bd. dirs. Juvenile Diabetes Found. Westchester County. Mem. NOW, Nat. Women's Polit. Caucus. E-mail: matusow@assembly.state.ny.us.

MATUSZEK, JOHN MICHAEL, JR., environmental scientist, educator, consultant; b. Worcester, Mass., Apr. 16, 1935; s. John Michael and Felicia Martha (Shandruk) M.; m. Roberta Eva Coonan, Nov. 30, 1957; children: Debra-Jane Y., John Michael III, Kevin P., Jennifer R. BS in Chemistry with distinction, Worcester Poly. Inst., 1957; PhD in Nuclear Chemistry, Clark U., 1962. Dept. mgr. Teledyne Isotopes, Westwood, N.J., 1964-71; rsch. scientist in nuclear chemistry, radioactive waste mgmt., radiological health, environ. radioactivity and radiation N.Y. State Health Dept., Albany, 1971-2000; cons., owner JMM Cons. Svcs., Delmar, N.Y., 1992—. Adj. prof. Rensselaer Poly. Inst., Troy, N.Y., 1977-2003; prof. SUNY, Albany, 1996-99. Lt. comdr. USPHS, 1962-64. Mem. Internat. Commn. Radionuclide Metrology. Avocations: skiing, music. Home and Office: JMM Cons Svcs 10 Fieldstone Dr Delmar NY 12054 E-mail: jmatuszek@att.net.

MATUSZKO, ANTHONY JOSEPH, research chemist, administrator; b. Hadley, Mass., Jan. 31, 1926; s. Joseph Anthony and Katherine (Narog) M.; m. Anita Colley, Oct. 26, 1956; children— Martha, Mary, Stephen, Richard. BA, Amherst Coll., 1946; MS in Chemistry, U. Mass., 1951; PhD in Chemistry, McGill U., 1953. Demonstrator in chemistry McGill U., Montreal, Que., Can., 1950-52; from instr. to assoc. prof. chemistry Lafayette Coll., Easton, Pa., 1952-58; head fundamental process div. Naval Propellant Lab., Indian Head, Md., 1958-62; program mgr. in chemistry Air Force Office Sci. Research, Washington, 1962-89; rsch. steering com. Dept. Def. Biotech., 1986-89; cons., Annandale, Va., 1989—. Contbr. articles to tech. jours. Patentee in field. Pres. Forest Heights PTA, Md., 1967. Served with U.S. Army, 1946-48. Named Hon. Fellow in Chemistry, U. Wis.-Madison, 1967-68, recipient Superior Performance award USAF, Outstanding Career Svc. award U.S. Govt. Fellow AAAS, Am. Inst. Chemists (life); mem. Am. Chem. Soc., Cosmos Club, Sigma Xi. Home: 4210 Elizabeth Ln Annandale VA 22003-3654

MATWICZAK, KENNETH MATTHEW, university educator, consultant; b. Milw., Sept. 26, 1948; s. Matthew T. and Dorothy M. Matwiczak; m. Barbara A. Larsen, June 12, 1971; 1 child, Brynn E. BS, U.S. Mil. Acad., 1971; MS, Purdue U., 1979; MBA, L.I. U., 1982; PhD in Indsl. Engring., Tex. A&M U., 1990. Commd. 2d lt. U.S. Army, 1971, advanced through grades to lt. col., 1990; air def. platoon leader, exec. officer 2 Bn. 56th ADA, Pirmasens, Fed. Rep. Germany, 1971-74; air def. battery comdr. 2/5 ADA, 2nd AD, Ft. Hood, Tex., 1975-76; asst. dean acad. computing U.S. Mil. Acad., West Point, N.Y., 1979-82, assoc. prof., 1989-93; chief studies and analysis Forward Area Air Def. Joint Test Force, Ft. Bliss, Tex., 1982-85; bn. exec. officer staff and faculty battalion U.S. Army Air Def. Sch., Ft. Bliss, 1985-86; adj. assoc. prof. U. Tex., Austin, 1993-99, sr. lectr., 1999—. Statis. cons., 1994—; owner, proprietor Fare Choice Vending Svcs., Austin, 1996-99; guest lectr. Ctr. Pub. Mgmt., San Marcos, Tex., 1997-. Admissions rep. U.S. Mil. Acad.-W. Point, Austin, 1997—. Mem. ASPA (bd. dirs. Centex chpt. 1999—), Inst. Ops. Rsch. and Mgmt. Sci., W. Point Soc. Ctrl. Tex. (pres. 1995-97, bd. dirs.), KC. Replblican. Roman Catholic. Avocations: bowling, travel, golf, reading, softball. Office: U Tex LBJ Sch Pub Affairs Drawer Y University Sta Austin TX 78713 E-mail: kmat@mail.utexas.edu.

MATYJASZEWSKI, KRZYSZTOF, chemist, educator; b. Konstantynow, Poland, Apr. 8, 1950; came to U.S., 1985; s. Henryk and Antonina (Styss) M.; m. Malgorzata Kowalska, July 15, 1972; children: Antoni, Maria. BS, MS, Tech. U., Moscow, 1972; PhD, Polish Acad. Scis., Lodz, 1976; DSc, Lodz Poly., 1985. Postdoctoral fellow U. Fla., 1977-78; rsch. assoc. Polish Acad. Scis., 1978-84, CNRS, France, 1984-85; asst. prof. chemistry Carnegie Mellon U., Pitts., 1985-89, assoc. prof., 1989-93, prof., 1993—, head dept. chemistry, 1994-98, J.C. Warner prof., 1998—. Invited prof. U. Paris, 1985; vis. prof. U. Freiburg, 1988, U. Paris, 1990, 97, 98, U. Bayreuth, 1991, U. Strasbourg, 1992, U. Bordeaux, 1996, 2004, U. Ulm, 1999, U. Pisa, 2000; adj. prof., U. Pitts., 2000-, Polish Acad. Sci., 2000-; cons. Dow Corning, Midland, Mich., 1988-89, Arco, Phila., 1990-92, GE, Schenectady, 1992—, Amoco, Naperville, Ill., 1994-97, Reilly Ind., Indpls., 1994—, Air Products, Allentown, Pa., 1994-97. Author 8 books; mem. editorial bd. Macromolecules, Macromolecular Synthesis, Jour. Polymer Sci., Jour. Macromolecular Sci.-Pure and Applied

Chemistry, Jour. Inorganic and Organometallic Polymers, Polymer, others; editor Progress Polymer Sci.; contbr. chpts. to books, more than 600 articles to profl. jours.; 27 U.S. and 75 internat. patents in field. Recipient award Polish Acad. Sci., 1981, Presdl. Young Investigator award NSF, 1989, Humboldt award for Sr. U.S. Scientists, 1999, Pitts. award, 2001. Fellow: Internat. Union Pure and Applied Chemistry (corr. mem. polymer nomenclature), Polymer Materials Sci. Engring., Am. Chem. Soc. (Carl S. Marvel award 1995, Polymer Chemistry award 2002, Coop. Rsch. award 2004); mem.: French Acad. Sci. (Elf chair 1998). Achievements include research in synthesis of well defined macromolecules via living and controlled polymerizations; organometallic polymers. Home: 9 Queens Ct Pittsburgh PA 15238-1519 Office: Carnegie Mellon U 4400 5th Ave Pittsburgh PA 15213-2617

MATZ, DEBORAH, federal agency administrator; m. Marshall Matz; children: Hayley, Peter. BS, Cornell U.; MA, George Washington U. Cmty. devel. rep. U.S. Dept. Housing and Urban Devel.; legis. asst. Congressman Peter Peyser; dir. Office Tech. Assessment, U.S. Congress; economist Joint Econ. Com.; exec. officer Liaison Office N.Am. Food and Agrl. Orgn., UN; numerous positions including deputy asst. sec. adminstrn., chair loan resolution task force, chiaf of staff adminstrs. Farm Svc. Agy and Farmers Home USDA, 1993—2001; mem. Nat. Credit Union Adminstrn., Alexandria, 2002—. Office: Nat Credit Union Adminstrn 1775 Duke St Alexandria VA 22314-3428

MATZ, JAMES RICHARD, municipal official; BA with honors, U. Tex., 1961; postgrad., Mexico city Coll., 1961-62. Mktg. exec. Fluor Corp.; mem. diplomatic corps Dept. of State; commr. City of Harlingen, Tex., Cameron County. Mem. Pres.'s Exec. Interchange Program, Bank of Am.; mayor Palm Valley, Tex. Contbr. articles to profl. jours. Founder Harlingen Proud; founder, chmn. Valley Proud Environ. Coun., 1990; mem. citizen's exec. adv. coun. Rio Grande State Mental Health and Retardation Ctr.; bd. dirs. Harlingen, South Padre Island, San Benito Emergency Med. Svcs.; chmn. Tex. Reg. Cmty. Devel. Grant Rev. Com.; mem. Met. Planning Orgn., Cameron County; mem. exploration com. World Birding Ctr.; bd. dirs. Tex. Urban Forestry Coun.; mem. Tex. Energy Coord. Coun., Govt. Adv. Com. to U.S. Rep. to N.Am. Commn. for Environ. Coop.; past vice chmn. legis. policy com. on utility regulation and environment Tex. Mcpl. League; past chmn. City of Harlingen Utility Rate Rev. Bd., pub. works com. Harlingen Capital Improvement Adv. Bd.; past. bd. dirs. Rio Grande basin Sustainable Devel. Initiative, Border Trade Alliance, Area Health Edn. Ctr. South Tex., Keep Tex. Beautiful; former commr. Cameron County; past exec. com. Rio Grande Valley Emergency Mgmt. Coord. Coun., numerous others. Recipient Rotary Found. Dist. Svc. award, 1990, Svc. Above Self award Harlingen Rotary, 1991, Tex. Urban Forestry Individual Accomplishment award, 1992, Harlingen Proud, Chairman's award, 1992, Outstanding Dist. Gov., Keep Tex. Beautiful, 1995, Leadership award, 1995, Pres.'s Nat. Svc. award, 1995, Outstanding tex. Urban Forester award, 1996, State of Tex. Senate Resolution #989, 1995, Joint Resolution of Appreciation, San Benito City Commn. and San Benito Area C. of C., 1997, Tex. Environ. Excellence award Tex. Commn. Environ. Quality, 2004. Mem. Harlingen Area C. of C. (past dir.), Assn. for Local Control of Utility Rates (past officer, dir.). Office: 900 Palm Valley Dr W Harlingen TX 78552

MATZICK, KENNETH JOHN, hospital administrator; b. Chgo., May 31, 1943; married. B, U. Iowa, 1965, MHA, 1967. Adminstrv. resident VA Med. Ctr., Iowa City, 1966, Morristown (N.J.) Meml. Hosp., 1967-68, asst. to exec. v.p., 1968-69; asst. dir. William Beaumont Hosp., Royal Oak, Mich., 1969-76, dir. Troy, Mich., 1976-83, v.p., COO Royal Oak, 1983-97, exec. v.p., COO, 1997—. Home: 22500 Lavon St Saint Clair Shores MI 48081-2076 Office: William Beaumont Hosp 3601 W 13 Mile Rd Royal Oak MI 48073-6712

MATZIORINIS, KENNETH N. economist; b. N.Y.C., May 4, 1954; s. Neocles N. and Popi (Gregoratos) Matziorinis; m. Catherine Marina Astrakianakis, July 27, 1985; children: Anna Maria, Angela Ellen Fylitsa. BA, McGill U., 1976, MA, 1979, PhD, 1988. Cert. mgmt. cons. Asst. economist Nat. Bank Greece (Can.), Montreal, 1978-81; lectr. econs. McGill U., Montreal, 1977—; prof. econs. John Abbott Coll., Montreal, 1981—. Pres. Canbek Econ. Cons., Inc., Montreal, 1983—; econs. adviser to bd. dirs. Internat. Orgn. Psychophysiology, 1982-89; bd. dirs. Nat. Bank of Greece, Can., Hellenic Bd. of Trade of Met. Montreal; dir. Hellas Capital, Inc. (Canada), 2001—. Author: Introduction to Macro Economics: An Applied Approach, 1988, 2d edit., 1994, 3d edit., 2000, Business Economics: Theory and Practice, 2d edit., 2000; editor: Vital Graphs of Canadian Economy, 1984; contbr. articles to profl. jours. V.p. Westmount Liberal Riding Assn., Montreal, 1975-77; bd. govs. McGill U., 1978-81, John Abbott Coll., 1988-91; chmn. bd. dirs. Cmty. Svc. Ctr. St. Louis, Montreal, 1978-80; bd. trustees Trafalgar Sch. for Girls, 2002—. Recipient of "The distinguished Teaching Award", McGill U, 1993. Mem. Am. Econ. Assn., Am. Hellenic Ednl. and Progressive Assn., Can. Assn. Bus. Economists, Can. Econ. Assn., Que. Inst. Cert. Mgmt. Cons., Nat. Assn. Bus. Economists, St. James Club. Greek Orthodox. Home: Laval 615 67th Ave Montreal QC Canada H7V 3N9 E-mail: canbekeconomics@spint.ca.

MATZKE, JAY, internist; b. Sidney, Nebr., Oct. 2, 1956; m. Ann Matzke, Feb. 13, 1982; children: Alex, Jered, Sloan. B Medicine, U. Nebr. Med. Ctr., 1979, MD, 1983. Diplomate Am. Acad. Family Physicians. Resident in family practice U. Nebr. Med. Ctr., Nebr., 1984—86; ptnr. Martin Med. Clinic/Sidney Meml. Hosp., 1987—90; med. dir. Sidney Meml. Hosp. Addiction Ctr., 1987—89; staff physician Omaha Family Practice, 1990—96; ptnr. Immanuel Clinic/Immanuel Med. Ctr., 1990—96; med. dir. Immanuel/Alegent Health Sports Medicine, 1995—96; staff physician Meml. Health Care Sys., Seward, Nebr., 1997—, chief med. staff, 1999; med. dir. S.W. Rural Fire Dept., Nebr., 1998—; med. advisor Lancaster County Red Cross, Nebr., 1999—. Chmn. emergency cardiac care com. for Nebr. Am. Heart Assn., 1995—, instr. ACLS, 1984—; instr. ATLS ACS, 1986—. Dist. chmn. Boy Scouts Am., 2000—, pack com. chmn., 1997—98; trustee Nebr. Children's Home Soc., Nebr., 1999—; bd. dirs. Emergency Med. Svcs., 1998—; mem. pres.' adv. com. U. Nebr., 1997—2000; den leader Boy Scouts Am., 1985—87; chmn. ACLS Task Force, Nebr., 1992—95; pres., v.p., treas. Millard Sch. Bd., 1993—97; mem. Sidney City Coun., 1988—90; pres., charter mem. Cheyenne County Cmty. Ctr. Found., Inc., 1988—90; mem. bd. mission outreach, trustee Faith Luth. Ch., 1997—. Named Outstanding Young Nebraskan, Nebr. Jaycees, 1989, Outstanding Chamber Mem., Cheyenne County C. of C., 1988; recipient award of achievement, Nebr. Assn. Sch. Bds., 1995, 1996. Mem.: Am. Med. Soc. Sports Medicine.

MATZKE, REX KAY, education educator; b. York, Neb., Dec. 28, 1947; s. Robert Keith and Jacie Edith Matzke; m. Genice Dolores Uelentrup, Oct. 3, 1992; children: Jacie, Kateri; m. Sally Ann Schulz, May 31, 1971. BME, U. Neb., 1971, MM, 1974; DA, U. No. Colo., 1993—95. Mem. faculty U. Mo., St. Louis, 1976—93; exec. dir. Grand Valley Music Festival, Grand Junction, Colo., 1997—2002; mem. faculty Pikes Peak C.C., Colo. Springs, Colo., 2002—, Colo. Jazz Workshop, 2002—, Adams State Coll., Alamosa, Colo., 2003—; faculty Colo. Coll., Colorado Springs, 2004—. Pres. T-Rex Productions, 1976—; co-founder Almagre Saxophone Quartet; leader Jazz Express Quartet. Contbr. articles to profl. publs. Recipient winner, Wichita Jazz Festival, 1978, 1982, Oustanding Big Band, Mid-West Collegiate Jazz, 1978—80. Mem.: Colo. Music Educators Assn., Internat. Assn. Jazz Edn. (mem. exec. bd.), Colo. Bandmaster Assn. Republican. Meth. Avocations: golf, hiking, racquetball. Home: 7859 Potomac Dr Colorado Springs CO 80920

MATZKE, RICHARD H. oil industry executive; Mem. Chevron Corp., San Francisco, 1961, corp. v.p., 1990, dir., 1997, vice chmn. worldwide oil and gas exploration and prodn., 2000; dir. Dynegy, Inc. Office: Chevron Corp 575 Market St San Francisco CA 94105

MATZKO, JOHN AUSTIN, historian; b. Audubon, N.J., Sept. 18, 1946; s. John Frank and Evelyn Austin Matzko; m. Rachel Grace Smith, May 27, 1976; 1 child, Austin Joel. BA, Bob Jones U., 1968; MA, U. of Cin., 1972; PhD, U. of Va., Charolottesville, 1984. Chair divsn. of social sci. Bob Jones U., Greenville, SC, 1998—. Historian Nat. Pk. Svc. Author: (hist. monograph) Reconstructing Fort Union, 2001; contbr. articles to profl. jours. With U.S. Army, 1969—70. Mem.: Am. Soc. for Legal History, Orgn. of Am. Historians. Conservative. Free Presbyterian. Avocations: singing (tenor), playing the violin and viola. Home: 17 Profs Pl Greenville SC 29609 Office: Bob Jones U 1700 Wade Hampton Blvd Greenville SC 29614

MAU, BENJAMIN, artist; b. Sien, China, Dec. 25, 1944; came to U.S., 1962; s. James K. and Sue Y. Mau; m. Sonya Chu Mau, July 14, 1972. AA, Southwest Bapt. U., Bolivar, Mo., 1964; BS, Ouachita Bapt. U., 1967; MS, Memphis State U., 1969. Paintings featured in books, including Artists of Illinois, 1995, The Best of Watercolor, 1995, The Best of Watercolor 2, 1997, Painting Color, 1997, Floral Inspirations, 1997, Landscape Inspirations, 1997, The Watercolor Expressions, 1999, The Collected Best of Watercolor, 2001. Recipient Permanent Collection awards Ea. Ill. U., Charleston, 1975, Caterpillar, Decatur, Ill., 1975, Carson P. Scott, Quincy, Ill., 1978, Best of Show award Ill. State Fair, 2001, award of distinction Mo. Watercolor Soc. 2d Ann., 2002. Mem. Nat. Watercolor Soc. (signature, regional rep.), Am. Watercolor Soc. (signature). Home: 1 Lateer Dr Normal IL 61761-3925 E-mail: maucorp@aol.com.

MAU, BOB, statistician; b. Sheboygan, Wis., Sept. 1, 1950; s. Robert W. Mau and Lydia Welsch; m. Lynn Ellen Deschler, Sept. 29, 1979. BA, Lawrence U., Appleton, Wis., 1973; PhD, U. Wis., 1996. Rsch. program mgr. Wis. Survey Rsch. Lab., Madison, 1980—90; sr. scientist U. Wis., Madison, 1996—. Contbr. articles to profl. jours. Postdoctoral fellow in Computational Molecular Biology, Sloan Found. / DOE, 1999—2001. Fellow: Royal Statis. Soc.; mem.: Inst. of Math. Stats., Am. Statis. Soc. Achievements include research in the identification of genomic reaarangements using Markov chain Monte Carlo; Bayesian phylogenetic inference using Markov chain Monte Carlo. Home: 207 E Racine Jefferson WI 53549 Office: Univ Wis - Madison 1656 Linden Dr Madison WI 53706 E-mail: robertm@genome.wisc.edu.

MAU, C. S. See SALERNO, CHERIE

MAUBERT, JACQUES CLAUDE, retired school superintendent; b. Provins, France, May 19, 1932; s. Jean Pierre and Simone Jeanne (Bocqueho) M.; m. Micheline Josephine Lathuille, June 16, 1956; children: Eric, Sandrine. MA, Dakar U., Senegal, 1969; CAPES, U. Bordeaux (France), 1971. Tchr. French Ministry Edn., Morocco, 1952-62, 1962—73, councellor and tchr., 1973-75, Lome, Togo, 1975-77, headmaster LeMans, France, 1977-79, headmaster Lycee Francais of San Francisco, 1979-85, headmaster, 1985-86, headmaster Lyceum Kennedy N.Y.C., 1986-2000; ret., 2000. Mem., pres. Commn. Reform for Tchg. French in Africa, Dakar, 1973—75; pedagogic councellor U. Benin, Togo, 1975—77. Author: French Literature for 11th Grade, 1975. Pres. Union des Francais de l' Etranger, San Francisco, 1983-85. Decorated officer The Acad. Palms (France). Roman Catholic. Avocations: swimming, tennis, classical music, jazz, opera. Home: 80 Longfellow Rd Mill Valley CA 94941-1591 E-mail: jacques.m@comcast.net.

MAUCH, ROBERT CARL, energy executive; b. Cleve., Dec. 7, 1939; s. Otto Herman and Clara M.; m. Rita Marie Szucs, Aug. 25, 1964 (div. Jan. 1980); children: David O., Martin L., Karolyn L.; m. Drusilla Ann Tesch, Feb. 18, 1989. AMP, Harvard U., 1983; MS, U. Calif., Berkeley, 1965; BSChemE, Cleve. State U., 1962. V.p., gen. mgr., LP gas divsn. Amerigas Inc., Valley Forge, Pa., 1978-83; v.p. UGI Corp., Valley Forge, 1978-87, sr. v.p., 1987-90; dir. Ansutech, Inc., Valley Forge, 1981-82, Matheson Gas Products, Inc., Valley Forge, 1981-82; pres., dir. AP Propane Inc., Valley Forge, 1983-90, Amerigas Propane, Valley Forge, 1983-96; pres., CEO, dir. AmeriGas Inc., Valley Forge, 1991-96, Petrolane, Inc., Valley Forge, 1993-96, Amerigas, Inc. subs. UGI Corp., Valley Forge, 1990-96, AmeriGas Propane Inc. (gen. ptnr. AmeriGas Ptnrs. L.P.); chmn., CEO Anthem Holdings Corp., Valley Forge, 1997-98, AllianceOne Inc., Exton, 1998—. Bd. govs. Pa. Economy League, Phila., 1985-91; mem. World Affairs Coun., Phila., 1980-95. Mem.: Am. Collectors Assn., Propane Vehicle Coun. (chmn. 1994—), Waynesborough C. of C., Nat. Propane Gas Assn. (bd. dirs., exec. com., pres. 1978—95), Healthcare Fin. Mgmt. Assn. Lutheran. Avocations: tennis, reading, skiing, running, weight training. Office: AllianceOne Inc 717 Constitution Dr Ste 202 PO Box 556 Exton PA 19341-0556

MAUCK, HENRY PAGE, JR., medical and pediatrics educator; b. Richmond, Va., Feb. 3, 1926; s. Henry Page and Harriet Hutcheson (Morrison) M.; m. Janet Garrett Horsley, May 14, 1955; children— Henry Page III, John Waller. BA, U. Va., 1950, MD, 1952. Diplomate: Am. Bd. Internal Medicine. Intern Henry Ford Hosp., Detroit, 1952-53; resident Med. Coll. Va., Richmond, 1953-56, asst. prof. medicine and pediatrics, 1961-66, assoc. prof., 1966-72, prof., 1972—. Fellow in cardiology Am. Heart Assn., 1956-57; cons. cardiology Langley Field Air Force Hosp., Hampton, Va., McGuire's VA Hosp., Richmond. Contbr.: chpt. to Autonomic Control of Cardiovascular System, 1972; contbr. articles to sci. jours. Served with U.S. Army, 1944-46. Fellow ACP, Am. Coll. Cardiology (former gov. Va.); mem. Am. Physiol. Soc., So. Soc. Clin. Investigation, Am. Fedn. Clin. Research, So. Soc. Clin. Research. Presbyterian. Home: 113 Oxford Cir W Richmond VA 23221-3224 Office: Med Coll Va PO Box 281 Richmond VA 23218-0281

MAUCK, WILLIAM M., JR., retired executive recruiter, small business owner; b. Cleve., Mar. 30, 1938; s. William M. and Elizabeth Louise (Stone) M.; m. Paula Jean Mauck, Aug. 15, 1969 (div. Mar. 1983); children: Brian, David; m. Jeanne Lee Mauck, May 21, 1987. BS in Bus., Ind. U., 1961. Sales engr. Inland Container Corp., Louisville, 1961-69; sales mgr. Dixie Container Corp., Knoxville, Tenn., 1969-70, gen. mgr., 1970-75; v.p., ptnr. Heidrick & Struggles, Inc., Houston, 1975-81; pres. Booker & Mauck, Inc., Houston, 1981-85; ptnr. Ward Howell Internat. Inc., Houston, 1985-88; prin. William M. Mauck, Jr., Houston, 1988-2001; owner Pepe Engring., Inc., Houston, 1990-2001; ret., 2001. Mem. adv. bd. Women's Sports Found., N.Y.C., 1985-96. Mem. Plaza Club (Houston) (chmn. bd. govs. 1987-88), Sertoma Club (Knoxville 1972-75) (pres. 1974-75). Republican. Methodist. Office: 9950 Cypresswood Dr Ste 300 Houston TX 77070-3412 Home: 6318 E Dusty Coyote Cir Scottsdale AZ 85262-7202

MAUCKER, EARL ROBERT, newspaper editor, newspaper executive; b. St. Louis, Sept. 20, 1947; s. Robert Buffem and Linette (Meloy) M.; m. Betsy Ann Johnson, May 21, 1977; children: Eric Robert, Michael Earl. BA in Mass Communications, So. Ill. U., 1972. Reporter Alton (Ill.) Telegraph, 1969-73; reporter, city editor, news editor, asst. mng. editor Rockford (Ill.) Morning Star, 1973-79; mng. editor Springfield (Mo.) Daily News, 1979-80, Ft. Lauderdale (Fla.) Sun-Sentinel, 1990-95, v.p. editorial, 1995—. Sgt. SUAF, 1966-69. Mem. Am. Soc. Newspapers Editors, Fla. Soc. Newspapers Editors, Associated Press Mng. Editors Assn. (bd. dirs. 1989-93). Home: 3511 NE 26th Ave Lighthouse Point FL 33064-8105 Office: Sun-Sentinel 200 E Las Olas Blvd Fort Lauderdale FL 33301-2293

MAUDERLY, JOE LLOYD, pulmonary toxicologist; b. Strong City, Kans., Aug. 31, 1943; s. Joseph Park and Violet May (Cox) M.; m. Cheryl Gaines, Jan. 31, 1965; children: Laurie Jean, Jameson Lynn. BS, Kans. State U., 1965, DVM, 1967. Respiratory physiologist Inhalation Toxicology Rsch. Inst., Albuquerque, 1967-89, supr. pathophysiology group, 1976-89, dir., 1989-96; rsch. prof. medicine U. N.Mex., Albuquerque, 1988—, clin. prof. pharmacy, 1990—; sr. scientist, dir. external affairs Lovelace Respiratory Rsch. Inst., Albuquerque, 1997-99; v.p., dir. Nat. Environ. Respiratory Ctr., 1999—. Cons. in field; mem. EPA Clean Air Scientific Adv. Com., 1992-96, chair, 1997-2000. Assoc. editor Fundamental Applied Toxicology, 1989-94, editl. bd. exptl. lung rsch., 1983-2003; mem. editl. bd. Inhalation Toxicology, 2004—; contbr. articles to profl. jours., chpts. to books. Served to capt. USAF, 1967-69. Mem. Am. Thoracic Soc. (chmn. assembly of environ. and occupational health 1991-93, long-range planning com. 1991-94, sci. adv. com. 1993-96), Am. Physiol. Soc., Am. Vet. Med. Assn., N.Mex. Vet. Med. Assn., Soc. Toxicology (pres. inhalation specialty sect. 1994-95, career achievement award 1999). Republican. Home: 4517 Banff Dr NE Albuquerque NM 87111-2829 Office Phone: 505-348-9432. Business E-Mail: jmauderl@lrri.org.

MAUDLIN, ROBERT V. economics and government affairs consultant; b. Washington, June 8, 1927; s. Cecil V. and Eva Jane (Wright) M.; m. Carole M. Jackson, Sept. 3, 1949; children: Lynda C., David V., Tim W.E. Student, MIT, 1945; BS, Am. U., 1951. Ptnr. C.V. & R.V. Maudlin, Washington, 1952-72, owner, 1972—. Mng. dir. Bur. Applied Econs., Washington, 1960—; sec. Nat. Assn. Scissors and Shears Mfrs., 1970-97; exec. dir. Joint Govt. Liaison Com., 1973-81; mem. Industry Sector Adv. Com. U.S. Dept. Commerce and U.S. Trade Rep., Washington, 1975-97; commr. Adv. Neighborhood Commn. of D.C., 1999—. Author econ. and statis. reports. Pres. Forest Hills Citizens Assn., Washington, 1964; chmn. Boy Scouts Am., Washington, 1972. 2nd lt. C.E., AUS, 1945-47, USAR, 1947-55. Republican. Home: 2906 Ellicott Ter NW Washington DC 20008-1023 E-mail: maudlin@alum.mit.edu.

MAUDSLEY, RONALD R. finance company executive; With Transamerica Title, Sacramento, 1975—88, Fidelity Nat. Title Ins. Co., 1988—2002; exec. v.p. Fidelity Nat. Fin., Santa Barbara, Calif., 2002—, co-COO, 2002—. Office: Fidelity National Financial 4050 Calle Real Santa Barbara CA 93110

MAUER, ALVIN MARX, physician, medical educator; b. LeMars, Iowa, Jan. 10, 1928; s. Alvin Milton and Bertha Elizabeth (Marx) M.; m. Theresa Ann McGivern, Dec. 2, 1950; children: Stephen James, Timothy John, Daria Maureen, Elizabeth Claire. BA, State U. Iowa, 1950, MD, 1953. Intern Cin. Gen. Hosp., 1953-54; resident in pediatrics Children's Hosp. Cin., 1954-56; fellow in hematology dept. medicine U. Utah, Salt Lake City, 1956-59; dir. div. hematology Children's Hosp. Cin., prof. dept. hematology, 1959-73; prof. dept. pediatrics U. Cin. Coll. Medicine, 1959-73; prof. pediatrics U. Tenn. Coll. Medicine, Memphis, 1973-97, prof. medicine, 1983-97, prof. emeritus, 1997—; dir. cancer program U. Tenn. Coll. Health Scis.; dir. St. Jude Children's Research Hosp., Memphis, 1973-83. Mem. hematology study sect. NIH; mem. clin. cancer investigation rev. com. Nat. Cancer Inst.; mem. com. on maternal and infant nutrition NRC. Author: Pediatric Hematology, 1969; editor: The Biology of Human Leukemia, 1990. Served with U.S. Army, 1946. Mem. Am. Soc. Hematology (pres. 1980-81), Assn. Am. Cancer Insts. (pres. 1980), am. Acad. Pediatrics (com. on nutrition), Am. Assn. Cancer Edn., Am. Soc. Clin. Investigation, Am. Fedn. Clin. Rsch., Assn. Am. Physicians, Am. Pediatric Soc., Cen. Soc. Clin. Investigation, Cen. Soc. Clin. Rsch., Internat. Soc. Hematology (pres. 1988-90, chmn. 1992-96, bd. councilors 1992-96), Am. Cancer Soc. (pres. Tenn. divsn. 1992-93), Midwest Soc. Pediat. Rsch., N.Y. Acad. Scis., Soc. Pediat. Rsch., Am. Assn. Cancer Rsch., Phi Beta Kappa, Sigma Xi, Alpha Omega Alpha. Democrat. Roman Catholic. Office: U Tenn Ctr for Health Scis Rm 808 910 Madison Ave Memphis TN 38103 Business E-Mail: amauer@utmem.edu.

MAUGANS, JOHN CONRAD, lawyer; b. Miami County, Ind., May 10, 1938; s. Willis William and Evelyn Jeannette (Mills) M.; m. Judith M. Gallagher, Jan. 24, 1960 (dec. June 1984); children: Lisa Denise, Stacy Erin, Kristen Cherie; m. Jo Ella Middlekauff, June 7, 1985. AB, Manchester Coll., 1960; LLB with distinction, Ind. U., 1962, JD, 1969. Bar: Ind. 1962. Assoc. Barnes, Hickam, Pantzer & Boyd, Indpls., 1962-63; atty. pvr. practice, Kokomo, Ind., 1966—; ptnr. Bayliff, Harrigan, Cord & Maugans, Kokomo, Ind., 1969—. Guest lectr. Coll. Bus. Manchester Coll., 1966-80 Contbr. articles to profl. jours. Chmn. Howard fund dr. Manchester Coll., 1971; bd. dirs. Tribal Trials coun. Girl Scouts U.S.A., 1977-85, Vols. in Cmty. Svc., 1978-84, Home Health Care of Ctrl. Ind., Inc., 1983-89; trustee Western Sch. Corp., 1986—, pres., 1991-93, 2003—; bd. dirs. kokomo Park Band, Inc., 1989—; chmn. Christian Edn. com., Main St. Christian Ch., 1993—; mem. asset devel. and mktg. com. Cmty. Found. Howard County, Inc., 1994—. Capt. AUS, 1963-66. Fellow Am. Trial Lawyers Assn. (Roscoe Pound chpt.), Ind. Bar Found.; mem. Assn. Trial Lawyers Am., Ind. Bar Assn., Howard County Bar Assn. (pres. 1989), Ind. Trial Lawyers Assn., Manchester Coll. Alumni Assn. (chmn. area chpt. 1970, 88, 89, 90, 91), Manchester Coll. M. Alumni Assn. (pres. 1972), Am. Legion, Order of Coif, Phi Delta Phi. Home: 3274 Woodhaven Trl Kokomo IN 46902-5062 Office: PO Box 2249 123 N Buckeye St Kokomo IN 46904-2249 Office Phone: 765-459-4861. Business E-Mail: connie.maugans@bhcmlaw.com.

MAUGANS, TODD ALLEN, pediatric neurosurgeon; b. Harrisburg, Pa., Oct. 2, 1961; s. Emmert and Marie Maugans; m. Karen Ellingwood, Dec. 19, 1993; 1 child, Ayla. MD, Temple U., 1985. Diplomate Nat. Bd., Am. Bd. Family Practice, Am. Bd. Neurol. Surgery. Asst. prof. family medicine U. of Va., Charlottesville, 1993—95; pediat. neurosurgeon Edwards and Ciricillo Med. Group, Sacramento, 1999—2000; asst. prof. neurosurgery, pediat., family practice Chip U. Vt. Coll. Medicine, Burlington, 2000—03; dir. pediat. neurosurgery U. of Vt. Coll. of Medicine, 2000—; pediat. neurosurgery The Children's Med. Ctr., Dayton, Ohio, 2004—. Frymoyer scholar U. of Vt. Coll. of Medicine, Burlington, 2002—04; med. dir. Madi's Fund for Hydrocephalus and Related Neurosurg. Disorders, Burlington, 2000—04. Author: (archives of family medicine) The Spiritual History; contbr. articles to profl. jours. Lt. col. Air N.G., 1989—99. Decorated Meritorious Svc. Medal USAF. Mem.: Joint Sect. of Pediat. Neurol. Surgery, Vt. Med. Soc., Am. Assn. of Neurol., Congress of Neurol. Surgeons. Achievements include first to Spiritual History methodology for medical practitioners. Avocations: aviation, scuba diving, bicycling, kayaking. Office: Children's Med Ctr Dept Neurosurgury One Children's Plz Dayton OH 45404 Office Phone: 937-641-5900. E-mail: maugans t@childrensdayton.org.

MAUGERE, DANNIS PAUL, historian, educator; b. Newark, Sept. 3, 1946; s. William John and Virginia Webb Maugere; m. Joanne Maria Cella, Sept. 21, 1974; children: Lisa Marie, Anthony Paul, lauren Michelle. AS cum laude, Broward Jr. Coll., 1966; BA in hist., polit. sci., U. Fla., 1969, MA in tchg., am. hist., polit. sci., social found. of edn., 1976. Cert. profl. social studies educator State Dept. Edn., Fla and NY. Human rels. specialist Broward County Comm. Govt., Ft. Lauderdale, Fla., 1977—80, Broward Employ. Tng. Admin., 1981—82; adj. prof., hist. govt. Broward CC, Pembroke Pines, Fla., 1984—99; hist. prof. Cooper City (Fla.) HS, 1984—. Chmn. Broward County Adv. Bd. for Disabled, Ft. Lauderdale, 1979—81; keynote spkr. South Fla Second Conf. on Handicapped, Hollywood, Fla., 1979. Author: (social studies course) The Warren Commission Report and The Assassination of John F. Kennedy, 1998; performer: (talk show host) Concerns of the Disabled, 1977; author: Hotline for the Disabled, 1978. Guest spkr. various comm. functions for handicapped issues. Recipient US Citizen Ambassador, Hist. Edn. Del. to Russia and Latvia selectee, Ariz. State U., 1993, Citation of Merit award, Muscular Dystrophy Assn., Inc., 1978, Physically Handicapped, Inc., 1978, Award of Excellence, Nat. Assn. County Organ., 1978. Mem.: Southern Poverty Law Ctr., Am. Hist. Assn., Phi Alpha Theta, Internat. Roman Catholic. Achievements include first to South Fla's 1st annual conf. on handicapped; development of numerous county ordinances for the rights of the handicapped. Office: Cooper City HS 9401 Stirling Rd Cooper City FL 33328 Office Phone: 954-680-7200. Office Fax: 954-680-7275. E-mail: maugered@aol.com.

MAUGHAN, SIR DERYCK, bank executive; Degree earned, King's Coll., Univ. of London, 1969, Stanford U., 1978. With Treasury Dept., United Kingdom, 1969—79, Goldman Sachs, 1979—83, Salomon Bros. Inc., 1983—97; mng. dir. Salomon Bros. Inc, 1986—91, COO, 1991-92, chmn., CEO, 1992—97; vice-chmn., CEO Citigroup, N.Y.C., 1998—; vice-chmn. NYSE, 1996—2000. Knighted for svcs. to Brit. bus. her majesty, The Queen, 2002. Office: Citigroup 399 Park Ave New York NY 10043-0001*

MAUGHAN, REX, natural healthcare products company executive; Founder Forever Living Products, Phoenix, 1978, pres., CEO.

MAUGHAN, WILLARD ZINN, dermatologist; b. Riverside, Calif., Apr. 21, 1944; s. Franklin David and Martha Charlotte (Zinn) M.; m. Rona Lee Wilcox, Aug. 20, 1968; children: Julie Anne, Kathryn Anita, Willard Wilcox, Christopher Keith. Student, Johns Hopkins U., Balt., 1962-64; BS, U. Utah, 1968, MD, 1972. Diplomate Am. Bd. Dermatology. Intern Walter Reed Army Med. Ctr., Washington, 1972-73; fellow Mayo Clinic, Rochester, Minn., 1976-79; pvt. practice Ogden, Utah, 1979—. Contbr. articles to profl. jours. Commr. Boy Scouts Am., Weber County, Utah, 1980-84, dist. chmn., 1993-94, assoc. mem. bd. dirs. Trapper Trails coun., 1995-99, v.p., mem. exec. bd., 1999—;

pres. Am. Cancer Soc., Weber County, 1985-86. Maj. U.S. Army, 1971-76. Recipient Dist. award of merit Boy Scouts Am., 1985, Silver Beaver award 1994. Fellow ACP, Am. Acad. Dermatology, Royal Soc. Medicine (London); mem. N.Y. Acad. Scis., Kiwanis Club, Alpha Omega Alpha, Phi Sigma Iota. Republican. Mem. Lds Ch. Avocations: woodcarving, camping. Home: 2486 W 4550 S Roy UT 84067-1944 Office: 3860 Jackson Ave Ogden UT 84403-1956

MAUKE, OTTO RUSSELL, retired college president; b. Webster, Mass., Jan. 26, 1924; s. Otto G. and Florence (Giroux) M.; m. Leah Louison, June 18, 1950. AB, Clark U., 1947, A.M., 1948; PhD (Kellogg fellow), U. Tex., 1965. Tchr. history, acad. dean Endicott Jr. Coll., Beverly, Mass., 1948-65; acad. dean Cumberland County Coll., Vineland, N.J., 1966-67; pres. Camden County Coll., Blackwood, N.J., 1967-87, pres. emeritus. Served with U.S. Army, 1943-46, PTO. Home: 2119 E Lakeview Dr Sebastian FL 32958-8519

MAUKSCH, INGEBORG GROSSER, nursing educator; b. Austria; d. Frederick and Claire (Tauber) G.; children from previous marriage: Lawrence Bernard, Valerie. PhD, U. Chgo., 1969; D.Sc. (hon.), Syracuse U., 1979. Valere Potter disting. svc. prof. nursing Vanderbilt U. Sch. Nursing, Nashville, sr. program cons. Robert Wood Johnson nurse faculty fellowships in primary care program, 1976—. Mem. Presdl. Com. on Nat. Health Inst. Author: (with M. Miller) Implementing Change in Nursing, 1981, Systematic Patient Medication Record Review, 1980; mem. editorial bd.: Nursing Outlook, Nurse Educator. Mem. U.S. Holocaust Meml. Council. Recipient Alumni Achievement award Columbia U., 1979 Mem. Am. Nurses Assn. (hon.), Am. Acad. Nursing, Nat. Acad. Scis., Tenn. Nurses Assn. Office: Sch Nursing Vanderbilt Hospital Nashville TN 37232-0001

MAUL, CAROL ELAINE, small business owner; b. Joliet, Ill., Feb. 28, 1953; d. Donald James and Virginia Olive (Wilson) Johnson; m. Richard Kester Maul, June 16, 1979. Student, Met. State Coll., 1971-76. Mgr. So-Fro Fabrics, Elgin, 1976-79; owner, operator Port Arthur Pie Co., Denver, 1985-87; freelance musician Denver, 1987—; owner CAMA Creative Mktg. Bus. Promotion, Profl. Voice Work. Prin. flutist Elgin Symphony Orch., 1976-79; mem. Denver Botanic Gardens. Mem. Colo. Rail Passenger Assn., Nat. Trust Hist. Preservation, Citizens for Classical FM Radio (bd. dirs.), Colo. Water Garden Soc., Denver Garden Railway Soc., Rocky Mtn. Koi Club. Independent. Episcopalian. Lodge: Job's Daughters (Honored Queen 1970-71). Avocations: needlepoint, calligraphy. Home and Office: 387 S Pontiac Way Denver CO 80224-1335

MAUL, KEVIN JAY, financial consultant; b. York, Pa., Jan. 11, 1968; s. Peter Henry Jr. and Patricia Louise (Young) M. BA, Shippensburg U., 1990; MA, U. Va., 1992. Economist USDA Econ. Rsch. Svc., Washington, 1991-92; fin. cons. Pricewaterhouse Coopers LLP, Washington, 1992-99, Resources Connection, McLean, Va., 1999-2000, Deloitte & Touche LLP, Washington, 2000—03. Author: The Handbook of Mortgage Banking, 1993. Mem. Am. Econ. Assn. Lutheran. Avocations: music, travel, gardening, stamp collecting/philately. Home: 13 Hawthorne Ct NE Washington DC 20017

MAUL, TERRY LEE, psychologist, educator; b. San Francisco, May 6, 1946; s. Chester Lloyd and Clella Lucille (Hobbs) M.; m. Gail Ann Retallick, June 27, 1970 (div. Dec. 1986); 1 child, Andrew Eliot. Student, Coll. San Mateo, 1964-65; AB, U. Calif., Berkeley, 1967, MA, 1968, PhD, 1970. Prof. psychology San Bernardino Valley Coll., San Bernardino, Calif., 1970—, chmn. dept., 1979—83, 1996—2002, 2003—, honors program coord., 2002—. Rschr. self-actualization. Author: (with Eva Conrad) Introduction to Experimental Psychology, 1981; (with Gail Maul) Beyond Limit: Ways to Growth and Freedom, 1983; contbg. author other psychol. texts. Mem. APA, AAUP (chpt. pres. 1971-73), Audubon Soc., Mensa, Nature Conservancy, Wilderness Soc., Sierra Club. Democrat. Office: San Bernardino Valley Coll 701 S Mount Vernon Ave San Bernardino CA 92410-2705

MAULDIN, JOHN INGLIS, public defender; b. Atlanta, Nov. 6, 1947; s. Earle and Isabel (Inglis) M.; m. Cynthia Ann Balchin, Apr. 15, 1967 (div. Dec. 1985); children: Tracy Rutherford, Abigail Inglis; m. Linda W. Farmer, Nov. 7, 1998. BA, Wofford Coll., 1970; JD, Emory U., 1973. Bar: S.C. 1974, U.S. Ct. Appeals (4th cir.) 1974, U.S. Dist. Ct. S.C. 1975, U.S. Supreme Ct. 1978. Asst. pub. def. Defender Corp. Greenville County, S.C., 1974-76; ptnr. Mauldin & Allison, Greenville, 1977-92; pub. defender Greenville County, S.C., 1992—. Chair S.C. Commn. on Indigent Def., 1993-96; adj. prof. Greenville Tech. Coll., 1975-80; sec., treas. Def. Corp. Greenville County, 1979-92, bd. dirs. Bd. dirs. Speech Hearing & Learning Ctr., Greenville, 1977-90, pres., 1982; bd. dirs. Save Our Sons, 1995—. Named S.C. Atty. Yr. ACLU, S.C., 1986. Mem.: SC Pub. Defender Assn. (bd. dirs. 1992—), SC Assn. Criminal Def. Lawyers (bd. dirs. 1997—99), SC Trial Lawyers Assn., Nat. Legal Aid and Defender Assn. (defender policy group 1999—, bd. dirs. 2002—), Nat. Assn. Criminal Def. Attys., Rotary, Sigma Delta Phi. Democrat. Methodist. Office: PO Box 10264fs Greenville SC 29603

MAULDIN, RICHARD DANIEL, mathematics professor; b. Longview, Tex., Jan. 17, 1943; s. Stanley Hubert Mauldin and Helen Jane Dowling; stepfather: Cloyd James Dowling; m. Diana Rogers Block, June 24, 1985; children: Christopher, Catherine. BA, U. Tex., 1965, MA, 1966, PhD, 1969. From asst. prof. to assoc. prof. U. Fla., Gainesville, 1969-77; assoc. prof. U. North Tex., Denton, 1977-79, prof., 1979-88, Regents prof., 1988—. Cons. Los Alamos (N.Mex.) Nat. Lab., 1980-92, Ctr. for Comms. Rsch., San Diego, 1999—. Editor: Advances in Mathematics, 1994—, Real Analysis Exchange, 1994—; author: TransAMS, Japan Jour. Math.; contbr. articles to profl. jours. Rsch. grantee NSF, 1978-2003. Mem. Am. Math. Soc. (editor procs. 1988-92), Math. Assn. Am., Inst. Math. Stats., Assn. Symbolic Logic, Sigma Xi. Office: U North Tex Math Dept Box 311430 Denton TX 76203-1430 Fax: 940-565-4805. Office Phone: 940-565-3321. E-mail: mauldin@unt.edu.

MAULDIN, ROSETTA JOHNSON, dean, social work educator; b. Bedford County, Va. d. Perroneau and Edna Johnson; m. Charles A. Pinder, May 20, 1995; children: Lee, Michael, Adrienne Mauldin Oliver, Mark. BS, Hampton Inst., 1957; MSW, Ohio State U., 1968, PhD, 1990. Lic. ind. social worker, Ohio. Social worker Hamilton County Welfare Dept., Cin., 1959-70; exec. dir. Careers in Social Work, Cin., 1970-72; dir. children's svcs. Ctrl. Cmty. Health Bd., Cin., 1972-77; prof. social work No. Ky. U., Highland Heights, 1977—, interim dean Coll. Profl. Studies, 1985-87, 98—, assoc. provost, 1994-97. Chairperson dept. social work No. Ky. U., Highland Heights, 1982-85; bd. mem. Counselor and Social Worker Bd., State Ohio, 1990-93; adj. prof. U. Ky., Lexington, 1990—; presenter in field. Contbr. chpt. to book. Mem. bd. regents No. Ky. U., Highland Heights, 1990-93; pres., sec., commr. Nat. Accreditation Coun. for Agys. Serving the Blind and Visually Impaired, N.Y.C., Cin., 1990—; bd. mem. United Way, Cin., 1991—; alumnae Class 17 Leadership Cin., 1994. Recipient Career Woman of Achievement award YWCA, Cin., 1986, Cmty. Svc. award U.S. Postal Svc., 1994, Top Achiever award Successguide, Cin., 1995. Mem. NAACP, NASW (state bd. mem., state sec., state membership chair), Acad. Cert. Social Workers. Baptist. Avocations: reading, singing. Fax: 606-572-6176. E-mail: mauldin@nku.edu.

MAULE, JAMES EDWARD, law educator, lawyer; b. Phila., Nov. 26, 1951; s. Edward Randolph George and Jennie Elisabeth (Zappone) M.; m. Susan Margaret Noonan, June 26, 1982 (div. May 1988); children: Charles Edward, Sarah Margaret; m. Susan K. Garrison, Apr. 7, 1990 (div. 1991). BS cum laude, U. Pa. Wharton Sch., 1973; JD cum laude, Villanova U., 1976; LLM with highest honors, George Washington U., 1979. Bar: Pa. 1976, U.S. Tax Ct. 1986. Atty.-adv. Office Chief Counsel to IRS Legis. and Regulations Divsn., Washington, 1976-78; atty.-adv. judge U.S. Tax Ct., Washington, 1978-80; asst. prof. law Dickinson Sch. Law, 1981-83, lectr. and tax program chmn. continuing legal edn., 1981-83; assoc. prof. Villanova Sch. Law, 1983-86, prof., 1986—. Lectr. continuing legal edn. Pa. Bar Inst., Harrisburg, Continuing Legal Edn. Satellite Network, Inc., 1988; lectr. state and local taxes Georgetown U. Law Ctr. Inst., 1992; sr. tax and tech. ptnr. Ctr. Info. Law and Policy, 1993—99; owner JEMBook Pub. Co., TaxJEM Inc.; co-owner Starjem LLC, 2001—04; lectr. continuing legal edn. Phila. Tax Conf., 1996, 2001. Author: Cases and Materials in Federal Income Taxation, 1981, 24th edit., 2004, Materials in Partnership Law and Taxation, 1985, 6th edit., 1991, Materials in Partnership Taxation, 1987, 26th edit., 2004, Materials in Introduction to Taxation, 1987, Cases and Materials in Introduction to the Taxation of Business Entities, 1992, 12th edit., 2004, Materials in Taxation of Fundamental Wealth Transfers, 1986;: 2d edit., 1988, Materials in Tax Consequences of Disposition of Property, 1983, Materials and Problems in Taxation of Property Disposition I, 1987, Materials in Tax Planning for Real Estate, 1986, Materials in Estate and Gift Tax, 1983;: 3d edit., 1985, Materials in Taxation of Real Estate Transactions, 1986, 3d edit., 1992, Taxation of Residence Transactions, 1985, S Corporations: State Law and Taxation, 1989, (supplemental edits.), 1989, 1990, 1991, 1992, 1993, Materials and Problems in Computer Applications in the Law, 1990, 6th edit., 1995, Materials in Tax Policy, 1990, Materials in Digital Legal Practice Skills, 1996, Materials and Problems in Computer Applications in Tax Law, 1991, 8th edit., 1998, Better That 100 Witches Should Live, 1995, Materials in Decedents Estates and Trusts, 1997, 6th edit., 2002; author: (with A. Clay) Preparing the 1065 Return, 1992, 1993; author: Continuing Legal Edn. Publs., 1981—; contbg. author: Federal Tax Service, 1989, Tax Practice Series, 1989—; contbr. articles to profl. jours., chapters to books, monographs; author, developer: Computer Assisted Legal Edn. Programs in Taxation, owner, author, editor: computer assisted tax law instruction TaxJEM Inc., cons., prin. author: ABA Section of Taxation Model S Corporation Income Tax Act and Commentary, 1989, author, editor: Report of the Subcommittee on Comparison of S Corporations and Partnerships, 1990, 1991, case and comment editor: Villanova Law Rev., 1975—76, columnist, mem. editl. bd.: S Corps. Jour., 1987—91, Jour. of Ltd. Liability Cos., 1994—98, BNA Tax Mgmt., 1994—. Recipient Disting. Author award, BNA Tax Mgmt., 1993; Nat. Merit scholar, 1969—73. Mem. ABA (chair and reporter phaseout Elimination Project, Tax Simplification and Restructuring Com., sect. of taxation, cons., ex-officio mem. subcom. on state law, S Corp. com., chmn. subcom. on comparison of partnerships, mem. task force on pass-through entities, tax sect., former chmn. subcom. manuscripts and unpublished tchg. material, com. tchg. tax), Phila. Bar Assn. (lectr. tax sect. state and local tax CLE program 1991, fed. income taxes 1992—), Ctr. Info. Law and Policy, Order of Coif, Friars Sr. Soc. (Phila), Beta Alpha Psi. Home: 219 Comrie Dr Villanova PA 19085-1402 Office: Villanova U Sch Law Villanova PA 19085 E-mail: maule@law.villanova.edu.

MAULE, THERESA MOORE, lawyer; b. Winner, S.D., Jan. 20, 1966; d. Robert James and Serrilyn Rae (Belmer) M.; m. Brian Lee Kramer, Nov. 25, 1996. BA summa cum laude, Dakota Wesleyan U., 1988; MA, U. S.D., 1990, JD, 1994. Bar: S.D., U.S. Dist. Ct. S.D., Lower Brule Sioux Tribal Ct., Rosebud Sioux Tribal Ct. Prosecutor Rosebud (S.D.) Sioux Tribal Ct., 1994-96; ptnr. Maule & Maule Law Offices, Winner, S.D., 1995—; prosecutor Lower Brule (S.D.) Sioux Tribal Ct., 1996—; states atty Tripp County, Winner, 1997—. Mem. Tripp County Child Protection Team, Winner, S.D., 1997—. Mem. ABA, S.D. Bar Assn., Nat. Dist. Attys. Assn., S.D. Trial Lawyers Assn., Bus. and Profl. Women (Young Careerist 1996), Phi Kappa Phi, Phi Alpha Theta. Republican. Episcopalian. Avocations: camping, ceramics.

MAULL, GEORGE MARRINER, music director, conductor; b. Phila., Oct. 14, 1947; s. Frederick Dunlap and Helen Norbury (Jordan) M.; m. Marcia Eileen Korn, Aug. 13, 1984. MusB, U. Louisville, 1970, MusM, 1972; postgrad., Juilliard Sch. Music, 1976-78. Condr. Louisville Ballet Co., 1971-75; asst. condr. Opera Orch. N.Y., N.Y.C., 1976-78, N.J. Symphony Orch., Newark, 1979-80; music dir., condr. Bloomingdale Chamber Orch., N.Y.C., 1980-83, N.J. Youth Symphony, Summit, 1979—97, Philharm. Orch. N.J., Warren, 1987—; Condr. Laureate N.J. Youth Symphony, 1997. Conductor: Carnegie Hall, N.Y.C., 1989, Lincoln Ctr., N.Y.C., writer, host, condr.: Philharmonic Orch. of N.J., Discovery Concert Bach to the Future, Am. Pub. TV, 2003 (Emmy nomination, 2004), Nat. Polish Radio Symphony Orch., 2001—02, featured in WNET mini-documentary Art Effects: Young and Noteworthy, 1988. Named Disting. Alumnus, U. Louisville, 1994. Mem. Am. Fedn. Musicians, Am. Symphony Orch. League (conducting fellow 1978, Nat. Cert. Merit 1980), Condr's. Guild. Episcopalian. Home: 79 Stone Run Rd Bedminster NJ 07921-1711 Office: Philharm Orch of NJ PO Box 4064 Warren NJ 07059-0064

MAULSBY, ALLEN FARISH, lawyer; b. Balt., May 21, 1922; AB, Williams Coll., Williamstown, Mass., 1944; LL.B., U. Va., 1946. Bar: Md. 1947, N.Y. 1950. Law clk. to judge U.S. Circuit Ct. Appeals 4th Circuit, 1946-47; assoc. firm Cravath Swaine & Moore, N.Y.C., 1947-57, ptnr., 1958-95. Vestryman St. James' Episcopal Ch., N.Y.C., 1962-68, 80-85, warden, 1986-87; trustee Greer-Woodycrest Child Care, 1961-82; bd. dirs. Episc. Ch. Found., 1973-86. Mem. Am. Bar Found., N.Y. Bar Found., Am. Coll. Trial Lawyers, Am. Bar Assn., N.Y. State Bar Assn., Fed. Bar Assn., Assn. Bar City N.Y., N.Y. County Lawyers Assn. Office: Cravath Swaine & Moore 825 8th Ave New York NY 10019-7475 E-mail: amaulsby@cravath.com.

MAULTSBY, MARILYN D. health science association administrator; b. Balt., 1953; BA, Case Western Res. U., 1975; MS, U. Cin., 1976. Dir. planning Md. Health Planning Commn., 1977—86; dir. regional policy Greater Balt. Com., 1986—88; dir. pub. policy BlueCross BlueShield Md., 1988—93, v.p. strategic planning and adminstrn., 1993—95; dir. devel. and mgmt. svcs. Fidelity Health Sys. Inc., 1996—98; exec. dir. Md. Health Care Found., 1998—. Chair Role Network 2000, Inc., 1995—; mem. Balt. City Bd. Fin., 1997—; mem., pres. Md. State Bd. Edn., 2002—; bd. mem. Md. Assn. Health Underwriters, N.W. Hosp. Ctr. Vice chair Bd. Associated Black Charities, 1996—98; chair nominating com. Md. Com. for Children, 1997—99; mem. Govs. Task Force on Charitable Giving, 1997—; chair, bd. mem. Associated Black Charities, 1998—; mem. audit and compliance com. LifeBridge Health, 1999—. Recipient Md. Top 100 Women award, Daily Record, 1998, 2000, 2002. Mem.: Omega Psi, Delta Sigma Theta. Office: Md State Bd Edn 200 W Baltimore St Baltimore MD 21201 also: Md Health Care Found 6470-C Dobbin Rd Columbia MD 21045

MAUMENEE, IRENE H. ophthalmology educator; b. Bad Pyrmont, Germany, Apr. 30, 1940; MD, U. Gottingen, 1964. Cert. Am. Bd. Ophthalmology, Am. Bd. Med. Genetics. Rsch. asst. U. Hawaii, 1968; vis. geneticist Population Genetics Lab., 1968-69; fellow dept. medicine Johns Hopkins U., 1969-71; ophthalmology preceptorship Wilmer Inst. Johns Hopkins Hosp., 1969-71, from asst. prof. to assoc. prof. Wilmer Ophthalmology Inst., 1972-87; prof. ophthalmology and pediatrics Wilmer Ophthalmology Inst., 1972—; dir. Johns Hopkins Ctr. Hereditary Eye Disease, Wilmer Inst., 1979—. Cons. John F. Kennedy Inst. Visually & Mentally Handicapped Children, 1974—; dir. Low Vision Clinic, Wilmer Inst., 1977-88; vis. prof. French Ophthalmology Soc., Paris & French Acad. Medicine, 1988; advisor Nat. Eye Inst. Task Forces, 1976, 81. Mem. AMA, Am. Soc. Human Genetics, Am. Acad. Ophthalmology, Assn. Rsch. Vision & Ophthalmology, Internat. Soc. Genetic Eye Disease, Am. Ophthal. Soc., Pan Am. Assn. Ophthalmology. Achievements include research in nosology and management of ophthalmic and general medical genetics; population genetics; computer application to genetic analysis; molecular genetics; over 200 publications on human genetics and eye diseases. Office: Johns Hopkins Ctr Hereditary Eye Diseases 600 N Wolfe St # 517 Baltimore MD 21287-0005 E-mail: jhched@jhmi.edu.

MAUN, MARY ELLEN, computer consultant; b. N.Y.C., Dec. 18, 1951; d. Emmet Joseph and Mary Alice (McMahon) M. BA, CUNY, 1977, MBA, 1988. Sales rep. N.Y. Telephone Co., N.Y.C., 1970-76, comml. rep., 1977-83, programmer, 1984-86; systems analyst Telesector Resources Group, N.Y.C., 1987-89, sr. systems analyst, 1990-95; pres. Sleepy Hollow (N.Y.) Techs., Inc., N.Y., 1995—. Corp. chmn. United Way of Tri-State Area, N.Y.C., 1985; recreation activities vol. Pioneers Am., N.Y.C., 1982—; active Sleepy Hollow Hist. Soc.; founder Mary Ellen Maun Philanthropic Found., 1998; Dem. dist. leader for Philipse Manor. Recipient Outstanding Community Service award, Calvary Hosp., Bronx, N.Y., 1984. Mem. N.Y. Health and Racquet Club, Road Runners. Avocations: antique restoration, classical music, skiing, running. Office: Sleepy Hollow Techs Inc 539 Martling Ave Tarrytown NY 10591-4719 Home: 539 Martling Ave Tarrytown NY 10591-4719

MAUNDER, ADDISON BRUCE, agronomic research company executive; b. Holdrege, Nebr., May 13, 1934; s. Addison Haynes and Marie Sophia (Luebs) M.; m. Katherina Marlene Blum, Sept. 8, 1978; children: Lynda Diane, Christopher Allen. B.Sc., U. Nebr., 1956; M.Sc., Purdue U., 1958, PhD, 1960; DSc (hon.), U. Nebr., 1991; DAgr (hon.), Purdue U., 2003. With DeKalb AgResearch, Inc., Lubbock, Tex., 1960-96, sorghum breeder, 1960-61, dir. sorghum research, 1961-76, v.p. sorghum research, 1976-78, v.p. rsch., 1978-82; v.p. DeKalb-Pfizer Genetics, DeKalb, Ill., 1982-89; v.p. agronomic research DeKalb Plant Genetics, DeKalb, Ill., 1989-91; sr. v.p. DeKalb Genetics Corp., DeKalb, Ill., 1991-96; rsch. advisor Nat. Grain Sorghum Prodrs. Assn., 1997—. Bd. dirs. Diversity Mag., Washington, 1984-95; adj. prof. Tex. Tech. U., 1992—. Contbr. 13 chpts. to books and more than 70 articles to profl. jours. Mem. deans adv. com. Tex. Tech. U., Lubbock, 1983-86; chmn. external rev. INTSORMIL of U.S. AID, Lincoln, Nebr., 1980-2001; bd. dirs. Tex. Tech. U. Rsch. Found., 1986-92; mem. Nat. Plant Genetic Resources Bd., 1991-92, Nat. Plant Variety Protection Bd., 1991-94. Recipient Gerald Thomas award Tex. Tech. U., 1974, Prodn. award Grain Sorghum Producers Assn., 1985, Genetics and Plant Breeding award for Industry, 1987, Indsl. Agronomy award, 1988, Purdue Disting. Alumni award, 1997, Monsanto Crop Sci. Disting. Career award, 2000, President's Disting Svc. award ASTA (Am. Seed Trad Assn.), 2001. Fellow AAAS, Am. Soc. Agronomy (bd. dirs. 1991-92), Crop Sci. Soc. Am. (bd. dirs. 1991-92, pres. 1995-96); mem. Am. Seed Trade Assn., Sigma Xi, Alpha Zeta. Republican. Achievements include development of plant products (150 hybrids) emphasizing yield, improved drought and insect resistance as well as nutritional quality. E-mail: texasgreenburg@aol.com.

MAUNEY, JAMES THOMAS, JR., music educator, musician; b. Atlanta, Ga., Apr. 15, 1963; s. Mary Lee and James Thomas Mauney; m. June Rogers June Vermeer, Oct. 12, 1998; children: Michelle Parrimore, Kristina Warren. MusB in Music Edn., U. Ga., 1985. Cert. performance based T4 music tchr. Profl. Practices Commn., Ga., 1987. Tchr. music/band Stewart County Bd. Edn., Lumpkin, Ga., 1987—89; tchr. band Taylor County Bd. Edn., Butler, Ga., 1989—96; tchr., dir. of bands Upson-Lee H.S., Thomaston-Upson Bd. of Edn., Ga. Musician saxophone/voice, Ga., 1981—. Mem. Thomaston-Upson Arts Coun., Ga., 1996, Upson-Lee Athletic Booster Club, Thomaston, Ga., 1996; dir. Upson-Lee Band Booster Club, Thomaston, Ga. Nominee Disney Hand Tchr. awards, Walt Disney Found., 2004; recipient Outstanding Young Band Dir. award, Albany State U., Ga., 1988, Tchr. award, Coca Cola, 2002, Tchr. of Excellence award, Mfrs. Roundtable-Thomaston C. of C., 2004; Educators grant, Wal Mart Found., 2002 and 2003. Mem.: Ga. Music Educators Assn., Music Educators Nat. Conf., Ga. Assn. of Educators, Nat. Educators Assn., North Am. Saxophone Alliance. Home: 136 Crescent Rd Thomaston GA 30286 Office: Upson-Lee HS 268 Knight Tr Thomaston GA 30286 Business E-Mail: jmauney@upson.k12.ga.us.

MAUNEY, THOMAS LEE, theater designer; b. Lexington, N.C., May 29, 1967; s. Thomas Pete and Iris Elnita (Washburn) M. BFA, U. N.C., Greensboro, 1990; MFA, U. Mont., 1995. Asst. tech. dir., designer Raleigh (N.C.) Little Theatre, 1989-90; tech. dir. U. Mont., Missoula, 1990-92; designer Big Fork (Mont.) Summer Playhouse, 1994-98; prodn. mgr., tech. dir. Raleigh Meml. Auditorium, 1998—2002, BTI Ctr. Performing Arts, 1998—2002. Freelance designer theatre and spl. events.

MAUPIN, A. WILLIAM, state supreme court justice; children: Allison, Michael. BA, U. Nev., 1968; JD, U. Ariz., 1971. Atty., ptnr. Thorndal, Backus, Maupin and Armstrong, Las Vegas, 1976—93; judge 8th Jud. Dist. Clark County, 1993—97; assoc. justice Supreme Ct. Nev., 1997—; chief justice Supreme Ct., Nev., 2001—02. Bd. govs. Nev. State Bar, 1991—95. Mem.: Nev. Supreme Ct. (study com. to review jud. elections, chmn. 1995, alternate dispute resolution implementation com. chmn. 1992—96). Office: Nev Supreme Ct 201 S Carson St Carson City NV 89701-4702

MAUPIN, ARMISTEAD JONES, lawyer; b. Raleigh, N.C., Nov. 10, 1914; s. Alfred McGhee and Mary Armistead (Jones) M.; m. Diana Jane Barton, May 16, 1942 (dec.); children: Armistead Jones, Anthony Westwood, Jane Stuart; m. Cheryl Leigh Erhard, July 31, 1982. AB, U. N.C., 1936; JD, George Washington U., 1940. Bar: N.C. 1939. Ptnr. Maupin Taylor PA, Raleigh. Pres. Occoneechee coun. Boy Scouts Am., 1962-64; pres. Carolina Charter Corp., 1976-80, 93—; former chancellor Episcopal Diocese of N.C.; former sr. warden Christ Ch. Parish; vice chmn. Am. Battle Monuments Commn., 1981-90. Comdr. USNR, WWII, PTO. Decorated chevalier French Legion of Honor. Fellow: Am. Bar Found.; mem.: ABA (ho. of dels. 1960—72), Soc. of Cin. (v.p. gen. 1968—70, pres. gen. 1971—74, pres. N.C. soc. 1964—67), N.C. State Bar (coun. 1955—60, pres. 1959—60), Triangle Fox Hounds, Cir. Club, Carolina Country Club. Republican. Episcopalian. Home: 2005 Banbury Rd Raleigh NC 27608-1121 Office: Highwoods Tower One 3200 Beech Leaf Ct Raleigh NC 27604-1085

MAUPIN, ARMISTEAD JONES, JR., writer; b. Washington, May 13, 1944; s. Armistead Jones and Diana Jane (Barton) M. BA, U. N.C., 1966. Reporter News and Courier, Charleston, S.C., 1970-71, AP, San Francisco, 1971-72; account exec. Lowry Russom and Leeper, Pub. Rels., San Francisco, 1973; columnist Pacific Sun mag., San Francisco, 1974; publicist San Francisco Opera, 1975; serialist San Francisco Chronicle, 1976-77, 81, 83; commentator Sta. KRON-TV, San Francisco, 1979; serialist San Francisco Examiner, 1986. Author: (novels) Tales of the City, 1978, More Tales of the City, 1980, Further Tales of the City, 1982, Babycakes, 1984, Significant Others, 1987, Sure of You, 1989, (omnibus) 28 Barbary Lane, 1990, (omnibus) Back to Barbary Lane, 1991, Maybe the Moon, 1992; co-author: The Essential Clive Barker, 1999; librettist musical Heart's Desire, 1990; exec. prodr. (TV program) Armistead Maupin's Tales of the City, 1993; contbr. articles to N.Y. Times, L.A. Times, others. Lt. (j.g.) USN, 1967-70, Vietnam. Recipient Freedom Leadership award Freedoms Found., Valley Forge, Pa., 1972, Comms. award Met. Elections Com. L.A., 1989, Exceptional Achievement award ALA, 1990, Best Dramatic Serial award Royal TV Soc., 1994, Peabody award 1994, Outstanding Miniseries award, Gay and Lesbian Alliance Against Defamation, 1994, Best Miniseries award Nat. Bd. of Rev., 1994. Office: ICM Care Amanda Urban 40 W 57th St Fl 16 New York NY 10019-4098 Address: c/o Literary Bent PO Box 4109990 Ste 528 San Francisco CA 94141 E-mail: inquiries@literarybent.com.

MAUPIN, ELIZABETH THATCHER, theater critic; b. Cleve., Oct. 21, 1951; d. Addison and Margaret (Thatcher) M.; m. Jay Yellen, Dec. 29, 1995. BA in English, Wellesley (Mass.) Coll., 1973; M in Journalism, U. Calif., Berkeley, 1976. Editorial asst. Houghton Mifflin Co., Boston, 1973-74; reporter, movie critic Times-Standard, Eureka, Calif., 1976-78; theater and movie critic Chronicle-Telegram, Elyria, Ohio, 1978-79; movie critic Ledger-Star, Norfolk, Va., 1979-82; feature writer Va.-Pilot and Ledger-Star, Norfolk, 1982-83; sr. theater critic Orlando (Fla.) Sentinel, 1983—. Fellow Nat. Arts Journalism program Columbia U., 1995-96. Fellow Nat. Critics Inst.; mem. Am. Theatre Critics Assn. (exec. com. 1993-99, chair 1996-99). Office: Orlando Sentinel 633 N Orange Ave Orlando FL 32801-1349

MAUPIN, JOHN E., JR., college president; b. L.A., Oct. 28, 1946; m. Eilene; three children. Diploma, San Jose State Coll.; DDS, Meharry Med. Coll., 1972; MBA, Loyola Coll., Balt., 1979; LLD (hon.), Va. Union Univ., 1996; DSc (hon.), Morehouse Sch. Medicine, 1995. Dentistry resident Provident Hosp., Balt., 1973; dentist, capt. then advanced through grades to lt. col. U.S. Army Dental Corps/Walter Reed Med. Ctr., Washington, 1974-97; various health/dental positions including dep. commr. Balt. City Health Dept., 1981-87; CEO Southside Healthcare, Inc., Atlanta; exec. v.p. Morehouse Sch. of Medicine, Atlanta; pres. Meharry Med. Coll., Nashville, 1994—. Mem. adv. groups Nat. Com. on Fgn. Med. Edn. and Accreditation, Bd. of Scientific Counselors, Nat. Ctr. for Infectious Diseases, Managed Care Task Force, others; bd. dirs. Monarch Dental Corp., Am. Gen. Series Portfolio Co., U.S. Life Mut. Funds, others. Exec. coun. Boy Scouts of Mid. Tenn.; bd. dirs. Nashville Cmty. Found., BellSouth Sr. Classic at Opryland; former chair bd. dirs. United Way of Mid. Tenn.; former mem. bd. govs. Nashville Area C. of C., others. Recipient A.B. Cooper award North Ga. Dental Soc., 1994, Dentist of Yr. award, 1991, Mayor's Citation for outstanding pub. svc., Balt., 1987,

others. Mem. Nat. Dental Assn. (past pres.), Nat. Med. Assn., Ga. State Med. Assn., Nat. Assn. Cmty. Health Ctrs., Nat. Assn. Health Care Execs., others. Office: Meharry Med Coll 1005 DB Todd Blvd Nashville TN 37208

MAUPIN, LARRY D. retired music educator, musician; b. Kansas City, Feb. 11, 1942; s. Dan W. and Ruth M. Maupin; m. Judy A. Bartzatt, Sept. 1, 1963; children: Cynthia A., Lisa R. MusB Edn., Nebr. Wesleyan U., Lincoln, Nebr., 1965; MusM, U. Nebr., Lincoln, Nebr., 1969. String specialist, dir. orch. Grand Island Pub. Schools, Grand Island, Nebr., 1965—2003. Founder, condr.,music dir. Nebr. Tri-City Area Youth Symphony, Grand Island, Nebr., 1972—97; concertmaster, asst. condr. Hastings Symphony Orch., Hastings, Nebr., 1965—. Contbr. articles to profl. jour. Served on over a dozen com.; mem. ch. choir Trinity United Meth. Ch., Grand Island, Nebr., 1965—2003; bd. dirs., scholarship chmn. Grand Island Concert Assn., Nebr., 1997—2003; nebr. dist. iv rep. Nebr. Coalition for Music Edn., Nebr., 1993—2003; fund-raising chmn. to establish statewide pub. radio network Pub. Radio Nebr. Found., Lincoln, Nebr., 1991—95. Recipient Arts Educator of the Yr., Moonshell Arts Coun., Grand Island, 2002, Hastings Symphony Orch. Hall of Fame, Hastings Symphony Orch., 2001, Outstanding Music Alumni, Nebr. Wesleyan U., 1984. Mem.: NEA, Am. String Teachers Assn., Nebr. Chpt. (Outstanding String Tchr. of the Yr. 1991—92), Nebr. Music Educators Assn. (chmn., orch. affairs 1988—89, Hall of Fame 1995), Grand Island Edn. Assn. (pres. 1970—72, Outstanding Young Educator 1974), Nebr. State Edn. Assn., Nat. Rlwy. Hist. Soc. Achievements include summer motorcoach operator, arrow stage lines (tours and charters throughout USA and Can.). Home: 1603 North Oak St Grand Island NE 68801-2558 Personal E-mail: jlmaupin@charter.net. Business E Mail: lmaupin@gips.org.

MAURER, ALAN HARVEY, nuclear medicine physician; b. Atlantic City, N.J., Jan. 17, 1947; s. Franklin E. and Ruth L. (Cohen) M.; m. Marilyn Erber, May 21, 1981; children: Joshua, Benjamin, Molly. AB, ScB, Brown U., 1969; MS, U. Pa., 1971; MD, Temple U., 1975. Diplomate Am. Bd. Nuclear Medicine, Am. Bd. Internal Medicine. Dir. nuclear medicine Temple U. Hosp. and Sch. Medicine, Phila., 1981—. Contbr. sci. papers to profl. publs. Mem. Soc. Nuclear Medicine (pres. 2001-02), Radiologic Soc. N.Am., Tau Beta Pi, Sigma Xi, Alpha Omega Alpha. Achievements include invention of medical imaging devices. Office: Temple Univ Hosp Broad & Ontario Sts Philadelphia PA 19140

MAURER, DAVID LEO, lawyer; b. Evansville, Ind., Oct. 31, 1945; s. John G. Jr. and Mildred M. (Lintzenich) M.; m. Diane M. Kaput, Aug. 11, 1973; children: Eric W., Kathryn A. BA magna cum laude, U. Detroit, 1967, Cert. in Teaching, 1971; JD, Wayne State U., 1975. Bar: Mich., U.S. Dist. Ct. (ea. and we. dist.) Mich., U.S. Ct. Appeals (6th cir.) Cin. Law clk. Mich. Ct. Appeals, Detroit, 1976, Supreme Ct. Mich., Lansing, 1977-78; asst. U.S. atty. civil div. U.S. Dept. Justice, Detroit, 1978-81; assoc. to ptnr. Butzel, Long, Gust, Klein & Van Zile, Detroit, 1981-85; ptnr. Pepper, Hamilton & Scheetz (now Pepper Hamilton LLP), Detroit, 1985—. Guest lectr. Practicing Law Inst., 1988—, Nat. Bus. Inst., 1989—, U. Mich. Law Sch., U. Detroit Law Sch., 1990, Hazardous Waste Super Conf., 1986-87. Co-author: Michigan Environmental Law Deskbook, 1992; contbr. articles to profl. jours. and chpts. in books. Mem. Energy & Environ. Policy Com., 1988—, chairperson, 1989-90; mem. Great Lakes Water Resources Commn., 1986. Mem. State Bar Mich. (environ. couns. 1986-91, sec., treas., chairperson-elect, chairperson 1991-93). Office: Pepper Hamilton LLP 100 Renaissance Ctr Ste 3600 Detroit MI 48243-1157 Office Phone: 313-393-7448. Business E-Mail: maurerd@pepperlaw.com.

MAURER, FREDERIC GEORGE, III, banker; b. Grand Rapids, Mich., May 15, 1952; s. Frederic George and Rhea Marie (Annesser) M. BA, St. Louis U., 1974, MBA, 1977. Dir. residence Marguerite Hall St. Louis U., 1977-79; internat. banking analyst Merc. Trust Co., St. Louis, 1979-80, banking rep. Latin Am., 1980-81, internat. officer, 1981-83, asst. v.p., 1983, Union Bank, L.A., 1983-86; asst. v.p. internat. sect. Centerre Bank, N.A., St. Louis, 1986-87, asst. v.p. portfolio mgmt. sect., 1987-88; with pvt. banking dept. Boatmen's Nat. Bank, St. Louis, 1988-90, v.p., 1990-97, Nations Bank, St. Louis, 1997-99, Bank of Am., St. Louis, 1999-2001, Commerce Trust Co., St. Louis, 2001—. Bd. dirs. Downtown/Marquette YMCA, 2003—. Bd. dirs. Assocs. St. Louis U. Librs., 1975-79, Friends of Forum, St. Louis, NCCJ, 1992—, Franciscan Missionary Union, 1996-2001; mem. dir.'s assn. Mo. Bot. Garden, 1986—; mem. World Affairs Coun., St. Louis, DuBourg Soc. Internat. Bus. fellow, 1975-77. Mem. Ctr. Internat. Banking Studies, U. Va., Charlottesville, Robert Morris Assocs., Alumni Council St. Louis U., Opera Guild, Performing Arts Council-In the Wings, L.A., English-speaking Union, American Club, (London), Noonday Club. Roman Catholic. Home: 849 Aldan Dr Saint Louis MO 63132-3501 Office: 1 Met Sq 211 N Broadway Saint Louis MO 63102-2733 Office Phone: 314-746-8921. E-mail: rick.maurer@commercebank.com.

MAURER, HAROLD MAURICE, pediatrician; b. N.Y.C., Sept. 10, 1936; s. Isador and Sarah (Rothkowitz) M.; m. Beverly Bennett, June 12, 1960; children: Ann Maurer Rosenbach, Wendy Maurer Rausch. AB, NYU, 1957; MD, SUNY, Bklyn., 1961. Diplomate Am. Bd. Pediatrics, Am. Bd. Pediatric Hematology-Oncology. Intern pediatrics Kings County Hosp., N.Y.C., 1961-62; resident in pediatrics Babies Hosp., Columbia-Presbyn. Med. Center, N.Y.C., 1962-64; fellow in pediatric hematology/oncology Columbia-Presbyn. Med. Center, 1966-68; asst. prof. pediatrics Med. Coll. Va., Richmond, 1968-71, asso. prof., 1971-75, prof., 1975—, chmn. dept. pediatrics, 1976-93; dean U. Nebr. Coll. Medicine, Omaha, 1993-98; chancellor U. Nebr. Med. Ctr., Omaha, 1998—. Chmn. Intergroup Rhabdomyosarcoma Study, 1972-98; exec. com. Pediatric Oncology Group. Editor: pediatrics, 1983, Rhabdomyosarcoma and Related Tumors in Children and Adolescence, 1991; mem. editorial bd. Am. Jour. Hematology, Journal Pediatric Hematology and Oncology, Medical and Pediatric Oncology, 1984-99; contbr. articles to profl. jours. Mem. Youth Health Task Force, City of Richmond., Gov.'s Adv. Com. on Handicapped., Gov.'s Homeland Security Policy Group, Nebr., 2002-; mem. coun. biodefense Assn. of Academic Health Ctr., 2003—, coun. global health, 2003—, gov.'s homeland security policy group 2002—; mem. nat. com. on childhood cancer Am. Cancer Soc., bd. dirs. Va. div.; mem. bd. Nebr. Med. Ctr., 1997—. Served to lt. comdr. USPHS, 1964-66. NIH grantee, 1974-98. Mem. Am. Acad. Pediatrics (com. oncology-hematology), Am. Soc. Hematology, Soc. Pediatric Rsch., Am. Pediatric Soc., Va. Pediatric Sic. (exec. com.), Assn. Med. Sch. Pediatric Dept. Chmn., Internat. Soc. Pediatric Oncology, Am. Soc. Clin. Oncology, Va. Hematology Soc., Am. Assn. Cancer Rsch., Am. Cancer Soc., Am. Soc. Pediatric Hematology-Oncology (v.p. 1990-91, pres. 1991-93, Lifetime Achievement award children's oncology group 2003), Sigma Xi, Coun. Deans AAMC, Gov.'s Blue Ribbon Commn., Alpha Omega Alpha. Republican. Jewish. Home: 9822 Ascot Dr Omaha NE 68114-3848 Office: U Nebr Med Ctr 986605 Nebraska Med Ctr Omaha NE 68198-6605 Business E-Mail: hmmaurer@unmc.edu.

MAURER, JEFFREY STUART, finance executive; b. N.Y.C., July 9, 1947; s. Herbert and Phoebe Maurer; m. Wendy S. Nemerov. BA, Alfred U., 1969; MBA, NYU, 1975; JD, St. John's U., 1976. With U.S. Trust Co. N.Y., 1970—, pres., 1990; COO U.S. Trust Co., N.Y.C., 1994-2001, CEO, 2001—02, chmn., CEO, 2002—03, Neuberger Berman Trust Co., N.A., N.Y.C., 2003—. Bd. dirs. Greater N.Y. Ins. Cos. Trustee Alfred (N.Y.) U., 1984, North Shore L.I. Jewish Health Sys.; bd. dirs., treas. Children's Health Fund, N.Y.C., 1988; bd. dirs. Hebrew Home Aged, Riverdale, N.Y., 1992, Roundabout Theatre Co. Mem. ABA, N.Y. State Bar Assn., Glen Head Country Club, Harmonie Club. Jewish. Avocations: skiing, golf. Office: Neuberger Berman Trust Co NA 605 Third Ave New York NY 10158 Business E-Mail: jmaurer@nb.com.

MAURER, RICHARD HORNSBY, physicist; b. Reading, Pa., Apr. 27, 1942; s. Samuel Forest and Marian E. (Hornsby) M.; m. Marian Ross Harvey, May 3, 1975; children: Jonathan, Andrew. BS, L.I. U., 1964; PhD, U. Pitts., 1970. Postdoctoral fellow Bartol Rsch. Found., Swarthmore, Pa., 1970-73; environ. engr. AMP Inc., Harrisburg, Pa., 1973-81; physicist Applied Physics Lab. Johns Hopkins U., Laurel, Md., 1981—, reliability group supr. test and evaluation sect., 1986-94, instr. Whiting Sch. Engring., 1988—. Contbr. chpt. to: Space Systems Reliability and Survivability, 1994; contbr. articles to Jour. IEEE Transactions Nuclear Sci., Jour. Spacecraft and Rockets, Internat. Reliability Physics Symposium. Baseball mgr. Howard County Youth Program, Ellicott City, Md., 1985-97; lector St. John's Episcopal Ch., 1994-98. Mem. IEEE, Am. Soc. Quality Control, Am. Phys. Soc., Sigma Xi. Achievements include patent for fabrication of thermal batteries by multi-layer ceramic of organic printed circuit board methods; research on effects of radiation on electronic devices, on reliability of electronic packaging designs and gallium arsenide devices; development of portable neutron spectrometer. Office: Johns Hopkins U Applied Physics Lab 11100 Johns Hopkins Rd Laurel MD 20723-6005

MAURER, RICHARD MICHAEL, investment company executive; b. Bethlehem, Pa., June 4, 1948; s. Richard Thomas and Anna Theresa (Bold) M.; m. Karen Coe, June 13, 1970; children: Christopher Coe, Mark Emerson. Student, Pa. State U., 1966 68; BS, Point Park Coll., 1971, MBA, U. Pitts., 1982. CPA Pa. Staff acct. Price Waterhouse, Pitts., 1972-74, tax acct., 1974, sr. tax acct., 1974-77, tax mgr., 1977-78; dir. taxes The Hillman Co., Pitts., 1978-85; pres. Maurer Ross & Co., Inc., Pitts., 1985—; co-mng. ptnr. Wesmar Ptnrs., Pitts., 1985—; chmn., CEO Admatic Industries, Inc., Pitts., 1998—. Bd. dirs. Women's Golf Unlimited, Inc., Admatic Industries, Inc., Maurer Ross & Co., Inc., Maurer & Ross, Inc. Bd. trustees Pa. State McKeesport U. Point Park U. Alumni. Mem. AICPA, Assn. Corp. Growth, Pa. Inst. CPAs, Rotary (past dir., past pres.), Oakmont Country Club, Duquesne Club, Lake Nona Golf Club. Office: PO Box 106 Murrysville PA 15668-0106 E-mail: rmaurer@alltel.net.

MAURER, VIRGINIA GALLAHER, law educator; b. Shawnee, Okla., Nov. 7, 1946; d. Paul Clark Gallaher and Virginia Ruth (Watson) Abernathy; m. Ralph Gerald Maurer, July 31, 1971; children: Ralph Emmett, William Edward. BA, Northwestern U., 1968; MA, Stanford U., 1969, JD, 1975. Bar: Iowa 1976. Tchr. social studies San Mateo (Calif.) H.S. Dist., 1969-71; spl. asst. to pres. U. Iowa, Iowa City, 1976-80, adj. asst. prof. law, 1979-80; affiliate asst. prof. law U. Fla., Gainesville, 1981, asst. prof. bus. law, 1980-85, assoc. prof., 1985-93, prof., 1993—, Huber Hurst prof., 1997—. Dir. Poe Bus. Ethics Ctr., 1998—, MBA program U. Fla., 1987, chair dept. mgmt., 1994-2003; vis. scholar Wolfson Coll., Cambridge, 1994; vis. prof. SDA Bocconi U., Milan, 1994-96, Helsinki Sch. Econs. and Bus., 1998, U. Catania, Sicily, 1999, 2002 03; cons. Gov.'s Com. on Iowa 2000, Iowa City, 1976-77, Fla. Banker's Assn., Gainesville, 1982, various law firms, 1995—; bd. dirs. Water & Air Rsch., Inc. Contbr. articles to profl. jours.; jr. editor Am. Bus. Law Jour., 1989-90, mng. editor, 1990-91, editor-in-chief, 1992-94. Bd. dirs. Gainesville Chamber Orch., 1990-93; fundraising com. Pro Arte Musica, Gainesville, 1980-84; sr. warden, vestry Holy Trinity Episc. Ch., 1991-93, 99—, jr. warden, 2000-02; bd. dirs. Holy Trinity Found., Gainesville, 1991-93; com. charter and canon law Episc. Diocese Fla., 1994-96; bd. dirs. Samaritan Ctrs. of North Ctrl. Fla., Inc., 1995-97. Fellow Soc. Advanced Legal Studies (UK); mem. ABA, AAUW, Acad. Legal Studies in Bus. (ho. of dels. 1989-90, exec. com. 1992, 98—, sec.-treas. 1998-99, v.p. 1999-2000, pres-elect 2000-01, pres. 2001-02), Southeastern Bus. Law Assn. (proc. editor 1984-87, treas. 1985-86, v.p. 1986-87, pres.-elect 1987-88, pres. 1988-89), Iowa Bar Assn., LWV, U. Fla. Athletic Assn. (bd. dirs. 1982-88, v.p. chmn. fin. com.), Gainesville Womens' Forum (bd. dirs. 1988-91), Fla. Women' Network (bd. dirs. 1995-99), Univ. Woman's Club (Gainesville, Fla.), Rotary (bd. dirs. 1989-91, dist. scholarship com. 1997-99, regional scholarship com. 2000, chair 2001), Beta Gamma Sigma, Kappa Alpha Theta, Delta Sigma Pi. Home: 2210 NW 6th Pl Gainesville FL 32603-1409 Office: U Fla Grad Sch Bus Gainesville FL 32611 E-mail: virginia.maurer@cba.ufl.edu.

MAURER, WILLIAM C. mining company executive; Pres. Maurer Engring., Inc., Houston. Mem. NAE. Office: Maurer Engineering Inc 13135 Dairy Ashford Rd Ste 800 Sugar Land TX 77478-3686 E-mail: maurer@maurereng.com.

MAURICE, PAUL, former professional hockey coach; b. Sault Ste. Marie, Ont., Canada, Jan. 30, 1967; m. Michelle; 1 child, Sydney. Asst. coach Detroit Jr. Red Wings, 1988-93, head coach, 1993-94, Carolina Hurricanes, 1995—2003; asst. coach All-Star Game NHL, 1997. Named runner up Coach of Yr. nominamtion OHL, 1995. Mem. Compuware Hockey Orgn.

MAURIN, JAMES E. real estate executive; Grad. in aerospace engring., La. State U., 1970; MBA, Tulane U., 1972. Acct. Ernst and Ernst, New Orleans; mng. ptnr. Maurin-Ogden Properties, Covington, La., 1975—; chmn. Stirling Properties, Covington, La., 1975—. Bd. dirs. Ochsner Found. Hosp. Mem.: Internat. Coun. Shopping Ctrs. (chmn. 2004—), World Pres.'s Orgn., Urban Land Inst. Office: Stirling Properties 109 Northpark Blvd Covington LA 70433-5005 E-mail: jmau@stirlingprop.com.

MAURO, ANTHONY PETER, small business owner; b. Red Bank, NJ, Feb. 20, 1955; s. Peter Anthony and Dolores Joyce Mauro; m. Carol Jean Albanese, Sept. 22, 1985. BA, Montclair State U., 1977; MBA, Monmouth U., 1985. Dist., gen. mgr. Gen. Med. Corp., Edison, NJ, 1988—93; v.p. Eldercare Co., Edison, NJ, 1993—95; owner, pres. Camtec Industries, Inc., Colts Neck, NJ, 1995—. Author: Take Me On Safari!, 2003. Avocations: writing, hunting. Office: Camtec Industries Inc 28 Saddle Ridge Colts Neck NJ 07722

MAURO, RICHARD FRANK, lawyer, investment manager; b. Hawthorne, Nev., July 21, 1945; s. Frank Joseph and Dolores D. (Kreimeyer) M.; m. LaVonne M. Madden, Aug. 28, 1965; 1 child, Lindsay Anne. AB, Brown U., 1967; JD summa cum laude, U. Denver, 1970. Bar: Colo. 1970. Assoc. Dawson, Nagel, Sherman & Howard, Denver, 1970-72, Van Cise, Freeman, Tooley & McClearn, Denver, 1972-73, ptnr., 1973-74, Hall & Evans, Denver, 1974-81, Morrison & Forester, Denver, 1981-84; of counsel Parcel & Mauro, P.C., Denver, 1984—; pres. Parcel, Mauro & Hultin, P.C., Denver, 1988-90; of counsel Parcel, Mauro P.C., Denver, 1992-99; pres. Sundance Oil Exploration Co., 1985-88; exec. v.p. Castle Group, Inc., 1992-97, pres., 1998—, Richard F. Mauro, P.C., 1999—; ptnr. Moye, Giles, O'Keefe, Vermeire & Gorrell, 1999—. Adj. prof. U. Denver Coll. Law, 1981-84. Symposium editor: Denver Law Jour., 1969-70; editor: Colorado Corporation Manual; contbr. articles to legal jours. Pres. Colo. Open Space Coun., 1974; mem. law alumni coun. U. Denver Coll. Law, 1988-91. Francis Wayland scholar, 1967; recipient various Am. jurisprudence awards Mem. ABA, Colo. Bar Assn., Denver Bar Assn., Colo. Assn. Corp. Counsel. (pres. 1974-75), Am. Arbitration Assn. (comml. arbitrator), Order St. Ives, Denver Athletic Club (bd. dirs. 1986-89). Home: 2552 E Alameda Ave Unit 128 Denver CO 80209-3330 Office: 1225 17th St Fl 29 Denver CO 80202-5534 E-mail: dick.mauro@moyelaw.com.

MAURSTAD, DAVID INGOLF, federal agency administrator, insurance company executive; b. North Platte, Nebr., Aug. 25, 1953; s. Ingolf Byron and Marilyn Sophia (Gimble) M.; m. Karen Sue Micek, Sept. 7, 1974; children: Ingolf, Derek, Laura. A. in Fine Arts, Platte Community Coll., Columbus, Nebr., 1973; BSBA, U. Nebr., 1989, MBA, 2000. Asst. golf profl. Country Club of Lincoln (Nebr.), 1973-76; head golf profl. Westward Ho Country Club, Sioux Falls, S.D., 1977; ins. agt. Maurstad/Zimmerman Ins., Beatrice, Nebr., 1978-84; ins. agy. mgr. Maurstad Ins. Svcs., Inc., Beatrice, 1984-90, pres., 1990—; mayor City of Beatrice, 1991-94; mem. Nebr. Senate from dist. 30, 1995—99; lt. gov. State of Nebr., 1998—2001; regional dir. FEMA, 2001—. Pres. Beatrice YMCA, 1982-83, Gage County United Way, Beatrice, 1985, founding trustee, 1st pres. Beatrice Ednl. Found., 1988-96; del., Rep. Nat. Conv., 2000; state vice chmn., Bush Cheney, 2000; mem. Nebr. Rep. State Cen. Com., Lincoln, 1985-90, 95-97, elected Bd. Edn. Sch. Dist. #15, Beatrice, 1988-90; candidate Nebr. Legislature, Lincoln, 1986; chmn. Highway 77 Improvement Assn., 1991-94; chair Nebr. Info. Tech. Commn., 1999-2001; trustee Beatrice Libr. Found., 1996-2001; bd. dirs. Madonna Found., 1997-2001. Named Outstanding Young Man of Am., Beatrice Jaycees, 1985, Citizen of Yr. Beatrice C. of C., 1993, Outstanding Amateur Golfer Nebr. Golf Assn., 1981, Harold Sieck Pub. Ofcl. of Yr., Arc of Nebr., 1998; recipient Young Alumnus award U. Nebr. Alumni Assn., 1993, Disting. Svc. award Nat. Fedn. Interscholastic Ofcls. Assn., 1989, Disting. Svc. award League of Nebr. Municipalities, 1998, Outstanding Alumnus award Ctrl. C.C. Platte Campus, Coll. Alumni Assn., 1998, Disting. Alumni award Nebr. C.C. System, 2000. Mem. Ind. Ins. Agts. Nebr. (Young Agt. of Yr. 1985), Blue Valley Life Underwriters (bd. dirs. 1988-94), Beatrice C. of C. (bd. dirs. 1985-87), U. Nebr.-Lincoln Coll. Bus. Adminstrn. Alumni Bd. (bd. dirs. 1989-96, pres. 1994-95, Leadership award 1994). Republican. Lutheran. Avocations: golf, reading, spectator sports. Office: Fed Emergency Mgmt Agy PO Box 25267 Bldg 710 A Denver Fed Ctr Denver CO 80225-0267

MAU-SHIMIZU, PATRICIA ANN, lawyer; b. Jan. 17, 1953; d. Herbert G. K. and Leilani (Yuen) Mau; 1 child, Melissa Rose. BS, U. San Francisco, 1975; JD, Golden Gate U., 1979. Bar: Hawaii 1979. Law clk. State Supreme Ct., Honolulu, 1979-80; atty. Bendet, Fidell & Sakai, Honolulu, 1980-81; legis. atty. Honolulu City Coun., 1981-83, House Majority Staff Office, Honolulu, 1983-84, dir., 1984-93; chief clk. Hawaii Ho. of Reps., 1993—. Mem. Hawaii Bar Assn., Hawaii Women Lawyers, Jr. League Hawaii. Democrat. Roman Catholic. Home: 7187 Hawaii Kai Dr Honolulu HI 96825-3115 Office: State House Reps 415 S Beretania St Rm 027 Honolulu HI 96813-2407 Office Phone: 808-586-6400.

MAUSKOPF, ROSLYNN R. prosecutor; b. Washington, 1957, BA, Brandeis U., 1979; JD, Georgetown U., 1982. Asst. dist. atty. N.Y. County Dist. Atty.'s Office, 1982—95, dep. chief spl. prosecution bur., 1992, chief frauds bur., 1993; insp. gen. State of N.Y., 1995—2002; U.S. atty. U.S. Dept. Justice, Ea. Dist. N.Y., Bklyn., 2002—. Chair Moreland Commn. N.Y.C. Schs., 1999. Office: Ea Dist NY 147 Pierrepont St Brooklyn NY 11201

MAUZ, HENRY HERRWARD, JR., retired naval officer; b. Lynchburg, Va., May 4, 1936, s. Henry Herrward and Rene C. (Ball) M.; m. Margaret Catherine O'Neill, June 6, 1959; children: Sheila, David, Lynn, Daniel. BS, U.S. Naval Acad., 1959; BSEE, U.S. Naval Postgrad. Sch., 1965; MBA, Auburn U., 1970. Commd. ensign USN, 1959, advanced through grades to adm., 1992, various ships and shore duty assignments, 1977-80; strategy and concepts officer Office of Chief Naval Ops. Washington, 1980-82; comdg. officer USS England, San Diego, 1980-82, chief of staff Carrier Group One, 1982-83; ops./readiness officer SHAPE Belgium, 1983-85; comdr. Cruiser/Destroyer Group 12, 1985-86; ops./plans officer to comdr. in chief Pacific Fleet, Pearl Harbor, Hawaii, 1986-88; comdr. Seventh Fleet Yokosuka, Japan, 1988-90; dep. chief Office Naval Ops., Washington, 1991 92; comdr. in chief U.S. Atlantic Fleet, 1992-94; ret. USN, 1994. Pres. Naval Postgrad. Sch. Found. Decorated D.S.M. with four gold stars, Def. Superior Svc. medal, Legion of Merit, Bronze Star with combat V device. Mem. U.S. Naval Inst., U.S. Naval War Coll. Found., Naval Hist. Found., Monterey Peninsula Country Club, Army-Navy Country Club. Avocations: golf, skiing. Home: 1608 Viscaino Rd Pebble Beach CA 93953-3303

MAVES, MICHAEL DONALD, medical association executive; b. East St. Louis, Ill., Oct. 14, 1948; BS, U. Toledo, 1970; MD, Ohio State U., 1973; MBA, U. Iowa, 1988. Lic. physician, Iowa, Mo., Ill., D.C.; diplomate Am. Bd. Otolaryngology. Rsch. fellow Ohio State U. Coll. Medicine, Columbus, 1977; fellow head and neck surgery Columbia-Presbyn. Med. Ctr., N.Y.C., 1978, U. Iowa Hosps. and Clinics, Iowa City, 1980-81; asst. prof. otolaryngology, head and neck surgery Ind. U. Sch. Medicine, Indpls., 1981-84, U. Iowa Hosps. and Clinics, Iowa City, 1984-87, assoc. prof., 1987-88; chmn. dept. otolaryngology St. Louis U. Sch. Medicine, St. Louis, 1988-94; exec. v.p. Am. Acad. Otolaryngology, Head and Neck Surgery, Alexandria, Va., 1994—2001; pres. Consumer Healthcare Products Assn., Wash., DC, 1999—2001; exec. v.p., CEO Am. Medical Assn., Chicago, 2002—. Lectr. in field. Contbr. articles to profl. jours. Capt. U.S. Army, 1974-76. Recipient numerous awards including Honor award and Pres.'s award Am. Acad. Otolaryngology-Head and Neck Surgery; named one of Best 1000 Physicians in U.S., 1992, 94, One of Best 400 Cancer Doctors in Am., Good Housekeeping, 1992. Fellow ACS; mem. AMA (RBRVS update com.), Am. Cancer Soc., Am. Acad. Facial & Plastic Reconstructive Surgery. Office: Am Med Assn 515 N State St Chicago IL 60610*

MAVIMA, PAUL, finance educator; b. Kwekwe, Zimbabwe, Sept. 25, 1963; arrived in U.S., 1994; s. Gabriel Tranos and Theresa Mavima; m. Sienna Ruregerero Juta, Dec. 2, 1989; children: Shingirirai, Michelle, Rumbidzai, Takunda. BS, U. Zimbabwe, Harare, 1986; MPA, U. Zimbabwe, 1991; PhD in Pub. Adminstrn., Fla. State U., 2000. Adminstrn. officer Govt. Zimbabwe, Harare, 1987—88; lectr. U. Zimbabwe, Harare, 1988—94; legis. policy analyst Fla. Legislature, Tallahassee, 2000; asst. prof. Grand Valley State U., Grand Rapids, Mich., 2000—. Cons. State of Fla., Tallahassee, 1996—98, Mich. Assn. United Ways, Lansing, 2002—. Contbr. articles to profl. jours. Initiator, founding bd. mem. Grand Rapids Food Sys. Coun., 2001. Fulbright fellow, U.S. Govt., 1994. Mem.: ASPA, S.E. Evaluation Assn., Acad. Mgmt. (Best Conf. Paper award 1997). Office: Grand Valley State Univ 401 W Fulton St Grand Rapids MI 49504 Home: 2673 Woodlake Rd SW 5 Wyoming MI 49509

MAVIS, DARRELL, lawyer, educator; SB, MIT, Cambridge, Mass., 1984—88; JD, Harvard Law Sch., Cambridge, Mass., 1988—91. Bar: Calif. 1992. Criminal prosecutor L.A. County Dist. Atty., 1991—; adj. prof., law Southwestern U. Sch. Law, L.A., 1996—; instr. UCLA, 1996—. Contbr. articles to profl. jours. Mem.: Calif. State Bar Assn. (sec., treas., criminal law sect. exec. com. 2004). Office: LA County Dist Attorney 210 W Temple Ste 1800 Los Angeles CA 90012

MAVRIDES, GREGORY, computer scientist, psychoanalyst, computer engineer, computer company executive; b. Flushing, N.Y., Jan. 17, 1955; s. George and Antoinette (Karamanol) M.; m. Nicole Witteboon, Feb. 14, 1977 (div. Jan. 1996); m. Doreen A. Diem, Apr. 25, 1998. BA, SUNY, Stony Brook, 1978; MS, Columbia U., 1980, PhD, 1990; certificate in Sys. Engring., Intense Sch., Ft. Lauderdale, Fla., 2001. Diplomate in clin. social work. Clin. social worker Pride of Judea Mental Health Ctr., Douglaston, N.Y., 1980-84, dir. computer rsch., 1985-89; asst. prof. social work U. S.C., Columbia, 1989-91, chmn. computer com. Coll. Social Work, 1989-91; assoc. prof. social work Barry U., Miami, Fla., 1991-94; clin. social work psychotherapist Emerald Hills Med. Sq., Hollywood, Fla., 1994-97; program dir. Am. Family Counseling Ctr., Boca Raton, Fla., 1997-98; exec. dir., CEO Lifeskills of Boca Raton, 1998-2000; CEO Elite Compusys., 2000—, microsoft cert. sys. engr., owner, 2001. Mem. Nat. Assn. Social Workers (chmn. clin. issues S.C. chpt. 1990-91), S.C. Soc. for Clin. Social Workers. Republican. Greek Eastern Orthodox. Avocations: chess, bridge, computer technology. Office: Elite Compusystems Ste 3 990 S Congress Ave Delray Beach FL 33445

MAVROUDIS, JOHN M. lawyer; b. N.Y.C., July 24, 1947; s. Michael and Anna (Hariton) Mavroudis; m. Anne Drogaris; children: Michael, Lauren. JD cum laude, Syracuse Coll. Law, 1972. Bar: Fla. 1972, N.Y. 1973, N.J. 1975. Assoc. Patterson, Belknap & Webb, N.Y.C., 1972—74; sole practice N.Y.C., 1974—77; sr. ptnr. Nicolette & Mavroudis, P.A., Hackensack, NJ, 1978—83, Klinger, Nicolette, Mavroudis & Honig, P.A., 1984—89, Mavroudis & Rizzo, 1990—. Editor: Syracuse Law Rev., 1972. Trustee The Greek Orthodox Cathedral of St. John the Theologian, NJ, Hellenic Coll. and Holy Cross Greek Orthodox Sch. Theology, Brookline, Mass., 1987—91; gen. counsel Greek Orthodox Archdiocese Am., 1997—2000. Served to capt. USAR. Recipient Ellis Island Medal Hon., 1999; Archon of the Ecumenical Patriarchate Constantinople. Mem.: Bar Assn. City N.Y., Justinian Soc. Office: 690 Kinderkamack Rd # 300 Oradell NJ 07649-1524

MAVROVIC, IVO, chemical engineer; b. Fiume, Italy, Dec. 5, 1927; came to U.S., 1959; s. Janko and Milica (Gregorina) M.; m. Erna Gallian, oct. 14, 1955; 1 child, Paul. BSChemE, U. Zagreb, Yugoslavia, 1952, MSChemE, 1955. Registered profl. engr, N.Y. Chem. engr. Dorr-Oliver, Milan, Italy, 1956-59, Chemico, N.Y.C., 1960-65; cons. N.Y.C., 1965-77; pres. UTI/UTI Constrn. Inc., Hackensack, N.J., 1977—. Patentee in field; contbr. articles to profl. jours. Mem. AICE. Roman Catholic. Home: 530 E 72nd St Apt 15-c New York NY 10021-4863 Office: UTI Constrn Inc 112 Temple Ave Hackensack NJ 07601-6001

MAWARDI, OSMAN KAMEL, plasma physicist; b. Cairo, Dec. 12, 1917; arrived in U.S., 1946, naturalized, 1952; s. Kamel Ibrahim and Marie (Wiennig) M.; m. Betty Louise Hosmer, Nov. 23, 1950. BS, Cairo U., 1940, MS, 1945; A.M., Harvard U., 1947, PhD, 1948. Lectr. physics Cairo U., 1940-45; asst. prof. Mass Inst. Tech., 1951-56, asso. prof., 1956-60; prof. engring., dir. plasma research program Case Inst. Tech., Cleve., 1960-88; dir. Energy Research Office, Case Western Res. U., 1977-82. Pres. Collaborative Planners, Inc.; mem. Inst. Advanced Study, 1969-70; also cons. Contbr. articles to profl. jours. Past trustee Print Club Cleve., Cleve. Inst. Art. Recipient Biennial award Acoustical Soc. Am., 1952; CECON medal of achievement, 1979 Fellow AAAS, Acoustical Soc. Am., IEEE (Edison lectr. 1968-69, Centennial award 1984, Cleve. sect. Engr. of Yr. 1994); mem. N.Y. Acad. Scis., Sigma Xi, Eta Kappa Nu. Home: 15 Mornington Ln Cleveland OH 44106 Office: 2490 Lee Rd Cleveland OH 44118-4125 Office Phone: 216-932-9550. *I never cease to be amazed that the goals I really believe in invariably materialize.*

MAWBY, RUSSELL GEORGE, retired foundation executive; b. Grand Rapids, Mich., Feb. 23, 1928; s. Wesley G. and Ruby (Finch) M.; m. Ruth E. Edison, Dec. 16, 1950 (dec. 2000); children: Douglas, David, Karen. BS in Horticulture, Mich. State U., 1949, PhD in Agrl. Econs., 1959, LL.D. (hon.), 1972; MS in Agrl. Econs, Purdue U., 1951, D.Agr. (hon.), 1973; L.H.D. (hon.), Luther Coll., Decorah, Iowa, 1972, Alma (Mich.) Coll., 1975, Nazareth Coll., 1976, Madonna Coll., 1983, N.C. Central U., 1986; LL.D. (hon.), N.C. A&T State U., Greensboro, 1974, Tuskegee Inst., 1978, Kalamazoo Coll., 1980; D.P.A. (hon.), Albion Coll., 1976; D.C.L. (hon.), U. Newcastle, Eng., 1977; D.Sc. (hon.), Nat. U. Ireland, 1980; D.Pub. Service (hon.), No. Mich. U., 1981; D.H.L. (hon.), So. Utah State Coll., 1983; HHD (hon.), Grand Valley State U., 1988; ScD (hon.), Calif. State U., 1989; LLD (hon.), Adrian Coll., 1990; LittD (hon.), Olivet Coll., 1991. Ext. specialist Mich. State U., East Lansing, 1952-56, asst. dir. coop. ext. svc., 1956-65; dir. div. agr. W.K. Kellogg Found., Battle Creek, Mich., 1965-66, mem., trustee, 1967—, v.p. programs, 1966-70, pres., 1970-82, chmn., CEO, 1982-95, chmn. emeritus, 1995—. Bd. dirs. Detroit br. Fed. Res. Bank Chgo., 1980-85, J.M. Smucker Co., 1983—; fellow Inst. for Children, Youth and Families Mich. State U., 1993; hon. fellow Kellog Coll., U. Oxford, Eng., 1990; mem. chancellor's ct. of benefactors U. Oxford, Eng., 1991; Disting. Vis. Prof. Inst. for Children, Youth and Families and Coll. of Edn., Mich. State U., 1996—. Trustee Youth for Understanding, 1973-79, Mich. State U. Coll. of Agr. and Natural Resources Alumni Assn., 1977-80, pres. 1978-79; trustee Arabian Horse Trust, 1978-90 (emeritus 1990—), Starr Commonwealth, 1987-97, 98—, (chmn. bd. trustees 1993-95), Found. Ctr., 1988-94 (chmn. bd. trustees 1989-94), Mich. Non-profit Assn., 1990-94 (chmn. bd. trustees 1990-94, emeritus 1994—), Mich. State U., 1992-96 (chmn. bd. trustees 1995); founding chmn. Coun. of Mich. Founds., 1972-74, chmn. emeritus 1994—; bd. dirs. Coun. on Founds., 1978-84, Mich.'s Children, 1995-98, emeritus 1998—; mem. Joint Coun. on Food and Agrl. Scis., USDA, 1984-88; mem. Com. on Agrl. Edn. in Secondary Schs., NRC, 1985-88, Gov.'s Task Force on Revitalization of Agr. Through Rsch. and Edn., 1986; mem. rural bus. partnership adv. bd. Mich. Dept. Commerce, 1989-90, Mich. Coop. Ext. Svc. Study Com., 1989; mem. pres.'s adv. coun. Clemson U., 1987-95; vis. com. Med. U. of S.C., 1990-95; steering com. Econ. Devel. Forum of Calhoun County, Mich., 1991—; mem. policy bd. Calhoun County Cmtys. in Schs., 1995-98; mem. Lt. Gov.'s Children's Commn., State of Mich., 1995-96; mem. leadership adv. coun. Olivet Coll., 1995—; trustee Battle Creek Community Found., 1996—, Mich. 4-H Found., 1996—, hon. trustee, 1996—; scholar-in-residence Ind. U. Ctr. on Philanthropy, 1996—; mem. State Officers compensation Commn., State of Mich., 1996-98; mem. bd. govs. Ind. U. Ctr. on Philanthropy, 2000—; bd. visitors Coll. of Nursing Mich. State U., 1997—; bd. dirs. Mich. State U. Found., 1998—. With AUS, 1953-55. Decorated knight 1st class Royal Order St. Olaf Norway, 1974; knight's cross Order of Dannebrog 1st class Denmark, 1976; comdr.'s medal Order of Finnish Lion Finland, 1981; recipient Disting. Service award U.S. Dept. Agr., 1963, Disting. Alumni award Mich. State U., 1971, Nat. Alumni award 4-H Clubs, 1972, Disting. Eagle Scout award Boy Scouts Am., 1973, Meritorious Achievement award Fla. A&M U., 1973, Nat. Ptnr. in 4-H award Dept. Agr. Ext. Svc., 1976; named hon. fellow Spring Arbor (Mich.) Coll., 1972; recipient Walter F. Patenge medal for pub. service Coll. Osteo. Medicine, Mich. State U., 1977, Disting. Service award Coll. Agr. and Natural Resources, 1980, Seaman A. Knapp Meml. lectr. U.S. Dept. Agr., 1983; recipient George award for cmty. svc. City of Battle Creek, 1986, Disting. Service award Rural Sociol. Soc., 1986, Centennial Alumnus award for Mich. State U. Nat. Assn. State Univs. and Land Grant Colls., 1988, Pres.'s award Clemson U., 1989, Disting. Citizen award Southwest Mich. Coun. Boy Scouts Am., 1989, Disting. Svc. award 1890 Land-Grant Colls. and Univs., 1990, Vol. of Yr. award Clemson U., 1990, Disting. Grantmaker award Coun. on Founds., 1992, Disting. Svc. award Nat. Assn. Homes and Svcs. for Children, 1992, Merit award Nat. Soc. Fund Raising Execs. West Mich. chpt., 1992, Red Rose award Rotary Club of Battle Creek, 1993, George W. Romney award Nat. Soc. Fund Raising Execs. Greater Detroit chpt., 1993, Director's award Arabian Horse Assn. of Mich., 1994, Disting. Svc. award Mich. Hort. Soc., 1994, Michiganian of Yr. The Detroit News, 1995, Gerald G. Hicks Child Welfare Leadership award Mich. Fedn. Private Child and Family Agys., 1995, Leon Bradley Humanitarian for Youth award No. Area Assn., Detroit, 1995, award of Honor Am. Hosp. Assn., 1995, Spirit of the Drum award, Nat. Youth Leadership Coun., 1996, Crystal Apple award Featherstone Soc. Coll. Edn. Mich. State U., 1996, Nat. Govs. Assn. award for disting. svc. to state govt., 1997, Nat. Interfraternity Conf. Gold Medal award, 1998, Govs. award for stewardship State of Mich., 1999; named Friend of the Coll., Mich. State U. Coll. Human Ecology, 1996, Internat. Adult and Continuing Edn. Hall of Fame, 1996, Owner of Yr. Mich. Harness Horsemen's Assn., 1999; Louis Harris fellow Rotary Club Battle Creek, 1998. Mem. Mich. Soc. Architects (hon.), Am. Agrl. Econ. Assn., Mich. State U. Alumni Assn. (bd. dirs. 1984-88), Alpha Gamma Rho (dir. 1976-82, grand pres. 1980-82, Man of Year Chgo. Alumni chpt. 1976, Hall of Fame 1986), Alpha Zeta, Phi Kappa Phi (Disting. Mem. award Mich. State U. 1978), Epsilon Sigma Phi (certificate of recognition 1974, Nat. Friend of Ext. 1982), Gamma Sigma Delta, Delta Sigma Pi (hon. mem., 1995). Home: 8400 N 39th St Augusta MI 49012-9713 Office: Heritage Tower 25 Michigan Ave W Ste 1701 Battle Creek MI 49017-7023

MAWN, LOUISE ANN, ophthalmologist, educator; b. Woburn, Mass., June 4, 1963; d. James Joseph and Rita Marie Mawn; m. Gregg Thomas Tarquinio, July 27, 1991; children: Jonathan Tarquinio children: Abigail Tarquinio, Christopher Tarquinio. MD, Wake Forest U., 1990. Diplomate Am. Bd. Ophthalmology. Asst. prof. ophthalmology U. Nebr. Med. Ctr., Omaha, 1997—98, Vanderbilt U. Med. Ctr., Nashville, 1998—, asst. prof. neurol. surgery, 2003—. Prin. investigator rsch. grant Nat. Eye Inst., Bethesda, 2001—. Author: (book) Preseptal and Orbital Cellulitis, 2002; contbr. articles to profl. jours. Fellow: Am. Acad. Ophthalmology; mem.: Can. Soc. Oculplastic Surgeons, Europeon Soc. Ophthalmic Plastic and Reconstructive Surgeons. Office: Vanderbilt U Med Ctr 8014 Medical Center East Nashville TN 37232 Office Phone: 615-936-1960. Business E-Mail: louise.mawn@vanderbilt.edu.

MAX, BUDDY (BORIS MAX PASTUCH), musician; b. Jan. 25; m. Freda Max; 1 child, John. *Buddy Max is President of the Chamber of Commerce of Lecanto, Florida, and is Master of Ceremonies at the Cowboy Junction Opry, America's No. 1 country western music show and legend. Buddy Max was born on the Orange Blossom Special Steam Locomotive, the most powerful and fastest train from 1921 to 1959. Some of the original coal used and a picture of the Orange Blossom Steam Locomotive can be seen on the wall of the Cowboy Junction Opry.* Musician, performer as America's Singing Flea Market Cowboy: albums include: Many Styles and Sounds of Buddy Max, 1980, The Great Nashville Star, 1984, The Story of Freda and Bud, 1985, Cowboy Junction Stars, 1985, Tribute to Challenger's Crew of 7, 1986, With Our Friends at Cowboy Junction, 1989, Little Circle B, 1990, Together-Our Masterpiece, 1991, The Life to Fame and Fortune, 1992, Orange Blossom Special, 1996, Hall of Fame, Gold Record Award Winning Buddy Max, 1996, Hall of Fame; composer songs include When the Magnolia Tree Blooms in Lecanto, The Story of Barney Clark, Hang My Guitar on the Wall, John F. Kennedy, The Challenger, Where the Maple Syrups Flow, Little Circle B, Way Up on the Mountain, Desert Storm, When Do I Love You, The Pretty Girl on TV. Recipient World Hall of Fame award and gold medalion, 1997, numerous trophies, awards for benefit and non-profit shows Am. Heart Assn., Am. Lung Assn., Girl Scouts Am., Citizens of Citrus County Fla., Deaf Svcs. of Citrus County, Statue of Liberty trophy and coin award Cowboy Junction Opry Country Music Show, 2000 for song I Love Miss America, cert. Young Marines of Citrus County, 2002; named Ky. Col., Gov. Paul E. Patton, 2001. Address: care Cowboy Junction 3949 W Hwy 44 & Jct 490 Lecanto FL 34461-9232 Office Phone: 352-746-4754.

MAX, CLAIRE ELLEN, physicist; b. Boston, Sept. 29, 1946; d. Louis William and Pearl (Bernstein) M.; m. Jonathan Arons, Dec. 22, 1974; 1 child, Samuel. AB, Harvard U., 1968; PhD, Princeton U., 1972. Postdoctoral rschr. U. Calif., Berkeley, 1972-74; physicist Lawrence Livermore (Calif.) Nat. Lab., 1974—; dir. Livermore br. Inst. Geophysics and Planetary Physics, 1984-93, dir. univ. rels., 1993-2000; assoc. dir. Ctr. for Adaptive Optics, U. Calif., Santa Cruz, 2000—. Mem. Math.-Sci. Network Mills Coll., Oakland, Calif.; mem. com. on fusion hybrid reactors NRC, 1986, mem. com. on internat. security and arms control NAS, 1986-89, mem. com. on phys. sci., math. and applications NRC, 1991-94, mem. policy and computational astrophys. panels, astron. and astgrophys. survey NRC, 1989-91; mem. sci. steering com. W.M. Keck Obs., 1992-96, mem. adaptive optics sci. team, 1994—; mem. vis. com. Space Telescope Sci. Inst., 1996-2000, Hubble Space Telescope Second Decade Com., 1998-2000. Editor: Particle Acceleration Mechanisms in Astrophysics, 1979; contbr. numerous articles to sci. jours. Fellow AAAS (coun. rep. physics sect. 2001—), Am. Phys. Soc. (exec. com. divsn. plasma physics 1977, 81-82); mem. Am. Astron. Soc. (exec. com. divsn. high energy astrophysics 1975-76), Am. Geophys. Union, Internat. Astron. Union, Phi Beta Kappa, Sigma Xi. Achievements include rsch. on adaptive optics and laser guide stars for astronomy; astrophys. plasmas. Office: Lawrence Livermore Nat Lab PO Box 808 7000 East Ave # L413 Livermore CA 94550-9516 E-mail: max1@llnl.gov.

MAX, ELIZABETH, educator; b. Fort Worth, Oct. 9, 1924; d. Frederick Ward and Alice Louise (Matthews) Maxwell; m. Herbert Jones McCorkle, Sept. 22, 1945 (div. Oct., 1969); children: Anne McCorkle Moore, Louise Kate McCorkle, Bruce Ward McCorkle, Sallie Matthews McCorkle. BS, Tex. Woman's U., 1944; MS in L.S., U. North Tex., 1966; PhD in Edn., Okla. State U., 1974. Cert. secondary, elementary tchr., Tex., Okla.; cert. sch. librarian, Tex., Okla. Copy clerk, beginning writer UPI, NBC, N.Y.C., 1944—45; elementary and secondary tchr. various schs., Tex., 1950-69; instr. library sci. Western Ill. U., Macomb, 1969-70; asst. prof., fine arts libr. Okla. State U., Stillwater, 1970-72, asst. prof., coord. Library Sci. Dept., 1972-76, assoc. prof., 1976-82, supervisor, English Edn., 1982-90, prof. emerita, 1990—. Cons. Skelly Oil Co., Tulsa, Okla., 1976, The Ctr. for Local Govt. Tech., 1983-84, Stillwater Library Sys. Bd., 1985, media reviewer, previews, book revs. Sch. Libr. Jour., 1976-77. Author (with others): Teaching the Short Story, 1996; mem. reader panel New York Times, 1996—, mem. New York Times Online Panel, 2002—; contbr. articles to profl. jours. and publs. Pres. Meml. Soc. Central Pa., 1994, 96-99; vol. Nat. Disaster Relief, ARC, 1991-96; mem. Dem. Nat. Com.; women's rights activist. Mem. NEA, ALA, Nat. Women's Studies Assn. (founder), Okla State U. Women's Coun. (founder, 2d chair), Okla. Adult and Continuing Edn., Nat. Collegiate Players, Stillwater Okla. Writer's Club (pres., 1985-89), Greek Sabbatical, Nat. Coun. Tchrs. of English (mem. comparative and world lit. com. 1990-97), Gen. Soc. Mayflower Descs., Parents and Friends of Lesbians and Gays, Emily List, NARAL, ACLU, Phi Delta Kappa, Phi Kappa Phi, Beta Phi Mu. Home and Office: 463 Kemmerer Rd State College PA 16801-6408 E-mail: elizabethmax@earthlink.net.

MAX, ERNEST, surgeon; b. Vienna, Mar. 3, 1936; m. Silvia Neger, Mar. 18, 1964; children: Yvette Rosa, Oliver Fredrick. MD, U. Chile, 1961. Diplomate Am. Bd. Surgery, Am. Bd. Colon and Rectal Surgeons, Am. Bd. Laser Surgery. Intern Hosp. San Borja, Santiago, Chile, 1960-61, resident, 1962-63; fellow in gen. surgery, colon and rectal surgery Lahey Clinic Found., Boston, 1969-70; resident Sinai Hosp., Balt., 1971-72, The Western Pa. Hosp., Pitts., 1972-74; resident in colon and rectal surgery Hermann Hosp., Houston, 1974-75, staff, 1975—, Park Plz. Hosp., 1975—, Meml. Hosp. Southwest, 1975—, Meml. NW Hosp., 1975—, Diagnostic Ctr. Hosp., 1975—, The Methodist Hosp., 1976—, Meml. City Hosp., 1976—, Houston NW Med. Ctr., 1976—, St. Luke's Episcopal Hosp., 1981—, Cypress Fairbanks, 1983—; chief of staff Meml. Hosp., 1983; staff HCA Med. Ctr., 1986—; CEO Colon and Rectal Clinic PA, 1989—. Clin. assoc. prof. surgery Baylor Coll. Medicine; clin. instr. surgery U. Tex. Med. Sch., Houston. Author: (with others) Current Diagnosis, 1971. Recipient Walter A. Fansler Travel Edn. award Am. Soc. Colon and Rectal Surgeons, 1974, Harriet Cunningham award Tex. Med. Assn., 1988, Best of the Best award Tex. Med. Assc., 1989; The Purdue Fredrick fellow Am. Soc. Colon and Rectal Surgeons, 1974. Mem. Am. Coll. Surgeons, Tex. Med. Soc., Harris County Med. Soc., Tex. Soc. Colon and Rectal Surgeons (pres. 1982-83), Am. Soc. Laser Medicine and Surgery, Internat. Soc. Univ. Colon and Rectal Surgeons, Lahey Clinic Alumni Assn., Am. Soc. Colon and Rectal Surgeons, Tex. Gulf Coast Colon and Rectal Surgical Soc. (sec. treas. 1992—), Colombian Soc. Colo-Proctology (hon. mem.). Office: Colon & Rectal Clinic PA 6550 Fannin St Ste 2307 Houston TX 77030-2723

MAXCY, SPENCER JOHN, education educator; b. Chgo., June 22, 1939; s. Spencer Thomas and Marian Adele (Davis) M.; m. Doreen Kay Oliver, Sept. 6, 1970; children: Colleen Shivaun, Spencer Oliver. BA in History, Blackburn Coll., 1961; MA in History, Loyola U., 1965; PhD in Philosophy of Edn., Ind. U., 1972. Cert. tchr. social studies, Ill. Substitute tchr. Chgo. Pub. Schs., 1962-63; social studies tchr. Dist. 218, Blue Island, Ill., 1963-67; assoc. instr. Ind. U., Bloomington, 1969-72; asst. prof. La. State U., Baton Rouge, 1972-76, assoc. prof., 1976-85, full prof., 1985—. Author: Educational Leadership, 1991, Democracy, Chaos, and the New School Order, 1995, Ethical School Leadership, 2002; editor: (book) Postmodern School Leadership, 1994, (3 vols.) John Dewey and American Education, 2002; mem. editorial bd. Record in Ednl. Adminstrn. and Supervision, 1981-91, Internat. Jour. of Ednl. Reform, 1992—. Basketball coach YMCA, Baton Rouge, 1993, 94, 95. NDEA fellow U. Chgo., 1966-67, Ind. U. fellow, 1967-68. Fellow Philosophy of Edn. Soc.; mem. Am. Ednl. Rsch. Assn., S.W. Philosophy of Edn. Soc. (pres. 1974-93). Avocations: weightlifting, fishing. Home: 251 E Woodgate Ct Baton Rouge LA 70808-5408 Office: La State U Peabody Hall 111 Baton Rouge LA 70803-0001

MAXEY, DAVID WALKER, lawyer; b. Scranton, Pa., May 17, 1934; s. Paul Harold and Margaret (Walker) M.; m. Catharine Eglin, June 6, 1968; children: Paul Eglin, Margaret Wilson. AB, Harvard U., 1956, LLB cum laude, 1960. Bar: Pa. 1961, U. S. Dist. Ct. (ea. dist.) Pa. 1961, U.S. Ct. Appeals (3d cir.) 1963. Assoc. Drinker Biddle and Reath LLP, Phila., 1960-66, ptnr., 1967-2000, chmn. real estate dept., 1970-88, mng. ptnr., 1977-91, co-chmn., 1988-91, of counsel, 2000—. Vis. faculty Villanova (Pa.) U. Law Sch., 1987-95. Contbr. articles to profl. jours. Chmn. internat. adv. com. Greater Phila. First, 1994-98; chmn. bd. dir. Hist. Soc. Pa., Phila., 1991-93; sec., bd. dir. Greater Phila. Internat. Network, 1981-94; bd. dir. Libr. Co., Phila., 1993-2000, sec., 1997-2000; bd. dir. Gladwyne (Pa.) Libr., 1991-98, pres., 1996-98; bd. dir. Young Audiences Ea. Pa., Phila., 1985-95, Phila. Soc. Preservation Landmarks, 2002-2003, Jewish-Cath. Inst., St. Joseph's U., 2003—. Recipient Hughes-Gossett award U.S. Supreme Ct. Hist. Soc., Washington, 1991. Mem. ABA, Pa. Bar Assn., Phila. Bar Assn., Am. Coll. Real Estate Lawyers, Harvard Club Phila. (pres. 1970-72), Merion Cricket Club. Avocation: historical research and publication. Home: 829 Black Road Rd Gladwyne PA 19035 Office: One Logan Sq 18th and Cherry Streets Philadelphia PA 19103-6996 Personal E-mail: cdmmax@aol.com. Business E-Mail: david.maxey@dbr.com.

MAXEY, RANDALL W. medical researcher, health science association administrator; BPharm, U. Cin., 1966; MD, PhD in Cardiovascular Pharmacology, Howard U., 1972. Chmn. bd. trustees Nat. Med. Assn., Washington, 2001—02; med. dir. Pacific Rim Dialysis Ctr., L.A., Calif. Supr. med. dir. hosp. in Guam. Office: Nat Med Assn 1012 Tenth St NW Washington DC 20001

MAXFIELD, FREDERICK ROWLAND, medical educator; b. Bklyn., Oct. 21, 1949; s. Allen F. and Marjorie Grant Maxfield; m. Christine Meredith Kiley, Aug. 21, 1971; children: Laura, Andrew. BS, Union Coll., Schenectady, N.Y., 1971; PhD, Cornell U., 1977. From asst. prof. to prof. pharmacology NYU Sch. Medicine, N.Y.C., 1979—87; prof. pathology and physiology Coll. Physicians and Surgeons Columbia U., 1987—95; prof., chmn. dept. biochemistry Weill Med. Coll. Cornell U., N.Y.C., 1995—. Mem.: N.Y. Soc. Exptl. Microscopists (pres. 1996—97), Biophysical Soc., Am. Soc. Cell Biology, Harvey Soc. (pres. 2002—03). Office: Cornell U Weill Med Coll 1300 York Ave New York NY 10021 Business E-Mail: frmaxfie@med.cornell.edu.

MAXFIELD, GUY BUDD, lawyer, educator; b. Galesburg, Ill., May 4, 1933; s. Guy W. and Isabelle B. Maxfield; m. Carol Tunick, Dec. 27, 1970; children: Susan, Stephen, Karen. AB summa cum laude, Augustana Coll., 1955; JD, U. Mich., 1958. Bar: N.Y. 1959. Assoc. White & Case, N.Y.C., 1958-63; prof. law NYU, N.Y.C., 1963—; of counsel August & Kulunas, P.A. Author: Tennessee Will and Trust Manual, 1982, Federal Estate and Gift Taxation, 8th edit., 2002, Florida Will and Trust Manual, 1984, Tax Planning for Professionals, 1986; contbr. articles to law jours. Trustee Acomb Found., Newark, 1974—. With U.S. Army, 1958-64. Fellow Am. Coll. Tax Counsel; mem. ABA, Am. Law Inst., N.Y. State Bar Assn., Order of Coif, Phi Beta Kappa. Office: NYU Sch Law 40 Washington Sq S New York NY 10012-1099 Office Phone: 212-998-6164.

MAXFIELD, JOHN EDWARD, retired university dean; b. Los Angeles, Mar. 17, 1927; s. Chauncey George and Rena Lucile (Cain) M.; m. Margaret Alice Waugh, Nov. 24, 1948; children— Frederick George (dec.), David Glen, Elaine Rebecca, Nancy Catherine, Daniel John. BS, Mass. Inst. Tech., 1947; MS, U. Wis., 1949; PhD, U. Oreg., 1951. Instr. U. Oreg., 1950-51; mathmatician U.S. Naval Ordnance Test Sta., China Lake, Calif., 1949-56, head computing br., 1956-57, head math. div., 1957-60; lectr. UCLA, 1951-60; head prof. dept. math. U. Fla., 1960-67; prof., chmn. dept. math. Kans. State U., 1967-81; dean Grad. Sch. and univ. research La. Tech. U., 1981-92, dean emeritus, 1992—; ret. La. Tech. U., 1992. Mem. Am. Math. Soc., Math. Assn. Am., Soc. Indsl. and Applied Math., Sigma Xi. Home: 209 E Louisiana Ave Ruston LA 71270-4417

MAXFIELD, MARY CONSTANCE, management consultant; b. Washington, Mar. 16, 1949; d. Orville Eldred and Rose Mary (Stiarwalt) Maxfield; m. Robert Charles Kneip III, Aug. 21, 1971 (div. Apr. 1981); 1 child, Stephanie Alexandra; m. Richard Howard Cowles, May 16, 1981 (dec.); m. Phillip Walker, July 25, 1985 (div. June 1991); m. Michael Lee Beeman, Sept. 28, 2002. BA in History and Spanish, Va. Tech., 1970; MS in Occupl. Tech., U. Houston, 1996. Clk.-typist HEW, Social Security Adminstrn., New Orleans, 1971—72, svc. rep., 1972-73; mgmt. analyst Office Comptr. of Currency Treasury Dept., Washington, 1974-77, dir. mgmt. analysis divsn. U.S. Customs New Orleans, 1978-80, mgmt. analyst Houston, 1980-81, program analyst, 1981-82, chief data processing br., 1982-83, chief mgmt. analysis br., 1983-85; pres. Constance Walker Assocs., Inc., 1985-91, Maxfield Productivity Cons., Inc., 1991—; co-founder Inspired Learning Adventures, L.C., 2002; founder, pres. Anam Cara (handmade jewelry), 2002—. Co-founder Supplier Registry; co-designer Kitchen 101 CD-ROM learning program. Author (with others): Team Approach to Problem Solving, 1991; author: Quality School Facilitator Training, 1992, Interpersonal Communications Skills, 1992, Introduction to Total Quality Schools, 1992, Tex. Leadership Ctr. DuPont LDP Tng., TQM Module, 1999, Total Quality Management, 1999, Strengthening Team Development, 1995, Internal Auditing to ISO 9000 Standards, 1995, Essential Facilitation Skills, 2000, Personnel Management in Food Service, 1995, Successfully Leading Change, 1996, Leading Change Through Site-Based Teams, 1996, Quality Tools 101, 1996, Introduction to ISO 9000, 1999, Benchmarking, 1999, Advanced Facilitation Skills, 2000, Developing and Evaluating Training, 2000, Presentation Skills for Change Agents, 2000, Successfully Managing Projects, 2001, Coaching for Performance, 2001, Everyday Creativity, 2001, Appreciative Inquiry, 2001, Kitchen 101, 2002, Conducting Value Added Assessments, 2002, Child Nutrition Course New Managers PlayBook, 2004; contbr. numerous articles to profl. jours. Named Customs Woman of Yr., U.S. Customs, 1979, Fed. Exec. Bd. Woman of Yr., 1979, Cora Bell Wesley scholar, UDC, 1969; recipient Outstanding Performance award, 1979—85, Outstanding Svc. award, Office of Sec. of Treasury, 1976, Key to City, New Orleans, 1990. Mem. DAR, ASTD, Assn. Psychol. Type, Am. Soc. Quality, Assn. Quality and Participation (past pres. Houston chpt.), Treasury Hist. Assn., Daus. Rep. of Tex., Daus 1812, UDC, Va. Tech. Alumni Assn., Austin's Old 300 (founding), Delta Zeta. Episcopalian. Home and Office: Maxfield Productivity Cons Inc 8007 Liberty Elm Ct Spring TX 77379-6125

MAXFIELD, PETER C. state legislator, law educator, lawyer; b. 1941; AB, Regis Coll., 1963; JD, U. Denver, 1966; LLM, Harvard U., 1968. Bar: Colo. 1966, Wyo. 1969. Trial atty. Dept. Justice, 1966-67; assoc. Hindry, Erickson & Meyer, Denver, 1968-69; asst. prof. U. Wyo. Coll. Law, 1969-72, assoc. prof., 1972-76, prof., 1976-96, dean, 1979-87, prof. emeritus, 1996—. Vis. assoc. prof. U. N.Mex., 1972-73; Raymond F. Rice Disting. prof. U. Kans., 1984; Chapman Vis. Disting. prof., U. Tulsa, 1987; vis. prof. U. Utah, 1992. Author: (with Garr Houghton) Cases and Materials on the Taxation of Oil and Gas and Natural Resources Transactions, 1990, (with Allen Houghton) Taxation of Mining Operation, 1981, 97, 2002; (with Trelease and Dietrich) Natural Resources Law on American Indian Lands, 1977. Coord. Wyo. State Planning 1988-89; spl. asst. Gov. Wyo. 1989-90; Dem. nominee U.S. Ho. Reps., 1990; mem. Wyo. Environ. Quality Coun., 1991-93; mem. Wyo. Senate, Laramie, 1993-97. Mem. Omicron Delta Kappa, Pi Delta Phi. Home: 1159 Escalera St Laramie WY 82072-5020 Office: U Wyo Coll Law PO Box 3035 Laramie WY 82071-3035 E-mail: petemaxfield@earthlink.net., petemax@uwyo.edu.

MAXIMOS, METROPOLITAN (MAXIMOS DEMETRIOS AGHIORGOUSSIS), bishop, metropolitan; b. Callimassia, Chios, Greece, Mar. 5, 1935; s. Evanghelos G. and Lemonia G. (Rythianou) A. Licentiate, Patriarchal Sch. Theology, Halki, 1957; Baccalaureate, Th.D., U. Louvain, Belgium, 1964. Ordained to ministry Greek Orthodox Ch., 1957; chaplain U. Louvain, 1957-64; pastor chs. Brussels, Rome, Brookline, Mass., Manchester and Newport, N.H., 1960-78; observer-del. II Vatican Council, 1964-65; chaplain Holy Cross Sem., Brookline, 1967-76; prof. systematic theology Holy Cross Sch. Theology, Brookline, 1967-79, Christ Savior Sem., Johnstown, Pa., from 1979; bishop Greek Orthodox Diocese Pitts., 1979-97, metropolitan, 1997—. Mem. Orthodox-Roman Cath. Consultation, from 1967; v.p. Nat. Council Chs. Christ U.S., 1979-81; ecumenical officer Greek Orthodox Archdiocese N. and S. Am., 1978-79, chmn. synodal coms. ecumenical affairs, spiritual renewal and youth, 1979-. Author: In the Image of God, 1998; contbr. articles in field. Mem. Orthodox Theol. Soc. Am., AAUP, Christian Assos. Pitts., Pa. Coun. Chs., W.Va. Coun. Chs., Ohio Coun. Chs. Greek Orthodox. Office: Greek Orthodox Diocese Pittsburgh 5201 Ellsworth Ave Pittsburgh PA 15232-1421 *My ministry is such that it requires a total commitment to its goals, but first of all a total commitment to Christ. In my childhood, I was fortunate to be guided by excellent parents and grandparents, who gave me not only the necessary security and stability, but also the inspiration to imitate their personal commitment to the Lord. I fully trust in the grace of the Lord, but I also have always accepted my responsibility for everything I have done.*

MAXMAN, SUSAN ABEL, architect; b. Columbus, Ohio, Dec. 30, 1938; d. Richard Jack Abel and Gussie (Brenner) Seiden; m. Rolf Sauer; children: Andrew Frankel, Thomas Frankel, Elizabeth Frankel, Melissa, Abby, William Jr. Student, Smith Coll., 1960; MArch., U. Pa., 1977; HHD, Ball State U., 1993, U. Detroit Mercy, 1997. Registered profl. architect, Pa., Ohio, N.J., N.Y., Md., W.Va., Va., Maine, Mo., N.C., S.C. Project designer Kopple Sheward & Day, Phila., 1978-80; ptnr. Maxman & Sutphin, Phila., 1980-83; prin. Susan Maxman & Ptnrs., Phila., 1984—. Mem. bd. overseers Grad. Sch. Fine Arts U. Pa.; mem. corp. vis. com. MIT; mem. Planning and Design Commn., Ga. Inst. Tech. Works include design of Women's Humane Soc. Animal Shelter, Bensalem, Pa. (Northeastern Sustainable Energy Assn.'s Comml. Bldg. award, 1994, Metal Constrn. Assn. award 1995, Gov.'s Award for Environ. Excellence 1997, AIA Pa. Hon. award 1997), Camp Tweedale-Freedom Valley Girl Scouts USA (AIA honor award, 1991), Cusano Environ. Edn. Ctr. at John Heinz Nat.

Wildlife Refuge at Tinicum, Phila. (award) including U.S. Dept. Energy Fed. Energy Saver Showcase award, U.S. Dept. Interior Environ. Achievement award,restoration Vernon House (honorable mention Remodeling Mag.), Germantown, Robert Lewis House (McArthur award 1985), Phila., Restoration Pennock Farmstead (Grand Prize Nat. Trust Historic Preservation 1995), Feasibility Study and Renovation of Old Main Pa. Hist. and Mus. Commn. Historic Preservation award, 1998, Kutztown U., Pa., sisters Servants of the Immaculate Heart of Mary Renovation of the Motherhouse (Mich. Hist. Preservation Network bldg. award 2003), Renovation of U. Pa. Nursing Edn. Bldg., Phila., Barbara C. Harris Camp and Conf. Ctr., Greenfield, N.H., Chestnut Hill Nat. Bank, Phila., Somerset (Pa.) Hist. Ctr., Seneca Rocks Visitor Ctr., Seneca Rocks, W.Va., Fort Necessity/Nat. Rd. Interpretive Edn. Ctr., Farmington, Pa., The Woods Residence Hall at Pa. State-Berks, Reading, Renovation to Roberts Hall U. Pa., others. Mem. Eco-Efficiency Task Force Pres. Coun. Sustainable Devel.; past chair Environ. Coun., Urban Land Inst.; mem. trustee's coun. for Pa. Women, U. Pa. Recipient Disting. Dau. Pa. award Gov. Tom Ridge, 1995, Excellence citation Engrng. News Record, Shattering the Glass Ceiling award Women's Nat. Dem. Club, Mayor's commendation City Phila., citation Pa. Ho. Reps., Gov.'s award Environ. Excellence, 1997; named to Pa. Honor Roll of Women, Pa. Commn. for Women, 1996, named 1 of Pa.'s Best 50 Women in Bus. 1996. Mem. AIA (nat. pres. 1993, Pa. chpt. Honor award 1997, Top Ten Green Bldg. award 2003), Pa. Women's Forum, Forum Exec. Women, Carpenter's Co. Phila. Avocation: sailing. Office: 1600 Walnut St Fl 2D Philadelphia PA 19103-5405 Office Phone: 215-985-4410. Personal E-mail: sam@maxhahpartners.com.

MAXSON, LINDA ELLEN, biologist, educator; b. N.Y.C., Apr. 24, 1943; d. Albert and Ruth (Rosenfeld) Resnick; m. Richard Dey Maxson, June 13, 1964; 1 child, Kevin. BS in Zoology, San Diego State U., 1964, MA in Biology, 1966; PhD in Genetics, San Diego State U./U. Calif., Berkeley, 1973. Instr. biology San Diego State U., 1966-68; tchr. gen. sci. San Diego Unified Sch. Dist., 1968-69; instr. biochemistry U. Calif., Berkeley, 1974; asst. prof. zoology, dept. genetics and devel. U. Ill., Urbana-Champaign, 1974-76, asst. prof. dept. genetics, devel. and ecology, ethology & evolution, 1976-79, assoc. prof., 1979-84, prof., 1984-87, prof. ecology, ethology and evolution, 1987-88; prof., head dept. biology Pa. State U., State College, 1988-94; assoc. vice chancellor acad. affairs/dean undergrad. acad. affairs, prof. ecology and evolutionary biology U. Tenn., Knoxville, 1995-97; dean Coll. Liberal Arts & Scis., prof. biol. scis. U. Iowa, Iowa City, 1997—. Exec. officer biology programs Sch. Life Scis., U. Ill., 1981-86, assoc. dir. acad. affairs, 1984-86, dir. campus honors program, 1985-88; vis. prof. ecology and evolutionary biology U. Calif., Irvine, 1988; mem. adv. panel rsch. tng. groups behavioral biol. scis. NSF, 1990-94. Author: Genetics: A Human Perspective, 3d edit., 1992; mem. editl. bd. Molecular Biology Evolution; exec. editor Biochem. Sys. & Ecology, 1993-2001; contbr. numerous articles to scientific jours. Recipient Disting. Alumni award San Diego State U., 1989, Disting. Herpetologist award Herpetologists' League, 1993. Fellow: AAAS; mem.: Herpetologists League, Soc. Molecular Biology and Evolution (treas. 1992—94, sec. 1992—95), Soc. Study Evolution, Soc. for Study of Amphibians and Reptiles (pres. 1991), Am. Men and Women in Sci., Phi Beta Kappa. Office: U Iowa 240 Schaeffer Hall Iowa City IA 52242-1409 Business E-Mail: linda-maxson@uiowa.edu.

MAXSON, ROBERT C. university president; Former sr. v.p. acad. affairs U. Houston Systems, Houston; pres. U. Nev., Las Vegas, 1984-94, Calif. State U., Long Beach, 1994—. Office: Calif St Univ Long Beach BH 300 1250 N Bellflower Blvd Long Beach CA 90840-0006

MAXWELL, ANDERS JOHN, investment banker; b. San Francisco, Oct. 3, 1946; s. John L. and Deborah A. M.; m. Carlene S. Maxwell, 2000; children by previous marriage: Lauren A., Colin A., Ian W., Erin C., Ryan N. BArch, U. Calif.-Berkeley, 1969; MBA, U. Pa., 1971. Analyst GE, 1971-73; v.p. GE Credit Corp., Stamford, Conn., 1973-83; mng. dir. Dean Witter Reynolds Inc., N.Y.C., 1983-87; v.p. Kidder Peabody & Co., Inc., N.Y.C., 1987-88; prin. L.F. Rothschild & Co., N.Y.C., 1988; v.p. Smith Barney, Harris Upham & Co., Inc., 1989-91, Lazard Frères & Co., N.Y.C., 1991-92; ptnr. Benedetto, Gartland & Greene, N.Y.C., 1992-94; v.p., gen. mgr. GE Capital Corp., Stamford, Conn., 1994-96; dir. Salomon Smith Barney Inc., N.Y.C., 1997-98; mng. dir. Barington Capital Group, N.Y.C., 1998; mng. dir., ptnr. Peter J. Solomon Co., N.Y.C., 1999—. Served to capt. U.S Army, 1971. Office: Peter J Solomon Co 520 Madison Ave New York NY 10022 Office Phone: 212-508-1683. E-mail: amaxwell@pjsolomon.com.

MAXWELL, ARTHUR EUGENE, oceanographer, marine geophysicist, educator; b. Maywood, Calif., Apr. 11, 1925; s. John Henry and Nelle Irene M.; m. Colleen O'Leary, July 1, 1988; children: Delle, Eric, Lynn, Brett, Gregory, Sam Wade, Henry Wade. BS in Physics with honors, N.Mex. State U., 1949; MS in Oceanography, Scripps Instn. Oceanography, 1952, PhD in Oceanography, 1959. Jr. rsch. geophysicist Scripps Instn. Oceanography, La Jolla, Calif., 1950-55; head oceanographer Office Naval Rsch., Washington, 1955-59, head br. geophysics, 1959-65; assoc. dir. Woods Hole (Mass.) Oceanographic Instn., 1965-69, dir. rsch., 1969-71, provost, 1971-81; prof. dept. geol. scis., dir. Inst. Geophysics U. Tex., Austin, 1982-94, prof. emeritus dept. geol. sci., 1994—. Chmn. bd. govs. planning com. deep earth sampling, 1968-70, chmn. exec. com. deep earth sampling, 1971-72, 78-79, 91-92; mem. joint U.S./USSR com. for coop. studies of the world ocean NAS/NRC, 1973-80, chmn. U.S. nat. com. to Internat. Union Geodesy and Geophysics, 1976-80, vice chmn. outer continental shelf/environ. studies rev. com., 1986-93; chmn. U.S. nat. com. on geology NAS, 1979-83, chmn. geophysics rsch. bd. geophysics study com., 1982-87; nat. sea grant rev. panel NOAA, 1982-85, 90-2000, sci. adv. bd., 1998—; mem. vis. com. Rosenstiel Sch. Marine and Atmospheric Studies U. Miami, 1982-86, dept. physics N.Mex. State U., 1986-94; acad. adv. com. Com. Exch. CIA, 1983-96; mem. Gulf of Mexico Regional Marine Rsch. Bd., 1992-96. Editor: The Sea, Vol. 4, Parts I and II, 1970; editorial adv. bd. Oceanus, 1981-92; contbr. articles to profl. jours. Chmn. tech. adv. com. Navy Thresher Search, 1963; mem. Mass. Gov.'s. Adv. Com. on Sci. and Tech., 1965-71. With USN, 1942-46, PTO. Recipient Meritorious Civilian Svc. award Chief Naval Rsch., 1958, Albatross award AMSOC, 1959, Superior Civilian Svc. award Assn. Sec. of Navy, 1963, Disting. Civilian Svc. award Sec. of Navy, 1964, Disting. Alumni award N.Mex. State U., 1965, Bruun Meml. Lecture award Intergovtl. Oceanographic Commn., 1969, Outstanding Centennial Alumnus award N. Mex. State U., 1988. Fellow Am. Geophys. Union (pres. 1976-78, pres. oceanography sect. 1970-72); mem. Marine Tech. Soc. (charter, pres. 1981-82), Cosmos Club. Achievements include research in heat flow through the ocean floor, in structure and tectonics of the sea floor. Home: PO Box 31249 Santa Fe NM 87594 Office: Univ Tex Inst Geophysics Bldg 600 4412 Spicewood Springs Rd Austin TX 78759 Business E-Mail: art@utig.ig.utexas.edu.

MAXWELL, CARLA LENA, dancer, choreographer, educator; b. Glendale, Calif., Oct. 25, 1945; d. Robert and Victoria (Carbone) Maxwell. Student, Bennington Coll., 1963-64; BS, Juilliard Sch. Music, 1967. Mem. Jose Limón Dance Co., N.Y.C., 1965, prin. dancer, 1969—, acting artistic dir., 1977-78, artistic dir., 1978—. Lectr., tchr. in field. Dancer soloist Louis Falco Dance Co., 1967—71, Harkness Festival at Delacorte Theater, N.Y.C., 1964—, artist-in-residence Gettysburg Coll., 1970—, Luther Coll., Decorah, Iowa, 1971—, U. Idaho, 1973—, choreographer Function, 1970—, Improvisations on a Dream, 1970—, A Suite of Psalms, 1973—, Homage to José Linón, Place Spirit, 1975, Aadvark Brothers: Schwartz and Columbo Present Please Don't Stone the Clowns, 1975, Blue Warrior, 1975, Sonata, 1980, Keeping Still Mountain, 1987, dancer toured East and West Africa, 1969. Recipient Dance Mag. award, 1995; N.Y. State Cultural Coun. grantee, 1971. Home: 7 Great Jones St New York NY 10012-1135 Office: Jose Limon Dance Fedn 611 Broadway Fl 9 New York NY 10012-2608

MAXWELL, CHIP, state legislator; b. Omaha, Aug. 10, 1962; m. Pam Maxwell; children: Tomas, Oto. B in Polit. Sci., Boston Coll., 1984; M in Am. History, Oxford U., 1987; JD, U. Nebr., 1992. Law clk. Nebr. Ct. Appeals; editl. writer Omaha World-Herald; spl. asst. to U.S. Senater Chuck Hagel; devel. dir. Jesuit Mid. Sch., Our Lady Guadalupe & St. Agnes Mission Sch.; mem. Nebr. Legislature from 9th dist., 2001—. Mem. Nebr. BAr Assn. Home: 3835 California St Omaha NE 68131 Office: Rm 1115 State Capitol Lincoln NE 68509

MAXWELL, DAVID E. academic executive, educator; b. NYC, Dec. 2, 1944; s. James Kendrick and Gertrude Sarah (Bernstein) M.; children: Justin Kendrick, Stephen Edward. BA, Grinnell Coll., 1966; MA, Brown U., 1968, PhD, 1974. Instr. Tufts U., Medford, Mass., 1971-74, asst. prof., 1974-78, assoc. prof. Russian lang. and lit., 1978-89, dean undergrad. studies, 1981-89; pres. Whitman Coll., Walla Walla, Wash., 1989-93; dir. Nat. Fgn. Lang. Ctr., Washington, 1993-99; pres. Drake U., Des Moines, 1999—. Chmn. steering com. Coop. Russian Lang. Program, Leningrad, USSR, 1981-86, chmn. 1986-90; cons. Coun. Internat. Edni. Exch., 1974-94, bd. dirs., 1988-92, 93-94, vice chair, 1991-92, cons. Internat. Rsch. Exchs., 1976-83; mem. adv. bd. Israeli Lang. Policy Inst. Contbr. articles to scholarly jours. Cmty. bd. dirs. Wells Fargo; bd. dirs. Iowa Wellness Coun.; bd. dirs. Greater Des Moines Partnership; pres. Des Moines Higher Edn. Collaborative, 2000—; bd. dirs. Downtown Cmty Alliance, Des Moines. Fulbright fellow, 1970-71, Brown U., 1966-67, NDEA Title IV, 1967-70; recipient Lillian Leibner award Tufts U., 1970; citation Grad. Sch. Arts and Scis., Brown U., 1991. Mem. MLA, Am. Coun. Edn. (commn. on internat. edn., pres.'s coun. on internat. edn.), Am. Assn. Advancement of Slavic Studies, Am. Assn. Tchrs. Slavic and E. European Langs., Assn. Am. Colls., Am. Assn. Higher Edn., Am. Coun. Tchg. Fgn. Langs., Brown U. Alumni Assn., Phi Beta Kappa.; mem. Bus. Higher EDn. Forum. Democrat. Avocations: tennis, running, music. Office: Drake Univ Office of the Pres 2507 University Ave Des Moines IA 50311-4505 Office Phone: 515-271-2191. Business E-Mail: david.maxwell@drake.edu.

MAXWELL, DAVID OGDEN, former government official and financial executive; b. Phila., May 16, 1930; s. David Farrow and Emily Ogden (Nelson) M.; m. Joan Clark Paddock, Dec. 14, 1968. BA, Yale U., 1952; LLB, Harvard U., 1955. Bar: Pa. 1955, D.C. 1955. From assoc. to ptnr. Obermayer, Rebmann, Maxwell & Hippel, Phila., 1959-67; from ins. commr. to adminstrn. and budget sec. State of Pa., 1967-70; gen. counsel HUD, Washington, 1970-73; pres., CEO Ticor Mortgage Ins. Co., 1973-81; CEO Fannie Mae, Washington, 1981-91; dir. bus. and non-profit orgns. Bd. dirs. Centre Ptnrs., L.P., Fin Security Assurance Holdings, Ltd. Bd. dirs. Sta. WETA-TV; trustee Nat. Gallery Art. With USNR, 1955-59. Office: 5335 Wisconsin Ave NW Ste 440 Washington DC 20015-2052

MAXWELL, DIANA KATHLEEN, early childhood education educator; b. Seminole, Okla., Dec. 16, 1949; d. William Hunter and ImoJean (Mahurin) Rivers; m. Clarence Estel Maxwell, Jly 3, 1969; children: Amanda Hunter, Alexandra Jane. BS, U. Md., 1972; M of Secondary Edn., Boston U., 1974; PhD, U. Md., 1980. Cert. tchr., counselor, Tex. Tchr. Child Garden Presch., Adelphi, Md., 1969-71; tchr., dir. PREP Edn. Ctr., Heidelberg, Germany, 1972-74; tchr. N.E. Ind. Schs. Larkspur, San Antonio, 1974-77, 89-90, Headstart, Boyds, Md., 1978; dir., founder First Bapt. Child Devel. Ctr., Bryan, Tex., 1982-84; instr. English lang. Yonsei Med. Ctr., Seoul, Republic of Korea, 1985-87; asst. prof. Incarnate Word Coll., San Antonio, 1987-89; tchr. kindergarten Fairfax County Pub. Schs., Kings Park, Va., 1990-94; tchr. Encino Park, San Antonio, Tex., 1994-95; lectr. U. Tex., San Antonio, 1995-96; multi-age tchr., theater arts tchr. Ft. Sam Houston Elem. Sch., San Antonio, 1996—. Cons. Sugar N'Spice Child Devel. Ctr., Kilgore, Tex., 1980-90; bd. dirs. Metro Area Assn. for Childhood Edn. Internat., 1991-93. Author: (book revs.) Childhood Education, 1979, 80, 92. Block chairperson March of Dimes, 1991, 92, 93,, 2000-, 01, 02, Am. Heart Assn., Fairfax, Fa., 1991, 92, San Antonio, 2000, 01, 02, Am. Diabetes Assn., Fairfax, 1992; judge speaking com. Burke Optomists, 1992, 93, judge writing competition N.E. Ind. Sch. Dist., 1996; sec. Cole H.S. Cougar Club, Ft. Sam Houston, San Antonio, 1996-97, v.p., 1997-2002, chair project graduation, 2002—; Bible tchr. 1st Bapt. Ch., Alexandria, Va., 1993-95; tchr. kindergarten Trinity Bapt. Ch., San Antonio, 1995-99, tchr. 1st grade, 2001—. Named one of Outstanding Young Women of Am., 1983; Md. fellow State of Md., 1978, 79; Tech. grantee Tex. Edn. Agy., San Antonio, 1990, State of Va. and Fairfax County, Springfield, 1991; recipient Yellow Rose of Tex. vol. award Gov. of Tex., 1996, Dean's Outstanding Tchg. award U. Tex., San Antonio, 1995-96, Ft. Sam Houston Hero award, 2001, 02. Mem. ASCD, Internat. Reading Assn., Assn. Profl. Tchr. Educators, Edn. Internat., Assn. for Childhood Edn. Internat. (v.p., pres.-elect), Tex. Assn. Childhood Edn., Bexar County and Surrounding Areas Assn. Childhood Edn. Avocations: oriental brush painting, singing, collecting butterflies, children/teacher advocate. Home: 2602 Country Square St San Antonio TX 78209-2235 Office: Ft Sam Houston Elem Sch 3370 Nursery Rd San Antonio TX 78234-1479

MAXWELL, DONALD MALCOLM, clergyman, religious educator; b. Watford, Eng., Apr. 6, 1934; s. Arthur S. and Rachel Elizabeth (Joyce) M.; m. Eileen J. Bolander, Aug. 25, 1955; children: Wendy E. Maxwell Henderson, D. Kevin. BA in Theology and Biblical Langs., Pacific Union Coll., 1956; MA in Systematic Theology, Andrews U., 1958; PhD in Biblical Studies New Testament, Drew U., 1968. Ordained to ministry Seventh-Day Adventist Ch., 1960. Pastor No. Calif. Conf. Seventh-Day Adventists, Oakland, Calif., 1956-64; instr. religion Union Coll., Lincoln, Nebr., 1964-65; prof. religion Walla Walla Coll., College Place, Wash., 1965-78, v.p. acad. affairs, 1978-83; pres. Pacific Union Coll., Angwin, Calif., 1983—2001, pres. emeritus, 2001—, chmn. dept. religion, 2004—; pastor Pacific Union Coll. Ch., 2002—03. Trustee Redbud Cmty. Hosp., Clearlake, Calif., 2002—. Recipient Charles Elliot Weniger award of excellence, 1996, Edn. award of excellence, 2001; Rockefeller fellow, 1967-68; Drew U. scholar, 1967-68; named Tchr. of Yr., Wash. State Auto Assn., 1971. Mem. Soc. Biblical Lit. Seventh-Day Adventist. Avocations: golf, boating, gardening. Office: Pacific Union Coll 1 Angwin Ave Angwin CA 94508-9713 Office Phone: 707-965-6206. Business E-Mail: mmaxwell@puc.edu.

MAXWELL, DOROTHEA BOST ANDREWS, volunteer; b. Greenville, Ill., Apr. 20, 1911; d. Samuel Washington and Viola Maud (Bost) Andrews; m. Richard Wesley Maxwell, June 1, 1935; children: Andrea Judith Maxwell Platz, Anne Dorothea Maxwell Walsh. BA with honors, diploma in piano, Greenville Coll., 1933; MusM, Northwestern U., 1937. Cert. primary and secondary tchr., music tchr., Mo. Dir. sch. music Spring Arbor (Mich.) Jr. Coll., 1933-34; tutor orthopedic handicapped children St. Louis Pub. Schs., 1950-56. Tour guide Mo. Bot. Garden, St. Louis, 1975—87; pres. The Wednesday Club St. Louis, 1983—85, archivist, 1985—92; guide tours of distinction St. Louis Symphony Soc., 1980—85; pres. Women's Assn., 2d Presbyn. Ch., St. Louis, 1956—58. Mem. Clan Maxwell Soc. U.S.A., Mo. Hist. Soc., St. Louis Genealogy Soc., Piano Club St. Louis, Washington U. Faculty women's Club, Mu Phi Epsilon. Republican. Congregationalist.

MAXWELL, FLORENCE HINSHAW, civic worker; b. Nora, Ind., July 14, 1914; d. Asa Benton and Gertrude (Randall) Hinshaw; m. John Williamson Maxwell, June 5, 1936; children: Marilyn Maxwell Grissom, William Douglas. BA cum laude, Butler U., 1935. Coord., bd. dirs. Sight Conservation and Aid to Blind, 1962-73, nat. chmn., 1969-73; active various fund drives; chmn. jamboree, hostess coms. North Ctrl. H.S., 1959, 64, Girl Scouts USA, 1937-38, 54-56; mus. chmn. Sr. Girl Scouts USA Regional Coun., 1956-57; scorekeeper Little League, 1955-57; vision screening Indpls. inner city pub. sch. kindergartens, pre-schs., 1962—69, 1981—2000; vision screener Headstart, 1967—98; trainer Indpls. inner city pub. sch. kindergartens, pre-schs., 1968—1992, Headstart, 1988—98. Asst. Glaucoma screening clinics Gen. Hosp., Glendale Shopping Ctr., City County Bldg., Am. Legion Nat. Hdqrs., Ind. Health Assn. Conf., 1962—73; chmn. sight conservation and aid to blind Nat. Delta Gamma Found., Indpls., Columbus, Ohio, 1969—73; mem. telethon team Butler U. Fund, 1964; symphoguide hostess Internat. Conf. on Cities, 1971, Nat. League of Cities, 1972; mem. health adv. com. Headstart, 1976—98, sec., 1980—98, mem. social svcs. com., 1987—98, coord. vision rescreening and referrals, assessment team of compliance steering com., 1978—79, 1984, 86, 1987—88, 1991—92, 1994, 96, 98; founder People of Vision Aux., 1981, bd. dirs., 1981—, v.p., 1990—92, mem. coord. vision and glaucoma screenings and office svcs., 1990—92, sec. emeritus, 1997; initiated vision screening and eye safety edn. Jameson Camp for Children, 1987. Recipient Key to City of Indpls., 1972, Those Spl. People award Women in Comm., 1980, Appreciation award Headstart, 1983, Jefferson award for Disting. Pub. Svc. Indpls. Star, 1991, Cmty. Action Head Start Outstanding Vol. award, 1996, Health/Social Svcs. award Family Devel. Svcs., 1998, Appreciation award Prevent Blindness, 1999. Mem.: People of Vision, Ind. State Symphony Soc. Women's Com. (vol. Indpls. symphony orch.'s discovery concerts, vol. Indpls. noontime concerts, vol. Yuletide, coffee concerts), Jameson Camp Aux., Ind. Soc. to Prevent Blindness (now Prevent Blindness Ind.) (dir. 1962—99, sec. 1971—83, exec. com. 1971—95, v.p. 1983—86, life hon. v.p. 1983—, Ind. del. to nat. 3-yr. program planning conf. 1985—, internal analysis task force for svcs. 1987, asst. sec.-treas. 1987—92, adv. bd. 1999—, Sight Saving award 1974, Svc. Appreciation award 1999, Lifetime Achievement award 2000), Ind. Hist. Soc., Ind. Audubon Soc., Nat. Soc. to Prevent Blindness (now Prevent Blindness Am.), Eastwood Jr. H.S. Triangle Club, Delta Gamma (chpt. golden ann. celebration decade comm. chmn. 1975, treas. Alpha Tau house corp. 1975—78, nat. chmn. Parent Club Study Com. 1976—77, instr. province leadership sem. workshop 1989, Cable award 1969, Outstanding Alumna award 1973, Svc. Recognition award 1977, Shield award 1981, scholarship hon. 1981, Stellar award 1986, Oxford award 1992). Republican. Address: 1502 E 80th St Indianapolis IN 46240-2706

MAXWELL, J. B. financial consultant, marketing professional, consultant; b. Clarksburg, W.Va., Sept. 30, 1944; s. J. B. and Martha (Hornor) Maxwell; m. Valerie Ronson, Oct. 13, 1983; 1 child, Jennifer. BS, Salem (W.Va.) Coll., 1967; M in Mktg., Harvard U., 1970. Lic. real estate sales, ins., securities, registered commodity rep., accredited mgmt. cons. and fin. planner, registered fin. planner, investment advisor, accredited asset mgmt. specialist. Exec. v.p. Textron Inc., Providence, 1968-71; pres. Martech Inc. and 6 other cos., Portland, Maine, 1968—; v.p. E. F. Hutton Co., Portland, 1976-83; 1st v.p. fin. planning Dean Witter, Boston, 1983-90; pres. Planning Svcs. Corp., Boston, 1990-92; 1st v.p. Gruntal & Co., Inc., Boston, 1992—2003; with Ryan Beck & Co., Wellesley, Mass., 2003—. Author: handbooks, booklets; contbr. articles to profl. jours., Portland Coll. Art, 1980—93. Bd. dirs. Wellness Inst., Boston, 1990—91. Recipient Bronze award, Nat. Acad. Scis., 1962. Mem.: Nat. Assn. Security Dealers (former br. office mgr.), World Affairs Coun., Inst. Mgmt. Cons., Am. Mktg. Assn., Am. Mgmt. Assn., Internat. Assn. Fin. Planning, Boston C. of C., Rotary. Avocations: golf, woodworking, travel, literature. Home: 15 Bailey Road Arlington MA 02476 Office: Ryan Beck 20 Williams St Wellesley MA 02481 Office Phone: 800-223-8166. E-mail: j.b.maxwell@ryan.becz.com.

MAXWELL, JACK ERWIN, manufacturing executive; b. Cleve., July 17, 1926; s. Fred A. and Gertrude F. (Haug) M.; m. Martha Jane Miller, Dec. 28, 1966; children by previous marriage: Laura Jane, Fredric, Elizabeth Grant, Carla Moore, Linda Hanson. BS, Case Inst. Tech., 1949; MBA, Harvard U., 1952. Indsl. engr. Lincoln Electric Co., Cleve., 1952-53; mgr. purchase analysis Ford Motor Co., Dearborn, Mich., 1953-57; v.p. Booz, Allen & Hamilton, Inc., Detroit, 1957-69; v.p. corp. devel. Am. Motors Corp., Detroit, 1969-71, v.p. adminstrn., 1971-76, v.p. non-automotive subsidiaries, 1976-79, v.p. diversified ops., 1979-80; chmn., pres. Wheel Horse Products, Inc., South Bend, Ind., 1974-80; chmn., CEO Ingersoll Products Corp., Chgo., 1980-86; pres. Wellmax, Inc., 1976—. Served with USNR, 1944-46. Mem. Case Inst. Tech. Alumni Assn., Harvard Bus. Sch. Alumni Assn., Detroit Athletic Club, Detroit Econ. Club, Chgo. Club, Old Club, Tau Beta Pi, Theta Tau. Address: 3541 Bradway Blvd Bloomfield Village MI 48301-2409 Office Phone: 248-646-3554. E-mail: wellmaxx@earthlink.net.

MAXWELL, JEROME EUGENE, corporate executive; b. Princeton, Ill., June 2, 1944; s. Emmett Eugene and June (Erickson) M.; m. Cynthia Jane O'Connell, July 30, 1977; children: Eric Vaughn, Christina Dawn, Jeremy Emmett, Jason Daniel, Nicholas Mark. BSEE, So. Meth. U., 1967, MSEE, 1971. Maintainability engr. product support divsn. Collins Radio Co., Richardson, Tex., 1965-67, jr. engr. computer sys. divsn., 1967-70; sr. engr. TRW Electronics Products, Inc., Colorado Springs, Colo., 1970-73, mgr. engring., 1973-79, mgr. program mgmt. office, 1979-81, gen. mgr. space electronics mfg. divsn., 1981-86; pres., CEO G&S Sys., Inc., Bedford, Mass., 1986-87, Atec, Inc., Houston, 1987-91; v.p., divsn. dir. Nat. Sys. & Rsch. Co., Colorado Springs, 1992-94; pres., chmn. bd. dirs. Tech. Assocs. of Colo., Inc., Colorado Springs, 1994-96; pres., CEO Advanced Profl. Tng., Inc., Colorado Springs, 1996—. Patentee in field. Mem. adv. coun. U. Colo., Colorado Springs, 1973-86, U. So. Colo., Pueblo, 1974-78; Webelo leader, asst. pack leader Boy Scouts Am., 1976-77; fin. chmn. Ascension Luth. Ch., 1981-86; cons. to cmty. edn. coord. for computer sys. and equipment, 1980-86; mem. Soli Deo Gloria Choir, 1999—. Mem. AIAA (sr.), Assn. Old Crows (pres. space chpt.), Mesa Sertoma (charter, bd. dirs.). Republican. E-mail: maxsquared@adelphia.net.

MAXWELL, JOE EDWIN, lieutenant governor; b. Kirksville, Mo., Mar. 17, 1957; s. Robert E. and Molly B. Maxwell; m. Sarah Baker; children: Megan, Shannen. BS in Secondary Edn., Social Studies, U. Mo., 1986, JD, 1990. Farmer, Rush Hill, Mo., 1976-78; ptnr., operator Maxwell Svc., Laddonia, Mo., 1978-84; rural mail carrier U.S. Postal Svc., Rush Hill, 1980-84; outstate field coord. Travis Morrison's Campaign for State Auditor, Mo., 1986; Mo. state field coord. Richard Gephardt for Pres., 1986-87; atty. Mexico, Mo., 1992—; mem. Mo. House, 1990-94, Mo. Senate, 1995—2001; Lt. gov. State Mo., 2001—. Mem. Senate Appropriations, Judiciary, Labor and Indsl. Rels., Pub. Health and Welfare coms.; vice chair Elections, Corrections, and Vet.'s Affairs coms.; chair Commerce and Environment Com. Assoc. editor-in-chief Mo. Jour. of Dispute Resolution, 1989. Mem. Am. Legion, 1982—, adj. Post 510, 1982-84; mem. Young Dem. Clubs Mo., 1982—, jud. coun. Young Dems. Am., 1985, pres., 1984-87, 9th Congl. Dist. chmn., 1982; mem. Laddonia Bapt. Ch., 1975—, Sunday Sch. tchr., 1990-91, pulpit com.; bd. dirs. Handi-Shop Inc., Mexico, 1981-84, chmn. mfg. and mktg. com., 1982-84; bd. dirs. Boy Scouts Am. Troop 94, 1980-82. Recipient St. Louis Globe Dem. award for outstanding achievement, 1979, Cert. of Appreciation, Troop 94, Boy Scouts Am., 1982, Mo.'s Outstanding Male Young Dem. award, 1987, George B. Freeman award for outstanding svc., 1987, Appreciation award Mo. Bar, 1992, Mo. Ho. of Reps. Resolution # 624 for exceptional svc. Mo., 1987, Mo. State Senate Resolution # 382 for exceptional svc. Mo., 1987; named one of Outstanding Young Men of Am., 1983, 85. Mem. Moose, Jaycees (Laddonia chpt. pres. 1978-79, coord. Laddonia Area Blood Drive, coord. Laddonia City Clean-up Day, chmn. Mexico Soybean Festival 1989, chmn. Lenten Breakfast 1990, Presdl. award of honor 1979), Kappa Delta Pi, Golden Key Nat. Honor Soc. Democrat. Office: Office of Lt Gov Rm 121 Capitol Bldg Jefferson City MO 65101

MAXWELL, JOHN E. priest, educator; b. Floydada, Tex., July 15, 1930; s. John Wallace Maxwell and Irene Cardinal. BA, Don Bosco Coll., 1952; MA in English, Loyola U., 1965; MA/MFCC in Counseling, U. San Francisco, 1977. Tchr. Salesian H.S., Richmond, Calif., 1960—64, prin., 1964—68; pastor St. Andrew's Ch., Oakland, Calif., 1968—94, St. John, El Cerrito, Calif., 1994—. Author: (book) Worship in Action, 1981. Mem. OXFAM, 1996—2004; treas. Oakland (Calif.) Cmty. Housing, 1985—2004; pres. Greater Richmond Interfaith Program, Richmond, 1994—2004; mem. Amnesty Internat., 1990—2004, Common Cause, 1979—2004; dean Diocese of Oakland, 1986—2004. Mem.: Oakland Senate of Priests (chmn., bd. dirs. 1970—2001), NAACP, Smithsonian Instn., Sierra Club, Knights of St. Peter Claver (chaplain 1985—2004, 4th degree). Democrat. Roman Catholic. Avocations: fishing, travel. Home: 11150 San Pablo Ave El Cerrito CA 94530 Office: St John the Bapt Cath Ch 1150 San Pablo Ave El Cerrito CA 94530

MAXWELL, JUDITH, think-tank executive, economist; b. Kingston, Ont., Can., July 21, 1943; d. James Ruffee and Marguerite Jane (Spanner) McMahon; m. Anthony Stirling Maxwell, May 8, 1970; 2 children. B in Commerce, Dalhousie U., 1963, LLD, 1991; postgrad., London Sch. Econs., 1965-66; LLD, Queen's U., 1992. Researcher Combines Investigation Br. Consumer and Corp. Affairs, Ottawa, Can., 1963-65; econs. writer, mem. editorial bd. Fin. Times, Montreal, Que., Can., 1966-72; dir. policy studies C.D. Howe Inst., Montreal, 1972-80; cons. Esso Europe Inc., London, Eng., 1980-82, Coopers & Lybrand, Montreal, Que., 1982-85; chmn. Econ. Council Can., Ottawa, Ont., 1985-92; exec.-dir. Queen's-U. Ottawa Econ. Projects, 1992—. Dir. Can. Found. for Econ. Edn., 1985-88, Inst. for Rsch. on Pub.

Policy, 1987-88. Author: Energy From the Arctic, 1973; (with C. Pestieau) Economic Realities of Contemporary Confederation, 1980; (with S. Currie) Partnership for Growth: Corporate University Education in Canada, 1984. Active Ont. Premier's Coun., 1988-90, Nfld. and Labrador Sci. and Tech. Adv. Coun., 1988-90. Mem. Can. Assn. Bus. Econs. (pres. 1976-77), Montreal Econs. Assn. (pres. 1975-76). Office: Canadian Policy Rsch Networks 600-250 Albert St K1P 6M1 Ottawa ON Canada Office Phone: 613-567-7500. E-mail: jmaxwell@cprn.org.

MAXWELL, KATHLEEN ELIZABETH, art historian; b. Elmhurst, Ill., Aug. 19, 1952; d. Francis William and Kathleen Margaret (Kane) M.; m. Paul Missiroli Sullam, July 24, 1982; children: Juliana, Angelica, Mariella. Student, Denison U., 1970-72, U. Aberdeen, Scotland, 1972-73; BFA, So. Meth. U., 1974; MA, U. Chgo., 1977, PhD with honors, 1986. Lectr. Santa Clara (Calif.) U., 1983-93, asst. prof., 1994—2001, assoc. prof., 2001—. Contbr. articles to profl. jours., abstracts. Grantee NEH, Parma, Italy, 1988; recipient fellowship Samuel H. Kress, Europe, 1980. Mem. Coll. Art Assn., Internat. Ctr. for Medieval Art, Byzantine Studies Conf. (sec. 1998-2001), Medieval Assn. of the Pacific, Medieval Acad. Am., AAUP. Roman Catholic. Office: Santa Clara U Dept Art and Art History 500 El Camino Real Santa Clara CA 95053-0264

MAXWELL, KENNETH ROBERT, historian; b. Wellington, Somerset, U.K., Feb. 3, 1941; s. Kenneth Bruce Maxwell and Jean Anderson. BA, Cambridge U., 1963, MA, 1967, Princeton (N.J.) U., 1967, PhD, 1970. Prof. history Columbia U., N.Y.C., 1976-84, dir. Camoes Ctr., 1988-99; program dir. Tinker Found., N.Y.C., 1979-85; dir. Latin Am. Coun. on Fgn. Rels., N.Y.C., 1989—2004, v.p., dir. studies, 1996, Nelson and David Rockefeller sr. fellow, 1995—2004; sr. fellow David Rockefeller Ctr. for Latin Am. Studies Harvard U., 2004—. Vis. prof. history and L.Am. studies Princeton U., N.J., 1985-86; vis. prof. history Yale U., New Haven, Conn., 1991-92; consultative coun. Luso-Am. Found., Lisbon, Portugal, 1996—; bd dirs. Tinker Found., Inc. Author: Conflicts and Conspiracies: Brazil and Portugal, 1973, rev. edits. 2004, Pombal: Paradox of Enlightment, 1995, The Making of Portuguese Democracy, 1995, Naked Tropics: Essays on Empire and other rogues, 2003; co-author: The New Spain, 1994; book review editor: Foreign Affairs, 1993-2004; contbr. articles to profl. jours. and publs.; columnist no.com.br., 2000-02, Folha de S. Paulo, 2001-, Epoca, 2002-04. Bd. trustees Latin Am. Scholarship, Cambridge, Mass., 1991-97; founding mem. Com. for Internat. Grantmakers, Washington, 1981-86; adv. com. Ams. Watch, N.Y.C., 1996—; adv. Dwight D. Eisenhower Exch. Fellowship, Phila., 1996; selection com. Hubert H. Humphery fellowship, 1985. Recipient Grand Cross Order of Merit, 1996; named Comdr. Order of Rio Branco, 1997, Grand Official, order of Prince Henry the Navigator, 2004; Herodotus fellow Inst. for Advanced Study, 1971-75, Guggenheim fellow, 1976-77, hon. fellow Romance Inst. London U., 1993—. Mem. Century Assn., Norfolk Country Club, Am. Hist. Assn., Coun. on Fgn. Rels., Instituto Historico Geografico Brasileiro. Avocations: swimming, drawing. Home: 20 Prescott St Apt 43 Cambridge MA 02138 Office: Harvard University David Rockefeller Ctr 61 Kirkland St Cambridge MA 02138 Office Phone: 617-496-4780.

MAXWELL, MARK, music educator; s. Duane and Judith Maxwell; m. Christine Maxwell; children: Nicole Crase, Melody. BMus in Edn., Vander-Cook Coll. of Music, 1980; MA in Edn., Coll. of Mt. St. Joseph, 1992. Cert. Permanent Tchg. State of Ohio, 1992. Assoc. band dir. Union Co. Pub. Schools, Morganfield, Ky., 1980—81; mid. sch. band dir. Bucyrus City Schools, Bucyrus, Ohio, 1981—85; band dir. Loudonville Perrysville Schools, Loudonville, Ohio, 1985—89; mid. sch. band head dir. Mansfield City Schools, Mansfield, Ohio, 1989—99; dept. chmn., dir. H.S. band Lexington Local Schools, Lexington, Ohio, 1999—. Mem.: Internat. Assn. Jazz Educators, Am. Fedn. Musicians, Nat. Band Assn., Music Educators Nat. Conf., Ohio Music Educators Assn. Office: Lexington Local Schools Music Department 103 Clever Ln Lexington OH 44904 E-mail: lexhs_mam@ncocc-k12.org.

MAXWELL, MARY ELLEN, school system administrator; Grad., St. Mary's Acad., 1961, N.C. Sch. Bds. Assn. Acad. Ret. child devel. adminstr. U.S. Naval Security Group Activity N.W., Chesapeake, Va.; chmn., mem. at large Currick County Bd. Edn., 1982—. Chairperson Currituck County Alcohol and Drug Task Force; bd. dirs. Colonial Coast Girl Scouts Coun.; mem. Edn. and Tng. Voluntary Partnership; active Albemarle Hopeline, Currituck County Relay for Life. Mem.: Nat. Coun. for the Accreditation of Tchr. Edn. (mem. exec. com.), Nat. Sch. Bds. Assn. (former pres. bd. dirs.), N.C. Sch. Bds. Assn. (bd. dirs.), Nat. Bd. for Profl. Tchg. Stds. (bd. mem.), Moyock Woman's Club, Currituck Christian Women's Club.

MAXWELL, MAX ANTHONY, language educator; b. Duncans, Trelawny, Jamaica, Aug. 27, 1937; s. John William Maxwell and Zelma Cynthia Thelwell; m. Barbara M. Durham, Feb. 27, 1965; children: Megan Christine, Maritza Joan. BA, L.I. U., 1963; MA, Rutgers U., 1970. Asst. instr. Rutgers U., New Brunswick, NJ, 1964—68; instr. L.I. U., New York, NY, 1968—69; tchr. English, Henry C. Woods Family Disting. Tchg. chair The Lawrenceville Sch., Lawrenceville, NJ, 1969—. Faculty cons. Ednl. Testing Svcs., Princeton, NJ, 1970—. Avocations: writing, photography, coaching cricket & soccer, carpentry. Office: The Lawrenceville School Main Street Lawrenceville NJ 08648 Office Phone: 609-895-2028. E-mail: mamaxwel@lawrenceville.org.

MAXWELL, PATRICIA JOY, fund raising executive; b. Belle Plaine, Iowa, Feb. 7, 1937; d. Verne Edwin and Julia Inez (Beem) M. Student, Pepperdine Coll., 1954-55; BS, Iowa State Tchrs. Coll., 1958; MPA, Roosevelt U., 1982. Cert. fund raising exec. Dir. resource devel. Boys Clubs Am., 1978-81; exec. dir. Westlake Health Svcs. Found., 1981-84; assoc. dean devel. and alumni affairs U. Ill. Coll. Medicine, 1984-91; sr. maj. gifts officer U. Ill., 1991-93; v.p. devel. Orlando (Fla.) M.D. Anderson Cancer Ctr., 1993; assoc. dir. nat. hdqrs. Alzheimer's Assn., Chgo., 1994; dir. devel. N.Y. Acad. Scis., N.Y.C., 1997; sr. dir. devel. Calif. State U., Long Beach, 1997—2003; sr. exec. dir. maj. gifts Sch. Medicine U. Miami, Fla., 2003—04. Cons. Ency. Britannica Ednl. Corp., Prentice Hall Inc., U.S. State Dept. Mem. N.Y. Acad. Scis., Am. Mktg. Assn. (co-founder Acad. of Health Svcs. Mktg. 1980), Chgo. Area Pub. Affairs Group, Univ. Club (Chgo.), Balboa (Calif.) Bay Club, Lake Nona Club (Orlando).

MAXWELL, RAYMOND ROGER, retired accountant; b. Parmer County, Tex., Jan. 7, 1918; s. Frederick W. and Hazel Belle (Rogers) M.; m. Jeanne Hollarn, June 16, 1945 (dec. Dec. 1987); children: Donald R., Bruce Edward, Sabrina G. Ed.B., Western Ill. State Tchrs Coll., 1941; MBA in Acctg., U. Fla., 1949; postgrad., UCLA, 1965-68. CPA, Fla., Calif. Asst. to bus. mgr. Western Ill. State Tchrs. Coll., Macomb, 1939-41; apprentice acct. Charles H. Lindfors, CPA, Ft. Lauderdale, Fla., 1946-48; acct./auditor Frederic Dunn-Rankin & Co. CPA, Miami, Fla., 1948-49; CPA staff Charles Costar, CPA, Miami, 1951; resident auditor/CPA prin. Raymond R. Maxwell CPA, Ft. Lauderdale, 1951-56; supt. pub. instrn. Broward County, Ft. Lauderdale, 1956-61; staff asst. in fin. North Am. Aviation, Inc., El Segundo, Calif., 1961-65; acctg. prin. Raymond R. Maxwell, CPA, Whittier, Calif., 1968-2000. Part-time rsch. asst. UCLA, 1965, teaching asst., 1966, 67; instr. Calif. Poly., 1967. Active precinct election bds., Whittier, L.A. County, 1989, 98-2000; 1st reader First Ch. of Christ, Scientist, Whittier, 1990-92, 96-98, exec. bd., 1989, exec. bd. chmn., 1993, participant Bible Explorations, 1991-92. 1st lt. USAAF, 1942-46. Recipient Am. Medal of Honor, Am. Bibliog. Inst., 2002. Republican. Avocations: dance, swimming, computers. *One, with God, is a majority.*

MAXWELL, RICHARD ANTHONY, retail executive; b. N.Y.C., Apr. 1, 1933; s. Arthur William and Mary Ellen (Winestock) M.; m. Jacqueline Ann Creamer, Oct. 27, 1962. Student, NYU, 1957-58, Acad. Advanced Traffic, 1959. Import ops. mgr. Associated Merchandising Corp., N.Y.C., 1950-52, 56-65; v.p. Associated Dry Goods Corp., N.Y.C., 1965-86, sr. v.p. mktg., 1980-82, exec. v.p. mktg., 1982-86; pres. A.D.G. Export Mktg., Florence, Italy, 1982-86, Associated Dry Goods Ltd., Hong Kong, 1983-86, Inter Textyle Corp., 1987-89; with Matol Botanical Internat. Ltd.; exec. v.p. Matol World Corp., Montreal, Canada, 1992-94; dir. Matol Botanical New Zealand, 1994-96; v.p. internat. ops. L'Aprina Internat. Inc., 1994-96; chief internat. officer Camelot Concept Co., Montreal, 1995-96; CFO Showcase Prodns., Phoenix, 1996; exec. v.p. Harmony House Internat., Phoenix, 1996-97, IGW Trust, Phoenix, 1997-99, Pre-Paid Legal Svcs., Inc., 1999—; pres. Team 39, Inc., Dunedin, Fla., 2000-2001; dir. Presley Promotions Inc., Memphis, 2001—02; pres., COO Home Farms Techs. Inc., Brandon, Canada. Mem. industry sector adv. com. Dept. Commerce, 1984-93; mem. shippers adv. com. Nat. Maritime Coun. Served with USAF, 1952-56. Recipient Silver medal for contbns. to trade expansion, Republic of China, 1980; appt. to rank of comdr. in Order of Merit in recognition of improvement of trade between Italy and U.S., Republic of Italy, 1985. Mem. Am. Assn. Exporters and Importers (past pres., dir.), Shippers Conf. Greater N.Y. (past pres., dir.), Nat. Retail Mchts. Assn. (vice chmn. fgn. trade com.), Nat. Com. Internat. Trade Documentation (past vice chmn. gen. bus. com.), Transp. Assn. Am., Italy-Am. C. of C. (past pres., dir.), Am. Soc. of Italian Legion of Merit (dir.). Home: 2408 Stag Run Blvd Clearwater FL 33765-1832 Personal E-mail: rmaxwel2@tampabay.rr.com.

MAXWELL, RICHARD CALLENDER, retired lawyer, educator; b. Mpls., Oct. 7, 1919; s. Bertram Wayburn and Blossom (Callender) M.; m. Frances Lida McKay, Jan 27, 1942; children: Richard Callender, John McKay. BSL, U. Minn., 1941, LLB, 1947; LLD (hon.), Calif. Western U., 1983, Southwestern U., 1993. Assoc. prof. U. ND, 1947-49, U. Tex., 1949-51, prof., 1951-53; counsel Amerada Petroleum Corp., 1952-53; prof. UCLA, 1953-81; dean UCLA Sch. Law, 1959-69, Connell prof., 1979-81, Connell prof. emeritus, 1981—; Chadwick prof. Duke U. Sch. Law, 1981-89, Chadwick prof. emeritus, 1989—. Vis. prof. Columbia U., 1955; vis. Alumni prof. U. Minn., 1970-71; Fulbright lectr. Queen's U., No. Ireland, 1970; vis. Ford Found. prof. U. Singapore, 1971; Thompson prof. U. Colo., 1982; vis. prof. Hastings Coll. Law, 1976, Duke U., 1979-80, U. Tex., 1985; pres. Minn. Law Rev., 1946; chmn. Coun. Legal Edn. Opportunity, 1971-72; pres. Assn. Am. Law Schs., 1972; chmn. adv. com. law Fulbright Program, 1971-74, chmn. adv. com. U.K., 1974-77; mem. com. on gas prodn. opportunities NRC, 1977-78; mem. law sch. editl. and adv. bd. West Pub. Co., 1971-94. Author: (with S. A. Riesenfeld) Cases and Materials on Modern Social Legislation, 1950, (with H.R. Williams and C.J. Meyers) Cases on Oil and Gas Law, 1956, 7th edit., (with Patrick H. Martin, Bruce M. Kramer), 2002, (with S.A. Riesenfeld) California Cases on Security Transactions, 1957, 4th edit. (with S.A. Riesenfeld, J.R. Hetland, W.D. Warren), 1991; West Coast editor Oil and Gas Reporter, 1953-. Mem. LA Employee Rels. Bd., 1971-74; bd. dirs. Constl. Rights Found., 1963-81; trustee Calif. Western U., 1979-81; bd. visitors Duke U. Sch. Law, 1973-79, chmn. bd. Pvt. Adjudication Ctr., 1984-89; bd. visitors Southwestern U. Sch. Law, 1981—. Served to lt. comdr. USNR, 1941-46. Recipient Clyde O. Martz Tchg. award Rocky Mountain Mineral Law Found., 1994. Mem. ABA (com. on youth edn. for citizenship 1975-79, spl. com. on pub. understanding about the law 1979-84), Order of Coif. (nat. exec. com. 1980-86). Office: Duke U Sch Law Durham NC 27708-0362 E-mail: rcmaxwell@mindspring.com.

MAXWELL, ROBERT EARL, federal judge; b. Elkins, W.Va., Mar. 15, 1924; s. Earl L. and Nellie E. (Rexstrew) M.; m. Ann Marie Grabowski, Mar. 29, 1948; children— Mary Ann, Carol Lynn, Ellen Lindsay, Earl Wilson. LLD (hon.), Davis and Elkins Coll., 1984; LLB, W.Va. U., 1949. Bar: W.Va. 1949. Practiced in, Randolph County, 1949; pros. atty., 1952-61; U.S. atty. for No. Dist. W.Va., 1961-64; judge U.S. Dist. Ct. (no. dist.) W.Va., Elkins, 1965—94, sr. judge, 1994—; judge Temp. Emergency Ct. of Appeals, 1980-89. Past chmn. budget com. Jud. Conf. U.S.; former mem. exec. com. Nat. Conf. Fed. Trial Judges; former mem. adv. bd. W.Va. U. Mem. bd. advisors W.Va. U., past chmn.; bd. advisors Mary Babb Randolph Cancer Ctr. Recipient Alumni Disting. Svc. award Davis and Elkins Coll., 1969, Religious Heritage Am. award, 1979, Outstanding Trial Judge award W.Va. Trail Lawyers Assn., 1988, Order of Vandalia award W.Va. U., Outstaning Alumnus award, 1992, Tenured Faculty Mem. Recognition award Bd. Govs., Def. Trail Coun., W.Va., 1992, Cert. of Merit, W.Va. State Bar, 1994, Justitia Officium award Coll. of Law, W.Va. U., 1994; fellow W.Va. Bar Found., 1999; Melvin Jones fellow Lions Internat. Found., 2001. Mem. Nat. Conf. Federal Trial Judges, Dist. Judges Assn. 4th Cir. (past pres.), Moose (life), Lions (life), Beta Alpha Beta (merit award), Elkins-Randolph County C. of C. (citizen of yr. 1994). Office: US Dist Ct No Dist PO Box 1275 Elkins WV 26241-1275 E-mail: rmaxwell@sunlitsurf.com.

MAXWELL, ROBERT WALLACE, II, lawyer; b. Sept. 6, 1943; s. Robert Wallace and Margaret Maxwell; m. Mamie Lee Payne, June 18, 1966; children: Virginia, Robert, William. BS magna cum laude, Hampden-Sydney Coll., 1965; JD with honors, Duke U., 1968. Bar: Ohio 1968. Assoc. Taft, Stettinius & Hollister, Cin., 1968—75, ptnr., 1975—88, Keating, Muething & Klekamp, Cin., 1988—. Instr. U. Cin. Sch. Law, 1975—76. Elder Wyoming Presbyn. Ch.; bd. dir. Contemporary Arts Ctr. of Cin., Cin. Ballet Co. Mem.: ABA, Am. Assn. Mus. Trustees. Republican. Home: 535 Larchmont Dr Cincinnati OH 45215-4215 Office: Keating Muething & Klekamp 1 E 4th St Ste 1400 Cincinnati OH 45202-3752 Office Phone: 513-579-6594.

MAXWELL, SARA ELIZABETH, psychologist, educator, speech pathologist, director; b. DuQuoin, Ill., Jan. 23; d. Jean A. (Patterson) Green; m. David Lowell Maxwell, Dec. 27, 1960 (div. Mar. 1990); children: Lisa Marina, David Scott; m. James F. Manning, July 19, 1997 (div. Aug. 1998). BS, So. Ill. U., 1963, MS, 1964, MS in Edn., 1965; MEd, Boston Coll., 1982, PhD, 1992; postgrad., Harvard U., 1983. Cert. and lic. speech.-lang. pathologist, early childhood specialist, guidance counselor, sch. adjustment counselor, behavior specialist, EMT. Clin. supr. Clin. Ctr. So. Ill. U., Carbondale, 1964-65, grad. clin. instr., 1965-66; speech/lang. pathologist, sch. adjustment counselor Westwood (Mass.) Pub. Schs., 1967-93; grad. faculty Emerson Coll., Boston, 1979-81; cons. Mass. Dept. Mental Health, Boston, 1979-82; grad. clin. supr. Robbins Speech/Hearing Ctr., Emerson Coll., Boston, 1979-82; predoctoral intern in clin. psychology South Shore Mental Health Ctr., Quincy, Mass., 1985-86, devel. and clin. staff psychologist Hingham and Quincy, 1989-93, emergency svcs. team and respite house manager Quincy, 1990-93; cons. Westwood Nursery Preschs., 1986-93; pvt. practice Twin Oaks Clin. Assocs., Westwood, 1986-88, South Coast Counseling Assocs., Quincy, 1989-93. Cons. local collaboratives and preschs., Westwood, 1980-83; profl. workshops presenter Head Start, 1980; program specialist speech, lang., learning Broward County (Fla.) Schs., 1993-96, exceptional student edn. specialist, 1996-98; behavior specialist, 1999—; adj. prof. grad. sch. of psychology Nova Southeastern U., 1995—; chmn Broward County Action Rsch. Grant Project 2002-03; presenter Head Start, ASHA, CEC, APSC, IALP and other profl., nat. and state confs., 1980-99; invited del. to Sino-Am. Conf. on Exceptionality, Beijing Normal U., China, 1995. Contbr. articles to profl. jours., chpts. to textbooks. Mem. adv. coun. Westwood Bd. Health, 1977-80; emergency med. technician Westwood Pub. Schs. Athletic Dept., 1981. Vocat. Rehab. fellow So. Ill. U., 1964; Merit scholar Perry County, Ill., 1959-64, Credi meml. scholar So. Ill. U., 1964. Mem. Am. Speech & Hearing Assn. (nat. schs. com., nat. chairperson Pub. Sch. Caucus 1985-87), Am. Psychol. Assn., Assn. Psychiat. Svcs. for Children, Coun. Exceptional Children, Internat. Assn. of Logopedics, Rio Vista Civic Assn., Boston Coll. Alumni Assn., Harvard Club. Episcopalian. Avocations: squash, sailing, skiing. Office: Nova Southeastern U Ctr Psychol Studies Maxwell Maltz Psych Bldg 3301 College Ave Fort Lauderdale FL 33314-7796 Office Phone: 754-323-7200 ext. 225.

MAXWELL, W(ILBUR) RICHARD, retired management consultant; b. Troy, Ohio, June 20, 1920; s. Wilbur D. and Gertrude (McDowell) M.; m. Roberta Mae Kennedy, June 29, 1942; children: Douglas R., Jean Ann. Student, Ohio Wesleyan U., 1938-41; BS, Richmond Profl. Inst. of Coll. William and Mary, 1955. Sec. Troy C. of C., 1948-50, Va. C. of C., 1950-55; asst. to pres./chmn. bd. Reynolds Metals Co., 1955-64; v.p., dir. Reynolds Fgn. Sales Inc., 1964-68; pres. Nat. Better Bus. Bur., 1968-70; pres., chief exec. officer Jr. Achievement, Inc., Stamford, Conn., 1970-82. Instr. Richmond Profl. Inst., part-time 1955-57; sponsor-trustee U. Va. Grad. Bus. Sch., 1963-72. Pres. Lancaster County Libr., 1984-85, Rappahannock Gen. Hosp. Found., 1988-90, Northern Neck Vocat.-Tech. Edn. Ctr., 1991-93; bd. dirs. Rappahannock Gen. Hosp., 1988-90, Richmond (Va.) Cmty. H.S., 1989-91; chmn. Northumberland County (Va.) Econ. Devel. Commn., 1994-97. Civilian specialist USAAC, USN, 1942-46. Recipient Albert Schweitzer award Hugh O'Brien Youth Fedn., 1982; inducted Jr. Achievement Profl. Hall of Fame, 1986. Mem. Indian Creek Yacht and Country Club (v.p., 1991-93, bd. dirs. 1991-93). Home: 13715 Richmand Pk Dr N #1203 Jacksonville FL 32224

MAXWELL, WILLIAM LAUGHLIN, retired industrial engineering educator; b. Phila., July 11, 1934; s. William Henry and Elizabeth (Laughlin) M.; m. Judith Behrens, July 5, 1969; children: Deborah, William, Judith, Keely BMechE, Cornell U., 1957, PhD, 1961. Andrew Schultz Jr. prof. dept. indsl. engring. Cornell U., Ithaca, N.Y., 1961-98. Author: Theory of Scheduling, 1967. Recipient Disting. Teaching award Cornell Soc. Engrs., 1968, Ralph S. Watts Tchg. award, 1997. Fellow Informs, Inst. Indsl. Engrs.; mem. Nat. Acad. Engring. Home: 106 Lake Ave Ithaca NY 14850-3537

MAXWELL, WILLIAM STIRLING, retired lawyer; b. Chgo., May 2, 1922; s. W. Stirling and Ethel (Bowes) Maxwell Reineke. AB with distinction, U. Mich., 1947, postgrad., 1946-49, JD, 1949. Bar: Ill. 1949, U.S. Ct. Mil. Appeals 1951, U.S. Supreme Ct. 1952. Assoc. Sidley & Austin, Chgo., 1949-60, 61, ptnr., 1962-84; now ret.; sr. legis. counsel U.S. Treasury, Washington, 1960-61. Trustee Mid-North Animal Shelter Found., Chgo., 1971— . Mem. Order of Coif, Phi Beta Kappa Clubs: Lawyers Club. Republican. Episcopalian. Home: PO Box 1839 Brookings OR 97415-0048

MAXWELL-BROGDON, FLORENCE MORENCY, school administrator, educational consultant; b. Spring Park, Minn., Nov. 11, 1929; d. William Frederick and Florence Ruth (LaBrie) Maxwell; m. John Carl Brogdon, Mar. 13, 1957; children: Carole Alexandra, Cecily Ann, Daphne Diana. BA, Calif. State U., L.A., 1955; MS, U. So. Calif., 1957; postgrad., Columbia Pacific U., San Rafael, Calif., 1982-86. Cert. tchr., Calif. Dir. Rodeo Sch., L.A., 1961-64; lectr. Media Features, Culver City, Calif., 1964—; dir. La Playa Sch., Culver City, Calif., 1968-75; founding dir. Venture Sch., Culver City, Calif., 1974—, also chmn. bd. dirs. Bd. dirs., v.p. Parent Coop. Preschools, Baie d'Urfe Que., Can., 1964—; del. to Ednl. Symposium, Moscow-St. Petersburg, 1992, U.S./China Joint Conf. on Edn., Beijing, 1992, Internat. Confedn. of Prins., Geneva, 1993, Internat. Conf., Berlin, 1994, Internat. Confedn. of Sch. Prins., Helsinki, Finland, 2000, Edinburgh, Scotland, 2003. Author: Let Me Tell You, 1973, Wet'n Squishy, 1973, Balancing Act, 1977, (as Morency Maxwell) Framed in Silver, 1985; (column) What Parents Want to Know, 1961—; editor: Calif. Preschooler, 1961-74; contbr. articles to profl. jours. Treas. Dem. Congl. Primary, Culver City, 1972. Mem. NASSP, Calif. Coun. Parent Schs. (bd. dirs. 1961-74), Parent Coop. Preschs. Internat. (advisor 1975—), Pen Ctr. USA West, Mystery Writers of Am. (affiliate), Internat. Platform Assn. Libertarian. Home: 10814 Molony Rd Culver City CA 90230-5451 Office: Venture Sch 11477 Jefferson Blvd Culver City CA 90230-6115 Office Phone: 310-559-2678. Personal E-mail: morencee@aol.com. Business E-Mail: vntrschl@comcast.net.

MAXWELL-DIAL, ELEANORE, foreign language educator; b. Norwich, Connecticut, Feb. 21, 1929; d. Joseph Walter and Irene (Beetham) Maxwell; m. John E. Dial, Aug. 27, 1959. BA, U. Bridgeport, Conn., 1951; MA in Spanish, Mexico City Coll., 1955; PhD, U. Mo., 1968. Mem. faculty U. Wis., Milw., 1968—75, Ind. State U., Terre Haute, 1975—78, Bowling Green State U., Ohio, 1978—79; asst. prof. dept. fgn. lang. and lit. Iowa State U., Ames, 1979—85, assoc. prof., 1985—96, emerita assoc. prof., 1996—. Cons. pub. companies; participant workshops; del. First World Congress Women Journalists and Writers, Mex., 1975, mem. edn. commn. Contbr. articles, anthologies, and reviews to scholarly journals. Active governor's commn. on fgn. lang. and internat. studies, 1988-95. NDEA grantee, 1967, Ctr. Latin Am. grantee, 1972, NEH summer seminar UCLA, 1981, U. Calif., Santa Barbara, 1984. Mem. MLA, Am. Assn. Teachers Spanish and Portuguese, Midwest MLA, N. Ctrl. Coun. Latin Americanists, Midwest Assn. Latin Am. Studies, Clermont County Geneal. Soc., Ohio Geneal. Soc., Story County Iowa Geneal. Soc., Caribbean Studies Assn., P.G. Wodehouse Soc., Phi Beta Delta, Phi Sigma Iota, Sigma Delta Pi. Home: 190 North St Batavia OH 45103-2911 Office: Iowa State U Ames IA 50011-0001

MAXWORTHY, TONY, mechanical and aerospace engineering educator; b. London, May 21, 1933; came to U.S., 1954, naturalized, 1961; s. Ernest Charles and Gladys May (Butson) M.; m. Emily Jean Parkinson, June 20, 1956 (div. 1974); children: Kirsten, Kara; m. Anna Barbara Parks, May 21, 1979 BS in Engring. with honors, U. London, 1954; MSE, Princeton U., 1955; PhD, Harvard U., 1959. Rsch. asst. Harvard U., Cambridge, Mass., 1955-59; sr. scientist, group supr. Jet Propulsion Lab., Pasadena, Calif., 1960-67, cons., 1968—; assoc. prof. U. So. Calif., L.A., 1967-70, prof., 1970—, Smith Internat. prof. mech. and aero. engring., 1988—, chmn. dept. mech. engring., 1979-89; cons. BBC Rsch. Ctr., Baden, Switzerland, 1972-82, J.P.L., Pasadena, Calif., 1968-80; lectr. Woods Hole Oceanographic Inst., Mass., summers 1965, 70, 72, 83. Forman vis. prof. aeronautics Technion Haifa, 1986; vis. prof. U. Poly., Madrid, 1988, Inst. Superiore Tech., Lisbon, 1988, Swiss Fed. Inst. Tech., Lausanne, 1989; assoc. prof. IMG, U. Joseph Fourier, Grenoble, 1980—, Ecole Superieure Physics and Indsl. Chemistry, Paris, 1995—; Shimizu vis. prof. Stanford U., 1996—. Mem. editorial bd. Geophys. Fluid Dynamics, 1973-79, 88-96, Dynamic Atmospheric Oceans, 1976-83, Phys. Fluids, 1978-81, Zeitschrift fuer Angewandte Mathematik und Physik, 1987-96; contbr. articles to profl. jours. Recipient Humboldt Sr. Scientist award, 1981-93, G.I. Taylor medal Soc. Engring. Sci., 2003; life fellow Clare Hall, Cambridge U., 1974, 93—, Australian Nat. U., 1978, Nat. Ctr. Atmospheric Rsch., 1976, Glennon fellow U. Western Australia, 1990, F.W. Mosey fellow, 1993, Sr. Queen's fellow in marine scis. Commonwealth of Australia, 1984; sr. visitor DAMTP, Cambridge U. Fellow: Am. Phys. Soc. (chmn. exec. com. fluid dynamics divsn. 1974—79, Otto Laporte award 1990), Am. Acad. Arts and Scis.; mem.: NAE, European Geophys. Soc., Am. Geophys. Union. Office: U So Calif Dept Aerospace & Mech Engr Exposition Park Los Angeles CA 90089-1191 Business E-Mail: maxworth@usc.edu.

MAXYMUK, JOHN MICHAEL, librarian, writer; b. Atlantic City, Nj, Feb. 7, 1957; s. Walter Onofrey and Treva Maxymuk; m. Suzanne Sanders, Aug. 22, 1982; children: Juliane, Katie. MLS, Drexel U., Phila., PA, 1982—84; BA English, Oreg. State U., Corvallis, OR, 1975—79. Reference libr. Ramapo Coll., Mahwah, NJ, 1984—85; law libr. Del. Law Sch., Wilmington, Del., 1985—86; coord. of computerized reference Temple U., Philadelphia, Pa., 1988—91; libr. Paul Robeson Libr./Rutgers U., Camden, NJ, 1991—. Author: Govt. Online: One-Click Access to 3, 400 Fed. and State Web Sites., Using Desktop Pub. to Create Newsletters, Handouts, and Web Pages: A How-To-Do-It Manual for Librarians, Finding Govt. Info. on the Internet: A How-To-Do-It Manual for Librarians., Govt. CD-ROMs: A Practical Approach to Searching Electronic Doc. Databases.; editor: (annual special issue) Jour. of Govt. Info.; author: (internet columnist) The Bottom Line: Mng. Libr. Finances, Packers by Numbers: Jersey Numbers and the Players Who Wore Them. Mem.: ALA (chair of lita's desktop pub. interest group 1995—96), Profl. Football Researchers' Assn., Soc. for Am. Baseball Rsch. Christian. Avocations: sports research, travel. Office: Robeson Library Rutgers Univ 300 N 4th Street Camden NJ 08101 E-mail: maxymuk@camden.rutgers.edu.

MAY, ADOLF DARLINGTON, civil engineering educator; b. Little Rock, Mar. 25, 1927; s. Adolf Darlington and Inez (Shelton) M.; m. Margaret Folsom, Dec. 23, 1948; children— Dolf, Barbara, David, Larry. B.Sc. in Civil Engring, So. Meth. U., 1949; M.Sc., Iowa State U., 1950; PhD, Purdue U., 1955. Asst. prof., then assoc. prof. Clarkson Coll. Tech., 1952-56; assoc. prof. Mich. State U., 1956-59; research engr. Thompson-Ramo Wooldridge, 1959-62; project dir. Ill. Div. Hwys., 1962-65; mem. faculty U. Calif., Berkeley, 1965—, prof. civil engring., 1965-91, prof. emeritus, 1991—. Guest prof. numerous univs., 1965—, cons. to industry, 1965— Contbr. to profl. jours., books. Served with USNR, 1944-47. Recipient Disting. Engring. Alumnus award Purdue U., 1978, Transp. Sci. and Ethics Internat. award, 1995; Fulbright scholar to Netherlands, 1977; German Humboldt scholar, 1980. Mem. ASCE (Turner award 1994), Transp. Rsch. Bd. (Disting. Lectr. award 1994), Nat. Acad. Engring. (Matson Transp. Rsch. award 1992), Am. Soc. Engring. Edn. (hon.), Inst. Traffic Engrs. (award 1995), Sigma Xi, Tau Beta Pi. Home: 1645 Julian Dr El Cerrito CA 94530-2011 Office: U Calif Dept Civil Engring 106 Mclaughlin Hall Berkeley CA 94720-1720 E-mail: amay@uclink4.berkeley.edu.

MAY, ALAN ALFRED, lawyer; b. Detroit, Apr. 7, 1942; s. Alfred Albert and Sylvia (Sheer) M.; m. Elizabeth Miller; children: Stacy Ann, Julie Beth. BA, U. Mich., 1963, JD cum laude, 1966. Bar: Mich. 1967, D.C. 1976; former reg. nursing home adminstr., Mich. Ptnr. May and May PC, Detroit, 1979—2001; ptnr., shareholder Kemp Klein, Umphrey and May, P.C., Troy, Mich., 2001—. Spl. asst. atty. gen. State of Mich., 1970—; pres., instr. Med-Leg Seminars, Inc., 1978; lectr. Wayne State U., 1974; instr. Oakland U., 1969. Chmn. Rep. 18th Congrl. Dist. Com., 1983-87, now chmn. emeritus; chmn. 19th Congrl. Dist. Com., 1981-83; mem. Mich. Rep. Com., 1976-84; del. Rep. Nat. Conv., 1984, rules com., 1984; del. Rep. Nat. Conv., 1988, platform com., 1988; former chmn. Mich. Civil Rights Commn.; mem., vice chair Mich. Civil Svc. Commn., 1984-88; former trustee, mem. exec. bd., vice chmn. nat conf. for cmty. and justice NCCJ; trustee Temple Beth El Birmingham, Mich., past pres. exec. bd.; mem. Electoral Coll.; former bd. dirs. ADL, Mich.; bd. dirs. exec. bd., past pres. Detroit Region/Nat. Conf. Cmty. and Justice, Charfoos Charitable Found. Mem. Nat. Conf. Cmty. and Justice (exec. bd., vice chmn.), Detroit Bar Assn., Oakland County Bar Assn., Victors Club, Franklin Hills Country Club (past pres., bd. dirs.), President's Club (trustee). Home: 4140 Echo Rd Bloomfield Hills MI 48302 1941 Office: Kemp Klein Umphrey Endelman & May PC 201 W Big Beaver Rd Ste 600 Troy MI 48084

MAY, ANDREW, technology company executive; BS in Econs., U. N.H. Dir. mktg. CompuServe, Inc., 1984-92; v.p. mktg. Primary Access Corp., 1992-95; v.p., gen. mgr. 3Com Corps. Network Svc. Provider Divsn.; pres., CEO Paradyne, Largo, Fla., 1996-2000, CEO, 2000—. Office: Paradyne Corp PO Box 2826 8545 126th Ave Largo FL 33779

MAY, ARTHUR W. retired academic administrator, educator; b. St. John's, Nfld., Can., June 29, 1937; s. William J. and Florence (Dawe), M.; m. Sonia Susan Streeter, Aug. 18, 1958; children: Stephen J., Heather E., Maria S., Douglas W. BSc with honors, Meml. U., St. John's, 1958; MSc, Meml. U., 1964; PhD, McGill U., Montreal, Que., Can., 1966; D of Univ. (hon.), U. Ottawa, 1988, DSc (hon.), Meml. U. Nfld., 1989; LLD (hon.), Brock U., 1992. Sci. adviser internat. fisheries Dept. Fisheries, Ottawa, Ont., Can., 1971-73, dir. Nfld. biol. sta. St. John's, 1973-75, dir. gen. resource services Ottawa, 1975-78; asst. dep. minister Atlantic Dept. Fisheries and Oceans, Ottawa, 1978-82, dep. minister, 1982-86; pres. Natural Sci. and Engring. Rsch. Coun. Canada, 1986-90; pres., vice chancellor Meml. U. Nfld., St. Johns, 1990-99, ret., 1999—. V.p. Internat. Coun. for Exploration of Seas, Copenhagen, 1977-79; mem. Task Force on Atlantic Fisheries, Ottawa, 1982, Nat. Adv. Bd. Sci. and Tech., 1988-90, 94-95; Canadian rep. to NATO Sci. Com., 1990-97; bd. dirs. Canadian Millenium Scholarship Found., World Wildlife Can.; chmn. bd. One Ocean, 2001—. Contbr. articles to profl. jours. Served to sub. lt. Can. Navy, 1955-58 Decorated officer Order of Can.; recipient Gov.-Gen.'s medal Nfld. Dept. Edn., 1954, Meml. U. Nfld., 1958; named Alumnus of Yr., Meml. U. Nfld., 1983. Mem. N.W. Atlantic Fisheries Orgn. (pres. 1977-80) Anglican. Avocations: gardening, stamp collecting/philately. Office: Meml Univ Nfld 4003 Spencer Hall Saint John's NF Canada A1C 5S7 Home: PO Box 112 Cupids NL AOA 2BO Canada

MAY, AVIVA RABINOWITZ, music educator, linguist, musician; b. Tel Aviv; naturalized, 1958; d. Samuel and Paula Pessia (Gordon) Rabinowitz; children: Chelley Mosoff, Alan May, Risa McPherson, Ellanna May/Gassman. AA, Oakton C.C., 1977; BA in Piano Pedagogy, Northeastern Ill. U., 1978. Folksinger, educator, musican Aviva May Studio/Piano and Guitar, 1948—; Sunday sch. dir. Canton (Ohio) Synagogue, 1952-54; nursery sch. tchr. Allentown (Pa.) Jewish Cmty. Ctr., 1954-56; Hebrew music tchr. Brith Shalom Cmty. Ctr., Bethlehem, Pa., 1954-62; Hebrew tchr. Beth Hillel Congregation, Wilmette, Ill., 1964-83; tchr. B'nai Mitzva, 1978; music dir. McCormick Health Ctrs., Chgo., 1978-79, Cove Sch. Perceptually Handicapped Children, Evanston, 1978-79; prof. Hebrew and Yiddish, Spertus Coll. Judaica, Chgo., 1980-89; Hebrew tchr. Anshe Emet Day Sch., 1989—, West Suburban Temple Har Zion, Oak Park, Ill., 1993—; music studio tchr. Cosmopolitan Sch., Chgo., 1992—. Tchr. continuing edn. Northeastern Ill. U., 1978-80, Niles Twp. Jewish Congregation, 1993—, also Jewish Cmty. Ctrs.; with Office Spl. Investigations, Dept. Justice, Washington; music dir. Temple Emanuel Rosenwald Sch. Composer classical music for piano, choral work, folk songs; developer 8-hour system for learning piano or guitar; contbr. articles to profl. jours. Recipient Magen David Adom Pub. Svc. award 1973; grantee Ill. State, 1975-79, Ill. Congressman Woody Bowman, 1978-79. Mem. Music Tchrs. Nat. Assn., Ill. Music Tchrs. Assn., Organ and Piano Tchrs. Assn., Am. Coll. Musicians, Ill. Assn. Learning Disabilities, North Shore Music Tchrs. Assn. (charter mem., co-founder), Sherwood Sch. Music, Friends of Holocaust Survivers, Nat. Yiddish Book Exch., Nat. Ctr. for Jewish Films, Chgo. Jewish Hist. Soc., Oakton C.C. Alumni Assn., Northeastern Ill. U. Alumni Assn. Office: Aviva May Studio 410 S Michigan Ave Ste 920 Chicago IL 60605-1471 Office Phone: 773-348-8700.

MAY, BENJAMIN TALLMAN, securities specialist, administrator; b. N.Y.C., Dec. 22, 1957; s. Joseph Leserman and Natalie Maria (McCuaig) M.; m. Kaaren Todd Clark, Sept. 1, 1985; children: Caroline Todd, Emily Applegate, Suzannah Tallman. BA, Yale U., 1980; MBA, NYU, 1985. Corp. bond trader, v.p. Drexel Burnham Lambert, N.Y.C., 1980-84; high yield bond trader, sr. v.p. Dillon Read, Inc., N.Y.C., 1984-95; mng. dir. high yield bond dept. 1st Union Corp., Charlotte, N.C., 1995-2000, mng. dir. fixed income sales, trading and rsch., 2000—. Mem. Alexis de Toqueville Soc., United Way, Charlotte, 1997-2003; trustee Charlotte Arts and Sci. Coun. Mem. Yale Club N.Y. (Yale Alumni Recruiter), The Bond Market Assn. (bd. dirs. 2001-03), Montgomery Bell Acad. (adv. bd. 2004-). Republican. Jewish. Home: 2420 Lemon Tre Ln Charlotte NC 28211 Office: 1st Union Corp 301 S College St Charlotte NC 28202-6000

MAY, BRIAN THOMAS, mathematician, educator; MS in Math., Calif. State U., 2003. Single Subject Tchg. Credential State of Calif. Commn. on Tchr. Credentialing, 1989. Tchr. math. Temecula Valley Unified Sch. Dist., Calif., 1990—, Mt. San Jacinto C.C., Menifee, 1995—. Office: Temecula Valley High Sch 31555 Rancho Vista Rd Temecula CA 92591 Home: 44361 Kingston Dr Temecula CA 92592 Personal E-mail: bmay@pe.net. E-mail: bmay@tvusd.k12.ca.us.

MAY, CECIL RICHARD, JR., academic administrator; b. Memphis, June 13, 1932; BA in biblical langs. magna cum laude, MA in New Testament, MTh, Harding U.; LLD (hon.), Freed-Hardeman U., 1984. Min., Holly Springs, Miss., 1954-57, Ripley, Miss., 1957-59, Pine Bluff Ch., Ctrl. Acad. Ch., Miss., 1959-60; dist. scout exec. Yocona Area Coun. Boy Scouts Am., Oxford, Miss., 1959-60; min. Ashland, Miss., 1961, Fulton, Miss., 1962-67, Eastside Campus Ch., Portland, Oreg., 1967-69; Bible tchr. Columbia Christian Coll., Portland, 1967-69; min. Vicksburg, Miss., 1969-76; dean Internat. Bible Coll., Florence, Ala., 1977-80; pres. Magnolia Bible Coll., Kosciusko, Miss., 1980-97; dean bibl. studies Faulkner U., Montgomery, Ala., 1998—, dir. annual Bible lectureship. Lectr. in field. Editor: Preacher Talk; assoc. editor: Magnolia Messenger; contbr. articles to profl. jours. Elder Vicksburg (Miss.) Ch., 1971-76, South Huntington St. Ch., Kosciusko, 1981-97, University Ch., Montgomery; active Boy Scouts Am., 1954-76; com. chair Kosciusko-Attala County C. of C., 1992; bd. dirs. Am. Cancer Soc., 1971-74, fin. campaign chmn., 1971; bd. dirs. Miss. Econ. Coun., 1985-86, 89-92, area vice-chmn., 1991-92; chmn. Attala County Med. Study Task Force, 1991-92. Recipient Disting. Christian Svc. award, Harding U., 2003. Mem. Nat. Assn. Ind. Coll. and Univs., Miss. Assn. Ind. Colls. (bd. dirs.), Evang. Theol. Soc., Miss. Assn. Colls. (bd. dirs.), Rotary Club (bd. dirs. 1983-85, pres. 1985-86). Office: Faulkner Univ 5345 Atlanta Hwy Montgomery AL 36109-3390 E-mail: cmay@faulkner.edu.

MAY, CLIFFORD DANIEL, director of communications, newspaper editor, journalist; m. Lou Ann Brunwasser; children: Miranda Rose, Evan Phillip Barr. Cert. in Russian lang. and lit., U. Leningrad, 1972; BA, Sarah Lawrence Coll., 1973; M Journalism, M Internat. Affairs, Columbia U., 1975. Assoc. editor Newsweek, 1975-78; roving fgn. corr. Hearst Newpapers, 1978-79; spl. corr. Bill Moyers' Jour./Internat. Report-PBS-TV CBS Radio News, 1978-79; sr. editor Am. edit. Geo mag., 1979-80; gen. editor Sunday Mag., Washington corr. N.Y. Times, 1980-89, chief West Africa bur., 1984; assoc. editor Rocky Mountain News, Denver, 1989-97; comms. dir. Rep. Nat. Com., Washington, 1997—. Host, prodr. Roundtable, Sta. KRMA, Colo.; freelance writer, 1979-89. Contbg. editor World Press Rev. Mag.; host, prodr. Roundtable Sta. KRMA, Denver, 1994-97; host Race for the Presidency TCI News, 1995-96. Avocations: downhill skiing, outdoor activities. Office: Rep Nat Com 310 1st St SE Washington DC 20082-0001

MAY, DONALD ROBERT LEE, ophthalmologist, retina and vitreous surgeon, educator, farmer; b. Spring Valley, Ill., Nov. 26, 1945; BS in Liberal Arts & Scis. with high honors and distinction, U. Ill., 1968, MD, 1972. Diplomate Am. Bd. Ophthalmology, Nat. Bd. Med. Examiners. Rsch. fellow dept. ophthalmology U. Ill. Eye and Ear Infirmary, Chgo., 1971—72; intern Northwestern U. Sch. Medicine Meml. Hosps., Chgo., 1972—73; resident in ophthalmology U. Ill. Eye and Ear Infirmary, Chgo., 1973—76, instr. dept. ophthalmology, 1974—77, attending surgeon dept. ophthalmology, 1976—77, fellow in diabetic retinopathy study, diabetic retinopathy vitrectomy study, and retina and vitreous surgery, 1976—77; founder, dir. retina svc., dept. ophthalmology Wilford Hall USAF Med. Ctr., San Antonio, 1977—79; asst. prof. ophthalmology, founder, dir. Retina/Vitreous/Ocular Trauma Svc. U. Calif. Davis Sch. Medicine, Calif., 1979—81; assoc. prof., dir. retina, vitreous and ocular trauma svc. U. Calif. Sch. Medicine, Davis, 1981—84; prof. ophthalmology Tulane U. Sch. Medicine, New Orleans, 1984—89, dir. med. student edn. dept. ophthalmology, 1985—89, dir. ophthalmology Charity Hosp., 1985—89; prof. Tex. Tech U. Health Scis. Ctr., Lubbock, Tex., 1989—2001, chmn. dept. ophthalmology and visual scis., 1989—94, prof. dept. health orgn. mgmt., 1993—2001, assoc. dean Sch. Medicine, 1991—96. Co investigator in the intraocular gentamicin prophylaxis study Govt. Erskine Hosp., Madurai, India, 1975, Dept. Ophthalmology, Audie Murphy VA Hosp., San Antonio, 1977—79, Martinez VA Hosp., Calif., 1979—84, VA Hosp., New Orleans, 1984—89, VA Med. Ctr., Big Spring, Tex., 1989—93, 1996—2001, VA Ctr., Lubbock, Tex., 1989—92, Lubbock, 1996—2001; vis. prof., Germany, 1984, Switzerland, 87; 1st v.p. U.S. Eye Injury Registry, 1990—92, pres.-elect, 1992—94, pres., 1994—96; founder, med. dir. Tex. Eye Injury Registry, 1991—2001; cons. in field. Contbg. editor: Outcome/Fragmatome Newsletter, 1978—81; assoc. editor: Vitreorentinal Surgery and Tech., 1989—98, mem. editl. bd.: Jour. Eye Trauma, 1996—2001; contbr. articles to profl. jours.; appeared in numerous TV and radio programs. Com. mem. Sch. Medicine U. Calif., Davis, Tulane U. Sch. Medicine, New Orleans, Sch. Medicine Tex. Tech. U. Health Scis. Ctr.; bd. dirs. Lubbock Internat. Cultural Ctr., Inc., 1997—, chmn. ways and means com., 1998—2000; planning com., chmn. medicine and history com., liaison Vatican Mus. Exhbn. Found., 2001—02. Maj. USAF, 1973—80. Decorated Air Force Commendation medal. Mem.: AMA, ACS, Tex. Farm Bur., Mil. Officers Assn. Am., Ill. Farm Bur., Ill. Agrl. Assn., Am. Farm Bur. Fedn., Soc. Med. Cons. Armed Forces, World Eye Found. (bd. dirs. 1982—2004), Vitreous Soc. (charter), Retina Soc., Pan-Am. Assn. Ophthalmology, Schepens Internat. Soc., Rsch. Prevent Blindness, Tex. Tech. Rsch. Found. (bd. dirs. 1993—96), Tex. Ophthal. Assn. (chair edn. com. 1990—93, coun. 1990—93, nominating com. 1991—93), So. Retina Study Group, Tex. Med. Assn. (com. continuing edn. 1993—96, bd. dirs. TEXPAC 2000—02), So. Med. Assn. (vice-chmn. sec. ophthalmology 1995—96, chmn. sec. ophthalmology 1996—97), Christian Med. Soc., Assn. Rsch. Vision and Ophthalmology (pub. rels. com. 1997—2000), Am. Acad. Ophthalmology (bylaws and rules com. 1990—95, com. internat. ophthalmology 1991—95), Sigma Xi (sec. Tex. Tech. chpt. 1990—91, v.p., pres.-elect 1999—2000, pres. 2000—01). Republican. Lutheran. Avocations: travel, photography, bicycling, hiking. Home: PO Box 1678 Lubbock TX 79408-1678 *If we are to survive as a free society, we must each accept responsibility. The individual must function on the premise that personal rewards come with the investment of hard, honest work and not as a right mediated by government at the expense of others. Our legislative bodies must enact laws for the common good and not for individual self-interest. Our judicial systems must provide for the just enforcement of our laws. Our leadership must be the watchdog to ensure the indivdual has the opportunity to life without unreasonable danger, the freedom to follow one's dreams, and the ability to pursue happiness through individual achievement. Security comes with the contribution of all who are able.*

MAY, EDGAR, former state legislator, nonprofit administrator; b. Zurich, Switzerland, June 27, 1929; arrived in U.S., 1940, naturalized, 1954; s. Ferdinand and Renee (Bloch) May. B.J. with highest distinction, Northwestern U., 1957. Reporter, acting editor Bellows Falls (Vt.) Times, 1951-53; reporter Fitchburg (Mass.) Sentinel, 1953; part time reporter Chgo. Tribune, 1955-57; reporter Buffalo Evening News, 1958-61; dir. pub. welfare projects State Charities Aid Assn., 1962-64; mem. President's Task Force on War Against Poverty, 1964; spl. asst. to dir., asst. dir. Office Econ. Opportunity, 1964; spl. adviser to Ambassador Sargent Shriver, 1968-70; cons. Ford Found., 1970-75; mem. Vt. Ho. of Reps., 1975-82, Vt. Senate, 1983-91, chmn. com. appropriations; project dir. Vt. Jud. Mgmt. Study, 1992; COO Spl. Olympics Internat., Washington, 1993-96; cons. New Eng. Culinary Inst., 1996—2001; chmn. So. Vt. Recreation Ctr. Found., 1998—. Author: The Wasted Americans, 1964. With AUS, 1953-55. Recipient Page One award Buffalo Newspaper Guild, 1959, Walter O. Bingham award, 1959, Pulitzer prize for local reporting, 1961, Merit award Northwestern U. Alumni Assn., 1962; named Citizen of Yr., C. of C., 2003.

MAY, ELAINE, actress, theatre and film director; b. Phila., Apr. 21, 1932; d. Jack Berlin; m. Marvin May (div.); 1 child, Jeannie Berlin; m. Sheldon Harnick, Mar. 25, 1962 (div. May 1963). ed. high sch., studied Stanislavsky method of acting withMarie Ouspenskaya. Stage and radio appearances as child actor; performed with Playwright's Theatre, in student performance Miss Julie, U. Chgo.; appeared with improvisational theatre group in night club The Compass, Chgo., 1954-1957, (with Mike Nichols) appeared N.Y. supper clubs, Village Vanguard, Blue Angel, also night clubs other cities; TV debut on Jack Paar Show, 1957; also appeared in Omnibus, 1958, Dinah Shore Show, Perry Como Show, Laugh Line, Laugh-In, TV spls.; comedy albums include Improvisations to Music, An Evening with Mike Nichols and Elaine May, Mike Nichols and Elaine May Examine Doctors; weekly appearance NBC radio show Nightline; appeared (with Mike Nichols) NBC radio show, N.Y. Town Hall, 1959, An Evening with Mike Nichols and Elaine May, Golden Theatre, N.Y.C., 1960-61; theater appearances include The Office, N.Y.C., 1966, Who's Afraid of Virginia Woolf?, Long Wharf Theatre, New Haven, Conn., 1980; dir. plays The Third Ear, N.Y.C., 1964, The Goodbye People, Berkshire Theater Festival, Stockbridge, Mass., 1971, various plays at Goodman Theatre, Chgo., 1983; dir., author screenplay, actress film A New Leaf, 1972; dir. films The Heartbreak Kid, 1973, Mikey and Nicky, 1976 (writer, dir. remake 1985), Ishtar, 1987 (also writer); appeared in films Luv, 1967, California Suite, 1978 (Acad. award Best Supporting Actress 1978), In The Spirit, 1990; co-author screenplay Heaven Can Wait, 1978, Birdcage, 1996, Primary Colors, 1998; author plays A Matter of Position, 1962, Not Enough Rope, 1962, Adaptation, 1969, Hot Line, 1983, Better Part of Valor, 1983, Mr. Gogol and Mr. Preen, 1991, (one act) Death Defying Acts, 1995; stage revue: (with Mike Nichols) Telephone, 1984; co-recipient (with Mike Nichols) Grammy award for comedy performance, Nat. Acad. Recording Arts & Scis., 1961; actress (film) Small Time Crooks, 2000. Office: care Julian Schlossberg Castle Hill Prodns Ste 1502 1414 Ave of the Americas New York NY 10019-2514

MAY, ERNEST DEWEY, university administrator, musician, executive; b. Jersey City, May 8, 1942; s. Ernest Max and Harriet Elizabeth (Dewey) M.; m. Eileen Marie Mayhew, Jan. 29, 1963 (div. 1984); children: Ernest Jr., Elizabeth May Goodell, Katherine May Waite, Caroline, Christopher, Abigail May Robles, Deirdre; m. Mary L. Milkey, June 29, 1985. AB, Harvard U., 1964; MFA, Princeton U., 1968, PhD, 1975. Asst. prof. music Amherst (Mass.) Coll., 1969-75; from asst. prof. to prof. music dept. music and dance U. Mass., Amherst, 1976-88, prof. music, chmn. dept. music and dance, 1988-2000, presiding officer faculty senate, 1997-2000, sec. faculty senate, 2000—. Faculty rep. Bd. Trustees, U. Mass., 1988-97; chair Intercampus Faculty Coun., 2001—; organist, dir. mus. South Congl. Ch., Springfield, Mass., 1983—. Rec.: Music for Trumpet and Organ, 1979, 2001; co-editor: J.S. Bach: Neve Ausgabe Samtlicher Werke Vol. I/20, 1986, J.S. Bach as Organist, 1986; contbr. New Harvard Dictionary of Music, 1986. Mem.: Am. Musicological Soc. (pres. New Eng. chpt. 1988—90), Am. Guild Organists, Am. Assn. Higher Edn. Home: 44 Amherst Rd Pelham MA 01002-9700 Office: U Mass Faculty Senate Amherst MA 01003 Business E-Mail: secretary@senate.umass.edu.

MAY, FRANK BRENDAN, JR., lawyer; b. Bronx, NY, Oct. 17, 1945; s. Frank Brendan and Margaret May; m. Mary Frances Fitzsimmons, June 19, 1976; children: David Brendan, Brian Christopher. BA in Econs., NYU, 1973, postgrad., 1973-75; JD, John Marshall Law Sch., Chgo., 1978. Bar: Ill. 1979, U.S. Dist. Ct. (no. dist.) Ill. 1979, U.S. Ct. Appeals (7th cir.), 1979, U.S. Supreme Ct. 1995, lic. Ill. real estate broker 1994. Legal intern criminal div. Cook County State's Atty.'s Office, Chgo., 1977-78; legal intern juvenile div. DuPage County State's Atty.'s Office, Wheaton, Ill., 1978; sr. assoc. atty. Lillig, Kemp & Thorness, Ltd., Oak Brook, Ill., 1978-81; v.p., gen. counsel Coldwell Banker, Oak Brook, 1981-90, Prudential Preferred Properties, Des Plaines, Ill., 1991-98, Law Offices, Frank B. May, Jr., Wheaton, Ill., 1999-2001; sr. corp. atty., asst. sec. Budget Rent a Car Corp., Lisle, Ill., 2001—03; sr. v.p., gen. coun. Coldwell Banker Primus Realty, Oswego, Ill., 2003—, Arbitrator 18th Jud. Cir. Ct., Dupage County, Ill., 1993—. Dir. Ray Graham Found. for People with Disabilities, 1999-2004. Sgt. USAF, 1963-67. NYU Coun. scholar, 1971-73; David Davis Meml. scholar, 1970-71. Mem. DuPage County Bar Assn., Medinah Country Club (membership com. 1997—, chmn. PGA credentials com. 1999, nominating com. 2004), Ill. Assn. Realtors (mem. large brokers coun. 1996-98, exec. com., fin. com. 1998-1999, lic. law rewrite task force, nominating com. 1998-99), Realtor Assn. Western Suburbs (legal counsel 1999-2000). Avocations: golf, music, gourmet cooking, wine collector. Home: 2064 Stonebridge Ct Wheaton IL 60187-7177 Office: Coldwell Banker Primus Realty 15 W Merchants Dr Oswego IL 60543 Business E-Mail: fmay@cbprimus.com.

MAY, GEORGIANA, biologist, educator; PhD, U. Calif., Berkeley, 1987. Assoc. prof. dept. plant biology U. Minn., St. Paul. Contbr. articles to profl. jours. Recipient Alexopoulos prize Mycological Soc. Am., 1997. Achievements include research on the interactions of fungi with plants, evolution of fungal populations and their interactions with other organisms, evolution of gene structure and function in mating compatibility loci, determining the genetic basis of smut resistance in maize, the impact of agricultural practice on host/pathogen interactions. Office: U Minn Dept Plant Biology 220 Biological Sci Ctr 1445 Gortner Ave Saint Paul MN 55108 Fax: 612-625-1738. E-mail: gmay@maroon.tc.umn.edu.

MAY, GITA, language educator, literature educator; b. Brussels, Sept. 16, 1929; came to U.S., 1947, naturalized, 1950; d. Albert and Blima (Sieradska) Jochimek; m. Irving May, Dec. 21, 1947. BA magna cum laude, CUNY-Hunter Coll., 1953; MA, Columbia U., 1954, PhD, 1957. Lectr. French CUNY-Hunter Coll., 1953-56; from instr. to assoc. prof. Columbia U., N.Y.C., 1956—68, prof., 1968—, chmn., 1983-93, mem. senate, 1979-83, 86-88, chmn. Seminar on 18th Century Culture, 1986-89. Lecture tour English univs., 1965 Author: Diderot et Baudelaire, critiques d'art, 1957, De Jean-Jacques Rousseau à Madame Roland: essai sur la sensibilité préromantique et révolutionnaire, 1964, Madame Roland and the Age of Revolution, 1970 (Van Amringe Disting. Book award), Stendhal and the Age of Napoleon, 1977, Encyclopedia of Aesthetics, 1998, Dictionnaire de Diderot, 1999, French Women Writers, 1991, The Feminist Encyclopedia of French Literature, 1999; co-editor: Diderot Studies III, 1961; mem. editl. bd. 18th Century Studies, 1975-78, French Rev., 1975-86, 98—, Romanic Rev., 1959—, Women in French Studies, 2000—; contbg. editor: Oeuvres complètes de Diderot, 1984, 95; gen. editor: The Age of Revolution and Romanticism: Interdisciplinary Studies, 1990—, extensive essays on Diderot and George Sand in European Writers, 1984, 85, and on Rebecca West, Anita Brookner and Graham Swift in British Writers, 1996, 97, 99, Bayle, Fontenelle and Fénelon in Dictionary of Literary Biography, 2003, Voltaire's Candide (in Barnes and Noble Classics), 2003; contbr. articles and revs. to profl. jours. Decorated chevalier and officier Ordre des Palmes Acad.; recipient award Am. Coun. Learned Socs., 1961, award for outstanding achievement CUNY-Hunter Coll., 1963; named Outstanding Mentor, Women in French, 2003; Fulbright rsch. grantee, 1964-65; Guggenheim fellow, 1964-65, NEH fellow, 1971-72. Mem. AAUP, MLA (del. assembly 1973-75, mem. com. rsch. activities 1975-78, mem. exec. coun. 1980-83), Am. Assn. Tchrs. French, Am. Soc. 18th Century Studies (pres. 1985-86, 2nd v.p. 1983-84, 1st v.p. 1984-85, One of Gt. Tchrs. award 1999, Outstanding Mentor 2003), Soc. Française d'Etude du Dix-Huitième Siècle, Soc. Diderot, Am. Soc. French Acad. Palms, Soc. des Etudes Staëliennes, N.Am. Soc. for the Study of Jean-Jacques Rousseau, Soc. des Professeurs Français et Francophones d'Amérique, Phi Beta Kappa. Office: Columbia U Dept French/Romance Philol 516 Philosophy Hall MC4918 New York NY 10027 Office Phone: 212-854-3905. Business E-Mail: gm9@columbia.edu.

MAY, HAROLD EDWARD, chemical company executive; b. N.Y.C., Oct. 18, 1920; s. Charles Edward and Mollie (Flax) M.; m. Margaret June Hochman, June 27, 1943; children: Charles S., Michael E., Suzanne E. AB, Columbia U., 1941, BS in Mech. Engring, 1942. With E.I. duPont de Nemours & Co., Inc., 1942—, v.p. materials and logistics, 1977-82, sr. v.p. corp. staff, 1982-85, ret., 1985. Recipient Illig medal Columbia U., 1942 Mem. Phi Beta Kappa, Tau Beta Pi. Jewish. Home: 36 Southridge Dr Kennett Square PA 19348-2714

MAY, HENRY STRATFORD, JR., lawyer; b. Greensboro, N.C., May 12, 1947; s. Henry Stratford and Doris (Richardson) M. BA, U. Tex., 1969, JD, 1971. Bar: Tex. 1972, U.S. Ct. Appeals (D.C. cir.) 1974, U.S. Supreme Ct. 1977, U.S. Ct. Appeals (5th and 11th cirs.) 1981, U.S. Dist. Ct. (so. dist.) Tex. 1985. Law clk. to judge U.S. Ct. Appeals (D.C. cir.), Washington, 1972-73; assoc. Vinson & Elkins, Houston, 1973-79, ptnr., 1979—, head energy sect., 1990—. Adj. prof. U. Houston Law Sch., 1994—. Author: Natural Gas Contracts. Mem. ABA, Tex. Bar Assn. Republican.

MAY, JAMES HARVEY, communications educator; s. Rhoudy and Ruby Mae May; m. Margit Röder, June 10, 1967; children: James Richard, Anika Nikol; 1 child, Tanja Babette Youngs. BS, Stanford U., 1958; MBA, Harvard U., 1964; certificate in radio and TV, NYU, 1966; DLS, Columbia U., 1973—78, advanced certificate in librarianship, 1977. Econ. engr. Gilbert Associates, Inc., NYC, 1964—67; v.p., treas. Pandex, Macmillan Info. Corp., NYC, 1967—72; dir., ctr. comm. and info. rsch. U. Denver, 1972—74; assoc. libr. dir., acting libr. dir. Sonoma State U., Rohnert Pk., Calif., 1974—83; vice provost info. resources Calif. State U., Chico, 1983—94; prof. comm. sci. and tech. Calif. State U. Monterey Bay, Seaside, 1994—, founding dean instrn., 1994—96, asst. to the pres., 1996—98. Ofcl. historian, bd. mem. Soc. Computer Simulation, 1991—97; panelist with US v.p. Al Gore Unity '99, Seattle, 1999; treas. Calif. Faculty Assn., 1999—2003, chpt. pres., 1998—2001, 2004—; ednl. effectiveness panel Am. Distance Edn. Consortium, 2000—; keynote spkr. Open Learning 2000, Brisbane, Queensland, Australia, 2000; bd. dir. Am. Indian Sci. and Engring. Soc., 2002—; co-chair, vice chair, bd. mem. Native Am. Pub. Telecom. Contbr. articles to jour. and chpt. to books. Lt. JG USN, 1959—62, Las Vegas and No. Ireland. Recipient outstanding leadership in libr. services for Am. Indian People and founding the Am. Indian Libr. Assn., Am. Indian Libr. Assn., 1994, Svc. to Am. Indians in Field of Tech., Stanford U. Am. Indian Alumni Assn., 1995, Union Mem. Yr., Monterey Ctrl. Labor Coun., AFL-CIO, 2000, Trade Unionist Yr., Monterey Bay Ctrl. Labor Coun., AFL-CIO, 2002. Mem.: Am. Indian Sci. and Engring. Soc. (life; bd.dir. 2002—, Ely S. Parker Medal 2000), United Keetoowah Band of Cherokee Indians (life). Achievements include created first computerized bibliographic database. Office: Calif State Univ Monterey Bay 100 Campus Ctr Seaside CA Home: 3704 Clubside Ln Sacramento CA 95835 E-mail: jameshmay@yahoo.com.

MAY, JAMES M. medical educator, medical researcher; b. Oklahoma City, Aug. 20, 1947; married; 2 children. BS, Yale Coll., 1969; MD, Vanderbilt U., 1973. Diplomate Am. Bd. Internal Medicine, Am. Bd. Endocrinology and Metabolism. Intern Vanderbilt U., Nashville, 1973—74, assoc. prof. medicine, 1986—, assoc. prof. molecular physiology and biophysics, 1993—; resident in medicine Johns Hopkins Hosp., Balt., 1974—75; fellow in endocrinology U. Wash., Seattle, 1975—78; asst. prof. medicine Med. Coll. Va., Richmond,

1978—83, assoc. prof. medicine, 1983—86. Mem. awards com. dept. medicine Vanderbilt U., 1992—; mem. awards com. Summer Diabetes Program Diabetes Rsch. and Tng. Ctr., 1994—. Mem. editl. bd.: Metabolism, 1996—; contbr. articles to profl. jours. Recipient Nat. Rsch. Svc. award, NIH, 1975—78, Poncin Fund award, 1975—78; grantee, NIH, 1993, 1995. Mem.: Southern Soc. Clin. Investigation, Am. Soc. Clin. Investigation, Am. Fedn. Clin. Rsch. (sec.-treas. Southern sect. 1983—86, nat. councilor 1983—88, pres.-elect and pres. 1986—88), Am. Diabetes Assn. (pres. Va. affiliate 1985—86, chmn. rsch. com. Tenn. affiliate 1990—92, Rsch. award 1996), Alpha Omega Alpha. Home: 44 Concord Park E Nashville TN 37205-4705 Office: Vanderbilt U Med Ctr Divsn Endocrinology & Diabetes 2220 Pierce Ave Bldg 2 Nashville TN 37232-0001

MAY, JANET SUE, playwright, lyricist; b. Bloomington, Ill., Dec. 24, 1946; d. James Woolston and Josephine Elisabeth (Ferguson) Grubb; children: John, Darbi, Heather, Brandy. Student, Lincoln Coll., 1965, Wabash Coll., 1965, St. Joseph's Hosp., 1966, Indian River C.C., 1983, Bloomington Sch. Practical Nursing, 1984; cert. in food svc. sanitation, Ill. State U., 1988. Chem. lab. tech. Ereka Williams, Bloomington, 1966; histology tech. St. Joseph's Hosp., Bloomington, 1966—67; activity dir. McLean County Nursing Home, Normal, Ill., 1968—70; rsch. asst. U. Fla. Med. Entomology Lab., Vero Beach, Fla., 1974—85; activity dir., meal supr. Bloomington Housing Authority, 1987—89; pub. rels. mgr. Miracle Ear, Peoria, Ill., 1990—92. Songwriter: Ice Age; playwright: More Than Just A Man, 2001; co-author (with James Kitzmiller): Patronymics of Mosquitoes, 2d edit., 1986. Achievements include co-inventor, tissue vacuum pump; invention of jeweled perfumed hair tie; blinking hair tie. Avocations: art, poetry, singing, Eqyptology. Home: 2112 W Malone Peoria IL 61605

MAY, JOAN VERNER, nursing consultant; b. Asheville, NC, Apr. 21, 1934; d. Oliver A. and Mildred Mills Verner; children: Jan, Cathy, Mark. BS, S.W. Baptist U., Bolivar, Md., 1980. RN Mather Sch. Nursing, New Orleans, 1955. Asst. adminstr. S.E. Hosp., Cape Girardeau, Md., 1968—72; asst. dir. nurses St. John's Regional Med. Ctr., Springfield, Mo., 1973—77; v.p. St. John's Hosp., Joplin, Md., 1977—79; dir. nurses Citizen's Meml. Hosp., Bolivar, Md., 1983—84; regional supr. Kemper Nat. Svcs., St. Louis, 1996—2001; case mgr. Aetna Ins., St. Louis; CCM Crawford & Assoc., 1987—89; with Ellis & Assoc., St. Louis, 1989—95.

MAY, JOHN RAYMOND, clinical psychologist; b. Rahway, NJ, Jan. 31, 1943; s. John Y. and Aline (Eichorn) M.; m. Brenda Lee Berg, June 17, 1967; children: Stacey Anne, John Jeffrey. BA in Psychology, Colgate U., 1965; PhD in Clin. Psychology, U. N.C., 1970. Clin. intern U. Wis. Med. Ctr., 1967-68; staff psychologist to chief, clin. svcs. divsn. Nat. Security Agy., Ft. Meade, Md., 1969-72; cons., 1972—92, 2003—; pvt. practice, 1972—. Exec. dir. Psychol. Health Svcs., Inc., Columbia, 1976—84, 1993—2001, Columbia Psychol. Svcs., 1984—91, Cmty. Counseling Assocs., 1991—; co-dir. Columbia Addictions Ctr., 1994—98; adj. prof. Loyola Coll., 1970—72. Co-author films on mental health tng., articles in profl. jours. and manuals. Recipient Wallach award U. N.C., 1969, Humanitarian award Citizens Against Spousal Assault, 1989; USPHS fellow, 1966-69; VA fellow, 1965-66. Mem. APA, Md. Psychol. Assn. (exec. coun., various coms. 1977-91, treas. 1985-88, pres.-elect 1988, pres. 1989-90, past pres. 1990-91, Outstanding Profl. Contbn. to Psychology award 1993), Am. Bd. Sexology (diplomate), Assn. Advancement of Psychology, Am. Soc. Clin. Hypnosis, Am. Assn. Sex Educators, Counselors, and Therapists (cert. sex. therapist), Anxiety Disorders Assn. Am., Howard County Psychol. Soc. (pres. 1975-76). Office: 10774 Hickory Ridge Rd Columbia MD 21044-3646 Home: 1310 Harmony Ln Annapolis MD 21401-5719 Office Phone: 410-992-7288. Personal E-mail: cca21044@msn.com.

MAY, JOHN T. college president; m. Shelly May. BS, U.S. Air Force Acad.; MS in Physics, PhD in Physics, N.C. State U. Prof. physics, head dept. Air Force Acad., 1980-84, vice dean faculty, chmn. basic sci. divsn., 1984-86; vis. prof. physics N.C. State U., 1987-88; dean spl. and career curriculum Atlantic Cape C.C., 1988, dean academics, 1989-94, pres., 1994—. Officer USAF, 1962-68, Vietnam. Address: 5100 Black Horse Pike Mays Landing NJ 08330-2623

MAY, JOSEPH LESERMAN (JACK MAY), retired lawyer; b. Nashville, May 27, 1929; s. Daniel and Dorothy (Fishel) M.; m. Natalie McCuaig, Apr. 12, 1957 (dec. May 1990); children: Benjamin, Andrew, Joshua, Maria; m. Lynn Hewes Lance, June 10, 1994. BA, Yale U., 1951; JD, NYU, 1958; postgrad., Harvard Bus. Sch., 1969. Bar: Tenn. 1959. Prodr. Candied Yam Jackson Show, 1947-51; with CIA, 1951-55; pres. Nuweave Socks, Inc., N.Y.C., 1955-59, May Hosiery Mills, Nashville, 1960-83, Athens Hosiery Mills, Tenn., 1966-83; v.p. Wayne-Gossard Corp., Chattanooga, 1972-83; dir. pvt. practice law Nashville, 1984—; ret., 2004. Mem. adv. bd. Asian Strategies Group, 1994; founding dir. Nashville Bank and Trust, 2003; chmn. Guardianship and Trust Corp., 1994—96; bd. dirs. Nashville Bank and Trust Co. Bd. dirs. Vanderbilt Cancer Ctr., 1994-99; pres. Jewish Cmty. Ctr., 1969; chmn. Campus for Human Devel., 2000-02; mem. AAA panel of neutrals. With USN, 1947-53, U.S. Army, 1954. Mem. Tenn. Bar Assn., Nashville Bar Assn., Am. Arbitration Assn. Panel of Neutrals, Tenn. Hist. Soc. (trustee, pres. 2000-02), Eagle Scout Assn., Belle Meade Country Club, Shamus Club, Old Oak Club, Old Goats, Zodiac, Yale Club N.Y., Rotary (pres. Nashville 1971). Republican. Jewish. Home: 133 Abbottsford Nashville TN 37215-2442

MAY, KENNETH NATHANIEL, food industry consultant; b. Livingston, La., Dec. 24, 1930; s. Robert William and Mary Hulda (Caraway) M.; m. Patsy Jean Farr, Aug. 4, 1953; children: Sherry Alison (dec.), Nathan Elliott. BS in Poultry Sci., La. State U., 1952, MS in Poultry Sci., 1955; PhD in Food Tech., Purdue U., 1959, DAgr, 1988. Asst. prof. U. Ga., Athens, 1958-64, assoc. prof., 1964-67, prof., 1967-68, Miss. State U., State College, 1968-70; dir. rsch. Holly Farms Poultry, Wilkesboro, N.C., 1970-73, v.p., 1973-85, pres., 1985-88, chmn., CEO, 1989. Adj. prof. N.C. State U., 1975. Contbr. over 60 articles to profl. jours.; patentee treatment of cooked poultry. Bd. trustees Appalachian State U., 1987-94, chmn., 1989-90. Recipient Industry Service award Poultry and Egg Inst. Am., 1971, Meritorious Service award, Ga. Egg Commn., 1964, Disting. Service award Agribus. N.C., 1986; named to Am. Poultry Hall of Fame, 1992. Fellow Poultry Sci. Assn.; mem. Nat. Poultry Hist. Soc. (bd. dirs. 1982-83), Inst. Food Technologists. Methodist. Avocations: reading, stained glass. Office: 113 La Maison Belle Dr Denham Springs LA 70726

MAY, LAWRENCE EDWARD, lawyer; b. N.Y.C., Aug. 7, 1947; s. Jack and Ann Marie (Schnell) M.; m. Rosalind Marsha Israel, Feb. 3, 1979; children: Jeremy, Lindsey. BA, UCLA, 1969, JD, 1972. Bar: Calif. 1972, N.Y. 1973. Assoc. Paul, Weiss, Rifkind, Wharton & Garrison, N.Y.C., 1972-76, Levine, Krom & Unger, Beverly Hills, Calif., 1976-79, Weissburg & Aronson, L.A., 1979-81, Valensi & Rose, L.A., 1981-83; prin. Lawrence E. May, P. C., L.A., 1983—. Bd. dirs. Pub. Counsel, 1989-97; pres., 1995-96. Mem. editorial adv. bd. L.A. Jewish Jour., 1985-91, exec. com. Pacific S.W. Region Anti-Defamation League, 1985—; bd. dirs. L.A. Youth, 1997-2002. Mem. State Bar Calif., Los Angeles County Bar Assn. (trustee 1987-88, pro bono coun. 1995-98), Beverly Hills Bar Assn. (bd. govs. 1981-90, pres. 1988-89, chmn. bus. law sect. 1984-85). Democrat. Avocations: current events, golf, family activities. Office: Ste 350 10350 Santa Monica Blvd Los Angeles CA 90025-5075 E-mail: lmay@maylaw.com.

MAY, MISTY, Olympic athlete; b. July 30, 1977; Majored in Kinesiology & Physical Ed., Long Beach State U. Mem. U.S. National Indoor Team, 1998, 1999; beach volleyball player Team USA, Sydney Olympic Games, 2000, Team USA, Athens Olympic Games, 2004. Named BVA Rookie of the Yr., 2000, AVP Team of the Yr. (with Kerri Walsh), 2003. Achievements include mem. NCAA nat. championship team, 1998; one of only three players to be named a two-time AVCA Nat. Player of the Yr., 1997, 1998; FIVB Tour champion with teammate Kerri Walsh, 2002, 2003; Gold medal (with Kerri Walsh), Beach Volleyball, Athens Olympic games, 2004. Office: c/o USOC One Olympic Plz Colorado Springs CO 80909*

MAY, MITCHELL JOHNSON, controller; b. San Antonio, Apr. 22, 1964; s. James Mitchell and Dicksie Ray May; m. Maria Hilda May (div.); children: Alexander Mitchell, Catherine Yvette. AA, San Antonio Coll.; BBA in Acctg., U. Tex., San Antonio. Retail acct. Fleming Foods, Ft. Worth, 1993—94; dir. acctg. Stockyards Sta. Partnership, Ft. Worth, 1994—98; sr. acct. Harris Meth. Hosp., Ft. Worth, 1998—2001; contr. Universal Health Svcs., Eagle Pass, Tex., 2001—. Treas. Leadership Eagle Pass, 1994. Capt. Tex. Army NG, 1987—. Home: 1760 Paseo de Encinal Apt D Eagle Pass TX 78852 Office: Universal Health Svcs 350 S Adams Eagle Pass TX 78852

MAY, PHILIP ALAN, sociology educator; b. Bethesda, Md., Nov. 6, 1947; s. Everette Lee and Marie (Lee) M.; m. Doreen Ann Garcia, Sept. 5, 1972; children: Katrina Ruth, Marie Ann. BA in Sociology, Catawba Coll., 1969; MA in Sociology, Wake Forest U., 1971; PhD in Sociology, U. Mont., 1976. NIMH predoctoral fellow U. Mont., Missoula, 1973-76; dir. health stats. and rsch. Navajo Health Authority, Window Rock, Ariz., 1976-78; from asst. prof. to prof. U. N.Mex., Albuquerque, 1978—89, prof., 1989—, from dir. Ctr. on Alcoholism, Substance abuse and Addictions to sr. rsch. scientist, 1990—2000, sr. rsch. scientist Ctr. on Alcoholism, Substance abuse and Addictions, 2000—, assoc. dir. Ctr. on Alcoholism, Substance abuse and Addictions, 2002—04, interim dir. Ctr. on Alcoholism, Substance abuse and Addictions, 2004—. Fetal alcohol syndrome study com. Inst. Medicine of NAS, 1994-96; dir. Nat. Indian Fetal Alcohol Syndrome Prevention Program, Albuquerque, 1979-85; adv. bd. Nat. Orgn. on Fetal Alcohol Syndrome, Washington, 1990—; rsch. assoc. Nat. Ctr. for Am. Indian and Alaska Native Mental Health Rsch., 1986—; mem. U.S. Surgeon Gens. Task Force on Drunk Driving, 1988-89; prin. investigator fetal alcohol syndrome epidemiology rsch. in South Africa, 1997—; com. on pathophysiology and prevention of adolescent and adult suicide Inst. Medicine of NRC, NAS, 2000-02; cons. in field. Contbr. chpts. to books, articles to profl. jours. V.p. Bd. Edn., Laguna Pueblo, N.Mex., 1998—2002, pres., 2002—. Lt. (s.g.) USPHS, 1970—73. Recipient Spl. Recognition award U.S. Indian Health Svc., 1992, award Navajo Tribe and U.S. Indian Health Svc., 1992, Human Rights Promotion award UN Assn., 1994, Program award for Contbns. to Mental Health of Am. Indians, U.S. Indian Health Svc., 1996, O.B. Michael Outstanding Alumnus award Catawba Coll., 2000. Mem. APHA, Am. Sociol. Assn., Am. Assn. Suicidology, Population Ref. Bur., Coll. on Problems of Drug Dependence, Rsch. Soc. Alcoholism. Methodist. Home: 4610 Idlewilde Ln SE Albuquerque NM 87108-3422 Office: U NMex CASAA 2650 Yale Blvd Albuquerque NM 87106-3202 Office Phone: 505-925-2307. E-mail: pmay@unm.edu.

MAY, PHYLLIS JEAN, financial executive; b. Flint, Mich., May 31, 1932; d. Bert A. and Alice C. (Rushton) Irvine; m. John May, Apr. 24, 1971 (dec. 1997). Grad., Dorsey Sch. Bus., 1957; cert., Internat. Corr. Schs., 1959; MBA, Mich. U., 1970; cert., Nat. Tax Inst., 1978. Registered real estate agt; lic. life, auto and home ins. agt. Office mgr. Comml. Constrn. Co., Flint, 1962-68; bus. mgr. new and used car dealership Flint, 1968-70; contr. various corps., 1970-75; fiscal dir. Rubicon Odyssey Inc., Detroit, 1976-87, Wayne County Treas.'s Office, 1987-93; exec. fin. office Grosse Pointe (Mich.) Meml. Ch., 1993—. Acad. cons. acctg. Detroit Inst. Commerce, 1980-81; pres. small bus. specializing in adminstrv. cons. and acctg., 1982—; supr. mobile svc. stat., upholstery and home improvement businesses; owner retail bus. Pieces and Things. Pres. PTA Westwood Heights Schs., 1972; vol. Fedn. of Blind, 1974-76, Probate Ct., 1974-76; mem. citizens adv. bd. Northville Regional Psychiat. Hosp., 1988, sec., 1989-90; pres. La'Renaissance Condominium Assn., Atlantic City, 1996-2000, sec., 2000-02, 04-. Recipient Meritorious Svc. award Genesee County for Youth, 1976, Excellent Performance and High Achievement award Odyssey Inc., 1981. Mem. NAFE (bd. dirs.), Am. Bus. Women's Assn. (treas. 1981, rec. sec. 1982, v.p. 1982-83, Woman of Yr. 1982), Womens Assn. Dearborn Orch. Soc., Dearborn Cmty. Art Ctr., Mich. Mental Health Assn., Internat. Platform Assn., Guild of Carillonneurs in N.Am., Pi Omicron (officer 1984-85, treas. 2002—). Presbyterian.

MAY, RICHARD WARREN, writer, consultant, inventor; b. Marlboro, Mass., Mar. 1, 1944; s. Richard and Lavinia (Crane) M. BS in Psychology, U. Mass., 1968; MA in Humanities and Philosophy, Calif. State U., Dominguez Hills, 1991. Lic. real estate broker. Tchr. Boston Pub. Schs., 1970-89; pres., founder The Aleph (formerly Promethean Pastimes), Boston, 1975—. Adv. bd. mem. and rsch. assoc. Point One Adv. Group, Inc., Madisonville, Ky. Author: (games of strategy) Game of the Gods, 1984, Trihex, 1985, Aliens and Amazons, The Game of Tetra, 1994; contbr. (anthology) Thinking on the Edge, 1993; patentee game bd. and pieces TriHex, 1988. Mem. Assn. Advance Ethical Hypnosis, West Orange, NJ, 1974-75, Boston Tchrs. Union, 1984-89, Point One Adv. Group. Fellow Internat. Soc. Philos. Enquiry (assl. historian 1981-82, diplomate); mem. Nat. Coalition of Ind. Scholars, Prometheus Soc. (past first jour. editor, ombudsman 1984-94, pres. 1991-98), Hoeflin Rsch. Group, The Mega Soc., One-in-Million Soc., Triple Nine Soc. (membership officer 1983-84, regent 1987-90), Mensa, Intertel, Am. Acad. Religion, Internat. Acad. Philosophy (bd. dirs., founder Found.), The Jewish Geneal. Soc. Office: Point One Adv Group PO Box 1111 Madisonville KY 42431-0022 E-mail: ferdlilac@yahoo.com.

MAY, ROBERT GEORGE, dean, accounting educator; b. Detroit, Nov. 11, 1943; s. George Joseph and Winifred Marie (Donnelly) M.; m. Carol Ann Rogers, June 18, 1965; children: Gregory Charles, Lynn Marie. BBA, Mich. State U., 1965, PhD, 1970. Asst. prof. U. Wash., Seattle, 1970-73, assoc. prof., 1973-79; prof. acctg. U. Tex., Austin, 1979—, chmn. dept. acctg., 1988-92, assoc. dean, 1992-95, interim dean, 1995-2001, dean McCombs Sch. Bus., 2001—. Vis. asst. prof. Stanford U., 1972-73; dir. Fedn. Schs. Accountancy, Athens, Ga., 1982. Co-author: Accounting, 1995, Financial Accounting, 1995, Managerial Accounting, 1995, Corporate Financial Accounting, 1995; assoc. editor: the Accounting Review Recipient Notable Contbn. to Acctg. Lit. award AICPAs, 1976; named Outstanding Alumnus, Mich. State U. Dept. Acctg., 1995. Mem. Am. Acctg. Assn. (chmn. audit sect. 1988-89, pres., adminstrs. of acctg. programs 1993-94, Innovation in Acctg. Edn. award 1991, 93). Home: 7137 Valburn Dr Austin TX 78731-1812 Office: McCombs Sch Bus U Tex Deans Office 21st and Speedway GSB2 104 Austin TX 78712

MAY, ROBERT M. retired obstetrician, gynecologist, educator; b. Camberg, Germany, Feb. 17, 1926; came to U.S., 1940; s. Herman and Flora May; m. Anita S. Wynne, Sept. 6, 1953; children: Harvey, Ann, Julie. MD, La. State U., 1948. Diplomate Am. Bd. Ob-Gyn. Intern Touro Infirmary, New Orleans, 1948-49, resident in ob-gyn., 1949-53; practice medicine specializing in gynecology Birmingham, Ala., 1954-97; mem. staff Bapt. Med. Ctr., pres. med. staff, 1985-86, chmn. dept. ob-gyn., 1980-86; assoc. clin. prof. ob-gyn. U. Ala., Birmingham, 1975-97. Served to capt. USAFR, 1950-52. Mem. Ala. Med. Soc., Am. Soc. Study Infertility, Am. Coll. Ob-Gyn. E-mail: rmaymd@aol.com.

MAY, ROBERT MCCREDIE, biology educator; b. Sydney, Australia, Jan. 8, 1936; s. Henry W. and Kathleen (McCredie) M.; m. Judith Feiner, Aug. 3, 1962; 1 child, Naomi Felicity. BSc, Sydney U., 1956, PhD, 1959; DSc (honoris causa) (hon.), City U. London, 1989, Uppsala U., 1990; DSc (hon.) (hon.), Yale U., 1993, Heriot-Watt U., 1994, U. Edinburgh, 1994; DSC (hon.) (hon.), U. Sydney, 1995. Gordon Mackay lectr. applied math Harvard U., Cambridge, Mass., 1959—61, mem. vis. faculty, 1966; theoretical physics lectr. Sydney U., 1962—64, reader, 1964—69, personal chair, 1969—73; prof. biology Princeton U., NJ, 1973—88; Royal Soc. rsch. prof. U. Oxford, England, 1988—95, fellow Merton Coll., 1989—. Chief sci. adviser to U.K. Govt., head U.K. Office Sci. and Tech., 1995—2000; vis. faculty Calif. Inst. Tech., 1967; vis. prof. Imperial Coll., England, 1975—95, UKAEA Culham Lab., 1971, Magdalen Coll., 1971; pres. Royal Soc., 2000—. Editor: Stability and Complexity in Model Ecosystems, 1973, Population Biology of Infectious Diseases, 1982, Theoretical Ecology: Principles and Applications, 1976, Perspectives in Ecological Theory, 1989, Infectious Diseases of Humans: Dynamics and Control, 1991, Extinction Rates, 1995. Decorated Order of Australia, Knighthood; recipient MacArthur award, 1984, Crafoord prize, Royal Swedish Acad. Scis., 1996, Life Peerage, Ho. of Lords Appointments Commn., 2001, Order of Merit, 2002. Fellow Royal Soc. (pres.), Am. Acad. Arts and Scis.; mem. NAS, Athenaeum Club. Office: U Oxford Dept Zoology Oxford OX13PS England also: The Royal Society 6-9 Carlton House Terrace SW1Y 5AG London England E-mail: robert.may@zoo.ox.ac.uk.

MAY, ROBERT P. health facility company executive; b. May 1949; married; 5 children. Student, Harvard U. Former CEO Intelogistics divsn. Intelligence Electronics; former COO Towne Air Freight; sr. exec. FedEx Corp., 1973—94; COO, dir. Cablevision Sys. Corp., 1997—99; pres., CEO PNV Inc., 1999—2000; pvt. investor, strategic cons. for telecom. and logistics cos.; bd. mem. HealthSouth Corp., Birmingham, Ala., 2002—03, interim CEO, 2003—04, chmn., 2004—. With USMC. Office: HealthSouth Corp One HealthSouth Pkwy Birmingham AL 35243

MAY, RON, state senator; b. Sherman, Tex., Sept. 16, 1934; m. Onilla May. BGS, U. Nebr. Commd. 2d lt. USAF, 1953, advanced through grades, 1974; pres., owner The May Corp., Colorado Springs; Rep. rep. dist. 15 Colo. Ho. of Reps., 1980-2000; Rep. senator dist. 10 Colo. State Senate, 2000—. Mem. bus. affairs and labor and transp. and energy coms. Colo. Ho. of Reps.; mem. govt., vets. and mil. rels. and transp. coms. Colo. State Senate. Mem. Colorado Springs City Coun., 1981-85; charter pres. Acad. Blvd. Sertoma Club; mem. adv. bd. Colorado Springs Internat. Airport; mem. Village Seven Presbyn. Ch. Office: Colo State Senate State Capitol 200 E Colfax Rm 274 Denver CO 80203 also: 6609 Showhorse Ct Colorado Springs CO 80922-3303 E-mail: ronmay@sni.net.

MAY, RONALD ALAN, lawyer; b. Waterloo, Iowa, Sept. 8, 1928; s. John W. and Elsie (Finlayson) M.; m. Naomi Gray, Aug. 18, 1950 (div. Feb. 1974); children: Sarah, Jonathan, Andrew, Rachel; m. Susan East Gray, May 9, 1975. BA, U. Iowa, 1950; LL.B., Vanderbilt U., 1953. Bar: Ark. 1953. Atty. Daggett & Daggett, Marianna, 1953-57, Wright, Lindsey & Jennings LLP, Little Rock, 1957-84, sr. ptnr., 1984-96; of counsel Wright, Lindsey & Jennings, LLP, 1996—. Editor: Automated Law Research, 1972, Sense and Systems in Automated Law Research, 1975; contbg. editor Fifty State Construction Lien and Bond Law, 1992, Fifty State Public Construction Contracting, 1996; assoc. editor Jour. Irreproducible Results. Pres. Spl. Com. on Pub. Edn., Ark. Assn. for Mental Health, Friends of Library, Central Ark. Radiation Therapy Inst.; chmn. Ark. Cancer Research Ctr., 1990-92; bd. dirs. Nat. Assn. for Mental Health, Ark. State Hosp., Gaines House, State Bd. Architects; bd. dirs. State Bd. Bar Examiners, chmn. 1987-88, Ark. ethics com., 1991-93; trustee Mus. Sci. and Natural History, Little Rock, chmn., 1973; mem. profl. adv. bd. sch. architecture U. Ark., 1990-96, mem. profl. adv. bd. sch. urban studies and design, 1993—; mem. human rsch. adv. com. U. Ark. for Med. Scis., 2000—. Served with AUS, 1946-47. Mem. ABA (chmn. sci. and tech. sect. 1975-76), Ark., Pulaski County Bar Assns., Internat. Assn. Def. Counsel, Am. Inns of Ct. (Master of the Bench), Assn. for Computing Machinery, Order of Coif, Phi Beta Kappa. Episcopalian. Home: 821 Ash St Little Rock AR 72205-2051 Office: Wright Lindsey & Jennings LLP 200 W Capitol Ave Ste 2300 Little Rock AR 72201-3699 Office Phone: 501-212-1231. Business E-Mail: rmay@wlj.com.

MAY, STEPHEN, writer, former government official; b. Rochester, NY, July 30, 1931; s. Arthur J. and Hilda (Jones) M. Grad., Wesleyan U., 1953; LLB, Georgetown U., 1961. Bar: NY 1963. Exec. asst. to Rep. and Senator Kenneth B. Keating, 1955-64; assoc., mem., then ptnr. Branch, Turner & Wise, Rochester, 1965-81; city councilman-at-large Rochester, 1966-73; mayor, 1970-73; chmn. and commr. N.Y. State Bd. Elections, Albany, 1975-79; asst. sec. for legis. and Congl. rels. Dept. Housing and Urban Devel., 1981-88; ind. historian, writer, lectr. for mags. and newspapers, 1988—. Vice chmn. Temporary State Commn. on Powers of Local Govt., 1970-73; mem. 20th Century Fund Task Force on Future of N.Y.C., 1979, Nat. Adv. Commn. Higher Edn. for Police Officers, 1977-79, Joint Com. Assn. Bar City N.Y. and Drug Abuse Coun. on N.Y. Drug Law Evaluation, 1977-78; chmn. Rochester Interfaith Com. on Israel, 1973-81; del.-at-large Rep. Nat. Conv., 1972; mem. N.Y. State Crime Control Planning Bd., 1970-73 Contbr. numerous articles on Am. art, culture and hist. preservation to newspapers and periodicals. Bd. dirs. Police Found., 1970-81, Nat. Com. for Labor Israel, 1977-81, Empire State Report, 1974-81, Inst. Mediation and Conflict Resolution, 1973-81. Served with U.S. Army, 1953-55. Mem. Phi Beta Kappa. Home and Office: 4101 Cathedral Ave NW Washington DC 20016-3585 also: 270 Mt Pleasant Rd Union ME 04862-3003 Office Phone: 202-362-2399., 207-785-4178.

MAY, STEPHEN JAMES, communications educator, writer; b. Toronto, Ont., Can., Sept. 10, 1946; s. Thomas and Claire (Thompson) M.; m. Caroline Casteel, Sept. 27, 1947; 1 child, Trevor. BA, Calif. State U., Carson, 1975; MA, Calif. State U., L.A., 1977; DLitt, Internat. U., London, 1990. Prof. and chair dept. of Englist and Lit. Pikes Peak C.C., Colorado Springs, Colo., 1980-91; prof. Colo. N.W. C.C., Craig, 1992-98; chair dept. of English and Lit. Pikes Peak C.C., Colorado Springs, Colo., 1998—2001; vis. prof. U. No. Colo., 2001—. Advisor Internat. Biog. Ctr., Cambridge, Eng., 1989-95; vis. prof. U. Colo., 2000—. Author: Pilgrimage, 1987, Fire From the Skies, 1990, Footloose, 1993, Zane Grey, 1997, Maverick Heart, 2000, Rascals, 2002; contbr. to profl. jours. including SouthWest Art, Ohio Review. Mem. Western Writers Am., Colo. Authors League, Zane Grey Soc., Soc. S.W. Authors, C.C. Humanities, James A. Mitchener Soc. Avocations: travel, writing, drawing. Home: 731 Peregrine Run Fort Collins CO 80524 Personal E-mail: stepkm@msn.com.

MAY, STERLING RANDOLPH, health association executive; b. Muskogee, Okla., Dec. 27, 1946; s. Sterling May William and Mary Catherine (Griffith) May. BA with honors, U. Kans., 1968; MS, U. Mich., 1969, PhD, 1977; M in Bus., Johns Hopkins U., 1995. Coord. Skin Bank St. Agnes Med. Ctr., Phila., 1977-79, assoc. dir. Burn Rsch., 1980, dir. Burn Rsch., 1981-83; dir. Southeastern Burn Rsch. Inst., Augusta, Ga., 1983-87; v.p. LifeCell Corp., The Woodlands, Tex., 1987-91; chief oper. officer ARC Nat. Hdqs., Arlington, Va., 1991-2000. Rsch. asst. prof. Hahnemann U. Sch. Medicine, Phila., 1979-82, rsch. assoc. prof., 1983; assoc. clin. prof. Med. Coll. Ga., 1984-87; adj. prof. U. Tex. Med. Sch., Houston, 1987-91. Editor: Care of the Burn Wound, 1985; author 84 published articles in biomed. lit., 1974—; mem. editorial bd. Jour. Burn Care and Rehab., 1982-90, Burns, 1985-92, Cryobiology, 1987-93. Mem. Soc. for Cryobiology (pres. 1989-91, chmn. 23d ann. meeting, 1986), Am. Burn Assn. (chmn. rsch. com. 1998-2000), Internat. Soc. For Burn Injuries (mem. gen. coun. 1982-90), Am. Assn. Tissue Banks (sec. 1991-93, v.p. 1993-95, pres. 1995-97, bd. govs. 1989-93), Nat. Trust for Hist. Preservation. Avocations: antique furniture, music, archaeology. Office: Health Care Rsch 1501 Crystal Dr Ste 828 Arlington VA 22202-4125 Home: 2318 River Cliff DR Gainesville GA 30501-1685 E-mail: srmayphd@aol.com.

MAY, THOMAS J. electric company executive; BS, Stonehill Coll.; MS in Fin., Bentley Coll. Various positions Boston Edison Co., 1976-90, exec. v.p., 1990-93, pres., CEO, 1993-94, chmn., CEO, 1994-99, NStar, Boston, 1999—. Office: NStar MSC P 1600 800 Boylston St Boston MA 02199

MAY, TIMOTHY JAMES, lawyer; b. Denver, Aug. 3, 1932; s. Thomas Henry and Helen Frances (O'Conner) M.; m. Monica Anita Gross, Aug. 24, 1957; children: Stephanie, Maureen, Cynthia, Timothy, Anthony. BA, Cath. U. Am., 1954; LLB, Georgetown U., 1957, LLM, 1960. Bar: D.C. 1957, U.S. Supreme Ct. 1961. Law clk. to judge U.S. Ct. Appeals, D.C. Cir., 1957-58; assoc. Covington & Burling, Washington, 1958-61; cons. Exec. Office of Pres. U.S., Washington, 1961-62; chief counsel subcom. on stockpile Armed Svcs. Com., U.S. Senate, Washington, 1962-63; mng. dir. Fed. Maritime Commn., Washington, 1963-66; gen. counsel U.S. Post Office Dept., Washington, 1966-69; sr. ptnr. Patton Boggs, L.L.P., Washington, 1969—. Bd. dirs. Legal Aid Soc. D.C., 1984—; pres. Coun. for Ct. Excellence, Washington, 1999—, Marine Corps Law Enforcement Found., 1996—2003; chmn. bd. regents Cath. U. Am., 1988-93, trustee, 1993—; pres. Holy Family of Bethlehem Found., 1997-99. Recipient Servant of Justice award Legal Aid Soc. D.C., 1997, St. Elizabeth Ann Seton award SOAR!, 1998, Caritas award Archdiocese D.C., 1998. Fellow Am. Bar Found. (life); mem. ABA (House of Dels.), Fed. Bar Assn., Bar Assn. of D.C. (pres. 1991-92, Lawyer of the Yr. award 1999), Congl. Country Club (bd. govs. 1992-98, sec. 1994-97), Nat. Christian

Leadership Conf. for Israel (exec. com. 1992-2003), Met. Club, Indian Creek Country Club (bd. dirs. 1999—, v.p. 2001—), Fed. City Coun., Econ. Club D.C. (bd. dirs. 2001—), Knight of Malta, Constantinian Order St. George (knight). Democrat. Roman Catholic. Home: 3828 52nd St NW Washington DC 20016-1924 Office: Patton Boggs LLP 2550 M St NW Washington DC 20037-1350 Home (Winter): 286 Bal Bay Dr Miami FL 33154 Office Phone: 202-457-6050. E-mail: tmay@pattonboggs.com.

MAY, WILLIAM FRANCIS, ethicist, educator; b. Chgo., Oct. 25, 1927; s. Harry Stuart and Leontine Frances (Torczynski) M.; m. Beverly Wilson May, June 28, 1952; children: Catherine, Theodore, David, Elisabeth. AB, Princeton U., 1948; BD, Yale U., 1952, PhD, 1962. Ordained minister Presbyn. Ch. From lectr. to assoc. prof. Smith Coll., Northampton, Mass., 1952—66, chmn. dept., 1959-62, 64-66; prof. Ind. U., Bloomington, Ind., 1966—80, chmn., founder religious studies dept., 1971-76; J.P. Kennedy prof. Christian ethics Georgetown U., Washington, 1980-85; Cary M. Maguire prof. ethics So. Meth. U., Dallas, 1985—2001, dir. Cary M. Maguire Ctr. for Ethics and Pub. Responsibility, 1995—98. Founding fellow Hastings Ctr. Author: A Catalogue of Sins, 1967, The Physician's Covenant, 1983, 2d edit., 2000, The Patient's Ordeal, 1991, Testing the Medical Covenant: Active Euthanasia and Health Care Reform, 1996, The Ethics of Giving and Receiving, 2000, Beleaguered Rulers: The Public Obligation of the Professional, 2001. Mem. work group on ethical founds., Clinton task force on health care reform The White House, Washington, 1993; mem. pres.'s coun. on bioethics, White House, 2002—. Lilly open faculty fellow, 1976-77, Guggenheim Found. fellow, 1978-79. Mem. Am. Acad. Religion (pres. 1974-75, Outstanding Tchr. in Religious Studies award 1993), Soc. for Values in Higher Edn., Soc. for Christian Ethics (pres. 2002). Democrat. Presbyterian. Avocations: golf, hiking, music. Home: RR 1 Box 1440 Berlin NH 03570-9716 also: 417 Heritage CT Charlottesville VA 22903-7888

MAY, WILLIAM FREDERICK, manufacturing executive; b. Chgo., Oct. 25, 1915; s. Arthur W. and Florence (Hartwick) M.; m. Kathleen Thompson, June 14, 1947; children: Katherine Hartwick (Mrs. Edward W. Bickford), Elizabeth Shaw. BS, U. Rochester, 1937; grad. Advanced Mgmt. Program, Harvard U., 1950; D in Engring., Clarkson U.; LLD, Okla. Christian Coll.; LHD, Livingstone U.; LLD, Lafayette U. Rsch. worker E.I. Du Pont de Nemours Co., 1937-38, with Am. Can Co., Greenwich, Conn., 1940-80, mgr., 1957-58, v.p., 1958-64, exec. v.p., 1964-65, vice chmn. bd. dirs., 1965, chmn. bd. dirs., CEO, 1965-80, mem. exec. com., 1960—. Dean Grad. Sch. Bus. Adminstrn., NYU, 1980-84; chmn. and CEO Statue of Liberty Found., 1984—. Bd. dirs. Lincoln Ctr.; trustee Am. Ditchley Found., Am. Mus. Natural History, Columbia-Presbyn. Hosp., U. Rochester; mem. corp. Poly. Inst. N.Y.; chmn. pub. policy coun. Advt. Coun. Mem. Nat. Order of Merit (France, officier), Econ. Club, Round Hill Club, Megunticook Golf Club, Indian Harbor Yacht Club, Camden Yacht Club, Phi Beta Kappa, Alpha Delta Phi. Episcopalian. Home: 84 Indian Harbor Dr Greenwich CT 06830-7148 Office: Statue of Liberty Found 292 Madison Ave New York NY 10017-7769 Office Phone: 212-561-4514. Personal E-mail: w.k.may@aol.com.

MAYDEN, BARBARA MENDEL, lawyer; b. Chattanooga, Sept. 18, 1951; d. Eugene Lester Mendel and Blanche (Krugman) Rosenberg; m. Martin Ted Mayden, Sept. 14, 1986. AB, Ind. U., 1973; JD, U. Ga., 1976. Bar: Ga. 1976, N.Y. 1980. Assoc. King & Spalding, Atlanta, 1976-79, Willkie Farr & Gallagher, N.Y.C., 1980, Morgan Lewis & Bockius, N.Y.C., 1980-82, White & Case, N.Y.C., 1982-89; spl. counsel Skadden, Arps, Slate, Meagher & Flom, N.Y.C., 1989-95; mem. Bass, Berry & Sims PLC, Nashville, 1996—; lectr. Vanderbilt U. Sch. Law, Nashville, 1995-97. Mem. bd. visitors U. Ga. Sch. Law, Athens, 1986—89; mem. Leadership Nashville, 1999—2000; mem. adv. bd. Women's Fund of the Cmty. Found. of Mid. Tenn., 2001—; bd. dirs. YWCA, 2001—, Jewish Cmty. Ctr., 2001—02. Fellow Am. Bar Found. (life); mem. ABA (chair young lawyers divsn. 1985-86, ho. of dels. 1986—, commr. commn. on women 1987-91, commr. commn. opportunities for minorities in profession 1986-87, select com. of the house 1989-91, chmn. assembly resolutions com. 1990-91, membership com. of the house 1991-92, bd. govs. 1991-94, chair com. on rules and calendar 1996-98, chair bd. govs. ops. com., exec. com. 1993-94, task force long range fin. planning 1993-94, com. scope correlation of work 1998-2003, chair 2001-02, sec. bus. law sect. 2001-02, vice-chair 2002-03, chair-elect 2003-04, chair 2004—), Nat. Assn. Bond Lawyers (bd. dirs. 1985-86), Bond Attys.' Workshop (chmn. 1986), N.Y. State Bar Assn. (ho. of dels. 1993-95), Assn. of Bar of City of N.Y. (internat. human rights com. 1986-89, 2d century com. 1986-90, com. women in the profession, 1989-92), N.Y. County Lawyers Assn. (com. spl. projects, chair com. rels with other bars), Am. Law Inst. Democrat. Jewish. Home: 4414 Herbert Pl Nashville TN 37215-4544 Office: Bass Berry & Sims PLC 315 Deaderick St Ste 2700 Nashville TN 37238-0002 Office Phone: 615-742-6208. E-mail: bmayden@bassberry.com.

MAYER, ALLAN, crisis communications consultant, writer; b. N.Y.C., Mar. 15, 1950; s. Theodore H. and Phyllis (Zwick) M. BA, Cornell U., 1971. Staff reporter Wall Street Jour., N.Y.C., 1972-73; assoc. editor, gen. editor Newsweek mag., N.Y.C., 1973-77, fgn. corr. London, 1977-80, sr. editor N.Y.C., 1980-82; editl. dir. Arbor House Pub., N.Y.C., 1986-88; sr. editor Simon & Schuster, N.Y.C., 1988-89; editor-in-chief Buzz mag., L.A., 1990-95, editor-in-chief, pub., 1996; sr. ptnr. Sitrick and Co., L.A., 1997—. Author: Madam Prime Minister, 1980, Gaston's War, 1987; co-author: Spin, 1998. Recipient award Overseas Press Club, 1974, Nat. Mag. award Am. Soc. Mag. Editors, 1978, William Allen White award City and Regional Mag. Assn., 1995-96. Mem. Writers Guild Am. Office Phone: 310-788-2850. E-mail: allan_mayer@sitrick.com.

MAYER, ANTHONY JOHN, investment company executive; b. Milw., Apr. 21, 1936; s. Anton J. and Mary (Plesnk) M. *Father Anton and head of family was a career government employee and successful business person. Brother Robert is a retired career government employee, college trained, a business person, and is currently chairman, vice-president, and registered investment advisor of a well-known investment company.* BS, Marquette U., 1958, postgrad., 1965. Registered investment adv.; cert. nutritionist. Ins. claims exec., 1962—65; founder Fixed Income Mutual Fund, Milw., 1968—; motel exec., 1968—80; pres. Anthony J. Mayer, Inc., Milw., 1994—; v.p. Banc One Investment Mgmt. Group, Chgo., 2001—. Chmn. Westridge Investors, 1998—, New Berlin Investors, 1998—, Millionaire Investor Entities Guidance.Com, 2000—, Hungarian Investors Com., 2003; country music seminar host, 1995. Anthony J. Mayer Investment Parables, 1995, Anthony J. Mayer Investment Advisory Book, 2003; author, editor, newsletter: Anthony J. Mayer Investment Bible, 1995;; columnist: Alaska newspapers, 1959—60; contbr. articles to profl. jours.; investment radio personality, 1990—93. Trustee Anthony J. Mayer Trust, 1991—, Jesuit Ptnrs., 1998—; active Ignatius Loyola Inner Circle, 1999—; pres. Pub. Lands Decor Classics, 2000—; bd. dirs. West Allis Food for Milw., First Mcpl. Credit Union, 1996-2001; del. Adv. Coun. Nat. Rep. Congl. Com., 2001—; chmn. adv. bd. Nat. Rep. Party, 2004—; hon. sponsor Pres. Bush victory dinner, 2001; grassroots leader Rep. Campaign, 2004. With U.S. Army, 1958-60. Named Successful Investor of Yr., Sta. WGN, 1996, Notable Pulaskian, Milw. Pub. Sch. Sys., 1999; recipient VIP award, Speedway-Super Am., 1995, 2000, Cleve. Meadows Achievement award, 1998, Commendation cert., State of Wis., 2002, Animal Stewardship award, 2002, Cmty. Svc. award, Jerusalem Christian, 2003. Mem.: N.Am. Investors Alliance (founder, chmn. 1993), Rep. Govs. Assn., Aircraft Owners Assn., Acad. Country Music, Country Music Assn., KC. Roman Catholic. Avocation: reading. Office Phone: 414-321-7126.

MAYER, CARL JOSEPH, prosecutor, lawyer; b. Boston, Apr. 23, 1959; s. Arno Joseph and Nancy Sue (Grant) M. AB magna cum laude, Princeton U., 1981; JD, U. of Chgo., 1986; LLM, Harvard U., 1988. Bar: N.J. 1986, Mass. 1988, N.Y. 1989, D.C. 1989. Writer for Ralph Nader, Washington, 1981-83; law clk. to presiding justice U.S. Dist. Ct., Wilmington, Del., 1986-87; law assoc., prof. Hofstra Law Sch., Hempstead, N.Y., 1989-94; atty. Milberg, Weiss, Bershad, Hynes and Lerach, N.Y.C., 1995-96; spl. counsel N.Y. State Atty. Gen.'s Office, N.Y.C., 1999—. Cons. U.S. Senate Com., Washington, 1988-89. Author: Shakedown, 1998; co-author: Public Domain, Private Dominion, 1985; contbr. articles to profl. jours. Town committeeman, Princeton, N.J., 1995-98. NYU fellow, 1988-89. Mem. ABA, N.Y. Bar Assn., N.J. Bar Assn., Mass. Bar Assn. Avocations: marathon running, squash, tennis. Home: 58 Battle Rd Princeton NJ 08540-4902 Office: NY State Atty Gen Office 120 Broadway New York NY 10271-0002 E-mail: carlmayer@aol.com.

MAYER, CHARLES ARTHUR, management consultant, musician; b. Salt Lake City, Oct. 6, 1949; s. Robert C. and Barbara (Arthur) M.; m. Carolyn Familetti, June 21, 1975 (div. June 1989); 1 child, George. BS in Indsl. Mgmt., Purdue U., 1971; MBA, Temple U., 1978. Cert. mgmt. cons. Systems analyst Burroughs Corp., Detroit, 1972-76; cons. Pinkerton Computer Cons., Phila., 1976-79, Coopers & Lybrand, Phila., 1979-82, Deloitte Haskins & Sells, Phila., 1982-85; prin. Mayer Computer Solutions, Merion Station, Pa., 1985—. Pres. Merion Park Civic Assn., Merion Station, Pa., 1979-80; Uptown String Band, (treas., 1999—). Mem. Inst. Mgmt. Cons. (chpt. pres. 1987-89), Cynwyd Club (treas. 1986-94). Office: PO Box 368 Merion Station PA 19066-0368

MAYER, FRANK D., JR., lawyer; b. Dec. 23, 1933; BA, Amherst Coll., 1955; student, Cambridge U.; JD, U. Chgo., 1959. Bar: Ill. 1959. Ptnr. Mayer, Brown, Rowe & Maw, Chgo. Mem. ABA, Chgo. Bar Assn., Order of Coif, Phi Beta Kappa. Office: Mayer Brown Rowe and Maw 190 S La Salle St Ste 3100 Chicago IL 60603-3441 E-mail: fmayer@mayerbrown.com.

MAYER, GEORGE ROY, education educator; b. National City, Calif, Aug. 28, 1940; s. George Eberly and Helen Janet (Knight) M.; m. Barbara Ann Fife, Sept. 9, 1964 (div. June 1986); children: Kevin Roy, Debbie Rae Ann; m. Jocelyn Volk Finn, Aug. 3, 1986 (div. July 2003). BA, San Diego State U., 1962; MA, Ind. U., 1965, EdD, 1966. Cert. sch. psychologist; bd. cert. behavior analyst. Sch. counselor, psychologist Ind. U., Bloomington, 1964-66; asst. prof. guidance and ednl. psychology So. Ill. U., Carbondale, 1966-69; profl. edn. Calif. State U., L.A., 1966—. Cons. in field; adv. bd. Dept. Spl. Edn., L.A., 1986-90, Jay Nolan Ctr. for Autism, Newhall, Calif., 1975 86; lectr. in field; study group on youth violence prevention Nat. Ctr. for Injury Prevention and Control, Divsn. Violence Prevention of the Ctrs. for Disease Control and Prevention, 1998. Author: Classroom Mgmt.: A Calif. Resource Guide, 2000, Teaching Alternative Behaviors Schoolwide: Preventing Schoolwide Behavior Problems, 2003; co author: Behavior Analysis for Lasting Change, 1991; contbr. articles to profl. jour. Recipient Outstanding Prof. award Calif. State U.-L.A., 1988; U.S. Dept. Edn. grantee, 1996—. Mem. Assn. for Behavior Analysis, Nat. Assn. Sch. Psychologists, Calif. Assn. Behavior Analysis (hon. life, pres., conf. chmn., Outstanding Contbr. to Behavior Analysis award 1997), Cambridge Ctr. for Behavioral Studies (adv. bd.), Calif. Assn. Sch. Psychologists (chmn. practitioners conf. 1994—). Avocations: horseback riding, fishing, swimming. Home: 10735 Frank Daniels Way San Diego CA 92131- Personal E-mail: grmayer@aol.com.

MAYER, HALDANE ROBERT, federal chief judge; b. Buffalo, N.Y., Feb. 21, 1941; s. Haldane Rupert and Myrtle Kathleen Mayer; m. Mary Anne McCurdy, Aug. 13, 1966; children: Anne Christian, Rebecca Paige. BS, U.S. Mil. Acad., 1963; JD, Coll. William and Mary, 1971. Bar: Va. 1971, D.C. 1980, U.S. Ct. Appeals (4th cir.) 1972, U.S. Dist. Ct. (ea. dist.) Va. 1972, U.S. Ct. Mil. Appeals 1973, U.S. Supreme Ct. 1977, U.S. Ct. Claims 1984. Law clk. U.S. Ct. Appeals (4th cir.), Richmond, Va., 1971—72; atty. McGuire Woods & Battle, Charlottesville, Va., 1975—77; spl. asst. to chief justice U.S. Supreme Ct., Washington, 1977—80; atty. Baker & McKenzie, Washington, 1980—81; acting spl. counsel U.S. Merit Systems Protection Bd., Washington, 1981—82; judge U.S. Claims Ct., Washington, 1982—87, U.S. Ct. Appeals (fed. cir.), Washington, 1987—97, chief judge, 1997—. Adj. prof. U. Va. Sch. Law, 1975—77, 1992—94, George Washington U. Law Sch., 1992—96. Bd. dirs. William and Mary Law Sch. Assn., 1979—85. Maj. U.S. Army, 1963—75, ret. lt. col. USAR. Decorated Bronze Star. Mem.: West Point Soc. D.C., Army Athletic Assn., West Point Assn. Grads., Omicron Delta Kappa. Office: US Ct Appeals for Fed Cir 717 Madison Pl NW Washington DC 20439-0002 Office Phone: 202-633-6556.

MAYER, IRA EDWARD, gastroenterologist; b. Bklyn., July 31, 1951; s. Elias M. and Mollie (Taxerman) M.; m. Celeste Ann Sivak, Mar. 13, 1976; children: Madelaine Rose, Amanda Beth. BS, Bklyn. Coll., 1972; MD, N.Y. Med. Coll., 1975. Diplomate Am. Bd. Internal Medicine, Am. Bd. Gastroenterology, Nat. Bd. Med. Examiners. Asst. resident in internal medicine N.Y. Med. Coll./Met. Hosp. Ctr., N.Y.C., 1975-76, resident in internal medicine, 1976-78; fellow digestive diseases divsn. Emory U., Atlanta, 1978-80; attending gastroenterologist Maimonides Med. Ctr., Bklyn., 1980—; clin. instr. medicine SUNY Health Sci. Ctr., Bklyn., 1980-81, instr. medicine, 1981-83, clin. asst. prof. medicine, 1983—2002, chmn. patient care com., 1984-99; clin. asst. prof. medicine Mt. Sinai Sch. Medicine, 2003—. Co-chmn. operative invasive and noninvasive procedures com., Maimonides Med. Ctr., pres.-elect med. staff, 2003--. Author: (with others) Digestive Diseases, 1983, Medicine, 1983; contbr. articles to profl. jours. Fellow ACP, Am. Coll. Gastroenterology; mem. Am. Gastroent. Assn., Am. Soc. for Gastrointestinal Endoscopy, N.Y. Acad. Scis., N.Y. Acad. Gastroenterolgy, N.Y. Soc. for Gastrointestinal Endoscopy, Med. Soc. for the State of N.Y. Jewish. Office: 2560 Ocean Ave Brooklyn NY 11229-4521

MAYER, JAMES HOCK, mediator, lawyer; b. Neptune City, N.J., Nov. 1, 1935; s. J. Kenneth and Marie Ruth (Hock) M.; m. Carol I. Keating, Sept. 20, 1958 (div. Feb. 1981); children: Craig, Jeffrey; m. Patrisha Renk, Mar. 28, 1981 (div. July 2001); m. Judith Courtemanche, Mar. 23, 2004. AB with distinction, Dartmouth Coll., 1957; JD, Harvard U., 1964. Bar: Calif. 1965, U.S. Dist. Ct (no. dist., so. dist.) Calif. 1965, U.S. Ct. Appeals (9th cir.) 1965, U.S. Supreme Ct. 1974. Assoc. Pillsbury, Madison & Sutro, San Francisco, 1964-72, ptnr., 1973—; ind. mediator, 1992—. Rear adm. USNR, 1957-93. Rufus Choate scholar Dartmouth Coll., 1956-57. Mem. Newcomen Soc., Navy League, Naval Order of U.S., Harvard Club. Office: Mayer Mediation Svcs 1476 Sierra Linda Dr Escondido CA 92025 Home: 2370 Avenida de La Playa La Jolla CA 92037 E-mail: just-results@msn.com.

MAYER, JAMES JOSEPH, retired corporate lawyer; b. Cin., Nov. 27, 1938; s. Cletus Joseph and Berna Mae (Schroeder) M.; m. Margaret Ann Hobbs, Oct. 24, 1964; children: Kimberly, Susanne, Terri. BEE, U. Cin., 1961; JD, No. Ky. U., 1969. Registered profl. engr., Ohio. Bar: Ohio 1969, Ky. 1975. Engr. Cin. Gas & Electric Co., 1961-69, atty., 1969-85, gen. counsel, 1986-91, v.p., gen. counsel, 1991-95, ret., 1995; of counsel Taft, Stetinius & Hollister, Cin., 1995—. With USAFR, 1961-64. Mem. Ohio Bar Assn., Ky. Bar Assn., Cin. Bar Assn., Terrace Park Country Club. Republican. Roman Catholic. Avocations: home remodeling, sports, golf. Business E-Mail: mayer@taftlaw.com.

MAYER, JOHN, vocalist; b. Oct. 16, 1977; Student, Berklee Coll. Music. Singer: (albums) Inside Wants Out, 1999, Room for Squares, 2001 (Grammy award Best Male Pop Vocal Performance for song "Your Body is A Wonderland", 2002), Any Given Thursday, 2003, Heavier Things, 2003. Office: Mick Mgmt c/o Michael McDonald 157 Chambers St 12th Fl New York NY 10007 also: Creative Artists Agy c/o Scott Clayton 3310 West End Ave 5th Fl Nashville TN 37203*

MAYER, JOHN M. medical researcher, educator; DC, Nat. Coll. of Chiropractic, 1988—91; PhD, Syracuse U., 1995—2000. Dir. of rsch. U.S. Spine & Sport Found., San Diego, 2001—; adj. rsch. prof. San Diego State U., 2002—. Com. mem. Internat. Collegiate Commn. of Exercise Sci., Boston, 2001—. Recipient Doctoral Prize Sch. of Edn., Syracuse U., 2001. Mem.: Soc. of Clin. Rsch. Associates (licentiate). Mailing: 8532 Via Mallorca La Jolla CA 92037

MAYER, JOHN WILLIAM, lawyer; b. Houston, Nov. 17, 1941; s. Maurice William and Julie Eldee (Borddofsky) Mayer; m. M. Ann Jodoin, July 30, 1972; children: Norbert, Kristin, Mara. BA in Econs., Vanderbilt U., 1963; JD, U. Chgo., 1966; postgrad., Nat. Jud. Coll., 1984. Bar: Ill. 66, Colo. 87, Ala. 87, US Ct. Mil. Appeals 71. Assoc. Lorenz & Stamler, Newark, 1963—66; estate tax atty. IRS, Chgo., 1966—67; commd. 2d lt. USAF, 1967, advanced through grades to lt. col., 1980, judge advocate, 1967—87; dep. dist. atty. 15th Jud. Dist. Ala., Montgomery, 1987—90, chief dep. dist. atty., 1991—98; dep. atty. gen. State of Ala., 1990—91; pvt. practice, 1998—. Adj. prof. Jones Coll. Law, 1998—. Recipient Nat. Pub. Defender's award, Chgo., 1966; Nat. Honor scholar, U. Chgo., 1963. Mem.: ATLA, ABA (chmn. mil. judges com. 1984—85), Phi Delta Phi, Zeta Beta Tau. Jewish.

MAYER, JOYCE HARRIS, artist; b. N.Y.C., May 7, 1935; d. Harold and Dorothy Harris; m. Bernard Charles Mayer, Mar. 15, 1969; 1 child, Robert Charles. AAS, Inst. of Applied Art and Sci., N.Y.C., 1957. Sketcher Merrylen Cartooning Studio, 1952. Client contact, layout artist, Haire Publ., N.Y.C., 1957-59; art dir., Real Estate Forum, N.Y.C., 1959-60; Denhard and Stewart, N.Y.C., 1960-67; Herb Lubalin Graphic Art Award, 1964; self employed N.Y.C., 1967-71; co curator, New Orleans Mus. of Art, 1985. Among first women to have work pub. in Art Direction, 1964, exhibitions include N.Y. Inst. of Applied Arts and Sci., New Orleans Mus. of Art, 2003, Horizon Gallery, Royal Typographers, N.Y., Nat. Arts Club, Tulane Univ., Dominican Coll., Robinson Gallery, Mario Villa and Arthur Roger, New Orleans, TWEED Gallery, Plainfield, N.J., Barbara Gillman Gallery, Miami, Contemporary Art Ctr., New Orleans, Bruce Mus., Conn., Represented in permanent collections paintings, mono prints, and digital photographs in numerous collections in Europe and. U.S., Digital La., Contemporary Art Ctr., New Orleans, 2002, Biennale Internazionale dell Arte Contemporanea, Florence, Italy, 2003, N.C. Mus. Art, numerous others. Mem. Bd. Edn., Greenwich, Conn., 1978; art advisor Freeport McMoRan Art Collection, New Orleans, 1985; curator Mario Villa Gallery, New Orleans, 1989; juror Arts Coun., New Orleans, 1990. Recipient N.Y. Graphic Soc. award, 1976, medal in photography, Florence Biennale, 2003. Coll. Art Assn. Avocations: reading, theater, ballet, birdwatching. Home: 8 Golfview Dr Medford NJ 08055 Address: 34 Castle Rock Branford CT 06405 Office Fax: 609-953-2390. E-mail: joycehmayer@aol.com.

MAYER, LLOYD DEWALD, allergist, immunologist, physician, medical educator; b. Bklyn., Nov. 6, 1921; s. Morris and Leonore (Solomon) M.; m. Marie Faith Puntney, Feb. 2, 1957 (dec. Sept. 1981); children: Michael, Fredrick, Loren, Lee; m. Carol Smith, Dec. 21, 1985. BA, U. Louisville, 1941, MD, 1944. Diplomate Am. Bd. Internal Medicine, Am. Bd. Internal Medicine Alergy, Am. Bd. Allergy and Immunology. Rotating intern Coney Island Hosp., Bklyn., 1944-45; resident in contagious diseases Kingston Ave Hosp., Bklyn., 1945-46; resident in pathology Long Island Coll. Hosp., Bklyn., 1946-47; resident in medicine Montefiore Hosp., Pitts., 1947-48; teaching fellow in allergy U. Pitts., 1948-49; resident in medicine VA Hosp., Pitts., 1949-50; instr. in allergy medicine U. Pitts., 1950-52; staff St. Joseph Hosp., Good Samaritan Hosp., Ctrl. Baptist Hosp., chmn. dept. internal medicine, 1972-74; clin. prof. medicine, allergy U. Ky. Med. Ctr., Lexington, Ky., 1963—2004; prof. emeritus Med. Sch. U. Ky., 2004—. Cons. in allergy medicine VA Hosp.; chmn. respiratory therapy com. Good Samaritian Hosp., Ctrl. Baptist Hosp., 1970-74; chmn. nursing care com. Ctrl. Baptist Hosp., 1979; bd. dirs. Allergy Clinic, VA Hosp., Adult Allergy Clinic, U. Ky. Med. Ctr. 1954—, prof. emeritus 2003. Contr. to profl. jours. Pvt. US Army, 1942-46. Recipient cert. Appreciation Coll. Allied Health and Nursing Eastern Ky. U., Am. Acad. Family Practice award, 1979. Fellow Am. Coll. Physicians, Am. Acad. Allergy, Am. Coll. Allergists; mem. AMA, Fayette County Med. Soc., Ky. State Med. Assn., Ky. Thoracic Soc. (sec. 1962), Am. Assn. Cert. Allergists, Mason (pres. 1961), Scottish Rite Masonic Shriner (pres. 1962). Home and Office: 470 Woodlake Way Lexington KY 40502-2570

MAYER, MARILYN GOODER, steel company executive; b. Chgo. d. Seth MacDonald and Jean (McMullen) Gooder; m. William Anthony Mayer, Nov. 14, 1959; children: William Anthony Jr., Robert MacDonald. Grad., Career Inst., Chgo., 1941; student, Lake Forest Coll., Ill., 1942. Adminstrv. asst. Needham, Louis & Brorby, Chgo., 1949-53; v.p. RMB Corp., Chgo., 1963-71, Mayer Motors, Ft. Lauderdale, Fla., 1965-74, Gooder-Henrichsen, Chicago Heights, Ill., 1975—. Dir. Barnett Bank, West Palm Beach, Fla. Trustee Gulf Stream (Fla.) Sch.; trustee emeritus St. Andrew's Sch., Boca Raton, Fla.; bd. dirs. Bethesda Hosp. Assn., Boynton Beach, Fla., pres. 1981-82; bd. dirs. Gulf Stream Civic Assn. Mem. Soc. Four Arts, Little Bath and Tennis Club (gov. of Gulf Stream). Avocation: travel. Home: 2925 Polo Dr Delray Beach FL 33483-7331

MAYER, MARTIN PRAGER, writer; b. N.Y.C., Jan. 14, 1928; s. Henry and Ruby (Prager) M.; m. Ellen Moers, June 23, 1949 (dec. Aug. 1979); children: Thomas, James; m. Karin Lissakers, Oct. 25, 1980; children: Fredrica, Henry. AB, Harvard U., 1947; D.Litt. (hon.), Wake Forest U., 1977, Adelphi U., 1981. Reporter, N.Y. Jour. Commerce, 1947-48; asst. editor Labor and Nation, 1948-49; editor Hillman Periodicals, 1949-51; assoc. editor Esquire mag., 1951-54, record critic, 1952-75; freelance writer, 1954—; N.Y. critic Opera Mag. (Eng.), 1985—2004; columnist American Banker, 1987-89. Rsch. dir. study of internat. secondary edn. Twentieth Century Fund, 1965-66; cons. Am. Council Learned Socs., 1961-63; consultant, Twentieth Century Fund, Carnegie Found., Ford Found., Sloan Kettering Found. Author: (novel) The Experts, 1955; Wall Street, Men and Money, 2d edit., 1960, Madison Avenue, USA, 1958, (novel) A Voice That Fills the House, 1959, The Schools, 1961, Where, When and Why, Social Studies in American Schools, 1963, The Lawyers, 1967, Emory Buckner, 1968, Diploma, 1968, (with Cornell Capa) New Breed on Wall Street, 1969, Bricks, Mortar and the Performing Arts, 1970, All You Know Is Facts, 1970, The Teachers Strike, 1970, About Television, 1972, The Bankers, 1975, Conflicts of Interest: Broker-Dealer Firms, 1975, Today and Tomorrow in America, 1976, The Builders, 1978, (novel) Trigger Points, 1979, The Fate of the Dollar, 1980, The Met: One Hundred Years of Grand Opera, 1983, The Diplomats, 1983, The Money Bazaars, 1984, (with G. Fitzgerald) Grandissimo Pavarotti, 1986, Making News, 1987, Markets, 1988, The Greatest Ever Bank Robbery, 1990, Whatever Happened to Madison Avenue?, 1991, Stealing the Market, 1992, Nightmare on Wall Street, 1993, (with Elizabeth Luessenship) Risky Business, 1995, The Bankers: The Next Generation, 1997, Risk Reduction in the New Financial Architecture, 1999, The Fed, 2001. Mem. Pres.'s Panel on Ednl. Research and Devel., 1961-66; mem. edn. com. Music Critics Assn., 1978-82; chmn. N.Y.C. Local Sch. Bd., 1962-67; commr. Nat. Commn. on Reform Secondary Edn., 1972-73; bd. visitors Wake Forest U., 1972-87; mem. Pres.'s Commn. on Housing, 1981-82. Guest scholar Brookings Instn., 1993—. Mem.: Century (N.Y.C.); Gardiner's Bay (Shelter Island, N.Y.). Democrat. Jewish. Address: PO Box 478 Shelter Island NY 11964-0478

MAYER, MORRIS LEHMAN, marketing educator; b. Demopolis, Ala., Dec. 14, 1925; s. Lehman M. and Anne (Rochotsh) M.; m. Judith Marian Morton, Dec. 22, 1957; children: Susan Morton, Elizabeth Anne. BS in Bus. Adminstrn, U. Ala., 1949, DHL (hon.), 1994; MS in Retailing, N.Y. U., 1950; PhD in Bus. Orgn, Ohio State U., 1961. Buyer Goldblatts Dept. Store, Chgo., 1951-55; mem. faculty U. Ala., 1955—, prof., 1960—, chmn. dept. mktg., 1969-74, dir. Hess Inst. Retailing, 1985-92, Bruno prof. mktg., 1986-92; Bruno prof. mktg. emeritus, 1992—; instr. Ohio State U., Columbus, 1956-60. Cons. Mgmt. Horizons Co., Columbus, 1966-70, N.C.R. Co., Dayton, Ohio, 1967-75. Co-author: Modern Retailing, 1978, 6th edit., 1993, Retailing, 1981, 5th edit., 1993. Served with AUS, 1944-46, 50-51. Recipient Teaching Excellence award Burlington No. Found., 1986, Distinctive Image award Jewish Childrens Regional Svc. Bd., 1997, Circle of Honor award Direct Selling Edn. Found., 1997; Ford Found. fellow, 1962-63, So. Mktg. fellow, 1986; named to U. Ala. Bus. Faculty Hall of Fame, 1995, Retail Patronage Acad. Hall of Fame, 1995; Morris Mayer Endowed scholarship established 1992; Morris L. Mayer award established U. Ala., 1993; Morris L. Mayer Outstanding Sutdent award established Sales and Mktg. Execs., 1993, others. Mem. Am. Mktg. Assn. (Morris L. Mayer Outstanding Mem. award estab. Birmingham chpt. 1993), So. Mktg. Assn. (pres.), Ala. Retail Assn. (bd. dirs.), Am. Coll. Retail Assn. (pres., Hall of Fame 1992, Mortar Bd., Beta Gamma Sigma, Eta Mu Pi, Pi Sigma Epsilon, Omicron Delta Kappa, Zeta Beta Tau (chpt. trustee). Jewish (temple trustee). Home: 1321 Montclair Cir Tuscaloosa AL 35404-4241 Office: U Ala PO Box 870225 Tuscaloosa AL 35487-0154

MAYER, NEAL MICHAEL, lawyer; b. N.Y.C., Dec. 4, 1941; s. Joseph Henry and Cele (Brodsky) M.; m. Jane Ellen Greenberg, Aug. 24, 1963; children: Andrew Warren, Amy Lynn, Rebecca Ann, Jenny Leigh. BA in History with honors, Kenyon Coll., 1963; JD, Georgetown U., 1966. Bar: D.C.

1967, U.S. Dist. Ct. D.C. 1967, U.S. Ct. Appeals (D.C. cir.) 1967, U.S. Customs Ct. 1967, U.S. Supreme Ct. 1970, U.S. Ct. Appeals (5th cir.) 1975. Assoc. Coles & Goertner, Washington, 1966-71, ptnr., 1971-82; sr. ptnr. Hoppel, Mayer & Coleman, Washington, 1982—. Trustee Kenyon Coll., 1995-2002. Mem. ABA, D.C. Bar Assn., Maritime Adminstrv. Bar Assn. (pres. 1979), Assn. for Transp. Law, Logistics and Policy, Propeller Club of U.S. (Washington), Kenyon Coll. Alumni Assn. (pres. 1993-94). Office: Hoppel Mayer & Coleman 1000 Connecticut Ave NW Washington DC 20036-5302 E-mail: nmayer@hmc-law.com.

MAYER, RAYMOND RICHARD, business administration educator; b. Chgo., Aug. 31, 1924; s. Adam and Mary (Bogdala) M.; m. Helen Lakowski, Jan. 30, 1954; children: Mark, John, Mary, Jane. BS, Ill. Inst. Tech., 1948, MS, 1954, PhD, 1957. Indsl. engr. Standard Oil Co., Whiting, Ind., 1948-51; orgn. analyst Ford Motor Co., Chgo., 1951-53; instr. Ill. Inst. Tech., Chgo., 1953-56, asso. prof., 1958-60; asst. prof. U. Chgo., 1956-58; Walter F. Mullady prof. bus. adminstrn. Loyola U., Chgo., 1960—. Author: Financial Analysis of Investment Alternatives, 1966, Production Management, 1962, rev. edit., 1968, Production and Operations Management, 1975, rev. edit., 1982, Capital Expenditure Analysis, 1978. Served with USNR, 1944-46. Ingersoll Found. fellow, 1955-56; Machinery and Allied Products Inst. fellow, 1954-55; Ford Found. fellow, 1962 Mem. Acad. Mgmt., Am. Econ. Assn., Am. Statis. Assn., Am. Inst. for Decision Scis., Nat. Assn. Purchasing Mgmt., Polish Inst. Arts and Scis. in Am., Alpha Iota Delta, Alpha Kappa Psi, Beta Gamma Sigma. Home: 730 Green Bay Rd Winnetka IL 60093-1912 Office: 820 N Michigan Ave Chicago IL 60611-2147

MAYER, RENEE G. lawyer; b. Elizabeth, N.J., Apr. 17, 1933; d. Harry and Bertha Sheinblatt Miller; m. Joseph C. Mayer, June 19, 1955; children: Douglas, Julia, Amy, Andrew. BS, Cornell U., 1955; JD, Hofstra U., 1978. Bar: N.Y. 1979, U.S. Dist. Ct. (ea. dist.) N.Y. 1979, U.S. Ct. Appeals (2d cir.) 1983, U.S. Supreme Ct. 1982. Assoc. atty. Meyer, English & Cianciulli, Mineola, N.Y., 1978-79; pvt. practice Mineola, N.Y., 1979-89; ptnr. Riebesehl, Mayer, Keegan & Horowitz, Garden City, N.Y., 1989-97; pvt. practice law Mineola, N.Y., 1997-2001, Port Washington, N.Y., 2001—. Mem. N.Y. State Bar Assn., Nassau Lawyers Assn. Long Island, Inc. (pres. 1996-97, first vice chancellor conf. of continuing legal edn.), Nassau County Women's Bar Assn. (pres. 1985-86), Nassau County Bar Assn. (dir. 1984-87, asst. dean acad. law 1987-91), Cornell Club (bd. govs. 1980-90), Democratic Com. (zone leader, Port. Washington, N.Y., 1980-93). Avocations: reading, theater, travel. Home and Office: 7 Leeds Dr Port Washington NY 11050-4116

MAYER, RICHARD EDWIN, psychology educator; b. Chgo., Feb. 8, 1947; s. James S. and Bernis (Lowy) M.; m. Beverly Linn Pastor, Dec. 19, 1971; children: Kenneth Michael, David Mark, Sarah Ann. BA with honors, Miami U., Oxford, Ohio, 1969; MS in Psychology, U. Mich., 1971, PhD in Psychology, 1973. Vis. asst. prof. Ind. U., Bloomington, 1973-75; asst. prof. psychology U. Calif., Santa Barbara, 1975-80, assoc. prof., 1980-85, prof., 1985—, pres., chmn. dept., 1987-90. Vis. scholar Learning Rsch. and Devel. Ctr., U. Pitts., 1979, Ctr. for Study of Reading, U. Ill., 1984. Author: Foundations of Learning and Memory, 1979, The Promise of Cognitive Psychology, 1981, Thinking, Problem Solving, Cognition, 1983, 2d edit., 1992, BASIC: A Short Course, 1985, Educational Psychology, 1987, The Critical Thinker, 1990, 2d edit., 1995, The Promise of Educational Psychology, 1999; editor: Human Reasoning, 1980, Teaching and Learning Computer Programming, 1988; editor jours. Instructional Sci., 1983-87, Educational Psychologist, 1983-89. Sch. bd. officer Goleta (Calif.) Union Sch. Dist., 1981—. NSF grantee, 1975-88. Fellow APA (divsn. 15 officer 1987—, G. Stanley Hall lectr. 1988), Am. Psychol. Soc.; mem. Am. Ednl. Rsch. Assn. (divsn. C officer 1986-88), Psychonomic Soc. Democrat. Jewish. Avocations: computers, hiking, bicycling, reading, dogs. Office: U Calif Dept Of Psychology Santa Barbara CA 93016 Office Phone: 805-893-2472. Business E-Mail: mayer@psych.ucsb.edu.

MAYER, ROBERT ANTHONY, retired college president; b. N.Y.C., Oct. 30, 1933; s. Ernest John and Theresa Margaret (Mazura) M.; m. Laura Wiley Christ, Apr. 30, 1960. BA magna cum laude, Fairleigh Dickinson U., 1955; MA, NYU, 1967. With N.J. Bank and Trust Co., Paterson, 1955-61, mgr. advt. dept., 1959-61; program supr. advt. dept. Mobil Oil Co., N.Y.C., 1961-62; asst. to dir. Latin Am. program Ford Found., N.Y.C., 1963-65, asst. rep., 1965-67; asst. to v.p. adminstrn., 1967-73; officer in charge logistical services Ford Found., 1968-73; asst. dir. programs N.Y. Community Trust, N.Y.C., 1973-76; exec. dir. N.Y. State Council on the Arts, N.Y.C., 1976-79; mgmt. cons. N.Y.C., 1979-80; dir. Internat. Mus. Photography, George Eastman House, Rochester, N.Y., 1980-89, mgmt. cons., 1989-90; pres. Cleve. Inst. of Art, 1990-97; ret., 1997. Author: (plays) La Borgia, 1971, Alijandru, 1971, They'll Grow No Roses, 1975; mem. editl. adv. bd. Grants mag., 1978—80, exhibited profl. photography, 1993—. Mem. state program adv. panel NEA, 1977—80; mem. Mayor's Com. on Cultural Policy, N.Y.C., 1974—75; mem. pres.'s adv. com. Bklyn. campus L.I. U., 1978—79; bd. dirs. Fedn. Protestant Welfare Agys., N.Y.C., 1977—79, Arts for Greater Rochester, 1981—83, Garth Fagan's Dance Theatre, 1982—86; trustee Internat. Mus. Photography, 1981—89, Lacoste Sch. Arts, France, 1991—96, sec., 1994—96; mem. dean's adv. com. Grad. Sch. Social Welfare, Fordham U., 1976; mem. N.Y. State Motion Picture and TV Devel. Adv. Bd., 1984—87, N.Y. State Martin Luther King Jr. Commn., 1985—90, Cleve. Coun. Cultural Affairs, 1992—94; chmn. Greater Cleve. Regional Transit Authority Arts in Transit Com., 1992—95; bd. dirs. Friends of Ariz. State U. Ctr. for Latin Am. Studies, 1997—99, Villa Solana Townhouse Assn., 2001—, pres., 2000. Recipient Nat. award on advocacy for girls Girls Clubs Am., 1976 Mem. Nat. Assembly State Art Agys. (bd. dirs. 1977-79, 1st vice chmn. 1978-79), Alliance Ind. Colls. Art (bd. dirs. 1983-91, vice chmn. 1986-87, sec. 1987-89), N.Y. State Assn. Museums (bd. councilors 1983-86, pres. 1986-89), Assn. Ind. Colls. Art and Design (bd. dirs. 1991-97, exec. com. 1991-93, 96-97). Home: 500A E 87th St Apt 3G New York NY 10128-7624

MAYER, ROSEMARY, artist; b. Ridgewood, N.Y., Feb. 27, 1943; d. Theodore Albert and Marie Anne (Stumpf) M. AB magna cum laude, U. Iowa, 1964; postgrad., Bklyn. Mus. Art Sch., 1964-65, Sch. of Visual Arts, N.Y.C., 1967-69. Model Raphael Soyer, N.Y.C., 1968-74; writer Arts Mag., N.Y.C., 1972-75, Art in Am., N.Y.C., 1974-75. Vis. artist many schs. including Hartwick Coll., Oneonta, N.Y., 1976, Art Inst., Chgo., 1974; guest artist Nat. Endowment Workshop, Tyler Sch. Art, Phila., Mpls. Acad. Art and Design, 1981; adj. lectr. La Guardia C.C., CUNY, 1992—; adj. prof. L.I. U., 1988—; writer, speaker A.I.R. Gallery, N.Y.C., 1972-74. Translator: Pontormo's Diary 1983; author: Swatches, 1969, Surroundings, 1977. Grantee numerous orgns. including NEA, CAPS, 1976—. Democrat. Home: 55 Leonard St New York NY 10013-2928

MAYER, SUSAN, telecommunications company executive; b. Providence, Feb. 15, 1950; d. Frederick Augustus and Margaret Patience (Elvin) Cluck; m. James Douglas Mayer, Sept. 4, 1976; children: Catherine Paige, Julia Christina. BA, Boston U., 1971; MBA, Harvard U., 1979. Social worker Mass. Dept. Pub. Welfare, Boston, 1973-75, project mgr., 1975-77; cons. Boston Cons. Group, Boston, Munich, 1979-83, mgr., 1983-86; v.p. Communications Satellite Corp., Washington, 1986-91; gen. mgr. Comsat Video Svcs., 1988-90; cons., 1991-93; sr. v.p. MCI Comms. Corp., 1993—; pres. Sky MCI, 1996-97, MCI WorldCom Venture Fund, 1998—. Bd. dirs. Caliber Learning Network, Inc., Rhythms NetConnections, Inc., STG, Inc., WAM!NET, Inc., Sta. WETA, Channel 26. Active Connelly Sch. of the Holy Child. Mem.: Harvard (Boston). Home: 12429 Rivers Edge Dr Potomac MD 20854-1069 Office: MCI WorldCom Venture Fund 1133 19th St NW Washington DC 20036-3604

MAYER, SUSAN LEE, nurse, educator; b. N.Y.C., Feb. 10, 1946; d. Hans and Frieda (Schein) Abramson; m. Steven Mayer, June 24, 1973; children: Jason, Stuart, Richard, Deborah. BSN, Hunter Coll., 1968; MA, NYU, 1974; EdD, Columbia U., 1996; postgrad., Yeshiva U., 1986, Adelphi U., 1987. RN, N.Y.; cert. in gerontology; cert. tchr., N.Y. Staff nurse ICU-CCU Montefiore Hosp., Bronx, N.Y., 1968; organizer CCU Jewish Meml. Hosp., N.Y.C., 1968; supr., adminstr. Morrisania City Hosp., N.Y.C., 1969-76; instr. Adelphi U., Garden City, N.Y., 1977-78; substitute nurse Great Neck (N.Y.) Pub. Schs., 1980-90; rsch. asst. to dean Adelphi U. Sch. Nursing, 1987-88; dir. ambulatory edn. North Bronx Healthcare Network, 2001—. Staff nurse Winthrop U. Hosp., Mineola, NY, 1987—90, per diem nurse, 1987—90; instr. dept. nursing edn. Bronx Mcpl. Hosp. Ctr. (now Jacobi Med. Ctr.), 1990—96; asst. prof. Helene Fuld Coll. Nursing, 1996—2001; adj. instr. Bronx C.C., 1992, Queensborough C.C., 1987—89; adj. asst. prof. Iona Coll. Sch. Nursing; adj. assoc. prof. Tchrs. Coll./Columbia U., 1997—; field nurse coord. RN Home Care Winthrop U. Hosp., Mineola, 1996—2001; lectr. and presenter in field. Contbr. articles to profl. jours. including Nursing and Health Care. Bd. dirs. Great Neck Synagogue, 1981-91, v.p. Sisterhood, 1978-79, pres., 1979-81; former bd. dirs. Russell Gardens Assn.; founder Work for Share Zedek Hosp., 1977—; past pres., fin. sec. L'Chaim chpt. Hadassah Nurse Coun. N.Y. State Regents scholar, 1963. Mem. ANA, Assn. Orthodox Jewish Scientists, Am. Assn. Ambulatory Care Nurses, N.Y. Counties Registered Nurses Assn., N.Y. State Nurses Assn. (dist. 13 bd. dirs., past chmn. nurse practice com., past treas., past chair coun. ethical practice), Am. Assn. for History of Nursing, Nurses Edn. Alumni Assn. (past historian), Sigma Theta Tau, Kappa Delta Pi. Democrat. Home: 28 Laurel Dr Great Neck NY 11021-2827 Office Phone: 718-515-1438. E-mail: sm192@columbia.edu., susan.mayer@nbhn.net.

MAYER, SUSAN MARTIN, art educator; b. Atlanta, Oct. 25, 1931; d. Paul McKeen and Ione (Garrett) Martin; m. Arthur James Mayer, Aug. 9, 1953; 1 child, Melinda Marilyn. Student, Am. U., 1949-50; BA, U. N.C., Greensboro, 1953; postgrad., U. Del., 1956-58; MA, Ariz. State U., 1966. Artist-in-residence Armed Forces Staff Coll., Norfolk, Va., 1968-69; mem. art faculty U. Tex., Austin, 1971—2003. Co-editor: Museum Education: History, Theory and Practice, 1989; author various mus. publs.; contbr. articles to profl. jours. Recipient award Austin Ind. Sch. Bd., 1985. Mem. Nat. Art Edn. Assn. (bd. dirs. 1983-87, award 1987, 91), Tex. Art Edn. Assn. (mus. edn. chair 1982-83, Mus. Educator of Yr. 1986), Tex. Assn. Mus. (mus. edn. chair), Austin Visual Arts Assn., Am. Assn. Mus.

MAYER, VICTOR JAMES, geologist, educator; b. Mayville, Wis., Mar. 25, 1933; s. Victor Charles and Phyllis (Bachhuber) M.; m. Mary Jo Anne White, Nov. 25, 1965; children: Gregory, Maribeth. BS in Geology, U. Wis., 1956; MS in Geology, U. Colo., 1960, PhD in Sci. Edn., 1966. Tchr. Colo. Pub. Schs., 1961-65; asst. prof. SUNY Coll., Oneonta, 1965-67, Ohio State U., Columbus, 1967-70, assoc. prof., 1970-75, prof. ednl. studies, geol. scis. and natural resources, 1975-95, prof. emeritus, 1995—. Co-organizer symposa at 29th and 31st Internat. Geol. Congresses; internat. sci. edn. assistance to individuals and orgns. in Japan, Korea, Taiwan, Russia, and Venezuela; dir. NSF Insts., program for leadership Earth Sys. Edn., 1990-95; dir. Korean Sci. Tchrs. Insts., 1986-88, 95; keynote spkr. U.S.A. rep. Internat. Conf. on Geoscis. Edn., Southampton, Eng., 1993; co-convenor Second Internat. conf. on Geosci. Edn., Hilo, Hawaii, 1997; disting. vis. prof. SUNY, Plattsburg, 1994; vis. rsch. scholar Hyogo U., Japan, 1996; sr. Fulbright rschr. Shizuoka U., Japan, 1998; vis. prof. Korea Nat. U. of Edn., 2000; Fulbright prof. Pusan Nat. U. Korea, 2003-04. Contbr. articles to profl. jours. Served with USAR. Recipient Lifetime Disting. Svc. award to the Internat. Earth Sci. Edn. Cmty., 1997; named Disting. Investigator Ohio Sea Grant Program, 1983. Fellow AAAS (chmn. edn. 1988-89), Ohio Acad. Sci. (v.p. 1978-79, exec. com. 1993-94, outstanding univ. educator 1995); mem. NSTA (bd. dirs. 1984-86), Sci. Edn. Coun. Ohio (pres. 1987-88), Sigma Xi, Phi Delta Kappa. Roman Catholic. Avocation: photography. Home: 8483 Sand Dollar Dr Windsor CO 80528 Office: Ohio State U Dept Geol Scis 125 S Oval Mall Columbus OH 43210-1308 E-mail: mayer.4@osu.edu.

MAYER, WILLIAM EMILIO, investor; b. N.Y.C., May 7, 1940; s. Emilio and Marie Mayer; m. Katherine Mayer, May 16, 1964; children: Kristen Elizabeth, William Franz. BS, U. Md., 1966, MBA, 1967. Pres., CEO First Boston Corp., N.Y.C., 1967-91; dean Coll. Bus. and Mgmt. U. Md., College Park, 1992-96; ptnr. Devel. Capital, 1996-99, Park Ave. Equity Ptnrs., 1999—. Bd. dirs. First Health Group Corp., Lee Enterprises, Inc., Columbia Fund Group, Sunrise Med., Inc., Readers Digest Corp. Trustee U. Md.; chmn. Aspen Inst. 1st lt. USAF, 1961—65. Mem. Annapolis Yacht Club, Manhasset Bay Club (N.Y.), Univ. Club (N.Y.C.), Mashomack Fish & Game Club, Met. Club (Washington). Home: 172 Long Neck Point Rd Darien CT 06820-5816 Office: 399 Park Ave Ste 3204 New York NY 10022-1606

MAYERI, BEVERLY, artist, ceramic sculptor, educator; b. N.Y.C., Nov. 2, 1944; d. Bernard and Cora (Wisoff) Howard; m. Earl Melchior Mayeri, Sept. 1, 1968; 1 child, Rachel Theresa. BA, U. Calif., Berkeley, 1967; MA in Art and Sculpture, San Francisco State U., 1976. Tchr. Foothill Coll., Los Altos Hills, 1990, Natsoulas Gallery, 1992, U. Minn., Mpls., 1993, Sonoma State U., Rohnert Park, Calif., 1994, Mendocino (Calif.) Art Ctr., 1995, Fresno State U., 1996, CCAC, Oakland, Calif., 1996, Edinboro (Pa.) U., 1997, Scropps Coll., Claremont, Clif., 1999, Cuesta Coll., San Luis Obispo, Calif., 2001, San Diego State U., 2002. Artist: solo exhibitions include Palo Alto (Calif.) Cultural Ctr., 1979, Ivory/Kimpton Gallery, San Francisco, 1981, 83, Garth Clark Gallery, N.Y., 1985, 87, Esther Saks Gallery, Chgo., 1988, 90, Dorothy Weiss Gallery, San Francisco, 1990, 92, 94, 96, 98, 2000, San Jose Inst. Contemporary Art, 1990, Robert Kidd Gallery, Birmingham, Mich., 1993, Perimeter Gallery, Chgo., 1998, Susan Cummins Callery, Mill Valley, Calif., 2002; group exhibitions include San Francisco Mus. of Art, Northern Calif. Clay Routes: Sculpture Now, 1979, Smithsonian Instn., Renwick Gallery, 1981, Prieto Meml. Gallery, Mills Coll., Oakland, Calif. 1982, Crocker Art Mus., San Francisco, 1983, Euphrate Gallery, De Anza Coll., Cupertino, Calif., 1984, 88, Fisher Gallery, U. So. Calif., L.A., traveled to Pratt Inst., N.Y.C., 1984, Arts Commn. Gallery, San Francisco, 1984, Signet Arts Gallery, St. Louis (two person show), 1984, Garth Clark Gallery, N.Y., 1985, Robert L. Kidd Gallery, Birmingham, Mich., Animals Contemporary Vision, Major Concepts: Clay, 1986, Fresno (Calif.) Arts Ctr. and Mus., 1987, Canton (Ohio) Art Inst., 1991, Soc. for Contemporary Crafts, Pitts., 1992, Triton Mus. of Art, Santa Clara, Calif., 1992, Nat. Mus. of History Taipei, Taiwan, 1993, Lew Allen Gallery, Santa Fe, New Mex., 1993, Perimeter Gallery, 1995, Duane Reed Gallery, St. Louis, 1997, Scripps Coll., 1999, LACMA, L.A., 2000, Calif. State U., Chico, 2001, Clay Studio, Phila., 2001; works in pub. and private collections include: Nat. Mus. History, Taipei, Canton Art Inst., Long Beach (Calif.) Parks and Recreation, L.A. Arts Commn., Mr. and Mrs. Eric Lidow, L.A., Alfred Shands, Louisville, Mrs. Audrey Landy, Atlanta, Karen Johnson Boyd, Racine, Wis., Alan and Esther Saks, Chgo., Gloria and Sonny Kamm, L.A. County Mus. Art. Founder Marin Women Artists, Marin County, Calif., 1974-84. Recipient fellowship visual artist NEA, Washington, 1982, 88; grantee: Marin Arts Coun., 1987, Virgina A. Groot Found., 1991. Avocations: painting, hiking, skiing, gardening, environmentalist. Office: Dorothy Weiss Gallery 3 Indian Gulch Rd Piedmont CA 94611-3527

MAYERS, DANIEL KRIEGSMAN, lawyer; b. Scarsdale, N.Y., July 10, 1934; s. Chauncey Maurice and Helen P. (Kriegsman) M.; m. Karen E. Silverman, Sept. 30, 1956, children: Peter D., Leslie H. Shroyer. AB, Harvard U., 1955, LLB, 1960. Bar: D.C. 1961, U.S. Supreme Ct. 1961. Law clk. to Justice Felix Frankfurter, U.S. Supreme Ct., Washington, 1960-61; spl. asst. U.S. Dept. Justice, Washington, 1961-62; assoc. Wilmer Cutler & Pickering, Washington, 1962-65, ptnr., 1967-99, of counsel, 2000—; exec. asst. to undersec. U.S. State Dept., Washington, 1965-66. Vis. com. Harvard Law Sch., Cambridge, Mass., 1982-89, chmn., 1986-89; chmn. Legal Action Ctr., N.Y.C., 1998—, Washington Ednl. TV Assn., 1993-97, Survivors Fund for Pentagon Victims, 2001--; bd. dirs. Hypres Corp., Netscan, Inc. Pres. Nat. Symphony Orch., Washington, 1987-89; chmn. Sidwell Friends Sch., Washington, 1979-81; mem. Ams. for Peace Now, 1991—, Fed. City Coun., Washington, 1981—; trustee Cmty. Found. for Nat. Capital Area, 1997—; counsel, dir. Ctr. for Nat. Policy, Washington, 1984-93. With U.S. Army, 1955-57. Recipient Sears prize Harvard Law Sch., 1959 Mem. ABA, Met. Club, Burning Tree Woodstock Country Club. Democrat. Jewish. Avocations: tennis; fishing. Home: 3222 Woodland Dr NW Washington DC 20008-3547 Office: Wilmer Cutler & Pickering 2445 M St NW Washington DC 20037-1487

MAYERS, EUGENE DAVID, retired philosopher, educator; b. N.Y.C., July 30, 1915; s. Sylvester and Estelle (Weinstein) M.; m. Odette Julia Marguerite Gilchriest, Dec. 30, 1950; children: David Allan, Marilyn Anne, Judith Odette, Peter Michael. AB, Yale U., 1936, LLB, 1940; PhD, Columbia U., 1956. Bar: N.Y. State bar 1941. With Nat. Bur. Econ. Research, N.Y.C., 1941, Office Gen. Counsel, Navy Dept., 1946; mem. faculty Carleton Coll., Northfield, Minn., 1950-61, Columbia, 1959-60, Mills Coll., Oakland, Calif., 1961-63; prof. philosophy Calif. State U., Hayward, 1963-92, prof. emeritus, 1992—, chmn. dept. philosophy, 1963-73, acting head div. humanities, 1966-67. Adj. prof. Calif. State U., 1996-97. Author: Some Modern Theories of Natural Law, 1957; Contbr. articles to profl. jours. Served to capt. (field artillery) AUS, 1941-46, 51-52; lt. col. judge adv. gen. USAR ret. Fellow Soc. Values in Higher Edn.; mem. AAUP, Am. Philos. Assn. (chmn. conf. dept. chmn. Pacific divsn. 1973-75, Pacific divsn. exec. com. 1976-80, chmn. exec. com. 1978-80), Am. Soc. Polit. and Legal Philosophy, Pacific Coast Theol. Soc. (sec. 1984-86), Internat. Assn. Philosophy Law and Social Philosophy, Am. Acad. Religion, Soc. Advancement Am. Philosophy, Soc. Study Process Philosophies (Pacific Coast rep. 1987-97, jurisprudence 3d internat. Whitehead conf. 1998). Home: 3191 Frye St Oakland CA 94602-4040 Fax: 510-336-0514. E-mail: edmayers@ix.netcom.com.

MAYERS, STANLEY PENROSE, JR., public health educator; b. Phila., Nov. 9, 1926; s. Stanley Penrose and Margaret Amelia (Thorpe) M.; m. Virginia Lee Lytle, Aug. 25, 1951 (dec. Oct. 1990); children: Douglas Lytle, Kenneth Stanley, Daniel John, Andrew William; m. Patricia Ann Harne Hulsey, Mar. 6, 1993. BA, U. Pa., 1949, MD, 1953; MPH, Johns Hopkins U., 1958. Diplomate Am. Bd. Preventive Medicine. Intern Phila. Gen. Hosp., 1953-54; resident Arlington County Health Dept., Va., 1954-55; health dir. Henry-Martinsville-Patrick Health Dist., Martinsville, Va., 1955-57; regional dir. Va. State Health Dept., Richmond, 1958-59; dist. state health officer N.J. State Dept. of Health, Trenton, 1959-62; asst. prof. and asst. dean Johns Hopkins Sch. Hygiene and Pub. Health, Balt., 1962-65; dir. Arlington County Dept. of Human Resources, Arlington, Va., 1965-71; prof. health policy and adminstrn. Pa. State U., University Park, 1971-97, prof. emeritus, 1997—, chmn., 1979-88, assoc. dean undergrad. studies Coll. Health and Human Devel., 1989-92, assoc. dean acad. studies Coll. Health and Human Devel., 1992-95, assoc. dean emeritus, 1997—. Interim dir. internat. edn. programs and studies Pa. State U., 2000-2001; faculty assoc. Johns Hopkins U. Sch. Hygiene and Pub. Health, Balt., 1965-75; clin. assoc. prof. Georgetown U. Sch. Medicine, Washington, 1965-71; cons. VA, 1985—. Contbr. articles to profl. jours. Pres. Arlington Optimist Club, 1970-71; bd. dirs. Centre County Family Planning Svcs., Bellefonte, Pa., 1972-79. With USN, 1945-46. Recipient Outstanding Achievement award Dept. Community Medicine, Georgetown U. Sch. Medicine, 1968, Saubel award Coll. of Human Devel., Pa. State U., 1985, Pioneer Achievement award Frankford H.S., Phila., 1999. Fellow Am. Coll. Preventive Med., APHA (chmn. membership com. health officer's sect. 1968-70, mem. nominating com. health adminstrn. sect. 1970-72, chmn. com. to draft a statement on local health agy. responsibilities 1973-74); mem. AMA, Arlington County Med. Soc. (Wellborn award 1971), Centre County Med. Soc. (pres. 1978), Med. Soc. Va., Met. Washington Health Officers Assn. (sec. 1967-71), Am. Assn. Pub. Health Physicians (pres. Va. chpt. 1970-71), Pa. Med. Soc. (mem. Ho. of Dels. for Centre County 1974-76, 81-97, treas. 1973-74, 85—, sec. 1974-76, v.p. 1976, pres. elect 1977, pres. 1978), Mt. Nittany Soc., Univ. Club (State College, Pa.), Phi Beta Kappa. Episcopalian. Avocations: fishing, boating, hiking. Home: 648 Wiltshire Dr State College PA 16803-1450 Office: Pa State U Human Devel Bldg Rm 115 University Park PA 16802 E-mail: spm1@psu.edu. *Never attempt to promote something or someone that you do not believe in yourself.*

MAYERSOHN, NETTIE, state legislator; m. Ronald Mayersohn; children: Jeffrey, Lee. BA, Queens Coll., 1978. Exec. dir. N.Y. State Crime Victims Bd.; mem. N.Y. State Assembly, 1982—, chairperson assembly ho. ops. com., mem. legis. women's caucus, mem. various coms. Dist. leader 27th N.Y. State Assembly Dist.-Part A, 1972—. Past mem. Cmty. Bd. # 8, former chairperson youth com.; past chairperson Pomonok Cmty. Ctr.; founder, organizer Pomonok Neighborhood Ctr., Inc.; active Electchester Jewish Ctr., Israel Ctr. of Hillcrest Manor; N.Y. state del. Internat. Women's Conf., 1977; bd. dirs. Harry Van Arsdale, Jr. Meml. Assn. Recipient Builders of Brotherhood award Nat. Conf. Christians and Jews, 1977, Legislator of Yr. award N.Y. State chpt. NOW, 1989. Mem. Stevenson Regular Dem. Club, Inc. (exec. mem.), Alpha Sigma Lambda. Home: 67-11 Parsons Blvd Flushing NY 11365-2961 Office: NY State Assembly State Capitol Albany NY 12224

MAYERSON, HY, lawyer; b. Phila., June 29, 1937; s. Henry and Gertrude Mayerson; m. June 13, 1964 (div. 1973); children: Merrie Joy, Benjamin, Erin Megan, Stephnie Dawn; m. Colleen Koos. BS, Temple U., 1958, JD, 1961. Bar: Pa. 1961, Phila. Ct. Common Pleas 1962, Pa. Supreme Ct. 1968, U.S. Ct. Appeals (3d cir.) 1980, U.S. Ct. Appeals (4th cir.) 1986, U.S. Dist. Ct. (ea. dist.) Pa. Pvt. practice, Phila., 1961-65; sr. ptnr. Hy Mayerson Law Offices, 1965-81, Mayerson, Schniper & Gerasimowicz, Spring City, Pa., 1981-87, Mayerson, Gerasimowicz & Munsing, Spring City, 1987-91, Mayerson, Munsing, Corchin & Rosato, P.C., Spring City, 1991-95; pvt. practice The Mayerson Law Offices, P.C., Spring City, 1995—. Coord. Nat. Forklift Litigation, 1978-91; lead counsel Agent Orange Product Liability Litigation. Contbr. articles to profl. jours. Mem. ATLA (emeritus chair sect. on Indsl. & Agrl. Eqipment, Product Liability adv.bd.), Pa. Trial Lawyers Assn. Home: Sky Farm Birchrunville PA 19421 Office: Rt 724 Spring City PA 19475 E-mail: hy@mayerson.com.

MAYERSON, PHILIP, classics educator; b. N.Y.C., May 20, 1918; s. Theodore and Clara (Fader) M.; m. Joy Gottesman Ungerleider, Nov. 25, 1976 (dec. Sept. 9, 1995); children: Miriam Mayerson, Clare Mayerson. AB, NYU, 1947, PhD, 1956. With Puritan Fed. Clothing Stores, N.Y.C., 1935-42; instr. NYU, 1948-56, asst. prof., 1956-60, assoc. prof., 1960-66, prof. classics, 1966—, vice dean, 1969-71, acting dean, 1971-73, dean Washington Sq. and U. Coll. Arts and Scis., 1973-78. Author: The Ancient Agricultural Regime of Nessana and the Central Negeb, 1961, Classical Mythology in Literature, Art and Music, 1971, Monks, Martyrs, Soldiers and Saracens, 1994; contbr. articles in field of papyrology to profl. jours. Served with USN, 1942-45. Rockefeller Found. grantee, 1956-57; Am. Coun. of Learned Socs. fellow, 1961-62. Mem. Am. Philol. Assn., Am. Schs. of Oriental Rsch. Home: 720 Walton Ave Mamaroneck NY 10543-4437 Office: NYU Dept Classics 25 Waverly Pl New York NY 10003

MAYERSON, SANDRA ELAINE, lawyer; b. Dayton, Ohio, Feb. 8, 1952; d. Manuel David and Florence Louise (Tepper) M.; m. Scott Burns, May 29, 1977 (div. Oct. 1978); 1 child, Katy Joy. BA cum laude, Yale U., 1973; JD, Northwestern U., 1976. Bar: Ill. 1976, N.Y. 1997, U.S. Ct. Appeals (7th cir.) 1976, U.S. Dist. Ct. (no. dist.) Ill. 1977, U.S. Dist. Ct. Md. 1989, U.S. Ct. Appeals (5th cir.) 1994, U.S. Dist. Ct. (so. and ea. dists.) N.Y. 1997, U.S. Ct. Appeals (2nd Cir.) 1997, U.S. Dist. Ct. (ea. dist.) Mich. 2000. Assoc. gen. counsel JMB Realty Corp., Chgo., 1979-80; assoc. Chatz, Sugarman, Abrams et al, Chgo., 1980-81; ptnr. Pollack, Mayerson & Berman, Chgo., 1981-83; dep. gen. counsel AM Internat., Inc., Chgo., 1983-85; ptnr. Kirkland & Ellis, Chgo., 1985-87; ptnr., chmn. bankruptcy group Kelley Drye & Warren, N.Y.C., 1987-93; ptnr., chmn. N.Y. bankruptcy group McDermott, Will & Emery, N.Y.C., 1993-99; ptnr., bankruptcy nat. practice group leader Holland and Knight, N.Y.C., 1999—. Examiner Interco chpt. 11, 1991. Contbr. articles to profl. jours. Bd. dirs. Jr. Med. Rsch. Inst. coun. Michael Reese Hosp., Chgo., 1981-86, Self Help Inc., 2000-; met. divsn. Jewish Guild for Blind, 1990-92; nat. legal afffairs com. Anti-Defamation League, 1990-; lawyers' exec. com. United Jewish Appeal; chair Holland & Knight Nat. Bankruptcy & Creditors Rights Group, 2001-. Named one of Top 50 Women Litigators, Nat. Law Jour., 2001; assoc. fellow, Branford Coll., Yale U., 1993—. Mem. ABA (bus. bankruptcy com. 1976—, sec. 1990-93, chair avoiding powers subcom. 1993-96, chair claims trading subcom. 1997-2000, chair strategic planning subcom., 2000-), Ill. State Bar Assn. (governing council corp. and securities sect. 1983-86), Chgo. Bar Assn. (current events chmn. corp. sect. 1980-81), 7th Cir. Bar Assn., Yale Club (N.Y.C.). Democrat. Jewish. Office: Holland and Knight 195 Broadway Fl 24 New York NY 10007-3100

MAYES, ILA LAVERNE, minister; b. Eldorado, Okla., Dec. 23, 1934; d. Thomas Floyd and Irene Elizabeth (Buchanan) Jordan; m. Forrest Clay Mayes, July 2, 1954; children: Barbara, Marian, Cynthia, Janice. BA, U. Tex., El Paso,

1973; MSW, U. Mich., 1976; MDiv, Austin Presbyn. Sem., 1986. Ordained to ministry Presbyn. Ch. (U.S.A.), 1986; cert. social worker. Pastor First Presbyn. Ch., Childress, Tex., 1986-97; interim pastor Trinity Presbyn. Ch., Iowa Port, Tex., 1999—, First Presbyn. Ch., Iowa Port, 1999—; med./social worker Childress Regional Med. Ctr., 1996-97; parish assoc. Westminster Presbyn. Ch., Ann Arbor, Mich. Mem. Austin Sem. Alumni Bd., 1991-94, Synod of the Sun Evangelism Com., Denton, 1990-93, Transition Coordinating Agy., 1991-97 Chmn. ARC, Childress, 1990; bd. dirs. Am. Cancer Soc., Childress, 1988-89; vice moderator, Palo Duro Presbytery, 1996-98. Mem. AAUW, Mortarboard, Rotary Internat., Alpha Chi, Alpha Lambda Delta. Home and Office: Trlr 251 6655 Jackson Rd Ann Arbor MI 48103-9674 E-mail: ilamaz@comcast.net. *You and I live in a wonderful tension between the past and the future. As our Faith in God helps us to reinterpret the past and reshapes our future, we grow and change. I like that*

MAYES, MICHELE COLEMAN, lawyer; b. Los Angeles, Calif., July 9, 1949; BA, U. Mich., 1971, JD, 1974. Bar: Mich. 1974, U.S. Dist. Ct. 1974, Ea. Dist. of Mich. 1976, Ill. 1980, U.S. Supreme Ct. 1988, Pa. 1988. Adj. prof. Wayne State U., 1981—87; in-house counsel Colgate-Palmolive, 1992—2003; sr. v.p., gen. counsel Pitney Bowes Inc., 2003—. Mem.: ABA (mem. commn. on women in the profession 1992, co-chair, arbitration com. 1990—92). Office: Pitney Bowes Inc World Hdqs 1 Elmcroft Rd, Mail Stop MSC 6411 Stamford CT 06926-0700

MAYES, PAUL EUGENE, engineering educator, consultant; b. Frederick, Okla., Dec. 21, 1928; s. Robert Franklin and Bertha Ellen (Walter) M.; m. Lola Mae Davis, June 4, 1950; children: Gwynne Ellen, Linda Kay, Stuart Franklin, Patricia Gail, Steven Lee, David Thomas. BS in Elec. Engring., U. Okla., 1950; MS in Elec. Engring., Northwestern U., 1952, PhD, 1955. Rsch. asst. Northwestern U., Evanston, Ill., 1950-54; asst. prof. U. Ill., Urbana, 1954-58, assoc. prof., 1958-63, prof., 1963-93, prof. emeritus, 1994—. Tech. cons. Author: Electromagnetics for Engineers, 1965; contbr. articles to profl. jours.; inventor in field. Fellow IEEE. Avocations: woodworking, hiking, camping. Home: 1508 Waverly Dr Champaign IL 61821-5002 Office: U Ill 1406 W Green St Urbana IL 61801-2918

MAYES, WENDELL WISE, JR., former broadcasting company executive; b. San Antonio, Mar. 2, 1924; s. Wendell Wise and Dorothy Lydia (Evans) M.; m. Mary Jane King, May 11, 1946; children: Cathey, Sarah, Wendell Wise, III. Student, Schreiner Inst., 1941-42, U. Tex., 1942, Daniel Baker Coll., 1946; BS, Tex. Tech. Coll., 1949; BA summa cum laude, St. Edward's U., 2002. Program dir., sta. mgr. Sta. KBWD, Brownwood, Tex., 1949-57; mgr. Sta. KCRS, Midland, Tex., 1957-63, pres., 1965-84, chmn., 1984-96; pres. Sta. KNOW, Austin, Tex., 1970-81, Stas. KVIC and KAMG, Victoria, Tex., 1970-84, chmn., 1984-98, Sta. KCRS-FM, Midland, 1984-96; pres. Sta. KCSW, San Marcos, 1976-81; sec.-treas. Sta. KSNY-AM-FM, Snyder, 1952-94; mem. bd. mgrs. Sta. KLBJ/KHHT-AM-FM, Austin, 1991-97. Lectr. Coll. Communications, U. Tex., Austin, 1978-81 Chmn. bd. Am. Diabetes Assn., 1974—77; mem. Nat. Diabetes Adv. Bd., 1977—84; v.p. Internat. Diabetes Fedn., 1980—88, pres.-elect, 1988—91, pres., 1991—94, hon. pres., 1997 ; pres. Tex. Broadcast Edn. Found., 1973—76, dir., 2002—; mem. Tex. Diabetes Coun., 1983—86, chmn., 1983—86, exec. dir., 1999; bd. regents Tex. Tech U., 1985—91, chmn., 1987—88. With USNR, 1943—46. Recipient Addison B. Scoville award Am. Diabetes Assn., 1977, first Wendell Mayes Jr. award, 1986, Josiah K. Lilly award, 1991, Harold Rifkin award, 1994, Masaji Takeda medal Kobe, Japan Colloquium Med. Sci., 1994; named to Tex. Tech. Mass Comm. Hall of Fame, 1978, Hall of Fame Tex. affiliate Am. Diabetes Assn., 1994; named Disting. Alumnus Tex. Tech. U., 1981, Disting. Engr., 1985. Mem. Tex. Assn. Broadcasters (pres. 1964, named Pioneer Broadcaster of Year 1978), Nat. Assn. Broadcasters (dir. 1969-72), Am. Council on Edn. in Journalism (dir. 1977-80), Broadcast Edn. Assn. (dir. 1973-77), AP Broadcasters (bd. dirs. 1988-91), Tex. Tech. Elec. Engring. Acad. Episcopalian (vestryman 1966-69, 86-88; sr. warden 1988). Home: 2834 Montebello Rd Apt 1 Austin TX 78746-6820 Office: 1907 N Lamar Blvd Austin TX 78705-4992 Office Phone: 512-477-6866. E-mail: wmayes@swbell.net.

MAYEUX, RICHARD, hospital administrator, neurologist; b. New Orleans, 1946; MD, U. Okla., 1972. Diplomate Am. Bd. Psychiatry and Neurology. Intern Boston City Hosp., 1972—73, resident in internal medicine, 1973—74; resident in neurology Columbia Presbyn. Med. Ctr., N.Y.C., 1974—77; fellow in neurology Boston U., 1977—78; neurologist Sergievsky Ctr., N.Y.C.; staff neurologist Columbia Presbyn. Med. Ctr., N.Y.C.; prof. Columbia Coll. Physicians and Surgeons, N.Y.C.; dir. Taub Inst., N.Y.C. Mem.: ARNMD, ANA, Am. Acad. Neurology, Inst. of Medicine of NAS. Office: Sergievsky Ctr 630 W 168th St New York NY 10032-2603

MAYFIELD, JEREMY, race car driver; b. Owensboro, Ky., May 27, 1969; m. Shana Mayfield. Profl. race care driver NASCAR Winston Cup, 1993—. Raced go-karts, OWensboro, 1982—86. Named Rookie of Yr. and Most Improved Driver, Ky. Motor Speedway, 1986, Rookie of Yr., ARCA, 1993, winner, Pocono 500, 1998, NAPA Auto Parts 500, 2000. Office: Evernham Motorsports 320 Aviation Dr Statesville NC 28677 Address: PO Box 3998 Mooresville NC 28117

MAYFIELD, ROBERT CHARLES, university official, geography educator; b. Abilene, Tex., Oct. 15, 1928; s. Percy Anderson and Fay (Hicks) M.; m. Loraine Poindexter, Sept. 3, 1952; children: Julie Barnes, Jennifer Manley, Mark Stanley, Malcolm Randall. BA, Tex. Christian U., 1952; MS, Ind. U., 1953; PhD, U. Wash., 1961. Chmn. geography dept. Tex. Christian U., Ft. Worth, 1960-64, U. Tex., Austin, 1967-71, Boston U., 1972-77, acad. v.p. external programs, 1977-83, provost, 1979-84. Cons. Coun. for Econ. Action, Boston, 1980—; adj. prof. U. Tex., Austin, 1987—; lectr. U.S. Info. Svc., Bangladesh, 1994; seminar dir. U. Tex. Seminars for Adult Growth and Enrichment, 1995-2004; mem. faculty rev. bd. Bangladesh U. Engring. and Tech., Dacca, 1996—. Editor, contbg. author: Man, Environment and Space, 1972. With USAF, 1946-49. Rsch. fellow Nat. Acad. Sci. No. India, 1957-58, Fulbright-Hays fellow Office Edn., Bangalore, Mysore, India, 1966-67; Rsch. grant Agrl. Devel. Coun., 1968. Mem. Assn. Am. Geographers. E-mail: rmayfield@mail.utexas.edu.

MAYFIELD, RONALD KEITH, endocrinologist, educator; b. Morgantown, W.Va., July 15, 1950; s. Albert Keith and Mary Kathleen (Lemley) M.; m. Karen Elizabeth Gaspar, Dec. 27, 1970; children: Douglas Keith, Cortnie Anne. MD, W.Va. U., 1975. Diplomate Am. Bd. Internal Medicine (cert.), Am. Bd. Endocrinology and Metabolism. Intern W.Va. U. Sch. Medicine, Charleston Area Med. Ctr., 1975-76, resident internal medicine, 1976-78; fellow in endocrinology-metabolism and nutrition Med. U. S.C., Charleston, 1978-80, instr. medicine, 1980-81, asst. prof., 1981-86, asst. prof. lab. medicine, 1983-86, assoc. prof. medicine, pathology and lab. medicine, 1986-92, prof. medicine, pathology and lab. medicine, 1992—. Staff physician, 1980—; cons. in endocrinology Med. U. Hosp., Charleston VA Med. Ctr., Charleston Meml. Hosp.; dir. specialized diagnostic and therapeutic unit VA Med. Ctr., 1984—2000, chief of endocrinology, 1984—; assoc. dir. gen. clin. rsch. Med. Ctr. U. S.C., 1988—95, dir. fellowship tng. endocrinology, 1995—; bd. dir. Diabetes Initiative S.C. Contbr. articles to profl. jours. Recipient Spl. Emphasis Rsch. Career award NIH, 1980-85; bd. govs. scholar W.Va. U. Sch. Medicine, 1971-75, Mosby scholar, 1972, Health Scis. Developing scholar Med. U. S.C., 1988; named America's Top Physician, Consumer Rsch. Coun. Am., 2003. Fellow ACP; mem. Assn. Subspecialty Profs., Am. Diabetes Assn. (rsch.-rev. com. 1986-89, Outstanding Profl. Svc. award S.C. affiliate 1983, bd. dirs. S.C. affiliate 1981-88), Am. Fedn. Med. Rsch., So. Soc. for Clin. Investigation, Endocrine Soc., Assn. Program Dirs. in Endorrinology and Metabolism, Alpha Epsilon Delta. Republican. Home: 537 Rice Planters Ln Mount Pleasant SC 29464 Office: 96 Jonathin Lucas St Ste 816 CSB Charleston SC 29425-0001 Office Phone: 843-792-2529. E-mail: mayfielr@musc.edu.

MAYFORTH, LEE J. finance company executive, consultant; b. NYC, Feb. 11, 1915; s. Fredrick and Rose (Weip) Mayforth; m. Kathryn Khan, Apr. 14, 1946; 1 child, Leland. Degree in bus. adminstrn., Rutgers U., 1938; degree in mktg., NYU, 1961. Lic. ins. broker, NY. Acct. exec. Walter E. Heller & Co., NYC, 1961—67; CFO Air Express Internat., NYC, 1967—68; contr. Transamerica Comml. Corp., NYC, 1968—69; pres. Leasing Cons., Inc., NYC, 1969—72; fin. cons. Ingersoll Fin. Corp., Cliffwood Lake, NJ, 1972—73; pres. Varilease, Inc., NYC, 1973; dir. mktg. United Va. Factors, NYC, 1974—75; prs. Lee Mayforth Co, NYC, 1976—. Author: Leasing Manual, 1972, History, Procedures and Advantages of Factoring and Commercial Financing, 1974. With res. USAF, 1942—43. Avocation: antique weapons. Office: Lee Mayforth Co 1700 York Ave 9R New York NY 10128 Office Phone: 212-427-0919.

MAYGARDEN, JERRY LOUIS, health care foundation executive; b. Pensacola, Fla., Dec. 22, 1948; s. Louis Ameal and Jean (Saxon) Maygarden; m. Rhonda Delene Fosha, June 25, 1977; children: Louis Ameal III, Morgan Lora. AA in Liberal Arts, Pensacola Jr. Coll., 1972; BA in Communications Arts, U. West Fla., 1974, MA in Communication, 1975. V.p. U. West Fla., Pensacola, 1980-83; exec. v.p. Sacred Heart Found., Pensacola, 1983-89; pres. Bapt. Health Care Found., Pensacola, 1989—. Bd. dirs. Bank of Pensacola; mem. Fla. House of Reps., 1994—. City councilman Pensacola City Coun., 1985-92, mayor pro tem, 1989-91, mayor, 1991-94; bd. dirs. C. of C. Com. 100, Pensacola, 1989—. With USN, 1968-74, Viet Nam. Recipient George Washington Honor medal, Freedoms Found. of Valley Forge, 1992, Paul Harris fellow, Rotary Found Internat., 1993; named Cmty. Leader of Yr. C. of C., Pensacola, 1988, Outstanding Young Man Am. U.S. Jaycees, 1977, Nat. Soc. Fund Raising Execs., Assn. for Health Care Philanthropy, Rotary Internat. Mem. Fla. League Cities, Nat. League Cities, Nat. Soc. Fund Raising Execs., Assn. for Health Care Philanthropy, Rotary Internat. Democrat. Methodist. Avocations: tennis, sailing, hiking, biking, fishing. Office: Bapt Health Care Found PO Box 17500 Pensacola FL 32522-7500 Home: 516 E Zarragossa St Pensacola FL 32502-6155

MAYHAR, ARDATH FRANCES (FRANK CANNON), author; b. 1930; Ind. book cons., 1979—; dairyman, 1947-57; prin. East Tex. Bookstore, Nacogdoches, 1958-62; proofreader Capital Jour., Salem, Oreg., 1968-75; chicken farmer, 1976-78; proofreader Daily Sentinel, Nacogdoches, 1979-82; writer, 1982—; co-mgr. View From Orbit Bookstore, Nacogdoches, 1984—99; writing instr. Writer's Digest, 1982—. Author: How the Gods Wove in Kyrannon, 1979, The Seekers of Shar Nuhn, 1980, Soul Singer of Tyrnos, 1981, Warlock's Gift, 1982, Khi to Freedom, 1982, Runes of the Lyre, 1982, Golden Dream, 1983, Lords of the Triple Moons, 1983, Exile on Vlahil, 1984, The Saga of Grittel Sundotha, 1985, The World Ends in Hickory Hollow, 1985, Medicine Walk, 1985, Carrots and Miggle, 1986, The Wall, 1987, Makra Choria, 1987, Feud at Sweetwater Creek (as Frank Cannon), 1988, A Place of Silver Silence, 1988; (collaboration with Marylois Dunn) The Absolutely Perfect Horse, 1983; (collaboration with Ron Fortier) Trail of the Seahawks, 1987, Monkey Station, TSR, 1989; (as John Killdeer) Wild Country, The Untamed, Wilderness Rendezvous, Blood Kin, People of the Mesa, 1992, Island in the Lake, 1993, Towers of the Earth, 1994, Passage West, 1994, Far Horizons, 1994, Hunters of the Plains, 1995, (as Frances Hurst) High Mountain Winter, 1996, Riddles and Dreams, 2003, elec. and paperback edits., 2004. Home: 533 CR 486 Chireno TX 75937

MAYHEW, AUBREY, music industry executive; b. Washington, Oct. 2, 1927; s. Aubrey and Verna June (Hall) M.; m. Carol de Onis, May 10, 1962 (div. 1971); children: Lawrence Aubrey, Michael Aubrey, Parris Mitchell, Casey Aran. Student, Wilson Tchs. Coll., 1948. Dir. WWVA, Wheeling, W.Va., 1947-54, WCOP, Boston, 1954-56; asst. to pres. MGM Records, N.Y.C., 1957-58; v.p. mktg. Capitol Records, LA, 1958-60; prodr., dir. KCAM-TV Prodns., Nashville, 1981—. Pres., founder John F. Kennedy Meml. Ctr., 1968; authority on John F. Kennedy life and memorabilia. Author: (books) Commandants Marine Corps, 1953, World Tribute to John F. Kennedy, 1965; composer (music) Touch My Heart, 1966 (Broadcast Music, Inc. award, 1967); record producer, artist mgmt., 1947—; music pub., 1954—; developed careers numerous entertainers including Johnny Paycheck, Jeannie C. Riley, Bobby Helms. Served to cpl. U.S. Army Signal Corps, 1945-48. Named Govs. Aide, Nashville, 1978. Mem. Country Music Assn., Broadcast Music Inc., Manuscript Soc., N.Y. Numismatic Soc., Gospel Music Assn. Republican. Episcopalian. Avocations: collector, historian, author. Office: Amcorp Music Group 827 Meridian St Nashville TN 37207-5856

MAYHEW, DAVID RAYMOND, political science educator; b. Putnam, Conn., May 18, 1937; s. Raymond William and Jeanie (Nicholson) M. BA, Amherst Coll., 1958; PhD, Harvard U., 1964. Tchg. fellow Harvard U., 1961-63; from instr. to asst. prof. polit. sci. U. Mass., Amherst, 1963-67; vis. asst. prof. Amherst Coll., 1965-66; faculty Yale U., 1968-77, prof. polit. sci., 1977—, chmn. dept., 1979-82, Alfred Cowles prof. govt., 1982-98, Sterling prof. polit. sci., 1998—. Olin vis. prof. Am. govt. Nuffield Coll., Oxford (Eng.) U., 2000-01. Author: Party Loyalty Among Congressmen, 1966, Congress: The Electoral Connection, 1974 (Washington Monthly ann. polit. book award 1974), Placing Parties in American Politics, 1986, Divided We Govern, 1991, America's Congress, 2000, Electoral Realignments, 2002. Recipient Richard E. Neustadt prize 1992, James Madison award, 2002, Yale Grad. Student Mentor award, 2002, Samuel J. Eldersveld award, 2004; Woodrow Wilson fellow, 1958-59, vis. fellow Nuffield Coll., Oxford, 1978, Guggenheim fellow, 1978-79, Hoover Nat. fellow, 1978-79, Sherman Fairchild fellow, 1990-91, fellow Ctr. for Advanced Study in Behavioral Scis., 1995-96. Fellow Am. Acad. Arts and Scis.; mem. Am. Polit. Sci. Assn. (nat. council 1976-78, Congl. fellow 1967-68), So. Polit. Sci. Assn., New Eng. Polit. Sci. Assn. Home: 100 York St Apt 5C New Haven CT 06511-5611 Office: Yale U Polit Sci Dept Box 208301 New Haven CT 06520-8301 Office Phone: 203-432-5237. Business E-Mail: david.mayhew@yale.edu.

MAYHEW, ERIC GEORGE, medical researcher, educator; b. London, Eng., June 22, 1938; came to U.S., 1964; s. George James and Doris Ivy (Tipping) M.; m. Barbara Doe, Sept. 28, 1966 (div. 1976); 1 child, Miles; m. Karen Caruana, Apr. 1, 1978 (div. 1994); children: Ian, Andrea; m. Ludmila Khatchatrian, June 29, 1995. BS, U. London, 1960, MS, 1963, PhD, 1967, DSc, 1993. Rsch. asst. Chester Beatty Rsch. Inst., London, 1960—64; cancer rsch. scientist Roswell Pk. Meml. Inst., Buffalo, 1964—68, sr. cancer rsch. scientist, 1968—72, assoc. cancer rsch. scientist, 1979—83, dep. dir. exptl. pathology, 1988—93; prin. scientist The Liposome Co., Princeton, NJ, 1993—99, May Pharm Consulting, 2000—. Assoc. rsch. prof. SUNY, Buffalo, 1979-93; ad-hoc mem. NIH study sects., 1982-94; cons. to industry, 2000—; mem. sci. adv. bd. NeoPharm Inc. Editor jour. Selective Cancer Therapeutics, 1989-91; contbr. articles to Jour. Nat. Cancer Inst., Cancer Rsch. and many other profl. jours. Grantee NIH, Am. Heart Assn., and pvt. industry, 1972-93. Mem. Am. Assn. Cancer Rsch., N.Y. Acad. Sci. Achievements include development of liposomes for drug delivery and patents for new chemical entities and liposome delivery. Office: May Pharm Consulting 1782 S Seaview Ave Coupeville WA 98239 Personal E-mail: eailkmay@aol.com.

MAYHEW, KENNETH EDWIN, JR., transportation company executive; b. Shelby, N.C., Sept. 27, 1934; s. Kenneth Edwin and Evelyn Lee (Dellinger) M.; m. Frances Elaine Craft, Apr. 7, 1957; 1 dau., Catherine Lynn Prince. AB, Duke U., 1956. CPA, N.C. Sr. auditor Arthur Andersen & Co., Atlanta, 1956-58, 60-63; controller Trendline, Inc., Hickory, NC, 1963-66; with Carolina Freight Corp., Cherryville, 1966-93, treas., 1969-74; v.p. Carolina Freight Carriers Corp., Cherryville, 1971-72, exec. v.p., 1972-85, pres., COO, 1985-89, dir., 1968-93, chmn., pres., CEO, 1989-93. Pres., dir. Robo Auto Wash Shelby Inc., 1967-73, Robo Auto Wash Cherryville, Inc., 1968-73; dir. Cherryville Nat. Bank, Kenmar Bus. Group, Inc. Mem. Bus. Adv. Bd., Fuqua Sch. Bus., Duke U.; bd. dirs., vice-chmn. Gaston Meml. Hosp.; trustee Pfeiffer U. With AUS, 1958-60. Mem. AICPA, Am. Trucking Assn. (dir., v.p.), N.C. Trucking Assn. (dir., chmn.), Gaston County C. of C. (v.p. pub. affairs), Lions (pres. Cherryville 1972-73), Phi Beta Kappa, Omicron Delta Kappa, Phi Eta Sigma. Methodist. Home: 507 Spring St Cherryville NC 28021-3540

MAYHUE, RICHARD LEE, provost, dean, pastor, writer; b. Takoma Park, Md., Aug. 31, 1944; s. J. Richard Mayhue and Myrtle Lorraine (Hartsell) Lee; m. Lois Elaine Nettleingham, June 18, 1966; children: Lee, Wade. BS, Ohio State U., 1966; MDiv, Grace Theol. Seminary, Winona Lake, Ind., 1974, ThM, 1977, ThD, 1981. Ordained pastor. Asst. pastor Grace Brethren Ch. of Columbus (Ohio), 1975-77; asst. prof. New Testament and Greek, Grace Theol. Seminary, Winona Lake, 1977-80; assoc. pastor Grace Cmty. Ch., Sun Valley, Calif., 1980-84, 89—; sr. pastor Grace Brethren Ch., Long Beach, Calif., 1984-89; sr. v.p., dean, prof. systematic theology and pastoral mins. The Master's Seminary, Sun Valley, 1989—; sr. v.p., provost The Master's Coll., Santa Clarita, Calif., 2000—. Bd. dirs. Grace Theol. Sem., 1987-89. Author: (booklets) The Biblical Pattern for Divine Healing, 1979, 2002, Snatched Before the Storm, 1980, 2002, (books) Divine Healing Today, 1983, How to Interpret the Bible for Yourself, 1986, A Christian's Survival Guide, 1987, Unmasking Satan, 1988, (2d edit., 2001), Spiritual Intimacy, 1990, Spiritual Maturity, 1992, The Healing Promise, 1994, What Would Jesus Say About Your Church?, 1995, 2d edit., 2001, Fight the Good Fight, 1999, 1 and 2 Thessalonians, 1999, Seeking God, 2000, Practicing Proverbs, 2003; contbr., co-editor: Rediscovering Expository Preaching, 1992, Rediscovering Pastoral Ministry, 1994; contbr. A Festschrift In Honor of Homer A. Kent, 1991; contbr., assoc. editor MacArthur Study Bible, 1997; contbr.: The Master's Perspective on Difficult Texts, 1998, The Master's Perspective on Contemporary Issues, 1998, Tim LaHaye Prophecy Study Bible, 2000; contbr., co-editor: The Master's Perspective on Pastoral Ministry, 2002, The Master's Perspective on Biblical Prophecy, 2002; contbr., assoc. editor Think Biblically!, 2003; contbr. articles to profl. jours. Bd. dirs. Capitol Ministries, 1996—, Slavic Gospel Assn, 1993-2002; bd. elders Grace Cmty. Ch., 1989—; mem. bd. of ref. Coun. on Bibl. Manhood and Womanhood, 1991—. Recipient Bronze Star with Combat V USN, 1969. Mem. Evang. Theol. Soc., Nat. Fellowship Grace Brethren Ministers (pres. 1988), Far West Region Evang. Theol. Soc. (pres. 1995), Evang. Homiletics Soc. Avocations: n-gauge model railroading, U.S. stamp collecting. Office: The Master's Seminary 13248 Roscoe Blvd Sun Valley CA 91352-3739 also: The Master's Coll 21726 Placerita Canyon Rd Santa Clarita CA 91321-1200

MAYKA, STEPHEN PAUL, lawyer; b. Rochester, N.Y., Sept. 18, 1946; m. Judith Holley Aitkin, July 26, 1981; 4 children. BA, U. Mich., 1968; JD, Union U., 1973. Bar: N.Y. 1973, N.J. 1996, Pa. 1996, U.S. Dist. Ct. (we. dist.) N.Y. 1973, U.S. Supreme Ct. 1982, U.S. Dist. Ct. (ea. and so. dists.) N.Y. 1984, U.S. Ct. Appeals (2d cir.) 1984, U.S. Dist. Ct. (no. dist.) N.Y. 1985, U.S. Dist. Ct. (we. dist.) N.C. 1987, U.S. Dist. Ct. N.J. 1996, U.S. Dist. Ct. (ea. and we. dists.) Pa. 1996. Assoc. Nixon & Hargrave, Rochester, 1973-75; gen. counsel Cen. Trust Co., Rochester, 1975-78; ops. counsel GE Capital, Stamford, Conn., 1978-80; ptnr. Lacy, Katzen, Ryen & Mittleman, Rochester, 1980-97; nat. practice in creditors' rights and bankruptcy, 1985—. Mem.: NY Trial Lawyers Assn., NY State Bar Assn. Office: 111 Knollwood Dr Rochester NY 14618-3514

MAYLAND, KENNETH THEODORE, economist; b. Miami, Fla., Nov. 17, 1951; s. Herbert and Vera (Bob) M; m. Gail Fern Bassok, Apr. 14, 1984. BS, MIT, 1973; MS, U. Pa., 1976, PhD, 1979. Cons. economist Data Resources, Inc., Lexington, Mass., 1973; economist, then chief economist First Pa. Bank, Phila., 1973-89; sr. v.p., chief economist Soc. Nat. Bank, Cleve., 1989-94; sr. v.p., chief fin. economist Key Corp., Cleve., 1994-96, sr. v.p., chief economist, 1996-2000; pres. ClearView Econs., LLC, 2000—. Econs. instr., Chartered Fin. Aanalysts Assn., Phila, 1984—; econ. adv. com. Phila. Econ. Devel. Coalition, 1984-86; chmn. econ. adv. com. Pa. Bankers Assn., Harrisburg, 1982-84; mem. Gov.'s Econ. Adv. Com., Ohio, 1989—. Contbr. semi-monthly periodical Money Markets, 1981-85, quar. periodical Regional Report, 1980-89, EconViewpoint/KeyViewpoint biweekly periodical, 1989-2000, Regional Rev. quar. periodical, 1989-94, ClearView on the Economy, 2000—. Mem. curriculum adv. com. Widener U., 1986-89. Named 2d Best Forecaster for 2003, USA Today survey panel. Mem. Am. Bankers Assn. (econ. adv. com. 1990-93), Internat. Econ. Roundtable (vice chmn. 1987-88, chmn. 1988-90), Nat. Assn. Bus. Economists (New Face for the Eighties award 1979), Phila. Coun. Bus. Economists (pres. 1982-84), Cleve. Bus. Economist Club (sec.-treas. 1990-91, v.p. 1991-92, pres. 1992-93). Avocations: fishing, badminton, gardening, camping. Office: 3237 Fox Hollow Dr Cleveland OH 44124-5426 Office Phone: 216-595-9931.

MAYNARD, CATHERINE, medical researcher; BS, U. Manchester. Mgr. core transgenic svcs. Imperial Cancer Rsch. Fund, 1988-92; various positions most recently assoc. dir. Animal Rsch. Svcs. and Microembryology, 1992-96; assoc. dir. animal rsch. svcs. & microembryology Abgenix, Inc., Fremont, Calif., 1996-98, dir. ops., 1998—. Office: Abgenix Inc 7601 Dumbarton Cir Fremont CA 94555-3616

MAYNARD, CHARLES DOUGLAS, radiologist; b. Atlantic City, Sept. 11, 1934; m. Mary Anne Satterwhite; children: Charles D., Deanne, David. BS, Wake Forest U., 1955, MD, 1959. Diplomate Am. Bd. Radiology (trustee 1987-99, sec.-treas., v.p. 1992-94, pres. 1994-96, guest examiner). Intern U.S. Army Hosp., Honolulu, 1959—60; resident N.C. Baptist Hosp., 1963—66; dir. Nuclear Medicine Lab., 1966—77; asst. dean admissions Bowman Gray Sch. Medicine, 1966—71, asso. dean student affairs, 1971—75, prof. radiology, chmn. dept., 1977—2000. Mem. Am. Bd. Med. Specialists; acting dean Wake Forest U. Sch. Medicine, 2001—02. Author: Clinical Nuclear Medicine, 1969; mem. editl. bd.: Yearbook of Diagnostic Radiology, Contemporary Diagnostic Radiology. Mem. Leadership Winston-Salem, Triad Leadership Network; bd. dirs. Downtown Devel. Corp., 1995—2000, Winston-Salem Bus., Inc., 1995—99. Mem.: AMA, Greater Winston-Salem C. of C. (bd. dirs.), Acad. Radiology Rsch. (pres. 1999—2001), Soc. Chairmen Radiology Depts. (past pres.), Assn. Univ. Radiologists, Radiol. Soc. N.Am. Rsch. and Edn. Found. (chmn. bd. 1999), Radiol. Soc. N.Am. (pres. 1999—2000), Am. Coll. Radiology (past bd. chancellors, past chmn. commn. on nuc. medicine), Soc. Nuc. Medicine (past pres.). Office: Wake Forest U Sch Medicine Dept Radiology Medical Center Blvd Winston Salem NC 27157-1088 Business E-Mail: dmaynard@wfubmc.edu.

MAYNARD, ELLIOTT, state supreme court justice; b. Williamson, W.Va., Dec. 8, 1942; BS in Psychology, Fla. So. Coll., 1967; JD, W.Va. U., 1974. Judge W.Va. Cir. Ct. 30th Jud. Cir., 1982-97; justice W.Va. Supreme Ct. Appeals, Charleston, 1997—, chief justice, 2000. Prosecuting atty., Mingo County, 1976, 80. Mng. dir. Tug Valley C. of C., 1968-70; active Boy Scouts Am.; dist. chmn. Mingo-Pike Dist., Chief Cornstalk Dist.; bd. dirs. Buckskin Coun. With USAF, 1961-66. Recipient Silver Beaver award Boy Scouts Am. Office: State Capital State Ct Appeals Bldg 1 Rm E306 Charleston WV 25305

MAYNARD, JOHN RALPH, lawyer; b. Mar. 5, 1942; s. John R. and Frances Jane (Mitchell) Maynard Kendryk; m. Meridee J. Sagadin, Sept. 10, 1995; children: Bryce James, Pamela Ann. BA, U. Wash., 1964; JD, Calif. Western U., San Diego, 1972; LLM, Harvard U., 1973. Bar: Calif. 1972, Wis. 1973. Assoc. Whyte & Hirschboeck, Milw., 1973-78, Minahan & Peterson, Milw., 1979-91, Quarles & Brady, Milw., 1991-2000, Davis & Kuelthau, Milw., 2000—. Bd. dirs. Am. Heart Assn., 1979—82, Transitional Living Svcs., Inc., 1999—2003; pres. Milw. Chamber Orch., 2000—02; mem. Wis. Adv. Coun. to U.S. SBA, 1987—89; bd. dirs. Found. Internal Medicine Exchange, 2004—. Mem.: ABA, Milw. Yacht Club, Harvard Club (Wis.). Home: 809 E Lake Forest Ave Milwaukee WI 53217-5377 Office: Davis & Kuelthau 111 E Kilbourn Ste 1400 Milwaukee WI 53202 Office Phone: 414-225-1467.

MAYNARD, JOHN ROGERS, English educator; b. Williamsville, N.Y., Oct. 6, 1941; s. Atherton Rogers and Olive (Fisher) M.; m. Florence Michelson, July 1, 1967 (div. 1980); 1 child, Alex Stevens; m. Ursula Krammer, Oct. 17, 1992 (div. 1995). BA, Harvard U., 1963, PhD, 1970. Asst. prof. Harvard U., Cambridge, Mass., 1969-74, NYU, N.Y.C., 1974-76, assoc. prof., 1976-84, prof. English, 1984—, chmn. English dept., 1983-89. Chmn. Faculty Council NYU, 1983-84; vis. prof. U. Venice, Italy, 1991. Author: Brownings Youth, 1977 (Wilson prize 1977), Charlotte Bronte and Sexuality, 1984, Victorian Discourses on Sexuality and Religion, 1993, Browning Re-Viewed, 1998; editor: Literature and Sexuality, 1991-2004; series of books on sexuality and lit.; editor: (with Lockridge and Stone) Nineteenth Century Lives, 1989, (with Bloom) Shankman's Anne Thackeray Ritchie: Journals and Letters, (with Munich) Victorian Literature and Culture, 1991—. Organizer Concord Sq. Assn., Boston, 1972-74. NEH grantee, 1972-73; Guggenheim fellow, 1979-80. Mem. IAUPE, MLA, PEN, Browning Inst. (bd. dirs.), Signet

Soc., Fly Club, Andiron Club (pres. 1983-84), Brooklyn Heights Assn. Democrat. Avocation: bicycling. Office: NYU Dept of English 5th Fl 19 University Pl New York NY 10003-4556

MAYNARD, KENNETH IRWIN, medical educator, researcher; b. San Fernando, Trinidad, Jan. 17, 1963; Student, Howard U., 1982; BSc with honors, Univ. Coll., London, 1986, MSc, 1987, PhD, 1991. Cert. design and conduct of clin. trials. Postdoctoral rsch. assistantship Univ. Coll., London, 1991; postdoctoral rsch. fellow Stroke Rsch. Lab. Neurosurg. Svc. Mass. Gen. Hosp., Harvard Med. Sch., Boston, 1991—93, postdoctoral rsch. fellow neurophysiology lab. Neurosurg. Svc., 1993—97; tchg. fellow dept. neurobiology Harvard Med. Sch., Boston, 1992, instr. in surgery, 1995—98, asst. prof., 1998—2001; asst. neuroscientist Mass. Gen. Hosp., 1998—2001; section head, cerebrovascular disorders Aventis Pharms., Inc., 2000—. Ad hoc reviewer Jour. Vascular Rsch., 1991, Neurosci. Letters, 1995, Vision Rsch., 1996, Neurosurgery, 1998, others; presenter in field; tutor dept. of neurobiology, 1998—2000; asst. prof. surgery, 1998; steering com. Boston Area Neurosci. Group, 1998—2000; ad hoc reviewer Ministry of Health, Internal Grant Agy., Czech Republic, 1998; med. rsch. grant program Jewish Hosp. Found., 2000; cons. neurosurgery Mass. Gen. Hosp., 2001—02; lectr. Harvard U. Med. Sch., 2001—02. Contbr. articles to med. jours. including Neurosci. Letters, articles to med. jours. including Stroke, articles to med. jours. including Exptl. Neurology, articles to med. jours. including Jour. Neurol. Rsch. Mem. parish pastoral coun. St. Joseph's Cath. Ch., Boston, 1992—95, chmn. stewarship commn., 1997; advisor regional com. ctrl. region on stewardship Archdiocese of Boston, 1995—97. Recipient Travel fellowship for minority neuroscientists, Nat. Inst. Neurol. Disease and Stroke, 1995, travel award, FASEB MARC, 1998; scholar, Autumn Sch. Caen France, 1996, Tokyo, 1998. Fellow: Am. Heart Assn. (minority scientist devel. award 1996, nat. affiliate brain/stroke study sect. 1999—, stroke coun. 2002, minority affairs com.); mem.: AAAS, Internat. Soc. Cerebral Blood Flow and Metabolism (Young Scientist Bursary award 1993), Congress of Neurosurg. Surgeons, Am. Assn. Neurosurg. Surgeons (adj. assoc. mem. joint sect. on cerebrovascular surgery 1995), Soc. for Neurosci. (minority neurosci. fellowship program 2000—, minority edn., tng. and profl. advancement com. 2000—03, membership com. 2002, steering com.), N.Y. Acad. Sci., Am. Stroke Assn. (affiliate brain rsch. peer rev. group 1999—2003). Office: Aventis Pharm Inc Rte 202-206 JR-2-303A Bridgewater NJ 08807-0800 E-mail: Kenneth.Maynard@aventis.com.

MAYNARD, OLIVIA P. foundation administrator; m. S. Olof Karlstrom. BA, Geroge Washington U., 1959; MSW, U. Mich., 1971. Dir. Mich. Office Svcs. to Aging, 1983—90; tchr. Sch. Social Work U. Mich., Mich. State U.; tchr. Ctr. for Aging Edn. Lansing (Mich.) C.C.; pres. Mich. Prospect for Renewed Citizenship, Flint, Mich. Del. White House Conf. on Aging, 1995. Regent U. Mich., Ann Arbor; chmn. Mich. Dem. Party, 1973—82; candidate Lt. Gov. of Mich., 1990. Democrat. Office: Northbank Ctr Ste 406 432 N Saginaw St Flint MI 48502

MAYNARD, ROBERT HOWELL, retired lawyer; b. San Antonio, Feb. 15, 1938; s. William Simpson Sr. and Lillian Isabel (Tappan) M.; m. Joan Marie Pearson, Jan. 6, 1962; children: Gregory Scott, Patricia Kathryn, Alicia Joan, Elizabeth Simms. BA, Baylor U., 1959, LLB, 1961; LLM, Georgetown U., 1965. Bar: Tex. 1961, D.C. 1969, Ohio 1973. Trial atty. gen. litigation sect. lands div. U.S. Dept. Justice, Washington, 1964-65; spl. asst. to solicitor U.S. Dept. Interior, Washington, 1965-69; legis. asst. U.S. Senate, Washington, 1969-73; ptnr., dept. head Smith & Schnacke, Dayton, Ohio, 1973-83; dir. Ohio EPA, Columbus, Ohio, 1983-85; ptnr., environ. policy and strategy devel., tech. law Vorys, Sater, Seymour and Pease, Columbus, 1985-2000; ret., 2000; pres. Tappan Woods LLC, 2001—. Trustee Ohio Found. for Entrepreneurial Edn., Bus. Tech. Ctr., 1994-2000, Episcopal Cmty. Svcs. Found., 1990-96, Columbus Technology Coun., 1992-2001, Johnson's Island Preservation Soc. USNR, 1962-65. Episcopalian.

MAYNARD, TERRELL DENNIS, minister; b. Paducah, Ky., Dec. 10, 1944; s. Claude and Euda (Finley) M.; m. Mary Jacqueline Chappell, Sept. 3, 1965; children: Terrell Geoffrey, Christopher Dennis. BA, Bethel Coll., 1966; MDiv, Memphis Theol. Sem., 1969. Pastor Cumberland Presbyn. Ch., Searcy, Ark., 1969-72, Hohenwald, Tenn., 1972-76, Swan Cumberland Presbyn. Ch., Centerville, Tenn., 1972-76, Elliottsville Presbyn. Ch., Alabaster, Ala., 1976-94, 1st Cumberland Presbyn. Ch., Jackson, Tenn., 1994—2002, Clarksville (Tenn.) Cumberland Presbyn. Ch., 2002—. Pres. Bd. Christian Edn., Memphis, 1976-85; chair Gen. Assembly's Exec. Com., Memphis, 1987-93. Bd. dirs., pres. Shelby Emergency Assistance, Montevallo, Ala., 1990-94; bd. dirs. Developing Ala. Youth Found., Alabaster, 1989-94, Shelby County Hosp. Authority, Alabaster, 1993-94, Area Relief Ministry, Jackson, 1996-2002. Recipient Disting. Alumni award Bethel Coll., McKenzie, Tenn., 1992; named Outstanding Vol. Shelby County Chpt. ARC, Alabaster, 1989. Mem. Assn. Cumberland Presbyn. Ch. Educators. Presbyterian. Avocations: fishing, golf, huntung, reading, college basketball. Home: 154 Village Way Clarksville TN 37043 Office: Cumberland Presbyn Ch 1410 Golf Club Ln Clarksville TN 37040 Office Phone: 931-648-0817.

MAYNARD, VIRGINIA MADDEN, foundation administrator; b. New London, Conn., Jan. 29, 1924; d. Raymond and Edna Sarah (Madden) Maynard. BS, U. Conn., 1945; postgrad., Am. Inst. Banking, 1964-66, Cornell U., 1975. With Nat. City Bank (now Citibank), N.Y.C., 1954-79, asst. cashier, 1965-69, asst. v.p., 1969-74, v.p. internat. banking group, 1974-76, comptroller's div., 1976-79; v.p. First Women's Bank, N.Y.C., 1979-80; rep. Internat. Fedn. Univ. Women UN, 1982—2003. Rep. UN, 1997—; trustee fellowships endowment fund AAUW Ednl. Found., Washington, 1977—80, Va. Gildersleeve Internat. Fund Univ. Women, Inc., pres., 1987—93, bd. dirs., 1994—2000, Conf. Nongovtl. Orgns. Found., Inc., 1997—2004, treas., 1999—2004. Mem.: AAUW (fin. chmn. N.Y.C. br. 1976—79, bylaws chmn. 1979—83, adminstr. Meml. Fund 1983—92, 2000—, bd. dirs. 1992—94, 1996—99, Woman of Achievement 1976). Republican. Congregationalist. Home: 601 E 20th St New York NY 10010-7622

MAYNE, LUCILLE STRINGER, finance educator; b. Washington, June 6, 1924; d. Henry Edmond and Hattie Benham (Benson) Stringer; children: Patricia Anne, Christine Gail, Barbara Marie. BS, U. Md., 1946; MBA, Ohio State U., 1949; PhD, Northwestern U., 1966. Instr. fin. Utica Coll., 1949-50; lectr. fin. Roosevelt U., 1961-64, Pa. State U., 1965-66, asst. prof., 1966-69, assoc. prof., 1969-70; assoc. prof. banking and fin. Case-Western Res. U., 1971-76, prof., 1976-94, prof. emerita, 1994—, grad. dean Sch. Grad. Studies, 1980-84. Sr. economist, cons. FDIC, 1977-78; cons. Nat. Commn. Electronic Fund Transfer Sys., 1976; rsch. cons. Am. Bankers Assn., 1975, Fed. Res. Bank of Cleve., 1968-70, 73; cons. Pres.'s Commn. Fin. Structure and Regulation, 1971, staff economist, 1970-71; analytical statistician Air Materiel Command, Dayton, Ohio, 1950-52; asst. to promotion mgr. NBC, Washington, 1946-48; expert witness cases involving fin. instns. Assoc. editor: Jour. Money, Credit and Banking, 1980-83, Bus. Econs., 1980-85; contbr. articles to profl. jours. Vol. Cleve. Soc. for Blind, 1979-2004, Benjamin Rose Inst., 1995—; mem. policyholders nominating com. Tchrs. Ins. and Annuity Assn./Coll. Retirement Equities Fund, 1982-84, chair com., 1984; bd. dirs. Women's Cmty. Found., 1994-96. Grad. scholar Ohio State U., 1949; doctoral fellow Northwestern U., 1963-65. Mem. LWV (bd. dirs. Shaker Heights chpt. 1999--), Midwest Fin. Assn. (pres. 1991-92, bd. dirs. 1975-79, officer 1988-93), Phi Kappa Phi, Beta Gamma Sigma. Episcopalian. Home: 3723 Normandy Rd Cleveland OH 44120-5246 Office: Case Western Res U Weatherhead Sch Mgmt U Circle Cleveland OH 44106-7235 Office Phone: 216-368-2151. Business E-Mail: lucille.mayne@case.edu.

MAYNE, RICHARD, educator; b. Oxford, Eng., May 10, 1942; arrived in U.S., 1968, naturalized, 2002; s. Robert John and Dorothy Emma Mayne; m. Pauline Maynard Oakley, July 27, 1966; children: Rebecca, Lucy. BA, U. Oxford, 1964, MA, DPhil, U. Oxford, 1967. Assoc. U. Pa., Phila., 1971—72, asst. prof., 1972—74, U. Ala., Birmingham, 1974—78, assoc. prof., 1978—83, prof., 1983—. Contbg. author Arthritis and Allied Conditions: A Textbook of Rheumatology, 1996; editor: Structure and Function of Collagen Types, 1987. Recipient Merit award, Nat. Inst. Arthritis, Musculoskeletal and Skin Diseases, NIH, 1993—2003. Mem.: Am. Soc. for Cell Biology, Am. Soc. for Biochemistry and Molecular Biology. Achievements include research in osteoarthritis; retinal detachment; muscle development. Avocations: gardening, travel, literature. Office: U Ala Birmingham MCLM Box 55 1530 3rd Ave South Birmingham AL 35294-0005

MAYNE, WILEY EDWARD, lawyer; b. Sanborn, Iowa, Jan. 19, 1917; s. Earl W. and Gladys (Wiley) M.; m. Elizabeth Dodson, Jan. 5, 1942; children—Martha (Mrs. F.K. Smith), Wiley Edward, John. S.B. cum laude, Harvard, 1938; JD, State U. Iowa, 1941. Bar: Iowa 1941, US Supreme Ct. 1950. Practiced in Sioux City, 1946-66, 75—; mem. Shull, Marshall, Mayne, Marks & Vizintos, 1946-66, Mayne and Berenstein, 1975-87, Mayne & Mayne, 1988-99, Mayne, Marks and Madsen, Sioux City, 1999—. Spl. agt. FBI, 1941-43; Mem. 90th-93d Congresses, 6th Dist. Iowa; mem. judiciary com., agr. com. Commr. from Iowa Nat. Conf. Commrs. Uniform State Laws, 1956-60; chmn. grievance commn. Iowa Supreme Ct., 1964-66; del. FAO, 1973; chmn. Woodbury County Compensation Bd., 1975-80 Chmn. Midwest Rhodes Scholar Selection Com., 1964-66; pres. Sioux City Symphony Orch. Assn., 1947-54, Sioux City Concert Course, 1947-54; vice-chmn. Young Republican Nat. Fedn., 1948-50; bd. dirs. Iowa Bar Found., 1962-68. Lt. (j.g.) USNR, 1943-46. Fellow Am. Coll. Trial Lawyers; mem. ABA (ho. of dels. 1966-68), Iowa Bar Assn. (pres. 1963-64), Sioux City Bar Assn., Internat. Assn. Def. Counsel (exec. com. 1961-64), Harvard Club (N.Y.C.), Sioux City Country Club, Masons (Scottish Rite/33 deg.). Home: 2728 Jackson St Sioux City IA 51104 Office: Pioneer Bank Bldg 701 Pierce St Ste 405 Sioux City IA 51101 Fax: 712-252-1535. Office Phone: 712-252-3220. E-mail: jmayne@maynelaw.com.

MAYNES, CHARLES WILLIAM, foundation executive; b. Huron, S.D., Dec. 8, 1938; s. Charles William and Almira Rose (Summers) M.; m. Gretchen Schiele, July 17, 1965; children: Stacy Kathryn, Charles William. BA, Harvard U., 1960; MA, Oxford (Eng.) U., 1962. UN polit. affairs ofcl. Dept. State, Washington, 1962-65; chief monetary economist AID, Laos, 1965-67; econ. officer Am. Embassy, Moscow, 1968-70; sec. Carnegie Endowment Internat. Peace, 1971-76; sr. legis. asst. to Sen. Fred R. Harris, 1972; mem. issues Sargent Shriver's Vice-Presdl. campaign, 1972; mem. Carter-Mondale Transition team, 1976-77; asst. sec. for internat. orgn. affairs Dept. State, 1977-80; editor Fgn. Policy mag., 1980-97; mem. Clinton-Gore Transition team, 1992-93, 96-97; pres. Eurasia Found., Washington, 1997—. Mem. Coun. Fgn. Rels., Washington Inst. Fgn. Affairs, UN Assn., Overseas Devel. Coun., Nat. Acad. Pub. Adminstrn., Internat. Inst. Strategic Studies. Contbr. articles to profl. jours. Recipient Meritorious Service award Dept. State; congl. fellow Rep. F. Bradford Morse, 1971, Sen. Fred R. Harris, 1971; Rhodes scholar. Mem. Phi Beta Kappa. Democrat. Office: Eurasia Found 10th Fl 1350 Connecticut Ave NW Washington DC 20036-1722 Home: 3914 Leland St Chevy Chase MD 20815-5036 E-mail: bmaynes@eurasia.org.

MAYO, ALEX T., JR., lawyer; b. Portsmith, Va., Apr. 18, 1943; s. Alex T. and Margaret Jackson (Eaton) Mayo; m. Nancy Cattlett, June 26, 1965; children: A. Taylor, Nancy Ellen. BA, Princeton U., 1966; JD, T.C. Williams Sch. Law, 1970. Ptnr. Hofheimer, Nusbaum, McPhaul & Brenner, Norfolk, Va., 1970—82, Kaufman & Canoles, Norfolk, 1982—; lectr. legal medicine Ea. Va. Med. Sch., 1976—80; trustee Norfolk Acad., 1980—. Mem.: Va. State Bar Assn., So. Conf. Bar Pres., Nat. Conf. Bar Presidents, ABA, Mcpl. Fin. Commn., Portsmouth Area United Way, Elizabeth Manor Golf and Country (Portsmouth), Cedar Point, Town Point, Town Point, Harbor (Norfolk). Democrat. Presbyn. Office: McGuire Woods & Battle Sovran Center PO Box 3767 Norfolk VA 23514

MAYO, CAROLYN, marketing professional, public relations executive; BA in Journalism, La. State U. Pub. rels. mgr. Houston dist. J.C. Penny; pvt. practice; shareholer, pres. Vollmer, 2002—. Supporter arts orgns., Gulf Coast area. Named 1 of city's top 50 woman bus. owners. Mem.: Pub. Rels. Soc. Am. Counselor's Acad., Pub. Rels. Soc. Am. (accredited mem.). Office: 808 Travis Ste 501 Houston TX 77002-5706

MAYO, CLYDE CALVIN, psychologist, educator; b. Robstown, Tex., Feb. 2, 1940; s. Clyde Culberson and Velma (Oxford) Mayo; m. Jeanne Lynn McCain, Aug. 24, 1963; children: Brady Scott, Amber Camille. BA, Rice U., 1961; BS, U. Houston, 1964, PhD, 1972; MS, Trinity U., 1966. Lic. psychologist Tex., La. Mgmt. engr. LWFW, Inc., Houston, 1966-72, sr. cons., 1972-78, prin., 1978-81; ptnr. Mayo, Thompson, Bigby, Houston, 1981-83; founder Mgmt. and Pers. Systems, Houston, 1983—. Counselor Interface Counseling Ctr., Houston, 1976—79; dir. Mental Health HMO Group, 1985—87; instr. St. Thomas U., Houston, 1979—, U. Houston Downtown Sch., 1972, 2002—, U. Houston, Clear Lake, 1983—88, U. Houston-Ctrl. Campus, 1984—; dir. mgmt. devel. insts. U. Houston Woodlands and West Houston, 1986—91; adj. prof. U. Houston, 1991—. Author: LWFW Annual Survey of Manufacturers, 1966—81, Bi/Polar Inventory of Strengths, 1978. Coach, mgr. Meryerland Little League, 1974—78, So. Belles Softball, 1979—80, S.W. Colt Baseball, 1982—83, Friends of Fondren Libr. Rice U., 1988—; charter mem. Holocaust Mus. Mem.: APA, Houston Area Indsl. Orgnl. Psychologists (bd. dirs. 1989—92), Am. Psychol. Soc., Tex. Psychol. Assn., Houston Psychol. Assn. (membership dir. 1978, sec. 1984), Tex. Indsl. Orgnl. Psychologists (founder, bd. dirs. 1995—, pres. 1999—2002), Soc. Indsl. Orgn. Psychologists, Found. Contemporary Theology, Meyerland Club (bd. dirs. 1988—92, pres. 1991), Forum Club. Home: 8723 Ferris Dr Houston TX 77096-1409 Office: Mgmt and Personnel Systems 4545 Bissonnet St Bellaire TX 77401-3121 Office Phone: 713-667-9251. Personal E-mail: mpsmayo@aol.com.

MAYO, DANA WALKER, chemistry professor; b. Bethlehem, Pa., July 20, 1928; s. Dana Harrat Nickerson and Ethel Marie (Chapman) M.; m. Odile Jeanne d'Arc Mailhiot, Jan. 12, 1962; children: Dana Lawrence, Chapman Scott, Sara Walker. BS, MIT, 1952; PhD, Ind. U., 1959. Asst. prof. chemistry Bowdoin Coll., Brunswick, Maine, 1962-65, assoc. prof. chemistry, 1965-68, prof. chemistry, 1969-70, Charles Weston Pickard prof. chemistry, 1970-91, Charles Weston Pickard rsch. prof. chemistry, 1991—. Pres. Microscale Organic Lab. Co., New Castle., N.H., 1985—. Author: Microscale Organic Laboratory, 1986, 2d edit., 1989, 3d. edit., 1994, 4th edit., 2000, Microscale Techniques for the Organic Laboratory, 1991, 2d edit., 2001, Course Notes on the Interpretation of Infrared and Raman Spectra, 2004; patentee microscale spinning band distillation column. Capt. USAF, 1956-61. Fellow MIT, 1959-62; recipient Charles A. Dana Found. award, N.Y.C., 1986, John A. Timm award New Eng. Assn. Chemistry Tchrs., 1987, Catalyst nat. award Chem. Mfr. Assn., Washington, 1989. Fellow AAAS, mem. Nat. Inst. Chemists (cert.), Am. Chem. Soc. (health and safety award 1987, James Flack Norris award New Eng. sect. 1988, chair Maine sect. 1971-72), Soc. Applied Spectroscopy, Coblentz Soc. (bd. dirs. 1977-79). Avocations: book collecting, genealogical research, forest management, swimming.

MAYO, DAVID WAYNE, sportswriter; b. San Diego, Dec. 28, 1960; s. Derwood Crandle and Shirley Ann (Jester) M. BA, Henderson State U., 1982. Sportswriter The Amarillo (Tex.) Globe-News, 1982-85, The Grand Rapids (Mich.) Press, 1985-87, sports columnist, 1989—; baseball beat writer Detroit Tigers Newhouse/Booth Newspapers, Lansing, Mich., 1987-89. Heisman Trophy elector, 1996—. Contbg. writer: Ring Mag., 1999—. Recipient first place Mich. Sustained Sports Coverage, Mich. AP, Detroit, 1989; named Mich. Sports Feature of the Yr., Mich. Press Assn., Detroit, 1994, 95, 98, Sports Columnist of Yr., Mich. Press Assn., 1998. Mem. Football Writers Assn. Am., Basketball Writers Assn. Am., Boxing Writers Assn. Am. (Best Investigative award 2003), Phi Sigma Kappa. Democrat. Baptist. Office: The Grand Rapids Press 155 Michigan St NW Grand Rapids MI 49503-2353 E-mail: davidwmayo@yahoo.com.

MAYO, GEORGE WASHINGTON, JR., lawyer; b. Waycross, Ga., Dec. 23, 1946; s. George Washington and Perrie R. (Ling) M.; m. Katherine Louise Boland, Nov. 15, 1977; children: Regan L.B., Taylor L.B. BA, Emory U., 1967; JD, U. Va., 1973. Bar: Va. 1973, D.C. 1974. Assoc. Hogan & Hartson, Washington, 1973—80, ptnr., 1980—. Contbr. articles. Bd. dirs. Vietnam Vets Meml. Fund, Inc., 1978—, Earth Conservation Corps, 1990—; bd. dirs. coll. coun. advisors Emory U., 1994—; bd. dirs. Deafness Rsch. Found., 1997—2001. 1st lt. U.S. Army, 1969—71, Vietnam. Mem.: ABA, D.C. Bar Assn., Congl. Country Club (Washington), City Club (Washington), Met. Club (Washington), Order of the Coif. Democrat. Methodist. Home: 26 Holly Leaf Ct Bethesda MD 20817-2652 Office: Hogan & Hartson 555 13th St NW Ste 800E Washington DC 20004-1161 Office Phone: 202-637-5679. Business E-Mail: gwmayo@hhlaw.com.

MAYO, JOHN SULLIVAN, telecommunications company executive; b. Greenville, N.C., Feb. 26, 1930; s. William Louis and Mattie (Harris) M.; m. Lucille Dodgson, Apr. 1957; children: Mark Dodgson, David Thomas, Nancy Ann, Lynn Marie. BS, N.C. State U., 1952, MS, 1953, PhD, 1955; hon. doctorate (hon.), Rutgers U., Stevens U., Lehigh U. With AT&T Bell Labs., Murray Hill, N.J., 1955-95, exec. dir. toll electronic switching div., 1973-75, v.p. electronics tech., 1975-79, sr. v.p. network systems and network svcs., 1979-91, pres., 1991-95, pres. emeritus, 1995—. Bd. dirs. Johnson and Johnson, Found. for Nat. Medals of Sci. and Tech., The Kenan Inst. for Engring., Tech. and Sci. at N.C. State U. Contbr. articles to profl. jours.; patentee in field. Trustee emeritus Polytech U., The Kenan Inst. for Engring., Tech. and Sci. at N.C. State U., Liberty Sci. Ctr. Recipient Indsl. Rsch. Inst. medal, 1992, Navy League N.Y. Coun. Roosevelts gold medal for sci., 1993, Engring. Mgr. of Yr. award Am. Soc. for Engring. Mgmt., 1992, N.J. Sci./Tech. medal, 1994; named Outstanding Engring. Alumnus N.C. State U., 1977; Internat. Engring. Consortium fellow, 1994. Fellow IEEE (Alexander Graham Bell award 1978, Simon Ramo medal 1988, C&C prize 1988, Nat. Medal of Tech. 1990), mem. NAE, Royal Swedish Acad. Engring. Scis., Sigma Xi, Phi Kappa. Avocations: fishing, gardening, bicycling, jogging.

MAYO, JOHN W. dean, educator, researcher; BA in econs., Hendrix Coll.; MA in Econs., PhD in econs., Washington U., St. Louis. Tchr. U. Tenn., Wash U., Va. Tech.; prof. econs., bus., pub. policy and dir. Ctr. for Bus. and Pub. Policy McDonough Sch. Bus., Georgetown U., 1997—, sr. assoc. dean, 1999—2001, dean, 2002—. Adv., cons. pub. and pvt. agys. including U.S. Dept. Justice, Fed. Trade Commn., Tenn. Valley Authority, U.S. Dept. Energy, Oak Ridge Nat. Lab.; former chief economist U.S. Senate Small Bus. Com. Co-author (with David L. Kaserman): Government and Business: The Economics of Antitrust and Regulation, 1995; contbr. numerous articles to profl. jours. Zaeslin Fellowship in law and econs., U. Basel, Switzerland. Mem.: Antitrust Law and Econs. Assn., Western Econ. Assn., So. Econ. Assn., Am. Econ. Assn. Office: Georgetown U McDonough Sch Bus 37th and O Sts NW Washington DC 20057

MAYO, MARTI, museum director, curator; b. Bluefield, W.Va., Oct. 17, 1945; d. Robert J. and Kathryn Ann (Kearns) Kirkwood; m. Edward K. Mayo, May 13, 1974 (div. 1983); 1 child, Nesta. BA, Am. U., 1970, MFA, 1974. Asst. dir. Jefferson Place Gallery, Washington, 1973-74; coord. exhbns. Corcoran Gallery Art, Washington, 1974-80; curator Contemporary Arts Mus., Houston, 1980-86; dir. Blaffer Gallery U., Houston, 1986—94; dir., chief curator Contemporary Arts Museum, Houston, 1994—. Mem. review panel, Inst. of Museum & Library Services; panelist Nat. Endowment for Arts, Texas Commn. on Arts. Author: Robert Morris Selected Works; 1970-80, 1981, Other Realities: Installations for Performance, 1981, Arbitrary Order: Paintings by Pat Steir, 1983, (with others) Robert Rauschenberg, Work from Four Series: A Sesquicentennial Exhibition, 1985, Joseph Glasco 1948-86: A Sesquicentennial Exhibition, 1986, Six Artists/Six Idioms, 1988. Mem. Am. Assn. Mus., Coll. Art Assn.; bd. mem. Houston Museum District Assn. (vice pres. 1998-99, pres. 2001-02), Cultural Arts Council of Houston/Harris County (v.p.); bd. trustees Am. Federation of Arts, Assn. of Art Museum Directors. Office: Contemporary Arts Museum 5216 Montrose Blvd Houston TX 77006-6598*

MAYO, ROBERT N. computer science researcher; b. Washington, Aug. 23, 1959; s. Robert P. and Marian A. Mayo. BS in Computer Sci., Washington U., St. Louis, 1981; MS in Computer Sci., U. Calif., Berkeley, 1983, PhD of Computer Sci., 1987. Asst. prof. U. Wis., Madison, 1988; staff Digital Equipment Corp./Compaq Computer/Hewlett Packard, Palo Alto, Calif., 1989—. Mem. IEEE, Assn. Computer Machinery. Home: 407 W Dana St Mountain View CA 94041-1337 Office: Hewlett Packard 1501 Page Mill Rd MS 1146 Palo Alto CA 94304 Office Phone: 650-857-2212. E-mail: wwbob@bobmayo.com.

MAYOCK, ROBERT LEE, internist; b. Wilkes-Barre, Pa., Jan. 19, 1917; s. John F. and Mathilde M.; m. Constance M. Peruzzi, July 2, 1949; children: Robert Lee, Stephen Philip, Holly Peruzzi Luff. BS, Bucknell U., 1938; MD, U. Pa., 1942. Diplomate Am. Bd. Internal Medicine. Intern Hosp. U. Pa., Phila., 1943-44, resident in internal medicine, 1944-45, chief med. resident, 1945-46, attending physician, 1946—; chief pulmonary disease Phila. Gen. Hosp., 1955-72, chief pulmonary disease sect., 1959-72, sr. cons. pulmonary disease sect., 1972—; asst. prof. clin. medicine U. Pa., 1949-59, assoc. prof., 1959-70, prof. medicine, 1970-87, prof. emeritus, 1987—. Med. adv. com. for Tb Commonwealth of Pa., 1965-74, med. adv. com. on chronic respiratory disease, 1974-92, chmn. adv. com., 1981-90; mem. subsplty bd. pulmonary disease Am. Bd. Internal Medicine, 1965-76; nat. bd. dirs. Am. Lung Assn., 1983-92, local bd. dirs., 1961, local pres., 1966-69, dir. at large, 1983—. Contbr. articles to profl. jours. Capt. U.S. Army, 1952-54. Robert L. Mayock-David A. Cooper Prof. of Medicine Endowed Chair named in his honor U. Pa. Sch. Medicine, 1997. Fellow ACP, Am. Coll. Chest Physicians (regent 1972-79), Phila. Coll. Physicians; mem. AMA, Am. Thoracic Soc., Am. Fedn. Clin. Rsch., Pa. Lung Assn. (dir. 1976—), N.Y. Acad. Scis., Pa. Med. Soc., Phila. County Med. Soc., Physiology Soc. Phila., Laennec Soc. Phila., Merion Cricket Club, Westmoreland Club, Swiftwater Res., Sigma Xi. Home: 244 Gypsy Ln Wynnewood PA 19096-1113 Office: U Penn Ravdin Bldg 3d Fl Ste F Philadelphia PA 19104

MAYOR, HEATHER DONALD, medical educator, molecular biologist; b. Melbourne, Victoria, Australia, July 6, 1930; d. Joseph A. L. and Elizabeth Emily (Boyd) Donald; m. Richard Blair Mayor, May 28, 1956; children: Diana Boyd (Mrs. Russell Hawkins), Philip Hastings. BS, U. Melbourne, Australia, 1949; MS, U. Melbourne, 1951, DSc, 1970; PhD, U. London, 1954. Electron microscopist Nat. Inst. for Med. Research, London, 1952-55; postdoctoral fellow Walter and Eliza Hall Inst., Melbourne, 1955-56; post doctoral fellow Harvard U. Med. Sch., Boston, 1956-60; from asst. prof. to prof. Baylor Coll. Medicine, Houston, 1960—, prof., 1970-96, prof. emeritus, 1996—. Cons. AEC, Washington, 1971—, Nat. Cancer Inst., Bethesda, Md., 1975—, U. Tex. Med. Sch., Houston, 1975—. Contbr. articles and papers to profl. jours.; artist, coordinator Life Shapes, Contemporary Arts Mus. Houston, Tex. art exhbn., 1974. Recipient Disting. award Ctr. for Interaction Man-Sci.-Soc., Houston, 1973, Sir Hiram Maxim award, 1990; named Scientist of Yr., Ency. Britannica, 1992; scholar in residence Rockefeller Inst. and Found., Bellagio, Italy, 1983. Mem. Am. Assn. Immunologists, Biophysical Soc. (program chmn.), Am. Soc. for Cell Biology (program chmn.), Houstonian Club, Houston Harpsichord Soc. (bd. dirs.). Avocations: piano, harpsichord. Home: 6 N West Oak Dr Houston TX 77056-2120 Office: Baylor Coll of Medicine 1 Baylor Plz Houston TX 77030-3411 E-mail: hmayor@bcm.tmc.edu.

MAYORAS, DONALD EUGENE, corporate executive, writer, consultant, educator; b. Danville, Ill., Aug. 25, 1939; s. Andrew John and Katherine Ann (Shelato) M.; m. JoAnna Marie Kacmer, June 9, 1962; children: D. Tyler, Stacie J. BS in Edn., Purdue U., 1962; postgrad., Northwestern U., 1968-71; MBA, So. Ill. U., 1977. Regional mgr. Pacific Intermountain Express, Akron, Ohio, 1972-74; v.p. United Van Lines, Fenton, Mo., 1974-78; pres. Bekins Van Lines, L.A., 1978-83; pres., CEO Sun Carriers, Inc., Holliston, Mass., 1983-90, chmn. bd. dirs.; vice-chmn., CEO Builders Transport, Camden, S.C., 1990-91. Chmn., CEO Truckload Holding Inc., Chester, N.Y., 1995-97, Cloverleaf Transp., Inc., Chester, 1997—; spkr. in field. Trustee Ross Ade Found., West Lafayette, Ind., 1962—2002. Capt. U.S. Army, 1962-68; Europe, Vietnam. Decorated Bronze Star. Mem. Am. Trucking Assn. (v.p. 1983—, trustee Found. 1983-91), Nat. Spkrs. Assn., Nat. Coun. Logistics, Nat. Pvt. Truck Coun., Purdue U. Alumni Assn., Nat. Def. Transp. Assn., Aronomink

Golf Club (Newton Sq., Pa.), Orange County Golf Club, Delta Nu Alpha, Beta Gamma Sigma, Omicron Delta Kappa. Republican. Roman Catholic. Avocations: golf, antiques, classic automobiles. E-mail: clor@aol.com, dmayoras@cloverleaftransport.com.

MAYPOLE, JOHN FLOYD, real estate holding company executive; b. Chgo., May 17, 1939; s. John James and Althea Floyd M.; m. Anne White, 1961; children: Cynthia, John, Kimberly. BA in Econs, Yale U., 1961. With Arthur Andersen & Co., 1961-62, 65-66; mgr. corp. acctg. Interpace Corp., 1966, asst. treas., 1967-68, treas., 1968-70, treas., controller, 1970-73, v.p. fin., 1973-77, sr. v.p., 1977-80, exec. v.p., 1980-81, pres., 1981-83; pres., chief operating officer Clevepak Corp., 1983-84; mng. ptnr. Peach State Real Estate Holding Co., Toccoa, Ga., 1984—. Bd. dirs. Dan River, Inc., Mass. Mut. Fin. Group, Meridian Automotive Sys., Inc., Church & Dwight Co., Inc., Nat. Captioning Inst., Inc. Bd. adjustment Borough of Mountain Lakes, N.J., 1971-81, chmn., 1980-81. Served with USMC, 1962-65. Mem. Yale Club, Ivy League Club (Sarasota), Rockaway River Country Club, Laurel Oak Country Club. Republican. Office: PO Box 1223 Toccoa GA 30577-1421

MAYR, ERNST, retired zoologist, philosopher; b. Kempten, Germany, July 5, 1904; came to U.S., 1931; s. Otto and Helene (Pusinelli) M.; m. Margarete Simon, May 4, 1935; children: Christa E., Susanne. Cand. med., U. Greifswald, 1925; PhD, U. Berlin, 1926; PhD (hon.), Uppsala U., Sweden, 1957; D.Sc. (hon.), Yale U., 1959, U. Melbourne, 1959, Oxford U., 1966, U. Munich, 1968, U. Paris, 1974, Harvard U., 1980, Guelph U., U. Cambridge, 1982, U. Vt., 1984; DSc (hon.), U. Mass., 1993; PhD (hon.), U. Vienna, 1994; DPhil (hon.), U. Konstanz, 1994; DSc (hon.), U. Bologna, 1995, Rollins Coll., 1997; Dr. ner. nat. (hon.), U. Berlin, 2000. Asst. curator zool. mus. U. Berlin, 1926-32; mem. Rothschild expdn. to Dutch New Guinea, 1928, expdn. to Mandated Ty. of New Guinea, 1928-29, Whitney Expdn., 1929-30; research asso. Am. Mus. Natural History, N.Y.C., 1931-32, asso. curator, 1932-44, curator, 1944-53; Jesup lectr. Columbia U., 1941; Alexander Agassiz prof. zoology Harvard U., 1953-75, emeritus, 1975—; dir. Mus. Comparative Zoology, Harvard U., 1961-70. Messenger lectr. Cornell U., 1985; Hitchcock prof. U. Calif., 1987; hon. fellow Ctr. for Philosophy of Sci., U. Pitts. Author: List of New Guinea Birds, 1941, Systematics and the Origin of Species, 1942, Birds of the Southwest Pacific, 1945, Birds of the Philippines, (with Jean Delacour), 1946, Methods and Principles of Systematic Zoology, (with E.G. Linsley and R.L. Usinger), 1953, Animal Species and Evolution, 1963, Principles of Systematic Zoology, 1969, 2d edit., 1991, Populations, Species and Evolution, 1970, Evolution and the Diversity of Life, 1976, (with W. Provine) Evolutionary Synthesis, 1980, Biologie de l'Evolution, 1981, The Growth of Biological Thought, 1982, Toward a New Philosophy of Biology, 1988, One Long Argument, 1991, This is Biology, 1997, What Evolution Is, 2001, (with J. Diamond) The Birds of Northern Melanesia, 2001; editor: Evolution, 1947-49. Pres. XIII Internat. Ornith. Congress, 1962. Recipient Leidy medal, 1946, Wallace Darwin medal, 1958, Brewster medal Am. Ornithologists Union, 1965, Daniel Giraud Elliot medal, 1967, Nat. Medal of Sci., 1970, Molina prize Accademia delle Sci., Bologna, Italy, 1972, Linnean medal, 1977, Gregor Mendel medal, 1980, Balzan prize, 1983, Darwin medal Royal Soc., 1987, Disting. Scientist award UCLA, 1993, Salvin Godman medal, 1994, Japan prize, 1994, Benjamin Franklin medal 1995, 96, Lewis Thomas prize, 1998, Crafoord prize, 1999, Golden Plate Am. Acad. Achievement, 2001; establishment of the Ernst Mayr Lectureship of the Berlin-Brandenburgische Akademie. Fellow Linnaean Soc. N.Y. (past sec. editor), Am. Ornithol. Union (pres. 1956-59), N.Y. Zool. Soc.; mem. NAS, Am. Philos. Soc., Am. Acad. Arts and Scis., Am. Soc. Zoologists, Soc. Systematic Zoology (pres. 1966), Soc. Study Evolution (sec. 1946, pres. 1950); hon. or corr. mem. Royal Soc., Royal Australian, Brit. ornithol. unions, Zool. Soc. London, Soc. Ornithol. France, Royal Soc. New Zealand, Bot. Gardens Indonesia, S. Africa Ornithol. Soc., Linnean Soc. London, Deutsche Akademie der naturforsch Leopoldina, Accad. Naz. dei Lincei, Royal Soc., Academie des Sci., Ctr. for Philosophy of Sci. (Pitts.), Russian Acad. Sci., Berlin-Brandenburgische Akademie, N.Y. Acad. Scis., Darwin Sci. Berlin, Muellleriana. Office: Harvard U Mus Comparative Zoology 26 Oxford St Cambridge MA 02138-2902

MAYR, JAMES JEROME, fertilizer company executive; b. Beaver Dam, Wis., Aug. 19, 1942; s. Alfred A. and Maxine E. (Kuehl) M.; m. Carol Ann Kaufman, Sept. 4, 1965; children: Christin and Carin (twins), Cathy, Conni. BS in Agrl. Econs., U. Wis., 1964. Mgr. trainee Oscar Mayer, Madison, Wis., 1964-65; v.p. Mayr's Seed and Feed, Beaver Dam, 1966-78; product mgr. Chem. Enterprises, Houston, 1978-80; gen. mgr. Coash, Inc., Bassett, Nebr., 1981-88, v.p., 1989; mgr. Blicks Agri-Farm Ctr., Inc., Scott City, Kans., 1990-91; area mgr. Rosen's Inc., Fairmont, Minn., 1992-95, Helena Chem. Co., Rochester, Minn., 1995—. Cons. Beaver Dam, 1971-75; spkr. fertilizer orgns., Wis. Advisor U. Wis. Coll. Agriculture; mem. com. Upper Elk Horn Natural Resources Dist., Oneill, Nebr., 1985-86. Mem. Wis. Fertilizer Assn. (bd. dirs. 1970-74), Nat. Fertilizer and Solutions Assn., Nebr. Fertilizer and Chem. Assn. Lodges: KC (dep. grand knight 1978-80, 81-85, Man of Yr. 1982). Republican. Roman Catholic. Avocations: target shooting, hunting, fishing, teaching target shooting. Home: 2550 Oak Hills Dr SW Rochester MN 55902-1263 Personal E-mail: jmayrusa@charter.net.

MAYRON, LEWIS WALTER, clinical ecology consultant; b. Chgo., Sept. 20, 1932; s. Max and Florence Minette (Brody) M.; married; children: Leslie Hope Mayron Coff, Eric Brian. BS in Chemistry, Roosevelt U., 1954; MS in Biol. Chemistry, U. Ill., 1955, PhD in Biol. Chemistry, 1959. Rsch. assoc. dept. biochemistry and nutrition U. So. Calif., L.A., 1959-61; asst. biochemist dept. biochemistry Presbyn.-St. Luke's Hosp., Chgo., 1961-62; instr. dept. biol. chemistry U. Ill., Chgo., 1961-62; biochemistry group leader Tardanbek Labs., Chgo., 1962-63; sr. devel. chemist Abbott Labs., Chgo., 1963-64; asst. attending physician, mem. spl. staff Michael Reese Hosp. and Med. Ctr., Chgo., 1964-66, rsch. assoc. Dept. Allergy Rsch., 1964-66; asst. prof. in biochemistry and physiology Sch. Dentistry Loyola U., Chgo., 1968-71; guest investigator Argonne (Ill.) Nat. Lab., 1973-79; rsch. chemist V.A. Hosp., Hines, Ill., 1968-79; chief clin. radiobiochemist nuclear medicine svc. V.A. Wadsworth Hosp. Ctr., L.A., 1979-83; cons. in clin. ecology, 1980—. Contbr. articles to profl. jours. Mem. AAAS, Am. Assn. Clin. Chemists, Soc. for Exptl. Biology and Medicine, Sigma Xi. Home: 823 S 1850 West Cedar City UT 84720-8237

MAYS, BETTY JEAN, retired automotive executive; d. Carl Well Henderson and Hattie Louise Lammie; m. James Mays (dec. 1972); 1 child, James; m. Larry Sumner, 1960; children: Larry, Tina. Student in Interdisciplinary Tech., Ea. Mich. U. Sec. state reps. Okla. State Capital, Okla. City, 1967—71; from adminstrv. asst. to engring. mgmt. cons., internal auditor Gen. Motors Corp., Detroit, 1972—98, engring. mgmt. cons. Pontiac, Mich., 1998—2001, internal auditor, 1998—2001, ret., 2001. Democrat. Roman Cath. Avocations: astrology, writing, painting, chess.

MAYS, CAROL JEAN, state legislator; b. Independence, Mo., July 16, 1933; m. Ronald H. Mays; children: Terri, Melanie, Hugh. Student, Baker U. State rep., chmn. consumer protection edn. appropriations com., mem. transp., ways & means & comm. coms. Mo. Ho. of Reps., Jefferson City. Restaurant owner. Mem. Mo. Restaurant Assn., Independence C. of C., Fairmount Comml. Club, Alpha Chi Omega. Democrat. Methodist. Home: 3603 S Hedges Ave Independence MO 64052-1167 Office: Mo Ho of Reps State Capitol Bldg 201 W Capitol Ave Rm 206A Jefferson City MO 65101-1556

MAYS, CAROLENE, state representative; 1 child, Jada. BA in Bus. Mgmt. and Mktg., Ind. State U. Various pos. in sales, corp. acct. mgmt., customer svc., and product distbn. Occidental Chem. Co., San Francisco, Dallas, and Mpls.; mgr. customer svc. and nat. accts. Mays Chem. Co.; pres., gen. mgr. The Indianapolis Recorder, 1998—; state rep. dist. 94 Ind. Ho. of Reps., Indpls., 2002—, mem. human affairs, judiciary, pub. health, and ways and means coms. Host, weekly TV news segment Community Link WISH-TV Ch. 8, Ctrl. Ind. Bd. dirs. Ind. Sports Corp. Bd., U. Indpls.; mem. Ind. Supreme Ct. Commn. for Racial and Gender Fairness; bd. dirs. Indpls. Downtown Mktg., Inc.; apptd. by mayor Indpls. Neighborhood Housing Partnership Bd.; adv. bd. Julian Ctr., NCAA Citizenship Through Sports Alliance/Common Ground; bd. dirs. Shrewsberry & Assocs., Peyton Manning's PeyBack Found.; apptd. by mayor Greater Indpls. Progress Com.; past bds. and coms. 2001 World Police and Fire Games Exec. Com., Indy Jazz Fest, Ind. Repertory Theatre, Ind. Sch. Champions, Ind. Pvt. Industry Coun., Girls, Inc., United Way's Ardeth Burkhart Series exec. com., Freetown Village Bd., chair Circle City Classic Coaches Lunchion 2000 NCAA Final Four Com., chair comm. World's Largest Christmas Tree, coord. Ind. Sch. Champions Camp, numerous other planning coms., workshops and speaking engagements. Named one of Women to Watch, Indpls. Bus. Jour.; recipient Disting. Alumni award, Ind. State U., Martin Luther King Ctr. Living the Legacy award, 2002, Media award, Ind. Black Expo, 2002, Trailblazer award, Women's Expo, 2001, Presdl. citation, Nat. Newspaper Pubs. Assn., 2000. Mem.: Nat. Coun. Negro Women (named Woman in the Bethune Tradition 2001), United Way Minority Key Club, Alpha Kappa Alpha (Regional Comm. award 2002). Democrat. Avocations: skiing, cooking. Office: Ind Ho of Reps 200 W Washington St Indianapolis IN 46204-2786

MAYS, GEORGE WALTER, JR., educational technology educator, consultant, tutor; b. Decatur, Ill., July 1, 1926; s. George Walter Sr. and Ida May (Lookabaugh) M.; children: Richard, Steven, John, James. BS in Edn., U. Ill., Champaign, 1950, MS in Edn., 1952; BSEE, U. md., 1960; cert., Calif. State U., Carson, 1987. Tchr. math. and physics Mahomet (Ill.) High Sch., 1950-52, prin., 1952-55; br. chief engring studies Nat. Security Agy., Ft. Meade, Md., 1955-62; sr. engr. Jet Propulsion Lab., Pasadena, Calif., 1962-71; tchr. math.-sci., chair Aviation High Sch., Redondo Beach, Calif., 1971-82; tchr. math. and physics, dept. chair Redondo Union High Sch., 1982-89; cons. edni. tech. Apple Valley, Calif., 1989—; math. coord. Sci. and Tech. Ctr., Apple Valley, Calif., 1990—. Part-time instr. electronics Pasadena City Coll., 1963-72, Pepperdine U., 1975-76, math. Victor Valley Coll., 1991-97; instr. math. Acad. for Acad. Excellence, Apply Valley, 1998—. Author: Educational Technology Application Notes, 1989-90. With USN, 1944-46. Recipient Appollo Achievement award NASA, 1969. Mem. IEEE (life), Calif. Tchrs. Assn. (WHO award 1988-89), Nat. Coun. Tchrs. of Math., Computer Using Educators, Apple Valley Country Club, Victor Valley Aero Club. Avocations: reading, sports, computer usage, flying. Home and Office: 13458 Sunset Dr PO Box 745 Apple Valley CA 92307-0013

MAYS, JANICE ANN, lawyer; b. Waycross, Ga., Nov. 21, 1951; d. William H. and Jean (Bagley) M. AB (hon.), Wesleyan Coll., Macon, Ga., 1973; JD, U. Ga., 1975; LLM in Taxation, U. Georgetown, 1978. Bar: Ga. 1976. Tax counsel com. on ways and means U.S. Ho. Reps., Washington, 1975-88, chief tax counsel com. on ways and means, staff dir. subcom. select revenue measures, 1988-93, chief counsel, staff dir. com. on ways and means, 1993-95, minority chief counsel, staff dir. com. on ways and means, 1995—. Recipient Disting. Achievement in Profession Alumnae award Wesleyan Coll., 1998. Mem. Tax Coalition (past chair). Office: Ways & Means Com 1106 Longworth Office Bldg Washington DC 20515-0001

MAYS, J.C. automotive executive; b. 1955; Grad., Art Ctr. Coll. of Design, 1980. Worked for BMW, Calif.; chief designer Volkswagon of Am., Simi Valley, Calif., 1989—93; v.p. design devel. SHR Perceptual Mgmt., Scottsdale, 1995—97; cons. Ford Motor Co., group v.p. design, 1997—. Office: Ford Motor Co One American Rd Dearborn MI 48126-1899

MAYS, JEFFERSON, actor; BA, Yale U.; MFA, UCSD. Actor: (TV series) Dynaman, 1988; (TV miniseries) Liberty! The American Revolution, 1997; (films) The Killing Box, 1993, Some Folks Call It a Sling Blade, 1994, The Low Life, 1995, Hudson River Blues, 1997, Cousin Bette, 1998, The Big Brass Ring, 1999, (regional theater) Rosencrantz & Guildenstern Are Dead, Misalliance, The Importance of Being Earnest, The Beauty Part, Not Suitable for Children, The Cherry Orchard, The Winter's Tale, She Stoops to Conquer, Servant of Two Masters, Macbeth, Miss Julie, Private Lives; (Broadway plays) I Am My Own Wife, 2003— (Theater World award, 2004, Drama Desk award outstanding solo performance, 2004, Obie award outstanding performance, 2004, Tony award best actor in a play, 2004). Office: Lyceum Theatre 149 W 45th St New York NY 10036*

MAYS, JILL DUNCAN, social services administrator, counselor; b. Louisville, Apr. 17, 1966; d. Charles Henry Sr. and Ruth Ella (Bohannon) Duncan; m. Samuel Aaron Mays Sr., Dec. 28, 1991; children: Shelby Amaris, Samuel Aaron Jr., Jayce Allan. BA in Psychology, Emory U., 1988; MS in Cmty. Counseling, Ga. State U., 1992. Lic. profl. counselor, Ga.; master addiction counselor, nat. cert. counselor Nat. Bd. Cert. Counselors, Inc. Rsch. interviewer Emory U. Sch. Pub. Health, Atlanta, 1990-92; evening outpatient coord. Decatur (Ga.) Hosp., 1992-94; counselor The Atlanta Union Mission, 1992-94, dir. women and children's svcs., 1994—, Atlanta City Mission, 2000—. Cons. Intracultural Comm., Decatur, 1993-95, DeKalb County Dept. Youth Svcs., Decatur, 1993; com. mem. Atlanta Summit Against Poverty, 1997; bd. dirs. Zion Hill Cmty. Devel. Corp.; mem. com. DeKalb County Bd. Health/Divsn. Health Assessment and Promotion, 2002-03. Olympic Force coord. Atlanta Com. for the Olympic Games, 1995—96; mem. Atlanta Women Making a Mark, 2002. Mem.: Coun. Vol. Adminstrs., Assn. Gospel Rescue Missions, Am. Assn. Christian Counselors, Nat. Assn. for the Edn. Young Children, Alpha Kappa Alpha Sorority, Inc. Democrat. Baptist. Avocations: singing, reading, acting/playwriting. Office: Vlge Atlanta Union Mission 921 Howell Mill Rd NW Atlanta GA 30318-5547 Office Phone: 404-532-1929. Personal E-mail: samnjam1@prodigy.net.

MAYS, K. J. writer, musician; b. Lake Station, Ind. m. Lee Mays; 1 child, Mitchell. AA, Harold Washington, Chgo. Composer: (songs) Plan, Call, Stand Up, 1999. Mem.: Golden Key. Achievements include invention of K.J. Mallet for cymbal, timpani, vibraphone, bells, bass drum, xylophone. Office: JLM Enterprises PO Box 79 West Brooklyn IL 61378-0079

MAYS, LARRY W. civil engineering educator, hydrologist; b. Pittsfield, Ill., Feb. 7, 1948; s. Fred W. and Lola M. Mays; children: Travis, Elyssa, Tyler. BSCE, U. Mo., Rolla, 1970, MSCE, 1971; PhD in Civil Engring., U. Ill., 1976. Registered profl. engr., Ariz., Okla., Calif., Ill., Mo. Ark., La.; registered prof. hydrologist Am. Inst. Hydrology. Asst., then assoc., then prof. civil engring. U.Tex., Austin, 1976-89, Engring. Found. endowed prof., 1987-89, dir. Ctr. for Rsch. in Water Resources, 1988-89; prof. civil engring. Ariz. State U., Tempe, 1989—, chmn. dept., 1989-96. Pres. Univs. Coun. on Water Resources, 1994; cons., lectr. in field. Co-author: Applied Hydrology, 1988, Hydrosystems Engineering and Management, 1992, Groundwater & Hydrology, 2004; author: Optimal Control of Hydrosystems, 1997, Water Resources Engineering, 2000; editor-in-chief: Water Resources Handbook, 1996, Water Distribution Systems Handbook, 2000, Hydraulic Design Handbook, 2000, Stormwater Collection Systems Design Handbook, 2001, Urban Water Supply Handbook, 2002, Urban Water Supply Management Tools, 2003, Urban Stormwater Management Tools, 2003, Water Supply Systems Security, 2004. With U.S. Army, 1970-73. Recipient cert. of commendation Nat. Assn. Water Inst. Dirs., 1989, Engr. of Yr. in Edn. award Ariz. Soc. Profl. Engrs., 1992, Quentin Mees rsch. award Ariz. Water Pollution Control Assn., 1993, Disting. Alumnus award dept. civil engring. U. Ill., 1999,. Fellow ASCE, Internat. Water Resources Assn.; mem. Am. Water Resources Assn., Internat. Assn. Hydraulic Rsch., Am. Water Works Assn. Avocations: skiing, fly fishing, scuba diving, gardening, photography, hiking. Home: 6064 E Cholla St Scottsdale AZ 85254-4905 Office: Ariz State U Dept Civil Engring Tempe AZ 85287

MAYS, LESLIE A. human resources specialist; b. Houston; BA, Tex. So. U. Pers. dir., city mgr. Peoples Express Airline; cons. Jane C. Edmonds and Assocs.; human resources dir. Reebok Internat. Ltd., 1989—94; mem. diversity dept. Gen. Mills, 1994—96; exec. dir. diversity Royal Dutch/Shell Oil Co., 1996—99, v.p., Global Group Diversity, 1999—. Mem.: Nat. Coalition 100 Black Women (bd. mem. 1997—2001, pres. 2001—). Office: Ste 1610 38 W 32nd St New York NY 10001-3816

MAYS, L(ESTER) LOWRY, broadcast executive; b. Houston, July 24, 1935; s. Lester T. and Virginia (Lowry) M.; m. Peggy Pitman, July 29, 1959; children: Kathryn Mays Johnson, Linda Mays McCaul, Mark P., Randall T. BS in Petroleum Engring., Tex. A&M U., 1959; MBA, Harvard U., 1962. Comml. recorder, San Antonio; with Sta. KTTU-TV, Tucson, Sta. KOKI/KTFO-TV, Tulsa, Sta. WMPI/WJTC-TV, Mobile and Pensacola, Okla., Sta. WAWS-TV, Jacksonville, Fla., Sta. KSAS-TV, Wichita, Kans., Sta. KLRT/KASN-TV, Little Rock, Sta. WFTC-TV, Mpls., Sta. WFTC-TV, WLMT/WMTU-TV, WLMT/WMTU TV, Memphis, Sta. WXXA, Albany, Sta. WQUE-AM-FM, New Orleans, Clear Channel Sports, Des Moines, Okla. News Network, Oklahoma City, Va. News Network, Stas. KJYO and KTOK, Oklahoma City, Sta. KEBC, Oklahoma City, Sta. WELI, New Haven, Sta. WKCI-WAVZ, New Haven, Sta. KPEZ, Austin, Tex., Stas. KHYS, KALO, KBXX, KMJQ, KPRC, KSEV and KYOK, Houston and Point Arthur, Tex., KMOD & KAKC, Tulsa, KTAM & KORA, Bryan and College Station, Tex., WHAS & WAMZ, Louisville; with radio and TV broadcasting WOAI, KQXT, and KAJA, San Antonio; chmn., CEO Clear Channel Comms., Inc., San Antonio, 1975—. Past chmn. bd. CBS Radio Affiliates Bd. Bd. dirs., trustee Tex. Rsch. Pk.; bd. dirs., mem. exec. com. United Way; chmn. United Way San Antonio and Bexar County, 1995; regent emeritus Tex. A&M U. Sys.; trustee Tex. Rsch. and Tech. Found.; mem. deve. bd. U. Tex. Health Sci. Ctr.; adv. dir. Permanent Univ. Fund Tex. Mem. Nat. Assn. Broadcasters (past chmn. joint bd.), Greater San Antonio C. of C. (past chmn.), Rotary. Home: 400 Geneseo Rd San Antonio TX 78209-6127 Office: Clear Channel Comms Inc PO Box 659512 San Antonio TX 78265-9512

MAYS, LINDA, performing arts association administrator; Pres. Am. Guild Musical Artists, N.Y.C. Office: Am Guild Musical Artists 14th Fl 1430 Broadway New York NY 10018*

MAYS, M. DOUGLAS, state legislator, financial consultant; b. Pittsburg, Kans., Aug. 18, 1950; s. Marion Edmund and Lilliemae Ruth (Norris) M.; m. Lena M. Krog, June 10, 1971; children: Jessica, Aaron. BFA, Pittsburg State U., 1972; postgrad., Washburn U., 1973—. Registered rep. Waddell & Reed, Inc., Topeka, 1981-83, Paine Webber Jackson & Curtis, Topeka, 1983-85, Columbian Securities, Topeka, 1985-87; commr. securities State of Kans., Topeka, 1987-91; pres. Mays & Assocs., Topeka, 1991—; mem. Kans. Ho. Reps., Topeka, 1993—, asst. majority leader, 1997-99, spkr. pro tem, 1999—2001, spkr., 2003—. Adminstrv. law judge various securities proceedings, 1987—; with securities and commodities fraud working group U.S. Dept. Justice, 1988-90; with penny stock task force SEC, 1988-90; del. Commonwealth Secretariat Symposium Comml. Crime, Cambridge, Eng., 1989; securities arbitrator, 1991—. Rep. precinct committeeman Shawnee County, Kans., 1976—, county chmn., 1978-82; mem. 2d Dist. Rep. State Com., Kans., 1976-86, 92—; mem. Kans. Rep. State Com., 1976-87; Senate steering com. Kassebaum for Senate campaign, 1978; chmn., mgr. Hoferer for Senate campaign, 1984; campaign coord., dir. fin. Hayden for Gov., 1986; mem. pub. bldg. commn. City of Topeka, 1985-86, bldg. and fire appeals bd., 1986-89, dep. mayor, 1987-88; mem. Topeka City Coun., 1985-89; exec. bd. Topeka/Shawnee County Interngovtl. Coun., 1986-89; adv. bd. Topeka Performing Arts Ctr., 1989-90; active Topeka/Shawnee County Met. Planning Commn., 1992—, chmn., 1994-97. Mem. North Am. Securities Adminstrs. Assn. (chmn. enforcement sect. 1988-89, pres.-elect, bd. dirs. 1989-90, pres. 1990-91), Nat. Assn. Securities Dealers, Nat. Futures Assn. (bd. arbitrators), Internat. Orgn. Securites Commns. (inter-Am. activities consultative com. 1990, pres.'s com. 1990, del. 1990). Methodist. Home: 1920 SW Damon Ct Topeka KS 66611-1926 Office: Kans Ho Reps State Capitol Topeka KS 66612

MAYS, MARK PITMAN, communication company executive; b. San Antonio, Aug. 2, 1963; BA in Econs. and Math., Vanderbilt U.; MBA, Columbia U. V.p., treas. Clear Channel Comms., San Antonio, sr. v.p. ops., 1993—96, pres., COO, 1996—, interim CEO, 2004. Bd. dirs. NAB Radio Bd. Bd. dirs. Jr. Achievement San Antonio Chap., Alamo Area Coun. Boy Scouts Am., United Way San Antonio, SW Found. Biomedical Rsch. Office: Clear Channel Comms 200 E Basse Rd San Antonio TX 78209-8328 Fax: 210-822-2299.*

MAYS, RANDALL T. broadcast executive; b. 1966; married. BA with honors, Univ. Tex., Austin, Tex.; MBA, Harvard Bus. Sch. With Trammell Crow Co. Real Estate Firm, Goldman, Sachs & Co., NY; v.p., treas. Clear Channel Commn., San Antonio, 1993—97, CFO, exec. v.p., 1997—. Bd. dirs. XM Satelitte Radio. Adv. coun. Univ. Tex McCombs Bus. Sch. Mem.: Broadcast Cable Fin. Mgmt. Assn. (CFO of the Yr. 2002), Nat. Assn. of Broadcasters. Office: Clear Channel Commn Svc & Broadcasting & Cable TV San Antonio TX 78209

MAYS, WILLIAM G. chemical company executive; MBA, Ind. U. Test chemist Linkbelt Facility, Indpls.; acct. mgr. Procter & Gamble; market planning Eli Lilly and Co.; asst. to pres. Cummins Engine Co.; founder, pres. Mays Chem. Co., Indpls., 1980—. Bd. dirs. NBD-Inc. Mem. exec. com., bd. dirs. United Way Ctrl. Ind., Ind. Conv. and Visitors Assn.; bd. dirs. Associated Group, Corp. Cmty. Coun., Ind. Univ. Found., Cmty. Leaders Allied for Superior Schs.; mem. dean's adv. coun. Ind. U. Sch. Bus.; mem. pres.'s coun. Ind. U.; co-chmn. Coca-Cola Circle City Classic; elder Witherspoon Presbyn. Ch. Recipient Man of Yr. award B'Nai B'Rith Isidora Feibleman award, 1990, Elder Watson Diggs Achievement award Kappa Alpha Psi, 1991, Ind. Minority Small Bus. Advocate of Yr. award, 1991, Sagamore of Wabash award Gov. Ind., 1991, Ind. Enterprise award, 1992, Ind. Christian Leadership Conf. Businessman of Yr. award, 1992, Disting. Hooser, 1992, 13th in Black Enterprise Mag. Top 100 Indsl./Svc Cos., 'Above and Beyond' award Ind. Black Expo, 1992, Pres.'s award Black Pres.'s Roundtable Assn., 1992, Vol. Fund Raiser award, 1992, Anti-Defamation League Americanizm award, 1993, Charles Whistler award, 1993, Indpls. Edn. Assn.'s Human Rights award, 1994, Ind. State Conf. NAACP Labor and Industry award, 1994, Robert W. Briggs Humanitarian award, 1995, and numerous others; carried Olympic flame during trip through Indpls., 1995. Mem. Ind. C. of C. (bd. dirs.), Indpls. C. of C. (exec. com., bd. dirs.). Office: Mays Chemical Co Inc PO Box 50915 Indianapolis IN 46250-0915

MAYS, WILLIAM GAY, II, lawyer, real estate developer; b. Washington, Mo., Apr. 8, 1947; s. Frank G. and Geneva Pauline (Brookhart) M.; m. Judith Ann Kriete, Oct. 5, 1974; 1 son, Daniel Brookhart. AB, U. Mo., 1969, JD, 1972. Bar: Mo. 1972, U.S. Dist. Ct. (we. dist.) Mo. 1972. Legis. rschr. State of Mo., 1972; pub. defender 13th Jud. Cir. Mo., 1973-77; ptnr. Holt, Mays & Brady, Columbia, Mo., 1977-98; ptnr. and gen. counsel comml. real devel. firm. Mem. Jud. Planning Commn., Mo., 1977. Served to capt. USAFR, 1969-82. Named Outstanding Young Man of Am., 1974. Mem. Mo. Bar Assn., Boone and Callaway County Bar Assn., Mo. Trial Lawyers Assn., Mo. Pub. Defender Assn. (pres. 1976-77), Assisted Living Fedn. Am., Beta Theta Pi. Clubs: Masons. Republican. Office: The Mays Bldg PO Box 10013 Columbia MO 65205-4001

MAYS, WILLIE HOWARD, JR., (SAY HEY KID), former professional baseball player; b. Westfield, Ala., May 6, 1931; s. William Howard and Ann M.; m. Mae Louise Allen, Nov. 27, 1971; 1 adopted son, Michael. Baseball player Birmingham Black Barons, 1948-50, Trenton Inter-State League, 1950-51, Mpls. Millers, Am. Assn., 1951, N.Y. Giants, 1951-57, San Francisco Giants, 1958-72, N.Y. Mets, 1972-73; with Bally's Park Place, Atlantic City, 1980—; pub. rels. exec. San Francisco Giants, 1986-98, retired, 1998. Author: Willie Mays: My Life In and Out of Baseball, 1966, Say Hey: The Autobiography of Willie Mays, 1988. Served with AUS, 1952-54. Named Most Valuable Player Nat. League, 1954, 65; named Player of Yr. Sporting News, 1954, Baseball Player of Decade Sporting News, 1970, Male Athlete of Yr. AP, 1954, Rookie of the Yr., 1951, Sporting News Player of the Year award, 1954, All-Star Game, 1954-73; recipient Hickok belt, 1954, Golden Bat award to commemorate 600 home runs, Gold Glove award (12 times), 1st Commissioner's award, 1970, Golden Plate award to America's Captains of Achievement by Am. Acad. Achievement, 1976, Spirit of Life award City of Hope, 1988, Sportsman of Decade, Cong. Racial Equality, 1991, Legendary Star award HBO Video; inducted into Ala. Sports Hall of Fame, Baseball Hall of Fame, 1979, Black Hall of Fame, 1973, Calif. Sports Hall of Fame.

Achievements include being the holder of 4th place in major league homeruns (660); lifetime batting average of .302; signed lifetime pub. rels. contract with San Francisco Giants, 1993. Office: Baseball Hall of Fame PO Box 590 Cooperstown NY 13326-0590

MAYSILLES, ELIZABETH, speech communication professional, educator; b. Sleepy Creek, W.Va. d. Evers and Rose (Scott) M. AB, W.Va. U.; MA, Hunter Coll., 1963; PhD, NYU, 1980. Announcer Radio Sta. WAJR, Morgantown, W.Va.; broadcaster Radio Sta. WGHF-FM, Rural Radio Network, N.Y.C.; group leader GMAC, N.Y.C.; instr. NYU, N.Y.C.; adj. prof. speech comm. Pace U., N.Y.C., 1978—2002; exec. adminstr. Am.-Scottish Found., N.Y.C., 1980-90; adminstrv. asst. Brit. Schs. and Univs. Found., Inc.; numerous radio and television appearances; cons. home equities, 2002—. Cons., lectr. in field. Vol. counselor Help Line, N.Y.C., 1971-75. Recipient Disting. Svc. award NYU Grad. Orgn., 1970-71. Mem. Internat. Platform Assn. (bd. govs. 1980—), N.Y. Acad. Scis., English-Speaking Union, Caledonian Club N.Y. (bd. dirs. 1994-96, chieftain 2001-02). Avocations: reading, swimming, gardening, travel in England and Scotland. Home: 155 E 77th St Apt 6F New York NY 10021-1955

MAYSLES, ALBERT H. filmmaker; b. Boston, Nov. 26, 1926; s. Philip and Ethel (Epstein) M.; m. Gillian Walker, Sept. 14, 1976; children: Rebekah, Philip, Sara. BA, Syracuse U., 1949; MA, Boston U., 1953. Rsch. fellow in anesthesia Mass. Gen. Hosp., Boston, 1951-52; instr. social rels. Boston U., 1953-55; pres. Maysles Films, Inc., N.Y.C., 1962—. Filmmaker, prodr. Psychiatry in Russia, 1955, (with others) Primary, 1960, Showman, 1963, What's Happening: The Beatles in the USA, 1964, Salesman, 1967, Gimme Shelter, 1970, Christo's Valley Curtain, 1974, (Blue Ribbon award 1975, Acad. award nomination), Grey Gardens, 1976, Running Fence, 1978 (Blue Ribbon award, 1978), Ozawa, 1985, Vladimir Horowitz: The Last Romantic, 1985, Islands, 1986 (Blue Ribbon award, Emmy award), Horowitz Plays Mozart, 1987, Christo in Paris, 1990, Soldiers of Music: Rostropovitch Returns to Russia, 1990 (Emmy award), Abortion: Desparate Choices, 1995 (Peabody award), Letting Go, A Hospice Journey, 1996 (Ace Cable award), Concert of Wills: The Making of the Getty Art Center, 1997. Served as pvt. U.S. Army, 1944-46. Named one of 100 World's Finest Cinematographers, Eastman Kodak, 1999; recipient Career Achievement award, Internat. Documentary Assn., 1994, John Grierson award for Documentary, SMPTE, 1997, Pres.'s award, Am. Soc. Cinematographers, 1998, Vision award, The Boston Film and Video Found., 1998, The Doubletake Career Achievement award, 1998, Lifetime Achievement award, Toronto's Hot Docs, 1999, Flaherty award, 1999, award for documentaries, Sundance Film Festival Cinematography, 2001, Dupont award, 2004; Guggenheim fellow, 1965. Mem. The Reality Club. Home: One West 72nd St New York NY 10023 Office: 250 W 54th St New York NY 10019-5515 E-mail: amaysles@mayslesfilms.com.

MAYSON, PRESTON B., JR., retired lawyer; b. Spartanburg, S.C., June 18, 1932; s. Preston Brooks and Sophie Rowena (Morgan) M.; m. Sara Dudley Heaton, June 16, 1955; children: Brooks, James. BS, U.S. Mil. Acad., West Point, 1955; MD, George Washington U., 1962; JD, Washington and Lee U., 1991. Bar: Va. Diplomate Am. Bd. Radiology. Physician Letterman Hosp., San Francisco, 1962-66, 93rd Evacuation Hosp., Vietnam, 1966-67, Walter Reed Army Hosp., Washington, 1967-70, Radiology Assocs., Roanoke, Va., 1970-88; law student Washington & Lee U., Lexington, Va., 1988-91; sr. atty. Woods, Rogers & Hazlegrove, Roanoke, 1991-95; pres. Preston B. Mayson, PC, Roanoke, 1995-2000; ret., 2000. Decorated Bronze Star medal. Mem. ABA, Va. State Bar Assn., Va. Trial Lawyers Assn. Presbyterian. Avocation: painting. E-mail: pdoctorlaw@aol.com.

MAYTHAM, THOMAS NORTHRUP, art and museum consultant; b. Buffalo, July 30, 1931; s. Thomas Edward and Margaret (Northrup) M.; m. Daphne Chace, Dec. 30, 1960 (div.); 1 child, T.F. Gifford; m. Gloria Goode Evans, June 11, 1994. BA in Art History, Williams Coll., Williamstown, Mass., 1954; MA in Art History, Yale U., 1956; cert. in German, Colby Coll., 1954. Intern Wadsworth Atheneum, 1955; rsch. asst. Yale U., 1956; head dept. paintings Boston Mus. Fine Arts, 1957-67; assoc. dir., acting dir. Seattle Art Mus., 1967-74; dir. Denver Art Mus., 1974-83; art cons., pub. Artadvisors LLC, Denver, 1983—. Mus. accreditation program evaluator Am. Assn. Museums; past trustee, mem. exhbns. adv. com. Am. Fedn. Arts, N.Y.; past mem. mus. program panel, grants reviewer Nat. Endowment for Arts, Washington; reviewer Nat. Endowment for Humanities, Washington; mem. adv. panel, grants reviewer Nat. Mus. Act, Smithsonian Instn.; past mem. policy panel and adv. com., econ. impact of arts study Colo. Coun. Arts and Humanities; co-founder Consortium of Rocky Mountain Regional Conservation Ctr., U. Denver; founder dirs. assn. Denver cultural agys.; del. Inter-Am. Museums Conf., Oaxaca, Mexico; co-founder United Arts Fund, Seattle; mem. art adv. com. Airport Art Program, Port of Seattle; vis. faculty Leadership Denver program, Pres.'s Leadership class U. Colo.; cons. Aspen Ctr. Visual Arts, Sangre de Cristo Arts Ctr., Pueblo, Western States Arts Found., Santa Fe, BBHC, Cody, Wyo.; lectr. museums, colls., corporate groups and art assns. Exhbns. organized include Ernst Ludwig Kirchner Retrospective, Seattle, Pasadena and Boston museums, 1968-69, Am. Painting from the Boston and Met. Museums, Nat. Gallery, St. Louis and Seattle museums, 1970-71; contbr. articles to profl. jours.; presenter TV programs on collections and exhbns. Boston Pub. TV, WGBH-TV. Trustee Internat. Exhbns. Found., Washington. Recipient Gov.'s Arts award Seattle Airport Art Program, 1972, Denver Art mus., award Downtown Denver Inc., 1978. Mem. Assn Art Mus. Dirs. (officer, trustee, ops. com. sec., future directions. com. chmn.) Office: Maytham Artadvisors 3882 S Newport Way Denver CO 80237-1246

MAZAHERI, ALI REZA, engineer, researcher; b. Monterey, Calif., July 27, 1975; s. Mohammad Bagher and Sedigheh Mazaheri; m. Mahzad Bastaninejad, Jan. 9, 2000. PhD, Clarkson U., Potsdam, N.Y., 2003. Rsch. asst. Clarkson U., Potsdam, NY, 2000—03; postdoctoral rsch. assoc. NAS/ Nat. Energy Tech. Lab., Morgantown, W.Va., 2003—. Assoc. Nat. Rsch. Coun. Author. Nat. Acads. postdoctoral fellow, 2003, U.S. Dept. Energy PhD fellow, 2000—04. Mem.: ASME (assoc.). Home: Apt 208 3290 Univ Ave Morgantown WV 26505 Office: Nat Energy Tech Lab Collins Ferry Morgantown WV 26507 Office Phone: 304-285-0906. Personal E-mail: ali_r_mazaheri@yahoo.com. E-mail: mazaheri@netl.doe.gov.

MAZANKOWSKI, DONALD FRANK, Canadian government official; b. Viking, Alta., Can., July 27, 1935; s. Frank and Dora (Lonowski) M.; m. Lorraine Poleschuk, Sept. 6, 1958; children: Gregory, Roger, Donald. Student, pub. schs., 1987; PhD in Engring (hon.), N.S. Inst. Tech.; LLD (hon.), U. Alta., 1993. MP Ho. of Commons, 1968—, chmn. com. transp., 1972-74, mem. com. govt. ops., 1976-77, mem. com. trans. and communication, 1977-79; min. of transp., min. responsible for Can. Wheat Bd. Govt. of Can., 1979-80, min. of transp. (re-drafted Nat. Transp. Act), 1984-86, dep. prime min., 1986—, govt. house leader, 1986-88, pres. Privy Coun., 1986-91, pres. Treas. Bd., 1987-88, min. responsible for privatization and regulatory affairs, 1988-91, min. of agriculture, 1988-91, min. of fin., 1991-93; chmn. Inst. of Health Econs. Former mem. bd. govs. U. Alta; bd. dirs. Power Corp. Can., Power Fin. Corp., Great West Life Assurance, The Investors Group, Shaw Comms. Inc., Weyerhauser Co., IMC Global Inc., Can. Oilsands Trust, ATCO Ltd., London Life Ins., Yellow Pages Group; chmn. Can. Genetic Diseases Network. Apptd. chmn. Premier's Adv. Coun. on Health. Apptd. officer Order of Can., 2000, Alta. Order of Excellence, 2003; Paul Harris fellow Rotary Internat., 2002; honoree Pub. Policy Forum Can., 2003; named one of Alta.'s 50 Most Influential People, 2002. Mem. Royal Can. Legion (life). Clubs: Vegreville Rotary (past dir.). Lodges: KC. Roman Catholic. Fax: 780-632-4737. E-mail: maz1@agt.net.

MAZE, BILL, state representative; b. Woodlake, Calif. m. Becky Maze; 5 children. BS in Agribusiness, Calif. Poly. State U. Staff insp. gen. U.S. Army, 1968—70; mem Calif. Assembly, 2002—. Chair United Way Tulare County; county supr. Tulare County Bd. Suprs., 1992—2002, chair, 1997, Kings-Tulare Area Agy. on Aging, 1993—95; founder Citizens Adv. Com. Govt. Assistance Reform; candidate Calif. Assembly, 1998; bd. dirs. Pro-Youth Visalia, Tulare County Econ. Devel. Corp., Tulare County Workforce Coalition, Visalia Econ. Devel. Coun. Mem.: San Joaquin Valley Supr. Assn. (pres. 1998), Calif. Farm Bur., Aircraft Owners Pilots Assn., Back Country Horsemen Calif. Republican. Office: 942849 Rm 2002 Sacramento CA 94249 Address: 5959 S Mooney Blvd Visalia CA 93277

MAZEL, JOSEPH LUCAS, publishing executive, consultant; b. Paterson, N.J., Oct. 1, 1939; s. Joseph Anthony and Anne (Kidon) M.; m. Joyce Virginia Kronenberger; children: Joseph William, Jeanne Eileen. BME, Newark Coll. Engring., 1960. Mech. engr. Austin Co., Roselle, NJ, 1960-61; engr. Western Electric Co., Newark, Atlanta, 1961-62; asst. assoc., sr. editor Factory Mag., N.Y.C., 1962-71; editor-in-chief, sr. editor 33 Metal Producing mag., McGraw-Hill Publs. Co., Newark and Summit, NJ, N.Y.C., 1971—85; chmn. editl. bd. McGraw-Hill Publs. Co., N.Y.C., 1980-82; pub. rels. account supr. Hammond Farrell, Inc., N.Y.C., 1985-87; mgr. corp. publs. Siemens Corp., Iselin, NJ, 1987-92; pres. Mazel Editl. Assocs., Fair Lawn, NJ, 1992—; group editor Inst. Mgmt. and Adminstrn., Inc., N.Y.C., 1993—. Guest lectr. Writers Conf. N.J. Inst. Tech., 1972—83. Property maintenance com. Borough of Fair Lawn, NJ, 1996—97; employment assistance response network mem. St. Catharine's Ch., Glen Rock, NJ, 1993—99. With Nat. Guard, 1963—69. Recipient Apolloneer award, GE Co., 1966, Jesse H. Neal Cert. of Merit, 1977, 1979, 1983, Jesse H. Neal Editl. Achievement award, 1979, Disting. Alumni award for Outstanding Achievement, N.J. Inst. Tech., 1979, Steuben Wise Old Owl award, U.S. Steel Corp., 1981. Mem.: KC (grand knight 1967—68, trustee 1968—71), Inst. Supply Mgmt., Inst. Indsl. Engrs., Coun. Logistics Mgmt., Materials Handling and Mgmt. Soc., Am. Prodn. and Inventory Control Soc., Inc., Am. Soc. Engring. Mgmt., Soc. Profl. Journalists, Sigma Delta Chi. Home: 40-22 Tierney Pl Fair Lawn NJ 07410-5141 Office Phone: 646-424-3857. Business E-Mail: jmazel@ioma.com.

MAZGALEV, TODOR NIKOLOV, health science association administrator, research scientist; b. Munich, Oct. 21, 1942; arrived in U.S., 1984; s. Nikola D. and Maria Mazgalev; m. Tatiana D. Zheltuhin, Feb. 28, 1972; 1 child, Victoria. BS, Sofia Poly. U., 1964; MS summa cum laude, St. Petersburg Electrotech. Inst., 1969, PhD, 1972. Rsch. assoc. Bulgarian Acad. Scis., Sofia, 1972-84; sr. scientist Lankenau Med. Rsch. Ctr., Phila., 1984-90; rsch. assoc. prof. U. Pitts., 1991-94; dir. basic cardiac electrophysiology rsch., dir. Cleve. Clinic Found., 1994—, assoc. staff in cardiology, 2000—02, prof. cardiovascular medicine and molecular cardiology, 2002—. Presenter and lectr. in field. Editor: Electrophysiology of the Sinoatrial and Atrioventricular Nodes, 1988, Atrial-AV Nodal Electrophysiology, 2000; contbr. articles to profl. jours. Grantee, NIH, 2000—. Fellow Am. Coll. Cardiology; mem. Internat. Cardiac Electrophysiology Assn., N.Am. Soc. Pacing and Electrophysiology, Am. Heart Assn. (grant-in-aid 1998-2000). Achievements include research in the propagation of cardiac electric impulses and arrhythmics, electrophysiology of atriventricular node in norm and pathology. Avocation: shorthand. Home: 29149 Bryce Rd Pepper Pike OH 44124-5767 Office: Cleve Clinic Found 9500 Euclid Ave Bldg Ff1-2 Cleveland OH 44195-0001 Fax: (216) 445-4168. E-mail: mazgalt@ccf.org.

MAZIAR, CHRISTINE M. academic administrator; BSEE, MSEE, PhD in Elec. Engring., Purdue U. Faculty mem. U. Minn., Mpls., 1998—, v.p. for rsch., dean Grad. Sch., 1998—2002, exec. v.p., provost, 2002—. Contbr. articles to profl. jours. Recipient Presdl. Young Investigator award, NSF, 1990, Tech. Excellence award, Semiconductor Rsch. Corp., 1992. Office: Office Sr VP for Acad Affairs 234 Morrill Hall 100 Church St SE Minneapolis MN 55455*

MAZLEN, ROGER GEOFFREY, physician, clinical pharmacologist, nutritionist; b. Bklyn., Nov. 23, 1937; s. Henry Gershwin and Ann Kurland (Shapero) M.; m. Sandra Phyllis Kuritzky, Aug. 7, 1960; children: James Edward, Vivien Gayle. BS in Biology, Rensselaer Poly. Inst., 1959; MD, SUNY, Bklyn., 1963. Intern maimonides Med. Ctr., Bklyn., 1963-64, resident in medicine, 1964-65; rsch. assoc. NIH, Bethesda, Md., 1965-67; resident in med. ophthalmology Mt. Sinai Med. Ctr., N.Y.C., 1967-69; assoc. med. dir. Pfizer Inc., N.Y.C., 1970-71; asst. dir. clin. rsch. Ayerst Labs., N.Y.C., 1971-75; assoc. dir. clin. rsch. Schering Corp., Bloomfield, N.J., 1975-78; adj. asst. prof. medicine N.Y. Med. Coll.; sr. clin. asst. prof. Mt. Sinai Sch. Medicine; sr. faculty, sr. attending div. endocrinology and metabolism Mt. Sinai Med. Ctr. Mem. cons. Profl. Children's Sch.; cons. in clin. nutrition and metabolism South Oaks Hosp. Author: A New Manifesto for Middle America, 1972; author: (with others) Nutrition and Health Care; contbr. (chpt.) Quick Reference to Clinical Nutrition, mem. editl. staff Jour. of the Chiropractic Coun. on Nutrition. Founder, chmn. Queens County (N.Y.) Common Cause, 1972—75, vice chmn. for N.Y. State, 1974—75; bd. dirs. Bayside Hills Civic Assn., 1970—80; adv. mem. bd. dirs. U.S.A., Inc., 1970—72; chmn. hyperalimentation com. Astoria (N.Y.) Gen. Hosp.; former dir. Clin. Rsch. N. Am. Immunatee Ltd., Montreal; nutrition dir. Cernitin Am. Nutritional, 1983—88, also mem. eating disorder adv. bd.; pres. The Inst. for the Study of CFS and Related Disorders; mem. Stealth Virus Task Force CCID. Served with USPHS, 1965—67. Fellow: Am. Coll. Nutrition (chmn. coun. on nutrition and cardiovasc. diseases 1976—85, sec.-treas.); mem.: N.Y. State Soc. Internal Medicine, Soc. for Natural Immunity, Am. Coll. Cardiology (constituent mem. N.Y. State chpt.), Am. Soc. Clin. Pharmacology and Therapeutics, Muhammad Ali Internat. Sport Youth Athletic Found. Inc. (bd. dirs.). Republican. also: 148 Tulip Ave Fl 2 Floral Park NY 11001-2705 E-mail: rgm1@aol.com.

MAZO, MARK ELLIOTT, lawyer; b. Phila., Jan. 12, 1950; s. Earl and Rita (Vane) M.; m. Fern Rosalyn Litman, Aug. 19, 1973; children: Samantha Lauren, Dana Suzanne, Ross Elliott, Courtney Litman. AB, Princeton U., 1971; JD, Harvard U., 1974. Bar: D.C. 1975, U.S. Dist. Ct. D.C. 1975, U.S. Claims Ct. 1975, U.S. Ct. Appeals (D.C. cir.) 1976, U.S. Supreme Ct. 1979. Ptnr. Hogan & Hartson, L.L.P., Washington and Paris, 1990—. Contbr. articles to profl. jours. White House intern Exec. Office of Pres., Washington, 1972. Capt. USAR, 1971-79. Mem. ABA, Harvard Law Sch. Assn., D.C. Bar Assn., Columbia Country Club, Princeton Club (N.Y.C.), Colonial Club, City Club, Phi Beta Kappa. Republican. Home: 3719 Cardiff Rd Chevy Chase MD 20815-5943 Office: Hogan & Hartson LLP 555 13th St NW Washington DC 20004-1161 also: Hogan & Hartson MNP 45 Ave Kleber 75016 Paris France Office Phone: 202-637-5673., 202-637-5673. Business E-Mail: memazo@hhlaw.com.

MAZO, ROBERT MARC, retired chemistry educator; b. Bklyn., Oct. 3, 1930; s. Nathan and Rose Marion (Mazo) M.; m. Joan Ruth Spector, Sept. 5, 1954; children: Ruth, Jeffrey, Daniel. BA, Harvard U., 1952; MS, Yale U., 1953, PhD, 1955. Rsch. assoc. U. Chgo., 1956-58; asst. prof. Calif. Inst. Tech., 1958-62; assoc. prof. U. Oreg., Eugene, 1962-65, prof. chemistry, 1965-95, prof. emeritus, 1996, head chemistry dept., 1978-81, dir. Inst. Theoretical Sci., 1964-67, 84-87, assoc. dean Grad. Sch., 1967-71; program dir. NSF, 1977-78. Alfred P. Sloan fellow, NSF Sr. Postdoctoral fellow, vis. prof. U. Libre de Bruxelles, Belgium, 1968-69; vis. prof. Technische Hochschule Aachen, Weizmann Inst., Rehovoth, Israel, 1981-82, U. New South Wales, Australia, 1989. Author: Statistical Mechanical Theories of Transport Processes, 1967, Brownian Motion, 2002, also rsch. articles. NSF Postdoctoral fellow U. Amsterdam, Netherlands, 1955-56. Fellow Am. Phys. Soc. Home: 2460 Charnelton St Eugene OR 97405-3214 Office: U Oreg Inst Theoretical Sci Eugene OR 97403 Office Phone: 541-346-5224. E-mail: mazo@uoregon.edu.

MAZON, MARGARET FAUSOLD, language educator; b. Windber, Pa., Dec. 26, 1946; d. George McLelland and Ann (Shank) Fausold; m. José Antonio Mazón, Apr. 21, 1973 (div. June 1985); children: David José Mazón, Daniel Eladio Mazón. Student, U. Valladolid, 1967; BS in Spanish Edn., Ind. U. Pa., 1968; MA in Spanish, W.Va. U., 1973, EdD, 1992. Tchr. Spanish McGuffey St. Jr.-Sr. H.S., Claysville, Pa., 1968—70; tchr. ESL Briam Inst., Madrid, 1970—71; adj. prof., asst. prof. St. Bonaventure U., Olean, NY, 1979—2002, assoc. prof., Dept. Chair, 2002—. Contbr. articles to profl. jours.; translator: Olean Gen. Hosp., 2000—. Vol. Interfaith Caregivers, Olean, 1999—. Mem.: Modern Lang. Assn. Democrat. Presbyterian. Avocations: swimming, bicycling, cooking, gardening. Office: Modern Lang Dept St Bonaventure Univ Olean NY 14778

MAZUMDER, JYOTIRMOY, mechanical and materials engineering educator; b. Calcutta, India, July 9, 1951; came to U.S., 1978; s. Jitendra Mohan and Gouri (Sen) M.; m. Aparajita, June 17, 1982; children: Debashis, Debayan. B in Engring., Calcutta U., 1973; diploma, PhD, Imperial Coll., London U., 1978. Rsch. scientist U. So. Calif., L.A., 1978-80; asst. prof. mechanical and indsl. engring. U. Ill., Urbana, 1980-84, assoc. prof., 1984-88, prof., 1988-96, co-dir. ctr. laser aided materials processing, 1990-96; Robert H. Lurie Prof. Engring. U. Mich., Ann Arbor, 1996—, dir. ctr. laser aided intelligent mfg., 1996—. Co-dir. ctr. laser aided material processing U. Ill., 1990-96; dir. Quantum Laser Corp., Edison, N.J., 1982-89; pres. Laser Scis., Inc., Urbana, 1988—; dir., CEO POM Inc., Plymouth, Mich.; vis. scholar physics dept. Stanford (Calif.) U., 1990. Author: (with others) Laser Welding; editor and co-editor more than 9 books including co-editor: Laser Materials Processing, 1984, 88; more than 250 technical papers; contbr. numerous articles to profl. jours. Fellow Am. Soc. of Metals and Laser Inst. of Am. (life, pres. 2000, editor-in-chief Jour. Laser Application); mem. Am. Inst. Metallurgical Engrs. (phys. mets. com. 1980—), Optical Soc. Am. Achievements include patent: weld pool visualization system for measurement of free surface deformation, apparatus and method for monitoring and controlling multi-layer cladding. Office: U Mich Dept Mech Engrng & Mechs 2041 GG Brown Ann Arbor MI 48109-2125 E-mail: mazumder@umich.edu.

MAZUMDER, SANDIP, engineer, researcher; b. Calcutta, India, Feb. 23, 1969; came to U.S., 1991; s. Satya and Amita Mazumder; m. Srirupa Dhar, Nov. 25, 1998. BTech with honors, Indian Inst. Tech., 1991; MS, Pa. State U., 1993, PhD, 1997. Project engr. CFD Rsch. Corp., Huntsville, Ala., 1997-98, sr. engr., 1999-2000, group leader, 2000—. Reviewer NSF, Arlington, Va., 1999—, Jour. Heat Transfer, 1997—, Numerical Heat Transfer, 1999—. Contbr. over 20 articles to profl. jours. including Internat. Jour. Heat and Mass Transfer, Jour. Heat Transfer, Internat. Jour. Numerical Method Fluids, Numerical Heat Transfer, others. Grantee NSF, 1999—. Mem. ASME, AIAA. Avocations: piano, guitar. Office: CFD Rsch Corp 215 Wynn Dr Huntsville AL 35805 E-mail: sm@cfdrc.com.

MAZUR, ALLAN CARL, sociologist, engineer, educator; b. Chgo., Mar. 20, 1939; s. Joseph and Esther (Markowitz) M.; m. Minnette Albrecht, Jan. 21, 1968; children— Julie Elizabeth, Rachel Lee. BS, Ill. Inst. Tech., 1961; MS, UCLA, 1964; PhD, Johns Hopkins U., 1969. Research engr. North Am. Aviation Co., Los Angeles, 1961-64; instr. polit. sci. Mass. Inst. Tech., 1966-67; ops. research analyst Lockheed Missile & Space Corp., Sunnyvale, Calif., 1967-68; asst. prof. sociology Stanford U., 1968-71; mem. faculty Syracuse U., N.Y., 1971—, prof. pub. affairs, 1992—. Author: Dynamics of Technical Controversy, 1981, Global Social Problems, 1991, A Hazardous Inquiry: The Rashomon Effect at Love Canal, 1998, True Warnings and False Alarms, 2004; co-author: Biology and Social Behavior, 1972; contbr. articles to profl. jours. Fellow AAAS. Jewish. Office: Syracuse U 400 Eggers Maxwell Sch Syracuse NY 13244 E-mail: amazur@syr.edu.

MAZUR, BARRY CHARLES, mathematician; b. N.Y.C., Dec. 19, 1937; 1 child. PhD in Math., Princeton U., 1959. Jr. fellow Harvard U., Cambridge, Mass., 1959—62, from asst. prof. to prof., 1962—82, William Petschek prof. math., 1982—, Gerhardt Gade univ. prof., 1998—. Recipient Veblen prize in Geometry, Am. Math. Soc., Cole prize in Number Theory, Chauvenet prize, Math. Assn. Am., 1994. Mem.: AAAS, NAS. Office: Harvard U Dept Math 1 Oxford St Cambridge MA 02138-2901

MAZUR, DEBORAH JOAN, school system administrator; b. Highland Park, Mich., Apr. 22, 1958; d. Frank J. and Joan A. (Cader) M.; m. Michael J. Baker, Sept. 20, 1986 (div. Apr. 1997); children: Adam Joseph, John Michael, Ryan Francis. BS, Western Mich. U., 1981; MA, Oakland U., 1989, EdS, 2002. Spl. edn. resources room tchr. Capac Cmty. Schs., Mich., 1981-82; supr. group home Blue Water Devel. Housing, Port Huron, Mich., 1982-83; unit adminstr. group home Luth. Social Svcs. Mich., Detroit, 1983-85; mgr. sales Fin. Svcs. Am., Inc., Madison Heights, Mich., 1985-86; clinician, case mgr. Ditty, Lynch and Assocs., Birmingham, Mich., 1986-87; spl. edn. tchr. Pontiac (Mich.) Sch. Dist., 1987-96; counselor Warren (Mich.) Consol. Schs., 1996—2002; asst. prin. Warren Consol. Schs., 2002—04, program adminstr., 2004—. Mem.: ASCD, ACA, Mich. Assn. Sec. Sch. Prins., Nat. Assn. Sec. Sch. Prins., Mich. Counseling Assn., Warren YMCA (bd. dirs.), Western Mich. U. Alumni Assn.

MAZUR, EDWARD JOHN, JR., financial planner; b. Lowell, Mass., Mar. 5, 1948; s. Edward John Sr. and Mary Annette (Terry) M.; m. Sheila MacDonald, Dec. 13, 1969 (div. Nov. 1984); 1 child, Kristen Leigh; m. Anna Maria Maia, May 18, 1985; children: Edward John III, Kara Maia Mazur. BA in History, U. Mass., 1969. CLU, Chartered Fin. Cons., Life Underwriters Tng. Coun. Fellow. From agt. to dir. agys. John Hancock Mut. Life Ins. Co., Boston, 1973—84, gen. agt. Hartford, 1984-89; founder Mazur Fin., Farmington, Conn., 1990—2000, Profl. Investors Exch., LLC, Farmington, 2000—. Team coord. Team Conn., 1998—. Recipient Raymond T. Wilbur award, Mass. Jaycees, 1982-83; named President of Yr., Mass. Jaycees, 1982-83, Outstanding Young Men of Am., Mass. Jaycees, 1984. Mem. Million Dollar Round Table, Nat. Assn. Ins. and Fin. Advisors (pres. Conn. chpt. 2000-01), Hartford Life Underwriters Assn. (pres. 1995-97), US Racquetball Assn., Conn. Racquetball Assn. (pres. 1985-94). Avocations: racquetball, coaching, hiking. Home: 48 Knollwood Ln Avon CT 06001-2701

MAZUR, JAY J. trade union official; BA in Indsl. Relations, CUNY, 1965; MA in Labor Studies, Rutgers U., 1977. Dir. orgn. local 40 Internat. Ladies Garment Workers Union, N.Y.C., 1955-59, dir. orgn. local 23, 1959-64, asst. mgr. local 23-25, 1964-77, mgr. sec. local 23-25, 1977-83, gen. sec.-treas., 1983-86; pres. Unite, N.Y.C., 1986—2001. V.p. exec. council AFL-CIO, Washington, 1986-2001, N.Y. State exec. council, Albany; mem. exec. council Indsl. Union Dept., Washington, 1984-2001; mem. exec. bd. Fiber, Fabric and Apparel Coalition, Washington, 1986-2001; bd. dirs. Occupational Health Legal Rights Fund, Washington. V.p. Nat. Immigration Refugee and Citizenship Forum, Washington; bd. dirs. Regional Plan Assn., N.Y.C., 1983, Spl. Contbn. Fund NAACP, Balt., 1987. Avocations: music, jogging, gardening.

MAZUR, LEONARD L. pharmaceutical company executive; b. Ansbach, Germany, Jan. 23, 1945; came to U.S., 1949; s. Walter and Maria (Zatwarnitsky) M.; m. Helena Maria Olijnyk, Nov. 1966; children: Maria, Michael, Irene. BA, Temple U., 1968, MBA, 1975. Mktg. mgr. Cooper Labs., Inc., Fairfield, N.J. and Palo Alto, Calif., 1971—81; dir. product mgmt. Knoll Pharm. Corp. divsn. BASF, Whippany, NJ, 1981—84; v.p. ICN Pharm. Corp., Costa Mesa, Calif., 1984—88; pres., COO Chantal Pharm. Corp., L.A., 1988—89; exec. v.p. Medicis Pharm. Corp., N.Y.C., 1989—93; vice chmn. Cabot Labs., Inc., N.Y.C., 1994—96; chmn., CEO Genesis Pharm., Inc., Parsippany, NJ, 1996—. Ptnr. Mazier Ptnrs. LLC, Morristown, N.J., 1995—. Patentee in field. Mem. adv. bd. Manor Coll., Jenkintown, Pa., 1972-78, trustee, 2000—; ind. observer Referendum for Independence, Ukraine, 1991. Roman Catholic. Office: Genesis Pharm Inc 9 Campus Dr Parsippany NJ 07054

MAZUR, MICHAEL, artist; b. N.Y.C., Nov. 2, 1935; s. Burton Boris and Helen (Isaacs) M.; m. Gail Lewis Beckwith, Dec. 28, 1958; children: Daniel Isaac, Kathe Elizabeth. BA, Amherst Coll., 1958; BFA, Yale U., 1959, MFA, 1961; degree (hon.), Lesley U. Asst. prof. fine arts Brandeis U., Waltham, Mass., 1965-76; instr. RISD, 1962-65. Vis. prof. Yale U. Sch. Art and Arch., 1972, 81, Queens Coll., CUNY, 1973, U. Calif., Santa Barbara, 1974-75, Boston U., 1982, Mass. Coll. Art, 1994, 95; lectr. Mus. Fine Arts, Boston, Brown U., U. Calif., Berkeley, New Sch. for Social Rsch., Bennington Coll., U. Iowa, Boston U., 1994-95, Katonah Mus., N.Y. Studio Sch., 1994; vis. lectr. Carpenter Ctr., Harvard U., 1976, 78, 89, 92, 94, 95, 97, others; illustrator Fleur du Mal, 1984, The Inferno of Dante, Farrar, Strans & Giroux, 1994, Genesis, 1996; co-chair bd. Fine Arts Work Ctr., Provincetown, Mass., 1996—. Exhibited in one-man shows at Kornblee Gallery, N.Y.C., 1960, 63, 66, Boris Mirski, Boston, 1963, 65, Phila. Print Club, 1964, Silvermine Guild, 1964, Fla. State U., 1966, Shoemaker Gallery Juniata Coll., 1966, Alpha Gallery, Boston, 1967, 68, 74, OGL Gallery, Los Angeles, Calif., 1968, Rose

Art Mus., Brandeis U., 1969, A.A.A. Gallery, 1969, Inst. Contemporary Art, Boston, 1970, Terry Dintenfass, N.Y.C., 1974, 76, Picker Gallery, Colgate U., 1973, Trinity Coll., 1976, Ohio State U., 1975, Robert Miller Gallery, N.Y.C., 1977, 80, Harkus-Krakow, Boston, 1977, 79, 80, Pace Gallery, N.Y.C., 1980, John Stoller, Mpls., 1981, 85, 88, 91, William and Mary Coll., 1981, Ronald Greenberg, St. Louis, 1981, Janus Gallery, L.A., 1982, 84, 88, Barbara Mathes Gallery, N.Y.C., 1984, 86, Barbara Krakow Gallery, Boston, 1984, 86, 89, 91, 93, 95, 97, 98, 2000, Art Club Chgo., 1985, Beaver Coll., 1985, Joe Fawbush, N.Y., 1987, 88, Jan Turner Gallery, L.A., 1988, Butler Gallery, Houston, 1989, Mary Ryan Gallery, N.Y.C., 1990, 94, 95, 96, 97, 98, 99, 2000, Mus. Fine Arts, Boston, 2000, Cantor Ctr.-Stanford U., 2000, Zimmerli Art Mus., New Brunswick, N.J., 2000, Mus. di Castelvecchio, Verona, Italy, 2000, Am. Acad. Rome, 2000—; exhibited group shows at, Mus. Modern Art, 1964, 75, Bklyn. Mus., 1960, 62, 64, 66, 76, 80, 84, 86, Fogg Art Mus., 1966, 76, 94, Art. Inst. Chgo., 1964, Pa. Acad., 1966, 93, Phila. Mus., 1966, 88, Boston Mus. Fine Arts., 1967, 68, 76, 77, 80, 88, 90-91, 92, DeCordova Mus., Lincoln, Mass., 1965-67, 75, 86, 87, Whitney Mus. Am. Art, 1965, 81, 90, 92, Nat. Inst. Arts and Letters, 1965, 74, 80, 86, Sivermine Guild, 1965, Print Biennial of Americas, Santiago, Chile, 1965, Paris Biennale, 1969, Venice Biennale, 1970, Finch Coll. Mus., 1971-72, 2d and 3d Biennial Graphic Art, Cali, Colombia, N.A.D. Ann., 1974, Butler Inst., Youngstown, Ohio, 1974, Ball State U., 1974, America-1976, Sense of Place, Met. Mus., N.Y.C., 1979, 80, Montreal Mus. Fine Arts, 1977, Palais Royale, Brussels, 1979, Claude Bernard, Paris, 1980, Alan Frumkin, N.Y.C., 1981, 82, Madison Art Ctr., 1989, Nat. Gallery of Art, Washington, 1990, Pratt Mus., N.Y.C., 1990, Nat. Mus. Am. Art, 1997; traveling exhbns. include, Bicentennial Exhbn., 1976, State Arts Councils, Iowa, Kans., Mo., Nebr., 1973, Am. Monotypes, Smithsonian Instn., 1977; represented in permanent collections, Met. Mus., N.Y.C., Mus. Modern Art, Smith Coll. Art Mus., Library Congress, Fogg Art Mus., Art Inst. Chgo., Whitney Mus., Los Angeles County Art Mus., Mus. R.I. Sch. Design, Oreg. Art Mus., U. Maine, Mpls. Inst., Pa. State U., Toledo Art Mus., Phila. Art Mus., U. Ohio Westminster Found., Boston Mus. Fine Arts, Boston Pub. Library, Bklyn. Mus., Addison Gallery, Andover Acad., Yale Art Gallery, Montreal Mus. Fine Arts; commd. Fed. Res. Bank, Boston, 1998, USB-Warburg-Dillon, Stanford, Conn., 1999; (Recipient 2d prize Soc. Am. Graphic Artists 1963, Nat. Inst. Arts and Letters award 1965). Co-founder Artists Against Racism and the War, 1968; bd. dirs. Artists Found., co-chair, 1995—; bd. dirs. Fine Arts Work Ctr., Provincetown, Mass.; mem. Mass. Coun. on Arts and Humanities; mem. Pennell com. Libr. of Congress, 1983-93; founder, dir. Art for Nuc. Weapons Freeze, 1983-84, New Provincetown Print Project, 1990-95; chmn. bd. Provincetown Fine Arts Work Ctr.; overseer Mus. Fine Arts, Boston. Grantee Tiffany Found., 1964, Tamarind Lithography Workshop, 1968; Guggenheim Found. fellow, 1964-65; winner numerous purchase awards. Home: 5 Walnut Ave Cambridge MA 02140-2706 also: 5 Walnut Ave Cambridge MA 02140-2706

MAZUR, PETER, cell physiologist, cryobiologist; b. NYC, Mar. 3, 1928; s. Paul M. and Adolphia (Kaske) M.; m. Drusilla Stevens, May 28, 1953 (dec. May 1982); 1 child, Timothy Stevens; m. Sara Jo Bolling, June 16, 1984 (dec. Apr. 2003). AB magna cum laude, Harvard U., 1949, PhD, 1953; DSc (hon.), Wilson Coll., 1998. NSF postdoctoral fellow Princeton (N.J.) U., 1957-59; rsch. staff biology divsn. Oak Ridge Nat. Lab., 1959-98. Group leader fundamental and applied cryobiology Oak Ridge Nat. Lab., 1966-98, sci. dir. biophysics and cell physiology, biology div., 1974-75, corporate fellow, 1985; chmn. ORNL Corp. Fellows Coun., 1995-96; mem. vis. com. biology Harvard U. Bd. Overseers 1972-77; rsch. prof. dept. biochem. and cellular and molecular biology U. Tenn., 1998—; mem. Space Sci. Bd. of Nat. Acad., 1975-77; Sigma Xi nat. lectr., 1980. Trustee Wilson Coll., Pa., 1984-93, trustee emeritus, 2003; bd. dirs. Meth. Hosp. Found., Oak Ridge, 1997—2003. Capt. USAF, 1953-57. Recipient Author of Yr. award, Martin-Marietta Energy Sys., 1985, Disting. Svc. award, Am. Assn. Tissue Banks, 1993, R&D 100 award, R&D Mag., 1993, Disting. Achievement award, Am. Soc. Reproductive Medicine, 2000; fellow Lalor fellow, Harvard U., 1952, John Harvard fellow, 1951. Fellow AAAS; mem. Soc. Cryobiology (pres. 1973-74, bd. govs. 1979-96), Rotary Club Oak Ridge, Phi Beta Kappa, Cosmos Club (Washington). Current work includes cryobiology and the mechanisms of freezing injury in living cells and tissues. Subspecialties are cell biology and biophysics. Home: 125 Westlook Cir Oak Ridge TN 37830-3856 Office: Dept Biochemistry and Cellular and Molecular Biology M407 Walters Life Sci Bldg Knoxville TN 37996-0001 Office Phone: 865-974-9960. E-mail: pmazur@utk.edu.

MAZUR, RHODA HIMMEL, community volunteer; b. Bklyn., July 4, 1929; d. Morris and Gussie (Nadler) Himmel; m. Marvin Irwin Mazur, June 7, 1952; children: Jody, Amy, Leslie, Eric. Student, CCNY, CUNY. Bd. dirs. Newport News Social Svcs. Adv. Bd., 1979-84, Gov.'s Commn. Status Women, Richmond, 1981-84, Coun. Jewish Fedns., N.Y.C., 1985-87, Nat. Coun. Christians and Jews, 1985-89, Rodef Sholom Endowment Com., 1996—; v.p. Anti-Defamation League Regional Bd., Richmond, 1983-85, bd. dirs., 1985—; pres. Newport News Hadassah, 1984-85, United Jewish Cmty. Va. Peninsula Inc., Newport News, 1985-88, Rodef Sholom Sisterhood, 1997-98; active Newport News Task Force on Emergency Housing, 1984-85; chair fin. com. Peninsula Peace Edn. Ctr., Newport News, 1984-85; adv. bd. Friends of the Homeless, Inc., 1987-2000, pres., 1993-98, v.p., 1998-99; adv. bd. Associated Marine Inst., 1988-92; mem. social svcs. com. United Jewish Cmty. Va. Peninsula, 1995—, mem. campaign coun., 1999—; chair social action com. Rodef Sholom Temple, 1993-96, endowment com., 1998—; cmty. activist; bd. dirs., Peninsula Camp Fund, 2001—, Fed. Emergency Mgmt. Agy., 2001. Recipient Young Leadership award Jewish Fedn. Newport News, 1968, Brotherhood citation Nat. Conf. Christians and Jews, 1984, Anti-Defamation Leadership award, 1997. Democrat. Avocations: hand crafts, reading, music, photography. Home: 114 James River Dr Newport News VA 23601-3604

MAZUREK, JOSEPH P. lawyer, former state legislator; b. San Diego, July 27, 1948; m. Patty Mazurek; 3 children. BA, U. Mont., 1970, JD, 1975. Bar: Mont. 1975. Atty. Gough, Shanahan, Johnson, and Waterman, Helena, Mont., 1975—93; mem. Mont. Senate from 23d Dist., 1981—92, pres., 1991—92; atty. gen. State of Mont., 1993—2000; ptnr. Crowley, Haughey, Hanson, Toole & Dietrich, PLLP, Helena, Mont., 2000—. Mem. Revenue Oversight Com., 1983—92; chmn. Senate Judiciary Com. Mem. editl. bd.: Mont. Law Rev., 1974—75. With U.S. Army, 1970—72. Mem.: ABA, Phi Delta Theta, Phi Delta Phi, Beta Gamma Sigma. Democrat. Office: PO Box 797 Helena MT 59625-0797 also: 100 N Park Ave Helena MT 59601-6263

MAZZA, RICHARD T. state legislator, small business owner; b. Colchester, Vt., Sept. 4, 1939; m. Dorothy D. Hinds; two children. Grocer; mem. Vt. Ho. of Reps., Montpelier, 1972-76; mem., Grand Isle County Vt. Senate, Montpelier, 1985—. Mem. transp. com., forest com., chmn. legis. coun., Vt. Ho. of Reps., 1974-76; chmn. transp. com., 1991-92, vice chmn. instns. com., mem. joint transp. oversight com., Vt. Senate. Trustee Vt. State Coll.; mem. Dem. Town Com.; pres. Fanny Allen Hosp. Assn. Office: Vt Senate State Capitol Montpelier VT 05602

MAZZA, TERILYN MCGOVERN, finance executive; b. Troy, N.Y., Apr. 25, 1952; d. Edward Joseph and Mary Elizabeth (Ryan) McGovern; m. Mario G. Mazza, Oct. 6, 1978. Student, Royal Acad. Dramatic Art, London, U. London Westfield Coll., 1972-73; BA with honors, Marymount Coll., 1974; MA, SUNY, Albany, 1976; MS, Pace U., 1989. Tchg. fellow SUNY, Albany, 1974-76; co. mgr. Cohoes (N.Y.) Music Hall, 1976-78; pub. rels. dir. Lake George (N.Y.) Opera Festival, 1978; promotion/rsch. dir. Capital Newspaper Group, Albany, N.Y., 1979-81; promotion dir., columnist Editor & Pub., N.Y.C., 1981-83; sr. v.p., dir. pub. rels. Am. Bus. Press, 1983-94; pub. adv. bd. Pace U.; adv. bd. Dyson Coll.; mag. adv. bd. Pace U./Fed. Farm Credit Banks Funding Corp., 1990—, v.p., dir. corp. devel., 1998, cons. corp. devel., 1995—, dist. legis. officer, 1995—2002. Trustee Co. Bank Pension Plan, 1995-98. Recipient Weyerhauser Craftmanship award Weyerhauser Paper Co., 1980, Design award Strathmore Paper Co., 1980, Design award Strathmore Paper Co., 1980, Telly award Local/Regional TV Comml. Festival, 1982, Pub. award Pace U., 1989, Dyson Fellowship award for excellence Pace U., 1989. E-mail: tmcgovern2@comcast.net.

MAZZA-DEBLAUWE, TANIA SUE, software engineer, technology educator; b. Belton, Tex., July 14, 1963; d. Anthony Charles and Fronia Irene (Tubbs) Mazza; m. Francis Gilbert George Deblauwe, May 7, 1989; children: Hannah, Anton, Miranda. BA in English, Baylor U., 1985; MEd, Boston U., 1993. Vol., English tchr. Peace Corps, Yemen, 1986-88; lectr. Cambria English Inst., L.A., 1988-90; dir. ESL Program Pacific States U., L.A., 1990-91; lectr. U. Md.-College Park, Brussels, 1993-94; assoc. prof. DeVry, Kansas City, Mo., 1994-97; quality assurance engr., software developer, software documentation specialist Kansas City, 1997—. Mem. Am. Soc. for Quality. Democrat. Unitarian-Universalist. Avocations: writing, internet, star trek memorabilia collecting. Home: 101 E 113th Ter Kansas City MO 64114-5449

MAZZAFERRI, ERNEST LOUIS, endocrinologist, educator; b. Cleve., Sept. 27, 1936; s. Joseph and Nanetta (Marinelli) M.; m. Florence Mildred Marolt, Nov. 23, 1957; children: Patricia Marie Atchison, Michael Louis, Sharon Lynne Brown, Ernest Louis. BS cum laude, John Carroll U., 1958; MD, Ohio State U., 1962. Diplomate Am. Bd. Internal Medicine. Intern Ohio State U. Hosps., Columbus, 1962-63, resident, 1963-64, 66-68; asst. prof. medicine Ohio State U., 1968-70, assoc. prof., 1973-76, prof., 1976-79, dir. div. endocrinology and metabolism, 1975-78; acting dean U. Nev., Reno, 1979-81, prof., chmn. dept. medicine, 1978-84, prof. physiology, 1982-84; prof., chmn. dept. medicine, prof. physiology Ohio State U., Columbus, 1984-99, prof. emeritus, 1999—; pres. Dept. of Medicine Found., 1986-99; chmn. bd. Ohio State Practice Group, 1996-99; clin. prof. medicine U. Fla., Gainesville, 2001—. Bd. dirs. The Ohio State U. Hosps., 1997—99; mem. com. on exposure of Am. people to I-131 from Nev. atomic bomb tests Nat. Acad. Sci. Inst. of Medicine, 1997—99, mem. com. on health effects assoc. with exposures experienced during the Gulf War, 1999—2000; mem. com. guidelines for thyroid cancer screening Inst. Medicine, 1997—99; chmn. Nat. Cancer Ctr. Network Com. on Thyroid Cancer Guidelines; mem. com. on health effects associated with exposures during the Gulf War Inst. of Medicine Nat. Academies of Sci., 1999—2000. Author: Endocrinology Case Studies, 3d edit., 1985, Internal Medicine Pearls, 1993; editor: Textbook of Endocrinology, 3d edit., 1986, Contemporary Internal Medicine, 1988, 3d edit., 1990, Advances in Endocrinology and Metabolism, Vol. 6, 1995, Endocrine Tumors, 1993, Morning Report, 1999, Yearbook of Endocrinology, 1999—; Endocrine editor Yearbook of Medicine, 1999—, mem. sci. adv. bd. Western Jour. Medicine, 1993; mem. editl. bd. Jour. Lab. Clin. Medicine, 1987-97, Hosp. Practice, Jour. of Clin. Endocrinology and Metabolism, Thyroid, 1999—; contbr. articles to profl. jours. Chmn. Gov.'s Com. on Radiation Fallout in Nev., 1980-84, hosp. ethics com. Ohio State U., 1994-98; mem. Sec. of Energy Dose Assessment Adv. Com., 1980-84, Agy. for Health Care Policy, Rsch. Cataract Guideline Com., 1991-92, Inst. of Medicine Guideline for Thyroid Cancer Screening com., 1997-99; mem. rsch. coun. com. on expense of Am. People to I-131 from Nev. Atomic Bomb Tests: Implications for Public Health, 1997-99. Lt. col. USAF, 1964-72; col. USAR, 1985-91. Recipient Earl N. Metz Disting. Physician award, Ohio State U., 1998, Light of Life award, Light of Life Found. N.Y., 1999, Graves' award, Thyroid Soc. for Rsch. and Edn., 2001. Master: ACP (gov. for Nev. 1984—85, chmn. clin. efficacy assessment program com. 1992—95, edn. policy com. 1992—95, mem. health and pub. policy com.); mem.: AMA, Am. Coll. Clin. Endocrinology (bd. dis. 1995—96, Disting. Clinician award 2002), Ctrl. Soc. Clin. Rsch., Am. Clin. and Climatol. Assn., Endocrine Soc., Am. Diabetes Assn. (pres. Ohio affiliate 1988—89), Am. Thyroid Assn. (Paul Star award), Am. Bd. Internal Medicine (chmn. Endocronology and Metabolism 1999—2003, bd. dirs. 1999—2003, cert. in endocrinology and metabolism, gen. internal medicine, cert. in geriatrics, continuous profl. devel.), Alpha Omega Alpha. Roman Catholic. Achievements include research in thyroid cancer. Home: 4020 SW 93rd Dr Gainesville FL 32608-4653 Personal E-mail: mazz01@bellsouth.net. *Success, like every other human experience, is relative, measured against shifting standards and subject to the scrutiny of time. One must strike a fine balance—self certainty against external review— that permits the full expression of new ideas enriched by the best and time-worn thoughts of others.*

MAZZAFERRI, KATHERINE AQUINO, lawyer, bar association executive; b. Phila., May 14, 1947; d. Joseph William and Rose (Aquino) M.; m. William Fox Bryan, May 5, 1984 (div.); 1 child, Josefa Mazzaferri Bryan. BA, NYU, 1969; JD, George Washington U., 1972. Bar: D.C., 1972. Trial atty. EEOC, Washington, 1972-75; dir. litigation LWV Edn. Fund, Washington, 1975-78; dep. asst. dir. for advt. practices FTC, Washington, 1978-80, asst. dir. for product liability, 1980-82, asst. dir. for advt. practices, 1982; exec. dir., v.p. pub. svcs. activities corp. D.C. Bar, Washington, 1982—. Bd. dir. regulatory analysis project U.S. Regulatory Coun.; mediator D.C. Mediation Svc., 1982; vis. instr. Antioch Law Sch., Washington, 1985; mem. Bd. of Women's Bar Assn. Found., 1990-93; mem. FBA Meml. Found., 1991-96. Bd. dirs. River Rd. Unitarian Ch., 2001—, bd. dir., 2001—. Recipient Superior Service award FTC, 1979 Mem. ABA (rep. of the homeless project steering com. 1988-90), D.C. Bar, Womens Legal Def. (pres. 1972-73, bd. dirs. 1971-75, 76-79), FBA Meml. Found. Home: 5832 Lenox Rd Bethesda MD 20817-6070 Office: DC Bar 1250 H St NW Lbby 6 Washington DC 20005-5906

MAZZAFERRO, JAMES JOSEPH, music educator; b. San Francisco, Calif., Apr. 19, 1956; s. James John and Marilyn Jean Mazzaferro; m. Anita Marie Piccone, Nov. 27, 1976; children: Cherylyn, Joseph, Jeanette. Bachelors Music Edn., San Francisco State U., San Francisco, CA, 1978; Masters in Music Conducting, Calif. State U., Sacramento, 1995. San Francisco Archdiocese Archbishop Riordan HS, San Francisco, 1979—89; tchr. music Florin H.S. Elk Grove Unified, Sacramento, 1989—97, Sacramento City Coll. Los Rios CC, Sacramento, 1997—2001, Sheldon HS Elk Grove Unified, Sacramento, 1997—, Cosumnes River Coll. Los Rios CC, Sacramento, 1999—. Bd. directors Cazadero Performing Arts, Cazadero, Calif., 1995—2001, Calif. Band Directors, Fresno, Calif., 1999—2001. Mem.: Calif. Music Educators Assn. (band rep. 1994—98), Musician's Union Local 6, Music Educators Nat. Conf., Phi Kappa Lambada (hon.), Phi Kappa Phi (hon.). D-Liberal. Avocation: music performance. Home: 9068 Shetland Court Elk Grove CA 95624 Office: Sheldon High School 8333 Kingstridge Drive Sacramento CA 95829 Personal E-mail: jmazz@earthlink.net.

MAZZAFRO, JOSEPH D. international adoption agency executive, web designer; b. Phila., Dec. 26, 1949; s. Joseph E. and Joan Mazzafro; m. Carole Peden, Jan. 5, 1972 (div. Feb. 1985); children: Michael, Tuan, Son, Brandon, Richard, Mikie. BA, Temple U., 1972; MA, Liberty U., Lynchburg, Va., 1994, BS in Theology. Cert. internat. lic. adoption agy. adminstr. Restaurant mgr. Marriott, Phila., 1972-82; restaurant owner Longhorne Ranch, Glenn Mills, Pa., 1982-84; vocat. coord. Applied Skills Industries, Willow Grove, Pa., 1984-89; CEO, owner Adoption World, Inc., Phila., 1989—. Author in field. Child advocate Luth. Children and Family Svcs., Phila., 1989-94; advocate for spl. needs children Adoption World, 1990—. Republican. Christian. Avocations: special needs kids, web page building, piano, travel. Office: Adoption World Inc PO Box 16269 Philadelphia PA 19114-0269 E-mail: adoption@adoptionworld.org.

MAZZA MORIARTY, ROSEMARIE, municipal official; b. Springfield, Mass., Mar. 8, 1964; d. Joseph Salvatore and Marie Grimaldi Mazza; m. Daniel Matthew Moriarty, Dec. 31, 1992; children: Cole Thomas Moriarty, Max Matthew Moriarty, Jake Daniel Moriaty. B, Elms Coll., 1986; M, Western New Eng. Coll., 1992. Dir. Mass. Career Devel. Inst., Springfield, 1996—98; tchr. H.S. of Commerce, Springfield, 1998—2000; city councilor City of Springfield, 2002—. Mem. Ward 2 Dem. Com., Springfield, 2002; bd. dirs., v.p. Springfield Tchrs. Credit Union, 2003—. Roman Catholic. Avocations: family activities, physical fitness. Home: 95 Osborne Ter Springfield MA 01104 Office: City of Springfield 36 Court St Springfield MA 01104 Office Phone: 413-787-6170. E-mail: romrmor@aol.com.

MAZZARELLA, DAVID, newspaper editor; b. 1938; With AP, Lisbon, N.Y.C., Rome, 1962—70, Daily American, Rome, 1971—75, Gannett News, DC, 1976—77, The Bridgewater, Bridgewater, NJ, 1977—83; editor USA Today, Arlington, Va., sr. v.p., 1999—. Office: USA Today 7950 Jones Branch Dr Mc Lean VA 22108-0001

MAZZARELLA, JAMES KEVIN, business administration educator; b. Phila., Sept. 22, 1955; s. Samuel Charles and Rosemary C. (Queenan) M. BA, St. Joseph's U., 1977; MBA, La Salle U., 1981, cert., 2001; MA, Temple U., 1987; PhD, Columbia-Pacific U., 1987; DBA, Pacific-Western U., 1988; cert. in acctg., Thomas Edison State Coll., 1994; BS, SUNY, 1996; cert. in e-Bus. & e-Commerce, U. Ill., 2003; cert. human rels. and law, Cornell U., 2004. Cert. mgmt. acct.; cert. in fin. mgmt. Asst. mgr. Olney Oil & Burner Co., Phila., 1977-80; data processing Craig Fuel Co., Phila., 1980-84; supr. M. Kelley Son's Inc., Phila., 1984-86; adj. instr. Holy Family Coll., Phila., 1987-88, instr., 1989, asst. prof., 1989—. Adj. instr. Phila. (Pa.) Coll. Textiles, 1984-86, La Salle U., Phila., 1985—, Rosemont (Pa.) Coll., 1988-91. Mem. Acad. Fin. Svcs., Am. Econs. Assn., Am. Fin. Assn., Am. Statis. Assn., Nat. Assn. Bus. Econs., Am. Risk and Ins. Assn., Inst. Mgmt. Accts., Math. Assn. Am., Fin. Mgmt. Assn., Prodn. and Ops. Mgmt. Soc., Midwest Fin. Assn., Western Econs. Assn. Internat., Ea. Econ. Assn., Ea. Fin. Assn., Am. Mgmt. Assn., So. Fin. Assn., Multinat. Fin. Soc., Am. Math. Soc., Am. Law and Econs. Assn., Nat. Coun. Tchrs. Math. Roman Catholic. Home: 5101 N Fairhill St Philadelphia PA 19120-3126 Office: Holy Family College Grant & Frankford Ave Philadelphia PA 19114

MAZZARESE, MICHAEL LOUIS, executive coach, consultant; b. S.I., Jan. 25, 1941; s. Louis John and Helen Ermenia (Mazzei) M.; m. Maureen Ann Starace, Oct. 3, 1970 (div. May 1998); children: Lauren, Adrienne BA, St. Joseph's Sem. and Coll., 1962; MS, CUNY, 1971, profl. dipl., 1973; PhD, Fordham U., 1980. Tchr. high sch., N.Y. and Maine, 1963-73; prof. CUNY, 1973-78; asst. dir. med. edn. St. Barnabas Med. Ctr., Livingston, N.J., 1978-79; staff supr. AT&T, Bedminster, N.J., 1979-84, mgr. Johnson and Johnson, New Brunswick, N.J., 1984-86; dir. EQUICOR, N.Y.C., 1986-87; exec. dir. Dun & Bradstreet, Murray Hill, N.J., 1987-92; v.p. Hoechst Celanese Corp., Somerville, N.J., 1992-94; pres. Mazzarese & Assocs., Westfield, N.J., 1994—; adjunct prof. bus. ethics N.Y.U. Stern Sch. Bus., 1999—; prof. bus. mgmt. Berkley Coll., 2002—. Translator: Letters from Paris (Teilhard J. Chardin), 1966. Recipient Excellence in Human Resources Devel. award Brigham Young U., 1985. Mem. Am. Psychol. Assn., Am. Soc. Tng. and Devel., Am. Evaluation Assn., Am. Evaluation and Rsch. Assn., Soc. Human Resource Mgmt., Human Resources Planning Soc. Home: 213 Scotch Plains Ave Westfield NJ 07090-4437 Office: Mazzarese & Assocs 213 Scotch Plains Ave Westfield NJ 07090-4437 E-mail: mmazzarese@aol.com.

MAZZARIELLO, MARY C. state representative; b. Rutland, Vt., Oct. 18, 1944; LPN, Fanny Allen Sch. Nursing, Vt., 1964; postgrad., Castleton State Coll. Justice of the peace, Rutland; state rep. Vt. Ho. of Reps., 1996—. Cons. in field; long-term care ombudsman, Bennington/Rutland County Office on Aging. Bd. dirs. Civil Authority, Rutland; mem. Rutland City Dem. Com., Rutland County Dem. Com. Office: 6 Tuttle Meadow Dr Rutland VT 05701-2543

MAZZE, EDWARD MARK, marketing educator, consultant; b. N.Y.C., Feb. 14, 1941; s. Harry Alan and Mollie (Schneider) M.; m. Sharon Sue Hastings, Sept. 9, 1967; children: Candace, Thomas. BBA, City U. N.Y., 1961, MBA, 1962; PhD, Pa. State U., 1966. Lectr. bus. adminstrn. CCNY, 1961-62; bus. cons., 1961—; instr. bus. Pa. State U., 1963-66; assoc. prof. mktg. U. Detroit, 1966-68; assoc. prof., dir. spl. programs W.Va. U., 1968-70; prof. bus. adminstrn., coordinator mktg. program Va. Poly. Inst. and State U., Blacksburg, 1970-75; v.p. adminstrv. services, dean Sch. Bus., Seton Hall U., South Orange, N.J., 1975-79; dean sch. bus. adminstrn. Temple U., Phila., 1979-86, prof. mktg. and internat. bus., 1979-93; dean Belk Coll. Bus. Adminstrn., prof. mktg. U. N.C.-Charlotte, Charlotte, 1993-98; co.-dir. Frank Hawkins Kenan Inst. Pvt. Enterprise U. N.C., Charlotte, 1997—98; dean Coll. Bus. Adminstrn., Alfred J. Verrecchia-Hasbro Inc. Leadership chair in bus. U. R.I., Kingston, 1998—. Chmn. bd. William Penn Bank, Phila., 1985-87; bd. dirs. Technitrol, Inc., Washington Trust Bancorp, Inc., Barrett Growth Fund; mem. dist. export coun. U.S. Dept. Commerce, 1978-80, 83-93; mem. panel trustees U.S. Bankruptcy Ct., 1984-96; adv. bd. McGettigan Ptrns., 1997-99, Radiator Specialty Co., 1997-99, Piedmont Venture Ptrns., 1997-98; mem. faculty cert. spl. studies in adminstrn. and mgmt. program Harvard U., 2003—. Author: International Business: Articles and Essays, 1963, Readings in Organization and Management, 1963, Marketing in Action, 1963, Case Histories in Sales Management, 1965, Sales Management: Theory and Practice, 1965, International Marketing Adminstration, 1967, Introduction to Marketing, 1970, Marketing in Turbulent Times: The Challenges and the Opportunities, 1975, Personal Selling: Choice Against Chance, 1976, The Food Marketing Wars: Marketing Triumphs and Blunders, 1998, Specialty Retailers: Marketing Triumphs and Blunders, 2001, Lifestyle Marketing: Reaching the New American Consumer, 2003; mem. editl. bd. Jour. Econs. and Bus., 1976-80, Indsl. Mktg. Mgmt., 1977—, Jour. Internat. Bus. Studies, 1978-82, Jour. Acad. Mktg. Sci., 1980-91, Jour. Mktg. Edn., 1985-94, Jour. Global Mktg., 1987—; contbr. articles to profl. jours. Trustee Phila. Home Care, 1984-89, Manor Coll., 1985-92, Thomas A. Edison State Coll. Found., 1987-89, Delaware Valley Coll. Sci. and Agr., 1991-97, Pa. Inst. Tech., 1992-93; chmn. econ. devel. adv. com. Village South Orange, 1977-80; mem., vice-chmn. Bd. Suprs. Doylestown Twp., 1980-81. Ford. Found. fellow, 1962-63 Mem. Am. Mktg. Assn., Acad. Internat. Bus., Nat. Assn. Corp. Dirs., Acad. Mktg. Sci., Beta Gamma Sigma, Pi Kappa Alpha. Home: 52 Horizon Dr Saunderstown RI 02874-2402 Office: U RI Coll of Business 350 Bellentine Hall Kingston RI 02881 Office Phone: 401-874-4348. Business E-Mail: emazze@uri.edu.

MAZZE, ROGER STEVEN, medical educator, researcher; b. N.Y.C., May 14, 1943; s. Harry Alan and Mollie (Schneider) M.; m. Rochelle Linda March, Dec. 28, 1969; children— Aaron, Rebekkah BA, Queens Coll., 1965, MA, 1967; PhD, U. Ill., 1971. Fellow in social psychiatry Brandeis U., Waltham, Mass., 1971; chmn. urban studies Fordham U., N.Y.C., 1970-75; from assoc. to full prof. epidemiololgy and social medicine Einstein Coll. Medicine, N.Y.C., 1975-87, exec. dir. Diabetes Research and Tng. Ctr., 1980-88; sr. v.p. research and devel. Internat. Diabetes Ctr., Mpls., 1988—; clin. prof. U. Minn. Med. Sch., 1988—; v.p. Inst. for Rsch. and Edn., Health Sys. Minn., Mpls., 1993—. Adv. bd. Nat. Diabetes Info. Clearinghouse, Washington, 1980-84, Pa. Diabetes Acad., Harrisburg, 1982—; co-dir. WHO Coll. Ctr. in Diabetes Care, Edn. and Computer Sci., Mpls., 1988—. Author: Narcotics, Knowledge and Nonsense, 1977, Professional Education in Diabetes, 1983, Frontiers of Diabetes Research, 1990, Staged Diabetes Management, 1995, Stage Diabetes Management: A Systemic Approach, 2000; editor: Practical Diabetes, 1987-89; contbr. articles to profl. jours. Active Internat. Diabetes Fedn., European Assn. for Study of Diabetes; chmn. Am. Diabetes Assn. Named Disting. vis. Scientist CDC, 1983-84; Hoechst lectr. Australian Diabetes Soc., 1985, 87, Japanese Diabetes Assn., 1983, 88, 93, 94, 99, Polish Diabetes Assn., 1993, 94, 95, 96, 99; named Best Spkr. of Yr., Soc. for Clin. Chemistry, 1991, Minn. Med. Alley award for excellence in rsch. and devel., 1995; grantee NIH, 1977—, ADA, 1991—, Juvenile Diabetes Found., 1992—; recipient Rschr. of Yr. award Inst. for Rsch. and Edn., 2000. Mem. Am. Diabetes Assn. (chmn.), Internat. Diabetes Fedn., European Assn. for Study Diabetes. Home: 5870 Boulder Bridge Ln Excelsior MN 55331-7969 Office: Internat Diabetes Ctr 3800 Park Nicollet Blvd Minneapolis MN 55416-2527 E-mail: mazzer@hsmnet.com.

MAZZEO, ANTHONY R. chemist; b. Buffalo, N.Y., May 2, 1958; s. George J. and Louise C. M.; m. Darlene Van Eseltine, May 21, 1988; children: Victoria, Seth. BS, SUNY, Brockport, 1980; PhD, Syracuse U., 1991. Chemist DuPont, Aiken, S.C., 1980-84; rsch., tchg. asst. Syracuse (N.Y.) U., 1984-88; mgr. quality assurance/tech. support New Methods Rsch., Syracuse, 1988-93; quality assurance scientist Bayer Corp., Spokane, Wash., 1993-99; sr. quality assurance scientist Hollister-Stier Labs., Spokane, 1999-2000; R&D stability mgr. DuPont Pharm. Co., Wilmington, Del., 2000—02; rsch. assoc. Pfizer Global Rsch. and Devel., 2002—. Contbr. articles to profl. jours. Mem. AAAS, Am. Chem. Soc. (chair Inland N.W. sect. 1998-2000, sec. treas. 1996), Am. Assn. Pharm. Scientists. Home: 25395 Crown Point Ct Farmington Hills MI 48335 Office: Pfizer Global Rsch and Devel 2800 Plymouth Rd Ann Arbor MI 48105

MAZZEO, DANIEL PATRICK, aerospace engineer, aviation consultant; b. N.Y.C., Apr. 18, 1949; s. Gennaro and Marie Grace (Mazzei) M.; m. Belva Faye Musick, Sept. 10, 1977; children: Gennaro, Jina Marie. BS in Aerospace Engring., Poly. Inst. Bklyn., 1971; grad. in Aviation Safety, U.S. Naval Postgrad. Sch., Monterey, Calif., 1981. Commd. ensign USN, 1969, advanced through grades to comdr., 1982, aviator, 1969-91; aviation program mgr. BDI Engring., Pensacola, Fla., 1991-95; aviation project mgr. DH Engrs., Sarasota, Fla., 1995-99; pres., CEO Aerocomm Group, Pensacola, Fla., 1999—. Airline transport pilot rating FAA, 1979; mem. State Aviation Planning Process, Fla., 1990—; completed over 150 major airport improvement projects; instr. civil engring. and engring. graphics Pensacola Tech. Acad., 2003—. Contbr. articles to profl. jours. Tech. advisor in aviation County Govt., Escambia, Fla., 1985, Santa Rosa, Fla., 1987, Tallahassee, Fla., 1994. Decorated Navy commendation medal, Navy expdn. medal, Navy Mertourous Citation Ribbon (four bronze stars), Navy Battle Ribbon (battle E), Navy Sea Svc. Ribbon (one bronze star), Navy Expert Pistol Ribbon, Def. Svc. medal with one bronze star; recipient Sci. grant N.Y.C., 1965, 68, Innovative Environmental award FAA, 1997, Airport of the Year award Fla. Dept. Transp., 1997. Mem. ASCE (section pres.), AIAA (sect. treas.), Soc. Am. Mil. Engrs., Aircraft Owners and Pilots Assn. (advisor 1997). Achievements include invention of electrophotographic imaging machine and invention of the respirograph employed in medical research. Home: PO Box 614 Gulf Breeze FL 32562-0614 Office: Aerocomm Group Pensacola FL 32502 E-mail: OneGoodEngineer@aol.com., Aerocomm@aol.com.

MAZZEO-MERKLE, LINDA LOU, legal administrator; b. Washington, Apr. 6, 1947; d. Robert Clifton Shreeves II and Esther A. (Harrison) Shreeves; m. John T. Mazzeo; children: Christina L. Schneider, Regina L. Hodges; stepchildren: John T. Mazzeo Jr., Christina M. Mazzeo. Lic. real estate salesperson, Prince Georges C.C., Largo, Md., 1972. Various secretarial positions, 1964-65, 67-72; real estate saleswoman, 1973-74; divsn. sec. Prince Georges C.C., 1974-75; real estate saleswoman Harvest Realty Inc., Clinton, Md., 1974-75; legal adminstr., property mgr., investment mgr. Tucker, Flyer, Sanger, Reider & Lewis, P.C., Washington, 1975-84; legal adminstr. Anderson, Heibey, Nauheim & Blair, Washington, 1984-85; v.p. fin. and adminstrn. Barnes, Morris, Pardoe & Foster, Inc., Washington, 1985-93; former CFO, chief adminstrv. officer Barnes, Morris & Pardoe, Inc.; legal adminstr. Payne, Negroni & Winston, Washington, 1994-95, Buckmaster & Assocs., Washington, 1996-98; cert. NIA instr. Vicksburg, Miss., 1998—; designer, owner Instant Ancestor, Jewelry Co., 2000—. Cons. and spkr. in field. Mem. Assn. Legal Adminstrs. (chmn. new adminstrs. and gen. adminstrn. sect. 1984-85). Home: 100 Lakewood Hls Vicksburg MS 39180-5343

MAZZETTI, ROBERT F. real estate manager, retired orthopedic surgeon; b. San Francisco, Sept. 29, 1930; children: Mark, Robert Alan, Michelle. BA, U. Calif., San Francisco, 1952, MD, 1955. Diplomate Am. Bd. Orthop. Surgery. Pvt. practice orth. surgeon, Santa Barbara, Calif., 1962-98; owner, pres. Mazat (Real Estate Mgmt. Co.) LLC, 1994—; owner Brushy Creek, Ltd., 1998. Mem.: Abbott Orthopedic Soc. (emeritus), Calif. Orthopedic Assn. (emeritus), Western Orthopedic Assn. (emeritus), Am. Acad. Orthopedic Surgeons (emeritus). Office: 11615 Angus Rd Ste 104 Austin TX 78759-4064 Office Phone: 512-343-1835. Personal E-mail: olmazz@aol.com.

MAZZILLI, LEE, professional baseball coach; b. N.Y., Mar. 25, 1955; Baseball player N.Y. Mets, 1976—81, Tex. Rangers, 1982, N.Y. Yankees, 1982, Pitts. (Pa.) Pirates, 1983—86, N.Y. Mets, 1986—89, Toronto (Can.) Blue Jays, 1989; coach Tampa (Fla.) Yankees, 1997—98, Norwich (Conn.) Yankees, 1998—2000; asst. coach N.Y. Yankees, 2000—03; mgr. Balt. (Md.) Orioles, 2004—. Named to All Star Game, 1979. Office: 333 W Camden St Baltimore MD 21201*

MAZZO, KAY, ballet dancer, educator; b. Evanston, Ill., Jan. 17, 1946; d. Frank Alfred and Catherine M. (Hengel) M.; m. Albert C. Bellas, 1978; children: Andrew, Kathryn. Student, Sch. Am. Ballet, 1959-61. Co-chair faculty Sch. Am. Ballet. Profl. debut in ballets U.S.A. 1961, touring Europe with co., performing for Pres. Kennedy at White House, 1961, joined N.Y.C. Ballet, 1962-80, soloist, 1965-69, prin. ballerina, 1969-80, prin. roles in world premiere of ballets including Tschaikowsky Suite No. #3, 1970, PAMTGG, 1971, Stravinsky Violin Concerto, 1972, Scherzo A La Russe, 1972, Duo Concertant, 1972, Sheherazade, 1975, Union Jack, 1976, Vienna Waltzes, 1977, Davidsbundlertanze, 1980; ballet tchr. Sch. Am. Ballet, 1980—; appeared as guest artist in leading roles with numerous cos. including Boston Ballet, Washington Ballet, Berlin Ballet, Geneva Ballet; appeared on TV in U.S., Can., Fed. Republic Germany. Recipient Mademoiselle Merit award 1970 Office: Sch Am Ballet 70 Lincoln Center Plz New York NY 10023-6548

MAZZOCCO, ANGELO, language educator, cultural historian, linguist; b. Cerreto di Vastogirardi, Isernia, Italy, May 13, 1936; arrived in U.S.A., 1954; naturalized, 1957; s. Giuseppe and Ida (Rotolo) M.; m. Elizabeth (Hunt-Davis), Oct. 7, 1990; children: Michael Ray, Marco Angelo. BS, BA, Ohio State U., 1959, MA, 1963; PhD in Romance Lang. and Lit., U. Calif., Berkeley, 0973. Instr. Spanish John Carroll U., Cleve., 1962—65; teaching asst. Italian U. Calif., Berkeley, 1966—69; asst. prof. Italian No. Ill. U., DeKalb, 1970—75; asst. prof. Spanish and Italian Mt. Holyoke Coll., South Hadley, Mass., 1975—78, assoc. prof., 1978—83, prof., 1983—, chair dept., 1981—84, chair Romance langs. and lits., 1989—93, chair dept., 1993—96, chair Romance lang. and lit., 1999—2002. Assoc. Columbia U. Renaissance Seminar, 1981-90; fellow-in-residence Inst. for Advanced Study, Ind. U., Bloomington, 1998; mem. editl. adv. bd. Renaissance Quart.; interviewer NPR, 2000. Author: Linguistic Theories in Dante/Humanists, 1993; contbr. numerous chapters to books, articles and reviews to profl. journals. Travel grantee Am. Coun. Learned Societies, 1985, Gladys Krieble Delmas Found. Rsch. grantee, 1993-94, 96-97; Italian, Am. traveling fellow U. Calif., 1969-70, NEH Italian Humanism summer sem. fellow, 1981, NEH/NSF Award, 1995-98. Mem. MLA (exec. com. Medieval and Renaissance Italian Lit. 1981-85, assembly del. 1985-87), Am. Assn. Teachers Italian, Dante Soc. Am. (coun. assoc. 1985-90, coun. 1994-97), Medieval Acad., Renaissance Soc. Am. (discipline rep. Italian lit., 2000—, mem. nominating com. 2004, chmn. Nelson Prize com. 2003, mem. Gordan Prize com. 2004), Internat. Assn. Neo-Latin Studies, N.Am. Assn. History Lang. Soc., Assn. Internat. Studi di Lingua e Letteratura Italiana, Internat. Soc. Classical Tradition, Am. Boccaccio Assn. (v.p. 1982-83), Am. Assn. Italian Studies, Nat. Assn. Scholars, Nat. Ital. Am. Found. Office: Mt Holyoke Coll Dept Spanish and Italian South Hadley MA 01075 Office Phone: 413-538-2347. Business E-mail: amazzocc@mtholyoke.edu.

MAZZOLA, ANTHONY THOMAS, editor, art consultant, designer, writer; b. Passaic, N.J., June 13, 1923; s. Thomas and Jennie (Failla) M.; m. Michele Morgan, Nov. 18, 1967; children: Anthony Thomas II, Marc Eden, Alisa Morgan. Grad., Cooper Union Art Sch., N.Y.C., 1948. Art dir. Street & Smith Publs., N.Y.C., 1948, Town and Country mag. (pub. by Hearst Corp.), N.Y.C., 1948-65, editor-in-chief, 1965-72, Harpers Bazaar, 1972-92; pres. Anthony Mazzola Design Corp., N.Y.C., 1963—; creative cons. Hearst Mags., 1992—. Editorial dir. 125 Great Moments of Harper's Bazaar, 1991-94, Town & Country 150th Anniversary, 1994—; cons. designer United Nations Childrens' Fund, Assn. Jr. Leagues Am., Columbia Pictures Corp., Sells Spltys., Gen. Foods, Paramount Pictures, Princess Marcella Borghese, Inc., Huntington Hartford, Ltd., N.Y. World's Fair, 1965 Exhibited, Art Dirs. Club. N.Y., ann. exhbns., 1948— . Served with AUS, 1943-46. Decorated Bronze Star, Knight Officer of Order of Merit Italy; recipient Cert. of Merit awards N.Y. Art Dirs. Club; medal Art Dirs. Club N.Y.C., 1955. Office: Town and Country 1790 Broadway New York NY 10019-1412

MAZZOLA, JOHN WILLIAM, former performing arts center executive, consultant; b. Bayonne, N.J., Jan. 20, 1928; s. Roy Stephen and Eleanor Burnett (Davis) M.; m. Sylvia Drulie, Mar. 7, 1959; children: Alison, Amy. AB, Tufts U., 1949; LLD, Fordham U., 1952. Bar: N.Y. 1956. Mem. firm Milbank, Tweed, Hadley & McCloy, N.Y.C., 1952-64; sec., exec. v.p. Lincoln Center for Performing Arts, N.Y.C., 1964-68, gen. mgr., chief exec. officer, 1969-70, mng. dir., chief exec. officer, 1970-77, pres., chief exec. officer, 1977-84. Cons. performing arts ctrs. in U.S. and abroad, also motion pictures, non-profit orgns. Bd. dirs. various charitable orgns.; mem. adv. bd. U. S.C. Koger Arts Ctr. With CIC, U.S. Army, 1953-55. Decorated cavaliere ufficiale Ordine al Merito della Repubblica Italiana; Ordre des Arts et des Lettres France; Benjamin Franklin fellow Royal Soc. Arts. Mem. Watch Hill Yacht Club, Misquamicut Club (R.I.). Episcopalian. Home: 12 Beekman Pl New York NY 10022-8059

MAZZOLA, MARIO, computer company executive; married; 3 children. MSEE, Bologna (Italy) U. Founder, v.p. engring. David Systems, 1982—90; co-founder, pres., CEO Crescendo, 1990—93; v.p., gen. mgr. Workgroup Bus. Unit (formerly Crescendo) Cisco Systems, Inc., San Jose, Calif., 1993—97, sr. v.p. new bus. ventures, sr. v.p. Enterprise Line of Bus., 1997—2001, sr. v.p., chief devel. officer, 2001—. Office: Cisco Systems Inc 170 W Tasman Dr San Jose CA 95134

MAZZOLA, MICHAEL, lighting designer; Resident lighting designer Oreg. Ballet Theatre, 1986—. Lighting designer Bebe Miller Co., N.Y.C. Improvisational Festival. Recipient Bessie Ward award, 2002. Office: 4931 NE 36th Ave Portland OR 97211-7621

MAZZONE, JASON, law educator; b. Devonport, Australia, Feb. 26, 1970; s. Rocco Frederick Benito and Elaine Mazzone. BA, Harvard U., 1993, JD, 1997; MA, Stanford U., 1994; LLM, Yale U., 2001, JSD, 2004. Bar: N.Y. 1998. Law clk. to Hon. Robert D. Sack U.S. Ct. of Appeals (2d cir.), N.Y.C., 1998—99; law clk. to Hon. John G. Koeltl, U.S. Dist. Ct. (so. dist.) N.Y., N.Y.C., 1999—2000; grad. fellow Yale Law Sch., New Haven, 2000—03; asst. prof. law Bklyn Law Sch., 2003—. Mem.: Am. Judicature Soc., Phi Beta Kappa. Office Phone: 718-780-7514. Business E-Mail: jason.mazzone@brooklaw.edu.

MAZZONI, KERRY, former state agency administrator; b. 1951; children: Casey, Peter. BS in Child Devel., U. Calif., Davis. Mem. Calif. State Assembly, Sacramento, 1994—2000, mem. various coms. including edn., sch. facilities fin., banking and fin., utilities and commerce, and housing and cmty. devel.; sec. of edn. State of Calif., Sacramento, 2000—03. Trustee Novato Unified Sch. Dist. Bd., 1987—, pres., 1990, 1993. Named Marin County Sch. Trustee of Yr., 1992.

MBAH, CHRIS H.N. business educator; b. May 1, 1956; BBA, Sul Ross State U., 1979, MBA, 1980. Lectr. U. Jos, Nigeria, 1982-89; sr. lectr. U. Tech., South Pacific, 1991-95; adj. prof. Ferris State U., Big Rapids, Mich., 1996-97; assoc. prof. Cornerstone U., Grand Rapids, Mich., 1997—. Adj. prof. Ferris State U., Big Rapids, 1996—. Office: Cornerstone U Business Divsn Grand Rapids MI 49505 E-mail: cmbah@cornerstone.edu.

MBARIKA, VICTOR W. information technology educator; s. George M and Regina M Mbarika. BS, U.S. Internat. U., Nairobi, 1995; MS, U. Ill., 1997; PhD, Auburn U., 2000. Info. sys. prof. Columbus State U., Ga., 1999—2001, La. State U., Baton Rouge, 2001—. Founder, pres. Cameroon Computer and Learning Ctr., Yaounde, Cameroon, 2001—. Contbr. articles various profl. jours. Recipient Outstanding Young Man of Am. award, OYA, 1998, LSU Outstanding Faculty Award, Delta Sigma Theta Sorority, 2003; KPMG scholar, KPMG Found., 2000, SREB scholar, So. Regional Ednl. Bd., 2000. Mem.: IEEE, Assn. for Info. Systems, Assn. for Computing Machinery.

MCABEE, THOMAS ALLEN, psychologist; b. Spartanburg, S.C., Mar. 31, 1949; s. Thomas Walker and Doris Lee (Gillespie) McA. Student, Ga. Inst. Tech., 1967-69; BA, Furman U., 1971; MA, U. S.C., 1975, PhD, 1979. Clin. counselor Adolescent Inpatient Svc. William S. Hall Psychiat. Inst., Columbia, S.C., 1971-73; counselor children's therapeutic camp Columbia Area Mental Health Ctr., 1974; co-dir. cmty. problems survey Eau Claire Cmty. Project, Columbia, 1975; asst. aging svcs. planner Ctrl. Midlands Regional Planning Coun., Columbia, 1976; instr. U. S.C., 1976; NSF intern S.C. State Legislature, 1978; rsch. dir. S.C. Legis. Gov.'s Com. Mental Health and Mental Retardation, Columbia, 1979-80; co-dir. TV project "Feelings Just Are" Columbia Area Mental Health Ctr., 1980-89; psychologist S.C. Dept. Mental Retardation, 1982-93, S.C. Dept. Disabilities and Spl. Needs, 1993—2003, S.C. Vocat. Rehab. Dept., 2004—. Cons. S.C. Protection and Advocacy System for Handicapped Citizens, 1980, 81, S.C. Dept. Mental Health, 1981; mem. deinstitutionalization task force S.C. Developmental Disabilities Coun., 1979-80; mem. subcom. State Commr.'s Ad Hoc Com. to Study and Develop Work/Lodge System for S.C., S.C. Dept. Mental Health, 1979-80; mem. Media Task Force of Gov.'s Adv. Com. on Early Childhood Devel. and Edn., 1980-81; chmn. primary prevention public media com. S.C. Dept. Mental Health, 1979-81; adj. faculty U. S.C., Spartanburg, 2003. Recipient Palmetto Pictures Photography award, 1977; NIMH fellow, 1976-77. Mem. APA, S.C. Psychol. Assn. Home: 353 Palmer Dr Lexington SC 29072-7476 Office: SC Vocat Rehab Dept 353 S Church St Spartanburg SC 29304 Office Phone: 864-585-3693. Business E-Mail: tmcabee@scvrd.state.sc.us.

MCADAM, DOUGLAS JOHN, sociologist, educator, director; s. Donald Neer McAdam and Merilyn Patricia Tapscott; m. Tracy Lee Stevens, Feb. 20, 1988; children: Taylor Stevens, Molly Stevens. BA, Occidental Coll., 1973; MA, SUNY, Stony Brook, 1977, PhD, 1979. Asst. prof. sociology U. Ariz., Tucson, 1983—98, assoc. prof. sociology, prof. sociology, Stanford (Calif.) U., 1998—, dir. Ctr. for Advanced Study in the Behavioral Scis., 2001—. Mem. adv. bd. Inst. Social Rsch., Ann Arbor, Mich., 2001—; trustee Social Sci. Rsch. Coun., N.Y.C., 2002—. Author: Political Process and the Development of Black Insurgency, 1982, Freedom Summer, 1988 (C. Wright Mills award, 1990), Dynamics of Contention, 2001. Fellow, Ctr. for Advanced Study in the Behavioral Scis., 1991—92, 1997—98; Fellowship, Guggenheim Found., 1984—85. Mem.: Am. Acad. Arts and Scis. Office: Ctr for Advanced Study Behavioral Scis 75 Alta Rd Stanford CA 94305

MCADAM, PAUL EDWARD, retired library administrator; b. Balt., Jan. 30, 1934; s. Joseph Francis Jr. and Irene Cecile (Heineck) McA. BA in Romance Langs., Johns Hopkins U., 1955, MA, 1956; MLS, Drexel U., 1970. Libr. Free Libr. Phila., 1969-81; br. mgr. Phila. City. Inst. Libr., 1974-81; dir. Am. Libr., Paris, 1981-85; libr. collection devel., libr. tech. svcs. Catonsville (Md.) C.C., 1986-89; assoc. v.p. learning resources Carroll C.C., Westminster, Md., 1989-99, assoc. v.p. emeritus, 1999—; adj. libr. C.C. of Baltimore County, Catonsville, Md., 1999—2002, instr. continuing edn., 2003—; adj. libr. Balt. Internat. Coll., 2000—; rschr. Transform, Inc., Columbia, Md., 2003—. Mem. adv. bd. Coop. Librs. Ctrl. Md., Annapolis, 1992-96, State Libr. Resource Ctr., Balt., 1994-95; bd. dirs. Renew, 1995—; del. Internat. Fedn. Libr. Assn, 1993, 95. Vol. MPT, 1989-2000, Walters Art Mus., 1991—, Md. Fine Arts Festival, 1991-97 AIRS, 1999—, Drexel U., 2002—. 1st lt. U.S. Army, 1956-58. Mem. ALA (membership com. 1996-98), Coll. Air Consortium, Congress Acad. Libr. Dirs. (treas. 1998-2000), Md. Libr. Assn. (hon.; membership chair 1993-96, awards chair 1996-97, 1999-2000, treas. 1997-99, chair fundraising task force 2001-02), Consortium Md. C.C. Libr. Dirs. (treas. 1998-2000), Beta Phi Mu. Democrat. Home: 524 Academy Rd Baltimore MD 21228-1814 Personal E-mail: PaulMcAd@aol.com.

MCADAM, WILL, electronics consultant; b. Wheeling, W.Va., Oct. 22, 1921; s. Will and Elizabeth Margaret (Wickham) McA.; m. Evelyn Virginia Warren, Sept. 22, 1945; children: Elizabeth Ruth, Margaret Evelyn. BSEE, Case Inst. Tech., 1942; MSEE, U. Pa., 1959. Rsch. technologist Leeds & Northrup Co., Phila., 1945-57, head elec. sect. R&D dept. North Wales, Pa., 1957-68, assoc. dir. rsch. ops., 1968-76, mgr. devel. and engring. adv. devel., 1977-79, prin. scientist rsch. dept., 1979-82, ret., 1982; cons. in electronics, 1982—. Contbr. articles to profl. jours., chpts. to handbooks; 30 patents in field. 1st lt. AUS, 1942-45, ETO. Decorated Bronze Star. Fellow IEEE (life, chmn. subcom. on elec. and high frequency measurements 1957-59, com. indsl. electronic and control instruments 1961-65, Prize Paper award 1958), Eta Kappa Nu, Tau Beta Pi. Republican. Presbyterian. Avocations: amateur radio, woodworking/cabinetmaking. Home: 3321 Twin Silo Dr Blue Bell PA 19422

MCADAMS, FRANK JOSEPH, III, communications educator; b. Chgo., Nov. 18, 1940; s. Frank Joseph Jr. and Mary Irene (Geary) McA.; m. Patty Ann Rafferty, Dec. 27, 1966. BS, Loyola U., Chgo., 1967; MFA, UCLA, 1979. Instr. UCLA, 1981—, U. Calif., Irvine, 1989—. Adj. prof. Sch. of Cinema, U. So. Calif., L.A., 1991—; mem. judging panel Diane Thomas Awards, UCLA, 1986—; vis. lectr. screenplay structure U. Navarra, Pamplona, Spain, 1990; vis. lectr. Southampton Coll., L.I. U., 1997; mem. screenwriting adv. bd. U. Calif.-Irvine Extension, 1995—. Screenwriter: California Rain, 1978, Stagecoach Bravo, 1979; author: The American War Film: History and Hollywood, 2002; co-author: Final Affair, 2002. Capt. USMC, 1966-72. Decorated Armed Forces Expeditionary medal (Laos), Vietnam Svc. medal, Rep. of Vietnam Campaign medal, Navy-Marine Corps medal, Navy Comm. medal with combat V, Presdl. Unit citation, Navy Unit citation, Meritous Unit commidation; recipient award for best newspaper col. Orange County Press Club, 1974, HM for Best Series, 1974, Sam Goldwyn Screenwriting award Sam Goldwyn Found., 1978, 79. Mem. Writers Guild of Am. W., UCLA Theater Arts Alumni Assn., PEN Ctr. USA West. Democrat. Roman Catholic. Office: MAGLA PO Box 1511 Hollywood CA 90078-1511 Office Phone: 818-244-2144. Business E-Mail: rushact@cox.net.

MCADAMS, H. T. statistician, researcher; b. Carrollton, Ill., Apr. 23, 1918; s. Hiram Ulysses Grant McAdams and Myrtle Mae Sherman; m. Catherine Conlee Jouett, Dec. 31, 1938; children: Constance, Dennis, Kay. EdB, Ill. State U., 1940; MA in Math., SUNY, Buffalo, 1956; postgrad., N.C. State U., 1961—62. Rsch. physicist Western Cartridge Co., East Alton, Ill., 1941—46; rsch. chemist Aluminum Co. Am., East St. Louis, Ill., 1946—53; prin. physicist Cornell Aeronautical Lab., Inc., Buffalo, 1953—64; spl. assignment engr. Bethlehem (Pa.) Steel Corp., 1964—65; staff scientist Calspan Corp., Buffalo, 1965—76; sr. rsch. analyst Falcon Rsch., Buffalo, 1976—81; pvt. statis. cons. Buffalo, 1981—86, Argenta, Ill., 1986—96, Carrollton, 1996—. Contbr. articles to profl. jours. Pres. bd. edn. Bethalto (Ill.) Pub. Schs., 1950—51; mgr. statis. survey Argenta Civic Club, 1990—91. Mem.: Am. Statis. Assn. Achievements include patents for air data computer system; method and apparatus for determining surface characteristics incorporating a scanning electron microscope; differential rate screening; agglomeration process using sewage sludge as a fuel; research in generalization of the Moebius Strip; method for precise control of size distributions of particulate material; means for maximizing packing density of aggregates; application of stochastic process theory to manufacturing processes, particularly metal cutting by grinding; off-road trafficability of the earth's surface; trafficability and visibility of the lunar surface; physico-geometric properties of surfaces affecting surface integrity; improved algorithm for cross-impact analysis; development of mathematical model for characterizing emissions and fuel economy of automotive vehicles; research in refinement and extension of random balance methodology; refinement of principal component regression. Avocations: music, poetry, creative writing, songwriting, gardening. Office: Accamath Svcs 333 Ninth St Carrollton IL 62016

MCADAMS, JOHN POPE, lawyer; b. Phila., June 5, 1949; s. Eugene P. and Mary (Miller) McA.; m. Anne Christina Connelly, Sept. 5, 1970; children: Emily Lane, Anne Connelly. BA, U. N.C., 1971; JD, Wake Forest U., 1976. Bar: Fla. 1976, N.C. 1976, U.S. Dist. Ct. (mid. dist.) Fla. 1977. Assoc. Carlton Fields, Tampa, Fla., 1976-82, ptnr., 1982—. Contbg. editor: The Developing Labor Law, 1983, Employee Duty of Loyalty, 1995; contbr. articles to profl. jours. Pres. Hillsborough Cmty. Mental Health Ctr., Tampa, 1983; trustee City of Temple Terrace (Fla.) Pension Plan, 1985-89; pres. Hyde Park Preservation, Inc., Tampa, 1993; bd. dirs., pres. Child Abuse Coun., Inc., Tampa Lighthouse for the Blind. Mem. ABA, ABA Equal Rights & Responsibilities Com., Fla. Bar Assn. (exec. coun. labor sect. 1987-89). Republican. Episcopalian. Home: 820 S Delaware Ave Tampa FL 33606-2915 Office: Carlton Fields PO Box 3239 Tampa FL 33601-3239 Office Phone: 813-223-7000. Business E-Mail: jmcadams@carltonfields.com.

MCADAMS, RACHEL, actress; b. London, Ont., Can., Oct. 7, 1976; d. Lance and Sandy. Actor: (films) My Name is Tanino, 2002, Perfect Pie, 2002, The Hot Chick, 2002, Mean Girls, 2004, The Notebook, 2004; (TV films) Guilt by Association, 2002; (TV series) Shotgun Love Dolls, 2001, Slings and Arrows, 2003. Office: The Gersh Agy 232 N Canon Dr Beverly Hills CA 90210 Office Phone: 310-274-6611.*

MCAFEE, CHERYL, architect; Grad, Ks. State Univ., 1979; grad., Harvard Univ. Grad. Sch. of Des., 1981. Prin./pres. Charles F. McAfee, Atlanta, 1998. Mem.: Atlanta Urban Design Commn. (bd. mem. 2002), AIA (chair of the Nat. 5th Annual Diversity Conference 1998), Nat. Org. of Minority Arch. (NOMA) (president 1998), Olympic Games in Atlanta (sr. mgr. arch. 1996). Office: Charles F McAfee 127 Peachtree St NE Atlanta GA 30303

MCAFEE, I. PAUL, III, editor; b. Denver, Oct. 23, 1955; s. I. Paul Jr. and Shirley Naomi McAfee; m. Aimee Suzanne Kepner, Apr. 9, 1976; children: Harmony, Megan, Tessie. BA in English, Biola U., 1978. City editor S.E. News-Signal, South Gate, Calif., 1983-85; asst. city editor City News Svc., Hollywood, Calif., 1986-87, Progress Bull., Pomona, Calif., 1988-89; city editor Inland Valley Daily Bull., Ontario, Calif., 1990, bus. editor, 1991-95; editor The Business Press, Ontario, Calif., 1996—. Mem. Soc. Profl. Journalists (pres. Inland chpt. 1999-00, Best Bus. Story 1994, Best Feature Story 1996, Best Tech./Sci. Story 1998, Best Legal Affairs Story 1999), Soc. Am. Bus. Editors and Writers. Avocations: internet research, book writing, competitive rollerskating. Office: The Business Press 1650 S E St San Bernardino CA 92408-2752 E-mail: paulmac@linkline.com.

MC AFEE, WILLIAM, government official; b. Port Royal, Jan. 25, 1910; s. French and Willietta (Anderson) McA. BA, Coll. of Wooster, 1932; MA in Am. History, Pa. State U., 1941; student, Oxford, Eng., summer 1937. Wooster in India rep. on faculty Ewing Christian Coll., Allahabad, India, 1932-35; tchr. pub. high schs. and prep. sch. Pa., 1935-42; joined State Dept., 1946; country specialist (Office Chinese Affairs), 1946-50; coordinator current intelligence (Bur. Intelligence and Research), 1950-56, spl. asst. to dir., 1956-60, dir. ops. staff, 1960-66, asst. dep. dir. coordination, 1966-72, dep. dir. coordination, 1972-80, dep. asst. sec. intelligence coordination, 1980—; dir. (Office of Intelligence Liaison), 1981-86, ret. Adviser Griffin Econ. Aid Mission to S.E. Asia, 1950 Served to lt. col. AUS, 1942-46, CBI. Decorated Legion of Merit; Order Brit. Empire; Precious Tripod Chinese Nationalist Govt.; recipient Superior Honor award State Dept., 1964, Disting. Honor award, 1980 Mem. Am. Fgn. Service Assn., Delta Sigma Rho. Home: 4433 Brandywine St NW Washington DC 20016-4419

MCALEAVEY, DAVID, English educator; b. Mar. 27, 1946; s. Frank Leo and Jane Louisa (Ayers) McA.; m. Christina Dickson, Dec. 1969 (div. 1971); m. Katherine Ann Perry, Jan. 2, 1977; children: Maia Margaret, Andrew Athan. AB summa cum laude, Cornell U., 1968; MFA in Creative Writing, Cornell U., 1972; PhD, Cornell U., 1975; postgrad., U. Calif., Berkeley, 1968—69. Grad. tchg. asst. Cornell U., Ithaca, NY, 1970—73, non-tchg. fellowship, 1973—74; instr. George Washington U., Washington, 1974—75, asst. prof., 1975—82, assoc. prof., 1982—87, prof., 1988—; assoc. dean for student svcs. Columbian Coll. Arts and Scis., 1986—94, dir. creative writing, 1998—; faculty liaison for summer distance learning initiative, 2004—. Author: (poems) The Forty Days, 1975, Shrine, Shelter, Cave, 1980, Holding Obsidian, 1985, Greatest Hits 1971-2000, 2001, Huge Haiku, 2004; editor: Evidence of the Community, 1984, Washington and Washington Writing, 1986. Bd. dirs. Clarendon Child Care Ctr., Arlington, Va., 1984—85, Washington Poetry Com., 1986—88, mem., 1976—88; chmn. lit. panel D.C. Arts Commn., 1984—85, mem. lit. panel, 1985—86, mem. organizing com. ann. lit. conf., 1984—86. Recipient Kreymborg Poetry award, Poetry Soc. Am., 1984, Univ. Faculty fellowship, George Washington U., 1984, 1985. Mem.: MLA, Poetry Soc. Am., The Writer's Ctr. (bd. dirs. 1976—78), Assn. Writing Programs. Democrat. Avocations: photography, woodworking, gardening, bicycling. Home: 3305 N George Mason Dr Arlington VA 22207-1859 Office: George Washington U English Dept Rm 760 Washington DC 20052-0001 Office Phone: 202-994-6515. E-mail: dmca@gwu.edu.

MCALISTER, CYNTHIA SWENSEN, writer; b. Quonsit, RI, Nov. 5, 1950; d. Robert Abercrombie and Patricia Avent (Fletcher) Swensen; m. William Harold McAlister, June 29, 1975; children: Teri Cherie, William Robert. AA, Foothill Coll., Los Altos, Calif., 1972; BA New Coll., San Jose State U., Calif., 1979. Flight attendant Tran Internat./Transamerica Airlines, Oakland, Calif., 1972—86; property mgmt. self employed, San Jose, 1975—. Author: (book) Crisscrossing the Globe For Free: Memoirs of a Charter Flight Attendant, 2002, Crisscrossing the Globe: The Crazy Life of a Charter Flight Attendant, 2004. Vol. Santa Clara Aquamaids, Calif., 1990—97. Recipient Team Mom (tennis), Carol Kane, Los Gatos HS, 2000. Achievements include participating in charity events. Office: McAlister's Electronics 926 East Fremont Avenue Sunnyvale CA 94087 Office Phone: 408-739-2605. Office Fax: 408-280-0970. E-mail: planeanxiety@aol.com.

MCALISTER, MICHAEL H. architect; b. Calif. s. Doyle R. and Mary E. McAlister. AA, Bakersfield Coll.; BArch, Calif. Poly. U. Planning technician Bakersfield (Calif.) City Hall, 1963; carpenter Del Webb Corp., Kern City, Calif., 1964; archtl. draftsman Goss & Choy Archs., Bakersfield, 1965-67; arch., v.p. D.G.C. & Assocs., Bakersfield, 1971-80; dir. architecture, v.p. N.B.A. & Assocs., Archs., Bakersfield, 1980-83; arch. Michael H. McAlister, A.I.A., Bakersfield, 1983—. Nepthrology design cons. for various treatment groups and hosps., 1987—. Commr., archtl. advisor Hist. Preservation Commn., Bakersfield, 1986-87; bd. dirs. Camp Fire Coun., Kern County, Calif., 1980-84. Recipient Archtl. Pub. Bldg. Hist. award Beautiful Bakersfield Com., City of Bakersfield's City Coun. and Hist. Preservation Commn., 1985, 87, Exterior Environ. Design Excellence Bakersfield C. of C., 1988, Comml. Design Excellence award, 1984, Design Excellence and Beautification award City of Taft, Calif., 1989, Design Excellence award State of Nev., 1992, Beautiful Bakersfield Archtl. Comml. Remodel award, 2003. Mem. AIA (Calif. Coun., Golden Empire chpt.). Avocation: religious architecture and art. Office: 1302 Ironstone Dr Studio 201 Bakersfield CA 93312-4668

MCALLISTER, DEUCE, professional football player; b. Dec. 27, 1978; s. Carl and Cornelia McAllister. Attended, Morton HS. Football player New Orleans Saints, 2001—. Office: New Orleans Saints 5800 Airline Dr Metairie LA 70003

MC ALLISTER, GERALD NICHOLAS, retired bishop, clergyman; b. San Antonio, Feb. 23, 1923; s. Walter Williams and Leonora Elizabeth (Alexander) McA.; m. Helen Earle Black, Oct. 2, 1953; children— Michael Lee, David Alexander, Stephen Williams, Elizabeth. Student, U. Tex., 1939-42, Va. Theol. Sem., 1948-51, DD (hon.), 1977. Ordained to ministry Episcopal Ch. as deacon, 1953, as priest, 1954. Rancher, 1946-48; deacon, priest Ch. of Epiphany, Raymondville, Ch. of Incarnation, Corpus Christi, St. Francis Ch., Victoria, Tex., 1951-63; 1st canon Diocese of West Tex., 1963-70; rector St. David's Ch., San Antonio, 1970-76; consecrated Episcopal bishop of Okla., Oklahoma City, 1977-89, ret., 1989; bishop-in-residence Episcopal Theol. Sem., Austin, Tex., 1990-93. Trustee Episcopal Theol. Sem. of S.W., 1961-2000, adv. bd., 1974—; mem. Case Commn. Bd. for Theol. Edn., 1981-82; pres. Tex. Council Chs., 1966-68, Okla. Conf. Chs., 1980-83; bd. dirs. Presiding Bishop's Fund for World Relief, 1972-77, Ch. Hist. Soc., 1976—; chmn. Nat. and World Mission Program Group, 1973-76; mem. Structure of Ch. Standing Commn., 1979, mem. standing com. on Stewardship/Devel., 1979-85; founder Chaplaincy Program, Bexar County Jail, 1968; mem. governing bd. nat. council Ch. of Christ, 1982-85; chmn. standing commn. on stewardship Episcopal Ch., 1983-85; v.p., trustee The Episc., Episc. Theol. Sem. of Southwest, 1987-93, chmn. bd. trustees, 1993-97. Author: What We Learned from What You Said, 1973, This Fragile Earth Our Island Home, 1980. Bd. dirs. Econ. Opportunity Devel. Corp., San Antonio, 1968-69; mem. exec. com. United Way, 1968-70, vice-chmn., 1970. With U.S. Mcht. Marines, 1942; to 1st lt. USAAF, 1942-45. Recipient Agudas Achim Brotherhood award, 1968. Mem.: Alumni Coun. Va. Theol. Sem. Episcopalian. Address: 507 Bluffestates San Antonio TX 78216-7930

MCALLISTER, KENNETH WAYNE, lawyer; b. High Point, N.C., Jan. 3, 1949; s. John Calhoun and Ruth Welch (Buie) McA.; children: Katherine Owen, Kenneth Grey. BA, U. N.C., 1971; JD, Duke U., 1974. Bar: N.C. 1974, U.S. Dist. Ct. for Middle dist. N.C. 1974, U.S. Ct. Appeals for 4th circuit 1980, U.S. Supreme Ct. 1980. Ptnr. firm Fisher, Fisher & McAllister, High Point, 1974—81; former U.S. atty. for middle dist. N.C. U.S. Dept. Justice, Greensboro, 1981—86; sr. exec. v.p., gen. counsel Wachovia Corp., Winston-Salem, NC, 1988—2001. Bd. of visitors Wake Forest U. Sch. of Law, 1988-96, U. N.C. at Chapel Hill, 1989-93, Duke U. Law Sch., 1996—. Pres. High Point Drug Action Coun., 1977-78; chmn. High Point Rep.Com., 1976-78, 88-89; mem. adv. bd. Salvation Army, High Point, 197-79; bd. dirs. Sch. of Nursing Found., U. N.C., Chapel Hill, 1993-99; vice chair Attys. Gen. Adv. Com. U S Atty., 1985-86; govs. commn. Bus. Laws and the Economy, 1994—; bd. govs. Presbyn. Homes, 1997—, chmn. 2000—; permanent mem. Fourth Cir. Jud. Conf. John Motley Morehead scholar Morehead Found., 1967; Arthur Priest scholar Phi Delta Theta, 1971 Fellow Am. Bar Found.; mem. N.C. Bar Assn. (bd. govs. 2000—), Piedmont Triad Airport Authority (bd. dirs. 1998-2001), High Point Country Club, Phi Beta Kappa. Republican. Presbyterian. Home: 220 Cascade Dr High Point NC 27265-9685

MC ALLISTER, LESTER BELDEN, economics professor; b. Chgo., Feb. 21, 1921; s. Lester Belden and Bertha (Wulpi) McA.; m. Elaine Schneider, Feb. 17, 1945; 1 child, Margaret. BA, Coe Coll., 1942; MA, Northwestern U., 1947; PhD (Carnegie fellow 1950-52), U. Oreg., 1953. Instr. econs. Coe Coll., 1947-50, Oreg. State Coll., 1952-53; mem. faculty Beloit Coll., 1953-91, prof. econs., 1959-91, prof. emeritus, 1991—, chmn. dept. econs. and bus., 1960-74. Cons.-examiner, 1974-91; vis. prof. econs. U. Wis., 1968; prof. fgn. affairs Nat. War Coll., 1961-62; mem. Wis. Banking Rev. Bd., 1974-79, Beloit Bd. Edn., 1955-58 Author articles, essays. Served to maj. USAAF, 1942-46. Ford Found. fellow U. Wis., 1957 Mem. Phi Beta Kappa. Home: 1400 N Drake Rd Apt 255 Kalamazoo MI 49006-3918

MCALLISTER, WILLIAM HOWARD, III, newspaper reporter, columnist, public affairs consultant; b. Durham, N.C., Nov. 6, 1941; s. William Howard, Jr. and Dorothy Fisk (Tillett) McA.; m. Rena Catherine Farrell, June 13, 1965; children: William Howard IV, Christopher F., Jonathan T., Benjamin J. BA in Polit. Sci, U. N.C., Chapel Hill, 1964, MA in Journalism, 1966. Cecil Prince research asst. U. N.C., 1965; reporter The Virginian-Pilot, Norfolk, 1964-67; reporter, city editor Virginian-Pilot, 1972-75; reporter Wall St. Jour., San Francisco, 1968-72, Washington Post, 1975-78, Va. editor, 1978-86, nat. reporter, 1986-99, columnist stamp and coin sect., 1987-99, lobbying columnist, 1997-99; Washington bur. chief Denver Post and MediaNews Newspapers, 1999—2003; Washington corr. Linn's Stamp News, 1997—. TV cons. Ford Found., 1969-72; cons. The Newseum, Arlington, Va., 2003—. Capt. USNR, 1966-93. Decorated Navy Commendation medal, Meritorous Svc. medal, Gold Star; recipient Lidman prize for philatelic writing, 1990. Mem. Am. Soc. Newspaper Editors, Kappa Tau Alpha, Nat. Press Club. Presbyterian. Home: 10121 Ratcliffe Manor Dr Fairfax VA 22030-2427 Office: 10121 Ratcliff Manor Dr Fairfax VA 22030-2427 E-mail: bmcallister@cox.net.

MCALPIN, KIRK MARTIN, lawyer; b. Newark, Sept. 14, 1923; s. Aaron Champion and Margaret (Martin) McA.; m. Sarah Frances Morgan, Dec. 14, 1951; children: Kirk Martin Jr., Philip Morgan, Margaret Champion Margeson. LLB, U. Ga., 1948; postgrad., Columbia U., 1949. Bar: Ga. 1949. Asst. solicitor gen. Ea. Jud. Cir. Ct. Ga., 1951; assoc. Bouhan, Lawrence, Williams, Levy & McAlpin, Savannah, Ga., 1952-53, ptnr., 1954-63; sr. ptnr. King & Spalding, Atlanta, 1963-86; pvt. practice Savannah, 1987-97, Atlanta, 1998—. Chmn. Inst. Continuing Legal Edn., 1980-81, Inst. Continuing Jud. Edn. in Ga., 1981-84, Jud. Council Ga., 1979-82. Pres. Atlanta Legal Aid Soc., 1971. Fellow Am. Bar Found., Am. Law Inst., Am. Coll. Trial Lawyers, Internat. Acad. Trial Lawyers, Internat. Soc. Barristers; mem. ABA (Jr. Bar Conf. chmn. 1958-59, chmn. gen. practice sect. 1972-73, chmn. sr. lawyers div. 1986-87, ho. of dels. 1960-90, state del. 1970-90, bd. govs. 1973-76), State Bar Ga. Assn. (chmn. Young Lawyers 1953-54, bd. govs. 1953-63, pres. 1979-80), Atlanta Bar Assn., Savannah Bar Assn. (v.p. 1960-61), Nat. Conf. Bar Pres. (exec. com. 1981-83), Ga. Def. Lawyers Assn., Fed. Bar Assn., Am. Judicature Soc., Assn. R.R. Trial Counsel, Soc. of Cin., Sons Colonial Wars, St. Andrews Soc., Capital City Club, Piedmont Driving Club, Oglethorpe Club, Phi Delta Phi, Sigma Alpha Epsilon. Episcopalian. Office: 77 E Andrews Dr NW Apt 352 Atlanta GA 30305-1392 Fax: 404-467-0619. Office Phone: 404-467-8307. E-mail: kmcasratty@mindspring.com.

MCAMIS, EDWIN EARL, lawyer; b. Cape Girardeau, Mo., Aug. 8, 1934; s. Zenas Earl and Anna Louise (Miller) McAmis; m. Malin Eklof, May 31, 1959 (div. 1979); 1 child, Andrew Bruce; life ptnr. Gerson Gonzalez. AB magna cum laude, Harvard U., 1956, LLB, 1959. Bar: N.Y. 1960, U.S. Dist. Ct. (so. dist.) N.Y. 1962, U.S. Supreme Ct. 1965, U.S. Ct. Appeals (2d and 3d cirs.) 1964, U.S. Ct. Appeals (D.C. cir.) 1981. Assoc. law firm Webster, Sheffield & Chrystie, N.Y.C., 1959-61, Regan Goldfarb Powell & Quinn, N.Y.C., 1962-65, Lovejoy, Wasson, Lundgren & Ashton, N.Y.C., 1965-69, ptnr., 1969-77, Skadden, Arps, Slate, Meagher & Flom, N.Y.C., 1977-90, spl. ptnr., pro bono, 1990-93; adj. prof. law Fordham U., 1984-85, Benjamin N. Cardozo Sch. Law, N.Y.C., 1985-90. Mem. Lambda Legal and Edn. Fund, 1991—95; bd. dirs. Aston Magna Found. Music, Inc., 1982—93, Cmty. Rsch. Initiative N.Y., 1988—89. With U.S. Army, 1961—62. Mem.: ABA, Selden Soc. Office: 2476 Mor East Tiburon CA 94920

MCANALLY, DAVID F. distribution company executive; CFO Wesco Distbn. Inc., Pitts., 1997-98. Office: Wesco Distbn Inc 4 Station Sq Ste 700 Pittsburgh PA 15219-1151

MCANARNEY, ELIZABETH R. pediatrician, educator; b. N.Y.C., May 7, 1940; d. Henry Kellers and Kathryn (Blaney) McA. AB, Vassar Coll., 1962; MD, SUNY, Syracuse, 1966. Diplomate Am. Bd. Pediatrics in pediatrics and adolescent medicine. Intern, resident SUNY Upstate Med. Ctr., Syracuse, N.Y., 1966-68; fellow in behavioral pediatrics U. Rochester (N.Y.) Med. Ctr., 1968-70, sr. instr. pediatrics, 1969-71, asst. prof. pediatrics, 1971-77, assoc. prof. pediatrics, 1977-85, prof. pediatrics, 1985—, chair pediatrics dept., 1993 . Adv. com. Fertility and Maternal Health FDA, Bethesda, Md, 1987-92; mem. program adv. bd. Robert Wood Johnson Clin. Scholars Program, Princeton, N.J., 1995—. Editor: (books) Premature Adolescent Pregnancy, 1983, Identifying Social/ Psychological Antecedents of Adolescent Pregnancy, 1984, Textbook of Adolescent Medicine, 1992; co-author of nearly 200 papers, chpts., and comm. Recipient McNeil Outstanding Achievement award Soc. for Adolescent Medicine, 1989, Job Lewis Smith award Cmty. Pediat., Am. Acad. Pediat., 1990; named to Alumni Honor Roll, SUNY, 1998. Fellow AAAS; mem. Soc. for Pediatric Rsch., Am. Pediatric Soc. (mem. exec. coun. 1998—), Assn. for Med. Sch. Pediatric Chairs (pres. 1999—), Inst. Medicine, Nat. Acad. Sci. Achievements include determination of relationship between young maternal age and maternal/neonatal outcomes. Office: U Rochester Med Ctr Dept Pediatrics 601 Elmwood Ave Box 777 Rochester NY 14642-0001 E-mail: carole_berger@urmc.rochester.edu.*

MCANDREWS, JAMES PATRICK, lawyer; b. Carbondale, Pa., May 11, 1929; s. James Patrick and Mary Agnes (Walsh) McA.; m. Mona Marie Steinke, Sept. 4, 1954; children: James P., George A., Catherine McAndrews Hazel, Joseph M., Anne Marie, Michael P., Edward R., Daniel P. BS, U. Scranton, 1949; LL.B., Fordham U., 1952; grad., Real Estate Inst., NYU, 1972. Bar: N.Y. 1953, Ohio 1974. Assoc. James F. McManus, Levittown, N.Y., 1955; atty. Emigrant Savs. Bank, N.Y.C., 1955-68; counsel Tchrs. Ins. and Annuity Assn., 1968-73; assoc. Thompson, Hine & Flory, 1973-74, ptnr., 1974-84, Benesch, Friedlander, Coplan & Aronoff, Cleve., 1984-94. Mem. law faculty Am. Inst. Banking, N.Y.C., 1968-69; mem. faculty Lakeland C.C., 1995-97. Author: Commercial Real Estate Law Practice Manual with Forms, 2001. 1st lt. USAF, 1952-54. Fellow Am. Bar Found. (life); mem. Am. Coll. Real Estate Lawyers (gov. 1983-86, treas. 1986-88, chmn. membership devel. com. 1985-87), Ohio Land Title Assn. (life, trustee 1985-88), Bar Assn. Greater Cleve. (hon. life; past chmn. real estate sect.), Ohio State Bar Assn. (hon. life). Roman Catholic. Home: 6638 Duneden Ave Cleveland OH 44139-4048 Office Phone: 216-363-4427. E-mail: jpmsolon@aol.com.

MCANENY, DEBORAH H. insurance company executive; b. 1960; Staff John Hancock Life Ins. Co., Boston, 1985—98, v.p., 1998—2000; sr. v.p. John Hancock Fin. Svcs., Inc. & John Hancock Life Ins. Co., Boston, 2000—02; dir. and CEO John Hancock Natural Resource Group, Boston, 2001—; exec. v.p. John Hancock Fin. Svcs., Inc & John Hancock Life Ins. Co., Boston, 2002—; also bd. dirs. John Hancock Subsidiaries, Boston, 2002—. Office: John Hancock Fin Svcs Inc John Hancock Pl PO Box 111 Boston MA 02117

MCANIFF, EDWARD JOHN, lawyer; b. N.Y.C., June 29, 1934; s. John Edward and Josephine (Toomey); m. Jane Reiss, June 11, 1960; children: John E., Maura T., Anne T. Annick, Jane A., Peter J., Kathleen A. AB magna cum laude, Holy Cross Coll., 1956; LLB cum laude, NYU, 1961. Bar: N.Y. 1962, Calif. 1963, D.C. 1976. Law clk. to Justice A.T. Goodwin Supreme Ct. Oreg., Salem, 1961-62; ptnr., of counsel O'Melveny & Myers, L.A., 1962—. Adj. prof. Sch. Law Stanford U., 1974-75, 94-98, Boalt Hall Law Sch., 1992-95, UCLA Law Sch., 1996—; vis. prof. U. Oreg. Law Sch., 1999—; fgn. law counsel Freehill, Hollingdale & Page, Sydney, 1981-82; bd. dirs. Mellon Fin. Corp. Bd. dirs. L.A. Master Chorale, 1979-81, 87—, chmn., 1996—; dir., exec. com. Perf. Art Ctr. Los Angeles County, 1992—; bd. dirs. Music Ctr. Found., 1992—. Capt. USNR, 1956-87. Republican. Office: O Melveny & Myers 400 S Hope St Ste 1717 Los Angeles CA 90071-2899 E-mail: tmcaniff@omm.com.

MCANIFF, NORA P. publishing executive; BA, CUNY. From mktg. info. mgr. to pres. People Mag. Time Inc., N.Y.C., 1982—98, pres. People Mag., 1998—2002, pub. Life Mag., 1992—93, pub. Teen People, 1997—98, exec. v.p., 2002—. Office: Time Inc 1271 Avenue of the Americas New York NY 10020-1300

MCANINCH, JACK WELDON, urological surgeon, educator; b. Merkel, Tex., Mar. 17, 1936; s. Weldon Thomas and Margaret (Canon) McA.; m. Barbara B. Buchanan, Dec. 29, 1960 (div. Aug. 1972); m. Burnet B. Sumner, Dec. 29, 1987; children: David A., Todd G., Brendan J. BS, Tex. Tech U., 1958; MS, U. Idaho, 1960; MD, U. Tex., 1964. Diplomate Am. Bd. Urology (trustee 1991-97, pres. 1996-97). Commd. capt. U.S. Army, 1964-66, advanced through grades to col., 1977, ret., 1977; col. USAR; intern then resident Letterman Army Med. Ctr., San Francisco, 1964-69; chief urol. surgery San Francisco Gen. Hosp., 1977—; prof. urol. surgery U. Calif., San Francisco, 1977—. Editor: Urogenital Trauma, 1985, Urologic Clinics of North America, 1989, Smith's General Urology, 1995; section editor: Early Care of the Injured Patient, 1990, Traumatic and Reconstructive Urology, 1996. Col. US Army, 1964-72. Recipient Disting. Alumnus award Tex. Tech U., 1994; named Disting. Alumnus U. Idaho, 1997. Fellow ACS (gov. 1992-97, regent 1998—); mem. Am. Urol. Assn. (pres. we. sect. 1992-93, bd. dirs. 1990—, pres. 1996-97), Genitourinary Reconstructive Surgeons (pres.), Am. Assn. Surgery Trauma (v.p.), Soc. Univ. Urologists, Am. Bd. Urology (pres. 1996-97). Office: San Francisco Gen Hosp Dept Urology 1001 Potrero Ave San Francisco CA 94110-3594 Office Phone: 415-476-3372.

MC ANINCH, ROBERT DANFORD, philosophy and government affairs educator; b. Wheeling, W.Va., May 21, 1942; s. Robert Danford and Dorothy Elizabeth (Goudy) McA.; children: Robert Micha, Ashley DeRossett, Daniel DeRossett, Zachary Schul, Beta Risner. AB, West Liberty State Coll., 1969; MA, W.Va. U., 1970, Morehead State U., 1975; postgrad., U. Hawaii, U. Ky. Engrng. technician Hydro-Space Rsch. Inc., Rockville, Md., 1965-66; prof. govt., philosophy Prestonburg (Ky.) Cmty. Coll., 1970—. V.p. Calico Corner, Inc.; dir. Chase-Options, Inc., Medisin, Inc. Bd. dirs. Big Sandy Area Cmty. Action Program Inc., 1973-76; chmn. Floyd County Solid Waste Inc.; mem. War on Drug Task Force. Served with AUS, 1962-65. Named to Hon. Order Ky. Cols., 1977; recipient 1st Place award Ea. Ky. Karate Championship. Mem. Am. Polit. Sci. Assn., Am. Philos. Soc., Ky. Philosophy Assn., Ky. Assn. Colls.and Jr. Colls. Achievements include design of Cosmic ray chamber, artificial human circulatory system, Wilson type cloud chamber, TOTO 1, 2. Home: PO Box 164 Prestonsburg KY 41653-0164

MCARDLE, RICHARD JOSEPH, retired academic administrator; b. Omaha, Mar. 10, 1934; s. William James and Abby Marie (Menzies) McA.; m. Katherine Ann McAndrew, Dec. 27, 1958; children: Bernard, Constance, Nancy, Susan, Richard. BA, Creighton U., 1955, MA, 1961; PhD, U. Nebr., 1969. Tchr. pub. high schs., Nebr., 1955-65; grad. asst. romance langs. U. Nebr., 1965-66, instr. fgn. lang. methods, 1966-69; chmn. dept. edn. Cleve. State U., 1969-70; chmn. dept. elem. and secondary edn. U. North Fla., 1971-75; dean Coll. Edn. Cleve. State U., 1975-87, prof. edn., 1987-89, spl. asst. to pres. for campus planning, 1989-91, vice provost for strategic planning, 1991-92, acting provost, v.p. for acad. affairs, 1992-94, vice provost for strategic planning, 1994-96, prof. edn., 1996-2001, ret., 2001. Cons. in field. Author articles related to issues in tchr. edn. Mem. Am. Assn. Higher Edn. Office: CASAL Dept Cleve State U Cleveland OH 44115

MCARTHUR, ELDON DURANT, geneticist, researcher; b. Hurricane, Utah, Mar. 12, 1941; s. Eldon and Denise (Dalton) McA.; m. Virginia Johnson, Dec. 20, 1963; children: Curtis D., Monica McArthur Bennion, Denise McArthur Johnson, Ted O. AS with high honors, Dixie Coll., 1963; BS cum laude, U. Utah, 1965, MS, 1967, PhD, 1970. Postdoctoral rsch. fellow, dept. demonstrator Agrl. Rsch. Coun. Gt. Britain, Leeds, Eng., 1970-71; rsch. geneticist Intermountain Rsch. Sta. USDA Forest Svc., Ephraim, Utah, 1972-75, rsch. geneticist Shrub Scis. Lab., Intermountain Rsch. Sta. Provo, Utah, 1975-83, project leader, chief rsch. geneticist, 1983-97, Rocky Mountain Rsch. Sta., USDA Forest Svc., Provo, Utah, 1997—. Adj. prof. Integrative Biology Dept. Brigham Young U., Provo, 1976—. Author more than 370 rsch. papers; contbr. chpts. to books; editor symposium procs. Named USDA Forest Svc. Superior Scientist, 1990, Disting. Scientist, 1996; Sigma Xi grantee, 1970, NSF grantee, 1981, 85, 96, Coop. State Rsch., Svc. grantee, 1986, 91; recipient Eminent Sci. Publ. award Rocky Mtn. Rsch. Station, 2001, New Century of Svc. award 2002. Mem. Soc. Range Mgmt. (pres. Utah sect. 1987, Outstanding Achievement award 1992), Botan. Soc. Am., Soc. Study Evolution, Am. Genetic Assn., Shrub Rsch. Consortium (chmn. 1983—, Disting. Svc. award 2002), Intermountain Consortium for Aridlands Rsch. (pres. 1991—). Mem. Lds Ch. Avocations: hiking, bicycling, basketball. Home: 555 N 1200 E Orem UT 84097-4350 Office: USDA Forest Svc Shrub Scis Lab 735 N 500 E Provo UT 84606-1856 Office Phone: 801-356-5112. Personal E-mail: edmdixie@aol.com. Business E-Mail: dmcarthur@fs.fed.us.

MC ARTHUR, GEORGE, journalist; b. Valdosta, Ga., July 15, 1924; s. George and Ann (Johnson) McA.; m. Eva Kim, Sept. 17, 1979. BA in Journalism, U. Ga., 1948. With AP, 1948-69, corr., 1950-54, 1954-60, bur. chief Cairo, 1960-63, Manila, 1963-65, corr. Saigon, 1966-68, bur. chief, 1968-69; with Los Angeles Times, 1969-83, bur. chief, 1970-75, corr. for Southeast Asia Bangkok, 1975-79; diplomatic corr. U.S. News & World Report, 1983-85. Served with USNR, 1943-45. Recipient citation for fgn. reporting Overseas Press Club, 1973 Mem. Sigma Delta Chi. Clubs: Fgn. Corrs. (Hong Kong); Glen Arven Country (Thomasville, Ga.); River Bend Country (Gt. Falls, Va.). Address: 506 E Creek Ct Vienna VA 22180-3578 E-mail: kimparkcho@aol.com.

MCARTHUR, JOHN HECTOR, business educator; b. Vancouver, B.C., Can., Mar. 31, 1934; came to U.S., 1957; s. Hector and Elizabeth Lee (Whyte) McA.; m. Netilia Ewasiuk, Sept. 15, 1956; children: Jocelyn Natasha, Susan Patricia. B in Commerce, U. B.C., 1957, LLD (hon.), 1995; MBA, Harvard U., 1959, DBA, 1962; LLD (hon.), Simon Fraser U., 1982, Queens U., 1985, Middlebury Coll., 1988, U. Navarra, Spain, 1989, U. Western Ont., 1992. Prof. bus. adminstrn. Harvard U., Cambridge, Mass., 1962—79, Sylvan C. Coleman prof. fin. mgmt., 1972—80, George F. Baker prof. bus. adminstrn., 1980—96; dean Harvard Bus. Sch., 1980-96; sr. advisor to pres. World Bank Group, Washington, 1995—. Bd. dirs. AES Corp., Bell Can., Bell Can. Enterprises, Inc., Cabot Corp., HCA Inc., KOC Holdings A.S., Reuters Founders Share Co. Ltd., Telsat Can.; cons. numerous cos. and govt. agys. in Can., Europe, Asia and U.S. Recipient Harvard Statesman award, HBS Club, NYC, Mgmt. Achievement award, McGill U., Can. Bus. Leadership award, HBS Clubs of Can.; John and Natty McArthur Univ. chair established at, Harvard U., 1997, McArthur Hall named in his honor, Harvard Bus. Sch., 1999, John H. McArthur Can. Fellowship program, created at Harvard Bus. Sch., 2002. Mem. Harvard Club, Links Club, Comml. Club, Somerset Club, Willowbend Club, Varsity Club. Home: 140 Old Connecticut Path Wayland MA 01778-3202 Office: Harvard Univ Sch Bus Adminstrn Boston MA 02163

MCARTHUR, JOHN WILLIAM, economist, researcher; s. William James and Lynn McArthur. BA, U. of B.C., Vancouver, 1991—96; M in Pub. Policy, Harvard U., 1996—98; MPhil in Economics, Oxford U., Eng., 1998—2000. Project mgr., africa competitiveness report 2000-2001 Ctr. for Internat. Devel., Cambridge, Mass., 2000; rsch. fellow Ctr. for Internat. Devel. at Harvard U., 2000—02; mgr. UN Millennium Project, N.Y.C., 2002—; assoc. dir. Earth Inst. at Columbia U., 2002—. Project leader, global competitiveness report Harvard U., World Econ. Forum, 2000—02. Author: (report) Global Competitiveness Report 2001-2002. Mem. Can.25, Toronto, 2001—02. Scholar Mackenzie King Travelling Scholarship, Mackenzie King Scholarship Trust, 1997, Rhodes Scholarship, Rhodes Trust, 1998. Mem.: Am. Economics Assn.

MCARTHUR, LISA R. music educator, musician; d. Tremaine James and Judith Hammon McArthur. Ph.D. in Music Theory, U. of Ky., Lexington, Kentucky, 1995—99; MA in Music Theory, Kent State U., Kent, Ohio, 1990—94, MusM in Performance, 1990—93; MusB in Music Edn., SUNY Potsdam Coll., Crane Sch. of Music, Potsdam, New York, 1986—90. Grad. asst. Kent State U., Kent, Ohio, 1990—92; orch. dir., grades 4-12 Akron Pub. Schools, Akron, Ohio, 1993—95; grad. tchg. asst. U. of Ky., Lexington, Ky., 1995—98; assoc. prof. Campbellsville U., Campbellsville, Ky., 1998—. Clinician Emerson Flutes, Elkhart, Ind., 2000—; performer, Ky., and New York, 1990—; dir. Campbellsville U. Flute Ensemble, Campbellsville, Ky., 1998—. Author: (article) Flute Keys (periodical name), musician guest recital, (debut CD) Something Old, Something New, Something Borrowed, Something Blue, 2004; presenter at the National Flute Convention, at the In-Service Conference of the Kentucky Music Educators Association/Southern Division of the Music Educators National Conference. Named Coll./U. Educator of the Yr., Ky. Music Educators Assn., 2001; recipient Performer's cert., Crane Sch. of Music, 1990. Mem.: Nat. Assn. of Coll. Wind and Percussion Instructors, Nat. Flute Assn., Soc. for Music Theory, Coll. Music Soc., Music Educators Nat. Conf. (coll. chpt. advisor 1998—, state chpt. advisor 2003—), Ky. Music Educators Assn., Flute Soc. of Ky. (pres. 2000—), Sigma Alpha Iota (life). Achievements include Musical Composition for Flute and Percussion: Finding Peace (1998); Musical Composition:...but deliver us from evil for Flute Ensemble (2001). Office: Campbellsville University UPO 1346 Campbellsville KY 42718 E-mail: lrmcarthur@campbellsville.edu.

MCARTHUR, STEVEN FRANCIS, psychologist, educator; b. Grand Rapids, Mich., Aug. 12, 1954; s. George Harold and Evelyn Theresa McArthur; m. Barbara Louise Duch, Oct. 18, 1975; children: Ryan, Alan. BA in Psychology, Aquinas Coll., Grand Rapids, 1975; PhD in Psychology, So. Ill. U., 1990. Lic. psychologist, Mich. Staff psychologist St. John Hosp. and Med. Ctr., Detroit, 1990-95, Henry Ford Ctr. Human Sexuality, West Bloomfield, Mich., 1991-95; primary care provider VA Med. Ctr., Detroit, 1997—; asst. prof. dept. psychiatry and behavioral neuroscis. Wayne State U. Sch. Medicine. Mem. rev. panel behavior and performance NASA, Washington. Mem. APA, Nat. Register Health Svc. Providers Psychology, Mich. Psychol. Assn., N.Y. Acad. Scis. Office: Detroit Receiving Hosp 3-P 4201 St Antoine Detroit MI 48201 E-mail: smcarthu@med.wayne.edu.

MCATEE, DAVID RAY, lawyer; b. Rosebud, Tex., Nov. 20, 1941; s. Lee Ray and Florine (Davis) McAtee; m. Carole Kay Pendergraft, Jan. 28, 1967; children: David Ray, Kristin Carole. BBA(hon.), Baylor U., 1964; LLB, U. Tex., 1967. Bar: Tex. 1967, U.S. Dist. Ct. (no. dist.) Tex. 1968, U.S. Dist. (so. dist.) Tex. 1994, US Ct. Appeals (5th cir.) 1969, US Ct. Appeals (11th cir.) 1981, US Tax Ct. 1993. Briefing atty. Supreme Ct. Tex., Austin, 1967—68; ptnr. Thompson & Knight, Dallas, 1968—90, Gibson, Dunn & Crutcher, Dallas, 1990—95; with Akin, Gump, Strauss, Hauer & Feld, LLP, Dallas, 1995; founder, bd. dir. No. Hills Neighborhood Assoc., Inc., 1974—76; pres., bd. dir. Montessori Sch. of Pk. Cities, 1975—78. Mem.: ABA (antitrust sect.),

Tex. Bar Assn. (legal ethics com. 1975—81), Dallas Bar Assn. (legal ethics com. 1979—81), City of Dallas Plan Commn. (mem. 1979—83, vice chmn. 1981—83), City of Dallas Thoroughfare Com. (chmn. 1979—81), City of Dallas Citizens Safety Adv. Com., Goals for Dallas Com. Democrat. Meth. Office: Akin Gump Strauss Hauer & Feld 1700 Pacific Ave Ste 4100 Dallas TX 75201-4675

MCATEE, PATRICIA ANNE ROONEY, medical educator; b. Denver, Apr. 20, 1931; d. Jerry F. and Edna E. (Hansen) Rooney; m. Darrell McAtee, Sept. 4, 1954; 1 son, Kevin Paul. BS, Loretto Heights Coll., 1953; MS, U. Colo., 1961; PhD, Union of Univs., 1976. Supr. St. Anthony Hosp., Denver, 1952-55; pub. health nurse, edn. dir. Tri-County Health Dept., Colo., 1956-58; adminstr. sch. health program Littleton (Colo.) Pub. Schs., 1958-60; asst. prof. community health, acad. adminstr. continuing edn. U. Colo., 1968-70; project dir. Western Interstate Commn. for Higher Edn., 1972-74; asst. prof. pediatrics, project co-dir. Sch. Medicine U. Colo., 1975—; mem. profl. svcs. staff Mead Johnson & Co., 1981—. Cons. Colo. Safety Coun.; treas. Vista Nueva Assocs. Editor: Pediatric Nursing, 1975-77. Chmn. bd. dirs. Found. for Urban and Neighborhood Devel.; mem. Arapahoe Health Planning Coun. Mem. NAS, APHA, Inst. Medicine, Nat. Bd. Pediatric Nurse Practitioners and Assocs. (pres.), Nat. Assn. Pediatric Nurse Practitioners (v.p.), Am. Acad. Polit. and Social Scientist, Nat. League Nursing, Western Soc. Rsch., Am. Sch. Health Assn., Sigma Theta Tau. Home: 877 E Panama Dr Littleton CO 80121-2531 Office: 4200 E 9th Ave Denver CO 80220-3706

MCAULEY, THOMAS H. real estate executive; Chmn. CEO, Ewing S.E. Realty, Inc., Atlanta, 1988-93; regional ptnr. Faison Assocs., Inc. (acquired Ewing S.E. Realty, Inc.), Charlotte, N.C., 1993-95; pres. IRT Property Co., Atlanta, 1995—, CEO, 1997—, chmn., 1998—. Office: Equity One Realty & Management SE IN 1275 Powers Ferry Rd SE #100 Marietta GA 30067-9490

MCAULEY, VAN ALFON, aerospace mathematician; b. Travelers Rest, S.C., Aug. 28, 1926; s. Stephen Floyd and Emily Floree (Cox) McA. BA, U. N.C., Chapel Hill, 1951; postgrad., U. Ala., Huntsville, 1956-57, 60-63. Mathematician Army Ballistic Missile Agy., Huntsville, Ala., 1956-59; physicist NASA, Marshall Center, Huntsville, 1960-61, rsch. mathematician, 1962-70, mathematician, 1970-81. Contbr. articles to profl. jours.; patentee for aerospace control invention; publ. method for solution of polynomial equations; devised methods for numerical solution of heat flow using partial differential equations. Served with U.S. Army, 1944-46. Recipient Apollo achievement award NASA, 1969, cost savs. award, 1973, Skylab achievement award, 1974, Outstanding Performance award, 1976, NASA Cert. of Recognition, 1977. Mem. AAAS, Am. Math. Soc., N.Y. Acad. Scis., Phi Beta Kappa. Home: 3529 Rosedale Dr NW Huntsville AL 35810-2573

MCAULIFFE, JANE DAMMEN, religious studies and Islamic studies educator; BA in Classics and Philosophy, Trinity Coll., 1968; MA in Religious Studies, U. Toronto, 1979, PhD in Islamic Studies, 1984. Asst. prof. dept. religious studies U. Toronto, 1981-86, assoc. to full prof. dept. Middle East and Islamic studies, dept. study religion, 1992-99, chair dept. study of religion, dir. Ctr. Study of Religion, 1992-97; from asst. prof. to assoc. prof. history of religions and Islamic studies Candler Sch. Theology Emory U., Atlanta, 1986-92, assoc. dean Candler Sch. Theology, 1990-92; prof. Dept. for the Study of Religion, 1997-99; dean, prof. history and Arabic Georgetown Coll. Georgetown U., Washington, 1999—. Appointed Vatican Commn. for Religious Rels. with Muslims, 1994. Author: Qur'anic Christians: An Analysis of Classical and Modern Exegesis, 1991, 'Abbasid Authority Affirmed: The Early Years of al-Mansur, vol. 28, 1995; editor: Encyclopaedia of the Qur'an, 2001—; contbr. articles to profl. jours. Danforth Found. fellow, 1976-80, NEH Summer fellow, 1979-80, Charles Gordon Heyd fellow, 1980-81, Social Scis. and Humanities Rsch. Coun. doctoral fellow, 1981-84, Postdoctoral fellow, 1984-86, CASA II fellow, 1986, NEH Summer Faculty Travel fellow, 1989, NEH Rsch. fellow, 1992, Mellon fellow, 1994, Guggenheim fellow, 1996. Mem. Am. Soc. Study of Religion, Am. Acad. Religion, Am. Oriental Soc., Can. Soc. Study of Religion, Mid. East Studies Assn. (Thesis award 1985), Soc. Values in Higher Edn. Office: Georgetown Coll Georgetown U PO Box 571003 Washington DC 20057-1003 Home: 1321 36th St NW Washington DC 20007

MCAULIFFE, JOHN ANTHONY, hand surgeon; b. Miami, Dec. 11, 1952; s. William A. McAuliffe and Gertrude A. Rogers; m. Marilyn Wiegand, Dec. 31, 1977; children: Christopher, Jacob, Caitlin. BA, Columbia U., 1977; MD, U. Fla., 1982. Diplomate Am. Bd. Orthopedic Surgeons. Intern in gen. surgery Shands Hosp., U. Fla., 1982-83, orthopedic resident, 1983-88; fellow in hand surgery Jackson Meml. Hosp., U. Miami, 1988-89; assoc. prof. U. Miami, 1989-95; hand surgeon Cleve. Clinic Fla., Weston, 1995—. Contbr. chpts. to books and articles to profl. jours. Fellow Am. Acad. Orthopedic Surgeons; mem. AMA, Am. Soc. for the Surgery of the Hand, New Millennium Hand Study Group (pres. 1994-95), Fla. Hand Soc. (pres. 1994-96), Alpha Omega Alpha. Office: Cleve Clinic Florida 2950 Cleveland Clinic Blvd Weston FL 33331 Office Phone: 954-659-5594.

MCAULIFFE, JOHN C. health/medical products executive; b. 1959; With Gen. Physics Corp. GP Strategies Corp., N.Y.C., 1980—, pres. Gen. Physics Corp., 1997—, sr. v.p., 1998—. Office: GP Strategies Corp 777 Westchester Ave Fl 4 White Plains NY 10604-3520 Office Fax: 212-230-9545.

MCAULIFFE, ROSEMARY, state legislator; b. Seattle, Aug. 1, 1940; m. James McAuliffe; 6 children. BSN, Seattle U. Owner, mgr. Hollywood Sch. House; mem. Wash. Senate, Dist. 1, Olympia, 1993—; chair edn. com. Wash. Senate, mem. environ. quality and water resources com., mem. higher edn. com., co-chairperson joint select com. on edn. restructuring, mem. student conduct task force, mem. spl. edn. adv. coun., mem. food safety adv. com. Bd. dirs. Northshore Sch., 1977-91, bd. pres., 1981-82; mem. Northshore Econ. Devel. Com., Together for a Drug-Free Youth Com., 1989; chairwoman Bothell Downtown Mgmt. Assn., 1987-90; del. Main St. Revitalization, Pacific N.W.; mem. conf. com. and diversion com. Northshore Juvenile Ct., 1978-80; mem. Lake Health Com., 1997-98. Mem. Wash. Sch. Dir.'s Assn. (legis. network rep. 1990-91), Assn. Children with Learning Disabilities, Northshore and Woodinville C. of C. Democrat. Office: 402A John Cherberg Bldg Olympia WA 98504-0001

MCAULIFFE, STEVEN JAMES, federal judge; b. 1948; BA, Va. Mil. Inst., 1970; JD, Georgetown U., 1973. Capt. appellate coun. US Army JAGC, 1973-77; asst. atty. gen. Office NH Atty. Gen., 1977-80; ptnr. Gallagher, Callahan, Gartrell, P.A., Concord, NH, 1980-92; fed. judge US Dist. Ct. (NH dist.), Concord, 1992—. Chair Rhodes Scholarship Selection Com. for NH, 1998—. Trustee Univ. Sys. of NH, 1986-94; bd. dirs. NH Med. Malpractice Stabilization Res. Fund Trust, 1987-92, Office Pub. Guardian, 1980-92, Challenger Ctr. for Space Sci. Edn.; active NH Dem. Leadership Coun., 1988-92. Capt. US Army, 1970-77, USAR, 1977-80, NH Army NG, 1980-88. Decorated US Army Commendation medal. Fellow NH Bar Found.; mem. ABA, NH Bar Assn. (pres. 1991-92, pres.-elect 1990-91, v.p. 1989-90, mem. ex-officio NH Supreme Ct. com. profl. conduct 1989-90, mem. ethics com. 1984-86), Nat. Conf. Bar Pres., Merrimack County Bar Assn., DC Bar Assn., US Supreme Ct. Hist. Soc., NH Jud. Coun. (vice-chmn. 1991-92), Aircraft Owners and Pilots Assn., Concord Country Club. Office: US Dist Ct 55 Pleasant St Room 416 Concord NH 03301-3904

MCAULIFFE, TERRY (TERENCE RICHARD MCAULIFFE), political organization administrator; b. Syracuse, N.Y., 1957; m. Dorothy Swann, 1988; children: Dori, Jack, Mary, Sally, Peter. BA in Polit. Sci., Cath. U., 1979; JD, Georgetown U., 1984. Fin. dir. Gephardt for Pres. Campaign Com., 1988; amb., commr. gen. Internat. Expo., 1993; chmn. Dem. Bus. Coun., 1993; fin. chmn. Dem. Nat. Com., 1994, Bill Clinton/Al Gore Election Campaign, 1996; co-chair Presdl. Inaugural Com., 1997; chmn. Dem. Nat. Conv., L.A., 2000, Dem. Nat. Com., 2001—. Office: Dem Nat Com 430 S Capitol St SE Washington DC 20003*

MCAUSLAND, RANDOLPH M. N. arts consultant; b. Phila., Oct. 9, 1934; s. John Randolph and Helen (Neal) McA.; m. Marilynn Kemp, July 10, 1965 (div. 1976); children: Andrew, Sean; m. Jan E. Tribbey, May 9, 1986. AB, Princeton U., 1957. Copy editor Wall Street Journal, N.Y.C., 1960-61; editor, publisher Stowe Reporter, 1961-63; consulting editor Interpub. Group Cos., 1963-67; creative dir. The Progress Group, N.Y.C., 1967-70, gen. mgr., 1970-75; dir. mktg. Billboard Pubs., N.Y.C., 1975-77; asst. to pres. Macmillan Mag., Stamford, Conn., 1977-80; editor The New Satirist, New Canaan, Conn., 1980-82; pres. Design Pubs. Inc., N.Y.C., 1983-89; dir. Design Arts Program, NEA, Washington, 1989-90; dep. chmn. NEA, Washington, 1990-93; writer, arts cons. Richmond, Va., 1993—. Founder, dir. Design History Found., N.Y.C., 1988-89; Theatre IV, 2002—, Cin. Chamber Orch., 2002—. Author: Supermarkets: History of an American Institution, 1980; contbr. articles to profl. jours. Bd. dirs. Hand Wodkshop, Richmond, 1993-94, Richmond Choral Soc., 1994, Worldesign Found., 1994-97, Fla. Friends Librs., 1995-99, Fla. Ctr. for the Book, Broward County Vision Com., 1998-99, Cin. Chamber Orch., 2002—. With U.S. Army, 1957-60. Recipient Commendation N.Y.C. Police Dept., 1971, Pres. Cup Am. Comedy Club N.Y., N.Y.C., 1974, Bronze Apple award Indsl. Design Soc., 1987, Disting. Svc. award NEA, 1991-92. Mem. Am. Ctr. For Design (hon.), Coalition Ind. Scholars, Ivy Club. Home: 7405 Fair Oaks Dr Cincinnati OH 45237-2925 E-mail: RandyMCA@cinci.rr.com.

MCAVITY, JOHN GILLIS, museum director, association executive, museologist; b. St. John, N.B., Can., Oct. 30, 1950; s. J. Patrick H. and Catharine A. (McNeill) McA. BA, U. N.B., 1972. Cert. assn. exec. Asst. curator Kings Landing Mus., Fredericton, N.B., Can., 1972-73; provincial mus. adviser N.B. Mus., St. John, Can., 1973-76; exec. dir. Ont. Mus. Assn., Toronto, Can., 1976-81, Can. Mus. Assn., Ottawa, Ont., Can., 1981—. Bd. dirs. internat. mus. Mgmt. Com., Internat. Coun. Mus., Can. Soc. of the Decorative Arts; sec. treas. Intercom, 2001—. Editor INTERCOM News, 1997—. V.p. St. John Heritage Trust, 1974-76; exec. com. Can. Club, St. John, 1975, English Speaking Union, St. John, 1974-76; vol. fundraiser Kidney Found., Can.; bd. dirs. Centretown Citizens Corp.; founding dir. Mus. Found. Can., 1994—. Recipient Queen's Jubilee medal, 2002. Mem.: Internat. Coun. Museums (task force, legal affairs com. 2002—), Shefford Heritage Co-op (membership chair 1992—95, 2000—), Can. Art Mus. Dirs. Orgn., Can. Soc. Assn. Execs. (bd. dirs. 1993—96, Long Svc. Achievement award 2002), Can. Soc. Copyright Consumers, Ont. Assn. Art Galleries (bd. dirs. 1986—90), Nat. Mus. Assn. (chair internat. com. 2000—), Assn. Museums N.B. (founding), Tourism Industry Assn. Can. (bd. dirs.), Quaco Hist. and Libr. Soc. (hon. life), Assn. Cultural Execs. (bd. dirs. 1988—92, apptd. to senate 1995), Inst. Assn. Execs. (chmn. postal com., cert., bd. dirs. Ottawa chpt.), Mus. Found. Can. (founding dir. 1994—), Am. Assn. State and Local History (awards com. 1981—84, nominations com. 1985), Am. Assn. Museums. Anglican. Home: 300 Cooper St Apt 41 Ottawa ON Canada K2P 0G7 Home (Summer): 29 Kingshurst Ln Rothesay NB Canada E2H 1T3 E-mail: jmcavity@museums.ca.

MCAVOY, BRUCE RONALD, engineer, consultant; b. Jamestown, N.Y., Jan. 30, 1933; s. George Harold and Agda Amelia (Martinson) McA. BS in Physics, U. Rochester, 1954. Jr. engr. Westinghouse Air Arm Div., Balt., 1956-57, assoc. engr., 1957-58; rsch. engr. Westinghouse Rsch. Ctr., Pitts., 1958-69; sr. rsch. engr. Westinghouse R & D Ctr., Pitts., 1969-78, fellow engr., 1978-84, adv. scientist, 1984—. Mem. adv. bd. Nat. Ctr. Phys. Acoustics, U. Miss., 1987—88; lectr. elect. engring. dept. Carnegie Mellon U., 1968—70. Editor spl. issue IEEE Trans. Microwave Theory Tech., Ultrasonics Symposium procs., 1976-96; mem. editl. bd. jour. Microwave and Guided Wave Letters, 1990. With U.S. Army, 1954-56. Fellow IEEE (life, awards and recognition com. 1989—, def. R&D policy com. 1989-91, Centennial medal 1984, tech. program com. Internat. Microwave Symposium 1986-99); mem. DAV (life), Ultrasonic, Ferroelectric and Frequency Control Soc. of IEEE (pres. 1986-87, Disting. Svc. award 1999), Electromagnetics Acad., Microwave Theory and Techniques Soc. (chmn. microwave acoustics tech. com. 1988-99). Republican. Lutheran. Home: 926 Ivy St Pittsburgh PA 15232-2651 Office Phone: 412-621-2791. E-mail: brmcavoy@comcast.net.

MCAVOY, JOHN JOSEPH, lawyer; b. Worley, Idaho, June 28, 1933; s. Earl Francis and Florence Jewel (Mitchell) McA.; m. Joan Marjorie Zeldon, Sept. 20, 1964; children: Jason, Jon. BA, U. Idaho, 1954, LLB, 1958; LLM, Yale U., 1959. Bar: Idaho 1958, U.S. Supreme Ct. 1962, N.Y. 1963, U.S. Tax Ct. 1969, D.C. 1976. Asst. prof. law George Washington U., Washington, 1959-62; staff atty. stockpile investigating subcom. Armed Forces Com. U.S. Senate, Washington, 1962; assoc. White & Case, N.Y.C., 1963-71, ptnr., 1972-95; of counsel Lukas, Nace, Gutierrez & Sachs, Washington, 1995—. Adj. prof. Washington Coll. Law, Am. U., Washington, 1990; mem. D.C. com. on grievances U.S. Dist. Ct., 2003—. Bd. dirs. N.Y. Civil Liberties Union, 1975-77, commr. Uniform State Laws, 2001—; chmn. due process com. ACLU, 1971-75. With U.S. Army, 1954-56. Mem. D.C. Bar Assn. (ethics com. 1982-88, vice chmn. 1986-87, chmn. 1987-88), Phi Beta Kappa, Phi Alpha Delta. Democrat. Avocations: swimming, bicycling, fgn. travel. Personal E-mail: mcavoylaw@aol.com.

MCBARNETTE, BRUCE OLVIN, lawyer, corporate executive; b. N.Y.C., Oct. 7, 1957; s. Olvin R. and Yvette Fay (Francis) McB. BA, Princeton U., 1980; JD, NYU, 1983. Bar: N.Y. 1985, Hawaii 1987, D.C. 1989. Atty. Natural Resources Def. Coun., N.Y.C., 1984, U.S. Judge Adv.Gen.'s Corp., Aberdeen Proving Grand, Md., 1988-89, Schofield, Hawaii, 1985-88; legis. asst. U.S. Ho. of Reps., Washington, 1989; counsel impeachment trial com. U.S. Senate, Washington, 1989-90; sr. counsel Fed. Nat. Mortgage Assn., Washington, 1990-93; pres. Summit Connections, Inc., Washington, 1993—. Faculty George Washington U.; dir. devel. Charlies Pl., 1998—. Coord. Achieve Speakers Bur., Washington, 1990. Capt. U.S. Army, 1985-88. Mem. ABA (contbg. author newsletter for mil. pers.), SAG, D.C. Bar Assn., N.Y. Bar Assn., Hawaii Bar Assn. Democrat. Episcopalian. Avocation: track and field. Home: 248 Willow Ter Sterling VA 20164-1628 Office: Summit Connections Inc 248 Willow Ter Sterling VA 20164-1628

MCBEE, LUCY ARMIJO, retired elementary education educator, administrator, singer, actress, writer; b. Santa Fe, Feb. 26, 1931; d. Jose Alfonso and Celine (Chaves) Armijo; m. Robert Levi McBee, June 13, 1959; children: Martin Christopher, Mark Antony, Mathieu A.C. Music cert., Kansas City Conservatory Music, 1952; BA in Econs., Avila Coll., 1952; postgrad. in theater, U. Mo., Kansas City, 1962; MA in Tchg., Webster Coll., 1974. Cert. Montessori tchr. Sec., translator fgn. dept. Commerce Bank Kansas City, Mo., 1952-53; sec., with econ. rsch. dept. Farmland Industries, Kansas City, 1953-59; sec. Western Electric, Kansas City, 1961-62; drama resident theatre tchr. Jewish Cmty. Ctr., Kansas City, 1962-63; Montessori tchr. Wee Wisdom Sch., Unity Village, Mo., 1964-67; Montessori/Spanish tchr. Montessori Sch., Blue Springs, Mo., 1967-68; tchr., dir. St. Peter's Day Sch., Kansas City, 1968-71; tchr., prin./adminstr. Loretto Sch., Kansas City, 1974-83; writer plays San Antonio, 1985—87; comptroller Charles Feldstein Co., Chgo., 1990-94. Drama/voice tchr. Backstage Workshop for profl. actors and singers, 1979-84; theatre tchr. Visitation Sch. Kans. City, 1983. Co-editor: The Clan MacBean Register, 2001—02. Mem., cantor Visitation Cath. Ch. Choir, Kansas City, 1948-85; computer consultation, data processing VA, Marion, Ind., 1988; fundraising, data processing, trainer Dukakis/Bentsen Presdl. Campaign, Chgo., 1987-88; fundraising office mgr. Simon for Senate Campaign, Chgo., 1988-89; comptroller Pres. Cook County Bd. Fundraising office, 1989-90; mem. Early Childhood Edn. Com., 1973-78, Holy Name Cathedral Choir, Chgo., 1988-94. Recipient Best Actress award U. Kans. City Theatre, 1958, Silver Tray award, Notre Dame de Sion Montessori Sch., Kans. City, 1971, St. Peter's Annual medal St. Peter's Episcopal Ch., Kansas City, 1974, VA award for svc. during Golden Age Games, Marion, Ind., 1988, 1st place award Irish Cultural Soc. Poetry Awards; named Miss Congeniality Dukakis-Bentsen Presdl. Campaign, Chgo., 1988. Mem.: Scottish Soc., The Clan McBean, San Antonio Poets Assn. Roman Catholic. Avocations: acting, singing, poetry, plays and music. Home: 7118 Walnut Trace San Antonio TX 78239-3058

MCBEE, MARY LOUISE, state legislator, former academic administrator; b. Strawberry Plains, Tenn., June 15, 1924; d. John Wallace and Nina Aileen (Umbarger) McB. BS, East Tenn. State U., 1946; MA, Columbia U., 1951; PhD, Ohio State U., 1961. Tchr. East Tenn. State U., Johnson City, 1947-51; asst. dean of women, 1952-56, 57-60; dean of women, 1961-63, U. Ga., Athens, 1963-67; world campus afloat adminstr., 1966-67; assoc. dean of students, 1967-72; dean of students, 1972-74; asst. v.p. acad. affairs, 1974-76; assoc. v.p. acad. affairs, 1976-86; v.p. acad. affairs, 1986-88. Author: College Responsibility for Values, 1980; co-author: The American Woman: Who Will She Be?, 1974, Essays, 1979, 2d edit. 1981. Bd. dirs. Salvation Army, Athens, 1978—, United Way, Athens. Fulbright scholar, The Netherlands, 1956-57. Mem. Athens C. of C. (bd. dirs.). Democrat. Methodist. Avocations: gardening, tennis, hiking. Home: 145 Pine Valley Pl Athens GA 30606-4031 Office: Ga House of Reps State Capitol Atlanta GA 30334 E-mail: lmcbee@legis.state.ga.us.

MCBEE, ROBERT LEVI, retired federal government official, writer, consultant; b. Braymer, Mo., Aug. 25, 1927; s. Calvin Levi and Wavah E. (Tripp) McB.; m. Lucy Armijo, June 13, 1959; children: Martin Christopher, Mark Antony Christian, Mathieu Alfonso Calvin. BA, Westminster Coll., Fulton, Mo., 1952. Editor Take-Off Smoky Hill AFB, Salina, Kans., 1947-48; publicity writer Westminster Coll., Fulton, Mo., 1950-52; advt. mgr. Battenfeld Grease and Oil Corp., Kansas City, Mo., 1952-53; asst. to advt. mgr. Ash Grove Lime and Cement Co., Kansas City, Mo., 1953-57; publicity dir. Am. Campaign Svcs., Kansas City, Mo., 1957; freelance writer Chelan, Wash., 1957-58; reporter Kansas City (Mo.) Times Star, 1958-61; assoc. editor Bailey Publs., Independence, Mo., 1961-63; editor Nat. Cath. Register, Denver, 1963-64; mng. editor Pleasant Hill (Mo.) Times, 1964-67; community affairs specialist Region 7 Job Corps, Kansas City, Mo., 1967-69; pub. info. officer Region 7 Office Econ. Opportunity, Community Svc. Adminstrn., Kansas City, Mo., 1969-81; pub. affairs specialist Kansas City Dist. Army C.E., 1981-85; chief community rels. Fifth U.S. Army, San Antonio, 85-88; acting dir. Chgo. Regional Office Pub. Affairs Dept. Vet. Affairs, 1989-90, asst. dir., 1988-94; acting dir. Dept. Vets. Affairs Chgo. Regional Office Pub. Affairs, 1991. Co-editor: The Clan MacBean Register, 2001-02. Sec., asst. treas. Kansas City Area Transp. Authority, 1965-70; pres. Pleasant Hill (Mo.) C. of C., 1966-67; sec. City Planning and Zoning Commn., Pleasant Hill, 1966; bd. dirs. Cath. Info. Svcs., Kansas City, 1966-72; adv. trustee Rsch. Med. Ctr., Kansas City, 1967-82. Mem. Westminster Coll. Alumni Coun. (life), Skulls of Seven, The Clan MacBean, The Scottish Soc. San Antonio, Pi Delta Epsilon (charter pres.), Eta Sigma Phi, Kappa Alpha. Democrat. Roman Catholic. Avocations: reading, genealogy.

MCBEE, SUSANNA BARNES, retired journalist; b. Santa Fe, N.Mex., Mar. 28, 1935; d. Jess Stephen and Sybil Elizabeth (Barnes) McBee; m. Paul H. Recer, July 2, 1983. AB, U. So. Calif., 1956; MA, U. Chgo., 1962. Staff writer Washington Post, 1957-65, 73-74, 77-79, asst. nat. editor, 1974-77; asst. sec. pub. affairs HEW, 1979; articles editor Washingtonian mag., 1980-81; assoc. editor U.S. News & World Report, 1981-86; news editor Washington Bur., Hearst Newspapers, 1987-89, asst. bur. chief, 1990—2003, ret., 2003; Washington corr. Life mag., 1965—69; Washington editor McCall's mag., 1970—72. Bd. dirs. Washington Press Club Found., 1992-95. Recipient Penney-Missouri mag. award, 1969, Hall of Fame award, Soc. Profl. Journalists, 1996, Sigma Delta Chi Pub. Svc. award, 1969, Hearst Eagle award, 1994. Mem. Nat. Press Club, Cosmos Club. Home: 5190 Watson St NW Washington DC 20016-5329

MCBRAYER, SANDRA L. educational director, homeless outreach educator; AA, San Diego Mesa Coll., 1981; BA in Applied Arts and Scis., San Diego State U., 1986, MA in Edn., 1990. Cert. presch.-kindergarten, grs. 1-12, adult edn., Calif. Tchr. asst. group homes Oz, The Bridge, Gatehouse, 1984-87; tchr. Hillcrest Receiving Home, 1987-88, Juvenile Hall, 1987-88, Comprehensive Adolescent Treatment Ctr., 1987-88; head tchr. the Monarch HS, 1988-96; CEO The Children's Initiative, San Diego. Lectr., cons. Ctrs. Careers Edn., Sch. Tchr. Edn. San Diego State U., 1990—; collaborator sch. dists. State Dept. Edn., Equity/Homeless Office, 1992—; staff devel. tng.; adj. prof. Coll. Edn., San Diego (Calif.) State U. Recipient award Exceptional Vols. Svc. Family Care Ctr., 1988, San Diego's 10 Leadership award Sta. KGTV, 1991, Celebrate Literacy award Internat. Reading Assn., 1992, Women of Vision in Edn. award LWV San Diego, 1992, Disting. Alumna of Yr.-Edn. award San Diego State U., 1992, Golden Bell award Calif. Sch. Bds. Found., 1992, Coun. of State Sch. Officers Nat. Tchr. of Yr. award 1994; named San Diego County Tchr. of Yr. by San Diego County Office of Edn., 1993, Calif. Tchr. of Yr. by State Dept. Edn., 1993, Nat. Tchr. of Yr., Pres. Clinton, 1994, Tech. Tchr. of Yr., Coun. on Tech. Tchr. Edn., 1994, Exceptional Svc. award Calif. State PTA, Humanitarian award Youth Advocacy Assn., Living Legacy award Internat. Women's Ctr.; recognized by local and nat. news media. Mem. NEA, Calif. Tchrs. Assn., Assn. Educators, Nat. Dropout Prevention Network, Calif. Homeless Coalition, Phi Kappa Phi. Office: The Childrens Initiative 4438 Ingraham St San Diego CA 92109

MCBREEN, MAURA ANN, lawyer; b. N.Y.C., Aug. 18, 1953; d. Peter J. and Frances S. (McVeigh) McB. AB, Smith Coll., 1975; JD, Harvard U., 1978. Bar: Ill. 1978. Ptnr. Kirkland & Ellis, Chgo., 1978-86, Isham, Lincoln & Beale (merged with Reuben & Proctor), Chgo., 1986-88, Baker & McKenzie, Chgo., 1988—. Mem. ABA, Chgo. Bar Assn., Midwest Pension Conf. Office: Baker & McKenzie 1 Prudential Pla 130 E Randolph Dr Ste 3700 Chicago IL 60601-6342

MCBRIDE, ANGELA BARRON, nursing educator; b. Balt., Jan. 16, 1941; d. John Stanley and Mary C. (Szczepanska) Barron; m. William Leon McBride, June 12, 1965; children: Catherine, Kara. BS in Nursing, Georgetown U., 1962, LHD (hon.), 1993; MS in Nursing, Yale U., 1964; PhD, Purdue U., 1978; D of Pub. Svc. (hon.), U. Cin., 1983; LittD (hon.), Purdue U., 1998; LLD (hon.), Ea. Ky. U., 1991; DSc(hon.), Med. Coll. of Ohio, 1995; LHD (hon.), U. Akron, 1997. Asst. prof., rsch. asst. inst. Yale U., New Haven, 1964-73; assoc. prof., chairperson Ind. U. Sch. Nursing, Indpls., 1978-81, 80-84, prof., 1981-92, assoc. dean rsch., 1985—91, interim dean, 1991—92, univ. dean, 1992—2003, disting. prof., 1992—; sr. v.p. acad. affairs, nursing Clarian Health Ptnrs., 1997—2003; Am. Acad. Nursing scholar-in-residence Inst. Medicine, 2003—04. Mem. Nat. Adv. Mental Health Coun., 1987—91; mem. adv. com. NIH Office of Women's Health Rsch., 1997—2001, NIH Office of Women's Health Rsch. Specialized Ctrs. Rsch. on Sex and Gender Factors, 2003—; mem. Yale U. Coun., 2000—; ext. acad. advisor Sch. Nursing, Hong Kong Polytechnic U., 2000—; mem. adv. bd. Meth. Health Found., 2001—. Author: The Growth and Development of Mothers, 1973 (Best Book award 1973), Living with Contradictions, A Married Feminist, 1976, How to Enjoy A Good Life With Your Teenager, 1987; editor: Psychiatric-Mental Health Nursing: Integrating the Behavioral and Biological Sciences, 1996 (Best Book award 1996); compiler: Nursing and Philanthropy, 2000. Mem. adv. bd. Women's Fund Indpls., 2001—; bd. dirs. United Way of Ctrl. Ind., 2001—. Recipient Disting. Alumna award Yale U., Disting. Alumna award Purdue U., Univ. Medallion, U. San Francisco, 1993, Hoosier Heritage award, 2000, Disting. Nurse Educator award Coll. Mt. St. Joseph, Cin., 2000, Ross Pioneering Spirit award Am. Assn. Critical-Care Nurses, 2004; named Influential Woman in Indpls., Indpls. Bus. Jour./Ind. Lawyer, 1999, named HealthCare Hero Indpls. Bus. Jour., 2003; Kellogg nat. fellow; Am. Nurses Found. scholar, Salute to Women award Indpls. YMCA, 1999, Sagamore of Wabash, 1999; named to Yale Sch. Nursing Hall of Fame, 2004. Fellow: Nat. Acads. Practice, Am. Acad. Nursing (dir. leadership devel. Bldg. Acad. Geriatric Nursing Capacity program 2001—, past pres.), APA (nursing and health psychology award divsn. 38 1995); mem.: Nat. Acad. Scis., Inst. of Medicine, Soc. for Rsch. in Child Devel., Midwest Nursing Rsch. Soc. (Disting. Rsch. award 1985), Sigma Theta Tau (past pres., mentor award 1993, disting. lectr 1995—99, Melanie Dreher award for contbns. as a dean 2001), Chi Eta Phi (hon.). Home: 744 Cherokee Ave Lafayette IN 47905-1872 Office Phone: 317-274-1486. Business E-Mail: amcbride@iupui.edu.

MCBRIDE, BEVERLY JEAN, lawyer; b. Greenville, Ohio, Apr. 5, 1941; d. Kenneth Birt and Glenna Louise (Ashman) Whited; m. Benjamin Gary McBride, Nov. 28, 1964; children: John David, Elizabeth Ann. BA magna cum laude, Wittenberg U., 1963; JD cum laude, U. Toledo, 1966. Bar: Ohio 1966. Intern Ohio Gov.'s Office, Columbus, 1962; asst. dean women U. Toledo, 1963-65; assoc. Title Guarantee and Trust Co., Toledo, 1966-69; spl. counsel

Ohio Atty. Gen.'s Office, Toledo, 1975; assoc. Cobourn, Smith, Rohrbacher and Gibson, Toledo, 1969-76; v.p., gen. counsel, sec. The Andersons, Maumee, Ohio, 1976—. Exec. trustee, bd. dirs. Wittenberg U., Springfield, Ohio, 1980-83; trustee Anderson Found., Maumee, 1981-93; mem. Ohio Supreme Ct. Task Force on Gender Fairness, 1991-94, Regional Growth Partnership, 1994—; chmn. Sylvania Twp. Zoning Commn., Ohio, 1970-80; candidate for judge Sylvania Mcpl. Ct., 1975; trustee Goodwill Industries, Toledo, 1976-82, Sylvania Cmty. Svcs. Ctr., 1976-78, Toledo-Lucas County Port Authority, 1992-99; chair St. Vincent Med. Ctr., 1992-99; founder Sylvania YWCA Program, 1973; active membership drives Toledo Mus. Art, 1977-87. Recipient Toledo Women in Industry award YWCA, 1979, Outstanding Alumnus award Wittenberg U., 1981. Fellow Am. Bar Found.; mem. ABA, AAUW, Ohio Bar Assn., Toledo Bar Assn. (pres., treas., chmn., sec. various coms.), Toledo Women Attys. Forum (exec. com. 1978-82), Pres. Club (U. Toledo exec. com.). Home: 5274 Cambrian Rd Toledo OH 43623-2626 Office: The Andersons 480 W Dussel Dr Maumee OH 43537-1690

MCBRIDE, BRIAN, professional soccer player; b. Arlington Heights, Ill., June 19, 1972; Student, St. Louis U. Player Vfl Wolfsburg, German 2nd Divsn., 1994—95, Columbus Crew, 1996—, U.S. Nat. Team, 1996—. Named to, Ea. Conf. All Star Team, 1996, 1997. Office: c/o Columbus Crew 77 E Nationwide Blvd Columbus OH 43215-2539 also: US Soccer Fedn 1801 S Prairie Ave # 1811 Chicago IL 60616-1319

MCBRIDE, DARL, information technology executive; BS, Brigham Young U.; MS, U. Ill. at Urbana-Champaign. Networking leader Novell, 1988—96, v.p., gen. mgr., embedded systems divsn.; sr. v.p. IKON Office Solutions; founder, chmn., CEO SBI and Co.; CEO PointServe; pres. Franklin Covey; pres., CEO SCO Group, Inc., Lindon, Utah. Office: SCO Group Inc 355 S 520 West Ste 100 Lindon UT 84042-1911 Office Phone: 801-765-4999. Office Fax: 801-765-1313.*

MCBRIDE, DONNA JANNEAN, publisher; b. Kansas City, Kans., July 3, 1940; d. donald Merle and Hazel Frances (Williams) McBride; life ptnr. Barbara Grier. AB, Central Coll., 1962; MLS, U. Mo., Columbia, 1969. Tchr. Pilot Grove (Mo.) H.S., 1961-62; corr. Bus. Mens Assurance Co., Kansas City, Mo., 1962-66; acctg. clk. Prudential of Eng., Sydney, Australia, 1966-67; head tech. processes Kansas City (Mo.) Pub. Libr., 1967-77; customer rep. C.L. Sys., Inc., Newtonville, Mass., 1977-80; dir. support svcs. Leon County Pub. Libr., Tallahassee, 1980-82; v.p., CFO The Naiad Press, Inc., Tallahassee, 1982—. Publisher; b. Kansas City, Kans., July 3, 1940; d. Donald Merle and Hazel Frances (Williams) McBride; life ptnr. Barbara Grier, 1972. AB, Central Coll., 1962; MLS, U. Mo.-Columbia, 1969. Tchr., Pilot Grove (Mo.) H.S., 1961-62; corr. Bus. Men's Assurance Co., Kansas City, Mo., 1962-66; acctg. clk. Prudential of Eng., Sydney, Australia, 1966-67; head tech. processes Kansas City Pub. Library (Mo.), 1967-77; customer rep. C.L. Systems, Inc., Newtonville, Mass., 1977-80; dir. support services Leon County Pub. Library, Tallahassee, 1980-82; v.p., CFO The Naiad Press, Inc., Tallahassee, 1982-2003; dir. The Naiad Press, 1976—, Sappho's Libr., 1983—. Mem. ALA, Nat. Gay Task Force, Am. Booksellers Assn., Nat. Women's Studies Assn., NOW. Mem. ALA, NOW, Nat. Gay Task Force, Am. Booksellers Assn., Nat. Womens Studies Assn. Home: 1097 Alligator Dr Alligator Point FL 32346-5107 Office: The Naiad Press Inc PO Box 10543 Tallahassee FL 32302-2543 E-mail: naiadpress@aol.com.

MCBRIDE, ELIZABETH ANNE WILMORE, writer; b. Charlotte, N.C., Nov. 10, 1942; d. John Henry and Frances (Cox) Wilmore; divorced; children: John and Laura. BA in English, Rice U., 1964; MA in English & Creative Writing, U. Houston, 1982; student, Edward Albee Workshops, 1989-92. Instr. U. Houston, 1979—81, 1985—88; editor Lit. Mag., Houston, 1982-83, Domestic Crude, Houston, 1983-84; contbr. editor, columnist Artscene, 1989; editor rsch. papers for Naomi Kraus, U. Tex., Houston, 1990. Reader Houston Festival; judge Southwest Writers' Conf., 1984; bd. dirs. Lawndale Art and Performance Ctr.; panel mem. Seminar on Hispanic Art, U. Ariz., 1987-88. Guest curator Rice U., Houston, 1988, Glassel Sch., Houston, 1993, Houston Art League, 1997; contbr. author: (short stories) Her Work, Common Bonds, The Whole Story, Texas Short Stories II; reviewer The Houston Chronicle, 1980, ARTspace Mag., 1987-92, ARTnews, 1990-95, 2000, Pub. News, 1988-94, Sculpture Mag., 1989-90, Artscene Mag., 1984, Chelsea Mag., N.Y., and numerous others; poems: Vapor Trails, 1981, Diversions, 1982, Biloxi 1945, 1982, South Pacific Stars and Stripes, 1982, Kwajalein, 1983, Deep Sea Fishing With My Father, 1984, Everyday Places, 1985, Linguistics, 1987, Moctezuma's Headdress, 1992, I Bury My Father, 1993, Corazal, 1993, Inca Doves, 1993, O Corporeal, 1997; editor Ctr. for Big Bend Studies, Bosque Bonito, 2002; contbr. articles and short stories to profl. jours. and mags.; exhibited in group shows at Treebeards, 1995, The New Gallery, 1995, Lawndale Art Ctr., 1995, Diverse Works Alternative Space, 1996, Sally Sprout Gallery, 1996, Houston Pottery Guild and Gallery, 1997, 2000; one woman shows at Westenberg Gallery, Marfa, 2000, Big Bend Sentinel, Marfa, 2000, Devin Borden Hiram Butler Gallery, Houston, 2002, Terlingua Ho. Projects, Alpine, Tex., 2002, Highland Gallery, Marfa, 2003; represented in numerous pvt. collections, S.I. Assocs., Houston, Playwright, Long Island; writer-in-residence Chinati Found, 1995-96, art critic ArtLies Mag., Houston Tex. Vol. tchg. Hartman Jr. High, Roberts Elem. Sch., Valley of Peace, Belize, Marfa Tex. Libr.; mem. literacy events bd. Houston Festival, chmn. lit. arts panel, 1986; bd. dirs. lit. and humanities panel Cultural Arts Coun. Houston, 1987-88; mem. lit. panel Tex. Commn. Arts, 1988-89. Recipient Brazos for fiction prize, 1984; fellow MacDowell Colony, 1986, Edward Albee Found., 1990. Mem. Poets and Writers, League Women Voters (chmn. voters svc.); founding bd. mem. Zocalo Theater. Office: PO Box 5 Marfa TX 79843

MCBRIDE, GUY THORNTON, JR., college president emeritus; b. Austin, Tex., Dec. 12, 1919; s. Guy Thornton and Imogene (Thrasher) McB.; m. Rebekah Jane Bush, Sept. 2, 1942 (dec. Aug. 1998); children: Rebekah Ann, William Howard, Ellen M. Alsobrooks; m. Cordelia D. Rush, Aug. 7, 1999. BS in Chem. Engring., U. Tex., 1940; Sc.D., MIT, 1948; D.P.S. (hon.), Regis Coll., 1979; D.Engring. (hon.), Colo. Sch. Mines, 1984. Registered profl. engr., Tex. La., N.Y., Colo. Instr. chem. engring. Mass. Inst. Tech., 1942-44, research assoc., 1946-48; job engr. Standard Oil Co. Calif., 1944-46; asst. prof. chem. engring Rice Inst., 1948-55, assoc. dean students, 1950-57, dean, 1957-58, assoc. prof., 1955-58; cons. Tex. Gulf Sulphur Co., 1950-58, asst. mgr. research dept., 1958-59, mgr., 1959-60, v.p., mgr. research, 1960-63; v.p. Tex. Gulf Sulphur Co. (Phosphate div.), 1963-70, gen. mgr., 1966-70; pres. Colo. Sch. Mines, Golden, 1970-84; ret. Dir. Halliburton Co., Kerr-McGee Corp., Hercules, Inc.; hon. dir. Texasgulf Inc. Fellow Am. Inst. Chem. Engrs.; mem. Am. Chem. Soc., Nat. Soc. Profl. Engrs., Sigma Xi, Phi Lambda Upsilon, Tau Beta Pi. Clubs: Mile High (Denver). Home: 2615 Oak Dr Apt 13 Lakewood CO 80215-7182

MCBRIDE, JACK J. retired diversified financial services company executive; b. Orient, Iowa, June 24, 1936; s. Marvin Clair and Ruth (Jones) McBride; m. Mary Ann Garden, June 16, 1957; children: Jeffry J., Beth Ann, Kelley Lynn, Grant G. BA, Simpson Coll., Indianola, Iowa, 1958; postgrad., U. Conn., 1963, U. Ill., 1974. Cert. agy. mgmt. LIMRA, mgmt. devel. Aetna Inst. Spl. agt. Bankers Life Co., Des Moines, 1958-60; supr. Aetna Life and Affiliated Cos., Hartford, Conn., 1960-65; agy. mgr. Equitable Life Iowa and Affiliated Cos., Omaha, Davenport, Iowa, 1965-72; gen. agt. Aetna Fin. Svcs. (name now Ing), Springfield, Ill., 1972—77, Milw., 1977-82; supt. personal fin. security divsn. Aetna Inc. (name now Ing), Chgo., 1982-84; instr. Life Underwriters Tng. Coun., Quad Cities, 1968-69. Lectr. various univs. and colls. Contbr. articles to profl. jours. Charter chmn. stewardship faith UMC, Phoenix, 1965, St. Luke's Ch., Omaha, 1966; chmn. friends bd. So. Ill. Med. Sch., 1975—77; mem. steering com. devel. coun. Simpson Coll., 1960. Named Outstanding Young Man Am., 1966. Mem.: Adminstrv. Mgmt. Soc., Brain Injury Assn. Ill., Brain Injury Assn. Am., Sangamon Estate Planners Coun. (charter), Springfield Gen. Agts. and Mgrs. Assn. (past pres., dir.), Nat. Assn. Life Underwriters (past co-chmn. edn. com., chmn., dir. Iowa State com.), Iowa Pioneer Arledge Farm Family, Quad Cities C. of C. (sprks. bur.), Rotary, Scottish Rite, Masons.

MCBRIDE, JANET MARIE, small business owner; b. Fort Wayne, Ariz., Nov. 21, 1948; d. Robert W and Helen F Plasterer; m. Joey W McBride, July 26, 1976; children: Kenneth Schortgen, Jr., Christian Schortgen, Dawna McBride Ross, Brand. Grad., Phoenix Coll., 1995. Feng Shui practitioner Western Sch. of Feng Shui, Calif., 2000. Dod ednl. exec asst DOD Schools-Europe, Madrid, 1979—82; engring. project adminstr. Honeywell, Inc., Tempe, 1987—95; cons., coach Young Living, Salt Lake City, 2000—. Singer (songwriter/producer): (spiritual songs) Irish Girl with the Heart of a Jew; singer: (musician/producer) (messianic hymns) Irish Girl with Heart of a Jew. Office: Essential Opportunities Inc 16448 West Adams Street Goodyear AZ 85338 E-mail: essentialvitality@cox.net.

MCBRIDE, JONATHAN EVANS, executive search consultant; b. Washington, June 16, 1942; s. Gordon Williams and Martha Alice (Evans) McB.; BA, Yale U., 1964; m. Emilie Evans Dean, Sept. 5, 1970; children: Webster Dean, Morley Evans. Account exec. Merrill Lynch & Co., Washington, 1968-72; v.p. dept. mgr. Lionel D. Edie & Co., N.Y.C., 1972-76; v.p., exec. search cons. Simmons Assocs., Inc., Washington, 1976-79; pres. McBride Assocs., Inc., Washington, 1979—. Bd. dirs. Yale U. Alumni Fund, 1974-79; trustee Sidwell Friends Sch., Washington, 1996-2004, vice chair, 2002-04. Served to lt. USNR, 1964-68. Clubs: Yale (N.Y.C.); Met. (Washington); Chevy Chase (Md.). Office: 1742 N St NW Washington DC 20036-2907 Office Phone: 202-452-1150. E-mail: hearthunt@aol.com.

MCBRIDE, JUDITH, elementary school educator; BFA in Interior Design, Utah State U., 1963; MFA, U. Wyo., 1980. Art tchr. Beitel Elem. Sch., Laramie, Wyo., Spring Creek Elem. Sch., Laramie, Centennial Valley Elem. Sch., Laramie. Named Wyo. State Tchr. of Yr., 1993. Office: Spring Creek Elem Sch 1203 Russell St Laramie WY 82070-4682

MCBRIDE, JUDITH BLISS, lawyer, educator, writer; b. East Cleveland, Ohio, Nov. 11, 1959; d. Jack Clarence and Gene Marie (Dowd) Bliss; m. James Dominick McBride; children: Jean Marie, Madelyn Ann. BA cum laude, John Carroll U., 1982; JD, Case Western U., 1985. Bar: Ohio 1986, U.S. Dist. Ct. (no. dist.) Ohio 1988. Pvt. practice, Cleve., 1986—; staff instr. Mead Data Ctrl., Inc., Cleve., 1986-88, account rep., 1988, sr. account rep., 1989-91; atty. editor product devel. Banks-Baldwin Law Pub. Co., Cleve., 1991-93, product mgr. electronic svcs., 1992-93; rep. Primerica Fin. Svcs., Cleve., 1991-95; atty.-editor, cons., 1993—. Deacon Lyndhurst (Ohio) Bapt. Ch., 1986—88, bd. stewardship and missions, 1989—91, moderator, 1991—92, vice moderator, 1993—94; bd. Christian edn. Brecksville United Ch. of Christ, Christian Edn. Cmty., 1997—99, mem. bldg. land task force, 1997—2001, chair, 1999, Christian Edn. Sch. tchr., 1999—; mem. Our Ch.'s Wider Mission Cmty., 2000—, co-chair, 2001—02; mem. United Meth. Ch. Christian Edn. Cmty., 2004—. Mem.: Ohio State Bar Assn., Ohio Bar, Lambda Iota Tau (v.p. 1981—82), Alpha Sigma Nu. Republican. Home: 7886 Cambridge Dr Brecksville OH 44141-1063

MCBRIDE, MARTINA, vocalist; b. Medicine Lodge, Kans., July 29, 1966; d. Daryl and Jeanne Schiff; m. John McBride, May 15, 1988; children: Delaney Katherine, Emma Justine. Vocalist Schiffters, 1975-86, assorted bands, Wichita, Kans.; represented by RCA Records, 1991—; backup singer Garth Brooks, 1992—93, European tour, 1994. Singer: (albums) The Time Has Come, 1992, The Way That I Am, 1993 (Platinum), Wild Angels, 1995 (Platinum), Evolution, 1997 (Triple Platinum), Martina McBride Christmas, 1998, Emotion, 1999 (Platinum), White Christmas, 1999 (Platinum), (various artists) Girls Night Out, 1999, (Group recording) Safe In The Arms Of Love, 2000, Greatest Hits, 2001 (Dounble Platinum), Martina, 2003 (Gold), (songs) (Runaway Bride soundtrack) I Love You, 1999, (Backstage at the Grand Ole Opry) Wrong Again, 2000, (Where The Heart Is soundtrack) There You Are, 2000, (The Mercy Project) You'll Get Through This, 2000; performer: (tv appearances co-star Pat Benatar) CMT Crossroads, 2003, (tv appearances) Stand By You Man, 2003, (tv appearance) Nat. Anthem, NBA All Star Game, 2003, (presenter of award) CMT Flameworthy Awards, 2003, (tv biography) Lifetime Intimate portrait, 2002. Nominee Best Country Song for "Independence Day", Grammy, 1994, Video Yr. for "Independence Day", Acad. Country Music, 1994, Best Country Collaboration with Vocals for "Own My Own" with Reba McEntire, Linda Davis, and Trisha Yearwood, Grammy, 1995, Vocal Event Yr. for "On My Own" with Reba McEntire, Linda Davis, and Trisha Yearwood., Country Music Assn., 1996, Album Yr. for "Wild Angels", 1996, Best Country Female Vocal Performance for "Safe In The Arms of Love", Grammy, 1995, Vocal Event Yr. for "Still Holding On" with Clint Black, Country Music Assn., 1997, Best Country Collaboration with Vocals for "Still Holding You" with Clint Black, Grammy, 1997, Video Yr. for "A Broken Wing", Country Music Assn., 1998, Single Yr. for "A Broken Wing", 1998, Acad. Country Music, 1999, Song Yr. for "A Broken Wing", 1999, Video Yr. for "A Broken Wing", 1999, Best Country Female Vocal Performance for "I Love You", Grammy, 1999, Single Yr. for "Blessed", Country Music Assn., 2002, Best Female Country Vocal Performance for "Blessed", Grammy, 2002, Video Yr. for "Concrete Angel", Country Music Assn., 2003, Top Female Vocalist, Acad. Country Music, 1993, 1998, 2000, 2001, Horizon award, Country Music Assn., 1994, Female Vocalist Yr., 1996, 1998, 1999, 2001, Am. Music Awards, 2003; recipient Breakthrough Artist Video for "My Baby Loves Me", Music Row Ind. Summit Award, 1994, Music Video Yr. for "Independence Day", Country Music Assn. Awards, 1994, Best Video Yr. for "Independence Day", Gt. Brit. Music Awards, 1994, Video Yr. for "Independence Day", Nashville Music Awards, 1995, TNN Music City News Award, 1995, Gold Clio for Country Music Video Yr. for "Independence Day", Clio Awards, 1995, Best Southern Gospel, Country Gospel or Bluegrass Gospel for "Amazing Grace - A Country Salute To Gospel", Grammy Awards, 1995, Country Album Yr. for "Wild Angels", Nashville Music Awards, 1996, Video Yr. for "Safe In The Arms of Love", 1996, Female Video Yr. for "Blessed", CMT Flameworthy Awards, 2002, Female Video Yr. for "Concrete Angel", CMT Flameworthy Award, 2003, Top Female Vocalist, Acad. Country Music, 2002, Acad. Country Music award, 2003, 2004, Female Vocalist Yr., Country Music Assn. Award, 2002, Country Female Artist Yr., Billboard Music Award, 2002, Best Female Artist, Country Radio Music Awards, 1996, Favorite Female Artist, Country, Am. Music Awards, 2003, Favorite Female Artist, Country Weekly, 2003, Female Vocalist Yr. award, Country Music Assn., 2003. Address: RCA Records 1400 18th Ave S Nashville TN 37212-2809

MCBRIDE, MICHAEL FLYNN, lawyer; b. Milw., Mar. 27, 1951; s. Raymond Edward and Marian Dunne (McBride); m. Kerin Ann (O'Brien), Mar. 23, 1991; children: Raymond Erin, Barbara Marian. BS in Chemistry and Biology, U. Wis., 1972, JD, 1976; MS in Environ. Engring. Sci., Calif. Inst. Tech., 1973. Bar: Wis. 1976, DC 1976. Assoc. LeBoeuf, Lamb, Greene, and MacRae, Washington, 1976-84, ptnr., 1985—. Mem. Assn. for Transp. Law, Logistics and Policy (v.p., energy tranp., law inst. com. 1990, exec. com. 1990-, co-chmn. 1991—, pres. 1994-95, 2004-, chmn. program com. 1998-99), Chantilly Nat. Golf and Country Club. Avocations: golf, reading, travel. Home: 6648 Byrns Pl Mc Lean VA 22101-4419 Office: LeBoeuf Lamb Greene & MacRae LLP 1875 Connecticut Ave NW Washington DC 20009-5728 Office Phone: 202-986-8000. E-mail: Michael.McBride@llgm.com.

MCBRIDE, MILFORD LAWRENCE, JR., lawyer; b. Grove City, Pa., July 16, 1923; s. Milford Lawrence and Elizabeth B. (Douthett) McB.; m. Madeleine Coulter, Aug. 6, 1947; children: Marta, Brenda, Trip, Randy, Barry. AB, Grove City Coll., 1944; BS, NYU, 1944; JD, U. Pa., 1949. Bar: Pa. 1949, U.S. Dist. Ct. (we. dist.) Pa. U.S. Supreme Ct. Ptnr., McBride & McBride, Grove City, 1949-77, sr. ptnr., 1992—; ptnr. McBride and McNickle, Grove City, 1977-92; dir. Integra Fin. Corp., 1988-93; trustee Grove City Coll., 1995—. 1st lt. USAAF, 1943-46. Mem. Mercer County Bar Assn. (state treas. 1970-77), ABA, Am. Bar Found., Oakmont Country Club, Univ. Club (Pitts.). Republican Office: 211 S Center St Grove City PA 16127-1508

MCBRIDE, ROBERT ALBERT, training services executive; b. Woonsocket, R.I., Mar. 9, 1960; s. Albert and Leonora Anna McB.; m. Kathryn Moore, June 14, 1998; 1 child, Jordan. BA in Psychology, Providence Coll., 1982; MBA in Mgmt., Bryant Coll., 1994. Commd. ensign USN, 1985, advanced through grades to comdr.; sales rep. Aventis Pharms., Providence, 1991—96, regional trainer New England region, 1996—99, area mgr., 1999—2002; dir. global tng. Genzyme Corp., 2002—. Mem. adv. bd. Boy's & Girl's Club, Cumberland, R.I., 1995-99; instr. Literacy Vols. Am., Woonsocket, R.I., 1997-99. Decorated Navy & Marine Corp Commendation medal, Navy Achievement medal; recipient Global War on Terrorism Svc. medal. Mem. World Affairs Coun., U.S. Naval Res. Assn., Naval Inst. Roman Catholic. Avocations: golf, biking, reading, basketball. Home: 10 Cathedral Ct Cumberland RI 02864 Office: Genzyme Corp 500 Kendall St Cambridge MA 02142 Office Phone: 617-768-6024. E-mail: bob.mcbride@genzyme.com.

MCBRIDE, SHARON LOUISE, counselor, technical communication educator; b. Peoria, Ill., Dec. 5, 1939; d. Ralph Cannon and Joyce Eliz (Shoff) McB.; m. Armond B. Ciota, Jr., Apr. 23, 1960 (div.); children: Matthew Ciota, Eliz Faron, Thomas Ciota, Nathan Ciota. BA, Bradley U., 1960, MA, 1987. Various positions to undergrad. student adviser Bradley U., Peoria, 1972—; instr. Ill. Ctrl. Coll., East Peoria, 1987—. Chmn. bd. trustees Greater Peoria Mass Transit. Trustee West Peoria Twp., 1984-96; sec.-treas. Ill. Twp. Trustees, 1993-96; chairperson West Peoria Zoning Bd. Appeals; mem. policy com. Peoria Pekin Urbanized Area Transp. Study. Mem.: Am. Assn. Women in C.C., Am. Pub. Transit Assn. (transit bd., Region IV rep.), Am. Soc. Engring. Edn., Rotary Club (Peoria North), Lions (bd. dirs. West Peoria chpt. 1984—97, precinct com.). Republican. Avocations: travel, community volunteer. Home: 2413 W Kellogg Ave West Peoria IL 61604-5011

MCBRIDE, TERESA, information systems specialist; b. Grants, N. Mex., Sept. 8, 1962; 1 child. Mem. staff Family Restaurant, Grants, N. Mex.; founder, pres., CEO McBride & Assocs., Albuquerque, 1986—. Office: McBride & Assocs 5555 Mcleod Rd NE Albuquerque NM 87109-2408

MCBRIDE, WILLIAM HOWARD, JR., lawyer; b. Belleville, Ill., May 10, 1945; s. William Howard McBride and Patricia (Sullivan) Sweat; m. Adelaide Alexander Sink, July 10, 1986; children: William Albert, Cheryle Alexander. BA, U. Fla., 1967, JD, 1975. Bar: Fla. 1976, D.C. 1978. With Holland & Knight, Tampa, Fla., 1975—, mng. ptnr., 1992—. Bd. dirs. Lawyers Com. for Civil Rights Under Law. Chmn. United Way Campaign, Tampa, 1991, Community Needs Assessment, Tampa, 1990; pres. Hillsborough County Bar Assn., Tampa, 1983-84. Capt. USMC, 1968-71, Vietnam. Fellow Am. Bar Found.; mem. ABA, Am. Law Inst. Democrat. Avocations: fishing, history, science fiction. Home: PO Box 219 Thonotosassa FL 33592-0219 Office: Holland & Knight PO Box 1288 Tampa FL 33601-1288

MC BRIDE, WILLIAM LEON, philosopher, educator; b. N.Y.C., Jan. 19, 1938; s. William Joseph and Irene May (Choffin) McB.; m. Angela Barron, July 12, 1965; children: Catherine, Kara. AB, Georgetown U., 1959; postgrad. (Fulbright fellow), U. Lille, 1959-60; MA (Woodrow Wilson fellow), Yale U., 1962, PhD (Social Sci. Rsch. Coun. fellow), 1964. Instr. philosophy Yale U., New Haven, 1964-66, asst. prof., 1966-70, assoc. prof., 1970-73; lectr. Northwestern U., Evanston, Ill., summer 1972; assoc. prof. Purdue U., West Lafayette, Ind., 1973-76, prof., 1976-2001, Arthur G. Hansen disting. prof., 2001—. Lectr. Korcula Summer Sch., Yugoslavia, 1971, 73; Fulbright lectr. Sofia U., Bulgaria, fall 1997. Author: Fundamental Change in Law and Society, 1970, The Philosophy of Marx, 1977, Social Theory at a Crossroads, 1980, (with R.A. Dahl) Demokrati og Autoritet, 1980, Sartre's Political Theory, 1991, Social and Political Philosophy, 1994, Philosophical Reflections on the Changes in Eastern Europe, 1999, From Yugoslav Praxis to Global Pathos, 2001; editor: (with C.O. Schrag) Phenomenology in a Pluralistic Context, 1983, Sartre and Existentialism, 8 vols., 1997, (with M.B. Matustik) Calvin O. Schrag and the Task of Philosophy after Postmodernity, 2002, The Idea of Values, 2003. Decorated chevalier Ordre des Palmes Académiques. Mem. AAUP (pres. Purdue chpt. 1983-86, pres. Ind. conf. 1988-89), Am. Philos. Assn. (chmn. com. on internat. coop. 1992-95, bd. dirs. 1992-95), N.Am. Soc. Philosophy (v.p. 1997-2000, pres. 2000—), Am. Soc. Polit. and Legal Philosophy, Soc. Phenomenology and Existential Philosophy (exec. co-sec. 1977-80), Sartre Soc. N.Am. (chmn. bd. dirs. 1985-88, 91-93), Am. Soc. Philosophy in the French Lang. (pres. 1994-96), Fed. Internat. Soc. Philosophie (mem. steering com. 1998—, sec. gen. 2003—). Home: 744 Cherokee Ave Lafayette IN 47905-1872 Office: Purdue U Dept Philosophy 100 N Univ St West Lafayette IN 47907-2098 Office Phone: 765-494-4285. E-mail: wmcbride@purdue.edu.

MCBROOM, THOMAS WILLIAM, SR., aviation consultant; b. Atlanta, Mar. 29, 1963; s. William Ralph and Ethel Irene (Bradley) McB.; m. Susan H.; 1 child, Thomas William Jr. B in Mech. Engring., Ga. Tech., 1985, MS in Mech. Engring., 1987; JD, MBA, Ga. State U., 1992; postgrad., Embry-Riddle Aero. U. Registered profl. engr., Ga.; cert. ins. agt.-life, accident and sickness, property, casualty & surety Ga.; bar: Ga. 1993, D.C. 1994, U.S. Tax Ct. 1993, U.S. Supreme Ct. 1996; lic. comml. pilot and flight instr., registered mediator and arbitrator Ga. Mfg. engr. AT & T Techs., Norcross, Ga., 1985-86; energy systems engr. Atlanta Gas Light Co., 1987-89, sales engr., 1989-90, dir. power systems markets, 1991-94, sr. corp. planning analyst, 1994-95, mgr. major accounts, 1995-97, dir. major accts., 1997-99; atty., cons. Newnan, Ga., 1999—; pilot ground instr. Delta Air Lines, Atlanta, 2000—01; project mgr. Aviation Consulting, AIR, Inc., Atlanta, 2001—. Mem. Grad. Leadership Coweta, 1996, Grad. Coverdell Rep. Leadership Inst., 1997. With USAR, 1997—, capt. JAGC. Mem. Ga. Bar Assn., Coverdell Leadership Inst., Phi Delta Phi (exchequer 1991). Home: 15 Culpepper Way Newnan GA 30265-2217 E-mail: tmcbroom@charter.net.

MCBRYDE, JOHN HENRY, federal judge; b. Jackson, Oct. 9, 1931; m. Betty Vinson; children: Rebecca, Jennifer, John Blake. BS in Commerce, Tex. Christian U., 1953; LLB, U. Tex., 1956. Bar: Tex. 1956, U.S. Ct. Appeals (5th cir.) 1958, U.S. Dist. Ct. (no. dist.) 1958, U.S. Dist. Ct. (ea. dist.) 1989, U.S. Supreme Ct. 1972. Assoc. Cantey, Hanger, Johnson, Scarborough & Gooch, Ft. Worth, 1956-62; ptnr. Cantey & Hanger and predecessor firm, Ft. Worth, 1962-69, McBryde, Bennett and predecessor firms, Ft. Worth, 1969-90; judge U.S. Dist. Ct. (no. dist.) Tex., Ft. Worth, 1990—. Fellow Am. Bar Found. (life), Tex. Bar Found. (life), Am. Coll. Trial Lawyers. Office: US Dist Ct US Courthouse 501 W 10th St Ste 401 Fort Worth TX 76102-3642

MCBRYDE, NEILL GREGORY, lawyer; b. Durham, N.C., Jan. 11, 1944; s. Angus M. and Priscilla (Gregory) McBryde; m. Margaret McPherson, Aug. 1, 1970; children: Margaret Courtauld McBryde Young, Neill Gregory Jr. AB cum laude, Davidson Coll., 1966; JD with high honors, U. N.C., 1969. Bar: N.C. 1969., Ga. 1972. Assoc. King & Spalding, Atlanta, 1971-76; ptnr. Fleming, Robinson, Bradshaw & Hinson, Charlotte, NC, 1977-81, Helms, Mulliss & Johnston, Charlotte, 1981-86, Smith Helms Mulliss & Moore, Charlotte, 1986-90, Moore & Van Allen PLLC, Charlotte, 1990—. Lectr. in field; condr. workshops in field. Author, editor: First Union National Bank of North Carolina Will Book, 1986; contbr. articles to profl. jours. Elder and Deacon Myers Park Presbyn. Ch., Charlotte, 1980-86, 92-95, 2001-04; dir. sec. Presbyn. Home for Aged, Charlotte, 1978-82; trustee Charlotte Latins Schs., Inc., 1980-86, 87-93; past chmn., past trustee Mint Mus. Charlotte. Fellow Am. Coll. Trust and Estate Counsel (past mem. bd. regents, past pres.), Am. Coll. Tax Counsel; mem. ABA, Ga. Bar Assn., N.C. Bar Assn. (probate and fiduciary law sect.), Order of Coif, Phi Beta Kappa, Omicron Delta Kappa. Republican. Avocations: tennis, golf, fishing. Office: Moore & Van Allen PLLC Bank of Am Corp Ctr 100 N Tryon St Fl 47 Charlotte NC 28202-4003 Office Phone: 704-331-1094.

MCBURNETTE-ARGUELLES, SHANNON HEATHER, language educator; b. Baton Rouge, July 20, 1971; d. Michael Henry McBurnette and Mary Ellen Chase, Charles Chase (Stepfather); m. Porfirio Rodolfo Arguelles, Jan. 14, 1976. BA in English Lang. and Lit., Miss. Coll., 1997; MA in Tchg. English to Speakers of Other Languages, Murray State U., 1999. Instr. ESL Murray (Ky.) State U., 1999, Ctrl. Wash. U., Ellenburg, 2000, Tulane U., New Orleans, 2000; instr. ESL, internat. lang. inst. Tex. A & M. Internat. U., Laredo, Tex., 2000—. Mem. praise and worship group Ch. of Crossroads,

Laredo, 2001—03, mem. Ninos children edn. ministry, 2003. Mem.: TESOL, Tex. TESOL. Avocations: reading, travel, singing, movies. Office: TAMIU - Internat Lang Inst 5201 University Boulevard Laredo TX 78041 Business E-Mail: smcburnette@tamiu.edu.

MCBURNEY, CHARLES WALKER, JR., lawyer; b. Orlando, Fla., June 6, 1957; s. Charles Walker McBurney and Jeane (Brown) Chappell. BA, U. Fla., 1979, JD, 1982. Bar: Fla. 1982, U.S. Dist. Ct. (mid. dist.) Fla. 1983, U.S. Ct. Appeals (11th cir.) 1984. Assoc. Mathews, Osborne, McNatt, Gobelman & Cobb, Jacksonville, Fla., 1982-84; asst. state's atty. State's Atty.'s Office, Jacksonville, 1984-90, civil atty., 1987-88, sr. trial atty., 1988-90; ptnr. Fischette, Owen, Held & McBurney, Jacksonville, 1990—2004; pvt. practice Jacksonville, 2004—. Dir. Serious or Habitual Juvenile Offender Program, 1986. Mem. Mayor's Bicentennial Constnl. Commn., 1989—91; chmn. com. congl. campaigns Jacksonville, 1982, 1984, 1988; bd. dirs. Civic Round Table, 1988—92, treas., 1988—89, pres., 1989—90; dir. Internat. Devel. Commn. for Jacksonville, 1993—2003, treas., 1995—97; bd. dirs. Am. Heart Assn. N.E. Fla., 1990—92. Mem.: ABA, Comml. Law League (So. region exec. coun. 1998—, treas. 2000—), Jacksonville Bankruptcy Bar Assn. (bd. dirs. 1999—, treas. 2003), Jacksonville Bar Assn. (chmn. bankruptcy sect. 1998—2000, 2002—03), Duval County Rep. Club (treas. 2002—), S.E. CPAC (environ. sub-chmn. 2001—04, vice-chmn. 2004—), James Madison Inst., Summit Civitan (judge adv. 1991—93, 2001—02), Jacksonville Jaycees (pres. 1986, Jaycee of yr. 1984), Fla. Jaycees (legal counsel 1987—88, Most Outstanding Local Pres. award 1987), Jacksonville C. of C. (bd. govs. 1987, govtl. affairs com. 1998—), First Coast Tiger Bay Forum (bd. dirs. 2001—04, Leadership award 2004), Jacksonville Hist. Soc., Southside Bus. Men's Club (v.p. 2003—), Bull Snort Club (pres. 1995—96, chmn. bd. 1996—99, pres. 1999—2000), Masons, N.E. Fla. Phi Beta Kappa Alumni Assn. (v.p. 1998—2000, 2003—04). Republican. Presbyterian. Home: 6326 Christopher Creek Rd E Jacksonville FL 32217-2485 Office: Ste 11 6320 St Augustine Rd Jacksonville FL 32217 Office Phone: 904-731-0002. Personal E-mail: cmcburney@bellsouth.net.

MCBURNEY, ELIZABETH INNES, dermatologist, physician, educator; b. Lake Charles, La., Dec. 24, 1944; d. Theodore John and Martha (Caldwell) Innes; divorced, 1980; children: Leanne Marie, Susan Eleanor. BS, U. Southwestern La., 1965; MD, La. State U., 1969. Diplomate Am. Bd. Internal Medicine, Am. Bd. Dermatology. Intern Pensacola (Fla.) Edn. Program, 1969-70; resident in internal medicine Boston U. and Carney Hosps., 1970-72; resident in dermatology Charity Hosp., New Orleans, 1972-74; staff physician Ochsner Hosp., New Orleans, 1974-80; assoc. head of dermatology Ochsner Clinic, New Orleans, 1974-80; clin. asst. prof. La. Health Scis., New Orleans, 1976-79, clin. assoc. prof., 1979-90, clin. prof., 1990—; clin. asst. prof. Tulane Health Scis., New Orleans, 1976-88, clin. assoc. prof., 1988-91, clin. prof., 1991—. Mem. courtesy staff Northshore Regional Med. Ctr., Slidell, La., 1985—; mem. staff Slidell Meml. Hosp., 1988—, chmn. CME courses, 1988—, pres.-elect med. staff, 2000-01, pres., 2001—02; regional dir. Mycosis Fungoides Study Group, Balt., 1974-94. Contbr. articles to profl. jours. Bd. dirs. Slidell Art Coun., 1988—, Camp Fire, New Orleans, 1979-83, Cancer Assn. New Orleans, 1978-83; juror Art in Pub. Places, Slidell, 1989. Recipient Disting. Woman Physician award AMA, 1999, Ian G. Pearson edn. meml. award, 2004. Fellow ACP; mem. Am. Soc. Dermatologic Surgery (treas. 1991-94, bd. dirs. 1988-91, pres. elect 1995-96, pres. 1996-97, Samuel Stegman award 2000), Am. Acad. Dermatology (bd. dirs. 1994-98), Am. Bd. Laser Medicine and Surgery (bd. dirs. 1991-96), La. Dermatologic Soc. (pres. 1989-90), St. Tammany Med. Soc. (pres. 1988), Phi Kappa Phi, Alpha Omega Alpha. Avocations: reading, gardening, fine art, music, film. Office: 1051 Gause Blvd Ste 460 Slidell LA 70458-2985 Office Phone: 985-649-5880.

MCBURNEY, MARGOT B. librarian; b. Lethbridge, Alta., Can. d. Ronald Laurence Maness and R. Blanche (Lott) Hart; children: Margot Elisabeth McBurney Lane, James Ronald Gordon. BA with honours, Principia Coll., 1953; M.Sc. in L.S, U. Ill., 1969. Sec. Marshall Brooks Library, Principia Coll., Elsah, Ill., 1966-69, reference librarian, 1969-70; systems analyst trainee in library systems U. Alta. Library, Edmonton, 1970-71, undergrad. reference librarian, 1971-72, editor periodicals holdings list, 1972-73, serials cataloguer, 1973-74, head acquisitions div., 1974-77; chief librarian Queen's U. Library, Kingston, Ont., Can., 1977-90. Editor: Am. Soc. Info. Sci. Western Can. chpt. Proceedings, 1975, 76. Mem. ALA, Am. Soc. Info. Sci. (councilor-at-large 1976-79, past chmn. chpt.), Assn. Research Libraries (dir. 1978-81, chmn. task force on library edn. 1980-83), Can. Assn. Info. Sci., Can. Assn. Research Libraries, Can. Library Assn., Council on Library Resources (PETREL com. 1981-84), Phi Alpha Eta, Beta Phi Mu. E-mail: mbm@perth.net.

MCCAA, JAMES CURETON, III, lawyer; b. Memphis, Jan. 31, 1949; s. James Cureton McCaa Jr. and Madeleine Perkins Jehl; m. Betty Driver, Aug. 23, 1969; children: Hunter D., Margaret C. BSBA, U. Ark., 1971; JD, U. Memphis, 1974. Bar: Ark. 1974, Tenn. 1974, Va. 1985. Assoc. Skillman & Durrett, West Memphis, Ark., 1974-76; ptnr. Hightower & McCaa, West Memphis, 1977-85; asst. city atty. City of West Memphis, 1978-85; instr. East Ark. C.C., West Memphis, 1983-85; assoc. Preston Wilson & Crandley, Virginia Beach, Va., 1985-89, Vandeventer Black Meredith & Martin, Norfolk, Va., 1989-90; ptnr. Taylor & Walker, Norfolk, 1990—. Mem. Va. Assn. Def. Attys. Episcopalian. Avocations: golf, home. Office: Taylor & Walker PC 555 E Main St Ste 1300 Norfolk VA 23510-2235 E-mail: jmccaa@taylorwalkerlaw.com.

MCCABE, BROOKS FLEMING, JR., state legislator; b. Charleston, W.Va., Jan. 19, 1949; s. Brooks F. Sr. and Jane (Mason) McC.; m. Barbara Given McCabe; 1 child, Katherine Jane. BS in Mgmt. Engring., MEd in Adminstrn., U. Vt., 1972; EdD in Adminstrn., W.Va. U., 1975. Asst. to dir. Gov.'s Office Fed. and State Rels., Gov.'s Office Fed. and State Rels., Charleston, 1975-77; gov.'s housing coord. State of W.Va., Charleston, 1977-79; comml. real estate salesperson Home Finders, Inc., Charleston, 1979-80; mem. W.V. Senate, Charleston, 1998—. Bd. dirs. Charleston Renaissance Corp.; pres., bd. dirs. Silver Creek Properties, Inc., Slaty Fork, W.Va., 1988-92. Pres. Community Coun. of Kanawha Valley, Charleston, 1987-89; campaign chmn. United Way of Kanawha Valley, Charleston, 1988; trustee U. Vt., Burlington, 1976-82, The Grow Sch., South Wales, N.Y., 1988-97, W.Va. Wesleyan Coll., Buchanon, 2000—02; bd. dirs. W.Va. State Coll. Found., Inc., Charleston Area Med. Ctr. Found., 1992—98, Greater Kanawha Valley Found., 1988-91. Named Vol. of the Yr., United Way of Kanawha Valley, 1986-87. Mem. Am. Inst. Cert. Planners, Charleston Exec. Club (pres. 1983-84), W.V. Planning Assoc., Kanowha Valley Bd. of Realtors, W.V. Assoc. of Realtors, Urban Land Inst., Nat. Trust for Historic Preservation, Charleston Renaissance Corp., W.V. Roundtable, Charleston Chamber of Commerce., Democrat. Episcopalian. Avocations: reading, history, skiing. Office: McCabe Henley LP 107 Capitol St Charleston WV 25301-2609 Address: WV State Senate 1900 Kanawha Blvd E Rm 441M Charleston WV 25305-0009 Office Phone: 304-347-7500.

MCCABE, EDWARD R. B. academic administrator, educator, physician; b. Balt., Mar. 26, 1946; BA in Biology, Johns Hopkins U., 1967; PhD in Pharmacology, U. So. Calif., 1972, MD, 1974. Diplomate Am. Bd. Pediatrics. Resident in pediatrics U. Minn. Hosps., Mpls., 1974—76; pediatric metabolism fellow Sch. Medicine U. Colo., Denver, 1976—78, instr., asst. prof., assoc. prof. pediatrics Sch. Medicine, 1978—86; from assoc. prof. to prof. genetics, pediatrics Baylor Coll. Medicine, Houston, 1986—94; prof., chmn. dept. pediatrics David Geffen Sch. Medicine UCLA, 1994—. Physician-in-chief Mattel Children's Hosp. UCLA, 1995—; mem. med. genetics residency rev. com. Accreditation Coun. Grad. MEd. Edn., 1993—97; chmn. conf. gaucher disease NIH, Bethesda, Md., 1994—96; mem. NICHD Coun., 1995—99. Editor: Biochem. and Molecular Medicine, 1990—97, Molecular Genetics and Metabolism, 1998—. Chair sci. adv. bd. HEreditary Disease Found., L.A., 1998—99; chmn. Basil O'Connor award March Dimes, White Plains, NY, 1997—99. Mem.: Inst. Medicine, Soc. Pediatric Rsch. (E. Mead Johnson award 1993), Am. Coll. Med. Genetics (chair sec.'s adv. com. genetics, health and society 2002—, maternal and child health bur. 1999—2000, pres. 2001—02, co-chair newborn screening screening task force), Am. Soc. Biochem. and Molecular Biology, Am. Pediatric Soc., Am. Fedn. Clin. Rsch., Am. Soc. Human Genetics, Am. Bd. Med. Genetics (bd. dirs. 1992—97, pres. Bethesda 1995—96, diplomate), Am. Acad. Pediatrics (chmn. com. genetics Elk Grove Village, Ill. 1987—91, co-founder, chmn. sect. genetics Elk Grove Village 1990, 1993—95), Alpha Omega Alpha, Sigma Xi, Phi Kappa Phi. Achievements include First to describe the Continguous Gene Syndrome Complex Glyverol Kinase Deficiency; first to extract DNA from blood in newborn screening blotters; first to set up molecular genetic diagonosis for sickle cell disease as part of newborn screening; development of concept of molecular genetic triage of bacterial infection. Office: UCLA Sch Medicine Dept Pediatrics 22 412 MDCC 10833 Le Conte Ave Los Angeles CA 90095-3075

MC CABE, GERARD BENEDICT, retired library administrator; b. N.Y.C., Jan. 22, 1930; s. Patrick Joseph and Margaret Irene (McDonald) McC.; m. Jacqueline L. Maloney, Aug. 3, 1963 (dec. 1987); children: Theresa Marie, Rebecca Mary. BA in English, Manhattan Coll., 1952; A.M. in Library Sci. (scholar), U. Mich., 1954; MA in English, Mich. State U., 1959. Asst. acquisitions dept. U. Nebr. Library, Lincoln, 1954-56; chief bibliog. acquisitions dept. Mich. State U. Library, East Lansing, 1956-58; librarian Inst. Community Devel. and Service, Mich. State U., 1958-59; acquisitions librarian U. S. Fla., Tampa, 1959-66, asst. dir. planning and devel., 1967-70; assoc. dir. U. Ark. Library, Fayetteville, 1966-67; dir. univ. libraries Va. Commonwealth U., Richmond, 1970-82; dir. libraries Clarion U. of Pa., 1982-95; ret., 1995; libr. cons., 1995—. Editor: The Smaller Academic Library: A Management Handbook, 1988, Operations Handbook for Small Academic Library, 1989, Academic Libraries in Urban and Metropolitan Areas, 1992; co-editor ann. pub. Advances in Libr. Adminstrn. and Orgn., vols. 1-12, Insider's Guide to Libr. Automation: Essays of Practical Experience, 1993, Acad. Librs.: Their Rationale and Role in Am. Higher Edn., 1995, Introducing and Managing Academic Library Automation Projects, 1996, Leadership for Academic Librarians, 1998, Planning for a New Generation of Public Library Buildings, 2000, Planning the Modern Public Library Building, 2003; contbr. articles to profl. jours. Mem. ALA, Southeastern Libr. Assn. Home and Office: 2 Stayman Ct Apt J Baltimore MD 21228-6034 Office Phone: 410-302-5911. E-mail: bldlib@comcast.net. *Consideration for others is a guiding principle for my personal and professional behavior. I, as a librarian, must have concern for those I serve. Their needs are my first and only interest, not success, not notoriety, only their service and their satisfaction.*

MC CABE, JOHN CHARLES, III, writer; b. Detroit, Nov. 14, 1920; s. Charles John and Rosalie (Dropiewski) McC.; m. Vija Valda Zarina, Oct. 19, 1962 (dec. 1984); children— Linard Peter, Sean Cahal and Deirdre Rose (twins); m. Rosina Lawrence, June 8, 1987 (dec. June 1997); m. Karen Jackson, Apr. 16, 1998. Ph.B., U. Detroit, 1947; M.F.A. in Theatre, Fordham U., 1948; PhD in English Lit, Shakespeare Inst., U. Birmingham, Eng., 1954. Instr. theatre Wayne State U., 1948-51, CCNY, 1955; mem. faculty N.Y. U., 1956-68, prof. dramatic art, chmn. dept., 1962-68; chmn. dept. drama and theatre arts Mackinac Coll., Mackinac Island, Mich., 1968-70. Founder The Sons of the Desert (group devoted to works Laurel and Hardy), 1963 Profl. actor, 1928—, producer-dir., Milford (Pa.) Playhouse, summers, 1948-53, prodr., N.Y.U. Summer Theatre, Sterling Forest, N.Y., 1963-65, author-in-residence, Lake Superior State Coll., Sault Ste. Marie, Mich., 1970-86; author: Mr. Laurel and Mr. Hardy, 1961, rev. edit., 1986, George M. Cohan: The Man Who Owned Broadway, 1973, The Comedy World of Stan Laurel, 1974, Laurel & Hardy, 1975, (with G.B. Harrison) Proclaiming the Word, 1976, Charles Chaplin, 1978, Grand Hotel: Mackinac Island, 1987, Babe: The Life of Oliver Hardy, 1990, The High, 1992, Cagney, 1997; ghostwriter James Cagney's autobiography, Cagney by Cagney, 1976. Served with USAAF, 1943-45, ETO. Mem. Shakespeare Assn. Am., Actors Equity Assn., Catholic Actors Guild Am., Baker St. Irregulars. Clubs: The Players (N.Y.C.), The Lambs (N.Y.C.). Home: PO Box 363 Mackinac Island MI 49757-0363 *At fourteen I learned from the Jesuits that one who knows both the function and beauty of an English sentence will be blessed life-long.*

MCCABE, JOHN L. lawyer; b. Chgo., Oct. 17, 1941; BA, U. Notre Dame, 1963; LLB, Harvard U., 1966. Bar: Ill. 1967, Colo. 1967. Ptnr. Davis, Graham & Stubbs, Denver. Office: Davis Graham & Stubbs 1550 Seventeenth St Ste 500 Denver CO 80202 E-mail: john.mccabe@dgslaw.com.

MCCABE, JOHN LEE, engineer, educator; b. Fond du Lac, Wis., Mar. 26, 1923; s. Arthur Lee and Florence Gertrude (Molleson) McC.; m. M. Leora Harvey, Mar. 17, 1946; 1 child, Steven Lee. Student, Western Mich. U., 1941-42, U. Colo., 1946-47, C.C. Aurora, 1984-85. Designer project assignments, Denver, 1947-50; archtl. engr. The Austin Co., Denver, 1950-52; resident engr. Peter Kiewit Sons Co., Portsmouth, Ohio, 1953; dist. mgr. Hugh J. Baker Co., Evansville, Ind., 1953-56; engr. Lauren Burt Inc., Denver, 1956-58; project mgr. Denver Steel Products Co., Commerce city, Colo., 1958-66; pres. corp. McCabe and Co., Aurora, Colo., 1966-75; master tchr. h.s. Sch. Dist. 50, Westminster, Colo., 1975-83; tchr. Aurora Pub. Schs., 1983-92; subs. tchr. Lawrence (Kans.) Pub. Schs., 1993-99; math. instr. Lawrence Career Coll., 1999-2000. Writer Kans. Sr. Press Svc., 1996—. Columnist Lawrence Jour.-World, 1997-99; author: Word Problems Simplified, 1986, Everyday Algebra, Everyday Geometry, 1987, Everyday Mathematics-A Study Guide, 1988, Mathematics Workbook series for Technical Schools, Drafting, Machine Shop, Auto Body, Welding, Horticulture, 1987-88, Mathematics Workbook series for Middle Schools, Problem Solving, 1987, Whole Numbers, Fractions-Decimals-Percents, 1989, Measurments, Metrics, 1990, Basic Algebra, Basic Geometry, 1991, Everyday Metrics, 1992, How to Get Started as a Contractor, 2d edit., 1992, Essentials of Algebra, 1993, Applying Algebra, 1994, Metrics at Work, 1994, Basic Trigonometry, 1994, Algebra Word Problems, 1994, Personal Finance, 1995, Applied Trigonometry, 1996 (novel) The Survivors, 1998. With USAF, PTO, WWII. Mem. Colo. Soc. Engrs. (life), 20th Air Force Assn., Am. Legion. Roman Catholic. Home: 811 Moundridge Dr Lawrence KS 66049-3747

MCCABE, JOSEPH, JR., telecommunications industry executive; B in Mgmt., MBA in Quantitative Analysis, MBA in Acctg., St. John's U. With NY Tele.; from contr. to internat. v.p. AT&T Bus. Comm. Sys.; v.p., CFO strategy and new svcs. innovation divsn. AT&T, 1996—99, exec. v.p., CFO, 1999—. Office: AT&T Wireless Svcs Inc 7277 164th Ave NE Bldg 1 Redmond WA 98052

MCCABE, LINDA RAE, interior designer, artist, writer; b. Hobart, Okla., Dec. 28, 1943; d. Donald Rex Atchinson; 1 child, Cassady Velasco-Evers. BA, Okla. State U., Stillwater, 1965. Cert. secondary tchr. Okla., Ohio. Art tchr. State of Ohio, Dayton, 1969—71; interior designer Homestead Ho., Littleton, Colo., 1988—93, L.A., 1993—2002, Macy's Home Gallery, Monterey, Calif., 2002—. Sr. designer program dir. Homestead Ho., Thousand Oaks, Calif., 1999—2001, design seminar coord., L.A., 2001—02, Macy's Home Gallery, Monterey, 2003—. Exhibitions include acrylic on canvas, Kennedy Ctr., Living with Style (rep. designer in residence, 1990), John Steinbeck Movie Trilogy; author: (novel adaptation) Where Has the Champion Gone?. Fundraiser Am. Cancer Soc., Alexandria, 1976—80; blood dr. coord. ARC, Boston, 1982—86; christmas tree designer City of Denver Fundraiser, Denver, 1989; art project for sch. fundraiser Internat. Sch. of Monterey, Monterey, 2003—04. Mem.: Soc. of Children's Book Writers and Illustrators (assoc.), Am. Soc. of Interior Design (assoc.).

MCCABE, LOUISE BEACHBOARD, language educator; b. N.Y.C., Apr. 11, 1941; d. Walter William and Harriet Wood (Colby) Beachboard; m. James Laws McCabe, June 8, 1974; children: Sarah Beachboard, William Laws. B.A., Smith Coll., 1963; M.A.T., Yale U., 1966; Ph.D., Harvard U., 1978. Instr. Italian, Harvard U., 1969-70, Harvard U., 1971-72, Yale U., New Haven, 1974-75, Tyler Art Sch. Temple U., Elkins Park, Pa., 1984-87, Villanova (Pa.) U., 1987-91; Latin tchr. Roxbury Latin Sch., Mass., 1970-71; tchr. of eng. to speakers of other langs.(ESOL) Schl. Dist. Phila., 1992-93; adj. prof. Italian St. Joseph's U., Phila., 1993, Penn State U., 2003-04; instr. Italian & French, 2003-03. Asst. editor Chilton Books, Phila., 1963-65. Contbr. articles to profl. jours. Founding mem. Somerville Police Community Relations Com., Mass., 1973. Mem. MLA, Am. Assn. Tchrs. Italian, Colonial Dames Am., Internat. Womens Club of Phila. Republican. Episcopalian. Clubs: Acorn (Phila.), Smith Coll. (bd. dirs. 1989-91). Avocation: genealogy. Home: 701 Williamson Rd Bryn Mawr PA 19010-1830

MCCABE, MARGARET CLARK, family nurse practitioner; b. Washington, Feb. 21, 1956; d. Philip R. and Jeanne M. (Cushing) C. ADN, Marymount Coll. Va., 1981; BSN, Cath. U. Am., 1986; MSN, FNP, Wilmington Coll., 1999. RN, D.C., Del.; cert. CPR instr.; cert. family nurse practitioner. Staff nurse, charge nurse med.-surg. unit Providence Hosp., Washington, 1981-84, staff nurse CCU, 1984-86; staff nurse critical care unit Beebe Med. Ctr., Lewes, Del., 1986-88, asst. nurse mgr., 1988-89, nurse mgr., 1989-91, edn. specialist patient/community staff edn., 1991-94; nurse Millville (Del.) Family Health Ctr. & Beebe Home Health Agy., 1995-98; clin. coord. Beebe Physician Network Inc., 1998-99, family nurse practitioner, 2000—. V.p. Cape unit Am. Heart Assn., Del., 1990-92; chair pub. edn. com. Ea. unit Am. Cancer Soc., Sussex County, 1989-95; family nurse practitioner migrant worker program Delmarva Rural Ministries; mem. Planned Parenthood of Del., 1999—, Delmarva Rural Ministries, Dover, Del. Mem. NAN, Am. Coll. Nurse Practitioners, Am. Acad. Nurse Practitioners, Am. Assn. Nurse Practitioners, Am. Hosp. Assn., Internat. Patient Edn. Coun., Am. Soc. Healthcare Edn. and Tng., Del. Nurses Assn., Del. Soc. Healthcare Edn. and Tng. (pres. 1992-94), Sigma Theta Tau. Home: 203 Banks Rd Millville DE 19970-9795 Office: Delmarva Rural Ministries 26 Wyoming Ave Dover DE 19904-6922

MCCABE, MICHAEL J. insurance executive; b. Denver, June 19, 1945; s. Joseph J. and Mary J. (Kane) McC.; m. Catherine Corrine Marquette, July 21, 1978; children: Brian Michael, Shannon Marquette. BS, U. No. Colo., 1967; JD, Cath. U. Am., 1971. Bar: D.C. Air transport econ. analyst U.S. Civil Aeronautics Bd., Washington, 1967-71; Washington counsel Allstate Ins. Co., 1971-74, of counsel, 1974-82, asst. v.p. bus. planning, 1982-84, v.p. corp. planning, 1984-89, group v.p., gen. atty., 1989-95; v.p., gen. counsel Allstate Corp.; sr. v.p., gen. counsel Allstate Ins. Co., 1999—. Bd. advisors No. Ill. U. Sch. Bus., DeKalb, 1986—. Chmn. Gateway Found. Mem. ABA, Fed. Bar Assn., D.C. Bar Assn., Planning Forum, Sigma Chi, Pi Alpha Delta. Democrat. Roman Catholic. Office: Allstate Ins Co 2775 Sanders Rd Northbrook IL 60062

MCCABE, ROBERT HOWARD, college president; b. Dec. 23, 1929; s. Joseph A. and Kathryn (Greer) McC.; m. Arva Moore Parks, June 1992. BEd, U. Miami (Fla.), 1952, LLD (hon.), 1990; MS, Appalachian State U., Boone, N.C., 1959; PhD, U. Tex., 1963; LLD (hon.), Barry U., 1986, Fla. Internat. U., 1990. Asst. to pres. Miami Dade C. of C., Fla., 1963-65, v.p., 1965-67, exec. v.p., 1967—80, pres., 1980—95, Essex County Coll., Newark, 1967-69; sr. fellow League for Innovation in the C.C., 1995—; Disting. fellow Edn. Commn. of the States, 2000—. Exec. com. So. Regional Edn. Bd., Atlanta, 1981-83; trustee Coll. Bd., chmn., 1988-90; vice chair The Miami Coalition for a Drug-Free Cmty., 1989-94, chair, 1991—. Author: Man and Environment, 1971, No One to Waste, 2000, Yes We Can, 2002, several monographs; editor: Jour. Environ. Edn.; cons. editor Change Mag., 1980—94; contbr. articles to profl. jours. Bd. dirs. Nat. Ctr. Pub. Policy and Higher Edn., 1998—. Recipient Disting. Svc. award Fla. Congl. Del., 1983, Spirit of Excellence award The Miami Herald, 1988, Harold W. McGraw Jr. prize in Edn., 1991, The Coll. Bd. medal, 1995; named Outstanding Grad., Coll. Edn., U. Tex., 1982, named one of the 18 Most Effective Chief Exec. Officers in Am. Higher Edn. Bowling Green U., 1988; Disting. Svc. award Dade County, Fla., 1983; Kellogg fellow, 1962-63, MacArthur sr. fellow John D. and Catherine T. MacArthur Found., 1992. Fellow League for Innovation in the C.C. (sr. fellow, dir. exec. com. 1985—, Disting. Svc. award 1995); mem. Am. Assn. C.C. (bd. dirs. 1991—, Disting Svc. award 1995), Am. Assn. Higher Edn. (dir. on Higher Edn. Issues, Higher Edn. Consortium), Am. Coun. Edn. (dir. 1973-75), Am. Assn. for Environ. Edn. (pres. 1970-73), Am. Coun. on Edn. (bd. dirs. 1983-85, 92—), Southeast Fla. Edn. Consortium (chmn. bd. 1981-83). Episcopalian. Home: 1601 S Miami Ave Miami FL 33129-1103 Office Phone: 305-854-4428. E-mail: rmccabe@bellsouth.net.

MCCABE, STEVEN LEE, structural engineer; b. Denver, July 11, 1950; s. John L. and M. Leora (Shaw) McC.; m. Ann McCabe, Aug. 10, 1974; 1 child, Stephanie A. BSME, Colo. State U., 1972, MSME, 1974; PhD in Civil Engring., U. Ill., 1987. Registered profl. engr., Colo., Kans., Okla. Engr. Pub. Svc. Co. of Colo., Denver, 1974-77; sr. engr. R.W. Beck and Assocs., Denver, 1977-78; engr., project engr. Black & Veatch Cons. Engrs., Kansas City, Mo., 1978-81; asst. prof. civil engring. U. Kans., Lawrence, 1985-91, assoc. prof., 1991-98, prof., 1998—, chmn. dept. civil, and environ. engring., 1998—2001, tchg. fellow, 1994—, chmn. dept. civil, environ. and archtl. engring., 2001—02; program dir. NSF, Washington, 2002—. Vis. prof. structural engring. Norwegian Inst. Tech., Trondheim, 1995-96. Contbr. articles to profl. jours. Named Fulbright scholar U.S. Govt. to Norway, 1995-96, Ill. fellow, 1981-82; grantee Am. Inst. Steel Constrn., 1990-91, NSF, 1989-91, 91—, Civil Engring. Rsch. Found., 1991—; recipient Mech. Coupler Industry Testing Consortium Funding, 1992-95, Structural Rsch. Paper award Am. Concrete Inst., 1996. Fellow ACI (pres. Kans. chpt. 1992, reinforced concrete rsch. coun. 1999—, bldg. code com. 2002-); mem. ASME (pressure vessels and piping divsn. honor paper award 1989, cert. of recognition for svc. 1993), ASTM, ASCE (assoc. editor Jour. Structural Engring. 1992-94, chair com. concrete masonry structures, 2000—), Concrete Reinforcing Steel Inst., Am. Soc. Engring. Edn., Earthquake Engring. Rsch. Inst., Com. Euro-Internat. du Beton, Sigma Xi, Sigma Tau, Pi Tau Sigma, Phi Kappa Phi, Chi Epsilon. Republican. Roman Catholic. Achievements include development of relationships for bond and anchorage of reinforcing bars in conrete, industry specifications for headed reinforcing bars, improved damage mechanics techniques for prediction of earthquake effects on structures, seismic design criteria for power plants; research on inelastic cyclic behavior of reinforcing bars and mechanical splices, on structural dynamics and earthquake engineering as well as computational mechanics, on the evaluation of response and damage and predictions of reserve capacity in structures and members subjected to earthquake strong ground motion, on use of finite element analysis for the response of structures and machines to various types of loading. Office: U Kans 2006 Learned Hall Lawrence KS 66045-7526 E-mail: slmccabe@ku.edu.

MCCABE, THOMAS EDWARD, corporate lawyer, financial software executive; b. Washington, Jan. 22, 1955; s. Edward Aeneas and Janet Isabel McCabe; m. Kelly Marie McCarthy; children: Edward Charles, Benjamin Patrick, Adrienne Marie, Therese Eileen, Luke Stevens, Nicholas Joseph, Maximilian Karol, Eva Christina. AB, Georgetown U., 1977; MBA, JD, U. Notre Dame, 1981. Bar: D.C. 1982, U.S. Dist. Ct. D.C. 1983, U.S. Ct. Appeals (D.C. cir.) 1983, Va. 1989, U.S. Supreme Ct. 1990. Law clk. U.S. Dist. Ct. Judge Hon. Charles R. Richey, Washington, 1981-82; assoc. Reavis & McGrath, Washington, 1982-84, Venable Baetjer Howard & Civiletti, Washington, 1984-85, McCarthy & Durrette, Washington, 1985-88; ptnr. McCarthy & Burke, Washington, 1988-91; sr. v.p., dir. corp. devel., gen. counsel, sec. GRC Internat., Inc., Vienna, Va., 1992—2000; pres., CEO MicroBanx Sys., LLC, Great Falls, Va., 2001—. Republican. Roman Catholic. E-mail: tmccabe@microbanx.com.

MCCAFFERTY, JAMES ARTHUR, sociologist; b. Columbus, Ohio, Jan. 1, 1926; s. James A. and Marjorie Agatha (Gilchrist) McC.; m. Jane Roush, June 13, 1948 (dec. Oct. 1984); children: Lucinda Jane Martin, James Stanley Thomas, Bridget Anne Roush Green; m. Carolyn Ring Bradley, Nov. 7, 1987 (div. Apr. 1992); m. Irma Mae Prosser Nicholson, May 28, 1993 (dec. Nov. 1996). BS, Ohio State U., 1948, MA, 1954; postgrad., Am. U. Social rsch. analyst Ohio State Dept. Pub. Welfare, 1948-51; criminologist U.S. Bur. Prisons, Washington, 1951-63; ast. chief divsn. info. sys. Adminstrv. Office of U.S. Cts., Washington, 1963-77, chief statis. analysis and reports divsn., 1977-86; ret. Vis. lectr. Am. U., 1959, 62-64; adj. instr. Fordham U., 1978-89. Editor: Capital Punishment, 1972; contbr. articles on criminology and correctional stats. to profl. jours. Life mem. Md. State PTA; past pres. Potomac area coun. Camp Fire Girls of U.S., 1966-67; v.p. Prince George's County (Md.) Coun. PTAs, 1964-65; chmn. Prince George's County Youth Commn., 1970-72; past pres. Hypoglycemia Assn., past pres. Interfaith Cmty. Action

Coun., Inc., 1991-93. Cpl. USAAF, 1944-46. Recipient Vol. award Prince George's Co., Md., 1992. Mem. AAUP, Nat. Soc. SAR (v.p. gen. MidAtlantic dist. 2002-03), Md. Soc. SAR (life, past pres., trustee, color guard, vice commdr.), Am. Sociol. Assn., Am. Correctional Assn. (life), Assn. Correctional Rsch. and Info. Mgmt. (life, past pres., Ronald H. Beattie award 1997), Nat. Geneal. Soc., Nat. Assn. Retired Fedl. Employees (life), Am. Statis. Assn., Prince George's County Geneal. Soc. (life, past pres.), Ohio Geneal. Soc. (life), Nat. Capital Buckeye chpt., former editor newsletter), Judicature Soc., Md. State Beekeepers Assn. (life), DAV (life), Sons of Union Vets. Civil War (life, past camp comdr., former editor), Am. Legion (life), Army Airways Com. Sys. (life), Gallia County (Ohio) Hist. Geneal. Soc. (life), Nat. Congress Patriotic Orgns. (life, recorder, pres. 2003—), Germany Soc. SAR (sec. 2001—), Army and Navy Union, Garrison #65. Presbyterian. Home: 613 Rosier Rd Fort Washington MD 20744-5554 E-mail: jirma@aol.com.

MCCAFFERTY, LEO RAYMOND, plastic surgeon; b. Pitts., Nov. 24, 1953; s. Leo Garvey and Virginia Catherine (Ballard) McC.; m. Susan Mary Kimball, July 31, 1992; children: Leo Thomas, Kristin Rae, Kimberly Lynn. BS, Pa. State U., 1975; MD, Temple U., 1981. Diplomate Am. Bd. Plastic Surgery. Resident in gen. surgery Cedars-Sinai Med. Ctr., L.A., 1981-85; resident in plastic surgery Jackson Meml. Hosp. U. Miami (Fla.), 1985-87, asst. prof. plastic surgery, 1987-90; pvt. practice, vol. asst. prof. Plastic Surgery U. Pitts., Pitts., 1990—. Asst. clin. prof. Plastic Surgery U. Pitts. Sch. Medicine, Pitts., 1990—. Contbr. articles to profl. jours. Med. practitioner Govt. Jamaica, Jamaica, 1987. State Sen. scholar Temple U., 1977-78, Measey scholar Temple U., 1977-78. Mem. Am. Soc. Plastic Surgeons, Am. Soc. Maxillofacial Surgeons, Am. Cleft Palate Assn., Am. Burn Assn., Greater Pitts. Plastic Surgery Soc. Avocations: athletics, art, music. Office: Plastic Surgery 211532 S Aiken Ave Pittsburgh PA 15232

MCCAFFERTY, MICHAEL, corporate financial executive; CEO TTC Illinois, Kankakee, Ill.

MCCAFFREY, BARRY RICHARD, federal official, retired army officer; b. Taunton, Mass., Nov. 17, 1942; s. William Joseph and Mary Veronica (Curtin) McC.; m. Jill Ann Faulkner, June 8, 1964; children: Sean, Tara, Amy. BS, U.S. Mil. Acad., 1964; MA, Am. U., 1971; postgrad., Command and Gen. Staff Coll., Ft. Leavenworth, Kans., 1976, Army War Coll., Carlisle Barracks, Pa., 1982. Commd. 2d lt. U.S. Army, 1964, advanced through grades to full gen., 1994; co. comdr. 7th Cav. Div., Vietnam, 1968-69; assoc. prof. dept. social sci. U.S. Mil. Acad., West Point, NY, 1972-75; from chief ops. to comdr. 2d battalion 3d Inf. Div., Germany, 1976-81; from chief staff to comdr. 3d brigade 9th Inf. Div., Ft. Lewis, Wash., 1982-86, comdr. 3d brigade 1984-86; asst. comdt. U.S. Army Inf. Sch., Ft. Benning, Ga., 1986-88; dep. U.S. mil. rep. NATO, Brussels, 1988-89; div. comdr. 24th Inf. Div., Ft. Stewart, Ga., 1990-92; asst. to chmn. Joint Chiefs of Staff, Washington, 1992-93; dir. strategic plans and policy directory The Joint Staff, Washington, 1993-94; comdr. in chief U.S. So. Commd., Quarry Heights, Panama, 1994-96; dir. White Ho. Office Nat. Drug Control Policy, Washington, 1996—2001; Olin disting. prof. nat. security studies U.S. Mil. Acad., 2001—; pres. B.R. McCaffrey Assocs., LLC, Alexandria, Va., 2001—. Contbr. articles to mil. publs. Decorated D.S.C. with oak leaf cluster, D.M.S. with oak leaf cluster, Silver Star with oak leaf cluster, Def. Superior Svc. Medal. Mem. NAACP, Assn. of U.S. Army, Coun. of Fgn. Rels., Inter-Am. Dialogue, Legion of Valor of U.S. Independent. Avocations: hunting, reading military history. Office: BR McCaffrey Assocs Ste 600 1800 Diagonal Rd Alexandria VA 22314

MCCAFFREY, CARLYN SUNDBERG, lawyer; b. N.Y.C., Jan. 7, 1942; d. Carl Andrew Lawrence and Evelyn (Back) Sundberg; m. John P. McCaffrey, May 24, 1967; children: John C., Patrick, Jennifer, Kathleen. Student, Barnard Coll., 1963; AB in Econs., George Washington U., 1963; LLB cum laude, NYU, 1967, LLM in Taxation, 1970. Bar: N.Y. 1974. Law clk. to presiding justice Calif. Supreme Ct., 1967-68; teaching fellow law NYU, N.Y.C., 1968-70, asst. prof. law, 1970-74; assoc. Weil, Gotshal & Manges, N.Y.C., 1974-80, ptnr., 1980—. Prof. in residence Rubin Hall NYU, 1971-75; adj. prof. law NYU, 1975—, U. Miami, 1979-81; lectr. in field. Contbr. articles to profl. jours. Mem. ABA (chmn. generation-skipping transfer tax 1979-81, 93—, real property pro and trust law sect.), N.Y. State Bar Assn. (exec. com. tax sect. 1979-80, chmn. estate and gift tax com. 1976-78, 95—, life ins. com. 1983-85, trusts and estates sect.), Assn. of Bar of City of N.Y. (matrimonial law com., chmn. tax subcom. 1984-86, Am. College Trusts & Estates Counsel (bd. regents 1992—), mem. exec. com. 1995—, pres. 2002--). Home: PO Box 232 Waccabuc NY 10597-0232 Office: Weil Gotshal & Manges 767 5th Ave Fl Conc1 New York NY 10153-0119 E-mail: Carlyn.mccaffrey@weil.com.

MCCAFFREY, JUDITH ELIZABETH, lawyer; b. Providence, Apr. 26, 1944; d. Charles V. and Isadore Frances (Langford) McC.; m. Martin D. Minsker, Dec. 31, 1969 (div. May 1981); children: Ethan Hart Minsker, Natasha Langford Minsker. BA, Tufts U., 1966; JD, Boston U., 1970. Bar: Mass. 1970, D.C. 1972, Fla. 1991. Assoc. Sullivan & Worcester, Washington, 1970-76; atty. FDIC, Washington, 1976-78; assoc. Dechert, Price & Rhoads, Washington, 1978-82, McKenna, Conner & Cuneo, Washington, 1982-83; gen. counsel, corp. sec. Perpetual Savs. Bank, FSB, Alexandria, Va., 1983-91; ptnr. Powell, Goldstein, Frazer & Murphy, Washington, 1991-92, McCaffrey P.A., 1992—. Contbr. articles to profl. jours. Mem. Leadership Collier, 1998. Mem. ABA (chair subcom. thrift instns. 1985-90), D.C. Bar Assn. (bd. govs. 1981-85), Fla. Bar Assn. (chmn. fin. svcs. com. 1999-2000, exec. coun. bus. law sect. 1998-), Women's Bar Assn. D.C. (pres. 1980-81), Collier County Women's Bar Assn. (pres. 1997-98), Gulf Coast Venture Forum (pres. 2001-03). Episcopalian. Avocations: travel, reading, martial arts, Spanish. Home: PO Box 2081 Naples FL 34106-2081 Office: McCaffrey PA 568 9th St S Ste 255 Naples FL 34102-6620

MCCAFFREY, ROBERT HENRY, JR., retired manufacturing company executive; b. Syracuse, N.Y., Jan. 20, 1927; s. Robert Henry and May Ann (McGuire) McC.; m. Dorothy Anne Evers, Sept. 22, 1956; children: Michael Robert, Kathleen Mary. BS, Syracuse U., 1949. Sales asst. Sealright Corp., Fulton, N.Y., 1949-50; with TEK Hughes div. Johnson & Johnson, Metuchen, N.J., 1950-67, gen. sales mgr., 1958-59, v.p. sales, 1959-62, pres., 1962-67; gen. mgr. med. div. Howmet Corp., N.Y.C., 1967-70; group v.p. Howmedica, Inc., 1970-73, sr. v.p., 1973-74, exec. v.p., also bd. dirs., 1974-76; pres., CEO C.R. Bard, Inc., Murray Hill, N.J., 1976-78, chmn. bd. dirs., CEO, 1978-89, chmn. bd., 1989-91, also bd. dirs., chmn. exec. com., 1991—. Bd. dirs. Summit and Elizabeth Trust, Summit Bancorp, Thomas & Betts Corp. Trustee Found. for Univ. Medicine and Dentistry N.J., 1987-90, Syracuse U., 1979—, chmn. corp. adv. council, 1974-75. With AUS, 1945-46. Mem. Orthopedic Surg. Mfrs. Assn., Health Industry Mfrs. Assn. (bd. dirs., chmn. 1982-83), N.Y. Sales Execs. Club, Algonquin Club (Boston), Baltusrol Golf Club (Springfield, N.J.), Oyster Harbors Club (Osterville, Mass.), Sigma Chi. Republican. Roman Catholic. Avocations: reading, skiing, golf. Office: C R Bard Inc 730 Central Ave New Providence NJ 07974

MCCAGHY, CHARLES HENRY, sociology educator; b. Eau Claire, Wis., Apr. 29, 1934; s. Elmer and Anna Josephine (Soha) McC.; m. M. Dawn Ysebaert, June 10, 1961 BBA, U. Wis., 1956, MS, 1962, Ph.D, 1966. Instr. sociology U. Conn., 1964-66; asst. prof. sociology Case Western Res. U., Cleve., 1966-70; assoc. prof. sociology Bowling Green State U., Ohio, 1970-76, prof., 1976-94, prof. emeritus, 1994—. Vis. scholar Australian Inst. Criminology, 1984 Author: Deviant Behavior: Crime, Conflict and Interest Groups, 1976, 6th edit., 2003, Crime in American Society, 1980, 2d edit., 1987. Lt. (j.g.) USN, 1956-59 Mem. Am. Soc. Criminology (treas. 1978-82). Home: 221 Williams St Bowling Green OH 43402-3259

MCCAIG, JEFFREY JAMES, transportation company executive; b. Moose Jaw, Sask., July 5, 1951; s. John Robert and Anne Shorrocks (Glass) McC.; m. Marilyn Graves, July 7, 1983; children: Robbert Angus, Scott Thomas, Christa Mae. Student, Can. J. Coll. Lausanne, Switzerland, 1970; AB, Harvard Coll., 1973; LLB, Osgoode Hall Law Sch., Can., 1976; MSc in Mgmt., Leland Stanford Jr. U., 1984. Assoc. MacKimmie Matthews, 1976-81; owner, sr.

officer Jeffrey J. McCaig Profl. Corp., 1981-83; v.p. planning and corp. devel. Trimac, Calgary, Canada, 1983—87, exec. v.p., 1987—90, pres., 1990—94, pres., CEO, 1994—. Bd. dirs. Trimac Corp., Potash Corp. of Sask, EnerVest Group, Orbus Pharma Inc., Seamans Drilling. Mem.: World Presidents' Orgn., Law Soc. Alta., Glencoe Club, Calgary Petroleum Club, Calgary Golf and Country Club. Home: 708 Riverdale Ave SW Calgary AB Canada T2S OY3 Office: Trimac Corp 800 5 Ave SW Ste 2100 Calgary AB Canada T2P 5A3

MCCAIN, BETTY LANDON RAY (MRS. JOHN LEWIS MCCAIN), political party official, state official; b. Feb. 23, 1931; d. Horace Truman and Mary Howell (Perrett) Ray; m. John Lewis McCain, Nov. 19, 1955; children: Paul Pressly III, Mary Eloise. Student, St. Marys Jr. Coll., 1948—50; AB in Music, U. N.C., Chapel Hill, 1952, LLD (hon.), 1998; MA, Columbia U., 1953; LittD (hon.), U. N.C., Wilmington, 1997; HHD (hon.), Wake Forest U., 1999; LLD (hon.), Barton Coll., 1999. Courier, European tour guide Ednl. Travel Assocs., Plainfield, NJ, 1952-54; asst. dir. YWCA, U. N.C., Chapel Hill, 1953-55; chmn. N.C. Dem. Exec. Com. (1st woman), 1976-79; mem. Dem. Nat. Com., 1971-72, 76-79, 80-85, chmn. sustaining fund, 1981, 88-91, mem. com. on presdl. nominations (Hunt Commn.), 1981-82, mem. rules com., 1982-85, mem. cabinet Gov. James B. Hunt, Jr., 1993-2001, sec. dept. cultural resources, 1993-2001; mem. State Dem. Exec. Com., 1971—99, 2001—. Mem. Winograd Commn., 1977-78; pres. Dem. Women of N.C., 1971-72, dist. dir., 1969-72; pres. Wilson County Dem. Women, 1966-67; precinct chmn., 1972-76; del. Dem. Nat. Conv., 1972, 88; mem. Dem. Mid-Term Confs., 1974, 78, mem. jud. coun. Dem. Nat. Com., 1985-89; dir. Carolina Tel. & Tel. Co. (now Sprint), 1981-97 (1st woman) Contbg. editor: History of N.C. Med. Soc. Sunday sch. tchr. 1st Presbyn. Ch., Wilson, 1970—71, 1988—88, 1990—92, mem. chancel choir, 1985—, deacon, 1986—92, chmn. fin. com., 1990—91, chair, 1992—; treas. Wilson on the Move, 1990—92; mem. Coun. on State Goals and Policy, 1970—72, Gov.'s Task Force on Child Advocacy, 1975—78; chmn. Wilson-Greene Morehead scholarship com., 1986—89; mem. career and personal counseling svc. adv. bd. St. Andrews Coll.; charter mem. Wilson Edn. Devel. Coun.; active Arts Coun. of Wilson, Inc.; N.C. Art Soc.; N.C. Lit. and Hist. Assn.; pres. Wilson County Mental Health Assn., bd. dirs., legis. chmn.; bd. govs. U. N.C., 1975—81, 1985—93, pres. and tenure com., 1985—91, chmn. budget and fin. com., 1991—93; bd. regents Barium Springs Home for Children, 2003—, chair Founds. com. Capital Campaign; bd. dirs. N.C. Mus. History Assocs., 1982—83, pres., 1982—83, membership chair, 1987—88; co-chmn. Com. to Elect Jim Hunt Gov., 1976, 1980, co-chmn. senatorial campaign, 1984; mem. N.C. Adv. Budget Com. (1st woman), 1981—85; chmn. State Employees Combined Campaign N.C., 1993; bd. visitors Peace Coll., Wake Forest U. Sch. Law, 1980—83, U. N.C., Chapel Hill; co-chmn. fund dr. Wilson Cmty. Theater; elder 1st Presbyn. Ch., 1992—; state bd. dirs. Am. Lung Assn., 1985—88; bd. dirs. Roanoke Island Commn.; USS/NC Battleship Commn., 1993—2001. Recipient state awards N.C. Heart Assn., 1967, Easter Seal Soc., 1967, Cmty. Svc. award Wilson Downtown Bus. Assocs., 1977, award N.C. Jaycees, 1979, 85, Women in Govt. award N.C. and U.S. Jaycettes, 1985, Alumni Disting. Svc. award U. N.C., Chapel Hill, 1993, Flora Mac Donald Scottish Heritage award, 1995, Carpathian award N.C. Equity, 1995, Pinnacle award, 1997, 1st winner Holderness-Weaver award U. N.C., Greensboro, 1999, Citizen of Yr. award Wilson C. of C., 2000, Ruth Coltrane Cannon award for hist. preservation Preservation N.C., 2000, N.C. State U. Sch. of Design award, 2000; named to Order of Old Well and Valkyries, U. N.C., 1952; named Dem. Woman of Yr., N.C., 1976. Mem.: DAR, UDC (historian John W. Dunham chpt.), Rotary Internat. (Paul Harris fellow 2003), N.C. Inst. Medicine (bd. dirs. 1993—), N.C. Sch. Arts (trustee 1993—2001), N.C. Equity (bd. dirs.), N.C. Soc. Internal Medicine Aux. (pres.), N.C. Symphony (trustee 2002—), Info. Resources Mgmt. Commn. N.C. (bd. dirs. 1993—2001), N.C. Agy. Pub. Telecom. (bd. dirs. 1993—2001), N.C. Found. for Nursing (bd. dirs. 1989—92), St. Mary's Alumni Assn. (regional v.p.), U. N.C. Chapel Hill Alumni Assn. (chmn. 2001—02, dir.), Nat. Soc. Colonial Dames Am. NC (pres., local com. program co-chmn., dir., proposal preparation for parliamentarian med. auxs.), AMA Alliance (dir., nat. vol. health svcs. chmn., aux. liaison rep. AMA Coun. on Mental Health, aux. rep. Coun. on Vol. Health Orgns.), Wilson Country Club, Little Book Club, The Book Club (pres.), Pi Beta Phi. Home: 1134 Woodland Dr NW Wilson NC 27893-2122

MCCAIN, JOHN SIDNEY, III, senator; b. Panama Canal Zone, Aug. 29, 1936; s. John Sidney and Roberta (Wright) McCain; m. Carol, 1965 (div. 1980); 1 child Sidney Ann; m. Cindy Hensley, May 17, 1980; children: Doug, Andrew, Sidney, Meghan, Jack, Jimmy, Bridget. Grad. U.S. Naval Acad., 1958; grad., Nat. War Coll., 1973-74; degree (hon.), Johns Hopkins U., 1999, Colgate U., 2000, U. Penn., 2001, Wake Forest U., 2002, U. So. Calif., 2004. Dir. Navy Senate Liaison Office, Washington, 1977-81; mem. U.S. Ho. Reps. 98th-99th Congress from 1st Ariz. Dist., 1983—86; senator from Ariz. U.S. Senate, 1987—; mem. armed svcs. com., Indian affairs com., chmn. commerce, sci. and transp. com. Chmn. Internat. Republican Inst., 1993—; Republican candidate for presidential nomination, 2000; mem. Commn. on the Intelligence Capabilities of the US Regarding Weapons of Mass Destruction, 2004; speaker Republican Nat. Convention, NYC, 2004. Author (with Mark Salter): (nonfiction) Faith of My Fathers, 1999, Worth the Fighting For: What I Learned from Mavericks, Heroes, and Politics, 2002, Why Courage Matters: The Way to a Braver Life, 2004. Served in USN, 1958—81, prisoner of war, 1967—73, Vietnam, became captain USN, 1977. Excellence in Pub. Svc. award, Am. Acad. of Pediatrics, 1999, Friendship award, League of Latin Am. Citizens, 1999, Intrepid Freedom award, Intrepid Museum Found., 1999, Profile in Courage award, John F. Kennedy Library Found., 1999, Paul H. Douglas Ethics in Govt. award, Institute of Govt. & Pub. Affairs, U. Il, 2000, William Penn Mott Jr. Park Leadership award, Nat. Parks Conservation Assn., 2001; Decorated Legion of Merit, Silver Star, Bronze Star, Purple Heart, Disting. Flying Cross, Vietnamese Legion of Honor; named on of the 25 Most Influential People in Am., Time mag., 1997. Mem., Am. Legion, Society of the Cincinnati, VFW; bd. dirs. Community Assistance League, Phoenix, 1981-, Internat. Rep. Inst., 1993—; Nixon Ctr. for Peace and Freedom. Republican. Episcopalian. Co-sponsor of the McCain-Feingold Bill, 2002. Office: US Senate 241 Russell Office Bldg Washington DC 20510*

MCCALEB, ANNETTE WATTS, executive secretary; b. Darbfork, Ky., Dec. 11, 1931; d. Benjamin Taylor and Suzanna Elizabeth (White) Watts; m. John Henry McCaleb, Oct. 23, 1962; children: Jonathan Jeffrey, Suzanna Elizabeth McCaleb Woodhead, Sarah Leslie McCaleb James. BS, U. Ky., 1954. Med. technologist Good Samaritan, Lexington, Ky., 1953-54; lab. supr. Charleston (W.Va.) Mcml., 1954-58; chief med. technologist Meml. Hosp., Indpls., 1958-63; assoc. prof. UAMC, Little Rock, 1963-66; sec., treas., co-owner John H. McCaleb Constrn., Little Rock, 1966—. Justice of the peace Pulaski County Quorum Ct., Ark., 1989—; state bd. dirs. F.L.A.G., 1989-98. Mem. S.W. Kiwanis (pres. 1997-99), Pulaski County Property Owners Assn. (pres. 1999-2000). Democrat. Baptist. Avocations: reading, crossword puzzles, gardening, sewing. Home and Office: 3900 Annette Ln Little Rock AR 72206-5357 Office Phone: 501-888-4253. Personal E-mail: annmccaleb@sbcglobal.net.

MCCALEB, GARY DAY, university official; b. Anson, Tex., Nov. 2, 1941; s. Victor Earl and Vivian (Day) McC.; m. Sylvia Ravanelli, June 5, 1964; children: Cara Lee Cranford, Bryan Day. BA, Abilene Christian Coll., 1964; MBA, Tex. A&M U., 1975, PhD, 1979. Asst. dir. alumni rels. Abilene (Tex.) Christian U., 1964-65, dir. alumni rels., 1965-69, dir. coll. rels., 1969-73, asst. acad. dean, 1978-80, v.p. pub. rels., 1980-83, v.p., dean campus life, 1983-91, 1991—93, v.p., exec. dir. Ctr. for Bldg. Cmty., 1999—; asst. dir. devel. Tex. A&M U., Bryan, 1973-75. Leader internat. travel and goodwill groups; U.S. rep. to world exec. com. Internat. Union Local Authorities, 1996-99. Author: Community, The Gift of Community. Coun. mem. City of Abilene, 1985-90, mayor, 1990-99; bd. dirs. Taylor County Am. Cancer Soc., 1972-73; mem. adv. bd. United Way of Abilene, 1979-83, dir. pub. svc. divsn., 1987, chmn. consortium on drug and alcohol abuse, 1987-88; dir. Civic Abilene, Inc., 1981-83; treas. Abilene Task Force on Drug and Alcohol Abuse, 1984-86, active March of Dimes; mem. Tex. Sch. Health Coun., 1997-2000. Recipient Polit. Courage award John Ben Shepperd Pub. Leadership Forum, Austin, Tex., 1993, Tex. Urban Leadersip award U. Tex.-Arlington Sch. Urban and Pub. Affairs, 1995. Mem. Nat. League Cities (nat. steering com. on fin.,

adminstrn. and intergovtl. rels. 1989-90, adv. bd. 1994, bd. dirs. 1992-94), U.S. Conf. Mayors, Internat. Mcpl. Consortium (chmn. 1994-95), Tex. Mcpl. League (legis. policy com. Houston 1986, resolutions com. Dallas 1988, v.p. region 6 1988-89, bd. dirs. 1989-90, pres. 1992), Abilene C. of C. (aviation com. 1981, 94). Republican. Mem. Ch. of Christ. Avocations: art, baseball, jogging. Office: Abilene Christian Univ PO Box 29136 Abilene TX 79699-0001 E-mail: mccalebg@acu.edu.

MCCALEB, JOHN E. public health environmentalist, biologist; b. Brilliant, Ala., June 3, 1948; s. Houston and Lois A. (Dodd) McCaleb; m. Sheila D. Branch, Feb. 7, 1976 (div.); 1 child, Jesse Houston; m. Mary W. Whitmire, June 5, 1999; stepchildren: Mary Ann, Thomas W. BS in Biology, Florence State U., 1970; MS in Biology, Auburn U., 1973. Biologist Ichthyological Assocs., Pottstown, Pa., 1976—77, Radiation Mgmt. Corp., Pitts., 1977—79; engring. aide Wellborn Cabinets, Ashland, Ala., 1979—81; environmentalist Marion County Health Dept., Hamilton, Ala., 1981—82; environmentalist II Marion County Health Dept., Hamilton, 1982—85, 1989—92, Winston County Health Dept., Double Springs, Ala., 1985—89; pub. health environmentalist Madison County Health Dept., Huntsville, Ala., 1992—. Contbr. articles to profl. jours. Mem.: Ala. Environ. Health Assn. (nominee Sanitarian of Yr. State of Ala. 2002), Nat. Environ. Health Assn. (registered environ. health specialist), Coleopterists Soc., Soc. WWI Aviation Historians, Land Trust North Ala., World Wildlife Fund, Lions, Civitans. Achievements include discovery of new species of freshwater snail. Avocations: hiking, studying freshwater beetles, WWI aviation, native American history. Office: Madison County Pub Health Dept PO Box 467 311 Green St Huntsville AL 35804 Personal E-mail: mccaleb2001@hotmail.com.

MCCALEB, MALCOLM, JR., lawyer; b. Evanston, Ill., June 4, 1945; BA, Colgate U., 1967; JD, Northwestern U., 1971. Bar: Ill. 1971. Atty. McCaleb, Lucas & Brugman, Chgo., 1970—85; ptnr. Keck, Mahin & Cate, Chgo., 1985—95, Foley & Lardner, Chgo., 1995—2000, Barack Ferrazzano Kirschbaum Perlman & Nagelberg, LLC, Chgo., 2000—. Chmn. Northfield (Ill.) Village Caucus, 1981-82, active, 1977-82, Northfield Zoning Commn., 1985-88; pres. bd. dirs. Vols. Am., 1977-79; active Northfield Sch. and Park Bd. Caucus, 1980-87. Mem. Chgo. Bar Assn., Bar Assn. 7th Fed. Cir., Patent Law Assn. Chgo. Internat. Trademark Assn. Office: Barack Ferrazzano Kirschbaum Perlman & Nagelberg LLC 333 W Wacker Dr Chicago IL 60606 Business E-Mail: mac.mccaleb@bfkpn.com.

MCCALEB, MARGARET ANNE SHEEHAN, application developer; b. Washington, Jan. 15, 1956; d. Rourke Joseph and Anne Marie (Fahy) Sheehan; m. Michael Ray McCaleb, May 2, 1987. Bachelors cum laude, Rosemont Coll., 1978; Masters, Cath. U., 1980. Co-dir. Media Analysis Project, Washington, 1980—81; dir., litigation support staff Morgan Assocs., Washington, 1981—90; software devel. mgr. Adminstrv. Office of U.S. Cts., Washington, 1990—. Co-author: Over the Wire and On TV, 1983; contbr. articles to mags. and newspapers. Recipient scholarship, Cath. U., 1978—79, grant, Russell Sage Found., 1980—81. Roman Catholic. Office: Adminstrv Office US Cts 1 Columbus Cir NE Washington DC 20544

MCCALEB, NEAL A. former federal agency administrator; b. Oklahoma City; m. Georgann McCaleb; 4 children. BS in Civil Engring., Okla. State U. Sec. transp. Dept. Transp., Okla., 1987—91, 1995—2001; asst. sec. Bur. Indian Affairs, U.S. Dept. Interior, Washington, 2001—03. Mem. Okla. Ho. of Reps., minority floor leader, 1978.

MCCALL, CHARLES BARNARD, health facility administrator, educator; b. Memphis, Nov. 2, 1928; s. John W. and Lizette (Kimbrough) McCall; m. Carolyn Jean Rosselot, June 9, 1951; children: Linda, Kim, Betsy, Cathy. BA, Vanderbilt U., 1950, MD, 1953. Diplomate Am. Bd. Internal Medicine, Am. Bd. Pulmonary Diseases. Intern Vanderbilt U. Hosp., Nashville, 1953-54; clin. assoc., sr. asst. surgeon USPHS, Nat. Cancer Inst., NIH, 1954-56; sr. asst. resident in medicine U. Ala. Hosp., 1956-57, chief resident, 1958-59; fellow chest diseases Nat. Acad. Scis.-NRC, 1957-58; instr. U. Ala. Med. Sch., 1958-59; from asst. prof. to assoc. prof. medicine U. Tenn. Med. Sch., 1959-69, chief pulmonary diseases, 1964-69; mem. faculty U. Tex. Sys., Galveston, 1969-75, prof. med. br., 1971-73; assoc. prof. medicine Health Sci. Ctr., Southwestern Med. Sch., Dallas, 1973-75, also assoc. dean clin. programs, 1973-75; dir. Office Grants Mgmt. and Devel., 1973-75; dean, prof. medicine U. Tenn. Coll. Medicine, 1975-77, Oral Roberts U. Sch. Medicine, Tulsa, 1977-78; interim assoc. dean U. Okla. Tulsa Med. Coll., 1978-79; clin. prof. medicine U. Colo. Med. Sch., Denver, 1979-80; prof. medicine, assoc. dean U. Okla. Med. Sch., 1980-82; exec. dean and dean U. Okla. Coll. Medicine, 1982-85; v.p. patient affairs, prof. medicine U. Tex. M. D. Anderson Cancer Ctr., 1985-94; chief of staff VA Med. Ctr., Oklahoma City, 1980-82. Exec. dir. Worldwide Healthcare Svcs., Inc., Waco, Tex., 1998—2002; clinic dir. Claremore Family Medicine, 2002—04, cons., 2002; bd. dirs. Amigos Internacionales, Inc. Contbr. articles to med. jours. Fellow: ACP, Am. Coll. Chest Physicians; mem.: AMA, Am. Fedn. Clin. Rsch., So. Thoracic Soc. (pres. 1968—69), Am. Thoracic Soc., Sigma Xi, Alpha Omega Alpha. Baptist. Address: PO Box 701585 Tulsa OK 74170-1585 Home: 9168 S Florence Pl Tulsa OK 74137 E-mail: majormann@cox.net., mccallcharles@earthlink.net.

MCCALL, DUKE KIMBROUGH, clergyman; b. Meridian, Miss., Sept. 1, 1914; s. John William and Lizette (Kimbrough) McC.; m. Marguerite Mullinnix, Sept. 1, 1936 (dec. 1983); children: Duke, Douglas H., John Richard, Michael W.; m. Winona Gatton McCandless, Feb. 2, 1984. BA, Furman U., Greenville, S.C., 1936; MDiv, So. Bapt. Sem., Louisville, 1938; PhD, So. Bapt. Sem., 1943; LLD (hon.), Baylor U.; DD (hon.), Furman U., U Richmond, Stetson U.; LittD, Georgetown Coll. Ordained to ministry, Bapt. Ch., 1937. Pastor Broadway Bapt. Ch., Louisville; pres. New Orleans Bapt. Theol. Sem., 1943-46; exec. sec. So. Bapt. Exec. Com., Nashville, 1946-51; pres. So. Bapt. Theol. Sem., Louisville, 1951-82, chancellor, 1982-92. Pres. Bapt. World Alliance, Washington, 1980-85; chmn. bd. dirs. Covenant Life Ins. Co., 1989-90. Author: God's Hurry, 1948, Passport to the World, 1951, Broadman Comments, 1957, 2nd edit., 1958, A Story of Stewardship, 1996; editor: What is the Church, Duke K. McCall: An Oral History, 2001. Recipient E.Y. Mullins Denominational Svc. award. Avocations: golf, boating. Home: 3328 Devonshire Way Palm Beach Gardens FL 33418- E-mail: dukemccall@mindspring.com.

MCCALL, ELIZABETH KAYE, columnist, consultant, writer; b. Columbus, Ohio, Mar. 18, 1951; d. Frank and Patricia J. McCall. BA in Sociology, Miami U., Oxford, Ohio, 1973; MBA, Ryokan Coll., 1985. Writer horse industry, travel, entertainment, bus. and various spiritual publs., Malibu, Calif., 1981—; cons. Elizabeth Kaye McCall & Assocs., Malibu, 1990—; pres. Magic Horse Prodns., Malibu, 1991—. Pub. rels. advisor Equestrian Edn. Ctr. Pepperdine U., Malibu, 1986—2001, Inner City Slickers, LA, 1997—; mktg. and pub. rels. cons. Author: The Tao of Horses: Exploring How Horses Guide Us on Our Spiritual Path, 2004. Mem.: Am. Horse Publs., Am. Horse Coun. (affiliate mem.). Avocations: horseback riding, travel, drawing, perfume, films. Office: PO Box 2102 Malibu CA 90265-7102 E-mail: elizmccall@earthlink.net.

MCCALL, H. CARL, finacial services executive, former state comptroller; b. Boston, Oct. 17, 1935; m. Joyce Brown; 1 child, Marci. BA, Dartmouth Coll., 1958; student, Andover Newton Theol. Sch., U. Edinburgh. Senator upper Manhattan dist. N.Y. State Senate, 1975—79; pres. Citicorp/Citibank, 1984—93; pres. N.Y.C. Bd Edn., 1991—93; comptroller State of N.Y., 1993—2003; vice chmn., mng. dir. HealthPoint, LLC, 2003—. Bd. dirs. Tyco Internat. Ltd., 2003—. Amb. to UN; commr. Port Authority N.Y. and N.J.; commr. N.Y. State Divsn. Human Rights, 1983-85; mem. Coun. Fgn. Rels., Coun. Am. Ambs.; past bd. dirs. N.Y. State Commn. State and Local Fin., Harlem Internat. Trade Ctr. Corp. Office: Healthpoint LLC 505 Park Ave 12th Fl New York NY 10022*

MCCALL, JENNIFER JORDAN, lawyer; b. N.Y.C., Feb. 15, 1956; m. James W. McCall; children: Caroline, Hillary. BA cum laude in English Lit., Princeton U., 1978; JD, U. Va. Sch. Law, 1982; LLM in Taxation, NYU, 1988.

Bar: N.Y. 1983, Calif. 2002. Assoc. Lord Day & Lord, N.Y.C., 1982-92; ptnr. Lord Day & Lord, Barrett Smith, N.Y.C., 1992-94; ptnr. Pvt. Client Group Cadwalader, Wickersham & Taft, N.Y.C., 1994—2003; ptnr. Pillsbury Winthrop, LLP, N.Y.C., 2003—; Palo Alto, Calif., 2003—. Trustee Charitable Founds. and Trusts and advisor to numerous high net worth individuals; spkr. in field on estate and tax planning and adminstrn. Co-author: Estate Planning for Authors and Artists, 1998; contbr. chpt. to Estate Tax Techniques. Steering com., Planned Giving Adv. Com., The Mus. of Modern Art; mem. Profl. Advisor's Coun., Lincoln Ctr., Inc.; trustee League for the Hard of Hearing, N.Y.C., 1992-2003, East Side House Settlement, Bronx, N.Y., 1995-2002, Chapin Sch., N.Y.C., 1998-2001; chairperson Ethel Gray Stringfellow Art Case Com., N.Y.C.; bd. trustees San Francisco Ballet. Fellow Am. Coll. Trust and Estate Counsel; mem. ABA (real property, probate and trust law sects.), N.Y. State Bar Assn. (com. on trusts and estates adminstrn.; chairperson subcom. on proposed legislation on executor's commns.), Calif. State Bar Assn. Office: Pillsbury Winthrop LLC 2470 Hanover St Palo Alto CA 94304 also: Pillsbury Winthrop LLC 1540 Broadway New York NY 10038

MC CALL, JERRY CHALMERS, retired government official; b. Oxford, Miss., June 30, 1927; s. E. Forrest and Mariada (Huffaker) McC.; m. Margaret Denton, Nov. 28, 1951; children: Betsy, Lynn, Kim. BA, MA, U. Miss., 1951; MS, U. Ill., 1956, PhD, 1959. Tchg. asst. dept. math. U. Miss., 1950-51; instr. math., 1952-53, prof. math., 1973-76, exec. vice chancellor, 1973-76; rsch. assoc. U. Ill., 1953-57; applied sci. engr. IBM, Springfield, Ill., 1957-58, mgr. Bethesda, Md., 1966-68, Huntsville, Ala., 1968-71, Owego, N.Y., 1971-72; exec. v.p. Midwest Computer Service, Inc., Decatur, Ill., 1958-59; mem. sci. staff computation lab. Army Ballistic Missile Agy., Huntsville, 1959-60; asst. to dir. Marshall Space Flight Ctr., NASA, Huntsville, 1960-63; dep. dir. rsch. and devel. ops. Marshall Space Flight Ctr. NASA, Huntsville, 1963-66, dir. info. rsch. NASA Miss. Test Facility Bay St. Louis, 1972-73; pres. 1st State Bank and Trust Co., Gulfport, Miss., 1976-77; dir. Nat. Data Buoy Ctr., Miss., 1977-99; pres. McKool, Inc., Gulfport, Miss., 1982-94, Am. Mini Storage, Gulfport, 1985—, Am Crane Rentals, Inc., 1985-89, Cool-Power, Inc., 1988-93; ret., 1999; owns. EG & G Corp., 1999—2000; pres. Greentree Apts., 1999—; 6582. Head math dept. St. Bernard Coll., Cullman, Ala., part-time, 1960-65; asso. prof. math. U. Ala., Huntsville, 1960-62; pub. speaker, 1960-63; chmn. incorporators First State Bank & Trust Co., Gulfport, Miss., 1973-76; tech. cons. Gen. Electric Co., 1974-75 Editor: (with Ernst Stuhlinger) Astronautical Engineering and Science, 1963, From Peenemunde to Outer Space, 1963. Mem. Miss. Criminal Justice Standards Commn., 1974-75; mem. Miss. Marine Resources Council, 1974-76; bd. dirs. U. Miss. Found.; bd. advisers Sch. Engring., U. Miss., 1965-73; mem. indsl. advisors U. New Orleans; chmn. founders U. Ala. Research Inst., Huntsville, 1960-62. Mem. U.S. Dept. Commerce Sr. Exec. Assn. (bd. dirs.), Am. Judicature Soc. (lay mem.), U. Miss. Alumni Assn. (dir. 1966-73) Home: PO Box 7092 Gulfport MS 39506-7092

MCCALL, JOHN CLARK, JR., interior designer; b. Vidalia, Ga., Sept. 6, 1949; s. John Clark McCall and Carolyn Elizabeth Kay. BA, Ga. State U., 1972, MPA, 1980. Program coord. dept. music Ga. State U., Atlanta, 1972-73; adminstrn. supr. dept. music, 1973-78, asst. to dir. office acad. assistance Coll. Arts and Scis., 1978-81; dir. Ctr. for Career Devel. Winthrop U., Rock Hill, S.C., 1981-83, dir., founder Office Campus Planning and Design, 1983-85, asst. prof. interior design, 1985-89; pres. John Clark McCall, Jr. Design Cons., Inc., Rock Hill, S.C., Hahira, Valdosta, Moultrie, Ga., 1983—. Acting chair dept. interior design Winthrop U., Rock Hill, 1985-86. Author: (foreword) Frank McCall: A Complete Designer in the Class Tradition, 1985, (monograph) Atlanta Fox Album: Mecca on Peachtree Street, 1975; designer interiors for residential and non-residential projects. Dir. Friends of Albany (Ga.) Theatre, 1998-99; bd. trustees Valdosta (Ga.) Symphony Orch.; vol. Save the Atlanta Fox, 1974-80; project dir. Rylander Theatre Moller Pipe Organ Donation, Americus, Ga., 1998-99. Mem. Am. Soc. Interior Designers (allied mem., D. Brahms H. Presv. award 1985, Press.'s award 1987), Am. Theatre Organ Soc., Theatre Hist. Soc., Found. for Interior Design Edn. Rsch. (bd. visitors), Lincoln Continental Owners Club, Packard Club. Episcopalian. Avocations: antique automobiles, theater and theater organ history and research, watercolor painting. Office: John Clark McCall Jr Design Cons Inc 1415 Crescent Dr Moultrie GA 31768 E-mail: jcmdc@alltell.net.

MCCALL, JOHN PATRICK, college president, educator; b. Yonkers, N.Y., July 17, 1927; s. Ambrose V. and Vera E. (Rush) McC.; m. Mary-Berenice Morris, June 15, 1957; children: Claire, Anne, Ambrose, Peter. AB, Coll. of Holy Cross, 1949; MA, Princeton U., 1952, PhD, 1955; DHL, Knox Coll., Galesburg, Ill., 1993. Instr. Georgetown U., 1955-57, asst. prof. English, 1957-62, assoc. prof., 1962-66; prof. U. Cin., 1966-82, head dept. English, 1970-76, sr. v.p., provost, 1976-82; pres. Knox Coll., 1982-93, pres. emeritus and prof. emeritus English, 1993—; vol. Peace Corps, Turkmenistan, 1993-95. Vis. prof. Turkmen State U., 1994-95; vice chmn. Gov.'s Task Force on Rural Ill., 1986; pres. Associated Colls. Ill., 1986-88; chmn. Associated Colls. of M.W., 1991-92; mem. edn. com. Ill. Bd. Higher Edn., 1985, 90; mem. rural libr. panel, State of Ill., 1992. Author: Chaucer Among the Gods: the Poetics of Classical Myth, 1979; contbr. articles to profl. jours.; research in medieval lit. and Chaucer's poetry. Exec.-in-residence Xavier U. La., 1997—. With Signal Corps, U.S. Army, 1952-54. Am. Coun. Learned Socs. fellow, 1962-63; John Simon Guggenheim Meml. Found. fellow, 1975; Fulbright grantee, 1962. Mem. Medieval Acad. Am. MLA, AAUP, World Affairs Coun. New Orleans, Order of St. Louis, Archdiocese of New Orleans. Democrat. Roman Catholic. Home: 1404 3rd St New Orleans LA 70130-5746 Office: Xavier U La 1 Drexel Dr Box 66 New Orleans LA 70125-1098 E-mail: jmccall@xula.edu.

MC CALL, JULIEN LACHICOTTE, banker; b. Florence, S.C., Apr. 1, 1921; s. Arthur M. and Julia (Lachicotte) McC.; m. Janet Jones, Sept. 30, 1950; children: Melissa, Alison Gregg, Julien Lachicotte Jr. BS, Davidson Coll., 1942, LLD (hon.), 1983; MBA, Harvard U., 1947. With First Nat. City Bank, N.Y.C., 1948-71, asst. mgr. bond dept., 1952-53, asst. cashier, 1953-55, asst. v.p., 1955-57, v.p., 1957-71; 1st v.p. Nat. City Bank, Cleve., 1971-72, pres., 1972-79, chmn., 1979-85, chief exec. officer, from 1979, also bd. dirs.; pres. Nat. City Corp., 1973-80, chmn., chief exec. officer, 1980-86, also bd. dirs., cons. Mem. fed. adv. coun. Fed. Res. Bd., 1984-87. Trustee St. Luke's Found., United Way Services, Boy Scouts Am., Playhouse Sq. Found., Cleve. Mus. Natural History. Served with AUS, 1942-46, Africa, ETO. Mem. Pepper Pike Club, Chagrin Valley Hunt Club, Mountain Lake Club (Lake Wales, Fla.), Rolling Rock Club (Ligonier, Pa.). Home: Arrowhead 115 Quail Ln Chagrin Falls OH 44022 Office: 30195 Chagrin Blvd Ste 104W Pepper Pike OH 44124-5703

MCCALL, LOUIS CHARLES JOHN, financial advisor, executive, accountant; b. Irvington, N.J., Sept. 22, 1959; s. Louis C. and Joan M. (Zalewski) McC.; m. Vicki Lynn Braun; children: Heather Ashley, Louis, Christina Helen, Sean Thomas. BS, St. Joseph's U., 1981. CPA, N.J.; cert. fin. officer, mcpl. fin. officer. Pub. acct./auditor Merves & Co. CPAs, Phila., 1980-84; st. audit mgr. Ernst & Young, LLP, Phila., 1984-94; CFO County of Camden, N.J., 1994-98; v.p. Advanta, 1998; sr. v.p., corp. contr. GMAC Mortgage, 1999-2000; CFO Metris Bus. Svcs., 2000—. Pres. acctg. alumni bd. St. Joseph's U., 1993-94, acctg. alumni bd. 1993—, bd. govs., 1994—; bd. dirs. Vis. Nurse Svc. Sys., Inc. Bd. dirs. Wenonah Planning/Zoneing Bd., 1995—; mem. Wenonah Hist. Soc., 1996—; pres. Lions Club, Wenonah, N.J., 1997-98. Recipient Cmty. Svc. award Borough of Wenonah, 1994, Outstanding Svc. award Wenonah Police, 1994, 97. Fellow N.J. Soc. CPAs (S.W. chpt. chmn. members in industry comm. 1991-94), Pa. Inst. CPA (Phila. chpt. bd. dirs., fin. svc. com. 1990-92); mem. N.J. County Fin. Officers Assn., South Jersey Assn. County Fin. Officers (founder).

MCCALL, MADHAVI MICHAEL, social sciences educator; d. Hasmukh and Nalini Shah; m. Michael A. McCall, May 22, 1993; 1 child, Spencer Jordan. PhD, Wash. U., St. Louis, 1999. Asst. prof. San Diego State, 2001—. Contbr. articles to profl. jours. Grantee Rsch. Creative Activity and Scholarship, San Diego State U., 2001—02; Sr. Tchg. Fellowship, Wash. U., 1997, Dean's Dissertation Fellowship, 1998—99. D-Liberal. Business E-Mail: mccall@mail.sdsu.edu.

MCCALLA, SANDRA ANN, educational administrator; b. Shreveport, La., Nov. 6, 1939; d. Earl Gray and Dorothy Edna (Adams) McC. BS, La. State U., 1960; MA, U. No. Colo., 1968; EdD, Tex. A&M U., 1987. With Caddo Parish Sch. Bd., Shreveport, 1960-88; asst. prin. Capt. Shreve H.S., 1977-79, prin., 1979-88, 94—; dir., dean divsn. edn. Northwestern State U., Natchitoches, La., 1988-94; instr. math. La. State U., 1979-81. Mem. adv. bd. Sta. KDAQ Pub. Radio, 1985-89, Shreveport Women's Commn., 1983-89. Named Educator of Yr. Shreveport Times-Caddo Tchrs. Assn., 1966, La H.S. Prin. of Yr., 1985, 87; recipient Excellence in Edn. award Capt. Shreve H.S., 1982-83; Danforth fellow, 1982-83. Mem. nat. Assn. Secondary Sch. prins., La. Assn. Prins. (Prin. of Yr. 1985), Assn. Am. Sch. Execs. (Disting. Svc. award 1983), Times-Caddo Educators Assn. (Educator of Yr. 1984), Phi Delta Kappa, Kappa Delta Pi. Republican.

MCCALLISTER, MICHAEL B. managed health care executive; b. Indianapolis, May 27, 1952; m. Charlene Gray, 1985; children: Megan, Ryan. BA, La. Tech. U., 1974; MBA, Pepperdine U., 1983. Fin. specialist Humana Inc., Louisville, 1974—75, exec. dir. fin. Cmty. Hosp. Springhill, La., 1975; exec. dir. Humana Hosps. in, Huntington and West Anaheim, Calif., 1978—85, Humana Hosp. West Hills, Canoga Park, Calif., 1985—88; pres. Humana Hosp. Phoenix, 1988—89; v.p. Humana Health Care Plans, Phoenix, 1989—92, San Antonio, 1992—96; pres. divsn. 1 with responsibility for Tex., Fla. and P.R., 1996—97; sr. v.p. health sys. mgmt. Humana Inc., Louisville, 1997—99, sr. v.p. office chmn., 1999—2000, pres., CEO, 2000—. Recipient Tower Medallion Award, La. Tech. U., 2003. Mem.: Am. Assn. Health Plans (bd. dirs.). Office: Humana Inc Humana Bldg 500 W Main St Ste 300 Louisville KY 40202-4268*

MCCALLISTER, RICHARD ANTHONY, business consulting company executive; b. Newark, Ohio, Apr. 10, 1937; s. Ward C. and LeDema Mc.; m. Trina D. Gordon, Sept. 1, 1979; children: Todd, Mark. BS, Ill. State U., 1960; postgrad., U. So. Calif., 1960-62. Indsl. cons. Sci. Rsch. Assocs., 1964-66; v.p. Mgmt. Psychologists, Inc., Chgo., 1966-68; dir. Price Waterhouse & Co., Chgo., 1968-75; pres. William H. Clark Assocs., Inc., Chgo., 1975-89; sr. v.p., dir. Boyden Internat., Chgo., 1989-91; mng. dir. Boyden Midwest, Chgo., 1991—. Chmn. bd. DH2O, 2004—; chmn. WHCA Ptnrs., 1986—; bd. dir. Spirian Techs., Boyden World Corp., mng. dir.; bd. dir. Mid Am., sec., treas.; mem. adv. bd. Fiduciary Management, Inc., Lionheart Trust Co., 1988—93. Former pres. Dist. 113 Bd. Edn., Deerfield, Ill.; bd. dirs., exec. com. Grant Hosp., Chgo., House of Vision, 1975-82. Mem. Glen View Club, Racquet Club, Chgo. Club, Mid-Am. Club (bd. dirs., treas., pres. 1998—). Office: 180 N Stetson Ave Chicago IL 60601-6710

MCCALLUM, BENNETT TARLTON, economist, educator; b. Poteet, Tex., July 27, 1935; s. Henry DeRosset and Frances (Tarlton) McCallum; m. Sally Jo Hart, June 3, 1961. BA, Rice U., 1957, BSChemE, 1958, PhD, 1969; MBA, Harvard U., 1963. Chem. engr. Petro-Tex Chem. Corp., Houston, 1958-61; lectr. U. Sussex, England, 1965-66; asst. prof. to prof. U. Va., Charlottesville, 1967-80; prof. econs. Carnegie-Mellon U., Pitts., 1981-86, H. J. Heinz prof. econs., 1986—. Cons. Fed. Res. Bd., Washington, 1974—75; adviser Fed. Res. Bank, Richmond, Va., 1981—; rsch. assoc. Nat. Bur. Econ. Rsch., Cambridge, Mass., 1979—; mem. Shadow Open Market Com., 2000—; hon. advisor Inst. Monetary Econ. Studies, Bank Japan. Author: (book) Monetary Economics, 1989, International Monetary Economics, 1996; co-editor: Am. Econ. Rev., 1988—91, Carnegie-Rochester Conf. series pub. policy, 1995—; contbr. articles to profl. jours. Vis. scholar, IMF, Washington, 1989—90, Bank Japan, 1993, Victoria U. Wellington and Res. Bank New Zealand, 1995; NSF grantee, 1977—86. Fellow: Econometric Soc.; mem.: Am. Econ. Assn. Home: 219 Gladstone Rd Pittsburgh PA 15217-1111 Office: Carnegie-Mellon U Grad Sch Indsl Adminstrn 206 Pittsburgh PA 15213

MC CALLUM, CHARLES ALEXANDER, academic administrator; b. North Adams, Mass., Nov. 1, 1925; s. Charles Alexander and Mabel Helen (Cassidy) McC.; m. Alice Rebecca Lasseter, Dec. 17, 1955; children: Scott Alan, Charles Alexander III, Philip Warren, Christopher Jay. Student, Dartmouth Coll., 1943-44, Wesleyan U., Middletown, Conn., 1946-47; DMD, Tufts U., 1951; MD, Med. Coll. Ala., 1957; DSc (hon.), U. Ala., 1975, Georgetown U., 1982, Tufts U., 1988, Chulalongkorn U., Thailand, 1993, U. Medicine and Dentistry, N.J., 1993. Diplomate Am. Bd. Oral Surgery (pres. 1970). Intern oral surgery Univ. Hosp., Birmingham, Ala., 1951-52, resident oral surgery, 1952-54, intern medicine, 1957-58; mem. faculty U. Ala. Sch. Dentistry, 1956-96, prof., chmn. dept. oral surgery, 1959-65, dean sch., 1962-77; prof., dept. surgery U. Ala. Med. Center, Birmingham, 1977-87; pres. U. Ala. Med. Center, Birmingham, 1987-97; v.p. for health affairs, dir. U. Ala. Med. Center, Birmingham, 1987-93, chief sect. oral surgery Sch. Dentistry, 1958-65, 68-69; prof., 1959-93; disting. prof., 1992-2000; disting. prof. emeritus, dean emeritus, 2000—. Mem. nat. adv. dental sch. coun. NIH, 1968-72; mem. Joint Commn. on Accreditation of Hosps., 1980-91, vice chmn., 1985, chmn., 1986-88. Fellow Am. Coll. Dentists, Internat. Coll. Dentists; mem. ADA (council on dental edn. 1970-76), Am. Assn. Dental Schs. (pres. 1969), Ala. Acad. of Honor, AMA, Am. Soc. Oral Surgeons (trustee 1972-73, pres. 1975-76), Southeastern Soc. Oral Surgeons (pres. 1970), Inst. of Medicine of Nat. Acad. of Scis., Assn. Acad. Health Ctrs. (chmn. bd. dirs. 1984-85), Omicron Kappa Upsilon, Phi Beta Pi. Home: 2328 Garland Dr Birmingham AL 35216-3002 Office: Univ Ala Birmingham 120 Sdb Birmingham AL 35294-0001

MC CALLUM, CHARLES EDWARD, lawyer; b. Memphis, Mar. 13, 1939; s. Edward Payson and India Raimelle (Musick) McC.; m. Lois Ann Gowell Temple, Nov. 30, 1985; children: Florence Andrea, Printha Kyle, Chandler Ward, Sabra Nicole Temple. BS, MIT, 1960; JD, Vanderbilt U., 1964. Bar: Mich., Tenn. 1964. Assoc. Warner Norcross & Judd LLP, Grand Rapids, Mich., 1964-69, ptnr., 1969—, mng. ptnr., 1992-97. Rep. assemblyman State Bar Mich., 1973-78; chmn. Rsch. and Tech. Inst. West Mich., 1989-91; lectr. continuing legal edn. programs; mem. West Mich. World Trade Week Com., 1988-99, chmn., 1992-99; mem. Mich. Dist. Export Coun., 1990-99, chmn., 1992-97; exec. vice chmn., vice chmn. membership TerraLex, 2002—. Chmn. Grand Rapids Area Transit Authority, 1976-79, mem., 1972-79; regional v.p. Nat. Mcpl. League, 1978-86, mem. coun.; 1971-78; pres. Grand Rapids Art Mus., 1979-81, 96-98, trustee, 1976-83, 94-99; chmn. Butterworth Hosp., 1979-87, trustee, 1977-87; chmn. Butterworth Health Corp., 1982-89, dir., 1982-97, vice chmn., 1989-91, sec., 1991-97; chmn. Priority Health, 1995—, bd. dirs., 1995—2004. Woodrow Wilson fellow, 1960-61; Fulbright scholar U. Manchester, Eng., 1960-61. Fellow Coll. Law Practice Mgmt.; mem. ABA (sec. bus. law sect. 2004-, chair standing com. on ethics and profl. responsibility 2004-, com. on multijurisdictional practice 2000-02, task force on corp. responsibility, 2001-03), Am. Bar Found., Am. Law Inst., Tenn. Bar Assn., Mich. Bar Assn. (mem. coun. bus. law sect. 1983-89, sect. chmn. 1988-89), Grand Rapids Bar Assn., Internat. Bar Assn., Grand Rapids C. of C. (pres. 1975, bd. dirs. 1970-76), Univ. Club, Order of Coif, Sigma Xi. Home: 5410 Forest Bend DR SE Ada MI 49301-9005 E-mail: mccallce@wnj.com.

MCCALLUM, JOHN, Canadian government official; b. Montreal, Que., Can., Apr. 9, 1950; m. Nancy Lim; 3 children. BA, U. Cambridge, 1971; diplôme d'études supérieures, U. Paris, 1973; PhD in econ., McGill U., 1977. Asst. prof. econ. U. Manitoba, 1976—78; prof. econ. U. Québec, 1982—87, McGill U., 1987—94, dean, faculty of arts, 1992—94; sr. v.p., chief economist Royal Bank of Can., 1994—2000; mem. Parliament, 2000—; parliamentary sec. to the min. finance, 2001—02; sec. of state (internat. fin. instns.), 2002; min. nat. def., 2002—03; min. vet. affairs, 2003—. Mem. Treasury Bd., Cabinet Com. on Econ. Union, Cabinet Com. on Pub. Safety and Anti-Terrorism. Office: Vet Affairs Can Daniel J MacDonald Bldg 161 Grafton St PO Box 7700 C1A 8M9 Charlottetown PE Canada*

MCCALLUM, JOHN STUART, finance educator, columnist; b. Prescott, Ont., Can., Feb. 2, 1944; s. Donald Robinson and Margaret Louise (Hoeschen) McC.; m. Deborah Joan Howe, Nov. 7, 1985; children: Pamela Anne, James Andrew. BS, U. Montreal, Que., Can., 1965, BA, 1968; MBA, Queen's U., 1968; PhD, U. Toronto, Ont., Can., 1973. With Bank of Montreal, 1965-68; sr. analyst Shell Can., Toronto, 1968-70; prof. fin. U. Man., Can., 1973—. Vice chmn. Man. Hydro, 1988-91, chmn., 1991—; bd. dirs. Toromont Industries Ltd., Man. Energy Authority, 1988—, Acctg. Rsch. Adv. Bd., 1988—; cons. various Can. cos., 1977—; advisor Fed. Minister of Fin., 1984-2001. Columnist Bus. Quar, 1978—; Fin. Post., 1979—; author: The Term Structure of Interest Rates, 1974, The Canadian Chartered Banks and the Bond Market, 1976, The Changing Face of Canadian Finance, 1980, Canadian Finance and the Federal Deficit, 1983, Canada and Technological Change, 1985. Recipient Touche Ross Bus. Writing award, 1985, 86, 87. Mem. Am. Fin. Assn., Adminstrv. Studies Assn. Can. (v.p. 1975-79). Roman Catholic. Avocations: reading, jogging, minor hockey. Home: 26 Lake Lindero Rd Winnipeg MB Canada R3T 4P3 Office: Man Hydro PO Box 815 Winnipeg MB Canada R3C 2P4

MCCALLUM, LAURIE RIACH, state government lawyer; b. Virginia, Minn., Aug. 19, 1950; d. Keith Kelvin and Maybelle Louella (Hanson) Riach; m. J. Scott McCallum, June 19, 1979; children: Zachary, Rory, Cara. BA, U. Ariz., 1972; JD, So. Meth. U., 1977. Bar: Wis. 1977. Consumer atty. Office of Commr. of Ins., Madison, Wis., 1977-79; asst. legal counsel Gov. of Wis., Madison, Wis., 1979-82; mng. ptnr. Petri and McCallum Law Firm, Fond du Lac, Wis., 1979-80; exec. dir. Wis. Coun. on Criminal Justice, Madison, 1981-82; commr. Wis. Pers. Commn., Madison, 1982—2002, chairperson, 1988—2002; commr. Wis. Labor and Industry Rev. Commn., 2002—03, sr. rev. atty., 2003—. Mem. gov.'s jud. selection com. Supreme Ct., 1993; dir. State Bar Labor Law Sect., Madison, 1988-91; faculty U. Wis. Law Sch., Madison, 1992, 93. Dir. Prevent Blindness Wis., Madison Symphony Orch., Wis. Women in Govt. Republican. Office: LIRC PO Box 8126 Madison WI 53708-8126

MCCALLUM, RICHARD WARWICK, medical researcher, clinician, educator; b. Brisbane, Australia, Jan. 21, 1945; came to U.S., 1969; MD, BS, Queensland U., Australia, 1968. Rotating intern Charity Hosp. La., New Orleans, 1969-70; resident in internal medicine Barnes Hosp., Washington, 1970-72; fellow in gastroenterology Wadsworth VA Hosp., L.A., 1972-74, chief endoscopic unit, dept gastroenterology, 1974-76; dir. gastrointestinal diagnostic svcs. Yale-New Haven Med. Ctr., New Haven, 1979-85; asst. prof. medicine UCLA, 1974-76, Yale U., New Haven, 1977-82, assoc. prof., 1982-85; prof., chief div. gastroenterology, hepatology and nutrition U. Va., Charlottesville, 1985-95; dir. GI Motility Ctr. U. Va. Health Sci. Ctr., Charlottesville, 1990-96; Paul Janssen prof. medicine U. Va., Charlottesville, 1987-96; prof. medicine and physiology U. Kans. Med. Ctr., Kansas City, 1996—, chief div. gastroenterology and hepatology, 1996—, dir. Ctr. for Gastrointestinal, Nerve and Muscle Function and Motility Disorders, 1996—. Patentee catheter for esophageal perfusion, gastrointestinal pacemaker usingphased multipoint stimulation, esophageal protection by mastication. Fellow ACP, Am. Coll. Gastroenterology (gov. Kans. 1998—), Royal Australasian Coll. Physicians, Royal Australian Coll. Surgeons; mem. Australian Gastroenterology Soc., Am. Fedn. Clin. Rsch., Am. Assn. Study Liver Diseases, Am. Soc. Gastrointestinal Endoscopy, Am. Soc. for Clin. Investigation, Am. Gastroenterology Assn., Am. Motility Soc. (host-organizer 11th biennial meeting Kansas City 2000), So. Soc. for Clin. Investigation (pres. 1997-98), Internat. Electrogastrography Soc. (pres. 1998-2000), So. Med. Assn. (chmn. gastrointestinal 1996-97). Office: U Kans Med Ctr Dept Internal Medicine 3901 Rainbow Blvd Kansas City KS 66160-0001 Office Phone: 913-588-3842. Business E-Mail: rmccallu@kumc.edu.

MCCALLUM, ROBERT D., JR., federal agency administrator; BA, Yale U., 1968, JD, 1973; MA, Oxford U. Spl. asst. atty. gen. State of Ga., Atlanta, 1979—87; assoc. Alston & Bird LLP, Atlanta, 1973—79, ptnr., 1973—2001; asst. atty. gen. civil divsn. U.S. Dept. Justice, Washington, 2001—03, assoc. atty. gen., 2003—, acting dep. atty. gen., 2003—. Scholar Rhodes scholar. Office: Robert F Kennedy Bldg 10th St & Constitution Ave NW Rm 4633 Washington DC 20530

MCCALLUM, RODERICK EUGENE, dean, microbiologist; b. Denver, Aug. 14, 1944; s. Thomas H. and Elizabeth M. (Matheson) McC.; m. Cheryl A. Ortmann, Aug. 20, 1967; children: Christopher, David. BA, U. Kans., Lawrence, 1967, PhD, 1970; postdoctoral study, U. Tex., 1970-72. Instr. U. Tex., Austin, 1970-72; asst. prof. microbiology U. Okla., Oklahoma City, 1972-75, assoc. prof., 1975-84, prof., 1984-92; prof., head dept. med. microbiology and immunology Health Sci. Ctr. Tex. A&M U., College Station, 1992-97, dir. Inst. Molecular Pathogenesis and Therapeutics, 1993—; assoc. dean for rsch., dir. rsch. Ctrl. Tex. Vets. Health Care System, 1997—; interim dean, v.p. academic affairs Texas A&M Univ. Health Sci. Center, 1999—2000, assoc. dean for research and grad studies, 2000—02; interim dean Texas A&M Univ. Health Sci. Center Coll. of Med., 2002—. Guest prof. U. Heidelberg, Germany, 1980, 85; reviewer BM-2 study sect. NIH, Bethesda, Md., 1986-90; lectr. Mid-Am. States Univ. Assn., 1988. Contbr. articles to profl. jours. Coalition mem. Shots Across Tex., College Station, 1993—. Fellow Am. Acad. Microbiology; mem. AAAS, Am. Soc. Microbiology (editor Infection and Immunity 1992—), Internat. Endotoxin Soc., Tex. Infectious Disease Soc., Soc. Leukocyte Biology, Shock Soc. Democrat. Lutheran. Avocations: woodworking, gardening, golf, travel. Office: Tex A&M U Health Sci Ctr College Station TX 77843-0001

MCCALLUM, SHELLY YVONNE, marketing and international business educator, consultant; arrived in U.S., 1995; d. Richard Albert and Eleanor Irene McCallum. BA in Sociology, U. Western Ont., London, Can., 1991; M in Internat. Bus., St. Mary's U., Winona, Minn., 1996. Media specialist Larter Advt., Toronto, Canada, 1988—89; sr. media buyer, planner McCann-Erickson, Toronto, 1989—90; media supr. Harrod & Mirlin, Toronto, 1990—95; internat. mktg. mgr. Am. Legend Corp., Seattle, 1997—98; prof. St. Mary's U., Winona, 1998—. Cons. Southeastern Minn. Devel. Corp., Rochester, 2002—. Bd. dirs., v.p., treas., mem. fin. com. Women's Resource Ctr., Winona, 1999—. Mem.: Winona C. of C., Acad. Mgmt., Acad. Internat. Bus. Avocations: reading, music, running, painting. Office: Saint Marys U 700 Terrace Heights # 1439 Winona MN 55987

MCCALLY, CHARLES RICHARD, construction company executive, consultant, mathematician, educator; b. Dallas, Oct. 5, 1958; s. Richard Holt and Elizabeth Ann (Webster) McC.; m. Shirley Elizabeth Avant, Aug. 18, 1979 (div.); children: Charles Richard Jr., Meredith Holt; m. Judy Lynn Tackett, June 24, 1993. BSME summa cum laude, So. Meth. U., 1981; MS in Higher Edn. and Math., Tex. A&M U., 2003. Engr. McCally Co., Dallas, 1977-83; owner, v.p. DRT Mech. Corp., Dallas, 1983-95; owner McCally Svc. Co., Inc., Dallas, 1995-97; pres. C.R. McCally & Assocs., Inc., Dallas, 1997—. Prof. math. Navarro Coll., Corsicana, Tex., 1999—; cons. McCally Group, Inc., Lewisville, Tex., 2002—. Active Young Reps., Dallas, 1980—. Mem. NSPE, ASME, ASHRAE, Am. Soc. Plumbing Engrs. (membership com. 1983-89), Tex. Soc. Profl. Engrs., So. Meth. U. Alumni Assn., SMU Mustang Club, Bent Tree Country Club (Dallas), Oaktree Country Club (Garland, Tex.) (bd. dirs. 1986-89), Sigma Chi. Avocations: tennis, boating, travel, camping. Home: 203 Chinaberry Way Coppell TX 75019-2961 E-mail: crmsr@mccally.com., rick@mccallygroup.com.

MCCAMBRIDGE, JOHN JAMES, civil engineer; b. Bklyn., Oct. 27, 1933; s. John Joseph and Florence Josita (McDonnell) McC.; m. Dorothy Antoinette Cook, Mar. 17, 1962; children: Sharon J., John S., Patrick J., Kathleen C. BCE, Manhattan Coll., 1955; MS, Vanderbilt U., 1958; postgrad., UCLA, 1963—66. Civil engr. Raymond Concrete Pile Co., NYC, 1955; commd. 2d lt. USAF, 1955, advanced through grades to col., 1972; exec. sec. Def. Com. On Rsch., Washington, 1971-73, DOD-NASA Supportive Rsch. Tech. Panel, Washington, 1972-74; asst. dir. Def. Rsch. and Engring. (for Life Scis.) Office Dir. Def., Washington, 1974-75; dir. Air Force Life Support Systems Program Office, Wright Patterson AFB, Ohio, 1975-79; ret. USAF, 1979; prin. Booz, Allen & Hamilton, Inc., Bethesda, Md., 1979-86; v.p. Espey, Huston & Assoc., Inc., Falls Church, Va., 1986-90; mng. prin. JMC Cons. Group, McLean, Va., 1990—. Chmn. air panel on NBC Def., NATO, Evere, Belgium, 1970-71; def. dept. rep. to physics survey com., NAS, Washington, 1971. Contbr. articles to profl. jours. Decorated Legion of Merit with oak leaf cluster. Fellow Aerospace Med. Assn. (exec. coun. 1972-73), Inst. Hazardous Materials Mgmt. (Disting. Diplomate, dir. 1984—; chmn. 1988-94); mem. Coun. Engring. and Sci. Splty. Bds. (dir., exec. com. 1995—, v.p. 2000, pres. 2001),

Acad. Cert. Hazardous Materials Mgrs. (pres. 1984-86), Survival and Flight Equipment Assn. (nat. sec. 1977-78), Air Force Ret. Officers' Cmty. (dir. 1997-2003), The Washington Assembly, (treas. 2002-03, vice chmn 2003—), River Bend Golf and Country Club, Black Tie Club (treas. 2002-03, v.p. 2003-), Tower Club, KC, Sigma Xi, Chi Epsilon. Republican. Roman Catholic. Office: JMC Cons Group 9200 Falls Run Rd Mc Lean VA 22102-1028 E-mail: jjmccambridge@earthlink.net.

MC CAMERON, FRITZ ALLEN, retired university administrator; b. Nacogdoches, Tex., Oct. 8, 1929; s. Leland Allen and Gladys (Turner) Mc C.; m. Jeannine Young, June 11, 1957; 1 child, Mary Hartley. BBA, Stephen F. Austin State Coll., 1950, MA, 1951; PhD, U. Ala., 1954. C.P.A., La. Asso. prof. La. State U., 1959-62, prof., 1962-67, chmn. dept. accounting, 1967-71, asst. vice chancellor, 1971-73, dean continuing edn., 1973-95; ret., 1995. Cons. in field. Author: FORTRAN Logic and Programming, 1968, Cobol Logic and Programming, rev. edit, 1970, 5th edit., 1985, FORTRAN IV, 1970, rev. edit., 1974, 3d edit., 1977. Mem. numerous civic and charitable bds. including Salvation Army, Womens Hosp., Computer Rehab. Tng. and others. Mem. Am. Inst. C.P.A.'s, La. Soc. C.P.A.'s, Am. Accounting Assn. Home: 930 Rodney Dr Baton Rouge LA 70808-5867

MCCAMMON, JAMES ANDREW, chemistry professor; b. Lafayette, Ind., Feb. 8, 1947; s. Lewis Brown and Jean Ann (McClintock) McC.; m. Anne Elizabeth Woltmann, June 6, 1969. BA magna cum laude, Pomona Coll., 1969; MA, Harvard U., 1970, PhD, 1976. Research fellow Harvard U., Cambridge, Mass., 1976-78; asst. prof. U. Houston, 1978-81, M.D. Anderson prof. chemistry, 1981-94, dir. Inst. for Molecular Design, 1987-94, prof. biochemistry, 1989-94. Adj. prof. molecular physiology and biophysics Baylor Coll. Medicine, Houston, 1986-94, adj. prof. biochemistry, 1992-94; Joseph E. Mayer chair theoretical chemistry U. Calif., San Diego, 1995—, prof. pharmacology, 1995—; investigator Howard Hughes Med. Inst., 2000—. Author: Dynamics of Proteins and Nucleic Acids, 1987. Recipient Tchr. scholar award Camille and Henry Dreyfus Found., George H. Hitchings award Burroughs-Wellcome Fund, 1987, Computerworld Smithsonian Info. Tech. Leadership award for Breakthrough Computational Sci., 1995; named Alfred P. Sloan Rsch. fellow, 1980. Fellow AAAS, Am. Phys. Soc., Biophys. Soc.; mem. Am. Chem. Soc., Protein Soc., Phi Beta Kappa. Achievements include development of the molecular dynamics simulation method for proteins and nucleic acids, of the thermodynamic cycle perturbation method for studying molecular recognition, and of the Brownian dynamics method for simulating diffusion-controlled reactions. Office: U Calif San Diego Dept Chemistry La Jolla CA 92093-0365

MCCAMPBELL, ROBERT GARNER, prosecutor; b. Oklahoma City, Nov. 23, 1957; s. Stanley Reid and Joan Fontane (Garner) McC. BA in History with honors, Vanderbilt U., 1980; JD, Yale U., 1983. Bar: Okla. 1983. Assoc. Crowe & Dunlevy, Oklahoma City, 1983-87; asst. U.S. atty. Western Dist. Okla., 1987-94, chief fin. fraud unit, 1990-94; dir. Crowe & Dunlevy, 1994—2001; U.S. atty. We. Dist. Okla., 2001—. Dir. Ctr. for Advancement of Sci. and Tech., 1995, chmn., 1999—. Mem. ABA, Phi Beta Kappa. Republican. Episcopalian. Office: US Atty 210 W Park Ave Ste 400 Oklahoma City OK 73102

MCCAN, JAMES LAWTON, education educator; b. Plymouth, Ind., Aug. 10, 1952; s.Jean F. and Mildred P. (Hayn) McC.; m. Carolyn G. Splain, Jan. 16, 1971; children: Kendra, Brittany. B of Phys. Edn., Purdue U., 1974; MS in Edn., 1981, PhD, 1983. Tchr. reading and English Waynetown (Ind.) Mid. Sch., 1974-75, Yorkville (Ill.) H.S., 1979-80; reading specialist Purdue U., West Lafayette, Ind., 1983-89; program chair Basic Skills Advancement Ind. Voc-Tech. Coll., Lafayette, 1989-91; asst. prof., coord. student teaching Hillsdale (Mich.) Coll., 1991-95; dir. Student Achievement Zone, South Bend, Ind., 1995-96; assoc. prof. Nova Southeastern U., Ft. Lauderdale, Fla., 1996—. Contbr. articles and poetry to jours. Mem. Internat. Reading Assn., Fla. Reading Assn. Avocations: reading, music. Home: 1024 St Croix Ave Apopka FL 32703 Office: Nova Southeastern U Dept Edn Fort Lauderdale FL 33314

MCCANDLESS, BRUCE, II, aerospace engineer, retired astronaut; b. Boston, June 8, 1937; s. Bruce and Sue McCandless; m. Alfreda Bernice Doyle, Aug. 6, 1960; children: Bruce III, Tracy. BS, U.S. Naval Acad., 1958; MSEE, Stanford U., 1965; MBA, U. Houston, Clear Lake, 1987. Commd. ensign USN, 1958, advanced through grades to capt., 1979, naval aviator, 1960, with Fighter Squadron 102, 1960-64; astronaut Johnson Space Ctr., NASA, Houston, 1966-90; mem. Skylab 1 backup crew Johnson Space Center, NASA, Houston, mem. STS-11 shuttle crew, mem. STS-31 Hubble Space Telescope deployment crew; ret. USN, 1990; prin. staff engr. Lockheed Martin Astronautics, Denver, 1990-97, chief scientist Advanced Space Transportation Systems, 1997—. Decorated Legion of Merit; recipient Def. Superior Service medal, NASA Exceptional Service medal, NASA Spaceflight medal, NASA Exceptional Engring. Achievement medal, Collier Trophy, 1985, Haley Space Flight award AIAA, 1991. Fellow Am. Astron. Soc.; mem. U.S. Naval Inst., Nat. Audubon Soc., Houston Audubon Soc. (past pres.) Episcopalian. Achievements include executing 1st untethered free flight in space using Manned Maneuvering Unit. Office: Lockheed Martin Space Systems Co T3005 PO Box 179 Denver CO 80201-0179 E-mail: bruce2mc@logcabin.com.

MCCANDLESS, CAROLYN KELLER, retired human resources executive; b. Patuxent River, Md., June 6, 1945; d. Stevens Henry and Betty Jane (Bethune) Keller; m. Stephen Porter McCandless, Apr. 22, 1972; children: Peter Keller, Deborah Marion. BA, Stanford U., 1967; MBA, Harvard U., 1969. Fin. analyst Time Inc., NYC, 1969-72, mgr. budgets and fin. analysis, 1972-78, asst. sec., dir. internat. adminstrn., 1978-85, v.p., dir. employee benefits, 1985-90; v.p human resources and adminstrn. Time Warner, Inc., NYC, 1990—2001. Bd. dirs. Friends and Relatives of Institutionalized Aged, NY Svc. Program for Older People, Inc., Annie Eaton Soc.; adv. bd. Booker T. Washington Learning Ctr. and Pres. Coun. Nat. Pub. Radio. Democrat. Mem. Unitarian Ch.

MCCANLESS, ROSS W. retail executive; B in Acctg., U. N.C., Charlotte; JD, Wake Forest U. CPA. Pvt. practice, lawyer; various pos., to vice chmn. Delhaize Am., Inc.; sr. v.p., gen. counsel, sec. Lowe's Cos., Inc., 2003—. Office: Lowes Cos Inc 1605 Curtis Bridge Rd Wilkesboro NC 28697

MCCANN, CHRIS (CHRISTIAN DAVID MCCANN), application developer, educator; b. Springfield, Mass., June 5, 1929; s. James Millard and Helen (Joblin) McCann; children: Nicole Fitzgerald, Adrienne Bashe, Gary. Grad., GE Fin. Mgmt. Program, Schenectady, N.Y. With GE, Schenectady, 1947-66, indsl. educator in stats., probability, math., computers, 1966-80, work effectiveness instr., 1969-83, designer employee incentive programs, 1970-80, software designer, 1966-87; ret., 1987. Prodr., dir., stage mgr., performer, playwright, adminstr.: various cmty. theatre groups; Schenectady Light Opera Co., 1949—52, 1961—67; author: Master Pieces - The Art History of Jigsaw Puzzles, 1998; contbr. articles to mags.; designer computer database for golden age of jigsaw puzzles. Pres. N.Y. State Young Adult Civic Coun., 1952—54; mem., officer Schenectady Young Adult Civic Coun., 1951—57; pres. Schenectady Civic Ballet Co., 1965—68; founder Merrimoppets Children's Theater, Schenectady, exec. dir., 1968—71; mem. liaison bd. Schenectady GE/United Way, 1974—77, chmn., 1976; stage mgr. U.S. Bicentennail celebration Schenectady County, 1976. Named to Schenectady honor roll of outstanding citizens, 1990, Schenectady Honor Roll of Outstanding Citizens, 1990. Avocation: research on jigsaw puzzle artists. Home: 658 Macelroy Rd Ballston Lake NY 12019-2202

MCCANN, CLARENCE DAVID, JR., museum curator and director, artist; b. Mobile, Ala., Apr. 30, 1948; s. Clarence David and Theresa (Pope) McC.; m. Brenda Clemens (div. 1979); 1 child, Nathan; m. Robin Chiavaroli, 1980; children: Angela, John. BFA, U. South Ala., 1970; MFA, U. Cin., 1972; grad. cert., Mus. Mgmt. Inst., Berkeley, Calif., 1982. Art instr. Spring Hill Coll., Mobile, 1972-75, U. South Ala., Mobile, 1975-76; mem. staff, asst. registrar Fine Arts Mus. of South, Mobile, 1977-78, registrar, 1978-81, curator collection, 1981-84, asst. dir., 1985-86, 88-91, acting dir., 1986 88, mus. curator, 1988-91; asst. mgr. spl. events coord. City of Mobile, 1991—2003. Adj. lectr. U.S. Ala., 1990-91, adj. lectr. Bishop State Community Coll., 1991-2000, 2002--; adj. art instr. U. South Ala., 1999—. Author: (catalogues) The Ripening of American Art: Duveneck and Chase, 1979, The Artists of Barbizon: The Boone Collection, 1983, Enisled Visions: The Southern Nontraditional Folk Artist, 1987, The Acquisitive Eye: Selections From The Collection of James M. Younger, 1990. Pres. Contemporary Artists Consortium of Mobile, 1979—81, Mobile Art Assn., 2002—04; co-chair art adv. bd. Ctr. for the Living Arts Space 301, Mobile, 2003—; bd. dirs. Very Spl. Arts, Ala., 1997—2003. Recipient various painting awards Allied Arts Coun., Mobile, 1974; U. Cin. fellow, 1972. Mem. Am. Assn. Mus., Ala. Mus. Assn., Southeastern Mus. Assn. Democrat. Home: 9080 Rawhide Ct Semmes AL 36575-7275 E-mail: cdmccann@bellsouth.net.

MCCANN, COLLEEN MARY, public affairs specialist, lobbyist; b. Phila., June 28, 1964; d. John Francis and Agnetta Marie (McLaughlin) McC. BA, Rutgers U., 1986. Staff asst. subcom. on commerce, transp. and tourism U.S. Congress, Washington, 1986; staff asst., legis. corr. U.S. Rep. Jim Florio, Washington, 1986-88, legis. asst., 1988-89; policy analyst Gov.-elect Jim Florio's Transition Team, 1989-91; legis. liaison Dept. of State, Trenton, N.J., 1990-93; v.p. The MWW Group, Trenton, 1993-99. Active N.J. Women's Polit. Caucus, 1990—; mem. govt. affairs alumni com. Rutgers U., trustee, 1994—. Democrat. Roman Catholic. Home: 815 Delancey Pl Ocean City NJ 08226-4137 Office: 150 W State St Ste 220 Trenton NJ 08608-1105

MCCANN, DIANA RAE, secondary school educator; b. Huron, S.D., Nov. 16, 1948; d. Ralph Henry and Rosina Agnes (Rowen) Yager; m. Gregory Charles McCann, 1974; children: Grant Christopher, Holly Ann. BS, S.D. State U., 1972. Tchr. Bon Homme 4-2, Tyndall, SD, 1972-74, 1976—, Avon (S.D.) Sch., 1975-76. Math. curriculum adv. bd., SD, 1992—; coord. Presdl. awards in math., SD, 1998—. Leader 4-H Club, 1986—; sec.-treas. 4-H Leaders Assn., 1992—2000; tournament coord. Bon Homme Youth Wrestling Club, 1986—93. Recipient Elem. Math. Presdl. award for Excellence in Math. Tchgs., NSF, 1993, Disting. Svc. award for Math. in S.D., 2003. Mem.: S.D. Coun. Tchrs. Math. (pres.-elect 1990—92, pres. 1992—94, treas. 1999—), Nat. Coun. Tchrs. Math. Avocation: gardening.

MCCANN, ELIZABETH IRELAND, theater, television and motion picture producer, lawyer; b. N.Y.C., Mar. 29, 1931; d. Patrick and Rebecca (Henry) McC. BA, Manhattanville Coll., 1952, PhD hon., 1983; MA, Columbia U., 1954; LLD, Fordham U., 1966; ArtsD (hon.), Manhattanville Coll., 1987; LitD (hon.), Marymount Coll., 1993. Bar: N.Y. 1966. Assoc. firm Paul, Weiss, Rifkind, Wharton & Garrison, N.Y.C., 1965-66; assoc. numerous theater mgmts. Robert Joffrey, Hal Prince, Saint Suber, Maurice Evans, 1956-68; mng. dir. Nederlander Orgn., N.Y.C., 1968-76; pres. McCann & Nugent Prodns., Inc., N.Y.C., 1976-86; mng. prodr. Tony Awards, N.Y.C., 2001—. Bd. dirs. City Ctr. Music and Dance, Marymount Coll. Prodr.: (play) My Fat Friend, 1975, Dracula (Tony award for most innovative prodn. revival, 1978), The Elephant Man, 1978 (Tony award for best play, 1979, Drama Critics award, 1978, Drama Desk award, 1978, Outer Critics Circle award 1978, Obie award 1978), Night and Day, 1979, Home, 1980 (Adelco award, 1980), Morning's at Seven, 1980 (Tony award for reproduction play/musical, 1980), Amadeus, 1980 (Tony award for best play, 1981, Drama Desk award, 1980), The Philadelphia Sotry, 1980, Piaf, 1981, Rose, 1981, The Dresser, 1981, Mass Appeal, 1981, Macbeth, 1981, The Floating Light Bulb, 1981, The Life and Adventures of Nicholas Nickleby, 1981 (Tony award for best play, 1982, Drama Critics Circle award, 1981), Good, 1982, All's Well That Ends Well, 1983, The Glass Menagerie, 1983, Total Abandon, 1983, Painting Churches, 1983, The Lady and the Clarinet, 1983, Cyrano de Bergerac/Much Ado About Nothing, 1984, Pacific Overtures, 1984, Leader of the Pack, 1985, Les Liaisons Dangereuses, 1987 (Drama Critics Circle award, 1987), Stepping Out, 1987, Orpheus Descending, 1989, Nick & Nora, 1991, Three Tall Women, 1995, A Midsummer Night's Dream, 1995, In the West End with Robert Fox, Ltd., 1996, Who's Afraid of Virginia Woolf?, 1996, A Delicate Balance, 1997, A View from the Bridge, 1998 (Tony award for best revival play, 1998), The Unexpected Man, 1998, A View from the Bridge (Tony award), 1999, Copenhagen, 2000 (Tony award for best play, 2000), Cobb, 2000, The Play About the Baby, 2001, Tuesdays with Morrie, 2002, The Goat, or Who is Sylvia?, 2002 (Tony award for best play, 2002), The Smell of the Kill, 2002, Beckee/Albee, 2003; TV show Piaf, 1981, Morning's at Seven, 1982, Pilobolus Dance Theatre, 1982; assoc. prodr. Orpheus Descending, 1990. Recipient Entrepreneurial Woman award Women Bus. Owners of N.Y., 1981, 82, James J. and Jame Hoey award for Interracial Justice, 1981, Spl Drama League award for co-producing the Life and Adventures of Nicholas Nickleby on Broadway, 1982, Dr Louis M. Spadero award Fordham Grad. Sch. Bus., 1982 E-mail: liz@weproduce.biz.

MCCANN, GAIL ELIZABETH, lawyer; b. Boston, Aug. 25, 1953; d. Joseph and Ruth E. (Lagerquist) McC.; m. Stanley J. Lukasiewicz. AB, Brown U., 1975; JD, U. Pa., Phila., 1978. Bar: R.I. 1978, Mass. 1984, U.S. Dist. Ct. R.I. 1978, U.S. Dist. Ct. Mass. 1990. Ptnr. Edwards & Angell, LLP, Providence, 1978—. Bd. dirs. Caritas House, Inc.; mem. R.I. adv. coun. New Eng. Legal Found. Mem.: Am. Coll. Mortgage Attys., RI Bar Assn., Brown U. Alumni Assn. (past pres.). Avocations: hiking, travel, yoga. Office: Edwards & Angell LLP 2800 Financial Plz Providence RI 02903 Office Phone: 401-274-9200.

MCCANN, GREG, law educator, consultant; b. Mt. Lebanon, Pa., June 4, 1959; s. G. Norman and Rosemary McCann. BBA, Stetson U., 1981; JD, U. Fla., 1988. CPA Fla.; bar: (Fla.) 1988. Prof. Stetson U., Deland, Fla., 1989—2004, dir. family bus. ctr., 1995—; family bus. cons. McCann & Associates, Deland, 2000—. Editor: Rethinking the Role of the University-Based Family Business Center, Destroying Myths and Creating Value in Family Business. Recipient Leavey award, Freedom Found., Innovation in Pedagogy, Acad. Mgmt., Model Program award, U.S. Assn. Small Bus. and Entrepreneurship. Office: Stetson U 421 N Woodland Blvd Unit 8398 Deland FL 32723 Office Phone: 386-822-7425. Office Fax: 386-822-7446. Business E-Mail: gmccann@stetson.edu.

MCCANN, JAMES F. consumer products company executive; Creator chain of 14 flower shops, N.Y.C.; chmn., CEO 1-800-FLOWERS.COM, 1987—. Bd. dirs. Gateway 2000, OfficeMax, Inc., PETCO, Inc., Nat. Retail Fedn., Very Spl. Arts., Gtech Holdings, Boyd's Bears, Nat. Retail Federation. Author: Stop and Sell the Roses, 1998. Bd. dirs. Hofstra U., Winthrop-Univ. Hosp. Named Entrepreneur of Yr., Merrill Lynch and Inc. Mag., Retailer of Yr., Ernst & Young and L.I. Assn., one of top 100 Bus. Men, Irish Am. Mag., Direct Marketer of Yr., Direct Mktg. Day N.Y., 1996, Outstanding Bus. Spkr., Toastmaster Internat., 1997. Office: 1600 Stewart Ave Westbury NY 11590-6696*

MCCANN, JEAN FRIEDRICHS, artist, educator; b. N.Y.C., Dec. 6, 1937; d. Herbert Joseph and Catherine Brady (Ward) Friedrichs; m. William Joseph McCann, May 14, 1960; children: Kevin, Brian, Maureen McCann Breslin, William, James, Denis Gerard, Kathleen. Student, Caton-Rose Inst. Fine Arts, 1955-57; AAS, SUNY, Farmingdale, 1959; BS, SUNY-Empire State Coll., Binghamton, 1986; MA summa cum laude, Marywood Coll., 1987, MFA in Art summa cum laude, 1989; completed Kellogg Leadership Progam, Sch. Mgmt., SUNY, Binghamton, 1992; PhD, Nova Coll., 1995. Designer Patton Corp., N.Y.C., 1959-66; sub. art tchr. Owego-Apalachin Sch. Dist., 1968-88; tutor, evaluator Empire State Coll. SUNY, 1987—; dir. ArtSpace Gallery, Owego, N.Y., 1992-94. V.p. bd. dirs. Tioga County Coun. on Arts, 1990—91, pres., 1992—95; tchr. design and drawing Diàn Dà Shui Coll., Guiyang, Guizhou, China, 2001; demonstrator for various schs., ednl. TV and county museums. One-woman shows include IBM, Owego, 1972, Tioga County Hist. Soc. Mus., 1975, Nat. Hist. Ct. House, 1982, Visual Arts Ctr., Scranton, Pa., 1989—90, ArtSpace Gallery, 1991, MacDonald Art Gallery of Coll. Misericordia, Dallas, Pa., 1992, Plaza Gallery, Binghamton, 1992, Krembs Gallery, 1993, 2000, Wilson Gallery, Johnson City, N.Y., 1994, 2001, 2003, Countryside Gallery, Owego, N.Y., 1996, 2002, Meml. Gallery, SUNY, Farmingdale, 1998, exhibited in group shows at IBM, Owego, 1970, Roberson Ctr., Binghamton, 1972, Arnot Art Mus., Elmira, 1974, 1989, 1992, Nat. Exhibits at Arena, Binghamton, 1974—76, Riise Gallery, St. Thomas, 1975—78, Pennino's Gallery, Burlington, Vt., 1975—77, 1999, 2000, Visual Arts Ctr., Scranton, Pa., 1987, Tioga County Hist. Soc. Mus., 1990, ArtSpace Gallery, 1990, Contemporary Gallery, Scranton, 1992, 1996, Meml. Gallery, SUNY, Farmingdale, 1997, Artists Guild Gallery, 1993, 1999, 2000, Krembs Gallery, Binghamton, 1999, 2001, 2003, Schweinfurth Meml. Art Ctr., Auburn, N.Y., 2002, Represented in permanent collections Pres. George Bush, Congressman Matt McHugh, Sen. Tom Libous, Gov. George Pataki, pub. collections. Bd. dirs. Birthright of Owego, 1993—2003. Recipient N.Y. State Artisans award, 1982, Nat. Strathmore Silver award, 1989, 1st pl. in Graphic Arts award Jericho Arts Coun., 1994. Mem. Nat. Mus. Women in Arts (charter), Kappa Pi (pres. Zeta Omicron chpt. 1987-89, life), Artists Guild. Avocations: travel, read, visit museums. Home (Winter): 1776 Atwater Ct Kissimmee FL 34746-3588

MCCANN, JOHN DAVID, physician, educator; b. Waterloo, Iowa, Feb. 8, 1961; m. Rachel Weisman. BA in Chemistry, U. No. Iowa, 1984; med. degree, PhD, U. Iowa, 1991. Diplomate Am. Bd. Ophthalmology. Assoc. prof. ophthalmology David Geffen Sch. Medicine UCLA, L.A., 1996—2002, 2002. Attending physician ophthalmology VA Med. Ctr., L.A., 1996; co-dir. Aesthetic Reconstructive Surgery Svcs. UCLA, L.A., 1997, co-dir. Aesthetic Ctr., 97; chief ophthalmology sect. VA Med. Ctr., Sepulveda, L.A. Grantee grant, Joyce J. Cammilleri Family Fund, 2002, 2003, 2004; Grant to study Benign Essential Blepharospasm, Benign Essential Blepharospasm Rsch. Found., 1997. Fellow: Am. Acad. Ophthalmology (Achievement award 2002), Am. Soc. Ophthalmic Plastic and Reconstructive Surgery; mem.: AMA, Soc. Heed Fellows. Achievements include development of electronic medical records system; research in benign essential blepharospasm treatment; orbital volume augmentation. Office: Jules Stein Eye Inst 100 Stein Plz #2-267 Los Angeles CA 90095 Office Phone: 310-825-0206. Office Fax: 310-825-9263. E-mail: mccann@jsei.ucla.edu.

MCCANN, JOSEPH LEO, lawyer, former government official; b. Phila., Aug. 27, 1948; s. Joseph John and Christina Mary (Kirwan) McC.; m. Aida Laico Kabigting, Dec. 6, 1986; 1 child, Angela Kathleen. BA, St. Charles Sem., Phila., 1970, postgrad., 1970-71; MA, Temple U., 1975, JD, 1977. Bar: Pa. 1977, U.S. Dist. Ct. (ea. dist.) Pa. 1977, U.S. Dist. Ct. (mid. dist.) Pa. 1978, U.S. Ct. Appeals (3d cir.) 1978, D.C. 1986, U.S. Supreme Ct. 1986, Md. 1987, U.S. Ct. Appeals (Fed. cir.) 1988, U.S. Ct. Internat. Trade 1988. Law clk. to chief justice Pa. Supreme Ct., Phila., 1977-78; dep. atty. gen. Pa. Dept. Justice, Harrisburg, 1978-80; sr. atty. U.S. GAO, Washington, 1980-96; sr. asst. gen. counsel GSA, Washington, 1996-99; pres., counsel, headmaster The Kabigting-Kirwan Meml. Nonprofit Corp., 1997-2000; atty., 2001—. Mem. Pa. Bar Assn., Phila. Bar Assn., Md. State Bar Assn. Roman Catholic. Home and Office: 204 Bookham Ln Gaithersburg MD 20877-3789 Office Phone: 301-330-1585. E-mail: ajmccann1@msn.com.

MCCANN, LAWRENCE ALTON, music educator; b. Sikeston, Mo., Jan. 11, 1951; s. William Alton and Billie Sue (Thomas) McC.; m. Vickie Dean Brown, Apr. 14, 1979; children: Luke Adam, Mollie Elizabeth. B Music Edn., Southeast Mo. State U., 1976; M Ednl. Adminstrn., William Woods U., 2003. Cert. vocal music K-12 tchg. Interstate Sch. Leaders Licensure Consortium. Music/youth dir. First Bapt. Ch., Gideon, Mo., 1974-77, Red Star Bapt. Ch., Cape Girardeau, Mo., 1977-78; news dir., announcer KPBM-FM, Poplar Bluff, Mo., 1979; elem. music tchr. Doniphan (Mo.) Elem. Sch., 1979—; pvt. guitar tchr. Three Rivers C.C., Poplar Bluff, 1979-86; music/youth dir. Calvary Bapt. Ch., Dexter, Mo., 1982-87; music dir. Temple Bapt. Ch., Poplar Bluff, 1987—. Profl. devel. chmn. Doniphan R-I Sch. Dist., 1993—; owner Luke and Mollie Music. Composer, lyricist: Mo. Conservation Melodies, 1982, Opus One, 1988, Choral Praise, 1989, We Teach the Children, 1992, Sacred Music Quarterly/Hong Kong, 1993, Luke and Mollie Music, Dare to Live, 1993. Commr. planning and zoning, City of Poplar Bluff, 1982; team coach/youth soccer Optimist Soccer League, Poplar Bluff, 1988-96; team coach/youth baseball, Park and Recreation Dept., Poplar Bluff, 1993; bicentennial choir dir., Gideon (Mo.) Bicentennial Com., 1976. Recipient Cmty. Svc. award Mo. N.G., 1991; Outstanding Contbr. DARE and Drug Consortium, Ripley County, Mo., 1993. Mem. Mo. State Tchrs. Assn. (state exec. bd. 1994-2000, pres. S.E. dist. 1992-93, CTA pres. 1984-85, 91-92, Medium Sized Sch. Outstanding Leadership award for state, dist. and local svc., SE Region meritorious svc. edn. award 2001), Music Educators Nat. Conf., Mo. Music Educators Assn. Baptist. Avocations: photography, sports card collecting, record collecting, ornament collecting. Office: Doniphan Elem Sch 603 E Summit St Doniphan MO 63935-1142 Office Phone: 573-996-3523, 573-785-1250. E-mail: mccannmusic69@netscape.net.

MCCANN, LEE I. psychology educator; BS, MS, PhD, Iowa State U. Prof. psychology U. Wis., Oshkosh, assoc. vice chancellor, 1992-97. Co-author: Recruiting Good College Faculty, 1996; co-editor: Lessons Learned: Practical Advice for the Teaching of Psychology, 1999, Lessons Learned, vol. 2, 2004.

MCCANN, MARGARET ANN, sister, educator; b. Port Arthur, Tex., June 3, 1953; d. Donald Joseph and Elizabeth Ann McCann. BA, Coll. of St. Elizabeth, 1996; MA, Montclair State U., 2002; postgrad., Marquette U., 2003—04. Cert. bereavement counselor Archdiocese of Newark, 2001; secondary edn. tchr. N.J., 1996. Tchr. H.S. English, Marylawn Acad. of the Oranges, South Orange, NJ, 1996—97, Acad. of Sacred Heart, Hoboken, NJ, 1997—98; adj. instr. English, Montclair State U., NJ, 1998—2002; instr. English composition, intro. to lit. Coll. of St. Elizabeth, Convent Station, NJ, 2001—02; tchr. H.S. English, Marylawn Acad. of the Oranges, South Orange, NJ, 2002—03. Panelist, presenter Mid-Atlantic Popular/Am. Culture Assn., Syracuse, NY, 1995, 17th Ann. Nat. Conf. of Peer Tutoring in Writing, Merrimack Coll., North Andover, Mass., 2000, 9th Ann. Meeting of the Group for Early Mod. Cultural Studies, Phila., Ctrl. NY Conf. on Lang. and Lit., SUNY, Cortland, 2002. Sister of charity, tchr. Sisters of Charity of St. Elizabeth, Convent Station, NJ, 1990—2004; mem. catechetical team Gesu Roman Cath. Ch., Milw., 2003—04. Grad. assistantship, Montclair State U., 1998-2000. Mem.: Nat. Coun. Tchrs. of English, Kappa Gamma Pi (assoc.). Republican. Roman Catholic. Avocations: teaching, writing, poetry, travel, film. Home: 833 N 14th St Milwaukee WI 53233 Personal E-mail: sistermccann@hotmail.com.

MCCANN, PETER PAUL, biology researcher, educator; s. Peter F. and Kathleen (Burnett) McC.; m. Danielle Soury, July 31, 1971. AB in Zoology, Columbia U., 1965; PhD, Syracuse U., 1970. Fellow NIH, Bethesda, Md., 1970-73; sr. scientist Ctr. of Rsch. Merrell Internat., Strasbourg, France, 1973-79; sr. biochemist Merrell Dow Rsch. Ctr., Cin., 1979-82; rsch. assoc. scientist Merrell Dow Rsch. Inst., Cin., 1982-84, dir. scientific and acad. liaison, 1984-90, dir. sci. adminstrn., 1988-90; prof. U. Cin. Coll. Medicine, 1981—; sr. dir., ctr. dir. Marion Merrell Dow Inc., Indpls., 1990-93; pres. Brit. Biotech Inc., Annapolis, Md., 1993-98; interim pres. U. Md. Biotech. Inst., College Park, Md., 1998-99; pres., CEO Oncostasis, Inc., 1999—2001, Mymetics Corp., 2001—03; GG. Co-vice chmn. Gordon Rsch. Conf. on Polyamines, 1987, co-chmn., 1989. Chief editor, co-author Inhibition of Polyamine Metabolism, 1987; co-editor, co-author: Enzymes as Targets for Drug Design, 1989; contbr. articles to profl. jours. Mem. Am. Soc. Cell Biology, Am. Soc. Tropical Medicine and Hygiene, Am. Soc. Biochemistry and Molecular Biology, Biochem. Soc. (editl. adv. bd. 1986-92, editor 1992-99), Soc. Protozoologists (editl. bd. reviewers 1989-95), Am. Philat. Congress, Inc. (pres. 1990-95), Am. Philat. Soc. (v.p. 1995-99, pres. 1999-2003). Achievements include patents for method of inhibiting the growth of protozoa, method of controlling phytopathogenic fungus. Personal E-mail: p103226706@cs.com.

MCCANN, RENETTA, advertising executive; married; 2 children. BS in Speech, Northwestern U., 1978. Client svc. trainee Starcom, 1978, v.p., 1988, media dir., 1989, sr. v.p., 1995; CEO Starcom N.Am., Chgo., 1999—2004; CEO Americas Starcom MediaVest Group, 2004—. Bd. mem. Audit Bur. Circulations Northwestern U., mem. adv. bd. Media Mgmt. Ctr.; bd. mem. Chgo. United. Named Media Maven, Advt. Age, 2001, Corp. Exec. of Yr.,

Black Enterprise, 2002, Advt. Woman of Yr., Women's Advt. Club Chgo., 2002; named one of 50 Women Who Are Changing the World, Essence, 2003; recipient Outstanding Women in Comm. award, Ebony, Vanguard award, Chgo. Mags. Assn., Media Strategies award, Bus. Week. Mem.: Am. Advt. Fedn. (mem. multicultural bus. practices leadership coun.), Am. Assn. Advt. Agys. (chair media policy com.). Office: Starcom NAm 35 W Wacker Dr Chicago IL 60601

MCCANN, RICHARD EUGENE, retired lawyer; b. Billings, Mont., Aug. 14, 1939; s. Oakey O. and Edith May (Miller) McC.; m. Mona N. Miyagishima, Apr. 27, 1964; children: Tami, Todd (dec.), Jennifer. BA magna cum laude, Rocky Mountain Coll., 1965; JD with highest honors, U. Mont., 1972. Bar: Mont. 1972, Washington 1977, Alaska 1982. Law clk. to Judge W. Jameson U.S. Dist. Ct., Billings, 1972-73; assoc. Crowley, Haughey, Hansen, Toole & Dietrich, Billings, 1973-77, Perkins Coie, Seattle, 1977-80, ptnr., 1981—2002, sr. counsel, 2003—. Contbr. articles to profl. jours. Trustee Rocky Mountain Coll., Billings., 1973-77. Served with USMC, 1957-61. Mem. ABA, Mont. Bar Assn., Wash. Bar Assn., Alaska Bar Assn. Office: Perkins Coie 1201 3rd Ave Fl 40 Seattle WA 98101-3029 Business E-Mail: rmccann@perkinscoie.com.

MCCANN, RICHARD STEPHEN, lawyer; b. Wilmington, Del., Dec. 26, 1938; s. Francis E.B. and Naomi H. (Riley) McC.; m. Gloria M. Baum (div. 1973); 1 child, Heather Marie; m. Sharon R. Cannon. BA, Georgetown U., 1960, JD, 1963; MA in City Planning, U. Pa., 1965. Bar: Del. 1964. Alderman City of Newark, Newark, 1964-66, pvt. practice law, 1970—; city planner Dover, Del., 1966-70. Atty. Del. Police Chief's Coun., Dover, 1971—, Del. Police Chief's Found., Dover, 1983—. Atty. Aetna Hose, Hook & Ladder Co., Newark, 1975—. Mem. ABA, Del. Bar Assn. Avocations: skiing, gardening, cannons. Home: PO Box 4706 Newark DE 19715-4076 Office: 125 E Delaware Ave Newark DE 19711-4644 E-mail: rsmccannesq@aol.com.

MCCANN, ROBERT J. investment company executive; Bachelor degree, Bethany Coll.; MBA, Tex. Christian U.; advanced mgmt. program, Harvard Bus. Sch. With Merrill Lynch & Co., 1982—, head US Equities, 1995—98, COO corp. and instl. client group (now global markets and investment banking), 2000—01, head rsch., 2001—03, exec. v.p., vice chmn. wealth mgmt. group, 2003—. Office: Merrill Lynch 4 World Fin Ctr New York NY 10080

MCCANN, VONYA B. federal agency administrator, telecommunications industry executive; BA, U. Calif., L.A., 1976; MPP, U. Calif., Berkeley, 1979, JD, 1980. Bar: D.C. Law clk. Commr. Tyrone Brown, Fed. Comm. Commn.; policy analyst Nat. Telecom.; ptnr. Arent, Fox, Kintner, Plotkin and Kahn; amb., dep. asst. sec. internat. comm. & info. policy Dept. State, 1994—99, prin. dep. asst. sec. of state for econ. and bus. affairs, 1997—99; sr. v.p., fed. external affairs Sprint Corp., Overland, Kans., 1999—. Office: Sprint World Hdqrs 6200 Sprint Pkwy Overland Park KS 66251

MCCANNON, TRICIA ANN, multi-media specialist, writer, photographer, educator; b. Detroit, Dec. 26, 1953; d. John R. McCannon and Carolyn Hayes. BA, Fla. State, Tallahassee, 1975. Multi-media specialist Fla. Dept. of Human Resources, 1976—78; photographer and art dir. Haus Publs., Atlanta, 1978—80; pres. Horizons Unlimited Prodns., Inc., Atlanta, 1980—. Prof. art South Ea. Ctr. Arts, Atlanta, 1987—90; master of ceremonies and headliner Whole Life Expo, L.A., 1991—96; appearances on radio and TV including Unsolved Mysteries and Strange Universe; keynote spkr. in internat. venues and confs. Author: Dialogues with the Angels, 1996, Landscape of the Inner Planes, 1997, UFO's in Am., 1997. Bd. dir. Atlanta Writers Guild, 1985—87; pres. bd. dir. Atlanta UFO Forum, 1988—96. Named a Bishop, Madonna Ministries/L.A., 1998, Priestess, The Iseum of the Eagle and the Dove/Ireland, 1999. Mem.: Assn. of Past Life Therapies, Lightstreamers, Theosophical Soc. Unitarian-Universalist. Avocation: animals. Office: Horizons Unlimited Inc Ste E 2135 Defoors Hills Rd Atlanta GA 30318 Office Phone: 404-355-2211.

MCCANTS, CLYDE TAFT, retired clergyman; b. Jan. 9, 1933; s. Edwin Clyde and Mary Rachel (Taft) McC. AB, Erskine Coll., 1954; MA, Duke U., 1956; MDiv, Erskine Theol. Sem., 1970; D of Ministry, Columbia Theol. Sem., 1987. Ordained to ministry, 1970. English faculty Elon Coll., N.C., 1955-60, Erskine Coll., Due West, S.C., 1960-65; faculty English, dept. chmn. Gaston Coll., Gastonia, N.C., 1965-67; pastor Lauderdale Ch., Lexington, Va., 1970-73; dir. ch. ext. Gen. Synod, Assoc. Ref. Presbyn. Ch., 1973-77; pastor 1st A.R. Presbyn. Ch., Burlington, N.C., 1977-78; asst. and assoc. prof. ministry Erskine Theol. Sem., 1978-82; pastor Greenville (S.C.) A.R.P. Ch., 1982-93, Bethel A.R.P. Ch., Winnsboro, S.C., 1993-98. Trustee Erskine Coll., 1973-78; moderator Gen. Synod of Assoc. Ref. Presbyn. Ch., 1978-79; chmn. Presbyn. Coun. on Chaplains and Mil. Personnel, Washington, 1983-84; chmn. bd. Friends of Fairfield County Libr., 1995-96, sec. 1997-99, Fairfield County Libr. Bd., 1996—2003, chmn., 1997—2003; vice-chmn. Friends of S.C. Libraries, 1998-99, chmn., 1999-2000; adv. coun. Palmetto Book Alliance, 1998—. Author: The God Who Makes History, 1976, David, King of Israel, 1978, Opera for Libraries, 2003; contbr. articles to profl. jours. Democrat. Home: 120 Walnut St Winnsboro SC 29180-1040

MCCARBERG, BILL HAROLD, physician; b. Seattle, Apr. 4, 1948; s. Harold Carl and Elizabeth Ann Mehlberg; m. Peggy J. McCarthy McCarberg. BA summa cum laude, U. Calif., Berkeley, 1972; MD, Northwestern U., Chgo., 1976. Diplomate Am. Bd. Family Practice, Am. Coll. Pain Medicine; cert. in geriatrics. Residency Highland Hosp., Rochester, N.Y., 1979; physician in charge Kaiser Permanente, Escondido, Calif., 1982—; asst. clin. prof. U. Calif. Sch. Medicine, San Diego, 1983—2003; coord. of pain svcs. Kaiser Permanente, San Diego, 1974—2002, dir. chronic pain mgmt. program, 1984—2003; founding mem. managed care task force Am. Pain Soc., 1990—; program chair Western Pain Soc., 1999—. Adv. bd. Knoll Pharma, Olive Mt., N.J., 1998—. Author: (monograph) Chronic Pain Management: Perspective for Primary Care Physicians, 1998, (book chpt.) A Sample of Existing Managed Care Organizations Pain Programs, 1999; contbr. articles to profl. jours. Recipient K Star for Outstanding Svc., Kaiser Permanente, San Diego, 1985, 92, Award of Excellence Southern Calif. Cancer Pain Initiative, L.A., 1999. Mem. Am. Acad. Pain Medicine, Am. Pain Soc. (chair managed care com. 2000—, bd. dirs. 2000—, Elizabeth Narcessian award 2003), Western Pain Soc., Appraisal of Physician Svcs., Phi Beta Kappa. Avocations: running, guitar, golf. Office: Kaiser Permanente 732 N Broadway Escondido CA 92025 Fax: 760-839-7096. E-mail: bill.h.mccarberg@kp.oag.

MCCARDELL, JAMES ELTON, retired naval officer; b. Daytona Beach, Fla., Jan. 22, 1931; s. J. Elton and Margaret Almira (Payne) McC.; m. Nancy Ann Chandler, July 9, 1955; children: Jenise, Patrick. Student, U. Fla., 1948-50; BA, U.S. Naval Postgrad. Sch., 1965. Commd. ensign U.S. Navy, 1952, advanced through grades to rear adm., 1980; exec. officer USS Forrestal, 1972-73; dep. chief of staff Air Readiness Staff, Chief Naval Res., New Orleans, 1973-76; comdg. officer NAS, Key West, Fla., 1976-78; chief of staff Staff of Chief Naval Res., New Orleans, 1978-80; def. and naval attache U.S. Embassy, Brasilia, Brazil, 1981-83; dir. Inter-Am. Def. Coll., Fort L.J. McNair, Washington, 1983-85; ret., 1985. Decorated Legion of Merit with cluster, Bronze Star medal, Air medal with 12 clusters, Def. Disting. Service medal, Def. Superior Performance medal Republican. Roman Catholic. Home: PO Box 719 Pass Christian MS 39571-0719 *The absolute measure of successful leadership has always been reflected by performance of subordinates in the achievement of unit goals.*

MCCARDELL, JOHN MALCOLM, JR., former academic administrator; b. Frederick, Md., June 17, 1949; s. John Malcolm and Susan (Lane) McCardell; m. Bonnie Greenwald, Dec. 30, 1976; children: John Malcolm III, James Benjamin Lee. AB, Washington and Lee U., 1971; postgrad., John Hopkins U., 1972-73; PhD, Harvard U., 1976; Litt.D., Washington and Lee U., 1997. Asst. prof. history Middlebury (Vt.) Coll., 1976-80, assoc. prof. history, 1982-87, dean for academic devel., 1985-88, prof. history, 1987—2004, dean facuty, 1988-89, provost, v.p for academic affairs, 1989-91, acting pres., 1991-92, pres., 1992—2004, pres. emeritus, 2004—; sr. rsch fellow U. S.C., Columbia, 1980-81, 96. Bd. dirs. Nat. Bank Middlebury. Author: The Idea of a Southern Nation, 1979 (Allan Nevins award, 1977); editor: A Master's Due, 1985. Sgt. USAR, 1971—77. Recipient Algernon Sydney Sullivan prize, Washington and Lee U., 1971, Charles Eliot medal, Eliot House Harvard U., 1976; fellow, NEH, 1980, Am. Philosophical Soc., 1979. Mem.: Vt. Hist. Soc., Am. Studies Assn., So. Hist. Assn., Orgn. Am. Historians, Am. Hist. Assn., Lambda Chi Alpha, Phi Beta Kappa, Omicron Delta Kappa.

MCCARDELL, KEENAN, professional football player; b. Jan. 6, 1970; Attended, Univ. Las Vegas. Wide receiver Tampa Bay Buccaneers, 2002—, Jacksonville Jaguars, 1996—2001, Cleveland Browns, 1992—95. Office: Tampa Bay Buccaneers 1 Buccaneer Pl Tampa FL 33607

MCCARGAR, ELEANOR BARKER, artist; b. Presque Isle, Maine, Aug. 30, 1913; d. Roy and Lucy Ellen (Hayward) Barker; m. John Albert McCargar, Feb. 18, 1947; children: Margaret, Lucy, Mary. Cert. elem. sch. tchg., Aroostook State Normal Sch., Presque Isle, 1933; student, Acadia U., 1935-36; B of Sociology, Colby Coll., 1937; summer student, Harvard U., 1939; and, Cambridge Sch. Art, 1939; studied portrait painting with Kenneth Washburn, Thomas Leighton, Maria von Ridelstein, Jean Henry, 1957-67. Ltd. svc. credential in fine and applied arts and related techs. Calif. C.C. Tchr. sci. and geography Limestone (Maine) Jr. H.S., 1937-41; ins. claim adjuster Liberty Mut. Ins. Co., Boston, 1941-42, Portland, Maine, 1943; ARC hosp. worker 20th Gen. Hosp., Ledo, Assam, India, 1944-45; portrait painter Burlingame and Apple Valley, Calif., 1958—. Commns. include more than 800 portraits in 10 states and 4 fgn. countries. Recipient M. Grumbacher Inc. Merit award for outstanding contbn. to arts, 1977; named Univ. of Maine Disting. Alumnus in Arts, 1981. Avocations: canoeing, camping, travel, studying.

MCCARGAR, JAMES GOODRICH, diplomat, writer; b. San Francisco, Apr. 20, 1920; s. Jesse B. and Addie May (Goodrich) McC.; m. Geraldine Claudia Cooper-Key, Aug. 2, 1948 (div. 1954); m. Emanuela Butculescu, Dec. 22, 1973. BA, Stanford U., 1942. Commd. Fgn. Svc. Officer, 1942; Dept. State, Moscow, 1942, 43; Vladivostok, 1942-43; Santo Domingo, 1943-44; sec. of legation, chief polit. sect. Budapest, Hungary, 1946-47; vice consul Genoa, Italy, 1948; chief div. Southeastern European Affairs Office of Policy Coordination, Washington, 1948-50; sec. of embassy, mem. U.S. Del. to Allied Coordinating Com., Paris, 1950-53; asst. to v.p. Free Europe Com., Inc., N.Y.C., 1955, European dir. polit. ops. Paris, 1956-58, cons. to pres., 1959-60, 71-76; spl. asst. to chmn. NEH, Washington, 1978-82; U.S. del. UNESCO confs., 1978, 80, 82; alt. rep. U.S.-Japan Friendship Commn., 1979-82; U.S. del. U.S.-Mexico Commn. on Cultural Coop., 1980, Sem. on Funding of Culture, Madrid, 1982; cons. BBC-TV, London, 1984, Nat. Dem. Inst. Internat. Affairs, Washington, 1984, African-Am. Labor Ctr., Washington, 1984-85, Am. Inst. Free Labor Devel., Washington, 1985, Dept. Internat. Affairs, AFL-CIO, Washington, 1986-95, Free Trade Union Inst., Washington, 1993-95, U.S. Info. Agy., Washington, 1998; editl. advisor Interco Press, Washington, 1988-96. Panelist internat. conf. Hungary and the World 1956, Budapest, 1996; bd. dirs. Ams. for Universality of UNESCO, Washington. Author: A Short Course in the Secret War, 1963, rev. edit., 1988, 4th edit., 2001, El Salvador and Nicaragua: The AFL-CIO Views on the Controversy, 1985, Ferenc Nagy: Smallholder or Statesman?, 1995; co-author: Three-Cornered Cover, 1972, Lost Victory, 1989; contbr. articles and book revs., 1940-70; ghostwriter, 1964-96. Co-founder, sec. Ams. Abroad for Kennedy, Paris, 1960. Ensign USNR, 1944-46. Recipient Cert. of Appreciation Internat. Ctr. for Free Trade Unions in Exile, 1958, Fed. Outstanding Performance award NEH, 1979, 81; decorated Knight First Class Royal Norwegian Order St. Olav, 1983, Silver Medallion of the Hungarian Parliament, 1991, Officer's Cross Order of the Hungarian Republic, 1992, Officer's Cross Order of Merit of the Rep. of Poland, 1993. Mem. Polish Inst. Arts and Scis. Am. (elected), Diplomatic and Consular Officers Retired, Oss Soc. (hon.), Authors' Guild, Cosmos Club (Washington). Democrat. Home and Office: 4201 Cathedral Ave NW Washington DC 20016-4948

MCCARL, HENRY NEWTON, economics and geology consultant, venture capitalist; b. Balt., Jan. 24, 1941; s. Fred Henderson and Mary Y. McCarl; m. Louise Becker Rys, June 8, 1963 (div. 1998); children: Katherine Lynne(dec.), Patricia Louise, Fredrick James; m. Mary Frederica Rhinelander, Jan. 31, 1987; 1 stepchild, Francesca C. Morgan. BS in Earth Sci., MIT, 1962; MS in Geology, Pa. State U., 1964, PhD in Mineral Econ., 1969. Lic. profl. geologist Ala., N.H. Market rsch. analyst Vulcan Materials Co., 1966-69; asst. prof. econ., asst. prof. geology U. Ala., Birmingham, 1969-72, assoc. prof. econ., 1973-77, assoc. prof. econ. and geology, 1978-91, prof. econs. and geology, 1991-95, prof. econ., edn. and geology, 1995-2001, prof. emeritus, 2001—, dir. Ctr. for Econ. Edn., Sch. Bus., 1987-2001; chief econ. div. Ala. Energy Mgmt. Bd., Montgomery, 1973-74; sr. lectr. in energy econs. Fulbright-Hays Program, Bucharest, Romania, 1977-78; ret., 2001. Mng. dir. McCarl & Assocs., Gloucester, Mass., 1969—; vis. fellow Grad. Sch. Arts and Scis. Harvard U., Cambridge, Mass., 1987; v.p., ptnr. Economagic, 1999—. Co-author: Energy Conservation Economics, 1986, Introduction to Energy Conservation, 1987; contbr. articles to profl. jours. Mem. Birmingham Planning Commn., 1974—86, chmn., 1980—86; dist. commr. Boy Scouts Am., Birmingham, 1988—94, asst. coun. Com. Greater Ala. Coun., 1999—2001; mem. edn. coun. MIT, 1974—. Recipient George B. Morgan award, MIT Alumni Assn., 1999. Mem.: SAR (life; nat. trustee 1996—97, investment com. 1999—2001, treas. gen. 2000—03, pres. gen. 2004—, sec. gen. 2003—04, chmn. found. bd. 2004—), Ala. Geol. Soc., Mineral Econ. and Mgmt. Soc. (pres. 1992—93), Am. Inst. Profl. Geologists (sect. pres. 1981—83, registered profl. geologist), Soc. Mining Engr. of AIME (bd. dirs. 1978—80, Disting. Mem. award 2000), St. Andrews Soc. Mid-South (life; sec. 1996—97), Sovereign Mil. Order the Temple Jerusalem. Republican. Episcopalian. Avocations: amateur radio, woodworking, beekeeping, model railroading. Home: 28 Old Nugent Farm Rd Gloucester MA 01930-3167 Office: 112 Eastern Ave Gloucester MA 01930

MCCARLEY, CAROLINE, state legislator; b. Birmingham, Ala., May 11, 1952; m. Dan Harkinson; three children. BA, Davidson Coll., 1974. Mem. Dist. 6 N.H. Senate, Concord, 1996—. Mem. econ. devel., edn., wildlife and recreation, pub. inst., HHS coms., vice-chair pub. affairs com. N.H. State Senate. Chmn. Rochester Sh. Bd., 1988—; incorporator N.H. Charitable Found., 1991—; founder, v.p. Rochester Lilac Family Fun Festival, 1993—. Mem. Rochester Vis. Nurse Assn. (pres. bd. dirs. 1995—). Office: NH State Legis State House Concord NH 03301 also: 5 Woodland LN Rochester NH 03867-3227

MCCARRICK, EDWARD R. magazine publisher; married; 2 children. Degree, Manhattan (N.Y.) Coll., 1971. From sales trainee to pub. Time Mag., NYC, 1973—99, pub., 1999—; sales dir. Life Mag., NYC, 1988—91, pub., 1993—99. Vol. Cath. Charities; bd. dir. YMCA/YWCA. Avocations: golf, squash, tennis. Office: Life Time Inc Time & Life Bldg 1271 Avenue of the Americas New York NY 10020-1300

MCCARRICK, THEODORE EDGAR CARDINAL, archbishop; b. N.Y.C., July 7, 1930; s. Theodore Egan and Margaret (McLaughlin) McCarrick. AB, St. Joseph's Sem., 1954, AM, 1958; MA, Cath. U., 1960, PhD, 1963. Elevated to cardinal Roman Cath. Ch., 2001, Ordained priest Roman Cath. Ch., 1958. Asst. chaplain Cath. U. Am., Washington, 1959—61, dean students, 1961—63, asst. to rector, dir. devel., 1963—65, instr. dept. sociology, 1961—65; domestic prelate, 1965; pres. Cath. U. P.R., 1965—69; assoc. dir. edn. Archdiocese of N.Y., 1969—71; sec. to Cardinal-Archbishop N.Y., 1971—77; aux. bishop, 1977—81; 1st bishop Diocese of Metuchen, NJ, 1981—86; archbishop Newark, 1986—2000; superior Turks & Caicos, Antilles, 1998—2000; archbishop Washington, 2001—. Mem. Fed. Commn. for Study of Migration and Econ. Devel., 1989; policy bd. Washington Consortium, Peace Corps, 1962—63, Pontifical Commn. for Migrants and Refugees, 1987; chmn. U.S. Bishops Com. on Migration, 1986—89, 1992—95, Gov.'s Commn. for Higher Edn. in P.R., 1968, P.R. Adv. Coun. on Tech. and Vocat. Edn., 1968—69; active U.S. Sec. of State's Adv. Com. on Religious Freedom Abroad, 1996—99, U.S. Com. for Internat. Religious Freedom, 1999—2001, Synod for Am. and Post Synod Coun.; Episcopal promoter Apostleship of the Sea, 1989—92; chmn. Com. Aid to Ch. in Ctrl. and Ea. Europe, U.S. Conf. of Cath. Bishops, 1992—96, chmn. internat. policy com., 1996—99, chmn. domestic policy com., 2002—. Sec.-treas. Papal Found., 1988—96, pres., 1997—. Decorated officer, knight grand cross Holy Sepulchre, Order of Cedars of Lebanon. Mem.: Knights Malta (chaplain 1978—82). Roman Catholic. Office: Archdiocese of Washington PO Box 29260 Washington DC 20017

MCCARROLL, KATHLEEN ANN, radiologist, educator; b. Lincoln, Nebr., July 7, 1948; d. James Richard and Ruth B. (Wagenknecht) McC.; m. Steven Mark Beerbohm, July 10, 1977 (div. 1991); 1 child, Palmer Brooke; m. Lawrence Albert Weiss, Aug. 28, 2004. BS, Wayne State U., 1974; MD, Mich. State U., 1978. Diplomate Am. Bd. Radiology. Intern/resident in diagnostic radiology William Beaumont Hosp., Royal Oak, Mich., 1978-82, fellow in computed tomography and ultrasound, 1983, dir. divsn. emergency radiology, 2001—; radiologist, dir. radiologic edn. Detroit Receiving Hosp., 1984-2001, vice-chief dept. radiology, 1988-96, chief dept. radiology, 1996-2001. Pres.-elect med. staff Detroit Receiving Hosp., 1992-94, pres., 1994-96; mem. admissions com. Wayne State U. Coll. Medicine, Detroit, 1991-2001; trustee Detroit Med. Ctr., 1996-2001, dir. med. staff consolidation, 1996-97, mem. consol. med. exec. com., 1998-2001, chmn. credentials com., 1998-99, joint conf. com., 1998-99; officer bd. dirs. Dr. L. Reynolds Assoc., P.C., Detroit, 1991-94, 96-2001; presenter profl. confs.; assoc. prof. radiology Wayne State U. Sch. Medicine, Detroit, 1995—; health care cons./med. staff affairs, 1998—. Editor: Critical Care Clinics, 1992; mem. editorial bd. Emergency Radiology; contbr. articles to profl. publs. Named to Crain's Bus. Detroit, Detroit's 100 Most Influential Women, 1997. Mem.: AMA, Wayne/Oakland County Med. Soc., Mich. State Med. . Soc., Am. Soc. Emergency Radiologists (bd. dirs. 1996—2001, mem. exec. com. 1998—2001, bylaws com. 2001—), Am. Roentgen Ray Soc., Radio. Soc. N.Am., Am. Coll. Radiology (Mich. chpt. sec. 1995—98, alt. councilor 1999—2002, councilor 2002—, plain film and fluoroscopy accreditation com. 2003—), Phi Beta Kappa. Avocations: travel, skiing, reading. Office: Wm Beaumont Hosp Dept Diag Radiology 3601 W 13 Mile Rd Royal Oak MI 48073

MCCARRON, DOUGLAS J. labor union administrator; b. L.A., Sept. 23, 1950; V.p., sec.-treas. L.A. County Dist. Coun.; pres. United Brotherhood of Carpenters and Joiners Am., Washington, 1995—. Former bd. mem. ULLICO Inc.; mem. S. Calif. Council of Carpenters; trustee S. California Pension Fund. Office: United Brotherhood of Carpenters and Joiners 101 Constitution Ave NW Washington DC 20001-2133 also: 1221 Massachusetts Ave Washington DC 20005 Office Phone: 202-546-6206.*

MCCARRON, JOHN FRANCIS, editor; b. Providence, Jan. 20, 1949; s. Hugh Francis and Katherine Anne (Brooks) McC.; m. Janet Ann Velsor, Sept. 3, 1971; children: Veronica, Catherine. BS in Journalism, Northwestern U., 1970, MS in Journalism, 1973. Gen. assignment reporter Chgo. Tribune, 1973-80, urban affairs writer, 1980-91, fin. editor, 1991-92, editorial bd. columnist, 1992-2000; v.p. strategy and comms. Met. Planning Coun. Chgo., 2000—02; adj. prof. Medill Sch. Journalism Northwestern U., 2002—. Contbr. to Planning mag., World Book Ency., Preservation mag. Lt. USNR, 1970-72. Recipient Editors award AP, 1983, 84, Ann. Journalism award Am. Planning Assn., 1983, Heywood Broun award Am. Newspaper Guild, Washington, 1989, Peter Lisagor award Soc. Profl. Journalists, 1994. Home: 1425 Noyes St Evanston IL 60201-2639 E-mail: j.mccarron@att.net.

MC CARTAN, PATRICK FRANCIS, lawyer; b. Cleve., Aug. 3, 1934; s. Patrick Francis and Stella Mercedes (Ashton) Mc Cartan; m. Lois Ann Buchman, Aug. 30, 1958; children: M. Karen, Patrick Francis III. AB magna cum laude, U. Notre Dame, 1956, JD, 1959. Bar: Ohio 1960, U.S. Ct. Appeals (6th cir.) 1961, U.S. Ct. Appeals (3rd cir.) 1965, U.S. Ct. Appeals (DC cir.) 1980, U.S. Ct. Appeals (5th cir.) 1981, U.S. Ct. Appeals (4th cir.) 1989, U.S. Ct. Appeals (7th cir.) 1992, U.S. Supreme Ct. 1970. Law clk. to Hon. Charles Evans Whittaker, U.S. Supreme Ct., 1959; assoc. Jones Day, Cleve., 1961—65, ptnr., 1966—93, mng. ptnr., 1993—2002, sr. ptnr., 2003—. Trustee U. Notre Dame, 1989—, chair, 2000—; trustee Cleve. Clinic Found.; chair Greater Cleve. Roundtable; mem. standing com. on rules of practice and procedure Jud. Conf. of U.S. Fellow: Internat. Acad. Trial Lawyers, Am. Coll. Trial Lawyers; mem.: ABA, Bar Assn. Greater Cleve. (pres. 1977—78), Ohio Bar Assn., 6th Cir. Jud. Conf. (life), U.S.-Japan Bus. Coun., Coun. on Fgn. Rels., Greater Cleve. Growth Assn. (chmn. 1997—2000), Musical Arts Assn. (trustee). Roman Catholic. Office: Jones Day North Point 901 Lakeside Ave E Cleveland OH 44114-1190 E-mail: pmccartan@jonesday.com.

MCCARTER, CHARLES CHASE, lawyer; b. Pleasanton, Kans., Mar. 17, 1926; s. Charles Nelson and Donna (Chase) McC.; m. Clarice Blanchard, June 25, 1950; children: Charles Kevin, Cheryl Ann. BA, Principia Coll., 1950; JD, Washburn U., 1953; LLM, Yale U., 1954. Bar: Kans. 1953, U.S. Supreme Ct. 1962, Mo. 1968. Asst. atty. gen. State of Kans., 1954-57; lectr. law sch. Washburn U., 1956-57; appellate counsel FCC, Washington, 1957-58; assoc. Weigand, Curfman, Brainerd, Harris & Kaufman, Wichita, 1958-61; gen. counsel Kans. Corp. Commn., 1961-63; ptnr. McCarter, Frizzel & Wettig, Wichita, 1963-68, McCarter & Badger, Wichita, 1968-73; pvt. practice law St. Louis, 1968-76; ptnr. McCarter & Greenley, St. Louis, 1976-85; mng. ptnr. Gage & Tucker, St. Louis, 1985-87, Husch and Eppenberger, St. Louis, 1987-89, McCarter & Greenley, LLC, St. Louis, 1990—. Prof. law, assoc. dir. law sch. Nat. Energy Law and Policy Inst. Tulsa U., 1977-79; prof. law, coach nat. moot ct. coll. of law Stetson U. Coll., St. Petersburg, Fla., 1980-84; mem. govtl. adv. coun. Gulf Oil Corp., 1977-81; legal com. Interstate Oil Compact Commn.; mem. adv. bd. Allegiant Bank, 1997—. Co-author: Missouri Lawyers Guide; assoc. editor Washburn U. Law Rev., 1952-53; contbr. articles to profl. jours. Chmn. Wichita Human Rels. Devel. Adv. Bd., 1967-68; bd. dirs. Peace Haven Assn.; active St. Louis Estate Planning Coun., 1987—; mem. bequests and endowment com. Salvation Army, 1995—; mem. YMCA endowment com., 1996—; mem. gifts and endowment bd. TV Channel 9, KETC, St. Louis, 2004—. With USNR, 1944-46. Recipient Excellent Prof. award U. Tulsa, 1979; vis. scholar Yale U., 1980 Mem. ABA (sect. real property, probate and trust law, bus. law sect.), Kans. Bar Assn., Mo. Bar Assn. (probate and trust com., tax com.), Am. Legion, VFW, Native Sons and Daus. Kans (pres. 1957-58), Kappa Sigma, Delta Theta Phi, Principia Dads Club (bd. dirs.) Republican. Office: One Metropolitan Sq Ste 2100 Saint Louis MO 63102-2797 Office Phone: 314-436-2100. E-mail: cmccarter@mccartergreenley.com.

MCCARTER, JAMES PHILIP, biotechnology company executive, researcher; b. Chgo., Aug. 27, 1967; s. John Wilbur and Judith (West) McC.; m. Rosalie M. Truong, Oct. 19, 1996. AB in Biology, Princeton U., 1989; MD, PhD in Devel. Biology, Washington U., St. Louis, 1998. Pres., chief sci. officer Divergence Inc., St. Louis, 1998—; postdoctoral fellow, group leader parasitic nematode project Washington U. Genome Sequencing Ctr., 1998—2002, rsch. instr. genetics, 2002—. Co-founder young scientist program and www.mad-sci.org, St. Louis. Contbr. articles to sci. jours., including Devel. Biology, Jour. Cell Biology, Jour. Molecular Evolution, Genetics, Jour. Nematology, Genome Biology, Trends in Parasitology, Genome Research, Nucleic Acids Research. Olin predoctoral fellow Washington U., 1997-98, postdoctoral fellow Nat. Human Genome Rsch. Inst., NIH, 1998-99, Merck postdoctoral fellow Helen Hay Whitney Found., 1999-2002, Henry Crown fellow Aspen Inst., 2002-2004; named one of 40 Under 40 Bus. Leaders, St. Louis Bus. Jour., 2002; recipient Innovation award, St. Louis Acad. of Sci., 2003. Mem. AAAS, Soc. Nematology, Am. Soc. Parasitologists, Am. Soc. Tropical Medicine and Hygiene, Am. Phytopathological Soc., Am. Assn. of Veterinary Parasitologists. Avocations: science education, urban restoraton, basketball, rowing. Office: 893 N Warson Rd Saint Louis MO 63141 Personal E-mail: mccarter@divergence.com.

MC CARTER, JOHN WILBUR, JR., museum executive; b. Oak Park, Ill., Mar. 2, 1938; s. John Wilbur and Ruth Rebecca McC.; m. Judith Field West, May 1, 1965; children: James Philip, Jeffrey John, Katherine Field. AB, Princeton U., 1960; postgrad., London Sch. Econs., 1961; MBA, Harvard U., 1963. Cons., assoc., v.p. Booz Allen and Hamilton, Inc., Chgo., 1963-69; White House fellow Washington, 1966-67; dir. Bur. Budget and Dept. Fin., State of Ill., Springfield, 1969-73; v.p. DeKalb AgResearch, Ill., 1973-78, dir.,

1975-86, exec. v.p., 1978-80, pres., 1981-82; pres., chief exec. officer DeKalb-Pfizer Genetics, 1982-86; pres. DeKalb Corp., 1985-86; sr. v.p. Booz Allen & Hamilton Inc., 1987-97; pres., CEO Field Mus., Chgo., 1996—. Bd. dirs. A.M. Castle & Co., Divergence Inc., W.W. Grainger, Inc., Janus and Harris Insight Funds. Trustee Chgo. Pub. Television, 1973—, chmn., 1989-96, trustee Princeton U., 1983-87, U. Chgo., 1993—. Office: Field Museum 1400 S Lake Shore Dr Chicago IL 60605-2496

MCCARTER, KATHERINE SAUTER, association executive; b. Nov. 12, 1942; d. William Charles and Josephine RFosina (Schoenie) Sauter; m. Robert James McCarter, Dec. 6, 1969; 1 child, Emily Katherine. BA in Biology, Cedar Crest Coll., Allentown, Pa., 1964; MHA (EPA trainee), Johns Hopkins U., 1973. Chmn. sci. dept. Arundel (Md.) Jr. H.S., 1964—68; assoc. career devel. program Am. Lung Assn., N.Y.C., 1968; air conservation cons. Mass. Lung Assn., 1968—69; exec. dir. Met. Boston Citizen's Coalition Clean Air, 1968—69; cmty. health educator Environ. Health Adminstrn., Md. Dept. Health, 1971—76; dir. govt. rels. APHA, Washington, 1976—80, asst. exec. dir., 1980—83, assoc. exec. dir., 1984—97; exec. dir. Ecol. Soc. Am., Washington, 1997—. Mem. nat. air pollution manpower devel. adv. com. EPA, 1973—76. Mem. editl. adv. bd.: The AIDS Reference Guide, 1987. Bd. dirs. Nat. Coalition Health and Environment, 1980—82, Coalition for Health Funding, 1983—, treas., 1983—86, v.p., 1987—88, pres., 1989—94, past pres., 1994—97. Mem.: APHA, Coun. Engring. and Sci. Soc. Execs. (bd. dirs. 2003—). Home: 9027 Billow Row Columbia MD 21045-2343 Office: 1707 H St NW Washington DC 20006

MCCARTER, THOMAS NESBITT, III, investment counseling company executive; b. NYC, Dec. 16, 1929; s. Thomas N. Jr. and Suzanne M. (pierson) McC. Student, Princeton U., 1948-51. Chartered investment counselor. Sales exec. Mack Trucks, Inc., NYC, 1952—59; ptnr. Kelly, McCarter, D-Arcy Investment Counsel, NYC, 1959—62; v.p., sec., dir. D-Arcy McCarter & Chew, NYC, 1962—66; v.p., dir. Trainer, Wortham & Co., Inc., NYC, 1967—71, exec. v.p., 1971—75; chmn. bd., dir. Island Security Bank Ltd., 1976—78; pres. Knottingham Ltd., NYC, 1976—84; gen. ptnr. W.P. Miles Timber Properties, New Orleans, 1974—; exec. v.p. Yorke McCarter Owen & Bartles, Inc., NYC, 1985—89. Cons. Laidlaw Holdings, Inc., 1990—92; pres. Mentor Mgmt. Group, Inc., NYC, 1986—90; chmn. bd. dirs. Ramapo Land Co., Sloatsburg, NY, 1990—, Stillrock Mgmt., Inc., NYC, 1992—96, Pendragon Tech., 1996—98, Dir Anker Coal Group Inc., Hyseq, Inc., Nitvelo, Inc.; bd. advisors Knowledge Delivery Sys. Inc.; vice chair Runnymede Capital Mgmt., Inc.; dir. Inst. Scientific Investment and Governance KCK Tokyo. Chmn. bd. trustees Christodora Found., Inc., NYC, 1970-93; charter trustee Dalton Sch., NYC, 1969-76, v.p., 1972-76; pres., trustee Civil War Libr. and Mus., Phila., 1985-92; chmn. bd. trustees ASPCA, 1984-95; chmn. loyal Legion Found., NYC; trustee Children's Aid Soc. NYC, 1973-94, Joffrey Ballet, Found. for Am. Dance, 1973-77; pres., trustee NYC Marble Cemetery Assn., 1990-2002; mem. Nat. Com. for Preservation of US Treasury Bldg., 1988-92; trustee Nat. Symphony Orch., Washington, 1990-94; chmn. Gibraltar Am. Coun., 1998-2002; bd. assocs. Whitehead Inst., Cambridge, Mass., 2000—. Mem. Loyal Legion US (comdr. NY State 1964-66, nat. comdr. in chief 1977-81), Racquet and Tennis Club, Brook Club, Links Club, River Club, St. Nicholas Soc., Pilgrims of US (NYC), Meadow club (Southampton, NY), Ivy Club (Princeton, NJ). Republican. Home and Office: PO Box 2380 Palm Beach FL 33480

MCCARTHY, BEA, state legislator; b. Great Falls, Mont., Apr. 17, 1935; d. Robert Joseph and Rose Mary (Krier) McKenna; m. Edward Joseph McCarthy, June 27, 1959; children: Colleen, Mary, Edward Jr., Patrick, John. BS in Elem Edn., Mont. State U., 1957. Tchr. 1st grade, Anaconda, Mont., 1968—; mem. Mont. Ho. of Reps., Dist. 66, 1991-94, Mont. Senate, Dist. 29, Helena, 1997—. Mem. Mont. Bd. Regents, 1983-90, Mont. Bd. Edn., 1983-90. Mem. AAUW, Am. Legion Aux., Ladies Ancient Order Hibernians (past pres.), Phi Beta Phi, Delta Kappa Gamma. Democrat. Roman Catholic. Avocations: needlecrafts, painting, reading. Home: 1906 Ogden St Anaconda MT 59711-1706 Address: Capitol Station Helena MT 59620

MCCARTHY, CAROLYN, congresswoman; b. Brooklyn, Jan. 5, 1944; LPN. With St. Francis and Winthrop Hosp., 1964—93; gun safety activist, 1994—97; mem. U.S. Congress from 4th N.Y. dist., 1997—. Mem. edn. and workforce com., fin. svcs., subcom. on fin. inst. and consumer credit, 21st century competitiveness. Recipient numerous awards, including being named one of Newsday's 100 L.I. Influentials, Congl. Quarterly's 50 Most Effective Legislators in Congress, one of nine Redbook Mag.'s "Mothers and Shakers", Ladies' Home Jour. list of America's 100 Most Important Women, and Advertising Age's list of Most Impact by Women in 1999; also honored by U.S. Women's Soccer Team and Oprah Winfrey. Democrat. Office: US Ho of Reps 106 Cannon Ho Office Bldg Washington DC 20515-3204

MCCARTHY, CHARLES R. bioethicist, consultant; b. St. Paul; s. Frederic D. and Florence Ruth (Milton) McC.; m. Estelle Rountree, July 23, 1971. BA, U. St. Thomas, St. Paul, 1947; MA, U. Toronto, 1956, PhD, 1961. Ordained priest, 1956. Priest Paulist Fathers; tchr. St. Paul's Coll., Cath. U. Am., George Washington U., Washington; program analyst NIH Divsn. Legis. Analysis, Bethesda, Md., 1971-74, chief legis. devel. br., 1975-78; dir. Office for Protection from Rsch. Risks NIH, Bethesda, Md., 1978-92; sr. rsch. fellow Kennedy Inst. Ethics Georgetown U., Washington; cons. to rsch. instns., 1992—98; dir. Office Rsch. Compliance Va. Commonwealth U., Richmond, 2000—. Fellow Hastings Ctr. Ethics, 1987—; bd. dirs. Pub. Responsiblity in Medicine and Rsch. Contbr. articles to profl. jours., chpts. to books; mem. editl. bd. Inst. Lab. Animal Rsch. Nat. Acad. Scis., 1995-99, issue editor, 1998. Group leader No. Ireland Peace Missions, Belfast, 1993, 96; mem. State of N.Y. Dept. Health Adv. Group on Human Subjects Rsch. Involving Protected Classes, N.Y.C., 1997-98. Recipient Exptl. Achievement award, Asst. Sec. for Health, 1983, Pub. Health Superior Achievement award, Surgeon Gen. of U.S., 1989, Spl. citation for 15 yrs. of leadership in protection of humans, Commr. FDA, 1992, Outstanding Achievement award, Sec. HHS, 1991, Harry C. Rowsell award, Scientists Ctr. for Animal Welfare, 1999, Lifetime Achievement award, ARENA, 2000, Pub. Responsibility in Medicine and Rsch., 2003. Mem. Nat. Acad. Scis. Inst. Medicine (com. on legal and ethical issues relating to the inclusion of women in rsch. 1993-94), Scientists Ctr. for Animal Welfare (bd. trustees, v.p., 1993—), Am. Fertility Soc. (mem. ethics com. 1989-94), Acad. Medicine, Kiwanis Internat. North Ctrl. Richmond (charter). Roman Catholic. Avocations: fishing, golf, carpentry, travel. Home: 3613 Hawthorne Ave Richmond VA 23222-1823 Fax: 804-321-6478. E-mail: chamcc@erols.com.

MCCARTHY, CORMAC, writer; b. Providence, R.I., July 20, 1933; s. Charles Joseph and Gladys (McGrail) McC.; m. Lee Holleman, 1961 (div.); 1 child, Cullen; m. Anne deLisle, 1967 (div.). Author: (novels) The Orchard Keeper, 1965 (William Faulkner Found. award 1965), Outer Dark, 1968, Child of God, 1974, Suttree, 1979, Blood Meridian, or The Evening Redness in the West, 1985, All the Pretty Horses, 1992 (Nat. Book award for fiction 1992, Nat. Book Critics Circle award for fiction 1993), The Crossing, 1994, Cities of the Plain, 1998; (teleplays) The Gardner's Son, 1977; (plays) The Stonemason: A Play in Five Acts, 1994. Ingram-Merrill Found. creative writing grantee, 1960, Am. Acad. Arts and Letter traveling fellow, 1965-66, Rockefeller Found. grantee, 1966, Guggenheim fellow, 1976, MacArthur Found. grantee, 1981; recipient Jean Stein award Am. Acad. and Inst. Arts and Letters, 1991.

MCCARTHY, DANIEL WILLIAM, management consultant; b. Syracuse, N.Y., Apr. 15, 1952; s. William Cornelius and Ruth Francis (Geller) McC.; m. Mary Coleen Kisil, Jan. 17, 1987; children: Katherine M., Kevin D., Patrick W. BA in Polit. Sci., SUNY, Geneseo, 1974; MBA, NYU, 1982. Asst. buyer Abraham & Straus, Bklyn., 1976—78; buyer Lord & Taylor, N.Y.C., 1978—80; cons. Touche Ross, Newark, 1982—87; sr. mgr. Deloitte & Touche, N.Y.C., 1987—93; dir. Coach Leatherware, N.Y.C., 1993—94; prin. Greenvale Consulting Group, Poughkeepsie, NY, 1994—2000; pres. Retex Cons. Group, N.Y.C., 2000—02, Greenvale Cons. Group, LLC, NY, 2002—03; dir. spl. projects Island Pacific, Inc., 2003—. Author: Point of Sale - Current Trends and Beyond, 1986; contbr. articles to profl. jours. Mem. Town of Poughkeepsie Hist. Planning Commn. Named Open Foil Champion, North Atlantic Veterans, 2000, 2001. Mem. Nat. Retail Fedn., Inst. Mgmt. Cons. Roman Catholic. Avocations: wine collecting, ballet, fencing, architecture, investing. E-mail: danmed@msn.com.

MCCARTHY, DENNIS M. military officer; b. Cleveland, Ohio, Feb. 1, 1945; m. Rosemary Mccarthy; children: Sean, Michael. Grad., Univ. Dayton, 1967. Communications officer 1st Battalion 13th Marines, Vietnam, 1968-69; asst. ops. officer Schs. Demo. Troops, Quantico, Va.; judge advocate, military judge Camp Lejeune, N.C., 1978; pvt. practice law Columbus, Ohio, 1979—; dir. tactical exercise evaluation, control group Marine Corps. Air Ground Combat Ctr., 29 Palms, Calif.; brigadier gen., 1993; commanding gen. Marine Corps. Res. Support Command, 1993-95, IMACE, 1995-97; major gen., 1995; commanding gen. 3d Marine Divsn., 1997; deputy dir. Ops. U.S. Atlantic Command, 1997-99, dir., 1999; dir. reserve affairs U.S. Marine Corps, Quantico, Va., 2000—01; promoted lt. gen., 2001; comdr. Marine Forces Reserve, New Orleans, 2001—. Office: Marine Forces Reserve 5020 Lakeshore Dr New Orleans LA 70146

MCCARTHY, DESMOND FERGUS, English literature educator; b. Boston, Oct. 18, 1959; s. Desmond Christopher and Agnes McCarthy. BA, Framingham State Coll., 1981; MA, Brandeis U., 1984, PhD, 1992. Lectr. Brandeis U., Waltham, Mass., 1987-88; instr. Simmons Coll., Boston, 1989-91, Northeastern U., Boston, 1990; asst. prof. English Framingham (Mass.) State Coll., 1991-99, assoc. prof. English, 1999—. Adviser The Gatepost, Framingham, 1992—. Author: Reconstructing the Family in Contemporary American fiction, 1997, 2d edit., 1998. Recipient 1997 Disting. Four Yr. Coll. Newspaper Advisor, presented by CMA. Office: Framingham State Coll 100 State St Framingham MA 01702-2460 E-mail: dmccart@frc.mass.edu.

MC CARTHY, EUGENE JOSEPH, writer, former senator; b. Watkins, Minn., Mar. 29, 1916; s. Michael John and Anna (Baden) McC.; m. Abigail Quigley, June 1945; children— Ellen, Mary, Michael, Margaret. AB, St. John's U., Collegeville, Minn., 1935; A.M., U. of Minn., 1939. Tchr. pub. schs., 1935-40, 45; prof. econ. edn. St. John's U., 1940-42; civilian tech. work with Mil. Intelligence Div., War Dept., 1944; instr. sociology and econs. St. Thomas Coll., St. Paul, 1946-48; mem. 81st-85th Congresses from 4th Minn. dist., 1949-59, mem. ways and means com.; U.S. senator from Minn., 1959-70; mem. senate finance, fgn. relations and govt. ops. coms.; Adlai Stevenson prof. polit. sci. New Sch. for Social Research, 1973-74; syndicated columnist, 1977—. Dir. Harcourt Brace Jovanovich, Inc. Author: Frontiers in American Democracy, 1960, Dictionary of American Politics, 1962, A Liberal Answer to the Conservative Challenge, 1964, The Limits of Power, 1967, The Year of the People, 1969, Other Things and The Aardvark, 1970, Up 'Til Now, 1987; also, The Hard Years, 1975, Mr. Raccoon and His Friends, 1977, America Revisited, 1978, Ground Fog and Night, 1979, The Ultimate Tyrany, 1980, Gene McCarthy's Minnesota, 1982, Complexities and Contraries: Essays of Mild Discontent, 1982, The View from Rappahannock, 1984; co-author: A Political Bestiary, 1978, Up 'Til Now, 1987, Required Reading, 1988, 89, The View from Rappahannock II, 1989, Up Til Now, 1991, Colony of the World, 1993, Required Reading, 1994, Selected Poems, 1997, No Fault Politics, 1999, Am. American Bestiary, 1999. Roman Catholic. Office: 271 Hawlin Rd Woodville VA 22749-1721

MC CARTHY, FRANK MARTIN, oral surgeon, surgical sciences educator; b. Olean, N.Y., Aug. 27, 1924; s. Frank Michael and Joan (Quinn) McC.; m. Julia Richmond, Nov. 24, 1949; children: Robert Lee, Joan Lee. BS, U. Pitts., 1943, DDS, 1945, MD, 1949; MS in Oral Surgery, Georgetown U., 1954; ScD (hon.), St. Bonaventure U., 1956. Med. intern Mercy Hosp., Pitts., 1949-50; practice oral surgery L.A., 1954-75; tchg. fellow Georgetown U., 1952-53; rsch. fellow NIH, 1953-54; prof. oral surgery U. So. Calif. Sch. Dentistry, 1966-75, prof., chmn. sect. anesthesia and medicine, 1975-90, prof. emeritus, 1990—, chmn. dept. surg. scis., 1979-84, assoc. dean adminstrv. affairs, 1977-79, asst. dean hosp. affairs, 1979-84. Dir. anesthesiology U.So. Calif. oral surgery sect. L.A. County Hosp., 1958-89; clin. supr., lectr. dental hygiene program Pasadena City Coll., 1992—; v.p. Am. Dental Bd. Anesthesiology, 1984-89; lectr. in field; mem. adv. panel on dentistry sect. anesthesizing agts. Nat. Fire Protection Assn., 1971-79; mem. Am. Nat. Stds. Com., 1974-86, 95—; cons. in field. Author: Emergencies in Dental Practice, 1967, rev., 1972, 79, Medical Emergencies in Dentistry, 1982, Safe Treatment of the Medically Compromised Patient, 1987, Essentials of Safe Dentistry for the Medically Compromised Patient, 1989; mem. editorial bd.: Calif. Dental Assn. Jour; contbr. articles to profl. publs. Bd. councilors Sch. Dentistry, U. So. Calif., 1972-75. Served as lt., M.C. USNR, 1950-52. Fellow Internat. Assn. Oral Surgeons (founder), Am. Coll. Dentists, Internat. Coll. Dentists; mem. ADA (editl. bd. jour.), Am. Dental Soc. Anesthesiology (Heidbrink award 1977), Am. Assn. Oral-Max Surgeons (chmn. anesthesia com. 1971), So. Calif. Soc. Oral Surgeons (pres. 1974), Calif., L.A. County Dental Assns., Delta Tau Delta, Psi Omega, Phi Rho Sigma, Omicron Kappa Upsilon. Home and Office: 480 S Orange Grove Blvd Apt 11 Pasadena CA 91105-1720

MCCARTHY, G. DANIEL, lawyer; b. Butte, Mont., Mar. 23, 1949; s. George Denis and Mary Agnes (Kiely) McC.; m. Carolyn M. Scully, June 19, 1976; children: Brendan, Katie, Kelly, Sean. BA, U. Dayton, 1971; JD, U. Notre Dame, 1974; AMP, Harvard U., 1994. Bar: Md. 1974, D.C. 1975, U.S. Ct. Appeals (D.C. cir.) 1976, Pa. 1977, N.Y. 1985, U.S. Ct. Appeals (10th cir.) 1985. Assoc. Bilger & Blair, Washington, 1974-77, 79-80; asst. U.S. atty. U.S. Dist. Ct. (ea. dist.) Pa., Phila., 1977-78; assoc. Abourezk, Shack & Mendenhall, Washington, 1980-83; atty. AT&T, N.Y.C., 1983-85; v.p., gen. counsel and sec. AT&T Credit Corp., Morristown, NJ, 1985-89; sr. v.p., gen. counsel, sec., chief risk mgmt. officer. AT&T Capital Corp., Morristown, NJ, 1990-96; v.p., gen. counsel, sec. Compaq Fin. Svcs. Corp., Murray Hill, NJ, 1996—2002; v.p. govt. affairs, dep. gen. counsel Compaq Computer Corp., Houston, 2001—02; v.p., gen. counsel, sec. Hewlett-Packard Fin. Svcs. Co., Murray Hill, NJ, 2002—. Vis. lectr. Marymount Coll., Arlington, Va., 1979-83; mem. adv. coun. U. Dayton, Coll. of Arts and Scis., 1993-97, chmn., 1994-96; bd. dirs. Compaq Fin. Svcs. Europe, LLC, Tandem Computers Credit Corp., Hewlett-Packard Internat. Bank PLC. Mem.: DC Bar Assn., Fairmount Country Club (Chatham, NJ) (bd. dirs. 2002—). Avocations: golf, fly fishing. Office: HP Fin Svcs Co 420 Mountain Ave New Providence NJ 07974-0006 Office Phone: 908-898-4003. E-mail: dan.mccarthy@hp.com.

MCCARTHY, GLORIA M, insurance company executive; Various leadership positions Empire Blue Cross Blue Shield, 1974—97; sr. v.p. Empire Blue Cross Blue Shield (WellChoice, Inc became the parent holding co. in 2002), 1997—2002, WellChoice, Inc., 2002, sr. v.p. ops., managed care and medicare services, 2002—03, exec. v.p., COO, 2003—. Office: WellChoice 11 West 42nd St New York NY 10036*

MCCARTHY, HAROLD CHARLES, retired insurance company executive; b. Madelia, Minn., Dec. 5, 1926; s. Charles and Merle (Humphry) McC.; m. Barbara Kaercher, June 24, 1949; children: David, Susan. BA, Carleton Coll., Northfield, Minn., 1950; postgrad. With Federated Mut. Ins. Co., Owatonna, Minn., 1950-67; with Meridian Mut. Ins. Co., Indpls., 1967-91, exec. v.p., then exec. v.p., gen. mgr., 1972-75, pres., 1975-90, bd. dirs., past chmn. bd., 1990-91; past pres. North Meridian Bus. Group; past pres., chmn. bd. Meridian Ins. Group, Inc. Chmn. bd., dir. Meridian Life Ins. Co.; past chmn., exec. com., bd. dirs. Ind. Ins. Inst.; mem. adv. bd. Harbor Fed. Savs. Bank. Former mem. Met. Devel. Commn., Corp. Community Council; bd. dirs. Meth. Health Found., Family Services Assn., Boy Scouts Am.; trustee Butler U.; mem. adv. bd. Harbor Fed. Bank. With USNR, 1944-46. Named Sagamore of the Wabash. Mem. Skyline Club (Indpls.), Indian River Golf Club. Republican. Congregationalist. Office: 2955 N Meridian St Indianapolis IN 46208-4714

MCCARTHY, IAN J. construction executive; Pres., CEO Beazer Homes USA, Inc., Atlanta, 1989—. Office: Beazer Homes USA Inc Ste B200 5775 Peachtree Dunwoody Rd NE B200 Atlanta GA 30342-1509

MCCARTHY, J. THOMAS, lawyer, educator; b. Detroit, July 2, 1937; s. John E. and Virginia M. (Hanlon) McC.; m. Nancy Irene Orrell, July 10, 1976 BS, U. Detroit, 1960; JD, U. Mich., 1963. Bar: Calif. 1964. Assoc. Julian Caplan, San Francisco, 1963—66; prof. law U. San Francisco, 1966—; counsel Morrison and Foerster, 2001—. Founding dir. McCarthy Inst. Intellectual Property and High Tech. Law; mem. Trademark Rev. Commn., 1986—88; cons. in field. Author: McCarthy on Trademarks and Unfair Competition, 6 vols., 4th edit., 1996, McCarthy on Rights of Publicity and Privacy, 1987, 2d edit., 2000, McCarthy's Desk Encyclopedia of Intellectual Property, 3d edit., 2004. Recipient Jefferson medal N.J. Intellectual Property Assn., 1994, Ladas award Brand Names Ednl. Found., 1997, Pattishall medal Brand Names Found., 2000, Pres.'s award Internat. Trademark Assn., 2003. Mem. IEEE, Am. Intellectual Property Law Assn. (Watson award 1965, Centennial award in Trademark law 1997), Internat. Assn. for Advancement of Tchg. and Rsch. in Intellectual Property, Am. Law Inst. (adv. com. on restatement of law of unfair competition).

MCCARTHY, JACK D. oil industry executive; CFO, sr. v.p. The Williams Cos., Tulsa, Okla., 1991—. Office: The Williams Cos One Williams Ctr Tulsa OK 74172

MCCARTHY, JEAN JEROME, retired physical education educator; b. St. Paul, Sept. 11, 1929; s. Joseph Justin and Florence (Quirin) McC.; m. Norma Louise Shermer, July 30, 1955; children: Patrick J., Anne L., Kevin M. BS, U. Minn., 1956, PhD, 1986; MS, Wash. State U., 1958. Tchg. asst. Wash. State U., 1956-57, U. Minn., 1957-59, adminstrv. asst., 1959-60; asst. prof. phys. edn. U. South Fla., 1960-62, Mankato State U., 1962-71, assoc. prof., 1971-86, prof., 1986-91, ret., 1991, baseball coach, 1962-77. Cons. AAU. Contbr. articles to profl. jours. Mem. Minn. Gov.'s Phys. Fitness Adv. Com. With USAF, 1950-54. Recipient Outstanding Faculty award Mankato State U., 1979; named Region 2 Coach of Yr., NCAA, 1971, Outstanding Educators Am., 1970; named to Mankato State U. Athletic Hall of Fame, 1993; U. Minn. Grad. Sch. fellow, 1959-60; Lilly Found. scholar, 1974—; Rsch. Consortium fellow. Mem. AAPHER, Minn. Assn. Health, Phys. Edn., Recreation and Dance, Mensa, Phi Delta Kappa, Phi Epsilon Kappa (scholarship award 1972), Phi Kappa Phi. Roman Catholic.

MCCARTHY, JENNY, actress; b. Chgo. m. John Asher. Student Sch. Nursing, So. Ill. U. Appeared in films Things to Do in Denver When You're Dead, 1995, The Stupids, 1996, Basketball, 1998, Diamonds, 1999, Scream 3, 2000, TV shows The Jenny McCarthy Show, 1997, Jenny, 1997-98; host game show Singled Out, MTV, 1995-96; featured photographs in Playboy mag., including as Miss Oct. 1993, then as Playmate of Yr. Address: c/o United Talent Agy 9560 Wilshire Blvd Ste 500 Beverly Hills CA 90212-2427

MCCARTHY, JOHN, computer scientist, educator; b. Boston, Sept. 4, 1927; s. Patrick Joseph and Ida McCarthy; children: Susan Joanne, Sarah Kathleen, Timothy Talcott. BS, Calif. Inst. Tech., 1948; PhD, Princeton U., 1951. Instr. Princeton U., 1951—53; acting asst. prof. math. Stanford U., 1953—55; asst. prof. Dartmouth Coll., 1955—58; asst. and assoc. prof. communications scis. M.I.T., Cambridge, 1958—62; prof. computer sci. Stanford U., 1962—2001, Charles M. Pigott prof. Sch. Engring., 1987—94, prof. emeritus computer scis., 2001. Served with AUS, 1945-46. Recipient Kyoto prize, 1988, Nat. Medal of Sci., NSF, 1990. Mem.: NAE, NAS, Am. Assn. Artificial Intelligence (pres. 1983—84), Am. Math. Soc., Assn. for Computing Machinery (A.M. Turing award 1971), Am. Acad. Arts and Scis. Home: 885 Allardice Way Stanford CA 94305-1050 Office: Stanford U Dept Computer Sci Stanford CA 94305 E-mail: mccarthy@stanford.edu.

MCCARTHY, JOHN DAVID, mathematician, educator; b. Salem, Mass., June 12, 1955; s. James Joseph and Joanne McCarthy; m. Catherine Rose McCarthy; children: David Michael, Steven Matthew, Ethan Joseph, Colin Patrick. BS, Stevens Inst. Tech., Hoboken, N.J., 1977; PhD, Columbia U., 1983. Moore instr. MIT, Cambridge, Mass., 1983—85; asst. prof. math. Mich. State U., East Lansing, 1985—90, assoc. prof. math., 1990—98, prof. math., 1998—. Rsch. visitor Max Planck Institut fur Mathematik, Bonn, Germany, 1984, Univerite de Louis Pasteur, Strasbourg, 1986, Max Planck Institut fur Mathematik, Bonn, 1988, Université de Louis Pasteur, Strasbourg, 1996. Co-author: (book) Casson's invariant for oriented homology 3-spheres. An exposition, 1990; contbr. articles to profl. jours. Grantee, NSF, 1986—88, 1993—95. Avocation: outdoor sports (e.g. orienteering). Home: 4943 Holt Rd Holt MI 48842-1033 Office: Mich State U A228 Wells Hall East Lansing MI 48824-1027 Business E-Mail: mccarthy@math.msu.edu.

MCCARTHY, JOHN F. healthcare administrator; BA, St. Patrick's Coll.; MSW, Cath. U.; MPA, Harvard U. Asst. dir. Cath. Charities, San Francisco; dir. Refugee Cath. Relief Svcs., Nigeria, econ. devel. planner Mayor's Office, San Francisco; regional program dir. Adminstrn. on Aging, San Francisco; dep. commr. on aging, acting commr. Dept. Health and Human Svcs., Washington, dep. asst. sec., dir. mgmt., 1994—. Office: Dept Health and Human Svcs Mgmt 330 Independence Ave SW Washington DC 20201-0002

MCCARTHY, JOHN ROBERT, real estate company officer; b. Carlisle, Pa., May 29, 1945; s. James Francis and Eleanor Marie (Harrington) McC.; m. Cathleen Ann Rice, Oct. 25, 1975; children: Kevin James, Michael John. BA in Bus. & Polit. Sci., St. Leo Coll., Fla., 1969. Mktg. rep. R.H. Donnelley Corp., NYC, 1969—70; employee benefits rep. Marsh & McLennan Corp., NYC, 1970—73; overseas sales rep. AMF, Inc., White Plains, NY, 1973—79; ptnr., sr. v.p. Rostenberg-Doern Co., White Plains, 1979—90; ptnr. pres. McCarthy Assoc., Inc., White Plains, 1990—. Mem. Con Edison Sports Hall of Fame Com., White Plains, 1981—, St. Agnes Hosp. Children's Com., 1983-90; bd. dirs. Am. Diabetes Assn. Westchester, 1987-94, adv. bd. St. Vincents Hosp., Harrison, N.Y., 1998—, Lighthouse West County, 1999—; mem. Cardinals Com. of Laity, Westchester; pres. Archbishop Stepinac H.S. Crusader Mens Club, 1998-2000; fund raising chmn. Gt. Hunger Meml. Westchester County, 1999-2001; Grand Marshal White Plains St. Patrick's Parade, 2000; mem. St. Patrick's Parade Com., 1997—. Mem. Exch. Club (hon., past pres. Downtown chpt.), Friendly Sons St. Patrick (officer Westchester chpt. 1984-91, pres. 1990-91, bd. stewards 1990—), Orienta Beach Club (chmn. children's com. 1987-92, bd. dirs. 1992-98, pres. 1995-98), Winged Foot Golf Club. Roman Catholic. Avocations: sports, charitable fund raising. Home: 16 Ridgeway Cir White Plains NY 10605-4119 Office: 1 N Broadway White Plains NY 10601-2310 Office Phone: 914-948-8900. Personal E-mail: jrmcc222@aol.com. Business E-Mail: john@mcoc.com.

MCCARTHY, JONATHAN PAUL, economist; b. Britt, Iowa, Dec. 8, 1957; s. Henry Felix and Lucille McC.; m. Diana Marie Shaw, Aug. 23, 1997. BS summa cum laude, U. Wis., Parkside, 1980, MS, 1991; PhD, U. Wis., Madison, 1992. Teaching asst. U. Wis., Madison, 1986-87, rsch. asst., 1987-90, lectr. Whitewater, 1990-91; economist Fed. Res. Bank, N.Y.C., 1992—. Vis. economist Bank Internat. Settlements, Basel, Switzerland, 1997-98 Contbr. articles to profl. jours. Mem. Am. Econ. Assn., Nat. Assn. Bus. Economists. Avocations: running, basketball, softball. Home: 395 S End Ave Apt 14E New York NY 10280-1029 Office: Fed Res Bank 33 Liberty St New York NY 10045-1003

MCCARTHY, JOSEPH HAROLD, consultant, former retail food company executive; b. Derby, Conn., Dec. 21, 1921; s. Joseph Harold and Kathryn (Feeley) McC.; m. Jean K. Ryan, June 7, 1947; children: Timothy J., Maureen, Barbara, Richard, Joseph Harold. BS in Econs., Villanova U., 1944. Sr. v.p. First Nat. Stores Inc., Boston, 1947-76, Grand Union Co., Elmwood Park, N.J., 1976-80; exec. v.p., chief oper. officer Great Atlantic and Pacific Tea Co., Inc., Montvale, N.J., 1980-90, ret., 1990, cons. North Chatham, Mass., 1990-92. Served to capt. USMC, 1943-46, PTO; served to capt. USMC, 1951-52, Korea. Named to Villanova Football Hall of Fame, 1989. Home: 2030 Imperial Golf C Blvd Naples FL 34110 Office: 2030 Imperial Golf Course Blvd Naples FL 34110-1025

MCCARTHY, KAREN P. congresswoman, former state legislator; b. Mass., Mar. 18, 1947; BS in English, Biology, U. Kans., 1969, MBA, 1985; MEd in English, U. Mo., Kansas City, 1976. Tchr. Shawnee Mission (Kans.) South High Sch., 1969-75, The Sunset Hill (Kans.) Sch., 1975-76; mem. Mo. House of Reps., Jefferson City, 1977-94; cons. govt. affairs Marion Labs., Kansas City, Mo., 1986-93; mem. U.S. Congress from 5th Mo. dist., Washington, 1995—; mem. commerce com.; mem. Ho. Select Com. on Homeland Security. Rsch. analyst pub. fin. dept. Stearn Bros. & Co., 1984-85, Kansas City, Mo.; rsch. analyst Midwest Rsch. Inst., econs. and mgmt. scis. dept., Kansas City, 1985-86. Del. Dem. Nat. Conv., 1992, Dem. Nat. Party Conf., 1982, Dem. Nat. Policy Com. Policy Commn., 1985-86; mem. Ho. Commerce Com. Energy and Power, Telecom., Trade and Consumer Protection; co-chair Dem. Caucus Task Health Care Reform. Recipient Outstanding Young Woman Am. award, 1977, Outstanding Woman Mo. award Phi Chi Theta, Woman of Achievement award Mid-Continent Coun. Girl Scouts U.S., 1983, 87, Annie Baxter Leadership award, 1993; named Conservation Legislator of Yr., Conservation Fed. Mo., 1987. Fellow Inst. of Politics; mem. Nat. Inst. of Politics; mem. Nat. Conf. on State Legis. (del. on trade and econ. devel. to Fed. Republic of Germany, Bulgaria, Japan, France and Italy, mem. energy com. 1978-84, fed. taxation, trade and econ. devel. com. 1986, chmn. fed. budget and taxation com. 1987, vice chmn. state fed. assembly 1988, pres.-elect 1993, pres. 1994), Nat. Dem. Inst. for Internat. Affairs (instr. No. Ireland 1988, Baltic Republics 1992, Hungary 1993). Democrat. Office: US House Reps 1436 Longworth HOB Washington DC 20515-2505

MCCARTHY, KEVIN, state representative; b. Bakersfield, Calif., Jan. 26, 1965; m. Judy McCarthy; children: Connor, Meghan. BS in Bus. Adminstrn., Calif. State U., Bakersfield, 1989, MBA, 1994. Owner Bakersfield Batting Range, Kevin O's Deli; dist. dir. Rep. Bill Thomas; mem. Calif. Assembly, 2002—. Bd. dirs. Kern Econ. Opportunity Corp. Trustee dist. bd. Kern C.C., 2000—; exec. dir. McCarthy Found., 2000—; coach YMCA, 1999—; mem. Kern County Rep. Ctrl. Com., 1992—; bd. dirs. First Book, 2001—, Head Start, Kern County Food Bank. Mem.: Rotary. Republican. Office: PO Box 942849 Sacramento CA 94249 Address: 4900 California Ave Ste 140-A Bakersfield CA 93309

MCCARTHY, KEVIN A. state representative; b. Chgo., Dec. 5, 1950; m. Judy McCarthy; children: Amy, Kevin John. BA, Chgo. State U., 1972; MA in Edn. Adminstrn. and Supr., DePaul U., 1976. Tchr. Chgo. Pub. Schs.; territory mgr. Am. Acad. Supplies; mem. Ill. Ho. of Reps., 1996—. Sch. bd. St. Michael, 1986—89, pres. sch. bd., 1987—89, endowment chair, 1989—91, head coach jr. varsity soccer, 1993—94, head coach varsity, 1995—96; mgr. girls' softball Orland Youth Assn., 1986—90, commr. girl's softball, 1990, mgr. boys' baseball, 1990—92. With USAR, 1971—77. Democrat. Office: 271-S Stratton Office Bldg Springfield IL 62706 Address: 8951 W 151st St Orland Park IL 60462

MCCARTHY, KEVIN BART, lawyer; b. Washington, May 7, 1948; s. Frank Jeremiah and Frances Patricia (Bilderback) McC.; m. Patrice Borders, Apr. 3, 1971; children: Kevin Patrick, Charles Ryan, Molly Virginia, Bridget Louise, Moira Patrice. BBA, U. Notre Dame, 1970; JD, Ind. U., Indpls., 1973. Bar: Ind. 1973, U.S. Dist. Ct. (so. dist.) Ind. 1973, U.S. Ct. Appeals (7th cir.) 1974, Ill 1976, U.S. Dist. Ct. (cen. dist.) Ill. 1985, U.S. Ct. Appeals (6th cir.) 1985. Bail commr. Mcpl. Ct. Marion County, Indpls., 1972-73; asst. regional counsel Fed. Hwy. Adminstrn., Homewood, Ill., 1973-75; 1st asst., chief counsel Ill. Dept. Transp., Springfield, 1975-77; counsel com. on interstate and fgn. commerce, subcom. on transp. and commerce Ho. Reps., Washington, 1977-79, asst. counsel com. on pub. works and transp., 1979-82, counsel com. on pub. works and transp., 1982; pvt. practice law Springfield, 1982-87; acting U.S. trustee Dept. Justice, Springfield, 1987-88, U.S. trustee Indpls., 1988—. Pvt. practice Indpls. and Springfield. Mem. Ill. State Bd. Agrl. Advisors, 1987-88. Home: 5619 Surrey Hill Rd Indianapolis IN 46226-1561

MCCARTHY, KEVIN E. library director, consultant; b. Albany, N.Y., Jan. 29, 1952; s. Gerald D. and Virginia M. McCarthy; m. Ann-Teresa Foy, June 20, 1976; 1 child, Anne H. AS in Bus. Adminstrn., U. Maine, Portland, 1976, BA in Polit. Sci., 1978; MPA, SUNY, Albany, 1982; MLS, Rutgers U., 1995. Libr. adminstr. Ferguson Libr., Stamford, Conn., 1984—96; libr. dir. Old Bridge (N.J.) Pub. Libr., 1996—98, Perrot Meml. Libr., Old Greenwich, Conn., 1998—. Libr. bldg. design cons. Lushington Assocs., Hartford, Conn., 1998—, Libr. Devel. Solutions, Princeton Junction, NJ, 2000—. Mem.: Lions Internat. (v.p. 2003—04). Office: Perrot Meml Libr 90 Sound Beach Ave Old Greenwich CT 06870

MCCARTHY, LISA, communications executive; m. Sean McCarthy; children: Caroline, Tara. BS, Georgetown U., 1988. With UBS Securities, Paramount TV, Turner Broadcasting, JMW Consultants; sr. v.p. Viacom Plus, 1998—2002, exec. v.p., 2002—. Named to, Crain's New York Bus. "40 under 40", 2004; recipient Women to Watch award, N.Y. Advt. Age and Advt. Women N.Y., 2003. Office: Viacom Inc 1515 Broadway New York NY 10036*

MCCARTHY, MARIANNE, government agency administrator; BA, UCLA; MA in Edn., U. No. Colo.; PhD in Psychology, UCLA. Prin. Woodview Calabasas Sch., Erikson H.S.; dir. edn. program NASA, 1996—. Vol. tchrs. asst. UCLA Neuropsychiat. Inst. Office: NASA Dryden Rsch Ctr PO Box 273 MS 4839 Edwards CA 93523-0273

MCCARTHY, MARK FRANCIS, lawyer; b. Boston, July 8, 1951; s. William Alfred and Martha Louise (Blodgett) McC.; m. Karen Marie Umerley; children: Kevin Francis, Daniel Henry. AB in Theology, Georgetown U., 1973, JD, 1976. Bar: Ohio 1976. Assoc. Sweeney, Mahon, & Vlad, Cleve., 1976-80; ptnr. Tucker Ellis & West LLP, Cleve. Atty. asst. to bd. pres. Bd. Cuyahoga County Commrs., Cleve., 1976-80; adj. prof. Case Western Reserve Law Ctr., Cleve., 1986—. Active Greater Cleve. Growth Assn. Leadership Cleve., 1979-80; trustee Parmadale, Parma, Ohio, Western Res. Hist. Soc., 1978-80, Cath. Charities Found.; chmn. Cath. Charities Svcs. Corp.; trustee, sec. Caritas Connection; sec., gen. counsel St. Martin De Porres H.S., Cleve., Inc. Mem. Ohio Assn. Civil Trial Attys. (chmn. product liability sect. 1989—), Fedn. Ins. & Corp. Counsel, Ct. of Nisi Prius, Rowfant Club. Democrat. Roman Catholic. Avocations: book collecting, fly fishing, upland shooting. Home: 363 Britannia Pky Avon Lake OH 44012-2180 Office: Tucker Ellis & West LLP 1150 Huntington Bldg 925 Euclid Ave Cleveland OH 44115-1475 Office Phone: 216-696-3290. E-mail: Mark.McCarthy@tuckerellis.com.

MCCARTHY, MARY ELIZABETH (BETH) CONSTANCE, conductor, educator, music educator; b. Chgo., Apr. 8, 1961; d. Thomas Joseph and Loretta Ann McCarthy. BA, North Ctrl. Coll., 1983; postgrad., Goethe Inst., 1991, Ea. Ill. U., 1993; MusM in Choral and Instrumental Edn. and Cognition and Vocal Performance, Northwestern U., 1999. Profl. cantor Joliet/Rockford Dioceses, Ill., 1979—; assoc. condr. Chorus Orch. Band Ill. Math. and Sci. Acad., Aurora, 1989—2000; site coord. gifted program Ill. Math. and Sci. Acad. at Ea. Ill. U., Charleston, 1990—95; soloist Lincoln Opera Co., Chgo., 1991—94; chmn. Dept. Fine Arts Rosary H.S., Aurora, 1993—; dept. chair music Aurora U., 1995—; condr., artistic dir. Fox Valley Festival Chorus, Aurora, 1999—. Profl. role coach pvt. students, Ill., 1989—; condr., music dir. dinner theatres, summer stock, Ill., 1990—; artistic cons. oratory and recitals, Ill., 1993—; adjudicator orchs., chorus, bands, Ill., 1993—; cons. to critique Nat. Stds. for the Arts, Ill., 1994; master class clinician various choral orgns., Ill., 1995—; guest condr. fine arts festivals, Ill., 2001—; host Cath. Conf. Fine Arts Festival Rosary H.S., Aurora, 2002. Sec. The Beta Fin. Group, Sycamore, Ill., 1995—2002; conservation mem. Salmon Unlimited-Ill. chpt., 1997; religious edn. tchr. St. Peter and Paul Ch., Naperville, Ill., 1980—, cantor, 1976—, Rite of Christian Initiation for Adults sponsor, 1995. Recipient Internat. Bel-Canto Vocal Competition Opera award, Bel-Canto Found., 1995; fellow Richter fellow for internat. rsch./study, North Ctrl. Coll., 1982. Mem.: AAUW, Lyric Opera Chgo., Ill. Music Educators' Assn., Music Educators' Nat. Conf., Fox Valley Music Educators' Assn., North Ctrl. Coll. Alumni Assn., Northwestern U. Music Sch. Alumni Assn. (bd. dirs. 1998—2001), Northwestern Club Chgo., Alpha Psi Omega, Beta Beta Beta, Phi Alpha Theta. Avocations: art, travel, running, boating, reading. Office: Aurora Univ Music Dept 347 S Gladstone Aurora IL 60506

MCCARTHY, MICHAEL JAMES, military intelligence officer; b. Columbus, Ohio, July 29, 1962; s. James Patrick and Alice Marie (Gartner) McC.; m. Muriel Ruth Levine, Oct. 8, 1987. BA, Ohio State U., 1984; diploma, Pushkin Inst., Moscow, 1984; MA, Cath. U. Am., Washington, 1996; M in Mil. Sci. with distinction, USMC Command and Staff Coll., Quantico, Va., 2000. Commd. 2d lt. USAF, 1986, advanced through grades to lt. col., 2002; staff intelligence officer 31st Tactical Fighter Wing, Homestead AFB, Fla., 1987, chief intelligence sect., 1987-89, chief target intelligence, 1989-90; watch officer Hdqrs. US Air Forces in Europe, Ramstein AB, Germany, 1990, command briefer, 1990-93; sr. analyst Nat. Air Intelligence Ctr., Washington, 1993-95; plans and requirements officer Hdqrs. U.S. Air Force, Washington, 1995-96, exec. officer, 1996-97; ops. officer Joint Intelligence Ctr. Ctrl., MacDill AFB, Fla., 1997-98, team chief Ctrl. Asia Analysis, 1998—99; detailed to US Marine Corps Command and Staff Coll., 1999—2000; ops. officer 23d Info. Ops. Squadron, Kelly AFB, Tex., 2000—02; UN mil. observer Tbilisi, Georgia, 2001—02; country dir. Office of Internat. Affairs, Hdqrs. USAF, Washington, 2002—. Contbr. articles to mil. publs. Mem. Am. Assn. Advancement Slavic Studies, Nat. Mil. Intelligence Assn., Air Force Assn. Republican. Roman Catholic. Avocations: running, weightlifting, travel, military history. Office: SAF/IARE 1500 Wilson Blvd Ste 801 Rosslyn VA 22209

MCCARTHY, MICHAEL M. construction executive; CEO McCarthy, St. Louis, chmn., 1976—. Office: McCarthy Bldg Cos 1341 N Rock Hill Rd Saint Louis MO 63124-1441

MCCARTHY, MICHAEL SHAWN, health care company executive, lawyer; b. Evergreen Park, Ill., May 16, 1953; s. Martin J. and Margaret Anne (McNeill) McC.; m. Jane F. Alberding, Oct. 28, 1988; children: Caroline Margaret, Nicholas Michael, Claire Patricia. BA, Georgetown U., 1975; MS, U. Ill., 1976; JD, Loyola U., 1980. Bar: Ill. 1980, U.S. Dist. Ct. (no. dist.) Ill. 1980. V.p., sec., gen. counsel Luth. Gen. Health Care System, Park Ridge, Ill., 1980-85, sr. v.p., sec., gen. counsel, 1985-91, sr. v.p. corp. svcs., sec., gen. counsel, 1990-93; chmn., CEO Parkside Sr. Svcs., LLC, Skokie, Ill., 1993—. Life trustee Lake Forest Acad.; mem. coun. of regents Loyola U., Chgo., Ill. Mem. ABA, ASHA (exec. bd.), Ill. Hosp. Assn., Ill. Pub. Health Assn., Chgo. Bar Assn., ALFA Leadership Coun. Roman Catholic. Avocations: golf, travel. Home: 1026 Pine St Winnetka IL 60093-2024 Office: Parkside Sr Svcs LLC 5215 Old Orchard Rd Skokie IL 60077-1035 E-mail: McCarthy@parkside-sr.com.

MCCARTHY, NOBU, actress, performing company executive, educator; Adj. prof. Calif. State U. Artistic dir.: East West Players in Los Angeles, As The Crow Flies (Drama-Logue award), Sarcophagus, Come Back Little Sheba; dir. The Chairman's Wife, Webster Street Blues, And the Soul Shall Dance, (TV) China Beach, Island Son, Magnum P.I., Quincy, Farell to Manzanar, Playhouse 90, (feature films) Geisha Boy, Wake Me When It's Over, Karate Kid II, Pacific Heights. Office: Mark Taper Forum 5905 Wilshire Blvd Los Angeles CA 90036-4504

MCCARTHY, PAMELA MAFFEI, magazine editor; b. N.Y.C., May 28, 1952; d. Rudolph Paul Maffei and Mary Frances Maresca; m. Joseph Matthews McCarthy, Sept. 16, 1978; 2 children. Student, Trinity Coll., Dublin, Ireland, 1972-73; BA, Mt. Holyoke Coll., 1974. Mem. editorial staff Esquire mag., N.Y.C., 1974-76, copy editor, 1976-79, exec. editor, 1978-84; mng. editor Vanity Fair mag., N.Y.C., 1984-92, The New Yorker, N.Y.C., 1992-95, dep. editor, 1995-99, mng. editor, 1999—. Mem. Am. Soc. Mag. Editors Office: The New Yorker Advance Publications Inc 4 Times Sq New York NY 10036-6561

MCCARTHY, PATRICE ANN, lawyer; b. New Haven, Jan. 23, 1957; d. Robert Edmund and Faith Arline (Augur) McC.; m. Donald Allen Kirshbaum, Oct. 25, 1986; children: Lynn Anne, Sara. BA, Mt. Holyoke Coll., 1978; JD, U. Conn., 1981. Bar: Conn. 1981, U.S. Dist. Ct. Conn. 1981. Staff assoc. Conn. Conf. Municipalities, New Haven, 1981-83; legal counsel Conn. Assn. Bds. Edn., Hartford, 1983-88, gen. counsel, assoc. exec. dir. for govt. rels., 1988-91; dep. dir., gen. counsel, 1991—. Editor: Conn. Manual Bd. Policy Regulations and By-laws, 1987; contbr. articles to profl. jours. Mem. ABA, Nat. Sch. Bds. Assn. Coun. Sch. Attys. (bd. dirs. 1990-94), Am. Soc. Pub. Adminstrn. (coun. 1988—), Nat. Orgn. for Legal Problems in Edn., Conn. Bar Assn., Conn. Sch. Attys. Coun. (pres. 1988-89), Conn. Pub. Employers Labor Rels. Assn. (bd. dirs. 1985-88), Mt. Holyoke Club (v.p. 1986-88, pres. 1990-94). Office: Conn Assn Bds Edn 81 Wolcott Hill Rd Hartford CT 06109-1242

MCCARTHY, PATRICK, magazine publishing executive; Joined Women's Wear Daily, 1977, reporter, bur. chief, Paris, editor N.Y.C., 1985-88, exec. editor, 1988-92; editor W, N.Y.C., 1985-88, exec. editor, 1988-92; exec. v.p. Fairchild Publs., N.Y.C., 1992-97; chmn., editl. dir., 1997—. Recipient Eugenia Sheppard award for fashion journalism CFDA, 1994. Office: Fairchild Publs Seven West 34th St New York NY 10001

MCCARTHY, PAUL FENTON, aerospace executive, former naval officer; b. Boston, Mar. 3, 1934; s. Paul Fenton and Jane Gertrude (O'Connor) McC.; m. Sandra Williams, June 20, 1959; children: Paul Fenton III, Susan Stacy. BS in Marine and Elec. Engring., Mass. Maritime Acad., 1954; MS in Mgmt., U.S. Naval Postgrad. Sch., 1964; D of Pub. Adminstrn. (hon.), Mass. Maritime Acad., 1987. Commd. ensign U.S. Navy, 1954, advanced through grades to vice adm., 1985; 7 command tours have included Aircraft Carrier USS Constellation, Carrier Group One, Task Force Seventy; commdr. U.S. 7th Fleet, 1980-82; dir. R & D USN, Washington, 1980-83; negotiator Naval Air, Incidents at Sea Agreement, Moscow, 1980; ret., 1990; cons. in field, 1990-92; pres. McCarthy and McCarthy, Ltd.; v.p., chief engr., dep. gen.mgr. McDonnell Douglas Aerospace/Boeing, St. Louis, 1992-95; v.p. processes and sys. integration McDonnell Douglas Aerospace, St. Louis, 1995-97, dir. naval systems integration, 1997-2000; vis. disting. prof. Peter Conrad chair Naval Post Grad. Sch., 2000-02; sr. ptnr. McCarthy and McCarthy, LLC, 2002—. Trustee Naval Mus., 1990; bd. visitors Mass. Maritime Acad., 1993. Decorated D.S.M., Legion of Merit, D.F.C., also by govts. of South Vietnam, Korea, Japan. Mem. Mass. Maritime Acad. Alumni Assn. Episcopalian. Avocations: research, development and acquisition, aircraft and missile systems, financial management. Office Phone: 619-922-9494. E-mail: mcandmc@aol.com.

MCCARTHY, RHODA ANN, nursing administrator, medical/surgical nurse; b. N.D., Apr. 6, 1928; d. Roy Leavitt and Emma (Norby) Hall; m. James L. McCarthy, Oct. 1, 1949; children: Kathryn, Margaret, Shirley, John, Patrick. Diploma, Sisters of St. Joseph, 1949; BS in Sociology, Valley City (N.D.) State Coll., 1983; BSN, U. Albuquerque, 1986; B in Psychology, Calif. Coast U., 1987, M in Psychology, 1998, D in Psychology, 2003. Dir. of nurses Trinity Hosp., Jamestown, ND; asst. dir. nurses forensic unit N.D. State Hosp., Jamestown, asst. dir. nurses substance abuse unit; nurse mgr. orthops. unit VA Med. Ctr., Albuquerque; staff nurse St. Joseph Med. Ctr., U. N.Mex.

MCCARTHY, ROBERT EMMETT, lawyer; b. Bklyn., May 26, 1951; s. John Joseph and Leona Mary (Hart) McC.; m. Elizabeth Anne Naumoff, May 20, 1978; children: John Philip, Emily Jane. BS in Fgn. Studies, Georgetown U., 1973, MS in Fgn. Studies, JD, 1978. Bar: N.J. 1978, U.S. Dist. Ct. (ea. and so. dists.) N.Y. 1979. Assoc. Patterson, Belknap et al, N.Y.C., 1978-84; gen. counsel MTV Networks Inc., N.Y.C., 1984-86; v.p., counsel/communications Viacom Internat., N.Y.C., 1986-87; exec. v.p. Nelson Vending Tech., Ltd., N.Y.C., 1987-89; exec. v.p., gen. counsel Cateret Savs. Bank FA, Morristown, N.J., 1989-91; cons. McCarthy Comms., Elizabeth, N.J., 1991-95; sr. v.p., gen. counsel Time, Inc., N.Y.C., 1996—. Cons. UN Ctr. on Transnat. Corps., N.Y.C., 1979; exec. dir. Spl. Master Reapportionment of N.Y., 1982; term mem. Council Fgn. Relations, N.Y.C., 1980-84. Founder, pres. Elizabeth (N.J.) Dem. Assn., 1980; coordinator Florio for Gov., Union County, N.J., 1981. Mem. ABA, N.Y. State Bar Assn., N.J. State Bar Assn., Assn. Bar City N.Y. Roman Catholic. Home: 3 Woods Ln Chatham NJ 07928-1760 Office: Time Inc 33rd Fl 1271 Avenue Of The Americas New York NY 10020-1300 E-mail: RobertMcCarthy1@aol.com.

MCCARTHY, ROGER LEE, mechanical engineer; AB in Philosophy with high distinction, BS in Mech. Engring. summa cum laude, U. Mich., 1972; MS in Mech. Engring., MIT, 1973, D in Mech. Engring., 1975, PhD in Mech. Engring., 1977. Registered profl. engr., Calif., Ga., Ariz. Project engr. machine design and devel. engring. divsn. Proctor & Gamble, Inc., Cin., 1973-74; program mgr. Spl. Machinery Group Foster-Miller Assocs., Inc., Waltham, Mass., 1976-78; prin. design engr. Failure Analysis Assocs., Inc. (became Exponent Failure Analysis Assocs., Inc. in 1998), Menlo Park, Calif., 1978—, chmn. bd. dirs., 1988—; CEO The Failure Group, Inc., Menlo Park, 1988-96, chief tech. officer, 1996-98; chmn. Exponent Failure Analysis Assocs., Inc., Menlo Park, 1998—. Co-contbr. numerous articles to profl. jours. Mem. Pres.' Commn. on Nat. Medal of Sci., 1992-94. Recipient Outstanding Civilian Svc. Gold medal U.S. Army, 1998; NSF fellow, 1972-75. Mem. ASME, ASHRAE, ASTM, NAE, Am. Soc. Metals, Soc. Automotive Engrs., Am. Welding Soc., Human Factors Soc., Nat. Fire Protection Assn., Phi Beta Kappa, Sigma Xi (James B. Angell scholar). Office: Exponent Failure Analysis Assn Inc 149 Commonwealth Dr Menlo Park CA 94025 Office Phone: 650-688-7100. Office Fax: 650-688-7366. E-mail: sfrlm@exponent.com.

MCCARTHY, THOMAS EDWARD, retired telecommunications executive; b. Sacramento, July 18, 1925; s. James Daniel and Lorene Margaret McCarthy; m. Joyce Elaine Reilly, June 28, 1952 (dec. Nov. 1987); children: Thomas E. Jr., Sharon E., Lisa A. McCarthy Harding; m. Gloria Adair Radford, Dec. 30, 1989. BS in Journalism with distinction, Northwestern U., 1950. Cert. Pub. Rels. Soc. Am. Reporter UP, San Francisco, 1951-54, Wall St. Jour., N.Y.C., 1954-56; pub. rels. project mgr. Sylvania Electric, N.Y.C., 1956-62; mgr. pub. info. GTE Corp., N.Y.C., 1962-72, dir. pub. info. Stamford, Conn., 1972-80, v.p. pub. affairs, 1980-86; ret., 1986. Cons. in field. Author: The History of GTE Corp., 1990 (Assn. Bus. Comms. award 1991), Irish Jubilee, 1997. With USAAC, 1943-46. Mem. Sigma Delta Chi, Kappa Tau Alpha, Zeta Psi. Roman Catholic. Avocations: reading, writing, travel, walking, history. Home: 9885 Mill Station Rd Sebastopol CA 95472-9662

MCCARTHY, THOMAS JAMES, JR., lawyer; b. Pulaski, Va., Nov. 24, 1943; s. Thomas James and Jane (Osborne) McC.; m. Sally Stockdale, July 25, 1987. BA in Econs., Washington and Lee U., 1967; JD, U. Va., 1970. Bar: Va. 1970, U.S. Dist. Ct. (we. dist.) Va. 1974, U.S. Supreme Ct. 2000. Assoc. Gilmer, Sadler, Ingram Sutherland & Hutton, Pulaski, 1970-75, ptnr., 1975—; county atty. Pulaski County, Pulaski, 1983—. Adminstrv. hearings officer Commonwealth of Va., 1983—; commr. of accts. Pulaski County, 1989—. Bd. dirs. New River C.C., 1980-88, 96-2004, vice-chair, 1981-88, 2000-02, chair 2002-2004, found. bd., 1989-91, 2004-. Col. JAGC, U.S. Army Res., ret., 1997. Decorated Legion of Merit, Meritorious Svc. medal, Army Commendation medal. Mem. Va. Bar Assn., 27th Jud. Cir. Bar Assn. (pres. 1978-81), Pulaski County Bar Assn.; fellow Va. Law Found., Sigma Chi, Phi Alpha Delta. Democrat. Episcopalian. Home: PO Box 818 Pulaski VA 24301-0818 Office: Gilmer Sadler et al 65 E Main St Pulaski VA 24301-5013

MCCARTHY, THOMAS STEPHEN, manufacturing executive; s. John Charles and Jean M. McCarthy; m. Michele Lee McCarthy, May 9, 1993. B, Northeastern U., 1986. Cert. EMT N.H. Mng. dir. New Eng. Arms Co., Kittery Point, Maine, 1988—2000; gen. mgr. ops. W. A. Tompkins Co. Inc., Hathorne, Mass., 2000—. Fundraiser Rep. Nat. Com., Portsmouth, 1990—2000; active mem. N.H. Rep. Party, Concord, 1995—2003; bd. dirs. Nat. Shooting Sports Found., Newtown, Conn., 1995—2000. Mem.: Minuteman Sportsman's Assn. (assoc.). Republican. Roman Catholic. Avocations: hunting, travel. Home: 169 Lafayette Rd Portsmouth NH 03801 Office: W A Tompkins Co Inc 598 Maple St Hathorne MA 01937 E-mail: steve@watompkins.com.

MCCARTHY, VINCENT PAUL, lawyer; b. Boston, Sept. 25, 1940; s. John Patrick and Marion (Buckley) McC.; children: Vincent, Sybil, Hope. AB, Boston Coll., 1962; JD, Harvard U., 1965. Bar: Mass. 1965. Ptnr. Hale and Dorr LLP, Boston, 1965—; sr. ptnr. Hale and Dorr, Boston, 1976—. Bd. dirs., sec. Robert F. Kennedy Action Corps, Inc.; bd. dirs. Boston Alcohol Detoxification Project, Inc.; mem. Mass. Gov.'s Adv. Coun. on Alcoholism, Boston, 1984-94, Gov.'s Jud. Nominating Com., 1991—; chmn. Mass. Housing Partnership Fund, 1991—; past chmn. Boston Ctr. for Arts; mem. adv. coun. Harvard Internat. AIDS Inst.; trustee, sec. Franklin Square House; past pres. Mass. Assn. for Mental Health; bd. dirs., past sec.-treas. Human Rights Campaign Found.; chmn. Gov.'s Commn. on Gay and Lesbian Youth, 2001—. Recipient Vols. of Am. Outstanding Svc. award, 1989. Mem. ABA (Pro Bono Publico award 1987), Mass. Bar Assn., Boston Bar Assn. (mem. jud. nominating com. 1991-99, Pub. Svc. award 1995). Office Phone: 617-526-6933. E-mail: vincent.mccarthy@wilmwehale.com.

MC CARTHY, WALTER JOHN, JR., retired utility executive; b. N.Y.C., Apr. 20, 1925; s. Walter John and Irene (Trumbl) McC.; m. Linda Lyon, May 6, 1988; children by previous marriage: Walter, David, Sharon, James, William. B.M.E., Cornell U., 1949; grad., Oak Ridge Sch. Reactor Tech., 1952; D.Eng. (hon.), Lawrence Inst. Tech., 1981; D.Sc. (hon.), Eastern Mich. U., 1983; LHD, Wayne State U., 1984; LLD, Alma (Mich.) Coll., 1985. Engr. Public Service Electric & Gas Co., Newark, 1949-56; sect. head Atomic Power Devel. Assos., Detroit, 1956-61; gen. mgr. Power Reactor Devel. Co., Detroit, 1961-68; with Detroit Edison Co., 1968-90, exec. v.p. ops., 1975-77, exec. v.p. divs., 1977-79, pres., chief operating officer, 1979-81, chmn., chief exec. officer, 1981-90. Bd. dirs. Energy Conversion Devices Inc. Author papers in field. Past chmn., bd. dirs. Inst. Nuclear Power Ops.; past pres. Monterey County Symphony Orch. Fellow Am. Nuc. Soc., Engring. Soc. Detroit; mem. ASME, NAE. Methodist.

MCCARTHY, WILLIAM ROBERT, minister; b. Tacoma, Nov. 17, 1941; s. Denward Sylvester and Florence Elizabeth (Lohan) McC.; m. Bernice Bigler, Apr. 22, 1962; children: Brian Edward Earl, Sean David. BS, Oreg. State U., 1966; MDiv, Nashotah House, 1975. Ordained deacon Episcopal Ch., 1975, priest, 1975. Curate St. Michael's Ch., Barrington, Ill., 1975-77; vicar St. Anselm's Ch., Park Ridge, Ill., 1977-81; rector Christ Ch. Parish, Waukegan, Ill., 1981-89, Ch. of Good Samaritan, Corvallis, Oreg., 1989—. Diocesan cursillo officer Diocese Chgo., 1975—85; spiritual dir. Ecumenical Cursillo Cmty., Chgo., 1977—83; mem. steering com. Happenings in Christianity, Chgo., 1978—80; chmn. Bishop's Adv. Commn. on Renewal & Evangelism, Chgo., 1983—85; mem. diocesan coun. Diocese of Oreg., 1991—93, 2000—02; bd. dir. Oreg. Episcopal Clergy Assn., pres., 2003—; standing com. Diocese of Oreg., 1994—97; bd. dir. Intercmty. HealthNetwork, 1994—. Founder, exec. dir. Share/Food Waukegan Area, 1985—89; bd. dirs. YMCA of Lake County, 1985—89; trustee Good Samaritan Reg. Med. Ctr., Corvallis, 1989—; founding mem. Samaritan Health Svc., 1997—, vice chair, 1997—2001; chmn. bd. dirs. Samaritan Health Svcs., 2001—03, past chair, 2003—; bd. mem. Waukegan Crime Stoppers, 1982—85; founder, chmn. FOCUS 90 Com. for Downtown Devel., 1988—89; charter bd. dirs. Waukegan Downtown Assn., 1983—89, v.p., 1986—87, pres., 1987—88. With USNR, 1962—65. Mem. Assn. for Psychol. Type, Rotary, Masons, Phi Sigma Kappa. Office: Ch of the Good Samaritan 333 NW 35th St Corvallis OR 97330-4908 Office Phone: 541-757-6647. E-mail: rector@goodsamchurch.com., BernieBill@comcast.net.

MCCARTHY-ALLEN, MARY FRANCES, medical foundation administrator, not-for-profit fundraiser, consultant; b. Washington, Apr. 16, 1937; d. Joseph Francis and Frances (Oddi) McGowan; m. Charles M. Sappenfield, Dec. 14, 1963 (div. June 1990); children: Charles Ross, Sarah Kathleen; m. Daniel Fendrich McCarthy, Jr., Aug. 25, 1990 (dec. Apr. 1999); m. Cary Walter Allen, Nov. 30, 2002. BA, Trinity Coll., Washington, 1958; cert. in bus. adminstrn., Harvard U.-Radcliffe Coll., 1959; MA, Ball State U., Muncie, Ind., 1984. Systems engr. IBM, Cambridge, Mass., 1959-61; editl. asst. Kiplinger Washington Editors, 1961-63; feature writer pub. info. dept. Ball State U., 1984-85, coll. editor Coll. Bus., 1985-86, coord. alumni and devel.,

1986-88, dir. major gift clubs and donor rels., 1988-90; dir. devel. Sweet Briar (Va.) Coll., 1990-91; adminstr. St. Mary's Hosp. and Med. Ctr. Found., Grand Junction, Colo., 1991—. Editor: A History of Maxon Corporation, 1986, Managing Change, 1986, Indiana's Investment Banker, 1987; assoc. editor Mid-Am. Jour. Bus., 1985-86. Participant Leadership Lynchburg, 1990, Jr. League; regional dir. IX Assn. for Healthcare Philanthropy, 1996—98, found. bd., 1997—; bd. dirs. Sr. Companions, Grand Junction, 1992—; mem. steering com. Mesa County Health Cmtys., 1992—; bd. dirs. Grand Junction Musical Arts, 1997—; trustee Women's Found. of Colo., 2000—; bd. dirs. Grand Valley Hospice, 2002—; mem. Mesa County Health Assessment, 1994—. Recipient Golden Broom award Muncie Clean City, 1989; svc. of distinction award Ball State U. Coll. Bus., 1990. Mem. Coun. for Advancement and Support of Edn., Assn. of Healthcare Philanthropy (regional 9 cabinet 1992—, bd. dirs. 1997—), Nat. Soc. Fundraising Execs. (cert., Colo. chpt. bd. dirs. 1994—), Rotary. Republican. Avocations: biking, walking, cross country skiing, gardening.

MCCARTIN, BRIAN JAMES, mathematician, educator; b. Providence, Aug. 26, 1951; s. James Dominic and Dorothy Frances (Kelly) McC.; 1 child, Sean Colin. BS in Applied Math. with highest distinc., U. R.I., 1976, MS in Applied Math., 1977; PhD in Applied Math., NYU, 1981; BMus in Music Theory summa cum laude, U. Hartford, 1994. Sr. rsch. mathematician United Technologies Corp., East Hartford, Conn., 1977-89; prof. computer sci. Rensselaer Poly. Inst., Hartford, 1989-92; prof. applied math. Kettering U., Flint, Mich., 1993—. Vis. lectr. high schs., 1997—. Contbr. articles to profl. jours., chpts. to books. Named Disting. Vis. Prof., N.J. Inst. Tech., 1997. Mem. Math. Assn. Am. (dept. liaison, Mich. sect. Disting. Tchg. award 2004), Soc. Indsl. and Applied Math. (founder spl. interest group on numerical methods for partial differentiation equations Great Lakes sect. 1997-98, sec. 1998-2000, v.p. 2000-02), Kappa Mu Epsilon (faculty advisor 1997-98), Pi Kappa Lambda, Phi Kappa Phi, Alpha Chi, Pi Mu Epsilon (Kettering U. Outstanding Rschr. award 2000, Kettering U. Outstanding Tchg. award 2001). Avocation: classical pianist. Home: 2310 Crestbrook Ln Flint MI 48507-2209 Office: Kettering Univ Applied Math 1700 W 3d Ave Flint MI 48504-4832 E-mail: bmccarti@kettering.edu.

MCCARTIN, JOSEPH ANTHONY, historian, educator; b. Chelsea, Mass., May 12, 1959; s. Joseph Vincent and Marybeth (Maier) McCartin; m. Diane Mary Reis, Aug. 3, 1996; children: Mara Claire, Elisa Reis. AB, Coll. Holy Cross, 1981; MA, SUNY-Binghamton, 1985, PhD, 1990. Lectr. U. R.I., Kingston, 1990—92; asst. prof., assoc. prof. SUNY-Genesco, 1992—99; assoc. prof. Georgetown U., Washington, 1999—. Author: Labor's Great War, 1997 (Taft prize, 1999). Fellow, NEH, 1993, 2002; Charles Warren fellow, Harvard U., 2003. Democrat. Roman Catholic. Office: Georgetown Univ History Dept 3700 O St NW Washington DC 20057

MCCARTIN, THOMAS JOSEPH, advertising executive; b. Rockville Centre, N.Y., Sept. 6, 1957; s. John Francis and Agnes (Farrell) McC.; m. Louise Ann Cuccurullo, Mar. 10, 1990; children; Thomas Joseph, Sean Cody. BS in Mktg., N.Y. Inst. Tech., 1979. Bus. devel. officer Mfrs. Hanover Trust, N.Y.C., 1981-83; asst. sec. Dollar Dry Dock Savs. Bank, N.Y.C., 1983-84; sr. v.p. IMC Mktg. Group, N.Y.C., 1984-86; pres. McCartin & Kunin, Inc., N.Y.C., 1986-95, M&K West, Phoenix, 1993-95; exec. v.p. Lipman, Richmond, Greene Advt., N.Y.C., 1995—2000; pres. Warren, Kremer, Paino, N.Y.C., 2001—. Bd. dirs. Delta Dental of N.Y., N.Y.C. Mem. NRA, Distributive Edn. Clubs Am. (life), Direct Mktg. Assn., Bus. Coun. N.Y. State, Sierra Club, Vet. Corps of Arty. Conservative. Roman Catholic. Avocations: hunting, camping. Office: Warren Kremer Paino 2 Park Ave New York NY 10016 E-mail: tmccartin@wkpadv.com.

MCCARTNEY, CHAD EDWARD, music educator; b. Gettysburg, Pa., June 22, 1972; s. Edward Berlin and Marjorie Ann McCartney; m. Andrea Michelle Mickey, Oct. 9, 1999. BS in Music Edn., Pa. State U., 2000, MS in Music Edn., 2004. Cert. tchr. Pa. Tchr. Littlestown (Pa.) Bands, 1995—96; band dir. Upper Dauphin Area Schs., Elizabethville, Pa., 1996. Performer Fink's Constant, Harrisburg, Pa., performer, composer, 2000—. Composer: (songs) I Can't Complain, 2001, One Day, 2002, Seuss, 2002. Mem.: Nat. Judges Assn. (judge 1999—, individual analysis music judge), Music Educators Nat. Conf. (sec. 1997—99), Pa. Music Educators Assn., Masons (life). Office: Upper Dauphin Area High School 220 North Church Street Elizabethville PA 17023 Home: 228 Shell St Harrisburg PA 17109-4731 Personal E-mail: mccartneychad@aol.com.

MCCARTNEY, CHARLES PRICE, retired obstetrician-gynecologist; b. Barnesville, Ohio, Aug. 18, 1912; s. Jesse Thomas and Carrie (Price) McC.; m. Phyllis Helen Graybill, Sept. 27, 1940; children— Marilyn B., Ann E. BS, U. Chgo., 1942, MD, 1943. Diplomate: Am. Bd. Obstetricians and Gynecologists. Intern U. Chgo. Clinics, 1943-44, resident, 1947-50; mem. faculty U. Chgo. Med. Sch., 1950 71, prof. obstetrics and gynecology, 1960-71, Mary Campeau Ryerson prof., 1967-71; clin. prof. obstetrics and gynecology U. Ill., 1971-80, prof. emeritus, 1980—. Attending gynecologist and obstetrician Chgo. Lying-In Hosp., 1950— Mem. Cook County Com. Maternal Welfare, 1965— . Served to maj., M.C. AUS, 1944-46. Fellow Am. Gynecol. Soc.; mem. Am. Gynecol. and Obstetrical Soc., Chgo. Gynecol. Soc. (pres. 1967), Chgo. Med. Soc. (councillor 1960—, pres. 1973, chmn. bd. trustees 1973), Am. Coll. Obstetricians and Gynecologists (chmn. Ill. sect. 1965—), Cen. Assn. Obstetricians and Gynecologists. Home: 200 Wyndemere Cir W-218 Wheaton IL 60187-2445

MCCARTNEY, DAN G. theology studies educator, musician; b. Clarksburg, W. Va., Jan. 27, 1950; s. James M. and Janet S. McCartney; m. Helen Kathleen Capcara, June 5, 1971; children: Christopher J., Cara E. BFA in Music Performance, Carnegie-Mellon U., 1971; MDiv, Gordon-Conwell Theol Sem., South Hamilton, Mass., 1974; ThM, Westminster Theol. Sem., Glenside, Pa., 1977, PhD, 1989. Ordination Presbyn. Ch. in Am., 1987. Lectr. in bible Manna Bible Inst., Phila., 1978—81; lectr. in Greek Westminster Sem., Glenside, Pa., 1983—86, adj. prof., 1986—87, asst. prof., 1987—92, assoc. prof., 1992—99, prof., 1999—. Bd. trustees Phila. Montgomery Christian Acad., Erdenheim, Pa., 1989—94. Author: Let the Reader Understand, 1993, Why Does it Have To Hurt, 1996; musician: (CD recording) Praise God in His Sanctuary, 2001. Fellow: Inst. for Biblical Rsch.; mem.: Evangelical Theol. Soc., Soc. for Biblical Lit. Avocations: photography, horn playing, genealogy. Home: 22 Elliot Ave Willow Grove PA 19090 Office: Westminster Theol Sem 2960 W Ch Rd Glenside PA 19038

MCCARTNEY, FRANK HOWARD, III, lawyer; b. Maysville, Ky., Sept. 30, 1949; s. Frank Howard and Gladys E. McCartney; m. Marsha Jane McNeill, Aug. 14, 1971; children: Rachael Evans, Laura Anne. BA, U. Ky., 1971, JD, 1973. Bar: Ky. 1974, U.S. Dist. Ct. (ea. dist.) Ky. 1975, U.S. Ct. Appeals (6th cir.) 1983, U.S. Supreme Ct. 1994. Ptnr. Suit, McCartney & Price, PLLC, Flemingsburg, Ky., 1974—. Atty. County of Fleming, Flemingsburg, 1977-90. Contbg. author: Kentucky Health Law Handbook, also 2d and 3d edits; mem. staff Ky. Law Jour., 1973-74 (Cite and Substance award 1974). Mem. Ky. Child Support Commn., 1987-91; bd. dirs. Lime Stone YMCA, 1991-99, pres., 1997-99. Recipient Disting. Svc. award Ky. Atty. Gen., 4th Ann. Kentuckians Involved with Dependent Support award. Mem. ABA (health law sect.), Am. Health Lawyer Assn., Am. Acad. Hosp. Attys., Nat. Dist. Attys. Assn., Ky. Bar Assn., Ky. Acad. Hosp. Attys. (pres. 1986-87, co-editor Jour., headnote editor 1980-90), Ky. County Attys. Assn. (bd. dirs. 1977-90), Flemingsburg Jaycees (State Speak-up award 1975, past pres.), Lions, Order of Coif. Democrat. Office: Suit McCartney & Price 207 Court Sq Flemingsburg KY 41041-1364 Office Phone: 606-849-2338.

MCCARTNEY, JAMES HAROLD, newspaper columnist, journalist, educator; b. St. Paul, July 25, 1925; s. Floyd Allen and Cora Jeanette (Heilig) McC.; m. Jule Ann Graham, Jan. 19, 1952 (div. 1983); children: Robert, Sharon; m. Molly Kathleen Bowers, Sept. 8, 1984. BA, Mich. State U., 1949; MSJ, Northwestern U., 1951. Reporter South Bend (Ind.) Tribune, 1949-50, Chgo. Daily News, 1952-60, Washington corr., 1960-66, city editor, 1966-68; Washington corr. Knight-Ridder Newspapers, Miami, Fla., 1968-90, columnist, 1985-96, Bradenton (Fla.) Herald, 2000—; 1990lectr. Georgetown U., 1990—2003. With U.S. Army, 1943-45, ETO. Mem. Nat. Press Club, Gridiron Club (pres. 1987). Avocation: golf. Home: 600 Manatee Ave W Unit 106 Holmes Beach FL 34217

MC CARTNEY, RALPH FARNHAM, lawyer; b. Charles City, Iowa, Dec. 11, 1924; s. Ralph C. and Helen (Farnham) McC.; m. Rhoda Mae Huxsol, June 25, 1950; children: Ralph, Julia, David. JD, U. Mich., 1950; B. Sci., Iowa State U., 1972. Bar: Iowa 1950. Mem. firm Miller, Heuber & Miller, Des Moines, 1950-52, Frye & McCartney, Charles City, 1952-73, McCartney & Erb, Charles City, 1973-78; judge Dist. Ct. Iowa, Charles City, 1978-87; chief judge 2d Judicial Dist., 1987-92; sr. judge Ct. Appeals, 1992—. Mem. jud. coordinating com. Iowa Supreme Ct. Chmn. Supreme Ct. Adv. Com. on Adminstrn. of Clks. Offices; mem. Iowa Ho. of Reps., 1967-70, majority floor leader, 1969-70; mem. Iowa Senate, 1973-74. Bd. regents U. Iowa, Iowa State U., U. No. Iowa, Iowa Sch. for Deaf, Iowa Braille and Sight Saving Sch. Served with AUS, 1942-45. Mem. Iowa Judges Assn. Home: 1828 Cedar View Dr Charles City IA 50616-9129

MCCARTNEY, ROBERT CHARLES, retired lawyer; b. Pitts., May 3, 1934; s. Nathaniel Hugh and Esther Mary (Smith) McC.; m. Janet Carolyn Moore, June 16, 1956; children: Ronald K., Sharon S., Carole J. AB, Princeton U., 1956; JD, Harvard U., 1959. Bar: D.C. 1959, Pa. 1960, U.S. Dist. Ct. (we. dist.) Pa. 1960, U.S. Ct. Appeals (3d dist.) 1960, U.S. Supreme Ct. 1966. Assoc. Eckert Seamans Cherin & Mellott, LLC, Pitts., 1959—64, ptnr., 1965—93, mem. exec. com., 1991—93, of counsel, 1993—. Sec., gen. counsel Ryan Homes, Inc., 1969-93; bd. dirs. United Meth. Found. of Western Pa., 1971— v.p., 1981-85, chmn., 1985-86; sec., gen. counsel Rimoldi of Am., Inc., 1989-99. Solicitor North Pitts. Cmty. Devel. Corp., 1968-76, alt. dir., 1968-80; mem. McCandless Twp. Govt. Study Commn., 1973-74, Princeton U. Leadership Devel. Coun., 2002—; solicitor, asst. sec. McCandless Indsl. Devel. Authority, 1972-98; exec. com. Princeton U. Alumni Coun., 1966-70, 76-85, vice-chmn., 1981-83, chmn., 1983-85, co-chair spl. com. 250th Anniversary Princeton U., 1994-97, nat chmn. class planned giving program, 2002—, mem. steardship adv. coun., 2004—; trustee Otterbein Coll., 1975-83, Pa. S.W. Assn., 1992-96, Pitts. Cultural Trust, 1992-99; chmn. conf.-wide endowment program United Meth. Conf. We. Pa., 1985-87; bd. dirs. Pitts. Civic Light Opera Assn., 1984 , v.p., 1987-92, pres., 1992-99; dir. The Ireland Inst. Pitts., 1991—, vice-chmn., 1996—; mem. No. Ireland Partnership, 1991—; bd. dirs. Pitts. Concert Chorale, 1997-2003, Pitts. Irish and Classical Theater, 2000—. Princeton fellow Harvard U., 1956-59. Mem. Princeton U. Alumni Assn. West Pa. (pres. 1976-78), Duquesne Club, Nassau Club. Republican. Home: 9843 Woodland Rd N Pittsburgh PA 15237-4347 Office: Eckert Seamans 600 Grant St Ste 44th Fl Pittsburgh PA 15219-2703

MCCARTOR, SHEILA SMITH, secondary school educator; b. Raymondville, Tex., May 4, 1941; d. M.D. Smith and Mae (Sansom) Jessie; m. Gary Don McCartor, July 20, 1999; m. Ira Yale Levanthal, Aug. 5, 1966; 1 child, Adam Yale. BS, N. Tex. State U., 1963, MEd, 1965; postgrad., Nova U., 1972, MIT, 1979. Elem. tchr. Grapevine (Tex.) Pub. Schs., 1963—65; tchr., team leader Lamplighter Sch., Dallas, 1965—. Task force for diversity Lamplighter Sch., 2002, mem. steering com., computer staff, 1979—84, sci. com., 1990—, chair, sci. com., 1993—94; presenter Internat. Conf. Tech. in Edn., U. London, 1994; pub. Internat. Conf. Tech. in Edn., 1993—94; staff Ind. Sch. Assn. of S.W. Beginning Tchr. Inst., 1993—94; presenter Internat. Coop. Learning Conf., Columbus, Ohio, 1996; pub. Dallas Opera Instrl. Series. Staff mem. Episc. Sch. Spirituality, Dallas, 1983, dir., 1989—. Mem.: Women of St. Francis (v.p. Dallas 1983, mem. task force diversity 2002). Office: Lamplighter Sch 11611 Inwood Rd Dallas TX 75229-3098

MCCARTY, DARREN, professional hockey player; b. British Columbia, Canada, Apr. 1, 1972; With Detroit Red Wings, 1993—. Office: Detroit Red Wings Joe Louis Arena 600 Civic Center Detroit MI 48226

MCCARTY, DORAN CHESTER, religious organization administrator; b. Bolivar, Mo., Feb. 3, 1931; s. Bartie Lee and Donta Marian (Russell) McC.; m. Gloria Jean Laffoon, June 14, 1952; children: Gaye, Risë, Marletta, Leslie. AA, Southwest Bapt. Coll., 1950; AB, William Jewell Coll., 1952; BD, So. Bapt. Theol. Sem, 1956, PhD, 1963. Pastor 1st Bapt. Ch., Switz City, Ind., 1956-62, Pleasant Hill, Mo., 1962-65, Susquehanna Bapt. Ch., Independence, Mo., 1965-67; prof. Midwestern Bapt. Theol. Sem., Kansas City, Mo., 1967-81, Golden Gate Bapt. Theol. Sem., Mill Valley, Calif., 1981-87; coord. Northeastern Bapt. Sch. Ministry, N.Y.C., 1987-94; exec. dir. Sem. Ext., Nashville, 1988-94; pres. McCarty Svcs., Nashville, 1994—. Cons. Bapt. Home Mission Bd., 1981—; assoc. dean So. Bapt. Theol. Sem., Louisville, 1989; pres. McCarty Svcs., St. Augustine. Author: Rightly Dividing trhe Word, 1973, Teilhard de Chardin, 1976, The Supervision of Ministry Students, 1978, The Supervision of Mission Personnel, 1983, The Inner Heart of Ministry, 1985, Working With People, 1987, Leading the Small Church, 1991, Supervision: Developing and Directing People on Mission, 1994, Making the Most of Your Time, 1996, Making the Most of Conflict, 1997, Making the Most of Change, 1998, Making the Most if Empowerment, 1999, Making the Most of Coping, 2000, Making the Most of Pastoral Leadership, 2002, Hallowed Be Thy Name, 2002; editor: Key Resources, 5 vols., Broadman Leadership Series, 16 vols., The Practice of Ministry: A Sourcebook, 1995. Recipient Life Service award Southwest Bapt. U., Bolivar, 1973, William Jewell Coll. Achievement citation, 1987. Mem. Assn. for Theol. Field Edn. (chairperson 1979-81), Inst. Theol. Reflection (exec. dir. 1978-86), Fellowship In Service Guidance Dirs. (pres. 1986-87, Lewis Newman award 1988). Home: 116 Del Lago Ln Saint Augustine FL 32080 *As I have experienced life, grace affords priviledge, priviledge calls forth duty, duty depends on transcendence, and transcendence provides enrichment.*

MCCARTY, FREDERICK BRIGGS, electrical engineer, consultant; b. Dilley, Tex., Aug. 11, 1926; s. John Frederick Briggs and Olive Ruth (Snell) Briggs McCarty; m. Doris Mary Cox, May 3, 1950 (div. 1970); children: Mark Frederick, David Lambuth, Jackson Clare; m. Nina Lucile Butman, Aug. 17, 1973. BSEE, U. Tex., 1949. Registered profl. engr., Calif. Design engr. GE, Schenectady, N.Y., 1949-51; sr. design engr. Convair, Ft. Worth, 1951-55; sr. engr. Aerojet Gen., Azusa, Calif., 1955-61; sr. engring. specialist Garrett Corp., Torrance, Calif., 1961-91; v.p., founder Patio Pacific, Inc., Torrance, 1973-84; owner, operator Textiger Co., Torrance, 1980-91; cons., 1991—. Author computer software, Textiger word processor, Tiger Tools, Big Mag and Roundrot generator synthesizers. Served with USNR, 1944—46, PTO. Mem.: IEEE (sr.), Eta Kappa Nu, Tau Beta Pi. Democrat. Achievements include patents in field; design of superconducting acyclic motor for USN and high speed elec. machines for aerospace and transp. Home and Office: 1366 Stonewood Ct San Pedro CA 90732-1550

MCCARTY, JOHN ALBERT, advertising and marketing educator, consultant; b. Nashville, May 28, 1951; s. Justin Hunter and Emily Lavender (Lacy) McC. BA, Vanderbilt U., 1973; MA, U. Ill., 1979, PhD, 1986; MA, U. Chgo., 1981. Rsch. assoc. Needham Harper Worldwide Advt., Chgo., 1983-85; asst. prof. dept. advt. and bus. adminstrn. U. Ill., Urbana, 1986-93; asst. prof. dept. mktg. Am. U., Washington, 1993—98, George Mason U., Fairfax, Va., 1998—2001; asst. prof. sch. bus. The Coll. of N.J., Ewing, NJ, 2001—. Vis. lectr. dept. advt. U. Ill., 1985-86. Contbr. chpts. in books: Advances in Non Profit Marketing, 1990, Global and Multi-National Advertising, 1994, Marketing and Consumer Research in the Public Interest, 1996, Integrated Communication: Synergy of Persuasive Voices, 1996, Values, Lifestyles and Psychographics, 1997, The Psychology of Entertainment Media, 2003, also articles to profl. jours.; reviewer Jour. of Advt., 1988—. Lt. (j.g.) USN, 1973-76. Mem. Am. Mktg. Assn. (workshop coord. 1987-88), Assn. for Consumer Rsch., Am. Acad. Advt., Am. Assn. Pub. Opinion Rsch. Office: The College of New Jersey 2000 Pennington Rd Ewing NJ 08628 E-mail: mccarty@tcnj.edu.

MCCARTY, JUDY, councilman; b. June 4, 1940; m. Curt McCarty; 2 children. BS, Ind. U. Aide to Assemblyman Larry Stirling; del. UN Program for Local Environ. Initiatives, White House Conf. on Libr. and Info. Svcs.; city councilwoman 7th Dist., San Diego, 1985—. Chair select com. on govt. effeciency, fiscal reform, Mission Traisl Regional Pk. Task Force, natural resources, culture com., city rep. Pk. and Recreation Bd., San Diego Processing Corp., alt. rep. Met. Transit Devel. Bd., San Diego City Coun. Pres. Navajo Cmty. Recipient Local Legislator of Yr. award, Kate Sessions award Industry Environ. Assn. Methodist. Office: City San Diego 202 C St Fl 10 San Diego CA 92101-3860

MCCARTY, MACLYN, medical scientist; b. South Bend, Ind., June 9, 1911; s. Earl Hauser and Hazel Dell (Beagle) McC.; m. Anita Alleyne Davies, June 20, 1934 (div. 1966); children: Maclyn, Richard E., Dale, Colin; m. Marjorie Steiner, Sept. 3, 1966. AB, Stanford U., 1933; MD, Johns Hopkins U., 1937; ScD (hon.), Columbia U., 1976, U. Fla., 1977, Rockefeller U., 1982, Med. Coll. Ohio, 1985, Emory U., 1987, Wittenberg U., 1989; MD (hon.), U. Cologne, Germany, 1988; LHD (hon.), Mount Sinai Sch. of Medicine, 1995; DMS (hon.), Thomas Jefferson U., 1999; ScD (hon.), Harvard U., 2000; LHD (hon.), Johns Hopkins U., 2001. House officer, asst. resident physician Johns Hopkins Hosp., 1937-40; assoc. Rockefeller Inst., 1946-50, prof., 1957-81, v.p., 1965-78, physician in chief to hosp., 1961-74, prof. emeritus, 1981—. Cons. USPHS, NIH. Author: The Transforming Principle: Discovering That Genes are Made of DNA, 1985 Mem. distbn. com. N.Y. Cmty. Trust, 1966-74; chmn. Health Rsch. Coun. City N.Y., 1972-75; Mem. bd. trustees Helen Hay Whitney Found; chmn. bd. dirs. Pub. Health Rsch. Inst. of N.Y., 1985-92. Served with Naval Med. Rsch. Unit, Rockefeller Hosp. USNR, 1942-46. Fellow medicine N.Y. U. Coll. Medicine, 1940-41; NRC fellow med. scis. Rockefeller Inst., 1941-42; recipient Eli Lilly award in bacteriology and immunology, 1946, 1st Waterford Biomed. Rsch. award, 1977, Wolf Found. prize in medicine, Israel, 1990, Lasker Spl. Pub. Health award, 1994, David Rockefeller award, 2003, Lifetime Achievement award Nature Botech. and Miami U., 2004. Mem. Am. Soc. for Clin. Investigation, Am. Assn. Immunologists, Soc. Am. Bacteriologists, Soc. for Exptl. Biology and Medicine (pres. 1973-75), Harvey Soc. (sec. 1947-50, pres. 1971-72), N.Y. Acad. Medicine (Acad. medal 1979, John Stearns award for lifetime achievement in medicine 1993), Assn. Am. Physicians (Kober medal 1989), Nat. Acad. Scis. (Kovalenko medal 1988), Am. Acad. Arts and Scis., N.Y. Heart Assn. (1st v.p. 1967, pres. 1969-71), Am. Philos. Soc. Home: 400 E 56th St New York NY 10022-4147 Office: Rockefeller U 66th St and York Ave New York NY 10021

MCCARTY, PERRY LEE, civil and environmental engineering educator; b. Grosse Pointe, Mich., Oct. 29, 1931; m. Martha Davis Collins, Sept. 5, 1953; children: Perry Lee, Cara L., Susan A., Kathleen R. BSCE, Wayne State U., 1953; MS in San. Engring., MIT, 1957, ScD, 1959; DEng (hon.), Colo. Sch. Mines, 1992. Field engr. Edwin Orr Co., Dearborn, Mich., 1951-52; engr. Pate & Hirn, Detroit, 1952-53; field engr. Hubbell, Roth & Clark, Detroit, 1953; instr. civil engring. Wayne State U., 1953-54; field engr. George Jerome & Co., Detroit, 1954; engr. Civil Engrs., Inc., Detroit, 1956; assoc. Rolf Eliassen Assocs., Winchester, Mass., 1958-61; asst. prof. san. engring. MIT, 1958-62; faculty Stanford (Calif.) U., 1962—, prof. civil engring., 1967-75, Silas H. Palmer prof., 1975-99, Silas H. Palmer prof. emeritus, 1999—, chmn. dept. civil engring., 1980-85. Chmn. Gordon Rsch. Conf. Environ. Scis., 1972; vice chmn. environ. studies bd. NRC-NAS, 1976-80, mem. com. on phys. scis., math. and resources, 1985-88, bd. on radioactive waste mgmt., 1989-96, mem. com. geoscis., environment, resources, 1994-97. Co-author: Chemistry for Environmental Engineering and Science, 5th edit., 2003, Environmental Biotechnology Principles and Applications, 2001. Served with AUS, 1954-56. Recipient Tyler Prize for Environ. Achievement, 1992, Clarke Prize Outstanding Achievement Water Sci. and Tech., 1997; NSF faculty fellow, 1968-69. Fellow AAAS, Am. Acad. Microbiology, Am. Acad. Arts and Scis.; mem. ASCE (Walter L. Huber Rsch. prize 1964, Simon W. Freese Environ. Engring. award 1979, James R. Croes medal 1995), NAE, Am. Water Works Assn. (hon., life, chmn. water quality divsn. 1972-73, trustee rsch. divsn. 1980-85, Best Paper award 1985, A.P. Black Rsch. award 1989), Am. Soc. for Microbiology, Water Environment Fedn. (hon. 1989, Harrison P. Eddy award 1962, 77, Thomas Camp award 1975), Assn. Environ. Engring. Sci. Profs. (Disting. Faculty award 1966, Oustanding Publ. award 1985, 88, 98, 2003, Founders award 1992), Am. Soc. Engring. Edn.(vice-chmn. environ. engring. divsn. 1968-69), Sigma Xi, Tau Beta Pi (fellow 1957-58). Home: 823 Sonoma Ter Stanford CA 94305-1024 Office: Stanford U Civil Environ Engring Dept Stanford CA 94305-4020 Office Phone: 650-723-4131. Business E-Mail: pmccarty@stanford.edu.

MCCARTY, RICHARD CHARLES, psychology educator, university dean; b. Portsmouth, Va., July 12, 1947; s. Constantine Ambrose and Helen Marie (Householder) McC.; m. Sheila Adair Miltier, July 15, 1965; children: Christopher Charles, Lorraine Marie, Ryan Lester, Patrick James. BS in Biology, Old Dominion U., 1970, MS in Zoology, 1972; PhD in Pathobiology, Johns Hopkins U., 1976. Rsch. assoc. NIMH, Bethesda, Md., 1976-78; asst. prof. U. Va., Charlottesville, 1978-84, assoc. prof., 1984-88, prof., 1988-2001, chair psychology, 1990-98, chair Coun. of Grad. Depts. Psychology, 1996-97; exec. dir. sci. directorate APA, Washington, 1998-2001; dean arts and sci. Vanderbilt U., Nashville, 2001—. Co-editor: Development of the Hypertensive Phenotype, vol. 19, Handbook of Hypertension, 1999; editor: Am. Psychologist, 2000—01. Lt. comdr. USPHS, 1976-78. Recipient Rsch. Scientist Devel. award NIMH, 1985-90; sr. fellow Nat. Heart Lung Blood Inst., NIH, 1984-85. Fellow AAAS, APA, Soc. Behavioral Medicine, Acad. Behavioral Med. Rsch., Am. Psychol. Soc., Am. Inst. Stress, Coun. for High Blood Pressure Rsch., AHA; mem. Internat. Soc. for Investigation of Stress (exec. bd. 1996-2001). Roman Catholic. Avocations: sports, gardening. Office: Office of the Dean Vanderbilt U Coll Arts and Sci 301 Kirkland Hall Nashville TN 37240

MCCARTY, ROBERT CLARKE, mathematician; b. Mountain View, Calif., Apr. 29, 1922; s. John Emmet and Eldora Lydia (Freeman) McC.; m. Netta Cassen, July 29, 1945 (div. Oct. 1968) 1 child, Stephanie Ann; m. Rita Ransier, July 29, 1969; children: Michael Wayne, Teresa Kay, Kathleen Gail. BA in Math., San Jose State U., 1950; MS in Math. and Statistics, U. Wash., 1957; PhD in Math., Pacific Western U., 1990. Staff mathematician Boeing Rsch. Labs., Seattle, 1952-59; rsch. mathematician Stanford Rsch. Inst., Menlo Park, Calif., 1959-70; pres., cons. McCarty and Assocs., Gilroy, Calif., 1976—; sr. staff scientist ESL-TRW Corp., Sunnyvale, Calif., 1984-87; prin. staff scientist ARGO Systems, Sunnyvale, 1987-93. Cons. in math., orchard mgmt.; sci. advisor to Congresswoman Zoe Lofgren, sci. com. US Congress, 1994—; rsch. proxy for Prof. A.S. Paulraj, Dept. Elec. Engring., Info. Scis., Stanford U., 1993-95; sr. rsch. mathematician Ares Corp., Arlington, Va., 1994-96. Contbr. articles to profl. jours. Lt. USCGR, 1941—52, ret. lt. USCGR-Ret 3, 1965—. Mem. Sigma Xi. Avocations: amateur radio, rifle and pistol marksmanship, swimming. Home and Office: 9425 Marcella Ave Gilroy CA 95020-9085

MCCARTY, SHIRLEY CAROLYN, aerospace executive; b. Minot, N.D., May 2, 1934; d. Harry and Cecelia Marie (Engene) Wolhowe; m. John Myron McCarty, Apr. 3, 1958. BS in Bus. Adminstrn., U. N.D., 1958. Mem. tech. staff Douglas Aircraft, El Segundo, Calif., 1960-62, The Aerospace Corp., El Segundo, 1962-72, mgr., 1972-73, dir., 1973-79, prin. dir., 1979-89; gen. mgr., 1989—. Mem. adv. council Calif. State U., Northridge, 1979—, chmn., 1984-86; mem. indsl. adv. bd. Purdue U. Soc. Women Engrs., West Lafayette, Ind., 1979-82, 1985—. Named Woman of Yr. The Aerospace Corp., 1976, Pres.'s award, 1987; recipient Spl. Judges Award for Leadership, Los Angeles YWCA, 1977, Sioux Alumni Award, U. N.D, 1982, Achievement award Los Angeles County Commn. for Women, 1987. Mem. IEEE, Assn. for Computing Machinery, Soc. Women Engrs., Bus. and Profl. Women (Woman of Achievement 1984, Golden Nike award 1985), Women in Bus.(corp. achievement award, 1987), Women in Computing (founding mem., bd. dirs.). Avocations: raising and training siberian huskies, travel, writing. Home: 357 Valley St El Segundo CA 90245-2932 Office: The Aerospace Corp 2350 E El Segundo Blvd El Segundo CA 90245-4691

MCCARTY, THOMAS JOSEPH, publishing company executive; b. Waltham, Mass., June 10, 1938; s. Raymond Anthony and Mary Agatha (Riley) McC; m. Colette Ann Koechley, Aug. 3, 1963; children: Matthew Thomas, Brendan James, Sarah Katherine. BA, Holy Cross Coll., 1960; cert.,

Harvard U., 1961. Various mgmt. positions Oxford U. Press, N.Y.C., 1960-71, mgr. ops., 1971-79, dir. distbn., 1980-81, v.p. distbn., 1982-84, v.p. distbn. and info. systems, 1985-88, sr. v.p., 1988-90; sr. v.p., gen. mgr. Oxford U. Press, Cary, N.C. ops., 1990-98, spl. cons. to pres., 1998-2000. Chmn., bd. advs. Carolina Pub. Inst. U. N.C., Chapel Hill, 1995-98. Trustee N.C. Symphony Found., v.p., 1998—; mem. adv. bd. Sch. Info. and L.S., U. N.C., Chapel Hill; mem. City of Cary Unified Devel. Ordinance Adv. Commn., 1999—; mem. bd. advisors Open Mind Publ. Group, 2000; mem. N.C. Mus. Art; bd. dirs. Shakti for Children Found., 1994—98, English Speaking Union of Research Triangle, pres., 1998—2002. Mem.: Exec. Svc. Corps., Fine Arts League Cary, Am. Mgmt. Assn., Svc. Corps Ret. Execs., Am. Assn. Pubs., U. N.C. Faculty Club (Chapel Hill), McGregor Downs Country Club (Cary). Personal E-mail: tjm2@mindspring.com.

MCCARTY, V.K. publisher, chaplain, librarian; b. Boston, June 26, 1948; d. Charles Osner and Dorothy June (McAlister) Long. BM, Mich. State U., 1969; MM, U. Louisville, 1972; cert. in theatre arts, U. London, 1972; intern in clin. pastoral edn., St. Luke's Roosevelt Hosp., 1989, resident in clin. pastoral edn., 1995; student, Congl. Devel. Inst. Tng., Dioceses of Newark, 2003. Advt. asst. Lansing (Mich.) State Jour., 1968-69; market rsch. cons. Sta. WKLO, Louisville, 1969-70; libr. Louisville Free Pub. Libr., 1970-72; v.p. assoc. pub. Gen. Media Inc., N.Y.C., 1979-2000; acquisitions libr. Gen. Theol. Sem. St. Mark's Libr., N.Y.C., 2000—; part-time acquisitions libr. United Theol. Sem. Burke Libr., N.Y.C., 2001—02; dir. Christian Formation, St. Paul's Ch., Chatham, NJ, 2002—03. Bd. dirs. B.F.T., Inc., N.Y.C. Dance editor Saturday Review Mag. Online, 1993-95. Master of ceremonies St. Ignatius of Antioch, N.Y.C., 1984-98; chaplaincy coord. St. Luke's Roosevelt Hosp., N.Y.C. Mem. N.Y. Liturgical Music Found. (steering com. 1982-84), N.Y. Ch. Club. Avocations: riding, ballet, preservation of Benedictine monasticism, Byzantine art. Office: Gen Theol Sem St Mark's Libr 175 9th Ave New York NY 10011-4977

MCCARTY, WILLIAM MICHAEL, JR., lawyer; b. Trenton, N.J., 1938; AB, Am. U., Dickinson Coll., 1964; JD, Dickinson Sch. Law, 1967. Bar: Vt. 1967, U.S. Dist. Ct. Vt. 1967, U.S. Ct. Appeals (2d cir.) 1973, U.S. Supreme Ct. 1978. Assoc. Fitts & Olson, Brattleboro, Vt., 1967-71; sole practice Brattleboro, 1971-76; ptnr. McCarty & Rifkin, Brattleboro, Wilmington, Vt., 1976-80; sr. ptnr., pres. McCarty Law Offices, P.C., Brattleboro, Wilmington, 1980—. Presenter in various fields; dir. various corps. Mem. Brattleboro Zoning Bd. Adjustment, 1968-75; trustee Vt. Legal Aid, 1970-82, pres., 1979-80; pres. Brattleboro Winter Carnival, 1971-72; rep. Windham Regional Planning & Devel. Com., 1968-70, chmn. ch. coun., bench bar com., 1992-97, moderator Congl. Ch., 1990-94. With USMC, 1956-60. Mem. ABA, ATLA, Am. Bd. Trial Advocates, Vt. Bar Assn., Windham County Bar Assn. (pres. 1991-93, chair bench bar com. 1989-97), Am. Jud. Soc., Am. Law Student Assn. (nat. v.p., bd. govs. 1966-67), Nat. Coun. Sch. Attys., Vt. Trial Laywers Assn. (outstanding litigation achievement award 1994), Am. Bd. Trial Advocates (advocate), Inns of Ct., Vt. Criminal Def. Attys. Assn., Brattleboro C. of C. (bd. mgrs. 1971-72), U.S. Supreme Ct. Hist. Soc. (Vt. state chair 1999-). Republican. Office: 76 High St Brattleboro VT 05301-6074

MCCASH, JUNE HALL, retired language educator; b. Newberry, S.C., June 8, 1938; d. James DeLeon and Williemaye Stone Hall; m. Marvin Hampton Martin (div. June 1971); children: Michael Hall Martin, Christopher Brenden Martin; m. William Barton McCash, July 3, 1974 (dec. Feb. 1991); m. Richard Douglas Gleaves, Jr., May 21, 1994. BA, Agnes State Coll., 1960; MA, Emory U., 1963, PhD, 1967. Instr. dept. romance langs. Emory U., Atlanta, 1964—66; from asst. to assoc. prof. Mid. Tenn. State U., Murfreesboro, 1967—75, from assoc prof. to prof., 1966—70, prof. emerita, 2004, founding dir. honors program, 1973—80, prof. dept. fgn. langs., 1975—, chair dept. fgn. langs., 1980—92, grad. dir. dept. fgn. langs. and lits., 1996—2004, prof. emerita, 2004—. Presenter in field; fellow Am. Coun. Edn., 1986—87; elderhostel instr. W. Ga. Coll., Ga., 1992; interpreter for vis. French del. C. of C., Murfreesboro, 1992; exec. bd. Tenn. Humanities Coun., 1987—89, chair grant program com., 1987—88, vice-chair, 1988—89; chair So. Humanities Media Fund, 1989—91, Tenn. Humanities Coun., 1989—91, exec. bd., 1991—92; local coord. ESL Inst. Tenn. Dept. Edn., 1992; trustee Jekyll Island Found., 2000—; coord. various profl. workshops. Author: Love's Fools: Aucassin, Troilus, Calisto and the Parody of the Courtly Lover, 1972; co-author: Jekyll Island Club Historic District 100 Years, The Jekyll Island Club: Southern Haven for America's Millionaires, 1989; editor: The Cultural Patronage of Medieval Women, 1996; author: The Jekyll Island Cottage Colony, 1998; contbr. articles to profl. jours.; mem. editl. bd. Le Cygne: A Jour. on Marie de France. Hon. life mem. Jekyll Island Mus. Assocs., Friends of Linebaugh; trustee Jekyll Island Found., 2000—; layreader St. Paul's Episcopal Ch., Murfreesboro; chair adv. bd. So. Festival Books, 1988—92, mem. author's com., 1988—94. Fellow, Am. Coun. Edn., 1986—87; Young Humanists fellow, NEH, 1975, Mellon grantee for workshop on medieval culture, Vanderbilt U., 1982. Mem.: AAUP (chair com. on status of women 1969—70, sec. MTSU chpt. 1970—71, mem. exec. com. 1970—74, v.p. 1971—72), Medieval Acad. Am., Internat. Marie de France Soc. (mem. exec. bd. 1993—95, mem. adv. coun. 2001—), Southeastern Medieval Assn. (mem. exec. coun. 1991—94, v.p. 1995—97, pres. 1997—99,), Internat. Courtly Lit. Soc. (internat. treas. 1980—86, v.p. N.Am. br. 1990—92, pres. N.Am. br. 1992—95, internat. v.p. 2001—04, internat. pres. 2004—), Soc. Rencesvals, Phi Sigma Iota, Phi Kappa Phi (pres. elect 1997—98, pres. 1998—99, MTSU chpt.), Alpha Mu Gamma. Democrat. Avocations: writing, photography, reading. Office: Dept Fgn Langs Mid Tenn State U Box 79 Murfreesboro TN 37132

MCCASKEY, MICHAEL B. professional football team executive; b. Lancaster, Pa., Dec. 11, 1943; s. Edward B. and Virginia (Halas) McCaskey; m. Nancy McCaskey; children: John, Kathryn. Grad., Yale U., 1965; PhD, Case Western Res. U. Tchr. UCLA, 1972-75, Harvard U. Sch. Bus., Cambridge, Mass., 1975-82; pres., chief exec. officer Chgo. Bears (NFL), 1983-99, chmn. bd., 1999—. Author: The Executive Challenge: Managing Change and Ambiguity. Named Exec. of Yr. Sporting News, 1985. Office: Chgo Bears Halas Hall 250 Washington Rd Lake Forest IL 60045-2459 also: 1000 Football Dr Lake Forest IL 60045-4829

MCCASKEY, RAYMOND F. insurance company executive; b. 1944; m. Judy McCaskey. With Continental Assurance Co., Chgo., 1963-73; assist v.p. Health Care Service Corp., 1973—79, chief actuary, 1979—82, CFO, 1982—91, pres., COO, 1991—98, pres., CEO, 1998—. Former bd. chmn. Lincoln Found. for Bus. Excellence. Office: Health Care Service Corp 300 E Randolph St Chicago IL 60601-5014 Office Phone: 312-938-6000.*

MCCASKILL, CLAIRE, auditor; b. Houston, July 25, 1953; Auditor State of Mo., Jefferson City, 1999—. Democrat. Office: Mo State Auditors Off PO Box 869 Jefferson City MO 65102-0869 Fax: 573-751-6539.

MCCASLIN, DAVID E. hotel executive; BS in Hotel Mgmt., U. Mo., 1979. Gen. mgr. Lincoln Hotels, Dallas; hotel gen. mgr. CapStar, 1987-88, v.p. ops., COO, 1988; pres. MeriStar Hotels & Resorts, Inc. Office: 4501 Fairfax DR #800 Arlington VA 22203-1656 Fax: 202-995-2187.

MCCASLIN, KATHLEEN DENISE, child abuse educator; b. Poughkeepsie, N.Y., Aug. 4, 1962; d. Nancy Ann Gosselin; m. David Wayne McCaslin, Sept. 27, 1986 (dec. Oct. 1990); 1 child, LeAnn; m. Larry Thomas Ward, July 14, 1998. BA, Adelphi Coll., 1984. Pub. speaker Impact Seminars, Littlestown, Pa., 1987-96; exec. dir. McCaslin Internat., Guffey, Colo., 1994—; pub. speaker The Family Advocate, Guffey, Colo., 1997—. Founder We the People, Colorado Springs, Colo., 1982; vol. counselor/facilitator Beginning Experience, Harrisburg, Pa., 1991-94. Author: (books) Trusting in God, 1993, Respecting Yourself, 1993, Loss and Recovery, 1992, (cd audio) One Child's Journey to Freedom, 1998. Troop leader Girl Scouts U.S., Guffey, Colo., 1998-2000. Recipient Outstanding Grad. award Adelphi Coll., Colorado Springs, 1984. Mem. ASCPA, World Wildlife Fedn., Arbor Day Found., S.W. Indian Found. Avocations: reading, hiking, needlecrafts, gourmet cooking, gardening. Office: McCaslin Internat 932 Clover Ave Canon City CO 81212 Office Phone: 719-276-0152.

MCCASLIN, RICHARD BRYAN, history educator; b. Atlanta, Feb. 21, 1961; s. Jerry L. and Ann Elizabeth (Sharman) McC.; m. Jana Dawn Maryovich, Apr. 5, 1979; 1 child, Christina Michele. BA, Delta State U., 1982; MA, La. State U., 1983; PhD, U. Tex., 1988. Tchg. asst. La. State U., 1982-83, grad. asst. La. Bus. Rev., 1983; tchg. asst. U. Tex., Austin, 1983-87, rsch. assoc., 1984-87; rsch. asst. prof. U. Tenn., Knoxville, 1988-90; asst. prof. history High Point U., NC, 1990-94, assoc. prof., 1994-2000, prof., 2000—. Instr. Pellissippi State C.C., 1988-89, Roane State C.C., 1989; adj. prof. Corpus Christi (Tex.) State U., 1989; lectr. East Tenn. Hist. Soc., 1990; rsch. cons. Tex. Senate, 1986-89, Nat. Pk. Svc., 1989-90, Tex. State Historical Assn., 2000—; assoc. historian Futurepast: History Co., Spokane, Wash., 1987-89; presenter Southwestern Social Sci. Assn., AAAS, Soc. for Mil. History. Author: (with Earnest F. Gloyna) Commitment to Excellence: One Hundred Years of Engineering Education at The University of Texas at Austin, 1986, Andrew Johnson: A Bibliography, 1992, Portraits of Conflict: A Photographic History of South Carolina in the Civil War, 1994, Tainted Breeze: The Great Hanging at Gainesville, Texas, October 1862, 1994 (Tullis prize Tex. State Hist. Assn., commendation Am. Assn. for State and Local History), Remembered Be Thy Blessings: High Point University—The College Years, 1924-1991, 1995, Portraits of Conflict: A Photographic History of North Carolina in the Civil War, 1997, Lee in the Shadow of Washington, 2001, The Last Stronghold: The Fort Fisher Campaign, 2003; contbr. chpt. to: 100 Years of Science and Technology in Texas: A Sigma Xi Centennial Volume, 1986; columnist Greensboro News and Record, 1993-94; referee Southwestern Hist. Quar., La. State U. Press, U. Nebr. Press, U.S.C. Press, Tex. A&M U. Press; asst. editor, then assoc. editor Papers of Andrew Johnson, U. Tenn., 1988-90; contbr. articles and book revs. to various profl. publ. U. Tex. dissertation fellow, 1987-88, Clara H. Driscoll fellow in Tex. history Daus. of Republic of Tex., 1985-87; James H. and Minnie M. Edmonds Ednl. Found. scholar, 1983-85, Colonial Dames Am. grad. scholar, 1987; Slatten award Va. Hist. Soc., Laney prize Austin Civil War Roundtable. Mem. So. Hist. Assn. (presenter), Soc. Civil War Historians (presenter), Tex. State Hist. Assn. (presenter), Hist. Soc. NC (treas. 2000). Episcopalian. Home: 221 Pine Ridge Dr High Point NC 27262-8204 Office: High Point Univ Dept History and Polit Sci High Point NC 27260 E-mail: rmccas@highpoint.edu.

MCCASLIN, TERESA EVE, human resources executive; b. Jersey City, Nov. 22, 1949; d. Felix F. and Ann E. (Golaszewski) Hrynkiewicz; m. Gary A. McCue. BA, Marymount Coll., 1971; MBA, L.I. U., 1981. Adminstrv. officer Civil Service Commn., Fed. Republic Germany, 1972-76; personnel dir. Oceanroutes, Inc., Palo Alto, Calif., 1976-78; mgr., coll. relations Continental Grain Co., N.Y.C., 1978-79, corp. personnel mgr., 1979-81, dir. bus. redesign, internal cons., 1981-84; dir., human resources Grow Group, Inc., N.Y.C., 1984-85, v.p. human resources, 1985-86, v.p. adminstrn., 1986-89; corp. v.p. human resources Avery Dennison Corp., Pasadena, Calif., 1989-94; v.p. human resources Monsanto Co., St. Louis, 1994-97; sr. v.p. human resources, mem. mgmt. com. Conti Group Cos. (formerly Continental Grain Co.), N.Y.C., 1997—, exec. v.p. human resources & info. tech., 1999—. Mem. global adv. bd. Am. Grad. Sch. Internat. Mgmt. Mem. Am. Mgmt. Assn. (chair bd. trustees, fin. and exec. com., chair compensation com.), Human Resources Coun. Roman Catholic. Avocations: skiing, travel, golf. Office: Conti Group Cos 277 Park Ave New York NY 10172-0003

MCCASLIN, W.C. products and packaging executive; Owner, CEO Douglas Products and Packaging. Office: Douglas Products & Packaging 1550 E Old 210 Hwy Liberty MO 64068

MCCAUGHEY ROSS, ELIZABETH P. (BETSY MCCAUGHEY), former lieutenant governor; b. Oct. 20, 1948; d. Albert Peterkin; m. Thomas McCaughey, 1972 (div. 1994); children: Amanda, Caroline, Diana. BA, Vassar Coll., 1970; MA, Columbia Univ., 1972, PhD, 1976. Public policy expert Manhattan Inst., N.Y.C.; lt. gov. State of N.Y., 1995—99. Asst. prof. Vassar Coll., 1979, Columbia U., 1980-84; chmn. Governor's Medicaid Task Force, 1994. Author: From Loyalist to Founding Father, 1980, Government By Choice, 1987; also articles including an article in The New Republic (Nat. Mag. award for Pub. Policy 1995). Recipient Bancroft Dissertation award, Richard B. Morris prize; Woodrow Wilson fellow, Herbert H. Lehman fellow, Honorary Vassar fellow, John Jay fellow, Post Doctoral Rsch. fellow NEH, 1984, John M. Olin fellow Manhattan Inst., 1993, sr. fellow Ctr. Study of the Presidency. Republican.

MCCAUL, ELIZABETH, investment advisor, former state agency administrator; BA in econ., Boston U., 1985; postgrad., Georgetown U. Congl. intern, 1981; investment banker, v.p. Goldman, Sachs & Co., 1985—95; chief of staff N.Y. State Banking Dept., 1995—96, first dep. supt. banks, 1996—97, acting supt. banks, 1997-2000, supt. banks, 2000—03; ptnr. Promontory Fin. Group, 2003—. Dir. Empire State Devel. Corp., State N.Y. Mortgage Agy., N.Y. State Job Devel. Authority, Harlem Cmty. Devel. Corp.; statutory mem. Cmty. Facilities Project Guarantee Fund. Scholar European Econ. Cmty., Inst. European Studies, Freiburg, Germany. Mem. Conf. State Bank Suprs. (bd. dirs., supervisory chmn., 2001-02, internat. bankers adv. bd.), Fed. Fin. Inst. Examination Coun., 2002-03. Office: Promotory Fin Group 1201 Pennsylvania Ave NW Ste 617 Washington DC 20004

MCCAUL, JOSEPH PATRICK, chemical engineer; b. N.Y.C., May 11, 1952; s. Joseph and Marion (Sheehan) McCaul; m. Kathleen Anne Crowley, Aug. 3, 1974 (div.); children: Kenneth, Christine; m. Nancy Marie Powell, May 28, 2000. BSChemE, Poly. Inst. Bklyn., 1973, M in Polymer Sci. and Engring., 1977; MBA, Case Western Res. U., 1987. Registered ofcl. baseball umpier Ill. HS Assn. Prodn. supr. Mobay Chem. Corp., Bayonne, NJ, 1973—77; process engr. Borg Warner Chems., Parkersburg, W.Va., 1977—78, process control engr. Ottawa, Ill., 1978—79, process control mgr. Linmar plant, 1979—82; mgr. tech. svc. Std. Oil Co., Cleve., 1982—87; mgr. internat. sales and tech. svc. Barex Group BP Chems., Cleve., 1987—96, dir. sales and licensing, 1996—98; group v.p. sales and mktg. EVAL Co. Am., Lisle, Ill., 1998—2001, v.p. rsch. and bus. devel., 2001; founder, pres. Joseph Assoc. Internat., Inc., Naperville, Ill., 2002—. Contbr. articles to profl. jours., mags., ency. Exec. bd. dirs. Mentor Lake Area Baseball, Mentor on the Lake, Ohio, 1988—89; pres. Mentor McMinn Area Baseball League, 1989—91; trustee Pinegate Homeowners Assn., Mentor, Ohio, 1988—89. Recipient award, Soc. Plastics Engrs., 1987. Mem.: Midwest Bus. Brokers and Intermediaries, Internat. Bus. Brokers Assn., DuPage Exec. Network, Naperville C. of C. (com. chair, mem. spkrs. bur. 2004), Am. Mensa. Republican. Roman Catholic. Achievements include patents in field. Avocations: fishing, boating, exercise, baseball, travel. Home: 1612 Pennsylvania Ct Naperville IL 60563-2600 Office: Joseph Assoc Internat Inc 55 S Main St Ste 355 Naperville IL 60540 Office Phone: 630-355-6061. Business E-Mail: jmccaul@josephassociates.biz.

MCCAULEY, BRUCE GORDON, financial consultant; b. St. Louis; s. William Maurice and Evylin Adele (Halbert) McC.; m. Barbara Allen Stevens, Mar. 16, 1945 (dec.); children: David S., Sharon; m. Gwen Crumpton Cummings, Nov. 25, 1967. Student, U. Mo., 1939-41, Yale U., 1944; BS in Engring., U. Calif., Berkeley, 1948, MBA, 1949, MS in Indsl. Engring., 1952. Registered profl. engr., N.Y., Calif., Hawaii. Asst. purchasing agt. Curtis Mfg. Co., St. Louis, 1941—43; teaching asst. U. Calif., Berkeley, 1948—49, asst. prof. mech. engring., 1950—56, chmn. indsl. engring. inst., 1954—55; design engr. Standard Oil Co. of Calif., 1949—50; sr. ptnr. McCauley & Dunmire, San Francisco, 1952—56; v.p. Shand & Jurs Co., Berkeley, 1956—58, exec. v.p., 1958—60; asst. to pres. Honolulu Star-Bulletin, 1960—62; gen. mgr. Christian Sci. Pub. Soc., Boston, 1962—69; gen. mgr. N.Y. Daily News Inc., N.Y.C., 1969—74, v.p., 1971—73, sr. v.p., 1973—75, asst. to pres., 1974—75, dir., 1971—75; v.p. Daseke & Co. Inc., Westport, Conn., 1975—77, sr. v.p., 1977—86, mgr. West Coast office, 1978—86; vis. scholar Principia Coll., Elsah, Ill., 1988—91; pres. Rossmoor Mut. 48 Corp., Walnut Creek, 1994—97. Bd. dirs. Better Bus. Bur., N.Y.C., 1973-77, N.Y.C. Conv. and Visitors Bur., 1974-77, Albert Baker Found., 1979-90, Asher Found., 1983-93, Sopac Energy Corp., 1986-92. Capt. USAAF, 1943-46, PTO. Mem. ASME (life), NSPE (life), Am. Inst. Indsl. Engrs. (life), Nat. Assn. Accts. (life), U. Calif. Alumni Assn., Principia Alumni Assn., Rossmoor Golf Club, Masons (32 degree), Kiwanis, Sigma Xi, Tau Beta Pi, Beta Gamma Sigma, Pi Mu Epsilon. Christian Scientist. Home: 3266 Ptarmigan Dr Apt 3B Walnut Creek CA 94595-3149

MCCAULEY, CLEYBURN LYCURGUS, lawyer; b. Houston, Feb. 8, 1929; s. Reese Stephens and Elizabeth Ann (Burleson) McC.; m. Elizabeth Kelton McKoy, June 7, 1950; children: Stephens Francis, Lillian Elizabeth, Cleyburn, Lucy Annette. BS, U.S. Mil. Acad., 1950; MS in Engring. Econ., Statistical Quality Control and Indsl. Engring., Stanford U., 1959; JD, Coll. William and Mary, 1970. Bar: D.C. 1971, Va. 1970, Tex. 1970, U.S. Ct. Claims 1971, U.S. Tax Ct. 1971, U.S. Supreme Ct. 1973. Commd. 2d lt. U.S. Air Force, 1950, advanced through grades to lt. col., 1971, ret., 1971; pvt. practice law, Washington, 1975—. Mem. Fed. Bar Assn., Va. Bar Assn., Tex. Bar Assn., D.C. Bar Assn., IEEE, AIAA, Am. Soc. Quality Control, Phi Alpha Delta. Home: 402 S 3rd St Wilmington NC 28401-5102

MCCAULEY, DAN PAUL, dentist; b. Pittsburg, Tex., Nov. 13, 1949; s. Loyd Cecil McCauley and Claudia Aletha Moore; m. Sandra Scott Kraemer, Sept. 14, 1974; children: Jennifer, Rebecca, Crissy. BA in Psychology, So. Meth. U., 1974; DDS, U. Tex., 1977. Pvt. practice, Mt. Pleasant, Tex., 1977—. Sec. N.E. Tex. CC, 1994—2001. Active Boy Scouts Am., 1977—; trustee N.E. Tex. CC Found., 1989—, pres., 1989—2001; bd. dirs. Red River Girl Scouts, 1986—89; chmn. Titus county Reps., Mt. Pleasant, 1980; deacon First Bapt. Ch., Mt. Pleasant, 1977—. Named Tex. Dentist of the Yr., Tex. Acad. General Dentistry, 2004; named one of Am. Top Dentists, Rsch. Coun. Am.; recipient Fraternal Achievement award, Psi Omega Dental Fraternity, 1976, Sandy Niforus Humanitarian award. Fellow: Am. Acad. Dentists, Pierre Fauchard Soc.; mem.: ADA, Acad. Gen. Dentistry, 1st Dist. Dental Soc. (pres. 1986—87, 2001—02, v.p. 2002, dir. 2002—), Tex. Dental Assn. (del. 1995—, dir. 2002—, sr. dir. 2003—04, v.p. 2004—), N. Tex. Optimists (gov. 1985—86, Optimist Lifetime Achievement 1995). Republican. Baptist. Avocations: tennis, travel, skiing. Home: 1403 S Florey Ave Mount Pleasant TX 75455-5813 Office: 1603 N Jefferson Ave Mount Pleasant TX 75455-2366 Office Phone: 903-572-3981. Personal E-mail: drdansmu@hotmail.com.

MCCAULEY, GERARD FRANCIS, literary agent; b. Pitts., Apr. 9, 1934; s. John Edward and Beatrice (McNally) McCauley; m. Kerstin E. Borg, Apr. 24, 1965; children: Peter, Brian. BA, U. Pitts., 1956. Editor Alfred A. Knopf Publishing, N.Y.C., 1961—62, Little Brown, Boston, 1962—63; literary agt. Curtis Brown Ltd., N.Y.C., 1964—70, Gerard McCauley Agy., Katonah, NY, 1970—2003. Editor: (book) Playing Around, 1973. Petty officer 3d class USN, 1956—58, Key West, Fla. Mem.: Orgn. of Am. Historians, Assn. of Authors Reps., Dutch Treat Club. Democrat. Episcopalian. Home: 7 Outpost Rd Katonah NY 10536

MCCAULEY, JANE REYNOLDS, journalist; b. Wilmington, Del., Oct. 22, 1947; d. John Thomas and Helen (Campbell) McC. BA, Guilford Coll., 1969. Editor, sr. writer Nat. Geographic Soc., Washington, 1970-90; freelance writer, editor, artist, 1990-96; exec. editor AM Quilter's Soc., 1996-97; freelance editor, writer, 1997—. Former owner Unique Native Crafts; tropical bird specialist. Author of 15 children's books; co-author award-winning travel books, art revs. Mem.: Children's Book Soc. E-mail: ritstuff4u@aol.com.

MC CAULEY, R. PAUL, criminologist, educator; b. Highspire, Pa., Jan. 13, 1943; s. Paul Herbert and Frances Vaden (Harper) McC.; m. Gail Lee Gummo, Jan. 30, 1965; 1 child, Brent Clayton. A.S., Harrisburg Area Community Coll., 1968; BS, Va. Commonwealth U., 1969; MS, Eastern Ky. U., 1971; PhD (fellow), Sam Houston U., 1973; certificate Home Office Detective Tng. Course, Eng., 1967. Diplomate Am. Coll. Forensic Examiners, Am. Bd. Law Enforcement Experts. Police officer Highspire Police, 1964-69; adminstr. Burns Internat. Security Services Inc., 1969-71; prof. police sci. and adminstrn., dir. grad. studies in adminstrn. of justice U. Louisville, 1973-82; prof., chmn. dept. criminology Indiana U. of Pa., 1982—; co-founder Sempas Security and Safety Technologies, 1980; advisor Reagan Presdl./Congressional Task Force on Criminal Justice, 1980; mem. staff So. Police Inst., 1973-82, Nat. Crime Prevention Inst., 1973-82. Researcher, ptnr. McShan Assocs., 1974-85; cons. U.S. Congress Com. on Emergency Communications, 1967. Co-author: The Criminal Justice System, 1976, 3d edit., 1984; co-founder, editor: Criminal Justice Policy Rev., 1984-86; contbr. chpts. to books, articles to profl. jours.; patents. Active Metro Child Abuse Program, Crime Clinic of Greater Harrisburg, 1965-74; mem. Lower Swatara Twp. Police Civil Service Commn., 1967-69. Served with USMC, 1962-66 Recipient Mayor's Citation, City of Louisville, 1982, Gold medal Educator of the 1980's; honoree Silliman Coll., Yale U., 1984; Fulbright scholar, lectr., Australia, 1987. Mem. Acad. Criminal Justice Scis. (exec. bd. 1980-83, pres. 1985), Navy League (award for disting. community service) Home: 4620 Lucerne Rd Indiana PA 15701-6003 Office: Indiana U of Pa G-1 McElhaney Hall Indiana PA 15705-0001 Office Phone: 724-357-5605. E-mail: mccauley@iup.edu. *One's philosophy, spirit, and drive contributes more to his relative success than do economic resources, social position, planning, or timing.*

MCCAUSLAND, MARGARET A. lawyer, educator; b. Bryn Mawr, Pa., Feb. 2, 1950; d. Joseph Edward and Margaret Mary O'Donnell; m. Paul Joseph McCausland, June 22, 1968; children: Patricia, Joseph. BS summa cum laude, St. Joseph's U., Phila., 1984; JD cum laude, Villanova U., 1987. Bar: Pa. 1987, U.S. Dist. Ct. (ea. dist.) Pa. 1987, U.S. Dist. Ct. (we. dist.) Mich. 1995, U.S. Ct. Appeals (3d cir.) 1997, U.S. Supreme Ct. 2002. Sec. Bankers Life, Bala Cynwyd, Pa., 1968—70, 1975—77, Frederick Brown & Assoc., Newton Square, Pa., 1977—84; assoc. Dechert LLP, Phila., 1987—93, Blank, Rome, Comisky & McCauley, Phila., 1993—97; ptnr. Blank Rome LLP, Phila., 1997—. Adj. faculty Villanova (Pa.) U. Law Sch., 1999—, mem. bd. advisors, 2001—. Vol. atty. Support Ctr. Child Advs., Phila., 1987—; tutor Phila. Reads, 2001—; mem. bd. advisors Archbishop Prendergast HS Girls, Phila., 2001—; bd. dirs. Robin's Nest, Inc., Glassboro, NJ, 1995—; pres., bd. dirs. CeaseFire Pa., Phila., 2002—. Named Disting. Adv., Support Ctr. Child Advs., 1996, Woman of Distinction, Phila. Bus. Jour., 2001, Pa. Super Lawyer, Law and Politics Mag., 2004. Mem.: ABA, AAUW, Pa. Bar Assn., J. Willard O'Brien Inn Ct., Phila. Bar Assn., Forum Exec. Women, Order of the Coif. Office: Blank Rome LLP One Logan Sq Philadelphia PA 19103 Office Phone: 215-569-5548. Business E-Mail: mccausland@blankrome.com.

MCCAUSLAND, PETER, technology company executive; b. 1950; BA, U. S.C.; JD, Boston U. Bar: Pa. 1974. Gen. counsel MG Industries, Inc.; chmn., CEO Airgas, Inc., Radnor, Pa., 1982—. Bd. dirs. Metrocall, Inc. Fax: 610-687-1052.

MCCAUSLAND, THOMAS JAMES, JR., brokerage house executive; b. Cleve., Nov. 27, 1934; s. Thomas James and Jean Anna (Hanna) McC.; m. Kathryn Margaret Schacht, Feb. 9, 1957; children: Thomas James III, Andrew John, Theodore Scott. BA in Econs., Beloit (Wis.) Coll., 1956. V.p. A.G. Becker & Co., Inc., Chgo., 1959-74; v.p. The Chgo. Corp., 1974-76, sr. v.p., dir., 1976-83, exec. v.p., 1983-90, vice chmn., 1991-96; pres. The Chgo. Corp. Internat., 1990-96. Treas. The LaSalle St. Coun., Chgo., 1990-95. V.p. Hospice the North Shore, Evanston, Ill., 1986-90; bd. dirs. McCormick Theol. Sem., Chgo., 1971-79, Presbyn. Home, Evanston, 1968-74; trustee Beloit Coll., 1987-90. Lt. USN, 1956-59. Mem. Union League, United Presbyn. Found. (trustee, vice-chmn. 1980-86), Skokie Country Club (bd. dirs. 1983-85, pres. 1993), Pelican Bay Club (Naples, Fla.)(chmn. 2001-03), Forum Club of Naples (bd. dirs.), Royal Poinciana Golf Club (Naples). Republican. Avocations: travel, Am. history, golf.

MCCAW, CRAIG O. communications executive; b. Centralia, Wash., 1949; s. John Elroy and Marion McCaw. Grad., Stanford U., 1971. Pilot; chmn., CEO McCaw Communications, 1968-88; chmn. bd. dirs., CEO McCaw Cellular Comm., Inc. (acquired MCI's cellular and paging operations in 1986

sold to AT&T in 1994), Kirkland, Wash., 1982-94; chmn., CEO Lin Broadcasting Co., 1990—; founder, chief, co-exec. officer Teledesic Corp., Kirkland, 1990—; chmn., CEO NEXTLINK Comm. Inc. (now XO Communications), 1994—2002, Eagle River Inc.; acquired Clearwire Holdings Inc., 2004—, NextNet Wireless Inc, Minneapolis, 2004—. Bd. dirs. RadioFrame Networks, Inc., China Unicom Ltd., China, 2000—; mem. Nat. Security Telecommunications Advisory Com. Avocation: boating.

MCCAW, JOHN E., JR., professional sports team executive; Co-founder, bd. dirs. McCaw Comm., McCaw Cellular Comm., Inc.; owner, bd. dirs. Seattle Mariners, 1992; co-chmn. Orca Bay Sports and Entertainment, Vancouver, B.C.; chmn., gov. Vancouver Canucks. Office: Vancouver Canucks 800 Griffiths Way Vancouver BC Canada V6B 6G1

MCCAWLEY, AUSTIN, psychiatrist, educator; b. Greenock, Scotland, Jan. 17, 1925; arrived in U.S., 1954; s. Austin and Anna Theresa (McBride) McC.; m. Gloria Klein, Feb. 15, 1958; children: Joseph, Tessa. MBCHB, U. Glasgow, 1948. Diplomate Am. Bd. Psychiatry and Neurology; DPM Royal Coll. London. Intern Glasgow Royal Infirmary, Scotland, 1948; resident Inst. Living, Harford, Conn., 1954-57, clin. dir., 1960-66; med. dir. Westchester br. St. Vincent's Hosp., N.Y.C., 1966-72; dir. psychiatry St. Francis Hosp., Hartford, 1972-88; prof. psychiatry U. Conn. Med. Sch., Farmington, 1983-93; pvt. practice, West Hartford, Conn., 1988—. Dir. psychiatry Kaiser Permanente of Conn., 1996-99. Co-author: The Physician, 1983; contbr. articles to profl. jours. Chmn. Bd. Mental Health, State of Conn., 1981-84, Search Com. for Commr. Mental Health, Conn., 1981; mem. Gov.'s Spl. Task Force on Mental health Policy, Conn., 1982. With RAF, 1948-50. Fellow: Am. Coll. Psychiatry (charter fellow, founder), Am. Psychiat. Assn.; mem.: Conn. Psychiat. Soc. (pres. 1978—79). Democrat. Roman Catholic. Avocation: music. Home and Office: 20 Worthington Dr Farmington CT 06032 Office Phone: 860-677-0109.

MCCHESNEY, MICHAEL C. computer network security company executive; b. Atlanta; BSBA magna cum laude, Vanderbilt U.; MBA in Fin. and Multinat. Enterprise, U. Pa. Sr. assoc. Investments Orange Nassau, Boston; v.p. corp. devel Lantech Sys., Inc., Dallas; co-founder, CEO SecureWare, Security First Techs. (formerly Five Paces and SecureWare), Atlanta, 1995-2000; chmn. Security First Network Bank, Atlanta, 1995-96; founder Webtone, Atlanta, 2000—. Office: Webtone Technologies 3535 Piedmont Rd Ne #800 Atlanta GA 30305-4535

MCCHESNEY, ROBERT MICHAEL, SR., political science educator; b. Effingham, Ill., Oct. 5, 1942; s. J.D. and Helen Grace (Russell) McC.; m. Laraine Freeman, Aug. 28, 1965; children: Robert M. Jr., Todd Patrick, Jennifer Laraine, Grant Russell, Brent Steven. BA, U. La., Lafayette, 1964; MA, U. Va., 1967, PhD, 1969. Asst. instr. U. Va., Charlottesville, 1967-68; chmn. dept. polit. sci. U. Ctrl. Ark., Conway, 1971-76, dean coll. scis. and humanities, 1976-82, v.p. for acad. affairs, 1982-89, disting. prof., 1989-90; provost U. Montevallo, Ala., 1990-92, pres., 1992—. V.p. Survey Rsch., Inc., Conway, 1989-92; spl. cons. U. Ark. System, Little Rock, 1989. Mem. Carmichael Found., Conway, 1975-79; exec. bd. Quapaw coun. Boy Scouts Am., Little Rock, 1982-88; Greater Ala. Area Coun., 1995—; chair Ala. Higher Edn. Partnership, Pres. Adv. Coun., 1999-2001. Capt. Med. Svc. Corps U.S. Army, 1968-71. Grantee State Justice Inst./Adminstrv. Office of Cts., Ark., 1989. Mem. Ala. Coun. Univ. and Coll. Pres. (chmn. 1993-95), So. Com. Colls. and Schs. (exec. coun. 1996-99), Birmingham C. of C., Montevall C. of C., Rotary (pres. Conway Club 1987-88, Paul Harris fellow 1986), Phi Beta Kappa, Phi Kappa Phi, Alpha Chi, Golden Key, Phi Alpha Theta, Phi Eta Sigma, Blue Key. Mem. Lds Ch. Avocations: hunting, fishing, golf. Office: U Montevallo Station 6001 Montevallo AL 35115

MCCHESNEY, ROBERT PEARSON, artist; b. Marshall, Mo., Jan. 16, 1913; s. John and Ruby (Pearson) McC.; m. Mary Ellen Fuller, Dec. 17, 1949. Student, Sch. Fine Arts, Washington U., 1931-34, Otis Art Inst., Los Angeles, 1936-37. Represented by Annex Galleries, Santa Rosa, Calif., Robert Green Fine Arts, Mill Valley, Calif., Thomas McCormick Gallery, Chgo., Claire Carlevaro Art Exchange, San Francisco, Michael Rosenfeld Gallery, NYC. Instr. art Calif. Sch. Fine Arts, San Francisco, 1949-51, Santa Rosa Jr. Coll., 1957-58; trustee San Francisco Art Inst., 1965-67. One-man shows include San Francisco Mus. Modern Art, 1949, 53, San Francisco Art Inst., 1957, 20th Century West, 1965, Bolles Gallery, N.Y., 1962, Nev. Mus., 1994, also others; one-man retrospective Fresno (Calif.) Mus. Art, 1996, Calif. State U., Fresno, 1999, City Visions Gallery, Santa Rosa, Calif., 2000, Art Exch., San Francisco, 2002; group shows include Art Inst. Chgo., 1947, 3d Biennial Sau Paulo, Brazil, 1955, Whitney Annual, 1955, Corcoran, 1957, Provincetown, 1957, Chgo., 1959, Osaka, Japan, 1970, Whitney, 1980, Robert Green Fine Arts, Mill Valley, Calif., also others; represented in permanent collections, Fresno Art Mus., Art Inst. Chgo., Worcester (Mass.) Art Mus., Whitney Mus., N.Y., San Francisco Mus. Modern Art, Utah State Mus., Nev. Art Mus., Laguna Beach Art Mus., Cleve. Art Mus. Hugh-Cherna Silvert Collection, 2003, San Jose Mus. Art, others; executed mural San Francisco Social Svcs. Bldg., 1978; (photo biography) Robert McChesney-An American Painter, 1996. Address: 2955 Sonoma Mountain Rd Petaluma CA 94954-9559 *The desert wilderness, which I truly love to be in as much as possible, has influenced me a great deal. Of course, the artist is no different from anyone else in that he is influenced by everything around him visually and psychologically, but he has the ability to digest this, you might say, and then transform it into art.*

MCCHESNEY, SAMUEL PARKER, III, real estate executive; b. Oakland, Calif., July 30, 1945; s. Samuel Parker and Edna Margaret (McCorkle) McC.; m. Vicki Storrie, June 21, 1969; children: Nathan, Amanda, Jed. BA, Washington and Lee U., 1967; JD, Case Western Res. U., 1970. Lic. real estate broker, Mo., Kans. Urban intern and multifamily housing rep. HUD, Chgo., 1970-71; project loan mgr. 1st Home Investment Corp., Overland Park, Kans., 1971-72; v.p. devel. Northland Bldg. Corp., Gladstone, Mo., 1973-74; cons. Urban Equities, Kansas City, Mo., 1975; pres., co-owner McChesney Devel. Co., Inc., Edwardsville, Kans., 1976-78; pres., owner McChesney, Inc., Kansas City, 1978—, Managed Maintenance Inc., 1990-97; owner Painted M Ranch LLC, Olathe, Kans., 2004—. Pres. Lake Quivira (Kans.) Homeowners Assn. Inc., 1983-85; mem. planning and zoning com. City of Lake Quivira, 1983, mem. planning commn., 1992—; mem. real estate com. Quivira, Inc., 1986, nominating com., 1987-88, 90, restrictions & covenants update com., 1993-95; mem. patron's com. Tom Watson Golf Classic, Kansas City, 1984-85; mem. Lake Quivira Long Range Planning Com., 1987-88. Recipient cert. Nat. Assisted Housing Profl. Exec. Level. Mem. Kans. City Regional Bd. Realtors, Affordable Housing Mgrs. Assn. (dir. region 7 1995—, v.p. region 7, mem. fin. com. 1995-96, chmn. 1995-96, mem. membership com. 1997—, mem. edn. com. 1997—), Lake Quivira Country Club (pres. 1983-85), Saddle and Sirloin Club. Avocations: golf, reading, gardening, travel, horseback riding. Home: 510 Hillcrest Rd E Lake Quivira KS 66217-8781 Office: 6870 W 105th St Overland Park KS 66212 Office Phone: 913-385-1400. E-mail: sam@mcchesneyinc.com.

MCCHRISTIAN, JOSEPH ALEXANDER, international business executive; b. Chgo., Oct. 12, 1914; s. Robert Lee and Lillian (Alexander) McC.; m. Dempsie Catherine Van Fleet, Sept. 26, 1940; children: Joseph Alexander, Anne, Lillian. BS in Mil. Sci., U.S. Mil. Acad., 1939; grad., Command and Gen. Staff Coll., 1942, Armed Forces Staff Coll., 1951, Army War Coll., 1955, Army Lang. Sch., 1956. Enlisted U.S. Army, 1933, commd. 2d lt., 1939, advanced through grades to maj. gen., 1961, various assignments, 1933-44, successively armored inf. bn. comdr., ast. chief staff plans and ops., chief staff 10th Armored, 1944-45; asst. chief staff intelligence Hdqrs. 3d U.S. Army, Germany, 1945-47; dep. dir. intelligence U.S. Forces, Austria, 1947-48; comdg. officer 2d Bn.; 3d Inf. "The Old Guard" U.S. Army, Ft. McNair, D.C., 1948-49; spl. asst. to chief JUSMAG, Greece, 1949-50; S3 dept. tactics U.S. Mil. Acad., 1951-53; comdg. officer 1st Regt. U.S. Corp Cadets, 1953-54; attache U.S. Army, Greece, 1956-60; comdg. officer 1st Armored Regt. (tng.), also comdg. officer U.S. Army Tng. Ctr. Armor, Ft. Knox, Ky., 1960-61; chief western divsn. Office Asst. Chief Staff-Intelligence, Dept. Army, 1962-63. Asst. chief staff intelligence Hdqrs. U.S. Army Pacific, 1963-65; chief Army, Navy, Air Force and Marine Corps Intelligence, Hdqrs. U.S. Mil. Assistance Command, Vietnam, 1965-67; comdg. gen. 2d Armored Divsn., also III Corps, Ft. Hood, Tex., 1967-68; asst. chief of staff for intelligence Dept. Army, 1968-71; v.p. Overseas Basic Industries, Fla., 1972-74; v.p., gen. mgr. Société des Eaux, Athens, 1972 74; v.p. Ulen Mgmt. Co., Fla., 1972-75, Van Fleet Estates, Inc., Fla., 1970-77. Commr., Town of Jupiter Island, Fla., 1975-83. Decorated D.S.M. with oak leaf cluster, Silver Star, Legion of Merit, Bronze Star with 3 oak leaf clusters, Air medal, Army Commendation medal, Am. Def., Am. Campaign, ETO Campaign with 3 bronze stars, WWII Victory, Nat. Def. with bronze oak leaf cluster, Vietnam Svc. with 4 oak leaf clusters, Vietnam Campaign, Combat Inf. badge; Croix de Guerre with gold star and bronze star (France); comdr. Royal Order King George 1st, also Disting. Svc. meda. (Greece); Nat. Order 5th class and Disting. Svc. Order 1st class (Republic Vietnam); Mil. Merit medal, Chung Mu, Korea, Grand Cross of Mil. Merit with white ribbon (Spain), Medal of Metz (France), Gen. Patton Meml. award, 2000. Mem. Mil. Order World Wars, Alumni Assn. U.S. Mil. Acad., Army and Navy Club, Hobe Sound Yacht Club, Jupiter Island Club, Ends of the Earth Club. Home: 365 S Beach Rd Hobe Sound FL 33455-2613 E-mail: general@mcchristian.net.

MCCLAIN, CURTIS KEITH, JR., religious studies educator, minister; b. Muskogee, Okla., Sept. 10, 1955; s. Curtis Keith Sr. and Dorothy Lee Scarborough McClain; m. Patsy Marlene Cater, Aug. 23, 1980; children: Elisabeth Ruth, Meredith Lee. BA, Howard Payne U., 1977; MDiv, Southwestern Bapt. Theol. Sem., 1980; PhD, Mid-Am. Bapt. Theol. Sem., 1995. Asst. tchr. Dean's Sch., Ft. Worth, 1980-81; adj. instr. Mid-Am. Bapt. Theol. Sem., Memphis, 1984-87; prof. Bible, chair humanities divsn. Mo. Bapt. Univ., St. Louis, 1988—. Preacher various chs., Mo., 1988—. Contbr. articles to profl. jours. Trustee Christian Civic Found., St. Louis; chmn. steering com. So. Bapt. Founders Conf. Midwest, St. Louis. Named Parkway Disting. prof. Parkway Bapt. Ch., 1991. Mem. Evangelical Theol. Soc., His Way Evangelistic Assn. (bd. dirs. 1995—). Baptist. Avocations: computers, cross-stitch. Home: 2813 Mcclay Valley Blvd Saint Peters MO 63376-7136 Office: Mo Bapt Univ 1 College Park Dr Saint Louis MO 63141-8660 Fax: (314) 434-7596. Office Phone: 314-392-2312. E-mail: mcclain@mobap.edu.

MCCLAIN, DENNIS DOUGLAS, advertising executive; b. Portsmouth, Va., Aug. 9, 1948; s. Merl Lane and Bonnie May (Herrick) McC.; m. Claudia Trammell, Oct. 6, 1979; children: Matthew, Cameron. ABJ., Henry Grady Sch. Journalism, U. Ga., 1970. Account supr. Leber Katz Ptnrs., 1974-76, group account supr., 1976-78, dir. creative svcs., 1978-81, exec. v.p. creative svcs., 1981—; pres. Southwest Bozell, 1985—; chmn., exec. creative dir. The Bloom Agy., 1983-85; pres. Temerlin McClain, Irving, Tex., 1985-2000, CEO, 2000—. Named Alumni of Yr. Henry Grady Sch. Journalism, U. Ga., 1983 Office: Temerlin McLain Inc 6555 Sierra Dr Irving TX 75039-2479

MCCLAIN, EDWARD FIFER, JR., retired physicist; b. Carrolton, Mo., Aug. 22, 1921; s. Edward Fifer and Corrine Carrie (Rahmoeller) McC.; m. Louise Cherry Shelby, Dec. 9, 1943; children: Deanna Louise, William Edward, Robert Jay. BSEE, George Washington U., 1950. With Naval Rsch. Lab., Washington, 1942-68, head radio astronomy br., 1956-68; ret., 1968. Past chmn. commn. radio astronomy Internat. Scientific Radio Union; past adv. com. Nat. Radio Astronomy Obs.; cons. Nat. Acad. Sci., Interdept. Radio Adv. Com., Nat. Radio Astronomy Obs.; astronomy panel NSF. Contbr. articles to profl. jours.; patentee in field. Fellow AAAS, Washington Acad. Scis.; mem. IEEE (sr., life), Internat. Astron. Union, Am. Astron. Soc., Scientific Rsch. Soc. Am., Sigma Tau. Achievements include conducting sea trials ST periscope radar in submarine; designed AN/APN67 self-contained doppler automatic navigator for aircraft; determined correct distance to radio source Cass A using galactic hydrogen absorption. Home: 4133 Maple Rd Morningside MD 20746-3514

MCCLAIN, GEORGE NELSON, economist, lawyer; b. New Haven, Aug. 10, 1952; s. James and Trina (George) McC.; m. Lisa Crossley, May 5, 1982. BS in Econs., U. Conn., 1975; JD, Yale U., 1978. Pres. McClain Internat., Washington, 1990—. Office: 6923 Storck CIR Lanham MD 20706-2129

MCCLAIN, GREGORY DAVID, chaplin; b. Anderson, SC, June 6, 1957; s. Lemuel David and Mary Josephine (Hawkins) McC.; m. Anne Leigh (Blackwell), May 21, 1983; children: Jonathan David and Sean Gregory. AS, Anderson Coll., 1977; BA, Erskine Coll., 1979; MDiv, Southeastern Bapt. Theol. Sem., Wake Forrest, N.C., 1982; D of Ministry, Wesley Theol. Sem., Washington, 1996. ordained Boulevard Bapt. Ch., 1983. Chaplain extern Bapt. Med. Ctr., Columbia, SC, 1982; assoc. pastor First Bapt. Ch., South Boston, Va., 1983-86; min. Corrottoman Bapt. Ch., Lancaster, Va., 1986-93, Colonial Beach Bapt. Ch., 1993-98, Neill's Creek Bapt. Ch., Angier, NC, 1998—2001; CCR tchr. Harnett Ctrl. Mid. Sch., 2001—02; chaplain Duke U. Med. Ctr., Durham, NC, 2002—03, Wake Med, Raleigh, NC, 2003—04, NC Dept. Corrections, Lillington, 2004—. Pres. Dan River Bapt. Pastors, Halifax, Va., 1984-85; preacher jr. high weekend Va. Bapt. Gen. Assn., 1986, faculty youth week, 1984-88; v.p. Lancaster Ministerial Assn., 1987-88; v.p. Little River Bapt. Pastor's Conf., Lillington, N.C., 2000. Active CROP walk, South Boston, Va., 1984-85; coach youth soccer, South Boston, 1985, Westmoreland County, Va., 1995-97, Buics Creek, N.C., 1998; merit badge counselor Boy Scouts Am., Lancaster, 1990-93; mem. Lancaster Ednl. Task Force, 1988. Mem. Ruritan Club (chaplain 1990-93). Office: Harnett Correctional Instn PO Box1569 Lillington NC 27546 *The Kingdom of God exists wherever God is king.*

MCCLAIN, LENA ALEXANDRIA, protective services official; b. Toledo, Ohio, Aug. 15, 1966; d. Lee Earl McClain, Mattie May Roberts-McClain; m. David Angelo Neyland, Aug. 4, 1990 (div. July 1995). AAS in Criminal Justice Adminstrn., Pikes Peak C.C., Colorado Springs, Colo., 1994; postgrad., U. Colo., 1994—95; BS in Criminology, U. So. Colo., 1996; postgrad., Spring Arbor U., Mich., 2001—02; postgrad. in Social Work, Lourdes Coll., Toledo, OH, 2003—. Corrections officer Colo. Dept. Corrections, Colorado Springs, 1994—96, sgt., 1996—97, case mgr./lt., 1997—99; sr. resident specialist coord. N.W. Cmty. Corrections Ctr., Bowling Green, Ohio, 1999—2000; shift supr. Lucas County Dept. Wk. Release, Toledo, 2000—. Employee counsel, bd. dirs. Delta Correctional Ctr., 1998—99. Mem. Colo. Grievance Team, 1998; bd. dirs. Pub. Arts Commn., Delta, Colo., 1999; bd. dirs., liaison Nat. Assn. Blacks in Criminal Justice, Delta, 1998. With U.S. Army, 1987—90. Mem.: Am. Correctional Assn., Correctional Peace Officers Found., Social Work Nat. Honor Soc., Phi Theta Kappa. Democrat. Avocations: golf, basketball, softball, chess, writing.

MCCLAIN, MICHAEL H. writer; b. Middletown, Ohio, Aug. 30, 1940; s. Thomas H. and Blanche (Hamilton) McC. BA in History, U. of Ohio; MA in History, U. Granada, Spain. Staff columnist El Correo Gallego, Santiago de Compostela, Spain, 1974-84. Spkr. in field. Author: Spain & Persia: Aryium & Iran, numerous essays; contbr. articles to Cath. and Islamic jours. internationally. With U.S. Army, 1963-67. Recipient letter of thanks and congratulations for rsch. on St. John of the Cross, The Vatican, 1993. Mem. Nat. Assn. Scholars, Nat. Alumni Forum, Am. Muslim Coun. (nat. adv. bd. 1994—), Assn. Art History, Caths. United for the Faith (sec. Dayton chpt. 1990—), Coun. of Shia Islamic Orgn., Valaam Soc. Am., Ameer Khusro Soc. Am., Assn. of Literary Scholars and Critics, Great War Soc., Am. Tradition Family and Property, The 1745 Assn., Order of the White Rose, Archconfraternité du Archange St. Michel, ComuniÓn Tradicionalista, Mensa. Avocations: hunting, fishing, travel. Home: 4518 Bonita Dr Apt 130 Middletown OH 45044-6759

MCCLAIN, PAULA DENICE, political scientist, educator; b. Louisville, Jan. 3, 1950; d. Robert Landis and Mabel (Molock) McC.; stepdau. of Annette Williams McClain; m. Paul C. Jacobson, Jan. 30, 1988; children: Kristina L., Jessica A. BA, Howard U., Washington, 1972; MA, Howard U., 1974, PhD, 1977; postgrad., U. Pa., 1981-82. Asst. prof. dept. polit. sci. U. Wis., Milw., 1977-82; assoc. prof. and prof. pub. affairs Ariz. State U., Tempe, 1982-91; prof. govt. and fgn. affairs U. Va., Charlottesville, 1991-2000, chair govt. and fgn. affairs, 1994-97; prof. dept. polit. sci. Duke U., Durham, N.C., 2000—. Co-author: Can We All Get Along? Racial and Ethnic Minorities in American Politics, 1995, 3d edit. 2001, Race, Place and Risk: Black Homicide in Urban America, 1990; editor: Minority Group Influence, 1993; co-editor: Urban Minority Administrators, 1988. Mem. Nat. Conf. Black Polit. Scientists (pres. 1989-90), Am. Polit. Sci. Assn. (exec. coun. 1985-87, v.p. 1993-94), So. Polit. Sci. Assn. (exec. coun. 1992-95, v.p. 2002-03, pres.-elect 2004), Internat. Polit. Sci. Assn. (exec. com. 1997-2003, v.p. 1997-2003), Midwest Polit. Sci. Assn. (v.p. 2002-04). Office: Duke U Dept Polit Sci Perkins Libr PO Box 90204 Durham NC 27708-0204 Office Phone: 919-660-4303. E-mail: pmcclain@duke.edu.

MCCLAIN, RICHARD STAN, cinematographer; b. Los Angeles, Oct. 7, 1951; m. Kim Girard, Nov. 7, 1987. Founder Pasadena Camera Sys., Inc., Expendol.com. Aerial cameraman: (feature films) On Any Given Sunday, The Client, Contact, Man on the Moon, I Love Trouble, Tombstone, Falling Down, Heart and Soul, So, I Married an Axe Murderer, The Good Son, Made in America, This Boy's Life, Fearless, Passenger 57, Wind, At Play in the Fields of the Lord, The Iceman, Rambo, Firebirds, Wind, Basic Instinct, Innerspace, U2 Rattle and Hum, Crazy People, The Hunt for Red October, The Doors, Flatliners, Nell, Murder in the First, Drop Zone, Get Shorty, The Money Train; (TV shows) Magnum P.I., Airwolf; editor: Operating Cameraman Mag. Recipient Best Cinematography award London Internat. Advt. Awards, 1993, Telly award (2), 1993, (1), 1994, N.Y. Festival Silver award, 1993, Telly award (2) 1994, (4) 1995, (2), 1996. Mem. Internat. Cinematographers Guild, Screen Actors Guild, Dirs. Guild Am., Soc. Operating Cameramen (past pres.).

MCCLAIN, THOMAS EMERSON, communications executive; b. East Liverpool, Ohio, July 26, 1950; s. Thomas E. and Helen Marie (Polinski) McC. BA, Case Western Reserve, Cleve., 1972; MA, Kans. State U., 1973. With intergovtl. rels. Ohio EPA, Columbus, 1974-77; legis. liaison Ohio Consumers Counsel, Columbus, 1977-80, dep. dir., 1980-81; press sec. Ohio Atty. Gen., Columbus, 1982-83; asst. dir. Pub. Utilities Commn., Columbus, 1983; with instnl. rels. dept. Battelle Project Mgmt. Div., Chgo., 1983-84, mgr. instl. rels., 1984-86; mgr. comms. Battelle, Columbus, 1986-88, dir. corp. comm., 1989-95, v.p. corp. comms., 1995—. Sec. devel. bd. Children's Hosp., Columbus, 1990-91. Vol. Ohio Youth Commn., Columbus, 1975-76; active ARC-Cen. Ohio chpt., 1986-87; mem. design rev. com. Ohio State U. Sci. and Tech. Park. Mem. Rotary (chmn. program com. 1991-93, bd. dirs. 1994-95, 2d v.p. 1996-97), Roman Catholic. Avocations: basketball, golf. Home: 2607 Wexford Rd Columbus OH 43221-3215 Office: Battelle 505 King Ave Columbus OH 43201-2693

MCCLAIN, TIM S. federal agency administrator; Grad., U.S. Naval Acad., 1970; JD, Calif. We. Sch. Law, San Diego, 1978. Commd. Navy JAG Corps USN, ret., 1990, mil. def. counsel Navy Legal Svc. Office, head claims officer Navy Legal Svc. Office, head legal assistance officer Navy Legal Svc. Office, staff judge adv. for the commanding officer Naval Air Station Miramar, 1981—83, dept. head, instr. Naval Justice Sch., 1981—86, gen. court-martial mil. judge Navy-Marine Trial Judiciary, S.W., 1986—90; with litigation law firm, San Diego, 1990—96; joined internat. mgmt. cons. firm, dir. opers., 1996—99; gen. counsel Dept. Vet. Affairs, Washington, 2001—; pvt. practice, 1999—2001. Office: US Dept Vet Affairs Gen Counsel 810 Vermont Ave NW Washington DC 20420

MCCLAIN, VEDA, education educator, department chairman; BA in English, Wesleyan U., 1979; MS in Edn., U. Ctrl. Ark., 1992; PhD in Reading Edn., U. Ga., 1997. Elem. sch. tchr., Little Rock; reading instr. Upward Bound Project U. Ga., Philander Smith Coll., Little Rock; tchg. asst., rsch. asst. Nat. Reading Rsch. Ctr. U. Ga., Athens; instr. dept. reading edn. Ark. State U., State University, asst. prof. reading, assoc. prof. reading edn., dir. Minority Tchr. Scholars Program, chair dept. edn., 2001—. Reviewer Reading Excellence Grants Ark. Dept. Edn. Mem.: Ark. Literacy Tchr. Educators, Ark. Reading Assn. (chair student membership com.), S.E. Literacy Consortium, Nat. Coun. Tchrs. English, Nat. Reading Conf., Internat. Reading Assn., S.W. Ednl. Lab. (bd. mem. 2003—). Office: Ark State Univ PO Box 2350 State University AR 72467

MCCLAIN, WILLIAM ANDREW, lawyer; b. Sanford, N.C., Jan. 11, 1913; s. Frank and Blanche (Leslie) McC.; m. Roberta White, Nov. 11, 1944. AB, Wittenberg U., 1934; JD, U. Mich., 1937; LLD (hon.), Wilberforce U., 1963, U. Cin., 1971; LHD, Wittenberg U., 1972. Bar: Ohio 1938, U.S. Dist. Ct. (so. dist.) Ohio 1940, U.S. Ct. Appeals (6th cir.) 1946, U.S. Supreme Ct. 1946. Mem. Berry, McClain & White, 1937-58; dep. solicitor, City of Cin., 1957-63, city solicitor, 1963-72; mem. Keating, Muething & Klekamp, Cin., 1972-73; gen. counsel Cin. br. SBA, 1973-75; judge Hamilton County Common Pleas Ct., 1975-76; judge Mcpl. Ct., 1976-80; of counsel Manley, Burke, Lipton & Cook, Cin., 1980—; adj. prof. U. Cin., 1963-72, Salmon P. Chase Law Sch., 1965-72. Mem. exec. com. ARC, Cin., 1978—; bd. dirs. NCCJ, 1975—. Served to 1st lt. JAG, U.S. Army, 1943-46. Decorated Army Commendation award; recipient Nat. Layman award, A.M.E. Ch., 1963; Alumni award Wittenberg U., 1966; Nat. Inst. Mcpl. Law Officers award, 1971, Ellis Island Medal of Honor, 1997. Fellow Am. Bar Found.; mem. ABA, FBA, Am. Judicature Soc., Cin. Bar Assn., Ohio Bar Assn., Nat. Bar Assn., Friendly Sons St. Patrick, Bankers Club, Masons (33d degree), Alpha Phi Alpha, Sigma Pi Phi. Republican. Methodist. Home: 2101 Grandin Rd Apt 904 Cincinnati OH 45208-3346

MCCLAIR, ANNETTE, protective services official; d. Willie Jay Jones and Lottie Mae Anthony; m. Moses McClair, Mar. 30, 1977 (div.); children: Stephanie Nikole, Amber Grace Louise. Cert. Owens Police Acad., Ohio peace officer basic tng. State of Ohio Office of Atty. Gen. Campus protection officer Toledo (Ohio) Pub. Sch. Sys., 1992—; aux. dep. sheriff Sheriff's Aux., Toledo, 2002; spl. dep. sheriff Lucas County Sheriff's Dept., Toledo, 2003. Author: various poems. Democrat. Avocations: poetry, writing, art, singing, public speaking. Home: 3411 Gibralter Heights N6 Toledo OH 43609

MCCLANAHAN, DAVID M. energy executive; B in Math., U. Tex.; MBA, U. Houston. Various exec. capacities Reliant Energy, 1986—; pres., COO electric utility divsn. Reliant Energy HL&P, 1997—99; pres., COO delivery group Reliant Energy, 1999—2000, vice-chmn., 2000—02; pres., CEO, dir. CenterPoint Energy, Houston, 2002—. Chmn. bd. dirs. ERCOT; bd. dirs. Edison Electric Inst., Am. Gas Assn., Interstate Natural Gas Assn. Am. Chmn. bd. Univ. St. Thomas. Office: CenterPoint Energy PO Box 4567 Houston TX 77210-4567

MCCLANAHAN, LELAND, university director; b. Hammond, Ind., Mar. 14, 1931; s. Alonzo Leland and Eva (Hermanson) McC.; m. Lavaughn Adell Meyrer, June 5, 1954; children: Lindel, Loren. Diploma, Ctrl. Bible Coll., 1954; PhBB, Nat. Postgrad. Bible Acad., 1969; BA, Southwestern Coll., 1973; MA, Fla. State Christian Coll., 1964, ThD, 1970; PhD, Faith Bible Coll. and Sem., Ft. Lauderdale, Fla. and Marina, Lagos, Nigeria, 1969; MA, Bapt. Christian U., 1988; PhD, Freedom U., 1989; ThD, Bapt. Christian U., 1989, DLitt, 1990, PsyD, 1991; PhD, Hawaii U., 1995; DEd, Bapt. Christian U., 1994, 2002, D in Bus. Adminstrn., 1993; DD (hon.), Internat. Evangelism Crusades, 1969, Trinity Union Coll., 1991; LLD, La. Bapt. U., 1994; StD, PhD, Trinity Internat. U., 1994; HHD (hon.), La. Bapt. U., 1995; LittD (hon.), Cambridge Theol. Sem., 1995; PhD, LittD, PsyD, DBA, LLD, EdD, U. Hawaii, 1995; LittD(hon.), The Messianic Coll. of Rabbinical Studies; MA, Am. Bible Coll. & Sem., 1998; MDiv, Chapel Christian U., 1991; PhD, Midwestern U., 1998; D in Min., Am. Bible Coll. and Sem., 1999. Diplomate Nat. Bd. Christian Clin. Therapists; ordained pastor, Christian Ch., 1950; archbishop Hierarchical Christian Ch., 2000. Founder, pastor Evangel Temple, Griffith, Ind., 1954-73, Abundant Life Temple, Cocoa, Fla., 1974-77; mgr. ins. divsn. United Agys., Cocoa, Fla., 1979-81; assoc. pastor Merritt Assembly of God, Merritt Island, Fla., 1982-85, Palm Chapel, Merritt Island, 1987-89, 1990-93; founder Hawaii U., Merritt Island Offices, Merritt Island, Fla., 1990-97; chancellor Hawaii U. Merritt Island Offices, 1995-97; dir. Fla. Hawaii U. Schs., 1994-97; dir., founder Chapel Christian U., Merritt Island, Fla., 1990—; founder People's Ch. Internat., Inc., 2000—. Founder, dir. Griffith Youth Ctr., 1960-70, Todd Nursery Sch., Griffith, 1971-73; founder, chancellor Ind. Bible Coll., Griffith, 1971-73; dir. Chapel Counseling Ctr., Merritt Island, 1990-94; mem. national accreditation com. Hawaii U.; founder, pres. Brevard Humanity Ctr., Inc.,

2002; founder Mini Job Link, 2002, Adult Edn., 2003. Author: Is Divine Healing For Today?, 1989, Truths From the Gospel of St. John, 1991, An Outline of the Revelation, 1993, Numbers in the Bible, 1994, An Outline of the Acts of the Apostle, 1995, An Outline of the Book of Proverbs, 2000; author 142 coll. courses and books. Recipient Disting. Svc. award U.S. Jaycees, 1966, Govs.'s Points of Light award, Fla., 2003; named Hon. Lt. Col., Gov. Guy Hunt, 1988, Archbishop, Hierarchical Christ Ch., 2000. Fellow Am. Biog. Inst. (life); mem. Internat. Platform Assn., Order of Internat. Fellowship (life), Am. Inst. Clin. Psychotherapists, Am. Assn. christian Counselors, Nat. Christian Counseling Assn. (assoc., lic.), Internat. Assn. Pastoral Psychologists (lic.), Order of St. John, Knight of Malta (comdr. 1990). Republican. Avocations: reading, walking, watching sports, watching television adventures, weightlifting. Office: Chapel Christian Univ 870 Australian St Merritt Island FL 32953-4676 Office Phone: 321-633-7008. Personal E-mail: myccu@yahoo.com.

MCCLANAHAN, MICHAEL NELSON, systems analyst; b. Cin., Oct. 28, 1953; s. Roland Nelson and Jeanne Ann McC.; m. Tina Rosanne Swiecki, Mar. 8, 1986; children: Sean G., Elena R. Student, U. Cin., 1972-73, Goldenwest Coll., 1979-80, Riverside Community Coll., 1980-83, 90-92. Pres. Riverside (Calif.) Mktg., 1983-88; digital systems analyst Wyle Labs., Norco, Calif., 1988-93; systems analyst Ctr. for Environ. Rsch. and Tech. U. Calif., Riverside, 1993—. Author: (software) SDAS, 1989, HCSS DAS System, 1990, (book) HCSS Systems Operation, 1990, (manual) Software Quality Assurance, 1991. Recipient Svc. award Wyle Labs., 1991. Mem. IEEE, Assn. Computing Machinery, Instrument Soc. of Am., Soc. Automotive Engrs. Achievements include design of numerous software systems and integration of these with data acquisition hardware systems for the purposes of acquiring rsch. data from unique test systems in environ., aerospace, nuclear and def. industries; rsch. in ULEV hydrogen-powered vehicle devel. Office: U Calif Riverside CE-CERT 1200 Columbia Ave Riverside CA 92507-2129

MCCLANE, ROBERT SANFORD, former bank holding company executive, entrepreneur; b. Kenedy, Tex., May 5, 1939; s. Norris Robert and Ella Addie (Stockton) McC.; m. Sue Nitschke, Mar. 31, 1968; children: Len Stokes McClane Brown, Norris Robert. BS in Bus. Adminstrn., Trinity U., San Antonio, 1961. With Ford Motor Co., Detroit, 1961-62; with Frost Nat. Bank, San Antonio, 1962-97, mem. staff, 1962-68, v.p., 1968-78; exec. v.p. Cullen/Frost Bankers, Inc., 1976—85, pres., 1985-97, dir., 1985—, Benefit Planners, Inc., 1997-2001; advisor, dir. Ellison Grandchildren Trust, 1996—; pres., owner McClane Ptnrs., LLC, 1997—; dir., vice chmn. Tobin Internat., 1998—. Bd. dirs. Frost Nat. Bank, San Antonio, Princeton eCom., CCI Telecom, Inc. Crusade chmn. Bexar County chpt. Am. Cancer Soc., 1974; bd. dirs. Bexar County ARC, 1969-72; sr. warden St. Luke's Episopal Ch., San Antonio, 1980; trustee Alamo Pub. Telecomms. Coun., San Antonio, 1981-88, Trinity U., 1990, chmn., 2001—; chmn. San Antonio Econ. Devel. Found., 1987-89, exec. com. 1985-91; chmn. bd. trustees Trinity U., 2001-. Mem. Greater San Antonio C. of C. (chmn. leadership San Antonio 1975-76, bd. dirs. exec. com. 1994-97, chmn. 1996), Trinity U. Alumni Assn. (pres. 1968-69, disting. alumnus 1987), Free Trade Alliance San Antonio (bd. dirs., exec. com. 1997—, chmn. 1998-2000), Southwest Rsch. Inst. (trustee 1997—), San Antonio German Club, Order Alamo, Tex. Cavaliers, Argyle Club, Club Giraud, Plaza Club (bd. dirs. 1973-92). Episcopalian. Office: 1616 Frost Bank Tower 100 W Houston St San Antonio TX 78205-1414 E-mail: bmcclane@frostbank.com.

MCCLARD, JACK EDWARD, lawyer; b. Lafayette, La., May 13, 1946; s. Lee Franklin and Mercedes Cecile (Landry) McClard; m. Marilyn Kay O'Gorman, June 3, 1972; 1 child, Lauren Minton. BA in History, Rice U., 1968; JD, U. Tex., 1974. Bar: Va. 1974, U.S. Dist. Ct. (ea. and we. dists.) Va. 1974, U.S. Ct. Appeals (4th cir.) 1978, DC 1981, U.S. Dist. Ct. DC 1981, U.S. Ct. Appeals (DC cir.) 1981, N.Y. 1985, U.S. Dist. Ct. (so. and ea. dists.) N.Y. 1985, U.S. Ct. Appeals (5th cir.) 1993, Tex. 1996, U.S. Dist. Ct. (ea. dist.) Tex. 1998, U.S. Ct. Appeals (7th cir.) 2001. Assoc. Hunton & Williams, Richmond, Va., 1974-81, ptnr., 1981—. Contbr. articles to profl. jours., chapters to books. Served to lt. (j.g.) USN, 1968—71. Mem.: ABA, Nat. Assn. R.R. Trial Ct., Lewis F. Powell, Jr. Inns Ct. (exec. com.), 5th Cir. Bar, Richmond Bar Assn., Va. Bar Assn. Democrat. Episcopalian. Avocations: bridge, gardening, wine. Home: 100 Trowbridge Rd Richmond VA 23238 Office: Hunton and Williams Riverfront Plz E Tower 951 E Byrd St Richmond VA 23219-4074 Office Phone: 804-788-8490. E-mail: jmcclard@hunton.com.

MCCLARY, GLEN DAVID, education educator; b. Lackawanna, NY, Apr. 10, 1945; 1 child, David Henry. EdD, U. at Buffalo, NY, 1962—78. Biology, chem., physics, social studies and bus. NY State, 1974. Tchr. Buffalo Pub. Schs., 1970—2000; asst. prof. edn. D'Youville Coll., Buffalo, 1989—. Volleyball coach, Buffalo, 1977—99. Mem.: NSTA (assoc.), Sci. Tchrs. Assn. NY (assoc.), NY State Social Studies Assn. (assoc.), Nat. Assn. Tchr. Educators (assoc.). Home: 4825 Tonawanda Ck Rd N Pendleton NY 14120 Office: D'Youville Coll 320 Porter Ave Buffalo NY 14201 Personal E-mail: vbdoc@adelphia.net. Business E-Mail: mcclary@dyc.edu.

MCCLARY, JIM MARSTON, accounting executive, consultant; b. Nashville, Feb. 26, 1949; s. Joseph Patrick and Daisy Wynell (Marston) McC.; m. Billie Sue Gwinn, Feb. 27, 1970; children: Traci Gwinn, Matthew Ryan. BSBA with honors, U. Tenn., 1974. CPA, Tenn.; cert. personal fin. specialist. Staff acct. Price Waterhouse & Co. CPAs, Nashville, 1974-76; sr. acct. Bradley & Crenshaw, CPAs, Nashville, 1976-77; controller Holder & No. Lumber Sales, Inc., Nashville, 1977-78; pres. Retirement Plans, Inc., Nashville, 1978-80; ptnr. McClary, Yeary & Howell, CPAs, Brentwood, Tenn., 1980-85; cons. Franklin, Tenn., 1985—; pres. Employee Benefit Svcs. Inc., Brentwood, 1985—. Ops. prin. Thoroughbred Fin. Svcs., LLC, Brentwood, 1985—, cons. 1985—. Served with USAF, 1968-69. Mem. AICPA, Tenn. Soc. CPAs, U.S. C. of C. Republican. Avocation: athletics. Office: Employee Benefit Svcs Inc 5038 Thoroughbred Ln Brentwood TN 37027-4225 E-mail: jmcclary@thoroughbredfinancial.com.

MCCLARY, LORETTA MARY, accountant; b. Boston, July 18, 1957; d. Loretto J. and Mary L. (Rufo) Salvucci; m. Richard E. McClary, May 17, 1980 (dec. Apr. 1997); children: Loretta, Robert, Gina. BA, Regis Coll., 1979; MA, Boston U., 1980; MBA, Suffolk U., 1984; MS in Taxation, advanced taxation cert., Bentley Coll., 1990; postgrad., Suffolk U. Law Sch. CPA, Mass. With fin. dept. GSA, Boston, 1979-84; acct. Feeley & Driscoll PC, Boston, 1986-97; prof. acctg. LaSell Coll., Newton, Mass., 1996—2000; sole practice Waltham, Mass., 1999—. Mem. fin. com. Our Lady's Parish, Waltham, Mass., 1996-97. Mem. AICPA, Mass. Soc. CPA's. Avocation: golf. Home: 438 Main St Waltham MA 02452-6129 Office: 520 Main St Waltham MA 02452

MCCLARY, PATRICIA ANN, lawyer; b. Rockville Centre, N.Y., Apr. 20, 1957; d. Francis Griffith and Edna Margaret (Maher) McC. AB, Princeton (N.J.) U., 1979; JD, Harvard U., 1982. Bar: N.Y. 1983, D.C. 1984, U.S. Dist. Ct. (no. dist.) N.Y. 1987, U.S. Ct. Appeals (D.C. cir.) 1985, U.S. Ct. Appeals (3d cir.) 1986, U.S. Ct. Appeals (2d cir.) 1992. Jud. clk. to presiding justice Alaska Supreme Ct., Anchorage, 1982-83; assoc. Chadborne & Parke, Washington, 1983-86; asst. counsel Cornell U., Ithaca, N.Y., 1986-88, assoc. counsel, 1988—. Mem. Nat. Assn. Coll. and Univ. Attys. Avocation: sports. Home: 414 Elm St Ithaca NY 14850-3021 Office: Cornell U 300 CCC Bldg Ithaca NY 14853-2801

MCCLATCHY, J. D. editor, writer, educator; b. Bryn Mawr, Pa., Aug. 12, 1945; s. J. Donald and Mary Jane (Hayden) McC. BA summa cum laude, Georgetown U., 1967; PhD, Yale U., 1974. Instr. English dept. LaSalle Coll., Phila., 1968-71; asst. prof. English dept. Yale U., New Haven, 1974-81, lectr. English dept., 1983, 86-87; writer-in-residence CCNY, 1982; writer-in-residence Poetry Ctr. 92d St. YMCA, N.Y.C., 1983-84, workshop leader Poetry Ctr., 1982-91; lectr. Creative Writing program, English dept. Princeton U., 1981-87, 89-93; editor The Yale Rev., New Haven, 1991—; prof. English Yale U., 2001—. Poet-in-residence Southampton Writers Conf., 1988; lectr. MFA Parsons/New Sch., 1989, English dept. Rutgers U., 1989, writing divsn. Columbia U., 1989, 92; vis. prof. English dept. UCLA, 1990, 92; selection com. Conn. Poetry Cir. Author: (poetry) Scenes from Another Life, 1981, (London 1983), Lantskip, Platan, Creatures Ramp'd, 1983, Stars Principal, 1986, Kilim, 1987, The Rest of the Way, 1990, Ten Commandments, 1998, Hazmat, 2002; librettist: A Question of Taste, 1989, Mario and the Magician, 1994, Orpheus Decending, 1994, Emmeline, 1996; editor: The Yale Review, 1991—, (books) Anne Sexton: The Artist and Her Critics, 1978, For James Merrill: A Birthday Tribute, 1986, Recitative: Prose by James Merrill, 1986, Poets on Painters: Essays on the Art of Painting by Twentieth Century Poets, 1988, The Vintage Book of Contemporary American Poetry, 1990, Woman in White: Selected Poems of Emily Dickinson, 1991, The Vintage Book of Contemporary World Poetry, 1996, Twenty Questions, 1998, Christmas Poems, 1999, On Wings of Song, 2000, The Magic Flute (translation) 2000, Longfellow, Selected Poetry and Prose, 2000, Poems of the Sea, 2001, Love Speaks its Name, 2001, Bright Pages: Yale Writers, 1701-2001, 2001, James Merrill: Collected Poems, 2001, James Merrill: Collected Novels and Plays, 2002, Horace: The Odes, 2002, Division of Spoils, 2002; translator Carmen, 2001; assoc. editor Four Quarters, 1968-71; contbg. editor Am. Poetry Review; poetry editor The Yale Review, 1981-91; trans. articles, contbr. poems, stories, articles, reviews to various jours. Fellow Am. Acad. Arts and Scis., 1998—; mem. Am. Acad. Arts and Ltrs., 1999—; bd. dirs. Ingram Merrill Found., 1986-99; chancellor The Acad. of Am. Poets, 1996—. Recipient gold medal Vergilian Acad., 1967, O. Henry award, 1972, prize Am. Acad. Poets,1972, Chase Going Woodhouse Poetry prize, 1976, Michener award, 1982, Gordon Barber Meml. award Poetry Soc. Am., 1984, Eunice Tietjens Meml. prize Poetry Mag., 1985, Witter Bynner Poetry prize Am. Acad. and Inst. Arts and Letters, 1985, award in lit., 1991, Oscar Blumenthal prize Poetry Mag., 1988, Levinson prize, 1990, Melville Cane award Poetry Soc. Am., 1991, Literary Lion N.Y. Pub. Libr., 1992; grantee Ingram Merrill Found., 1979, Conn. Commn. Arts, 1981; fellow NEA, 1987, John Simon Guggenheim Meml. Found., 1988; fellow lit. Acad. Am. Poets, 1991; artist resident Djerassi Found., 1988; Woodrow Wilson fellow 1967-68; Yale U. fellow, 1971-72; Ethel Boise Morgan fellow, 1972-74; artist's fellow N.Y. Found. Arts, 1986; artist resident Yaddo, 1991, MacDowell Colony, 1991. Mem. Acad. Am. Poets (chancellor 1996-2003, bd. dirs. 2003-), Phi Beta Kappa, Alpha Sigma Nu. Home: 15 Grand St Stonington CT 06378-1340 Office: The Yale Review Yale Univ PO Box 208243 New Haven CT 06520-8243

MCCLATCHY, JAMES B. newspaper publisher, editor; b. Sacramento; s. Carlos K. and Phebe (Briggs) McC.; m. Susan Brewster; children: Carlos F., William B. BA, Stanford U.; MS, Columbia U. Pub. The McClatchy Co., Sacramento. Past pres., dir. InterAm. Press Assn.; dir. Capital Region Inst., Sacramento; pres. Ctrl. Valley Found. Trustee Nat. Ctr. Internat. Schs. Office: McClatchy Co 21st & Q Sts Sacramento CA 95816

MCCLATCHY, KEVIN S. professional sports team executive; b. Sacramento, Jan. 13, 1963; Diploma in Polit. Sci., U. Calif., Santa Barbara. Sport producer WPLG-TV, Miami; mktg. profl. Knight-Ridder Newspapers; nat. sales mgr. Newspaper Network (subs. McClatchy Newspapers); CEO, mng. gen. ptnr. Pittsburgh Pirates, 1996—; bus. opers. mgr. Amador Ledger-Dispatch, Calif., 1990. Co-owner Modesto A's, Oakland Athletics. Trustee Trinity-Pawling H.S., Pawling, N.Y., U. Calif. Santa Barbara; active United Way, Roberto Clemente Found., Extra Mile Found., U. Pitts. Cancer Inst., also Catholic charities. Office: Pittsburgh Pirates 115 Federal St Pittsburgh PA 15212

MCCLAUGHERTY, JOE L. lawyer, educator; b. June 1, 1951; s. Frank Lee and Elease (Terrell) McClaugherty. BBA with honors, U. Tex., 1973, JD with honors, 1976. Bar: Tex. 1976, N.Mex 1976, U.S. Dist. Ct. N.Mex 1976, U.S. Ct. Appeals (10th cir.) 1976, U.S. Supreme Ct. 1979, Colo. 1988. Assoc. Rodey, Dickason, Sloan, Akin & Robb, P.A., Albuquerque, 1976-81, ptnr., dir., 1981-87, resident ptnr. Santa Fe, 1983-87, mng. ptnr., 1985-87; ptnr. Kemp, Smith, Duncan & Hammond, P.C., 1987-92, mng. ptnr., 1987-92; ptnr. McClaugherty & Silver, P.C., Santa Fe, 1992—. Adj. prof. law U. N.Mex, Albuquerque, 1983—; faculty Nat. Inst. Trial Advocacy, So. Meth. U. Law Sch., 1983—, Hastings Ctr. Trial and Appellate Advocacy, 1985—, U. Denver Law Sch., 1986—, U. Colo. Law Sch., 1987; bd. dirs. MCM Corp., Brit.-Am. Ins. Co., Ltd., Nassau, 1985—91. Mem.: N.Mex Assn. Def. Lawyers (pres. 1982—83, bd. dirs. 1982—85), N.Mex Bar Assn. (bd. dirs. trial practice sect. 1976—85, chairperson 1983—84, dir. young lawyers divsn. 1978—80). Office: McClaugherty & Silver PC PO Box 8680 Santa Fe NM 87504-8680 Office Phone: 505-988-8804.

MCCLAVE, DONALD SILSBEE, academic administrator; b. Cleve., May 7, 1941; s. Charles Green and Anne Elizabeth (Oakley) McC.; m. Christine Phyllis Mary Tomkins, Feb. 19, 1966; children: Andrew Green, Susan Elizabeth (dec.). BA, Denison U., 1963. Mktg. rsch. officer Bank of Calif., San Francisco, 1968-70; v.p. Cen. Nat. Bank, Chgo., 1970-75, First Interstate Bank, Portland, Oreg., 1975-77, sr. v.p., 1977-79, exec. v.p., 1979-86; pres., CEO Portland Met. C. of C., 1987—2002; asst. to pres. Portland State U., 2002—. Instr. Pacific Coast Sch. Banking, Seattle, 1976-78, Grad. Sch. Mktg. and Strategic Planning, Athens, Ga., 1982-84; dir., mem. exec. com. Bank Mktg. Assn., 1976-82; bd. dirs. Oreg. Nanosci. and Microtechs. Inst. Pres. Oreg. Episc. Sch. Bd., Portland, 1983-84; pres. Assn. Oreg. Industries Found., Salem, 1984-85; pres., co-chmn. Japan-Am. Conf. Mayors and C. of C., Portland, 1985, trustee, 1991-98, exec. com., 1992-97; trustee YMCA of Columbia-Willamette, 1990-92, Portland Student Svcs. Corp., 1991-93; mem. METRO Urban Growth Mgmt. Adv. Com., 1989-92; mem. adv. com. Downtown Housing Preservation Partnership Adv. Com., 1989-94; mem. City of Portland Mayoral Transition Team, 1992, Mayor's Bus. Roundtable, 1993—; bd. dirs. Oreg. Trail chpt. ARC, 1994-95, Tri-Met, 1994—, chair fin. com., 1995—; bd. dirs. United Way Columbia Willamette, 1978-83, 2000-01, Urban League Portland, 2000-01. Capt. USAF, 1963-68. Mem. Oreg. Chamber Execs. Assn. (pres. 1998-2002). Avocations: reading, travel, golf, model building. Office: Portland State U PO Box 751 PO Portland OR 97207-0751

MCCLAVE, WILKES, III, lawyer, business executive; b. N.J., Apr. 22, 1947; BA cum laude, Yale U., 1969; JD, U. Denver, 1976. Bar: Colo. 1977, Calif. 1983. Atty. U.S. EPA, 1979-81; asst. gen. counsel, v.p. Tosco Corp., Stamford, Conn., 1981-91, sr. v.p., gen. counsel, 1991—. Mem. ABA, Conn. Bar Assn., Colo. Bar Assn., State Bar Calif., Los Angeles County Bar Assn. Office: Tosco Corp 72 Cummings Point Rd Ste 1 Stamford CT 06902-7922

MCCLEAN, LENORA JAMES, nursing educator, dean; b. Jesup, Ga., Apr. 22, 1937; d. Ealey and Mary (Howard) Hayes; m. Robert William McClean, July 13, 1963; children: Anne-Marie St. John, Sharman Danielle, Tara Lauren, Marshall Hayes. Asst. prof. nursing Fla. State U., Tallahassee, 1963-64; asst. prof. nursing Tchrs. Coll. Columbia U., N.Y.C., 1964-73; clinician Bronx Psychiat. Center, 1966-73; asst. prof., dean graduate studies Sch. Nursing Health Scis. Ctr., Stony Brook, 1973-79, prof., 1979—, assoc. dean academic affairs, 1979-80, acting dean, 1981—; chief nursing officer U. Med. Ctr. Cons. in field; chair subcom. alternative healthcare delivery patterns Cmty. Health Plan Suffolk, 1977; mem. search com. for chmn. OB/GYN Nassau County Med. Ctr., 1977-78, for chief of nursing V.A. Hosp., Northport, N.Y., 1983, planning com. rsch. and edn., 1983-86; planning group L.I. State Vets. Home, 1986-91, adv. group multidisciplinary opers., 1992; nursing adv. com. N.Y. State pub. svc. tng. program, 1988; faculty Comparative Health Care clin. study tour, U.S.-Morocco, 1990, Comparative Health Sys. Sino-Am. clin. study tour, China, 1982-91, Pediatric Nursing Soviet-Am. clin. study tour, 1981; researcher, presenter in field. Author: (with Dorothy Anderson) Identifying Suicide Potential, 1976; contbg. author: Comprehensive Psychiatric Nursing, 1979, 2d edit., 1982; contbr. numerous articles to profl. jours. Bd. dirs. Response Suffolk County, 1973-76; mem. cmty. adv. bd. transitional svcs., 1977, prof. adv. bd. chpt. Nat. Found.-March of Dimes Birth Defects, L.I. chpt., 1978-84, Blue Ribbon panel Suffolk County Infirmary, chair patient care subcom., 1989-90. Vis. fellow Sturt Coll. Advanced Edn., Bedford Park, South Australia, 1981-82; grantee. Mem. Am. Assn. Colls. Nursing (chair spl. interest group academic health sci. ctrs. 1990-93), Nat. League Nursing (coun. baccalaureate and higher degree programs), N.Y. State Nurses Assn. (v.p. 1980-82, reelected 1982, chair edn. com. 1978-80), Am. Nurses Assn., Coun. Deans of Nursing, Sr. Colls. and Univs. N.Y. State (-res. 1992), Sigma Theta Tau (Kappa Gamma chpt. 1988—). Democrat. Episcopalian. Home: 70 Washilngton St Setauket NY 11733-4029

MCCLEARY, BENJAMIN WARD, investment banker; b. Washington, July 9, 1944; s. George William and Nancy (Grim) McCleary; m. Dierdre Marsters, May 6, 1967 (div. 1977); children: Benjamin, Katherine; m. Jean Muchmore, Oct. 15, 1983. AB, Princeton U., 1966. With Chemical Bank, N.Y.C., 1969-81, trainee, asst. sec., asst. v.p., v.p.; sr. v.p. Lehman Bros. Kuhn Loeb, N.Y.C., 1981-83; mng. dir. Shearson Lehman Bros., 1983-87, Shearson Lehman Hutton Internat., London, 1987-88, Shearson Lehman Hutton, Inc., N.Y.C., 1988-89; ptnr. McFarland Dewey & Co., LLC, N.Y.C., 1989—. Bd. dirs. Detrex Corp., Harvel Plastics. Lt. (j.g.) USN, 1966—69. Office: McFarland Dewey & Co LLC 420 Lexington Ave Ste 2650 New York NY 10170 E-mail: mccleary@mcfd.com.

MCCLEARY, HENRY GLEN, geophysicist; b. Casper, Wyo., June 4, 1922; s. Raymond and Wyoma N. (Posey) McCleary Grieve; m. Beryl Tenney Nowlin, May 28, 1950; children: Gail, Glenn, Neil, Paul. Geol. Engr., Colo. Sch. Mines, 1948. From geophysicist to party chief seismic Amoco, various locations, 1948-53; exploration mgr. Woodson Oil Co., Fort Worth, 1953-60; resident mgr. NAMCO, Tripoli, Libya, 1961-62; chief geophysicist to staff geophys. assoc. Amoco Internat. Oil Co., 1963-86, 1963-73, Chgo., 1973-84, Denver, 1983-84, Houston, 1984-86; internat. geophys. cons., 1986—. Served with USN, 1943-46. Named Hon. Admiral Tex. Navy, 1968. Mem. Soc. Exploration Geophysicists, Soc. Petroleum Engrs., AAAS, Houston Gem and Mineral Soc., Profl. Oil People, Sigma Alpha Epsilon, Theta Tau. Clubs: Adventurers, Meml. Forest (Houston). Republican. Episcopalian. Home: Apt F209 2501 Westerland DR Houston TX 77063-2276

MCCLEARY, LLOYD E(VERALD), education educator; b. Bradley, Ill., May 10, 1924; s. Hal and Pearl McC.; m. Iva Dene Carter, June 13, 1971; children: Joan Kay, Victoria Lea, Karen Ann. Student, Kans. U., 1941—42; BS, U. Ill., 1948, MS, 1950, EdD, 1956; postgrad., Sorbonne U., Paris, 1946. Tchr., asst. prin. Portland (Oreg.) Pub. Schs., 1949-51; asst. prin. Univ. H.S., Urbana, Ill., 1951-52, prin., 1953-56; asst. supt. Evanston Twp. (Ill.) H.S., 1956-60; assoc. Roosevelt U., 1957-69; mem. faculty U. Mich., summers, 1958-59; prof. ednl. adminstrn. U. Utah, 1969—, chmn. dept., 1969-74. Assoc. CFK Ltd. Found., 1971-76; dir. projects in L.Am. for AID, World Bank, Ford Found., Bolivian Govt.; dir. Nat. Sch. Prin. Study, 1976-79, 86-89, res. project Families in Edn., 1992-94; edn. rep. to Utah People to People Program; keynoter Asian Conf. Edn., 1985; edn. adviser Office of the Queen, Jordan, 1985-86; advisor Nat. Commn. on Stds. in the Principalship; U.S. del. Conf. on Status Children, Senegal, 1992, Yr. of the Family, Malta, 1993; J. Lloyd Trump lectr., New Orleans, 1994. Author: Organizational Analysis X-Change, 1975, Politics and Power in Education, 1976, The Senior High School Principalship, 1980, Educational Administration, Today, 1984, High School Leaders and Their Schools, vols. 1 and 2, 1990, Leadership, 1996; editor Western Hemisphere Edn. Sch. Orgn., 1989—. Served with inf. AUS, 1941-46. Decorated Bronze Star with oak leaf cluster, Army Commendation medal; S.D. Shankland fellow, 1956; grantee Ford Found., 1968, 72, AID, 1966, 67, 70, 72, 74, 76, CFK Ltd., 1970-74, Rockefeller Family Found., 1979-80, U.S. Dept. State, 1981, 86-87, U.S. Dept. Def., 1986—; recipient Hatch Prize, 1988-89. Mem. Nat. Assn. Secondary Sch. Prins. (cert. of merit 1978, scholar-in-residence fall 1989, grantee 1969, 77, 86—), Assn. Supervision and Curriculum Devel., Nat. Assn. Elem. Sch. Prins., Phi Delta Kappa, Kappa Delta Pi. Methodist. Home: 1470 Wilton Way Salt Lake City UT 84108-2549 Office: U Utah 339 MBH Salt Lake City UT 84112 E-mail: www.birdsphoto@aol.com.

MCCLEERY, WINSTON THEODORE, computer consulting company executive; b. Mobile, Ala., Sept. 6, 1935; s. Robert Alton and Theadora K. (Kiebel) McC.; m. Sandra Thoss, Dec. 28, 1958; children: Winston T., Jacqueline McCleery McNeely. BS, Springhill Coll., 1957; postgrad., U. Ala., 1957-58. Logic design engr. Autonetics N.Am. Aviation, Anaheim, Calif., 1960—64; dir. info. sys. Litton Industries, L.A., 1965—69; founder, owner Winston T. McCleery, Cons., 1969—; pres., CEO Mgmt. Software Systems, Inc., Mobile, 1979—. Patentee in field. With U.S. Army, 1958-60. Recipient Cert. for Heroism Boy Scouts Am., 1949. Mem. Data Processing Mgmt. Assn., Assn. Computer Machinery, Am. Mgmt. Assn., Ind. Computer Cons.'s Assn., Optimists (pres. 1972). Republican. Achievements include contributions to the design and development of the U.S. Army Field Artillery's first digital fire direction computer; member of design team of the centaur missile's guidance system that made the first soft landing on the moon; design and development of the first seamless, integrated, on-line and instant-time computer application system for main frame class computers; inventor of computer power and temperature enviroment control system, development of first automatic documentation system used to document computer programs written in the Cobol language. Home: 5213 Janekyn Dr Mobile AL 36693-4142 Office: PO Box 9365 Mobile AL 36691-0365 Office Phone: 251-345-9960.

MCCLELLAN, BARRY DEAN, city manager; b. Parsons, Kans., Sept. 20, 1946; s. Don Leonard and Doris Elaine (Hamsher) McC.; m. Marshal Ellen Neuber, May 14, 1978 (div. Apr. 1990); children: Yvette, Scott, Jennie, Brian; m. Jeanne Lochart, Dec. 1, 2002. BS, U. San Francisco, 1986; MPA, Calif. State U., San Bdrnardino, 1994. Registered engr., Calif. Assoc. engr. City of Riverside, Calif., 1969-78; mng. engr. Kicak & Assocs., Redlands, Calif., 1978-80; pub. works dir. City of Palm Desert, Calif., 1980-85; regional mgr. Neste, Brudin & Stone, Inc., Palm Springs, Calif., 1985-86; pub. works dir. City of Irvine, Calif., 1995-96, City of Moreno Valley, Calif., 1986-95, asst. city mgr., 1996—. Curriculum advisor U. Calif. Extension, Riverside, 1993-94. Chair regional steering com. United Way of Inland Valley, Riverside, 1997-2000, bd. dirs., 2000—; dir. Riverside County Regional Med. Ctr. Found., program adv. bd. pub. adminstrn. dept. Calif. State U., San Bernardino; dir. Riverside C.C. Found., 2003—. Served with USAF, 1964-68. Named Outstanding Campaign Vol., United Way, 1998-99, 99-2000. Mem. Am. Soc. Pub. Adminstrn., Internat. City Mgmt. Assn., Rotary (bd. dirs. 1998-2001), Victoria Club, Moreno Valley Rotary Club (pres. 2000-2001). Republican. Avocations: exercise, travel, reading, golf. Home: 15600 Oliver St Moreno Valley CA 92555 Office: 26559 Chamomile St Murrieta CA 92562 E-mail: barrym@moval.org.

MC CLELLAN, CATHARINE, anthropologist, educator; b. York, Pa., Mar. 1, 1921; d. William Smith and Josephine (Niles) McClellan; m. John Thayer Hitchcock, June 6, 1974. AB magna cum laude in Classical Archaeology, Bryn Mawr Coll., 1942; PhD (Anthropology fellow), U. Calif. at Berkeley, 1950. Vis. asst. prof. U. Mo. at Columbia, 1952; asst. prof. anthropology U. Wash., Seattle, 1952-56; anthrop. cons. USPHS, Arctic Health Research Center, Alaska, 1956; asst. prof. anthropology, chmn. dept. anthropology Barnard Coll., Columbia U., 1956-61; asso. prof. anthropology U. Wis. at Madison, 1961-65, prof., 1965-83, prof. emeritus, 1983—, John Bascom prof., 1973. Vis. lectr. Bryn Mawr (Pa.) Coll., 1954; vis. prof. U. Alaska, 1973, 87. Assoc. editor: Arctic Anthropology, 1961; editor, 1975-82; assoc. editor: The Western Canadian Jour. of Anthropology, 1970-73. Served to lt. WAVES, 1942-46. Margaret Snell fellow AAUW, 1950-51; Am. Acad. Arts and Scis. grantee, 1963-64, Nat. Mus. Can. grantee, 1948-74 Fellow Am. Anthrop. Assn., Royal Anthrop. Inst. Gt. Britain and Ireland, AAAS, Arctic Inst. N.Am.; mem. Am. Ethnol. Soc. (sec.-treas. 1958-59, v.p. 1964, pres. 1965), Kroeber Anthrop. Soc., Am. Folklore Soc., Am. Soc. Ethnohistory (exec. com. 1968-71), Sigma Xi. Achievements include rsch. in archaeol. and ethnographic field investigations in Alaska and Yukon Territory in Can. E-mail: cmclellan@rivermead.org.

MCCLELLAN, CRAIG RENE, lawyer; b. Portland, Oreg., June 28, 1947; s. Charles Russell and Annette Irene (Benedict) McC.; m. Susan Armistead Nash, June 7, 1975; children: Ryan Alexander, Shannon Lea. BS in Econs., U. Oreg., 1969; JD magna cum laude, Calif. We. U., 1976. Bar: Calif. 1976, U.S. Dist. Ct. (so. dist.) Calif. 1976, U.S. Dist. Ct. (ea., ctrl., no. dists.) Calif. 1991, U.S. Supreme Ct. 1991. Compliance specialist Cost of Living Coun. and Price Commn., Washington, 1972-73, dir. Oil Policy subcom., 1973; ptnr. Luce, Forward, Hamilton & Scripps, San Diego, 1976-87; owner McClellan & Assocs., San Diego, 1987—. Chmn. annual fundraising auction KPBS, 1984.

Capt. USMC, 1969-72. Fellow Am. Coll. Trial Lawyers; mem. Assn. Trial Lawyers Am., Am. Bd. Trial Advocates, Am. Inns of Ct. (master), Calif. State Bar Assn., San Diego County Bar Assn., Calif. Trial Lawyers Assn. (bd. govs. 1985-87), San Diego Trial Lawyers Assn. (bd. dirs. 1983-90), Nat. Forensics League, Phi Gamma Delta, Phi Alpha Delta. Presbyterian. Avocations: reading, running, tennis, chess, civic activities. Office: McClellan & Assocs 1144 State St San Diego CA 92101-3529 Office Phone: 619-231-0505. E-mail: craig@mcclellanlaw.com.

MCCLELLAN, EDWIN, Japanese literature educator; b. Kobe, Japan, Oct. 24, 1925; came to U.S., 1952; s. Andrew and Teru (Yokobori) McC.; m. Rachel Elizabeth Pott, May 28, 1955; children: Andrew Lockwood, Sarah Rose. MA, U. St. Andrews, Scotland, 1952; PhD, U. Chgo., 1957. Instr. English, U. Chgo., 1957-59, asst. prof. Japanese lang. and lit., 1959-63, assoc. prof., 1963-65, prof., 1965-70, Carl Darling Buck prof., 1970-72, chmn. dept. Far Eastern langs. and civilizations, 1966-72; prof. Japanese lit. Yale U., New Haven, 1972-79, Sumitomo prof. Japanese studies, 1979-98, Sterling prof. Japanese lit., 1998-2000, Sterling prof. emeritus Japanese lit., 2000—, chmn. dept. East Asian langs. and lits., 1973-82, 88-91, chmn. council humanities, 1975-77, chmn. council East Asian studies, 1979-82. Vis. lectr. Far Eastern langs. Harvard U., spring 1965; mem. adv. coun. dept. Oriental studies Princeton U., 1966-71; mem. Com. to Visit East Asian Studies, Harvard U., 1982-88; mem. Am. adv. com. Japan Found., 1985-95; mem. bd. Coun. for Internat. Exch. Scholars, 1981-84. Translator: Kokoro (Natsume Soseki), 1957, Grass on the Wayside (Soseki), 1969, A Dark Night's Passing (Naoya Shiga), 1976, Fragments of a Past (Eiji Yoshikawa), 1992; author: Two Japanese Novelists: Soseki and Toson, 1969, Woman in the Crested Kimono, 1985; mem. bd. editors Jour. Japanese Studies, 1986-99; contbr. articles to profl. jours. Liason intelligence officer Royal Air Force, Washington, 1945-47; bd. trustees Society Japanese Studies U. Wash., 1992-99. Served with Royal Air Force, 1944—48. Recipient Kikuchi Kan prize for contbn. to study of Japanese lit., Tokyo, 1994, Noma Lit. Translation prize, 1995, Order of the Rising Sun, Gold Rays with Neck Ribbon, Japanese Govt., 1998. Fellow Am. Acad. Arts and Scis. Home: 641 Ridge Rd Hamden CT 06517-2516

MCCLELLAN, LARRY ALLEN, minister, educator; b. Buffalo, Nov. 3, 1944; s. Edward Lurelle McClellan and Helen (Denison) Greenlee; m. Diane Eunice Bonfoey, Aug. 19, 1973; children: Kara E., Seth C. Student, U. Ghana, 1964-65; BA in Psychology, Occidental Coll., 1966; MTh, U. Chgo., 1969, D Ministry, 1970. Ordained to ministry Presbyn. Ch. (U.S.A.), 1970. Prof. of sociology and community studies Govs. State U., University Park, Ill., 1970-86; interim pastor Presbyn. Ch. (U.S.A.), Chgo. area, 1980-86; sr. pastor St. Paul Community Ch., Homewood, Ill., 1986-96; adj. prof. Govs. State U., University Park, Ill., 1987-96; dir. South Met. Regional Leadership Ctr., Govs. State U., University Park, Ill., 1996—2001; cmty. rels. dir. Northeastern Ill. Planning Commn., 2001—; pastor First Christian Ch. (Disciples), Chicago Heights, Ill., 2003—. Newspaper columnist Star Publs. Chgo., 1993—; trustee Internat. Coun. Community Chs., 1989-91, pres., 1991-93. Author: Local History South of Chicago, 1988; developer social simulation games; contbr. articles to profl. pubs. Mayor Village of Park Forest South (name now University Park), Ill., 1975-79; co-organizer S. Region Habitat for Humanity, Chgo. area, 1989; pres. S. Suburban Heritage Assn., Chgo. area, 1988-91. Fellow Layne Found., 1966-70, NEH, 1979. Mem. Am. Assn. State and Local History, Ill. State Hist. Soc. (Spl. Achievement award 1989). Office Phone: 708-754-3792. E-mail: larryamcclel@msn.com.

MCCLELLAN, MARK B. federal agency administrator; BA, BS, U. Tex., 1985; MA, MPA, Harvard U., 1991, MD, 1992; PhD, MIT, 1993. Cons. The Rand Corp., Santa Monica, Calif., 1989—91; rsch. assoc. Harvard Med. Sch. Dept. of Health Care Policy, Boston, 1991—95; attending physician Stanford U. Health Svcs.; asst. prof. dept. econs. and dept. medicine Stanford U., 1995—99; dir. program on health outcomes rsch. Stanford Med. Sch.; dep. asst. sec. for econ. policy U.S. Dept. Treasury, Washington, 1998—99; mem. Coun. of Econ. Advisors Exec. Office of the Pres., Washington, 2001—02; commr. FDA, Rockville, Md., 2002—04; CEO, adminstr., Ctrs. for Medicare & Medicaid Svcs. U.S. Dept. Health & Human Services, Washington, 2004—. Mem.: Inst. Medicine, 2004. Office: Ctrs for Medicare & Medicaid Svcs Hubert H Humphrey Bldg 200 Independence Ave SW Rm 314G Washington DC 20201*

MCCLELLAN, MARY ANN, pediatric nurse practitioner; b. Mar. 29, 1942; BS, Tex. Woman's U., 1964; MN, U. Wash., 1968-69; cert., U. Tex., Arlington, 1997. Cert. family life educator, CPNP, pediatric nurse practitioner; advanced RN practitioner, Okla. Charge nurse Baylor U. Med. Ctr., Dallas, 1964—65; pub. health staff nurse Dallas County Health Dept., Dallas, 1965—68; supervising nurse Okla. State Dept. Health, Oklahoma City, 1969—70, maternal-child health nurse cons., 1971; asst. prof. U. Okla. Coll. Nursing, Oklahoma City, 1971—72; from instr. to asst. prof. Harris Coll. Nursing Tex. Christian U., Ft. Worth, 1972—75; asst. prof. continuing edn. U. Okla. Coll. Nursing, Oklahoma City, 1976—79, asst. prof. baccalaureate program, 1979—96, mem. grad. faculty, 1991—. Cons. and lectr. in field. Contbr. chpts. to books, articles to profl. jours. Mem. Nat. Coun. on Family Rels., Okla. Family Resources Coalition, Nat. Assn. Pediatric Nurse Assocs. and Practitioners (Okla. chpt.), Assn. Faculty of Pediat. Nurse Practitioner Programs, So. Early Childhood Assn., Okla. Coun. on Family Rels., Okla. Early Childhood Assn., Sigma Theta Tau., Phi Kappa Phi. Office: U Okla Coll Nursing PO Box 26901 Oklahoma City OK 73126-0901 Office Phone: 405-271-2302.

MCCLELLAN, RICHARD AUGUSTUS, retired small business owner; b. Gainesville, Fla., Sept. 13, 1930; s. Marion Theodore Sr. and Cornelia (Hampton) McC.; m. Thelma Watson, May 19, 1947 (dec. Mar. 1980); children: Richard A., Wayne Theodore, Viola Patricia, Michael Ray; m. Betty Lee Snow, Dec. 12, 1980 (div. July 1991); children: Claranell Y., Juanita F., Johnnie C.; m. Geraldine C. Williams, Aug. 14, 1993. Diploma, Nat. Inst. Drycleaning, 0975, Napoleon Hill Found., 1994. Drycleaner S & S Cleaners, Gainesville, 1958-97; ret., 1997. Mem. Am. Soc. Notaries (govt. rels. com. 1984, pub. rels. com. 1989), Notary Pub. Assn. State Fla., Nat. Notary Assn., Internat. Order St. Luke the Physician. Democrat. Mem. United Methodist Ch. Avocations: reading, radio, jazz music. Home and Office: 625 SE 15th St Gainesville FL 32641-3123

MCCLELLAN, ROBERT EDWARD, civil engineer; b. Atlanta, Feb. 27, 1922; s. Robert Edward and Maria Elizabeth (Ameln) McC.; m. Mary Margaret Billetter, Oct. 21, 1944; children: Kathleen Mary, Mary Elizabeth, Patricia Maura, Eileen Mary, Robert Edward III, Mary Margaret, Thomas Francis. BCE, U. So. Calif., 1947, MSCE, 1956, PhD in Engring., 1970. Registered profl. civil and structural engr., Calif. Gen. supr. design Rocketdyne, Canoga Park, Calif., 1959-62; mem. tech. staff The Aerospace Corp., El Segundo, Calif., 1962-69, mgr. strategic studies, 1980-85; chief tech. staff The Ralph M. Parsons Co., Pasadena, Calif., 1969-80; v.p. research and devel. Apollo Systems Tech., Canyon Country, Calif., 1985-88, also bd. dirs. Served to lt. (j.g.) USN, 1943-46, PTO. Recipient Outstanding Civil Engring. Grad. award U. So. Calif., 1977. Mem. AIAA, Am. Def. Preparedness Assn., AAAS, N.Y. Acad. Scis., L.A. Athletic Club, Sigma Xi, Tau Beta Pi, Chi Epsilon. Republican. Roman Catholic.

MCCLELLAN, ROGER ORVILLE, toxicologist; b. Tracy, Minn., Jan. 5, 1937; s. Orville and Gladys (Paulson) McC.; m. Kathleen Mary Dunagan, June 23, 1962; children: Eric John, Elizabeth Christine, Katherine Ruth. DVM with highest honors, Wash. State U., 1960; M of Mgmt., U. N.Mex., 1980. Diplomate Am. Bd. Vet. Toxicology, Am. Bd. Toxicology. From biol. scientist to sr. scientist Gen. Electric Co., Richland, Wash., 1957-64; sr. scientist biology dept. Pacific N.W. Labs., Richland, Wash., 1965; scientist med. rsch. br. divsn. biology and medicine AEC, Washington, 1965-66; asst. dir. rsch., dir. fission product inhalation program Lovelace Found. Med. Edn. and Rsch., Albuquerque, 1966-73; v.p., dir. rsch. adminstrn., dir. Lovelace Inhalation Toxicology Rsch. Inst., Albuquerque, 1973-76, pres., dir., 1976-88; chmn. bd. dirs. Lovelace Biomed. and Environ. Rsch. Inst., Albuquerque, 1988-96; pres., CEO Chem. Industry Inst. Toxicology Rsch., Triangle Park, NC, 1988-99, pres. emeritus, 1999—; pvt. advisor Toxicology and Human Health Risk Analysis, 1999—. Mem. rsch. com. Health Effects Inst., 1981-92; bd. dirs. Toxicology Lab. Accreditation Bd., 1982-90, treas., 1984-90; adj. prof. Wash. State U., 1980-95, U. Ark., 1970-88; clin. assoc. U. N.Mex., 1971-85, adj. prof. toxicology, 1985—; adj. prof. toxicology and occupl. and environ. medicine Duke U., 1988—; adj. prof. toxicology U. N.C., Chapel Hill, 1989-2000; adj. prof. toxicology N.C. State U., 1991—; cons. faculty Colo. State U., 2002—; regents lectr. UCLA, 1999-2000; mem. dose assessment adv. group U.S. Dept. Energy, 1980-87, mem. health and environ. rsch. adv. com., 1984-85, 1999-2004; mem. exec. com. sci. adv. bd. EPA, 1974-95, mem. environ. health com., 1980-83, chmn., 1982-83, chmn. radionuclide emissions rev. com., 1984-85, chmn. Clean Air Sci. Adv. Com., 1987-92, Diesel Exhaust Panel, 1996-2001, chmn. rsch. strategies adv. com., 1992-94, mem. Particulate Matter Panel, 1993-97, 99—; mem. com. on toxicology NAS-NRC, 1979-87, chmn., 1980-87; mem. com. risk assessment methodology for hazardous air pollution NAS-NRC, 1991-94, com. biol. effects of Radon NAS NRC, 1994-98, com. rsch. priorities for airborne particulate matter, 1998-2004; mem. Environ. Roundtable, Inst. Medicine, 1998-2002; mem. com. on environ. justice Inst. of Medicine, 1996-99, trustee toxicology excellence in risk assessment, 2000—, chmn. bd. trustees, 2002-04, mem. coord. com. strengthening sci.-based decision making, 2002—; pres. Am. Bd. Vet. Toxicology, 1970-73; mem. adv. coun. Ctr. for Risk Mgmt., Resources for the Future, 1987-2001; mem. Nat. Coun. for Radiation Protection, 1970-2001, hon. mem., 2002—; bd. dirs. N.C. Assn. Biomed. Rsch., 1989-91, N.C. Vet. Med. Found., 1990-95, pres., 1993-94; bd. govs. Rsch. Triangle Inst., 1994-2001; mem. adv. com. alternative toxicol. methods Interagy. Ctr. Evaluation Alternative Methods, Health and Human Svcs., 1998-2001; mem. sci. adv. bd. strategic environ. rsch. strategies program Dept. Def./Dept. Energy/EPA, 1997-99; mem. adv. com. Ctr. for Environ. Health, Agy. for Toxic Substances and Disease Registry, CDC, 2002-04; mem. bd. sci. counselors Ctr. for Environ. Health/Agy. for Toxic Substances Disease Registry, 2004—. Jour. Toxicology, 1984—89, assoc. dir., 1987—89; editor: Critical Revs. in Toxicology, 1987—; mem. editl bd.: Regulatory Toxicology and Pharmacology, 1993—, Risk Analysis, 1998—, Ullman's Ency. of Indsl. Chemistry, 1999—, Non-Linearity in Biology-Toxicology-Medicine, 2003—; contbr. articles to profl. jours. Trustee Wash. State U. Found., 2001—. Recipient Herbert E. Stokinger award Am. Conf. Govtl. Indsl. Hygienists, 1985, Alumni Achievement award Wash. State U., 1987, Disting. Assoc. award Dept. Energy, 1987, 88, Arnold Lehman award Soc. Toxicology, 1992; co-recipient Frank R. Blood award Soc. Toxicology, 1989; Internat. Aerosol fellow Internat. Aerosol Rsch. Assembly, 1998; named Disting. Vet. Medicine Alumnus Wash. State U., 1999, Robert Leader Meml. lectr. Mich. State U., 1999; named to Hall of Fame Robert O. Anderson Schs. of Mgmt., U. N.Mex., 2002. Fellow: AAAS, Acad. Toxicol. Sci., Gesellschaft fur Zerosolforschung, Health Physics Soc. (chmn. program com. 1972, Elda E. Anderson award 1974), Am. Acad. Vet. and Comparative Toxicology, Soc. Risk Analysis; mem.: Am. Vet. Med. Assn., Internat. Soc. Aerosols in Medicine (Thomas Mercer Joint prize for Aerosol Rsch. 1997), Am. Assn. Aerosol Rsch. (bd. dirs. 1982—94, treas. 1986—90, v.p. to pres. 1990—93), Toxicology Edn. Found. (founding pres. 1990—91), Internat. Congress Toxicology VII (treas. 1995), Soc.Toxicology (chmn. 1983—85, inhalation splty. sect. v.p. to pres. 1983—86, bd. publs. 1983—86, v.p.-elect to pres. 1987—90), Am. Conf. Govtl. Indsl. Hygienists, Internat. Regulatory Pharmacology and Toxicology (Internat. Achievement award 1999), Am. Assn. Cancer Rsch., Am. Thoracic Soc., Radiation Rsch. Soc. (chmn. fin. com. 1979—82, sec.-treas. 1982—84), Inst. Medicine (elected 1990, chair other health professions sect. 1999—2001), Am. Chem. Soc., Phi Zeta, Phi Kappa Phi, Sigma Xi. Republican. Lutheran. E-mail: roger.o.mcclellan@att.net.

MC CLELLAN, WILLIAM MONSON, library administrator, retired; b. Groton, Mass., Jan. 7, 1934; s. James Lewis and Ruth Caldwell (Monson) McC.; m. Jane Muir, Sept. 3, 1955; children— Jennifer, Anne, Margaret, Amy. BA, Colo. Coll., 1956, MA, 1961; A.M. in L.S, U. Mich., Ann Arbor, 1959. Music librarian U. Colo., Boulder, 1959-65; dir. Music Library, U. Ill., Urbana, 1965-97. Cons. music library resources and services to colls. and univs.; co-dir. Inst. Music Librarianship, Kent State U., 1969 Editor: Music Library Assn. Notes, 1977-82; Contbr. articles to profl. jours. Council on Library Resources fellow, 1976-77 Mem. Internat. Assn. Music Librs., Music. Libr. Assn. (pres. 1971-73, conf. panelist, chmn. stats. subcom. 1990-93). Home: 451 Boardwalk Dr Apt 1306 Fort Collins CO 80525-3230 Personal E-mail: muirmack@frii.com. *To commit myself daily to giving and opening myself to others in all professional and other contexts.*

MCCLELLAND, EMMA L. state legislator; b. Springfield, Mo., Feb. 26, 1940; m. Alan McClelland; children: Mike, Karen. BA, U. Mo., 1962. mem. appropriations, natural and econ. resources com., budget com., elem. and secondary edn. com., mcpl. corps. com., rules, joint rules and bills perfected and printed com., social services com., medicaid and elderly com. Dir. field office, corp. divsn. Mo. Sec. of State, St. Louis; committeewoman Gravois Twp.; mem. St. Louis County Rep. Cent. Com., Mo. Rep. State Com., Mo. Ho. of Reps., Jefferson City, 1991—; mem. appropriations, budget, edn., mcpl. corps., rules, joint rules and bills perfected and printed, social svcs., medicaid and the elderly coms. Bd. dirs. Ct. Apptd. Spl. Advocates, Family Support Network; elder Webster Groves Presbyn. Ch.; mem. Leadership St. Louis. Recipient Leadership award for govt. YWCA of St. Louis, Spirit of Enterprise award Mo. C. of C., Mental Health Assn. award for legis. svc., 1998, Mo. Child Adv. of Yr. award Mo. Child Care Assn., 1998. Mem. Webster Groves C. of C., Pi Lambda Theta. Republican. Presbyterian. Home: 455 Pasadena Ave Webster Groves MO 63119-3126 Office: Mo Ho of Reps State Capitol Building Jefferson City MO 65101-1556

MCCLELLAND, FRANK, chef, restaurant owner; m. Catherine McClelland; children: Keppler, Annie, James. Chef The Harvest, Cambridge, Mass., L'Espalier, Boston, exec. sous chef, 1986—, owner, 1988—; exec. chef The Country Inn, Princeton, Mass., 1984—86; owner, exec. chef Sel de la Terre, Boston, 2000—. Named one of Top 25 New Chefs, Food & Wine Mag., 1985. Office: L'Espalier 30 Gloucester St Boston MA 02115

MCCLELLAND, GEORGE DUNCAN, business executive; b. Washington, July 8, 1946; s. Glenn Bryan and Elizabeth (Bliss) McC.; m. Jacquelyn Elaine Gaudion, Apr. 26, 1969; children— Lindsay Robyn, Geordie Gaudion BA in Econs. cum laude, Trinity Coll., Hartford, Conn., 1968; MBA with distinction, Harvard U., 1970. Internat. analyst Data Gen. Corp., Southboro, Mass., 1972—73, controller internat. ops., 1973—75, mgr. treasury ops., 1975—77, dir. treasury svcs., 1977—80, treas., 1980—83, v.p., treas., 1983—87; corp. v.p., treas. FMR Corp. (Fidelity Investments), 1987; pres. FACS, 1988, OAA, 1989; mng. dir. Fidelity Capital, 1992—93; sr. v.p., COO Kendall Sq. Rsch., 1993; sr. v.p. United Asset Mgmt., 1994—2001; founder, chmn. bd. eSeeLanding, 2000. Chmn. bd. dirs. U. Mass. Hosp., Worcester, 1985-1998, mem. fin. and investment coms., 1992-1998; vice chair, exec. com. Big Brothers Mass. Bay, 1995-2003. W. T. Grant and George Baker fellow, Harvard Bus. Sch., 1969 Mem. Harvard Bus. Sch. Assn. (bd. govs. 1984—)

MCCLELLAND, HAROLD FRANKLIN, economics professor; b. Omaha, Mar. 8, 1918; s. Frank Melanchthon and Nellie (Hawthorne) McC.; m. Marion Lois Ludlow, July 3, 1941; children— Donald G., Nancy J., Jeanne L. BA, Hastings Coll., 1939; MA, U. Nebr., 1940; MS, Denver U., 1942; PhD, Harvard, 1959. Research asso. Govtl. Research Inst., St. Louis, 1942-43; treas. McClelland-Rose Motors, Inc., Hastings, Neb., 1946-55; from instr. to prof. econs. Claremont (Calif.) McKenna Coll. and Claremont Grad. Sch., 1958-65, James G. Boswell prof. econs., 1976-88, ret., 1988; dean faculty Claremont (Calif.) Men's Coll., 1963-70. Author: State and Local Finance, Nebraska, 1962, (with others) Essays in Federalism, 1961, The American Property Tax, 1965; also articles. Mem. Calif. Constn. Revision Commn., 1969-72. Served to lt. USNR, 1943-46. Mem. Am. Econ. Assn., Western Econ. Assn., Nat. Tax Assn. (bd. dirs. 1978—) Clubs: Commonwealth of Calif, University. Republican. Presbyterian. Home: 4630 23rd St N Arlington VA 22207-3507

MCCLELLAND, HELEN, music educator; b. Chgo., Dec. 5, 1951; d. Leon Leroy and Willie Jo (Darnell) McC.; (div. Sept. 1981); 1 child, Tasha Renee. Diploma in arts, Kennedy-King Coll., 1971; cert. in voice, Sherwood Music Coll., 1971-73; BS, Chgo. State U., 1975, MA in Adminstrn., 1983; D in Adminstrn. and Supervision, U. Calif., 1993. Tchr. Faulkner Sch., Chgo., 1975-78; tchr. music Harvey (Ill.) Pub. Sch. Dist. 152, 1978—. Dir. music Pleasant Green Missionary Bapt. Ch., Chgo., 1971—; mem. sch. bd. New World Christian Acad., Chgo., 1988—; bd. dirs. South Shore Drill Team, Chgo. Author: operetta So You Want to Be a Star, 1987. Cmty. worker People United to Save Humanity, Chgo., 1973, Harold Washington Orgn., Chgo., 1987; cmty. educator Chgo. Planned Parenthood, 1988; cmty. counselor Lincoln Cmty. Ctr., Chgo., 1975; mem. sch. bd. Dist. 160, 1994, now v.p.; mem. Ill. State Sch. Bd., 1997-98; bd. dirs. Operation P.U.S.H.; vice chmn. Ill. Assn. Sch. Bds., Ill. State Assn. Bd.; bd. dirs. Ill. State Assn. Bd., So. Cook Div., 2003-; v.p. Sch. Dist. #160;; mem. Grace M.B. Ch. Named Tchr. of the Yr., Faulkner Sch., 1976; recipient Nat. Sch. Bd. award for Disting. Svc., Ill. State Assn. Bd., 2003. Mem. Ill. Edn. Assn., NEA, Harvey Edn. Assn., Tennis Club, Traveling Club, Phi Delta Kappa, Pi Lambda Theta. Democrat. Baptist. Avocations: singing, bowling, piano. Home: 18029 Ravisloe Ter Country Club Hills IL 60478-5169

MCCLELLAND, JAMES RAY, lawyer; b. Eunice, La., June 21, 1946; s. Rufus Ray and Homer Florene (Nunn) McClelland; m. Sandra Faye Tate, Feb. 6, 1971; children: Joseph Ray, Jeffrey Ross. BS, La. State U., 1969, MBA, 1971, JD, 1975. Bar: La. 1975, US Ct. Appeals (5th cir.) 1976, US Dist. Ct. (ea. dist.) La. 1976, US Dist. Ct. (we. dist.) La. 1976, US Dist. Ct. (mid. dist.) La. 1994. Assoc. Aycock, Horne & Coleman, Franklin, La., 1975—78, ptnr., 1978—. Bd. dirs. Bayou Bouillon Corp., Cotten Land Corp. Exec. com. Dem. Party; del. La. Dem. Party, 1982, 1984; Exec. com. St. Mary Parish, 1980—88. Mem.: St. Mary Parish Bar Assn. (pres. 1978—79), La. State Bar Assn. (ho. of dels. 1982—95, law reform com. 1984—86, bd. govs. 1995—2002, ho. of dels. 1998—99, sec. 2003—), Rotary (pres. 1981—82), Order of Coif. Home: PO Box 268 Franklin LA 70538-0268 Office: PO Box 592 Franklin LA 70538-0592 Office Phone: 337-828-1880.

MCCLELLAND, PATRICIA G. minister; b. Warsaw, Mo., July 12, 1944; d. Gail Raymond and Martha Carolyn (Lewis) Easton; m. Lester E. McClelland, Aug. 18, 1974; 1 child, Melody. BS, U. Mo., 1968; MA, Drury Coll., 1972. Cert. tchr., Mo., Kans., Ill.; lic. counselor; ordained to ministry Unity Ch., 1986. Instr. U. Mo., Kansas City, 1968, 71-74, Park Coll., Parkville, Mo., 1968-70; spl. cons. Kansas City Pub. Schs., 1970-71; author edn. materials, 1975-70, instr. U. Wis., 1970-79, min. Milw., 1979-81, instr. Sem. Unity Sch. Christianity, 1983-85; co-min. Unity Ch. Pitts., 1985-86; sr. min. Unity Ch., Anderson, Ind., 1986-87, sr. minister Warren, Ohio, 1987-88, Massillon, Ohio, 1988-90; dir. housing Southwestern Coll., Winfield, Kans., 1990-91; min. specializing in ministry to women, cons., Lincoln, Nebr., 1991-93; co-min. Lindenwood Union Ch., Rockford, Ill., 1993—. Founding min. Council Bluffs Unity Ch.; tchr. pub. schs., Rochelle, Ill., 1994—2000; instr. Rockford (Ill.) Coll.; tchr., facilitator Skylight grad. program Rock Valley Coll., Janesville, Wis., 2001—02; tchr. Belvidere Pub. Schs., 2002—, St. Xavier U., 2002—. Mem. NAFE, ASCD, TESOL, Nat. Assn. Self-Employed, Internat. New Thought Alliance, Internat. Platform Assn. Methodist/Unity. Home and Office: 7399 Bermuda Dr Rockford IL 61108-4486 E-mail: revpatmcc@yahoo.com. *Our inheritance as Children of God is a world where everything necessary is available for every human being to live a happy, healthy, peaceful, abundant life. The choice to do so, as well as the work to fulfill that choice, is up to us both individually and collectively.*

MCCLELLAND, RICHARD LEE, dentist; b. Pitts., May 18, 1927; s. William Noble and Pauline Elizabeth (Lee) McC.; m. Elizabeth Anne Michon, Dec. 6, 1958; children: Richard Scott, William Alfred, Robert Craig. BA, Princeton U., 1950; DDS, U. Pa., 1954. Pvt. practice, Princeton, N.J., 1958-92. Clin. instr. U. Pa. Dental Sch., Phila., 1958-62; mem. exec. com. Med. Ctr. Princeton, 1971-72, past chmn. dental dept.; elected Nat. Dental Surgeon Res. Officers Assn. of U.S., 1972-73. With USN, 1945-46, WWII, lt. Dental Corps, USNR, 1954-57, capt., ret. Fellow: Acad. Gen. Dentistry, Internat. Coll. Dentists, Am. Coll. Dentists; mem.: ADA, Fedn. Dentaire Internat., Princeton Officers' Soc., Res. Officers Assn., Princeton Club (N.Y.C.), Nassau Club, Rotary (pres. Princeton 1978—79). Republican. Episcopalian. Avocations: sailing, photography. Home: 58 Governors Ln Princeton NJ 08540-3671

MC CLELLAND, ROBERT NELSON, surgeon, educator; b. Gilmer, Tex., Nov. 20, 1929; s. Robert Hilton and Verna Louise (Nelson) McC.; m. Connie Logan, May 5, 1958; children: Robert Christopher, Alison, Julie. BA, U. Tex., Austin, 1952; MD, U. Tex., Galveston, 1954. Diplomate Am. Bd. Surgery. Rotating intern U. Kans. Med. center, 1954-55; resident in gen. surgery Parkland Hosp., Dallas, 1957-59, 60-62; instr. surgery Southwestern Med. Sch., U. Tex., Dallas, 1962-63, asst. prof., 1963-67, asso. prof., 1967-71, prof., 1971—, Alvin Baldwin prof. surgery, 1977—. Examiner Nat. Bd. Med. Examiners Editor Audio Jour. Rev. Gen. Surgery, 1971-82, Selected Readings in Gen. Surgery, 1974—; contbr. numerous articles to profl. jours., chpts. to books. Served to capt. M.C. USAF, 1955-57. Fellow ACS (mem. grad. edn. com.); mem. AMA, Am. Surg. Assn., Western Surg. Assn., Soc. Surgery of Alimentary Tract, Am. Gastroent. Assn., Southwestern Surg. Soc., So. Surg. Assn., Dallas Soc. Gen. Surgeons (pres. 1987-88), Tex. Surg. Soc., Tex. Med. Assn., Dallas Country Med. Soc., Soc. Internatale de Chiurgie (bd. dirs. Am. chpt.), Phi Beta Kappa, Alpha Omega Alpha. Republican. Lutheran. Home: 3601 Potomac Ave Dallas TX 75205-2110 Office: 5323 Harry Hines Blvd Dallas TX 75390-7208

MCCLELLAND, SHEARWOOD JUNIOR, orthopaedic surgeon; s. Shearwood and Zenobia McClelland; m. Yvonne Shirley Thornton, 1974; children: Shearwood III, Kimberly. AB, Princeton U., 1969; MD, Columbia U., 1974; MPH, 1996. Diplomate Am. Bd. Orthopaedic Surgery. Intern St. Luke's Hosp., N.Y.C., 1974-75; resident, 1975-76; asst. resident in orthopaedic surgery N.Y. Orthopaedic Hosp., 1976-79; lt. comdr. USNR, 1979-82; staff orthopaedic surgeon Nat. Naval Med. Ctr., Bethesda, Md., 1979-82; asst. prof. surgery Uniformed Svcs. U. Health Scis., 1980-82; acting chief orthopaedic surgery Harlem Hosp. Ctr., 1983-84; assoc. dir. orthopaedic surgery, 1985-92; acting dir., 1992-94; dir., 1994—; asst. prof. clin. orthopaedic surgery Columbia U., 1983-94; assoc. prof. clinic, 1994—. Oral examiner Am. Bd. Othopaedic Surgery, 1993—; mem. N.Y. State Bd. of Profl. Med. Conduct, 1989-98. Annie C. Kane fellow in orthopaedic surgery, 1978-79; fellow in total joint implant surgery Ohio State U., 1982. Fellow ACS, AMA, Am. Acad. Orthopaedic Surgeons, N.Y. Acad. Medicine; mem. Assn. Mil. Surgeons of U.S., Am. Coll. Phys. Execs., N.Y. Orthopaedic Hosp. Alumni Assn., Mensa, No. N.J. Princeton Alumni Assn., Columbia P&S Alumni Assoc. (pres. 2002-2004). Office: Harlem Hosp Ctr Dept Orthopaedic Surgery 506 Lenox Ave New York NY 10037-1802 Office Phone: 212-939-3510. E-mail: sjm2@columbia.edu.

MCCLELLAND, W. CARTER, bank executive; BS in Aero. Engring., Stanford U., 1967, MBA, 1973. Engr. NASA-Jet Propulsion Lab., Calif.; various positions including dir. corp. fin. Morgan Stanley, chief adminstrv. officer, mem. oper. com., 1993—95; pres., CEO Deutsche Bank N.Am., 1995—98, also bd. dirs.; sr. mng. dir., co-dir. investment banking NationsBanc Montgomery Securities LLC (now Banc of Am. Securities LLC), San Francisco, 1998—; head banking and equities Banc of Am. Securities LLC, 2001—, pres., 2001—; mng. dir. Bank of Am. Corp., market pres., 2003—. Bd. dirs. United Way N.Y., Nat. Coun. on Econ. Edn., NYC2012. Office: Bank Am Securities LLC 9 W 57th St New York NY 10019

MCCLELLAND, WILLIAM CRAIG, paper company executive; b. Orange, N.J., Apr. 21, 1934; s. William N. and Pauline (Lee) McClelland; m. Alice Garrett, Dec. 28, 1956; children: Suzanne, Alice Elizabeth, Heather. BS in Econs., Princeton U., 1956; MBA, Harvard U., 1965. Salesman, br. mgr. PPG Industries, Cleve. and Erie, Pa., 1960—63; pres. Watervliet Paper Co. divsn. Hammermill Paper Co., Mich., 1969—73; product, mktg. mgr. Hammermill Paper Co., Erie, Pa., 1965—69, v.p., 1973—80, sr. v.p., 1980—83, exec. v.p., dir., 1983—85, pres., CEO, 1985—88, also bd. dirs.; sr. v.p. Internat. Paper Co., 1986—87, exec. v.p., 1987—88, also bd. dirs.; exec. v.p. Union Camp Corp., Wayne, NJ, 1988—89, chmn., pres., COO, 1989—94, chmn., CEO, 1994—99. Bd. dirs. Quaker State Corp., PNC Fin. Corp., Allegheny Ludlum

Corp., Allegheny Techs. Inc., Pitts., PNC Bank Corp., Pitts. Mem. Coun. Fellows Behrend Coll. of Pa. State U., 1980—88; dir. Pitts. Theol. Sem., 1988—. Lt. j.g. USN, 1956—59. Home: 7 Ridge Crest Rd Saddle River NJ 07458-3107

MCCLENDON, FRED VERNON, real estate professional, business consultant, equine and realty appraiser, financial consultant; b. Vernon, Tex. s. Guy C. and Lexie M. (Johnson) Mc C.; m. Dorothy J. Seibert, June 1943 (div. 1953); children: Cathy, Kent, Tracy; m. Ethel R. Cherry, Sept. 15, 1959; children: Tess, Rob, J.T. Assoc. in Commerce, Hannibal La Grange Coll., 1947; BBA, Baylor U., 1949; MBA, postgrad. in law, Harvard U., 1951; postgrad. in banking, Colo. U., 1951-52; postgrad., Denver U., 1951-52. Lic. ins. agt., Tenn.; cert. real estate broker, Tenn.; cert. internat. financier. Asst. cashier U.S. Nat. Bank, Denver, 1951; gen. mgr. Nat. Paper Band Co., Denver, 1952-53; personnel mgr. Houston Fire & Casualty Co., Ft. Worth, 1954-56; gen. sales mgr. City Lincoln/Mercury, Dallas, 1957-58; owner INS-Bank Personnel Agy., Dallas, 1959-61; mng. ptnr. Allen & Mc Clendon Ins., Dallas, 1959-63; owner, broker Mc Clendon Real Estate, Dallas, 1959-63; pres. Mc Clendon Realty Co., Hampton, Tenn., 1961-2001; gen. mgr. Eagle Nest Ranch, Roan Mountain, Tenn., 1963-88, Mile High Ranch, Roan Mountain, 1988-99; pres. FMV Appraisal Co., Hampton, 1988-99, Amerifund Ventures, Internat., Tex., 2000—. Cons. Gen. Adjustments Bur., 1981—, Debourdieux Corp., 1985—, Wachesaw Corp., 1985—, Hidden Lakes Devel. Corp., various ins. cos. and law firms in U.S. and Can., IRS, U.S. Marshals Svc., U.S. Customs, 1993—, Heartland Presbyn. Ctr.; exec. cons. El Dorado Ranch, 1991-98; cons. IRS; lectr. to lodges and assns.; gen. ptnr. Flexnet Investments, Ltd., Dallas, 1988-91; pres. Bus. Realty Internat. Cons., Hillsboro, Tex., 2000-; exec. v.p. OmniVue, Inc., S.C., 1992-95; chmn. AmeriFund Ventures, Internat., Tex., 1995-99, Tex., 2000—; pres. U.S. Med-Am. Bus. Svcs., 1995—. Contbr. articles to profl. jours. Recipient W.T. Grant fellow Harvard U., 1950-51. Mem. Am. Quarter Horse Assn. (life), Australian Appaloosa Assn., Appaloosa Horse Club U.S., Tenn. Walking Horse Breeders Assn., Am. Paint Horse Assn., Am. Soc. Equine Appraisers, Am. Horse Coun., Am. Soc. Appraisers (Accredited sr. appraiser, bd. examiners 1990—), Internat. Real Estate Inst., Nat. Assn. Real Estate Appraisers, Environ. Assessment Assoc. (cert. insp. 1991—), Appraisers Assn. Am. (cert. sr. appraiser), Internat. Soc. Financiers (cert. internat. financier). Republican. Mem. Seventh Day Adventists. Avocations: boating, travel, fishing, swimming. Home: Eagle Nest West Ranch 1580 Hwy 77 N Hillsboro TX 76645 Office: Amerifund Ventures Internat PO 1209 Hillsboro TX 76645-1209 Office Phone: 254-632-4441. Personal E-mail: fredmcclendon@hillsboro.net.

MCCLENDON, IRVIN LEE, SR., business owner, writer, editor, proofreader, tutor; b. Waco, Tex., June 12, 1945; s. Irvin Nicholas and Evelyn Lucile (Maycumber) McC.; divorced; children: Michael Boyd, Irvin Lee Jr., Laura Ann, Paul Nicholas, Richard Lester. Student, El Camino Coll., 1961-63, U. So. Calif., 1962-66; BA in Math., Calif. State U., Fullerton, 1970, postgrad. in bus. adminstrn., 1971-76; cert. nat. security mgmt., Indsl. Coll. Armed Forces, 1974; postgrad. in religion, Summit Sch. Theology, 1982-84; student, Fullerton Coll., 1998, student, 2004—05; postgrad., Trinity Coll. Grad. Studies, 2005—. Engring. lab. asst. Rockwell Internat. Corp., Anaheim, Calif., 1967-68, test data analyst, 1968-70, mem. tech. staff, 1970-82; systems programmer A-Auto-trol Tech. Corp., Denver, 1982-84; sr. tech. writer, editor Colo. Data Systems, Inc., Englewood, Colo., 1986-87; engring. writer III CalComp subs. Lockheed Co., Hudson, N.H., 1987; sr. tech. writer CDI Corp., Arvada, Colo., 1987-88; staff cons. CAP GEMINI AM., Englewood, 1989; sr. tech./instrnl. writer & editor TTS Inc., Aurora, Colo., 1990-96, sr. multimedia developer, 1996-97; gen. mgr., chief editor The Berkeley Group, LLC, Denver, 1997-99; writer Am. Resume Ctr., Northglenn, Colo., 1997-98; info. processing technician County of Orange, Health Care Agy., Santa Ana, Calif., 1998—2002; vol. The David Bohnett Cyber Ctr., The Ctr. Orange County, Garden Grove, Calif., 2002—04; copy editor The Orange County and Long Beach Blade, Laguna Beach, Calif., 2003—04; owner, gen. mgr., writer, editor, proofreader, tutor McClendon Profl. Svcs., Garden Grove, Calif., 2004—. Sec. of governing bd. Yorba Linda Libr. Dist., 1973-78; mem. First United Meth. Ch. of Orange, 1998—; mem. Men Alive, The Orange County Gay Men's Chorus, 2004-; trustee Ch. of God (Seventh Day), Bloomington, Calif., 1979-81, treas., 1980-81, mem. Calif. State U. and Coll. Statewide Alumni Coun., 1976-77; 2d v.p. Orange County chpt. Calif. Spl. Dists. Assn., 1976, pres., 1977; mem. Adams County Rep. Ctrl. Com., 1984-90, Denver County Rep. Ctrl. Com., 1992-95, Scouting for All, Petaluma, Calif. 1998- (vol., copy editor, 1998-, asst. southwestern regional dir. for Ariz., Calif., Colo., Hawaii, NNex., and Utah, grassroots organizerm Garden Grove, Calif., Alliance for Human Rights, 2003-); tech. support adviser to chmn. Colo. Rep. Com., 1997-98, mem. Soulforce, Orange County, 2004-. With USAFR, 1967-71. USAF Nat. Merit scholar, 1963-67. Mem. Calif. Assn. Libr. Trustees and Commrs. (exec. bd., So. Calif. rep. 1976-78), Nat. Eagle Scout Assn. (life), Bible Sabbath Assn. (life), Calif. State U.-Fullerton Alumni Assn. (dir. 1975-77). Republican. Business E-Mail: OCLBBlade@cox.net., McClendonSr@scoutingforall.org.

MCCLENDON, MAXINE NICHOLS, artist; b. Leesville, La., Oct. 21, 1931; d. Alfred Harry and Clara (Jackson) McMillan; m. Edward Edson Nichols, Mar. 28, 1967; children: Patricia Ann, Joan Terri, Christopher, Jennifer. Student, Tex. U., 1948—50, Tex. Woman's U., 1950—51, Pan Am. U., 1963—64. Instr. McAllen Internat. Mus., 1987—90; artist, owner in studio, Mission, Tex., 1991—. Pvt. practice drawing tchr., Mission, 1990. Artist: one woman shows include: Art Mus. S. Tex., Corpus Christi, 1971, McAllen (Tex.)Internat. Mus., 1976, Amarillo (Tex.) Art Ctr., 1982, U. Tex., Pan American, 1994; group shows in Wichita, Kans., 1972, Marietta, Ohio, 1975, Dallas, 1977, represented in permanen collections: Mus. Internat. Folk Art, Santa Fe, Ark., Mus. Fine Art, Little Rock, McAllen Internat. Mus., Lauren Rogers Mus., Laurel, Miss.; commns.: Caterpiller Corp., Peoria, Ill., Union Bank Switzerland, N.Y.C., Crocker Bank, L.A., Tarleton U., Tex., Hyatt Regency, Ft. Worth, Forbes, Inc., San Francisco, First Savs. & Loan, Shreveport, La., Continental Plaza, Ft. Worth.; curator folk art McAllen Internat. Mus., 1974-80. Recipient judges' award 4th Nat. Marietta, 1975, numerous others. Mem. World Crafts Coun., Am. Crafts Coun. (Tex. rep. 1976-80), Tex. Designer/Craftsmen (pres. 1973-74). Christian Scientist. Home: 2018 Sharyland St Mission TX 78572 E-mail: enichols@rgv.rr.com.

MC CLENDON, WILLIAM HUTCHINSON, III, retired lawyer; b. New Orleans, La, Feb. 19, 1933; s. William H. and Eleanor (Eaton) McC.; m. Eugenia Mills Slaughter, Feb. 6, 1960; children: William Hutchinson, IV, Virginia Morris, Eleanor Eaton, Bryan Slaughter. BA, Tulane U., 1956, LLB, 1958. Bar: La. 1958, US Supreme Ct. 1964. Atty. Humble Oil & Refining Co., 1958-60; with firm Taylor, Porter, Brooks & Phillips, Baton Rouge, 1960—, ptnr., 1966-2001, mem. exec. com., 1987-2001; mediator, assoc. Mediation Arbitration Profl. Sys., Inc., 1999—2001. Instr. comml. law and negotiable instruments Am. Inst. Banking, 1963-74; lectr. movable Property La. Bar Assn. Bridging the Gap Inst., 1965; lectr. La. State U. LAw Sch. and Real Estate Seminar chmn., 1972, 74, 76, 80, 82, 85, 87, 95, La. Soc. of Profl. Surveying, 1989, La. Soc. CPA's, 1991, Banking Seminar, 1995; adj. prof. La. State U. Legal Negotiation, 1983—, U. Tenn., 2003-, Western Carolina U., 2003-; mem. faculty Profl. Edn. Group, Inc., We. Carolina U. Contbr. articles to legal jour. Bd. dir. Cancer Soc. Baton Rouge, 1968-71; trustee Episcopal HS, 1976-78; mem. Dean's council Tulane U. Law Sch., 1984-88. Served to capt. AUS. Recipient Preservation award Found. for Hist. La., 1997. Mem. ABA, Am. Judicature Soc., La. Bar Assn. (chmn. sect. trust estates, probate and immovable property law 1969-70, Meml. award article 1987), Baton Rouge Bar Assn. (chmn. title standards com. 1968-69), Tulane Alumni Assn. Greater Baton Rouge (pres. 1968-69), Baton Rouge Green (bd. dir. 1991-93), Hilltop Aboretum (bd. dir. 1993-95), La. Civil Svc. League (pres. 1992-94), La. Tulane Law Alumni (treas., 2d v.p. 1964-65), Baton Rouge Assembly (treas. 1983, ball chmn. 1997, chmn. 1999), Toastmasters (pres. 1970), Baton Rouge Country Club, Camelot Club, Pickwick Club, Rotary (bd. dir. Baton Rouge club 1972), Kappa Alpha, Baton Rouge Symphony (bd. dir. 2001-02). Republican. Episcopalian (vestry, sr. warden 1975, 81, 84, diocesan standing com. 1985-89). E-mail: wh.mcclendon@verizon.net.

MCCLENNEN, CRANE, judge; b. July 31, 1946; s. Louis McClennen and Dorothy (Petrovich) Johnson; m. Deborah Ann Hass, Feb. 19, 1995. BS, Ariz. State U., 1968, JD cum laude, 1972. Bar: Ariz. 1972, U.S. Dist. Ct. (Ariz.) 1972, U.S. Ct. Appeals (9th cir.) 1977, U.S. Supreme Ct. 1977. Atty. Snell & Wilmer, Phoenix, 1972-75; asst. atty. gen. Ariz. Atty. Gen.'s Office, 1975-97; judge Ariz. Superior Ct., Maricopa County, 1997—. Lectr. State Bar of Ariz., 1987—, continuing legal edn. commn., 1987—, chair, 1996-97, appellate handbook com., 1985—, criminal jury inst. com., 1996—, bd. legal specialization, 1991-96, chair, 1993-95, peer review com., 1992-95, criminal rules com., 1990-94, alternative dispute resolution com., 1984-86, criminal justice sec., 1980-87, chair, 1984-86; editl. bd. Ariz. Atty., 1987-98; spkr. in field. Author: Arizona Courtroom Evidence Manual, 3rd edit., 1998, Arizona Legal Forms, Criminal Procedure, 1990. Named Disting. Public Lawyer, State Bar Ariz., 1991, Mem. of Yr. State Bar of Arizona, 1995. Fellow Ariz. Bar Found.; mem. Phi Delta Theta. Office: 201 W Jefferson St SPC 47 Phoenix AZ 85003-2244

MC CLENNEN, LOUIS, lawyer, educator; b. Cambridge, Mass., May 29, 1912; s. Edward F. and Mary (Crane) Mc C.; m. Miriam Jacobs, Apr. 25, 1969; children by previous marriage: Adams, James, Helen, Persis, Crane, Emery. AB cum laude, Harvard U., 1934, JD, 1937. Bar: Mass. 1937, Ind. 1940, Ariz. 1947. Pvt. practice, Boston, 1937-39, Indpls., 1940-42, Phoenix, 1946-95; pres. McClennen & Fels, P.C., 1974—2002; adj. prof. law fed. taxation Ariz. State U., 1974-80, pres. Law Soc., 1981-83. Author: Arizona Estate Tax, 1953, (with J.T. Melczer Jr.) Arizona Income Tax Regulations, 1954; contbr. articles to profl. jours. Pres. Ariz. Bd. Edn., 1965-69; trustee No. Ariz. Mus.; pres. Maricopa County Legal Aid Soc.; bd. dirs. Phoenix Symphony Assn., 1950-70, pres., 1952-54; v.p., bd. dirs. Phoenix United Fund; founder, sec., bd. dirs. Phoenix Country Day Sch.; bd. dirs. Ariz. Acad.; regional dir. Harvard Alumni Assn. Maj. USAAF, 1942-46. Mem. ABA, Am. Law Inst., Ariz. Bar Assn., Maricopa County Bar Assn. (dir., past v.p.), Harvard Law Sch. Assn. (v.p.) Lawyers Club Phoenix (pres.), Phoenix Country Club, Eastward Ho Country Club (Chatham, Mass.). Unitarian Universalist. Home and Office: 5311 N La Plaza Cir Phoenix AZ 85012-1415

MCCLENNEN, MIRIAM J. former state official; b. Seattle, Sept. 16, 1923; d. Phillip and Frieda (Golub) Jacobs; m. Louis McClennen, Apr. 25, 1969; stepchildren: Adams Peter, James C.A., Helen, Persis, Crane, Emery. BA, U. Wash., 1945; MBA, Northwestern U., 1947. Exec. trainee Marshall Field & Co., Chgo., 1945-47; buyer Frederick & Nelson (subs. of Marshall Field), 1949-57, Goldwaters, Phoenix, 1963—67; adminstrv. asst. to pres. Ariz. State Senate, Phoenix, 1973-76; dir. publs. Office of Sec. of State, Phoenix, 1976-87. Chairwoman legis. subcom. adminstrv. procedure Ariz. State Legislature, Phoenix, 1984-85. Original compiler, codifier, editor publ. Ariz. Adminstrv. Code, 1973-87, Ariz. Adminstrv. Register, 1976-87. Bd. dirs., mem. Phoenix Art Mus. League, 1972—90; bd. dirs., mem. exec. bd. Phoenix Symphony Guild, 1969—88; bd. dirs., sec. Combined Met. Phoenix Arts and Scis., 1974—90, mem. adv. bd., 1990—95; bd. dirs. Phoenix Art Coun., 1973—78, Master Apprentice Programs, 1980—83; bd. dirs., mem. exec. bd. Heard Mus., 1982—88, 1990—; mem. adv. bd. Ariz. State Hist. Records, 1987—90, Ariz. Commn. on Arts, 1989—96, Phoenix Art Mus., 1966—; bd. dirs. Arizonans for Cultural Devel., 1996—2002; mem. Cape Mus. Fine Arts, 1996—. Recipient Disting. Svc. award Atty. Gen. Ariz., 1987, Outstanding Svc. to People, Ariz. State Senate, 1987, Nat. Assn. Secs. of State award, 1987. Mem.: Univ. Club, Ariz. Club, Phoenix Country Club, Charter 100 (bd. dirs. 1981—85). Home: 5311 N La Plaza Cir Phoenix AZ 85012-1415 also: 2267 Rt 28 Harwich MA 02645 E-mail: mjmlm@earthlink.net.

MC CLENNEY, BYRON NELSON, community college administrator; b. San Antonio, Dec. 14, 1939; s. Thomas B. and Lorene Holley McC.; children: Mark Nelson, Don Alan; m. Kay McCullough, May 17, 1986. BS, U. Tex., 1961, MEd, 1963, EdD, 1969. Asst. dean evening divsn. San Antonio Coll., 1966-68; dean instrn. McLennan C.C., Waco, Tex., 1968-70, Eastfield Coll., Dallas County, Tex., 1970-71, pres., 1971-78, Parkersburg (W.Va.) C.C., 1978-81, San Antonio C.C. Dist., 1981; chancellor Alamo C.C. Dist., 1982-86; pres. C.C. Denver, 1986-2000, Kingsborough C.C., 2000—. Author: Management for Productivity, 1980. Mem. steering com. Pres. Clinton's Am. Reads Challenge, 1997-2000. Recipient PBS O'Banion prize, 2002; NDEA fellow, 1965-66; recipient Disting. Alumni award U. Tex. Coll. Edn., 1982-83, Thomas J. Peters Nat. Leadership award League for Innovation, 1989. Mem. Am. Assn. Cmty. and Jr. Colls. (chmn. pres.'s acad. 1983-84, mem. urban commn. 1987-90), Commn. on Instns. of Higher Edn. Clubs: Rotary (past dist. gov.). Presbyterian. Office: 2001 Oriental Blvd Brooklyn NY 11235 Home: 4711 Hickory Hollow Austin TX 78731-3605

MCCLENON, JOHN RAYMOND, retired chemistry educator; b. Grinnell, Iowa, May 1, 1937; s. Raymond Benedict and Erika (Weber) McC.; m. Mary Alice Thornton, June 7, 1959; children: Anne Jeanette, Marca Kay, Maureen. BA, Grinnell Coll., 1959; PhD, UCLA, 1964. Asst. prof. Milton Coll., Wis., 1963-65; asst. prof. chemistry Sweet Briar (Va.) Coll., 1965-72, assoc. prof., 1972-76, prof., 1976-82, Charles A. Dana prof., 1982—2002. Head FBN Microcomputing, Lynchburg, Va., 1980—. Johnny McClenon Big Band, Lynchburg, Va., 1978— Editor: (newsletter) Macintosh User's Group, Sweet Briar Coll. Chmn. ACLU local chpt., 1966-75; prin. clarinettist Lynchburg Symphony, Va., 1976—. Mem. AAUP (chmn. Sweet Briar chpt. 1982-83) Democrat. Unitarian Universalist. Home: 712 Riverside Dr Lynchburg VA 24503-1327 E-mail: mcclenon@cstone.net.

MCCLESKEY, JERRY MICHAEL, retired chemical company executive; b. Ft. Worth, July 3, 1933; s. Ray Emmett McCleskey and Nelle Ileta Canuteson; m. Margaret Elaine Milton, July 19, 1957; children: Claire McCleskey Dubit, Catherine McCleskey Gassman. BA, Rice U., 1955, BSChE, 1956. Chief engr. Conoco, Inc., Ponca City, Okla., 1960-67; plant mgr. Conoco Chems., Balt., 1967-72, mgr. mfg. Saddle Brook, N.J., 1972-74, v.p. Houston, 1974-80; pres. Conoco Coal Devel. Co., Stamford, Conn., 1980-82; dir. chems. dept. El Du Pont de Nemours, Wilmington, Del., 1982-92; ret., 1992. Trustee, chmn. fin. com. Kosciuszko Found., N.Y.C., 1984-94; bd. govs. Rice U., Houston, 1985-89, gov. advisor, 1990—; mem. fine arts com. U. Del., 1988-92. Lt. USN, 1956-60. Avocation: woodworking. Home: 211 Heritage Oaks Ln Houston TX 77024 Fax: 713-977-1951. E-mail: jmcc33@swbell.net.

MCCLIMON, TIMOTHY JOHN, lawyer; b. Clinton, Iowa, July 17, 1953; s. Leonard James and Celeste Margaret (Borman) McC.; m. Suzanne Berman, Jan. 30, 1994. BA magna cum laude, Luther Coll., 1975; MS, St. Cloud State U., 1976; JD, Georgetown U., 1986. Bar: N.Y. 1987. Asst. dir. student activities St. Cloud State U., Minn., 1975-76; performing arts coordinator Western Ill. U., Macomb, 1976-79; program specialist Nat. Endowment for the Arts, Washington, 1979-82, program adminstr., 1982-86, law clk., 1985-86; assoc. Webster and Sheffield, N.Y.C., 1986-88; v.p. AT&T Found., 1988-96, exec. dir., 1996—2003, Second Stage Theatre, 2003—. Adj. prof. NYU, 1990—; bd. dirs. N.Y. Regional Assn. Grantmakers, N.Y.C., Second Stage Theatre, N.Y.C., BBB Found., N.Y.C., New Vision Pub. Schs., N.Y.C., Times Square Alliance, N.Y.C., Field Papers, Inc., N.Y.C.; spkr. confs. on arts mgmt., fundraising and nonprofit mgmt., 1979—; cons. NEA, Washington, 1986—; mem. mayor's cultural affairs adv. commn. City of N.Y.C., 1992-94. Author: (textbook chpt.) Audiences and the Arts, 1981; contbr. articles to Jour. of Law and the Arts, 1986, other publs., 1989—. Recipient Eagle Scout award Boy Scouts Am., 1967, Faculty award Blue Key Nat. Honor Frat., 1979. Mem. N.Y.C. Bar Assn. (com. mem. 1987-92), ABA (com. mem. 1986-88), N.Y. State Bar Assn., Vol. Lawyers for the Arts. Avocations: photography, bicycling, travel, reading. Home: 222 Riverside Dr Apt 14A New York NY 10025-6809 Office: Second Stage Theatre 307 W 43d St New York NY 10036 Office Phone: 212-787-8302 ext. 106.

MCCLINTIC, JAMES A. lab administrator; BS in Mktg., Calif. State U., San Diego. From sales rep. to v.p., mktg. & planning to v.p., sales Bristol Myers Squibb; pres. SciCor Inc.; regional pres., eastern opers. Corning MetPath, Teterboro, NJ; pres., CEO Esoterix Inc., Austin, 1999—. Office: Esoterix Inc 4509 Freidrich Ln Bldg 1 Ste 100 Austin TX 78744*

MC CLINTOCK, ARCHIE GLENN, lawyer; b. Sheridan, Wyo., Mar. 26, 1911; s. James Porter and Martie E. (Glenn) McC.; m. Ina Jean Robinson, May 27, 1939 (dec. 1974); children: Ellery, Jeffry, Kathleen. BA, U. Wyo., 1933, LLB with honor, 1935. Bar: Wyo. 1935, Calif. 1982. Pvt. practice law, Cheyenne, Wyo., 1935-73, 81-83, 87—; justice Wyo. Supreme Ct., Cheyenne, 1973-81; atty. gen. State of Wyo., 1982-87; semi-ret. Adj. prof. law U. Wyo., 1988, 90-92. Mem. Wyo. Fair Employment Practices Commn., 1965-71. Served with USNR, 1944-45. Mem. Wyo. State Bar (pres. 1950-51), Am. Judicature Soc., Order of Coif (hon. mem.) Sigma Nu. Clubs: Elks. Democrat. Home: 4010 N College Dr #121 Cheyenne WY 82001-1960

MCCLINTOCK, GEORGE DUNLAP, retired lawyer; b. Pocatello, Idaho, Nov. 30, 1920; s. George Dunlap and Jessie (McCabe) McC.; m. Aileen McHugh, Sept. 19, 1945 (dec. Jan. 2000); children— Jessie Kelly, Catharine, George, Jane Wyatt, Michael, Anne AB cum laude, Dartmouth Coll., 1942; LLB, Harvard U., 1948. Bar: Minn. 1948. Ptnr. Faegre & Benson, Mpls., 1948-90. Dir. Merchants Bank, Rugby, N.D.; trustee Douglas Rees Trust, 1966—, Paul R. Held Testamentary Trusts, 1980—. Trustee, mayor City of Woodland, Minn., 1970-79; exec. bd., Viking council Boy Scouts Am., Mpls., 1959-74, pres., 1966-67; gen. campaign chmn. United Way of Mpls., 1972, bd. dirs., 1973-81, pres., 1976; trustee Convent of Visitation Sch., St. Paul, 1975-81; trustee North Meml. Med. Ctr., Robbinsdale, Minn., 1959-75; trustee, sec. Minn. Med. Found., Mpls., 1982-90. Served to lt. USNR, 1942-46 Recipient Disting. Eagle Scout award Boy Scouts Am., 1982 Mem. Mpls. Club (governing com. 1983-89, pres. 1987), Woodhill Country Club (trustee 1985-94). Republican. Presbyterian. Avocations: golf, waterfowl hunting.

MCCLINTOCK, JESSICA, fashion designer; b. Frenchville, Maine, June 19, 1930; d. Rene Gagnon and Verna Hedrich; m. Frank Staples (dec. 1964); 1 child Scott. BA, San Jose State U., 1963. Elem. sch. tchr., Marblehead, Mass., 1966-68, Long Island, N.Y., 1968, Sunnyvale, Calif., 1964-65, 68-69; fashion designer Jessica McClintock, Inc., San Francisco, 1969—. Active donor, AIDS and Homeless programs; scholarship sponsor Fashion Inst. Design and Merchandising. Recipient Merit award Design, 1989, Dallas Fashion award, 1988, Tommy award, 1986, Pres. Appreciation award, 1986, Best Interior Store Design, 1986, Calif. Designer award, 1985, Earnie award, 1981, numerous others. Mem. Coun. Fashion Designers of Am., Fashion Inst. Design & Merchandising (adv. bd. 1979—), San Francisco Fashion Industry (pres. 1976-78, bd. dirs. 1989). Office: Jessica McClintock Inc 1400 16th St San Francisco CA 94103-5181

MCCLINTOCK, MARTHA K. biologist, educator; AB, Wellesley College, 1969; MA in Psychology, U. Penn., 1972, Ph.D. in Psychology, 1974. With U. Chgo., 1976—, asst. prof., psychology and human devel., 1976, David Lee Shillinglaw Distinguished Svc. Prof. Psychology, dir., Inst. Mind & Biology. Chmn. biopsychology com., 1986—99; mem. neurobiology com., evolutionary biology com., human develop. com. Contbr. articles to profl. jours. Recipient Disting. Sci. Award for Early Career Contbn. to Psychology, APA, 1982, MERIT Award, NIMH, 1992, Edith Krieger Wolf Disting. Vis. Prof., Northwestern Univ., 2000, Henry G. Walter Sense of Smell Award, Sense of Smell Inst., 2001. elected mem., Inst. of Medicine, 1999, Acad. of Arts and Sciences, 1999. Office: U Chgo 5730 S Woodlawn Ave Chicago IL 60637

MCCLINTOCK, RICHARD POLSON, dermatologist; b. Lancaster, N.H., Dec. 16, 1933; s. Richard P. and Dorothy Grace McClintock; m. Barbara Wyatt, June 1959 (div. Mar. 1970); children: Peter, Pamela; m. Mary Joy Fitzgerald, Mar. 21, 1970; children: Wayne, Patrick. BA, Dartmouth Coll., 1956; MD, Harvard U., 1960. Diplomate Am. Bd. Dermatology, Am. Bd. Dermatopathology. Intern in medicine U. N.C., Chapel Hill, 1960-61; resident in dermatology Stanford U., Palo Alto, Calif., 1964-67; pvt. practice Ukiah, Calif., 1967—; clin. instr. dermatology Stanford U., Palo Alto, 1967-78, clin. asst. prof., 1978-86, assoc. clin. prof., 1986-92, lectr., 1992-98, assoc. clin. prof., 1998—. Mem. hosp. staff Ukiah Valley Med. Ctr., chief of staff, 1974; bd. dirs. IPA and Found. Med. Care Mendocino and Lake Counties. Contbr. articles to profl. jours. Trustee Found. for Med. Care for Mendocino and Lake Counties, 1990-94, pres., 1992-94. Lt. Med. Corps, USN, 1961-64. Mem. San Francisco Dermatol. Soc. (Practitioner of Yr. 2004), Pacific Dermatol. Assn., Am. Acad. Dermatology, Calif. Med. Soc., Mendocino Lake County Med. Soc., Internat. Soc. Dermatopathology. Office: 723 S Dora St Ukiah CA 95482-5335 E-mail: fitzmac@pacific.net.

MCCLINTOCK, THOMAS LEE, lawyer; b. Lake Bluff, Ill., July 5, 1948; s. Harold B. and Sarah O. (Durbin) M.; children: Ryan Arthur, Andrew Smith, Max Thomas. AA, Ill. Valley C.C., 1968; BS, No. Ill. U., 1970, MBA, 1971; JD, Valparaiso U., 1974. Bar: Ill. 1974, U.S. Dist. Ct. (no. dist.) Ill. 1975, U.S. Supreme Ct. 1977. With Ill. Defender Project, Ottawa, 1973; asst. states atty. LaSalle County, Ottawa, 1974-79; ptnr. McClintock & Steele, LaSalle, Ill., 1979-83, McClintock, Steele & Barry, LaSalle, 1983-84; pres. Aplington, Kaufman, McClintock, Steele & Barry, Ltd., LaSalle, 1984—. Dem. candidate for State's Atty., 1980. Named among Outstanding Young Men of Am., Jaycees, 1980-84. Fellow Phi Beta Lambda (Ill. Bus. Exec. award 1971); mem. ATLA, Ill. State Bar Assn., Ill. Trial Lawyers Assn., Sigma Iota Epsilon. Methodist. Home: 207 Shooting Park Rd Peru IL 61354-1966 Office: 160 Marquette St La Salle IL 61301 E-mail: tmcclintock@theramp.net.

MCCLINTOCK, WILLIAM THOMAS, health care administrator; b. Pittsfield, Mass., Oct. 23, 1934; s. Ernest William and Helen Elizabeth (Clum) M.; m. Wendolyn Hope Eckerman, June 22, 1963; children: Anne Elizabeth, Carol Jean, Thomas Daniel. BA, St. Lawrence U., Canton, NY, 1956; MBA, U. Chgo., 1959, MHA, 1962. Prodn. planner Corning (NY) Glass, 1959-60; adminstrv. resident Alameda County Med. Instns., Oakland, Calif., 1961-62; adminstrv. asst. Univ. Hosps. of Cleve., 1962-65; asst. adminstr. Presbyn. Hosp., Whittier, Calif., 1965-68; regional asst. Kaiser Found. Hosps., Oakland, 1968-70; assoc. dir., exec. dir. Conn. Hosp. Planning Commn., New Haven, 1970-75; project dir., lectr. sch. health studies U. N.H., Durham, 1975-77; regional mgr. Tex. Med. Found., Austin, 1977-81; adminstr. Schick Shadel Hosp., Ft. Worth, 1981-87; mgmt. cons. George S. May Internat. Co., Park Ridge, Ill., 1987-88; mgr. Nat. Ctr. Rsch. Programs Am. Heart Assn., Dallas, 1988-89; adminstr. Ambulatory Svcs. Health Care of Tex., Ft. Worth, 1990-92; CEO Boundary Cmty. Hosp., Bonners Ferry, Idaho, 1992-2000; healthcare cons., 2000—02; exec. dir. Oceanview Convalescent Ctr., Long Beach, Wash., 2002—. 1st lt. U.S. Army, 1957. Fellow Am. Coll. Health Care Execs. (life, Sr.-Level Healthcare Exec. Regent's award 2000); mem. Am. Hosp. Assn. (life), Am. Heart Assn. (bd. dirs. Idaho/Mont. affiliate 1993-95), Idaho Hosp. Assn. (bd. dirs. 1995-2000, sec.-treas. 1998, chmn.-elect 1998, chmn. bd. dirs. 1999, Recognition of Retirement award 2000), Masons (Unity Lodge No. 9). Avocations: book collections, gardening, photography, fly fishing. Home: PO Box 1221 Long Beach WA 98631-1221 Address: County Rd 62C PO Box 1226 Bonners Ferry ID 83805 Office Phone: 360-642-3123. E-mail: wtmcclintock@centurytel.net.

MCCLINTON, DONALD GEORGE, retired diversified holding company executive; b. Pitts., June 30, 1933; s. Donald K. and Ethel M. McC.; m. Jane Ann Knoebel, Apr. 12, 1958; children: Catherine, D. Scott. BS, Miami U., Oxford, Ohio, 1955. Audit mgr. Arthur Andersen & Co., Cleve., 1955-62; mgr. accounting E. Ohio Gas Co., Cleve., 1962-66; exec. v.p. Nat. Industries, Inc., Louisville, 1966-79; pres. Yellow Cab Co., Louisville, 1979-94; owner, chmn. bd. Interlock Industries, Inc., 1982-94; pres. Skylight Thoroughbred Tng. Ctr., Inc., 1994—2002. Bd. dirs. Almost Family, Clifton Ctr., MidAm. Bancorp, 1980-2002; trustee Jewish Hosp. Health Care Systems, Inc., 1983—. Mem. Louisville-Jefferson County Bicentennial Commn., 1976-77; mem. coun., treas. Old Kentucky Home. coun. Boy Scouts Am., 1976-94; mem. Citizens at Large Jefferson County Budget Com., 1978-84; bd. overseers Bellarmine Coll., 1978-84; bd. dirs. Ky. Derby Festival, 1978—, Jewish Hosp., Louisville, 1980-; trustee Spalding U., 1985-91. Mem.: Fin. Execs. Inst.

MCCLINTON, JAMES LEROY, city administrator; b. Longview, Wash., Oct. 14, 1949; s. James Delmer and Norma Jean (Ammons) McC.; m. Carmen Lassaphine Amador, Nov. 7, 1983; children: James Andrew, Ian Tyler, Kevin Riley. AA, SUNY, Albany, 1973; BA, Upper Iowa U., 1974; MA, Calif. State

U., Carson, 1984; PhD, Calif. Coast U., 1985. Cert. mgr. Inst. Cert. Profl. Mgrs. With USCG, 1967-89, commd. officer, 1981-83, advanced through grades to comdr., 1987, ret., 1989; bur. mgr. adminstrv. svcs. Charleston (S.C.) County Sheriff's Office, 1989—2003; chief dep. clk. of ct. Berkeley County, SC, 2003—. Spkr. pro tem S.C. Criminal Justice Acad., Columbia, 1989—; mem. auditor selection com. Charleston County Govt., 1989—, computer users action com., 1989—; mem. various coms. County Govt. and Sheriff's Office, Charleston, 1989—; chief dep. clerk of ct. Berkeley County, S.C., 2003-. Editor (newsletter) The Badge, 1989—; newspaper columnist; contbr. articles to profl. jours. and mags. Mem. Charleston Police Pipes and Drums, 1994—; grad. Leadership S.C., 1993, Leadership Charleston, 1997. Recipient Achievement award Nat. Assn. Counties, Washington, 1993, 96, Golden Pen award The Post and Courier Newspaper, Charleston, 1996. Mem. ASPA, S.C. Law Enforcement Officers Assn., Rotary Internat. (bd. dirs. North Charleston). Republican. Avocations: bagpipes, writing. Office Phone: 843-719-4508. Personal E-mail: ag4nm@comcast.net. Business E-Mail: jmcclinton@co.berkeley.sc.us.

MCCLINTON, JOANN, state legislator; m. Emory McClinton; 2 children. Grad., Washington High Sch. State rep. Ga. Ho. of Reps., Atlanta, 1992—, mem. children and youth, health and ecology state planning com., chmn. com. for arts and humanities. Democrat. Office: Ga House of Reps State Capitol SE Atlanta GA 30334

MCCLINTON, WENDELL C. religious organization administrator; b. Waco, Tex., Jan. 10, 1933; s. Clyde E. and Gertrude (Cotton) McC.; m. Beverly A. Harrison, Oct. 19, 1954; children: Kent, Jana, Lori, Meg. BBA, Baylor U., 1960. Exec. dir. Gideons Internat., Nashville, exec. dir. emeritus, 1997—.

MCCLOSKEY, J(OHN) MICHAEL, retired association administrator; b. Eugene, Oreg., Apr. 26, 1934; s. John Clement and Agnes Margaret (Studer) McC.; m. Maxine Mugg Johnson, June 17, 1965; stepchildren: Claire, Laura, James, Rosemary Johnson. BA, Harvard U., 1956; JD, U. Oreg., 1961. N.W. rep. Sierra Club, Eugene, 1961-65, asst. to pres. San Francisco, 1965-66, conservation dir., 1966-69, exec. dir., 1969-85, chmn. Washington, 1985-99, acting exec. dir., 1986-87; vice-chmn. Commn. on Environ. Law and Policy (Internat. Union for Conservation of Nature), Gland, Switzerland, 1978-88; mem. Pres.'s Commn. on Agenda for 1980's, Washington, 1979-80; co-chmn. OSHA-Environ. Conf., Washington, 1983-87; vice chmn. Am. Com. on Internat. Conservation, 1988-90; mem. Internat. Union for Conservaton of Nature World Commn. on Protected Areas, 1988—. Mem. adj. faculty Sch. Natural Resources, U. Mich., 1988—; chmn. Mineral Policy Ctr., 1998-2001, Nat. Resources Coun. of Am., 1992-93; co-chmn. environ. policy task force Pres.'s Coun. Sustainable Devel., 1997-99; pres. Fedn. of Western Outdoor Clubs, 2000-03. Contbr. articles to profl. jours. Bd. dirs. Nat. Resources Coun. Am., 1988-94, vice chmn., 1989-91, chmn., 1992-93, chmn. Advocacy Forum, 1989-91; bd. dirs. Ind. Sector, 1990-96, Mineral Policy Ctr., 1988-2001, Coalition for Environmentally Responsible Economies, 1989-99, OMB Watch, 1998—; bd. trustees Sierra Club Found., 2000—; mem. steering com. Blueprint for Environ., 1987-88; nominated candidate Oreg. Ho. of Reps., 1962. Recipient award Calif. Conservation Coun., 1969, John Muir award Sierra Club, 1979, UN Environ. Program Global 500 award, 1992, Lifetime Achievement award Wild Found., 1998, Honor award Natural Resources Coun. Am., 1999, Packard award Internat. Union for Conservation of Nature Parks Commn., 2003. Mem. Univ. Club (Portland, Oreg.), Explorers Club (N.Y.C.). Democrat. E-mail: jmmccloskey@aol.com.

MCCLOUD, ANECE FAISON, academic administrator; b. Dudley, N.C., May 29, 1937; d. J.D. Faison and Nancy Jane (Simmons) Faison-Cole; m. Verable Lancaster McCloud, June 1, 1959; children: Aja Siobhan, Carla Danette. BS, Bennette Coll., Greensboro, N.C., 1959; MA, U. Nebr., Omaha, 1989; Basic Mediations Skills, Ea. Mennonite Coll., 1994. Tchr. Lincoln Jr. High Sch., Greensboro, N.C., 1959-60, Woodbridge Airforce Base (Eng.), 1961-62; resident advisor and ednl. coord. Child Saving Inst., Omaha, 1967-71; asst. registrar for acad. records U. Nebr. Med. Ctr., Omaha, 1972-76, first dir. minority student affairs, 1976-85; assoc. dean of students Washington and Lee U., Lexington, Va., 1985—. Cons. Deans Forum on Revitalizing Health Profl. Edn., Dept. of Health and Human Svcs., 1985, Campus Alcohol Initiative, N.C. Gov.'s Inst. Alcohol and Substance Abuse, 1999—, Peer Rev., Health Careet Opportunity Program, 1982, 1984; cons. on simulated minority admissions Assn. Am. Med. Colls., Washington, 1979. Bd. mem., v.p. Rockbridge Area Housing Corp., Lexington, 1988-95; mem. Va. adv. com. U.S. Commn. on Civil Rights, 1995—; mem. Va. Identification Program for Advancement of Women in Higher Edn., 1995-96; treas. Mayor's Commn. on Status of Women, Omaha, 1977-78. Recipient Plaque for Outstanding Svc. to Washington and Lee Comty., 1994, Cert. Acknowledgement of Contbn. to Edn., Omaha Pub. Schs., 1984, Cert. Black History Month Spkr., VA Hosp., Omaha, 1983, Vol. Program award Girls Club of Omaha, 1977; grantee Health Career Opportunity, Disadvantaged Assistance Office, Dept. Health and Human Svcs., 1976, 80, 83. Mem. Am. Assn. for Higher Edn., Nat. Assn. For Women in Edn., Am. Coll. Personnel Assn., Assn. of Am. Med. Colls., Am. Assn. of Counseling and Devel., Nebr. Assn. for Non-White Concerns (past sec.), Nebr. Assn. of Collegiate Registrars and Admissions Officers (chairperson sub.-com. on minority affairs 1978-89), Nat. Assn. of Med. Minority Educators (vice coord. 1982-83). Democrat. Avocations: social research, writing, interior decorating. Office: Washington & Lee U Payne Hall 3 Lexington VA 24450

MCCLOUD, MELODY THERESA, obstetrician-gynecologist, surgeon; b. N.Y.C., Sept. 11, 1955; BA, Boston U., 1977, MD, 1981. Intern Emory U. Affiliated Hosps., Atlanta, 1981-82, resident in ob-gyn., 1982-85; pres., founder, CEO Atlanta Women's Health Care, 1985—. Bd. dirs. Vis. Nurses Health Sys., Atlanta; med. cons. Greeley Co., Wis., 1994—; spkr. Nat. Dental Assn.-Atlanta Bus. League, 1995, Women-On-Tour Conf., Nat. Coalition 100 Black Women, Congl. Black Caucus-Women, others; cons. health WXIA-TV, Atlanta, 1995, 99. Author: Medical Bloopers!! Amusing, Amazing Stories, 1994, The Health Diary for Women, 1999, Blessed Health, 2003, Melodies of the Heart, 2004; med. advisor Body and Soul, 1994; health columnist: Women Looking Ahead, 1995—. Mem. med. support group Com. Olympic Games, Atlanta, 1996; chair selection com. YWCA Acad., Atlanta, 1999 Inductee Leadership Atlanta, 1992, YWCA Acad. for Women Achievers, 1992; named Bus. Woman of Yr. Am. Bus. Women's Assn., 1994, Atlanta's Top 100 Black Women of Influence Atlanta Bus. League, 2003; recipient Cmty. Health Svc. award Black Pages. Mem. Med. Assn. Ga., Ga. Ob-Gyn Soc., Med. Assn. Atlanta, Atlanta Med. Assn., Soc. Laparoendoscopic Surgeons. Baptist. Avocations: tennis, bowling, water sports, theater, travel. Office: Melody T McCloud MD PO Box 344 Roswell GA 30077-0344 E-mail: mtm@drmccloud.com.

MCCLOUD, SAMUEL ALFRED, lawyer; b. Chgo., Feb. 24, 1943; s. Walter Hall and Jeraldine Mae McCloud; children: Eric, Daniel, Christina, Amber, Samantha, Cassondra, Cheyenne, Rockel, Travis, Johnna. JD, Wm. Mitchell Coll. Law, 1977. Pvt. practice, Shakopee, Minn. With U.S. Air Force, 1962-66. Mem. Nat. Assn. Criminal Def. Lawyers. Office: PO Box 216 Shakopee MN 55379

MCCLOW, ROGER JAMES, labor lawyer; b. St. Johns, Mich., July 23, 1947; s. Jack Gordon and Madalene V. (Mahaffy) McC.; m. Suzanne Terese Posler, July 13, 1978. BA in Polit. Sci. with distinction, U. Mich., 1969; JD magna cum laude, Wayne State U., 1976. Bar: Mich. 1977, U.S. Dist. Ct. (ea. dist.) Mich. 1977, U.S. Ct. Appeals (6th cir.) 1985, U.S. Ct. Appeals (8th cir.) 1987, U.S. Supreme Ct. 1988. Assoc. Miller, Cohen, Martens & Sugerman, Detroit, 1977-81, Klimist, McKnight & Sale, P.C., Southfield, Mich., 1981-83; ptnr. Klimist, McKnight, Sale, McClow & Canzano, P.C., Southfield, 1983—. Bd. dirs. Hemid (Sr. Citizen's Agy.), Detroit, 1982-2002; tutor Children's Ctr., Detroit, 1990-93; vol. Hospice Legal Aid, Detroit, 1991—, Patient Advocate Found., 1998—; mem. gun safety com. Alliance for Greater, Safer Detroit, 1993-95. Recipient Outstanding Vol. Svc. award Children's Ctr. Detroit, 1993. Mem. State Bar Mich. (coun. mem., labor law and employment sect. 1992-96), Detroit Bar Assn., Oakland County Bar Assn., Assn. Trial Lawyers Am., Mich. Trial Lawyers Assn., Indsl. Rels. Rsch. Assn., Phi Sigma Alpha. Democrat. Avocations: antiques, tennis, historic home restoration, landscaping. Office: Klimist McKnight Sale McClow & Cazano 400 Galleria Officentre Ste 117 Southfield MI 48034-2161 Business E-Mail: rmcclow@kmsmc.com.

MCCLOY, ELIZABETH K. lawyer; b. 1959; BA, Dartmouth Coll., 1981; JD, Northwestern U., 1984. Bar: Ill. 1984. With Sidley Austin Brown & Wood, Chgo., 1984—, ptnr., 1993—. Office: Sidley Austin Brown and Wood Bank One Plz 10 S Dearborn St Chicago IL 60603

MCCLUGGAGE, KERRY, film and television executive; Grad., U. So. Calif., 1976, Harvard U., 1978. With MCA, 1979—90; chmn. Paramount TV Group, Viacom, 1991—2002; founder, CEO Craftsman Films, 2002—. Office: Craftsman Films 5555 Melrose Ave Los Angeles CA 90038

MCCLUNG, A(LEXANDER) KEITH, JR., retired lawyer; b. Gallipolis, Ohio, Sept. 13, 1934; s. Alexander Keith and Florence (Juhling) McC.; m. Sandra B. Foley, Aug. 17, 1957; children: Alexander Keith III, Martha E. AB, W.Va. U., 1956; JD, Harvard U., 1959. Bar: W.Va. 1959, Md. 1970, Mich. 1972. Assoc. Jackson, Kelly, Holt & O'Farrell, Charleston, W.Va., 1959-69; assoc. counsel Comml. Credit Corp., Balt., 1969-70; v.p., counsel McCullagh Leasing, Inc., Roseville, Mich., 1970-73, Comml. Credit Corp., Balt., 1973-82, gen. atty., 1982-85; sr. gen. atty. Comml. Credit Co., Balt., 1985-89, sr. v.p., gen. counsel, 1989-98. Bd. dirs. Travelers Bank; trustee Roland Park Found.; mem. adv. coun. Coll. Arts and Sci., W.Va. U. Lt. U.S. Army, 1961-62, capt. Res. Mem. ABA (subcom. uniform comml. code, com. equipment leasing). Democrat. Home: 13 Devon Hill Rd Baltimore MD 21210-1044 E-mail: campussandy@aol.com.

MCCLUNG, HUGO JUHLING, pediatrician, educator; b. Gallipolis, Ohio, Feb. 27, 1941; s. A. Keith and Florence E. (Juhling) McC.; m. Helen K. Peters, Aug. 22, 1964; children: William J., Andrew P., Matthew A. BA, W. Va. U., 1963, MD, 1967. Diplomate Am. Bd. Pediatrics in Gen. Pediatrics, Pediatric Gastroenterology. Intern, then resident U. Wis.; rsch. fellow Hosp. for Sick Children, Toronto, Canada, 1972—74; chief pediatric gastroenterology Ohio State U., Columbus, Ohio, 1974—; assoc. med. dir. Columbus Children's Hosp., 1983—2000, prof. pediatrics Ohio State U., Columbus, 1992—. Med. dir. Children's Homecare Svcs., 1992—. Elder Presbyn. Ch., Blacklick, Ohio. Maj. U.S. Army, 1969-72. Mem. Am. Gastroenterology Assn., N. Am. Soc. Pediat. Gastroenterology and Nutrition, Pediat. Acad. Assn. (pres. 1992-99). Avocation: genealogy. Home: 6470 Havens Rd Blacklick OH 43004-9671 Office: Columbus Children's Hosp 700 Childrens Dr Columbus OH 43205-2664

MCCLUNG, J(AMES) DAVID, corporate executive, lawyer, academic administrator; b. Lamesa, Tex., July 16, 1943; s. Jack Weldon Sr. and Ruby (Brown) McC.; m. Linda Nelson, Feb. 12, 1966; children: LeEtta McClung Felter, Dennis, Pamela McClung Frazier, Jennifer McClung Panicker. Student, N.E. La. State Coll., 1961-62, McNeese State Coll., 1963; BSBA cum laude, Bethany Nazarene Coll., 1965; postgrad., U. Okla., 1967-68; JD cum laude, Baylor U., 1973. Bar: Tex. 1973, U.S. Dist. Ct. (no. dist.) Tex. 1975, U.S. Ct. Appeals (5th cir.) 1974. Assoc. Jackson & Walker, Dallas, 1973-76; exec. v.p. Austin Industries, Inc., Dallas, 1976-88; pres., chief exec. officer, chmn. bd. Green Internat., Inc., Denver, 1988—; owner NazNet.Com, 1999—. Arbitrator Am. Arbitration Assn., 1978—; bd. dirs. Green Holdings, Inc., Denver; chmn. bd. Green Construction Co., Green Mining, Inc., Green Alaska, Inc., GEM Investors, Inc., Green Overseas Corp., Northland Maintenance Co., Northland Alaska, Inc., Green Investments, Inc., Denver, 1988—; pres. Triton Marine Cons., 1994-2000; chmn. Triton Marine Cons., 2000—; pres. Ea. Nazarene Coll., 2002—. Contbr. articles to profl. jours. Trustee So. Nazarene U., Bethany, Okla., 1978-2003; mem. gen. bd. Ch. of the Nazarene, Kansas City, 1985-89, sec. Commn. Report, 1989. Capt. USAF, 1965-71, Vietnam. Decorated 6 Air medals; recipient Young Grads. award of merit Baylor U., 1983, Outstanding Alumni award So. Nazarene U., 1989, Disting. Svc. award Ch. of the Nazarene, 1989. Mem. ABA, Tex. Bar Assn., The Beavers. Republican. Avocations: digital photography, fishing. Home: 3504 C St NW Gig Harbor WA 98335-7801 Office: Ea Nazarene Coll 23 E Elm Ave Quincy MA 02170-1663 E-mail: mcclung@naznet.com.

MC CLUNG, JIM HILL, light manufacturing company executive; b. Buena Vista, Ga., Nov. 8, 1936; s. Jim Hill and Marjorie (Oxford) McC.; m. Jo Patrick, July 5, 1958; children: Jim Hill, Karen Mareese. BA, Emory U., 1958; MBA, Harvard U., 1964. With Lithonia Lighting divsn. Nat. Svc. Industries, Inc., Conyers, Ga., 1964—, chmn., CEO, 1976, assoc. dir., 1986—. With USAF, 1958-62. Mem. Illuminating Engring. Soc. N.Am. (vice chmn. lighting rsch. and edn. fund), Nat. Elec. Distbrs. Assn. (mfrs. bd.), Nat. Elec. Mfrs. Assn. (nat. lighting bur., bd. dirs., chmn. bd. govs.), Intelligent Bldgs. Inst. (bd. dirs.), Lighting Rsch. Inst. (bd. dirs.), Data Exchange Assn. (bd. gov. industry), Elec. Mfrs. Club, World Pres.'s Orgn. Methodist. Office: Lithonia Lighting Div PO Box A Conyers GA 30013-9912

MCCLUNG, KENNETH AUSTIN, JR., training executive, performance consultant; b. Decatur, Ga., Apr. 11, 1947; s. Kenneth Austin Sr. and Marianne (Conklin) McC.; m. Christina June Palensar, Mar. 21, 1975. BA, North Ga. Coll., 1969; MS, EdD, U. So. Calif., 1976. Commd. 2d lt. U.S. Army, 1969, advanced through grades to maj., 1980; col. USAR; sr. ptnr. Instrl. Design Group, Inc., Morristown, N.J., 1981-99; v.p., nat. learning dir. Jack Morton Worldwide, 1999-2000, nat. learning dir., 2000—02; ptnr. McClung, McClung & Assoc., Hertford, NC, 2002—. Bd. dirs. Nat. Productivity Ctr., Boulder, Colo., Price Waterhouse Learning Bd.; author/mgr. over 150 mgmt., sales, and tech. tng. programs; cons. in field. Author: Microcomputers for Medical Professionals, 1984, Microcomputers for Legal Professionals, 1984, Microcomputers for Investment Professionals, 1984, Microcomputers for Insurance Professionals, 1984, Personal Computers for Executives, 1984, French edit. 1985; co-author: Sales Training Handbook, 1989. Mem. ASTD, Internat. Soc. for Performance Improvement (pres. N.J. chpt. 1986-88, N.E. regional cons. 1989-90, nat. nomination chmn. 1990-91, nat. emerging tech. chmn. 1991-92). Avocations: sailing, tennis, bicycling, running, skiing. Home: 128 Back Creek Dr Hertford NC 27944 Office: McClung McClung & Assoc 128 Back Creek Dr Hertford NC 27944

MCCLUNG, SAMUEL BRENTON, music educator, consultant; b. Parkersburg, W.Va., Feb. 2, 1954; s. Asa Maples (Stepfather) and Dorothy Faith Reece; life ptnr. Margarita Maria Vera; m. Julie Ann Illingworth, Aug. 16, 1975 (div. Oct. 2, 2000); children: Catherine Faith McClung - Smith, Leta Marie Mcclung. MusB, Stetson U., 1976; MusM, Mich. State Univ., 1979, PhD, 1981. Cert. tchr. Am. Orff-Schulwerk Assn., MN, 1998. Instr. Mich. State U., East Lansing, Mich., 1980—81; music dir. Dade County Pub. Schs., Miami, Fla., 1982—84, Cedar Grove HS, Atlanta, 1984—85; music specialist Gwinnett County Pub. Schs., Norcross, Ga., 1985—. Cons. Ga. State Univ., Atlanta, 1999—. Composer: (songs) God With Us. Fellow: AOSA (life; pres. 1994—96, Hon. Six). Liberal. Roman Catholic. Avocations: squash, reading, swimming, folk instr.'s, poetry. Home: 3501 Grovewood Lane Duluth GA 30096 Personal E-mail: levelbor@bellsouth.net.

MCCLUNG, WILLIAM ALEXANDER, foundation administrator, educator; b. Norfolk, Va., Jan. 22, 1944; s. William Alexander and Winifred (Boggs) McC. BA, Williams Coll., 1966; AM, Harvard U., 1967, PhD, 1972. Asst. prof. English, Miss. State U., Mississippi State, 1971-76, assoc. prof., 1976-84, prof., 1984-2001; exec. dir. Theta Delta Chi Ednl. Found., Inc. Vis. assoc. prof. Conn. Coll., New London, 1980; vis. prof. Ga. Tech, 1986, UCLA, 1989, Meisei U., Tokyo, 1990-91. Author: The Country House in English Renaissance Poetry, 1977, The Architecture of Paradise, 1983, Landscapes of Desire, 2000 (L.A. Times Best Nonfiction book award 2000); contbr. numerous articles on architecture and lit. to profl. jours. Mem.: St. Botolph Club, Williams Club NY, Harvard Faculty Club, Harvard Club N.Y.C., Theta Delta Chi (editor 1967—88, 1998—, trustee Ednl. Found. 1984—). Avocation: photography. Office: 214 Lewis Wharf Boston MA 02110 E-mail: execdir@tdx.org.

MCCLURE, BROOKS, management consultant; b. N.Y.C., Mar. 8, 1919; s. Walter Harsha and Angelica (Mendoza) McClure; m. Olga Beatrice Gallik, Oct. 15, 1949; 1 child, Karen (dec.). AB summa cum laude, U. Md.; disting. grad., U.S. Naval War Coll. N.Y. corr. Western Press Ltd., Australia, 1939-42; copy editor Washington Eve. Star, 1946-51; joined State Dept. Fgn. Service, 1951; information officer, attache embassy Copenhagen, 1951-53; press attache embassy Vienna, 1953-55; information officer, attache embassy Cairo, 1956—57, Seoul, 1957-60, Bonn, 1960-63; policy officer Europe USIA, 1963-66; pub. affairs officer 1st sec. embassy, Copenhagen, 1967-72; spl. asst. policy plans and nat. security council affairs, internat. security affairs Dept. Def., 1972-76; internat. security adviser USIA, 1976-77; program coordinator Crisis Assessment Staff, Dept. Commerce, 1977-78; dir. ops. Internat. Mgmt. Analysis and Resources Corp., 1978-81, v.p., 1982—; sec. Cross-Continent Assocs. Ltd., 1994-99. Various spl. assignments Europe, Mid. East, Asia, Africa; detailed to Vietnam, 1967—70; mem. working group Cabinet Com. to Combat Terrorism, 1973—77; lectr. FBI Acad., Fgn. Svc. Inst., Inter-Am. Def. Coll., Army War Coll., Navy War Coll., NJ Police Acad., NY State Police Acad. Contbg. author: book Modern Guerrilla Warfare, 1962, International Terrorism in Contemporary World, 1978, Corporate Vulnerability and How to Assess it: Political Terrorism and Business, 1979, Business and the Middle East, 1981, Political Terrorism and Energy, 1981; author (treatise) Dynamics of Terrorism, 1977; contbr. articles to profl. jours.; author: report to Senate Judiciary Com. on internat. terrorism and hostage def. measures; testifier on internat. security, hostage behavior, def. of Alaskan pipeline, FBI charter U.S. Senate, 1975—79. With AUS, 1942—46, ETO. Recipient Presdl. medal, Slovak Republic, 2002. Mem.: DACOR, Nat. Press Club, Assn. Diplomatic Studies, Am. Fgn. Svc. Assn., Alpha Sigma Lambda, Phi Kappa Phi. Home: 6204 Rockhurst Rd Bethesda MD 20817-1756 Office: IMAR Corp PO Box 34528 Bethesda MD 20827-0528 E-mail: imarmgtsvcs@mindspring.com., b-kmcclure@mindspring.com.

MCCLURE, CHARLES G. automotive executive; BS in Mech. Engring., Cornell U.; MBA, U. Mich. Heavy truck sales engr., product engr. Ford Motor Co.; v.p., gen. mgr. automotive sys. groups for the Ams. Johnson Controls, Inc., pres., Detroit Diesel Corp., 1997—2003, CEO, 1999—2003; CEO, pres. Federal-Mogul Corp., 2003—; also bd. dirs. Bd. dirs. R.L. Polk and Co., Intermet Corp., Detroit Renaissance, Cornell U. Coun. Lt. (j.g.) USN, 1975—79. Office: Federal Mogul Corp 26555 Northwestern Hwy Southfield MI 48034

MCCLURE, DANIEL M. lawyer; b. Enid, Okla., Feb. 5, 1952; s. Larry M. and Marie Dolores (Sarver) McC.; m. Judy Lynn Pinson, Jan. 3, 1976; children: Andrew Mead, Mark William, Kathleen Claire. BA with highest hons., U. Okla., 1974; JD cum laude, Harvard U., 1978. Bar: Tex. 1978, U.S. Dist. Ct. (so. dist., ea. dist.) Tex. 1979, U.S. Ct. Appeals (5th cir., 10th cir., 11th cir.) 1981, U.S. Supreme Ct., 2003. Assoc. Fulbright & Jaworski, LLP, Houston, 1978-86, ptnr., 1986—. Fellow Tex. Bar Found.; mem. ABA, Nat. Health Lawyers Assn., Nat. Assn. R.R. Trial Counsel, Tex. Bar Assn., Houston Bar Assn. (cert. civil trial law), Am. Inns of Ct., Harvard Law Sch. Assn. Avocation: tennis. Home: 2 Long Timbers Ln Houston TX 77024-5445 Office: Fulbright & Jaworski LLP 1301 McKinney St Houston TX 77010-3031 E-mail: dmcclure@fulbright.com.

MCCLURE, DAVID H. utilities company analyst; b. Kennesaw, Ga., Apr. 29, 1948; s. Benjamin H. and Katherine E. (Reece) McC.; m. Judy King McClure; children: Christina Aldridge, John Robert Aldridge, Lori K. Aldridge, Charissa Diane Thomas. B in Indsl. Engring. Tech., So. Poly. U., 1976. Assoc. engr. Western Electric Co., Atlanta, 1972-75; jr. acct. Jack McPherson, CPA, Acworth, Ga., 1975-76; div. materials planner Southwire Co., Carrollton, Ga., 1976-78, indsl. engr., 1978-79; process engr. Alcan Cable, Tucker, Ga., 1979-82; rsch. specialist Ga. Power Co., Forest Park, 1982-86, staff rep., 1986-87, staff services engr., 1987-91, head of quality assurance sect., 1982-91, mgr. quality and support, 1991-94; bus. cons., 1994-96; bus. analyst, 1996—. Chmn. bd. dirs. Am. Diabetes Assn. Ga. Affiliate, Inc., Atlanta, 1985-87, nat. bd. dirs., 1988-91, mem. nat. com. on affiliate assocs., 1986-89, vice chmn., 1988-89, chmn. 1991-92, nat. So. region liaison, 1987-89; chmn. Nat. Com. on Fund Raising, 1989-91; nat. bd. mentor, 1989—, chmn. nat. bd. dirs., 1995-96, chmn. nat. strategic planning steering com., 1994-95, chmn. nat. nominating com., 1996-97, chmn. nat. alumni assn., 1996-97, ctr. for quality excellence adv. coun., 1987-92, chmn., 1989-90; chmn. Southeastern Quality Conf. Program, 1989, 90, 91, chmn. arrangements, 1992; mem. Ga. Dept. Human Resources Diabetes adv. com., 1989-92; chmn. bd. dirs. Am. Diabetes Rsch. Found., 1997-98, chmn. rsch. found. nominating com., 1998-99; nat. bd. dirs. Combined Health Appeal of Am., 1993-99, chmn. agy. rels., 1996-99. Staff sgt. USAF, 1968-72. Named Vol. of Yr., Am. Diabetes Assn. Ga. Affiliate, Inc., 1983-84, 84-85; recipient Ga. Power Co. R.W. Scherer award for leadership in cmty. svc., 1991, Am. Diabetes Assn. Charles H. Best award for disting. svc., 1996. Mem. Inst. Indsl. Engrs. (sec. 1976-77, v.p. seminars 1977-78), Am. Soc. Quality Control (cert. quality engr. 1983—, chmn. bd.-elect Greater Atlanta sect. exec. bd. 1989-92), Nat. Mgmt. Assn. (LDR chpt., profl. devel. com. 1989-91), Capital Area Kiwanis Club (bd. dirs. 1989—, pres. elect 1990-91, pres. 1991-92). Baptist. Home: 706 Singley Dr Lawrenceville GA 30044-5972

MCCLURE, GROVER BENJAMIN, management consultant; b. Houstonia, Mo., Oct. 15, 1918; s. Grover B. and Sue F. (Cook) McC. BA, U. Richmond, 1939. Pres. internat. div. Richardson-Merrell, N.Y.C., 1954-62; pres. Europe and Africa divs. Paris, 1960-81; exec. v.p., dir. Richardson-Vicks, Inc., Wilton, Conn., 1981-85; cons. New Canaan, Conn., 1985—. Bd. dirs., chmn. emeritus Silvermine Art Guild. Served to lt. comdr. USNR, 1941-46. Mem. Silver Springs Club (Ridgefield, Conn.). Republican. Presbyterian. Avocations: tennis, golf, travel, yachting. Home: 1321 Meadow Ridge Redding CT 06896

MCCLURE, HAL H. film producer; b. Indpls. s. Harold Alonzo and Betty (Zemah Hays) McClure; m. Dorothea Vernell Millar, Jan. 15, 1949 (dec. 1994). AA, L.A. City Coll., 1941. Journalist various newspapers, Calif., 1949-56; newsman AP, L.A., 1956-58, N.Y.C., 1959-60, fgn. corr., 1961-76, bur. chief N.J., 1976-77; prin., travel film prodr. Hal McClure Prodns., Laguna Woods, Calif., 1978—. Adj. asst. prof. journalism Seton Hall U., South Orange, NJ, 1976—77. Co-author: (book) Lighting Out of Israel, 1967; co-editor: Fire Over Suez, 1971; prodr.: (films) Istanbul-Travels in Turkey, 1990, Land of Legend-England Scotland and Wales, 1993, Adventure Holland, 1994, Mystery Tales of Europe, 1996, Dracula-Travels in Transylvania, 1997, Story Book England, 1999, Magic of Malaysia, 2001, Casablanca-Travels in Morocco, 2003; editor, co-owner Travel Adventure Cinema mag., 1978—, leader in move to digital prodn. travel fun field. Capt. USAFR, 1942—56. Named to Travelogue Hall of Fame, 1994; recipient Rising Star award, 1978; Ogden Reid Found. fellow, 1959. Mem.: Travel Adventure Cinema Soc. Home and Office: 686 Avenida Sevilla # C Laguna Woods CA 92637-3838

MCCLURE, HELEN PLAYFAIR, writer; b. L.A., Aug. 28, 1926; d. Edward Baker and Kathleen (Shuford) Anderson; m. Drexel Eugene McClure, June 30, 1950 (dec. Mar. 15, 1977). BA, UCLA, 1948. Author: A Kiss to Remember, 1995, Flying High, 1995. Democrat.

MCCLURE, HOWARD JEAN, JR., advocate; b. High Point, NC, June 15, 1959; s. Howard Jean McClure Sr. and Mary Elizabeth McClure. Author: Conflict Of Interest, 1999. Chmn. polit. action com. Carolina Advocates for Legal Reform, Charlotte, NC, 2001—02, v.p., 2001—02; active Charlotte Mecklenburg Cmty. Rels. Com., 2002—; chmn. membership and cmty. rels. com. Western Region NC Black Leadership Caucus, 2003; active Black Polit. Caucus Charlotte-Mecklenburg, 1998; founder Citizens Coun. for Equal Opportunity, 2003; elected vice chair 29th Precinct for Mecklenburg County Dem. Party, 2004. Recipient Outstanding Svc. award, Black Polit. Caucus of Charlotte Mecklenburg, 2003, chmn. award Dem. of the Month, Mecklenberg County Dem. Party, 2004. Mem.: NAACP (chmn. legal redress com. 1999—, edn. com. 2001—, labor & industry com. 2003—). Conservative. Avocations: music, writing, fishing, travel, football. Home: 3621 B Central Ave Charlotte NC 28205 Office: Charlotte Mecklenburg NAACP Charlotte NC 28229-5774 Office Phone: 704-537-3139. Personal E-mail: theebonysaint@webtv.net. E-mail: theebonysaint2@msn.com.

MCCLURE, JAMES FOCHT, JR., federal judge; b. Danville, Pa., Apr. 6, 1931; s. James Focht and Florence Kathryn (Fowler) McC.; m. Elizabeth Louise Barber, June 14, 1952; children: Holly McClure Kerwin, Kimberly Ann Pacala, Jamee McClure Sealy, Mary Elizabeth Hudec, Margaret McClure Persing. AB, Amherst Coll., 1952; JD, U. Pa., 1957. Bar: D.C. 1957, Pa. 1958, U.S. Dist. Ct. D.C. 1957, U.S. Dist. Ct. (ea. and mid. dist.) Pa. 1958, U.S. Ct. Appeals (3d cir.) 1959. Atty., advisor Dept. State, Washington, 1957-58; assoc. Morgan, Lewis & Bockius, Phila., 1958-61; atty. Merck & Co., Inc., N.Y.C., 1961-65; ptnr. McClure & McClure, Lewisburg, Pa., 1965-77, McClure & Light, Lewisburg, 1978-84; pres., judge Ct. Common Pleas, 17th Jud. Dist. Pa., Lewisburg, 1984-90; sr. dist. judge U.S. Dist. Ct. (mid. dist.) Pa., Williamsport, Pa., 1990—. Dist. atty. Union County, Lewisburg, 1974-75. Pres. bd. sch. dirs. Lewisburg Area Sch. Dist., 1969-74. Cpl. U.S. Army, 1952-54. Mem. Pa. Bar Assn., Union County Bar Assn., Bucknell U. Golf Club, Susquehanna Valley Chorale, Order of Coif, Phi Beta Kappa. Republican. Presbyterian. Office: US Dist Ct 240 W 3rd St Ste 320 Williamsport PA 17701-6466 E-mail: gary_palmer@unc.edu.

MCCLURE, JAMES JULIUS, JR., lawyer, former city official; b. Oak Park, Ill., Sept. 23, 1920; s. James J. and Ada Leslie (Baker) McC.; m. Margaret Carolyn Phelps, Apr. 9, 1949; children: John Phelps, Julia Jean, Donald Stewart. BA, U. Chgo., 1942, JD, 1949. Bar: Ill. 1950. Ptnr. Gardner, Carton & Douglas, Chgo., 1962-91, of counsel, 1991—; mem. Oak Park Plan Commn., 1966-73, Northeastern Ill. Planning Commn., 1973-77, pres., 1975-77, Village of Oak Park, 1973-81, Oak Park Exch. Congress Inc., 1978—2002. Mem. Bus. Leaders for Transp., 1998—. Pres. United Christian Cmty. Svcs., 1967-69, 71-73, Erie Neighborhood House, 1953-55, Oak Park-River Forest Cmty. Chest, 1967; moderator Presbytery Chgo., 1969; mem. Gov.'s Spl. Com. on MPO, 1978-79; bd. dirs. Leadership Coun. of Met. Open Cmtys., 1981-2002, sec., 1990-98; bd. dirs. Met. Planning Coun., 1982-93, hon. dir., 1993—; bd. dirs. Cmty. Renewal Soc., 1982-91, v.p., 1984-88, treas. 1988-91; bd. dirs. Christian Century Found., 1972—, chmn., 1981—; trustee McCormick Theol. Sem., 1981—, chmn. bd. 1987-90. hon. trustee, 1990—; mem. vocation agy., 1973-82; mem. ch. vocations unit, 1987-92, vice chair 1990; mem. gen. assembly coun. Presbyn. Ch. U.S.A., 1987-90, mem. gen. assembly Permanent Jud. Commn., 1997-2003; bd. dirs. Oak Park Edn. Found., 1991-96, Oak Park River Forest Cmty. Found., 1991-2002; mem. Vision 2000 (Oak Park) Coordinating Com., 1995. With USNR, 1942-46. Recipient Disting. Citizen award Oak Park, 1976; Silver Beaver award; Disting. Eagle Scout award Boy Scouts Am., Carl Winters Cmty. Svc. award Oak Park Rotary Club, 1996, William Staczak award Oak Park Edn. Found., 1997, Rita Johnson award Oak Park Family Svc. and Mental Health Ctr., 1997, Public Svc. award U. Chgo. Alumni Assn., 1997, Tradition of Excellence award Oak Pk. River Forest H.S., 1998, Alumni Service Medal, Alumni Svc. medal, 2003, U. Chgo. Alumni Assn., 2003, Gutenberg Award Chgo. Bible Soc., 2003; named one of 100 disting. Oak Parkers for Millenium, Wed Jour., 2002. Mem. ABA, Am. Coll. Trust and Estate Counsel, Ill. State Bar Assn., Chgo. Bar Assn., Am. Law Inst., Order of the Coif, Lambda Alpha. Clubs: Univ. (Chgo.). Home: One Calvin Cir # C 309 Evanston IL 60201 Office: Gardner Carton & Douglas 191 N Wacker Dr Chicago IL 60606-4719 *Love of God, love of family, awareness of both the uniqueness and the contribution of every other human being, a sense of the wholeness of life with my religious faith, my profession of law, my family and my community service each playing an important part and complimenting each other.*

MCCLURE, LAURA, state legislator; b. Hays, Kan., May 11, 1950; m. John D. McClure. Kans. state rep. Dist. 119, 1993—. Democrat. Friends Church. Office: Kans Ho of Reps State Capitol Topeka KS 66612

MCCLURE, RICHARD P. transportation executive; m. Sharon McClure; children: Ryan, Lindsay. Degree in Mgmt., Southwest Mo. State U.; MPA, U. Syracuse. Chief of staff Gov. Mo., John Ashcroft, 1985—92; in corp. svcs. Ctrl. Bancompany; COO United Van Lines and UniGroup WorldWide; various pos., to group exec. v.p. corp. fin. svcs. UniGroup, Inc., St. Louis, pres., COO, 2002—. Office: UniGroup Inc 1 Premier Dr Fenton MO 63026

MCCLURE, THOMAS EDWARD, lawyer; b. Urbana, Ill., Nov. 8, 1954; s. William Leslie McClure and Carolyn Jean (Hovey) McClure Byrnes; m. Karen Leah Zinn, Dec. 14, 1985. BS, Ill. State U., 1976; JD, DePaul U., 1979; MS, Ill. State U., 2001. Bar: Ill. 1979, U.S. Dist. Ct. (no. dist.) Ill. 1979, U.S. Ct. Appeals (7th cir.) 1980, U.S. Dist. Ct. (cen. dist.) Ill. 1983, U.S. Dist. Ct. (no. dist.) Ind. 1991, U.S. Supreme Ct. 1993. Law clk. to presiding justice Ill. Ct. Appeals (1st dist.), Chgo., 1979-81; assoc. Elliott & McClure, Bourbonnais and Momence, Ill., 1981-88; ptnr. Elliott & McClure P.C., Bourbonnais and Momence, Ill., 1988—. Legal counsel Ill. Jaycees, 1985-86, individual devel. v.p., 1987-88, regional dir., 1988-89; atty. Village of Bourbonnais, 1989-93, Village of Chebanse, 1993-97, Village of Manteno, 1999-2001; bd. mem. Bourbonnais Elem. Sch. Dist., 2001—, pres., 2003-2004. Editor DePaul Law Rev., 1978-79; contbr. articles to profl. jours. Recipient Outstanding Instrn. award Dale Carnegie & Assocs., 1982, 83, Dennis Hamilton Meml. award U.S. Jaycees, 1988. Mem. ABA, Ill. Bar Assn. (cert. of recognition 1983), 7th Cir. Bar Assn. (cert. of recognition 1994), Chgo. Bar Assn., Kankakee County Bar Assn., Appellate Lawyers Assn., Ill. Jaycees (individual devel. v.p. 1987-88, Outstanding Local Pres. 1985, Outstanding Local Dir. East Region 1984, Outstanding Portfolio V.P. 1987-88, Outstanding Regional Dir. 1988-89), Kankakee Jaycees (pres. 1984-85, bd. dirs. 1983-86), Ill. Jaycees Charitable Found., Inc. (bd. dirs., mem. and legal counsel 1986-89), Ill. Jaycees Charitable Camp, Inc. (bd. dirs., legal counsel 1989-91). Office: Elliott & McClure 18 Briarcliff Prof Ctr Bourbonnais IL 60914-1775

MCCLURE, THOMAS JAMES, lawyer; b. Chgo., Feb. 19, 1955; BA in Humanities cum laude, St. Norbert Coll., 1977; JD, Marquette U., 1980. Bar: Wis. 1980, U.S. Dist. Ct. (we. dist.) Wis. 1980, U.S. Dist. Ct. (ea. dist.) Wis. 1981, U.S. Ct. Appeals (7th cir.) 1984. Asst. dist. atty. Washington County, West Bend, Wis., 1980-81, Milwaukee (Wis.) County, 1982, Rock County, Janesville and Beloit, Wis., 1982-85; assoc. deVries, Vlasak & Schallert, Milw., 1985-88, McLario Law Offices S.C., Menomonee Falls, Wis., 1988-92; ptnr. Osinga & McClure, Milw., 1992-97; pres. McClure Law Offices, S.C., Delafield, Wis., 1997—. Instr. Am. jurisprudence Am. Inst. Paralegal Studies Alverno Coll., Milw., 1986; legal counsel city of Delafield Promotional and Tourism Coun., Inc. Elder, bd. dirs. Kettle Moraine Evang. Free Ch., Delafield, Wis., 1987—; mem. police fire commn. City of Delafield, 1988, planning commn., 1988-90; alderman city coun. City of Delafield, 1988-90, pres. city coun., 1989-90. Named One of Outstanding Young Men in Am. U.S. Jaycees, 1984. Mem. Milw. County Bar Assn., Assn. Trial Lawyers Am., Wis. Acad. Trial Lawyers, Wis. State Bar (young lawyers div. subcom. mem. and presenter, Law Day for Clergy 1991), The Rutherford Inst.(Wis. state coord., 1993—), Delafield C. of C., Waukesha County Bar Assn. Home: W318 737 Partridge Run Delafield WI 53018-2820 Office: McClure Law Offices SC 15 Crossroads Ct Delafield WI 53018-2035

MCCLURE, WESLEY C. academic administrator; Instr. Lynchburg (Va.) Sch. Bd., 1964-66, U. Va., Charlottesville, Va., 1970; asst. to pres. Lane Coll., Jackson, Tenn., 1970-78, pres., 1992—; coord. U. S.C., 1974-77; prof. Memphis State U., 1974-78; dean faculty and instrn. Clark Coll., Atlanta, 1978-79; exec. asst. pres. St. Augustine's Coll., Raleigh, N.C., 1979-81; vice chancellor acad. affairs, chancellor Baton Rouge campus So. U. and Agrl. and Mech. Coll., 1985-88; pres. Va. State U., Petersburg, 1988-92. Office: Lane College Office Pres 545 Lane Ave Jackson TN 38301-4598

MCCLURE, WILLIAM F. agricultural studies educator; Prof. biol. & agrl. engring. dept. N.C. State U., Raleigh. Am. Socl. Agrl. Engrs. fellow, 1994. Office: NC State U Dept Biol & Agrl Engring Box 7625 Raleigh NC 27695

MCCLURE, WILLIAM OWEN, biologist; b. Yakima, Washington, Sept. 29, 1937; s. Rexford Delmont and Ruth Josephine (Owen) McC.; m. Pamela Preston (Harris), Mar. 9, 1968 (div. 1979); children: Heather Harris, Rexford Owen; m. Sara Joan (Rorke), July 27, 1980. BS, Calif. Inst. Tech., 1959; PhD, U. Wash., 1964. Postdoctoral fellow Rockefeller U., NYC, 1964-65, asst. prof., 1965-68, U. Ill., Urbana, 1968-75; assoc. prof. U. So. Calif., LA, 1975-79, prof. biology, prof. neurology, 1979—, dir. program. neurol. info. sci., 1982-92, dir. program in psychobiology, 1991—; v.p. sci. affairs Nelson Rsch. and Devel. Co., Irvine, Calif., 1981-82, acting v.p. rsch. and devel., 1985-86. Dir. cellular biology U. So. Calif., 1979-81; dir. neurobiology, 1982-88; dir. program psychobiology, 1991—; cons. in field; dir. Marine & Freshwater Biomed. Ctr., U. So. Calif., 1982-83; co-dir. Baja Calif. Expdn. of the R/V Alpha Helix, 1974, others; chmn. Winter Conf. on Brain Rsch., 1979-80, others; lectr. in field; sci. adv. bd. Nelson R and D, 1972-91; bd. commentators Brain and Behavioral Sci., 1978—. Co-editor: Wednesday Night at the Lab, 1972; patentee in field; mem. editl. bd. Neurochem. Rsch., 1975-81; Jour. Neurochemistry, 1977-84; Jour. Neurosci. Rsch., 1980-86; contbr. over 150 articles to profl. jours. Bd. dirs. San Pedro and Peninsula Hosp. Found., 1989-95; San Pedro Health Svc., 1992-97. Recipient John R. Hubbard award Univ. Assoc., 1993; Assoc. award for outstanding tchg., 1994, Peer Achievement award, 2003, Presdl. medallion, 2003; Scripps Inst. fellow, 1958; NIH fellow, 1959-65; Alfred P. Sloan fellow, 1972-76; West Coast Coll. Biol. Psychiatry fellow, 1983; Intersci. Rsch. Inst. fellow, 1989; others; recipient numerous rsch. grants. Mem. AAAS, Am. Soc. Neurochemistry, Soc. for Neurosci., Am. Soc. Biol. Chemistry and Molecular Biology, Internat. Soc. Neurochemistry, Assn. Neurosci. Dept. and Programs, Univ. Park Investment Group, Bay Surg. Soc., Univ. Club U. So. Calif., (bd. dirs. 1991-95, 2000—), NY Acad. Sci, Phi Beta Kappa, Phi Kappa Phi. Republican. Presbyterian. Avocations: travel, photography, computing. Home: 30533 Rhone Dr Palos Verdes Peninsula CA 90275-5742 Office: U So Calif Dept Biol Sci Los Angeles CA 90089-0101 Office Phone: 213-740-6090. E-mail: wmcclure@usc.edu.

MCCLURE, WILLIAM PENDLETON, lawyer; b. Washington, May 25, 1925; s. John Elmer and Helen Newsome (Pendleton) McC.; children: Marilyn Alexander, Helen Pendleton, Elizabeth Ruffin, Melinda Geoghegan. BS, U. Pa., 1949; JD, George Washington U., 1951, LLM, 1954; postgrad., The Hague (Netherlands) Acad. Internat. Law, 1952. Bar: D.C. 1951. Sr. ptnr. McClure & Trotter, Washington, 1952-91, McClure, Trotter & Mentz, Washington, 1991-93, McClure, Trotter & Mentz, chartered, Washington, 1993-95; of counsel White & Case, Washington, 1995—. Chmn. D.C. div. Crusade Against Cancer, Am. Cancer Soc., 1966, 67. Served from pvt. to 1st lt., inf. U.S. Army, 1943-46, PTO. Mem. Am. Bar Assn., Bar Assn. D.C., Am. Judicature Soc., Order of Coif, Phi Delta Phi, Phi Delta Theta. Clubs: Metropolitan (Washington), Columbia Country (Washington). Office: 601 13th St NW Ste 600 S Washington DC 20005-3807

MCCLURE-BIBBY, MARY ANNE, former state legislator; b. Milbank, S.D., Apr. 21, 1939; d. Charles Cornelius and Mary Lucille (Whittom) Burges; m. D.J. McClure, Nov. 17, 1963 (dec. Apr. 1990); 1 child, Kelly Joanne Kyro; m. John E. Bibby, May 1, 1993 (dec. July 2003). BA magna cum laude, U. S.D., 1961; postgrad., U. Manchester, Eng., 1961-62; M of Pub. Adminstrn., Syracuse (N.Y.) U., 1980. Staff asst. U.S. Senator Francis Case, Washington, 1959-61; sec. to lt. gov. State of S.D., Pierre, 1963, with budget office, 1964; exec. sec. to pres. Frontier Airlines, Denver, 1963-64; tchr. Pub. High Schs., Pierre and Redfield, S.D., 1965-66, 68-70; mem. S.D. State Senate, Pierre, 1975-89, pres. pro tem, 1979-89, vice chmn. coun. of state govts., 1987, chmn. coun. of state govts., 1988; spl. asst. to Pres. Bush for intergovernmental affairs, 1989-92; exec. dir. S.D. Bush-Quayle Campaign, 1992. Vice chmn. sch. bd. Redfield Ind. Sch. Dist., 1970-74. Fulbright scholar, 1961-62, Bush Leadership fellow, 1977-80. Mem. Phi Beta Kappa. Republican. Congregationalist. Home: 822 8th Ave Brookings SD 57006-1314

MCCLURG, PATRICIA A. minister; b. Bay City, Tex., Mar. 14, 1939; d. T.H. and Margaret (Smith) McC. BA, Austin Coll., 1961; M in Christian Edn., Presbyn. Sch. of Christian Edn., 1963; BD, Austin Presbyn. Theol. Sem., 1967; postgrad., So. Meth. U., 1971-73; DD (hon.), Austin Coll., 1978. Dir. Christian edn. 2d Presbyn. Ch., Newport News, Va., 1963-65; asst. pastor Westminster Presbyn. Ch., Beaumont, Tex., 1967-69; assoc. pastor 1st Presbyn. Ch., Pasadena, Tex., 1969-71; assoc. exec. Synod of Red River, Denton, Tex., 1973-75; dir. gen. assembly mission bd. Presbyn. Ch., Atlanta, 1975-86; assoc. exec. for mission The Presbytery of Elizabeth, Plainfield, N.J., 1986-91; exec. presbyter Presbytery of New Castle, Newark, Del., 1992—2001. Pres. Nat. Coun. Chs. of Christ in the U.S.A., N.Y.C., 1988-89, v.p., 1985-87; del., budget com. chmn. World Coun. Chs. Assembly, Vancouver, Can., 1985; sect. leader World Coun. Chs. Mission and Evang. Confs., Melbourne, Australia, 1980. Contbr. articles to prof. jours. Mem. chs. spl. commn. on South Africa, N.Y.C., 1985—, Anti-Pollution Campaign, Pasadena, 1970. Recipient Disting. Alumni award Austin Coll., 1979. Mem.: Rotary. Democrat. Presbyterian. Avocations: shell collecting, reading, minor house repairs.

MCCLURG, ROBERT JAMES, emergency nurse practitioner, educator; b. Warsaw, N.Y., Sept. 5, 1958; s. Robert and Elizabeth (Castiglia) McC.; m. Tina Marie Crawford, July 15, 1984; 1 child, Rose Marie. AAS, SUNY, Morrisville, 1978; ASN, SUNY, Albany, 1987; AAS, C.C. of the Air Force, Maxwell AFB, Ala., 1988; BSN, Brockport State coll., 1996; MS, U. Buffalo, 1999. RN, N.Y.; cert. paramedic. Enlisted USAF, 1980, advanced through grades to maj., 2000; med. technician 390 Tactical Fighter Squadron, Mountain Home AFB, Idaho, 1981-83; supr., shift leader David Grant USAF Med. Ctr., Travis AFB, Calif., 1983-84, USAF Hosp., Kirtland AFB, N.Mex., 1984-85; ind. duty med. technician USAF Survival Sch., Spokane, Wash., 1985-86, supr., field med. br., 1986-88; staff nurse St. Luke's Hosp., Spokane, 1987-88, Wyo. County Cmty. Hosp., Warsaw, N.Y., 1988-89; flight nurse, med. crew dir. USAFR, Niagara Falls, N.Y., 1989—; EMS coord. St. Jerome Hosp., Batavia, N.Y., 1989-96; emergency nurse practitioner Strong Meml. Hosp., Rochester, 1999—; clin. assoc. faculty U. Rochester, N.Y., 2000—; family nurse practitioner Wyo. County Cmty. Health Sys., 2000—. Chmn. prehosp. adv. com. Western Regional EMS System, Buffalo, N.Y., 1993-95; mem. Wyo.-Erie Regional EMS Coun. Buffalo, 1993—; vice-chmn. Genesee County EMS Coun., Batavia, 1994-96; EMS coord. World Univ. Games, Buffalo, 1994; alternate rep. to N.Y. State EMS Coun.; mem. legis. com., regional activities com. N.Y. State EMS Coun. Vol. paramedic Perry Emergency Ambulance, N.Y., 1978-79, 88—; mem. Wyo. Co. Paramedic Task Force. Mem. Res. Officer Assn. (life), Air Force Assn. (life). Avocations: kayaking, backpacking, camping. Office: Strong Meml Hosp Emergency Dept 601 Elmwood Ave Rochester NY 14642-0002 E-mail: robert_mcclurg@urmc.rochester.edu.

MCCLUSKEY, FRANK BRYCE, director; b. Orange, N.J., July 28, 1949; s. Frank Bryce and Angela McCluskey; life ptnr. Marguerite Walker; children: Brandon Albert McLuskey, Kelly Bryce. BA in Philosophy, Bloomfield (N.J.) Coll., 1972; PhD in Philosophy, New Sch. U., N.Y.C., 1977. Prof. philosophy Mercy Coll., Dobbs Ferry, NY, 1977—, dean of online learning, 2000—; postdoctoral fellow Yale U., New Haven, 1978. Cons. Am. Mgmt. Assn., N.Y.C., 1994—2001; spkr. in field. Author: Thoughts on Fire; Life Lessons of a Volunteer Firefighter (Readers Choice award Writers Advantage, 2003), Burning for Success; contbr. articles to profl. jours. V.p. Putnam County Fire Chiefs, Carmel, NY, 1995—2004. Named Firefighter of Yr., Mahopac Falls (N.Y.) Vol. Fire Dept., 1990; fellow, NEH, 1978. Mem.: Internat. Assn. Fire Chiefs, Nat. Assn. Vol. Firefighters, N.Y. State Assn. Fire Chiefs. Republican. Roman Catholic. Avocation: travel. Home: 456 N Lake Blvd Mahopac NY 10541 Office: Mercy Coll 555 Broadway Mahopac NY 10522 E-mail: fmccluskey@mercy.edu.

MCCLUSKEY, JAMES FRANCIS, music educator, musician; b. Boston, Mass., Sept. 1952; s. Joan Dolan and William John McCluskey; m. Christine Elizabeth Stern, Jan. 4, 1985; children: Sean Vincent, Maura Joan. MusM, New Eng. Conservatory, 1982, MusB, 1979; M Theol. Studies, Weston Jesuit Sch. Theology, 1993; Cert. of Advanced Study in Humanities, Harvard U., 1984. Music educator St. Johns H.S., Shrewsbury, Mass., 2000—; faculty Guitar dept. New Eng. Conservatory Preparatory Sch., and New Eng. Conservatory Sch. Continuing Edn., Boston, 1989—; music educator Malden Cath. H.S., Malden, Mass., 1995—99; music dir. Holy Spirit Chapel Loyola Marymount U., L.A., 1993—95. Cons. Boston Music Edn. Collaborative, 1998—99. Composer: Hymn of the Universe - Quintet for Guitar and String Quartet, Irish Song Suite for Solo Guitar, Fantasy on Karl Bellmann's Songs for Solo Guitar; author: (music theory) An Analysis of Irish Traditional Music, (theology) Aesthetics and Theology, (music theory) The Development Section in Mozart's Symphonies. Recipient award, Frank Huntington Beebe Found., 1981—83. Mem.: Internat. Assn. Jazz Educators, Music Educators Nat. Conf. Roman Catholic. Avocations: ornithology, gardening. Office: St John's High School 378 Main St Shrewsbury MA 01545-2204 Personal E-mail: jmccluskey@stjohnshigh.org. E-mail: jmccluskey@stjohnshigh.org.

MCCLUSKEY, JOHN ASBERRY, JR., literature educator, writer; b. Middletown, Ohio, Oct. 25, 1944; s. John Asberry and Helen Mildred (Harris) McC.; m. Audrey Louise Thomas, Dec. 24, 1969; children: Malik Douglass, Jerome Patrice, John Toure. BA in Social Rels., Harvard U., 1966; MA in English, Stanford U., 1972. Lectr. Miles Coll., Birmingham, Ala., 1967-68, Valparaiso (Ind.) U., 1968-69; from lectr. to asst. prof. Case-Western Res. U., Cleve., 1969-77; from assoc. prof. to prof. Ind. U., Bloomington, 1977-85, prof., 1985—, assoc. dean Grad. Sch., 1983-88, chair Afro-Am. studies, 1995-2000. Dir. Com. Instl. Cooperation Minorities Fellowship, Bloomington, 1983-88. Author: (novels) Look What They Done to My Song, 1974, Mr. America's Last Season Blues, 1983; editor: (story collection by Rudolph Fisher) City of Refuge, 1987; co-editor: Black Men Speaking, 1997. Mem. Bd. Pub. Safety, Bloomington, 1983-88; life mem. Monroe County NAACP. Named one of Outstanding Educators of Am., 1976; Yaddo fellow, 1984, 86. Mem. MLA, Am. Studies Assn., Midwest MLA, Authors' Guild. Avocations: master swimmer, jogging, mini-triathlons, gardening. Home: 3300 E Moores Pike Bloomington IN 47401-7102 Office: Ind U Afro-Am Studies Memorial Hall E-28 Bloomington IN 47405 Office Phone: 812-855-0143.

MCCLUSKEY, LOIS THORNHILL, photographer; b. Boston, Apr. 7, 1945; d. Fred S. and Mary (Evans) Thornhill; m. Edward J. McCluskey, Feb. 14, 1981. BA, Middlebury Coll., 1966; postgrad., U. St. Thomas, Houston, 1967-69; MA, NYU, 1971; cert. in graphic design, U. Calif., Santa Cruz, 1983. Rsch. technician dept. virology Baylor Sch. Medicine, Houston, 1966-68; with Kelly Girls, Palo Alto, Calif., 1971-72; slide curator dept. art Stanford (Calif.) U., 1972-80; founder, pres. Stanford Design Assocs., Palo Alto, 1981—. Cons. copy and museum photography; graphic designer. Mem. Smithsonian Assocs. Home: 895 Northampton Dr Palo Alto CA 94303-3434 Office: Stanford Design Assocs PO Box 60451 Palo Alto CA 94306-0451

MCCLUSKEY, NEIL GERARD, gerontologist, educator, literary agent; b. Seattle, Dec. 15, 1920; s. Patrick John and Mary Genevieve (Casey) McC.; m. Elaine Lituchy, June 5, 1977. AB, Gonzaga U., 1944, MA, 1945; Lic. in Sacred Theology, Gen. Theol. Union, Berkeley, 1952; PhD, Columbia U., 1957. Assoc. editor Am. (Nat. Cath. Weekly), N.Y.C., 1955-60; dean sch. edn. Gonzaga U., Spokane, 1960-62, dir. hons. program, 1963-65, v.p. acad., 1963-66; prof. U. Notre Dame, South Bend, Ind., 1966-71, dean, dir. Inst. Studies in Edn., 1968-71; prof., dean profl. studies Lehman Coll. CUNY, 1971-75; dir. Ctr. Gerontol. Studies CUNY Grad. Sch., 1975-81; exec. dir. BHRAGS Social Svcs. Ctr., Bklyn., 1981-84; sr. cons. Retirement Advisors, Inc., N.Y.C., 1985—. Pres. Westchester Lit. Agy., 1991—. Author: Public Schools and Moral Education, 1958, Catholic Viewpoint on Education, 1959, Catholic Education Faces Its Future, 1969; author, editor: Aging and Society, 1980, Aging and Retirement, 1981. Bd. dirs. Cath. Big Bros. N.Y., 1985—. Home: 2533 Egret Lake Dr West Palm Beach FL 33413-2161 E-mail: neilagency@adelphia.net.

MCCLUSKEY, SUSAN D. lawyer; b. Osmond, Nebr. d. Earle R. and Deloris C. (Olson) M.; m. Charles D. Gray, Feb. 17, 1980; children: Charles W., Johanna M. BA, U. Denver, 1973; JD, Cornell U., 1977; cert. sr. mgrs. in govt., Harvard U., 1992. Bar: D.C., 1977, U.S. Supreme Ct., 1993. Asst. counsel Nat. Treasury Employees Union and Panel Assoc., 1984-86, Fed. Svc. Impasses Panel, 1984-86; spl. asst. to exec. dir. Fed. Labor Rels. Authority, 1984-86, exec. asst. to chmn., 1986-89, chief counsel to chmn., 1989—. Methodist. Office: Fed Labor Relations Authority 607 14th St NW Ste 410 Washington DC 20005-2000

MCCOART, JANICE GREENBERG, art educator; b. Hartford, Conn., July 4, 1952; d. Bennett and Hilda (Podnetsky) Greenberg; m. Edward Scott Rosenthal, Nov. 11, 1978 (div. Dec. 1991); children: Amy Dawn Rosenthal, Lindsey Jean Rosenthal, Samantha Robyn Rosenthal; m. James John III McCoart, Aug. 20, 1995 (div. Apr. 2003). BS, Skidmore Coll., Saratoga Springs, N.Y., 1974; MFA, George Washington U., 1986. Buyer, visual presentation dir. Blake's Dept. Stores, Springfield, Mass., 1974—77; instr. bus. Bay Path Coll., Longmeadow, Mass., 1977—78; from lectr. to prof. fine and applied arts Marymount U., Arlington, Va., 1980—, chair fashion design, fashion merchandising. Cons. to exhibit "Between a Rock and a Hard Place: A Dialogue on Sweatshops, 1820 to the Present Smithsonian Instn., Washington, 1998; organizer, grantee Contemporary Bulgarian Art Exhibit Marymount U., 2002; cons. Fashion Industry Forum U.S. Dept. Labor, Washington, 1996; conf. chair An Acad. Search for Sweatshop Solutions Marymount Coll., 1997. Editor: (conf. proc.) An Academic Search for Sweatshop Solutions, 1997; contbr. articles to profl. jours. Sr. Scholar grantee, Fulbright Scholarship Bd., 2001—02. Mem.: Internat. Textile and Apparel Assn., Costume Soc. Am., Coll. Art Assn. Am., So. Assn. of Colls. and Schs. Commn. on Colls. Office: Marymount Univ 2807 N Glebe Rd Arlington VA 22207

MCCOBB, ALLAN PAUL, not-for-profit organization executive; b. Russell, Kans. s. Boyden and Doris Marie (Marsh) McC.; m. Ursula Seubert Fox, June 25, 1983 (div. Sept. 1991). BS in Phys. Edn., Kans. State U., 1967, BS in Bus. and Acctg., 1971; MS in Exercise Sci., Ft. Hays State U., 1986. Staff acct. Arthur Young & Co., Kansas City, 1972-74; gen. mgr., part owner McCobb Inc., Russell, Kans., 1974-80; grants mgr. N.W. Kans. Area Agy. on Aging, Hays, 1980-81; exec. dir. S.W. Kans. Area Agy. on Aging, Dodge City, Kans., 1981-85; grants mgr. N.W. Area Agy. on Aging, Hays, 1985-86; exec. dir. United Way of Enid and N.W. Okla., Enid, 1990—. Exec. dir. Wheatbelt Girl Scout Coun., Hutchinson, Kans., 1987-90; presenter, group facilitator Meth. Divorce Support Group and Workshop, Enid, 1993—; youth coord. Enid Cmty. Children's Choir, 1994—; mem. initial bd. Enid Cmty. Free Health Clinic, Enid, 1996-99, Enid Cmty. Found., 1998—, Gar. County Child Advocacy Coun., 1997-2002; small claims mediator N.W. Okla. Early Settlement, Fairview, 1998—. With U.S. Army, 1968-70, Vietnam. Decorated Bronze Star U.S. Army, 1970; inductee Lake Atwood 10 Mile Hall of Fame, 1984. Mem. Garfield County Area C. of C., Enid Rotary Club. Methodist. Avocations: running, genealogy, youth work. Home: PO Box 771 Enid OK 73702-0771 Office: United Way Enid NW Okla 321 W Cherokee Ave Ste C Enid OK 73701-5603

MCCOBB, JOHN BRADFORD, JR., lawyer; b. Oct. 14, 1939; s. John Bradford and Dorothea Joyce (Hoffman) M.; m. Maureen Kelly, Oct. 6, 1973; 1 child, Carrie Elizabeth. AB cum laude, Princeton U., 1961; JD, Stanford U., 1966; LLM, NYU, 1973. Bar: Calif. 1967. Assoc. IBM, Armonk, NY, 1966—74, gen. counsel Tokyo, 1974—77, lab. counsel Endicott, NY, 1977—79, sr. atty. White Plains, NY, 1979—81, regional counsel Dallas, 1981—83; counsel, sec. IBM Instruments, Inc., Danbury, Conn., 1983—87; area counsel European Labs., Hursley, England, 1987—90; counsel govtl. programs IBM, Washington, 1990—97. Princeton-in-Asia tchg. fellow Chinese U. Hong Kong, 1963—65. Contbr. articles to profl. jours. Trustee Princeton-in-Asia, Inc., 1970—86. Mem.: ABA, State Bar of Calif., Phi Beta Kappa.

MCCOID, DONALD JAMES, bishop; b. Wheeling, W.Va., Dec. 31, 1943; s. Roy Conrad and Alberta Virginia (Sturm) McC.; m. Saundra Ernette Piisila, Oct. 20, 1973; children: Kimberly, Elizabeth. AB, West Liberty (W.Va.) State Coll., 1965; MDiv, Luth. Theol. Sem., Phila., 1968; DD (hon.), Thiel Coll., 1983. Ordained to ministry Evang. Luth. Ch. in Am., 1968. Pastor St. Luke's Luth. Ch., Monessen, Pa., 1968-72; assoc. pastor St. John's Luth. Ch. Highland, Pitts., 1972-74; area Luth. coord. Western Pa.—W.Va. synod, Luth. Ch. Am., Clarksburg, W.Va., 1974-77; sr. pastor Trinity Luth. Ch., Latrobe, Pa., 1977-87; bishop Southwestern Pa. synod, Evang. Luth. Ch. in Am., Pitts., 1987—. Chmn. Pa. Coun. Chs., Harrisburg, Inst. for Mission, 1997-2002; co-chmn. Luth.-Orthodox Nat. Dialogue, 1997—, Internat. Dialogue, 2004—; del. Luth. World Fedn. Assembly, 1997, Luth. Sem. at Gettysburg, 2003—; bd.

dir. Faith and Order Conf. Bd. dirs. Religious Leadership Forum, Pitts., 1988—, Luth. Svcs. in Am., 1997-2003; exec. com. Christian Assocs. S.W. Pa., Pitts., 1988—, chair coun., 1994-96; chair Conf. Bishops, Evangel. Luth. Ch. Am., 1999-2003. Lutheran. Office: Evang Luth Ch in Am SW Pa Synod 9625 Perry Hwy Pittsburgh PA 15237-5555 Office Phone: 412-367-8222. Business E-Mail: donald.mccoid@ecunet.org.

MC COIN, JOHN MACK, social worker; b. Sparta, N.C., Jan. 21, 1931; s. Robert Avery and Ollie (Osborne) McC. BS, Appalachian State Tchrs. Coll., Boone, N.C., 1959-60; MS in Social Work, Richmond (Va.) Profl. Inst., 1962; postgrad., U. N.C., 1959-60; PhD, U. Minn., 1977. Lic. master social worker; cert. social worker, N.Y. Social svc. worker Broughton State Hosp., Morganton, N.C., 1958-59, John Unstead State Hosp., Butner, N.C., 1960-61; clin. social worker Dorothea Dix State Hosp., Raleigh, N.C., 1962-63; child welfare case worker Wake County Welfare Dept., Raleigh, 1963-64; psychiat. social worker Toledo Mental Hygiene Clinic, 1964-66; sr. psychiat. social worker N.Y. Hosp.-Cornell U. Med. Ctr. Westchester divsn., White Plains, 1966-68; social worker VA Hosp., Montrose, N.Y., 1968-73; also vol. mental health worker Westchester County Mental Health Assn. and Mental Health Bd., White Plains; seminar instr. Grad. Sch. Social Work U. Minn., Mpls., 1973-74; social worker F.D.R. VA Health Care Facility, Montrose, 1975-77; asst. prof. social work U. Wis., Oshkosh, 1977-79, chmn. dept. cmty. liaison com., 1978-79; assoc. prof. social work Grand Valley State Colls., Allendale, Mich., 1979-81; social worker VA Med. Ctr., Battle Creek, Mich., 1981-83, supr. social worker dept. Leavenworth, Kans., 1983-94. Cons. 44th Gen. Hosp., USAR, Menasha, Wis., 1978-79, 5540th Support Command, USAR, Grand Rapids, Mich., 1979-83; cons. in field; adj. faculty mem. social scis. dept. Kansas City C.C., 1985-89, St. Mary Coll., 1984, Kellogg C.C., Battle Creek, 1981-83; adj. faculty mem. sch. social welfare U. Kans., Lawrence, 1992; presenter in field. Author: Adult Foster Homes: Their Managers and Residents, 1983; founder (with Human Scis. Press), editor Adult Foster Care Jour., 1987-88, Adult Resdl. Care Jour., 1989-91, ind. jour., 1992-96; contbr. articles to profl. jours. With USMC, 1948-52, USMCR, 1957-72; lt. col. USAR, 1972-91. Recipient Outstanding Performance award VA, 1971, 83, Superior Performance award, 1982; grantee NIMH, 1974. Mem. NASW (social action com. West Mich. br. 1980-81), Alpha Delta Mu. Democrat. Baptist. Home and Office: 4913 Colonial Way Lawrence KS 66049-3599

MCCOLL, HUGH LEON, JR., former bank executive; b. Bennettsville, S.C., June 18, 1935; s. Hugh Leon and Frances Pratt (Carroll) McC.; m. Jane Bratton Spratt, Oct. 3, 1959; children: Hugh Leon III, John Spratt, Jane Bratton. BS in Bus. Adminstrn, U. N.C., 1957. Trainee NCNB Nat. Bank, Charlotte, 1959-61, officer, 1961-65, sr. v.p., 1965-68, div. exec., 1969, exec. v.p., 1970-73, vice chmn. bd., 1973-74, pres., 1974-83, also dir.; CEO Bank of Am. (formerly NationsBank Corp.), Charlotte, 1983—; CEO,pres. Barnet Banks, Miami, Fla., 1998—; Pres., CEO, chmn. Bank of America Corp., Charlotte, NC, 1983—2001, Chmn. Emeritus, 2001—. Bd. dirs. Sonoco Products Inc., Hartsville, S.C. Trustee Heineman Found., Charlotte, 1976—, Queens Coll., Charlotte; bd. visitors Grad. Sch. Bus. U. N.C. at Chapel Hill; chmn. Charlotte Uptown Devel. Corp., 1978-81, 85. 1st lt. USMCR, 1957-59. Mem. Bankers Roundtable (mem. trialateral commn.), Am. Bankers Assn., N.C. Bankers Assn. (pres. 1974). Democrat. Presbyterian.

MCCOLLAM, CRAIG A. manufacturing executive; b. 1960; Dir. fin., corp. controller Dionex Corp, Sunnyvale, Calif., 1993-99, v.p. fin. & adminstrn., CFO, 1999—. Office: PO Box 3603 1228 Titan Way Sunnyvale CA 94085-4015

MCCOLLAM, MARION ANDRUS, consulting firm executive, educator; b. New Orleans, Feb. 8, 1931; d. Gerald Louis and Lucile Gordon (Isacks) Andrus; m. Andrew McCollam, Jr., Jan. 29, 1955 (div. 1978); children: Andrew III, Gerald Andrus, Marion Cage. BA, Tulane U., 1952; M. Urban and Reg. Planning, U. New Orleans, 1978. Human affairs coord. Office of the Mayor, City of New Orleans, 1978, arts coord., 1978-80; dir. planning, prin. cons. Duncan Plaza Design Project, New Orleans, 1978-80; dir. planning Downtown Devel. Dist., New Orleans, 1980-81; pres. Andrus and Roberts Inc., Phoenix, New Orleans, 1980-84; exec. dir. Arts Coun. New Orleans, 1981-90, Cultural Arts Coun. of Houston and Harris County, 1991-98; pres. McCollam Cons., LLC, 1998—. Cons. in field; adj. lectr. in arts adminstrn. Goucher Coll., 1998—. Mem. nat. adv. com. Working Capital Fund, Mpls., 1995-99, Nat. Arts Stabilization, Balt., 1998—; adv. panel design Nat. Endowment for the Arts, Washington, 1995, adv. and chair local arts agencies, 1992-94; bd. dirs., sr. fellow Am. Leadership Forum, Houston, 1994-2000; mem. cmty. assessment com. United Way of Tex. Gulf Coast, 1995-99; bd. dirs. Urban League of New Orleans, 1984-89; pres. Jr. League of New Orleans, 1969-70. Recipient Arts Adminstr. of Yr. award Arts Mgmt. Inst./Nat. News Svc., 1987, Award for Sustained Mgmt. Excellence, Greater New Orleans Found., 1989. Mem. Am. Inst. Cert. Planners, AIA (hon.), U.S. Urban Arts Fedn. (pres. 1988), Nat. Assembly of Local Arts Agencies (vice chmn. bd. dirs. 1988-94, Chairman's award 1992). Avocations: music, art, reading, travel, family activities. Office: 1914 Bissonnet St Houston TX 77005-1645

MCCOLLAM, SHARON L. retail executive; BS in Acctg. CPA. Former acctg. Ernst and Young; divisional v.p., CFO Dole Food Co., Inc., 1993—2000; v.p. fin. Williams-Sonoma, Inc., San Francisco, 2000—01, sr. v.p., CFO, 2001—03, exec. v.p., CFO, 2003—. Office: Williams-Sonoma Inc 3250 Van Ness Ave San Francisco CA 94109*

MCCOLLAM, WILLIAM, JR., utility company executive; b. New Orleans, Mar. 15, 1925; s. William and Marie (Mason) McC.; m. Hope Flower Joffrion, Apr. 20, 1947; children: Ellendale McCollam Hoffman, William Cage, Stephen Mason. BS, La. State U., 1943; BS in Engring., U.S. Mil. Acad., 1946; MS in Civil Engring., MIT, 1954. Registered profl. engr., N.Y. Commd. 2d lt. U.S. Army, 1946; advanced through grades to lt. col. U.S Army; resigned U.S. Army, 1961; with Ark. Power and Light Co., Little Rock, 1961-70, exec. asst., 1961-64; v.p. Ark Power and Light Co., Little Rock, 1964-68; sr. v.p. Ark. Power and Light Co., Little Rock, 1968-70; exec. v.p. New Orleans Pub. Service, 1970-71, pres., 1971-78, Edison Electric Inst., Washington, 1978-90, pres. emeritus, 1990—. Cons. energy mgmt., Washington, 1990—; bd. dirs. Burns and Roe Group, Inc., Oradell, NJ; trustee Thomas Alva Edison Found., Detroit, 1978—89; past chmn. S.W. Power Pool, Little Rock, 1973—74, Nat. Elec. Reliability Coun., Princeton, NJ, 1975—78; bd. dirs., exec. com. U.S. Mem. Com., World Energy Coun., Washington, 1978—94; bd. dirs. McDermott Internat., Inc., 1990—99. Past pres. Greater New Orleans area C. of C., 1974-75; former dir. Loyola U., New Orleans, 1975-78; pres.'s council Tulane U., 1982-86. Named to La. State U. Alumni Hall of Distinction, 1985; recipient U.S. Energy award in recognition of outstanding contbn. to world energy coun., 1991. Mem. La. Soc. Profl. Engrs. (A.B. Paterson award 1975) Clubs: Chevy Chase, Metropolitan (Washington); Boston, New Orleans Country. Republican. Episcopalian. Home: 2411 Tracy Pl NW Washington DC 20008-1628 Office: Edison Electric Inst 701 Pennsylvania Ave NW Fl 3 Washington DC 20004-2696

MC COLLISTER, JOHN CHARLES, writer, clergyman, educator, executive producer; b. Pitts., June 1, 1935; s. John Charles and Caroline Jesse (Hall) Mc C.; m. Beverly Ann Chase, Aug. 6, 1960; children: Beth Ann, Amy Susan, Michael John. BA, Capital U., 1957; MDiv, Luth. Theol. Sem., Columbus, Ohio, 1961; PhD, Mich. State U., 1969. Ordained to ministry Luth. Ch., 1961. Pastor Zion Luth. Ch., Freeland, Mich., 1961-65, Bethlehem Luth. Ch., Lansing, Mich., 1965-71; prof. religion and Greek Olivet (Mich.) Coll., 1970-74; prof. religion and philosophy Bethune-Cookman Coll., Daytona Beach, Fla., 1974-76, Embry-Riddle Aero. U., 1976-82, dir. profl. programs, 1979-80, cons. to pres., 1980-82. Pres. Wright Advt. Co., Daytona Beach, 1975-76; CEO New Arran Prodns., Inc., Daytona Beach, 1993—, Yongestreet Prodns., Ormond Beach, Fla., 1986, arbitrator Fed. Mediation and Conciliation Svc., 1978; spl. master Fla. Pub. Employees Rels. Commn., 1975—; mgmt. cons. Hoover Ball and Bearing, Charlotte, Mich.; pres. Am. Writers Inst., 1982—. Host Open Phone Forum, radio sta. WROD, Daytona Beach, 1974—76; author: A Philosophy of Flight, 1981, So Help Me, God, 1981, The Christian Book of Why, 1983; Problem Solving for Executives, 1984; author: The Sky is Home, 1986; co-author: The Sunshine Book, 1979, Day by Day, 1990; editor and compiler A Child is Born, 1972, Portraits of the Christ, 1974, Writing for Dollars, 1995, The Story of the Pittsburgh Pirates, 1998, The Tigers and Their Den, 1999, The Best Baseball Games Ever Played, 2002, Tales from the Pirates Dugout, 2003, Tales from the Cockpit, 2003, Echoes from the Smithsonian, 2004; contbr. articles to various mags. Vol. probation officer, Mich., 1961-71, hearing officer, 1970-74; commr. Mich. Dept. Commerce, 1969-72; speaker Nat. Lincoln Day Observance, Washington, 1982; internat. adviser Han Nam U., Taejon, Republic of Korea, 1989. Recipient Outstanding Am. award Daytona Beach Jaycees, 1974. Mem. Am. Arbitration Assn. Home and Office: 26 Lazy Eight Dr Daytona Beach FL 32128-6775 Office Phone: 386-767-9999. E-mail: writerdoc@aol.com.

MCCOLLOUGH, NEWTON CLARK, III, orthopaedic surgeon; b. Butler, Pa., July 17, 1934; s. Newton C. and Margaret Elizabeth (Mattocks) McC.; m. Mary Eva Semanski, Feb. 22, 1968; children: Peter Scott, Amy Marie. BA, Duke U., 1956; MD, U. Pa., 1959. Diplomate: Am. Bd. Orthopaedic Surgery. Intern Jackson Meml. Hosp., Miami, Fla., 1959-60; resident in orthopaedic surgery, 1960-64; dir. orthopaedic resident edn. Orange Meml. Hosp., Orlando, Fla., 1965-66; asst. prof. orthopaedics and rehab. U. Miami Sch. Medicine, 1968-72, assoc. prof., 1972-76, prof., vice chmn. dept., 1976-78, prof., chmn. dept., 1978-86; dir. rehab. Jackson Meml. Hosp., Miami, 1972-82, chief orthopedics and rehab., 1978-86; dir. med. affairs Internat. Shriners Hosps. Children, Tampa, Fla., 1986-2001, 2001—, mem. med. adv. bd., 2001—, dir. med. affairs emeritus, 2001—, med. adv. bd., 2001—. Dir. Am. Bd. for Certification in Prosthetics/Orthotics, 1974-77; mem. Health Planning Council So. Fla. Task Force on Long Term Patient Care, 1974-77; asst. med. dir. Div. of Children's Med. Services, State of Fla., 1975-86; chmn. Statewide Com. for Spinal Cord Injury, 1976-78 Trustee Jour. Bone and Joint Surgery, 1992-98, vice chmn., 1996-98; contbr. articles to med. jours. Served to lt. comdr. M.C. USNR, 1966-68. Decorated Legion of Merit. Mem. ACS, AMA, Am. Acad. Orthopaedic Surgeons (bd. dirs. 1978-79, 87-92, 2d v.p. 1987-88, 1st v.p. 1988-89, pres. 1989-90), Am. Burn Assn. (Disting. Achievement award 2001), Fla. Orthopaedic Soc. (mem. exec. com. 1978-79), Miami Orthopaedic Soc. (v.p. 1978-79), Am. Acad. Orthotists and Prosthetists (hon.), Fla. Med. Soc. Hillsborough County Med. Assn., Am. Congress Rehab. Medicine, Nat. Rehab. Assn., Scoliosos Rsch. Soc., Internat. Soc. Prosthetics and Orthotics, Am. Orthopaedic Assn., Orthopaedic Rsch. and Edn. Found. (trustee 1991-97, sec. 1995-97), Internat. Soc. Prosthetics and Orthotics (dir. 1980-83), Assn. Children's Prosthetic and Orthotic Clinics (pres. 1983-84), Rehab. Engring. Soc. N.Am. (dir. 1980-83), Am. Spinal Injury Assn., Internat. Med. Soc. Paraplegia, Pediatric Orthopaedic Soc. (dir. 1983-84, pres. 1984-85, Disting. Achievement award 2000), 20th Century Orthopaedic Assn. (treas. 1984-89), Am. Acad. Pediatrics, Phi Beta Kappa, Alpha Omega. Republican. Lutheran. Home: 602 Juan Anasco Dr Longboat Key FL 34228-1425 Office: Internat Shriners Hosps for Crippled Children 2900 N Rocky Point Dr Tampa FL 33607-1435 Office Phone: 813-281-0300.

MCCOLLOUGH, W. ALAN, electronics retail executive; Gen. mgr. corp. ops. Circuit City Stores Inc., Richmond, Va., 1988, asst. v.p., 1989-91, pres. ctrl. operating divsn., 1991-95, sr. v.p. merchandising, 1995-97, pres., COO, 1997—2000, chmn., pres., CEO, 2000—. Office: Circuit City Stores Inc 9950 Maryland Dr Richmond VA 23233

MCCOLLUM, BETTY, congresswoman; b. July 12, 1954; m. Douglas McCollum; 2 children. BS in Edn., Coll. St. Catherine. Retail store mgr., Minn.; mem. Minn. Ho. Reps., 1992-2000, mem. edn. com., environ. and natural resources com., mem. gen. legis. com., vet. affairs and elections com., mem. transportation and transit com., asst. majority leader, chair legis. commn. on econ. status of women, mem. rules and adminstrv. legis. com.; mem. U.S. Congress from Minn. 4th Dist., Washington, 2001—; mem. edn. and workforce com., resources com.; mem. Com. on Internat. Relations. Mem. St. Croix Valley Coun. Girl Scouts. Mem. VFW Aux., Am. Legion Aux. Democrat. Office: US Ho of Reps 1029 Longworth HOB Washington DC 20515

MCCOLLUM, CLIFFORD GLENN, college dean emeritus; b. South Gifford, Mo., May 12, 1919; s. William Henry and Aultie V. (Westfall) McC.; m. Alice Elizabeth Erickson, Aug. 18, 1940; children: Eric Edward, Lisa Buren. Student, Central Coll., 1935-37; BS, U. Mo., 1939, MA, 1947, EdD, 1949. Tchr. pub. schs., Monett, Mo., 1938-39, Poplar Bluff, Mo., 1939-41, Boonville, Mo., 1941-42; asst. prof. sci. U. No. Iowa, 1949-55, assoc. prof., 1956-59, prof., 1959-84, prof. emeritus, 1984—, head dept. sci., 1957-68; dean U. No. Iowa (Coll. Natural Scis.), 1968-84, dean emeritus, 1984—. Prof. State U. N.Y. at Oneonta, 1955-56; Dir., instl. rep. Central States Univs., Inc.; cons. Coronet Instrnl. Films; cons. on sci. curricula to pub. schs. and colls.; speaker in field. Contbr. articles to profl. jours. Served with USAAF, 1943-46. Fellow AAAS (nat. committeeman 1964-67), Iowa Acad. Sci. (pres. 1979-80); mem. Am. Inst. Biol. Scis., Nat. Assn. Biology Tchrs. (regional dir. 1963-65), Nat. Assn. Research in Sci. Teaching, Nat. Sci. Tchrs. Assn., Sigma Xi, Phi Delta Kappa. Home: 6511 N Revere Ave Kansas City MO 64151-3989 E-mail: cmccollum1@kc.rr.com. *My personal response to the philosophical conditions in which we live today is one of preparing to live rather consistently with crises. It is my conviction that the mood of our time is toward a growing pessimism, and much of this is associated with the concomitants of a galloping technology. Yet we are not willing at this point to give up our human condition to the natural evolution that would result from basic environmental mechanisms. We will still try to condition that destiny.*

MCCOLLUM, EVERETT, retired school system administrator, music educator; b. Reidsville, NC, July 10, 1928; s. Roy and Carrie Lee McCollum; m. Mary Helen Barganier; children: Connie, Karen, Evette, Lisa. BA, Youngstown Coll., 1957; MA, Westminster Coll., 1964. Pvt. tchr. piano, voice, Youngstown, 1953—; tchr. West Jr. H.S., Youngstown, Ohio, 1957—61, Volney Rogers Sch., Youngstown, 1961—68; prin. Hillman Jr. H.S., Youngstown, 1968—71, South H.S., Youngstown, 1971—76; ret., 1976. Author: How to Play Gospel Music, 1961. Bd. dirs. Penn Ohio Coll., Youngstown, 1990—94; choir dir. Mahoning United Meth. Choir, 1957—88. Cpl. U.S. Army, 1953—57. Mem.: Youngstown Kiwanis Club (youth svc. dir. 1980). Home: 2122 Kimmel St Youngstown OH 44505 Fax: 330-746-4403. E-mail: emccoll@earthlink.net.

MC COLLUM, IRA WILLIAM, JR., (BILL MC COLLUM), former congressman; b. Brooksville, Fla., July 12, 1944; s. Ira William and Arline Gray (Lockhart) McC.; m. Ingrid Maria Seebohm, Sept. 25, 1971; children: Douglas Michael, Justin Randolph, Andrew Lockhart. BA, U. Fla., 1965, JD, 1968. Bar: Fla. 1968, D.C. 2001. Ptnr. Pitts, Eubanks & Ross (P.A.), Orlando, Fla., 1973-80; mem. 97th-102nd Congresses from 5th Dist. Fla., 1981-92, 103d-106th Congresses from 8th Dist. Fla., 1993-2001; former vice chmn. banking/fin. svcs. com.; former chmn. judiciary subcom. on crime; former mem. select com. on intelligence; ptnr. Baker & Hostetler LLP, Orlando, Fla. and Washington, D.C., 2001—. Vice chair House Rep. Conf. 101st-103d Congresses. Chmn. Rep. Exec. Com. Seminole County, Fla., 1976-80; county chmn.'s rep. 5th Dist. Fla. State Rep. Exec. Com., 1977-80; co-chmn. rep. platform com., 1992. With USN, 1969-72. Mem. Fla. Bar, Naval Res. Assn., Res. Officers Assn., Orange County Bar Assn. (exec. coun. 1975-79), Am. Legion, Mil. Order World Wars, Fla. Blue Key, Phi Delta Phi, Omicron Delta Kappa, Kiwanis. Republican. Episcopalian.

MCCOLLUM, JAMES FOUNTAIN, lawyer; b. Reidsville, NC, Mar. 24, 1946; s. James F. and Dell (Frazier) McC.; m. Susan Shasek, Apr. 26, 1969; children: Audra Lynne, Amy Elizabeth. BS, Fla. Atlantic U., 1968; JD, Fla. State U., 1972. Bar: U.S. Ct. Appeals (5th cir.) 1973, Fla. 1972, U.S. Ct. Appeals (11th cir.) 1982. Assoc. Kennedy & McCollum, 1972-73; prin. McCollum & Rinaldo, P.A., 1973-77, McCollum & Oberhausen, P.A., 1977-80, McCollum, Oberhausen & Tuck, L.L.P. (and predecessor firm), Sebring, Fla., 1977—. Bd. dirs. Comml. Bancorp, Inc., Comml. Bank Highlands County; pres. Highlands Devel. Concepts, Inc., Sebring, 1982—; sec. Focus Broadcast Comm., Inc., Sebring, 1982-87; mng. ptnr. Highlands Investment Service; pres. Am. Svc. Title & Escrow, Inc., 2001-; campaign chmn. George W. Bush for Pres., 2000, 04. Treas. Highlands County chpt. ARC, 1973-76; vestryman St. Agnes Episcopal Ch., 1973—, chancellor, 1978—; mem. Fla. Sch. Bd. Atty.'s Assn., 1974-2001, bd. dirs., 1989-97, pres., 1995-96; mem. Com. 100 of Highlands County, 1975-83, bd. dirs., 1985-87, chmn., 1991-92; chmn. Highlands County High Speed Rail Task Force; chmn. bd., treas. Ctrl. Fla. Racing Assn., 1976-78; chmn. Leadership Sebring; life mem., past pres. Highlands Little Theatre, Inc.; bd. dirs. Palms of Sebring Nursing Home, 1988-90, Palms Estate Mobile Home Park, Sebring Airport Authority, 1988-90, treas., 1988, chmn. indsl. com., 1988, vice-chmn., 1989-90, chmn., 1990-91, Highlands County High Speed Rail Task Force, 1986-89; bd. dirs. Highlands County Family YMCA, 1985-93, pres. Sebring br., 1992-93, chmn. bldg. com., 1992-94; bd. dirs. Good Shepherd Hospice, Inc., v.p., 2000—, chmn. bd. dirs., 2003—; campaign chmn. Jeb Bush for Gov., Highlands County, 1998, 2002. Recipient ARC citation, 1974, Presdl. award of appreciation Fla. Jaycees, 1980-82, 85, Outstanding Svc. award Highlands Coun. of 100, 1988, Most Valuable Player award Highlands Little Theatre, Inc., 1986, Zenon Significant Achievement award, 1991, Best Set award, 2002; named Jaycee of Year, Sebring Jaycees, 1981, Outstanding Local Chpt. Pres., U.S. Jaycees, 1977. Mem. ABA, ATLA, Comml. Law League Am., Am. Arbitration Assn. (comml. arbitration panel), Nat. Assn. Retail Credit Attys., Fla. Bar (jour. com.), Highlands County Bar Assn. (past chmn. legal aid com.), Fla. Sch. Bd. Attys. Assn. (bd. dirs. 1989-97, v.p. 1993-94, pres. 1994-95), Greater Sebring C. of C. (dir. 1982-89, pres. 1986-87, chmn. transp. com. 1986—, Most Valuable Dir. award 1986-87), Fla. Jaycees (life, internat. senate 1977—), Lions (bd. dirs. 1972-73, v.p. 1994-95, Disting. award 1984). Republican. Episcopalian. Office: 129 S Commerce Ave Sebring FL 33870-3602 Office Phone: 863-385-5188. Personal E-mail: jimmccollum@earthlink.com.

MCCOLLUM, JEAN HUBBLE, medical assistant; b. Peoria, Ill., Oct. 21, 1934; d. Claude Ambrose and Josephine Mildred (Beiter) Hubble; m. Everett Monroe Patton, Sept. 4, 1960 (div. Jan. 1969); 1 child, Linda Joanne; m. James Ward McCollum, Jan. 2, 1971; 1 child, Steven Ward. Student, Bradley U., Ill. Cen. Coll. Stenographer Caterpillar Tractor Co., Peoria, 1952-53, supr. stenographer pool, 1953-55, adminstrv. sec., treas., 1955-60, sec., asst. dept. mgr., 1969-71; med. staff sec. Proctor Cmty. Hosp., Peoria, 1978-82; med. asst. Drs. Taylor, Fox and Morgan, Peoria, 1982-84; freelance med. asst. Meth. Hosp. and numerous physicians, Peoria, 1984-89; office mgr. bus. office Dr. Danehower, McLelland and Stone, Peoria, 1989—. Vol. tutor Northmoor Sch., Peoria, 1974-78; bd. dirs., mem. exec. com., chmn. patient rels. com., com. chmn. Planned Parenthood, Peoria, 1990-92; judge scholarship com. Bradley U., 2004, Region 2 Ill. State History Fair; hon. mem. scholarship com. Am. Indian Edn. Found. Recipient Outstanding Performance award Proctor Hosp., 1981, also various awards for svc. to schs., ch. and hosps. for mentally ill. Mem. Nat. Wildlife Fedn., Mensa Internat. (publs. officer, scholarship com., editor 1987-89, csholar com. 1993), Mothers League (treas. 1977), Willow Knolls Country Club (social com. 1989-90), Nature Conservancy (Seasons of the River event com. 2000—), World Wildlife Fund, Forest Park Found., Jacques Cousteau Soc., Wilderness Soc., Nat. Trust for Historic Preservation, Natural Resources Def. Coun., Religious Coalition for Reproductive Rights, USO, Am. Indian Educators Found. (hon., scholar com. 2004). Methodist. Avocations: socializing, reading, travel, theater, yoga. Home: 6501 N Brookwood Ln Peoria IL 61614-2401

MCCOLLUM, JOHN MORRIS, tenor; b. Coalinga, Calif., Feb. 21, 1922; s. Fay James and Ingabord Telette (Mason) McC.; m. Mary Margaret Wilson, Jan. 23, 1944; children: Kristi Elizabeth, Timothy James. Student, Coalinga Coll., 1939-40; BA in Journalism, U. Calif. at Berkeley, 1947; student voice and acting, Am. Theatre Wing, 1951-53. Reporter, city editor Coalinga Record, 1947-50; editor agrl. news U. Calif. Coll. Agr., 1950-51. Prof. music and chmn. voice faculty U. Mich.; dir. U. Mich. div. Nat. Music Camp; faculty Aspen Music Festival and School, 1963-76 Concert and opera singer, 1951—, soloist, Fifth Ave. Presbyn. Ch., N.Y.C., 1953-56, debut, Town Hall, N.Y.C., 1952, with, Boston Symphony Orchestra, Tanglewood, Mass., summer 1952, engagements with Symphony Orchestras in, N.Y.C., Chgo., Phila., San Francisco, Cleve., Washington, St. Louis, Detroit, New Orleans, Toronto, London, Mexico; with opera companies of, Boston, Washington, Toronto, Ft. Worth, Central City, Colo., also, NBC-TV, music festivals and oratorio societies, European debut, Festival of Two Worlds, Spoleto, Italy, summer 1958, Santa Fe Opera Co., leading tenor, N.Y.C. Opera Co., performing mem., Music Assos. of Aspen. (Recipient award Atwater Kent Auditions 1950, Am. Theatre Wing award 1952). Mem. Rep. Ctrl. Com., Fresno County, Calif., 1950; pres. Ann Arbor Civic Theatre, 1987-88; mem. Sarasota County Rep. exec. com.; mem., bd. dirs. Sarasota Concert Assn.; bd. dirs. Univ. Mich. Alumni Club. Served with U.S. Navy, 1942-49. Mem. U. Calif. Alumni Assn., Nat. Assn. Tchrs. Singing, Am. Acad. Tchrs. Singing, Alpha Tau Omega, Sigma Delta Chi, Pi Kappa Lambda. Episcopalian (lay reader). Clubs: Rotary (pres. 1977, Paul Harris fellow), Ann Arbor Golf and Outing (pres. 1979), The Meadows Country Club (Sarasota, Fla.). Home: 3380 W Chelmsford Ct Sarasota FL 34235-0947

MCCOLLUM, ROBERT WAYNE, physician, educator; b. Waco, Tex., Jan. 29, 1925; s. Robert Wayne and Minnie (Brown) McC.; m. Audrey Talmage, Oct. 16, 1954; children: Cynthia, Douglas Scott. AB, Baylor U., 1945; MD, Johns Hopkins, 1948; DPH, London Sch. Hygiene and Tropical Medicine, 1958; MA (hon.), Yale U., 1965, Dartmouth Coll., 1985. Intern in pathology Columbia-Presbyn. Med. Center, N.Y.C., 1948-49; intern in internal medicine Vanderbilt Hosp., Nashville, 1949-50; asst. resident in internal medicine Yale-New Haven Med. Center, 1950-51; faculty Yale Sch. Medicine, 1951-81, prof. epidemiology, 1965-81, chmn. dept. epidemiology and public health, 1969-81; dean Sch. Medicine Dartmouth Coll., Hanover, N.H., 1982-90, prof. epidemiology, 1982-95, dean emeritus, 1990—; prof. emeritus, 1995—. Assoc. physician Yale-New Haven Hosp., from 1954; v.p. Dartmouth-Hitchcock Med. Ctr., 1983-90, acting v.p. for devel., 1999; cons. WHO, 1962-79; surgeon gen. U.S. Army, from 1960. Contbr. articles on epidemiology and control infectious diseases to profl. jours. Bd. sci. advisers Merck Inst., 1981-85; trustee Mary Hitchcock Meml. Hosp., Hanover, 1982-90. Capt. M.C., AUS, 1952-54. Mem. Assn. Tchrs. Preventive Medicine, Am. Epidemiological Soc., Internat. Epidemiological Assn., Infectious Diseases Soc. Am., Conn. Acad. Sci. and Engring., Am. Coll. Epidemiology Office: Dartmouth Med Sch Dartmouth-Hitchcock Med Ctr Lebanon NH 03756

MCCOLLUM, RUDOLPH C., JR., mayor; BA in Econs., Howard U.; JD, U. Md. Asst. to pres. for govtl. rels. and pub. affairs Va. Union U.; mayor Richmond, Va., 2001—. Elected mem. City Coun., 1996, chmn. orgnl. devel. com., mem. edn. com., mem. pub. utilities subcom. Chmn. Richmond Renaissance, Va. First Cities; mem. Cmty. Criminal Justice Bd., Greater Richmond Partnership, Maymont Found., Richmond Regional Planning Dist. Commn. Office: Ste 200 900 E Broad St Richmond VA 23219

MCCOLLUM, SUSAN, elementary school educator; Grad., Butler County C.C.; BA in Edn., Emporia State U., 1974, MA in Edn., 1979. Nat. bd. cert. tchr. 1998. Tchr. Santa Fe Trail Sch. Dist., Carbondale (Kans.) Sch. Named Disting. Alumni, Emporia State U., 2002. Mem.: NEA, Nat. Bd. for Cert. Tchrs. in Kans. (state chair 2003—), Nat. Bd. for Profl. Tchg. Stds. (bd. mem. 2002—). Office: Carbondale Attendance Ctr 315 N 4th Carbondale KS 66414

MCCOLLUM, W. LEE, chemical company executive; CFO SC Johnson & Son, Inc., Racine, Wis. Office: SC Johnson & Son Inc 1525 Howe St Racine WI 53403

MCCOLM, GEORGE LESTER, international agricultural consultant, journalist; b. Colby, Kans., Aug. 2, 1911; s. Theodore Harrison and Jane (Speirs) McC.; m. Emma Victoria Davis, Aug. 9, 1936 (dec. Sept. 1959); children: Carol Ann, Patricia Alice; m. Elizabeth Jane Gunder Funderburg, May 1, 1975. BS in Agr., Kans. State U., 1935; postgrad., U. Ariz., 1961-64. Cert. profl. agronomist Am. Soc. Agronomy. Jr. del. Rep. Nat. Conv., 1928; various soil conservation, agrl. positions, 1935-41; dir. crop. prodn. War Relocation Authority, Topaz, Utah, 1942-43; chief agrl. officer planning invasion, occupation Japan Joint Chief's of Staff, 1944-45; sr. officer, civilian govt. Ponape Island USN, 1946; soil conservationist Bur. Indian Affairs, Shiprock, N.Mex., 1949—52, dir. nursery, 1953-57; dir. B Square Ranch Expt. Sta., Farmington, 1958-61; educator U. Ariz., 1961-64; with US Dept. State, India,

1964-66, tech. rep. internat. Mekong River devel. com., 1966—67; agrl. advisor CORDS, 1968—72; rancher Lewiston, Calif., 1973-87; owner Lewiston Nursery, 1987-95. Part-time agrl. advisor Mex. Govt., 1976-81; with Office Strategic Svcs. in WWII conf., Washington, DC, 1991; bd. dirs. San Juan Co., NM Fair Assn., 1957-61, v.p., 1961; pres. San Juan co. Farm Bureau, 1961. Contbr. articles to sci. jours. Bd. dirs. Trinity County California Fair Assn., 1987-99. Lt. USNR, 1944-46, PTO; USN officer directing civilian govt. Ponape Island, 1946. Mem. NRA, CAST, Am. Soc. Agronomy and Soil Sci., Calif. Soc. Agronomy and Soil Sci., Am. Asst. Ret. Persons, Am. Legion, Alpha Gamma Rho, mem., Kansas 4H Club; Edison Medal, The Outstanding 4H Club, 1929. Republican. Methodist. Achievements include direction of first US Soil survey made with aerial photographs, 1936; development of method of taking water from a flowing stream without a diversion dam in stream channel, 1939; perfection of method of constructing a stable roadbed or airfield through a swampy area, without limiting movement of ground water, 1939; wrote original draft of Japanese Land Reform Law, 1945. Home: 925 South St Redding CA 96001

MCCOLMAN, WILLIAM ERNEST, construction company executive; b. Chgo., Oct. 8, 1947; s. William Walter and Irene Laverne (Wildes) McC.; m. Caridad S. Jorajuria, Sept. 19, 1981; children: William Patrick, Scott Mariano. BS in Agrl. Bus., Colo. State U., 1970. Leadman R&D Theil, Chgo., 1972-74; foreman Carpenter Contractors Am., Ft. Lauderdale, Fla., 1974-75; pres. Bamco Constrn., Inc., Pompano Beach, Fla., 1975—, Bamco Homes Fla., Pompano Beach, 1980—, McColman Crane & Equipment Lease, Pompano Beach, 1981—, Bamco Constrn. South Fla., Pompano Beach, 1983—, New Image Homes, Inc., Pompano Beach, 1986—, Cardinal Custom Builders, Pompano Beach, 1988—. Bd. dirs. TRNPK Comml. Plaza, Pompano Beach (pres. 1985-86), Tropical Life Style Bldrs., Inc.; adv. Planning and Zoning Bd., Ocean Ridge, Fla., 1987-91. Editor computer program, 1983. Coach North Lauderdale Little League, 1979-82, flag football coach Boynton Beach (Fla.) Little League, 1988—; active Margate (Fla.) Girl Scouts, 1982-87, Palm Beach (Fla.) Boy Scouts, 1980—. Recipient Outstanding Service cert. Broward County (Fla.) Girl Scout Council, 1984. Mem. Nat. Small Bus. Assn. (cert. merit, 1977), Fla. Atlantic Builders Assn. (outstanding contbns., 1982, apprenticeship bd. 1979-82, Bronze award 1991), South Fla. Builders Assn. (apprenticeship bd. 1977-78), Nat. Assn. Home Builders, Fla. C. of C. Clubs: Boat/U.S., Royal Holiday, Mexico. Avocations: boating, snorkeling, skiing, travel, whitewater rafting.

MCCOMAS, DAVID JOHN, science administrator, space physicist; b. Milw., May 22, 1958; s. Harrold James and Hazelyn (Melconian) McC.; m. Richelle Wolff, May 30, 1981; children: Random A., Koan I., Orion G. BS in Physics, MIT, 1980; MS in Geophysics and Space Physics, UCLA, 1985, PhD in Geophysics and Space Physics, 1986. Mem. staff Los Alamos (N.Mex.) Nat. Lab., 1980-91, sect. leader space plasma and planetary physics, 1991-92, group leader for space and atmospheric scis., 1992-98, founding dir. Ctr. for Space Sci. and Exploration, NASA prog, 1998-2000; exec. dir. space sci. and engring. divsn. S.W. Rsch. Inst., San Antonio, 2000—03, sr. exec. dir., 2004—. Mem. strategic planning com. earth and space scis. divsn. Los Alamos Nat. Lab, 1986; mem. advanced composition explorer phase A study team NASA, 1988-89, mem. space physics data system steering com., 1990-91, mem. inner magnetosphere imaging study team, 1991-94, prin. investigator Ulysses Solar Wind Observations Over the Poles of the Sun Experiment, Two Wide-Angle Imaging Neutral-Atom Spectrometers, Explorer Mission-of-Opportunity, Solar Wind Electron Proton Alpha Monitor (instrument on the Advanced Composition Explorer, co-investigator Medium Energy Neutral Atom instrument on IMAGE Midsized Discovery Mission, plasma instrument for Cassini mission to Saturn, GENESIS Discovery mission, ISTP Polar Spacecraft's Thermal Ion Dynamics Experiment, Cluster plasma electron instrument, team mem. New Millennium Plasma Experiment for Planetary Exploration, mem. Space Sci. Adv. Com., chmn. Sun-Earth Connections Adv. Subcom.; mem. com. solar-terrestrial rsch. Nat. Rsch. Coun., 1991-94, mem. com. space sci. tech. planning Aeronautics and Space Engring. Bd./space studies bd., 1992, mem. task group rsch. prioritization future space sci. space studies bd., 1994—; former prin. investigator series of 10 magnetospheric plasma analyzer instruments at geosynchronous orbit Dept. Energy; mem. coms. and panels Nat. Acad. Sci.'s Nat. Rsch. Coun., U. Calif., State of N.Mex., others. Assoc. editor Jour. Geophys. Rsch.-Space Physics, 1993-94; contbr. over 300 sci. papers to profl. jours.; patentee in field. Grad. fellow Inst. Geophysics and Planetary Physics, 1983-84. Fellow Am. Geophys. Union (James B. Macelwane award 1993). Office: SW Rsch Inst PO Drawer 28510 San Antonio TX 78228-0510

MCCOMB, DAVID GLENDINNING, history educator; b. Kokomo, Ind., Oct. 26, 1934; s. John Floyd and Jennie (Glendinning) McC.; m. Mary Alice Collier, Sept. 6, 1957; children: Katherine, Susan, Joseph. BA, So. Meth. U., 1956; MBA, Stanford U., 1958; MA, Rice U., 1962; PhD, U. Tex., 1968. Purchasing agt. McRan Co., Houston, 1958-60; instr. South Tex. Jr. Coll., Houston, 1962, U. Houston, 1966-68; asst. prof. San Antonio Coll., 1962-66; rsch. assoc. U. Tex., Austin, 1968-69; asst. prof. history Colo. State U., Ft. Collins, 1969-72, assoc. prof., 1972-77, prof., 1977—2002, chmn. dept., 1975—80, emeritus prof., 2002—. Interviewer, dir. Oral History of Colo. Project, 1973-77, Big Thompson Disaster Oral History, 1976-78, Olympic Tng. Ctr. Oral History, 1983-87. Author: Houston, a History, 1969, rev. edit., 1981 (Tullis award 1969), Galveston, a History, 1986 (Tex. history 1987), Texas, a Modern History, 1989, Texas, an Illustrated History, 1995, Historic Seacoast of Texas, 1999, Travels with Joe, 2001, also others; editor: World History Ann. Edits., 1987, 89, 92, 96, 98, 2000, 01; contbr. articles to hist. jours. Recipient award of merit Am. Assn. for State and Local History, 1980, Disting. Svc. award Colo. State U., 1986; Danforth Found. grantee, 1978, Sigma Xi, 2001, also others, 1966-85. Fellow Tex. Hist. Assn.; mem. Oral History Assn. (program chmn. 1980), N.Am. Assn. for Sports History, World History Assn. (exec. coun. 1997-99), Western History Assn. (program chmn. 1979), Rocky Mountain World History Assn. (chmn. 1988-92). Democrat. Unitarian Universalist. Avocation: master swimming competition. Office: Colo State U Dept History Fort Collins CO 80523-0001 E-mail: david.mccomb@colostate.edu.

MCCOMBS, BILLY JOE (RED MCCOMBS), professional football team executive; m. Charlene McCombs; 3 daughters. Founder, dir. Clear Channel Communications, Inc, 1972—; former owner, chmn. bd. Denver Nuggets, 1982—86, San Antonio Spurs; chair. bd of trustees Southwestern Univ.; owner, chair., pres. Minnesota Vikings, Eden Prairie, 1998—. Chmn. bd. trustees Southwestern U.; former chmn. United Way of San Antonio, Hemis-Fair World's Fair '68. Named to Bus. Hall of Fame. Mem. San Antonio C. of C. (former chmn.), Nat. Ford Dealers, U. Tex. Longhorn Club. Office: Winter Pk Admin Office 9520 Viking Dr Eden Prairie MN 55344-3898

MCCOMBS, CHARLINE, professional sports team executive; m. Red McCombs, 1950; children: Lynda, Marsha, Connie. DH(hon.), Southwestern U. Owner Minn. Vikings, Inc. Co-host Tex. Tuxedo fundraiser U. Minn., 1999; vol. Salvation Army, Cris Carter Viking Super Challenge; mentor San Antonio elem. schs.; mem. adv. bd. Friends of Ronald McDonald; bd. dirs. Las Casas Found., San Antonio, Susan G. Komen Breast Cancer Found., nat. adv. bd.; bd. dirs. Cancer Ctr. Coun.; former bd. dirs. Friends of Ronald McDonald, San Antonio; bd. dirs. McNay Art Mus., mem. art and edn. coms. Named Mother of Yr., Advance orgn.; recipient Trfoil award, Girl Scouts U.S., 1999, Spirit of Youth award, Boys Town, Sch. Arch. and Design award, U. Tex., Outstanding Philanthropist award, NAFE, Civic Virtue award, Freedom of Info. Found., Spirit of Philanthropy award, Non-Profit Resource Ctr. Office: 9520 Vikings Dr Eden Prairie MN 55344

MCCOMBS, JEFFREY SCOTT, economist, educator; b. San Diego, Calif., Feb. 1, 1948; s. James Winfield and Bernice Edith (Grote) McCombs; m. Mary Anne Fioretta, July 6, 1974; children: Christiian James, Michael Vincent, Mark Jeffrey. PhD, UC San Diego, La Jolla, 1973—81. Social sci. rsch. analyst Health Care Financing Adminstrn., Office Rsch. and Demonstrations, Balt., 1983—87; assoc. prof. Dept. Pharm. Economics and Policy, Los Angeles, Calif., 1987—. Asst. prof. Dept. Mental Hygiene, Sch. Hygiene and Pub. Health, Johns Hopkins U., Balt., 1980—83. Comdr. USCG, Long Beach, Calif., 1970—96. Republican. Lutheran. Avocation: golf. Office: Dept Pharmacuetical Economics and Poli RM CHP 140 1540 E Alcazar Los Angeles CA 90033 Business E-Mail: jmccombs@usc.edu.

MCCOMBS, RED, automotive sales executive; b. 1927; m. Charline Hamblin, 1950; children: Lynda, Marsha Shields, Connie McNab. Student, Southwestern U., U. Tex. Automobile salesman, Corpus Christi, Tex., 1950; from ptnr. to owner Red McCombs Automotive, San Antonio, 1958; CEO McCombs Automotive, San Antonio. Co-founder Forney-McCombs Oil, Clear Channel Comm.; former owner Denver Nuggets, San Antonio Spurs. Chmn. bd. trustess Southwestern U.; chmn. numerous fund drives and cmty. svc. orgns. Recipient San Antonio Citizenship award; inducted into San Antonio Bus. Hall of Fame, Nat. Automobile Dealers Hall of Fame. Office: McCombs Family Ltd 755 E Mulberry Ave Ste 600 San Antonio TX 78212

MC COMIC, ROBERT BARRY, real estate development company executive, lawyer; b. Selmer, Tenn., Nov. 6, 1939; s. Richard Donald and Ila Marie (Prather) McC.; children: Thomas Christopher, Robert Geoffrey. BS, Union U., 1961; LLB, Tulane U., 1964; postgrad. in law, U. Freiburg, W. Ger., 1964-65, Hague (Netherlands) Internat. Acad. Law, 1965. Bar: Tenn. 1964, N.Y. 1966, Calif. 1971. Assoc. Donovan Leisure Newton & Irvine, N.Y.C., 1965-68; assoc. gen. counsel Avco Corp., Greenwich, Conn., 1968-70; exec. v.p., pres., CEO Avco Cmty Developers, Inc., 1973-82; chmn., CEO R.B. McComic, Inc., 1982-92, McComic Consolidated, Inc., 1992—; CEO Trans West Housing, Inc., 1994—, Globelink, LLC, 1995—. Pres. emeritus U. Calif. San Diego Found.; bd. dirs. World Affairs Coun. Honoree Human Relations Inst. Am. Jewish Com., 1981, Kellog's Celebrity Tribute, 1988. Mem. ABA, Calif. Bar Assn., San Diego County Bar Assn., Assn. of Bar of City of N.Y., San Diego Bldg. Industry Assn., San Diego Yacht Club, Order of Coif, Sigma Alpha Epsilon, Omicron Delta Kappa, Lambda Alpha. Office: McComic Consolidated Inc 7979 Ivanhoe Ave Ste 550 San Diego CA 92037 Home: 7180 Fairway Rd La Jolla CA 92037-5623 E-mail: bMcComic@Yahoo.com.

MCCONAHEY, STEPHEN GEORGE, retired securities company executive; b. Fond du Lac, Wis., Nov. 8, 1943; s. George and Charlotte McC.; m. Kathleen Louise Litten, Aug. 19, 1967; children: Heather, Benjamin. BS, U. Wis., 1966; MBA, Harvard U., 1968. Assoc. McKinsey & Co., Washington, 1968-72; White House fellow Washington, 1972-73; program adminstr. Dept. Transp., Washington, 1973-75; spl. asst. to Pres. Gerald Ford The White House, 1975-77; underwriter, ptnr. Boettcher & Co., Inc., Denver, 1977-80, mgr. pub. fin., 1980-82, mgr. corp. fin., 1982-84, pres., chief exec. officer, 1984-86, chmn. bd., 1986-87, Boettcher Investment Corp., Denver, 1987-90; sr. v.p. for corp. and internat. devel. Kemper Corp., Chgo., 1991—; exec. v.p. Kemper Fin. Svcs., Inc., Chgo., 1991—; pres., COO EVEREN Capital Corp., Chgo., from 1994. Chmn. oper. com. EVEREN Securities, Chgo., 1994—; trustee Amli Properties, Ill. Inst. Tech. Trustee Denver Symphony Assn., 1986, Ill. Inst. Tech., Chgo. Field Mus., U.S. Ski Team Found.; chmn. Greater Denver Corp., 1987; bd. dirs. The Denver Partnership; bd. fellows U. Denver; nat. trustee Boys and Girls Clubs Am. Mem. Young Presidents Orgn., Greater Denver C. of C. (bd. dirs.), Denver Club, Colo. Harvard Bus. Sch. Club (Denver), Cherry Hills Country Club (Englewood, Colo.), Castle Pines Country Club (Castle Rock, Colo.), Chgo. Club, Econ. Club Chgo. Home: 100 E Huron St Chicago IL 60611-2932 Office: EVEREN Securities Inc 77 W Wacker Dr Chicago IL 60601-1651

MCCONAUGHY, JOSEPH C. surgeon; b. Berwyn, Ill., Jan. 14, 1947; MD, U. Ill., 1973. Diplomate Am. Bd. Surgery. Intern U. Cin. Group Hosps., 1973-74, resident, 1974-80; active staff Hinsdale (Ill.) Hosp., 1980—, chief of staff, 1999—2001; active staff Good Samaritan Hosp., Downers Grove, Ill., 1980—; asst. clin. prof. surgery U. Ill., 1994—. Fellow ACS; mem. Ill. State Med. Soc., Dupage County Med. Soc. Office: Ste 310 908 N Elm St Hinsdale IL 60521-3625

MCCONKEY, JAMES RODNEY, English educator, writer; b. Lakewood, Ohio, Sept. 2, 1921; s. Clayton Delano and Grace (Baird) McC.; m. Gladys Jean Voorhees, May 6, 1944; children: Lawrence Clark, John Crispin, James Clayton. BA, Cleve. Coll., 1943; MA, Western Res. U., 1946; PhD, U. Iowa, 1953. Teaching fellow, instr. Cleve. Coll., 1945-46; teaching asst. U. Iowa, Iowa City, 1949-50; asst. prof. Morehead State Coll., Ky., 1950-54, assoc. prof., 1954-56; asst. prof. Cornell U., Ithaca, N.Y., 1956-62, assoc. prof., 1962-67, prof., 1967-87, Goldwin Smith prof. English lit., 1987-92; Goldwin Smith prof. emeritus, 1992—. Dir. Morehead Writers Workshop, 1951-56, Antioch Seminar in Writing and Pub., Yellow Springs, Ohio, 1957-59 Author: The Novels of E.M. Forster, 1957, Night Stand, 1965, Crossroads, 1968, Journey to Sahalin, 1971, The Tree House Confessions, 1979, Court of Memory, 1983, To a Distant Island, 1984, Kayo: The Authentic and Annotated Autobiographical Novel From Outer Space, 1987, Rowan's Progress, 1992, Stories From My Life With the Other Animals, 1993, The Telescope in the Parlor, 2004; editor: The Structure of Prose, 1963, Chekhov and Our Age, 1984, The Anatomy of Memory, 1996. Served with U.S. Army, 1943-45. Guggenheim fellow, 1970; Eugene Saxton Meml. Trust Fund fellow, 1962; recipient Nat. Endowment of Arts essay award, 1968, Am. Acad. and Inst. Arts and Letters award in lit., 1979 Democrat. Home: 402 Aiken Rd Trumansburg NY 14886-9733 Office: Cornell Univ Goldwin Smith Hall Dept English Ithaca NY 14853 E-mail: jrm9@cornell.edu.

MCCONN, WILLIAM EVERETT, music educator; b. Patuxent River, Md., Mar. 2, 1953; s. William Harley and Edwina Wyche McConn; m. Polly Claire Berry, Aug. 28, 1976; children: Ryan Everett, Matthew David, Amy Elizabeth, Patrick Berry, Susanna Joy. B in music edn., U. of Fla., 1974—77. Teacher State of Fla., 1977. Dir. of bands P.K. Yonge Lab. Sch., Gainesville, Fla., 1977—80, Howard Bishop Mid. Sch., Gainesville, Fla., 1980—84; prin. Living Faith Fellowship Christian Sch., Gainesville, Fla., 1984—95; dir. of bands C. H. Price Mid. Sch., Interlachen, Fla., 1996—98, Ft. Clarke Mid. Sch., Gainesville, Fla., 1998—. Band dir. Gainesville Cmty. Christian Band, 1996—; french horn Gainesville Brass Quintet, 1990—2003; 2nd horn Gainesville Chamber Orch.; music dir. Living Faith Fellowship, Gainesville, 1990—. Mem.: Nat. Band Assn., Music Educators Nat. Conf., Fla. Band Masters Assn. Christian. Avocations: skiing, water sports, bicycling. Office: Fort Clarke Middle School 9301 NW 23rd Ave Gainesville FL 32606

MCCONNAUGHEY, GEORGE CARLTON, JR., retired lawyer; b. Hillsboro, Ohio, Aug. 9, 1925; s. George Carlton and Nelle (Morse) McC.; m. Carolyn Schlieper, June 16, 1951; children: Elizabeth, Susan, Nancy. BA, Denison U., 1949; LL.B., Ohio State U., 1951, JD, 1967. Bar: Ohio 1951. Sole practice, Columbus; ptnr. McConnaughey & McConnaughey, 1954-57, McConnaughey, McConnaughey & Stradley, 1957-62, Laylin, McConnaughey & Stradley, 1962-67, George, Greek, King, McMahon & McConnaughey, 1967-79, McConnaughey, Stradley, Mone & Moul, 1979-81, Thompson, Hine & Flory (merger McConnaughey, Stradley, Mone & Moul with Thompson, Hine & Flory), Cleve., Columbus, Cin., Dayton, Washington, N.Y.C., and Brussels, 1981—93; ret. ptnr. Thompson Hine LLP, Columbus, 1993—. Bd. dirs. N.Am. Broadcasting Co. (Sta. WMNI, WBZX and WEGE Radio); asst. atty. gen. State of Ohio, 1951-54. Pres. Upper Arlington (Ohio) Bd. Edn., 1967-69, Columbus Town Meeting Assn., 1974-76; chmn. Ohio Young Reps., 1956; U.S. presdl. elector, 1956; trustee Buckeye Boys Ranch, Columbus, 1967-73, 75-81, Upper Arlington Edn. Found., 1987-93; elder Covenant Presbyn. Ch., Columbus. With U.S. Army, 1943-45, ETO. Fellow Am. Bar Found., Ohio Bar Found., Columbus Bar Found.; mem. ABA, Ohio State Bar Assn., Columbus Bar Assn., Am. Judicature Soc., Scioto Country Club, Athletic Club, Rotary, Masons. Home: 1993 Collingswood Rd Columbus OH 43221-3741 Office: Thompson Hine LLP One Columbus 10 W Broad St Ste 700 Columbus OH 43215-3435

MCCONNAUGHEY, JAMES WALTER, economist; b. Washington, May 8, 1951; s. William Eugene and Eunice (Ensor) McC.; m. Rosemarie Fuchs, June 23, 1984. BS in Econs. with high honors, U. Md., 1973; MA in Econs., George Washington U., 1979; MPA with high honors, Harvard U., 1992. Industry economist FCC Common Carrier Bur., Washington, 1973-80, sr. economist, 1981-83; sr. assoc. Bolter and Nilsson, Bethesda, Md., 1983; mgr. rsch. studies div. Bethesda Rsch. Inst., 1983-89; sr. economist office policy analysis and devel. U.S. Dept. Commerce Nat. Telecommunications and Info. Adminstrn., Washington, 1989—. Mem. rsch. bd. advisors Am. Biographical Inst., 1994—; presenter in field of telecomms. policy. Author: (with others) Telecommunications Policy for the 1980's: The Transition to Competition, 1984, Telecommunications Policy for the 1990's and Beyond, 1990, U.S. Telecommunications in a Global Economy: Competitiveness at a Crossroads, 1990, Telecommunications in the Age of Information, 1991, NII Field Hearings on Universal Service and Open Access: America Speaks Out, 1994, Falling Through the Net and a Nation Online: Reports on the "Digital Divide," 1995, 1998-2004, (with others) Structure of American Industry, 2000, 2d edit., 2004. Campaign worker, contbr. nat. and local elections; coach Bowie (Md.) Boy's Club; mem. Neighborhood Open Space Com.; worker, contbr. numerous environ. and consumer orgns.; awards evaluator Ford Found./Harvard U. Recipient certs. of appreciation for leadership Prince George's County (Md.) Pub. Sch. System, 1986, Nat. Found. Cancer Rsch., 1990, U.S. Dept. Commerce Gold medal, 1998, 2000, Silver medal for leadership/excellence, 2000, 2001; Robert Seamans tech. fellow, Lucius Littauer fellow John F. Kennedy Sch. Govt., Harvard U., 1991-92. Mem. Am. Econ. Assn. (pub. utilities group), Ea. Econ. Assn., So. Econ. Assn., Soc. Govt. Economists, Indsl. Orgn. Soc., DAV Comdrs. Club, Phi Eta Sigma, Omicron Delta Epsilon, Beta Gamma Sigma, Phi Kappa Phi. Avocations: hiking, reading. Home: 8380 Sweet Cherry Ln Laurel MD 20723-1062

MCCONNELL, ALBERT LYNN, dean; b. Springfield, Ohio, Oct. 20, 1946; s. Jack Pershing and Betty Ann (Venema) McConnell; m. Rannette Oledge, Dec. 21, 2001; 1 child, Ciara Lynn 1 stepchild, Joshua Hooper. BA, Ctrl. State U., 1969; MA, Webster U., 1983; MS, USACGSC, 1984. Commd. 2d. lt. U.S. Army, 1969, advanced through grades. to maj., 1980; ret., 1989; served as inf. bn. intelligence officer, 1970-71; inf. co. comdr., asst. ops. officer, inf. bn., 1971; intelligence analyst and briefer U.S. Mil. Assistance Command, Schofield Barracks, 1972-73; instr. U.S. Army Intelligence Sch., Ft Huachuca, Ariz., 1973-77; served in 3rd Armored Divsn., Frankfurt, Germany, 1980-81; project officer Combined Arms Ctr., Ft. Leavenworth, Kans., 1981-83, comdr. spl. security detachment, 1981-83; dir. intelligence, asst. chief staff for intelligence U.S. Army South, Ft. Clayton, Panama, 1984-85, mng. exec. officer Ft. Davis, Panama, 1985-86; tactical intelligence officer, chief adminstrv. svcs. U.S. Army Air Def. Arty. Sch., Ft. Bliss, Tex., 1986-87, dep. directorate chief, 1987-88, sr. intelligence officer, dept. divsn. chief, 1988-89; ops. analyst RAM Inc., Sierra Vista, Ariz., 1989-92; prof. bus. adminstrn. and mgmt. So. Ohio Coll., Columbus, 1992, Bliss Coll., Columbus, 1993; store mgr. Circle K Corp., Yuma, Ariz., 1993-94; tchr. Glendale (Ariz.) Union HS, 1994-95; mgr. Dexter Book Store, 1995-96; dean students Ariz. Inst. Bus. and Tech., Phoenix, 1996-98, campus dir. Mesa, Ariz., 1998-2000, prof. Phoenix, 2002—03; dir. edn. High Tech Inst., Phoenix, 2000—02; dean students Internat. Inst. Ams., Phoenix, 2003—. Adj. prof. Chapman U., Sierra Vista, 1990—92; tax preparer H&R Block, Sierra Vista, 1990—92; br. mgr. Jackson Hewitt Tax Svc. Met. Ctr., Phoenix, 2002—. Voter registration ofcl. Maricopa County, Ariz., 2002; treas. Antioch Missionary Bapt. Ch., Huachuca City, Ariz., 1991—92. Decorated Bronze Star. Mem.: Assn. Old Crows, Ret. Officers Assn., Assn. U.S. Army, Air Force Assn., Scabbard and Blade, Iota Beta Sigma, Phi Alpha Theta. Republican. Baptist. Avocations: photography, reading, coaching youth football and baseball. Office: Internat Inst Ams 6049 N 432 Ave Phoenix AZ 85019-1600 Office Phone: 602-242-6265 220.

MCCONNELL, ANDREA MARIE, elementary school educator; b. Champaign, Ill., Feb. 24, 1972; d. John T. and Peggy Leigh Geeves; m. Tim J McConnell, June 18, 1971; children: Owen James, Paige Lauren. BA, Monmouth Coll., Ill., 1990—94. Cert. elem. edn. tchr. State of Ill., 1994. Third grade tchr. Erie Elem., Ill., 2002—; fourth and sixth grade tchr. ROWVA Sch. Dist., Altona, Oneida, Ill., 1994—2002. Personal E-mail: owenpaige@iwon.com.

MCCONNELL, BRUCE WILLIAM, information technology executive; b. Washington, Oct. 26, 1949; s. John Paul McConnell and Sally Dean McConnell Breul; m. Margaret Reagan Anderson. BS, Stanford U., 1971; MPA, U. Wash., 1985. Registered professional engr., Wash. Engr. Austin-Mac, Inc., Seattle, 1980—83; analyst U.S. Office of Mgmt. and Budget, Washington, 1985—92, chief info. policy and tech., 1992—99; dir. Internat. Y2K Cooperation Ctr., Washington, 1999—2000; co-chair encryption policy com. U.S. Nat. Security Coun., Washington, 1996—2000; pres. McConnell Internat. LLC, Washington, 2000—. Mem. bd. visitors RH Smith Sch. of Bus., U. Md., College Park, 2000—; mem. policy group on network-enabled svcs. and govt. Harvard U. Kennedy Sch. Government, Cambridge, Mass., 1997—. Bd. trustees Charles Babbage Found., 2003—; tenor Thomas Cir. Singers, Washington, 1990—. Recipient Eagle award, Fed. Computer Week, 2000, Elmer B. Staats award for accountability in govt., Am. Soc. Pub. Adminstrn., 2000. Mem.: Nat. Press Club. Office: McConnell Internat LLC 1341 G St NW Ste 1100 Washington DC 20005 Business E-Mail: mcconnell@mcconnellinternational.com.

MCCONNELL, CHRISTOPHER F. technology company administrator; Grad., Dartmouth Coll., Harvard Coll. Founder, chmn. bd. CFM Technologies Inc., Exton, Pa., 1984—. Bd. dirs. V-SPAN, Inc., Gemini Ventures, Inc., Batteries Batteries, Inc. Fax: 610-280-8309.

MCCONNELL, DAVID KELSO, lawyer; b. N.Y.C., July 12, 1932; s. David and Caroline Hanna (Kelso) McC.; m. Alice Schmitt, Dec. 26, 1953; children: Elissa Anne McConnell Henebry, Kathleen Anne, David Willet. BCE, CCNY, 1954; LLB, Yale U., 1962. Bar: Conn. 1962, U.S. Dist. Ct. Conn. 1963, U.S. Ct. Appeals (2d cir.) 1964, U.S. Ct. Appeals (3d cir.) 1966, U.S. Sup. Ct. 1970, U.S. Dist. Ct. (ea. dist.) Pa. 1971, Pa. 1975, N.Y. 1986. Asst. counsel N.Y.N.H. & H. R.R., New Haven, 1962-65, counsel, 1966-68; asst. atty. gen. U.S. V.I., 1965-66; asst. gen. atty. Pa. Cen. Transp. Co., New Haven, 1969-70, asst. gen. counsel Phila., 1970-71, sr. reorganization atty., 1971, adminstrv. officer, spl. counsel to trustees, 1971-76, gen. atty., 1977-78; asst. to chmn., CEO The Penn Cen. Corp., N.Y.C., 1979-80, corp. sec., 1980-82; v.p., gen. counsel Gen. Cable Co., Greenwich, Conn., 1982-85; pvt. practice Stamford, Conn., 1985-86, Pelham, N.Y., 1989-91, Greenwich, Conn., 1991-98. Of counsel McCarthy, Fingar, Donovan, Drazen & Smith, White Plains, N.Y., 1986-89. Dep. supr., councilman Town of Pelham, N.Y., 1986-90, budget officer, 1996; dep. mayor, trustee Village of Pelham, 1992-95, village atty., 1995-96; clk. of session, elder, trustee, deacon Huguenot Meml. Ch., Pelham N.Y. With U.S. Navy, 1954-59, USNR, 1959-79. Mem.: Yale Law Sch. Assn. (exec. com. 1988—91, dir. New Eng. 2001—), Assn. Bar City NY, NY Bar Assn., Conn. Bar Assn., Quindecim, St. Andrews Soc. NY (bd. mgrs. 1986—89, chmn. bd. mgrs. 1988—89, bd. mgrs. 1996—99), The Corinthians (mem. afterguard, dir. The Corinthians Assn., fleet capt. New Eng. fleet, trustee, pres., treas., sec. The Corinthians Endowment Fund), Little Ship Club, Newport Sail and Power Squadron, Rotary Club of Newport RI (dir. 2001—), Rotary Club of The Pelhams NY (pres. 1993—94). Home: 68 1/2 Roseneath Ave Newport RI 02840-3849 E-mail: david.mcconnell.law.62@aya.yale.edu.

MCCONNELL, DONALD PATRICK, research institute executive; b. Oceanside, N.Y., Mar. 6, 1950; s. Frederick Joseph and Frances Dorothy (Demeo) McC.; m. Suzanne Yorke, Aug. 8, 1976; children: Jessica Lauren, Christopher Robert. BS in Aero. and Astron. Engring., NYU, 1971, MME, 1973. Engring. aide Ralph M. Parsons Co., N.Y.C., 1970; rsch. assoc. NYU, University Heights, 1970-73; program mgr. U.S. Dept. Transp., Boston, 1973-81; gen.mgr. Battelle Petroleum Tech. Ctr., Houston, 1981-85; group v.p. Battelle Meml. Inst., Columbus, Ohio, 1985—. Tech. expert U.S.-USSR Tech. Del., Moscow, 1976. Contbr. articles to profl. jours. Trustee Ohio Dominican Coll., 1991—. Recipient Silver medal U.S. Sec. Transp., 1980. Mem. ASME, Soc. Exptl. Mechanics, Engrs.' Found. Ohio (trustee 1987—), Tau Beta Pi, Sigma Gamma Tau, bd. dirs., Brookhaven Sci. Assocs. Episcopalian. Office: Battelle Meml Inst Design & Manufacturing Engring 505 King Ave Columbus OH 43201-2681

MCCONNELL, E. HOY, II, advertising/public policy executive; b. Syracuse, N.Y., May 14, 1941; s. E. Hoy and Dorothy R. (Schmitt) McC.; m. Patricia Irwin, June 26, 1965; children: E. Hoy, III, Courtney. BA in Am.

Studies magna cum laude, Yale U., 1963; MBA in Mktg, Harvard Bus. Sch., 1965. With Foote, Cone & Belding, Chgo., 1965-76, v.p. account supr., 1971—76; with D'Arcy-MacManus & Masius, Chgo., 1976-85, sr. v.p., dir. client services, then vice chmn., 1978-80, pres., 1980-84, chmn., 1984-85; mng. dir. D'Arcy Masius Benton & Bowles, Chgo., 1986-96, also bd. dirs.; sr. v.p., account dir. Leo Burnett Co., Chgo., 1996-98; exec. dir. Bus. and Profl. People for the Pub. Interest, 1999—. Bd. dirs. Evanston (Ill.) United Way, 1980-83, Evanston Youth Hockey Assn., 1980-89, pres. 1981-83; bd. dirs. Off-the-Street Club, 1980-90, Bus. Profl. People for Pub. Interest, 1981-, v.p. 1984-89, pres. 1990-95; co-chair Housint Ill., 2002—; bd. dirs. Harvard Bus. Sch. Club, 1990-92, The Cradle Soc., 2000—; mem. Chgo. Coun. on Fgn. Rels., 1989-95, Wayfarers Club, 2001-. Mem. Am. Assn. Advt. Agys. (gov.-at-large Chgo. coun. 1984, sec. 1986, vice chmn. 1987, chmn. 1988-89), Glen View Country Club (bd. dirs. 1992-96), Dairymen's Country Club, Yale Club Chgo. (bd. dirs. 1996-99). Democrat. Unitarian Universalist. Home: 2703 Colfax St Evanston IL 60201-2035 Office: BPI 25 E Washington St Ste 1515 Chicago IL 60602-1804 Office Phone: 312-759-8259. E-mail: hmcconnell@bpichicago.org.

MCCONNELL, EDWARD BOSWORTH, legal organization administrator, lawyer; b. Greenwich, Conn., Apr. 3, 1920; s. Raymond Arnott and Anna Bell (Lee) McC.; m. Jeanne M. Rotton (dec. 1984); children: Annalee, Marilyn, Edward, Barbara, William; m. Florence M. Leonard, (dec. 1994); stepchildren: Susan L. Little, William R. Leonard, Molly M. Leonard. AB, U. Nebr., 1941, LLB, 1947; MBA with distinction, Harvard U., 1943. Bar: Nebr. 1947, N.J. 1950. Mem. faculty Rutgers U. Sch. Bus. Adminstrn., Newark, 1947-53; assoc. firm Toner, Speakman and Crowley, Newark, N.J., 1949-50; adminstrv. asst. and law sec. to Chief Justice of N.J., 1950-53; adminstrv. dir. Cts. of N.J., Trenton, 1953-73; also standing master Supreme Ct., 1953-73; pres. Nat. Center for State Cts., Williamsburg, 1973-90, bd. dirs., 1980-90, pres. emeritus, 1990—, cons. on ct. mgmt., 1990—. Mem. U.S. Dept. Justice Coun. on Role of Cts. in Am. Soc., 1978-83; mem. adv. com. Dispute Resolution Policy Study, Social Sci. Rsch. Inst., U. So. Calif., 1975-79, Civil Litigation Rsch. Project, U. Wis. and U. So. Calif., 1979-83, nat. judg. edn. program to promote equality for men and women in the cts., 1980—; mem. Nat. Inst. Criminal Justice Task Force, Urban Consortium, 1979-83; participant Access To Justice Colloquium, European Univ. Inst., Florence, Italy, 1979; nat. adv. coun. Ctr. Adminstrn. Justice, Wayne State U., 1973-77; nat. project com. State Jud. Info. Sys. Project SEARCH Group, 1973-76; lectr. Inst. of Local and State Govt. Wharton Sch. U. Pa., 1955-65, Appellate Judges Seminar, Inst. Jud. Adminstrn., NYU, 1962-75; vis. expert UN Asia and Far East Inst., Tokyo, 1971; mem. Cts. Task Force Nat. Adv. Commn. Criminal Justice Standards and Goals, 1971-73; nat. adv. com. D.C. Ct. Mgmt. Project, 1966-70; trustee Inst. Ct. Mgmt., 1969-73, 84-86; chmn. Nat. Conf. Ct. Adminstrv. Officers, 1956; mem. nat. task force on gender bias in cts. Nat. Assn. Women Judge's 1985-90; mem. adv. bd. Nat. Ctr. for Citizen Participation in Adminsrtn. of Justice, 1984-90; mem. Nat. Commn. Trial Ct. Performance Standards, 1991-95. Mem. adv. com. on article III Commn. on the Bicentennial of the Constitution, 1989-91; adv. com. Judicary Leadership Coun., 1990-95. Maj. C.E., AUS, 1943-46. Decorated Bronze Star medal; recipient Warren E. Burger award for greatest contbn. to improvement of ct. adminstrn. Inst. for Ct. Mgmt., 1975, Herbert Lincoln Harley award for efficient adminstrn. justice Am. Judicature Soc., 1973, Glenn R. Winters award for outstanding service in jud. adminstrn. Am. Judges Assn., 1974, Tom C. Clark award for outstanding contbns. to field of ct. adminstrn. Nat. Conf. Met. Cts., 1983, Award of Merit Nat. Assn. Ct. Mgmt., 1987, Spl. award, Nat. Assn. Women Judges, 1989, Paul C. Reardon award for disting. svc. Nat. Ctr. for State Cts., 1991, Alumni Achievement award U. Nebr., 1991, Robert B. Yegge award ABA Jud. Divsn. Lawyers Conf., 1997. Fellow Nat. Acad. Pub. Adminstrn. (mem. panel on evaluation budget decentralization project of fed. cts. 1989-91, chmn. panel long range planning in fed. cts. 1991-92, mem. panel for study of fed. trial ct. adminstrv. structure 1995-96); mem. ABA (fellow-at-large, coun. mem. 1960-66, 71-80, house of dels., 1977-80, chmn. com. on oversight and goals 1975-76, chmn. com. on jud. compensation jud. adminstrn. div. 1984-89, chmn. jud. adminstrn. div. 1976-77, sect. of litigation task force on excess litigiousness in Am. 1986-88, task force on reduction of litigation cost and delay, jud. adminstrn. dir. 1984-94, chmn. 1991-94, mem. long range planning com. 1989-94), N.J. Bar Assn., Nebr. Bar Assn., Fellows of Am. Bar Found. (life), Warren E. Burger Soc., Kingsmill (Va.) Golf Club, Kingsmill Tennis Club (pres. 2001), Kingsmill Yacht Club, Order of Coif (hon.), Delta Upsilon, Sigma Delta Phi, Phi Delta Phi. E-mail: ebm80@aol.com.

MCCONNELL, GLENN F. state legislator, lawyer, art gallery executive; b. Charleston, SC, Dec. 11, 1947; s. Samuel W. and Evelyn (McDaniel) McC. BS, Coll. of Charleston, 1969; JD, U. S.C., 1972. Bar: SC 1972. Pres. CSA Galleries, Inc., Charleston; mem. S.C. Senate, Columbia, 1981—, pres. pro tem, 2001—, chmn. judiciary com., mem. banking and ins. com., ethics com., judiciary com., labor, commerce and industry com., rules com. Chmn. Charleston County Rep. Com., 1978-82; del. Rep. Nat. Conv., 1980, 84, 88; bd. dirs. Neighborhood Legal Assistance Program, 1977-80, S.C. Battle Ground Preservation Trust, Inc.; mem. Am. Legis. Exch. Coun.; chair African Am. History Monument Commn.; chmn. Hunley Commn. Recipient Outstanding Achievement award S.C. Rep. Com., 1980. Mem. SCV, Scottish Soc. Charleston, Palmetto Bn., 27th S.C. Eutaw Vols., 19th Ind. Vols., Pi Kappa Phi. Episcopalian. Office: 101 Gressette Bldg PO Box 142 Columbia SC 29202

MCCONNELL, HARDEN MARSDEN, biophysical chemistry researcher, chemistry educator; b. Richmond, Va., July 18, 1927; s. Harry Raymond and Frances (Coffee) McConnell; m. Sophia Milo Glogovac, Oct. 6, 1956; children: Hunter, Trevor, Jane. BS, George Washington U., 1947; PhD, Calif. Inst. Tech., 1951; DSc (hon.) (hon.), U. Chgo., 1991, George Washington U., 1993. NRC fellow dept. physics U. Chgo., 1950—52; research chemist Shell Devel. Co., Emeryville, Calif., 1952—56; asst. prof. chemistry Calif. Inst. Tech., 1956—58, prof. chemistry and physics, 1963—64; prof. chemistry Stanford U., Calif., 1964—79, Robert Eckles prof. chemistry, 1979—, chmn. dept., 1989—2000, chmn. emeritus, 2000; founder Molecular Devices Corp., 1983—. Cons. in field. Contbr. Pres. Found. for Basic Rsch. in Chemistry, 1990—96; hon. assoc. Neurosci. Rsch. Program. Named Sherman Fairchild Disting. scholar, 1988; recipient Calif. sect. award, Am. Chem. Soc., 1961, award in pure chemistry, 1962, Harrison Howe award, 1968, Irving Langmuir award in chem. physics, 1971, Pauling medal, Puget Sound and Oreg. sects., 1987, Peter Debye award in phys. chemistry, 1990, Am. Achievement award, George Washington U., 1971, Disting. Alumni award, Calif. Inst. Tech., 1982, Dickson prize for sci., Carnegie-Mellon U., 1982, Wolf prize in chemistry, 1984, ISCO award, 1984, Wheland medal, U. Chgo., 1988, Nat. Medal Sci., 1989, Brucker prize, 1995, Gold medal, Internat. ESR Soc., Zavoisky award, 2000. Fellow: AAAS, Biophys. Soc.; mem.: NAS ((award in chem. scis. 1988), Serbian Acad. Scis. and Arts (fgn. mem.), Am. Chem. Soc (award in Surface Chemistry 1997, Welch award in Chemistry 2002), Am. Soc. Biol. Chemists, Am. Acad. Arts and Scis., Am. Phys. Soc., Internat. Acad. Quantum Molecular Scis. Achievements include patents in field. Office: Stanford U Dept Chemistry Stanford CA 94305 Office Phone: 650-723-4571.

MCCONNELL, JACK B. physican, retired corporate executive; b. Crumpler, W.Va., Feb. 1, 1925; s. Enoch L. and Mattie (Davidson) McC.; m. Mary Ellen Rhodes, Nov. 29, 1958; children: Steven Rhodes, Katherine Marie, Page Samuel. Student, U. Va., 1943-45, U. Miss., 1945-47; MD, U. Tenn., 1949; postgrad., Columbia U., 1963, Harvard U., 1972; DSc (hon.), Emory & Henry Coll., 1982; HHD (hon.), Presbyn. Coll. of SC, 1998. Dir. clin. investigation Lederle Labs., Pearl River, N.Y., 1953-61; v.p. comml. devel. McNeil Labs., Ft. Washington, Pa., 1961-68; corp. dir. advanced tech. Johnson & Johnson, New Brunseick, NJ, 1968—89. Bd. trustees Morristown (N.J.) Meml. Hosp., 1977-87; bd. dirs. African Med. and Rsch. Found., NYC. Author: The Story of the Volunteers in Medicine Clinic, 1998. Mem. bd. health, Basking Ridge, N.J., 1972-74; cons. U.S. Senate, Washington, 1987—. With USN, 1943-46; founder, chmn. emeritus, Volunteers in Medicine Clinic, Hilton Head, SC., 1994-, Volunteers in Medicine Inst. Recipient Disting. Scientist award Tenn. Tech. Found., 1985, Humanitarian award, 1988, Disting. Svc. to State Govt. Award, Nat. Gov.'s Assn., 1993, Outstanding Svc. Award, Hilton Head Chpt. NAACP, 1993, Award of Achievement, Gleitsman Found., 1994, Cmty. Svc. Award, SC Hosp. Assn., 1994, Citizen of Yr. Award, Presbyn. Men's Club of Hilton Head, 1995, Nat. Assn. Cmty. Health Centers Award, 1997, Disting. Svc. Award, SC Rural Health, 1999, Humanitarian Award, Watson Clinic Found., Lakeland, FL, 2000, Pride in Profession Award, AMA Found., 2004; Named Humanitarian of Yr., Kidney Found. of NJ, 1988, Disting. Alumnus of Yr., U. Tenn. Coll. Med., 1990, Physician of Yr., Nat. Assn. Hospice and Home Care, 1995; Named one of 200 Disting. Graduates, U. Tenn., 1994; Named to Order of the Palmetto, State of SC, 1999. Mem. AMA, Royal Instn., Soc. Magnetic Resonance in Medicine, Acad. Med. Dirs, Soc. for Analytical Cytology. Republican. Avocations: sports, jazz, travel, bridge.

MCCONNELL, JOHN EDWARD, electrical engineering company executive; b. Minot, N.D., July 28, 1931; s. Lloyd Waldorf and Sarah Gladys (Mathis) McC.; m. Carol Claire Myers, July 4, 1952 (dec. Feb. 1989); children: Kathleen Anne, James Mathis, Amy Lynn; m. Heidi Banziger, Sept. 29, 1990. BSME, U. Pitts., 1952; MS, Drexel Inst. Tech., 1958. Registered profl. engr., Pa. With mktg. and design depts. for turbomachinery Westinghouse Electric Corp., Lester, Pa., 1954-60, 63-67, Pitts., 1960-63; mgr. power generation equipment activities in U.S. ASEA, Inc., White Plains, N.Y., 1967-79, regional mgr. power equipment activities Middle Atlantic and Southeastern U.S. regions, 1967-79, mgr. turbine generator dept., 1979-83, mgr. internat. ops. Power Sys. divsn., 1983-84, mgr. transmission substas. dept., 1984-85; mgr. Ea. U.S. ops. ASEA Power Sys., Inc., 1985-86, mgr. ea. ops. measurement divsn. GEC, 1986-91; mgr. ea. region Protection and Control divsn. GEC Alsthom T&D Inc., 1991-98; prin. JEMTECH Co., 1998—, v.p. ATG Exodus, 2000—02. Adviser on energy matters to U.S. congressman 1968-74; spkr. in field. Contbr. articles on energy and electric power to profl. jours. 1st lt. C.E., U.S. Army, 1952-54. Mem. IEEE (life, sr., energy com., past chmn. subcom. energy conservation and cogeneration, hon. mem. power sys. relay com.), IEEE Power Engring. Soc. (sr., past chmn. chpts. pub. affairs subcom.), ASME. Republican. Achievements developer analytical techniques for power systems performance characteristics and economics of cogeneration systems. Home: 173 Remington Rd Ridgefield CT 06877-4324 Office: JEMTECH PO Box 229 Ridgefield CT 06877-0229 Personal E-mail: mcconnell173@cs.com. Business E-Mail: j.e.mcconnell@ieee.org. *1) If it doesn't produce revenue, is it worthwhile? 2) Problem solving begins with careful listening. 3) Keep people informed. If they don't know, they'll assume the worst. 4) The truth is the most credible explanation you'll find.*

MCCONNELL, JOHN HENDERSON, metal and plastic products manufacturing executive, professional sports team executive; b. New Manchester, W.Va., May 10, 1923; s. Paul Alexander and Mary Louise (Mayhew) McC.; m. Margaret Jane Rardin, Feb. 8, 1946; children— Margaret Louise, John Porter BA in Bus., Mich. State U., 1949; Dr. Law (hon.), Ohio U., 1981. Sales trainee Weirton Steel Co., W.Va., 1950-52; sales mgmt. Shenango-Steel Co., Farrell, Pa., 1952-54; founder, chmn. bd. Worthington Industries, Inc., Columbus, Ohio, 1955—, also past CEO; bd. dirs. Pitts. Pirates; owner, NHL Franchise Columbus Blue Jackets, Worthington, Ohio, 1998—. Dir. Alltel Corp., Hudson, Ohio, Anchor Hocking, Lancaster, Ohio, Nat. City Corp., Cleve. Bd. dirs. Children's Hosp., Columbus; trustee Ashland Coll., Ohio. Served with USN, 1943-46 Recipient Ohio Gov.'s award Gov. State of Ohio, 1980; Horatio Alger award Horatio Alger Assn., 1983; named Outstanding Chief Exec. Officer, Fin. World Mag., 1981 Mem. Columbus Area C. of C. (chmn. 1978) Clubs: Golf (New Albany, Ohio) (pres. 1983—); Brookside Country (Columbus) (pres. 1964-65). Lodges: Masons. Republican. Presbyterian. Avocations: flying; golf. Address: Columbus Blue Jackets 150 E Wilson Bridge Rd Ste 235 Columbus OH 43085-2328 Office: Worthington Industries Inc 1205 Dearborn Dr Columbus OH 43085-4769

MCCONNELL, JOHN HOWARD, personnel management consultant, writer; b. Highland Park, Mich., June 18, 1933; s. Melvin William and Dorothy Marie (Miller) McC.; m. Dolores Ann Cooper, Oct. 29, 1955; children: Keith Ernest, Brian Howard, Eric William. BS, Wayne State U., 1957, MEd, 1963. Tchr. Detroit Bd. Edn., 1957-59, Highland Park Bd. Edn., 1959-60; personnel mgr. Wolverine Tube Co., Allen Park, Mich., 1960-69; personnel dir. Garan, Inc., N.Y.C., 1970-71; cons. Morristown, N.J., 1971-74; cons. human resource mgmt., pres. McConnell, Simmons & Co., Inc., Morristown, 1974—. Bd. dirs. Circus Royale, Inc., Morristown. Author: How To Audit, 8 vols., 1974-85, Introduction to Human Resources, 1982, A Ring, A Horse and A Clown, 1994, Shrine Circus, 1998, Hunting Heads, 1999, Auditing the Human Resources Department, 2000, How to Identify Training Needs, 2002, How to Design, Implement and Interpret an Employee Survey, 2003, How to Develop Essential HR Policies and Procedures, 2004; prodr. Player's Theater in Concert, 1989, 90, London Follies, 1994, 96; contbr. articles to various publs. Pres. Morristown Civic Assn., 1980. Mem. Am. Psychol. Assn., Am. Mgmt. Assn., Acad. Magical Arts, Magic Castle Club (L.A.), Circus Hist. Soc. (bd. dirs.), Masons. Democrat. Methodist. Avocation: producing entertainment events. Home: 1 Skyline Dr Morristown NJ 07960-5146 Office: 73 E Hanover Ave Morristown NJ 07960-3161 Office Phone: 973-539-6481. E-mail: john@circusroyale.org.

MCCONNELL, JOHN THOMAS, newspaper executive, publisher; b. Peoria, Ill., May 1, 1945; s. Golden A. and Margaret (Lyon) McC.; 1 child, Justin. BA, U. Ariz., 1967. Mgr. Fast Printing Co., Peoria, 1970-71; mgmt. trainee Quad-Cities Times, Davenport, Iowa, 1972-73; asst. gen. mgr., then v.p., gen. mgr. Peoria Jour. Star, 1973-81, pub., 1981—, pres., 1987—; v.p. The Copley Press, Inc., Peoria, 1997—. Bd. dirs. Peoria Downtown Devel. Council, Peoria Devel. Corp.; past trustee Methodist Hosp., Peoria. Served with USAR, 1967-69. Named Young Man of Year Peoria Jaycees, 1979 Mem. Peoria Advt. and Selling Club, Peoria C. of C. Clubs: Peoria Country, Mt. Hawley C.C. Congregationalist. Office: Peoria Jour Star Inc 1 News Plz Peoria IL 61643-0001 E-mail: mac@pjstar.com.

MCCONNELL, JOSEPH PAUL, lab administrator, researcher, biochemist, consultant; b. Lapeer, Mich., June 29, 1965; s. Harry P. and Anna M. McConnell; m. Suzanne Jean Bloecker, Feb. 21, 1987; children: Joshua Paul, Katheryn Suzanne. BS in Biology with honors, U. Mich., Flint, 1987; MS in Chemistry, Cleve. State U., 1990, PhD in Clin. Chemistry, 1993. Medical Technologist Am. Soc. of Clin. Pathologists, 1989, diplomate Am. Bd. Clin. Chemistry Am. Assn. for Clin. Chemistry, 1998. Post-doctoral fellow in clin. chemistry The Mayo Clinic, Rochester, Minn., 1993—95; asst. prof. allied health scis. and pathology Ind. U. Sch. of Medicine, Indpls., 1995—98; assoc. dir. thrombosis and hemostasis svcs. Ind. U. Med. Ctr., Indpls., 1995—98; dir. lipoprotein and cardiovasc. risk assessment sect., biochemical genetics lab. The Mayo Clinic, Rochester, 1998—, dir. porphyrins and nutritional biochemistry sect. biochemical genetics lab., 1998—, assoc. dir. immunochemical core lab. dept. of rsch. svcs., 1999—, asst. prof. lab. medicine med. sch., 2001—, med. dir. clin. lab. scis. program sch. of health scis., 2003—. Cons. - divsn. of lab. genetics, dept. of lab. medicine and pathology The Mayo Clinic, Minn., 1998—. Contbr. articles to profl. jours. Chair staff pastor parish rels. Evang. United Meth. Ch., Rochester, 2001—02. Recipient Outstanding Poster award, Am. Assn Clin. Chemistry, 2001. Mem.: AAAS, Internat. Fedn. of Clin. Chemistry, Am. Porphyria Found., Am. Heart Assn., Am. Soc. for Clin. Pathology, Nat. Acad. of Clin. Biochemistry, Am. Assn. for Clin. Chemistry, Student Assn. for Clin. Chemistry (pres. 1992—93, mem. standardization total plasma homocysteine measurements group), Sigma Xi. Office: The Mayo Clinic 200 First St SW Rochester MN 55901 E-mail: mcconnell.joseph@mayo.edu.

MCCONNELL, MICHAEL ARTHUR, lawyer; b. Ft. Worth, Jan. 15, 1947; BA, Loyola U., New Orleans, 1969; JD, U. Tex., 1975. Bar: Tex. 1976, U.S. Dist. Ct. (no. dist.) Tex. 1976, U.S. Dist. Ct. (ea. dist.) Tex. 1981, U.S. Dist. Ct. (we. dist.) Tex. 1982, U.S. Dist. Ct. (so. dist.) Tex. 1989, U.S. Ct. Appeals (5th cir.) Tex. 1980, U.S. Ct. Appeals (10th cir.) 1987. Briefing atty. U.S. Dist. Ct. Hon. Eldon B. Mahon, Ft. Worth, 1976-77; assoc. atty. Cantey, Hanger, Gooch, Munn and Collins, Ft. Worth, 1977-81, ptnr., 1981-83; judge no. dist. U.S. Bankruptcy Ct., Ft. Worth, 1983-86; ptnr. Kelly, Hart & Hallman, Ft. Worth, 1986-88, Jackson & Walker, Ft. Worth, 1988-95, McConnell & Goodrich, Ft. Worth, 1995-2000, Winstead, Sechrest, and Minick, P.C., Ft. Worth, 2000—. Sgt. USAF, 1969-73. Mem. Nat. Conf. Bankruptcy Judges. Office: Winstead Sechrest & Minick PC 777 Main St Ste 1100 Fort Worth TX 76102

MCCONNELL, MICHAEL THEODORE, lawyer; b. San Francisco, June 18, 1954; s. Lawrence V. and Ann McConnell. BS, U. Oreg., 1977; JD, U. Denver, 1980. Bar: Colo., Wyo., U.S. Dist. Ct. Colo., U.S. Ct. Appeals (10th cir.), U.S. Supreme Ct., U.S. Dist. Ct. Wyo. Ptnr. Long & Jaudon, Denver, 1980—2001; founding mem., CEO McConnell Siderius Fleischner Houghtaling & Craigmile, LLC, Denver, 2002—. Fellow Am. Coll. Trial Lawyers; mem. ABA, Colo. Bar Assn., Denver Bar Assn., Colo. Def. Lawyers Assn. Office: McConnell Siderius Fleishner Houghtaling & Craigmile, PC 4700 S Syracuse St, Ste 200 Denver CO 80237 Office Fax: 303-458-9520. E-mail: mmcconnell@msfhc.com.

MCCONNELL, MICHAEL V. medical educator, researcher; b. N.Y.C. SB, MIT, 1983, SM in Elec. Engring., 1985; MD, Stanford U., 1990. Intern medicine Brigham and Women's Hosp., Boston, 1990-91, jr. asst. resident in internal medicine, 1991-92, cardiology fellow, 1992-96, assoc. physician medicine, 1996—; cardiovasc. imaging fellow Brigham and Women's Hosp., Beth Israel Hosp., Boston, 1995-96; clin. fellow in medicine Harvard Med. Sch., Boston, 1990-93, rsch. fellow in medicine, 1993-96, instr. medicine, 1996—. Tech. intern pacing rsch. divsn. Medtronic, Inc., 1982, 83; bioengring. apprentice Micro-Med, Paris, 1985. Contbr. articles to profl. jours. Recipient Undergrad. Rsch. award Uniroyal, 1981, Individual Nat. Rsch. Svc. award NHLBI, 1994, fellowship award for rsch. in cardiac imaging Bracco Diagnostics, Inc.-Soc. for Cardiac Angiography and Interventions, 1995. Mem. Am. Coll. Cardiology, Am. Heart Assn. Coun. Clin. Cardiology (student rsch. fellow 1987, clinician scientist award 1996), Internat. Soc. Magnetic Resonance Medicine, Mass. Med. Soc., Eta Kappa Nu, Sigma Xi, Tau Beta Pi. Achievements include research in magnetic resonance angiography of coronary artery disease, magnetic resonance imaging of atherosclerotic plaque. Office: Brigham and Women's Hospital 75 Francis St Boston MA 02115-6106

MC CONNELL, MICHAEL W. judge, law educator; b. 1955; BA, Mich. State U., 1976; JD, U. Chgo., 1979. Bar: D.C. 1981. Law clk. to Hon. J. Skelly Wright U.S. Ct. Appeals (D.C. cir.), 1979-80; law clk. to Hon. William J. Brennan Jr. U.S. Supreme Ct., Washington, 1980-81; asst. gen. counsel U.S. Office of Mgmt. and Budget, Washington, 1981-83; asst. to the solicitor gen. U.S. Dept. Justice, Washington, 1983-85; asst. prof. U. Chgo., 1984-89, prof., 1989—97; Presdl. prof. U. Utah Coll. Law, 1997—2002; visiting prof. Harvard Law School, 1999; special consultant Mayer, Brown & Platt, 1989—2002; circuit judge U.S. Ct. Appeals (10th Cir.), 2002—. Mem. Am. Acad. Arts and Scis., Order of Coif, Phi Beta Kappa, Phi Kappa Phi. Office: 1oth Circuit Ct Appeals 125 S State St # 6404 Salt Lake City UT 84138

MCCONNELL, MICHAEL W. investment company executive; Gen. ptnr. Brown Bros. Harriman & Co., N.Y.C. Office: Brown Bros Harriman & Co 59 Wall St New York NY 10005-2808

MCCONNELL, MITCHELL, JR., (MITCH MCCONNELL JR., ADDISON MITCHELL MCCONNELL JR.), senator, lawyer; b. Tuscumbia, AL, Feb. 20, 1942; s. Addison Mitchell and Julia (Shockley) McC.; children: Eleanor Hayes, Claire Redmon, Marion Porter; m. Elaine Chao, Feb. 6, 1993. BA with honors, U. Louisville, 1964; JD, U. Ky., 1967. Bar: Ky. 1967. Chief legis. asst. to Senator Marlow Cook, Washington, 1968-70; sole practice Louisville, 1970-74; dep. asst. U.S. atty. gen. Washington, 1974-75; judge Jefferson County, Louisville, 1978-85; U.S. Senator from Ky., 1985—; chmn. Nat. Republican Senatorial Com. 105th and 106th Congress; asst. maj. leader, 2002—. Mem. agr., nutrition, and forestry com., appropriations com., rules and adminstrn. com. Chmn. Jefferson County Republican Com., 1973-74; co-chmn. Nat. Child Tragedies Coalition, 1981; chmn., founder Ky. Task Force on Exploited and Missing Children, 1982; mem. Pres.'s Partnership on Child Safety Recipient commendation Nat. Trust on Hist. Preservation in U.S., 1982, Conservationist of Yr. award League Ky. Sportsmen, 1983, cert. of appreciation Am. Correctional Assn., 1985 Mem. Ky. Assn. County Judge Execs. (pres. 1982), Nat. Inst. Justice (adv. bd. 1982-84) Republican. Baptist. Avocations: fishing; cooking. Office: Russell Office Bldg # 361A Washington DC 20510-0001

MCCONNELL, NICHOLAS STILLWELL, lawyer; b. Chgo., May 25, 1946; s. James Millholland and Emily (Robinson) McC.; m. Nancy Haines Fifield, Dec. 14, 1968; children: Abigail Haven, Rebecca Fifield. BA, Bowdoin Coll., 1968; JD, George Wash. U., 1972. Bar: Va. Supreme Ct. 1972, U.S. Supreme Ct. 1973, U.S. Ct. Appeals D.C. 1973, D.C. Ct. Appeals 1973, U.S. Dist. Ct. D.C. 1973, Md. Ct. Appeals 1978. Assoc. Jackson, Gray & Laskey, Washington, 1972-78; prin., Jackson & Campbell, P.C., Washington, 1978—, dir. Mem. faculty Nat. Inst. Trial Advocacy, South Bend, Ind., 1984—; dir. Sauls Lithograph Co., Inc., Washington, 1986—, Am. Hospice Found., 1997-2003. Pres., dir. Combined Health Appeal Nat. Capital Area, Washington, 1980-93; dir. Combined Health Appeal Am., Atlanta, 1993-94; pres. Albert L. and Elizabeth T. Tucker Found, 1996-. With U.S. Army, 1969-71. Recipient Young Lawyer of Yr. award Bar Assn. D.C., 1982. Fellow Am. Coll. Trial Lawyers; mem. Health Lawyers Assn., D.C. Def. Lawyers, Def. Rsch. Inst., Barristers (pres. 1998), Counsellors, Bar Assn. D.C. (pres.-elect 2002-03, pres. 2003-04), Cosmos Club, Lawyers Club Congregationalist. Avocations: tennis, squash, golf, sailing. Home: 5004 Warren St NW Washington DC 20016-4370 Office: Jackson & Campbell PC 1 Lafayette Ctr 300 S Tower 1120 20th St NW Washington DC 20036-3437 Office Phone: 202-457-1628.

MCCONNELL, ROBERT EASTWOOD, architect, educator; b. Spokane, Wash., July 15, 1930; s. Robert Ervie and Alma (Eastwood) Mc C.; m. Beverly Ann Vincent, Sept. 12, 1953; children: Kathleen Ann, Karen Eileen, Terri Lynn. B in Archtl. Engring., Wash. State U., 1952; MArch, Mass. Inst. Tech., 1954. Project architect John W. Maloney (Architect), Seattle, 1956-62; asst. prof. architecture Ariz. State U., Tempe, 1962-66, asso. prof., 1966-67; prof. U. Kans., Lawrence, 1967-69; prof., head dept. art and architecture U. Idaho, Moscow, 1969-71; prof. U. Ariz., Tucson, 1971-92, dean Coll. Architecture, 1971-77, prof. emeritus, dean emeritus, 1992—, acting assoc. dean, 1994; partner McConnell & Peterson, Architects, Tempe, 1963-66; pvt. practice architecture, 1962-96. Author, project dir.: Land Use Planning for Ariz., Ariz. Acad, 1974; Contbr. articles to profl. jours. Chmn. Idaho Gov.'s Awards Program in Arts and Humanities, 1970; project dir. Rio Salado Conceptual Study, Phoenix, 1966; bd. dirs. Tucson Regional Plan, 1972-79. Served with USAF, 1954-56. Fellow AIA (awards 1969, 76, pres. So. Ariz. chpt. 1975-76, bd. dirs. 1971-77); mem. AIA Ariz. (mem. coun. of dels. 1971-77, chmn. honor awards jury 1975), Phi Kappa Phi, Scarab, Tau Beta Pi, Sigma Tau. Home: 930 East Camino Corrida Oro Valley AZ 85737-7652

MCCONNELL, ROGER, investment representative, political party official; b. Aug. 3, 1954; m. Susan Butler; children: Mellissa, Jonathan. BA, Livingston U., 1976. Investment rep. George M Wood & Co., A.G. Edwards & Sons, Edward D. Jones & Co., Mobile, Ala., 1991—. Fin. chmn. Bill Cabaniss senate campaign, 1990; chmn. Mobile County Exec. Com., Ala. State Rep. Party, 1995—. Baptist. Office: 4452 Airport Blvd Mobile AL 36608-2209

MCCONNELL, WILLIAM F., JR., medical products executive; b. LaGrange, Ill. BS in sys. analysis, Miami U., Ohio, 1971. Cert. CPA. Staff mem. Arthur Andersen, 1971—75; mgr. Arthur Andersen LLP, 1983—89, mng. ptnr., bus. cons., 1983—89; CFO Resort Condo. Internat., 1989—90, COO, 1990—96, info. officer, worldwide, 1996—97; rejoined Arthur Andersen, 1997; v.p., COO Guidant, Indpls., Ill., 1998—. Former chmn. Children's Mus. of Indpls., Am. Red Cross of Greater Indpls., Red Cross of Conner Prairie; former bd. mem. Acordia Personal Ins. Svcs. Office: Guidant PO Box 44906 111 Monument Cir 2900 Indianapolis IN 46244 Mailing: PO Box 44906 Indianapolis IN 46244

MCCONNELL, WILLIAM THOMPSON, commercial banker; b. Zanesville, Ohio, Aug. 8, 1933; s. William Gerald and Mary Gladys McC.; m. Jane Charlotte Cook, Aug. 25, 1956; children: Jennifer Wynne, William Gerald. BA, Denison U., 1955; MBA, Northwestern U., 1959. Pres. Park Nat. Bank, Newark, Ohio, 1979-83, pres., chief exec. officer, 1983-93, chmn., chief exec. officer, 1993-98, also bd. dirs., chmn., 1999—; pres., chief exec. officer Park Nat. Corp., Newark, 1987-94, chmn., CEO, 1994-98, chmn., 1999—. Mem. Newark Area C. of C. (past pres., dir. 1977-83), Ohio Bankers Assn. (pres., chmn. 1981-83), Am. Bankers Assn. (pres. 1997-98). Office: Park Nat Bank PO Box 3500 Newark OH 43058-3500

MCCONNELL SERIO, SUZIE THERESA, former professional basketball player, professional basketball coach; b. Pitts., July 29, 1966; married; 4 children. BA, Pa. State U., 1988. Coach Oakland Cath. High Sch., Pitts.; guard Cleve. Rockers, WNBA, 1998—2000; head coach Oakland Cath. H.S., 1990—2003, Minn. Lynx, WNBA, 2003—. Recipient Gold medal Olympic Games, Barcelona, 1988, Bronze medal Olympic Games, Seoul, 1992, Sportsmanship award WNBA, 1998, 1999, Newcomer award, 1998; named to All-WNBA 1st team, 1988. Office: Minn Lynx 600 First Ave North Minneapolis MN 55403

MCCONNEY, MARY E. information technology executive; BA in physics & Environ. Studies, Whitman Coll., 1976; M in Econ., U. Pa., 1979, M in Urban Planning, 1980, PhD in Spatial Econ., 1983. Applied statistician U. Wash., 1977—85, U. Pa., 1977—85; applied statistician & database design NAS, 1985—88; pres. HiroSoft Internat. Corp., 1988—; CFO Sunhawk.com, Seattle, 1992—99, treas., 1999—. Contbr. articles to profl. jours. Office: Sunhawk.com Corp 1463 E Republican St Seattle WA 98112-4517

MCCONNICO, JOHN, photojournalist; BJ, U. Tex., 1987, MA, 1994. Recipient Pulitzer prize, 1999. Office: c/o Photo Dept AP New Delhi 50 Rockefeller Plaza New York NY 10020

MCCONOMY, JAMES HERBERT, lawyer; b. Pitts., Mar. 24, 1937; s. Murray Michael and Catherine Elizabeth (Herbert) McC.; m. Jeanne Margaret Cronin, Sept. 3, 1960 (div. Apr. 1989); children: Margaret Jeanne, Michael Murray; m. Roberta L. Cavanaugh, June 30, 1989. AB cum laude, Harvard U., 1959, LLB, 1962. Bar: Pa. 1963, U.S. Ct. Appeals (3d cir.) 1972, U.S. Supreme Ct. 1977. Ptnr. Reed, Smith, Shaw & McClay, Pitts., 1962-92; mng. ptnr. Titus & McConomy, Pitts., 1992—. Fellow Am. Coll. Trial Lawyers; mem. ABA, Pa. Bar Assn. Allegheny County Acad. Trial Lawyers. Clubs: Duquesne, Harvard-Yale-Princeton (Pitts.). Roman Catholic. Avocations: photography, travel. Home: 1117 Harvard Rd Pittsburgh PA 15205-1726 Office: Titus & McConomy Four Gateway Ctr 20th Fl Pittsburgh PA 15222

MCCONVILLE, EDWARD PATRICK, lawyer; b. Albany, N.Y., Nov. 5, 1932; s. Edward Patrick McConville and Anne Dolores Leonard; m. Lois Anne Bessette, June 30, 1956 (div. Aug. 1982); 1 child, Stephen Patrick; m. Michelle Cristin Coderre, Mar. 17, 1984; 1 child, Collin William. BA, U. Notre Dame, 1954; JD, Union U., 1956. Bar: N.Y., INd., D.C., U.S. Supreme Ct. Investigator U.S. Civil Svc. Commn., N.Y.C., 1956—59; asst. divsn. counsel bowling divsn. Am. Machine and Foundry Co., N.Y.C., 1959—63; asst. counsel Lincoln Nat. Life Ins. Co., Ft. Wayne, Ind., 1963—66; asst. chief counsel U.S. Dept. Commerce, Econ. Devel. Adminstrn., Portland, Maine, 1966—68, Washington, 1966—68; v.p. First Nat. Bank, Washington, 1968—70, sr. v.p., 1970—73, exec. v.p., 1973, Cmty. State Bank, Albany, NY, 1973—75; sr. v.p. Union nat. Bank, Albany, 1975—77; ptnr. Maney McConville & Liccardi, P.C., East Greenbush, NY, 1977—, Valatie, NY, 1977—; pres. People Comml. Bank, Albany, 1984—86. Instr. Hudson Valley C.C., 1978—85, 1992; lectr. fin. Siena Coll., 1989; instr. bus. law and internat. bus. St. Rose Coll., 1991—98; chmn. bd. Evergreen Bank, Albany, NY, 1991—92. Vol. probation officer Albany County Probation Dept., 1981; dir. Cath. Youth Orgn., Washington, 1971—73; bd. dirs. Model Cities Econ. Devel. Corp., Washington, 1972—73. With U.S. Army, 1956—58, with USAR, 1958—60. Mem.: Albany Currach Rowing Club (dir. 1987—), Ft. Orange Club. Democrat. Roman Catholic. Avocations: rowing, horseback riding. Home: 55 Fordham Rd Valatie NY 12184 Office: Maney McConville and Liccari 22 Troy Rd East Greenbush NY 12061 Office Phone: 518-758-6296.

MCCONVILLE, RITA JEAN, finance executive; b. Chgo., July 7, 1958; d. Daniel Joseph and Rosemary (Smolinski) McC. BA, Northwestern U., 1979; MBA, U. Chgo., 1982. CPA, Ill. Fin. analyst Miami Valley Hosp., Dayton, Ohio, 1982-85; sr. cons. Health Facilities Corp., Northfield, Ill., 1985-87; sr. fin. analyst Lyphomed, Inc., Rosemont, Ill., 1987-88, mgr. fin. planning, 1988-90; controller Videocart, Inc., Chgo., 1990-93, OptionCare, Inc., Bannockburn, Ill., 1993-97; v.p., CFO, sec. Akorn, Inc., Buffalo Grove, Ill., 1997—. Mem. Ill. CPA Soc. Office: Akorn Inc 2500 Millbrook Dr Buffalo Grove IL 60089-4694 Home: 177 Willow Blvd Willow Springs IL 60480-1644

MCCOOK, KATHLEEN DE LA PEÑA, university educator; b. Chgo. d. Frank Eugene and Margaret L. (de la Peña) McEntee; m. Philip G. Heim, Mar. 20, 1972 (div.); 1 child, Margaret Marie; m. William Woodrow Lee McCook, Oct. 12, 1991; stepchildren: Cecilia, Billie Jean, Nicole. BA, U. Ill., Chgo.; MA, Marquette U., U. Chgo.; PhD, U. Wis.-Madison. Reference librarian Elmhurst Coll. Libr., Ill.; dir. pub. svcs. Dominican U., River Forest, Ill.; lectr. U. Wis., Madison; asst. prof. library sci. U. Ill., Urbana; dean, prof. La. State U. Sch. Libr. and Info. Sci., Baton Rouge; dean grad. sch. La. State U.; dir. Sch. Libr. and Info. Sci., U. South Fla., 1993-99, prof., 1993—, coord. cmty. outreach, 2000—02, disting. univ. prof., 2002—; McCusker lectr. Dominican U., 2003—. Author: (wth K. Weibel) Role of Women in Librarianship, 1978, (with L. Estabrook) Career Profiles, 1983, (with William E. Moen) Occupational Entry, 1989, Adult Services, 1990, (with Gary O. Rolstad) Developing Readers' Advisory Services, 1993, Toward a Just and Productive Soc., 1994, Opportunities in Library and Information Science, 1997, (with B. Ford) Global Reach: Local Touch, 1998, Women of Color in Librarianship, 1998, (with B. Immroth) Library Services to Youth of Hispanic Heritage, 2000, A Place at the Table, 2000, Introduction To Public Libraries, 2004; contbr. essays to books, articles to profl. jours. Chmn. Equal Rights Amendment Task Force, Ill., 1977-79. South Count Coalition for Cmty. Concerns, 1996-; mem. Eugene McCarthy campaign, U. Ill., Chgo., 1968; mem. La. Gov.'s Commn. for Women, 1985-88; bd. dirs. La. Endowment for Humanities, 1991-92; mem. exec. bd. Rural Social Svcs. Partnership, Hillsborough County, 1998-2001; mem. dem. exec. com., Hillsborough County, 2001-; dem. del. Fla. State Convention, 2002-03. Recipient Disting. Alumnus award U. Wis., 1991, award of merit Trejo Foster Found., 1999; named Bradshaw scholar Tex. Woman's Univ., 1994, Outstanding Rsch. award AUA, 2004; named scholar in residence Chgo. Pub. Libr., 2003. Mem. ALA (com. chmn. 1980—, editor RQ jour. 1982-88, Pub. Librs. Jour. 1989-90, Am. Librs. adv. com. 1994-96, contbg. editor Am. Librs. 1999-2001, column editor RUSQ 2000—, REFORMA (bd. dirs. 1997-98, Latino Libr. of Yr. 2002, Equality award 1987, Adult Svc. award 1991, Futas Catalyst for Change award 1998, Achievement in Diversity Rsch. award 2004), Assn. for Libr. and Info. Sci. Edn. (com. chmn. 1981—, pres. 1987-88, Pres. award 1997), Fla. Libr. Assn. (bd. dirs. 1995-98, Transformer award 1996), Tampa Bay Libr. Consortium (bd. dirs. 1994-97), Women Libr. Workers, Ruskin Civic Assn. (sec. 1997-99), Ill. Libr. Assn. (treas. 1981-83), Beta Phi Mu (50th Anniversary Disting. Mem. 1999, Dist. Lectr. award 2002, Disting. Svc. to Edn. of Librarianship 2003), Cath. Libr. Assn. (Brubaker award for Outstanding Artid 2003). Democrat. Roman Catholic. Avocation: reading. Office: U South Fla Sch Libr and Info Sci 4202 E Fowler Ave Stop Cis1040 Tampa FL 33620-7800 Home: PO Box 1027 Ruskin FL 33575 Personal E-mail: kmccook@tampabay.rr.com.

MCCOOK, RICHARD PAUL, grocery chain financial executive; b. Miami, Fla., Mar. 15, 1953; s. Leon Ennis and Ruth Erminor (Davenport) McC.; m. Anne Thackerson, Mar. 22, 1975; children: Ryan Wesley, Kelly Lauren. BS in Acctg., Fla. State U., 1975, M in Accountancy, 1976. CPA, Fla. Sr. audit mgr. Peat, Marwick, Mitchell & Co., Jacksonville, Fla., 1976-84; fin. v.p., CFO Winn-Dixie Stores, Inc., 1984—, sr. v.p., CFO. Participant Leadership Jacksonville, 1986-87. Mem. Am. Inst. CPA's, Fla. Inst. CPA's, Fin. Execs. Inst. Clubs: River (Jacksonville). Democrat. Methodist. Avocations: hunting, fishing, tennis. Office: Winn-Dixie Stores Inc 5050 Edgewood Ct Jacksonville FL 32254-3601

MCCOOK, THOMAS H. savings and loan association executive; Chmn. First Liberty Fin. Corp., Macon, Ga., 1990—; also bd. dirs. V.p., sec., treas. Macon Concrete Pipe Co., Macon. Office: First Liberty Fin Corp 201 2nd St Macon GA 31201-8293

MCCOOL, COURTNEY, Olympic athlete; b. Kansas City, Apr. 1, 1988; Mem. U.S. Nat. Gymnastics Team, 2002—; gymnast Team USA, Athens Olympic Games, 2004. Achievements include mem. U.S. Championship Team, Pan Am. Games, 2003; invention of Athens Test Event, 1st in all-around, 2004. Office: c/o USOC One Olympic Plz Colorado Springs CO 80909*

MCCOOLE, ROBERT F. construction company executive; b. St. Louis, Mar. 26, 1950; BS, St. Louis U., 1972. Project mgr. J.S. Alberici Constrn. Co. Inc., St. Louis, 1981-84, v.p. bus. devel., 1987-93, sr. v.p. bus. devel., 1993-96, pres., 1996—. Mem. Assoc. Gen. Contractors (chair 1997—). Office: JS Alberici Constrn Co Inc 2150 Kienlen Ave Saint Louis MO 63121-5505

MCCORD, GUYTE PIERCE, JR., retired judge; b. Tallahassee, Sept. 23, 1914; s. Guyte Pierce and Jean (Patterson) McC.; m. Laura Elizabeth Mack, Dec. 1, 1939 (dec. Oct. 8, 2000); children: Florence Elizabeth, Guyte Pierce III, Edward LeRoy; m. Elizabeth Rogers Green, May 24, 2002. Student, Davidson Coll., 1933-34; BA, JD, U. Fla., 1940. Bar: Fla. 1940. Summer ranger Yosemite Nat. Park, 1936-39; rsch. aide Fla. Supreme Ct., summer 1940; pvt. practice Tallahassee, 1940-48; dep. commr. Fla. Indsl. Commn., 1946-47; pros. atty. Leon County, 1947-48; asst. gen. counsel Fla. Pub. Svc. Commn., 1949-60; judge 2d Jud. Cir. Fla., Tallahassee, 1960-74, Ct. Appeals 1st Dist. Fla., 1974-83, chief judge, 1977-79. Mem. Fla. Senate Pres.'s Council on Criminal Justice 1972; mem. appellate ct. rules com. Fla. Supreme Ct., 1977-78, mem. appellate ct. structure commn. 1978-79. Pres. Murat House Assn., Inc., 1967-69; bd. dirs. Fla. Heritage Found., 1969-70, mem. exec. com., 1965-69; mem. Andrew Jackson staff of Springtime Tallahassee, 1973-74, 84-86, Andrew Jackson, 1987. Commdr. USNR, 1942—64, WWII, Korea. Mem. ABA, Mil. Officers Assn. Am., Fla. Bar, Fla. Conf. Cir. Judges (sec.-treas. 1970, chmn. 1972), Fla. State U. Pres. Club, Kiwanis (dir. 1958-59). Presbyterian (elder 1960—, ch. trustee 1981-86). Home: 2718 Timbertrail Cir Tallahassee FL 32308-5745

MCCORD, JAMES RICHARD, III, chemical engineer, mathematician; b. Norristown, Ga., Sept. 2, 1932; s. Zachariah Thigpen Houser Jr. and Neilie Mae (Sumner) McC.; m. Louise France Manning, Oct. 1956 (div. 1974); children: Neil Alexander, Stuart James, Valerie France, Kent Richard. Student, Abraham Baldwin Agrl. Coll., Tifton, Ga., 1949-50; BChE with honors, Ga. Inst. Tech., 1955; postgrad., U. Pitts., 1955-56, Carnegie Inst. Tech., 1956-57; MS, MIT, 1959, PhD in Math, 1961. Asst. chem. engr. TVA, Wilson Dam, Ala., 1951-54; assoc. engr. Westinghouse Electric Corp., Pitts., 1955-57; rsch. asst. ops. rsch. MIT, Cambridge, Mass., 1957-59, tchg. asst. dept. math., 1959-61, rsch. assoc. dept. math., 1961-62, asst. prof., postdoctoral fellow dept. chem. engring., 1962-64; sr. engr., project analyst Esso Research and Engring. Co., Florham Park, N.J., 1964-68; asst. prof. Emory U., Atlanta, 1968-71; pvt. practice math. cons. Atlanta, 1971-80; instr. in math. Ga. So. Coll., Statesboro, 1980-81; inventory control Lovett & Tharpe, Inc., Dublin, Ga., 1981-84; Norristown-Adrian; farmer, businessman, 1984—. Contbr. numerous articles to sci. and math. jours. WEBELOS den leader Boy Scouts Am., Dunwoody, Ga., 1969-70; mem., vol. worker Key Meml. Found., Adrian-Norristown, Ga., 1965—. Mem. AIChE, Ga. Tech. Alumni Assn., MIT Alumni Assn., Sigma Xi, Tau Beta Pi. Republican. Methodist. Avocations: music, fishing, gardening, mathematical puzzles. Home and Office: PO Box 549 Dublin GA 31040-0549

MCCORD, JEAN ELLEN, secondary art educator, coach; b. Ilion, NY, Oct. 20, 1952; d. Harold Shepard and Marian Alice (Bernier) Shepard; m. Colin McCord, May 10, 1977 (div. Sept. 1993). AA, Mohawk Valley C.C., Utica, NY, 1972; BA, SUNY, New Paltz, 1975, postgrad., 1976—77; student, Coll. Santa Reparata Sch. Art, Florence, Italy, 2001. Cert. art educator, NY. Jr. kindergarten tchr. Norfolk (Va.) Naval Base, 1978-79; jr. kindergarten and art tchr. Sunnybrook Day Sch., Virginia Beach, Va., 1979-81; tchr. art Fisher Elem. Sch., Mohawk, NY, 1982-84, Mechanicstown Sch., Middletown, NY, 1984-88, Middletown Start Ctr., 1986-87; tchr. art, synergetic edn. Middletown Tchr. Ctr., 1986-87; pvt. portfolio tutor Middletown, 1989-91; tchr. art Middletown Elem. Summer Sch., 1989—, Middletown H.S., 1987-97; tchr. Maple Hill Elem., 1997—. Sec. of policy and exec. bds. Middletown Tchr. Ctr., 1988—91, chmn. policy and exec. bds., 1991—92; com. mem. Bicentennial of Edn.; advisor Nat. Art Honor Soc., 1989—97; coord. After Sch. Program for Youth at Risk, 1995—; tchr., curriculum writer for interdisciplinary art, 1992—94; author 3-vol. curriculum companion, 2004; internat. com. for commn. Cambridge U., 2001, Cultural Ednl. Exch., Japan, U.S., 2004; coord. 1st child's sculpture garden by children Marble Hill Elem. Sch. Actress, vocalist, designer in regional theatre, 1970—; artistic designer sch. plays and Creative Theatre Group; writer, dir. for local cabarets and charities; local muralist and portraitist, 1990—; set designer (off broadway) in NYC including Mother Posture, Seedless Grapes, The Pelican, New Village Prodns. benefit for AIDS, marquee 1st Theatre Mus. Village, Monroe, NY; performer Cancer Soc. Fundraiser, 1997, for John Brigham Meml. Scholarship Fundraiser, Ruthie Dino Marshall Fundraiser, others; prodr., dir. Follies/Toys for Tots Campaign, 1997; exhibited in shows Lisbon, Portugal, 2001, Paramount Theatre, Middletown, Cambridge, Eng., 2001, Vancouver, 2002, Middletown Ctr., 2004, Middletown Culture Ctr., 2004; executed mural Middletown H.S., 2001; set designer, Dracula, 2003. County svc. coord. Orange County Youth-In-Govt. (adv. 1988-91), Goshen, NY, 1991-93; Odyssey of the Mind Coach, 1984-92; chair edn. and cultural sem., Lisbon, Portugal, 1999; chair edn. and culture comm., Vancouver, Can.; art and music comm., Vancouver; chmn., internat. comm. com. Internat. Edn. Culture Com.; mem. Internat. Art and Music Com., Vancouver, 2002, mem. multi-cultural com., 2002-03, edn. and culture chairperson Dublin, Ireland, 2004; curriculum writer Middletown City Schs., 2003; founding mem. Nat. Campaign for Tolerance, Birmingham, Ala., 2003. Named for outstanding set design Times Herald Record, 1994; honored by Bd. Edn. Outstanding Educator, 1992, Apple award, 1999; named in S.W. Arts Mag., 2001, named Educator Yr. Am. Biog. Inst., 2003. Mem. Marine Corps League (hon.), NJROTC (hon. cadet 1997, Outstanding Contbn. to Arts award, Millenium Medal of Honor 2000), Am. Biog. Inst. (chmn. ednl. culture com., 1999, mem. comm. com., chmn. edn. and culture com., 2002, art and music com., 2002, multicultural com., 2002), World Peace Diplomacy Forum. Episcopalian. Avocations: theatrical design, singing, calligraphy. Home: PO Box 4429 Middletown NY 10941-8429 Office: Middletown City Schs Wisner Ave Middletown NY 10940 Office Phone: 845-346-4900.

MC CORD, JOHN HARRISON, lawyer, educator; b. Oceanside, N.Y., Dec. 22, 1934; s. John Francis and Elsie (Powers) McC.; m. Maureen Ursula Maclean, Dec. 30, 1961; children: John F.X., Paul V., David G., Maureen E. AB, Fordham Coll., 1957; JD magna cum laude, St. John's U., 1960; LLM, U. Ill., 1965. Bar: N.Y. 1960, Ill. 1964. Atty. U.S. Dept. Justice, Washington, 1960-61; mem. faculty U. Ill. Coll. Law, Champaign, 1964—, prof. law, 1965—, assoc. dean for acad. affairs., 1990-92; of counsel Meyer Capel PC, 1998—; auditor/notary Cath. Diocese of Peoria, 2000—. Acad. cons. Ill. Inst. Continuing Legal Edn., 1968-72; vis. prof. law U. N.C., 1975, U. Hawaii, 1976 Author: (with Keeton and O'Connell) Crisis in Car Insurance, 1967, Buying and Selling Small Businesses, 1969, (with O'Byrne) Deskbook for Illinois Estate Planners, 1969, Closely Held Corporations, 1971, (with O'Neill, Pearlman and Stroud) Buying, Selling and Merging Businesses, 1975, (with McKee) Federal Income Taxation-A Summary Analysis, 1975, (with Kramer) Problems for Federal Estate and Gift Taxes, 1976, Estate and Gift Tax Reform, 1977, Estate and Gift Tax Summary, 15th edit. 1993, Estate, Gift and Generation-Skipping Taxes, 1999; editor: Dimensions and Academic Freedom, 1969, With All Deliberate Speed: Civil Rights Theory and Reality, 1969, Ill. Law Forum, 1965-69; contbr. articles to profl. jours.; author computer programs for estate planning, 1984—. Served to capt. JAGC, USAF, 1961-64. St. Thomas More fellow St. John's U., 1960. Fellow Am. Coll. Trust and Estate Counsel; mem. ABA (com. CLE and chief reporter for study outline on buying, selling and merging businesses sect. fed. tax 1969-73, com. estate and gift taxes 1973-84, chmn. subcom. gross estate issues 1976-78, subcom. tax reform 1978-84), Ill. Bar Assn. (exec. coun. fed. tax sect. 1966-73, chmn. sect. 1971-72, exec. coun. bus. planning sect. 86-91), Champaign County Bar Assn., Am. Arbitration Assn. (nat. panel arbitrators 1969-90), Eastern Ill. Estate Planning Coun. (pres. 1970-71), U. Miami Inst. Estate Planning (adv. coun. 1979-87), Assn. Am. Law Schs. (fed. taxation roundtable coun. 1969-72), Ill. Inst. CLE (bd. dirs. 1991-2000, estate planning adv. com. 2000—), U.S. Navy League, Order of Coif. Home: 104 E Sherwin Dr Urbana IL 61802-7133 Office: U Ill Coll Law Champaign IL 61820 E-mail: jmccord@law.uiuc.edu.

MCCORD, MICHAEL DAVID, anesthesiologist; b. Gary, Ind., Mar. 22, 1959; BS in Pharmacy, Purdue U., 1984; MD, Ind. U., 1989. Diplomate Am. Bd. Anesthesiology; cert. pharmacist. Intern Mayo Clinic, Rochester, Minn., 1989-90, resident, 1990-93; staff mem. St. Elizabeth Hosp., Beaumont, Tex., 1993—, Bapt. Hosp. (now Meml. Hermann Bapt. Hosp.), Beaumont, 1993—. Mem. Am. Soc. Anesthesiologists, Tex. Soc. Anesthesiology, Tex. Med. Assn. Office: 6440 Wellington Pl Beaumont TX 77706-3206

MCCORISON, MARCUS ALLEN, librarian, cultural organization administrator; b. Lancaster, Wis., July 17, 1926; s. Joseph Lyle and Ruth (Mink) McC.; m. Janet Buckbee Knop, June 10, 1950 (dec. 1998); children: Marcus Allen II, Judith McC. Gove, Andrew Buckbee, Mary McC. Rosenbloom (dec. 2001), James Rice, Peter Gardner. AB, Ripon Coll., 1950; MA, U. Vt., 1951, LittD (hon.), 1992; MS, Columbia U., 1954; LHD (hon.), Assumption Coll., Worcester, Mass., 1987, Coll. of the Holy Cross, 1992; LittD (hon.), Clark U., 1992. Librarian Kellogg-Hubbard Library, Montpelier, Vt., 1954-55; chief of rare books dept. Dartmouth Coll. Library, Hanover, N.H., 1955-59; head spl. collections dept. State U. Iowa Libraries, 1959-60; libr. Am. Antiquarian Soc., Worcester, Mass., 1960-91, editor Procs., 1960-67, dir., 1967-89, pres., 1989-92, pres. emeritus, 1993—; cons. Christie, Manson & Woods, Internat., 1993-96, N.Y. Hist. Soc., 1994-95, Libr. Congress, Hist. Soc. of Pa., 1996, U. Kans., 1998-99. Mem. N.Am. steering com. 18th Century Short Title Catalogue, 1977—; mem. Com. for a New Eng. Bibliography, 1968-90, treas., 1970-77; mem. adv. com. Eleutherian Mills-Hagley Found., 1971-74, 87-89; chmn. Ind. Rsch. Librs. Assn., 1972-73, 78-80; mem. adv. coun. Princeton U. Libr., 1988-92; bd. govs. Rsch. Librs. Group, 1980-91, chmn. preservation com., 1982-85, chmn. governance com., 1989-91, chmn. Writings of James Fenimore Cooper, 1991-2002. Author: Vermont Imprints 1778-1820, 1963, The 1764 Catalogue of the Redwood Library, 1965; contbr.: The Pursuit of Knowledge in the Early American Republic, 1976, Publishing and Readership in Revolutionary France and America, 1993; editor: History of Printing in America by Isaiah Thomas, 1970. Trustee Fruitlands Mus., 1978-89, Old Sturbridge Village, 1981-92, Hist. Deerfield, Inc., 1991—2002; mem. bd. mgrs. Lewis Walpole Libr., Yale U., 1995—; nat. trustee Newberry Libr., 1995—; mem. Cultural Commn. City Worcester, Mass., 1999—, Mass. Hist. Commn., 1999—; mem. com. of mgmt. Wm. L. Clements Libr., U. Mich., 2001—. Recipient Samuel Pepys medal Ephemera Soc., London, 1980, Disting. Alumni award Ripon Coll., 1989, Columbia U. Sch. Libr. Svc., 1992, Rickards medal Ephemera Soc. Am., 2000. Fellow Pilgrim Soc.; mem. Am. Antiquarian Soc., Coll. and Rsch. Librs. Assn. (chmn. rare books sect. 1965-66), Bibliog. Soc. Am. (pres. 1980-84, del. to ACLS 1985—2002), Am. Printing Hist. Assn. (trustee 1998—2004, laureate 1998), Vt. Hist. Soc. (trustee 1956-66), Worcester Hist. Mus. (exec. com. 1967-80), Ctr. for Rsch. on Vt. (assoc.), N.E. Am. Soc. 18th Century Studies (pres. 1978-79), Colonial Soc. Mass., Club of Odd Vols., Grolier Club (councillor 1979-82, 83-84), Zamorano Club (hon.), Roxburghe Club (San Francisco), Century Assn. Democrat. Congregationalist. Home and Office: 3601 Knightsbridge Close Worcester MA 01609-1161

MCCORKINDALE, DOUGLAS HAMILTON, lawyer, publishing executive; b. N.Y.C., June 14, 1939; s. William Douglas and Kathleen (Miles) McC.; m. Nancy Walsh, Dec. 24, 1991; children by previous marriage: Laura Ann, Heather Jean. BA, Columbia U., 1961, LLB cum laude (Harlan Fiske Stone scholar), 1964. Bar: N.Y. 1964. Assoc. Thacher Proffitt & Wood, N.Y.C., 1964-70, ptnr., 1970-71; gen. counsel, sec. Gannett Co., Inc., Arlington, Va., 1971-72, v.p., gen. counsel, sec., 1972-77, sr. v.p. fin. and law, 1977-79, sr. v.p., chief fin. officer, 1979-83, pres. diversified media div., 1980-83, exec. v.p., 1983, vice chmn., CFO, 1984—, chief adminstrv. officer, 1986—, vice chmn., pres., 1997—, CEO, 2000—, chmn., pres., CEO, 2001—. Bd. dirs. AP, Continental Airlines Inc., Lockheed Martin Corp., Mut. Ins. Co. Ltd. Mem. ABA (chmn. com. Exch. Art of 1934 1971-73), Newspaper Assn. Am., Pine Valley Golf Club, Mid Ocean Club, Burning Tree Club. Office: Gannett Co Inc 7950 Jones Branch Dr Mc Lean VA 22102

MCCORKLE, RUTH, oncological nurse, educator; BS, U. Md., 1968; MA, U. Iowa, 1972, PhD, 1975. Staff nurse CCU Vancouver (Wash.) Med. Hosp., 1968-69; oncological clin. nurse specialist U. Iowa Hosps. and Clinics, Iowa City, 1971-73; instr. psychiat. nursing and oncological nursing Sch. Nursing, U. Iowa, Iowa City, 1974-75; from asst. prof. to prof. dept. cmty. health care sys. U. Wash., Seattle, 1975-85; prof. adult health and illness divsn. Sch. Nursing, U. Pa., Phila., 1986—, chairperson, 1988-89, dir. Ctr. Advancing Care in Serious Illness, 1989—, dir. cancer control Cancer Comprehensive Ctr., 1990-98; prof. nursing, chmn. doc program, dir. Ctr. Chronic Illness Sch. Yale U., New Haven, 1998—. Mem. nursing sci. rev. com. Nat. Ctr. Nursing Rsch., 1988-92. Contbr. articles to profl. jours. Fellow Am. Acad. Nursing; mem. ANA, NAS, Internat. Soc. Nurses Cancer Care (dir.-at-large 1983-89), Am. Assn. Cancer Edn., Oncology Nursing Soc. (charter mem., mem. rsch. com. 1981-82, dir.-at-large 1983-85). Office: Yale U 100 Church St S PO Box 9740 New Haven CT 06536-0740

MCCORKLE, WILLIAM LITTLETON, journalism educator, writer; b. St. Louis, June 16, 1926; s. Carroll Grey and Ruth (Warren) McCorkle; m. Patricia Josephine Kenepaske, June 1959; 1 child, Melissa. AA, Harris Tchrs. Jr. Coll., St. Louis, 1946; BA, Ctrl. Coll., Fayette, Mo., 1948; MA, U. Kansas City, Mo., 1958; PhD, U. Tex., Austin, 1968. Reporter, sports editor Borger (Tex.) News-Herald, 1948—50; copy editor, war corr. Pacific Stars and Stripes, Japan, Korea, 1951—52; statehouse reporter AP, Jefferson City, Mo., 1952—53; newsman Kansas City (Mo.) Star, 1953—58, 1962—78; assoc. prof. journalism S.D. State U., Brookings, 1978—82; prof. journalism Baylor U., Waco, Tex., 1982—93; adj. prof. journalism U. Tex., Arlington, 1994—96; ret., 1996. Writing critic Mobridge (S.D.) Tribune, 1979—80. Contbr. articles to various jours. and periodicals, 1982—93. Sgt. U.S. Army, 1950—52, Tokyo, Korea. Recipient Disting. Reporting of Pub. Affairs award, Am. Polit. Sci. Assn., 1963. Mem.: Kans. Hist. Soc., Mo. Hist. Soc., Am. Hist. Assn., Lions (pres. Woodway, Tex. chpt. 1989). Presbyterian. Home: 10015 Sandalwood Dr Woodway TX 76712

MC CORMAC, JOHN WAVERLY, judge; b. Zanesville, Ohio, Feb. 8, 1926; s. Samuel D. and Phyllis (Murray) McC.; m. Martha Ann Cunningham, June 22, 1952; children: Michael Paul, John Mark, James Samuel. BS, Muskingum Coll., 1951; JD, Capital U., 1961. Bar: Ohio 1961. Fire protection engr. Ohio Insp. Bur., 1951—60; pvt. practice Columbus, 1961—65; prof. law Capital U., Columbus, 1965-66, 71-74, dean Law Sch., 1966—71; judge 10th Dist. Ct. Appeals, 1975—92; prof. law Ohio State U., Columbus, 1993—2001. Mem. staff cons. rules adv. com. Supreme Ct. Ohio; chmn. adv. bd. Vols. in Probation, 1972-74; chmn. ohio Jud. Conf., 1982-84; commr. Ohio Dispute Resolution Com., 1989-96, chmn., 1993-95; chief justice Ohio Ct. Appeals Assn., 1989-91. Author: Ohio Civil Rules Practice, 1970, 2nd edit., 1992, Anderson's Ohio Civil Practice, Vol. 1, 1971, Vol. 2, 1976, Vol. 3, 1977, Wrongful Death in Ohio, 1982. Served with USNR, 1943-46. Fellow Ohio Bar Assn. Found.; mem. League Ohio Law Schs. (pres. 1969-70), ABA, Ohio Bar Assn. (council of dels. 1973-77), Columbus Bar Assn. (bd. govs. 1968-72, sec.-treas. 1973-74, pres. 1975-76), Am. Judicature Soc., Phi Alpha Delta. Clubs: Masons (33 deg.). Republican. Home: 395 Longfellow Ave Columbus OH 43085-3024 E-mail: johnmccormac46@hotmail.com.

MC CORMAC, WESTON ARTHUR, retired educator, retired career officer; b. Tacoma, Mar. 5, 1911; s. Jesse Carney and Jessie (Myron) McC.; m. Mary Jeanne Rapinac, Sept. 5, 1941. BA, Golden Gate U., MBA, 1968; diploma, Nat. War Coll., 1956; MPA, U. So. Calif., 1972; MA, Calif. Poly. State U., 1975. Acct. exec. Merrill, Lynch, Pierce, Fenner & Beane, Tacoma, Seattle, 1929-40; commd. lt. U.S. Army, 1940, advanced through grades to col., 1946, comdg. officer 35th F.A. Group, 1958, dep. chief staff V Corps, 1958-60, asst. chief staff G 1 Pacific, 1962-65, ret., 1966; prof. bus., dept. chmn. Calif. Poly. State U., San Luis Obispo, 1968-80, ret., 1980. Decorated Legion of Merit with 2 oak leaf clusters, Silver Star, Bronze Star medal, Commendation medal with oak leaf cluster. Fellow Fin. Analysts Fedn.; mem. L.A. Soc. Fin. Analysts. Home: 16732 Lew Allen Cir Riverside CA 92518-2909 E-mail: fivone@aol.com.

MCCORMACK, DAN, photographer, educator; s. John H. and Catherine F. McCormack; m. Wendy M. Gessel, Dec. 30, 1968; children: Sean B., Orrin R., Maya V., Leah K. BS Photography, Ill. Inst. Tech. - Inst. of Design, Chgo., 1967; MFA Photography, Sch.of Art Inst., Chgo., 1970. Instr. of photography Purdue U., West Lafayette, Ind., 1969; photography prof. Pratt Inst., Brooklyn, NY, 1969—70, SUNY New Paltz, New Paltz, NY, 1970—71, Columbia-Greene C.C., Hudson, NY, 1972—79, Somerset County Coll., Somerville, NJ, 1976—85, Jr. Coll. of Albany, NY, 1979—80, Mercy Coll., Dobbs Ferry, NY, 1982—89; artist Internat. Ctr. for Photography, New York, NY, 1992—93; instr. of photography Ramapo Coll., Mawah, NJ, 1994—94; artist - seminar leader Ctr. for Photography, Woodstock, NY, 1999—2002; head of photography Marist Coll., Poughkeepsie, NY, 1991—. Office mgr. Gerald T. O'Buckley Assoc., Accord, NY, 1973—; artist - v.p. Artists Coop, Woodstock, NY, 1975—76; bd. of directors - founder Ctr. for Photography, Woodstock, NY, 1977—87, Level Three Gallery, Philadelphia, Pa., 1987—88; vis. artist Suny New Paltz Art Dept., 1997; artist mentor Fine Arts Masters program Boston Inst. Art, 2003. Exhibitions include digital photography Internat. Festival of Digital Imaging, Novosbirsk, Russia, 2003, exhibitions include labyrinth of light: zone zero Nat. Ctr. of the Arts, Mexico City, 2003, exhibitions include digital fine art Eleanor Bliss Ctr. for the arts, Steamboat Springs, Colo., 2003, exhibitions include phillips' mill photographic e Rural Poughkeepsie, 2003. Seminar of advanced photography Barrett Art Ctr., Poughkeepsie, NY, 2003. Recipient Art on the Net 1000 (Tokyo), MCMOGATK (Machida City Mus. of Graphic Arts), 1999; fellow Creative Arts Pub. Svc., NY Sate Coun. of the Arts, 1982, Exhbn. Support, Andy Warhol Found., 1991, Workplace Fellowship, Woodstock Sch. of Art, 1993. Mem.: Soc. for Photographic Edn. Office: Marist College 3399 North Rd Poughkeepsie NY 12601 Office Phone: 845-575-3000 2128.

MCCORMACK, DONALD PAUL, newspaper consultant; b. Brockton, Mass., Jan. 15, 1926; s. Everett G. and Esther (Lufkin) McC.; m. Petronella Ruth Seger, Apr. 28, 1951; 1 son, Christopher Paul. BA, U. Pitts., 1949. Corr. U.P.I., 1949-52; asst. city editor Pitts. Sun-Telegraph, 1952-56; pub. relations exec., 1956-64; copy reader N.Y. News, 1964-67, editorial writer, 1967-72, chief editorial writer, 1972-82; cons., 1982—. With USAAF, 1944-46, Pa. N.G., 1952-57. Home and Office: PO Box 3539 Westport CT 06880-8539

MC CORMACK, FRANCIS XAVIER, lawyer, former oil company executive; b. Bklyn., July 9, 1929; s. Joseph and Blanche V. (Dengel) Mc C.; m. Margaret V. Hynes, Apr. 24, 1954; children: Marguerite, Francis Xavier, Sean Michael, Keith John, Cecelia Blanche, Christopher Thomas. AB cum laude, St. Francis Coll., Bklyn., 1951; LLB, Columbia U., 1954. Bar: N.Y. 1955, Mich. 1963, Calif. 1974, Pa. 1975. Assoc. Cravath, Swaine & Moore, N.Y.C., 1956-62; sr. atty. Ford Motor Co., 1962-64, asst. gen. counsel, 1970-72; v.p., gen. counsel, sec. Philco-Ford Corp., 1964-72; v.p., gen. counsel Atlantic Richfield Co., 1972-73, sr. v.p., gen. counsel, 1973-94. Editor Columbia U. Law Rev., 1954. Decorated commendatore Ordine al Merito (Italy); Stone scholar Columbia U., 1954. Mem. Calif. Club, Chancery Club, Annandale Golf Club.

MCCORMACK, GRACE LYNETTE, civil engineering technician; b. Dallas, Nov. 2; d. Audley and Janice Meredith (Metcalf) McC. Tech. degree, Durham's Coll., 1958; grad. in civil engring., El Centro Coll., 1972; grad. in advanced surveying, Eastfield, 1975. Cert. sr. engr. technician. Contract design technician various engring firms, Dallas, 1958-70; sr. design engr. technician City of Dallas Survey Div., 1970-80, street light div., 1980-95, ret. 1995. Mem. Unity Ch. Avocations: numerology, astrology, metaphysics, Egyptian-Arabian horses, lighting and designing black and white portrait photography. Home: 1428 Meadowbrook Ln Irving TX 75061-4435

MCCORMACK, JOHN BRENDAN, bishop; b. Winthrop, Mass., Aug. 12, 1935; s. Cornelius and Eleanor (Noonan) McC. Student, Cardinal O'Connell Sem. Coll., Brighton, Mass., St. John's Sem.; MSW, Boston Coll., 1969. Ordained priest Roman Cath. Ch., 1960, consecrated bishop, 1995. Exec. dir. North Shore Cath. Charities Ctr., Peabody, Mass., 1967-81; pastor Immaculate Conception Parish, Malden-Medford, Mass., 1981—85; cabinet sec., vicar for religious and priests Archdiocese of Boston, 1984-94; pastor St. Francis Xavier Parish, South Weymouth, Mass., 1995; consecrated aux. bishop, 1995; regional bishop so. region Archdiocese of Boston, 1995-98; bishop Diocese of Manchester, N.H., 1998—. Roman Catholic. Office: PO Box 310 153 Ash St Manchester NH 03105

MCCORMACK, JOHN JOSEPH, JR., insurance executive; b. Morristown, NJ, Aug. 22, 1944; s. John Joseph and Marion Loretta (Smith) McC.; m. Judith Gail Harvey, July 20, 1968; children: Brendan, Matthew, Margaret. BBA, St. Bonaventure U., 1966. From group underwriter to exec. v.p. Tchrs. Ins. and Annuity Assn.-Coll. Retirement Equities Fund, N.Y.C., 1966-98; pres. TIAA-CREF Enterprises, 1998-99, group pres., 1999-2001; chmn. McCormack's Retirement and Fin. Svcs. Cons., 2001—. Trustee Am. Psychol. Assn. Ins. Trust, Washington, 1980-90, chmn., 1985-86, trustee investment com., 1990-98, 2001—; trustee Employee Benefit Rsch. Inst., Washington, 1983—, treas., 1986-90, vice-chmn., 1997-98, chmn., 1999-2001; mem. adv. bd. Andrew W. Mellon Found., N.Y.C., 1997-2001. Pres.'s coun. St. Bonaventure U., 1986—, chmn., 1986-89, trustee, 1996—, chmn. investment com., 1999—; bd. visitors Ctr. for Study Future Mgmt. U. Md., 1987-92; trustee Coll. and Univ. Pers. Assn. Found., 1992-94; bd. govs. Investment Co. Inst., 1994-2000; trustee Fenimore Asset Mgmt. Funds, 2004-. Roman Catholic. Office: PO Box 432 New Vernon NJ 07976-0432 Office Phone: 908-415-0104. E-mail: jmccsbu@aol.com.

MCCORMACK, JOHN ROBERT, lawyer; b. Middletown, Conn., Mar. 30, 1962; s. John Francis and Ann Jane (Monarca) McC.; m. Cristina Dorthea Dwyer, Sept. 27, 1986; children: Kevin, Cara. BS, Univ. Conn., 1984; JD, Stetson Univ., 1990. Assoc. Kelly & McKee, P.A., Tampa, Fla., 1990-92; ptnr. Wiggins & McCormack, Clearwater, Fla., 1992-94; sole practitioner J. Robert McCormack, P.A., Clearwater, Fla., 1994-00; ptnr. Persante & McCormack, P.A., 2000—. Editor: Labor and Employment in Florida, 1990, Critical Issues in Labor and Employment Labor, 1990. Mem. ABA (labor and employment law sect.), Fla. Bar Labor and Employment Law Sect., Barney Masterson Inn of Ct. (treas. 1998-99), Clearwater Bar Employment Law Com. (co-chair 1997-99). Office: Persante & McCormack P A 2555 Enterprise Rd Bldg 15 Clearwater FL 33763

MCCORMACK, MICHAEL, state supreme court justice; b. Omaha, July 20, 1939; JD, Creighton U., 1963. Asst. pub. defender, Douglas County, Nebr., 1963-66; pvt. practice Omaha, 1966-97; justice Nebr. Supreme Ct., 1997—. Office: State Capitol Bldg Rm 2218 Lincoln NE 68509 also: PO Box 98910 Lincoln NE 68509

MCCORMACK, ROBERT CORNELIUS, investment banker; b. N.Y.C., Nov. 7, 1939; m. Mary Lester, Dec. 14, 1963; children: Robert Cornelius Jr., Walter, Scott. BA, U. N.C., 1962; MBA, U. Chgo., 1968. V.p. Dillon Read & Co. Inc., 1968-81; mng. dir. Morgan Stanley & Co., Inc., Chgo., 1981-87; dep. asst sec. def. prodn. support U.S. Dept. Def., Washington, 1987-88, dep. under sec. def. indsl. and internat. programs, 1988-89, acting dep. under sec. of def. acquisition, 1989-90, asst. sec. Navy fin. mgmt., 1990-93; founding ptnr. Trident Capital L.P., Chgo., 1993—. Served to lt. USNR, 1963-66. Office: 277 83RD St #B2 Burr Ridge IL 60527-5846

MCCORMACK, STANLEY EUGENE, financial consultant; b. Olney, Ill., Oct. 15, 1949; s. Donald Eugene and Patricia Louise (Dickerson) McC.; m. Janis Eileen Bush; m. Jeffrey Daniel, Erin Louise, Evan Stuart. Student, DePauw U., 1967-68, Ohio State U., 1968-71; MS in Fin. Svc., The Am. Coll., 1991, MS in Mgmt., 1996. CLU; chartered fin. cons. Ins. agt. Art Holtzman Assocs., Rochester, N.Y., 1973-75, ins. sales mgr., 1975-82; fin. cons., pres. Assoc. Fin. Cons., Rochester, 1983—. Instr. Am. Coll., Rochester, 1988, Empire State Coll. Moderator Webster (N.Y.) Bapt. Ch., 1985-88, mem. fin. com., 1994-2000; com. mem. Webster Rep. Com., 1978-81; mem. fin. com. Webster Swim Assn., 1993-95, treas., 1989-91. Mem.: Estate Planning Coun. Rochester, Internal Assn. Fin. Planners (bd. dirs. 1989—95, v.p. chmn. symposium 1990, pres. 1993—94, pres. adv. bd. 1994—96), Am. Soc. Chartered Life Underwriters and Charterred Fin. Cons., Phi Delta Theta (pres. Beta West 1999—2001). Avocations: voice, bridge. Home: 622 Fairmont Dr Webster NY 14580-8967 Office Phone: 585-381-5820. E-mail: smccorm123@aol.com.

MCCORMACK, THOMAS JOSEPH, playwright, retired publishing company executive; b. Boston, Jan. 5, 1932; s. Thomas Joseph and Lena Carolyn (Allen) McC.; m. Sandra Harriet Danenberg, Aug. 21, 1964; children: Daniel Aaron, Jed Charles (dec.), Jessie Ann. Student, U. Conn., 1950-51; AB summa cum laude (James Manning scholar), Brown U., 1954; postgrad. (G.H. Palmer scholar, Woodrow Wilson fellow), Harvard U., 1956. Writer radio news WSTC, Stamford, Conn., 1957-59; editor Doubleday & Co., Inc., N.Y.C., 1959-64, Harper & Row, N.Y.C., 1964-67; edn. editor New Am. Library, N.Y.C., 1967-69; dir. trade dept. St. Martin's Press, N.Y.C., 1969-70, pres., 1970-87, chief exec. officer, editorial dir., 1970-96, chmn., 1987-97. Pres., chmn. bd. St. James Press, Ltd., London, 1973-79; v.p., treas. Sandra D. McCormack, Inc. (Interior Designer.); chmn., chief exec. officer Tor Books, N.Y.C., 1987-96; exec. com. Holtzbrinck GmbH, Stuttgart, Germany, 1995-97. Author: Afterwords, Novelists on Their Novels, 1969, The Fiction Editor, the Novel and the Novelist, (plays) American Roulette, 1969, Endpapers, 2002; columnist: The Cheerful Skeptic, 1997—99. Mem. Play Devel. Coun., Manhattan Theater Club, 1995-2001, Dramatists Gild, 1997—. With AUS, 1954-56. Mem. Assn. Am. Pubs. (dir. 1973-76, freedom to read com. 1974-77, Curtis Benjamin award 1997, LMP Lifetime Achievement award 1997), Phi Beta Kappa. Clubs: The Players (N.Y.C.), Century Assn. (N.Y.C.). Home: 50 Central Park W New York NY 10023-6028 E-mail: cheerskep@aol.com.

MCCORMACK, WILLIAM ARTHUR, lawyer; b. Rochester, N.Y., Sept. 18, 1951; s. Austin Francis and June Ann (Doyle) McC. AB in Polit. Sci. magna cum laude, St. Louis U., 1973; cert., Sorbonne, Paris, 1974; JD, Georgetown U., 1977. Bar: Tex. 1978, D.C. 1979. Assoc. Crutcher, Hull, et al., Dallas, 1978-82, Hughes & Luce, Dallas, 1982-83, ptnr., 1983—, mem. mgmt. com., exec. com., sect. head, 1993-97, mgn. ptnr., chm., 1997—. Bd. dirs. Engles Capital Corp., McCormack Corp.; speaker and author on legal topics. Contbr. articles to profl. jours. Bd. dirs. Alliance Francaise Found., Dallas, Jesuit Found., St. Anthony Found., Dallas Epilepsy Found., pres., 1992, Dallas Citizens Coun.; bd. advisors Jesuit Prep., Bishop Dunne H.S., Bus. Com. for the Arts, Dallas; coun. mem., exec. comm. circle ten coun. Boy Scouts Am.; leadership coun. Dallas Chamber. Mem. ABA, State Bar Assn. Tex. (chmn. minority com.), Dallas Bar Assn. (chmn. legal ethics com., mem. minority commn.), Pi Sigma Alpha, Alpha Sigma Nu. Roman Catholic. Office: Hughes and Luce 1717 Main St Ste 2800 Dallas TX 75201-4685

MCCORMALLY, KEVIN JAY, editor; b. Boston, Mar. 13, 1950; s. John Patrick and Marguerite Louise (Wichert) McC.; m. Anne Louise Long, May 27, 1972; children: Niamh Anna, Patrick Henry. BA with honors, U. Iowa, 1972. Area editor Burlington (Iowa) Hawk Eye, 1969-70; city editor Daily Iowan, Iowa City, 1971-72; press sec. U.S. Rep. Edward Mezvinsky, Washington, 1972-77; assoc. editor Changing Times Mag., Washington, 1977-85, sr. editor, 1985-90; exec. editor Kiplinger's Personal Fin. Mag. (formerly Changing Times), Washington, 1991-2000; editl. dir. Kiplinger's Personal Fin. mag., 2000—. Commentator Nightly Bus. Report PBS and ABC Radio. Author: Successful Tax Planning, 1988, Sure Ways to Cut Your Taxes, 1989-94, Cut Your Taxes, 1996, 97, 98, 99; co-author: A Term to Remember, 1977; editor: Get More for Your Money, 1981. Mem. Nat. Press Club (best consumer journalism award 1986, 88), Sigma Delta Chi. Democrat. Roman Catholic. Avocation: photography. Home: 161 D St SE Washington DC 20003-1809 Office: Kiplingers Personal Fin Mag 1729 H St NW Washington DC 20006-3925

MCCORMICK, BARNES WARNOCK, aerospace engineering educator; b. Waycross, Ga., July 15, 1926; s. Barnes Warnock and Edwina (Brogdon) McC.; m. Emily Joan Hess, July 18, 1946; 1 dau., Cynthia Joan. BS in Aero. Engring, Pa. State U., 1948, MS, 1949, PhD, 1954. Research assoc. Pa. State U., University Park, 1949-54, assoc. prof., 1954-55, prof. aero. engring., 1959-92, Boeing prof. aero. engring., 1985-92, prof. emeritus, cons., 1992—, head dept. aerospace engring., 1969-85. Assoc. prof., chmn. aero. dept. Wichita U., 1958-59; chief aerodynamics Vertol Helicopter Co., 1955-58; mem. Congl. Adv. Com. Aeros., 1984-86; U.S. coord. flight vehicle integration panel Adv. Group for Aerospace R&D, 1988—; cons. to industry. Author: Aerodynamics of V/Stol Flight, 1967, Aerodynamics, Aeronautics and Flight Mechanics, 1979, 2d edit., 1995; co-author: (with M.P. Papadakis) Aircraft Accident Reconstruction and Litigation, 1996; contbr. articles to profl. jours.; patentee in field. Served with USNR, 1944-46. Recipient joint award for achievement in aerospace edn. Am. Soc. Engring. Edn.-Am. Inst. Aeros. and Astronautics, 1976 Fellow Am. Inst. Aeros. and Astronautics; mem. ASEE, Am. Helicopter Soc. (hon. fellow), Sigma Xi, Sigma Gamma Tau, Tau Beta Pi. Clubs: Masons. Home: 611 Glenn Rd State College PA 16803-3475 Office: Pa State U Coll Engring University Park PA 16802 Office Phone: 814-863-0602. E-mail: bwmaer@engr.psu.edu.

MCCORMICK, DALE, state treasurer; b. N.Y., Jan. 17, 1947; BA, U. Iowa, 1970. Mem. Maine State Senate from 18th dist, 1991-96; treas. State of Maine, Augusta, 1999—. Author: Against the Grain, a Carpentry Manual for Women, 1977. Address: Maine State Treasury 39 St House Station Augusta ME 04333-0001

MCCORMICK, DAVID ARTHUR, lawyer; b. McKeesport, Pa., Oct. 26, 1946; s. Arthur Paul and Eleanor Irene (Gibson) McC. BA, Westminster Coll., 1967; JD, Duquesne U., 1973; MBA, U. Pa., 1975. Bar: Pa. 1973, D.C. 1978, U.S. Ct. Appeals (3d cir.) 1977, U.S. Ct. Appeals (4th and D.C. cirs.) 1980, U.S. Supreme Ct. 1980. Asst. commerce counsel Penn Cen. R.R., Phila., 1973-76; assoc. labor counsel Consol. Rail Corp., Phila., 1976-78; atty. Dept. Army, Washington, 1978—. Author various geneal. and hist. works; contbr. articles to profl. jours. Mem. ATLA, Pa. Bar Assn., Phila. Bar Assn., D.C. Bar Assn., Assn. Transp. Practitioners, Soc. Petroleum Engrs., Soc. Cin. (Del. chpt.), SAR (Pitts. chpt.), Am. Legion, Res. Officers Assn., Masons, Phi Alpha Delta, Theta Chi. Presbyterian.

MCCORMICK, DONALD BRUCE, retired biochemist, educator; b. Front Royal, Va., July 15, 1932; s. Jesse Allen and Elizabeth (Hord) McC.; m. Norma Jean Dunn, June 6, 1955; children: Susan Lynn, Donald Bruce, Michael Allen. BA, Vanderbilt U., 1953, PhD, 1958. Postdoctoral fellow U. Calif., Berkeley, 1958—60; asst. prof. Cornell U., 1960-63, assoc. prof., 1963-69, prof. nutrition, biochemistry and molecular biology, biol. scis., 1969-79, Liberty Hyde Bailey prof. nutritional biochemistry, 1978-79; chmn. dept. biochemistry Emory U., Atlanta, 1979-94, Fuller E. Callaway prof. biochemistry, 1979-99, prof. emeritus, 1999—; exec. assoc. dean sci. Emory U. Sch. Medicine, 1985-89. Vis. lectr. U. Ill, 1963; Wellcome vis. prof. U. Fla., 1986, Med. Coll. Pa., 1989; Hurley lectr. U. Calif., Davis, 1992; O'Dell lectr. U. Mo., Columbia, 1993; biochem. cons. Interdepartmental Com. on Nutrition for Nat. Def., Spain, 1958; mem. and chmn. nutrition study sect. NIH, 1977-81; mem. diet and health com., dietary guidelines implementation com., vice chmn. food and nutrition bd. NRC, Inst. Medicine of NAS; exec. com., chmn. dept. med. biochemistry, Coun. Acad. Soc., Am. Assn. Med. Colls., 1984-87; mem. biology panel U.S. Civilian R&D Found., 1998-2001. Author: (with others) Spain: Nutrition Survey of the Armed Forces, 1958, Molecular Associations in Biology, 1968, Flavins and Flavin Enzymes, 1968, Flavins and Flavoproteins, 1980, 82, 84, 88, 89, 91, Comprehensive Biochemistry, Vol. 21, 1971, Riboflavin, 1974, Metal Ions in Biological Systems, Vol. 1, 1974, Present Knowledge in Nutrition, 1976, 84, 90, 2001, Natural Sulphur Compounds, 1979, Vitamin B6, Metabolism and Role in Growth, 1980, Ann. Rev. of Nutrition, Vol. 1, 1981, Vol. 9, 1989, Vol. 24, 2004, Mechanisms of Enzymatic Reactions: Stereochemistry, 1986, Chemical and Biological Aspects of Vitamin B6 Catalysis, Part A, 1984, Biochemistry of Vitamin B6, 1987, Biochemistry and Molecular Biology of Vitamin B6 and PQQ-Dependent Proteins, 2000, Tietz Textbook of Clinical Chemistry, 1986, 94, 99, Fundamentals of Clinical Chemistry, 1987, 95, 2000, Vitamins and Biofactors in Life Science, 1992, Encyclopedia of Food Science, 1993, 2003, Encyclopedia of Molecular, Biology and Molecular Medicine, 1996, 97, Modern Nutrition in Health and Disease, 1988, 94, 99, New Trends in Biological Chemistry, 1990, Chemistry and Biochemistry of Flavins, 1991, Encyclopedia of Human Biology, 1991, 97, Liver, 1994, Molecular Biology and Biotechnology, 1995, Biochemical and Physiological Bases of Human Nutrition, 2000, Nutrition in Space Flight and Weightlessness Models, 1999; editor: Vitamins and Hormones, Vitamins and Coenzymes, Ann. Rev. of Nutrition, Handbook of Vitamins. Recipient award Bausch and Lomb, 1950, award Mead Johnson, 1970, award Osborne and Mendel, 1978, award Ga. Nutrition Coun., 1989, award Bristol-Myers Squibb/Mead Johnson, 1999; Westinghouse Sci. scholar, 1950; fellow NIH, 1957-58, 58-60; Guggenheim fellow, 1966 67. Fellow AAAS, Am. Inst. Nutrition (now Am. Soc. Nutrition Sci., pres. 1991); mem. Am. Soc. Biochemistry and Molecular Biology, Soc. Exptl. Biology and Medicine, Am. Chem. Soc., Am. Inst. Biol. Sci., Biophysics Soc., Fedn. Am. Socs. Exptl. Biology (bd. dirs., LSRO sci. steering group), Microbiol. Soc., Photobiol. Soc., N.Y. Acad. Sci., Protein Soc., Sigma Xi. Office Phone: 770-270-5508. Business E-Mail: biocdbm@emory.edu.

MCCORMICK, DOUGLAS WALTER, Internet company executive; b. N.Y.C., Dec. 15, 1949; s. Howard George and Hazel Frances (Sullivan) McC.; m. Karen J. Lane, Dec. 9, 1980; children: Douglas Jr., Luke Patrick. BA, U. Dayton; MBA, Columbia U., 1990. Rsch analyst TeleRep Inc., L.A., 1970; account exec. Sta. KCOP-TV, L.A., 1970-71, Petry TV, N.Y.C., 1971-80; composer, staff writer The Entertainment Co., N.Y.C., 1980-82; v.p. ea. sales, mgr. Lifetime Cable TV, N.Y.C., 1982-85; v.p. TV sales The Samuel Goldwyn Co., L.A., 1985-86; sr. v.p. sales Lifetime TV Network, L.A., 1986-90, exec. v.p., 1990-95, pres., CEO, 1995-99; pres. iVillage, Inc., 2000, CEO, 2000—, chmn., 2001—. Bd. dirs. iVillage, Inc., 1999—, Ad Coun. Composer popular songs for artists including Paul Anka, Gladys Knight, Dusty Springfield, others. Bd. dirs., treasurer Child Care Action Campaign; bd. dirs. Women's Sports Found., Cancer Rsch. and Treatment Fund, Parent Action. Mem. Internat. Radio and TV Soc. (bd. dirs.), Nat. Acad. Cable Programming. Office: iVillage Inc 500-512 7th Ave New York NY 10018*

MCCORMICK, EDGAR LINDSLEY, language educator, writer; b. Wadsworth, Ohio, Mar. 12, 1914; s. Thomas Edward McCormick and Carrie Belle Van Sickle; m. Cora Lee Morrow, Aug. 11, 1945; 1 child, Carol Helen. BA, Kent State Univ., Kent, Ohio, 1936; MA, Univ. Mich., Ann Arbor, Mich., 1937, PhD, 1950. Tchg. fellow Univ. Mich., Ann Arbor, 1939—41, 1945—46; head dept. of English Florence State Coll., Florence, Ala., 1946—50, Bethany Coll., Bethany, W.Va., 1950—54; chair freshman English Kent State U., Kent, Ohio, 1956—60, asst. dean and assoc. dean, Coll. Arts and Sci., 1964—70, coord. Am. studies, 1966—78, prof. emeritus English, 1979—. Editor English Assn. Ohio Bull., 1959—62; dir. curator Kelso House Mus., Brimfield, Ohio, 1963—96. Author: Brimfield and Its People...1816-1941, 1988, Determined Lives...(Family History), 1989, Yesterday's Scholars...1932-1979, 2001, They Also Served: Citizen Soldiers (WWII), 1993, Fond Recollection, Country Life, 1918-1941, 2003. Staff sgt. USAF, 1942—45, N. Africa. Recipient Outstanding Achievement award, Ohio Assn. Hist. Soc., 1996. Mem.: Modern Language Assn. Democrat. Meth. Achievements include the first detailed account of the 1839-1855 Nantucket migration to Portage County, Ohio. Avocations: history, poetry, photography, travel. Home: 1106 Old Forge Rd Kent OH 44240-7404

MCCORMICK, FLOYD GUY, JR., agricultural educator, college administrator; b. Center, Colo., July 3, 1927; s. Floyd Guy and Gladys (Weir) McC.; m. Constance P. Slane; children: Angela Lynn, Craig Alan, Kim Ann, Robert Guy. BS, Colo. State U., 1950, MEd, 1959; PhD, Ohio State U., 1964. Tchr. vocat. agr. State of Colo., 1956-62; asst. prof. agrl. edn. Ohio State U., 1964-67; mem. com. agr. edn. com. edn. in agr. and natural resources Nat. Acad. Scis., 1967-69; prof. agrl. edn., head dept. U. Ariz., 1967-89, prof. emeritus, dept. head emeritus, 1990—. Cons. in-svc. edn., div. vocat. edn. Ohio Dept. Edn., 1963-64; vis. prof. Colo. State U., 1973, U. Sierra Leone, Njala Univ. Coll., 1989; external examiner U. Sierra Leone, 1984, 85, 87; adv. trustee Am. Inst. Cooperatives, Washington, 1985-88; mem. Nat. Coun. Vocat. and Tech. Edn. in Agr., Washington, 1985-88. Co-author: Teacher Education in Agriculture, 1982, Supervised Occupational Experience Handbook, 1982; author: The Power of Positive Teaching, 1994, also instrl. units, tech. bulls., articles in profl. jours.; spl. editor: Agrl. Edn. mag., 1970-74. Trustee Nat. FFA Found. Served with USNR, 1945-46. Named hon. state farmer Colo., 1958, Ariz., 1968, Am. farmer, 1972; recipient Centennial award Ohio State U., 1970, E.B. Knight award NACTA Jour., 1980, Regional Outstanding Tchr. award Nat. Assn. Coll. Tchrs. Agr., 1989, also fellow, 1988, VIP citation Nat. FFA Assn., 1990, Diamond Anniversary award Ohio State U., 1992. Mem. Am. Vocat Assn. (mem. policy com. agrl. edn. divsn. 1976-79, v.p. divsn. 1985-88, chmn. membership com. 1980-83, sec. agrl. edn. divsn. 1983-86, pres. 1985-88, outstanding svc. awrd 1989), Nat. Vocat. Agr. Tchrs. Assn. (life, Outstanding Svc. award Region I 1974, 83, 96), Am. Assn. Tchr. Educators in Agr. (disting. lectr. 1984, editor newsletter 1975-76, pres. 1976-77, Disting. Svc. award 1978, 88, Rsch. award western region rsch. 1988), Alpha Zeta, Alpha Tau Alpha (hon.), Gamma Sigma Delta, Phi Delta Kappa, Epsilon Pi Tau. Home: 6933 E Paseo San Andres Tucson AZ 85710-2203

MCCORMICK, HAROLD J. music educator; b. Dover, N.J., Sept. 22, 1954; s. Harold Joseph and Dorothy McCormick; m. Patricia Anne McCormick, Oct. 4, 1980; children: Harold J. IV, Timothy Vincent, Caroline Constance, Cecilia James. B in Music Edn., Kean U., 1979. Band dir. Red Bank (N.J.) Cath. H.S., 1981—83, Jackson (N.J.) Twp. Meml. H.S., 1984—. Adjudicator Drum Corps Assocs., Monmouth Beach, NJ, 1987—, Music Showcase Festivals, 1994—; drum corps arranger; marching band music arranger. Active Jackson Coun. of the Arts, 2000—02. Mem.: Ea. Marching Band Assn., U.S. Scholastic Band Assn., Music Educators Nat. Conf. Office: Jackson Meml HS 101 Don Connor Blvd Jackson NJ 08527

MCCORMICK, HOMER L., JR., lawyer; b. Frederick, Md., Nov. 11, 1928; s. Homer Lee McCormick and Rosebelle Irene Biser; m. Jacquelyn R.; children: Deidre Ann and Thomas Lee. Student, George Washington U., 1946-48; AB, San Jose State U., 1951; JD, U. Calif., San Francisco, 1961. Bar: Calif. 1961, U.S. Dist. Ct. Ctrl. Dist. Calif. 1972, U.S. Dist. No. Calif. 1961, U.S. Dist. Ct., So. Dist. Calif. 1976, U.S. Dist. Ct. of Appeals (9th cir. 1961), U.S. Tax Ct. 1977, U.S. Ct. Claims 1977, U.S. Supreme Ct. 1977. Atty. Holiway Jones State of Calif., 1961-63; atty. assoc. Rutan & Tucker, Santa Ana, Calif., 1963-66, atty. ptnr., 1966-70, atty., sr. ptnr. Costa Mesa, Calif., 1970-88, dept. head pub. law, 1974-88, mng. ptnr., 1984-88; founding ptnr., sr. ptnr. McCormick, Kidman & Behrens, Costa Mesa, 1988—. Arbitrator Am. Arbitration Assn., 1966-88; judge pro tem Orange County Superior Ct., 1975, 81, 84; spkr., lectr. Cal. Continuing Edn. of the Bar, 1976-88; profl. designation Internat. Right of Way Assn., 1971-; elected mem. Cal. Condemnation Lawyers, 1994—. Contbg. author: Real Property Remedies, 1982; contbr. articles to profl. jours. Mem. bd. govs. Bus. Com. Arts, Orange County Philharm. Soc. Lt. USMCR, 1951-56; pilot, Korea. Named Alumnus of Year Hastings Law Sch., 1992. Mem. ABA (com. chair 1991), Am. Bd. Trial Adv. (pres. O.C. chpt. 1973), Orange City Atty. Assn. (pres. 1972), Fed. Bar Assoc., Consumer Attys. Calif., Am. Judicature Soc., Orange County Bar Assn. (com. chair 1991-92), Orange County Bus. Trial Lawyers, Order Coif, Thurston

Soc., Hastings Alumni Assn. (pres. 1973), Springs Country Club, Delta Theta Pi. Republican. Episcopalian. Avocations: boating, fishing, flying, golf, foreign travel. Office Phone: 714-755-3100. E-mail: mmcormick@mkblawyers.com.

MCCORMICK, HUGH THOMAS, lawyer; b. McAlester, Okla., Nov. 24, 1944; s. Hugh O. and Lois (McGucken) McC.; m. Suzanna G. Weingarten, Dec. 5, 1975; 1 child, John B. BA, U. Mich., 1968; JD, Rutgers U., 1977; LLM in Taxation, Georgetown U., 1980. Bar: N.Y. 1977, D.C. 1979, Maine 1981. Atty. office chief counsel interpretative divsn. IRS, Washington, 1977-81; assoc. Perkins, Thompson, Hinkley & Keddy, Portland, Maine, 1981-83, LeBoeuf, Lamb, Leiby & MacRae, N.Y.C., 1983-88, counsel, 1989-91; ptnr. LeBoeuf, Lamb, Greene & MacRae, L.L.P., N.Y.C., 1992—. Dir. Ins. Tax. Conf., 1993—, pres., 2002—. Mem. bd. contbrs. and advisors Jour. of Taxation of Investments; contbr. articles to profl. jours. Trustee U.S. Team Handball Found., N.J., 1985-95. Fellow Am. Bar Found.; mem. ABA (chmn. com. on taxation of ins. cos. 1989, chmn. subcom. sect. of taxation 1989-96, mem. torts and ins. practice sect., sect. on taxation), D.C. Bar Assn. Democrat. Home: 555 Pelham Manor Rd Pelham NY 10803-2525 Office: LeBoeuf Lamb Greene MacRae LLP 125 W 55th St New York NY 10019-5369 E-mail: hmccormi@llgm.com.

MCCORMICK, JAMES HAROLD, academic administrator; b. Indiana, Pa., Nov. 11, 1938; s. Harold Clark and Mary Blanche (Truby) McCormick; m. Maryan Kough Garner, June 7, 1963; children: David Harold, Douglas Paul. BS, Indiana U. of Pa., 1959; MEd, U. Pitts., 1961, EdD, 1963, postdoctoral, 1966, Columbia U., U. Mich., 1966-67, Harvard U., 1982. Tchr. Punxsutawney (Pa.) Area Joint Sch. Dist., 1959-61; adminstr. Baldwin-Whitehall Schs., Pitts., 1961-64; grad. asst. U. Pitts., 1962-63; asst. supt. instrn. Washington (Pa.) City Schs., 1964-65; prof. dept. edn. and psychology, asst. dean acad. affairs, acting dean acad. affairs, acting dean tchr. edn., asst. to pres., v.p. adminstrn. and fin. Shippensburg (Pa.) U., 1965-73; pres. Bloomsburg (Pa.) U., 1973-83, pres. emeritus, 1983—; chancellor Pa. State System Higher Edn., Harrisburg, 1983—2001, Minn. State Colls. and Univs., 2001—. Falk intern in politics, 1959; mem. adv. bd. Pa. Ednl. Policy Seminar; mem. Gov.'s Econ. Devel. Partnership Bd.; mem. higher edn. adv. coun. pa. State Bd. Edn.; past commr. Edn. Commn. of the States. Contbr. articles profl. jours. Named One of 10 Outstanding Young Men of Yr., Pa. Jr. C. of C.; recipient Young Leader in Edn. award Phi Delta Kappa, 1981, Disting. Alumnus award Indiana U. Pa., 1981, Outstanding Alumni award Bloomsburg U., 1984, Outstanding Alumnus award U. Pitts., 1985, Adler award Pa. Edn. assn., 1992; selected CIVITAS Prague mission, 1995, Presdl. Lectures, Kuwait U., 1993, Svc. Awd., Coll. and Univ. Pub. Rels., Assn. of PA (CUPRAP), 1999, Distig. Svc. Awd., PA Assn. of Councs. of Trustees (PACT), 1998, Alumni Assn. Leadership Awd., Bloomsburg Univ. PA, 1999.; McCormick Human Svcs. Ctr. named in his honor Bloomberg U., 1983; McCormick Ho. named in his honor Dixon U., 1994. Mem. Am. Assn. State Colls. and Univs. (Pa. state rep. 1988-93, former chmn. acad. and student pers. com., mem. com. on state rels. and task force on ednl. equity, chmn. policies and purposes com. 1996), Am. Coun. on Edn. (commn. on women in higher edn.), Nat. Assn. Sys. Heads, (exec. com., past pres.), Commn. State Colls. and Univs. (mem. and past chmn. govt. rels. and student rels. coms.), Assn. Governing Bds. (adv. coun.), Am. Assn. for Affirmative Action, Am. Assn. Higher Edn., Am. Assn. Sch. Adminstrs., Am. Assn. Univ. Adminstrs. (Tosney Leadership award 1993), Pa. Assn. Colls. and Univs. (bd. dirs., chair 1982), Natl. Ctr. for the Study of Sport in Soc., Pa. Black Conf. on Higher Edn., State Higher Edn. Ofcrs. (SHEEO), exec. com., fed. rels. liaison, Pers. Assn., Bloomsburg Area C. of C. (pres. 1983), Rotary (bd. dirs. through 1992), Phi Delta Kappa. Office: 500 Wells Fargo Pl 30 East 7th St Saint Paul MN 55101 Home: 2817 Oakwood Dr Harrisburg PA 17110-3903

MCCORMICK, JAMES K. application developer; BS in Acctg. summa cum laude, Fla. State U., 1984. CPA, Ga., 1985. Sr. auditor emerging bus. divsn. Arthyr Andersen & Co., Atlanta, 1984-89; cons. mgr. strategic svcs. divsn. Andersen Cons., Melbourne, Australia, 1989-91; dir. fin. Am. Sign & Mktg. Svcs., Inc., 1991-92; corp. controller, treas. United Dairy Farmers, Inc., 1992-97; mgr. acctg., fin. MIS & human resources depts. Knology, 1997-99; chief fin. officer Harbinger Corp., Atlanta, 1999—. Office: Harbinger Corp 11720 Amberpark Dr Ste 100 Alpharetta GA 30004-2271

MCCORMICK, JOHN HOYLE, lawyer; b. Pensacola, Fla., July 30, 1933; s. Clyde Hoyle and Orrie Brooks (Fink) McC.; m. Patricia McCall, Dec. 27, 1974. BS, U. Fla., 1955; JD, Stetson U., 1958. Bar: Fla. 1958. Ptnr. McCormick, Drury & Scaff, Jasper, Fla., 1958-74; county atty., 1973—; sr. ptnr. McCormick, Drury & Scaff, Jasper, 1974-91; pvt. practice Jasper, 1991—. County judge, Hamilton County, Fla., 1960-72; local counsel So. Ry. System, 1968—, CSX, Ry., 1972—; atty. Hamilton County Devel. Authority, 1970-91; bd. dirs. 1st Fed. Savs. Bank Fla.; bd. dirs., v.p., atty. Hamilton County Bank. Mayor City of White Springs, Fla., 1959; pres. Hamilton County C. of C., Jasper, 1961. Mem. Masons, Phi Delta Phi. Democrat. Methodist. Avocations: gardening, motorhome camping, college football. Home: 403 2nd Ave NW Jasper FL 32052-6687 Office: 215 2nd St NE Jasper FL 32052-6616 Address: PO Drawer O Jasper FL 32052-0695

MCCORMICK, JOHN OWEN, retired comparative literature educator; b. Thief River Falls, Minn., Sept. 20, 1918; s. Owen Charles and Marie Antoinette Beauchemin (Smith) McC.; m. Helen Manuel, 1942; m. Mairi Clare MacInnes, 1954; children: Jonathan, Peter, Antoinette, Fergus. BA magna cum laude, U. Minn., 1941; MA, Harvard U., 1947, PhD, 1951. Dean, lectr. Salzburg Seminar in Am. Studies, 1951-52; lectr., prof. Free U., Berlin, 1952-59; prof. comparative lit. Rutgers U., 1959-87, prof. emeritus, 1987—. Vis. prof. Nat. U. Mexico, 1961-62, Hachioji (Tokyo) seminar, 1979; Christian Gauss Seminar lectr. Princeton, 1969; resident fellow Sch. Letters of Ind. U., 1970 Author: The Middle Distance: a Comparative History of American Imaginative Literature, 1919-32, 1971, The Complete Aficionado, 1967, 2d edit., 1998, (with Mairi MacInnes McCormick) Versions of Censorship, 1962, Der moderne amerikanische Roman, 1960, Amerikanische Lyrik, 1957, Catastrophe and Imagination, 1957, 2d edit., 1998, Fiction as Knowledge, 1975, 2d edit., 1999, George Santayana: A Biography, 1987, 2003, Wolfe, Malraux, Hesse, 1987, American and European Literary Imagination: 1919-1932, 2000; editor: (with G. Core) Sallies of the Mind: Essays of Francis Fergusson, 1998, Seagoing: Essay-Memoirs, 2000. With USNR, 1941-46. Recipient prize for non-fiction Longview Found., 1960, Am. Acad. and Inst. Arts and Letters award, 1988; Gugenheim fellow, 1964-65, 79-80, Bruern fellow Leeds (Eng.) U., 1975-76, NEH fellow, 1983-84, hon. fellow U. York, 1992. Mem. Taurino Club (London), Harvard Club (N.Y.C.).

MCCORMICK, KAREN LOUISE, savings and loan association executive; b. San Jose, Calif., Nov. 22, 1954; d. Clifford Kaye Jr. and Margaret Elizabeth (Bigler) McC.; children: Crystal DeAnne, Sheralyn Rose McCormick. Grad. high sch., Mountain View, Calif., 1973; cert. Inst. Fin. Edn., Ariz. State U., 1987. Cashier, loan officer Santa Clara County Employees' Credit Union, San Jose, 1973-77; teller, loan officer First Fed. Savs. & Loan Assn. Port Angeles, Wash., 1977-83, v.p., br. mgr., 1983-87, v.p., adminstr. loan prodn., 1987-89, v.p., ass. dir. lending, 1989-90, sr. v.p., dir. lending, 1990—97, pres., CEO, 1997—. Bd. dirs., chair opns. com. Wash. Community Reinvestment Assn., Seattle, 1992-95.; mem. Wash. Savs. League Affordable Housing com., 1991; vice chair Wash. Fin. League, 2003-; chair bd. dirs. WFL Services (subsid. corp. of Wash. Fin. League), 2003-; past bd. mem. & pres. Thrift Inst. Adv. Coun. Contbr. articles to newspapers, 1989-91. Bd. dirs. Clallam County YMCA, 1992-95, Diversified Industries, Inc., Port Angeles, 1985-87, Port Angeles C of C; mem. Queen of Angels sch. bd., 1988-90; co-founder Olympic Peninsula Housing Coalition, 1992—; treas. Peninsula Coll. Found., past pres. Nor'Wester Rotary Club of Port Angeles. Named one of The Top 25 Most Powerful Women in Banking, US Banker mag., 2003. Mem.: America's Cmty. Bankers (pres. 2003). Avocations: creative writing, reading, music, travel. Office: First Fed Savs Port Angeles PO Box 351 Port Angeles WA 98362-0055

MCCORMICK, KATHLEEN ANN KRYM, geriatrics nurse, computer information specialist, federal agency administrator; b. Manchester, N.H., June 27, 1947; BSN, Barry Coll., 1969; MSN, Boston U., 1971; MS, U. Wis., 1975, PhD, 1978. Capt. nurse officer USPHS, COSTEP nurse, 1968, staff nurse, instr. Brighton, Mass., 1970; staff nurse Mercy Hosp., Miami, 1969, St. Elizabeth's Hosp., Brighton, 1970—71; clin. nurse specialist Boston U. Hosp., 1970—71; clin. nurse specialist, instr. U. Wis., Madison, 1971—72; asst. rsch. to chief nursing clin. ctr., dept. Nursing NIH, Bethesda, 1978—83; rsch. nurse, co-dir. inpatient geriatric continence project, Lab. Behavioral Scis., Gerontology Rsch. Ctr. Nat. Inst. Aging, Balt., 1983—88, dir. nursing rsch., 1988—91; dir. office forum quality and effectiveness health care Agy. Health Care Policy and Rsch., Rockville, Md., 1991—93, sr. sci. adviser, 1993—. Adj. asst. prof. Cath. U., Washington, 1979, Washington, 82; faculty assoc. U. Md., Balt., 1979—81; ad hoc reviewer biomed. rsch. grants NIH, 1979—80, divns. nursing rsch. and tng. HRA, 1979—82; instr. Found. Advanced Edn. in Scis., 1981—82; exec. com. Bat. Inst. Aging Liaison Ctr. Nursing Rsch., 1986—91; Surgeon Gen.'s rep. Sec. Alzheimer's Task Force19089, 1989—; Surgeon Gen. alt. to Bd. Regents Nat. Libr. Medicine, 1989—; co-chair panel guidelines for urinary incontinence in adult, 1990—91; spkr. in field. Editor: Nursing Outlook, 1988—90; mem. editl. staff: Mil. Medicine, 1985—93, assoc. editor: Internat. Jour. Tech. and Aging, 1985—87. Recipient award, Jour. Acad. Sci., 1965, travel award, NSF, 1973, J.D. Lane Jr. Investigator award, USPHS Profl. Assn., 1979, Excellence in Writing award, Nat. League Nursing/Humana, 1983, award Spl. Recognition Rsch., U. Pa. Sch. Nursing, 1986, Fed. Svc. Nursing award, 1987, Surgeon Gen.'s medallion, 1989; grantee, U. Wis. Grad. Sch., 1977, Upjohn Co., 1977; scholar Queen's Vis. scholar, Royal Adelaide (Australia) Hosp., 1990. Fellow: NAS Inst. Medicine, Gerontologic Soc. Am. (clin. med. sect., computer program coord. 1985—87, clin. medicine rep. publs. com., Nurse of Yr. 1992), Coll. Am. Med. Informatics, Royal Coll. Nursing (Australia), Am. Acad. Nursing; mem.: AACN (strategic planning com. 1987—89, Disting. Rsch. award 1986), ANA (editor newsletter coun. nurse rschrs. 1980—85, vice chairperson exec. com. coun. computer applications in nursing 1984—86, sec.), Md. Lung Assn. (awards and grants subcom. 1978, 1992, v.p. exec. bd. dirs. 1980—87), Met. Area Nursing Rsch. Consortium, Commd. Officers Assn., Assn. Mil. Surgeons (Sustaining Mem. award 1982), Internat. Med. Informatics Assn. (working group 8, program com. 1984—), Acad. Medicine, Am. Med. Informatics Assn. (bd. dirs.), Am. Lung Assn./Am. Thoracic Soc. (chairperson 1983—84, nominating com. 1989, nat. rsch. rev. com., cert. appreciation mid.-Md. chpt. 1982, 1983, 1984), Capital Spkrs. Club (10M), Am. News Women's Club, Sigma Theta Tau (grantee 1976), Sigma Delta Epsilon (Eloise Gerry grant-in-aid fellow 1979—80), Lambda Sigma. Office: 540 Gaither RD Rockville MD 20850-6649

MCCORMICK, KENNETH L. pediatrics educator, researcher; BS in Chem. Engring., U. Pa., 1970; MD, U. Rochester, 1974. Diplomate Am. Bd. Pediat., Am. Bd. Pediatric Endocrinology. Intern in pediat. U. Hosp. Cleve., Case Western Reserve U., 1974—75, resident in pediat., 1975—76; instr., rsch. and clin. fellow in pediat. metabolism/diabetes Brown U., R.I. Hosp., Providence, 1976—79; asst. prof. pediat. U. Rochester (N.Y.), 1979—85, assoc. prof. pediat., 1985—88, SUNY Health Sci. Ctr., Syracuse, 1988—92; assoc. prof. pediat., dir. metabolism and diabetes Med. Coll. of Wis., Milw., 1993—98; dir. pediat. endocrinology, diabetes and metabolism So. Ill. U., Peoria, 1998—. Editl. bd. Endocrinology, 1993—, reviewer Metabolism, Am. Jour. Diseases in Children, Endocrinology, Am. Jour. of Physiology, contbr. articles and revs. to profl. jours., chpts. to books. Fellow NIH, 1978—79; grantee Kroc Found., 1981—83, NIH, 1982—87, 1993—, Wilson Found., 1984—85, Upjohn Co., 1985, Squibb Novo, 1994—95, Am. Heart Assn., 1995—. Mem.: Endocrinology Soc., Am. Diabetes Assn. (bd. dirs. Rochester affiliate 1980—88, grantee 1994—96, Rsch. award 1995).

MCCORMICK, KIMBERLY A, elementary school educator; d. Russell Kerr and Sydney Shumaker; m. Rodney W. McCormick, Aug. 25, 1979; children: Kaycee L, Nicolette F. BS, Slippery Rock U., 1984—87; M, Westminster Coll., 1988—92. Elem. tchr. New Wilmington Ele. Sch., New Wilmington, PA 16142, Pa., 1988—. Sec. Lawrence Co. Reading Coun., New Castle, Pa., 2000—03. Author The Way I See It. R-Consevative. Bapt. Avocations: walking, writing, singing, acting. Office: Wilmington Ele School 450 Wood St New Wilmington PA 16142

MCCORMICK, MARIE CLARE, pediatrician, educator; b. Haverhill, Mass., Jan. 7, 1946; d. Richard John and Clare Bernadine (Keleher) McC.; m. Robert Jay Blendon, Dec. 30, 1977. BA magna cum laude, Emmanuel Coll., 1967; MD, Johns Hopkins U., 1971, ScD, 1978; MA, Harvard U., 1991. Diplomate Am. Bd. Pediat. Pediatric resident, fellow Johns Hopkins Hosp., Balt., 1971-75, rsch. fellow, 1972-75; asst. prof. U. Ill. Schs. Medicine & Pub. Health, Chgo., 1975-76; pediat. instr. Johns Hopkins Med. Sch., Balt., 1976-78; asst. prof. healthcare orgn. Johns Hopkins Sch. Hygiene & Pub. Health, 1978-81; asst. prof. pediat. U. Pa., Phila., 1981-86, assoc. prof. pediat., 1986-87, Harvard Med. Sch., Boston, 1987-91, prof. pediat., 1992—, 1st Sumner and Esther Feldberg prof. maternal/child health, 1996—; prof. Harvard Sch. Pub. Health, Boston, 1992—2003, chair maternal and child health, 1992—2003, prof. Soc., Human Devel. and Health, 2003—. Adj. assoc. prof. pediat. U. Pa., 1987-92; active attending physician, Johns Hopkins Hosp., 1976-81, asst. physician Children's Hosp. Phila., 1981-84, assoc. physician, 1984-86, sr. physician, 1986-87, assoc. pediatrician Brigham & Women's Hosp., 1987—; sr. assoc. in medicine Children's Hosp., 1987—; sr. assoc. in pediat. Beth Israel Deaconess Med. Ctr., 1987—; vis. prof. Wash. U., St. Louis, 1993; editl. bds. Health Svcs. Rsch., 1985-94, Pediat. in Rev., 1986-91, Pediat., 1993-99; assoc. editor Jour. Ambulatory Pediatric Assn., 1999—; adv. coun. Ctr. Perinatal & Family Health Brigham & Women's Hosp., 1991—; cons. to numerous coms., orgns. and bds. Contbr. articles to profl. jours. Adv. The David and Lucile Packard Found., 1993-95; bd. dirs. Family Planning Coun. S.E. Pa., 1984-87; chair com. child health Mayor's Commn. Phila., 1982-83. Named Henry Strong Denison scholar Johns Hopkins Sch. Medicine, 1971, Leonard Davis Inst.; Health Econs. fellow U. Pa. 1984, recipient Johns Hopkins U. Soc. Scholars award, 1995. Fellow Am. Acad. Pediat.; mem. AAAS, Inst. Medicine of NAS, Ambulatory Pediat. Assn. (Rsch. award 1996), Soc. Pediatric Rsch. (sr.), Am. Pediatric Soc., Am. Pub. Health Assn., Internat. Epidemiol. Assn., Assn. Health Svcs. Rsch., Ea. Soc. Pediatric Rsch., Soc. Pediatric Epidemiologic Rsch., Assn. Tchrs. Maternal and Child Health, Mass. Med. Soc., Norfolk Dist. Med. Soc., Mass. Pub. Health Assn., Johns Hopkins U. Soc. Scholars, NAS (nat. assoc.). Office: Harvard Sch Pub Health 677 Huntington Ave Boston MA 02115-6096 E-mail: mmccormi@hsph.harvard.edu.

MCCORMICK, MICHAEL JERRY, retired judge; b. Fort Lewis, Wash., Oct. 17, 1945; s. Thaddeus Charles and Geraldine (Fogle) McC.; m. Katleen Karen Kelley, Sept. 2, 1967; children: Patrick Kelley, Karen Michelle. BA, U. Tex.-Austin, 1967; JD, St. Mary's U., 1970. Bar: Tex. 1970. Briefing atty. Tex. Ct. Criminal Appeals, 1970-71; asst. dist. atty. Travis County, Tex., 1971-72; exec. dir. Tex. Dist. and County Attys. Assn., Austin, 1972-80; judge Tex. Ct. Criminal Appeals, Austin, 1981—2001, chief presiding judge, 1988-2000, sr. judge, 2001—; of counsel Law Office Kelley McCormick, Lockhart, Tex., 2002—. Dir. Tex. Ctr. for Judiciary, 1983; vice-chmn. Tex. Commn. on Sentencing, 1984; mem. Tex. Jud. Budget Bd., 1983; co-chair Tex. Jud. Coun., 1997—. Author: Branch's Annotated Penal Code, 3d edit., Criminal Forms and Trial Manual, 10th edit., Tex. Justice Court Deskbook, Tex. Constables Civil Process Handbook. Pres. Joslin (Tex.) P.T.A., 1981-82. Served with U.S. Army, 1966-72. Named Rosewood Gavel Outstanding Jurist, St. Mary's U. Sch. Law, 1984, Disting. Law Grad., 1992. Mem. State Bar Tex., Tex. Dist. and County Attys. Assn. Office: 119 W San Antonio St Lockhart TX 78644

MCCORMICK, RICHARD, retired telecommunications company executive; b. Fort Dodge, Iowa, July 4, 1940; s. Elmo Eugene and Virgilla (Lawler) McC.; m. Mary Patricia Smola, June 29, 1963; children: John Richard, Matthew David, Megan Ann, Katherine Maura. BS in Elec. Engring., Iowa State U., 1961. With Bell Telephone Co., 1961-85; N.D. v.p., CEO Northwestern Bell Telephone Co., Fargo, 1974-77; asst. v.p. human resources AT&T, Basking Ridge, N.J., 1977-78; sr. v.p. Northwestern Bell, Omaha, 1978-82, pres., CEO, 1982-85; exec. v.p. U S West Inc., Englewood, Colo., 1985-86; pres., COO U S West Inc. (now Qwest), Englewood, Colo., 1986-90, pres., CEO, 1990-91, chmn., pres., CEO, 1992—, chmn. emeritus; bd. mem., pres.-elect Internat. C. of C.; ret. Bd. dirs. Norwest Corp., United Airlines Corp., Health Trio. Mem. Phi Gamma Delta. Office: Health Trio Corp Office 102 Woodmont Blvd Ste 200 Nashville TN 37205

MCCORMICK, RICHARD LEVIS, academic administrator; b. New Brunswick, N.J., Dec. 26, 1947; s. Richard Patrick and Katheryne Crook (Levis) McCormick; m. Suzanne Dee Lebsock, Aug. 30, 1984; children: Elizabeth, Michael. BA in Am. Studies, Amherst Coll., 1969; PhD in History, Yale U., 1976. From asst. prof. to prof. Rutgers U., New Brunswick, NJ, 1976—92, dean Faculty Arts and Scis., 1989—92; exec. vice chancellor, provost, vice chancellor acad. affair U. N.C., Chapel Hill, 1992—95; pres. U. Wash., Seattle, 1995—2002, Rutgers U., New Brunswick, NJ, 2002—. Author: From Realignment to Reform: Political Change in New York State 1893-1910, 1981, The Party Period and Public Policy: American Politics from the Age of Jackson to the Progressive Era, 1986. Fellow, Am. Coun. Learned Socs., 1978—79, John Simon Guggenheim Meml. Found., 1985. Mem.: Phi Beta Kappa. Home: 1245 River Rd Piscataway NJ 08854 Office: Rutgers Univ New Brunswick NJ 08901

MC CORMICK, RICHARD PATRICK, history professor; b. N.Y.C., Dec. 24, 1916; s. Patrick Austin and Anna (Smith) McC.; m. Katheryne Crook Levis, Aug. 25, 1945; children: Richard Levis, Dorothy Irene. BA, Rutgers U., 1938, MA, 1940, LittD (hon.), 1982; PhD, U. Pa., 1948. Historian, Phila. Q.M. Depot, 1942-44; instr. U. Del., 1944-45; mem. faculty Rutgers U., 1945—, univ. historian, 1948—; dean Rutgers Coll., 1974-77, Univ. prof. history, 1977-82, Univ. prof. emeritus, 1982—. Research adviser Colonial Williamsburg, 1953-61; Fulbright lectr. Cambridge (Eng.) U., 1961-62; Commonwealth lectr. U. London, 1971; chmn. N.J. Hist. Commn., 1967-70 Author: Experiment in Independence, 1950, History of Voting in N.J, 1953, N.J. From Colony to State, 1964, Second American Party System, 1966, Rutgers: a Bicentennial History, 1966, The Presidential Game, 1982, The Black Student Protest Movement at Rutgers, 1990; co-author: The Case of the Nazi Professor, 1989. Mem. N.J. Tercentenary Commn., 1958-60, Am. Revolution Bicentennial Commn., 1971-74. Social Sci. Research Council fellow, 1956-57 Mem. Am. Hist. Assn. (scholarly distinction award 2003), Soc. Historians of Early American Republic (pres. 1988-89), N.J. Hist. Soc. (pres. 1950-57), Phi Beta Kappa. Mailing: 115 Monroe St Bridgewater NJ 08807

MCCORMICK, ROBERT JUNIOR, former government official, air transportation executive; b. Boone, Iowa, Aug. 1, 1929; s. Ivyl Robert and Darlene Adel (Bowes) McC.; m. Shirley May Zerbe, Dec. 24, 1950; children: Elaine McCormick Newland, Kathleen, Michael, Tara McCormick Wieting, Tammy McCormick Kirby. Grad., Flying Sch., Williams Field, Ariz., 1951, Parachute Jump Sch., 1964, Armed Forces Staff Coll., Norfolk, Va., 1966, Def. Systems Mgmt. Coll., Ft. Belvoir, Va., 1975; BS in Mech. Engring., Tex. Tech. U., 1963; cert., Harvard U. Def. Studies Program, 1984. Served as enlisted man USAF, 1948—51, commd. 2d lt., 1951, advanced through grades to col., 1971, pilot, fighter pilot Korean War, 1951—52; exec. officer to Gen. George Brown 7th Air Force, Saigon, Vietnam, 1969—70; mil. asst. to asst. sec. of Air Force for research and devel. USAF, Washington, 1970—74, ret., 1975; exec. officer NASA, Washington, 1976—80; adminstrv. asst. to sec. of Air Force USAF, Washington, 1980—94; mem. U.S. Sr. Exec. Service, 1979—84; pres. McG, Ltd., Fairfax, Va. Mem. Pres.'s transition team Dept. of Def., 2001. Decorated Air Force Legion of Merit, Bronze star, Air medal, Meritorious Svc. medal, Air Force Exceptional Civilian Svc. medal, NASA Exceptional Svc. medal, 1980; recipient Presdl. Meritorious Rank, 1989, Disting. Civilian Svc. medal Dept. Def., 1994, Commendation medal State of Calif., 2001. Mem. ASME, DAV, Air Force Assn., Nat. Def. Indsl. Assn., Order of Daedalians, St. Andrews Soc. Washington, Mil. Order of Carabao, Chevaliers du Testevin. Clubs: Army-Navy Country (Fairfax, Va.). Office: 4035 Hadley Ln Fairfax VA 22032-1308 Fax: 703-978-1035. E-mail: mcgltd1@aol.com.

MCCORMICK, ROBERT MATTHEW, III, newspaper executive; b. N.Y.C., Dec. 31, 1938; s. Robert Matthew Jr. and Rita Patricia (McGuinness) McC.; m. Janet Severin Ahrens, Apr. 27, 1957; children: Susan Anne Heisler, Mary Teresa Berrier, Robert M. IV, Mark P. BA, Georgetown U., 1960; grad. advanced mgmt. program, Harvard U., 1978. Various sales and mktg. positions The Washington Post, 1962-76, v.p. sales, 1976-82; exec. v.p. Chgo. Sun-Times, 1982-83; sr. v.p., sales and mktg. San Francisco News Agy., 1984-86, pres., CEO, 1987-93; exec. v.p. South Jersey Pub. Co., Atlantic City, 1994—; pub. Press of Atlantic City. Bd. dirs. Noyes Mus., 1995—. Mem. Newspaper Assn. Am. (bd. dirs. 1998—), Burning Tree Club, Champion Hills Club, N.J. Press Assn. (bd. dirs. 1998—), Shoprite LPGA Classic (bd. dirs. 1998—). Home: 80 Old Hickory Trl Hendersonville NC 28739-8977

MCCORMICK, ROD, sculptor, art educator; b. Battle Creek, Mich., Sept. 2, 1952; s. Rodney Lawrence and Joan (Kaminsky) McC.; m. Barbara Mail, Dec. 29, 1985; children: Anna, Sonya. BFA, Tyler Sch. Art, 1974; MFA, RISD, 1978. Sculptor and metalsmith, Phila., 1974—; vis. prof. Kent State U., Ohio, 1978-79; prof. U. Arts, Phila., 1981—, chmn. crafts dept., 1993-94, 95-96. One-man shows include Owen Patrick Gallery, Phila., 1990, U. Arts, 1993, John Elder Gallery, N.Y.C., 1998, Design Arts Gallery, Drexel U., Phila., 1999; exhibited in group shows at Phila. Mus. Art, 1990, Pa. State U., 1991, Meredith Gallery, Balt., 1991, Leo Kaplan Modern Gallery, N.Y.C., 1992, Paley Design Ctr., Phila., 1993, Peter Joseph Gallery, N.Y.C., 1994, Md. Art Place, Balt., 1996, Pentimenti Gallery, Phila., 1996, Stedman Gallery-Rutgers, Camden, N.J., 1997, James Michener Art Mus., Doylestown, Pa., 1997, Art in City Hall, Phila., 1997, Ellipse Art Ctr., Arlington, Va., 1998. Recipient Young Americans Metal exhbn. award Am. Craft Mus., 1980; grantee Nat. Endowment Arts, 1990, Pa. Coun. Arts, 1991. Mem. Soc. N.Am. Goldsmiths, Internat. Sculpture Ctr. Home: PO Box 29578 Philadelphia PA 19144-0578 Office: University of the Arts 320 S Broad St Philadelphia PA 19102-4994

MCCORMICK, RODGER JOHN, biologist, educator, minister; b. Greensburg, Pa., Feb. 15, 1940; s. John Leander and Elizabeth Irene McCormick; m. Dixie Jean Helmick, June 13, 1964; children: Laurie Jean, Shawna Erin Populorum. BSc, Shippensburg (Pa.) U., 1962; MSc, U. of Md., 1965; EdD, The Pa. State U., 1973. Asst. prof. of biology Rocky Mountain Coll., Billings, Mont., 1966—69; adj. asst. prof. U. Ill., Champaign-Urbana, 1974—77; prof. biology W.Va., Buckhannon, 1977—2003; tchr. HS sci. Upshut County Bd. Edn., Buckhannon, 2003—. Content specialist Med. Sch. U. Ill., Champaign-Urbana, 1974—77. Contbr. articles to profl. jours. Dir. Champaign-Urbana Jaycees, 1975—76; chaplain troop 128 Boy Scouts Am., Buckhannon, 1993—2002; pastor United Meth. Ch., Tallmansville, W.Va., 1998—2002; W.Va. prayer adv. United Meth. Men, Buckhannon, 1990—; track (javelin) coach W.Va. Wesleyan Coll., Buckhannon, 1998—2002. Grantee, NSF, 1980, W.Va. Wesleyan Coll., 1994—95. Mem.: Soc. For Coll. Sci. Teachers (corr.), NSTA (corr.), W.Va. Sci. Teachers Assn. (corr.), W.Va. Acad. of Sci. (life; dir. symposium 1985—2002), Phi Sigma Soc. (corr.), Omicron Delta Kappa (life). Conservative. Methodist. Avocations: hiking, travel, carpentry, birdwatching. Home: 46 North Tenney Drive Buckhannon WV 26201 Personal E-mail: mccormick@3wlogic.net.

MCCORMICK, STEVEN THOMAS, insurance company executive; b. Phila., Dec. 18, 1955; s. Howard C. and Ruth Marion (Stahl) McC.; m. Helene Mary Trommler, Nov. 21, 1981; children: Matthew Thomas, Bria Helene. BBA, U. Ky., 1978; gen. ins cert., Ins. Inst. Am., 1980. Cert. adminstrv. mgr., purchasing mgr., ins. agt., Ky., 1980. Supr. trainee Ky. Farm Bur. Ins. Cos., Louisville, 1978-79, supr. micrographics dept., 1979-83, supr. adminstrv. svcs., 1983-85, mgr. adminstrv. svcs., 1985-89; asst. v.p. ops., 1989—. Named to Hon. Order Ky. Cols., Outstanding Employee of Yr., Nat. Assn. of Mut. Ins. Cos., 1986; recipient Cert. of Excellence, Jefferson County Bd. Edn. Mem. Adminstrv. Mgmt. Soc. (internat. top recruiter 1985, chpt. pres. 1988, internat. dir. area 7 1990-91, internat. v.p. profl. devel. 1992-93), Acad. Adminstrv. Mgmt. (mem. bd. regents 1991-92, internat. v.p. 1992-93, internat. pres. 1993-94), U. Ky. Alumni Assn., Sigma Nu. Republican. Home: 706 Elsmere Cir Louisville KY 40223-2764 Office: Ky Farm Bur Ins Cos PO Box 20700 Louisville KY 40250-0700

MCCORMICK, TERRI, state legislator; b. Waupun, Wis., Oct. 24, 1956; married; 3 children. BS, U. Wis., 1980; postgrad., U. Windsor, Ont., Can., 1982, Lawrence U., 1993; MA, Marian Coll., 2000. Former edn. cons.; mem. Wis. State Assembly, Dist. 56, Madison, 2000—, mem. edn. reform, ins., judiciary, labor and workforce devel., pub. health and state/local fin. coms. Coach Xavier Mock Trial Team; mem. Winnebago County r. Mem.: Am. Legion Aux. Republican. Office: State Capitol Rm 127W PO Box 8953 Madison WI 53708-8953 Address: 3328 W Parkridge Ave Appleton WI 54914

MCCORMICK, THOMAS A., JR., city attorney; BBA, U. N.C., 1967, JD, 1973. Asst. to spkr. N.C. House Reps., 1973-74; city atty. Office of the City Atty., Raleigh, N.C., 1976—. Office: Office of City Attorney Raleigh Mcpl Bldg Rm 218 222 W Hargett St Raleigh NC 27601-1316

MCCORMICK, WILLIAM CHARLES, manufacturing executive; b. Glendale, Ohio, Oct. 24, 1933; s. Warren Starling and Helen Catherine (Haering) McC.; children— William Charles II, Timothy L., Anthony R. BS in Math., U. Cin., 1968. Mfg. engring. mgr. Gen. Electric Co., Evendale, Ohio, 1972-74, plant mgr. Lynn, Mass., 1974-76, mfg. mgr. Detroit, 1976-80, gen. mgr. Plainville, Conn., 1980-85; pres. Precision Castparts Corp., Portland, Oreg., 1985—. Served to sgt. U.S. Army, 1952-54; Korea Avocations: tennis; jogging; golf; reading. Address: Precision Castparts 4650 SW Macadam Ave Portland OR 97201

MCCORMICK, WILLIAM THOMAS, JR., electric and gas company executive; b. Washington, Sept. 12, 1944; s. William Thomas and Lucy Valentine (Offutt) McCormick; m. Ann Loretta du Mais, June 13, 1969; children: Christopher, Patrick. BS, Cornell U., 1966; PhD, M.I.T., 1969. Mem. staff Inst. for Def. Analysis, Arlington, Va., 1969—72; mem. staff Office of Sci. and Tech., Exec. office of the Pres., Washington, 1972—73; sr. staff mem. Energy Policy Office, The White House, 1973—74; chief sci. and energy tech. br. Office Mgmt. and Budget, Exec. Office of the Pres., 1974—75; dir. commercialization U.S. Energy Rsch. and Devel. Adminstrn., 1975—76; v.p. policy and govt. relations Am. Gas Assn., 1976—78; v.p., asst. to chmn. Am. Natural Resources Co., Detroit, 1978—80; exec. v.p. Mich. Wis. Pipeline Co., Am. Natural Resources System, Detroit, 1980—82; pres. Am. Natural Resources Co., Detroit, 1982—85; chmn., chief exec. officer Consumers Power Co., Jackson, Mich., 1985—92, chmn., 1992—2002, chmn., CEO CMS Energy Corp., 1985—2002. Bd. dirs. Bank One Corp., Rockwell Inst., Schlumberger Ltd. Prin. author, editor Commercialization of Synthetic Fuels in the U.S., 1975. Bd. dirs. McGregor Fund, St. John Hosp. Alfred P. Sloan scholar, 1962—66. Mem.: Detroit Club, Country Club Detroit, Detroit Athletic Club, Econ. Club Detroit (bd. dirs.). Roman Catholic. Office: CMS Energy Corp 1 Energy Plaza Dr Jackson MI 49201-2357

MCCORMICK, YUMI, language educator, translator; b. Yokkaichi, Mie, Japan, Aug. 16, 1958; arrived in U.S., 1990; d. Izaemon and Toyoko Moriguchi; m. Michael James McCormick, June 15, 1996; 1 child, Julie. BA, Notre Dame Women's Coll., Kyoto, Japan, 1981; MEd, Holy Names Coll., 1993; EdD, U. San Francisco, 1999. Lang. coord. Mie YMCA, Yokkaichi, 1983—90; instr. Linfield Coll., McMinnville, Oreg., 1990—91, Soko Gakuen Sch., San Francisco, 2000—, De Anza Coll., Cupertino, Calif., 2002—. Author: Y color in Colorado, 1995; translator: Showa Teihon, 1998. Home: 1865 Bush St #106 San Francisco CA 94109 Office: De Anza College 21250 Stevens Creek Blvd Cupertino CA 95014

MCCORQUODALE, J. ALEXANDER, civil and environmental engineer, educator; BA, U. Western Ont., Can.; MA in Fluid Mechanics, U. Glasgow, Scotland; PhD in Hydraulics, U. Windsor. With H.G. Acres Ltd., Niagara Falls, N.Y., 1964-66; prof. dept. civil and environ. engring. U. Windsor; FMI prof. dept. civil engring. Univ. New Orleans, 1996—. Recipient Harrison Prescott Eddy medal Water Environment Fedn., 1998. Fellow Can. Soc. Civil Engring. (past chair hydrotechnical divsn., Camille A. Dagenais award 1995). Office: Univ New Orleans Coll of Engring Dept Civil Engring 2000 Lakeshore Dr New Orleans LA 70122-3520

MCCOTTER, THADDEUS G. congressman; b. Detroit, Aug. 22, 1965; s. Dennis and Joan McCotter; m . Rita Michel; children: George, Timothy, Emilia. BA summa cum laude, U. Detroit, 1987, JD, 1990. Bar: Mich. 1991. Trustee Schoolcraft C.C., 1989; commr. Wayne County, Mich., 1992-98; mem. 9th dist. Mich. Senate, Lansing, 1998—2002; mem. U.S. Ho. of Reps from 3rd Mich. dist., 2003—. Rep. precinct del., 1986; chair Wayne County Rep. com. Republican. Office: 415 Cannon House Office Bldg Washington DC 20515-2211 also: 17197 N Laurel Pk Dr Ste 161 Livonia MI 48152-7908

MCCOURT, FRANK (FRANCIS MCCOURT), writer; b. Bklyn., Aug. 19, 1931; s. Malachy and Angela McCourt; m. Ellen McCourt. Bachelors, Masters, NYU. Tchr. McKee Vocat. and Tech. Sch., Peter Stuyvesant H.S., N.Y.C. Author: Angela's Ashes, 1996 (National Book Critics Circle award 1997, Pulitzer prize 1997), Tis: A memoir, 2000, Through Irish Eyes: Visual Companion to Angela in Court's Ireland, 2001, Brotherhood, 2001; (films) The McCourts of Limerick, 1998, The McCourts of NY, 1999. Address: Simon & Schuster Trade Division 1230 Avenue Of The Americas New York NY 10020-1513

MCCOVEY, WILLIE LEE, former professional baseball player; b. Mobile, Ala., Jan. 10, 1938; s. Frank and Ester (Jones) McC. Minor league baseball player, 1955-59; first baseman San Francisco Giants, 1959-73, 77-80, active in pub. rels., 1981-86, spl. asst. to pres., 1986-94; mem. San Diego Padres, 1974-76, Oakland Athletics, 1976-81. Named Nat. League Rookie of Year, 1959, Most Valuable Player, 1969; Home Run Champion, 1963, 68, 69; Runs Batted In Leader, 1968, 69; Comeback Player of Year, 1977; 10th on All-Time Major League List of Career Home Runs (521); All-Time Nat. League leader in grand slam home runs (18); mem. Nat. League All-Star Team, 1963, 66, 68-71; inducted into Baseball Hall of Fame, 1986 Office: c/o San Francisco Giants 24 Willie Mays Plz San Francisco CA 94107 also: Baseball Hall Fame PO Box 590 Cooperstown NY 13326-0590

MCCOWAN, OTIS BLAKELY, mathematics professor; b. Monterey, Tenn., June 17, 1934; s. Burton and Martha Catherine (Phipps) McC. BS, Tenn. Tech. U., 1959; MA, La. State U., 1966; PhD, Vanderbilt U., 1975. Mathematician Missile Devel. Ctr., Holloman AFB, N.Mex., 1962-63; math. tchr. Rhea Ctrl. H.S., Dayton, Tenn., 1963-65; math. instr. Kilgore (Tex.) Coll., 1966-67; asst. prof. math. Belmont U., Nashville, 1967-72, assoc. prof. math., 1972-75, prof. math., 1975—2004, prof. emeritus, 2004—. With U.S. Army, 1959-62. Named Outsting Young Educator in Rhea County, Dayton C. of C., 1964. Mem. Nat. Coun. Tchrs. Math., Math. Assn. Am., Tenn. Math. Tchrs. Assn., Kappa Delta Pi, Kappa Mu Epsilon, Pi Mu Epsilon, Omicron Delta Kappa, Alpha Chi (Region III v.p. 1980-82, pres. 1982-84, nat. v.p. 1991-93). Democrat. Baptist. Avocations: travel, gardening, reading, attending concerts and theatre. Home: 2205 18th Ave S Nashville TN 37212-5001 Office: Belmont Univ Dept Math and Computer Sci Nashville TN 37212 E-mail: mccowano@mail.belmont.edu.

MCCOWEN, ALEC, actor; b. Tunbridge Wells, May 26, 1925; s. Duncan and Mary (Walkden) McC., Ed. Skinners Sch., Tunbridge Wells, and Royal Acad. Dramatic Art. Appeared as Touchstone, Ford, Richard II, Mercutio, Malvolio, Oberon at Old Vic Theatre, 1959-60; appeared with R.S.C. as Fool in King Lear, 1964, Hadrian VII, 1968, The Philanthropist, 1970, The Misanthrope, 1972, as Dr. Dysart in Equus, 1972, as Henry Higgins in Pygmalion, 1974, as Ben in The Family Dance, 1976, Someone Who'll Watch Over Me, 1992, as Prospero in The Tempest, 1994, as Gaev in The Cherry Orchard, 1995; appeared with Prospect Co. as Antony in Antony and Cleopatra, 1977, in solo performance of St. Mark's Gospel, 1978, 81, as Frank in Tishoo, 1979, as Malvolio in Twelfth Night (TV), 1980, of Kipling, 1984, as Reilly in The Cocktail Party, 1986, as Nicolai in Fathers and Sons, 1987, as Vladimir in Waiting for Godot, 1987; appeared with Nat. Theatre and Abbey Dublin as Jack in Dancing at Cughnasa, 1990; appeared with Nat. Theatre as Crocker-Harris in The Browning Version, Arthur in Harlequinade, Capt. Corcoran in H.M.S. Pinafore, 1981, Adolf Hitler in The Portage to San Cristobal of AH, PTO, 1982, Reginald, in 2000 Quartet; films: Frenzy, 1971, Travels with My Aunt, 1973, Stevie, 1978, Personal Services, Cry Freedom, 1987, The Age of Innocence, 1992, Gangs of New York, 2000; TV: Private Lives, 1976; author: Young Gemini,1979, Double Bill, 1980, Personal Mark, 1984. Named Best Actor, Evening Standard (now New Standard), 1968, 73, 82, Variety Club Stage Actor, 1970. Office: care Conway Van Gelder 18-21 Jermyn St London SW1 Y6HB England

MCCOWN, GEORGE E. venture banking company executive; b. Portland, Oreg., July 1, 1935; s. Floyd Conly and Ada Elizabeth (Stephens) McC.; m. Karen Stone, Mar. 22, 1986; children: Taryn, Daniel, David; stepchildren: Bryan, Norman, Mark, Amy. BSME, Stanford U., 1957; MBA, Harvard U., 1962. Assoc. Am. Rsch. & Devel. Corp., 1962-63; from asst. to the pres. to sr. v.p. Boise (Idaho) Cascade, 1963-80; pres. Boise Cascase Home & Land Corp., 1974-80; chmn. Sequoia Corp., Boise, 1981—. Co-founder, mng. gen. ptnr. McCown De Leeuw & Co., Menlo Park, Calif., 1984—; chmn. bd. BMC West Corp., Vans, Inc.; bd. dirs. Specialty Paperboard Inc., Fitness Holding Inc. Trustee Stanford U., chmn. fin. com. and investment policy subcom., 1980-85; dir. Packard Childrens Hosp. Ctr. Econ. Policy Rsch., Stanford; trusteeNeuva Learning Ctr., Pacific Crest Outward Bound Sch.; chmn. bd. govs. Wyo. Centennial Everest Expdn.; mem., past chmn. policy adv. bd. Harvard Joint Ctr. Housing Studies, Ctr. Real Estate and Urban Econs., U. Calif. Berkeley; chmn. World Bus. Acad.; overseer Hoover Inst. War, Revolution and Peace. Capt. USAF, 1957-60. Mem. Harvard Bus. Assn. No. Calif. (chmn.), Chief Execs. Orgn., World Pres. Orgn., Explorers Club, Bus. Execs. Nat. Security, Bohemian Club. Republican. Avocations: classical piano, mountain climbing, adventure travel, aviation, tennis, skiing. Home: 250 Greer Rd Woodside CA 94062-4206 Office: McCown De Leeuw & Co Bldg 3-290 3000 Sand Hill Rd Menlo Park CA 94025-7141 E-mail: gmccown@mdcpartners.com.

MCCOWN, HALE, retired judge; b. Kansas, Ill., Jan. 19, 1914; s. Ross S. and Pauline (Collins) McC.; m. Helen Lanier, July 15, 1938; children: Robert B., William L., Mary Lynn. AB, Hastings Coll., 1935; LLB, Duke U., 1937. Bar: Oreg. 1937, Nebr. 1942. With firm Carey, Hart, Spencer & McCulloch, Portland, 1937-42; pvt. practice Beatrice, Nebr., 1942-65; ptnr. McCown, Baumfalk & Dalke; justice Supreme Court Nebr., 1965-83. Author articles in legal jours. Served to lt. USNR, 1943-45. Recipient Disting. Alumnus award Hastings Coll., 1981, Charles S. Murphy award Duke U., 1986, Legal Pioneer award Nebr. Bar Found., 1996, Alumni Appreciation award Duke U., 1981. Fellow Am. Coll. Trial Lawyers, Am. Coll. Trust and Estate Counsel; mem. ABA (legal ethics com. 1957-62), Nebr. Bar Assn. (chmn. ho. dels. 1955-56, pres. 1960-61), Am. Law Inst. (mem. council 1969—2000, emeritus 2000—), Am. Judicature Soc. Presbyterian.

MCCOY, CHARLES SHERWOOD, university president, former theology educator; b. Laurinburg, N.C., June 27, 1923; s. Clarence Latimer and Lutie Heber (Walker) McC.; m. Marjorie Louise Casebier, Dec. 28, 1971 (dec. Feb. 1985); children: Carroll, Marsha, Priscilla, Celia, Stephanie, Elizabeth. AS, Presbyn. Jr. Coll., Maxton, N.C., 1942; BA, U. N.C., 1943; MDiv, Duke U., 1945; PhD, Yale U., 1957; LHD (hon.), U. Hawaii, 1966; DLitt (hon.), St. Andrews Coll., Laurinburg, N.C., 1996. Ordained to ministry Meth. Ch., 1945. Pastor Creedmore (N.C.) United Meth. Ch., 1946-47; dir. Wesley Found., Raleigh, N.C., 1947-49; assoc. prof. religion U. Fla., Gainesville, 1954-59; Sproul prof. theol. ethics Grad. Theol. Union, Berkeley, Calif., 1967-98, Sproul prof. emeritus, 1998—; organizer, pres. Pan Pacific U., Oakland, Calif., 1999—. Vis. prof. U. N.C., Chapel Hill, Fresno (Calif.) State U., U. Calif., Santa Cruz, U. Tübingen, Germany, U. Münster, Germany; lectr. numerous univs., colls., including Danforth lectr. Assn. Am. Colls., Washington, 1963-64, 66-67; Fulbright sr. lectr., Germany, 1977-78; also U. Pacific, U. Puget Sound, Harvard U., Colo. State U., Syracuse U., Calif. State U., Bakersfield, San Francisco Theol. Sem., Kent State U., John Carroll U., U. Heidelberg and Bremen, Germany, Basel and Bern, Switzerland, also in Czech Republic, Japan, China, Republic of Korea; mem. exec. com. Fellowship So. Churchmen, Chapel Hill, N.C., 1944-52; founding exec. sec. Christian Action, New Haven, 1951-52; founder, sr. fellow dir. Ctr. for Ethics and Social Policy, Berkeley, 1974-81, Trinity Ctr. for Ethics and Corp. Policy, N.Y.C., 1981-90. Author: When Gods Change: Hope for Theology, 1980, Management of Values, 1985, Fountainhead of Federalism, 1991, The Greatness of America: People, Promise, Dream, 1994, also others; co-author: Ethics in the Corporate Policy Process, 1975. Frederick Buechner: Novelist/Theologian of the Lost and Found., 1988, also others; contbr. over 150 articles to theol. jours., chpts. to books. Pres. coun. on Human Rels., Gainesville, Fla., 1956-59; chmn. (with M.L. King, Jr.) Mission to Miss., Jackson, 1961; mem. Robert Kennedy Campaign Com., Calif.,1 968. Lt. USN, 1943-46, 52-54. Recipient Univ. medal U. Pacific, 1988; Lilly fellow Duke U., 1958. Mem. Am. Acad. Religion, Soc. Christian Ethics (sect. chmn. 1987), Pacific Coast Theol. Soc. (chmn., sec. 1979-81), Polanyi Soc. (Centennial lectr. 1991). Democrat. Avocations: tennis, golf, chess, reading. Home: 1191 Glen Ave Berkeley CA 94708 Office: Pan Pacific U 2362 Bancroft Way Berkeley CA 94704 E-mail: aenglert@psr.edu.

MCCOY, DOUGLAS LEON, lawyer; b. Atlanta, Mar. 15, 1957; s. Johnny L. and Nell (Wilson) McC.; m. Karen Delchamps, Jan. 3, 1987. BS, U. Tenn., 1979; JD, Duke U., 1982. Bar: Ala. 1982, U.S. Ct. Appeals (2d, 5th and 11th cirs.). Assoc. Hand, Arendall, LLC, Mobile, Ala., 1982—87, ptnr., 1987—. Lectr. in field. Mem. ABA (litig. sect.), Mobile Bar Assn. Methodist. Office: Hand Arendall LLC 107 St Francis St Ste 2600 Mobile AL 36602 Office Phone: 251-694-6255. E-mail: dmccoy@handarendull.com.

MCCOY, DOUGLAS MICHAEL, social services administrator, clergyman; b. Altadena, Calif., Jan. 29, 1945; s. Burton Douglas and Margaret Ellen (Ledbetter) McC.; m. Edna Catherine DeChambeau, Mar. 23, 1968; children: Douglas Arthur, Robert Carl, Lewis Aaron. AA, Sacramento City Coll., 1964; BA in Am. History, Literature, Univ. Calif., 1966; MDiv., Pacific Sch. Religion, 1969. Ordained elder Meth. Ch. Youth dir. First United Meth. Ch., Redwood City, Calif., 1967-68; assoc. pastor 1st United Meth. Ch., Redwood City, 1968-69; pastor Cmty. United Meth. Ch., Georgetown, Calif., 1969-71, Christ United Meth. Ch., Sacramento, 1971-73; assoc. pastor 1st United Meth. Ch., Reno, 1973-82; exec. dir. Kairos Outreach, Inc., Reno, 1982-88, Nome (Alaska) Cmty. Ctr., Inc., 1988-2000; pastor Susanville (Calif.) United Meth. Ch., 2000—. Founder, spiritual dir. Nev. Kairos Prison Ministry, Reno, 1981-87. Pres. No. Nev. Sponsoring Com., Reno, 1975-78, AGENET, 1998-99; pres. Planned Parenthood, Reno, 1981-85, Mental Health Adv. Com., Nome, 1988-91, Nome Visitor's Assn., 1990-94; chmn. Interagy. Child Advocates, Nome, 1988-91; active Action for Alaska Children, 1990-97; chmn. exec. com., Alaska Food Coalition, 1999-2000; chmn. Lassen County Children and Family Commn., 2002—. Mem.: Rotary. Democrat. Office: Susanville United Meth Ch 70 S Lassen St Susanville CA 96130 E-mail: divenome@aol.com.

MCCOY, FREDERICK JOHN, retired plastic surgeon; b. McPherson, Kans., Jan. 17, 1916; s. Merle D. and Mae (Tennis) McC.; m. Mary Bock, May 17, 1972; children: Judith, Frederick John, Patricia, Melissa, Steven. BS, U. Kans., 1938, MD, 1942. Diplomate Am. Bd. Plastic Surgery (dir. 1973-79, chmn. 1979). Intern Lucas County Hosp., Toledo, 1942-43; resident in plastic surgery U. Tex. Med. Sch., Galveston, 1946; preceptorship in surgery Grand Rapids, Mich., 1947-50; practice medicine specializing in plastic and reconstructive surgery Kansas City, Mo., 1950-93; staff St. Mary's Hosp., 1950-83, St. Joseph's Hosp., 1950—, N. Kansas City Meml. Hosp., 1955—; mem. staff, chief plastic surgery Kansas City Gen. Hosp. and Med. Center, 1952-72, Children's Mercy Hosp., 1954-93, Research Hosp., 1950—, St. Luke's Hosp., 1951—, Baptist Hosp., 1958—, Menorah Hosp., 1950—; chief div. plastic surgery Truman Med. Ctr., 1972-91; chmn. maxillo-facial surgery U. Kansas City Sch. Dentistry, 1950-57; assoc. prof. surgery U. Mo. Med. Sch., Kansas City, 1964-69, clin. prof. surgery, 1969—; pres. McCoy Enterprises, Kansas City, Mo. Contbr. articles to, profl. jours.; editor: Year Book of Plastic and Reconstructive Surgery, 1971-88. Bd. govs. Kansas City Mus., 1959-93, pres., 1973-74. Served to maj. M.C. U.S. Army, 1943-46. Mem. ACS (pres. Mo. chpt. 1973), AMA, Am. Acad. Pediatrics, Am. Soc. Plastic and Reconstructive Surgeons (sec. 1969-73, dir. 1973-76, pres. 1976, chmn. bd. 1977, Spl. Achievement award 1988), Am. Soc. Pediat. Plastic Surgeons, Pan Pacific Surg. Soc., Singleton Surg. Soc. (v.p. 1965), Am. Assn. Plastic Surgeons (founder plastic surgery rsch. coun.), Internat. Soc. Aesthetic Plastic Surgery, Am. Soc. Aesthetic Plastic Surgery, Jackson County Med. Soc. (pres. 1964-65), Kansas City Southwest Clin. Soc. (pres. 1971), Mo. Med. Assn. (v.p. 1975), Internat. Coll. Surgeons (v.p. 1969), Royal Soc. Medicine (London), U. Tex. Sys. Chancellors Coun., Kansas City C. of C., Conservation Fedn. Mo., Natural Sci. Soc. (founder, chmn. 1973), Citizens Assn. Kansas City, Explorer's Club, Mission Hills Country Club, Boone and Crocket Club, Phi Delta Theta, Nu Sigma Nu. Republican. Mem. Christian Ch. Office: 801 W 47th St Ste 421 Kansas City MO 64112-1253 Home: 542 S Anemone Drive Four Seasons MO 65049-9495

MCCOY, GORDON R. minister; s. Herman G. and Dorothy McCoy; life ptnr. Eugene M. Thomas. BA, Macalester Coll., St. Paul, 1961; MDiv, McCormick Theol. Sem., Chgo., 1964. Ordained minister Met. Cmty. Ch., 1991. Grants adminstr. Ill. Dept. of Mental Health and Devel. Disabilities, Chgo. and Elgin, 1972—84, Ctr. on Deafness, Northbrook, Ill., 1984—97, dir., cmty. outreach programs, 1997—99; sr. pastor Ch. of the Resurrection MCC, Chgo., 1984—97; pastor Met. Cmty. Ch. of the Fox Valley, Elgin, Ill., 2002—; dir. of program devel. Mental Health and Deafness Resources, Inc., Northbrook, Ill., 2000—03. Editor: Ill. Railgram, 2004—. Dir. at large NARP, 2004; editor Ill. Railgram, 2004—; west area coord. Gt. Lakes Dist., UFMCC, Chgo., 1998—2002; regional dir. Nat. Assn. R.R. Passengers, Washington, 2002; bd. dirs. Ill. Assn. R.R. Passengers, Chgo., 2001—. Named Clergyperson of the Yr., Gt. Lakes Dist., Met. Cmty. Chs., 1994. Avocations: travel, reading. Personal E-mail: grmchitown@aol.com.

MCCOY, JEANIE SHEARER, analytical chemist, consultant; b. Mancelona, Mich., May 27, 1921; d. Theophil R. and Goldie Margaret (Halladay) Schroeder; m. Theodore R. Shearer, June 14, 1958 (div. 1964); 1 child, Blair Barnett; m. George Altha McCoy, July 23, 1966. AA, North Pk. coll., 1941; BS, Northwestern U., 1944; MS, No. Ill. U., 1970. Jr. analytical chemist Buick Motor divsn. GM, Melrose Park, Ill., 1944—45; asst. rsch. chemist Hodson Oil Corp., Chgo., 1945—47; asst. analytical chemist Internat. Harvester Co., Melrose Park, 1947—49, analytical chemist, 1949—60, prin. chemist, 1968—74, supr. metal process control, 1974—82; cons. cutting fluid mgmt. divsn. IMT Inc., Lombard, Ill., 1983—2003; cons. Cutting Fluid Mgmt. Co., Lombard, 2004—. Editor: Lubrication Engring. Mag., 1979-2000; author: (monograph chpt.) Metalworking Fluids, 1993 Fellow Soc. Tribologists and Lubrication Engrs. (Allan Mantafel award Chgo. sect. 1987, P.M. KU award, 1991, Internat. award 2000); mem. AAUW, Soc. Automotive Engrs., Am. Chem. Soc., Abrasive Engring. Soc., Soc. Mfg. Engrs. Avocations: shell and stamp collecting, fitness activities. Home and Office: 654 N West Rd Lombard IL 60148-1547 E-mail: j10mccoy@aol.com.

MCCOY, JOHN BONNET, retired bank executive; b. Columbus, Ohio, June 11, 1943; s. John Gardner and Jeanne Newlove (Bonnet) McC.; m. Jane Deborah Taylor, Apr. 21, 1968; children: Tracy Bonnet, Paige Taylor, John Taylor. BA, Williams Coll., 1965; MBA, Stanford U., 1967; LLD (hon.), Williams Coll., 1991; D of Bus. Adminstrn. (hon.), Ohio State U., 1993; LLD (hon.), Kenyon Coll., 1994. With Banc One Corp., Columbus NA, Columbus, Ohio, 1970—, banking officer, 1970-73, v.p., 1973-77, pres., 1977-83; pres., COO Banc One Corp., Columbus, Ohio, 1983-84, pres., CEO, 1984-87, chmn., CEO, 1987-99, also bd. dirs., past chmn., CEO Chgo., 1999. Pres., COO Banc One Corp., Columbus, Ohio, 1983-84, pres., CEO, 1984-87, chmn. CEO, 1987—, also bd. dirs.; pres. Bank One Trust Co., 1979-81; bd. dirs. Cardinal Health, Inc., Fed. Home Loan Mortgage Corp., SBC Corp., Choice Point, Inc., InsLogic, Loews Cineplex Entertainment; fed. adv. coun. Fed. Res. Sys., 1991-93. Active Boy Scouts Am.; trustee, chmn. bd. dirs. Kenyon Coll., 1992-95; trustee Stanford U., 1986-96, Williams Coll., 1996-2001, Battelle Meml. Inst.; bd. dirs. PGA Tour; past pres. Columbus Area Growth Found.; chmn. Capitol South Urban Redevel. Corp. Capt. USAF, 1967-70. Recipient Ernest C. Arbuckle award Stanford U., 1994. Mem. Columbus C. of C. (past chmn., trustee), Am. Bankers Assn., Bankers Roundtable (bd. dirs. 1989-94), Assn. Bank Holding Cos., Young Pres. Orgn. (chmn. Columbus chpt. 1982-83), Cypress Point Club, Seminole Golf Club, Links Club N.Y.C. Episcopalian. Office: Banc One Corp 191 W Nationwide Blvd Ste 625 Columbus OH 43215

MCCOY, JOHN DENNY, artist; b. Columbus, Ohio, Dec. 13, 1945; s. Robert William and Dorothy Louise (Denny) McC.; children: Melinda Rene and Nathan Robert. Cert. of Grad., Columbus Coll. Art and Design, 1967; MFA, Washington U., St. Louis, 1969. Instr. Columbus Coll. Art and Design, Ohio, 1969—73; program dir. Presidio of Monterey, Calif., 1975—78; gallery dir. Richard Danskin Gallery, Carmel, Calif., 1978—79, Bleich Gallery West, Carmel, Calif., 1979—80. One person shows include: Brunswick Gallery, Columbus, 1973, Seaside, Calif. City Hall, 1978, Bleich Gallery, Carmel, Calif., 1980, Angles Gallery, Santa Monica, Calif., 1987, Hagger Gallery, Dallas, 1999, Flatbed Gallery, Austin, Tex., 2000, O2 Gallery, Austin, Tex., 2004; exhibited in group shows at Columbus Mus. Art, 1965, Laclede Town Gallery, St. Louis, 1967, Merton Boyd Gallery, Columbus, 1970, Changing Scene Gallery, 1971-72, Gallery Five, Columbus, 1972, Monterey Peninsula Mus. Art, 1976-77, Angles Gallery, Santa Monica, 1989, Richard Bennett Gallery, L.A., 1991, Arlington Mus. Art, 1998, Meridian Internat. Ctr., Washington, Vietnam, China, Singapore, Indonesia, 1999-2000, Haggerty Gallery, Dallas, 2000, David Berman Gallery, Austin, Tex., 2002 Columbus Coll. Art and Design scholar, 1963; Ford Found. grantee, 1966; Washington U. fellow, 1968-69. Home: 4606 Ave C Austin TX 78751-3026

MCCOY, JOHN JOSEPH, lawyer; b. Cin., Mar. 15, 1952; s. Raymond F. and Margaret T. (Hohmann) McC. BS in Math. summa cum laude, Xavier U., 1974; JD, U. Chgo., 1977. Bar: Ohio 1977, D.C. 1980. Ptnr. Taft, Stettinius & Hollister, Cin., 1977—, exec. com., 2002—. Lectr. Greater Cin. C. of C., 1984. Pro bono rep. Jr. Achievement Greater Cin., 1978; fund raiser Dan Beard coun. Boy Scouts Am., 1983; fund raising team leader Cin. Regatta, Cin. Ctr. Devel. Disorders, 1983; account mgr. United Appeal, Cin., 1984; mem. green areas trust adv. com. Village of Indian Hill, 1994-98. Mem. ABA, Ohio State Bar Assn. (banking, comml. and bankruptcy law com., corp. law com., fed. ct. practice com.), Cin. Bar Assn. (fed. cts., common pleas cts. and negligence law coms., trustee Vol. Lawyers for the Poor Fund. 1994—, chmn. 1996-97), Cin. Inn. of Ct. (barrister 1984-86), Cin. Athletic Club (pres. bd. trustees 1986-89, nominating com. 1989—), Rhodesian Ridgeback Club of the U.S. (bd. dirs. 2000—).

MCCOY, LOIS CLARK, emergency services professional, retired county official, magazine editor; b. New Haven, Oct. 1, 1920; m. Herbert Irving McCoy, Oct. 17, 1943; children: Whitney, Kevin, Marianne, Tori, Debra, Sally, Daniel. BS, Skidmore Coll., 1942; student, Nat. Search and Rescue Sch., 1974. Asst. buyer R.H. Macy & Co., N.Y.C., 1942-44, assoc. buyer, 1944-48; instr. Mountain Medicine & Survival, U. Calif., San Diego, 1973-74; cons. editor Search & Rescue Mag., 1975, Rescue Mag., 1988-97, editor, 1992-94, Press On Newsletter, 1992—2000. Coord. San Diego Mountain Rescue Team, La Jolla, Calif., 1973-75; exec. sec. Nat. Assn. for Search and Rescue, Inc., Nashville, La Jolla, 1975-80, comptr., 1980-82; disaster officer San Diego County, 1980-86, Santa Barbara County, 1985-91, ret.; pres. Nat. Inst. Urban Search & Rescue, Inc., 1987—; assoc. dir. Armed Forces Commns. and Electronics Assn., 2003—. Author: Search and Rescue Glossary, 1974; contbr. editor Rescue Mag., 1989-97; editor-in-chief Response! mag., 1982-86; editor Press On! Electronic mag., 1994—; mem. adv. bd. Hazard Monthly, 1991-99; contbr. articles to profl. jours. Cons. law enforcement divsn. Calif. Office Emergency Svcs., 1976-77; pres. San Diego Com. for L.A. Philharm. Orch., 1957-58; bd. dirs. Search and Rescue of the Californias, 1976-77, Nat. Assn. for Search and Rescue, Inc., 1980-87, pres., 1985-87, trustee, 1987-90, mem. Calif. OES strategic com., 1992-96; CEO Nat. Inst. for Urban Search, 1989—; mem. Gov.'s Task Force on Earthquakes, 1981-82, Earthquake Preparedness Task Force, Seismic Safety Commn., 1982-85, Army Sci. and Tech. Commn., 2003; mem. adv. coun. Nat. Meml. Inst. for the Protection from Terrorism. Recipient Hall Foss award for outstanding svc. to search and rescue, 1982, Diamond Safety award for outstanding work in emergency svcs., 1996; named to "The Fed. 100", 2002. Mem.: IEEE, Armed

Forces Comm. and Electronics Assn. (named to Army Sci. and Tech. com. for Homeland Def. 2003—04, bd. dirs. 2003—04), San Diego Mountain Rescue (life), Nat. Assn. Search and Rescue (life Svc. award 1985, 2002), Santa Barbara Amateur Radio Club. Episcopalian. Office: PO Box 91648 Santa Barbara CA 93190-1648 Office Phone: 800-767-0093. Personal E-mail: niusr@cox.net.

MCCOY, MARY ANN, state official; b. Duluth, Minn., Oct. 13, 1924; d. Homer Burke and Avis (Woodworth) Hursh; m. Charles Ramon McCoy, June 11, 1949; children: Jeffrey, Mary, Jeremy. BA, Grinnell Coll., 1946; postgrad., Laval U., 1946, Mankato State U., 1964-65. Cert. neutral mediator Minn. Supreme Ct. 1996—. Exec. trainee Younkers, Inc., Des Moines, 1946; advt. copywriter Des Moines Register & Tribune, 1947; field dir. Duluth (Minn.) Girl Scout Coun., 1947-49; with merchandising dept. Dayton's Inc., Mpls., 1966-75; dir. election and legis. manual divsn. Office of Sec. of State of Minn., St. Paul, 1975-81; exec. dir. Minn. State Ethical Practices Bd., St. Paul, 1981-95, cons., 1996—. Mem. Minn. Supreme Ct. Bd. for Continuing Legal Edn., 1981-87; sec. State Rev. Bd. for Nominations to Nat. Register, 1976-89. Editor Minn. Legis. Manual, 1975-81. Mem. Minn. Hist. Soc. (life, hon. coun., exec. coun. 1972-81, 82-90), Coun. on Govt. Ethics Laws (steering com. 1986-89, treas. 1987-88, hon. life), Minn. Assn. Pub. Adminstrs., Am. Judicature Soc., Internat. Assn. Facilitators, Women Historians of Midwest, Am. Assn. State and Local History. E-mail: mamccoy4@juno.com.

MCCOY, MATTHEW WILLIAM, state legislator, human resource manager; b. Des Moines, Mar. 29, 1966; s. William Paul and Mary Ann (Kenneally) McC.; m. Jennifer Ann Stitt, May 29, 1993; 1 son, Jack William. BA in History and Polit. Sci., Briar Cliff Coll., 1988. V.p. industry rels. Ruan Transp. Mgmt. Systems, Des Moines, 1989-92; mem. Iowa Ho. of Reps., Des Moines, 1992-96, Iowa Senate from 34th dist., Des Moines, 1996—. Bd. dirs. Polk County (Iowa) Conservation Bd.; vice chair YMCA Bd. Mgrs.; mem. Youth Emergency Svcs. & Shelter Bd.; fundraising chair, Boy Scouts of Am. Democrat. Roman Catholic. E-mail: mmccoy@ruan.com. Also: mmcoy@mccoyfor congress.com. E-mail: mmccoy@ruan.com.

MCCOY, MAUREEN B. music educator; b. Chgo., Sept. 3, 1974; d. Robert George and Eileen Marie (O'Sullivan) Boyda; m. Jason Michael McCoy, June 21, 1997; 1 child, Maura. BS in Cmty. Health, U. Ill., 1996; MusB in Music Edn., DePaul U., 2004. Mktg. asst. Blue Cross Blue Shield Assn., Chgo., 1997, client svcs. assoc., 1998, assoc. cons., 1998—2000; piano instr. Music Makers of Western Springs, Ill., 2000—02, Gold Coast Music Sch., Chgo., 2001—02. Accompanist Ill. Grade Sch. Music Assn., 2001—. Fundraising vol. VH1 Save the Music Found., Western Springs, 2001, New Mom's Benefit Concert, Chgo., 2001; family choir accompanist, children's choir dir. St. Alphonsus Cath. Ch., Lemont, Ill., 1999—. Mem.: Am. Orff Schulwerk Assn., Chgo. Area Kodaly Educators, Am. Choral Dirs. Assn., Music Educators Nat. Conf. Office Phone: 630-254-1579. E-mail: mccoyjm@prodigy.net.

MCCOY, MICHAEL J. food products company executive; BS in Acctg., Loras Coll., 1969. With Hormel Foods Corp., Austin, Minn., 1992—, mem. staff treas.' office, co. treas., 1996-97, v.p., 1997-2000, sr. v.p. adminstrn., CFO, 2000—. Office: Hormel Foods 1 Hormel Pl Austin MN 55912-3680

MCCOY, STUART SHERMAN, manufacturing executive; b. Little Rock, Dec. 16, 1958; s. Gene Guy and Idella Maria Theresa (Brown) McC.; m. Juliet Kathryn Goens, Sept. 9, 1977 (div. Apr. 1986); children: Ashley Nicole, Christopher Sean. Student, U. Ark., Little Rock, 1976, 78. Various positions Ad Craft Ark., Inc., Little Rock, 1976-80, prodn. supr., 1980-82, v.p. prodn., 1982-86, v.p. ops., 1986-93, exec. v.p., 1993—. Bd. dirs. Subiaco Acad. Alumni Assn. Photojournalist. Team mgr. Red Elk Motorsports, 1990-93, pres., 1991—; v.p. Ark. Dirt Riders, 1991-92, pres., 1992-93. Mem. Am. Advt. Fedn. (10th dist Addy award com. 1989-96, 10th dist. student competition com. 1994—, Nat. Addy com., 1994-96, constrn. and bylaws com. 1991—), Screen Print Assn. Internat., Ark. Advt. Fedn. (bd. dirs. 1992—), Jaycees (state dist. bd. dirs. Ark. chpt. 1983, state bd. dirs. pub. rels. com. 1984-85), Masons., Sabiaco Acad. Alumni Assn. (bd. dirs. 1991-95). Republican. Episcopalian. Avocations: sports, computers, photography, writing short stories, camping, hunting, motorcycle riding. Home: 11940 Southridge Dr Little Rock AR 72212-1740 Office: Ad Craft Ark Inc 1122 W 3rd St Little Rock AR 72201-2008

MCCOY, THOMAS, information technology executive; BA, Stanford U.; JD, U. So. Calif. Assoc., ptnr. O'Melveny and Meyers, 1977—95; gen. counsel Advanced Micro Devices, Sunnyvale, Calif., 1993—95, sec., 1995—2003, sr. v.p., gen. counsel, 1998—2003, exec. v.p., chief adminstrv. officer, 2003—. Office: Advanced Micro Devices One AMD Pl PO Box 3453 Sunnyvale CA 94088-3453*

MC COY, TIDAL WINDHAM, former government official; b. Gainesville, Fla., Apr. 25, 1945; Grad., U.S. Mil. Acad., 1967; MA in Bus. Fin, George Washington U., 1975. Officer U.S. Army, 1967-72; mem. long-range planning and net assessment group Office of Sec. Def., Washington, 1972-73; mem. staff Nat. Security Council, 1973; staff asst. and then dep. asst. to Sec. Def., 1973-77; sci. asst. to asst. sec. for research, engring. and systems Dept. Navy, 1977-78; dir. policy research, office of under sec. for policy Dept. Def., 1978-79; asst. for nat. security affairs to Sen. Jake Garn, 1979-81; asst. sec. for manpower, res. affairs and installations Dept. Air Force, Washington, 1981-87; asst. sec. for readiness support USAF, Washington, 1987-88, acting sec. and undersec., 1981-88; sr. assoc. Hecht, Spencer & Assocs., 1988-89; v.p. govt. rels. Thiokol Corp., 1989—2002; chmn., CEO Washington Capital Ptnrs., 1998—. Chmn. Washington Capital Ptnrs., 1998—. Recipient DOD Outstanding Civil Svc. medal, USAF Exceptional Civilian Svc. medal. Mem. Space Transp. Assn. U.S.A. (dir., chmn. 1996—), Def. Forum Found. (vice-chmn.).

MCCOY, VERL EUGENE, JR., physical chemist, consultant; b. Chgo., July 7, 1933; s. Verl Eugene and Dorothy Adelaide McCoy; m. Mary Lee Wetterholm, Dec. 28, 1957; children: Sharon Lee, Linda Ann, Lisa Kay. BA, Princeton U., 1955; PhD, Harvard U., 1964. Rsch. assoc. EI DuPont DeNemoans & Co., Wilmington, Del., 1963—98, textile cons., 1998—. Pres. Wilmington (Del.) Sister Cities, 1969—; mem. exec. com. Coun. Civic Orgns. of Brandwine Hundred; elder Trinity Presbtn. Ch.; chmn. Planning Bd. New Castle (Del.) County, 1968—93; bd. dir. Wilmington (Del.) Sister Cities, 1969—. Lt. USN, 1955—58. Mem.: Am. Chem. Soc., Textured Yarn Assn. Am. (pres. 1988—95, bd. dir. 1988—95), Civic League New Castle (Del.) County (v.p. 1995—, dir. 1995—). Presbyn. Avocations: tennis, golf, photography. Home and Office: 2641 Majestic Drive Wilmington DE 19810-2428 E-mail: McCoy.Gene@worldnet.att.net.

MCCOY, WESLEY LAWRENCE, musician, conductor, educator; b. Memphis, Jan. 27, 1935; s. Harlan Eftin and Gladys (Coggin) McC.; m. Carolyn June Noble, Aug. 26, 1960; children: Jill Laurene McCoy Kurtz, Scott Edward. B of Music Edn., La. State U., 1957, PhD, 1970; M of Music Edn., U. Louisville, 1958; M of Sacred Music, So. Bapt. Theol. Sem., 1960. Min. of music Beechmont Bapt. Ch., Louisville, 1959-62; also instr. music So. Bapt. Theol. Sem., Louisville; asst. prof. music, dir. bands Carson Newman Coll., Jefferson City, Tenn., 1962-67; asst. prof. music U. S.C., Columbia, 1969-72; assoc. prof. music U. Ark., Little Rock, 1972-77, prof., 1977-80, asst. dean for pub. svc. Coll. Fine Arts, 1978-79; condr. Wind Ensemble, River City Cmty. Band, 1972-80, Oklahoma City Youth Symphony, 1985-89; chmn. dept. music Phillips U., Enid, Okla., 1980-82, chmn. fine arts divsn., 1982-84; music tchr. Bishop Sullivan H.S., 2003—04. Min. music 1st United Meth. Ch., Edmond, Okla., 1983-2000; owner WJ Travel, Oklahoma City, 1985-2002. French horn player, Knoxville (Tenn.) Symphony Orch., 1962-67, Columbia Philharm. Orch., 1969-72, Ark. Symphony Orch., 1972-80, Enid-Phillips Symphony, 1980-84; contbr. to Ch. Musician, 1974-76, 85-86. Co-chmn. Jefferson County (Tenn.) Com. for Goldwater for Pres., 1962; mem. Pulaski County (Ark.) Rep. Com., 1977-81; mem. Oklahoma County Rep. exec. Com., 1995-97; pres. Ctrl. Okla. La. State U. Alumni, 1997-98. Mem. S.C. Music Educators Assn. (pres. coll. divsn. 1971-73), Ark. Music Edn. Assn. (chmn. rsch. 1975-80), Phi Mu Alpha, Pi Kappa Lambda, Phi Delta Kappa, Alpha Tau Omega. Republican. Baptist. Home and Office: 8548 Kaylynn Ave Baton Rouge LA 70810 Personal E-mail: wesleymccoy@yahoo.com.

MCCOY, WILLIAM O. former academic administrator, retired telecommunications executive; b. Snow Hill, N.C., Oct. 26, 1933; s. Marcus Cicero and Anna Kathleen (Shirley) McC.; m. Sara Jane Hart, Dec. 18, 1955; children—Laura Jo McCoy Foster, Kathleen Sue. BS, U. N.C., 1955; MS, MIT, 1968. Gen. mgr. South Central Bell, New Orleans, 1973—76, v.p. Nashville, 1978, exec. v.p. Birmingham, Ala., 1978—82, vice chmn., 1982—83; asst. v.p. Am. Tel & Tel, Basking Ridge, 1976—78; vice chmn. BellSouth Corp., Atlanta, 1993—95; v.p. fin. U. N.C., 1995—99, interim chancellor, 1999—2000; dir. U N. C. Health Care System, 1999—. Dir. First Am. Corp., Nashville, Liberty Corp., Greenville. Chmn. Middle Tenn. Heart Assn., Nashville, 1971; div. chmn. Greater New Orleans Fedn. of Chs., 1974; gen. vice chmn. New Orleans Symphony Campaign, 1975; co-chmn. Ala. United Way Campaign, Birmingham, 1982; adv. council Coll. Bus. Adminstrn., Ga. State U., 1983—. Served to capt. USMC, 1955-59. Served to capt. USMC, 1955—59. Republican. Methodist. Office: U NC 103 South Bldg PO Box 9100 Chapel Hill NC 27599-0001 also: U NC Systemsrp PO Box 2688 Chapel Hill NC 27515-2688

MCCRABB, DONALD RAYMOND, pastoral field educator; m. Barbara Humphrey; 1 child, Andrew Thomas. BA in Religion, BA in Polit. Sci., Wright State U., 1975; MA in Theology, U. Dayton, 1978; DMin, United Theol. Sem., 1998. Cert. catechetical leader, Roman Cath. Ch. Campus min. Newman Ctr., Wright State U., Dayton, Ohio, 1975-76; grad. asst. U. Dayton, 1976-78; pastoral assoc. St. Raphael Cath. Ch., Springfield, Ohio, 1978-82; Cath. campus min. Cen. State U., Wilberforce U., 1982-85; exec. dir. Cath. Campus Ministry Assn., 1985-98; dir. devel. Sojourners, Washington, 1998-99; assoc. dir. pastoral field edn. Dominican House of Studies, Washington, 1999—, dir. adminstrn. Mem. planning com. Cath. Edn. Futures Project, 1985-88; bd. dirs., site visitor Commn. on Cert. and Accreditation, U.S. Cath. Conf., 1986-92. Office: Dominican House of Studies 487 Michigan Ave NE Washington DC 20017-1585*

MCCRACKEN, CARON FRANCIS, information technology consultant; b. Detroit, Jan. 12, 1951; d. WIlliam Joseph and Constance Irene (Kramer) McC. AS, Mott C.C., 1971; BS, Ctrl. Mich. U., 1973; MA, U. Mich., 1978; MBA in Fin. with hons., Wayne State U., 2003. Tchr. Elkton, Pigeon, Bayport (Mich.) High Sch., 1973—74, Davison (Mich.) Jr. High Sch., 1974-75; instr. Mott C.C., Flint, Mich., 1974-78; planning and rsch. specialist Flint Police Dept., 1977-79; campus coord., programmer Systems & Computer Tech. Corp. (now SunGard Data Sys., Inc.), Detroit, 1981-82; acad. specialist computing systems Systems & Computer Tech. Corp., Detroit, 1982-83, mgr. acad. computing systems, 1983-84, mgr. adminstrv. computing systems, 1984-85; communications analyst Fruehauf Corp., Detroit, 1985-86, sr. comms. analyst, 1986-87; account tech. cons. US Sprint Communications Co., Detroit, 1987-89; account mgr. US Sprint Communications Corp., Detroit, 1989-90; sr. mgr. Technology Specialists, Inc., Phila., 1990-91; sr. cons. info. tech. practice, tech. delivery svcs. PriceWaterhouseCoopers LLP, Detroit, 1992—; Sun Guard Data boardwalk. Adv. bd. CONTEL Bus. Networks, Atlanta, 1987. Contbr. articles to profl. jours. Vol. charitable and homeless orgns. including Coalition on Temporary Shelter, Core Cities, Paint the Town; undergrad. computer lab. cons., student mgr. computer sci. dept. Wayne State U., 1993-95, vol. computer cons. Bus. Sch., 1997-98; vol. tech. advisor on 1992 elections project City of Detroit; vol. St. Joseph's Mercy Hosp., Pontiac, Mich., 1995; chair of bd., pres., treas. Bloomfield Courts Condominium Assn., 1996-98; vol. Pub. TV WTVS, Detroit, 1996-99, vol., Pub. Radio Sta. WDET, Detroit, 1996-98; elected precinct del. for 4th precinct Bloomfield Twp., 2002—; vol. State Senatorial and U.S. Congressional re-election campaigns, 2002—. Named to Beta Gamma Sigma MBA Hon. Soc., 2001. Mem.: Detroit Zool. Soc., Detroit Inst. Arts, Assn. Computing Machinery, Data Processing Mgmt. Assn., Alumni Assn. Wayne State U., Smithsonian Instn. (assoc.), Alumni Assn. U. Mich., Adventure Cycling Assn. (Missoula, Mont.), Women's Econ. Club of Met. Detroit (fin. com. 1999), Beta Gamma Sigma. Avocations: reading, athletics, personal research, international travel. Home: 100 W Hickory Grove H4 Bloomfield Hills MI 48304-2169 Office: PricewaterhouseCoopers LLP 400 Renaissance Ctr Ste 780 Detroit MI 48243-1501

MCCRACKEN, DOUGLAS M. consultant company executive; m. Naomi McCracken; children: Doug, Kristi. BA in Econs., Norwich U.; MA in Econs., Northeastern U.; MS in Mgmt., Rensselaer Polytechnic Inst. Cert. mgmt. cons. Various positions Deloitte Consulting, Detroit, 1977-82, ptnr., 1982-91, Boston, 1991-96, mng. dir.-Ams., 1996—, bd. dirs., 1996—; chmn. bd. Deloitte & Touche LLP, Wilton, Conn., 1999—. Mem. Inst. Mgmt. Conss. Office: Delotte & Touche LLP PO Box 820 Wilton CT 06897-0820

MCCRACKEN, EDWARD R. electronics executive; b. Fairfield, Iowa, 1943; children: Kathi, David. BSEE, Iowa State U., 1966; MBA, Stanford U., 1968. With Hewlett Packard Co.; pres., CEO Silicon Graphics, Inc., 1984—98, chmn., CEO, 1994—98. Bd. dirs. Digital Rsch., Inc.; chmn. bd. The PRASAD Project, 1992—; dir. Nat. Semiconductor Corp., Tularik, Inc., Acumen Internat. Recipient Disting. Info. Scis. award, Data Processing Mgmt. Assn., 1994, Nat. Tech. medal, 1995, Exec. of Yr., R&D Mag., 1995, Disting. Achievement award, Iowa State Alumni Assn., 1995.

MCCRACKEN, EUGENE LUKE, lawyer; b. Savannah, Ga., Aug. 9, 1932; s. John and Estelle (Powers) M.; m. Helen Kelly Morekis, May 9, 1964; A.A., Armstrong State Coll., 1952; BA, Mercer U., 1954; LLB, U. Ga., 1957. Bar: Ga. 1958, U.S. Dist. Ct. (so. dist.) Ga. 1959, U.S. Ct. Appeals (11th cir.) 1961, U.S. Supreme Ct. 1978. Assoc. Brannen, Clark & Hester, Savannah, 1958-64; sole practice, Savannah, 1964—; asst. dist. atty. Chatham County, Ga., 1963-64; asst. city atty. City of Savannah, 1970-74; judge pro tem Juvenile Ct. of Chatham County, 1974-80. Bd. dirs. United Way of Savannah, 1973-74; mem. Chatham County Zoning Bd. Appeals, 1967-70; chmn. Chatham County Reps., 1985-87, chmn. 1st congl. dist. Ga. Rep. Party, 1987-89. Named Savannah's Outstanding Young Man of Yr., Jaycees, 1966; recipient Sword of Hope award Am. Cancer Soc., 1968. Mem. State Bar of Ga., Savannah (Ga.) Bar Assn., Armstrong State Coll. Alumni Assn. (pres. 1973, 83), Hibernian Soc. of Savannah (pres., 2004—), St. Andrews Soc. Savannah, First City Club. Roman Catholic. Home: 16 Brightwater Dr Savannah GA 31410-3301 Office: 223 W York St Savannah GA 31401-3636 Office Phone: 912-232-4106.

MCCRACKEN, KENNETH DONALD, retired education educator; b. Hiattville, Kans., Feb. 18, 1930; s. Joseph Andrew and Elinor Nellie (Peelle) McC.; m. Janis Erline Houghton, Dec. 24, 1961 (dec. Sept. 2000); children: Schuyler Lowe, Vance. BS, Pittsburg, Kans., 1955, MS, 1956; EdD, Fayetteville, Ark., 1966. Prof. edn. U. Tenn., Martin, 1962-99; ret., 1999. Contbr. chpts. to books and articles to profl. jours. With U.S. Army, 1952-54. Mem. Phi Delta Kappa. Home: 119 Elm Martin TN 38237 E-mail: dmccrack@utm.edu.

MC CRACKEN, PAUL WINSTON, retired economist, business educator; b. Richland, Iowa, Dec. 29, 1915; s. Sumner and Mary (Coffin) McC.; m. Emily Ruth Siler, May 27, 1942; children— Linda Jo, Paula Jeanne. Student, William Penn Coll., 1937; MA, Harvard U., 1942, PhD, 1948. Faculty Found. Sch., Berea Coll., Ky., 1937-40; economist Dept. Commerce, Washington, 1942-43; fin. economist, dir. research Fed. Res. Bank of Mpls., 1943-48; assoc. prof. Sch. Bus. Adminstrn., U. Mich., 1948-50, prof., 1950-66, Edmund Ezra Day Univ. prof. bus. adminstrn., 1966-86, prof. emeritus, 1986—, ret. Dir. emeritus Nat. Bur. Econ. Rsch.; trustee Earhart Found. Author: monographs Can Capitalism Survive?; articles on financial, econ. subjects. Fellow Am. Statis. Assn.; mem. Am. Econ. Assn., Am. Finance Assn., Royal Econ. Soc., Harvard Grad. Soc. (coun.). Clubs: Cosmos (Washington); Harvard (N.Y.C.). Presbyterian. Home: 2564 Hawthorne Rd Ann Arbor MI 48104-4032

MC CRACKEN, PHILIP TRAFTON, sculptor; b. Bellingham, Wash., Nov. 14, 1928; s. William Franklin and Maude (Trafton) McC.; m. Anne MacFetridge, Aug. 14, 1954; children— Timothy, Robert, Daniel. BA in Sculpture, U. Wash., 1954. Asst. to Henry Moore, England, 1954. One-man shows: Willard Gallery, N.Y.C., 1960, 65, 68, 70, Seattle Art Mus., 1961, Wash. State Capitol Mus., Olympia, 1964, Art Gallery of Greater Victoria, B.C., 1964, LaJolla (Calif.) Mus. Art, 1970, Anchorage Hist. and Fine Arts Mus., 1970, Tacoma Art Mus., 1980, Kennedy Galleries, N.Y.C., 1985, Lynn McAllister Gallery, Seattle, 1986, 89, Valley Mus. N.W. Art, La Conner, Wash., 1993, Whatcom Mus., Bellingham, Wash., 1994, Schneider Mus. Art, 1994, So. Oreg. State Coll., 1994, Monterey Mus. Art, 1999, Mus. N.W. Art, La Conner, 2004, others; group shows include: Mus. Art, Ogunquit, Maine, 1957, Chgo. Art Inst., 1958, Detroit Inst. Arts, 1958, Pa. Acad. Fine Arts, 1958, Contemporary Art Gallery, Houston, 1958, DeYoung Meml. Mus., San Francisco, 1960, Los Angeles Mcpl. Art Mus., 1960, Galerie Claude Bernard, Paris, 1960, Phillips Gallery, Washington, 1966, Corcoran Gallery, 1966, Mus. Art, Akron, 1967, Finch Coll., N.Y.C., 1968, Rutgers U., 1968, Whitney Mus. Art, 1978, Portland Art Mus., 1976, Mont. State U., Bozeman, 1979, Brigham Young U., 1980, Bellvue (Wash.) Art Mus., 1986, Lynn McAllister Gallery, 1986, Am. Acad. Arts and Letters, N.Y.C., 1986, Schmidt Bingham Gallery, N.Y.C., 1987, Wash. State Capital Mus., 1987, 89, Cheney-Cowles Mus., Spokane, Wash., 1988, Smithsonian Instn., 1991—, Nat. Mus., Ottawa, Can., 1991-92, Gallery Three-Zero, N.Y.C., 1993, Seattle Art Mus., 1994, SA Gallery Christ Ch., New Zealand, 1996, Art and Cultural Ctr., Fallbrook, Calif., 2002, others; sculptures represented: Norton Bldg., Seattle, Kankakee (Ill.) State Hosp., Swinomish Indian Tribal Center, LaConner, UN Assn., N.Y.C., King County King Dome, Seattle, City Hall, Everett, Wash., others. (Recipient numerous prizes, awards). Address: 5029 Guemes Island Rd Anacortes WA 98221-9039

MCCRACKEN, THOMAS JAMES, JR., lawyer; b. Chgo., Oct. 27, 1952; s. Thomas J. Sr. and Eileen (Brophy) McC.; children: Catherine, Michael, Amanda, Quinn. BA, Marquette U., 1974; JD, Loyola U., 1977. Bar: Ill. 1977, U.S. Dist. Ct. (no. dist.) Ill., U.S. Ct. Appeals (7th cir.) 1984. Asst. state's atty. DuPage County State's Atty.'s Office, Wheaton, Ill., 1977-81; assoc. atty. McCracken & Walsh, Chgo., 1981-84; ptnr. McCracken, Walsh deLaVan & Hetler, Chgo., 1984—. Commr. Nat. Conf. of Commns. on Uniform State Laws, 1989—; bd. dirs. Oak Trust and Savs. Bank, Chgo. Contbr. articles to profl. jours. State rep. Ill. Gen. Assembly, Springfield, Ill., 1983-93, state senator, 1993; chmn. Regional Trans. Authority, Chgo., 1993-2004. Named Top Ten Legislators Chgo. Mag., 1990. Mem.: Chgo. Bar Assn., Ill. State Bar Assn. Avocations: skiing, fishing, hunting, coaching children's sports. Office: McCracken Walsh & deLaVan 134 N La Salle St Ste 600 Chicago IL 60602-1079

MCCRACKEN, URSULA E. museum director; Degree in Art History, Wellesley Coll.; Masters Degree, Johns Hopkins U. With Coll. Notre Dame, Balt., Walters Art Gallery, Balt.; curatorial asst. Albright-Knox Art Gallery, Balt.; dir. Textile Mus., Washington, 1987—. Office: Textile Mus 2320 S St NW Washington DC 20008-4088*

MCCRADY, BARBARA SACHS, psychologist, educator; b. Evanston, Ill., May 7, 1949; d. James Frederick and Margaret Maxine (Miller) Sachs; m. Dennis D. McCrady, June 13, 1969; 1 child, Eric Paul. BS, Purdue U., 1969; PhD, U. R.I., 1975. Lic. clin. psychologist. Clin. project evaluator Butler Hosp., Providence, 1974-75, chief psychol. assessment program, 1975-76, chief problem drinkers' project, 1976-83; assoc. prof. psychology Rutgers U., Piscataway, N.J., 1983-89, prof. psychology, 1989-2000, prof. II, 2000—. From instr. to assoc. prof. psychiatry Brown U., Providence, 1975-83; acting dir. Rutgers Ctr. Alcohol Studies, Piscataway, 1990-92; reviewer Nat. Inst. on Alcohol Abuse and Alcholism, Washington, 1979-82, extramural scientific adv. bd., 1989-93; cons. Inst. Medicine, Washington, 1988-89. Author: The Alcoholic Marriage, 1977; editor: Marriage and Marital Therapy, 1978, Directions in Alcohol Abuse Treatment Research, 1985, Research on Alcoholics Anonymous: Opportunities and Alternatives, 1993, Addictions: A Comprehensive Guidebook, 1999. Grantee Nat. Inst. on Alcohol Abuse and Alcoholism, 1979-83, 1988—. Fellow Am. Psychol. Assn. (past pres. divsn. addictions); mem. Assn. for Advancement Behavior Therapy, Rsch. Soc. on Alcoholism (bd. dirs., 1999-2003). Avocations: horseback riding, skiing, piano. Office: Rutgers U Ctr Alcohol Studies 607 Allison Rd Piscataway NJ 08854-8001 Office Phone: 732-445-0667. E-mail: bmccrady@rci.rutgers.edu.

MCCRADY, JAMES DAVID, veterinarian, educator; b. Beaumont, Tex., June 26, 1930; s. James Homer and Lucyle (Ward) McC.; m. Mary Elizabeth McDougald, Sept. 8, 1951; children— David, Diane, Darla. BS, Tex. A. and M. Coll., 1952, D.V.M., 1958; PhD, Baylor U., 1965. Instr., then asst. prof. Tex. A. and M. Coll., 1958- 62; dir. animal rsch., instr. Baylor U. Coll. Medicine, 1962-64; mem. faculty Tex A&M U., 1964—; prof., head dept. vet. physiology and pharmacology Tex. A. and M. Coll., 1966-90, prof., dir. spl. programs, 1990—. Dir. Russian-Am. Tng. Partnership, 1995—; adj. prof. Baylor Coll., Medicine, M.D. Anderson Hosp. and Tumor Inst. Served with USAF, 1952-54. Mem. AVMA, Tex. Acad. Sci., Am. Physiol. Soc., Sigma Xi, Phi Kappa Phi, Phi Zeta. Achievements include research on comparative cardiovascular and respiratory physiology. Home: 511 Olive St Bryan TX 77801-3506 Office: Tex A&M U College Station TX 77843-0001 Office Phone: 979-845-7261. Business E-Mail: jd-mccrady@tamu.edu.

MCCRAE, KEITH R. medical educator, researcher; b. Springfield, Mass., Dec. 4, 1956; m. Jo Ann McCrae; children: Brett, Kristen Ann. BA in Biochemistry summa cum laude, Dartmouth Coll., 1978; MD, Duke U., 1982. Diplomate Am. Bd. Internal Medicine, Am. Bd. Med. Oncology, Am. Bd. Hematology. Resident in internal medicine Duke U. Med. Ctr., Durham, 1982—85; fellow in hematology and oncology U. Pa., Phila., 1985—89, postdoctoral fellow, 1986—88, co-dir. clin. coagulation lab., 1991-93, dir. clin. coagulation course, 1992—93; rsch. assoc. U. Pa. Sch. Medicine, 1989, lectr. bridge curriculum, 1989—93, asst. prof. medicine, 1990—93, asst. prof. pathology and lab. medicine, 1991—93; lectr. basic curriculum U. Pa. Dental Sch., 1989—92; attending physician Hosp. of U. Pa., 1989—93, Phila. VA Hosp., 1990—93, Temple U. Hosp., 1993—; asst. prof. medicine Temple U. Sch. Medicine, 1993—96, lectr. bridge curriculum, 1993—, assoc. prof. medicine, 1996—. Tchg. attending hematology consult svc. U. Pa., 1989—93, tchg. attending hematology oncology inpatient unit, 1992—93; with hematology/oncology outpatient clinic, 1989—93; attending staff mem. hematology consult svc. Temple U. Sch. Medicine, 1993—, attending staff mem. hematology sickle cell outpatient clinic, 1993—, attending staff mem. gen. internal medicine svc., 1993; lectr. in field. Co-author (with M.D. Feldman): Blood: Hemostasis, Transfusion and Alternatives in the Perioperative Period, 1995; jour. reviewer: Blood, 1990—, Thrombosis and Haemostasis, 1991—, Annals of Internal Medicine, 1991—, Jour. Biol. Chem., 1992—, Placenta, 1992—, Jour. Exptl. Medicine, 1992—, Platelets, 1992—, Jour. Allergy and Clin. Immunology, 1992—, Cancer Rsch., 1993—, Am. Jour. Hematology, 1993—, Jour. Clin. Oncology, 1994—, Jour. Histochemistry and Cytochemistry, 1994—, Am. Jour. Physiol., 1995—, Thrombosis Rsch., 1995—; contbr. articles to profl. jours., chpts. to books. Mem.: AAAS, Am. Fedn. Clin. Rsch., Am. Soc. Hematology, Am. Heart Assn. (mem. thrombosis coun. 1994—, mem. arteriosclerosclerosis coun. 1994—, mem. southeastern Pa. peer rev. com. B 1995—), Phi Beta Kappa. Office: Case Western Res U Sch Med 2109 Adelbert Rd Cleveland OH 44106-2624

MCCRAIN, MICHAEL WILLIAM, accountant, financial advisor; b. Bklyn., Apr. 25, 1952; s. William Joseph Sr. and Penelope (Malarios) McC.; m. Kathleen Jean O'Donnell, June 9, 1974; children: Michael Walter, Kevin O'Donnell, Christopher William. AS in Computer Sci. with honors, Suffolk County C.C., Selden, N.Y., 1973; BBA in Pub. Acctg. cum laude, Hofstra U., 1975; MS in Bus., Columbia U., 1988. CPA, N.Y. Supervising sr. acct. Peat, Marwick, Mitchell Co., Jericho, N.Y., 1974-79; corp. acctg. mgr. Pall Corp., Glen Gove, N.Y., 1979-81; v.p. CFO North Atlantic Industries, Inc., Hauppauge, N.Y., 1981-88; v.p. fin. Loral Fairchild Sys., Syosset, N.Y., 1988-89; pres. MKC Assocs., Inc., Islandia, NY, 1989—. Trustee Sachem Schs. Dist., Lake Ronkonkuma, N.Y., 1992-93; v.p. Sachem Athletic Booster Club, Lake Ronkonkuma, 1993-94, pres., 1994-95; vice chairperson Sachem Cmty. Adv.

Coun., Lake Ronkonkuma, 1994-95, chairperson, 1995-97. Mem. AICPA, N.Y. Soc. CPAs, Beta Gamma Sigma. Avocations: racquetball, skiing, golf, computers, coaching lacrosse. Office: 1747 Veterans Hwy Ste 12 Central Islip NY 11749-1537

MCCRAKEN, VICKIE DARLENE, nursing assistant; b. Glendale, W. Va., Oct. 20, 1966; d. Robert Lonnie McCraken and Pearl Ruth Purnty-McCraken; 1 child, Angelica Leah. Diploma, Northeastern Bus. Coll., 1985—86, Stratford Career Inst., 2001—02; student, Writers Digest Sch. CNA McGraws Nursing Home, Adena, Ohio, 1990—91, Valley View Nursing Home, Colerian, Ohio, 1992, Heartland Nursing Home, Lansing, Ohio, 1992—96, Advanced Home Health, Bridgeport, Ohio, 1996—97, Valley View Nursing Home, Colerian, 1997; rep. Telespectrum Worldwide Inc., Wheeling, W.Va., 1997—98; CNA Good Shepherd Nursing Home, Wheeling, 1998—. Avocations: fishing, hunting, gardening, crafts. Home: RR 3 Box 384 Moundsville WV 26041

MCCRARY, EUGENIA LESTER (MRS. DENNIS DAUGHTRY MC-CRARY), civic worker, writer; b. Annapolis, Md., Mar. 23, 1929; d. John Campbell and Eugenia (Potts) Lester; m. John Campbell Howard, July 15, 1955 (dec. Sept. 1965); m. Dennis Daughtry McCrary, June 28, 1969; 1 child, Dennis Campbell. AB cum laude, Radcliffe Coll.-Harvard U., 1950; MA, Johns Hopkins U., 1952; postgrad., Harvard U., 1953, Pa. State U., 1953-54, Drew U., 1957-58, Inst. Study of USSR, Munich, 1964. Grad. asst. dept. Romance langs. Pa. State U., 1953-54; tchr. dept. math. The Brearley Sch., N.Y.C., 1954-57; dir. Sch. Langs., Inc., Summit, N.J., 1958-69, trustee, 1960-69. Co-author: Nom de Plume: Eugenia Campbell Lester, (with Allegra Branson) Frontiers Aflame, 1987; film script adaptation (with John Gallagher) Frontier, 1998. Dist. dir. Ea. Pa. and N.J. auditions Met. Opera Nat. Coun., N.Y.C., 1960-66, dist. dir. publicity, 1966-67, nat. vice chmn. publicity, 1967-71, nat. chmn. public rels., 1972-75, hon. nat. chmn. pub. rels., 1976-99; bd. govs., chmn. Van Cortlandt House Mus., 1985-90. Mem. Nat. Soc. Colonial Dames Am. (bd. mgrs. N.Y. 1985-90), Met. Opera Nat. Coun., Soc. Mayflower Desc. (former bd. dirs. N.Y. soc., chmn. house com. 1986-89), Soc. Daus. Holland Dames (bd. dirs. 1982-87, 96—, 3d directress gen. 1987-92, directress gen. 1992-96), L'Eglise du St.-Esprit (vestry 1985-88, sr. warden 1988-90), Huguenot Soc. Am. (governing coun. 1984-90, 2000-03, 2004-, asst. treas. 1990-91, sec. 1991-95, 2d v.p. 1995-2000), Colonial Dames Am. Daus. of Cin., Colony Club (bd. govs. 1988-96), Causeries du Lundi, The Acorn Found. (bd. mem.). Republican. Episcopalian. Home: 24 Central Park S New York NY 10019-1629 Personal E-mail: elmccrary@aol.com.

MCCRARY, LARRY DALE, minister, religious studies educator; b. Memphis, Sept. 22, 1952; s. James Reginald and Margaret Kathleen McCrary; m. Janice Elaine Tucker; children: Virginia Anne (McCrary) Hodges, Margaret Alice, Matthew Thomas. BA, Blue Mountain (Miss.) Coll., 1974; MDiv, Southwestern Bapt. Theol. Sem., Ft. Worth, 1977, PhD, 1985. Ordained minister Bapt. Ch., 1988. Pastor First Bapt. Ch., St. Francis, Kans., 1988—92, Burlington, Kans., 1992—94, Grace So. Bapt. Ch., Goddard, Kans., 1994—98; adj. instr. religion Friends U., Wichita, Kans., 1998—; adj. instr. New Testament/Greek Midwestern Bapt. Theol. Sem., Kansas City, Mo., 2000—; pastor N.W. Cmty. Bapt. Ch., Wichita, 2002—. Dir. theol. studies Heart of Kans. So. Bapt. Assn., Wichita, 1995—98. Cubmaster Cub Scouts Am., St. Francis, 1991—92; cookie chmn. Girl Scouts of Am., St. Francis, 1991; pres. St. Francis Ministerial Alliance, 1991—92. Baptist. Avocations: swimming, camping, reading, chess, board games. Home: 626 S Spruce Goddard KS 67052-9430 Office: Friends University 2100 W University St Wichita KS 67213 Personal E-mail: lmccrary74@earthlink.net. E-mail: larrym@friends.edu.

MCCRAVEN, CARL CLARKE, health service administrator; b. Des Moines, May 27, 1926; s. Marcus Henry and Buena Vista (Rollins) McC.; m. Eva Louise Stewart, Mar. 18, 1978; 1 child, Carl B. BS in Elec. Engring., Howard U., 1950; MS in Health Svcs. Adminstrn., Calif. State U., Northridge, 1976. Radiation physicist Nat. Bur. Standards, 1951-55; rsch. engr. Lockheed Calif. Co., 1955-63; mem. tech. staff TRW Sys., 1963-72; assoc. adminstr. Pacoima Meml. Hosp., Lake View Terrace, Calif., 1972-74; founder, CEO Hillview Mental Health Ctr. Inc., Lake View Terrace, 1974—; asst. prof. Calif. State U., Northridge, 1976-78. Regent Casa Loma Coll.; bd. dirs. San Fernando Valley Girl Scout Coun., Pledgerville Sr. Citizens Villa, ARC; treas. San Fernando Valley Mental Health Assn.; developer, mgr. Hillview Village Housing Project. Recipient citation Calif. Senate, 1971, 88, Resolution of Commendation, 1988, Calif. Assembly, 1971, 88, commendation, 1989, City of L.A., 1971, 78, 88, commendation, 1989, County of Los Angeles, 1988, commendation, 1989, Mayor of L.A. commendation 1989; named in honor Carl. C. McCraven Bldg. (formerly Hillview Mental Health Ctr.). Fellow Assn. Mental Health Adminstrs.; mem. NAACP (pres. so. area Calif. conf. 1967-71, nat. dir. 1970-76), Am. Pub. Health Assn., Am. Mgmt. Assn., Nat. Assn. Health Svcs. Execs., Assn. Cmty. Mental Health Agys. (pres.), North San Fernando Valley Rotary (pres. 1983), Sigma Pi Phi.

MCCRAVEN, EVA STEWART MAPES, health service administrator; b. L.A., Sept. 26, 1936; d. Paul Melvin and Wilma Zech (Ziegler) Stewart; m. Carl Clarke McCraven, Mar. 18, 1978; children: David Anthony, Lawrence James, Maria Lynn Mapes. ABS magna cum laude, Calif. State U., Northridge, 1974; MS, Cambridge Grad. Sch. Psycholoy, 1987, PhD, 1991. Dir. spl. projects Pacoima Meml. Hosp., 1969-71, dir. health edn., 1971-74; ast. exec. dir., v.p. Hillview Cmty. Mental Health Ctr., Lakeview Terrace, Calif., 1974-99, exec. dir., 1999—, former dir. clin. svcs. Past dir. dept. consultation and edn. Hillview Ctr., developer, mgr. long-term residential program, 1986-90; former program mgr. crisis residential program, transititional residential program and day treatment program for mentally ill offenders, past dir. mentally ill offenders svcs.; former program dir. Valley Homeless Shelter Mental Health Counseling Program; dir. Integrated Svcs. Agy., Hillview Mental Health Ctr., Inc., 1993-98, dir. clin. programs, 1996-99, exec. dir. 1999—. Former pres. San Fernando Valley Coordinating Coun. Area Assn., Sunland-Jujunga Coordinating Coun.; bd. advisors Pacoima Sr. Citizens Multi-Purpose Ctr.; bd. dirs. N.E. Valley Health Corp., 1970-73, Golden Gate Cmty. Mental Health Ctr., 1970-73. Recipient resolution of commendation State of Calif., 1988, commendation award, 1988, spl. mayor's plaque, 1988, commendation awards for cmty. svcs. City of L.A., 1989, County of Los Angeles, 1989, Calif. Assembly, 1989, Calif. Senate, 1989, award Sunland-Tujunga Police Support Coun., 1989, Women of Achievement award Sunland-Tujunga Bus and Profl. Women, 1990. Mem. Health Svcs. Adminstrn. Alumni Assn. (past v.p.), Sunland-Jujunga Bus. and Profl. Women, LWV, Valley Philharm. Soc. Office: Hillview Cmty Mental Health Ctr 11500 Eldridge Ave Lake View Terrace CA 91342-6523

MCCRAW, MICHAEL K. construction executive; CFO Pacific USA, Plano, Tex., 1989—. Office: 2901 Dallas Pkwy Ste 100 Plano TX 75093-5981

MCCRAW, THOMAS KINCAID, business history educator, editor, author; b. Corinth, Miss., Sept. 11, 1940; s. John Carey and Eugenia Olive (Kincaid) McC.; m. Susan Morehead, Sept. 22, 1962; children: Elizabeth, Thomas Kincaid Jr. BA, U. Miss., 1962; MA, U. Wis., 1968, PhD, 1970; MA (hon.), Harvard U., 1978. Tchg. asst. U. Wis., Madison, 1968-69; asst. prof. U. Tex., Austin, 1970-74, assoc. prof., 1974-78; vis. assoc. prof. Bus. Sch., Harvard U., Boston, 1976-78, prof., 1978-89, Straus prof. bus. history, 1989—, dir. research, 1985-87, co-chmn. bus. govt. and internat. economy unit, 1986-97. Ednl. cons. to cos., U.S., Japan, 1977-95. Author: Morgan versus Lilienthal, 1970, TVA and the Power Fight, 1971, Prophets of Regulation, 1984, American Business, 1920-2000: How it Worked, 2000; co-author, editor: Management Past and Present, 1996, Creating Modern Capitalism, 1997; editor: Regulation in Perspective, 1981, America Versus Japan, 1986, The Essential Alfred Chandler, 1988; editor: Bus. History Rev., 1994—; co-editor: The Intellectual Venture Capitalist, 1999; contbr. numerous articles to various publs., chpts. to books. Trustee Bus. History Conf., 1986-95, pres., 1989; mem. coun. Mass. Hist. Soc., 1989-92. Lt. USN, 1962-66. Recipient Lyons Master's Essay award Loyola U., Chgo., 1969, Younger Humanist award NEH, 1975, Pulitzer prize in history Columbia U., 1985, Thomas Newcomen Book award, 1986; Woodrow Wilson fellow, 1966-67; named to Alumni Hall of Fame, U. Miss., 1986; Newcomen fellowship Harvard U., 1973-74. Mem. Orgn. Am. Historians, Econ. Hist. Assn., Am. Econ. Assn. Democrat. Roman Catholic. Office: Harvard U Bus Sch Soldiers Fld Boston MA 02163-1317

MCCRAY, ALEXA T. health science association administrator, director; PhD, Georgetown U., Washington, 1981. Faculty Georgetown U., Washington, 1981—84; rsch. staff mem. IBM T.J. Watson Rsch. Ctr., 1984—86; with Lister Hill Nat. Ctr. for Biomed. Comms., a divsn. Nat. Libr. of Medicine, NIH, Bethesda, Md., 1986—, dir. Contbr. articles to profl. jours.; co-editor-in-chief Methods of Information in Medicine, mem. editl. bd. Jour. Am. Med. Informatics Assn. Fellow: AAAS, Am. Coll. Med. Informatics; mem.: Internat. Med. Informatics Assn., Am. Med. Informatics Assn. (bd. dirs.), Inst. Medicine of NAS. Achievements include research in medical informatics. Office: Nat Library Medicine 8600 Rockville Pike Bethesda MD 20894

MCCRAY, CURTIS LEE, academic administrator; b. Wheatland, Ind., Jan. 29, 1938; s. Bert and Susan McCray; m. Mary Joyce Macdonald, Sept. 10, 1960; children: Leslie, Jennifer, Meredith. BA in psychology, Knox Coll., Galesburg, Ill., 1960; postgrad., U. Pa., 1960-61; PhD in English, U. Nebr., 1968. Mem. faculty Saginaw Valley Coll., Univ. Ctr., Mich., 1968—77, chmn. dept. English, 1972-73, dean arts and scis., 1973-75, v.p. acad. affairs, 1975-77; provost, v.p. acad. affairs Govs. State U., Chgo., 1977-82; pres. U. North Fla., Jacksonville, 1982-88, Calif. State U., Long Beach, 1988-93, Millikin U., Decatur, Ill., 1993-98, Nat.-Louis U., Chgo., 1998—. Chmn. high tech and industry coun., SUS, 1986-88; mem. state rels. and undergrad. edn. com., Am. Assn. State Colleges and Universities, 1985-88. Bd. dirs. Jacksonville United Way, 1982-88, campaign chmn., 1987; bd. dirs. Sta. WJCT Channel 7 and Stereo 90, Jacksonville, 1982-88, Jacksonville Art Mus., 1983-88, Meml. Med. Ctr., Jacksonville, 1983-88, Jacksonville Cmty. Coun. Inc., 1982-88, Arts Assembly Jacksonville, 1984-88, Jacksonville Urban League, 1985-88; hon. dir. Jacksonville Symphony Assn., 1983; mem. Dame Point Bridge Commn., Jacksonville, 1982; mem. Jacksonville High Tech. Task Force, 1982. George F. Baker scholar, 1956; Woodrow Wilson fellow, 1960-61; Johnson fellow, 1966; Ford Found. grantee, 1969; recipient Landee award for excellence in tchg. Saginaw State Coll., 1972. Mem. AAUP, Torch Club. Office: Nat-Louis U 122 S Michigan Ave Chicago IL 60603-6191

MCCRAY, DOROTHY WESTABY, artist, printmaker, educator; b. Madison, S.D., Oct. 13, 1915; d. Robert Spencer and Annie Mary (Otter) Westaby; m. Francis F. McCray, Aug. 6, 1938 (dec. Jan. 1960); 1 child, Peter Michael. BA, State U. Iowa, 1937, MA in Painting, 1939; MFA in Printmaking, Calif. Coll. Arts and Crafts, Oakland, 1955; DHL (hon.), We. N.Mex. U., 2001. Prof. art Western N.Mex. U., Silver City, 1948-81, prof. emeritus, 1981—; profl. painter/printmaker McCray Studios, Silver City. Solo exhbns. include Mezzanine Gallery, Oakland, Calif., Art Directions Gallery, N.Y.C., Lebanon Valley Coll., Pa., Coralles Art Assn., N.Mex., Richard Levy Gallery, Albuquerque, numerous others; group exhbns. include Art Inst. Chgo., 1940-41, Phila. Acad., 1941, Kansas City Art Inst., 1941, 42, Smithsonian Inst., Washington, 1941, 58, Am. Fine Arts Gallery, N.Y.C., 1943, Joslyn Meml. Art Mus., Omaha, 1947, Mus. Fine Arts, Santa Fe, 1950, 51, 52, 53, 54, 56, 57, 58, 59, 63, 66, Oakland (Calif.) Art Mus., 1955, Cin. Art Mus., 1956, 58, NAD, Newton, Kans., 1956, Dallas Mus. Fine Arts, 1956, 58, Roswell (N.Mex.) Art Mus., 1958, Bradley U., Peoria, Ill., 1960, Highlands U., Las Vegas, 1960, Bklyn. Mus., 1961, Pa. Acad. Art, Phila., 1965, Museo de Arte Historia, Juarez, Mexico, 1978, The Shellfish Collection, Silver City, N.Mex., 1990, 91, Deming (N.Mex.) Ctr. for Arts, 1991, Grant County Art Guild, Pinos Altos, N.Mex., 1991, 92, Carlsbad (N.Mex.) Mus. and Art Ctr., 1992, Richard Levy Gallery, Albuquerque, 1992, Jonathon Green Gallery, Naples, Fla., numerous others; represented in pvt. and mus. collections throughout the United States. Named Hon. Citizen of S.D., 1983; Western N.Mex. U. Art Building named Dorothy McCray Art Building, 1982; recipient N.Mex. Gov.'s Award for Excellence and Contbns. to the Arts, 1992, numerous art awards in exhbns. Office: PO Box 322 Silver City NM 88062-0322

MCCRAY, LORA, real estate developer; b. Donalsonville, Ga., Nov. 5, 1963; d. Robert and Eula Mae McCray. BA in Polit. Sci., U. Ga., 1985; JD, U. Wash., 1988; MA in Applied Anthropology, U. Memphis, 1998. Bar: Md. 1988. Sr. case supr. DSZ & Assocs., Arlington, Va., 1990—96; rsch. assoc. Ctr. Urban Rsch. and Ext., Memphis, 1996—98; bus. developer Fannie Mae, Washington, 1998—2002; sr. devel. assoc. McAuley Inst., Silver Spring, Md., 2002—. Dir. Lamont Productions, Washington, 1996—; leadership awards com. mem. Washington Area Womens Found., 2002—03. Literacy tutor Washington Literacy Coun., Washington, 1999—2002. Fellow, U. Wash., 1985—88; scholar, Nat. Merit Scholar Program, 1981—85. Mem.: ABA, Am. Anthrop. Assn., Md. State Bar Assn. (licentiate), Phi Kapp Phi. Avocations: travel, reading, literature. Office: McAuley Inst 8380 Colesville Rd Ste 420 Silver Spring MD 20910 Personal E-mail: java2jo@aol.com. E-mail: lmccray@mcauley.org.

MCCRAY, NIKKI KESANGAME, professional basketball player; b. Collierville, Tenn., Dec. 17, 1971; BA, U. Tenn., 1995. Basketball player USA Women's Nat. Team, 1996, Washington Mystics, 1998—. Office: Washington Mystics MCI Ctr 601 F St NW Washington DC 20004-1605

MCCREADY, GUY MICHAEL, lawyer; b. Tulsa, Okla., Mar. 21, 1960; s. John McCready and Patsy Ann (Xander) Ryman; children: Sean, Loren. BA, Ft. Hays State U., 1984; JD, Washburn Law Sch., 1987; diploma, Nat. Inst. for Trial Advocacy, 1992. Bar: Colo. 1987, U.S. Dist. Ct. Colo. 1989, U.S. Ct. Appeals (10th cir.) 1990. Pvt. practice, Colorado Springs, 1987—. Prof. ethics U. So. Colo., Colorado Springs, 1991; mem. jud. com. to reform juvenile ct. procedure, 2000. Author: Manitou, 2002; author: (asst.) Yearbook of School Law, 1987; contbr. articles to profl. jours. Vol. Pikes Peak Legal Svcs., Colorado Springs, 1987—. Mem. Assn. Trial Lawyers Am., Colo. Trial Lawyers Assn., Colo. Bar Assn., El Paso County Bar Assn., Order of Barristers. Avocations: skiing, hiking, jogging. Office: Ste 1100 2 N Cascade Ave Colorado Springs CO 80903 Home: 102 Alpine Trl Manitou Springs CO 80829

MCCREADY, KENNETH FRANK, former electric utility executive; b. Edmonton, Alta., Can., Oct. 9, 1939; s. Ralph and Lilian McCready; children: John, Janet, Brian. BSc, U. Alta., 1963. Supr. data processing and systems Calgary (Alta.) Power Ltd., 1965-67, supr. rates and contracts, 1967-68, adminstrv. asst. to exec. v.p., 1968-72, asst. mgr. mgmt. cons. div., 1972-75; mgr. mgmt. systems dept., gen. mgr. Montreal Engring. Co., Calgary, 1975-76; v.p. adminstrn. Calgary (Alta.) Power Ltd., 1976-80; sr. v.p. ops. TransAlta Utilities, Calgary, 1980-85, pres., COO, 1985-89, also bd. dirs., 1988-96; pres., CEO TransAlta Corp., 1989-96; CEO TransAlta Energy Corp., 1989-96; pres. K. F. McCready & Assocs. Ltd., Calgary, 1996—. Bd. dirs. Encana Corp., Calgary, Biosphere Refineries Corp., Calgary, Canada, Biosphere Technologies, Inc., Edmonton, Canada, Computer Modelling Group, Calgary, Can. Environ. Tech. Advancement Corp., Calgary, Nexterra Energy Corp., Vancouver, Naikun Wind Devel. Inc., Vancouver, Canada, NABEST, Innovest Strategic Value AdvisorsInc., N.Y., Minister's Adv. Coun. on Sci. and Tech., Ottawa; policy advisor Energy Coun. Can., Ottawa; past chmn. Conf. Bd. Can.; past chmn. bd. Advanced Computing Techs., Inc.; past adv. bd. Tata Energy Rsch. Inst., Washington, Internat. Inst. for Sustainable Devel., Airborne Techs. Inc., Calgary; past moderator Premier's Forum, Govt. of Alta.; past environ. adv. bd. ABB Asea Brown Boveri, Zurich; adv. bd. energy, sci. and tech. NRCAN, Ottawa, Canada; chmn. ministers adv. coun. sci. and tech. MACST, Ottawa. Past dep. chmn. bd. govs. So. Alta. Inst. Tech.; past chair Alta. Round Table on Environment and Econ.; past mem. com. on trade and environment Govt. Can. Internat. Trade Adv.; past pres. Western Electric Power and Light Assn.; past chair environ. task force Bus. Coun. Nat. Issues. Mem. Assn. Profl. Engrs., Geologists and Geophysicists of Alta., Ranchmen's Club. Avocations: computers, bicycling, photography. E-mail: ken.mccready@telus.net.

MCCREADY, MATT, music educator; s. Karon and Thomas McCready. B of Mus. Edn., U. Kans., 1997. Asst. band dir. Blue Valley N.W. Band, Overland Park, Kans., 1998—2000, dir. of bands, 2000—. Office: Blue Valley Northwest HS 13260 Switzer Overland Park KS 66213

MCCREADY, SAM, theatre educator, actor, director, writer; b. Belfast, No. Ireland, Nov. 22, 1936; s. David James and Sarah Elizabeth (Howlett) McC.; m. Joan Carslake, Mar. 16, 1962; children: Marcus Diarmuid Julian, Richard Alastair. MA, U. N. Wales, U.K., 1976. Advt. mgr. Berkshire Internat., Ireland, 1961-63; head dept. theatre Orangefield Boys Sch., Belfast, Ireland, 1963-67, head English dept., 1967-69; lectr. U. North Wales, Bangor, England, 1969-78; artistic dir. Lyric Theatre, Belfast, Ireland, 1980-81; head dept. theatre Stranmillis Coll., Belfast, Ireland, 1978-83; assoc. prof. theatre U. Md., Catonsville, 1984-99, prof., 1999—2001; artistic dir. Shakespeare On Wheels, 1985-96. Examiner Guildhall Sch. Music and Drama, London, 1969—; trustee Lyric Theatre, Belfast, 1978-82; adjudicator Hong Kong Speech and Drama Festival, 1980, 84, 87, 93, 96, 2001; actor Tartuffe, Md. Stage Co., Ctr. Stage, Balt., 1997, 98, Serebriakov, Round House Theatre, Washington, 1997, Songs of Wandering Aengus, NYC, Sligo, Ireland, 1999, 2000, Krapp's Last Tape, Trinity Coll., Hartford, Conn., 1999, That Time, 2000, Early Memories, NY, 2001; The Great Yeats, 2002, Elizabeth the Queen, 2003, Folger Theatre, Washington, 2003; Heartbreak House, Roundhouse, DC, 2003; lectr. Yeats Internat. Summer Sch., Sligo, Ireland, 1998, 99, 2000, 03, 04. Author: Lucille Lortel: The Queen of Off-Broadway, 1993, Yeats Encyclopedia, 1997, Theatre in the North of Ireland, 1969-99, 2000; adaptor, dir. play: Spring's Awakening, 1987 (Best Dir. award 1987), No Country for Old Men, 1985, Picture of Dorian Gray, 1988, Salome, 1989, The Tutor, 1992, The Widening Gyre, 1994, The Shadow of a Gunman, 1995, Diary of a Scoundrel, 1996 (Best Dir. award 1997), On the Verge, 1997, Deirdre, 1997, What the Butler Saw, 1998, Yerma, 2000, Macbeth, 2001, The Belfast Carmen, 2002, Death of Cuchulain, Sligo, 2003, Coole Lady (Irish tour), 2004; contbr. articles to profl. jour. Named Outstanding Dir. Am. Coll. Theatre Festival, 1986, 87, 93, 97. Mem. Brit. Actors Equity, Am. Actors Equity, East Ctrl. Theatre Conf., Am. Conf. Irish Studies, Phi Kappa Phi. Episcopalian. Avocations: painting, music, photography, reading, gardening. E-mail: akwadux@yahoo.com.

MCCREARY, BILL, state representative; b. Joplin, Mo., Apr. 28, 1932; m. Natalie McCreary; 3 children. Student, Joplin City U., Kans. City U., Ottawa U. Former supermarket owner; mem. Kans. Ho. of Reps., 1997—. Employer's com. Kans. Job Svc. With USAF. Mem.: Wellington C. of C. (past pres.), Kiwanis. Republican. Office: 182-W State Capitol 300 SW 10th Ave Topeka KS 66612 Home: 1423 N C St Wellington KS 67152

MC CREARY, JAMES FRANKLIN, lawyer, mediator; b. Farmington, Mo., June 15, 1942; s. Frank J. and Bernice E. (Dugal) McCreary; m. Martha Jean Tucker, June 30, 1962; children: James Franklin, III, Jason Tucker, Josh Adam. BSBA, U. Evansville, 1964; JD, Nashville Law Sch., 1969; MBA, Vanderbilt U., 1980. Bar: Tenn. 1969, rule 31 listed mediator: Tenn. With Old Nat. Bank, Evansville, Ind., 1960-64; with First Am. Corp., Nashville, 1972-80, exec. v.p., corp. sec., gen. counsel, 1974-80; with First Am. Nat. Bank Nashville (N.A.), 1964-72, 80-86, exec. v.p., 1980-86; ptnr. Borod & Huggins Attys., Memphis, 1986-87, Gerrish & Mc Creary, Memphis, 1988, of counsel, 1988-92, dir., 1993—. Pres. Met. Fed. Bank, 1988-91; vis. prof. bus. law David Lipscomb U., 1975-77; instr. law and banking Am. Inst. Banking, 1969-75. Mem. Beta Gamma Sigma Mem. Ch. of Christ. Office: Gerrish & Mc Creary PC 5214 Maryland Way Brentwood TN 37027 E-mail: fmccreary@gerrish.com.

MCCREDIE, JAMES ROBERT, fine arts educator; b. Chgo., Dec. 31, 1935; s. William and Mareta (Black) McC.; m. Marian Lucille Miles, Sept. 3, 1960; children: Miles William, Meredeth Black Winter. AB in History and Literature summa cum laude, Harvard U., 1958, AM, 1961, PhD, 1963; student, Am. Sch. Classical Studies, Athens, Greece, 1958-59, 61-62; LittD (hon.), U. Athens, 2004. Instr. NYU, 1963-64, asst. prof., 1965-66, assoc. prof., 1967-70, prof., 1970, 78-88, Sherman Fairchild prof. fine arts, 1988—2002, Sherman Fairchild prof. emeritus fine arts, 2002—, dep. dir. Inst. Fine Arts, 1967-69, acting dir., 1982-83, dir., 1983—2002, trustee, 2003—, asst. field dir. Excavations in Samothrace, 1962, field dir., 1963-65, dir. excavations, 1966—. Dir. Am. Sch. Classical Studies at Athens, Greece, 1969—77, chmn. mng. com., 1980—90, trustee, 1980—, pres., 2001—; vis. mem. Inst. Advanced Study, Princeton, NJ, 1977—78; mem. vis. com. dept. classical and Near Ea. archaeology Bryn Mawr Coll., 1982; mem. vis. com. dept. European paintings Met. Mus. Art, 1983—2003; mem. vis. com. Ctr. Old World Archaeology and Art Brown U., Providence, 1985; mem. adv. bd. Alexander S. Onassis Ctr. for Hellenic Studies NYU, 1990—97; cons. in field. Author: Fortified Military Camps in Attica, Hesperia, 1966, Samothrace, 7, The Rotunda of Arsinoe, 1992; mem. adv. bd. Am. Jour. Archaeology, 1969-81; contbr. articles to prof. jours. Bd. dirs. Hellenic-Am. Union, Athens, 1973-77, vice chmn., 1974-77, U.S. Ednl. Found., Greece, 1969-75; active Pres. Adv. Com. on Cultural Property, 1992-95. Charles Norton fellow, 1961-62; named hon. citizen Community of Samothrace, 1976. Mem. Am. Philos. Soc., Archaeol. Inst. Am. (life, trustee 1972-75, mem. exec. com. 1978-81), Archaeol. Soc. Athens (hon.), Deutsches archaeologisches Inst. (corr.). Home: 30 Battle Rd Princeton NJ 08540-4902 also: Palaiopolis GR-680 02 Samothrace Greece Office: NYU Inst Fine Arts 1 E 78th St New York NY 10021-0119 Office Phone: 212-992-5805. E-mail: jrm1@nyu.edu.

MCCREE, PAUL WILLIAM, JR., systems design and engineering company executive; b. St. Louis, Oct. 27, 1926; s. Paul William and Hazel Elfrieda (Wilson) McC.; m. Carolyn Williams, Sept. 7, 1955; children: Brian, Paula, Ross. BS in Biochem. Scis., Harvard U., 1950. Mem. tech. staff System Devel. Corp., Santa Monica, Calif., 1956-62, Mitre Corp., Bedford, Mass., 1966-67; prin. engr. equipment divsn. Raytheon Co., Sudbury, Mass., 1963-66, 67-72; mem. tech. staff MIT Lincoln Labs., Lexington, Mass., 1972-76; mgr. Aerospace Systems divsn. Input Output, Waltham, Mass., 1976-79, tech. dir., 1979-80; mem. tech. staff Mitre Corp., Bedford, Mass., 1980-82; founder, pres. BPR Co., Profl. Cons. Svcs., 1981—. Sr. mem. tech. staff, mgr. subsystem design and devel. dept. GTE Strategic Systems Div., 1982-84; tech. dir. HH Aerospace and Design Co. Inc., Bedford, 1984-86; prin. engr., mem. tech. staff Raytheon equipment div. Software Systems Lab., Sudbury, 1986-87; v.p. HH Aerospace and Design Co. Inc., Bedford, 1986-91. Mem. NAACP, Urban League. Served with U.S. Army, 1944. Recipient Black Achiever award, Greater Boston YMCA, 1977. Mem. AAAS, IEEE, Math. Assn. Am., Am. Math. Soc., N.Y. Acad. Scis. Democrat. Home: 173 Goodman's Hill Rd PO Box 77 Sudbury MA 01776-0077 Office Phone: 978-440-9268. Personal E-mail: pmccree@worldnet.att.net.

MCCREEDY, EDWIN JAMES, lawyer; b. Atlanta, Dec. 29, 1939; s. Harold D. McCreedy and Annette Raymond (Denton) Chapman; m. Linda Jandora, Mar. 20, 1965; children: James M., Matthew B. BA, Columbia U., 1961; JD, Fordham U., 1968. Bar: N.J. 1968, U.S. Supreme Ct. 1982, cert. civil trial atty. N.J. Supreme Ct. 1982. Ptnr. McCreedy & Cox, Cranford, NJ, 1984—. Pres. Richard J. Hughes Inn of Court, 1991-92; mem. civil practice com. Supreme Ct. N.J., 1985-96. Fellow ABA, Internat. Soc. Barristers, Internat. Acad. Trial Lawyers, Am. Coll. Trial Lawyers (chair state com, 1995-97); mem. N.J. State Bar Assn. (trustee 1997-2001, chmn. jud. adminstrn. com. 1994-96, treas. 2001, 1st v.p. 2002, pres. elect 2002-03), Trial Attys. N.J. (trustee), Union County Bar Assn. (pres. 1987). Avocations: golf, travel. Office: McCreedy & Cox 6 Commerce Dr Ste 13 Cranford NJ 07016-3551

MCCREIGHT, JOHN A. management consultant; b. Phila., Jan. 29, 1938; s. John A. and Marion R. (Vetter) McC.; m. Kim Amet Healey; children: Laura, Cindy, Brian, Kimberly. BS in Mgmt. Scis., Northeastern U., 1968. Cert. mgmt. cons. Chief systems devel. AVCO Apollo Systems, Boston, 1964-68; sr. mgmt. cons. Touche, Ross & Co., Detroit, 1968-72, ptnr. Detroit and N.Y.C., 1972-80, nat. dir., mem. exec. com. N.Y.C., 1980-83; mng. dir. Hayes Hill, N.Y.C., 1983; pres. McCreight & Co., Inc., Phila. and New Canaan, Conn., 1983-85; mng. dir. Hay Group, Inc., N.Y.C., 1985-91; chmn. McCreight & Co., Inc., New Canaan, Conn., 1991—; co-founder, mng. ptnr. CIO Group, LLC, 2002—, Bd. Effectiveness Ptnrs., LLC, 2002—. Mem. Presdl. Task Force to Reduce Cost and Improve Effectiveness of USN; advisor Dept. Sec.

Def.; dir. officer Inst. Mgmt. Cons. Adv.; Carnegie Hall Bd. Trustee NIH, N.Y. Mayor's Office, Salvation Army; past chmn. N.Y. Corp. Fund Raising, NIMH; mem. N.Y. Ireland U.S. Coun. With USNR, 1955-63. Mem. University Club (N.Y.C.). Office: McCreight & Co Inc 36 Grove St New Canaan CT 06840

MCCRERY, JAMES (JIM MCCRERY), congressman; b. Shreveport, La., Sept. 18, 1949; m. Johnette Hawkins, Aug. 3, 1991; children: Claiborne Scott, Otis Clark. BA, La. Tech. U., 1971; JD, La. State U., 1975. Bar: La. 1975. Pvt. practice, Leesville, La., 1975-78; asst. city atty. City of Shreveport, 1979-80; staff U.S. Rep. Buddy Roemer, 1981-84; regional mgr. Ga.-Pacific Corp., 1984-88; mem. U.S. Congress from 4th La. dist., 1988-93, 97—, U.S. Congress from 5th La. dist., 1993-97; mem. ways and means com. Republican. Office: US Ho of Reps 2104 Rayburn House Ofc Bldg Washington DC 20515-1804

MCCRIE, ROBERT DELBERT, editor, publisher, educator; b. Sarnia, Ont., Can., Oct. 8, 1938; s. Robert Newton and Evelyn May (Johnston) McC.; m. Fulvia Madia, Dec. 22, 1965; children: Carla Alexandra, Mara Elizabeth. BA, Ohio Wesleyan U., 1960; MS, U. Toledo, 1964; postgrad., U. Chgo., 1962-63; MA, Hunter Coll., 1994; MPhil, CUNY, 1994, PhD, 1995. Cert. protection profl. Researcher Connective Tissues Research Lab., Copenhagen, 1963; copywriter numerous advt. agys., 1965-70; owner, editor Security Letter, N.Y.C., 1970—; editor, pub. HBJ Publs., N.Y.C., 1973-76; pres. Mags. for Medicine, Inc., N.Y.C., 1972-81. Faculty John Jay Coll. Criminal Justice, 1985—, adj. to full prof., chair Law, Police Sci. and Criminal Justice Adminstrn., 1997—2003; cons. in field; spkr. at numerous meetings. Editor: Behavioral Medicine, 1978—81, Security Letter Source Book, 1983—, Security Jour., 1989—98; author: Security Operations Management, 2001, Readings in Security Management, 2002; contbr. books and articles on security and urban crime and policing. Mem.: AAUP, Accolade, Internat. Assn. Profl. Security Cons. Disting. Svc., Internat. Security Mgmt. Assn. (Brennan award 1993), Nat. Coun. Investigation and Security Svcs. (Duffy Meml. Achievement award 1992), ASIS Internat. (pres.'s cert. of merit 1990), Am. Hist. Assn., Urban History Assn. (life), Union League Club, Pi Delta Epsilon, Delta Sigma Rho, Alpha Tau Omega. Presbyterian. Home: 49 E 96th St New York NY 10128-0782 Office: 166 E 96th St New York NY 10128-2565 also: John Jay Coll Criminal Justice 899 10th Ave New York NY 10019-1069 Office Phone: 212-237-8386. E-mail: rmccrie@mindspring.com.

MCCRIMMON, BARBARA SMITH, writer, librarian; b. Anoka, Minn., May 3, 1918; d. Webster Roy and Jessie (Sargeant) Smith; m. James McNab McCrimmon, June 10, 1939; Children: Kevin Mor, John Marshall. BA, U. Minn., 1939; MSL.S., U. Ill., 1961; PhD, Fla. State U., 1973. Asst. librarian Ill. State Nat. Hist. Survey, Champaign, Ill., 1961-62; research assoc. Bur. Community Planning, U. Ill., Champaign, 1962-63; librarian Ill. Water Survey, Champaign, 1964-65, Am. Meterol. Soc., Boston, 1965-67; edit. asst. Jour. Library History, Tallahassee, 1967-69, 73-74. Adj. asst. prof. Sch. Library Sci., Fla. State U., Tallahassee, 1976-77. Author: Power, Politics and Print, 1981, Richard Garnett: The Scholar as Librarian, 1989; editor: American Library Philosophy, 1975; contbr. articles to profl. jours. Mem. ALA, Pvt. Libraries Assn., Beta Phi Mu, Manuscript Soc. Democrat. Home: The Colonnades C30 2600 Barracks Rd Charlottesville VA 22901

MCCRONE, ALISTAIR WILLIAM, retired academic administrator; b. Regina, Can., Oct. 7, 1931; BA, U. Sask., 1953; MSc, U. Nebr., 1955; PhD, U. Kans., 1961. Instr. geology NYU, 1959-61, asst. prof., 1961-64, assoc. prof., 1964-69, prof., 1969-70, supr. Rsch. Ship Sea Owl on L.I. Sound, 1959-64, asst. dir. univ. program at Sterling Forest, 1965-66, resident master Rubin Internat. Residence Hall, 1966-69, chmn. dept. geology, 1966-69, assoc. dean Grad. Sch. Arts and Scis., 1969-70; prof. geology, acad. v.p. U. Pacific, 1970-74, acting pres., 1971; prof. geology, pres. Calif. State U. Sys. Humboldt State U., Arcata, 1974—2002. Exec. coun. Calif. State U. Sys., 1974-2002, acad. senate Humboldt State U., 1974-2002, mem. chancellor's com. on innovative programs, 1974-76, trustees' task force on off-campus instrn., 1975-76, exec. com. Chancellor's Coun. of Pres., 1976-79, Calif. state del. Am. Assn. State Coll. and Univ., 1977-80; mem. Commn. on Ednl. Telecomm., 1983-86; chair Calif. State U. Statewide Task Force on Earthquake and Emergency preparedness, 1985-88, 95-97; chmn., mem. accreditation teams Western Assn. Sch. and Coll.; chair com. on energy and environ. Am. Assn. State Coll. and Univ., 1980-84; chair program com. Western Coll. Assn., 1983-84, panelist, 1983; chair. bd. dirs. Assn. Am. Coll., 1992-93. Contbr. articles to profl. jour.; lectr. on geology Sunrise Semester program CBS Nat. Network, 1969-70; various appearances on local TV stas. Bd. trustees Presbyn. Hosp.-Pacific Med. Ctr., San Francisco, 1971-74; mem. Calif. Coun. for Humanities, 1977-82; mem. local campaign bd. United Way, 1977-83; mem. Am. Friends Wilton Park, 1980—; bd. dirs. Humboldt Convention and Visitors Bur., 1980-87, Redwood Empire Assn., 1983-87; bd. dirs. Calif. State Automobile Assn., 1988—, Am. Automobile Assn., 1990-93; bd. trustees Calif. State Parks Found., 1994-2000. Recipient Erasmus Haworth Disting. Alumnus award U. Kans., 2000; Shell fellow in geology U. Nebr., 1954-55; Danforth assoc. NYU, 1964. Fellow Calif. Acad. Sci.; mem. AAAS, Geol. Soc. Am., Am. Assn. U. Adminstrs. (nat. bd. 1986-89, 96-99, 2001-2002), St. Andrews Soc. NY (life), Rotary, Sigma Xi (pres. NYU chpt. 1967-69), Phi Kappa Phi. Avocation: golf. Office: Humboldt State U Univ Campus Arcata CA 95521

MCCRORY, JOHN BROOKS, retired lawyer; b. St. Cloud, Minn., Oct. 23, 1925; s. John Raymond and Mary Lee (Rutter) McC.; m. Margaret Joan Dickson, Sept. 4, 1954 (dec. Apr. 1957); 1 child, William B.; m. Elizabeth Ann Quick, June 27, 1959; children: John B., Ann Elizabeth. BA, Swarthmore Coll., 1948; JD, U. Pa., 1951. Bar: N.Y. 1952, D.C. 1985. Assoc. Donovan, Leisure, Newton, Lumbard & Irvine, N.Y.C., 1951-52, Nixon, Hargrave, Devans & Doyle, Rochester, N.Y., 1952-62, ptnr., 1963-92; ret. 1992. Author: Constitutional Privilege in Libel Law, 1977-90. Served to lt. comdr. USNR, 1943-47, PTO Fellow Am. Coll. Trial Lawyers; mem. ABA, Monroe County Bar Assn., N.Y. State Bar Assn., D.C. Bar Assn. Democrat. Quaker. Address: 25 Kendal Dr Kennett Square PA 19348-2321 Office: Nixon Peabody LLP Clinton Sq PO Box 31051 Rochester NY 14603-1051 Office Phone: 585-263-1000.

MCCRORY, PATRICK, mayor; b. Columbus, Oct. 17, 1956; m. Ann Gordon McCrory. BA in Polit. Sci. and Edn., Catawba Coll., 1978, doctorate (hon.), 2001. With Duke Power Co., NC, 1978—, now mgr. bus. rels., Charlotte City Coun., NC, 1989—95, mayor protem, 1993-95, mayor, 1995—. Co-chmn. Charlotte's Fighting Back Commn.; mem. Children Svcs. Network; hon. chmn. Cystic Fibrosis Found., Arthritis Found.; former chmn. United Way Corp. Campaign; former mem. U. NC-Charlotte Bus. Adv. Com., Charlotte Bond Campaign, ARC Pers. Recruitment Com.; HS basketball ofcl.; former bd. dirs. Drug Free Workplace Alliance Com.; founder Uptown Crime Prevention Coun., Mayor's Mentoring Alliance, 1995; leader Homeland Security; mem. adv. coun. President's Homeland Security; pres. Republican Mayors and Local Ofcls.; bd. dir. US Conf. of Mayors, chair, Hosing and Cmty. Develop. Com.; chair NC Metropolitan Coalition; hon. chair Charlotte chpts., Alzheimer Found., Cystic Fibrosis Found., Arthritis Found. Recipient Governor's Outstanding Local Ofcl. award, 2001. Mem.: Mayor's Mentoring Alliance (founder 1995), Republican Mayors and Local Ofcls. Orgn. (pres.), U.S. Conf. Mayors. Office: Office of the Mayor Govt Ctr 600 E 4th St Charlotte NC 28202-2816 Business E-Mail: mayor@ci.charlotte.nc.us.

MC CRORY, WALLACE WILLARD, pediatrician, educator; b. Racine, Wis., Jan. 19, 1920; s. Willard L. and Beulah (St. Clair) McC.; m. Sylvia E. Hogben, Feb. 6, 1943; children— Pamela, Michael, Christine. BS, U. Wis., 1941, MD, 1944. Diplomate: Am. Bd. Pediatrics. Rotating intern Phila. Gen. Hosp., 1944-45; resident pediatrics Children's Hosp., Phila., 1945-46, chief resident physician, 1948-49, asso. pediatrician, 1953-55, sr. pediatrician, 1955-58; provisional asst. pediatrician to out-patients, Lewis Cass Ledyard, Jr. fellow pediatrics N.Y. Hosp., 1949-50, pediatrician-in-chief, 1961-80, sr. pediatrician, chief pediatric nephrology, 1980—. Chief pediatric service Univ. Hosp., Iowa City, 1958-61; instr. pathology U. Wis. Med. Sch., 1942-43; instr. pediatrics U. Pa. Sch. Medicine, 1948-49, instr., research fellow pediatrics, 1950-53, asst. prof., 1953-55, asso. prof., 1955-58; prof. pediatrics, chmn. dept. State U. Iowa Coll. Medicine, 1958-61; prof. pediatrics Cornell U. Med. Coll., 1961— Pres. Nat. Kidney Found., 1964-66. Served to capt., M.C. AUS, 1946-48. Fellow N.Y. Acad. Medicine, Royal Soc. Medicine; mem. Am. Pediatric Soc., Am. Acad. Pediatrics, Soc. Pediatric Research, Am. Soc. Nephrology, Am. Soc. Pediatric Nephrology, AAAS, Sigma Xi, Alpha Omega Alpha. Home: 61 Carrs Tavern Rd Clarksburg NJ 08510-1506 Office: NY Hosp Cornell Med Ctr 525 E 68th St New York NY 10021-4885 E-mail: wallacemccrory@msn.com.

MCCRUM, ROBERT TIMOTHY, lawyer; b. Pitts., Nov. 4, 1958; s. Robert Terrence and Gertrude Callanan McCrum; m. Andrea Nourie, Mar. 19, 1960; children: Megan, Kelsey, Brian, Colleen, Shane. BA in Geology, Franklin & Marshall Coll., 1980; JD, Lewis & Clark Coll., 1983. Atty. U.S. Dept. Interior, Washington, 1984-86; ptnr. Crowell & Moring LLP, Washington, 1986—, vice chmn. natural resources and environ. group. Co-author: RCRA Hazardous Waste Handbook, 2001, Superfund Manual, 1998, Natural Resources Law Manual, 1995. Mem. Bush-Cheney Transition Adv. Com., 2000-2001. Mem. ABA (chmn. mining com. sect. environment, energy and resources 1997-99), Rocky Mt. Mineral Law Found. (bd. trustees 2000-03). Republican. Roman Catholic. Avocation: prestidigitation. Office: Crowell & Moring LLP 1001 Pennsylvania Ave NW Washington DC 20004-2505

MCCUAN, WILLIAM PATRICK, real estate company executive; b. Muskogee, Okla., Oct. 28, 1941; s. Lee L. and LaRee A. (Beverage) McC.; m. Jill Pamela Thomas, May 5, 1982; children: LaRee, Megan. Student, U. Tulsa, 1961-62; BA in Psychology, Baylor U., 1965; MRE, So. Sem., Louisville, 1967; MS, U. Louisville, 1969; postgrad., U. Md., 1971-73. Prof., asst. dean grad. sch. U. Md., Balt., 1969-73; lobbyist, cons. Washington, 1973-76; CEO KMS Group, Inc., Columbia, Md., 1976-84, MDG Cos. of Md., 1984—, MDG-Capital Corp., Naples, Fla., 1992—, MDG Cos. of W.Va., Berkeley Springs, 1991—, McCuan Family Found. Adj. prof. Cmty. Coll., Balt., 1969-72, U. Md. College Park, 1969-71; lectr. Univ. Coll.-Univ. Md., Balt., 1970-71, Howard C.C., Columbia, 1987-88; CEO Pet Holiday, Inc., Toledo, 1973-94; CEO Uniglobe Columbia Travel Ctr., 1986-94; non-lawyer mem. Atty. Grievance Commn., Md., 1990-96. Contbr. to numerous publs. Chmn., bd. dirs. Concert Soc. Md., 1988-98; chmn. United Way, Howard County, Md., 1984, Am. Presdl. Inaugural Com., Md., 1988, Howard County Cmty. Partnerships; fin. chmn. Rep. Ctrl. Com., Howard County, 1988-92; trustee Columbia Found.; mem. Pres.'s Commn. on Food, Nutrition and Health, Washington, 1970, Howard County Environ. Affairs Bd.; mem. bus. adv. coun. Howard C.C.; bd. dirs. Congl. Commn. on Mental Health of Children, Washington, 1973-75, Human Svcs. Inst. for Children and Families; pres., chairman & trustee McCuan Family Found., 1997—; active Nat. Rep. Eagles, 2002—; bd. govs. St. Margarets Sch. Recipeint Alumni Fellows award U. Louisville, 1996. Mem. Nat. Assn. Home Builders (bd. dirs. 1979-87, fed. govt. affairs com.), Md. Builders Assn. (pres. 1981-82), Home Builders Assn. Md. (bd. dirs. 1977-82, Award of Honor 1979, Award of Excellence 1980, Presdl. award 1982), Howard County Home Builders Assn. (pres. 1978-80), Howard County C. of C. (pres. bd. dirs. 1984-86). Home: 4256 Snowberry Ln Naples FL 34119-8513 Office: MDG Bldg 5550 Sterrett Pl Columbia MD 21044-2611: 3416 Shady Ln Glenwood MD 21738-9513 E-mail: pmccuan@aol.com.

MCCUBBIN, SHARON A, elementary school educator; b. Fullerton, Calif., Nov. 20, 1948; children: Julie, Adrian, Matthew; m. Robert Patrick McCubbin BA, U. Calif., 1973; MEd, Cleve. State U., 1993. Cert. Mid. Childhood Generalist NBCT, 2000, Early Childhood Generalist NBCT, 2003, English as a new Language NBCT, 2002, Clear Crosscultural, Lang. and Acad. Devel. Tchr. Primanti Montessori, Orange, Calif., 1977-81; tchr., adminstr. Montessori of Orange, 1981-83, Tustin Hills Montessori, Santa Ana, Calif., 1983-89; tchr., cons. for Montessori programs Irvine (Calif.) Unified Sch. Dist., 1990—; Montessori elem. mentor tchr., 1990—. Cons. title VII programs Irvine Unified Sch. Dist., 1990—, GATE adv. bd. mem.; cons. for early childhood programs to local corps. Asst. Jr. Disabled Programs, Orange, 1988—. SBD fellow Johns Hopkins U., 1999. Mem. ASCD, AAUW, Assn. Montessori Internat., Assn. Montessori Internat./U.S.A., Assn. Montessori Internat. Elem. Alumni Assn., N.Am. Montessori Tchrs. Assn., Pvt. Sch. Adminstrs., U. Calif.-Irvine Alumni Assn., Calif. Tchrs. Assn., Irvine Tchrs. Assn., Nat. Coun. Tchrs. Math., Nat. Coun. for Social Studies, Nat. Assn. for Edn. of Young Children, Pi Lamda Theta Home: PO Box 616 Tustin CA 92781-0616 Office: Irvine Unified Sch Dist 5050 Barranca Pkwy Irvine CA 92604-4698 also: Santiago Hills Elem 29 Christman W Irvine CA 92620-1836 E-mail: smccubbi@iusd.k12.ca.us., smccubbi@iusd.org.

MCCUE, ARTHUR HARRY, artist, educator; b. N.Y.C., Sept. 27, 1944; s. Raymond Noel and Alice (Cassidy) McC.; m. Lorraine Havel Bingham, Nov. 18, 1989. BFA, Pratt Inst., N.Y.C., 1967; MFA, U. Colo., 1969. Instr. art SUNY, Geneseo, 1969-72; instr. printmaking and drawing Ithaca (N.Y.) Coll., 1973-77, assoc. prof., 1987-2001, chmn. dept. art, 1977—, prof., 2001—. Guest speaker sch. supt.'s seminar Ithaca Coll., 1990; guest artist N.Y. State Pastel Artists Assn., Cooperstown, 1990, 92, Schweinfurth Meml. Art Ctr., 1990; cons., interpreter on wheelwrighting Onondaga County Parks, Salt Mus., Liverpool, N.Y., 1989-90; guest lectr. dept. art Tompkins Cortland Community Coll., 1987. One-man shows include Univ. Club, Boulder, Colo., 1968, David Gallery, Rochester, N.Y., 1973, Ithaca Coll., 1977, 79, 97, Art Gallery Adelphi U., Garden City, N.Y., 1980, Wagner Gallery, Lodi, N.Y., 1983, Ithaca House Gallery, 1984, 85, Schwein Furth Meml. Mus., Auburn, N.Y., 1986, Johnson Mus. Art, Ithaca, 1987, Upstairs Gallery, Ithaca, 1992, Lamoreaux Landing Wine Cellars Gallery, Lodi, N.Y., 1993, 97, 99, Trumanburg Conservatory Fine Arts, 1993, Wells Coll., Aurora, N.Y., 1995; exhibited in two-person shows at Harry McCue/David Smyth, Ithaca House, 1980, Hackworth/McCue, U. Pa., Edinboro, Grippi/McCue, Handwerker Gallery, Ithaca, McCue/Licht, Upstairs Gallery, Ithaca; exhibited in group shows at Internat. Gallery, Denver, 1969, Double U. Gallery, N.Y.C., 1977, Handwerker Gallery, 1980, 82, 84, 85, 86, 87, 89, 90, 91, 92, 93, 94, 95, 97, 98, 99, 2000, 2003, Upstairs Gallery, 1983—, Everson Mus., Syracuse (2d prize printmaking 1987), New Visions Gallery, Ithaca, 1987-90, Elmira Coll., 1991, Cazenovia Coll., 1993, Cooperstown Nat., 1993, 96, 97, 01, Old Forge Art Assn., 1992, West End Gallery, Corning, N.Y., 1996, 97, 2001—, Galeria Mesa, Ariz., 1998, Wright State U., Dayton, Ohio, 2000, Wichita (Kans.) Ctr. for Arts, 2001, Purdue U., Lafayette, Ind., 2004, U. Wis., Parkside, Wis., 2003; nat. exhbns.: Fall River Art Show, Mass., 1973, 74, 76, Marietta (Ohio) Coll., 1974, 76, Arnot Mus., Elmira, N.Y., 1977, 96, 2001, Ft. Hays State U., 1984, 2003, U. Maine, 1985, 92, 93, 96-99, Everson Mus., 1985; included in book The American History Supply Catalogue, 1983, N.Y. Art Rev., 3d edit.; invited spl. guest at spl. showing Christie's Auction House, N.Y.C., 1984, Roch Meml. Art Gallery, 1991; commd. by Cornell U./Statler Hotel to design art work for hotel, 1988. Lodestar grantee, 1984. Home: 2423 Skinner Rd Lodi NY 14860-9739 Office: Ithaca Coll Dept Art Danby Rd Ithaca NY 14850-5736

MCCUE, DAVID J. information systems specialist, entrepreneur; b. Phila., Mar. 28, 1956; s. Earl E. and A. Kathleen McCue; m. Nicole E. Schumacher, Aug. 16, 1981; 1 child, Christopher D. BSc, Rider U., 1978; MBA, NYU, 1980. Cons. Human Sys. Inc., New Vernon, NJ, 1980-81; from cons. to regional dir. tech. Andersen Consulting, NJ, 1981-93; chief info. and resource officer Am. Practice Mgmt., Inc., N.Y.C., 1993-96; chief info. officer Computer Scis. Corp., N.Y.C., 1996-2001; corp. dir. global applications Computer Scis. Corp. Worldwide, N.Y.C., 2001—03; v.p. applications portfolio mgmt. Computer Scis. Corp., Falls Church, Va., 2003—. Mem. adv. bd. Coll. Edn., Rider U., Lawrenceville, N.J., 1997-99. Mgr. Somerset County 4-H Fair, 1998—99; mem. Air Safety Found.; bd. dirs. Rider U. Alumni Assn., 1984—. Mem. Inst. Mgmt. Cons. (cert.), Assn. MBA Execs., Am. Prodn. and Inventory Control Soc. (cert. prodn. and inventory mgr.). Am. Soc. Indsl. Security, Aircraft Owners and Pilots Assn., Exptl. Aircraft Assn., NRA, NRCC (bus. adv. coun.). Republican. Roman Catholic. Avocations: commercial aviation pilot, equestrian sports. Home: PO Box 909 21580 Lower Woodchuck Rd Fairview MT 59833-0909 Office: CSC Corp Office VTC-C 630 MC 320 3170 Fairview Park Dr Falls Church VA 22042 Office Phone: 706-641-3076. E-mail: djmccue@mccue.org.

MCCUE, HOWARD MCDOWELL, III, lawyer, educator; b. Sumter, S.C., Jan. 4, 1946; s. Howard McDowell and Carolyn Hartwell (Moore) McC.; m. Judith Weiss, Apr. 3, 1972; children— Howard McDowell IV, Leigh AB, Princeton U., 1968; JD, Harvard U., 1971. Bar: Mass. 1971, Ill. 1975, U.S. Tax Ct. 1977. Assoc. Hale and Dorr, Boston, 1971-72; assoc. Mayer, Brown & Platt, Chgo., 1975-77, ptnr., 1977—. Adj. prof. law master in tax program Chgo. Kent Coll. Law, 1981— Author: (with others) Drafting Wills and Trust Agreements, 1979, 82, 85, 87, 90; mem. editorial adv. bd. Trusts and Estates mag., 1981-2000; contbr. articles to profl. jours. Bd. dirs. Art Inst. Chgo.; former chmn. bd. govs. Northwestern U. Libr. Coun.; bd. dirs., past vice-chmn. Ravinia Festival Assn.; chmn. Lloyd A. Fry Found. Lt. USN, 1972-75. Princeton U. scholar, 1965 Mem. ABA, Ill. Bar Assn., Chgo. Bar Assn. (fed. tax com., past chmn., exec. coun.), Chgo. Bar Found. (past pres.), Am. Coll. Tax Counsel, Am. Coll. Trust and Estate Counsel (regent, chair charitable planning and exempt orgns. com.), Harvard Law Soc. Ill., Internat. Acad. Estate and Trust Law, Chgo. Club, Phi Beta Kappa.

MCCUE, JUDITH W. lawyer; b. Phila., Apr. 7, 1948; d. Emanuel Leo and Rebecca (Raffel) Weiss; m. Howard M. McCue III, Apr. 3, 1971; children: Howard, Leigh. BA cum laude, U. Pa., 1969; JD, Harvard U., 1972. Bar: Ill. 1972, U.S. Tax Ct. 1984. Ptnr. McDermott, Will & Emery LLP, Chgo., 1995—. Dir. Schawk, Inc., Des Plaines, Ill.; past pres. Chgo. Estate Planning Coun. Trustee Chgo. Symphony Orch., 1995—, vice chair, 1998—2001. Fellow: Am. Coll. Trust and Estate Counsel (com. chair 1991—94, regent 1993—2000, com. chair 1998—2001, pres.-elect 2004—); mem.: Chgo. Bar Assn. (chmn. probate practice com. 1984—85, chair estate and gift tax divsn. of fed. tax com. 1988—89). Office: McDermott Will & Emery LLP 227 W Monroe St Ste 3100 Chicago IL 60606-5096 E-mail: jmccue@mwe.com.

MCCUEN, JOHN FRANCIS, JR., lawyer; b. N.Y.C., Mar. 11, 1944; s. John Francis and Elizabeth Agnes McCuen; m. Christine McCuen; children: Sarah, Mary, John. AB, U. Notre Dame, 1966; JD, U. Detroit, 1969. Bar: Mich. 1970, Fla. 1970, Ohio 1978. Legal counsel Kelsey-Hayes Co., Romulus, Mich., 1970-77; corp. counsel Sheller-Globe Corp., Toledo, 1977-79, v.p., gen. counsel, 1979-86, sec., 1982-87, sr. v.p. gen. counsel, 1986-89; ptnr. Marshall & Melhorn, Toledo, 1989-92; pvt. practice Law Offices John F. McCuen, Toledo, 1992-93; counsel Butzel Long, Ann Arbor, Mich., 1994; v.p. legal Kelsey Hayes Co., Livonia, Mich., 1994-98, v.p., gen. counsel, 1998-99; of counsel Butzel Long, 1999—2001. Trustee Kidney Found. N.W. Ohio, 1979-88, pres., 1984-86. Mem. Mich. Bar, Forest Lake Country Club. Home: 1668 Trading Post Ln Bloomfield Hills MI 48302-1868

MCCUEN, JOHN JOACHIM, finance company executive, columnist, educator; b. Washington, Mar. 30, 1926; s. Joseph Raymond and Josephine (Joachim) McCuen; m. Gloria Joyce Seidel, June 16, 1949; children: John Joachim Jr., Les Seidel. BS, U.S. Mil. Acad., 1948; M of Internatl. Affairs, Columbia U., 1961; grad., U.S. Army War College, 1968. Commd. 2d. lt. U.S. Army, 1948, advanced through grades to col.; dir. internal def. and devel. U.S. Army War Coll., Carlisle Barracks, Pa., 1969-72; chief U.S. Def. Liaison Group, Jakarta, Indonesia, 1972-74; chief field survey office U.S. Army Tng. and Doctrine Command, Ft. Monroe, Va., 1974-76; ret. U.S. Army, 1976; mgr. tng. Chrysler Def., Center Line, Mich., 1977-82; mgr. modification ctr. Land Systems div. Gen. Dynamics, Sterling Heights, Mich., 1982-83, mgr. field ops. Warren, Mich., 1983-94; pres. Mich. Econ. Devel. Corp., Birmingham, 1994—, The Magic Christmas Tree, Inc., Birmingham, 1994—; pres., CEO Laminar, Inc., Southfield, Mich., 1996—; owner Adventure and Exotic Travel Outfitters, Inc., Birmingham, 1995—; past pres. First Internat. Corp., Birmingham, 1995-97. Ptnr. East West Connection, Birmingham; past pres. Energy Resource Mgmt. Sys., Inc., Birmingham; armor advisor 3d Royal Thai Army, 1957—58; U.S. rep. users' com. NATO Missile Firing Installation Crete, Paris, 1964—66; advisor Vietnamese Nat. Def. Coll., Saigon, 1968—69; spkr., writer terrorism and counter insurgency. Author: The Art of Counter Revolutionary War-The Strategy of Counter Insurgency, Faber, 1966, Stackpole, 1967, Circulo Militar, 1967; columnist: Army Times, 2002—. Bd. dirs. Troy and Mt. Clemens (Mich.) Cmty. Concert Assn., 1982—, pres., 1985—; past pres. Mich. Oriental Art Soc., Brimingham; pres. Grander View Found. Sr. Housing and Nursing, Milford, Mich., 1984—89; past chmn. region VI N.E. unit Detroit United Way Campaign; 1st reader First Ch. of Christ Scientist, Birmingham, 1989—92, chmn. bd. dirs., 2000—01. Mem.: Nat. Mgmt. Assn., Soc. Logistics Engrs., Oriental Art Soc., Assn. U.S. Army. Republican. Avocations: oriental antiques, national security, writing. Home: 1530 Northlawn Blvd Birmingham MI 48009 Office: Laminar Inc 999 Haynes Suite 345 Birmingham MI 48009-6703 also: Mich Econ Devel Corp 999 Haynes Suite 345 Birmingham MI 48009-6703 Office Phone: 248-644-3485.

MCCUISTION, PEG OREM, retired hospice administrator; b. Houston, July 28, 1930; d. William Darby and Dorothy Mildred (Beckett) Orem; m. Palmer Day McCuistion, Sept. 4, 1949 (div. 1960); 1 child, Leeanne E. BBA, Southwest Tex. State, 1963; MBA, George Washington U., 1968; EdD, Wayne State U., 1989. Patient care adminstr. Holy Cross Hosp., Silver Spring, Md., 1968-79; exec. dir. Hospice of S.E. Mich., Southfield, 1979-86, Hospice Austin, Tex., 1987-94; CEO EMBI, Inc., Arlington, Tex., 1994—98; gen. mgr. Hospice Home Care, San Antonio, 2001—04, ret., 2004. Bd. dirs. Cmty. Home for the Elderly, Austin, 1989-92. Fellow Am. Coll. Health Care Execs. (membership com.); mem. Internat. Hospice Inst. (assoc.), Nat. Hospice Orgn. (chair standards and accreditation com.), Tex. Hospice Orgn. (pres. 1993-94), exec. com., standards and ethics com., edn. com., chair legis. com.), Mich. Hospice Orgn. (chair edn. com., bd. dirs.). Personal E-mail: pegomc@wimberley-tx.com.

MCCUISTION, ROBERT WILEY, hospital administrator, management consultant, lawyer; b. Wilson, Ark., June 15, 1927; s. Ed Talmadge and Ruth Wiley (Bassett) McC.; m. Martha Virginia Golden, June 11, 1949 (dec. Nov. 1991); children: Beth, Dan, Jed.; m. Sudola M. Getz, Feb. 12, 1994. AB in History, Hendrix Coll., Conway, Ark., 1949; JD, U. Ark., 1952. Bar: Ark. 1952, U.S. Dist. Ct. (we. dist.) Ark. 1953. Practice in, Dermott, Ark., 1952-57; dep. pros. atty. 10th Jud. Dist. Ark., 1952-57; bus. mgr. St. Mary's Hosp., Dermott, 1953-56, asst. adminstr., 1956-57; adminstr. Stuttgart (Ark.) Meml. Hosp., 1957-60, Forrest Meml. Hosp., Forrest City, Ark., 1960-68; assoc. adminstr. St. Edward Mercy Hosp., Ft. Smith, Ark., 1968-70; pres. Meml. Med Center, Corpus Christi, Tex., 1970-79; adminstr. Methodist Hosp., Mitchell, S.D., 1979-85, cons., 1985-86; mgmt. cons., owner Creative Leadership Concepts, Granbury, Tex., 1985—; adminstr. Cen. United Meth. Ch., Fayetteville, 1986-91. Sec. Ark. Hosp. Adminstrs. Forum, 1958-59, pres., 1959-60; pres. Ark. Hosp. Assn., 1964-65, Areawide Health Planning, 1970; pres. Ark. Conf. Cath. Hosps., 1970; chmn. Twin City Hosp. Coun. West Ark., 1968; v.p. Ark. Assn. Mental Health, 1966-70. Div. chmn. Forrest City United Cmty.Svcs., 1961, Corpus Christi United Way Cmty. Svcs., 1972, DeSoto coun. Boy Scouts Am., Explorer advisor, 1954-57; vice chmn., sec. ofcl. bd. Meth. Ch., 1957, lay del. S.D. ann. conf., 1980-85, cert. lay spkr., 1960—. With USAAF, World War II. Recipient Eminent Leadership award DeSoto Area council Boy Scouts Am., 1956 Mem. Am. Assn. Hosp. Accountants (pres. Ark. chpt. 1957), S.D. Hosp. Assn. (dist. chmn. 1980-81), Mid-West Hosp. Assn. (trustee 1963-65), Am. Coll. Health Execs. (life), Rotary (pres. Forrest City 1964-65). Home and Office: 2133 Savannah Trail Denton TX 76205

MCCULLAGH, GRANT GIBSON, retired architect; b. Cleve., Apr. 18, 1951; s. Robert Ernest and Barbara Louise (Grant) McC.; m. Suzanne Dewar Folds, Sept. 13, 1975; children: Charles Weston Folds, Grant Gibson Jr. BArch, U. Ill., 1973; MArch, U. Pa., 1975; MBA, U. Chgo., 1979. Registered architect, Ill. Dir. mktg. The Austin Co., Chgo., 1977-83, asst. dist. mgr., 1983-84, dist. mgr., 1984-88, v.p., 1987-88; chmn., CEO McClier Corp., Chgo., 1988—; chmn. Holmes & Narver, Orange, Calif., 1997-2001; exec. v.p. AECOM, L.A., 2000—03, vice chmn., 2003—04, ret., 2004. Trustee Chgo. (Ill.) Libr. Found., 2004—. Contbr. articles to various indsl. publs. Bd. dirs. Friends of Prentice Hosp.; trustee Newberry Libr. Fellow: AIA; mem.: Design/Build Inst. Am., Calif. Club, Comml. Club, Indian Hill Country Club, Univ. Club, Casino Club, Chgo. Club, Econ. Club. Republican. Episcopalian. Home: 43 Locust Rd Winnetka IL 60093-3725 Office: AECOM 555 S Flower Ste 3700 Los Angeles CA 90071-2300

MCCULLAR, MICHAEL D. pastor; b. Jasper, Ala., Dec. 8, 1954; s. Dewaine and Jean (Parvin) McC.; m. Lisa Davis, Dec. 15, 1978; children: Mallory, Jacob. BS, U. Ala., 1977; M of Christian Edn., 1982; DPhil, Oxford (Eng.) Grad. Sch., 1992. Min. of edn. First Bapt. Ch., Covington, La., 1982-88, Cullman, Ala., 1988-94; exec. pastor Johns Creek Bapt., Alpharetta, Ga., 1994—. Lead cons. Ctr. for Christian Edn., Charlotte, N.C., 1998—. Author: Sessions with James, 1999, A Guide to Innovative Adult Education, 2000; contbr. articles to Baptist Today. Mem. coun. Coop. Bapt. Fellowship Ga., 2000—. Recipient Grail award Oxford Grad. Sch./Ctr. Religion Soc. Studies, 1992; Tynedalef fellow. Fellow Oxford Soc. Scholars; mem. Am. Acad. Ministry, Atlanta Bapt. Assn. (ednl. cons. 1995—). Avocations: tennis, golf, jogging, writing. Office: Johns Creek Bapt Ch 7500 McGinnis Ferry Rd Alpharetta GA 30005 Home: 212 Ashton Lake Ct Sugar Hill GA 30518

MCCULLEN, JOSEPH T., JR., venture capitalist; b. Phila., Mar. 15, 1935; s. Joseph Thomas and Sara Ellen (Berryman) McC.; m. Eleanor Joan Houder, July 5, 1958; children: Geoffrey, Jennifer, Justin. BA, Villanova U., 1957, PhD (hon.), 1976. Mgr. planning & acquisitions Merck & Co., Inc., Rahway, N.J., 1961-65; sr. v.p., ptnr. Spencer Stuart & Assocs., N.Y.C., 1965-71; spl. asst. to Pres. Richard M. Nixon, Washington, 1971-73; asst. sec. of The Navy, Washington, 1973-77; sr. v.p., sec. New Eng. Mut. Life, Boston, 1977-80; pres. McCullen Ptnrs. Inc., Boston, 1980—; mng. dir. OneLiberty Ventures, Boston, 1986-99, Whitney & Co., Boston, 1999—2002; chmn. McCullen Capital, 2002—. Bd. dirs. MetroPCS, Inc., Dallas, EXTRAPRISE Group, Boston, Atlantis Wireless, Inc., Washington, TeleCorp WCS Inc., Washington; advisor Heritage Capital, Atlanta, 2001—, Carrott Capital, N.Y.C., 2001—; advisor transition team Mass. Port Authority, 2002—03; sr. advisor Key Prin. Ptnrs., Cleve., 2001—, Key Venture Ptnrs., Waltham, Mass., 2003—. Mem. selection com. White House Fellows Program, 1979-96; bd. dirs. World Affairs Coun., 1977-95, Boston Ballet, 1978-85, chmn., 1980-85; bd. trustees Goodwill Industries, 1979-95, Boston Biomed. Rsch. Inst., 1989-95; assoc. dir. Pres. Reagan Transition Team, 1980; advisor Pres. Bush Transition Team, 1988, Presdl. Bus. Commn., 2003—. Served with U.S. Navy, 1952-53; lt. U.S. Army, 1958-61. Recipient Disting. Pub. Svc. medals Exec. Office of Pres., 1973, U.S. Dept. Def., 1977. Home: 97 Essex Rd Chestnut Hill MA 02467-1316 Office: One Liberty Sq 12th Fl Boston MA 02109-4825

MCCULLEN, MICHAEL JOHN, retired advertising executive; b. Phila. Aug. 12, 1937; s. Joseph Thomas and Sara Ellen (Berryman) McC.; m. Kathleen Carol Flynn, Sept. 14, 1968; 1 child, Kelly Ann. BS in Mktg., Temple U., Phila., 1963. Creative liaison Phila. Inquirer, 1963-66; artist/writer The Phila. Bull., 1966-71; pres. Creative Creatures, Inc., Phila., 1971-79; advt. mgr. Eckerd Drug Co., Newark, Del., 1979-83; advt./sales promotion mgr. Eljo Products, Inc., Pennsauken, N.J., 1983-93; owner, operator McCullen & Assocs., Marlton, NJ, 1993—2001; ret., 2001. Mem. Rep. Nat. Com., Washington, 1985-86, Heritage Found., 1999—. With USN, 1957-59. Mem. Am. Soc. Advt. and Promotion, Nat. Assn. Desktop Pubs., Mktg. Color Group, Phila. Advt. Club, The Heritage Found. Republican. Roman Catholic. Avocations: drawing, painting, reading, sports. Home: 268 Grisscom Ct Marlton NJ 08053-2011

MCCULLOCH, ANNE MERLINE JACOBS, college dean; b. L.A., Mar. 20, 1948; d. Merlin Lee and Edna (Rammell) J.; m. Arlyn Cecil McCulloch, Sept. 17, 1977 (div. Mar. 1993); children: Justin Jacobs, Caroline Ranawn. BA, Coll. of Charleston, 1971; D of Arts, Idaho State U., 1975. Cert. secondary tchr., Idaho; cmty. coll. cert., Calif. Caseworker Dept. Social Svcs., Newport News, Va., 1970-71; asst. prof., then assoc. prof. polit. sci. Idaho State U., Pocatello, 1975-86, prof., 1986-89, grad. dir. polit. sci. dept., 1977-87; prof. Columbia (S.C.) Coll., 1989—, chmn. dept. history and polit. sci., 1991-98, interim dir. Leadership Inst., 1990-91, dean evening coll. and external programs, 1998—. Cons. Shoshone/Bannock Tribes, Ft. Hall, Idaho, 1986-87, 97; cons. S.C. ednl. TV film Snowbird Cherokee, 1993-95. Contbg. author: Native Americans and Public Policy, 1992; editor Native Am. Policy Network Newsletter, 1995—; assoc. editor Ency. Minorities in American Politics, 1999; contbr. articles to profl. jours. Mem. Idaho Gov.'s Blue Ribbon Econ. Commn., 1982-83; co-program chmn. Elizabeth Cady Stanton Conf., Columbia, 1995. Mem. Am. Polit. Sci. Assn. (coord. Native Am. studies 1995-96), So. Polit. Sci. Assn., So. Polit. Sci. Assn., Phi Kappa Phi, Pi Sigma Alpha, Phi Alpha Theta. Democrat. Mem. Lds Ch. Avocations: gardening, running, home remodeling. Home: 437 Southlake Rd Columbia SC 29223-6601 Office: Columbia Coll Evening Coll Columbia SC 29203 E-mail: amcculloch@colacoll.edu.

MC CULLOCH, ERNEST ARMSTRONG, internist, educator; b. Toronto, Ont., Can., Apr. 27, 1926; s. Albert E. and Letitia (Riddell) McC.; m. Ona Mary Morganty, 1953; children: James A., Michael E., Robert E., Cecelia E., Paul A. MD with honors, U. Toronto, 1948, DSc (hon.), 2004. Intern Toronto Gen. Hosp., 1949-50, sr. intern, 1951-52; NRC fellow dept. pathology U. Toronto, 1950-51; asst. resident Sunnybrook Hosp., Toronto, 1952-53; pvt. practice specializing in internal medicine Toronto, 1954-67; clin. tchr. dept. medicine U. Toronto, Toronto, 1954-60, asst. prof. dept. med. biophysics, 1959-64, assoc. prof., 1964-66, prof., 1966, asst. prof. dept. medicine, 1967-68, assoc. prof., 1968-70, prof., 1970—, Univ. prof., 1982-91, Univ. prof. emeritus, 1991—; mem. grad. faculty U. Toronto (Inst. Med. Sci.), 1968—, dir., 1975-79; asst. dean Sch. Grad. Studies U. Toronto, 1979-82. Physician Toronto Gen. Hosp., 1960-67; sr. scientist, sr. physician Ont. Cancer Inst., 1957-91, head divsn. biol. rsch., 1982-89, head divsn. cell and molecular biology, 1989-91, sr. scientist emeritus, 1991-93; vis. prof. U. Tex. Med. Ctr. Anderson Cancer Ctr., Houston, 1992-93, adj. prof., 1993-98; cons. Nat. Cancer Plan, 1972—; mem. standing com. on health rsch. and devel. Ont. Coun. Health, 1974-82. Author numerous articles on rsch. in hematology; mem. editl. bd.: Blood, 1969-80, Biomedicine, 1973, Clin. Immunology and Immunopathology, 1972-76; assoc. editor: Jour. Cellular Physiology, 1966-68; editor, 1968-91. Trustee Banting Rsch. Found., 1975-84, hon. sec.-treas., 1958-74, v.p., 1977-79. Decorated officer Order of Can., 1988; recipient William Goldie prize U. Toronto, 1964, Ann. Gairdner award Internat. Gairdner Found., 1969, Starr Medallist award Dept. Anatomy U. Toronto, 1957; Thomas W. Eadie Medal, 1991, Royal Soc. Canada, Nat. Cancer Inst. Can. fellow, 1954-57; named to Can. Med. Hall of Fame, 2004. Fellow Royal Soc. Can. (pres. Acad. Sci. 1987-90, Thomas W. Eadie Medal 1991, Golden Jubilee Medal), Royal Coll. Physicians and Surgeons Can., Royal Soc. London, Can. Acad. Sci.; mem. Am. Soc. Exptl. Pathology, Am. Assn. Cancer Rsch., Can. Soc. Cell Biology, Can. Soc. Clin. Investigation, Am., Internat. Socs. Hematology, Internat. Soc. Exptl. Hematology, Inst. Acad. Medicine (charter mem.), Badminton Club, Racquet Club. Home: 480 Summerhill Ave Toronto ON Canada M4W 2E4 Office: 610 University Ave Toronto ON Canada M5G 2M9 E-mail: mcculloch@oci.utoronto.ca. *Research success depends on associating with agreeable and talented people.*

MCCULLOCH, GEORGE MCQUILLAN, retired foundation executive, fundraiser; b. Glasgow, Scotland, Aug. 22, 1931; came to the U.S., 1949; s. William John and Margaret (McQuillan) McC.; m. Marian Gabriel, Jan. 19, 1954; children: William, David, Clifford, George. Student, Seton Hall U. Asst. credit mgr. Kraft Food Corp., Hillside, N.J., 1950-53; acctg. dept. staff FYR-Fyter Corp., Newark, 1953-64; scout exec. Boy Scouts Am., Rutherford and Elizabeth, N.J., 1965-75; exec. dir. United Cerebral Palsy, East Orange, N.J., 1975-80; exec. housekeeper various hotels, N.J./Mich., 1980-86; dir. housekeeping North Caldwell Bd. of Edn., 1986-91; pres. Scotty's Janitorial, Bloomfield, N.J., 1991-94. Cons. McQuillan and Apgar, Elizabeth; fund raising cons. Rahway (N.J.) Food Bank. Mem. Young Reps., Elizabeth, 1954-64; state chmn. N.J. Conservative Party, State of N.J., 1964-66; mem. Rep. Nat. Com., Washington, 1994-96. Mem. Free and Accepted Masons, Friends of Nat. Pks., Assn. Preservation Civil War, Libr. Congress Assn., Civil War Trust, Hospitalized Vets. Avocations: civil war buff, golf, travel, politics. Home: 107 Franklin St Bloomfield NJ 07003-5757

MCCULLOCH, JAMES CALLAHAN, corporate executive; b. Pittsfield, Mass., Aug. 20, 1947; s. G. Robert and Marion Elizabeth (Callahan) McC.; m. Patricia A. Greene, Dec. 28, 1970; children: William Brennan, Patrick Callahan, Daniel Daly, Peter Brennan, James Callahan II. BS in Commerce, St. Louis U., 1969, MS in Commerce, 1970. With Ford Motor Co., 1970-72; group contr. Chemetron Corp., 1972-80; corp. contr. Six Flags Corp., L.A., 1980-82; v.p. fin. and planning Indsl. Controls Group Allen-Bradley Co., Milw., 1982-86; v.p., chief fin. officer and treas. Sybron Corp., Saddle Brook, N.J., 1986-87, also bd. dirs.; pres. McCulloch Investments, Madison, N.J., 1987-98. Pres. McCulloch Investments, Madison, NJ, 1987—98; bd. dirs. Summit Industries, Chgo., Fraud-Check, Inc. Mem. Fin. Exec. Inst., Morris County Golf Club. Republican. Office: Fraud-Check Inc 70 W Red Oak Ln White Plains NY 10604 E-mail: JMcCulloch@fraud-check.com.

MCCULLOCH, LINDA, state official; b. Mont., Dec. 21, 1954; m. Bill McCulloch, 1978. BA in Elem. Edn., MA in Elem. Edn., U. Mont. Tchr. Pub. Schs, Mont., Ashland, Missoula, Bonner, 1978—95; rep. Mont. Ho. of Reps., Boise, 1995—2001; supt. pub. instrn. Mont., 2002—. Mem. juvenile justice, mental health, judiciary, Indian Affairs coms. Mont. Ho. Reps., 1997; minority caucus leader Ho. Reps., Helena, Mont., 1999; vice chair edn. com. Mont. Ho. Reps., 1999. Mem., officer PTA Assn., Helena, 1985—; bd. dirs. Missoula Developmental Svcs. Corp.; mem. adv. com. Missoula Youth Homes Foster Care. Recipient Mike and Maureen Mansfield Libr. scholaship, 1995, J.C. Penny Vol. Program award, 1998. Mem.: AAUW, LWV, Five Valleys Reading Assn., Mont. State Reading Coun., Mont. Fedn. Tchrs., Mont. Ednl. Assn., Mont. Libr. Assn. (Legislator of Yr. award 1997), Mont. Family Union, Montana Dem. Womens Club. Office: Mont Office Pub Instruction 1227 11th Ave Helena MT 59620-2501

MCCULLOCH, RACHEL, economics researcher, educator; b. Bklyn., June 26, 1942; d. Henry and Rose (Offen) Preiss; m. Gary Edward Chamberlain; children: Laura Chamberlain Gehl, Neil Dudley Chamberlain. BA, U. Pa., 1962; MA in Teaching, U. Chgo., 1965, MA, 1971, PhD, 1973; student, MIT, 1966-67. Economist Cabinet Task Force on Oil Import Control, Washington, 1969; instr., then asst. prof. Grad. Sch. Bus. U. Chgo., 1971-73; asst. prof., then assoc. prof. econs. Harvard U., Cambridge, Mass., 1973-79; assoc. prof., then prof. econs. U. Wis., Madison, 1979-87; prof. Brandeis U., Waltham, Mass., 1987—, Rosen Family prof., 1989—, dir. Lemberg Program in Internat. Econs. and Fin., 1990-91, dir. PhD program Grad. Sch. Internat. Econs. and Fin., 1994—2001. Mem. Pres.'s Commn. on Indsl. Competitiveness, 1983-84; mem. adv. coun. Office Tech. Assessment, U.S. Congress, 1979-88; cons. World Bank, Washington, 1984-86; mem. com. on internat. rels. studies with People's Republic of China, 1984-91; rsch. assoc. Nat. Bur. Econ. Rsch., Cambridge, 1985-93; mem. adv. com. Inst. for Internat. Econs., Washington, 1987—; faculty Advanced Mgmt. Network, La Jolla, Calif., 1985-92; mem. com. examiners econs. test Grad. Record Exam. Ednl. Testing Svc., 1990-96, chair, 1992-96; mem. discipline adv. com. for Fulbright scholar awards in econs. Coun. Internat. Exch. Scholars, 1991-93, chair, 1992-93; mem. adv. com. for Fulbright Chairs Program, 1997; cons. Global Economy Project, Edn. Film Ctr., 1993-94; mem. study group on pvt. capital flows to developing and transitional economies Coun. Fgn. Rels., 1995-96, acad. adv. panel, Fed. Reserve Bank of Boston, 1999—; faculty assoc. Harvard Inst. for Internat. Devel., 1997-2000; fellow Internat. Leadership Forum, 2001-; AGIP prof. internat. econs. Sch. Advanced Internat. Studies, Bologna Ctr., Johns Hopkins U., 2004-05. Author: Research and Development as a Determinant of U.S. International Competitiveness, 1978; contbr. articles to profl. jours. and books. Grantee NSF, 1975-79, Hoover Inst., 1984-85, German Marshall Fund of U.S., 1985, Ford Found., 1985-88, U.S. Dept. Edn., 1990-91, Schulhof Found., 2001-02. Mem. Am. Econ. Assn. (dir. summer program for minority students 1983-84, mem. executive com., 1997-2000), Internat. Trade and Fin. Assn. (bd. dirs. 1993-95). Home: 10 Frost Rd Lexington MA 02420-1904 Office: Brandeis U Dept Econs MS 021 Waltham MA 02454 E-mail: mcculloch@brandeis.edu.

MC CULLOCH, SAMUEL CLYDE, history professor; b. Ararat, Australia, Sept. 3, 1916; came to U.S., 1936, naturalized, 1944; s. Samuel and Agnes Almond (Clyde) McC.; m. Sara Ellen Rand, Feb. 19, 1944; children: Ellen (Mrs. William Henry Meyer III), David Rand, Malcolm Clyde. AB with highest honors in History, UCLA, 1940, MA (grad. fellow history), 1942; PhD, U. Calif. at Los Angeles, 1944. Asst. U. Calif. at Los Angeles, 1943-44; instr. Oberlin Coll., 1944-45; asst. prof. Amherst Coll., 1945-46; vis. asst. prof. U. Mich., 1946-47; mem. faculty Rutgers U., 1947-60, prof. history, assoc. dean arts and scis., 1958-60; dean coll., prof. history San Francisco State Coll., 1960-63; dean humanities, prof. history U. Calif. at Irvine, 1963-70, prof., 1970-87, prof. emeritus, 1987—, coordinator Edn. Abroad Program, 1975-85, dir. Australian Study Ctr., 1986, 87. Vis. summer prof. Oberlin Coll., 1945, 46, U. Calif. at Los Angeles, 1947, U. Del., 1949; Fulbright Research prof. Monash U., Melbourne (Australia) U., 1970; Am. Philos. Soc. grantee, 1970 Author: British Humanitarianism, 1950, George Gipps, 1966, River King: The Mc Culloch Carrying Company and Echura, 1865-1898, 1986, Instant University: A History of U.C.I., 1957-1993, 1995, William McCulloch, 1932-1909, 1997, A Collection of Book Reviews, 1948-93, 2000; contbr. numerous articles, revs. to profl. jours.; assoc. editor Jour. Brit. Studies, 1960-68, bd. advisors, 1968-70; bd. corrs. Hist. Studies: Australia and New Zealand, 1949-83. Mem. Calif. Curriculum Commn., 1961-67, Highland Park (N.J.) Bd. Edn., 1959-60. Grantee Am. Philos. Soc., Social Sci. Research Council and Rutgers U. Research Council to Australia, 1951; Fulbright research fellow U. Sydney, Australia, 1954-55; grantee Social Sci. Research Council to Eng., summer 1955 Fellow Royal Hist. Soc.; mem. Am. Hist. Assn., Church, Royal Australian hist. socs., A.A.U.P., Conf. Brit. Studies (exec. sec. 1968-73, pres. 1975-77), English Speaking Union (pres. New Brunswick 1957-59), Phi Beta Kappa, Pi Gamma Mu. Episcopalian (vestry). Home: 2121 Windward Ln Newport Beach CA 92660-3820

MCCULLOCH, SCOTT ANDREW, sales executive; b. Orange, N.J., June 18, 1957; s. Robert Patton and Jane Ruth McCulloch. Attended, Am. Coll. of Switzerland, 1976—77; BA, U. Miami, 1979; MS, Western Conn. State U., 1988. Nat. account/bus. mgr. United Parcel Service (UPS), Hartford, Conn., 1988—90; fin. cons./analyst Shearson Lehman Brothers, Sunnyvale, Calif., 1991—92, Merrill Lynch, Inc., San Francisco, 1991—92; mortgage cons. Citibank, FSB, Los Altos, Palo Alto, Atherton, Menlo Park, Calif., 1992—93; sr. internat. corp. credit analyst/mgr. Maxtor Corp., San Jose, 1994; project mgr. No. Calif regional sales mgr. At&T, San Francisco, 1994—95; corp. account rep. Hewlett Packard, Sunnyvale, Calif., Stamford, Conn., 1995—98; sr. corp. account mgr./project mgr. Saturn Bus. Systems Inc., New York, NY, 1999—2000; fin./mktg. analyst Robert Half Accountemps Internat., Danbury, Conn., 2001—, GE-VFS Inc., Boehringer Ingelheim Inc., The Innovation Group. Vol. Newtown Hook & Ladder Co. #1, 1973—75, Conn. Special Olympics, 1975. Mem.: The Mayflower Soc. Protestant. Avocations: skiing, running, hiking, sailing, travel.

MCCULLOCH, WILLIAM LEONARD, trade association administrator; b. Providence, Mar. 11, 1921; s. William Fraser and Elsie Cornelia (Westeberg) McC.; m. Dolores Ione Collier, July 26, 1952; children— William Fraser, II, Bruce Collier. BS, U.S. Naval Acad., 1945; MA in Internat. Relations, Georgetown U., 1958. Commd. 2d lt. USMC, 1944, advanced through grades to brig. gen., 1971; service in Okinawa; comdg. gen. (1st Marine Div.), 1974-75; congl. aide, 1975-76; exec. dir. Am. Assn. Orthotists and Prosthetists, Washington, 1976-86; pres. nat. office Orthotics and Prosthetics, 1986-88; pres. Assn. Communications and Mktg. Svcs., Washington, 1988—. Bd. dirs. Hanger Orthopedic Group. Decorated Legion of Merit with 2 stars, Bronze Star. Mem. Am. Soc. Assn. Execs., U.S. Naval Acad. Class of 1945 Assn. (pres. 1979-80), U.S. Naval Acad. Athletic Assn., Ret. Officers Assn., Capitol Hill Club (Washington), Army-Navy Country Club (Arlington, Va.), Marine Meml. Club (San Francisco), Army and Navy Club (past pres.), Washington, D.C. Club. Republican. Presbyterian. Home and Office: 528 Ft Williams Pky Alexandria VA 22304-1849 E-mail: acms-mcculloch@erols.com.

MCCULLOH, JUDITH MARIE, editor; b. Spring Valley, Ill., Aug. 16, 1935; d. Henry A. and Edna Mae (Traub) Binkele; m. Leon Royce McCulloh, Aug. 26, 1961. BA, Ohio Wesleyan U., 1956; MA, Ohio State U., 1957; PhD, Ind. U., 1970. Asst. to dir. Archives of Traditional Music, Bloomington, Ind., 1964-65; asst. editor U. Ill. Press, Champaign, 1972-77, assoc. editor, 1977-82, sr. editor, 1982-85, exec. editor, 1985—, dir. devel., 1992—2003; asst. dir., 1997—. Advisor John Edwards Meml. Forum, Los Angeles, 1973—. Mem. Editorial Bd. Jour. Am. Folklore, Washington, 1986-90; co-editor Stars of Country Music, 1975; editor (LP) Green Fields of Ill., 1963, (LP) Hell-Bound Train, 1964, Ethnic Recordings in America, 1982; gen. editor Music in American Life series. Trustee Am. Folklife Ctr., Libr. of Congress, Washington, 1986-2004, chair, 1990-92, 96-98. Fulbright grantee, 1958-59; NDEA grantee, 1961, 62-63; grantee Nat. Endowment for the Humanities, 1978; recipient Disting. Achievement citation Ohio Wesleyan U. Alumni Assn., Disting. Svc. award Soc. for Am. Music, Lifetime Achievement award Belmont U. Curb Music Industry, Disting. Achievement award Internat. Bluegrass Music Assn. Fellow: Am. Folklore Soc. (exec. bd. 1974—79, pres. 1986—87, exec. bd. 2001—03); mem.: Am. Musicological Soc., Am. Anthropol. Assn., Soc. Am. Music (1st v.p. 1989—93), Soc. for Ethnomusicology (treas. 1982—86). Democrat. Office: U Ill Press 1325 S Oak St Champaign IL 61820-6903 E-mail: jmmccull@uillinois.edu.

MCCULLOUGH, BENJAMIN FRANKLIN, transportation researcher, educator; b. Austin, Mar. 25, 1934; s. Benjamin Franklin and Mabel Comelia (Kitteridge) McC.; m. Norma Jean Walsh, Sept. 1, 1956; children: Michael Wayne, Bryan Scott, Steven Todd, Franklin Norman, Melanie Jean. MSCE, U. Tex., 1962; PhD of Civil Engring., U. Calif., Berkeley, 1969. Registered profl. engr., Tex. Testing engr. Covair Aircraft Co., Ft. Worth, 1957; design and rsch. engr. Tex. Hwy. Dept., Austin, 1957-66; rsch. engr. Materials R&D, Inc., Oakland, Calif., 1966-68; from asst. to prof. U. Tex., Austin, 1969—, dir. transp. rsch., 1980-99. Contbr. articles to profl. jours. Mem. ASCE (Outstanding Paper award 1987), Transp. Rsch. Bd., Coun. Univ. Transp. Ctrs., Univ. Transp. Ctrs. Program, Am. Concrete Inst. Mem. Lds Ch. Avocations: coaching, sports, golfing, U.S. and Tex. history. Office: U Tex Transp Rsch Ctr 3208 Red River St Ste 200 Austin TX 78705-2650

MCCULLOUGH, COLLEEN, author; b. Wellington, N.S.W., Australia, June 1, 1937; m. Ric Robinson, Apr. 13, 1984. Student, U. Sydney, Australia, London U.; LittD (hon.), Macquarie U., Sydney, 1993. Neurophysiologist Sydney, London, Yale U. Sch. Medicine, 1967-77. Author: Tim, 1974, The Thorn Birds, 1977, An Indecent Obsession, 1981, Cooking with Colleen McCullough and Jean Easthope, 1982, A Creed for the Third Millennium, 1985, The Ladies of Missalonghi, 1987, The First Man in Rome, 1990, The Grass Crown, 1991, Fortune's Favorites, 1993, Caesar's Women, 1996, Caesar, 1997, The Song of Troy, 1998, Roden Cutler, V.C. (The Biography), 1998, Morgan's Run, 2000, The October Horse, 2002, The Touch, 2003. Office: PO Box 333 Norfolk Island Australia Fax: (6723) 23313.

MCCULLOUGH, DAVID, writer, educator; b. Pitts., July 7, 1933; s. Christian Hax and Ruth (Rankin) McC.; m. Rosalee Ingram Barnes, Dec. 18, 1954; children: Melissa (Mrs. John E. McDonald, Jr.), David, William Barnes, Geoffrey Barnes, Doreen Kane (Mrs. Timothy Lawson). BA, Yale U., 1955; HLD, Skidmore Coll., 1983, Rensselaer Poly. Inst., 1983; D of Engring. (hon.), Villanova U., 1984; hon. doctorate, Worcester Poly. Inst., 1984; LittD (hon.), Allegheny Coll., 1984; LHD (hon.), Wesleyan U., Middletown, Conn., 1984, Colo. Coll., 1985; LittD (hon.), Middlebury Coll., 1986, U. Indiana at Pa., 1991, U. S.C., 1993; HLD (hon.), U. N.H., 1991; LittD (hon.), U. Pitts., 1994, Union Coll., 1994, Washington Coll., 1994; LHD (hon.), Chatham Coll., 1994. Writer, editor Time, Inc., N.Y.C., 1956-61, USIA, Washington, 1961-64, Am. Heritage Pub. Co., N.Y.C., 1964-70; sr. contbg. editor Am. Heritage mag.; free-lance author, 1970—. Newman vis. prof. American civilization, Cornell U., fall 1989; mem. Bennington (Vt.) Coll. Writers Workshop, 1978-79; scholar-in-residence U. N. Mex., 1979, Wesleyan U. Writers Conf., 1982, 83; mem. adv. bd. Ctr. for the Book, Libr. of Congress; past vis. prof. Dartmouth Coll., Wesleyan U.; spkr. and lectr. in field. Author: The Great Bridge, 1972, The Path Between the Seas, 1977, The Johnstown Flood, 1968, Mornings on Horseback, 1981, Brave Companions, 1992, Truman, 1992 (Pulitzer Prize for biography 1993), John Adams, 2001 (Pulitzer prize for biography 2002); host TV series: Smithsonian World, 1984-88, The American Experience, 1988—; narrator numerous TV documentaries including The Civil War, Napoleon, 2000, Abraham & Mary Lincoln: A House Divided, 2001. Mem. Harry S. Truman Centennial Commn.; trustee Nat. Trust Hist. Preservation, Harry S. Truman Libr. Inst., Hist. Soc. Western Pa., Jefferson Meml. Found., Boston Pub. Libr.; hon. trustee Carnegie Inst.; founding mem. Protect Hist. Am. Guggenheim fellow; recipient N.Y. Diamond Jubilee award, 1973, cert. of merit Mcpl. Art Soc. N.Y., 1973, Nat. Book award for history, 1978, Francis Parkman prize, 1978, 93, Samuel Eliot Morison award, 1978, Cornelius Ryan award, 1978, Civil Engring. History and Heritage award, 1978, L.A. Times prize for biography, 1981, Am. Book award for biography, 1982, Harry S. Truman Pub. Svc. award, 1993, St. Louis Lit. award, 1993, Pa. Gov.'s award for excellence, 1993, Pa. Soc. Gold Medal award, 1994, Charles Frankel prize contributions to humanities Endowment Humanities and U.S. Govt., 1995, Disting. Contbns. to Am. Letters award. Nat. Book Found., Lit. Lion award N.Y. Pub. Libr., Emmy award for work in pub. TV, Gold medal Pa. Soc. Fellow Soc. Am. Historians (pres.); mem. ASCE (hon.), Am. Acad. Arts and Scis., Soc. Am. Historians (pres. 1991—). Avocations: travel, reader, landscape painter, sunday night spaghetti chef. Office: Janklow & Nesbit Associates 445 Park Ave # 13th New York NY 10022-2606

MCCULLOUGH, DAVID L. urologist; b. Chattanooga, 1938; MD, Bowman Gray, 1964. Intern U. Hosps. Case Western Res. U., Cleve., 1964-65, resident in surgery, 1965-66; fellow urology Baylor U. Coll. Medicine, Houston, 1968-69; resident in urology Mass. Gen. Hosp., Boston, 1969-72; chief urologist N.C. Bapt. Hosp., Winston-Salem, 1983—; prof., former chmn. urology Wake Forest U. Coll. Medicine, Winston-Salem. Past pres. Am. Bd. Urology. Mem. ACS, AMA, Am. Urol. Assn. (past pres. southeastern sect., past pres., bd. dirs., chair for edn.), Am. Assn. Genitourinary Surgeons (v.p.), Clin. Soc. Urol. Surgeons, Halsted Soc.

MCCULLOUGH, EDWARD EUGENE, patent consultant; b. Baldwin, N.D., June 4, 1923; s. Elmer Ellsworth and Emma Izelda (Nixon) McC. BA, U. Minn., 1957; postgrad., Utah State U., 1965. Machine designer Sperry Rand Corp., Mpls., 1952-58; patent adminstr. Thiokol Corp., Brigham City, Utah, 1958-86, patent cons., 1986; pvt. practice, 1986—. Patentee 34 U.S. patents including instruments for making perspective drawings, apparatus for forming ignition surfaces in solid propellant motors, passive communications satellite or similar article, flexible bearings and process for their manufacture, rocket nozzel support and pivoting system, cavity-shaping machine, others. Pianist Aldersgate Meth. Ch., Brigham City, 1959—. Staff Sgt. U.S. Army, 1949-52. Decorated Korean War Svc. medal, two battle stars. Avocations: philosophy, music composition, hiking in the mountains. E-mail: edmccullough@msn.com.

MCCULLOUGH, FRANK WITCHER, III, lawyer; b. New Orleans, Dec. 13, 1945; s. Frank Witcher, Jr. and Kathleen Elizabeth (Van Pelt) McCullough; m. Barry Jean Bock, Mar. 7, 1981; children: William David Oat, Frank Witcher IV, Elizabeth Layton. BA, Stetson U., 1967; JD, W.Va. U., 1970. Bar: W.Va. 1970, Tex. 1970, U.S. Dist. Ct. (so. dist.) W.Va. 1970, U.S. Dist. Ct. (so. dist.) Tex. 1972, U.S. Ct. Appeals (5th cir.) 1972, U.S. Supreme Ct. 1980, U.S. Dist. Ct. (no. dist.) Calif. 1983, U.S. Dist. Ct. (we. dist.) Tex. 1987, U.S. Dist. Ct. (ea. dist.) Tex. 1993. Indsl. rels. specialist Continental Oil Co., Houston, 1970-72; asst. U.S. atty. U.S. Atty.'s Office, Houston, 1972-75; assoc. Baker & Botts, Houston, 1975-76, Austin, Tex., 1985-89; ptnr. Weiner Strother & Lamkin, Houston, 1983-85; regional counsel GATX Leasing Corp., Houston, 1976-78; ptnr. Walsh Squires Tompkins & McCullough, Houston, 1978-82; shareholder Sheinfeld, Maley & Kay, Austin, 1989-2001, Diamond McCarthy Taylor & Finley, Austin, 2001—04, Haynes and Boone, lLP, Austin, 2004—. Spl. commr. Harris County, Houston, 1982; mem. Bellaire (Tex.) Bd. Adjustments, 1982; bd. dirs. Big Bros. and Big Sisters Austin, 1991—94. Mem.: SAR, State Bar Tex. (mem. grievance com. 1979—87, 1995—2001, panel chair 2000—01, chmn. unauthorized practice law com. 1984—87), Austin Country Club. Republican. Episcopalian. Home: 6707 Bridge Hill Cv Austin TX 78746-1338 Office: Haynes and Boone LLP 600 Congress Ave Ste 1300 Austin TX 78701 *Notable cases include: Univ. Savs. Assn. vs. Springwoods Shopping Ctr., 1982, in which the Tex. Supreme Ct. created significant exception to the rule of law that the terms and provisions of deed of trust must be strictly followed in foreclosure proceeding.*

MCCULLOUGH, GLENN L., JR., electric power industry executive; b. Tupelo, Miss. m. Laura White; children: Vance, Glenn Thomas. Degree in agrl. econ., Miss. State U., 1977. Dir. Appalachian Regional Commn. (ARC), Miss., 1992—97; mayor Tupelo, Miss., 1997—99; chmn., bd. dirs. Tenn. Valley Authority, 1999—. Mem. Nat. Electric Adv. Bd., Dept. Energy; mem. bd. Miss. Partnership Econ. Devel., Econ. Devel. Partnership, Ala.; mem. governing bd. Electric Power Rsch. Inst., Inst. Nuc. Power Ops., Nuc. Energy Inst. Governing bd. United Way; mem. Big Bros./Big Sisters Orgn.; governing bd. Cmty. Devel. Found., Commn. Future Northeast Miss. Recipient All-Am. City award, Nat. Civic League, 1999. Office: Tenn Valley Authority 400 W Summit Hill Dr Knoxville TN 37902-1499 Office Phone: 865-632-2101. Business E-Mail: tvaineot@va.gov.

MC CULLOUGH, J. LEE, industrial psychologist; b. Bryn Mawr, Pa., Oct. 3, 1945; s. Leo Francis and Margaret Mary (Hart) McC.; m. Bonnie R. Goldberg, Jan. 14, 1979. AB, Villanova U., 1967; MA, Ohio State U., 1968, PhD, 1971. Tchg. asst. Ohio State U., 1967-68, rsch. assoc., 1968-69; assoc. O.P.S. Assocs., Columbus, 1970-71; assoc., sr. assoc., sr. prin., v.p Hay Group, N.Y.C., 1971-90, v.p., dir. fin. svcs. cons., 1990-94; prin. William M. Mercer, Inc., N.Y.C., 1994—. Adj. prof. Fordham U. Grad. Sch. Bus., 1984-89. Served with AUS, 1972. NSF fellow, 1969; NDEA Title IV fellow, 1970; Univ. Dissertation Year fellow, 1971. Mem. Am. Psychol. Soc., Met. Psychol. Assn. Home: 6 Hereford Dr Princeton Junction NJ 08550-1514 Office: 30th Fl 1166 Avenue Americas New York NY 10036-2708 Office Phone: 212-345-7844. E-mail: LeeMcCullough@comcast.net.

MCCULLOUGH, JEFFERSON WALKER, industrial engineering consultant; b. Hartford, Conn., Nov. 2, 1944; s. Sam Walker and Beula (Adams) McC. Grad. Williston Sch., 1963; student Rutgers U., 1963-69, Greater Hartford Coll., 1979-80; postgrad. Oxford U., Eng. With Textron, Inc., United Technologies, Royal Bus. Machines, Colt Industries, Ill. Tool Works, ALCO Corp., Ingersoll Rand, Combustion Engring., Cooper Industries, Allied Signal, Becton-Dickinson; cons. indsl. engring. and fin., Rocky Hill, Conn., 1950—; cons. Select Equity Assn. Friend (hon.) of Bodleian Libr, Friend of Rewley House (Oxon.); active Wadsworth Atheneum, Hartford, City Spirit Artists, Artspace, New Haven, Campaign for Oxford. Mem. Internat. Platform Assn. Avocations: art, music, classical languages. Home: 140 Hayes Rd Rocky Hill CT 06067-1010

MCCULLOUGH, JOHN PHILLIP, management consultant, educator; b. Lincoln, Ill., Feb. 2, 1945; s. Phillip and Lucile Ethel (Ornellas) McC.; m. Barbara Elaine Carley, Nov. 29, 1968; children: Carley Jo, Ryan Phillip. BS, Ill. State U., 1967, MS, 1968; PhD, U. N.D., 1971. Adminstrv. mgr. McCullough Ins. Agy., Atlanta, Ill., 1963-68; ops. supr. Stetson China Co., Lincoln, 1967; asst. mgr. Brandtville Svc., Inc., Bloomington, Ill., 1968; instr. in bus. Ill. Ctrl. Coll., 1968-69; rsch. asst. U. N.D., Grand Forks, 1969-71; assoc. prof. mgmt. West Liberty State Coll., 1971-74, prof., 1974—. Chmn. dept. mgmt., West Liberty State Coll., 1974-82, dir. Sch. Bus., 1982-86, dean, 1986—, provost, 1998—, interim pres., 2001, dir. Small Bus. Inst., 1978—; mgmt. cons., Triadelphia, W.Va., 1971—; instr. Am. Inst. Banking, 1971—; lectr. W.Va. U., 1971—; adj. prof. MBA program Wheeling Coll., 1972—, U. Steubenville, 1982—; lectr. Ohio U., 1982—; profl. assoc. Inst. Mgmt. and Human Behavior, 1975—; v.p. West Liberty State Coll. Fed. Credit Union, 1976—; rep. W.Va. Bd. Regents Adv. Coun. of Faculty. Author: (with Howard Fryette) Primer in Supervisory Management, 1973; contbr. articles to profl. jours. Team leader Wheeling divsn. Am. Cancer Soc.; coord. Upper Ohio Valley United Fund, 1972-74; instr. AFL-CIO Cmty. Svcs. Program, Wheeling; project dir. Ctr. for Edn. and Rsch. with Industry; bd. dirs. Family Svc.-Upper Ohio Valley, Ohio Valley Indsl. and Bus. Devel. Corp., Inc., Labor Mgmt. Inst. Wheeling Salvation Army, Progress, Inc., Ohio Valley Health Svcs. and Edn. Corp. Recipient Svc. award Bank Adminstrn. Inst., 1974, United Fund, 1973, Acad. Achievement award Harris-Casals Found., 1971. Mem. Soc. Humanistic Mgmt. (nat. chmn.), ORgn. Planning Mgmt. Assn. (exec. com.), Spl. Interest Group for Cert. Bus. Educators (nat. dir.), Soc. Advancement Mgmt. (chpt. advisor), Acad. Mgmt., Adminstrv. Mgmt. Soc. (cert.), Am. Soc. Pers. Adminstrn. (cert.), Nat. Bus. Honor Soc. (Excellence in Tchg. award 1976, dir. 1974—), Alpha Kappa Psi (Dist. Svc. award 1973, Civic award 1977, chpt. advisor 1971—), Merit Found. W.Va. (Ednl. Excellence award), Delta Mu Delta, Delta Pi Epsilon, Delta Tau Kappa, Phi Gamma Nu, Phi Theta Pi, Pi Gamma Mu, Pi Omega Pi, Omicron Delta Epsilon. Home: 68 Elm Dr Triadelphia WV 26059-9620 Office Phone: 304-336-8004. Business E-Mail: mcculljp@ulsc.edu.

MCCULLOUGH, JOHN PRICE, retired oil company executive; b. Dallas, May 10, 1925; s. John A. and Alta (McGee) McC.; m. Mary Ann Calvert, Aug. 5, 1946; children: Sherri, Cathryn, Patricia. Student, U. Denver, 1942-43; BS in Chem. Engring, U. Okla., 1945; MS, Oreg. State U., 1948, PhD in Chemistry, 1949. With U.S. Bur. Mines, Bartlesville, Okla., 1949-63, phys. chemist, 1949-57, chief thermodynamics br., 1958-63; mgr. central research div. Mobil Oil Corp., Princeton, N.J., 1963-69, mgr. applied research and devel. Paulsboro, N.J., 1969-71; gen. mgr. research and devel. Mobil Chem. Co., Edison, N.J., 1971-78; v.p. environ. health and safety Mobil Research & Devel. Corp., Princeton, N.J., 1978-89. Adj. prof. chemistry Okla. State U., Stillwater, 1961-63; vis. fellow Woodrow Wilson Found., 1991-95; dir. Internat. Petroleum Industry Environ. Conservation Assn., 1981-89, chmn., 1985-88; dir. Mobil Found., Inc., 1987-89. Co-author: (with Donald Scott) Experimental Thermodynamics, Volume I: Calorimetry of Non-reacting Systems, 1968; contbr. 90 articles on thermodynamics, molecular structure and energetics, environ. and health policy to profl. jours. Mem. adv. com. Mercer County (N.J.) C.C., 1968-69; bd. dirs. Chem. Industry Inst. Toxicology, 1977-89, chmn., 1986-88; bd. dirs. United Cmty. Fund, Princeton, 1963-69, Middlesex-Somerset-Mercer Regional Study Coun., 1968-69, 86-89, World Environ. Ctr., 1986-89; mem. adv. bd. Georgetown U. Inst. Health Policy Analysis, 1986-89; trustee Stony Brook-Millstone Watershed Assn., 1989-95, vice chmn., 1991-93, adv. bd., 1996-99; trustee Friends of Art Mus. Princeton U., 1994-2000, treas., 1997-2001; elder Nassau Presbyn. Ch. Lt. (j.g.) USNR, 1943-54. Recipient Meritorious Svc. award U.S. Dept. Interior, 1959, Disting. Svc. award, 1962; DuPont fellow, 1947-48. Mem. AAAS, Gordon Rsch. Conf. (trustee, chmn. bd. trustees, mem. coun.), Am. Chem. Soc. (editl. bd. Jour. Chem. and Engring. Data, Jour. Phys. Chemistry, mem. coun. com. on chemistry and pub. affairs 1984-92, chmn. 1987-89, award for petroleum chemistry 1963, Chemtech. award 1977), Internat. Calorimetry Conf. (chmn. 1960, Huffman award 1963), Am. Inst. Chemists, Sigma Xi. Home: 7 Fringe Tree Ct Princeton NJ 08540-5061 E-mail: jmccullough55@comcast.net.

MCCULLOUGH, JOSEPH, college president emeritus; b. Pitts., July 6, 1922; s. Joseph Phillip and Margaret (List) McC.; m. Elizabeth Cramer, Mar. 31, 1945; children— Marjorie Ann, Warren BFA, Yale U., 1949-50, MFA, 1951; Diploma, Cleve. Sch. Art, 1948; DFA (hon.), U. Evansville, Ind., 1980; DA (hon.), Cleve. Inst. Art, 1996. Instr. San Jose State Coll., Calif., 1948-49; asst. instr. Yale U., New Haven, 1949-51; asst. dir. Cleve. Inst. Art, 1952-54, dir., 1954-74, pres., 1974-88. Artist paintings, nat. regional and local exhbns., 1948— Chmn. Fine Arts Adv. Com., Cleve. Planning Commn., 1963-91; trustee Mpls. Coll. of Art and Design, 1988-98, Sculpture Ctr. Cleve., 1990-98; trustee, sec. Access to the Arts, Cleve., 1991-95. Capt. USAAF, 1943-46, ETO. Recipient Cleve. Arts prize Women's City Club, 1971, Centennial medal John Carroll U., 1987, medal for excellence Cleve. Inst. of Art, 1997. Mem.: Coll. Art Assn. ((past dir.)). Home: 20101 North Park Blvd Cleveland OH 44118-5006

MCCULLOUGH, KATHRYN T. BAKER, social worker; b. Trenton, Tenn., Jan. 5, 1925; d. John Andrew and Alma Lou (Wharey) Taylor; m. John R. Baker, Sept. 30, 1972 (dec. Oct. 1981); m. T.C. McCullough, May 14, 1988. BS, U. Tenn., 1945, MSW, 1954; postgrad., U. Chgo., 1950, Vanderbilt U., 1950-51. Lic. social worker, Tenn.; emeritus diplomate in clin. social work Am. Bd. Examiners. Home demonstration agt., agrl. extension svc. U. Tenn., Hardeman County, 1946-49; Dyer County, 1949-50; dir. med. social work dept. Le Bonheur Children's Hosp., Memphis, 1954-57; chief clin. social worker clinic mentally retarded children U. Tenn. Dept. Pediatrics, Memphis, 1957-59; clin. social worker Children's Med. Ctr., Tulsa, 1959-60; dir. med. social work dept. Coll. of Medicine U. Tenn., Memphis, 1960-69; dir. community svcs. regional med. program Coll. of Medicine, 1969-76; dir. regional clinic program Child Devel. Ctr. Coll. of Medicine, 1976-85; mem. faculty Coll. of Medicine, Coll. of Social Work U. Tenn., Memphis, 1960-85; social worker admissions rev. bd. Arlington Devel. Ctr., Memphis, 1976-98. Cons. Tenn. Dept. Children's Svcs., 1999—2003. Author 14 books. Commr. Dist. I, Gibson Utility Dist., Shelby County, Tenn., 1990—98; former bd. dirs. Am. Heart Assn., Am. Cancer Soc., Am. Lung Assn., United Cerebral Palsy, Goodwill Industries, AGAPE Child and Family Svcs., Health and Welfare Planning Coun., Shelby County Child Head Start, Greater Memphis Day Care Assn.; advisor AGAPE Child and Family Svcs., 1998—2001, field. rep., 2003—; mem. bd. visitors U. Tenn. Coll. Social Work, Knoxville, 2000—; active Gibson County Fedn. Dem., 1985—98, Dem. Party orgns., 1946—. Fellow: Am. Assn. Mental Retardation (life); mem.: AAUP, Tenn. Conf. on Social Welfare, Acad. Cert. Social Workers, Sigma Kappa Sorority (life). Mem. Ch. of Christ. Avocations: piano, organ, symphony. Home: 627 Riverside Yorkville Rd Trenton TN 38382-5917

MCCULLOUGH, M. BRUCE, judge; b. Princeton, N.J., July 26, 1944; s. Malcolm S. and Ruth S. (Strandness) McC.; m. Kathleen M. Ryan, Apr. 12, 1985. BA in Polit. Sci. and Econs., Whitworth Coll., 1966; JD, U. Mich., 1969. Bar: Pa., Fla., D.C. Ptnr. Buchanan Ingersoll P.C., Pitts., 1969-95; judge U.S. Bankruptcy Ct., Pitts., 1995—. Chmn. ARC (southwest Pa., 1994-96). With USAR, 1969-75. Mem. Chartiers Country Club, Duquesne Club. Avocations: golf, boating, hunting. Office: US Bankruptcy Ct 600 Grant St Pittsburgh PA 15219-2702

MCCULLOUGH, RALPH CLAYTON, II, lawyer, educator; b. Daytona Beach, Fla., Mar. 28, 1941; s. Ralph C. and Doris (Johnson) McC.; m. Elizabeth Grier Henderson, Apr. 5, 1986; children from previous marriage: Melissa Wells, Clayton Baldwin. BA, Erskine Coll., 1962; JD, Tulane U., 1965. Bar: La. 1965, S.C. 1974. Assoc. Baldwin, Haspel, Maloney, Rainold and Meyer, New Orleans, 1965-68; asst. prof. law U. S.C., 1968-71, assoc. prof., 1971-75, prof., 1975—, chair prof. of advocacy, 1982—, asst. dean Sch. Law, 1970-75, instr. Med. Sch., 1970-79, adj. prof. law and medicine Med. Sch., 1979—; adj. prof. medicine Med. U. SC, 1984—; of counsel Finkel & Altman, 1978—. Adj. prof. pathology Med. U. S.C., 1985—; asst. dean U. S.C. Sch. Law 1970-75, Disting. prof. law, 2001, Disting. prof. law emeritus, 2003—; mem. fourth cir. adv. com. on rules and procedures U.S. Ct. Appeals, 2001—. Author: (with J.L. Underwood) The Civil Trial Manual, 1974, 7th supplement, 1987, The Civil Trial Manual II, 1984, 87, (with Myers and Felix) New Directions in Legal Education, 1970, (with Finkel) S.C. Torts II, 1986, III, 1990, IV, 1995; co-reporter S.C. Criminal Code, 1977, S.C. Study Sentencing, 1977. Trustee S.C. dist. U.S. Bankruptcy Ct., 1979—; exec. dir. S.C. Continuing Legal Edn. Program.; bd. visitors Erskine Coll.; reporter S.C. Jury Charge Commn., 1991-95. Mem. ATLA, ABA, La. Bar Assn., S.C. Bar (sec. 1975-76, exec. dir. 1972-76, award of service 1978), New Orleans Bar Assn., Am. Law Inst., Am. Coll. Trial Lawyers, Southeastern Assn. Am. Law Schs. (pres.), S.C. Trial Lawyers Assn. (bd. govs. 1984-88), Forest Lake Club, Phi Alpha Delta. Republican. Episcopalian. Home: PO Box 1799 Columbia SC 29202-1799 Office: 1201 Main St Ste 1800 Columbia SC 29201-3294 Office Phone: 803-765-2935.

MCCULLOUGH, RICHARD LAWRENCE, advertising agency executive; b. Chgo., Dec. 1, 1937; s. Francis John and Sadie Beatrice McCullough; m. Julia Louise Kreimer, May 6, 1961; children: Stephen, Jeffery, Julie. BS, Marquette U., 1959. Commd. U.S. Army, 1959, advance through grades to sgt., 1966; account exec. Edward H. Weiss Advt., Chgo., 1960-66; account supr. Doyle Dane Bernbach, N.Y.C., 1966-68; sr. v.p. J. Walter Thompson Co., Chgo., 1969-86; pres. E.H. Brown Advt., Chgo., 1986-97; exec. v.p. Space-Time Media Mgmt., Chgo., 1997—; ptnr. Callahan Group, Chgo., 2000—. Developer Mktg. with Country Music nat. seminar, 1996. Author: Building Country Radio, 1986, A New Look at Country Music Audiences, 1988, (video) Country Music Marketing, 1989. Bd. dirs. Gateway Found., Chgo., 1976—, chmn., 1988-91; bd. dirs., chmn. mktg. com. Cath. Charities, Chgo. Recipient Nat. Cmty. Svc. award, Gateway Found., 2002, Dennis Kelly Honor award, Cath. Charities, 2002. Mem. Country Music Assn. (Nashville bd. dirs. 1979—, pres. 1983-85, Pres.'s award 1987, elector Country Music Hall of Fame), NARAS (Nashville chpt.), North Shore Country Club (Glenview, Ill.), Dairymen's Country Club (Boulder Junction, Wis.), Quail Creek Country Club (Naples, Fla.). Roman Catholic. Home: 2720 Lincoln St Evanston IL 60201-2043 Office: Space-Time Media Mgmt Inc 35 E Wacker Dr Chicago IL 60601-2103 Home: 2720 Lincoln St Evanston IL 60201-2043 E-mail: dick@spacetimemedia.com., relchar@aol.com.

MCCULLOUGH, ROBERT, management consultant, information technology executive; s. Ralph W. McCullough and Becky W. Morris. BBA, Ga. State U., 1994. Pres., CEO IT Mgmt. Ptnrs., Duluth, Ga., 2002—. Corp. dir. BIG, Atlanta, 2003—03. Mem.: Nat. Assn. Corp. Dirs. (assoc.). Office: IT Management Ptnrs 2180 Pleasant Hill Rd Ste A-5 Duluth GA 30096 Personal E-mail: contactus@itmpinc.com. E-mail: contactus@itmpinc.com.

MCCULLOUGH, ROBERT DALE, II, osteopath; b. Tulsa, June 2, 1937; s. Robert Dale and Roberta Maud (Purdy) McC.; m. Lindell Arlene Wilcox, Sept. 28, 1963; children: Robert Mark, Lori Lindell. Student, Wheaton (Ill.) Coll., 1955-57; BS, N.E. Mo. State U., 1958; DO, Kansas City (Mo.) Coll. Osteopathy, 1958-62. Diplomate in internal medicine and med. oncology Am. Osteo. Bd. Internal Medicine. Gen. practice McCullough Clinic, Tulsa, 1963-68; internal medicine resident Detroit Osteo. Hosp., 1968-71; internal medicine Baker-Todd-McCullough-Sutton, Tulsa, 1971-74; fellow med. oncology M.D. Anderson Hosp., Houston, 1974-75; internal medicine-med. oncology Baker-Todd-McCullough-Sutton, Tulsa, 1975-90; pvt. practice Tulsa, 1990-93; attending staff mem. VA Outpatient Clinic, Tulsa, 1993-94; assoc. med. dir. Blue Cross/Blue Shield of Okla., Tulsa, 1994—. Trustee Tulsa Regional Med. Cttr., 1983-88, 90-93; bd. dirs. Okla. Blue Cross Blue Shield, Tulsa, 1983-92, vice chmn., 1991-92; mem. adv. coun. Okla. State U. Coll. Osteo. Medicine, 1988-94, chmn., 1988-90. Mem. bd. of editors Patient Care Magazine, Montvale, N.J., 1988-93. Mem. Okla. State Bd. Health, Oklahoma City, 1983-87, Tulsa City/County Bd. Health, 1988-95, chmn., 1993; bd. mem., Cmty. Health Found., 1997—, chmn., 2003-04. Mem. Nat. Osteo. Found. (trustee 1993-2000, treas. 1998-2000), Am. Osteo. Assn. (vice speaker Ho. of Dels. 1986-92, trustee 1993-2000), Am. Coll. Osteo. Internists, Am. Soc. Clin. Oncology, Okla. Osteo. Assn. (pres. 1982-83), Tulsa Downtown Lions Club, Soc. for Preservation and Encouragement of Barbershop Quartet Singing in Am. Republican. Baptist. Avocation: barbershop quartet singing. Home: 2477 E 73rd Pl Tulsa OK 74136-5520 Office: 1400 S Boston Ave Tulsa OK 74119-3613 Office Phone: 918-631-6670. Personal E-mail: RMccull207@aol.com. Business E-Mail: rmccullough@bcbsok.com.

MCCULLOUGH, ROSS A., JR., delivery service executive; b. Decatur, Ill., Mar. 18, 1966; s. Ross A. and Laura K. McCullough; m. Cindy E. Mullinax, June 11, 1992; children: Ross, III, Gracie. MBA, Emory U., Atlanta, 1996; BS in Indsl. Tech., Ea. Ill. U., 1987. Mgr. strategic planning UPS, Atlanta, 1994—96, v.p. electronic commerce, 1996—2001, v.p. corp. strategy Brussels, 2001—03, v.p. mktg. supply chain solutions Alpharetta, Ga., 2004—. Mem.: Coun. Logistics Mgmt. Office: UPS Supply Chain Solutions 12380 Morris Rd Alpharetta GA 30005

MCCULLOUGH, V. BETH, pharmacist, educator; b. Harrison, Ark., May 15, 1953; d. A. G. and Willene L. (McLain) McC.; m. David Mark Pearson, Oct. 25, 1980; children: Colin McCullough-Pearson, Emily McCullough-Pearson. BS in Edn. cum laude, S.W. Mo. State U., 1976; BS in Pharmacy, U. Mo., 1981. Registered Pharmacist, Mo. Chief pharmacist Mt. Vernon Park Pharmacy, Springfield, Mo., 1981-89; dir. pharmacy Foster Health Care Group, Springfield, 1989-96; chief pharmacy ops. Balanced Care Corp./Foster Health Care Group, Springfield, 1996-97; cons. pharmacist Managed Healthcare Pharmacy divsn. Omnicare Corp., Springfield, 1997-2001; owner Med. Park Pharmacy, Eureka Springs, Ark., 2001—. Long term care pharmacy cons. Foster Health Care Group, Springfield, 1981-83, Managed Healthcare Pharmacy, Springfield, 1997-2001. Mem. NOW, Springfield, 1982—, assoc. mem. Animal Shelter League of the Ozarks, Nixa, Mo. Mem. Am. Soc. Cons. Pharmacists, Southwest Mo. Humane Soc., Mo. Equine Coun., Mo. Pharmacy Assn., Long Term Care Acad., Biokinetics (instnl. rev. bd. 1999-2001). Avocations: watercolor painting, jewelry making, horse breeding and showing. Office: 146 Passion Play Rd Eureka Springs AR 72632-9495 Home: 146 CR 238 Berryville AR 72616

MCCULLOUGH, WILLARD G. retired biochemist; b. Brighton, Mich., Nov. 13, 1914; s. George W. and Florence Bird McCullough; m. Barbara Isabel McMullen, Sept. 23, 1944; children: Andrew Scott, Robin Nelson. BS in Chemistry, Mich. State U., 1941, MS in Bacteriology, 1942; PhD in Biochem., U. Wis., 1949. Instr. U. Mich., Ann Arbor, 1949—50; from asst. to assoc. prof. Wayne State U., Detroit, 1950—60; rsch. biochemist USDA ARS Nat. Animal Disease Ctr., Ames, Iowa, 1960—78. Contbr. scientific papers to profl. jours. Capt. chem. br. U.S. Army, 1943—46. Fellow: AAAS; mem.: Am. Soc. for Microbiology, Am. Chem. Soc. Home: 1310 50th Ave Sears MI 49679-8725

MCCULLOUGH, WILLIAM LAWRENCE, medical readiness consultant; b. Norfolk, Va., Mar. 18, 1951; s. William Lawrence, Jr. and Anne Laurie McC.; m. Marilyn Jane Greer, Sept. 5, 1971 (div. Nov. 1974); m. Carolyn Elizabeth Buckley, Oct. 9, 1976; children: Ross, Mark, Jena. BBA in Personnel Mgmt., St. Mary's U., San Antonio, Tex., 1973; MS in Healthcare Adminstrn., Trinity U., San Antonio, 1977. Cert. med. adminstr. Commd. 2d lt. U.S. Army, 1974; exec. officer/detachment comdr. U.S. Army dental activity, Ft. McLellan, Ala., 1978-81; commd. lt. USN, 1981; various to head, deployable med. systems Chief of Naval Ops., Washington, 1990-92; head, med. strategic plans and policies The Joint Staff, Washington, 1992-96; chief, med. plans and policies Chief of Naval Opers., Washington, 1996-97; ret. USN, 1997; sr. rsch. scientist Battelle Meml. Inst., Falls Church, Va., 1997-2000; with Integrated Mgmt. Svcs., Inc., 2000—. Vestry mem. Aquia Episc. Ch., Stafford, Va., 1999; com. chmn. Cub Scout Pack 324, Boy Scouts Am., Stuttgart-Vaihingen Germany, 1987-90, cubmaster Pack 840, Stafford, 1991-93, com. mem. 1992-94. Decorated Def. Meritorious Svc. awards (2) Dept. of Def., Meritorious Svcs. awards (3) USN, Army Commendation medal; named to Outstanding Young Men of Am., 1990. Mem. Am. Assn. Med. Adminstrs. Episcopalian. Avocations: sports cars, sailing. Office: 5109 Leesburg Pike Falls Church VA 22041 E-mail: william.mccullough@tma.osd.mil.

MCCULLY, EMILY ARNOLD, illustrator, writer; b. Galesburg, Ill., 1939; d. Wade E. and Kathryn (Maher) Arnold; m. George E. McCully, 1961 (div. 1975); children: Nathaniel, Tad. BA, Brown U., 1961; MA, Columbia U., 1964; LittD (hon.), Brown U., 2002. Author: How's Your Vacuum Cleaner Working? O'Henry Collection, 1977, A Craving, 1982, (novel) Picnic, 1984 (Christopher award), First Snow, 1985, (novel) Life Drawing, 1986, The Show Must Go On, 1987, School, 1987, You Lucky Duck!, 1988, New Baby, 1988, The Grandma Mix-up, 1988, The Christmas Gift, 1988, Zaza's Big Break, 1989, Grandma's at the Lake, 1990, The Evil Spell, 1990, Speak Up, Blanche!, 1991, Mirette on the Highwire, 1992 (Caldecott medal 1992), Grandma's at Bat, 1993, The Amazing Felix, 1993, My Real Family, 1994, Crossing The New Bridge, 1994, Little Kit, or: The Industrious Flea Circus Girl, 1995, The Pirate Queen, 1995, The Ballot Box Battle, 1996, The Bobbin Girl, 1996, Popcorn at the Palace, 1997, Starring Mirette and Bellini, 1997, an Outlaw Thanksgiving, 1998, Beautiful Warrior, 1998, Mouse Practice, 1999, Monk Camps Out, 2000, The Orphan Singer, 2001, Four Hungry Kittens, 2001; illustrator: Sea Beach Express, 1966, The Seventeenth Street Gang, 1966, Rex, 1967, Luigi of the Streets, 1967, That Mean Man, 1968, Gooney, 1968, Journey From Peppermint Street, 1968 (Nat. Book award 1969), The Mouse and the Elephant, 1969, The Fisherman, 1969, Tales from the Rue Brocca, 1969, Here I Am, 1969, Twin Spell, 1969, Hobo Toad and the Motorcycle Gang, 1970, Slip! Slop! Gobble!, 1970, Friday Night is Papa Night, 1970, Maxie, 1970, Steffie and Me, 1970, The Cat and the Parrot, 1970, Gertrude's Pocket, 1970, Go and Hush the Baby, 1971, Finders Keepers, 1971, Ma n Da La, 1971 (Bklyn. Mus. award 1976, N.Y. Pub. Libr. award 1976), Hurray for Captain Jane!, 1971, Michael Is Brave, 1971, Finding Out With Your Senses, 1971, Henry's Pennies, 1972, Jane's Blanket, 1972, Grandpa's Long Red Underwear, 1972, Girls Can Too!, 1972, The Boyhood of Grace Jones, 1972, Black Is Brown Is Tan, 1973, Isabelle the Itch, 1973, When Violet Died, 1973, That New Boy, 1973, How To Eat Fried Worms, 1973, Jenny's Revenge, 1974, Her Majesty, Grace Jones, 1974, Tree House Town, 1974, I Want Mama, 1974, Amanda, the Panda and the Redhead, 1975, The Bed Book, 1976, My Street's A Morning Cool Street, 1976, Professor Coconut and the Thief, 1977, Martha's Mad Dog, 1977, That's Mine, 1977, Where Wild Willie, 1978, No Help At All, 1978, Partners, 1978, The Twenty-Elephant Restaurant, 1978, What I Did Last Summer, 1978, The Highest Hit, 1978, I and Spraggy, 1978, Edward Troy and the Witch Cat, 1978, My Island Grandma, 1979, Whatever Happened to Beverly Bigler's Birthday?, 1979, Last Look, 1979, Ookie-Spooky, 1979, The Black Dog Who Went Into the Woods, 1980, How I Found Myself at the Fair, 1980, How We Got Our First Cat, 1980, Oliver and Allison's Week, 1980, Pajama Walking, 1981, The April Fool, 1981, I Dance in My Red Pajamas, 1982, The Halloween Candy Mystery, 1982, Go and Mush the Baby, 1982, Mitzi and the Terrible Tyrannosaurus Rex, 1983, Best Friend Insurance, 1983, Mail-Order Wings, 1984, Gertrude's Pocket, 1984, Fifth Grade Magic, 1984, The Ghastly Glasses, 1985, Fourth of July, 1985, The Explorer of Barkham Street, 1985, Wheels, 1986, Lulu and the Witch Baby, 1986, Richard and the Vratch, 1987, Molly, 1987, Molly Goes Hiking, 1987, Jam Day, 1987, The Boston Coffee Party, 1988, The Take-Along Dog, 1989, Selene Goes Home, 1989, The Magic Mean Machine, 1989, It Always Happens to Leona, 1989, The Grandpa Days, 1989, Dinah's Mad, Bad Wishes, 1989, Stepbrother Sabotage, 1990, Lulu Goes to Witch School, 1990, The Day Chubby Became Charles, 1990, The Christmas Present Mystery, 1990, Sky Guys to White Cat, 1991, Meatball, 1991, Leona and Ike, 1991, The Butterfly Birthday, 1991, Yankee Doodle Drumsticks, 1992, One Very Best Valentine's Day, 1992, Meet the Lincoln Lions Band, 1992, Jingle Bells Jam, 1992, In My Tent, 1992, Anne Flies the Birthday Bike, 1993, Amzat and His Brothers, 1993, Leo the Magnificent, 1996, Old Home Day, 1996, The Divide, 1997, Rabbit Pirates, 1999, Sing a Song of Piglets: A Calender in Verse, 2002.

MC CUNE, BARRON PATTERSON, retired federal judge; b. West Newton, Pa., Feb. 19, 1915; s. James Patterson and Lyda Barron (Hammond) McC.; m. Edna Flannery Markey, Dec. 23, 1943; children: Edward M., James H., Barron Patterson. AB, Washington and Jefferson Coll., 1935; LLB, U. Pa., 1938. Bar: Pa. bar 1939. Practiced in, Washington, Pa., 1939-64; judge 27th Jud. Dist. Ct. Common Pleas, Washington, Pa., 1964-71, U.S. Dist. Ct., Western Dist. Pa., Pitts., 1971-95, sr. fed. judge; ret., 1995. Trustee emeritus Washington and Jefferson Coll.; bd. dirs. emeritus Washington (Pa.) Hosp. Served with USNR, 1942-45. Home: 144 Lemoyne Ave Washington PA 15301-3636

MCCUNE, ELLIS E. retired university system chief administrator, higher education consultant; b. Houston, July 17, 1921; s. Ellis E. and Ruth (Mason) McC.; m. Hilda May Whiteman, Feb. 8, 1946; 1 son, James Donald. Student, Sam Houston State U., 1940-42; BA, UCLA, 1948, PhD, 1957; LHD, Golden Gate U., 1994. Teaching asst. UCLA, 1949-51; from instr. to assoc. prof. polit. sci. Occidental Coll., Los Angeles, 1951-59, chmn. applied politics and econs. curriculum, 1951-56; asst. prof. Calif. State U., Northridge, 1959-61, assoc. prof., chmn. dept. polit. sci., 1961-63, prof., 1963, dean letters and sci., 1963; dean acad. planning Calif. State Univs. and Colls., 1963-67, pres. Calif. State U., Hayward, 1967-90, pres. emeritus, 1991—; acting chancellor The Calif. State U. System, 1990-91, ret., 1991. Cons. govtl. units and agys.; lectr., panelist; mem. Calif. State Scholarship and Loan Commn., 1964-68, chmn., 1967-68; pres. Govtl. Adminstrn. Group Los Angeles, 1959; chair planning com., mem. exec. com., bd. dirs. Eden Med. Ctr. Found., 1994-2003, pres.-elect, 1995-97, pres., 1997-99. Chmn. univs. and colls. div. United Bay Area Crusade, 1969-70, 73-74; bd. dirs. Oakland (Calif.) Museum Assn., 1974-77, 86-88, Hayward Area Hist. Soc., 1998-2004; vice chmn. higher edn. div., East Bay United Way, 1989-90; mem. arts adv. council, 1986-87, devel. com., 1988-89, Bay Area Urban League, bd. trust Calif. Coun. Econ. Edn. No. sect., Emergency Shelter Program Adv. Coun., Hayward Area Hist. Assn., NAACP Hayward chpt.; trustee Calif. Council Econ. Edn.; sec. bd. dirs. Eden Community Found., 1978-79; rsch. fellow Haynes Found, 1957. With US-AAF, 1942-46. Mem. Am. Coun. Edn. (adv. com. 1970-72, inst. coll. & univ. adminstrs. 1973-74, bd. dirs. 1985-86), Western Assn. Schs. and Colls.

(accrediting commn. sr. colls. and univs. 1974-78, chmn., 1978-82, pres. 1979-81), N.W. Assn. Schs. and Colls. (commn. colls. 1974-80), Assn. Am. Colls. (bd. dirs. 1972-75, vice chmn. 1975-76), Assn. Western Univs. (bd. dirs.), Coun. Postsecondary Accreditation (bd. dirs. 1977-88, exec. com. 1979-88, chmn. 1985-87, immediate past chmn., 1988-89, chmn. com. recognition 1982-84), Am. Assn. State Colls. and Univs. (chmn. accreditation com. 1983-86, com. acad. pers. and acad. freedom 1987-88, com. on acad. affairs 1988-91), Calif. Coun. Edn. (trustee), Western Polit. Sci. Assn. (exec. coun. 1958-61), Hayward C. of C. (dir. 1968-71, 73-76, 77-80, 82-85, 86-90), Regional Assn. East Bay Colls. and Univs. (exec. com. 1974-90, sec. 1975-76, 87-88, vice chmn. 1976-77, 84-85, chmn. 1977-79, 85-86), Rotary, Phi Beta Kappa, Pi Gamma Mu, Pi Sigma Alpha. Clubs: Bohemian (San Francisco). Home: 22012 Sevilla Rd # 85 Hayward CA 94541-2735 Home Fax: 510-537-5674. E-mail: EMcCune@worldnet.att.net.

MCCUNE, GREG E. communications media executive; Bur. chief Reuters Am., Inc., Washington, 1996—. Office: Reuters Am Inc 1333 H St NW Ste 410 Washington DC 20005-4707

MCCUNE, JOHN BRIAN, broadcast engineer; b. Richmond, Va., Aug. 17, 1960; s. Horace Glenn Jr. and Mamie Ray (Potts) McC. Student, J. Sargeant Reynolds Community Coll., Richmond, 1979-80, 85-86, No. Va. Coll., 1984. Lic. 2d class radiotelephone operator. Engr. Sta. WRVA, Richmond, 1975, Sta. WLEE, Richmond, 1979-86, Sta. WCVE-TV, Richmond, 1980-82, Sta. WTVR-TV, Richmond, 1982-83, Richmond Subscription TV, 1982-84, Sta. WXGI, Richmond, 1984-86, Sta. WXEX-TV, Richmond, 1986-87, Sta. WRGF, Richmond, 1986-88; rec. engr. Audio Communications, Richmond, 1986—; with Ray Sports Network Sta. WRLH-TV, Richmond, 1988—; with dept. media svcs. Richmond Pub. Schs., Richmond, 1990—. Mem. Soc. Broadcast Engrs. (cert.). Avocations: amateur radio, rebuilding old broadcast equipment. Home: 1000 Pond View Ln Richmond VA 23231-4643 Office: Richmond Pub Schs Dept Media Svcs 2907 North Ave Richmond VA 23222-3612

MCCUNE, PHILIP SPEAR, lawyer; b. Spokane, Wash., Sept. 14, 1965; s. Calmar A. McCune and Katrina Y. Spear; children: Emma Sophia, Jackson Spear. BA magna cum laude, Dartmouth Coll., 1987; JD cum laude, U. Mich., 1991. Bar: Wash. 1991, U.S. Dist. Ct. (we. dist.) Wash. 1991, U.S. Dist. Ct. (ea. dist.) Wash. 1996, U.S. Ct. Appeals (9th cir.) 1991, U.S. Dist. Ct. (no. dist.) Utah 1996. Law clk. Hon. John C. Coughenour chief judge U.S. Dist. Ct. (we. dist.) Wash., Seattle, 1991—93; with Heller, Ehrman, White and Maculliffe, Seattle, 1993—97; ptnr., founder Summit Law Group, Seattle, 1997—. Author: The Forest Practices Act, Washington Environmental Law and Practice, 1997; sr. editor U. Mich. Jour. Law Reform, 1989-91; contbr. articles to profl. jours. Bd. dirs. Friends of Ind. Schs. and Better Edn., Seattle Repertory Theater; pres. bd. dirs. Am. Friends St. Michaels U. Sch. Recipient Wash. Law and Politics mag. Rising Star awards. Mem. ABA, Wash. State Bar Assn., King County Bar Assn., Wash. Athletic Club, U. Mich. Law Sch. Barristers. Avocations: hiking, running. Office: Summit Law Group 315 Fifth Ave S Ste 300 Seattle WA 98104-2682 E-mail: philm@summitlaw.com.

MCCUNE, SARA MILLER, foundation executive, publisher; b. N.Y.C., Feb. 4, 1941; d. Nathan M. and Rose (Glass) M.; m. George D. McCune, Oct. 16, 1966 (dec. May 1990). BA, Queens Coll., 1961. Asst. to v.p. sales Macmillan Pub. Co., N.Y.C., 1961-63; sales mgr. Pergamon Press Ltd., Oxford, England, 1963-64; pres., pub., founder Sage Publs. Inc., N.Y.C., 1965-66, pres., pub. Beverly Hills, Calif., 1966-83, pub., chmn. Newbury Park, Calif., 1984—; bd. dirs. Sage Publs. Ltd., London, chmn., 1990-95; bd. dirs. Sage Publs. India, New Delhi; pres. McCune Found., Newbury Park, Calif., 1990—. Mem. bd. dirs. UCSB Comm. Dept. Adv. Bd., Santa Barbara, Calif., 1994—, USCB Bd. Trustees, 1994—, The Fielding Inst., 1994—, Am. Acad. Pol. Scis., Phila., 1994—. Bd. dirs. USCB Found. Bd. Trustees, 1994—, sec., 1996-97, treas., 1997-98, vice-chair, 1998—. Mem. Am. Evaluation Assn. (spl. award for disting. contbns. 1988). Office: Sage Publications Inc 2455 Teller Rd Newbury Park CA 91320-2234

MCCURDY, DONNA T. food products company executive; Degree in math., Case Western Res. U.; MBA, James Madison U. CPA, Va. Dir. acctg. Delmonte Corp., Charlottesville, Va.; CFO pvt. found. Charlottesville; corp. contr. Rocco Inc., Harrisonburg, Va., 1990-95, sr. v.p., CFO, 1996—. Mem. Phi Beta Kappa. Office: 1 Kratzer Ave Harrisonburg VA 22801-3939

MCCURDY, GILBERT GEIER, retired retailer; b. Rochester, N.Y., May 25, 1922; s. Gilbert J.C. and Virginia (Geier) McC.; m. Katherine W. Babcock, Nov. 9, 1946; children— Gilbert Kennedy, Lynda Babcock (Mrs. Hotra). BA, Williams Coll., 1944. With McCurdy & Co., Inc., Rochester, 1946—, controller, asst. treas., 1953-55, v.p., 1956-59, exec. v.p., 1959-62, pres., gen. mgr., 1962-80, chief exec. officer, 1969-80, chmn. bd., chief exec. officer, 1980-92, chmn. exec. com. of bd., 1993—. Chmn. bd. Frederick Atkins, 1968-70. Bd. dirs. Pathway Houses of Rochester, Boys and Girls Club, Rochester; former mem. bd. dirs. United Way of Greater Rochester; life trustee U. Rochester. 1st lt. Signal Corps AUS, 1943—46. Mem. Rochester C. of C. (pres. 1975) Baptist. Home: 1 Whitney Ln Rochester NY 14610-3551 Office: 1465 Jefferson Rd Rochester NY 14623

MCCURDY, HARRY WARD, otolaryngologist; b. Branchton, Pa., Aug. 15, 1918; s. Adam Oscar and Sarah Fern (Hindman) McC.; m. Joan Jacqueline Talty, Dec. 10, 1955; children: Bridget Elizabeth, Peter Adam. AB, Allegheny Coll., 1940; MD, U. Pa., 1943. Diplomate: Am. Bd. Otolaryngology. Intern Geisinger Meml. Hosp., Danville, Pa., 1944, resident in otolaryngology, 1944-45, 48-49; resident in pathology Hamot Hosp., Erie, Pa., 1945-48; mem. staff Geisinger Med. Center, Danville, 1948-50; commd. 2d lt. U.S. Army, 1945, advanced through grades to col., 1962-74; mil. cons. Surgeon Gen., U.S. Army, 1964-74; ret., 1974; exec. v.p. Am. Acad. Otolaryngology-Head and Neck Surgery, Washington, 1974-84; mem. staff Walter Reed Army Hosp. Mem. resources council Gallaudet Coll., 1975-80; mem. nat. adv. council Sertoma Found., 1976-84; chmn. FDA Panel on Otolaryngologic Med. Devices, 1974-78, cons., 1978-84 Mem. ACS, AMA, Royal Soc. Medicine (U.K.), Am. Acad. Otolaryngology, Mil. Surgeons Assn., Am. Soc. Assn. Execs., Soc. Med. Consultants to Armed Forces, AAAS, Am. Soc. Facial Plastic Surgery, Soc. Mil. Otolaryngologists, Am. Acad. Facial Plastic and Reconstructive Surgery, Am. Laryngol., Rhinol. and Otol. Soc., Anglo-Am. Med. Soc., Am. Audiology Soc., Royal Soc. Health, Osler Med. Soc., Acad. Medicine, Soc. Univ. Otolaryngologists, Am. Council Otolaryngology, Pan-Am. Soc. Bronchoesophagology., Internat. Fedn. Otolaryngol. Socs. (sec. gen. 1981—), Soc. Mil. Cons. to Armed Forces (sec. 1993—). Clubs: Army Navy, Press, Mil. Attaches of London, Les Chevaliers du Tastevin. Republican. Methodist. Home and Office: 6006 Dellwood Pl Bethesda MD 20817-3812

MCCURDY, LARRY WAYNE, automotive parts company executive; b. Commerce, Tex., July 1, 1935; s. Weldon Lee and Eula Bell (Quinn) McC.; m. Anna Jean Ogle, June 2, 1956; children: Michael, Kimberly, Laurie. BBA, Tex. A&M U., 1957. Jr. acct. Tenneco Inc., Houston, 1958-60; sr. acct. Tenneco Oil Co., Houston, 1960-64; acctg. supr. Tenneco Chems., Houston, 1964-69, from divsn. controller to v.p. fin. Saddle Brook, N.J., 1970-78; sr. v.p. fin. Tenneco Automotive, Deerfield, Ill., 1978-80; pres. Walker Mfg. Co., Racine, Wis., 1980-81; exec. v.p. N.Am. ops. Tenneco Automotive, Deerfield, 1981-82; v.p. fin. Echlin Inc., Branford, Conn., 1983; pres., COO Echlin, Inc., Branford, Conn., 1983-85, pres., 1997—; pres., CEO Moog Automotive Inc., St. Louis, 1985-94; exec. v.p. ops. Cooper Industries, Houston, 1994-97; chmn. bd., pres., CEO Echlin, Inc., Branford, Conn., 1997-98; pres. Dana Automotive Aftermarket Group, 1998-2000; ret., 2000. Bd. dirs. Lear Corp., Mohawk Industries, Inc., Am. Axle and Mfg. Co., Gen. Parts, Inc. Trustee Somerset County Coll., Somerville, N.J., 1974-78, Millikin U., Decatur, Ill., 1991-97, St. Raphaels's Hosp., New Haven, Conn., 2002—; former mem. bd. dirs. Jr. Achievement, Chgo.; bd. dirs. Sam Houston coun. Boy Scouts Am., 1995-97; mem. adv. coun. Tex. A&M U. Engring. Sch., 1995-97; dir. New Haven Symphony Orch., 2002—. Mem. Fin. Execs. Inst., Nat. Assn. Accts., Motor Equipment Mfrs. Assn. (chmn. bd. dirs. 1989). Personal E-mail: larrywmccurdy@aol.com.

MCCURDY, LAYTON, medical educator; b. Florence, SC, Aug. 20, 1935; m. Gwendolyn A. McCurdy, 1958; children: Robert Jr., David Barclay. BS, U. NC, 1956; MD, Med. U. SC, 1960. Resident in psychiatry NC Meml. Hosp., Chapel Hill, 1961—64; with psychiatry tng. br. NIMH, Bethesda, Md., 1964—66; asst. prof. dept. psychiatry Sch. Medicine Emory U., Atlanta, 1966—68; prof., chmn. dept. psychiatry and behavioral scis. Med. U. SC, 1968—82, v.p. med. affairs, dean, 1990—2001, dean emeritus, prof. psychiatry, 2001—; prof. psychiatry Sch. Medicine U. Pa., Phila., 1982—90; psychiatrist-in-chief Inst. of Pa. Hosp., Phila., 1982—90. Vis. colleague Inst. Psychiatry, U. London, 1974—75; nat. adv. mental health coun. NIMH, 1980—83; apptd. Pa. Adv. Com. for Mental Health and Mental Retardation, 1984—87; chmn. consensus panel on panic disorder NIH, 1991. Recipient Disting. Alumnus award, Med. U. SC, 1988, George C. Ham. Soc., 1990, rsch. fellowship, NIMH, 1974—75. Fellow: Am. Coll. Psychiatrists (bd. regents 1987—90, v.p. 1990—93, pres. 1993—94, Bowis award 1997); mem.: AMA, Royal Coll. Psychiatrists (U.K.), Waring Libr. Soc. (pres. 1979—80, exec. com. 1991—99), S.C. Med. Assn., Assn. for Acad. Psychiatry, So. Psychiat. Assn. (bd. regents 1977—90, chmn. bd. regents 1979—80), Am. Psychiat. Assn. (joint commn. pub. affairs 1981—84, chmn. com. on diagnosis and assessment 1988—94), VA CARES Commn., Cosmos Club (Washington), Alpha Omega Alpha. Office: Med U SC Coll Medicine 96 Jonathan Lucas St 601CSB PO 250617 Charleston SC 29425-0001 Office Phone: 843-792-2084. Business E-Mail: mccurdy@musc.edu.

MCCURDY, MICHAEL CHARLES, illustrator, author; b. N.Y.C., Feb. 17, 1942; s. Charles Errett and Beatrice (Beatson) McC.; m. Deborah Lamb, Sept. 7, 1968; children: Heather, Mark. BFA, Tufts U., 1964, MFA, 1971. Dir. Penmaen Press, Lincoln, Mass., 1968-85; instr. Concord (Mass.) Acad., 1972-75, Wellesley (Mass.) Coll., 1976. Illustrator: The Man Who Planted Trees, 1985, American Tall Tales, 1991, American Buffalo, 1992, The Way West: Journal of a Pioneer Woman, 1993, Giants in the Land, 1993, The Gettysburg Address, 1995, The Seasons Sewn, 1996; author, illustrator: Hannah's Farm, 1988, Trapped by the Ice, 1997, The Sailor's Alphabet, 1998, An Algonquian Year: The Year According to the Full Moon, 2000; editor, illustrator: Escape From Slavery: The Boyhood of Frederick Douglass in His Own Words, 1994, American Fairy Tales, 1996, War and the Pity of War, 1998, Tarzan, 1999, The Wizard of Oz, 1999, Iron Horses, 1999, The Signers: The 56 Stories Behind the Declaration of Independence, 2002, Walden by H.D. Thoreau, 2004. Mem. Great Barrington (Mass.) Housing Authority, 1990-93. Small press grantee Nat. Endowment Arts, 1978, Mass. Arts and Humanities, 1978. Mem. Soc. Printers, St. Botolph Club. Democrat. Episcopalian.

MC CURDY, PATRICK PIERRE, editor, consultant; b. Angers, France, Sept. 14, 1928; s. Joseph Alexander and Constance Yolande (Hillairet de Boisferon) McC.; m. Eiko Yamada, May 30, 1953; children: Alan J., Wendy C., Alec J., Jeffrey R. BS in Chem. Engring., Carnegie Inst. Tech., 1949. Chem. engr. tech. service dept. Humble Oil & Refining Co., Baytown, Tex., 1949-50; chem. engr. Callery Chem. Co., Pa., 1954-56; sr. chem. engr. U.S. Army Engr. R & D Labs., Ft. Belvoir, Va., 1956-60; asst. editor Chem. & Engring. News, Washington, 1960-61, N.Y.C., 1961-62, bur. head Frankfurt, Germany, 1962-64, Tokyo, 1964-67, mng. editor Washington, 1967-69, editor, 1969-73; editor in chief Chemical Week, 1973-80, 84-87, editor-in-chief, assoc. pub., 1987-88; dir. communications Am. Chem. Soc., 1988-91, dir. industry rels., 1991-93, founding editor Today's Chemist at Work, 1989-97; cons. American Chemical Soc., 1993-97; pub. issues mgr. Dow Chem. Co., Midland, Mich., 1980-82, dir. tech. communications, 1982-84. Cons. in field, 1997—; editl. cons. Chem. Heritage mag., 1997—. Served U.S. Coast Guard, Great Lakes, 1945, first lt. C.E. AUS, 1950-54. Recipient Jesse H. Neal award, 1979, finalist 1985; recipient Carnegie Mellon Univ. Alumni Merit award, 1988. Mem.: Societe de Chimie Industrielle (past pres. Am. sect.), Chemists Club, Fgn. Corrs. Club Japan, Am. Chem. Soc., Tokyo Am. Club, Tau Beta Pi, Phi Kappa, Theta Tau, Phi Kappa Phi. Home and Office: 11717 Chauncey Ln Mason Neck VA 22079-4140 Personal E-mail: mccurdypp@aol.com.

MCCURLEY, CARL MICHAEL, lawyer; b. Denton, Tex., July 15, 1946; s. Carl and Geneva McCurley; m. Mary Jo Trice, June 5, 1983; 1 child, Melissa Renee. BA, N. Tex. State U., 1968; JD, So. Meth. U., 1972. Bar: Tex. 1972, US Dist. Ct. (no. dist.) Tex. 1972, US Dist. Ct. (ea. dist.) Tex. 1974, US Supreme Ct. 1977. Ptnr. McGuire, Levy & McCurley, Irving, Tex., 1972—82, Koons, Fuller, McCurley & Vanden Eykel, Dallas, 1982—92, McCurley, Orsinger, McCurley, Nelson & Downing, Dallas, 1992—. Contbr. articles to profl. jours. Mem.: Dallas Bar Assn., Internat. Acad. Matrimonial Lawyers, Am. Acad. Matrimonial Lawyers (treas. 1990—93, v.p. 1993—96, pres.-elect 1997, pres. 1998), Family Law Coun. (chmn. 1991—93). Home: 4076 Hanover Ave Dallas TX 75225-7009 Office: McCurley Orsinger McCurley Nelson & Downing 5950 Sherry Ln Ste 800 Dallas TX 75225-6533

MCCURLEY, MARY JOHANNA, lawyer; b. Baton Rouge, La., Oct. 3, 1953; d. William Edward and Leora Elizabeth (Block) Trice; m. Carl Michael McCurley, June 6, 1983; 1 stepchild, Melissa Reneé McCurley. BA, Centenary Coll., 1975; JD, St. Mary's U., 1979. Bar: Tex. 1979; cert. family law. Assoc. Martin, Withers & Box, Dallas, 1979-82, Raggio & Raggio, Inc., Dallas, 1982-83; ptnr. Bruner, McColl, McColloch & McCurley, Dallas, 1983-87; assoc., ptnr. Selligson & Douglass, Dallas, 1987-90; jr. ptnr. Koons, Fuller, McCurley & VanderEykel, Dallas, 1990-92; ptnr. McCurley, Orsinger, McCurley,. Nelson & Downing, Dallas, 1992—. Contbr. articles to profl. jours. Adv. Women's Service League, Dallas, 1993—. Mem.: Annette Stewart Am. Inn. Ct. (master, sec.-treas. 2003—04), Dallas Bar Assn., Tex. Acad. Family Law Specialist, Tex. State Bar Assn. (sec. 2001, vice-chair 2001, treas. 2001, chair 2003—, family law coun.), Dallas Bar Assn. (chair family law sect. 1985), Am. Acad. Matrimonial Lawyers (treas. Tex. chpt. 1993—95, sec. 1995—96, pres. 1997, pres. Tex. chpt. 1997—98, bd. govs. 2000, nat. sec. 2000—01, nat. v.p. 2003, nat. bd. dirs.). Methodist. Avocations: golf, travel, jogging, horseback riding. Home: 4076 Hanover Ave Dallas TX 75225-7009 Office: McCurley Orsinger McCurley Nelson & Downing LLP 5950 Sherry Ln Ste 800 Dallas TX 75225-6533 Office Phone: 214-273-2400.

MCCURLEY, ROBERT LEE, JR., lawyer, educator; b. Gadsden, Ala., Sept. 7, 1941; s. Robert Lee and Nellie Ruth McC.; m. Barbara; 1 child, Allison Leah. BS, U. Ala., 1963, JD, 1966. Bar: Ala. 1966, D.C. 1973, U.S. Ct. Mil. Appeals 1966, U.S. Supreme Ct. 1970, U.S. Ct. Appeals (5th cir.) 1972, U.S. Ct. Appeals (11th cir.) 1973, U.S. Ct. Appeals (fed. cir.) 1981. Asst. to dir. Fed. Savs. & Loan Ins. Corp., Washington, 1966-67; partner firm Rains, Rains, McCurley & Wilson, Gadsden, Ala., 1967-75; city judge Southside, Ala., 1970-75; dir. Ala. Law Inst., 1975—; assoc. dir. U. Ala. Center Public Law and Service, 1981-82; asst. dean Sch. Law U. Ala., 1978-81. Panelist White House Conf. on Volunteerism; pres. Gadsden Jaycees, 1972; mem. White House Fifty States Project; Henry Toll fellow Coun. State Govt., 1992. Editor: Divorce, Alimony and Child Support Custody, 3d edit., 1993, Land Laws of Alabama, 7th edit. rev., 2001, The Legislative Process, 8th edit., 2003, Alabama Law Office Practice Deskbook, 9th edit., 2001, Federally Mandated State Legislation, 1990, Alabama Legislation, Cases and Statutes, 5th edit., 2003, Alabama Election Handbook, 11th edit., 2004. Pres. Gadsden Boys Club, 1971, Kiwanis Internat. Found., 1998—2000; mem. Nat. Dem. Charter Commn., 1974. Fellow ABA, Ala. Bar Assn., mem. Am. Law Inst. (life), Order of Coif, Scribes, Farrah Law Soc., Commn. Uniform State Laws, Kiwanis (pres. Tuscaloosa club 1976, gov. Ala. dist. 1984), v.p. 1998-2000, internat. found. pres.), Indian Hills County Club, Univ. Club. Baptist. Office Phone: 205-348-7411.

MCCURN, NEAL PETERS, federal judge; b. Syracuse, N.Y., Apr. 6, 1926; LL.B., Syracuse U., 1952, JD, 1960. Bar: N.Y. 1952. Ptnr. Mackenzie Smith Lewis Mitchell & Hughes, Syracuse, 1957-79; judge U.S. Dist. Ct. (no. dist.) N.Y., 1979-88; chief judge U.S. Dist. Ct. (no. dist.), N.Y., 1988-93; sr. judge, 1993—. Del. N.Y. State Constl. Conv., 1976; mem. 2d Cir. Jud. Council, 1987-93. Pres. Syracuse Common Coun., 1970-78. Mem. ABA, N.Y. State Bar Assn. (chmn. state constn. com.), Onondaga County Bar Assn. (past pres.), Am. Coll. Trial Lawyers, Am. Judicature Soc. (bd. dirs. 1980-84). Office: US Dist Ct 100 S Clinton St Rm 344 Syracuse NY 13261-6100

MCCURRY, MARGARET IRENE, architect, educator, furniture designer, interior designer; b. Chgo., Sept. 26, 1942; d. Paul D. and Irene B. McC.; m. Stanley Tigerman, Mar. 17, 1979. BA, Vassar Coll., 1964. Registered architect, Ill., Mass., Mich., Tex., Wis., Pa., Ind., Fla.; registered interior designer, Ill. Design coord. Quaker Oats Co., Chgo., 1964-66; sr. interior designer Skidmore, Owings & Merrill, Chgo., 1966-77; pvt. practice architect Margaret I, Chgo., 1977-82; ptnr. Tigerman, McCurry, Chgo., 1982—. Vis. studio critic Art Inst. Chgo., 1985-86, 88, 98, lectr., 1988, 98; vis. studio critic U. Ill., Chgo., Miami U., Oxford, Ohio, 1990; juror Internat. furniture awards Progressive Architecture mag., N.Y.C., 1986, advt. awards, 1988; juror design grants Nat. Endowment for Arts, Washington, 1983; NEA Challenge Design Rev., 1992; peer reviewer design excellence program Gen. Svcs. Administrn., 1992—; juror, Wis., Minn., Calif., Va., Washington, Pitts., Ky., Ga. Conn. Soc. Architects, Detroit, N.Y.C., Memphis, Austin, L.A. chpts. AIA, Am. Wood Coun., AIA Students Design Competition, 1993. Author: Margaret McCurry: Constructing 25 Short Stories, 2000; contbr. Chgo. Archtl. Club Jour.; designer, contbr. archtl. exhibit Art Inst. Chgo., 1983-85, 93, 99, Chgo. Hist. Soc., 1984, Gulbenkian Found., Lisbon Portugal, 1989, Chgo. Athenaeum, 1990, Gwenda Jay Gallery, 1992, Women of Design Traveling Exhbn., 1992-96; archtl. drawings and models in permanent collection Art Inst. Chgo. and Deutsches Architektur Mus., Frankfurt. Chmn. furniture sect. fundraising auction Sta. WTTW-TV, PBS, Chgo., 1975-76; mem. Chgo. Beautiful Com., 1968-70; pres. alumni coun. Grad. Sch. Design, Harvard U., 1997-2000; bd. dirs. Architecture and Design Soc. Art Inst. Chgo., 1988-97, mem. textile adv. bd. textile dept. Loeb fellow Harvard U., 1986-87; recipient Builders Choice Grand award Builders Mag., 1985, Interior Design award Interiors Mag., 1983, Dean of Architecture award Chgo. Design Source and the Merchandise Mart, 1989, Designer of Distinction award ASID, 2002; inducted into Interior Design Hall of Fame, Interior Design Mag., 1990. Fellow AIA (mem. coll. fellows, v.p. bd. dirs. Chgo. chpt. 1984-89, chair 1993, nat. design com., lectr. Colo. chpt. 1985, nat. conv. 1988, 97-98, Monterey Design Conf. 1989, Washington Design Ctr. 1989, Nat. Honor award 1984, Nat. Interior Architecture award 1992, 98, Disting. Bldg. award Chgo. chpt. 1984, 86, 91, 94, 99-2000, Disting. Interior Architecture award 1981, 83, 88, 91, 97, product display Neocon award 1985, 88, Gold award best of Neocon 1998, Associated Licensed Archs. Silver Medal Design award 2003), Internat. Interior Design Assn., Chgo. Network, Am. Soc. Interior Designers (v.p. bd. dirs. Chgo. chpt., Nat. Design award 1992, 94, Ill. chpt. Design award 1994, Ill. chpt. Merit award 1994, Designer Distinction award, 2002), Chgo. Archtl. Club, Arts Club Chgo., Womens Athletic Club, Harvard Alumni Assn. (dir. 2000—). Episcopalian. Avocations: drawing, writing, travel, golf, gardening. Office: Tigerman McCurry Archs 444 N Wells St Chicago IL 60610-4501 Office Phone: 312-644-5880. Business E-Mail: mimccurry@tigerman-mccurry.com.

MCCURRY, STEPHANIE, historian, educator; BA, U. Western Ont., 1981; MA, U. Rochester, 1983; PhD, SUNY, Binghamton, 1988. Asst. prof. U. Calif., San Diego, 1988—94, assoc. prof., 1994—98, Northwestern U., Evanston, Ill., 1998—. Mem. grad. student award com. CCHWP-CGWH/Berkshire Conf. Women Historians, 1993, 94; mem. award selection com. NEH, 1995; dir. Calif. History Project U. Calif., San Diego, 1996—98; dir. Alice Berline Kaplan Ctr. for the Humanities Northwestern U., Evanston, 2002—03; reviewer Oxford U. Press, U. N.C. Press, Harvard U. Press, U. Ill. Press, Johns Hopkins U. Press, U. Ga. Press; referee Am. Hist. Rev., Jour. Am. History, Gender and History, Jour. So. History, Ark. Hist. Quarterly; lectr. in field. Author: Masters of Small Worlds: Yeoman Households, Gender Relations and the Political Culture of the Antebellum South Carolina Low Country, 1995 (nominated for Pulitzer prize in history, 1995); contbr. articles to profl. jours. Recipient Frances Weir prize for history and lit., U. Western Ont., 1981, John Hope Franklin prize, Am. Studies Assn., 1996; fellow, John Simon Guggenheim Meml. Found., 2003; grantee, Am. Coun. Learned Socs., 1990; Rush Rhees and History Dept. fellow, U. Rochester, 1981—83, Doctoral fellow, Social Scis. and Rsch. Coun. Can., 1983—85, Smithsonian Instn., 1985—86, AAUW, 1986—87, Vis. scholar, Inst. for Rsch. on Women and Gender, Stanford U., 1994—95. Mem.: Am. Hist. Assn. (mem. Joan Kelly prize com. 1997—99), So. Assn. Women Historians (chair Willie Lee Rose prize 1999, mem. A. Elizabeth Taylor prize com. 1996, Willie Lee Rose prize 1997), So. Hist. Assn. (chair Francis B. Simkins award com. 1999—2001, mem. program com. ann. meeting 1997, Charles Sydnor prize 1996, Francis Butler Simkins prize 1997), Orgn. Am. Historians (co-chair program com. 2003). Office: Northwestern Univ Dept History Harris Hall #202 1881 Sheridan Rd Evanston IL 60208

MCCUSKER, PAUL DONALD, lawyer, educator; b. Niagara Falls, N.Y., Sept. 23, 1921; s. Alexander J. and Catherine (Barron) McC.; m. Joan Gross, Aug. 28, 1948; children: Karen, Mary, Paul Alexander, Ian. BA, Holy Cross Coll., 1943; JD, Cornell U., 1949; JD, U. Rome, Italy, 1952. Bar: N.Y. 1949. Counselor of embassy U.S. Fgn. Svc., Dept. State, Washington, 1950-69; prin. officer UN, N.Y.C., 1969-82; ptnr. Garrity & McCusker, N.Y.C., 1982-94. Adj. prof. L.I. U., 1982-99. With MC U.S. Army, 1943—46. Fulbright fellow, Italy, 1949-50. Mem. Am. Soc. Internat. Law. Home: 32 Glenmore Dr Durham NC 27707-3980

MCCUSKER, THOMAS J. lawyer, insurance company executive; b. 1943; BA, JD, U. Notre Dame. Bar: Nebr. 1970. Exec. v.p., gen. counsel Mutual of Omaha Ins. Co. Mem. ABA. Office: Mutual of Omaha Ins Co Mutual Of Omaha Plz Omaha NE 68175-1008

MCCUSKEY, JOHN F. lawyer; b. Clarksburg, W.Va., Nov. 7, 1947; BS, W.Va. Wesleyan Coll., 1969; BSEE, U. Pa., 1970; JD, W.Va. U., 1973. Bar: W.Va. 1974, U.S. Dist. Ct. (no. dist.) W.Va., U.S. Dist. Ct. (so. dist.) W.Va., U.S. Ct. Appeals (4th cir.). Mem. W.Va. Ho. of Dels., 1972—76, 1978—82; justice Supreme Ct. Appeals W.Va., 1998; atty. Shuman, McCuskey & Slicea, Charleston, W.Va. Capt. USAR, 1974—80. Recipient Disting. Faculty award, Def. Trial Counsel of W.Va. Mem.: ABA, W.Va. State Bar, Kanawha County Bar Assn., W.Va. Bar Assn. (pres.-elect), Omicron Delta Kappa. Office: Shuman McCuskey and Slicea PO Box 3953 405 Capitol St Ste 1007 Charleston WV 25301

MCCUTCHAN, GORDON EUGENE, retired lawyer, insurance company executive; b. Buffalo, Sept. 30, 1935; s. George Lawrence and Mary Esther (De Puy) McC.; m. Linda Brown; children: Lindsey, Elizabeth. BA, Cornell U., 1956, MBA, 1958, LLB, 1959. Bar: N.Y. 1959, Ohio 1964. Pvt. practice, Rome, N.Y., 1959-61; atty., advisor SEC, Washington, 1961-64; ptnr. McCutchan, Druen, Maynard, Rath & Dietrich, 1964-94; mem. office of gen. counsel Nationwide Mut. Ins. Co., Columbus, Ohio, 1964-94, sr. v.p., gen. counsel, 1982-89, exec. v.p., gen. counsel, 1989-94; exec. v.p. Law and Corp. Svcs., Nationwide Ins. Enterprise, 1994-98; ret., 1998. Trustee, bd. govs. Franklin U., 1992-97; trustee Ohio Tuition Trust Authority, 1992-97. Mem. Columbus Bar Assn., Ohio Bar Assn., Am. Corp. Counsel Assn., Assn. Life Inst. Counsel (bd. govs. 1990-94), Fedn. Ins. and Corp. Counsel, Am. Coun. Life Ins. (chair legal sect. 1992-93). Home: 2376 Oxford Rd Columbus OH 43221-4011 E-mail: tunkpa@columbus.rr.com.

MCCUTCHEN, TAMMY DEE, federal agency administrator; b. Kewanee, Ill., Oct. 20, 1965; BA, Western Ill. U.; JD, Northwestern U. Clk. U.S. Ct. Appeals (7th cir.), 1991—92; assoc. Skadden, Arps, Slate, Meagher and Flom, Chgo., 1992—95, Matkov, Salzman, Madoff anf Gunn, 1995—99; sr. counsel Hershey Foods Corp., 1999—2001; adminstr. wage and hour divsn. U.S. Dept. Labor, Washington, 2001—. Office: US Dept Labor 200 Constitution Ave NW Washington DC 20210

MCCUTCHEN, WILLIAM WALTER, JR., management educator; b. Hamlet, N.C., Aug. 26, 1940; s. William Walter and Edith Wall (Rucker) McC.; m. Irene Katherine Lilly, June 16, 1962; 1 child, William Walter III. BS in Civil Engring., Duke U., 1962; MBA, Harvard U., 1967; PhD, Ind. U., 1988. Sales rep. Eli Lilly and Co., San Francisco, 1967-69, analyst econ. studies Indpls., 1969-70, mgr. econ. studies, 1970-72, mgr. personnel (mktg.), 1972-73; dir. nat. sales Elizabeth Arden, N.Y.C., 1973-76; mng. dir. Lilly Industries Pty. Ltd., Sidney, Australia, 1976-79; dir. corp. communications Eli Lilly & Co., Indpls., 1980-83; assoc. prof. mgmt. Zicklin Sch. of Bus., Baruch Coll., CUNY, N.Y.C., 1988—, dep. chmn. dept. mgmt., 1995—. Capt. USMC,

1962-65. Mem. Acad. Mgmt., Am. Econ. Assn., Woodstock Club, Univ. Club, Shorehaven Golf Club, Phi Delta Theta, Beta Gamma Sigma. Congregationalist. Office: CUNY Baruch Coll Zicklin Sch of Bus 17 Lexington Ave New York NY 10010-5518

MCCUTCHEON, ALLAN LEE, sociology educator; b. Clarinda, Iowa, Mar. 15, 1950; s. Merle Marvin and Margaret Lucille (Larabee) McC.; m. Nancy Ann Cooper, June 13, 1970 (div. May 1975); 1 child, Jennifer; m. Elisabeth Jean Crockett, May 25, 1985. BS, Iowa State U., 1972; MA, U. Chgo., 1977, PhD, 1982. Asst. prof. sociology U. Del., Newark, 1982-88, assoc. prof. sociology, 1988-96, assoc. chair dept. sociology, 1989-95; Donald O. Clifton disting. prof. survey rsch. U. Nebr., Lincoln, 1996—, dir. Gallup Rsch. Ctr., 1996—; sr. scientist Gallup Orgn., 1996—. Cons. Disaster Rsch. Ctr., Newark, 1986-88; vis. scientist Max Planck Inst., Freiburg, Germany, 1988-89; dozent U. Cologne (Germany), 1989, 96, 2001; instr. European Consortium for Polit. Rsch. U. Essex (Eng.), 1990—; mem. sci. adv. coun. German Ctr. for Survey Rsch. and Methodology, 1998—. Author (book) Latent Class Analysis, 1987; editor (newsletter) States and Societies, 1988-95; contbr. articles to profl. jours. Resource cons. Leadership Del. United Way, Wilmington, 1991-92. U. Chgo. rsch. fellow, 1974-77; Deutscher Akademischer Austauschdienst scholar, 1990; Fulbright scholar, The Netherlands, 1995-96. Mem. World Assn. for Pub. Opinion Rsch. (sec.-treas. 2000-03), Coun. for European Studies, Am. Assn. for Pub. Opinion Rsch., Midwest Assn. for Pub. Opinion Rsch. (v.p., 2003—), Am. Statis. Assn., Am. Sociol. Assn., Sigma Xi. Avocations: German culture, literature. Office: U Nebr Gallup Rsch Ctr 200 N 11th St Lincoln NE 68508-1406 E-mail: AMcCutcheon1@unl.edu.

MCCUTCHEON, JOHN TINNEY, JR., retired journalist; b. Chgo., Nov. 8, 1917; s. John Tinney and Evelyn (Shaw) McC.; m. Susan Dart, Feb. 1, 1943; children: Anne McCutcheon Lewis, Mary, John Tinney III. BS, Harvard U., 1939. Reporter City News Bur., Chgo., 1939-40, Chgo. Tribune, 1940-51, editor column A Line O' Type or Two, 1951-57, editorial writer, 1957-71, editor editorial page, 1971-82, columnist, 1967-70. Pres. Lake Forest (Ill.) Libr., 1970-72. Served with USNR, 1941-46. Mem. Soc. Midland Authors, Am. Soc. Newspaper Editors, Nat. Conf. Editorial Writers, Geog. Soc. Chgo. (pres. 1955-57), Chgo. Zool. Soc. (hon. trustee), Chgo. Hist. Soc. (life trustee), Inter Am. Press Assn. (dir., freedom of press com. 1978-87), Wayfarers Club (Chgo.), Tryon (N.C.) Country Club, Sigma Delta Chi. Home: 10 Fox Paw Ln Saluda NC 28773-9527

MCCUTCHEON, STEVEN CLIFTON, environmental and ecological engineer, hydrologist; b. Decatur, Ala., Oct. 29, 1952; s. Bernard Clifton and Rosa May (Askenburg) McC.; m. Sherry Lynn Sharp; children: Michael Ian, Alexander Tavis. BS, Auburn U., 1975; MS, Vanderbilt U., 1977, PhD, 1979. Hydrologist U.S. Geol. Survey, Bay St. Louis, Miss., 1977-86; sr. environ. engr. U.S. EPA, Athens, Ga., 1986—. Adj. asst. prof. Tulane U., New Orleans, 1984-85; panel mem. Nat. Rsch. Coun., Washington, 1989-92; adj. prof. Forestry U. Ga., Athens, 1994—; asst. prof. Clemson (S.C.) U., 1990-97; program evaluator Accreditation Bd. Engring. & Tech., 1992—. Author: Water Quality Modeling, vol. 1, 1989, Water Quality, Handbook of Hydrology, 1993; editor and author: (with others) Manual for Performing Estuarine Waste Load Allocations, 1990, Hydrodynamics and Transport for Water Quality Modeling, 1999, Phytoremediation, 2003, 226 papers, articles, reports, chpt. and books; editor Jour. Environ. Engring., 1992—94, mem. editl. bd. Ecol. Engring., 1995—, Internat. Jour. Phytoremediation, 2000—, vice-chair editl. bd. Hazardous Toxic and Radioactive Waste Mgmt., 1996—97, co-editor Environ. Sci. and Pollution Rsch. Mem. Zoning Commn., St. Tammany Parish, La., 1984-85; vice=chmn. Planning Adv. Bd., St. Tammany Parish, 1985; asst. den leader Cub Scouts Am., Athens, pack 83, 1991-92, pack 96, 1998-99, den leader, 1999-2001. Co-recipient EPA Sci. Achievement award in waste mgmt., Air and Waste Mgmt. Assn., 1995, EPA Sci. Achievement award in Chemistry, Am. Chem. Soc., 1997, Sci. and Tech. Achievement award, EPA, 1999, Bronze medal, 2001, 2002; recipient medal and plaque, Korea Soc. Water Pollution Rsch. and Control, Seoul, 1986, Engr. of Yr. award in EPA, NSPE, 1992, Richard R. Torrens award, ASCE, Engr. of Yr. in Govt. award, Ga. Engr. Week Com., 2004. Mem.: ASCE (br. pres. 1983—84, sect. dir. 1984—85, 1995—2001, sect. v.p. 2001—03, sect. pres.-elect 2003—04, rep. Dist. 14 coun., nat. dir. Dist. 14, Young Civil Engr. of Yr. award 1984, Torrens award 1994, Govt. Civil Engr. of Yr. award 2004), Water Environ. Fedn., Internat. Assn. Hydrologic Scis., Internat. Water Assn., Internat. Soc. Environ. Ethics (charter), Am. Geophys. Union, Am. Ecol. Engring. Soc. (charter, chair com. registration and certification 2001—04, v.p. and pres.-elect 2004—), Phi Theta Kappa, Phi Kappa Phi, Sigma Xi (chpt. sec. 1982—84, membership com. 1984—85). Achievements include pioneering work in phytoremediation and ecological engineering to clean up federal facilities and response to Exxon Valdez oil spill. Home: 147 Spalding Ct Athens GA 30605-3716 Office: US EPA Nat Exposure Rsch Lab 960 College Station Rd Athens GA 30605-2720 Office Phone: 706-355-8235. Business E-Mail: McCutcheon.Steven@epa.gov. E-mail: EnvironHyd@aol.com.

MCDADE, HERBERT H., III, finance company executive; m. Martha McDade, 1989. BA, Duke U.; MBA, U. Mich., 1983. Corp. bond trader Lehman Brothers Holdings Inc., 1983—91, head, corp. bond dept., 1991—95, head, high grade credit bus., 1995—98, global head, debt capital markets, 1998—2000, co-global head, fixed income divsn., 2000—02, head, global fixed income divsn., 2002—. Mem. exec. com. Lehman Brothers Holdings Inc. Mem.: Bond Market Assn. (v. chmn.), Winged Foot Golf Club (bd. govs.). Office: Lehman Brothers Holdings Inc 745 Seventh Ave New York NY 10019

MCDADE, JAMES RUSSELL, management consultant; b. Dallas, Jan. 15, 1925; s. Marion W. and Jeannette (Reneau) McD.; m. Elaine Bushey, Sep. 10, 1955. BSEE, So. Meth. U., Dallas, 1947; MBA, Northwestern U., Evanston, Ill., 1950. Asst. to pres. Davidson Corp., Chgo., 1951-52, Mergenthaler Linotype Co., Bklyn., 1952-53, comml. works mgr., 1953-56; chief indsl. engr. Tex. Instruments, Inc., Dallas, 1956-57, product gen. mgr., 1958-60, v.p., 1961-64; chmn. bd. McDade Properties Co., Aspen (Colo.), Denver, Dallas, 1964—. Bd. dirs. Pitkin County Bank, Aspen; chmn. bd. dirs. Harley-Davidson Tex., Westec Security of Aspen, Aspen Security, Inc. Founding mem. Aspen Art Mus., 1980; mem. Ballet Aspen, 1980—; pres. club Aspen Valley Hosp., 1984—. Served to 1st lt. USAF, 1943-46. Mem.: Presidents Assn., Am. Mgmt. Assn., Rep. Senatorial Inner Circle. Avocations: skiing, horseback riding, camping, swimming.

MCDADE, JOSEPH MICHAEL, former congressman; b. Scranton, Pa., Sept. 29, 1931; s. John B. and Genevieve (Hayes) McD.; children: Joseph, Aileen, Deborah, Mark; m. Sarah Scripture, May 1988; 1 child, Jared. BA in Polit. Sci. with honors, U. Notre Dame, 1953; LL.B., U. Pa., 1956; LL.D. (hon.), St. Thomas Aquinas Coll., 1968, U. Scranton, 1969, Misericordia Coll. and Kings Coll., 1981, Mansfield State Coll., 1982; H.H.D., Kings Coll. Bar: Pa. bar 1957. Clk. to fed. judge, 1956-57; pvt. practice law, 1957—; city solicitor, 1962; mem. 88th-105th Congresses from 10th Pa. dist., Washington, 1963—99; former mem. appropriations com. Chmn., Ford Theater, Washington; chmn. ETA Cons.; lectr.; bd. dirs. Kennedy Ctr. Mem. Am., Pa., Lackawanna County bar assns., Scranton C. of C. Clubs: K.C; James Wilson Law (Phila.). Republican. Roman Catholic.

MCDADE, MARK, biotechnology company executive; BS, Dartmouth Coll.; MBA, Harvard U. With Sandoz Ltd.; COO Boehringer Mannheim Therapeutics, divsn. of Corange Ltd.; co-founder, exec. v.p., COO Corixa, pres., COO, 1999—2000; CEO Signature BioSci., Inc., Hayward, Calif., 2000—. Bd. dirs. Corixa Corp., Valentis Inc.

MCDADE, SANDY D. manufacturing executive; BA, Whitman Coll., 1974; JD cum laude, Seattle U., 1979. Mem. law dept., gen. counsel Weyerhaeuser Co., 1980—2000, corp. sec., 1993—2000, v.p. strategic planning, 2000—03, sr. v.p. Can., 2003—. Mem. camping svcs. bd. Seattle Met. YMCA; mem. Wash. State Corp. Act Revision Com. Mem.: Wash. State Bar Assn. (past chmn. corp. law dept. sect.), Am. Soc. Corp. Secs. Office: Weyerhaeuser Co 33663 Weyerhaeuser Way S Federal Way WA 98063-9777

MCDANIEL, DAVID HENRY, physician; b. Clarksburg, W.Va., May 12, 1952; s. Hubert Harold and Ada Virginia (Henry) McD.; m. Sheila Marie Travis, Sept. 17, 1994. BS in Chemistry cum laude, W.Va. U., Morgantown, 1974, MD, 1978. Diplomate Am. Bd. Dermatology, 1983. Emergency physician Monongalia Gen. Hosp., Morgantown, 1979—82; dir. Laser Skin and Vein Ctr. of Va., Virginia Beach, Va., 1982—; asst. prof. clin. dermatology Ea. Va. Med. Sch., Norfolk, 1991—, asst. prof. clin. plastic surgery, 1992—; command cons. dept. plastic surgery Naval Med. Ctr., Portsmouth, Va., 1994—; dir. rsch. and innovation Light BioSci., LLC, 2002—. Adj. asst. prof. dept. biol. scis. Old Dominion U., 2001-; pres. The Ctr. for Disfigurement, Virginia Beach, 1993—; adv. coun. mem. Disfigurement Guidance Ctr., Scotland, 1994—; pres. David H. McDaniel Cons., Internat., Virginia Beach, 1995—. Contbr. numerous articles to sci. jours. Fellow Am. Acad. Dermatology, Am. Soc. Laser Medicine and Surgery, Am. Soc. Dermatologic Surgery (com. practice mktg. and pub. rels. 1993-96, chair 1996), Internat. Soc. Dermatologic Surgery; mem. Tidewater Dermatology Soc. (pres. 1987-88), Space Dermatology Found. (founding), Va. Space Bus. Roundtable (charter), Phi Lambda Upsilon. Avocations: nature and wildlife photography, bicycling, gardening, hiking, church and charitable activities. Office: Laser Skin & Vein Ctr Va 933 First Colonial Rd Ste 113 Virginia Beach VA 23454-3172

MCDANIEL, GEORGE M. pediatrician; b. Augusta, Ga., Apr. 29, 1963; BA in Math. and Computer Sci., Emory U., Atlanta, 1985; MS in Biochemistry, U. of Ga., 1998; MD, U. S.C., 1992. Diplomate Am. Bd. of Pediat., 1996. Pediatrician Pediat. Assocs. of Anderson, SC, 1997—98; attending physician and dir. AnMed Child Health Ctr., Anderson, 1998—2001; sr. fellow MCG Pediat. Cardiology, Augusta, Ga., 2001—. Bd. dirs. Anderson/Oconee Child Advocacy, Anderson, SC, 2000—01. Grantee H. Victor Moore Rsch. award, Children's Heart Program Vol. Coun., 2002—03. Fellow: Am. Academy of Pediat. Presbyterian. Avocations: gardening, exercise, shooting sports, music. Office: Medical College of Georgia 1120 15th St Augusta GA 30912 E-mail: gmcdaniel@mail.mcg.edu.

MCDANIEL, JAMES EDWIN, lawyer; b. Dexter, Mo., Nov. 22, 1931; s. William H. and Gertie M. (Woods) McD.; m. Mary Jane Crawford, Jan. 22, 1955; children: John William, Barbara Anne. AB, Washington U., St. Louis, 1957, JD, 1959. Bar: Mo. 1959. Assoc. firm Walther, Barnard, Cloyd & Timm, 1959-60, McDonald, Barnard, Wright & Timm, 1960-63, ptnr., 1963-65, Barnard, Timm & McDaniel, St. Louis, 1965-73, Barnard & Baer, St. Louis, 1973-82, Lashly & Baer, St. Louis, 1982—2002, of counsel, 2002—; pros. atty. Glendale, Mo., 1968—. City atty. City of Glendale, Mo., 1996—; bd. dirs. Eden. Theol. Sem.; lectr. Latvian U., Riga, Inst. Fgn. Rels., Banking in Am., 1992-93. Leader legal del. Chinese-Am. Comparative Law Study, China, 1988, Russian-Am. Comparative Law Study, Russia, 1990; trustee, past chmn., past treas. 1st Congl. Ch. St. Louis. With USAF, 1951-55. Fellow Am. Bar Found. (life), St. Louis Bar Found. (life); mem. ABA (bd. govs. 1997-2000, ho. of dels. 1976-80, 84-92, 97-2000, state del. 1986-92, chmn. lawyers conf., jud. adminstrn. divsn. 1992-95, 8th cir. rep. standing com. on fed. jud. 1995-98, mem. standing com. on jud. qualification, tenure and compensation 1996-97), The Mo. Bar (pres. 1981-82, bd. govs. 1974-83), Mo. Assn. Def. Counsel, Bar Assn. Met. St. Louis (pres. 1972), Internat. Assn. Ins. Counsel, Assn. Def. Counsel St. Louis (past pres.), Phi Delta Phi. Home: 767 Elmwood Ave Saint Louis MO 63122-3216 Office: Lashly & Baer 714 Locust St Saint Louis MO 63101-1699 Office Phone: 314-621-2939.

MCDANIEL, JAMES MARK, JR., health care executive; b. Harrisonburg, Va., Mar. 18, 1953; s. James Mark and Mary (Jones) McD.; m. Lynne Stewart, Mar. 21, 1981; children: Diane Marie, Laura Elizabeth. BA, U. N.C., Greensboro, 1975. Pres. Rock-O-Lawn Mfrs., High Point, N.C., 1976-81; ins. exec. R.P.M. Assocs., Raleigh, N.C., 1981-84; adminstr. White Eye Clinic, Greenville, N.C., 1984-85; pres. S.I.S.I., Greensboro, N.C., 1988—; chief exec. officer Southeastern Eye Ctr., Greensboro, N.C., 1985—. Pres. Salem Optical Co., Winston-Salem, N.C., 1988—. Football coach Lewisville (N.C.) Titans Athletic Assn., 1982-83, 85-87, Pfafftown (N.C.) Packers Football Assn., 1988—; basketball coach Clemmons (N.C.) Basketball Assn., 1981-84; elder Community in Christ Presbyn. Chr., Forest Oaks, N.C., 1976. Republican. Avocation: coaching football and basketball. Office: Southeastern Eye Ctr 3312 Battleground Ave Greensboro NC 27410-2400 also: 146 Sycamore Ridge Dr Advance NC 27006-7476

MCDANIEL, JAN, television station executive; b. St. Louis, June 27, 1951; BA in Journalism, U. Mo., 1973. Pres., gen. mgr. Sta. KAKE-TV, 1991-96; gen. mgr. Sta. WCCO-TV, Mpls., 1996—. Mem. Women in Comm. Office: Sta WCCO-TV 90 S 11th St Minneapolis MN 55403-2414

MCDANIEL, JARREL DAVE, lawyer; b. Clovis, N. Mex., Oct. 17, 1930; s. Raymond Lee and Blanch (Booth) McD.; m. Anne Louise McAllister; children: Jarrel Dave Jr., Julia Anne. AA, Riverside Coll., 1951; BA, U. Tex., 1956, LL.B., 1957. Bar: Tex. 1957. Assoc. Vinson & Elkins, Houston, 1957-69, ptnr., 1969-96; of counsel Sheinfeld, Maley & Kay, Houston, 1997-2001; sr. counsel Akin, Gump, Strauss, Hauer & Feld, L.L.P., Houston, 2001—. Author, lectr. in field. Served with USAF, 1950-54. Mem.: ABA, Am. Bankruptcy Inst., State Bar Tex., Am. Coll. Bankruptcy, Houston Club. Roman Catholic. Home: 1217 Potomac Dr Houston TX 77057-1919 Office: Akin Gump Strauss Hauer & Feld LLP 1111 Louisana St 44th Fl Houston TX 77002 Business E-Mail: jmcdaniel@akingump.com.

MCDANIEL, JOANAVA B. medical/surgical nurse; b. Belmont Land, Barbados, May 22, 1948; d. Charles Herbert and Etheline Odessa Griffith; 1 child, Shelley Johnson. A in Liberal Arts with honors, Delaware County C.C., Media, Pa., 1986; BA in Orgnl. Mgmt. with honors, Ea. U., St. Davids, Pa., 1993. Cert. health mgmt. nurse, Barbados, pub. health nurse, W.I. Sch. Pub. Health, midwife, Tercentenary Sch. Nursing, Barbados, RN Eng.l. Staff nurse Ministry of Health, Barbados, 1972—77, pub. health nurse, 1977—83; pvt. duty nurse Lansdale Agy., Newtown Square, Pa., 1984—88; pvt. duty and vis. nurse PRN Health Care Svcs., Inc., Ardmore, Pa., 1986—88, dir. profl. svcs., 1988—91; asst. dir. clin. svcs. Home Nurse, Inc., Wayne, Pa., 1992—2001; clin. support specialist Bayada Nurses, Moorestown, NJ, 2001—. Missionary nurse Project Word Found., Inc., Pa., 1995—, pres., 2000—; bd. dirs. Life Bible Inst., Ardmore, 2002. Avocations: reading, sewing, cooking, gardening, Scrabble. Office: Bayada Nurses 286 Chester Ave Moorestown NJ 08057 Office Phone: 856-778-5300. E-mail: sparkles227@juno.com.

MCDANIEL, JOHN MARK, lawyer; b. Decatur, Ala., Nov. 5, 1951; s. John Lester and Helen Juanita McD.; m. Henri Butler, Jan. 19, 1973; children: Henri Jo, John Benjamin. BS, Athens Coll., 1972; JD, Birmingham Sch. of Law, 1976. Bar: Ala. Ptnr. McDaniel & McDaniel, Huntsville, Ala., 1976—; prosecuting atty. Town of New Hope, Ala., 1976-83. Pres. McDaniel Media, Inc., Huntsville, 1995—; legal counsel Congressman Cramer, Huntsville, 1991—; trial counsel Gov. Hunt, Montgomery, Ala., 1994; spl. atty. gen., Montgomery, 1984, 90; legal advisor to dir. emergency mgmt., State of Ala., Montgomery, 1984-87; assoc. prof. Faulkner U., Huntsville, 1976—; instr. People's Law Sch., Huntsville, 1993—, Athens State Coll., 1998; adv. bd. Jones Sch. of Law, Montgomery, 1984-87. Bd. dirs. Boys Club, Huntsville, 1994-97, Huntsville Stars, 1995—, Indsl. Devel. Named to County Sports Hall of Fame, Huntsville, 1996, Alumni of Yr., Athens State Coll., 1993. Mem. ABA, Ala. State Bar (pres. criminal law sect. 1985-86), Madison County Bar, Mensa. Mem. Ch. of Christ. Avocation: jogging.

MCDANIEL, MIKE, former political association executive; b. Muncie, Ind., Feb. 11, 1951; m. Gail McDaniel, 1978. BS, Ball State U., 1973, MPA, 1979. Legis. intern Rep. Caucus Ind. State Senate, 98th Session, Ind. Gen. Assemply; rsch. dir. City County Coun., Indpls., 1974-75; adminstrv. asst. to Pres. ProTem Ind. State Senate, 1975-76, minority caucus adminstr., 1977-78, spl. asst. to majority caucus, 1978-79; campaign dir. Rep. State Senate Campaign com., 1978; campaign mgr. John Mutz for Lt. Gov. campaign, 1980, 87-88; asst. to gov.-elect Hon. Judge Robert D. Orr, Ind.; chief of staff Lt. Gov. Ind., Hon. John M. Mutz, 1981-87; chmn. Ind. State Rep. Party; pub. rels. account exec. Caldwell Van Riper, Indpls. Instr. polit. sci. Ball State U., 1984—; exec. asst. to v.p. for bus. affairs, 1988-94, dir. govt. rels., 1994-95; exec. dir. Ind. State Election Bd., 1988; writer, producer, dir., editor video module series Ind. Gen. Assemply, 1990; bd. dirs. Bowen Inst. for Practical Politics. Recipient Sagamore of Wabash prize Gov. Otis R. Bowen, 1979, Gov. Robert D. Orr, 1981.

MCDANIEL, MYRA ATWELL, lawyer, former state official; b. Phila., Pa, Dec. 13, 1932; d. Eva Lucinda (Yores) Atwell; m. Reuben Roosevelt McDaniel Jr., Feb. 20, 1955; children: Diane Lorraine, Reuben Roosevelt III. BA, U. Pa., 1954; JD, U. Tex., 1975; LLD, Huston-Tillotson Coll., 1984, Jarvis Christian Coll., 1986. Bar: Tex. 1975, U.S. Dist. Ct. (we. dist.) Tex. 1977, U.S. Dist. Ct. (so. and no. dists.) Tex. 1978, U.S. Ct. Appeals (5th cir.) 1978, U.S. Supreme Ct. 1978, U.S. Dist. Ct. (ea. dist.) Tex. 1979. Asst atty. gen. State of Tex., Austin, 1975-81, chief taxation div., 1979-81, gen. counsel to gov., 1983-84, sec. of state, 1984-87; asst. gen. counsel Tex. R.R. Commn., Austin, 1981-82; gen. counsel Wilson Cos., San Antonio and Midland, Tex., 1982; assoc. Bickerstaff, Heath & Smiley, Austin, 1984, ptnr., 1987-96; mng. ptnr. Bickerstaff, Heath, Smiley, Pollan, Kever & McDaniel, Austin, Tex., 1996—2000, of counsel, 2003. Mem. asset. mgmt. adv. com. State Treasury, Austin, 1984-86; mem. legal affairs com. Criminal Justice Policy Coun., Austin, 1984-8, Inter-State Oil Compact, Oklahoma City, 1984-86; bd. dirs. Austin Cons. Group, 1983-86; mem. Jud. Efficiency Coun., Austin, 1995-96; lectr. in field. Contbr. articles to profl. jours., chpts. to books Del. Tex. Conf. on Librs. and Info. Sci., Austin, 1978, White House Conf. on Librs. and Info. Scis., Washington, 1979; mem. Libr. Svcs. and Constrn. Act Adv. Coun., 1980-84, chmn., 1983-84; mem. long range plan task force Brackenridge Hosp., Austin, 1981; clk. vestry bd. St. James Episcopal Ch., Austin, 1981-83, 89-90; bd. visitors U. Tex. Law Sch., 1983-87, vice chmn., 1983-85; bd. dirs. Friends of Ronald McDonald House Ctrl. Tex., Women's Advocacy, Inc., Capital Area Rehab. Ctr.; trustee Episcopal Found. Tex., 1986-89, St. Edward's U., Austin, 1986—, chmn. acad. com., 1988-2002, vice chair, 2002-04, chmn. 2004—; chmn. divsn. capital area campaign United Way, 1986; active nat. adv. bd. Leadership Am.; trustee Episcopal Sem. S.W., 1990-96, Assn. Governing Bds. Univs. and Colls., Leadership Edn. Arts Program, 1995-2004; adv. bd. mem. Women Basketball Coaches Assn., 1996-99; bd. dirs. U.Tex. Law Sch. Found., 1997-98, Wells Fargo Cmty. Bd., Ctrl. Tex., 2000-03; trustee Episcopal Health Charities, 1997—. Recipient Tribute to 28 Black Women award Concepts Unltd., 1983; Focus on women honoree Serwa Yetu chpt. Mt. Olive grand chpt. Order of Eastern Star, 1979, Woman of Yr. Longview Metro C. of C., 1985, Woman of Yr. Austin chpt. Internat. Tng. in Communication, 1985, Citizen of Yr. Epsilon Iona chpt. Omega Psi Phi, Lone Star Girl Scout Coun. Women of Distinction, 1997, Profiles in Power Austin Bus. Jour., 1999, Silent Samaritan award Samaritan Counseling Ctr., 2000. Master Inns of Ct.; mem. ABA, Am. Bar Found., Tex. Bar Found. (trustee 1986-89), Travis County Bar Assn., Travis County Women Lawyers' Assn., Austin Black Lawyers Assn., State Bar Tex. (chmn. Profl. Efficiency & Econ. Rsch. subcom. 1976-84), Golden Key Nat. Honor Soc., Longhorn Assocs. for Excellence in Women's Athletes (adv. coun. 1988—), Order of Coif (hon. mem.), Omicron Delta Kappa, Delta Phi Alpha. Democrat. Office: Bickerstaff Heath Smiley Pollan Keever & McDaniels 1700 First Bank Plz 816 Congress Ave Austin TX 78701-2443 Office Phone: 512-472-8021. Business E-Mail: mmcdaniel@bickerstaff.com.

MCDANIEL, NORWOOD ALLAN, insurance broker; b. Pitts., Dec. 16, 1928; children: Norwood Jr., Cherie Suzanne, Thomas Cavin. Student, Washington and Lee U., 1948-50; PhD (hon.), C.C. Allegheny County. Gen. ins. broker, Pitts., 1949—. Adv. bd. Union Nat. Bank, Pitts. Asst. treas. C.C. Allegheny County, 1980-90. Recipient citation Pa. Senate, 1987, Pa. Ho. of Reps., 1987, tribute Congl. Record, Pres. Ronald Reagan, 1987; inducted into Pa. Sports Hall of Fame, 1973. Mem. Fellows Club (pres.), City Club, Ins. Club Pitts., Profl. Ins. Agts. Assn., Amen Corner (pres.), Masons, Shriners (potentate Syria Temple Shrine 1978), Variety Club (chief barker), The Shrine Treas. Assn. N.Am. (sec.-treas. 1985-98). Home and Office: 26319 Feathersound Dr Punta Gorda FL 33955 E-mail: woodymcdaniel@earthlink.net.

MCDANIEL, RANDALL CORNELL, retired professional football player; b. Phoenix, Dec. 19, 1964; BPE, Ariz. State U., 1988. Offensive guard Minn. Vikings, 1988-98, Tampa Bay Buccaneers, 1998—2002. Named NFL All-Pro Team Guard by Sporting News, 1991-93. Achievements include playing in Pro Bowl, 1988-93. Office: Tampa Bay Bucs 1 W Buccaneer Pl Tampa FL 33607-5701

MCDANIEL, RAYMOND W., JR., financial information company executive; Degree in polit. sci., Colgate U.; degree in Law, Emory U. Sch. Law. Bar: NY 1984. Mng. dir. internat. Moody's Corp., 1996—2001; sr. mng. dir. global ratings and rsch. Moody's Investors Svc., 2001; sr. v.p. internat. Moody's Corp., 2000—01, sr. v.p. global ratings and rsch., 2001—03, exec. v.p. global ratings and rsch., 2003—04, bd. dirs., 2003—; pres. Moody's Investors Svc., NYC, 2001—; COO Moody's Corp., NYC, 2004—. Mem. bd. dirs. Nat. Coun. Econ. Edn. Mem.: Fixed Income Analysts Soc. Office: Moodys Corp 99 Church St New York NY 10007 Office Phone: 212-553-0300. Office Fax: 212-553-7194.

MCDANIEL, RHONDA LOUISE, literature educator; d. Thomas Jefferson and Jewel Marie McDaniel; m. Monte Brent Unger, Oct. 25, 1986 (div. Apr. 19, 1995). AA in Music, Miami (Fla.)-Dade C.C., 1983; B of Music Therapy, Shenandoah Conservatory Music, 1986; MA, U. Tenn., Chattanooga, 1998; PhD, Western Mich. U., 2003. Inventory contr./bookkeeper Brown's Furniture and Majestic Industries, Chattanooga, 1989—95; office mgr. Benefit Plans Adminstrs., Chattanooga, 1995—98; editl. asst. Tenn. Philol. Bull. U. Tenn., Chattanooga, 1996—98; academic advisor Coll. Arts and Scis. Western Mich. U., Kalamazoo, 1998—2000, doctoral assoc. dept. English and Medieval Inst., 2000—03; asst. prof. English, Middle Tenn. State U., Murfreesboro, 2003—. Contbr. articles to profl. jours. Pianist Cmty. Presbyn. Ch., Kalamazoo, 2000—03, dir. children's music camp, 2001—03. Grantee, Mellon Found., 2001, The Erasmus Inst., 2002; Mathilde Steckelberg scholar in Latin, Western Mich. U., 2002. Mem.: MLA, Medieval Acad. Am. (John Leyerle-CARA award 2002), Phi Theta Kappa, Sigma Tau Delta, Phi Beta Kappa. Avocations: singing, acting, canoeing. Office: Middle Tenn State U Dept English Box 70 Murfreesboro TN 37132

MCDANIEL, RODERICK ROGERS, petroleum engineer, consultant; b. High River, Alta., Can., 1926; s. Dorsey Patton and Daisy (Rogers) McD.; m. Trudy Ethier, Apr. 15, 2000; children: Nancy, Leslie. BS, U. Okla., 1947. Petroleum reservoir engr. Creole Petroleum Corp., 1947, Imperial Oil Ltd., 1948-52, chief reservoir engr., 1952-55; founder McDaniel Cons., Calgary, Canada, 1955—; chmn. Can. Airlines Ltd., Calgary, 1974-91, Can. Regional Airlines, Calgary, 1991-92. Hon. dir. Calgary Exhbn. and Stampede, 1979-88, hon. bd. dirs., 1988—; dir. Calgary Stampeder Football Team, 1988. Mem. Assn. Profl. Engrs. Alta (hon. life), Can. C. of C. (bd. dirs. 1973), Calgary C. of C. (past pres.), Calgary Petroleum Club (past pres.), Calgary Highlanders (hon. col. ret.), Calgary Golf and Country Club, Outrigger Club (Honolulu), Mission Hills Country Club. Home: # 2200 255 5 Ave SW Calgary AB Canada T2P 3G6 Office: McDaniel & Assoc 2200 255 5th Ave SW Calgary AB Canada T2P 3G6 Office Phone: 403-262-5506.

MCDANIEL, SUE POWELL, writer, speaker; b. Jefferson City, Mo., Mar. 13, 1946; d. Ernest Gayle and Ruth Angeline (Raithel) Powell; m. Walter Lee Zimmerman, Aug. 14, 1966 (div. 1980); m. Olin Cleve McDaniel, June 23, 1985 (div. 2002). BS in Edn., U. Mo., 1968, MEd in Edn., 1977, EdS, 1980, PhD, 1985. Cert. tchr., Mo. Tchr. Jefferson City Pub. Schs., 1968-80; fiscal assoc. Mo. Coordinating Bd. for Higher Edn., Jefferson City, 1980-90; exec. dir. Mo. Women's Coun., Jefferson City, 1990-99; exec. dir. Skillpath Seminars, 2000—03; pres. Alternatives, Jefferson City, Mo., 1999—; dir. Heisinger Hope Found., 2004. Author: (with C. Dixon) Learning, Changing, Leading: Keep to Success in the 21st Century, 1998, I.M. Heart, 2004; co-author: Missouri Women Today, 1993, Status of the Women, 1994,. Mem. Zonta Internat. Avocations: reading, music, drawing, flower garden, photography. Home: 1600 Stadium Blvd Jefferson City MO 65109-2418

MCDANIEL, THOMAS R. utilities executive; BS in Civil Engring., UCLA; postgrad., Calif. State U., L.A., U. So. Calif. Joined So. Calif. Edison, 1971; CEO, dir. Edison Capital, 1987—; CEO, pres. Edison Mission Energy, Irvine, Calif., 2002—, chmn., 2003—. Active Huntington Youth Shelter; dir. Sr. Care Action Network. Office: Edison Mission Energy 18101 Von Karman Ave Irvine CA 92612

MCDANIEL, THOMAS ROBB, academic administrator, educator; b. Washington, Jan. 30, 1941; s. Noble Ashby and Emilie (Robb) McD.; m. Suzanne H. McDaniel, June 12, 1965; children: Robb Ashby, Kathryn Noble. BA, Hampden-Sydney Coll., 1963; MAT, Johns Hopkins U., 1964, MLA, 1968, PhD, 1971. Tchr. The Gilman Sch., Balt., 1964-65; administr. Johns Hopkins U., Balt., 1965-71; prof. Converse Coll., Spartanburg, S.C., 1971—, dean Coll. Arts and Scis., 1986-90, v.p. for acad. affairs, 1990-93, interim pres., 1993-94, provost, 1994—2002, sr. v.p., 2002—. Author: At Home in South Carolina, 1991, rev. edit., 2000, Dr. Luke's Prescriptions for Spiritual Health, 2000, Dean's Dialogue, 2002; author, editor: Public Education in South Carolina, 1984; exec. editor The Clearing House, 1999—; cons. editor Acad. Leader, 1999—. Chmn. Spartanburg County Bd. Elections, 1981-83; pres., bd. dirs. Charles Lea Ctr., Spartanburg, 1979-81, 89-91; chmn. policy bd. dirs. S.C. Ctr. for Tchr. Recruitment, Rock Hill, S.C., 1994-96; elder First Presbyn. Ch., Spartanburg, 1977—; chmn. Spartanburg County Commn. on Excellence in Edn., Spartanburg, 1984; mem. Spartanburg Human Rels. Commn., 1996-2000; chmn. Weekday Sch. First Presbyn. Ch., 1978—. Mem. Spartanburg C. of C. Phi Beta Kappa (pres. Piedmont chpt. 1998-2001), Phi Delta Kappa (pres. Greenville-Spartanburg chpt. 1989-90, Svc. award 1992). Avocations: reading, writing, consulting, golf. Home: 169 Mills Ave Spartanburg SC 29302 Office: Converse Coll 580 E Main St Spartanburg SC 29302 E-mail: tom.mcdaniel@converse.edu.

MCDANIELS, JOHN LOUIS, retired mathematics educator; b. Alton, Ill., Oct. 3, 1933; s. John Clarence and Carrie Elizabeth (Kortkamp) McD.; m. Betty Lou Verble, June 20, 1964. BS, U. Mo., Rolla, 1960; MS, So. Ill. U., 1977. Registered profl. engr., Ill.; Mo. Engr. McDonnell Douglas Corp., St. Louis, 1960-74; prof. Lewis and Clark Community Coll., Godfrey, Ill., 1975-96. Dist. TEAMS competition coord. Ill. Jr. Engring. Tech. Soc., Lewis and Clark C.C., 1987-96, pre-engring. coord., 1975-96, water tech. coord., 1975-92. Bd. dirs. Alton (Ill.) Mus. History and Art, 1984-86, With U.S. Army, 1954-56. Mem. Ill. Math. Assn. Cmty. Colls., Kiwanis (Alton-Godfrey pres. 1989-90, Alton-Godfrey Svc. 1997—, Disting. Pres. award 1990), Service Corps of Ret. Execs., Sigma Pi Sigma, Tau Beta Pi, Kappa Delta Pi. Presbyterian. Home: 3208 Greenwood Ln Godfrey IL 62035-1815 E-mail: jlmcdaniels@charter.net.

MCDANIELS, WILLIAM E. lawyer; b. Needham, Mass., July 1, 1941; BA, Williams Coll., 1963; JD, Georgetown U., 1966. Bar: D.C. 1967, Md. 1983. Grad. fellow criminal law, litigation U. Pa., Phila., 1966-68; pub. defender Phila. Pub. Defender's Office, 1966-68; adj. prof. evidence, criminal law, advanced criminal procedure Georgetown U. Law Ctr., Washington, 1970-87; mem. Williams & Connolly, Washington, 1968—. Instr. Nat. Inst. Trial Advocacy, 1975—. Fellow Am. Coll. Trial Lawyers; mem. ABA, Md. State Bar Assn, D.C. Bar. Office: Williams & Connolly 725 12th St NW Washington DC 20005-5901

MC DANNALD, CLYDE ELLIOTT, JR., management consultation company executive; b. June 29, 1923; s. Clyde E. and Evelyn (Tunison-Morgan) McD.; m. Virginia Malachrick, Apr. 25, 1953; children: Leslie Ann McDannald Malarchick, Clyde Elliott III, Bruce Robert, Bonnie Washington McDannald Jefferis, Brian Christopher (dec.), Laura Leigh. Market rsch. analyst J. Walter Thompson Co., N.Y.C., 1948-50; asst. dir. market rsch. Nat. Lead Co., N.Y.C., 1950-51; product rsch. supr., account exec. Foote, Cone & Belding, Inc., N.Y.C., 1951-52; product mgr., asst. advt. mgr. Am. Safety Razor Corp., N.Y.C., 1953-54; account exec., account supr. Meldrum & Fewsmith, Inc., Cleve., 1954-56; sr. account exec. Young & Rubicam, N.Y.C., 1956-58; exec. asst. to v.p., advt. mgr. Brown & Williamson Tobacco Corp. subs. Brit.-Am. Tobacco Co., Ltd., Louisville, 1959-63; dir. advt. and mktg. svcs., dir. mktg. Miller Brewing Co., Milw., 1963-65; divsn. gen. mgr., v.p. consumer products, corp. v.p. Revere Copper & Brass Inc., N.Y.C., 1966-71; pres., COO H.H. Pott Distillers Ltd. U.S. subs. H.H. Pott NFGR, N.Y.C., 1972-80, also bd. dirs.; pres., CEO Oxbridge Cons., Inc., N.Y.C., 1981—; ptnr. Hilbert, Peers and Young, Inc., N.Y.C., 1984—. Bd. dirs. West Indies Distillers, Ltd., Distilled Spirits Inst., Washington, McFrank & Williams Inc. and Cooperating Cons. Corp., N.Y.C.; vis. prof. mktg. Fairfield U. Sch. Bus., 1975-77. Apptd. to staff Col. Ky. Govs., 1959-63, 92—; mem. Ky. Hwy. Commn., 1960-63, N.Y. Gov.'s Indsl. Comn., 1967-72; bd. govs. N.Y. Mil. Acad., 1970-76, trustee, 1975-92. Capt. Inf. USAAF, 1942-45, ETO. Decorated D.F.C., Air medal with 4 oak leaf clusters; recipient Conspicuous Svc. Cross State of N.Y. with 5 oak leaf clusters, Valor medal UDC, Knickerbocker Greys City of N.Y., War Cross, Sons of Confederate Vets., Medaille de la France Liberee, Croix de Guerre (Belgium, France), Roi Leopold III, Battle of Britain, Knight Mil. Order of Malta, Knight Sovereign Mil. Order Temple Jerusalem. Mem. SAR, SR (bd. mgrs. 1988—), Alumni Fedn. Columbia U., Am. Mgmt. Assn., NAM (mktg. com.), Audit Bur. Circulation, Navy League, St. Andrews Soc. State of N.Y., Am. Revolution Round Table, Am. Legion, VFW, N.Y. Soc. Mil. and Naval Officers World Wars, Sons of Confederate Vets., Soc. Colonial Wars, St. George Soc., Soc. Mayflower Descs., Nat. Huguenot Soc., St. Nicholas Soc. of City of N.Y. Columbia U. Club, Explorers Club, Univ. Club, Sigma Chi (life), Alpha Chi Sigma. Democrat. Presbyterian. Home: Clarendon Gardens 5 Red Fox Run Pinehurst NC 28374-9031 E-mail: cmcdann398@aol.com.

MCDARRAH, FRED WILLIAM, photographer, writer; b. Bklyn., Nov. 5, 1926; s. Howard Arthur and Elizabeth (Swahn) McD.; m. Gloria Schoffel, Nov. 5, 1960; children: Timothy Swann, Patrick James. BA in Journalism, NYU, 1954. Mem. staff Village Voice Newspaper, N.Y.C., 1959—, picture editor, 1971—; book reviewer ASMP Infinity Mag., 1972-73, Photo Dist. News, 1985-88, The Picture Profl., 1990—2002. Exhibited in Soho Photo Gallery, 1973, Whitney Mus., 1974, 76-77, Dallas Mus. Art, 1974, San Francisco Mus. Art, 1975, Wadsworth Atheneum, 1975, Sidney Janis Gallery, 1976, Basel (Switzerland) Art Fair, 1976, Alfred Stieglitz Gallery, 1976, Empire State Mus., Albany, N.Y., 1978, Lightworks Gallery, Syracuse, N.Y., 1981, Cape Cod Gallery, Provincetown Mass., 1982, Galleria di Franca Mancini, Pesaro, Italy, 1983, Musée du Quebec, 1987, Anita Shapolsky Gallery, N.Y., 1988, Hartnett Gallery U. Rochester, N.Y., 1989, G. Ray Hawkins Gallery, L.A., 1989, Read Gallery Antioch (Ohio) Coll., 1989, Mus. Art/Sci./Industry, Bridgeport, Conn., 1989, N.Y.C. Gallery Queens Mus., 1989, Ctr. Photography, Woodstock, 1989, Frumkin/Adams Gallery, 1990, Musée d'Art Moderne De La Ville de Paris, 1990, Musée d'Art Contemporain, Montreal, 1990, Pollack-Krasner Mus., East Hampton, N.Y., 1990, Found. Cartier, Paris, 1990, Marty Carey Pictures Gallery, Woodstock, N.Y., 1992, Galerie Gilles Ringuet, Belfort, France, 1992, Galerie Contre Jour, Belfort, France, 1992, Galleria La Pescheria, Cesena, Italy, 1994, Whitney Mus. Am. Art, 1995—, Nat. Portrait Gallery, 1996, Candice Perich Gallery, 1996; exhbns. include Jack Kerouac Visions of the Road, Les Rencontres D'Arles, Arles, France, 1991, Jack Kerouac Travelling Writers, Saint-Malo (France) Internat. Festival, 1991, 97, Images of Greenwich Village N.Y. Camera Club, 1992, Walker Art Ctr., Mpls., 1996, M.H. de Young Meml. Mus., San Francisco, 1996, Whitney Mus. Am. Art, 1997-98, New York Stories, Chiostro del Bramante, Rome, 1999, Detroit Inst. Arts, 2000, Great Modern Pictures, N.Y., 2000, MOCA, Wexner Ctr., Parrish Mus., 2000, Mus. Nat. Modern Art 2001, Gallerie Comunale d'Arte Moderna, Rome, 2001, Mus. City of N.Y., 2001, Centre Pompidou, Paris, 2001, Albright-Knox Art Gallery, 2002, Mus. Contemporary Art, L.A., 2002, Fahey/Klein Gallery, L.A., 2002, Grimaldi Forum, Monaco, 2003 others; author: The Beat Scene, 1960, The Artist's World in Pictures, 1961, rev. edit. 1988, Greenwich Village, 1963, New York, New York, 1964, Sculpture in Environment, 1967, Museums in New York, 1973, French edit., 1979, 5th edit., 1990, Photography Marketplace, 2d edit., 1977, Stock Photo and Assignment Source Book, 1977, 2d edit., 1984, Gay Pride: Photographs from Stonewall to Today, 1994, Frommer's Virginia Guide, 2d edit., 1994, Fodor's Cancun, Cozumel, Yucatan Peninsula, 1996, Kerouac and Friends: A Beat Generation Album, 1984, Japanese edit, 1990, 2nd edit, 2002, Frommer's Atlantic City and Cape May, 4th edit., 1991, 5th

edit., 1993, New York Stories, 2001, Anarchy, Protest & Rebellion & the Counter Culture that Changed America, 2003; co-author: The New Bohemia, 1967, 2d edit., 1990, Guide for Ecumenical Discussion, 1970, Greenwich Village Guide, 1992, Frommer's Virginia, 1992, 2d edit. 1994; author: (with Timothy S: LA Pop Art Negli Anni '60 Chiostro del Bram Ante, 1999; author: (with Gloria S. McDarrah) Beat Generation: Glory Days in Greenwich Village, 1998; The Beat Generation: Glory Days in Greenwich Village, editor, 1996; editor: (with Gloria S. McDarrah and Timothy S. McDarrah) The Photography Encyclopedia, 1999; author: (with Gloria S. McDarrah) The Artist's World in Pictures, 2d edit., 1988; Saturday Rev. Executive Desk Diary, 1962-64; photographer: Personality Posters, Fotofolio (post cards) (polit. and social figures); contbr. articles, picture features to various publs. including N.Y. Mag., Vanity Fair. Paratrooper U.S. Army, 1944-47. Recipient numerous photography awards including 1st place spot news photo award. N.Y. Press Assn., 1964, 68; recipient 1st place feature photo award N.Y. Press Assn., 1967, 1st place picture story award N.Y. Press Assn., 1969, 2nd place spot news photo award N.Y. Press Assn., 1967, 70, 3d place spot news photo award N.Y. Press Assn., 1965, 3d place feature photo award N.Y. Press Assn., 1965, 3d place picture story award N.Y. Press Assn., 1966, Page One award Newspaper Guild N.Y., 1971, 80; Guggenheim fellow in photography, 1972. Mem. N.Y. Press Photographers Assn., Authors Guild, N.Y. Press Club, Am. Soc. Picture Profls. Office: 36 Cooper Sq New York NY 10003-7118

MCDARRAH, GLORIA SCHOFFEL, editor, author; b. Bronx, N.Y., June 22, 1932; d. Louis and Rose Schoffel; m. Fred W. McDarrah, Nov. 5, 1960; children: Timothy, Patrick. BA in French, Pa. State U., 1953; MA in French, NYU, 1966. Editorial asst. Crowell-Collier, N.Y.C., 1957-59; reading asst. to pub. Time Inc., N.Y.C., 1959-61; libr., tchr. N.Y.C. Pub. Schs. and St. Luke's Sch., 1972-76; exec. asst. to pres. Capital Cities Communications Inc., N.Y.C., 1972-76; analyst N.Y.C. Landmarks Preservation Commn., 1976-79; project editor Grosset & Dunlap Inc., N.Y.C., 1979-80; sr. editor Prentice Hall trade div. Simon & Schuster Inc., N.Y.C., 1980-88; pres. McDarrah Media Assocs., N.Y.C., 1988—. Editor book rev. The Picture Profl., 1989—; book reviewer Pub.'s Weekly, 1994—. Author: Frommer's Guide to Va., 1992, Frommer's Guide to Va. 2d edit., 1994—95, Frommer's Atlantic City and Cape May, 1984, Frommer's Atlantic City and Cape May 4th edit., 1991, Frommer's Atlantic City and Cape May 5th edit., 1993—95, The Artist's World 2d edit., 1988, Photography Encyclopedia, 1999; co-author: Museums in N.Y. 5th edit., 1990, Photography Marketplace, 1975, The Beat Generation: Glory Days in Greenwich Village, 1996, Anarchy, Protest and Rebellion and the Counter-Culture That Changed Am., 2003; co-editor: Exec. Desk Diary Saturday Rev., 1962—64; contbg. editor (quar.): Dollarwise Traveler, Fodor's Cancun, Cozumel, Yucatan Peninsula, Fodor's Ariz.

MCDAVID, ANDREW J. health facility administrator, medical educator; BA, U. Tex., Austin, 1980; MD, U. Tex., 1984. Diplomate Am. Bd. Anesthesiology, Am. Bd. Anesthesiology Pain Mgmt. Resident in anesthesiology Scott & White Regional Clinics, Temple, Tex., dir. anesthesiology and pain mgmt., dir. anesthesiology pain clinic, asst. prof. anesthesiology. Contbr. articles to profl. jours. Office: 1402 W Avenue H Temple TX 76504-5342

MCDAVID, DOUGLAS WARREN, executive research consultant; b. San Francisco, Feb. 25, 1947; s. James Etheridge and Elizabeth Rae (Warren) McD.; m. Nancy Kathleen Somers, June 1968 (div. 1982); 1 child, Amy Kemp; m. Carleen Ann Richmond, Feb. 14, 1987; 1 child, Amanda Claire. BA in Sociology, U. Calif., Santa Cruz, 1969; MA in Libr. Sci., San Jose State U., 1972. Libr. Palo Alto (Calif.) City Libr., 1969-81; systems analyst Tymnet (Tymshare), Cupertino, Calif., 1981-84; mgr. systems architecture Tymnet McDonnell Douglas, San Jose, Calif., 1984-86; data modeling cons. Fireman's Fund Ins., Terra Linda, Calif., 1986-87, Bank of Calif., San Francisco, 1988; systems cons. Pacific Bell, San Ramon, Calif., 1989-93; prin. Integrated Info., 1993—; exec. cons. IBM Global Svcs., 1995—, IBM Almaden Rsch Ctr., 2002—. Mem. IBM Acad. Tech., 2000—; spkr. Entity/Relationship Conf. Internat., Burlingame, Calif., 1991, DAMA Internat. Conf., 1994—; cons. in bus. semantic modeling for object oriented applications IBM Corp., 1994—; 1996 spkr. Bus. Rules Conf. OOPSLA, IBM Object Technology Conf., Intl. Labor & Mgmt. Coun.; cons. IBM, 1994-98, mgr. knowledge devel., 1999—; spkr. in field. Assoc. editor: Handbook of Object Technology. Mem. IEEE, Assn. for Computing Machinery, Data Adminstrn. Mgmt. Assn. (San Francisco bd. dirs. 1987-91, Sacramento bd. dirs. 1992, speaker 1991, 92), Data Processing Mgmt. Assn. (speaker 1992), Am. Assn. Artificial Intelligence (speaker 1993), Internat. Soc. Sys. Sci. (speaker 1999). Avocations: golf, gardening, creative writing, investing, swimming. Home and Office: 8611 Kingslynn Ct Elk Grove CA 95624-3135 Office Phone: 408-927-1565. Business E-Mail: mcdavid@us.ibm.com.

MCDAVID, GEORGE EUGENE (GENE MC DAVID), retired newspaper executive; b. McComb, Miss., June 30, 1930; s. O. C. and Inez S. McDavid; m. Betty Ernestine Tinsley, Sept. 24, 1949; children: Carol, Martha Gene Newman. BBA cum laude, U. Houston, 1965. Owner, pub. Wilk Amite Record, Gloster, Miss., 1949-58; with Houston Chronicle, 1958—, prodn. mgr., 1967-74, v.p. ops., 1974-85, v.p., gen. mgr., 1985-90, pres., 1990-98, ret., 1998. Mem. adv. bd. Am. Press Inst.; past pres., bd. dirs. S.W. Wch. Printing Mgmt. Chmn. Greater Houston chpt. ARC, 1st vice-chmn.; pres.'s counsel Houston Bapt. U; vice-chmn. Sam Houston Boy Scouts Am., United Negro Coll. Fund, Asia Soc. Goodwill Industries, YMCA; chmn. Houston Forum Houston region Am. Cancer Soc., bd. regents, 1997—; spl. deacon Second Bapt. Ch., Houston.; bd. dirs. Nat. Conf. Christians and Jews; nat. bd. govs. Greater Houston chpt. ARC; bd. dirs. Greater Houston Partnership; bd. dirs., pres. Houston Symphony; bd. dirs., v.p. Books of the World; vice-chmn. devel. bd. U. Houston, chair bd. regents, 2003. Recipient Franklin award, U. Houston, 1961, Disting. Alumnus award, 1990, 1997, Taggart award, Tex. Newspaper, 1992, Man of Yr. award, NCCJ, 1993, named Outstanding Ex-Citizen Gloster, 1973, Hon. Father of Yr., 1996, named to Miss. Jour. Hall of Fame, 2002. Mem.: So. Newspaper Pubs. Assn. (pres.), Am. Newspaper Pubs. Assn. (chmn. newsprint com.), Pine Forest Country Club, Tex. Daily Newspaper Assn. (pres.), Houston C. of C. (Houston Citizen's Cmty. Svc. award 1993, named Houston Cultural Leader of Yr. 1998), Coronado Tex. Club, Houstonian Club, Houston Club, Beta Gamma Sigma, Phi Kappa Phi. Home: 403 Hunters Park Ln Houston TX 77024-5438 Office: 801 Texas St Houston TX 77002-2904

MCDAVID, JANET LOUISE, lawyer; b. Mpls., Jan. 24, 1950; d. Robert Matthew and Lois May (Bratt) Kurzeka; m. John Gary McDavid, June 9, 1973; 1 child, Matthew Collins McDavid. BA, Northwestern U., 1971; JD, Georgetown U., 1974. Bar D.C. 1975, U.S.Ct. Appeals (fed.) 1975 (D.C. cir. 1976), U.S. Supreme Ct. 1980, U.S. Ct. Appeals (5th cir.) 1983, (9th cir.) 1986. Assoc. Hogan & Hartson, Washington, 1974-83, ptnr., 1984—. Gen. counsel ERAmerica, 1977-83; mem. antitrust task force Dept. Defense, 1993-94, 96-97; mem. antitrust coun. U.S. C. of C., 1994—; advisor Bush adminstrn. transition team, 2001. Contbr. articles to profl. jours. Participant Clinton and Bush adminstrn. transition team FTC. Mem. ABA (antitrust sect., vice chmn. civil practice com. 1989-89, sect. 2 com. 1989-90, chmn. franchising com. 1990-91, coun. mem. 1991-94, program officer 1994-97, vice chair 1997-98, chair-elect 1998-99, chair 1999-2000, immediate past chair, governing com. of forum on franchising 1991-97), ACLU, U.S. C. of C. (antitrust coun. 1995—), Washington Coun. Lawyers, D.C. Bar Assn., Fed. Bar Assn., Womens Legal Def. fund. Democrat. Office: Hogan & Hartson 555 13th St NW Washington DC 20004-1109 Office Phone: 202-637-8780. E-mail: jlmcdavid@hhlaw.com.

MCDAVID, WILLIAM HENRY, lawyer; b. NYC, May 10, 1946; m. Sylvia Noin, Dec. 21, 1984; children: Andrew, Madeline, William, Flora. AB, Columbia Coll., N.Y.C., 1968; JD, Yale U., 1972. Assoc. Debevoise & Plimpton, N.Y.C., 1972-81; asst. gen. counsel Bankers Trust Co., N.Y.C., 1981-83, assoc. gen. counsel, 1983-84, v.p., 1984-85, v.p., counsel, 1986-88; gen. counsel J.P. Morgan & Co., N.Y.C., 1988—2000, J.P. Morgan Chase & Co., N.Y.C., 2000—03, chief legal officer, 2003—. Office: JP Morgan Chase & Co Office Gen Coun 270 Park Ave Fl 8 New York NY 10017-2014*

MCDAVIS, RODERICK J. academic administrator; b. Dayton, Ohio, Oct. 17, 1948; m. Deborah Moses; children: Ryan, Tony. BS in Social Scis. in Secondary Edn., Ohio U., 1970; MS in Student Pers. Adminstrn., U. Dayton, 1971; PhD in Counselor Edn., U. Toledo, 1974. Asst. prof. edn. grad. divsn. Siena Heights Coll., Adrian, Mich., 1973—74; asst. prof. edn. dept. counselor edn. Coll. Edn. U. Fla., Gainesville, 1974—79, assoc. prof. edn. dept. counselor edn. Coll. Edn., 1979—82, prof. edn. dept. counselor edn. Coll. Edn., 1982—89, acting asst. dean for grad. studies Grad. Sch., 1984—85, assoc. dean Grad. Sch. and Minority Programs Grad. Sch., 1986—89, prof. edn. dept. counselor edn. Coll. Edn., 1994—99, dean Coll. Edn., 1994—99; prof. counselor edn. dept. edn. leadership, counseling and founds. Coll. Edn. U. Ark., Fayetteville, 1989—94, dean Coll. Edn., 1989—94; prof. edn. divsn. ednl. studies Sch. Edn. Va. Commonwealth U., Richmond, 1999—2004, provost, v.p. acad. affairs, 1999—2004; pres. Ohio U., Athens, 2004—. Vis. prof. edn. dept. counselor edn. and human svcs. Grad. Sch. Edn. U. Mass., 1979—83, 1992. Named Person of Yr. in Edn., The Gainesville Sun, 1995; recipient Disting. Svc. award for cmty. outreach through TV media, Fla. Assn. for Counselor Edn. and Supervision, 1978, Key to the City, City Commn., Gainesville, 1995, Outstanding Alumnus award, Ohio U. Coll. Edn., 1996, Black Achiever's award in edn., Fla. Conf. Black State Legislators, Tallahassee, 1997. Mem.: Nat. Alliance Black Sch. Educators, Am. Coll. Pers. Assn., Phi Kappa Phi, Phi Delta Kappa (Post-secondary Outstanding Educator award North Ctrl. Fla. chpt. 1996). Office: Office of the Pres 108 Cutler Hall Athens OH 45701*

MCDEMMOND, MARIE VALENTINE, academic administrator, consultant; b. New Orleans, Feb. 4, 1946; d. George Graham and Marie Valentine (Prudeaux) McD.; m. Louis Saulny, June 15, 1966 (div. 1972); children: Alan Peter, Eric W. Reid; m. Roy Russell Mouton, Sept. 18, 1987. BA, Xavier U., 1968; MEd, U. New Orleans, 1971; postgrad, SUNY, Albany; EdD, U. Mass., 1985. Tchr. Kohn Jr. High Sch., New Orleans, 1968-70; dir. Community Leadership Program, New Rochelle, N.Y., 1970-72, Community Leadership Consortium, Westchester County, N.Y., 1972-73; assoc. Higher Edn. Opportunity Program Office, Albany, N.Y., 1973-74; instr. dept. edn. Ithaca (N.Y.) Coll., 1974; with bus. office, dept. acctg. Bronx (N.Y.) Phychiatric Ctr., 1974-77; assoc. higher edn. N.Y. State Bd. Regents, Albany, 1977-78; dir. fin. Mass. Bd. Regional Community Colls., Boston, 1979-80; assoc. vice chancellor U. Mass., Amherst, 1980-84; v.p. budget & fin. Atlanta U., 1984-85; asst. v.p. for fin. Emory U., Atlanta, 1983-80, pres. McDemmond & Assoc., Boca Raton, Fla., 1986-89; asst. prof. edn. U. New Orleans, 1987-88; asst. v.p. adminstrn. & fin. Fla. Atlantic U., Boca Raton, 1988-89, v.p. adminstrn. & fin., 1990-96; pres. Norfolk (Va.) State U., 1996—. Adj. asst. prof. Coll. New Rochelle, N.Y., 1971-73; adj. prof. edn. U. Mass., Amherst, 1984; hostess Sta. WTCC, Springfield, Mass., 1983-84; lectr. in economic redevel., 1989. Author tng. course. Civil svc. examiner State N.Y., Albany, 1976-78; precinct coord. Democrats for Jackson, Amherst, 1984; advisor Palm Beach Judicial Bldg., West Palm Beach, Fla., 1991. Named Fla. Woman Who Makes a Difference Nat. Assn. Women Bus. Owners, 1990. Mem. Bus. and Profl. Women's Club Am. (Woman of Achievement award 1991), New England Minority Women (pres. 1982-84), So. Assn. Coll. and Bus. Officers (exec. com. 1991—), Nat. Assn. Coll. and Univ. Bus. Officers, Coun. Minority Edn. (pres. 1982-84). Roman Catholic. Avocations: gardening, reading. Office: Norfolk State U 700 Park Ave Norfolk VA 23504-8090

MCDERMID, MARGARET E. information technology executive, engineer; B in bus., Mary Baldwin Coll.; MBA, U. Richmond. With Stone and Webster Engring. Corp.; joined Va. Power, 1982, various positions engring. & construction dept., 1982—86, dir. adminstrv. svcs., 1986—98; v.p. info. tech., CIO Dominion Resources Inc., 1998—2000, sr. v.p. info. tech., CIO, 2000—. Mem. apptd. by Gov. Gilmore CIO Adv. Bd., 2000. Active with United Way, Big Brothers, Big Sisters; bd. trustees Mary Baldwin Coll.; found. bd. J. Sargeant Reynolds Cmty. Coll.; bd. dirs. Greater Richmond Tech. Coun., Children's Mus. Richmond Bus. Com., CIO Forum; mem. Va. Rsch. and Tech. Adv. Coun. Achievements include first woman to enter the Apprentice Program at Newport News Shipyard where she completed the Patternmaker's program. Office: Dominion Resources Inc 120 Tredegar St Richmond VA 23219 Office Phone: 804-819-2000.

MCDERMOTT, AGNES CHARLENE SENAPE, philosophy educator; b. Hazelton, Pa., Mar. 11, 1937; d. Charles G. and Conjetta (Ranieri) Senape; children: Robert C., Lisa G., Jamie C. BA, U. Pa., 1956, PhD, 1964; postgrad., U. Calif.-Berkeley, 1960—61, U. Amsterdam, Netherlands, 1965, U. Wis., 1967—69. Instr. math. Drexel Inst. Tech., Phila., 1962-63; asst. prof. philosophy SUNY-Buffalo, 1964-65, Hampton Inst., Va., 1966-67; asst. prof. U. Wis.-Milw., 1967-70; assoc. prof. philosophy U. N.Mex., Albuquerque, 1970-80, prof., dean grad. studies, 1981-86; dean in residence Coun. of Grad. Schs., Washington, 1985-86; provost, v.p. acad. affairs, cons. Albuquerque Acad., 1991-93; ind. cons. Corrales, N.Mex., 1993—. Vis. assoc. prof. U. Wash., Seattle, 1974, U. Calif.-Berkeley, 1973-74, U. Hawaii, Honolulu, 1975; vis. prof. U. Calif.-Berkeley, 1980; vis. prof. Semester at Sea, U. Pitts., fall 1994; bd. dir. Juvenile Diabetes Rsch. Found.; lectr., panelist in field. Author: An Eleventh Century Buddhist Logic of 'Exists', 1969, Boethius' Treatise on the Modes of Signifying, 1980; compiler, editor anthology: Comparative Philosophy: Selected Essays, 1983; rev. editor Phil. East West, 1986—; contbr. articles and stories to profl. and literary jours. Active Albuquerque Care Alliance, 1988-2000. AAUW postdoctoral fellow, 1965-66; NEH Younger Humanist fellow, 1971-72; faculty rsch. fellow U. N.Mex., 1978, 79, 80; U. Pa. grad. fellow, 1961-62; S. Fels Found. fellow, 1963-64; U. Pa. tuition scholar; Pa. Hist. Soc. scholar Mem. N.Y. Acad. Scis., Am. Philos. Soc., Am. Philos. Assn. (exec. com. 1977-80), Assn. Asian Studies (exec. com. 1977-80), Am. Oriental Soc., Western Assn. Grad. Schs. (pres. 1986-87), N.Mex. Juvenile Diabetes Rsch. Found., Phi Beta Kappa, Pi Mu Epsilon. Democrat. Avocations: skiing, fly-fishing. E-mail: mcdcott@netzero.net.

MCDERMOTT, ALAN, newspaper editor; b. Kansas City, Mo., Sept. 5, 1951; Sr. editor Universal Press Syndicate, Kansas City, Mo., 1996—. Office: Universal Press Syndicate 4520 Main St Ste 700 Kansas City MO 64111-7701

MCDERMOTT, ALICE, writer; b. Bklyn., June 27, 1953; married; 3 children. BA, SUNY, Oswego, 1975; MA, U. N.H., 1978. Instr. U. Calif., San Diego, Am. U., Washington; lectr. in English U. N.H.; writer-in-residence Lynchburg Coll., Va., Hollins Coll., Va., Johns Hopkins U., Balt. Author: A Bigamist's Daughter, 1982, That Night, 1987 (Pulitzer Prize finalist, Nat. Book Award finalist, L.A. Times Book Prize finalist), At Weddings and Wakes, 1992, Charming Billy, 1998 (Nat. Book Award); contbr. short stories to numerous profl. publs. Recipient Whiting Writers award. Office: Farrar Straus and Giroux 19 Union Sq W New York NY 10003

MCDERMOTT, DAVID (JOHN), writer, marketing professional, artist; b. Wrangell, Alaska, Apr. 8, 1958; s. A. W. and Margaret McDermott; children: Amy, Rachel, Kelly. Student, Seattle Pacific Coll., 1976-77. Nat. registered and cert. emergency med. technician; cert. instr. NRA; lic. 3rd class boiler operator. Pres. owner Mut. Forest Co., Ketchikan, 1980—; facilities supr. U. Alaska, 1995—2000; internet mktg. profl. Daisy, Tenn., 2000—. Fireman, emergency med. technician Ketchikan Vol. Fire Dept., 1989-91; contbg. cons. bodybldg. books and mags., 1986—; feature article Musclemag Internat. mag., 1990. Artist ltd. edit. art print series, 1997—. Recipient Expert Rifleman award U.S. Govt., 1973, 1st, 2d & 3d Profl. Painting prizes Arts Guild Show, 1995. Mem. NEA (del. state/nat. governing assemblies), Ketchikan Emt. Assn. (bd. 1992-94, pres. 1994), Am. EMTs, Nat. Soc. EMT-Paramedics, Nat. Soc. EMS Adminstrs., Soc. EMT Tech. Instr/Coords. Avocations: weightlifting, motorcycling, target shooting. Home and Office: 1975 Darby Dr Apt A2 Florence AL 35630-2637

MCDERMOTT, DENNIS MICHAEL, trade association executive; b. Akron, Ohio, Jan. 9, 1947; s. Gerard Joseph and Irene Cathryn McDermott; m. Margaret Mary Hayden, Dec. 14, 1968 (div. July 1981); children: Martin Jerome, Kathleen Marie; m. Margaret Amberg Egan, Apr. 30, 1983; 1 stepson, Michael Amberg. BS in Journalism, Kent (Ohio) State U., 1969; postgrad. in edn., Chapman Coll., 1972; postgrad. in pub. rels., Kent (Ohio) State U., 1975.

Reporter Akron Beacon Jour., 1967-69; conv. mgr. Am. Sch. of Health, Kent, 1973-74, asst. exec. dir., 1974-77; exec. dir. Emergency Dept. Nurses Assn., Chgo., 1977-80; exec. v.p. Oakland (Calif.) Bd. Realtors, 1980-83; v.p. Calif. Assn. of Realtors, L.A., 1983-87; exec. v.p. Mo. Assn. of Realtors, Columbia, 1988—. Vis. lectr. journalism Kent State U., 1973-77; cons. 30 trade assns., 1977-87. Contbg. editor Jour. of Sch. Health, 1973-77; exec. editor Jour. of Emergency Nursing, 1977-80, Oakland Realtor mag., 1980-83, Missouri Realtor mag., 1988—. Life mem. Realtors Polit. Action Com., Washington, 1984—. Sgt. USAF, 1969-73. Scholar Knight Found., 1965-69. Mem. Am. Soc. of Assn. Execs., Pub. Rels. Soc. of Am. Avocations: travel, photography. Home: 3812 Barrington Dr Columbia MO 65203-4453 Office: Mo Assn of Realtors PO Box 1327 Columbia MO 65205-1327

MCDERMOTT, DYLAN, actor; b. Waterbury, Conn., Oct. 26, 1962; m. Shiva Afshar, 1995; 1 child, Colette. BA in Drama, Fordham U., 1983. Appeared in films: Hamburger Hill, 1987, Twister, 1988, Steel Manolias, 1989, In The Line Of Fire, 1993, The Cowboy Way, 1994, Miracle on 34th Street, 1994, Destiny Turns On The Radio, 1995, Home For The Holidays, 1995, 'Til There Was You, 1996, Texas Rangers, 2000, Three to Tango, 1999, Party Monster, 2003, Wonderland, 2003; TV series: The Practice, 1997-2003, The Grid, 2004, dir. 1997; TV guest appearances Ally MacBeal, 1997, Tales from the Crypt, Will & Grace, 1998. Recipient Golden Globe award, 1999. also: 3 Arts Entertainment 20th Century Fox 1325 Sixth Ave New York NY 10019 Address: William Morris Agy 151 El Camino Dr Beverly Hills CA 90212*

MCDERMOTT, FRANCIS OWEN, retired lawyer; b. Denver, Feb. 25, 1933; s. Paul Harkins and Agnes (Clark) McD.; divorced; children: Diana, Daniel, Christopher, Anthony, Justine; m. Estella Marina Idiaquez, June 6, 1986; stepchildren: Bernard, Michael, Nicole, Marie, Steven. JD, Am. U., 1960. Bar: D.C. 1960, U.S. Dist. Ct. D.C., 1960, U.S. Ct. Appeals (D.C. cir.) 1960, u.S. Tax Ct. 1961, U.S. Supreme Ct. 1964. Trial atty. office regional counsel IRS, Washington, 1961-65; mem. profl. staff com. on fin. U.S. Senate, Washington, 1965-68; tax counsel Assn. Am. R.R.s, Washington, 1968-73; assoc. Hopkins & Sutter, Washington, 1973-76, ptnr., 1976-98, ret., 1999; ret. ptnr. Foley & Lardner, Washington, 2001—02. Gen. counsel Inst. Ill., Washington, 1987-96. Mem. ABA, Fed. Bar Assn., Nat. Def. Transp. Assn. (v.p., gen. counsel 1974—). Roman Catholic. Avocation: tennis. Home: 1 S Montague St Arlington VA 22204-1007 Office Phone: 202-945-6092. E-mail: fmcdermott@foley.com.

MCDERMOTT, IRENE ELIZABETH, librarian, columnist; b. Pasadena, Calif., June 26, 1959; d. Patrick Henry and Jean Irene (Ramsell) Brandenburg; m. Philip Hurt McDermott, June 20, 1992; 1 child, Peter James. AB in Theatre Arts and Rhetoric, Occidental Coll., L.A., 1981; MLIS, UCLA, 1995. Assoc. rsch. editor Salem Press, Pasadena, 1986—96; reference libr. U. So. Calif., L.A., 1996—97; reference libr., sys. mgr. San Marino (Calif.) Pub. Libr., 1997—. Columnist, searcher mag. Info. Today, Medford, NJ, 1997—. Author: Librarians' Internet Survival Guide. Recipient Luminary Lectures at Your Libr., Libr. of Congress, 2002. Mem.: Calif. Libr. Assn., Phi Beta Kappa. Democrat. Roman Catholic. Avocations: gardening, writing, home repair. Office: San Marino Pub Libr 1890 Huntington Dr San Marino CA 91108 Office Phone: 626-300-0776. E-mail: irene@ci.san-marino.ca.us.

MCDERMOTT, JAMES A. congressman, psychiatrist; b. Chicago, Dec. 28, 1936; children: Katherine, James. BS, Wheaton Coll., 1958; MD, U. Ill., 1963. Intern Buffalo Gen. Hosp., 1963-64; resident in adult psychiatry U. Ill. Hosps., Chgo., 1964-66; resident in child psychiatry U. Wash. Hosps., Seattle, 1966-68; asst. clin. prof. dept. psychiatry U. Wash., Seattle, 1970-83; mem. Wash. Ho. of Reps., 1971-72, Wash. Senate, 1975-87; regional med. officer U.S. Fgn. Svc., 1987-88; mem. U.S. Congress from 7th Wash. dist., 1989—; former chmn. standards of ofcl. conduct com.; mem. ways and means com., budget com. Mem. exec. and edn. com. Nat. Conf. State Legislatures, chair ethics com.; co-chmn. congressional task force internat. HIV/AIDS, Congl. Caucus on India and Indian Ams., Africa Trade and Investment Caucus, Congl. Kidney Caucus. Mem. Wash. State Arts Commn., Wash. Coun. for Prevention Child Abuse and Neglect; Dem. nominee for gov., 1980. Lt. comdr. M.C., USN, 1968-70. Mem. Am. Psychiat. Assn., Wash. State Med. Assn., King County Med. Soc. Democrat. Episcopalian. Office: US Ho Reps 1035 Longworth Ho Office Bldg Washington DC 20515

MC DERMOTT, JOHN FRANCIS, psychiatrist, physician; b. Hartford, Conn., Dec. 12, 1929; s. John Francis and Camilla R. (Cavanaugh) McD.; m. Sarah N. Schemm, Dec. 27, 1958; children: Elizabeth C., John Francis III. AB, Cornell U., 1951; MD, N.Y. Med. Coll., 1955. Diplomate in psychiatry and child psychiatry Am. Bd. Psychiatry and Neurology. Intern Henry Ford Hosp., Detroit, 1955-56; resident in psychiatry U. Mich. Med. Center, 1956-58, resident in child psychiatry, 1960-62; practice medicine, specializing in psychiatry and child and adolescent psychiatry Honolulu, 1969-95; instr., asst. prof., asso. prof. psychiatry U. Mich. Sch. Medicine, 1962-69; prof., chmn. dept. psychiatry U. Hawaii Sch. Medicine, 1969-95, prof. emeritus, 1995—; scholar-in-residence Rockefeller Found. Study Ctr., Bellagio, Italy, 1985, 92. Chmn. com. cert. in child psychiatry Am. Bd. Psychiatry and Neurology, 1974-78, bd. dirs., 1983-91, chmn. R&D com., 1985-91; sr. vis. scientist dept. exptl. psychology Oxford (Eng.) U., 1993; sr. vis. fellow Inst. Criminology Cambridge U., Eng., 1998, 2000; vis. prof. numerous univs.; cons. numerous mental health clinics and orgns. Author: Psychiatry for the Pediatrician, 1970, Childhood Psychopathology, 1972, Mental Health Education in New Medical Schools, 1973, Roles and Functions of Child Psychiatrists, 1976, Psychiatric Treatment of the Child, 1977, New Directions in Childhood Psychopathology, vol. I, 1980, vol. II, 1982, Raising Cain (and Abel Too), 1980: People and Cultures of Hawaii, 1980, Culture Mind and Therapy: An Introduction to Cultural Psychiatry, 1982, Japanese edit., 1984, The Complete Book on Sibling Rivalry, 1987, German edit., 1991; editor Jour. Am. Acad. Child and Adolescent Psychiatry, 1987-97; contbr. over 150 articles to profl. jours.; mem. editorial bds. numerous psychiat. jours. Served with USN, 1958-60. Named Disting. Alumnus N.Y. Med. Coll., 1976; life mem. Clare Hall, Cambridge (Eng.) U. Fellow Am. Psychiat. Assn. (disting. life, Agnes Purcell McGavin award 1998), Am. Orthopsychiat. Assn. (life), Am. Acad. Child and Adolescent Psychiatry (life), Am. Coll. Psychiatrists, World Psychiat. Assn. (chmn. child and adolescent psychiatry 1977-89), Benjamin Rush Soc. (sec.-treas. 2000-02, v.p. 2002-04, pres. 2004—), Cosmos Club, Outrigger Canoe Club. Home: 67-1003 N Alulike Rd Kamuela HI 96743

MCDERMOTT, JOHN H(ENRY), lawyer; b. Evanston, Ill., June 23, 1931; s. Edward Henry and Goldie Lucile (Boso) McD.; m. Ann Elizabeth Pickard, Feb. 19, 1966; children: Elizabeth A., Mary L., Edward H. BA, Williams Coll., 1953; JD, U. Mich., 1956. Bar: Mich. 1955, Ill. 1956. Assoc. McDermott, Will & Emery, Chgo., 1958-64, ptnr., 1964-99, of counsel, 2000—. Bd. dirs. Patrick Industries Inc. 1st lt. USAF, 1956-58. Mem. ABA, Chgo. Bar Assn. Clubs: Commerical of Chgo., Econ. of Chgo., Legal Chgo. (pres. 1981-82), Law Chgo. (pres. 1986-87). Home: 330 Willow Rd Winnetka IL 60093-4130 Office: McDermott Will & Emery 227 W Monroe St Ste 3100 Chicago IL 60606-5096 Office Phone: 312-984-7562. Personal E-mail: mcdermott330@cs.com.

MCDERMOTT, KEVIN R. lawyer; b. Youngstown, Ohio, Jan. 26, 1952; s. Robert J. and Marion D. (McKeown) McD.; m. Cindy J. Darling, Dec. 11, 1976; children: Ciara, Kelly. AB, Miami U., Oxford, Ohio, 1974; JD, Ohio State U., 1977. Bar: Ohio 1977, U.S. Dist. Ct. (so. dist.) Ohio 1978, U.S. Dist. Ct. (no. dist.) Ohio 1988, U.S. Dist. Ct. (we. dist.) Mich. 1993, U.S. Supreme Ct. 1990, U.S. Ct. Appeals (3rd cir.) 1996, U.S. Ct. Appeals (6th cir.) 1988. Assoc. ptnr. Murphey Young & Smith, Columbus, Ohio, 1977-88; ptnr. Squire Sanders & Dempsey, Columbus, Ohio, 1988-90, Schottenstein Zox & Dunn, Columbus, Ohio, 1990—. Adv. bd. mem. Capitol U. Legal Asst. Program, Columbus, Ohio, 1988—. Bd. pres. Easter Seal Soc. Ctrl. Ohio, Columbus, 1992-94, bd. mem. 1988-92; pres. Upper Arlington Civic Svc. Commn., Columbus, Ohio, 1988-93. Office: Schottenstein Zox & Dunn 250 West St Columbus OH 43215 Office Phone: 614-442-5001.

MCDERMOTT, LARRY ARNOLD, newspaper publisher, newspaper editor; b. Parkin, Ark., Apr. 27, 1948; s. John Allen and Ila Mae (Harris) McD.; m. Linda Louis Lancaster, Mar. 20, 1969; children: Marshall, Kelly, Amanda. BS, Ark. State U., 1970. Reporter Jonesboro (Ark.) Sun, 1968-70, AP, Richmond, Va., 1970-71, 72-75, Norfolk, Va., 1975-76, polit. correspondent Lansing, Mich., 1976-78, bur. chief Little Rock, 1978-80, Mpls., 1980-84, Detroit, 1984-87, asst. to the pres. N.Y.C., 1987-88; info. specialist UN Command, Seoul, Republic of Korea, 1971-72; copy editor Korea Times, Seoul, 1971-72; editor, bur. chief Booth Newspapers, Lansing, 1988-90; pub. Bay City (Mich.) Times, 1990-91; exec. editor Springfield Union News, Mass., 1991-98, editor, assoc. pub., 1998-99, pub., 1999—. V.p., bd. dirs. Mich. State News, East Lansing, 1990-91. Bd. dirs. Bay Area Econ. Growth Alliance, Bay City, 1990-91. With U.S. Army, 1970-72. Presbyterian. Avocations: fly fishing, golf, camping, horseback riding. Home: 135 Chilson Rd Wilbraham MA 01095-1225 Office: Union-News 1860 Main St Springfield MA 01103-1073

MCDERMOTT, MARY ANN, nursing educator; b. La Junta, Colo., June 23, 1938; d. George O. and Alice Agnes (Nohelty) Kelley; m. Dennis J. McDermott; children: Dennis, Michael, Sarah, William. BSN, Loyola U., 1960, MSN, 1969; EdD, No. Ill. U., 1980. RN Ill. Staff nurse Evanston (Ill.) Vis. Nurse Assn., 1960-63, St. Francis Hosp., Sch. Nursing, Evanston, 1963-67; nurse, tchr. Head Start, Chgo. Bd. Edn., 1967-68; faculty mem. Niehoff Sch. Nursing Loyola U., Chgo., 1969—. Dir. Ctr. Faith and Mission, Loyola U., Chgo., 1998—2002; bd. dirs. Park Ridge Ctr. Study Health, Faith and Ethics, Advocate Health Care, 1995—2003; mem. adv. coun. Chgo. Dept. Aging, 1995—99. Co-editor: Parish Nursing: The Developing Practice, 1990, Parish Nursing: Promoting Whole Person Health Within Faith Communities, 1998. Adv. bd. St. Scholastica Acad., Chgo., 1996-2002; adv. coun. Chgo. Schweizer Urban Fellows, 1996-99; chair Civic Affairs com. Univ. Club. of Chgo., 2001-2003. Recipient Ill. Nurse Leader/Power of Nursing award, 2002. Fellow: Am. Acad. Nursing; mem.: ANA, Health Ministries Assn. (adv. bd. 1989—99), Ill. Nurses Assn., Nat. League Nursing, Am. Hosp. Assn. (nominating com. 1995—97). Democrat. Roman Catholic. Office: Loyola U Sch Nursing Damen Hall 6525 N Sheridan Rd Chicago IL 60626-5344

MCDERMOTT, MORGAN, secondary school educator, writer; s. Michael Charles and Paulette T. McDermott; m. Wendy A. Parks, June 29, 2002. BA, U. Iowa, 1990; MA, Nat. Louis U., Chgo., 2000. Creative writing tchr. Adlai E. Stevenson HS, Lincolnshire, Ill., 2000—. Assoc. editor: Story Quar., 2003—. Recipient 1st pl. for fiction, Dogwood Prize, 2002, Nebr. Rev. Award, 2002, H. E. Francis Award, 2002, River City Award, 2002, Grand Prize award, Random House, Inc., 2002, 1st pl. for fiction, Tobais Wolff Award, 2002, New Millennium Award, 2002, Dana Short Fiction Award, 2002, 1st pl., Speakeasy Prose Prize, 2003, Phoebe Winter Fiction Award, 2003, Swink Editor's Prize for Emerging Writers, 2003, Meridian Editors' Prize, 2004; fellow, Ill. Arts Coun., 2004. Personal E-mail: mcdermottmorgan@yahoo.com.

MCDERMOTT, PATRICIA ANN, nursing administrator; b. Bklyn., July 10, 1943; d. John J. and Lillian J. (Sweeney) Skelly; m. Joseph Kevin McDermott, Oct. 5, 1963; children: Colleen Mary, John Joseph. Diploma, Kings County Hosp Sch. Nursing, Bklyn., 1963; BS in Health Care Adminstrn., St. Francis Coll., Bklyn., 1979. Staff nurse Kings County Hosp., Bklyn., 1963-66, head nurse outpatient dept., 1966-74; evening supr. Park Nursing Home, Rockaway Park, N.Y., 1974-83; day supr. Hyde Park Nursing Home, Staatsburg, NY, 1984-85, DON, 1985—96, Victory Lake Nursing Ctr., Hyde Park, N.Y., 1996-97. NY State evaluator for nurses aides, 1988—; PRI assessor; MDS coord. Active local Girl Scouts U.S.A., 1971-78, Boy Scouts Am., 1978-82, Stella Maris Parents Club, 1978-82, St. Francis de Sales Altar and Rosary Soc., 1970-83; active St. Francis de Sales Little League, 1978-80, also softball coach, 1974-77; elected tax collector Town of Clinton, N.Y., 1999—; dance com. chair St. Peter's, Hyde Park, N.Y., 1998-2002. Dutchess County Salute to Women honoree, 1997. Home: 184 Shadblow Ln Clinton Corners NY 12514-2834

MCDERMOTT, RAYMOND, JR., physician; b. Chgo., Apr. 20, 1924; s. Raymond A. and Helen (Furlong) M.; m. Audrey H. Bergt, Feb., 1995; children: Kathy, Mary Anne, Raymond III, Thomas, Laura, Sharon, Jean, Michael, Trish. MD, Loyola U., 1947. Bd. cert. Obstertrics and Gynocology. Assoc. attending Cook County Hosp., Chgo., 1954-61; asst. prof. obgyn. Northwestern U. Med. Sch., Chgo., 1958—; med. reviewer Healthcare Compare, Oakbrook, Ill., 1978-88, CIMRO, Champaign, Ill., 1988—2003; med. dir. Wellmark (Health Network), Oakbrook, 1992—. Staff pres. Grant Hosp. Chgo., 1976-78, staff v.p., 1974-76. Lt. U.S. Navy, 1941-53. Avocation: sailing. Home: 3950 W Bryn Mawr Ave Chicago IL 60659-3156

MCDERMOTT, RENÉE R(ASSLER), lawyer; b. Danville, Pa., Sept. 26, 1950; d. Carl A. and Rose (Gaupp) Rassler; m. James A. McDermott, Jan. 1, 1986. BA, U. So. Fla., 1970, MA, 1972; JD, Ind. U., 1978. Bar: Ind. 1978, N.C. 1999, U.S. Dist. Ct. (so. and no. dists.) Ind. 1978, U.S. Ct. Appeals (7th cir.) 1979, U.S. Ct. Appeals (9th cir.) 1985. Law clk. to presiding judge U.S. Dist. Ct. (no. dist.) Ind., Ft. Wayne, 1978-80; assoc. Barnes & Thornburg, Indpls., 1980-84, ptnr., 1985-93; pvt. practice Nashville, Ind., 1994-99, Tryon, NC, 1999—. County atty. County of Brown, Ind., 1994-98. Editor-in-chief Ind. U. Law Jour., 1977-78. Bd. visitors Ind. U. Law Sch., Bloomington, 1979—; bd. dirs. Pacolet Area Conservancy, 1999—, v.p., 2000-02, pres., 2003; bd. dirs. Foothills Equestrian Trail Assn., 1999-2002. Fellow Ind. Bar Found. (chair 1998-99), Am. Bar Found. (life); mem. ABA (bus. sect. coun. 1995-98, chmn. environ. controls com. 1991-95, liaison to standing com. on environ. law bus. law sect. 1991-98), Ind. State Bar Assn. (chmn. young lawyers sect. 1985-86, chmn. environ. law sect. 1989-91), Fellows of Ind. Bar. Found. (chair 1998-99), Polk County Cmty. Found. (bd. dirs. 2000-, chair exceptional distbns. com. 2000-02), Order of Coif. Avocations: scuba diving, horseback riding, music, reading, hiking. Home and Office: 845 Fox Run Ln Tryon NC 28782-9758 E-mail: rmcdermott@alltel.net.

MCDERMOTT, RICHARD FRANCIS, judge; b. Seattle, Feb. 18, 1948; s. Richard F. Sr. and Madeline (Frison) McD.; m. Susan Lynn Brandt, Feb. 19, 1977; children: Kelsey Anne, Megan Marie, Michael Brandt. BA in Polit. Sci., Seattle U., 1970; JD, U. Wash., 1973; grad., Nat. Jud. Coll., 2002. Bar: Wash. 1973, U.S. Dist. Ct. (we. dist.) Wash. 1973, U.S. Ct. Appeals (9th cir.) 1973, U.S. Supreme Ct. 1981. Atty. King County, Seattle, 1973-76; assoc. Parks, Johnson & East, Bellevue, Wash., 1976-78; ptnr. Revelle, Ries & McDermott, Bellevue, 1978-86, McDermott & Jones, Bellevue, 1986—93, Richard F. McDermott, Jr. P.S., 1993—2000; King County Superior Ct. judge, 2000—. Mem. Minorities and Justice Commn., 1993—; adj. prof. law Seattle U. Sch. Law, 1999—; mem. Bd. Ct. Edn., 2003. Author: (with others) Best of CLE Seminar, 1986, Auto Accident Deskbook, 1988. Served to 1st lt. USAR, 1970-78. Named Wash. Super Lawyer, Wash. Law and Politics, 1999. Mem. Wash. State Bar Assn. (spl. disciplinary counsel 1993-99), Seattle King County Bar Assn., East King County Bar Assn., Assn. Trial Lawyers Am., Wash. State Trial Lawyers Assn. (bd. dirs. 1982-90), Superior Ct. Judge's Assn. (spring conf. chair 2002). Lodges: Rotary. Roman Catholic. Avocations: golf, baseball. Office: King County Superior Ct 401 4th Ave No Kent WA 98032 Office Phone: 206-296-9115. E-mail: richard.mcdermott@metrokc.gov.

MCDERMOTT, ROBERT B. lawyer; b. Washington, June 16, 1927; s. Edward H. and Goldie Lucile (Boso) McD.; m. Julia Wood, Nov. 16, 1950; children: John, Jeanne, Charles; m. Jane S. Whitman, July 31, 1973; m. Sarah Jaicks, Jan. 6, 1996. AB, Princeton U., 1948; LL.B., Harvard U., 1951. Bar: D.C. 1951, Ill. 1955. Atty. Office Gen. Counsel, Navy Dept., Washington, 1951-52; assoc McDermott, Will & Emery, Chgo., 1954-60, ptnr., 1961-92, chmn., 1986-91. Trustee Ill. Inst. Tech., Chgo., 1985—, The Mather Found., Evanston, Ill., 1988—; bd. dirs. Ct. Theatre. Lt. USNR, 1945-46, 52-54. Mem. Chgo. Club, Econ. Club, Univ. Club (Chgo.). Home: 990 N Lake Shore Dr Apt 31E Chicago IL 60611-1386 E-mail: bobmcder61@aol.com.

MCDERMOTT, THOMAS JOHN, JR., lawyer; b. Santa Monica, Calif., Mar. 23, 1931; s. Thomas J. Sr. and Etha Irene (Cook) McD.; m. Yolanda Amante Jatap; children: Jodi Friedman, Kimberly E., Kish S. BA, UCLA, 1953, JD, 1958. Bar: Calif. 1959. Ptnr. Gray, Binkley and Pfaelzer, L.A., 1964-67, Kadison, Pfaelzer, Woodward, Quinn and Rossi, L.A., 1967 87, Rogers & Wells, L.A., 1987-93, Bryan Cave, L.A., 1993-95, Manatt, Phelps & Phillips, LLP, L.A., 1995-99, Shanks and Herbert, San Diego, 1999—2003. Served with U.S. Army, 1953-56, Korea, 1999-2003. Fellow Am. Coll. Trial Lawyers; mem. ABA, Assn. Bus. Trial Lawyers (pres. 1980-81, mem. exec. com. 9th cir. jud. conf. 1993—, chair 1997), State Bar Calif. (chair litigation sect. 1993-94), UCLA Law Alumni Assn. (pres. 1961-62), Order of Coif. Office: McDermott & DeLalteur LLP 74-770 Highway 111 Ste 201 Indian Wells CA 92210 Office Phone: 760-346-8200. E-mail: tmcdermottjr@earthlink.net.

MCDEVITT, BRIAN PETER, history professor, educational consultant; b. Jersey City, Dec. 29, 1944; s. Bernard Aloysius and Veronica Sabina (Decker) McD.; m. Dorothy Helen Gilligan, Oct. 19, 1968; children: Peter David, Timothy Bernard. BS, Seton Hall U., 1966; MA, Columbia U., 1971; DLitt, Drew U., 2001. Tchr. history St. Patrick's High Sch., Elizabeth, N.J., 1966-68, Vail Deane High Sch., Elizabeth, N.J., 1968-70; fed. grant writer Alexian Bros. Hosp., Elizabeth, N.J., 1970-72, Union County Coll., Cranford, N.J., 1972-76; prin., owner Ednl. Svcs., Westfield, N.J., 1976—. Adj. prof. history Union County Coll., Cranford, N.J., 1976—; adj. prof. classics Montclair (N.J.) State U., 1990—. Author: The Irish Librists, 1988, The Irish Librists and the Scrolls of Aristotle, 1993, A Historian's Thematic Study of Western Civilization, 1994, Evidence of an Ancient Greek Navigation System, 1995, The Irish Librists and The Vatican Library Mystery, 1996, A Definition of Western Civilization, 1997, Ancient Greeks: First Navigators, 2000, Ten Historical Odes, 2001, Twenty-Five Sonnets, 2001, Arthur Brooke's Poem: The Tragic HIstory of Rome and Juliet, revised, 2002, (video) The Minoans According to Sir Arthur Evans; contbr. articles to profl. jours. N.J. Dept. Higher Edn. grantee. Mem. Trireme Trust U.S.A. (internat. rowing team 1990), Friends of Trireme (London), Soc. Naval Architects and Marine Engrs., Assn. Ancient Historians, Soc. Ancient Greek Philosophy, Assn. Muslim Social Scientists, Classical Assn. of Atlantic States, Keats-Shelley Meml. Assn. (London and Rome), Am. Soc. Naval Engrs., Westfield United Fund, Westfield P.A.L., Westfield Basketball Assn., Westfield Baseball Assn., Boy Scouts Am. Roman Catholic. Avocations: golf, rowing, basketball, playing piano, stamp collecting/philately. Home: 607 S Chestnut St Westfield NJ 07090-1369

MCDEVITT, CHARLES FRANCIS, retired state supreme court justice, lawyer; b. Pocatello, Idaho, Jan. 5, 1932; s. Bernard A. and Margaret (Hermann) McD.; m. Virginia L. Heller, Aug. 14, 1954; children: Eileen A., Kathryn A., Brian A., Sheila A., Terrence A., Neil A., Kendal A. LLB, U. Idaho, 1956. Bar: Idaho 1956. Ptnr. Richards, Haga & Eberle, Boise, 1956-62; gen. counsel, asst. sec. Boise Cascade Corp., 1962-65; mem. Idaho State Legislature, 1963-66; sec., gen. counsel Boise Cascade Corp., 1965-67, v.p., sec., 1967-68; pres. Beck Industries, 1968-70; group v.p. Singer Co., N.Y.C., 1970-72, exec. v.p., 1973-76; pub. defender Ada County, Boise, 1976-78; co-founder Givens, McDevitt, Pursley & Webb, Boise, 1978-89; justice Idaho Supreme Ct., Boise, 1989-97, chief justice, 1993-97; ptnr., founder McDevitt & Miller, LLP, Boise, 1997—. Served on Gov.'s Select Com. on Taxation, Boise, 1988-89; mem. State Select Com. on Campaign Ethics and Campaign Finances, State Select Com. on Legis. Compensation. Chair Idaho Jud. Coun., 1993-97, Cts. Advisors Coun., 1994-98; mem. Multi-State Tax Com. Home: 4940 Boise River Ln Boise ID 83716-8816 Office: MC McDevitt Miller 420 W Bannock Boise ID 83702-6034 Business E-Mail: chas@McDevitt.org.

MCDEVITT, HUGH O'NEILL, immunologist, educator; b. Cin., Aug. 26, 1930; MD, Harvard U., 1955. Diplomate: Am. Bd. Internal Medicine. Intern Peter Bent Brigham Hosp., Boston, 1955-56, sr. asst. resident in medicine, 1961-62; asst. resident Bell Hosp., 1956-57; research fellow dept. bacteriology and immunology Harvard U., 1959-61; USPHS spl. fellow Nat. Inst. Med. Research, Mill Hill, London, 1962-64; physician Stanford U. Hosp., Calif., 1966—; assoc. prof. Stanford U. Sch. Medicine, Calif., 1969-72, prof. med. immunology, 1972—, prof. med. microbiology, 1980—2001, Burt and Marian Avery Prof. Immunology, 1988—2001. Cons. physician VA Hosp., Palo Alto, Calif., 1968— Served as capt. M.C., AUS, 1957-59. Mem. NAS, AAAS, Am. Fedn. Clin. Rsch., Am. Soc. Clin. Investigation, Am. Assn. Immunologists, Transplantation Soc., Inst. Medicine, Royal Soc. (fgn.). Office: Sherman Fairchild Bldg Stanford U Sch of Medicine 299 Campus Dr MC5124 Stanford CA 94305-5124 Business E-Mail: hughmcd@stanford.edu.

MCDEVITT, JAMES A. lawyer; b. July 1943; Bachelor, U. Wash.; MBA, JD, Gonzaga U. Asst. atty. gen. State of Wash., Office of Atty. Gen., 1975—77; from sr. ptnr. to mng. ptnr. Reed & Geisa, Spokane, Wash., 1977—94; ptnr. Preston, Gates & Ellis, Spokane, Wash., 1994—2002; U.S. atty. Ea. Dist. Wash., 2002—. With USAF, 1965—71, brig. gen. Wash. Air Nat. Guard, ret. Office: PO Box 1494 Spokane WA 99210

MCDEVITT, JOHN, delivery service executive; b. Upper Darby, Pa., Aug. 15, 1958; m. Lori McDevitt; children: Kelly, Tara, Shannon, John. BS in Polit. Sci., Rutgers U., 1980; grad., U. Mich., 1999. Part-time loader UPS, Edison, NJ, 1976—77, part-time supr. Bound Brook, 1977—80, package car driver, 1980—81, supr., 1981—84, mgr. Parsippany, 1984—87, divsn. mgr. Meadowlands, 1987—92, dist. mgr. East Long Island, NY, 1992—94, West Long Island, 1994—96, v.p. corp. compliance Atlanta, 1996—98, mgr. corp. labor rels., 1998—99, v.p. air ops., 1999—2003, sr. v.p. strategic integration, 2003—. Office: UPS 55 Glenlake Kwy NE Atlanta GA 30328

MCDEVITT, SHEILA MARIE, lawyer, energy company executive; b. St. Petersburg, Fla., Jan. 15, 1947; d. Frank Davis and Marie (Barfield) McD. AA, St. Petersburg Jr. Coll., 1966; BA in Govt., Fla. State U., 1968, JD, 1978. Bar: Fla. 1978. Research asst. Fla. Legis. Reference Bur., Tallahassee, 1968-69; adminstr., research assoc. Constitution Revision Commn. Ga. Gen. Assembly, Atlanta, 1969-70; adminstrv. asst., analyst Fla. State Sen., Tallahassee, Tampa, 1970-79; assoc. McClain, Walkley & Stuart, P.A., Tampa, Seminole, Fla., 1979-81; govtl. affairs counsel Tampa Electric Co., 1981-82, corp. counsel, 1982-86; sr. corp. counsel TECO Energy, Inc., Tampa, 1986-89, asst. v.p., 1989-92, v.p., asst. gen. counsel, 1992-99, corp. compliance officer, 1993-99, v.p., gen. counsel, 1999—2001, sr. v.p., gen. counsel, chief legal officer, 2001—. Mem. Worker's Compensation adv. coun. Fla. Dept. Labor, Tallahassee, 1984-86; trustee St. Leo U., 1999—, vice chair, 2001; mem. bd. visitors Fla. State U. Coll. Law, 1996—, chmn., 2003; mem. bd. advisors The Centre for Women, 1998—, Met. Ministries, 1996—; mem. ethics adv. bd. U. Tampa Ctr. for Ethics, 1997-99; mem. jud. nominating commn. 13th Jud. Cir., 2001—; mem. Fla. bd. govs. State Univ. sys., 2004. Bd. dirs. Vol. Ctr. Hillsborough County, Tampa, 1984-85, Fla. Aquarium, 1999-2000; bd. dirs. Lowry Park Zoo Soc., 1999—2004, chmn., trustee, 1986-94, also legal advisor; bd. dirs. Hillsborough County Easter Seal Soc., 1994-95; mem. Fla. Rep. Exec. Com., Tallahassee, 1974-75, Hillsborough County Rep. Exec. Com., 1974-75; mem. transition team for Fla. Gov. Bob Martinez, 1986-87; mem. Fed. Jud. Adv. Commn., 1989-93; mem. Fla. Humanities Coun., 2000—04; mem. WW Women's Leadership, 2004—. Mem ABA, Fla. Bar (vice chmn., then chmn. energy law com. 1984-87, jud. nominating procedures com. 1986-91, jud. adminstrn. selection and tenure com. 1991-93), Hillsborough Bar Found. (trustee 2002-), Hillsborough County Bar Assn. (chmn. law week com. 1990, corp. counsel com. 1986-87, internat. law com. 1994-95) corporate counsel of the yr. award, 2001-02, Am. Corp. Counsel Assn. (bd. dirs. Ctrl. Fla. chpt. 1986-87), Hillsborough County Bar Found., Tampa Club, Tiger Bay Club, Tampa Yacht and Country Club. Roman Catholic. Avocations: photography, bicycling, reading, boating. Office: TECO Energy Inc PO Box 111 702 N Franklin St Fl 5 Tampa FL 33602-4440 Business E-Mail: smmcdevitt@tecoenergy.com.

MCDIARMID, LUCY, English educator, author; b. Louisville, Mar. 29, 1947; m. Harris B. Savin, Oct. 13, 1984; children: Emily Clare, Katharine Eliza. BA, Swarthmore (Pa.) Coll., 1968; MA, Harvard U., 1969, PhD, 1972. Asst. prof. Boston U., 1972-74; from asst. prof. to assoc. prof. Swarthmore Coll., 1974-81; asst. prof. U. Md. Baltimore County, Balt., 1982-84; prof. Villanova (Pa.) U., 1984—. Vis. prof. English Princeton U., 1995; Carole and Gordon Segal vis. prof. Irish lit. Northwestern U., 2004—; mem. exec. com. Am. Conf. for Irish Studies, 1987-91, v.p., 1995-97, pres., 1997-99, past pres.,

internat. rep., 1999—2001. Author: Saving Civilization: Yeats, Eliot and Auden Between the Wars, 1984, Auden's Apologies for Poetry, 1990; co-editor: Selected Writings of Lady Gregory, 1995, High and Low Moderns: Literature and Culture, 1889-1939, 1996, The Irish Art of Controversy, 2005; contbr. articles to profl. jours. NEH fellow, 1981-82; ACLS grantee, 1976, Bunting Inst. fellow, 1981-82, Guggenheim fellow, 1993-94; vis. fellow N.Y. Inst. Humanities, 1993-95. Mem. MLA (exec. com. Twentieth Century Lit. divsn.), Internat. Assn. for Study Anglo-Irish Lit. (Am. sec.-treas. 1994-96), Phi Beta Kappa. Home: 1931 Panama St Philadelphia PA 19103-6609 Office: Villanova U Dept Of English Villanova PA 19085

MCDIARMID, ROBERT CAMPBELL, lawyer; b. N.Y.C., July 13, 1937; s. Norman Hugh and Dorothy (Shoemaker) McD.; m. Ruth Sussman, 1963 (div. 1996); children: Jennifer, Alexander Samuel; m. Frances Enseki Francis, 1996. BS in Mech. Engring., Swarthmore Coll., 1958; MS in Engring. Physics, Cornell U., 1960; LLB, Harvard U., 1963. Bar: D.C. 1964, Va. 1964, U.S. Supreme Ct. 1967, U.S. Ct. Appeals (4th, 6th and 9th cirs.) 1965, U.S. Ct. Appeals (3d, 5th and 10th cirs.) 1966, U.S. Ct. Appeals (7th, 8th and D.C. cirs.) 1967, U.S. Ct. Appeals (2d cir.) 1970, U.S. Ct. Appeals (1st cir.) 1979, U.S. Ct. Appeals (11th cir.) 1981. Assoc. Weaver & Glassie, Washington, 1963-64; trial atty. civil divsn. appellate sect. Dept. Justice, Washington, 1964-68; asst. to gen. counsel Fed. Power Commn., Washington, 1968-70; assoc. Law Office of George Spiegel, Washington, 1970-73; ptnr. Spiegel & McDiarmid, Washington, 1973—. Mem. alumni coun. Swarthmore Coll., 1986-89. Mem. ABA, Va. State Bar, Bar Assn. D.C., D.C. Bar, Energy Bar Assn. (exec. com. 1982-83, bd. dirs. 1997-2000). Democrat. Mem. Soc. Of Friends. Home: 3625 Fulton St NW Washington DC 20007-1452 Office: Spiegel & McDiarmid 1333 New Hampshire Ave NW Washington DC 20036 E-mail: robert.mcdiarmid@spiegelmcd.com.

MC DONAGH, EDWARD CHARLES, sociologist, university administrator; b. Edmonton, Alta., Can., Jan. 23, 1915; came to U.S., 1922, naturalized, 1936; s. Henry Fry and Aletta (Bowles) McD.; m. Louise Lucille Lorenzi, Aug. 14, 1940 (dec.); children: Eileen, Patricia. AB, U. So. Calif., 1937, A.M., 1938, PhD, 1942. Asst. prof. So. Ill. U., Carbondale, 1940-46, asst. to pres., 1942-44; asst. prof. U. Okla., Norman, 1946-47, U. So. Calif., L.A., 1947-49, assoc. prof., 1949-56, prof., 1956-69, head dept., 1958-62, chmn., acad. univ. affairs com., 1963, assoc. dean divsn. social scis. and comms., 1960-63, head dept. sociology U. Ala., 1969-71; chmn. dept. sociology Ohio State U., Columbus, 1971-74, acting dean Coll. Social and Behavioral Scis., 1974—, dean Coll. Social and Behavioral Scis., 1975-78, chmn. coordinating coun. deans Colls. Arts and Scis., 1977-78, prof. emeritus Colls. Arts and Scis., 1981—. Smith-Mundt prof., Sweden, 1956-57; vis. prof. U. Hawaii, summer 1965; cons. Los Angeles and related sch. dists.; mem. Region XV Woodrow Wilson Selection Com., 1961-62 Author: (with E.S. Richards) Ethnic Relations in the U.S. 1953, (with J.E. Nordskog, M.J. Vincent) Analyzing Social Problems, 1956, (with Jon Simpson) Social Problems: Persistent Challenges, 1965, rev., 1969; Assoc. editor: Sociology and Social Research, 1947-69; editorial cons.: Sociometry, 1962-65; Contbr. articles to profl. publs. Served with AUS, 1944-46. Fellow Am. Sociol. Assn. (co-chmn. nat. conf. com. 1963, budget and exec. office com. 1975-78); mem. AAUP, AAAS, Am. Assn. Pub. Opinion Rsch., Alpha Kappa Delta (pres. united chpts. 1965-66), Phi Beta Kappa (chpt. pres. 1959-60), Humanist, Blue Key, Skull and Dagger. Democrat. Home: 201 Spencer Dr Amherst MA 01002-3362

MCDONALD, ALAN ANGUS, federal judge; b. Harrah, Wash., Dec. 13, 1927; s. Angus and Nell (Britt) McD.; m. Ruby K., Aug. 22, 1949; children: Janelle Jo, Saralee Sue, Stacy. BS, U. Wash., 1950, LLB, 1952. Dep. pros. atty. Yakima County, Wash., 1952—54; ptnr. Halverson, Applegate & McDonald, Yakima, 1954—85; judge U.S. Dist. Ct. (ea. dist.) Wash., Yakima, 1985—95, sr. judge, 1995—. Fellow Am. Coll. Trial Lawyers; mem. Yakima Country Club, Royal Duck Club (Yakima). Office: US Dist Ct PO Box 2706 Yakima WA 98907-2706

MCDONALD, ALAN THOMAS, lawyer; b. Aug. 16, 1949; s. James Francis and Jennie Eloise (Thomits) McDonald; m. Joyce Ann Martin, Feb. 28, 1981. BSCE, Rutgers U., 1971; JD, U. Houston, 1973; LLM in Patent and Trade Regulation Law, George Washington U., 1976. Bar: Tex. 1974, Pa. 1977, Va. 1980, U.S. Ct. Customs and Patent Appeals 1974. Patent examiner U.S. Patent and Trademark Office, Arlington, Va., 1974—75; patent atty. PPG Industries, Inc., Pitts., 1975—78, Reynolds Metals Co., Richmond, Va., 1978—97, Honda of Am. Mfg., Inc., 1998—. Mem. adminstrv. bd. Dutilh United Meth. Ch., Cranberry, Pa., 1977—78; sunday sch. tchr. Providence United Meth. Ch., Chesterfield County, Va., 1981—84, mem. adminstrv. bd., 1985—, chmn. fin. com., 1988—90; mem. coun. on ministries Reveille United Meth. Ch., 1994—95. Mem.: Am. Intellectual Property Law Assn., ABA, Mensa (vice local sec. Richmond chpt. 1981—82, adminstr. 1980—81), Phi Delta Phi. Republican. Achievements include patents for method for producing slubbed yarn. Home: 23920 N Darby Coe Rd Milford Center OH 43045-9775 Office Phone: 937-644-6621.

MC DONALD, ANDREW JEWETT, securities firm executive; b. Cin., Sept. 7, 1929; s. Matthew Arnold and Jane (Jewett) Mc D. Grad., Hotchkiss Sch., 1947, Yale U., 1951. With Paine, Webber, Jackson & Curtis Inc., Boston, 1955—; dir. Paine, Webber, Jackson & Curtis Inc. (New Eng. region), 1972-73; sr. v.p., dir. Paine, Webber, Jackson & Curtis Inc. (Eastern div.), 1973—; dir. F. W. Paine Found., 1973—. Pvt. trustee and investor, 1985—; allied mem. N.Y. Stock Exch., 1971—. Mem. Flight Safety Found., 1971—. Served with USAF, 1951-55. Mem. Am. Farmland Trust (life), Am. Aviation Hist. Soc. (life). Clubs: Aero of New Eng. (Boston), Fed. (Boston), Down Town (Boston), Yale (Boston). Home: 5 Stonehill Dr Stoneham MA 02180-3927

MCDONALD, ANGUS WHEELER, farmer; b. Washington, Apr. 21, 1927; s. John Yates and Dorothy Helen (Bosworth) McD.; m. Mary Joan Montgomery, May 8, 1952 (div. Sept. 1958); children: Mary Ann Hetzer, Paul Yates. BA, Columbia Union Coll., 1974. Farmer, owner Pleasant View Farm, Charles Town, W.Va., 1953—. Presdl. candidate Democratic Party, 1987-88, 92, 2000. With U.S. Army, 1946-47. Mem. AARP, Jefferson County Farm Bur., W.Va. State Hort. Soc., No. W.Va. Automobile Club, Am. Legion, The Moose. Avocations: photography, travel, attending historical events. Home and Office: Pleasant View Farm RR 3 Box 142 Charles Town WV 25414-9413 Office Phone: 304-725-7238.

MCDONALD, ANNE B. state legislator; b. Syracuse, N.Y. BS, LeMoyne Coll.; MS, Syracuse U. Mem. Commn. on Aging, Stamford, Conn., 1969-76, chair, 1972-76; mem. State Adv. Coun. on Aging, 1977-80, Bd. of Edn., Stamford, 1980-87, pres., 1984-85; chmn. Housing Authority, Stamford, 1988-90; mem. Conn. Ho. of Reps., Hartford, 1991—. Democrat. Home: 53 Courtland Hill St Stamford CT 06906-2306 Office: Conn Ho of Reps Legislative Bldg Capitol Ave Hartford CT 06106

MCDONALD, AUDRA ANN, actress; b. Berlin, July 3, 1970; d. Stanley and Kathryn McDonald; m. Peter Donovan, Sept. 10, 2000; 1 child, Zoe Madeline Donovan. BFA in Voice, Juilliard Sch., 1993; attended, Sch. Arts., Calif. Stage appearances include (regional) Man of La Mancha, Evita, The Wiz, A Chorus Line, Grease, Anything Goes, The Real Inspector Hound, (Broadway) The Secret Garden, Man of La Mancha, 1989, Carousel, 1994 (Tony award best featured actress in a musical, 1994, Outer Critics Circle award outstanding actress in a musical, 1994), Master Class, 1995-97 (Tony award best featured actress in a musical, 1996, L.A. Ovation award best featured actress in a musical, 1996), Ragtime, 1998-99 (Tony award best featured actress in a musical, 1998), Sweeney Todd, 2000, A Raisin in the Sun, 2004 (Tony award best featured actress in a play, 2004, Drama Desk award best featured actress in a play, 2004); (TV series) Bill Cosby pilot, 1996, Mister Sterling, 2003 (TV Movies) Having Our Say: The Delaney Sisters' First 100 Years, 1999, Annie, 1999, The Last Debate, 2000, Wit, 2001 (Emmy award nom. best supporting actress, 2001) (Films) Seven Servants, 1996, The Object of My Affection, 1998, Cradle Will Rock, 1999, It Runs in the Family, 2003, The Best Thief in the World, 2004; concert performances include S'Wonderful, Some Enchanted Evening, Christa Ludwig and James Levine Recital, Revelation in Courthouse Park, Requiem Canticles. Recipient Theatre World award, 1994, Drama League award distinguished achievement in musical theatre, 2000. Office: Gersh Agency Inc 41 Madison Ave Fl 33 New York NY 10010-2210*

MCDONALD, BARBARA ANN, retired psychotherapist; b. Mpls., July 15, 1932; d. John and Georgia Elizabeth (Baker) Rubenzer; m. Lawrence R. McDonald, July 27, 1957 (dec. Sept. 1993); children: John, Mary Elizabeth. BA, U. Minn., 1954; MSW, U. Denver, 1977. Diplomate Am. Bd. Social Work; lic. psychotherapist. Day care cons. Minn. Dept. Pub. Welfare, St. Paul, 1954-59; social worker Cmty. Info. Ctr., Mpls., 1959-60; exec. dir. Social Synergistics Co., Littleton, Colo., 1970—. Cons. to cmty. orgns., Indian tribes; family therapist, 1979—. Author: Selected References on the Group Day Care of Pre-School Children, 1956, Helping Families Grow: Specialized Psychotherapy with Hearing Impaired Children and Their Families, 1984. Bd. dirs. Vol. Bur. Sun Cities, Ariz., 1988, 89, 90. Named 1 of 8 Women of Yr. and featured on TV spl. Ladies Home Jour., 1974; Clairol scholar, 1974; Am. Bus. Women's Assn. scholar, 1974; Alpha Gamma Delta scholar, 1974. Mem. Minn. Pre-Sch. Edn. Assn. (hon. life), NASW, Ariz. Assn. Social Workers, Assn. Clin. Social Workers, Am. Bus. Women's Assn., Alpha Gamma Delta (Disting. Citizen award 1975), Altrusa Club (hon.). Office: 3921 W Meadow Dr Glendale AZ 85308-4122

MCDONALD, BERNARD ROBERT, retired federal agency administrator; b. Kansas City, Kans., Nov. 17, 1940; s. Bernard Luther and Mabel McD.; m. Jean Graves, June 7, 1963 (div. 1996); children: Aaron Michael, Elizabeth Kathleen; m. Joann Huffaker, Aug. 2, 1997. BA, Park Coll., Parkville, Mo., 1962; MA, Kans. State U., 1964; PhD, Mich. State U., 1968. Prof. math. U. Okla., Norman, 1968-83, chmn. math. dept., 1981-83; program dir. div. math. scis. NSF, Washington, 1983-86, program dir. spl. projects, 1986-88, dep. dir. div. math. scis., 1988—2004; ret., 2004. Author: R-linear Endomorphism, 1983, Geometric Algebra, 1976, Finite Rings, 1974, Ring Theory III, 1980. Mem. AAAS, Am. Math. Soc., Math. Assn. Am., Soc. Ind. and Applied Math., Assn. Women Math., Sigma Xi. Home: 5016 35th St N Arlington VA 22207-2816

MCDONALD, BRADLEY G. lawyer; m. Ann Gilbert, Sept. 3, 1964; 1 child, Perry. BA, U. Okla.; JD, Georgetown U., 1961. Bar: D.C. 1961, U.S. Ct. Appeals (D.C., 11th and 4th cirs.), U.S. Supreme Ct. With McDonald & Karl, Washington. Guest lectr. Wash. Coll. of Law, Am. Univ., Washington. Mem. nat. alumni adv. coun. U. Okla; mem. Arlington Com. of 100; bd. dirs gen. counsel, sec. Close Up Found.; trustee Randolph Macon Acad.; bd. dirs. Montessori Sch. of McLean. 1st lt. USMC, 1956-58. Recipient 1st Regent's Alumni award U. Okla. Mem. Sigma Nu (trustee Ednl. Found.). Office Phone: 202-293-3200. E-mail: abmcdonal7@aol.com.

MCDONALD, CAPERS WALTER, biomedical engineer, manufacturing executive, educator; b. Georgetown, S.C., Nov. 29, 1951; s. WalBern and Cecilia (Lockwood) McD.; m. Marion E. Kiper, Aug. 23, 1975; child, Adam Capers. BS in Engring. magna cum laude, Duke U., 1974; MS in Mech. Engring., MIT, 1976; MBA, Harvard U., 1983. EIT N.C., 1977. Dir. mktg. Becton Dickinson Co., Sunnyvale, Calif., 1978-81; cons. Booz, Allen & Hamilton, San Francisco, 1982-84; v.p. Siegen Corp., Mountain View, Calif., 1984, HP Genenchem, South San Francisco, Calif., 1984-87; bio-analytic systems mgr. Hewlett-Packard Corp., Palo Alto, Calif., 1986—87; v.p. Orion Instruments, Inc., Redwood City, Calif., 1987-89, Spectroscopy Imaging Systems Corp., Fremont, Calif., 1989-90, pres., bd. dirs., 1991—92; pres., CEO, bd. dirs. BioReliance Corp., Rockville, Md., 1992—2004; pres., CEO MAGENTA Corp., Rockville, 1993—2000; chmn., dir. MAGENTA Svcs., Ltd., Stirling, Scotland, 1994-2000; dir. BioReliance Holdings GmbH, Heidelberg, Germany, 1996—2004, Q-One Biotech Group Ltd., Glasgow, Scotland, 2003—04; exec. in residence, faculty mem. Johns Hopkins U., 2004—. Bd. dirs. EXPION, Inc., Olney, Md.; chmn. Md. Health Care Products Devel. Corp.; guest lectr. Weizmann Inst. Sci., Rehovot, Israel, 1977, All-Union Cardiology Ctr., Moscow, 1978, Inst. Hematology Munich, 1978, Thomas Jefferson U., Phila., 1979, Christchurch (New Zealand) Clin. Sch., 1980, U. Sydney, 1980, Flinders U., Adelaide, Australia, 1980, U. Edinburgh, 1981, CDC, Atlanta, 1981, Stanford Rsch. Inst., Menlo Park, Calif., 1983, Duke U., Durham, N.C., 2003, others; co-founder, chmn. Md. Biosci. Alliance, 1995-98; bd. visitors U. Md. Biotech. Inst., 1996-2000, Duke U. Sch. Engring., 2001—; bd. advisors Md. Partnership for Workforce Quality, 1996-98; vice chmn. High Tech. Coun. Md., 1998-2001; chmn. Tech. Coun. Md., 2001-2004; mem. industry adv. bd. Chesapeake Bay Area chpt. ISPE, 1998-2000; bd. dirs. Greater Washington Bd. Trade, 2002-03; mem. bd. advisors Washington Bus. Jour., 2003—. Contbr. chpts. to books; patentee flow microfluorometer; contbr. articles to profl. jours. Asst. scoutmaster Boy Scouts Am., Georgetown, SC, 1965-66; trustee Bethesda Acad. Performing Arts, 1998-2001; mem. oversight bd. advanced tech. consortium Montgomery Coll., 1998-2001; mem. steering com. Biotech. Industry Orgn., 2003 Ann. Meeting, 2002—03; mem. econ. adv. coun. Montgomery County, 1998—; mem. founding exec. bd. Greater Washington Regional Partnership, 1998-2001; mem. leadership coun. Treatment and Learning Ctrs., 1998-2000; mem. Md. Advanced Tech. Bus. Devel. Commn., 2003; mem. state planning com. for postsecondary edn. Md. Higher Edn. Commn., 2004; chmn. Md. Adv. Tech. del. to Peoples Republic China, 2004; chmn. Eagle Career Day, Greater Washington, 2002-03, Capstone Co., Johns Hopkins U., 2003-04. Duke U. scholar, 1970-74, MIT scholar, 1974-76; NSF (hon.) fellow, 1974; recipient High Tech. Firm of Yr. award Md. High Tech. Coun., 1995, Leadership in Tech. award Md. High Tech. Coun., 1996, Employer of Yr. award Md. Pvt. Industry Coun., 1996, Region's Most Admired Bosses award Washington Techway Mag., 2000, Good Scout award Nat. Capital Area Coun., 2000, Nat. Disting. Eagle Scout award Boy Scouts Am., 2001, Emerging Firm of Yr. award Montgomery C. of C., 2001, Export award Scottish Coun. Devel. and Industry, 2001, Gemstone award for ann. report, 2002, Stevie award Am. Bus. Awards, 2003, others; named Greater Washington Entrepreneur of Yr. in Life Scis., 2002, No. 1 Earnings growth Forbes 200 Entrepreneurial Hot Shots, 2003, No. 11 among Fortune 100 Fastest Growing Small Cos. Am., 2003. Mem. AAAS, Acad. Mgmt., Biomed. Engring. Soc., N.C. Acad. Sci., Md. C. of C. (bd. dirs. 1996-2000), Harvard U. Alumni Assn., Duke U. Alumni Assn., MIT Alumni Assn., Congl. Country Club, Sigma Xi, Tau Beta Pi, Phi Eta Sigma, Pi Mu Epsilon. Methodist. Avocations: fresh and salt water fishing, travel. Office: 14920 Broschart Rd Rockville MD 20850-3349

MCDONALD, CHARLES EDWARD, lawyer; b. El Paso, Tex., Nov. 13, 1957; s. Carlos and Armida (Adauto) McD.; 1 child, Miranda Lee. BA in Philosophy, U. St. Thomas, Houston, 1980; JD, South Tex. Coll. Law, 1985. Bar: Tex. 1985, U.S. Ct. Appeals. (5th cir.) 1991, U.S. Supreme Ct. 1992. Prin. Law Office Charles E. McDonald, El Paso, 1985-2000, McDonald and Assocs, El Paso, 2000—. Comms. liaison Coleman Re-election Congl. Campaign, El Paso, 1984, 86. Mem. ATLA, Tex. Trial Lawyers Assn., State Bar Tex., El Paso County Bar Assn. (ethics com. 1997-98, rules com. 1997-98, clin. law coun. 1997-98), Nat. Assn. Cave Divers. Roman Catholic. Avocations: cave diving, chess, travel, foreign language (spanish). Office: 106 Santo Ysidro Rd Santa Teresa NM 88008-9622 E-mail: cemassoc@yahoo.com.

MC DONALD, CHARLES J. dermatologist, educator; b. Tampa, Fla., Dec. 6, 1931; s. George B. and Bertha C. (Harbin) McDonald; m. Maureen McDonald; children: Marc S. McDonald, Norman D. McDonald, Eric S. McDonald. BS magna cum laude, A and T Coll. NC, 1951; MS, U. Mich., 1952; MD with highest honors, Howard U., 1960. Diplomate Am. Bd. Dermatology. Rotating intern Hosp. St. Raphael, New Haven, 1960-61, asst. resident in medicine, 1961-63; asst. resident, dermatology Yale U., 1963-65, spl. USPHS rsch. fellow, chief resident dermatology, 1965-66, instr. medicine, pharmacology, 1966-67, asst. prof. medicine, pharmacology, 1967-68; asst. prof. med. sci. Brown U., Providence, 1968-69, assoc. prof., 1969-74, prof., 1974—, dir. dermatology program, 1970-74, head subsect. dermatology, 1974-82, dir. divsn. dermatology, 1982—96, chair dept. dermatology, 1996—; dir. dermatology Roger Williams Gen. Hosp., 1968-97; physician in chief, dept. dermatology RI Hosp., 1989—. Mem. com., task force, chmn. task force minority affairs Am. Acad. Dermatology, 1975—80; mem. dermatology adv. panel Fed. Drug Adminstrn., 1975—78, cons., 1978—; chmn. com. pub. edn., dir., v.p. RI divsn. Am. Cancer Soc., 1978—80, pres., 1980—83, bd. dir. nat. soc., 1983—, nat. dir. at large, 1990—95, mem. nat. exec. com., 1991, nat. officer, 1995—2001, pres. elect, 1997—98, pres., 1998—99; mem. pharm. scis. rev. commn. NIH, 1979—83; mem. residency rev. com. dermatology ACGME, 1992—97; vice chmn. RRC dermatology, 1996—97; mem. adv. com. Arthritis, Muscular, Skeletal, Skin Disease Inst., NIH, RI, 1993—95. Editor: Post Grad. Med. Jour., 1970—85; contbr. numerous articles to med. publs. Trustee Howard U., 1993—, chair health affairs com., 1994—98, mem. exec. com., 1994—98; chair bd. advisors Sch. Medicine, 1998—; bd. dirs. Providence Health Care Found., chmn. mem. adv. com., 1976—87; bd. dirs. Providence Fund for Edn., Providence Pub. Libr., 1987—2000, sec., 1991—96; mem. R.I. State Bd. Edn., 1970—72; bd. dirs. R.I. Cancer Coun., 1999—2001. Maj. USAF, 1952—56. Recipient Disting. Svc. award, Hosp. Assn., RI, 1971, Disting. Alumni award, Howard U. Coll. Medicine, 1983, St. George medal, Nat. Divsn. award, Am. Cancer Soc., 1992. Mem.: Assn. Profs. Dermatology (bd. dirs. 1991—94), Dermatology Found. (chmn. sci. com. 1972—76), New Eng. Dermatology Soc., Am. Soc. Clin. Oncology, Nat. Med. Assn. (chmn. sect. dermatology 1973—75), Am. Acad. Dermatology (bd. dirs. 1987—91), Am. Fedn. Clin. Rsch., Soc. Investigative Dermatology, Noah Worcester Dermatol. Assn. (bd. dirs. 1983—86), RI Dermatol. Assn., New Eng. Cancer Soc., New Eng. Dermatol. Assn. (v.p. 1983—84, pres. 1984—85), Am. Dermatol. Assn. (bd. dirs. 1995, pres elect 2002, pres. 2003—04), AAAS, Beta Kappa Chi, Alpha Kappa Mu, Alpha Omega Alpha, Sigma Xi. Democrat. Office: RI Hosp Dept Dermatology 593 Eddy St Providence RI 02903-4971 Office Phone: 401-444-7137.

MCDONALD, CHRISTIE ANNE, Romance languages and literature educator, writer; b. N.Y.C., May 4, 1942; d. John Denis and Dorothy (Eisner) McD.; m. Eugene Augustus Vance, June 11, 1965 (div. June 1986); children: Adam Vance, Jacob Vance; m. Michael David Rosengarten, Dec. 4, 1987. AB, Mt. Holyoke Coll., 1964; PhD, Yale U., 1969; MA (hon.), Harvard Coll., 1994. Acting instr. Yale U., New Haven, 1968-69; asst. prof. French U. Montreal, Que., Can., 1969-77, assoc. prof. French, 1977-83, prof., 1983, 86-93; prof. modern langs. Emory U., Atlanta, 1984-86; prof. romance langs. and. lits. Harvard U., Cambridge, Mass., 1994—, chmn. romance langs. and lits., 2000—. Author: The Dialogue of Writing, 1985, Dispositions, 1986, The Proustian Fabric, 1991; editor: The Ear of the Other, 1988, Transpositions, 1994. Recipient Clifford prize Am. Assn. 18th-Century Studies, 1994-95. Mem. Royal Soc. Can., Chevalier Palmes Académiques. Office: Harvard U 431 Boylston Hall Cambridge MA 02138 Office Phone: 617-495-2547.

MCDONALD, CRAYDON DEAN, psychologist; b. Denver, Dec. 22, 1946; s. Donald D. and Irene (Dunlavy) McD.; children: Ian, Brendan, Tavis, Morgynne. BFA, Parsons Sch. Design, N.Y.C., 1970; MDiv cum laude, St. Paul Sch. Theology, Kansas City, Mo., 1979; D of Ministry, Wesley Theol. Sem., Washington, 1982; PhD, Boston U., 1987. Diplomate Am. Bd. Profl. Psychology; lic. psychologist, Mass., Wis., Ill., Ariz.; approved supr. Am. Assn. Marriage & Family Therapy; ordained to ministry United Meth. Ch., 1982. Psychologist Worcester (Mass.) Pastoral Counseling Ctr., 1982-87; assoc. prof., asst. program dir. Loyola U., Chgo., 1987-88; clin. psychologist Lake Geneva, Wis., 1987-93. Psychology faculty No. Ariz. U., 1993—; chief psychologist Dr. McDonald & Assocs., Inc., 1982—; examiner Am. Bd. Profl. Psychology. Author: Personality and Cognitive Theology, 1982, Type A Coronary Prone Behavior and Narcissism, 1987. Fellow The Acad. Family Psychology; mem. APA (program com. divsn. 43), Human Factors Soc., Am. Assn. Pastoral Counselors. Democrat. Office: 1100 N San Francisco St Ste C Flagstaff AZ 86001-3260 Office Phone: 928-774-1100. *I have seldom found what a person does to be as significant as the motivation for doing it.*

MCDONALD, DAVID EUGENE, transportation operator; b. Decatur, Ill., July 6, 1956; s. Robert Alexander McDonald and Ida Jane (Varvil) Crowell; m. Lynda Jean Christensen McDonald, Apr. 23, 1983; children: Melanie Ann, Joshua Glen and Jordan David (twins). BS in History, Ill. State U., Normal; student, Parkland C.C., Champaign, Ill. Asst. mgr. Gen. Cinema Corp., Decatur, Champaign, Chgo., 1978-81; mgr. Classic Cinemas, Elmhurst, Ill., 1981-83, World Mgmt. Inc., Downers Grove, Ill., 1983-87; driver UPS, Addison, Ill., 1987—. Active Jr. Achievement, 1971-75, Dupage County Rep., Wheaton, Ill., 1993-2002; treas. Local Luth. Laymans League, 2000—. Named Mr. Exec. Jr. Achievement, Decatur, Ill., 1975; recipient Internat. Literary award Manuscripts Internat., Dayton, Wash., 1988. Republican. Lutheran. Avocations: politics, photography, reading, writing. Home: 841 Prospect Ave Elmhurst IL 60126-4862 Office: UPS 150 S Lombard Rd Addison IL 60101-3020

MCDONALD, DONALD C. lawyer; accountant, corporation executive. B.B.A., U. Tex., 1950, LL.B., 1958. Bar: Tex. 1958. Assoc., Fulbright & Jaworski, Houston, 1958-63; acct. Collier, Johnson & Woods, 1950-51, 53-55; v.p. legal Anderson, Clayton & Co., Houston, 1967— . Office: PO Box 2538 3800 Inter First Plaza 1100 Louisiana St Houston TX 77002-5227

MCDONALD, DOUGLAS ROBERT, non profit agency executive; b. San Francisco, May 27, 1949; s. Robert Angus and Shirley Anne (Beine) McD.; m. Karen Bachanas, June 24, 1978; children: Jennifer, Cameron. AB, Stanford Univ., 1971; MBA, Santa Clara Univ., 1974. Dist. exec. Boy Scouts Am., San Mateo, Calif., 1971-74, exec. Palo Alto, Calif., 1974-76; regional sales mgr. Baron Data Systems, San Leandro, Calif., 1976-81; field dir., COO Boy Scouts Am., San Mateo, Calif., 1981-86, assoc. reg. dir. Sunnyvale, Calif., 1986-88, scout exec., CEO Stockton, Calif., 1988-92, San Jose, Calif., 1992-99, Sacramento, 1999—2003, scout exec., COO Redlands, Calif., 2003—. Recipient Paul Harris fellow Rotary Internat., 1990, St. George award Roman Cath. Diocese of Sacramento, 2000; James E. West fellow Boy Scouts Am., 1993. Mem. Nat. Soc. Fund Raising Execs., Sigma Alpha Epsilon, Alpha Phi Omega, Silicon Valley Planned Giving Coun., Rotary Internat., Scouting Heritage Soc. Republican. Roman Catholic. Avocations: travel, computers, investments.

MCDONALD, FORREST, historian, educator; b. Orange, Tex., Jan. 7, 1927; s. John Forrest and Myra (McGill) McD.; m. Ellen Shapiro, Aug. 1, 1963; children from previous marriage: Kathy, Forrest Howard, Marcy Ann, Stephen, Kevin. BA, MA, U. Tex., 1949, PhD, 1955; MA (hon.), Brown U., 1962; LHD (hon.), SUNY, Geneseo, 1989. Exec. sec. Am. History Research Ctr., Madison, Wis., 1953-58; assoc. prof. history Brown U., Providence, 1959-63, prof., 1963-67, Wayne State U., Detroit, 1967-76, U. Ala., Tuscaloosa, 1976-87, disting. univ. rsch. prof., 1987—2002, prof. emeritus, 2002—. James Pinckney Harrison prof. Coll. of William and Mary, Williamsburg, Va., 1986-87; presdl. appointee Bd. Fgn. Scholarships, Washington, 1985-87; mem. fellowship selection com. Richard M. Weaver Fellowships, Bryn Mawr, Pa., 1980—. Author: We The People, 1958, Insull, 1962, E Pluribus Unum, 1965, Alexander Hamilton, 1979 (Frances Tavern Book award 1980), Novus Ordo Seclorum, 1985, Requiem, 1988, The American Presidency: An Intellectual History, 1994, States Rights and the Union, 2000, Recovering the Past: A Historian's Memoir, 2004. Trustee Phila. Soc., North Adams, Mich., 1983-86, 87-90, pres. 1988-90; co-chmn. New Eng. for Goldwater, 1964. Served with USN, 1945-46. Recipient George Washington medal Freedom's Found., Valley Forge, Pa., 1980, Best Book award Am. Revolution Round Table, N.Y., 1986, Richard M. Weaver award Ingersoll Found., 1990, First Salvatori award Heritage Found., 1992, Salavatori Book award Intercollegiate Studies Inst., 1994; Guggenheim fellow, N.Y., 1962-63; Jefferson lectr. NEH, 1987. Republican. Avocations: horticulture, tennis.

MCDONALD, FRANCES D. government official, editor, lawyer; b. Washington, July 6, 1949; BA, U. Va., 1971; JD, Cath. U. Am., 1981. Bar: Va. 1982. Legal publs. specialist Office Fed. Register. Nat. Archives and Records Adminstrn., Washington, 1980-82, atty., 1982-86, dir. legal svcs., 1986-91, dir. presdl. and legis. divsn., 1991-96, mng. editor, 1996—. Mem. Pi Gamma Mu. Office: Office Fed Registr Nat Archives-Recs Adminstrn 800 N Capitol St Rm 700 Washington DC 20408-0001 Office Phone: 202-741-6002. Business E-Mail: frances.mcdonald@nara.gov.

MCDONALD, FRANCIS MICHAEL, judge trial referee, retired state supreme court justice; b. Waterbury, Conn., Jan. 22, 1931; s. M. Francis and Margaret (Kelly) McD.; m. Mary Kelly, Jan. 28, 1956; children: Michael, Mary Ann, John K. AB, Holy Cross Coll., 1953; LLB, Yale U., 1956. Bar: Conn. 1956. Spl. agt. FBI, Washington, 1956-57; asst. U.S. atty. Dist. of Conn., New Haven, 1958-60; asst. prosecutor Cir. Ct., Waterbury, 1961-68; state's atty. Waterbury, 1968-84; judge Superior Ct., Waterbury, 1984-96; assoc. justice Conn. Supreme Ct., Hartford, 1996-99, chief justice, 1999-2001, judge trial referee, 2001—. Avocations: fishing, skiing, fly tying. Home: 257 Christian Rd Middlebury CT 06762-2908 Office: Superior Ct 400 Grand St Waterbury CT 06702-1900

MC DONALD, FRANK BETHUNE, physicist; b. Columbus, Ga., May 28, 1925; s. Frank B. and Lucy (Kyle) McD.; m. Virginia Ballew, June 15, 1951 (dec. 1977); children: Kyle Louise McDonald Jossi, Robert Kyle, Douglas Frank; m. Irene Negosh Kelejian, Nov. 7, 1987. BS, Duke U., 1948; MS, U. Minn., 1951, PhD (AEC fellow), 1955. Rsch. assoc. State U. Iowa, Iowa City, 1953-56, asst. prof. physics, 1956-59; chief lab. for high energy astrophysics Goddard Space Flight Ctr. NASA, Greenbelt, Md., 1959-82, mem. phys. scis. com. space program adv. coun., 1974-76; the NASA chief scientist, 1982-87; assoc. dir., chief scientist Goddard Space Flight Ctr. NASA, 1987-89; sr. policy analyst Office Sci. and Tech. Policy, Exec. Office of Pres., Washington, 1982; sr. rsch. scientist Inst. for Phys. Sci. and Tech. U. Md., College Park, 1989—. Part-time prof. U. Md., College Park, 1963-82; mem. Geophysics Rsch. Forum, 1985-88; Internat. Union Pure and Applied Physics mem. Internat. Commn. on Cosmic Rays, 1981-84, sec. to commn., 1984-87, chmn., 1987-90; NASA rep. to NASA Adv. Coun., 1984-89. Editor: High Energy Particles and Quanta in Astrophysics, 1974; assoc. editor: Jour. Geophys. Research, 1964-67; mem. editorial bd.: Space Sci. Revs.; Research in cosmic ray physics With USNR, 1942-45. Recipient Exceptional Sci. Achievement award NASA, 1964, 78, 86, Outstanding Leadership medal, 1981; Presdl. Mgmt. Improvement cert., 1971; Presdl. rank of meritorious exec. Sr. Exec. Service, 1980, 89, W. Randolph Lovelace II award Am. Astronautical Soc., 1986. Fellow Am. Phys. Soc. (chmn. div. cosmic physics 1973-74, mem. council 1982—, mem. exec. com. 1983), Am. Geophys. Union; mem. Am. Inst. Physics (council, governing bd. 1983-86), Washington Philos. Soc., Am. Astronom. Soc., Nat. Acad. Sci., Sigma Xi, Phi Beta Kappa. Office: U Md IPST Rm 3245 Computer Sci Spc Bui College Park MD 20742-0001

MC DONALD, GAIL FABER, musician, educator; b. Jersey City, Oct. 24, 1917; d. Samuel and Jennie (Weiss) Faber; m. George Walther, Nov. 17, 2000; children from previous marriage: Lora McDonald Ferguson, Charles McDonald, Henry McDonald. Diploma, Mannes Music Sch., N.Y.C., 1938; BA, U. Md., 1962; MusM, Cath. U., 1968; DMus Arts, U. Md., 1977. Legis. asst. Capitol Hill, 1943-46; pvt. tchr. piano and music theory Washington and Md., 1950—. Piano soloist Nat. Gallery Art, 1977; rec. artist Educo Records; lectr., performer Bach Sinfonias and Mendelssohn's Complete Songs Without Words; recorded complete solo piano works of Daniel Gregory Mason. Author: Muzio Clementi and the Gradus Ad Parnassum, 1968. Mem. D.C. Music Tchrs. Assn., Md. Music Tchrs. Assn. (pres. 1977—), D.C. Fedn. Music Clubs, Nat. Guild Piano Tchrs. (adjudicator 1972-2003), Friday Morning Music Club (performing mem.). Address: 801 N Monroe St Apt 602 Arlington VA 22201-2372

MCDONALD, GREGORY CHRISTOPHER, author; b. Shrewsbury, Mass., Feb. 15, 1937; s. Irving Thomas and Mae (Haggerty) M.; m. Susan Aiken, Jan. 12, 1963 (div. Oct. 1990); children: Christopher Gregory, Douglas Gregory; m. Cheryle Higgins, May 25, 2001. BA, Harvard U., 1958. Bd. dirs. Camaldon Corp. Author: (novels) Running Scared, 1964, Fletch, 1974, Confess, Fletch, 1976, Flynn, 1977, Love Among the Mashed Potatoes, 1978, Fletch's Fortune, 1978, Fletch Forever, 1978, Who Took Toby Rinaldi, 1980, Fletch and the Widow Bradley, 1981, The Buck Passes Flynn, 1981, Fletch's Moxie, 1982, Fletch and the Man Who, 1983, Carioca Fletch, Flynn's In, 1984, Fletch Won, Safekeeping, 1985, Fletch, Too, 1986, (non-fiction) The Education of Gregory Mcdonald, 1985, Fletch Chronicle, Vol. 1, (drama) Bull's Eye, 1986, A World Too Wide, 1987, Exits and Entrances, 1988;: Fletch Chronicle, Vol. 3, 1988, Merely Players, 1988, The Brave, 1991, Son of Fletch, 1993, Fletch Reflected, 1994, Skylar in Yankeeland, 1997, Flynn's World, 2003; editor: Last Laughs, 1986; dir.: Bach Cantata Singers, 1973—80; author: (stage play) CDI pour SDF, 2003. Mem. vis. com. Boston Mus. Fine Arts, 1970-73, 85—; mem. Lincoln Recreation Com., 1977, 78; mem. Winthrop House Sr. Commons Harvard Coll. 1982—. Recipient Humanitarian of Yr. award Tenn. Assn. Fed. Execs., 1989, Citizen of Yr. award Nat. Assn. Social Workers, 1990, Roger William Straus award NCCJ, 1990, Alex Haley award, 1992. Mem. Authors Guild, Dramatists Guild, Mystery Writers Am. (dir. 1977—, pres. 1985-86, Poe award 1975, 77), Crime Writers Eng., Writers Guild Am., Mass. Chiefs Police Assn., Giles Countians United, Mid-Tenn. Harvard-Radcliffe Assn. Clubs: Harvard (Boston); Overseas Press (N.Y.C.); Hillcrest Country (Pulaski, Tenn.). Office: care Arthur Greene Esq 101 Park Ave New York NY 10178-0002

MCDONALD, JACKSON, ambassador; b. Fla., Jan. 1956; married; 3 children. Grad., Georgetown U., Inst. d'Etudes Politiques, Paris, Ecole Nat. d'Adminstrn. 3rd sec., vice consul Am. Embassy Dhaka Dept. of State, Bangladesh, 1980—82, country officer for Bangladesh, 1982—84, 2nd sec. for polit. affairs Am. Embassy Beirut, 1984—86, 1st sec. for polit. affairs Am. Embassy Paris, 1987—89, 1st sec. for polit. affairs Am. Embassy Moscow, 1990—91, from chargé d' affaires to dep. chief of mission Am. Embassy Almaty Kazakhstan, 1992—94, consul gen. Marseille, France, 1994—97, dep. chief of mission Am. Embassy Abidjan Cote d'Ivoire, 1998—2001, U.S. amb. to Gambia, 2001—. Office: 2070 Banjul Pl Washington DC 20521

MCDONALD, JAMES H. anthropologist, educator; b. Chgo., Feb. 13, 1957; s. James H. and Dorothy L. McDonald; m. Jan L. Carey, Apr. 18, 1986. B.A., U. Ariz., 1979; MS, U. Wis., Milw., 1981; Ph.D., Ariz. State U., 1991. From asst. prof. anthropology to prof. U. Mich., Flint, 1992—95; prof. anthropology U. Tex., San Antonio, 1995—. Jour. editor Culture and Agr., Am. Anthrop. Assn., Washington, 1998—. Editor: The Applied Anthropology Reader; contbr. articles to profl. jours. Model OAS com. World Affairs Coun. San Antonio, 1998—2003; mem. ethics bd. Vitas Hospice, San Antonio, 1996—98; bd. trustees Greater Flint Arts Coun., 1993—95. Recipient Chancellor's Coun. Outstanding Tchg. award, U. Tex. Sys., 2000; Extending the Reach Faculty Rsch. grantee, NEH, 2001. Fellow: Soc. Applied Anthropology; mem.: Soc. Econ. Anthropology, Am. Anthrop. Assn. Home: 8624 Espanola Dr Helotes TX 78023 Office: U Tex San Antonio 6900 N Loop 1604 W San Antonio TX 78249-0649 E-mail: jmcdonald@utsa.edu.

MCDONALD, JAMES S. investment company executive; b. Titirangi, New Zealand, 1953; arrived in U.S., 1960; AB, Harvard Coll., 1974; JD, U. Va., 1977. With Choate, Hall & Stewart, 1977—86, Boston Harbor Trust Co., N.A. (now Pell Rudman), 1988—; pres. Boston Harbor Trust N.A. (formerly Pell Rudman Trust Co. N.A.), 1988; COO Pell Rudman Trust Co., N.A., 1993—98, CEO, 1998—2000, Rockefeller & Co., Inc., N.Y.C., 2000—. Bd. dirs. N.Y. Stock Exch. Office: Rockefeller & Co Inc 30 Rockefeller Plaza New York NY 10112*

MCDONALD, JINX, interior designer; b. Kingston, Jamaica, Aug. 5, 1946; d. Leonard Fraser and Norma Dawn (Phillips) McConnell; m. C. John McDonald, Dec. 20, 1965 (div. Nov. 1993); children: Sarah, Minka. Interior design/journalism, St. Godric's Coll., Hampstead, Eng., 1967; interior design, Tuxedo Ctr., Atlanta, 1986. Owner/pres. Internat. Accents, Inc., Atlanta, 1986—91; interior designer Style, Inc., Naples, 1991—95, Forum Design group, Inc., Naples, Fla., 1995—2000; prin., owner Jinx McDonald Designs, Inc., Naples, Fla., 2000—. Cons. interior design. Recipient Sand Dollar award, Collier Bldg. Industry Assn., 1999, 2002, 2003, Design of Distinction, Naples Illustrated, 2002, Pinacle award, 2003. Mem. Am. Soc. Interior Design (allied mem.), Interior Design Soc., Nat. Abortion and Reproductive Rights Action League, Natural Resources Def. Coun. Democrat. Anglican. Home and Studio: 7536 San Miguel Way Naples FL 34109-7162 Office: Jinx McDonald Designs Inc 5603 Naples Blvd Naples FL 34109-2023 E-mail: jinxmcdonald@yahoo.com.

MCDONALD, JOHN FRANCIS PATRICK, electrical engineering educator; b. Narberth, Pa., Jan. 14, 1942; s. Frank Patrick and Lulu Ann (Hegedus) McD.; m. Karen Marie Knapp, May 26, 1979. BSEE, MIT, 1963; MS in Engring., Yale U., 1965, PhD, 1969. Instr. Yale U., New Haven, 1968-69, asst. prof., 1969-74; assoc. prof. Rensselaer Poly. Inst., Troy, N.Y., 1974-86, prof., 1986—. Founder Rensselaer Ctr. for Integrated Electronics, 1980—. Contbr. more than 250 articles to profl. publs.; patentee in field. Recipient numerous grants, 1974—. Mem. ACM, IEEE (sr., assoc. editor Transactions on VSLI Design 1995—), Optical Soc., Acoustical Soc., Vacuum Soc., Materials Rsch. Soc. Office: Rensselaer Poly Inst Ctr for Integrated Electronics Troy NY 12181

MCDONALD, JOHN GREGORY, financial investment educator; b. Stockton, Calif., 1937; m. Melody McDonald. BS, Stanford U., 1960, MBA, 1962, PhD, 1967. Mem. faculty Grad. Sch. Bus. Stanford U., Calif., 1968—, now The IBJ prof. fin. Grad. Sch. Bus. Vis. prof. U. Paris, 1972, Columbia Bus. Sch., 1975, Harvard Bus. Sch. 1986; gov., vice chmn., bd. govs. NASD/NASDAQ Stock Market, 1987-90; mem. adv. bd. InterWest Venture Capital; dir. Growth Fund Am., New Perspective Fund, Inc., Scholastic Corp., Varian Inc., EuroPacific Growth Fund. Contbr. articles to profl. jours. Bd. overseers vis. com. Harvard U. Bus. Sch., Cambridge, Mass., 1994-2000. Fulbright scholar, Paris, 1967—68. Office: Stanford U Grad Sch Bus 518 Memorial Way Stanford CA 94305 Office Phone: 650-723-4037.

MCDONALD, JOHN JOSEPH, electronics executive; b. NYC, Apr. 18, 1930; s. John J. and Margaret (Shanley) McD.; m. Tessa de R. Greenfield, Aug. 22, 1956; children: Kathryn, Elizabeth, Andrew. BA, Bklyn. Coll., 1951. With Sperry Rand Corp., Blue Bell, Pa., 1954-75, v.p., 1972-75; mng. dir. Casio Electronics Ltd., London, 1975-78, pres. Casio Europe, 1975-78; pres., CEO Casio, Inc., Dover, NJ, 1978-99, also bd. dirs.; chmn. Casio Can. Ltd., 1988—99; pres., CEO McDonald Assoc., Dover, NJ, 1999—, Electric Fuel Corp. (Instant Power subs.), 2002. Mem. exec. com. Electronic Ind. Found., 1994—. Chmn. Electronics Industries Found., 1997-98; trustee Bklyn. Coll., CUNY, 1997—. Served with US Army, 1952-54. Mem. Electronic Industries Assn. (bd. gov.), Electronic Industries Found. (trustee 1987—), Consumer Electronics Assn.(dir.). Home and Office: PO Box 322 Hope NJ 07844-0322 Office Phone: 908-459-5386.

MCDONALD, JOHN W. oil industry executive; b. Ont., Can. BS in Geophysics with honors, U. Western Ont., 1975. Geophysicist Texaco, Calgary, Canada, 1975—91, strategic adviser, asst. to chmn., 1992—94; asst. divsn. mgr. Texaco Exploration and Prodn., New Orleans, 1994—96, v.p. exploration and prodn. offshore divsn., 1996—98; v.p. prodn. Texaco Internat., London, 1998—99; mng. dir. Texaco Ltd., 1998—2001, ChevronTexaco Upstream Europe, Aberdeen, Scotland, 2001—02; v.p. strategic planning ChevronTexaco Corp., San Ramon, Calif., 2002—. Mem.: U.K. Industry/Govt. Forum, U.K. Offshore Operators Assn. (past pres, exec. officer), Soc. Exploration Geophysicists, Am. Assn. Petroleum Geologists. Office: ChevronTexaco Corp 6001 Bollinger Canyon Rd San Ramon CA 94583-2324

MCDONALD, JOHN W. internist; MD, U. Western Ont., 1961; PhD in Biochem., UWO, 1966. Resident McGill U.; asst. prof. UWO, 1970—78, prof., 1978—85; chair dept., chief medicine U. Hosp., 1985—94; internist London Health Scis. Ctr., 1994—. Chair rsch. com. Heart and Stroke Found. Ont. Co-author: Evidence-Based Gastroenterology and Hepatology, 1999. Mem.: Royal Coll. Physicians and Surgeons Can. (pres. 2002—04). Office: Royal Coll Physicians & Surgeons Canada 774 Echo Dr Ottawa ON K1S 5N8 Canada

MC DONALD, JOHN WARLICK, diplomat, global strategist; b. Coblenz, Germany, Feb. 18, 1922; s. John Warlick and Ethel Mae (Raynor) McD.; m. Barbara Jane Stewart, Oct. 23, 1943 (div.); children: Marilyn Ruth, James Stewart, Kathleen Ethel, Laura Ellen; m. Christel Meyer, Oct. 24, 1970. AB, U. Ill., 1943, JD, 1946; PhD (hon.), Mt. Mercy Coll., 1989, Teikyo Marycrest U., 1991, Salisbury State U., 1993. Bar: Ill. 1946, U.S. Supreme Ct. 1951. With legal div. Office Mil Govt., Berlin, 1947; asst. dist. atty. U.S. Mil. Govt. Cts., Frankfort, Germany, 1947-50; with Allied High Commn., Bonn, Germany, 1950-52; U.S. mission to NATO and OEEC, Paris, 1952-54; fgn. affairs officer Dept. State, Washington, 1954-55; exec. sec. to dir. ICA, Washington, 1955-59; U.S. econ. coord. for CENTO affairs Ankara, Turkey, 1959-63; chief econ. and comml. sect. Am. Embassy, Cairo, 1963-66; student Nat. War Coll., Washington, 1966-67; dep. dir. office econ. and social affairs Bur. Internat. Orgn. Affairs, Dept. State, 1967-68, dir., 1968-71; coord. UN Multilateral Devel. Programs, Dept. State, 1971-74, acting dep. asst. sec. econ. and social affairs, 1971, 73; dep. dir. gen. ILO, Geneva, 1974-78; pres. INTELSAT Conf. Privileges and Immunities, 1978; U.S. coord. Tech. Coop. among Developing Countries, 1978; rep. with rank of amb. to UN Conf., 1978—. Sec. gen. 27th Colombo Plan Ministerial Meeting, 1978; U.S. coord. UN Decade on Drinking Water and Sanitation, 1979; U.S. coord., amb. Third World Conf. on Indsl. Devel., 1979, World Assembly on Aging, 1980-82; chmn. fed. inter-agy. com. Internat. Yr. of Disabled Persons, 1980-81; U.S. rep. Internat. Youth Yr., 1981-83; coord. multilateral affairs Ctr. Study of Fgn. Affairs, 1983-87; profl. lectr. in law George Washington U. Nat. Law Ctr., 1987-88, lectr. in conflict resolution, multilateral diplomacy and art of negotiation; pres. Iowa Peace Inst., Grinnell, 1988-92; prof. polit. sci. Grinnell Coll., 1989-92; Disting. vis. prof. George Mason U., Fairfax, Va., 1992-93; chmn., CEO Inst. for Multi-Track Diplomacy, Washington, 1992—; mem. Fgn. Affairs Res. Corps., 1993—; adj. prof. Union Inst., 1993-94, 97-98. Author: The North-South Dialogue and the UN, 1982, How to Be a Delegate, 1984, 2nd edit., 1994; co-editor: International Negotiation, 1985, Perspectives on Negotiation, 1986, Conflict Resolution: Track Two Diplomacy, 1987, 2nd edit., 1995, U.S. Soviet Summitry, 1987, US Bases Overseas: Negotiations with Spain, Greece and The Philippines, 1990, Multi-Track Diplomacy, 1991, revised, 1993, 3rd edit., 1996, Defining A U.S. Negotiating Sytle, 1996; contbr. articles on aging, terrorism, water conflict resolution. Bd. dirs. Global Water, 1982-, chair, 1982—, Touchstone Theatre, 1982-88, World Com.-UN Decade of Disabled Persons, 1987—, Countdown 2001, 1987-93, People-to-People Com. on Disability, 1987—2003, Am. Impact Found., 1987-89, chmn. bd., 1988-89; dir. Am. Assn. Internat. Aging, 1983—2003, chmn., 1983—2003; v.p. nat. capital area UN Assn., 1993-98, mem., 1978—. Recipient Superior Honor award, State Dept., 1972, Presdl. Meritorious Service award, State Dept., 1984; named Patriot of Yr., Kansas City, 1987, Alumni Achievement award U. Ill., 2004; nominee Nobel Peace prize, 1994. Mem. ABA, Am. Fgn. Svc. Assn., U.S. Assn. for Club of Rome (chair 2002-), People to People Internat. (bd. trustees 2003-), Soc. Profls. in Dispute Resolution, Consortium of Peace Rsch., Edn. and Devel., Cosmos Club, Delta Kappa Upsilon, Phi Delta Phi. Office: IMTD 1901 Fort Myer Drive Ste 405 Arlington VA 22209 Office Phone: 703-528-3863. Business E-Mail: imtd@imtd.org.

MCDONALD, JOSEPH ANDREW, information services director, consultant, writer; b. Buenos Aires, July 10, 1942; came to the U.S., 1955; s. Joseph Andrew and Vera Ruth (Brown) McD.; m. Julianna Sue Adams, Oct. 11, 1962 (div. Nov. 1995); children: J. Andrew, Timothy Robert, Jonathan David; m. Kathryn Jean Baehr, Dec. 9, 1995; children: Gabriel Joseph, William Joseph, Peter Joseph. AB, Ea. Coll., 1963; MS, Drexel U., 1966, PhD, 1987. Asst. dir. libs. Stockton State Coll., Pomona, N.J., 1972-75; edn. materials adminstr. Triton Coll., River Grove, Ill., 1975-77; libr., asst. dir. univ. libs. SUNY, Albany, 1978-80; dir. univ. libs. L.I. U., Bklyn., 1981-85; dir. libr. svcs. Holy Family Coll., Phila., 1985-89; dir. univ. libs. Pepperdine U., Malibu, Calif., 1989-92; v.p. info. svcs. Dordt Coll., Sioux Center, Iowa, 1992-93; ind. cons., author St. Louis, 1994-97; dir. libr. Fontbonne Coll., St. Louis, 1997-98; head info. & learning svcs. Benedictine Coll., Atchison, Kans., 1998—. Rschr. Pa. Hist. and Mus. Commn., Harrisburg, 1971-89; cons., coll. visitor Middle States Assn., Phila., 1989-92; cons. City of Thousand Oaks, Calif., 1991, Impact Technologies, St. Louis, 1995—. Author: Public Library Architecture, 1967, Academic Libraries, 1994; contbr. articles to profl. jours. Cons. LWV, Harrisburg, 1967-70; pres. PTO, Vineland, N.J., 1973-74; mem., WEB site adv. com. Luth. Ch.-Mo. Synod, 1997—. Rsch. grantee Drexel U., Phila., 1980-81, Coun. on Libr. Resources, Washington, 1985-89, Pa. Hist. and Mus. Commn., Harrisburg, 1987-89. Mem. ALA (bldgs. for coll. and univ. librs. com. 1979-81), Cath. Libr. Assn. (bd. dirs., fin. com. 1987-89), Tri-State Libr. Coop. (bd. dirs. 1985-89), Consortium for Health Info. (bd. dirs. 1985-89), Acad. Librs. Bklyn. (bd. dirs. 1981-85). Avocations: sailing, hiking, music, painting. Office: Benedictine Coll 1020 N 2d St Atchison KS 66002

MCDONALD, JOSEPH VALENTINE, neurosurgeon; b. N.Y.C., June 7, 1925; m. Carolyn Alice Patricia Petersen, Apr. 30, 1955; 5 children. AB, Coll. Holy Cross, 1945; MD, U. Pitts., 1949. Intern St. Vincent's Hosp., N.Y.C., 1949-50; rsch. fellow neuroanatomy Vanderbilt U., 1950-51; gen. surgery asst. resident Cushing VA Hosp., Boston, 1951-52; neurology extern Lenox Hill Hosp., 1952; asst. resident neurosurgery Johns Hopkins Hosp., 1953-55, resident neurosurgeon, 1955-56; practice medicine specializing in neurol. surgery Rochester, N.Y., 1956—; emeritus prof. neurosurgery U. Rochester Med. Sch. Mem. Soc. Neurol. Surgeons, A.C.S., Am. Assn. Neurol. Surgeons, Congress Neurosurgeons. Home: 800 Allens Creek Rd Rochester NY 14618-3412

MCDONALD, KIRK, publishing executive; b. LaJolla, Calif. m. Kathleen McDonald; 1 child, Meghan. Sports reporter The Blade Tribune, 1974—76, asst. sports editor, 1976—79, dir. retail advt., 1985—87; pub. The Citizen, 1979—84; retail adv. mgr. San Antonio Light, 1987—88, display advt. dir., 1988—89; advt. dir. Denver Post, 1989, v.p. advt., 1989—93, sr. v.p. sales and mktg., 1993—95, exec. v.p., gen. mgr., 1995—98; v.p. newspapers Hearst Newspapers, 1998—2000; pres., CEO Denver Newspaper Agy., 2000—. Active Legatus; bd. mem. Regis U., Webb-Waring Inst., Denver Metro C. of C. Office: Denver Newspaper Agy 400 W Colfax Ave Denver CO 80204

MCDONALD, LARRY WILLIAM, neuropathologist educator; b. Louisville, Nebr., May 25, 1928; s. Clifford Marion and Tessie Margaret (Higgens) McD.; m. Dorothy Ann Baumgartner, Dec. 26, 1955; children: Laura Ann (dec.), Susan Helen, Lawrence Clifford. BA, U. Calif., Berkeley, 1950; MD, Northwestern U., 1955. Resident Chgo. Wesley Meml. Hosp., 1956; resident in pathology Pondville State Hosp., Walpole, Mass., 1959-60; instr. Harvard U. Med. Sch., Boston, 1961-62; rsch. assoc. U. Calif., Berkeley, 1963-67, assoc. prof. of pathology Davis, 1968-74; prof. Wright State U., Dayton, Ohio, 1975-77; prof. neuropathology U. Ill., Chgo., 1978-94, ret., 1994, prof. emeritus, 1994—. Contbr. articles to Jour. of Neurosurgery, Lab. Investigation, Exptl. and Molecular Pathology, Am. Jour. Pathology. Capt. USAF, 1957-58. Recipient 1st place award Electron Micro Exhibit, Electron Microscopy Soc. of N.Am., 1967. Mem. Internat. Acad. Pathology, AMA (Gold Medal Hektoen award 1968), Am. Assn. Neuropathologists, Coll. Am. Pathologists. Achievements include demonstration that blood in space around the brain causes permanent reduction of internal diameter of arteries, that late effects of radiation on the brain produce changes in the walls of small blood vessels of the brain. Office: Univ Ill Dept Pathology M/C 847 1819 W Polk St Rm 446 Chicago IL 60612-7331

MCDONALD, LOIS ALICE, elementary school educator; b. Grand Rapids, Mich., Feb. 19, 1930; d. Embert and Ruth Alfareta (Priest) Grooters; m. Ronald Gerard McDonald, July 17, 1954; children: Rodney Mark, Wendy Louise. BS, Western Mich. U., 1952, MA, 1974. Cert. elem. permanent tchr., Mich. Kindergarten and elem. tchr. Chalmers Sch., Algoma Twp., Sparta, Mich., 1952-54; elem. tchr. Loucks Sch., Peoria, Ill., 1955-56, Lakeside Sch., East Grand Rapids, Mich., 1957-58, Clyde Park Sch., Wyoming, Mich., 1958-63, 64-76; tchr. kindergarten Gladiola Sch., Wyoming, 1963-64; elem. tchr. Pinery Park Elem. Sch., Wyoming, 1976-85, Rogers Lane Sch., Wyoming, 1985-91; ret., 1991. Dir. John Knox Food Pantry, 1991—96; vol. Red Cross & West Mich. Trails of Girl Scouts, 1998—2002; ch. sch. supt. John Knox Presbyn. Ch., 1968—73; mem. Chancel Choir, 1977—98; bd. of dir. Second Harvest Gleaners of West Mich., 1993—2001. Mem.: MEA-NEA (life), Beta Sigma Phi Internat. Sorority (life). Home: 33 13 Mile Rd NE Sparta MI 49345-9342

MCDONALD, MACKEY J. apparel company executive; With VF Corp., Wyomissing, Pa., 1983—, pres., 1993—, CEO, 1996—, chmn., 1998—. Bd. dirs. Hershey Foods Corp., 1st Union Corp., Tyco Internat. Ltd. Trustee Davidson Coll. Mem.: Am. Apparel Mfrs. Assn. (bd. dirs.). Office: VF Corp PO Box 21488 Greensboro NC 27420-1488*

MCDONALD, MALCOLM WILLIS, retired real estate company executive; b. Mpls., Nov. 17, 1936; s. Malcolm Blanchard and Ruth Virginia (Stees) McD.; m. Judy Glynn Ballard, Aug. 22, 1959 (dec. 2003); children: Malcolm Scott, Margaret Alice, Philip Brian. BA magna cum laude with high honors and high orations, Yale Coll., 1958; MBA, Harvard U., 1960. V.p. First Nat. Bank of St. Paul, 1960-77; dir., sr. v.p., trustee Space Center, Inc., St. Paul, 1977—2002. Adj. prof. grad. programs in mgmt. U. St. Thomas, St. Paul, 1975—94; mem. adv. bd. Firstar Bank of Minn., St. Paul, 1999—2001; bd. dirs. Scherer Bros. Lumber Co., Mpls.; vice chair adv. com. Minn. State Bd. of Investment, St. Paul, 1982—; mem. adv. bd. Sherbrooke Capital, 2002—, Hill Monastic Manuscript Libr., St. John's U., Collegeville, Minn., 1980—97; bd. dirs. HMN Fin., Inc. Mem. North Oaks Home Owners Assn., 1996; trustee, sec., chmn. audit com., investment com. Amherst H. Wilder Found., St. Paul, 1971—; trustee Bigelow & FR Bigelow Found., St. Paul, 1967-98, Lee and Rose Warner Found., 1990-2002, Manitou Fund, 1990-2002, Adelaide and Harry G. McNeely Found., St. Paul, 1980-98, Minn. State Fair Found., 2002—, Episcopal Diocese Minn., 2004-; trustee, treas. mem., Grotto Found., St. Paul, 1980—; pres. Minn. Taxpayers Assn., 1994-96; former bd. dirs. Guthrie Theater, Minn. Orchestral Assn.; chmn. Minn.landmark, Minn. Kids First, 2004—. Mem. Mpls. Club (bd. govs. 2002—), North Oaks Golf Club, White Bear Racquet & Swim Club, St. Paul C. of C. (Bravo awards), Colony Found., Phi Beta Kappa, Phi Beta Kappa Fellows, Phi Gamma Delta. Republican. Episcopalian. Avocations: physical fitness, gardening, travel, encouraging 3, 4 and 5 yr. olds to want to read. Home: 21 E Oaks Rd North Oaks MN 55127-2527 Office Phone: 651-484-7714. Personal E-mail: malcolmmcdonald@comcast.net.

MCDONALD, MARIANNE, classicist; b. Chgo., Jan. 2, 1937; d. Eugene Francis and Inez (Riddle) McD.; children: Eugene, Conrad, Bryan, Bridget, Kirstie (dec.), Hiroshi. BA magna cum laude, Bryn Mawr Coll., 1958; MA, U. Chgo., 1960; PhD, U. Calif., Irvine, 1975; doctorate (hon.), Am. Coll. Greece, 1988; diploma (hon.), Am. Archaeol. Assn.; DLitt (hon.), U. Athens, 1994, U. Dublin, 1994, Aristotle U., 1997, U. Thessalonika, 1997, Nat. U. Ireland, 2001. Instr. Greek, Latin, English, mythology, cinema U. Calif., Irvine, 1975-79; founder, rsch. fellow Thesaurus Linguae Graecae Project, 1975-97. Tchg. asst. U. Calif., Irvine, 1974; vis. prof. U. Ulster, Ireland, 1997, U. Dublin, 1990—, Univ. Coll. Dublin, 1999, 2002; adj. prof. theatre U. Calif., San Diego, prof. theatre and classics, 1994—; bd. dirs. Centrum. Author: (novels) Terms for Happiness in Euripides, 1978, Semilemmatized Concordances to Euripides' Alcestis, 1977, Cyclops, Andromache, Medea, 1978, Heraclidae, Hippolytus, 1979, Hecuba, 1984, (critical books) Hercules Furens, 1984, Electra, 1984, Ion, 1985, Trojan Women, 1988, Iphigenia in Taurus, 1988, Euripides in Cinema: The Heart Made Visible, 1983, The Living Art of Greek Tragedy, 2003; translator: The Cost of Kindness and Other Fabulous Tales (Shinichi Hoshi), 1986, Views of Clytemnestra, Ancient and Modern, 1990, Classics and Cinema, 1990, Modern Critical Theory and Classical Literature, 1994, A Challenge to Democracy, 1994, Ancient Sun/Modern Light: Greek Drama on the Modern Stage, 1990, Star Myths: Tales of the Constellations, 1996, Sole Antico Luce Moderna, 1999, Mythology of the Zodiac: Tales of the Constellations, 2000, Antigone by Sophocles, 2000, Mythology of the Zodiac, 2000, Sing Sorrow: Classics, History, Heroines in Opera, 2001; translator: (with Michael Walton) Euripides Andromache, 2001; translator: Eurinides Electra, 2004; editor (with M. McDonald and Michael Walton): Six Greek Tragedies, 2002; editor: (with Michael Walton) Amid Our Troubles: Irish Versions of Greek Tragedy, 2002, Canta la tua Pena, 2002. Bd. dirs. Am. Coll. of Greece, 1981-90, Scripps Hosp., 1981, Am. Sch. Classical Studies, 1986-; mem. bd. overseers U. Calif., San Diego, 1985-; nat. bd. advisors Am. Biog. Inst., 1982—; pres. Soc. for the Preservation of the Greek Heritage, 1990-, Asian Am. Repertory Theatre, 2003; founder Hajime Mori Chair for Japanese Studies, U. Calif., San Diego, 1985, McDonald Ctr. for Alcohol and Substance Abuse, 1984, Thesaurus Linguarum Hiberniae, 1991-, Hiroshi McDonald Mori Performing Arts Ctr. Recipient Ellen Browning

Scripps Humanitarian award, 1975, Disting. Svc. award U. Calif., Irvine, 1982, 2001, Irvine medal, 1987; named one of the Cmty. Leaders Am., 1979-80, Philanthropist of Yr., 1985, Headliner San Diego Press Club, 1985, Philanthropist of Yr. Honorary Nat. Conf. Christians and Jews, 1986, Woman of Yr. AHEPA, 1988, San Diego Woman of Distinction, 1990, Woman of Yr. AXIOS, 1991; recipient Bravissimo gold medal San Diego Opera, 1990, Gold Medal Soc. Internationalization of Greek Lang., 1990, Athens medal, 1991, Piraeus medal, 1991, award Desmoi, 1992, award Hellenic Assn. of Univ. Women, 1992, Acad. of Achievement award AHEPA, 1992, Woman of Delphi award European Cultural Ctr. Delphi, 1992, Civis Universitatis award U. Calif., San Diego, 1993, Hypatia award Hellenic U. Women, 1993, Am.-Ireland Fund Heritage award, 1994, Contbn. to Greek Letters award Aristotle U. Thessaloniki, 1994, Mirabella Mag. Readers Choice One of 1000 Women for the Nineties, 1994, citations from U.S. Congress and Calif. Senate, Alexander the Gt. award Hellenic Cultural Soc., 1995, made hon. citizen of Delphi and gold medal of the Amphiktuonon, Del. Bus. award for Fine Arts San Diego Bus. Jour., 1995, Vol. of Decade Women's Internat. Ctr., 1994, 96, Gold Star award San Diego Arts League, 1997, Golden Aeschylus award Inst. Nat. Drama Antkg. Siracusa, 1998, Women Who Mean Bus., Fine Arts award San Diego Bus. Jour., 1998, Fulbright award, 1999, Ellis Island award, 1999, Spirit of Scripps award 1999; Theatre Excellence award KPBS Patte, 2001, Laud and Laurels, U. Calif. Disting. Alumni award Hellenic Cultural Soc. San Diego, 2003, Sledgehammer Theatre award, 2003, New Path award, 2003, Egeria award Women's Internat. Ctr., 2004. Mem. MLA, AAUP, Am. Philol. Assn. (disting. svc. award 1999), Soc. for the Preservation of the Greek Heritage (pres.), Libr. of Am., Am. Classical League, Philol. Assn. Pacific Coast, Am. Comparative Lit. Assn., Modern and Classical Lang. Assn. So. Calif., Hellenic Soc. (coun. award 2000), Calif. Fgn. Lang. Tchrs. Assn., Internat. Platform Assn., Royal Irish Acad., Greece's Order of the Phoenix (comdr. 1994), KPBS Prodrs. Club, Hellenic Univ. Club (bd. dirs.). Avocations: Karate, harp (medieval), skiing, diving. Home: PO Box 929 Rancho Santa Fe CA 92067-0929 Office: U Calif at San Diego Dept Theatre La Jolla CA 92093 Office Phone: 858-481-0107. E-mail: mmcdonald@ucsd.edu.

MCDONALD, MARK DOUGLAS, electrical engineer; b. Princeton, NJ, Aug. 3, 1958; s. James Douglas and Jacquelyn (Milligan) McD.; m. Patricia Joann Watson, Sept. 12, 1980. BSE, Duke U.; MS, N.C. State U. Product engr. Exide Electronics, Raleigh, N.C., 1981-84; rsch. asst. N.C. State U., Raleigh, 1985-86; tech. staff Avantek (Hewlett Packard), Newark, Calif., 1987-90; prin. engr. Nat. Semiconductor, Santa Clara, Calif., 1990-92, engring. project mgr., 1992-95; design engring. mgr. Linear Tech. Corp., Milpitas, Calif., 1995—2001; dir. RF/Analog Bermai Inc, Palo Alto, Calif., 2001—02; dir. McDonald Watson and Assocs., Campbell, Calif., 2002—; v.p. design engring. Altierre Corp., Los Gatos, 2003—. Session chmn. Wireless Symposium, Santa Clara, 1993-2002, RF and Microwave Applications Conf., Santa Clara, 1992; mem. com. Symposium on VLSI Circuits Program, 1995-97. Contbr. articles to profl. jours. Precinct capt. various polit. campaigns, Fremont, Calif., 1988. Mem. IEEE (sr.), Cairn Terrier Club of No. Calif. (asst. chairperson 1995, specialty show chairperson 1996-97, bd. govs. 1996-99), Cairn Terrier Club Am., Sacramento Valley Cairn Terrier Club, No. Calif. Terrier Assn. (bd. govs. 2002—) Achievements include U.S. and foreign patents in area of high-speed analog circuits; designed front-end integrated circuits in first wireless digital European cordless telecomm. transceiver (DECT) for voice comm.; design of first selective frequency trip circuit for parallel uninterruptible power supplies; ownership of # 1 Cairn Terrier in the world. Personal E-mail: markm@altierre.com.

MCDONALD, MARY HELEN, special education educator; b. Killeen, Tex., Jan. 21, 1953; d. Eugene W. and Shirley A. (Clem) Toifl; m. Randy C. McDonald, Feb. 26, 1972; children: Brent McDonald, Mistie McDonald Boyle. BA, U. Tex. San Antonio, 1980; MA, Incarnate Word U., 1990. Cert. tchr. spl. edn. adminstrn., Tex. Tchr. Concordia Luth., San Antonio, 1980-88; tchr., adminstr. Northside Ind. Sch. Dist., San Antonio, 1989-97; spl. edn. adminstrn. N.E. Ind. Sch. Dist., San Antonio, 1997—, asst. prin., 1998—. Vol. Conservation Soc., San Antonio, 1985—. Mem. Zonta (mem. chair 1995—), Phi Delta Kappa (historian 1989—). Republican. Christian. Avocations: walking, reading, skydiving. Home: 23 Greens Clf San Antonio TX 78216-7879

MC DONALD, MEG, public relations executive; b. Santa Monica, Calif., Oct. 11, 1948; Dir. radio & TV svcs. Fran Hynds Pub. Rels., 1969-75; owner, CEO Mc Donald Media Svcs., 1975—. Recipient Buccaneer award PIRATES, 1980, 82, Prisms award Pub. Rels. Soc. Am., 1981, Pro awards Publicity Clubs. of L.A. Mem. Pub. Rels. Soc. Am. (sec. 1985), Radio ane TV News Assn. of So. Calif. (mem. bd. dirs. 1973-88), Publicity Club of L.A. (pres. 1979-80), L.A. Advt. Women (v.p. 1984-85), Print Interactive Radio and TV Ednl. Soc. (pres. 1998-00), Radio and TV News Assn. Office: Mc Donald Media Svcs 11076 Fruitland Dr Studio City CA 91604-3541

MCDONALD, MICHAEL EUGENE, lawyer, educator, clergyman; b. Buffalo, N.Y., Aug. 13, 1956; s. Ned and Margaret (Hereford) McD.; m. Darlene Carver, July 1, 1989; 1 child, Miranda Danielle. AA, BS, Middle Tenn. State U., 1979; MPA, So. Ill. U., 1984; JD, John Marshall Sch. Law, Chgo., 1987; MDiv, Vanderbilt U., 1989—91. Bar: Ill. 1986, Tenn. 1990; cert. adminstr. elections, Tenn., 1994; cert. civil mediator; ordained to ministry United Meth. Ch., 1996. Legis. intern Office of the Speaker, Ill. Ho. of Reps., Springfield, 1982-83; fellow Exec. Office of the Gov., State of Ill., Springfield, 1983-84; law clk. intern U.S. Dist. Ct. No. Dist. Ill., Chgo., 1984-85; adminstrv. asst. to dir. Ill. Dept. State Police, Chgo., 1984-87; asst. atty. gen. Ill. Atty. Gen.'s Office, Chgo., 1986-87; spl. asst. to mayor Exec. Office of the Mayor, Nashville, 1987-90; assoc. King & Ballow, Nashville, 1991-93; election adminstr. Davidson County Election Commn., Nashville, 1993—. Adj. prof. polit. sci., bus. law and paralegal studies program Middle Tenn. State U., Murfreesboro, 1987—; gen. counsel Gov.'s Alliance for a Drug Free Tenn., Davidson County, 1987—; asst. prof. The Honors Program, Tenn. State U., 1996—; instr. U. Tenn. Ctr. for Govt. Tng., 1995—' instr. Ptnrs. in Policymaking, Tex., Kans., Mo., Tenn., N.J., Ga.; mediator U.S. EEOC, 1998-99. Vol. Buddies of Nashville, 1988—; loaned exec. United Way Mid. Tenn., 1990; mem. Leadership Nashville, 1990-91, Citizens Police Acd., 1997; ordained deacon Bethlehem Ctrs. of Nashville, 2000—; mem. design com. Internat. Convocation of Deacons and Diaconate Mins., Dalals, 2003. Recipient Disting. Young Alumni Achievement award Middle Tenn. State U., 1987, Disting. African Am. Alumni Achievement award; Coun. on Legal Edn. Opportunity fellow, Thurgood Marshall scholar, 1984-87. Mem. ABA (del. ho. of dels.), Nat. Bar Assn., Ill. State Bar, Alpha Phi Alpha, Phi Alpha Delta. Avocations: basketball, running, Karate, sport card collecting, playing guitar. Home: 1603 Benjamin St Nashville TN 37206-2511 Office: Election Commn Met Govt of Nashville Howard Sch Bldg Rm 153 2d Ave S Nashville TN 37210-0650

MCDONALD, NANCY E. retired secondary school educator; d. Paul E. McDonald and Bernice Leach. BS in Edn. magna cum laude, Marywood Coll., 1962, MS in European History magna cum laude, 1968. Cert. tchr. Pa. History tchr. Scranton Sch. Dist., 1962—99. Mem. curriculum coun. Scranton Sch. Dist., 1985—2001; owner Bern Paul Pub. Author: If You Can Play Scranton, 1981, Today at SF7-The History of The Scranton Federation of Teachers, 2002. Mem. Scranton Singers Guild, 1983—88, bd. dirs., 1990—94; choir mem., cantor St. Mary Mount Carmel, Dunmore, Pa., 1975—90; active Cathedral Choir, Scranton, 1990—2003, N.E. Choral Soc. Finalist Pa. Tchr. of Yr., State of Pa., 1983. Mem.: PASR (Ret. Tchrs.) (assoc. editor, sec.), Pa. Ret. Sch. Employees Assn., Pa. Assn. Sch. Retirees (sec. 2003—), Scranton Fedn. Tchrs. (mem. negotiating coms. 1965—2001, v.p.), Pa. Fedn. Tchrs. (govtl. appointee profl. stds. and practices commn. for state of Pa.), Broadway Theater League, Marywood Alumna Assn., Lackawanna Hist. Soc., St. Mary's Women's League, Audubon Soc., Cmty. Concert Assn., N.E. Philharm. Chorus, Northeastern Philharm. Soc., Sierra Club, Phi Alpha Theta. Democrat. Roman Catholic. Avocations: music, travel, birdwatching, writing, sports. Office: Bernpaul Pub Box 378 Dunmore PA 18512

MCDONALD, PATRICIA ANN, legislative administrator; d. Alfred Keith and Mercelene (Eberlee) McD. BA with distinction, U. Mich., 1973. Writer, photographer Jackson (Wyo.) Hole Guide, 1974; asst. mktg. mgr. Grand Targhee Ski Area, Alta, Wyo., 1975; back country ranger Grand Teton Nat. Pk., Moose, Wyo., 1973-76; legis. dir. U.S. Sen. Malcolm Wallop, Washington, 1977-84; spl. asst., western field rep. to sec. Dept. of Interior, Denver, 1984-85; dir. comm. Steve Schuck for Gov., Denver, 1985-86; exec. dir. pub. lands coun., dir. pub. lands Nat. Cattlemen's Assn, Washington, 1986-90; pres. McDonald and Assocs., Washington, 1990, 95-96; chief of staff for U.S. Sen. Malcolm Wallop, Washington, 1991-94; Rep. staff dir. U.S. Senate Com. on Energy and Natural Resources, Washington, 1994; chief of staff U.S. Rep. Barbara Cubin, Washington, 1996-2000, Sen. Conrad Burns, Washington, 2000—. Republican. Avocations: dance, skiing, snowboarding, hiking, boating. Home: 4525 Macomb St NW Washington DC 20016-2752 Office: US Senate Senate Office 187 Dirksen Rd Ofc Washington DC 20510-0001

MCDONALD, PEGGY ANN STIMMEL, retired automobile company official; b. Darbyville, Ohio, Aug. 25, 1931; d. Wilbur Smith and Bernice Edna (Hott) Stimmel; m. George R. Stich, Mar. 7, 1953 (dec.); 1 child, Mark Stephen (dec.); m. Joseph F. McDonald Jr., Feb. 1, 1986 (dec.). Missionary diploma with honor, Moody Bible Inst., 1952; BA in Econs. cum laude (scholar), Ohio Wesleyan U., 1965; MBA with distinction, Xavier U., 1977. Lic. capt. USCG. Missionary in S.Am. Evang. Alliance Mission, 1956-61; cost acct. Western Electric Co., 1965-66; acctg. mgr. Ohio Wesleyan U., 1966-73; fin. specialist NCR Corp., 1973-74, systems analyst, 1974-75, supr. inventory planning, 1975, mgr. material planning and purchasing control, 1976-78; materials mgr. U.S. Elec. Motors Co., 1978; with Gen. Motors Corp., 1978-92, shift supt. materials, 1979-80, gen. ops. supr. material data base mgmt. Ctrl. Office Warren, Mich., 1980, dir. material mgmt. GM Truck and Bus divsn. Balt., 1980-91; dir. edn. and tng. GM Truck and Bus, Linden, N.J., 1991-92; ret., 1992. Founder Creaciones Peggy Sport Jeans Mfg., Venezuela, 1993; vis. lectr. Inst. Internat. Trade, Jiao Tong U., Shanghai, China, 1985, Inst. Econs. and Fgn. Trade, Tianjin, China, 1986-87; part time instr. Towson (Md.) State U., 1986-87. Founder, pres. Capt.'s Challenge Corp., Global Christian Ministry of Econ. Devel., 1998; mem. 1st United Meth. Ch., Dunedin, Fla.; vol. missionary/tchr. Susana Wedey Instn. with Missionary Meth. Ch., Bogota, Colombia, 2000-2001. Mem. AAUW, Am. Prodn. and Inventory Control Soc., Am. Soc. Women Accts., Balt. Exec. Women's Network, Balt. Coun. on Fgn. Rels. Methodist. Avocation: sailing. Home: PO Box 884 Sarasota FL 34236 E-mail: jpmcdonald@ozline.net.

MCDONALD, PETER D, airline executive; m. Diane McDonald; children: Megan, Katie. B, Judson Coll., 1976. Various positions United Airlines Corp., 1969—, v.p., op. svcs., 1999—2001, sr. v.p. airport ops., 2001—02, exec. v.p. ops., 2002—.

MCDONALD, REBECCA ANN, natural gas company executive; b. Phoenix, June 14, 1952; d. William Robert and Regenia Lucille (Hall) Kennedy; m. John Edward McDonald Sr., May 26, 1977; 1 child, John Edward Jr. BS, Stephen F. Austin State U., 1973. Project procurement mgr., buyer Fluor Engrs. and Constructors, Houston, 1974-79; pvt. practice cons. Houston, 1979-81; devel. mgr. Panhandle Ea. Pipeline, Houston, 1981-82, mgr. customer rels., 1982-84, mgr. sales, 1984-85; mgr. gas sales Panhandle Trading Co., Houston, 1985-88, v.p., gen. mgr., 1988-90; v.p. Strategic Planning Tenneco Gas Co., 1990—. Cert. power trainer Situation Mgmt. Systems, Plymouth, Mass., 1981—. Pres. bd. trustees The Chinquapin Sch., Highlands, Tex., 1986—; mem. Houston Jr. Forum, 1986—. Mem. Natural Gas Men of Houston (bd. dirs. Houston chpt.), Am. Soc. Tng. & Devel. (membership chair 1975-76, Most Valuable Mem. award 1976), Am. Bus. Women (hon. nom. bd.). Episcopalian. Office: Tenneco Gas Co 1010 Milam St Houston TX 77002-5312

MCDONALD, REGINALD ADRIAN, musician, educator; b. Columbus, Ohio, Mar. 16, 1968; s. Charlie Alf McDonald, Jr. and Muriel Paulette McDonald; m. Coretta Craddock, July 14, 2000; m. Mia Rochelle Bell, Sept. 7, 1991 (div. Sept. 22, 1995). BA Music Ed., Ala. State Univ., Montgomery, AL, 1991; M. Music, State Univ. West Ga., Carrollton, GA, 1997. Cert. Education Specialist Clark Atlanta Univ., 2002. Band dir. McNair Mid. Sch., College Park, Ga., 1991—96; band dir./music dept. chair SW DeKalb H.S., Decatur, 1996—2001; assoc. dir. of bands/asst. music prof. Tenn. State Univ., Nashville, 2001. Saxophone/clarinet clinician Precision Camp, Inc., Atlanta, 1996—2001; band cons. Milestone, Inc., Atlanta, 1996—2001; band adjudicator/clinician Ga. Music Educators Assn., Atlanta, 1995—; assoc. condr. Tenn. State Univ., Nashville, 2002—. Pres. student govt. Albama State Univ., Montgomery, Ala., 1990; saxophonist/mem. Ga. Afro-American All-Star Band, Atlanta, Ga., 1994—99. Recipient Tchr. of the Yr., McNair Mid. Sch., Coll. Pk., GA, 1996-1997, Expert Tchr. Citation, Fulton County Bd. of Edn., Atlanta, GA, 1996, Medal of Excellence, Coll. Pk. Bus. Cmty. Mem.: Alpha Phi Alpha, Inc., Music Educators Nat. Conf., Phi Mu Alpha Sinfonia (pres. delta beta 1988—90). Democrat-Npl. Methodist. Avocations: golf, golf. Home: 1420 Brentwood Terrace Nashville TN 37211 Office: Tennessee State Univ 3500 John A Merritt Blvd Nashville TN 37209 Personal E-mail: mcdonaldreginald@hotmail.com.

MCDONALD, ROBERT DELOS, manufacturing executive; b. Dubuque, Iowa, Jan. 30, 1931; s. Delos Lyon and Virginia (Kolck) McD.; m. Jane M. Locher, Jan. 16, 1960 (div. Jan. 1970); children: Jean, Trish, Maria, Sharon, Rob; m. Marilyn I. Miller, July 4, 1978. BA in Econs., U. Iowa, 1953. From salesman to pres. A.Y. McDonald Mfg. Co., Dubuque, 1956—85, pres., 1985-95, CEO, 1987-2001, chmn. emeritus, 2004—. Sr. v.p. A.Y. McDonald Industries, Inc., Dubuque, 1983—; chmn. emeritus, A.Y.M. Inc., Albia, Iowa, 1988—; pres., CEO, 1988-2001. Trustee, bd. dirs. A.Y. McDonald Mfg. Co. Charitable Found., 1977—, pres., 1982—; bd. dirs. Stonehill Care Ctr., Dubuque, 1984-92, chmn. bd., 1991-92; mem. Stonehill Renovation and Financing Task Force, 1994-97; bd. dirs. Boys and Girls Club of Greater Dubuque, 1989-2004, Dubuque Bank & Trust Co., 1994-2002, Save Iowa's Civil War Monument Restoration Fund, 1995—, Dubuque County Hist. Soc., 1996—, Grand Opera House Found., 1997—, Terrace Hill Found., 1997—; bd. govs. Iowa Coll. Found., 1997-2001; trustee United Way Svcs., Inc., Dubuque, 1989-2003; bd. dirs. Stonehill Benevolent Found., Dubuque, 1998-2000, vice chmn., 1989-92; mem. regional adv. coun. SBA, Cedar Rapids, 1984-89; mem. adv. bd. Jr. Achievement Tri-States, Inc., 1991—, Iowa State Fair Blue Ribbon Found., 1993—. Lt. USNR, 1953-56, Korea. Mem. Am. Mgmt. Assn., Am. Supply Assn., Am. Water Works Assn., Nat. Assn. Mfrs., Dubuque Area C. of C., Am. Legion, Dubuque Shooting Soc., Dubuque Golf and Country Club, Sigma Alpha Epsilon. Republican. Roman Catholic. Home: Fountain Hill 3399 Eagle Point Dr Dubuque IA 52001-8320 Office: AY McDonald Mfg Co PO Box 508 Dubuque IA 52004-0508

MCDONALD, ROSA NELL, engineering executive; b. Boley, Okla., Feb. 12, 1953; d. James and Beatrice Irene (Hayes) McDonald. BS, Calif. State U., Long Beach, 1975; MBA, Calif. State U., Dominquez Hills, 1980, postgrad., 1988; BS in Computer Info. Sys., Chapman Coll., 1988. Acct. Aerospace Corp., El Segundo, Calif., 1976-77, analytical acct., 1977-79, budget analyst, 1979-81, sr. budget analyst, 1981-84, budget adminstr., 1984-86, mgr. indirect budgets, 1986-91, head budgets and pricing dept., 1991-95, dir. budgets, pricing and fin. planning, 1996—2001, ops. bus. mgr., 2001—. Vol. Youth Motivation Task Force, El Segundo, 1980—, Holiday Project, El Segundo, 1984, 1985, Recording for the Blind and Dyslexic. Named Woman of Achievement, NAACP Legal Def. Fund, 1988. Mem.: NAFE, Am. Bus. Women's Assn., Beta Gamma Sigma. Democrat. Avocations: dance, aerobics, reading, contests. Office: MI-009 2350 E El Segundo Blvd El Segundo CA 90245-4609

MCDONALD, SANDRA ANN, surgical pathologist; b. Phila., Mar. 5, 1965; d. John William and Barbara McDonald. AB in Chemistry with high honors, Princeton U., 1986; MD, Duke U., 1990. Diplomate Am. Bd. Pathology in anatomic and clin. pathology. Resident in anatomic and clin. pathology Duke U. Med. Ctr., Durham, N.C., 1990-95; asst. prof. pathology St. Louis U. Med. Ctr., 1995—2001; pathologist St. Vincent's Med. Ctr., 2001—02, Pfizer Corp., 2002—. Contbr. articles to profl. jours. Recipient award NIH rsch. festival, 1992. Fellow Coll. Am. Pathologists, Am. Soc. Clin. Pathology.

MCDONALD, STEPHEN DOUGLAS, banker; b. Cambridge, Ontario, Can., Oct. 17, 1956; came to U.S., 1984; s. William C. and Evelyn V. (Dakin) McD.; m. Donna Eva Dauneckas, Sept. 28, 1984. LLB, U. Western Ont., London, Ont., Can., 1980, MBA, 1983. Real estate lending officer Toronto Dominion Bank, Atlanta, 1984-86, dir. N.Y.C., 1986-87, mng. dir. communications fin., 1987-90; pres. Toronto Dominion Securities (USA), Inc. (now TD Waterhouse), 1991—98; CEO TD Waterhouse Group, N.Y.C., 1998—2002; vice-chmn., corp. TD Bank Fin. Group, 2002—. Office: TD Waterhouse Group 100 Wall St New York NY 10005-3701

MC DONALD, STEPHEN LEE, economics professor; b. Arkadelphia, Ark., Aug. 8, 1924; s. Claud Bethel and Ruth Jane (Gresham) McD.; m. Elizabeth Gene Brewer, Aug. 14, 1945; children: Martha Elizabeth Mc Donald Worchel, Kathryn Ann Mc Donald McGlothlin. BA, La. Poly. Inst., 1947; MA, U. Tex., 1948, PhD, 1951. Asst. prof. U. Tex., Austin, 1950-56, prof. econs., 1961—, Josey prof. in energy studies, 1983-85, Duncan prof. econs., 1985-94, chmn. dept., 1972-76, 78-79, 88-89, emeritus, 1997. Sr. fellow Bur. Bus. Rsch., 1990-97; economist Humble Oil & Refining Co., 1956-57; assoc. prof., prof., chmn. dept. La. State U., 1957-61; faculty Stonier Grad. Sch. Banking; staff assoc., Brookings Instn., 1961-63; econs. adv. panel NSF, 1962-64; cons. in field. Author: Federal Tax Treatment of Income from Oil and Gas, 1963, Petroleum Conservation in the United States, 1971, The Leasing of Federal Lands for Fossil Fuels Production, 1979; mem. editorial bds.: So. Econ. Journal, 1961-64, Energy Jour., 1979-86; contbr. articles to profl. jours. Served with USNR, 1943-46. Recipient Citation for Excellence Am. Bankers Assn.; Ford Found. grantee, 1964; Resources for Future grantee, 1967, 76; Pres. Assocs. award teaching excellence, 1982 Mem. Am. Econ. Assn., So. Econ. Assn. (v.p. 1969-70), Southwestern Econ. Assn. (pres. 1964-65), Internat. Assn. Energy Econs., Gamma Epsilon, Phi Kappa Phi. Democrat. Methodist. Home: 4002 Sierra Dr Austin TX 78731-3914

MCDONALD, STEVEN L. controller; b. Sacramento, Apr. 6, 1960; s. Jack L. and Donna L. McD.; m. Cheryl Ann; children: Jilliam, Danielle. BBA in Acctg., So. Meth. U., 1982. Mgr. Ernst & Young, Dallas, 1982-88; sr. v.p. First USA, Inc., Dallas, 1988-96; mng. dir., corp. controller Household Internat., Inc., Prospect Heights, Ill., 1996—. Mem. Controllers Conf. Bd., 1997—. Avocation: photography. Office: Household Internat Inc 2700 Sanders Rd Prospect Heights IL 60070-2701

MCDONALD, SUSAN, publishing executive; V.p., CFO San Jose (Calif.) Mercury News. Office: San Jose Mercury News 750 Ridder Park Dr San Jose CA 95190-0001

MCDONALD, TANNY, actress; b. Princeton, Ind. d. Douglas Hewitt and Irene Elizabeth (Codding) McD.; m. Robert D. Currie, Mar. 5, 1966 (div. Mar., 1986). BA cum laude, Vassar Coll., 1958. Actress Am. Savoyards, N.Y.C. and Tour, 1961—. Actress: (film) Hercules in New York, 1970, (plays) Broadway: Fiddler on the Roof, 1964, The Lincoln Mask, 1972, Clothes for A Summer Hotel, 1980, Macbeth (First Witch and Nurse), 1988, Man of La Mancha, 1992 and nat. tour, 1996-97, Medea (Woman of Corinth), 1994; Off-Broadway: Chelsea Theater Ctr. - the Beggar's Opera, 1972, Total Eclipse, 1974, Gorky, 1975, N.Y. Shakespeare Festival - Temptation, 1989, Titus Andronicus, 1989, Hamlet (Player Queen) also Great Performances, 1995; L.O.R.T. maj. roles (select): A Little Night Music, 1977, Three Penny Opera, 1979, Pal Joey, 1980, Tintypes, 1982, A Lesson From Aloes, 1982, Cloud Nine, 1984, Heartbreak House, 1986, The Bakkhai, 1995, Orpheus Descending, 1995, House of Bernarda Alba, 1997, Vassar to Vassar Cabaret, Road to Mecca, Long Day's Journey Into Night, 1998, WIT=NYC, Jekyll & Hyde, 1999, NYC: Sitting Pretty, La Bonne Dame (George Sand) 2001; Nat. Tour Copenhagen, 2002; CBS Kate and Allie, NBC The Doctors, 1973, NCR spl. Duty Bound (Emmy award 1973). Reid Hall fellow, Paris, 1958, 59; recipient Frances Walker Prize for Excellence, Vassar Coll., 1958; named Best Actress Richmond (Va.) News Leader in 1978.

MCDONALD, THERESA BEATRICE PIERCE (MRS. OLLIE MCDONALD), church official, minister; b. Vicksburg, Miss., Apr. 11, 1929; d. Leonard C. Pierce and Ernestine Morris Templeton Pierce; m. Ollie McDonald, Apr. 23, 1966. Student, Tougaloo Coll., 1946-47, U. Chgo. Indsl. Rels. Ctr., 1963-64; BA in Sociology with deptl. honors, Roosevelt U., 1997; student, Chgo. Theol. Sem., 1997—. Ordained to Gospel Ministry, 1997. Vol. rep. Liberty Bapt. Ch., Am. Legion Aux., VA West Side Hosp., Chgo., 1971-73; nat. instr. ushers dept. Prog. Nat. Bapt. Conv. Inc., Washington, 1973-75, nat. sec. ushers dept., 1975-76, v.p. at large, 1980-82, chmn. pers. com., 1982-84; mem. faculty Congress of Christian Edn., 1978-85; mem. pub. rels. staff Liberty Bapt. Ch., Chgo., 1973-79, trustee, 1987-91; asst. Christian edn. dir. Maryland Ave. Bapt. Ch., Chgo., 1995-99; assoc. min. Md. Ave. Bapt. Ch., Chgo., 1997—, dir. Christian edn., 2000—02. Cons., lectr. in field; Sunday ch. sch. tchr.; bible class instr.; guest speaker TV and radio programs. Participant White House Regional Confs., 1961. Recipient Christian Svc. award Prog. Nat. Bapt. Conv. Inc., 1986, 92, 94, Disting. Svc. award, 1990-94, Dedicated Svc. award, 1998. Mem. VFW (life mem. Hunt aux. 2024), Bethlehem Bapt. Dist. Assn. Chgo. (asst. sec. 1982-84), Ch. Women United in Greater Chgo. (Ecumenical Actions com. 1981-83), Am. Legion (Outstanding Svc. award 1972, 73), Bapt. State Conv. Ill. (life), Order Ea. Star. Address: 9810 S Calumet Ave Chicago IL 60628-1432

MCDONALD, THOMAS ALEXANDER, lawyer; b. Chgo., Aug. 20, 1942; s. Owen Gerard and Lois (Gray) McD.; m. Sharon Diane Hirk, Nov. 25, 1967; children: Cristin, Katie, Courtney, Thomas Jr. AB, Georgetown U., 1965; JD, Loyola U., Chgo., 1968. Bar: Ill. 1969, U.S. Dist. Ct. (no. dist.) Ill. 1969. Ptnr. Clausen Miller, PC, Chgo., 1969—2001, McDonald & McCabe, LLC, Chgo., 2001—. Mem. ABA, Ill. Bar Assn., Chgo. Bar Assn. Office: McDonald & McCabe LLC 300 S Wacker Dr Ste 1600 Chicago IL 60606 Office Phone: 312-845-5199. Business E-Mail: tmcdonald@mcdonaldmccabe.com.

MCDONALD, THOMAS EDWIN, JR., retired electrical engineer; b. Wapanucka, Okla., June 19, 1939; s. Thomas Edwin and Roasamond Bell (Enoch) McDonald; m. Myrna Kay Booth, Sept. 10, 1961; children: Stephen Thomas, Jennifer Kay, Sarah Lynn. BSEE, U. Okla., 1962, MSEE, 1963; PhDEE, U. Colo., 1969. Registered profl. engr., N.Mex. Asst. prof. elec. engring. U. Okla., Norman, 1969—70; planning engr. Okla. Gas and Electric Co., Oklahoma City, 1970—72; staff mem. Los Alamos (N.Mex.) Nat. Lab., 1972—2003, group leader, 1974—80, program mgr., 1980—92, program mgr. Centurion program, 1986—90, dep. program dir. inertial confinement fusion program, 1990—92, program coord. mine detection and laser tech., 1992—93, project mgr. Nat. Ctr. Advanced Mfg. Tech., 1993—96, project leader high-speed electronic imaging tech. devel. Nat. Ctr. Advanced Mfg. Tech., 1996—2003; ret., 2003. Adj. prof. elec. engring. U. Okla., 1970—72; cons. Los Alamos Tech. Assocs., 1980—, mgr. design sect., 1980—81. Contbr. articles to profl. jours. Bd. dirs., v.p. Sombrillo Care Facility; mem. Los Alamos High Speed Network Study Com., 2002—04; treas. Com. Study Constrn. Civic Ctr., Losa Alamos, 2003—04; bd. dirs. United Ch. Los Alamos, 1987—, chmn. fin. bd., chmn. bd. elders, 1992. Served to capt. U.S. Army, 1963—67. Mem.: AAAS, IEEE (chmn. Los Alamos sect.), Soc. Photo-Optical Instrumentation Engrs., Soc. Info. Display, Los Alamos Gymnastic Club (treas., bd. dirs. 1980—88), Rotary, Sigma Xi, Eta Kappa Nu. Republican. Achievements include research in inertial confinement fusion; high-speed electronic imaging and neutron radiography. Avocation: computer science. Home: 910 Circle Dr Los Alamos NM 87544 Personal E-mail: mhmtem@msn.com.

MCDONALD, THOMAS PAUL, controller; b. Williamsport, Pa., Aug. 13, 1949; s. Paul Tripp and Ethel Mary (Cowden) McD.; m. Debra Ann Rosamilia, July 17, 1976; children: Kevin, Gail. BS in Acctg., U. Scranton, 1971. CPA, N.Y. Auditor Coopers & Lybrand, N.Y.C., 1971-79; internal audit dir. Ward Foods, N.Y.C., 1979-81; contr. Mallory Randall Corp., N.Y.C., 1981-83,

Sullivan & Cromwel, LLP, N.Y.C., 1983—. Mem. AICPA, N.Y. State Soc. CPAs. Avocations: golf, coaching recreational sports. Home: 34 Dawson Dr West Caldwell NJ 07006-8128 Office: Sullivan & Cromwell LLP 125 Broad St Fl 20 New York NY 10004-2489

MCDONALD, WALTER J. internist; b. Rochester, Minn., May 1, 1938; MD, U. Mich. Sch. Medicine. Diplomate Am. Bd. Internal Medicine, Am. Bd. Pulmonary Diseases. Intern internal medicine U. Oreg. Med. Sch.; prof. medicine, assoc. dean edn. and student affairs, dir. grad. med. edn. Oreg. Health Scis. U., Portland; chief med. svcs. VA Med. Ctr., Portland, Oreg.; CEO, exec. v.p. ACP-Am. Soc. Internal Medicine, Phila. With U.S. Army, 1965—67. Fellow endocrinology fellow, NIH, 1967—69. Mem.: ACP-Am. Soc. Internal Medicine. Office: ACP Am Soc Internal Medicine 1900 N Independence Mall W Philadelphia PA 19106-1572

MCDONALD, WARREN GEORGE, retired accountant, former savings and loan executive; b. Oakland, Calif., Feb. 14, 1939; s. George Daniel and Barbara (Sainsot) McD.; m. Roberta Anne Peterson, Apr. 27, 1968; children: Edward Bruce, Deborah Lynn. BA, San Francisco State Coll., 1962. CPA, Calif. Ptnr. Main Lafrentz & Co., CPAs, San Francisco, 1969-74; v.p., treas. Imperial Corp. Am., San Diego, 1975-80; v.p. fin. No. Calif. Savs. & Loan, Palo Alto, 1980-82; sr. v.p. fin. Unified Mortgage Co., Santa Clara, Calif., 1982-85; pres. Saratoga Savs., 1985-89; pvt. practice cons. San Francisco, 1989—2003; ret., 2003. Co-author: Power Above The Law, 1990. Served to capt. USCGR. Mem. AICPA, Calif. Soc. CPAs, Inst. Mgmt. Accts., Res. Officers Assn., Naval Inst., Navy League. Home: 1430 Wendy Way Menlo Park CA 94025-6022

MCDONALD, WESLEY S. retail executive; b. 1962; Bachelor Degree cum laude, Bucknell U.; MBA, Wharton. Various fin. positions Target Corp., 1988—2000; CFO Abercrombie & Fitch, 2000—03; exec. v.p., CFO Kohl's, 2003—. Office: Kohls Corp N56 W17000 Ridgewood Dr Menomonee Falls WI 53051-5660

MCDONALD, WILLIAM BRICE, educational association administrator; b. Greenville, Ky., June 16, 1957; s. James Marlin and Joyce Rudale (Cox) M. BS in Polit. Sci., Loyola U., Chgo., 1976, MA in Internat. Rels., 1973; MA in Media, Northeastern U., Chgo., 1985; postgrad., Northwestern U., 1993; DD, St. Johns, Saskatchewan, 1995. Tchr. Chgo. Pub. Schs., 1967-69, libr., 1969-85; coordinator Edn. Service Ctr. 6, 1986-92; coord. Bur. of Librs. Chgo. Pub. Schs., 1992—; CEO Pax Vobiscum, Inc., 1993—. Cons. bd. examiners Chgo. Pub. Schs., 1987; judge, participant Ill. Young Authors, Chgo., 1987-99; advisor Chgo. Tchrs. Libr. Assn., 1988; advisor High Sch. Libr. Media Assn., 1988, treas., 1992—; treas. Chgo. Libr. Club, 1992—; bd. dirs. No. Ill. U. Children's Lit. Inst., 1992-99; edn. cons., 2001—. Author: Alliance for Progress, 1981, Library Networking, 1985, Illinois School Library Media Program Guidelines, 1992. Del. Chgo. Tchrs. Union, 1968-81; bd. dirs. McDonald Charitable Trust, 2002—. George M. Pullman Found. scholar, Chgo., 1966, Kiwanis Internat. scholar, Chgo., 1974, State of Ill. scholar, Chgo., 1978; grantee Northeastern U., Chgo., 1984. Mem. Oriental Inst. Chgo., Breasted Soc., Am. Rsch. Ctr. Egypt (life), Citizens Sch. Com., Friends Chgo. Pub. Libr., Newberry Libr. Assocs., Soc. Sch. Librs. Internat. (nominating com.), Ill. Libr. Assn. (bd. dirs. 1990-92, north cen. evaluation team 1992), Ill. Coalition Libr. Advisors, Assn. Supervision and Curriculum Devel. (Midwest authors selection com. 1993, Chgo. Pub. Libr.-Chgo. Pub. Schs. task force com. 1992—), Children's Reading Roundtable (bd. dirs. 1992—). Avocations: aviation, bibliophile, archeology, stamp collecting/philately. Home: 3750 N Lake Shore Dr Apt 9D Chicago IL 60613-4233 Office: CPS Bur Libr 1819 W Pershing Rd Chicago IL 60609-2300 also: Pax Vobiscum Inc 1820 Campbell La Salle IL 61301

MCDONALD, WILLIAM HECTOR, JR., writer; s. William Hector McDonald and Marcella A. Engelking; m. Carol Jean Henry, Jan. 3, 1970; children: Joshua U., Daya M. AA in Labor Studies, San Jose (Calif.) City Coll., 1976; BA in Pub. Svc. Adminstrn., U. San Francisco, 1978. Author: (non-fiction and poetry) A Spiritual Warrior's Journey: The Inspiring Life Story of a Mystical Warrior, 2003 (Gold medal Am. Authors Assn., 2003), Purple Hearts - Vietnam War Poetry, 2004, Sacred Eye: Poetry in Search of the Divine, 2004; contbr.; (mem. documentary team) In The Shadow of The Blade, radio talk show host KDVS FM 90.3, Davis, Calif. Wedding min. United Faith Ministries. Served with U.S. Army, 1965—68, Vietnam. Decorated DFC, Bronze Star, Purple Heart, 14 Air medals U.S. Army; recipient writing award, Parade Mag., 2002. Mem.: Am. Authors Assn. (life; founding dir., pres. 2003—04). Home: PO Box 2441 Elk Grove CA 95759-2441 Personal E-mail: angelnet@citlink.net.

MCDONALD, WILLIAM HENRY, financial executive; b. Ottawa, Ont., Can., Sept. 8, 1924; s. Joseph and Constance Mary (Gordon) McD.; m. D. Gwen Selkirk, July 8, 1950; 1 child, Barbara Elaine. Grad. high sch. Credit and operating mgr. B.F. Goodrich Co., Winnipeg, Man., Can., 1945-49; fin. adminstrn. officer Govt. Can., Ottawa, 1949-55; asst. gen. mgr. mortgages Bank of N.S., 1955-66; mng. dir. Boyd Stott & McDonald Ltd., Toronto, Ont., 1966-79; exec. v.p., dir. Morguard Trust Co., 1966-74; chmn. bd. Can. Comml. Bank, Toronto, 1976-81, chmn. exec. com., 1981-84; chmn. bd. Can. Comml. Bank Mortgage Investment Corp., 1983-84; pres., CEO, dir. Boyd Stott and McDonald Techs., Ltd., 1984—2003. Pres. Thornton McDonald Assocs., Inc. Mem. bd. govs. J. Douglas Ferguson Hist. Research Found., 1971—. Served with RCNVR, 1943-45. Mem. Can. Paper Money Soc. (hon. pres.), Internat. Bank Note Soc. (life), Can. Credit Inst., Classical & Medieval Numismatic Soc. (exec. sec.). Conservative. Anglican. E-mail: billmcdo@idirect.com.

MCDONALD, WILLIAM HENRY, lawyer; b. Niangua, Mo., Feb. 27, 1946; s. Milburn and Fannie M. McDonald; m. Janice E. Robinson, July 13, 1968; children: Melissa L., Meghan M. BS in Pub. Adminstrn., Southwest Mo. State U., 1968; JD, U. Mo., 1971. Bar: Mo. 1971, U.S. Dist. Ct. (we. dist.) Mo. 1973, U.S. Supreme Ct. 1978, U.S. Ct. Appeals (8th cir.) 1982. Ptnr., pres. Woolsey, Fisher, Whiteaker & McDonald, PC, 1973-95; pres. William H. McDonald & Assocs., PC, Springfield, Mo., 1995—. Chmn. blue ribbon task force on Delivery of Mental Health Services to Southwest Mo., Mo. Commn. Continuing Legal Edn.; pres. Tan Oaks Homeowners Assn.; mem. fin. com. Child Adv. Council, Rep. Nat. Com., Mo. Rep. Com., Greene County Nat. Com.; active various Southwest Mo. State U. Clubs; bd. dirs. Greene County div. Am. Heart Assn., Ozarks regional Am. Athletic Union Jr. Olympics; pres., bd. dirs. Springfield Little Theatre; v.p. pub. affairs Springfield Area C. of C., bd. dirs., 1995-98. Capt. U.S. Army, 1971-73. Named one of Outstanding Young Men Am., 1978, 81, Outstanding Young Men Springfield, 1980. Fellow ABA (life, antitrust and litigation and torts and ins. sects.); mem. ATLA, Fed. Bar Assn., Mo. Bar Assn. (chmn. spol. com. on mandatory continuing edn., various coms., Pres.'s award 1986), Mo. Assn. Trial Attys. (bd. govs. 1998-2001), Springfield Met. Bar Assn. (bd. dirs., chmn. pub. edn. speakers bur.), Met. Bar Assn. St. Louis, Def. Rsch. Inst., Am. Judicature Soc., Am. Bd. Trial Advs. (state coord.), Nat. Bd. Trial Advs., Am. Coll. Barristers, Million Dollar Forum, 31st Jud. Cir. Bar Com. (chmn.), Supreme Ct. Hist. Soc., U. Mo.-Kansas City Sch. Law Found., Springfield Claims Assn. (pres.), U.S. Cavalry Assn. (life), Am. Legion, 1st Inf. Divsn. Soc., K.T., Beta Omega Tau, Kappa Epsilon. Presbyterian. Home: 4857 E Royal Dr Springfield MO 65809-2425

MCDONALD-UMBAYEMAKE, LINDA, librarian, rehabilitation counselor; b. Cleve., Feb. 19, 1953; d. Charles Morgan and Helen Loretta (Ballard) McDonald; children: Manu, Kumar, Bari, Mayi, Thurayya, GlennChinua. AA, Cuyahoga C.C., Cleve., 1980; BA, Kent State U., 1984; MLS, Tex. Woman's U., 1989; MRC, U. Ky., 1998. Dir. African Am. Ctr. Toledo-Lucas County Pub. Libr., Toledo, 1989; libr. young adult, correctional and homebound Cuyahoga County Pub. Libr., Warrensville, Ohio, 1989-90; libr. supr. Western N.Mex. Correctional Facility, Grants, 1990; instr., libr. supr. Santa Fe C.C., 1990; libr. supr. Ga. Dept. Corrections, Buford, 1991; instr. head circulation Ky. State U., Frankfort, 1992-93, instr./ILL/reference libr., 1993-96; pub. svcs. asst. libr. Owensboro C.C., 1996; substitute tchr. Franklin County Pub. Schs., Frankfort, 1997—98; offender rehab counselor, substance abuse program Luther Luckett Correctional Ctr., 1998—99; collection devel. specialist Book Wholesalers Inc., 1999-2000; STAR program coord. U. Akron, Ohio, 2001—02; br. mgr. East Cleve. Pub. Libr. Caledonia Br., Cleve., 2001—. Founder Lumbay, 1997—; mem. Kent Ohio Cable Commn., 2003—. Apptd. to Ky. Foster Care Rev. Bd., 1999—2000; child support, visitation com. Franklin County Family Ct., Ohio, 1999—2000; mem. Bd. Elections Franklin County. Mem.: NAMI, Nat. Rehab. Assn., Black Caucus of ALA (chair new mem. orientation com. 1994—96, membership com. 1989—96, ALA Shirley Olofson com. 1993—96, mem. minority recruitment com. 1993—96), Chi Sigma Iota. E-mail: lumbay2001@yahoo.com.

MCDONALD-WEST, SANDI MACLEAN, headmaster, consultant; b. Lowell, Mass., May 8, 1930; d. Walter Allan and Celina Louise (Lalime) MacLean; m. Thomas D. McDonald, Sept. 8, 1951 (div.); children: Todd F., Brooke Goodfriend, Ned M., Reid A., Heather McDonald McLean. BA, DePauw U., 1951; MA, Fairleigh Dickinson U., 1966; MEd, North Tex. State U., 1980. Cert. in Montessori teaching. Tchr., adminstr. Hudson (Ohio) Montessori Sch., 1966-68, Berea (Ohio) Montessori Sch., 1968-70, Creative Learning Ctr., Dallas, 1970-71; tchr., head of lower sch. The Selwyn Sch., Denton, Tex., 1971-83; tchr., headmaster Cimarron Sch., Enid, Okla., 1983-87; cons. Corpus Christi (Tex.) Montessori Sch., 1987-89, Azlann-Eren Horn Montessori Sch., Denton, 1989-95, Highland Meadow Montessori Acad., Southlake, Tex., 1994-2001, various pub. and pvt. Montessori Schs., 1999—. Ednl. dir., pres. Southwestern Montessori Tchg. Ctr., Inc., Denton, 1974—; adj. prof. North Tex. State U., Denton, 1979-80; cons., lectr. Am. Montessori Soc., N.Y.C., 1970—, Japanese Montessori Soc., 1978—, also pub. and pvt. schs., 1972—; chair commn. for accreditation Montessori Accreditation Coun. Tchr. Edn., 1991-97, chair emerita, 1997—; cons. Public Montessori Programs, 1995-. Developer various Montessori materials; contbr. articles to profl. jours. Mem. Am. Montessori Soc. (life), No. Ohio Montessori Assn. (pres. 1968-70), Assn. Montessori Internat., N.Am. Montessori Tchrs. Assn., LWV, Concerned Scientists. Avocations: ecology, golf, reading, travel. Home: 2005 Marshall Rd Denton TX 76207-3316 E-mail: swest4smtc@aol.com.

MCDONELL, HORACE GEORGE, JR., instrument company executive; b. N.Y.C., Sept. 23, 1928; s. Horace Gustave and Anabel (Armstrong) McD.; m. Eileen Romar, Sept. 6, 1952; children: Victoria (dec.), Diane, Horace. AB, Adelphi Coll., 1952; postgrad., Harvard U., 1962; DHL, Adelphi Coll., 2002. Engr. Sperry Gyroscope Co., N.Y.C., 1952; with Perkin-Elmer Corp., Norwalk, Conn., 1963—, mgr. instrument group, 1967-77, v.p., 1966-69, sr. v.p., 1969-77, exec. v.p., 1977-80, pres., 1980-85, chmn., 1985-90, ret., 1990. Bd. dirs. Perkin Elmer, Ltd., U.K. UniRoyal, Inc., Perkin Elmer Internat., Inc., Harvey Hubbell, Inc., Ethan Allen Inc.; Mem. adv. task force on export controls U.S. Def. Sci. Bd., 1975—, chmn. instrumentation subcom., 1975—. Mem. Bd. Edn., Ridgefield, Conn., 1969; Bd. dirs. Conn. Sci. Fair.; Trustee, bd. dirs. Danbury (Conn.) Hosp.; trustee Adelphi U.; bd. dirs. Danbury Health Svcs. With AUS, 1946-48. Mem. Sci. Apparatus Maker Assn. (dir., chmn. analytical instrument sect.), Am. Inst. Physics, AAAS, Instrument Soc. Am., Am. Electronics Assn. (bd. dirs. 1984-89, chmn. 1987) Home: 740 Bald Eagle Dr Naples FL 34105-7409 E-mail: chatham28@aol.com.

MCDONELL, NEIL EDWIN, lawyer; b. Johnson City, N.Y., May 30, 1952; s. Alexander Edwin McDonell and Loretta Arlene Terry; m. Margaret Lynn Moline, June 18, 1978; children: Adam, Aaron. AB in Philosophy and English Lit., U. Mich., 1974; PhD in Philosphy, Harvard U., 1979; JD, Columbia U., 1983. Bar: N.Y. 1984. Asst. prof. philosophy Middlebury (Vt.) Coll., 1979-80; assoc. Battle Fowler, N.Y.C., 1983-89, Marks & Murase, N.Y.C., 1989-92, ptnr., 1992-96, Dorsey & Whitney LLP, N.Y.C., 1996—. Editor-in-chief Columbia Jour. Tranational Law, 1982-83, bd. dirs., 1989—; contbr. articles to profl. jours. Mem. ABA (internat., sci., tech., and antitrust sects.), N.Y. State Bar Assn., Internat. Trade Commn. Trial Lawyers Assn., Harvard Club, Phi Beta Kappa. Avocations: literature, history, poetry. Office: Dorsey & Whitney LLP 250 Park Ave New York NY 10177-0001

MCDONELL, ROBERT TERRY, magazine editor, novelist; b. Norfolk, Va., Aug. 1, 1944; s. Robert Meinard and Irma Sophronia (Nelson) McD.; m. Joan Raffeld Hitzig, June 15, 1981; Robert Nicholas Campbell, Thomas Hunter Campbell. Student, U. Calif., Berkeley, 1962-63, San Jose State U., 1963-64; BA in Art, U. Calif., Irvine, 1967. With AP, N.Y.C., 1970-72; reporter Los Angeles Weekly, 1972-73; asso. editor San Francisco mag., 1974-76, City mag., San Francisco, 1976-77; sr. editor San Francisco mag., 1977, Outside mag., San Francisco, 1978-79; founding editor Rocky Mountain mag., Denver, 1979-80; mng. editor Rolling Stone mag., N.Y.C., 1980-83; asst. mng. editor Newsweek Mag., N.Y.C., 1983-86; founder Smart mag., N.Y.C., 1986-90; editor-in-chief Esquire mag., N.Y.C., 1990-93; editor-in-chief, pub. Sports Afield Mag., N.Y.C., 1994-97; editor Men's Journal, 1997-99; v.p. Wenner Media, 1997—; editor-in-chief US Weekly, N.Y.C., 2000—02; mng. editor Sports Illustrated, N.Y.C., 2002—. Author: California Bloodstock, 1980, paperback edit., 1989; screenwriter: Miami Vice, China Beach. Office: US Weekly 1290 Avenue Of The Americas Fl 2 New York NY 10104-0298

MCDONELL, TERRY, publishing executive, writer, editor; b. Santa Cruz, Calif. m. Joanie McDonell; children: Robert Nicholas, Thomas Hunter. Attended, U. Calif. at Berkeley and Irvine. Worked on film in Tehran, Iran; began career in journalism as freelance photographer; writer, photographer NY Associated Press, 1971; founder, writer, editor Outside, 1977, Rocky Mountain, 1979; mng. editor Rolling Stone, 1981—83; asst. mng. editor Newsweek, 1983—88; founder, pres., editor Smart, 1988—90; editor-in-chief Esquire, 1990—93; editor-in-chief, publishing editor Sports Afield, 1993—97, publishing/editorial dir., 1997; editor Men's Jour., 1997—99, editor-in-chief, 1999—2000, US Weekly, 2000—02; mng. editor Sports Illustrated, 2002—; v.p. Wenner Media. Author: California Bloodstock, 1980; screenwriter: TV series Miami Vice, China Beach. Avocations: painting, surfing. Office: Sports Illustrated 135 West 50th St New York NY 10020 Office Phone: 212-522-4044. Office Fax: 212-467-4049.*

MCDONNELL, ARCHIE JOSEPH, environmental engineer; b. N.Y.C., June 3, 1936; s. Patrick and Margaret (O'Reilly) McD.; m. Nancy Carol Schaeffer, June 18, 1966; children: Patrick, Sean. BS in Civil Engring., Manhattan Coll., 1958; MS in Civil Engring., Pa. State U., 1960, PhD in Civil Engring., 1963. Prof. Pa. State U., University Park, 1963-96; asst. dir. Water Resources Rsch. Ctr., Pa. State U., 1969-82; dir. Inst. for Rsch. on Land and Water Resources, Pa. State U., 1982-86, Environ. Resources Rsch. Inst., Pa. State U., 1986—. Bd. dirs. Pa. Environ. Coun., 1989-92, Nat. Assn. State Univs. & Land Grant Colls., 1990-92, chmn. water resources com., 1985-91; mem. rsch. & modeling subcom. EPA Chesapeake Bay Program, 1984-86, sci. & tech. adv. com., 1984—, exec. com., 1988-92; U.S. rep. Internat. Joint Commn., 1976-79, 87-89; mem. Pa. State Conservation Com., 1988-89, water resources policy adv. com. Pa. Dept. Environ. Resources, 1979-82, air & water quality tech. adv. com., 1983—, chmn. water quality subcom., 1986-88; chmn. Northeast Assn. Water Inst. Dirs., 1973-74; mem. exec. com. Nat. Assn. Water Inst. Dirs., 1975-78. Contbr. articles to profl. jours. Fellow U.S. Pub. Health Svc., 1961-62; recipient Commendation cert. Internat. Joint Commn., Conservationist of Yr. award Chesapeake Bay Found., Washington, 1986, Outstanding Rsch. award Pa. State U. Engring. Soc., 1988, Outstanding Profl. Rsch. award Water Pollution Control Assn. Pa., 1990, Karl M. Mason medal Pa. Assn. Environ. Profls., 1991, Gabriel Narutowicz medal Ministry Environ. Protection and Natural Resources, Poland, 1991. Mem. ASCE (chmn. 1972-73, exec. com. 1976-80, J. James R. Croes Rsch. medal 1976, Outstanding Svc. award 1981), Water Environ. Fedn. (co-chmn. 1991—), Fed. Water Pollution Control Fedn., Internat. Assn. Water Pollution Rsch., Am. Soc. Limnology and Oceanography, Chi Epsilon, Sigma Xi, Phi Kappa Phi. Achievements include demonstration of low cost treatment method for renovation of acidmine waters. Office: Pa State U 100 Land Water Research University Park PA 16802-4900

MCDONNELL, BARBARA, lawyer; B, Univ. Ill.; M, Univ. Iowa; JD magna cum laude, Univ. Pa. Law Sch. With Sherman & Howard, 1982-87; staff atty. Colo. Ct. Appeals, 1988-89; law clerk Phila.; legal adv. Gov. Romer, dep. dir. policy and rsch., 1989-90; exec. dir. Colo. Dept. Human Svcs., 1991-99; chief dep. atty. gen. Office of Atty. Gen., Denver, 1999—. Rep. Nursing Adv. bd., team leader Policy Acad. Team on Families & Children At Risk. Office: Office Atty Gen 1525 Sherman St Denver CO 80203-1702

MCDONNELL, DAVID CROFT, diversified financial services company executive; Nat. mng. ptnr. Grant Thornton Internat. (UK office), 1989—2001; global CEO Grant Thornton Internat., 2001—. Office: Grant Thornton Internat 1 Prudential Plz Ste 800 130 E Randolph Dr Chicago IL 60601-6050

MCDONNELL, JOHN L., JR., lawyer; JD, U. San Francisco. Bar: Calif. 1964. With Crosby Heafey Roach & May; counsel Reed Smith, Oakland, Calif., 2003—. Lectr. in field; cons. in field. Contbr. articles to profl. jours. Trustee East Bay Cmty. Found., Holy Names Coll.; chair bd. trustees Oakland Mus. Calif. Found.; founder, bd. mem., sec. Calif. Patrons of the Arts in the Vatican Mus.; bd. counselors U. San Francisco Sch. Law. Fellow: Am. Coll. Trust and Estate Counsel (Calif. state chair, bd. regents); mem.: ABA (bd. govs. 14th dist. 2000—03, mem. drug adv. task force, chair estate planning, trust and probate law sect., chair probate com., advisor standing com. on lawyer competence), Internat. Acad. Estate and Trust Law (acaemician), State Bar Calif. (bd. govs., v.p., chair estate planning, trust and probate law sect. legal svcs. com., com. on profl. stds. and admissions, consortium on competence), Alameda County Bar Assn. Avocations: choral music, reading, foreign languages, fishing. Office: Reed Smith 26th Fl 1999 Harrison St Oakland CA 94612-3573

MC DONNELL, LORETTA WADE, lawyer; b. San Francisco, May 31, 1940; d. John H. and Helen M. (Tinney) Wade; m. John L. McDonnell, Jr., Apr. 27, 1963 (div.); children: Elizabeth, John L. III, Thomas. BA, San Francisco Coll. for Women, 1962; MA, Stanford U., 1963; grad., Coro Pub. Affairs Tng. Program for Women, 1976; JD, Golden Gate U., 1989. Bar: Calif. 1990. H.S. tchr. East Side Union H.S. Dist., San Jose, Calif., 1962-63; project coord. Inter Agy. Collaboration Effort, Oakland, Calif., 1977; legal asst. Pacific Gas and Elec. Co., San Francisco, 1980-89, coord., 1989-90, atty., 1990—. Assoc. editor The Antiphon, 1971-74. Chmn. spkrs. panel Focus on Am. Women, 1973-74; bd. dirs. Alameda County Vol. Bur., 1973-74, St. Paul's Sch., 1974-75, Carden Redwood Sch., 1975-77; budget panelist United Way of Bay Area, 1975-77; cmty. v.p. Jr. League, 1976-77, nat. conv. del., 1976. Mem. Jr. League Oakland-East Bay, Inc., Stanford Alumni Assn. Democrat.

MCDONNELL, MICHAEL R. communications executive; With Pricewaterhouse, 1986—89, mgr. high-tech. group, 1989—96; ptnr. Pricewaterhouse-Coopers LLP, 1996—2000; sr. v.p., CFO EchoStar Comms., Littleton, Colo., 2000—. Office: EchoStar Communications 5701 South Santa Fe Drive Littleton CO 80120

MCDONNELL, PETER, ophthalmologist, health facility administrator, medical educator, researcher; b. 1959; m. Jan Menefee McDonnell; 3 children. B in Chemistry, Dartmouth Coll., 1978; grad., Johns Hopkins U., 1982. Intern in pathology and emergency medicine John Hopkins U. Sch. Medicine, resident in ophthalmology; full prof. U. So. Calif., 1988; Irving H. Leopold prof. and chair ophthalmology dept. U. Calif., Irvine, 1999; dir. Wilmer Eye Inst. Johns Hopkins Hosp., Balt., 2003—. Mem. editl bd.: six ophthalmology jours. Recipient Honor award, Am. Acad. Ophthalmology, 1991, Sr. Achievement award, 2001, awards for ophthalmic rsch., CIBA Vision, Rsch. to Prevent Blindness, Alcon Rsch. Inst. Achievements include first physician to use excimer ("cool") lasers in the treatment of astigmatism in the 1990s; led the national clinical trials of the technology, which generates high-power, ultraviolet pulses that strip electrons from the nucleus of an atom, vaporizing tissue with shock waves. Office: Wilmer Eye Inst John Hopkins Hosp 600 North Wolfe St Baltimore MD 21287

MCDONNELL, SANFORD NOYES, aircraft company executive; b. Little Rock, Oct. 12, 1922; s. William Archie and Carolyn (Cherry) McD.; m. Priscilla Robb, Sept. 3, 1946; children: Robbin McDonnell MacVittie, William Randall. BA in Econs., Princeton U., 1945; BS in Mech. Engring., U. Colo., 1948; MS in Applied Mechanics, Washington U., St. Louis, 1954. With McDonnell Douglas Corp. (formerly McDonnell Aircraft Corp.), St. Louis, 1948—, v.p., 1959-66, pres. McDonnell Aircraft div., 1966-71, corp. exec. v.p., 1971, corp. pres., from 1971, chief exec. officer, from 1972, chmn., 1980-88, chmn. emeritus, 1988—. Active St. Louis United Way; mem. exec. bd. St. Louis and nat. councils Boy Scouts Am.; trustee, elder Presbyn. Ch.; chmn. bd. Character Edn. Partnership, Washington, 1993—. Fellow AIAA; mem. Navy League U.S. (life), Tau Beta Pi. Office: McDonnell Douglas Corp PO Box 516 Saint Louis MO 63166-0516

MCDONNELL, TIMOTHY ANTHONY, bishop; b. N.Y., Dec. 23, 1937; Ordained priest N.Y., ordained bishop 2001. Aux. bishop, N.Y.C., 2001; titular bishop of Semina, 2001; bishop Diocese of Springfield, 2004—. Office: Diocese of Springfield PO Box 1730 76 Elliot St Springfield MA 01101*

MCDONOUGH, ANN PATRICE, ice skater; b. Korea, May 29, 1985; Grad. high sch. Figure skater competing numerous events including State Farm U.S. Championships, 1999—, Jr. Grand Prix, Norway, Mex., 2000, World Jr. Championships, 2001—02, Four Continents Championships, 2002—03, Campbell's Classic, 2002—03, Smart Ones Skate Am., 2002, ABC Sports Internat. Figure Skating Challenge, 2003, Cup of China, 2003, numerous other competitions. Recipient numerous 1st place awards including, Gardena Spring Trophy, Southwestern Sectional, Midwestern Sectional, Jr. Grand Prix Final, Southwestern Regional, World Jr. Championships, numerous 2d place awards including, Jr. GLIrand Prix Norway, World Jr. Championships, Nebelhorn Trophy, Campbell's Class, Smart Ones Skate Am. Office: US Figure Skating Hdqrs 20 First St Colorado Springs CO 80906

MCDONOUGH, BRIDGET ANN, music theatre company director; b. Milw., June 19, 1956; d. James and Lois (Hunzinger) McD.; m. Gregory Paul Opelka, Sept. 20, 1986 (div. Aug. 1993); m. Robert Markey, Feb. 29, 2000. BS, Northwestern U., 1978. Bus. mgr. Organic Theater Co., Chgo., 1979-80; mng. dir., founder Light Opera Works, Evanston, Ill., 1980—. U.S. rep. European Congress Musical Theatre, 1995. Founder, mem. Chgo. Music Alliance, 1984—, pres., 1995-98; mem. Ill. Arts Alliance; bd. dirs., Nat. Alliance for Musical Theatre, 2001—, sec., 2001—04; bd. dirs. Evanston Convention Visitors Bur., 1999-2002; mem. alumni adv. bd. Northwestern U. Sch. Speech, 1999-2002. Recipient Women on the Move award Evanston YWCA, 1991. Mem. Evanston C. of C. (bd. dirs., 1993-99), Rotary (pres. Evanston chpt. 1999-2000). Avocation: birding. Office: Light Opera Works 927 Noyes St Evanston IL 60201-6206

MCDONOUGH, GERALD CLYDE, transportation leasing company executive; b. Cleve., 1928. B.B.A., Case Western Res. U., 1953. Treas. Molded Fiberglass Co., 1964-69, Rexnord Inc., 1969-74; v.p. and treas. Reliance Electric Co., 1974-79; exec. v.p., dir. Leaseway Transp. Corp., Cleve., 1979-82, chmn. and chief exec. officer, 1982-88, acting pres., chief operating officer, 1985, chmn., York Internat. Corp., York, Pa., 1999—; dir. AmeriTrust Corp., Brush Wellman Inc., York Internat. Corp, 1988—. Office: York Internat Corp 631 S Richland Ave York PA 17403

MCDONOUGH, JOHN J. household products company executive; V.p. fin. Litton med. products Litton Industries; v.p., treas. Am. TV and Comm., Denver; CFO, v.p. Blount, Inc., Montgomery, Ala.; sr. v.p. fin. Newell, 1981-83; founder, pres. GENDEX Corp. (merger with Dentsply Internat. 1993), 1983-93; vice chmn., CEO Dentsply Internat., 1993-95; CEO, vice chmn. bd. Newell Rubbermaid Inc., Freeport, Ill., 1997-2000, also bd. dirs. Chmn. bd. dirs. Juvenile Diabetes Found., 1998—, former mem. exec. and fin. coms., chmn. planned giving and vice chmn. $200 million internat. initiative. Named Man of Yr. Chgo. chpt. Juvenile Diabetes Found., 2000. Office: Newell Rubbermaid Inc 29 E Stephenson St Freeport IL 61032-4235

MCDONOUGH, JOHN MICHAEL, lawyer; b. Evanston, Ill., Dec. 30, 1944; s. John Justin and Anne Elizabeth (O'Brien) McD.; m. Susan J. Moran, Sept. 19, 1981; children: John E., Catherine Anne. AB, Princeton U., 1966;

LLB, Yale U., 1969. Bar: Ill. 1969, Fla. 1991. Assoc. Sidley & Austin, Chgo., 1969-75, ptnr., 1975—. Bd. dirs. Met. Planning Coun., 1978—, pres., 1982-84; bd. dirs. Ctr. Am. Archeology, 1980-85, chmn., 1982-84; bd. dirs. Leadership Greater Chgo., 1984-90, sec.-treas., 1987-90; bd. dis. Brian Rsch. Found., 1985—, pres., 1989-94. With JAGC, USAR, 1969-75. Mem. ABA, Ill. Bar Assn., Chgo. Bar Assn., Racquet Club, Saddle & Cycle Club, Commonwealth Club, Econ. Club, Phi Beta Kappa. Democrat. Episcopalian. Home: 1407 N Dearborn St Chicago IL 60610-1505 Office: Sidley & Austin 425 W Surf St Apt 605 Chicago IL 60657-6139

MC DONOUGH, JOHN RICHARD, lawyer; b. St. Paul, May 16, 1919; s. John Richard and Gena (Olson) McD.; m. Margaret Poot, Sept. 10, 1944; children— Jana Margaret, John Jacobus. Student, U. Wash., 1937-40; LLB, Columbia U., 1946. Bar: Calif. 1949. Asst. prof. law Stanford U., 1946-49, prof., 1952-69; assoc. firm Brobeck, Phleger & Harrison, San Francisco, 1949-52; asst. dep. atty. gen. U.S. Dept. Justice, Washington, 1967-68, assoc. dep. atty. gen., 1968; of counsel and ptnr. firm Keatinge & Sterling, L.A., 1969-70; ptnr. Ball, Hunt, Hart, Brown and Baerwitz, L.A., 1970-90, Carlsmith Ball Wichman Case & Ichiki, L.A., 1990-96, of counsel, 1996-98, Carlsmith Ball, L.A., 1998—2002. Exec. sec. Calif. Law Revision Commn., 1954-59, mem. commn., 1959-67, vice chmn., 1960-64, chmn., 1964-65. Served with U.S. Army, 1942—46. Mem.: Am. Coll. Trial Lawyers. Democrat.

MCDONOUGH, JOSEPH CORBETT, former army officer, aviation consultant; b. N.Y.C., Sept. 30, 1924; s. Joseph Walter and Catherine Loretta (Corbett) McD.; m. Mary Patricia Aaron, June 10, 1945; children— Joseph Corbett, Thomas Michael, Robert Timothy. BS, U.S. Mil. Acad., West Point, N.Y., 1945; MA, Georgetown U., Washington, 1957; grad., U.S. Command and Gen. Staff Coll., 1954, Brit. Staff Coll., Camberly, 1958, U.S. Army War Coll., 1965. Commd. 2d lt. U.S. Army, 1945, advanced through grades to maj. gen., 1973, served in Philippine Scouts, 1945-47, served with 82d Airborne Div., 1948-51, served with 40th Inf. Div., 1952-53; instr. U.S. Naval Acad., 1954-57; staff and command U.S. Army, Europe, 1958-61; with Office Personnel Mgmt., Dept. Army, Washington, 1961-64; mem. staff Office Under Sec. Army, Washington, 1965-67; bn. and brigade comdr. 1st Calvary Div. U.S. Army, Vietnam, 1967-68; with Joint Chiefs of Staff, Washington, 1968-71; brigade and asst. div. comdr. Vietnam, 1971-72; chief of staff CENTO, Turkey, 1972-73; comdg. gen. 8th Inf. Div. U.S. Army, Germany, 1973-75; U.S. Comdr. Berlin, 1975-78; ret. U.S. Army, 1978; cons. numerous govt. agys., 1978-79; v.p., gen. mgr. Butler Aviation, BWI Airport, Md., 1980-83; v.p. ops. Butler Aviation Internat., 1983-86; cons., 1986-88; exec. v.p. Butler Aviation Internat., 1988-90; cons., 1990—. Decorated D.S.M. with oak leaf cluster, Silver Star, Legion of Merit with oak leaf cluster, D.F.C., Bronze Star, Air medal with 32 oak leaf clusters, Army Commendation medal with 2 oak leaf clusters. Mem. Assn. U.S. Army, Army Aviation Assn. Address: Ste 306 19385 Cypress Ridge Ter Leesburg VA 20176-5164

MCDONOUGH, PATRICK DENNIS, academic administrator; b. Virginia, Minn., Jan. 30, 1942; s. James Morris and Vivian S. McDonough; children: Jeffrey, Anne; m. Karen Howe, June 27, 1981. BA cum laude, Moorhead State U., 1964; MA, U. Kans., 1969; PhD, U. Minn., 1972. Asst. prof. theatre Emporia (Kans.) State U., 1966-70; dir. sales, mktg. Guthrie Theater, Mpls., 1971, 72; asst. prof. speech, dir. of forensics Moorhead (Minn.) State U., 1972-73; assoc. prof., mng. dir., chair Marshall Performing Arts Ctr. U. Minn., Duluth, 1973-76; dean fine arts, prof. U. Evansville (Ind.), 1976-81; vice chancellor, prof. U. Wis., Stevens Point, 1981-84; program dir. (edn. and leadership) W.K. Kellogg Found., Battle Creek, Mich., 1984-89; 15th pres., prof. theatre and mgmt. Marietta (Ohio) Coll., 1989-95, exec. dir. McDonough Ctr. for Leadership and Bus.; assoc. vice chancellor planning and analysis Calif. State U. Sys., Long Beach, 1995-97, prof. theatre, 1997—; exec. v.p. higher edn. practice The Charitable Resources Group, Pitts. Pres. Emporia chpt. AAUP, 1969; cons. Lexington (Ky.) Children's Theatre, 1979; festival evaluator Am. Coll. Theatre Festival, 4 states, 1975-76; mem. theatre panel Ind. Arts Commn., Indpls., 1977-79; arts orgn. panel Mich. Arts Bd., Detroit, 1985-89; presenter in field. Producer, dir. 100 plays and musicals, 1964-84; contbr. articles to profl. jours. Bd. visitors U. Wis., Stevens Point, 1988-90; dist. organizer Eugene McCarthy Presdl. Campaign, Emporia, 1968; mem. leadership commn. Am. Coun. Edn., 1989-94; mem. exec. com. Campus Compact, 1990-95; bd. dirs. numerous civic and arts orgns., 1973-90; chmn. govs. adv. com. on vol. svc., Ohio, 1990-93; mem. leadership studies project U. Md., 1994—. Recipient Disting. Alumnus award Moorhead State U., 1989; grantee Minn. Arts Bd., 1974-76, Ind. Arts Commn., 1976-79. Mem. Am. Assn. Higher Edn., Univ. and Coll. Theatre Assn. (v.p. 1982-83), Marietta Country Club, Stevens Point Country Club, Athletic Club of Columbus. Democrat. Episcopalian. Avocations: travel, international relations, arts. Office: Dept Theatre 1250 N Bellflower Blvd Long Beach CA 90840-0006 E-mail: mcdonou@gte.net.

MCDONOUGH, PAUL GERARD, obstetrician-gynecologist, educator; b. Scranton, Pa., May 1, 1930; s. Gerard A. and Mary E. (Gannon) McD.; m. Nicole Moreau, Sept. 9, 1959; children: Diana, Michel, Jean Paul. BS in Biology magna cum laude, Holy Cross Coll., Worcester, Mass., 1952; MD, Thomas Jefferson U., 1956. Diplomate: Am. Bd. Ob-Gyn. Intern Phila. Gen. Hosp., 1956-57; resident in diagnostic and therapeutic radiology U. Calif. Med. Center, San Francisco, 1960-61; resident in ob-gyn Phila. Gen. Hosp., 1961-64; research fellow Med. Coll. Ga., 1964-66, asst. prof. ob-gyn, 1966-67, assoc. prof., 1970-75, prof., chief reproductive endocrine div., 1975-83, acting dir. Human Genetics Inst., 1983-99; now prof. emeritus. Cons. Dwight D. Eisenhower Army Med. Center, Univ. Hosp., Meml. Med. Center, Savannah, Ga., Columbus (Ga.) Med. Center, Greenville (S.C.) Gen. Hosp. Contbr. articles to profl. jours., chpts. in books. Served to capt. M.C. USAF, 1957-60. Recipient Billings Silver medal AMA, 1965, Aesculapius award Med. Assn. Ga., cert. of award So. Med. Assn., 1969 Fellow Am. Coll. Ob-Gyn; mem. Ga. Ob-Gyn Soc., Am. Fertility Soc. (dir.), Med. Assn. Ga., Richmond County Med. Soc., So. Med. Assn., Endocrine Soc., South Atlantic Assn. Obstetricians and Gynecologists, Am. Soc. Human Genetics, Am. Assn. Gynecol. Laparoscopists, Atlanta Genetics, Soc., AAUP, Ga. Perinatal Assn., Internat. Soc. Pediatric and Adolescent Gynecology (exec. com.), Internat. Fedn. Infantile and Juvenile Gynecology (v.p. U.S. sector), Alpha Omega Alpha. Roman Catholic. Office: Med Coll Ga Dept Ob-Gyn 1120 15th St Augusta GA 30912-0006

MCDONOUGH, PAUL H. corporate financial executive; Various fin. positions Sears Roebuck & Co., 1995—99; asst. treas. St. Paul Co., Inc., St. Paul, 1999—2002, v.p., corp. treas., 2002—. Office: St Paul Co Inc 385 Washington St Saint Paul MN 55102

MCDONOUGH, RICHARD ALOYSIUS, IV, investment banker; b. Ann Arbor, Mich., Oct. 20, 1966; s. Richard Aloysius McDonough III and Mary (Carlin) Camp; m. Gerda-Marie Kenyon, 1995; 1 child, Eliza Lily. AB, Dartmouth Coll., 1988; MBA, Harvard U., 1993. Fin. analyst Merrill Lynch & Co., N.Y.C., 1988-90, L.A., 1990-91; with corp. devel. RJR Nabisco, Inc., N.Y.C., 1992; dir. The Bridgeford Group, N.Y.C., 1993-97; mng. dir. The Beacon Group, N.Y.C., 1997-2000; mng. dir., group head So. Calif. group J.P. Morgan H&Q, 2001—. Merrill Lynch chmn. Fin. Analyst Fundraiser for N.Y. Times Neediest Cases Fund, N.Y.C., 1988-90 Mem. The Met. Club, Harvard Bus. Club Greater N.Y., Harvard Club of N.Y., Yale Club of N.Y.C., Dartmouth Club of N.Y. Republican. Roman Catholic. Avocations: creative writing, travel, recreational sports. Office: JP Morgan H&Q 10877 Wilshire Blvd Los Angeles CA 90024 Address: 253 26th St Santa Monica CA 90402-2545

MC DONOUGH, RICHARD DOYLE, retired paper company executive; b. St. Stephen, N.B., Can., May 8, 1931; s. Kenneth Paul and Mary (Doyle) McD.; m. Caroline Wilkins, July 7, 1956; children: Elizabeth Wilkins, Richard David, Philip Bradford. AB, Dartmouth Coll., 1952. Mgmt. trainee Gen. Electric Co., Lynn, Mass., 1953-56, various fin. positions lamp div. Monterrey, Mex., 1956-59, controller Mexican subs. Mexico City, 1959-63; cost supr. Singer Co., N.Y.C., 1964, fin. dir. Clydebank, Scotland, 1965-66, controller Eur. div. London, 1967-69; v.p. ops. Home Furnishings Group, 1969; v.p., corp. contr. Singer Co., N.Y.C., 1970-73, corp. v.p., pres. mail order div. Hanau, Fed. Republic of Germany, 1973-76, v.p. London, 1976-79; sr. v.p., CFO, dir. Bowater Inc., Darien, Conn., 1979-92, vice chmn., CFO, 1992-93, vice chmn., 1993-94, ret., 1994. Dir. Xylem Investments. Mem. Am. Forest and Paper Assn. (fin. com. 1980-94, steering com. 1987-94, vice chmn. 1989-91, chmn. 1991-93), Fin. Execs. Inst., Greenwich Country Club, Harbour Ridge Yacht and Country Club. Republican. Episcopalian. Avocations: scuba, opera.

MCDONOUGH, RICHARD MICHAEL, philosophy educator; b. Pitts., Jan. 29, 1950; s. Walter and Marilyn (Duman) McD.; m. Mary Lau, July 26, 1991. BA summa cum laude, U. Pitts., 1971; MA, Cornell U., 1974, PhD, 1975. Asst. prof. philosophy Bates Coll., Lewiston, Maine, 1975-82; sr. lectr. Nat. U. Singapore, 1982-91; asst. prof. philosophy U. Tulsa, 1991—; assoc. prof. philosophy, psychology U. Putra Malaysia, Selangor, 1997-98; prof. philosophy Overseas Family School: The College, Republic of Singapore, 1999—, lectr., 1999—. Author: The Argument of the Tractatus, 1986; contbr. articles to profl. jours. Woodrow Wilson fellow, 1971-72, NSF fellow, 1971-74; postdoctoral rsch. grantee NEH, Ind. U., 1980-81. Mem. Australasian Debating Fedn. (hon. life, adjudicator 1991—), Phi Kappa Phi. Achievements include prodn. of original interpretation of Wittgenstein's logical-metaphys. sys., original application Kantian Copernican Revolution to philosophy of lang.; significant interdisciplinary work logic, linguistics, psychology & philosophy. Office: Dept Philosophy OFS Coll 25F Paterson Rd Singapore 238515 Singapore

MCDONOUGH, RUSSELL CHARLES, retired state supreme court justice; b. Glendive, Mont., Dec. 7, 1924; s. Roy James and Elsie Marie (Johnson) McD.; m. Dora Jean Bidwell, Mar. 17, 1946; children: Ann Remmich, Michael, Kay Jensen, Kevin, Daniel, Mary Garfield. JD, George Washington U., 1949. Bar: Mont. 1950. Pvt. practice, Glendive, Mont., 1950-83; judge Gen. Jurisdiction State of Montana, Glendive, 1983-87; justice Mont. Supreme Ct., Helena, 1987-93, ret., 1993. City atty. City of Glendive, 1953-57; county atty. Dawson County, Mon., 1957-63; del. Mont. Constl. Conv., Helena, 1972. 1st lt. AC, U.S. Army, 1943-45, ETO. Decorated DFC. Mem. Mont. Bar Assn. Roman Catholic. Home: PO Box 60 Circle MT 59215-0060

MCDONOUGH, THOMAS P. health facility administrator; BBA, Northeastern U. COO Jardine Group Svcs. Corp., 1988—93; pres. Harrington Svcs. Corp., 1993—95; sr. v.p. MetraHealth Cos., Inc., 1995; sr. v.p. claim svcs. United HealthCare, Inc., 1995—97, exec. v.p. customer svc. group, 1997, CEO Uniprise, 1997—98; exec. v.p. Coventry Health Care, Bethesda, Md., 1998—, COO, 1998—. Bd. dir. FireLogic Homes. Office: Coventry Health Care 6705 Rockleged Drive Bethesda MD 20817

MCDONOUGH, WILLIAM J. banker; b. Chgo., 1934; married. BS, Coll. of Holy Cross, 1956; MA, Georgetown U., 1962. With Dept. of State, 1961-67, 1st Nat. Bank of Chgo., 1967-89, asst. v.p. internat. banking dept., 1967-70, v.p., gen. mgr. Paris, 1970-72, area head, Europe, Mid. East and Africa, 1972-73, sr. v.p., head internat. banking dept., 1973-75, exec. v.p., 1975-86, CFO, 1982-89, chmn. asset and liability mgmt. com., until 1989; vice chmn. 1st Chgo. Corp. and 1st Nat. Bank Chgo., 1986-89; exec. v.p., head markets group Fed. Res. Bank of N.Y., N.Y.C., 1992-93, pres., CEO, 1993—2003; chmn. Pub. Co. Acctg. Oversight Bd., Washington, 2003—. Bd. dirs. N.Y. Philharm. Orch., Fgn. Policy Assn., Inst. for Internat. Econs.; bd. dirs. Georgetown U.; bd. advisors Yale Sch. Mgmt. Mem.: Coun. Fgn. Rels. Office: Pub Co Acctg Oversight Bd 1666 K St NW Washington DC 20006 Business E-Mail: mcdonoughw@pcaobus.org.

MCDONOUGH-TREICHLER, JUDITH DIANNE, medical educator, consultant; b. L.A., Aug. 15, 1938; d. William Charles and Eleanor (Lewis) Anderson; m. Raymond Milan McDonough, Mar. 2, 1957 (div. Oct. 2, 1974); children: Joyce Churchill, Steven McDonough, Jill Cannon; m. John Rex Treichler, June 2, 1985. BS in Health Edn., Calif. State U., Long Beach, 1978; MS in Health Care Adminstrn., U. LaVerne, Calif., 1981; PhD in Pub. Health, Loma Linda U., Calif., 1991. Cert. registered nurse, Calif., health edn. specialist nat. Commn. for Health Edn. Credentialing. Dir. health edn. Nat. Med. Enterprises, Lakewood, Calif., 1972-80, Taif, Saudi Arabia, 1980-82, health educator Manila, Philippines, 1983; dir. health promotion and edn. Med. Ptnrs. US Family Care, Montclair, Calif., 1992-97; adj. faculty prof. U. LaVerne, Calif., 1986—, U. Phoenix, Ontario, Calif., 1996—, Crafton Hills Coll., Yucaipa, Calif., 1997—; owner, exec. v.p. JJS Health Edn. Cons., Rancho Cucamonga, Calif., 1996—. Rsch. asst. Loma Linda (Calif.) U., 1995-97; adv. bd. mem. Cerritos (Calif.) Coll., 1975-80, U. LaVerne, Calif., 1996—. Contbr. articles to profl. jours. Contbg. mem. La Liga Flying Samaritans, Rosario Mex., 1978-80, Friendship For Animals, Rancho Cucamong, Calif., 1995—. Recipient Dean's fellowship Loma Linda (Calif.) U., 1988. Mem. APHA, Calif. Scholarship Fedn., Nat. Coun. Against Health Fraud, World Clowns Assn., Clowns of Am. Internat., Calif. State U. Alumni Assn., Alpha Gamma Sigma. Avocation: clowning. Office: U LaVerne Dept Health Svcs Mgmt 1950 3d St La Verne CA 91750 Home: 5152 Breckinridge Ave Banning CA 92220-7153

MCDORMAND, FRANCES, actress; b. Ill., June 23, 1957; m. Joel Coen, 1984; 2 children. Student, Yale U. Sch. Drama. Stage appearances include Awake and Sing!, N.Y.C., 1984, Painting Churches, N.Y.C., 1984, The Three Sisters, Mpls., 1985, N.J., 1991, All My Sons, New Haven, 1986, A Streetcar Named Desire, N.Y.C., 1988, Moon for the Misbegotten, 1992, Sisters Rosensweig, N.Y.C., 1993, The Swan, N.Y.C., 1993, To You, the Birdie!, 2002, Far Away, 2002; TV appearances include The Twilight Zone, The Equalizer, Spencer: For Hire, Hill Street Blues, (series) Hunter, 1984, Legwork, 1986-87, Twilight Zone, 1986, State of Grace, 2001; film appearances include Blood Simple, 1984, Crime Wave, 1986, Raising Arizona, 1987, Mississippi Burning, 1988 (Academy award nominee), Chattahoochee, 1990, Darkman, 1990, Miller's Crossing, 1990, Hidden Agenda, 1990, The Butcher's Wife, 1991, Passed Away, 1992, Short Cuts, 1993, Beyond Rangoon, 1995, Plain Pleasures, 1996, Fargo, 1996 (Academy award for Best Actress in a Leading Role, 1997), Lone Star, 1996, Primal Fear, 1996, Palookaville, 1996, Paradise Road, 1997, Johnny Skidmarks, 1998, Madeline, 1998, Talk of Angels, 1998, Wonder Boys, 1999, Almost Famous (Academy award nominee, Brit. Acad. award nominee, Golden Globe nominee, SAG nominee), Man Who Wasn't There, 2001, City by the Sea, 2002, Something's Gotta Give, 2003, (TV movies) Scandal Sheet, 1985, Vengeance: The Story of Tony Cimo, 1986, Crazy In Love, 1992, Good Old Boys, 1995, Hidden in America, 1996. Office: Endeavor Talent Agy LLC 9701 Wilshire Blvd Fl 10 Beverly Hills CA 90212

MCDOUGAL, MARIE PATRICIA, retired educator, freelance writer and editor; b. Mt. Clemens, Michigan, Apr. 10, 1946; d. Allan Charles and Dorothy Nadine (Berger), Ling; m. Douglas Stevens McDougal, Aug. 23, 1969. BA, Central Mich. U., 1968; MA, Antioch U., Ohio, 1997. Lic. tchr., Mich., 1968. Tchr. L'Anse Creuse High Sch., Harrison Twp., Mich., 1969-97; retired, 1997. Mem. L'Anse Creuse High Crisis Team, 1988-93, S.A.F.E. Task Force, Harrison Twp., 1986-98; spkr. in field. Author: Mount Clemens: Bath City U.S.A. in Vintage Post Cards, 2000; columnist: The Jour. Newspaper, 1983—90, writer: Introspective Mag., 1996—98, writer, editor: Antiquities Guide, 1997—98; author: Harrison Township, Michigan, 2002. Mem., L'Anse Creuse Athletic Boosters; chair Harrison Twp. Hist. Commn., 1993-2002; historian Harrison Twp.; founder, dir. Tranquil Life Fibromyalgic Support Group. Recipient Appreciation Award Macomb County Hist. Soc., 1989, Pres. Award for Lit. Excellence The Nat. Authors Registry, 1994. Mem. Soc. Children's Book Writers and Illustrators, Romance Writers Am., Venice Shores Property Owners (bd. dirs. 1994-2000, corr. sec. 1994-98), Detroit Working Writers, Red Hat Soc., L'Anse Creuse Public Sch. Alumni Assn. (steering com. 1996-98), Am. Auto Immune-Related Diseases Assn. Lutheran. Avocations: boating, crafts, reading. E-mail: ratisboat@wideopenwest.com. *Personal philosophy: Strive for the pinnacles, but stop to pick up any stragglers along the way.*

MCDOUGAL, STUART YEATMAN, comparative literature educator, author; b. L.A., Apr. 10, 1942; s. Murray and Marian (Yeatman) McDougal; m. Menakka Weerasinghe, Apr. 29, 1967 (div. 1977); children: Dyanthe Rose, Gavin Rohan; m. Nora Gunneng, Aug. 4, 1979; children: Angus Gunneng, Tobias Yeatman. BA, Haverford Coll., 1964; MA, U. Pa., 1965, PhD, 1970. Lectr. U. Lausanne, Switzerland, 1965-66; asst. prof. Mich. State U., East Lansing, 1970-72; from asst. prof. to prof. English, comparative lit. and film /video U. Mich., Ann Arbor, 1972-85; dir. program in comparative lit. U. Mich., Ann Arbor, 1981-97, asst. to dean spl. projects, 1997-98; Dewitt Wallace prof. English, chair English Dept. Macalester Coll., St. Paul, Minn., 1998—. Vis. prof. film Aegean Inst., Greece, 1994; vis. scholar Senapulli, Brazil, 1996. Author: Ezra Pound and the Troubadour Tradition, 1972 (Bredvold prize 1973), 1973; Made into Movies: From Literature to Film, 1985, Korean edit., 2002; editor: Dante Among the Moderns, 1985, Stanley Kubrick's A Clockwork Orange, 2003; co-editor: Play It Again, Sam: Retakes on Remakes, 1998; contbr. articles to profl. jours. Am. Council of Learned Socs. fellow, 1974-75; U. Mich. Rackham Research grantee, 1975-76; Fulbright Assn. sr. lectr., Italy, 1978; recipient Faculty Recognition award, U. Mich., 1987. Fellow Dirs. Guild Am. (summr workshop, 1993); mem. MLA, Am. Comparative Lit. Assn. (sec.-treas. 1983-89, v.p. 1989-91, pres. 1991-93), Internat. Comparative Lit. Assn., Soc. Cinema Studies. Democrat. Office: Macalester Coll English Dept 1600 Grand Ave Saint Paul MN 55105-1801

MCDOUGAL, WILLIAM SCOTT, urology educator; b. Grand Rapids, Mich., 1942; s. William Julian and Verna Wilma (Pasma) McD.; m. Mary Stuart Logan, Sept. 19, 1992; 1 child, Molly Katherine. AB, Dartmouth Coll., 1964; MD, Cornell U., 1968. Intern in surgery U. Hosps., Cleve., 1968-69, resident in surgery, 1969-75, attending urologist, 1977-80; postdoctoral fellow in physiology Yale U., New Haven, 1971-72; postdoctoral fellow in surgery Case-Western Res. U., Cleve., 1972-75; chief, burn study div. Inst. Surg. Rsch. Brooke Army Med. Ctr., Ft. Sam Houston, 1975-77; instr. surgery U. Tex., San Antonio, 1975-77; asst. prof. urology Case Western Res. U., Cleve., 1977-78, assoc. prof., 1978-80, Dartmouth Coll., Hanover, N.H., 1980-84, chmn. dept. urology, 1982-84; prof., chmn. dept. urology Vanderbilt U., Nashville, 1984-90; Walter S. Kerr Jr. prof. urology Harvard Med. Sch., 1991—; chief urology Mass. Gen. Hosp., Boston, 1991—. Office: Mass Gen Hosp Dept Urology Fruit St Boston MA 02114

MCDOUGALL, DONALD BLAKE, retired government official, librarian; BA, BEd, U. Sask., 1966; BLS, U. Toronto, 1969; MLS, U. Alta., 1983, cert. pub. adminstrn., 1990. Classroom tchr. Regina Bd. Edn., Sask., 1960-63, vice prin., 1963-68; asst. chief libr. Stratford Pub. Libr., Ont., Can., 1969, chief libr., 1970-72; supr. info. svcs. Edmonton Pub. Libr., Alta., Can., 1972, head pub. svcs., 1973-74; legislature libr. Province of Alta., Edmonton, Can., 1974-87; asst. dep. min., legis. libr. Legis. Assembly Alta., 1987-93, ret., 1993. Editor microfilm: Alberta Scrapbook Hansard, 1906-1964, 1976; editor: A History of the Legislature Library, 1979; author: Princess Louise Caroline Alberta, 1988, Premiers of the Northwest Territories and Alberta, 1876-1991, 1991; co-author, editor: Lieutenant-Governors of the Northwest Territories and Alberta, 1876-1991; (pamphlet) Canadian Parliamentary Libraries, 1989; mem. editl. bd. Sask. Hist. Baseball Rev., 1998—. Govt. Sask. scholar, 1965; recipient Queen's Silver Jubilee medal Govt. Can., 1977; named Hon. Clk.-At-The-Table, Legis. Assembly Alberta, 1987-93. Mem. Alta. Govt. Librs. Coun. (chmn. 1975), Assn. Parliamentary Librs. in Can. (pres. 1980-82), Edmonton Libr. Assn., Hist. Soc. Alta. (v.p. Edmonton chpt. 1987), Libr. Assn. Alta., Can. Libr. Assn., Edmonton Jaguar Drivers Club, Edmonton Scottish Soc., Can. Vintage Motorcycle Assn., Beta Phi Mu. Presbyterian.

MC DOUGALL, DUGALD STEWART, retired lawyer; b. Indpls., May 15, 1916; s. George and Effie (Barclay) McD.; m. Carol Brueggeman, Aug. 1938; children: George, Duncan, Walter, Robert; m. Judith Stephen, Dec. 1967. AB, U. Chgo., 1935, JD, 1937. Bar: Ill. 1937. Since practiced in, Chgo.; sr. ptnr. McDougall, Hersh & Scott, 1961-87. Sec., dir. Aladdin Industries, Inc. Served with USNR, 1942-46. Fellow Am. Coll. Trial Lawyers; mem. ABA, Am. Patent Law Assn., Patent Law Assn. Chgo., Law Club Chgo., Union League (Chgo.). Clubs: Union League (Chgo.); Olympia Fields (Ill.) Country. Office: 25 Pine Forest Ln Haines City FL 33844-9675

MCDOUGALL, IAIN ROSS, nuclear medicine educator; b. Glasgow, Scotland, Dec. 18, 1943; came to U.S., 1976; s. Archibald McDougall and Jean Cairns; m. Elizabeth Wilson, Sept. 6, 1968; children: Shona, Stewart. MB, ChB, U. Glasgow, 1967, PhD, 1973. Diplomate Am. Bd. Nuclear Medicine (chmn. 1985-87), Am. Bd. Internal Medicine (gov. 1984-86). Lectr. in medicine U. Glasgow, 1969-76; fellow Harkness-Stanford Med. Ctr., 1972-74; assoc. prof. radiology and medicine Stanford (Calif.) U., 1976-84, prof. radiology and medicine, 1985—. Contbr. numerous articles to sci. jours. Fellow Royal Coll. Physicians (Glasgow), Am. Coll. Physicians; mem. Am. Thyroid Assn., Soc. Nuclear Medicine, Western Assn. for Clin. Research. Office: Stanford U Med Ctr Divsn Nuclear Medicine Stanford CA 94305 Office Phone: 650-725-4711. Business E-Mail: rossmcdougall@stanford.edu.

MCDOUGALL, RODERICK GREGORY, lawyer; BBA in Econs., JD, U. Ariz. Bar: Ariz. 1965, U.S. Ct. Claims 1965, U.S. Supreme Ct. 1970, U.S. Dist. Ct. Ariz. 1972, U.S. Ct. Appeals (9th cir.) 1972. Law clk. Ariz. Supreme Ct., 1964, Ariz. Ct. Appeals, 1965; dep. county atty. Maricopa County, 1965-67; staff atty. Ariz. State Senate, 1967; asst. atty. gen., 1967-74; chief asst. Atty. Gen., Ariz., 1974-84; city atty. City of Phoenix, 1984-2000. Advisor Ariz. Supreme Ct. Mem. ABA, Internat. Mcpl. Lawyers Assn. (bd. dirs. 1994-2000), Ariz. Bar Assn., Maricopa County Bar Assn. Office Phone: 602-274-0522. E-mail: rodmcdougall@excite.com.

MCDOUGALL, RONALD ALEXANDER, restaurant executive; b. Chgo., Aug. 12, 1942; s. John A. and Doris E. (Sengstock) McD.; m. Dale O. Ryser, Feb. 1, 1964 (div. July 1969); children: Timothy, Jonathan; m. Carolyn Kay Conley, Aug. 9, 1979; 1 child, Matthew. BBA, U. Wis., 1964, MBA, 1965. With Procter & Gamble, Cin., 1967-68, Sara Lee, Deerfield, Ill., 1969-72, The Pillsbury Co., Mpls., 1972-74, S&A Restaurant Corp., Dallas, 1974-82, Burger King, Miami, Fla., 1982-83; pres., CEO,& COO Brinker Internat., Dallas, 1983—. Bd. dirs. Brinker Internat., Excel Comm., Inc. With U.S. Army, 1965-67. Mem. Nat. Restaurant Assn., Am. Mgmt. Assn., Bent Tree Country Club, Aerobics Activity Ctr., Employment Policies Inst. Republican. Presbyterian. Avocations: running, bicycling, golf. Office: Brinker Internat 6820 L B J Fwy Dallas TX 75240

MC DOW, JOHN JETT, biosystems engineering educator; b. Covington, Tenn., Jan. 6, 1925; s. Robert Simpson and Lucy Ann (Cocke) McD.; m. Dorothy Virginia Glass, Dec. 22, 1946; children: Ronald Allan, Jane Virginia. Student, Franklin and Marshall Coll., 1944-45; BS, U. Tenn., 1948; MS, Mich. State U., 1949, PhD, 1957. Registered profl. engr., Tenn., La. Instr. Mich. State U., 1949; instr. Okla. State U., 1949-51, asst. prof. agrl. engring., 1951; assoc. prof. La. Poly. U., 1951-57, prof., 1957-62, head agrl. engring. dept., 1953-62; prof., head dept. agrl. engring. U. Tenn., Knoxville, 1962-73, dean admissions and records, 1973-83, prof. agrl. engring., 1983-92, prof. emeritus, 1992—. Cons./collaborator Agrl. Research Service, U.S. Dept. Agr., 1970-76; leader Rotary Internat. Found. Group Study Exchange Team to Philippines, 1984; mem. scholarship selection com. N.Am. Philips Corp., 1976-88. Contbr. articles to profl. jours. Mem. La. Engring. Coun., 1955-56; bd. dirs. Tenn.-Venezuela-Amazonas Partners, 1977-80; vol. Internat. Centennial Olympic Summer Games, Atlanta, 1996. Served with USN, 1943—46, comdr. USNR, to 1977. So. Fellowship grantee, 1957. Mem. Am. Soc. Agrl. Engring. (dir. 1973-75), Am. Soc. Engring. Edn. (sec. agrl. engring. div. 1971-72, vice chmn. 1972-73, chmn. 1973-74), Sigma Xi, Tau Beta Pi, Pi Mu Epsilon, Omicron Delta Kappa, Gamma Sigma Delta, Phi Kappa Phi (v.p. 1971-77, nat. pres. elect 1977-80, pres. 1980-83, pres. found. 1974-78). Lodges: Rotary (pres. 1989-90, chmn. dist. scholarship selection com., 1982-87, 88-91). Presbyterian. Home: 2008 Walnut Hills Dr Knoxville TN 37920-2946

MCDOWELL, CASSANDRA, multi-media specialist; b. Oklahoma City, Sept. 16, 1961; d. Zane Brown and Alice June Copenhaver, Eugene Lee Copenhaver (Stepfather) and Dorothy Brown(Stepmother); m. Richard Lane

McDowell, Jan. 29, 1983; children: Zachary Lynn, Robin Lyle. M. in Libr. Media, U. of Ctrl. Okla., 1997. Cert. libr. media specialist Dept. of Edn. State of Okla., 1997. Libr. media specialist Mid-Del Schools, Midwest City, Okla., 1997—. Mem.: ALA, NEA, Okla. Educators Assn., Assn. of Classroom Tchrs. (bldg. rep. 2002—03). Avocations: travel, reading, gardening. Office: Midwest City High School 213 Elm Drive Midwest City OK 73110 Office Phone: 405-739-1741 ext 152. Personal E-mail: cassimust@aol.com. Business E-Mail: cmcdowell@mid-del.k12.ok.us.

MCDOWELL, CHARLES EAGER, lawyer, retired military officer; b. Manchester, N.H., Sept. 9, 1923; s. Joseph Curry and Mildred (Eager) McD.; m. Carolyn A. Gibbons, June 21, 1947; children— Robin, Patricia. AB, Dartmouth Coll., 1947; JD, U. Va., 1950. Bar: Tex. 1950, Va. 1981, D.C. 1981. With land div. Shell Oil Co., Houston, 1950; commd. lt. (j.g.) USN, 1951, advanced through grades to rear adm., 1976; staff legal officer Comdr. Service Force, U.S. Pacific Fleet; staff judge adv., head internat. law div. Naval War Coll., 1963-66; staff legal officer, comdr. 7th Fleet, 1966-68; sr. Navy mem. ad hoc com., dep. asst. judge adv. gen. Office Judge Adv. Gen. Dept. Def., Washington, 1968-72; staff judge adv. on staff comdr. in chief U.S. Naval Forces, Europe, London, 1972-75; comdg. officer Naval Justice Sch., Newport, R.I., 1975-76; dep. judge adv. gen. Navy Dept., Washington, 1976-78, judge adv. gen., 1978-80; pvt. practice Dumfries, Va., 1981-96. Served to 2d lt. AUS, 1943-46. Decorated D.S.M., Bronze Star, Joint Service Commendation medal, Navy Commendation medal with Combat V, Purple Heart, Combat Inf. badge. Mem. FBA, Tex. Bar Assn., Va. Bar Assn., Judge Advs. Assn., Order of Coif, Chi Phi, Square Dancer Club. Methodist. Home: 1106 Croton Dr Alexandria VA 22308-2008 E-mail: cmcdowell@erols.com.

MCDOWELL, CHARLES S. lawyer; b. Norfolk, Va., June 20, 1945; AB cum laude, Princeton U., 1967; JD, U. Va., 1974. Bar: Del. 1975. Ptnr. Potter Anderson & Corroon LLP, Wilmington, Del. Counsel Del. Health Facilities Authority. Dir. WHYY, Inc. (Delaware Valley Pub. TV and Radio); mem. com. LPGA Urban Youth Golf Program. Mem.: ABA, Nat. Assn. Bond Lawyers, Del. State Bar Assn. (pres. 2003—). Office: Potter Anderson and Corroon LLP Hercules Plz PO Box 951 1313 N Market St Wilmington DE 19899-0951

MCDOWELL, DAVID MICHAEL, psychiatrist, educator, researcher; b. Middletown, Conn., Mar. 16, 1963; s. Arthur Vanall and Jacqueline Larson McDowell. MD, Columbia Coll. Physicians and Surgeons, 1989. Bd. cert. psychiatry Am. Bd. Psychiatry and Neurology, 1993, cert. addiction psychiatry Am. Bd. Psychiatry and Neurology, 1996. Fellow in addiction psychiatry NYU Med. Ctr., N.Y.C., 1993—95; instr. psychiatry Bellevue Hosp./NYU Med. Ctr., N.Y.C., 1995—; asst. prof. clin. psychiatry Columbia U. Coll. Physicians and Surgeons, N.Y.C., 1995—; dir. buprenorphine program Columbia U.; founder, med. dir. STARS the Substance Treatment and Rsch. Svc. Columbia U., N.Y.C., 1997—. Cons. Malinkrodt Pharmaceuticals, St. Louis, 2002—. Author: (textbook) Substance Abuse: From Principles to Practice; contbr. chapters to books, articles to profl. jours. Bd. mem. The Three Dollar Bill Theater Co., N.Y.C., 1995—99. Grantee, NIH/Nat. Inst. on Drug Abuse, 2000—. Mem.: Am. Psychiat. Assn. (vice chair sci. program com. 2000—, disting. life fellow), The Charaka Club. Achievements include Advisor for Creative work including the Golden Globe Award winning film Quills, and other plays and film scripts. Avocations: cooking, singing. Office: Stars 3 East 65th St New York NY 10019 Home: 160 W 86th St # 6 B New York NY 10024 Office Phone: 212-570-4166.

MCDOWELL, DONALD L. hospital administrator; b. Indpls., June 9, 1934; married; 5 children. BS Acctg., Ohio State U., 1956; grad. Edn. Adminstrn., U. Fla. Acctg. tng. program Chevrolet divsn. Gen. Motors Corp., Toledo, Ohio, 1956-58, acctg. asst. supr. Chevrolet divsn., 1958-59, acctg. supr. Chevrolet divsn. Atlanta, 1959-61; controller U. Fla., Gainesville, 1961-67; dir. mgmt. info. systems Fla. Bd. Regents, Tallahassee, 1967-68; v.p. adminstrv. affairs Fla. Internat. U., Miami, 1969-74; exec. dir. ops. Vanderbilt U., 1974-76, v.p. bus. affairs, 1976-80; exec. v.p., treas. Maine Med. Ctr., 1980-91, interim pres., 1990-91; pres. Main Med. Ctr., 1991-97, Main Health Ctr., 1997—. Bd. dirs. Maine Bank and Trust, Maine Med. Mutual Ins. Co.; com. mem. So. Assn. Colls. and Schs., program classification com. Nat. Ctr. Higher Edn. Mgmt. Systems; educator Fla. Internat. U.; city mgrs. adv. com. Portland; trustee U. Maine Sys. (v. chair). Mem. Bldg. com. YWCA Portland; chmn. Hosp. adv. com. Maine Health Care Fin. Commn.; at-large mem. House Dels. Am. Hosp. Assn.; Pres'. coun. visitors U. So. Maine; bd. dirs. ARC, Greater Portland United Way, Park Danforth Home for the Aged, Portland C. of C. (pres. 1990-91), Community Health Svcs., Portland Stage Co., Maine Hosp. Assn., Portland Symphony Orchetras (pres.), Voluntary Hosps. Am., New England (chair), Regional C. of C. (chmn.), Maine Devel. Found., Ptnrs. for Progress, New England Healthcare Assembly. Office: Maine Health Ctr 465 Congress St Ste 600 Portland ME 04101-3537

MCDOWELL, DONNA SCHULTZ, lawyer, educator; b. Cin., Apr. 23, 1946; d. Robert Joseph and Harriet (Parronchi) Schultz; m. Dennis Lon McDowell, June 20, 1970; children: Dawn Megan, Donnelly Lon. BA in English with honors, Brandeis U., 1968; MEd, Am. U., 1972; C.A.S. with honors in Reading, Johns Hopkins U., 1979; JD with honors, U. Md., 1982; MS, Hood Coll., 1995; postgrad., U. Md. Bar: Md. 1982; cert. tchr. reading K-12, D.C.; advanced profl. cert. in English, Biology and Reading, Md. Instr. Anne Arundel & Prince George's C.C., Severna Park and Largo, Md., 1977-78; coll. adminstr. Bowie State Coll. (Md.), 1978-79; assoc. Miller & Bortner, Lanham, Md., 1982-83; sole practice Lanham, 1983-87, Gaithersburg, Md., 1987—; sci. tchr. D.C. Pub. Schs., 1999-2000; chair dept. English Montgomery County Pub. Schs., 2000—, English lit. tchr., 2002—03. Ednl. cons.; presenter in field. Chmn. Housing Hearing Com., Bowie, 1981-83; trustee Unitarian-Universalist Ch., Silver Spring, Md., 1979-83; bd. dirs. New Ventures, Bowie, 1983, Second Mile (Runaway House), Hyattsville, Md., 1983; officer Greater Laytonsville Civic Assn., 1989; founding mem. People to Preserve, Laytonsville; mem. Solid Waste Adv. Com., Montgomery County, Md.; election judge; presenter NCTE, SOMIRA, NCPS. Recipient Am. Jurisprudence award U. Md., 1981; Michael Jordan grantee, 2000, D.C. Pub. Schs. grantee. Mem. Phi Kappa Phi. Democrat. Avocations: gardening, reading, bluebirds, movies. Home: 24308 Hipsley Mill Rd Gaithersburg MD 20882-3132 E-mail: DonnaSMcD@aol.com.

MCDOWELL, EDWARD R. H. chemical engineer; b. Cleve., Aug. 13, 1932; s. Blake and Lois (Held) McD.; m. Joyce Patricia Dudley, June 18, 1955; children: Edward R. H. Jr., James D. BSChemE, Cornell U., 1955; MS, Calif. Inst. Tech., 1960, PhD, 1964. Registered prof. chem. engr., Calif. Instr. Cornell U., Ithaca, N.Y., 1955; assoc. rsch. engr. Calif. Rsch. Corp., El Segundo, 1955-59; instr. Calif. Inst. Tech., Pasadena, 1959-63; rsch. engr. Chevron Rsch. Corp., La Habra, Calif., 1963-66, sr. rsch. engr., 1966-68; sr. engring. assoc. Chevron Oil Field Rsch. Co., La Habra, 1968-74, mgr., 1974-86; gen. ptnr. C. Blake McDowell Ltd. Partnership, Akron, Ohio, 1986—95. NSF fellow Calif. Inst. Tech., 1961-63; recipient Engring. Merit award Orange County Engring. Coun., 1985. Fellow Am. Inst. Chem. Engrs. (pres. 1989, v.p. 1988, dir. 1982-84, Civic Achievement award 1983, F.J. & Dorothy Van Anwepen award 1992), Inst. for Advancement of Engring.; mem. Soc. Petroleum Engrs., Am. Assn. Engring. Socs. (bd. govs.), King Harbor Yacht Club (commodore 1990, vice commodore 1989, rear commodore 1988), St. Francis Yacht Club (San Francisco), Transpacific Yacht Club (Long Beach, Calif.), Assn. Santa Monica Bay Yacht Clubs (commodore 1989, vice commodore 1988, rear commodore 1987), Nawiliwili Yacht Club (Lihue, Hawaii), Magic Castle Club, Manhattan Country Club, The Cornell Club (N.Y.C.). Avocations: offshore sailboat racing (winner uldb70 season sailing championship 1990, 92), magic. Home: 3700 Kilauea Rd Kilauea HI 96754

MCDOWELL, ELAINE, retired federal government executive, educator; b. Balt., June 28, 1942; d. McKinley and Lena (Blue) McDowell; children: Nathan H. Jr. Murphy, Michael W. Murphy. BA, Morgan State U., Balt., 1965; MSW, U. Md., 1971, PhD, 1988. Drug abuse adminstr., acting regional dir. State Md. Drug Abuse Adminstrn., Balt., 1971-72; social sci. analyst, pub. health advisor Nat. Inst. Drug Abuse, Rockville, MD, 1972-76, dep. dir., dir. div. community assistance, 1976-82, dep. assoc. dir. for policy devel., 1981-82, dir. div. prevention and communications, 1982-85; exec. asst. to adminstr. Alcohol, Drug Abuse & Mental Health Adminstrn., Rockville, Md., 1985; dep. dir. Nat. Inst. on Drug Abuse, Rockville, MD, 1985-88; dir. Ctr. for Substance Abuse Prevention, 1988-96; acting adminstr. Alcohol, Drug Abuse and Mental Health Adminstrn., Rockville, Md., 1992, Substance Abuse and Mental Health Svcs. Adminstrn., Rockville, Md., 1992-94. Expert cons. in substance abuse, treatment, and mental health fields; prof. Morgan State U., Balt. Chmn. non-alcoholic internat. gen. svc. bd. Alcoholics Anonymous, 2001—; active Presbyn. Ch. U.S.A., Balt., 1998—; bd. dirs. Rosalynn Carter Inst. for Human Devel. Recipient Outstanding Leadership in Improving Health Care in Black Cmty. award Nat. Med. Assn., 1989, Secretary's commendation HHS, 1989, Disting. Svc. award, 1990, Nat. Coun. on Alcoholism and Drug Dependence Ind., Pres. award for outstanding fed. leadership, 1991, Presdl. Meritorious Exec. Rank award, 1991, Presdl. Meritorious Disting. Rank award, 1993. Mem.: NASW, Sr. Execs. Assn. Personal E-mail: JLuvenia@aol.com.

MCDOWELL, ELIZABETH MARY, retired pathology educator; b. Kew Gardens, Surrey, Eng., Mar. 30, 1940; came to U.S., 1971; d. Arthur and Peggy (Bryant) McD. B Vet. Medicine, Royal Vet. Coll., London, 1963; BA, Cambridge U., 1968, PhD, 1971. Gen. practice vet. medicine, 1964-66; Nuffield Found. tng. scholar Cambridge (Eng.) U., 1966-71; instr. dept. pathology U. Md., Balt., 1971-73, asst. prof., 1973-76, assoc. prof., 1976-80, prof., 1980-96, ret., 1996. Co-author: Biopsy Pathology of the Bronchi, 1987; editor: Lung Carcinomas, 1987; contbr. over 120 articles to sci. jours., chpts. to books. Rsch. grantee NIH, 1979-92. Avocations: conservation education, gardening, swimming. Home: 9715 Branchleigh Rd Apt 3 Randallstown MD 21133-2158

MCDOWELL, FLETCHER HUGHES, physician, educator; b. Denver, Aug. 5, 1923; married BA, Dartmouth Coll., 1943; MD, Cornell U., 1947. From instr. to prof. neurology Cornell U. Med. Coll., N.Y.C., 1968—, assoc. dean, 1970-95, Winifred Masterson Burke prof. rehab. medicine; pres. Winifred Masterson Burke Rsch. Inst., White Plains, 1992—. Mem. Am. Acad. Neurology, Am. Neurol. Assn., Am. Fedn. Clin. Research Office: Burke Rehab Ctr 785 Mamaroneck Ave White Plains NY 10605-2523

MCDOWELL, JENNIFER, sociologist, composer, playwright, publisher; b. Albuquerque; d. Willard A. and Margaret Frances (Garrison) McD.; m. Milton Loventhal, July 2, 1973. BA, U. Calif., 1957; MA, San Diego State U., 1958; postgrad., Sorbonne, Paris, 1959; MLS, U. Calif., 1963; PhD, U. Oreg., 1973. Tchr. English Abraham Lincoln H.S., San Jose, Calif., 1960-61; free-lance editor Soviet field, Berkeley, Calif., 1961-63; editor, pub. Merlin Papers, San Jose, 1969-80, Merlin Press, San Jose, 1973—; rsch. cons. sociology San Jose, 1973—; music pub. Lipstick and Toy Balloons Pub. Co., San Jose, 1978—, Abbie & Dolley Records, 2003—; composer Paramount Pictures, 1982-88. Tchr. writing workshops; poetry readings, 1969-73; co-producer radio show lit. and culture Sta. KALX, Berkeley, 1971-72. Author: (with Milton Loventhal) Black Politics: A Study and Annotated Bibliography of the Mississippi Freedom Democratic Party, 1971 (featured at Smithsonian Inst. Spl. Event 1992), Contemporary Women Poets, 1977; co-author: (plays off-off Broadway) Betsy and Phyllis, 1986, Mack the Knife Your Friendly Dentist, 1986, The Estrogen Party To End War, 1986, The Oatmeal Party Comes to Order, 1986, (plays) Betsy Meets the Wacky Iraqi, 1991, Bella and Phyllis, 1994; contbr. poems, plays, essays, articles, short stories, and book revs. to lit. mags., news mags. and anthologies; rschr. women's autobiog. writings, contemporary writing in poetry, Soviet studies, civil rights movement, and George Orwell, 1962—; writer: (songs) Money Makes a Woman Free!, 1976, 2004, 3 songs featured in Parade of Am. Music, 1976-77; co-creator mus. comedy Russia's Secret Plot To Take Back Alaska, 1988, (CDs) Our Women Are Strong, 2002, The Wearing of the Green Burkas, 2003; (musical revs., CD) She, A Tapestry of Women's Lives, 2004. Recipient 8 awards Am. Song Festival, 1976-79, Bill Casey Award in Letters, 1980, ERFA Found. Award for SHE, Calif. State U., 2004, collected by Nobel Inst. for 2004 Nobel Peace Prize laureate Sharin Ebadi; doctoral fellow AAUW, 1971-73; grantee Calif. Arts Coun., 1976-77. Mem. AAUW, Am. Assn. for Advancement of Slavic Studies, Soc. Sci. Study of Religion, Am. Sociol. Assn., Dramatists Guild, Phi Beta Kappa, Sigma Alpha Iota, Beta Phi Mu, Kappa Kappa Gamma. Democrat. Office: c/o Merlin Press PO Box 5602 San Jose CA 95150-5602 E-mail: jeditorphd@earthlink.net.

MC DOWELL, JOHN B. bishop; b. New Castle, Pa, July 17, 1921; s. Bernard A. and Louise M. (Hannon) McD. BA, St. Vincent Coll., 1942, MA, 1944, Catholic U. Am., 1950, PhD, 1952; Litt.D. (hon.), Duquesne U., 1962; grad., St. Vincent Sem., Latrobe, Pa. Ordained priest Roman Cath. Ch., 1945, consecrated as titular bishop of Tamazuca and aux. bishop of Pitts., 1966—; asst. pastor St. Irenaeus Ch., Oakmont, 1945-49; asst. supt. schs. Diocese of Pitts., 1952-55, supt. schs., 1955-70, vicar for edn., 1970-85; vicar gen.; pastor Epiphany Parish, Pitts., 1969-96; ret., 1996. Papal chamberlain to Pope Pius XII, 1956, to Pope John XXIII, 1958; domestic prelate to Pope Paul VI, 1964; chmn. ad hoc com. on moral values in our soc. Nat. Conf. Cath. Bishops, from 1973, Bishops Com. for Pastoral on Moral Values, from 1976; mem. Internat. Council for Catechesis, from 1975 Author: The Life of Hugh C. Boyle, 6th Bishop of Diocese of Pittsburgh, 1999, Catholic Schools, Public Education, and American Culture, 2000, Giants Were On the Earth in Those Days, The Life of John Francis Regis Canevin, 5th Bishop, Diocese of Pittsburgh, 2000, Blessed Are the Poor in Spirit, For Theirs is the Kingdom of Heaven, the Life of Vincent Martin Leonard, the 9th Bishop of Diocese of Pittsburgh, 2001, Water, Death, and Grace: His Name is John, a tribute to his eminence John Cardinal Dearden, Coadjutor/Bishop, Diocese of Pittsburgh, Cardinal Archbishop, Archdiocese of Detroit, 2001, I Am Going To Tell You A Mystery, the life of the fourth Bishop, Diocese of Pitts., 2002, To Dwell in the House of the Lord All the Days of My Life, the life of Father Charles Bonaventure Maguire, O.F.M., 2003, Reflections on the Life of John Cardinal Wright, S.T.D. Eighth Biship of Pittsburg, 2003; co-author elem. sch. religions series, JHS lit. series, elem. sci. series and elem. reading series; contbr. ednl. articles to various publs.; former editor: Cath. Educator Mag. Bd. dir. Allegheny County Community Coll.; bd. dir. Western Pa. Safety Council, Duquesne U. Named Man of Yr. in Religion Pitts., 1970, 93, Educator of Yr., United Pvt. Acad. Schs. Assn., 1978, Man of Yr., Pitts. chpt. KC, 1989. Mem. Nat. Cath. Ednl. Assn., Cath. Ednl. Assn. Pa., Omicron Delta Kappa Gamma Circle (hon.) Roman Catholic. Address: Chancery Office 111 Blvd Of The Allies Pittsburgh PA 15222-1613

MCDOWELL, JOHN EUGENE, lawyer; b. Toledo, Nov. 22, 1927; s. Glenn Hugh and Evelyn (Millspaugh) McD.; m. Jean Ann Hepler, June 18, 1950; children: Jane Lynn McDowell Thummel, Sheila Lorraine McDowell Laing. BS, Miami U., Oxford, Ohio, 1949; JD, U. Mich., 1952. Bar: Ohio 1952. Assoc. Dinsmore & Shohl, Cin., 1952-59, ptnr., 1959-97, of counsel, 1997—. Bd. dirs. Structural Dynamics Rsch. Corp., Milford, Ohio. Mem. solicitation coms. United Appeal, Cin., NCCJ, Cin., Boy Scouts Am., Cin. Mem. ABA, Ohio Bar Assn., Cin. Bar Assn., Cin. Country Club, Queen City Club, Order of Coif, Sawgrass Country Club. Democrat. Episcopalian. Office: Dinsmore & Shohl 1900 Chemed Ctr 255 E 5th St Cincinnati OH 45202-4700

MCDOWELL, MALCOLM, actor; b. Leeds, Eng., June 13, 1943; m. Mary Steenburgen, 1980 (div.); 2 children; m. Kelley Kuhr, 1991; 1 child, Beckett Taylor; m. Margot Dullea (div.). Began career with: Royal Shakespeare Co., Stratford, Eng., 1965-66; early TV appearances include: role of Dixon of Dock Green in Z Cars, British TV; other TV appearances: Little Red Riding Hood, Faerie Tale Theatre, Showtime TV, 1983, Gulag, HBO, 1985, Our Friends in the North, 1996, Lexx: The Dark Zone, 1996, The Great War, 1996, Captain Simian and The Space Monkeys, 1996, The Little Riders, 1996, Pearl, 1996-97, Nazis: The Occult Conspiracy, 1998, Beings, 1998; stage appearance: Look Back in Anger, N.Y. Stage, 1980, In Celebration, N.Y.C., 1984, Hunting Cockroaches, L.A. Stage, 1987, Another Time - Stage, 1993; films include: Poor Cow, 1967, If...., 1969, Figures in a Landscape, 1970, The Raging Moon, 1971, A Clockwork Orange, 1971, O Lucky Man, 1973, Royal Flash, 1975, Aces High, 1976, Voyage of the Damned, 1977, Caligula, 1977, The Passage, 1978, Time After Time, 1979, Cat People, 1981, Britannia Hospital, 1984, Blue Thunder, 1983, Get Crazy, 1983, Cross Creek, 1983, Sunset, 1987, Buy and Cell, 1989, Class of 1999, 1989, Assassin of the Tsar, 1990, Bopha!, 1993, Milk Money, 1994, The Caller, Star Trek: Generations, 1997, Tank Girl, 1995, Yesterday's Target, 1996, Where Truth Lies, 1996, Asylum, 1996, Superman, 1996, Mr. Magoo, 1997, Hugo Pool, 1997, 2103 The Deadly Wake, 1997, The Gardener, 1998, Beings, 1998, World of Moss, 1998, Y2K, 1999, Southern Cross, 1999, My Life So Far, 1999, Love Lies Bleeding, 1999, Gangster #1, 2000, Island of the Dead, 2000, Just Visiting, 2001, Dorian, 2001, Between Strangers, 2001, I Spy, 2002, I'll Sleep When I'm Dead, 2003, Tempo, 2003, The Company, 2003, Red Roses and Petrol, 2003, Bobby Jones, Stroke of Genius, 2004, (voice) Pinocchio 3000, 2004, (voice) Dinotopia: Curse of the Ruby Sunstone, 2004; TV guest appearances Tales From the Crypt, 1989, Spider-Man, 1995, Superman, 1996, Ruby, 1999, (voice) South Park, 2000, numerous others.*

MCDOWELL, ROBERT E. animal science educator; b. Charlotte, N.C., June 27, 1921; s. Robert and Grace W. (Bradford) McD.; m. Dorothy Gill, Dec. 8, 1945; children: Jean G. McDowell Burke, Ann G. Hickey, Robert G. BS, N.C. State U., 1942; MS, U. Md., 1949, PhD, 1955. Tchr. VA, Charlotte, 1946; rsch. investigator U.S. Dept. Agr., Beltsville, Md., 1946-67; prof. emeritus internat. animal sci. Cornell U., Ithaca, N.Y., 1967-86; vis. prof. internat. programs N.C. State U., 1986—. Cons. FAO, Peace Corps, AID, Rockefeller Found., govts. of Venezuela, Dominican Republic, Taiwan, others. Author: Improvement of Livestock Production in Warm Cliamtes, 1972, Partnership for Humans and Animals, 1991, Dairying with Improved Breeds in Warm Climates, 1994, Potential for Commercial Dairying with Buffalo, 1995, others; contbr. chpts. to books and articles to profl. jours. Bd. dirs. Internat. Found. for Sci., Sweden; chmn. bd. dirs. Internat. Livestock Ctr. for Africa, 1979-85, Ethiopia. Col. USMC, 1942-46. Decorated Bronze Star. Mem. AAAS, Am. Dairy Sci. Assn. (Internat. Dairy Prodn. award 1988), Am. Soc. Animal Sci. (award 1979), Ret. Officers Assn., Alpha Zeta. Home: 911-104 Washington St Raleigh NC 27605 Office: Nc State U Raleigh NC 27695-0001

MCDOWELL, ROBERT JAMES, music educator, composer; b. Primghar, Iowa, Mar. 16, 1946; s. Jon Evans and Virginia Mae McDowell; m. Susan Carol Profilet, June 10, 1966; 1 child, Robert John. BA in Music Edn., U. of Sioux Falls, Sioux Falls, SD, 1964—68; BS in Bus. Adminstrn., Nat. Am. U., Sioux Falls, SD, 1980—82. Substitute tchr. Sioux Falls Pub. Schs., SD, 1973—76; pvt. horn instr. self-employed, Sioux Falls, SD, 1973—; v.p. K & M Music, Ltd., Sioux Falls, SD, 1976—98; adj. horn instr. Augustana Coll., Sioux Falls, SD, 1998—; staff mem. Midwest Ambassadors of Music, Brookings, SD, 1999—2001. Mem. Sioux Falls Mcpl. Band, SD, 1961—76, pres., 1974—76; mem. S.D. Symphony, Sioux Falls, SD, 1963—69; prin. horn Sioux Empire Brass Soc., SD, 2000—. Composer: (musical composition) Fanfare for Four. Pres. Sioux Empire Cosmopolitan Club, SD, 1987—88; bd. mem., worship and the arts Our Saviors Luth. Ch., Sioux Falls, SD. With USAF, 1969—73. Recipient Outstanding Young Men of Am., Jaycees of Am., 1970, Disting. Svc. award, Phi Beta Mu, Sigma Chpt., 2002. Mem.: Internat. Horn Soc. (assoc.), Assn. of Concert Bands (assoc.), S.D. Bandmaster's Assn. (assoc.), Music Tchrs. Nat. Assn. (assoc.), Sunrise Sertoma Club (assoc.; sec. 1998—2003). Lutheran. Avocations: golf, photography, gardening, travel. Home: 2611 W Minnehaha Dr Sioux Falls SD 57105-3325 Office: Augustana Coll Music Dept 2001 S Summit Ave Sioux Falls SD 57197 Personal E-mail: bob.mcdowell@yebb.com.

MCDUFF, ELAINE MARIE, sociologist, educator; b. Greensboro, N.C., Dec. 14, 1954; d. E. J. Johnson and Frances Virginia Anderson; m. D. Stephen McDuff, Dec. 27, 1975; children: Matthew, Sarah, Luke. BA, U. N.C., 1975; MDiv, Duke U., 1980; PhD, U. Iowa, 1998. Ordained to ministry United Ch. Christ, 1980. Tchr. jr. high sch. sci. U.S. Peace Corps, Gbarnga, Liberia, 1976—77; tchr. high sch. math. Mt. Silinda Inst., Zimbabwe, 1981—84; assoc. stewardship So. Conf. United Ch. Christ, Burlington, NC, 1986—88; tchr. adult high sch. edn. Ctr. Carolina C.C., Sanford, 1988—89; instr. sociology U. Iowa, Iowa City, 1995—96; asst. prof. Iowa State U., Ames, 1996—2001; asst. prof. sociology Truman State U., Kirksville, Mo., 2001—. Co-dir. Nat. Survey Clergy on Job Satisfaction & Work, 1996—98; presenter in field. Co-author: Research in the Sociology of Work Vol. 8, 2000; contbr. articles to profl. jours. Fellow, U. Iowa, 1991—95; grantee, Lilly Found., 1996—97, 2001—02. Mem.: Mo. Sociol. Assn. (pres. elect 2001—02, pres. 2002—03), Midwest Sociol. Soc. (chair nominations & elections 2001—03), Am. Sociol. Assn., Phi Beta Kappa. Avocations: reading, travel. Home: 1502 Buchanan Dr Ames IA 50010 Office: Truman State U 207 D Baldwin Hall Kirksville MO 63501

MC DUFFIE, MALCOLM, oil company executive; b. San Francisco, Nov. 14, 1915; s. William Chester and Mary (Skaife) McD.; m. Mary Sutherland de Surville, Dec. 8, 1951; children: Cynthia de Surville, Duncan de Surville. AB in Econs, Stanford U., 1940. With O.C. Field Gasoline Corp., 1940-41, Wilmington Gasoline Corp., 1941-42; with Mohawk Petroleum Corp., 1945-80, pres., dir., 1969-80; dir. Res. Oil & Gas Co., 1973-80, sr. v.p., 1977-80; sp. asst. to pres. Getty Oil Co., Los Angeles, 1980-82. Bd. overseers Huntington Library, Art Gallery and Bot. Gardens, 1972-98; bd. dirs. Calif. Inst. Tech. Assos., 1976-82. Mem. Nat. Petroleum Refiners Assn. (Dir. 1970-80), Ind. Refiners Assn. Calif. (pres. 1967-69, 77-78, dir. 1950-80), Rancheros Visitadores. Clubs: California (Los Angeles); Bohemian (San Francisco); Valley Hunt (Pasadena, Calif.), Annandale Golf (Pasadena, Calif.); Birnam Wood (Santa Barbara, Calif.), Valley (Montecito, Calif.). Republican. Episcopalian. Home and Office: 457 Eastgate Ln Santa Barbara CA 93108-2249

MCDUFFIE, MARCIA JENSEN, pediatrics educator, researcher; b. Phila., Apr. 10, 1949; d. John Calvin and Agnes Margaret (Jakob) J.; children: Kathryn Steere, Joanna Steere, Michael. Student, Duke U., 1967-69; BA cum laude with honors in Biochemistry, U. Pa., 1971; MD with honors, U. N.C., 1981. Diplomate Am. Bd. Pediat. Pediat. intern U. Colo. Health Scis. Ctr., Denver, 1981-82, resident in pediat., 1982-84, asst. prof., 1987-93, rsch. mem. Barbara Davis Ctr. for Childhood Diabetes, 1989-93; postdoctoral fellow div. basic immunology dept. medicine Nat. Jewish Ctr. for Immunology and Respiratory Medicine, Denver, 1984-87; assoc. prof. U. Va. Health Scis. Ctr., Charlottesville, 1993—. Assoc. editor Jour. Immunology, 1992-94; mem. editl. bd. Diabetes, 1995—; contbr. articles to profl. jours. Recipient career devel. award Juvenile Diabetes Found., 1992-95; rsch. grantee Juvenile Diabetes Found., 1991-95, 96—, Am. Diabetes Assn., 1994—, NIH, 1996—. Mem. Soc. for Pediatric Rsch., Am. Assn. Immunologists. Office: U Va Health System Dept Pharmacology Mr-4 Rm 5116 Charlottesville VA 22908-0001

MCDUFFIE, OTIS JAMES (O.J. MCDUFFIE), professional football player; b. Marion, Ohio, Dec. 2, 1969; Degree in labor in indsl. rels., Pa. State U. Wide receiver Miami (Fla.) Dolphins, 1993—. Named wide receiver, The Sporting News Coll. All-Am. 2d team, 1992. Achievements include shares NFL postseason career and single-game records for most 2-pt. conversions. Office: c/o Miami Dolphins 7500 SW 30th St Davie FL 33314-1020

MCDUFFY, ADITYA, lawyer; d. Louis and Brenda McDuffy. LLM in Corp. Law and Fin., Widener U., 1998; JD, Tex. So. U., 1995; BA, Howard U., 1990. Bar: Pa. 1996, cert.: mediator Justice Ctr., Atlanta 2000. Asst. counsel dept. def. Def. Logistics Agy., Phila., Def. Supply Ctr., Phila., 1998—. Presenter, organizer in field at seminars, tng. sessions, presentations. Creator, editor (legal edn. website) Blacks In Government's Online Legal Resources Center; editor (creator): (newsletter) EEO Flash. Vol. atty. Consumer Bankruptcy Advocacy Program, Phila., 1997—98; chair, nat. legal rev. com. Nat. Orgn. Blacks in Govt., Wash., 2000—; mem. Met. Wilmington Urban League, 2003; asst. chaplain Hillside Ch. Christ, Wilmington, Del., 1998—2003. Recipient Vol. award, Girls Inc., 1998, Cert. of Achievement, Fed. Exec. Bd., Ptnrs. In Equality, 2001, Achiever's award, Def. Supply Ctr., Phila., 2001, Spl. Act award, 2001. Mem.: NAACP, nat. Assn. Female Exec., Am. Constn. Soc., Am. Comm. Assn., Zeta Phi Beta Sorority, Inc. (chpt. v.p., chpt. sec. 2000—03, coord. state com. 2003—). Home Fax: 1-800-430-7848. Personal E-mail: asmcduffy@yahoo.com.

MCDYESS, ANTONIO, professional basketball player; b. Quitman, Miss. Forward Denver Nuggets, 1995—97, 1998—2002, Phoenix Suns, 1997—98, N.Y. Knicks, 2003—04, Phoenix Suns, 2004, Detroit Pistons, 2004—. Named

to NBA All-Rookie First Team, 1995—96, All-NBA Third Team, 1998—99. Avocations: bowling, rhythm and blues. Office: c/o Detroit Pistons Palace of Auburn Hills 2 Championship Dr Auburn Hills MI 48326*

MCEACHEN, RICHARD EDWARD, banker, lawyer; b. Omaha, Sept. 24, 1933; s. Howard D. and Ada Carolyn Helen (Baumann) McE.; m. Judith Ann Gray, June 28, 1969; children: Mark E., Neil H. BS, U. Kans., Lawrence, 1955; JD, U. Mich., 1961. Bar: Mo. 1961, Kans. 1982. Assoc. Hillix, Hall, Hasburgh, Brown & Hoffhaus, Kansas City, Mo., 1961-62; sr. v.p. First Nat. Bank, Kansas City, Mo., 1962-75; exec. v.p. Commerce Bank Kansas City, Mo., 1975-85, Centerre Bank of Kansas City N.A., 1985-87, Security Bank Kansas City, Kans., 1987-88; exec. v.p., trust officer UMB Overland Park Bank, 1988-93; atty. Ferree, Bunn, O'Grady & Rundberg, Chartered, Overland Park, 1994—. Gov. Am. Royal Assn., Kansas City, Mo., 1970-2002, amb., 1980-2004, com. mem., 1995—; bd. dirs. Harry S. Truman Med. Ctr., Kansas City, 1974-86, mem. fin. com., 1975-86, treas., 1979-84, bd. govs., 1986-2002, mem. bldg. and grounds com., 1993-2002, mem. pension com., 1976-93, 96-2000; trustee Clearinghouse for Midcontinent Founds., 1980-87; bd. dirs. Greater Kansas City Mental Health Found., 1963-69, treas., 1964-69, v.p., 1967-69; adv. bd. urban svcs. YMCA, Kansas City, 1976-83; cubmaster Kanza dist. Boy Scouts Am., 1982-83, dist. vice chmn., 1982-83, troop com., 1983-90, treas., 1986-88; bd. dirs. Scout Booster Club, Inc., 1989-94; mem. planned gift com. William Rockhill Nelson Gallery Art, Children's Mercy Hosp. Planned Gift Coun., 1991—; mem. adv. com. Legal Assistance Program Avila Coll., 1978-80, adv. coun. Future Farmers Am., 1972-82; mgr. Oppenstein Bros. Found., 1979-85; trustee Village Presbyn. Ch., 1987-90, chmn., 1989-90, elder, 1994-97; found. com. Am. Royal Charitable Found., 1995—; bd. dirs. Village Presbyn. Ch. Found., 1987-89, 94-97, chmn., 1996-97, mem. adv. bd., 1997-2001, bd. dirs. Estate Planning Coun., 1984-86; mem. Kansas City Fed. Estate Planning Symposium Com., 1992-98; bd. dirs. Shawnee Mission Med. Ctr. Found., 1988—, fin. com., 1989-92, 2002—, mem. planned giving com., 1996-, mem. investment com., 2000—; mem. adv. coun. Shawnee Mission Edn. Found., 2003. Mem. Nat. Assn. Securities Dealers Inc. (bd. arbitrators 1994—), Am. Arbitration Assn. (panel arbitrators 1994-96), Estate Planning Soc. Kansas City, Mo. Bar Assn., Kans. Bar Assn., Johnson County Bar Assn., Estate Planning Assn. (pres. 1974-75), Kansas City Jr. C. of C. (v.p. 1964-66), Ea. Kans. Estate Planning Coun., 40-Yrs. Ago Column Club (program com. 1999-2000, pres. 2001, bd. trustees 2001-), Indian Hills Club, Delta Tau Delta Alumni (v.p. Kansas City chpt. 1978 80). Republican. Home: 9100 El Monte St Shawnee Mission KS 66207-2627 Office: One Glenwood Pl 9300 Metcalf Ave Ste 300 Shawnee Mission KS 66212-6319

MCEACHERN, ALEXANDER, electronics company executive; b. Boston, Feb. 18, 1955; s. Alexander William and Elisabeth Helena McEachern; m. Barbara Ruth Pereira, Dec. 18, 1975; children: Alexander Wallis, Ian Wallis. V.p. Mac Systems, 1975-79; dir. R&D Lomac Corp., Santa Clara, Calif., 1979-80; chmn., founder Basic Measuring Instruments, Santa Clara, 1981-99; pres. Electrotek Concepts, Inc., 1996-97, Power Stds. Lab., 2000—. Dir. WPT, 1997—, Dranetz/BMI/Electrotek, 1997—; founder Infrastructure Instruments Inc., 1996—; bd. dirs. Basic Measuring Instruments. Author: Handbook of Power Signatures; contbr. articles to profl. jours. Mem. IEEE (sr.). Office: PSL 2000 Powell St Ste 1200 Emeryville CA 94608-1856

MCEACHERN, ALLAN, lawyer; b. Vancouver, B.C., Can., May 20, 1926; s. John A. and Blanche L. (Roadhouse) McE.; m. Gloria, July 17, 1953 (dec. Sept. 1997); children: Jean Williams, Joanne Evans; m. Mary Victoria Newbury. BA, U. B.C., Vancouver, 1949, LLB, 1950, LLM (hon.), 1990. Assoc., sr. ptnr., barrister, solicitor Messrs. Russell & DuMoulin, Vancouver, 1950-78; chief justice Supreme Ct. B.C., Vancouver, 1979-88, Ct. Appeals B.C., Vancouver, 1988—2001; assoc. counsel Faskin Martineaes, Vancouver, 2001—; chancellor U. B.C., 2002—. Pres. Kats Rugby Club, Vancouver, 1953-64, B.C. Lions Football Club, Vancouver, 1967, 68, 69, We. Football Conf., 1964, Can. Football League, 1967-68, commr. 1967-68. Mem. Can. Bar Assn. (bd. dirs.), Vancouver Bar Assn. (bd. dirs.), Legal Aid Soc. (pres. 1977-78), Law Soc. B.C. (bencher 1971-79). Avocations: sailing, gardening, walking, summer cottage. Office: Faskin Martineaes 1075 W George St Vancouver BC V6E 3G2 Canada

MCEACHERN, JOAN, medical association administrator; b. East Los Angeles, Calif., Feb. 28, 1937; d. Chester Manwell Biffi and Doris May Horrocks; m. Wayne Emery McEachern, Sept. 8, 1961 (dec. Mar. 1992); children: Marc Alan, David Wayne, Eric John. AA, East Los Angeles Coll., 1957. Sec. Flour Corp., City of Commerce, Calif., 1957-61; volunteer art tchr. Yorkville Schs., Yorkville, IL, 1975-1983; office supr. McKeoun-Dunn Ambulance, Oswego, Ill., 1992-97. Author: Illinois Association for Home and Community Education—An Aim for the Homemaker: 75 Years of Education and Outreach, 1999. Mem. Kendall County 4-H, various coms., 1975-2000, mem. Ill. 4-H Found., 1988-97, sec. exec. com. 1990-97; del. Ill. 4-H Salute to Excellence, Washington, 1985; mem. various state coms. in 4-H, 1979-94, developed 4-H project books; ext. adv. coun. U. Ill., 1994-97; pres. Kendall County Homemakers Ext. Assn., 1982-84; adv. coun. Yorkville Schs. Curriculum Com., 1974-76, pres. 1975-76; started Picture Person Art Appreciation program, Yorkville Schs., 1976, chmn., 1975-81; vol. art tchr., 1975-83, others. Recipient Yorkville Area Humanitarian award City of Yorkville Human Svcs. Com., 1983, Disting. Svc. award award Kendall County Homemakers Ext. Assn., 1985, Kendall County Friend of 4-H award, 1989, numerous others. Mem.: Am. Women for Internat. Understanding (bd. dirs. 2002—, membership chair 2003—), Associated Country Women of the World (pubs. and promotions com. 2001—04), Ill. Assn. Home and Cmty. Edn. (pres. 1994—97), Nat. Vol. Outreach Network (pres. 1998—2001), Kendall County Hist. Soc. (newsletter editor 1992—2001), Yorkville Women's club. Avocations: water color painting, skiing, photography, travel, reading. Home and Office: 137 Riverside Dr Yorkville IL 60560-9471 E-mail: mcskikat@usa.com.

MCEACHERN, STEPHEN MATTHEW, accountant; b. Nacogooches, Tex., Oct. 18, 1948; s. Maxie Neil and Exa Julia (Stephenson) McE.; m. Rebecca Brookshire, Dec. 29, 1968 (div. Sept. 1973); 1 child, Mathew Clayton; m. Sherry Jane Fears, Sept. 1, 1974. BBA in Acctg., Tex. A&M U. CPA, Tex. Staff acct. Ernst & Whinney, Houston, 1971-75; sr. acct. Fitts, Roberts & Co., Houston, 1975—77, ptnr., 1977—97, pres., mng. ptnr., 1997—. Deacon, chmn. personnel and bldg. fin. com. Met. Bapt. Ch., Houston, 1984-86; committeeman Houston Livestock Show and Rodeo., 1983—. Mem. Am. Inst. CPA's, Tex. Soc. CPA's (bd. dirs., v.p. Houston chpt. 1985-—). Lodges: Rotary (sec. 1985—). Republican. Home: 13010 Dogwood Blossom Trl Houston TX 77065-3320 Office: Fitts Roberts & Co Inc 3707 Fm 1960 Rd W Houston TX 77068-3526*

MCEACHRAN, ANGUS, retired editor; b. Memphis, Aug. 24, 1939; s. Angus G. and Maxine (Taylor) McE.; m. Ann Blackwell; children: Angus G. 111, Amanda Simmons. Student, George Washington U., 1958-59, Memphis State U., 1959-61. Reporter The Comml. Appeal, Memphis, 1960-63, asst. city editor, 1963-65, metro editor, 1965-69, asst. mng. editor, 1969-77; exec. editor Birmingham (Ala.) Post-Herald, 1977-78, editor, 1978-82; exec. editor The Pitts. Press., 1982-83, editor, 1983-92, The Commercial Appeal, Memphis, 1993-94, editor, pres., 1994—2002. Corr. N.Y. Times, Wall St. Jour., Newsweek, The Nat. Observer. Mem. Am. Soc. Newspaper Editors, Pa. Soc. Newspaper Editors (bd. dirs.), Sigma Delta. Roman Catholic. Avocations: fishing, hiking, reading, photography.

MCELDOWNEY, ROLAND CONANT, mining executive, photographer; b. Newton, Mass., Nov. 14, 1940; s. Richard Lancaster and Virginia Davis (Conant) McEldowney; m. Barbara Lynn Read, Mar. 26, 1966; children: Richard Read, Scott Roland, Kathryn Ramsay. AB in Geology, Franklin & Marshall Coll., 1963; MS in Geology, San Diego State U., 1971. Cert. geologist, Maine. Vol. geologist U.S. Peace Corps, Ghana, 1963-66; geologist U.S. Army C.E., San Francisco, 1966-68; sr. geologist Geodata Systems Inc., Orange, Calif., 1969-71; assoc. sr. geologist Dames & Moore, Denver, 1972-79; v.p. Apache Energy and Minerals Co., Lakewood, Colo., 1979-84; pres., owner Wolf Creek Exploration Co., Evergreen Colo., 1984—; sr. v.p. Internat. Gold Resources Corp., Houston, Tex., 1985-96; owner Image of Africa, Evergreen, Colo., 1999—. Mng. dir. Internat. Gold Resources, Inc., Bibiani, Ghana, 1990—96. Artist, prodr. silver proof coin World Cup Skiing, Breckenridge, Colo., 1991—92; contbr. articles to profl. jours. Mem.: Geol. Soc. Am., Metallurgy and Exploration, Soc. Mining, Kiwanis (past bd. dirs. Blue Spruce). Republican. Achievements include discovery of Bibiani Open Pit Gold Mine. Avocations: art, hunting, fishing, skiing, bicycling. Home: 29434 Greenwood Ln Evergreen CO 80439-7446 Personal E-mail: auexplore@aol.com.

MCELDOWNEY, TODD RICHARD, lawyer; b. Rhinelander, Wis., Apr. 7, 1955; s. Russell James and Donna Jo (Stoll) McE. BS with highest honors, U. Wis., Stevens Point, 1977; JD, Marquette U., 1980. Bar: Wis. 1980, U.S. Dist. Ct. (ea. dist.) Wis. 1980, U.S. Dist. Ct. (we. dist.) Wis. 1980. With O'Melia, Eckert, McEldowney & Mangerson, Rhinelander, 1981-85; ptnr. O'Melia & McEldowney, S.C., Rhinelander, 1985-89, O'Melia, Schiek & McEldowney, S.C., Rhinelander, 1989—. Commr., Rhinelander Basketball League, 1976—; mem., pres., Rhinelander Police and Fire Commn., 1982—; mem. Oneida County Hwy. Safety Commn., Rhinelander, 1983—. Mem. Def. Rsch. Inst., Wis. Acad. Trial Lawyers, Am. Jud. Soc., Oneida-Vilas-Forest County Bar Assn., Optimists Club (pres. local club 1981—), Lions Club, Rhinelander Basketball Assn. (pres. 1991-). Home: 705 Lake Shore Dr Rhinelander WI 54501-2310 Office: O'Melia Schiek & McEldowney PO Box 1047 Rhinelander WI 54501-0797 Office Phone: 715-369-5456. E-mail: Todd@Schieklaw.com.

MCELHANEY, JAMES WILLSON, lawyer, educator, author, trial consultant; b. N.Y.C., Dec. 10, 1937; s. Lewis Keck and Sara Jane (Hess) McE.; m. Maxine Dennis Jones, Aug. 17, 1961; children: David, Benjamin. AB, Duke U., 1960; LLB, 1962. Bar: Wis. 1962. Assoc. Wickham, Borgelt, Skogstad & Powell, 1966; asst. prof. U. Md. Law Sch., 1966-69, assoc. prof., 1969-72; vis. prof. So. Meth. U. Sch. of Law, Dallas, 1973-74, prof., 1974-76; Joseph C. Hostetler prof. trial practice and advocacy Case Western Res. U. Sch. of Law, Cleve., 1976—2002, Baker & Hostetler Disting. scholar in trial practice, 2002—; mem. faculty Nat. Inst. Trial Advocacy, Boulder, Colo., 1975—87; Fred Parks Disting. lectr. in trial advocacy South Tex. Coll. Law, Houston, 2002—. Vis. prof. U. Tulsa Coll. Law, summer 1977, 79, Ind. U. Law Sch., summer 1980; cons. to U.S. Atty. Gen. on Justice Dept. Advocacy Tng. Programs, 1979—; lectr. in field; litigation cons.; spl. cons. U. S.C. Sch. of Law Nat. Advocacy Ctr., 1998. Author: Effective Litigation: Trials, Problems and Materials, 1974, Trial Notebook, 1981, 3rd edit., 1994, Mc Elhaney's Litigation, 1994, Trial Notebook on Tape: The Basics, 1989, Mc Elhaney's Trial Notebook on Tape: Advanced Techniques, 1991, Mc Elhaney's Trial Notebook on Tape: Evidence, Foundations and Objections, 1992, Mc Elhaney's Trial Notebook on Tape: Winning Tactics, 1994, Mc Elhaney's Litigation, 1995, Mc Elhaney on Cross-Examination on Tape, 1997, Mc Elhaney on Depositions and Trial Preparation on Tape, 1999, McElhaney's Deposition Notebook on CD and audiotape, 2003; editor-in-chief Litigation mag., 1984-86, sr. editor, 1986—; columnist Trial Notebook, Litigation; contbr. articles to profl. jours. Mem. ABA (mem. coun. on litigation 1987—, author jour. column Litigation), Assn. Am. Law Schs. (chmn. sect. on trial advocacy 1974-76, chmn. sect. on evidence 1978). Home and Office: PO Box 367 Chama NM 87520-0367 *The lamp of doctrine is a flickering and unsteady guide; we are led more by facts than by theories.*

MC ELHANEY, JOHN HESS, lawyer; b. Milw., Apr. 16, 1934; s. Lewis Keck and Sara Jane (Hess) McE.; m. Jacquelyn Masur, Aug. 4, 1962; children— Scott, Victoria. BBA, So. Meth. U., 1956, JD, 1958. Bar: Tex. bar 1958. Pvt. practice law, Dallas, 1958—; pntr. Locke, Liddell & Sapp, L.L.C., Dallas, 1976—. Lectr. law So. Meth. U., 1967-76 Contbr. articles to legal jours. Trustee St. Mark's Sch. Tex., 1980-86. Fellow Am. Coll. Trial Lawyers; mem. Am. Bd. Trial Advs., ABA, Tex. Bar Assn., So. Meth. U. Law Alumni Assn. (pres. 1972-73, dir. 1970-73), Town and Gown Club (pres. 1981-82). Presbyterian. Home: 5340 Tanbark Dr Dallas TX 75229-5555 Office: Locke Liddell & Sapp 2200 Ross Ave Ste 2200 Dallas TX 75201-6776

MCELHANY, ANDY, state senator; b. San Francisco, Apr. 28, 1940; Student, Colo. Sch. Mines, 1958-59, U. Mo. Lic. real estate broker. Rep. rep. dist. 17 Colo. Ho. of Reps., 1994-2000; Rep. senator dist. 12 Colo. State Senate, 2000—. Mem. transp. and energy coms. Colo. Ho. of Reps., chair vets. and mil. affairs com.; mem. bus. affairs and labor, capitol devel. and pub. policy and planning coms. Colo. State Senate. Chmn. adv. bd. Colo. Springs Pk. and Recreation, 1992-94. Recipient Disting. Svc. award, 1989-90, Realtor of Yr. award, 1992. Mem. Pikes Peak Assn. Realtors. Office: 95 W Boulder Colorado Springs CO 80903 also: Colo State Senate State Capitol 200 E Colfax Rm 274 Denver CO 80203

MCELHINNEY, JAMES LANCEL, artist, educator; b. Abington, Pa., Feb. 3, 1952; s. James and Joan Howland (Carpenter) McE.; m. Victoria Maria Dávila, Sept. 12, 1981 (div.), m. M.L. Burnell Shively, May 14, 2003. Scholarship student, Skowhegan (Maine) Sch. of Art, 1973; BFA, Temple U., 1974; MFA, Yale U., 1976. Asst. prof. Moore Coll. Art, Phila., 1977-78, Skidmore Coll., Saratoga Springs, N.Y., 1979-87; adj. instr. UCLA, 1983, Moore Coll. Art, 1983, Tyler Sch. Art, Phila., 1983-86, U. of Arts, Phila., 1985-89; instr. Milw. Inst. Art and Design, 1991-93; vis. artist East Carolina U., Greenville, N.C., 1994-98; head painting and drawing program visual arts dept. U. Colo., Denver, 1998—; dir. study abroad program Feltre, Veneto, Italy, 2000—. Artist in residence Harper's Ferry Nat. Hist. Park, 1999; lectr. USAF Acad., 2001. One-man shows include Peninsula Ctr. for the Fine Arts, Newport News, Va., 1993, Danville (Va.) Mus., 1993, Second Street Gallery, Charlottesville, Va., 1995, F.A.N. Gallery, Phila., 1995, 1998, Greenville (N.C.) Mus. Art, 1996, Lee Hansley Gallery, Raleigh, N.C., 1996, 1998, 1999, Asheville (N.C.) Art Mus., 1996, William Havu Gallery, Denver, 2001—02, Mus. of the S.W., Midland, Tex., 2003, Letterkenny Arts Ctr., Donegal, Ireland, 2003, William Havu Gallery, 2001, Mus of Southwest, Midland, Tex., 2003, Letterkenny Arts Ctr., Donegal, Ireland, 2003, exhibited in group shows at Chrysler Mus., Norfolk, Va., 1999, Allen Sheppard Gallery, N.Y.C., 1999, Ucross Found., 2000, Nicolayseu Mus., 2000, Represented in permanent collections Chrysler Mus. Art, Denver Art Mus., Asheville Art Mus.; contbr. articles to various profl. mag., to profl. jours.; prin. works include multiple venues, 2003. Vol. Richmond (Va.) Nat. Battlefield Park, 1991—, Frontier Army Living History Corps of Discovery, U.S. Army C.E. Lewis and Clark Bicentennial, Topog. eng. 1st Divsn. Staff, Hdqs. Nat. Reft. (U.S.C.W.). Grantee painting, NEA, 1987—88, Ptnrs. in Arts, Richmond Arts Coun., 1995; rsch. grant, U. Colo., 2000, Faculty Devel. grant, 2003. Mem. Coll. Art Assn., SAR, Civil War Preservation Trust, Frontier Army L.H. Assoc.,Foote Family Assoc. Office: U Colo Coll Arts Media Box 177 PO Box 173364 Denver CO 80217-3364

MCELHINNY, HAROLD JOHN, lawyer; b. San Francisco, Jan. 5, 1947; s. Harold James and Margaret I. (Mahoney) McE.; m. Mary Ellen McElhinny, June 22, 1968; children: Hannah, Jennifer, William. BA in Polit. Sci., U. Santa Clara, 1970; JD, U. Calif., Berkeley, 1975. Bar: Calif. 1976, U.S. Supreme Ct. 1983. Vol. Peace Corps., Tripoli, Libya, 1968-69; juvenile counselor Santa Clara County (Calif.) Juvenile Hall, 1969-72; law clk. U.S. Dist. Ct., Hartford, Conn., 1975-76; ptnr. Morrison & Foerster, San Francisco, 1976—. Mem. ABA, Calif. Bar Assn., State Bar Calif. (rev. dept. 1986-89, chmn. 1988), San Francisco Bar Assn., Am. Intellectual Property Law Assn., Assn. Bus. Trial Lawyers (bd. govs. 1992-97, pres. 1997). Democrat. Roman Catholic. Office: Morrison & Foerster 425 Market St Fl 30 San Francisco CA 94105-2482 Office Phone: 415-268-7265. E-mail: hmcelhinny@mofo.com.

MCELHINNY, WILSON DUNBAR, banker; b. Detroit, July 27, 1929; s. William Dunbar and Elizabeth (Wilson) McE.; m. Barbara Cheney Watkins, June 6, 1952 (dec.); children: David Ashton, Ward Cheney, Edward Wilson, William Dunbar; m. Lisa Lesher, Mar. 27, 1993. BA, Yale U., 1953. With Union and New Haven Trust Co., 1952-63, Reading Trust Co., Pa., 1963-68, pres., 1968-70, Nat. Ctrl. Bank (formerly Reading Trust Co.), Pa., 1970-79, CEO, 1975-79; chmn. bd. dirs., pres., CEO Hamilton Bank (formerly Nat. Ctrl. Bank), Lancaster, Pa., 1979-81, chmn. bd. dirs., CEO, 1981-83, chmn. bd. dirs., 1981-90; pres. CoreStates Fin. Corp., Phila., 1983-86, vice chmn., 1986-90; pres., chmn. Hamilton Bank, Lancaster, 1988-90. Bd. dirs. Reading Eagle Co., 1st Bank Idaho, SIGCO, Portland, Maine. Mem. St. Luke's Wood River Found. Mem. Pa. C. of C. (chmn. 1990-92), Yale Club N.Y., The Valley Club. Home and Office: PO Box 3070 Ketchum ID 83340-3070

MCELLISTREM, MARCUS T. chemistry professor, semiconductor materials researcher; s. Marcus T. and Eleanor McEllistrem; m. Laurel J. Knott, Sept. 5, 1995; children: Marcus T., Michael M., Grace M. PhD, Univ. of Wis., 1985—93. Postdoctoral fellow chemistry U. of N. C., Chapel Hill, 1996—98; asst. prof. chemistry U. Wis., Eau Claire, 1998—2004; assoc. prof. chemistry U. Wis., Eau Claire, 2004—. Contbr. jour. publications. Grantee support of study of GaN surfaces; support for instrumentation, NSF, 1999—2003. Mem.: Am. Chem. Soc. Achievements include patents for piezoelectric inchworm controller. Avocation: bicycling. Office: Dept of Chemistry Univ of Wis 105 Garfield Ave Eau Claire WI 54702-4004 Office Phone: 715-836-4081. Office Fax: 715-836-4979. Business E-Mail: mcellimt@uwec.edu.

MCELLISTREM, MARCUS T. physics professor, nuclear researcher; b. St. Paul, Apr. 19, 1926; s. Marcus T. and Loretta Camille (Simard) McEllistrem; m. Eleanor DeMeuse, Aug. 17, 1957; children: Mary Ann, Marcus T., Rebecca, Joan, Catherine, Deborah. BA St. Thomas Coll., 1950; MS, U. Wis., 1951, PhD, 1955. Rsch. asst. U. Wis., Madison, 1952—55; rsch. assoc. Ind. U., Bloomington, 1955—57; asst. prof. U. Ky., Lexington, 1957—60, assoc. prof., 1960—65, prof. physics, 1965—94, univ. rsch. prof., 1979—80, prof. emeritus, 1994—. Sponsor U. Ky. Newman Ctr., 1960—70, pres., 1979—81; cons. Arnold AFB, Tullahoma, Tenn., 1968—70, Wright Patterson AFB, Dayton, Ohio, 1971—74; pres. Adena Corp., Lexington, 1971—75; Collaborateur Etr. CEA, Bruyeres-le-Chatel, France, 1974—75, 1978, 81, 84. Contbr. articles to profl. jours. Sec. bd. Lexington Catholic High Sch., 1983—85. Served with USNR, 1944—46. Fellow: Am. Phys. Soc.; mem.: AAAS, NSF (co-Principal Investigator 1994—, program. officer 1981—82), Sigma Xi. Roman Catholic. Office: Physics & Astronomy U. of Ky. Lexington KY 40506-0055 Business E-Mail: marcus@uky.edu.

MC ELRATH, RICHARD ELSWORTH, retired insurance company executive; b. Thompsontown, Pa., Oct. 11, 1932; s. Clayton Ellsworth and Jane Elizabeth (Shoop) McE.; m. Donna Gail Booher, Aug. 18, 1952; children— Leslie Jo, Jennifer Jo, Josie Arlene Elizabeth, Rebekah Clare. BS cum laude Elizabethtown (Pa.) Coll., 1955; MBA cum laude, Harvard U., 1961. Research asst. Harvard U., 1961-62; asst. to pres. Callaway Mills Co., LaGrange, Ga., 1963-65; with Irving Trust Co., N.Y.C., 1965-73, v.p., 1969-73; treas. Tchrs. Ins. Annuity Assn. and Coll. Retirement Equities Fund, 1973-81; v.p. Met. Life Ins. Co., 1982-95. Pres., dir. MetLife Funding, Inc., MetLife Credit, Inc., 1984-95. Author articles, case studies. Trustee Elizabethtown Coll.; mem. Society Valley Hosp., Ridgewood, N.J.; mem. Boston Rep. Com., 1961-63, Troup County (Ga.) Rep. Com., 1964-65; bd. dirs. Family Counseling Svc., Ridgewood, 1986-92. Lt. comdr. USNR, 1956-59. Mem. Assn. Gov. Bds. Univs. and Colls. Clubs: Harvard (N.Y.C.). Methodist. Home: 17 Cedar St Glen Rock NJ 07452-1608

MCELROY, EDWARD J. labor union administrator; b. Providence, Mar. 17, 1941; s. Edward J. Sr. and Clara (Angelone) McE.; m. Edwina Barbara Ricci, Apr. 20, 1963; children: Kathleen, Mary, Stephen, Elizabeth. AB, Providence Coll., 1962. Cert. tchr. Tchr. Lockwood Jr. High Sch., Warwick, R.I., 1962-72; pres. Warwick Tchrs. Union, Warwick, R.I., 1967-69, R.I. Fed. Tchrs., Am. Fed. Tchrs., Providence, 1971-92, R.I. AFL-CIO, Providence, 1977-92; v.p. Am. Fed. Tchrs., AFL-CIO, Providence, 1974-92, sec. treas. Washington, 1992—2004, pres., 2004—. Exec. com. mem. R.I. Democratic State Com., Providence, 1976-92; sec. exec. com. United Way So. New England, Providence, 1978-92; devel. commn. R.I. State, 1984-85, mem. Workforce 2000, 1987-92. Recipient Quirk Inst. award Providence Coll., 1980. Mem. Aurora Civic Assn, bd. dirs., Voices for Working Families, Amalgamated Bank of Chgo. Democrat. Roman Catholic. Avocations: golf, photography, reading. Office: Am Fed Tchrs AFL CIO 555 New Jersey Ave NW Washington DC 20001-2029*

MCELROY, HOWARD CHOWNING, lawyer; b. Shreveport, La., Mar. 26, 1946; s. Charles Imogene and Verna Mae (Snow) McE.; m. Heidi Margot Hansen, June 17, 1970; children: Andrew, Christopher, Karen. BS, U.S. Mil. Acad., 1968; JD, Georgetown U., 1977. Bar: Va. 1977, U.S. Dist. Ct. (we. dist.) Va. 1977, U.S. Ct. Appeals (4th cir.) 1977. Ptnr. Bundy McElroy Hodges, Abingdon, Va., 1995—. Mem. mandatory continuing legal edn. bd. Va. State Bar 1986-89, professionalism course faculty, 1991-94. Capt. M.I. U.S. Army, 1968-72, Vietnam. Fellow Am. Bar Found., Va. Law Found.; mem. ABA, Am. Bd. Trial Advocates (Va. chpt.), Def. Rsch. Inst., Va. Bar Assn. (exec. com. 1991-95, sec. 1993-95), Va. Assn. Def. Attys. (pres. 1995-96), Internat. Assn. Def. Counsel, Assn. Def. Trial Attys., Rotary (pres. local club 1983-84, Paul Harris fellow). Episcopalian. Home: 160 Crestview Dr NE Abingdon VA 24210-2010 Office: Bundy McElroy Hodges 330 Cummings St Abingdon VA 24210-3208 Office Phone: 276-628-9515. E-mail: hmcelroybmhlaw@naxs.net.

MCELROY, JEROME LATHROP, economics professor; b. St. Louis, Sept. 14, 1937; s. King Gerard and Audrey (Lathrop) McE.; m. Birdie Maria Rossow; children: Jacqueline, Christopher. BA, St. Louis U., 1961, PhL, 1962, MA in Econs., 1965; PhD in Econs., U. Colo., 1972. Instr. St. John's Coll., Belize City, Belize, 1962-65; grad. assoc. U. Colo., Boulder, 1971-72; asst. prof. econs. Coll. of V.I., St. Thomas, 1972-75, assoc. prof. econs., 1975-79; dir. planning Govt. of V.I., St. Thomas, 1979-80; assoc. prof. econs. U. Notre Dame, Ind., 1980-82, St. Mary's Coll., South Bend, Ind., 1982-86, prof. econs., 1986—, chmn. dept. bus. and econs., 1990-93. Rsch. fellow Island Resources Found., Washington, 1980—; expert adv. panel Office Tech. Assessment, U.S. Congress, 1985-86; econ. cons. U.S. AID, 1987-89, Govt. V.I., 1974-79, 89. Author: Consumer Expenditure Patterns, 1980, USVI Status Options, 1989; contbr. articles to profl. jours., poems to lit. mags. Mem. adv. bd. Ea. Caribbean Ctr., U. V.I., 1993-95. Recipient Maria Pieta Tchr. award, St. Mary's Coll., 1989, Tchr. of the Yr., Coll. of V.I., 1973, Spes Unica Svc. award, 1997. Mem. Am. Econ. Assn., Caribbean Studies Assn., So. Reg. Sci. Assn., Midwest Assn. Latin Americanists, Internat. Small Islands Studies Assn., Internat. Sci. Coun. for Island Devel. (founding mem.), Inst. for Devel. of Insular Economies and Socs. (founding mem.), Island Environ. Inst. (founding mem.). Democrat. Roman Catholic. Avocations: swimming, poetry. Home: 2036 Portage Ave South Bend IN 46616-2033 Office: Saint Mary's College 106 Madeleva Notre Dame IN 46556 Office Phone: 574-284-4488. E-mail: jmcelroy@saintmarys.edu.

MC ELROY, JOHN HARLEY, electrical and industrial engineering educator; b. Marion, Ohio, June 27, 1936; s. Francis and Alice Marie McElroy; m. Eleonore Hildegard Schmidt, Mar. 18, 1957. BS in Elec. Engring, U. Tex., Austin, 1966; M.E.E., Cath. U. Am., 1973, PhD, 1978. Instr. guided missles Air Defense Sch. U.S. Army, 1957-63; rsch. asst. Quantum Electronics rsch. Lab U. Texas, Austin, 1963-66; staff Goddard Flight Ctr., Greenbelt, Md., 1966-79, 80-82, chief comms. tech. div., 1978-79, dep. dir. ctr., 1980-82; dir. comms. programs NASA Hdqrs., Washington, 1979-80; asst. adminstr. NOAA, Washington, 1982-85; dir. spl. projects Hughes Aircraft Co., Los Angeles, 1985-86; v.p. tech. Hughes Comms., Inc., 1986-87; dean Coll. Engring., prof. elec. engring. U. Tex., Arlington, 1987-96, vice provost for rsch. and grad. studies, 1996-97, prof. elec. and indsl. engring., 1997-2000, dean emeritus Coll. Engring.; chair space studies bd. Nat. Rsch. Coun., 2000—03. Cons. satellite communications and earth observations. Contbr. articles to profl. jours. Served with AUS, 1954-63. Recipient Apollo Achievement award NASA, 1969, Applications Tech. Satellite award, 1975, Earth Resources Satellite award, 1973, Internat. Coop. in Space Sci. medal AIAA, 1997, Pub. Svc. medal NASA, 2003; named Wernher von Braun Meml. Lectr. Smithsonian Instn., Disting. Hon. Alumnus U. Tex., Arlington, 1998. Fellow AIAA, IEEE, Washington Acad. Scis.; mem. Nat. Acad. Engring. Home: 5687 Wild Olive St Las Vegas NV 89118-1956 Personal E-mail: jhmcelroy@worldnet.att.net.

MCELROY, LEO FRANCIS, communications consultant, journalist; b. Los Angeles, Oct. 12, 1932; s. Leo Francis and Helen Evelyn (Silliman) McE.; m. Dorothy Frances Montgomery, Nov. 3, 1956 (div. 1981); children: James, Maureen, Michael, Kathleen; m. Judith Marie Lewis, May 30, 1992. BS in English, Loyola U., L.A., 1953. News dir. KFI, KRLA, KABC Radio, L.A., 1964-72; pub. affairs host TV Sta. KCET, L.A., 1967-74; v.p. Sta. KROQ AM/FM, L.A., 1972-74; polit. editor Sta. KABC-TV, L.A., 1974-81; pres. McElroy Comm., Sacramento, 1981—. Pres. sec. Lt. Gov.'s Office, Sacramento, 1982-84; chmn. Calif. AP Broadcasters, 1972-74; cons. State Office Migrant Edn., Sacramento, 1974, Californians for Water, L.A., 1982, Calif. Water Protection Coun., Sacramento, 1982, Planning and Conservation League, Sacramento, 1984—, Common Cause, Sacramento, 1988—. Author: Uneasy Partners, 1984; author plays: Mermaid Tavern, 1956, To Bury Caesar, 1952 (Christopher award), Rocket to Olympus, 1960, The Code of Whiskey King, 1995. State del. Western Am. Assembly on Prison Reform, Berkeley, Calif., 1973; chmn. State Disaster Info. Task Force, Calif., 1973-74; campaign media cons. statewide issues, various candidates, Sacramento, L.A., 1981—; bd. dirs. Vols. in Victim Assistance, Sacramento, 1984, Rescue Alliance, Sacramento, 1987-92, Mental Health Assn., Sacramento, 1985-89, Leukemia Soc., 1992-97, Calif Fire Safe Coun., 2002—. Recipient Gabriel award Cath. Archdiocese, L.A., 1972, Golden Mike award Radio-TV News Assn., L.A., 1973; Hon. Resolution, Calif. State Assembly, Sacramento, 1981. Mem. ASCAP, AFTRA, Screen Actors Guild, Am. Assn. Polit. Cons. Roman Catholic. Home: 2262 Swarthmore Dr Sacramento CA 95825-6608 Office: Bouchard McElroy Comm Group 2410 K St Ste C Sacramento CA 95816-5002 E-mail: mcelcom@pacbell.net.

MCELROY, MICHAEL ROBERT, lawyer; b. Providence, Feb. 7, 1951; s. Gerald Robert and Jeannette (Belanger) McE.; m. Christine Anne O'Donnell, June 5, 1976; children: Brian Robert, Dianne Elizabeth, Erin Christine. BA with highest distinction, U. R.I., 1973; JD cum laude, Boston U., 1976; MS in Taxation cum laude, Bryant Coll., 1987. Bar: Tenn. 1976, Mass. 1985, U.S. Dist. Ct. (ea. dist.) Tenn. 1977, U.S. Ct. Appeals (5th cir.) 1977, U.S. Supreme Ct. 1979, U.S. Ct. Appeals (6th cir.) 1980, R.I. 1981, U.S. Dist. Ct. R.I. 1981, U.S. Ct. Appeals (1st cir.) 1981, U.S. Dist. Ct. Mass. 2000. Trial atty. TVA, Knoxville, 1976-81; counsel R.I. Pub. Utilities Commn., Providence, 1982-83; spl. asst. atty. gen. Office Atty. Gen., Providence, 1982-83; ptnr. O'Leary & McElroy, Providence, 1981-85; sole practice Providence, 1985-87; ptnr. Schacht & McElroy, Providence, 1987—. Pres. Utility Cons., Inc., Providence, 1983; ptnr. McElroy, Lawrence, Edge & Assocs., Providence, 1983-85. Legal counsel for candidate Congl. campaign, Providence, 1982; legal counsel Pawtuxet Valley Preservation and Hist. Soc., West Warwick, R.I., 1983—; chief speech writer for candidate gubernatorial campaign, R.I., 1984; chief legal counsel for candidate gubernatorial campaign, R.I., 1988, Gov. Bruce Sundlun's successful gubernatorial campaign, 1990; legal counsel to R.I. Pers. Appeal Bd., 1991—; arbitrator Superior Ct. R.I., 1992—; spl. master/commr., 1993—; mediator Superior Ct., 1999—; spl. legal counsel to R.I. Ethics Commn., 2000-02. Danforth Found. hon. fellow, 1973; Rhodes scholar nominee, 1973; honoree for life-saving CPR, TVA, 1980; nominated for judgeship Jud. Nom. Commn. Superior Ct., 1994. Mem.: ATLA, Million Dollar Advs. Forum, Assn. Trial Lawyers R.I., R.I. Bar Assn. (chmn.Superior Ct. Bench/Bar com. 2003—, mem. Supreme Ct. com., fed. ct. and superior ct. Bench/Bar coms.). Roman Catholic. Home: 345 Sharon St Providence RI 02908-2220 Office: PO Box 6721 Providence RI 02940-6721 Office Phone: 401-351-4100. E-mail: mcelroymik@aol.com.

MCELROY, MICHELLE MARIE, physician; b. Atchison, Kans., Jan. 25, 1968; d. James Patrick and Victoria Jane (DeGreeff) McE. BS, Mich. State U., 1990; DO, Kirksville Coll. Osteo., 1994. Bd. cert. ob-gyn. AOBOG / Am. Osteo. Assn. Intern Riverside Osteo. Hosp., Trenton, Mich., 1994-95, resident in ob-gyn., 1995-98; with Women's Health Assocs. of Mid. Ga., Dublin, 1998—2000; Cynthia J. Caputo, MD, PC, Blue Springs, Mo., 2001—. Clin. instr. dept. osteo. medicine Mich. State U., East Lansing, 1995-98. Mem. Am. Osteo. Assn., Am. Coll. Osteo. Obstetricians and Gynecologists, Mo. Assn. Osteo. Physicians and Surgeons. Roman Catholic. Avocations: aerobics, jogging, family and friends. Home: 5208 E 30th Ter S Blue Springs MO 64015-1114 Office: Cynthia J Caputo MD PC 1900 NW Copper Oaks Cir Bldg 1 Blue Springs MO 64015 Office Phone: 816-220-5550. E-mail: mobdo@msn.com.

MCELVAIN, DAVID PLOWMAN, retired manufacturing company financial executive; b. Chgo., Oct. 16, 1937; s. Carl R. and Ruth P. (Plowman) McE.; m. Mary Rosalind Hysong, Dec. 20, 1961; children: Jana, Jodi. BBA, U. Ariz., 1961, MBA, 1962. Cert. mgmt. acct. Consolidation acct., exec. divsn. Dresser Industries, Inc., Dallas, 1962-67, corp. fin. controller, 1973-76, dir. fin. svcs., 1976-78, staff v.p. fin. svc. and risk mgmt., 1978-82, exec. v.p. fin. svcs. group, 1982-83, pres. fin. svcs. group, 1984-86, v.p. fin., CFO, 1987-93; owner McElvain Oil Co., Dallas, 1993—. Controller crane, hoist & tower div., Muskegon, Mich., 1967-73. Mem. Nat. Assn. Accts., Beta Gamma Sigma, Phi Delta Theta. Episcopalian. Home: 14828 Bellbrook Dr Dallas TX 75254-7647

MCELVAINE, ROBERT STUART, writer, educator; b. East Brunswick, N.J., Jan. 24, 1947; s. Edward and Ruth Ludewig McElvaine; m. Anne Therese Lee, Aug. 24, 1968; children: Kerri Anne, Lauren Lee Itzkowitz, Allison Therese, Brett Edward. BA, Rutgers U., 1968; MA in History, SUNY, Binghamton, 1971; PhD, SUNY, 1974. Asst. prof. history Millsaps Coll., Jackson, Miss., 1973—79, assoc. prof. history, 1979—84, prof. history, 1984—, Elizabeth Chisholm prof. arts & letters, 1988—. Cons. PBS series, Blackside Productions, Boston, 1991—93; assoc. editor, Am. Nat. Biography Oxford U. Press, N.Y.C., 1997—2001; editor-in-chief, The Ency. of the Great Depression Macmillan Reference USA, 1999—2004. Author: The Great Depression: America, 1929-1941, The End of the Conservative Era: Liberalism After Reagan, Mario Cuomo: A Biography, What's Left? - A New Democratic Vision for America, Eve's Seed: Biology, the Sexes and the Course of History, Franklin Delano Roosevelt; editor: Down and Out in the Great Depression: Letters from the Forgotten Man, The Depression and New Deal: A History in Documents, The Encyclopedia of the Great Depression. Recipient Silver medal, Nat. Prof. of the Yr., Coun. Advancement & Support Edn., 1988, Miss. Prof. Yr., Carnegie Endowment Edn., 2002. Mem.: AAUP, Orgn. Am. Historians, Am. Hist. Assn. Liberal. Roman Catholic. Avocations: travel, sports, music, movies, photography. Home: 201 Concord Drive Clinton MS 39056 Office: Millsaps College 1701 N State Street Jackson MS 39210 Office Phone: 601-974-1291. Personal E-mail: mcelvrs@millsaps.edu. E-mail: mcelvrs@millsaps.edu.

MCELVEEN, JOSEPH JAMES, JR., journalist, author, educator, mass media executive; b. Sanford, Fla., Feb. 23, 1939; s. Joseph James Sr. and Genevieve (Stoll) McE.; m. Mary Louise Young, Aug. 18, 1979; 1 child, Ryan Leighton. BA, Furman U., 1961; MA, U. S.C., 1968. Editor, pub. West Ashley News, Charleston, S.C., 1951-57; reporter, photographer Charleston Post, 1955-57; tchr. English and journalism St. Andrew's Parish High Sch., Charleston, 1961-65; dir. info., prof. journalism Columbia Coll., S.C., 1965-68; prof. journalism U. S.C., Columbia, 1968-79; sr. pub. affairs specialist FCC, Washington, 1979-81; dir. pub. affairs adminstrn. Nat. Cable TV Assn., Washington, 1981-87; dir. internal communications Corp. for Pub. Broadcasting, Washington, 1987-92, dir. program adminstrn., 1992-96, sr. program officer, 1996-99; media/comms. cons. Vienna, Va., 1999—; tchr. English, Fairfax County Pub. Schs., Vienna, Va., 2002—. Ombudsman, columnist Alexandria Gazette, Va., 1981—88; pres. McElveen Seminars, Vienna, 2000—. Author: Introduction to Creative Writing, 1963, Modern Communications, 1964; contbr. chpt. to Dictionary of Literary Biography (Mencken), 1986, Words, Words, Words: A Journalist's Memoir, 1997, Effective Writing and Editing, 2000, 1940s: Decade on the Threshold, 2000. Mem. Orgn. of News Ombudsmen, Soc. Profl. Journalists, Mencken Soc. Episcopalian. Avocations: photography, reading, desktop pub. Office: 1807 Hursley Ct Vienna VA 22182-2105 Personal E-mail: jjmcelveen@aol.com.

MCELVEEN, JUNIUS CARLISLE, JR., lawyer; b. Rogersville, Tenn., Feb. 17, 1947; s. Junius Carlisle and Martha Kathleen (Harrison) McE.; m. Mary Wallace Pyles, Sept. 22, 1973; children: Kathryn Carlisle, Sarah Elizabeth. BA cum laude, U. Va., 1969, JD, 1972. Bar: Va. 1972, Calif. 1975, U.S. Dist. Ct. (ea. dist.) Va. 1976, D.C. 1978, U.S. Ct. Appeals (4th cir.) 1978, U.S. Ct. Appeals (Fed. cir.) 1986, U.S. Ct. Appeals (11th cir.) 1990. Rsch. assoc. Atlantic Richfield, Washington, 1972; assoc. Pender & Coward, Norfolk, Va., 1976-77; from assoc. to ptnr. Seyfarth, Shaw, Washington, 1977—83; ptnr. Jones Day, Washington, 1983—. Mem. adv. com., reproductive hazards in the workplace Office of Tech. Assessment, Washington, 1984-86; mem. adv. council Ctr. Environ. Health, U. Conn., 1986-95; mem. editorial bd. The Occupational and Environ. Medicine Report, 1986—, Human and Ecol. Risk Assessment, 1998—. Contbr. articles to legal jours. Elder Kirkwood Presbyn. Ch., Springfield, Va., 1984-86. Served as lt. USN, 1972-75. Mem. ABA, Va. State Bar, State Bar Calif., Phi Beta Kappa, Phi Delta Phi (sec. local chpt. 1971-72, Outstanding Grad. award 1972). Home: 318 S Pitt St Alexandria VA 22314-3712 Office: Jones Day 51 Louisana Ave NW Washington DC 20001 Office Phone: 202-879-3939. Business E-Mail: jcmcelveen@jonesday.com.

MCELVEEN, WILLIAM LINDSAY, broadcasting executive, lecturer; b. Columbia, S.C., Sept. 20, 1950; s. Henry Moody and Dorothy Butler (Sligh) McE.; m. Laurie Wells Boyle, Sept. 8, 1969 (div. 1976); 1 child, Earle Sligh; m. Catharine Elizabeth McCaslin, Aug. 13, 1992; 1 child, Kerry Elizabeth McCaslin. BA in English, U. of South, 1972. Acct. exec. Sta. WNOK-FM, Columbia, S.C., 1972-73, mng. dir., 1973-79; v.p., gen. mgr. Stas. WNOK-AM-FM, Columbia, 1979-84; pres. Audubon Broadcasting Co., Columbia, 1984-89, Radio South Carolina, Columbia, 1989—. Exec. dir. Bloomington Broadcasting Corp., 1998-2000; lectr. Internat. Media Fund, Washington, 1993—; v.p. s.e. region Citadel Broadcasting, 2000—. Chmn. bd. dirs. Columbia Urban League, 1983-85; bd. dirs. Crimestoppers of Midlands, 1984-88, S.C. Law Inst., Columbia, 1985-88, Helpline of Midlands, 1986-90; gen. campaign chair United Negro Coll. Fund, Columbia, 1985-86; mem. exec. com. United Way of Midlands, Columbia, 1987-88. Mem. Nat. Assn. Broadcasters (bd. dirs. 1988-92, 96—, v.p. 1997-98, chmn. 1998-2000), S.C. Broadcasters Assn. (exec. com., bd. dirs. 1980-87, pres. 1988-92, Hall of Fame inductee 1996), Columbia Advt. Fedn. (pres. 1980-81), Media Club of Columbia (bd. dirs., pres. 1983-84). Presbyterian. Avocations: golf, tennis, travel. Home: 263 Tombee Ln Columbia SC 29209-0804 Office: Radio SC 1801 Charleston Hwy Cayce SC 29033-2019

MCELVEEN-HUNTER, BONNIE, ambassador; b. S.C., Jan. 1945; m. Bynum M. Hunter, Sr.; 1 child, Bynum M. Hunter Jr. Pres., CEO, owner Pace Comm., Inc.; U.S. amb. to Finland Dept. of State, Helsinki, 2001—. Chmn. Alexis de Tocqueville Soc., United Way Greater Greensboro, NC; bd. mem. United Way Am., chair nat. women's leadership giving campaign; chair Women in Philanthropy Summit, Washington; internat. bd. mem. Habitat for Humanity; bd. mem. Internat. Women Build Habitat for Humanity, Habitat for Humanity First Ladies Build. Office: DOS Amb 5310 Helsinki Pl Washington DC 20521

MCELWEE, DENNIS JOHN, lawyer, former pharmaceutical company executive; b. New Orleans, July 30, 1947; s. John Joseph and Audrey (Nunez) McE. BS, Tulane U., 1970; JD, U. Denver, 1992. Clean room and quality control analyst Sci. Enterprises Inc., Broomfield, Colo., 1975-76; analytical chemist in toxicology Poisonlab. Inc., Denver, 1977; analytical chemist, then dir. quality control program Colo. Sch. Mines Rsch. Inst., 1977-79; dir. quality control, then dir. compliance Benedict Nuclear Pharms. Co., Golden, Colo., 1979-84; pres. MC Projections Inc., Morrison, Colo., 1985-86; dir. regulatory affairs Electromedics Inc., Englewood, Colo., 1986-89; pvt. practice, 1992—. Author: Mineral Research Chemicals, Toxic Properties and Proper Handling, 2d edit., 1979; mem. editl. bd. CF Network Mag.; contbr. articles to profl. jours. Bd. dirs. Denver chpt. Cystic Fibrosis Found., 1996, Assn. of Vols. for Children's Hosp., Denver, 1999, hon. lifetime mem., 2004. Recipient Sutton prize in internat. law U. Denver Sch. Law, 1991, Finest award Denver Charities, 1999. Mem. Colo. Bar Assn., 1st Jud. Dist. Bar Assn. Office: 7475 W 5th Ave #315 Lakewood CO 80226 E-mail: dionysius@prodigy.net.

MCELWREATH, SALLY CHIN, corporate communications executive; b. N.Y.C., Oct. 15, 1940; d. Toon Guey and Jean B. (Wong) Chin; m. Joseph F. Callo, Mar. 17, 1979; 1 child, R.J. McElwreath III. BA, Pace Coll., 1963; MBA, Pace U., 1969. Copywriter O.E. McIntyre, N.Y.C., 1963-65; editl. asst. Sinclair Oil Corp., N.Y.C., 1966-70; account exec. Muller, Jordan & Herrick, N.Y.C., 1970-71; regional mgr. pub. rels. United Airlines, N.Y.C., 1971-79; dir. corp. comm. Trans World Airlines, N.Y.C., 1979-86; v.p. pub. rels. TWA Mktg. Svcs., Inc., N.Y.C., 1986-88; ptnr. The Comm. Group, N.Y.C., 1988-90; gen. mgr. corp. comm. Ofcl. Airline Guides, 1990-91; v.p. corp. comm. Macmillan, Inc., 1991-93; cons. N.Y.C., 1993-94; sr. v.p. corp. comm. Utilicorp United, Inc., Kansas City, 1994—2001, Utilicorp United, Inc. (now Aquila Inc.), Kansas City, 2003—. Pub. affairs officer USNR, 1973-2000. Ret. Capt. Named Woman of Yr., YWCA, 1980, Alumnus of Yr., Pace U., 1976. Mem. N.Am. Pub. Rels. Assn. (vice chair 2003-04), N.Y. Airline Pub. Rels. Assn. (chmn. 1978-79), Wings Club (N.Y.C.). Avocations: sailing, skiing, harpsichord. Office: Aquila Inc 20 W 9th St Kansas City MO 64105-1704 E-mail: sallymc79@aol.com.

MCELYEA, JACQUELYN SUZANNE, accountant, real estate consultant; b. Dallas, July 19, 1958; d. Owen Clyde and Mary Lou (Cockerill) Harvey; m. James E. McElyea, June 11, 1983. BBS, Tex. A&M U., 1980. CPA, Tex. Acctg. mgr. Oxford Tex. Devel., Dallas, 1980-81; staff to dir. PriceWaterhouseCoopers, Dallas, 1981—. Pres. Nat. Assn. Corp. Real Estate, Dallas. Co-author: Real Estate Accounting Reporting, 1995. Bd. dirs. Am. Diabetes Assn., Dallas, 1996-97. Mem. AICPA, Nat. Assn. Real Estate Cos., Tex. Soc. CPAs. Presbyterian. Avocations: animals, cooking. Office: PriceWaterhouse Coopers 2001 Ross Ave Ste 1800 Dallas TX 75201-2933 E-mail: smcelyea@home.com.

MCELYEA, ULYSSES, JR., veterinarian; b. Ft. Collins, Colo., Oct. 29, 1941; s. Ulysses and Hazel (Hall) McE.; m. Rexanna Bell, Dec. 29, 1975 (div. 1980); m. Natalia B. Zarzosa, Apr. 29, 2000. BS in Pharmacy, U. N.Mex., 1963; DVM, Colorado State U., 1967, MS, 1968. Diplomate Am. Bd. Vet. Practicioners, cert. in companion animals. Owner Alta Vista Animal Clinic, Las Cruces, N.Mex., 1970—; attending vet. N.Mex. State U., 1995—. Bd. dirs. N.Mex. Acad. Vet. Practice, Albuquerque, bd. dirs. state of N.Mex. Bd. Vet. Examiners, v.p., 1988-98, vice chair, 1992, chair, 1992-96, Bank of the Rio Grande; adj. prof. N.Mex. State U., 1998—. Pres. Las Cruces Community Theater, 1974; founder, bd. dirs. Dona Ann Arts Coun., Las Cruces, 1976-80. Capt. U.S. Army, 1968-70. Mem. AVMA, Am. Assn. Feline Practitioners, Am. Soc. Vet. Ophthalmologists, N.Mex. Vet. Med. Assn. (bd. dirs. 1976-82), So. N.Mex. Vet. Assn. (pres. 1974, 84), N.Mex. State U. Athletic Assn. 9bd. dirs. 1976—, pres.-elect 1992-93, pres. 1993-94), N.Mex. State U. Pres.'s Assn. 9bd. dirs. 1988-91), U. N.Mex. Alumni Assn. (bd. dirs. 1976-80). Republican. Home: 2635 Fairway Dr Las Cruces NM 88011-5044 Office: Alta Vista Animal Clinic 725 S Solano Dr Las Cruces NM 88001-3244 Office Phone: 505-524-7176. Business E-Mail: umcelyea@zianet.com.

MCENANEY, SHERRIE JEANINE, writer, marketing professional, advertising executive; d. Jack Smith and Helen Livingston, Edy Livingston (Stepfather); m. Thomas J. McEnaney, Aug. 2, 1995; children: Chad William Burrell(dec.), Brandon Moore, Saira, Nikki, Tommy. A, U. Tulsa, 1986. Advt. cons. KXTD, Broken Arrow, Okla., 1988—89; ops. asst. Tulsa Fastbreakers Basketball Team, Tulsa, 1989—92; agt. Dave Travlin Davlin, 1992—94; cons. Branson, Mo., 1995—. Author: Another Clamente in the Making. Pres. The Burrell Found., Branson, Mo., 2002—03. Mem.: Kiwanis (hon.). Conservative. Achievements include research in Research for the cure of AIDS and assistance for it's victims and their families. Avocations: travel, theater, music, teaching, sports. Home: 2243 Mallard Creek Cir Kissimmee FL 34743-3537 Personal E-mail: cubfanmack@msn.com. E-mail: cubfanmack@msn.com.

MCENARY, JOHN WALTER, music educator; b. Minneapolis, Dec. 7, 1952; s. David Nye and Marilynn Sahlin M.; m. Allison Roberts, Mar. 25, 1988. BFA, U. Minn., Minneapolis, 1975; MFA, U. Minn., 1977. Cert. Calif. Cmty. Coll. Instr. Music. prof. Orange Coast Coll., Costa Mesa, Calif., 1978—, music dept. chair, 1984—2001, program coord., 1986—. Software developer Sound Source Unlimited, Agoura Hills, Calif., 1989-92, Midiman, Arcadia, Calif., 1989-98; content developer Coda Music Tech., Eden Prairie, Minn., 1992-94; midi cons. Roland Corp., L.A., 1990-96. Author: (books) Guide to Sequencers, 1992, Computers in Music, 2002, (software) Proteus Sound Manager, 1988, Interval, 1998. Mem. Bowers Mus., Santa Ana, Calif., 1999—; subscriber Globe Theatre, San Diego, 1991-98. Recipient Regents fellowship, U. Calif. San Diego, 1975. Mem. Music Assn. Calif. Cmty. Colls., (life) Orange Co. Guitar Cir. (pres. 1984-86). Avocations: reading, movies, theatre, tech., music. Office: Orange Coast Coll 2701 Fairview Rd Costa Mesa CA 92626-5563 E-mail: jmcenary@mail.occ.cccd.edu.

MCENIRY, ROBERT FRANCIS, education educator, researcher; b. Milw., Feb. 22, 1918; s. Frank Michael and Mary (Brown) McE. BA, St. Louis U., 1941, Philosophiae Licentiatus cum laude, 1944, Theologiae Licentiatus cum laude, PhL, ThL cum laude, St. Louis U., 1953; PhD, Ohio State U., 1972. Elem. sch. inst., 1938-40; tchr. Howdershell Grade Sch., 1939-40; radio announcer Sta. WOW, St. Louis, 1941-43; instr. classics St. Louis U. High Sch., 1944-47, Creighton Prep. Sch., Omaha, 1947-48; asst. prof., chmn. classics Rockhurst Coll., Kansas City, Mo., 1953-58; retreat dir. White House Retreat, St. Louis, 1958-68; assoc. research prof. Creighton U., Omaha, 1972-89; ret., 1989. Dir., facilitator Growth for Couples, 1975-89; lectr. Creighton Natural Family Planning Ctr.; facilitator groups Adult Children of Alcoholism and Dysfunctional Families, 1989-93; vis. lectr. San Francisco Sch. Theology, San Anselmo, Calif., 1985; more than 800 presentations (lectrs., papers, workshops and seminars) in 175 cities, 22 states and 12 fgn. countries on value decisions during high anxiety and stress in marriage, family, teaching and learning; exec. dir. Studies Adult Survivors of Abuse, 1993—; tchr., counselor in marriage and family issues. Editor and pub. Interaction Review, 1982-89; editor Scholar and Educator, 1974-76; mem. editorial bd. Counseling and Values, 1976-82; editor (book) Pastoral Counseling, 1977, Premarriage Counseling, 1978; contbr. over 180 articles to profl. jours.; literary agent, 1992-98. Mem. Bd. of Pastoral Ministry, Omaha, 1972-78. Research grantee Council for Theol. Reflection, 1975-77; recipient Research award Creighton U., 1977; 1st prize for "Pro and Con" in Queen's Work Play contest, 1945. Fellow Nat. Acad. Counselors and Family Therapists (editor book rev. 1979-91); mem. APA, Am. Assn. for Religious Values in Counseling (editor newsletter 1982-89, Outstanding Svc. award 1985, Meritorious Svc. award 1989, Edgar Dale award 1995), Phi Delta Kappa (exec. com. 1977-83, del. 1981-83). Avocations: barbershop quartets, photography, civil war sites, yoga.

MCENROE, JOHN PATRICK, JR., former professional tennis player, commentator; b. Wiesbaden, Fed. Republic Germany, Feb. 16, 1959; s. John Patrick and Kathy McEnroe; m. Tatum O'Neil, Aug. 1, 1986 (div. 1994); children: Kevin, Sean, Emily; m. Patty Smyth, 1997; children: Anna, Ava 1 stepchild, Ruby. Grad., Trinity Sch., N.Y.C., 1977; student, Stanford U. Winner numerous U.S. jr. singles and doubles titles; winner jr. titles French Mixed Doubles, 1977, French Jr. Singles, 1977; winner Nat. Coll. Athletic Assn. Intercollegiate U.S. Men's Singles title, 1978; professional tennis player, 1978-93; played on victorious U.S. Davis Cup Team, 1978, 79, 81, 82, 92; winner Grand Prix Masters Tournament, N.Y.C., 1979, U.S. Open Men's Singles Championship, 1979, 80, 81, 84, World Championship Tennis Championship, 1979, 83, Wimbledon Singles, 1981, 83, 84, Tournament of Champions, 1981, 83, Wimbledon Doubles, 1992; tennis sportscaster USA Network, 1993; host The Chair, 2002, McEnroe, 2004—. Owner John McEnroe Gallery. Co-author (with James Kaplan): (autobiography) You Cannot Be Serious, 2000; author: Serious, 2003. Inducted, Tennis Hall of Fame, 1999. Mem: Men's Seniors' Tour Circuit, 1994. Office: The John McEnroe Gallery 41 Greene St New York NY 10013-5916*

MCENROE, KATE, broadcast executive; BA in Advt., U. Colo.; MBA, NYU. Past mktg. dir., new product devel. mgr. Outward Bound Sch.; past gen. mgr., exec. v.p. Am. Movie Classics Rainbow Programming Holdings, Inc., from mktg. dir. to pres. Am. Movie Classics, 1981—. Recipient Pres.'s award for contbns. to prosoc. and ednl. programming, NATAS. Mem.: NAFE, CTAM, Women in Cable. Office: Rainbow Media Svc Holdings Inc 111 Stewart Ave Bethpage NY 11714-5310

MCENROE, MICHAEL LOUIS, lawyer; b. July 31, 1951; s. C. Louis and Mary C. (Cain) McEnroe. BA magna cum laude, Loras Coll., 1973; JD, Creighton U., 1976. Bar: Ill. 1976, Iowa 1977, U.S. Dist. Ct. (no. dist.) Iowa 1977, U.S. Dist. Ct. (so. dist.) Iowa 1988, U.S. Supreme Ct. 1992. Assoc. McMahon & Cassel, Algona, Iowa, 1977-78; ptnr. McMahon, Cassel, McMahon, McEnroe & MacDonald, Algona, Iowa, 1979—88; judicial magistrate 3rd Judicial Dist. State of Iowa, Algona, 1981-89; ptnr. Cook, Gotsdiner, McEnroe & McCarthy, Des Moines, 1988—98; shareholder McEnroe, McCarthy & Gotsdiner PC, West Des Moines, Iowa, 1998—. Mem.: bd. govs., Polk County Bar Assn., Iowa Assn. Trial Lawyers, Iowa State Bar Assn. (mem. agrl. law com. 1986—90, mem. exec. coun. young lawyers sect. 1986—88, mem. gen. practice com. 2000—03), Ill. State Bar Assn., Blackstone Inn of Ct., Delta Epsilon Sigma. Democrat. Roman Catholic. Home: 700 S 32nd Ct West Des Moines IA 50265-5701 Office: McEnroe McCarthy & Gotsdiner PC 1701 48th St Ste 100 West Des Moines IA 50266-6723 E-mail: mmcenroe@dwx.com.

MCENROE, PATRICK, former professional tennis player, sports commentator; b. Manhasset, N.Y., July 1, 1966; s. John Patrick Sr. and Katy McEnroe. Grad., Stanford U. Doubles winner French Open, 1989; winner ATP tournament, Sydney, Australia, 1995. Mem. US Davis Cup team, 1993, 94, 96, captain, 2001—04; commentator CBS Sports and ESPN, 1998—; bd. dir. US Tennis Assn, 1999—2000; player, partial owner NY Sportimes, World Team Tennis; US Olympics Men's Tennis coach, Athens, Greece, 2004. Author: (books) Tennis for Dummies, 1998. Achievements include ranked 12th, US Tennis Assn., 1991; ranked 664th, 1999. Office: Sportime at Harbor Island PO Box 783 Mamaroneck NY 10543*

MCENTEE, GERALD W. labor union official; b. Phila., Jan. 11, 1935; four children. B in Econs., LaSalle Coll., 1956; postgrad., Temple U., Harvard U. With Am. Fedn. State County and Mcpl. Employees, 1973—, former leader Dist. Coun. 13, union internat. v.p., mem. exec. bd., since 1974, internat. pres., 1981—; v.p., mem. exec. coun., chair polit. edn. com. AFL-CIO. Office: AFSCME 1625 L St NW Washington DC 20036-5687

MCENTIRE, BETTY, health facility administrator; Exec. dir. Am. SIDS Inst., Marietta, Ga. Office: Am SIDS Inst 509 Augusta Dr SE Marietta GA 30067-8205

MCENTIRE, BRAD, theater director, performing artist, educator; b. Houston, Sept. 16, 1975; s. David Lee and Linda Key McEntire. BFA in Theatre Arts, Coll. of Santa Fe, 1998; MFA in Theatre, Tex. Woman's U. Head, theatre arts dept. R.L. Turner H.S., Carrollton, Tex., 1999—2001; artistic dir. Audacity Theatre Prodns., Dallas, 1999—2004; theatre instr. Collin County CC, Plano, Tex., 2001—03, Richland CC, Dallas, 2001—04. Ensemble mem. Plano Children's Theatre, Tex., 2001—. Author: (plays) Arsenic and Roses, 1996, Red Pajama Blues, 1999, For the Love of an Anesthesiologist, 2004. Mem.: Dallas-Ft. Worth Playwrights Alliance, Theatre Comm. Group. Avocations: travel, architecture, Aikido, French. Business E-Mail: audacityproductions@hotmail.com.

MCENTIRE, REBA N. country singer; b. McAlester, Okla., Mar. 28, 1955; d. Clark Vincent and Jacqueline (Smith) McE.; m. Narvel Blackstock, 1989; 1 child, Shelby Steven McEntire Blackstock. Student elem. edn., music, Southeastern State U., Durant, Okla., 1976. Rec. artist Mercury Records, 1978-83, MCA Records, 1984—. Albums include Whoever's in New England (Gold award), 1986, What Am I Gonna Do About You (Gold award), 1987, Greatest Hits (Gold award, Platinum award, U.S., Can.), 1987, Merry Christmas To You, 1987, The Last One To Know (Gold award), 1988, Reba (Gold award 1988), Sweet 16 (Gold award 1989, U.S.), Rumor Has It (Gold award 1991, Platinum award 1992, Double Platinum 1992), Reba Live (Gold award 1990, Gold award 1991, Platinum award 1991), For My Broken Heart, 1991, Forever in Your Eyes, 1992, It's Your Call, 1992, Read My Mind, 1994,

Starting Over, 1995, Reba compilation video (Gold award, Platinum award 1992), Reba Live (video), 1995, What If It's You, 1996, Celebrating 20 Years (video), 1996, If You See Him, 1998, Forever Reba, 1998, Star Profile, 1999, So Good Together, 1999, Secret of Giving: A Christmas Collection, 1999; author: (with Tom Carter) Reba: My Story, 1994; actress: (films) Tremors, 1990, The Little Rascals, 1994, North, 1994, One Night at McCool's, 2000, (TV films) The Gambler Returns: The Luck of the Draw, 1991, The Man From Left Field, 1993, Is There Life Out There?, 1994, Forever Love, 1998, Secret of Giving, 1999; (TV series) Disney's Hercules, 1998, A Salute to Dustin Hoffman, 1999, Reba (also prodr.), 2001-; other TV appearances include Country Gold, 1982, Bob Hope Winterfest Christmas Show, 1987, (video) Wrestlemania VIII, 1992; appeared on TV series Evening Shade, 1993, Frasier, 1994, The Roseanne Show, 1998, One Life to Live,; (host) Acad. Country Music awards, 2004. Spokesperson Middle Tenn. United Way, 1988, Nat. and State 4-H Alumni, Bob Hope's Hope for a Drug Free Am.; Nat. spokesperson Am. Lung Assn., 1990-91. Recipient numerous awards in Country music including Disting. Alumni award Southeastern State U., Female vocalist award Country Music Assn., 1984, 85, 86, 87, Grammy award for Best Country Vocal Performance, 1987, 2 Grammy nominations, 1994, Grammy award, Best Country Vocal Collaboration for "Does He Love You" with Linda Davis, 1994, Entertainer of Yr. award Country Radio Awards, 1994, Female Vocalist award, 1994; named Entertainer of Yr., Country Music Assn., 1986, Female Vocalist of Yr. Acad. Country Music, 1984, 85, 86, 87, 92, Top Female Vocalist, 1984, 85, 86, 87, 1991, 94, Am. Music award favorite female country singer, 1988, 90, 91, 92, 93, Am. Music award, 1989, 90, 91, 92, Best Album, 1991, Favorite Female Vocalist, 1994, Favorite Female Vocalist, Peoples Choice Award, 1992, Favorite Female Country Vocalist, 1992, 93, Favorite Female Vocalist, TNN Viewer's Choice Awards, 1993, Favorite Female Country Artist, Billboard, 1994, Favorite Country Album award Am. Music Awards, 1995, Favorite Female Country Vocalist award Am. Music Awards, 1995, Favorite Female Vocalist award People's Choice Awards, 1995, Top Female Vocalist of Yr. award Acad. Country Music, 1995, Entertainer of Yr. award Acad. Country Music, 1995, Favorite Female Vocalist award TNN Viewer's Choice Awards, 1995, Star on the Walk of Fame, 1999. Mem. Country Music Assn., Acad. County Music, Nat. Acad. Rec. Arts and Scis., Grand Ol' Opry, AFTRA, Nashville Songwriters Assn. Inc. Avocations: golf, shopping, being with narvel and shelby, horse racing, raising horses.

MCEVOY, LORRAINE KATHERINE, oncology nurse; b. S.I., N.Y., Mar. 24, 1950; d. Edward Donald and Josephine (Boyle) McMahon; children: Kelly Ann, Kevin Michael. RN, St. Vincent's Sch. Nursing, 1970; BSN, Seton Hall U., 1994; MSN, Kean U. N.J., 1997. RN, N.J. Staff nurse St. Joseph's Hosp. and Med. Ctr., Paterson, N.J., 1981-88, nurse mgr. oncology, bone marrow transplant, 1988—, cons., educator devel. bone marrow, stem cell and cord blood transplant programs, 1995-98. Adj. prof. Kean U., 1997-98. Recipient Disting. Alumni award Kean U., 1999; Susan G. Komen Breast Cancer Found. grantee, 1997, 98, 99. Mem. Oncology Nursing Soc., Transcultural Nursing Soc., Tri-State Bone Marrow Transplant Nurses Assn., Breast Cancer Connection, Sigma Theta Tau. Office: St Joseph's Hosp and Med Ctr 703 Main St Paterson NJ 07503-2621

MCEVOY, NAN TUCKER, publishing company executive, olive rancher; b. San Mateo, Calif., July 15, 1919; d. Nion R. and Phyllis (de Young) Tucker; m. Dennis McEvoy, 1948 (div.); 1 child, Nion Tucker McEvoy. Student, Georgetown U., 1975. Newspaper reporter San Francisco Chronicle, 1944-46, N.Y. Herald Tribune, N.Y.C., 1946-47, Washington Post, 1947-48; rep. in pub. rels. John Homes, Inc., Washington, 1959-60; spl. asst. to dir. U.S. Peace Corps, Washington, 1961-64; mem. U.S. delegation UNESCO, Washington, 1964-65; dir. Population Coun., Washington, 1965-70; co-founder, dep. dir. Preterm, Inc., Washington, 1970-74; former chmn. bd. Chronicle Pub. Co., San Francisco, 1975-95, dir. emeritus, 1995—. Mem. nat. bd. dirs. Smithsonian Instn., Washington, 1994—; bd. dirs. Am. Farmland Trust; mem. coun. Brookings Instn., Washington, 1994—; mem. U. Calif. San Francisco Found., 1993—; dir. emeritus Nat. Mus. Am. Art; mem. Nat. Coun. Fine Arts Museums; formerly arbitrator Am. Arbitration Assn., Washington. Named Woman of Yr., Washingtonian Mag., 1973. Mem. Am. Art Forum, Burlingame Country Club, The River Club, Commonwealth Club of Calif., World Affairs Coun., Villa Taverna. Avocations: overseeing marin county, california olive grove ranch producing fine extra virgin olive oil. Office: 655 Montgomery St Ste 1430 San Francisco CA 94111-2635

MCEVOY, SHARLENE ANN, law educator; b. Derby, Conn., July 6, 1950; d. Peter Henry Jr. and Madaline Elizabeth (McCabe) McE. BA magna cum laude, Albertus Magnus Coll., 1972; JD, U. Conn., West Hartford, 1975; MA, Trinity Coll., Hartford, 1980, UCLA, 1982, PhD, 1985. Bar: Conn., 1975. Pvt. practice, Derby, 1984—; asst. prof. bus. law Fairfield (Conn.) U. Sch. Bus., 1986—92; adj. prof. bus. law, polit. sci. Albertus Magnus Coll., New Haven, 1978-80, U. Conn., Stamford, 1984-86; acting chmn. polit. sci. dept. Albertus Magnus Coll., 1980; assoc. prof. law Fairfield U., 1992-98, prof. bus. law, 1998—. Chmn. Women's Resource Ctr., Fairfield U., 1989-91. Staff editor Jour. Legal Studies Edn., 1989-94; reviewer Am. Bus. Law Assn. jour., 1988—, staff editor, 1995—; sr. articles editor N.E. Jour. Legal Studies in Bus., 1995-96. Active Derby Tercentennial Commn., 1973—74; justice of the peace City of Derby, 1975—83; alt. mem. Parks and Recreation Commn., Woodbury, 1995—99; v.p. N.E. Acad. Legal Studies in Bus., 2001—02, 2001—02, pres-elect., program chair, 2003, pres., 2003—; treas. Woodbury Dem. Town Com., 1995—96, corr. sec., 1996—98; bd. dirs. Valley Transit Dist., Derby, 1975—77. Recipient Best Paper award N.E. Regional Bus. Law Assn., 1990, Best Paper award Tri-State Regional Bus. Law Assn., 1991; Fairfield U. Sch. Bus. rsch. grantee 1989, 91, 92, Fairfield U. rsch. grantee, 1994. Mem. ABA, Conn. Bar Assn., Acad. Legal Studies in Bus., Mensa (coord. SINISTRAL spl. interest group 1977—). Democrat. Roman Catholic. Avocations: sailing, tennis, swimming. Office: 198 Emmett Ave Derby CT 06418-1258 E-mail: samcevoy@mail.fairfield.edu.

MCEVOY, THOMAS J. communications executive; BBA, Rollins Coll. Various pos. in fin., ops., bus. markets, consumer markets, and carrier markets bus. unit telecomm. industry, 22 yrs.; acct., so. ops. fin. area Sprint Corp., 1980, various other pos. in fin., including payroll mgr., oper. budgets mgr., and local exchange pricing and costing mgr., dir. consumer markets and carrier markets bus. units, v.p. sales and consumer care, local telecomm. divsn. consumer markets, pres., consumer markets, local telecomm. divsn., 2000—. Office: Sprint Corp 6200 Sprint Pkwy Overland Park KS 66251

MCEVOY-JAMIL, PATRICIA ANN, English language educator; b. Butler, Pa., June 26, 1955; d. Joseph Lawrence McEvoy and Janet Ann (McConnell) Beier; m. M. Jamal Jamil, Nov. 23, 1977; 1 child, Amirah M. MA in TESOL, Monterey Inst. Internat. Studies, 1984; MA in English, U. Notre Dame de Namur, 1995; EdD, U. San Francisco, 1996. Calif. C.C. credential for life. Instr. ESL City Coll. San Francisco, 1989—98, Can. Coll., Redwood City, Calif., 1989—98; lectr. ESL Stanford U., Calif., 1989—97, U. Notre Dame de Namur, 1991—98; co-owner, v.p. bd. MPA Co. Investments, Inc., Houston, 1998—. Presenter in field; vis. prof. English as Fgn. Lang., Georgetown U., Washington, summer 1999; adj. ESL instr. U. Houston-Downtown, 2000-02, Mus. Fine Arts, Houston. Mem. leadership coun. So. Poverty Law Ctr.-contributed to Jimmy Carter Ctr.; ptnr. mem. Habitat for Humanity Internat.; team leader Rep. Party. Recipient ELITE Patron of Honor award, ELITE Stanford Hosp., 1989, 1990, Wall of Tolerance award; faculty rsch. grant, U. Notre Dame de Namur, 1984, doctoral rsch. grant, U. San Francisco, 1992—93. Mem. AAUW, NAFE, Nat. Coun. Tchrs. English, Tchrs. English to Spkrs. Other Langs., Nat. Mus. Women Arts, Nat. Trust Hist. Preservation, Phi Delta Kappa. Avocations: tennis, swimming, bicycling. Office: 5850 San Felipe Ste 500 No 117 Houston TX 77057 E-mail: docpamjam@hotmail.com.

MCEWEN, ALEXANDER CAMPBELL, cadastral studies educator, former Canadian government official, land administration consultant; b. Ryde, Isle of Wight, Eng., Aug. 22, 1926; emigrated to Can., 1949; s. Walter Scott and Florence Lilian (Goodall) McE.; m. Patricia Stuart Richards, July 27, 1956 (div. 1988); m. Sherry Lee Wilson, June 13, 1993; children: Ann Florence, Sheila Jean, Laura Susan. LL.B., U. London, 1966, PhD, 1979; LL.M., U. East Africa, 1970. Sr. surveyor H. Wheeler Assocs., Toronto, Ont., Can., 1961-62; sec. treas. Assn. Ont. Land Surveyors, Toronto, 1963-64; prin. Survey Tng. Centre, Dar es Salaam, Tanzania, 1964-70; survey cons. Ottawa, Ont., Can., 1970-72; dir. lands and surveys Govt. Nfld., St. John's, 1972-76; commr. Internat. Boundary Commn., Ottawa, Ont., 1976 90; survey adviser Govt. Can., Jesselton, North Borneo, 1954-56, Lagos, Nigeria, 1989-90; tech. expert UN, Victoria, Seychelles, 1958-61; survey cons. Can. Exec. Svc. Orgn., Kingston, Jamaica, 1981, Quito, Ecuador, 1986, La Paz, Bolivia, 2002—03; prof. cadastral studies, dept. geomatics engrng. U. Calgary, Alta., Can., 1991-96; land. adminstrn. cons. Asian Devel. Bank, Ulaanbaatar, Mongolia, 2003; lant title registration cons. Inter-Am. Devel. Bank, Port of Spain, Trinidad and Tobago, 2004—. Author: International Boundaries of East Africa, 1971 In Search of the Highlands, 1988; contbr. articles to profl. jours. Served with Royal Armoured Corp. Mem. Can. Inst. Geomatics (mem. coun. 1977-81, 97-2002, Jim Jones award 1967, 83, 90, 99, Presdl. citation 1981), Western Can. Bd. Examiners for Land Surveyors (registrar, bd. dirs. 1991-96), Assn. Ont. Land Surveyors (sec.-treas. 1963-64), Assn. Nfld. Land Surveyors (bd. examiners 1975-76). Home: 2129 2d Ave NW Calgary AB Canada T2N OG8 E-mail: amcewen@telusplanet.net.

MCEWEN, BRUCE S. neuroendocrinology educator; Prof., head Lab. Neuroendocrinology, Rockefeller U., N.Y.C. E-mail: mcewen@mail.rockefeller.edu.

MCEWEN, CRAIG A. dean; AB, Oberlin Coll.; MA, PhD, Harvard U. Mem. faculty Bowdoin Coll., Brunswick, Maine, 1975—, Daniel B. Fayerweather prof. polit. economy and sociology; dean acad. affairs. Mediator Ct. Mediaton Svc., Maine. Author (with Nancy Rogers): Mediation: Law, Policy and Practice. Home: 15 Baxter Ln Brunswick ME 04011 Office: Bowdoin Coll 5800 College Sta Brunswick ME 04011-8449

MCEWEN, GERALD NOAH, JR., bio-scientist executive; b. Washington, 1943; s. Gerald Noah and Kathryn Lyle (Kimes) McE.; m. Carol Sue Edwards, Aug. 27, 1966; children: Jennifer Lyle, Kathleen Schofield. BS in Life Sci., Ind. State U., Terre Haute, 1966; MA in Life Sci., Ind. State U., 1968; PhD in Physiology and Biophysics, U. Ill., Urbana, 1973; JD, George Washington U., 1989. Vis. lectr. U. Ill., Urbana, 1973-74; research assoc. NASA-Ames Research Co., Moffett Field, Calif., 1974-76, research physiologist SRI-Internat., Washington, 1976-77; mgr. Biosci. Group SRI Internat., 1977-78; sr. bioscientist and dir. health hazard info. program, 1978-80; ingredient safety coordinator Cosmetic, Toiletry and Fragrance Assn., Washington, 1980-82, dir., 1982-86, v.p. sci., 1986—. Mem. tech. com. on cosmetics Health Can.; bd. dirs. Environ. Sensitivities Rsch. Inst. Industry liaison representive to cosmetic ingredients review expert panel and to the US FDA dental product panel. Contbr. Editor to several texts, frequent speaker at national and internat. seminars on personal care product safety regulation; Contbr. articles to profl. jours. Recipient Tech. Achievement award NASA, 1976, Superior Achievement award SRI Internat., 1978; NRC research grantee, 1974-76. Mem. FASEB, Am. Physiol Soc., Am. Acad. Dermatology, Am. Contact Dermatitis Soc., Va. Bar Assn., Theta Alpha Phi. Lodges: Masons. Methodist. Home: 2799 N Quebec St Arlington VA 22207-5212 Office: 1110 Vermont Ave NW Washington DC 20005-3544 E-mail: gnmcewen@hotmail.com.

MCEWEN, IRENE RUBLE, physical therapy educator; b. Columbus, Ohio, May 19, 1943; d. John Mitchell and Isabel (Ruble) McE. BS in Phys. Therapy, U. Wash., 1965, MEd in Ednl. Psychology, 1973; PhD in Spl. Edn., Purdue U., 1989. Cert. pediatric clin. specialist Am. Bd. Phys. Therapy Spltys. (pediatric splty. coun.); lic. phys. therapist, Okla., Wash. Phys. therapist St. Vincent Hosp., Portland, Oreg., 1965-69; head phys. therapist Lowell Sch., Seattle, 1970-76; physiotherapist Spastic Centre of New South Wales, Mosman, Australia, 1976-77; head phys. therapist Seattle Sch. Dist., 1977-84; phys. therapist Mesa Pub. Sch., Ariz., 1984, Roosevelt Sch. Dist., Phoenix, 1984-86; rsch. fellow Purdue U., West Lafayette, Ind., 1986-89; tech. specialist Ind. Augmentative and Alternative Communication Tech. Team, West Lafayette, 1988-89; assoc. prof. phys. therapy U. Okla. Health Sci. Ctr., Oklahoma City, 1989-97, prof. phys. therapy, 1997—, Presbyn. Health Found. Presdl. prof., 1998, George Lynn Cross rsch. prof., 2003. Rschr., presenter in field. Mem. editl. bd., dep. editor, editor: Case Reports Phys. Therapy; co-editor: Physical and Occupational Therapy in Pediatrics; contbr. Mem.: Rehab. Engring. and Assistive Tech. Soc. N.Am., Internat. Soc. Augmentative and Alternative Comm., Coun. Exceptional Children, Assn. for Persons with Severe Handicaps, Am. Phys. Therapy Assn. (Margaret L. Moore Outstanding New Acad. Faculty mem. award 1992, Dorothy Briggs Sci. Inquiry award 1993, sect. on pediat. rsch. award 1998, sect. on pediat. Bud DeHaven Svc. award 2001), Am. Assn. Mental Retardation, Am. Acad. Cerebral Palsy and Devel. Medicine, Alpha Eta, Sigma Xi, Phi Kappa Phi. Office: U Okla Dept Rehab Sci PO Box 26901 Oklahoma City OK 73190-1090 Office Phone: 405-271-2131 47125. E-mail: irene-mcewen@ouhsc.edu.

MCEWEN, JAMES WALLACE, JR., former publishing executive; m. Laura Ellen Cherensky, 1996. Assoc. pub., adv. dir. Family Cir., N.Y.C., 1993—94, sr. v.p., pub., 1994—95; group pub. Family Cir. and McCall's, N.Y.C., 1995—2001.

MCEWEN, JOAN GRACE (JOANIE LAWRENCE), actress, recording industry executive; b. Hopkinsville, Ky., Oct. 15, 1932; d. Joseph Thomas McEwen and Thelma Irene (Grace) Fox; m. John E. Bills Jr. (dec.); children: Jennifer Jones, John E. III, James L., Robert J. Student, U. Tenn., Knoxville, 1950-53, U. Tenn., Nashville, 1961-62, Aquinas Jr. Coll., 1962-63, Alvin Ailey Dance Theatre, NY.C., 1977, Lee Strasberg Theatre Inst., N.Y.C., Neighborhood Playhouse, 1995-97. Ballet instr., Nashville, 1960-68; adminstr. Shelby Singleton Records, Nashville, 1968-70; from adminstrv. asst. to gen. mgr. Sta. WLAC, Nashville, 1970-73; nat. dir. promotion Mercury Records, Chgo., 1973-76, Pvt. Stock Records, Inc., N.Y.C., 1976-78, Arista Records, Inc., L.A., 1978-87; pres. Joan Lawrence Entertainment, Nashville, 1987—. Active Nashville Symphony Guild. Mem. SAG, AFTRA, Nashville Symphony Assn., Cheekwood Arts. Republican. Avocations: skiing, tennis, horseback riding, golf.

MCEWEN, LAURA, publishing executive; m. James McEwen; 1 child, Sean. BA, Fordham U. Pub. New Woman, Snow Country Mag.; sr. pub. Harpers Bazaar, Family Circle; pub. YM Mag., 2000—03; v.p., pub. dir. Readers Digest Mag., 2003—. Mem., planning com. Mag. Pub. of Am., 2003. Mem.: Fragrance Found., N.Y. Advt. Club, Advt. Women of N.Y., Fashion Group Internat. (bd. dirs.), Cosmetic Exec. Women (bd. dirs.). Office: Readers Digest Mag Box 200 Pleasantville NY 10572-0200

MCEWEN, WILLARD WINFIELD, JR., lawyer, judge; b. Evanston, Ill., Dec. 26, 1934; s. Willard Winfield Sr. and Esther (Sprenger) McE.; children: Michael, Elizabeth, Allison. BS, Claremont Men's Coll., 1956; LLB, U. Calif., San Francisco, 1959. Bar: Calif. 1960, U.S. Dist. Ct. (no. and so. dists.) Calif. 1960, U.S. Supreme Ct. 1974. Commd. U.S. Army, 1956, advanced through grades to capt., 1965, resigned, 1968; dep. legis. counsel. City of Sacramento, Calif., 1960-61; asst. city atty. City of Santa Barbara, Calif., 1961-62; sole practice Santa Barbara, 1962—; judge U.S. Magistrate Ct., Santa Barbara County, 1973—; atty. Goleta Water Dist., 1986-87. Lectr. Santa Barbara Adult Edn. Program. Founder, bd. dirs., officer, gen. legal coun. Santa Barbara Coun. for Retarded, 1962-72; active WORK Workshop for Handicapped, Assn. Retarded Citizens, Santa Barbara City Landmarks Adv. Com., 1967-73; v.p. Santa Barbara Harbor Pageants and Exhibits Com., 1964; chmn. Citizens Save our Shoreline Com., 1964, Citizens Cmty. Master Plan Com., 1964, YMCA Membership Drive, 1964, Citizens Adv. Com. on Sch. Dist. Tax Needs, 1965; commr. Santa Barbara City Water Commn., 1965, City of Santa Barbara Recreation Commn., 1970-73; elected to founding bd. dirs. City Commerce Bank. Recipient Disting Svc. award Santa Barbara Jaycees, 1965; named Santa Barbara's Young Man of Yr. Sanata Barbara C. of C. 1983. Mem. Am. Heart Assn. (pres. Santa Barbara County chpt. 1981-82), Santa Barbara Heart Assn. (bd. dirs., pres. bd. dirs. 1981-82, chmn. Heart Sunday 1973, 75), Santa Barbara Malacological Soc., Santa Barbara Kiwanis (pres. 1967), C. of C. (com. on local govt., state legisaltion com., bd. dirs., past v.p. bd. dirs., pres. bd. dirs. 1981-82, chmn. several coms.). Republican. Roman Catholic. Avocations: golf, skiing. Office: US Courthouse 8 E Figueroa St Ste 210 Santa Barbara CA 93101-2745 E-mail: imannieo@aol.com.

MCFADDEN, DANIEL LITTLE, economist, educator; b. Raleigh, N.C., July 29, 1937; s. Robert S. and Alice (Little) McFadden; m. Beverlee Tito Simboli, Dec. 15, 1962; children: Nina, Robert, Raymond. BS in physics, U. Minn., 1957, PhD in econs., 1962; LLD, U. Chgo., 1992; degree (hon.), U. Coll. London, 2003. Asst. prof. econs. U. Pitts., 1962-63, U. Calif., Berkeley, 1963—66, assoc. prof. econs, 1966—68, prof., 1968—79, E. Morris Cox Chair, prof. econs. Coll. Letters & Sci., 1991—, dir. Econometrics Lab., 1991—95, 1996—, chmn. dept. of econ., 1995—96; vis. assoc. prof. U. Chgo., 1966—67; Irving Fisher research prof. Yale U., New Haven, 1977—78; prof. econs. MIT, Cambridge, Mass., 1978—91, James R. Killian Chair, 1984—91, dir. Stats. Rsch. Ctr., 1986—88; Sherman Fairchild Disting. Scholar Calif. Inst. Tech., 1990. Mem. econs. adv. panel NSF, 1969—71, Univs. Nat. Bur., 1974—77; chmn. NSF-NBER Conf. Econs. of Uncertainty, 1970—; bd. dirs. Nat. Bur. Econ. Rsch., 1976—77, 1980—83; mem. book com. Sloan Found., 1977—79; mem. rev. com. Calif. Energy Com. Forecasts, 1979; chmn. awards com. AEA, 1981—84. Editor: Jour. Statis. Physics, 1968—70, Economteric Soc. monographs, 1980—83; mem. bd. editors Am. Econ. Rev., 1971—74, Jour. Math. Econs., 1973—77, Transp. Rsch., 1978—80; assoc. editor: Jour. Econometrics, 1977—78; adv. com. Jour. Applied Econs., 1996—; co-editor: Essays on Economic Behavior Under Uncertainty, 1974, Production Economics, Vols. I and II, 1978, Structural Analysis of Discrete Data with Econometric Applications, 1981, Preferences, Uncertainty, and Optimality, 1990, Handbook of Econometrics Vol. IV, 1994; co-author: Urban Travel Demand: A Behavioral Analysis, 1975, Microeconomic Modeling and Policy Analysis, 1984. Mem. adv. com. Transp. Models Project, Met. Transp. Commn., 1975, City of Berkeley Coordinated Transit Project, 1975—76. Recipient Outstanding Tchr. Award, MIT, 1981, Nobel Prize in Econs., 2000, Nemmers prize in Econs., Northwestern U., 2000, Richard Stone prize in Applied Econs., Jour. Applied Economtrics, 2000—01; Ford Found. Behavioral Sci. Fellow, 1958—62, Earhart Fellow, 1960—61, Mellon Post-Doctoral Fellow, 1962—63, Ford Faculty Rsch. Fellow, 1966—67. Mem.: NAS (mem. com. basic rsch. social scis. 1982—87, mem. com. energy demand modelling 1983—84, mem. commn. behavioral and social scis. and edn. 1989—94, mem. commn. sci. engring., pub. policy 1995—, chair sect. 54 econ. scis. 2003—, chair com. forecasting demand/supply of doctoral scientists and engrs. 1997—2000), Transp. Rsch. Bd. (mem. exec. com. 1975—78), Math. Assn. Am., Am. Statis. Assn., Econometrics Soc. (Fisher-Schultz lectr. 1979, mem. exec. com. 1983—86, v.p. 1984, pres. 1985, fellow 1969, Frisch Medal 1986), Am. Econ. Assn. (mem. exec. com. 1985—87, v.p. 1994, pres.-elect 2004, John Bates Clark Medal 1975), Am. Acad. Arts and Scis. Democrat. Avocations: bicycling, tennis, squash, sailing, skiing. Home: 1370 Trancas St # 152 Napa CA 94558-2912 Office: U Calif Berkeley Dept Econs 549 Evans Hall # 3880 Berkeley CA 94720-3880*

MCFADDEN, DENNIS, experimental psychology educator; b. Oakland, Calif., Oct. 2, 1940; s. Samuel John and Evelyn (Dinnerson) McF.; m. Nancy L. Wilson, Dec. 28, 1960; children: Tracie Ann, Devin James. BA, Sacramento State Coll., 1962; PhD, Ind U., 1967. Asst. prof. U. Tex., Austin, 1967-72, assoc. prof., 1972-77, prof., 1977—, Piper prof., 1987, Ashbel Smith prof., 1998—. Contbr. articles to profl. jours. Recipient Jacob K. Javits Neurosci. Investigator award, NIH, 1984-89, Claude Pepper award of Excellence, 1989-91; NIH grantee. Fellow AAAS, Acoustical Soc. Am., Am. Psychol. Soc.; mem. Assn. for Rsch. in Otolaryngology, Com. Hearing, Bioacoustics & Biomechanics (NAS-NRC com. on hearing, bioacoustics and biomechanics), Soc. Neurosci., Soc. for Behavioral Neuroendocrinology, Internat. Acad. for Sex Rsch. Avocations: jogging, bicycling, birdwatching, travel. Office: U Tex Dept Psychology 1 University Station Seay Bldg A 8000 Austin TX 78712-0187 Business E-Mail: mcfadden@psy.utexas.edu.

MCFADDEN, FRANK HAMPTON, lawyer, business executive, former judge; b. Oxford, Miss., Nov. 20, 1925; s. John Angus and Ruby (Roy) McF.; m. Jane Porter Nabers, Sept. 30, 1960; children— Frank Hampton, Angus Nabers, Jane Porter. BA, U. Miss., 1950; LL.B., Yale U., 1955. Bar: N.Y. 1956, Ala. 1959. Assoc. firm Lord, Day & Lord, N.Y.C., 1955-58, Bradley, Arant, Rose & White, Birmingham, Ala., 1958-63, partner, 1963-69; judge U.S. Dist. Ct. No. Dist. Ala., Birmingham, 1969-73, chief judge, 1973-81; sr. v.p., gen. counsel Blount, Inc., Montgomery, Ala., 1982-91, exec. v.p. adminstrn. and govt. affairs, 1991, exec. v.p. legal affairs, 1991-93, exec. v.p., gen. counsel, 1993-95; mem. Capell & Howard, P.C., Montgomery, 1995—. Chmn. Blount Energy Resource Corp., Montgomery, 1983-88. Mem. jud. panel CPR Inst. for Dispute Resolution, 1985—. Served from ensign to lt. USNR, 1944-49, 51-53. Fellow Am. Coll. Constrn. Lawyers; mem. Am. Corp. Counsel Assn. (bd. dirs. 1984-93, chmn. 1989). Office: Capell & Howard PC 150 S Perry St Montgomery AL 36104-4227 Office Phone: 334-241-8041. Business E-Mail: fhm@chlaw.com.

MC FADDEN, GEORGE LINUS, retired army officer; b. Sharon, Pa., Oct. 16, 1927; s. George Linus and Frances Jane (Byrne) McF.; m. Floretta Theresa McFadden, Nov. 20, 1948; children: Kenneth William, Mark Edward (dec.), Mary Kathleen, Robert Bernard, George Linus, William. B.E., U. Omaha, 1961; MS, George Washington U., 1967; grad., Advanced Mgmt. Program, Harvard U., 1971. Pvt. U.S. Army, 1946, advanced through grades to maj. gen., 1976; comdg. officer (7th inf. div. arty.), Korea, 1969-70; dep. comdg. gen. U.S. Army Security Agy., Arlington, Va., 1972-74; dep. dir. for field mgmt. and evaluation, dep. chief central security service Fort George G. Meade, Md., 1975-78; dep. dir. ops. Nat. Security Agy., 1978-79; comdg. gen. U.S. Army So. European Task Force, Vicenza, Italy, 1979-82; corp. v.p. CompuDyne Corp., 1986-89; sr. v.p. The Abbott Group, Inc., Annapolis, Md., 1989-90; dir. Washington Studies and Analysis Group McDonnell Douglas Corp., 1985-86; dir. security affairs Dept. Energy, 1990-97, cons., 1999—. Pres., chmn. bd. Met. Washington chpt. Arthritis Found., 1986-95. Decorated D.F.C., D.S.M., Silver Star, Bronze Star, Purple Heart, others. Roman Catholic.

MCFADDEN, JAMES FREDERICK, JR., surgeon; b. St. Louis, Dec. 5, 1920; s. James Frederick and Olivia Genevieve (Imbs) McF.; m. Mary Cella Switzer, Sept. 15, 1956 (div. Sept. 1969); children: James Frederick, Kenneth Michael, John Switzer, Mary Cella, Joseph Robert; m. Deanne Nemec Puls, Apr. 29, 1989. AB, St. Louis U., 1941, MD, 1944. Intern Boston City Hosp., 1944-45; ward surgeon neorsurg. and orthopedics McGuire Gen. Hosp., Richmond, Va., 1945; ward surgeon in internal medicine Regional Hosp., Fort Knox, Ky., 1946; ward surgeon plastic surgery Valley Forge Gen. Hosp., Phoenixville, Pa., 1946-47; intern St. Louis City Hosp., 1947-48; resident in surgery VA Hosp., St. Louis, 1948-52; clin. instr. surgery St. Louis U., 1952-62; gen. practice medicine specializing in surgery St. Louis, 1952—; mem. staff St. Mary's Hosp., 1952-77, St. John's Mercy Hosp., 1952-74, St. Louis U. (Desloge) Hosp., 1952-62; Cardinal Glennon Children's Hosp., 1952-62; mem. staff Frisco RR Hosp., 1953-64, DePaul Hosp., 1954—, Christian Hosp., 1955-66, 83-91. Mem. St. Louis Ambassadors, 1979-81; officer St. Louis County Aux. Police, 1973-75. Served to capt. AUS, 1945-47. Recipient Eagle Scout award, Order of the Arrow Honor award Boy Scouts Am. Fellow ACS, Royal Soc. Medicine, Internat. Coll. Surgeons; mem. St. Louis Med. Soc., Am. Coll. Occupl. and Environ. Medicine, Am. Soc. Clin. Hypnosis, Internat. Soc. Hypnosis, Am. Assn. RR Surgeons, St. Louis U. Student Conclave, Alpha Sigma Nu, Phi Beta Pi. Roman Catholic. Avocations: hypnosis, photography. Home: PO Box 411933 Saint Louis MO 63141-1933

MCFADDEN, JOHN VOLNEY, retired manufacturing company executive; b. N.Y.C., Oct. 3, 1931; s. Volney and Mary Lucile (McConkie) McF.; m. Marie Linstead, June 27, 1953; children— Deborah, John Scott, David. BS in Commerce and Fin, Bucknell U., 1953; JD, Detroit Coll. Law, 1960. Pres., vice chmn. MTD Products, Inc., Cleve., 1960-92; pres. MTD Products Inc., Cleve., 1980-91, vice chmn., 1990-92; gen. ptnr. Camelot Ptnrs., Cleve.; pres. Parkside Acquisition Ptnrs. Ltd., Cleve., 1997—. Bd. dirs. C.E. White Co., Fusion Inc., Flambeau Corp., Hinkley Lighting, Inc.; past chmn. financing adv. bd. State of Ohio Devel.; past pres. Cleve. World Trade Assn.; chmn. Parkside

Acquisition Ptnrs. Ltd. Trustee Fairview Health Svcs, Cleve. Clinic. Lt. Supply Corps, USN. Mem. Cleve. Yachting Club. Office: Parkside Acq Ptnrs Ltd 20160 Parkside Dr Cleveland OH 44116-1347

MC FADDEN, JOSEPH MICHAEL, history educator; b. Joliet, Ill., Feb. 12, 1932; s. Francis Joseph and Lucille (Adler) McF.; m. Norma Cardwell, Oct. 10, 1958; children: Timothy Joseph, Mary Colleen, Jonathan Andrew. BA, Lewis Coll., 1954; MA, U. Chgo., 1961; PhD, No. Ill. U., 1968. Tchr. history Joliet Cath. High Sch., 1957-60; mem. faculty history dept. Lewis Coll., Lockport, Ill., 1960-70, asso. prof., 1967-70, v.p. acad. affairs, 1968-70; prof. history, dean sch. Nat. and Social Sci., Kearney (Nebr.) State Coll., 1970-74; prof. history, dean Sch. Social and Behavioral Scis., Slippery Rock (Pa.) State Coll., 1974-77; pres. No. State Coll., Aberdeen, S.D., 1977-82, U. S.D., Vermillion, 1982-88, U. St. Thomas, Houston, 1988-97, pres. emeritus, prof. history, 1997—. Served with USNR, 1954-56. Roman Catholic. Office: U St Thomas Office of Pres 3812 Montrose Blvd Houston TX 77006-4626 E-mail: mcfadden@stthom.edu.

MCFADDEN, MARGARET H. education educator, writer; b. Lafayette, Ind., Aug. 1, 1941; d. William Allen and Glenara English McFadden; m. Leslie Eldridge Gerber, Sept. 2, 1967 (div. Feb. 2002); 1 child, Leslie Noel McFadden-Gerber. BA summa cum laude, U. Denver, 1963; MA in English Lang. and Lit., Boston U., 1964; PhD in Humanities, Emory U., 1973. Instr. English No. Mich. U., Marquette, 1964—66, Clark Coll., Atlanta, 1966—67; from instr. to asst. prof. English Spelman Coll., Atlanta, 1969—71; lectr. English U. Md., 1971—73, U. Colo., Colorado Springs, 1974—75; from asst. prof. to prof. interdisciplinary studies and womens studies Appalachian State U., Boone, NC, 1975—. Editor: Nat Womens Studies Assn. Jour., 1997—2003, Women's Issues, 2000; author: Loren Eiseley, 1983, Golden Cables of Sympathy: The Transatlantic Sources of 19th Century Feminism, 1999. Fellow, Sallie Bingham Ctr. for Women's History and Culture, Duke U., 2004; Fulbright scholar, Finland, 1991—92, Austria, 2004. Mem.: AAUP, NOW. Episcopalian. Office: Appalachian State Univ Dept Interdisciplinary Studies 216 LLA Boone NC 28608 Business E-Mail: mcfaddenmh@appstate.edu.

MCFADDEN, MARY JOSEPHINE, fashion industry executive; b. N.Y.C., Oct. 1, 1938; d. Alexander Bloomfield and Mary Josephine (Cutting) McF.; m. Philip Harari; 1 child, Justine. Ed., Sorbonne, Paris, Traphagen Sch. Design, 1957, Columbia, 1959-62; DFA, Internat. Fine Arts Coll., 1984. Pub. rels. dir. Christian Dior, N.Y.C., 1962—64; merchandising editor Vogue South Africa, 1964—65, editor, 1965—69; polit. and travel columnist Rand (South Africa) Daily Mail, 1965—68; founder sculptural workshop Vukutu, Zimbabwe, 1968—70; spl. projects editor Vogue U.S.A., 1973; pres. Mary McFadden, Inc., N.Y.C., 1976—; ptnr. MMcF Collection by Mary McFadden, 1991—. Bd. dirs., advisor Sch. Design and Merchandising Kent State U., Eugene O'Neill Meml. Theatre Ctr.; mem. profl. com. Cooper-Hewitt Mus., Smithsonian Inst., Nat. Mus. of Design; designer Collection by Mary McFadden, 2000, Mary McFadden Collection, 2003, Earth-BOUND, N.Y.C., 2003; lectr. U. Phila., 2004, Dept. Ancient Near Eastern Art, Met. Mus. Art, 2004, Sackler Mus., Japan Soc., 2004. Fashion and jewelry designer, 1973—; maj. retrospective of fashion, textiles and jewels at Allentown (Pa.) Art Mus., 2004; author introduction Mary McFadden High Priestess of High Fashion, 2004. Advisor Nat. Endowment for Arts; active local Police Athletic League, We Care About N.Y., CFDA-Vogue Breast Cancer Initiative, Beth Israel Hosp., The Chemotherapy Found.; curator emeritus Cannan Found., 1973-85; founding trustee Robert Redford's Sundance Inst., 1978-83; trustee Devi Ahilya Bai Holkal Meml. Charitable Trust, Maheshwar, Indore, India. Recipient Am. Fashion Critics award-Coty award, 1976, 78, 79, Audemars Piguet Fashion award, 1976, Rex award, 1977, award More Coll. Art, 1977, Pa. Gov.'s award, 1977, Roscoe award, 1978, Pres.'s Fellows award RISD, 1979, Neiman-Marcus award of excellence, 1979, Design Excellence award Pratt Inst., 1993, award N.Y. Landmarks Conservancy, 1994, NU Breed Fashion award, 1996, Marymount Coll. Fashion award, 1996, Legends award N.Y., 2001, Lifetime Achievement award South Am. Press Assn., Miami, Fla., 2002, Pratt Legions award, 2002, Spirit of Design award Phila. U., 2004; named to Fashion Hall of Fame, 1979; fellow RISD. Mem. Fashion Group (bd. dirs. 1981-82), Council of Fashion Designers Am. (past pres.). Office: Mary McFadden Inc 525 E 72nd St New York NY 10021 Office Phone: 212-772-1125. E-mail: MMcFCouture@aol.com.

MCFADDEN, NANCY ELIZABETH, lawyer; b. Wilmington, Del., Oct. 20, 1958; d. William P. and Mary Elizabeth (Adams) McF. BA, San Jose State U., 1984; JD, U. Va., 1987. Judicial clk. Hon. John P. Wiese U.S. Claims Ct., Washington, 1987-88; atty. O'Melveny & Myers, Washington, 1988-91; deputy communications dir. Office of Pres.-Elect, Washington, 1992-93; asst. atty. gen. U.S. Dept. Justice, Washington, 1993, prin. deputy assoc. atty. gen., 1993-95; gen. counsel Dept. Transp., Washington, 1996—. Nat. deputy polit. dir. Clinton for Pres. Campaign, 1992, nat. surrogate dir. Clinton-Gore for Pres. Campaign, 1992.

MCFADDEN, PETER WILLIAM, retired mechanical engineering educator; b. Stamford, Conn., Aug. 2, 1932; s. Kenneth E. and Marie (Gleason) McF.; children: Peter, Kathleen, Mary. BSME, U. Conn., 1954, MS, 1956; PhD, Purdue U., 1959. Registered profl. engr., Ind. Asst. instr. U. Conn., 1954-56, prof. mech. engring., 1971-98, dean Sch. Engring., 1971-85, dir. devel., 1985-88, provost, v.p., 1988, exec. asst. to pres., exec. sec. to bd. trustees, 1989-98; mem. faculty Purdue U., 1956-71; prof. mech. engring., head Purdue U. (Sch. Mech. Engring.), 1965-71; postdoctoral research Swiss Fed. Inst., Zurich, 1960-61. Cons. to industry, 1959-98. Achievements include research in cryogenics, heat transfer, mass transfer.

MCFADDEN, ROBBYN KILBANE, interior designer, public policy specialist, artist, advocate; b. Chgo., Oct. 5, 1951; d. Robert Harrison and Adrienne Fay (Seyring) Kilbane; m. James E. McFadden Jr., Dec. 20, 1975; 1 child, Ryan James. BFA, U. Ill., 1969-74; Diploma in Interior Design, Harper Coll., Chgo., 1976. Designer Euromarket Designs, 1978-83; project cons. Volo Interiors, 1983-90; educator, art and design dept. Coll. of Lake County, 1981-83; owner, prin. Design Perspectives, 1983—. Design cons. Law Offices of Patricia Hogan, Monadnock Bldg., Chgo., 1989; project designer retail space Historic Harbor House, Waukegan, Ill., 1988, others. Pub. design commns. include Hunterdon Art Ctr. Archival Print System, 1994, Cleve. Edn. Fund. Historic Dallas Bldg., 1998, Kids First Festival, Lake County, Ill., 1998, numerous others; pvt. commns. include residences in Ill., N.J., Ohio, Calif. Mem. adv. com. to internat. programs LWV USA, Washington, 1994—; nat. bd. dirs. UNIFEM/UN Devel. Fund for Women, N.Y.C., 1999—; fundraiser, pub. policy advocate Ctr. for the Humanities and Environment, Jackson Hole, Wyo., 1992-95; adv. mem., cons. Com. for Pub. Art, Cleve., 1995-97; vis. svcs. cons. Art Inst. Chgo., 2003—; specialist advisor Lake County Women's Coalition Arts, 2003—; mem. women's bd. Hist. Genesee Theater, Lake County, Ill. Recipient Carrie Chapman Catt award LWV, Cleve., 1998. Mem. LWV (bd. dirs. Ill. chpt., Lake County pres. 2003—), Am. Soc. Interior Designers (allied), Interior Design Soc./Nat. Home Furnishings Assn., PEO, Lake County Dem. Women (bd. dirs.). Avocations: painting, golf. Personal E-mail: indezyn@aol.com.

MCFADDEN, ROBERT DENNIS, reporter; b. Milw., Feb. 11, 1937; s. Francis Joseph and Violet (Charleston) McF.; m. Judith Marian Silverman, June 20, 1971; 1 son, Nolan Seth. BS cum laude, U. Wis., 1960. Reporter Wisconsin Rapids (Wis.) Daily Tribune, 1957-58, Wis. State Jour., Madison, 1958-59, Cin. Enquirer, 1960-61; sr. writer, reporter N.Y. Times, 1961—. Mem. adv. coun. St. John's U. dept journalism, 1996—. Co-author: No Hiding Place, 1981, Outrage: The Story Behind the Tawana Brawley Hoax, 1990. With U.S. Army, 1960-61, Res. 1961-68. Recipient Pulitzer Prize for Spot News Reporting (N.Y. Times team), 1994, (individual) 1996; Byline award N.Y. Press Club, 1973, 74, 80, 87, 89, 92, Page One award Newspaper Guild N.Y., 1978, Spot News award Uniformed Firemen's Assn., 1967, Spot News award L.I. Press Club, 1984, 95, Chancellor's award for Disting. Svc. U. Wis., 1987, Man of Yr. award Alumni N.Y., 1997, Excellence in Local Reporting award N.Y. Newspaper Publ. Assn., 1988, Spot News award N.Y. Newspaper Publ. Assn., 1988, Spot News award N.Y. State Associated Press, 1989, 91, Continuing Coverage award, 1995, 99, In Depth Reporting award, 1989, 91, Feature Writing award, 1996, Ochs Prize in Journalism, 1989, Best News/Feature Story award Internat. Assn. Fire Fighters, 1991, Nat. Spot News award Asian-Am. Journalists Assn., 1994, Comprehensive Reporting award, N.Y. Uniformed Fire Officers Assn., 1995. Mem. N.Y. Soc. Silurians (Spot News Story award 1977, 2001, Peter Kihss award 1987, Investigative reporting award 1989, Excellence in Journalism award 1994, gov. 1988—). Office: NY Times 229 W 43rd St New York NY 10036-3959

MCFADDEN, ROSEMARY THERESA, lawyer, financial services executive; b. Oct. 1, 1948; came to U.S., 1951, naturalized, 1967; d. John and Winifred (Quinn) McFadden; m. Brian Doherty, May 26, 1973. BA, Rutgers U., 1970, MBA, 1974; JD, Seton Hall U., 1978; hon. doctorate, St. Elizabeth's Coll., Convent Station, N.J., 1985. Bar: N.J. 1978, U.S. Dist. Ct. N.J. 1978. Spl. asst. Office of the Mayor, Jersey City, 1973-76; exec. dir. Hudson Health Sys., Jersey City, 1976-81; assoc. legal counsel N.Y. Merc. Exch., N.Y.C., 1981-82, exec. v.p., 1982-84, pres., 1984-89, spl. policy advisor to bd. dirs., 1989-91; of counsel Shulman, Hanlon and Doherty, Jersey City and N.Y.C., 1989-97; sr. mgr. Price Waterhouse Internat. Practice Group, 1993-97; sr. v.p. Donaldson Lufkin & Jenrette/Pershing, Jersey City, 1997-98; mng. dir. global devel. CSFBdirect, Jersey City, 1999—. Mem. deans adv. coun. Rutgers U. Grad Sch. Mgmt., Newark, 1985. Bd. dirs. Jersey City Med. Ctr., 1985-87, UNICEF, 1989-92, Futures Industry Assn., 1989-90; St Anthony H.S. 2003—, Liberty Health Corp., 2003—. Named Alumna of Yr., Rutgers U., 1985, Seton Hall U. Mem. ABA, N.J. Bar Assn., Futures Industry Assn., Securities Industry Assn., Rutgers U. Alumni Assn. Roman Catholic. Avocations: travel, antiques. Office: CSFBdirect Harborside Plz II 5th Fl Jersey City NJ 07311

MCFADIN, HELEN LOZETTA, retired elementary education educator; b. Tucumcari, N.Mex., Sept. 7, 1923; d. Henry J. and LaRue Altha (Ford) Stockton; m. John Reece McFadin, July 3, 1946; 1 child, Janice Lynn McFadin Koenig. AB in Edn./Psychology, Highlands U., Las Vegas, N.Mex., 1956; MA in Teaching, N.Mex. State U., 1968; postgrad., U. N.D., 1965, St. Leo's Coll., St. Leo, Fla., 1970. Cert. tchr., K-12 reading/psychology specialist, N.Mex. Tchr. 1st and 2d grades Grant County Schs., Bayard, N.Mex., 1943-44; tchr. 4th grade Durango (Colo.) Pub. Schs., 1946-48; tchr. 2d grade Artesia Pub. Schs., Loco Hills, N.Mex., 1955; tchr. 3d grade Alamogordo (N.Mex.) Pub. Schs., 1957-66, h.s. reading specialist, 1966-72, elem. reading specialist, 1972-77, tchr. 4th grade, 1977-82, reading tchr. 7th grade, dept. chair, 1982-87; ret. N.Mex. State U., Alamogordo, 1987, instr. edn., 1987-90. Organizer reading labs. h.s., elem. schs., Alamogordo, 1966-77, designer programs and curriculum, 1957-89; presenter/cons. in field; cons. Mary Kay Cosmetics; rep. Excel Telecomms., Inc. Contbr. articles to profl. jours. Local and dist. judge spelling bees and sci. fairs Alamogordo Pub. Schs., 1987-98. Recipient Literacy award Otero County Reading Coun., 1986; named to Women's Hall of Fame, Alamogordo Women's Clubs, 1989. Mem. Am. Bus. Women's Assn. (pres. 1986-87, v.p. local chpt. 1999-00, named Woman of the Yr. 1988, 2003), NEA (del. 1957-87, Dedicated Svc. award 1987), N.Mex. Edn. Assn., Internat. Reading Assn. (mem. Spl. League of the Honored 1985, pres. 1975-76), N.Mex. Reading Assn. (bd. dirs. 1988-94, del. to 1st Russian reading conf. 1992, Dedicated Svc. award 1994), Tularosa Basin Hist. Soc., Beta Sigma Phi (pres. local chpt. 1998-99, formed new master chpt. 1999, Golden Cir. Anniversary award 2002), Kappa Kappa Iota (local pres. Kappa Conclave 1998-00, state officer, nat. com., co-chair nat. conv. 2000-02, Disting. Educator Emeritus Cert. of Merit 1988, VIP award 2000, 2002). Republican. Baptist. Avocations: reading, fashion modeling. Home: 2364 Union Ave Alamogordo NM 88310-3848

MCFADYEN, LIANE, state representative; m. Paul Ray; 1 child. BA, Adams State Coll., 1991, MS, 1993. State rep., dist. 45 Colo. House Rep., Denver, 2000—; owner Rocky Mountain Specialized Cleaning, Pueblo, Colo., Alliance Bus. Strategies, Pueblo. Mem. Info. and Tech. Com., Transp. and Energy Com. Democrat. Office: State Capitol #307 200 E Colfax Ave Denver CO 80203

MCFALL, CATHERINE GARDNER, poet, critic, educator; b. Jacksonville, Fla., July 10, 1952; d. Albert Dodge and Joan (Livingston) McF.; m. Peter Forbes Olberg, Oct. 21, 1978; 1 child, Amanda Olberg. Baccalaureat, U. Paris, 1973; AB magna cum laude, Wheaton Coll., Norton, Mass., 1974; MA, Johns Hopkins U., 1975; PhD, NYU, 1990. Editl. asst., short story editor Ladies' Home Jour., N.Y.C., 1975-77; adminstrv. dir. Poetry Soc. Am., N.Y.C., 1981-83; instr. writing NYU, N.Y.C., 1983-87, asst. dir. Poetics Inst., 1984-86; asst. prof. humanities Cooper Union, N.Y.C., 1990-98. Adj. asst. prof. English, Hunter Coll., N.Y.C. Author: Jonathan's Cloud, 1986, Discovery, 1989 (Nation award), Naming the Animals, 1994, The Pilot's Daughter, 1996; editor: Made with Words, 1998; contbr. poetry and revs. to mags. including Paris Rev., Atlantic Monthly, N.Y. Times, others. Bd. dirs. Yaddo, 2003—. MacDowell Colony fellow, 1980, 86, Yaddo fellow, 1981, 84, 91, 93, 97, 99, Nat. Arts Club Poetry scholar Bread Loaf Writers Conf., 1983. Mem. MLA, Poets and Writers, Poetry Soc. Am., Nat. Book Critics Cir. Personal E-mail: cathgm@nyc.rr.com.

MCFALL, DONALD BEURY, lawyer; b. Charleston, W.Va., Aug. 2, 1941; s. Henry Tucker and Elizabeth Katharine (Beury) McF.; m. Donna Glenn Binion, May 27, 1972; children: Katharine Atkinson, Mary Crawford. BA, Washington and Lee U., 1964, JD, 1969. Bar: Va. 1969, Tex. 1969, U.S. Supreme Ct. 1979, U.S. Dist. Ct. (we., no., so. and ea. dists.) Tex. 1969. Asst. U.S. atty. U.S. Dept. Justice, Houston, 1970-71; assoc. Butler & Binion, Houston, 1971-77, ptnr., 1977-85, McFall, Sherwood & Sheehy, Houston, 1985-2000; shareholder McFall, Sherwood & Breitbeil, P.C., Houston, 2000—. Trustee Humana Hosp.-Sharpstown, Houston, 1984—85, Southmore Med. Ctr., 1994—98; bd. dirs. Planned Parenthood Houston and S.E. Tex., 1978—88; trustee Woodberry Forest Sch., Orange, Va., 1984—90, Washington and Lee U., 1997—. 1st lt. U.S. Army, 1964—66. Fellow: Internat. Soc. Barristers, Am. Coll. Trial Lawyers, Houston Bar Found., Tex. Bar Found.; mem.: Am. Judicature Soc., Am. Bd. Trial Advocates (adv.), Fedn. Ins. and Corp. Counsel, Tex. State Bar Assn., Va. State Bar Assn., Internat. Assn. Def. Counsel, Garland Walker Inn, Am. Inns of Ct. Office: McFall Sherwood & Breitbeil PC 1250 Four Houston Ctr 1331 Lamar St Houston TX 77010 Office Fax: 713-590-9300. Personal E-mail: dbmcf@aol.com. Business E-Mail: dmcfall@mcfall-law.com.

MCFALL, JOHN, artistic director; b. Kansas City, Mo. Studies with Tatiana Dokoudovska, Conservatory of Music; student, San Francisco Ballet Sch., 1964-65. Formerly with San Francisco Ballet, prin. dancer, 1969; artistic dir. BalletMet, Columbus, Ohio, 1986-94; artistic dir., CEO Atlanta Ballet Co., 1994—. Choreographer Nat. Ballet Can., Am. Ballet Theatre, Dance Theatre Harlem, San Francisco, Hubbard St. Dance Co., Atlanta Ballet, for other artists, including Mikhail Baryshnikov, Cynthia Gregory. Choreographer Commd. 2 world premieres for 1996 Olympic Arts Festival; recently staged: 10 Atlanta prodns., including The Nutcracker. Ford Found. scholar San Francisco Ballet Sch., 1964, Nat. Endowment for Arts fellow, 1978, 1980, 1985. Office: Atlanta Ballet 1400 W Peachtree St Atlanta GA 30309-2906

MCFARLAN, FRANKLIN WARREN, business administration educator; b. Boston, Oct. 18, 1937; s. Ronald Lyman and Ethel Warren (White) McF.; m. Margaret Karen Nelson, Dec. 17, 1971; children: Andrew, Clarissa, Elizabeth. AB, Harvard Coll., 1959, MBA, 1961, D.B.A, 1965. Asst. prof. Harvard Bus. Sch., Boston, 1964-68, assoc. prof., 1968-73, prof. bus. adminstrn., 1973—, sr. assoc. dean, dir. rsch., 1991-95, sr. assoc. dean external rels., 1995-2000, sr. assoc. dean, dir. Asia Pacific, 2000—. Dir. Providian Fin. Corp., San Francisco, Li and Fung Corp., HOng Kong, Computer Sci. Corp., L.A. Author: (with Richard Nolan) Information Systems Administration, 1973; (with Linda Applegate and Robert Austin) Corporate Information Management, 6th edit., 2003, (with Linda Applegate and Robert Austin) Creating Business Advantages in Information Age, 2002, (with Cathleen Benko) Connecting the Dots, 2003; editor: (with Richard Nolan) Information Systems Handbook, 1973, Information Systems Research Challenge, 1984; sr. editor MIS Quar., 1986-88. Bd. dirs.; pres. Belmont (Mass.) Day Sch., 1982-86; bd. dirs. Dana Hall Sch., Wellesley, Mass., 1982-94, chmn. bd., 1990-93; trustee Mt. Auburn Hosp., 1991-99, ch mn. bd., 1995-98, trustee care group, 1996—; trustee Winsor Sch., 1994-2000, Milton Acad., 2001--. 1st lt. U.S. Army, 1962-67. Mem.: The Country (Brookline, Mass.). Republican. Episcopalian. Home: 37 Beatrice Cir Belmont MA 02478-2657 Office: Harvard Bus Sch Soldiers Field Rd Boston MA 02163-1317 E-mail: fmcfarlan@hbs.edu.

MCFARLAN, REBECCA COLLINS, secondary school educator, consultant; b. Middletown, Ohio, July 21, 1953; d. Thomas Paige and Treva Grigsby Collins; m. James Powell McFarlan III, Aug. 21, 1976; children: James Powell IV, Paige Lynne. BS in Mktg. and Textiles, Ea. Ky. U., 1976; BA in English, No. Ky. U., 1979; MA in English, Xavier U., 1988. Cert. adolescent/young adult English lang. arts Nat. Bd. Profl. Tchg. Stds., 1998. English tchr. Our Lady of Providence, Newport, Ky., 1977—83, Covington Cath. H.S., Park Hills, Ky., 1984—88; English tchr., dept. chair Indian Hill Bd. Edn., Cin., 1988—. Ednl. cons. The Coll. Bd., N.Y.C., 1998—; reader for advanced placement English exam Ednl. Testing Svc., Princeton, NJ, 2000—. Named Master Tchr., Martha Holden Jenning Found., Cleve., 2002; Rousseau Seminar fellow, NEH, 1993, Tchr. Practitioner grantee, Spencer Found., Chgo., 2000. Mem.: MLA, Ohio Conf. Tchrs. English Lang. Arts, Nat. Conf. Tchrs. English. Episcopalian. Avocations: reading, travel, gardening. Home: 225 Riverside Pkwy Fort Thomas KY 41075 Office: Indian Hills HS 6845 Drake Rd Cincinnati OH 45343

MCFARLAND, CAROL ANNE, lawyer; b. Eugene, Oreg., Aug. 25, 1951; d. Harvey John and Muriel Anne (Walker) McF.; children: Annette Catherine, Miles Patrick. BS, Oreg. State U., 1973; JD, Western State U., 1977. Bar: Calif. 1977, U.S. Dist. Ct. (so. dist.) Calif. 1977. Assoc. Sankary & Sankary, San Diego, 1977-81; pvt. practice San Diego, 1981-88; dep. dist. atty. Family Support divsn., Clackamas County, Oreg., 1990—. Vol. atty. Supervision Ctr. Women's Studies-Clinic Domestic Violence Restraining Orders, 1983-88, San Diego Vol. Lawyers Assn., 1986-88. Mem. ABA, Calif. Bar Assn., Oreg. State Bar Assn., Clackamas County Bar Assn., Oreg. Women Lawyers, Rotary Internat., Delta Theta Phi. Office: 619 Madison St # 106 Oregon City OR 97045 Office Phone: 503-722-6030.

MC FARLAND, H. RICHARD, food company executive; b. Hoopeston, Ill., Aug. 19, 1930; s. Arthur Bryan and Jennie (Wilkey) McF.; m. Sarah Forney, Dec. 30, 1967. BS, U. Ill., 1952. With Campbell Soup Co., Camden, N.J., 1957-67, mgr. purchasing, 1961-67; dir. procurement Keebler Co., Elmhurst, Ill., 1967-69; v.p. purchasing and distbn. Ky. Fried Chicken Corp., Louisville, 1969-74, v.p. food svcs., sales and distbn., 1974-75; pres., dir. Mid-Continent Carton Co., Louisville, 1974-75, Ky. Fried Chicken Mfg. Corp., Nashville, 1974-75; owner, pres., dir. McFarland Foods Corp., Indpls., 1975—. Chmn. processed foods com. World's Poultry Congress, 1974; mem. exec. coun., nat. franchise coun. Ky. Fried Chicken, 1979-85; dir. nat. advt. coun. Ky. Fried Chicken, 1985-91, exec. com., 1988-90, chmn., 1989-90; mem. devel. com. U. Ill., 1989—. Mem. U. Ill. Found., 1992—, bd. dirs., 1993—, vice chmn., 2001—; chmn. U. Ill. Nat. Advocates, 1992-2001; life pres. U. Ill. Sr. Class of '52; bd. dirs. Ind. Fedn. Children and Youth, 1983-84; Ind. bd. dirs. Fellowship Christian Athletes, 1997-98, Ind. bd. advisors, 1998—; chmn. campaign Ind. Ky. Fried Chicken March of Dimes, 1978-87; nat. trustee McCormick Theol. Sem., 1993-97, mem. adv. coun., 1998-2002. 1st lt. USAF, 1952-54, Korea. Recipient Award of Merit U. Ill. Coll. Agr., 1988, Achievement award U. Ill. Alumni Assn., 1996. Mem. Ky. Restaurant Asns. (bd. dirs. 1970-75), Nat. Broiler Coun. (bd. dirs. 1971-74), Ind. Restaurant Assn., Am. Shorthorn Breeders Assn., Great Lakes Ky. Fried Chicken Franchise Assn. (bd. dirs. 1975-91, 1st v.p. 1978-79, pres. 1979-80), Delta Upsilon. Clubs: Main Line Ski (Phila.) (pres. 1964); Hillcrest Country. Presbyterian. Home: 10720 Compass Ct Indianapolis IN 46256-9532

MCFARLAND, JAMES W. dean, finance educator; BA in econs./math., Texas A&M U., 1967, PhD in stats./econs./math., 1971. Instr. Inst. Stats. Texas A&M U., 1970—71; econometrician Nat. Water Commn., 1971; asst. prof. dept. math. U. La., Lafayette, 1971—73; asst. prof. dept. resource econs. U. RI, 1973—75; adj. prof. Robert O. Anderson Sch. Mgmt., U. N. Mex., 1975—76; staff mem. stats. and energy systems analysis Los Alamos Nat. Lab. U. Calif., 1975—76, vis. staff. mem., 1976—85; assoc. prof. Coll. Bus. Adminstrn., U. Houston, 1976—79, chmn. mgmt. scis., 1977—79, assoc. dean, 1979—85, prof., 1983—88, dean, 1985—88; dean and J.F. Jr. Seinsheimer Chair in Bus. A.B. Freeman Sch. Bus., Tulane U., New Orleans, 1988—. Bd. dirs. Am. Indemnity Fin. Corp., 1994—99, Petroleum Helicopters, Inc., 1996—2001, Sizeler Property Investors, Inc., 1994—, Stewart Enterprises, Inc., 1995—. Bd. dirs. New Orleans World Trade Ctr., 1990—. Recipient Disting. Svc. Award, Nat. Water Commn., 1971, Disting. Faculty Mem. Award, Coll. Bus. Adminstrn., U. Houston, 1983, Disting. Svc. Award, U. Houston Alumni Assn., 1988. Office: AB Freeman Sch Bus Tulane U 440 Goldring/Woldenberg New Orleans LA 70118-5669*

MCFARLAND, JANE ELIZABETH, librarian; b. Athens, Tenn., June 22, 1937; d. John Homer and Martha Virginia (Large) McFarland. AB, Smith Coll., 1959; M in Divinity, Yale U., 1963; MS in LS, U. N.C., 1971. Tchr. hist. and religion Northfield Schs., Mass., 1961-62; head librarian reference and circulation Yale Divinity Library, New Haven, Conn., 1963-71; head librarian Bradford (Mass.) Coll., 1972-77; reference librarian U. Tenn., Chattanooga, Tenn., 1977-80; head librarian reference dept Chattanooga-Hamilton County Bicentennial Library, Tenn., 1980-86, acting dir., 1986, dir., 1986—. Mem. Chattanooga Library Assn., Tenn. Library Assn., Southeastern Library Assn., Am. Library Assn., Phi Beta Kappa. Democrat. Roman Catholic. Avocations: reading, travel, needlecrafts. Home: 1701 Estrellita Cir Chattanooga TN 37421-5754 Office: Chattanooga-Hamilton County Libr 1001 Broad St Chattanooga TN 37402-2620

MCFARLAND, KAY ELEANOR, state supreme court chief justice; b. Coffeyville, Kans., July 20, 1935; d. Kenneth W. and Margaret E. (Thrall) McF. BA magna cum laude, Washburn U., Topeka, 1957, JD, 1964. Bar: Kans. 1964. Sole practice, Topeka, 1964-71; probate and juvenile judge Shawnee County, Topeka, 1971-73; dist. judge Topeka, 1973-77; assoc. justice Kans. Supreme Ct., 1977-95, chief justice, 1995—. Mem. Kans. Bar Assn., Women Attys. Assn. Topeka., Topeka Bar Assn. Office: Kans Supreme Ct Kans Jud Ctr 301 SW 10th Ave Topeka KS 66612-1507 Fax: (785) 291-3274.

MCFARLAND, KEVIN JOHN, foundation administrator; b. Mt. Clement, Mich., Mar. 18, 1958; s. Chuck Paul and Myrna (Bell) McFarland; m. Betty Ann Bolton, Nov. 26, 1976; children: Michelle, Michael, Melinda. BS in Bibl. Studies magna cum laude, Abilene Christian U., Tex., 1980; postgrad., Tex. Tech. U., 1980-81, Stanford U., 1982-83. Resident asst. Abilene (Tex.) State Sch., 1976-78; pvt. landscaping bus. Abilene, 1978-80; research assoc., home and family life dept. Tex. Tech. U., Lubbock, 1980-81; youth and family min. Redwood Ch., 1981-84; pres. Manna Internat. Relief and Devel. Corp., Redwood City, 1984—. Mem. Amnexty Internat., Bread for the World; bd. dirs. Am. Coun. Voluntary Internat. Action. Mem.: Internat. Devel. Network, Acad. Polit. Sci., Inst. Cultural Affairs, Inst. Coop. Interant. Devel. (bd. dirs., founder, exec. dir.), Soc. Internat. Devel. Global Affairs Coun., Evang. for Social Action, Cultural Survival, Nat. Assn. Scholars, Nat. Honor Soc., Alpha Chi. Home: 1193 Hudson St Redwood City CA 94061-2208 Office: Manna Internat PO Box 3507 Redwood City CA 94064-3507

MCFARLAND, MICHAEL C. academic administrator; b. Boston, 1948; AB in Physics, Cornell U., 1969; M in Elec. Engring., Carnegie M in Elec. Engring., PhD in Elec. Engring., Carnegie Mellon U.; MDiv, ThM in Social Ethics, Weston Sch. Theology. Ordained to ministry Jesuits, 1984. Cons. AT&T Bell Labs., 1985—86; assoc. prof. computer sci. Boston Coll., 1986—96, dept. chair; prof. computer sci., dean Coll. Arts and Scis. Gonzaga U., Spokane, 1996—2000; pres. Coll. of the Holy Cross, Worcester, Mass., 2000—. Bd. dirs. U. Scranton. Avocation: running. Office: Coll of the Holy Cross 1 College St Worcester MA 01610-2395

MC FARLAND, NORMAN FRANCIS, bishop; b. Martinez, Calif., Feb. 21, 1922; Student, St. Patrick's Sem. Ordained to ministry Cath. Ch., 1946, consecrated bishop Cath. Ch., 1970. Auxilliary bishop, San Francisco,

1970—74; apostolic adminstr. Diocese of Reno, 1974—76; bishop Diocese of Reno-Las Vegas, 1976—87, Diocese of Orange, Calif., 1987—98. Office: 200 W La Veta Ave Orange CA 92866-1936

MCFARLAND, PATRICK E. federal agency administrator; b. St. Louis; m. Kathy McFarland; 4 children. BS, St. Louis U., 1965; MPA, Am. U., 1986. Police officer, detective St. Louis Met. Police Dept.; spl. agt. Fed. Bur. Narcotics, Chgo.; with U.S. Secret Svc., Washington; inspector gen. Office Personnel Mgmt., 1990—. Mem. alumni adv. bd. Key Exec. Program Am. U. Mem.: Assn. Govt. Accts., Internat. Assn. Chiefs of Police, Fed. Investigators Assn. Office: OPM 1900 E St NW Washington DC 20415-1100

MCFARLAND, PHILIP JAMES, educator, writer; b. Birmingham, Ala., June 20, 1930; s. Thomas Alfred McFarland and Alice Lucile Sylvester; m. Patricia Katherin Connors, July 23, 1960; children: Philip James Jr., Joseph Thomas. BA, Oberlin Coll., 1951; MA, Cambridge U., 1957. Textbook editor Houghton Mifflin Co., Boston, 1958-64; tchr. English Concord (Mass.) Acad., 1965-95. Author: A House Full of Women, 1960, Sojourners, 1979, Seasons of Fear, 1984, Sea Dangers, 1985, A History of Concord Acad. 2 vols., 1986, 2000, The Brave Bostonians, 1998; sr. editor: Houghton Mifflin Literature Series, 6 vols., 1972, Focus on Literature, 7 vols., 1978; editor: Composition: Models and Exercises, 5 vols., 2d edit., 1971, Hawthorne in Concord, 2004. Lt. j.g. USN, 1951-55. Fellow Mass. Hist. Soc. Democrat. Avocations: bicycling, trekking. Home: 18 Independence Ave Lexington MA 02421-5939

MCFARLAND, RICHARD M. executive recruiting consultant; b. Sept. 10, 1923; s. George Fiske and Phyllis C. (Macomber) McF.; m. Virginia Fitz-Randolph Ripley, Dec. 6, 1947; children: Richard Macomber, Kirk, Jane. BChemE, Rensselaer Poly. Inst., 1944; postgrad., U. Mich., 1946-47. Prodn. supr. E. I. duPont, 1947-51; mgr. agrl. chem. market rsch. Brea Chem. (Calif.) subs. Union Oil Co., 1953-55; product mgr. chem. divsn. FMC Corp., N.Y.C., 1955-59; mgr. mktg. devel. Tex. Butadiene & Chem., N.Y.C., 1959-60; pres. Cumberland Chem. Corp., N.Y.C., 1960-67; gen. mgr. inorganic divsn. Wyandotte Chem. Co., Mich., 1967-69; assoc. Heidrick & Struggles, Inc., N.Y.C., 1969-72, v.p., 1972-81; founder, pres. Brissenden, McFarland, Wagoner & Fuccella, Inc. and predecessors, Stamford, Conn., 1981-94. Patentee in field. Ensign USNR, 1943-46, lt. comdr., 1951-53. Mem. Cedar Point, Yacht Club, Lambda Chi Alpha. Home: 16 Clover Ln Westport CT 06880-2626

MCFARLAND, RICHARD MACKLIN, retired journalist; b. Blockton, Iowa, Mar. 27, 1922; s. William Harold McFarland and Elsie (Sisson) McFarland Chavannes; m. Jacquelyn Jean Folske, Mar. 22, 1955; children: Bethany Rose, Scott Macklin, Elizabeth Ann McFarland Heyda, Kathryn Belle. BA, U. Iowa, 1944. Newsman UPI, Des Moines, 1944, Chgo., 1945, 46-47, bur. mgr. Bismarck, N.D., 1944-45, Herrin, Ill., 1945, Sioux Falls, S.D., 1947-49, Milw., 1949-51, legis. reporter Des Moines, 1947, Pierre, S.D., 1949, Iowa mgr. Des Moines, 1951-54, NW mgr. Mpls., 1954-55, Wis. mgr. Milw., 1956-57, regional exec. sales, 1958-59, bur. mgr. Chgo., 1960-61, Minn. mgr. Mpls., 1961-69, Mich. editor Detroit, 1969-71, Minn. editor Mpls., 1971-84, bur. mgr.-capitol reporter St. Paul, 1985-89. Bd. dirs. Minn. Press Club, 1981-84. Former deacon, Advent Luth. Ch., Roseville, Minn., 8 yrs; coun. mem. Redeemer Luth. Ch., Bradenton, Fla., 1996-98, pres. coun., 1998-99, coun. mem. 2001-. Served with USN, 1943-44 Avocations: reading, music, fishing, backpacking, golf. Home: 7312 5th Ave NW Bradenton FL 34209-1522 E-mail: rmcf@aol.com.

MCFARLAND, ROBERT EDWIN, lawyer; b. St. Louis, July 25, 1946; s. Francis Taylor and Kathryne (Stephens) McF.; m. Jeannine M. Ghekiere, Feb. 26, 1982. BA, U. Mich., 1968, JD, 1971. Bar: Mich. 1971, U.S. Dist. Ct. (ea. dist.) Mich. 1971, U.S. Ct. Appeals (6th cir.) 1974, U.S. Supreme Ct. 1975, U.S. Ct. Appeals (D.C. cir.) 1978, N.Mex. 2001. Law clk. to chief judge Mich. Ct. Appeals, 1971-72; assoc. William B. Elmer, St. Clair Shores, Mich., 1972-74, James Elsman, Birmingham, Mich., 1974-75; ptnr. McFarland, Schmier, Stoneman & Singer, Troy, Mich., 1975-77; sr. ptnr. McFarland & Bullard, Bloomfield Hills, Mich., 1977-90, McFarland & Niemer, Farmington Hills, Mich., 1990-91; shareholder Foster, Swift, Collins & Smith, P.C., Farmington Hills, 1992—, mem. exec. com., 1995—2003. Chmn. bd. govs. Transp. Law Jour., U. Denver Coll. Law, 1981-83. Mem. bd. control Intercollegiate Athletics, U. Mich., 1966-68; mem. rulemaking study com. Mich. Pub. Svc. Commn., 1983-84, Motor Carrier Adv. Bd., 1984-88. Capt. USAR, 1971-80. Mem. ABA, Transp. Lawyers Assn. (officer 1998—, pres. 2002-03, Disting. Svc. award 1997), Assn. Transp. Law, Logistics and Policy, State Bar Mich. (vice-chmn. transp. law com. adminstrn. law sect. 1990—, sect. coun. adminstrv. law sect. 1994, 99), Am. Judicature Soc., Mich. Trust Safety Commn. Office: Foster Swift Collins & Smith PC 32300 Northwestern Hwy Ste 230 Farmington MI 48334-1571 E-mail: rmcfarland@fosterswift.com.

MC FARLAND, ROBERT HAROLD, physicist, researcher; b. Severy, Kans., Jan. 10, 1918; s. Robert Eugene and Georgia (Simpson) McF.; m. Twilah Mae Seefeld, Aug. 28, 1940; children: Robert Alan, Rodney Jon. BS and BA, Kans. State Tchrs. Coll., Emporia, 1940; Ph.M. (Mendenhall fellow), U. Wis., 1943, PhD, 1947. Sci. instr., coach high sch., Chase, Kans., 1940-41; instr. navy radio sch. U. Wis., Madison, 1943-44; sr. engr. Sylvania Elec. Corp., 1944-46; faculty Kans. State U., 1947-60, prof. physics, 1954-60, dir. nuclear lab., 1958-60; physicist Lawrence Livermore Radiation Lab. U. Calif., 1960—69; dean Grad. Sch., U. Mo., Rolla, 1969-79, dir. instnl. analysis and planning, 1979-82; prof. physics U. Mo., Rolla, 1969-84, prof. emeritus physics dept., 1985—; v.p. acad. affairs U. Mo. System, 1974-75; Intergovtl. Personnel Act appointee Dept. Energy, Washington, 1982-84; vis. prof. U. Calif., Berkeley, 1980-81. Mem. Grad. Record Exams. Bd., 1971-75, chmn. steering com., 1972-73; cons. Well Surveys, Inc., Tulsa, 1953-54, Argonne Nat. Lab., Chgo., 1955-59, Kans. Dept. Pub. Health, 1956-57, cons. in residence Lawrence Livermore Radiation Lab., U. Calif., 1957, 58, 59, med. physics U. Okla. Med. Sch., 1971, grad. schs., PhD physics program, Utah State U., 1972; physicist, regional counselor Office Ordnance Research, Durham, N.C., 1955. Author McFarland Collections, 1985, Simpson Connections, 1987; co-author two family geneaol. books; contbr. over 113 articles to profl. jours.; patentee in field of light prodn., vacuum prodn., controlled thermonuclear reactions. Active Boy Scouts Am., 1952—, mem. exec. bd. San Francisco Bay Area council, 1964-68, Ozark Council, 1986—; chmn. Livermore (Calif.) Library Bond drive, 1964. Mem. Kans. N.G., 1936-40. Recipient Silver Beaver award Boy Scouts Am., 1968, Community Service award C. of C., 1965, Disting. Alumnus award Kans. State Tchrs. Coll., 1969. Fellow AAAS, Am. Phys. Soc., Kiwanis Internat.; mem. AAUP (chpt. pres. 1956-57), Am. Assn. Physics Tchrs., Mo. Acad. Sci., Mo. Assn. Phys. Sci. Tchrs., Am. Soc. Engring. Edn., Kiwanis (lt. gov. Mo.-Ark. dist. 1984-85, internat. accredited rep. 1985-92, Disting. Lt. Gov. 1985, Tablet of honor award 1997, 50 Yr. Perfect Attendance pin 2003), Sigma Xi, Lambda Delta Lambda, Xi Phi, Kappa Mu Epsilon, Kappa Delta Pi, Pi Mu Epsilon, Gamma Sigma Delta, Phi Kappa Phi. Home: 416 W Spring St Apt 3 Neosho MO 64850-1777 Office: U Mo Dept Physics Rolla MO 65401 *Continuation of the last hundred years of major progress in the quality of life for the human race will not only require the best of our educational systems and technological talents but a sincere interest in all of us to contribute positively toward our collective well-being.*

MCFARLAND, ROBERT N. federal agency administrator; BS in Bus. Mgmt., LeTourneau U. V.p. Asia Pacific andMid. East Regions AST Rsch., Inc.; sr. v.p. Cerplex Group, Inc., Calif., 1994—96; v.p., gen. mgr. Fed. Bus. Segment Dell, 1996—2004; asst. sec. info. and tech. Dept. Vets. Affairs, Washington, 2004—. With U.S. Army, Vietnam. Office: US Dept Vets Affairs 810 Vermont Ave NW Room 700 Washington DC 20420*

MCFARLAND, SAMUEL P., JR., psychologist; b. Atlanta, Oct. 16, 1957; s. Samuel P. and Gladys Blake (Pepper) McF. BA in Psychology, Mercer U., 1983; MA in Gen. and Exptl. Psychology, Fla. Atlantic U., 1987; MS in Clin. Psychology, Nova U., 1993; PhD in Clin. Psychology, Nova Southeastern U., 1998. Store mgr. Reeds Drugs Inc., Atlanta, 1973—81; mental health technician C.P.C. Parkwood Hosp., Atlanta, 1982—84; mental health asst. C.P.C. Ft. Lauderdale Hosp., Fla., 1985, N.M.E. Fair Oaks Hosp., Delray Beach, 1985-87; peer acad. advisor Fla. Atlantic U., Boca Raton, 1986-87; clin. counselor/supr. Henderson Mental Health Ctr./New Vistas, Ft. Lauderdale, 1987-88; adj. faculty instr. Art Inst. Ft. Lauderdale, 1992-93; case mgr., psychologist Bradley Ctr. of St. Francis, Columbus, Ga., 1993—. Therapist Biofeedback Clinic/Nova Clinic, Davie, Fla., 1992, The Family Ctr./Nova U., 1991-92, Child & Adolescent Anxiety Disorders Clinic/Nova Clinic, Coral Springs, 1988-89. Co-sponsor Al-Ateen Group, Atlanta, 1975-76. Mem. APA (nat. treas. 1988-90, mem. divsns. 12 and 37 1994—), Am. Psychol. Assn. Gread. Students (nat. treas. 1988-90), Am. Psychol. Soc., Columbus Psychol. Assn. Office: Bradley Ctr St Francis 2000 16th Ave Columbus GA 31901 Office Phone: 706-320-3766. E-mail: wolf444@charter.net.

MCFARLAND, WALTER GERARD, management consultant; b. Chicago Heights, Ill., June 28, 1952; s. Walter Louden and Rosemary (Voelker) McF. BA in Psychology, So. Ill. U., 1976, MPA, 1978; MA in Nat. Security, Georgetown U., 1991; EdD in Human Resource Devel., George Washington U., 1999. Program analyst USAF, San Antonio, 1978-82; program monitor CIA, Washington, 1982-85; spl. asst. to sec. of def. Dept. of Def., Washington, 1985-88; mgmt. cons. Hay Mgmt. Consultants, Washington, 1988-97; prin. rsch. scientist Am. Insts. Rsch., Washington, 1997—. Guest lectr. CIA, 1985-88, Georgetown U., 1995, Johns-Hopkins U., Washington, 1996. Elder Great Falls (Va.) Bible Ch., 1988-90; mem. Wakefield H.S. PTA, Arlington, Va., 1992-96. Mem. ASPA (nat. chpt. head 1985-86, chpt. dir. 1987), Acad. Mgmt. Republican. Baptist. Home: 4050 40th St N Arlington VA 22207-4608

MCFARLANE, BETH LUCETTA TROESTER, former mayor; b. Osterdock, Iowa, Mar. 9, 1918; d. Francis Charles and Ella Carrie (Moser) Troester; m. George Evert McFarlane, June 20, 1943 (dec. May 1972); children: Douglas, Steven (dec.), Susan, George. BA in Edn., U. No. Iowa, 1962, MA in Edn., 1971. Cert. tchr. Tchr. rural and elem. schs., Iowa, 1936-50, 55-56; elem. tchr. Oelwein Cmty. Schs., Iowa, 1956-64, jr. high reading tchr., 1964—71, 1983; city council Oelwein, 1981-82; mayor of Oelwein, 1982-89. Evaluator North Cen. Accreditation Assn. for Ednl. Programs; mem. planning team for confs. for Iowa Cities, N.E. Iowa, 1985; v.p. N.E. Iowa Regional Coun. Econ. Devel., 1986-89; mem. Area Econ. Devel. Com. N.E. Iowa, 1985, Legis. Interim Study Com. on Rural Econ. Devel., 1987-88; mem. policy com. Iowa League Municipalities, 1987-88. V.p. Fayette County Tourism Coun., 1987-88; mem. Iowa State steering com. on road use tax financing, 1988-89; chmn. bd. govs. Oelwein Cmty. Ctr., 1990-94, bd. govs., 2001—; chmn. bldg. and fin. com. Reorganized LDS/Cmty. of Christ Ch. Bldg., 1980—, dist. ch. fin. com., 1992-2001, dist. ch. revolving loan com., 1982-00. Named Iowa Reading Tchr. of Yr., Internat. Reading Assn. Iowa, 1978; recipient Outstanding Contbn. to Reading Coun. Activities award Internat. Reading Assn. N.E. Iowa, 1978, State of Iowa's Gov.'s Leadership award, 1988. Mem.: Oelwien Area C. of C. (bd. dirs. 1986—89, Humanitarian award 1987), Oelwein Area Ret. Sch. Pers. (pres. 1994—96), Oelwein Bus. and Profl. Women (Woman of Yr. 1983), MacDowell Music and Arts Orgn. (pres. 1978—80), N.E. Iowa Reading Coun. (pres. 1975—77), Area Univ. Women (pres. 1999—2000), Delta Kappa Gamma (pres. 1980—82). Republican. Mem. Cmty. Of Christ Ch. Avocations: hiking, refinishing antiques, gardening, walking, creative sewing. Home: 512 7th Ave NE Oelwein IA 50662-1326

MCFARLANE, DONOVAN ANTHONY, writer, poet, researcher; b. Manchester, Jamaica, Apr. 19, 1978; came to U.S., 1997; s. Merceline Agatha Wright. Cert., deCarteret Coll., Jamaica, 1995, Church Tchrs. Coll., 1997; PhD in Parapsychic Sci., Am. Inst. Theology, 2003; diploma in fitness and nutrition, Harcourt Learning Direct, Scranton, Pa., 1999; diploma in mgmt. restaurant and hotel, Profl. Career Devel. Inst., Atlanta, 2000; diploma in bus. mgmt. with highest honor, Stratford Career Inst., Washington, 2000; diploma in small bus. mgmt., Lifetime Career Sch., Archbald, Pa., 2000; BS in Geog. Sci., Bernadean U., North Hollywood, Calif., 2000; PhD in Metaphysics, Am. Coll. Metaphys. Theology, Golden Valley, Minn., 2000, PhD in Comparative Religion, 2002; cert. in paralegal studies, Blackstone Sch., 2002; BS in Parapsychic Sci., Am. Inst. Holistic Theology, 2003, MS in Parapsychic Sci., 2002; MBA, Frederick Taylor U., 2002; MBA in Mgmt., Barrington U., 2003; BSBA, Nova Southeastern U., Fla., 2003; diploma in writing, Inst. Childrens Lit., 2003; B in Metaphs. Sci., U. Metaphysics, Calif., 2003; diploma, U. Metaphysics, 2003; cert. metaphysical practitioner, U. Metaphysics Sem., 2003. Cert. in secondary edn. Tchr. trainee in Spanish and social studies Comprehensive H.S., Jamaica, 1997; tutor gen. sci. Church Tchrs. Coll., Jamaica; curriculum planner pvt. orgn., Fla., essayist, cons., 1998—; clk. Phillips and Phillips, Fort Lauderdale, Fla., 1997—98; supr. inventory and warehouse Lord's Supermarket, Oakland, Fla., 1999; with Corp. Edu. Rsch., 2001—. Author: numerous poems. With USMC, 2000. Recipient cert. excellence in spanish, social studies, geography, math., history, cert. diligence in spanish, religious edn., cert. outstanding achievement in social studies, cert. outstanding achievement in spanish, Internat. Poet of Merit award, 2002, Outstanding Achievement in Poetry Silver award, 2003, Commemorative award, 2003; named hon. alumni Oglata Lakota Coll., S.Dak., 2000. Mem. Nat. Libr. Poetry (Disting. Membership cert. and plaque 1998), Internat. Soc. Poets (Editor's Choice award 1998), Internat. Libr. Poetry (laureate cert. 2002). Avocations: dance, oratory, martial arts, singing, writing.

MCFARLANE, STEPHEN C. dean, researcher; BS, MS, Portland State U.; PhD, U. Wash. Chmn. dept. speech pathology and audiology, vice dean U. Nev. Sch. Medicine, 2001, dean, 2002—. Rschr. in field. Author: The Voice and Voice Therapy, 2000; contbr. articles to profl. jours. Office: Manville Bldg Mailstop 357 Reno NV 89557

MCFARLANE, WALTER ALEXANDER, lawyer, educator; b. Richlands, Va., May 4, 1940; s. James Albert and Frances Mae (Padbury) McF.; m. Judith Louise Copenhaver, Aug. 31, 1962. BA, Emory and Henry Coll., 1962; JD, U. Richmond, 1966. Bar: Va. 1966, U.S. Supreme Ct. 1970, U.S. Ct. Appeals (4th cir.) 1973, U.S. Ct. Appeals (D.C. cir.) 1977, U.S. Dist. ct. (ea. dist.) Va. 1973. Asst. atty. gen. Office Va. Atty. Gen., Richmond, 1969-73, dep. atty. gen., 1973-90; exec. asst., chief counsel, dir. policy Gov.'s Office Commonwealth of Va., 1990-94, supt. Dept. Correctional Edn., 1994—. Acting dir. Dept. Juvenile Justice, 1997, State Bd. Dept. Criminal Justice Svcs., 1994-; prof. adj. staff U. Richmond, 1978-2003, A.L.Philpott disting. prof. T.C. Williams Sch. Law, 2003; chmn. transp. law com. Transp. Rsch. Bd., Nat. Rsch. Bd. Nat. Acads. Sci. and Engring., Washington, 1977-85, 88-94, chmn. legal affairs com., 1978-85, chmn. environ., archeol. and hist. com., 1985-90; mem. State Water Commn., 1994-96, mem., Coun. of State Govts. Henry Toll Fell., 1988, Legal Task Force, 1988-2002. Contbr. articles to profl. jours. Mem. exec. com., bd. govs. Emory and Henry Coll., 1985-98; pres. Windsor Forest Civic Assn., Midlothian, Va., 1975-76; bd. dirs. Greater Midlothian Civic League, 1980-86, v.p., 1980; instr. water safety ARC, 1962-87; chmn. bldg. com. Mt. Pisgah United Meth. Ch., 1980-85, pres. men's club, 1980-81; bd. dirs. cen. Va. chpt. Epilepsy Assn. Va., 1988-91. Capt. JAGC, USAF, 1966-69. Recipient J.D. Buscher Disting. Atty. award Am. Assn. State Hwy. and Transp. Ofcls., 1983, John C. Vance legal writing award Nat. Acads. Sci. and Engring., 4th ann. outstanding evening lectr. award Student Body, U. Richmond, 1980. Mem. Chesterfield Bar Assn., Richmond Bar Assn. (bd. dirs. 1989-93), Richmond Scottish Soc. (bd. dirs. 1980-82), Emory and Henry Coll. Alumni Assn. (chpt. pres. 1971-73, regional v.p. 1974-77, pres. 1981-83), Meadowbrook Country Club (bd. dir. 2001-). Home: 9001 Widgeon Way Chesterfield VA 23838-5274 Office: 101 N 14th St Richmond VA 23219-3684 Office Phone: 804-225-3314. E-mail: wamcfarlane@dce.state.va.us.

MCFARLIN, DIANE HOOTEN, publisher; b. Lake Wales, Fla., July 10, 1954; d. Ruffie Denton Hooten and Anna Loraine (Peeples) Huff; m. Henry Briggs McFarlin, Aug. 28, 1976 (div. 1993). BS, U. Fla., 1976. Reporter Sarasota (Fla.) Jour., 1976-77, asst. news editor, 1977-78, city editor, 1978-82; asst. mng. editor Sarasota (Fla.) Herald Tribune, 1983-84, mng. editor, 1985-87; exec. editor Gainesville (Fla.) Sun, 1987-90; from exec. editor to assoc. publ. Sarasota Herald-Tribune, 1990-99, publ., 1999—. Adv. bd. U. Fla. Coll. Journalism and Comm., 1987—; Pulitzer juror Columbia U., 1995-96, 2001-02. Mem. accrediting coun. Edn. in Journalism and Mass Comms., 1994-96. Recipient Alumna of Distinction award U. Fla., 1999. Mem. Am. Soc. Newspaper Editors (com. chair 1992, 94, 96, 2000, bd. dirs. 1994—, treas., sec., v.p. 2001, pres. 2002), Fla. Soc. Newspaper Editors (sec.-treas. 1993, v.p. 1994, pres. 1995). Office: Sarasota Herald-Tribune PO Box 1719 Sarasota FL 34230-1719 also: 801 S Tamiami Trail Sarasota FL 34236-7824

MCFARLIN, RICHARD FRANCIS, retired industrial chemist, researcher; b. Oklahoma City, Oct. 12, 1929; s. Loy Lester and Julie Mae (Collins) McF.; m. Clare Jane Burroughs, Apr. 4, 1953; children: Robin Sue McFarlin Godwin, Richard Prescott, Rebecca Lynn McFarlin Bray, Roger Whitsitt. BS, Va. Mil. Inst., 1951; MS, Purdue U., 1953, PhD, 1956. Rsch. chemist Monsanto Chem. Co., St. Louis, 1956-60; supr. inorganic rsch. Internat. Minerals and Chems., Mulberry, Fla., 1961; mgr. Agr. Rsch. Ctr. Armour Agrl. Chem. Co., Atlanta, 1962; v.p. rsch., ops., devel. & adminstrn. div. agri-chems. U.S. Steel, Atlanta, 1986; tech. dir. Lester Labs. Inc., Atlanta, 1986-88; exec. dir. Fla. Inst. Phosphate Rsch., Bartow, 1988-96; ret., 1996. Mem. bd. advisors engring. coun. U. South Fla., Lakeland, 1990—, U. Fla., Gainesville, 1991—; mem. bd. advisors Inst. Recyclable Materials La. State U., Baton Rouge, 1990—. Capt. USAR, 1951-61. M. M. Cohn Found. scholar, 1947, L. D. Wall scholar, 1949, O. M. Baldinger scholar, 1950. Presbyterian. Achievements include eight U.S. and foreign patents for selective organic reducing agents, fertilizer processes and selective biocides. Home: 3239 Bridgefield Dr Lakeland FL 33803-7903 E-mail: rmcf203@aol.com.

MCFARREN, FREDDY E. military career officer; b. Cleburne, Tex., Oct. 13, 1943; s. Aubrey McFarren; children: Preston, William. BS, U.S. Mil. Acad., 1966; MEd, Duke U.; grad., Armed Forces Staff Coll., U.S. Army War Coll. Commd. 2d lt. US Army, 1966, advanced through grades to maj. gen., various positions, comdr. 18th Field Artillary Brigade, XVIII Airborne Corps, bn. comdr. 1st Bn. 319th Airborne Field Artillery 82d Divsn., exec. officer 155mm bn. 8th Inf. Divsn. Europe, advisor to Vietnamese Rangers, field arty. battery comdr. XVIII Airborne Corps Arty., asst. chief staff ops. G3 XVIII Airborne Corps, asst. divsn. comdr. 24th Inf. Divsn. (Mechanized) Ft. Stewart, Ga., dir. tng. Office of the Dep. Chief Staff for Ops. and Plans Washington, chief Office Mil. Cooperation Cairo, commdg. gen. 24th Inf. Divsn. (Mechanized) Ft. Riley, Kans., 1998—2000, commdg. gen., 5th US Army Fort Sam, Tex., 2000—; tactical officer US Mil. Acad., comdt. of cadets. Decorated Silver Star, Def. Superior Svc. medal, Legion of Merit with four oak leaf clusters, Bronze Star with V device and three oak leaf clusters, Purple Heart, Meritorious Svc. medal with two oak leaf clusters, Air medal, Army Commendation medal with oak leaf cluster, French Croix de Guerre with Gold Star, The Republic of Vietnam Cross of Gallantry with two Palms and the Honor medal first class. Office: Fort Sam-US Army Fort Sam Houston TX 78234*

MCFATE, KENNETH LEVERNE, trade association administrator; b. LeClaire, Iowa, Feb. 5, 1924; s. Samuel Albert and Margaret (Spear) McF.; m. Imogene Grace Kness, Jan. 27, 1951; children: Daniel Elliott, Kathryn Margaret, Sharon Ann. BS in Agrl. Engring., Iowa State U., 1950; MS in Agrl. Engring., U. Mo., 1959. Registered profl. engr., Mo. Agrl. sales engr. Ill. No. Utility Co., Aledo, 1950-51; extension agrl. engr. Iowa State U., Ames, 1951-53, rsch. agrl. engr., 1953-56; prof. agrl. engr. U. Mo., Columbia, 1956-86, prof. emeritus, 1986; dir. Mo. Farm Electric Coun., Columbia, 1956-75; exec. mgr. Nat. Farm Electric Coun., Columbia, 1975-86; pres. Nat. Food and Energy Coun., Columbia, 1986-91, pres. emeritus, 1991; mgr. Electrotechnology Rsch., 1991-93. Bd. dirs. Internat. Congress Agrl. Engrs., Brussels, 1989—94. Editor, author: (with others) Handbook for Elsevier Science, Electrical Energy in World Agriculture, 1989; mem. editl. bd. Energy in Agriculture for Elsevier Sci., Amsterdam, The Netherlands, 1981-88. Served with USAAF, 1943—45, 2d lt. USAAF, 1945. Recipient Outstanding Svc. awards Nat. Safety Coun., 1975, MOFEC, 1976, Nat. 4-H Coun., 1982, Nat. Hon. Extension Frat., 1984, Hon. Am. Future Farmers Assn. degree, 1991. Fellow Am. Soc. Agrl. Engrs. (George Kable elec. award 1974, Spl. Svc. award, 2000); mem. Alpha Epsilon, Gamma Sigma Delta. Republican. Presbyterian. Avocations: technical writing, gardening, woodworking.

MCFATE, PATRICIA ANN, foundation executive, science educator; b. Detroit, Mar. 19, 1936; d. John Earle and Mary Louise (Bliss) McF.; m. Sidney Norman Graybeal, Sept. 10, 1988. BA (Alumni scholar), Mich. State U., 1954; MA, Northwestern U., 1956, PhD, 1965; MA (hon.), U. Pa., 1977. Assoc. prof. English, asst. dean liberal arts and scis. U. Ill., Chgo., 1967-74, assoc. prof. English, assoc. vice chancellor acad. affairs, 1974-75; assoc. prof. folklore Faculty Arts and Scis., U. Pa., Phila., 1975-81; prof. tech. and soc. Coll. Engring. and Applied Sci., 1975-81, vice provost, 1975-78; dep. chmn. Nat. Endowment for Humanities, Washington, 1978-81; exec. v.p. Am.-Scandinavian Found., N.Y.C., 1981-82, pres., 1982-88; sr. scientist Sci. Applications Internat. Corp., Mc Lean, Va., 1988—, program dir. Ctr. for Nat. Security Negotiations, 1988—; cons. UN, 1994-95. Vis. assoc. prof. dept. medicine Rush U., Chgo., 1970-85; bd. dirs. First Union Corp.; mem. sr. adv. panel Dept. Def., 1998—. Author: The Writings of James Stephens, 1979, Uncollected Prose of James Stephens, 1983; exec. producer Northern Stars, 1985, Diego Rivera: I Paint What I See, 1989, The Bear in the Skies, 1998; contbr. articles in fields of sci. policy and lit. to various jours. Mem. Arms Control and Non-Proliferation Adv. Bd., Dept. of State, 1995-2001; mem. disting. adv. panel Sandia Nat. Labs.; bd. dirs. Raoul Wallenberg Com. of U.S., Swedish Coun. Am., Santa Fe Cmty. Found., Santa Fe Opera, Lensic Performing Arts Ctr. Decorated officer Order of Leopold II Belgium, comdr. Order Icelandic Falcon, comdr. Royal Order of Polar Star (Sweden), comdr. Order of Lion (Finland), comdr. Royal Norwegian Order Merit, Knight 1st class Royal Order Dannebrog (Denmark); U. Ill. Grad. Coll. faculty fellow, 1968; Swedish Bicentennial Fund grantee, 1981 Fellow N.Y. Acad. Scis.; mem. AAAS (chmn. com. on sci., engring. and pub. policy 1984-87, com. on sci. and internat. security 1976-79, 88-93), Coun. on Fgn. Rels., Acad. Scis. Phila. (founding mem., corr. sec. 1977-79), Theta Alpha Phi, Omega Beta Pi, Delta Delta Delta. E-mail: patricia.a.mcfate@saic.com.

MCFAYDEN, SHANNON, bank holding company executive; b. Sept. 21, 1960; BA in psychology, Davidson Coll. Head human resources Fla. Bank (merged with Wachovia); with Wachovia Corp., 1982—, dir. human resources client svc., 1998—2001, dir. cmty. affairs, 2001—04, sr. v.p., 2004—, head corp. and cmty. affairs, 2004—. Co-chair Nat. Bus. Strengthening Am. Initiative. Mem.: Davidson Coll. Alumni Assn. Office: Wachovia Corp 1 Wachovia Ctr Charlotte NC 28288

MCFEATTERS, ANN CAREY, journalist; b. Colorado Springs, Colo., June 27, 1944; d. Norman Cromer and Mildred Harriet Carey; m. Dale B. McFeatters, Sept. 27, 1969; children: Dale C., Matthew C., Kirsten C. BA, Marquette U., 1966. Reporter Evansville (Ind.) Press, 1966-68, Pitts. Press, 1969, Washington Daily News, 1969-70, Scripps Howard News Svc., Washington, 1970-99; Washington bur. chief The Pitts. Post-Gazette and The Toledo Blade, Washington, 1999—. Named to Hall of Fame Soc. Profl. Journalists, 1998; recipient Disting. Svc. award Scripps Howard News Svc., 1999. Mem. Nat. Press Found. (chmn. 1996-98), Washington Press Club (pres. 1980-81), The Gridiron Club. Office: Block News Alliance 529 14th St NW Ste 955 Washington DC 20045 E-mail: amcfeatters@nationalpress.com.

MCFEE, ARTHUR STORER, physician; b. Portland, Maine, May 1, 1932; s. Arthur Stewart and Helen Knight (Dresser) McF.; m. Iris Goeschel, May 13, 1967. BA cum laude, Harvard U., 1953, MD, 1957; MS, U. Minn., 1966, PhD, 1967. Diplomate: Am. Bd. Surgery. Intern U. Minn. Hosp., 1957-58, resident in surgery, 1958-65; asst. prof. surgery U. Tex. Med. Sch., San Antonio, 1967-70, asso. prof., 1970-74, prof., 1974-2001, ret., 2001, prof. emeritus, 2001—. With Univ. Health Sys., Bexar-County, 1968-2003; spl. cons. on emergency med. care text to AAOS. Contbr. articles to profl. jours. Served with USNR, 1965-67. Fellow ACS; mem. AMA, Am. Assn. History of Medicine, Assn. Acad. Surgery, Tex. Med. Assn., Bexar County Med. Soc., Tex. Surg. Soc., Western Surg. Assn., San Antonio Surg. Soc., Soc. Surgery Alimentary Tract, So. Med. Assn., N.Y. Acad. Scis., Royal Soc. Medicine, So. Surg. Assn., Internat. Surg. Soc., Halsted Soc., J. Bradley Aust Surg. Soc., Am. Surg. Assn. Home: 131 Brittany Dr San Antonio TX 78212-1721 Office: MC 7842 7703 Floyd Curl Dr San Antonio TX 78229-3900 Office Phone: 210-567-2164. Business E-mail: mcfee@uthscsa.edu. *Most of my life has been spent in training surgeons. It has been an informative experience.*

MCFEE, RICHARD, electrical engineer, physicist; b. Pitts., Jan. 24, 1925; s. William and Beatrice (Allender) McF.; m. Anne Stauffer, June 26, 1947 (div. 1960); m. 2d., Joanellen Lewis, Dec. 31, 1974. BEE, Yale U., 1947; MS in Physics, Syracuse U., 1949; PhDEE, U. Mich., 1955. Rsch. asst. Syracuse U. Med. Sch., 1947-48; instr. Syracuse U. elec. engring. dept., 1948-49; rsch. assoc. U. Mich. Med. Sch., 1949-51; engr. Electro-Mech. Rsch. Inc., Ridgefield, Conn., 1951-52; mem. tech. staff Bell Tel. Labs., Whippany, NJ, 1952-57; prof. elec. engring. Syracuse U., 1957-82; ind. rschr. Union Springs, NY, 1982—86, Hawi, Hawaii, 1986—. Contbr. articles on electronics, electrocardiography, magnetocardiography, superconductivity, circuit theory, thermodynamics, elec. measurements; patentee in field. Sgt. U.S. Army, 1943-46. Sci. Faculty fellowship NSF, Stanford U., 1970. Fellow IEEE; mem. AAAS, Sigma Xi. Home and Office: PO Box 989 Kapaau HI 96755-0989 Office Phone: 808-889-5778. E-mail: rjmcfee@earthlink.net.

MC FEE, THOMAS STUART, retired government agency administrator; b. Delafield, Wis., Nov. 19, 1930; s. Leon Worrick and Margurette Ella (Morris) McFee; m. Mary Virginia Butler, June 7, 1952; children: Richard Stuart, John Worrick, Charles Paxton. BS, U. Md., 1953, postgrad., 1956-60. Mathematician math. computation divsn. David Taylor Model Basin, Navy Dept., Washington, 1956-58, dir. sys. analysis br. ops. rsch. divsn., 1958-62; project leader weapons sys. evaluation group U.S. Dept. Def., 1962-65; tech. asst. to dir. Sci. and Tech. Office, Exec. Office of Pres., White House, 1965-66; dir. sys. devel. HEW, 1967-69, dep. asst. sec. for program sys., planning and evaluation, 1969-71, dep. asst. sec. for mgmt. planning and tech., 1971-77, dep. asst. sec. for mgmt., 1977-78; asst. sec. for pers. adminstrn. HHS, 1978-95. With USAF, 1954-56. Mem. Am. Soc. Pub. Adminstrn., Am. Consortium for Internat. Pub. Adminstrn., Nat. Acad. Pub. Adminstrn. (elected). E-mail: TomMcfee@aol.com.

MCFEE, WILLIAM WARREN, soil scientist; b. Concord, Tenn., Jan. 8, 1935; s. Fred Thomas and Ellen Belle (Russell) McF.; m. Barbara Anella Steelman, June 23, 1957; children— Sabra Anne, Patricia Lynn, Thomas Hallie. BS, U. Tenn., 1957; MS, Cornell U., 1963, PhD, 1966. Mem. faculty Purdue U., 1965—, prof. soil sci., 1973—, dir. natural resources and environ. sci. program, 1975-91, head dept. agronomy, 1991-2001. Vis. prof. U. Fla., 1986-87; cons. U.S. Forest Svc., Desert Rsch. Inst. Author articles in field, chpts. in books. Served with USAR, 1958-61. Alpha Zeta scholar, 1957; named Outstanding Agr. Tchr. Purdue U., 1972; recipient Am. Educator award Soil Sci. Soc., 1987. Fellow: Soil Sci. Soc. Am. (pres. 1991—92), Am. Soc. Agronomy (pres. 1996—97, resident edn. award 1989); mem.: Purdue Agrl. Alumni Assn. (cert. of distinction 2002), Ind. Seed Trade Assn. (hon.), Sigma Xi. Presbyterian. Home: 708 Mccormick Rd West Lafayette IN 47906-4915 Office: Purdue U Dept Agronomy West Lafayette IN 47907 E-mail: wmcfee@purdue.edu.

MC FEELEY, JOHN JAY, chemical engineer; b. Bklyn., Aug. 15, 1945; s. John Joseph and Maude May (Irvine) McF.; m. Jacquelyn Anne Ratzin, Oct. 30, 1971; children: Christine, John Jay. BS, Poly. Inst. Bklyn., 1966, MS, 1967, PhD, 1972. Engr. Polaroid Corp., Cambridge, Mass., 1971-72, sr. engr., 1972-74, sr. scientist, 1974-77, prin. engr. R&D, 1977-79, tech. mgr. chem. engring. devel., 1979-83, sr. mgr. chem. engring., 1983-99; tech. mgr. Arkwright, Inc., Fiskeville, RI, 1999—2003. Contbr. articles to profl. jours. Mem. water supply study com. Town of Norfolk, Mass., 1976-77, mem. adv. bd., 1979-81, mem. bicentennial com., 1975-76, chmn. adv. bd., 1980-81, selectman, 1981-84, 99—, chmn., 1983-84, 2001-03; registrar of voters, 1991-97, chmn., 1993-97; mem. Dem. Town Com., 1981—, vice-chmn., 1988—; mem. Norfolk Cmty. TV, 1989-98, pres., 1992-94, 95-98; mem. Norfolk Cable Adv. Com., 1998-99. NDEA fellow, 1969-71; NSF fellow, 1968-69, tchg. fellow, 1967-68, rsch. fellow, 1966-67. Mem. AAAS, Am. Chem. Soc., Am. Inst. Chem. Engrs., N.Y. Acad. Scis., Lions (pres. 1977-78, 89-90), Tau Beta Pi, Sigma Xi, Omega Chi Epsilon, Phi Lambda Upsilon. Democrat. Roman Catholic. Home: 10 Chicatabut Ave Norfolk MA 02056-1164 Office: 538 Main St Fiskeville RI 02823

MCFEELY, WILLIAM DRAKE, publishing company executive; b. Port Chester, N.Y., July 15, 1954; s. William Shield and Mary (Drake) McF.; m. Karen Gail Eliason, Aug. 12, 1978; children: Matthew Bensen, Eric Daniel, Laura Mae. BA cum laude, Amherst Coll., 1976. Coll. traveler W.W. Norton & Co., Inc., N.Y.C., 1976-80, asst. sales mgr., 1980-82, editor, 1982—, v.p., 1990-94, bd. dirs., 1990—, pres., 1994—, chmn., 2000—. Dir. W.W. Norton & Co., Ltd.; trustee Princeton Univ. Press, chmn., 2004—. Mem. Pubs. Lunch Club (pres. 1998-99), Seven Bridges Field Club (pres. 1989). Home: 106 Seven Bridges Rd Chappaqua NY 10514-1121 Office: WW Norton & Co 500 5th Ave Fl 6 New York NY 10110-0054

MC FEELY, WILLIAM SHIELD, historian, writer; b. N.Y.C., Sept. 25, 1930; s. William C. and Marguerite (Shield) Mc F.; m. Mary Drake, Sept. 13, 1952; children: William Drake, Eliza, Jennifer. BA, Amherst Coll., 1952, L.H.D., 1982; MA, Yale U., 1962, PhD, 1966; LD, Washington Coll., 1986. Asst. prof. history and Am. studies Yale U., 1966-69, assoc. prof., 1969-70; dean faculty Mount Holyoke Coll., 1970-73, prof. history, 1970-80, Rodman prof. history, 1980-82, Andrew W. Mellon prof. humanities, 1982-86; Richard B. Russell prof. Am. history U. Ga., Athens, 1986-94, Abraham Baldwin prof. humanities, 1994-97, prof. emeritus, 1997—; Cardozo vis. prof. history Yale U., 2001—. Tchr. Yale-Harvard-Columbia intensive summer studies program, 1967-69; vis. prof. history Univ. Coll. London, 1978-79, Amherst Coll., 1980-81, U. Mass., 1984-85, John J. McCloy prof., 1988-89; cons. to com. on judiciary U.S. Ho. of Reps., 1974 Author: Yankee Stepfather: Gen. O.O. Howard and the Freedmen, 1968, Grant: A Biography, 1981, Frederick Douglass, 1991, Sapelo's People, 1994, Proximity to Death, 1999, Ulysses S. Grant: An Album, 2004. Recipient Pulitzer Prize in biography, 1982, Francis Parkman prize, 1982, Lincoln prize, 1992, Avery O. Craven award, 1992; Morse fellow, 1968-69, fellow Am. Coun. Learned Socs., 1974-75, Huntington Library, 1976, 83, Guggenheim fellow, 1982-83, assoc. fellow Charles Warren Ctr., 1991-91, fellow Libr. Co. of Phila., 2002-03, vis. scholar W.E.B. Du Bois Inst., Harvard U., 1992—; NEH grantee, 1986-87 Mem. Am. Hist. Assn., So. Hist. Assn., Soc. of Am. Historians, Orgn. Am. Historians, PEN Ctr., Century Assn., Authors Guild. Home: 35 Mill Hill Rd Wellfleet MA 02667-7441

MC FERON, DEAN EARL, mechanical engineer, educator; b. Portland, Oreg., Dec. 24, 1923; s. Wallace Suitor and Ruth Carolyn (Fessler) McF.; m. Phyllis Grace Ehlers, Nov. 10, 1945; children: David Alan, Phyllis Ann, Douglas Dean, Donald Brooks. Student, Oreg. State Coll., 1942-43; BSME with spl. honors, U. Colo., 1945, MSME, 1948; PhD, U. Ill., 1956. Instr. U. Colo., Boulder, 1946-48; assoc. prof. U. Ill., 1948-58; rsch. assoc. Argonne (Ill.) Nat. Lab., 1957-58; prof. mech. engring., assoc. dean U. Wash., Seattle, 1958-82, prof. emeritus, 1983—. Cons. to industry, 1959-80 Served with USNR, 1942-46, to comdr. Res., 1946-72. Co-recipient Outstanding Tech. Applications Paper award ASHRAE, 1974; Ednl. Achievement award Soc. Mfg. Engrs., 1970; NSF faculty fellow, 1967-68 Mem. ASME, Am. Soc. Engring. Edn., U.S. Naval Inst. (life), Sigma Xi (nat. dir. 1972-80, nat. pres. 1978), Tau Beta Pi, Sigma Tau, Pi Tau Sigma. Home: 4008 NE 40th St Seattle WA 98105-5422 Office: U Wash Dept Mech Engring Seattle WA 98195-0001
What matters most in life is what you can do for others.

MCFERREN, CARL DAVIS, II, retired military officer, risk management consultant; b. Columbus, Ga., July 3, 1946; s. Carl Davis and Mary Homer McFerren; children: Carl Davis III, Mary Anne, Colleen. BA in Polit. Sci., The Citadel, 1968; MS in Counselling, L.I. U., 1978; MBA, Auburn U., 1981; grad., USAF Command and Staff Coll., 1981, Nat. War Coll., 1991. Comml. pilot's license FAA. Commd. 2d lt. U.S. Army, 1968, advanced through grades to col., 1990, brigade exec. officer Aviation Brigade, 1986-88, bn. commdr. 9th U.S. Inf. Ft. Wainwright, Alaska, 1988-90, chief environ. inspections U.S. Army Inspector Gen., Washington, 1991-93; ret., 1993; program mgr. Sys. Rsch. Applications, Arlington, Va., 1993-94; ITAM program mgr. U.S. Army Environ. Ctr., Aberdeen Proving Ground, Md., 1994-98, program mgr. green ammo, 1998-2000; program mgr. Innovative Emergency Mgmt., Salt Lake City, 2000—. Editor: The U.S. Army, 1981; contbr. articles to profl. jours. Commr. Boy Scouts Am., Ft. Riley, 1984. Decorated Silver Star medal Dept. of the Army, 1970, Legion of Merit award Dept. of the Army, 1993; recipient Hammer award Partnership for Reinventing Govt., 2000. Mem. Assn. Citadel Men, Assn. U.S. Army, Nat. War Coll. Alumni Assn., Am. Legion. Republican. Avocations: running, skiing. Home: 2192 E Country View Ln Salt Lake City UT 84121 Office: Innovative Emergency Mgmt Ste 2D 515 South 700 East Salt Lake City UT 84102 E-mail: dave.mcferren@iеminc.com.

MCFILLEN, JAMES MILTON, finance educator, consultant; b. Middletown, Ohio, Oct. 25, 1948; s. Clement Milton and Dorothy Mae McFillen; m. Karen Louise Cox, Nov. 4, 1948; children: Brian James, Kevin Douglas. BSBA, Miami U., 1970, MBA, 1973, Ind. U., 1975, DBA, 1976. Asst. prof. Ariz. State U., Tempe, Ariz., 1976—78, The Ohio State U., Columbus, Ohio, 1978—83; assoc. prof. Bowling Green (Ohio) State U., 1983—89, prof., 1989—2004, assoc. dean, 1998—. With U.S. Army, 1970—72. Mem.: Acad. of Mgmt. Independent. Office: Graduate Studies in Business Bowling Green State University Bowling Green OH 43403

MCGAFFEY, JERE D. retired lawyer; b. Lincoln, Nebr., Oct. 6, 1935; s. Don Larsen and Doris McG.; m. Ruth S. Michelsen, Aug. 19, 1956; children: Beth, Karen. BA, BSc with high distinction, U. Nebr., 1957; LLB magna cum laude, Harvard U., 1961. Bar: Wis. 1961. Mem. firm Foley & Lardner LLP, Milw., 1961—2004, ptnr., 1968—2004. Dir. Smith Investment Co., Northwestern Mut. Trust Co., Lord Balt. Corp., Wis. Gas Co., 1978-2000. Author works in field. Chmn. bd. dirs. Helen Bader Found.; former vice chmn. legis. Milw. Met. Assn. Commerce, 1984—2003; former chmn. Wis. Taxpayers Alliance, sec.-treas., 1994—; former chmn. bd. dirs. Aurora Health Care, 1986—2003; chmn. bd. advisors U. Wis. Nursing Sch., Milw. Mem. ABA (chmn. tax sect. 1990-91, ho. dels. 1995-2000), AICPA, Wis. Bar Assn., Wis. Inst. CPAs, Am. Coll. Tax Counsel (chmn. 1996-98), Am. Coll. Trust and Estate Counsel (chmn. bus. planning com. 1994-97, regent 2000—), Am. Law Inst., Univ. Club (Milw.), Milw. Country Club, Harvard Club N.Y.C., Univ. Club Washington, Phi Beta Kappa, Beta Gamma Sigma, Delta Sigma Rho. Home: 12852 NW Shoreland Dr Mequon WI 53097-2304 Office: Foley & Lardner 777 E Wisconsin Ave Ste 3600 Milwaukee WI 53202-5302 Office Phone: 414-297-5729. E-mail: jmcgaffey@foleylaw.com.

MCGAGH, WILLIAM GILBERT, financial consultant; b. Boston, May 29, 1929; s. Thomas A. and Mary M. (McDonough) McG.; m. Sarah Ann McQuigg, Sept. 23, 1961; children: Margaret Ellen, Sarah Elizabeth. BSBA, Boston Coll., 1950; MBA, Harvard U., 1952; MS, MIT, 1965. Fin. analyst Ford Motor Co., Dearborn, Mich., 1953-55; mem. staff treas. office Daimler-Chrysler, Detroit, 1955-64, compt., treas. Canadian divsn. Windsor, 1965-67, staff exec.-fin. Latin Am. ops. Detroit, 1967-68, asst. treas., 1968-75, treas., 1975-76, v.p., treas., 1976-80; sr. v.p. fin., dir. Northrop Grumman Corp., L.A., 1980-88; owner McGagh Assocs., Beverly Hills, Calif., 1988—. Chmn. bd. dirs. Pacific Am. Income Shares, Inc., We. Asset Premier Bond Fund, We. Asset Funds, Inc.; bd. adv. mem. Santa Monica-UCLA Med. Ctr. Mem. bd. regents Mt. St. Mary's Coll.; chmn. bd. dirs. L.A. Orthop. Hosp., John Tracy Clinic. Sloan fellow MIT, 1965. Mem. Fin. Execs. Inst. (pres. Detroit chpt. 1979-80), Harvard Club (N.Y.C. and Boston), Beach Club (Santa Monica, Calif.), L.A. Country Club, Calif. Club (L.A.), Eastward Ho Country Club (Chatham, Mass.). Home: 2189 Century Hl Los Angeles CA 90067-3516 Office: McGagh Assocs 9601 Wilshire Blvd Ste 560 Beverly Hills CA 90210-5208 Office Phone: 310-248-4395.

MCGAHAN, MARTIN J. health products executive; BA, Villanova U.; MBA, U. Va. Asst. treas. Chase Manhattan Bank; reg. v.p. HealthSouth Corp.; exec. dir. Alabama Sports Med. Inst.; CFO, sr. v.p. Saks Direct; with HealthMarket, Inc.; CFO HealthTronics Surgical Svcs. Office: 1841 W Oak Pkwy Ste A Marietta GA 30062

MCGAHREN, EUGENE DEWEY, JR., lawyer; b. Oct. 4, 1926; s. Eugene D. and Cecelia (Paulson) McGahren; m. Elizabeth M. Connellan, Oct. 19, 1957; children: Eugene, Thomas, Kevin, Brian, Paul, Peter. AB, Columbia U., 1949; JD, Columbia U., 1952; LLM, NYU, 1960. Bar: N.Y. 1955. Assoc. Willkie Farr & Gallagher, N.Y.C., NY, 1954—56, McGovern, Vincent & Connelly, N.Y.C., 1956—60; asst. divsn. counsel Sperry Corp., N.Y.C., 1960—69, divsn. counsel, 1969—72, asst. gen counsel, 1972—80, staff v.p., assoc. gen. counsel, 1980—87; pvt. practice N.Y.C., 1988—. Arbitrator Am. Arbitration Assn., 1988—, N.Y. Stock Exchange, 1988—, NASD, 1988—; adminstrv. law judge, N.Y.C., 1993—2003. V.p. Lincoln Park Taxpayers Assn., Yonkers, NY, 1974—78.

MCGANN, JEROME JOHN, English language educator; b. N.Y.C., July 22, 1937; s. John Joseph and Marie Violet (Lecouffe) McG.; m. Anne Patricia Lanni, July 26, 1938; children: Geoffrey, Christopher, Jennifer. BS, Le Moyne Coll., 1959; MA, Syracuse U., 1962; PhD, Yale U., 1966; LHD (hon.), U. Chgo., 1996. From asst. prof. to prof. U. Chgo., 1966-75; prof. Johns Hopkins U., Balt., 1975-80; Dreyfuss prof. humanities Calif. Inst. Tech., Pasadena, 1980-86; John Stewart Bryan univ. prof. U. Va., Charlottesville, 1987—. Author: Swinburne: An Experiment in Criticism, 1972 (Melville Cane award 1972), The Romantic Ideology, 1983, The Beauty of Inflections, 1985, Social Values and Poetic Acts, 1987, Towards a Literature of Knowledge, 1989, The Textual Condition, 1991, Black Riders: The Visible Language of Modernism, 1993; editor: The New Oxford Book of Romantic Period Verse, 1993, Poetics of Sensibility: A Revolution in Literary Style, 1996, Byron: Complete Poetical Works, 7 vols., 1980-93, Dante Gabriel Rossetti and the Game That Must Be Lost, 2000, The Complete Writings and Pictures of Dante Gabriel Rosetti: A Hypermedia Research Archive, 2000—, Radiant Textuality, Literature after the World Wide Web, 2001, Byron and Romanticism, 2002, D.G. Rosetti. Collected Poetry and Prose, 2003, Swinburne, Selected Poetry and Prose, 2004; author, editor 24 scholarly books and 4 poetry books. Recipient Mellon Achievement award, 2003, Richard Lyman award, 2002; Fulbright fellow, Fels Found. fellow, Eng., 1965-66; Guggenheim fellow, Eng., 1970-71, 74-75; NEH fellow, Eng. and Europe, 1975-76, 87-88, 2003—. Fellow Am. Acad. Arts and Scis.; mem. MLA. Address: English Department Bryan Hall U VA Charlottesville VA 22903

MCGANN, LISA B. NAPOLI, language educator; b. West Hartford, Conn., Sept. 07; d. James Napoli; m. Edward Harrison McGann, Jr. BA, Vassar Coll., 1980; MA, Columbia U., 1983, postgrad., 1991-95; MA, Middlebury Coll., 1987. Cert. tchr. French, ESL and Italian, Conn. Cmty. English program coord. Tchrs. Coll. Columbia U., N.Y.C., 1982-83; mgr. English tchg. com. Jr. League N.Y., N.Y.C., 1983-84; asst. dir. ESL Fordham U., N.Y.C., 1988-89; ESL instr. Laguardia C.C., CUNY, Long Island City, NY, 1983—, Columbia U., 1983-96. ESL instr. Yale U., 1988, 89; ESL specialist, tchr. UN, N.Y.C., 1990. Big sister Highland Hts., New Haven, 1976-77; ESL tchr. Boys and Girls Club, Astoria, N.Y., 1992. Recipient awards and scholarships. Mem. Nat. TESOL Soc., Am. Assn. Tchrs. Italian, Italian-Am. Hist. Soc., Nat. Italian Am. Found. (coun.), The Statue of Liberty-Ellis Island Found., Inc. Roman Catholic. Avocations: ballet, reading, travel, real estate, tennis.

MCGANNEY, THOMAS, lawyer; b. San Mateo, Calif., Mar. 12, 1938; s. Daniel James and Mary Irene (West) McGanney; m. Mildred Kalik McGanney; children: Jennifer, Abigail, Melanie, Juliana. BA, Stanford U., 1959; LLB, Harvard U., 1962. Bar: N.Y. 1963, U.S. Dist. Ct. (so. and ea. dists.) N.Y. 1965, U.S. Ct. Appeals (2d cir.) 1966, U.S. Ct. Appeals (3d cir.) 1969, U.S. Ct. Appeals (10th cir.) 1970, U.S. Supreme Ct. 1971, U.S. Ct. Appeals (9th cir.) 1990. Law clk. U.S. Dist. Ct., So. Dist. N.Y., 1962—64; assoc. White & Case, N.Y.C., 1964—72, ptnr., 1973—. Adj. prof. NYU Law Sch., 1984—86. Mem.: ABA, Assn. Bar City of N.Y., Fed. Bar Coun., N.Y. State Bar Assn., Am. Coll. Trial Lawyers. Office: White & Case Bldg Ll 1155 Avenue Of The Americas New York NY 10036-2787 E-mail: tmcganney@whitecase.com.

MCGARITY, MARGARET DEE, federal judge; b. 1948; BA, Emory U., 1969; JD, U. Wis., 1974. Bar: Wis. 1974. Pvt. practice, 1974-87; bankruptcy judge U.S. Dist. Ct. (ea. dist.) Wis., 1987—. Lectr. on marital property, bankruptcy and family law Fed. Judicial Ctr., Nat. Conf. Bankruptcy Judges, State Bar Wis., Nat. Child Support Enforcement Assn., others. Co-author: Marital Property Law in Wisconsin, 2d edit. 1986, Collier Family Law and the Bankruptcy Code, 1991. Mem. Nat. Conf. Bankruptcy Judges, State Bar Wis., Nat. Assn. Women Judges, Milw. Bar Assn., Assn. Women Lawyers, Thomas E. Fairild Inn, Am. Bankruptcy Inst. Office: 162 US Courthouse 517 E Wisconsin Ave Milwaukee WI 53202-4500

MCGARR, ARTHUR FRANCIS, geophysicist; b. San Francisco, Calif., May 24, 1940; s. Arthur Francis and Elizabeth (Radius) McGarr; m. Annette Bilger McGarr, Feb. 9, 1971; children: Philip, Timothy. BS, Calif. Inst. Tech., 1962, MS, 1963; PhD, Columbia U., 1968. Sr. rsch. fellow U. Witwatersrand, Johannesburg, 1968—70, sr. rsch. officer, 1970—77; geophysicist U.S. Geol. Survey, Menlo Pk., Calif., 1977—. Assoc. editor: Jour. Geophys. Rsch., 1983—85, author, editor: Induced Seismicity, 1993. Scoutmaster Boy Scouts Am. Troop 52, Palo Alto, Calif., 1987—93. Mem.: AAAS, Seismological Soc. Am. (assoc. editor bulletin 1994—), Am. Geophys. Union. Avocations: rock climbing, tennis, windsurfing. Office: US Geological Survey MS 977 345 Middlefield Rd Menlo Park CA 94025

MCGARR, FRANK JAMES, retired federal judge, dispute resolution consultant; b. Feb. 25, 1921; married; 6 children. BA cum laude, Loyola U., Chgo., 1942, JD, 1950, hon. degree, 2002. Bar: Ill. 1950. Assoc. Dallstream Schiff Stern & Hardin, Chgo., 1952—54; asst. U.S. atty., chief criminal divsn. No. dist. of Ill., 1954—55, first asst. U.S. atty., 1955—58; ptnr. McKay Solum & McGarr, Chgo., 1958—68; first asst. atty. gen. State of Ill., 1969—70; judge U.S. Dist. Ct. for No. Ill., 1970—88, chief judge, 1981—86, sr. judge, 1986—88; of counsel Phelan Cahill & Quinlan, Chgo., 1988—96, Foley & Lardner, Chgo., 1996—2001; pvt. practice, 2001—. Instr. Eng. and pub. speaking Loyola U., 1946—48, administrv. asst. to pres., 1948—52; instr. law Loyola U. Law Sch., 1950—52, instr. criminal law, 1953—57, prof. admiralty and maritime law, 1953—57; instr. legal ethics John Marshal Law Sch., 1985—86. Chmn. law observance com. Chgo. Crime Comm., v.p., bd. dirs.; chmn. Law Enforcement Week Com.; pres. Constl. Rights Found., 1994; chmn. Ill Gov.'s Comm. on Death Penalty, 2000. With USN, 1942—45, Pacific Fleet. Named Man of Yr., Cath. Lawyers Guild Chgo., 1985; recipient Alumni Medal of Excellence, Loyola Law Alumni, 1964, Mother Cabrini award, Columbus-Cuneo-Cabrini Med. Ctr., 1978, Dei Gloriam award, St. Ignatius Coll. Prep, 1984. Fellow: Am. Coll. Trial Lawyers; mem.: Soc. Trial Lawyers, Chgo. Bar Assn., Fed. Bar Assn. (pres. chgo. chpt. 1962—63, mem. exec. com.), 7th Cir. Bar Assn. Office: 4146 Venard Rd Downers Grove IL 60515-1908 Office Phone: 630-960-4655.

MCGARRELL, JAMES, artist, educator; b. Indianapolis, Feb. 22, 1930; s. James and Gretchen (Heermann) McG.; m. Anna (Harris), June 24, 1955; children: Andrew Rider, Flora Raven. BA, Ind. U., 1953; MA, U. Calif. at Los Angles, 1955. Artist in residence Reed Coll., Portland, Oreg., 1956—59; prof. fine arts, dir. grad. painting Ind. U., Bloomington, Ind., 1959—80; prof. fine arts Washington U., St. Louis, 1981—93, prof. emeritus, 1993—; artist in residence Dartmouth Coll., 1993, Roswell, N. Mex. Found., 1999. Exhibitions include Frumkin, Adams Gallery, N.Y.C., 1961, 1964, 1966, Gallery Claude Bernard, Paris, 1967, Gallery Il Fante de Spade, Rome and Milan, 1967, Frumkin, Adams Gallery, N.Y.C., 1968, Gallery Claude Bernard, Paris, 1970, Gallery Il Fante de Spade, Rome and Milan, 1971, Frumkin, Adams Gallery, N.Y.C., 1971, Gallery Il Fante de Spade, Rome and Milan, 1972, Utah Mus. Art, Salt Lake City, 1972, Frumkin, Adams Gallery, N.Y.C., 1973, Gallery Il Fante de Spade, Rome and Milan, 1974, Gallery Claude Bernard, Paris, 1974, Gallery Il Fante de Spade, Rome and Milan, 1976, Frumkin, Adams Gallery, N.Y.C., 1977, Gallery Il Fante de Spade, Rome and Milan, 1979, Frumkin, Adams Gallery, N.Y.C., 1980, Galeria Gian Ferrari, Milan, 1981, Art Mus. Univ. N.Mex., Albuquerque, 1982, Gallery Gian Ferrari, Milan, 1983, Frumkin, Adams Gallery, N.Y.C., 1984, St. Louis Art Mus., 1985, Frumkin, Adams Gallery, N.Y.C., 1986, More Gallery, Phila., 1987, Frumkin, Adams Gallery, N.Y.C., 1988, 1988, Struve Gallery, Chgo., 1988, Frumkin, Adams Gallery, N.Y.C., 1989, Gallery Simonne Stern, New Orleans, 1989, Frumkin, Adams Gallery, N.Y.C., 1989, More Gallery, Phila., 1989, Frumkin, Adams Gallery, N.Y.C., 1990, Struve Gallery, Chgo., 1990, Printworks Gallery, 1990, Gallery Simonne Stern, New Orleans, 1991, Frumkin, Adams Gallery, N.Y.C., 1991, 1993, More Gallery, Phila., 1994, Gallery Simonne Stern, New Orleans, 1994, Frumkin, Adams Gallery, N.Y.C., 1995, Gallery Simonne Stern, New Orleans, 1995, George Adams Gallery, N.Y.C., 1997, Gallery Simonne Stern, New Orleans, 1998, The Art Gallery Univ. N.H., Durham, 1998, Art Mus. U. Ariz., Tucson, 1998, Printworks Gallery, Chgo., 1999, Gallery Simonne Stern, New Orleans, 2000, George Adams Gallery, N.Y.C., 2000, Sonia Zaks Gallery, Chgo., 2001, 2003, Heriard Cimino Gallery, New Orleans, 2003, Represented in permanent collections Mus. Modern Art, N.Y.C., Met. Mus. Art, Whitney Mus. Am. Art, Pa. Acad., Phila., Santa Barbara Mus. Art, Calif., San Francisco Art Mus., Art Inst., Chgo., Joseph Hirshborn Mus., Washington, St. Louis Art Mus., Hamburg Mus. Art, Germany, Centre Georges Pompidou, Paris, Rose Art Mus., Brandeis U. Bd. gov. Skowhegan Sch. Painting and Sculpture. Recipient Am. Acad. Arts and Letters Lifetime Achievement Award, 1995; Fulbright Fellow, 1955-56; Guggenheim Found. Fellow, 1965; Nat. Endowment for Arts grantee, 1967, 85; Bogliasco Found. Fellow, 2003; Rockerfeller Found. Bellagio Ctr. Fellow Mem. Coll. Art Assn. (bd. dir. 1969-73), Academie des Beaux Arts de L'Institut de France, Nat. Acad. Design. Home: PO Box 39 Newbury VT 05051-0039 Office Phone: 802-866-5447. E-mail: bluedeuce@charter.net.

MCGARRY, ALEXANDER BANTING, lawyer; b. Detroit, July 27, 1940; s. Patrick Joseph and Marne Elizabeth (Banting) McG.; m. Diane Lee Fisher, Feb. 10, 1940; children— Erin Kathleen, Molly Anne, Megan Catherine. B.S., Drake U., 1962; J.D., U. Minn., 1965. Bar: Minn. 1965, Mich. 1966, U.S. Supreme Ct. 1978. Asst. pros. atty. Oakland County (Mich.), 1967-69; assoc. Condit, Denison, Devine, Porter & Bartush, Bloomfield Hills, Mich., 1969-71; ptnr. Condit, McGarry & Schloff (formerly Condit & McGarry), Birmingham, Mich., 1971— . Chmn. City of Troy Irish Heritage Group and Bicentennial, 1976; citizens adv. com. Troy Sch. Bd., 1978; chmn. Oakland County Health & Welfare, 1995-98; mem. City of Rochester Hills Traffic Safety Adv. Bd., 1989-95. Recipient Disting. Service award Oakland County, 1970; named Master of the Bench, Oakland A.I.C. Mem. State Bar Mich., Oakland County Bar Assn. (dir., chair health and welfare com. 1993—, Disting. Svc. award 1994, Professionalism award 1998), Assn. Trial Lawyers Am., Inc. Soc. Irish Am. Lawyers (dir.), Cath. Lawyers Soc., Minn. Bar Assn. Lodges: Ancient Order Hibernians (state pres. 1972-76, nat. dir. 1976-78, nat. chmn. Notre Dame Fund 1978-82, Hibernian of Yr. 1980). Office: 6905 Telegraph Rd Ste 215 Bloomfield Hills MI 48301-3159

MCGARRY, CHARLES WILLIAM, lawyer; b. Mt. Kisco, N.Y., June 23, 1957; m. Lori J. Voss. BA in Philosophy, SUNY, Binghamton, 1979; JD, U. Tex., 1982. Bar: Tex. 1983. Law clk. Atty. Gen. of Tex., Austin, 1980-82; briefing atty. Tex. Ct. of Appeals, Dallas, 1982-83; pvt. practice Dallas, 1984-93, 95—; chief justice Tex. Ct. Appeals, Dallas, 1993-94. Mediator Dallas County Juvenile Dept., 1984-93; arbitrator Better Bus. Bur., Dallas, 1985-93. Editor: Aviation Litigation, 1986. Chmn. Irving (Tex.) Dems., 1987-91; pres. Dallas Jazz Orch., 1990-92. Mem. Tex. Bar Assn., Dallas Bar Assn., Irving Bar Assn. Democrat. Roman Catholic. Home: 4324 Twin Post Rd Dallas TX 75244-6743 Office: 701 Commerce St Ste 400 Dallas TX 75202 E-mail: cmcgarry@ix.netcom.com.

MCGARRY, DIANE E. marketing professional; b. Oakland, Calif., July 13, 1949; Doctorate (hon.), The Ryerson Sch. Bus. Mgmt.; D of Commerce (hon.), St. Mary's U., Halifax, Nova Scotia; LLD (hon.), U. Waterloo, Can. Sales rep. to sr. v.p./gen. mgr. ea. customer ops. group Xerox Corp., Ft. Wayne, Ind., 1973-99, corp. v.p. gen. mktg. Stamford, Conn., 2000—. Bd. dirs. Can. Life Fin. Inc., Toronto, Omnova Solutions, Fairlawn, Ohio; spkr. in field. Office: 800 Long Ridge Rd Stamford CT 06902-1227

MCGARRY, FRANCES LORRAINE, education educator; b. Northport, NY, Aug. 5, 1951; d. Louis Joseph Beccaria and Philomena Marie Barile; m. Donald L. McGarry, July 31, 1976; 1 child, Donald P. BS, SUNY, Oneonta, NY, 1973; MA, SUNY, Stony Brook, NY, 1979; PhD, NYU, 2001. Cert. speech and theater edn. NY, Eng. secondary edn. NY. English/theater faculty Northport-East Northport Sch. Dist. 4, Northport, NY, 1975—2004; adj. faculty Nassau CC, Garden City, NY, 2001—, NYU, 2003—. Actress various

stage, screen, TV roles, NYC, 1997—. Vol. NYU Breakout Com., NYC, 2003; choir St. Anthony of Padua Ch., East Northport, NY, 1999—; vol. Ecumenical Lay Coun., Northport, NY, 2004. Mem.: Drama League, Assn. Theater in Higher Edn. (awards com. 1997—2004), Am. Alliance for Theater and Edn. (adjudicator awards com. 1993—95, John C. Barrer Theater Tchr. of Yr. 1993). Achievements include successfully marketing theatrical program into an on-going event; planning, coordinating and producing an interdisplinary program and a children's theater company for secondary school students. Avocation: boating. Home: 2 Heather Dr Northport NY 11768

MCGARRY, JOHN PATRICK, JR., retired advertising agency executive; b. Elizabeth, N.J., Nov. 22, 1939; s. John Patrick and Elizabeth (Weber) McG.; m. Gilda R. Spurio, Oct. 24, 1964; children: Victoria Elizabeth, John Patrick, III. BS in Mktg. Econs, Villanova U., 1961. Salesman Exxon Corp., Elizabeth, 1961-64; advt. exec. Young and Rubicam Inc., N.Y.C., 1965-69, sr. v.p., mgmt. supr., 1969-87, pres., mem. ops. com., advt. exec. com., 1987—; vice chmn. Young and Rubicam Advt. Worldwide, N.Y.C., 1990—; chmn. Client Svcs. Worldwide, N.Y.C., 1987—; pres., CEO Young and Rubicam N.Am., N.Y.C., 1992-94; pres. Young & Rubicam Inc., N.Y.C., 1996-98; ret., 1998. Bd. dirs. Caramoor; mem. corp. exec.'s com. Young and Rubicam, 1992. Bd. dirs. New Youth Performing Theatre, Bedford, N.Y., Regional Rev. League, Westchester, 4 A's, Louisville Opera Assn., 1981-83, Dominican Coll., Drop-out Prevention Fund, United Negro Coll. Fund, 1994—; bd. dirs. N.Y. coun. Boy Scouts Am., 1992; head parents fund St. Lawrence U. Mem. Internat. Advt. Assn. (pres. U.S. and Can.), Proprietory Assn. (bd. dirs.), Bedford Club, Golf and Tennis Club, N.Y. Athletic Club, The Roundabout Theater (adv. bd. 1994—). Democrat. Roman Catholic. Office: Young & Rubicam Inc 285 Madison Ave New York NY 10017-6486 Home: PO Box 445 Bedford Hills NY 10507-0445

MCGARRY, LISA COUGHLIN, language educator; b. Phila., June 10, 1963; d. Neil G. and Nancy V. Coughlin; m. Patrick J. McGarry, Apr. 5, 1986; 1 child, Neil Patrick. BA in English, Temple U., 1986; MA, Villanova U., 1992; PhD, Lehigh U., 2002. V.p. mktg. Universal Svc. Agy., Fort Washington, Pa., 1987—91; lectr. Gwynedd-Mercy Coll., Gwynedd Valley, Pa., 1992—98, dir. acad. resource ctr., 1998—2002, asst. prof., dir., 2002—03, asst. prof., 2003—. Co-chair mission and values com. Gwynedd-Mercy Coll., Pa., 2000—02, mem. strategic planning steering com., 2003—; chair Gwynedd-Mercy Coll. Middle States Self-Study Work Group, 2004—. Mem.: Nat. Coun. Tchrs. English, Coll. Reading and Learning Assn., MLA, Kappa Delta Pi (hon.). Office: Gwynedd-Mercy Coll 1325 Sumneytown Pike Gwynedd Valley PA 19437 E-mail: mcgarry.l@gmc.edu.

MCGARRY, MARCIA, retired community service coordinator; b. Washington, Dec. 9, 1941; d. Emil Sylvester and Bernice B. (Bland) Busey. BS, Morgan State U., 1964. Cert. tchr., law enforcement officer, Fla. Payroll clk., jr. acct. U.S. Dept. Labor, Washington, 1964-65; English tchr. Taiwan, 1968-70; tchr. Monroe County Sch. Bd., Key West, Fla., 1971-81; exec. dir. Monroe Assn. Retarded Citizens, Key West, 1977-79; dep. sheriff Monroe County Sheriff's Dept., Key West, 1979-83, 86-90; probation/parole officer Fla. State Dept. Corrections, Key West, 1983-91; law enforcement instr. Fla. Keys C.C., 1983-91; cmty. svc. coord. City of Bradenton, 1991-2000; domestic violence specialist II Broward County Sheriff Dept., 2001—. Mem. rev. bd. City of Bradenton Police Dept., 1996—2000, mem. cmty. rels. com., 1996—2000. Active local polit. campaigns; co-founder day schs. for under-privileged children; former mem. Big Bros./Big Sisters Am., mem. com., 1985-86, former bd. dirs., Spouse Abuse, former bd. dirs.; bd. dirs. Adv. Coun. Orange-Ridge Elem., 1991-93; bd. dirs. mayor's com., chmn. task force Drug Free Cmtys., 1991-94, bd. dirs., 1996-2001; bd. dirs. Human Rels. Commn., 1991-93, Drug Free Schs. and Cmty. Adv. Coun., 1991-98, T.O.T.S. (These Our Tots), Inc., 1998-2000; former mem. adv. coun. Byrd Edn. Found., Sweet Adelines Internat., 1992-94, commr. 12th Jud. Nominating Commn., 1992-99, cons., facilitator Cultural Diversity Conflict Resolution Workshops, Manatee County High Schs. and Bradenton Police Dept.; attendance adv. com. Bayshore High, 1993, multicultural com., 1994, former rep. Women's Forum; former dir. choir Luth. Ch.; founding mem. Comprehensive Neighborhood Support Network; mem. adv. bd. Manatee County Sheriff's Dept., 1994-2000, mem. hiring rev. bd., 1997-2000. Recipient Appreciation cert., Lions Club, 1978, 1979, Career Week award, Harris Elem. Sch., 1981, Glynn Archer Elem. Sch., 1989, Trainers award, Probation/Parole Acad., 1987, Cert. of Acknowledgement for Cmty. Svc., AAUW, 1995, awadrd, Vol. Army for the War on Drugs, 1989. Mem. NAFE, Fla. Police Benevolent Assn., Fla. Women in Govt. (mem. Manatee County chpt.), Ecumanical Luth. Ch. of Am. (elected consultation conm. Fla. Synod 1989), Key West Profls., Luth. Ch. Women, Delta Sigma Theta (v.p. 1990-91, corr. sec. 1993-95). Office Phone: 954-831-7045. Personal E-mail: marciadnc@aol.com.

MCGARRY, RICHARD LAWRENCE, lawyer; b. Flushing, N.Y., Jan. 12, 1960; s. Richard J. and Loretta (McCarthy) McG.; m. Lynda R. Jones, Dec. 21, 1987; children: Abraham A. Eichelberger, Chelsea Eichelberger St. Clair, David B. Eichelberger. BS, Hampden Sydney Coll., 1982; JD, Washington and Lee U., 1989. Bar: Va. 1989, U.S. Dist. Ct. (we. dist.) Va., U.S. Supreme Ct., 1993. Assoc. Jeffrey H. Krasnow and Assocs., Roanoke, Va., 1989-93; ptnr. Johnson & McGarry, P.C., Charlottesville, Va., 1993-94; pvt. practice Roanoke, 1994—. Bd. dirs. Roanoke Valley SPCA. Mem. Va. Trial Lawyers Assn., Assn. Trial Lawyers Am., Roanoke Bar Assn., Va. Bar Assn. Office: PO Box 21565 2320 Electric Rd SW Roanoke VA 24018 E-mail: rick.mcgarry@att.net.

MCGARRY, SANDRA ALETHEA, elementary school educator; arrived in U.S., 1965; d. Victor Theodore and Sixta McGarry. BA, N.W. Nazarene, 1977; EdM, U. Tex., Tyler, 2001. Cert. tchr. Tex. Edn. Agy., reading specialist Tex. Edn. Agy. Educator Tyler Ind. Sch. Dist., 1979—, dept. chair Dogan Middle Sch., 2000—. Dist. campus performance com. Tyler Ind. Sch. Dist., 1997—2000, team leader Dogan Middle Sch., 1999—2000, curriculum author, 2001—02. Project Continue grantee, U. Tex. Tyler-Tyler Ind. Sch. Dist., 2000. Republican. Avocations: reading, writing, calligraphy, guitar, cross stitch. Home: 21224 CR 3124 Chandler TX 75758 Office: Dogan Middle Sch 2621 N Border Tyler TX 75702

MCGARRY, W. DAVID, real estate company executive; BA in Urban and Regional Planning, Fairfield U.; MS, Va. Tech.; MBA, Dartmouth Coll. Joined Spaulding & Slye Colliers, Washington, 1984—, pres., 2004—. Office: Spaulding & Slye Colliers Ste 1000 1717 Pennsylvania Ave NW Washington DC 20006*

MCGARVEY, JOSEPH F. X., SR., cardiologist; b. Darby, Pa., Sept. 8, 1936; MD, U. Pa., 1962. Diplomate Am. Bd. Internal Medicine, Am. Bd. Cardiovasc. Disease. Intern Fitzgerald Mercy Hosp., Darby, 1962-63; resident Hahnemann U., Phila., 1963-66; fellow in cardiology Cin. Gen. Hosp., 1968-69; mem. staff Doylestown (Pa.) Hosp.; pvt. practice Doylestown, 1969—. Fellow ACP, Am. Coll. Cardiology. Office: 14 Memorial Dr Ste B Doylestown PA 18901-3529 Office Phone: 215-345-6050.

MC GAUGH, JAMES LAFAYETTE, psychobiologist; b. Long Beach, Calif., Dec. 17, 1931; s. William Rufus and Daphne (Hermes) McG.; m. Carol J. Becker, Mar. 15, 1952; children: Douglas, Janice, Linda. BA, San Jose State U., 1953; PhD (Abraham Rosenberg fellow), U. Calif. - Berkeley, 1959; sr. postdoctoral fellow, NAS-NRC, Istituto Superiore di Sanitá, Rome, 1961-62; DSc (hon.), So. Ill. U., 1991. Asst. prof., assoc. prof. psychology San Jose State U., 1957-61; assoc. prof. psychology U. Oreg., 1961-64; assoc. prof. U. Calif., Irvine, 1964-66, founding chmn. dept. psychobiology, 1964-67, 71-74, 86-89, prof., 1966-94; rsch. prof., 1994—; dean Sch. Biol. Sci. U. Calif., Irvine, 1967-70, vice chancellor acad. affairs, 1975-77, exec. vice chancellor, 1978-82, founding dir. Ctr. Neurobiology of Learning and Memory, 1983—. Mem. adv. coms. NIMH, 1965-78, Mental Health Coun. NIMH, 1992-95. Author: (with J.B. Cooper) Integrating Principles of Social Psychology, 1963, (with H.F. Harlow, R.F. Thompson) Psychology, 1971, (with M.J. Herz) Memory Consolidation, 1972, Learning and Memory: An Introduction, 1973, (with R.F. Thompson and T. Nelson) Psychology I, 1977, (with C. Cotman) Behavioral Neuroscience, 1980; editor: (with N.M. Weinberger, R.E. Whalen) Psychobiology, 1966, Psychobiology-Behavior from a Biological Perspective, 1971, The Chemistry of Mood, Motivation and Memory, 1972, (with M. Fink, S.S. Kety, T.A. Williams) Psychobiology of Convulsive Therapy, 1974, (with L.F. Petrinovich) Knowing, Thinking, and Believing, 1976, (with R.R. Drucker-Colín) Neurobiology of Sleep and Memory, 1977, (with S.B. Kiesler) Aging, Biology and Behavior, 1981, (with G. Lynch and N. M. Weinberger) Neurobiology of Learning and Memory, 1984, (with N.M. Weinberger and G. Lynch) Memory Systems of the Brain, 1985, Contemporary Psychology, 1985, (with C.D. Woody and D.L. Alkon) Cellular Mechanisms of Conditioning and Behavioral Plasticity, 1988, (with N.M. Weinberger and G. Lynch) Brain Organization and Memory: Cells, Systems and Circuits, 1990, (with R.C.A. Frederickson and D.L. Felten) Peripheral Signaling of the Brain, 1991, (with L. Squire, G. Lynch and N.M. Weinberger) Memory: Organization and Locus of Change, 1991; (with N.M. Weinberger and G. Lynch) Brain and Memory: Modulation and Mediation of Neuroplasticity, 1995; author over 400 sci. papers; founding editor Behavioral Biology, 1972-78, Behavioral and Neural Biology, 1979-94, Neurobiology of Learning and Memory, 1995-98, Plasticity in the Central Nervous System; Learning and Memory, 1995, Brain Processes and Memory, 1996. Recipient medal U. Calif., Irvine, 1992; recipient John P. McGovern award, 1996. Fellow AAAS, Am. Acad. Arts and Scis., Soc. Exptl. Psychologists, Am. Psychol. Soc. (William James fellow 1989, pres. 1989-91), Western Psychol. Assn. (pres. 1992-93); mem. NAS (chmn. psychol. secat. 1992-95), APA (chief sci. advisor 1986-88, Sci. Contbn. award 1981), Internat. Brain Rsch. Orgn., Soc. Neurosci., Am. Coll. Neuropsychopharmacology, Brazilian Acad. Sci. (fgn. mem.), Collegium Internat. Neuropsychopharmacologicum, Psychonomic Soc., European Behavioral Pharmacology Soc., Phi Beta Kappa, Sigma Xi. Office: U Calif Dept Neurobiology Behavior Ctr Neurobiology Learning Irvine CA 92697-0001

MCGAUGHEY, CHARLES GILBERT, retired research biochemist; b. San Diego, Sept. 8, 1925; s. Gilbert Arthur and Louisa Ellen (Inskeep) McG. BA, U. Calif., Berkeley, 1950; MA, U. So. Calif., 1952. Diplomate Am. Inst. Oral Biology. Scientist radiol. hazards evaluation U.S. Naval Radiol. Def. Lab., San Francisco, 1952; rsch. biochemist VA Med. Ctr., Long Beach, Calif., 1953-81; prin. investigator studied dental caries, plaque and oral cancer Oral Diseases Rsch. Lab., 1978-81. Contbr. articles to profl. jours. Grantee Nat. Inst. Dental Rsch., 1965. Mem. AAAS. Republican. Home: 337 N Winnipeg Pl Long Beach CA 90814-2561

MCGAVICK, MICHAEL S. insurance and financial services company executive; b. Seattle, Wash. BA, U. Wash., 1983. V.p. The Rockey Comp., Wash. Round Table, 1986—88; chief of staff for Sen. Slade Gorton, 1989—91; ptnr. The Gallatin Group, Seattle, 1991—92; dir. Superfund Improvement Project, Am. Insurance Assn., 1992—95; pres. & COO CNA Fin. Corp., Chicago, 1995—2001; CEO, pres., bd. dirs. SAFECO Corp., 2001—. Office: 4333 Brooklyn Ave NE Seattle WA 98185

MCGAW, BRIDGER E. management consultant; s. Robert E. and Eloise S. McGaw. AB in Govt., cum laude, Harvard Coll., 1993—98; M in Pub. Policy, John F. Kennedy Sch. Govt., Harvard U., 2002—04. White ho. advance staff The White Ho., Wash., DC, 1996—2001; nat. advance staff Clinton Gore 1996 Presdl. Campaign, Wash., DC, 1996; pub. affairs officer, def. fellow Office of Sec.Def., Wash., DC, 1998—2000; asst. press sec. The White Ho., Office of the V.P., Wash., DC, 1999—2000; nat. media advance coord. Gore Lieberman Presdl. Campaign, Nashville, 2000—00; press sec. Office of Congressman Marty Meehan (D-MA), Wash., DC, 2001—03; mayoral policy fellow City of Chgo., 2003; sr. cons. Booz Allen Hamilton, McLean, Va., 2004—. Founder Student Police Adv. Bd., Cambridge, Mass., 1993—97. Researcher team franken (rsch. nat. best seller) Lies and the Lying Liars who Tell Them: A Fair And Balanced Look at the Right. Mem. fgn. policy staff John Kerry for Pres., 2004—; mem. Dem. Town Com., Belmont, Mass., 1996—99. Decorated Office of Sec. Def. award for Outstanding Achievement Asst. Sec. Def. for Pub. Affairs, award for Exceptional Pub. Svc. Sec. of Def. Mem.: Hugh O'Brian Youth Found., Ky. Colonels (hon.). Democrat. Unitarian Universalist. Home: 23 Louise Rd Belmont MA 02478 Personal E-mail: bridger_mcgaw@ksg04.harvard.edu.

MCGEADY, SISTER MARY ROSE, retired religious organization administrator; b. Hazelton, Pa., June 28, 1928; d. Joseph James and Catherine Cecilia (Mundie) McG. BA in Sociology, Emmanuel Coll., 1955; MA in Clin. Psychology, Fordham U., 1961; DHL (hon.), St. John's U., Queens, N.Y., 1982, Coll. New Rochelle, N.Y., 1991, Fordham U., 1991, Niagara U., 1991, Coll. St. Rose, Albany, N.Y., 1991, DePaul U., 1991. Joined Daus. of Charity St. Vincent De Paul, Roman Cath. Ch., 1946. Dir. Astor Home Clinics, Rhinebeck, N.Y., 1961-66; exec. dir. Nazareth Child Care Ctr., Boston, 1966-71; dir. mental health Cath. Charities Bklyn., 1971-79, assoc. exec. dir., 1987-90; dir. Kennedy Child Study Ctr., N.Y.C., 1979-81; provincial supr. Daus. of Charity St. Vincent DePaul, Albany, 1981-87; pres., chief exec. officer Covenant House, N.Y.C., 1990—2003. Bd. dirs. Cardinal Cooke Health Care Ctr., N.Y.C., Meninger Found., Kans., Ctr. for Human Devel., Washington. Author: Catholic Special Education, 1979. Mem. N.Y. State Mental Health Svcs. Coun., Albany, 1983-90, N.Y. State Mental Health Planning Coun., Albany, 1986-91, Cath. Charities USA, 1966—. Recipient svc. award N.Y.C. Dept. Mental Health, 1988, Encouragement award Cath. U. Am., 1991. Roman Catholic. Home: 75 Lewis Ave Brooklyn NY 11206-7015 Office: Covenant House 346 W 17th St New York NY 10011-5089

MCGEE, BRUCE D. evangelist; b. Lenoir, NC, Nov. 29, 1943; s. Julian B. and Lorece M. McGee(Stepmother), Dorothy I. McGee; m. Ann E. Saxon, Nov. 29, 1945; children: Robert L., Melissa A. Flow. BA, U. La., Monroe, 1974. Pastor Columbia Heights Bapt., Columbia, La., 1997—, Good Hope Bapt., West Monroe, La., 1988—97, Ctr. Point Bapt., West Monroe, 1981—88; store mgr. Safeway Stores, Inc., Texarkana, Ark., 1974—78; asst. mgr. Safeway Stores Inc., West Monroe, 1968—74. Chaplain Caldwell Sheriff's Dept., Columbia, La., 200—; exec. bd. mem. La. Bapt. Conv., Columbia, La.; pastoral ministries dir. Caldwell Bapt. Assn., Columbia, La., 1999—. Composer (writer): (book) Born To Grow In Jesus, Sealed In His Spirit. Bd. dirs. Crossover Ministries, Columbia, La., 1999—2003. Sgt. USAF, 1963—67. R-Consevative. Christian. Avocation: golf. Home: 205 Adams Columbia LA 71418 Personal E-mail: mcge3582@bellsouth.net.

MCGEE, CARRIE L. artist; BA, Immaculate Heart Coll., L.A., 1976. One-woman shows include Penine Hart Gallery, N.Y.C., 1989, The Greater Nashville Arts Found., 1995, Cheekwood Mus. Art, Nashville, 1996, Internat. Austausch Ateliers Region Basel, Basel, Switzerland, The Lowe Gallery, Atlanta, 1998; group shows at Penine Hart Gallery, N.Y.C., 1989, 90, 93, Cheekwood Mus. Art, Nashville, 1993, The Gallery on Broadway, Nashville, 1993, Bell Gallery, Memphis, 1994, AKA Gallery, Nashville, 1994, Zeitgeist, Nashville, 1995, 96, Southeastern Ctr. for Contemporary Art, Winston-Salem, N.C., 1997, Cumberland Gallery, Nashville, 1998, others. Fellow MacDowell Colony, N.H., 1989-90; fellow NEA/So. Arts Fedn. Visual Arts, 1996; named Internat. Austausch Ateliers Basel Exchange Artist, Christoph Merian Found., 1997.

MCGEE, CHAD ALAN, historian, educator; b. McMinnville, Tenn., June 22, 1972; s. Clark Rhea and Marilyn Ann McGee; m. Rachel Martha Jones, Feb. 21, 1969; children: Lucy Katherine Ruth, Abigail Cora Morgan. BA, Rhodes Coll., 1994—94; MA, Tenn. Technol. U., 2000. Project dir. Tchg. Am. History Grant Cumberland River Valley Consortium, McMinnville, Tenn., 2002—04; instr. advanced placement history Warren County HS, McMinnville, 2000—. Bd. mem. Pk. Theatre Restoration Group, McMinnville. Tchg. Am. History Grant, US Dept. of Edn., 2002—05. Mem.: Nat. Coun. Tchrs. Social Studies, Orgn. Am. Historians. Home: 307 Morrison St Mc Minnville TN 37110 Office: Warren County High School 199 Pioneer Lane Mc Minnville TN 37110 Personal E-mail: chadmcgee@charter.net. E-mail: mcgeec3@k12tn.net.

MCGEE, DAN(IEL) W. state legislator; b. Shreveport, La., Sept. 30, 1947; m. LaRae McGee; 3 children. BS, La. State U. Land surveyor, geologist; mem. Mont. Ho. of Reps., 1995—2003, speaker, 2001—03; mem. Mont. Senate, 2003—. Lt. USAF. Republican. Home: 1925 Pinyon Dr Laurel MT 59044

MCGEE, HAROLD JOHNSTON, former academic administrator; b. Portsmouth, Va., Apr. 13, 1937; s. Harold Valentine McGee and Clara Mae (Johnston) Webber; m. Mary Frances Eure, Mar. 22, 1959; children: Harold Johnston, Mary Margaret, Matthew Hayden; m. Linda Gayle Stevens, Apr. 3, 1976; 1 child, Andrew Meade. BS, Old Dominion U., 1959; MEd, U. Va., 1962, EdD, 1968; HumD, James Madison U., 1999. Tchr. Falls Church (Va.) City Schs., 1959-62; asst. dean, then dean of admissions Old Dominion U., Norfolk, Va., 1962-65; field rep., program officer, sr. program officer U.S. Office Edn. Bur. Higher Edn., Charlottesville, 1965-70; provost Tidewater Community Coll., Portsmouth, 1970-71; founding pres. Piedmont Va. Community Coll., Charlottesville, 1971-75; various offices including dean grad. sch., asst. to pres., v.p. student affairs, v.p. adminstrv. affairs, sec. bd. visitors James Madison U., Harrisonburg, Va., 1975-86; pres. Jacksonville (Ala.) State U., 1986-99, pres. emeritus, 1999—. Bd. dirs. Marine Environ. Scis. Consortium, Dauphin Island, Ala., Gulf South Conf., chmn., 1990—92, Ala. Coun. Univ. Pres., 1991—92; bd. dirs. Trans America Athletic Conf., chmn., 1998—99. Author: Impact of Federal Support, 1968, The Virginia Project, 1976. Mem. United Way Calhoun County Ala., 1986—92, Knox Concert Series Adv. Bd., Anniston, Ala., Leadership Ala., Anniston Mus. Natural History Found.; bd. dirs. Southland Athletic League. Mem. NCAA (coun. 1991-95), ACA, Soc. Coll. and Univ. Planning Am. Assn. Higher Edn., Capital City Club (Montgomery, Ala.), Rotary, Phi Delta Kappa. Episcopalian.

MCGEE, HENRY ALEXANDER, JR., university official; b. Atlanta, Sept. 12, 1929; s. Henry Alexander and Arrie Mae (Mallory) McG.; m. Betty Rose Herndon, July 29, 1951; children: Henry Alexander, Charles Nelson, Kathy Nan. BChemE, Ga. Inst. Tech., 1951, PhD, 1955; postgrad., U. Wis., 1955-56. Rsch. scientist Army Rocket and Guided Missile Agy. and NASA, Huntsville, Ala., 1956-59; from assoc. prof. to prof. chem. engring. Ga. Inst. Tech., Atlanta, 1959-71; prof. Va. Poly. Inst. and State U., Blacksburg, 1971-94, head dept. chem. engring., 1971-82; assoc. provost for engring. Va. Commonwealth U., Richmond, 1994-95, founding dean engring., 1995-99, founding dean emeritus, prof. chem. engring., 1999—. Vis. prof. Calif. Inst. Tech., 1984; dir. chem. and transport sys. div. NSF, Washington, 1990-93; cons. in field. *While at NSF, he created the first federally supported program of research on environmentally conscious chemical processing now called "green engineering." He led the design and implementation of a new school of engineering at VCU. His design emphasized entrepreneurship, synthesis or creativity, industrial practice, business skills, multidisciplinary teaching and research, communication skills, and teamwork. "Molecular Engineering" (McGraw-Hill) was the first textbook to teach the useful aspects of molecular theory to engineers in language, while highly mathematical, nonetheless unencumbered by the jargon and esoteric arguments of specialists. His research centered upon chemistry at cryogenic temperatures.* Author: Molecular Engineering, 1991; editorial adv. bd.: Chemical Abstracts; contbr. numerous articles to profl. publs. Bd. dirs. Greater Richmond Tech. Coun. Recipient Cmty. Svc. award Richmond Joint Engrs. Coun., 2000, Leadership award Greater Richmond Tech. Coun., 2002; various rsch. grants NSF, NASA, Air Force Office Sci. Rsch.; named one of five Outstanding Young Men of Yr. Atlanta, 1964, Acad. Disting. Engring. Alumni, Ga. Tech., 1994; Danforth assoc. Fellow AIChE (chmn. nat. program com., mem. editl. bd. jour), AAAS (chmn. sect. on engring. 1985-86); mem. Am. Chem. Soc.; mem. Sigma Xi. Republican. Home: 6 River Court Ln Richmond VA 23238-5581 Office: Va Commonwealth U Richmond VA 23284 Business E-Mail: hmcgee@vcu.edu.

MCGEE, HUMPHREY GLENN, architect; b. June 26, 1937; s. James Gladney and Elizabeth Adams (Williams) McG. BArch, Clemson U., 1960. Designer Clark, McCall & Leach, Hartsville-Kingstree, S.C., 1961; designer prodn. A. G. Odell & Assocs., Charlotte, N.C., 1962; chief designer Clark, McCall & Leach, Hartsville-Kingstree, 1963; sr. designer LBC & W, Inc., Columbia, SC, 1965—76, sr. v.p. client svcs. and design, 1976; pres. CEDA, Inc., Columbia, S.C., 1976-86; pres., treas. McGee-Howle & Assocs., Vero Beach, Fla., 1986—2002; pvt. practice Indian River Shores, Fla., 2002—, Chattanooga, 2002—, 2004—. Pub.: Who's Who in Interior Design, 1993-95; cited in 100 Designer's Favorite Rooms, 1993, 94, 95. With USAR, 1961-67. Mem. AIA, Nat. Soc. Interior Designers (award 1972), Am. Soc. Interior Designers (chmn. S.C. chpt. com. on Found. Interior Design Edn. and Rsch. 1976). E-mail: hglennmcgee@aol.com.

MCGEE, JAMES SEARS, historian, educator; b. Houston, July 12, 1942; s. William Sears and Mary Elizabeth (Peterson) McG.; m. Mary Arnall Broach, Aug. 20, 1966; children: Elizabeth, Claude. BA, Rice U., 1964; MA, Yale U., 1966, M in Philosophy, 1968, PhD, 1971. Asst. prof. Ga. So. Coll., Statesboro, 1969-71; asst. prof. history U. Calif., Santa Barbara, 1971-78, assoc. prof., 1978-84, prof., 1984—, chmn. dept., 1990-95. Pres. Pacific Coast Conf. on Brit. Studies, 1998-2000. Author: The Godly Man in Stuart England, 1976; co-author: The West Transformed, 2000; editor: The Miscellaneous Works of John Bunyan, Vol. 3, 1987. Named Disting. Tchr. in Soc. Scis., U. Calif., Santa Barbara, 1989; fellow Abraham Found., 1962-63; Woodrow Wilson fellow, 1964-65; recipient summer stipend NEH, 1975. Fellow Royal Hist. Soc.; mem. Am. Soc. Ch. History, Am. Hist. Assn., N.Am. Conf. on Brit. Studies. Democrat. Episcopalian. Avocation: gardening. Office: U Calif Dept History Santa Barbara CA 93106

MC GEE, JOSEPH JOHN, JR., former insurance company executive; b. Kansas City, Mo., Dec. 2, 1919; s. Joseph J. and Margaret (Cronin) McG.; m. Anne Cunningham, Apr. 30, 1949; children: Sally, Peter, Mary, John, David, Julie, Simon. Attended, Rockhurst Coll., Kansas City, Georgetown U. Asst. sec. Old Am. Ins. Co., Kansas City, Mo., 1939-45, v.p., 1946-51, exec. v.p., 1952-55, pres., 1956-87; ins. cons. Kansas City, Mo., 1987-91. Bd. dirs. Truman Med. Ctr., Truman Libr. Inst. for Nat. and Internat. Affairs; trustee emeritus Rockhurst Coll.; pres. McGee Found. Office: 1045 W 54th St Kansas City MO 64112

MCGEE, KIMBERLEY, editor, writer; d. Debbie Stuck and Patrick McGee. BA, U. Nev., 1992. Reporter Las Vegas Sun, 1998—2002; editor What's On Mag., Las Vegas, 2002—. Freelancer People Mag., Nev., 2000—.

MCGEE, LINDA MACE, judge, lawyer; b. Marion, N.C., Mar. 20, 1949; d. Cecil Adam and Norma Jean (Hogan) Mace; m. B. Gary McGee, Dec. 19, 1970; children: Scott Adam, Jeffrey Sean. BA, U. N.C., 1971, JD, 1973. Bar: N.C. 1973. Exec. dir. N.C. Acad. Trial Lawyers, Raleigh, 1973-78; assoc. Finger, Watson & di Santi, Boone, N.C., 1978-80; ptnr. Finger, Watson, di Santi & McGee, Boone, 1980-89, di Santi, Watson & McGee, Boone, 1989-95; judge N.C. Ct. of Appeals, 1995—. Mem. trustee panel U.S. Bankruptcy Ct., Greensboro, N.C., 1980-82; bd. dirs. Legal Services of N.C., Raleigh, 1980-84; mem. N.C. Bd. Law Examiners, 1986-93. Vice-chairperson Watauga County Coun. on Status of Women, Boone, 1979-82; trustee Caldwell C.C. and Tech. Inst., Hudson, N.C., 1980-89; mem. exec. bd. N.C. Assn. C.C. Trustees, 1983-85; trustee Caldwell C.C., 1981-89; mem. Pub. Edn. Commn., 2000—. Mem. ABA, ATLA, AAUW, LWV, ABA Found., Am. Law Inst., N.C. Assn. Women Attys. (charter, treas. 1980-84, chair jud. divsn. 1997, Gwyneth B. Davis award 1997, Outstanding Judge of Yr. award 1999), N.C. Bar Assn. (bd. govs. 1983-86, co-chair lawyers in schs. com., Pro Bono Svc. award, 1992, jud. divsn. Outstanding Judge of Yr. award 1999), N.C. Acad. Trial Lawyers (bd. govs. 1993-95), N.C. State Bar, Boone C. of C. (bd. dirs. 1982-85), N.C. Bus. and Profl. Womens Clubs (chair polit. action com. 1982-83, Young Career Woman 1980), Boone Bus. and Profl. Women's Club (Woman of Yr. 1980), N.C. Women's Forum. Democrat. Presbyn. Home: PO Box 9068 Hickory NC 28603-9068 Office: PO Box 888 Raleigh NC 27602-0888

MCGEE, MICHAEL JAY, protective services official, educator; b. Ft. Worth, June 9, 1952; s. Cecil Carl McGee and Helen Ruth (Peeples) McGee-Furrh; m. Carol Lee Garbarino, Sept. 18, 1982; children: Megan Rose, John Michael, Molly Caitlin. Student, U. Tex., 1970-73, Western Oreg. State U., 1983; AAS in Fire Protection Tech., Colo. Mountain Coll., 1990. Lic. fire suppression systems insp., Colo., vocat. educator, Colo.; cert. hazardous materials technician, Colo., 1992, EMT, Colo.; cert. fire investigator, 2002, fire safety hazardous materials instr., evaluator. Driver Massengale Co., Austin, Tex., 1970-73; gen. mgr. Sundae Palace, Austin, 1973-74; staff mem. Young

Life, Colorado Springs, Colo., 1970-75; mgr. Broadmoor Mgmt. Co., Vail, Colo., 1974-76; technician Vail Cable Communications, 1976-77; dep. chief, fire marshal Vail Fire Dept., 1977—, fire sci. coord., 1995—, emergency med. program coord., 1996—2002; 2000v.p. HAZPRO (Hazardous Materials and Fire Safety Consulting Firm), 1996; pres. Fire Protection Tng. & Consulting, Inc., 1999; v.p. OTB, LLC, 2002—. Dist. rep. Joint Coun. Fire Dist. Colo., 1983-85; co-chmn. Eagle County Hazardous Materials, 1984-85, mem. planning com., 1987-90; mem. accountability com. Eagle County Sch. Dist., 1991-96, mem. budget rev. com., 1991-93, vice chair accountability com. 1992-93, chmn. accountability com., 1993-96; mem. policy rev. com., 1993-96, bldg. coord., team coach Odyssey of the Mind at Eaglevalle Elem. Sch., 1995; invited dir. workshops Colo. Dept. Edn. Dist. Accountability Convention, Colo. Springs, 1995; pres. Fire Protection Tng. and Cons., Inc.; instr., trainer EMP Am. Inc. Chmn. Eagle County chpt. ARC, 1980-83, disaster chmn., 1977-80; tng. officer Eagle Vol. Fire Dept., 1988-90; mem. parish coun. St. Mary's Parish, Eagle County, 1989-90; mem. citizen's adv. com. Colo. Mountain Coll., 1990-91, bd. dirs. 1990; bldg. coord., team coach Odessey of the Mind, Eagle Valley Elem. Sch., 1994-95, 97-98, 98-99, coach Destination Imagination, 1999-2000; mem. facilities master planning com. Engle County Sch. Dist., 1996-97; mem. planning com. 1999 World Alpine Ski Championships; program coord. Eagle County Driver's Edn. Named Alumnus of the year, Co. Mountain Coll., 2001. Mem.: KC (trustee 2003—, charter Grand Knight, Eagle Count chpt.), Nat. Inst. Cert. Engring. Tech. Cert., Glendale Fire Safety Inst., Colo. State Fire Chiefs Assn., Colo. State Fire Marshals Assn., Nat. Fire Protection Assn., Internat. Assn. Arson Investigators (Colo. chpt.), Internat. Platform Assn. Office: Vail Fire Dept 42 W Meadow Dr Vail CO 81657-5000 E-mail: mmcgee@vailgov.com.

MCGEE, MICHAEL VANHOOK, writer; b. Ft. Smith, Ark., July 23; s. Lillard Harold Weatherman and Hila VanHook Mcgee; m. Evelyn Elizabeth Weber; children: Michael VanHook Jr.(dec.), Patricia Lynn Mc Gee Gunderson, Sarah Valerie McGee Cannon. AB polit. sci., Univ. of the South, 1950; LLB, Southern Law U., 1957; MFA, U. Alaska, 1982. Clk. and announcer Radio Sta. WMPS, Memphis, 1948; bank clk. Union Planters Bank, Memphis, 1950—51, bank teller, 1953—56; real estate ins. sales Galbreath Co., Memphis, 1956—62; writer, 1979—. Contbr. articles publ. to profl. jour. 2nd lt. USAF, 1951—53, ret. as maj. USAF, 1962—79. Mem.: Shriners, Masons. Anglican. Avocations: fishing, camping, painting. Home: PO Box 56116 North Pole AK 99705

MCGEE, PATRICIA K. state legislator; m. Mike McGee, 1960; foster children: Ann, Carol, Norma. AA, Alfred State Coll. Asst. to the dean Jamestown C.C., Cattaraugus, N.Y.; mem. N.Y. State Assembly, Albany, 1987-98, vice chmn. minority joint conf. com., ranking minority mem. assembly higher edn. com., assembly intern com., ranking minority mem. assembly transportation com., mem. assembly standing com. on environ. conservation and higher edn. com., appointed asst. minority wip.; mem. dist. 56 N.Y. Senate, Albany, 1998—. Mem. legis. commn. on Hazardous and Toxic Waste and Rural Resources Commn.; rep. task force mem. on Econ. Devel. and the Future of SUNY; guest speaker Chautauqua Inst. Mem. 219 Liaison Com., Farm Bur., Portville Parent Tchr Assn., Cattaraugus County Tourist Bur. Mem. Am. Legis. Exchange Coun., Nat. Conf. State of State Legis., Nat. Order of Women Legis., N.Y. State Fire Safety Consortium, VFW, Am. Legion, Disabled Am. Vets. Office: Westgate Plz 700 W State St Olean NY 14760-2346 also: 814 Legislative Office Bldg Albany NY 12247

MCGEE, RICHARD K. energy executive; b. Houston, 1961; m. Kris McGee; 4 children. BA in Econ., Polit. Sci. and Managerial Studies, Rice U., 1983; JD, U. Tex., Austin, 1986. Ptnr. Vinson & Elkins LLP, Houston, 1986—98; sr. v.p., gen. counsel energy svcs. divsn. Duke Energy, Charlotte, NC, 1999—2001, pres. internat. divsn., 2001—. Bd. dirs., exec. com. Houston Ballet Found., Houston, Coun. of Overseers, Jones Grad. Sch. Mgmt., Rice U., M.D. Anderson Cancer Prevention Ctr. Advance Team. Office: Duke Energy Corp 526 S Church St Charlotte NC 28202-1803

MCGEE, ROBERT MERRILL, oil company executive; b. Laramie, Wyo., Dec. 15, 1946; s. Gale William and Loraine (Baker) McG.; m. Mary Louise Lehman, July 26, 1969; children: Kirk Lehman, Scott Baker. BA in Polit. Sci., Allegheny Coll., 1969. Bus. assoc. B.F. Goodrich Co., Akron, Ohio, 1969-70; dir. of info. Nat. Petroleum Coun., Washington, 1970-73; asst. dir. pub. rels. Occidental Internat. Corp., Washington, 1973-74, exec. asst. to pres., 1974-76, v.p., 1976-78, exec. v.p., 1978-82, sr. exec. v.p., 1982-91, pres., 1991—; v.p. Occidental Petroleum Corp., 1994—. Mem. Pres.'s Commn. on White House Fellowships, Washington, 1993—2001, Meridian Internat. Ctr., Washington, 1994—98; mem. bd. advisors Pan Am. Devel. Found., Washington, 1985, pres., 1991—93; bd. govs. Ford's Theatre, Washington, 1991—; bd. govs. Karl Landegger Program in internat. bus. diplomacy Sch. Fgn. Svc., Georgetown U., Washington, 1991—2000; bd. dirs. Decatur House, Washington, 1998, vice chmn. bd., 2000, chmn. bd. dirs., 2001—04. Mem. The Econ. Club of Washington, Met. Club Washington, Nat. Press Club. Office: Occidental Internat Corp Ste 400 1717 Pennsylvania Ave NW Washington DC 20006-4614

MCGEE, SHERRY, retail executive; b. Honolulu, Hawaii, Nov. 16, 1957; d. Winnie R. Johnson; 1 child, Michael L. BS, Wayne State U., 1987, MBA, 1991. Divsn. sales mgr. CDI Corp., 1978-89; sales tng. cons. McGee & Co., 1990-92; dir. mktg. Bartech, Inc., 1992-97; founder, pres. Apple Book Ctr., 1996—. Vol. Jr. Achievement.: Apple Book Center 18843 Gainsborough Rd Detroit MI 48223-1341 E-mail: apple001@aol.com.

MCGEE, WILLIAM HOWARD JOHN, librarian, administrator; b. Rochester, N.Y., May 15, 1942; s. William Peter and Cecilia Matilda (Kuhn) McG.; m. Sheila Anne Drumm, Sept. 4, 1965; children: Kathleen Moira, Margaret Frances. BA with honors, U. Toronto, Ont., Can., 1965; MEd, U. Toronto, 1973; MLS, U. Western Ont., London, 1980. Tchr. Mimico (Ont.) High Sch., 1966-67; tchr., libr. Applewood Secondary Sch., Mississauga, Ont., 1967-71; libr. Crestwood Secondary Sch., Peterborough, Ont., 1971-74; libr. cons. Cayman Islands Edn. Dept., Grand Cayman, B.W.I., 1975-79; adminstrv. asst. Lake Erie Regional Libr., London, Ont., 1980-83; chief libr. Ft. Erie (Ont.) Pub. Libr., 1983-86; asst. dir. McAllen (Tex.) Pub. Libr., 1986-89; coord. Hidalgo County Libr. System, McAllen, 1989—2001; libr. br. mgr. Lark Cmty. Ctr. Library, McAllen, 2001—. Cons. Grand Ct. Libr., Grand Cayman, 1974-79; mem. Tex. State Libr. Task Force, Austin, Tex., 1991-93; adv. coun. Libr. Svcs. Tech. Act, Austin, 1993—. Editor InTraLogue jour., 1980-83; assoc. editor Can. Jour. Info. Sci., 1980. Bd. dirs. C-ME-CU Credit Union, 1994-99, chmn., 1999. Mem. ALA, Ont. Libr. Assn., Tex. Libr. Assn. (chmn. dist. 4 1994-95, 96-97, intellectual freedom com. 1995-96, profl. rights, responsiblities, and recruitment, 1996—, centennial celebration com. 2000—), Bibliothecaires Francophones Internat. Roman Catholic. Avocations: gourmet cooking, music, travel, reading. Office: Lark Cmty Ctr Libr 2601 Lark Ave Mcallen TX 78504 Office Phone: 956-688-3320. E-mail: billmcgee@mcallen.lib.tx.us., liam_magee@hotmail.com.

MCGEE, WILLIAM TOBIN, intensive care physician; b. Port Chester, NY, May 23, 1957; s. James R. and Mary (Delzotto) McG.; m. Sarah McGrath; children: Erin, Kelly, Mary, Kate. BA in Physics, Dartmouth Coll., 1979; MD, N.Y. Med. Coll., 1983; M in Health Adminstrn., Clark U., 1997. Diplomate Am. Bd. Internal Medicine with spl. qualifications in Critical Care. Resident in internal medicine Baystate Med. Ctr., Springfield, Mass., 1983-86, intensivist, acting dir. surg. ICU, 1990-95; fellow in critical care St. Louis U./St. John's Mercy Med. Ctr., St. Louis, 1986-88; intensivist critical care divsn. Baystate Med. Ctr., Springfield, MA, 1990-98, dir. ICU quality improvement, 1998—. DeWitt Wallace fellow rehab. medicine Rusk Inst. NYU Med. Ctr. Fellow Coll. Chest Physicians (Cecile Lehman Mayer award 1993); mem. AMA, Soc. Critical Care Medicine (presdl. citation 2000, internal medicine specialty award 2000), Am. Soc. Parenteral and Enteral Nutrition. Roman Catholic. Avocations: skiing, biking, hiking, sailing, windsurfing. Office: Baystate Med Ctr 759 Chestnut St Springfield MA 01199-1001 Business E-Mail: william.t.mcgee@bhs.org.

MCGEER, EDITH GRAEF, neurological science educator; b. NYC, Nov. 18, 1923; d. Charles and Charlotte Annie (Ruhl) Graef; m. Patrick L. McGeer, Apr. 15, 1954; children: Patrick Charles, Brian Theodore, Victoria Lynn. BA, Swarthmore Coll., 1944; PhD, U. Va., 1946; DSc (hon.), U. Victoria, 1987, U. B.C., 2000. Rsch. chemist E.I. DuPont de Nemours & Co., Wilmington, Va., 1946-54; rsch. assoc. divsn. neurol. sci. U. B.C., Vancouver, Canada, 1954-74, assoc. prof., 1974-76, prof., acting head, 1976-83, prof., head, 1983-89, prof. emerita, 1989—. Author: (with others) Molecular Neurobiology of the Mammalian Brain, 1978, 2d edit., 1987; editor: (with others) Kainic Acid as a Tool in Neurobiology, 1978, Glutamine, Glutamate, and GABA, 1983; contbr. articles to profl. jours. Decorated officer Order of Can.; recipient citation, Am. Chem. Soc., 1958, Rsch. award, Clarke Inst., 1992, Lifetime Achievement award, Sci. Coun. B.C., 1995, Hon. Alumnus award, 1996, cert., Internat. Sci. Inst., 2001, medal of svc., Dr. Cam Coady Found., 2003. Fellow Can. Coll. Neuropsychopharmacology, Royal Soc. Can.; mem. Can. Biochem. Soc., Internat. Brain Rsch. Orgn., Internat. Soc. Neurochemistry, Soc. Neurosci., Am. Neurochem. Soc. (councilor 1979-83), North Pacific Soc. Neurology and Psychiatry (hon. fellow), Lychnos Soc., Sigma Xi, Phi Beta Kappa. Office: U BC Divsn Neurol Sci 2255 Wesbrook Mall Vancouver BC Canada V6T 1Z3 E-mail: mcgeer@interchange.ubc.ca.

MCGEER, JAMES PETER, research executive, consultant; b. Vancouver, B.C., Can., May 14, 1922; s. James Arthur and Ada Alice (Schwenger) McG.; m. Catherine Pearson Deas, June 22, 1948; children: Mary, Allison, James, Thomas. BA, U. B.C., 1944, MA, 1946, Princeton U., 1948, PhD, 1949; DSc, Queens U., Kingston, Ont., Can., 1996. Researcher Alcan R & D, Arvida, Que., Can., 1949-52, group leader, 1952-59, pilot plant dir., 1960-67; dept. head Alcan Smelters, Arvida, Que., Can., 1968-71, asst. div. head, 1972-73; mgr. tech. transfer Alcan Smelter Svcs., Montreal, Que., 1973-77; dir. rsch. Alcan Internat. Ltd., Kingston, Ont., Can., 1978-82, dir. lab., 1983-87; mng. dir. Ont. Ctr. Materials, Kingston, 1988—; cons. Materials & Mfg. Ont. Chmn. bd. Can. Rsch. Mgmt. Assn., Toronto, Ont., 1990-91, Welding Inst. Can., Mississauga, Ont., 1988-90, Can. U. Ind. Coun. Advanced Ceramics, Ottawa, Ont., 1986-88; dir. Metall. Soc., Pitts., 1987-89; Can. Coun. lectr. Am. Soc. Metals, 1985-86; disting. lectr. Can. Inst. Mining Metallurgy, 1987. Contbr. articles to profl. jours. Chmn. bd. Que. Assn. Protestant Sch. Bds., Montreal, 1968-70. Recipient Airey award Can. Inst. for Mining and Metallurgy, 1993, Forum award Xerox Can., 1994. Mem. Anglican Ch.

MCGEGAN, NICHOLAS, music director; b. Eng. Student, Cambridge U., Oxford U. Music dir. San Francisco's Phila. Baroque Orch., 1985—; artistic dir. Göttingen Handel Festival, Germany, 1990; prin. guest condr. Scottish Opera, 1992-98; prin. condr. Drottningholm Ct. Theatre, 1993-95; founder, dir., harpsichordist The Arcadian Acad. Guest condr. San Francisco, St. Louis, Houston, Detroit, Indpls., Minn., Nat. Symphony orchs., City of Birmingham Symphony Orch., Halle Orch., Acad. of St. Martin-in-the-Fields in Breat Britain, Montreal Symphony, Nat. Arts Ctr. Orch., Ottawa, Orchestra de la Suisse Romande, Jerusalem Symphony; condr. Hanover Band, Freiburg Baroque Orch., Orch. of the Age of Enlightment; condr. over 40 operas in Europe and U.S.

MC GEHEE, H(ARRY) COLEMAN, JR., bishop; b. Richmond, Va., July 7, 1923; s. Harry Coleman and Ann Lee (Cheatwood) McG.; m. June Stewart, Feb. 1, 1946; children: Lesley, Alexander, Harry III, Donald, Cary. BS, Va. Poly. Inst., 1947; JD, U. Richmond, 1949; MDiv, Va. Theol. Sem., 1957, DD, 1973. Bar: Va. 1949, U.S. Supreme Ct. 1954; ordained to ministry Episcopal Ch., 1957. Spl. counsel dept. hwys. State of Va., 1949-51, gen. counsel employment svc., 1951, asst. atty. gen., 1951-54; rector Immanuel Ch.-on-the-Hill, Va. Sem., 1960-71; bishop Diocese of Mich., Detroit, 1971-90. Adv. bd. Nicaraguan Network, Ctr. for Peace and Conflict Studies, Wayne State U.; bd. dirs. Mich. Religious Coalition for Abortion Rights, 1976-84; trustee Va. Theol. Sem., 1978-93; pres. Episc. Ch. Pub. Co., 1978-85. Columnist: Detroit News, 1979-85; weekly commentator pub. radio sta. WDET-AM, Detroit, 1984-90. Mem. Gov.'s Commn. on Status of Women, 1965-66, Mayor's Civic Com., Alexandria, 1967-68; sponsor Nat. Assn. for ERA, 1977-85; pres. Alexandria Legal Aid Soc., 1969-71; bd. dirs. No. Va. Fairhousing Corp., 1963-67; pres. Mich. Coalition for Human Rights, 1980-89 (Humanitarian award 2001); chmn. Citizens' Com. for Justice in Mich., 1983-84; sponsor Farm Labor Orgn. for Children, 1983-85; bd. dirs. Pub. Benefit Corp., Detroit, 1988-90, Mich. Citizens for Personal Freedom, 1989-92, Poverty and Social Reform Inst., Detroit, 1989—, Bread for the World, 1990-94, Ams. United for Separation of Ch. and State, 1990, ACLU Oakland County, Mich., 1991-94; co-chair Lesbian-Gay Found. Mich., 1991—. 1st lt. C.E., U.S. Army, 1943-46. Named Feminist of Yr., Detroit NOW, 1978, Person of Yr., Econ. Justice Commn. Mich., 1997; recipient Humanitarian award ACLU, 1984, Phillip Hart medal Mich. Women's Studies Assn., 1984, Sayre award for justice and peace Episc. Peace Fellowship, 1988, Spirit of Detroit award, 1989, Archbishop Romero award Mich. Labor Com., 1990, Brotherhood award AME Ch., Detroit, 1993, Ira Jayne award Detroit br. NAACP, 1993, Martin Luther King, Jr. award United Ch. of Christ, 1995, William Scarlett award Episc. Ch. Pub. Co., 1997, Humanitarian award Mich. Coalition for Human Rights, 2001. Mem.: Detroit Econ. Club (bd. dirs.). Episcopalian. Home: 1496 Ashover Dr Bloomfield Hills MI 48304-1215 Office: Diocese of Mich 4800 Woodward Ave Detroit MI 48201-1399

MCGEHEE, LARRY THOMAS, university administrator; b. Paris, Tenn., May 18, 1936; s. George Eugene and Margaret Elizabeth (Thomas) McG.; m. Elizabeth Hathhorn Boden, Aug. 26, 1961; children: Elizabeth Hathhorn, Margaret Thomas. BA, Transylvania Coll., 1958; BD, Yale U., 1963, MA, 1964, PhD, 1969. Dir., asst. v.p. for univ. relations U. Ala., 1966-68, exec. asst. to pres., 1968-69, exec. v.p., 1969-71; lectr., assoc. prof. dept. Am. studies, 1969-71, acad. v.p., 1971; chancellor U. Tenn., Martin, 1971-79; spl. asst. to pres. U. Tenn. Sys., Knoxville, 1979-82; v.p. coll., prof. religion Wofford Coll., Spartanburg, S.C., 1982—. Syndicated columnist Southern Seen, 1982—. Danforth fellow Yale U., 1960-66. Home: 1047 Woodburn Rd Spartanburg SC 29302-2867 Office: Wofford Coll 429 N Church St Spartanburg SC 29303-3663 E-mail: mcgeheelt@wofford.edu.

MCGEHEE, ROBERT B. energy executive; Grad., Nuclear Power Sch. and Submarine Sch., U.S. Naval Acad.; law degree, U. Tex. Atty. Wise Carter Child & Caraway, Jackson, Miss.; sr. v.p., gen. counsel Carolina Power & Light Co., 1997—99, exec. v.p., gen. counsel, chief adminstrv. officer, 1999—2000; pres., CEO Progress Energy Svc. Co., LLC, 2000—02; exec. v.p. Carolina Power & Light Co. and Fla. Progress Corp., 2000—, Progress Energy, Inc., Raleigh, NC, 2000—02, pres., COO, 2002—04, pres., CEO, chmn., 2004—. Lt. USN. Office: Progress Energy PO Box 1551 411 S Wilmington St Raleigh NC 27601-1748 E-mail: bob.mcgehee@pgnmail.com.

MCGEHEE, SHARON, school system administrator; Tchr. Ramona Elem. Sch.; prin. Berlyn Elem. Sch., Lehigh Elem. Sch.; with personnel svcs. Ontario-Montclair Sch. Dist., Calif., dir. certificated personnel and staff devel., asst. supt., dep. supt., 1998—2000, supt., 2000—. Office: Ont-Montclair Sch Dist 950 W D St Ontario CA 91762

MCGEORGE, DON W. retail executive; With Kroger Co., Cin., 1977, sr. v.p., 1997—2000, exec. v.p., 2000—03, pres., COO, 2003—. Office: Kroger Co 1014 Vice St Cincinnati OH 45202-1100

MCGEOUGH, ROBERT SAUNDERS, lawyer; b. Aug. 30, 1930; s. Edward James and Florence Isabelle (Saunders) McG.; m. Janet James, Nov. 24, 1961; children: Maureen, Michael, Molly. AB, Duke U., 1952; JD, U. Mich., 1959. Assoc. Hoppe, Frey, Hewitt & Milligan, Warren, Ohio, 1965-70, ptnr., 1970-98; of counsel Harrington, Hoppe & Mitchell, Warren, Ohio, 1999—. Dir. First Pl. Bank, 1973-2003; state trustee Jaycees, Warren, 1963; pres. Warren Exchange Club, 1965; pres. Children's Rehab. Ctr. Found., Warren, 1979, trustee, 1983-97; trustee First Fed. Cmty. Found., 1999—. Editor Lawyer's Desk Book, 1978, 98. Recipient award of merit Ohio Legal Ctr. Inst., 1978. Mem. Ohio State Bar Assn., Trumbull County Bar Assn. Republican. Avocation: golf. Home: 3264 Crescent Dr NE Warren OH 44483-6306 Office: Harrington Hoppe & Mitchel Ltd 108 Main Ave SW Ste 500 Warren OH 44481-1010 Office Phone: 216-392-1541. E-mail: BobMcGeo@webtv.com.

MCGETTIGAN, CHARLES CARROLL, JR., investment banker; b. San Francisco, Mar. 28, 1945; s. Charles Carroll McGettigan and Molly (Fay) McGettigan Pedley; m. Katharine Havard King, Nov. 1, 1975 (div. 1981); m. Meriwether Lewis Stovall, Aug. 6, 1983; 1 child, Meriwether Lewis Fay. AB in Govt., Georgetown U., 1966; MBA in Fin., U. Pa., 1969. Assoc., asst. v.p., v.p. Blyth Eastman Dillon, N.Y.C., 1970-75, 1st v.p., 1975-78, sr. v.p. San Francisco, 1978-80, Dillon, Read & Co., San Francisco, 1980-83; gen. ptnr. Woodman Kirkpatrick & Gilbreath, San Francisco, 1983-84; prin. corp. fin. Hambrecht & Quist, Inc., San Francisco, 1984-88; mng. dir., founder McGettigan, Wick & Co., Inc., San Francisco, 1988—; gen. ptnr., founder Proactive Ptnrs., L.P., San Francisco, 1990—, Proactive Investment Mgrs., L.P., San Francisco, 1991—. Gen. ptnr. Fremont Proactive Ptnrs., 1991—2001; bd. dirs. Cuisine Solutions, Inc., Alexandria, Va.; chmn. Modtech, Inc., Perris, Calif., Onsite Energy Corp., Carlsbad, Calif.; adv. dir. Chesapeake Ventures, Balt., 1984—94. Trustee St. Francis Meml. Hosp., San Francisco, 1980-86; mem. United San Francisco Rep. fin. com., 1983—, steering com., 1986—; adv. bd. dirs. Leavey Sch. Bus. Adminstrn., Santa Clara U., Calif., 1984-90. With USN, 1966. Mem. The Brook, Racquet and Tennis Club (N.Y.), The Pacific Union Club, Bohemian Club (San Francisco), San Francisco Golf Club, Burlingame Country Club (Hillsborough, Calif.), Boston (New Orleans), White's (London). Republican. Roman Catholic. Home: 3375 Clay St San Francisco CA 94118-2006 Office: McGettigan Wick & Co Inc 50 Osgood Pl San Francisco CA 94133-4622 Office Phone: 415-986-4433. E-mail: Chas@McGettigan-Wick.com.

MCGHEE, CARLA RENEE, professional basketball player; b. Peoria, Ill., Mar. 6, 1968; Degree in Sports Mgmt. with honors, U. Tenn., 1990. Basketball player USA Women's Nat. Team Olympics, 1996; profl. basketball player Orlando (Fla.) Miracle, 1999—.

MCGHEE, HERSCHEY, public relations executive, writer, poet; Cert. program, Diversitas N.Y., 1996; cert. program in pub. rels., NYU, 1996; cert. in profl. devel. legal svs., Holt Profl. Devel. Corp., 1998. Dir. office svs. Coun. U.S. and Italy, 1987—89; adminstr. corp. rels. ITT Corp., 1989—95; cons. Your Opportunities Untapped Pub. Rels., 1996; supr. word processing Stroock and Stroock and Lavan LLP, 1997—2000; CEO Pub. Rels Co., N.Y.C.; prodn. mgr. Document Techs., Inc., 2000; cons. Herschey McGhee Inc., 2000—. Former pub. Y.O.U. Create Newsletter; spkr. On Radio and Cable TV shows and at various orgns. which help youths.; seminar leader. Author (1 anthology and 4 books of poetry). Mem.: NAFE, Am. Women's Self-Defense Assn. Office: Park West Sta PO Box 20577 New York NY 10025 Office Phone: 917-903-2231. E-mail: herscheymcghee@aol.com.

MCGHIE, MICHAEL, real estate company executive; Cert. property mgr. Inst. Real Estate Mgmt., lic. real estate broker Mich. Joined Midwest Mgmt., Milford, Mich., 1978—, fin. supr., contr., dir. payroll svcs., exec. v.p., pres., 1986—. Office: Midwest Mgmt Ste 100 950 Corporate Office Dr Milford MI 48381*

MCGIBBON, MURRAY LEWIS JAMES, theater educator, theater director; b. Durban, Natal, South Africa, June 26, 1957; s. James William and Amelia Jean McGibbon; m. Ashley Peche Fisher, June 26, 1993; children: James William, Catherine Elizabeth. MFA, So. Ill. U., Carbondale, 1984—87. Higher Diploma in Education U. of Natal, Pietermaritzburg, 1979. Artistic dir. drama The Playhouse Co., Durban, South Africa, 1990—96; prof. acting, directing Ind. U., Bloomington, 1996—. Dir.: (numerous theatre productions). Recipient Young Artist of the Yr. award, South African Airways, 1989. Mem.: Internat. Brotherhood of Magicians. Office: Ind U 275 N Jordan Ave Bloomington IN 47405

MCGIBBON, PHYLLIS ISABEL, art educator, artist; b. Madison, Wis., Jan. 9, 1961; d. W. Henry and G. Louise McGibbon. BFA, U. Wis., 1983, MFA, 1988. Luther Gregg Sullivan vis. artist Wesleyan U., Middletown, Conn., 1989-91; asst. prof. art Pomona Coll., Claremont, Calif., 1991-94, Wellesley (Mass.) Coll., 1994-97, assoc. prof., 1997—. Artist residency Bemis Ctr. for Contemporary Art, Omaha, 1995, Millay Colony, Austerlitz, N.Y., 1996, Va. Ctr. Creative Arts, Sweet Briar, 1997. Solo art installations include Davison Art Ctr., Middletown, Conn., 1990, Orange County Ctr. for Contemporary Art, Santa Ana, Calif., 1992, Sushi Performance and Visual Art, Inc., San Diego, 1994, Davis Mus. and Cultural Ctr., Wellesley, 1996, John Michael Kohler Arts Ctr., Sheboygan, Wis., 1998. Recipient award Elizabeth Greenshields Found., Montreal, Can., 1991, award Western States Arts Found. NEA, 1992, award Art Matters, Inc., N.Y.C., 1994; fellow Kala Inst., Berkeley, Calif., 1992-93, individual artist fellow Nat. Endowment for Arts 1995. Mem. Coll. Art Assn., Am. Print Alliance. Office: Wellesley Coll Dept of Art Jewett Arts Ctr Wellesley MA 02481

MC GIFFERT, DAVID ELIOT, lawyer, former government official; b. Boston, June 27, 1926; s. Arthur Cushman and Elizabeth (Eliot) McG.; m. Enud De Kibedi-Varga, Jan. 21, 1966; children: Laura, Carola.; m. Nelse Greenway, Apr. 9, 1983. Student, U. Calif.-Berkeley, 1944; BA, Harvard U., 1949, LL.B., 1953; postgrad., Cambridge (Eng.) U., 1950. Bar: D.C. 1954. With firm Covington & Burling, Washington, 1953-55, 57-61, ptnr., 1969-77, 81—. Lectr. law U. Wis., 1956; asst. to sec. def. for legis. affairs Dept. Def., 1962-65, undersec. army, 1965-69, asst. sec. for internat. security affairs, 1977-81 Served with USNR, 1944-46. Mem. Am. Bar Assn., Council Fgn. Relations, Alpha Delta Phi. Clubs: Metropolitan (Washington). Office: Covington & Burling PO Box 7566 1201 Pensylvania Ave NW Washington DC 20044-7566 Home: 3113 38th St NW Washington DC 20016

MCGIFFERT, MICHAEL, retired history educator, editor; b. Chgo., Oct. 5, 1928; s. Arthur Cushman and Elisabeth (Eliot) McG.; m. Genevieve White Mischel, Aug. 13, 1960; m. Elizabeth Eastman, June 19, 1949 (div. 1960). BA, Harvard Coll., 1949; B.D., Yale U., 1952, PhD, 1958; postgrad., Union Theol. Sem., N.Y.C., 1949-50. Instr. history Colgate U., Hamilton, N.Y., 1954-55, 56-60, U. Md., College Park, 1955-56; asst. prof. history U. Denver, 1960-64, assoc. prof., 1964-69, prof. history, 1969-74; editor William and Mary Quar., Inst. Early Am. History and Culture, prof. history, Coll. William and Mary, Williamsburg, Va., 1972-97; ret. Author: The Higher learning in Colorado, 1964; editor: The Character of Americans, 1964 (rev. edit.), 1969, Puritanism and the American Experience, 1969, (with Robert A. Skotheim) American Social Thought, 1972, God's Plot: The Paradoxes of Puritan Piety, 1972, God's Plot: Puritan Spirituality in Thomas Shepard's Cambridge, 1994. Faculty rsch. grantee U. Denver, 1970, Coll. William and Mary, 1981-82, 89; rsch. fellow NEH, 1977-78. Mem. Am. Hist. Assn., Orgn. Am. Historians, Confr. of Hist. Jours. (pres.1987-89), Am. Antiquarian Soc., Mass. Hist. Soc. Home: 102 Old Glory Ct Williamsburg VA 23185-4914 Personal E-mail: mcgiff@widomaker.com.

MC GILL, ARCHIE JOSEPH, venture capitalist; b. Winona, Minn., May 29, 1931; s. Archibald Joseph and Anne (Lettner) McG.; m. Jeanne Sullivan, Mar. 17, 1974; children: Archibald Joseph, III, Mark E., Gregory P., Debora, Susan, Brian. BA in Econs., St. Mary's Coll., Winona, 1956. With IBM Corp., 1956-69, v.p. market ops., 1956-69; founder, pres. McGill Assocs., White Plains, 1970-73; dir. market mgmt. AT&T Co., 1973-78, v.p. bus. mktg., 1978-83; pres. Advanced Info. Systems Am. Bell, Inc., 1983; pres., chief exec. officer Rothschild Ventures, Inc., 1983; now pres. Chardonnay, Inc. Dir. various cos. Bd. dirs. Steadman/Hawkins Found. With USAF, 1951-54. Named Mktg. Statesman of Year Sales Execs. Club, 1978 Home and Office: 10216 E Venado Trl Scottsdale AZ 85262-2961 E-mail: archmgill@cox.net.

MCGILL, DAN MAYS, insurance business educator; b. Greenback, Tenn., Sept. 27, 1919; s. John Burton and Jane (Mays) McG.; m. Elaine Kem, June 22, 1952; children: Douglas Russell, Melanie Mays BA, Maryville Coll., 1940, LLD (hon.), 1982; MA, Vanderbilt U., 1941; PhD, U. Pa., 1947. Assoc.

prof. fin. U. Tenn., Knoxville, 1947-48; Julian Price assoc. prof. ins. U. N.C., Chapel Hill, 1948-51; assoc. prof. ins. U. Pa., Phila., 1952-56, Frederick H. Ecker prof. life ins., 1959-90. Trustee N.W. Mut. Life Ins. Co., Milw., 1978-90; bd. dirs. NRG Life Reassurance Corp., Phila., 1984-94, Phila. Reins. Corp., 1990—, Independence Blue Cross, 1990—; exec. dir. S.S. Huebner Found., 1954-75, 78-86, chmn., 1965-94; dir. rsch. Pension Rsch. Coun., 1952-90; chmn., mem. governing bd. Leonard Davis Inst. Health Econs., 1967-90; 1st chmn. adv. commn. Pension Benefit Guaranty Corp., 1975-78, mem. 1978-81. Author: An Analysis of Government Life Insurance, 1949, The Fundamentals of Private Pensions, 7th edit., 1996, Legal Aspects of Life Insurance, 1959, Fulfilling Pension Expectations, 1962, Life Insurance, 1967, Preservation of Pension Benefit Rights, 1972, others; editor: (with others) World Insurance Trends, 1959, others. Trustee Presbyn. Med. Ctr., Phila., 1987—96; chmn. Boettner Inst. Fin. Gerontology, 1993—2002; mem. retirement bd. Mass. Bay Transp. Authority, 1980—96; chmn. bd. pensions Presbyn. Ch. U.S.A., 1977—88; trustee Presbyn. Found. for Phila., 1996—2001. Maj. USAF, 1942—46, Maj. USAF, 1951—52. Recipient Disting. Alumni award Maryville Coll., 1962, Huebner Gold medal award Am. Coll., 1977, Gold medal Internat. Ins. Soc., 1987. Mem.: Am. Risk and Ins. Assn. (pres. 1959, Elizur Wright award 1955, 1981), Merion Cricket Club, Union League. Republican. Presbyterian. Avocations: music, travel, sports. Home: 50 Belmont Ave Bala Cynwyd PA 19004-2437

MCGILL, GILBERT WILLIAM, lawyer; b. Glen Cove, N.Y., Mar. 28, 1947; BS, L.I. U., 1972; JD, Hofstra U., 1975. Bar: N.Y. 1975, U.S. Dist. Ct. 1976, U.S. Supreme Ct. 1979. Pvt. practice, Huntington, N.Y., 1975-76; ptnr. Dunne & McGill, Huntington and Sea Cliff, N.Y., 1976-81; pvt. practice Sea Cliff, N.Y., 1981—. Citizens adv. com. North Shore Schs., Glen Head, N.Y., 1977-79, mem. local waterfront revitalization com. Town of Oyster Bay, 1988—; chmn. legal adv. com. Sea Cliff Civic Assn., 1978-79; adv. com. North Shore Republican Club, Glen Head, 1979-81; trsutee Sea Cliff Village Libr., 1980-86; trustee Angelo J. Melillo Ctr. for Mental Health, 1986—, pres., 1986—. Mem. ABA, N.Y. State Bar Assn., Nassau County Bar Assn., Nassau County Lawyers Assn., North Shore Lawyers Assn. (chmn. 1977-78), Sea Cliff Bus. Assn. (pres. 1979-85), Rotary (pres. Glen Head 1983-84, 97-99).

MCGILL, HENRY COLEMAN, JR., pathologist, educator, researcher; b. Nashville, Oct. 1, 1921; s. Henry Coleman and Thursa (Lowry) McG.; m. Cloace Laurite Perguson, Sept. 12, 1945; children: Margaret Ann, Laurilynn, Elizabeth Gail. BA, Vanderbilt U., 1943, MD, 1946. Intern Vanderbilt Hosp., Nashville, 1946-47; asst. prof. pathology La. State U. Med. Ctr., New Orleans, 1950-55, assoc. prof., 1955-61, prof., chmn. dept., 1961-66; prof. pathology U. Tex. Health Sci. Ctr., San Antonio, 1966-92, chmn. dept., 1966-72; sci. dir. S.W. Found. for Biomed. Rsch., San Antonio, 1978-92, sr. scientist, 1992-96, sr. scientist emeritus, 1996—. Contbr. articles to med. jours. Capt. M.C., U.S. Army, 1948-50. Mem. Phi Beta Kappa, Sigma Xi, Alpha Omega Alpha. Home: 4102 Fawnridge Dr San Antonio TX 78229-4212 Office: PO Box 760549 San Antonio TX 78245-0549 Office Phone: 210-258-9408. Business E-Mail: hmcgill@icarus.sfbr.org.

MCGILL, J. YANCEY, state legislator, real estate broker, homebuilder; b. Kingstree, S.C., Sept. 18, 1951; s. Frank H. and Peggy (Tomlinson) McG.; m. Pamela Jean Fennell, May 18, 1974; children: Lisa, John, Maggie. Student, The Citadel, hon. degree, 1994; student, Francis Marion Coll. Mem. S.C. Senate, Columbia, 1989—. Mem. agr. and natural resources com., fin. com., fish, game and forestry com., invitations com., rules com., transp. com. Chmn., deacon Kingstree 1st Bapt. Ch., 1987-88; past pres. Kingstreee Jaycees; mem. Kingstree Town Coun., 1976-79, mayor pro tem, 1978-79, mayor, 1984-88; bd. dirs. Waccamaw Regional Planning and Devel. Coun.; past chmn. Waccamaw Indsl. Revolving Loan Commn.; former mem. S.C. Dem. Com. Exec. Com.; mem. select com. Edn. Improvement Act; mem. Am. Legis. Exch. Coun.; bd. visitors Med. U. S.C., 1990-91. Named Legislator of Yr., S.C. Assn. Counties, 1993. Mem. Kingstree C. of C. (past pres.). Democrat. Office: 508 Gressette Bldg Columbia SC 29202

MCGILL, JAY, magazine publisher; With Hearst Magazines, 1979—; pub. Country Living, N.Y.C., 1993—97; v.p. pub. Popular Mechanics, 1997—2003; dir., digital integration Hearst Corp., 2001—03; senior v.p. and pub. SmartMoney, N.Y.C., 2003—. Office: Attn Jay McGill Hearst Mags 224 W 57th St New York NY 10019-3212 also: SmartMoney Mag 1755 Broadway New York NY 10019*

MCGILL, JENNIFER HOUSER, non-profit association administrator; b. Abingdon, Va., Mar. 3, 1957; d. Mason L. and Margaret Jane Houser; m. James B. McGill, July 15, 1978; children: Melissa Diane, Mark James. AA, Va. Highlands C.C., Abingdon, 1978; BA, U. S.C., 1980. Reporter, editor Sumter (S.C.) Daily ITEM, 1980-81; assoc. editor Sandlapper Mag., Columbia, S.C., 1981-82; membership editor Assn. for Edn. in Journalism/Mass Comm., Columbia, 1982-83, adminstrv. asst., 1984-85, exec. dir., 1985—. Mem. nat. steering com. Journalist-in-Space Project, Columbia, 1985-86; mem. exec. com. Coun. Nat. Journalism Orgns., 2003—; co-exec. dir. Coun. Comm. Assocs., 2003—. Mem. Lioness Club (3d v.p. 1990-91, 2d v.p. 1991-92). Avocations: reading, cooking, biking. Office: Assn Schs Journalism & Mass Comm 234 Outlet Pointe Blvd Columbia SC 29210-5667

MCGILL, JOHN J. radiologist; b. Denver, Nov. 26, 1965; BA, U. Calif., Berkeley, 1988; MD, Creighton U., Omaha, Nebr., 1992. Diplomate Am. Bd. Radiology. With Associated Radiologists, Ltd., Scottsdale, Ariz. Office: Associated Radiologists Ltd 1125 E Southern Ave # 300 Mesa AZ 85204-5011

MCGILL, JOHN KNOX, lawyer; b. Charlotte, N.C., Aug. 25, 1956; s. John Charles and Mabel (Hamilton) Mc.; m. Elizabeth Roxanne Bondurant. BS in Bus. cum laude, Erskine Coll., 1978; MBA, JD, U. N.C., 1982. Bar: N.C. 1983; CPA, N.C. Ptnr., tax atty. Garland & Alala, P.A., Gastonia, N.C., 1982-86; tax atty., pub. Blair, McGill & Co., Inc., Charlotte, N.C., 1986—. Chmn., bd. dirs. Blair, McGill & Co., Inc., Charlotte; bd. dirs., founder, Advanced Pension Systems, Inc., Charlotte. Tax editor: Dental Economics Mag., 1982—; editor-in-chief: (newsletter) The Blair, McGill Advisory; contbr. editor: (textbook) Contemporary Marketing (4th edition, 1983. Bd. trustees Erskine Coll., 1998—; treas. 1st Assoc. Reformed Presbyn. Ch., Gastonia, N.C., 1989-94, deacon, 1989-94, elder, 1995-98. Recipient Tax Law scholarship, Touche, Ross & Co., CPA's, 1982. Mem. ABA, N.C. Bar Assn., Am. Inst. CPA's, N.C. Assn. CPA's, Sertoma Club (Disting. Svc award, Kings Mt. N.C., 1983). Republican. Avocations: jogging, basketball, baseball, skiing, card/stamp collecting. Home: 905 Cloister Dr Gastonia NC 28056-6629 Office: Blair McGill & Co Inc 2810 Coliseum Centre Dr Ste 360 Charlotte NC 28217-4622

MCGILL, KENNETH, JR., mental health services professional; b. Paterson, N.J., Aug. 22, 1965; s. Kenneth and Shirley A. McG.;m. Barbara Joan, Dec. 27, 1989; children: Megan Elizabeth, Shannon Eileen BA, William Paterson Coll., 1989; MA in Edn., Seton Hall U., 1995; Ednl. Specialist, 1999. Social Worker N.J., cert. Hypnotherapist Am. Bd. Clin. Hypnotherapy, lic. Marriage and Family Therapist. Mental health worker Wayne (N.J.) Gen. Hosp., 1989-90; case supr. N.J. Superior Ct. Essex County, Newark, 1990-95; adj. prof. psychology William Paterson U., Wayne, 1995—; asst. dir. admissions, evalns., 1996-99; marriage and family therapist St. Mary's Counseling Svcs., Pompton Lakes, N.J., 1998—; owner, pres., therapist Bergen-Passaic Psychol. Assocs., LLC, North Haledon, N.J., 1999—. Bd. dirs. Apraxia Network Bergen County, Paramus, N.J., 2000—. Reviewer books. Asst. soccer coach North Haledon Soccer Assn., 2000. Mem. APA, ACA, Am. Assn Marriage and Family Counselors, Mental Health Assn. Passaic County (bd. dirs. 1993-96, 2000—), Assn. Christian Counselors, KC (1st, 2nd degree 1995, 3rd degree 1996, Knight of the Month 1997), Ancient Order Hibernians, Psi Chi. Democrat. Roman Catholic. Avocations: mountain biking, hiking, sketching, writing. Office: Bergen-Passaic Psychol Assocs LLC 552 High Mountain Rd North Haledon NJ 07508-2660 E-mail: mcgillkb@bellatlantic.net.

MCGILL, MAURICE LEON, financial executive; b. Malden, Mo., Aug. 22, 1936; s. William Howard and Iris (Phillips) McG.; m. Wanda Coral Wirt, Feb. 2, 1957; children— Melany, Melinda, William Shannon BS, U. Mo., 1958, MA, 1959. C.P.A., Mo., Iowa, Ariz. Mgr. Touche, Ross, Bailey & Smart, Kansas City, Mo., 1959-64; fin. v.p., treas. Iowa Beef Packers, Inc., Dakota City, Nebr., 1964-69; exec. v.p., treas. Spencer Foods, Inc., Iowa, 1969-71, also dir.; sr. v.p. Diamond Reo Trucks, Inc., Lansing, Mich., 1971-72; fin. v.p. Ariz. Colo. Land & Cattle Co., Phoenix, 1972-75; ptnr. Touche Ross & Co., Phoenix, 1975-81; exec. v.p. fin. and adminstrn., treas., bd. dirs. IBP, Inc., Dakota City, Nebr., 1981-89; pres., bd. dirs. Wirmac Corp., Garland, Tex., 1989—. Bd. dirs. Premium Std. Farms, Kansas City, Mo. Mem.: AICPA. Home: 3318 S Country Club Rd Garland TX 75043-1314 E-mail: mandwmcgill@msn.com.

MCGILL, ROBERT ERNEST, III, retired manufacturing company executive; b. San Francisco, Apr. 30, 1931; s. Robert Ernest and Madeleine Melanie (Ignace) McG.; m. Daphne Urquhart Driver, Apr. 26, 1958; children: Robert Ernest, Meredith Louise, Christina Elizabeth, James Alexander. BA, Williams Coll., 1954; MBA, Harvard U., 1956. With Morgan Stanley & Co. (investment bankers), N.Y.C., 1956-63; mem. fin. staff Air Products & Chems., Inc., Allentown, Pa., 1963-64, dir. corp. planning and devel., 1964-68; v.p. Gen. Interiors Corp., N.Y.C., 1968-70, exec. v.p., 1970-73; v.p. fin. Ethan Allen, Inc., Danbury, Conn., 1973-75; v.p. fin., sec. Dexter Corp., Windsor Locks, Conn., 1975-83, sr. v.p. fin. and adminstrn., 1983-88, exec. v.p., 1989-94; pres. Kettlebrook Ins. Co. Ltd., 1983-93, chmn., 1993-94; pres. Dexter Credit Corp., 1982-88; dir. Landmark Tech. Ptnrs., Inc. Bd. mgrs. Travelers Funds for Variable Annuities; trustee Travelers Mut. Fund. Trustee Assn. des Amis L'Abbaye Valmont, Atlanta Art Conservation Ctr.; pres. bd. trustees Williamstown Arts Conservation Ctr.; mem. vestry St. Johns Episcopal Ch., Williamstown. Home: 295 Hancock Rd Williamstown MA 01267-3005

MCGILL, STUART R. oil industry executive; b. Australia; BAChemE, DSChemE, Sydney U., Australia. Engr. prodn. dept. Esso Australia Ltd., 1969, engr., Longford, Long I. Point, Australia, Exxon Co. USA, Exxon Prodn. Rsch., Houston; mng. dir. Esso Prodn. Malaysia, Kuala Lumpur, 1980; dir. Esso Australia Ltd., 1983, chmn. and mng. dir., 1985; v.p. Exxon Co. Internat., 1988; CEO Esso Holding Co. Holland Inc., 1991, Esso B.V., 1991; exec. v.p. Exxon Co. Internat., 1994—2003, pres., 1998; v.p. ExxonMobil Corp., 1999—2003. Office: ExxonMobil Corp 800 Bell St Houston TX 77002

MCGILL, WILLIAM JAMES, JR., university official, writer; b. St. Louis, Mar. 25, 1936; s. William James Sr. and Ethel (Williams) McG.; m. Ellen Buck, June 18, 1960; children: Sara Louise, Susan Elizabeth, Alison Marcia. BA, Trinity Coll., 1957; MA, Harvard U., 1958, PhD, 1961, grad. Inst. Ednl. Mgmt., 1989; LHD (hon.), Lebanon Valley Coll., 1998. Instr. history Western Md. Coll., Westminster, 1960-62; asst. prof. history Alma (Mich.) Coll., 1962-68, assoc. prof., 1968-72; dean of coll. Washington & Jefferson Coll., Washington, Pa., 1972-75, prof. history, 1972-84; asst. dir., div. edn. programs NEH, Washington, 1984-86; v.p., dean faculty Lebanon Valley Coll., Annville, Pa., 1986-98, acting pres., 1987-88. Author: Maria Theresa, 1972, The Rock Springs Chronicles, 1999, George Herbert, R.S. Thomas and the Argument with God, 2003; contbr. 70 articles to profl. jours., 53 book revs., 19 short stories, numerous poems; poetry editor Spitball Mag., 1993—, mng. editor, 2000—. Assoc. to rector St. Luke's Episc. Ch., Lebanon, Pa., 1986-98; priest-in-charge St. George's Episc. Ch., Waynesburg, Pa., 1974-83; actor Washington Theater Wing, 1984-86, Gretna Playhouse, Mt. Gretna, Pa., 1987-90; bd. dirs. Lebanon County United Way, 1987-95, Gretna Prodns., Mt. Gretna, 1986-90, 91-92, Concertante, 1999-2001; trustee Penn Sch. Art and Design, 1992—. Mem. Phi Beta Kappa. Avocations: sailing, writing, acting. Home and Office: PO Box 333 Annville PA 17003-0333 E-mail: wjmcgill@earthlink.net.

MCGILL, WILLIS ALEXANDER, anesthesiologist; b. Cairo, July 1, 1941; s. Willis Alexander and Anne (McAuley) M.; m. Robin Louise Blake, Aug. 2, 1965; children: Margaret Anne McGill Mantz, Leslie Marie McGill Dale, Erin Suzanne. MD, U. Pitts., 1967. Cert. anesthesiology. Intern York Hosp., 1967-68; resident in anesthesiology Naval Hosp., Phila., 1970-73; fellow in pediatric anesthesiology Children's Hosp., Phila., 1973; attending anesthesiologist Children's Nat. Med. Ctr., Washington, 1976—, chmn., 1985-97. Prof. anesthesiology George Washington U. Sch. Medicine, 1990—; pres. Children's Faculty Assocs., Washington, 1987-88. Mem. AMA, Am. Soc. Anesthesiologists, MDDS CA, Acad. Anesthesiology (pres. 1991-92). Office: Childrens Nat Med Ctr 111 Michigan Ave NW Washington DC 20010-2916 E-mail: wmcgill@cnmc.org.

MC GILLICUDDY, JOHN FRANCIS, retired banker; b. Harrison, N.Y., Dec. 30, 1930; s. Michael J. and Anna (Munro) McG.; m. Constance Burtis, Sept. 9, 1954; children: Michael Sean, Faith Burtis Benoit, Constance Erin Mc Gillicuddy Mills, Brian Munro, John Walsh. AB, Princeton, 1952; LL.B., Harvard, 1955. With Mfrs. Hanover Trust Co. subs. Mfrs. Hanover Corp., N.Y.C., 1958-91, v.p., 1962-66, sr. v.p., 1966-69, exec. v.p., asst. to chmn., 1969-70, vice chmn., dir., 1970, pres., 1971-79, chmn., chief exec. officer, 1979-91; chmn. bd., chief exec. officer Chem. Banking Corp., N.Y.C., 1992-93, ret., 1994. Chmn. Wellchoice, Inc.; bd. dirs. Kelso, Inc. Bd. dirs. life trustee, chmn. emeritus N.Y. Presbyn. Hosp.; trustee emeritus Princeton U.; pres. Boy Scouts Am., Greater N.Y. Couns. Lt. (j.g.) USNR, 1955-58. Mem. Westchester Country Club (Rye, N.Y.), Blind Brook Club (Port Chester, N.Y.), Princeton Club (N.Y.C.), Augusta Nat. Golf Club (Ga.), Pine Valley Golf Club (N.J.), Laurel Valley Golf Club (Ligonier, Pa.), Seminole Golf Club (north Palm Beach, Fla.), Links Club (N.Y.C.), Sky Club (N.Y.C.). Roman Catholic. Office: JP Morgan Chase Corp 270 Park Ave New York NY 10017-2014

MCGILLIVRAY, DONALD DEAN, seed company executive, agronomist; b. Muscatine, Iowa, Aug. 28, 1928; s. Walter C. and Pearl E. McG.; m. Betty J. Anderson, June 24, 1951; children: Ann E., Jean M. BS in Agronomy, Iowa State U., 1950. Asst. mgr. Iowa, Minn., Wis. sect. Funk Seeds Internat., Belle Plaine, Iowa, 1965-69, mgr., 1969-70, mgr. hybrid corn ops. Bloomington, Ill., 1970-75, v.p. ops., 1976-82, pres., 1982-88; assoc. Smart Seeds, Inc., Bloomington, 1989—. Dir. U.S. Grains Coun., Washington, 1984-87. Bd. dirs. Ill. Agrl. Leadership Found., Macomb, 1985—, chmn. bd., 1990-2000; bd. dirs. Ill. Wesleyan Assocs., 1986-89, Ill. 4-H Found., 1996—; mem. adv. bd. Bro-Menn Hosp., 1985—, pres., 1989-90. Sgt. U.S. Army, 1951-53. Mem. Am. Seed Trade Assn. (bd. dirs. 1986-, divsn. chmn. 1978-79, 2d v.p. 1986-87, 1st v.p. 1987-88, pres. 1988-89), Am. Seed Rsch. Found. (bd. dirs. 1982-95, pres. 1984-87), Exch. Club, Masons.

MC GIMSEY, CHARLES ROBERT, III, anthropologist; b. Dallas, June 18, 1925; s. Charles Robert, Jr. and Ellen Randolph (Parks) McG.; m. Mary Elizabeth Conger, Dec. 20, 1949; children— Charles Robert, Brian Keith, Mark Douglass. Student, Vanderbilt U., 1942-43, U. of South, 1943-44; BA, U. N.Mex., 1949; MA, Harvard U., 1954, PhD, 1958. Instr. U. Ark., Fayetteville, 1957, asst. prof., 1958-62, assoc. prof., 1962-67, prof. anthropology, 1967-90, prof. emeritus, 1990—, chmn. dept., 1969-72; asst. curator U. Ark. Mus., 1957-59, dir., 1959-83, Ark. Archeol. Survey, 1967-90, dir. emeritus, 1990—. Cons. archeology U.S. GAO, 1979-87, U.S.-Internat. Com. on Monuments and Sites; Rep. to Internat. Com. on Archeol. Heritage Mgmt., 1988-95. Author: (with G.R. Willey) Monagrillo Culture of Panama, 1954, Mariana Mesa, 1980, Indians of Arkansas, 1969, Public Archeology, 1972, Archeology and Archeological Resources, 1973, (with H.A. Davis) The Management of Archeological Resources, 1977; assoc. editor Am. Antiquity, 1972-80; Co-editor (with H. A. Davis) Southeastern Museums Conf., 1964-73; Contbr. articles to profl. jours. Mem. Ark. Rev. Com., Historic Preservation Program, 1968-76; collaborator Nat. Park Service, 1971-74, adviser, 1974-77; mem. Com. on Recovery Archeol. Remains, 1971-78; mem. adv. bd. dirs. Red River Mus., 1975-76; mem. adv. bd. Am. Indian Archeol. Inst., 1975-80, Ark. Natural and Cultural Heritage Dept., 1976-90. Served to lt. (j.g.) USNR, 1943-47. Recipient Cert. Recognition State of Ark., 1990; rsch. grantee Am. Philos. Soc., Am. Acad. Arts and Scis., Andean Rsch. Inst., Nat. Park Service, NSF, Smithsonian Instn., Wenner-Gren Found.; rsch. fellow dept. archaeology U. Cambridge, 1985-86, assoc. mem. Darwin Coll., 1985— Fellow: Am. Anthrop. Assn.; mem.: Am. Assn. State and Local History (award of merit 1985), Am. Assn. Mus., Soc. Profl. Archeologists (founder, bd. dirs. 1976—79, pres. 1983—84, emeritus, life, Seiberling 1989, presidential recognition award 1997), Am. Soc. Conserv. Archeology (founding, outstanding contrib. 1980), Southeastern Mus. Conf. (coun. 1962—71, editor 1964—77), Ark. Archeol. Soc. (editor 1960—83, Preservationist 1989), Soc. Am. Archeology (pres. 1974—75, Distinguished Serv. 1975, excellence in cultural resource mgt. 1995), Registered Prof. Archeologists. Home: 435 W Hawthorn St Fayetteville AR 72701-1935 Office: Ark Archeol Survey 2475 N Hatch Ave Fayetteville AR 72704-5590

MCGINITY, JAMES W. pharmacy educator; BPharm, U. Queensland, 1967; PhD, U. Iowa, 1972. Johnson & Johnson Centennial chair in pharmacy U. Tex., Austin. Office: U Tex Coll Pharmacy Austin TX 78712-1157

MCGINLEY, JACK L. healthcare company executive; B in Mktg. Adminstrn., U. N.D. With Baxter Healthcare, 1970—, various sales and mktg. positions, v.p. Baxter Can., 1982, gen. mgr. Baxter U.K., 1984, v.p. mktg. and mfg. Baxter's World Trade Corp., pres. Baxter Japan, pres. drug adminstn. divsn., corp. v.p., pres. IV systems divsn., group v.p., group v.p. IV systems/med. products. Office: RoundTable Healthcare Partners 272 East Deerpath Road Suite 350 Lake Forest IL 60045

MCGINLEY, JOHN REGIS, JR., lawyer; b. Pitts., Nov. 26, 1943; s. John R. and Marie E. (Rooney) McGinley. BS, St. Bonaventure U., 1965; JD, Duquesne U., 1968. Bar: Pa. 1968, U.S. Dist. Ct. (we. dist.) Pa. 1968, U.S. Ct. Appeals (3d cir.) 1973, U.S. Supreme Ct. 1983. Asst. dist. atty. Allegheny County, Pa., 1960-70, ptnr. Eckert Seamans Cherin & Mellott, assoc. Duff Grogan & Doyle & Duff, Grogan Graffam, Pitts., 1970—71; chmn. Grogan, Graffam, McGinley, 1971—2002; ptnr. Eckert Seaman Cherin & Mellott, 2002—. Mem. disciplinary bd. Pa. Supreme Ct.; mem., chmn. Pa. Ind. Regulatory Rev. Commn.; adj. prof. law Duquesne U. Sch. Law. Contbr. Duquesne U. Law Rev., 1968, articles to legal jours. Chmn., trustee Mercy Hosp. Found., Pitts. Mercy Health Sys., Pitts. Mercy Hosp., St. Bonaventure U. Fellow: Am. Coll. Trial Lawyers; mem.: ABA, Duquesne U. Law Alumni (pres. 1998), Acad. Trial Lawyers, Allegheny County Bar Assn., Pa. Bar Assn. Office: 4th Fl US Steel Tower 600 Grant St Pittsburgh PA 15219 Office Phone: 412-566-6000. E-mail: jmcginley@eckertseamons.com.

MCGINLEY, PAUL ANTHONY, JR., lawyer; b. Allentown, Pa., Apr. 24, 1948; s. Paul A. Sr. and Mary (McGurl) McG.; m. Deborah C. Reinhart; children: Paige, Laura, Paul Anthony III, Jonathan. AB, Princeton U., 1970; JD, Georgetown U., 1974. Bar: Pa. 1974, U.S. Dist. Ct. (ea. dist.) Pa. 1974, U.S. Supreme Ct. 1987. Assoc. Gross & Brown, Allentown, 1974-76; asst. pub. defender Lehigh County, Allentown, 1976-77, asst. county solicitor, 1977-78; ptnr. Gross, McGinley & McGinley, Allentown, 1976-83, Gross, McGinley, McGinley & LaBarre, Allentown, 1983-86, Gross, McGinley & LaBarre, Allentown, 1986-87, Gross, McGinley, LaBarre & Eaton, Allentown, 1987—. Mem. legal affairs com. Mag. Pubs. Am., 1994—; chmn. hearing com. disciplinary bd. Supreme Ct. of Pa., 1986-90, 1997-2003. Bd. dirs. Swain Sch., Allentown, 1984-89, Cedar Crest Coll. Bd. Assocs., Allentown, 1986-88; trustee Allentown YWCA, 1985-88. Mem. ABA, Pa. Bar Assn., Lehigh County Bar Assn. (bd. dirs. 1978-84, pres. 1987), Pa. Trial Lawyers Assn., Allentown-Lehigh County C. of C., Princeton Quadrangle Club (bd. dirs.), Velodrome Fund (dir., sec. 1995—), Rodale Inst. (dir. 1998—), Rodale Inc. (asst. sec. 1999—, gen. counsel, 2000-). Democrat. Roman Catholic. Avocations: skiing, tennis. Office: Gross McGinley LaBarre & Eaton 33 S 7th St Allentown PA 18101-2436 Office Phone: 610-820-5450.

MCGINN, BERNARD JOHN, religious educator; b. Yonkers, N.Y., Aug. 19, 1937; s. Bernard John and Catherine Ann (Faulds) McG.; m. Patricia Ann Ferris, July 10, 1971; children: Daniel, John. BA, St. Joseph's Sem., Yonkers, N.Y., 1959; Licentiate in Sacred Theology, Gregorian U., Rome, 1963; PhD, Brandeis U., 1970. Diocesan priest Archdiocese N.Y., N.Y.C., 1963-71; prof. U. Chgo., 1969—, Naomi Shenstone Donnelly prof., 1992—2003, emeritus, 2003—. Program coord. Inst. for Advanced Study of Religion, Divinity Sch., U. Chgo., 1980-92. Author: The Calabrian Abbot, 1985, Meister Eckhart, 1986, Foundations of Mysticism, 1991, Growth of Mysticism, 1994, Antichrist, 1994, Flowering of Mysticism, 1998; editor: (series) Classics of Western Spirituality, 1978, (book) God and Creation, 1990. Fellow Medieval Acad. Am., Am. Acad. Arts and Scis. Home: 5701 S Kenwood Ave Chicago IL 60637-1718 Office: U Chgo Divinity Sch 1025 E 58th St Chicago IL 60637-1509 Business E-Mail: bmcginn@uchicago.edu.

MCGINN, CHERIE M. secondary school educator; b. Oil City, Pa., Feb. 5, 1949; d. Rendall Baxter amd Helen Joyce (Kunselman) Agnew; 1 child from previous marriage, Joshua Edward; m. Stephen James McGinn, Jan. 1, 1983; 1 child, Kathleen Erin. BS, Clarion (Pa.) U., 1971. Cert. secondary tchr., Md. Grad. asst. Clarion U., 1971—72; tchr. Montgomery County Pub. Schs., 1972—. Chmn. Montgomery Blair H.S., Silver Spring, Md., 1994—; program dir. G.B.T.L.A., Inc., 2002—; cons. curriculum, Upper Marlboro, Md.; panelist Odyssey 1984, Excellence in Edn., Md. Humanities Coun., Balt., 1984; vol. reader grant proposal Coun. for Basic Edn., fellow, 1983, 91, NEH, Washington, 1984—. Fellow NEH, 1989, 92, 95, 2000. Mem.: NEA, ASCD, Montgomery County Educators Assn., Md. Tchrs. Assn., Montgomery County Social Studies Coun., Md. Social Studies Assn., Nat. Coun. for Social Studies, U.S. Capitol Hist. Soc. Democrat. Unitarian Universalist. Home: 14228 Rutherford Rd Upper Marlboro MD 20774-8564 Office: Montgomery Blair HS 51 University Blvd E Silver Spring MD 20901-2451 E-mail: Cherie_McGinn@fc.mcps.k12.md.us.

MCGINN, DANIEL F. journalist; b. Flemington, N.J., Oct. 23, 1970; 2 children. BS, Boston Coll., 1993; MBA, Auburn U., 2000. Nat. corr. Newsweek, Boston, 1999—. Office: Newsweek 800 Boylston St Ste 1525 Boston MA 02199

MCGINN, DANIEL G. public relations executive; B in Congl. Studies, Georgetown U. Staff mem. for 2 W.Va. congressmen House Ways and Means Com.; founder Ryan McGinn, 1987—98; dep. chmn. Weber Pub. Rels. Worldwide, Cambridge, 1998; pres. & CEO The McGinn Group, 2001—. Founder, "Cause for Celebration," provides birthday parties to homeless and needy children. Office: The McGinn Group Ste 901 2300 Clarendon Blvd Arlington VA 22201

MCGINN, DENNIS VINCENT, career officer; b. Attleboro, Mass. m. Kelly Harris; children: Susan, John, David, Daniel. Grad., U.S. Naval Acad., 1967. Commnd. ensign USN, 1967, advanced through grades to vice adm., 1998; served in combat deployments USS Ranger; landing signal officer, weapons officer Squadron 113; ops. & maintenance officer Attack Squadron 146 USS Constellation; exec. officer USS Coral Sea; air warfare officer VX-5, China Lake, Calif.; chief test pilot strike directorate Naval Air Test Ctr., Patuxent River, Md.; chief naval ops. fellow Strategic Studies Group; chief info. sys., chief negotiator Supreme Hdqs. Allied Powers, Europe, Casteau, Belgium; commdg. officer Light Attack Weapons Sch., Attack Squadron 27, F/A-18 Replacement Air Group Strike Fighter Squadron 125, USS Ranger, 1991-93; commdr. Carrier Group 1 Pacific Fleet Carrier Battle Groups; dir. Air Warfare Divsn. Office Chief Naval Ops., 1996-98; comdr. U.S. Navy Third Fleet, 1998-2000, DCNO Warfare Requirements and Programs, 2000—02. Decorated Def. Superior Svc. Medal, 2 Legion Merit awards, DFC, DSM, others. Office: OPNAV N7 2000 Navy Pentagon Washington DC 20350-2000

MCGINN, RICHARD A. telecommunications company executive; Bachelor's degree, Grinnell Coll. With Ill. Bell, 1969; exec. positions internat. and computer sys. groups AT&T, 1978, CEO network sys.; CEO, pres. Lucent Techs., chmn., CEO, 1997-2000. Bd. dirs. Lucent Techs., Oracle Corp., Am. Express Co. Bus. Coun. Office: Lucent Technologies 600 Mountain Ave New Providence NJ 07974-2008

MCGINN, TERENCE JAMES, business consultant, minister; b. Rochester, N.Y., Oct. 18, 1950; s. James Edward III and Diane Edwina (Jewell) Ging; m. Kathie Jo Stirk, June 26, 1976 (div. 1984); 1 child, John F. Terris. BA, St. John

Fisher Coll., 1972; MDiv, Colgate Rochester Div. Sch., 1975; PhD, U. Mich., 1986, MBA, 1995. Ordained to ministry Am. Bapt. Ch., 1976. Campus min. Am. Bapt. Campus Found., Ann Arbor, Mich., 1980-84; Employee Assistance Prog. mgr. NBD Bank, Detroit, 1988-90, regional mgr. human resources, 1991-93; adj. faculty U. Mich., Ann Arbor, 1990—; pastor Northside Cmty. Ch., Ann Arbor, 1992—2001; cons. Career Directions, Ann Arbor, 1994—, Orion Internat., Ann Arbor, 1996—. Bd. dirs. Eden Found., Fairmount, Ind. Avocations: vocal performance, Gaelic studies. Home: 300 Briarcrest Dr Apt 147 Ann Arbor MI 48104-6762 Office: Orion Internat 101 N Main St Ste 850 Ann Arbor MI 48104-1491

MCGINNIES, ELLIOTT MORSE, psychologist, educator; b. Buffalo, Sept. 19, 1921; s. Elliott Morse and Mabel Christina (Hussong) McG.; m. Bessie Yeh, Jan. 27, 1967; children: Michelle, Lisa, Amy. BA, SUNY-Buffalo, 1943; MA, Brown U., 1944; PhD, Harvard U., 1948. Teaching fellow Harvard U., 1944-47; asst. prof. U. Ala., 1947-52; assoc. prof., then prof. U. Md., 1952-70; prof., chmn. dept. psychology Am. U., 1970-86, prof. emeritus, 1987—; vis. scholar U. Calif., Berkeley, 1987-88; Fulbright prof. Nat. Taiwan U. With AUS, 1943. Fellow Am. Psychol. Assn.; mem. Eastern Psychol. Assn., Psychonomic Soc., Sigma Xi. Author: Social Behavior: A Functional Analysis, 1970, The Reinforcement of Social Behavior, 1971, Attitudes, Conflict and Social Change, 1972, Perspectives on Social Behavior, 1994. Office: Am Univ Dept Psychology 4400 Massachusetts Ave NW Washington DC 20016-8001

MCGINNIS, BARRY EUGENE, music educator, musician; s. Calvin G. and Martha S. McGinnis; m. Amy McGinnis. BS, Towson State U., Md., 1984—91; MusM - Woodwind Specialist, East Carolina U., Greenville, N.C., 1991—93; D of Musical Arts - Saxophone Performance, U. Ga., Athens, 1993—2002. Instr. of music Ga. Coll. & State U., Milledgeville, Ga., 1995—97; instr., music Piedmont Coll., Demorest, Ga., 1997—2000; vis. asst. prof., music Adams State Coll., 2000—01, instr., music, 2001—02; asst. prof., music, dir. woodwinds, dir. jazz combo Newberry Coll., SC, 2002—. Author: (profl. journal articles) Nat. Assn. of Coll. Wind and Percussion Instructors. Mem.: S.C. Band Dirs. Assn., S.C. Music Educators Assn., Music Educators Nat. Conf., College Music Soc., Nat. Assn. of Coll. Wind and Percussion Instructors, Internat. Clarinet Assn., North Am. Saxophone Alliance, Delta Omicron, Pi Kappa Lambda, Kappa Kappa Psi. Home: 763 Pope St Apt D3 Newberry SC 29108 Office: Newberry College Music Department 2100 College St Newberry SC 29108 Office Phone: 803-321-5178. Personal E-mail: barry.mcginnis@newberry.edu.

MCGINNIS, CHARLES IRVING, civil engineer; b. Kansas City, Mo., Jan. 31, 1928; s. Paul Sherman and Sidney (Bacon) McG.; m. Shirley Ann Meyer, Nov. 5, 1955; children: Gail B., Ann K., James P. BS, Tex. A & M Coll., 1949, M.Engring., 1950; grad., Army Engr. Sch., 1955, Command and Gen. Staff Coll., 1959, Armed Forces Staff Coll., 1962, Army War Coll., 1969. Registered profl. engr., Tex., Mo. Enlisted as pvt. U.S. Army, 1945, advanced through grades to maj. gen., 1976; area engr. Ethiopia and Somalia, 1962-65; dist. engr., 1969-71; dir. engring. and constrn. bur. Panama Canal Co., 1971-72, v.p., 1972-74; lt. gov. C.Z., 1972-74; div. engr. southwestern div. C.E., Dallas, 1974-77; dir. civil works Office Chief of Engrs. U.S. Army, Washington, 1977-79; civil engr., 1979—; exec. v.p. Fru-con Corp.; pres. Fruco Engrs., Inc., 1983-87; assoc. dir. Constrn. Industry Inst. U. Tex., 1987-93, sr. lectr. civil engring. dept., 1992-97; vice chmn. chem. weapons stockpile com. NRC, 2000—04. Vis. com. dept. civil engring. MIT, 1978-81; mem. Mississippi River Commn., 1975-77, Bd. Engrs. for Rivers and Harbors, 1975-77; chmn. water policy task force NSPE, 1979-81. Chmn. Combined Fed. Campaign coordinating com., C.Z., 1972-74; pres. C.Z. coun. Boy Scouts Am., 1973-74; mem. exec. bd. St. Louis area coun., 1983-87, Capitol area coun., 1987-90, Stonewall Jackson area coun., 1999—; mem. com. mgmt. Balboa YMCA, 1973-74; trustee C.Z. United Way, 1972-74. Decorated D.S.M., Legion of Merit with oak leaf cluster, Joint Svcs. Commendation medal, U.S. Army Commendation with oak leaf cluster, Chuong My medal 1st class Vietnam; named Disting. Grad. Civil Engring. Dept., Tex. A&M U., 2002. Fellow ASCE, Soc. Am. Mil. Engrs. (past pres. Twin Cities post and Panama post); mem. Assn. U.S. Army, Mil. Order of the World Wars, Tau Beta Pi, Chi Epsilon. Address: 50 Gooseneck Ln Charlottesville VA 22903-9712 *The simple four-part philosophy that has well served three generations of my family requires an uncompromising commitment to honesty in all things, industry, concentration on the job and on personal objectives, and economy of all resources, both natural and man-made.*

MCGINNIS, DAVE, former professional football coach; b. Independence, Kansas, Aug. 7, 1951; Attended, Tex. Christian U. Freshmen coach Tex. Christian U., 1973—74, defensive backfield coach, 1982; grad. asst. Missouri U., 1975, def. backs coach, 1976—77; secondary coach Ind. State U., 1978; defensive ends, linebackers coach Kansas State U., 1983—85; linebackers coach Chgo. Bears, 1986—95; defense coord. Ariz. Cardinals, 1996—2000, coach, 2000—03. Avocations: travel, golf, jazz, reading.

MCGINNIS, JAMES MICHAEL, physician; b. Columbia, Mo., July 12, 1944; s. Leland Glenn and Lillian Ruth (Mackler) McG.; m. Patricia Anne Gwaltney, Aug. 4, 1978; children— Brian, Katherine AB, U. Calif., Berkeley, 1966; MA, MD, UCLA, 1971; M.P.P., Harvard U., 1977. House officer in internal medicine Boston City Hosp., 1971-72; internat. med. officer HEW, 1972-74; dir. Office for Asia and Western Pacific, 1974-75; state coordinator smallpox eradication program WHO, India, 1974-75; fellow Harvard Center for Community Health and Med. Care, Boston, 1976-77; cons. to sec. HEW, Washington, 1977, dep. asst. sec. for health, dir. office disease prevention, 1977-95, asst. surgeon gen., 1980-95, acting dir. office of rsch. integrity, 1992-93; scholar-in-residence NAS, Washington, 1995-99; sr. cons. Robert Wood Johnson Found., Princeton, 1996-99, sr. v.p., dir. Health Grp., 1999—2004, counselor to pres., 2004—. Instr. medicine George Washington U. Med. Sch., 1973-75; adj. prof. pub. policy Duke U., 1979-81, 99—; chair, sec. task force on smoking and health; chair exec. com. HHS Environ. Health Policy Com.; mem. U.S. Japan Leadership program; chair World Bank/European Commn. Task Force on Reconstrn. of Health Sector, Bosnia, 1996-97; sr. scholar Assn. of Acad. Health Ctrs., 1997-99. Mem. editl. bd. Jour. Med. Edn., 1975-78, Jour. Preventive Medicine, 1987—, Jour. Health Promotion, 1992-98; editor-in-chief: Healthy People, Healthy People 2000, Surgeon General's Report on Nutrition and Health, Determining Risks to Health. Bd. dirs. United Way of Nat. Capital. With USPHS U.S. Army, 1972—75, with USPHS U.S. Army, 1977—95. Recipient Arthur S. Flemming Pub. Svc. award, 1979, USPHS Disting. Svc. medal, 1989, Surgeon Gen.'s medallion, 1995, Fed. Profile in Leadership award, 1989, Wilbur Cohen award, 1995, award for excellence APHA, 1995, Health Leader of Yr. award, 1996. Fellow Am. Coll. Epidemiology, Am. Coll. Preventive Medicine; mem. Inst. Medicine/Nat. Acad. Scis., NIH Office: PO Box 2316 Princeton NJ 08543 Office Phone: 202-293-4296.

MCGINNIS, MICHAEL BOYD, chemistry professor; b. Balt., Mar. 3, 1970; s. Phyllis Lee (Miller) McG.; m. Maryann Lampart, Oct. 23, 1993. BS in Chem., Elizabethtown Coll., 1992; PhD in Organic Chemistry, U. Tenn., 1997. Postdoctoral rsch. assoc. U. Tenn., Knoxville, 1997, instr. chemistry, 1997; assoc. prof. chemistry, faculty assoc. Ga. Coll. and State U., Milledgeville, 1997—. Contbr. to profl. jours. Instr. ARC, Milledgeville, 1997—; active in various sci. fairs; bd. dirs., exec. dir. Ga. Jr. Acad. Sci. Recipient Sci. Outreach award, Hoechst Celanese Corp., 1996, Excellence in Tchg. award, Ga. Jr. Acad. Sci. Mem.: Am. Chem. Soc. (pub. outreach, mid. Ga. chair younger chemists com.), Sigma Xi. Democrat. Methodist. Avocations: whitewater canoeing, kayaking. Home: 1307 Clack Rd Madison GA 30650-4812 Office: Ga Coll and State U Dept Chemistry and Physics Milledgeville GA 31061 Office Phone: 478-445-2989. Business E-Mail: michael.mcginnis@gcsu.edu.

MCGINNIS, PATRICIA GWALTNEY, nonprofit organization executive; b. Goldsboro, N.C., July 19, 1947; d. Thomas McKim Gwaltney and Patricia Anne (Watkins) Schools; m. James Michael McGinnis, Aug. 4, 1978; children: J. Brian, Katherine B. BA, Mary Washington Coll., 1969; MPA, Harvard U., 1975. Dir. spl. studies U.S. Dept. Commerce, Washington, 1975-76; prof. staff mem. U.S. Senate Budge Com., Washington, 1976-77; dep. assoc. dir. U.S. Office Mgmt. and Budget, Washington, 1977-81; sr. cons. Cresap, McCormick and Paget, Inc., Washington, 1981-82; prin. The FMR Group, Inc., Washington, 1982-94; pres., CEO Coun. for Excellence in Govt., Washington, 1994—. Mem. exec. alumni coun. Kennedy Sch. Govt., Harvard U., Cambridge, Mass., 1992-96; dir. Primark Corp., Waltham, Mass., 1995-2000; mem. assoc. coun. George Washington Sch. Bus. and Pub. Adminstrn., 1996-99; bd. dirs. Brown Shoe Co., St. Louis, Imagitas, Inc., Newton, Mass.; bd. visitors U. Md. Sch. Pub. Affairs; dir. Logistics Mgmt. Inst., McLean, Va. Contbr. articles to profl. jours. Fellow: Nat. Acad. Pub. Adminstrn. Office: Coun for Excellence in Govt 1301 K St NW Ste 450W Washington DC 20005-3397

MCGINNIS, ROBERT E. lawyer; b. Caldwell, Ohio, May 1, 1931; s. Earl Peregoy and Mary Ethel (Richner) McG.; m. Jane Ann Lindenmeyer, Sept. 12, 1953; children: Sharon Ann, David E. BA, Ohio Weslayan U., 1952; JD summa cum laude, Ohio State U., 1954. Bar: Ohio 1954, Calif. 1956. Asst. judge advocate USAF, 1954-56; sr. ptnr. Luce, Forward, Hamilton, & Scripps, San Diego, 1956—. Counsel to pub. utilities, pub. agys., savs. and loan instns., ins. cos. and contractors. Trustee Wesley Meth. Ch., San Diego, Fine Arts Soc., First Meth. Ch., La Mesa, Calif.; counsel Kensington Community Ch.; dir. San Diego Opera Assn., corp. sec., v.p. Mem. Order of Coif. Republican. Mem. United Ch. Christ. United Ch.Of Christ. Office: Luce Forward Hamilton & Scripps 600 W Broadway Ste 2600 San Diego CA 92101-3372 E-mail: rmcginnis@luce.com.

MCGINNIS, ROBERT WILLIAM, electronics company executive; b. Modesto, Calif., Oct. 31, 1936; s. George Crawford and Lola May (Provis) McG.; m. Sondra Elaine Hurley, Mar. 1, 1964; children: Michael Fredrick, Traci Anne, Patrick William. BSEE with highest honors, U. Calif., Berkeley, 1962; postgrad., NYU, 1962-63. Mem. tech. staff Bell Tel. Labs., Murray Hill, NJ, 1961—63; devel. engr., engring. mgr., product mgr., ops. mgr. Motorola Semicondr. Group, Phoenix, 1963—73, ops. mgr. for hybrid circuits group comm. divsn. Ft. Lauderdale, Fla., 1973—76, solar ops. mgr., 1976—79; v.p., gen. mgr. Photowatt Internat., Inc., Tempe, Ariz., 1979—83; gen. mgr. SAFT Electronic Sys. Divsn., 1983—85; pres. Safe Power Sys., Inc., 1985—88; gen. mgr. advanced energy sys. Acme Electric Corp., 1988—93; product mgr. energy products divsn. Motorola Worldwide, Plantation, Fla., 1993—97, Motorola, Lawrenceville, Ga., 1993—97; quality dir. computer group Motorola Computer Group, Tempe, 1997—2002. Mem. Ariz. Solar Energy Commn., 1977-83; chmn. photovoltaic subcom. Am. Nat. Stds. Inst., 1978-83; mem. coordinating coun. Solar Energy Rsch. Inst. Stds., 1977-82. Contbr. articles to profl. jours. With USNR, 1955-58. Mem. Phi Beta Kappa, Tau Beta Pi, Eta Kappa Nu. Republican. Methodist. Home: 5771 W Gail Dr Chandler AZ 85226 Personal E-mail: rmcginnis2002@yahoo.com.

MCGINNIS, W. PATRICK, diversified company executive; BA in Political Science, Univ. Denver, 1970; MBA, Washington Univ, St. Louis, 1972. With Ralston Purina (now Nestle Purina), St. Louis, 1972—; dir. mktg, cons. prod. Ralston Purina Internat., 1978—80; exec. v.p., dir., grocery products Canadian div. Ralston Purina Co., Canada, 1980—83, div. v.p., dir. mktg., grocery products, 1983—84; pres., COO, grocery products group Ralston Purina, St. Louis, 1989—92; pres., CEO, grocery products group Ralston Purina Co., St. Louis, 1992—99, pres., CEO, 1999—2001, Nestle Purina, St. Louis, 2001—; corp. v.p., exec. v.p. Ralston Purina, St. Louis, 1984—89. Bd. dir Brown Shoe Co. Recipient Disting. Alumni Award, Olin Sch Bus., Washington Univ., 1993. Office: Nestle Purina Co Checkerboard Sq Saint Louis MO 63164-0001*

MCGINTY, BRIAN DONALD, lawyer, author; b. June 22, 1937; s. Donald Bruce and Natalia Vallejo (Haraszthy) M. AB, U. Calif., Berkeley, 1959, JD, 1962. Bar: Calif. 1963. Assoc. Twohig, Weingarten & Haas, Seaside, Calif., 1962-63; ptnr. Weingarten & McGinty, Seaside, Calif., 1963-70; sole practice Monterey, Calif., 1970-73, San Francisco, 1973-83; writer, editor Matthew Bender & Co., San Francisco, Oakland, Calif., 1984-93. Author: Haraszthy at the Mint (Famous Calif. Trials Series), 1975, The Palace Inns, 1978, We the People, 1987, Strong Wine: The Life and Legend of Agoston Haraszthy, 1998; contbg. author: The Craft of the Essay, Historical Times Illustrated Encyclopedia of the Civil War, Portrait of America, 5th edit., 1990, California Real Estate Law and Practice, California Forms of Pleading and Practice, California Legal Forms, California Insurance Law, California Probate Law and Practice, California Public Agency Law and Practice, California Wills and Trusts; editor: Napa Wine (Rounce and Coffin Club award 1975), 1974; contbr. articles to profl. jours. Recipient Excellence in Writing award Nat. Hist. Soc., 1976, Editor's award for Hist. Scholarship, Sonoma County Hist. Soc., 1999.

MC GINTY, JOHN MILTON, architect; b. Houston, Apr. 24, 1935; s. Milton Bowles and Ruth Louise (Dreaper) McG.; m. Juanita Jones, May 4, 1957; children: Christopher Harold, Jacqueline Ruth McGinty Carlson. BS, Rice U., 1957; M.F.A., Princeton U., 1961. With archtl. firm Barnes, Landes & Goodman, Austin, Tex., 1957-58, Ingram & Harris, Beaumont, Tex., 1958-59; prin. McGinty Partnership, Architects, Inc., Houston, 1961-89, City Assocs., Inc., 1979-91, Bovay-McGinty, Inc., engrs. & architects, Houston, 1989-91; founder, pres. Am. Constrn. Investigations Inc., Houston, 1991-2000. Instr. archtl. design U. Houston, 1965-67; White House fellow, asst. to Sec. of Interior, 1967-68; vis. prof. architecture Rice U., 1969-70 Named Disting. Alumnus Rice U., 1986. Fellow AIA (mem. U.S. delegation to USSR 1972, pres. Houston chpt. 1973, nat. pres. 1977) Home: 1650 County Rd 312 Palacios TX 77465 Office: Am Constrn Investigations Ste 200 602 Sawyer St Houston TX 77007-7510 E-mail: jmginty@acico.com.

MCGIRR, DAVID WILLIAM JOHN, pharmaceutical executive; b. Glasgow, Scotland, May 19, 1954; arrived in US, 1991; s. Edward McCombie and Diane Curzon (Woods) McG.; m. Margaret Joslin Richardson, May 9, 1981; children: William David, Katherine Joslin, Lucy Ann, Elizabeth Margaret. BSc(hon.), U. Glasgow, 1976; MBA, U. Pa., 1978. Assoc. S.G. Warburg & Co. Ltd., London, 1978—80, exec. dir., 1981—86; mng. dir. S.G. Warburg & Co. Inc., NYC, 1991—95, CFO, 1992—95; assoc. Warburg Paribas Becker Inc., N.Y.C., 1980—81; exec. dir. S.G. Warburg Securities, London, 1986—87; CEO S.G. Warburg Securities Ltd., Toronto, Canada, 1987—89; COO, CFO Bunting Warburg Inc., Toronto, 1989—91; pres. GAB Robins North Am. Inc., Parsippany, NJ, 1996—99, CEO, 1997—99; COO hippo, Inc., New Haven, 1999—2002, pres., 2001—02; sr. v.p., CFO Cubist Pharm., Inc., Lexington, Mass., 2002—, treas., 2002—03. Selection com. Thouron Scholarship. Bd. dirs. Friends of Glasgow U., Inc., 2003—. Thouron scholar, 1976-78. Mem. Apawamis Club (Rye, N.Y.). Avocations: collecting cars, family, golf. Office: 65 Hayden Ave Lexington MA 02421 Office Phone: 781-860-8526. Business E-Mail: david.mcgirr@cubist.com.

MCGIVERIN, ARTHUR A. former state supreme court chief justice; b. Iowa City, Iowa, Nov. 10, 1928; s. Joseph J. and Mary B. McG.; m. Mary Joan McGiverin, Apr. 20, 1951; children: Teresa, Thomas, Bruce, Nancy. BSC with high honors, U. Iowa, 1951, JD, 1956. Bar: Iowa 1956. Pvt. practice law, Ottumwa, Iowa, 1956; alt. mcpl. judge, 1960-65; judge Iowa Dist. Ct. 8th Jud. Dist., 1965-78; assoc. justice Iowa Supreme Ct., Des Moines, 1978-87, chief justice, 1987-2000, sr. judge, 2000—. Mem. Iowa Supreme Ct. Commn. on Continuing Legal Edn., 1975. Served to 1st lt. U.S. Army, 1946-48, 51-53. Mem. Iowa State Bar Assn., Am. Law Inst. Roman Catholic. Avocation: golf. Office: Iowa Supreme Court State Capitol Building Des Moines IA 50319-0001

MCGIVNEY, JOHN JOSEPH, lawyer; b. Boston, Oct. 31, 1956; s. William A. and Mary Angela (Wall) McG. AB magna cum laude, Boston Coll., 1978, JD cum laude, 1981. Bar: Mass. 1981, U.S. Dist. Ct. Mass. 1982, U.S. Ct. Appeals (1st cir.) 1983, U.S. Supreme Ct. 1990. Assoc. Burns & Levinson, Boston, 1981-87, ptnr., chief appellate sect., 1988-96; ptnr. Rubin and Rudman, Boston, 1997—. Sec. Lynnfield (Mass.) Dem. Town Com., 1974-75, chmn., 1976-77. Mem. Mass. Acad. Trial Attys., Mass. Def. Lawyers Assn. (bd. dirs.), Algonquin Club of Boston. Home: 47 Doncaster Cir Lynnfield MA 01940-2255

MC GLAMERY, MARSHAL DEAN, crop scientist, weed science educator; b. Mooreland, Okla., July 29, 1932; s. Walter Gaiford and Bernice (Gardner) McG.; m. Marilyn Hudson, June 2, 1957; children: Paul, Steve. BS, Okla. State U., 1956, MS, 1958; PhD, U. Ill., 1965. Instr. Panhandle A. and M. Coll., 1958-60; agronomist Agribus. Co., Lawrence, Kans., 1960-61; teaching asst. U. Ill., 1961-63, research fellow, 1963-65, asst. prof. weed sci., 1965-70, assoc. prof., 1970-76, prof., 1976-2000, prof. emeritus, 2002—, ext. crop scientist, 1965-2000, ret., 2000. Served with U.S. Army, 1953-55. NSF fellow, 1963 Mem. Weed Sci. Soc. Am., Coun. Agr. and Tech. Baptist. Home: 35 Lange Ave Savoy IL 61874-9705 Office: 1102 S Goodwin Ave Urbana IL 61801-4730 Business E-Mail: mmcglame@uiuc.edu.

MCGLAMRY, MAX REGINALD, lawyer; b. Wilcox County, Ga., Sept. 12, 1928; s. Edgar Lee and Allie Bea (Faircloth) McG.; m. Jean Louise Hilyer, Dec. 28, 1950; children: Sharon Kay McGlamry Hendrix, Michael Lee. BS, Auburn U., 1948; LLB cum laude, Mercer U., 1952, JD cum laude, 1970. Bar: Ga. 1953, U.S. Dist. Ct. (mid. dist.) Ga. 1954, U.S. Ct. Appeals (5th cir.) 1964, U.S. Supreme Ct. 1972, U.S. Ct. Appeals (11th cir.) 1981, U.S. Ct. Appeals (4th cir.) 1985, U.S. Dist. Ct. (no. dist.) Calif. 1988, U.S. Dist. Ct. (no. dist.) Ga. 1989. Pvt. practice, Columbus, Ga., 1953-64; from ptnr. to officer Swift, Pease, Davidson & Chapman (name changed to Page, Scrantom, Harris, McGlamry, & Chapman, P.C.), Columbus, 1964-85; ptnr. Pope, Kellogg, McGlamry, Kilpatrick & Morrison, Columbus, 1985-90, Pope, McGlamry, Kilpatrick & Morrison, LLP, Columbus, 1990-2000; pres. Max R. McGlamry, P.C., Columbus, 2000—04. Exec. com. Muscogee County Dem. Orgn., Columbus, 1956-60; bd. dirs. Columbus Jr. C. of C. Ens. USN, 1948-49, Ens. USNR, 1949-59. Am. Coll. Trust & Estate Counsel fellow, 1973, Lawyers Found. Ga. fellow, 1983. Mem. ABA, ATLA, State Bar Ga., Ga. Trial Lawyers Assn., Assn. U.S. Army, Ga. Sr. Golfers Assn., Valley Sr.'s Golf Assn. (pres. 2003), Urban League of Greater Columbus, Inc., Columbus Lawyers Club (pres. 1964-65), Lions (Columbus chpt. pres. 1967-68), Green Island Country Club, Phi Kappa Phi, Alpha Epsilon Delta, Phi Alpha Delta, Pi Kappa Alpha. Democrat. Methodist. Avocations: golf, fishing. Home: 6941 Wethersfield Rd Columbus GA 31904-3317

MCGLASHAN, AMY GIBANS, educational association administrator, consultant; b. San Francisco, May 19, 1960; d. James David and Nina (Freedlander) Gibans; m. Roland Scot McGlashan, Aug. 10, 1991; children: Kelsey, Cody. AB in Edn., U. Mich., 1983; MEd, Harvard U., 1987. Organizer Pub. Interest Rsch. Groups, Ann Arbor, Mich., Boston, 1986; supr. Philbrook Spl. Edn. Sch., Concord, NH, 1987—89; dir. Portland (Maine) Partnership Program, 1989—90; assoc. dir. N.H. AllianceEffective Schs., Concord, 1990—94; project dir. N.H. Coll. & Univ. Coun., Bedford, 1994—97; exec. dir. Campus Compact N.H., Bedford, 1997—99, Vt. Campus Compact, Middlebury, 1999—. Facilitator N.H. Dept. Edn., Concord, 1999—2002; program dir. Found. Excellent Schs., Cornwall, Vt., 2001; instr. CC Vt., Middlebury, 2003—; cons. Measured Progress, Dover, NH, 2004—. Bd. dirs. N.H. Commn. Nat. and Cmty. Svc., Concord, 1994—99, Campus Compact, Providence, 1998—2000, Vt. Commn. Nat. and Cmty. Svc., Monpelier, 1999—, chair, 2004—. Home: PO Box 52 Ripton VT 05766 Office: Vt Campus Compact 152 Maple St Ste G1 Middlebury VT 05753 Office Phone: 802-443-2510. Business E-Mail: agibansm@middlebury.edu.

MCGLASHAN, THOMAS HAMEL, psychiatry educator; b. Rochester, N.Y., Oct. 20, 1941; BA in Chemistry magna cum laude, Yale U., 1963; MD, U. Pa., 1967. Diplomate in psychiatry Am. Bd. Psychiatry and Neurology. Intern Mary Hitchcock Meml. Hosp., Hanover, N.H., 1967-68; resident, chief resident psychiatry Mass. Mental Health Ctr., 1968-71; officer in psychiatry, sr. asst. surgeon USPHS, 1971-73; chief clin. rsch. unit psychiat. assessment sect. NIMH, Adult Psychiatry Br., Bethesda, Md., 1973-75; staff psychiatrist Chestnut Lodge, Rockville, Md., 1975-90, dir. adult studies Rsch. Inst., 1977-81, dir. rsch., 1982-90; prof. dept. psychiatry Yale U. Sch. Medicine, 1990—; exec. dir. Yale Psychiat. Inst., New Haven, Conn., 1990-2000. Spl. and invited faculty, supr. Washington Sch. Psychiatry, 1978, 81, 82, 83; instr. Washington Psychoanalytic Inst., 1982-89, Western New Eng. Psychoanalytic Inst., 1992-93; clin. assoc. prof. dept. psychiatry Uniformed Svcs. U. of the Health Scis., 1983-88, clin. prof. dept. psychiatry, 1988-90; rsch. prof. dept. psychiatry U. Md. Sch. Medicine, 1986-90; bd. dirs. Parents Found. for Transitional Living, 1991-97; cons. and grant cons. in field; presenter in field; many others. Author: The Documentation of Clinical Psychotropic Drug Trials, 1973, The Borderline: Current Empirical Research, 1985, Schizophrenia: Treatment, Process and Outcome, 1989. Early Intervention in Psychosis, 2001, A Developmental Model of Borderline Personality Disorder, 2003; editl. cons.: Schizophrenia Bull., 1980-82, 84—, Archives of Gen. Psychiatry, 1982—, Am. Jour. Psychiatry, 1982—, Hosp. and Cmty. Psychiatry, 1984—, Jour. Personality Disorders, 1987—, Schizophrenia Rsch., 1987—, Acta Psychiatrica Scand., 1999—, Jour. Abnormal Psychology, 1988, Psychiatry Rsch., 1988—, others; mem. editl. bd.: Jour. Personality Disorders, 1989—, Schizophrenia Bull., 1989—; contbr. chpts. to books, over 200 articles to profl. jours. Recipient Gary Morris Rsch. award Washington Psychoanalytic Soc., 1980, Presdl. award for rsch. Nat. Assn. Pvt. Psychiat. Hosps., 1988, Silvano Arieti award Am. Acad. Psychoanalysis, 1990, Psychiat. Inst. Am. Found. award for rsch. devel. in hosp. psychiatry, 1990, Alexander Granlick award Am. Psychiat. Found., 1997, Established Investigator award Nat. Alliance Rsch. Schizophrenia & Depression, 1997-98; grantee Fund for Psychoanalytic Rsch. Am. Psychoanalytic Assn., 1978, 79, NIMH, 1996—, Norwegian Rsch. Coun., 1997—. Fellow Am. Psychiat. Assn., Am. Psychopathol. Assn.; mem. Western New Eng. Psychoanalytic Inst. and Soc., Soc. for Psychotherapy Rsch., Assn. for Clin. Psychosocial Rsch., Psychiat. Rsch. Soc., Internat. Soc. Study Personality Disorders, Internat. Early Psychosis Assn. Office: Yale Psychiat Rsch PO Box 208098 New Haven CT 06520-8038

MCGLATHERY, JAMES MELVILLE, foreign language educator; b. New Orleans, Nov. 22, 1936; s. Samuel Lyon and Mary Jackson (Garrott) McG.; m. Nancy Judith Beyer, June 1, 1939; children: Samuel Lyon, Daniel Beyer, Andrew James, Benjamin Kim. AB, Princeton U., 1958; AM, Yale U., 1959, PhD, 1964. Instr. German Phillips Andover (Mass.) Acad., 1959-60; lectr. German Harvard U., 1963-64, instr. German, 1964-65; from asst. prof. to assoc. prof. U. Ill. at Urbana-Champaign, 1965-84, prof. German, 1984-2000, prof. emeritus, 2000—, acting dept. head, spring 1985, dept. head, 1985-95. Instr. Colby Coll. Summer Lang. Sch., 1964, Harvard U. Summer Lang. Sch., 1965-66, 70, U. Ill., Urbana-Champaign, 1972, 74, 76, 78, 80, 82, 87, 90, U. Göttingen, Germany, 1993-94, 2001; lectr., presenter in field. Author: Mysticism and Sexuality: E. T. A. Hoffmann, Part One: Hoffmann and His Sources, 1981, Desire's Sway: The Plays and Stories of Heinrich von Kleist, 1983, Mysticism and Sexuality: E. T. A. Hoffmann, Part Two: Interpretations of the Tales, 1985, Fairy Tale Romance: The Grimms, Basile, Perrault, 1991, Grimms' Fairy Tales: A History of Criticism on a Popular Classic, 1993, E.T.A. Hoffmann, 1997, Wagner's Operas and Desire, 1998; editor: German Source Readings in the Arts and Sciences, 1974, Journal of English and Germanic Philology, 1976, The Brothers Grimm and Folktale, 1988, 91, Music and German Literature: Their Relationship since the Middle Ages, 1992; contbg. author: Reader in German Literature, 1969, Molière and the Commonwealth of Letters: Patrimony and Posterity, 1975, Fairy Tales as Ways of Knowing: Essays on Märchen in Psychology, Society, and Literature, 1981, Reflection and Action: Essays on the Bildungsroman, 1991, A Companion to the Nibelungenlied, 1998; mng. editor: Jour. English and Germanic Philology, 1972-2000; contbr. articles and book revs. to profl. jours. Princeton U. scholar, 1954-58; undergrad. rsch. assistantship Princeton U., 1956-58; Woodrow Wilson Nat. fellow Yale U., 1958-59, Jr. Sterling fellow Yale U., 1960-61, Nat. Def. Edn. Act fellow in Russian, Yale U., 1961-63; grad. rsch. bd. grantee U. Ill. Urbana-Champaign, 1975, 79-80, 86, 89, 92. Mem.: N.Am. Heine Soc., E.T.A. Hoffmann Assn. Home: 1204 Thomas Dr Champaign IL 61821-1632 Business E-Mail: mcglath@uiuc.edu.

MCGLAUCHLIN, TOM, artist; b. Turtle, Wis., Sept. 14, 1934; s. Charles Orion and Frances Lenore (Cadman) McG.; m. Patricia Ann Smith, Aug. 5, 1961; children: Christopher, Jennifer (dec.), Patrick (dec.). BS in Art, U. Wis., 1959, MS in Art, 1960; studied pottery with James McKinnell, 1962. Instr. dept. art and art edn. U. Wis., Madison, 1960-61; instr. art dept. Cornell Coll., Mt. Vernon, Iowa, 1961-64, asst. prof. art dept., 1964-68, assoc. prof., chmn. art dept., 1968-71; instr. Toledo Mus. Art, 1971-82, prof., dir. glass program, 1982-84. One-man exhbns. include Habatat Gallery, Dearborn, Mich., 1979, Glass Art Gallery, Toronto, 1981, 85, Glass Gallery, Bethesda, Md., 1981, 85,

87, 91, Heller Gallery, N.Y.C., 1983, B.Z. Wagman Gallery, St. Louis, 1983, Running Ridge Gallery, Santa Fe, 1990; selected group exhbns. include Toledo Mus. Art, 1972, 88, Glasmuseum Frauenau, Franenau, Germany, 1977, Habatat Gallery, 1980, 84, The Hand and the Spirit Gallery, Scottsdale, Ariz., 1980, Gallery of Contemporary Crafts, Detroit, 1980, The Naples (Fla.) Art Gallery, 1981, The Craftsman's Gallery, Scarsdale, N.Y., 1981, 84, The Nat. Mus. Modern Art, Kyoto and Tokyo, 1981, Perception Gallery, Houston, 1985, The AirLoft Gallery, Honolulu, 1986, The Corning (N.Y.) Mus. Glass, 1987; selected competitive exhbns. include Everson Mus. Art, Syracuse, N.Y., 1961, 62, Mus. Contemporary Crafts, N.Y.C., 1962, Corning Glass Mus., Met. Mus. Art, N.Y.C., Victoria and Albert Mus., London, Musee Ars Decoratif, Paris; public collections include Toledo Mus. Art, The Smithsonian Collection, Washington, Portland (Oreg.) Art Mus., New Orleans Mus. Art, Mus. Contemporary Crafts, Musee des arts decoratifs de la Ville de Lausanne, Switzerland, Minn. Mus. Art, St. Paul, Kunstmuseum, Dusseldorf, Germany, Corning Glass Mus. Grantee Associated Colls. Midwest, 1966-67; recipient First Jury award Toledo Glass Nat. II, 1968. Mem. Am. Crafts Coun., Internat. Sculpture Soc., Ohio Designer-Craftsmen, Glass Art Soc. Office: The Glass Studio 1940 W Central Ave Toledo OH 43606-3944 Office Phone: 419-461-4097. E-mail: tom@mcglauchlin.com.

MCGLAUGHLIN, THOMAS HOWARD, publisher, retired naval officer, marine surveyor; b. Cin., Jan. 12, 1928; s. George Godden and Cordelia (Herrlinger) McG.; m. Moana Maharam-Stone, Jan. 4, 1984. BS in Elec. Engring., U.S. Naval Acad., 1950. Lic. master mariner. Commd. ensign U.S. Navy, 1950, advanced through grades to capt., 1970; White House aide to Pres. John F. Kennedy, Washington 1960-63; exec. officer USS Prichett, Long Beach, Calif., 1963-65; comdg. officer USS Maddox, Long Beach, 1965-67; exec. officer USS Boston, Boston, 1967-70; chief naval ops. Comdr.-in-Chief, Pacific, Honolulu, 1970-74; chief of staff Mil. Sealift Command, N.Y.C., 1974-79; ret. U.S. Navy, 1979; pres. Falmouth Press, Honolulu, 1983—. Marine surveyor R.W. Dickieson Internat., Inc., Honolulu, 1982—; master Motor Vessel Rella Mae, Honolulu, 1981-90, Royal Taipan, Cebu, Philippines, 1990. Hon. police chief Boston Police Dept., 1969. Decorated Bronze Star, Navy commendation medal with combat "v", combat action ribbon, Vietnamese Disting. Svc. order; recipient medal for Outstanding Svc., Am. Legion, Pitts., 1942. Mem. Nat. Def. Transp. Assn., VFW (life), U.S. Naval Acad. Alumni Assn. (life), The Mil. Officers Assn. Republican. Presbyterian. Avocations: flying, scuba diving, tennis, golf. Home: 118 Kiionioni Pl Honolulu HI 96816-4248 Office: RW Dickieson Internat Inc 46-208 Kahuhipa St Kaneohe HI 96744-3905

MCGLOCKTON, CHESTER, professional football player; b. Whiteville, N.C., Sept. 16, 1969; Student, Clemson U. Defensive tackle Oakland Raiders, 1992-97, Kansas City Chiefs, 1998—2000, Denver Broncos, 2001—. Named to Sporting News NFL All-Pro Team, 1994, to NFL Pro Bowl Team, 1994. Office: Denver Broncos 13655 Broncos Pkwy Englewood CO 80112

MCGLONE, MICHAEL ANTHONY, lawyer; b. New Orleans, Jan. 6, 1951; s. James Godfrey and Dorothy (Barta) McG.; m. Suzanne Blanchard, Nov. 27, 1976; children: Kevin, Kathleen, Meghan. BBA cum laude, Loyola U., New Orleans, 1972, JD, 1975. Bar: La. 1975, U.S. Dist. Ct. (ea. dist.) La. 1975, U.S. Ct. Appeals (5th and 11 cirs.) 1975, U.S. Dist. Ct. (we. dist.) La. 1978, U.S. Dist. Ct. (mid. dist.) La. 1979, U.S. Supreme Ct. 1981. Law clk. to Hon. Herbert W. Christenberry U.S. Dist. Ct., New Orleans, 1975-76; ptnr. Lemle and Kelleher, New Orleans, 1976—. Mem. ABA, ALA, FBA (bd. dirs. New Orleans chpt. 1986—, pres. 1995-96), La. Bar Assn., Southeastern Admiralty Law Inst., New Orleans Bar Assn., Maritime Law Assn., St. Thomas More Inn of Ct. (master barrister), Alpha Sigma Nu, Beta Gamma Sigma. Democrat. Roman Catholic. Home: 4708 N Turnbull Dr Metairie LA 70002-1447 Office: Lemle and Kelleher 601 Poydras St New Orleans LA 70130-6029 Office Phone: 504-584-9112. E-mail: MMcGlone@lemle.com.

MCGLOTHLIN, JAMES W. wholesale distribution executive; b. 1940; Grad., William & Mary Coll. Bar: Va. 1964. CEO United Co., Big Rock, Va. Office: United Co Inc PO Box 1280 Bristol VA 24203-1280

MCGLYNN, MARGARET G. pharmaceutical executive; BS in Pharmacy, SUNY, Buffalo, 1982, MBA in Mktg., 1983. Profl. rep. Merck & Co., Inc., Whitehouse Sta., NJ, 1983—84, mktg. analyst, 1985—86, promotion mgr., 1986, product mgr., 1987—89, dir. bus. devel., 1987—89, 1989—90, sr. dir. mkt. planning, 1990—91, exec., dir. nat. consumer mktg. U.S. human health, 1991—93, v.p. bus. mgmt. and devel. U.S. human health, 1993, sr. v.p. managed care U.S. human health, 1994—95, sr. v.p. bus. planning proposals and analysis Merck-Medco Managed Care, 1994, sr. v.p. health and utilization mgmt., Merck-Medco Managed Care L.L.C., 1995—98, sr. v.p. world wide human health mktg., 1998—2001, exec. v.p. customer mktg. and sales U.S. human health, 2001—02, pres. U.S. human health, 2003—. Mem. dean's adv. coun. U. Buffalo Sch. Mgmt. Office: Merck & Co Inc One Merck Dr PO Box 100 Whitehouse Station NJ 08889-0100

MCGLYNN, MARTIN M, biotechnology company executive; B Commerce, Univ. Coll., Dublin, 1968; diploma indsl. engring., Irish Inst. Indsl. Engring., 1970; diploma prodn. planning, U. Birmingham, England, 1971. Pres., CEO, dir. StemCells, Inc., Palo Alto, Calif., 2001—; pres., CEO Pharmadigm, Inc., Salt Lake City, 1994—2001. Office: StemCells Inc 3155 Porter Dr Palo Alto CA 94304

MC GLYNN, SEAN PATRICK, physical chemist, educator; b. Dungloe, Ireland, Mar. 8, 1931; arrived in U.S., 1952, naturalized, 1957; s. Daniel and Catherine (Brennan) Mc Glynn; m. Helen Magdalena Salacz-von Dohnanyi, Apr. 11, 1955 (div.); children: Sean Ernst, Daniel Julian, Brian Charles, Sheila Ann, Alan Patrick; m. Maureen G. Potts, Oct. 23, 1985; children: Shane Joseph, Brennan John, Colin Patrick. BS, Nat. U. Ireland, 1951, MS, 1952; PhD, Fla. State U., 1956. Fellow Fla. State U., 1956, U. Wash., 1956-57; mem. faculty La. State U., 1957—, prof. chemistry, 1964—, Boyd prof. chemistry, 1967—, dean Grad. Sch., 1981-82, vice chancellor rsch., 1981-91. Assoc. prof. biophysics Yale U., 1961; Humboldt prof. physics U. Bonn, Germany, 1979—80; cons. to pvt. cos. Author (with others): (book) Molecular Spectroscopy of the Triplet State, 1969, Introduction to Applied Quantum Chemistry, 1971, Photophysics and Photochemistry in the Vacuum Ultraviolet, 1985, The Geometry of Genetics, 1988; editor: Wiley-Interscience Monographs in Chem. Physics; contbr. articles to profl. jours., chapters to books. Recipient award, Baton Rouge Coun. Engring. and Sci. Socs., 1962—63, Sr. Scientist award, Alexander von Humboldt Found., 1979, Disting. Rsch. medal, U. Bologna, Italy, 1979; fellow, Rsch. Corp., 1960—63; Sloan fellow, 1964—68. Mem.: AAAS, Am. Phys. Soc., Am. Chem. Soc. (S.W. Regional award 1967, Fla. sect. award 1970, Coates award 1977). Achievements include research in molecular electronic spectroscopy; electronic structure; energy transfer; molecular genetics; bioenergetics; mathematical biology; optoacoustics; optogalvanics. Home: 12048 Pecan Grove Ct Baton Rouge LA 70810-4835 E-mail: chspm@lsu.edu., maureen.potts@wcox.net.

MCGLYNN, WILLIAM CHARLES, brokerage house executive; b. Hazelton, Pa., Apr. 4, 1944; s. William Charles and Mary McGlynn; m. Phyllis Marie Fotia, May 28, 1967; children: William Jason, Devon Laura, Robert Ryan, Kirsten Ann. BS in Bus. Mgmt., Farleigh Dickenson U., Madison, N.J., 1968, postgrad. studies in Fin. and Econs., 1968-69. V.p. William D. Witter, Inc., N.Y.C., 1970-75, Dillon Read & Co., Inc., N.Y.C., 1975-79, Tucker Anthony R. L. Day, N.Y.C., 1979-81; mng. dir. L.F. Rothschild, Inc., N.Y.C., 1982-88, Bear, Stearns & Co., Inc., N.Y.C., 1988—2002, sr. mng. dir., 2002—. Fundraiser Wall St. Charity Fund, N.Y.C., 1971—75; benefits com. Cath. Charities Home Bur., N.Y.C., 1980—90; trustee, exec. com. mem. Oak Knoll Sch. Holy Child, Summit, NJ, 1989—; fundraiser, mem. Fathers and Friends Delbarton Sch., 1993—98, Morristown Bearcd Sch. Assn., 1998—99; advisor, mem. Oak Knoll Fathers Bd., 1989—; trustee, chmn. fin. com. Chubb Found., 2001—. Republican. Roman Catholic. Avocations: skiing, tennis, boating, reading. Home: 151 Deer Run Watchung NJ 07069-6255 Office: Bear Sterns & Co Inc 245 Park Ave New York NY 10167-0002

MCGOLDRICK, JOHN LEWIS, lawyer; b. Plainfield, N.J., Mar. 2, 1941; s. John Leslie and Sarah (Walker) McG.; m. Ann Chapman Puffer, Oct. 1, 1966; children: Scott Runyon, Jennifer Winslow. BA cum laude, Harvard U., 1963, LLB, 1966. Bar: N.J. 1966, N.Y. 1985. Assoc. McCarter & English, Newark, 1966-73, ptnr., 1974-95; exec. v.p. Bristol-Myers Squibb Co., N.Y.C., 1995—, gen. counsel, 2001—. Vice-chmn., bd. dirs. N.J. Transit Corp., Newark; bd. dirs. Bristol-Myers Squibb Found., Zimmer Holdings, Inc., HealthCare Inst. N.J., Regional Plan Assn., bd. mem. N.J. Network, Trustee Essex-Newark Found. Legal Svcs. N.J.; mem. com. to visit The Coll., mem. com. to visit Sch. Pub. Health, Harvard Bd. Overseers. Fellow Am. Coll. Trial Lawyers, Am. Bar Found., Am. Acad. Appellate Lawyers; mem. ABA, World Econ. Forum, Legal Svcs. N.J. (bd. dirs.), N.J. Bar Assn., N.Y. Bar Assn., Assn. Bar City of N.Y., Assn. Fed. Bar N.J. (former pres., mem. adv. bd.), Am. Law Inst., Assn. Gen. Counsel, Chief Legal Officers Roundtable, Coun. of Chief Legal Officers (The Conf. Bd. Inc.), CPR Inst. for Dispute Resolution (mem. exec. com.), Aspen Inst. on the World Economy, Coun. on Fgn. Rels., Harvard Law Sch. Assn. N.J. (former pres.), mem. Coun. for the U.S. and Italy, Mem. Nat. Panel of Arbitrators, Am. Arbitration Assn. Home: 25 Vandeventer Ave Princeton NJ 08542-6937 Office: Bristol-Myers Squibb Co 345 Park Ave New York NY 10154-0004*

MCGOLDRICK, KATHRYN ELIZABETH, anesthesiologist, educator, writer; b. Worcester, Mass., 1946; MD, Cornell U., 1970. Diplomate Am. Bd. Anesthesiology. Intern N.Y. Hosp.-Cornell Med. Ctr., 1970—71; resident anesthesiology Peter Bent Brigham Hosp., Boston, 1971—73; fellow pediat. anesthesiology Children's Hosp. Med. Ctr., Boston, 1973—74; prof. anesthesiology Yale U., New Haven, 1992—2001; prof., chmn. dept. anesthesiology N.Y. Med. Coll., Valhalla, 2001—. Med. dir. ambulatory surgery Yale-New Haven Hosp., 1991—2001. Editor-in-chief Survey of Anesthesiology, 1995—; mem. editl. bd. Anesthesia Wkb, 1999—. V.p., trustee Wood Libr.-Mus. Anesthesiology, 1998—2001, pres., 2001—. Fellow Am. Coll. Anesthesiology; mem. AMA, Am. Soc. Anesthesiologists, Conn. State Soc. Anesthesiologists (pres. 1998-2000), Assn. Univ. Anesthesiologists, Acad. Anesthesiology, Soc. Ambulatory Anesthesia (pres-elect 2003, pres. 2004). Office: Dept Anesthesiology NY Med Coll Valhalla NY 10595 Office Phone: 914-493-7693.

MCGONAGLE, DUNCAN FRANCIS, mental health nurse, substance abuse counselor; b. Bklyn., May 6, 1939; s. John and Kathleen (Rooney) McGonagle; m. Gloria Maria Carrubba, Dec. 5, 1987. AA, Allan Hancock, 1964; AAS in Nursing, CUNY, 1992. Cert. psychiat. and mental health nurse, addictions RN. Substance abuse counselor Pritikin Longevity Ctr., Santa Monica, Calif., 1978-84; paramedic N.Y.C. Emergency Med. Svc., 1987-92; psychiatric nurse Bellevue Hosp. Ctr., N.Y.C., 1992-99; adminstr. Methadone Maintenance Treatment Program, St. Barnabas Hosp., Bronx, NY, 1999—2001; nurse mgr. Methadone Maintenance Treatment Program, Beth Israel Med. Ctr., N.Y.C., 2001—. Founder Methadone Anonymous, N.Y. Aux. police officer N.Y.C. Police Dept., 1985—. With USN, 1956-60, 1961-62, Vietnam. Recipient Nat. award for Clin. Excellence in Nursing, Nat. Nurses Soc. on Addictions, 1995. Mem. Blue Knights, Knights of Life, Rolls Royce Owners Club, Harley Owners Group. Roman Catholic. Avocations: computers, sailing, motorcycling, antique autos. Home: 73 Verona St Brooklyn NY 11231-1612 Office: Beth Israel Med Ctr 215 Park Ave S New York NY 10003 E-mail: duncan73@aol.com.

MCGONIGLE, JAMES GREGORY, financial consultant; b. Bklyn., Nov. 17, 1945; s. William John and Helen Bernadette (Dennin) McG.; m. Francine Anne Falango, May 27, 1972; children: MarieElena, Lauren Anne. AAS in Acctg., CUNY, 1972; BS in Fin. summa cum laude, L.I. U., 1980. Cert. fin. planner Internat. Bd. Cert. Fin. Planners. Account exec. Coburn Credit Corp., Rockville Centre, N.Y., 1965-66; asst. credit mgr. UNI-CARD, Greatneck, N.Y., 1966-68; accounts receivable mgr. Granite Leasing Corp., Garden City, N.Y., 1968-73; v.p. Citicorp., N.Y.C., 1973-88; cons. O/E Learning, Inc., Detroit, 1988-90; regional dir. Ednl. Techs., Inc., Troy, Mich., 1989—. Adj. faculty Coll. for Fin. Planning, Denver. Vol. Family Svc. Assn., Nassau, N.Y., 1981-84, Better Bus. Bur., Farmingdale, N.Y., 1987—; vol., career advisor L.I. U., Brookville, N.Y., 1990—; treas. W. Tresper Clarke Friends of Arts, 1988-89. Mem. ABA (assoc.), Fin. Mgmt. Assn., Internat. Assn. Fin. Planning, Adelphi Soc. Cert. Fin. Planners, Internat. Assn. Registered Fin. Planners (speaker's bur.), Nat. Assn. Life Underwriters, Nat. Panel Consumer Arbitrators, Nat. Ctr. for Fin. Edn., Inst. Cert. Fin. Planners (bd. dirs. L.I. 1989-92), N.Y. State Assn. Cert. Fin. Planners, Delta Mu Delta. Republican. Roman Catholic. Avocations: bicycling, public speaking, travel, writing, gardening. Home: 2167 Plum Tree Rd N Westbury NY 11590-6029 Office: 33 Willis Ave Mineola NY 11501-4423

MCGONIGLE, THOMAS, writer, humanities educator; b. Bklyn., Oct. 25, 1944; s. Hugh A. McGonigle and Marion C. Whitney; m. Anna C. Saar, Oct. 12, 2002; m. Ruth K. Josimovich; children: Elizabeth, Lorcan. BA, Beloit (Wis.)Coll., 1966; MA, Hollins (Va.)Coll., 1970. Adj. asst. prof. NYU, 2002—, John Jay Coll. Criminal Justice, NYC, 1988—, Borough of Manhattan C.C., NYC, 1995—, Rutgers U., Newark, 1998—. Author: (books) Corpse Dream of N. Petkov, 1988, Going to Patchogue, 1992; editor: Adrift Mag., 1980; contbr. articles to newspapers. Home: 46 E First Street # 3D New York NY 10003 Personal E-mail: tmcgonigle@hotmail.com.

MCGOUGH, BRIAN EDWARD, investment banker, lawyer; b. NYC, Feb. 18, 1964; s. George V. McGough Sr. and Mary Elizabeth (Keaveny) Covell; m. Tamra Ann Pearce, Aug. 1, 1987; children: Michael Christopher, Christopher Thomas, Matthew Steven. BS, Bradley U., 1986; JD, No. Ill. U., 1990. Bar: Ill. 1991, U.S. Dist. Ct. (no. dist.) Ill. 1990, U.S. Tax Ct. 1993, U.S. Ct. Appeals (7th cir.) 1991, U.S. Supreme Ct. 1993. Assoc. Katten Muchin & Zavis, Chgo., 1990-96; v.p. JP Morgan & Co., Chgo., 1996-98; sr. mng. dir. Bank One Capital Markets, Chgo., 1998—2003; mng. dir. RBC Dain Rauscher, Inc., Chgo., 2003—. Spl. asst. atty. gen. State Ill., Chgo., 1992-96. Bd. dirs. Naperville (Ill.) Cmty. Outreach, 1990—; trustee No. Ill. U., DeKalb, 1993, mem. law sch. adv. bd., 1993. Recipient Disting. Alumnae award No. Ill. U., DeKalb, 1998.

MCGOUGH, DUANE THEODORE, economist, consultant, retired government official; b. Rice Lake, Wis., Aug. 3, 1932; s. James Patrick and Josephine Margaret (Huerth) McG.; m. Donna Mae Jones, June 13, 1959 Student, Wis. State Coll., Eau Claire, 1950-52, U. Wis., 1952-54, 56-60, BS in Light Constrn. Industry, 1959, MBA in Urban Land Econs., 1962; postgrad., U. So. Calif., 1968-69. Housing mgmt. officer Pub. Housing Adminstrn. Atlanta, 1960-62; program planning analyst Pub. Housing Adminstrn. Phila., 1962-67; program analyst HUD, Washington, 1967-68, 69-70, industry economist, 1970-73, supervisory economist, 1973-77, dir. housing and demographic analysis, 1977-97, govt. tech. rep. ann. housing survey, 1977-83; govt. tech. rep. Am. Housing Survey, 1984-97; acting dep. asst. sec. for econ. affairs (chief economist) HUD, Washington, 1977, 82, 84-85, ret., 1997. U.S. rep housing subcom. UN Econ. Commn. for Europe, Geneva, 1976, 79, 82; HUD rep. Interagy. Com. on Population Rsch., 1978-97, Interagy. Forum on Aging-Related Stats., 1986-97; mem. Fed. Task Force on Household Survey Redesign, 1988-97; mem. policy com. Year 2000Census; coord. PRSC Ctr. U.S./Mex. Sem. Housing Stats., Mexico City, 1997. Editor: President's Report on Housing Goals, 1974-78, Nat. Housing Prodn. Report, 1980, 82; U.S. Housing Market Conditions Report, 1994-97, FEMA National Emergency Management Program, 1967-97, Housing Consultant, 1997—; tenor, Washington Choral Ensemble, 2002. With U.S. Army, 1954-56; saxophonist 7th Army Band. Fellow NAt. Inst. Pub. Affairs, 1969; recipient Outstanding Performance award Pub. Housing Adminstrn., Phila., 1966, HUD, 1984, 92, 97, Career Edn. award Nat. Inst. Pub. Affairs, 1968-69, Cert. Spl. Achievement, HUD, 1978, 83, 84, 96, Cert. Superior Svc., HUD, 1988, 95, Cert. Appreciation, Bur. Census, 1990. Mem. Am. Econ. Assn., Am. Real Estate and Urban Econ. Assn., Lambda Alpha Internat. (v.p. programs 1987-89, chmn. real estate and fin. com. George Washington chpt. 1990-92, dir.-at-large 1992-93), Lambda Chi Alpha. Avocations: music, gardening, rockhounding, web-surfing. E-mail: duanetm@aol.com.

MCGOUGH, WALTER THOMAS, JR., lawyer; b. Pitts., Nov. 7, 1953; s. Walter Thomas and Jane (Fitzpatrick) McG.; m. Rebecca Gai Frazier, June 24, 1978; children: Emily Ann, Walter Thomas III. BA, Princeton U., 1975; JD, U. Va., 1978. Bar: Pa., D.C., U.S. Dist. Ct. (we. dist.) Pa. 1980, U.S. Ct. Appeals (3d cir.) 1983, U.S. Ct. Appeals (6th cir.) 1984, Pa. Supreme Ct. 1978, U.S. Supreme Ct. 1983. Law clk. to judge U.S. Ct. Appeals 3d Cir., Wilmington, Del., 1978-79; law clk. to Hon. William H. Rehnquist U.S. Supreme Ct., Washington, 1979-80; asst. U.S. atty. We. Dist. Pa., 1980-82; assoc. Reed Smith LLP, Pitts., 1982-86, ptnr., 1987—, head of litigation dept., 1999—. Assoc. counsel Sen. Select Com. on Secret Mil. Asst. to Iran and the Nicaraguan Opposition, Washington, 1987; mem. lawyers adv. com. U.S. Ct. Appeals (3d cir.), 1987-89, chmn., 1989; mem. appellate rules com. U.S. Jud. Conf., 1998-2004. Co-author: federal Appellate Procedure, 3rd Circuit, 1996; contbr. articles to profl. jours. Trustee Sta. WQED, Pitts., 1996-2002, vice chmn, 1997-99, chmn., 1999-2002; mem. 3d Cir. Task Force on Rule 11, 1987-89. Mem. Am. Coll. Trial Lawyers, Am. Acad. Appellate Lawyers, Allegheny County Bar Assn. (ethics com. 1983-86, bd. govs. 1994-2001, pres. 1999-2000), Allegheny County Acad. Trial Lawyers, Duquesne Club, Ross Mountain Club. Office: Reed Smith LLP 435 6th Ave Ste 2 Pittsburgh PA 15219-1886 Office Phone: 412-288-3088.

MCGOVERN, DONALD A. diversified financial services company executive; Chmn. high tech. industry practice Price Waterhouse L.L.P.-U.S., N.Y.C. Office: Price Waterhouse LLP US 11 Madison Ave New York NY 10010

MCGOVERN, GEORGE STANLEY, former senator; b. Avon, S.D., July 19, 1922; s. Joseph C. and Frances (McLean) McG.; m. Eleanor Stegeberg, Oct. 31, 1943; children: Ann, Susan, Teresa (dec.), Steven, Mary. BA, Dakota Wesleyan U., 1945; MA, Northwestern U., 1949, PhD, 1953. Prof. history and polit. sci. Dakota Wesleyan U., 1949-53; exec. sec. S.D. Dem. Party, 1953-55; mem. 85th-86th Congresses, 1st Dist. S.D.; spl. asst. to Pres., dir. Food for Peace, 1961-62; U.S. senator from S.D., 1963-81; chmn. senate select com. on nutrition and human needs; pres. Middle East Policy Coun.; amb. to U.S. Mission UN Agys., Rome, Italy, 1998—. Chmn. Ams. for Common Sense, Washington, 1981-82; guest lectr. Northwestern U., Evanston, Ill., Duke U., Columbia U., Cornell U., Munich, Berlin, and numerous others in U.S. and Europe, from 1981 Author: The Colorado Coal Strike, 1913-14, 1953, War Against Want, 1964, Agricultural Thought in the Twentieth Century, 1967, A Time of War, A Time of Peace, 1968, (with Leonard Guttridge) The Great Coalfield War, 1972, An American Journey, 1974, Grassroots, 1978, Terry: My Daughter's Life and Death Struggle with Alcoholism, 1996, The Third Freedom: Ending Hunger in Our Time, 2001. Democratic nominee for Pres. U.S., 1972; candidate for presdl. nomination Dem. Party, 1984. Served as pilot USAAF, World War II. Decorated D.F.C.; recipient Presdl. Medal of Freedom, 2000, Food for Life award World Food Program, 2000. Mem. Am. Hist. Assn.; Clubs: Mason (33 deg., Shriner), Elk, Kiwanian. Methodist. E-mail: jedelhoff@usaid.gov.

MCGOVERN, JAMES P. congressman; b. Worcester, Mass., Nov. 20, 1959; m. Lisa Murray. BA, Am. U., 1981, MA in Pub. Administration, 1984. Aide U.S. Senator George McGovern (Dem. South Dakota); spokesman, legis. dir., sr. aide U.S. Congressman Joe Moakley (Dem. South Boston); mem. U.S. Congress from 3rd Mass dist., 1997—; elected regional whip, mem. transp. & infrastructure com., house rules com. Mgr. George McGovern for Pres., 1984; delivered McGovern presdl. nomination speech Dem. Nat. Convention, San Francisco, 1984; leader Congressional Investigation on El Salvador, 1989 Candidate for U.S. Congress, 1996; vol. Mt. Carmel House; bd. dirs. Jesuit Internat. Vols. Democrat. Home: 34 Mechanic St Worcester MA 01608-2424 Office: Ho of Representatives 430 Cannon House Office Bldg Washington DC 20515-0001

MCGOVERN, JENNIFER ANNE, education educator; b. Lawrence, Kans., July 9, 1975; d. Jana Lynne and Daniel Joseph McGovern. BA, The U. of Chgo., 1993—97; MA student, PhD student, The U. of Iowa, 1997—. Rsch. asst. English dept. U. Chgo., 1996—97, U. Iowa, Iowa City, 1997—98, rhetoric instr., 1998—2000, speaking ctr. instr. rhetoric dept., 1999, writing ctr. instr. rhetoric dept., 1999—2000, lit. instr. English dept., 2002—, writing ctr. instr. rhetoric dept., 2002—; English instr. Garden City (Kans.) C.C., 2000—01. Program assoc. Univ. of Iowa, English Dept., 2003—; profl. devel. program co-leader Univ. of Iowa, Rhetoric Dept., 1999. Textbook com. rhetoric dept. U. Iowa, 1999, sen. Grad. Student Senate, 1997—98. Mem.: Am. Culture Assn., Mid-Am. Am. Studies Assn., Film and History Assn., SW Tex. Popular Culture Assn., MLA. Home: 1200 23rd Ave #7 Coralville IA 52241 Office: University of Iowa English Dept 308 English-Philosophy Bldg Iowa City IA 52242 Personal E-mail: jenmcgovern2001@yahoo.com. E-mail: jennifer-mcgovern@uiowa.edu.

MCGOVERN, JOHN FRANCIS, former financial executive; b. Port Chester, N.Y., June 4, 1946; s. Charles William and Jeanette Mary (Farrell) McG.; m. Gertrude Anne Mills, June 21, 1969; children: Robert Francis, Sarah Mills BS in Econs., Fordham U., 1968. Asst. treas. Chase Manhattan Bank, N.Y.C., 1973-74, 2d v.p., 1974-76, v.p., 1976-80, v.p. div. treas. forest products, 1980-81; v.p. project fin Ga.-Pacific Corp., Portland, Oreg., 1981-83, v.p., 1983—99, exec. v.p. fin., CFO, 1995—99. Bd. dirs. fibermarket.com, Atlanta, 2000-01. Fund raiser Am. Heart Assn., Atlanta, 1985—; adviser Atlanta Ballet, 1985. Served with U.S. Army, 1968-70 Mem. Fin. Execs. Inst. Clubs: Atlanta Country. Republican. Roman Catholic. Avocations: golf, tennis, skiing, jogging.

MCGOVERN, MICHAEL BARBOT, lawyer; b. N.Y.C., Mar. 6, 1947; s. Michael Malachy and Annette (Barbot) McG.; m. Christine Anne Beaudet, Sept. 2, 1972; children: Kathleen, Ellen, Maura. AB, Georgetown U., 1969, JD, 1972; LLM in Taxation, George Washington U., 1987. Bar: D.C. 1973, Md. 1978. From assoc. to ptnr. Wilkes & Artis, Washington, 1973-79; sole practice Washington, 1980, 84-87; ptnr. Lambert, Griffin & McGovern, Washington, 1981-84, Venable, Baetjer, Howard & Civiletti, Washington, 1987-93, Montedonico, Hamilton & Altman, Washington, 1994-98, Hanson & Molloy, Washington, 1998—. Bd. dirs. Hist. Soc. Washington, 1984-93, Montgomery County Hist. Soc., 1997-; co-founder, vice-chair, bd. dirs., mem. Greater Bethesda-Chevy Chase Coalition Inc., 1986—; pres. Westmoreland Citizens Assn. Inc., 1988-90; mem. Leadership Washington, 1987—. Served to capt. USAFR, 1969-82. Recipient Disting. Svc. award Fed. Bar Assn., 1978. Mem. Columbia Country Club (Chevy Chase), Met. Club (Washington), Barristers, John Carroll Soc. Republican. Home: 5414 Albemarle St Bethesda MD 20816-1825 Office: Hanson & Molloy 1320 19th St NW Ste 300 Washington DC 20036

MCGOVERN, PATRICK J. communications executive; BA in Physics, M.I.T. With Internat. Data Corp., Framingham, Mass., 1964—, chmn., 1976—; with IDG Comm. Inc., Framingham, 1987—, CEO, 1999. Trustee Mass. Inst. Tech., Whitehead Inst. RecipientThe Bus. Pub. of the Year award Delaney Report, The Communicator of the Year award N.Y. Chpt. Bus. Profl. Advertisers Assn., The Entrepreneur of the Year award Ernst & Young. Office: Internat Data Group 1 Exeter Plz Fl 15 Boston MA 02116-2848

MCGOVERN, PETER JOHN, law educator; b. N.Y.C., Dec. 6, 1938; s. John Phillip and Helen Marie (Gaisser) McG.; m. Catherine Bigley, Aug. 31, 1963; children: Brian Peter, Sean Daniel. AB, Notre Dame U., 1961; JD, Fordham U., 1964; EdD, U. S.D., 1980. Bar: N.Y. 1964, S.D. 1972, Ind. 1983, Ill. 1990, U.S. Supreme Ct. 1968. Atty. criminal divsn. Dept. Justice, 1971-72; prof. law U. S.D., Vermillion, 1972-83; from asst. dean to assoc. dean U. S.D. Sch. Law, Vermillion, 1972-77, dir. programs and planning, 1979-83; dean Valparaiso (Ind.) U. Sch. Law, 1983-85, St. Thomas U. Sch. Law, Fla., 1985-87, John Marshall Law Sch., Chgo., 1987-90, prof. law, 1990—. Dir. Ctr. for Internat. Bus. and Trade Law, 2000; dir. continuing legal edn. State Bar S.D., 1972-83; past chmn. S.D. Family Law Com.; bd. dirs. Legal Svcs. of Greater Gary Inc. Past pres. Vermillion Area Arts Coun., Nat. Anti-Vivisection Soc.; bd. dirs. Lawyer for Creative Arts, 1990-92. Lt. comdr. JAGC, USN, 1965-71. Recipient Legal Writing award Fed. Bar Assn., 1969. Fellow Ind. Bar Found.; mem. ABA, bd. dirs., mediator, arbitrator, Internat. Acad. Dispute

Resolution Democrat. Roman Catholic. Home: 2 East Erie St Apt 2705 Chicago IL 60611-7679 Office: John Marshall Law Sch 315 S Plymouth Ct Chicago IL 60604-3968 Office Phone: 312-987-2369. Business E-Mail: mcgover@jmls.edu.

MCGOVERN, THOMAS BOARDMAN, physician, pediatrician; b. St. Louis, Sept. 26, 1940; s. John Thomas and Hazel Marie (Boardman) McG.; m. Jane Emly Keyes, June 17, 1967 (dec.); children: John Thomas, Erin Kathleen, Ann Michal, Robert Andrew. AB, Dartmouth Coll., Hanover, N.H., 1962; MD, U. Mo., Columbia, 1966. Diplomate Am. Bd. Pediatrics, 1976, 89. Maj. USAF, 1966-72; rotating intern M. Co. Gen. Hosp., Indpls., 1966-67; flight med. officer USAF, Korea, Calif., 1967-69; pediatric resident USAF Hosp., K. AFB, Miss., 1969-71; pediatrician USAF, Westover AFB, Mass., 1971-72, partnership, Binghamton, N.Y., 1972-86, Assocs. in Medicine, Johnson City, N.Y., 1986-91, United Med. Assocs., Johnson City, N.Y., 1991—, chmn. pediat. sect., 1999—. Pediatric dept. chmn. Binghamton Gen. Hosp., 1980-82, sec.-treas. med. staff, 1982-84; pediatric dept. chmn. Lourdes Hosp., Binghamton, 1984-86, 93-95; clin. asst. prof. pediatrics Health Science Ctr., Syracuse, N.Y., 1980—. Cons. pediatrician Handicapped Children's Assn., Johnson City, 1973-78, mem. bd. dirs. 1980-91. Fellow Am. Acad. Pediatrics; mem. N.Y. State Med. Soc., Broome County Med. Soc. (bd. dirs. 1992-93). Republican. Roman Catholic. Home: 4 Cornell Ave Binghamton NY 13903-2020 Office: United Med Assocs PC 601 Riverside Dr Johnson City NY 13790-2544

MC GOVERN, WALTER T. federal judge; b. Seattle, May 24, 1922; s. C. Arthur and Anne Marie (Thies) McG.; m. Rita Marie Olsen, June 29, 1946; children: Katrina M., Shawn E., A. Renee. BA, U. Wash., 1949, LL.B., 1950. Bar: Wash. 1950. Practiced law in, Seattle, 1950-59; mem. firm Kerr, McCord, Greenleaf & Moen; judge Municipal Ct., Seattle, 1959-65, Superior Ct., Wash., 1965-68, Wash. Supreme Ct., 1968-71, U.S. Dist. Ct. (we. dist.) Wash., 1971-87, chief judge, 1975-87, sr. judge, 1987—. Mem. subcom. on supporting personnel Jud. Conf. U.S., 1981-87, chmn. subcom., 1983, mem. adminstrn. com., 1983-87, chmn. jud. resources com., 1987-91. Mem. Am. Judicature Soc., Wash. State Superior Ct. Judges Assn., Seattle King County Bar Assn. (treas.), Phi Delta Phi. Clubs: Seattle Tennis (pres. 1968). Office: US Dist Ct US Courthouse 5th Fl 1010 5th Ave Ste 215 Seattle WA 98104-1189

MCGOWAN, BERNARD W. venture capitalist, writer; b. Stonington, Colo., May 22, 1925; s. Neal and Lena Elton (Dean) McGowan; m. Betty B. Neill, Apr. 2, 1944; children: Wava K. Morris, Darwin L., Marla G. Grad., Walsh H.S., Colo., 1943. Farmer, rancher, Walsh, 1943—50; rancher Cotopaxi, Colo., 1951—61; ptnr. Paul & McGowan Constrn. Co., Cotopaxi, 1955—62; owner Auto/Aircraft Financing & Leasing, Denver, 1962—66; pres., pub. Aircraft Bluebook-Price Digest, Oklahoma City, 1967—86; ptnr. McGowan Investment Co., Oklahoma City, 1986—2001; pres. TIVY Games Inc., Oklahoma City, 1991—2000; writer. Owner Cotopaxi Garage, 1953—60; mgr., v.p. Insured Aircraft Title Svc., Okla. City, 1970—74. Past editor, pub.: Jour. Aviation Finance. With U.S. Army, 1944—45. Mem.: Okla. Auctioneers Assn., Nat. Auctioneers Assn., Aircraft Fin. Assn., Internat. Flying Bankers Assn., Aviation Writers Assn., Aircraft Appraisal Assn. (pres. 1967—82). Achievements include patents for (2) math game to raise students average math computation scores. Home: 8205 Brownsville Ln Bethany OK 73008-3038

MCGOWAN, GERALD S. diplomat; b. Birmingham, Mich., 1946; married Susan Anne Brophy; seven children. BSBA, Georgetown U., 1968, JD, 1974. Bar: D.C.; U.S. Ct. Appeals (D.C.), U.S. Dist. Ct. D.C., U.S. Supreme Ct. Founding prin. Lukas, McGowan, Nace & Gutierrez, Washington; amb. to Portugal U.S. Dept. of State, 1998—. Founder Integrated North Coast, Inc; developer cellular system ea. Ohio, 1992; bd. dirs. Overseas Pvt. Investment Corp. 1st lt. U.S. Army, Vietnam, 1970-71. Mem. D.C. Bar, Fed. Comms. Bar Assn. Office: Avenida das Forcas Armadas Psc 83 APO AE 09726-9998

MCGOWAN, HAROLD, real estate developer, investor, scientist, author, philanthropist; b. Weehawken, N.J., June 23, 1909; s. Sylvester and Grace (Kalbfleish) McG.; m. Anne Cecelia McTiernan, Jan. 15, 1938; children—Linda Anne, Harold Charles, Janice Marie. Ed., Bklyn. Poly. U., Pratt Inst., N.Y. U.; student, N.Y. Tech.; ed., Hubbard U. (Eng.); D.Sc., Coll. Fla. Chmn. bd. Atomic Rsch. Inc.; pres. Harold McGowan Builders; owner, developer Central Islip Shopping Center, Central Islip Indsl. Center; developer, builder Brinsley Gardens, Rolling Green, Slater Park, Clover Green, Maple Acres, Wheeler Acres; owner-donor Little League Baseball Pks., 1950—. Sculptures include: Bless Them; Victory, Eternity, Love and Hate, Triumph; author: Green Flight, (originator) The Thoughtron Theory of Life and Matter, Race with Death across the Sahara, The Incorrigibles, The Frigid Trap, The Shah's Swiss Secret, Another World for Christmas, The Spirit of Christmas in Words and Sculpture, The Making of a Universalist, The Journeyman, $800,000 for Love, Beyond the Visible, Shock after Shock, Christmas Stories, Short Stories, Born Again, You Are Forever, Black Shroud Over Bagdad, The Gold Mine; mural Back to Creation; holder U.S. patent to form one-piece plywood corner units, U.S. patent apparatus for forming one-piece plywood corner units. Hwy. commr., Suffolk County; chmn. Recreation & Parks-Islip; past dir. Suffolk County Girl Scouts; land donor St. John of God R.C. Ch., The Episcopal Ch. of the Messiah, Ctrl. Islip Sch. Dist. Recipient Winston Churchill Medal of Wisdom, 1986, Wisdom Hall of Fame, Beverly Hills, Calif., 1970; Churchill fellow, 1989. Mem. AAAS, IEEE, Explorers Club, Mensa Internat. Avocations: sculpture, art, philanthropy. Address: 28 2nd Ave Central Islip NY 11722-3012 *To become a really whole and successful person, one should recognize the efforts and good will of those living and dead who developed the culture, the fruits of which he enjoys, and repay his benefactors by contributing more to that society than he takes and also by doing good deeds to make the society better than he found it. He must also strive to understand the world and his relationship to it and know that the universe is neither capricious nor mysterious, that miracles do not happen. Everything and every action can only occur within the bounds of the laws of physics, chemistry, biology and communication. He must further realize that he is eternal and the basic purpose of human life is to become aware of and to live by these universal laws. The acme of a person's accomplishments would be his comprehension of the structure of the physical universe, the processes of life, and the nature of his mind. When he comprehends the Universe, Life and Mind, he will understand his own immortality.*

MCGOWAN, IAN DUNCAN, retired librarian; b. Liverpool, Eng., Sept. 19, 1945; s. Alexander and Dora (Sharp) McG.; m. Elizabeth Ann Weir, Oct. 30, 1971; children: Catherine, Margaret. BA, Exeter Coll., Oxford, 1967. FRSA, 1999. Asst. keeper Nat. Libr. of Scotland, Edinburgh, 1971-78, keeper, 1978-88, sec. of libr., 1978-90, libr., 1990—2002. Editor: Alexandria, 2003—. Chmn. U.K. Nat. Preservation Adv. Com., 1995-96; chmn. Britain-Russia Ctr., Scotland, 1999-2002, hon. treas., 2003—. Recipient Internat. Fedn. Libr. Assns. medal, 2002. Mem. Scottish Libr. Assn. (v.p. 1996-97, pres. 1998), Edinburgh Bibliog. Soc. (v.p. 2004—).

MCGOWAN, JOAN YUHAS, development researcher; b. Trenton, N.J., Feb. 13, 1955; d. Bernard Joseph and Estelle (Gray) Yuhas; children: Matthew Sheehan, Allison Joo Ok. BA summa cum laude, The Coll. N.J. (formerly Trenton State Coll.), 1977. Cert. tchr. N.J., 1977. Tchr. Blessed Sacrament Sch., Trenton, 1977; intake officer Mercer County Juvenile Ct, Trenton, 1978-82; rsch. dir. Audits and Surveys, Princeton, N.J., 1982-85; project dir. The Gallup Orgn., Princeton, 1985-86, Hase/Schannen Rsch. Assocs., Princeton, 1986; devel. rschr. Coll. NJ, 1986—2003; ind. rsch. cons. J.A.M.S. Cons., 2002—. Guest lectr., Thomas Jefferson U., Rutgers U., Helene Fuld Sch. Nursing; guest speaker local television programs. Author: Waiting: The Hopes and Frustrations of a Childless Couple, 1983; contbr. articles to various publs. Pres. Resolve, Inc., Phila, 1982; mem. Holt Internat. Children's Svcs., Trenton, 1984-85, Incarnation Altar Rosary Soc., Trenton, 1988—, Holy Name Soc., Trenton, 1989—; treas, area contact, Homeward Bound, Inc., 1996-2000. Recipient Think and Suggest award State of N.J., 1977, Meritorious award Trenton State Coll., 1989. Mem.: New Eng. Devel. Rschrs. Assn. (mentor), Assn. Profl. Rschrs. for Advancement, Am. Fedn. Tchrs., Villa Park Civic Assn., Operation Scarlet (assoc.). Democrat. Roman Catholic. Avocations: reading, family activities, rescue dogs, piano, music. Home: 941 Lyndale Ave Trenton NJ 08629-2409 E-mail: sadiemae@snip.net.

MCGOWAN, PATRICK FRANCIS, lawyer; b. N.Y.C., July 23, 1940; s. Francis Patrick and Sonia Veronica (Koslow) M.; m. Patricia Neil, June 6, 1964; children: Susan Claire, Kathleen Anne. BA, Rice U., 1962; JD, U. Tex., Austin, 1965. Bar: Tex. 1965, U.S. Ct. Appeals (5th cir.) 1969, U.S. Tax Ct. 1972, U.S. Supreme Ct. 1970, U.S. Ct. Appeals (11th cir.) 1981, U.S. Ct. Appeals (fed. cir.) 1993. Briefing atty. Tex. Supreme Ct., Austin, 1965-66; ptnr. Strasburger & Price, Dallas, 1966-98, Akin, Gump, Strauss, Hauer & Feld, Dallas, 1998—. Pres., chmn. bd. Tex Lex, Inc., 1991-98. Contbr. numerous articles on internet, trademark, copyright and franchise law. Bd. advisors Dallas Ft. Worth Sch. Law. Fellow Coll. State Bar Tex. (faculty Franchising Inst. 1987, Intellectual Property Inst. 1992, S.W. Legal Found. Patent Law Inst. 1992, Practising Law Inst. 1996, Ctr. for Am. and Internat. Law I.P. Inst. 2001-03); mem. ABA (alt. dispute resolution, forum com. on franchising, trademark and unfair competition com., patent, trademark and copyright law sect.), State Bar Tex. (alt. dispute resolution, intellectual property sect., com. continuing legal edn.), Dallas Bar Assn. (dir. intellectual property law sect. 1994—, chmn. I.P. Basics seminar 1999, sect. vice chmn. 2001, chmn. 2002), ALFA Internat. Tel. Symposium, Internat. Anti-Counterfeiting Assn., Tex. Law Rev. Editors Assn., Phi Delta Phi. Office: Akin Gump 1700 Pacific Ave Ste 4100 Dallas TX 75201-4675

MCGOWAN, ROSE, actress; Actor: (films) Encino Man, 1992, The Doom Generation, 1995, Bio-Dome, 1996, Kiss & Tell, 1996, Scream, 1996, Going All The Way, 1997, Nowhere, 1997, Lewis & Clark & George, 1997, Seed, 1997, Phantoms, 1998, Southie, 1998, Devil in the Flesh, 1998, Jawbreaker, 1999, Sleeping Beauties, 1999, Ready to Rumble, 2000, The Last Stop, 2000, Monkeybone, 2001, Strange Hearts, 2001, Vacuums, 2002; (TV films) God Is In the T.V., 1999, The Killing Yard, 2001; (TV series) Charmed, 2001—, (TV appearances) True Colors, 1990—, What About Joan, 2001—. Office: Internat Creative Mgmt 8942 Wilshire Blvd Beverly Hills CA 90211-1934

MCGOWAN, THOMAS RANDOLPH, retired religious organization administrator; b. Balt., Apr. 19, 1926; s. Robert and Mary (Miller) McGowan; m. Bernice A. Bernard, May 20, 1967 (dec. Nov. 1981); children: Howard, James, Terry; m. Roedean Olivia Oden, Feb. 9, 1985; children: Karen White, Kevin, Kurt. AA, Oakland Jr. Coll., 1964; postgrad., San Francisco State Coll., 1964-68; BS, U. Md., 1978. Lt. security police Oakland (Calif.) Army Base, 1955-60; chief motor pool San Francisco Procurement Agy., Oakland, 1960-64, contract specialist, 1964-68, Harry Diamond Labs., Washington, 1968-79, br. chief procurement divsn., 1972-79; chief procurement directorate Yuma (Ariz.) Proving Ground, 1979-82; dir. ecumenism Roman Cath. Diocese of Oakland, 1983—, dir. African Am. Cath. Pastoral Ctr., 1991—. Bd. dirs. Columbia (Md.) Found., 1972—74, chmn., 1975—79; convenor Interreligious Coun. Oakland, 1988—; trustee Greater Oakland Interfaith Network, 1989—92; bd. dirs. Thea Bowman Manor, Oakland, 1989—, St. Mary's Ctr.; mem. E. Oakland Renewal Task Force, 1990—; div. Bd. Cons., Graymoor, NY, 1990—. With U.S. Army, 1944—46. Mem.: Rotary, Knights Peter Claver. Democrat. Avocations: tennis, woodworking. Home: 139 Pinto Dr Vallejo CA 94591-8451 E-mail: ThomDean@pacbell.net.

MCGOWAN, WILLIAM ANDREW, lawyer; b. N.Y.C., Apr. 29, 1918; s. Andrew J. and Kathryn A. (Sweeney) McG.; m. Manuela Marie Corey, July 11, 1946; children— Susan C. McGowan Turner, Andrew J., Mary Louise McGowan Manifold, William E. B.A., Manhattan Coll., 1938; LL.B., Bklyn. Law Sch., 1941. Bar: N.Y. 1942, Ind. 1958, D.C. 1964. Sole practice, N.Y.C., 1946-48; atty. NLRB, 1948-54; asst. gen. counsel United Brotherhood of Carpenters and Joiners Am., Washington, 1954-69, gen. counsel, 1969— . Served with AUS, 1942-46; World War II. Democrat. Roman Catholic.

MCGOWEN, GERALD ELLIS, biologist; b. Muskegon, Mich., Dec. 27, 1946; s. Gerald Edward and Helen Lorraine McGowen. BS in Biology, San Diego State U., 1970, MS in Biology, 1977; PhD in Biology, U. So. Calif., L.A., 1987. Assoc. environ. specialist Occidental Coll., L.A., 1974-78; rsch. assoc. U. So. Calif., L.A., 1978-80; asst. rsch. curator Natural History Mus. L.A. County, 1978-92; lectr. Calif. State U., Long Beach, 1990; water biologist environ. monitoring divsn. City of LA, 1992—2001, water biologist regulatory affairs divsn., 2001—. Cons. Tenera, San Francisco, 1996-2000. Author: (book chpts.) Ontogeny and Systematics of Fishes, 1984; contbr. articles to books and profl. jours. Mem. Soc. Environ. Toxicologists and Chemists (mem., bd. dirs. So. Calif. chpt. 1999-2002), So. Calif. acad. Scis., So. Calif. Toxicity Assessment Group. Avocations: fishing, hiking, camping, diving, pool. Office: City of LA Regulatory Affairs 433 S Spring St Los Angeles CA 90013 E-mail: gem1440@adelphia.net., gem@san.lacity.org.

MC GOWIN, WILLIAM EDWARD, artist; b. Hattiesburg, Miss., June 2, 1938; s. William Edward and Emily (Ratliff) Mc G.; m. Claudia DeMonte, May 28, 1977; children: Leah, Jill. BS, U. So. Miss., 1961; MA, U. Ala., 1964. Prof. art SUNY, Old Westbury, 1978—, Coll. Old Westbury; mem. faculty Corcoran Gallery Art, 1966-77, head sculpture dept., 1967-74; lectr. in field. One-man shows include Corcoran Gallery Art, Washington, 1962, 71, 75, Martha Jackson Gallery, N.Y.C., 1968, Am. Cultural Ctr., Paris, 1974, Mus. Modern Art, Paris, 1978, Brooks Jackson Gallery, Iolas, N.Y.C., 1978-80, Fendrick Gallery, Washington, 1977-80, U. Colo., New Orleans Contemporary Art Ctr., 1982, Project Studios 1, L.I., N.Y., Cranbrook Acad., Bloomfield Hills, Mich., 1983, Art Park, Lewiston, N.Y., 1984, Gracie Mansion Gallery, N.Y.C., 1985, 86, 89, Mus. Fine Arts, Miami, Jones, Troyer Gallery, Washington, 1987, 89, 91, Boca Raton (Fla.) Mus., 1991, Margulis-Taplin Gallery, Miami, 1993, Paris-New York-Bangkok Gallery, Bangkok, Thailand, 1994, Grey Art Gallery, NYU, 1995, Siipakorn U., Bangkok, 1997, Genkan Gallery, Tokyo, 1997, Miss. Mus. Art, 2000; group shows include Contemporary Mus., Houston, Miss. Mus. Art, Whitney Mus., N.Y.C., Detroit Inst. Art, Guggenheim Mus., Speed Mus., Ky., Cologne (Germany) Art Fair, Zurich (Switzerland) Art Fair; represented in permanent collections Phillips Collection, Washington, Indpls. Mus. Art, Addison Mus. Art, Andover, Mass, Corcoran Gallery Art, Nat. Collection Fine Arts, Washington, New Orleans Mus. Art, Whitney Mus. Am. Art, N.Y.C., Guggenheim Mus., N.Y.C., Hirshorn Gallery and Sculpture Garden; permanent commn. U.S. Gen. Svc. Adminstrn., 1979, VA, Indpls., 1985, Percent for Art, N.Y.C., 1992, City of Jubai, Saudi Arabia, 1993, Dallas Rapid Transit Authority, 1994, Queens Co. N.Y. Supreme Ct., 1996, Art in Pub. Places, Socorro, N.Mex., 1997, Met. Transit Authority State of N.Y., Bayside, 1998, Inst. for Internat. Econs., Washington, 2000, St. Marks Gates, Plan de Grass, France, 2002, U. Iowa, Cedar Falls, 2003. Recipient Oscar for painting, 1977, Painting prize 9th Internat. Painting Festival, Cagnes-sur-Mer, France, 1977, Miss. Arts and Letters award for visual arts, 1980, Art Commn. Design award N.Y.C., 1998; Nat. Endowment for Arts grantee, 1967-68, 79-80, pub. outdoor sculpture grantee, 1977, Cassandra Found. grantee. Home and Office: 96 Grand St New York NY 10013-2633 Office Phone: 212-966-4496. Personal E-mail: mcmonte2@aol.com.

MCGOWN, JOHN, JR., lawyer; b. Bowling Green, Ky., June 15, 1949; s. John Stanley and Margaret (Deatherage) McG.; m. Mary Grunewald, Apr. 20, 1978; children: Erin Margaret, Brenna Kathryn. BS, U. Ky., 1971; JD, U. Colo., 1974; LLM in Taxation, U. Denver, 1981. Bar: Colo. 1975, U.S. Tax Ct. 1981, Idaho 1982; cert. mediator tax disputes Multistate Tax Commn., 2004. Dep. dist. atty. Weld County, Colo., 1974-78; assoc. Montgomery, Little, Young, Campbell, & McGrew, Denver, 1979-80; rschr. appellate divsn. IRS, Denver, 1980-81; mem. staff tax dept. Price Waterhouse, Denver, 1981-82; ptnr. Hawley Troxell Ennis & Hawley, LLP, Boise, Idaho, 1982-99, of counsel, 2000—. Adj. prof. Boise State U., 1983, assoc. prof., 2000-02; guest lecturer U. Idaho Coll. Law, Moscow, 1990, 2003; guest speaker various tax seminars, 1983—. Contbr. over 85 articles to profl. jours. Bd. dirs. Assn. for Retarded Citizens Ada County, Inc., 1987-93, pres. 1991-92, Assoc. Taxpayers Idaho, Inc., 1993-2002, exec. com., 1995-2002; audit review panel United Way Ada County, 1986-91; IRS vol. tax asst. program 1982, 87. Fellow Am. Coll. of Trust and Estate Counsel; mem. ABA (taxation sect.), Idaho State Bar Assn. (founding mem., taxation probate and trust law sect.), Idaho Soc. CPAs (fed. and state taxation com. 1984-89, bus. legis. com. 1989-91, pers. fin. com. 2000—), Boise Bar Assn., Toastmasters (pres. 1991), Beta Gamma Sigma, Sigma Chi. Home: 282 S Mobley Ln Boise ID 83712-8329 Office: Hawley Troxell Ennis & Hawley LLP 877 Main St Ste 1000 Boise ID 83702-5883

MCGRADY, CORINNE YOUNG, design company executive; b. N.Y.C., May 6, 1938; d. Albert I. and Reda (Bromberg) Young; m. Michael Robinson McGrady; children: Sean, Siobhan, Liam. Student, Bard Coll., Annandale-on-Hudson, N.Y., 1960, Harvard U., 1968—69. Founder, pres. Corinne McGrady Designs; designer Corinneware (joint venture Corinne McGrady Designs and Boston Warehouse Trading Corp.), East Northport, NY, 1970—. Exhibited in group shows at Mus. Contemporary Crafts, N.Y.C., 1969—70, Smithsonian Instn., 1970—71, Pompidou Ctr., Paris, 1971, Mus. Sci. and Industry, 1970, exhibitions include Guild Hall Show, Southampton, N.Y., 1968, Hecksher Mus., 1968; patentee cookbook stand. V.p. Women's Internat. League for Peace and Freedom, Huntington, NY, 1971; mem. bldg. com. Timberland Lib Hoodsport, 1996—97. Recipient Design Rev. award, Indsl. Design, 1969, 1970, Instant Supergraphic Indsl. Design Rev. award, 1971. Home and Office: PO Box 27 Lilliwaup WA 98555-0027

MCGRADY, PHYLLIS, television producer; Exec. prodr. PrimeTime Live, N.Y.C., Turning Point; with ABC, 1977—; v.p. and exec. prodr. spl. programming ABC News, 1998—2000; exec.-in-charge Good Morning Am., 1999—; sr. v.p. primetime, early morning and news program devel. ABC News, 2000—. Office: PrimeTime Live 147 Columbus Ave Fl 3D New York NY 10023-5900

MCGRADY, TRACY, professional basketball player; b. May 24, 1979; Forward Toronto Raptors, 1997—2000, Orlando Magic, 2000—04, Houston Rockets, 2004—. Active NBA's Reading Time-Out program. Named to NBA All-Star Game, 2000—04, All-NBA First Team, 2002, 2003. Achievements include NBA scoring champion, 2003. Office: c/o Houston Rockets 1510 Polk St Houston TX 77002 Office Phone: 407 89M AGIC.*

MCGRAIL, JEANE KATHRYN, artist, educator, poet, curator; b. Mpls., May 1, 1947; d. Robert Vern and Mary Virginia (Kees) McGrail. BS, U. Wis.-River Falls, 1970; MFA, Cranbrook Acad. Art, 1972; postgrad., Sch. of Art Inst. of Chgo., 1985, Ill. Inst. Tech., 1993. *The Anishinaabeg Mokaun Series, centered in awareness of Jeane's Ojibwe heritage, combines the technique of the work, with the philosophy of healing. Her philosophical vision is for healing the mind, emotions and the spirit. The technique of the art work originates with a meshed linear field of space. The colors of the forest-browns and greens are given dimension by multiple impressions. Then, creating the images on both sides of the paper makes a bark-like material. In addition, bones, beads, sinew and quills form and bind transformed paper. Therefore, the essences are recreated in the etched-reliefs and further enhanced in photoshop-the digital medium.* Group exhbn. include Saginaw Art Mus., Mich., 1972, Met. Mus. Art, Miami, Fla., 1974, Lowe Mus. Art, Coral Gables, Fla., 1974, 76, Miller Galleries, Coconut Grove, Fla., 1978, 80, Cicchinelli Gallery, NYC, 1980-82, Harper Coll., 1984, Contemporary Art Ctr. Arlington, Arlington Heights, Ill., 1984, 85, 86, 94, Evanston Art Ctr., 1985, South Shore Cultural Ctr., Chgo., 1990, N.A.M.E. Gallery, 1990, Artemisia Gallery, Chgo., 1991, 92, 93, 94, North Lakeside Art Ctr., Chgo., 1991, 94, 95, Ceres Gallery, NYC, 1992, Harper Coll., Ill., 1993, Environ. Concerns, Chgo., 1993, North Pk. Coll., Chgo., 1993, Franklin Square Gallery, Chgo., 1994, 95, 96, Space 900 Gallery, Chgo., 1994, 95, 96, 97, 98, 99, Chuck Levitan Gallery, NYC, 1995, Riverwest Art Ctr., Milw., 1995, Nat. Mus. Women in the Arts, Wash., 1996, Gallery 1040, 1997-, "Red", Chgo., 1998, Oakton Coll. Gallery, Ill., 1999-, Women's Works, Woodstock, Ill., 1999, "Paint It Siver", ARC Gallery, Chgo., 1999, Past/Present, Chgo., 1999, "Blue", Northeastern Ill. U.,Chgo., 2000, Then and Now, Chgo., 1999, Norris Cultural Ctr., St. Charles, Ill., 1999, others; represented in permanent collections at Chgo. Mus. Sci. and Industry, U. Chgo., Mus. Photography, Chgo., Miami-Dade Pub. Libr., U. Wis.-River Falls, MacGregor Found., Printmakers Workshop, NYC, Norman R. Eppnik Art Gallery Emporia State U., Kans., 2000, Mini Print Internat. Exhbn., Binghamton, NY, 2000, Yale U. Med. Libr., 2000, Columbia U. Med. Ctr., 2000, Mini Print Internat. of Cadaques, Spain, Macy Gallery, Providence, RI, 2000, Brickton Gallery, Pk. Ridge, Fla., 2001, Mini Print Internat. of Cadaques, Spain, 2001-04, Last of Primaries, Coll. of Lake Co., 2003-, Ukrainian Mus. Contemporary Art, Chgo., 2003, Chautauqua Nat. Exhbn., N.Y., others; solo exhbn. include Gallery at the Commons, Chgo., 1982, Truman Coll. Gallery, Chgo., 1991, C.G. Jung Inst., Evanston, Ill., 1992, Carlson Tower Gallery, Chgo., 1994, Olcott Ctr. Gallery, Theosophical Soc. Am., Wheaton, Ill., 2001; pub. "Mosaic", 1992, The Best of Printmaking, 1997; contbr. publ. to profl. jour. Cranbrook Acad. Art scholar, 1971; CAAP grantee Dept. Cultural Affairs City Chgo, 1992; recipient Poster Competition award Vizcaya Mus., 1974; Print award Auction WPBT, 1979. Mem. Coll. Art Assn., Chgo. Women's Caucus for Art (bd. dirs. 1992-95, sec.), Chgo. Artists Coalition. Democrat. Studio: 1040 W Huron St LL5 Chicago IL 60622-6591 Office Phone: 312-882-8512. E-mail: whoswho@jeanemcgrail.com.

MCGRANE, MILES A., III, lawyer; b. Oct. 3, 1947; m. Patricia Lea McGrane; children: Miles IV, Ashley, Blake. AS in Bus. Adminstrn., Jr. Coll. Broward County, 1968; BS in Bus. Adminstrn., Fla. Atlantic U., 1970; JD, Samford U., 1975. Bar: Fla. 1975, D.C. 1982, U.S. Dist. Ct. (so. dist.) Fla. 1976, U.S. Dist. Ct. (so. dist. trial bar) Fla. 1976, U.S. Ct. Appeals (5th cir.) 1976, U.S. Tax Ct. 1977, U.S. Supreme Ct. 1979. Assoc. Adams, George, Wood, Lee & Schulte, 1975—78, George & Thompson, P.A., 1978—80; ptnr. Kubicki, Draper, Gallagher & McGrane PA, 1980—93, McGrane & Nosick, P.A., Miami, Fla., 1993—. Adj. prof. trial program sch. law U. Miami, 1980—; mem. Judicial Nominating Comsn., 11th Cir., 1990-1994. Bd. govs. Fla. Med. Malpractice Joint Underwriting Assn., 1982-85, 88-90, 90-92, 1992-2002; bd. dirs. Legal Svcs. Greater Miami, Inc., 1984-90, v.p., 1987-88, pres., 1988-90; mem. bldg. com. U. Miami Law Sch., com. of 100; bldg. com. St. Thomas Episcopal Parish Sch. Recipient Leadership Award, Legal Svcs. Greater Miami Inc., 2001, Dist. Alumni Award, Broward Community Coll., 2002. Mem. Am. Coll. Legal Medicine, Am. Soc. Law and Medicine, Am. Acad. Hospital Attys., Internat. Assn. Def. Counsel (legal malpractice com. 1994-96, med. malpractice com. 1994-96, casualty insurance com. 1994-96), Fla. Def. Lawyers Assn., The Fla. Bar (pres. 2002-03, various coms. and positions), D.C. Bar, Dade County Bar Assn. (various coms. and positions), Dade County Def. Bar Assn.; diplomate Am. Bd. Trial Advocates (exec. com. Miami chpt. 1994-2000, treas. 1999, sec. 2000, v.p. 2001, pres. 2002, Nat. Bd. mem 1994-96.) Office: McGrane & Nosich PA 2801 Ponce de Leon Blvd 12th Fl Coral Gables FL 33134

MCGRANERY, REGINA C. judge; b. Phila., Nov. 7, 1945; BA magna cum laude, Trinity Coll., 1967; JD, U. Va., 1970. Law clk. to Chief Judge Edward M. Curran U.S. Dist. Ct. DC Dist., 1971-73; asst. U.S. atty. Washington, 1973-84; asst. gen. counsel for litigation U.S. Cath. Conf., 1984; adminstrv. appeals judge benefits rev. bd. Dept. Labor, Washington, 1995—. Contbr. articles to profl. jours. Mem. Am. Inns of Ct., Fed. Bar Assn. (disting. svc. award 1990). Roman Catholic. Office: Dept Labor Benefits Rev Bd 800 K St NW Ste 500 Washington DC 20001-8004

MCGRATH, DON JOHN, banker; b. Springfield, Ill., June 15, 1948; s. Donald John and Wilma P. (Beck) McG.; m. Patriaia Ratti, May 7, 1983. BS in Mktg., U. Ill., 1970; MBA, Boston U., 1973. Investment officer Banque Nationale de Paris, San Francisco, 1975-76, treas. San Francisco and L.A., 1976-78, v.p., treas., 1978-80, Bank of the West, San Francisco, 1980, v.p., CFO, 1980-81, sr. v.p., CFO, 1981-84, sr. exec. v.p., CFO, 1984-87, sr. exec. v.p., COO, 1987-91, pres., COO, 1991-95, pres., CEO, 1996—; pres., COO, dir. BancWest Corp., 1998—. Bd. dirs. Commonwealth Club Calif., Nature Conservancy Calif., Dominican Coll. San Rafael, Calif. Mem. Calif. Bankers Assn., Univ. Club, St. Francis Yacht Club (San Francisco), Diablo (Calif.) Country Club. Office: BancWest Corp 1450 Treat Blvd Walnut Creek CA 94596-7579

MCGRATH, EILEEN MARIE, pediatric nurse; b. N.Y.C., June 13, 1961; d. Patrick J. and Bridget K. (Dolphin) McG. BS in Nursing, Coll. New Rochelle (N.Y.), 1983, M in Nursing Adminstrn., 1990. Cert. pediatric nurse. Staff pediatric nurse Montefiore Med. Ctr., Bronx, N.Y., 1983-86; lic. practical nurse med./surg. New Rochelle Hosp., 1982-83; pvt. duty nurses aide Kingsbridge Jewish Nursing Home, Bronx, N.Y., 1978-80; patient care coord. Montefiore Med. Ctr., Bronx, 1986—; exec. dir. Am. Med. Women's Assoc, Alexandria, Va., 2001—02, exec. v.p., CEO, 2002—. Mem. Am. Assn. Nurses Network, Inc., N.Y. State Nurses Assn.

MCGRATH, ELEANOR BURNS, editor, writer; b. Gloucester, Mass., July 28, 1952; d. Edward James and Julia Ann (Holloran) McG.; m. Paul Allen Witteman, May 5, 1984; 1 child, Katharine McGrath Witteman. AB magna cum laude, Mt. Holyoke Coll., 1974. Rschr. Time-Life Books, N.Y.C., 1974-76; reporter, staff writer, edn. editor Time Mag., N.Y.C., 1976-86; sr. editor Women's Sports and Fitness Mag., San Francisco, 1986-87; spl. corr. Time Mag., San Francisco, 1988; sr. editor, articles editor Self Mag., N.Y.C., 1991-98; editor Time Mag./Princeton Rev. Coll. Guide, 2000—02; editor and pub. McWitty Press, 2004—. Journalist-in-residence U. Mich., Ann Arbor, 1984-85. Author: My One and Only: The Special Experience of the Only Child, 1989; editor: One Earth, 1990. Trustee Mt. Holyoke Coll., South Hadley, Mass., 1976-79; pres. Greater N.Y. Athletic Assn., N.Y.C. 1980-84. Time fellow Duke U., 1981. Mem. N.Y. Rd. Runners Club. Home: 110 Riverside Dr New York NY 10024-3715 Personal E-mail: elliemcgra@aol.com.

MCGRATH, EUGENE R. utility company executive; b. N.Y.C., 1942; BSME, Manhattan Coll., 1963; MBA, Iona Coll., 1980. With Consol. Edison Co. N.Y., N.Y.C., 1963—, v.p., 1978-82, exec. v.p., 1982-89, pres., COO, 1989-90, chmn. pres., CEO, 1990—, also bd. dirs. Mem. NAE. Office: Consol Edison Co NY Inc 4 Irving Pl New York NY 10003

MCGRATH, JAMES CHARLES, III, financial services company executive, lawyer, consultant; b. Davenport, Iowa, May 25, 1942; s. James Charles and Genevieve (Clarke) McG.; m. Sherbourne Everett, Apr. 11, 1970. BA, U. Notre Dame, 1964; JD, U. Iowa, 1967. Bar: Iowa 1967, U.S. Supreme Ct. 1970, D.C. 1971, U.S. Ct. Appeals (D.C. cir.) 1971, U.S. Ct. Mil. Appeals 1974. Spl. agt. FBI, Balt., N.Y.C., 1967-71; trial atty. Dept. Justice, Washington, 1971-75; dir. investigations Am. Express Co., N.Y.C., 1975-77, v.p. corp. security, 1978-82, sr. v.p. security, 1982-89; pres. McGrath Internat., Inc., 1989—. Overseas security adv. coun. U.S. State Dept., 1985-88. Mem. Soc. Former Spl. Agts. FBI, Am. Soc. Indsl. Security (chmn. white collar crime com. 1985-88), Internat. Assn. Credit Card Investigators (exec. adv. bd. 1985-88), Iowa State Bar Assn., D.C. Bar Assn., U.S. C. of C. (white collar crime adv. panel 1979—), Debordieu Club (Georgetown, S.C.), Phi Delta Phi. Office: McGrath Internat Inc PO Box 1384 Georgetown SC 29442-1384

MCGRATH, JAMES THOMAS, real estate investment company executive; b. N.Y.C., Nov. 10, 1942; s. Thomas James and Mary Ita (Finnegan) McG.; m. Paulette L. Franck, Aug. 16, 1980; 1 child, Tara (dec.). BS in Acctg., Providence Coll., 1964. CPA, N.Y. Sr. auditor Coopers & Lybrand, N.Y.C., 1968-72, mgmt. cons., 1972-74; group contr. IU Internat. Corp., Phila., 1974-77; v.p. fin. Taylor Engring. Corp. subs. IU Internat., Detroit, 1977-78; controller Pool Co. subs. Enserch Corp., Houston, 1978-85; sr. v.p. fin., treas. Lone Star Gas Co. subs. Enserch Corp., Dallas, 1985-91; pres. McGrath & Assocs., Inc., Dallas, 1991—. Ct. Apptd. Spl. Advocate. Bd. dirs. ARC, Dallas chpt., 1990-93. Lt. USN, 1964-68. Mem. AICPA, Dallas Athletic Club, St. Vincent de Paul Soc. Libertarian. Roman Catholic. Avocations: golf, cooking, skiing, scuba diving, sailing. Home and Office: 2838 Colleen Dr Garland TX 75043-1215 E-mail: pjmcgrath2@comcast.net.

MCGRATH, JOHN FRANCIS, retired utilities executive; b. Freeport, N.Y., May 4, 1925; s. John Francis and Catherine Frances (Maune) McG.; m. Catherine Elizabeth Zainor, June 22, 1946; children— Joseph R., Susan M., Martha J., Thomas J. BS, U.S. Mcht. Marine Acad., 1944; AB, Muhlenberg Coll., Allentown, Pa., 1948; JD, St. John's U., Bklyn., 1952; grad. bus. exec. program, U. Minn. Grad. Sch., 1973. Bar: N.Y., 1952, Minn., 1958, Fla.-Emeritus, 1991. Atty. firm Casey, Lane & Mittendorf, N.Y.C., 1953-58; jud. inquiry asst. counsel N.Y. State Supreme Ct., 1957-58; atty. U.S. Steel Corp., Duluth, Minn., 1958-64; with Minn. Power & Light Co., Duluth, 1964-83, sr. v.p., 1978-83, gen. counsel, 1975-83, sec., 1979-84; v.p., dir. USICO Ins. Co., Bermuda. Adj. prof., gen. counsel Coll. St. Scholastica, Duluth; vol. atty. Bay Area Legal Svcs., Tampa, Fla. Bd. dirs. emeritus Duluth Cathedral H.S., 1972, St. Anne's Residence, Duluth, 1963-83; commr. Seaway Port Authority, Duluth, 1966-76, pres., 1970, 75; bd. dirs., sec. Good Samaritan Fund Greater Sun City Center, Fla., 1987—; mem. Hillsborough County Bd. Zoning Adjustment, 1992-94; pro bono atty. Bay Area Legal Svcs., Tampa, 1991—. With Mcht. Marine, 1943-46, USNR, 1943-68, lt. ret. Mem. Minn. Bar Assn., St. Louis County Bar Assn. Democrat. Roman Catholic. Home: 2036 Hampstead Cir Sun City Center FL 33573-7350 E-mail: cjm2036@tampabay.rr.com.

MCGRATH, JOSEPH PATRICK, lawyer; b. Jersey City, Mar. 28, 1938; s. Thomas Acquinas and Mary Josephine (Keane) McG.; m. Kathleen Andrea Crummy, June 23, 1962; children— Joseph P., Sheila K., Brian T., Colleen M. A.B. cum laude, Coll. of Holy Cross, 1958; LL.B. cum laude, Harvard U., 1961. Bar: N.Y. 1964. Assoc. Dewey Ballantine, Bushby, Palmer & Wood, N.Y.C., 1962-69, ptnr., 1969— . Served with USAR, 1961-65. Mem. ABA, N.Y. State Bar Assn. (tax exempt bond com. 1978-79), Assn. Bar City of N.Y. (com. on taxation 1974-77). Roman Catholic. Clubs: Baltusrol Golf (Springfield, N.J.); Downtown Assn. (N.Y.C.). Home: 21 Rolling Hill Ct Madison NJ 07940-2747

MCGRATH, JOSEPH W. information technology executive; Bachelor's, Rutgers U. V.p. and svc. dir. Gartner Group, worldwide info. tech. cons. firm; with Xerox Corp., 1989—98, v.p. N.Am. sys. sales, v.p. mktg., integrated sys. ops., v.p. strategy and mktg. Xerox Prodn. Sys. Group, v.p. and gen. mgr. Xerox Prodn. Color Sys.; joined Unisys Corp., 1999, sr. v.p. maj. accounts sales and chief mktg. officer, 1999—2000, exec. v.p. and pres. Global Industries, 2000—02, exec. v.p. and pres. Enterprise Transformation Svcs., 2002—04, pres. and COO, 2004—. Office: Unisys Corp Unisys Way Blue Bell PA 19424*

MCGRATH, JUDITH, broadcast executive; b. Scranton, PA, 1952; BA English, Cedar Crest Coll., Allentown, PA. Copy chief Glamour mag.; sr. writer Mademoiselle; copywriter Nat. Advt., Phila.; copywriter, on-air promotion Warner Amex Satellite Entertainment Corp. (predecessor to MTV), 1981; editl. dir. MTV, sr. v.p., creative dir., 1988—92, exec. v.p., creative dir., 1992—93, co-pres., creative dir., 1993—94, pres., 1994—96, MTV, MTV2, 1996—2000, pres. MTV Group, chmn. Interactive Music, 2000—02; pres. MTV Networks Music Group, 2002—04, chmn., CEO, 2004—. Trustee emeritus Nat. Campaign to Prevent Teen Pregnancy; bd. dirs. Rock the Vote. Named Humanitarian of Yr., T.J. Martell Found. Leukemia, Cancer and AIDS Rsch., 2003; recipient Cable Ace Award, 1993, Founders award, Rock the Vote, 2001, Friend of the Children award, Harlem Children's Zone, 2001. Office: MTV 1515 Broadway Fl 25 New York NY 10036-8901*

MCGRATH, KATHRYN BRADLEY, lawyer; b. Norfolk, Va., Sept. 2, 1944; d. James Pierce and Kathryn (Hoyle) Bradley; children: Ian M., James D. AB, Mt. Holyoke Coll., 1966; JD, Georgetown U., 1969. Ptnr. Gardner, Carton & Douglas, Washington, 1979-83; dir. div. investment mgmt. SEC, Washington, 1983-90; ptnr. Morgan Lewis, Washington, 1990—2002, Crowell & Moring, LLP, Washington, 2002—. Named Disting. Exec. Pres. Reagan, 1987. Mem. Fed. Bar Assn. (exec. council securities law com.). Office: Crowell & Moring LLP 1001 Pennsylvania Ave NW Washington DC 20004 Office Phone: 202-624-2944. E-mail: kmcgrath@crowell.com.

MCGRATH, MARY HELENA, plastic surgeon, educator; b. N.Y.C., Apr. 12, 1945; d. Vincent J. and Mary M. (Manning) McG.; children: Margaret E. Simon, Richard M. Simon. BA, Coll. New Rochelle, 1966; MD, St. Louis U., 1970; MPH, George Washington U., 1994. Diplomate Am. Bd. Surgery, Am. Bd. Plastic Surgery, lic. physician Calif. Resident in surg. pathology U. Colo. Med. Ctr., Denver, 1970-71, intern in gen. surgery, 1971-72, resident in gen. surgery, 1971-75, chief resident in gen. surgery, 1975-76; resident in plastic and reconstructive surgery Yale U. Sch. Medicine, New Haven, 1976-77, chief resident plastic and reconstructive surgery, 1977-78; fellow in hand surgery U. Conn.-Yale U., New Haven, 1978; instr. in surgery divsn. plastic and reconstructive surgery Yale U. Sch. Medicine, New Haven, 1977-78, asst. prof. plastic surgery, 1978-80; attending in plastic and reconstructive surgery Yale-New Haven Hosp., 1978-80, Columbia-Presbyn. Hosp., N.Y.C., 1980-84, George Washington U. Med. Ctr., Washington, 1984-2000, Children's Nat. Med. Ctr., Washington, 1985-2000, Loyola U. Med. Ctr., 2000—02, Hines VA Hosp., 2001—02, U. Calif., San Francisco, 2003—, San Francisco (Calif.) VA Ctr., 2003—, San Francisco (Calif.) Gen. Hosp., 2003—; asst. prof. plastic surgery Columbia U., N.Y.C., 1980-84; assoc. prof. plastic surgery Sch. Medicine, George Washington U., Washington, 1984-87, prof. plastic surgery, 1987-2000, Loyola U. Med. Ctr., 2000—02, U. Calif., San Francisco, 2003—. Attending physician VA Hosp., West Haven, Conn., 1978-80; attending in surgery Hosp. Albert Schweitzer, Deschapelles, Haiti, 1980; historian., bd. dirs. Am. Bd. Plastic Surgery, 1991-95; guest examiner certifying exam., 1986-88, 95-2003; specialist site visitor Residency Rev. Com. for Plastic Surgery, 1985, 87, 91, 94; presenter, cons. in field; senator med. faculty senate George Washington U., bd. govs. Med. Faculty Assocs. Co-editor: (with M.L. Turner) Dermatology for Plastic Surgeons, 1993; assoc. editor: The Jour. of Hand Surgery, 1984-89, Annals of Plastic Surgery, 1984-87, Plastic and Reconstructive Surgery, 1989-95, Contemporary Surgery, 1999—, Annals of Surgery, 2004—; advt. editor Plastic and Reconstructive Surgery, 2003—; contbr. book chpts.: Problems in General Surgery, 1985, Human and Ethical Issues in the Surgical Care of Patients with Life-Threatening Disease, 1986, Problems in Aesthetic Surgery, Biological Causes and Clinical Solutions, 1986; guest reviewer numerous jours.; contbr. articles to profl. jours. Recipient numerous rsch. grants, 1978—. Fellow ACS (D.C. chpt. program ann. meeting chmn., 1992, pres. 1994-95, bd. govs. 1995-98, exec. com. 1996-97, chmn. adv. coun. for plastic surgery 1995-98, regent 1997—); mem. AAAS, Am. Surg. Assn., Am. Assn. Hand Surgery (exec. sec. 1988-90, 1st prize ann. resident contest 1978, other coms.), Am. Assn. Plastic Surgeons (trustee 1997-2000), Am. Burn Assn., Am. Soc. for Aesthetic Plastic Surgery, Am. Soc. Maxillofacial Surgeons, Am. Soc. Plastic and Reconstructive Surgery (chmn. ethics com. 1985-87, chmn. device/tech. evaluation com. 1993-94, chmn. workforce task force 1997-2000, bd. dirs. 1994-96, chmn. endowment bd. dirs. 2000—, ednl. found. bd. dirs. 1985-96, treas. 1989-92, v.p. 1992-93, pres.-elect 1993-94, pres. 1994-95), Am. Soc. Reconstructive Microsurgery (edn. com. 1992-94), Am. Soc. Surgery of Hand (chmn. 1987 ann. residents' and fellows conf. 1986-87, rsch. com. 1988-90), Assn. Acad. Chmn. Plastic Surgery (bd. dirs. 1999—), Assn. Acad. Surgery, Chgo. Soc. Plastic Surgeons (treas. 2001-02), Calif. Soc. Plastic Surgeons, San Francisco Surg. Soc., Chgo. Surg. Soc., Internat. Soc. Reconstructive Surgery, Met. D.C. Soc. Surgery Hand (pres. 1995-97), N.Y. Surg. Soc., Northeastern Soc. Plastic Surgeons (chmn. sci. program com. 1991, treas. 1993-96, pres. 1997-98), Plastic Surgery Rsch. Coun. (chmn. 1990), Surg. Biology Club III, The Wound Healing Soc. Office Phone: 415-476-3727. Business E-Mail: mcgrathm@surgery.ucsf.edu.

MCGRATH, MICHAEL G. finance company executive; CFO, mng. ptnr. Accenture, Chgo. Office: Accenture 161 N Clark St Fl 11 Chicago IL 60601-3362

MCGRATH, MIKE, attorney general, lawyer; b. Aug. 22, 1947; BS, U. Mont., 1970; JD, Gonzaga U., 1975. Bar: Wash. 75, Mont. 77, U.S. Ct. Appeals (9th cir.) 80, U.S. Supreme Ct. 80. Reginald Heber Smith cmty. lawyer fellow; atty. Washoe County Legal Svcs., Reno, 1975—76; asst. atty. gen. State of Mont., Helena, 1977—82, atty. gen., 2001—; county atty. Lewis and Clark County, Helena, 1983—2001. Bd. dirs. Mont. Legal Svcs. Assn., 1980—2003, pres., 1984—85, 1995—96; bd. dirs. Mountain chpt. Nat. Com. for Prevention of Child Abuse, 1985—90, Big Bros. Sisters, Helena, 1977—83, Friendship Ctr. Helena, 1989—, pres., 1995—97; chmn. Conf. We. Atty. Gens., 2003—. With USAF, 1970—72. Mem.: Mont. County Attys. Assn. (pres. 1996—97), Nat. Dist. Attys. Assn., Mont. Bar Assn. Democrat. Home: 514 Hayes Ave Helena MT 59601-6106 Office: 215 N Sanders PO Box 201401 Helena MT 59620

MCGRATH, MURRAY FRANKLIN, publishing executive; b. San Francisco, July 3, 1943; s. Daniel Charles and Catherine Eileen (Murray) McGrath; m. Gloria Lee Wong, Nov. 27, 1982 (dec. Aug. 1995). AA, El Camino Coll., 1969. Sgt. USAF, 1964, advanced through grades to staff sgt., 1971; electronic tech. U.S. Post Office, San Francisco, 1979—86, Las Vegas, 1986—92; publisher, writer Murray McGrath Pub., Stockton, Calif., 1995—. Author: The Author of Us All, 1996, On the Road to Paradise, 1998, Escape Velocity, 1999. Tchr. maritime navigation USCG Aux., Dayton, 1966. Avocation: gardening. Home: PO Box 4653 Stockton CA 95204

MCGRATH, ROBERT EDWARD, psychology educator; b. Woodside, NY, Aug. 31, 1956; s. Vincent McG.; m. Deborah Ellen Bernstein, July 20, 1986; children: Megan, Brian. BA, Hartwick Coll., 1978; MS, Auburn Univ., 1981, PhD, 1984. Lic. psychologist, N.Y., N.J. Asst. prof. Fairleigh Dickinson U., Teaneck, N.J., 1984-91, assoc. prof., 1991—98, prof., 1998—. Author: Understanding Statistics, 1997. Mem. AAUP (pres. Teaneck-Hackensack chpt. 1986-95), Am. Psychol. Assn., Soc. for Personality Assessment, Ea. Psychol. Assn., N.J. Psychol. Assn. Office: Fairleigh Dickinson Univ 1000 River Rd Teaneck NJ 07666-1996 Office Phone: 201-692-2300. Business E-Mail: mcgrath@fdu.edu.

MCGRATH, ROBERT L. academic administrator; PhD, U. Iowa, 1965. V.p. for Brookhaven affairs SUNY, Stony Brook, dir. Nuc. Structure Lab., prof. physics, acting provost, 1999—2000, provost, exec. v.p. for acad. affairs, 2000—. Bd. dirs. Brookhaven Sci. Assocs. Office: SUNY Stony Brook Adminstrn 407 Stony Brook NY 11794

MCGRATH, THOMAS J. lawyer, writer, film producer; b. N.Y.C., Oct. 8, 1932; children: Maura Lee, J. Connell; m. Diahn W. McGrath, Sept. 28, 1974; 1 child, Courtney C. BA, NYU, 1956, JD, 1960. Bar: N.Y. 1960. Assoc. Milbank, Tweed, Hadley & McCloy, N.Y.C., 1960-69; ptnr. Simpson, Thacher & Bartlett, N.Y.C., 1970-95; retired, 1995. Lectr., writer Practicing Law Inst., 1976—, Am. Law Inst. ABA, 1976-81. Author: Carryover Basis Under Tax Reform Act, 1977; contbg. author: Estate and Gift Tax After ERTA, 1982; producer: feature film Deadly Hero, 1977. Bd. dirs. N.Y. Philharm.; pres. Am. Austrian Found. With U.S. Army, 1953-54, Korea. Fellow Am. Coll. Trust and Estate Coun.; mem. ABA, N.Y. State Bar Assn., Assn. Bar City N.Y. Office: Simpson Thacher & Bartlett 425 Lexington Ave New York NY 10017-3954 Office Phone: 212-355-2232.

MCGRATH, WILLIAM ARTHUR, arbitrator, mediator, lawyer; b. Hackensack, NJ, Jan. 31, 1941; s. Donald Marble and Elinor (Peck) McGrath; m. Diane Gurley, Apr. 25, 1965 (div. Nov. 1976); children: Philip M., Christian P.; m. Jackie Wynne, Aug. 10, 2002. BS, Calif. U., Long Beach, 1963; JD, U. Pacific, 1972. Bar: Colo. 1972, U.S. Dist. Ct. Colo. 1972. Pvt. practice, Breckenridge, Colo., 1972—82, Aurora, Colo., 1982—84; ptnr. McGrath & Callan, P.C., Breckenridge, 1975—80, McGrath & Lavenhar, Esq., Denver, 1984—85; prin. William A. McGrath & Assocs., Denver, 1985—88; pvt. practice San Diego, 1988—, Sacramento, 1993—. Vocat. instr. Colo. Mountain Coll., 1972—80; instr. Sacramento City Coll., 2004—. Mem.: ABA, Colo. Assn. Realtors, Colo. Trial Lawyers Assn. Republican. Episcopalian. Home: 1916 Bidwell Way Sacramento CA 95818 Office Phone: 916-715-8667. Personal E-mail: wmcgrathppl@aol.com.

MCGRATTAN, MARY K. state legislator; b. N.Y.C. RN, St. Catherine's Hosp. Sch. of Nursing. Mem. town coun. Town of Ledyard, Conn., 1977-83, mayor, 1983-91; pres. Conn. Conf. of Municipalities, 1990-91; mem. Conn. Ho. of Reps., Hartford, 1993—. Mem. Ledyard Dem. Town Com. Address: 13 Lynn Dr Ledyard CT 06339-1312 Office: Conn Ho of Reps State Capitol Hartford CT 06106 Fax: 860-464-7079. E-mail: Mary.McGrattan@po.state.ct.us.

MCGRAW, BENJAMIN F., III, biotechnology executive; Chmn., pres., CEO Valentis, Inc., Burlingame, Calif. Office: Valentis Inc 863A Mitten Rd Burlingame CA 94010

MCGRAW, BRYAN KELLY, military officer; b. Ironton, Mo., Sept. 10, 1962; s. Robert Lee and Francine Clara McGraw; m. Elizabeth Adair Keck, Jan. 24, 1987; children: Kaitlyn Adair, Brendan Kelly, Shaun Kelly. BS, S.E. Mo. State U., 1984; MPA, U. Okla., 1990; postgrad., St. Louis U., 1996—. Lic. residential contractor, N.C. Commd. 2d lt. USAF, 1984, advanced through grades to maj., 1998, svcs. officer, mgr., 1985-87, Kadena AB, Okinawa, Japan, 1987-91; dep. chief svcs. K.I. Sawyer AFB, Mich., 1991-92; v.p. McGraw Builders, Inc., Goldsboro, N.C., 1992-95; exec. officer USAFR, Mitchell ARS, Wis., 1995-96; mgr. total quality Deutsche Fin. Svcs., St. Louis, 1998-99, dir. quality and process innovation, 1999—2001, def. fin. & acctg. svc., 2003—. Mem. urban planning and real estate com. St. Louis U., 1997-98; coach U.S.A. Youth Hockey, St. Louis, 1998-2000; mem. Heritage Found., Washington, 1996—. Recipient Young Alumni merit award S.E. Mo. State U., 1999. Mem. DAV, Assn. for Quality and Participation (bd. dirs. 1998—99), Am. Soc. for Quality, Nat. Geog. Soc., Res. Officers Assn., U.S.A. Hockey. Republican. Roman Catholic. Avocations: hockey, racquetball, music, outdoors, military history. Home: 5346 Old Lemay Ferry Rd Imperial MO 63052-1919 E-mail: bkmgraw@swbell.net.

MC GRAW, DARRELL VIVIAN, JR., state attorney general; b. Mullens, W.Va., Nov. 8, 1936; s. Darrell Vivian and Julia (ZeKany) Mc Graw; m. Jorea Marple; children: Elizabeth, Sarah, Darrell, Elliott. AB, W.Va. U., 1961, JD, 1964, MA, 1977. Bar: W.Va. 1964. Gen. atty. Fgn. Claims Settlement Commn., U.S. Dept. State, 1964; counsel to gov. State of W.Va., 1965—68; pvt. practice Charleston, Shepherdstown and Morgantown, 1968—76; judge W.Va. Supreme Ct. Appeals, Charleston, 1977—88, chief justice, 1982—83; atty. gen. State of W.Va., Charleston, 1993—. With U.S. Army, 1954—57. Fellow, W.Va. U., Nat. Ctr. Edn. in Politics/Ford Found. Fellow: Am. Polit. Sci. Assn., Rotary. Democrat. Office: Office of Atty Gen 1900 Kanawha Blvd E Rm E-26 Charleston WV 25305-0009

MCGRAW, DONALD JESSE, biologist, science historian, writer; b. Altadena, Calif., Oct. 27, 1943; s. Jesse E. and Mary L. (Hajostek) McG.; m. Laura Lee Hansen, July 13, 1968; children: Adrienne, Holly, Rachel. BS in Biol. Scis., Calif. State Poly. Coll., 1965; MS, Utah State U., 1967; PhD, Oreg. State U., 1976. Registered microbiologist Am. Acad. Microbiology. Research asst. microbiology Utah State U., 1965-66, teaching asst. food and aquatic microbiology, 1966-67; grad. teaching asst. gen. biology Oreg. State U., 1970-72, instr., 1972-73; tchr. phys. and biol. scis. U.S. Bur. Indian Affairs Boarding Sch., Shonto, Ariz., 1974-75; asst. prof. biology Franklin Coll., Ind., 1975-78; adj. asst. prof. biology Ind. Central U., Indpls., 1977-78; adj. asst. prof. Ind. U.-Purdue U., Columbus, 1978; mem. faculty Yavapai C.C., Prescott, Ariz., 1978-79; assoc. dir. Ute Research Lab., Ft. Duchesne, Utah, 1980-81, dir., 1981-82; vis. prof. biology Coll. St. Thomas, Minn., 1985-87; asst. prof. biology U. San Diego, 1988—2004, prof., 2001—, assoc. provost, 2001—. Adj. prof. biology U. San Diego, 2001—; summer ranger, naturalist U.S. Nat. Park Svcs., 1970—79, 1983—86. Author: (book) Andrew Ellicott Douglass and the Role of the Giant Sequoia in the Development of Dendrochonology, 2001; contbr. over 85 articles to profl. jours. Commr. San Diego County Columbian Quincentenary Commn., 1990-93, chmn. edn. com., 1990-93; mem. pres.'s adv. com. San Diego Zool. Soc., 1995-97; trustee Quail Bot. Gardens Found., 1995-98. Capt. (0-6) USPHS Ready Res. Recipient Disting. Alumnus award, Calif. State Poly. U., 1991, Monrovia H.S., 1991, Meritorious Pub. Svc. award USN, 2003; Eli Lilly doctoral grantee Oreg. State U., 1973-74; NSF grantee, 1998. Mem. AAAS, Cabrillo Hist. Assn. (bd. dirs. 1989-94, vice chair 1992, chair 1993, 94), History of Sci. Soc., Tree Ring Soc., Alpha Scholastic Honor Soc. of Franklin Coll. (pres. 1976-78), Sigma Xi (sec. San Diego chpt. 1996-97, v.p. 1997-98, pres. 1999-2000, assoc. dir. S.W. region 2000-02, Silver medal of achievement 2002), Beta Beta Beta. E-mail: granttree@yahgoo.com.

MCGRAW, HAROLD WHITTLESEY, JR., publishing executive; b. Bklyn., Jan. 10, 1918; s. Harold Whittlesey and Louise (Higgins) McG.; m. Anne Per-Lee, Nov. 30, 1940; children: Suzanne, Harold Whittlesey III, Thomas Per-Lee, Robert Pearce. Grad., Lawrenceville (N.J.) Sch., 1936; AB, Princeton U., 1940. With G.M. Basford (advt. agy.), N.Y.C., 1940-41, Brentano's Bookstores, Inc., 1946; with McGraw-Hill Book Co., Inc., N.Y.C., 1947—, successively promotion mgr., dir. co. advt. and trade sales, 1947-55, dir., v.p. charge trade book, indsl. and bus. book depts., co. advt., 1955-61, sr. v.p., 1961-68, pres., 1968-74, McGraw-Hill, Inc., 1974-81, CEO, 1975-83, chmn., 1976-88; chairman emeritus, 1988—. Bd. dirs. McGraw Hill, Inc., 1954-88. Founder, pres., bd. dirs. Bus. Council Effective Literacy and Bus. Press Ednl. Found. Served as capt. USAAF, 1941-45. Mem.: Wee Burn Club (Darien, Conn.), Blind Brook Club (Purchase, N.Y.). Home: Watch Tower Rd Darien CT 06820 Office: The McGraw-Hill Cos 1221 Avenue Of The Americas New York NY 10020-1095

MCGRAW, HAROLD WHITTLESEY, III, (TERRY MCGRAW), information company executive; b. Summit, N.J., Aug. 30, 1948; s. Harold W. McGraw Jr.; m. Nancy Goodrich, Sept. 22, 1973; children: Harold W. IV, Megan G. BA, Tufts U., 1972; MBA, U. Pa., 1976. Fin. mgmt. staff GTE; asst. v.p. pension investment GTE Mgmt. Corp., McGraw-Hill, Inc., N.Y.C., 1980-83, dir. corp. planning systems, 1983-84, v.p. corp. planning, 1984-85, also bd. dirs.; group v.p., pub. transp. group McGraw-Hill Publs. Co., N.Y.C., 1985-86, group v.p., pub. transp., aerospace and def. group, 1986-87, pres., 1987-88, McGraw-Hill Fin. Svcs. Co., N.Y.C., 1988-89; exec. v.p. The MHP Companies, N.Y.C., 1989-93, pres., COO, 1993-98, pres., CEO, now chmn., 1998—. Bd. dirs. Mag. Publ. Am., Am. Bus. Press. Bd. dirs. Hartley House, N.Y.C., 1983—, Prep for Prep, Black Execs. Exchange Program, Nat. Actors Theatre; co-chmn. Carnegie Hall's Corp. Fund. Mem. Assn. Am. Publ. (bd. dirs.). Office: The McGraw Hill Companies Ste C3A 49th Fl 1221 Avenue Of The Americas New York NY 10020-1095

MCGRAW, JACK WILSON, federal agency administrator; b. Balt., May 19, 1943; s. P.W. and Nina (Gwinn) McG.; m. Nancy F. Foster, Aug. 31, 1974; children— David, Mark BA, Morris Harvey Coll., 1964; B.Div., Tex. Christian U., 1967. Ordained minister Christian Ch. (Disciples of Christ). Dir. temporary housing HUD, Washington, 1979-82; asst. assoc. dir. Fed. Emergency Mgmt. Agy., Washington, 1982, dep. asst. dir., 1982-83; dep. asst. adminstr. EPA Office Solid Waste and Emergency Response, Washington, 1983-88, acting asst. adminstr.; dep. regional adminstr. EPA Regional Office, Denver, 1988—. Nominee William H. Jump award HUD, 1972; recipient Presdl. Meritorious award, Presdl. Disting. Exec. award. Presbyterian. Home: 8074 S Oneida Ct Englewood CO 80112-3128 Office: EPA Regional Office 8074 S Oneida Ct Englewood CO 80112

MCGRAW, LAVINIA MORGAN, retired retail company executive; b. Detroit, Feb. 26, 1924; d. Will Curtis and Margaret Coulter (Oliphant) McG. AB, Radcliffe Coll., 1945. Mem. Phi Beta Kappa. Home: 2501 Calvert St NW Washington DC 20008-2620

MCGRAW, PHILLIP C. psychologist, television personality; b. Vinita, Okla., Sept. 1, 1950; s. Joseph and Jerri McGraw; m. Debbie Higgins, 1970 (div. 1973); m. Robin Jameson, 1976; children: Jay, Jordan. Student U. Tulsa, BA Midwestern State U.; MA exptl. psychology, U. North Tex., 1976, PhD clin. psychology, 1979. Clin. psychologist, behavioral medicine practitioner; co-founder Courtroom Scis., Inc. (litigation consulting firm), Irving, Tex., 1989; regular commentator Oprah Winfrey Show, 1986—; host The Dr. Phil Show, 2001—; monthly columnist O, the Oprah Magazine. Pub. spkr. in field. Author: Life Strategies: Doing What Works, Doing What Matters, 1999, Relationship Rescue: A Seven-Step Strategy for Reconnecting with Your

Partner, 2000, Self Matters: Creating Your Life from the Inside Out, 2001, The Ultimate Weight Solution: The 7 Keys to Weight Loss Freedom, 2003; contbr. articles to profl. jours. Founder Dr. Phil Foundation, 2003—. Named one of Most Intriguing People of 2002, People mag., Ten Most Fascinating People, Barbara Walters TV special, 2002. Avocations: golf, tennis, scuba diving, coaching Little League baseball. Office: The Dr Phil Show 5482 Wilshire Blvd 1902 Los Angeles CA 90036*

MCGRAW, TIM, country music singer; b. Delhi, La., May 1, 1967; s. Tug McGraw; m. Faith Hill; children: Gracie Katherine, Maggie Elizabeth, Audrey Caroline. Albums include Tim McGraw, 1993, Not a Moment Too Soon, 1994 (triple-platinum), All I Want, 1995, Everywhere, 1997, A Place in the Sun, 1999, Set the Circus Down, 2001, Tim McGraw and the Dancehall Doctors, 2002, Live Like You Were Dying, 2004; (single) Welcome to the Club, 1992. Recipient Country Music Association award, 1997, 98, 99, 2000, 2001, Grammy award, 2001, nominee, 2004 Office: care Curb Records 3907 W Alameda Ave Burbank CA 91505-4332*

MCGRAW, WARREN RANDOLPH, state supreme court justice; b. Wyoming County, W.Va., May 10, 1939; m. Peggy Shufflebarger; children: W. Randolph, H. Suzanne, Rebecca L. AB, U. Charleston, 1960; postgrad., W.Va. U.; JD, Wake Forest U., 1963. Bar: W.Va. 1963. Trial atty. U.S. Dept. Justice, Washington; legal svc. atty.; elected W.Va. Ho. of Dels., 1968, 70, W.Va. Senate, 1972, 76, 80; elected prosecuting atty. Wyoming County, 1996; justice W.Va. Supreme Ct. Appeals, 1998—, chief justice, 2001. Instr. W.Va. U. Ext. Agy.; W.Va. del. Dem. Nat. Conv., 1972, 74; mem. Del. and Senatorial Dist. Exec. Coms.; del. State Dem. Jud. Conv. and State Dem. Conv.; elected pres. W.Va. Senate, 1980, 82; co-chmn. Crime Commn.; mem. Nat. Conf. Lt. Govs. Featured on Nat. Pub. TV series Bill Moyers Journal. Trustee 1st United Meth. Ch., Pineville; participant Marshall U.'s Taft Lectr. Series; elected W.Va. del. Dem. Nat. Conv., 1972, 74, Wyo. County Bd. Edn., 1986, 44th pres. W.Va. Sen., 1980, 82; del. State Dem. Jud. Conv., State Dem. Conv.; past pres. Jaycees; mem. Nat. Conf. Lt. Govs., Heart Fund, Wyoming County Cancer Fund, Del. and Sen. Dist. Exec. Coms.; past chmn. Wyoming County Dem. Exec. Com.; co-chmn. Crime Commn. Named one of nation's Outstanding Legislators, Rutgers U.; recipient Friend of Edn., Margaret Baldwin award W.Va. Edn. Assn. Mem. Wyo. Bar Assn., Raleigh County Bar Assn., Rotary Internat. Office: Bldg 1 Rm E-302 Capitol Complex Charleston WV 25305

MCGREEVEY, JAMES EDWARD, governor; b. Jersey City, N.J., Aug. 6, 1957; s. Jack and Veronica McGreevey; m. Karen J. Schutz, 1991 (div. 1997); 1 child, Morag Veronica; m. Dina Matos, 2000; 1 child, Jacqueline Matos. BA, Columbia U., 1978; JD, Georgetown U., 1981; MEd, Harvard U., 1982; LLD (hon.), Rider U., 2002. Mem. NJ State Assembly (19th dist), Middlesex, 1990—91; mayor City of Woodbridge, NJ, 1992—2001; mem. NJ State Senate (19th dist.), 1994—97; gov. State of NJ, Trenton, 2002—; announced Nov. 15th resignation on August 12th, 2004. Atty., regional mgr. Merck & Co., Rahway, N.J., 1987-91. Campaign com. vol. state Legis. Campaigns, 1983, 85, 87; campaign vol. Middlesex County Freeholder reelection campaigns, 1983-88; atty., policy counsel Assembly Dem. Majority Office, 1983-84; campaign vol. speaker for Congressman Bernard J. Dwyer, 1984, 86, 88, Senator Frank R. Lautenberg, 1988, 94; former chmn. Ctrl. Jersey chpt. ARC. Mem. Nat. Conf. Christians and Jews (former chmn.), Middlesex County Cult and Heritage Commn. (former chmn.), N.J. League Nursing (former trustee), Diocese of Metuchen Cath. Lawyers Guild (past pres.). Democrat. Office: Office Gov, Attn: Cathy McLaughlin PO Box 001 125 W State St Trenton NJ 08625

MCGREEVY, MARY SHARRON, former psychology educator; b. Kansas City, Kans., Nov. 10, 1935; d. Donald and Emmy Lou (Neubert) McG.; m. Phillip Rosenbaum (dec.); children: David, Steve, Mariya, Chay, Allyn, Jacob, Dora. BA in English with honors, Vassar Coll., 1957; postgrad., New Sch. for Social Rsch., NYU, 1958-59, Columbia U., 1959-60, U. P.R., 1963-65, U. Mo., 1965-68, U. Kans.; PhD with distinction, U. Calif., Berkeley, 1969. Exec. Doubleday & Co., N.Y.C., 1957—60; chief libr. San Juan Sch., PR, 1962—63; NIMH drug rschr. Russell Sage Found., Clinico de los Addictos, Rio Piedras, PR, 1963—65; psychiat. rschr. U. PR Med. Sch., PR, 1963—65; psychiat. researcher U. Kans. Med. Ctr., Kansas City, 1966—68; rsch. assoc. Ednl. Rsch., 1965—69; from assoc. prof. to disting. prof. U. Calif., Berkeley, 1968—69, ret., 1969. Yacht owner Encore; lectr. in philosophy; founder Simone de Beauvoir Cir., Inc. Author: (poetry) To a Sailor, 1989, Dreams and Illusions, 1993, Wedding: A Celebration, 1998, The Red Hibiscus, 2000, Irish Poems, 2000, The Swan, 2001, Sea Poems, 2002, Memoir of Annette Van Howe, 2002; contbr. articles to profl. jours. Mem. U.S. Holocaust Meml. Mus., Women in the Arts. Nat. Gallery, Jewish World Congress, 2000—, Friends Everglades, Nat. Wildlife Assn., Nat. Coun. Jewish Women (photographer 2000-), 1999—; publicity chair Nat. Coun. Jewish Women, 2000—02; vol. Broward County Hist. Commn., Friends of the Libr., Ft. Lauderdale Libr., 1969—, Broward County Libr. Found., FAU Wimberly Libr. Found.; mem. (donor for archives) Naval Air Sta. Ft. Lauderdale Hist. Assn., 1994—; mem. Am. Friends of Bodleian Libr., Oxford, England, Irish Cultural Inst., Ft. Lauderdale, Ft. Lauderdale Hist. Soc., Nat. Trust Hist. Preservation, Frances Loeb Lehman Art Gallery, Vassar Col., Ctr. de las Artes, Miami, Friends of Modern Mus. Art, Friends of the Guggenheim, Friends of Met. Mus. Art, Nelson-Atkins Mus. Art, Nat. Gallery of Art of Ireland, Norton Mus. Art, Palm Beach, Friends of Mus. of Art, Ft. Lauderdale, Friends of U. Mo. Libr., Johnson County Mental Health Assn.; mem. (scholarship donor) Pine Crest Columns Soc.; mem. Ft. Lauderdale Philharm. Soc., Menninger Found., 1997—, Navy League Broward County; founder Dora Achenbach McGreevy Poetry and Philosophy Found., Inc., 1989—, exec. dir., 1989—, Plus X Cath. Women's Club; active donor various scholarships Fla. Atlantic U. Found., 1993—. Recipient Cert. for Svc. Broward County Hist. Commn., 1994, Nat. Women's History Project award, 1995; honored by Broward County Women's Hist. Coalition, 1996; Sproul fellow, Bancroft Libr. fellow, Russell Sage Found. fellow; postdoctoral grant U. Calif. Mem.: NOW, AAUW (corr. sec. 1991—95, bd. dirs. 1991—2001, Jeanne Faiks meml. scholarship fund com. 1992—98, Nat. Ednl. Found. book brunch com. 1994—98, chair cultural events 1995—. chair 1998, rec. sec. 1998—2002, book brunch com. 2000—01, photographer, honoree Ednl. Found. Fund 1993, cert. appreciation 2000), Fla. Women's Consortium, Southwestern Philosophy Assn., Soc. Phenomenology and Existentialism, Nietzsche Soc., Fla. Philosophy Assn. (spkr. 1991, 1993, chair self in philosophy 1994), Mo. Sociol. Assn., Poets of the Palm Beaches (yearly poetry anthology 1992—, 1st prize free verse ann. contest 1996), South Fla. Poetry Inst. (yearly poetry anthology 1991—98), Union of Concerned Scientists, Women in Psychology, Nat. Acad. Poets, Nat. Women's History Project Orgn., Internat. Soc. Universal Dialogue, Am. Philos. Assn., Nat. Women's Political Caucus, Pem-Hill Alumni Assn., Vassar Alumni Assn., Secular Humanists (bd. dirs. 1992—98, program chair 1995—98, publicity chair 1998—99), Oxfam Am., Smithsonian Instn., Fla. State Poets Assn., Inc., Broward Women's Hist Coalition (bd. dirs. 1991—98, archivist 1991—98, ad hoc com., Hall of Fame Women's History awards 1989—98), Fla. Atlantic U. Chamber Music Soc., Libr. Congress, Sierra (conservation com. 1979—, co-chair beach clean-up 1993, archivist 1993—95, Redwoods chpt. 1997, newspaper reporter, environ. com.), Vassar Club (N.Y., Kansas City, South Fla. and Palm Beach chpts.). Democrat. Roman Catholic. Achievements include first to use methodone treatment and rehabilitation at drug clinic in Puerto Rico. Avocations: poetry, painting, sailing, tennis, the beach.

MCGREGOR, DOUGLAS A. real estate company executive; Exec. v.p., dir. devel. & ops. The Rouse Co., Columbia, Md., 1989—. Office: The Rouse Co 10275 Little Patuxent Pkwy Columbia MD 21044-3455

MCGREGOR, DOUGLAS HUGH, pathologist, educator; b. Temple, Tex., Aug. 28, 1939; s. Harleigh Heath and Joyce Ellen (Lambert) McG.; m. Mizuki Kitani, July 6, 1969; children: Michelle Sakuya, David Kenji. BA, Duke U., 1961, MD, 1966; postgrad., U. Edinburgh, Scotland, 1961-62. Diplomate Am. Bd. Pathology. Intern, chief resident in pathology UCLA Med. Ctr., 1966-68; surgeon, lt. comdr. Atomic Bomb Casualty Commn., Hiroshima, Japan, 1968-71; chief resident in pathology Queens Med. Ctr., Honolulu, 1971-73; asst., assoc. prof. pathology U. Kans. Med. Ctr., Kansas City, 1973-82, prof., 1982—. Dir. anat. pathology VA Med. Ctr., Kansas City, Mo., 1975-94, chief pathology and lab. medicine, 1994-2003, dir. surg. pathology, 2003—. Contbr. numerous articles to profl. jours., chpts. to books. Leader YMCA Indian Princess Program, Overland Park, Kans., 1977-79, Indian Guide Program, 1978-80, Cub Scout Am., Overland Park, 1980-82, Boy Scouts Am., Leawood, Kans., 1982—. Lt. comdr. USPHS, 1968-71, Japan. Grantee Merck, Sharp and Dohme, 1980. Fellow Coll. Am. Pathologists, Am. Soc. Clin. Pathologists; mem. Am. Assn. Pathologists, Internat. Acad. Pathologists, Soc. Exptl. Biology and Medicine, N.Y. Acad. Scis., AAAS, Kansas City Soc. Pathologists (sec.-treas. 1982-83, pres. 1983-84), Leawood Country Club. Achievements include research in ultrastructure and pathobiology of neoplasms, radiation carcinogenesis, and morphogenesis of atherosclerosis. Home: 9400 Lee Blvd Shawnee Mission KS 66206-1826 Office: VA Med Ctr 4801 E Linwood Blvd Kansas City MO 64128-2226 Business E-Mail: douglas.mcgregor@med.va.gov.

MCGREGOR, EWAN GORDON, actor; b. Crieff, Scotland, Mar. 31, 1971; m. Eve Mavrakis, 1995; 2 children. LLD, U. Ulster, 2001. Motion picture actor; stage actor. Film appearances include Being Human, 1993, Shallow Grave, 1994, Blue Juice, 1995, Emma, 1996, Trainspotting, 1996 (Brit. Actor of Yr., 1996), Brassed Off, 1996, A Life Less Ordinary, 1997, Velvet Goldmine, 1998, Little Voice, 1998, Nora, 1999, Eye of the Beholder, 1999, Star Wars: Episode I-The Phantom Menace, 1999, Moulin Rouge, 2001 (European Film award for Achievement in World Cinema, 2001), Black Hawk Down, 2001, Star Wars II- Attack of the Clones, 2002, Down With Love, 2003, Young Adam, 2003, Big Fish, 2003, others, (TV films) Lipstick on Your Collar, 1993, Doggin' Around, 1994, TV guest appearances include Tales from the Crypt, 1989, ER, 1994. Recipient ALFS award, 1997. Office: care Lindy King Drury House 34-43 Russell St Peters etc London WC2B 5HA England*

MCGREGOR, JOHN JOSEPH, lawyer; b. Fort Knox, Ky., Nov. 18, 1946; s. Arden Durham and Ruth Marguerite (Funkner) McG.; m. Rebecca Lounsbury, 1989. AB, U. San Francisco, 1968; JD, U. Calif. Hastings Coll. Law, 1971; LLM, NYU, 1974. Bar: Calif. 1972, U.S. Dist. Ct. (no. dist.) Calif. 1972, U.S. Ct. Appeals (9th cir.) 1979, U.S. Dist. Ct. (ea. dist.) Calif. 1988; cert. specialist in taxation law. Sports info. dir. U. San Francisco, 1966-68; staff atty. Community Legal Svcs., San Jose, Calif., 1972-73; cons. IRS Project, Washington, 1974-75; assoc. Thomas, Snell, Jamison, Russell, Williamson & Asperger, Fresno, Calif., 1975-78; shareholder Thomas, Snell, Jamison, Russell & Asperger, Fresno, 1978-91, McGregor, Dahl, Sullivan & Klug, Fresno, 1991—. Asst. sec., gen. counsel The Vendo Co., Fresno, 1985-88; mem. Fresno County Assessment Appeals Bd., 1993-98. Author: Taxation of Real Property Transfers, 1981. Bd. dirs. Fresno (Calif.) Storyland, 1976-81; mem. Fresno Ski Patrol, 1976-93, Sierra Summit Ski Patrol, Lakeshore, Calif., 1985-93, The Acad., Fresno, 1981—. Named Vol. Atty. of the Year Fresno County Bar Assn., 1983. Mem. Am. Law Inst., Calif. State Bar Assn. (dir. taxation sect., exec. com. 1983-86, chair standards of tax practice com. 1995, 98), Fresno County Bar Assn. (dir. 1982-86). Roman Catholic. Avocations: skiing, golf, reading. Home: 4774 N Wishon Ave Fresno CA 93704-3144 Office: McGregor Dahl Sullivan & Klug 7080 N Whitney Ave Fresno CA 93720-0154 Business E-Mail: jmcgregor@mdsklaw.com.

MCGREGOR, RUTH VAN ROEKEL, state supreme court justice; b. Le Mars, Iowa, Apr. 4, 1943; d. Bernard and Marie Frances (Janssen) Van Roekel; m. Robert James McGregor, Aug. 15, 1965. BA summa cum laude, U. Iowa, 1964, MA, 1965; JD summa cum laude, Ariz. State U., 1974. Bar: Ariz. 1974, U.S. Dist. Ct. Ariz. 1974, U.S. Ct. Appeals (9th cir.), U.S. Supreme Ct. 1982. Assoc. Fennemore, Craig, von Ammon, Udall & Powers, Phoenix, 1974-79, ptnr., 1980-81, 82-89; law clk. to justice Sandra Day O'Connor U.S. Supreme Ct., Washington, 1981-82; judge Ariz Ct. Appeals, 1989-98, vice chief judge, 1993-95, chief judge, 1995-98; justice Ariz. Supreme Ct., 1998—, vice chief judge, 2002—. Mem. disciplinary commn. Ariz. Supreme Ct., 1984-89, City of Mesa jud. adv. bd., 1997—. Mem., newsletter editor Charter 100, Phoenix, 1981—; bd. dirs., mem. Ctr. for Law in Pub. Interest, Phoenix, 1977-80. Mem. ABA (chmn. state memberships 1985—), Ariz. Bar Assn. (disciplinary com. 1984—), Ariz. Judges Assn. (exec. com. 1990—, sec. 1991-92, v.p. 1992-93, pres. 1993-94), Nat. Assn. Women Judges (chair first time attendees com. 1990-91, 1994 conv. com.; exec. com. 1995—). Lodges: Soroptomists. Democrat. Lutheran. Office: Arizona Supreme Court 1501 W Washington St Phoenix AZ 85007-3231

MCGREGOR, WENDOLYN SUZANNE, elementary school educator, mathematician; b. The Dalles, Oreg., Aug. 25, 1964; d. Delbert Eugene and Mary Ann Trowbridge; m. Brian Lee McGregor, Sept. 10, 1983 (dec. Apr. 28, 2003); children: Stephanie Nicole, Nathan Jeffrey. AA in Edn., Coll. So. Idaho, 1998, AA in History, 1999; BA in History, Idaho State U., 1999, BS in Elem. Edn., 2001. Cert. elem. and secondary tchr. Idaho, 2000. Computer operator Coll. So. Idaho, Twin Falls, Idaho, 1987—88; payroll clk. Amalgamated Sugar, Twin Falls, 1989—90; 5th grade tchr. Kimberly (Idaho) Sch. Dist., 2000—03; 4th grade tchr. Twin Falls (Idaho) Sch. Dist., 2003—. Bookkeeper Garnard Mktg., Twin Falls, 1987—89; tutor Coll. So. Idaho, 1997—99; mem. math. curriculum com. Kimberly (Idaho) Sch. Dist., 2000—03, mem. tech. com., 2000—03. Asst. leader Girl Scouts Am., Filer, 1992—94; leader Cloverlands 4-H, Filer, 1991—92; bible club dir. Filer (Idaho) First Bapt. Ch., 1991—96; children's leader Bible Study Fellowship, Twin Falls, 1993—96. Scholar Zobell-Albion scholar, Idaho State U., 1999. Mem.: Golden Key Nat. Honor Soc. (Peat Marwick scholar 1999), Nat. Job Corp. Alumni Assn. (Outstanding Student scholar 1999), Phi Theta Kappa. Avocations: reading, time with family, computers, astronomy, college classes. Office: Bickel Elem 607 2nd Ave E Twin Falls ID 83301 Business E-Mail: mcgregorwe@tfsd.k12.id.us.

MCGRIFF, CHERYL RENEE, medical products executive; d. Herb Hightower and Georgie Luvern Burnett, Julius Burnett (Stepfather) and Mai Bach Hightower(Stepmother); children: Georgina Janelle Greene, Christina Marie Grayson, Felicia Renee Holley, Dorian Gerard, Destinee Gerard, Delilah Grayson. BA in Bus., Eckerd Coll., St. Petersburg, 1998; BSN, MS in Healthcare Adminstrn., PhD in Pub. Health, Rochville U., 2004. Indsl. nurse, safety mgr. Lykes Pasco, Inc., Tampa, Fla., 1991—95; COO Global Internat. Med. and Safety Supply, Tampa, 2004—. Minority bus. coun. mem. Lakeland C. of C., 1999—2000; cmty. svc. chair Imperial Assn. of Life Underwriters, Lakeland, 1999—2000. Mem.: Am. Bus. Women's Assn., Gamma Sigma Sigma, Kappa Epsilon (life). Office: Global Int'l Medical & Safety Supply PO Box 82725 Tampa FL 33682-2725 Office Phone: 813-382-5967. Office Fax: 813-931-8881. Business E-Mail: globalmednsafety@aol.com.

MCGRIFF, FRED (FREDERICK STANLEY MCGRIFF), professional baseball player; b. Tampa, Fla., Oct. 31, 1963; Grad., H.S., Tampa. Baseball player Toronto Blue Jays, 1982—90, San Diego Padres, 1990—93, Atlanta Braves, 1993—97, Tampa Bay Devil Rays, Fla., 1997—. Named Am. League Home Run Leader, 1989, Nat. League Home Run Leader, 1992; named to All-Star Team, Sporting News, 1989, 1992, 1993, Nat. League, 1992, 1994; recipient Silver Slugger award, 1989, 1992, 1993. Achievements include being a mem. of World Series Championship team, 1995. Office: Tropicana Field 1 Tropicana Dr Saint Petersburg FL 33705-1703

MCGRORY, MARY KATHLEEN, retired academic administrator, humanities educator; b. N.Y.C., Mar. 22, 1933; d. Patrick Joseph and Mary Kate (Gilvary) McG. BA, Pace U., 1957; MA, U. Notre Dame, 1962; PhD, Columbia U., 1969; DHL, Albertus Magnus Coll., 1984; LLD, Briarwood Coll., 1990; DHL, Trinity Coll., 1991. Prof. English Western Conn. State U., Danbury, 1969-78; dean arts and scis. Ea. Conn. State U., Willimantic, 1978-80, v.p. for acad. affairs, 1981-85; pres. Hartford (Conn.) Coll. for Women, 1985-91; sr. fellow U. Va. Commonwealth Ctr., Charlottesville, 1991-92; exec. dir. Soc. Values in Higher Edn./Georgetown U., Washington, 1992-96; chair dept. rhetoric, lang. and culture U. Hartford, dir. profl. and tech. writing. Pres. MKM Assocs., Holland, Mass., 1983—. Author: Yeats, Joyce & Beckett, 1975. Bd. dirs. Hartford Hosp., 1985-93; chmn. bd. govs. Greater Hartford Consortium Higher Edn., 1989-90. Fels Found. fellow, 1966-67, NEH summer fellow, 1975; Ludwig Vogelstein Found. travel grantee, 1973. Mem. New Eng. Jr. Community and Tech. Coll. Coun. (v.p. 1988-91), Am. Assn. Higher Edn., Med. Acad. of Am., Greater Hartford C. of C. (bd. dirs. 1989-91), Hartford Club (bd. dirs. 1988-91). Avocations: writing, swimming, piano. Address: 44 Forest Dr Holland MA 01521-9702

MCGROTTY, CAROLE WEAVER, elementary school educator, parochial school educator; d. Earl Arthur and Mary Marjory (Darland) Weaver; children: Kevin, Heather McGrotty Shade, Sean, Erin McGrotty Russell. BA, N.Mex. Highlands U., 1961. Cert. English tchr. grades K-12 Fla., N.C. 5th and 6th grade tchr. St. Theresa Cath. Sch., Coral Gables, Fla., 1959—61; 5th grade tchr. Starr Elem., Richmond, Ind., 1961—62; 5th and 6th grade tchr. Dade County Schs., Miami, Fla., 1962—65; 6th - 8th grade English tchr. St. Francis Cath., Ft. Myers, Fla., 1982—83. Author: Watch Out: Mother's on the Road, 2002, Woman's World "A Fair to Remember", 2004; corr. The Catholic News & Herald, Charlotte, N.C.; contbr. articles to newspapers. Active Kennedy for Pres. Campaign, Miami, 1962. Mem.: Writer's Coffee. Republican. Roman Catholic. Avocations: cross stitch, painting, drawing, sewing. Home: 209 Crowell Sq Ct #313 Asheville NC 28806

MCGUANE, FRANK L., JR., lawyer; b. White Plains, N.Y., July 10, 1939; s. Frank L. and Dorothy P. (McGrath) McG.; m. Carla L. Miller; children: Lauri Elizabeth, Molly Elizabeth. BA, U. Notre Dame, 1961; JD, U. Cin., 1968. Bar: Colo. 1968, U.S. Dist. Ct. Colo. 1968, U.S. Ct. Appeals (10th cir.) 1970, U.S. Supreme Ct. 1971. Shareholder McGuane and Malone, P.C., Denver, 1981-95; pres. Frank McGuane & Assocs., P.C., Denver, 1995—; ptnr. McGuane & Hogan, LLP, Denver, 1997—. Mem. faculty Nat. Inst. for Trial Advocacy, 1987—; lectr. in field. Author: Domestic Relations-Colorado Methods of Practice, 1983; co-author: Colorado Family Law and Practice, 2 vols., 1999; contbr. articles to profl. jours. Chmn. Denver area chpt. Nat. Eagle Scout Assn. Boy Scouts Am,. 1980-82. With USMC, 1961-63. Fellow Am. Acad. Matrimonial Lawyers (jour. editor 1990-95, 2000-01, bd. govs. 1988-95, pres. Colo. chpt. 1988-89), Internat. Acad. Matrimonial Lawyers (founding fellow, bd. govs. 1997—); mem. ABA, Colo. Bar Assn. (chmn. family law sect. 1977-78), Denver Bar Assn., Arapahoe County Bar Assn., Douglas-Elbert County Bar Assn., Pitkin County Bar Assn., Am. Coll. Family Trial Lawyers (diplomate), Cath. Lawyers Guild. Office: Ste 950 Ptarmigan Pl 3773 Cherry Creek N Dr Denver CO 80209 Office Phone: 303-691-9600. E-mail: flm@mcguanehogan.com.

MCGUFFEY, CARROLL WADE, JR., lawyer; b. Decatur, Ga., Dec. 1, 1951; s. Carroll Wade and Dorothy (Landers) McG.; m. Virginia Elizabeth Miller, Aug. 12, 1972; children: Carroll Wade, III, Michelle Elizabeth, Jennifer Lanier. BBA, U. Ga., 1973, JD cum laude, 1976. Bar: Ga. 1976, Fla. 1977, U.S. Dist. Ct. (mid. dist.) Ga. 1976, U.S. Supreme Ct. 1980. Capt. Chief Claims Tort Litigation Div. USAF, Eglin AFB, Fla., 1976-80; assoc., ptnr. Savell and Williams, Atlanta, 1980-90; mng. ptnr., CEO Goodman McGuffey Aust & Lindsey LLP, Atlanta, 1990—2003; CEO Goodman McGuffey Lindsey & Johnson, LLP, Atlanta, 2003. Lectr. in field. Editor: Employers Guide to Workers Compensation in Georgia, Employee Leasing: An Employer's Guide. Ward capt. Athens Mayoral Campaign (Ga.), 1975; commr., dir. Stone Mountain Dixie Youth Baseball, 1982-87; cubmaster Boy Scouts Am., 1986-88, scoutmaster, 1988-90, troop chmn., 1991-92, dist. chmn., 1993-95; mgr., coach Murphy Candler Girls Softball Assn., 1996-2003. Recipient Dist. Award of Merit, Boy Scouts Am., 1995. Mem. ABA, Fla. Bar Assn., Atlanta Bar Assn. (workers compensation seminar chmn. 1993, 97, fundraising chmn. Kid's Chance Found. Race, 1992, workers compensation section, bd. dirs. 1994-01, sec.-treas. 1997, chair-elect 1998, chair 1999), Ga. Def. Lawyers Assn. (trial acad. instr. 1987), Def. Rsch. Inst., Ind. Ins. Agts. of Ga. (hon. life, young agents com.), Ga. Mental Health Assn. (bd. dirs. 1987). Clubs: Athens Boat (dir. 1982-90), Lawyers (Atlanta), UGA Pres. Club. Methodist. Business E-Mail: wmcguffey@gmlj.com.

MCGUINN, EDWIN J. chemicals executive; b. 1953; BA in Math. and Econ., Colgate U.; MA in Acctg., N.Y. U. cert. CPA. Mng. dir. Lehman Brothers; mgmt. Mabon Securities, Rodman & Renshaw Capital Group, Inc.; exec. v.p., head ops. InterVest Securities, Inc.; pres., CEP Automated Trading Sys., Inc, eLot, Inc., Milford, Conn., 2000—.

MCGUINN, MARTIN GREGORY, banker, lawyer; b. Phila., Sept. 9, 1942; s. Martin G. and Rita (Horgan) McG.; m. Ann M. Muldoon, Sept. 17, 1977; children: Patrick J., Christopher M. AB, Villanova U., 1964, JD, 1967. Bar: Pa. 1967, N.Y. 1970. Assoc. Sullivan & Cromwell, N.Y.C., 1970-77; mng. counsel The Singer Co., Stamford, Conn., 1977-80; chmn., CEO Mellon Bank, Pitts., 1998—; CEO, chmn. Mellon Fin. Corp, Pitts., 1999—. Bd. consultors Villanova Law Sch., 1972—, chmn. 1985-87; bd. dirs. U.S.-Japan Bus. Coun., Inc., Allegheny Conf. on Cmty. Devel. Editor in chief Villanova Law Rev., Vol. 12, 1966-67. Bd. dirs. UPMC Health Sys.; trustee Carnegie Mus. of Pitts.; chmn. Hist. Soc. Western Pa. Mem. ABA, N.Y. State Bar Assn., Pa. Bar Assn., Allegheny County Bar Assn., Am. Law Inst., The Fin. Svcs. Roundtable, Am. Soc. Corp. Secs. (chmn. 1990-91). Home: 714 Amberson Ave Pittsburgh PA 15232-1446 Office: Mellon Fin Corp 1 Mellon Bank Ctr Pittsburgh PA 15258-0001

MCGUINN, MICHAEL EDWARD, III, retired army officer; b. Spartanburg, S.C., Feb. 22, 1925; s. Michael Edward Jr. and Margaret Cordelia (Shackleford) McG.; m. Betty Gay Corn, 1948 (div. 1951); m. Phyllis Fryer, Oct. 7, 1952 (dec. July 1997); children: Michael Edward IV, Carol Anne McGuinn Branch. Student, Clemson U., 1941-43, 46, Coll. William and Mary, 1962-63. Served with U.S. Navy, PTO, 1943-46; commd. 2d lt. U.S. Army, 1949, advanced through grades to col., 1971; asst. mil. attache Am. Embassy, Copenhagen, 1958-61; posted to svc. British Army, Longmoor, Eng., 1964-66; served on U.S. Dept. Army Gen. Staff, Washington, 1966-68; comdr. 10th Transp. Bn. U.S. Army, Vietnam, 1968-69; chief transp. div. U.S. Readiness Command, MacDill AFB, Fla., 1969-72; ret. U.S. Army, 1972; state govt. svc. various locations, 1972-82; chief of staff Ga. State Def. Force, an Agy. of the State of Ga., Atlanta, 1987-95, 2002—; orgnl. cons. Ga. Dept. Def. Decorated Legion of Merit (2), Army Commendation medal (2), Naval Commendation medal. Mem.: U.S. Army Transp. Mus. Avocations: military history, photography, home workshop. Home and Office: 6420 Tanacrest Ct NW Atlanta GA 30328-2837 E-mail: sdftrooper@aol.com. *Since boyhood when a young cadet, I have lived by one code "Duty, Honor and Country". In good times and bad, it has kept me faithful to principles of personal responsibility, personal integrity, and the importance of service to something greater than oneself. The code has never failed our nation nor has it ever failed me.*

MCGUIRE, BRIAN LYLE, educator, consultant; b. Mobile, Ala., June 13, 1959; m. Jean Ellen Marler, June 18, 1983. BS in Acctg., U. S. Ala., 1982, MBA, 1990; PhD, U. Ctrl. Fla., 1996. CPA, Ala.; cert. mgmt. acct.; cert. bus. mgr. Staff acct. Smith, Dukes & Buckalew, CPA's, Mobile, 1983-86; corp. acct. So. Med. Health Systems, Mobile, 1986, dir. corp. ops, 1987-88; exec. dir. Med. Arts Clinic, Inc. subs. So. Med. Health Systems, Foley, Ala., 1986-88; adminstr. Mobile Heart Ctr., 1988-91; acctg. instr. U. Ctrl. Fla., Orlando, 1991-95; assoc. prof. acctg. U. So. Ind., Evansville, 1995—. Unit commr. Boy Scouts Am., Buffalo Trace Coun., 1996-97, pack com. chair, 1995-98. Recipient Eagle Scout Order of Arrow Boy Scouts Am., 1977, Faculty Rsch. award, 1001, Faculty Svc. award, 1999, 2001; named to Outstanding Young Men of Am., 1982. Mem. AICPA, Inst. Mgmt. Accts. (chpt. bd. dirs. 1983-85, pres. 1987-88, nat. bd. dirs. 1989-91, 92-93, 98—, pres. regional coun. 1992-93, 98-99, Award of Excellence 1993, 99, chair regional ops. com. 1998-00, chair com. on ethics 2000-01, exec. com. 2003—). Methodist. Avocations: travel, camping, fishing, golf. Office: U So Ind Dept Acctg and Bus Law 8600 University Blvd Evansville IN 47712-3534

MCGUIRE, CAROLE BAKER, legislative staff member; b. Seattle, Dec. 26, 1951; BA, Western Wash. U., 1974. Staff aide Sen. Warren Magnuson, 1974-76; legis. analyst Budget Com., 1976-81, legis. and budget analyst, 1981-85, dir. appropriations activities, 1985—, asst. staff dir., 1995—. Office: Budget Com 621 Senate Dirksen Office Bldg Washington DC 20510-0001

MCGUIRE, EDWARD DAVID, JR., lawyer; b. Waynesboro, Va., Apr. 11, 1948; s. Edward David and Mary Estelle (Angus) McG.; m. Georgia Ann Charuhas, Aug. 15, 1971; children: Matthew Edward, Kathryn Ann. BS in Commerce, U. Va., 1970; JD, Coll. William and Mary, 1973. Bar: Va. 1973, D.C. 1974, Md. 1990, Pa. 1995, U.S. Dist. Ct. (ea. dist.) Va. 1974, U.S. Dist. Ct. D.C. 1974, U.S. Dist. Ct. Md. 1990, Ct. Appeals (4th cir.) 1974, U.S. Ct. Appeals (D.C. cir.) 1974, U.S. Supreme Ct. 1993. Assoc. Wilkes and Artis, Washington, 1973-78; gen. corp counsel Mark Winkler Mgmt., Alexandria, Va., 1978-80; sr. contracts officer Amtrak, Washington, 1980-81; sr. real estate atty., asst. corp. sec. Peoples Drug Stores, Inc., Alexandria, 1981-88; of counsel Cowles, Rinaldi & Arnold, Ltd., Fairfax, Va., 1989-91; sr. assoc. Radigan, Rosenberg & Holmes, Arlington, Va., 1991; pvt. practice, Annandale, Va., 1992-97; sr. assoc. Stein, Sperling, Bennett, DeJong, Driscoll, Greenfeig Metro, Rockville, Md., 1997-99; of counsel Hodes, Ulman, Pessin & Katz, P.A., Annandale, 1999-2000; atty. pvt. practice, Alexandria, Va., 2000—; mng. dir., personal trust adminstr. Riggs Bank, N.A., Washington, 2000—. Co-author: Legacy: Plan, Protect and Preserve Your Estate, 1995, Generations: Planning Your Legacy, 1998. Bd. dirs. Dist. XVI Va. Student Aid Found., 1978-85, George Washington dist. Boy Scouts Am., 1986; active William and Mary Law Sch. Assn., bd. dirs., 1983-96, pres., 1987-88, treas., 1990-91. Capt. JAGC, USANG, 1973-79. Mem. ABA, Va. Bar Assn., Va. State Bar, D.C. Bar, Md. State Bar Assn., Fairfax Bar Assn., Am. Trial Lawyers Am., Arlington County Bar Assn., Va. Trial Lawyers Assn., No. Va. Estate Planning Coun., William and Mary Alumni Soc. (bd. dirs. D.C. chpt. treas. 1992-94), U. Va. Club of Washington (schs. com. chmn. 1995—, v.p. outreach 1997-99, pres.-elect 1998-99, bd. dirs. 1996-99), Rotary (treas. Springfield chpt. 1985-86, sec. 1986-87, pres.-elect 1987, chmn. World Affairs Conf. 1985-88, bd. dirs. 1984-88, 96-97, Dist. 7610 youth leadership awards chmn. 1994-97, Outstanding Rotarian award 1985). Greek Orthodox. Avocations: racquetball, coaching youth sports. Home and Office: 31 W Myrtle St Alexandria VA 22301-2422

MCGUIRE, GARRY K., SR., communications executive; b. Rochester, N.Y. BS in Econs., U. Dayton; student in Exec. Edn. Program, U. Pa. With Detroit (Mich.) Bank & Trust Co., 1969—83; from dir. ops. and adminstrn. to v.p. strategic planning No. Telecom Fin. Corp., 1983—90; v.p. strategic planning No. Telecom Inc., 1991—95; pres. NORTEL Comms. Sys. Inc., 1995—2002; sr. v.p. Avaya, Basking Ridge, NJ, 2002—, CFO, 2002—; pres., CEO Williams Comms. Solutions LLC. Bd. dir. Globespan Virata, Inc., chmn. audit com.; bd. trustees U. Dayton. With USAF. Office: Avaya 211 Mount Airy Rd Basking Ridge NJ 07920

MCGUIRE, GEORGE R. lawyer, educator; b. Binghamton, N.Y., June 8, 1969; s. Charles S. McGuire and Anita J. Mangiaracina; m. Tanya M. Harlec, July 30, 1994; children: Grace E., Abigail E. BS in Aerospace Engring., Syracuse U., 1991, JD magna cum laude, 1996. Bar: NY 1997, registered: U.S. Patent and Trademark Office (Patent Agent) 1993. Patent agt., patent atty. McGuire Law Offices, Syracuse, NY, 1991—97; ptnr. Hancock & Estabrook, LLP, 1997—2003; mem. Bond, Schoeneck & King, PLLC, 2003—. Adj. prof. Syracuse U., 1997—. Dir. Make-A-Wish Found. of Ctrl. N.Y., Inc., Syracuse, 2003, Everson Mus. of Art, Syracuse, 2003; pres. Ctrl. N.Y. Patent Law Assn., Syracuse, 2000. Recipient 40 Under 40, M&T Bank, 2003. Mem.: N.Y. State Bar Assn. (assoc.; co-chair trademark com 2004—), Am. Intellectual Property Law Assn. (assoc.). Home: 6910 Kassonta Dr Jamesville NY 13078 Office: Bond Schoeneck & King PLLC One Lincoln Center Syracuse NY 13202 Office Phone: 315-218-8515. E-mail: gmcguire@bsk.com.

MCGUIRE, HUNTER HOLMES, JR., retired surgeon, educator; b. Richmond, Va., Dec. 13, 1929; s. Hunter Holmes and Catharine Skelton (Bemiss) McG.; m. Alice Burwell Reed, Apr. 23, 1960; children: Alice McGuire Massie, Hunter III, William Reed. BA, U. Va., 1951, MD, 1955. Cert. Am. Bd. Surgery. Asst. dean of medicine Med. Coll. Va., Richmond, 1964-76, prof. surgery, 1973-2000; chief surg. svc. VA Hosp., Richmond, 1976-2000, ret., 2000. Trustee Va. Hist. Soc., Richmond, 1970-90. Lt. USNR, 1956-58. Mem. So. Surg. Assn. (v.p. 1994), Med. Soc. Va. (v.p. 1965), Assn. Va. Surgeons (pres. 1994, Disting. Svc. award 1996), Ea. Surg. Soc. (sec. 1975-80), Va. Surg. Soc. (pres. 1976).

MCGUIRE, JOHN FRANCIS, JR., construction company executive; b. NYC, May 28, 1941; s. John Francis and Ann Helena (Hoey) McG.; m. Dorann Rastetter (dec. July 1968); 1 child, Sean Philip; m. Jan Barbara Close, Oct. 18, 1969; 1 child, Seth Adrian. Student, Marist Coll., Poughkeepsie, N.Y., 1976, Dutchess C.C., Poughkeepsie, 1976, 90-97, 99—. Founder, owner, mgr., pres. McGuire Constrn. Co., Rhinebeck, N.Y., 1966—; pres., owner Olde Mill Wine & Spirits Inc., Rhinebeck, NY, 1994-99. Mem. Rhinebeck Town/Village Shared Svcs. study com., 1991. Trustee Rhinebeck Theater Soc., asst. treas., chmn. fin. com., bd. dirs., 1987-98, v.p. 1990-93, pres. 1994-98, fin. com., chmn. phys. plant & grounds Wilderstein Preservation Inc.; coach, instr., referee, umpire Rhinebeck Little League Baseball and Basketball, Jr. League Baseball, Girls Softball League; co-founder, coach Rhinebeck Soccer League, 1972-85; Rhinebeck Cub Scouts, Boy Scouts asst, 1974-80; former vice chmn. sch. bldg. needs com. Rhinebeck Cen. Sch. Dist., 1980, facilities study com., 2003; chief fire officer Hillside Fire Dist., 1963-75; former Rhinebeck Town Natural Disaster Coord.; co-author Town of Rhinebeck, Town of Hyde Park Fire Codes, Dutchess County Fire Mutual Aid Plan; asst. to mgr. Dutchess County Fair, 1976-85; past pres., past bd. mem. Rhinebeck Alumni Assn.; co-chmn. Rhinebeck Bicentennial, 1974-77; mem. Rhinebeck Rep. Com., 1977—, vice chmn., 1984-88, chmn., 1989-95; mem. Dutchess County Rep. Com., exec. com.; coord. coun. Dutchess County Criminal Justice; mem. Friends of Clermont, Mills Mansion Hist. Sites; merger study com. No. Dutchess Hosp., Kingston Hosp. and Benedictine Hosp., 1997-99; sales tax rev. com. Dutchess County, 1998-99; trustee Quitman Hist. Resource Ctr., 2000—, pres., 2003—. Named to Hall of Fame, Dutchess County Sports Mus., Poughkeepsie, 1989; recipient Life Saving award Hillside Fire Dist., Hometown Hero award Dutchess County Red Cross, 2004, Spirit of Dutchess County award United Way, 2004. Mem.: Rhinebeck C. of C. (bd. dirs. 1968—92, mem. Blue Ribbon com. 2000—02), Huguenot Hist. Soc., Dutchess County Agricultural Soc., Alpha Beta Gamma, Phi Theta Kappa. Avocations: tennis, cross country skiing, running, reading. Home and Office: 42 Ackert Hook Rd Rhinebeck NY 12572-2605 Office Phone: 845-876-6666.

MCGUIRE, JOHN LAWRENCE, pharmaceutical executive; b. Kittanning, Pa., Nov. 3, 1942; s. Lawrence F. and Florence G. (Jones) McG.; m. Pamela Hale, Aug. 2, 1969; children: Megan L., Christa H. BS, Butler U., 1965; MA, Princeton U., 1968, PhD, 1969; postgrad., Columbia Sch. Bus., 1981. Asst. in instrn. Princeton U., 1967-69; pharmacologist Ortho Pharm. Corp., Raritan, NJ, 1969-72, sect. head molecular biology, 1972-75, exec. dir. rsch., 1975-80, v.p. preclin. R&D, 1980-88; sr. v.p. global rsch. and devel., bd. dirs. R.W. Johnson Pharm. Rsch. Inst., Raritan, 1988-92; corp. v.p. bus. devel., pharm./diagnostics group Johnson & Johnson, New Brunswick, NJ, 1992—2004; pres. Ferring Rsch. Insts., Copenhagen, 2004—, San Diego, 2004—, Lausanne, Switzerland, 2004—. Adj. assoc. prof. dept. medicine M.S. Hershey Sch. Medicine Pa. State U., 1978—; adj. prof. dept. animal sci. Rutgers U., 1983-92; adj. prof. ob-gyn. East Va. Med. Sch., 1987—; adj. prof. ob-gyn. and reproductive endocrinology U. Medicine and Dentistry of N.J., 1988—; cons. NASA, 1985-87; cons. Nat. Tech. Transfer Ctr., 1997-2000. Mem. editl. bd. Ullman's Ency. Indsl. Chemistry, 1987—; editor numerous books; contbr. articles to profl. jours.; patentee in field. Trustee Hunterdon Med. Ctr. Found., 1986—, chmn., 2002—; trustee N.J. State Hosp. Assn., 2002—, NJ State Theater, New Brunswick, 2002—, August Found., 1997—, pres., 1997—; trustee Raritan Valley C.C., North Branch, NJ, 1986—, vice chmn., 1990—; trustee Hunterdon Med. Ctr., Flemington, NJ, 1978—2002, vice chmn., 1984—86, chmn., 1988—98; trustee Hunterdon Health Care Sys., Flemington, NJ, 1986—, chmn., 1989—2002; trustee Atlantic Health Sys., Morristown, NJ, 1991—93, vice chmn., 1992—93; trustee The Pennington (N.J.) Sch., 1995—, pres., CEO, 1996—; exec. bd. Keystone Area coun. Boy Scouts Am., Harrisburg, Pa., George Washington Coun., Boy Scouts Am., Trenton, NJ, 1980—86, 1995—99, Ctrl. N.J. coun. Boy Scouts Am., Princeton, 1999—, pres., 2000—; mem. N.E. Region bd. Boy Scouts Am., 2004—; bd. dirs. United Way of Hunterdon County, NJ, 1983—97, pres., 1985—87; bd. dirs. Tri-State United Way, NY, 1987—94, Hunterdon County (NJ) YMCA, 1982—87, Mid Jersey Health Corp., 1986—88, chmn., 1986—88; bd. visitors Butler U., Indpls., 2004—. Named N.J. Hosp. Trustee of Yr., 2001; recipient Silver Beaver award, Boy Scouts Am., 1984, Disting. Eagle Scout award, 2000, Johnson medal for rsch. and devel., 1990; Population Coun. fellow, 1969. Mem. Am. Soc. Pharmacology and Exptl. Therapeutics, Soc. Exptl. Biology and Medicine, Am. Physiol. Soc., Endocrine Soc., Am. Coll. Ob-Gyn, Am. Soc. Clin. Pharmacology and Therapetics, Soc. Gynecol. Investigation, Licensing Execs. Soc., Biochemistry Soc. Great Britain, Royal Soc. Medicine (U.K.), Am. Chem. Soc. Clubs: Princeton (N.Y.C.). Home: 10 Club House Dr Whitehouse Station NJ 08889-3378 Personal E-mail: John.McGuire@Ferring.com.

MCGUIRE, JOHN THOMAS, lawyer, educator; b. Bronx, N.Y., Oct. 12, 1966; s. Thomas John and Irene McGuire. BA in History magna cum laude, MA in History, U. Scranton, 1988; JD cum laude, U. Buffalo, 1991; PhD in Am. History, Binghamton U., 2001. Bar: N.Y. 1991. Trial atty. U.S. Dept. of Justice, Washington, 1991-95; pvt. practice Vestal, NY, 1995—. Bd. dirs. Legal Svcs. of Ctrl. N.Y., 2004—, Legal Aid Soc. of Mid. N.Y., 2004—; adj. prof. SUNY, Oneonta, 2000—, Broome C.C., 2001-03. Reviewer American Jewish History, 1998, Left History, 2001, Labor History, 2004; author: Making the Democratic Party a Partner: Eleanor Roosevelt the WJLC and the Women's Division of the New York State Democratic Party, 2001; contbr.: Historical Dictionary of the Gilded Age, Encyclopedia of New York State, 2003, Historical Encyclopedia of the Gilded Age and Progressive Era, 2003; author: From The Courts to The State Legislatures: Social Justice Feminism, Labor Legislation and The 1920's, 2004. V.p. Peace Action of N.Y., 2003—; pres. Broome County Peace Action, 2004—. James A. Finnegan fellowship, 1987, Albert M. Greenfield Rsch. fellowship, 2003, Archie K. Davis Rsch. fellowship, 2004; recipient Rsch. grant State Hist. Soc. of Iowa, 2004. Mem. N.Y. State Bar Assn., Am. Hist. Assn., Orgn. Am. Historians, Order of Barristers, Alpha Sigma Nu. Home: 422 Clubhouse Rd Vestal NY 13850-3727 E-mail: johnmcguireus@yahoo.com.

MCGUIRE, JOHN W., SR., advertising executive, marketing professional, writer; b. Chgo., May 12, 1952; s. Eugene H. Sr. and Marjorie (Bolger) McG.; m. Mary Sue Roper, June 17, 1972 (div. 1977); 1 child, John William Jr.; m. Lynn L. Rembos, June 21, 1984 (div. April 1991); children: Kelly Lynn, Ryan Michael. AA, Chgo. City Colls., 1972; BA, Northeastern Ill., Chgo., 1974. Janitor Bd. of Edn., Chgo., 1970-74; sales rep. Motorola Comms., Inc., Schaumburg, Ill., 1974-76, Pattis Group, Chgo., 1976-77; midwest sales mgr. Harcourt Brace Jovanovich Pub. Co., N.Y.C., 1977-79; account sales mgr. Cosmopolitan Mag. Hearst Pub. Co., N.Y.C., 1979-81; midwest acct. mgr. Psychology Today Mag. Ziff-Davis Pub. Co., N.Y.C., 1981-82; midwest regional mgr. Pennwell Pub. Co., Tulsa, Okla., 1982-84; western regional sales mgr. Nursing Mgmt. Mag. SN Pub. Co., West Dundee, Ill., 1984-91; western regional sales mgr., midwest regional sales mgr. U.S. Pharmacist Mag. Jobson Pub. Co., N.Y.C., 1991-98; v.p. SK&A Info. Svcs., Irvine, Calif., 1998-99; assoc. pub. Health Mgmt. Technology Mag. Nelson Pub., Nokomis, Fla., 1999; pres., CEO Blossom Pub. Co., Wasco, Ill., 2000—. Author: (book) One Man's Life: A Poetic Review, 1995; co-author: (with Scott Mennie) The Original Parent and Family Logbook, 2002; singer (cassette tapes), designer (creative posters). With USN, 1970. Mem. VFW, Midwest Healthcare Mktg., Arlington Poetry Project. Republican. Roman Catholic. Avocations: writer, scuba, horsemanship, travel, skydiving.

MCGUIRE, JOSEPH, Canadian government official; b. Morell, Can. s. Louis and Etta McGuire; m. Mary Cain; children: Moira, Matthew. Student, Prince Wales Coll. Tchrs. Tng., U. N.B.; BA, St. Dunstans U., 1968. Tchr. Tracadie (Prince Edward Island) Sch.; vice prin. Sioux Lookout (Ont.) Elem. Sch.; with Cmty. Employment Strategy, O'Leary Svc. Ctr., George Henderson, MP, Egmont Constituency Office; asst. to Joe Ghiz Office of Premier of Prince Edward Island; asst. campaign mgr. George Henderson for Mem. Parliament campaign, 1980, campaign mgr., 1984; mem. parliament for Egmont Can. House of Commons, 1988—, mem. standing com. Fisheries, Oceans and Natural Resources; chair standing com. Fisheries and Oceans; chair standing com. Agr.; vice-chair Atlantic Caucus; parliamentary sec. to minister of agr. and agri-food, 1998-2000; mem. standing com. human resources devel./disabled persons, 2000—; min. Atlantic Can. opportunities agy. Govt. Can., Ottawa, 2003—. Bd. dirs. West Prince Forestry, Tyne Valley Sports Ctr.; mem. St. Patrick's Parish Coun., Grand River. Avocations: sports, historical novels, golf, hiking. Office: House of Commons 807 Confederation Bldg Ottawa ON Canada K1A 0A6 E-mail: mcguij@parl.gc.ca.

MCGUIRE, LESIL L. state representative; b. Portland, Oreg., Jan. 22, 1971; m. Scott McCracken. Degree in Speech Comm. and Polit. Sci., Willamette U., 1993, JD, 1998. Legis. and press aide U.S. Senator Ted Stevens, 1993—95; legal intern U.S. Atty., 1996; law clk. Oreg. Dept. Justice, 1996—98; mem. Alaska Ho. of Reps., 2000—, judiciary com. Vol. Habitat for Humanity; mentor Bush Elem. Sch. Mentor Program; vol. Salem's Women's Crisis Ctr. Mem.: Young Rep., Anchorage Rep. Women's Club, Am. Diabetes Assn. Republican. Avocations: fishing, skiing, flying, scuba diving, reading. Office: Rm 118 State Capitol Juneau AK 99801-1182 Address: 716 W 4th Ave Ste 430 Anchorage AK 99501-2133 Office Phone: 907-465-2995.

MCGUIRE, MARY JO, state legislator; b. Mpls., 1956; BA in Bus. Adminstrn., Coll. of St. Catherine, 1978; JD, Hamline U., 1988; postgrad., Harvard U., 1995-97. Mem. Minn. Ho. of Reps., 1988—, mem. judiciary com., judiciary fin. divsn., vice chair family and early childhood edn. fin. divsn., mem. govt. ops., chair data practices subcom., lead minor mem. Democrat. Home: 1529 Iowa Ave W Saint Paul MN 55108-2128 Office: Minn Ho of Reps State Ho Office Bldg Saint Paul MN 55155-0001

MCGUIRE, MICHAEL FRANCIS, plastic surgeon; b. St. Louis, Oct. 4, 1946; s. Arthur Patrick and Virginia Claribel (Gannon) McG. BA, Columbia U., 1968, MD, 1972. Diplomate Am. Bd. Surgery, Am. Bd. Plastic Surgery. Intern UCLA, 1972-73, resident in gen. surgery, 1973-77, resident in plastic surgery, 1978-80; fellow in plastic surgery rsch. Stanford (Calif.) U., 1977-78; traveling fellow in plastic surgery Gt. Britain, 1980; chief plastic surgery L.A. County-Olive View Med. Ctr., Sylmar, Calif., 1980-85; pvt. practice Santa Monica, Calif., 1980—; chief plastic surgery St. John's Health Ctr., 1990—; asst. clin. prof. surgery UCLA, 1980-97, assoc. clin. prof., 1998—. Bd. dirs. Calif. Med. Rev., Inc., sec.-treas., 1997, v.p., 1997-99, chmn. bd. dirs. 1999—2003; chmn. surg. rev. St. Johns Health Ctr., 1996-98; pres. Pacific Coast Plastic Surgery Ctr., 1988—. Charter patron L.A. Music Ctr. Opera, 1983—; sponsoring patron Los Angeles County Art Mus., 1986—; patron Colleague Helpers in Philanthropic Svc., Bel Air, Calif., 1987, 93, 95; pres. Found. for Surg. Reconstrn., 1996—. Fellow ACS, Royal Soc. Medicine; mem. Am. Soc. Plastic Surgeons (membership chmn. 1997-2000, bd. dirs. 2002-), Am. Soc. Aesthetic Plastic Surgery (ethics chmn. 1998-99, bd. dirs. 2004—, pub. edn. chmn. 2004—), Am. Health Quality Assn. (bd. dirs. 1999—), L.A. County Med. Assn. (v.p. 1995-97, sec.-treas. 1997-99), Calif. Med. Assn. (del., exec. com., splty. delegation 1994-99), Calif. Soc. Plastic Surgery (exec. com., auditor 1988-89, program chmn. 1990, exec. coun. 1991-94, treas. 1994-97, v.p. 1997-98, acting pres. 1997, pres.-elect 1998-99, pres. 1999-2000, nominating com. chmn. 2000-01, strategic planning com. chmn. 2001—), Am. Assn. Accreditation of Ambulatory Surgery Facilities (ops. com. 1995-96, bd. dirs. 1996, treas. 1996-98, sec. 1998-2000, v.p. 2000-02, pres. 2002-), Alpha Omega Alpha. Avocations: golf, travel, collecting antique irish glass, opera, modern art. Office: 1301 20th St Ste 460 Santa Monica CA 90404-2054 Office Phone: 310-315-0121.

MCGUIRE, MICHAEL JOHN, environmental engineer; b. San Antonio, June 29, 1947; s. James Brendan and Opal Mary (Brady) McG.; m. Deborah Marrow, June 19, 1971; children: David, Anna. BS in Civil Engring., U. Pa., 1969; MS in Environ. Engring., Drexel U., 1972, PhD in Environ. Engring., 1977. Diplomate Am. Acad. Environ. Engring.; registered profl. engr., Pa., N.J., Calif., Ariz. San. engr. Phila. Water Dept., 1969-73; rsch. assoc. Drexel U., Phila., 1976-77; prin. engr. Brown & Caldwell Cons. Engrs., Pasadena, Calif., 1977-79; water quality engr. Met. Water Dist. of So. Calif., L.A., 1979-84, water quality mgr., 1984-86, dir. water quality, 1986-90, asst. gen. mgr., 1990-92; pres. McGuire Environ. Cons., Inc., Santa Monica, Calif., 1992—. Cons. to subcom. on adsorbents, safe drinking water com. Nat. Acad. Scis., 1978-79, NRC, Drinking Water Contaminants (comm. mem.), 1998-99; cons. mem. Techs. Workgroup U.S. EPA, DBP Reg. Neg., 1992-93, 97, 98 2000. Editor: (with I.H. Suffet) Activated Carbon Adsorption of Organics from the Aqueous Phase, 2 vols., 1980, Treatment of Water by Granular Activated Carbon, 1983, (with J.L. McLain and A. Obolensky) Information Collectoin Rule Data Analysis; contbr. articles to profl. jours. Mem. ASCE, Internat. Water Assn. (specialist group on taste and odor control 1982—, chmn. organizing com. 1991, off-flavor symposium 1987-91), Internat. Ozone Assn. (internat. bd. dirs. 1992-95), Am. Water Works Assn. (Calif.-Nev. sect. chmn. water quality and resources divsn. 1982-83, governing bd. 1984-87, 89-96, exec. com. 1989-96, chmn. 1991-92, nat. edn. divsn. chmn. 1982-83, dir. 1994-96, chair taste and odor com. 1993-98, exec. com. 1994-96, Acad. Achievement award 1978, Fuller award 1994, Publs. award 2001), Am. Chem. Soc., Sigma Xi, Sigma Nu, Sigma Tau. Office: McGuire Environ Cons Inc # 200 1919 Santa Monica Blvd Santa Monica CA 90404-1954

MCGUIRE, PATRICIA A. lawyer, academic administrator; b. Phila., Nov. 13, 1952; d. Edward J. and Mary R. McGuire. BA cum laude, Trinity Coll., 1974; JD, Georgetown U., 1977. Bar: Pa. 1977, D.C. Ct. Appeals 1979. Program dir. Georgetown U. St. Law Clinic, Washington, 1977-82; asst. dean for devel. and external affairs Georgetown U. Law Ctr., Washington, 1982-89; pres. Trinity Coll., Washington, 1989—. Adj. prof. law Georgetown U., 1977-82, Georgetown Law Ctr., 1987—; commr. Mid. States Commn. on Higher Edn., 1991—; bd. dirs. Acacia Group, Elderhostel, Inc. Editor: Street Law Mock Trial Manual, 1984; contbr. articles to profl. jours. Trustee Trinity Coll., 1986—; bd. dirs. Assn. Cath. Colls. and Univs., 1991—, Eugene and Agnes Meyer Found.; mem. adv. bd. Merion Mercy Acad. and Sisters of Mercy, 1990—; bd. dirs. Nat. Assn. Ind. Colls. and Univs.; mem. commn. govt. rels. Am. Coun. Edn.; bd. dirs. Women's Coll. Coalition; adv. bd. Nat. Coll. Access Network; mem. dollar coin design adv. com. U.S. Mint; bd. vis. Joint Mil. intelligence Coll. Recipient Daytime Emmy, TV Acad., N.Y.C., 1979-80. Mem. ABA, Assn. Am. Law Schs. (instl. advancement 1985—), Coun. for the Advancement and Support of Edn., Trinity Coll. Alumnae Assn. (pres. 1986-89) Democrat. Roman Catholic. Office: Trinity Coll Office of the President 125 Michigan Ave NE Washington DC 20017-1091 E-mail: president@trinitydc.edu.

MCGUIRE, ROBERT C. retired federal bankruptcy judge; b. 1935; AB, Dartmouth Coll., 1957; JD, Boston Coll., 1960. Bar: Mass. 1960, Tex. 1961. Assoc. Turner, White, Dallas, 1961-64, Ungerman, Hill, Angrist & Dolginoff, 1965-78; probate judge Dallas County, 1979-80; ptnr. Skibell & McGuire, 1981-83; judge U.S. Bankruptcy Ct., Dallas, 1983—2002, chief judge, 1985—2002. Mem.: John C. Ford Am. Inn of Ct. (pres. 2000—01), Dallas Bar Assn., Tex. Bar Assn., Nat. Conf. Bankruptcy Judges. Home: 4729 Alta Vista Ln Dallas TX 75229-2923

MCGUIRE, ROGER ALAN, retired foreign service officer; b. Troy, Ohio, July 1, 1943; s. Charles M. and Mary L. (Coppock) McG.; m. Harriet H. Cooke, July 12, 1969; children: Sara, Casey. BA, Beloit Coll., 1965; MA, U. Wis., 1967. Country desk officer Dept. State, Washington, 1974-78; dep. chief of mission Am. Embassy, Maputo, Mozambique, 1978-80; congl. fellow Am. Polit. Sci. Assn., Washington, 1980-81; polit. officer Am. Embassy, Asuncion, Paraguay, 1981-83, Lusaka, Zambia, 1983-86; dep. dir. Office of West African Affairs Dept. of State, Washington, 1986-88; chief of mission Am. Embassy, Windhoek, Namibia, 1988-90; consul Am. Consulate, Porto Alegre, Brazil, 1990-92; U.S. amb. to Guinea-Bissau, 1992-95; counselor for polit. affairs Am. Embassy, Canberra, Australia, 1995-97; ret., 1997. Vol. Am. Couns. Internat. Edn. Recipient Superior Honor award U.S. Agy. for Internat. Devel., 1969. Mem. Rotary Internat., Phi Beta Kappa. Home: 3007 Russell Rd Alexandria VA 22305-1719

MCGUIRE, SANDRA LYNN, nursing educator; b. Jan. 28, 1947; d. Donald Armstrong and Mary Lue (Harvey) Johnson; m. Joseph L. McGuire, Mar. 6, 1976; children: Matthew, Kelly, Kerry. BSN, U. Mich., 1969, MPH, 1973, EdD, 1988, MSN, 1997. Staff nurse Univ. Hosp., Ann Arbor, Mich., 1969; pub. health nurse Wayne County Health Dept., Eloise, Mich., 1969-72; instr. Madonna Coll., Livonia, Mich., 1973; pub. health coord. Plymouth Ctr. for Human devel., Northville, Mich., 1974-75; asst. prof. cmty. health nursing U. Mich., Ann Arbor, 1975-83; asst. prof. U. Tenn., Knoxville, 1983-88, assoc. prof., 1990—, gerontol. nurse practitioners program coord., 1998—, chair MSN program Coll. Nursing. Dir. Kids Are Tomorrow's Srs. Program, 1988—; resource person Gov.'s Com. Unification of Mental Health Svcs. in Mich.; spkr. profl. assns. and workshops. Author (with S. Clemen-Stone and D. Eigsti)): Comprehensive Community Health Nursing, 1981, Comprehensive Community Health Nursing, 5th edit., 1998, Comprehensive Community Health Nursing, 6th edit., 2002. Bd. dirs. Ctr. Understanding Aging, 1987-93, v.p., 1995; bd. dirs. Mich. chpt. ARC, 1980-83, Knoxville chpt., 1984-85; founder Knoxville Intergenerational Network, 1989. Recipient John W. Runyan, Jr. Cmty. Health Nursing award U. Tenn. Memphis, 2002; USPHS fellow, 1972-73, Robert Woodruff fellow Emory U., 1996-97, Hewlett Innovative Tech. fellow U. Tenn., Knoxville, 1999-00, Profl. Devel. awardee U. Tenn. Knoxville, 1996-97, 99-2000. Mem. ANA, Tenn. Nurses Assn., Nat. Conf. Gerontol. Nurse Practitioners, Nat. Gerontol. Nursing Assn., Mich. Pub. Health Assn. (chmn. mental health sect. 1976, dir., co-chmn. residential svcs. com. 1976-79, chmn. health svcs. 1979-82), Nat. Assn. Retarded Citizens, Mich. Assn. Retarded Citizens, Nat. Coun. on Aging, Ctr. for Understanding Aging (v.p. 1994-95), Plymouth (chmn. residential svcs. com. 1975-77), Tenn. Assn. Retarded Citizens, So. Nursing Rsch. Soc., Sigma Theta Tau, Pi Lambda Theta, Phi Kappa Phi. Home: 11008 Crosswind Dr Knoxville TN 37922-4011 Office: 1200 Volunteer Blvd Knoxville TN 37996 Office Phone: 865-974-7589. Business E-Mail: smcguire@utk.edu.

MCGUIRE, SUSAN GRAYSON, legislative staff member; BA in Polit. Sci., U. Mich., 1962. Legis. asst. select com. on equal ednl. opportunity U.S. Senate, Washington, 1970-73; staff dir. subcom. on employment opportunities U.S. Ho. of Reps., Washington, 1973-84, staff dir. com. on edn. and labor, 1984-91; pub. policy cons. McGuire & Assocs., Cedar Crest, N.Mex., 1991-93; exec. dir. Indian Arts and Crafts Assn., Albuquerque, 1995-98; state dir. U.S. Senator Jeff Bingaman, Albuquerque, 1998—. Pres. N.Mex. Arts and Crafts Fair, Albuquerque; sec. bd. dirs. Albuquerque Literacy Program; active N.Mex. Clinton for Pres. Com., 1992. Office: 625 Silver Ave SW Ste 130 Albuquerque NM 87102-3185 Fax: 505-346-6780. E-mail: Susan_McGuire@Bingaman.senate.gov.

MCGUIRE, THOMAS G. economist, educator, mental health services professional, researcher; PhD. Asst. prof Boston U., 1976—83, assoc. prof., 1983—87, prof. econs., 1897—2001; prof. hlth. econs. Harvard Med. Sch., 2001—. Rsch. dir. tng. program in Econs. and Mental Health Heller Sch. at Brandeis, 1981—. Author: (book) Financing Psychotherapy, 1982 (Elizur Wright award from Am.Risk and Ins. Assn.), two other books and over 100 articles. Co-recipient Investigator award (with Richard Frank), Robert Wood Johnson Found, Kenneth J. Arrow award (with Ching-to Albert Ma), Internat. Health Econs. Assn., 1998; recipient Carl Taube award, Am. Pub. Health Assn., 1991. Office: Harvard Med Sch Dept Hlth Care Policy 180 Longwood Ave Boston MA 02115 E-mail: mcguire@hcp.med.harvard.edu.

MCGUIRE, THOMAS PETER, show boat captain, secondary school educator; b. N.Y.C., Apr. 27, 1945; s. Thomas Edward and Susan Rose (Cafarelli) McG. BA, Calif. State U., 1979, postgrad., 1979-83, MA in English CUNY, 1993. co. mgr. Vaudeville Driftwood Floating Theatre, 1963-75; Tchr., St. Philip's Sch., Pasadena, Calif., 1981-83; prodr. Driftwood Floating Theatre, 1968-75; owner, capt. Driftwood ShowBoat, Kingston, N.Y., 1983-98; pres. Driftwood Showboat Co., 1983—; tchr. English John F. Kennedy H.S., N.Y.C., 1986—2003; mem. faculty, founding mem. adv. com. Bronx Theatre H.S., 2003—; guest lectr. Hayden Planetarium, N.Y.C., 1960-64. Contbr. articles to profl. jours. Activist in human rights and equal rights. Served with USN, 1966-68. Mem. Am. Guild Variety Artists, Soc. Am. Magicians, Lesbian and Gay Tchrs. Assn. N.Y.C. (pres. 1998—). Roman Catholic. Avocations: writing, ballooning, astronomy. Home and Office: Driftwood Showboat PO Box 1032 Kingston NY 12402-1032

MCGUIRE, THOMAS ROGER, distribution company executive; b. Marshfield, Wis., Aug. 29, 1943; s. James Gilbert and Gene Elizabeth (Connor) McG.; m. Patricia Mae Ainsworth, Aug. 25, 1962; children: Elizabeth Anne, Amy Lynn. Chief exec. officer, chmn. bd. dirs. Coast Fabrication, Inc., San Jose, Calif., 1964-83, Coast R.V., Inc., San Jose, 1977—. Republican. Methodist. Avocation: basketball. Home: 1480 Calaveras Ave San Jose CA 95126-2502 Office: Coast Distbn System PO Box 1449 Morgan Hill CA 95038-1449

MCGUIRE, TIM, editor; Editor, sr. v.p. Star Tribune, Mpls., 1993—2002. Juror Pulitzer Prize, 2002. Mem.: Am. Soc. Newspaper Editors (pres. 2001—02). Roman Catholic. Office: Star Tribune 425 Portland Ave Minneapolis MN 55488-0002

MCGUIRE, TIMOTHY JAMES, lawyer, editor, columnist; b. Mount Pleasant, Mich., Mar. 24, 1949; s. James Edward and Anita Matilda (Starr) McGuire; m. T. Jean Fannin, May 10, 1975; children: Tracy, Jason, Jeffrey. BA, Aquinas Coll., Grand Rapids, Mich., 1971; JD cum laude, William Mitchell Coll. Law, St. Paul, 1987. Bar: Minn. 1987. Mng. editor Ypsilanti Press, Mich., 1973—75, Corpus Christi Caller, Tex., 1975—77, Lakeland Ledger, Fla., 1977—79, Mpls. Star, 1979—82; mng. editor features and sports Mpls. Star and Tribune, 1982—84, mng. editor, 1984—91, exec. editor, 1991—93, editor, sr. v.p., 1993—2002; syndicated columnist, spkr. on workplace spirituality, ehtics and values. Pulitzer Prize juror, 1988—89, 1995—2002. Lay preacher at St. Joseph Roman Cath. Ch., Mpls., 1995—. Mem.: Minn. State Bar Assn., Am. Soc. Newspaper Editors (bd. dirs. 1992—, chmn. change com. 1994—95, chmn. program com. 1996—97, treas. 1998—99, sec. 1999—2000, v.p. 2000—01, pres. 2001—02). Roman Catholic. Home: 3645 Rosewood Ln N Minneapolis MN 55441-1127

MCGUIRE, TIMOTHY WILLIAM, economics and management educator, dean; b. Englewood, N.J., Nov. 30, 1938; s. Charles James and Marie (McCarthy) McG.; children: Timothy William Jr., Gretchen Elizabeth, Michael Joseph; m. Nancy Paule Melone, 1991. BS in Indsl. Mgmt., Carnegie Inst. Tech., 1960, MS in Econs., 1961; PhD in Econs., Stanford U., 1968. Staff mem. Coun. Econ. Advisors, 1963-64; rsch. assoc. in econs. Grad. Sch. Indsl. Adminstrn., Carnegie Mellon U., Pitts., 1964-66, asst. prof. econs., 1966-69, assoc. prof., 1969-75, prof., 1975-79, prof. mgmt. and econs., 1982—, dep. dean, 1983-90; prof. social scis. and econs. Dept. Social Scis. Carnegie Mellon U., Pitts., 1981-82; prof. econs., chmn. dept. U. Iowa, Iowa City, 1979-80; dean, Harry B. Miller prof. bus. Charles H. Lundquist Coll. Bus., U. Oreg., Eugene, 1994-98; sr. exec. v.p., chief operating officer Mgmt. Sci. Assocs., Inc., Pitts., 1998—. Sr. visitor U. Cambridge, Eng., summer, 1970; bd. dirs. Mgmt. Sci. Assocs., Inc., Pitts.; bd. visitors Joseph M. Katz Grad. Sch. Bus., U. Pitts. Contbr. articles to profl. jours. Bd. trustees, mem. bus. adv. coun. Point Park Coll.; chmn. corp. adv. bd. Pitts.(Pa.) Ctr. Sports, Arts and Entertainment Mgmt. Woodrow Wilson Nat. Hon. fellow Carnegie Inst. Tech., 1960-61; Stanford U. fellow, 1961-62; fellow Ford Found., 1962-63, 70-71. Mem.: Soc. Judgment and Decision Making, Internat. Soc. Bayesian Analysis, Omicron Delta Kappa, Tau Beta Pi. Home: 118 Lakeland Dr Mars PA 16046-2114 Office: Mgmt Sci Assocs Inc RockPointe Bus Airpark 400 MSA Dr Tarentum PA 15084-2808 Office Phone: 412-362-2000. Personal E-mail: tmcguire@msa.com.

MCGUIRE, WILLIAM, civil engineer, educator; b. S.I., N.Y., Dec. 17, 1920; s. Edward Joseph and Phoebe (Sellman) McG.; m. Barbara Weld, Feb. 5, 1944; children: Robert Weld, Thomas Rhodes. BSCE, Bucknell U., 1942; MSCE, Cornell U., 1947. Structural designer Jackson & Moreland (engrs.), Boston, 1947-49; faculty Cornell U., Ithaca, 1949—, prof. civil engring., 1960-90, prof. emeritus of civil engring., 1990—; dir. Cornell U. (Sch. Civil Engring.), 1966-68; vis. prof. civil engring. Asian Inst. Tech., Bangkok, Thailand, 1968-70. Vis. research engr. Nat. Bur. Standards, 1972; Gledden vis. sr. fellow U. Western Australia, 1973; cons. structural engr., 1951—; vis. prof. U. Tokyo, 1979, U. Strathclyde, 1986 Author: Steel Structures, 1967; author: (with R.H. Gallagher and R.D. Ziemian) Matrix Structural Analysis, 1979, 2d edit., 2000. Served to lt. USNR, 1942-45. Recipient Naval Letter of Commendation, award for Outstanding Achievement, Bucknell U., 1987, T.R. Higgins Lectureship award Am. Inst. Steel Constrn., 1992, G. Haaijer awrd Am. Inst. Steel Constrn., 2000. Fellow ASCE (pres. Ithaca 1964, Norman medal 1962, 94, Hardesty award 1992, honorary mem. 1994); mem. Internat. Assn. Bridge and Structural Engring., Nat. Acad. Engring., Sigma Xi, Chi Epsilon, Kappa Delta Rho. Congregationalist. Home: 121 Simsbury Dr Ithaca NY 14850-1728

MCGUIRE, WILLIAM ALBERT, humanities educator; b. St. Louis, Mar. 18, 1944; s. William Albert and Virginia Marie (Grant) McGuire. BA, St. Louis U., 1966; MA, San Francisco State U., 1976. Instr. De Andreas H.S., St. Louis, 1966—69, Presentation H.S., San Francisco, 1977—91, U. San Francisco, 1992—97, San Francisco State U., 1995, City Coll. of San Francisco, 1975—. Coord. humanities City Coll. of San Francisco, 1998—. Mem. Soc. for the Preservation of San Francisco Archl. Heritage, 1986—. E-5 U.S. Army, 1969—71. Mem.: C.C. Humanities Assn., Calif. Humanities Assn., ACLU, UNICEF, Friends of Urban Forest, Amnesty Internat., Vets. for Peace, Sierra Club. Democrat. Roman Catholic. Avocations: music, gardening, cooking, writing. Office: City Coll of San Francisco 50 Phelan Ave San Francisco CA 94112 Office Phone: 415-452-5757 x 257.

MCGUIRE, WILLIAM B(ENEDICT), lawyer; b. Newark, Feb. 14, 1929; children: Joan Ellen, Ralph R., James C., Keith P., Grant W. BS, Fordham U., 1950; JD, Seton Hall U., 1958; LLM in Taxation, NYU, 1963. Bar: N.J. 1958, U.S. Dist. Ct. N.J. 1958, U.S. Supreme Ct. 1971, U.S. Ct. Appeals (3d cir.) 1980, N.Y. 1982. Chief acct. Hanover Fire Ins. Co., N.Y.C., 1950-58; sr. ptnr. Lum, Biunno & Tompkins, Newark, 1958-83, Tompkins McGuire Wachenfeld & Barry LLP, Newark, 1984—, mng. ptnr. Asst. prosecutor Essex County, N.J., 1964-65; bd. dirs. Ind. Coll. Fund of N.J.; trustee St. Barnabas Corp., St. Barnabas Med. Ctr. and Irvington Gen. Hosp.; mem. Essex County Ethics Com., 1974-77; mem. com. to review State Commn. of Investigation, 1982. Fellow Am. Coll. Trial Lawyers, Am. Bar Found. (state chmn.), Am. Bd. Trial Advocates, Internat. Acad. Trial Lawyers, Internat. Soc. Barristers; mem. ABA, N.J. State Bar Assn. (trustee 1982-89, sec. 1989-90, treas. 1990-91, 2d v.p. 1991-92, 1st v.p. 1992-93, pres.-elect 1993-94, pres. 1994-95), N.J. State Bar Found. (pres. 1988-89), Essex County Bar Assn. (pres. 1975-76), Internat. Assn. Ins. Counsel, Fedn. Ins. Counsel, Def. Rsch. Inst., Maritime Law Assn., U.S. Am. Arbitration Assn., Trial Attys. N.J., Assn. Fed. Bar N.J. (pres. 1985-88), Essex County Country Club (pres. 1983), Newark Club. Roman Catholic. Office: Tompkins McGuire Wachenfeld & Barry LLP 4 Gateway Ctr 100 Mulberry St Newark NJ 07102-4007 E-mail: WMcGuire@tompkinsmcguire.com.

MCGUIRE, WILLIAM DENNIS, health facility administrator; b. Glen Ridge, N.J., Sept. 24, 1943; s. John William and Kathleen Mary (Sexton) McG.; m. Nancy Katherine Hoyne, Aug. 13, 1966; chldren: Kathleen Anne, Colleen Dempsey. BA, U. Notre Dame, 1965; M.H.A., U. Mich., 1968. Asst. adminstr. U. Wis. Hosps., Madison, 1971-74; adminstr. Children's Med. Ctr., Dayton, Ohio, 1974-79; COO Mercy Cath. Med. Ctr., Phila., 1979-80; CEO Wills Eye Hosp., Phila., 1980-85; pres., CEO Mercy Health Care Sys., Scranton, Pa., 1985-89, Mt. Carmel Health, Columbus, Ohio, 1989-92, Incarnate Word Health Svcs., San Antonio, 1992-95, Cath. Med. Ctrs. of Bklyn, and Queens, N.Y.C., 1996—2000; health care cons., 2000—02; pres., CEO Kaleida Health, Buffalo, 2002—. Adj. faculty dept. health care Trinity U., 1992-95; asst. prof. Ohio State U., 1990-92; asst. clin. prof. Wright State U. Sch. medicine, Dayton, Ohio, 1978-79; instr. U.Wis. Madison, 1972-73; mem. Wilkes Coll. Health Adminstrn. Adv. Com, 1988-89; bd. dirs. Coll. Misericordia Health Care Task Force, 1988-89; bd. govs. League Vol. Hosps., 1996-2000, sec., 1997-2000; mem. bd. govs. Fidelis Care N.Y., 1996-2000, Queensbrook Ins. Ltd., 1996-2000, vice chmn., 1996-97, chmn., 1997-2000; trustee Cmty. Blood Ctr., 1977-79; trustee Cath. Social Svcs., 1976-79, pres., 1978-79; bd. dirs. Coop. Purchasing Corp., 1974-79; mem. Dayton Pub. Schs. Lay Adv. Com. on Vocat. Edn., 1974-79; pres. Dayton Area Young Adminstrs. Group, 1977; pres. elect Greater Dayton Area Hosp. Assn., 1979; mem. allied health technologies adv. com. Sinclair Community Coll. 1974-79. Bd. dirs. Covenant Health Sys., 1992-2003, chmn. finance com. 2001-2003, Fletcher Allen Health Care, 2002-2003, Consol. Cath. Risk Retention Group, 1992-95, Cath. Charities, 1996-2000, Primary Care Devel. Corp., 1997-2000. Buffalo Niagara Partnership, 2002—, D'Youville Coll., 2004—; active Health Policy Forum, United Hosp. Fund, United Way, ARC. Mem. Am. Coll. Healthcare Execs., Acad. for Cath. Health Care Leadership, Mercy Leadership Group. (nat. commn. Cath. health care ministry), Turnaround Mgmt. Assn., Maj. Cath. Health Alliance (sec. 1990-95, chmn. 1997-99), Health Care Fin. Mgmt. Assn., Am. Assn. Univ. Profs. Ophthalmology, Am. Soc. Law and Medicine, Am. Hosp. Assn., Am. Assn. Eye and Ear Hosps. (pres.-elect 1984-85), Health Mgmt. Edn. Assn. (pres. 1987-88), Hosp. Assn. N.Y. State (bd. dirs. 1998-2000, 2002—), Greater N.Y. Hosp. Assn. (mem. bd. govs. 1997-2000, 2002—), Tex. Hosp.Assn., We. N.Y. Hosp. Assn. (bd. dirs. 2002—), Ohio Hosp. Assn., Hosp. Assn. Pa., Cath. Health Assn., Am. Pub. Health Assn., Pa. Pub. Health Assn., Del. Valley Hosp. Council, Pa. Emergency Health Svcs. Coun., Del. County Emergency Health Svcs. Coun., Nat. Union Hosp. and Health Care Employees (plan trustee), Pa. Hosps. Ins. Co. Adv. Coun., 1988-89. C. of C., U. Notre Dame Alumni Assn., U. Mich. Alumni Assn., U. Wis. Med. Sch. Alumni Assn., Wills Eye Soc., Sorin Soc., Badin Guild, Notre Dame Club (pres. 1971, v.p. 1983-84), Dominion Country Club, Buffalo Club, Country Club of Buffalo. Home: 9624 Cobblestone Dr Clarence NY 14031 Office: 100 High St Buffalo NY 14203 Office Phone: 716-859-2732. Personal E-mail: billmcg@together.net.

MCGUIRE, WILLIAM JAMES, social psychology educator; b. N.Y.C., Feb. 17, 1925; s. James William and Anne M. (Mitchell) McG.; m. Claire Vernick, Dec. 29, 1954; children: James William, Anne Maureen, Steven Thomas. BA, Fordham U., 1949, MA, 1950; PhD, Yale U., 1954; PhD (hon.), Eötvös U., Budapest, Hungary, 1990. Postdoctoral fellow U. Minn., 1954-55; assoc. prof. psychology U. Ill., 1958-61; prof. Columbia U., 1961-67, U. Calif., San Diego, 1967-70; vis. prof. London Sch. Econs., 1970-71; asst. prof. Yale U., New Haven, 1955-58, prof., 1970—, chmn. dept. psychology, 1971-73. Mem. adv. panel for sociology and social psychology NSF, 1963-65; mem. review panel for social scis. NIMH, 1968-72, cons., 1974-95. Author: Content and Processes in the Experience of Self, 1988, A Perspectivist Approach to Strategic Planning, 1989, Structure of Attitudes and Attitude Systems, 1989, The Content, Structure, and Operation of Thought Systems, 1991, Explorations in Political Psychology, 1993, Creative Hypothesis Generating in Psychology, 1997, Constructing Social Psychology: Creative and Critical Processes, 1999, After a Half Century of Election Studies: Whence, Where and Whither, 2001; contbr. to Ency. Brit.; editor Jour. Personality and Social Psychology, 1967-70; cons. editor European Jour. Social Psychology, 1978—, Jour. Applied Social Psychology, 1983—, Jour. Exptl. Social Psychology, 1994—, Comm. Rsch., 1988—, Human Comm. Rsch., 2001—, Jour. Commn., 2002—, Applied Psychology in Hungary, 2002—; contbr. Ency. Psychology. With AUS, 1943-46. Recipient Ann. Social Psychology award AAAS, 1964, Gen. Electric Found. awards, 1963, 64, 66, Disting. Scientist award Soc. Exptl. Social Psychology, 1992, Disting. Sci. award Internat. Soc. Political Psychology, 1999; grantee NSF, 1960-79, NIH, 1979-99; Fulbright fellow Louvain (Belgium) U., 1950-51, Ctr. for Advanced Study in Behavioral Scis. fellow, 1965-66, Guggenheim fellow, 1970-71, William James fellow Am. Psychol. Soc., 1989—. Fellow APA (pres. divsn. personality and social psychology 1973-74, Disting. Sci. Contbn. award 1988), Am. Acad. Arts and Scis.; mem. Am. Sociol. Assn., Am. Assn. Pub. Opinion Rsch., Sigma Xi. Home: 225 St Ronan St New Haven CT 06511-2313 Office: Yale U Dept Psychology PO Box 208205 New Haven CT 06520-8205 Office Phone: 203-432-4535. Business E-Mail: william.mcguire@yale.edu.

MCGUIRE, WILLIAM W. insurance company executive; b. Troy, N.Y., 1948; Grad., U. Tex., 1970, grad., 1974. Exec. v.p. United Healthcare Corp., Minnetonka, Minn., 1988—89, pres., 1989—98; chmn., CEO United Healthcare Corp., Minnetonka, 1991—98; pres., CEO, chmn., dir. UnitedHealth Group, Minnetonka, 1991—2000, CEO, chmn., dir., 2000—. Bd. dirs. Minn. Bus. Partnership. Trustee Mpls. Inst. Arts; dir. Minn. Orch. Assn. Office: UnitedHealth Group PO Box 1459 Minnetonka MN 55343-9664*

MCGUIRE-RIGGS, SHEILA, chairman Democratic party; Chmn. Iowa Democrat Party, Iowa. Democrat. Mailing: 5661 Fleur Dr Des Moines IA 50321 E-mail: smriggs@iowademocrats.org.

MCGUIRK, RONALD CHARLES, retired bank executive, economic advisor; b. Balt., Dec. 9, 1938; s. Charles F. and Grace E. (Delcher) McG.; m. Katherine Sauer, Oct. 1, 1960; children: Frank D., Ann E. Student, St. John's Coll., Annapolis, Md., 1956-59. Sr. data processing officer 1st Nat. Bank, Balt., 1966-72, v.p. data processing, 1972-76, v.p. mktg., 1976-80, sr. v.p. mktg., 1980-90, sr. v.p. corp. plan, chief of staff to CEO, 1990-94; sr. v.p., corp. sec. 1st Md. Bancorp, Balt., 1995-99; sr. econ. advisor Anne Arundel County, Md., 1999—. Bd. dirs., treas. North Arundel Hosp., Glen Burnie, Md., 1974—, v.p., 1999—; bd. dirs., treas. Internet, Inc., 1990-95, Glen Burnie Town Ctr. Com., 1995—, AACO Conf. and Vis. Bd., 1999—, Annapolis Symphony, 1991-92; trustee Mt. Washington Pediat. Hosp., 1997—2004; mem. adv. bd. Hist. Annapolis Found., 1982-85, dir., 1985-90; chmn. Annapolis Boundary Commn., 1983-84; mem. Anne Arundel County Coun., 1974-82, Anne Arundel County Libr. Bd., 1974-84; pres. Anne Arundel County Scholarship for Scholars/Bd. Edn., 1983-85, treas., 1985-88; mem. Anne Arundel County Charter Rev. Commn., 1986, Anne Arundel County Govt. Salary Commn., 1985, 89; chmn. Anne Arundel County Impact Fee Study Task Force, 1987; pres. Anne Arundel County YMCA, 1987-89, bd. dirs., 1982-87, 89-90; mem. Commn. for Ednl. Excellence, 1988-90; vice chmn. Ft. Meade Coordinating Coun., 1989-91; mem. Exec. Com. Md. Bus.-Industry PAC, 1991-99, Anne Arundel County Charter and Orgn. Transition Group, 1991; corp. ptnr. Sch. Bus. and Mgmt. Morgan State U., 1991-92; trustee Md. Hist. Soc., 1995-96; co-chair Anne Arundel County transition fin. com., 1998-99; chair adhoc Fire Dept. Com., 2003-04. Mem. Ctr. Club. Democrat. Roman Catholic. Office: Arundel Ctr Calvert St Annapolis MD 21401 Business E-Mail: rmcguirk@aacounty.org. E-mail: rmz1061@aol.com.

MCGUIRK, TERRENCE, former broadcasting company executive; b. Bklyn., Apr. 2, 1925; s. William Edward and Loretta Beatrice (Lanigan) McG.; m. Gloria Helen Geoghan, June 17, 1950; children: Terence F., Sara McGuirk Duncan, Susan McGuirk Blank, Elizabeth McGuirk Magee, Melissa McGuirk Bowman, Bryan, Michelle McGuirk O'Connor. BS, Fordham U., 1950. Nat. sales mgr. St. WAGA-TV, Atlanta, 1966-68; mgr. Sta. WAGA-TV, Atlanta, 1970-75; eastern sales mgr. Storer TV Sales, N.Y.C., 1968-70; pres., gen. mgr. Sta. WTEN-TV, Albany, N.Y., 1976-82; pres. Knight-Ridder Broadcasting, Inc., 1982-85; ret. Assoc. trustee Siena Coll., Loudonville, N.Y., 1979-83; trustee Meml. Hosp. Found., 1980-83; dir. Albany chpt. ARC, 1987-91. Served with U.S. Army, 1943-46. Mem. Mariner Sands Country Club, Babylon Yacht Club (hon.).

MCGUIRL, MARLENE DANA CALLIS, law librarian, educator; b. Hammond, Ind., Mar. 22, 1938; d. Daniel David and Helen Elizabeth (Baludis) Callis; m. James Franklin McGuirl, Apr. 24, 1965. AB, Ind. U., 1959; JD, DePaul U., 1963; MALS, Rosary Coll., 1965; LLM, George Washington U., 1978; postgrad., Harvard U., 1985. Bar: Ill. 1963, Ind. 1964, D.C. 1972. Asst. DePaul Coll. of Law Libr., 1961-62, asst. law libr., 1962-65; ref. law librarian Boston Coll. Sch. Law, 1965-66; libr. dir. D.C. Bar Libr., 1966-70; asst. chief Am.-Brit. Law Divsn. Libr. of Congress, Washington, 1970, chief, 1970-90, environ. cons., 1990—; counsel Cooter & Gell, 1992-93; adminstr. Washington Met. Transit Authority, 1994—. Libr. cons. Nat. Clearinghouse on Proverty Law, OEO, Washington, 1967-69, Northwestern U. Nat. Inst. Edn. in Law and Poverty, 1969, D.C. Office of Corp. Counsel, 1969-70; instr. law librarianship Grad. Sch. of U.S. Dept. of Agr., 1968-72; lectr. legal lit. Cath. U., 1972; adj. asst. prof., 1973-91; lectr. environ. law George Washington U., 1979—; judge Nat. and Internat. Law Moot Ct. Competition, 1976-78, 90—; pres. Hamburger Heaven, Inc., Palm Beach, Fla., 1981-91, L'Image de Marlene Ltd., 1986-92, Civilance de Beaute Inc., 1987-92, Heads & Hands Inc., 1987-92, Horizon Design & Mfg. Co., Inc., 1987—; dir. Stoneridge Farm Inc., Gt. Falls, Va., 1984—. Contbr. articles to profl. jours. Mem. Georgetown Citizens Assn.; trustee D.C. Law Students in Ct.; del. Ind. Democratic Conv., 1964. Recipient Meritorious Svc. award Libr. on Congress, 1974, letter of commendation Dirs. of Pers., 1976, cert. of appreciation, 1981-84. Mem. ABA (facilities law libr. Congress com. 1976-89), Fed. Bar Assn. (chpt. council 1972-76), Ill. Bar Assn., Women's Bar Assn. (pres. 1972-73, exec. bd. 1973-77, Outstanding Contbn. to Human Rights award 1975), D.C. Bar Assn., Am. Bar Found., Nat. Assn. Women Lawyers, Am. Assn. Law Libraries (exec. bd. 1973-77), Law Librarians Soc. of Washington (pres. 1971-73), Exec. Women in Govt. Home: 3416 P St NW Washington DC 20007-2705 Personal E-mail: marlenemcguirl@aol.com.

MCGUNIGLE, DOROTHY GREENE, interior designer, artist; b. Providence, Jan. 24, 1914; d. Dutee Thomas and Carrie May (Stewart) Greene; m. Douglas Campbell McGunigle, June 14, 1941 (dec. 1958); children: Jane Douglas (dec.), Bruce Campbell. Grad., R.I. Sch. Design, 1935, BFA (hon.), 1990. Interior designer Healy & Helgeson, Providence, 1935-36, Merriam Co., Providence, 1936-43; mgr. interior decorating dept. Shepard Co., Providence, 1960-70; owner Dorothy McGunigle Interiors, East Greenwich, R.I., 1970-95. Tchr. adult edn. Providence YMCA, 1958-59, Cranston High Sch., 1962, Warwick High Sch., 1964, East Greenwich High Sch., 1970-71; art shows include: Providence Art Club, 1972, 74, 76, 78, 80, 82; Indsl. Nat. Bank, Providence, 1974, 76; Warwick Pub. Library, 1980; cons. hist. restoration Varnum House Mus., 1963— . Paintings represented in permanent collection R.I. Hist. Soc. Bd. dirs. East Greenwich Preservation Soc., 1972—77, chmn. consultation com. hist. restoration. Recipient Hon. Mem. award Continental Ladies, Varnum House Mus., 1970; top 3% interior designers in Am., 1989, top 1% internat. designers, 1990. Mem. AID and ASID (visited fgn. designers in Greece, Spain, Portugal, Turkey, Austria, Italy, Switzerland, France, England, Sweden, Denmark, Finland, Norway, Russia to exchange ideas on projects), Providence Art (picture custodian 1974-85, chmn. ladies bd. 1978-79), Providence Pottery and Porcelain (pres. 1981-83), Colonial Dames, Mayflower Descendants, DAR, R.I. Sch. Design Alumni Assn.

MCGUNNIGLE, GEORGE FRANCIS, judge; b. Rochester, N.Y., Feb. 22, 1942; s. George Francis and Mary Elizabeth (Curran) McG.; m. Priscilla Ann Lappin, July 13, 1968; children: Cynthia A., Brian P. AB, Boston Coll., 1963; LLB, Georgetown U., 1966; LLM, George Wash. U., 1967. Bar: Conn. 1971, Minn. 1972, U.S. Dist. Ct. D.C. 1967, U.S. Dist. Ct. Conn. 1971, U.S. Dist. Ct. Minn. 1972, U.S. Ct. Appeals (2d cir.) 1971, U.S. Ct. Appeals (8th cir.) 1977, U.S. Supreme Ct. 1986. Asst. U.S. atty. Office of U.S. Atty., Bridgeport, Conn., 1971—72; assoc. Leonard, Street and Deinard, Mpls., 1972—73, ptnr., 1974—2000; judge Fourth Jud. Dist., Mpls., 2000—. Editor: Business Torts Litigation, 1992. Bd. dirs. Cath. Charities, 1997—, Minn. chpt. Arthritis Found., Mpls., 1986-92, 94—, mem. exec. com., 1988-92, 2001—. Lt. JAGC, USN, 1967-71. Recipient Nat. Vol. Svc. citation Arthritis Found., 1992. Mem. ABA (litigation sect., chmn. bus. torts litigation com. 1988-91, divsn. dir. 1991-92, 97-98, coun. 1992-95, sect. of dispute resolution coun. 2000-01). Avocations: reading, boating. E-mal. Office: Fourth Judicial Dist C-1251 Hennepin County Govt Ctr Minneapolis MN 55487-0422 E-mail: george.mcgunnigle@co.hennepin.mn.us.

MCGURK, CHRISTOPHER J. film company executive; BS, Syracuse U.; MBA, U. Chgo. Various positions including CFO Pepsico, 1982—88; sr. v.p. fin. Walt Disney Studios, 1988-90, exec. v.p., CFO, 1990—94, pres. motion pictures group, 1994—96; various positions including pres., CEO Universal Pictures, 1996—99; vice-chair, COO Metro-Goldwyn-Mayer Inc., 1999—. Office: Metro-Goldwyn-Mayer Studios Inc 2500 Broadway Santa Monica CA 90404-3065 Fax: 310-264-8690.*

MC GURK, JAMES HENRY, consultant company executive; b. Phila., July 24, 1936; s. James Henry and Ednah Mae (Kleinsmith) McG.; m. LaVerne M. Kraynek, 1960; children: Healther, Melanye. BS, Pa. State U., 1957; postgrad. in Econs., Temple U., 1960-62. Cons. mfg., various states, 1968-72; ops. chief mfg. cons. Manatech Internat., Westmont, N.J., 1970-72, A.T. Oxford Inc., N.Y.C., 1972-74; mem. corp. staff mfg. cons. Aspro Inc., Westport, Conn., 1974-77; cons. LHM, Inc., Rochester, Mich., 1977-79, also dir.; exec. v.p. Morse Hemco Inc., Holland, Mich., 1978-83; pres. Western Pegasus, Inc., 1983—, also bd. dirs. Dir. Pegasus Spline, Birmingham, Eng. Served with USAF, 1957-59. Mem. Am. Mgmt. Assn. Republican. Home: 326 Spyglass Dr Coppell TX 75019-5429 Office: 728 E 8th St Holland MI 49423-3080

MC GURN, BARRETT, communications executive, writer; b. N.Y.C., Aug. 6, 1914; s. William Barrett and Alice (Schneider) McG.; m. Mary Elizabeth Johnson, May 30, 1942 (dec. Feb. 1960); children: William Barrett III, Elizabeth (Mrs. Jerry Phelps), Andrew; m. Janice Ann McLaughlin, June 19, 1962; children: Summers, Martin Barrett, Mark Barrett. AB, Fordham U., 1935, LittD, 1958. Editor-in-chief Fordham Ram, 1934-35; with N.Y. Herald Tribune, 1935-66, asst. corr., 1939, bur. chief, 1946-52, 55-62, reporting staff, 1935-42, 62-66, bur. chief, 1952—55, acting chief bur. Moscow, 1958; with, assignments in Morocco, Algeria, Tunisia, Hungary (1956 revolution), Egypt, Greece, Yugoslavia, Poland, Cen. Africa, Gaza Strip.; press attache Am. Embassy, Rome, 1966-68, counselor for press affairs Saigon, 1968—69; U.S. consular officer, sec. appointed by Pres., 1969; dir. U.S. Govt. Press Ctr., Vietnam, 1968-69; White House and Pentagon liaison for State Dept. spokesman Washington, 1969-72; World Affairs commentator, 1972-73; dir. pub. info. U.S. Supreme Ct., Washington, 1973-82; dir. communications Cath. Archdiocese of Washington, 1984-87; pres. Carroll Pub. Co. pub. Cath. Standard and El Pregonero, 1987-91; dir. Our Sunday Visitor Pub. Co., 1988-98. Mem. Italian-Am. com. to select Italian fellowship winners for study in U.S., 1950-52; mem. U.S. Nat. Cath. Com. on Comm. Policy, 1970-74, White House Com. on Drug Control Info., 1970-72; mem. interdept. com. on U.S. govt. press info. policy, 1970, interdept. U.S. govt. task force to rescue 100 Ams. kidnapped in Jordan, 1970, one-man U.S. Presdl. mission to Cambodia on media news problems, 1970; archivist John Carroll Soc., Washington, 1990-97. Author: Decade in Europe, 1959, A Reporter Looks at the Vatican, 1962, A Reporter Looks at American Catholicism, 1967, America's Court, The Supreme Court and The People, 1997, The Pilgrim's Guide to Rome, 1999, Yank, Reporting the Greatest Generation, 2004; contbg. author: The Best from Yank, 1945, Yank, the GI Story of the War, 1946, Combat, 1950, Highlights from Yank, 1953, Overseas Press Club Cook Book, 1962, I Can Tell it Now, 1964, U.S. Book of Facts, Statistics and Information, 1966, New Catholic Treasury of Wit and Humor, 1967, How I Got that Story, 1967, Heroes for Our Times, 1968, Newsbreak, 1975, Saints for all Seasons, 1978, Informing the People, 1981, The Courage to Grow Old, 1989, Am. Peoples Encyclopedia Yearbook, Close To Glory: Yank Correspondents Untold Stories of World War II, 1992; contbr. articles to profl. jours. Trustee Corrs. Fund, 1965-68; mem. bd. Anglo-Am. Charity Fund in Italy, 1967-68; v.p. Citizens Assn., Westmoreland Hills, Md., 1984-86. Sgt. AUS, 1942-45. Decorated Purple Heart; grand knight Italian Order of Merit; Vietnam Psychol. Warfare medal 1st class; recipient Polk award for outstanding fgn. reporting L.I. U., 1956; named best press corr. abroad Overseas Press Club, 1957; recipient N.Y.C. Fire Dept. Essay Silver Medal, 1924, N.Y. Times Oratorical Contest Bronze Medal, 1930; Christopher award for one of ten most inspiring books of year, 1959; named Man of Year Cath. Inst. Press, 1962, Fordham U. Alumnus of Year in communications, 1963; co-winner ann. Golden Typewriter award N.Y. Newspaper Reporters Assn., 1965, nominated by N.Y. Herald Tribune for Journalism Pulitzer Prize, 1965; outstanding pub. service award N.Y. chpt. Sigma Delta Chi, 1965; recipient Page One award N.Y. Newspaper Guild, 1966, Silurians award, 1966, award N.Y. Newspaper Reporters Assn., 1966, Citation for pub. service N.Y.C. Citizens Budget Commn., 1966, pres. commendation for Cambodia mission on news problems, 1970, Meritorious Honor award Dept. State, 1972; Lifetime Achievement award Fordham U. Club, Washington, 1986 Mem. Fgn. Press Assn. Italy (v.p. 1951-52, pres. 1961-62), SHAPE Corrs. Assn. Paris (treas. 1955), Authors Guild, Am. Fgn. Svc. Assn., Pax Romana Soc. for Cath. Intellectuals, Overseas Press Club (pres. 1963-65), Nat. Press Club, Diplomats and Consular Officers, Ret., Kenwood Club, Cosmos Club, Fordham U. Club Washington (bd. govs. 1980—99). Roman Catholic. Home: 5229 Duvall Dr Bethesda MD 20816-1875 E-mail: jmcgurn@erols.com. *Providing information to our democratic public has been the work of my life both as a foreign correspondent, as a government spokesman, and as a lecturer. The newsman and the person who speaks for government share the same objective of explaining government*

policy. The spokesman has an added responsibility— to help government policy succeed. The reporter and the spokesman sometimes are at war with one another, but it is a war in behalf of the same beneficiary: the people.

MCGURN, WILLIAM BARRETT, III, lawyer; b. N.Y.C., Apr. 3, 1943; s. Barrett and Mary Elizabeth (Johnson) McGurn; m. Catherine Roche, June 17, 1972; children: Mary Anne, Edward Johnson. BA, Yale U., 1965; JD, Harvard U., 1972. Bar: DC 1973, Paris 1992. Ptnr. Cleary, Gottlieb, Steen & Hamilton, Washington, Paris, Rome, 1972—. Gov. Am. Hosp. Paris, 1991—; chmn. Dem. Abroad, France, 1987—89. Lt. USNR, 1967—69. Mem.: ABA, Am. C. of C. France (bd. dirs. 1996—, v.p. 1998—2000, pres. 2000—02), Am. Club Paris. Democrat. Home: via del Pié di Marmo 16 00186 Rome Italy Office: Cleary Gottlieb Steen and Hamilton Piazza di Spagna 15 00187 Rome Italy

MCGUYER, FRANK, construction executive; Chair, CEO McGuyer Home Improvement, Houston, 1987—. Office: McGuyer Home Improvement 7676 Woodway Dr Ste 104 Houston TX 77063-1521

MCGWIRE, MARK DAVID, retired professional baseball player; b. Pomona, Calif., Oct. 1, 1963; s. John and Kathy McGwire; 1 child, Matthew. Student, U. So. Calif. With Oakland Athletics, Calif., 1984—97, St. Louis Cardinals, 1997—2001. Named Am. League Rookie of Yr., 1987; named to All-Star Team, 1987—92, 1995—2000, MLB All-Century Team, 1999; recipient Gold Glove award, 1990. Achievements include being a member of U.S. Olympic Baseball Team, 1984; mem.of World Series Championship Team, 1989; led Am. League in Home Runs, 1987 (49), 1996 (52); led Nat. League in Home Runs, 1998 (70), 1999 (65); led Nat. League in RBI's (147), 1999.*

MCHALE, EDWARD ROBERTSON, retired lawyer; b. Chgo., Jan. 24, 1921; s. Edward F. and Martha (Robertson) McH.; m. Helen Louise Lindgren, Aug. 28, 1953; children: Nancy Ellen McHale Kaufman, Sally Jane McHale Cutler, John Robertson. BSS., Northwestern U., 1942; LL.B., Harvard U., 1948. Bar: Calif. 1949. Asst. U.S. atty. U.S. atty. So. Dist. Calif., 1949—61, chief tax div., 1954—61; assoc. Mitchell, Silberberg & Knupp, Los Angeles, 1961—64, ptnr., 1965—86, mgr. litigation dept, 1978—82; pres. Edward R. McHale, P.C., 1979—86; ret., 1986. Lectr. U. So. Calif. Law Center, 1958-61 Co-author: Handling Federal Tax Litigation, 1961. Served to lt. USNR, 1943-46. Mem. Fed. Bar Assn. (past pres. Los Angeles chpt., past nat. v.p. for 9th Circuit), Assn. Bus. Trial Lawyers (bd. govs. 1981-83), State Bar Calif., Delta Sigma Rho. Clubs: South Hills Country (West Covina); Clan Donnachaidh Soc. Lutheran. Home: 1116 S Serena Dr West Covina CA 91791-3754 E-mail: casu8@earthlink.net.

MC HALE, JOHN JOSEPH, baseball club executive; b. Detroit, Sept. 21, 1921; s. John Michael and Catherine M. (Kelly) McH.; m. Patricia Anne Cameron, Feb. 15, 1947; children: Patricia Cameron II, John Joseph, Jr., Kevin K., Anne F., Brian F., Mary M. AB cum laude, U. Notre Dame, 1947. Profl. baseball player, 1941-42, 45-47; asst. dir. minor league clubs Detroit Tigers Baseball Club, 1948, asst. farm dir., 1948-53, dir. minor league clubs, 1954-55, dir. player personnel, 1956-57, gen. mgr., 1957-58; v.p., gen. mgr. Milw. Braves Baseball Club (became Atlanta Braves Baseball Club 1961), 1957-61, pres., gen. mgr., 1961-67; dep. commr. N.Y.C., 1968—82; pres., gen. mgr. Montreal Expos Baseball Club, 1968-87, dep. chmn., CEO, 1987—; ret. Japan Sports Systems. Dir. Perini Corp. Ret. trustee, Intracoastal Hosp. Corp., West Palm Beach, Fla., 1986—; dir. emeritus Schwartz Investment Trust, Ave Maria Fund., 2001; bd. dirs. Nat. Baseball Hall of Fame and Mus. Mem. Nat. Monogram Club (U. Notre Dame), Assn. Ret. Ball Players Am. (pres.), Harbour Ridge Club. Address: Harbour Ridge 2014 NW Royal Fern Ct Palm City FL 34990-8025

MCHALE, JUDITH A. (JUDITH OTTALLORAN), broadcast executive, lawyer; b. N.Y.C., 1947; m. Michael McHale; 2 children. B in politics, U. Nottingham, Eng.; JD, Fordham U.Law Sch., 1979. Atty. Battle, Fowler, N.Y.C.; gen. counsel MTV networks, Discovery Comm., Inc., 1987, sr. v.p. and gen. counsel, exec. v.p. and gen. counsel, pres. and COO, 1995—. Mem. Md. State Bd. of Edn., 1997—2001; bd. dirs. Polo Ralph Lauren, John Hancock Co., Potomac Electric Power Co., Host Marriott Corp., Cable in the Classroom, Vital Voices Global Partnership, Africa Soc., Africare, Sister-to-Sister Everyone Has a Heart Found. Office: Discovery Comm 7700 Wisconsin Ave Bethesda MD 20814

MCHALE, KEVIN EDWARD, former professional basketball player, sports team executive; b. Hibbing, Minn., Dec. 19, 1957; m. Lynn McHale; children: Kristyn, Michael. Student, U. Minn., 1976-80. Basketball player Boston Celtics, 1980-93; v.p. basketball ops. Minn. Timberwolves, 1995—. Named to NBA All Rookie Team, 1981, NBA All-Defensive First Team, 1986-88, All-NBA First Team, 1987, NBA All-Star Game, 1984, 86-91; recipient NBA Sixth Man award, 1984, 85. Achievements include playing on NBA Championship Team, 1981, 84, 86. Office: Minn Timberwolves 600 1st Ave N Minneapolis MN 55403-1416

MCHALE, PAUL F., JR., federal official, former congressman; b. Bethlehem, Pa., July 26, 1950; m. Katherine McHale; children: Matthew, Mary, Luke. BA in Govt. sigma cum laude, Lehigh U., 1972; JD, Georgetown U. Law Sch., 1977. Atty., Bethlehem, 1977—82; mem. Pa. Ho. of Reps., 1983—92, 103rd-105th Congresses from 15th Pa. dist., 1993—99; former mem. nat. security com., mem. sci. com.; mem. Tallman, Hudders and Sorrentino, Allentown, Pa., 1999—2003; asst. sec. of Defense for Homeland Defense U.S. Dept. Homeland Security, Washington, 2003—. Infantry officer USMC, 1972—74, Okinawa, Philippines, maj. USMCR, 1990—92, Persian Gulf. Decorated Navy Commendation medal. Mem.: Phi Beta Kappa. Democrat. Office: Dept Homeland Security 3801 Nebraska Ave NW Washington DC 20016

MCHALE, VINCENT EDWARD, political science educator; b. Jenkins Twp., Pa., Apr. 17, 1939; m. Ann Barbara Cotner, Nov. 8, 1963; 1 child, Patrick James. A.B., Wilkes Coll., 1964; M.A., Pa. State U., 1966, Ph.D. in Polit. Sci., 1969. Asst. prof. polit. sci. U. Pa., Phila., 1969-75, dir. grad. studies, 1971-73; assoc. prof. Case Western Res. U., Cleve., 1975-84, prof., 1984-2003, chmn. dept. polit. sci., 1978—03; vis. lectr. John Carroll U., summer 1980, Beaver Coll., spring 1975. Author: (with A.P. Frognier and D. Paranzino) Vote, Clivages Socio-politiques et Developpement Regional en Belgique, 1974. Co-editor; contbr.: Evaluating Transnational Programs in Government and Business, 1980; Political Parties of Europe, 1983; edtl. adv. bd. Worldmark Ency. of Nations, 1994—. Contbr. chpts. to books, articles to profl. jours. Project cons. Council Econ Opportunity in Greater Cleve., 1978-81; mem. Morris Abrams Award Com., 1977—. Recipient Outstanding Prof. award Lux chpt. Mortar Bd., 1989, 90; named one of Most Interesting People of 1988, Cleve. Mag.; NSF grantee, 1971-72; HEW grantee, 1976-78; Woodrow Wilson fellow, 1968, Ruth Young Boucke fellow, 1967-68; All-Univ. fellow, 1967-68. Mem. Phi Kappa Phi. Home: 3070 Coleridge Rd Cleveland OH 44118-3556 Office: Case Western Res U Cleveland OH 44106 Office Phone: 216-368-2425. Business E-Mail: vem@case.edu.

MCHALE-HENDRICKS, CYNTHIA, writer; b. Waterbury, Conn., Feb. 1, 1972; d. Robert Paul and Anne Theresa McHale; m. Guy Theodore Koch Hendricks, Sept. 28, 2002. BA in English, Albertus Magnus Coll., New Haven, Conn., 1994; MA in English and Creative Writing, Trinity Coll., Hartford, Conn., 2004. News reporter WATR 1320 AM Radio, Waterbury, 1997—98; creative svcs. asst. Waterbury Republican, 1996—98; copywriter Mason & Kirchar/MK Design, Woodbridge, Conn., 1998—2001; freelance writer Write On, Woodbury, Conn., 2001—. Editor Author Karl Koch III, Oyster Bay, NY, 2003—. Author: (poetry) One Small Step/Icarus Internat., 2002, The View From 100/Icarus Internat., 2003, New Millennium Writings, 2003. Mem. Humane Soc. of U.S., 1998—. Grantee Tuition grantee, Trinity Coll., 2002—; scholar Honors scholar, Albertus Magnus Coll., 1990. Mem.: Greater Waterbury C. of C. (mem. sml. bus. coun. 2001—), Nat. Writers Union. Avocations: reading, art enthusiast, web developer. Home and Office: PO Box 630 Woodbury CT 06798

MCHARD, JAMES LORIN, corporate financial executive; b. Bay City, Mich., June 23, 1942; s. James Alvah and Daisy Evelyn McHard; m. Jerilee Miles, June 6, 1964 (div. May 15, 1985); m. Alice Brallie Dekle, May 24, 1997; children: Maureen Day, Clair James Ian. BS, U. Mich., 1964. Cert. secondary sch. tchr. Mich. Engrng. fin. analyst Ford Motor Co., Livonia, Mich., 1964—97; pres. J & A Music Enterprises, Mich. Author: The Future of Modern Music, 2001; composer: Tremors, 1991, Virtuals, 1992; lectr. music theory, editor Voice of Reason newsletter, 1980—82; author: Julio Estrada, Five Years of ONCE. Mem.: Electronic Music Found., S.E. Mich. Horn Club (assoc.; sec. 1985—88). Home: 28860 Richland Livonia MI 48150 Office Phone: 734-525-6265. Personal E-mail: release10@sbcglobal.net.

MC HARGUE, CARL JACK, research laboratory administrator; b. Jan. 30, 1926; s. John David and Virginia (Thomas) McH.; m. Edith Trovillion, Aug. 28, 1948; children: Anne Odell McHargue Diegel, Carol Virginia Hornberger, Margaret Katherine McHargue; m. Betty Ford, Sept. 30, 1960. BS in Metall. Engrng., U. Ky., 1949, MS, 1951, PhD, 1953. Instr. U. Ky., Lexington, 1949-53; with Oak Ridge Nat. Lab., 1953-90, sect. head, 1960-80, program mgr. for materials scis., 1961-88, sr. rsch. staff, 1980-90; prof. metall. engrng. U. Tenn., Knoxville, 1991—. Vis. prof. U. Newcastle upon Tyne, Eng., 1987; adj. prof. Vanderfilt U., 1988—; bd. dirs. Accreditation Bd. for Engrng. and Tech., 1998—; bd. dirs. The Minerals, Metals and Materials Soc. Contbr. numerous articles in field to profl. jours. With AUS, 1944-46. Recipient Disting. Svc. award The Minerals, Metals and Materials Soc., 2001; named to Engrng. Hall of Distinction, U. Ky., 1995. Fellow Metall. Soc. AIME, Am. Soc. for Metals; mem. Materials Rsch. Soc., Sigma Xi, Tau Beta Pi. Republican. Presbyterian. Home: 7201 Sheffield Dr Knoxville TN 37909-2414 Office: U Tenn 514 E Stadium Hill Knoxville TN 37996-0750 Office Phone: 865-974-7680. Business E-Mail: crl@utk.edu.

MCHENRY, BARNABAS, lawyer; b. Harrisburg, Pa., Oct. 30, 1929; s. William Cecil and Louise (Perkins) McH.; m. Marie Bannon Jones, Dec. 13, 1952; children: Thomas J.P., W.H. Davis, John W.H. AB, Princeton U., 1952; LLB, Columbia U., 1957. Bar: N.Y. 1957. Assoc. Lord, Day, & Lord, N.Y.C., 1957-62; gen. counsel The Reader's Digest Assn., Inc., N.Y.C., 1962-85; exec. dir. Wallace Funds, N.Y.C., 1985-86; chmn. N.Y. state orgns., 1986—. Trustee, pres. Boscobel Restoration, Inc., 1964; trustee Am. Conservation Assn. 1977, Saratoga Performing Arts Ctr., 1984, Aperture Found., 1986; trustee emeritus Met. Mus. Art, 1980; coun. mem. Villa I Tatti, Harvard Sch. Renaissance Studies, 1982; regent emeritus Smithsonian Instn., 1985; commr. Palisades Interstate Park Commn., 1987; chmn. Hudson River Valley Greenway Coun., 1989; co-chair Hudson River Valley Nat. Heritage Assn., 1996. Home: 164 E 72nd St New York NY 10021-4363 Office Phone: 212-681-4550. Fax: 212-681-4552.

MCHENRY, HENRY MALCOLM, anthropologist, educator; b. Los Angeles, May 19, 1944; s. Dean Eugene and Emma Jane (Snyder) McH.; m. Linda Jean Conway, June 25, 1966; children: Lindsay Jean, Annalisa Jane. BA, U. Calif., Davis, 1966, MA, 1967; PhD, Harvard U., 1972. Asst. prof. anthropology U. Calif., Davis, 1971-76, assoc. prof. anthropology, 1976-81, prof. anthropology, 1981—, chmn. dept. anthropology, 1984-88. Fellow Am. Anthrop. Assn., Calif. Acad. Sci.; mem. Am. Assn. Phys. Anthropologists (exec. com. 1981-85), Soc. Study Evolution, Soc. Vertebrate Paleontology, Phi Beta Kappa, Phi Kappa Phi. Democrat. Buddhist. Avocation: winemaker. Home: 330 11th St Davis CA 95616-2010 Office: U of Calif Davis Dept Of Anthropology Davis CA 95616 Office Phone: 530-752-1588. E-mail: hmmchenry@ucdavis.edu.

MCHENRY, JULIE, communications executive; BJ, U. Mo.; MBA in Mktg., U. Portland. Adv. prog. supr. Tektronix, Inc., Beaverton, Oreg.; acct. exec. Regis McKenna Inc., Portland, Oreg.; co-founder, v.p. The Waggener Group; co-founder Global Tech. Comm., Wilson McHenry Co. Spkr. in field. Office: Wilson McHenry Co 393 Vintage Park Dr Ste 140 Foster City CA 94404-1172

MCHENRY, LEEMON BENTON, education educator, writer; b. Camp Lejeune, N.C., Sept. 1, 1956; s. Leemon and Joyce McHenry. BA, U. So. Miss., 1978, MA, 1981; PhD, U. Edinburgh, Scotland, 1984. Lectr. Calif. State U., Northridge, 1997, Loyola Marymount U., LA, 1997—2002. Lectr. U. Edinburgh, 1983—84, Old Dominion U., Norfolk, Va., 1984—86; rsch. assoc. Johns Hopkins U., Balt., 1986—88; lectr. Davidson Coll., NC, 1886—1988, Ctrl. Mich. U., Mt. Pleasant, 1988, Wittenberg U., Springfield, Ohio, 1990—95; vis. scholar UCLA, 1996—97. Author: Whitehead and Bradley: A Comparative Analysis; editor: Reflections on Philosophy, American Philosophers, 1950-2000, American Philosophers to 1950, British Philosophers: 1800-2000; author: Bradley's Conception of Metaphysics, Metaphysics, 1910, Alfred North Whitehead, Timothy L. S. Sprigge, Quine and Whitehead: Ontology and Methodology; contbr. articles to profl. jours. Recipient Overseas Rsch. Students award, Com. of Vice-Chancellors and Principals of the Univs. of U.K., 1982—84; grantee Fellowship, Nat. Endowment for the Humanities, 1989, Conf. on the Philosophy of W. V. Quine, Matchette Found., 1992; scholar Vans Dunlop Scholarship in Logic and Metaphysics, U. of Edinburgh, 1981—84, Profl. Degree Scholarship, Bd. of Trustees of State Insts. of Higher Learning, 1981—84. Mem.: Ctr. for Process Studies (rev. editor 1997—2004). Home: 4900 Overland Ave # 121 Culver City CA 90230 Office: Calif State U Dept Philosophy 18111 Nordhoff St Northridge CA 91330 Personal E-mail: leemon.mchenry@csun.edu.

MCHENRY, MARTIN CHRISTOPHER, physician, educator; b. Feb. 9, 1932; s. Merl and Marcella (Bricca) McH.; m. Patricia Grace Hughes, Apr. 27, 1957; children: Michael, Christopher, Timothy, Mary Ann, Jeffrey, Paul, Kevin, William, Monica, Martin Christopher. Student, U. Santa Clara, 1950-53; MD, U. Cin., 1957; MS in Medicine, U. Minn., 1966. Diplomate Am. Bd. Internal Medicine. Intern Highland Alameda County (Calif.) Hosp., Oakland, 1957-58; resident, internal medicine fellow Mayo Clinic, Rochester, Minn., 1958-61, spl. appointee in infectious diseases, 1963-64; staff physician Henry Ford Hosp., Detroit, 1964-67, Cleve. Clinic, 1967-72, chmn. dept. infectious diseases, 1972-92, sr. physician infectious diseases, 1992-98. Cons. infectious diseases, 1998—; asst. clin. prof. Case Western Res. U., 1970-77, assoc. clin. prof. medicine, 1977-91, clin. prof. medicine, 1991—; assoc. vis. physician Cleve. Met. Gen. Hosp., 1970-00; cons. VA Hosp., Cleve., 1973-74. Contbr. more than 100 articles to profl. jours., also chpts. to books. Chmn. manpower com. Swine Influenza Program, Cleve., 1976. With USNR, 1961-63. Named Disting. Tchr. in Medicine, Cleve. Clinic, 1972, 90; recipient 1st ann. Bruce Hubbard Stewart award Cleve. Clinic Found. for Humanities in Medicine, 1985, Nightingale Physician Collaboration award Cleve. Clinic Found. Divsn. Nursing, 1995, Clinician of Yr. award Acad. Medicine of Cleve./No. Ohio Med. Assn., 2002. Fellow ACP, Infectious Diseases Soc. Am. (Clinician award 2000), Am. Coll. Chest Physicians (chmn. com. cardiopulmonary infections 1975-77, 81-83), Royal Soc. Medicine of Gt. Britain; mem. Am. Soc. Clin. Pharmacology and Therapeutics (chmn. sect. infectious diseases and antimicrobial agts. 1970-77, 80-85, dir.), Am. Thoracic Soc., Am. Soc. Clin. Pathologists, Am. Fedn. Clin. Rsch., Am. Soc. Tropical Medicine and Hygiene, Am. Soc. Microbiology, N.Y. Acad. Scis., Assn. for Profls. in Infection Control and Epidemiology, So. Med. Assn. Home: 2779 Belgrave Rd Pepper Pike OH 44124-4601 Office: 9500 Euclid Ave Cleveland OH 44195-0001

MCHENRY, ROBERT (DALE), editor; b. St. Louis, Apr. 30, 1945; s. Robert Dale and Pearl Lenna (Nalley) McH.; m. Carolyn F. Amundson, Oct. 2, 1971; children: Curran, Zachary. BA in English Lit., Northwestern U., 1966; MA in English Lit., U. Mich., 1967; MBA in Mgmt., Northwestern U., 1987. Proofreader, prodn. editor Ency. Britannica, Inc., Chgo., 1967-69, editor, 1974-75, dir. yearbooks, 1985-86, mng. editor, 1986-90, gen. editor, v.p., 1990-92, editor-in-chief, 1992-97, editor-at-large, 1997—. Editor: Documentary History of Conservation in America, 1972, Webster's American Military Biographies, 1978, Liberty's Women, 1980, Webster's New Biographical Dictionary, 1983. Mem. United Ch. of Christ.

MCHOES, ANN MCIVER, academic administrator, computer systems consultant; b. San Diego, June 17, 1950; d. Donald Anthony and Ann Mae McIver; children: A. Genevieve, Katherine Marie. BS in Math., U. Pitts., 1973, MS in Info. Sci., 1986. Tech. writer Westinghouse Electric Corp., Pitts., 1973—79; pres. McHoes & Assocs., Pitts., 1981—; dir. enrollment svcs. Chatham Coll., Pitts., 2002—. Mem. adj. faculty computer sci., Carlow Coll., Pitts., 1992—, Duquesne U., 1997-99; cons. Westinghouse Electric Corp., 1988-99, PNC Bank, Pitts., 1988—, CBS Corp., 1996-99, Intel, 1998—, McDonalds Corp., 1998-2001, commonwealth of Pa. Healthy Women Project, 1998—; vis. lectr. Pa. State U., State College, 1990-91; judge Pa. Jr. Acad. Sci., Pitts., 1993—; vol. tutor Greater Pitts. Literacy Coun., 1996-98; webmaster NVR Mortgage, 1998-2000; bd. dirs. Pitts. Playback Theatre, 2000-2001. Co-author: Understanding Operating Systems, 1991, 2d edit., 1997, 3d edit., 2000 (used in colleges and univs., North Am., Europe, Africa, Asia and Australia); assoc. editor: (4-vol. ency.) Computer Science for Students, 2002. Recipient 2001 Texty Excellence award Text and Academic Authors Assn., 2001. Mem. IEEE Computer Soc., Assn. Computing Machinery, Info. Sys. Security Assn. (chpt. sec. 1991-94, v.p. 1995-96, membership chair 1994—), Pa. Mid. Sch. Assn. (conf. exhibit chair 1996-97). Avocations: travel, tennis, golf. Office: Chatham Coll Braun Hall Woodland Rd Pittsburgh PA 15232

MCHOSE, ALISON LITTELL, assemblywoman; b. May 24, 1965; BS in govt. and politics, U. of Md. Assemblywoman N.J. Gen. Assembly, 2003—. Mem. Franklin Econ. Devel. Com., 1995—; adv. bd. Sussex County Office of Aging, 1997—; mem. Sussex County 250th Com., 2002—. Republican. Office: 13 Main St Sparta NJ 07871-1911 E-mail: AswMcHose@njleg.org.

MCHUGH, CARIL EISENSTEIN DREYFUSS, art dealer, art gallery director, consultant; b. New Haven, Conn. d. Irving and Gertrude (Lax) Eisenstein; m. Barney Dreyfuss II (div.); children: Caryn, Barney III (Terry), Andrew, Evan; m. James Marshall McHugh Jr., Dec. 31, 1976. BA, Smith Coll. Libr. archivist, mem. staff art rental Washington Gallery of Modern Art, 1963-67; asst. to curator of prints and drawings Nat. Mus. Am. Art, Washington, 1967-69; dir. Studio Gallery, Washington, 1970-75; dir., ptnr. Parsons-Dreyfuss Gallery, N.Y.C., 1976-80; dir. Frank Marino Gallery, N.Y.C., 1981, Humphrey Fine Art, N.Y.C., 1988-90, Gregory Gallery, N.Y.C., 1995-96, freelance curator, adv. bd. Hugo de Pagano Gallery, 1997—2000, rschr. Barnett Newman Found., N.Y.C., 2001—. Art cons., writer, N.Y.C., 1982—; arranger exhbns. Nat. Mus. Am. Art, Washington, 1968-69, USIA, Washington, 1976, Automation House, N.Y.C., 1983. An Homage to Betty Parsons exhbn., 2000, Portraits by Tom Block/Amnesty Internat. Exhbn., 2002, essays to catalogs, articles to profl. mags. Bd. dirs. Women's Nat. Dem. Club, Washington, 1972-76, Friends of the Corcoran, Washington, 1972-76, Smith Club of Washington, 1974-76; Sophia Smith Assoc. Smith Coll., Northampton, Mass., 1985, 90, 95, 2000, Women in the Arts, 1995—. Avocations: reading, hiking, swimming, designing accessories, poetry. Home: 241 Central Park W Apt 9C New York NY 10024-4545

MCHUGH, DONALD P. insurance company executive, lawyer; b. 1917. A.B., Bucknell U.; J.S.D., Georgetown U., 1943. Bar: D.C. 1943. Atty., U.S. Dept. Treasury, 1943-44; atty. antitrust div. U.S. Dept. Justice, 1944-53; pvt. practice, 1953-55; chief counsel, staff dir. U.S. Senate Antitrust and Monopoly Subcom., 1955-61; v.p., gen. counsel State Farm Ins. Co., Bloomington, Ill., 1961— . Office: 1 State Farm Plz Bloomington IL 61701-4300

MCHUGH, GERALD C. bank executive; Chmn. Alliance Bank, Broomall, Pa., 1989—. Office: Alliance Bank 541 Lawrence Rd Broomall PA 19008-3501

MCHUGH, HEATHER, poet; b. Calif., Aug. 20, 1948; BA, Radcliffe Coll., 1970; MA, U. Denver, 1972. Assoc. prof. English SUNY, Binghamton, 1976-82; prof. English, Milliman writer-in-residence U. Wash., Seattle, 1983—. Vis. prof. Columbia U., 1987; Holloway lectr. U. Calif., Berkeley, 1987; judge Nat. Poetry Series book award, 1986, 95. Author: (poetry) Dangers, 1977, A World of Difference, 1981, To the Quick, 1987, Shades, 1988, Hinge & Sign: Poems, 1968-93, 1994 (Nat. Book award nomination 1994), The Father of the Predicaments, 1999, Eyeshot, 2003, (essays) Broken English: Poetry and Partiality, 1993; translator: D'Apres Tout: Poems by Jean Follain, 1981; (with Nikolai Popov) Because the Sea Is Black: Poems by Blaga Dimitrova, 1989, (with Nikolai Popov) Glottal Stop: 101 Poems by Paul Celan, 2000, (with David Konstan) Cyclops of Euripides, 2000. Recipient Harvard U./Pollock prize, 1995, Lila Wallace/Reader's Digest Writer's award, 1996, PEN Voelcker prize, 2000. Mem. Acad. Am. Poets (chancellor 1999), Am. Acad. Arts and Scis. Office: U Washington Dept English Box 354330 Seattle WA 98195-4330

MCHUGH, JAMES JOSEPH, lawyer; b. Phila., Sept. 15, 1961; s. James Joseph and Helene Anne (Kiernan) McHugh; m. Colette Marie McHugh, May 20, 1989; children: Albert Taylor, James Joseph III, Cole Michael, Sophia Kiernan. BSME, Drexel U., 1985; JD magna cum laude, Villanova (Pa.) Law Sch., 1992. Bar: Pa. 1992, N.J. 1992, U.S. Dist. Ct. (ea. dist.) Pa., U.S. Dist. Ct. N.J. Ptnr. McHugh Plumbing & Heating, Phila., 1984-89; project mgr. Fluidics Mech Contractors, Phila., 1989-92; assoc. Pepper, Hamilton & Scheetz, Phila., 1992-94; ptnr. The Beasley Firm, LLC, Phila., 1994—. Author, editor case notes. Mem. adv. com. Penn Pub. Svc. Program, Sch. Law, U. Pa. Named to Order of the Coif, Villanova Law Sch., 1992. Mem. ATLA, Pa. Bar Assn., Phila. Bar Assn. Home: 65 Brooks Rd Moorestown NJ 08057-3855 Office: The Beasley Firm 1125 Walnut St Philadelphia PA 19107-4918 Office Phone: 215-592-1000. Business E-Mail: jjm@beasleyfirm.com.

MCHUGH, JAMES LENAHAN, JR., lawyer; b. Pitts., June 28, 1937; s. James Lenahan and Annette (Dalton) McH.; m. Mary-Ann Curto, Feb. 16, 1963 (div. 1988); children: Angela Dalton Sherrill, Hillary Lenahan Clagett; m. Rosa Lamoreaux, Sept. 8, 1991. BA, Duquesne U., 1959; LLB, Villanova U., 1962. Bar: DC 1963. Law clk. U.S. Dist. Ct. (ea. dist.) Pa., Phila., 1962-63; law clk. to Assoc. Justice Tom C. Clark, U.S. Supreme Ct., Washington, 1963-64; assoc. Steptoe & Johnson, Washington, 1967-70, ptnr., 1970-94; gen. counsel APA, Washington, 1994—2001, sr. counsel, 2001—. Mem. bd. consultors Law Sch., Villanova (Pa.) U., 1973—; dir. Higher Achievement Program, Washington, 1984-87; coord. Washington Lawyers' Project, Robert F. Kennedy Meml. Found., Washington, 1972-75. Editor-in-chief Villanova Law Rev., Vol. VII, 1961-62; chmn. editl. adv. bd. Fed. Comm. Law Jour., 1981-84. Bd. dirs. Columbia Hosp. for Women's Found., Washington, 1985-96, Children's Radio Theatre, Washington, 1983-86; chmn. exec. giving Archbishop's Appeal, Archdiocese of Washington, 1982-84; mem. bd. visitors Ctr. for Study of Orgns. and Mgmt., U. Md. Univ. Coll., 1987-92; bd. dirs. Human Resources Rsch. Orgn., Inc., 1978—; chmn. bd. dirs., 1991—; mem. adv. bd. Inst. for Conflict Analysis and Resolution, George Mason U., 1990-94. Capt. U.S. Army, 1964-67. Mem. ABA (sect. on health law, tax, antitrust, intellectual property and legal edn.), D.C. Bar Assn., Am. Soc. Assn. Execs. (chmn. Washington Legal Symposium 2003, vice chmn. legal sect. coun. 2003-04, chmn. 2004—), Choral Arts Soc., Villanova Law Alumni Assn. (pres. Greater Balt./Washington area chpt. 2002—), Order of Coif, Confrerie des Chevaliers du Tastevin. Home: 4112 Fessenden St NW Washington DC 20016-4227 Office: APA 750 1st St NE Washington DC 20002-4242 Office Phone: 202-336-6089. Business E-Mail: jmchugh@apa.org.

MCHUGH, JOHN MICHAEL, congressman, former state senator; b. Watertown, N.Y., Sept. 29, 1948; s. Donald and Jane (O'Neill) McH. BA in Polit. Sci., Syracuse U., 1970; MPA, Nelson A. Rockefeller Grad. Sch. Pub. Affairs, 1977. Asst. city mngr. Watertown, 1968-73; confidential asst. Watertown City Mgrs. Office, 1971-76; chief of research, liaison with local govts. Office of N.Y. State Senator H.D. Barclay, 1976-84; U.S. senator from 46th N.Y. dist., 1984-93; chmn. joint legis. commn. on dairy industry devel., 1987-92; mem. U.S. Congress from 23th N.Y. dist., 1993—; mem. armed svcs. com., internat. rels. com., govt. reform com., chmn. subcom. on military pers. Mem. Legis. Commn. on Modernization of the Tax Code, Nat. Conf. State Legis., Commerce & Econ. Devel. Com., Commerce, Labor and Regulation

Com. of the State Fed. Assembly, Coun. State Govt. Eastern Regional Conf. Com. on Fiscal Affairs. Recipient 40 Outstanding Alumni awards Syracuse U., Individual Achievement award N.Y. State Dept. Econ. Devel.; named to Hon. First Citizen, City of Watertown, 1976. Mem. Legis. on State Legislators (nat. conf. state legislators), Nat. Conf. State Legislators (vice chmn. agrl. and internat. trade com. State-Fed. Assembly), Am. Soc. Young Polit. Leaders. Republican. Roman Catholic. Avocations: boating, skiing, music. Office: US Ho of Reps 2441 Rayburn Ho Office Bldg Washington DC 20515

MC HUGH, MARGARET ANN GLOE, retired psychologist; b. Salt Lake City, Nov. 8, 1920; d. Harold Henry and Olive (Warenski) Gloe; m. William T. McHugh, Oct. 1, 1943; children: Mary Margaret McHugh-Shuford, William Michael, Michelle McHugh Sprague. BA, U. Utah, 1942; MA in Counseling and Guidance, Idaho State U., 1964; PhD in Counseling Psychology, U. Oreg., 1970. Nat. cert. counselor. Tchr. kindergarten, Idaho Falls, Idaho, 1951-62; tchr. high sch. English, 1962-63; counselor Counseling Ctr., Idaho State U., Pocatello, 1964-67; instr. U. Oreg., Eugene, 1967-70; asst. prof. U. Victoria, B.C., Can., 1970-76; therapist Peninsula Counseling Ctr., Port Angeles, Wash., 1976-81, Sequim, Wash., 1976-81; psychologist McHugh & Assocs. Counseling Ctr., Sequim, 1981-95; ret., 1995. Ensign with WAVES, 1943-44. Recipient Recogniton award for 25 yrs. vol. svc. to Hospice. Mem. APA, ACA, Am. Assn. Marriage and Family Therapy, Wash. Psychol. Assn. (rsch. women issues, depression and women, sexual abuse, adults with childhood and abuse trauma). Achievements include research in stress management. Home: 1175 Cameron Rd Sequim WA 98382-7501 E-mail: whugh@olypen.com.

MCHUGH, MAURA, professional basketball coach; b. Worcester, Mass. m. Greg Olson. Grad. magna cum laude, Old Dominion U., 1975; MS in Phys. Edn., Pa. State U., 1977. Grad. asst. Pa. State U., Univ. Pk., 1977, asst. basketball coach, 1978-80; basketball coach U. Okla., Norman, Ariz. State, Tempe, 1988-93; exec. dir. Bus. Coun. for Alcohol Edn., Phoenix, 1993-97; head basketball coach Long Beach (Calif.) StingRays, 1997—. Named Big Eight Coach of Year, 1977, Converse Nat. Coach of Year, 1977. Achievements include being awarded one of first ever women's basketball scholarships at Old Dominion U.; No. 1 ranking academically at Old Dominion U.; advancing to NCAA Sweet 16 postseason play in 1986. Address: Long Beach Stingrays 1900 Embarcadero Rd Ste 110 Palo Alto CA 94303-3310 also: Long Beach Stingrays 230 California St Ste 510 San Francisco CA 94111-4331

MCHUGH, PAUL R. psychiatrist, neurologist, educator; b. Lawrence, Mass., May 21, 1931; s. Francis Paul and Mary Dorothea (Herlihy) McH.; m. Jean Barlow, Dec. 27, 1959; children: Clare Mary, Patrick Daniel, Denis Timothy. AB, Harvard U., 1952, MD, 1956. Diplomate: Am. Bd. Psychiatry and Neurology. Intern Peter Bent Brigham Hosp., Boston, 1956-57; resident in neurology Mass. Gen. Hosp., 1957-60, fellow in neuropathology, 1958-59; teaching fellow in neurology and neuropathology Harvard, 1957-60; clin. asst. psychiatry Maudsley Hosp., London, Eng., 1960-61; mem. neuropsychiatry div. Walter Reed Army Inst. Research, Washington, 1961-64; asst. prof. psychiatry and neurology Cornell U., N.Y.C., 1964-68, assoc. prof., 1968-71, prof., 1971; dir. electroencephalography N.Y. Hosp., 1964-68; founder, dir. N.Y. Hosp. Bourne Behavioral Rsch. Lab., 1967-68, clin. dir., supr. psychiat. edn., founder, dir. Weschester divsn. dept. psychiatry, 1968-73; prof., chmn. dept. psychiatry U. Oreg. Health Sci. Center, Portland, 1973-75; Henry Phipps prof. psychiatry Johns Hopkins, Balt., 1975—2003, chmn. dept. psychiatry, 1975—2003, prof. dept. mental hygiene, 1976—; psychiatrist-in-chief Johns Hopkins Hosp., 1975—2003; dir. Blades Ctr. for Clin. Practice and Rsch. in Alcoholism Johns Hopkins Med. Inst., 1992—2001; chmn. med. staff Johns Hopkins Hosp., 1983-89, trustee, 1983—89. Author: The Perspectives of Psychiatry, 1983; (with Phillip R. Slavney) Psychiatric Polarities, 1987, Genes, Brain and Behavior, 1990; contbg. author: Cecil-Loeb Textbook of Medicine; mem. editorial bd. Am. Jour. Physiology, Jour. Nervous and Mental Disease, Comprehensive Psychiatry, Medicine, Psychol. Medicine, 1976—, Am. Scholar; contbr. articles to profl. jours. Mem. Md. Gov.'s Adv. Com., 1977—80, U.S. Conf. Cath. Bishops Nat. Rev. Bd. Office of Child and Youth Protection, 2002—. Grantee NIH, 1964-68, 67-70, 70-74, 75—; recipient William C. Menninger award ACP, 1987. Fellow: Am. Psychiat. Assn., Royal Coll. Psychiatry; mem.: Am. Coll. Psychiatrists (Disting. Svc. award 2002), Pavlovian Soc., Am. Psychopath. Assn. (Joseph Zubin award 1995), Am. Coll. Neuropsychopharmacology, Harvey Soc., Am. Physiol. Soc., Am. Neurol. Assn., Inst. Medicine-NAS, W Hamilton St. Club. Home: 3707 St Paul St Baltimore MD 21218-2403 Office: Johns Hopkins Med Insts Meyer 127 600 N Wolfe St Baltimore MD 21287

MCHUGH, ROBERT DANIEL, bank executive, writer; b. Bridgeport, Conn., Aug. 23, 1954; s. Robert Daniel McHugh and Joan Norine Mycock; 5 children. BS in Acctg., Villanova U., Pa.; MBA in Fin., St. Joseph's U., Phila. Cert. CIA, CBA. Exec. v.p., CFO Main St. Bancorp, Reading, Pa.; v.p. fin. Nat. Penn Bankshares, Boyertown, Pa.; cons. Grant Thornton, CPAs, Phila.; prof. St. Joseph's U., Phila., Albright U., Phila. Advisor U.S. Sec. of Commerce, 1994. Author: Bank Operations Management, 1989, (novels) Portal to Power, 2003; contbr. articles to profl. jours. Twp. auditor East Vincent Twp., Pa., 2003. Mem.: Author's Guild, Alpha Sigma Lambda. Republican. Avocation: coaching baseball.

MCHUGH, STUART LAWRENCE, materials engineer; b. San Francisco, Nov. 7, 1949; s. James and Ruth McHugh. BSc in Geophysics with high distinction, U. Nev., 1971, BSc in Geol. Engring. with high distinction, 1972; MS in Geophysics, Stanford U., 1974, MS in Materials Sci., 1976, PhD in Geophysics, 1977. Seismol. asst. U. Nev., Reno, 1971-72; intern, student geophysicist Humble Oil Co., New Orleans, summer 1972; geophysicist U.S. Geol. Survey, Menlo Park, Calif., 1973-77, SRI, Internat., Menlo Park, 1977-81; materials engr. Lockheed Martin Missiles & Space Co., Palo Alto, Calif., 1981—. Contbr. articles to profl. jours. Recipient traineeship NSF, 1972-73; named MacKay Sch. Mines Outstanding Geologist, U. Nev., Reno, 1972. Mem. AAAS, AIAA, Am. Geophys. Union, Am. Phys. Soc., Inst. Molecular Modeling, Phi Kappa Phi. Avocation: fgn. lang. studies. Office: Lockheed Martin Space Systems Co Bldg 204 O/ABBS 3251 Hanover St Palo Alto CA 94304-1121

MCILRATH, THOMAS, physicist, researcher; b. Dowagiac, Mich. s. William Frederick and Leora Lewis McIlrath; m. Valerie Hoy McIlrath, June 30, 1962; children: Christine, Laura. BS in Physics, Mich. State U., 1960; PhD in Physics, Princeton U., 1966. Rsch. assoc., instr. Harvard Coll. Obs., Cambridge, Mass., 1967-73; from assoc. prof. to prof. U. Md., College Park, 1973-98, assoc. dean for rsch. and grad. studies, 1995-96, prof. emeritus, 1998—; physicist Nat. Inst. Stds. and Tech., Gaithersburg, Md., 1974-97. Cons. AT&T Bell Labs., Holmdel, N.J., 1984-93, Princeton (N.J.) Plasma Physics Lab., 1984-90; program officer NSF, Washington, 1993-95; spkr. in field. Contbr. papers to profl. jours. Recipient Silver medal U.S. Dept. Commerce, 1980, IR-100 award Indsl. Rsch. Mag., 1981. Fellow Am. Phys. Soc. (treas. and pub. 1996—), Optical Soc. Am. (bd. dirs. 1993-95), Am. Assn. Advanced Sci. Office: Am Phys Soc One Physics Ellipse College Park MD 20740 Fax: (301) 209-0844. E-mail: mcilrath@aps.org.

MCILROY, ALAN F. manufacturing executive; b. 1950; Internat. contr. Wheelabrator Corp., 1983-87; bus. unit contr. Gen. Chem., 1987-90; sr. v.p. Harris Chem.; head Greenock Group; CFO Dayton Superior Corp., Miamisburg, Ohio, 1997—. Office: Dayton Superior Corp Ste 130 7777 Washington Village Dr Dayton OH 45459

MCILWAIN, CARL EDWIN, physicist; b. Houston, Mar. 26, 1931; s. Glenn William and Alma Ora (Miller) McI.; m. Mary Louise Hocker, Dec. 30, 1952; children— Janet Louise, Craig Ian. BA, N. Tex. State Coll., Denton, 1953; MS, State U. Iowa, 1956, PhD, 1960. Asst. prof. State U. Iowa, 1960-62; assoc. prof. physics U. Calif.-, San Diego, 1962-66; prof. U. Calif., 1966—. Mem. space scis. steering com., fields and particles subcom. NASA, 1962-66; mem. anti-submarine warfare panel President's Sci. Adv. Com., 1964-67; mem. com. potential contamination and interference from space expts. Space Sci. Bd., Nat. Acad. Scis.-NRC, 1964-71; mem. advisory com. for radiation hazards in supersonic transports FAA, 1967-71; mem. Fachbeirat Inst. Extraterrestrial Physics, Max Planck Inst., Garching, Fed. Republic Germany, 1977-83, Space Sci. Bd., NRC, 1983-86. Author; patentee in field. Guggenheim fellow, 1968, 72; recipient Space Sci. award Am. Inst. Aeros. and Astronautics, 1970, Computer Art award U.S. Users Automatic Info. Display Equipment, 1971, Sr. U.S. Scientist award Alexander von Humboldt Found., Ger., 1976, Hannes Alfven medal European Geogphys. Soc., 2000. Fellow Am. Geophys. Union (John A. Fleming award 1975); mem. Am. Phys. Soc., Am. Astron. Soc. Home: 6662 Avenida Manana La Jolla CA 92037-6228 Office: U Calif San Diego Cass 0424 La Jolla CA 92093-0424 E-mail: cmcilwain@ucsd.edu.

MCILWAIN, JOHN KNOX, housing policy fellow; b. NYC, Nov. 9, 1943; s. Knox and Emily Edey (Woods) McI.; m. Wende Lillian Sheffield, Oct. 28, l972; l child, Knox. AB, Princeton U., 1966; JD, NYU, l970. Bar: N.Y. 1970, D.C. 1979. Assoc. Dewey, Ballantine, Bushby, Palmer & Wood, N.Y.C., 1970-73; dep. dir. Maine State Housing Authority, Augusta, 1976-77; exec. asst. to asst. sec. for housing Fed. Housing Commn., HUD, Washington, 1977-79; ptnr. Cohen & Uretz, Washington, 1979-84; sr. v.p. Nordheimer Bros. Co., Arlington, Va., 1984-85; ptnr. Powell, Goldstein, Frazer & Murphy, Washington, 1985-96, mng. ptnr. Washington Office, 1988-92; mng. dir. Fannie Mae Am. Cmtys. Fund, 1996-97; pres., CEO Fannie Mae Found., Washington, 1997-98; sr. mng. dir. Fannie Mae Am. Cmtys. Fund, Washington, 1998—2001; sr. resident fellow Urban Land Inst., Washington, 2001—, J. Ronald Terwilliger chair for housing, 2001—. Mem. DC Comprehensive Housing Strategy Task Force, 2004—. Bd. dirs., exec. com. Ctr. for Housing Policy, 1992—, editl./policy rev. com., 2000-02, v.p. 2002—; bd. dirs., exec. com. Nat. Housing Conf., Washington, 1980-90, treas., 1985-90, vice chmn., 1990-93, pres., 1993-97; bd. dirs. Praugue Inst. for Global Urban Devel., co-chair, sub com. on Urban Devel., 2002—, Nat. Inst. for Cmty. Empowerment, 1998-2003; vestryman St. Mark's Episc. Ch., Washington, 1982-86; pres. Insight Mediation Comm. of Washington, 2001—, bd. dirs., v.p. Nat. Housing and Rehab. Assn., Washington, 1988-93, pres., 1993-95; bd. dirs., exec. com. Cmty. Preservation and Devel. Corp., 2001—, Washington Area Housing Partnership, 1991-96, Coun. for Excellence in Govt., 1989-92, Children's Hosp. Found., 1997—, mem. Princeton U. Alumni Coun. Cmty. Svc. Com., 1995-96; DC Agenda, 1997-98; bd. dirs., sec. Found. for Cmty. Leadership, Inc., 1995-2002. Mem. ABA, D.C. Bar Assn. (steering com. real estate sect. 1980-82), Cosmos Club (Washington), Lambda Alpha Internat. Democrat. Avocations: sailing, music, Maine. Home: 1737 New Hampshire Ave NW Apt 4 Washington DC 20009-2522 Office: Urban Land Inst 1025 Thomas Jefferson Se NW Ste 500W Washington DC 20007-5201 Office Phone: 202-624-7071.

MC ILWAIN, WILLIAM FRANKLIN, newspaper editor, writer; b. Lancaster, S.C., Dec. 15, 1925; s. William Franklin and Docia (Higgins) McI.; m. Anne Dalton, Nov. 28, 1952 (div. 1973); children: Dalton, Nancy, William Franklin III; m. K. L. Brelsford, June 5, 1978 (div. 1983). BA, Wake Forest Coll., 1949; postgrad., Harvard, 1957-58. Various positions with Wilmington (N.C.) Star, 1943, Charlotte (N.C.) Observer, 1945, Jacksonville (Fla.) Jour., 1945, Winston-Salem (N.C.) Jour.-Sentinel, 1949-52, Richmond (Va.) Times-Dispatch, 1952-54; chief copy editor Newsday, Garden City, N.Y., 1954-57, day news editor, 1957-60, city editor, 1960-64, mng. editor, 1964-66, editor, 1967-70; writer-in-residence Wake Forest U., 1970-71; dorm leader Alcoholic Rehab. Ctr., Butner, N.C., 1971; dep. mng. editor Toronto Star, 1971-73; mng. editor The Record, Hackensack, N.J., 1973-77; editor Boston Herald Am., 1977-79; dep. editor Washington Star, 1979-81, exec. mng. editor, 1981; editor Ark. Gazette, 1981-82; founding editor N.Y. Newsday, 1982-84; exec. editor Sarasota (Fla.) Herald-Tribune, 1984-90; sr. editor N.Y. Times Regional Newspaper Group, 1991-92; chmn. Bill Mc Ilwain, Inc., 1993—. Author: The Glass Rooster, 1960, (with Walter Friedenberg) Legends of Baptist Hollow, 1949; collaborator: (with Newsday staff) Naked Came The Stranger, 1969, A Farewell to Alcohol, 1973; contbr. to: Reader's Digest, Harper's, Esquire, Atlantic Monthly; editor N.C. Writer's Workshop. Mem. Pres. Johnson's Commn. on Civil Rights; mem. adv. bd. Pulitzer Prize, 1982. With USMC, 1944. Named to N.C. Journalism Hall of Fame. Mem. Am. Soc. Newspaper Editors, Soc. Nieman Fellows. Home and Office: 305 N Channel Dr Wrightsville Beach NC 28480-2723 *As Fats Waller said, "One never knows, do one?".*

MC INDOE, DARRELL WINFRED, retired nuclear medicine physician; b. Wilkinsburg, Pa., Sept. 28, 1930; s. Clarence Wilbert and Dorothy Josephine (Morrow) McIndoe; m. Carole Jean McClain, Aug. 23, 1952; children: Sherri L. McIndoe, Wendy L. McIndoe, Darrell B. McIndoe, Ronald S. McIndoe, Holly B. McIndoe. BS, Allegheny Coll., 1952; MD, Temple U., 1956, MS, 1960. Commd. 2d lt. M.C. US Air Force, 1956, advanced through grades to col., 1971; intern Brooke Army Med. Ctr., San Antonio, 1956-57; resident in medicine Temple U. Med. Ctr., Phila., 1957-60; chief internal medicine and Hosp. svc. Norton AFB, 1960-64; dir. divsn. nuc. medicine St. Joseph Hosp., Towson, Md., 1992-2000; chief internal medicine and hosp. services 7520 U.S. Air Force Hosp., England, 1964-68; vis. rsch. fellow Royal Post Grad. Med. Sch., London, 1968-69; chief endocrinology svcs., chmn. dept. nuc. medicine USAF Med. Ctr., Keesler AFB, Miss., 1969-75; dep. dir. Armed Forces Radiobiology Rsch. Inst., Def. Nuc. Agy., Bethesda, Md., 1975-77, dir., 1977-79; staff physician nuc. medicine br., dept. radiology Nat. Naval Med. Ctr., Bethesda, Md., 1979-82; sr. lectr. mil. medicine Uniformed U. of Health Scis., Bethesda, Md., 1975-80; asst. prof. radiology/nuc. medicine and rsch. program coord. Uniformed U. of Health Sci., 1980-82; assoc. divsn. nuc. medicine St. Joseph Hosp., Towson, Md., 1982-91, dir. divsn. nuc. medicine, 1991—2000; ret, 2000. Med. advisor Nev. ops. office Dept. Energy, Las Vegas; cons. in field. Fellow: Am. Coll. Nuc. Physicians (regent ea. USA), Fellow royal Soc. Medicine; mem.: AMA, Soc. Med. Cons.'s to Armed Forces, Assn. Mil. Surgeons U.S., Health Physics Soc. (dir. Balt., Washington chpt.), Md. Soc. Nuc. Medicine (past pres.), Soc. Nuc. Medicine (ho. of dels.), Uniformed Svcs. Nuc. Medicine Assn. (pres. 1975), Air Force Soc. Physicians (bd. govs. 1973—77), Alexander Graham Bell Soc. Home: 15510 Foxpaw Trail Woodbine MD 21797-8000

MC INERNEY, DENIS, lawyer; b. N.Y.C., May 31, 1925; s. Denis and Anne (Keane) McI.; m. Mary Irene Murphy, Nov. 14, 1953; children: Kathleen Mc Inerney O'Hare, Denis J., Maura Mc Inerney Romano. BSS, Fordham U., 1948, JD cum laude, 1951, LLD (hon.), 1996. Bar: N.Y. 1951, D.C. 1961. Instr. philosophy Fordham U., 1948-51; assoc. Cahill Gordon & Reindel, N.Y.C., 1951-61, ptnr., 1961-90, sr. counsel, 1991—. Vice chmn. Com. Character and Fitness Admission State Bar N.Y., 1st Jud. Dept., 1979-97, chmn. Departmental Disciplinary Com., 1st Jud. Dept., 1997-2003; lectr. in field. Co-author: Practitioners Handbooks for Appeals to the Appellate Divisions of the State of New York, 1979, and to the Court of Appeals of the State of New York, 1981. Bd. dirs. Vols. of Legal Svc., Inc., 1985-2001, Cath. Youth Orgn., 1975—; mem. adv. bd. St. Vincent's Hosp., Westchester, N.Y., 1988—; chmn. bd. visitors Fordham Law Sch., 1989—; trustee Fordham U., 1988-94. Sgt. 82d Airborne Divsn. U.S. Army, 1943-46, ETO. Decorated Knight of Malta, Knight of the Holy Sepulcher; recipient Achievement in Law award Fordham U., 1977, St. Thomas More award Archdiocese NY Cardinal's Com. of Laity Lawyers' Divsn., 2001, Second Harvest award Fordham U. Sch. Law, 2003. Fellow Am. Coll. Trial Lawyers (state chmn. 1980-82); mem. ABA, N.Y. State Bar Assn., Bar Assn. City N.Y., New York County Lawyers Assn. (pres. 1982-84), N.Y. County Lawyers Assn. Inn of Ct. (pres. 1996-2002), Fordham U. Law Alumni Assn. (pres. 1968-72, medal of achievement 1975). Clubs: Westchester Country, Univ. Roman Catholic. Office: Cahill Gordon & Reindel 80 Pine St Fl 20 New York NY 10005-1790 E-mail: d.mcinerney@cahill.com.

MCINERNEY, JAMES EUGENE, JR., trade association executive; b. Springfield, Mass., Aug. 3, 1930; s. James Eugene and Rose Elizabeth (Adikes) McI.; m. Mary Catherine Hill, July 17, 1963; children: Anne Elizabeth, James Eugene, III. BS, U.S. Mil. Acad., 1952; MS in Engring., Princeton U., 1960; postgrad., Royal Air Force Staff Coll., 1964; MS in Internat. Affairs, George Washington U., 1970. Commd. 2d lt. USAF, 1952, advanced through grades to maj. gen., 1976, fighter pilot, comdr. tactical fighter squadron S.E. Asia, 1967, tactical fighter wing, 1971; sr. US adviser Turkish Air Force, 1973—75; dir. mil. assistance and sales Hdqrs. USAF, 1975-78; comdt. Indsl. Coll. Armed Forces, 1978-79; dir. programs Hdqrs. USAF, 1979-80, asst. dep. chief of staff for programs and evaluation, 1980; dir. legis. liaison McDonnell Douglas Corp., Washington, 1980-83, dir. internat. affairs, 1983-86; from v.p. to exec. v.p. Am. League for Exports and Security Assistance, 1986-92, exec. v.p., 1989-92; v.p. Am. Def. Preparedness Assn., 1992-97, Nat. Def. Indsl. Assn., 1997—. Decorated Air Force Cross, D.S.M. (2), Silver Star (3), D.F.C. (7), Bronze Star, Air medal (18), Meritorious Svc. medal (2), Air Force Commendation medal, Vietnamese Crosses of Gallantry with palm and star, Republic of Korea Cheongsu medal, comdr. Order of the Brit. Empire (CBE). Mem. Air Force Assn. (citation of honor 1968, Medal of Merit, 2002), Brit.-Am. Bus. Assn.-Washington (pres. 1982-94, chmn. 1994-96), Brit.-Am. Bus. Coun. (chmn. 1996-97), Am.-Air Mus. in Britain (exec. dir. 1984—), The Jefferson Islands Club, Capitol Hill Club, Congl. Country Club. Roman Catholic. Home: 1031 Delf Dr Mc Lean VA 22101-2009 Office Phone: 703-247-2562.

MCINERNEY, JOSEPH ALOYSIUS, hotel executive; b. Oak Park, Ill., Sept. 2, 1939; s. Joseph Aloysius and Helene (Mustari) McI.; m. Ruth McClelland, Aug. 29, 1969; children— Joseph A., Susan B. Student, Loyola U., Chgo., 1959-61; BA cum laude, Boston Coll., 1974. With Sheraton-Chgo. Hotel, 1961-65, regional dir. franchise ops., 1966-67, dir. franchise devel., 1968-69; gen. mgr. Sheraton-Winston, Salem, 1969-70; v.p., asst. to pres. Sheraton Corp., 1970-73, sr. v.p., dir. franchise ops., 1973-79; sr. v.p. Sheraton Corp., pres. Sheraton Corp. (Franchise div.), 1979-86; pres. Hawthorn Suites, 1986-91; pres., chief exec. officer Travelodge Internat., 1991-92; pres., CEO, chmn. Forte Hotels, Inc., 1992-96; CEO Pacific Asia Travel Assn., 1997-2001; pres., CEO Am. Hotel & Lodging Assn., 2001—. Guest lectr. Cornell Hotel Sch., Boston U. Hotel Sch., U. N.H. Hotel Sch., Mich. State U., San Diego State U., Okla. State U. Former mem. industry sect. adv. com. U.S. Dept. Commerce, also U.S. trade rep.; mem. adv. bd. Master Sci. degree program in hospitality industry studies at NYU; mem. hospitality adv. bd. N.Mex. State, Calif. Poly. Hosp.; former trustee Boston U. Med. Ctr., Bethune-Cookman Coll.; bd. trustees St. Vincent de Paul Village; exec. com. CEO San Diego Roundtable. Mem. Am. Hotel & Motel Assn. (govtl. affairs com.), Am. Hotel & Motel Ednl. Inst. (former chmn.). Office: Am Hotel & Lodging Assn 1201 New York Ave NW Washington DC 20005-3931 Fax: 202-289-3106. E-mail: joe@ahla.com.

MCINERNEY, NOREEN LINDA, lawyer; b. Evergreen Park, Ill., Sept. 27, 1971; d. Patrick Joseph and Florence Murphy; m. Michael Joseph McInerney, June 4, 1995; children: Cortney Marie, Neive Renee. BAS in Econs., U. Ill., 1993; JD, Ill. Inst. Tech., 1996. Bar: Ill. 1996. With First Chgo., Chgo., 1997; atty. Griffin & Gallagher, Palos Hills, Ill., 1997—. Mem.: ABA, Clare Assn., Ill. State Bar Assn. Roman Catholic. Avocations: running, bicycling, reading. Office: Griffin & Gallagher 10001 S Roberts Rd Palos Hills IL 60465 Office Phone: 708-598-6800. Business E-Mail: linda@griffingallagher.com.

MCINERNY, RALPH MATTHEW, philosopher, educator, writer; b. Mpls., Feb. 24, 1929; s. Austin Clifford and Vivian Gertrude (Rush) McI.; m. Constance Terrill Kunert, Jan. 3, 1953; children: Cathleen, Mary, Anne, David, Elizabeth, Daniel. BA, St. Paul Sem., 1951; MA, U. Minn., 1952; PhD summa cum laude, Laval U., 1954; LittD (hon.), St. Benedict Coll., 1978, U. Steubenville, 1984; DHL (hon.), St. Francis Coll., Joliet, Ill., 1986; DHL, St. John Fisher Coll., 1994, St. Anselm Coll., 1995, Holy Cross Coll., New Orleans, 2001. Instr. Creighton U., 1954-55; prof. U. Notre Dame, Ind., 1955—, Michael P. Grace prof. medieval studies, 1988—, dir. dept., 1978-85. Vis. prof. Cornell U., 1988, Cath. U., 1971, Louvain, 1983, 95; founder Internat. Catholic Univ.; disting. vis. prof. Truman State U., Mo., 1999; Joseph lectr., Rome, 2003. Author: (philos. works) The Logic of Analogy, 1961, History of Western Philosophy, vol. 1, 1963, vol. 2, 1968, Thomism in an Age of Renewal, 1966, Studies in Analogy, 1967, New Themes in Christian Philosophy, 1967, St. Thomas Aquinas, 1976, Ethica Thomistica, 1982, History of the Ambrosiana, 1983, Being and Predication, 1986, Miracles, 1986, Art and Prudence, 1988, A First Glance at St. Thomas: Handbook for Peeping Thomists, 1989, Boethius and Aquinas, 1989, Aquinas on Human Action, 1991, The Question of Christian Ethics, 1993, Aquinas Against the Averroists, 1993, The God of Philosophers, 1994, Aquinas and Analogy, 1996, Ethica Thomistica, 1997, Student Guide to Philosophy, 1999, Vernunftgemässes Leben, 2000, Characters in Search of Their Authors, 2001, Conversion of Edith Stein, 2001, John of St. Thomas, Summa Theologiae, 2001, Defamation of Pius XII, 2001, Very Rich Hours of Jacques Maritain, 2003, Aquinas, 2003; (novels) Jolly Rogerson, 1967, A Narrow Time, 1969, The Priest, 1973, Gate of Heaven, 1975, Rogerson at Bay, 1976, Her Death of Cold, 1977, The Seventh Station, 1977, Romanesque, 1977, Spinnaker, 1977, Quick as a Dodo, 1978, Bishop as Pawn, 1978, La Cavalcade Romaine, 1979, Lying Three, 1979, Abecedary, 1979, Second Vespers, 1980, Rhyme and Reason, 1981, Thicker than Water, 1981, A Loss of Patients, 1982, The Grass Widow, 1983, Connolly's Life, 1983, Getting Away with Murder, 1984, And Then There Were Nun, 1984, The Noonday Devil, 1985, Sine Qua Nun, 1986, Leave of Absence, 1986, Rest in Pieces, 1985, Cause and Effect, 1987, The Basket Case, 1987, Veil of Ignorance, 1988, Abracadaver, 1989, Body and Soil, 1989, Four on the Floor, 1989, Frigor Mortis, 1989, Savings and Loan, 1990, The Search Committee, 1991, The Nominative Case, 1991, Sister Hood, 1991, Judas Priest, 1991, Easeful Death, 1991, Infra Dig, 1992, Desert Sinner, 1992, Seed of Doubt, 1993, The Basket Case, 1993, Nun Plussed, 1993, Mom and Dead, 1994, The Cardinal Offense, Law and Ardor, 1995, Let's Read Latin, 1995, Aquinas and Analogy, 1996, The Tears of Things, 1995, Half Past Nun, 1997, On This Rockne, 1997, Penguin Classic Aquinas, 1997, The Red Hat, 1998, What Went Wrong With Vatican II, 1998, Lack of the Irish, 1998, Irish Tenure, 1999, Grave Undertakings, 1999, Heirs and Parents, 2000, Shakespearean Variations, 2000, Book of Kills, 2001, Triple Pursuit, 2001, Still Life, 2001, Sub Rosa, 2001, Emerald Aisle, 2001, John of St. Thomas, Summa Theologiae, 2001, Law and Ardor, 2001, As Good as Dead, 2002, Celt and Pepper, 2002, Prodigal Father, 2002, Last Things, 2002, Ablative Case, 2003, Irish Coffee, 2003, Requiem For A Realtor, 2004; editor The New Scholasticism, 1967-89; editor, pub. Crisis, 1982-96; pub. Catholic Dossier, 1995—, Fellowship of Cath. Scholars Quar., 2003—. Exec. dir. Wethersfield Inst., 1989-92; bd. govs. Thomas Aquinas Coll., Santa Paula, Calif., 1993-2001; bd. dirs. Southern Cross Found., 1999—. With USMC, 1946-47. Fulbright rsch. fellow, Belgium, 1959-60, NEH fellow, 1977-78, NEA fellow, 1983, Catholic Scholars fellow; Fulbright scholar, Argentina, 1986, 87, Outstanding Philosophical scholar Delta Epsilon Sigma, 1990; recipient Thomas Aquinas medal U. Dallas, 1990, Thomas Aquinas Coll., 1991, Maritain medal Am. Maritain Assn., 1994, P.G. Wodehouse award CRISIS Mag., 1995; Gifford lectr. Glasgow U., Scotland, 1999-2000, Joseph lectr. Pontifical Gregorian Inst., Rome, 2003. Fellow Pontifical Roman Acad. St. Thomas Aquinas; mem. Am. Philos. Assn., Am. Cath. Philos. Assn. (past pres., St. Thomas Aquinas medal 1993), Cath. Acad. Scis., Am. Metaphys. Soc. (pres. 1992), Internat. Soc. for Study Medieval Philosophy, Medieval Acad., Mystery Writers Am. (Lifetime Achievement award 1993), Authors Guild, Fellowship Cath. Scholars (pres. 1992-95, pres.'s com. arts and humanities 2002--, Cardinal Wright award 1996, Premio Roncevalles de Navarre 2002). Office: U of Notre Dame Jacques Maritain Ctr 714 Hesburgh Notre Dame IN 46556-5677 Home: Holy Cross Village 1010 E Village Dr PO Box 839 Notre Dame IN 46556

MCINNES, DONALD GORDON, railroad executive; b. Buffalo, Nov. 6, 1940; s. Milton Gordon and Blanche Mac (Clunk) McI.; m. Betsy Campbell, Mar. 18, 1967 (dec. Feb. 1995); children: Campbell Gordon, Cody Milton; m. Carol Anne Haverty, Oct. 12, 1996; stepchildren: Molly Caroline, Lawrence Joseph. BA, Denison U., 1963; MS, Northwestern U., 1965; Cert. in Transp., Yale U., 1965. Budget mgr. operating AT&SF R.R. Co., Chgo., 1969-71; v.p., COO Burlington No. Santa Fe Corp., 1995—; from asst. trainmaster to sr. v.p., COO AT&SF R.R. Co., San Bernardino, Calif., 1971—94, sr. v.p., COO Chgo., 1994—95; COO Burlington No. Santa Fe Corp., 1995—2000. Bd. dirs. AT & SF Railway Co., TTX Corp., Kervik Corp., founding mem. Intermodal Assn. N.Am., 1st chmn., 1991-93; bd. dirs. Thrall Car Mfg., Chgo. Trustee Vt. Acad., Saxtons River; chmn. bd. Found. for Intermodal Rsch. and Edn., Washington. Served to 2d lt. USAF, 1965-67; capt. U.S. Army, 1967-69.

Decorated Bronze Star. Mem. Ballymeade Country Club (North Falmouth, Mass.), Falmouth Yacht Club. Home: 75 Waterside Ave Falmouth MA 02540-3825 Personal E-mail: dgmc@flash.net.

MC INNES, WILLIAM CHARLES, priest, academic administrator; b. Boston, Jan. 20, 1923; s. William Charles and Mary (Byrne) Mc Innes. BS, Boston Coll., 1944, AB, 1950, MA, 1951; STL, Weston Coll., 1958; PhD, N.Y. U., 1955. Joined Soc. of Jesus, 1946; ordained priest Roman Cath. Ch., 1957; prof. mktg. and bus. ethics Sch. Bus. Adminstrn. Boston Coll., 1959-63, assoc. dean Sch. Bus. Adminstrn., 1961-63, dir. honors program, 1963-64, mem. citizens seminar planning com., 1959-63, dir. Nat. Jesuit Honor Soc., 1997—2003; pres. Fairfield (Conn.) U., 1964-73, prof. urban problems, 1969-72; pres. U. San Francisco, 1972-77, Assn. Jesuit Colls. and Univs., 1977-89; campus min. U. Conn., Storrs, 1990-96. Vis. fellow Woodstock Theol. Ctr., 1990—91. Life mem. United Cerebral Palsy Assn. Fairfield County; mem. adv. com. Conn. Dept. Social Svcs., 1993—96; chaplain Boston Coll. Alumni Assn.; past chmn. bd. dirs. ABCD (cmty. action agys.); bd. dirs. Nat. Better Bus. Bur.; past pres. Conn. Assn. Cmty. Action Programs; founder Fairfield County Cmty. Forum Conn. Charter Oak Coll.; vice chmn. Nat. Better Bus. Bur. Found.; chmn. Calif. Coun. Humanities. Served to capt. USAF, 1942—46, CBI. Mem.: Alpha Epsilon Delta, Phi Kappa Theta, Delta Sigma Pi, Alpha Sigma Nu, Beta Gamma Sigma. Home: Jesuit Cmty Boston Coll Chestnut Hill MA 02467 E-mail: mcinnewi@bc.edu.

MCINNIS, SCOTT STEVE, congressman, lawyer; b. Glenwood Springs, Colo., May 9, 1953; s. Kohler McInnis and Carol Kreir; m. Lori McInnis; children: Daxon, Tessa, Andrea. BA, Ft. Lewis Coll., 1975; JD, St. Mary's Law Sch., 1980. Atty. Delaney & Balcomb P.C., Glenwood Springs, Colo., 1981—; mem. Colo. State Ho. of Reps., 1984-93, chmn. agrl. livestock and natural resources com., 1986-90, majority leader, 1990-92; mem. U.S. Ho. Reps. 103d-108th Congresses from 3rd Colo. Dist., 1993—; mem. rules com. U.S. Ho. Reps., 1998, mem. house ways and means com., 2001—, chmn.resources subcom. on forests and forest health. Recipient Florence Sabin award, 1984, Guardian of Small Bus. award Nat. Fed. Ind. Bus., 1990, Lee Atwater Leadership award, 1991, and various awards from United Vets. Commn.; named Legislator of Decade and Legislator of Yr by Colo. Ski Country and Colo. Wildlife Found. Mem. Elks, Rotary, Phi Delta Phi. Republican. Roman Catholic. Office: US Ho Reps 320 Cannon Hob Washington DC 20515

MCINTIER, RUSSELL J. retired writer; s. Ralph E. and Caroline M. McIntier; m. Gladys F. VanZandt, Sept. 12, 1965; children: Debbra F. Burchett, Russell J.(dec.). Br. chief US ATSC, Corpus Christi Army Depot, Tex., 1988—94, site mgr. Ft. Sill, Okla., 1980—88; team leader US ACRC, Pueblo Army Depot, Colo., 1966—80; airman/sgt. USAF, McConnell AFB, 1955—64. Survey officer US ATSC, Corpus Christi Army Depot, Tex., 1963—64. Author: (novel) Hardscrabble, (short story) The Denver City No Girls Club (Cert. Of Exellence, 1997), (book of short stories) Peace Officer: A Collection of Short Stories. Achievements include Caregiver.

MCINTIRE, LARRY VERN, biomedical engineering educator; b. St. Paul, June 28, 1943; s. James Lawrence and Lenore Vineal (Converse) McI.; m. Suzanne G. Eskin, June 27, 1997. BChemE, MS, Cornell U., 1966; MA, Princeton U., 1968, PhD, 1970. Registered profl. engr., Tex. Asst. prof. Rice U., Houston, 1970-74, assoc. prof., 1974-78, prof. chem. engring., 1978—2003, E.D. Butcher prof., 1983—2003, chmn. dept., 1981-91, chmn. Bioscis. and Bioengring. Inst., 1991—2003, chmn. rsch. coun., 1988-91, dir. Biomed. Engring. Lab., 1980—, chmn. dept. biomed. engring., 1997—2003; spke faculty coun., 1994-95. Adj. prof. medicine Baylor Coll. Medicine, Houston, 1982—, U. Tex. Med. Sch., Houston, 1982—, M.D. Anderson Cancer Ctr., 2001—; chmn. dept. biomed. engring. Ga. Tech., 2003—; chmn. blood/materials working group NIH, Bethesda, Md., 1982-85; mem. surgery and bioengring. study sect. NIH, 1984-88, 99—; mem. com. on bioprocessing NRC, 1991-94; chmn. rheology subcom. Internat. Coun. on Thrombosis and Hemostasis, 1985-89. Contbr. over 250 articles to profl. jours. Recipient Merit award NIH, 1989; NSF fellow Cornell U., Princeton U., 1965-69, NATO-NSF postdoctoral fellow Imperial Coll., London, 1976-77. Fellow Am. Inst. Med. Biol. Engring. (sec., treas. 1993-96, pres. 1997-98), AIChE (officer local sect. 1980-81, 86, Food Pharm. and Bioengring. divsn. award 1992, divsn. chair 1998), AAAS; mem. Biomed. Engring. Soc. (bd. dirs. 1992-97, pres. 1995-96, Disting. lectr. 1992), N.Am. Soc. Biorheology (v.p. 1992-94, pres. 1994-96), N.Y. Acad. Scis., Am. Heart Assn. (coun. on thrombosis, exec. com. 1994—), Faculty Club Rice U. (bd. dirs., chmn. 1982-84), Sigma Xi (nat. lectr. 1993-96), Nat. Acad. Engring. Presbyterian. Avocations: tennis, squash, classical music, hiking. Office: Ga Tech Dept Biomed Engring Atlanta GA 30332-0535

MCINTIRE, T. BRYAN, lawyer, councilman; s. Theodore Bryan and Anna Lleigh McIntire; m. Doris L. Poehler, Aug. 14, 1979; m. Carole Lee Wood, June 26, 1954 (div.); children: Lee Anne Wildemann, Carole Leslie, Laurel Gordon Penn, Lynnette Wood Hansel, Lisa Digges. BA, Johns Hopkins U., 1952; LLB, U. Balt., 1955. Sr. ptnr. McIntire, Johnson, Levin & Webb, Westminster, Md., 1956—2003; elected official Balt. County Coun., Towson, Md., 1994—. Maj. Army N.G., 1949—69. Mem.: Md. State Bar Assn. (bd. govs. 1994—96). Office: Balt County Coun 400 Washington Ave Towson MD 21204

MCINTIRE, WILLIAM TREDICK, II, municipal official, investment banker; b. Red Bank, N.J., Dec. 18, 1925; s. Frank and Elizabeth Bel (Ewing) McI.; m. Patricia Marie Mickleburgh, May 22, 1954; children: William Tredick III, Henry Dickson. AB, Harvard U., 1947; cert., U. Geneva, 1949. Salesman Dominick & Dominick, N.Y.C., 1949-57; asst. v.p. R.S. Dickson & Co., N.Y.C., 1957-63; v.p. Shearson Hammill, N.Y.C., 1963-66, White Weld & Co., N.Y.C., 1966-70; pres. Kleinwort Benson Inc., N.Y.C., 1970-86; treas. Town of Darien, Conn., 1987—. Vol. exec. Internat. Exec. Svc. Corp., Stamford, Conn., 1987-93. Pres. Darien Red Cross, 1972-74, Darien Hist. Soc., 1976-80. Lt. USN, 1965-75. Recipient Congl. Cert. of Appreciation, U.S. Congress, 1993, Svc. award Gov. of Conn., 1997. Mem. Tokeneke Club, Harvard Club of N.Y.C., Rep. Club of Darien. Home: 9 Hickory Ln Darien CT 06820-3211 Office: Town of Darien 2 Renshaw Rd Darien CT 06820-5397

MCINTOSH, ANITA JANE, retired administrative assistant; b. Huntington, W.Va., Mar. 5, 1937; d. Harold Herbert and Edwinna Work (Barnhart) Boyd; m. Melvin Dwight McIntosh, June 21, 1958; children: Kevin Neal, Menita Lynn. Art and Illustration cert. Famous Artists Schs., Conn., 1965. Sec. Life Ins. Co. of Ga., Atlanta, 1955—59, adminstrv. asst. Charlotte, 1982—99; sec. Santee Sales, High Point, NC, 1968—73; tchrs. aide Burke County Dept. Social Svcs., Morganton, NC, 1974—82; art instr. Myers Pk. United Meth. Ch., Charlotte, NC, 1988, Charlotte, NC, 2002. Author: (poem) Teacher in the Church Today, 1991, (devotions) Upper Room Devotional Book, 2002. Mem.: Charlotte Mecklenburg Sr. Games, First Flight Soc., Watercolor Soc. N.C. United Methodist. Avocations: watercolors, water-skiing, swimming. Home: 2832 Morris Ln Denver NC 28037 Home Fax: 704-483-9270. E-mail: waterwood@charter.net.

MCINTOSH, CAROLYN LEIGH, lawyer; b. Boulder, Colo., Dec. 10, 1955; d. Glen Elvis and Alice Joy McIntosh; m. Roger Alan Bucholz, Oct. 4, 1980 (div. Dec. 1998); m. Leland Kioshi Marable, Dec. 11, 1998. BA cum laude, Middlebury Coll., 1978; JD, U. Colo., 1981. Bar: Colo. 1981, U.S. Dist. Ct. Colo. 1981, Mon. 1988 (specially admitted), U.S. Dist. Ct. Mont. 1989, U.S. Ct. Appeals 2000. Rsch. asst. Rocky Mountain Mineral Law Found., Boulder, 1979-80; assoc. Sisk, Foley, Hultin & Driver, Denver, 1981-83, Hultin, Driver & Spaanstra, Denver, 1983-85; asst. atty. gen. Colo. Dept. of Law, Denver, 1986-88; assoc. Cogswell & Wehrle, Denver, 1988-89, shareholder, 1989-90; spl. asst. atty. gen. State of Mont., 1988-90; sr. assoc. Patton, Boggs & Blow, Denver, 1990-92; ptnr. Patton Boggs, LLP, Denver, 1992—, mng. ptnr. Denver office, 1993—2002. Assoc. adj. prof. Colorado Sch. Mines, 1991-2000; mem., atty. program to provide legal svcs. to indigent, Denver, 1982-86. Mem. procedural rules subcom. Colo. Air Quality Control Commn., 1983-84; mem. Lafayette Planning Commn., 1986-87, 95-99, Lafayette City Coun., 1987-99, mayor pro tem, 1989-91, mayor, 1995-99; mem. bd. Denver Regional Coun. Govts., 1990-99; mem. Regional Air Quality Coun., 1992-99, mem. exec. com., 1996-99; mem. Colo. Water Conservation Bd., 2001—, Urban Drainage and Flood Control Bd., 1995-99. Mem. ABA (natural resources sect.), Colo. Bar Assn., Denver Bar Assn. (legal fees arbitration com. 1983 84, 86 87), Alliance Profl. Women (bd. dirs. 1986-90), Internat. Inst. Environ. Risk Mgmt. (bd. govs. 1996—). Office: Patton Boggs 1660 Lincoln St Ste 1900 Denver CO 80264-1901 E-mail: cmcintosh@pattonboggs.com. *Notable cases include: Environ. Def. Fund vs. Colo. Dept. Health, 1986, defending against unsuccessful challenge to the State of Colo.'s prevention of significant deterioration air quality regulations; State of Colo. vs. Idarado Mine Co., 1989, prosecution of superfund clean up claims against Idarado; Denver vs. Adolph Coons Co., et al, superfund cost recovery action.*

MCINTOSH, CAROLYN MEADE, retired educational administrator; b. Waynesburg, Ky., Oct. 21, 1928; d. Clarence Hobert and Sarah Letitia (Bentley) Meade; m. Edgar G. McIntosh, Aug. 21, 1948; children: Wayne, Jeanne, Penny, Jimmi, Carol. BS, Miami U., Oxford, Ohio, 1962; MEd, Xavier U., Cin., 1966. Elem. tchr., Ohio, 1961-79; prin. New Richmond (Ohio) Sch. Dist., 1980-91, ret., 1991. Tchr. Clermont County Adult Edn. Program, 1970-95, Clermont County dir.of Headstart 1971-72, Clermont County Rep. to Ohio elem. adminstr., 1985-87, Pres. Clermont and Brown County adminstr., 1988-89; apptd. student achievement liaison team, New Richmond Bd. Edn. Editor Ret. Tchrs. Newsletter. Pres. New Richmond Bd. Edn.; v.p. U.S. Grant Vocat. Sch. Bd. Edn.; mem. Clermont County Excellence in Edn. Com.; mem. edn. adv. com. Clermont Coll., mem. long range planning com., 1999;; mem. adv. bd. Bethany Children's Home; mem. Clermont 2001 Com.; mem. Rep. Ctrl. Com. of Clermont County; mem. New Richmond Continuous Improvement Com., 1999; mem. Clermont County Kids Voting Com.; mem. com. Renaissance New Richmond; judge Clermont/Brown County Lit. Coun. Ann. Spelling Bee. Recipient New Richmond Adminstr. of the Yr. award City of New Richmond, 1989; named citizen of yr. Monroe Twp., 1996; selected for sr. leadership charter class, Clermont 2000—. Mem. AAUW, ASCD, NAESP, Nat. Sch. Bd. Assn., Ohio Sch. Bd. Assn., Ohio Assn. Elem. Sch. Adminstrs. (all county legis. liaison), Ohio County Ret. Tchrs. Assn., Clermont County Ret. Tchrs. Assn. (pres.), Order Eastern Star, Clermont County Comm. Svcs. Bd. (apptd. 1998), Phi Delta Kappa, Delta Kappa Gamma (pres. chpt.). Baptist.

MCINTOSH, CATHLEEN ANNE, small business owner, educator; d. Joseph Kimbal Goforth and Mary Elizabeth Jordan; m. Charles David McIntosh, June 9, 1994; children: Amy Lee Vest, Elizabeth Page Henley, Michael Dow Busby, Dee Candelaria. MA with distinction, U. of N.Mex, 2002. Tchr. Ruidoso H.S. and ENMU-Ruidoso, Ruidoso, N.Mex., 1993—; drama, choreography, French, English, pilates tchr. Ruidoso Mcpl. Schs., Ea. N.Mex U./Ruidoso, Ruidoso, N.Mex., 1994—; co-owner Action Ski & Snowboard, Pro Action Sports, Action Scooters, Ruidoso, N.Mex., 1999—, Ruidoso Lifestyle Mag., Ruidoso, N.Mex., 1995—. Founder Lincoln County Cmty. Theatre, Ruidoso, N.Mex., 2004—. Editor: Ruidoso Lifestyle Mag. Mem. Ruidoso Arts Commn., Ruidoso, N.Mex., 1995—2001, Alamgordo Music Theatre, Alamogordo, N.Mex., 1985—90. Recipient Meritorious Svc. to Dance Edn., Dept. of Theatre and Dance and Coll. of Fine Arts, NDEO, 2003. Mem.: Ruidoso Chamber of Commerce (bd. dirs. 1999—2002), AFAA (licentiate; mem. 1989—2004), Nat. Dance Educators Assn. (assoc.; mem., Meritorious Svc. to Dance Edn. 2003), P.E.O. (assoc.; mem. 1986—2004). R-Consevative. Methodist. Avocations: skiing, dance, racquetball, travel. Home: 410 Snowcap Ruidoso NM 88345 E-mail: mcintoshc@ruidoso.k12.nm.us.

MCINTOSH, DAVID M. former congressman; b. June 8, 1958; m. Ruthie McIntosh. Grad., Yale Coll., 1980, U. Chgo., 1983. Bar: Ind., U.S. Supreme Ct. Spl. asst. domestic affairs to Pres. Reagan; spl. asst. to Atty. Gen. Meese; liaison Pres.'s Commn. on Privatization; spl. asst. to V.P. Quayle, dep. legal counsel to; exec. dir. Pres.'s Coun. on Competitiveness; sr. fellow Citizens for a Sound Economy; founder Federalist Soc. for Law & Pub. Policy, now co-chmn.; mem. U.S. Congress from Ind., Washington, 1995-2001; ptnr. Mayer, Brown, Rowe and Maw, 2002—; prof., dept of econ. Ball St. Univ. Sch. of Bus., 2002—. Mem. State Bar of Ind. Republican. Office: PO Box 3300 Muncie IN 47307 also: Mayer Brown Rowe and Maw 1909 K St NW Washington DC 20006 E-mail: dmcintosh@mayerbrown.com.

MCINTOSH, DENNIS KEITH, veterinarian, consultant; b. Newark, June 12, 1941; s. Sheldon Weeks and Enid Nicholson (Casey) McI.; children: Kevin, Jamie. BS in Animal Sci., Tex. A&M U., 1963, BS in Vet. Sci., 1967, DVM, 1968. Asst. county agrl. agt., Cleburne, Tex., 1963—65; owner, operator Park North Animal Hosp., San Antonio, 1970—75, El Dorado Animal Hosp., San Antonio, 1973—. Co-chmn. vet. tech. adv. coun. Palo Alto Coll., 1995—, tchr. Animal Health Tech., San Antonio Coll., 1985-95; pres., mgr. Bexar County Emergency Animal Clinic, Inc., 1978-81; cons. vet. practice mgmt., mktg., client rels.; spkr. for vet. meetings, assns.; co-host Ask the Vet, Adopt a Pet, Sta. KENS-TV, 1980-93; vet. mem. Tex. Bd. Health, 1984-89, chmn. disease control com., pers. com.; mem. environ. health, hosps. com. Team capt. Alamo Roundup Club and Pres.' Club of San Antonio C. of C., 1970-75; mem. Guadalupe County Youth Fair Bd., 1978-80. Contbg. author: Mosby's Review Questions and Answers for Veterinary Boards, 1998, Chicken Soup for the Pet Lover's Soul, 1998; contbr. articles to profl. jours. With Vet. Corps, USAF, 1968-70. Recipient Alumnus award Guadalupe County 4-H Club, 1979, Outstanding Svc. award San Antonio Coll., 1986-87, Outstanding Bus. Ptnrs. award N.E. Ind. Sch. Dist., 1995-96. Mem. AVMA, Tex. Vet. Med. Assn. (pres., chmn. bd. dirs.), Tex. Acad. Vet. Practice (pres.), San Antonio C. of C. (life), Tex. County Agrl. Agts. Assn. (4th v.p. 1964), Am. Legion, Tex. Old Time Fiddler's Assn., Delta Soc. (pres. San Antonio chpt. 1989-90). Office: 13039 Nacogdoches Rd San Antonio TX 78217-1960 Office Phone: 210-656-1444. Personal E-mail: dennis.mcintosh@att.net.

MCINTOSH, ELAINE VIRGINIA, nutrition educator; b. Webster, S.D., Jan. 30, 1924; d. Louis James and Cora Boletta (Bakke) Nelson; m. Thomas Henry McIntosh, Aug. 28, 1955; children: James George, Ronald Thomas, Charles Nelson. BA magna cum laude, Augustana Coll., Sioux Falls, S.D., 1945; MA, U. S.D., 1949; PhD, Iowa State U., 1954. Instr., asst. prof. Sioux Falls Coll., 1945-48; instr. Iowa State U., Ames, 1949-53, rsch. assoc., 1955-62; postdoctoral rsch. assoc. U. Ill., Urbana, 1954-55; asst. prof. human biology U. Wis., Green Bay, 1968-72, assoc. prof., 1972-85, prof., 1985-90, emeritus prof., 1990—, writer, cons., 1990—, chmn. human biology dept., 1975-80, asst. to vice chancellor, asst. to chancellor, 1974-76. Author 3 books including American Food Habits in Historical Perspective, 1995, Lewis and Clark: Food, Nutrition, and Health, 2003; contbr. numerous articles on bacterial metabolism, meat biochemistry and nutrition edn. to profl. jours. Fellow USPHS, 1948-49. Avocation: travel. Office: U Wis Green Bay ES 307A Human Biology 2420 Nicolet Dr Green Bay WI 54311-7001

MC INTOSH, JAMES EUGENE, JR., interior designer; b. Dadeville, Ala., Nov. 13, 1938; s. James Eugene and Jessie (Latimer) McI. B.Interior Design, Auburn (Ala.) U., 1961. Designer contract div. Rich's Dept. Store, Atlanta, 1961-64; assoc. William Trapnell & Assocs., Atlanta, 1964-70; dir. Interior Concepts, Inc., Atlanta, 1970-72; dir. design comml. design div. Rich's Dept. Store, 1972-80; v.p. Comml. Interior Designs, Inc., 1980-82; exec. staff Rollins Inc., 1982—; pres. Gene Mc Intosh & Assocs., 1985—. Fellow Am. Soc. Interior Designers (Presdl. citation 1974); mem. Nat. Trust Hist. Preservation, Ala. Hist. Soc., High Mus. Art, Soc. Archtl. Historians. Home: Gene McIntosh & Assocs 130 Church St Decatur GA 30030 E-mail: cmeneg@earthlink.net.

MCINTOSH, JON CHARLES, illustrator, graphics designer, painter; b. Alliance, Ohio, Aug. 8, 1947; s. John Cowles and Lucile Tipple (Ketcham) McI.; 1 child, Forgan Cowles; m. Jean Bogart Goodman, Apr. 24, 1993; stepchildren: Buffy Trott, Hays Spangler Trott. Student, Hobart Coll., 1965-67; BFA, R.I. Sch. of Design, 1974. Pres. McIntosh Ink, Inc., Vineyard Haven, Mass., 1971—. Bd. ov overseers New Eng. Conservatory of Music, Boston, 1989-95; bd. dirs. Sail Martha's Vineyard. Illustrator: (book) The Foolish Dinosaur Fiasco, 1978, The Mysterious Zetabet, 1980, The Doctor's Handbook, 1982, Witch Way to The Country, 1995, Witch Way to the Beach, 1997, The Longest Hair in the World, 1999; author, illustrator: Hooked On Golf, 1986, Fineart Gingerbread Sq. Gallery, Grannary Gallery. Artwork contbr. Ducks Unltd; art for advt. Bose, Wang, Digital, NASA. Recipient Silver medal V.I. Internat. Film Festival, 1976, Gold medal Soc. of Newspaper Designers, 1985, First place Francis Hatch Advt. Awards, 1987, First place New Eng. Newspaper Awards, 1998, Silver award Soc. Newspaper Designers, 2000. Mem. Soc. of Illustrators (Silver Funny Bone 1991), The Country Club, The West Chop Club. Republican. Episcopalian. Avocations: musician, ski racing, tennis, fishing, skeet shooting. Office: McIntosh Ink Inc 620 Elizabeth St Key West FL 33040 Office Phone: 305-295-2533.

MCINTOSH, KATHLEEN ANN, music educator; b. Portland, Oreg., Nov. 29, 1944; d. Norman Bankson and Geraldine Mattos McIntosh; m. Sam Adams, Nov. 23, 1986; m. David Farr, June 18, 1968 (div. Apr. 1, 1976). MusB, U. of Oreg., 1962—66; Cert. of Advanced Musical Studies, King's Coll., U. of London, 1966—67; MusM, U. of Wash., 1967—68; Performer's Cert., U. Oreg., 1966. Harpsichord instr. Calif. State U. at Long Beach, 1980—85; prof. Los Angeles Valley Coll., 1975—2000. Harpsichordist Santa Fe Chamber Music Festival, N.Mex., 1996—; harpsichordist and organist Santa Fe Pro Musica, 1989—; harpsichordist Vail Valley Bravo Festival, Beaver Creek, Colo., 1999—. Soloist (harpsichordist) Chamber Orch. Kremlin, recitalist Art of Fugue (J.S. Bach), Deya internat. festival, harpsichordist San Francisco Consortium Antiquum (dance group). Recipient Lillian and Paul Petri award, Oreg. State U., 1966. Home: 1301 Calle Ramon Santa Fe NM 87501

MCINTOSH, L(ORNE) WILLIAM, marketing executive; b. Kingston, Ont., Can., May 1, 1945; s. Jack Lorne and Lillian (Oaks) McI.; m. Siobhan McAfee, May 18, 1998. BSBA, Lehigh U., 1967, MBA, 1968. Asst. prof. Union Coll., Cranford, NJ, 1968-72; sr. market rsch. analyst Merck, Sharp & Dohme, West Point, Pa., 1972-75, advt. copywriter, 1975-77, product mgr., 1977-80, assoc. dir. advt., 1980-82, dir. licensing and acquisitions, 1982, sr. dir. mktg., 1983-86; exec. v.p. mktg. Medco Containment Svcs., Inc., Fair Lawn, NJ, 1987-88; v.p. mktg. and bus. devel. Boehringer Mannheim Pharms., Rockville, Md., 1988-92; chmn. bd., CEO Target Mktg. Systems, Inc., Blue Bell, Pa., 1992-93; sr. v.p. bus. devel. and com. ops. Zynaxis, Inc., Malvern, Pa., 1993 95, sr. cons. SmithKline Beecham, Phila., 1995 97; sr. v.p. bus. devel. and fin., CFO VIMRx Pharms. Inc., 1997—98; pres., CEO Nexell Therapeutics, 1998—2000; pres., chief bus. officer FASgen, Inc., Balt., 2001—03; CEO, Q-RNA, Inc., N.Y.C., 2004—. Mem. Am. Econ. Assn., Am. Mktg. Assn., Lic. Execs. Soc., Antique Automobile Club Am., Model A Ford Club Am., Vintage Chevrolet Club Am., Pontiac Oakland Owners Club, Beta Gamma Sigma. Avocations: antique automobiles, woodworking, antique furniture restoration, music. Home: 1711 Cannongate Rd Forest Hill MD 21050-2203 Office Phone: 212-568-0365. E-mail: mcamci@msn.com.

MCINTOSH, MAGGIE, state legislator; b. Quinton, Kans., Dec. 22, 1947; AA, Independent Jr. Coll., 1967; BAE, Wichita State U., 1970; MS, ABS, Johns Hopkins U., 1987. Adminstr., tchr. Balt. City Pub. Schs., 1972-78; adj. instr. continuing edn. Cantonville (Md.) C.C., 1978-79; cmty. svc. planner, grants analyst Commn. on Aging and Retirement Edn., Balt., 1979-85; del. Dist. 44 Md. State Delegation, 1992-94, del. Dist. 42, 1995—, mem. appropriations com., 1993—, mem. econ. matters com., 1992—. Del. Dem. Nat. Conv., 1980; mem. Dem. State Ctrl. Com., 1986—; state dir. U.S. Senator Barbara A. Mikulski, 1988-92. Office: Md Ho of Reps State Capitol Annapolis MD 21401 also: Lowe House Office Bldg 84 College Ave Rm 141B Annapolis MD 21401-1693 Address: 6615 Reisterstown Rd Ste 301 Baltimore MD 21215-2689

MCINTOSH, MOLLY, interior designer; b. Spokane, Wash., Feb. 4, 1951; d. Keith L. and Dolores J. (Hensel) Yates; m. Forrest E. McIntosh, Dec. 18, 1971; children: Jennifer, Brandon. Student, N.W. Christian Coll., 1971. Archtl. signage salesperson Clarke & Assoc., Santa Ana, Calif., 1983-84; interior designer Precept Design, Worthington, Ohio, 1984-85, Gracious Living, Redmond, Wash., 1985—. Recipient Silver award Master Builder Assn., 1994. Mem. Am. Soc. Interior Designers (allied mem., showhouse com. 1998), N.W. Soc. Interior Designers (profl. mem., 2d pl. for residential design 1994). Mem. Christian Ch. (Disciples Of Christ). Avocation: travel. Fax: 360-243-6717.

MCINTOSH, TERRIE TUCKETT, lawyer; b. Ft. Lewis, Wash., July 20, 1944; d. Robert LeRoy and Elda (Perry) Tuckett; m. Clifton Dennis McIntosh, Oct. 13, 1969; children: Alison, John. BA, U. Utah, 1967; MA, U. Ill., 1970; JD, Harvard U., 1978. Bar: N.Y. 1979, Utah 1980. Assoc. Hughes, Hubbard & Reed, N.Y.C., 1978-79, Fabian & Clendenin, Salt Lake City, 1979-84, shareholder, 1984-86; staff atty. Questar Corp., Salt Lake City, 1986-88, sr. atty., 1988-92, sr. corp. counsel, 1992—. Instr. philosophy Douglass Coll. Rutgers U., New Brunswick, N.J., 1971-72; mem. adv. com. civil procedure Utah Supreme Ct., Salt Lake City, 1987—; mem. jud. nominating com. 5th Cir. Ct., Salt Lake City, 1986-88. Mem. Utah State Bar (ethics and discipline screening panel 1989-96, vice chair ethics and discipline com. 1996-99, co-chair law related edn. com. 1985-86), Women Lawyers of Utah (chair exec. com. 1986-87), Salt Lake Legal Aid Soc. (trustee 1999—), Harvard Alumni Assn. Utah (bd. dirs. 1987—), Phi Beta Kappa, Phi Kappa Phi. Office Phone: 801-324-5532.

MCINTURFF, FLOYD M. retired state agency administrator; b. Greenback, Tenn., May 1, 1923; s. Samuel Floyd and Hazel Agnes (Vaden) M.; m. Merle Celeste Sosna, May 27, 1950; children: Judith Margaret, Laura Ellen, Melissa Ann. BS, U. Tenn., Knoxville, 1950. Asst. to the chief engr., missiles Rockwell Internat., Columbus, 1957-73; chief, targeted jobs tax credit program Ohio Bur. Employment Svcs., Columbus, 1974-88; ret., 1988. Commd. officer U.S. Army Signal Corps, 1942-46, 51-52. Mem. Opera Columbus, Columbus Astron. Soc., Am. Atheists, Sons of Revolution, First Families of Tenn. Avocations: music, astronomy, photography, elderhostel. Home: 4985 Beatrice Dr Columbus OH 43227-2114

MCINTYRE, ANITA GRACE JORDAN, lawyer; b. Louisville, Ky., Jan. 29, 1947; d. Blakely Gordan and Shirley Evans (Grubbs) Jordan; m. Kenneth James McIntyre, Oct. 11, 1969; children: Abigail, Jordan Kenneth. BA, Smith Coll., 1969; JD, U. Detroit, 1975. Bar: Mich. 1975, U.S. Dist. Ct. (ea. dist.) Mich. 1975, U.S. Dist. Ct. (we. dist.) Mich. 1979, U.S. Ct. Appeals (6th cir.) 1979. Ptnr. Rollins White & Rollins, Detroit, 1975-79; vis. assoc. prof. Detroit Coll. Law, 1979-81; assoc. Tyler & Canham, Detroit, 1981-82; prin. Anita G. McIntyre, P.C., Grosse Pointe, Mich., 1982-87, 91—; of counsel Nederlander Dodge & Rollins, Detroit, 1987-90; assoc. Damm & Smith, P.C., Detroit, 1990-91. Hearing panel chmn. Atty. Discipline Bd., 1985—. Editor, author (case notes) U. Detroit Jour. Urban Law, 1975; contrbr. articles to profl. jours. Sec. Berry Subdivsn. Assn., Detroit, 1975-77; pres. Smith Coll. Club Detroit, 1982-86; mem. parents bd. U. Liggett Sch., Grosse Pointe, Mich., 1991,95; vice chair state pub. affairs com. Mich. State Coun. Jr. Leagues, 1998-2000, chair, 2001-. Mem.: Wayne County Juvenile Trial Lawyers Assn., Wayne County (Mich.) Probate Bar Assn., State Bar Mich., Edgemont Park Assn. (sec.), Jr. League Detroit (chair pub.affairs com. 1998—2001, vice chair Mich. state pub. affairs com. 1999—2001, chair 2001—02). Episcopalian. Avocations: skiing, swimming, needle point. E-mail: agmcintyr@cs.com.

MCINTYRE, BERNICE KAY, lawyer, management consultant; b. Worcester, Mass., Aug. 9, 1950; d. William James and Theodora Grace (McCullough) M.; m. Michael Henry Pete, June 25, 1994. BA, Oberlin Coll., 1972; JD, Boston U., 1977. Bar: Mass. 1977. Asst. gen. counsel Dept. Pub. Welfare, Boston, 1977-78, Coastal Zone Mgmt., Boston, 1978-79, gen. counsel, 1979-81, Exec. Office Environ. Affairs, Boston, 1981-83, asst. sec., 1982-83; commr. Dept. Pub. Utilities, Boston, 1983—; appointed by gov. chmn. Pub. Utilities Commn., Boston, 1987-90. Active Clinton Gore Energy Transition Team, 1992-93; mgr., sr. cons. Arthur D. Little, Inc., 1991-95; prin., pres. B.K. McIntyre & Assocs., Inc., 1995—; assoc. prof. mgmt. dept. Southeastern U., Washington. Contbr. chpts. to books. Office: BK McIntyre & Assocs Inc 1250 24th St NW Ste 350 Washington DC 20037-1124

MCINTYRE, BRUCE HERBERT, media and marketing consultant; b. Takoma Park, Md., Jan. 24, 1930; s. Orrin Raymond and Leila Hazel (Olmsted) McI.; m. Natalie Ann Wolff, Oct. 10, 1953; children: Douglas A., Elizabeth W., Emily O., Catherine N., Jane A. Student, Gannon Coll., 1954-57, U. Akron, 1958-61. Reporter, city editor Erie (Pa.) Times and News, 1949-57; reporter, city editor, asst. to exec. editor Akron (Ohio) Beacon Jour., 1958-67; with Battle Creek (Mich.) Enquirer & News, 1967-71, asst. mng. editor, 1967-68, mng. editor, 1968-71; exec. v.p., editor Oakland Press, Pontiac, Mich., 1971-77, pub., 1977-95; v.p., pub. div. Capital Cities/ABC Inc., 1987-96; chmn. Great Lakes Media Inc., 1995-96; pre. McIntyre Media LLC, West Bloomfield, Mich., 1997—; sec., dir. Clarkston State Bank, Clarkston, Mich., 1998—; councilman City of Orchard Lake Village, Mich., 1998—2004, mayor, 2001—04. Lectr. Am. Press Inst., 1968—; journalism juror Pulitzer Prizes, 1972— Served with AUS, 1951-53; lt. col. Res. ret. Mem. Soc. Profl. Journalists. Clubs: Pine Lake Country (Bloomfield, Mich.). Episcopalian. E-mail: bhmcintyre@comcast.net.

MCINTYRE, DOUGLAS CARMICHAEL, II, (MIKE MCINTYRE), congressman; b. Lumberton, N.C., Aug. 6, 1956; s. Douglas Carmichael and Thelma Riley (Hedgpeth) McI.; m. Lola Denise Strickland, June 26, 1982; children: Joshua Carmichael, Stephen Christopher. BA, U. N.C., 1978, JD, 1981. Bar: N.C. 1981, U.S. Dist. Ct. (ea. dist.) N.C. 1984, U.S. Dist. Ct. (mid. dist.) N.C. 1985., U.S. Ct. Appeals (4th cir.) 1987, U.S. Supreme Ct., 1987. Assoc. Law Office Bruce Huggins, Lumberton, 1981-82, McLean, Stacy, Henry & McLean, Lumberton, 1982-86; ptnr. Price & McIntyre P.A., Lumberton, 1987-89; prin. McIntyre Law Firm, P.A., Lumberton, 1989-96; congressman U.S. Ho. of Reps., 1997—. Mem. law-focused edn. adv. com. N.C. Dept. Pub. Instrn., 1986-87; mem. U.S. Ho. Com. on Agr., 1997—, Nat. Security Com., 1997—; co-chmn. Coalition Task Force on Edn., 1997-98, Congrl. Task Force on Promotion of Fatherhood, Rural Health Care Coalition, 1999-2002, Democratic Task Force on Children, 1999-2000, Coalition Task Force on Bus. and Tech., Spl. Forces Caucus, 2002—; mem. President's Summit on Am.'s Future, 1997. Del. Dem. Nat. Conv., N.Y.C., 1980, N.C. Dems., Raleigh, 1974—; pres. Robeson County Young Dems., Lumberton, 1982; sec.-treas. 7th Congl. Dist. Young Dems., N.C., 1983, chmn., 1984; 2d vice chmn. 7th Congl. Dist. Dems. So. N.C., 1986-89, 1st vice chmn., 1989; mem. state adv. bd. North Carolinians Against Drug and Alcohol Abuse, Raleigh, 1984-85; chmn. Morehead Scholarship Selection Com., Robeson County, 1985-94; deacon, elder, clk. of session Presbyn. Ch.; active Boy Scouts Am., Lumberton, 1983; mem. N.C. Commn. on Children and Youth, 1987-89, N.C. Commn. on the Family, 1989-91; mem. Young Life Lumberton com., 1987-89; chmn. Robeson County U.S. Constn. Bicentennial com., 1986-87; mem. lawyers' adv. com. to N.C. Commn. on Bicentennial of U.S. Constn., 1986-89; bd. dirs. Robeson County Group Home, Lumberton, 1984-87, Lumberton Econ. Advancement for Downtown, Inc., 1987-90, pres., 1988-89, 89-90; chmn. legis. affairs com. C. of C., 1991, 92, 93, bd. dirs., 1992-94; mem. N.C. Mus. of History Assocs., 1987-89; mem. regional selection com. Gov.'s Award for Excellence in Teaching Social Studies, 1991. Morehead Found. scholar, 1974-78; named one of Outstanding Young Men in Am., 1981, 84, 85, 88; Outstanding Young Dem. Robeson County Young Dems., 1984-85; one of State's Outstanding Young Dems. Young Dems. N.C., 1984, 85; recipient Algernon Sydney Sullivan award U. N.C., 1978, Outstanding Young North Carolinian award N.C. Jaycees, 1988, Outstanding Young North Carolinians, Heart Robeson Jaycees, 1988, Nat. Bicentennial Leadership award for Individual Achievement Coun. for Advancement of Citizenship and Ctr. for Civic Edn., Washington, 1987, Gov.'s Outstanding Vol. Svc. award, 1989, Thomas Jefferson award Food Distbrs. Internat., 1998, 2002, Guardian of Small Bus. award, Nat. Fedn. Independent Bus., 1997-99, Nat. Rural Health Legislative award, 1999, 2003, Outstanding Health Svc. award Cmty. Ptnrs. Health Net, 2000, Spirit of Enterprise award, U.S. C. of C., 1997-98, Super Hero award Nat. Assn. Cmty. Health Ctrs., 2001, 02, 03, Internat. Pub. Policy award Internat. Assn. Pers. Employment, 2002, Law Enforcement award, N.C. Narcotics Officers Assn., 2002, Quality Pub. Svc./Pub. Edn. and Health Care award Am. Fedn. Tchrs., 2001, Charles Dick Medal of Merit Nat. Guard Assn., 2000, Disting. Svc. to Agriculture award Robeson County Crop Promotion Assn., 2001, Congrl. Partnership award Nat. Assn. Devel. Orgns., 2002; named to Legis. Honor Roll So. Econ. Devel. Coun., 1997, 2001, 02. Mem. ABA (exec. com. citizenship edn. com. 1985-87, nat. cmty. law week com. 1982-83), Internat. Platform Assn., N.C. Bar Assn. (chmn. youth edn. and constn. bicentennial com. 1986-87, youth edn. com., exec. coun. young lawyers divsn. 1986-87), Robeson County Bar Assn. (founder, chmn. citizenship edn. com. 1982-94, law day com.), 16th Jud. Dist. Bar Assn., N.C. Acad. Trial Lawyers, N.C. Coll. Advocacy, Christian Legal Soc. (state adv. bd. 1986-90, state pres. 1987), Lumberton C. of C. (bd. dirs. 1992-94), The Ret. Officers' Assn. (hon. life), Order of Old Well, Lumberton Rotary Club (bd. dirs. 1995-96), Phi Beta Kappa, Phi Eta Sigma. Democrat. Avocations: tennis, skiing, softball, dance, bible study. Home: 1701 N Chestnut St Lumberton NC 28358-3839 Office: 228 Cannon Washington DC 20515-3307 E-mail: congmcintyre@mail.house.gov.

MCINTYRE, EDWARD J. power company executive; BBA, Minot State U., 1973. Jr. acct. No. States Power Co., Minot, N.D., 1973, rate analyst Mpls., 1975, gen. mgr. revenue requirements, 1983, dir. gas supply and storage, dir. gas supply and bus. ops., pres., CEO Wis. subs., v.p., CFO, 1993-2000; with Xcel Energy Inc., Mpls. Bd. dirs. Greater Mpls. Met. Housing Corp., Jr. Achievement, Como Zoo & Conservatory Soc. Office: Xcel Energy Inc 800 Nicollet Mall #3000 Minneapolis MN 55402-2023

MCINTYRE, ELIZABETH JONES, retired multi-media specialist, educator; b. Teaneck, N.J., July 17, 1939; d. Paul J. Jones and Ann Cecilia O'Leary; m. John Peter McIntyre, Jan. 30, 1960; children: John P. III, Paul M., Patricia M., Maura M. Student, Rosemont Coll., 1957—59; BS in Edn., Seton Hall U., 1961; degree, Caldwell Coll., 1976. Cert. Tchr. N.J., 1976, Libr. N.J., 1976. Tchr. 4th grade Corpus Christi Sch., Hasbrouck Heights, NJ, 1960—61; media specialist Gould & Grandview Sch., North Caldwell, NJ, 1961—63, Parsippany Twp. Sch., Parsippany, NJ, 1974—2000; ret., 2000. Grantee, Parsippany Bd. Edn., 1981, 1989. Mem.: AAUW, Women of Irish Heritage. Republican. Roman Catholic. Avocations: gardening, reading. Home: 12 South Tamarack Drive Brielle NJ 08730

MCINTYRE, JAMES OWEN, insurance executive; b. Cleve., July 21, 1958; s. Owen Eugene and Carole Diane (Saladin) McI.; m. Marina Zeccardi, Dec. 4, 1981 (div.); children: Antoinette, Owen, Helen, Robert; m. Enid Draviczky, Apr. 4, 1998. BS, Pa. State U., 1980, M of Mgmt., 1992. CLU. Sales rep. Liberty Mutual Ins. Co., Boston, 1982-89; sales mgr. Prudential Ins. Co., Blue Bell, Pa., 1989-94, adv. coun. agents Ft. Washington, Pa., 1989; mgr. Del. Valley Fin. Group (agy. of Provident Mutual), Radnor, Pa., 1994-96; sales support and competition cons. Provident Mut. Ins. Co., Valley Forge, Pa., 1996-97, dir. competition and sales support officer, 1997-99, regional v.p., 1999—. Author: Economic Effect of Banks Entering the Insurance and Financial Services Industry, 1992. Mgr. Hatfield Area Little League, Pa., 1991-97; den leader Boy Scouts of Am., Hatfield, Pa., 1994-96. Recipient Pa. Life Roundtable award Pa. Assn. Life Underwriters, 1991. Fellow Life Underwriting Tng. Coun.; mem. Nat. Assn. Life Underwriters, Am. Soc. CLU & ChFC, Gen. Agt. and Mgrs. Assn. Republican. Lutheran. Avocation: golf. Home: 354 Carlyn Ct Downingtown PA 19335-4207 Office: Provident Mut Ins Co 1000 Chesterbrook Blvd Berwyn PA 19312-2421 E-mail: JamesMcIntyre@providentmutual.com.

MCINTYRE, JERILYN SUE, university administrator; b. June 24, 1942; d. Frank Otto and Maxine (Ward) McIntyre; m. W. David Smith. Student, Stanford U., Italy, 1962; AB in History with distinction, Stanford U., 1964, MA in Journalism, cert. Summer Radio-TV Inst., Stanford U., 1965, tchrs. cert., 1968; PhD in Comms., U. Washington, 1973; postgrad. Inst. Ednl. Mgmt., Harvard U., 1993. Corr. World News Bureau McGraw-Hill Pub. Co., L.A., 1965-67; asst. prof. dept. mass comm. Chico (Calif.) State Coll., 1968-70; asst. prof. Sch. Journalism U. Iowa, Iowa City, 1973-77; assoc. prof., prof. dept. comm. U. Utah, Salt Lake City, 1977-2000, assoc. dean Coll. Humanities, 1984-88, assoc. v.p. acad. affairs, 1988-90, interim pres., 1997, v.p. acad. affairs, 1990-98; pres. Ctrl. Wash. U., Ellensburg, 2000—. Dir. Wall St. Jour. Publs. Workshop, Chico State Coll., 1968; mem. edn. adv. bd. NFL, 1996; mem. exec. com. coun. acad. affairs Nat. Assn. State Univs. and Land Grant Coll., 1995—98, chair, 1997; mem. steering com. Utah Edn. Network, 1995—98. Editl. asst. Chemical Week Mag., 1965-66, World News Bureau, 1966-67; mem. editl. bd. Journalism History; co-author: Symbols & Society; contbr. articles to profl. jours., chpts. to books. Mem. Utah Women's Forum. Named a David P. Gardner fellow, 1984; recipient Yesterday's Girl Scout Today's Successful Woman, Utah Girl Scout Coun., 1996. Mem.: AAUW (Salt Lake City chpt. Disting. Woman 1994), Assn. Edn. in Journalism and Mass Comm. Office: 400 E University Way Ellensburg WA 98926-7501

MCINTYRE, JERRY L. lawyer; b. Atlantic City, July 1, 1941; AB, Columbia U., 1963; JD, Fordham U., 1969. Bar: N.Y. 1969, R.I. 1970. Mem. McIntyre, Tate, Lynch & Holt, Providence. Com. mem. Family Ct. Bench/Bar Com., 1985—. Pres. town coun., Town of Jamestown, R.I., 1983-89. Fellow Am. Acad. Matrimonial Lawyers; mem. ABA (sect. family law), N.Y. State Bar Assn. (sect. trusts and estates law), R.I. Bar Assn., R.I. Bar Found. Office: McIntyre Tate Lynch & Holt 321 S Main St Providence RI 02903-7108

MCINTYRE, JOHN ARMIN, physics educator; b. Seattle, June 2, 1920; s. Harry John and Florence (Armin) McI.; m. Madeleine Forsman, June 15, 1947; 1 son, John Forsman. BS, U. Wash., 1943; MA, Princeton U., 1948, PhD, 1950. Mem. faculty elec. engring. Carnegie Inst. Tech., Pitts., 1943; radio engr. Westinghouse Elec. Co., Balt., 1944; research asso. Stanford, 1950-57; mem. faculty Yale, 1957-63, asso. prof., 1960-63; prof. physics Tex. A&M U., College Station, 1963-95, emeritus prof., 1995—; asso. dir. Cyclotron Inst., 1965-70. Mem. council Oak Ridge Asso. Univs., 1964-71 Fellow Am. Phys. Soc., Am. Sci. Affiliation (exec. council 1968-73); mem. AAAS. Presbyterian. Achievements include research and publs. on scintillation counters for gamma ray spectroscopy; determination of nuclear charge distbns. by electron scattering; study of nuclear structure by neutron transfer reactions; devel. variable energy gamma ray beams, gamma ray cameras. Home: 2316 Bristol St Bryan TX 77802-2405 Office: Tex A&M U Dept Physics College Station TX 77843-0001 E-mail: jmcintyre@physics.tamu.edu.

MCINTYRE, JOHN GEORGE WALLACE, real estate development and management consultant; b. Toronto, Ont., Can., July 26, 1920; s. George Crerar and Gwendolyn Alberta (Wallace) McI.; m. Ruth Elizabeth Wilson, July 26, 1945 (dec.); children: Angus, Heather, Robert, Anne. B of Commerce, U. Toronto, 1941; MBA, Harvard U., 1947. Budget acct. Abitibi Paper Co., Toronto, 1947-51; budget mgr., asst. gen. mgr. Ford of Can., Windsor, Ont., 1951-58, gen. mgr. mfg. ops., 1963-65; asst. mng. dir., mng. dir. Ford of Australia, Melbourne, 1958-63; exec. v.p., pres. Columbia Cellulose Ltd., Vancouver, B.C., Can., 1965-67; v.p. retail devel. and distbn. Hudson's Bay Co., Toronto, 1967-84; pres. Rupert's Land Tng. Co., Hudson's Bay Co. Devels. Ltd.; trustee Internat. Council of Shopping Ctrs., 1970-84; v.p., gen. mgr. Broadcast Ctr. Devel. Project Can. Broadcasting Corp., 1984-88; cons., 1988—. Chmn. Soldiers' Tower Com., U. Toronto, 1998. Served to capt. Royal Can. Ordnance Corps., 1942-45, ETO. Address: Ste 412 Richview Residence 105 Clement Rd Etobicoke ON Canada M9R 4C2

MCINTYRE, JUDY, social worker, state representative; b. Tulsa, Okla., May 31, 1945; d. Garland O. Eason, Del (Stepfather) and Jeanne (Hughes) Phillips; BS in Social Work, U. Okla., 1967, MS in Social Work, 1979. Social worker Dept. Human Svcs. in Child Welfare, Okla.; rep. Ho. Reps., State of Okla., Okla. City, 2002—. Mem. speaker's leadership team Okla. Ho. Reps., Okla. City, 2002—, mem. common edn., higher edn., human svcs., pub. health coms., 2002—. 1921 Race Riot Design Com.; Greenwood Redevel. Authority; mem., pres. Tulsa Sch. Bd. Named Fellow, Ctr. for Am. Women and Politics/Eagleton Inst. Politics, Rutgers U. Leadership Inst., 2002. Mem.: Com. Workers of Am., NAACP. Democrat. Office: 2300 N Lincoln Blvd Rm 301 Oklahoma City OK 73105 Home and Office: PO Box 48548 Tulsa OK 74148 E-mail: mcintyreju@lsb.state.ok.us.

MCINTYRE, LOLA MAZZA, music educator; b. Hammond, Ind., Sept. 23, 1955; d. Tony and Isabell Emma Mazza, Wanda Marie Mazza (Stepmother); m. William Russell McIntyre; children: William, Alexander. BMus, Hope Coll., Holland, Michigan, 1978; MMus, U. Tenn., 1989. Cert. nat. cert. piano 1991, Mich. Music Tchg. K-12 1978, Ind. applied music tchg. 2002. Music tchr. Saugatuck (Mich.) Pub. Schs., 1978—79; owner, tchr. The Studio of Holland, Holland, Mich., 1979—81; parish dir. music ministries Lafayette Diocese of Ind., Carmel, Ind., 1991—97; pvt. piano tchr. Carmel, Ind., 1976—; assoc. adj. prof. piano U. Indpls., 2001—. Prodr.: (Audio Recording) Alleluia!, 1996; author: (Multi-media Instructional CD-ROM) Bach's Musette, 2000. Friend Mus. Miniature Enthusiasts, Carmel, 2001—; docent Indpls. Symphony Orch., 1999. Recipient Concerto Competition award, Hope Coll., 1977. Mem.: Ind. Piano Tchrs. Guild (web designer, webmaster 2001—), Gtr. Indpls. Piano Tchrs. Assn. (v.p., theory chmn. 2000—02), Ind. Music Tchrs. Assn. (state advisor, music tech. 2001—02), Music Tchrs. Nat. Assn., Delta Omicron (life; chpt. pres. 1977—78, Star of Delta Omicron 1978). Roman Catholic. Avocations: miniatures, golf, quilting, travel, concerts. Office: U Indpls Music Dept 1400 E Hanna Ave Indianapolis IN Office Phone: 317-788-3255. Personal E-mail: lmcintyre@indy.rr.com. Business E-Mail: lmcintyre@uindy.edu.

MCINTYRE, LOUISE S. income tax consultant; b. Cin., Jan. 29, 1924; d. George Washington and Bertha (McDaniels) Sullivan; m. Harry McIntyre Jr., Jan. 18, 1947; children: Carol L., Patricia A., Harriet L., Harry J., Brenda R. AA, Mira Costa Coll., Oceanside, Calif., 1972; grad. in auditing, Nat. Tax Practice Inst., 1989. Enrolled agt. Hydraulic tester Paterson Field, Fairfield, Ohio, 1942-45; control clk. Hickam Field, Honolulu, 1945-47; clk.-typist Patterson Field, Fairfield, 1947-49, Camp LeJeune, Jacksonville, N.C., 1951-56; sec., bookkeeper Mission Bowl, Oceanside, 1973-79; income tax cons. Oceanside, 1974—. Mem. Oceanside Human Rels. Commn., 1970; bd. dirs. Armed Forces YMCA, Oceanside, 1969-71, Oceanside Christian Women's Club, 1988-91, North County Concert Assn. Aux., 1993-96; active PTA, Girl Scout U.S. Mem. Inland Soc. Tax Cons. (bd. dirs. 1988—), Am. Soc. Women Accts. (v.p. 1989-90), Enrolled Agts. Palomar, Nat. Assn. Enrolled Agts., Nat. Soc. Pub. Accts., Calif. Assn. Ind. Accts., Palmquist PTA (hon. life). Avocations: bowling, dance, crafts, interior decorating, cake decorating. Home: 328 Camelot Dr Oceanside CA 92054-4515

MCINTYRE, MARY MAUREEN, social services consultant; b. Decatur, Ill. d. Leo M. and Madge Eleanor (Daniels) McInroe; m. David McIntyre (dec. Sept. 1978); children: Laura, Kathy, Michael, Ellen, Paul. AA in Journalism/Comm., Cosumnes River Coll., 1994. Founder, dir. Sheltering Wings, Elk Grove, Calif., 1984-94, Washougal, Wash., 1996-97, Merimac Enterprises (a/k/a Sheltering Wings), Elk Grove, Calif., 1997—. Communicator, cons. on prevention of child abuse and homelessness; coord./conduct seminars/workshops on conflict resolutions, getting organized and successful living. Author: 8 Steps to Successful Living, 1987, (puppet prodn. script) Rochester Betsy, 1989, songs; contbr. articles to newspapers. Bd. dirs. Calvary Chapel, Camas, Wash., sec.-treas., 1996. Avocations: gardening, writing, music, travel. Home and Office: Merimac Enterprises 8698 Elk Grove Ste 3 #218 Elk Grove CA 95624 E-mail: merimac@cwo.com.

MCINTYRE, OSWALD ROSS, physician; b. Chgo., Feb. 13, 1932; m. Jean Geary, June 5, 1957; children— Margaret Jean, Archibald Ross, Elizabeth Geary. AB cum laude, Dartmouth Coll., 1953, postgrad, 1953-55; MD, Harvard U., 1957. Intern U. Pa. Hosp., 1957-58; resident in medicine Dartmouth Med. Sch. Affiliated Hosps., 1958-60; instr. medicine Dartmouth Coll., 1964-66, asst. prof. medicine, 1966-69, assoc. prof., 1969-75, prof., 1976—, James J. Carroll prof. oncology, 1980-95, dir. Norris Cotton Cancer Center, 1975-92, prof. emeritus, 1995—; attending physician VA Hosp., White River Junction, Vt., 1964. Cons. in hematology and oncology; acting chmn. dept. medicine Dartmouth-Hitchcock Med. Ctr., 1987-89; chmn. Cancer and Leukemia Group B.; 1990-95. Mem. Am. Soc. Hematology, Am. Assn. Cancer Rsch., Am. Soc. Clin. Oncology, Assn. Cancer Inst. (pres. 1988-89), New Eng. Cancer Soc. (pres. 1989-90). Home: 34 Lamphire Hill Ln Lyme NH 03768-3109

MCINTYRE, PATRICIA BOWNE, councilman; b. Yonkers, N.Y. d. Hubert L. and Margaret Connelly Bowne; m. Hugh B. McIntyre, July 11, 1958; children: Anne Louise, Hugh Cameron. BA cum laude, U. Fla., 1957; MA in Libr. Sci., U. Mich., 1958; JD, Northrup U., 1987. English tchr. Beverly Hills (Calif.) Unified Sch. Sys., 1962—65, The Chadwick Sch., Palos Verdes, Calif., 1966—86; contract adminstr. The Salvation Army, Long Beach, Calif., 1987—. Libr. commr. City of Torrance, Calif., 1983—91, civil svc. commr., 1991—99, planning commr., 2000—01, councilwoman, 2002—; bd. mem. Torrance Symphony, 2001—, Far Eastern Arts Coun./LA County Mus. of Art, L.A., 2003—. Mem.: AAUW (sec. 1997—), Kiwanis Club Torrance (pres. 1991—). Home: 3024 El Dorado Torrance CA 90503

MCINTYRE, ROBERT WHEELER, retired conservation organization executive; b. Chgo., Aug. 26, 1936; s. Henry Langenberg and Winifred (Wheeler) McI.; m. Emily Beardsley Taylor, Oct. 12, 1961 (div. 1985); children: W. Burley, Nancy T., Oliver W., Shanna L., Amanda K.; m. Miriam de Jesus Zarate, June 23, 1990 (div. 1998); m. Myung Sook Son, Jan. 6, 2001. AB in Sociology, Stanford U., 1959; MBA, Harvard U., 1964. Loan analyst Wells Fargo Bank, San Francisco, 1964-65; supr. budget analysis Ford Aerospace, Palo Alto, Calif., 1965-69; controller Allied Life Scis., San Leandro, Calif., 1969-70; ptnr. Diplomat Mfg. Co., Palo Alto, 1970-71; staff cons. Opportunity Through Ownership, San Francisco, 1971-72; gen. mgr. Quality Metal Finishers, San Francisco, 1972-73; sr. v.p., chief fin. officer The Trust for Pub. Land, San Francisco, 1973—2003, ret., 2003. Mem. adv. bd. Peninsula Open Space Trust, Menlo Park, 1978—; mem. Marin Headlands Adv. Com., 1978—81, Resource Renewal Inst., Sausalito, 1988—98, Water Heritage Trust, Sausalito, 1988—98, Dorothy Erskine Open Space Fund, San Francisco, 1978—; bd. dirs. Environ. Vols., Palo Alto, 1980—; bd. dirs., treas. Robert C. Wheeler Found., Palo Alto, 1965—95; chair, bd. dirs. Families Adopting Interracially, San Jose, 1971—74; adv. Jr. Achievement, 1966; bd. dirs. Sempervirens Fund, Mountain View, 2002—, treas., 2003—. Lt. USN, 1959—62, hon. discharge USN, 1964. Recipient Presdl. Citation award, The Trust for Pub. Land, 1988, Spl. Svc. award, Environ. Vols., 1989. Mem. Harvard Club N.Y., Harvard Club Boston, San Francisco Tennis Club, USS Coral Sea Assn., Palo Alto Tennis Club. Avocations: hiking, backpacking, tennis, travel. Home: 1061 Fulton St Palo Alto CA 94301-3313

MC INTYRE, VONDA NEEL, writer; b. Aug. 28, 1948; d. H. Neel and Vonda Barth (Keith) McI. BS, U. Wash., Seattle, 1970. Author: The Exile Waiting, 1976, 85, Dreamsnake, 1978 (Hugo award, Nebula award), Fireflood and Other Stories, 1979, The Entropy Effect, 1981, The Wrath of Khan, 1982, Superluminal, 1983, The Search for Spock, 1984, Barbary, 1986, Enterprise: The First Adventure, 1986, The Voyage Home, 1986, Starfarers, 1989, Transition, 1991, Metaphase, 1992, Nautilus, 1993, Star Wars: The Crystal Star, 1994, The Moon and the Sun, 1997 (Nebula award); editor: (with Susan Janice Anderson) Aurora: Beyond Equality, 1976. Mem. ACLU. Recipient Nebula award, 1973, 78 Mem. Sci. Fiction Writers Am., Planetary Soc., Cousteau Soc., NOW, Space Studies Inst., Authors Guild, Greenpeace, Nature Conservancy.

MCINTYRE-IVY, JOAN CAROL, data processing executive; b. Port Chester, N.Y., Mar. 1, 1939; d. John Henry and Molly Elizabeth (Gates) Daugherty; m. Stanley Donald McIntyre, Aug. 24, 1857 (div. Jan. 1986); children: Michael Stanley McIntyre, David John McIntyre, Sharon Lynne McIntyre; m. James Morrow Ivy IV, June 1, 1988. Student, Northwestern U., 1956-57, U. Ill., 1957-58. Assoc. editor Writer's Digest, Cin., 1966-68; instr. creative writing U. Ala., Huntsville, 1974-75; editor Strode Pubs., Huntsville, 1974-75; paralegal Smith, Huckaby & Graves (now Bradley, Arant, Rose & White), Huntsville, 1976-82; exec. v.p. Micro Craft, Inc., Huntsville, 1982-85, pres., 1985-89, ceo, chmn. bd., 1989—; also bd. dirs., co-owner. Author: numerous computer operating manuals for law office software, 1978—; co-author: Alabama and Federal Complaint Forms, 1979; editor: Alabama Law for the Layman, 1975; contbr. numerous articles to profl. jours. Hon. scholar Medil Sch. Journalism Northwestern U., 1956. Mem. Huntsville Literary Soc. (bd. dirs. 1976-77). Republican. Methodist. Office: 123 Fairington Rd NW Huntsville AL 35806-2249 Office Phone: 256-830-9746. Business E-Mail: verdictsales@aol.com. E-mail: verdictsos@aol.com.

MC ISAAC, GEORGE SCOTT, retired management consultant, government official; b. Auburn, N.Y., July 25, 1930; s. Robert Scott and Agnes Congalton (Aitchison) McI.; m. Betsy Clark, Sept. 11, 1954; children: Ian Scott, Christopher Clark (div. 2000); m. Mary Olds Post, Feb. 2001. BS, Yale U., 1952; MS, U. Rochester, 1961. In mfg. mgmt. Eastman Kodak Co., Rochester, N.Y., 1954-62; dir. McKinsey & Co. (Mgmt. Consultants), N.Y.C., Dusseldorf, Ger., Washington, 1962-78; asst. sec. of energy for resource applications U.S. Dept. Energy, Washington, 1978-80; sr. v.p. ops. Schlegel Corp., Rochester, 1980-85. AT&T resident mgmt. fellow; exec. prof. bus. and pub. policy William E. Simon Grad. Sch. Bus. Adminstrn., U. Rochester, 1985-97; cons. various govts., mfg. cos., fin. instns., non-profit enterprises. Contbr. articles to bus. jours. Bd. dirs. Rochester Hosp. Corp., 1987-94, vice chmn., 1991-93, Rochester Gen. Hosp., 1983-89, chmn., 1986-88; trustee emeritus Internat. Mus. Photography, George Eastman House, chmn. 1987-90; trustee Fort Hill Assn., 2003-. Lt. USMC, 1952-54. Mem.: Met. (Washington), Genesee Valley (Rochester), Owasco (Auburn).

MCIVER, BARBARA BASORE, language educator; b. Oklahoma City; d. George Milroy and Eleanor (Irvin) Basore; m. William Wood McIver. BA, U. Ark., 1968, MA, 1988, PhD, 1994. Tchr. St. Paul H.S., Ark., 1968—69, Ctrl. H.S., Kansas City, Mo., 1970—71; office mgr. AMC, Inc. Mech. Contractors, Fayetteville, Ark., 1972—85; grad. tchg. asst., lectr. U. Ark., Fayetteville, 1985—94; asst. prof., assoc. prof. Claflin U., Orangeburg, SC, 1994—. Dir. Writing Ctr. Claflin U., Orangeburg, 2000—. Contbr. articles to profl. jours.; editor: Claflin Rev., 2003—. Faculty advisor Friends of Earth, Orangeburg, 1998—. Grantee, NEH, 2000—03. Mem.: S.C. Coun. on Langs., South Ctrl. Modern Lang. Assn., Sigma Tau Delta. Office: Claflin Univ 400 Magnolia Orangeburg SC 29115

MCIVOR, DONALD KENNETH, retired petroleum company executive; b. Winnipeg, Man., Can., Apr. 12, 1928; s. Kenneth MacIver and Nellie Beatrice (Rutherford) McI.; children: Gordon, Deborah, Duncan, Donald, Daniel. BS with honors in Geology, U. Man., 1950; postgrad., Nat. Def. Coll., 1973. Geophysical trainee seismic crew Imperial Oil Ltd., Alta., 1950, various operational and rsch. positions in exploration, 1950-58, held various positions including asst. to exploration mgr., suprv. exploration planning, mgr. exploration rsch., 1958-68, with Jersey Prodn. Rsch. Co. Angola, France and Tulsa, Okla.; asst. mgr., mgr. corp. planning Toronto HO, 1968-69, mgr. exploration, 1970-72, sr. v.p., dir., 1973, exec. v.p., 1975; v.p. oil and gas exploration and prodn. Exxon Corp., 1977-81; dep. chmn., dir. Imperial Oil Ltd., 1981, chmn., chief exec. officer, 1982-85; dir., sr. v.p. Exxon Corp., Dallas, 1985-92. Bd. dirs. Nat. Coun. on Econ. Edn., Internat. Exec. Svc. Corps., N.W. Oil Co. Mem. Can. Soc. Petroleum Geologists, Am. Petroleum Inst. Home: 79 Lukes Wood Rd New Canaan CT 06840-2202 E-mail: mcivordon@aol.com.

MCJUNKIN, SHIRLEY ANNE, writer; b. Billings, Mont., Sept. 14, 1935; d. Adam Frank Lambrecht and Theresa Marie Thomas; m. Keith Eldon McJunkin, May 3, 1957; children: Lorena Anne, Keith Joseph, Daniel Allen. Student, Ea. Mont. Coll., 1980—82. Bookkeeper Mont. Nat. Bank, Billings, 1954—58, Billings Clinic, 1958—59; ward clk. St. Vincent's Hosp., Billings, 1970—72; clk. Ea. Mont. Coll., Billings, 1980—82; bookkeeper McJunkin Svc., Red Lodge, Mont., 1983—. Author: Homesteading on the Kenai, 2001, Montana Mountain Fugitives, 2004, short stories. Mem. State Arts Coun., Helena, Mont., 1998—. Avocations: writing, reading, sewing, cooking, gardening. Home: 803 N Hauser Red Lodge MT 59068 Personal E-mail: mcjn@att.net.

MCKAGUE, SHIRLEY, state representative; b. Nampa, Idaho, Dec. 4, 1935; m. Paul McKague; children: Rhonda, Van, Dan, Randy, Rick, Robert. Grad., Nampa H.S., 1953. Legal sec. Carey Nixon, 1964—78; columnist Valley Times, 1980—82; co-owner Paul's Meridian Stinker, 1970—; state rep. dist. 20B Idaho Ho. of Reps., Boise, 1996—, mem. commerce and human

resources, and transp. and def. coms., vice chmn., revenue and taxation com. Mem. Miss Meridian Pageant com.; mem. Rep. Precinct Com., 1986—. Mem.: Meridian C. of C., Idaho Farm Bur. Republican. Office: State Capitol PO Box 83720 Boise ID 83720-0038

MCKAIN, MARY MARGARET, musician; b. Spokane, Wash., June 11, 1940; d. Neil Dunn and Elinore (Bien) McK. BA in Music and Police Sci., Calif. State U., L.A., 1968; studied trumpet with Rafael Mendez, Jane Sager, Sidney Lazar, and others. Trumpet player Peter Meremblum Jr. Symphony, 1954-59, Jack Benny at Greek Theater, 1963, Highland Park Symphony, L.A., 1955-66, Beverly Hills (Calif.) Symphony, 1960-66, South East Symphony, Downey, Calif., 1957-70, Santa Monica (Calif.) Elks Club, 1965-70, The Foresters, 1965-69, Latin Am. Symphony, L.A., 1961-63, L.A. Concert Band, Mexican Tipica Orch. Symphony, West Covina (Calif.) Symphony, 1976-79, Monterey Park (Calif.) Band, 1970-81, Calif. Concert Band, 1978-81, L.A. Police Dept. Concert Band, 1956-65, San Fernando Valley (Calif.) Opera, 1955-61, Iturbi on Tour, 1961; leader, trumpet player Pieces of 8 Polka Band, L.A., 1961-96; band leader, dir. Elks 99 Concert Band, 1996—, Hollywood Showcase Orch., 1998—. 1st female dep. marshal, L.A. County, 1964-99; Sheriff, 1973; part time musician TV series Here Come The Brides, 1972; musician for film E.T., 1983, leader Elks 99 Concert Band; also numerous TV commls., recordings, 1980—. Mem. Quartz Hill Town Coun.; active Alads, Sheriff's Relief. Mem. Musicians Local 47 (life), Sons and Daughters Mont. Pioneers (life), Wild Life Fedn., U.S. Humane Soc., Marshals Assn. (sec., dir.), Internat. Police Assn. Avocations: fishing, bicycling, genealog. rsch. Home: 43212 45th St W Quartz Hill CA 93536-5523

MCKANE, DAVID BENNETT, business executive; b. Salem, Mass., July 10, 1945; s. Vernon Wilson and Barbara Inez (Bennett) McK.; m. Wilson Lineburgh Baldwin, Apr. 16, 1977; adopted daughters, Taylor A., Lee and Paige Baldwin. BA, Dartmouth Coll., 1967; MBA, Amos Tuck Sch., 1969. Product mgr. Church & Dwight Co. Inc. (Arm and Hammer Products), N.Y.C., 1969-72; v.p. NTA Inc. N.Y.C., Nanuet, N.Y., 1972-75; v.p., exec. asst. to chmn. Schick Inc., Westport, Conn., 1975-77, sr. v.p., 1977-79, COO, exec. v.p., 1979-84, treas., 1980-84; chmn., CEO A.I. Friedman, Inc., N.Y.C., 1985-87; chmn. McKane Robbins & Co. Inc., N.Y.C. and Westport, 1986-96; mng. gen. ptnr. Riverland and Indian Sun, L.C., Westport, 1996—. Bd. dirs. Oakhurst Dairy, Portland, Maine, Impax Corp., Westport. Bd. trustees Greens Farms (Conn.) Acad., 1991—. Mem. New Eng. Soc. in City N.Y., Mass. Mayflower Soc., Union Club (N.Y.C.), Country Club Fairfield, John's Island Club (Vero Beach, Fla.), RedStick Golf Club (Vero Beach, Fla.). Episcopalian. Home: 48 Owenoke Park Westport CT 06880-6833

MCKAUGHAN, HOWARD PAUL, linguistics educator; b. Canoga Park, Calif., July 5, 1922; s. Paul and Edith (Barton) McK.; m. Barbara Jean Budroe, Dec. 25, 1943; children: Edith Santoro, Charlotte Barnhart, Patricia (Mrs. Stephen B. Pike), Barbara (Mrs. Ronald Chester Bell), Judith (Mrs. Verne A.Rudebusch). AB, UCLA, 1945; MTh, Dallas Theol. Sem., 1946; MA, Cornell U., 1952, PhD, 1957. Mem. linguistic rsch. team Summer Inst. Linguistics, Mexico, 1946-52, assoc. dir.; also assoc. dir. summer sessions U. N.D., 1952-57, dir. Philippine br., 1957-61; rsch. asst. prof. anthropology U. Wash., 1961-62, rsch. assoc. prof., 1962-63; assoc. prof. linguistics U. Hawaii, 1963-64, prof. linguistics, 1964-88, prof. emeritus, 1988—, chmn. dept., 1963-66, dir. Pacific and Asian Linguistics Inst., 1964, 66-69, assoc. dean grad. divsn., 1965-72, dean grad. divsn., dir. rsch., 1972-79, acting chancellor, 1979, interim vice chancellor acad. affairs, 1981-82, acting dir. rsch., 1982-84, acting dean grad. div., 1982-83, dean, 1984-87, dir. rsch. rels., 1987-88. Lectr. linguistics U. Philippines, summers, 1954, 60; Fulbright vis. prof. Philippine Normal Coll.-Ateneo-De La Salle Consortium, Philippines, 1977, De La Salle U., Philippines, 1992; vis. prof. linguistics Bukidnon State Coll., Malaybalay, Philippines, 1993, 94; linguistic cons. Summer Inst. Linguistics, Malaysia br., 1995-2002; prin. Wycliffe Sch. Linguistics, summers 1953, 61; vis. prof. Australian Nat. U., Canberra, 1970; adj. prof. linguistics U. Okla., summers 1984, 85, 86; vis. prof., head dept. linguistics Payap U., Chiang Mai, Thailand, 1989-90. Author: (with B. McKaughan) Chatino Dictionary, 1951; (with J. Forster) Ilocano: An Intensive Language Course, 1952; The Inflection and Syntax of Maranao Verbs, 1959, (with B. Macaraya) A Maranao Dictionary, 1967, rev. edit., 1996; editor: Pali Language Texts: Philippines, 21 vols., 1971; The Languages of the Eastern Family of the East New Guinea Highlands Stock, 1973, Maranao Stories, 1995; Stories from the Darangen, 1995, Iranun Word List from Traditional Narratives, 2002, Iranun Traditional Narratives, Vols. 1 & II, Short Texts from the Iranun of Sabah, 2002; contbr. articles, chpts. to books, sci. jours. Sr. scholar East-West Ctr., Honolulu, 1964; NDEA Maranao-Philippines rsch. grantee, 1963-65; Office of Edn. Hawaii English grantee, 1965-66; NSF Jeh Language of South Vietnam grantee, 1969-70, Maranao Linguistic Studies, 1971-72, numerous other rsch. grants. Mem. Am. Linguistic Soc., Philippines Linguistic Soc., Western Assn. Grad. Schs. (pres. 1978), Hawaii Linguistic Soc., Linguistic Circle N.Y., Philippine Assn. Lang. Tchrs., Hawaii Govt. Employees Assn., Phi Beta Kappa, Phi Kappa Phi. Home: 17921 Grand Island Rd Dayton OR 97114 E-mail: howard_mckaughan@sil.org.

MCKAY, ALEXANDER GORDON, classics educator; b. Toronto, Dec. 24, 1924; s. Alexander Lynn and Marjory Maude Redfern (Nicoll) McKay; m. Helen Jean Zulauf, Dec. 24, 1964; stepchildren: Julie Anne Stephanie Brott, Danae Helen Fraser. BA, U. Toronto, 1946; MA, Yale U., 1947, Princeton U., 1948, PhD, 1950; LLD (hon.), U. Man., 1986, Brock U., 1990, Queen's U., 1991; DLitt (hon.), McMaster U., 1992, U. Waterloo, 1993. Mem. faculty classics Wells Coll., 1949-50, U. Pa., 1950-51, U. Man., 1951-52, 55-57, Mt. Allison U., 1952-53, Waterloo Coll., 1953-55; mem. faculty McMaster U., 1957-90, prof., chmn. dept. classics, 1962-68, 76-79, dean humanities, 1968-73, mem. univ. senate, 1968-73, 85-87, prof. emeritus, 1990—; Disting. vis. prof. classics U. Colo., 1978; prof. in charge Intercollegiate Center for Classical Studies, Rome, 1975; vis. mem. Inst. Advanced Study, Princeton, 1979, 81. Vis. scholar U. Tex., Austin, 1987, Hardt, Vandoevres, Geneva, 88; vis. fellow Trinity Coll., Cambridge, 1988; adj. prof. humanities York U., 1990—96; Disting. vis. lectr. Concordia U., Montreal, 1992—93, prof. emeritus, 2001—; vis. scholar Rockefeller Study and Conf. Ctr., Bellagio (Como), Italy, 1993. Author: Naples and Campania: Texts and Illustrations, 1962, Roman Lyric Poetry: Catullus and Horace, 2d edit., 1974, Vergil's Italy, 1970, Cumae and the Phlegraean Fields, 1972, Naples and Coastal Campania, 1972, Houses, Villas and Palaces in the Roman World, 1975, reprint, 1998, Roman Satire, 1976, Vitruvius, Architect and Engineer, 1978, 2d edit., 1985, Römische Häuser, Villen und Paläste, 1980, Roma Antiqua: Latium and Etruria, 1986; co-author: Selections from Vergil, Aeneid I, IV and VI (Dido and Aeneas), 1988, Festschrift, The Two Worlds of the Poet: New Perspectives on Vergil, 1992, Tragedy, Love, and Change: Roman Poetic Themes and Variations, 1994, Arma Virumque: Heroes at War (Aeneid 10 and 12), 2 vols., 1998, Classics at McMaster (1890-2000), 2000, A Song of War: Readings from Vergil's Aeneid, 2003. Pres., bd. govs. Hamilton Philharm. Orch., 1967-96, Hamilton Chamber Music Soc., 1965-67, Hamilton br. Archtl. Conservancy Ont., 1965-67, Hamilton and Region Arts Coun., 1971-72; bd. dirs. Can. Fedn. Humanities, 1980-82; v.p., dir. Internat. Acad. Union, 1978-90; v.p. U. Bristol, Inst. Hellenic & Roman Studies, 1997—; trustee Hamilton Found., 1972-75; bd. govs. Art Gallery Hamilton; bd. govs., dir. Boris Brott Summer Music Festival, 1989-2000 (pres. 2001), Montreal Chamber Music Festival, 1997—; presdl. bd. trustees McMaster U. Art Gallery, 1985-91; pres. Sir Ernest MacMillan String Ensemble, 1988-90, pres. Nat. Acad. Orch., 2001—; mem. adv. bd. Inst. for Classical Tradition, Boston U., 1987-88; v.p., dir. Bach-Elgar Choral Soc., Hamilton, 1992-95. Decorated knight comdr. Order St. John of Jerusalem; officer Order of Can.; recipient Silver Jubilee medal Queen Elizabeth II, 1977, 125th Anniversary medal Can. Confedn., Golden Jubilee medal Queen Elizabeth II, 2002; Woodrow Wilson fellow, 1947-48, Can. Coun. fellow, 1973-74, Killam rsch. fellow, 1979-80, fellow Vanier Coll., York U., 1991—, vis. scholar, 1996—. Fellow Royal Soc. Can. (hon. editor 1970-83, pres. 1984-87, past pres. 1987-89, Centennial medal 1982); mem. Vergilian Soc. (pres. 1972-74, Hon. Pres. for Life 1988—, chmn. Villa Vergiliana mgmt. com. 1993—2004), Classical Assn. Mid. West and South (pres. 1972-73, award of merit com. 1989-91), Classical Assn. Can. (v.p. 1970-72, 76-78, pres. 1978-80), Ont. Classical Assn. (hon. pres. 1994—), Master Print and Drawing Soc. (Toronto) (v.p. 1998-2001, pres. 2001-04), Yale Club (N.Y.C.), Tamahaac Club (Ancaster), Arts and Letters Club (Toronto), X Club (Toronto), Univ. Club (McMaster). Home: 15 Inglewood Dr Hamilton ON Canada L8P 2T2 E-mail: ag.mckay@sympatico.ca.

MCKAY, DONALD A. retail company executive; b. 1945; married. BS, Univ. Ill., 1968. V.p., treas. J.C. Penney Co. Inc., Dallas, 1972—; treas. J.C. Penney Properties Inc., N.Y.C.; chmn. J.C. Penney Funding Corp., Dallas, CFO, sr. v.p., 1995-2000. Office: J C Penney Funding Corp 6501 Legacy Dr Plano TX 75024-3698

MCKAY, DONNA, legal association administrator; V.p. devel. U.S. Fund for UNICEF; dir. program funding Planned Parenthood, N.Y.C., devel. dir., v.p. for external affairs Chgo.; dir. devel. ACLU, N.Y.C. Office: ACLU 18th Fl 125 Broad St New York NY 10004

MC KAY, EMILY GANTZ, civil rights professional; b. Columbus, Ohio, Mar. 13, 1945; d. Harry S. and Edwina (Bookwalter) Gantz; m. Jack Alexander McKay, July 3, 1965. BA, Stanford U., 1966, MA, 1967. From pub. info. specialist to rsch. assoc. Cmty. Action Pitts., 1967-70; freelance cons., 1969-70; pub. rels. and materials specialist Met. Cleve. JOBS Coun., 1971-72; rsch. and mgmt. cons. BLK Group, Inc., Washington, 1970-73; dir. tech. products Am. Tech. Assistance Corp., McLean, Va., 1973-74; rsch. and mgmt. cons. CONSAD Rsch. Corp., Pitts., 1974-76, v.p., 1976-78; spl. asst. to pres. for planning and eval. Nat. Coun. La Raza, Washington, 1978-82, v.p. rsch., advocacy & legislation, 1981-88, exec. v.p., 1983-88, cons. to pres., 1988-90, v.p. instl. devel., 1991-93, sr. v.p. instl. devel., 1993-94. Pres. Mosaica: Ctr. for Nonprofit Devel. and Pluralism, 1994—; cons. resource devel. New Israel Fund, 1989-91; cons. City of Cleve., Nat. Assn. Cmty. Devel., Nat. Coun. La Raza, 1975-78, Ford Found., 1989, Nat. AIDS Network, 1988-89, Am. Cultural Ctr., Israel, 1990, 2000, Nat. Hispana Leadership Inst., 1993; vol. orgnl. cons. SHATIL, Jerusalem and cmty. based groups in Israel, 1987—; guest faculty Union Inst. Grad. Sch.; adj. faculty Sch. Internat. Svc. Am. U., Washington, 1995—; mem. faculty Salzburg (Austria) Seminar on Leadership, 2003. Author devel. tng. materials and HIV/AIDS tech. assistance materials. Co-chmn. Citizens Adv. Com. to D.C. Bar, 1986-87; mem. Mayor's Commn. Coop. Econ. Devel., 1981-83; non-lawyer bd. govs. D.C. Bar, 1982-85; exec. com., bd. dirs. Indochina Resource Action Ctr., 1982-92; bd. dirs. exec. com. Southeast Asia Resource Action Ctr., 1993-97; co-chmn. Citizens Commn. Adminstrn. Justice, 1982-84; exec com. Coalition on Human Needs, 1981-88; Washington area steering com. New Israel Fund, 1989-91; co-chmn. adv. com. to Washington dist. office dir. Immigration and Naturalization Svc., 1984-88; chair Refugee Women in Devel., 1987-90, vice-chair, 1990-94; nat. adv. bd. Project Blueprint United Way of Am., 1992-94, diversity com., 1994-96; vice-chair, treas. Fund for the Future of Our Children, 1994—; sec. bd. dirs. New Bosnia Fund, 1995-99, U.S. vice-chair, 1997-99; bd. advisors Internat. Ctr. for Residential Edn., 1994-96; bd. dirs. Mary's Ctr. Maternal and Child Care, 1995-2000, treas., 1996-2000; treas., bd. dirs. AVODAH: The Jewish Svc. Corps., 1996-99; bd. dirs. Acad. of Hope, 2001—; bd. dirs. Nat. Hispana Leadership Inst., 1997-2003, treas., 1998-2003, Hispanic Link Found., 2004—; working group Memorandum of Understanding between HHS and Israeli Ministry of Labour and Social Welfare, 1990-94, chair subcom Youth at Risk, 1992-94; adv. merit sel. panel Superior Ct. D.C., 1987-90; planning task force US-Israel Women to Women, 2000-01; bd. dirs. Hispanic Link Found., Washington, 2004—. Recipient I. Pat Rios award Guadalupe Ctr., 1988; Ford Found. nat. honors fellow, 1966-67. Mem. NAACP, Nat. Coun. La Raza, Phi Beta Kappa. Democrat. Home: 3200 19th St NW Washington DC 20010-1006 Office: 1522 K St NW Ste 1130 Washington DC 20005-1225 Office Phone: 202-887-0620. Business E-Mail: Emily@mosaica.org.

MCKAY, GEOFF, private equity investor; b. Hope, B.C., Canada, Aug. 13, 1967; s. Gordon McKay and Sharon Ferguson. BA, U. Victoria, B.C., Can., 1990; MBA, U. Pa., 1997. Chartered acct., Can. Inst. Chartered Accts., 1994. Mgr. Ernst & Young, Victoria, 1990—95; assoc. Goldman Sachs, N.Y.C., 1997—99, London, 1999—2000, Forstmann Little & Co., N.Y.C., 2000—. Office: Forstmann Little & Co 767 Fifth Ave New York NY 10153 E-mail: gmckay@forstmannlittle.com.

MC KAY, JIM, television sports commentator; b. Phila., Sept. 24, 1921; s. Joseph F. and Florence (Gallagher) McManus; m. Margaret Dempsey, Oct. 2, 1948; children: Mary Edwina, Sean Joseph. AB, Loyola Coll., Balt., 1943, HLD (hon.), 1981. Reporter Balt. Evening Sun, 1946-47; news and sports commentator sta. WMAR- TV, Balt., 1947-50; sports commentator CBS Network, 1950-61; host This is New York, 1958-59; sports commentator for Winter and Summer Olympics, 1960-88; host ABC Wide World of Sports, from 1961; now commentator ABC Sports. Chmn. "Maryland Million" Horse Racing Program, 1986—. Author: My Wide World, 1973, The Real McKay, 1998. Served to lt. USNR, 1943-46. Decorated Officer's Cross Order of Merit (Fed. Republic Germany), 1974; recipient 13 Emmy awards, George Polk Meml. award, 1973, Olympic medal Austria, 1977, Engelhard award Thoroughbred Breeders of Ky., 1978, 90, Humphrey S. Finney award Md. Racing Writers, 1985, Nat. Turf Writers award, 1987, Peabody Award, 1989, Olympic Order, 1998, Lifetime Achievement award Radio & TV News Dirs. Assn., 2001, U.S. Turfwriters award 2001, Lifetime Achievement award Eclipse, 2001; named to Sportscasters Hall of Fame, 1987, U.S. Olympic Hall of Fame, 1989, TV Acad. Hall of Fame, 1994. Mem.: Jockey, Balt. Country, Md., Caves Valley (Balt.) Golf, Pinetree (Fla.) Golf Club, Thoroughbred Club of Am. Avocation: raising and breeding race horses. Office: ABC Sports 47 W 66th St Rm 800 New York NY 10023-6290

MCKAY, JOHN, lawyer; b. Seattle, June 19, 1956; s. John Larkin and Kathleen (Tierney) M. BA, U. Wash., 1978; JD, Creighton U., 1982. Bar: Wash. 1982, U.S. Dist. Ct. (we. dist.) Wash. 1982, U.S. Supreme Ct. 1990, U.S. Ct. Appeals (9th cir.) 1990, D.C. 1999. Ptnr. Lane Powell Spears Lubersky, Seattle, 1982-92, Cairncross & Hempelmann, Seattle, 1992-97; pres. Legal Svcs. Corp., Washington, 1997—2001; U.S. atty. We. dist. Wash. U.S. Dept. Justice, 2001—. White House fellow, Washington, 1989-90. Mem. ABA (bd. govs. 1991-94), Wash. State Bar Assn. (pres. young lawyers divsn. 1988-89). Republican. Roman Catholic. Avocations: soccer, golf. Office: US Atty 601 Union St Ste 5100 Seattle WA 98101-3903

MCKAY, JOHN M. former state senator; b. Winter Haven, Fla., Sept. 23, 1948; m. Michelle Dodson; children: Mary Patricia, Sara Jane, Meredith. BS, Fla. State U., 1972. Real estate broker; mortgage broker; senator 26th dist. Fla. State Legislature, 1990—2003, pres., 2002—03. Mem. agr. com., children, families and srs. com., natural resources com., rules and calendar com., ways and means com., human svcs. subcom., WAGES Targeted Econ. Devel. select com., joint legis. mgmt. com., chmn. cmty. affairs com. Fla. State Senate. Chmn. Bradenton (Fla.) Downtown Devel. Authority, 1989-90, Bradenton Cmty. Redevel. Agy., 1989-90; bd. dirs. Habitat for Humanity, 1989-90; elder 1st Presbyn. Ch., Bradenton, Fla. With U.S. Army N.G., U.S. Army Res., 1969-75. Recipient Cornerstone of Fla. Bus. award Fla. C. of C., 1993, 95, Legis. Svc. award Fla. Assn. C.C.s, 1993, Legis. Leadership award Fla. Med. Assn., 1993, Legislator of Yr. award Fla. Alcohol and Drug Abuse Assn., 1994, Fla. Assn. Realtors, 1995, Internat. Coun. Shopping Ctrs., 1995, Friends of Agr. award Fla. Farm Bur., 1994, Honors award Fla. Educators of Hearing Impaired, 1995, Legis. award Fla. Sheriffs Assn., 1995, Organized Fishermen of Fla., 1995, Svc. award Tampa Bay Regional Planning Coun., 1996, Appreciation award Port Authority of Manatee County, 1996, Cmty. Comm. award Tampa Ednl. Cable Consortium, 1996, County Champion award Fla. Assn. of Counties, 1996. Mem. Learning Disability Assn. of Fla. (bd. dirs.), Manatee and Sarasota C. of C., Kiwanis. Republican. Avocations: golf, sailing.

MCKAY, JOHN PATRICK, history educator; b. St. Louis, Aug. 27, 1938; s. John Price and Eleanor Jeffrey McKay; m. JoAnn Ott, Apr. 21, 1961; children: John Philip, Thomas Jeffrey. BA, Wesleyan U., Middletown, Conn., 1961; MA, Tufts U., 1962; PhD, U. Calif., Berkeley, 1968. From instr. to assoc. prof. history U. Ill., Urbana, 1966-76, prof., 1976-99, prof. emeritus, adj. tchg. prof., 1999—. Mem. author's adv. bd. Houghton Mifflin Co., Boston, 1992-94. Author: Pioneers for Profit: Foreign Entrepreneurship and Russian Industrialization, 1985-1913, 1970 (Herbert Baxter Adams prize Am. Hist. Assn. 1970), Tramways and Trolleys: The Rise of Urban Mass Transit in Europe, 1976; co-author: (with B. Hill and J. Buckler) A History of Western Society, 1979, 7th edit., 2003, (with B. Hill, J. Buckler and P. Ebrey) A History of World Societies, 1983, 6th edit., 2004; mem. editl. bd. Bus. History Rev., 1980—. Fellow for western Europe, Fgn. Area Program, 1964-66, John Simon Guggenheim fellow, 1970, Internat. Rsch. Exch. fellow, USSR, 1970, fellow NEH, 1984. Mem. Am. Hist. Assn., Econ. History Assn., Bus. History Conf., World History Assn., French Hist. Soc. Avocations: hiking, travel, gardening, cooking. Office: U Ill Dept History 810 S Wright St Urbana IL 61801

MCKAY, KAY, academic administrator; Student, No. Ariz. U., 1961—65. Pres. Ariz. Bd. Regents, Phoenix, 1998—. Cons. in staff/mgmt. rehab. Exec. dir. Big Bros./Bis Sisters, Flagstaff, Ariz.; superior ct. mediator Conconino County, Ariz.; mem. jud. rev. and selection bd., Ariz.; bd. dirs. Flagstaff Med. Ctr., Ariz. Health Care, Inc. Office: Ariz Bd Regents Ste 230 2020 N Central Ave Phoenix AZ 85004

MCKAY, KENNETH GARDINER, physicist, electronics company executive; b. Montreal, Que., Can., Apr. 8, 1917; came to U.S., 1946, naturalized, 1952; s. James Gardiner and Margaret (Nicholas) McK.; m. Irene C. Smith, July 25, 1942; children— Margaret Craig, Kenneth Gardiner B.Sc., McGill U., 1938, M.Sc., 1939; Sc.D, MIT, 1941; D.Eng. (hon.), Stevens Inst. Tech., 1980. Research engr. Nat. Research Council Can., 1941-46; with Bell Telephone Labs., 1946-66, 73-80, dir. solid state device devel., 1957-59, v.p. systems engring., 1959-62, exec. v.p. systems engring., 1962-66, exec. v.p., 1973-80; v.p. engring AT&T, 1966-73; chmn. bd. Bellcomm Inc., 1966-73, Charles Stark Draper Lab., 1982-87. Advisor Min. of Transp. and Comms., Republic of China, 1982-95. Trustee Stevens Inst. Tech., 1974-87; bd. govs. McGill U., 1972-77, N.Y. Coll. Osteo. Medicine, 1980-89; mem. vis. com. for engring. Stanford U., 1974-87; mem. sci. and acad. adv. com. U. Calif., 1980-88; mem. Sci. and Tech. Adv. Group, Republic of China, 1982-96. Fellow IEEE, Am. Phys. Soc., N.Y. Acad. Scis.; mem. NAS, NAE (councillor 1970-73), Century Assn. Home and Office: 200 E 66th St Apt A1901 New York NY 10021-9179

MCKAY, MONROE GUNN, federal judge; b. Huntsville, Utah, May 30, 1928; s. James Gunn and Elizabeth (Peterson) McK.; m. Lucile A. Kinnison, Aug. 6, 1954; children: Michele, Valanne, Margaret, James, Melanie, Nathan, Bruce, Lisa, Monroe. BS, Brigham Young U., 1957; JD, U. Chgo., 1960. Bar: Ariz. 1961. Law clk. Ariz. Supreme Ct., 1960-61; assoc. firm Lewis & Roca, Phoenix, 1961-66, ptnr., 1968-74; assoc. prof. Brigham Young U., 1974-76, prof., 1976-77; judge U.S. Ct. Appeals for 10th Cir., Denver, 1977-91, chief judge, 1991-94, sr. judge, 1994—. Mem. Phoenix Community Council Juvenile Problems, 1968-74; pres. Ariz. Assn. for Health and Welfare, 1970-72; dir. Peace Corps, Malawi, Africa, 1966-68; bd. dirs., pres. Maricopa county Legal Aid Soc., 1972-74. Served with USMCR, 1946-48. Mem. Ariz. Bar Assn. Mem. Lds Ch. Office: US Ct Appeals 10th Cir Fed Bldg 125 S State St Ste 6012 Salt Lake City UT 84138-1181

MCKAY, NEIL, banker; b. East Tawas, Mich., Aug. 9, 1917; s. Lloyd G. and Rose (McDonald) McK.; m. Olive D. Baird, Nov. 11, 1950; children: Julia B., Lynn B., Hunter L. AB, U. Mich., 1939, JD with distinction, 1946. Bar: Mich. 1946, Ill. 1947. With firm Winston & Strawn, Chgo., 1946-63, partner, 1954-63, mem. mgmt. com., 1958-63; with First Nat. Bank of Chgo., 1963-83, from v.p. charge heavy industry lending div., gen. mgr. London br., to exec. v.p., cashier, 1970-75, vice chmn. bd., 1976-83, also dir. Exec. v.p., sec. First Chgo. Corp., 1970-75, vice chmn. bd., 1976-83, also bd. dirs.; bd. dirs. Baird & Warner, Inc., Chgo.; founding dir. Student Loan Mktg. Assn. Mem.: U. Mich. Law Rev; assoc. editor-in-chief: U. Mich. Law Rev., 1942, sr. editor, 1946. Trustee Morton Arboretum; former trustee Kalamazoo Coll. and Ill. Inst. Tech. Served with USNR, 1942-46. Mem. ABA, Ill. Bar Assn., Dunham Woods Riding Club, Chgo. Hort. Soc. (bd. dirs.), Chgo. Club, Mid-Day Club, Geneva Golf Club. Office: 21 S Clark St Ste 2590 Chicago IL 60603

MCKAY, RENEE, artist; b. Montreal, Que., Can. came to U.S., 1946, naturalized, 1954; d. Frederick Garvin and Mildred Gladys (Higgins) Smith; m. Kenneth Gardiner McKay, July 25, 1942; children: Margaret Craig, Kenneth Gardner. BA, McGill U., 1941. Tchr. art Peck Sch., Morristown, N.J., 1955-56. One woman shows include Pen and Brush Club, N.Y.C., 1957, Cosmopolitan Club, N.Y.C., 1958; group shows include Weyhe Gallery, N.Y.C., 1978, Newark Mus., 1955, 59, Montclair (N.J.) Mus., 1955-58, Nat. Assn. Women Artists, Nat. Acad. Galleries, 1954-78, N.Y. World's Fair, 1964-65, Audubon Artists, N.Y.C., 1955-62, 74-79, N.Y. Soc. Women Artists, 1969-80, Provincetown (Mass.) Art Assn. and Mus., 1975-79; traveling shows in France, Belgium, Italy, Scotland, Can., Japan; represented in permanent collections: Slater Meml. Mus., Norwich, Conn., Norfolk (Va.) Mus., Butler Inst. Am. Art, Youngstown, Ohio, Lydia Drake Libr., Pembroke, Mass., Nat. Arts Club, N.Y.C., Provinceton Mus.- Mass., Provincetown, many pvt. collections. Recipient Jane Peterson prize in oils Nat. Assn. Women Artists, 1954, Famous Artists Sch. prize in watercolor, 1959, Grumbacher Artists Watercolor award 1970, Solo award Pen and Brush, 1957, Sadie-Max Tesser award in watercolor Audubon Artists, 1975, Peterson prize in oils, 1980, Michael Engel prize Nat. Soc. Painters in Casein and Acrylic, 1983. Mem. Nat. Assn. Women Artists (2d v.p. 1969-70, adv. bd. 1974-76), Audubon Artists (pres. 1979, dir. oils 1986-88), Artist Equity (dir. 1977-79, v.p. 1979-81), N.Y. Soc. Women Artists, Pen and Brush, Nat. Soc. Painters in Casein and Acrylic M.J. Kaplan prize 1984, Nat. Arts Club, Provincetown Art Assn. and Mus., Key West Art Assn., Cosmopolitan Club.

MCKAY, RICHARD JAMES, lawyer; b. Eugene, Oreg., Mar. 16, 1959; s. John H. and Nancy Jean (Hunter) McK.; m. Terrin Lea Few, May 19, 1984; children: K. Hunter, John Crosby. BA, Princeton U., 1981; JD, Stetson Coll. Law, St. Petersburg, Fla., 1984. Bar: Fla. 1984, U.S. Dist. Ct. (mid. dist.) Fla. 1984. Law clk. Judge William Terrell Hodges U.S. Dist. Ct. (middle dist. Fla.), Tampa, 1984-86; ptnr. Hill, Ward & Henderson, Tampa, Fla., 1986-92, Tampa Bay Bucaneers, 1992—, gen. mgr. Adj. prof. Stetson Coll. Law, St. Petersburg, 1989-92; co-chmn. NFL Competition Com., 1994—. Office: Tampa Bay Buccaneers One Buccaneer Pl Tampa FL 33607 E-mail: mckayr@buccaneers.nfl.com.

MCKAY, ROBERT CONNALLY, lawyer; b. Tyler, Tex., Apr. 28, 1950; s. Connally and Glee (McCrary) McK.; m. Bonnie Swain, Mar. 31, 1979; children: Robert Connally, Sarah Catherine, Caroline Swain. BA, Baylor U., 1972, J.D., 1975. Bar: Tex., U.S. Dist. Ct. (so. dist.) Tex.; cert. in Oil, Gas and Mineral Law Tex. Bd. Legal Specializaiton. Asst. counsel com. on pub. works and transp. U.S. Ho. of Reps., Washington, 1975-77; dir. Scott, Robins, McKay, Smith & Rigsby, Victoria, Tex., 1977-85; chmn., chief exec. officer McKay, Smith, Robins, Russell & Rigsby, 1986-87; chmn., chief exec. officer McKay & Russell, P.C., 1987-92, McKay & Crain, P.C., 1992-96, Stephenson & McKay, L.L.P., 1996-2001, Cole, Cole & Easley, P.C., 2001——; pres. Victoria Savs. Assn., 1985; mem. Tex. State Ethics Adv. Commn., 1983-88. Bd. dirs. Victoria Regional Mus. Assn., 1981-84, Victoria Econ. Devel. Corp., 1983-89; mem. Mayor's Image Com., Victoria, 1983-84. Mem. Coll. of State Bar of Tex., Tex. Bar Found., Victoria County Bar Assn. (pres. 1989-90), Rotary. Presbyterian. Home: 303 Leisure Ln Victoria TX 77904-1670 Office: 302 West Forrest Victoria TX 77901 Office Phone: 361-575-0551.

MCKAY, WILLIAM PAUL, oncologist, health facility administrator; b. Buffalo, Mar. 28, 1952; s. Robert Leon and Elizabeth (Bono) McK.; m. Jan Tankersley, June 22, 1974; children: Jesse David, Christopher Andrew, Karis Paige. BS, Mercer U., 1977; MD, Med. Coll. Ga., 1981. Diplomate Am. Bd. Radiology. Resident Med. Coll. Ga., Augusta, 1986-88; med. dir. Judd Cancer Treatment Ctr., Dalton, Ga., 1989—; pvt. practice Hamilton Med. Ctr., Dalton, 1989—. Chmn. cancer com. Hamilton Med. Ctr., Dalton, 1989-96, chmn. exec. cancer com., 1991—, vice chair cancer com., 1997-99. Elder Fellowship Bible Ch., Dalton, 1997-99. Mem. AMA, Am. Coll. Radiology, Am. Soc. Therapeutic Radiation Oncology, Biology & Physics, Med. Assn. Ga. (pres. whitfield chpt. 1990-91). Avocations: sailing, skiing, water-skiing, road biking, mountain biking. Office: Hamilton Med Ctr 1200 Memorial Dr Dalton GA 30720-2529

MCKAY-WILKINSON, JULIE ANN, minister, marriage and family therapist; b. Washington, D.C., Feb. 26, 1953; d. Charles William and Evelyn Loretta (Starr) McKay; m. Grover Gene Wilkinson, Jan. 13, 1990; 1 child, Angela Starr Gotti. AS, Camden County Coll., 1975; BA, Rowan U., 1978; grad., Unity Sch. Christianity, Lee's Summit, Mo., 1997. Cert. pastoral addictions counselor, and lic. addictions counselor, co-dependency counselor. Probation officer York County Probation, Pa., 1983—86; therapist pvt. practice, York, 1985—90, New Insights, York, 1985—87, Clare Ctr., York, 1987—90; founder, min., therapist Unity Christ Ch., Lubbock, Tex., 1997—. Editor: (monthly newsletter) Spiritual Lifelines, 1997—. Chairperson Christmas toy dr. Unity Christ Ch., 1997—. Mem.: Lubbock Ecimenical Orgn. Democrat. Avocations: gardening, music, animals, movies. Office: Christ Unity Church 7300 Mallard Creek Rd Charlotte NC 28262 Home: 2540 Pickway Dr Charlotte NC 28269 Office Phone: 704-599-1180. Personal E-mail: revjulie3@bellsouth.net.

MCKEACHIE, WILBERT JAMES, psychologist, educator; b. Clarkston, Mich., Aug. 24, 1921; s. Bert A. and Edith E. (Welberry) McK.; m. Virginia Mae Mack, Oct. 30, 1942; children: Linda, Karen. BA, Mich. State Normal Coll., 1942; MA, U. Mich., 1946, PhD, 1949; LLD, Ea. Mich. U., 1957, U. Cin.; ScD, Northwestern U., 1973, Denison U., 1975, Nat. Acad. Edn., 1977, Alma Coll., 1995; DLitt (hon.), Hope Coll., 1985; LHD (hon.), Shawnee State U., 1994. Faculty U. Mich., 1946—, chmn. dept., 1961-71, dir. Center for Research in Learning and Teaching, 1975-83. Mem. nat. adv. mental health council NIMH, 1976-80; mem. spl. med. adv. group VA, 1967-72 Author: (with J.E. Milholland) Undergraduate Curricula in Psychology, 1961, (with Charlotte Doyle and Mary Margaret Moffett) Psychology, 1966, 3d edit., 1977 (also Spanish edit. and instr.'s manual), Teaching Tips, 11th edit., 2002. Trustee Kalamazoo Coll., 1964-77; trustee-at-large Am. Psychol. Found., 1974-84, 92-96, pres., 1979-82. Officer USNR, 1943-45. Recipient Outstanding Tchr. award U. Mich. Alumni Assn., Am. Coll. Testing-Am. Ednl. Rsch. Assn. award for outstanding rsch. on coll. students, 1973, career contbns. award, 1990, award for disting. teaching in psychology Am. Psychol. Found., 1985, Gold medal award Am. Psychol. Found., others. Mem. APA (sec., dir., pres. 1976-77, Disting. Career Contbn. to Edn. and Tng. in Psychology award 1987, E.L. Thorndike award for outstanding rsch., 1988), Internat. Assn. Applied Psychology (pres. div. ednl. instrn. and sch. psychology 1982-86), Am. Assn. Higher Edn. (dir. 1974-80, pres. 1978), AAUP (pres. U. Mich. chpt. 1970-71), AAAS (chmn. sect. on psychology 1976-77), Sigma Xi. American Baptist. Home: 4660 Joy Rd Dexter MI 48130-9706 Office: U Mich Dept Psychology 525 E University Ave Ann Arbor MI 48109-1109 E-mail: billmck@umich.edu.

MCKEACHNIE, GAYLE F. lieutenant governor; b. Vernal, Utah, Jan. 26, 1943; s. Colton Orville and Helen (Fletcher) McK.; m. Kathlene Argyle, Dec. 15, 1967; children: Brett, Michelle, Jared, Ashley, Dana Marie, Jonathon, Jacob. BA, Coll. So. Utah, 1967; JD, U. Utah, 1970. Bar: Utah 1970, U.S. Dist. Ct. Utah 1970, U.S. Ct. Appeals (10th cir.) 1970, U.S. Tax Ct. 1985, U.S. Supreme Ct. 1985. Assoc. Senior & Senior, Salt Lake City, 1970-72; adj. prof. Utah State U., 1972—2000; prin. Gayle F. McKeachnie & Assocs., Vernal, 1972-78; ptnr. McKeachnie & Allred, Vernal, 1978-81, Nielson & Senior, Vernal, 1981-89, pres., 1988-89, also bd. dirs.; adj. prof. BYU J. Reuben Clark Law School, 1996—2000; lt. gov. State of Utah, 2003—. Shareholder McKeachnie & Allred PC Vernal, Roosevelt, Utah, 1989—; atty. Daggett County, Manila, Utah, 1974-79; dep. atty. Uintah County, Vernal, 1976-79; appointed to Utah Commn. on Adminstrn. Justice in the Dist. Cts. 1986; chmn. Utah Constl. Review Commn., 1989-2001; mem. task force Mgmt. and Regulation of the Practice of Law, Utah Supreme Ct., 1990-92; bd. dirs. Utah Bar Commrs., 1990-94. Mem. Utah Ho. of Reps., Vernal, 1979-88; Utah Bd. State Lands and Forestry, 1992-94. Mem. Kiwanis (pres. 1977-78), Utah State U. (chmn., bd. trustees 1994-), BYU J. Reuben Clark Law School (bd. visitors), 1998-2000. Mem. Lds Ch. Office: 210 State Capitol Salt Lake City UT 84114

MCKEAGUE, DAVID WILLIAM, judge; b. Pitts., Nov. 5, 1946; s. Herbert William and Phyllis (Forsyth) McK.; m. Nancy L. Palmer, May 20, 1989; children: Mike, Melissa, Sarah, Laura, Elizabeth, Adam. BBA, U. Mich., 1968, JD, 1971. Bar: Mich. 1971, U.S. Dist. Ct. (we. dist.) Mich. 1972, U.S. Dist. Ct. (ea. dist.) 1978, U.S. Ct. Appeals (6th cir.) 1988. Assoc. Foster, Swift, Collins & Smith, Lansing, Mich., 1971-76, ptnr., 1976-92, sec.-treas., 1990-92; adj. prof. Thomas M. Colley Law Sch., 1995—96; judge U.S. Dist. Ct., Western Dist. Mich., Lansing, 1992—. Adj. prof. TDetroit Coll. of Law, Mich State U., 1998—. Nat. com. U. Mich. Law Sch. Fund, 1980-92; gen. counsel Mich. Rep. Com., 1989-92; adv. coun. Wharton Ctr., Mich. State U., 1996—; adv. bd. Corp. for Supportive Housing, 2002—. Mem. FBA (bd. dirs. Western Mich. chpt. 1991—), Mich. Bar Assn., Am. Inns of Ct. (pres. Mich. State U. Detroit Coll. of Law chpt. 1999-01), Country Club Lansing (bd. govs. 1988-92, 96—), The Federalist Soc. for Law and Pub. Studies (lawyers divsn. Mich. chpt. 1996—). Roman Catholic. Office: US Dist Ct 315 W Allegan St Lansing MI 48933-1500

MCKEAGUE, NANCY PALMER, trade association executive; b. Detroit, Apr. 12, 1955; d. Spencer Jay and Barbara Jeanne (Murray) Palmer; m. Ronald Martin Nowak, Oct. 23, 1971 (div. 1978); children: Michael M., Melissa J.; m. David William McKeague, May 20, 1989; stepchildren: Sarah E., Laura K., Elizabeth A., Adam D. AA, Oakland Community Coll., Bloomfield Hills, Mich., 1979; BA, Spring Arbor (Mich.) Coll., 1986; MS, Ctr. Mich. U., 1993. Cert. sr. profl. human resources. Reporter The Times Newspapers, Pontiac, Mich., 1979-81; legis. aide Ho. of Reps., Lansing, Mich., 1981-84, Mich. State Senate, Lansing, 1984-85, adminstrv. aide, 1985-86; exec. v.p. Mich. Ins. Fedn., Lansing, 1986-88, pres., 1988-91; dir. govt. rels. Mich. C. of C., 1991-95, v.p. human resources, 1995-2000, sr. v.p., 2000—. Apptd. by gov. as Chmn. Workers' Compensation Qualifications Adv. Com., 1991—. Contbr. articles to profl. jours. Commr. Meridian Twp. Parks Commn., Okemos, Mich., 1984-90; state com. mem. Mich. Rep. State com., Lansing, 1987-88; exec. com. Ingham County Rep. Party, 1984-90; devel. com. Lansing Symphony Orch., 1989, bd. dirs., 1990—, v.p. devel., 1991-92; bd. dirs. Accident Fund Co., 1995—, Sparrow Physicians Health Network, 1996—; trustee Ctrl. Mich. U., 2001—. Recipient Community Contbn. award, Ingham County Bd. Commrs., 1987. Mem. Mich. Soc. Assn. Execs., Soc. for Human Resource Mgmt. (legis. action com. 1997—). Republican. Lutheran. Office: Mich C of C 600 S Walnut St Lansing MI 48933-2209 E-mail: nmckeague@michamber.com.

MCKEAN, ERIN MARGARET, editor, writer; b. Charlotte, N.C., Aug. 12, 1971; d. Thomas Albert and Devon Craig McKean; m. Joseph Patrick Gerharz, July 4, 1993; 1 child, Henry Ludwig McKean Gerharz. AB/AM, U. Chgo., 1993. Editor VERBATIM: The Lang. Quar., Chgo., 1997—; editl. mgr. Thorndike-Barnhart dictionaries ScottForesman, Glenview, Ill., 1998—2000; editor in chief U.S. dictionaries Oxford U. Press, N.Y.C., 2000—04; editor in chief Linguistic Soc. Am., 2004—. Author: (dictionary) Weird and Wonderful Words, More Weird and Wonderful Words; editor: (magazine collection) VERBATIM. Mem.: Euralex, Soc. of Midwest Authors, Am. Name Soc., Am. Dialect Soc., Dictionary Soc. of N.Am. (bd. mem. 2001—03). Avocation: sewing from vintage patterns. Personal E-mail: editor@verbatimmag.com.

MC KEAN, JOHN ROSSEEL OVERTON, university dean; b. Cortland, N.Y., July 31, 1928; s. Norman Dodge and Janet (Passage) McK.; m. Ruth MacDonald, July 2, 1955; children: Janet, Annalise. BA, Coll. William and Mary, 1951; M.Ed., Cornell U., 1956, Ed.D., 1961. Tchr. Landon Sch. for Boys, Washington, 1952-53; tchr. Central Sch., Homer, N.Y., 1953-55; asst. prof. history, dean students Allegheny Coll., 1957-67; headmaster Kingswood Sch. for Girls, Cranbrook, Bloomfield Hills, Mich., 1967-68; dean Hobart Coll., 1968-73; v.p. Coll. Kenyon Coll., Gambier, Ohio, 1973-77; dean arts and scis. State U. N.Y. at Canton, 1977-92. Mem. SUNY Coun. Deans Arts and Scis., Nat. Assn. Student Personnel Adminstrs. (pres. Pa. 1958-59), SUNY Coun. Two-Yr. Bus. Adminstrs., Nat. Assn. Student Personnel Adminstrs. (dir. 1959-61), Am. Assn. Higher Edn., C.C. Gen. Edn. Assn., Middle States Assn. Colls. and Secondary Schs., Direct Descs. Signers Declaration Independence (historian), St. Lawrence County Hist. Soc., Geneva Concerts Assn., (dir. 1969-72), Am. Hist. Assn., Round Table, English-Speaking Union, St. Andrews Soc., Chapel Hill Tennis Club, Rotary, Phi Delta Kappa, Kappa Sigma. Home: 25 Flemington Rd Chapel Hill NC 27517-5638

MCKEAN, KEVIN S. editor-in-chief, writer; b. Ann Arbor, Mich; BA in English cum laude, Yale U. Police reporter City New Bur. Chgo., 1974; gen. assigment writer, broadcast editor Denver, New Orleans, 1975; nat. sci. writer, 1978; staff writer, sr. editor Discover mag., 1981—87; sr. editor, founding new media editor Money mag., 1987—97; exec. editor Forbes.com; editl. dir., v.p. PC World mag., 2000—03; editorial dir., CEO InfoWorld Media Group, San Francisco, 2003; CEO and editorial dir. Info World Media Group, 2002. Asst. mng. editor bus. and fin. Time Inc. New Media; spkr. in field. Sci. editor (3 hr. WGBH-produced pub. TV spl.) Living Against the Odds; contbr. chapters to books; appeared (TV programs) NBC'S Today show, CBS This Morning, CNN, CNBC, CNNfn. Office: InfoWorld Media Group 501 Second St San Francisco CA 94107

MC KEAN, MICHAEL, actor; b. N.Y.C., Oct. 17, 1947; s. Gilbert and Ruth McKean; m. Susan McKean; children: Colin Russell, Fletcher. Student, Carnegie Inst. Tech., NYU. Toured with satirical comedy group The Credibility Gap; TV appearances include The Goodtime Girls, More Than Friends, American Bandstand, The TV Show; regular on ABC-TV series Laverne and Shirley, 1976-83, Grand, 1989, Dream On, 1990, Sessions, 1991, Spinal Tap Anniversary Spl., 1992, Saturday Night Live, 1994, Road Rovers, 1996, Clerks: The Animated Series, 2000, Life's Too Short, 2000, The Lone Gunmen, 2001, Primetime Glick, 2002; actor: (films) 1941, 1979, Used Cars, 1980, Young Doctors in Love, 1982, This is Spinal Tap, 1984, Clue, 1985, D.A.R.Y.L., 1985, Jumpin Jack Flash, 1986, Light of Day, 1987, Planes, Trains, & Automobiles, 1987, Short Circuit II, 1988, Earth Girls Are Easy, 1989, Flashback, 1989, The Big Picture, 1989, Book of Love, 1991, True Identity, 1991, Memoirs of an Invisible Man, 1992, Man Trouble, 1992, Mojo Flats, 1993, Coneheads, 1993, Airheads, 1994, Radioland Murders, 1994, The Brady Bunch Movie, 1995, The Pompatus of Love, 1996, Jack, 1996, Still Breathing, 1997, That Darn Cat, 1997, Nothing to Lose, 1997, Small Soldiers (voice), 1998, Mystery, Alaska, 1999, Teaching Mrs. Tingle, 1999, True Crime, 1999, Best in Show, 2000, Beautiful, 2000, Little Nicky, 2000, My First Mister, 2001, Never Again, 2001, Dr. Doolittle 2, 2001, Teddy Bear's Picnic, 2001, The Guru, 2002, Auto Focus, 2002, 100 Mile Rule, 2002, A Mighty Wind, 2003, Haunted Lighthouse, 2003, Candor City Hospital, 2003; (Broadway) Accomplice, 1989; (TV movies) More Than Friends, 1978, Classified Love, 1986, Murder in High Places, 1991; (video) Casper: A Spirited Begining, 1997; rec. artist: (with David Lander) Lenny and the Squiggtones, This is Spinal Tap. Office: care William Morris Agy 151 S El Camino Dr Beverly Hills CA 90212-2704

MCKEAN, ROBERT JACKSON, JR., retired lawyer; b. N.Y.C., Dec. 21, 1925; s. Robert Jackson and Isabel (Murphy) McK.; m. Sally H. Ament; children from previous marriage: Katherine, Douglas, Lauren, Andrew. BA, Amherst Coll., 1950; LL.B., Harvard U., 1953. Bar: N.Y. 1954. Assoc. Simpson Thacher & Bartlett, N.Y.C., 1953-62, ptnr., 1962-85. Trustee Amherst Coll., Mass., Folger Shakespeare Library, Washington. Served with U.S. Army, 1944-46, ETO. Recipient medal for eminent service Amherst Coll., 1968 Mem. Phi Beta Kappa. Democrat.

MCKEAN, THOMAS B. company executive; b. Norwalk, Conn. s. Charles T. and Charlotte C. (Meisel) McK.; m. Kathryn Ann Taylor, Jan. 19, 1963; children: Pamela, Douglas, Gregory, Susan. BA in Econs., U. Conn., 1963; MA in Econs./Fin., Trinity Coll., Hartford, Conn., 1969. Fin. planning/analysis asst. to fin. dir. Office Document Products L.Am., Mexico City, 1976-78, mgr. group pricing/ops. analysis Stamford, Conn., 1978-81, mgr. inter-Am. affairs, program office, 1981-86, mgr. reprographics bus. ctr., 1986-89, mgr. bus. strategy L.Am., 1989-92, dir. office document products, 1992-96, v.p. mktg. integration, 1996—2001. Office: Xerox Corp 800 Long Ridge Rd Stamford CT 06902-1288

MCKEAN, THOMAS WAYNE, dentist, retired military officer; b. Adams County, Ind., May 18, 1928; s. Gorman F. and Elmira B. (Staley) McK.; m. Marilyn Kimberlin, Aug. 9, 1952; children: Thomas Wayne, Randall K., Dana K. D.D.S., Ind. U., 1953; grad., Naval Dental Sch., 1963. Diplomate: Am. Bd. Oral Surgery. Commd. ensign Dental Corps USN, 1949, advanced through grades to rear adm., 1980; stationed at Naval Tng. Ctr., Great Lakes, Ill., 1953; dental officer U.S.S. Randall, 1953-56; head dental svc., asst. dental officer U.S. Naval Acad./Naval Hosp., Annapolis, Md., 1956-59; dental officer FASRON III; asst. dental officer U.S. Naval Sta., Bermuda, 1959-63; postgrad. student Naval Dental Sch., Bethesda, Md., 1963-64; resident oral and maxillofacial surgery Naval Hosp., Great Lakes, Ill., 1964-66; dental officer U.S.S. America, 1966-68; chief oral surgery Naval Hosp., Orlando, Fla., 1968-70; dir. oral surgery and gen. practice residency tng. programs Naval Regional Med. Ctr., Great Lakes, 1970-74, chmn. dept. dentistry, 1970-74; cons., lectr. U.S. Army, Fort Sheridan, Ill., 1970-74; dir. oral surgery and gen. practice residency tng. programs Naval Regional Med. Ctr., Oakland, Calif., 1974-78, chmn., dept. dentistry, 1974-78; lectr. oral surgery Letterman Army Med. Ctr., San Francisco, 1974-78; clin. lectr. dept. oral surgery U. of Pacific Sch. Dentistry, San Francisco, 1974-78; comdg. officer Naval Regional Dental Ctr., Pensacola, Fla., 1978-80; lectr. oral surgery Pensacola (Fla.) Jr. Coll., 1978-80; cons., lectr. Dwight D. Eisenhower Army Regional Med. Ctr., Augusta, Ga., 1978-80; insp. gen. dental Bur. Medicine and Surgery, Dept. of Navy, Washington, 1980-81; comdg. officer Naval Regional Dental Ctr., San Diego, 1981-82; insp. gen. Naval Med. Command, Washington, 1983-85; ret. USN, 1985. Contbr. articles to profl. jours. Chmn. bd. trustees UMC, Winter Park, 1992, mem. bd. adminstrs. 1995-98; bd. dirs. Circle of Friends Fla. Hosp. Found., 1989-91, Fla. Hosp. Found., 1991—, chmn. bd., 1995-96; bd. dirs. Fla. Hosp. Found., 1996—; chmn. Fla. Hosp. Shares (Internat. Med. Missions), 1994—; mem. Fla. Hosp. Cmty. Benefits subcom., 1996—. Decorated Humanitarian Service medal, Legion of Merit with Gold Star, Meritorious Service medal, Nat. Def. Service medal with star, Vietnam Service medal, Republic of Vietnam Campaign medal with device, others; recipient Alumnus of Yr. award Ind. U. Sch.of Dentistry Alumnus Assn., 1988. Fellow Am. Dental Soc. of Anesthesiology, Internat. Coll. Dentists, Am. Coll. Dentists, Internat. Assn. Oral Surgeons; mem. Am. Assn. Oral and Maxillofacial Surgeons, ADA, Western Soc. Oral Surgeons, Assn. Mil. Surgeons U.S. (medal), Fla. Soc. Oral Surgeons, Delta Sigma Delta, Sigma Chi (Significant Sig award 1983). Home: 1309 Temple Grove Ct Winter Park FL 32789-2716

MCKEAND, PATRICK JOSEPH, newspaper publisher, educator; b. Anderson, Ind., June 10, 1941; s. William Dale and Iva Pearl (Shaw) McK. BA, Ind. U., 1963; MA, Ball State U., 1983. Staff writer The St. Petersburg (Fla.) Times, 1963; mng. editor The Anderson (Ind.) Herald, 1968-79; adminstr. analyst Ind. Medicaid Program, Indpls., 1980-81; assoc. prof. Defense Info. Sch., Ft. Ben Harrison, Ind., 1981-89; owner p.m. ink!, Indpls., 1989—. Pub. bd. dirs. Student Pub. at Ind. U., Purdue U. at Indpls., 1992—; bd. dirs. Miss Indpls. Scholarship Pageant, Indpls, 1994—. Capt. U.S. Army, 1964-68. Decorated Bronze Star, Army Commendation medal with 1 Oak leaf cluster. Mem. Soc. Profl. Journalists (bd. dirs.), Soc. Newspaper Design, Assn. Educators in Journalism and Mass Comm., Associated Press Mng. Editors Assn., Investigative Reporters and Editors, Ind. Collegiate Press Assn. (bd. dirs., exec. dir.), Coll. Media Advisors (Disting. Newspaper Adviser award 1998), Faculty Club IUPUI (bd. dirs. 2002—). Home: 4450 E 56th St Indianapolis IN 46220-5710 Office: Sch of Journalism 902 W New York St Indianapolis IN 46202-5197 E-mail: pmckeand@iupui.edu.

MCKECHNIE, JOHN CHARLES, gastroenterologist, educator; b. Louisville, Feb. 1, 1935; s. Albert Hay and Edna Scott (Johnson) M.; children: Steven Keith, Kevin Stuart. BA, U. Louisville, 1955; MD, Baylor Coll. Medicine, 1959. Diplomate Am. Bd. Internal Medicine, Am. Bd. Gastroenterology. Intern Jefferson Davis Hosp., Houston, 1959-60; resident in internal medicine Baylor Affiliated Program, Houston, 1960-61, 65-66; gen. practice medicine, Benham, Ky., 1964; practice medicine specializing in gastroenterology, Houston, 1966—; clin. instr. Baylor Coll. Medicine, Houston, 1966-69, asst. prof., 1969-72, assoc. prof., 1972-77, prof., 1977—; mem. staff Methodist Hosp.; cons. Ben Taub Hosp., St. Luke's Episcopal Hosp. Served to capt. USMC, 1962-64. Fellow Am. Coll. Gastroenterology (gov. Tex. 1979-80, trustee 1981-84), ACP; mem. AMA, So. Med. Assn., Tex. Med. Assn., Am. Gastroent. Assn., Digestive Disease Found., Am. Soc. Gastrointestinal Endoscopy, Tex. Soc. Gastrointestinal Endoscopy, Houston Gastroent. Soc. (pres. 1983), Alpha Omega Alpha. Republican. Presbyterian. Contbr. numerous articles to profl. jours. Office: 6560 Fannin St Ste 1630 Houston TX 77030-2734 Office Phone: 713-797-0916.

MCKEE, ADELE DIECKMANN, retired church music director, educator; b. Atlanta, Oct. 29, 1928; d. Christian William and Emma Pope (Moss) D.; m. Dean Greer McKee, Nov. 14, 1972 (dec. July 1987). BA summa cum laude, Agnes Scott Coll., 1948; MA, Wellesley Coll., 1949; M in Sacred Music magna cum laude, Union Theol. Sem., N.Y.C., 1955. Tchr. Latin and music theory, chapel organist The Northfield Schs., East Northfield, Mass., 1949-53; tchr. Latin and English Westminster Schs., Atlanta, 1955-58; dir. music, organist Trinity Presbyn. Ch., Atlanta, 1955-83; asst. organist Cathedral St. Philip, Atlanta, 1984-85; organist, choir master St. Luke's Presbyn. Ch., Atlanta, 1985-89; ret., 1989. Dir. Montreat Conf. on Worship and Music, 1968; chmn. new music commns. Am. Guild of Organists Nat. Convention, Atlanta, 1992—. Choral reviewer The Am. Organist, 1967-71; contbr. articles to Reformed Liturgy mag., 1970—. Mem. City of Decatur Hist. Preservation Task Force, 1989-90. Fellow Am. Guild Organists (nat. councillor 1967-70, dean 1964-66, 76-78, program chmn. nat. conv. 1966, chmn. cert. work Atlanta chpt., mem. exec. com. 1999—); mem. Choristers Guild (nat. bd. dirs. 1976-79), Decatur Book Lovers' Club, Atlanta Young Singers, Young Singers Callanwolde (bd. dirs. 1993—, pres. bd. dirs. 1994-98.

MCKEE, CATHERINE LYNCH, law educator, lawyer; b. Boston, June 7, 1962; d. Robert Emmett and Anne Gayle (Tanner) Lynch; m. Bert K. McKee Jr., Dec. 25, 1990; children: Timothy Kingston, Shannon Lancaster. BA in Biol. Sci., U. Calif. Berkeley, 1984; JD, U. San Diego, 1988. Bar: Calif. 1988, U.S. Dist. Ct. (cen., so. and ea. dists.) Calif. 1989, U.S. Ct. Appeals (9th cir.) 1989. Assoc. Parkinson, Wolf, Lazar & Leo, L.A., 1988-89, McCormick & Mitchell, San Diego, 1989-91; prof. Mt. San Antonio Coll., Walnut, Calif., 1994—, mock trial coach, 1994—2000, dir. paralegal program, 1999—2003. Cert. rev. hearing officer, Orange County, 1994—; legal counsel Imperial Valley Lumber Co., Valley Lumber and Truss Co., 1998—; coach nat. champion C.C. mock trial team, 2000; mem. acad. senate exec. coun. Mt. San Antonio Coll., 1996-2000, chmn. campus equivalency com., 1999, chair paralegal program adv. com., 1999-2003; mem. East San Gabriel Valley regional occupl. program adv. com., 2003—. Contbr. weekly newspaper column, 1993-99; prodr., star videos An Attorney's Guide to Legal Research on the Internet, 1998, 99; co-author: Jeff and Catherine's World's Best List of Legal (and Law-related) Internet Sites. Chair scholarship com. U. Calif. Alumni Assn., Berkeley, 1995—; capt. auction team SCATS Gymnastics, 2000—02. Named Cmty. Person of Yr. Diamond Bar C. of C., 1995. Mem. NEA, State Bar Calif. (probation monitor 1993—), Ea. Bar Assn. L.A. (trustee 2000—), Calif. Tchrs. Assn., Am. Inns of Ct., Calif. Assn. Lanterman-Petris-Short Hearing Officers. Avocations: weightlifting, photography, reading. Office: Mount San Antonio Coll 1100 N Grand Ave Walnut CA 91789-1341

MCKEE, CHRISTOPHER FULTON, librarian, historian, educator; b. Bklyn., June 14, 1935; s. William Ralph and Frances McKee; m. Ann Adamczyk, 1993; children: Sharon, David. AB, U. St. Thomas, Houston, 1957; AMLS, U. Mich., 1960. Catalogue libr. Washington and Lee U., Lexington, Va., 1958-62; social sci. libr. So. Ill. U., Edwardsville, 1962-66, book selection officer, 1967-69, asst. dir., 1969-72; libr. of coll. Grinnell Coll., Iowa, 1972—, Samuel R. and Marie-Louise Rosenthal prof. Sec. of Navy rsch. chair naval history Naval Hist. Ctr., Washington, 1990—91; trustee Bibliog. Ctr. Rsch., Denver, 1984—88. Author: (book) Edward Preble, 1972, A Gentlemanly and Honorable Profession: The Creation of the U.S. Naval Officer Corps 1794-1815, 1991, Sober Men and True: Sailor Lives in the Royal Navy 1900-1945, 2002. Recipient U.S. Naval History prize, 1985, John Lyman Book award, N.Am. Soc. Oceanic History, 1991, Samuel Eliot Morison Disting. Svc. award, USS Constn. Mus., 1992; fellow NEH-Newberry Libr., 1978—79, Newberry Libr.-Brit. Acad., 1995—96. Mem.: U.S. Naval Inst., Soc. Historians Early Am. Republic, Orgn. Am. Historians, Soc. Mil. History, Navy Records Soc., Can. Nautical Rsch. Soc., Am. Hist. Assn. Home: 2382 Willowbrooke Ln Iowa City IA 52246-1834 Office: Grinnell Coll Burling Libr 1111 6th Ave Grinnell IA 50112-1690

MCKEE, CHRISTOPHER FULTON, physicist, astronomer, educator; b. Washington, Sept. 6, 1942; m. Suzanne P. McKee; 3 children. AB in Physics summa cum laude, Harvard U., 1963; PhD in Physics, U. Calif., Berkeley, 1970. Physicist Lawrence Livermore (Calif.) Labs., 1969-70, cons., 1970—; rsch. fellow in astrophysics Calif. Inst. Tech., Pasadena, 1970-71; asst. prof. astronomy Harvard U., Cambridge, Mass., 1971-74; asst. prof. physics and astronomy U. Calif., Berkeley, 1974-77, assoc. prof., 1977-78, prof., 1978—, Miller Rsch. prof., 1984-85, 99, chair dept. physics, 2000—04; assoc. dir. Space Scis. Lab., Berkeley, 1978-83, acting dir., 1983-84, dir., 1985-98, Theoretical Astrophysics Ctr., Berkeley, 1985. Co-chair Astronomy and Astrophysics Survey com., NRC, 1998-2001. Fannie and John Hertz Found. fellow, 1963-69, Guggenheim fellow, 1998; Sherman Fairchild Disting. scholar, 1981, NAS, 1992. Fellow AAAS, Am. Phys. Soc. (exec. com. astrophysics divsn. 1986-88); mem. Am. Astron. Soc. (councillor 1981-84), Am. Acad. Arts and Scis., Internat. Astron. Union, Phi Beta Kappa. Office: U Calif Dept Physics Berkeley CA 94720-0001

MCKEE, DAVID CHARLES, physician, neurologist; b. May 19, 1961; m. Marie-Laure Mazquiain, Dec. 29, 1984; children: Tyvand, Camille, Charlotte, Alexanne. BA in Chemistry, Macalaster Coll., 1983; MD, U. Wis., 1987. Diplomate Am. Bd. Psychiatry and Neurology, Am. Bd. Electrodiagnostic Medicine. Resident in neurology Oreg. Health Scis. U., 1987—91; Jeanne Timmins fellow Montreal Neurol. Inst., 1991—92; clin. neurologist Northland Neurology and Myology, Duluth, Minn., 1992—; chief sect. neurology St. Lukes Hosp. and Regional Trauma Ctr., Duluth, 1993—; clin. assoc. prof. neurology U. Minn.-Duluth Med. Sch., 1993—; pres. Northland Med. Assocs., 2000—02. Chmn. bd. dirs. Care North Health Sys., 2001—02, Comdr. USNR med. corp., 1998—. Fellow: Am. Assn. Electrodiagnostic Medicine; mem.: European Neurol. Soc., Am. Acad. Neurology, Alpha Omega Alpha, Phi Beta Kappa. Office: 1000 E 1st St Ste 202 Duluth MN 55805-2297 Home: 2215 E Superior St Duluth MN 55812

MCKEE, DELBER L. retired education educator; b. Superior, Nebr., Jan. 15, 1923; s. John Knox and Lottie Frances (Touzalin) McKee; m. Margaret Coleman Carson, June 5, 1946; children: Richard Howard, Anne Leslie, Mary Frances. BA Hastings (Nebr.) Coll., 1946; MA, U. Wis., Madison, 1947; PhD, Stanford U., Calif., 1953. Instr. history Simpson Coll., Indianola, Iowa, 1947—50; asst. prof. history Westminster Coll., New Wilmington, Pa., 1952—55, assoc. prof. history, 1955—57, prof. history, 1957—89, chmn. dept. history, polit. sci. and sociology, 1956—79, acting dean of the coll., 1977, prof. emeritus, 1989—. Curator of cultural artifacts Westminster Coll., New Wilmington, 1991—2000; mem. editl. bd. Pacific Hist. Rev., Berkeley, Calif., 1991—93, Lawrence County Hist. Soc., New castle, Pa., 1992—95. Author: (Book) Chinese Exclusion Versus the Open Door Policy, 1900-06, 1977; contbr. articles to profl. jours., chapters to books on local Pa. history. Mem. sch. bd. Wilmington Area Schs., Pa., 1971—77. Cpl. USAAF, 1943—46. Grantee Fulbright grant, Taiwan, 1962. Mem.: Soc. for Historians of Am. Fgn. Rels., Pacific Hist. Assn., Rotary Club (pres. 1985—86, Disting. Citizen award (New Wilmington) 1987). Presbyterian. Avocations: camping, travel, writing. Home: 150 Waugh Ave Apt 4401 New Wilmington PA 16142

MCKEE, ELLSWORTH R. food products executive; BA in Bus. and Econs., So. Adventist U., 1954; postgrad., Andrews U., 1987. Shipping/receiving clk. Jack's Cookie Co., Charlotte, N.C., 1949-50; various positions McKee Foods, Collegedale, 1951-54, v.p. prodn. and fin., 1954-62, exec. v.p., treas., 1962-71, pres., CEO, 1971-96, also bd. dirs., 1954—, chmn. bd. dirs., 1997—. Bd. dirs. So. Adventist U., Collegedale, Andrews U., Berrien Springs, Mich., 1976—2000. Recipient Pvt. Sector Initiative Commendation, Pres. Ronald Reagan, 1988. Office: McKee Foods PO Box 750 Collegedale TN 37315-0750

MCKEE, FRANCIS JOHN, medical association consultant, lawyer; b. Bklyn., Aug. 31, 1943; s. Francis Joseph and Catherine (Giles) McK.; m. Antoinette Mary Sancis; children: Lisa Ann, Francis Dominic, Michael Christopher, Thomas Joseph. AB, Stonehill Coll., 1965; JD, St. John's U., 1970. Bar: N.Y. 1971. Assoc. Samuel Weinberg, Esquire, Bklyn., 1970-71, Finch & Finch, Esquire, Long Island City, N.Y., 1971-72; staff atty. Med. Soc. of State of N.Y., Lake Success, N.Y., 1972-77; prin. Francis J. McKee Assocs., Clinton, NY, 1984—2001; exec. dir. Suffolk Physicians Rev. Orgn., East Islip, N.Y., 1977-81, N.Y. State Soc. Surgeons, Inc., Clinton, N.Y., 1981-2000, N.Y. State Soc. Orthopaedic Surgeons, Inc., Clinton, NY, 1981—2000, Upstate N.Y. chpt. ACS, Inc., Clinton, N.Y., 1981-2000, N.Y. State Ophthalmol. Soc., 1984-92, N.Y. State Soc. Obstetricians and Gynecologists, 1985-2001, Orthopac of N.Y., 1986-2000, Nat. Com. for the Preservation Orthopaedic Practice, New Hartford, N.Y., 1989-2000; L.I. Ophthalmological Soc., 1994-2000. Coun. Suffolk County Med. Soc., Hauppauge, N.Y., 1977-81. With U.S. Army, 1966-68. Mem.: N.Y. State Bar Assn., Am. Legion. Conservative. Roman Catholic. Home and Office: Taberna Country Club 908 Taberna Cir New Bern NC 28562 E-mail: Frank4Mets@cox.net.

MCKEE, GEORGE MOFFITT, JR., civil engineer, consultant; b. Valparaiso, Nebr., Mar. 27, 1924; s. George Moffitt and Iva (Santrock) McK.; m. Mary Lee Taylor, Aug. 11, 1945; children: Michael Craig, Thomas Lee, Mary Kathleen, Marsha Coleen, Charlotte Anne. Student, Kans. State Coll. Agr. and Applied Sci., 1942—43, Bowling Green State U., 1943; BSCE, U. Mich., 1947. Registered profl. civil engr., Kans., Okla., land surveyor, Kans. Draftsman Jackson Constrn. Co., Colby, Kans., 1945-46; asst. engr. Thomas County, Colby, 1946; engr. Sherman County, Goodland, Kans., 1947-51; salesman Oehlert Tractor & Equipment Co., Colby, 1951-52; owner, operator George M. McKee, Jr.; cons. engrs. Colby, 1952-72; sr. v.p. engring. Contract Surety Cons., Wichita, Kans., 1974-2000; engring. cons. Wichita, 2000—. Adv. rep. Kans State U., Manhattan, 1957-62; adv. com. N.W. Kans. Area Vocat. Tech. Sch., Goodland, 1967-71; chmn. ofcl. bd. Meth. Ch., 1966-67. With USMCR, 1942-45. Mem. Kans. Soc. Profl. Engrs. (pres. N.W. profl. engrs. chpt. 1962-63, treas. cons. engrs. sect. 1961-63), Kans. County Engr.'s Assn. (dist. v.p. 1950-51), N.W. Kans. Hwy. Ofcls. Assn. (sec. 1948-49), Nat. Soc. Profl. Engrs., Kans. State U. Alumni Assn. (life, pres. Thomas County 1956-57), Am. Legion (Goodland 1st vice comdr. 1948-49), Alumni Assn. U. Mich. (life), Colby C. of C. (v.p. 1963-64), Goodland Jr. C. of C. (pres. 1951-52), Masons (32 degree, Shriner), Order of the Ea. Star. Home: 8930 Suncrest St Apt 502 Wichita KS 67212-4069

MCKEE, HARRY W. federal judge; b. 1940; PhB, U. N.D., 1963; LLB, George Washington U., 1966. Trial atty. U.S. Dept. Justice, Washington, 1966-79, spl. asst., 1979, asst. U.S. atty., 1979-82; apptd. magistrate judge ea. dist. U.S. Dist. Ct. Tex., 1982. Mem. ABA, State Bar Tex., Smith County Bar Assn. Office: 210 Federal Bldg 211 W Ferguson St Tyler TX 75702-7212

MCKEE, JACK, food products executive; BS, U. Tenn. CEO McKee Foods, Collegedale, Tenn. Office: McKee Foods 10260 McKee Rd Collegedale TN 37315 Fax: 423-238-7536.

MCKEE, JANATH DEBIN, medical researcher; d. Jesse Aurelius deBin and Marjorie Caroline Bennett; m. Homer James McKee, Jan. 5, 1987; m. Louis Michael Caldarera, June 13, 1959 (div.); children: Michael Bennett Caldarera, Louis Patrick Caldarera, Keith Matthew Caldarera. BA, U. of Ark. at Little Rock, 1956—86. Rsch. asst. U. Ark. Med. Sciences, 1987—. Roman Catholic. Avocations: travel, writing.

MCKEE, JOHN MORRISON, broadcast executive; b. Winnipeg, Man., Can., Sept. 2, 1951; s. Gordon John Frederick and Lee Rae (Morrison) M.; m. Susan Leslie Lewis, Apr. 13, 1974; children: Sean Adam, Jessica Lee, Trevor James. BA, U. Winnipeg, Can., 1975. Retail store mgr. Eaton's of Can., 1975-79; gen. mktg. mgr. Hudson Bay Co., Can., 1979-90; v.p. sales and mktg. CUC Broadcasting Ltd., Can., 1990-92; v.p. gen. mgr. DIRECTV Can., 1992-95; sr. v.p. spl. markets DIRECTV, Inc., El Segundo, Calif., 1995-99, sr. v.p., gen. mgr., 1999—2002; pres. Four Windows No Walls Cons., LLC, 2001—. Home: 2456 S Oak Ridge Rd Sedalia CO 80135 E-mail: jmckee@voom.com.

MCKEE, KEITH EARL, manufacturing technology executive; b. Chgo., Sept. 9, 1928; s. Charles Richard and Maude Alice (Hamlin) McK.; m. Lorraine Marie Celichowski, Oct. 26, 1951; children: Pamela Ann Houser, Paul Earl. BS, Ill. Inst. Tech., 1950, MS, 1956, PhD, 1962. Engr. Swift & Co., Chgo., 1953-54; rsch. engr. Armour Rsch. Found., Chgo., 1954-62; dir. design and product assurance Andrew Corp., Orland Park, Ill., 1962-67; dir. engring. Rsch. Ctr. Ill. Inst. Tech., Chgo., 1967-80, dir. mfg. prodn. ctr., 1977—. Prof. Ill. Inst. Tech., Chgo., 1979—; coord. Nat. Conf. on Fluid Power, Chgo., 1983-88; mem. com. on materials and processing Dept. Def., Washington, 1986-92. Author: Productivity and Technology, 1988; editor: Automated Inspection and Process Control, 1987; co-editor: Manufacturing High Technology Handbook, 1987; mng. editor: Manufacturing Competitiveness Frontier, 1977-97. Capt. USMC, 1950-54. Recipient outstanding presentation award Am. Soc. of Quality Control, Milw., 1983. Fellow World Acad. Productivity Scis.; mem. ASCE, Am. Def. Preparedness Assn. (pres. Chgo. chpt. 1972-95), Am. Assn. Engring. Soc. (Washington) (coor. com. on productivity 1978-88), Inst. of Indsl. Engrs., Soc. Mfg. Engrs. (Gold medal 1991), Am. Assn. for Artificial Intelligence, Robotic Industry Assn. (bd. dir. 1978-81), Assn. for Mfg. Excellence, Soc. for Computer Simulation. Democrat. Roman Catholic. Home: Ste 504 3115 S Michigan Ave Chicago IL 60616 Office: Illinois Inst Tech Mfg Productivity Ctr 3424 S State St Ste 4001 S Chicago IL 60616 Office Phone: 312-567-3650. Business E-Mail: mckee@iit.edu.

MCKEE, MARGARET JEAN, federal agency administrator; b. New Haven, June 20, 1929; d. Waldo McCutcheon and Elizabeth McKee. AB, Vassar Coll., 1951. Staff asst. United Rep. Fin. Com., N.Y.C., 1952, N.Y. Rep. State Com., N.Y.C., 1953—55, Crusade for Freedom (name later changed to Radio Free Europe Fund), N.Y.C., 1955—57; researcher Stricker & Henning Rsch. Assocs., Inc., N.Y.C., 1957—59; exec. sec. New Yorkers for Nixon (name later changed to N.Y. State Ind. Citizens for Nixon Lodge), N.Y.C., 1959—60; asst. to Raymond Moley, polit. columnist N.Y.C., 1961; asst. campaign com. Louis J. Lefkowitz for Mayor, N.Y.C., 1961; rsch. programmer, treas. Consensus, Inc., N.Y.C., 1962—67; spl. asst. to U. S. Senator Jacob K. Javits NY, 1967—73; adminstr. asst., 1973—75; dep. adminstr. Am. Revolution Bicentennial Adminstrn., 1976, acting adminstr., 1976—77; chief of staff Perry B. Duryea (minority leader) N.Y. State Assembly, 1978; pub. affairs cons., 1979—80; dir. govt. rels. Gen. Mills Restaurant Group, Inc., 1980—83; exec. dir. Fed. Mediation and Conciliation Svc., 1983—86; mem. Fed. Labor Rels. Authority, 1986—89, chmn., 1989—94; mem. Nat. Partnership Coun., 1993—94; chmn. adv. bd. Workplace Solutions, 1996—. Mem. U.S. Adv. Commn. on Pub. Diplomacy, 1972—82; dir. scheduling and spkrs.' bur. N.Y. Com. to Re-elect the Pres., 1972; mem. bd. govs. Women's Nat. Rep. Club, N.Y.C., 1963—66; mem. N.Y. State Bingo Control Commn., 1965—72; pres. Bklyn. Heights Slope Young Rep. Club, 1955—56; co-chmn. Bklyn. Citizens for Eisenhower-Nixon, 1956; chmn. 2nd Jud. Dist. Assn. N.Y. State Young Rep. Clubs, Inc., 1957—58, vice chmn., mem. bd. govs., 1958—60, v.p., 1960—62, pres., 1962—64; mem. exec. com. Fedn. Women's Rep. Clubs N.Y. State, Inc., 1960—64; asst. campaign mgr. Kenneth B. Keating for Judge Ct. Appeals, NY, 1965; dir. scheduling Gov. Rockefeller campaign, 1966, Sen. Charles E. Goodell campaign, 1970; dir. planning and strategy Conn. Reagan-Bush campaign, Hartford, 1980; mem annual fund adv. com. Vassar Coll., 1992—96, chmn. 50th Reunion, 2001. Mem.: Nat. Assn. Olmsted Parks (bd. trustees 2003—, bd. dirs.), New Eng. Hist. Geneal. Soc. (mem. adv. coun. 2001—03, bd. trustees 2003—), Nat. Women's Edn. Fund. (mem. bd.), Exec. Women on Govt. (chmn. 1986), Nat. Soc. Colonial Dames, Vassar Club (past dir., Bklyn.), Am. Newspaper Women's Club, Jr. League of Bklyn. (past dir.). Republican. Episcopalian. Home: 532 S Brooksvale Rd Cheshire CT 06410-3515 also: 3001 Veazey Ter NW Apt 1225 Washington DC 20008-5407

MCKEE, ROGER CURTIS, retired federal judge; b. Waterloo, Iowa, Feb. 11, 1931; s. James A. and Leonace (Burrell) McK.; m. Roberta Jeanne Orvis, Sept. 3, 1954; children: Andrea Jane, Brian Curtis, Paul Robert. BA, State Coll. of Iowa, 1955; MA, U. Ill., 1960; JD, U. San Diego, 1968. Bar: Calif. 1970, U.S. Dist. Ct. (so. dist.) Calif. 1969, U.S. Ct. Appeals (9th cir.) 1971. Telegrapher, agt. Ill. Cen. R.R., 1950-55; tng. asst. No. Ill. Gas Co., Aurora, 1959-60; with indsl. rels. dept. Convair div. Gen. Dynamics Corp., San Diego, 1960-68; contract adminstr. and supr. Datagraphix div. Gen. Dynamics Corp., San Diego, 1968-69, asst. counsel, 1969-70; ptnr. Powell & McKee, San Diego, 1970-75, Millsberg, Dickstein & McKee, San Diego, 1975-83; magistrate judge U.S. Dist. Ct. for So. Dist. Calif., San Diego, 1983-97; presiding magistrate judge, 1993-97. Bd. trustees So. Calif. Presbyn. Homes, L.A., 1979-81; moderator Presbytery of San Diego, 1980. Capt. USNR, 1949-85. Mem. Calif. Bar Assn., Fed. Magistrate Judges Assn., Navy League U.S., Naval Res. Officers Assn., Res. Officers Assn., Dixieland Jazz Soc. (bd. dirs. San Diego chpt. 1984—). Republican. Fax: (858) 277-0444. E-mail: rcmckee10@cs.com.

MCKEE, THEODORE A. federal judge; b. Rochester, NY, 1947; BA, SUNY, Cortland, 1969; JD magna cum laude, Syracuse U. Coll. of Law, 1975. Dir. of minority recruitment & admissions SUNY, Binghamton, 1969—72; atty. Wolf, Block, Schorr & Solis-Cohen, Phila., 1975—77; asst. U.S. atty., Eastern Dist. Pa., 1977—80; asst. U.S. atty., Eastern Dist. Gen. Crimes Unit, Narcotics and Firearms Unit, then Polit. Corruption Unit; lectr. Rutgers U. Coll. of Law, 1980—91; dep. city solicitor Law Dept., Phila., 1980—83; gen. counsel Phila. Parking Auth., 1983; judge Ct. of Common Pleas, 1st Jud. Dist, Pa., 1984—94, judge major felony program, 1986, judge orphans' ct. divsn., 1992; judge U.S. Ct. Appeals (3d cir.), Phila., 1994—. Bd. dirs. Diagnostic and Rehab. Ctr. of Phila. Trustee Edna McConnell Clark Found.; mem. adv. bd. City Yr. for Phila. Mem.: ABA, Pa. Bar Assoc., Phila. Bar Assoc., Temple Inn of Ct., Barristers' Assn. Phila., Am. Law Inst., Nat. Bar Assn., Crime Prevention Assn. (bd. dirs.). Office: 20614 US Courthouse 601 Market St Philadelphia PA 19106

MCKEE, THOMAS J. association administrator; b. Fairfax Station, Va. m. Patricia Rizzuto; children: Michelle, Catherine, Thomas McKee Jr. BA in Polit. Sci., S.E. Mo. State U., 1970; grad. Emerging Exec. Program, Pa. State U., 1983. Customer requirements rep. Grumman Aerospace Corp., Bethpage, NY, dir. Air Force requirements, corp. v.p. Washington; exec. br. customer rels. Northrop Grumman Corp., 1994; nat. sec. Air Force Assn., under 40 nat. dir., nat. pres., nat. chmn. bd., 2001—. Chmn. bd., past pres. Aerospace Edn. Found.; chmn. resolutions com. and indsl. assoc. task force, exec. com., comm. com. Air Force Assn.; chpt. v.p., pres., chmn. Nat. Air Force Salute Found.; bd. trustees Air Force Meml. Found., Falcon Found. With USAF. Recipient Presdl. citation; fellow, Doolittle. Office: c/o AFA Nat Hqrs 1501 Lee Hwy Arlington VA 22209-1198

MCKEE, THOMAS M. state representative; b. Cynthiana, Ky, Mar. 13, 1941; m. Sue McKee. BA, Centre Coll., 1963. State Rep. House of Rep., Dist. 78, Ky., 1996—; farmer, 1963—. Magistrate Harrison County, 1978—; del. State Dem. Convention, 1966; county chairperson Gubernatorial Candidate, 1967; mem. Animal Shelter Comm., Farm comm., Rd. comm., Scholarship Comm., Agr. & Natural Resources, Appropiation & Rev.; vice Chair Econ. Devel. & Tourism; chair Energy; mem. Tobacco Task Force. Mem.: Cynthiana Fifth Third Bank (adv. bd.), Nat. Bank of Cynthiana (past dir.), Am. Angus Assoc., Am./KY/Harrison County Cattleman's Assoc., Harrison County Farm Bur. (former pres.), Harrison Meml. Hosp. Democrat. Office: Capitol Capitol Annex Rm 324B Frankfort KY 40601 also: Dist 1053 Cook Rd Cynthiana KY 41031

MCKEE, TIMOTHY CARLTON, taxation educator; b. South Bend, Ind., Mar. 9, 1944; s. Glenn Richard and Laura Louise (Niven) McK.; m. Linda Sykes Mizelle, Oct. 13, 1984; children: Brandon Richard. BS in Bus. Econs., Ind. U., 1970, MBA in Fin., 1973, JD, 1979; LLM in Taxation, DePaul U., 1980. Bar: Ill. 1980, U.S. Dist. Ct. (no. dist.) Ill. 1980; CPA, Va.; cert. govt. fin. mgr. Procedures analyst Assocs. Corp., South Bend, 1969-71; asst. dir. fin. Ind. U., Bloomington, 1971-79; sr. tax mgr. Peat Marwick Mitchell & Co., Chgo., Norfolk, Va., 1979-84; corp. counsel K & K Toys, Norfolk, 1984; assoc. prof. acctg. Old Dominion U., Norfolk, 1985-98, chmn. dept., 1994-95, chmn. acctg., fin. and law dept., 1995, univ. prof. dept. acctg., 1998—. Computer coord. Peat, Marwick, Mitchell & Co., 1982-84; micro computer cons. Old Dominion U., 1985-91. Contbr. articles to profl. jours. Active Friends of Music, Bloomington, 1978, Art Inst., Chgo., 1981; loan exec. United Way, Chgo., 1981; telethon chmn. Va. Orch. Group, Norfolk, 1983. Mem. Assn. Govt. Accts., Am. Acctg. Assn., Am. Assn. Atty. CPAs, Inc., Am. Tax Assn., Fin. Execs. Inst. (pres. 1995-96), Hampton Rds. Tax Forum, Inst. Internal Auditors, Beta Alpha Psi, Beta Gamma Sigma. Home: 412 Rio Dr Chesapeake VA 23322-7144 Office: Old Dominion U Constant Hall Rm 2153 Norfolk VA 23529

MCKEEL, SETH DOUGLAS, real estate manager, commissioner; b. Lakeland, Fla., June 5, 1975; s. Seth Douglas and Ellen Tucker McKeel; m. Kim Green, Oct. 26, 2002. BA in Polit. Sci., U. Fla., 1997. Intern Publix Supermarkets, Lakeland, Fla., 1995—97; v.p. Lakeland (Fla.) Properties & Mgmt., Inc., 1997—99; real estate mgr. Heritage Equities, Inc., Lakeland, Fla., 1999—; city commr. City of Lakeland (Fla.), 2000—. Chairperson McKeel Acad. of Tech. Charter Schools, Lakeland, Fla., 2000—04; v.p. Imperial Symphony Orch., Lakeland, Fla., 2003. Mem.: Kiawanis Club of Lakeland. Office: City of Lakeland 228 S Massachusetts Ave Lakeland FL 33801-5012 Office Phone: 863-834-6005. Office Fax: 863-834-8402. E-mail: seth.mckeel@lakelandgov.net.

MCKEEN, ALEXANDER C. retired engineering executive, foundation administrator; b. Albion, Mich., Oct. 10, 1927; s. John Nisbet and Janet (Callander) McK.; m. Evelyn Mae Feldkamp, Aug. 18, 1951; children: Jeffrey, Brian, Andrew. BSME, U. Mich., 1950; MBA, Mich. State U., 1968. Registered profl. engr., Mich. From asst. supt. maintenance to supt. final assembly Cadillac Motor Car divsn. GM, Detroit, 1961-69; asst. dir. reliability cadillac motor car divsn. GM, Detroit, 1969-72, exec. engr. product assurance Warren, Mich., 1972-75, from asst. dir. to dir engring. analysis, 1975-87; pres., owner Engring. Analysis Assocs., Inc., Bingham Farms, Mich., 1987-99; cons. Detroit Exec. Svc. Corps, 1999—; pres. McKeen Found., 2002—. Pres. Dells of Bloomfield Home Owners Assn., Bloomfield Hills, Mich., 1987-88; trustee Kirk in Hills, Bloomfield Hills, 1990-93, 2003—, elder, 1995-97. Mem. Soc. Auto. Engrs., Am. Soc. Quality Control, Econ. Club Detroit, Detroit Athletic Club, Stonycroft Hills Golf Club, Pelican Nest Golf Club, Beta Gamma Sigma. Avocations: tennis, golf, photography, travel, gardening. Home: 5071 Champlain Cir West Bloomfield MI 48323-3530 Office: Detroit Executive Service Corps 16250 Northland Dr Ste 390 Southfield MI 48075

MC KEEN, CHESTER M., JR., retired business executive; b. Shelby, Ohio, Mar. 18, 1923; s. Chester Mancil and Nettie Augusta (Fox) McK.; m. Alma Virginia Pierce, Mar. 1946 (dec. Feb. 1998); children: David Richard, Karin, Thomas Kevin; m. Sally Ann Werst, Nov. 1999; 1 stepchild, Stephen Harry Werst. BS in Mil. Sci., U. Md., 1962; MBA, Babson Coll., Wellesley, Mass., 1962. Advanced through grades to maj. gen. U.S. Army, 1942-77; dir. logistics Bell Helicopter Internat., Tehran, Iran, 1977-79; v.p. procurement Bell Helicopter Textron, Ft. Worth, 1979-82, v.p. materiel, 1982-89; pres. Logistics Svcs. Internat., Arlington, Tex., 1990—2002; ret., 2002. Adv. bd. Salvation Army, Cancer Care Svcs. Decorated D.S.M., Legion of Merit (3), Commendation medal (3); named to U.S. Army Ordnance Hall of Fame. Mem. Nat. Def. Indsl. Assn., Assn. U.S. Army, Ridglea Country Club, Rotary, Masons (33 degree), Shriners, Sojourners, Sigma Pi. Home: 2310 Woodsong Trail Arlington TX 76016-1037 E-mail: cmmckeen@aol.com. *To live for oneself is to pursue emptiness. To live for others is to insure fulfillment.*

MCKEE-RYAN, FRANCES M. education educator; d. Sonja M and Stephen F McKee; m. David P Ryan, Sept. 27, 1997; children: Alexander D. Ryan children: William S. Ryan. PhD, Ariz. State U., 2002. Asst. prof. of mgmt. W.Va. U., 2000—02; asst. prof. of orgnl. behavior Oreg. State U., 2002—. Contbr. articles to profl. jours. Mem.: APA, Soc. for Human Resource Mgmt., Soc. for Indsl. and Orgnl. Psychology, Acad. of Mgmt., Sigma Iota Epsilon, Phi Kappa Phi, Golden Key Honor Soc., Beta Gamma Sigma, Alpha Gamma Delta (pres., leadership cons. 1991—93), Delta Sigma Pi. Christian. Avocations: reading, walking, hiking. Office: Oregon State University 200 Bexell Hall Corvallis OR 97331

MCKEEVER, JOHN EUGENE, lawyer; b. Phila., Oct. 24, 1947; s. John James and Marie Julia (Supper) McKeever; m. Kathleen Marie Wynne, Dec. 9, 1995; children: John Joseph, Jeannine Marie. BA magna cum laude with distinction, U. Pa., 1969, JD magna cum laude, 1972. Bar: Pa. 1972, U.S. Dist. Ct. (ea. dist.) Pa. 1972, U.S. Dist. Ct. (mid. dist.) Pa. 1977, U.S. Ct. Appeals (3d cir.) 1979, U.S. Ct. Appeals (DC cir.) 1981, U.S. Supreme Ct. 1981. Assoc. Schnader, Harrison, Segal & Lewis, Phila., 1972-80, ptnr., 1980-98, Piper Rudnick LLP, Phila., 1998—. Trustee Lawyers Com. Civil Rights Under Law, Washington, 2002, dir., 2003—. Mem. Bus. Leadership organized Cath. Schs., Phila., 1984—; bd. dirs. Jr. Achievement, Phila., 1986—; c-chair Oblates St. Francis De Sales Capital Campaign, 1998—99; capt. spl. gifts com. Cath. Charities Appeal, Phila., 1986—91; mem. pres.'s coun. De Sales U., Center Valley, Pa., 1980—; mem. adv. com. De Sales Sch. Theology, Washington, trustee, 1988—91. Mem.: Pro-Life Lawyers' Guild (bd. dirs. 1983—84, chancellor 1984—86), Phila. Bar Assn., St. Thomas More Soc. (gov. 1979—91, pres. 1981—82), Phi Beta Kappa, Order of Coif, Pi Gamma Mu. Republican. Roman Catholic. Office: Piper Rudnick LLP One Liberty Pl 1650 Market St Ste 4900 Philadelphia PA 19103 Office Phone: 215-656-3310. E-mail: john.mckeever@piperrudnick.com.

MCKEEVER, JOSEPH FRANCIS, III, lawyer; b. Weymouth, Mass., July 21, 1950; s. Joseph Francis Jr. and Virginia Agnes McK.; m. Janice Danielle Kearney, Oct. 17, 1970. BA, George Washington U., 1972, JD, 1978. Bar: D.C. 1978, U.S. Supreme Ct. 1989. Editor Congl. Rsch. Svc. Libr. Congress, Washington, 1974-78; law clk. Honorable Harry Wood U.S. Ct. Claims, Washington, 1978-79, Honorable Wilson Cowen U.S. Ct. Claims, Washington, 1979-80; atty. Sutherland, Asbill & Brennan, Washington, 1980-85; ptnr. Davis & Harman LLP, Washington, 1985—. Author, editor: Annuities Answer Book, 1999; contbr. articles to profl. jours. Mem. ABA (chair sect. on taxation com. on ins. cos. 2000-02); Nat. Assn. for Variable Annuities (chmn., 2002-2003) Avocations: gardening, bicycling. Home: 2812 34th Pl NW Washington DC 20007-1405 Office: Davis & Harman LLP Willard Office Bldg 1455 Pennsylvania Ave NW Washington DC 20004-1008

MCKEEVER, KENT, library director, law librarian; b. Southampton, N.Y., Sept. 6, 1952; BA, SUNY, Oswego, 1974; JD, La. State U., 1980. Bar: La. 1980. Ref. libr. Fordham U. Sch. Law Libr., 1981—82; internat., fgn. and comparative law libr. Columbia U. Law Sch. Libr., N.Y.C., 1982—83, assoc. law libr., head collection devel. and tech. svcs., 1983—93, acting law libr., 1994—95, dir. Diamond Law Libr., 1996—. Lectr. Fudan U., Shanghai, 1986, Columbia U. Sch. Libr. Svc., N.Y.C., 1986—91, Columbia Summer Program, Leiden, Netherlands, 1998—2000; cons. Beijing U., Dept. of Treaty and Law, China, MetaMetrics, Inc.; grant application evaluator NEH. Class of 1950 scholar, La. State U., Supr.'s scholar, Tullis-Herget scholar. Office: Diamond Law Libr 435 W 116th St New York NY 10027 Home: 456 Riverside Dr # 10B New York NY 10027 Business E-Mail: mckeever@law.columbia.edu.

MCKEEVER, MICHAEL PIERCE, SR., economics and business educator; b. Glendale, Calif., Mar. 3, 1941; s. Samuel Pierce and Martha Frances (Darby) McK.; m. Jeanetta Ross, Oct. 20, 1964 (div. June 1970); 1 child, Nancy; m. Marjorie Alice McKean, Dec. 17, 1970; (div. March, 2004); children: Michael P. Jr., Johnathan Brooks. BA with honors, Whittier (Calif.) Coll., 1963; MS in Econs., London Sch. Econs., 1966. Life credential bus., econs., social sci. Calif. C.C. Owner Counseling Brokerage Group, Santa Rosa, Calif., 1980-84, Bus. Plan Workshop, Santa Rosa, 1980-95; asst. prof. econs. and bus. Armstrong U., Berkeley, Calif., 1995-97; founder McKeever Inst. Econ. Policy Analysis, Berkeley, 1995—. Instr. Vista Coll., Berkeley, Calif., 1998—2002; CFO Platform Tech. Computer Svcs., Oakland, Calif., 1999—; instr. City Coll. San Francisco, 2003—. Author: How to Write a Business Plan, 1981, Conceptual Economics, 1993, Moral Economics, 2001. Dir. Inst. Small Bus. Dept. Sonoma State U., 1981; pres. We Care, Santa Rosa, 1984; chmn. adv. com. Suppression of Drug Abuse in Schs. Sonoma County, Santa Rosa, 1985. Recipient award Role Recognition-Downtown Devel., Santa Rosa City Coun., 1983; named Vol. of Yr. Santa Rosa City Schs., 1984. Avocation: men's senior baseball league player and coach. Home and Office: 1627 47th Ave San Francisco CA 94122 E-mail: mpmckeever@earthlink.net.

MCKEIGHEN, RONALD EUGENE, physicist; b. Marion, Ill., Oct. 17, 1942; s. George A. and Aileen (Reach) McK.; m. Loretta M. Ward, Sept. 3, 1966; children: Kevin, Christy. BS in Engring. Physics, U. Ill., 1964, MS in Nuclear Engring., 1965, PhD in Physics, 1971. Postdoctoral in cancer rsch. and nuclear medicine Oak Ridge Nat. Lab., 1972-73; sr. prin. rsch. scientist Searle/Siemens Ultrasound, Des Plaines, 1973-79; sr. R&D engr. KB-Aerotech, Lewistown, Pa., 1979-83; staff scientist Advanced Diagnostic Rsch., Tempe, Ariz., 1983-85; prin. staff engr. Motorola Space Elect, Scottsdale, Ariz., 1985-86; mgr. advanced devel. Advanced Tech. Labs., Bothel, Wash., 1986-93; dir. advanced devel. Acoustic Imaging inc., Phoenix, 1993—2001; prin. rsch. engr. Lockheed-Martin, Litchfield Park, Ariz., 2001—. Contbr. articles to profl. jours. and chpts. to books. Spl. fellow in nuclear engring. AEC. Mem. IEEE. Mem. Pentecostal Ch. Achievements include patent for concept of digital beamformer for ultrasonic phased array, developed ultrasonic transducer arrays and sensors. Office: Lockheed-Martin Litchfield Park AZ

MCKEITHEN, WALTER FOX, secretary of state; b. Columbia, La., Sept. 8, 1946; s. John Jesse and Marjorie (Funderburk) McK.; m. Yvonne May; children: Marjorie, Marianne, Rebecca, John Jesse. B in History and Social Studies, La. Tech. U., 1972. Owner, operator Apparel Mart Dept. Store, Columbia, 1974-83, McKeithen Chem. & Cementing, Columbia, 1979-88; mem. appropriation, natural resources and joint budged coms. La. Ho. of Reps., Baton Rouge, 1983-87; sec. of state State of La., Baton Rouge, 1987—. Tchr., coach Caldwell Parish High Sch., Grayson, La., 1975-78; past mem. La. Assn. Educators. Past v.p. Caldwell Parish Jaycees; trustee La. Sch. Employees' Retirement System; mem. La. Tourist Devel. Commn.; second injury bd. La. Workmen's Compensation; mem. State Bd. Election Supervisors and State Bond Commn., La. Farm Bur., Am. Petroleum Inst.; adminstrv. bd. Broadmoor Meth. Ch. Recipient Outstanding Legislator award La. Assn. Educators, 1985, Golden Apple award La. Fedn. Tchrs., 1986. Republican. Methodist. Office: Dept of State State Capitol 20th Fl PO Box 94125 Baton Rouge LA 70804-9125

MCKELDIN, WILLIAM EVANS, management consultant; b. Richmond, Va., Aug. 14, 1927; s. Robert A.W. and Mary E. (Burk) McK.; children: William Evans, Roberts Evans; m. Phyllis Shellhase, Jan. 23, 1982. BSBA, Temple U., 1951, postgrad., 1951-53, U. Pitts., 1953-54. Various mgmt. positions Westinghouse Corp., Pitts., 1950-62, Farrel Corp., Rochester, N.Y., 1963-66, Gen. Signal Corp., Norwalk, Conn., and Watertown, N.Y., 1966-71, Copperweld Steel Co., Warren, Ohio, 1971-75, Tenn. Forging Steel, Knoxville, 1975-77, Val Bradley Assocs., West Chester, Pa., 1977-79; pres., owner McKeldin Assocs., West Chester, 1979-95; founder, co-owner McKeldin Group, Bala Cynwyd, Pa., 1995—. Contbr. articles to profl. jours. Bd. dirs. United Fund, YMCA, ARC, Rochester Inst. Tech., Jefferson C.C., Kent State U. With USAAF, 1945-47. Mem. Inst. Mgmt. Cons., Am. Soc. Safety Engrs., Am. Soc. Personnel Adminstrn., C. of C. (bd. dirs.), Masons, Rotary. Republican. Presbyterian. Office: The McKeldin Group 24 Timber Ln Hilton Head Island SC 29926-1002 Office Phone: 843-837-6565. E-mail: mckeldin@webtv.net.

MCKELL, CYRUS M. retired college dean, plant physiologist; b. Payson, Utah, Mar. 19, 1926; s. Robert D. and Mary C. (Ellsworth) McK.; m. Betty Johnson; children: Meredith Sue, Brian Marcus, John Cyrus. BS, U. Utah, 1949, MS, 1950; PhD, Oreg. State U., 1956; postgrad., U. Calif., Davis, 1957. Instr. botany Oreg. State U., Corvallis, 1955-56; range rsch. plant physiologist

U. Calif. USDA-Agrl. Research Service, Davis, 1956—61; prof., dept. chmn. U. Calif., Riverside, 1961—69; prof. dept. head., dir. Utah State U., Logan, 1969-80; v.p. research NPI, Salt Lake City, 1980-88; dean Coll. of Sci. Weber State U., Ogden, Utah, 1988-94; pres., prin. Applied Ecol. Svcs. Inc., Logan, Utah, 1995—. Cons. Ford Found. 1968-72, Rockefeller Found., 1964-70, 89, UN, 1978, 90, NAS, 1980, 89, 91, 92, 93, USAID, 1972, UN Devel. Program, 1989; mem. faculty of sci. adv. bd. UAE Nat. U., 2000-02. Editor: Grass Biology and Utilization, 1971, Useful Wildland Shrubs, 1972, Rehabilitation of Western Wildlife Habitat, 1978, Paradoxes of Western Energy Development, 1984, Resource Inventory and Baseline Study Methods for Developing Countries, 1983, Shrub Biology and Utilization, 1989, Wilderness Issues, Arid Lands of the Western United States, 1992; contbr. over 230 articles to profl. jours. Chmn. Cache County Planning Commn., Logan, 1974-79; mem. Utah Energy Conservation and Devel. Coun., 1976-79, Gov.'s Sci. Adv. Coun., 1988-97, chmn., 1990-91, 96-97; mem. Commn. of the Californias, Riverside, 1965-68; mem. Holladay City Planning Commn., 2003—. Recipient Utah Gov.'s Sci. and Tech. medal, 1990, Gardner Prize in Sci., awarded by Utah Acad. Scis., Arts and Letters, 1999; Fulbright scholar Spain, 1967-68; World Travel grantee Rockefeller Found., 1964. Fellow AAAS (com. chmn. 1979-89, sci. exchange to China grantee 1984-85, 89, sci. panel U.S.-Chile 1987); mem. Am. Soc. Agronomy, Soc. Range Mgmt. (pres. Calif. sect. 1965, pres. Utah sect. 1982). Mem. Lds Ch. Avocations: travel, photography, history. Home: 2248 E 4000 S Salt Lake City UT 84124-1864 Office: 550 N Main St Ste 302 Logan UT 84321-3957 Business E-Mail: cmmc1@xmission.com.

MCKELLEN, SIR IAN, actor; b. Burnley, England, May 25, 1939; s. Denis Murray and Margery (Sutcliffe) McK. Student, St. Catharine's Coll., Cambridge. Prof. Oxford U., 1990-91. First stage appearance as Roper in A Man for All Seasons, Belgrade Theatre, Coventry, Eng., 1961; numerous other parts include title roles in Henry V, Luther, Ipswich, 1962-63, Aufidius in Coriolanus, Arthur Seaton in Saturday Night and Sunday Morning, title role in Sir Thomas More, Nottingham Playhouse, 1963-64; London debut as Godfrey in A Scent of Flowers, 1964, Claudio in Much Ado About Nothing, Andrew Cobham in Their Very Own and Golden City, 1966; title part in O'Flaherty, V.C. and Bonapart in The Man of Destiny, 1966, (Broadway debut) Leonidik in the Promise, London, 1966-67, Richard II, Edward II, Hamlet, Prospect Theatre Co., 1968-71; Captain Plume in The Recruiting Officer; founder-mem. Actors' Co., Edinburgh Festival, 1972 and touring as Giovanni in Tis Pity She's a Whore, Page-Boy in Ruling the Roost, title role Wood Demon; debut with R.S.C. as Dr. Faustus, Edinburgh Festival, 1974; title role in The Marquis of Keith, Philip the Bastard in King John, 1974-75, Young Vic Colin in Ashes, 1975; Royal Shakespeare Co.: Burglar in Too True to be Good, Romeo, MacBeth, Leontes in the Winter's Tale, Face in the Alchemist, Bernick in Pillars of the Community, Langevin in Days of the Commune, 1976-78, Ivanov in Every Good Boy Deserves Favour, Toby Belch in Twelth Night, Andrei in The Three Sisters, Max in Bent, 1979, Amadeus, N.Y.C., 1980, Iago in Othello, The Other Place, Stratford, 1989; European tour of one-man show Acting Shakespeare, 1983, also L.A., N.Y.C., 1984, one-man show A Knight Out at the Lyceum (devised especially for Gay Games IV U.K. and South Africa tour), 1994, An Enemy of the People, 1997, Peter Pan, 1998, The Seagull, 1998, Present Laughter, 1998, The Tempest, 1999, Dance of Death, N.Y.C, 2001-02, London, 2003, Sydney, 2004; assoc. dir. Nat. Theatre, London, 1984-86, plays include: Venice Preserved, Wild Honey, Coriolanus, Duchess of Malfi, The Cherry Orchard, King Lear, Richard III, Napoli Milionaria, Uncle Vanya, An Enemy of The People, Peter Pan, others; dir. first prodn. The Prime of Miss Jean Brodie, Liverpool Playhouse, 1969, A Private Matter, 1973, The Clandestine Marriage, 1975; films include: Alfrred the Great, 1969, The Promise, 1969, A Touch of Love, 1969, The Keep, 1982, Plenty, Zina, 1985, Scandal, 1988, The Ballad of Little Jo, 1992, I'll Do Anything, 1992, Last Action Hero, 1993, Six Degrees of Separation, 1993, The Shadow, 1994, Jack and Sarah, 1994, Restoration, 1994, Richard III, 1995, Bent, 1996, Swept From the Sea, 1997, Apt Pupil, 1998, Gods and Monsters, 1998, X-Men, 2000, Lord of the Rings: The Fellowship of the Ring, 2001 (Outstanding Performance by Male Actor in Supporting Role SAG award 2002, nominee Best Supporing Actor Acad. Award 2002, Best Supporting Actor Saturn award 2002; nominee Best Performance by Actor BAFTA Film award, Empire award, Golden Satellite award, MTV Movie award, and OFCS award 2002), Lord of the Rings: The Two Towers, 2002, X2: X-Men United, 2003, The Lord of the Rings: The Return of the King, 2003; TV appearances include: David Copperfield, 1965, Ross, 1969, Richard II, Edward II and Hamlet, 1970, Hedda Gabler, 1974, Macbeth, Every Good Boy Deserves Favour, Dying Day, 1979, Acting Shakespeare, 1981, The Scarlet Pimpernel, 1982, And the Band Played On, 1993 (Emmy nomination, Supporting Actor, 1993), Cold Comfort Farm, 1995, Rasputin, 1996(Emmy nomination, Supporting Actor,1996) David Copperfield, 1999. Recipient Clarence Derwent award, 1964, Variety and Plays and Players awards, 1966; Actor of Year, Plays and Players, 1976, Soc. of West End Theatres for Best Actor in Revival award, 1977, for Best Comedy Performance, 1978, for Best Actor in a New Play, 1979, Tony Award for Best Actor, Drama Desk award, Outer Critics Circle award, N.Y. Drama League award, 1981, Performer of the Yr. award Royal TV Soc., 1983; decorated comdr. Order Brit. Empire, knight Bachelor. Mem. Brit. Actors' Equity (coun. 1970-71).*

MCKELLIPS, TERRAL LANE, mathematics educator, university administrator; b. Terlton, Okla., Dec. 2, 1938; s. Raymond Orlando and Patrice Lillian (Fuller) McK.; m. Karen Kay Sweeney, Sept. 7, 1958; children: Marty Suzanne, Kyle Bret. BS in Edn., S.W. Okla. State U., 1961; MS, Okla. State U., 1963, EdD, 1968. Asst. prof. S.W. Okla. State U., Weatherford, 1962-66; prof., dept. chmn. Cameron U., Lawton, Okla., 1968-72, 73-83, prof., dean Sch. Math. Applied Scis., 1983-89, provost, 1989—2001. Vis. prof. Okla. State U., Stillwater, 1972-73. Contbr. articles to profl. jours. State coord. Dept. Leadership Inst., Am. Coun. Edn., 1982-83; chair Okla. State Regents for Higher Edn. Coun. on Instrn., 1997-98. NSF Sci. Faculty fellow, 1966-68. Mem. Math. Assn. Am. (cons. bur. 1975—), Nat. Coun. Tchrs. Math., Lawton Country Club (dir. 1982-89, pres. 1986-89), Pi Mu Epsilon, Phi Kappa Phi. Democrat. Avocations: golf, genealogy. E-mail: terralm@cameron.edu.

MCKELVEY, ALAN CURTIS, pharmacist; b. Dayton, Ohio, Mar. 29, 1958; s. Paul Laverne and Julia Curtis McKelvey; m. Linda Beckley, May 21, 1983; children: Jennifer, David. BS, Ohio No. U., 1981. Registered pharmacist Ohio, cert. smoking cessation facilitator Am. Lung Assn. Pharmacist Revco Drug Store, Xenia, Ohio, 1981—82, Wright State U., Fairborn, Ohio, 1982—. Pharmacist Howards Pharmacy, Huber Heights, Ohio, 1989—97, CVS, Huber Heights, Ohio, 1997—2002, Wal-Mart Pharmacy, Beavercreek, Ohio, 2002—03, 2002—; part-time pharmacist Walgreens, Kettering, Ohio, 2002—; pharmacy and therapeutics com. United Healthcare Ohio, Centerville, 1993—99; externship site preceptor Ohio No. U., Fairborn, 1991—, U. Cin. Coll. Pharmacy, 1994—, Ohio State Coll. Pharmacy, Fairborn, 1999—. Officer YMCA Indian Princesses, Kettering, Ohio, 1990—96; youth soccer coach YMCA, Kettering, 1995—2001; pharmacy advisor Reach Out Montgomery County, Dayton, 1999—. Named Pharmacist of the Yr., Miami Valley Pharm. Assn., 1986. Republican. Nazarene. Avocations: marching band pit crew member, swimming, gardening. Home: 2068 E David Rd Kettering OH 45440 Office: Wrigth State U Pharmacy 3640 Colonel Glenn Dayton OH 45435 Office Phone: 937-775-3414. Business E-Mail: alan.mckelvey@wright.edu.

MCKELVEY, ANDREW J. advertising executive; 1 son, Stuart J. McKelvey. BA, Westminster Coll. Chmn. bd. TMP Worldwide, Inc., NYC, 1967—; CEO TMP Worldwide, Inc. (now Monster Worldwide, Inc.), NYC, 1967—. Bd. dirs. Yellow Pages Pubs. Mem. Assn. Director Mktg. (bd. dirs. 1994-96). Office: Monster Worldwide Inc 622 3rd Ave Fl 36 New York NY 10017-6707*

MCKELVEY, GERALD, public relations executive; b. Waynesboro, Pa., June 27, 1943; s. Gerald Campbell and Mary Lou (Dunn) McK. BA, Wash. Coll., 1965. Reporter The Record Herald, Waynesboro, Pa., 1965-67; reporter, editor Phila. Inquirer, 1967-76; night city editor Newsday, Melville, 1976-81; dep. met. editor N.Y. Newsday, 1981-88; spl. asst. Manhattan Dist. Atty.'s Office, N.Y.C., 1988-96; sr. v.p. Rubenstein Assocs., Inc., N.Y.C., 1996-00, exec. v.p., 2000—. Trustee Ch. of St. Mary Virgin, N.Y.C., 1996-00. Mem. SAR, The Inner Cir. Office: Rubenstein Assocs Inc 1345 Avenue Of The Americas New York NY 10105-0302

MCKELVEY, JAMES MORGAN, chemical engineering educator; b. St. Louis, Aug. 22, 1925; s. James Grey and Muriel (Morgan) McK.; m. Edith Rothbauer, Dec. 28, 1957; children: James, Robert; m. Judith Hood Forgotson, Sept. 4, 1992. BS, U. Mo.-Rolla, 1945; MS, Washington U., St. Louis, 1947, PhD, 1950. Research engr. E.I. DuPont de Nemours & Co., Inc., 1950-54; asst. prof. chem. engring. Johns Hopkins U., Balt., 1954-57; mem. faculty Washington U., St. Louis, 1957—, dean Sch. Engring. and Applied Sci., 1964-91, prof. chem. engring., 1991-98, sr. prof. chem. engring., 1998—. Recipient Disting. Educator award Soc. Plastics Engrs., 1979 Home: 9861 Copper Hill Rd Saint Louis MO 63124-1063

MCKELVEY, JOHN CLIFFORD, mental health services professional; b. Decatur, Ill., Jan. 25, 1934; s. Clifford Venice and Pauline Lytton (Runkel) McK.; m. Carolyn Tenney, May 23, 1980; children: Sean, Kerry, Tara, Evelyn, Aaron. BA, Stanford U., 1956, MBA, 1958. Rsch. analyst Stanford Rsch. Inst., Palo Alto, Calif., 1959—60, indsl. economist, 1960—64; with Midwest Rsch. Inst., Kansas City, Mo., 1964—2000, v.p. econs. and mgmt. sci., 1970—73, exec. v.p., 1973—75, pres., CEO, 1975—2000, The Menninger Clinic, Topeka, 2001—. Chmn. Trustee Vis. Coms. The Menninger Clinic, Topeka, 1978—86, chmn. bd. dirs., 1988—94; chmn. bd. The Menninger Found., 1994—97. Trustee Rockhurst Coll., 1993, Hoover Presdl. Libr. Assn., West Branch, Iowa, 1997; mem. Civic Coun. of Greater Kansas City; bd. dirs. Yellow Corp., Mid-Am. Mfg. Tech. Ctr., 1991; trustee The Menninger Found., 1975. Mem.: Carriage, Mission Hills. Home: 1156 W 103d St # 232 Kansas City MO 64114-4511 Address: Menningers PO Box 809045 Houston TX 77280

MCKELVEY, JUDITH GRANT, lawyer, educator, university dean; b. Milw., July 19, 1935; d. Lionel Alexander and Bernadine R. (Verdun) Grant. BS in Philosophy, U. Wis., 1957, JD, 1959. Bar: Wis. 1959, Calif. 1968. Atty. FCC, Washington, 1959-62; adj. prof. U. Md., Europe, 1965; prof. law Golden Gate U. Sch. Law, San Francisco, 1968-99, dean, 1974-81. Mem. State Jud. Nominees Evaluation Commn., 1981-82. Contbr. to: Damages Book, 1975, 76. Bd. dirs. San Francisco Neighborhood Legal Assistance Found. Fellow Am. Bar Found.; mem. ABA, Wis. Bar Assn., Calif. Bar Assn., San Francisco Bar Assn. (dir. 1975-77, chmn. legis. com., sec.-treas., pres.-elect 1980-83, pres. 1984), Calif. Women Lawyers (1st pres.), Law in a Free Soc. (exec. com.), Continuing Edn. of Bar (chmn. real estate subcom., mem. joint adv. com.), Legal Svcs. to Children Inc. (pres. 1987-89), San Francisco Neighborhood Legal Assistance Found. (dir. and exec. com. 1985-87), Lawyers Com. for Urban Affairs (dir. and exec. com. 1985-87, co-chairperson 1988-90). Office: Golden Gate U Sch Law 536 Mission St San Francisco CA 94105-2921

MCKELVEY, VIRGINIA MAUDE, language educator; b. Pueblo, Colo., June 5, 1935; children: Daniel Helman, Nancy Schuessler. BA in English/Edn., U. So. Colo., 1994; MLS in Lang. Comm., Regis U., 1998; PhD in Philosophy/Edn., Walden U., Mpls., 2002. Acctg. and bus. adminstr., 1964-92; collector and seller rare and new books; tchr. English Sch. Dist. 60, Pueblo, 1994-2000, U.S. Peace Corps, Bangkok, 2001, Campina, Romania, 2003—. Mem.: Virginia Woolf Soc., Am. Acad. Poets, Humane Soc. Am., Sierra Club, Phi Delta Kappa. Democrat. Avocation: travel. Office: US Peace Corp 1111 20th St NW Washington DC 20526

MCKELVY, MICHAEL JOHN, materials chemist, research scientist; b. Berkeley, Calif., Apr. 19, 1954; s. Andy Milton and Dagmar Marie (Johnson) McK.; m. Margaret Knight Riddall, Aug. 2, 1975; children: Robin, Adam, Evan. BS in Chemistry, U. Calif., Berkeley, 1975; MS in Chemistry, Ariz. State U., 1981, PhD in Chemistry, 1985. Engr. crystal growing lab., ctr. solid state sci. Ariz. State U., Tempe, 1976-82, materials sci. engr. II, 1982-84, rsch. specialist, 1984-90, mgr. materials facility, 1986-94, assoc. rsch. scientist, 1990-99, affiliate assoc. prof. sci. & engring. of materials PhD program, 1993-99, dir. materials facility, 1994—, dir. Goldwater materials sci. labs., 1995—, acting dir. ctr. solid state sci., 1997, sr. rsch. scientist, 1999—, affiliate prof. sci. and engring. materials grad. program, 1999—. Invited asst. prof. Inst. des Matériaux de Nantes, U. Nantes, France, 1993; NRC sr. rsch. assoc. Albany (Oreg.) Rsch. Ctr., 2002; proposal reviewer Petroleum Rsch. Fund, Washington, 1992-94, U.S. Dept. Energy, 2000—. Contbr. articles to profl. jours.; manuscript reviewer Chemistry of Materials, 1994-2002, Jour. Physics and Chemistry of Solids, 1995, Jour. Solid State Chemistry, 1996—, Molecular Crystals and Liquid Crystals, 1997-98, Jour. Am. Chem. Soc., 1998-2001, Jour. Am. Ceramic Soc., 2001-2002, Environ. Sci. and Tech., 2003—. Coach Chandler (Ariz.) Youth Baseball, 1988-95, Chandler Am. Little League, 1996-97; com. chmn. cub scouts Boy Scouts Am., Mesa, Ariz., 1992, mem. Boy Scout com., Chandler, 1993-95. Recipient Outstanding Cmty. Impact award, Acad. Cmty. Engagement Svcs., ASU, 2002; rsch. grantee NSF, 1986—, Petroleum Rsch. Fund, 1992-95, Dept. Energy, 1995—; NRC sr. rsch. assoc., 2002. Mem. Am. Chem. Soc., Materials Rsch. Soc. Democrat. Presbyterian. Achievements include patents for method for detection of chemical components, chemical switch and method for detection of chemical compounds, and chemical switch for detection of chemical components; co-development of atomic-level imaging of lamellar intercalation reaction processes using dynamic high-resolution transmission electron microscopy and scanning tunneling microscopy/spectroscopy; research in new materials synthesis, materials reaction mechanisms, carbon dioxide mineral sequestration, intercalation chemistry, thermal chemistry and analysis, materials sci. edn. Office: Ariz State U Ctr for Solid State Science Tempe AZ 85287-1704 Office Phone: 480-965-4535. Business E-Mail: mckelvy@asu.edu.

MCKELWAY, ALEXANDER JEFFREY, religion studies educator; b. Durham, N.C., Dec. 8, 1932; s. Alexander Jeffrey and Alice (Gibbon) McK.; m. Adelaide Bullard, Sept. 17, 1960; children: Alexander J., Daniel, Matthew Phillip. AB, Davidson Coll., 1954; BD, Princeton Theol. Sem., 1957; ThD, U. Basel, 1963. Ordained to ministry Presbyn. Ch., 1957. Min. Vienna (Austria) Cmty. Ch., 1958-60; asst. prof. Dartmouth Coll., Hanover, N.H., 1963-65; Paul B. Freeland prof. religion Davidson (N.C.) Coll., 1965-98, faculty chair, 1991-94. Vis. prof. Princeton (N.J.) Theol. Sem., 1973, 86, 87, Duke U. Div. Sch., Durham, N.C., 1999; mem. Fulbright Commn., Vienna, 1958-60. Author: The Systematic Theology of Paul Tillich, 1964, The Freedom of God and Human Liberation, 1991; editor: The Context of Contemporary Theology, 1974. Chair jud. com. Synod of N.C., 1975; moderator Charlotte (N.C.) Presbytery, 1985; active Kincaid for Congress Com., Charlotte, 1980, Exec. Com. Dem. Party, Davidson, 1975-77. Fellow in theology Princeton Sem., 1957, Younger Scholars fellow NEH, 1969, Ctr. for Theol. Inquiry fellow, 1997—. Mem. Am. Acad. Religion, Calvin Studies Soc., Duodecim Theol. Soc. (sec.), Am. Theol. Soc.

MCKENDRY, JOHN H., JR., lawyer, educator; b. Grand Rapids, Mich., Mar. 24, 1950; s. John H. and Lois R. (Brandel) McK.; m. Linda A. Schmalzer, Aug. 11, 1973; children: Heather Lynn, Shannon Dawn, Sean William. BA cum laude, Albion Coll., 1972; JD cum laude, U. Mich., 1975. Bar: Mich. 1975. Assoc., then ptnr. Landman, Latimer, Clink & Robb, Muskegon, Mich., 1976-85; ptnr. Warner, Norcross & Judd, Muskegon, 1985—. Dir. debate Mona Shores High Sch., Muskegon, 1979-90; adj. prof. of taxation (employee benefits), Grand Valley State U., 1988—; debate instr. Muskegon C.C., 1999-2001. Pres. local chpt. Am. Cancer Soc., 1979; bd. dirs. West Shore Symphony, 1993-2000, v.p. 1995-97, pres., 1997-99; bd. dirs. Cath. Social Svcs., 1998—; chair profl. divsn. United Way, 1994, 98; chair bd. dirs. Deaf Hard of Hearing Connection, 2003—; bd. dirs. Mona Lake Watershed Coun., 2003—; chair Charter Commn. City of Norton Shares, 2003—. Recipient Disting. Service award Muskegon Jaycees, 1981; named 1 of 5 Outstanding Young Men in Mich., Mich. Jaycees. 1982; named to Hall of Fame, Mich. Speech Coaches, 1986, Diamond Key Coach Nat. Forensic League, 1987. Mem. ABA, Mich. Bar Assn., Muskegon County Bar Assn. (dir. 1992-98, pres. 1996-97), Muskegon C. of C. (bd. dirs. 1982-88), Mich. Interscholastic Forensic Assn. (treas. 1979-86), Optimists (pres. 1992). Republican. Roman Catholic. Home: 1575 Brookwood Dr Muskegon MI 49441-5276 Office: Warner Norcross & Judd LLP PO Box 900 400 Terrace Pla Muskegon MI 49443-0900 Office Phone: 231-727-2637. E-mail: mckendjh@wnj.com.

MCKENNA, ALVIN JAMES, lawyer; b. New Orleans, Aug. 17, 1943; s. Dixon N. Sr. and Mabel (Duplantier) McK.; m. Carol Jean Windheim, 1963; children: Sara, Alvin James Jr., Martha, Andrea, Erin, Rebecca. AB, Canisius Coll., 1963; JD, Notre Dame U., 1966. Bar: N.Y. 1966, Ohio 1967, U.S. Dist. Ct. (so. dist.) Ohio 1968, U.S. Dist. Ct. (no. dist.) Ohio 1978, U.S. Ct. Appeals (6th cir.) 1969, U.S. Supreme Ct. 1977. Law clk. to judge of U.S. Dist. Ct. (so. dist.), Columbus, Ohio, 1966-68; asst. U.S. atty., 1968-70; ptnr. Porter, Wright, Morris & Arthur, 1970—. Mem. Gahanna (Ohio) City Council, 1972-80, 82-84; chmn. Gahanna Charter Rev. Commn., 1981; pres. Community Urban Redevel. Corp., Gahanna, 1984—. Named one of Ten Outstanding Young Persons in Columbus, Jaycees, 1974. Mem. ABA, Ohio Bar Assn., Fed. Bar Assn. (pres. Columbus chpt. 1973-74), Columbus Bar Assn. (chair fed. cts. com. 1972-74). Home: 202 Academy Ct Columbus OH 43230-2104 Office: Porter Wright Morris & Arthur 41 S High St Ste 2800 Columbus OH 43215-6194 Office Phone: 614-227-1945. Business E-Mail: amckenna@porterwright.com.

MCKENNA, ANDREW JAMES, paper distribution and printing company executive, baseball club executive; b. Chgo., Sept. 17, 1929; s. Andrew James and Anita (Fruin) McK.; m. Mary Joan Pickett, June 20, 1953; children: Suzanne, Karen, Andrew, William, Joan, Kathleen, Margaret. BS, U. Notre Dame, 1951; JD, DePaul U., 1954. Bar: Ill. Chmn., CEO Schwarz Paper Co. (name now Schwarz), Morton Grove, Ill., 1964—; non-exec. chmn. McDonald's Corp., 2004—. Bd. dirs. Skyline Corp., AON Corp., Click Commerce, Inc., McDonald's Corp., 1991—. Chmn. trustees, emeritus U. Notre Dame; trustee Mus. Sci. and Industry, Chgo.; bd. dirs. Cath. Charities of Chgo., Children's Meml. Med. Ctr. Chgo.; founding chmn. Chgo. Metropolis 2020. Mem. Comml. Club Chgo.(chair civic com.), Econ. Club Chgo., Lyric Opera (bd. dirs.), Execs. Club Chgo., Civic Comm. (chair), Glenview Golf Club, Old Elm Club, Merit Club, Casino Club, The Island Club. Home: 60 Locust Rd Winnetka IL 60093-3751 Office: Schwarz 8338 Austin Ave Morton Grove IL 60053-3288 Office Phone: 847-967-4034.

MCKENNA, FRANK JOSEPH, lawyer; b. Apohaqui, N.B., Can., Jan. 19, 1948; s. Durward and Olive (Moody) McK.; m. Julie Friel; children: Tobias John, Christine Alice, James Durward. BA with honors, St. Francis Xavier U., 1970; postgrad., Queen's U., 1970-71; LLB, U. N.B., 1974; DSc (hon.), Université de Moncton, Can., 1988; LLD (hon.), University of N.B., Can., 1988, Mt. Allison U., 1991. Spl. asst. to pres. Privy Council, 1971; rsch. asst. Constl. Law Unit, 1973-74; v.p. U. N.B. Faculty of Law Liberal Assn., Fredericton, 1974; ptnr. Martin, Lordon, McKenna & Bowes, Chatham, 1974-87; mem. N.B. Liberal Party, 1982, leader, 1985; premier Province of N.B., Fredericton, 1987-97; with McInnes Cooper, Moncton, NB, Can. Dir. Bank of Montreal, Noranda Inc., Zenon Environ., Acier LeRoux, various provincial, nat. and internat. cos. Recipient Vanier award, 1988, Distinction award Can. Advanced Tech. Assn., 1994; named Econ. Developer of Yr., Econ. Developers' Assn. Can., 1993, Chair, Can. Quality Month, 1994. Mem. Can. Bar Assn., N.B. Bar Assn. Liberal. Avocations: jogging, baseball, hockey. Office: McInnes Cooper PO Box 1368 Moncton NB Canada E1C 8T6

MCKENNA, FREDERICK GREGORY, lawyer, consultant; b. Chgo., Oct. 4, 1952; s. Frederick Hilary and Jean Elizabeth (Henneberry) McK.; m. Cornelia Ann Burns, Nov. 17, 1984; children: Kieran Padraig, Conor Burns. BA with honors, Coll. Holy Cross, 1974; JD, Georgetown U., 1978; postgrad., U. Nev., Las Vegas, U. Denver. Bar: D.C. 1978, Md. 1981, Nev. 1986, U.S. Supreme Ct. 1987, Colo. 1993. Assoc. Joseph, McDermott et al, Washington, 1979-82, Hudson & Creyke, Washington, 1982-85; sr. counsel Reynolds Elec. & Engring. Co., Inc., Las Vegas, 1985-90; dep. gen. counsel EG&G Rocky Flats, Golden, Colo., 1990-92, v.p., gen. counsel, 1992-96; ptnr. Hall & Evans, Denver, 1996—. Mem. Community Svc. Commn., Md., 1984-85. Mem. ABA, D.C. Bar Assn. (D.C. procurement com.), Mensa. Republican. Roman Catholic. Avocation: history. Home: 5954 Wood Sorrel Way Littleton CO 80123-6758 Office: Hall & Evans 1200 17th St Ste 1700 Denver CO 80202-5817

MCKENNA, GEORGE LAVERNE, art museum curator; b. Detroit, Dec. 7, 1924; s. John LaVerne and Carolyn Georgia (Schwab) McK.; m. Janice Ballinger, July 22, 1966. Student, U. Oreg., 1943-44, U. Calif., Berkeley, 1948-49, U. Chgo., 1950; AB, Wayne State U., 1948, MA, 1951. Curator prints, drawings and photographs Nelson-Atkins Mus. Art, Kansas City, Mo., 1952-96, cons, 1997—. Cons. Hallmark Cards, Inc., Kansas City, 1974-76. Curator, author exhbn. and coll. catalogues. With U.S. Army, 1943-46. Mem. Am. Assn. Mus., Print Coun. Am. Office: Nelson-Atkins Mus Art 4525 Oak St Kansas City MO 64111-1873

MCKENNA, GEORGE NORTON, government educator; b. Chgo. s. Robert Emmet and Helen Elizabeth McK.; m. Sylvia Rhea McKenna, Aug. 29, 1964; childre: Laura, Maria, Christopher. AB, U. Chgo., 1959; MA, U. Mass., 1962; PhD, Fordham U., 1967. Lectr. CCNY, N.Y.C., 1963-67, asst. prof., 1967-75, assoc. prof., 1975-84, prof., 1984—. Author: The Drama of Democracy, 1998; co-editor: Taking Sides: Clashing Views on Controvesial Political Issues, 14th edit., 2003; contbr. articles to profl. jours. Candidate Clarkstown (N.Y.) Town Coun., 1975; pres. Save the Lake Assn., Clarkstown, 1970-73. Carnegie Found. fellow, 1963. Roman Catholic. Office: CCNY Dept Polit Sci 138th Convent Ave New York NY 10031

MCKENNA, JAMES RICHARD, agronomy educator; b. Orange, N.J., Feb. 27, 1942; s. John Frances and Esther Hope (Rice) McK.; m. Judith Ann Morse, June 21, 1969 (div. Nov. 1979); children: Catherine Jean, Jennifer Lynn; m. Debra Lynn Morris, Mar. 22, 1980. BS, U. R.I., 1964; MS, U. Maine, 1970; PhD, Va. Poly. Inst. and State U., 1988. Tchr. sci. Patton Acad., Sch. Dist. 25, Patten, Maine, 1964-68; rsch. asst. Dept. Plant and Soil Sci., Orono, Maine, 1968-70; tchr. biology Houlton (Maine) High Sch., Sch. Dist. 29, 1970-78; extension agt. Maine Coop. Extension Svc., Houlton, 1978-79, Va. Coop. Extension Svc., Harrisonburg, 1979-84; instr. dept. crop and soil environ. sci. Va. Poly. Inst. and State U., Blacksburg, 1984-88, prof., 1988—. Ind. farmer, Houlton and Patten, 1964-78; cons. Mali (W. Africa) Farming Systems Rsch/Extension Project, U.S. AID, 1988-91. Assoc. editor: Jour. Natural Resources and Life Scis. Edn.; contbr. articles to profl. jours. Chmn. Town Planning Bd., Houlton, 1977; master of ceremonies Mountain Acad. Coun., Blacksburg, 1989. Recipient Young Scientist award Am. Forage and Grassland, Springfield, Ill., 1987, Excellence in Acad. Advising award Alumni Assn. of Va. Poly. Inst. and State U., 1991; Nat. Assn. of Coll. & Teachers of Agrl. Fellow, 1993, Diggs Tchg. scholar 1996. Fellow Am. Soc. Agronomy (chair crops com. 1991, Agronomic Resident Edn. award 1997); mem. Crop Sci. Soc. Am. (vice chair collegiate crops judging 1990), Nat. Assn. Colls. and Tchrs. of Agr. (ea. regional dir., 2000, v.p. 2002, presdl. nominee 2003), Va. Poly. Inst. and State U. Faculty Assn. (sec. faculty affairs com. 1991), Gamma Sigma Delta (teaching award of merit 1990). Mem. Ch. of Brethren. Achievements include development of global orientations for course and curriculum in deptartments of crops and soil environmental science, of undergraduate BS degree in Environmental Science, of practice of using prolific (multiple ear) corn as part of sustainable production, of recommendations for rock phosphate use on sorghum/cowpea association in Mali of system for establishment of warm-season grasses no-till in Virginia. Office: Va Poly Inst and State Univ 235 Smyth Hall Blacksburg VA 24061 Home: 5000 Whitethorne Rd Blacksburg VA 24060-0882

MCKENNA, JOHN A., JR., data processing executive; b. 1955; Grad., Trinity Coll. Sales trainee IBM, head br. ops.; v.p. ops. Fisher Macleod Assocs.; v.p. bus. devel. JWP, 1989; sr. v.p., gen. mgr. JWP Info. Sys., pres. network and integration svcs. divsn.; pres. Entex Info. Svcs., Rey Brook, NY, 1993, CEO Rye Brook, NY. Bd. adv. Quality Inst. Internat. Office: Entex Information Svcs 6 International Dr Rye Brook NY 10573-1058

MCKENNA, MARGARET ANNE, university president; b. R.I., June 3, 1945; d. Joseph John and Mary (Burns) McK.; children: Michael Aaron McKenna Miller, David Christopher McKenna Miller. BA in Sociology, Emmanuel Coll., 1967; postgrad., Boston Coll. Law Sch., 1968; JD, So. Meth. U., 1971; LLD (hon.), U. Upsala, N.J., 1978, Fitchburg (Mass.) State Coll., 1979, Regis Coll., 1982; D Community Affairs, U. R.I., 1979; LLD (hon.),

Emmanuel Coll., 2000. Bar: Tex. 1971, D.C. 1973. Atty. Dept. Justice, Washington, 1971-73; exec. dir. Internat. Assn. Ofcl. Human Rights Agys., Washington, 1973-74; mgmt. cons. Dept. Treasury, Washington, 1975-76; dep. council to Pres. White House, Washington, 1976-79; dep. undersec. Dept. Edn., Washington, 1979-81; dir. Mary Ingraham Bunting Inst., Radcliffe Coll., Cambridge, Mass., 1981-85; v.p. program planning Radcliffe Coll., Cambridge, 1982-85; pres. Lesley U., Cambridge, 1985—. Bd. dirs. Dominion Resources, Inc., Cisco Learning Inst., The Jason Found. for Edn. Bd. dirs. Am. Assn. Coll. for Tchr. Edn., Coun. for Higher Edn. Accreditation, Datatel Scholars Found.; chmn. higher edn. task force Clinton Transition, 1992-93; chmn. edn. task force Mayor Thomas Menino Transition Com., 1994; bd. overseers Peabody Essex Mus. Recipient Outstanding Contribution award Civil Rights Leadership Conf., 1978; named Woman of Yr. Women's Equity Action League, 1979, Outstanding Woman of Yr. Big Sister Assn., 1986, Pinnacle award for Lifetime Achievement, Lelia J. Robinson award Women's Bar Assn. Mass., 1996, Valeria Addams Knapp award, The Coll. CLub, 1995; named Margaret A. McKenna Day, Gov. DePrete, R.I. Mem. Boys Scouts Am., Big Sisters Ass. Boston, Y.W.C.A. Cambridge, Women's Equity Action League, Nat. Women's Polit. Conf., Nat. Assn. Official Human Rights Agencies. Democrat. Office: Lesley Univ Office of the President 29 Everett St Cambridge MA 02138-2702

MCKENNA, MARIANNE, architect; b. Montreal, Que., Can., Sept. 25, 1950; d. Richard D. and Anna M. (Lohr) McK.; m. Ian Tudhope; children: Cameron Lohr, Portia McKinley. Attended, The Study Montreal, 1969; BA, Swarthmore Coll., 1972; MArch, Yale U., 1976. Asst. architect Bobrow & Fieldman, Montreal, Can., 1976-78; architect Denys Lasdun, Redhouse & Softley, London, 1978-79, Barton Myers Assocs., 1980-87, assoc., 1981—; founding ptnr. Kuwabara Payne McKenna Blumberg Archs., Toronto, 1987—. Assoc. prof. architecture U. Toronto, 1994—; guest critic, U. Toronto, U. Waterloo, McGill U., Yale U., 1975-87; exec. dir. Ont. Coll. of Art. Selected projects include Jackson Triggs Estate Winery, Niagara-on-the Lake, Hasbro Toy Co., N.Y.C., Mazzoleni Hall, RCM, Toronto, Indigo Books Music & Café, Toronto, Kingston, Burlington (Vt.), Mitchell Field Cmty. Ctr. and McKee Pub. Sch., Toronto; selected projects present firm York U. Ctr. Fine Arts 3, Tudhope Assocs. Design Studios Toronto, 35 E. Wacker Addition Chgo., Kitchener City Hall, Royal Conservatory of Music Master Plan, Grand Valley Instn. for Women, Kitchener, Home for the Aged Providence Ctr.; current projects include Concordia U., Montreal, Montreal Genomics and Proteomics Ctr. McGill U. Recipient Gov. Gen.'s award for Architecture, 1997, Royal Archtl. Inst. Can., 1994. Fellow Royal Architecture Inst. Can.; mem. Ont. Assn. Architects, Ordre des architectes de Québec, Ont. Coll. Art (past bd. dirs.). Office: Kuwabara Payne McKenna Blumberg Archs 322 King St W 3rd Fl Toronto ON Canada M5V 1J2

MCKENNA, MATTHEW MORGAN, lawyer; b. Apr. 29, 1950; s. James Aloysius and Rebecca (Rial) McK.; m. Nancy Fitzpatrick, Sept. 11, 1976; children: Matthew, James, Christine, Connor. BA, Hamilton Coll., 1972; JD, Georgetown U., 1975, LLM, 1978. Bar: N.Y. 1977. Clk. to Hon. Fred B. Ugast Superior Ct., Washington, 1975—76; assoc. Winthrop, Stimson, Putnam & Roberts, N.Y.C., 1979—83, ptnr., 1984—93; sr. v.p., treas. Pepsi Co., Inc., Purchase, NY, 1998—2001, sr. v.p. fin., 2001—. Adj. prof. Sch. Law Fordham U., N.Y.C., 1983—94, N.Y.C., 2002—. Trustee Merrill Lynch Found., 1986—95, Mt. St. Mary's Coll., Emmitsburg, Md., 1994—2002; bd. trustees SUNY, Purchase Found., NY, 2003—, Hamilton Coll., 2003—. Mem.: ABA (tax sect.), Assn. Bar of City of N.Y., N.Y. State Bar Assn. (chmn. com. on fgn. activities of U.S. taxpayers). Home: 35 Valley Rd Bronxville NY 10708-2226 Office: PepsiCo 700 Anderson Hill Rd Purchase NY 10577-1444

MCKENNA, PATRICK JAMES, management consultant; b. Edson, Alta., Can., Oct. 31, 1951; s. James Edward and Madeline (Watson) McKenna; m. Monique, 1 Child, David. CIM, Can. Inst. Mgmt., Toronto, Ont., 1979, P. Mgr., 1977, MBA, 1982, ICIA, 1985. Asst. div. mgr. Hudsons Bay Co., Edmonton, Alta., 1973-75; gen. mgr. Alta. C. of C. Edmonton, 1975-78; mng. dir. QCTV Ltd., Edmonton, 1978-81; v.p. Achieve Enterprises Ltd., Edmonton, 1981-83; ptnr. Edge Intl., Edmonton, 1983—; dir. Can. Inst. Mgmt., 1981-85. Author: Building Business Abroad, 1985; co-author: Creating the Marketing Mindset, 1989; contbg. author: The Lawyer's Handbook, 3d edit., 1992; co-author, Herding Cats, 1995, Beyond Knowing, 2000, First Among Equals, 2002 contbr. articles to profl. jours.; mem. publ. adv. bd. Partner-to-Partner Advisory, The Marcus Letter on Profl. Svcs. Mktg. Mem. ABA, Strategic Leadership Forum. Conservative. Home: 11226 60th St Edmonton AB Canada T5W 3Y8

MCKENNA, PETER DENNIS, lawyer; b. Amityville, N.Y., Aug. 15, 1937; s. John Paul and Margaret (Foley) McK.; children: Michael A., Suzanne E. AB cum laude, Coll. of the Holy Cross, Worchester, Mass., 1959; JD cum laude, N.Y.U., 1968. Bar: N.Y. 1968, U.S. Dist. Ct. (so. dist.) N.Y. 1970, U.S. Supreme Ct. 1973, U.S. Ct. Appeals (4th cir.) 1977, U.S. Ct. Appeals (7th cir.) 1979, U.S. Ct. Appeals (2nd cir.) 1983. Assoc. Wachtell, Lipton, Rosen & Katz, N.Y.C., 1968-71, ptnr., 1972-91, of counsel, 1992—2001. Mem. pres.'s coun. NYU, Weinfeld Ptnr. NYU Law Sch.; regent mem. pres.'s coun. Coll. Holy Cross. Editor-in-chief N.Y.U. Law Review, 1967-68; contbr. articles to profl. jours. Mem. Cmty. Sch. Bd. Dist. 26, Queens, N.Y., 1973-77; adv. bd. St. Aloyisius Sch. for Cen. Harlem Inner-City Children, 1992—, mem. exec. com., 1994-2001; founding dir. Ctrl. Harlem Initiative for Learning and Devel., 1994—; bd. dirs. Mt. St. Michael Acad., 1994-2001, mem. exec. com., 1994-99. Lt. USN 1959-65. MEM. ABA, Fed. Bar Coun., Am. Arbitration Assn. (comml. and securities panels), Am. Judicature Soc., N.Y. State Bar Assn., Assn. of Bar of City of N.Y., Order of Coif. Democrat. Roman Catholic. Avocations: history, public affairs, travel, swimming, golf. Address: 21205 NE 37th Ave Apt 1607 Aventura FL 33180-4056

MCKENNA, ROBERT E. automotive parts company executive; Grad., Ohio State U. With Genuine Parts Co., Atlanta, 1977—, pres. NAPA, 1983—, group v.p. GPC team, 1996—, chmn. bd. dirs. NAPA, pres. U.S. Automotive Parts group, 1998—. Office: Genuine Parts Co 2999 Circle 75 Pkwy Atlanta GA 30339

MCKENNA, SIDNEY F. retired technical company executive; b. Detroit, Nov. 27, 1922; s. Michael James and Elizabeth Josephine McK.; m. Helen Mary Spiroff, Sept. 20, 1944; children: Lynne Marie McKenna Hoss, Dennis Michael, Patrick Conlon, Mary Elizabeth McKenna Raimondi, Maureen T. McKenna Anderson, Christopher John. AB, U. Mich., Ann Arbor, 1947; MA, Wayne State U., 1948. With Ward Baking Co., Detroit, 1939-41; prodn. worker Cadillac Motor Co. (div. Gen. Motors Corp.), Detroit, 1941-42; mem. indsl. relations staff Ford Motor Co., Dearborn, Mich., 1942-79, v.p., 1974-79; sr. v.p. United Techs. Corp., Hartford, Conn., 1980-90. Bd. dirs. Schwartz Value Fund. Adv. bd. Providence Hosp., Detroit, 1972-80; bd. dirs. Brighton (Mich.) Hosp., 1976-80, Mercy Coll., Detroit, 1976-80, United Found., 1976-80, St. Francis Hosp., Hartford, Conn., 1983-89, St. Joseph's Coll., 1988-89. Served with USN, 1942-46. Decorated knight St. Gregory. Mem. Labor Policy Assn. (chmn.), Bus. Roundtable, Orgn. Resources Counselors, Nat. Assn. Mfrs. (bd. dirs. 1988-89), Bloomfield Hills Country Club, Birmingham Athletic Club, Mariner Sands Country Club, K.C. Roman Catholic. Home: 5680 SE Winged Foot Dr Stuart FL 34997-8642 E-mail: SFMcK@aol.com.

MCKENNA, TERENCE PATRICK, retired insurance company executive; b. Oldham, Lancashire, Eng., Sept. 3, 1928; came to U.S., 1929, naturalized, 1939; s. Patrick A. and Mary F. McK.; m. Patricia Buckley, Sept. 22, 1973. Student, St. Thomas Coll., Bloomfield, Conn., 1946—48. With John Hancock Mut. Life Ins. Co., 1951-87, gen. agt., 1963-67, field v.p. gen. agy. dept. Atlanta, 1967-69, field v.p. dist. agy. dept. Boston, 1969-73, 2d v.p. mktg. ops. dept., 1973-74, v.p. dept., 1974-76, sr. v.p. dept., 1976-83, sr. v.p. gen. agy. sales dept., 1983-87; ret., 1987. V.p., also bd. dirs. John Hancock Variable Life Ins. Co.; chmn. bd. mgrs. I.V.A.; bd. dirs. John Hancock Distbrs. Inc., John Hancock Property and Casualty Ins. Co. Served with USMC, 1952-54. Mem.: Am. Soc. CLUs, Am. Coll. Life Underwriters, Woods Hole Golf Club (Falmouth, Mass.), Palm Beach Gardens Club, Frenchman Creek Country Club.

MCKENNA, WILLIAM JOHN, textile products executive; b. N.Y.C., Oct. 11, 1926; s. William T. and Florence (Valis) McK.; m. Jean T. McNulty, Aug. 27, 1949 (dec. Nov. 1984); children: Kevin, Marybeth, Peter, Dawn; m. Karen Lynne Hilgert, Aug. 6, 1988; children: Katherine Lynne, William John IV. BBA, Iona Coll., 1949; MS (Univ. Store Service scholar), NYU, 1950. V.p. Hat Corp. Am., N.Y.C., 1961-63, v.p. mktg., 1961-63, exec. v.p., 1963-67; pres. Manhattan Shirt Co., N.Y.C., 1967-74; pres., dir. Lee Co., Inc., Shawnee Mission, Kans., 1974-82, Kellwood Co., St. Louis, 1982—, chief exec. officer, 1984—, also bd. dirs., chmn., CEO, 1991-97, chmn., 1991-99, chmn. emeritus, 1999—. Dir. United Mo. Bancshares, Kansas City, Mo., United Mo. Bank of St. Louis. Trustee emeritus St. Louis U., Boys Hope, St. Louis U. H.S.; permanent deacon Archdiocese St. Louis. With USN, 1944-46, PTO. Mem. Sovereign Mil. Order Malta, St. Louis Club, Bellerive Country Club. Roman Catholic. Office: Kellwood Co PO Box 14374 Saint Louis MO 63178-4374 E-mail: william_mckenna@kellwood.com.

MCKENNA, WILLIAM MICHAEL, advertising executive; b. Washington, Apr. 4, 1951; s. William H. and Betty Ann (Cashin) McK.; m. Lynn Stevenson, Dec. 18, 1976; children: James Langdon, Lee Stevenson. BA, Wesleyan U., 1973; MS in Journalism, Boston U., 1978. V.p., creative dir. Ingalls Quinn & Johnson, Boston, 1981-88; sr. v.p., creative dir. Young & Rubicam, N.Y.C., 1988-94; chief creative officer, exec. v.p. AF GL Internat., N.Y.C., 1994-95; mng. dir., chief creative officer Citigate Albert Frank, N.Y.C., 1996-99; mng. dir., COO, Marsteller, N.Y.C., 1999-2000; pres., CEO Marsteller Advt., N.Y.C., 2000—. Recipient CLIO, Hatch, N.Y. Film Soc. creative advt. awards, 1982-95. Home: 26 Wildwood Darien CT 06820-5231 Office: Burson Marsteller 230 Park Ave S New York NY 10003-1513 E-mail: michael_mckenna@bm.com

MCKENNON, KEITH ROBERT, chemical company executive; b. Condon, Oreg., Dec. 25, 1933; s. Russel M. and Lois E. (Edgerton) McK.; m. Patricia Dragon, Sept. 30, 1961; children: Brian, Marc, Kevin. BS, Oreg. State U., 1955. Rsch. chemist Dow Chem. Co., Pittsburg, Calif., 1955—67, sales mgr. Houston, 1967, from research mgr. to exec. v.p. Midland, Mich., 1968—87, bd. dirs., 1983—92, 2003—, exec. v.p., 1987-92; pres. Dow USA, 1987-90; chmn., chief exec. officer Dow Corning Corp., 1992-94, also bd. dirs.; chmn. PacifiCorp, Portland, Oreg., 1994-99, CEO, 1998-99. Patentee. Recipient Chemical Industry medal Soc. of Chemical Industry, 1994 Republican Presbyterian. Home: 6079 N Paradise View Dr Paradise Valley AZ 85253-3828

MCKENZIE, BRIAN BRUCE, finance educator; b. Kelowna, B.C., Canada, Nov. 23, 1948; arrived in U.S., 2003; s. Rex Bruce and Dorothy McKenzie; m. Molly Kathleen Farrend, Mar. 21, 1970. BA, U. B.C., Vancouver, Can., 1974; MBA, U. Victoria, Can., 1997, PhD, 2003. Cert. qualification - boatbuilding Province of BC, 1990. Pres. Brian McKenzie Boatbuilding, Inc, Victoria, Canada, 1982—97; lectr. U. Victoria, 1997—2002; asst. prof. U. Calif., Hayward, Calif., 2003—. Vis. instr. Worcester Poly. Inst., Mass., 1999—2000. Contbr. scientific papers (Entrepreneurship Theory and Practice Best Conceptual Paper Award, 2004), rsch. to profl. jours. Fellow: Students in Free Enterprise (Sam Walton fellow 2004); mem.: Small Bus. Inst., North Am. Case Rsch. Assn., Acad. of Mgmt. (chair nontraditional academics com.entrepreneurship divsn., Innovations in Pedagogy award 1999), U.S. Assn. of Small Bus. and Entrepreneurship (Model Undergraduate Program award 2000), Can. Anthrop. Assn., Oral History Assn. Office: Calif State Univ Hayward 25800 Carlos Bee Blvd Hayward CA 94542 Office Phone: 510-885-2858. Personal E-mail: brian@brian-mckenzie.com. E-mail: bmckenzie@csuhayward.edu.

MCKENZIE, CLIF ALLEN, Indian tribe official, accountant; b. Lawton, Okla., Sept. 29, 1942; s. Robert Allen and Rubie (Paukei) Williams; m. Michele Ann Martin, Aug. 4, 1972; children: Kasey Roberta, Kristen Marti. BS in Acctg., U. Okla., 1965; MBA, Pa. State U., 1976. Fin. analyst United Tribes of Okla., Shawnee, 1973-75; credit officer Bur. Indian Affairs, Dept. Interior, Horton, Kans., 1975-77; liaison officer Syracuse, N.Y., 1977-80; program analyst Denver, 1980-81; tribal administr. Kiowa Tribe of Okla., Carnegie, 1981-82; CEO tribal bus. mgr. Cheyenne and Arapaho Tribe of Okla., Concho, 1982-84; pres. Indian Devel. Corp., Oklahoma City, 1973—; prin. ptnr. McKenzie & Assocs., 1994—2001. Contracting officer Bur. Indian Affairs, Anadarko, Okla., 1984-89, agy. ops. officer, Concho, Okla.; contract specialist, Gen. Svc. Administr., Ft. Worth, 1989-92, Dept. Health Human Svc., Pub. Health Svc., supervisory contract specialist, Oklahoma City, 1992-94; asset mgr. HUD Loan Mgmt. Br., Oklahoma City, 1994-01, chmn. Kiowa Tribe, 2002, Carnegie, Okla. Police commr. City of Horton, 1976-77, city commr., 1976-77 dir. LECO, Inc., Tulsa. Capt. U.S. Amy, 1959-68. Recipient H.M. Hefner First Amendment award Playboy Found., 1985, Nat. Notary Pub. of the Yr. award Nat. Notary Assn., 1996. Mem. DAV (life), U. Olka. Alumni Assn.; mem. Kiowa Black Legging Soc., Nat. Assn. Accts., Am. Soc. Notaries (dir. govt. affairs 1975-80), Nat. Taxpayers Investigative Fund (Whistleblower award 1982), Elks, Moose Republican. Home: 3708 Epperly Dr Del City OK 73115-3610 Office: McKenzie & Assocs PO Box 15613 Oklahoma City OK 73155-5613 also: Kiowa Tribe Okla PO Box 369 Carnegie OK 73105 Office Phone: 405-740-6784. E-mail: clifmck@swbell.net.

MCKENZIE, ELIZABETH MCDANIEL, law librarian; b. Lexington, Ky., June 27, 1954; d. William E. and JoAnn E. (Harris) McDaniel; m. James A. McKenzie, May 20, 1978; children: Joseph D., E. Alexa. BA with distinction, Transylvania U., 1975; JD, U. Ky., 1981, MLS with distinction, 1984. Bar: Ky. 1981, U.S. Dist. Ct. (ea. dist.) Ky. 1981. Reginald Heber Smith community lawyer fellow Cen. Ky. Legal Svcs., Lexington, 1981-83; info. specialist Ky. Dept. for Environ. Protection, Frankfort, Ky., 1984-85; readers svcs. librarian St. Louis U. Law Library, 1986-96; dir. Suffolk U. Law Libr., Boston, 1996—. Owner, mgr. Juris Data Legal Rsch. Co., Lexington, 1985-86. Contbg. author: Libraries, Erotica and Pornography. Recipient Article of Yr. award Law Libr. Jour., 1999; Nat. Merit scholar Transylvania U., 1972-75. Mem. ABA, Ky. Bar Assn., Am. Assn. Law Libraries, Law Libraries New England, New England Law Library Consortium, Assn. Boston Law Libraries. Democrat. Roman Catholic. Office: Suffolk U Law Sch 120 Tremont St Boston MA 02108-4977 Office Phone: 617-573-8705. E-mail: emckenzi@suffolk.edu.

MCKENZIE, HARRY JAMES, cardiothoracic surgeon, surgical researcher; b. Meyersdale, Pa., Aug. 7, 1960; s. Henry Sadrus and Betty Elaine (Reiber) McK.; m. Judith Palmieri, July 6, 1985; children: Henry James, Anne Christine, Mark Angus. BS, Duquesne U., 1984; postgraduate, U. Pitts., 1986-87; MD, Hahnemann U., 1992. Surg. intern Temple U., Conemaugh Med. Ctr., Johnstown, Pa., 1992-93, surg. resident, 1993-97; cardiothoracic resident Med. Coll. Ga., Augusta, 1997-99. Mem. problem task force Conemaugh Med. Ctr., 1992-93. Contbr. articles to profl. jours.; presenter in field. Hosp. vol. Ctrl. Med. Pavilion, Pitts., 1981-84, Presbyn. Hosp., Pitts., 1986-87; med. exam. officer, Phila. Special Olympics, 1989-90; grad. banquet spkr. Salisbury (Pa.) H.S., 1993. Recipient 3d place rsch. competition award, ACS Region III com. on trauma, Norfolk, Va., 1993; recipient 1st place rsch. competition award ACS-Pa. com. on trauma, Hershey, 1993. Mem. ACS, AMA, Am. Soc. Gen. Surgeons, Soc. Am. Gastrointestinal Endoscopic Surgeons, Soc. Thoracic Surgeons. Avocations: skiing, golf, jogging, fishing, hiking. Home: 4130 N Tara Cir Wichita KS 67226-3367

MCKENZIE, JAMES FRANKLIN, lawyer; b. Mobile, Ala., May 3, 1948; s. Frank L. McKenzie and Mary K. (Crow) McKenzie O'Neal; m. Randy Jo Jones, June 25, 1977; children: Katherine J., J. Alistair. BA magna cum laude, U. W. Fla., 1970; JD with honors, U. Fla., 1973. Bar: Fla. 1973, U.S. Dist. Ct. (no. dist.) Fla. 1973, U.S. Ct. Appeals (5th cir.) 1975, U.S. Ct. Appeals (11th cir.) 1982, U.S. Supreme Ct. 1988. Lectr. bus. law U. Fla., Gainesville, 1972-73; assoc. Levin, Warfield et al, Pensacola, Fla., 1973-76; ptnr. Myrick & McKenzie, PA, Pensacola, Fla., 1976-82, McKenzie, Taylor & Zarzaur, P.A., Pensacola, Fla., 1982—. Contbr. chpts. to books, articles to profl. jours. Pres. N.W. Fla. Easter Seal Soc., Pensacola, 1975; bd. dirs. Five Flags Sertoma Club, 1977; trustee Fla. Lawyers Action Group, Tallahassee, 1996-97; adv. bd. Lupus Soc., N.W. Fla., 1992. Mem.: 1st Cir. Acad. Trial Lawyers (founding mem., pres. 1984), ATLA (bd. govs. 2001—, pres. club), ABA, Million Dollar Advocates Forum, Civil Justice Found. (founding sponsor), Nat. Bd. Trial Advocacy (cert. civil trial advocacy), Escambia-Santa Rosa Bar Assn., Fla. Bar Assn. (cert. in civil trial law), Acad. Fla. Trial Lawyers (bd. dirs. 1986—93, exec. com. 1990—91, bd. dirs. 2000—, coll. diplomates, Silver Eagle award 1989, 2002, ABCD award 1991), Pensacola Country Club, Order of Coif, Phi Delta Phi, Omicron Delta Kappa, Phi Kappa Phi. Republican. Methodist. Home: 12 Tristan Way Pensacola Beach FL 32561-5121 Office: McKenzie Taylor & Zarzaur PA 905 E Hatton St Pensacola FL 32503-3931 E-mail: jfm01@bellsouth.net.

MCKENZIE, JAMES W. lawyer; b. Oct. 3, 1959; AB, Dartmouth Coll., 1982; MBA, JD, U. Pa., 1987. Bar: Pa. 1987. Assoc. Morgan, Lewis & Bockius LLP, Phila. Office: Morgan Lewis & Bockius LLP 1701 Market St Philadelphia PA 19103-2903

MC KENZIE, JOHN MAXWELL, physician; b. Glasgow, Scotland, Nov. 13, 1927; came to U.S., 1980; s. Thomas Wilson and Isabell Connor (Spencer) McK.; m. Vieno Laine Kangas, June 29, 1957; children— Ann, Ian, Lesley, Gordon. M.B., Ch.B., U. St. Andrews, Scotland, 1950, MD, 1958. Intern U. St. Andrews, 1950-51, resident, 1953-55, fellow, 1955-56, 57-58; research trainee, fellow Tufts U., 1956-57, 58-59; clin. asst. medicine McGill U., Montreal, Que., Can., 1959-61, asst., then assoc. prof., 1961-68, prof., 1968-80, U. Miami, 1980—, chmn. dept. medicine, 1980-94. Contbr. numerous articles to profl. jours. Served with Royal Army Med. Corps, 1951-53. Recipient Killam award Can. Coun., 1980. Mem. Am. Thyroid Assn. (Parke-Davis disting. lectr. 1981, pres. 1983-84), Am. Soc. Clin. Investigation, Endocrine Soc. (Ayerst award 1961, Rorer Pharm. Clin. Investigator award 1990), Am. Physiol. Soc., Assn. Am. Physicians, Am. Fedn. Clin. Rsch., AAAS, Internat. Soc. Neuroendocrinology, European Thyroid Assn. (corr.) Home: 12505 SW 63rd Ave Miami FL 33156-5531 Office: U Miami Jackson Meml Med Ctr 1611 NW 12th Ave Miami FL 33136-1005 E-mail: jmckenzie@med.miami.edu.

MCKENZIE, KATHLEEN JULIANNA, artist; b. Jan. 20, 1957. Artist, Torrington, Conn., 1987—. Paintings featured in 7th, 9th and 11th Encyclopedia of Living Artist, Internat. Encyclopaedic Dictionary of Modern and Contemporary Art in Casa Editrice Alba. Address: 1655 Mountain Rd Torrington CT 06790-2750 E-mail: kj_mckenzie_studios@msn.com.

MCKENZIE, KAY BRANCH, public relations executive; b. Atlanta, Feb. 12, 1936; d. William Harllee and Katherine (Hunter) Branch; m. Harold Cantrell McKenzie, Jr., Apr. 11, 1958; children: Ansley, Katherine, Harold Cantrell III. Student, Sweet Briar Coll., 1955, Emory U., 1956-57. Account exec. Hill and Knowlton Inc., Atlanta, 1979-80, account supr./dir. S.E. govt. rels., 1981-83; ptnr. McKenzie, Gordon & Potter, Atlanta, 1983-85; pres. McKenzie & Assocs. Inc., Atlanta, 1986-89; sr. v.p. Manning Selvage & Lee, Atlanta, 1989-93; v.p. comm. and creative svcs. 1996 Atlanta Paralympic Games, 1993-96; v.p. comm. and devel. U.S. Disabled Athletes Fund, 1997—. Mem. Commn. on Future of South, 1974; co-chmn. John Lewis for Congress, Atlanta, 1986; regional bd. dirs. Inst. Internat. Edn., 1987-93. Fellow Soc. Internat. Bus. Fellows (bd. dirs. 1983-85, 92-93, v.p. 1986-88); mem. Pub. Rels. Soc. Am., Ga. C. of C. (bd. dirs. 1983-97), Leadership Atlanta, Ga. Internat. Horse Park Found. (bd. dirs. 1993-98). Democrat. Episcopalian. Office: 280 Interstate N Cir Ste 450 Atlanta GA 30339 Home: 209 N Forest Ave Marietta GA 30060 E-mail: kmckenzie@blazesports.com.

MCKENZIE, KEVIN PATRICK, artistic director; b. Burlington, Vt., Apr. 29, 1954; s. Raymond James and Ruth (Davison) McKenzie. Grad. high sch., Washington. Mem. corps de ballet Nat. Ballet of Washington, 1972-74; prin. Joffrey Ballet, N.Y.C., 1974-78, Am. Ballet Theatre, N.Y.C., 1979-91; artistic assoc. Washington Ballet, 1991-92; artistic dir. Am. Ballet Theatre, N.Y.C., 1992—. Pres. bd. dirs. Am. Ballet Theatre Dancers Fund, Inc., 1982—89; assoc. dir. New Amsterdam Ballet, N.Y.C., 1984—; founding bd. mem. Kaatsbaan Internat. Dance Ctr., 1991—. Performer: (films) Unicorn, 1971; dancer Houston Ballet, 1978, Spoleto Festival, 1980, 1984, Theatre des Champs Elysees, Paris, 1981, Sadler's Wells Theatre, London, 1981, Asami Maki Ballet Co., Tokyo, 1983, Aspen Festival, 1982, choreographer Groupo Zambaria Ballet, 1984, Liszt Etudes, 1991, Lucy and the Count, 1992, The Nutcracker, 1993, dancer La Bayadere, Carmen, Cinderella, Coppelia, Dim Lustre, Don Quixote, Giselle, The Garden of Villandry, Jardin aux lilas, The Leaves Are Fading, Pillar of Fire, Raymonda, Requiem, Rodeo, Romeo and Juliet, The Sleeping Beauty, Swan Lake, La Sylphide, Paquita, Sylvia Pas de Deux, Theme and Variations. Named Kevin McKenzie Day, City of Burlington, 1985; recipient Silver medal, Varna Internat. Ballet Competition, Bulgaria, 1972, Artistic Achievement medal, Dept. State, U.S. Govt., 1972, Mayor Burlington, Vt., 1984, Performing Arts award, Am. Ireland Fund, 1994. Office: Am Ballet Theatre 890 Broadway New York NY 10003-1211

MC KENZIE, LIONEL WILFRED, economist, educator; b. Montezuma, Ga., Jan. 26, 1919; s. Lionel Wilfred and Lida (Rushin) McK.; m. Blanche Veron, Jan. 2, 1943 (dec. July 1999); children— Lionel Wilfred (dec.), Gwendolyn Veron (dec.), David Rushin. AB, Duke U., 1939; MA, Princeton U., 1946, PhD, 1956; BLitt, Oxford (Eng.) U., 1949; postgrad., U. Chgo., 1950-51, LLD (hon.), 1991; D of Econs. (hon.), Keio U., Japan, 1998; DPhil (hon.), Kyoto U., Japan, 2004. Asst. economist WPB, 1942; instr. Mass. Inst. Tech., 1946; from asst. prof. to assoc. prof. Duke, 1948-57; prof. econs. U. Rochester, 1957-64, John Munro prof. econs., 1964-67, Wilson prof. econs., 1967-89, Wilson prof. emeritus, 1989—, chmn. dept., 1957-66. Taussig research prof. Harvard U., 1980-81; Mem. math. divsn. NRC, 1960-63, mem. behavioral scis. divsn., 1964-70; mem. math., social scis. bd. Center Advanced Study in Behavioral Scis., Palo Alto, Calif., 1964-70, chmn., 1969-70 Author: Classical General Equilibrium Theory, 2002; assoc. editor Internat. Econs. Rev., 1964-96, Jour. Econ. Theory, 1970-73, Jour. Internat. Econs., 1970-84, Econ. Theory, 1991-95; contbr. articles to profl. jours. Lt. (s.g.) USNR, 1943-45. Recipient Rising Sun award Japan, 1995; Rhodes scholar Oriel Coll. Oxford U., 1939; Guggenheim fellow, 1973-74, fellow Center for Advanced Study in Behavioral Scis., 1973-74. Fellow Econometric Soc. (coun. 1973-78, pres. 1977), Am. Acad. Arts and Scis., Am. Econ. Assn.; mem. NAS, Royal Econ. Soc., Am. Math. Soc., Am. Econ. Assn. (Disting. Fellow 1993), Phi Beta Kappa (chpt. v.p. 1968-70, chpt. pres. 1972-73). Home: 225 Dorchester Rd Rochester NY 14610-1322 Business E-Mail: mcke@mail.rochester.edu.

MCKENZIE, MARY BETH, artist; b. Cleve. d. William Jennings and Mary Elizabeth (McCray) McK.; m. Tony Mysak, May 8, 1974; children: Zsuzsa McKenzie Mysak, Maria McKenzie Mysak. Student, Mus. Fine Arts, Boston, 1964-65, Cooper Sch. Art, Cleve., 1965-67; diploma, NAD, N.Y.C., 1974. Painting instr. NAD, 1981—, Art Students League, 1995—. Author: A Painterly Approach, 1987; contbr. articles to profl. jours.; one-woman shows include Nat. Arts Club, N.Y.C., 1976, FAR Gallery, 1980, Perin and Sharpe Gallery, New Canaan, Conn., 1981, Frank Caro Gallery, N.Y.C., 1988—89, Joseph Keiffer Gallery, 1991, Union County Coll., 1998, exhibited in group shows at Sindin Gallery, N.Y.C., 1985—86, Ice Collection, 1995—96, Susan Conway Gallery, Washington, Galerie Yoramgil, Beverly Hills, Met. Mus. Art, 2001, Represented in permanent collections The Butler Mus. Am. Art, Met. Mus. Art, N.Y.C., Mus. City of N.Y., NAD, Art Students League of N.Y., Nat. Mus. Women in the Arts, Nat. Mus. Am. Art, Smithsonian Instn., Bklyn. Mus. Art, New Britain Mus. Am. Art, N.Y. Hist. Soc., Galerie Yoramgil, Beverly Hills, Calif., Spanierman Gallery, N.Y.C. Recipient Nat. Scholastic award Mus. Fine Arts, Boston, numerous awards including Thomas B. Clark prize and the Isaac N. Maynard prize Nat. Acad. Design, Greenshields Found. grantee, Stacey Found. grantee. Mem. Nat. Acad. Design, Pastel Soc. Am. (Best In Show, Award of Exceptional Merit, Exhbn. Com. award), Allied Artists Am. (Gold medal, The Jane Peterson award, Grumbacher Cash award, Silver medal), Audubon Artists (Pastel Soc. Am. award). Home: 525 W 45th St New York NY 10036-3414 E-mail: mbmckenzie525@yahoo.com.

MCKENZIE, MICHAEL K. wholesale company executive; Past pres., CEO G.S.C. Enterprises, Inc., Sulphur Springs, Tex., now chmn. bd., CEO, also bd. dirs. Office: GSC Enterprises Inc PO Box 638 Sulphur Springs TX 75483

MCKENZIE, STANLEY DON, academic administrator, English educator; b. Yakima, Wash., July 10, 1942; s. Don Guy and Jean Elizabeth McKenzie; m. Michal A. Koehler, Sept. 21, 1968 (div. Sept. 1974); 1 child, Thomas Charles. BS, MIT, 1964; MA, U. Rochester, 1967, PhD, 1971. Prof. lit. Rochester (N.Y.) Inst. Tech., 1967--, asst. to v.p. student affairs/judicial affairs, 1972-87, 92-94, acting dean, Coll. Liberal Arts, 1987-88, provost, v.p. acad. affairs, 1994--. Vice-chair bd. dirs. RIT Rsch. Corp., Rochester, 1994-2001; bd. dirs. CIMS Print, Rochester, Am. Coll. Mgmt. & Tech., Dubrovnik, Croatia. Author: Shakespeare Studies, 1987; (with others) The Practice of Theory, 1992, Other Voices, Other Views, 1999. Mem.: MLA, AAUP, ACLU. Democrat. Avocations: hiking, reading. Office: Rochester Inst Tech 6 Lomb Memorial Dr Rochester NY 14623-5604 E-mail: SDMPRO@RIT.edu.

MCKENZIE, STEVEN L. theology studies educator, writer; s. Maurice Wilfred and Germaine Lynn McKenzie; children: Christina Denise, Bonnie Lynn. BA, Abilene Christian Coll., 1975; MDiv, Abilene Christian U., 1978; ThD, Harvard U., 1983. Prof. dept. religious studies Rhodes Coll., Memphis, 1983—. Pres. bd. dirs. Inst Egyptian Art & Archaeology, Memphis, 1999—2002. Author: All God's Children: A Biblical Critique of Racism, 1997, King David: A Biography, 2000; co-editor (with John Kaltner): Beyond Babel: A Handbook for Biblical Hebrew and RElated Languages, 2002; mem. editl. bd. Jour. Biblical Lit., 1996—2002. Mem.: Cath. Biblical Assn., Soc. Biblical Lit. Office: Rhodes Coll Dept Religious Studies 2000 N Parkway Memphis TN 38112 Business E-Mail: mckenzie@rhodes.edu.

MCKENZIE, WESLEY MELVIN, JR., music educator, composer; b. LaGrange, Ga., Sept. 17, 1945; s. Wesley Melvin McKenzie, Sr. and Gladys Thompson McKenzie; m. Karen Sue Nichols, July 11, 1988; m. Sydney Rosalie Boone, Jan. 15, 1965 (div. Apr. 3, 1970); children: Dawn Elizabeth Rivera, Kimberley Sue, Eric Lee Riggs, Daniel Wesley. MusB, U. of Ga., 1963—66, MFA, 1966—68; Mus D in Composition, Fla. State U., 1974—78. Cert. tchr. Ga. State Bd. Edn., 1972, Fla. State Bd. Edn., 1974, Nev. State Bd. Edn., 1994. Dir. of bands Dawson County H.S., Dawsonville, Ga., 1968—69; assoc. dir. of bands Cairo H.S., Ga., 1969—71, dir. of bands, 1972—74; gen. music, beginning band instr. Washoe County Sch. Dist., Reno, 1994—98; assoc. dir. of bands Edward C. Reed H.S., Sparks, Nev., 1997—99; dir. of bands Edward C. Reed H.S., 1999—. Profl. performer Wes McKenzie Music Inc., Fla., 1974—98, Ga., 1974—98, Calif., 1974—98, Nev., 1974—98. Composer: (chamber music) Quintet for Brass, Sonatina for Alto Saxophone and Piano, (doctoral dissertation) Concerto for Alto Saxophone & Wind Band, (concert band composition) La Playa; editor: (music theory workbook) Basic Music Theory by Charles Douglas. Mem.: Internat. Assn. of Jazz Educators, Nev. Music Educators Assn. (nev. all-state jazz band chmn. 1998—99), NEA. Achievements include Led Outstanding Nevada Jazz Band, Reno Jazz Festival, 2000; Led Reed High School Wind Ensemble to Command Performance, Northern Nevada Band Festival, 2000; Guest Conductor, Northern Nevada Zone Honor Jazz Band, 2000. Avocations: scuba diving, computers, music performance. Home: 3829 Kings Row Reno NV 89503-1833 Office: Edward C Reed High School 1350 Baring Blvd Sparks NV 89434 Personal E-mail: wmckenzi@nvbell.net.

MCKEON, HOWARD P. (BUCK MCKEON), congressman, former mayor; b. L.A., Sept. 9, 1938; m. Patricia Kunz; 6 children. BS, Brigham Young U., 1985. Mem. Coun. City of Santa Clarita, Calif., 1987-92, mayor, 1987—92; mem. edn. and workforce, armed svcs. and vet. affairs 103rd-108th Congresses from 25th Calif. dist., 1993—. Founding dir., chmn. Valencia Nat. Bank; co-owner Howard & Phil's Western Wear, Inc., 1963-. Hon. chmn. Leukemia Soc. Celebrity program, 1990, Red Cross Community Support Campaign, 1992; active Dist. Com. Boy Scouts Am.; chmn., trustee William S. Hart Sch. dist., 1979-87; chmn., dir. Henry Mayo Newhall Meml. Hosp., 1983-88; mem. Calif. Rep. State Ctrl. Com., 1988-92; bd. dirs. Santa Clarita Valley Sml. Bus. Devel. Ctr., 1990-92, Canyon Country C. of C., 1988-92. Republican. Office: US Ho Reps 2351 Rayburn Ho Office Bldg Washington DC 20515-0525 E-mail: tellbuck@mail.house.gov.

MCKEON, JOHN ALOYSIUS (JACK MCKEON), professional baseball manager; b. South Amboy, N.J., Nov. 23, 1930; m. Carol McKeon; children: Kelly, Kasey, Kristi, Kori. BA in Phys. Edn. and Sci., Elon Coll. Baseball mgr. in 13 maj. and minor league cities; mgr. Kansas City Royals, Am. League, 1973-75, Oakland A's, 1977-78; v.p. baseball ops. San Diego Padres, Nat. League, 1980-93, mgr., 1988-90, Cincinnati Reds, 1997—2000, Fla. Marlins, Miami, 2003—. Bd. dirs. San Diego Make-a-Wish Found. NL Mgr. of the Year, 1999, 2003. Office: Fla Marlins Pro Player Stadium 2267 Dan Marino Blvd Miami FL 33028

MCKEON, JOHN C. publishing executive; BA in Polit. Sci., MBA, NYU. V.p. mktg. Times Mirror Nat. Mktg.; various advt. and mktg. positions Newsday, Melville, NY, 1986—98, retail advt. mgr., 1991—92, advt. dir., 1992—94, v.p. advt., 1994—98, sr. v.p. advt., chief innovation officer, 1998, exec. v.p., gen. mgr., 2004—; sr. v.p. advt. L.A. Times, 1998—2001; sr. v.p., gen. mgr. South Fla. Sun-Sentinel, 2001—04. Office: Newsday 235 Pinelawn Rd Melville NY 11747*

MCKEON, LARRY J. state representative; b. Nampa, Idaho, June 30, 1944; BA, Calif. State U., LA, 1967, MS, 1969; postgrad., U. Chgo. Project dir. U. So. Calif.; asst. to dean sch. social svc. adminstrn. U. Chgo.; lt. Sheriff's Dept., LA; instr. pub. adminstrn. Roosevelt U., Chgo., 1985—87; dir. United Charities Chgo., 1987—92; exec. dir. Commn. Human Rels., Chgo., 1992—96; mem. Ill. Ho. of Reps., 1996—. Adv. com. Horizons Cmty. Svcs., 2000—; hate crimes prosecution counsel Cook County State's Atty.; bd. dirs. Horizons Cmty. Svcs., 1985—87, Alexian Bros. Bonaventure Ho., 1993—96. 1st lt. USAR, 1971—74. Mem.: NOW, Cmty. Alliance Neighborhood Safety, Lakeview Citizens Coun., Ravenswood Cmty. Coun., Uptown Chgo. Commn., Uptown C. of C. (discrimination needs task force), Ravenswood C. of C., North Ctr. C. of C., Lincoln Sq. C. of C., Emily's List, Ind. Voter Ill. Ind. Precinct Orgn., People for Am. Way, Nat. Abortion Rights Action League Ill., Am. Separation Ch. and State, AARP. Democrat. Roman Catholic. Office: 279-S Stratton Office Bldg Springfield IL 62706 Address: 1967 W Montrose Ave Chicago IL 60613

MCKEOUGH, WILLIAM DARCY, investment company executive, director; b. Chatham, Ont., Can., Jan. 31, 1933; s. George Grant and Florence Sewell (Woodward) McK.; m. Margaret Joyce Walker, June 18, 1965; children: Walker Stewart, James Grant. BA, U. Western Ont., 1954; LLD (hon.), Wilfred Laurier U., 1980; DDiv, Huron Univ. Coll., 2003. Chmn. McKeough Supply Inc. Bd. dirs. Retirement Residential REIT, Can. Gen. Tower Ltd., CableServ Inc. Former mem. exec. com. Anglican Diocese of Huron; former mem. Gen. Synod, Anglican Ch., Can.; mem. Chatham City Coun., 1960-63; also mem. Planning Bd. and Lower Thames Valley Conservation Authority; former mem. Chatham-Kent adv. bd. Can. Nat. Inst. of the Blind; former bd. dirs. Chatham YMCA, Chatham Little Theatre; former chmn. and pres. bd. govs. pres. Ridley Coll.; former bd. govs. Stratford Shakespearian Festival, Wilfrid Laurier U.; former mem. Can. group Trilateral Commn.; mem. Ont. Legislature, 1963-78, minister without portfolio, 1966, minister mcpl. affairs, 1967; treas. and minister of econs., also chmn. Treasury Bd., 1971-72, minister mcpl. affairs, 1972, treas. and minister of econs. and intergovtl. affairs, 1972, parliamentary asst. to premier Ont., 1973, minister of energy, 1973-75, treas. and minister econs. and intergovtl. affairs, 1975-78; chmn. Ridley Coll. Found.; chmn. Huron Coll. Found. Decorated officer of Order of Can. Home and Office: PO Box 940 Chatham ON Canada N7M 5L3 Office Phone: 519-352-7110.

MCKEOWN, H. MARY, lawyer, law educator; b. West Palm Beach, Fla., Sept. 17, 1952; d. Honore Stephen McKeown and Margaret Berg McKeown Growney; m. Jon Henry Barber, Sept. 18, 1981; children: Sean Patrick, Mary Kathleen. AA, St. Petersburg Jr. Coll., Fla., 1970; BA in Polit. Sci. and Sociology, U. South Fla., 1972; JD cum laude, Samford U., 1976. Bar: Fla. 1976, U.S. Dist. Ct. (mid. dist.) Fla. 1977, U.S. Ct. Appeals (5th and 11th cirs.) 1981, U.S. Supreme Ct. 1992. Asst. state atty. 6th Jud. Ct., Clearwater, Fla., 1976-90; ptnr. Growney, McKeown & Barber, St. Petersburg, 1976—. Adj. prof. Stetson Coll. of Law, St. Petersburg, 1990—. Chairperson Child Welfare Std. and Tng. Coun., 1995—98; mem. nominee qualifications rev. com. Health and Human Svcs. Bd. Dist. 5, 1992—2000; mem. Study Commn. Child Welfare, 1990—91; leader Girl Scouts U.S., 1991—2001. Recipient Victim Advocacy award Pinellas County Victims Rights Coalition, 1984, Law and Order award Elks, Pinellas County, 1991. Mem.: St. Petersburg Bar Assn., Fla. Bar Assn., Acad. Fla. Trial Lawyers, Phi Alpha Delta. Office: 7455 38th Ave N Saint Petersburg FL 33710-1228

MCKEOWN, JAMES CHARLES, accounting educator, consultant; b. Cleve., Nov. 3, 1945; s. Charles Joseph and Dara Ferrol (Prew) McK.; m. Mary Alinda Park, Jan. 2, 1965 (div. May 1980); children— Jeffrey Charles, Pamela Lynn; m. 2d, Nancy Ann Stratton, Jan. 3, 1981 BS in Math. with high honors, Mich. State U., 1966, PhD in Bus. Adminstrn., 1969. Asst. prof. accountancy U. Ill., Urbana-Champaign, 1968-73, assoc. prof., 1973-76, prof., 1976-80, Weldon Powell prof. accountancy, 1980-83, A.C. Littleton prof. accountancy, 1983-89; disting. prof. acctg. Pa. State U., University Park, 1989-92, Ernst & Young prof. acctg., 1992-99, Mary Jean and Frank P. Smeal chaired prof. acctg., 1999—. Cons. research, computers; expert witness Editor: Inflation and Current Value Accounting, 1979; author computer-delivered acctg. course PLATO for Elementary Accounting, 1978; contbr. numerous articles to acad. jours. Recipient Instructional award U. Ill., Urbana-Champaign, 1970, Weldon Powell award, 1973; Fred Roedgers Research award U. Ill., 1978; Ford Found. fellow, 1967-68 Mem. Am. Acctg. Assn. (Manuscript award 1970, Outstanding Acctg. Educator 2003), Am. Statis. Assn., Decision Scis. Inst., Inst. Mgmt. Accts. Republican. Office: Pa State U 210 Beam Bus Adminstrn Bldg University Park PA 16802

MCKEOWN, LORRAINE LAREDO, travel company executive, writer; b. N.Y.C., Mar. 20, 1928; d. Frank A. and May (Collins) Laredo; m. William Taylor McKeown, July 9, 1964; children: Beth Ellison, Kate Taylor, Suzanne Harris. Talent agt. Carl Eastman, N.Y.C., 1960-65; cooking/travel columnist Camping Jour./Boating Jour., N.Y.C., 1968-70; travel agt. Beecher Travel, N.Y.C., 1968-70; founding ptnr. Computer Travel Info., N.Y.C., 1984, v.p., pres., 1985-90, CEO, 1990—. Contbr. articles to various publs. Bd. dirs. Chapin-Brearley Exch., N.Y.C., 1980, Howland Cultural Ctr., 2002—, Howland Cultural Ctr., 2002—. Mem. Freelance Assocs., Beacon Conservation Coun. Personal E-mail: mckeown@bestweb.net.

MCKEOWN, MARY ELIZABETH, educational administrator; m. James Edward McKeown, Aug. 6, 1955. BS, U. Chgo., 1946; MS, DePaul U., 1953. Supr. h.s. dept. Am. Sch., 1948-68, prin., 1968-99, trustee, 1975—, v.p., 1979, ednl. dir., 1979—2002, exec. v.p., 1992—2002; cons., 2002—. Author study guides for algebra, geometry, and calculus. Mem.: Distance Edn. and Tng. Coun. (chair person rsch. and edn. com. 1988—93), N. Ctrl. Assn. Colls. and Schs. (exec. bd. 1990—93), NASSP, LWV. Office: 2200 E 170th St Lansing IL 60438-1002

MCKEOWN, MARY MARGARET, federal judge; b. Casper, Wyo., May 11, 1951; d. Robert Mark and Evelyn Margaret (Lipsack) McKeown; m. Peter Francis Cowhey, June 29, 1985; 1 child, Megan Margaret. BA in Internat. Affairs and Spanish, U. Wyo., 1972; JD, Georgetown U., 1975. Bar: Wash. 1975, D.C. 1982. Assoc. Perkins Coie, Seattle, 1975—79, Washington, 1979—80; White House fellow U.S. Dept. Interior and White House, Washington, 1980—81; ptnr., mem. exec. com. Perkins Coie, Seattle, 1981—98, mng. dir. strategic planning and client rels., 1990—95; judge U.S. Ct. Appeals for 9th Cir., Seattle, 1998—2001, San Diego, 2001—. Trustee The Pub. Defender, Seattle, 1982—85; rep. 9th Cir. Judicial Conf., San Francisco, 1985—89; mem. gender bias task force, 1992—93; jud. conf. Com. on Codes of Conduct, 2001—; exec. com. 9th Cir., 2001—. Author: Girl Scout's Guide to New York, 1990; contbr. chpt. to book and articles to profl. jours. Nat. bd. dirs. Girl Scouts U.S., N.Y.C., 1976—87; mem. exec. com. Corp. Coun. for the Arts, Seattle, 1988—98; bd. gen. counsel Downtown Seattle Assn., 1986—89; mem. exec. com. Wash. Coun. Internat. Trade, 1994—; bd. mem. YMCA Greater Seattle, 1998—; bd. dirs. Family Svcs., Seattle, 1982—84. Named one of 100 Young Women of Promise, Good Housekeeping, 1985, Washington's Winningest Trial Lawyers, Washington Jour., 1992, Top 50 Women Lawyers, Nat. Law Jour., 1998; recipient Rising Stars of the 80's award, Legal Times Washington, 1983; fellow Japan leadership, 1992—93. Fellow: ABA (ho. of dels. 1990—); mem.: Am. Intellectual Property Law Assoc., Am. Law Institute, Nat. Assn. Iolta Programs (bd. dirs. 1989—91), Wash. Women Lawyers (bd. dirs., pres. 1978—79), Legal Found. Wash. (trustee, pres. 1989—90), Seattle-King County Bar Assn. (trustee, sec. 1984—85, Outstanding Lawyer award 1992), Wash. Bar Assn. (chmn. jud. recommendations 1989—90), Fed. Bar Assn. (trustee western dist. Wash. 1980—90), White House Fellows Found. (bd. dirs. 1998—, pres. 2000—01). Avocations: travel, classical piano, hiking, gourmet cooking, tennis. Office: US Ct Appeals 401 West A St Ste 2000 San Diego CA 92101-7908 E-mail: Judge_McKeown@ca9.uscourts.gov.

MCKEOWN, MICHAEL EUGENE, psychologist, consultant; b. Clovis, N.Mex., May 10, 1947; s. Julian Perry and Jean (Young) Keown; m. Elisabeth Anna McKeown, Sept. 26, 1997; children: Andrew Michael, Kimberly Anne. BA in Psychology, Pomona Coll., Claremont, Calif., 1969; M of Mgmt., Vanderbilt U., 1974; PhD in Psychology, Peabody/Vanderbilt U., 1976. Lic. psychologist, Wis., Colo., Tenn., Calif.; Erickson cert. in conflict and divorce mediation. Clin. psychologist VA Med. Ctr., Murfreesboro, Tenn., 1976-79, Grand Junction, Colo., 1979-83, Tomah, Wis., 1984-88; clin. psychologist in pvt. practice Ten., Wis., Colo., Calif., 1978-95; clin. psychologist Wis. Dept. Corrections, Racine, 1994-95, Naval Hosp. and Tng. Ctr., Great Lakes, Ill., 1995-97; dir. family advocacy Naval Air Facility, El Centro, Calif., 1997-2000, Naval Med. Ctr., San Diego, 2000—. Adj. instr. U. Ill., Chgo. Med. Sch., 1995-97, Sch. Profl. Psychology, Chgo., 1995-97, Mesa Coll., Adams State Coll., Grand Junction, 1982-83. Author, editor, developer various programs. Mem. APA, Nat. Register Health Svc. Providers in Psychology. Episcopalian. Avocations: fly fishing, woodworking, welding. Office: Mental Health Svcs Navel Med Ctr San Diego CA 92134 Home: 2847 Mary Ln Escondido CA 92025-7717

MCKEOWN, PETER PHILIP, medical center administrator, medical educator, cardiothoracic surgeon; b. Newcastle, NSW, Australia, Feb. 1, 1951; came to U.S., 1977; s. Arthur Lindsay and Phyllis Joyce McKeown. MB BS, U. Queensland, Australia, 1975, BA, 1976; MBA, U. South Fla., 1996; MPA, Harvard U., 1998, MPH, 1999. Asst. prof. surgery U. Wash., Seattle, 1984-88; assoc. prof. surgery U. South Fla., Tampa, 1989-98; dir. surgery VA Med. Ctr., Asheville, N.C., 1998—; cons. prof. surgery Duke U., Durham, 1999—. Dir. cardiovascular and thoracic surgery U. South Fla., 1989-94, mem. faculty coun., 1991-94, UMSA bd. dirs., 1991-94, univ. senate, 1993-96; pres. QMEDA, Inc., Tampa, 1993—, dir. Asheville Med. Edn. Rsch. Corp., 1999-. Author: (software) QMEDA H&P, 1994. Bd. dirs. Fla. Am. Heart Assn., St. Petersburg, 1992-94, chair pub. liason, 1996., bd. of regents, Am. Coll. Chest Physicians. Commonwealth Univ. scholarship Australian Govt., 1968, Alley-Sheridan scholarship Thoracic Surgery Found. for Rsch. Edn., 1997. Fellow Royal Coll. Physician and Surgeons Can., Royal Australasian Coll. of Surgeons; mem. Am. Coll. of Chest Physicians (state gov. 1997-99, gov. NC 2003-), Phi Kappa Phi, Beta Gamma Sigma. Office: Dept Surgery VA Med Ctr 1100 Tunnel Rd Asheville NC 28805-2043 Office Phone: 828-299-2540.

MCKEOWN, REBECCA J. principal; b. Wayne, Okla., Apr. 4, 1937; d. William S. and Ila Rebekah (Mitchell) Lackey; m. Loren Ferris, Apr. 5, 1958; children: Michael, Thomas, Nancy, David. BS, Okla. State U., 1966; MEd, U. Okla., 1976. Cert. elem. tchr., elem. prin. 6th grade tchr. Ponca City (Okla.) Pub. Schs., 1966-67; 1st and 6th grade tchr. Peru Elem. Sch., Auburn, Nebr., 1967-69; 4th grade tchr. Woodland Hills Sch., Lawton, Okla., 1971-76; asst. prin. Douglass Learning Ctr., Lawton, Okla., 1976-78; prin. Lincoln Elem. Sch., Lawton, Okla., 1978-84, Hugh Bish Elem., Lawton, Okla., 1984—. Recipient Disting. Achievement award Lawton Bd. Edn., 1992, Adminstr. of Yr. award Lawton Area Reading Coun., 1993, Arts Adminstr. of Yr. award Okla. Alliance for Arts, 1993, Nat. Blue Ribbon Sch. Recognition award 1993-94, D.A.R.E. Adminstrn. award Lawton Police Dept., 1993. Mem. ASCD, Okla. Reading Coun., Okla. ASCD, Lawton Area Reading Coun., Elem. Prins. Assn. (pres. 1986-87), PEO Sisterhood. Democrat. Methodist. Avocations: reading, walking, music, cooking. Home: 3122 NW Denver Ave Lawton OK 73505-3864 Office: Lawton Pub Schs 751 NW Fort Sill Blvd Lawton OK 73507-5421

MCKEOWN, WILLIAM PHILIP, lawyer; b. Quebec City, Que., Can., Mar. 10, 1936; m. Elizabeth McKeown; 4 children. B Comm., McGill U., Montreal, Que., 1956; LLB, U. Toronto, 1959. Queen's counsel Ont. 1983. Counsel Dept. Health, Province Ont., Toronto, 1962-63, McMillan Binch, Toronto, 1963-64, Can. GE, Toronto, 1965-74; dep. dir. investigation and rsch. Bur. Competition Policy, Ottawa, Ont., 1974-77; ptnr. Stephens French McKeown, Toronto, 1977-86; judge Supreme Ct. Ont., Toronto, 1986-90, Gen. Divsn., Ont. Ct. Justice, Toronto, 1990-93, Trial Divsn., Fed. Ct. Can., Ottawa, Canada, 1993—2002; judge, chmn. Competition Tribunal, Ottawa, 1993—2002; counsel Fasken, Martineau, DuMoulin, LLP, 2002—. Mem. Can. Bar Assn., Toronto Lawyers' Club. Office: Fasken Martineau DuMoulin LLP 4200 TD Bank Tower PO Box 20, Stn Toronto Dom Toronto ON Canada M5K1N6

MC KEOWN, WILLIAM TAYLOR, magazine editor, author; b. Ft. Collins, Colo., July 4, 1921; s. Stuart Ellison and Eunice Harris (Akin) Mc K.; m. Lorraine Laredo; children: Elizabeth Ellison, Katherine, Suzanne. AB, Bowdoin Coll., 1942; student, Columbia U. Grad. Sch., 1948. Editor Fawcett Library Series, 1953-56; founding editor True's Boating Yearbook, 1955-56, Popular Boating mag., 1956, editor-in-chief, 1956-62; CEO The Mc Keown Co., N.Y.C., 1993—; editl. dir. Computer Travel Info., 1994—. Travel editor Davis Publs.; outdoor/boating/travel editor Popular Mechanics, 1971-82; sr. editor Outdoor Life, 1983-93. Author weekly NEA syndicated newspaper column American Afloat, 1959-65; contbr. fiction, non-fiction to nat. mags., 1947—; author: Boating Handbook, 1956, Boating in America, 1960. Pilot USAAF, WW II, ETO. Mem. Am. Power Boat Assn., U.S. Power Squadrons, 357 FIghter Group Assn., N.Y. Yacht Club, Overseas Press Club, Royal Danish Yacht Club (Copenhagen), Turtles Internat. Avocation: international competitor in power and sail racing events. Office: The Mc Keown Co 52 Monell Pl Beacon NY 12508-1424

MCKERLEY, ANNETTE ELIZABETH, school system administrator; b. Nashville, Feb. 8, 1951; d. James and Dorothy Ann Shaub; m. Brian Joseph McKerley, May 24, 1997; stepchildren: Marc, Michael, Keith. BS in Educable Mentally Retarded and Psychology, U. Tenn., 1973; MEd in Spl. Edn. and Rehab., U. Memphis, 1979. Cert. tchr. Tenn. Spl. edn. resource tchr. Alcorn County Schs., Cornith, Miss., 1974—76, Decatur County Schs., Decaturville, Tenn., 1977—86; spl. edn. comprehensive devel. class tchr. Harrison County Tng. Ctr. for Exceptional Children, Gulfport, Miss., 1976—77; program/complaince cons. divsn. spl. edn. Tenn. Dept. Edn., Nashville, 1987—92, dir. programs and svcs. divsn. spl. edn., 1993—2000, dir. mgmt. svcs., 2000—; ednl. diagnostician Washington County Schs., Jonesborough, Tenn., 1992—93. Mem.: Delta Kappa Gamma (treas. Beta Mu chpt. 1982—84, pres. 1984—86). Office: Tenn Dept Edn Dvisn Spl Edn 710 James Robertson Pkwy 7th Fl Nashville TN 37243-0380 Fax: 615-532-9412.

MCKERROW, AMANDA, ballet dancer; b. Albuquerque; d. Alan and Constance McKerrow; m. John Gardner. Student, Met. Acad. Ballet, Bethesda, Md., Washington Sch. Ballet. With Washington Ballet Co., 1980-82, Am. Ballet Theatre, N.Y.C., 1982—, soloist, from 1983, prin. dancer, 1987—. Toured Europe with Washington Ballet; danced in Margot Fonteyn Gala at Metropolitan Opera House; featured in Pavlova Tribute film, also many guest appearances; leading roles in Ballet Imperial, La Bayadere, Manon, Birthday Offering, Dim Lustre, Donizetti Variations, Giselle, Graduation Ball, The Leaves Are Fading, Nine Sinatra Songs, The Nutcracker, Pillar of Fire, Requiem, Romeo and Juliet, The Sleeping Beauty, Les Sylphides, Push Comes to Shove, Symphony Concertante, Symphonic Variations, Theme and Variations, Stravinsky Violin Concerto, Swan Lake, Triad, Duets, Etudes, Coppelia, Voluntaries and Rodeo; created leading role in Bruch Violin Concerto No. 1, Some Assembly Required and Agnus De Mille's The Other. Recipient N.Y. Woman award for dance, 1991; co-winner gold prize for women Moscow Internat. Ballet Competition, 1981. Office: Am Ballet Theatre 890 Broadway New York NY 10003

MC KETTA, JOHN J., JR., chemical engineering educator; b. Wyano, Pa., Oct. 17, 1915; s. John J. and Mary (Gelet) McK.; m. Helen Elizabeth Smith, Oct. 17, 1943; children: Charles William, John J. III, Robert Andrew, Mary Anne. BS, Tri-State Coll., Angola, Ind., 1937; BSE., U. Mich., 1943, MS, 1944, PhD, 1946; D.Eng. (hon.), Tri-State Coll., 1965, Drexel U., 1977; Sc.D., U. Toledo, 1973. Diplomate: registered profl. engr., Tex., Mich. Group leader tech. dept. Wyandotte Chem. Corp., Mich., 1937-40, asst. supt. caustic soda div., 1940-41; teaching fellow U. Mich., 1942-44, instr. chem. engring., 1944-45; faculty U. Tex., Austin, 1946—, successively asst. prof. chem. engring., assoc. prof., then prof. chem. engring., 1951-52, 54—, E.P. Schoch prof. chem. engring., 1970-81, Joe C. Walter chair, 1981-94, prof. emeritus, 1994—. Asst. dir. Tex. petroleum research com., 1951-52, 54-56, chmn. chem. engring. dept., mem. bd. regents, Tri State Univ, 56-, disting. service in trusteeship, 2002, 1950-52, 55-63, dean Coll. Engring., 1963-69; exec. vice chancellor acad. affairs U. Tex. System, 1969-70; editorial dir. Petroleum Refiner, 1952-54; pres. Chemoil Cons., Inc., 1957-73; chmn. Tex. AEC, So. Interstate Nuclear Bd., 1963-70; mem. Tex. Radiation Adv. Bd., 1978-84; chmn. Nat. Energy Policy Com., 1970-72, Nat. Air Quality Control Com., 1972-85; mem. adv. bd. Carnegie-Mellon Inst. Research, 1978-84; pres. Reagans's rep. on U.S. Acid Precipitation Task Force, 1982-88; apptd. mem. Nuclear Waste Tech. Rev. Bd., 1992-97. Author: series Advances in Petroleum Chemistry and Refining (10 vols.); Chmn. editorial com.: series Petroleum Refiner; mem. adv. bd.: series Internat. Chem. Engring. mag; exec. editor: series Ency. of Chem. Processing and Design (68 vols.). Bd. regents Tri-State U., 1957—. Recipient Bronze plaque Am. Inst. Chem. Engrs., 1952, Charles Schwab award Am. Steel Inst., 1973, Lamme award as outstanding U.S. educator, 1976, Joe J. King Profl. Engring. Achievement award U. Tex., 1976, Gen. Dynamics Teaching Excellence award, 1979, Triple E award for contbns. to nat. issues on energy, environment and econs. Nat. Environ. Devel. Assn., 1976, Boris Pregal Sci. and Tech. award NAS, 1978, Internat. Chem. Engring. award, Italy, 1984, Pres. Herbert Hoover award for advancing well-being of humanity and developing richer and more enduring civilization Joint Engring. Socs., 1989, Centennial award exceptional contbn. Am. Soc. Engring. Edn., 1993; named Disting. Alumnus U. Mich Coll. Engring., 1953, Tri-State Coll., 1956; fellow Allied Chem. & Dye, 1945-46; named Disting. fellow Carnegie-Mellon U., 1978; Chem. Engring. Dept. at U. Tex. named The John J. McKetta Ctr. for Excellence in Chem. Engring. Edn. in his honor, 1995, Chem. Engring. Dept. at Tri State U. named The Dr. John J. McKetta Chem. Engring. Dept. in his honor, 1998. Mem. Am. Chem. Soc. (chmn. Central Tex. sect. 1950), Am. Inst. Chem. Engrs. (chmn. nat. membership com. 1955, regional exec. com., nat. dir., nat. v.p. 1961, pres. 1962, service to soc. award 1975), Am. Soc. Engring. Edn., Chem. Markets Research Assn., Am. Gas Assn. (adv. bd. chems. from gas 1954), Houston C. of C. (chmn. refining div. 1954, vice chmn. research and statistics com. 1954), Engrs. Joint Council (dir.), Engrs. Joint Countil Profl. Devel. (dir. 1963-85), Nat. Acad. Engring., Sigma Xi, Chi Epsilon, Alpha Psi Omega, Tau Omega, Phi Lambda Upsilon, Phi Kappa Phi, Iota Alpha, Omega Chi Epsilon, Tau Beta Pi, Omicron Delta Kappa. Home: 5227 Tortuga Trl Austin TX 78731-4501 Office Phone: 512-471-5227. Business E-Mail: mcketta@mail.utexas.edu.

MCKEWEN AMATO, MARY PATRICIA, musician; b. Balt., Jan. 26, 1954; d. Edward Joseph and Ethel Lillian McKewen; m. Samuel Chase Amato, Sept. 24, 1983; children: Elena Cecelia Amato, Antonette McKewen Amato, Angela Mira Amato. Cert. in lieder and chamber music, Am. Inst. Musical Studies, Graz, Austria, 1977; cert. in opera and chamber music, Am. Inst. Musical Studies, 1978; B in Music Edn. magna cum laude, Cath. U. of Am., 1976; MusM magna cum laude, U. Houston, 1979. Asst. music dir. Balt. Opera Co., 1980—85; music dir., condr., pianist Annapolis (Md.) Opera Co., 1986—; music dir., condr. Md. Lyric Opera, Frederick, 1991—98; dir. of music St. Thomas More Cath. Ch., Balt., 1991—; asst. condr., chorus master Washington Summer Opera, 1994—96; dir. choral activities Hood Coll., Frederick, 1995—2004; opera coach, music dir. Peabody Inst. of the Johns

Hopkins U., Balt., 2000—; staff accompanist Towson U., Balt., 2004—; instr., piano Essex Cmty. Coll., Balt., 2004—. Adjudicator Md. Music Educators Assn., 1998—; mem. adv. bd. Children's Chorus of Md., Towson, 1999—. The Messiah-50th Anniversary Performance, 1998, condr. (CDs) A Dream Within a Dream, 1999, conductor, pianist (CD) Instruments of Peace, 1999. Mem., builder Habitat for Humanity, Balt., 1990; mem. MADD, Balt., 1986, Md. Cath. Conf., Annapolis, 1995. Recipient 1st pl., Houston Chamber Music Soc. Competition, 1979. Mem.: Am. Guild Organists, Nat. Assn. Pastoral Musicians, Am. Choral Dirs. Assn., Sigma Alpha Iota (life; pres. coll. chpt. 1974—76, Province Leadership award, Ruby Sword of Honor 1976). Democrat. Roman Catholic. Avocations: running, hiking, travel, reading. Home: 7724 Babikow Rd Baltimore MD 21237 Office: Hood Coll 401 Rosemont Ave Frederick MD 21701 E-mail: pmcamato@comcast.net.

MCKEY, THOMAS J. retired lawyer; b. Detroit, Jan. 9, 1934; s. Thomas J. and Pauline H. (Feys) McK.; m. Lila W. Webber, Sept. 3, 1960; children: Tim, Christopher, Heather, Brenda. BS, USCG Acad., 1955; JD, U. Mich., 1962; MA in Psychology, Antioch U., 1995. Bar: Wash. 1962. With Bogle & Gates, Seattle, 1962-94, ptnr., 1970-94; arbitrator/mediator, pres., bd. dirs. North Pacific Dispute Resolution Svc., 1996—2001. Former chmn. N.W. Admiralty Law Inst., Seattle; mem. permanent adv. bd. Tulane Admiralty Law Inst., New Orleans, 1981—. Former bd. dirs. Bellevue (Wash.) Area Self-Improvement Coun., N.W. Seaport, Seattle, Coast Guard Mus. N.W., Seattle, Friends of Youth, Seattle, Resource Inst., Seattle. Comdr. USCGR, ret. Mem. Maritime Law Assn. U.S. (exec. com. 1979-82), Seattle C. of C. (former chmn. maritime steering com.).

MCKHANN, GUY MEAD, pediatrician, educator; b. Boston, Mar. 20, 1932; s. Charles Fremont and Emily (Priest) McKhann; m. Katherine E. Henderson, Nov. 30, 1957 (div. 1983); children: Ian, James, Emily, Guy, Charles; m. Marilyn S. Albert, Sept. 27, 1997; children: Joshua, Katie. Student, Harvard U., 1948—51; MD, Yale U., 1955. Intern N.Y. Hosp., 1955—56; asst. resident pediat. Johns Hopkins Hosp., Balt., 1956—57; clin. assoc. NIH, Bethesda, Md., 1957—60; resident neurology Mass. Gen. Hosp., Boston, 1960—63; asst. and assoc. prof. pediat. and neurology Stanford (Calif.) U., 1963—69; prof. neurology Johns Hopkins, Balt., 1969—, Kennedy prof. neurology, head neurology dept., 1969—88, prof. neurology, dir. Zanvyl Krieger Mind Brain Inst., 1988—2000; acting dir. for clin. activities Nat. Inst. Neurol. Diseases and Stroke NIH, 2000—01. Served with USPHS, 1957—60. Scholar, Markle, 1964—69, Joseph P. Kennedy Jr., 1963—69. Fellow: AAAS; mem.: Inst. Medicine, Soc. Neuroscis., Am. Neurochem. Soc., Am. Neurol. Assn., Alpha Omega Alpha. Achievements include research in on normal and abnormal human nervous system. Home: 6526 Montrose Ave Baltimore MD 21212-1023 Office: Zanvyl Krieger Mind/Brain Inst Johns Hopkins U 338 Krieger Hall Baltimore MD 21218 E-mail: guy.mckhann@jhu.edu.

MCKIBBEN, HOWARD D. federal judge; b. Apr. 1, 1940; s. James D. and Bernice McKibben; m. Mary Ann McKibben, July 2, 1966; children: Mark, Susan. BS, Bradley U., 1962; MPA, U. Pitts., 1964; JD, U. Mich., 1967. Assoc. George W. Abbott Law Office, 1967-71; dep. dist. atty. Douglas County, Nev., 1969-71, dist. atty., 1971-77; dist. ct. judge State of Nev., 1977-84; judge U.S. Dist. Ct. Nev., Reno, 1984—. Mem. Nev. Bar Assn., Am. Inns of Ct. (pres. Nev. chpt. 1986-88). Methodist. Avocations: tennis, golf, racquetball. Home: PO Box 588 Verdi NV 89439-0588 Office: US Dist Ct 400 S Virginia St Ste 804 Reno NV 89501-2197

MCKIBBIN, WILLIAM ALEX, artist; b. Phila., May 7, 1940; s. William A. and Jane Harrison (Pippin) McK.; m. Dorothy K. McKibbin, Jan. 26, 1963; children: Erin P., William Alex IV. Student, Barnes Found., Merion, Pa., 1958-59, 60-61; BFA, Temple U., Phila., 1963; MFA, The Claremont Grad. Sch., 1965; postgrad., U. Hartford, Conn., 1967-68. Instr. Mt. Pleasant (Del.) Jr. High Sch., 1965-66, U. Hartford Coll. Basic Studies, 1966-68; instr. evening divsn. Cen. Conn. State Coll., 1967-68; instr. Aegean Sch. Fine Arts, Paros, Greece, summers 1967-68; asst. prof. Western Coll., 1968-74, acting chair, 1968, 69, 70-71; instr. Cin. Art Acad., 1972-74; asst. prof. Miami U., Oxford, Ohio, 1974-77, assoc. prof., 1977-84, full prof., 1984—. Juried various exhbns. throughout U.S. One-man shows at Evansville (Ind.) Mus. Arts and Scis., Main Artist Gallery, 1985, Museum of the Maya Culture, Chetumal, Q.R., Mex., 2002, Casa de la Cultura de Cancun, Mex., 2001; exhibited in over 200 exhbns. including group shows at East Carolina U., Greenville, N.C., 1981, Second Crossing Gallery, Valley City, N.D., 1981, 93, Okla. Art Ctr., Oklahoma City, 1981-82, U. N.D., Grand Forks, 1982, 85, Art Chgo. Internat. Art Expo, 1982-90, Trenton (N.J.) State Coll., 1983, Fort Hays (Kans.) State U., 1984, 88, Owensboro (Ky.) Mus. Fine Arts, 1984, Middletown (Ohio) Fine Arts Ctr., 1985, Cameron U., 1986, Springfield (Mo.) Art Mus., 1988-90, 94, 2003, La Fond Galleries, Inc., Pitts., 1994, numerous others; represented by Zaks Gallery, Chgo., The Art Exch., Columbus, Boody Fine Arts, Inc., St. Louis, Nancy Mulle Assocs., Cleve., Steinway Gallery, Chapel, N.C., Yvonne Rapp Gallery, Louisville, Orbe Gallery, Cancun, Mex., Gallery Henoch, N.Y.C.; pub. collections include Pomona Coll., Claremont, Calif., Thomas More Coll., Ft. Mitchell, Ky., The Springfield Mus., Ind. U. East, Richmond, Evansville (Ind.) Mus. Art and Sci., Art Ctr., Inc., South Bend, Ind., Cin. Art Mus., Grinnell (Iowa) Coll., Ft. Hays State U., Hays, Kans., Des Moines Art Ctr., Charles H. MacNider Mus., Mason City, Iowa, Ohio State U., Columbus, Clark State U., Springfield, Ohio, U. N.C., Chapel Hill, Ohio State U. Law Sch., So. Alleghenies Mus. of Art, Loretto, Pa., Blanden Meml. Art Mus., Ft. Dodge, Iowa, Ark. Arts Ctr., Little Rock, Taos Art Mus., Taos, N.Mex., Casa de la Cultura de Cancun, Mex., Fitton Ctr. for Creative Arts, Hamilton, Ohio; pvt. collections, 70 corporate collections; reprodns. of work appear in (books) Watercolor Bold and Free, 1980, Figure Drawing, 5th edit., 2000, The Watercolor Solution Book, 1988, Splash I, 1990, The Art of Responsive Drawing, 1992, Splash II, 1993, Watercolor Step-By-Step, 1993, Watercolor School, 1993, Collins' Artist's Manual, 1995, Splash IV, 1995, The Encyclopedia of Watercolour Landscape Techniques, 1996, Painting Shapes and Edges, 1996, North Light Illustrated Book of Watercolor Techniques, Splash VIII, 2004; (mags.) Artist's Mag., The Bull., Jiangsu Pictorial, China, Watercolor Magic, Tropo a la una, Cancun, Mex., Internat. Artist, 2000; work included as cover art on CDs Music for Winds, The Miami Wind Quintet, Vol. 1, 1995, Vol. 2, 1996. Recipient Cert. of Merit Tyler Sch. of Art Temple U., Gen. Alumni Assn., 1991, First State Bank award for watercolor Vechten-Lineberry, Taos Art Mus., 17 cash and purchase awards from various orgns. Home: 34 Loch Lee Williamsville NY 14221 Studio: PO Box 31 77760 Akumal QR Mexico Office: 435 Tacoma Ave Buffalo NY 14216

MC KIE, TODD STODDARD, artist; b. Boston, Apr. 25, 1944; s. Roy Albert and Lois E. (Barwood) McK.; m. Judy Anne Kensley, Apr. 10, 1967; 1 son, Jesse Simon. BFA, RISD, 1966. Vis. artist RISD, 1977, Mass. Coll. Art, 1977-78, Sch. Mus. Fine Arts, Boston, 1979; artist-in-residence Isabella Stewart Gardner Mus., Boston, 2000; lectr. schs. and museums. Exhibited in one-man shows Harcus Krakow Gallery, Boston, 1977, 79, 83, Aquavella Gallery, N.Y.C., 1978, 79, 81, Hokin-Kaufman Gallery, Chgo., 1983, Helander Gallery, N.Y.C., 1990, 92, Toale Gallery, Boston, 1994, Barbara Singer Gallery, Boston, 1996, Greenville (S.C.) Mus. of Art, 1997, Littlejohn Contemporary Art, 1999, Clark Gallery, Lincoln, Mass., 2001, Victoria Munroe Gallery, Boston, 2003, 2004, Centre d'Art, Marnay-sur-Seine, France, 2003; exhibited in group shows including, Whitney Museum Am. Art, N.Y.C., 1975, Harcus Krakow Gallery, 1975, 78, Mus. Fine Arts, Boston, 1975, 77, 81, Acquavella Gallery, 1976, 78, 79, 81, Inst. Contemporary Art, Boston, 1979, Addison Gallery Am. Art, 1981; represented in permanent collections including Fogg Art Mus., Cambridge, Mass., M.I.T., Cambridge, Brockton (Mass.) Mus., Mus. Fine Arts, Boston, DeCordova Mus., Lincoln, Mass., Rose Art Mus. Brandeis U., Mus. of Modern Art, Fidelity Investments, Microsoft; also numerous pvt. collections. Recipient Blanch E. Colman award Colman Found., 1974; Artists fellowship Villa Montalvo, 1995; Artists Found. fellow Boston, 1975, 89. Home and Office: 82 Holworthy St Cambridge MA 02138-4579 Office Phone: 617-492-0471.

MCKILLIP, PATRICIA CLAIRE, operatic soloist; b. Milw., Apr. 28; d. Lester J. and Ruth J. (Lohneis) McK.; m. Mark Richard McKillip, June 16, 1990. BA in English-Drama, Creative Writing, Lit., Alverno Coll., 1980, MusB in Applied Music, 1981; postgrad., Wis. Conservatory of Mus., 1981-82; MS in Fine Arts Edn., U. Wis., Milw., 1996; postgrad., The Juilliard Sch., 1982-84, Am. Acad. Dramatic Arts, 1983-84, Adelphi U., 1984; MA in English-Creative Writing and Lit., U. Wis., Milw., 1997; postgrad., Milw. Inst. Art and Design, 2003—. Soloist Amadeus Opera Co.; instr. vocal music seminars various high schs., N.Y. Co-founder, co-dir. The Masque Consort, N.Y.C., 1990-91, exec. v.p., 1991; v.p., co-founder Creative Learning Assocs.; instr. Cardinal Stritch Coll., Milw., 1994—. Performed with numerous opera cos. including The Florentine Opera Co., Music Under the Stars Prodns., Milw. Opera Co., Westchester Lyric Opera Co., Profl. Opera Workshop at Lincoln Ctr., Met. Opera Co., N.Y. Grand Opera Co., Monteverdi Opera Guild Prodns., Republic Opera Co., La Puma Opera Co., and other chamber, theater and folk groups; puppeteer, costumer, designer Puppet Art Troupe; performed in over 50 mus. shows and prodns., 6 solo recitals, also medieval concerts, choruses, orchestras, oratorio; 42 other recitals; author: (poetry and artwork) Springdrift, 2003; contbr. poetry to lit. pubs. Exec. v.p. Masque Consort, a multi-media theatrical orgn. Music dept. scholar Alverno U.; named Woman of Yr., Am. Biographical Inst. Bd. Internat. Rsch., 2003. Mem. AFTRA, SAG, Nat. Assn. Music Tchrs., Music Educators Nat. Conf. (treas.), Internat. Platform Assn., Wis. Fedn. Music Clubs, Music Clubs Am., Am. Guild Mus. Artists, Q'ahal-Liturgical Music Soc., Acad. Am. Poets, Milw. Artists Resource Network, Walker's Point Ctr. for Arts, Delta Omicron (v.p., chaplain, warden Gamma Gamma chpt., WMA State and Regional Vocal award 1978, Star of Delta Omicron award 1980, 40 music medals from state and dist. WSMA), Alpha Sigma Tau. Democrat. Roman Catholic. Avocations: dance, creative writing, art. Home: 4860 S 69th St Greenfield WI 53220-4452 E-mail: pcmckil@aol.com.

MCKIM, PAUL ARTHUR, management consultant, retired petroleum executive; b. Milford, Conn., Feb. 1, 1923; s. Arthur Wheatley and Helen Agnes (Brennan) McK.; m. Daisy Flora Brown, June 18, 1945; 1 dau., Meredith Ann. Student, Lamar Inst. Tech., 1940-42; BS in Chem. Engring., La. State U., 1943, MS, 1947, PhD, 1949; grad. Advanced Mgmt. Program, Harvard, 1959; grad. Aspen Inst. Humanistic Studies Exec. Program, 1970. With Ethyl Corp., 1949-62, asst. gen. mgr. research and devel. operations, 1958-62; v.p., gen. mgr. rsch. and devel. Atlantic Refining Co., Phila., 1962-66; v.p. Atlantic Richfield Co., 1966-78; v.p. comml. devel. Arco Chem. Co., 1966-69, v.p. nuclear operations and comml. devel., 1969-73; exec. v.p. Sinclair Koppers Co., 1973; pres. Arco Polymers, Inc., 1974-78; asst. to pres. Tex. Eastern Corp., 1978-80, v.p., 1980-84, sr. v.p., 1985-88. Chmn. US Organizing com. for 12th World Petroleum Congress, Houston, 1987. Past bd. mgrs. Franklin Inst. Research Labs; past vice chmn. bd. mgrs. Spring Garden Coll., Phila. Coll. Art.; past vice chmn. World Affairs Council of Phila. Served to lt. (j.g.) USNR, 1944-46. Mem. AIChE, Merion (Pa.) Cricket Club, Houston Club, Shreveport (La.) Country Club, Alpha Chi Sigma, Omicron Delta Kappa, Tau Beta Pi, Phi Lambda Upsilon, Phi Kappa Phi, Delta Kappa Epsilon. Home: 5405 Holly Springs Dr Houston TX 77056-2021

MCKIM, RUTH ANN, financial planner; b. Keokuk, Iowa, Nov. 26, 1932; d. Carl Edward and Ruby Irene (Martin) McKim; m. William James Ashbrook, Aug. 15, 1959 (div. 1974); children: Leslie, Diane Hodges. BS, U. Louisville, 1955, MS in Cmty. Devel., 1977. Dir. art therapy Ky. Bapt. Hosp., Louisville, 1955—56; co-dir. art therapy Norton-Children's Hosps. Inc., 1956—57; dir. art therapy NKC Hosps., 1957—59; rschr. Bd. Aldermen, 1976; pub. rels. staff Dept. Consumer Affairs, 1976—78; realtor assoc. Century 21, 1979—86; fin. planner Nat. Life Vt., 1986—. Tutor Ky. Assn. Specific Perceptual-Motor Disability, Louisville, 1970—74. Author: Banking Survey, 1977. Arts festival com., 1975—77; coord. Louisville Food Day, 1978; vol. and art donor PBS, 1985—88; voter registration canvasser, 1976, 1978, 1982; active Rep. Nat. Com., Rep. Presdl. Task Force, Nat. Rep. Senatorial Com., Nat. Rep. Congl. Com. Com.; sec., treas. 2d Presbyn. Ch., Louisville, 1975—76. Recipient Rep. Presdl. Legion of Merit medal, Order of Merit; scholar Allen R. Hite Art Inst., 1952—54; Bd. Realtors scholar, 1979—. Mem.: Inst. Community Devel. Assn., Ky. Artists and Craftsmen, Louisville Craftsmans Guild (life), U. Louisville Alumni Assn. Republican. Avocation: oil and acrylic painting. Home: No 43 410 Mockingbird Valley Rd Louisville KY 40207-1318 Office Phone: 502-895-9514.

MCKIM, SAMUEL JOHN, III, lawyer; b. Pitts., Dec. 31, 1938; s. Samuel John and Harriet Frieda (Roehl) McK; children: David Hunt, Andrew John; m. Eugenia A. Leverich. AA cum laude, Port Huron Jr. Coll., 1959; BA cum laude, U. Mich., 1961, JD cum laude, 1964. Bar: Mich. 1965, U.S. Dist. Ct. (so. dist.) Mich. 1965, U.S. Ct. Appeals (6th cir.) 1969, U.S. Supreme Ct. 1994. Assoc. Miller, Canfield, Paddock and Stone, PLC, Detroit, Bloomfield Hills, 1964-71, sr. mem., 1971—, head state and local tax sect., 1985—, chmn. tax dept., 1989-94, mng. ptnr., 1979-85, chmn., mng. ptnr., 1984-85. Mem. tax coun. State Bar Mich., 1981-94, chmn. state and local tax com. real property sect., 1982-90; adj. prof. law sch. Wayne State U., 1993-. Assoc. editor Mich. Law Rev. Bd. dirs., past chmn. Goodwill Industries of Greater Detroit, 1970-2000; dir. Goodwill Industries Found., 1982-95; tchg. elder Presbyn. Ch., Stevens min. Fellow: Am. Coll. Tax Counsel; mem.: ABA, Barrister's Soc., Detroit Bar Assn., Mich. Bar Assn., Mariner Sands Country Club, Port Huron Golf Club, Nomads Club, Order of Coif, Phi Delta Phi. Home: 8351 Lakeshore Rd Lexington MI 48450 Address: 6403 SE Brandywine Ct # 124 Stuart FL 34994 Office: Miller Canfield Paddock & Stone 150 W Jefferson Ave Ste 2500 Detroit MI 48226-4416 Office Phone: 313-496-7546. Business E-Mail: mckim@millercanfield.com.

MCKINLEY, DOUGLAS WEBSTER (WEBB MCKINLEY), consultant; b. Bay City, Mich., May 26, 1917; s. Frank and Amelia Ingraham (Webster) McK.; m. Martha Slade, July 12, 1945; children: Judith Anne, Martha Webster (Mrs. Duane Kissick), Mary Slade (Mrs. Joel Bingham), Jane Elizabeth; m. Roberta Baughman Burton, Nov. 25, 1994; m. Peggy Lighter. BA, Amherst Coll., 1939. Reporter Ann Arbor News, 1940-41, 46-47; staff AP, Detroit, 1947-53, Rome, 1953—60, chief Middle East services, 1960-65, news editor world services, 1965-82; cons. to agys. in developing nations Zimbabwe, Malaysia, Morocco, Tunisia, 1982—. Author: Trouble in the Middle East. Served to maj. AUS, 1941-45. Mem. Phi Kappa Psi. Home: 619 Old Plantation Rd Jekyll Island GA 31527-0723

MCKINLEY, ELLEN BACON, priest; b. Milw., June 9, 1929; d. Edward Alsted and Lorraine Goodrich (Graham) Bacon; m. Richard Smallbrook McKinley, III, June 16, 1951 (div. Oct. 1977); children: Richard, Ellen Graham, David Todd, Edward Bacon. BA cum laude, Bryn Mawr Coll., 1951; MDiv, Yale U., 1976; STM, Gen. Theol. Sem., N.Y.C., 1979; PhD, Union Theol. Sem., N.Y.C., 1988. Ordained deacon Episcopal Ch., 1980, as priest Episcopal Ch., 1981. Intern St. Francis Ch., Stamford, Conn., 1976-77; pastoral asst. St. Paul's Ch., Riverside, Conn., 1979-80, curate, 1980-81; asst. St. Saviour's Ch., Old Greenwich, Conn., 1982-90; interim asst. Trinity Ch., Princeton, NJ, 1990—91; priest assoc. All Saints Ch., Princeton, NJ, 1992—97, St. Christophers Ch., Chatham, Mass., 1997—. Episc. election com. Diocese of Conn., 1986—87, com. on human sexuality, 1987—90, donations and bequests com., 1987—90; major chpt. mem. Trinity Cathedral, Trenton, NJ, 1992—96; interim rector All Saints Ch., Princeton, NJ, 1993. Sec. Greenwich Com. Drugs, 1970—71; active Episcopal Women's Caucus; bd. dirs. Greenwich YWCA, 1971—72, Chatham Old Village Assn., 1998—2004. Mem.: Colonial Dames Am.

MCKINLEY, JAMES FRANK, JR., retired manufacturing executive; b. Chgo., Feb. 17, 1943; s. James F. Sr. and Annabell I. (Williams) McK.; m. Sharon M., Dec. 7, 1968; children: James P., Scott J., Rebecca L. BS, Monmouth Coll., 1964; MS, Ill. Inst. Tech., 1966; MBA, Stanford U., 1987. Salesman Joseph T. Ryerson & Son, Chgo., 1961-66, Scot Forge Co., Cicero, Ill., 1966-71, v.p. sales, 1971-76, exec. v.p., 1976-85, pres., COO, 1985-92, pres., CEO, COO, 1992—; pres., bd. dirs. Ringmasters (formerly Ovaco Ajax), Wayne, Mich., 1996—; ptnr. N.Am. Forgemasters, 1997, vice-chmn., 2001, ret., 2002; owner Classic Electric Boats, 2004—. Dir. Fox Waterway Agy., state office, 1997—, chmn. 2000—. Capt. USCG Aux., Fox Lake, Ill., 1985—; dir. Allendale Sch., Lake Villa, Ill., 1983-96; regent Milw. Sch. Engring., 1995; McHenry County mem. Sheriff Merit Commn., 2000. Mem. Am. Soc. Metals, Forging Industry Rsch. Found., Forging Industry Assn. (bd. dirs. 1986—, gov. coun. 1990—, dir. 1998, v.p. 1999, pres. 2000—), Ill. St. Andrews Soc. (bd. govs., v.p. 1996-97), Profl. Capts. Assn., McHenry C. of C. (chmn. 1999). Republican. Avocations: boating, skiing, scuba diving, golf. Home: 5764 Staysail Ct Cape Harbour Preserve Cape Coral FL 33914-2572 Office Phone: 715-358-8326. E-mail: jmkinleyjr@msn.com.

MCKINLEY, JIMMIE JOE, business executive; b. Bertram, Tex., July 23, 1934; s. Joseph Crofford and Velma Anne (Barnett) McK. AA, Kilgore Coll., 1953; BJ, U. Tex., 1955; MS, U. Ky., 1964. Asst. libr. Bethel Coll., McKenzie, Tenn., 1961-63, reference libr., 1966-70, acting head libr., 1970-71; owner, mgr. Longview Book Co., Tex., 1974—. Former mem., bd. dirs. Longview-Piney Woods chpt. ARC; trustee Bethel Coll., 1977-86. Mem. East Tex. Hist. Assn., Gregg County Hist. Soc., Burnet County Heritage Soc., History Club East Tex., East Tex. Oil Mus. Guild (pres. 1996-97), U.S. Lighthouse Soc., Presbyterian. Home: PO Box 2106 Longview TX 75606-2106 Office: PO Box 1748 Longview TX 75606-1748

MC KINLEY, JOHN KEY, retired oil company executive; b. Tuscaloosa, Ala., Mar. 24, 1920; s. Virgil Parks and Mary Emma (Key) McK.; m. Helen Grace Heare, July 19, 1946; children: John Key Jr., Mark Charles. BS in Chem. Engring. U. Ala., 1940, MS in Organic Chemistry, 1941, LL.D. (hon.), 1972; grad., Advanced Mgmt. Program, Harvard U., 1962; LL.D. (hon.), Troy State U., 1974. Registered profl. engr., Tex. With Texaco Inc., 1941-86, asst. dir. research, 1957-59, asst. to v.p., 1959-60, mgr. comml. devel., 1960, gen. mgr. petrochem. dept., 1960-67, v.p. petrochem. dept., v.p. in charge supply and distbn., 1967-71, sr. v.p. worldwide refining, petrochems., also supply and distbn., 1971, pres., dir., 1971-80, pres., chief operating officer, chmn. exec. com., 1980, chmn. bd., pres., chief exec. officer, 1980-83, chmn. bd., chief exec. officer, 1983-86, ret., 1986. Bd. dirs. emeritus Federated Dept. Stores, Inc. Patentee for chem. processing. Hon. bd. dirs. Met. Opera Assocs.; nat. chmn. Met. Opera Centennial Fund, 1980; bd. dirs. The Ams. Soc.; mem. Bus. Coun. Maj. AUS, 1941-45, ETO. Decorated Bronze Star; recipient George Washington Honor medal Freedoms Found., 1972; Andrew Wellington Cordier fellow Columbia U.; named to Ala. Bus. Hall of Fame, 1982, Ala. Acad. Honor, 1983, State of Ala. Engring. Hall of Fame, 1992. Fellow Am. Inst. Chem. Engrs.; mem. Am. Petroleum Inst. (hon. dir.), Wee Burn Country Club, Links Club, Brook Club, Augusta Nat. Golf Club, Blind Brook Country Club, North River Yacht, Sigma Xi, Tau Beta Pi, Gamma Sigma Epsilon, Kappa Sigma. Office: 1 Canterbury Grn Stamford CT 06901-2032

MCKINLEY, PAUL, state legislator; Mem. Iowa State Senate, 2001—, mem. edn. com., ranking mem. transp. com., vice chair ways and means com., mem. small bus., econ. devel. and tourism com. Republican. Home: Rt 5 Box 101H Chariton IA 50049 E-mail: paul_mckinley@legis.state.ia.us.

MCKINLEY-HAAS, MARY, artist; b. St. Louis; d. Lee Carrington and Florence (Dowden) McK.; m. Saul Haas; children: Christopher, Matthew. BA, Smith Coll.; student, Art Students League, 1973-74, Nat. Acad. Design, 1965-66, Studio and Forum Stage Design. Head costume design dept. ABC-TV, NYC, 1968-73. Solo exhbns. include Tarlowe Gallery, Westhampton Beach, N.Y., 1974, Fontbonne Gallery, St. Louis, 1977, Gallery Yssa, N.Y.C., 1979, Vered Gallery, East Hampton, N.Y., 1981, Netherlands Bank & Ludlow-Hyland Gallery, N.Y.C., 1981, U. Tex., Austin, 1988, RVS Fine Art, Southampton, N.Y., 1990, TSS Gallery, N.Y.C., 1992, U. Tex., Austin, 1992, TAI Gallery, N.Y.C., 1999; group exhbns. include Guild Hall, East Hampton, N.Y., 1974, 75, 76, 78, 81, 85, 96, Parrish Art Mus., Southampton, 1975, 76, 78, 81, Water Mill Mus., 1983, 92, Vared Gallery, East Hampton, N.Y., 1985, Lincoln Ctr., N.Y.C., N.Y., 1989, 90, Queens Coll. Art Ctr., Flushing, N.Y., 1991, Dorothy Chandler Pavillion, L.A., Calif., 1993, Stony Brook U. Art Gallery, N.Y., 1994, Women in Art and Culture, Beijing, 1995, Elite Gallery, Moscow, 1995, Nat. Mus. Women in Arts, Washington, 1996, Soho 20 Gallery, N.Y.C., 1998—, Canajoharie (N.Y.) Libr. and Art Ctr., 2000, Weill Cornell Med. Libr., N.Y.C., 2002, others; represented in permanent collections at Nat. Mus. of Women in the Arts, Washington, Tari Women's Cultural Ctr., Papua, New Guinea, Fontbonne Coll., St. Louis, No. Trust Naples (Fla.); also numerous pvt. collections; costume designer for Broadway and network TV shows, Harkness Ballet, Holiday on Ice, others. Mem. United Scenic Artists, Women in the Arts, N.Y. Artists Equity. Address: 280 Lafayette St Loft5B New York NY 10012-3303

MCKINNELL, HENRY A. pharmaceutical company executive; BA, U. B.C.; MBA, PhD, Stanford U. Joined Pfizer, Inc., Tokyo, 1971; pres. Pfizer Asia, Hong Kong; chief fin. officer, pres. med. technology group Pfizer, Inc., exec. v.p., 1992—99; pres. Pfizer Pharms. Group, prin. oper. divsn., 1997—2001; COO Pfizer, Inc., NYC, 1999—2000, pres., 1999—2001, chmn., CEO, 2001—. Mem. Presidential Advisory Council on HIV/AIDS; bd. dirs. ExxonMobil Corp., Moody's Corp., John Wiley & Sons, Inc., Trilateral Commn., Bus. Coun.; chmn. emeritus Pharm. Rsch. and Mfrs. of Am.; vice chmn. Com. Econ. Devel.; chmn. Food and Drug Law Inst.; chmn. Bus. Roundtable. Bd. trustee NY Pub. Libr., NYC Police Found., Econ. Club of NY; chmn. Stanford U. Grad. Sch. of Bus. Adv. Coun.; chmn. emeritus, Bus.-Higher Edu. Forum. Fellow, NY Acad. of Medicine. Office: Pfizer Inc 235 E 42d St New York NY 10017-5755*

MCKINNELL, ROBERT GILMORE, retired zoology, genetics and cell biology educator; b. Springfield, Mo., Aug. 9, 1926; s. William Parks and Mary Catherine (Gilmore) McK.; m. Beverly Walton Kerr, Jan. 24, 1964; children: Nancy Elizabeth, Robert Gilmore, Susan Kerr. B in Naval Sci., U. Notre Dame, 1946; AB, U. Mo., 1948; BS, Drury Coll., 1949, DSc (hon.), 1993; PhD, U. Minn., 1959. Rsch. assoc. Fox Chase Cancer Ctr., Phila., 1958-61; asst. prof. biology Tulane U., New Orleans, 1961-65, assoc. prof., 1965-69, prof., 1969-70; prof. zoology U. Minn., Mpls., 1970—76, prof. genetics and cell biology St. Paul, 1976—99, prof. emeritus, 1999—. Vis. scientist Dow Chem. Co., Freeport, Tex., 1976; guest dept. zoology U. Calif., Berkeley, 1979; Royal Soc. guest rsch. fellow Nuffield dept. pathology John Radcliffe Hosp., Oxford U., 1981-82; NATO vis. scientist Akademisch Ziekenhuis, Ghent, Belgium, 1984; faculty rsch. assoc. Naval Med. Rsch. Inst., Bethesda, Md., 1988; secretariat Third Internat. Conf. Differentiation, 1978; organizer, secretariat 6th Internat. Conf. on Pathology of Reptiles and Amphibians, 2001; mem. amphibian com. Inst. Lab. Animal Resources, NRC, 1970-73, mem. adv. coun., 1974; mem. panel genetic and cellular resources program NIH, 1981-82, spl. study sect., Bethesda, 1990. Author: Cloning: Amphibian Nuclear Transplantation, 1978, Cloning, A Biologist Reports, 1979; sr. editor: Differentiation and Neoplasia, 1980, Cloning: Leben aus der Retorte, 1981, Cloning, of Frogs, Mice, and other Animals, 1985, (with others) The Biological Basis of Cancer, 1998, (with D.L. Carlson) Pathology of Reptiles and Amphibians, 2002, also symposium procs. in field; mem. editl. bd. Differentiation, 1973—; mem. bd. advisors Marquis Who's Who; contbr. articles to profl. jours. Served to lt. USNR, 1944-47, 51-53. Recipient Outstanding Teaching award Newcomb Coll., Tulane U., 1970; Disting. Alumni award Drury Coll., 1979, Morse Alumni Tchg. award U. Minn., 1992; Rsch. fellow Nat. Cancer Inst., 1956-58, Prince Hitachi award Japanese Found. Cancer Rsch., 1998; Sr. Sci. fellow NATO, 1974. Fellow AAAS, Linnean Soc. (London); mem. Am. Assn. Cancer Rsch. (emeritus), Am. Assn. Cancer Edn. (sr.), Am. Assn. History of Medicine, Indian Soc. Devel. Biology (lifetime emeritus), Internat. Soc. Differentiation (pres. 1994-96), Minn. Acad. Medicine, Gown-in-Town Club, Sigma Xi. Office: 140 Gortner Lab Biochemistry 1479 Gortner Ave Saint Paul MN 55108 Office Phone: 612-624-2285. Business E-Mail: mckin002@umn.edu.

MCKINNEY, ALEXANDER STUART, retired neurologist; b. N.Y.C., Feb. 3, 1933; s. John McDowell and Katherine Elizabeth (Morse) McK.; m. Carolyn Clifton Braman, Aug. 15, 1958 (div. July 1985); children: James, David, Mark; m. Susan Lowe Childress, July 30, 1985; children: Josephine, Mary, Jennifer. AB, Princeton U., 1955; MD, Columbia U., 1959. Diplomate Am. Bd. Neurology. Intern St. Luke's Hosp., N.Y.C., 1959-60; resident N.Y. Neurological Inst., 1960-63; prof. neurology Emory U., Atlanta, 1965-85; pvt. practice Mountain Med. Assocs., Clyde, N.C., 1985-95; chief of staff Haywood County Hosp., Clyde, N.C., 1989-90. Contbr. articles to profl. jours. Served to lt. comdr. USNR, 1963-65. Fellow Am. Acad. Neurology, Royal

Soc. Medicine; mem. N.C. Med. Soc. (vice councillor 1991-94), N.C. Neurol. Soc. (pres. 1992). Avocations: travel, gardening. Home: 9 Charles Wesley Dr Waynesville NC 28786-3066 E-mail: ssmck@charter.net.

MCKINNEY, BETSY, state legislator; b. Bangor, Maine, Mar. 24, 1939; BS, Bentley Coll., 1972. Accountant, N.H.; mem. dist. 24 N.H. Ho. Rep., mem. budget com., 1977-81, 87-88, mem. regulated revenues com. Del. N.H. Constl. Conv., 1984. Treas. Friends of the Libr., 1988—; chmn. Old Home Day, 1990, treas., 1978—; chmn. Rockingham County Exec. Com., 1991-92; mem. Londonderry Charter Commn., 1995; mem. Libr. Bldg. Com., 1995-96; treas. N.H. OWLs, 1994—. Recipient Citizen of the Yr. award City of Londonderry, 1987. Mem. Londonderry C. of C. (treas. 1980-88). Republican. Roman Catholic. Home and Office: 3 Leelynn Cir Londonderry NH 03053-2326

MCKINNEY, CAROLYN, educational association administrator, educator; BS in Early Childhood Edn., U. N.C., Greensboro; M in Elem. Edn., Gardner-Webb U. Elem. sch. tchr. Winston-Salem/Forsyth County Schs.; elem. tchr Sedge Garden Sch. Math. and Sci.; 2n and 3d gr. tchr. Kernersville Elem. Sch.; tchr. Gen. Greene Sch., Guilford County; pres. N.C. Assn. Educators, Raleigh, 2001—. Mem.: NEA (alt. dir. bd. dirs.), N.C. Assn. Educators (bd. dirs., Terry Sanford award for excellence in edn. 1997), Forsyth Assn. Classroom Tchrs. (pres.). Office: NC Assn Educators PO Box 27347 Raleigh NC 27611

MCKINNEY, CHARLES CECIL, investment company executive; b. Newdale, N.C., Nov. 30, 1931; s. Sherbert Day and Florence Van (Hall) McK.; children— Emry Lynn, Robin Ashley, Marc Jason; m. Suzanne Reeves, Apr. 3, 1988. Student, U. Tenn., 1950-52; BA, U. N.C., 1957. V.p., creative dir. J.T. Howard Advt., 1957-68; chmn. bd., chief exec. officer McKinney & Silver, Raleigh, N.C., 1968-90; chmn., pres., chief exec. officer Onyx Corp., 1991—. Trustee N.C. Symphony, Raleigh, 1983-87; bd. visitors U. N.C., Chapel Hill, 1989-91, Kenan Flagler Sch. Bus., 1985-94; mem. Nat. Trust for Historic Preservation Coun., 2002-04. Recipient profl. awards Mem. N.C. Mus. Art, Sphinx Club, Carolina Country Club, Figure Eight Yacht Club. Republican. Home: 1006 Harvey St Raleigh NC 27608-2332

MCKINNEY, CYNTHIA ANN, former congresswoman; b. Atlanta, Georgia, Mar. 17, 1955; d. Billy and Leola McKinney. BA, U. So. Calif., 1978; postgrad., Ga. State U., U. Wis.; Tufts U. Former instr. Clark Atlanta U., Atlanta Met. Coll.; mem. Ga. Ho. of Reps., 1988-92, U.S. Congress from 4th and 11th Ga. dist., 1993—2003; mem. banking and fin. svcs. com., com. housing and cmty. devel. 103rd Congress from 11th Ga. dist.; mem. internat. rels. com. internat. ops. and human rights 103rd-106th Congress from 11th Ga. dist., mem. nat. security com.; mem. NAACP, congress. black caucus and prog. caucus; Frank H.T. Rhodes Class of '56 prof. Cornell U., Ithaca, NY, 2003—. Vis. prof. Cornell U., Ithaca, NY, 2003—. Recipient Diplomatic fellow, Spellman Coll., 1984. Democrat. Office: Cornell U Rhodes Class of '56 Profs Ithaca NY 14853*

MCKINNEY, DONALD LEE, magazine editor; b. Evanston, Ill., July 12, 1923; s. Guy Doane and Cora Redfield (Brenton) McK.; m. Mary Frances Joyce, Dec. 14, 1958; children— Jennifer Joyce, Douglas Guy. AB, U. N.C., 1948. Salesman textbooks John Wiley & Sons, N.Y.C., 1949-52; freelance writer mostly comic books with some short articles and fiction, 1952-54; asst. mng. editor True mag., N.Y.C., 1955-62; editor articles Saturday Evening Post, 1962-69; spl. features editor N.Y. Daily News, 1969-70; mng. editor McCalls mag., N.Y.C., 1969-86; Gonzales prof. journalism U. S.C., Beaufort, 1986-90, prof. emeritus, 1990—. Author: Magazine Writing That Sells, 1994; reporter, book reviewer. Served with USNR, 1943-46. Democrat. Home: 10520 Shadowlawn Dr Raleigh NC 27614 *I learned early that it is important to speak up if you think you are being treated unfairly; sometimes it's true, and nobody else will complain if you don't. I also learned that in my business, and probably in most others, it is best to always say what you think. Truth is usually more helpful than any assortment of euphemisms, and it also saves a lot of worry over who you have lied to and just what you've said. Truth is not only the best policy— by all odds it's the easiest to keep track of.*

MCKINNEY, E. KIRK, JR., retired insurance company executive; b. Indpls., Mar. 27, 1923; s. E. Kirk and Irene M. (Hurley) McK.; m. Alice Hollenbeck Greene, June 18, 1949; children: Kirk Ashley, Alan Brooks, Nora Claire McKinney Hiatt, Margot Knight. AB, U. Mich., 1948. Asst. treas. Jefferson Nat. Life Ins. Co., Indpls., 1949-52, asst. to pres., asst. treas., 1952-53, treas., asst. to pres., 1953-55, v.p., treas., 1955-59, pres., 1959-90, chmn. bd., 1970-90; vice chmn. bd. Somerset Group Inc., 1986-89; ret., 1990. Corp. rels. com. U. Mich.; former pres., former CEO, bd. govs., treas., bd. dirs., exec. com. Indpls. Mus. Art; past bd. dirs. (hon.) Greater Indpls. Progress Com.; former vice chmn. Indpls.-Marion County Bd. Ethics; former dir. Park Tudor Sch., Cmty. Svc. Coun. Indpls., Hosp. Devel. Corp., Ind. Repertory Theater; past adv. com. Indpls. Retirement Home; former bd. dirs., and pres. Episcopal Cmty. Svcs., Inc.; former vice chmn., life trustee Nature Conservancy; mem. adv. bd. Ind. U., Purdue U.; active Indpls. Symphony Orch.; former bd. dirs. Ind. Pub. Broadcasting Soc.; bd. dirs. Indpls. Civic Theater, 2001—, Athenaeum Found., 2000—. Mem. Life Office Mgmt. Assn. (bd. dirs. 1981-83), Am. Coun. Life Ins. (state v.p. 1973-75, dir., exec. com. 1976-79), Assn. Ind. Life Ins. Cos. (pres. 1969-71), Indpls. C. of C., Sigma Chi. Clubs: Economic of Indpls. (bd. dirs.). Democrat. Home: 250 W 77th St Indianapolis IN 46260-3608 Office: 1330 W 38th St #100 Indianapolis IN 46208-4103 Office Phone: 317-925-2223. Personal E-mail: ekirkjr@earthlink.net.

MCKINNEY, FRANK, music educator; b. Dade City, Fla., Apr. 1, 1953; s. Henry McKinney and Lucille Beeson, William Lawrence Beeson (Stepfather); m. Cara Lynn Nereim, July 31, 1988; m. Mary Ramsey, Sept. 30, 1972 (div.); children: Maurice Ramsey, Brett. MusB Edn., Fla. State U., 1976. Cert. tchr. Fla. Band/music tchr. Columbia County Schools, Evans, Ga., 1976—82; band/chorus dir. Pasco H.S., Dade City, 1982—86; band dir. Raymond B. Stewart Mid. Sch., Zephyrhills, Fla., 1986—88, Jackson Heights Mid. Sch., Oviedo, Fla., 1988—92, Indian Trails Mid. Sch., Winter Springs, Fla., 1992—. Clinician Volusia All-County Band, Daytona Beach, Fla., 2001; clinician/guest condr. 10th Dist. Honor Band, Augusta, Ga., 2002; guest condr. Savannah River Winds, Augusta, 2002. Mem.: Music Educators Nat. Conf., Fla. Music Educators Assn. (Music Enrollment award 1996—98), Fla. Bandmasters Assn. (Music Enrollment award 1998—2001, Five Yr. Superior award 2000). Office: Indian Trails Mid Sch 415 Tuskawilla Rd Winter Springs FL 32708

MCKINNEY, GEORGE HARRIS, JR., training systems analyst; b. Birmingham, Ala., Nov. 23, 1943; s. George Harris and Elizabeth Dickey (Fikes) McK.; m. Lynda Jeanne Ponder, June 26, 1965 (div. Aug. 18, 1992; children: Michael Thomas, Carol Elizabeth; m. Tambri Sue Hillis, Aug. 19, 1992. BS in Polit. Sci., U.S. Air Force Acad., 1965; MS in Psychology, Troy State U., 1977. Commd. 2d lt. U.S. Air Force, 1965, advanced through grades to lt. col., 1981, fighter pilot, 1965-85, ret., 1985; tng. sys. cons. in pvt. practice, Milton, Fla., 1985—. Author tech. reports. Decorated D.F.C. (5), Air medal (26), Purple Heart, Meritorious Svc. medal (3). Mem. Order of Daedalians, USAFA Assn. Grads., Air Force, Assn., Am. Def. Preparedness Assn. Avocations: whitetail deer hunting, fishing. Home: 3101 Chippewa Dr Milton FL 32571-9603

MCKINNEY, HARRY WEBB, computer company executive; b. Upland, Calif. BS in Elec. Engring., MS in Elec. Engring., Univ. So. Calif. Sales engring. Hewlett-Packard Co., Palo Alto, Calif., 1969—70, various positions, 1970—88, gen. mgr., 1988—90, gen. mgr. PC software divsn. Sunnyvale, Calif., 1992—94, gen. mgr. home products divsn., 1994—99, pres. bus. customer orgn. Palo Alto, Calif., 1999—2002, exec. v.p. merger integration & orgnl. effectiveness, 2002—03, exec. v.p. strategic change & global excellence, 2003—. Office: Hewlett-Packard 3000 Hanover St Palo Alto CA 94304

MCKINNEY, JAMES CLAYTON, electronics executive, electrical engineer; b. Charleston, W.Va., June 3, 1940; s. George Clayton and Leona (Adams) McK. BSE.E., W.Va. Inst. Tech., 1963. Mem. staff Sta. WMON, Montgomery, W.Va., 1961-63; stringer AP, Charleston, W.Va., 1961-63; with FCC, Washington, 1963-87, chief ops. br., 1969-73, chief monitoring div., 1973, chief enforcement div., 1974, dep. chief Field Ops. Bur., 1974-80, chief Field Ops. Bur., 1980-81, chief Pvt. Radio Bur., 1981-83, chief Mass Media Bur., 1983-87; dep. asst. to Pres., dir. White House Mil. Office Washington, 1987-89; chmn. Advanced TV Systems Com., Washington, 1989-96; CEO Model HDTV Sta. Project, Inc., 1996-97. Chmn. U.S. del. UN Conf. on Radio, Geneva, 1986.; mem. U.S. Dels., Geneva, 1978-79, Can., 1984, Italy, 1985, Mexico, 1986, S.Am., 1986, Fed. Republic Germany, 1990; mem. presdl. dels., NATO, UN, Mexico, USSR, Can., Eng., Finland, Econ. Summit, 1987-88; U.S. Spokesman High Definition TV Conf., Geneva, 1989. Author: (with Eliot Maxwell) Future of Electronic Information Handling at the FCC—Blue Print for the 80's, 1980; (with G.A. Fehlner) Direct Broadcast Satellites in the United States, 1985; New Look at AM Radio, 1986, HDTV Approaches the End Game, 1991. Vice chmn. Montreux Medal Award Com., 1990-95; chmn. High Definition TV World Conf., 1990-93; chmn. strategic planning group for Internat. Consultative Com. for Radio, Dept. State, 1990-91; bd. dirs. Bowler Found., 1990-95, PICA Found., Inc., 1996-97, HDTV Sta. Project, Inc., 1996-97. Recipient Outstanding Fed. Exec. award FCC, 1979, 80, 82, 83, 85, 86; Presdl. Rank award for disting. exec. svc., 1985, Gold medal for disting. fed. svc., 1987, TV Engring. Achievement award, 1992, NAB award of honor, 1996, Broadcast Pioneers' Disting. Svc. award, 1996; W.Va. Broadcasters Disting. West Virginian, 1997. Fellow Radio Club Am., Soc. Broadcast Engrs. (sr.), Broadcast Pioneers, Soc. Motion Picture and TV Engrs. (presdl. proclamation 1991); mem. Fed. Exec. Assn., Cosmos Club of Washington. Episcopalian. Home: 10055 Heather Lake Ct W Jacksonville FL 32256-3595

MCKINNEY, JERRY WAYNE, retired journalist; b. Esperanza, Texas, Sept. 17, 1937; s. Lee Parker McKinney and Elsie Margaret Haass; m. Violet Elizabeth Davenport, Oct. 1959 (div. Oct. 1969); m. Valda Kay Cooper, Feb. 12, 1972; children: Kathleen Low, Ellen. Announcer, comml. mgr. Sta. KVOU Radio, Uvalde, Tex., 1959-62; announcer Sta. K-SIX Radio, Corpus Christi, Tex., 1962-66; reporter, editor Corpus Christi Caller-Times, 1966-74; polit. editor Albuquerque Tribune, 1974-79; mgr. pub. rels. Mountain Bell Telephone, Albuquerque, 1979-80; press sec. Congressman Joe Skeen Washington, 1980-85; Tokyo bur. chief Voice of Am., Washington, 1993-95, corr., 1985-93, 95-99, mng. editor news divsn., 1999—2001, ret., 2001; press sec. Congressman Joe Skeen, Washington, 2001—02. Mem. exec. com. Rep. Party N.Mex., Albuquerque, 1979-80; mem. exec. com. Chaparral chpt. Girl Scouts Am., Corpus Christi, 1972-74. With USN, 1955-59. Mem. Soc. Profl. Journalists (past pres. N.Mex. profl. chpt., past dep. dir. region 9), Corpus Christi Press Club (pres. 1971-72), Overseas Press Club Am., Fgn. Corr. Club Japan (hon. mem., fgn. corr.). Avocations: reading, travel.

MCKINNEY, JOHN ADAMS, JR., lawyer; b. Washington, Mar. 10, 1948; s. John A. and Cleo G. (Turner) McK., m. Carol A. Cowen, Dec. 22, 1970; children: John III, Thomas. BA, Principia Coll., 1970; JD, Coll. William and Mary, 1973. Bar: N.J. 1973. Assoc. Mason, Griffin & Pierson, Princeton, N.J., 1973-77; gen. atty. Nabisco, Inc., East Hanover, N.J., 1977-79; asst. counsel Republic Steel Corp., Cleve., 1979-84; atty. and sr. atty. AT&T, Berkeley Heights, N.J., 1984-90; ptnr. McCarter & English LLP, Newark, 1990—2003; mem. Wolff & Samson PC, West Orange, NJ, 2003—. Adj. prof. Sch. of Law, Seton Hall U., 1997—. Co-author: The RCRA Practice Manual, 2d edit., 2004; co-editor: CERCLA Enforcement, 1996. Trustee Hackettstown (N.J.) Free Pub. Libr., 1998—, Drumthwacket Found., 2003—. Mem. ABA (vice-chair sect. natural resources energy and environ. law solid and hazardous waste com. 1990-98, chair, teleconf. programs 1994-97), N.J. Bar Assn. (dir. environ. law sect. 1992-96, chair 1996-97). Office: Wolff & Samson PC One Boland Dr West Orange NJ 07052-3698 Office Phone: 973-530-2036.

MC KINNEY, JOSEPH CRESCENT, retired bishop; b. Grand Rapids, Mich., Sept. 10, 1928; s. Joseph Crescent and Antoinette (Theisen) McK. Student, Seminaire de Philosophie, Montreal, Can., 1948—50; STL, Collegio di Propaganda Fide, Rome, 1954. Ordained priest Roman Cath. Ch., 1953. H. s. prof. St. Joseph Sem., Grand Rapids, Mich., 1954—62; asst. pastor Sacred Heart Parish, Mt. Pleasant, Mich., 1962—65; pastor St. Francis Parish, Conklin, Mich., 1965—68; asst. chancellor Diocese of Grand Rapids, 1965—68; pastor St. Andrew Cathedral, Grand Rapids, 1968—69; ordained titular bishop of Lentini and aux. bishop Grand Rapids, 1968—85; vicar gen. Diocese of Grand Rapids, 1968—2001; pastor Our Lady Of Consolation, Rockford, Mich., 1985—98. Adminstr. Sede Vacante, 1969; pastor St. Stephen's Ch., Grand Rapids, 1971—77, Sacred Heart Parish, Muskegon Heights, Mich., 1977—.

MCKINNEY, JUDSON THAD, broadcast executive; b. Sacramento, Aug. 21, 1941; s. Judson Bartlet and Mildred Eoline (Taylor) McK. Student, Sacramento State U., 1959-61, Western Bapt. Bible Coll., 1961-62, Am. River Coll., 1962-63. Prodn. dir. Sta. KEBR, Sacramento, 1962-65; prodn. dir. Sta. KEAR, Merced, Calif., 1965-68; sta. mgr. Sta. KAMB, 1968-75, Sta. KEAR, San Francisco, 1975-78, 79-88, WFME, Newark, 1978; western regional mgr. Family Stas. Inc., 1988—. Pres. Abounding Love Ministries, 2000—. V.p. New Millennium Strings, 2003—; chmn. 1st. Bapt. Ch. San Francisco, 1985—91; recording engr. 1st Bapt. Ch. Los Altos, Calif. Mem. Gideons. Republican. Baptist. Office: Family Stations Inc 290 Hegenberger Rd Oakland CA 94621-1436

MCKINNEY, LARRY J. federal judge; b. South Bend, Ind., July 4, 1944; s. Lawrence E. and Helen (Byers) McK.; m. Carole Jean Marie Lyon, Aug. 19, 1966; children: Joshua E., Andrew G. BA, MacMurray Coll., Jacksonville, Ill., 1966; JD, Ind. U., 1969. Bar: Ind. 1970, U.S. Dist. Ct. (so. dist.) Ind. 1970. Law clk. to atty. gen. State of Ind., Indpls., 1969-70, dep. atty. gen., 1970-71; ptnr. Rodgers and McKinney, Edinburgh, Ind., 1971-75, James F.T. Sargent, Greenwood, Ind., 1975-79; judge Johnson County Cir. Ct., Franklin, Ind., 1979-87, U.S. Dist. Ct. (so. dist.) Ind., Indpls., 1987—, chief judge, 2001—. Presbyterian. Avocations: reading, jogging. Office: US Dist Ct 204 US Courthouse 46 E Ohio St Indianapolis IN 46204-1903

MCKINNEY, MICHAEL WAYNE, government and public affairs representative; b. Pomona, Calif., Aug. 30, 1967; s. Jerry D McKinney and Patricia Lee Hazleton; m. Linda Christine Van Zandt, Nov. 15, 2004. BA, Polit. Sci., Calif. Luth. U., Thousand Oaks, 1986—91. Mgr., govtl. affairs So. Calif. Edison/Edison Int., Rosemead, 1999—; corp. rep. So. Calif. Edison, Rosemead, 1991—99; legislative analyst/comm. GTE Calif., Thousand Oaks, 1990—91. Polit. cons., Anaheim Hills, Calif., 1991—. Author: (book: genealogy) The Family McKinney. Pres./chmn. Young Republicans, Pasadena, 1995—96. R-Consevative. Catholic. Home: 984 South Creekview Lane Anaheim Hills CA 92808 Office: Southern California Edison/Edison Intern 2244 Walnut Grove Avenue Rosemead CA 91770 Personal E-mail: mwlc_mckinney@hotmail.com.

MC KINNEY, MICHAEL WHITNEY, trade association executive; b. San Angelo, Tex., Aug. 23, 1946; s. Wallace Luster and Mitzi Randolph (Broome) McK.; m. Martha LaNan Hooker, Feb. 24, 1973; children: Wallace Blake, Lauren Brooke. BA in Govt., U. Tex., Austin, 1973. Adminstrv. asst. to lt. gov. State of Tex., Austin, 1968-69, adminstrv. asst. to gov., 1969-73; asst. to dir. Tex. Water Quality Bd., Austin, 1973-76; chief of staff Tex. Alcoholic Beverage Commn., 1976-83; v.p. for industry affairs Wholesale Beer Distbrs., Tex., 1984-88, exec. v.p., chief exec. officer, 1989—. Bd. govs. Keep Tex. Beautiful, 1997—98; mem. Travis County Zoo Task Force, 1986, Senate Com. on Fees and Grants, 1982—83; bd. dirs. Friends of Gov.'s Mansion, 1993—97, Bob Bullock Tex. State History Mus. Found., 2002—. Recipient Bert Ford award Tex. Alcholic Beverage Commn., 1996, Pres. award for legis. excellence Nat. Beer Wholesalers Assn., 1998, F.X. Matt award Brewers Assn. Am., 2002. Mem.: Nat. Wholesale Beer Assn. Execs. (pres. 2001—02, chmn. 2002—, Industry Svc. award 2002), Austin Assembly, Sam. Houston Soc., Knights of the Symphony, Austin Club (bd. dirs. 1989—, exec. com. 1994—, Mem. of Yr. 1994), Austin Country Club, Masons (32 deg., K.T.), Phi Kappa Psi. Home: 1708 Intervail Dr Austin TX 78746-7630 Office: 823 Congress Ave Ste 1313 Austin TX 78701-2434

MCKINNEY, PATRICIA J. automobile company executive; Student, Memphis State U. Various positions in automotive bus., 1968-96; pres., owner Nissan of Brandon, 1996—. Mem. Nat. Auto Dealers Assn., Auto Import Assn., Tampa New Car Dealers Assn., Brandon C. of C. Office: 9920 Adamo Dr Tampa FL 33619-2618

MCKINNEY, RENOVIA M. music educator; MusB, U. So. Maine, Gorham, 1996—2001. Cert. Profl. Tchr. Maine, 2001. Music tchr. Maine Sch. Adminstrv. Dist., South Berwick, 2001—03, Falmouth Sch. Dept., Maine, 2003—. Recipient William B. Wise Academic Athlete award, U. So. Maine, 1997. Mem.: Music Educators Nat. Conf., Maine Music Educators Assn. Republican. Avocations: stitchery, book binding, travel, golf, paper crafts. Personal E-mail: renovia@yahoo.com.

MCKINNEY, RONALD W. lawyer; b. Greenville, S.C., Mar. 23, 1948; s. William R. and Doris (Chadwick) McK.; m. Kathleen Crum, Jan. 13, 1979; children: William, Kathleen. BA, Furman U., 1970; MA, U. N.C., 1973; JD, U. S.C., 1978. Bar: S.C. 1978. Atty. S.C. Consumer Advocate's Office, Columbia, 1978-81; ptnr. Duggan, Reese & McKinney, Greer, S.C., 1981-95; city atty. City of Greenville, S.C., 1995—, interim city mgr., 2000. Chair Greenville County Transportation Com., 1994-95. Mem. ABA, S.C. Bar Assn., Internat. Mcpl. Lawyers Assn., S.C. Mcpl. Attys. Assn. (pres. 1997). Methodist. Avocations: travel, reading. Office: City of Greenville PO Box 2207 Greenville SC 29602-2207 E-mail: mckinnr@greatergreenville.com.

MCKINNEY, ROSS ERWIN, civil engineering educator; b. San Antonio, Aug. 2, 1926; s. Roy Earl and Beatrice (Saylor) McK.; m. Margaret McKinney Curtis, June 21, 1952; children: Ross Erwin, Margaret E., William S., Susanne C. BA, BSCE, So. Meth. U., 1948; SM, MIT, 1949, ScD, 1951. San. scientist S.W. Found. for Research and Edn., San Antonio, 1951-53; asst. prof. MIT, 1953-58, assoc. prof., 1958-60; prof. U. Kans., 1960-63, chmn. dept. civil engring., 1963-66, Parker prof. civil engring., 1966-76, N.T. Veatch prof. environ. engring., 1976-93, prof. emeritus, 1993—. Adj. prof. Tongji U., Shanghai, Peoples Rep. China, 1985; v.p. Rolf Eliassen Assocs., Winchester, Mass., 1954-60; pres. Environ. Pollution Control Services, Lawrence, Kans., 1969-73; adj. prof. environ. engring. Duke U., 1997-2002. Author: Microbiology for Sanitary Engineers, 1962, Environmental Pollution Control Microbiology, 2004; editor: Nat. Conf. on Solid Waste Research, 1964, 2d Internat. Symposium for Waste Treatment Lagoons, 1970. Mem. Cambridge (Mass.) Water Bd., 1953-59, Lawrence-Douglas County Health Bd., 1969-76, Kans. Water Quality Adv. Council, 1965-76, Kans. Solid Waste Adv. Council, 1970-76, Kans. Environ. Adv. Bd., 1976-85. Served with USNR, 1943-46. Recipient Harrison P. Eddy award, 1962, Rudolph Hering award, Water Pollution Control Fedn., 1964, U.S. Presdl. Commendation, 1971, Environ. Quality award, EPA Region VII, 1979, Chancellors Tchg. award, U. Kans., 1986, Lifetime Achievement award, Enviro.-Water Resources Inst./ASCE, 2001. Mem.: AAAS, NAE, ASCE (hon.), Am. Soc. Microbiologists, Am. Chem. Soc., Water Pollution Control Fedn. (Thomas R. Camp medal 1982), Am. Water Works Assn., Kans. Water Pollution Control Assn. (hon. Gordon M. Fair medal 1991), Tau Beta Pi, Chi Epsilon, Kappa Mu Epsilon, Sigma Tau, Sigma Xi. Achievements include patent for water treatment process. Home: 750 Weaver Dairy Rd # 248 Chapel Hill NC 27514-1493 E-mail: remck@mindspring.com.

MCKINNEY, SALLY VITKUS, state official; b. Muncie, Ind., Aug. 6, 1944; d. Robert Brookins and Mary (Mann) Gooden; m. Alan George Vitkus (div. Jan. 1979); m. James Larry McKinney, Feb. 1, 1986. AA, William Woods U., 1964; BS, U. Ariz., 1966; postgrad., U. Nev., Las Vegas, 1966-68. Tchr. Las Vegas Day Sch., 1972—76; salesperson Globe Realty, Las Vegas, 1976—79; owner, pres. Realty West, Las Vegas, 1979—96; chief investigator State of Nev. Real Estate Divsn., 1996—2000; prin., owner McKinney Realty, Las Vegas, 2000—; corp. broker, dir. bus. and devel. Real Estate Temps, Las Vegas. Rec. sec. Clark County Rep. Cen. Com., Las Vegas, 1982, 1st vice chmn., 1985; vice chmn. Nev. Rep. com., 1986, chmn., 1987-88; mem. Assistance League Las Vegas; state chmn. Nev. Rep. Party. Recipient award Nat. Assn. Home Builders, 1981, 82, 83. Mem. Nat. Assn. Realtors, Las Vegas Bd. Realtors, Greater Las Vegas C. of C., Gen. Fedn. Womens Clubs (nominee Outstanding Young Woman Am. 1979, exec. bd. 1980-82), Jr. League Las Vegas, Mesquite Club (chmn. pub. affairs com. 1986-87, past pres., secret witness exec. bd. 1994-96, vice chmn.). Presbyterian. Avocations: bridge, fly fishing. Home: 511 Mountain Dell Ave Henderson NV 89012-2509 Office Phone: 702-271-4611.

MCKINNEY, WILLIAM MARK, retired geology educator; b. Spring Valley, NY, Dec. 26, 1923; s. John and Mabel Genevieve (Munger) McKinney; m. Georgia Anna Coleman, June 2, 1951 (dec. Mar. 23, 2003); 1 child, Mark Warren (dec.). Student, U. NC, Raleigh and Chapel Hill, 1940—42; BA, New Sch. U., NYC, 1948; MA, U. Fla., 1949, PhD, 1958. Cons. Ga. Dept. Pub. Health, Atlanta, 1953—58; asst. prof. So. Oreg. U., Ashland, 1958—63; asst. prof. to prof. U. Wis., Stevens Point, 1963—88; ret., 1988. Guest rschr. Lowell Obs., Flagstaff, Ariz., 1969—78. Contbr. articles to profl. jours., chpts. to books. Pres. Unitarian Soc., Medford, Oreg., 1959—62, Stevens Point, Wis., 1970—73. With USN, 1943. Mem.: Geol. Soc. Am., Phi Kappa Phi. Unitarian Universalist. Avocations: comparative religion, astronomy, railroads. Home: 1540 NW Kings Blvd Corvallis OR 97330

MCKINNEY, WILLIAM T. psychiatrist, educator; b. Rome, Ga., Sept. 20, 1937; BA cum laude, Baylor U., 1959; MD, Vanderbilt U., 1963. Diplomate Nat. Bd. Med. Examiners (mem. psychiatry test com. 1982-87, chmn. 1984-87); cert. Am. Bd. Psychiatry and Neurology (sr. examiner 1979-90, bd. dirs. 1991—, mem. rsch. com., co-chair part I test com., chair added qualifications in geriatric psychiatry test com., mem. part II audio visual com., mem. disability accomodations com., rep. to residency rev. com.). Intern in medicine Bowman Gray Sch. Medicine, Wake Forest U., Winston-Salem, N.C., 1963-64; resident dept. psychiatry Sch. Medicine, U. N.C., Chapel Hill., 1964-66, Sch. Medicine, Stanford (Calif.) U., 1966-67; clin. assoc. psychosomatic sect. adult psychiatry br., tng. specialist, asst. br. chief NIMH, Bethesda, Md., 1967-69; asst. prof. psychiatry dept. psychiatry Sch. Medicine, U. Wis., Madison, 1969-72, assoc. prof. psychiatry, 1972-74, prof. psychiatry, 1974-93; Asher prof. of psychiatry dept. psychiatry and behavioral scis., dir. Asher Ctr. for Study and Treatment of Depressive Disorders Med. Sch., Northwestern U., Chgo., 1993—. Part-time clin. pvt. practice, Bethesda, 1967-69; NIMH rsch. career investigator Sch. Medicine, U. Wis., Madison, 1970-75, rsch. psychiatrist Primate Lab., 1974-93, affiliate sci. Wis. Regional Primate Rsch. Ctr., 1974-93, affiliate prof. psychology dept. psychology, 1974-93, chmn. dept. psychiatry, 1975-80, dir. Wis. Psychiat. Rsch. Inst. Ctr. Health Scis., 1975-80; sr. staff psychiatrist William S. Middleton Meml. VA Hosp., Madison, Wis., 1974-93; rschr. sub dept. animal behaviour U. Cambridge, Eng., 1974; mem. rsch. rev. com. VA Behavioral Scis., 1976-79; Abbott Sigma XI Club lectr., 1976; Milw. Psychiat. Hosp. lectr., 1977; mem. program adv. com. and workshop chmn. Dahlem Found. Internat. Conf. on Depression, Berlin, 1982; U. Minn. lectr. at Festshrift, 1982; cons. grad. sch. U. Minn., 1982; fellow Ctr. Advanced Study in Behavioral Scis., Stanford, Calif., 1983-84; mem. external adv. bd. Clin. Rsch. Ctr. Dept. Psychiatry U. N.C., Chapel Hill, 1984—, cons., bd. advisors clin. rsch. fellow tng. program dept. psychology, 1988—; William F. Orr lectr. Vanderbilt U., 1985; vis. prof. dept. psychiatry U. Tex. Health Scis. Ctr., Dallas, 1986, U. Utah Sch. Medicine, Salt Lake City, 1987, U. Minn. Sch. Medicine, Mpls., 1988; cons. biol. scis. tng. br. divsn. manpower and tng. programs NIMH, 1975-76, mem. psychiatry spl. tng. com. 1983, plenary lectr., Clearwater, Fla., 1987, cochairperson Workshop on Non-Human Primate Models of Psychopathology, 1987, mem. biol. psychopathology spl. rev. com., 1992—; mem. sci. core group MacArthur Found. Mental Health Rsch. Network I: The Psychobiology of Depression and Other Affective Disorders, 1988-93; vis. spkr. So. Calif. Psychiat. Soc., L.A., 1988; plenary lectr. Soc. Biol. Psychiatry ann. meeting, Montreal, 1988; vis. prof. Dalhousie U. Sch. Medicine, N.S., 1989, HCA Riveredge Hosp., Chgo., 1989, U. Pa., Phila., 1991, U. N.Mex., Albuquerque, 1992, Northwestern U., Chgo., 1992; invited spkr. Animal Models in Psychopharmacology Symposium, Duphar, Amsterdam, 1990; vis. spkr., cons. CIBA-GEIGY, Basel, Switzerland, 1990; mem. minority instns. rsch. devel. rev. com. Alcohol, Drug Abuse and Mental Health Adminstrn., 1990; guest

spkr. Inst. Pa. Hosp., Phila., 1991; reviewer Human Frontier Sci. Program, 1992—; external cons. dept. psychiatry Mental Health Clin. Rsch. Ctr. U. Tex. Southwestern Med. Ctr., Dallas, 1992—; presenter in field. Author: Animal Models of Mental Disorders: A New Comparative Psychiatry, 1988; co-author: Mood Disorders: Towards a New Psychobiology, 1984; mem. editl. bd. Archives of Psychiatry and Neurol. Scis., Contemporary Psychiatry, 1981-82, Ethology and Sociobiology, Experientia, 1982-89, Trends in Neurosciences, 1982-86, Neuropsychopharmacology, 1987-90; manuscript and book reviewer numerous sci. jours.; contbr. articles to profl. jours. USHPS fellow in biostats. Vanderbilt U., 1962; recipient Beauchamp award Vanderbilt U. Med. Sch., 1963, Rsch. Career Devel. award NIMH, 1975, Rsch. Leave award U. Wis., 1983-84, Am. Acad. Pediats. award, 1991. Fellow Am. Psychiat. Assn. (cons. psychiat. edn. consultation svc. 1983—), Am. Coll. Psychiatrists, Am. Coll. Neuropsychopharmacology (mem. constn. and rules com. 1985-87, mem. ethics com. 1987-89, mem. fin. com. 1990-92, panel chair San Juan, P.R. 1992, panel presenter 1992); mem. Am. Soc. Primatologists, Am. Psychosomatic Soc. (mem. program com. 1975-76), Internat. Primatology Soc., Internat. Coll. Neurobiology, Biol. Psychiatry and Psychopharmacology (lectr. Zurich 1985), Internat. Soc. Devel. Psychobiology, Internat. Soc. Ethological and Behavioral Pharmacology (bd. advisors 1983—), Collegium Internat. Neuro-Psychopharmacologicum, Psychiat. Rsch. Soc., Soc. Neuroscience, Wis. Psychiat. Assn. (chmn. program com. 1972, co-chairperson task force on sexual misconduct and membership edn. 1986-88, pres.-elect 1989-91, pres. 1991-93). Office: Northwestern U Med Sch Dept Psychiatry and Behavioral Scis 303 E Chicago Ave Bldg 9-217 Chicago IL 60611-3072

MCKINNIS, MICHAEL B. lawyer; b. St. Louis, May 31, 1945; s. Bayard O. and Doris (Lammert) McK.; m. Patricia Butow, Aug. 24, 1968; children: Scott, Christopher, Elizabeth. BS, Drake U., 1967; JD, U. Mo., 1970. Bar: Mo. 1970, U.S. Dist. Ct. (ea. dist.) Mo. Ptnr. Bryan Cave, St. Louis, leader firm litigation practice, mem. firm operating group. Editor U. Mo. Law Rev., 1969-70. Mem. ABA, Mo. Bar Assn., Order of Coif, Phi Delta Phi. Office: Bryan Cave 1 Met Sq 211 N Broadway Saint Louis MO 63102-2733

MCKINNISH, RICHMOND D. manufacturing executive; From mem. staff to pres., CEO Carlisle Cos. Inc., Charlotte, NC, 1974—2001, pres., 2001—, CEO, 2001—. Bd. dirs. Carlisle Cos. Inc. Office: Carlisle Cos Inc 13925 Ballantyne Corp Place Charlotte NC 28277*

MCKINNON, ARNOLD BORDEN, retired transportation company executive; b. Goldsboro, N.C., Aug. 13, 1927; s. Henry Alexander and Margaret (Borden) McK.; m. Oriana McArthur, July 19, 1950; children: Arnold Borden Jr., Colin McArthur, Henry Alexander. AB, Duke U., 1950, LLB, 1951; grad. Advanced Mgmt. Program, Harvard U., 1972. Bar: D.C. 1951, N.C. 1966. With Norfolk So. Corp. (formerly So. Ry. System), Norfolk, Va., 1951-2000, from v.p. law to chmn., 1971-92, chmn. exec. com., 1992-2000, ret., 2000. Bd. trustees Chrysler Mus. Art; active Mil. Civilian Liaison Group; bd. dirs. Norfolk Forum, Inc. With U.S. Army, 1946—47. Mem.: ABA, Am. Soc. Corp. Execs., D.C. Bar Assn., N.C. Bar Assn., Rotary, Norfolk German Club, Bonita Bay Club, Cedar Point Club, Met. Club, Chevy Chase Club, Norfolk Yacht and Country Club. Presbyterian. Home: 552 Mowbray Arch Norfolk VA 23507-2130 Office: Norfolk So Corp 3 Commercial Pl Norfolk VA 23510-2108

MCKINNON, CAROLYN ANN, child care center director; b. Bangor, Maine; d. Joseph Russell and Muriel Ann (Capen) Johnston; m. James Coolidge McKinnon, July 24, 1967; step-children: Michael, Ronald, Shaun, Jeannine; children: William, John. RN, D.C. Gen. Hosp., Washington. RN, N.Y., Colo., Maine. Nurse D.C. Gen. Hosp., Washington, Onondago Gen. Hosp., Syracuse, NY, Colo. Gen. Hosp., Denver, Bangor Mental Health Inst., Maine; dir., adminstr. A Small World Day Care Ctr., Bangor; ad copy writer Interactive Mktg. Group, Bangor. Spkr. TV and radio programs, 1997. Author: Insanity, Inc., 1996. Roman Catholic. Avocation: theater and musical organizations. Home: 287 Birch St Bangor ME 04401-4025 Office: A Small World Day Care Ctr 300 Forest Ave Bangor ME 04401-3947 also: Interactive Mktg Group 304 Hancock St Bangor ME 04401-5123

MC KINNON, CLINTON DAN, aerospace transportation executive; b. San Bernardino, Calif., Jan. 27, 1934; s. Clinton Dotson and Lucille V. (McVey) McK.; m. Janice Bernard; children: Holly Jean, Sherri Lynn, Clinton Scott, Lisa Caroline BA, U. Mo., 1956; honorary doctorate, Nat. U., 1987. Page U.S. Ho. of Reps., 1950-52; reporter, photographer, advt. salesman Sentinel Newspaper, San Diego, 1960-62; owner, pres. KSON Radio, San Diego, 1962-85, KSON-FM, San Diego, 1964-85; pub. La Jolla (Calif.) Light Jour., 1969-73; owner House of Hits (book and music pub.), San Diego, 1972—; co-owner KIII-TV, Corpus Christi, Tex., 1964—, KBMT-TV, Beaumont, Tex., 1976—, KUSI-TV, San Diego, 1992—; chmn. CAB, Washington, 1981-84; with spl. projects CIA, 1985-86; chmn., pres. North Am. Airlines, Jamaica, N.Y., 1989—. Author: Bullseye--One Reactor (aka Bullseye Iraq), 1986, The Ten Second Message, 1994, Words of Honor, 1995, Rescue Pilot, 2002, Safe Air Travel Companion, 2002. Chmn. exec. com. Greater San Diego Billy Graham Crusade, 1976. Served as aviator USNR, 1956-60. Recipient Advt. Man of Year award San Diego Advt. and Sales Club, 1971; Radio Sta. Mgr. of Year award Billboard Mag., 1973; Internat. Pres.'s award Youth for Christ, 1975; Man of Distinction award Mexican-Am. Found., 1976; George Washington Honor medal Freedoms Found., 1976; Headliner of Yr. (govt.), San Diego Press Club, 1985; named to Country Music Radio Hall of Fame, 2003. Mem. Country Music Assn. (pres. 1977, Pres. award 1980), C. of C. (dir.), Nat. Assn. Broadcasters (bd. dirs. 1970-74), Calif. Broadcasters Assn. (dir.), Navy League (Media Man of Yr. 1980), Wings Club (bd. govs. 1995-2003, pres. 2002-2003), San Diego Rotary. Achievements include setting Navy helicopter peacetime rescue record of 62 air/sea rescues, 1958; 1st person to close down fed. govt. regulatory agy., CAB, 1984. Office: JFK International N Am Air Ste 250 Bldg 75 Jamaica NY 11430 Office Phone: 718-656-2650.

MCKINNON, DANIEL WAYNE, JR., naval officer; b. St. Joseph, Mo., Apr. 26, 1934; s. Daniel Wayne and Esther Ruth McK.; m. Rae Lynne Hopper, Apr. 21, 1957; 1 child, Daniel W. III. BSBA, U. Mo., 1956; MBA with distinction, U. Mich., 1966; grad. (disting.), Indsl. Coll. Armed Forces, Washington, 1975. Commd. ensign USN, 1956, advanced through grades to rear adm., 1983; exec. asst. to comdr. Naval Supply Systems Command, Washington, 1970-74, dir. supply corps pers., 1982-83, dep. comdr. for inventory and systems integrity, 1983-84, vice comdr., 1984-86, comdr., 1988-91; ship supply readiness officer, supply systems ops. officer Naval Logistic Command, Pacific Fleet, Pearl Harbor, Hawaii, 1975-78; dir. shipbuilding contracts div. Naval Sea Systems Command, Washington, 1978-80; comdg. officer Naval Supply Depot, Subic Bay, The Philippines, 1980-82; dep. dir. for acquisition mgmt. Def. Logistics Agy., Cameron Station, Va., 1986-88; chief Navy supply corps, comdr. Naval Supply Systems, 1988-91; ret. USN, 1991—; pres., CEO NISH (formerly Nat. Industries for Severely Handicapped), Vienna, Va., 1992—. Chmn. Annandale (Va.) Ctrl. Bus. Dist. Planning Com., 1986-91, Pres.'s Com. for Purchase from the Blind and Other Severely Handicapped, Washington, 1986-91; mem. strategic devel. bd. U. Mo.; bd. dirs. Va. Industries for Blind, 1991—, Project Handclasp, 1994—. Decorated D.S.M., Legion of Merit. Recipient Disting. Svc. award Nat. Industries for Severely Handicapped, 1991; Capstone fellow Nat. Def. U., 1986. Mem. Navy Supply Corps Assn. (pres. 1988-91), Nat. Contract Mgmt. Assn. (bd. advisors 1986—), Navy Fed. Credit Union (vice chmn. 1998—), Navy Mut. Aid Assn. (bd. dirs. 1982-91), Comprehensive Tech. Internat. (bd. dirs. 1992—), Army and Navy Club, Beta Theta Pi, Beta Gamma Sigma, Phi Kappa Phi.

MCKINNON, FLOYD WINGFIELD, textile executive; b. Columbus, Ga., Dec. 1, 1942; s. Malcolm Angus and Sarah C. (Bullock) McK.; m. Barbara Evans Roles, June 18, 1966; children: James Wingfield, Sarah Elizabeth, Robert Kent. AB, Washington and Lee U., 1964. Lic. airplane pilot. Pres. Cotswold Industries, Inc., N.Y.C., 1966—, also bd. dirs.; v.p., corp. sec. Cen. Textiles, Inc., S.C., 1984—, also bd. dirs. Arbitrator Am. Arbitration Assn., 1983-2001; bd. dirs. Scarsdale Leasing Corp. Pres. Berkley-in-Scarsdale Assn., 1980; admissions rep. Washington and Lee U., 1979-89, 93-99. Mem. Aircraft Owner's and Pilot's Assn., St. Andrews Soc. N.Y., Union League Club (bd. govs. 1974-77, 88-91, 97—, sec. 1981-83, chmn. admissions com. 1996), (N.Y.C.); Scarsdale Golf Club (bd. govs. 1983-91, pres. 1990-91) (Hartsdale, N.Y.), Bras Coupe Club (exec. com. 1980—) (Maniwaki, Can.). Republican. Episcopalian. Home: 26 Taunton Rd Scarsdale NY 10583-5610 Office: Cotswold Industries 10 E 40th St Rm 3410 New York NY 10016-0367 Business E-Mail: wink@cotswoldindustries.com.

MCKINNON, F(RANCIS) A(RTHUR) RICHARD, utilities executive; b. Delburne, Alta., Can., Mar. 5, 1933; s. John Donald and Ruth Rebecca (Sundberg) McK.; m. Elma Lorraine Lebsack, June 1, 1957; children: Kenneth Richard, Stephen David, Karen Diane. B. Commerce, U. Alta., 1954; postgrad., Stanford Exec. Program, Stanford U., 1982. With Alta. Gas Trunk Line Co. Ltd., Calgary, 1960-75, treas., 1971-75; dir. fin. TransAlta Utilities Corp. (formerly Calgary Power Ltd.), 1975—, treas., 1976-81, v.p. fin., 1981—, Trans Alta Energy Corp., Trans Alta Corp.; pres. ELM FARMS CONS., INC., Calgary, 1996—. Bd. dirs. AEC Power Ltd. Past bd. dirs. Foothills Gen. Hosp., Calgary. Fellow Inst. Chartered Accts. of Alta.; mem. Can. Inst. Chartered Accts., Fin. Execs. Inst. Can. (past chmn., past pres., bd. dirs. Calgary chpt., v.p.), Fin. Execs. Inst. (bd. dirs.). Clubs: Calgary Petroleum, Canyon Meadows Golf and Country. Office: ELM FARM CONS INC 1412 Windsor St NW Calgary AB Canada T2N 3X3

MCKINNON, JAMES BUCKNER, real estate sales executive, writer, researcher; b. Tacoma, Dec. 5, 1916; s. James Mitchell and Rochelle Lenore (Buckner) McK.; m. Mary C. Corbitt, Dec. 1961 (div. June 1963); 1 child, James H.C.; m. Marylyn Adelle Coote, Mar. 12, 1967 (div. May 1977); 1 child, Michelyn; m. Martha Sackmann, June 12, 1977. BA in Internat. Studies, U. Wash., 1983, H.M. Jackson Sch. Police detective Los Angeles Police Dept., 1946-50; bn. security officer 1st med. bn. 1st Marine div. Fleet Marine Force, 1950-53; owner, operator, mgr., dir. promotional sales The Saucy Dog Drive-In, Venice, Calif., 1953-63; salesman new car sales and leasing Burien Mercury, Seattle, 1963-66; real estate salesman and appraiser various firms Seattle, 1966—; instr., lectr. U.S. Naval Support Activity, Sandpoint, Wash., 1964-74. Mem., lectr. NRC 11-8, Naval Postgrad. Sch., Monterey, Calif., 1975-76; Burien Mercury announcer KOMO TV. Author: (poetry) On the Threshold of a Dream, Vol. III, 1992, Best Poems of the 90's, 1992; contbr. to anthologies: Where Words Haven't Spoken, 1993, Fire From Within, 1994; contbr. articles to various newspapers and mil. jours. Mem. br. adv. com. Wash. State YMCA, Seattle, 1994—, treas., 1986-94, 95, mem. so. dist. fin. bd., 1989-93, 94, 95-96. With USN, 1939-53, PTO, Korea. Recipient Wilmer Culver Meml. award Culver Alumni Fictioneers, Seattle, 1979, Silver Poet award World of Poetry Press, 1986, Golden Poet award, 1987-92, Best Poet of the 90's Nat. Libr. of Poetry, 1992, First Place with Editor's Preference award Creative Arts and Scis. Enterprises, 1996; Occidental Coll. scholar, 1935; named to Honorable Order Ky. Cols., 1976; named One of Best New Poets, Am. Poetry Assn. Anthology, 1988; inducted into the Internat. Poetry Hall of Fame, 1996. Mem. Internat. Soc. Authors and Artists (1st place award for 1997 poem), Internat. Platform Assn., U.S. Naval Inst. (life), Internat. Soc. Poets (life), N.W. Writers Conf., Acad. Am. Poets, Ret. Officers Assn. (life), Mensa, Acad. Am. Poets, KP, Masons. Republican. Home: PO Box 4774 Spanaway WA 98387-4051 *Personal philosophy: To realize one's greatest potential pursue goals that hold the greatest meaning in life.*

MCKINNON, RUSSEL FRANCIS DANIEL, professional society administrator; b. Springfield, Mass., Feb. 11, 1944; s. John Phee Joseph McKinnon and Margret Louise Bates; m. Deborah Anne Oplinger, July 11, 1987; 1 child, John. AB in History, Coll. Holy Cross, 1966; M in Mgmt., George Washington U., 1988. Pres. The Mackinnon Co., Alexandria, Va., 1972—; exec. Nat. Rural Electric Coop. Assn., Arlington, Va., 1994—; pres. Internat. Theos Found., Alexandria, 1998—. Photographer Parade Mag., 1989. Lt. USNR, 1966-72. Mem. Am. Soc. Assn. Execs. (cert.), Assn. Meeting Planners. Avocations: skiing, golf. Office: Nat Rural Electric Coop Assn 4301 Wilson Blvd Arlington VA 22203-1867

MCKINNON, WILLIAM MITCHELL PATRICK, surgeon; b. Houston, Mar. 17, 1924; s. William M. and Rosina Mary McKinnon; m. Elizabeth Jean Beall, Oct. 3, 1953; children: William, Stuart, Mary, John, Fraser, David (dec.). Student, St. Michael's Coll., Toronto, Can., 1942, Tex. A&M State U., 1943, U. Tex., 1947; BS maxima cum laude, St. Edward's U., Austin, Tex., 1948; MD, Baylor U., 1952. Diplomate Am. Bd. Surgery; lic. physician, La., N.Y., Tex. Intern Royal Victoria Hosp., Montreal, Can., 1953; resident in surgery 2d surg. divsn. Bellevue Hosp., 1954; asst. resident thoracic surgery Triboro Hosp. for Chest Disease, 1955; asst. resident in surgery Queens Hosp. Ctr., Jamaica, N.Y., 1955, asst. resident in pathology, 1956, assoc. resident, 1957, asst. surgeon, 1959-61; chief resident surgery, fellow in surg. rsch. Maimonides Hosp. of Bklyn., 1958; asst. attending surgeon Flower & Fifth Ave. Hosps., 1961-64, attending surgeon, 1965-67; staff surgeon Alton Ochsner Found. Hosp., 1968-96; staff, dept. surgery Ochsner Clinic, 1968-96, assoc. dir., dept. surgery, 1979-84, co-dir., breast screening, 1982-92; dir. Breast Ctr., Ochsner Clinic, 1992-96. Clin. asst. in surgery SUNY Med. Ctr. Coll. Medicine, 1957-59; asst. surgeon Kew Gardens (N.Y.) Gen. Hosp., 1959-61, Jamaica Hosp., 1960-61; vis. surgeon Met. Hosp. and Bird S. Coler Hosp., 1961-66, Tulane divsn. Charity Hosp., 1968—; dist. med. cons. N.Y. State Edn. Dept. Vocat. Rehab., 1960-67; surg. cons. VA Hosp., Lyons, N.J., 1963-67, E.A. Conway Meml. Hosp., Monroe, La., 1968-79; asst. prof. to assoc. prof. surgery N.Y. Med. Coll., 1961-67; clin. assoc. prof. surgery Tulane U., 1968-92, clinical prof. dept. surgery, 1992—, Tulane U. Hosp. and Clinic, 1997—, Univ. Hosp., 1997—; chief clin. breast disease program, med. dir. Breast Health Ctr., Tulane Cancer Ctr., 1997—; prin. investigator Nat. Surg. Adjuvant and Breast Project Protocols, 1999—, Nat. Surg. Adjuvant Breast and Bowel Project. Contbr. articles to med. jours. Bd. dirs. Am. Cancer Soc., New Orleans, 1953, Komen Found., New Orleans, 1953. Capt. USAF, 1948-52. Recipient 1st prize for med. writing Queensborough Med. Soc., 1957; USPHS rsch. fellow Nat. Heart Inst., 1958. Fellow ACS; mem. AMA, Soc. for Surgery of Alimentary Tract, So. Med. Assn., Am. Gastroenterol. Assn., Societe Internationale de Chirugie, Collegium Internationale Chirugie Digestivae, So. Surg. Assn., New Orleans Surg. Soc. (pres. 1988), Orleans Parish Med. Soc., Tulane Surg. Soc., Alton Ochsner Surg. Soc. (pres. 1985). Avocations: duplicate bridge, woodworking, computers. Home: 1529 Nashville Ave New Orleans LA 70115-4254 Office: Tulane U Med Ctr Dept Surgery SL22 1430 Tulane Ave New Orleans LA 70112-2699 also: Tulane Metairie Clinic 4770 S I 10 Service Rd W Metairie LA 70001-1215 also: Tulane Uptown Clinic 200 Broadway St Ste 230 New Orleans LA 70118-3544 E-mail: wmpm@bellsouth.net., wmckinn@tulane.edu.

MCKINSEY, DAVID STEPHEN, infectious diseases specialist; b. Dallas, Oct. 24, 1955; s. John Jerome and Jacqueline (Ronay) McK. BS cum laude, Tulane U., 1977; MD, U. Mo., 1981. Diplomate Am. Bd. Internal Medicine, Am. Bd. Infectious Diseases. Intern, then resident in internal medicine U. Iowa Hosps. and Clinics, Iowa City, 1981-84; fellow in infectious diseases U. Tenn., Memphis, 1984-86; co-dir. dept. infectious disease Rsch. Med. Ctr., Kansas City, Mo., 1986—; clin. asst. prof. medicine U. Mo., Kansas City, 1986-90; clin. assoc. prof. medicine U. Kans., Kansas City, 1991—2002, clin. prof. medicine, 2002—; med. dir. Health Midwest Pharmacy, Kansas City, 1999—2002. Recipient Outstanding Young Physician award U. Mo., Columbia, 1999. Fellow ACP, Infectious Diseases Soc. Am. (Clinician of Yr. award 1998); mem. AMA, Am. Soc. Microbiology, Soc. Hosp. Epidemiologists Am., Kansas City S.W. Clin. Soc. (pres. 1992). Office: Ste 392 6400 Prospect Ave Kansas City MO 64132-1199 E-mail: david.mckinsey@hcamidwest.org.

MCKINSTRY, RONALD E. lawyer; b. Bakersfield, Calif., Aug. 11, 1926; s. Melville Jack and Lillian Agatha (Saner) McK.; m. Shirley Danner, June 19, 1948; children: Michael R., Jill I. McKinstry Epperson, Jeffrey A., Carol A. McKinstry Sundquist. BS, U. Wash., 1950, JD, 1951. Bar: Wash. 1951, U.S. Ct. Claims 1970, U.S. Ct. Appeals (D.C. cir.) 1981, U.S. Supreme Ct. 1982. Assoc. Evans, McLaren, Lane, Powell & Beeks, Seattle, 1951-55, Bogle, Bogle & Gates, Seattle, 1955-61; ptnr. Bogle & Gates, Seattle, 1962-91, chmn. litigation dept., 1970-91; sr. trial ptnr. Ellis Li & McKinstry, Seattle, 1992—. Apptd. spl. master by U.S. Dist. Ct. (we. dist.) Wash., 1976-81, apptd. settlement mediator, 1980—. Editor-in-chief Washington Civil Procedure Before Trial Deskbook, 1981, Supplement to Deskbook, 1986; contbr. articles to profl. jours. Attends Christ Meml. Ch., Poulsbo, Wash. With USN, 1944-46, PTO. Recipient Svc. award Western Ctr. for Law and Religious Freedom, 1990. Fellow Am. Coll. Trial Lawyers (regent 1978-82); mem. ABA, Internat. Assn. Def. Counsel (mem. exec. com. 1974-78), CPR Panels of Disting. Legal Neutrals, AAA Club Wash. (mem. exec. com. 1983-98). Avocations: golf, travel. Office: Ellis Li & McKinstry Two Union Square 601 Union St Ste 4900 Seattle WA 98101-3906 E-mail: rmckinstry@elmlaw.com.

MCKINZIE, CARL WAYNE, lawyer; b. Lubbock, Tex., Dec. 3, 1939; s. J. Clyde and Flora (Cates) McK.; m. Rowena Ann Williams; children: Wayne, Clinton, Morgan (dec.). BBA, Tex. Tech U., 1962, MBA, 1963; JD, So. Meth. U., 1966. From assoc. to ptnr. Nossaman, Guthner, Knox & Elliot, L.A., 1966-80; prin. Riordan & McKinzie, L.A., 1980—2003; ptnr. Bingham McCutchen (merged with Riordan & McKinzie), 2003—. Bd. dirs., mem. exec. com., Saint John's Health Ctr., Santa Monica, Calif., 2001—, vice chair, 2002-2003, chair, 2003-. Contbr. articles to law jours. Trustee Jaquish Found., Raymond Marshall Found., 1993-2003; bd. visitors Sch. Law So. Meth. U., Dallas, 1979-82, 90—, bd. dirs., 1970-73, 84-89, chmn. exec. com., 1996-98; bd. visitors Ariz State U. Coll. Law, 1990-98; bd. dirs. Riordan Found., 1992—; bd. dirs. Rx for Reading, 1992—; vice chair, bd. dirs., mem. exec. com. Libr. Found. L.A., 2002—, Pub. Counsel, 1996-99, Calif. Cmty. Found., 1994-98; bd. advisors Coll Law, U. Wyo., 1987-91, 2001—. Recipient disting. alumni award So. Meth. U., Dallas, 1994. Mem. ABA (chmn. current devel. subcom., com. tax problems 1978-80), Nat. Assn. Real Estate Investment Trusts (bd. govs. 1986-89), Calif. Bar Assn., Los Angeles County Bar Assn., Jonathan Club, City Club on Bunker Hill, L.A. Country Club. Republican. Home: 527 21st Pl Santa Monica CA 90402-3047 Office: Bingham McCutchen 44th Fl 355 S Grand Ave Los Angeles CA 90071-3106 Office Phone: 213-229-8484.

MCKIRAHAN, RICHARD DUNCAN, classics and philosophy educator; b. Berkeley, Calif., July 27, 1945; s. Richard Duncan and Helen Marion (Hixson) McK.; m. Voula Tsouna, June 3, 1961; 1 child, Helen Hamilton. AB, U. Calif., Berkeley, 1966; BA, U. Oxford, Eng., 1969; MA, Oxford U., Eng., 1979; PhD, Harvard U., 1973. Teaching fellow, tutor Harvard U., Cambridge, Mass., 1971-73; asst. prof. classics and philosophy Pomona Coll., Claremont, Calif., 1973-79, assoc. prof., 1979-87, E.C. Norton prof. classics and philosophy, 1987—, chair dept. classics, 1992—. Author: Socrates and Plato, A Comprehensive Bibliography, 1958-1973, 1978, Plato's Meno, 1986, Principles and Proofs: Aristotle's Theory of Demonstrative Science, 1992, Philosophy Before Socrates, 1994, A Presocratics Reader, 1996, Cicero, De Natura Deorum I, 1997, Simplicius, On Aristotle's Physics, book 8, chpts. 6-10, 2001; contbr. articles on Greek philosophy, math. and scis. Marshall Aid Commemoration Commn. scholar, U. Oxford, 1966-69, Fulbright Sr. scholar, 1999, Overseas Vis. scholar St. John's Coll., Cambridge, 1999; Woodrow Wilson Found. fellow, 1966-67; NEH grantee, 1975, 85, 90, 98, 2004. Mem. Am. Philol. Assn., Soc. Ancient Greek Philosophy, Phi Beta Kappa. Office: Pomona Coll Dept Classics 140 W 6th St Claremont CA 91711-4301 Business E-Mail: rmckirahan@pomona.edu.

MCKITTRICK, NEIL VINCENT, lawyer; b. Framingham, Mass., June 21, 1961; s. Harold Vincent and Dorothy Frances (Alexander) McK.; m. Karen Beth Hoffman, May 30, 1987; children: Kerry Alexandra, Brian Hoffman, Robert Hoffman. AB magna cum laude, Brown U., 1983; JD, U. Va., 1987. Bar: Mass. 1988, U.S. Dist. Ct. Mass. 1989, U.S. Ct. Appeals (1st cir.) 1989, U.S. Supreme Ct. 1999. Law clk. to Hon. Frank M. Johnson Jr. U.S. Ct. Appeals (11th cir.), Montgomery, Ala., 1987-88; assoc. Hill & Barlow, Boston, 1988-95, mem., 1995—2002; pub. defender Suffolk County (Mass.) Bar Advocate, 1990-91; asst. dir. White House sec. rev. U.S. Dept. Treasury, 1994-95; case conf./mediator Boston Mcpl. Ct. Alternative Dispute Resolution Program, 1997—; dir. Goulston & Storrs, Boston, 2002—. Editor U. Va. Law Rev., 1985-87. Bd. dirs. Lawyers' Com. for Civil Rights Under Law, 1998—, Bd. trustees, 2001—. Recipient Disting. Citizens award, Mass. Assn. for Retarded Citizens, 1996, Charles River Gala Benefit award, 2001; fellow Dillard fellow, U. Va., 1985—86. Mem.: FBA (Mass. chpt.exec. com. 1997—, treas. 2000—01, sec. 2001—02, v.p. 2002—03), ABA (Pro Bono Publico award 2001), Boston Bar Assn., Mass. Bar Assn. (coun. mem. Access to Justice Sect. Coun. 2001—, Access to Justice Pro Bono Publico award 2001), Order of the Coif, Theta Delta Chi, Phi Beta Kappa. Office: Goulston & Storrs 400 Atlantic Ave Boston MA 02110 E-mail: nmckittrick@goulsonstorrs.com.

MCKITTRICK, WILLIAM WOOD, lawyer; b. Mt. Carmel, Ill., July 11, 1915; s. Lafe E. and Mary Lynn (Wood) McK.; m. Carolyn Lenne Davis, Dec. 19, 1942; children: Lynn McKittrick Pond, Bruce W. AB, DePauw U., 1936; JD, Northwestern U., 1939. Bar: Ill. Assoc. Pope & Ballard, Chgo., 1939-48, ptnr., 1948-52; atty. Office Gen. Counsel, Panama C.Z., 1942; ptnr. Vedder, Price, Kaufman & Kammholz, Chgo., 1952-95; lectr. on labor law Northwestern U. Sch. Law, Chgo., 1961-62. Case note editor, mem. editorial bd. Ill. Law Rev., 1938-39. Life trustee Orchestral Assn. of Chgo. Symphony Orch., 1980—, Chgo. Symphony Musicians Pension Trust, 1987-98; bd. dirs. Am. Symphony Orch. League, 1986-93, mem. exec. com., 1988-91; trustee Newberry Libr., Chgo., 1984-98, life trustee, 1998—, exec. com., 1989-98; vice chmn. exec. bd. Libr. Coun., Northwestern U., 1984-96; chmn. Friends of Ryerson & Burnham Librs., Art Inst. Chgo., 1988-90, mem. com. on librs., 1982—. Lt. USNR, 1943-45, PTO. Recipient Svc. award Northwestern U., 1968. Mem. ABA, Ill. Bar Assn., Chgo. Bar Assn. (lectr. various programs 1940-70, bd. mgrs. 1961-63), Lawyers Club of Chgo., Univ. Club (Chgo.), Michigan Shores Club, Skokie Country Club, Caxton Club of Chgo. (v.p. 1982-83, pres. 1983-85). Home: 232 Essex Rd Kenilworth IL 60043-1122

MCKNIGHT, JOSEPH WEBB, law educator, historian; b. San Angelo, Tex., Feb. 17, 1925; s. John Banning and Helen Katherine (Webb) McK.; m. Julia Ann Dyer, July 20, 1957 (dec. Jan. 1972); children: John Banton, Joseph Adair; m. Mildred Katherine Virginia Payne, Aug. 9, 1975 BA, U. Tex., 1947, Oxford U., Eng., 1949, B.C.L., 1950, MA, 1954; LL.M., Columbia U., 1959. Bar: Tex. 1951, U.S. Ct. Appeals (5th cir.) 1982. Assoc. Cravath, Swaine & Moore, N.Y.C., 1951-55; asst. prof. So. Meth. U., Dallas, 1955-57, assoc. prof., 1957-63, prof. law, 1963—, acad. dean, 1977-80, Larry and Jane Harlan faculty fellow, 1991—. Vis. prof. various univs. Gen. editor Creditors' Rights in Texas, 1963, History of the Texas Supreme Court Project, 1998—; author: (with William A. Reppy, Jr.) Texas Matrimonial Property Law, 1983, 7th edit. 2003; contbr. articles to profl. jours. Pres., Tex. Old Missions and Forts Restoration Assn., 1977-79, 99-2001; bd. dirs. San Jacinto Mus. History Assn., 1976-99; mem. exec. coun. Tex. State Hist. Assn., 1988-91, fellow, 2004. Served to lt. USNR, 1942-47 Rhodes scholar, 1947-50; James Kent fellow Columbia Law Sch., 1958-59; Academico, Acad. Mexicana de Derecho Internat., 1988, Hall of Legends, State Bar of Texas Fam. Law Sec., 1997. Fellow, Soc. for Advanced Legal Studies (London), 1998; mem. ABA, State Bar Tex., Dallas Bar Assn., Tex. Bar Found. (v.p. 1959), Nat. Legal Aid and Defenders Assn. (bd. dirs. 1963-66), Selden Soc., Am. Soc. Legal History (v.p. 1967-68, bd. dirs. 1967-75), Inst. Texan Cultures (exec. bd. 1990-95), Oxford and Cambridge Club (London), Sigma Chi. Democrat. Episcopalian. Office: So Meth U Law Sch 3315 Daniel Ave Dallas TX 75275-0116 Office Phone: 214-768-2591., 214-768-3851. Business E-Mail: jmcknigh@smu.edu.

MCKNIGHT, JOYCE SHELDON, adult educator, community organizer, mediator; b. Meadville, Pa., Oct. 12, 1949; d. Seth Carlyle and Juanita Bessie (Sheets) Sheldon; m. Hugh Frank McKnight, Aug. 22, 1970; children: Frank Nathan, Joanna Michelle. BA in Psychology and Sociology, Allegheny Coll., 1971; MEd in Counseling, Gannon Coll., 1977; EdD, Pa. State U., 1995. Cert. nat. counselor. Asst. met. dir. Ecumenical Inst., Chgo. and Tulsa, 1970-73; health planner East Okla. Devel. Dist., Muskogee, 1973; juvenile counselor Tulsa County Aftercare Program, 1973; program specialist psycho-social rehab. Counseling Svcs. Ctr., Corry, Pa., 1975-77; counselor Adult Diploma Program, Corry, Pa., 1974-79; dir. Anchor House Agy., Corry, Pa., 1977-78; community programs dir. Warren-Forest Counties Econ. Opportunity Coun., Warren, Pa., 1979-80; dir. Corry Ctr. Mercyhurst Coll., Corry, Pa., 1981-87; cons. Pulaski, Pa., 1987-89. Adj. faculty Mercyhurst, 1981-87, program devel. cons., 1987-89, program devel. cons. for new ch. Heritage Hills Ch., 1988-89; adj. faculty Allegheny Coll., 1984, Jamestown C.C., 1991-93; planner Pa. State U., Shenango Valley, 1989; mentor Empire State Coll. SUNY, 1989-93; coord. adult svcs. Alfred State Coll., 1992-95, adj. faculty mem., 1994-95, distance edn. team, 1994-95; dir. Inst. for Support of Cmty. Initiative, 1995-97;

dir. McKnight Mediation, 1997-2002; mem. faculty Cambria County Area C.C., 1998-2002, adj. grad. faculty Pa. State U., 2000, dept. chair, Ctr. Distance Learning, Empire State Coll., SUNY; cons. higher edn., cmty. svc., ch. growth. Contbr. articles to profl. jours; co-author: Text Doing Democracy Workbook, 2003 Pres., Corry Concerned for Youth, Inc., 1975-77; pres. Community Care Coun. of Agys., Corry, 1976-79, sec., 1975; mem. steering com. Vol. Action Ctr., Corry, 1977, bd. dirs. Erie County Citizens Coalition for Human Svcs., Erie, 1979-80, Horizon House for Women, 1981-87; mem. coordinating bd. Corry Reindustrialization Coun. 1983-87; mem. Allegany County N.Y Gateway Project, 1993-95. Mem. NAACP (Johnstown chpt., adv. com. family ctr.), Pa. Assn. Pub. Continuing Adult Edn. (dir. 1977-78), Pa. Assn. for Adult Continuing Edn. (bd. dirs. 1985-90) Cambria County Cmty. Action (bd. dirs.), Coalition of the So. Alleghenies, SEAD, Saratoga Springs Women in Leadership, Saratoga Springs. Mennonite. Office: Ctr Distance Learning Empire State Coll Saratoga Springs NY 12866 Home and Office: McKnight %Kathys Motl 2354 Route 9 N #104 Lake George NY 12845 Business E-Mail: joyce.mcknight@esc.edu.

MCKNIGHT, LENORE RAVIN, child psychiatrist, educator; b. Denver, May 15, 1943; d. Abe and Rose (Steed) Ravin; m. Robert lee McKNight, July 22, 1967; children: Richard Rex, Janet Rose. Student, Occidental Coll., 1961-63; BA, postgrad., U. Colo., 1965-67; MD, U. Calif., San Francisco, 111969. Diplomate in adult and child psychiatry Am. Bd. Psychiatry and Neurology. Intern in pediat. Children's Hosp., San Francisco, 1969-70; resident in gen. psychiatry Langley Porter Neuropsychiat. Inst., 1970-73, fellow in child psychiatry, 1972-74, asst. clin. prof., 1974—; pvt. practice child psychiatry, Walnut Creek, Calif., 1974-93; child psychiatrist Kaiser Permanente Med. Group, 1993—. Child psychiatrist Youth Guidance Center, San Francisco, 1974-74; asst. clin. prof. psychiatry U. Calif. San Francisco Med. Ctr. Internat.; med. dir. CPC Walnut Creek (Calif.) Hosp., 1990-93. Insts. Edn. fellow U. Edinburgh, 1964; grantee to study childhood nutrition NIH, 1966. Fellow Am. Acad. Child and Adolescent Psychiatry, Internat. Arabian Horse Assn. Office: Kaiser Martinez Inpat Psych 200 Muir Rd Martinez CA 94553-4672 Office Phone: 925-372-1738.

MCKNIGHT, MAMIE, commissioner; Ret. H.S. and coll. educator; part-time dir.Tex. PreFreshman Engring. Program U. Tex., Dallas; commr. Tex. Hist. Commn., Austin, 1999—. Assoc. dir. Louis Stokes Alliance for Participation Program in Engring., Math. and Sci.; dir. re-opening and operation Juanita Craft Civil Rights House, Dallas, 2000—; chmn. Dallas Landmark Commn.; founding dir. Black Dallas Remembered, Inc. Office: PO Box 12276 Austin TX 78711-2276

MCKNIGHT, STEVEN LANIER, molecular biologist; b. El Paso, Tex., Aug. 27, 1949; s. Frank Gillespie and Sara Elise (Stevens) McK.; m. Jacquelynn Ann Zimmer, Sept. 16, 1978; children: Nell, Grace, Frances, John Stevens. BA summa cum laude, U. Tex., 1974; PhD, U.Va., 1977. Postdoctoral fellow Carnegie Instn. Washington, Balt., 1977-79, staff assoc., 1979-81, mem. staff, 1984-92; co-founder, dir., dir. rsch. Tularik Inc., 1991—. Prof., chmn. dept. biochemistry U. Tex. Southwestern Med. Ctr., 1995—; hon. prof. Johns Hopkins U., scientific rev. bd. Howard Hughes Med. Inst., 1997—; trustee Carnegie Inst., Washington, 2000—. Contbr. articles to jours. in field. With U.S. Army, 1969-71, Vietnam. Decorated ARCOM medal; recipient Eli Lilly prize Am. Soc. Microbiology, 1987, Newcomb-Cleveland prize Sci. mag., 1989, NAS Molecular Biology award Nat. Acad. Sci., 1991. Fellow Carnegie Inst. Washington (hon.), Am. Soc. Microbiology (hon.); mem. NAS, Am. Acad. Arts and Scis., Am. Soc. for Biochemistry and Molecular Biology, Am. Soc. for Cell Biology, Japanese Biochem. Soc. (hon.). Home: 3717 Euclid Ave Dallas TX 75205-3161 Office: U Tex Southwestern Med Ctr Dept Biochemistry 5323 Harry Hines Blvd Dallas TX 75390-7208 also: Tularik Inc Two Corp Dr South San Francisco CA 94080

MCKNIGHT, TERRANCE THALES, music educator; s. Edward and Katie Mae McKnight; m. Chanda Leigh Bailey, May 31, 2003. BA in liberal arts, Morehouse Coll., 1990; MA in piano pedagogy, Ga. State U., 1998. Piano instr. Neighborhood Music Sch., Atlanta, 1994—99; adj. prof. of music Morehouse Coll., Atlanta, 1998—; resident prodr. Nat. Pub. Radio, Washington, 1999—2000; prodr./announcer Ga. Pub. Broadcasting, Atlanta, 2000—; music prodr. Ga. Pub. Radio, Atlanta, 2000—. Cons. Nat. Pub. Radio, Washington, 2000—01. Prodr.: (radio feature) Singing in the Oral Tradition (Best Use of Sound - NABJ, 2000), (radio program) Musically Reclined, Studio GPR. Scholar, Morehouse Coll., 1987-1990. Office: Georgia Pub Broadcasting 260 14th St Atlanta GA 30318 Personal E-mail: tmcknight@gpb.org. E-mail: tmcknight@gpb.org.

MCKNIGHT, THOMAS FREDERICK, artist; b. Lawrence, Kans., Jan. 13, 1941; m. Renate Hödl. BA cum laude, Wesleyan U., Middletown, Conn., 1963; postgrad., Columbia U., 1963-64. One-man shows Basel (Switzerland) Art Fair, 1975-77, Tomic Galerie, Dusseldorf, Germany, 1976, Hartmann Gallery, Munich, 1977, Newport (R.I.) Art Assn., 1981, Kobe (Japan) Mcpl. Art Mus., 1993, R² Gallery, N.Y.C., 2002; exhibited in group shows Llubljana, Yugoslavia, 1981, Tokyo, 1989, Davison Art Ctr., Wesleyan U., 1988, 98, numerous others; represented in permanent collections Davison Art Ctr., N.Y. State Mus., Albany, Smithsonian Instn., Washington, Met. Mus. Art, N.Y.C.; represented in Art in Embassies program; commns. include poster and print U.S. Constn. Bicentennial, 1989, prints Am.'s Cup, 1992, paintings and prints Urban Fair, Kobe, Japan, 1991, White House Christmas card, 1994, 95, 96; author: Thomas McKnight: Voyage to Paradise, 1993. Recipient Disting. Alumni award Wesleyan U., 1998. Office Phone: 860-567-5571. E-mail: tmck@thomasmcknight.com.

MCKNIGHT, WILLIAM BALDWIN, physics educator; b. Macon, Ga., July 4, 1923; s. Gilbert Franklin and Exie (Baldwin) McK.; m. Helen Mabel Bowling, Oct. 1, 1955; children: Tandy Ringoringo, Linda McKnight Gibson. BS, Purdue U., 1950; PhD, Oxford U., 1968. Physicist Underwater Sound Reference Lab., Orlando, Fla., 1952-53, U.S. Army Missile Command, Redstone Arsenal, Ala., 1953-61, supervisory rsch. physicist, 1961-74; cons. Ballistic Missile Def. Advanced Tech. Ctr., 1975; rsch. prof. physics U. Ala., Huntsville, 1974—; pres. Tech. Rsch. Assocs. Inc., 1984—. Contbr. articles to profl. jours. Vice pres. Cotaco Cmtys. League, Somerville, Ala., 1964-65; mem. Madison County Rep. Exec. Com.; mgr. Gordo Area C. of C., 1993-97; chmn. transp./infrastructure com. Pickens County Strategic Planning, 1994-96; mem. North-South Hwy. Corridor, West Ala. Coalition Task Force, 1995-96; chmn. Citizens for the Improvement of Pickens County, 1997—; chmn. adv. coun. Pickens County Commn.; bd. dirs. West Ctrl. Partnership of Ala.; chair Gordo Area Indsl. Devel. Authority; pres. Gordo Area Cmty. Devel. Found.; mem. Ala. Silver-Haired Legislature, 2001-02. Decorated D.F.C., Air medal with three oak leaf clusters; recipient Research and Devel. award U.S. Army, 1961, 64, Presdl. Unit Citation with oak leaf cluster; Sec. of Army fellow, 1966-67. Fellow Optical Soc. Am.; mem. IEEE (sr.), Am. Phys. Soc., Rotary (pres. Gordo club 1997-98), Oxford and Cambridge Club, Tuscaloosa Univ. Club, Sigma Xi, Sigma Pi Sigma. Mem. Ch. of Christ. Home: 770 Clear Creek Rd Gordo AL 35466-4446

MCKNIGHT, WILLIAM EDWIN, minister; b. Grenada, Miss, Mar. 21, 1938; s. Leslie Spurgeon and Lucy Jennings (Sistrunk) McK.; m Sue Belle Roberts, Aug. 5, 1960; children: Susan Michele, William Roberts. BA, Millsaps Coll., 1960; BD, Lexington (Ky.) Theol. Sem., 1963. Ordained to ministry, 1964. Chaplain intern Grady Hosp., Atlanta, 1963-64; pastor First Christian Ch., Cleveland, Miss., 1964-67, Inverness, Miss., 1964-67, assoc. pastor Jackson, Miss., 1967-70; regional minister Christian Ch. (Disciples of Christ) in Miss., Jackson, 1971—2002. Bd. dir. Nat. City Christian Ch., Washington, DC, Christian Brotherhood Homes, Jackson, So. Christian Svc., Macon, Ga.; mem. Gen. Bd. the Christian Ch., Indpls., 1969—, bd. dir. fin. coun., 1979-82; mem. bd. higher edn., St. Louis, 1979-80. Named one of Outstanding Young Men Am. US Jaycees, 1976. Mem. Miss. Religious Leadership Conf. (pres. 1984-85), Conf. Regional Ministers and Moderators (pres. 1985-86), Coll. of regional Ministers, mem. Mem. Christian Ch. Office: Christian Church Po Box 192058 Little Rock AR 72219-2058 E-mail: bill@grr.cc.

MCKOWEN, DOROTHY KEETON, librarian, educator, consultant; b. Bonne Terre, Mo., Oct. 5, 1948; d. John Richard and Dorothy (Spoonhour) Keeton; m. Paul Edwin McKowen, Dec. 19, 1970; children: Richard James, Mark David. BS, Pacific Christian Coll., 1970; MLS, U. So. Calif., 1973; MA in English, Purdue U., 1985, PhD, 2003. Libr.-specialist Doheny Libr., U. So. Calif., L.A., 1973-74; asst. libr. Pacific Christian Coll., 1974-78; serials cataloger Purdue U. Librs., 1978-88; head children's and young adult svcs. Kokomo-Howard County Pub. Libr., Ind., 1988-89, coord. children's and tech. svcs., 1989-91; cataloger, network libr. Ind. Coop. Libr. Svcs. Authority, 1991-2001; libr. cons. and contractor, 2001—. Mem. adj. faculty.C.C. of Ind., 2001—. Mem. ALA, MLA, Soc. Early Americanists, Assn. for Libr. Collections and Tech. Svcs. (bd. dirs. 1986-90, 95-96, vice chair, chair-elect coun. of regional groups 1986-88, chair 1988-90, conf. program com. 1986-88, internat. rels. com. 1986-88, micropub. com. 1986-87, subject analysis com., membership com. 1988-90, planning and rsch. com. 1988-90, chair program initiatives com. 1991-93, orgn. and bylaws com. 1991-92, 99-2001), Network OCLC Svc. Mgrs. (MARC Task Force 2000-01), Ind. Coun. Libr. Automation (bibliog. stds. task force), Ind. Libr. Fedn. (chair tech. svcs. divsn. 1984-85), Ohio Valley Group Tech. Svcs. Libr. (chmn. 1985-86). Republican. Home: 7625 Summit Ln Lafayette IN 47905-9729 E-mail: mckowens2@yahoo.com.

MCKOWN, CHARLES HENRY, dean; b. Huntington, W.Va., Dec. 29, 1934; BS, W.Va. U., 1956; MD, Med. Coll. Va., 1960. Intern Med. Coll. Va., 1961; resident in radiology McGuire VA Hosp., 1961—62; fellow NIH, 1964—67; prof. radiology, chmn. dept. radiology Marshall U., Huntington, W.Va., 1975—88, v.p. health scis., dean Sch. Medicine, 1989—. Office: Marshall U Joan C Edwards Sch Medicine Ste 3400 1600 Medical Center Dr Huntington WV 25701-3655

MC KOY, BASIL VINCENT CHARLES, theoretical chemist, educator; b. Trinidad, W.I., Mar. 25, 1938; came to U.S., 1960, naturalized, 1973; s. Allan Cecil and Doris Augusta McK.; m. Anne Ellen Shannon, Mar. 18, 1967; 1 son, Christopher Allan. B.Chem. Eng., N.S. Tech. U., 1960; PhD in Chemistry (Univ. fellow), Yale U., 1964. Instr. chemistry Calif. Inst. Tech., 1964-66, asst. prof. chemistry, 1966-69, asso. prof., 1969-75, prof. theoretical chemistry, 1975—, chmn. of faculty, 1985-87. Cons. Lawrence Livermore Lab., U. Calif., Livermore, 1974—, Inst. Def. Analysis, 1984—; vis. prof. Max Planck Inst., Munich, Ger., 1976—, U. Paris, 1968—, U. Campinas, Brazil, 1976—; lectr. Nobel Symposium, Goteborg, Sweden, 1979. Contbr. articles to Jour. Physics, London, chem. Physics Lettters, Phys. Rev., Jour. Chem. Physics; bd. editors; Chem. Physics Jour., 1977-79, mem. adv. editoral bd., 1992—; co-editor: Electron-Molecule and Photon-Molecule Collisions, 1979, 83, Swarm Studies and Inelastic Electron-Molecule Collisions, 1986; co-author: Electron-Molecule Collisions and Photoionization Processes, 1982. Recipient medal Gov.-Gen. Can., 1960; Alfred P. Sloan Found. fellow, 1969-73; Guggenheim fellow, 1973-74 Fellow Am. Phys. Soc. Home: 3855 Keswick Rd La Canada Flintridge CA 91011-3945 Office: Calif Inst Tech Divsn Chemistry Pasadena CA 91125-0001 Office Phone: 626-395-6545. Business E-Mail: mckoy@caltech.edu.

MCKUSICK, VICTOR ALMON, geneticist, educator, physician; b. Parkman, Maine, Oct. 21, 1921; s. Carroll L. and Ethel M. (Buzzell) Mc K.; m. Anne Bishop, June 11, 1949; children: Carol Anne, Kenneth Andrew, Victor Wayne. Student, Tufts Coll., 1940-43; MD, Johns Hopkins U., 1946; DSc (hon.), N.Y. Med. Coll., 1974; MD (hon.), Liverpool U., 1976; DSc (hon.), U. Maine, 1978, Tufts U., 1978, U. Rochester, 1979, Meml. U., Nfld., 1979; DMCh (hon.), U. Helsinki, 1981; D Med. Sci. (hon.), Med. U. S.C., 1979; MD (hon.), Edinburgh U., 1984; DSc (hon.), Aberdeen U., 1988, Med. Coll. Ohio, 1988, Bates Coll., 1989; PhD (hon.), Tel Aviv U., 1989; MD (hon.), Zurich (Switzerland) U., 1990; DSc (hon.), Colby Coll., 1991, U. Chgo., 1991, Mt. Sinai Sch. Medicine, 1992; DSc (hon.), Med. Coll. Wis., 1998, Rockefeller U., 2002. Diplomate Am. Bd. Internal Medicine. Tng. in clin. medicine, lab. rsch. Johns Hopkins U./USPHS, 1946-52; instr. medicine Johns Hopkins Sch. Medicine, 1951-54, asst. prof., 1954-57, assoc. prof., 1957-60, chief divsn. med. genetics, dept. medicine, 1957-73, prof. medicine, 1960-85, prof. epidemiology, biology, 1969-78, William Osler prof. medicine, 1978-85, chmn. dept. medicine, 1973-85; physician-in-chief Johns Hopkins Hosp., 1973-85, Univ. prof. medical genetics, 1985—, chief div. med. genetics, 1957-73, 85-89. Mem. rsch. adv. com. Nat. Found., 1959—78; mem. adv. bd. Howard Hughes Med. Inst., 1967—83; com. mapping and sequencing of human genome Nat. Acad. Sci., 1986—88; pres. Internat. Med. Congress, Ltd., 1972—78; mem. Nat. Adv. Rsch. Resources Coun., 1970—74; mem. bd. sci. advisors Roche Inst. Molecular Biology, 1967—71; trustee Jackson Lab., 1979—; founding mem. Am. Bd. Med. Genetics, 1979—82; pres. 8th Internat. Conf. Human Genetics, Washington, 1991; mem. human genome adv. com. NIH, 1988—92, NIH/DOE work group on ethical, legal and societal implications of human genome project, 1990—95; co-chmn. Centennial of Johns Hopkins Hosp., 1989—90; co-founder, co-dir. ann. short course in med. and exptl. mammalian genetics, Bar Harbor, Maine, 1960—, European Sch. Med. Genetics Sestri Levante and Bertinoro, 1988—; chmn. com. on DNA tech. in forensic sci. NRC/NAS, 1989—92, adv. update com., 1993—96; mem. sci. adv. bd. Celera Genomics, 1998—; founding fellow Am. Coll. Med. Genetics. Author: Heritable Disorders of Connective Tissue, 1956, 60, 66, 72, 93, Cardiovascular Sound in Health and Disease, 1958, Medical Genetics 1958-60, 1961, Human Genetics, 1964, 69, On the X Chromosome of Man, 1964, Mendelian Inheritance in Man, 1966, 68, 71, 75, 78, 83, 86, 88, 90, 92, 94, 98, Medical Genetics Self-Instruction Guide, 1993, (with others) Osler's Textbook Revisited, 1967, Genetics of Hand Malformations, 1978, Medical Genetic Studies of the Amish, 1978, A Model of its Kind, 1989, Osler's Legacy, 1990, A Century of Biomedical Science at Johns Hopkins, 1993; author, editor: Online Mendelian Inheritance in Man, 1985—; editor-in-chief Medicine jour., 1985—; founding co-editor-in-chief Genomics jour. 1987—; editor med. textbook. Named hon. citizen of Genoa, 1997; named to Internat. Pediat. Hall of Fame, 1987; recipient Disting. Achievement award, Modern Medicine, 1965, John Phillips award, ACP, 1972, Silver medal, U. Helsinki, 1974, Gairdner Internat. award, 1977, Premio Internazionale Sanremo per le Ricerche Genetiche, 1983, Col. Saunders award, March of Dimes, 1988, Disting. Alumnus award, Johns Hopkins U., 1983, Alumnus Svc. award, Johns Hopkins Med. Sch., 1989, Passano award, 1989, Disting. Svc. award, Miami Biotech. Winter Symposium, 1991, Frank Bradway Rogers Info. Advancement award, Med. Libr. Assn., 1991, Silver Columbus medal, Comune di Genova, 1992, Maine prize (with twin), 1993, Mendel medal, Villanova U., 1995, Big "M" award, Maine State Soc. Washington, D.C., 1995, Coriell medal, Coriell Inst., Camden, N.J., 1997, Lasker award for lifetime achievement in med. sci., 1997, City of Medicine award, Durham, N.C., 1997, James P. McGovern Compleat Physician award, 2000, Albert Lasker award for Special Achievement in Medicine, Lasker Found., 2000, Nat. medal of sci., 2002, Rsch. Achievement award, Am. Heart Assn., 2002. Fellow AAAS (chair med. scis. sect. 1991), Am. Acad. Orthopedic Surgeons (hon.), Royal Coll. Physicians (London), Hastings Ctr., Am. Coll. Med. Genetics (hon.); mem. Nat. Acad. Sci. (James Murray Luck award 1982), Am. Philos. Soc. (v.p. 1996—, Benjamin Franklin medal for disting. achievement in scis. 1996), Am. Soc. Human Genetics (pres. 1975, Wm. A. Allan award 1977), Assn. Am. Physicians (Kober medal 1990), Am. Soc. Clin. Investigation (v.p. 1967), Human Genome Orgn. (founder pres. 1988-89), Am. Acad. Arts and Sci., Little People of Am. (hon. life), Acad. Nat. Médecine (France; corr.), Phi Beta Kappa, Alpha Omega Alpha, Johns Hopkins Club, West Hamilton St. Club, St. Andrew's Soc. Balt. Presbyterian (elder). Home: 221 Northway Baltimore MD 21218-1141 Office: Johns Hopkins Hosp Inst Genetic Medicine-Blalock 1007 600 N Wolfe St Baltimore MD 21287-4922*

MCKUSICK, VINCENT LEE, former state supreme court chief justice, lawyer, arbitrator, mediator; b. Parkman, Maine, Oct. 21, 1921; s. Carroll Lee and Ethel (Buzzell) McK.; m. Nancy Elizabeth Green, June 23, 1951; children: Barbara McKusick Liscord, James Emory, Katherine McKusick Ralston, Anne Elizabeth. AB, Bates Coll., 1943; SB, SM, MIT, 1947; LLB, Harvard U., 1950; LLD, Colby Coll., 1976, Nasson Coll., 1978, Bates Coll., 1979, Bowdoin Coll., 1979, Suffolk U., 1983; LHD, U. So. Maine, 1978, Thomas Coll., 1981. Bar: Maine 1952. Law clk. to Chief Judge Learned Hand, 1950-51; to Justice Felix Frankfurter, 1951-52; partner Pierce, Atwood, Scribner, Allen & McKusick and predecessors, Portland, Maine, 1953-77; chief justice Maine Supreme Jud. Ct., 1977-92; of counsel to Pierce Atwood (formerly Pierce, Atwood, Scribner, Allen, Smith, & Lancaster), Portland, Maine, 1992—. Mem. adv. com. rules civil procedure Maine Supreme Jud. Ct., 1957-59, chmn., 1966-75, commr. uniform state laws, 1968-76, sec. nat. conf., 1975-77; mem. Conf. Chief Justices, 1977-92, bd. dirs., 1980-82, 91-92, pres.-elect, 1989-90, pres., 1990-91. standing com. past pres., 1992—; dir. Nat. Ctr. for State Ctrs., 1988-89, chmn.-elect, 1989-90, chmn., 1990-91; spl. master U.S. Supreme Ct. Conn. v. N.H., 1992-93, La. v. Miss., 1994-96, Kans. v. Nebr., 1999-2003; spl. master Mass. S.J.C. Liquidation Am. Mutual Liability Ins. Co., 1995-96; leader Am. Judges Del. to China, 1983, USSR, 1988, U.S. State Dept. Rule of Law Del. to Republic of Ga., 1992; mem. permanent com. Oliver Wendell Holmes Devise, 1993-2001. Author: Patent Policy of Educational Institutions, 1947, (with Richard H. Field) Maine Civil Practice, 1959, supplements, 1962, 67, (with Richard H. Field and L. Kinvin Wroth) 2d edit., 1970, supplements, 1972, 74, 77; also articles in legal publs. Trustee emeritus Bates Coll.; mem. adv. com. on pvt. internat. law U.S. State Dept., 1980-85, Fed.-State Jurisdiction com., Jud. Conf. of U.S., 1987-89. With AUS, 1943-46. Recipient The Maine prize U. Maine Sys., 1993, Benjamin E. Mays award Bates Coll., 1994, Big M award Maine State Soc. Washington, 1995, Paul C. Reardon award Nat. Ctr. for State Ctrs., 1999. Fellow Am. Bar Found. (bd. dirs. 1977-87), Am. Philos. Soc. (coun. 1990-96, 97-02, v.p. 2002—); mem. ABA (chmn. fed. rules com. 1966-71, bd. editors jour. 1971-80, chmn. 1976-77, mem. study group to China 1978, ho. dels. 1983-87, coun. sr. lawyers divsn. 1997-01), Maine Bar Assn., Cumberland County Bar Assn., Am. Arbitration Assn. (bd. dirs. 1994—), Am. Judicature Soc. (dir. 1976-78, 92-98), Am. Law Inst. (coun. 1968—), Maine Jud. Coun. (chmn. 1977-92), Inst. Jud. Adminstrn., Supreme Ct. Hist. Soc. (trustee 1994—), Rotary Club (hon., past pres. Portland club), Phi Beta Kappa, Sigma Xi, Tau Beta Pi. Republican. Unitarian Universalist. Home: 1152 Shore Rd Cape Elizabeth ME 04107-2115 Office: 1 Monument Sq Portland ME 04101-1110 Office Phone: 207-791-1100. Business E-Mail: vmckusick@pierceatwood.com. E-mail: judgemac@maine.rr.com.

MCLACHLAN, SARAH, composer, musician; b. Halifax, Nova Scotia, Jan. 28, 1968; Founder, performer Lilith Fair. Albums include Touch, 1989, Solace, 1991, Live EP, 1992, Fumbling Towards Ecstasy, 1994, Freedom Sessions, 1995, Rarities, B-Sides, and Other Stuff, 1996, Surfacing, 1997, Mirrorball, 1999, Sarah McLachlan Remixed, 2001, Afterglow, 2003; appearances include Gravity, 1991, Island of Circles: A Nettwork C, 1991, No Alternative, 1993, Christmas at Mountain Stage, 1994, Testimonial Dinner: the Songs of Xt, 1995, Memories of the Soul Shack Survivor, 1996, Heroine, 1996; worked with Delerium, Donovan. Recipient Best Female Pop Vocal Performance award Grammy, 1997, 1999, Best Pop Instrumental Performance award, 1997. Office: c/o Arista Records 6 W 57th St New York NY 10019-3901 also: Nettwork Mgmt 1650 W 2nd Ave Vancouver BC V6J 4R3 Canada*

MCLACHLIN, BEVERLEY, Canadian supreme court chief justice; b. Pincher Creek, Alta., Can., Sept. 7, 1943; m. Roderick McLachlin (dec. 1988); 1 child, Angus; m. Frank E. McArdle, 1992. BA, MA in Philosophy, LLB, U. Alta., LLD (hon.), 1991, U. B.C., 1990, U. Toronto, 1995, York U., 1999, Law Soc. Upper Can., 2000, U. Ottawa, 2000, U. Calgary, 2000, Brock U., 2000, Simon Fraser U., 2000, U. Victoria, 2000, U. Alberta, 2000, U. Lethbridge, 2001, Bridgewater State Coll., 2001, Mt. St. Vincent U., 2002, U. PEI, 2002, U. Montreal, 2003, U. Man., 2004. Bar: Alta. 1969, B.C. 1971. Assoc. Wood, Moir, Hyde and Ross, Edmonton, Canada, 1969—71, Thomas, Herdy, Mitchell & Co., Fort St. John, Canada, 1971—72, Bull, Housser and Tupper, Vancouver, 1972—75; lectr., assoc. prof., prof. with tenure U. B.C., 1974—81; appointed to County Ct., Vancouver, 1981; justice Supreme Ct. of B.C., 1981—85, B.C. Ct. of Appeal, Canada, 1985—88; chief justice Supreme Ct. of B.C., Canada, 1988; justice Supreme Ct. Can., Ottawa, Canada, 1989—2000, chief justice Can., 2000—. Co-author: B.C. Supreme Court Practice, B.C. Court Forms, Canadian Law of Arch. and Engring.; contbr. articles to profl. jours. Office: Supreme Ct Bldg 301 Wellington St Ottawa ON Canada K1A 0J1

MCLAIN, CHRISTOPHER M. lawyer; b. San Luis Obispo, Calif., July 21, 1943; s. James Latane and Marjorie Patricia (McNalley) McL.; m. Barbara McFarland, Nov. 23, 1968; children: Beth, Brian, Amy. BS in Bus. Adminstrn., U. Calif.-Berkeley, 1965, JD, 1968. Assoc. Knox, Goforth & Ricksen, Oakland, Calif., 1968-69, Donahue, Gallagher, Thomas & Woods, Oakland, 1969-73, ptnr., 1973-83; sec., counsel Lucky Stores, Inc., Dublin, Calif., 1984-89, v.p., 1985-89; ptnr. Sonnenschein, Nath & Rosenthal, San Francisco, 1989-90; sr. v.p., gen. counsel, sec. Transam. Corp., San Francisco, 1990-94; of counsel Sonnenschein Nath & Rosenthal, San Francisco, 1994-95; sr. v.p., gen. counsel, sec. Crown Vantage Inc., Oakland, Calif., 1995-99; ptnr., sr. v.p., gen. counsel Sequoia Assocs., LLC, Menlo Park, Calif., 1999—2003; pres., CEO, Creativity Inc., Van Nuys, Calif., 2003—. Mem. ABA, State Bar Calif., San Francisco Bar Assn., Am. Soc. Corps. Secs. Avocation: skiing. Office: Creativity Inc 7855 Hayvenhurst Ave Van Nuys CA 91406

MCLAIN, DENNIS O. lawyer; b. Detroit, Aug. 11, 1945; s. Francis William McLain and Hazel Joyce (Owen) Hortop. BA, U. Mich., 1971; JD, Detroit Coll. Law, 1975. Bar: Mich. 1975. Assoc. Collins & McCormick, Ypsilanti, Mich., 1972—77; gen. ptnr. McLain & Winters, Ypsilanti, Mich., 1977—. Mem.: Ypsilanti C. of C., Ypsilanti Bar Assn., Wastenau County Bar Assn., Mich. Bar Assn., Fed. Bar Assn. Democrat. Roman Catholic. Office: McLain & Winters 61 N Huron St Ypsilanti MI 48197-2675 Office Phone: 734-481-1120.

MCLAIN, DONALD J. retired academic administrator, educational consultant; b. St. Louis, Sept. 15, 1935; s. Clyde and Genevieve Dwyer McLain; m. Geraldine Peach McLain, May 13, 1961; children: James P., Matthew J. BS, St. Louis U., 1958. Dir. United Fund, St. Louis, 1963-68; exec. dir. Am. Optometric Found., St. Louis, 1968-74; exec. v.p. Optometric Progress Fund, St. Louis, 1968-74; alumni dir. profl. schs. Washington U., St. Louis, 1974-77; v.p. instnl. advancement Maryville U., St. Louis, 1977-93, Logan Coll. Chiropractic, St. Louis, 1993—2003; campaign cons. Humane Soc. Mo., 2001—02; v.p. St. Louis Coll. Pharmacy, 2003—. Participant confs. in field. Mem. pub. rels. com. Christmas in St. Louis; mem. allocations com. United Way; past pres. Wedgewood Improvement Assn.; v.p. fair Pub. Rels. Com. Sgt. U.S. Army, 1957, USAR, 1957-62. Mem. Nat. Soc. Fund Raising Execs., Am. Soc. Assn. Execs., Nat. Coun. on Philanthropy, Chesterfield C. of C., Sales and Mktg. Club St. Louis, Advt. Club, St. Louis COUNTS, Deferred Giving Club of St. Louis, Kiwanis, Rotary (past pres. West County chpt.). Roman Catholic. Address: 2009 Long Gate Ct Chesterfield MO 63017

MCLAIN, WILLIAM TOME, principal, educator; b. Washington, July 10, 1935; s. Ronald Alpha and Dorothy Smithson (Tome) McL.; m. Meurial Claire Webb, Nov. 20, 1977; 1 child, Laura Louisa McLain. BA, U. Del., 1957, MEd, 1966. Secondary Prin. Cert., Del. Math. tchr. Newark Sch. Dist., 1957-69, high sch. adminstrv. asst., 1969-78; high sch. assoc. prin. New Castle County Sch. Dist., Newark, 1978-81; high sch. asst. prin. Christina Sch. Dist., Newark, 1981-84, middle sch. asst. prin., 1984-87, prin. adult edn. program, 1987—. Treas., past chmn. Del. Coalition for Literacy; past pres. Del. Assn. for Adult and Cmty. Edn. Recipient Tchrs. medal, Freedoms Found., 1968, Silver Beaver award, Boy Scouts Am., 1967, Walace Johnson Cmty. Svc. award, New Castle County C. of C., 1979, Adult and Family Lit. Outstanding Svc. award, State of Del., 1992, Pres.'s award, Del. Assn. for Adult and Cmty. Edn., 2001, Cross and Flame award for svc. to children and youth, United Meth. Men, 2003. Mem. Interagency Coun. on Adult Lit. United Methodist. Avocations: travel, history. Home: 95 Dallas Ave Newark DE 19711-5123 Office: Christina School District 925 Bear Corbitt Rd Bear DE 19701-1323

MCLANE, DAVID GLENN, lawyer; b. Dallas, Jan. 17, 1943; s. Alfred Ervin and Dixie Marie (Martin) McL.; m. Sally Ruth Payne, Apr. 5, 1963; children: Cynthia Lynn, Kathleen Michelle, Michael Scott; m. Beverly Anne Bledsoe, Feb. 5, 1983; children: Morgan Elizabeth, Nicholas Martin, Elizabeth Clark. BA, So. Meth. U., 1963, LLB, 1966. Bar: Tex. 1966, U.S. Supreme Ct. 1971. Briefing atty. Supreme Ct. Tex., 1966-67; assoc., then ptnr. Gardere Wynne Sewell LLP (and predecessor firm), Dallas, 1967—. Lectr. in field. Author: Texas Corporations - Law and Practice, 1984; editor: Incorporation Planning

in Texas, 1977. Bd. dirs. urban Svcs. br. YMCA, Dallas, 1977-84, Dallas Symphony assn., 1980-93; mem. Dallas County AIDS Planning Commn. Task Force, 1988; pres. Coun. Dallas Theol. Sem., 1994—; exec. bd. Law Sch. So. Meth. U., 1997—; mem. ministry coun. Josh McDowell Ministries, 1997—. Mem. ABA, Tex. Bar Assn., Dallas Bar Assn., S.W. Benefits Assn. (bd. dirs. 1975-80, prs. 1978-79), So. Meth. U. Law Alumni Assn. (sec., bd. dirs. 1981-85, Vol. of Yr. award 1984), So. Meth. U. Alumni Assn. (bd. dirs. 1972-77). Presbytrian. Office: 3000 Thanksgiving Tower Dallas TX 75201 E-mail: dmclane@gardere.com.

MCLANE, FREDERICK BERG, lawyer; b. Long Beach, Calif., July 24, 1941; s. Adrian B. and Arlie K. (Burrell) McL.; m. Lois C. Roberts, Jan. 28, 1967; children: Willard, Anita. BA, Stanford U., 1963; LLB, Yale U., 1966. Bar: Calif. 1967, U.S. Dist. Ct. (cen. dist.) Calif. 1967. Assoc. prof. law U. Miss., Oxford, 1966-68; assoc. O'Melveny & Myers LLP, L.A., 1968-74, ptnr., 1975—. Lectr. in field. Pres., bd. dirs. Legal Aid Found., L.A., 1974-83; deacon Congl. Ch., Sherman Oaks, Calif., 1979-83; vice-chair L.A. Music Ctr., Unified Fund, 1992-94; bd. dirs. Calif. Sci. Ctr. Found., 1991-2000. Mem. ABA (banking com., fed. regulation of securities com.), Calif. Bar Assn. (fin. insts. com., uniform comml. codes), L.A. Bar Assn., Order of Coif, Calif. Club (L.A.), L.A. Country Club (bd. dirs.), The Quarry at La Quinta. Democrat. Avocations: golf, walking, reading. Office: O'Melveny & Myers 400 S Hope St Los Angeles CA 90071-2899 Business E-Mail: fmclane@omm.com.

MCLANE, WILLIAM DELANO, mechanical engineer; b. Ralls, Tex., Aug. 22, 1936; s. Clyde and Lillian Helen (Earp) McL.; m. Mary Ann Clark, Feb. 17, 1962; children: William Devin, Keri, Kristi, Mandy. BSME, Tex. Tech. U., 1961. Profl. engr. Tex. Engr. Texaco Inc., Tulsa, 1961-63; plant engring. mgr. Owens-Corning Fiberglas Corp., Toledo, 1963-72; pres., CEO Tucker-McLane Tire Corp., Waxahachie, Tex., 1972-89; commr. County of Ellis, Waxahachie, 1989-93; engr. Morrison Knudsen Corp., Dallas, 1993-94, MK-Ferguson, Albuquerque, 1994-95, Parsons Brinckerhoff, Dallas, 1995-96; quality control mgr. Sedalco, Inc., Ft. Worth, 1996-97; engring. mgr. Fortra Fiber-Cement, LLC., Waxahachie, Tex., 1997-2001; constrn. mgr. FWTA commuter rail project Parsons Brinckerhoff Constrn. Svcs., Inc., Dallas, 2001—02, project mgr., Bush Internat. Airport Svcs. Improvement program, 2002—. Mem. adv. bd. Guaranty Fed. Bank, Waxahachie, 1993—, Citizens Nat. Bank, Waxahachie, 1991-92, City of Waxahachie, 1990-91, Tex. State Tech. Coll., Inc., Waco, 1998—, Navarro Coll., Corsicana, 1998—, Portland Cement Assn., Skokie, Ill., 1998—. Sec. bd. Waxahachie Sch. Dist., 1979-88; vice chmn. Ctrl. Tex. Econ. Devel. Dist., Waco, 1989-93; mem. adv. com. Tex. State Tech. Coll., Waco, 1998—. Mem. ASME, ASCE, NSPE, Tex. Soc. Profl. Engrs., So. Bldg. Code Congress Internat., Internat. Soc. Tribologists and Lubrication Engrs., Internat. Conf. Bldg. Officials, Waxahachie C. of C. (pres. 1977). Republican. Presbyterian. Avocations: civic and political volunteer work, golf, fishing, cooking. Home: 1612 Alexander Dr Waxahachie TX 75165-1902 Office: Parsons Brinckerhoff Constrn Svcs Ste 1333 2777 Stemmons Fwy Ste 1333 Dallas TX 75207 also: The PB Team 15333 JFK Blvd Ste 300 Houston TX 77032 Personal E-mail: delmclane@aol.com.

MCLAREN, ARCHIE CAMPBELL, JR., marketing executive; b. Atlanta, Sept. 25, 1942; s. Archie Campbell and Virginia Lynn (Sides) McLaren; m. Georgia Mae Blunt, 1969 (div. 1971); 1 child, Leslie Michelle; m. Yvette Rubio, June 17, 1995 (div. Dec. 2001). BA, Vanderbilt U., 1964; JD, Memphis State U., 1968. Clk. FBI, Memphis, 1965-66; tchr., tennis coach Memphis U. Sch., 1966-68; tchr. Hunt High Sch., Columbus, Miss., 1968-69; tennis coach Miss. State U., Starkville, Miss., 1968-69; concierge The Roosevelt Hotel, New Orleans, 1969-70; sales rep. West Pub. Co., St. Paul, 1970-84, adminstr. internat. mktg. The Orient, 1985-90; freelance wine cons., 1985—. Cons. Calif. Ctrl. Coast Wine Growers Assn., Santa Maria, 1987-91; lectr. advanced wine appreciation Calif. Poly. U. Extended Edn., San Luis Obispo, 1986-90; dir. KCBX Ctrl. Coast Wine Classic, San Luis Obispo, 1985—, KHPR Wine Classic, Honolulu, 1987-91, Winesong, Ft. Bragg, Calif., 1987-96, WETA Washington Wine Classic, 1989-90, KCRW Summerday, 1991, Santa Barbara Wine Auction, 1997-98, auction dir., 1992-94, 97, 98—03; auction cons. Am. Inst. of Wine And Food, 1994—; chmn. Edna Valley Arroyo Grande Valley Vintners Assn., 1999-2001, San Luis Obispo Vintners and Growers Assn., 2002-04. Host talk show Pub. Radio Sta. KCBX, San Luis Obispo, 1984—; columnist (newspaper) San Luis Obispo Telegram-Tribune, 1992-95, New Times San Luis Obispo, 1995-96; contbg. writer: Adventures in Dining, 1994-95, Santa Barbara Mag., 1998-2002. Dir. Internat. Festival Champagne and Sparkling Wine, 1992—98; mem. Avila Valley Adv. Coun., 1993—95, City of San Luis Obispo Tourism Coun., 2000—04; founder Avila Drum Day; chmn. Avila Beach Cmty. Arts Com., 2000—; bd. dirs. Avila Beach County Water Dist., 1992—95, pres., 1992—94; mem. San Luis Obispo (Calif.) Mozart Festival, 1988—92, pres., 1991—92, mem. festival devel. com., 2000—01; bd. dirs. Am. Inst. Wine and Food, 2002—, Guild South County Ctr. for Performing Arts, 1993—94, San Luis Obispo County Arts Coun., 2000—02. Recipient Tourism award, San Luis County Visitors and Confs. Bur., 2000, decorated Commandeur d'Honneur, Commanderie du Bontemps de Medoc on des Graves de Sauternes on Barsac, France, 2001. Mem.: Austrian Wine Brotherhood, Internat. Food, Wine and Travel Writers' Assn., Marin County Food and Wine Soc., Ctrl. Coast Chaine des Rotisseurs (chpt. pres. 1987—89), Avila Bay Wine Soc., Vintners Club San Francisco, German Wine Soc. Honolulu, Am. Soc. Wine Educators, Calif. Ctrl. Coast Wine Soc. (pres. 1985), San Luis Yacht Club, Avila Bay Club. Avocations: racquetball, tennis, hiking, collecting wine, basketball. Office: PO Box 790 Avila Beach CA 93424-0790

MCLAREN, JOHN EDWARD, economics professor; b. Wadsworth, Ohio, May 21, 1962; s. Edward and Marion (Rae) McL.; m. Alev Erisir, Nov. 14, 1997. BSc, McGill U., 1986; MA, U. Toronto, 1987; PhD, Princeton U., 1992. Asst. prof. Columbia U., N.Y.C., 1992-98, assoc. prof., 1998-2000; prof. U. Va., Charlottesville, 2000—. Vis. asst. prof. Yale U., New Haven, Conn., 1996, Princeton (N.J.) U., 1997. Contbr. articles to profl. jours.; mng. editor, co-editor Economics and Politics jour., 1999—. Rsch. grantee NSF, 1999; faculty rsch. fellow Nat. Bur. Econ. Rsch., Cambridge, Mass., 2000—. Mem.: Am. Econ. Assn. Office: Dept Econs U Va Rouss Hall Charlottesville VA 22903 Office Phone: 434-924-3994. Business E-Mail: jmclaren@virginia.edu.

MCLAREN, KAREN LYNN, advertising executive; b. Flint, Mich., Feb. 14, 1955; m. Michael L. McLaren, June 18, 1974. AA, Mott Community Coll., Flint, 1976; BA, Mich. State U., 1978. Writer Sta. WGMZ-FM, Flint, 1979-84; writer, producer Tracy-Stephens Advt., Flint, 1984-87; pres. McLaren Advt., Troy, Mich., 1987—. Contbr. articles to profl. jours. Mem. centennial com. Wolverine region ARC, 1981, pub. rels. com., 1981-84; vol. coord., pub. rels. tour guide Whaley Hist. Ho., Flint, 1980-91; home designer, tour guide Romeo (Mich.) Hist. Home Tour, 1992; mem. Nat. Trust for Hist. Preservation, 1991-95; com. chair Crim Festival of Races, Flint, 1992, 93, 94, 95; active Sta. WFUM-Pub. TV, Flint, 1980-91; panelist career fair Modona U., Livonia, Mich., 1994, 95, 96, 97; ad book chair Juvenile Diabetes Found./Detroit Evening of Brilliance, 1997; mem. Oakland Regional Bd. Barbara Ann Karmanos Cancer Instn., 1999. Recipient 3 awards, 2 Nat. Health Care Mktg. Competition awards, Women's Adv. Club Detroit Pres.'s award, 1994. Mem. NAFE, Women's Advt. Club Detroit (scholar chmn. 1988-88, bd. dirs. 1989, 92-93, chmn. scholarship fundraiser 1991, co-chmn. career fair 1989, 90, 92, career fair panelist 1993, v.p. 1990, pres. 1991, amb. 1992, chmn. woman of yr. award 1994-96, by-laws chmn. 1994), Women's Econ. Club Detroit (progam com. 1996, workplace of tomorrow com. 1996, vice chair 1997, chair 1999). Office: 3001 W Big Beaver Rd Ste 306 Troy MI 48084-3104

MCLAREN, RICHARD WELLINGTON, JR., lawyer; b. Cin., May 15, 1945; s. Richard Wellington and Edith (Gillett) McL.; m. Ann Lynn Zachrich, Sept. 4, 1971; children: Christine, Richard, Charles. BA, Yale U., 1967; JD, Northwestern U., 1973. Bar: Ohio 1973, Ill. 1997, U.S. Dist. Ct. (no. dist.) Ohio 1973, U.S. Dist. Ct. (no. dist.) Ill. 1997, U.S. Ct. Appeals (6th cir.) 1978, U.S. Ct. Appeals (7th cir.) 1997, U.S. Ct. Appeals (fed. cir.) 1997, U.S. Supreme Ct. 1981. Assoc. Squire, Sanders & Dempsey, Cleve., 1973-82, ptnr., 1983-87; prin., counsel Ernst & Whinney, Cleve., 1988-89; assoc. gen. counsel Ernst & Young, Cleve., 1989-93; prin. counsel Centerior Energy Corp., Cleve., 1994-96; prin. Welsh & Katz, Ltd., Chgo., 1997—. 1st lt. U.S. Army, 1967-70. Mem. ABA (litigation, intellectual property and corp. law), FBA, Am. Judicature Soc., Ohio Bar Assn., Ill. Bar Assn. Home: 638 S Monroe St Hinsdale IL 60521-3926 Office: 120 S Riverside Plz Fl 22 Chicago IL 60606-3913 Office Phone: 312-655-1500. Business E-Mail: rwmclaren@welshkatz.com.

MCLARTY, THOMAS F., III, (MACK MCLARTY), former governement advisor, business executive; b. Hope, Ark., June 14, 1946; s. Thomas Franklin and Helen (Hesterly) McL.; m. Donna Kay Cochran, June 14, 1969; children: Mark Cochran, Franklin Hesterly. BA, U. Arkansas, Fayetteville, 1968. Founder, pres. McLarty Leasing System Inc., Little Rock, 1969-79; pres. McLarty Cos., 1979-83; with Arkla Inc., Shreveport, from 1983, pres., CEO Arkla Gas divsn., 1983; pres., COO Arkla Gas divsn. Arkla, Inc., Shreveport, 1984, chmn. bd., pres., CEO, from 1985; chief of staff The White House, Washington, 1993-94, sr. adviser to President Clinton, 1994—, counselor to pres., spl. envoy for Ams.; vice chmn. Kissinger McLarty Assocs., Washington, D.C., 1998—. Chmn. Arkla Energy Mktg. Co., Shreveport, La., Arkla Chem. Corp., Shreveport, AER-Ark. Gas Transit Co., Shreveport; chmn., chief exec. officer, Miss. River Transmission Corp., St. Louis, MRT Energy Mktg. Co., St. Louis, Ark. La. Fin. Corp., Shreveport. Mem. Ark. Ho. of Reps., 1970-72; chmn. Ark. Dem. Com.; mem. Dem. Nat. Com., 1974-76; treas. David Pryor Gubernatorial Campaign, 1974, Gov. Bill Clinton campaign, 1978; bd. dirs. Hendrix Coll., Conway, Ark.; bd. visitors U. Ark., Little Rock; former chmn. United Negro Coll. Fund Campaign, fund-raising campaign Ark. Symphony Mem. Greater Little Rock C. of C. (pres. 1983) Office: Kissinger McLarty Assocs 1775 Pennsylvania Ave NW Washington DC 20006-4605 also: The McLarty Cos 425 W Capitol Ave Ste 3810 Little Rock AR 72201-3460

MCLAUCHLAN, SYLVIA JUNE, charity organization executive; b. Hornchurch, Essex, Eng., June 8, 1935; d. Sydney George and Muriel May (Treweek) Smith; m. Derek John A. McLauchlan, Aug. 6, 1960. MB, ChB, U. Bristol, Eng., 1959; MSc, U. Manchester, Eng., 1979. Gen. practitioner, Bristol, 1960-66; med. officer Portsmouth (Eng.) City Coun., 1970-76; pub. health physician Univ.-Regional Health Authority, Manchester, 1976-85, S.W. Thames Regional Health Authority, London, 1985-91; dir. pub. health Ealing (Eng.) Health Authority, 1991-93; dir. gen. The Stroke Assn., London, 1993-97. Cons. in pub. health medicine. Fellow Faculty Pub. Health Medicine.

MCLAUGHLIN, ALLAN D. information technology executive; BS in Math. and Computer Sci., W.Va. Wesleyan Coll.; MBA, U. Dayton. Joined LexisNexis, Miamisburg, Ohio, 1988; mng. dir. Reed Elsevier Tech. Group, Cambridge, Mass., 1997—2000; v.p. Reed Elsevier, Inc., Cambridge, 1997—2000; sr. v.p., CTO LexisNexis Group, Miamisburg, 2000—. Trustee Greater Dayton (Ohio) Info. Tech. Alliance, founder exec.-on-loan program, Va. Piedmont Tech. Coun., Charlottesville; mem. adv. bd. Write State U. Computer Sci. and Engring. Sch., Dayton; mem. CIO adv. bd. U. Dayton; mem. tech. task force City of Dayton, 2002—03. Office: LexisNexis 9443 Springboro Pike Miamisburg OH 45342*

MCLAUGHLIN, CALVIN STURGIS, biochemistry educator; b. St. Joseph, Mo., May 29, 1936; s. Calvin Sturgis and Agnes Jane McLaughlin; m. Chin Helen Moy, Sept. 7, 1960; children: Heather Chin Chu, Christine Leng Oy, Andrew Calvin Moy. BS, King Coll., 1958; postgrad., Yale U., 1958-59; PhD, MIT, 1964. Postdoctoral fellow Institut de Biologie Physico-Chimique, Paris, 1964-66; prof. biochemistry U. Calif., Irvine, 1966—, dir. Cancer Rsch. Inst., 1981-83; vis. prof. Sch. Botany Oxford U., Eng., 1976, 80. Mem. peer rev. panels Am. Cancer Soc., NSF, NIH, VA Contbr. numerous articles to profl. jours.; mem. editl. bds. Jour. Bacteriology, 1975-80, Exptl. Mycology, 1980-86; reviewer profl. jours. Bd. dirs. Am. Cancer Soc., Orange County, 1980-89; mem. Traffic Affairs Com., Newport Beach, Calif., 1972-78. Named Outstanding Tchr. U. Calif.-Irvine, 1978, Gabriel Lester Meml. Lectr. Reed Coll., 1979; fellow Rockefeller Found., 1958-59, Upjohn Found., 1959-60, Nutrition Found., 1960-61, NIH, 1961-64, Am. Cancer Soc., 1964-66 Mem. Genetics Soc. Am., Am. Soc. Biochemistry and Molecular Biology, Am. Soc. Microbiology, Am. Soc. Mycology, Am. Soc. for Cell Biology, Yeast Genetics and Molecular Biology Soc. Am. (co-chair 1986-88), Electrophoresis Soc. Presbyterian. Office: U Calif Irvine Dept Biol Chemistry Irvine CA 92697-1700 E-mail: cal@uci.edu.

MCLAUGHLIN, CATHERINE G. healthcare educator; AB, Randolph-Macon Woman's Coll., 1971; MS in Econs., U. Wis., 1978, PhD in Econs., 1980. Prof. health mgmt. and policy U. Mich., 1983—, dir. Econ. Rsch. Initiative on the Uninsured, prof. dept. health mgmt. and policy, dir. Robert Wood Johnson Found. Scholars in Health Policy Rsch. Program. Dir. U. Mich. component Agy. for Healthcare Rsch. and Quality's Ctr. of Excellence on Managed Care Markets and Quality. Contbr. articles to profl. jours.; sr. assoc. editor Health Svcs. Rsch. Office: U Mich Dept Health Mgmt and Policy 109 S Observatory M3166 SPH II Ann Arbor MI 48109-2029 Business E-Mail: cmcl@umich.edu.

MCLAUGHLIN, DANIEL R. display designer, lighting designer; b. Denver, Colo., Dec. 7, 1966; m. Mary Beth Sprankle, July 22, 1990. BA Design/Theatre Tech. Summa Cum Laude, Loretto Heights Coll., Denver, 1989. Prodn. stage mgr. Dayton Ballet, Ohio, 1991—; gen. ptnr. Scenic Solutions LLC, Dayton, Ohio, 1996—. Mem. IATSE Stagehands Local 66, Dayton, Ohio, 1997—. Head carpenter, NASCAR Winston Cup Awards Ceremony; builder (stage deisgn) Inventing Flight Centennial Celebration, tech. dir.,builder (stage design) Schuster Ctr. Opening Gala. Mem.: United Scenic Artists Local 829. Office: Scenic Solutions LLC 229 South Alex Rd West Carrollton OH 45449 Personal E-mail: dan@scenicsolutions.com. Business E-Mail: dan@scenicsolutions.com.

MCLAUGHLIN, DAVID, foundation administrator; Grad., M.B.A., Dartmouth Coll.; Ph.D. (hon.), Colby-Sawyer Coll. Pres. Dartmouth College, 1981—87; chmn. Aspen Institute, 1987—88; chmn., CEO Orion Safety Products, 1988—; former chmn. CBS Corp., N.Y.C.; mem. bd. of gov. American Red Cross, 1998—, chmn., 2001—. Mem.: Ausbon Sargent Land Preservation Trust, Lake Sunapee Protective Assoc., Friends of the John Hay National Wildlife Refuge, Colby-Sawyer Coll. Bd. of Trustees. Office: Amer Red Cross 6900 Georgia Ave NW Washington DC 20307

MCLAUGHLIN, DAVID, academic administrator; Asst. prof. math. NYU, N.Y.C., 1970, dir. Courant Inst. Math. Scis., 1994—2002, provost, 2002—; chmn. applied math. U. Ariz., 1974—89; dir. applied and computation math. Princeton U., 1989. Adj. prof. biomathematics Mt. Sinai Med. Sch. Editor: two books; contbr. articles to profl. jours. Recipient Lester Ford award, 1976, David Alcaraz Spinola award, 1995. Fellow: Am. Acad. Arts and Scis.; mem.: NAS, Soc. Indsl. and Applied Math. Office: NYU 70 Washington Sq South New York NY 10012*

MCLAUGHLIN, HARRY ROLL, architect; b. Indpls., Nov. 29, 1922; s. William T. and Ruth E. (Roll) McL.; m. Linda Hamilton, Oct. 23, 1954. Registered architect, Ind., Ohio, Ill., Nat. Coun. Archtl. Registration Bds. Past pres. James Assocs. Inc., Indpls. Specializing in restoration of historic bldgs. and domestic architecture. Restorations include Old State Bank State Meml, Vincennes, Ind., Andrew Wylie House, Bloomington, Ind., Old Opera House State Meml, New Harmony, Ind., Old Morris-Butler House, Indpls. (Merit award 1972), Market St. Restoration and Maria Creek Baptist Ch., Vincennes, Benjamin Harrison House, Old James Ball Residence, Lafayette, Ind. (1st Design award 1972), Lockerbie Sq. Master Plan Park Sch., Indpls., Knox County Ct. House, Vincennes, 1972, J.K. Lilly House, Indpls., 1972, Waiting Station and Chapel, Crown Hill Cemetery, Indpls., 1972, Blackford-Condit House Ind. State U., Terre Haute, several Indian houses Angel Mounds Archaeol. Site and Interpretative Ctr. near Evansville, Ind.; architect: Glenn A. Black Mus. Archaeology, Ind. U., Bloomington; Restoration Morgan County Ct. House, Indpls. City Market, Hist. Schofield House, Madison, Ind., Ernie Pyle Birthplace, Dana, Ind., Phi Kappa Psi Nat. Hdqrs, Indpls., 1980 (Design award), East Coll. Bldg, DePauw U., Greencastle, Ind., Pres.'s House Restoration, DePauw U., 1992; contbr. articles to profl. jours.; Illustrator: Harmonist Construction. Past chmn. bd., past pres., now chmn. emeritus Historic Landmarks Found., Ind.; bd. dirs., archtl. adviser, bd. advisers Historic Madison, Inc.; mem. adv. coun. Historic Am. Bldgs. Survey, Nat. Park Svc., 1967-73; past mem. Ind. profl. rev. com. for Nat. Register nominations, 1967-81; past adv. bd. Conner Prarie Mus., Patrick Henry Sullivan Found.; past adviser Indpls. Historic Preservation Commn.; past mem. preservation com. Ind. U.; past mem. Meridian St. Preservation Commn., Indpls., 1971-2001; hon. mem. Ind. Bicentennial Commn.; bd. dirs. Park-Tudor Sch., 1972-85; past nat. bd. dirs. Preservation Action; life bd. dirs. Historic New Harmony; trustee Masonic Heritage Found.; past bd. dirs. Ind. Masonic Home, 1984-91, Inpls. Pub. Libr. Found., treas. 1988, 95—, v.p., 1989, pres. 1990-97; past trustee Eiteljorg Mus. Western Art, mem. adv. and planning com., 1999; past mem. Hamilton County Tourism Commn., 1989-91. Recipient numerous award including gov.'s citation State of Ind., 1967, Sagamore of Wabash award, 1967, 80, 82; Mayor's citation for svcs. in preservation archtl. heritage City of Indpls., sec.'s citation U.S. Dept. Interior, design and environ. citation for work in preservation, 1975. Fellow AIA (nat. com. historic bldgs., chmn. historic resources com. 1970); mem. Ind. Soc. Architects (state preservation coord. 1960—, Biennial award 1972, Design award 1978), Nat. Trust Historic Preservation (past trustee, bd. advisers), Soc. Archtl. Historians (Wilbur D. Peat award Ctrl. Ind. chpt. outstanding contbns. to understanding and appreciation of archtl. heritage 1993, past bd. dirs.), Ind. Com. for Preservation of Archtl. Records, Indpls. Mus. Art. (trustee, chmn. bldgs. com., bd. govs. 1986-95), Zionsville C. of C. (hon. bd. dirs.), U.S. Capitol (hon. trustee), Ind. Hist. Soc. (pres. 1999, trustee, bldg. com.), Marion County Hist. Soc. (past v.p., bd. dirs.), Zionsville Hist. Soc. (hon. life), Navy League U.S. (life), Ind. State Mus. Soc. (life), English Speaking Union (past bd. dirs. Indpls.), Hamilton County Hist. Soc. (life), Woodstock Club (bd. dirs. 1982-86, pres. 1985, ex-officio 1986), Literary Club Found. (trustee), Amateur Movie Club, Skyline Club (life), Packard Club, Masons (33 deg.). Home and Office: 950 W 116th St Carmel IN 46032-8864

MCLAUGHLIN, JAMES DANIEL, architect; b. Spokane, Wash., Oct. 2, 1947; s. Robert Francis and Patricia (O'Connel) McL.; m. Willa Kay Pace, Aug. 19, 1972; children: Jamie Marie, Robert James. BArch, U. Idaho, 1971. Registered architect, 10 states including Idaho. Architect AIA, Sun Valley, Idaho, 1971-74, McMillan & Hayes, Architects, Sun Valley, 1974-75, now pres.; prin. McLaughlin Architects Chartered, Sun Valley. Prin. works include Oakridge Apts., Moscow, Idaho (Excellence in Design award AIA), Walnut Ave. Mall, Ketchum, Idaho (Excellence in Design award AIA 1987), McMahan Residence, Sun Valley (Excellence in Design award AIA 1987). Chmn. Ketchum Planning and Zoning Commn., Ketchum Planning Commn., Ketchum Zoning Commn.; chmn. Sun Valley Planning and Zoning Commn.; chmn. Idaho Archtl. Licensing Bd. 1st lt. U.S. Army. Mem. AIA, Nat. Coun. Archtl. Registration Bds., Nat. Home Builders Assn., Ketchum-Sun Valley C. of C. (dir.), Rotary. Roman Catholic. Home: PO Box 6 Lot # 5 Red Cliffs Subdivsn Ketchum ID 83340-0006 Office: McLaughlin Architects Chartered PO Box 479 Sun Valley ID 83353-0479

MCLAUGHLIN, JAMES PATRICK, lawyer, educator; b. Jamesport, Mo., June 2, 1953; s. Robert Lee and Doris Ruth (Cox) McL.; m. Lana Gale Linville, June 10, 1978; children: Jamie Megan, Erin Brianne. BSBA, Cen. Mo. State U., 1975; JD, U. Mo., Kansas City, 1978. Bar: Mo., U.S. Dist. Ct. Mo. Assoc. prof. N.W. Mo. State U., Maryville, 1978—, chmn. dept. acctg., econs. and fin., 1988—; pvt. practice Maryville, 1979—. Pros. atty. City of Maryville, 1979—; asst. pros. atty. County of Nodaway, Maryville, 1980—; judge Mcpl. Ct., City of Rock Port and Tarkio, Mo., 1985—; atty. City of Burlington Junction, Mo., 1988, Bolckow, Barnard and Ravenwood, Mo., Clyde and Skidmore, 1998, Rosendale, Clearmont, Arkoe. Avocation: golf. Office: 1250 Chick Ave Maryville MO 64468-2741 also: NW Mo State U 2120 Colden Hall Maryville MO 64468

MCLAUGHLIN, JEAN WALLACE, art director, artist; b. Charlotte, N.C., Dec. 19, 1950; d. John Mason and Caroline (Garner) McL.; m. Thomas Hudson Spleth, Jan. 1991. BA, U. N.C., 1972; postgrad., Calif. Coll. Arts & Crafts, 1983-85; MA, N.C. State U., 1994. Spl. projects coord. Divsn. of the Arts, Dept. Cultural Resources, Raleigh, N.C., 1975-77; arts program coord. Gov.'s Adv. Coun. for Persons with Disabilities, Raleigh, 1978-79; visual and literary arts coord. N.C. Arts Coun., Raleigh, 1979-82; pvt. practice arts cons. San Francisco, 1982-85; visual arts sect. dir. N.C. Arts Coun., Raleigh, 1985-98; dir. Penland (N.C.) Sch. Crafts, 1998—. Art educator Charlotte (N.C.) Latin Sch., 1973-75; panelist and spkr. in field. Author: The Arts in the Churches and Synagogues of North Carolina, 1976; prodr. (book) Public Art Dialogue: SE, 1988. Bd. mem. New Langton Arts, San Francisco, 1983-85, N.C. World Ctr., Raleigh, 1988-91; program com. mem. Fiberworks, Berkeley, 1984-85. Mem. Nat. Assn. Artists Orgns., N.C. Ats Advs., Am. Assn. Mus., Am. Crafts Coun., New Langton Arts, Internat Sculpture Ctr., Art Table, Inc., N.C. Mus. Art, Southeastern Ctr. for Contemporary Art, Mint Mus. Craft and Design, Smithsonian. Avocations: gardening, travel, reading, writing, making art.

MC LAUGHLIN, JEROME MICHAEL, lawyer, shipping company executive; b. St. Louis, Jan. 11, 1929; s. John Thomas and Mary Adelaide (White) McL.; m. Delphine M. McClellan, June 15, 1957; children— Margaret D., Mary Martha, Elizabeth O., Jerome Michael, John T. AB, St. Louis U., 1950, JD, 1954. Bar: Mo. 1954, U.S. Supreme Ct. 1972. V.p. Internat. Indemnity, St. Louis, 1955-56; asst. circuit atty. City of St. Louis, 1957-58; partner firm Willson, Cunningham & McClellan, St. Louis, 1958-78; v.p., gen. counsel Alexander & Baldwin, Inc., Honolulu, 1978-79; sr. v.p. Philippines, Micronesia & Orient Navigation Co., San Francisco, 1979-87, chmn. bd. dirs., 1996—. Instr. philosophy St. Louis U., 1955-60 Served to capt. USMC, 1951-53, Korea. Mem. Mo. Bar Assn. Republican. Roman Catholic. Home: 820 Smoketree Ct San Marcos CA 92078-4980 Office: 353 Sacramento St San Francisco CA 94111-3620

MCLAUGHLIN, JOHN E. federal agency administrator; b. McKeesport, PA, June 15, 1942; BA, Wittenberg U., 1964; MA, Johns Hopkins U., 1966; postgrad., SAIS Ctr., Bologna, Italy, U. Pa. With CIA, 1972—, with State Dept., Bur. European and Can. Affairs, 1984—85, deputy dir. Office European Analysis, 1985—89, dir. European analysis, 1989, dir. Slavic and Eurasian analysis, 1989—95, numerous diplomatic delegations, 1995—2000, deputy dir., 2000—, acting dir., 2004—. With U.S. Army, 1966—69. Office: CIA Office of Dir Washington DC 20505

MC LAUGHLIN, JOHN FRANCIS, civil engineer, educator; b. N.Y.C., Sept. 21, 1927; s. William Francis and Anna (Goodwin) McL.; m. Eleanor Thomas Trethewey, Nov. 22, 1950; children: Susan, Donald, Cynthia, Kevin. B.C.E., Syracuse U., 1950; MS in Civil Engring., Purdue U., 1953, PhD, 1957. Mem. faculty Purdue U., 1950-95, prof. civil engring., 1963-95, head Sch. Civil Engring., 1968-78, asst. dean engring. Sch. Civil Engring., 1977-80, assoc. dean engring., 1980-94, interim dean engring., 1994-95; ret. Sch. Civil Engring., 1995. Cons. in field. Served with USAAF, 1945-47. Fellow ASCE, Hwy. Rsch. Bd.; mem. ASTM (bd. dirs. 1984-86), Am. Concrete Inst. (hon. mem., bd. dirs., v.p. 1977-79, pres. 1979), Am. Nat. Stds. Inst. (bd. dirs. 1992-94), Sigma Xi, Tau Beta Pi, Chi Epsilon, Theta Tau. Home: 112 Sumac Dr West Lafayette IN 47906-2157 E-mail: JmackSumac@aol.com.

MCLAUGHLIN, JOHN J. broadcast executive, television producer, journalist, political commentator; s. Augustus Hugh and Eva Philomena (Turcotte) McL.; m. Ann Lauenstein, Aug. 23, 1975 (div. 1992); m. Cristina Vidal, Jun. 22, 1997. AB, Boston Coll., 1951, MA in Philosophy, 1952, BDiv, 1959, MA in English, 1961; PhD, Columbia U., 1967. Ordained priest Roman Catholic Ch., 1960. Mem. Jesuit Order, N.E., N.Y. and Washington; resigned order and active ministry, 1975; tchr., dir. communications Fairfield (Conn.) Univ. and Preparatory Sch., 1960-64; assoc. editor America Mag., N.Y.C., 1967-70; dep. spl. asst. to Pres. Richard Nixon and Gerald Ford, Washington, 1971-74; pres. McLaughlin and Co. Pub. Policy Cons., Washington, 1975-79; radio talk-show host Sta. WRC-AM, Washington, 1979-82; pres., chmn. bd. dirs. Oliver Prodns., Inc., Washington, 1983—. Lectr. numerous univs., corps. and orgns. nationwide and abroad, 1963—; host various TV series, Sta. WJAR-TV, Providence, 1962-63, Sta. WNHC-TV, New Haven, 1963, Sta. WTIC-TV,

Hartford, 1963, Sta. WOR-TV, N.Y.C., 1964; host, exec. producer Biafra Today report ABC-TV Network, 1969; radio commentator Sta. WSTC, Stamford, Conn., 1964, CBS Network Radio, N.Y.C., 1964, Nat. Pub. Radio All Things Considered, Washington, 1981-85; dir. film insts. Yale U., Holy Cross Coll., Manhattanville Coll.; juror Am. Film Festival, 1969; congressional testimony pub. broadcasting and TV license renewal, Washington, 1967, 69. Author: Love Before Marriage, 1970; editor National Review, Washington, 1981-89, columnist From Washington Straight, 1982-89; TV host and exec. producer The McLaughlin Group NBC and PBS TV stas., 1982—, John McLaughlin's One on One, 1984—, McLaughlin CNBC cable system, 1989-94; TV appearances (host spl. episode) Cheers, 1990, (cameo) Murphy Brown, 1995, Lateline, 1998; Motion picture appearances: Dave, 1993, Mission Impossible, 1996, Independence Day, 1996, Murder at 1600, 1997, Bulworth, 1998. Rep. candidate U.S. Senate, R.I., 1970. Recipient Excellence in Journalism award Cath. Press Assn., 1969, News Media award VFW, 1984; nominee Nat. Acad. Cable Programming ACE award, 1989, 90, 91, 94; The McLaughlin Group named Best Polit. Talk Show, Washingtonian mag., 1987-93, George Mag., 1998. Mem. NATAS (Emmy award 1984), Am. Fedn. TV and Radio Artists, Screen Actors Guild. Office: Oliver Prodns Inc 1211 Connecticut Ave NW Ste 810 Washington DC 20036-2703 E-mail: slucian@mclaughlin.com.

MCLAUGHLIN, JOHN MARK, lawyer, banker; b. Wichita Falls, Tex., Oct. 24, 1930; s. Clarence T. and Evelyn Claire (Littleton) McL.; m. Amy I. Johnson, June 25, 1954; children— Laure, Brian, Matthew. B.B.A., U. Tex.-Austin, 1952, LL.B., 1954. Bar: Tex. 1954. Asst. atty. gen. Tex., 1957-58; sole practice, Snyder, Tex., 1958-64; ptnr. Marschall, Hall & McLaughlin, San Angelo, Tex., 1965— . Chmn. bd. trustees Concho Valley Council Boy Scouts Am.; chmn. bd. trustees Angelo Community Hosp.; mem. Tex. Constn. Revision Commn., 1973; mem. Tex. Bd. Corrections, 1973-79. Served to capt. USAF, 1954-56. Fellow Am. Bar Found., Am. Coll. Probate Counsel, Tex. Bar Found. (chmn. fellows 1981-82); mem. State Bar of Tex. (v.p. 1976-77). Democrat. Episcopalian. Club: San Angelo Country. Office: PO Box 1170 San Angelo TX 76902-1170

MCLAUGHLIN, JOHN RICHARDSON, electric motor company executive; b. New Orleans, Sept. 8, 1929; s. Thomas Phillip and Louise (Fortier) McL.; m. Lorraine Bergstrom, Aug. 9, 1952; children: Elizabeth, Richard, Thomas. BSChemE, Tulane U., 1950, MBA in Mgmt., 1953. Gen. mgr. housewares mfg. dept. GE Co., Bridgeport, Conn., 1953-78; group v.p. Lear Siegler Co., Greenwich, Conn., 1978-85; pres. Electric Indicator Co. Inc., Norwalk, Conn., 1985—. Bd. dirs. Japanese Products Corp., Norwalk. Selectman Town of Easton (Conn.), 1997-99; chmn. ch. coun. Easton Congl. Ch., 2000—. Recipient Official Citation Gen. Assembly State of Conn., 1999. Mem. Easton Exch. Club. Republican. Congregationalist. Avocations: tennis, fishing, chess. Home: 105 Norton Rd Easton CT 06612-1550 Office: Elec Indicator Co Inc 120 Fiske St Fairfield CT 06432-6104

MCLAUGHLIN, JOHN SHERMAN, lawyer; b. Pitts., Apr. 1, 1932; s. John H. and Dorothy I. (Schrecongost) McL.; m. Suzanne Shaver, June 5, 1971; children— Dorothy, Sarah, Martha. AB, Harvard U., 1954, LLB, 1957. Bar: Pa. 1958, U.S. Supreme Ct. 1967. Assoc. Reed, Smith, Shaw & McClay, Pitts., 1957-71, ptnr., 1971—2002, of counsel, 2002—. Trustee Harmarville Rehab. Ctr., Inc., 1980-87; pres., trustee Western Pa. Sch. for the Deaf, 1985—; pres. Pa. NG Assn., 1976-78; justice of peace Borough of Edgewood, 1963-73; trustee Winchester Thurston Sch., 1987-2002; life trustee Carnegie Libr. of Pitts., Carnegie Inst., 1994—, Carnegie Mus. Art, 1997—; dir. Pitts. Symphony, 1985-95, adv. 1996-99. Lt. col. Air NG, 1957-79. Mem.: Allegheny County Bar Assn., Am. Law Inst., Rolling Rock Club (Ligonier, Pa.), Duquesne Club. Office: Reed Smith LLP 435 6th Ave Pittsburgh PA 15219-1886 E-mail: jmclaughlin@reedsmith.com.

MCLAUGHLIN, JOSEPH, lawyer; b. Newark, Aug. 1, 1941; s. Joseph Nicholas and Genevieve Veronica (Lardiere) McL.; m. Elisabeth Lippold, July 31, 1965; children: Elisabeth, Jessica, Emilie. AB, Columbia U., 1962, LLB, 1965. With Sullivan & Cromwell, N.Y.C., 1968-76; v.p., gen. counsel Goldman, Sachs & Co., 1976-88, cons., 1988-90; ptnr. Sidley Austin Brown & Wood, N.Y.C., 1993—. Adj. prof. law NYU Sch. Law, 1988-92; spkr., presenter in field. Author (with C.J. Johnson Jr.): Corporate Finance and the Securities Laws, 3d edit., 2004; contbr. articles to profl. jours. Trustee Greenwich (Conn.) Acad., 1988-2000; treas. Presbyn. Ch. Old Greenwich, 1988-91; bd. dirs. United Way, Greenwich, 1993-97; mem. Rep. Town com., Greenwich, 1993-96. Jervey fellow Parker Sch. Fgn. Comparative Law, Columbia Law Sch., U. Munich, 1966-68. Mem. ABA (sect. bus. law, fed. regulation securities com., subcom. broker-dealer matters 1985—, subcom. civil litigation and SEC enforcement matters 1989—, chair task force rule 10b-6 1995-97, co-chair task force sellers' due diligence and similar defenses under fed. securities laws 1989-92), Am. Law Inst., Assn. of Bar of City of NY (internat. law com. 1979-84, chair 1981-84, civil rights com. 1984-87, internat. arms control and security affairs com. 1988-90), NY Stock Exch. (legal adv. com. to bd. govs. 1985-88, subcom. corp. governance, subcom. internat. issues 1988—), Securities Industry Assn. (fed. regulations com. 1978-88, chair 1982-84), Nat. Assn. Securities Dealers, Inc. (corp. financing com. 1983-86), Am. Arbitration Assn. (dir. 1986-90). Republican. Congregationalist. Office Phone: 212-839-5312. Business E-Mail: jmclaughlin@sidley.com.

MCLAUGHLIN, JOSEPH MICHAEL, federal judge, law educator; b. Brooklyn, N.Y., Mar. 20, 1933; s. Joseph Michael and Mary Catherine (Flanagan) McLaughlin; m. Frances Elizabeth Lynch, Oct. 10, 1959; children: Joseph, Mary Jo, Matthew, Andrew. AB, Fordham Coll., 1954, LL.B., 1959; LL.M., NYU, 1964; LL.D., Mercy Coll., White Plains, N.Y., 1981; LLD, Fordham U., 1998. Bar: N.Y. 1959. Assoc. Cahill, Gordon, N.Y.C., 1959—61; prof. law Fordham U., N.Y.C., 1961—71, dean Sch. of Law, 1971—81, adj. prof., 1981—90; judge U.S. Dist. Ct. Eastern Dist. N.Y., Bklyn., 1981—90, U.S. Ct. Appeals (2nd Cir.), N.Y.C., 1990—98; sr. judge, 1998—; editor-in-chief Fed. Practice Guide. Adj. prof. St. John's Law Sch., N.Y.C., 1982—97; chmn. N.Y. Law Revision Commn., Albany, 1975—82. Author (with Peterfreund): New York Practice, 1964; author: Evidence, 1979, also articles. Capt. Corps of Engineers U.S. Army, 1955—57, Korea. Mem.: ABA, N.Y. State Bar Assn., Assn. of Bar of City of N.Y., Lotos Club. Roman Catholic. Office: US Courthouse US Ct Appeals 40 Foley Sq Rm 2402 New York NY 10007-1502

MCLAUGHLIN, LEIGHTON BATES, II, journalism educator, former newspaperman; b. Evanston, Ill., Apr. 10, 1930; s. Leighton Bates and Gwendolyn I. (Markle) McL.; m. Beverly Jean Jeske, May 5, 1962; children: Leighton Bates III, Jeffrey, Steven, Patrick. Student English lit., Kenyon Coll., Gambier, Ohio, 1948-50, Northwestern U., 1951; BA in English lit., UCLA, 1983; MA in communications, Calif. State U., Fullerton, 1990. Copyboy, reporter, rewriteman City News Bur., Chgo., 1957-58; reporter, rewriteman Chgo. Sun-Times, 1958-62; rewriteman, asst. city editor Ariz. Jour., Phoenix, 1962; reporter Miami (Fla.) Herald, 1962-64; successively rewriteman, night city editor, 1st asst. city editor, telegraph editor Chgo. Sun-Times, 1964-74; dir. Chgo. Daily News/Sun-Times News Service, 1974-79; editorial coord. electronics newspaper div. Field Enterprises, 1975-79; adminstr. reference libr. and communications ctr. Field Newspapers, 1976-79; editor News Am. Syndicate, Irvine, Calif., 1979-85; mng. editor San Gabriel Valley Daily Tribune, 1986; assoc. prof. journalism Riverside (Calif.) C.C., 1987-96, chmn. performing arts and media dept., 1993-96, coll. publs. editor, ret., 1996-99; lectr. in journalism Calif. State U.-Fullerton, 1984-96. Copy editor The Press-Enterprise, Riverside, Calif., 1988-95; lectr., condr. seminars in field. Author articles in field. Served to 1st lt. USMC, 1951-54. Recipient Stick-o-Type award for best feature story Chgo. Newspaper Guild, 1961, Best News story award Ill. AP and UPI, 1967 Mem. Chgo. (Ill.) Press Vets., Verban Soc., Psi Upsilon. Office: Riverside CC 4800 Magnolia Ave Riverside CA 92506-1242 *Reporting the news is like any other intellectual activity in that it involves research, verification, organization, and clarity of presentation. But news reporting is unique in that all this is done on a dead run, in time for the day's editions.*

MCLAUGHLIN, MARGUERITE P. state legislator, logging company executive; b. Matchwood, Mich., Oct. 15, 1928; d. Harvey Martin and Luella Margaret (Livingston) Miller; m. George Bruce McLaughlin, 1947; children: Pamela, Bruce Jr., Cynthia. Owner, operator contract logging firm, Orofino, Idaho; mem. Idaho Ho. of Reps., 1978-80, Idaho Senate, 1980—, asst. Dem. Leader, 1990-93, Dem. leader, 1997-98. Chair Democrat Caucus, 1995-96; mem. Senate Fin. Com., 1987—, Gov.'s Adv. Coun. Workers Compensation, 1990-96, State of Idaho Endowment Fund Investment Bd., 1991-95, legis. coun., 1989-94, 95—. Mem. State of Idaho Job Tng. Coun., 1989-98, State Ins. Fund Commn., 1998—; trustee Joint Sch. Dist. 171, 1976-80; pres. Oro Celebration, Inc. Office: Idaho State Senate State Capital Boise ID 83720-0001

MCLAUGHLIN, MICHAEL ANGELO, mortgage consultant, author; b. Medford, Mass., Mar. 13, 1950; s. Bernard Thadeus and Rose Francis (DiStasio) McL.; m. Karen Jean Parker, Nov. 19, 1972 (div. 1985); m. Claudia Chuber, June 29, 1985; 1 child, Camila; 1 stepchild, Sebastian Ortega. BS with honors, Northeastern U., 1975, MPA, 1978. Asst. juvenile supr. Dept. Youth Svcs., Boston, 1972-73; correction officer Dept. Correction, Billerica, Mass., 1974, Dept. Correction-MCI Walpole, Boston, 1974-80; facility mgr. 1st Security Svc. Corp., Boston, 1980-82; from sales mgr. to owner Solar Resources Internat., Danvers, Mass., 1982-84; account exec. New Eng. Rare Coin Galleries, Boston, 1985, Progressive Consumers Fed. Credit Union, 1985, br. mgr., 1988-90; mortgage broker McLaughlin Fin., Inc., 1991—; br. mgr. CitiMortgage, Inc., 2000-01; mortgage broker McLaughlin Fin., Inc., 1991—. Lectr. Northeastern U., Boston, 1981; pres. local chpt. Am. Fedn. State, County and Mcpl. Employees, Mass., 1977-79. Author: Screw: The Truth about Walpole State Prison by the Guard Who Lived It, 1989. Candidate, mem. Com. to Elect Mike McLaughlin Sheriff, Middlesex County, Mass., 1980; mem. Spl. Legis. Conf. Com., Boston, 1979, Joint Labor Mgmt. Com., Boston, 1978. MPA Assn. (activities com. 1982), Sigma Epsilon Rho. Roman Catholic. Avocations: golf, sailing, skiing, pocket billiards, tennis, racquetball. Home: 3 White St Salem MA 01970-5609 Office Phone: 800-500-6016. E-mail: mfiloans@mindspring.com., mike@mclaughlinfinancial.com.

MCLAUGHLIN, MICHAEL JOHN, retired insurance company executive; b. Cambridge, Mass., Feb. 14, 1944; s. Michael John and Evelyn Katherine (Quinn) McL. AB, Boston Coll., 1965; JD, N.Y. U., 1968. Bar: N.Y., Mass. With N.Y. Life Ins. Co., 1968—, sr. v.p. info. systems and services dept., 1982-88, sr. v.p., 1988-91, sr. v.p., dep. gen. counsel, 1991-95, sr. v.p., gen. counsel, 1995-2000. Mem. ABA, N.Y. State Bar Assn. E-mail: mmclau2260@aol.com.

MCLAUGHLIN, MIKE, race car driver; b. Waterloo, N.Y., Oct. 6, 1956; m. Katie McLaughlin. Race car driver, Busch Series Joe Gibbs Racing. Achievements include Featherlite Modified Series, NASCAR Touring champion, 1988. Mailing: Joe Gibbs Racing 13415 Reese Blvd West Huntersville NC 28078

MCLAUGHLIN, PATRICK MICHAEL, lawyer; b. Monahans, Tex., July 23, 1946; s. Patrick John and Ann (Donnelly) M.; m. Christine Manos, Aug. 21, 1970; children— Brian Patrick, Christopher Michael, Conor Andrew B.Gen. Studies, Ohio U., 1972; JD, Case Western Res. U., 1976. Bar: Ohio 1976, U.S. Dist. Ct. (no. dist.) Ohio 1978, U.S. Ct. Appeals (6th cir.) 1979, U.S. Supreme Ct. 1980; U.S. Dist. Ct. (so. dist.) Ohio 1989, U.S. Ct. Appeals (5th cir.). Dir. vets. edn. project. Am. Assn. Community and Jr. Colls., Washington, 1972-73; law clk. Common Pleas Ct., Cleve., 1976-77; law clk. to judge 8th Jud. Dist. Ct. of Appeals, Cleve., 1977-78; asst. U.S. atty. No. Dist. Ohio, Cleve., 1978-82, chief civil div., 1982-84, U.S. atty., 1984-88; ptnr. Janik & McLaughlin, Cleve., 1988-89, Mansour, Gavin, Gerlack & Manos Co., L.P.A., Cleve., 1989-97; apptd ind. spl. prosecutor Ohio Attorneys General, 1993-96; mng. ptnr. McLaughlin & McCaffrey, LLP, Cleve., 1997—. Cons. Nat. League of Cities, U.S. Conf. Mayors, 1971-72; co-creator Opportunity Fair for Veterans Concept, 1971 Editor-in-chief Case Western Res. Jour. Internat. Law, 1975-76 Chmn. North Ohio Drug Abuse Task Force, 1986-88; chmn. Law Enforcement Coordinating Commn., North Ohio, 1985-88; chmn. civil issues subcom. Atty. Gen.'s Adv. Com., 1986-88; exec. v.p. Greater Cleve. Vets. Meml., Inc., 1993, pres., 1994—. Decorated Silver Star, Bronze Star, Purple Heart, Army Commendation medal, Vietnamese Cross of Gallantry with Silver and Bronze Stars; named to Ohio Vets. Hall of Fame, 2003, Ohio Mil.Hall of Fame for Valor, 2004. Fellow Am. Coll. Trial Lawyers; mem. ABA, FBA, Ohio Bar Assn., Cleve. Bar Assn., Nat. Assn. Former U.S. Attys., Soc. 1st Divsn., 18th Inf. Regiment Assn., Order of Ahepa, Vietnam Vets. Am., Nat. Vietnam Vets. Network (Disting. Vietnam Vet. award 1985), Nat. Assn. Concerned Vets. (nat. v.p. external affairs 1971-72, exec. dir. 1972-73), Cuyahoga County Vets. (award 1985), Nat. Soc. SAR (law enforcement commendation medal 1989). Republican. Roman Catholic. Office: McLaughlin & McCaffrey LLP Eaton Ctr 1111 Superior Ave Ste 1350 Cleveland OH 44114-2500 Office Phone: 216-623-0900.

MCLAUGHLIN, PHILIP T. lawyer, former state attorney general; b. Nashua, N.H., Jan. 23, 1945; s. Philip J. and Pauline (Reilly) McLaughlin; m. Janice Livingston, 1968; children: Matthew, Timothy, Emily, Katherine, Philip. AB in History, Holy Cross coll., 1967; MPA, U. R.I., 1971; JD, Boston Coll., 1974. Bar: N.H. 1974. Atty. Belknap County, NH, 1979—81; ptnr. McLaughlin, Hemeon & Lahey, P.A., Laconia, NH, 1981—97; atty. gen. State of N.H., 1997—2002; pvt. practice law, 2002—. Past pres. Lakes Region Mental Health Ctr., Laconia; mem. Laconia City Coun., 1976—80, Laconia Sch. Bd., 1985—94, also chair; mem. prof. conduct com. N.H. Supreme Ct., 1983—92, 1994—97; del. N.H. Constl. Conv., 1984. Lt. USN, 1969—71. Democrat. Office: Atty Gen Office 33 Capitol St Concord NH 03301-6397

MCLAUGHLIN, PHILIP VANDOREN, JR., mechanical engineering educator, researcher, consultant; b. Elizabeth, N.J., Nov. 10, 1939; s. Philip VanDoren and Ruth Evans (Landis) McL.; m. Phoebe Anne Feeney, Aug. 19, 1961; children: Philip VanDoren III, Patrick Evans, Christi M. Barton. BSCE, U. Pa., 1961, MS in Engring. Mechanics, 1964, PhD in Engring. Mechanics, 1969. Assoc. engr. Boeing-Vertol, Morton, Pa., 1962-63, engr. II, 1963; rsch. engr. Scott Paper Co., Phila., 1963-65, rsch. project engr., 1965-69, sr. rsch. project engr., 1969; asst. prof. theoretical and applied mechanics U. Ill., Urbana, 1969-73, asst. dean engring., 1971-72; project mgr. Materials Scis. Corp., Blue Bell, Pa., 1973-76; assoc. prof. mech. engring. Villanova (Pa.) U., 1976-81, prof., 1981—2003, prof. emeritus, 2003—. Cons. Naval Air Engring. Ctr., Lakehurst, N.J., 1977-79, U.S. Steel Corp., Trenton, 1980-82, RCA Corp., Moorestown, N.J., 1986, Coal Tech Corp., Merion Station, Pa., Air Products and Chems., Inc., Allentown, Pa., 1988, Aircraft divsn. Naval Air Warfare Ctr., Patuxent River, Md., 1995-96, Christini Technologies, Phila., 1999—, Alpha Sci. Corp., Southeastern, Pa., 2000-01, Materials Rsch. & Design, Inc., Rosemont, Pa., 2002-, DETechs., King of Prussia, Pa., 2002—; vis. prof. dept. engring. U. Cambridge, Eng., 1990-91. Reviewer: for sci. and tech. jours.; contbr. numerous articles to profl. jours. Rsch. grantee NSF, 1970-72, Naval Air Engring. Ctr., 1978-84, Lawrence Livermore Nat. Lab., 1979-81, Naval Air Devel. Ctr., 1985-86, RCA Corp., 1986-87; sr. rsch. assoc. NRC, Washington, 1983-84; USN-Am. Soc. for Engring. Edn. sr. faculty fellow, 1995. Mem.: ASME (life; chmn. applied mechanics divsn. Phila. sect. 1981—83, mem. materials divsn. com. on composites 1992—), ASCE (life; chmn. engring. mechanics divsn. com. on inelastic behavior 1977—79, assoc. editor Jour. Engring. Mechanics Divsn. 1977—79, mem. aerospace divsn. com. on structures and materials 1986—95), Am. Soc. Composites, Am. Soc. Engring. Edn., Am. Acad. Mechanics, Sigma Xi. Achievements include research and consulting on composite materials and structures, structural analysis and design and inelastic behavior. Office: Villanova U Dept Mech Engring 800 Lancaster Ave Villanova PA 19085-1681 E-mail: philip.mclaughlin@villanova.edu.

MCLAUGHLIN, ROSEMARY, horse trainer, state representative; b. Royalton, Vt., July 15, 1952; m. Tom Wells; 1 child, Katie. Student, Vt. Tech. Coll., 1969—70, Reed Coll., 1971—73. Prin., owner Hitching Post Farm, Royalton, Vt., 1973—; rep. Vt. State Ho. Reps., 2003—. Mem. Royalton (Vt.) Selectboard, Royalton (Vt.) Sch. Bd., 1990—96. Democrat. Home: 273 Rousseau Rd South Royalton VT 05068

MCLAUGHLIN, SHERRY, association administrator; m. Art McLaughlin; 3 children. With Emil H. Dutler unit 177 Am. Legion Aux., 1956, unit pres., 3d dist. pres., Dept. of Iowa pres., 1985—86, nat. v.p., nat. pres., 2001—; counselor Iowa Girls State. Chmn. Aux. Emergency Fund; mem. numerous coms. Am. Legion Aux. Vol. Iowa Vets. Home, Iowa Braille, Vinton-Shellsburg Schs., Union Sch.; Ct. apptd. spl. advocate; confirmation tchr. Trinity Luth. Ch. Recipient Gov.'s Vol. of the Yr. award, 1999, 2000. Office: American Legion Auxiliary 777 N Meridian St 3rd Flr Indianapolis IN 46204

MCLAUGHLIN, SYLVIA CRANMER, volunteer, environmentalist; b. Denver, Dec. 24, 1916; d. George Ernest and Jean Louise (Chappell) Cranmer; m. Donald Hamilton McLaughlin, Dec. 29, 1948; children: Jean Katherine McLaughlin Shaterian, George Cranmer McLaughlin. AB, Vassar Coll., 1939. Co-founder Save San Francisco Bay Assn., Berkeley-Oakland, Calif., 1961-99, pres., 1993-95. Bd. dirs. Ptnrs. for Liveable Cmtys., Washington, 1975-78; mem. waterfront adv. com. City of Berkeley, Calif., 1964-68; sec., bd. dirs. Resource Renewal Inst., 1980—, Citizens for Eastshore State Park, 1980—; founder, bd. dirs. Pub. Trust Group, Oakland, Calif., 1997—; mem. awards com. Berkeley Cmty. Fund, 1998—; mem. adv. bd. Greenbelt Alliance, San Francisco, 1982—; mem. nat. adv. coun. Trust for Pub. Land, San Francisco, 1986—, Ecocity Builders, Berkeley, 1990—. Mem. Nat. Aubudon Soc. (bd. dirs. 1970-76), Nat. Recreation and Parks Assn. (bd. dirs. 1974-78), East Bay Conservation Corps (bd. dirs. 1985-97), Student Conservation Assn. (bd. dirs. 1979-84). Avocations: outdoor activities, adventure and travel, reading, children and grandchildren, working out. Home: 1450 Hawthorne Ter Berkeley CA 94708-1804

MCLAUGHLIN, T. MARK, lawyer; b. Salem, Mass., Apr. 20, 1953; s. Terrence E. and Mary E. (Donlon) McL.; m. Sandra L. Roman, Oct. 16, 1982; children: Daniel, Kathleen, Eileen. BA in Econs., U. Notre Dame, 1975, JD, 1978. Bar: Ill. 1978, U.S. Dist. Ct. (no. dist.) Ill. 1978, U.S. Dist. Ct. (cen. dist.) Ill. 1992, U.S. Dist. Ct. (ea. dist.) Wis. 1992, U.S. Ct. Appeals (7th cir.) 1982, U.S. Ct. Appeals (11th cir.) 1982, U.S. Ct. Appeals (8th cir.) 1998. Assoc. Mayer Brown Rowe & Maw LLP, Chgo., 1978-84, ptnr., 1985—. Adj. faculty law Loyola U., Chgo., 1983, 86-90. Bd. dirs. no. Ill. affiliate Am. Diabetes Assn., Chgo., 1985-94. Mem. ABA (franchising forum com. antitrust law sect.), Phi Beta Kappa. Office: Mayer Brown Rowe & Maw LLP 190 S La Salle Street Ste 3100 Chicago IL 60603-3441 Office Phone: 312-701-7066. E-mail: mmclaughlin@mayerbrownrowe.com.

MCLAUGHLIN, THOMAS KEITH, diversified financial services company executive; BS in Bus., Calif. State U., Northridge. CPA Grant Thornton, 1980—85; fin. analyst Countrywide Fin. Corp., Calabasas, Calif., 1986—87, treas. Countrywide Home Loans, 1989—96, mng. dir. fin., 1997—2000, CFO, 2000—, sr. mng. dir., 2001—. Office: Countrywide Fin Corp 4500 Park Granada Calabasas CA 91302-1613

MCLAUGHLIN, WILLIAM IRVING, space technical manager, writer; b. Oak Park, Ill., Mar. 6, 1935; s. William Lahey and Eileen (Irving) McL.; m. Karen Bjorneby, Aug. 20, 1960; children: William, Margot, Walter, Eileen. BS with highest honors, U. Calif., Berkeley, 1963, MA, 1966, PhD, 1968. Mem. tech. staff Bellcomm, Inc., 1968-71, Jet Propulsion Lab., Pasadena, Calif., 1971-99. Supr. terrestrial planets mission design group, 1981-83, mission design mgr. for Infrared Astron. Satellite, 1976-83, mgr. flight engring. office for Voyager/Uranus project, 1983-86; mgr. mission profile and sequencing sect., 1986-92; dep. mgr. astrophysics and fundamental physics program office, 1992-96, mgr. mission and syss. architecture sect., 1996-99. Served with USMC, 1957-60. Recipient Apollo Achievement award, 1969, Exceptional Svc. medal NASA, 1984, Outstanding Leadership medal NASA, 1986; asteroid 4838 Billmclaughlin named in his honor. Fellow Brit. Interplanetary Soc. (L.J. Carter Meml. lectr. London 2002, Space Achievement Bronze medal 1993); mem. Internat. Acad. Astros., Phi Beta Kappa, Sigma Xi.

MCLAURIN, HUGH MCFADDIN, III, military officer, historian consultant; b. Sumter, S.C., Jan. 30, 1936; s. Hugh McFaddin and Louise Mellette (Nettles) McL.; m. Virginia Anne Harvin, Aug. 22, 1958; children: Mary Louise, Virginia Harvin, Hugh IV. BS, Clemson U., 1959; grad. (hon.), Command & Gen. Staff Coll., Ft. Leavenworth, Kans., 1978. Commd. 2d lt. U.S. Army, 1958, advanced through grades to col., 1985; exec. officer 151st Field Arty. Brigade, Sumter, 1975-85; dir. pers. S.C. NG, Columbia, 1986-91, dir. logistics, 1991-95, rank of brig. gen., ret., 1996; owner McLaurin Farms, Wedgefield, SC, 1999—. Cons. S.C. Ednl. TV, Columbia, 1992-93; moderator Nat. Def. Seminar, Washington, 1978. Author: History of South Carolina National Guard and Militia, 1989. Elder, Presbyn. Ch., Wedgefield, 1961, moderator Presbytery Coun., 2001-04; v.p. Com. for Progress, Sumter, 1963; chmn. bd. dirs. S.C. NG Mus., Columbia, 1982-99; trustee Thornwell Home for Children. Fellow Coll. Mil. Historians; mem. Field Arty. Soc. S.C. (pres. 1987), SAR (historian), Sumter County Hist. Soc. (dir. 1996-99, pres. 2000), The Sumter Assembly (pres. 1991), Soc. of High Hills of Santee (steward 2002), Hon. Order St. Barbara, Fortnightly Club. Avocation: American Revolution research. Home: Stirling Plantation 6380 Mclaurin Rd Wedgefield SC 29168-9393

MCLAWHON, RONALD WILLIAM, pathology educator, biochemist; b. Chgo., Sept. 10, 1957; s. William Columbus and Esther Shirley (Bukowski) McL. AB in Biol. Scis., U. Chgo., 1979, MS in Biochemistry, 1980, PhD in Biochemistry, 1982; MD, Rush Med. Coll., 1986. Diplomate Am. Bd. Pathology. Rsch. assoc. pediat. Joseph P. Kennedy Jr. Mental Retardation Rsch. Ctr., Chgo.; rsch. assoc. pediatrics U. Chgo. Pritzker Sch. Medicine, 1982-83; resident in pathology Rush-Presbyn.-St. Luke's Med. Ctr., Chgo., 1986-87, pathologist, 1987-88; instr. Rush Med. Coll., Chgo., 1986-87, asst. prof., 1987-88; resident in pathology U. Chgo. Med. Ctr., 1988-90; asst. prof. U. Chgo. Pritzker Sch. Medicine, 1990-96, assoc. prof., 1996—; dir. clin. chemistry, attending physician U. Chgo. Med. Ctr., 1990—; dir. outreach and clin. support svcs. U. Chgo. Hosps. and Health Sys., 1997, dir. regional lab. svcs. and med. dir. of hosp. labs., 1998—. Contbr. articles to Jour. Biol. Chemistry, Molecular Pharmacology, Jour. Neurochemistry, Jour. Membrane Biology, Procs. of NAS, Am. Jour. Clin. Pathology, Clin. Chemistry. U.S. Pub. Health Predoctoral fellow NIH, 1981-82; James B. Herrick scholar Rush Med. Coll., 1986-87; recipient Young Investigator award Acad. Clin. Lab. Physicians and Scientists, 1990. Fellow Nat. Acad. Clin. Biochemistry, Coll. Am. Pathologists, Am. Soc. Clin. Pathologists,; mem. AAAS, Am. Assn. Clin. Chemistry, Am. Soc. Investigative Pathology, Am. Soc. for Biochemistry and Molecular Biology, Am. Soc. for Cell Biology, Sigma Xi. Achievements include research in biochemistry of cell membrane receptors and signal transduction in the nervous system, molecular pharmacology of opiates and opioid peptides, regulation of complex carbohydrate and lipid metabolism, clinical laboratory automaton and robotics. Office: U Chgo Pritzker Sch Medicine Dept Pathology 5841 S Maryland Ave MC0004 Chicago IL 60637-1470 Office Phone: 773-702-1318. E-mail: rm28@midway.uchicago.edu.

MCLEAN, ARTHUR FREDERICK, mechanical engineer; b. Bristol, Eng., Apr. 16, 1929; came to U.S., 1959; naturalized, 1966; s. Frederick Robert and Edith (Hawkings) McL.; m. Oriole R. Robinson, Aug. 30, 1952; children: Mark F., Peter A. Nat. and Higher Nat. degrees in Mech. Engring., Bristol Coll. Tech., 1952. Sr. engr. aircraft control sys. Bristol Aero.-Orenda Engines Can., 1954-59; sr. engr. power sys. rsch. Bendix Corp., Southfield, Mich., 1959-61; supr. turbine sys. sect. Ford Motor Co., Dearborn, Mich., 1961-66, mgr. turbine R & D, 1967-78, mgr. ceramic materials rsch., 1979-86, mgr. materials engring., 1987-88; pvt. practice Oceanside, Calif., 1988—. Patentee in field; contbr. articles to profl. jours. With RAF, 1951-54. Recipient Soichiro Honda medal. Fellow ASME (past chmn. vehicular com., ceramics com.), Am. Ceramic Soc.; mem. Soc. Automotive Engrs. (past turbine com.), Inst. Mech. Engrs. Home: 3764 Southridge Way Oceanside CA 92056-5428 Office Phone: 760-724-3102. Personal E-mail: artmcl@prodigy.net. E-mail: artmcl@cox.net.

MCLEAN, CHRISTOPHER ANTHONY, lawyer, former government official; b. Chgo., Mar. 21, 1958; s. Earl James and Joan A. (Wolski); m. Hae Kyung Oh. BSBA, Creighton U., 1980, JD, 1982; LLM, Georgetown U., 1985. Bar: Nebr. 1982, U.S. Dist. Ct. Nebr. 1982, D.C. 1983, U.S. Ct. Appeals (D.C. cir.) 1985, U.S. Supreme Ct. 1990. Sales clk. J.L. Brandeis Co., Omaha, 1975-82; legal counsel, legis. asst. Senator J.J. Exon, Washington, 1982—96; legis. counsel Senator Bob Kerrey, Washington, 1997; dep. adminstr. Rural Utilities Svc., Washington, 1998—2000, adminstr., 2000; pvt. practice Washington, 2001—; counsel ComCare Alliance, 2001—; v.p. Nat. Strategies, Inc., Wash., DC, 2001—; prin. e-Copernicus, Wash., DC, 2003. Vol. Dem. campaigns, Nebr., 1973—. Mem.: ABA, DC Bar Assn., Nebr. Bar Assn., Alpha Sigma Nu. Roman Catholic. Avocations: politics, photography, travel. Home: 4701 Davenport St NW Washington DC 20016-4405 also: 1620 S 138th St Omaha NE 68144-1135 Office: Ste 200 317 Massachusetts Ave NE Washington DC 20002 Office Phone: 202-292-4600.

MCLEAN, CRAIG ELLIOTT, retired non-commissioned officer; b. Muskegon, Mich., Dec. 12, 1950; s. Elliot Garber and Margaret Irene (Carlson) McL. Grad., Langley H.S., McLean, Va., 1969. Enlisted U.S. Army, 1971, advanced through ranks to sgt. first class; served in continental U.S., West Germany and West Berlin; ret., 1992. Contbr. short stories and poetry to profl. publs. Field rep. Law Enforcement Alliance Am., Falls Church, Va., 1998—; mem. Coun. Conservative Citizens, St. Louis, 1999—. Decorated French Commando Badge, French Army, 1981. Mem. DAV, Golden Key Nat. Honor Soc., U-Boot-Archiv (full friend), Sigma Tau Delta. Avocations: study of world war ii and u-boat history, writing.

MCLEAN, DENNIS EDGAR, lawyer; b. Portland, Oreg., July 11, 1954; s. Dennis A. and Wauneta M. (Jones) McLean; m. Bonnie Berk, Oct. 10, 1981. BA, U. Calif., Berkeley, 1976; JD, U. Calif., San Francisco, 1980. Bar: Wash. 1980, U.S. Dist. Ct. (we. dist.) Wash. 1980. Ptnr. Davis Wright Tremaine, LLP, Seattle, 1980—. Trustee, vice chmn. western Wash. chpt. Multiple Sclerosis Soc., Seattle, 1987—95; dir., sec. Seattle Habitat for Humanity, 1996—2001; trustee Bertschi Sch., 1999—2001. Mem.: ABA, Seattle-King County Bar Assn., Wash. State Bar Assn. Office: Davis Wright Tremaine LLP 2600 Century Sq 1501 4th Ave Ste 2600 Seattle WA 98101-1688 E-mail: dennismclean@dwt.com.

MC LEAN, DON, singer, instrumentalist, composer; b. New Rochelle, N.Y., Oct. 2, 1945; s. Donald and Elizabeth (Bucci) McL.; m. Patrisha Shnier, Mar., 1987. Student, Villanova U., 1964; BBA, Iona Coll., 1968. Pres., owner The Benny Bird Co., Inc., Fairfield, Conn.; recorded for United Artists, Artista Records, EMI Records. Star BBC-TV spls., 1973, 78. Albums include Tapestry, 1972, American Pie, 1972, Don McLean, 1972, Playin' Favourites, 1973, Homeless Brother, 1974, Solo, 1976, Prime Time, 1987, Chain Lightning, 1979, Very Best of, 1980, Believers, 1982, Dominion, 1983, The Best of Don McLean, 1987, Don McLean's Greatest Hits Then & Now, 1987, Love Tracks, 1988, For the Memories, 1989, Don McLean's Greatest Hits Live, 1990, Headroom, 1991, Classics, 1992, The River of Love, 1995, Solo, 1995, Greatest Hits Live, 1997, Don McLean's Christmas Dreams, 1997; singles include American Pie, 1971, Vincent, 1971, Crying, 1980; wrote Perry Como hit And I Love You So, 1973; performances include America's Millenium, Washington, Starry Starry Night (TV special). Mem. bd. Hudson River Sloop Restoration, World Hunger Yr., Advs. for Arts; fund raiser Scenic Hudson, Hudson River Fisherman's Assn. Recipient more than 30 gold and platinum records worldwide, 5 grammy award nominations and others; Israel Cultural award, 1981. Mem. Coffee House Club. Office: Atlantic Records 1290 Avenue Of The Americas New York NY 10104-0184 also: PO Box 307 Camden ME 04843-0307

MC LEAN, DONALD MILLIS, microbiology and pathology educator, physician; b. Melbourne, Australia, July 26, 1926; s. Donald and Nellie (Millis) McL.; married. BSc, U. Melbourne, 1947, MB, 1950, MD, 1954. Fellow Rockefeller Found., N.Y.C. and Hamilton, Mont., 1955; vis. instr. bacteriology U. Minn., Mpls., 1957; med. officer Commonwealth Serum Labs., Melbourne, 1957; virologist Research Inst., Hosp. for Sick Children, Toronto, Ont., Can., 1958-67; assoc. prof. microbiology, assoc. in pediatrics U. Toronto Med. Sch., 1962-67; prof. med. microbiology U. B.C. Med. Sch., Vancouver, Can., 1967-91, prof. emeritus Pathology, 1991—. Author: Virology in Health Care, 1980, Immunological Investigation of Human Virus Disease, 1982, Same-Day Virus Diagnosis, 1984, Virological Infections, 1988, Medical Microbiology Synopsis, 1991, Acute Viral Infections, 1991; contbr. articles to profl. jours. Fellow Royal Coll. Physicians (Can.), Royal Coll. Pathologists; mem. Am. Epidemiological Soc., Am. Soc. Tropical Medicine, Can. Med. Assn., Am. Soc. Virology, Soc. for Vector Ecology, Soc. for Gen. Microbiology. Home: 6-5885 Yew St Vancouver BC Canada V6M 3Y5 Office Phone: 604-263-9076.

MCLEAN, HON. WALTER FRANKLIN, executive, pastor, legislator; b. Leamington, Ont., Can., Apr. 26, 1936; s. J.L.W. McL.; m. Barbara Muriel Scott, Aug. 19, 1961; children: Scott, Chima, Ian, Duncan BA, Victoria Coll., U. B.C., 1957; M.Div., Knox Coll., U. Toronto, 1960; LLD (hon.), Wilfrid Laurier U., 1995; DD (hon.), Knox Coll., 2002. Ordained to ministry, Presbyterian Ch. Min. Knox Presbyn. Ch., Waterloo, 1971-79; mem. House of Commons, Ottawa, Ont., Can., 1979-93, Sec. of State of Can., 1984-85; sworn to Privy Coun., 1984; min. of immigration House of Commons, Ottawa, Ont., Can., 1985-86; min. responsible for status of women Govt. of Can., 1984-86. CUSO, Nigeria coord., 1962-67; chaplain U. Nigeria, 1962-67; dep. dir. Internat. Program Can. Centennial, 1967; exec. dir. Man. Assn. for World Devel., 1970; past chmn. World Concerns Comm. Canadian Coun. Chs.; Can. del. Gen. Assemblies UN, 1986-93; apptd. spl. rep. Commonwealth and South African affairs, 1989-93; Can. rep. So. Africa Devel. Coordination Conf., 1987-93; del. Commonwealth Fgn. Mins. Against Apartheid, 1987-93, African Devel. Bank, 1990-91, Assn. West European Parliamentarians Against Apartheid, 1988-89; leader fact finding mission to Mozambique, 1987, Can. delegation UN Conf. on Women, Nairobi, 1985; led Parliamentary del. to observe the pre-election process and attended Namibian Indpedence, Mar. 21, 1990; chmn. paliamentary Com. on Devel. and Human Rights; Commonwealth observer South African and Sri Lanka elections 1994; pres. Franklin Cons. Ltd., 1993—. Alderman City of Waterloo, Ont., 1976-79; co-founder UN based Parliamentarians Global Action; hon. consul of the Rep. of Namibia, 1994—; convenor Millenium Celebration Presbyn. Ch., 1998-2000; prin. The Osborne Group, 2000—. Chaplain 404 wing RCAF; mem. Ont. Criminal Injuries Compensation Bd., 2000-03. Recipient Can. U. Svcs. Overseas award, 1990, Can. Bur. Internat. Edn. award, 1994; Paul Harris fellow, 1984. Mem. UN Assn. Can. (chair human rights com.), Rotary. Progressive Conservative. Office Phone: 519-578-5932. E-mail: franklinltd@sympatico.ca., walter@mcleanandassociates.ca.

MCLEAN, IAN SMALL, astronomer, physics educator; b. Johnstone, Scotland, Aug. 21, 1949; s. Ian and Mary (Small) McL.; (div.); 1 child, Jennifer Ann; m. Janet Wheelans Yourston, Mar. 4, 1983; children: Joanna, David Richard, Graham Robert. BS with hons., U. Glasgow, Scotland, 1971, PhD, 1974. Rsch. fellow dept. astronomy U. Glasgow, 1974-78; rsch. assoc. Steward Obs. U. Ariz., Tucson, 1978-80; sr. rsch. fellow Royal Obs. U. Edinburgh, Scotland, 1980-81, sr. sci. officer Royal Obs., 1981-86; prin. sci. officer Joint Astronomy Ctr., Hilo, Hawaii, 1986-89; prof. dept. physics and astronomy UCLA, 1989—, dir. Infrared Imaging Detector Lab., 1989—; assoc. dir. UC Observatories, 2001—. Author: Electronic and Computer-Aided Astronomy: From Eyes To Electronic Sensors, 1989, Infrared Astronomy with Arrays: The Next Generation, 1994, Electronic Imaging in Astronomy: Detectors and Instrumentation, 1997; contbr. articles to profl. jours. Recipient Exceptional Merit award U.K. Serc, Edinburgh, 1989; NSF grantee, 1991, 93. Mem. Internat. Astron. Union (pres. com. Paris chpt. 1988-91, v.p. 1985-88), Am. Astron. Soc., Golden Key Honor Soc. (hon.) Achievements include discovery of relationship between polarization of light and orbital inclination of close binary stars; development of first CCD spectropolarimeter, first fully automated infrared camera for astronomy used to achieve images of faintest high redshift galaxies, first twin-channel infrared camera; first high resolution infrared spectrograph for studies of brown dwarfs, galactic center and high redshift galaxies; research in optical and infrared astronomy, use of CCDs and infrared array detectors. Office: UCLA Dept Physics and Astronomy 405 Hilgard Ave Los Angeles CA 90095-9000 Business E-Mail: mclean@astro.ucla.edu.

MC LEAN, JACKIE, jazz saxophonist, educator, composer, community activist; b. N.Y.C., May 17, 1932; Doctorate(hon.), Trinity Coll., Hartford, 1999. Bandmaster, counselor N.Y. State Correction Dept.; chmn., prof. Hartt Sch. Music, Hartford, Conn., from 1968; founder Artist Collective, Inc., Hartford, 1970; founder African Am. music program (jazz degree) Hartt sch. music U. Hartford. With Art Blakey's Jazz Messengers, performed with, Charles Mingus; actor: film The Connection; albums include Monuments, New York Calling, Antiquity, Live at Montmarte, Ode To Super, A Ghetto Lullaby, Lights Out, Dr. Jackle, The Meeting, Jack Knife, New and Old Gospel, Let Freedom Ring, Destination Out, One Step Beyond, Grachan Moncur III, (with Jackie McLean Quintet) Dynasty, 1990, Rites of Passage, 1991, Triloka: Rhythm of the Earth, 1992, Jackie MacAttack, 1993, Rhythm of the Earth, 1993, Jackie's Hat Trick, 1995, Swing, Swang, Swingin', 1997, Fire & Love, 1998, Nature Boy, 2000, Blue Note - Fire and Love; guest artist album by Jazz Messengers Midnight Session, 1993; led McLean Jazz Dynasty tour with son Rene in 6 countries in Southern Africa, 1993. Decorated officer of the Arts (France); recipient Bent award U. Hartford, State of Conn. Blue Book Registration Manual award, 1996, Jazz Master award Nat. Endowment for the Arts; named # 1 in Downbeat Mag. Critics Poll, 1993, 94, 95, # 1 in Jazz Times Mag. Readers' Poll, 1993, 94, 95; Jackie McLean Inst. of Jazz named in his honor Music Dept. Hartt Sch. Music. Univ. Hartford, 2000, Beacon award New Sch. Univ., N.Y.C., 2001. Office: Artists Collective 1200 Albany Ave Hartford CT 06112-2104

MCLEAN, JODIE W. investment company executive; b. Chgo. BS in Fin. and Mgmt. with honors, U. S.C. With Edens & Avants, Columbia, SC, 1990—, chief investment officer, 1997—, pres., 2002—. Office: Edens & Avant 900 Bank of America Plaza 1901 Main St Columbia SC 29201*

MCLEAN, JULIANNE DREW, concert pianist, educator; b. Stoneham, Mass., Sept. 12, 1928; d. Benjamin Drew and Elizabeth Anna McLean; m. Carmelo Addario, Oct. 18, 1958 (dec.); 1 child, Angela Elizabeth Addario. BMusic, Conservatory of Music, Kansas City, Mo., 1949, MMusic, 1950. Concert pianist NAC, U.S., Europe, Near and Far East, 1956—; tchr. pvt. classes, Kans., Hawaii, Va., 1956—; rec. artist Wichita State U., 1987—; lectr. in field. Musician: appearances on TV; musician: (invited pianist) Survivors of Andrea Doria Reunion; musician: live on Vatican Radio. Bd. dirs. Maud Powell Found., Falls Church, Va., 1995—. Recipient scholarships. Mem. Mu Phi Epsilon. Roman Catholic. Avocation: cooking.

MCLEAN, LYNNE MARIE, social worker; b. Sharon, Pa., Feb. 1, 1957; d. Merle Alfred and Grace Buckley Johnson; m. William Paul McLean, May 18, 1991. BSW, U. Tex., Arlington, 1979, MSW, 1981. Caseworker investigations Child Protective Svcs., Dallas, 1981-85, supr., 1985-90, cmty. coord., 1990-91, program dir., 1991-95; dir. family life edn. Child and Family Guidance Ctr., Dallas, 1995-99; exec. dir. CPS Cmty. Ptnrs., Dallas, 1999—2002, Greater Tex. Cmty. Ptnrs., Dallas, 2002—. Chmn. Sexual Abuse Intervention Network of Dallas, 1995-97; mem. Respite Care Coalition, Dallas, 1998—; mem. advocacy com. Child Abuse Prevention Ctr., 1999—, pub. awareness chmn., 1996; chmn. Sexual Abuse Group Treatment Bd., 1991-95; presenter tng. programs to numerous cmty. orgns. Chmn. social activities St. Thomas Episcopal Ch., Dallas, 1996-98, mem. team 50th anniversary celebration, 1999-2000. Democrat. Avocations: crochet, reading, gardening, genealogy. Office: Greater Tex Cmty Ptnrs 2801 Swiss Ave Ste 110 Dallas TX 75204 E-mail: gtcp@sbcglobal.net.

MCLEAN, R. BRUCE, lawyer; b. N.Y.C., Nov. 15, 1946; BS with honors, Ind. U., 1968, JD cum laude, 1971. Bar: Ind. 1971, DC 1974. Atty. appellate ct. br. Nat. Labor Rels. Bd., 1971—73; chmn. Akin, Gump, Strauss, Hauer & Feld L.L.P., Washington. Bd. visitors Ind. U. Sch. Law, 1989—, vice chair, 1998—; bd. visitors Georgetown Law Ctr., 2003—. Mem.: ABA, DC Bar, Fed. Bar Assn., Order of Coif, Phi Alpha Delta. Office: Akin Gump Strauss Hauer & Feld LLP 1333 New Hampshire Ave NW Washington DC 20036-1564 Office Phone: 202-887-4022. Business E-Mail: bmclean@akingump.com.

MCLEAN, ROBERT, III, real estate company executive; b. Balt., May 23, 1928; s. Robert Jr. and Mary Somerville (Iglehart) McL.; m. Elizabeth Madison Lewis, May 21, 1960; children: Elizabeth, Alexander, Mary, John. BA, Yale U., 1950; MA, U. Pa., 1965. Mktg. exec. Owens-Ill., Toledo, 1957-65; mktg. cons. Old Phila. Devel. Corp., Phila., 1966-70; 2001vice chmn. Cushman & Wakefield, N.Y.C., 1970—2001; chmn. directorate Cambridge Inst. of Applied Rsch., McLean, Va., 2001—. Mem. real estate investment com. Yale U., New Haven, Conn., 1982-90; mem. bd. Cushman & Wakefield, N.Y.C., 1986-2000. Author: Countdown to Renaissance II, The New Way Corporate America Builds, 1984. Chmn. Nat. Bldg. Mus., Washington, 1992-95; mem. bd. Washington Nat. Cathedral, 1980-88. S/Sgt. USMC, 1953-56. Mem. Rolling Rock Club, Metropolitan Club, Center Club, Gibson Island Club. Republican. Episcopalian. Avocations: tennis, golf, skiing. Home: 631 Stillwater Rd Gibson Island MD 21056 Office: Cambridge Inst 7008 Capital View Dr Mc Lean VA 22101 Office Phone: 703-893-0101. Personal E-mail: rmclean05@aol.com.

MCLEAN, ROBERT JAMES CAMERON, microbiologist, educator; b. Toronto, Sept. 18, 1956; came to U.S., 1993; m. Martha Elaine Law, May 21, 1988; children: Malcolm Albert Campbell, Alistair Ian Law. BSc, U. Guelph, Ont., Can., 1978; PhD, U. Calgary, Alta., Can., 1986. Asst. prof. Queens U., Kingston, Ont., 1988-93; from asst. prof. to assoc. prof. Tex. State U., San Marcos, 1993—. Cons. Kingston Techs., Trenton, N.J., 1991, Q-Life Systems, Inc., Kingston, 1992-93, ICET, Inc., Norwood, Mass., 1995, Sulzer Carbomedics Inc., Austin, Tex., 1999-2001. Author: (with I. A. Veliky) Immobilized Biosystems, 1994, (with A.W. Decho) Molecular Ecology of Biofilms, 2002; mem. editl. bd. Applied and Environ. Microbiology, 1999—, Bioresource Tech., 1997-2002, Geomicrobiology Jour., 1999—; contbr. articles to profl. jours. Recipient Pres. award Microscopical Soc. Can., 1986. Mem. Am. Soc. for Microbiology (pres. Tex. br. 2003—), Can. Soc. Microbiologists (chmn. morphology and structure sect. 1994-96), Internat. Soc. Microbial Ecology, Sigma Xi. Presbyterian. Achievements include first experimental bacterial biofilm formation during space flight; first experimental investigation of bacterial species interactions in space flight; co-discovery of quorum sensing signal molecules in naturally occurring biofilms; research on gene expression including slow growth, starvation survival and quorum sensing genes in biofilm growth. Office: Tex State Univ Dept Biology San Marcos TX 78666 E-mail: McLean@swt.edu.

MCLEAN, VINCENT RONALD, former manufacturing company financial executive; b. Detroit, June 1, 1931; s. Frederick Ronald and Bernice Mary (Vincent) McL.; m. Joyce Adrienne Koch, July 23, 1960; children— Judith Adrienne, Bruce Ronald BBA, U. Mich., 1954, MBA, 1955. Fin. analyst Ford Motor Co., Detroit, 1954—55, Mobil Oil Corp., N.Y.C., 1958—69; treas. Mobil Chem. Co., N.Y.C., 1966—69; v.p. fin., treas. NL Industries, N.Y.C., 1969—76, exec. v.p. fin. and planning, dir., 1976—82; exec. v.p., CFO, dir. Sperry Corp., N.Y.C., 1982—86; sr. advisor Wertheim Schroder & Co., N.Y.C., 1988—89. Bd. dirs. Legal and Gen. Am., Inc., William Penn Life Ins. Co. NY, Banner Life Ins. Co., Mad. Served with U.S. Army, 1955-57 Mem. N.Y. Soc. Security Analysts, Econ. Club N.Y. Home: 702 Shackamaxon Dr Westfield NJ 07090-3408

MCLEAN, WILLIAM RONALD, retired electrical engineer, consultant; b. Bklyn., Mar. 26, 1921; s. Harold W. and Helena Winifred (Farrell) McL.; m. Cecile L. Mills, Aug. 17, 1946 (div.); m. Evelyn Hupfer, Nov. 29, 1968. BA in Math., Bklyn. Coll., 1980, BS in Computational Math., 1981. Chief electrician U.S. Mcht. Marine, 1942-64, elect. designer, engr., 1965-76; sr. elect engr. M. Rosenblatt & Son, Inc., N.Y.C., 1976-86; cons., 1986-98; ret., 1996. Mem. AAAS, IEEE, Soc. Naval Archs. and Marine Engrs., Am. Soc. Naval Engrs. Home and Office: 57 Montague St Brooklyn NY 11201-3374 E-mail: mclnbill@aol.com.

MCLEAR, PATRICK EDWARD, education educator; b. Kans. City, Mo., July 19, 1944; s. William Joseph and Frances Louise Mclear. AA, Jr. Coll., Kans. City., Mo., 1963; BE, Northwest Mo. State Univ., 1965; MA, Univ. Mo., Kans. City, 1967; PhD, Univ. Mo., Columbia, 1974. Tchg. asst. history Univ. Mo., Kans. City, 1966—67, rsch. asst. history, 1968, prof. Columbia, 1972—73, vis. lectr. Kans. City, 1973—74; asst. prof. Mo. Western State Coll., St. Joseph, 1974—79, assoc. prof., 1979—83, prof., 1983—. Contbr. articles pub. to profl. jour., book reviews. YN3 USN, 1966—72. Mem.: State Hist. Soc. of Mus., So. Hist. Orgn., Orgn. of Am. Historians, Argl. History Soc. Democrat. Roman Cath. Home: 7797 Sebenner Lake Rd Dearborn MO 64439 Office: Mo Western State Coll 4525 Downs Dr Saint Joseph MO 64507

MCLEER, LAUREEN DOROTHY, drug development and pharmaceutical professional; b. N.Y.C., Feb. 5, 1955; d. William Myers and Una Lee (Massey) McLeer. BS, Columbia U., 1977; MBA, U. London, 1981. RN N.Y., D.C., state reg. nurse, Eng., registered state nurse, Wales. Staff nurse NYU Med. Ctr., N.Y.C., 1977-78; charge nurse Scripps Clinic and Rsch. Found., La Jolla, Calif., 1979-80; clin. rschr. Ayerst Labs., N.Y.C., 1982; sales rep. Pfizer, Inc., N.Y.C., 1983-87, Cahners Pub. Co., N.Y.C., 1988-89; dir. bus. devel. Pro Clinica, N.Y.C., 1990-91; account supr. Salthouse Torre Norton, Inc., Rutherford, N.J., 1992-93; dir. bus. devel. Med. & Tech. Rsch. Assocs. Inc., Wellesley, Mass., 1993-94, sr. project dir. Quilules Inc., Arlington, Va., 1994-99; project mgr. product devel. and commercialization Aventis Pharms., Inc., Berwyn, Pa., 1999—2002; clin. trial mgmt. leader AstraZeneca, LP, Wilmington, Del., 2002—. Mem. com. for healthcare issues and legis. United Hosp. Fund, N.Y.C., 1992—94. Chmn. Help Our Neighbors Eat Yr. 'Round, N.Y.C., 1987—89; trustee Murray Hill Com., N.Y.C., 1988—90; bd. dirs. East Midtown Svcs. for Older People, 1987—94; vol. nurse Whitman Walker Clinic, 1995—99; bd. dirs. Cecil Land Trust, 2002—, Eastern Shore Land Conservancy, 2003—. Mem.: Drug Info. Assn., Regulatory Affairs Profl. Soc. Home: PO Box 681 Chesapeake City MD 21915 Office: AstraZeneca LP 1800 Concorde Pike Wilmington DE 19802-4034 Office Phone: 302-885-5213. E-mail: laureen.mcleer@astrazeneca.com.

MCLEES, JOHN ALAN, lawyer; b. Mpls., Jan. 19, 1948; s. Alan L. and Marian G. (Melby) McL.; m. Bozena Nowicka, June 25, 1993; children: Alexandra, Thomas. BA, U. Chgo., 1970, MBA, 1973, JD, 1974; MS in Econs., London Sch. Econs., 1971. Bar: D.C. 1974, Ill. 1975. Assoc. Keck Mahin & Cate, Chgo., 1975-79; atty. advisor office of sec. U.S. Dept. Energy, Washington, 1979-81; mng. atty. Sidley & Austin, Muscat, Oman, 1981-83, assoc. Chgo., 1983-88, Morgan Lewis & Bockius, Washington, 1988-91; dir. Latin Am. tax svc. Coopers & Lybrand, Chgo., 1991-97; ptnr. Baker & McKenzie, Chgo., 1997—. Organizer, chmn. confs. on Mex. and Latin Am. tax laws, 1992—. Contbr. articles to profl. jours. Adv. bd. Com. for Pub. Autonomous Schs., Washington, 1989—; chmn. of bd. dirs. Mid Am. Chpt., U.S. Mex. C. of C., 1993-97. Named Leading Tax Advisor, Euromoney Guide to Leading U.S. Tax Lawyers, 1997, Euromoney Guide to the World's Leading Tax Advisors, 1999, Leading Advisor on Latin Am. Tax, Internat. Tax. Review, 1996-2003. Mem. ACLU, ABA, Internat. Fiscal Assn. Episcopalian. Home: 1434 S Plymouth Ct Chicago IL 60605-2729 Office: Baker & McKenzie 130 E Randolph Dr Ste 3700 Chicago IL 60601-6342 E-mail: john.a.mclees@bakernet.com.

MCLELLAN, A. ANNE, Canadian government official; b. Hants County, N.S., Can., Aug. 31, 1950; d. Howard Gilmore and Joan Mary (Pullan) McL. BA, Dalhousie U., LLB, 1974; LLM, King's Coll., U. London, 1975. Bar: N.S., 1976. Asst. prof. law U. N.B., Can., 1976-80; assoc. prof. law U. Alta., Edmonton, Can., 1980-89, assoc. dean faculty of law, 1985-87, prof. law, 1989-93, acting dean, 1991-92; M.P. for Edmonton West Ho. of Commons, Can., 1993—; min. of nat. resources Govt. of Canada, Ottawa, 1993—97, min. of energy, mines and resources, 1993—95, min. of forestry, 1993—95, fed. interlocator for metis and non-status Indians, 1993—97, min. justice and atty. gen. of Canada, 1997—2002, min. of health, 2002—03, dep. prime min., 2003—, min. of public safety and emergency preparedness, 2003—. Commentator on Can. Charter of Rights and Freedoms and on human rights issues. Contbr. articles to profl. publs. Past bd. dirs. Can. Civil Liberties Assn., Alta. Legal Aid; past v.p. U. Alta. Faculty Assn. Office: Office of the Prime Min Langevin Block 80 Wellington St K1A 0A2 Ottawa ON Canada E-mail: McLellan.A@parloge.ca.

MCLELLAN, ROBERT, gynecologist, oncologist, educator; b. Miami Beach, Fla., 1954; m. Krista E. McLellan, Sept. 1991; children: David John, James Robert. BS in Biology summa cum laude, Boston Coll., 1976; MD, U. Md., 1980. Diplomate Am. Bd. Ob-Gyn., Am. Bd. Gynecol. Oncology. Resident in ob-gyn. St. Agnes Hosp., Balt., 1980-84; fellow in ob-gyn. Johns Hopkins U. Hosp., Balt., 1987-89; sr. surgeon Lahey Clinic Med. Ctr., Burlington, Mass., 1989—, dir. sect. gynecol. oncology; clin. instr. Harvard U. Sch. Medicine, Boston. Adj. assoc. prof. ob-gyn. Dartmouth Med. Sch. Contbr. articles to sci. and profl. jours. Trustee Lahey Clinic, Burlington, 1994—, bd. govs., 1993-96. Lt. comdr. Med. Corps USNR. Mem. AMA, ACOG, Soc. Gynecol. Oncologists, New. Eng. Cancer Soc., Mass. Med. Soc., Obstetric Soc. Boston. Office: Lahey Clinic Med Ctr 41 Mall Rd Burlington MA 01805-0002

MCLEMORE, MICHAEL KERR, lawyer, minister; b. Atlanta, May 19, 1949; s. Gilbert Carmichael Sr. and Jeannie (Gulley) M.; m. Colleen Owen, Aug. 19, 1972; children: Megan, Shannon. BA, Haverford Coll., 1971; JD, U. Ga., 1974; MDiv, Candler Sch. Theology, 1997. Bar: Fla. 1974, U.S. Dist. Ct. (mid. and so. dists.) Fla. 1974, U.S. Ct. Appeals (5th cir.) 1974, U.S. Ct. Appeals (11th cir.) 1981, U.S. Supreme Ct. 1984; ordained deacon Methodist Ch., 1997, elder, 1999. Shareholder Kimbrell & Hamann P.A., Miami, Fla., 1974-91. Pres. Haverford Soc. South Fla., Miami, 1978-91; Fla. Alumni admissions rep. coord. Haverford Coll., 1978-91, alumni coun., 1980-91; lay leader 1st United Meth. Ch., South Miami, 1986-90; lay del. Fla. Ann. Conf., 1986-90, chmn. adminstrv. bd., 1991—, property and compensation com., 1988-90; co-chmn. Miami dist. Work Area on Stewardship, 1987—; chair deferred gifts Epworth Village, 1990-91; pastor Bishop Circuit United Meth. Ch., 1995-97, New Pentecost United Meth. Ch., 1997—. 1st lt. USAR, 1976-78. Mem. ABA, Fla. Bar Assn. (aviation sect.), Dade County Def. Bar Assn. (bd. dirs. 1989—, treas. 1990—), Nat. Transp. Safety Bd. Assn., Lawyer-Pilot Bar Assn. Democrat. Home: 268 Moss Side Dr Athens GA 30607-2109 Office: New Pentecost United Meth Ch 385 Pleasant Hill Church Rd Winder GA 30680

MCLEMORE-WHEELER, LINDA M. literature educator; b. Akron, Ohio, Oct. 26, 1970; d. Lee and Catherine White; m. William A. Wheeler, June 10; children: Elizabeth Wheeler, Jordan Wheeler, Austin Wheeler. BA in English, Jackson State U., Miss., 1988—92, MA in English, 1995—97. Computer instr. Johnson Elem., Jackson, Miss., 1992—96; English instr. Coahoma C.C., Clarksdale, Miss., 1998—2000, Jackson State U., Jackson, Miss., 2000—. Editor: (cookbook) Heart and Soul: Student Recipes for Everyday Living. Vol. Couples Ministry Outreach, Jackson, Miss., 2000—01. Mem.: Miss. Assn. for Devel. Edn., Nat. Coun. for the Teachers of English, Writer's Guild, Alpha Epsilon Lambda (sec. 1995), Phi Kappa Phi. Baptist. Avocations: piano, reading, singing, poetry. Office: Jackson State Univ 1400 John R Lynch St Jackson MS 39217 E-mail: linda.m.wheeler@jsums.edu.

MCLENDON, DOROTHY, school psychologist; b. Crawfordsville, Ind., Feb. 20, 1918; d. Joseph Newton and Dora (Ryall) Fullenwider; m. Hiram James McLendon, May 23, 1942; 1 child, Hiram James McLendon, Jr. AB, Olivet Coll., Kankakee, Ill., 1942; MA, Boston U., 1945, EdD, 1970. Diplomate Am. Bd. of Profl. Psychology. Spl. edn. tchr. Kingsley Schs., Belmont Jr. High, Boston, 1943-46, 56-57; lectr. Homerton Coll., Cambridge, England, 1946-47; sch. psychologist Alameda County Schs., Oakland, Calif.,

1949—51, Berkeley Pub. Schs., 1951—52, Paris Am. Army Dependent Sch., France, 1957-58, Brookline (Mass.) Pub. Schs., 1958-81; pvt. cons. Cambridge, Mass., 1981—; cons. Cocoa, Fla., 1981—. Home (Winter): 1660 Rosetine St Cocoa FL 32926-5502

MCLENDON, MELBURNE DEKALB, lawyer, arbitrator; b. Atlanta, Apr. 21, 1921; s. Jesse Martin and Elizabeth Lee (Sartain) McL.; m. Loyce Jacqueline Kirkland, Dec. 31, 1949; children: James Kirkland, Loyce Eloise McLendon Snyder. LLB, U. Ga., 1948. Bar: Ga. 1949, U.S. Dist. Ct. (no. dist.) Ga. 1949, U.S. Ct. Appeals (5th cir.) 1965, U.S. Supreme Ct. 1973, U.S. Dist. Ct. (mid. dist.) Ga. 1985. Law clk. Fulton County Superior Ct., Atlanta, 1949-50; ptnr. Carter Ansley Smith & McLendon, Atlanta, 1950-86; dir. Amica Mutual Ins. Co., 1976-96; cons. U.S. VA Hosp., Decatur, Ga., 1996—; pro bono. Arbitrator N.Y. Stock Exch., 1980-88, U.S. Dist. Ct. (mid. dist.) Ga., Macon, 1988—. Scout master Boy Scouts Am., Atlanta, 1959-70; active pro bono work for war vets., 1998—. Staff sgt. USAAF, 1942-45, ETO. Recipient Disting. Svc. award U. Ga., 1996, Exceptional Performance citation def. Rsch. Inst., 1985. Mem. Ga. Def. Lawyers Assn. (pres. 1984), Atlanta Bar Assn., Lawyers Club of Atlanta, Univ. Yacht Club, Buckhead Men's Garden Club (pres. 2002), Masons (32 deg.). Republican. Methodist. Avocations: gardening, woodwork, travel, fishing, spectator sports. E-mail: melburnem@aol.com.

MCLENDON, RICHARD CHARLES, music educator; b. Troy, Ala., July 9, 1953; s. Charles Elie and Doris Dean McLendon; m. Michelle Rene Buck, June 25, 1988 (div. July 2, 1996); children: Zachary, Ryan; m. Tatyana Klimentyevna Stepanova, June 4, 2003; 1 stepchild, Nikita. BS in Edn., Jacksonville State U., 1977; MusM, U. Southwestern La., 1979; Ednl. Specialist, Troy State U., 1997; postgrad., Argosy U., 2000—03. Cert. tchr. Ga. Grad. asst. U. Southwestern La., Lafayette, 1977—79; band dir. Murray (Ky.) Ind. Sch. Sys., 1979—80; program coord. Pride of Cin., Inc., 1981—83; instr. of percussion Murray (Ky.) State U., 1981—82; band dir. Colquitt County Jr. H.S., Moultrie, Ga., 1984—93; dir. of bands Colquitt County H.S., Moultrie, Ga., 1993—2001, adminstrv. asst., 2002—. Assoc. condr. European tour US Collegiate Wind Band, 1998; creative & instrnl. staff tour of Ecuador and Colombia US All-Star Marching Band, 1978. Composer: Medigated Goo II (3rd Pl., 11th Internat. Percussion Composition Contest, Percussive Arts Soc., 1984). Mem.: Music Educators Nat. Conf., Nat. Band Assn., Comparative and Internat. Edn. Soc., Am. Assn. for the Advancement of Slavic Studies, Ga. Music Educators Assn. (dist. chmn. 2002—04), Kappa Delta Pi, Pi Kappa Lambda, Phi Mu Alpha Sinfonia. Avocations: swimming, bicycling, hiking, travel. Home: 1725 Gatewood Circle Moultrie GA 31768 Office: Colquitt County HS 1800 Park Ave Moultrie GA 31768 Personal E-mail: rmclendon@alltel.net. E-mail: rmclendo@colquitt.k12.ga.us.

MCLENNAN, BARBARA NANCY, international tax specialist; b. N.Y.C., Mar. 25, 1940; d. Sol and Gertrude (Rochkind) Miller; m. Kenneth McLennan, Aug. 14, 1962; children: Gordon, Laura. BA magna cum laude, CCNY, 1961; MS, U. Wis., 1962, PhD, 1965; JD, Georgetown U., 1983. Bar: DC 1983, U.S. Ct. Internat. Trade 1988, U.S. Ct. Appeals (DC cir.) 1988, U.S. Supreme Ct. 1988, Va. 1991; cert. accredited valuation analyst Nat. Assn. Career Valuation Analysts, 2004. From asst. prof. to assoc. prof. Temple U., Phila., 1965—78; budget analyst Com. Budget, U.S. Ho. of Reps., Washington, 1978—81; legis. asst. fin. and budget Senator Dan Quayle, Washington, 1981—84; internat. tax specialist IRS U.S. Dept. Treasury, Washington, 1984—89; dep. asst. sec. trade, info. and analysis U.S. Dept. Commerce, Washington, 1989—91; prin., atty.-at-law Bitonti and Wilhelm, PC., McLean, Va., 1991—93; staff v.p. govt.-legal affairs consumer electronics group Electronic Industries Assn., Washington, 1993—94, staff v.p. tech. policy, consumer electronics group, 1994—95; v.p. Van Scoyoc Assocs., Washington, 1995—96; cons. on tax related issues in U.S., former Soviet Union, and West Bank and Gaza McLean, Va., 1996—. Sr. polit. scientist SRI-Internat., Arlington, Va., 1971—74; vis. prof. Am. Coll., Paris, 1975—76; cons. UNESCO, Paris, 1977—78. Author: (book) Comparative Political Systems, 1975; contbr. articles to profl. jours. Mem. parents adv. coun. Randolph-Macon Coll., Ashland, Va., 1989—92. Fellow NDEA, 1962—65. Mem.: ABA, Va. Bar Assn., Fed. Bar Assn., DC Bar Assn., Am. Soc. Assn. Execs., Phi Beta Kappa. Home: 1620 Harbor Rd Williamsburg VA 23185 E-mail: barb.mcl@cox.net.

MCLENNAN, BERNICE CLAIRE, human resources professional; b. Malden, Mass., Dec. 26, 1936; d. Ralph Cyril Worth and Alice Seaman (Hunter) Worth Barrett; m. Hubert Earle McLennan, Oct. 28, 1961; 1 child, Cynthia Alice. Student, Moody Bible Inst., 1958, Salem State Coll., 1988, Bentley Coll., 1989. Youth dir. Faith Evangelical Ch., Melrose, Mass., 1971-77; adminstrv. asst. Boston Redevel. Authority, 1977-85, adminstr. coord., 1985-87, asst. sec. authority, 1981—2002, dir. human resources, 1988-95, asst. dir., 1995-99, dep. dir. human resources, 1999—2002; human resources cons., 2003; ret., 2003. Moderator Faith Evangelical Ch., Melrose, 1985-88, Christian edn. chair, 1973-76. Sec. Melrose (Mass.) Sch. Com., 1983-85; vol. Boston (Mass.) Youth Campaign, 1989, 90; bd. dirs. Chime Time Children's Ctr., Melrose, 1998-99; mem. 1st Bapt. Ch. Melrose, 1999--. Mem. Internat. Pers. Mgmt. Assn., Assn. Affirmative Action Profls. Avocations: Christian edn., women's issues, drug/alcohol edn. Home: 31 Botolph St Melrose MA 02176-1126

MCLENNAN, ROBERT GORDON, asset management company executive; b. Chgo., Aug. 13, 1943; s. Robert G. and Grace (Anderson) McL.; m. Rebecca Ann Martin, Aug. 14, 1965; children: Robert Martin, Douglas Andrew. BA, Cornell Coll., 1965; JD, U. Ill., 1968. Bar: Ill. 1968. Atty. Amoco Oil Co., Chgo., 1968-70; ptnr. McLennan Co., Park Ridge, Ill., 1970-81; chmn. MTI Construction Svcs. LLC, 1982—; pres. Beacon Mgmt. Co., Wheeling, Ill., 1995—. Bd. dirs. Am. Health Care, Oak Brook, Ill., 1988—; trustee Village of Glenview, Ill., 1995-99; chmn. caucus Glenview Elem. Sch., 1972-73. Mem. Chief Execs. Orgn., World Presidents Orgn. (bd. dir.), Econs. Club. Avocations: running, skiing, tennis, scuba. Fax: 847-541-8855. Office Phone: 847-541-8400. E-mail: arem@aol.com.

MCLEOD, DAVID G. urologist, educator; BS, MD, U. N.C.; JD, No. Va. Law Sch. Chief urologic oncology Walter Reed Army Med. Ctr., Washington, 1984—. Prof. surgery Uniformed Svcs. U. of Health Scis., Bethesda, Md.; clin. prof. Surgery Dept. Georgetown U. Med. Ctr., Washington; prin. investigator Nat. Bladder Cancer Group; sr. rsch. investigator Ctr. for Prostate Disease Rsch. Contbr. chpts. in books, articles to profl. jours. Decorated Legion of Merit award with 2 Oak Leaf Clusters, Bronze Star, Air medal, Combat Med. Badge. Mem.: Nat. Prostate Cancer Project, Soc. Univ. Urologists, Am. Urol. Assn. (past pres. Mid-Atlantic sect.), Am. Found. Urol. Disease (pres. 2001—), Soc. Surg. Oncology, Am. Assn. Clin. Urologists, Soc. Urol. Oncology, Am. Soc. Clin. Urology. Office: Walter Reed Army Med Ctr Urology Svc 1600 Georgia Ave NW Washington DC 20307-5001 Address: Uniformed Svcs Univ 4301 Jones Bridge Rd Bethesda MD 20814

MCLEOD, DOUGLAS BAILEY, mathematician, educator; b. Wahpeton, ND, Apr. 15, 1941; m. Susan Margaret Herminghaus, Dec. 28, 1965; children: Alison Marie, Jonathan Mark. PhD, U of Wis., Madison, 1968—72, MA, 1963—65; BA, U of ND, Grand Forks, 1959—63. Prof. math. San Diego State U., San Diego, Calif., 1972—; program dir. NSF, Arlington, Va., 2000—01; prof. Wash. State U., Pullman, Wash., 1986—93; lectr. Haile Selassie I U., Addis Ababa, Ethiopia, 1966—68; instr. Tex. So. U., Houston, Tex., 1965—66; program mgr. NSF, Arlington, Va., 1979—81. Co-editor (with V.M. Adams): (book) Affect and Math. Problem Solving; author: (book chpt.) From Consensus to Controversy: The Story of the NCTM Standards; co-author (with Susan H. Mcleod): (book chapter) Beliefs and Math. Edn.: Implications for Learning, Tchg., and Rsch. Vol. US Peace Corps, Addis Ababa, Ethiopia, 1966—68. Grantee Math. Problem Solving: Affective Influences on Cognitive Processes, NSF, 1985 to 1989, Setting the Standards: A Case Study of NCTM's Role in Reform Movement, Wis. Ctr. for Ednl. Rsch., 1992 to 1996. Mem.: Nat. Coun. of Teachers of Math. (mem. of various editl. boards 1979—97). Unitarian. Avocation: choral singing. Office: CRMSE 6475 Alvarado Rd Ste 206 San Diego CA 92120

MCLEOD, E. DOUGLAS, real estate developer, lawyer; b. Galveston, Tex., Aug. 6, 1941; s. Vaughan Watkins McLeod and Dorothy (Milroy) Burton; m. Sarah Jackson Helms, Mar. 20, 1965 (div. 1979); children: Chanse, Alexandra, Lindsey; m. Joan Margaret Williams, Dec. 26, 1979; 1 child, Joanie stepchildren: Meg, Libbie. BBA, U. North Tex., 1965; postgrad., So. Meth. U., 1965-66; JD, South Tex. Coll. Law, 1990; LLM, U. Houston, 1993. Bar: Tex., U.S. Dist. Ct. (so. dist.) Tex.; lic. real estate broker. Pres., owner McLeod Properties & co., Galveston, 1967—; tchr. Galveston Ind. Sch. Dist., 1967-69, pres., trustee, 1969—73; banker W. L. Moody & Co., Galveston, 1969-72; developer, broker McLeod Properties/Builders, Galveston, 1972-82; developer Moody Found., Galveston, 1982—. Bd. dirs. Am. Nat. Ins. Co., Galveston, Nat. Western Life Ins. Co., Austin, Anrem Corp., Galveston, Colonel Inc., Galveston, Moody Gardens Inc., Galveston, chmn., 1984—. Mem. editl. bd.: Currents Internat. Trade Law Jour., 1992—. Mayor pro-tem, mem. city coun. City of Galveston, 1973—76; state legislator Tex. Ho. Reps., Austin, 1976—83; bd. visitors South Tex. Coll. Law, 1990—96, bd. dirs., 2000—; mem. adv. bd. U. Houston, 1986—95; bd. dirs. STCL, Ronald McDonald House, 1986—93, Trinity Episcopal Sch., 1990—96, Galveston Econ. Devel. Partnership, 1998—2002; vestryman, sr. warden, chancellor Episc. Ch. With USMC, 1961—67. Mem.: ABA, Am. Judicature Soc., Galveston County Bar Assn., Tex. Bar Assn., Marine Corps League. Avocations: physical fitness advocate, legal history collector, family archivist. Home: 53 Cedar Lawn Cir Galveston TX 77551-4631 Office: The Moody Found 2302 Post Office St Ste 704 Galveston TX 77550-1994 Office Phone: 409-797-1521. Business E-Mail: dmcleod@moodyf.org.

MCLEOD, HARRY O'NEAL, JR., retired petroleum engineer, consultant; b. Shreveport, La., Feb. 26, 1932; s. Harry O'Neal Sr. and Odelle Nan (Crow) McL.; m. Sandra Lou Mahaffey, Feb. 6, 1959; children: Kathleen Odelle, Bryan O'Neal. Degree in engring., Colo. Sch. of Mines, 1953; MS in Petroleum Engring., U. Okla., 1963, PhD in Engring. Sci., 1965. Registered profl. engr., Okla. Prodn. engr. Phillips Petroleum Co., 1953-58; rsch. engr. Jersey Prodn. Rsch. Co., Tulsa, 1963-64; sr. rsch. engr. Dowell divsn. Dow Chem. Co., Tulsa, 1965-69; dir. info. svcs. dept. U. Tulsa, 1969-75; from sr. prodn. engr. to sr. staff engr. Conoco, Inc., Houston, 1975-86, engring. profl., 1986-91, sr. engring. profl., 1992-97; pvt. practice cons. Houston, 1998—2003; ret., 2004. 1st lt. U.S. Army, 1954-56. Mem. Soc. Petroleum Engrs. (Prodn. Engring. award 1989, Disting. Mem. award 1995, disting. author, 1983, disting. lectr. 1987-88, 96-97), Sigma Xi. Republican. Methodist. Home: 2006 Southwick St Houston TX 77080-6315 E-mail: homcleod@aol.com.

MCLEOD, JOHN HUGH, JR., mechanical and electrical engineer; b. Hattiesburg, Miss., Feb. 27, 1911; s. John Hugh and Martha (Caldwell) McL.; m. Suzette Boutell, 1951; children: John Hugh III, Robert Boutell. BS, Tulane U., 1933. Registered profl. engr., Calif. Engr. various firms, 1933-39; field engr. Taylor Instrument Co., Rochester, N.Y., 1940-42; R&D engr. Leeds & Northrup, Co., Phila., 1943-47; sect. head guidance sys. and guided missiles U.S. Naval Air Missile Test Ctr., Point Mugu, Calif., 1947-56; design specialist Gen. Dynamics./Astronautics, San Diego, 1956-63; cons., 1963-64; pvt. practice mech. and elec. engring. cons., 1964—. Disting. vis. prof. Calif. State U., Chico, 1975; mem. exec. com. Fall Joint Computer Conf. Am. Fedn. Info. Processing Socs., 1965; co-founder San Diego Symposium Biomed. Engring., 1961. Author: Simulation: The Dynamic Modeling of Ideas and Systems with Computers, 1968; Computer Modeling and Simulation: Principles of Good Practice, 1982; editor, pub. Simulation Coun. Newsletter, 1952-55; editor: Simulation, 1963-74; assoc. editor Instruments & Control Systems, 1955-63, Behavioral Sci., 1973—; tech. editor Simulation in the Service of Soc., 1971—; co-author: Large-Scale Models for Policy Evaluation, 1977. With USN, 1942-43. Recipient Sr. Sci. Simulation award Electronic Assocs., Inc., 1965, TIMS award Inst. Mgmt. Scis., 1986; NEH, NSF grantee, 1983; McLeod Inst. Simulation Sci. named in his honor at 18 acad. instns. including Calif. State U., Chico, U. Calgary, Can., U. Ottawa, Can., U. Ghent, Belgium, Istituto per la Recerca, Naples, Italy, Polish Acad. Scis., Warsaw, U. Edinburgh, Scotland, Beijing U. Aeronautics and Astronautics, Riga Tech. U., Latvia, Hungarian Acad. Scis., Budapest. Mem. IEEE, AAAS, Soc. Computer Simulation (founder, chmn. com. on profl. ethics, publs. advisor, John McLeod award 1987). Home: 8484 La Jolla Shores Dr La Jolla CA 92037-3019 Office: Soc Computer Simulation PO Box 17900 San Diego CA 92177-7900 E-mail: jmcleod@scs.org.

MCLEOD, LORNA A. personnel director; d. Lois Mary Starr and Donald R. McLeod; m. Daniel J. Borich, Aug. 19, 1994. BA program, U. San Francisco, 1981. Cert. acad. coach Acad. Coaching Excellence, Calif., 2004. Pub. rels. dir./cmty. outreach Redwood Empire Pub. TV/PBS, Eureka, Calif., 1982—86; dir. programs and advocacy Calif. Confederation Arts, Sacramento, 1986—89; profl. devel. coach Creative Callings Coaching, Sedona, Ariz., 1990—; dir. dept. arts and culture City of Sedona, 1990—97. Found. mgr. New Earth Found., Inc., Sedona, 1999—; writer, presenter courses nonprofit leaders. Editor (pub.): (statewide newsletter) Art Matters. 4 county coord. Just Say No Anti-Drug Campaign/KEET TV, Eureka, Calif., 1984—86; co-founder Calif. Assn. Local Arts Agys., Sacramento, 1984—89; youth co-founder Calif. Indian Edn. Assn., Modesto, Calif., 1966—75; sec. Verde Valley Regional Econ. Devel. Coun., Cottonwood, Ariz., 1994—97. Grantee Cmty. Arts Leadership, Ariz. Commn. Arts, 1991-1996; Cmty. Arts Rsch. fellow City of Sedona, Nat. Endowment Arts, 1993. Mem.: Internat. Coach Fedn. (assoc.). Avocations: writing, hiking, gardening. Office: Creative Callings Coaching PO Box 3749 Sedona AZ 86336 Office Phone: 928-282-5196. Personal E-mail: lorna@creativecallings.com.

MCLEOD, PURSER L., JR., financial executive; Pres. Colonial, MOntgomery, 1981, Colonial Bank, Opp, Ala., 1983; exec. v.p. Colonial Retail Banking, Birmingham, 1984. Mem. bd. trustees Univ. Montevallo, 1990-96. Chmn. bd. dir. United Way; chmn. oOntgomery Area Food Bank, Together We Build Habitat for Humanity Devel. Project, West Montgomery, 1996; bd. dirs. YMCA Metro, Boy Scouts Am., Boys and Girls Club of Montgomery. Office: The Colonial Bancgroup Inc PO Box 1108 Montgomery AL 36101-1108

MCLEOD, STEPHEN GLENN, education educator, language educator; b. Pensacola, Fla., Mar. 30, 1949; AA, Pensacola Jr. Coll., 1969; BA, U. West Fla., 1971; MA, Vanderbilt U., 1973; EdD, Nova Southeastern U., 1992. Commd. 2d lt. U.S. Army, 1978, advanced through grades to capt., 1981, resigned, 1984; sr. assoc. prof. mil. edn. program St. Leo Coll., Hurlburt Field, Fla., 1984-92; adj. instr. Pensacola Jr. Coll., 1984—86, 1991—2003; West Fla. cluster adminstr. programs for higher edn. Nova Southeastern U., Pensacola/Ft. Lauderdale, Fla., 1994—2003; asst. prof. English Jackson State U., Miss., 2003—. Contbr. articles to profl. jours. Capt. U.S. Army, 1975-84. Recipient Rsch. award Phi Delta Kappa, 1989. Mem.: Coll. Lang. Assn., Nat. Coun. Tchrs. English, Two-Year Coll. English Assn. Southeast, Internat. Fellowship of Christians and Jews. Avocations: golf, travel, Israeli dance. Home: 1400 JR Lynch St PO Box 190411 Jackson MS 39217 Personal E-mail: mcleods@bellsouth.net.

MCLEOD, WALTON JAMES, lawyer, state legislator; b. Walterboro, S.C., June 30, 1937; s. Walton James Jr. and Rhoda Lane (Brown) M.; m. Julie Edwina Hamiter, Feb. 15, 1969; 1 child, Walton James IV. BA, Yale U., 1959; LLB, U. S.C., 1964. Bar: S.C. 1964, U.S. Supreme Ct. 1974. Law clk. to Chief Judge Clement Haynsworth U.S. Ct. Appeals (4th cir.), Richmond, Va., 1964-65; assoc. Pope and Schumpert, Newberry, S.C., 1965-67; asst. U.S. Atty. Columbia, S.C., 1967-68; gen. counsel S.C. Dept. Health & Environ. Ctrl., Columbia, 1968-94, spl. counsel, 1994-96; dep. S.C. atty. gen. Columbia, 1987-88. Magistrate Newberry County, Little Mountain, S.C., 1973-81; mcpl. judge Town of Little Mountain, 1981-83, mayor, 1983-89, 93-96; mem. S.C. Ho. of Reps., Columbia, 1996—. Author: Legal Perspectives of Environmental Health, 1973; co-author: Environmental Quality Law, 1975, Hospital Franchising Law and Regulation, 1979. Pres. Newberry (S.C.) Jaycees, 1967; bd. dirs. S.C. Housing Fin. & Devel. Authority, Columbia, 1977-96; chair Ctrl. Midlands Coun. Govts., Columbia, 1981-82, 2001—; trustee S.C. State Mus., Columbia, 1981-85. Lt. (j.g.) USN, 1959-61, served to Capt. USNR, 1961-92, ret. Recipient Outstanding Jaycee award Newberry Jaycees, 1967, Howell Excellence award Naval Res. Law Program, Washington, 1991; named Outstanding Freshman Rep. of Yr. Carolina Hist. Found. Soc., Inc., 1997. Fellow S.C. Bar Found.; mem. S.C. Magistrates Assn. (pres. 1976-77, Disting. Jud. Svc. award 1975, 77), Judge Advs. Assn. (nat. pres. 1991-92), S.C. Res. Officers Assn. (state pres. 1981-82, Res. Officer of Yr. 1998), S.C. Soc. (pres. 1990-93). Democrat. Luth. Avocations: jogging, reading. Home: 308 Pomaria St Little Mountain SC 29075-9003 Office: SC House of Reps PO Box 11867 Columbia SC 29211-1867 Fax: 803-345-0770.

MCLEOD, WILLIAM LASATER, JR., lawyer, former judge and state legislator; b. Marks, Miss., Feb. 27, 1931; s. William Lasater and Sara Louise (Macaulay) McL.; m. Marilyn Qualls, June 16, 1962; children: Sara Nelson Judson, Martha Ellen Livanec, Ruth Elizabeth Rohs. AB, Princeton U., 1953; JD, La. State U., 1958. Bar: La. 1958, U.S. Supreme Ct. 1980. Pvt. practice, Lake Charles, La., 1958—90, 1997—; ptnr. McLeod & Little, 1976—90; dist. judge Calcasieu Parish, 1991—96. Mem. La. Ho. of Reps., 1968-76; mem. La. Senate, 1976-90. Chmn. adv. bd. Lake Charles Salvation Army, 1965-66; pres. Calcasieu Area coun. Boy scouts Am., 1978; elder Presbyn. Ch. With U.S. Army, 1953-55. Recipient Disting. Svc. award Lake Charles Jaycees, 1963, Civic Svc. award S.W. La. C. of C., 1986. Mem. La. Bar Assn., S.W. La Bar Assn. (pres. 1980), Masons. Democrat. Office: 120 W Pujo St Lake Charles LA 70601-4257 Home: 3709 Holly Hill Rd A Lake Charles LA 70605-2526

MCLEOD, WILLIS B. academic administrator; m. Jacqueline Cumbo; 1 child, Jeffrey. BS in Math., MEd in Elem. Sch. Adminstrn., Fayetteville State U.; EdD in Sch. Adminstrn., U. Va. Pres. Fayetteville (N.C.) State U., 1995—.

MCLESKEY, CHARLES HAMILTON, anesthesiologist, educator, pharmaceutical executive; b. Phila., Nov. 8, 1946; s. W. Hamilton and Marion A. (Butts) McL.; m. Nanci S. Simmons, June 3, 1972; children: Travis, Heather. BA, Susquehanna U., 1968; MD, Wake Forest U., 1972. Diplomate Am. Bd. Anesthesiology. Intern Maine Med. Ctr., Portland, 1972-73; resident in anesthesiology U. Wash. Sch. Medicine, Seattle, 1973-76, NIH rsch. trainee, 1974-75; clin. teaching assoc. dept. anesthesiology U. Calif., San Francisco, 1976-78; asst. prof. anesthesiology Wake Forest U. Bowman Gray Sch. Medicine, Winston-Salem, N.C., 1978-83, assoc. prof., 1983-84, U. Tex. Med. Br., Galveston, 1985-87; assoc. prof. anesthesiology U. Colo. Health Sci. Ctr., Denver, 1987-91, prof., 1991-93, dir. acad. affairs, 1987-93; prof., chmn. dept. anesthesiology Tex. A&M U., 1993-2000; chmn. dept. anesthesiology, med. dir. perioperative svcs. Scott and White Clin. and Meml. Hosp., Temple, Tex., 1993-2000; assoc. med. dir. Scott and White Health Plan, 1995-2000; sr. dir. clin. devel. Abbott Labs., Abbott Park, Ill., 2000—02, global med. dir., global mktg. dir. anesthesia and sedation, 2002—. Cons., lectr. Janssen Pharmaceutica, Piscataway, N.J., 1980-98, Alza Corp., Palo Alto, Calif., 1986-99; cons. Glaxo-Wellcome Co., Research Triangle Park, N.C., Abbott Labs., Chgo., Hoechst, Marion, Roussel, Kansas City, Kans., Aspect Med., Natick, Mass., Baxter Labs., Chgo., Scott Labs., Lubbock, Tex.; lectr. to over 500 nat. and state med. orgns., 1982—; examiner Am. Bd. Anesthesiology; lectr. Ohmeda, Liberty Corner, N.J. Assoc. editor Anesthesiology Rev., Anesthesiology News, Pharmacy Practia News; editor Geriatric Anesthesiology, 1997; contbr. numerous articles to med. jours. Mem. choir Friendswood (Tex.) Meth. Ch., 1985-87; mem. Friendswood Fine Arts Commn., 1985-87; mem. Temple Chamber Arts Adv. Coun., 1997-99. Lt. comdr. M.C., USN, 1976-78. Woodruff-Fisher scholar, 1964-68. Mem.: Temple C. of C., Evergreen Newcomers, Soc. Acad. Anesthesia Chairs (councilman 1996—99), Soc. for Ambulatory Anesthesia (program chair 1999), Internat. Anesthesia Rsch. Soc., Colo. Soc. Anesthesiologists (past pres.), Soc. for Edn. in Anesthesiology (past v.p., past pres.), Am. Soc. Anesthesiologists (del. 1983—85, 1988—90), Assn. U Anesthetists, Nat. Spkrs. Assn., Internat. Platform Assn., Mensa, Alpha Omega Alpha. Republican. Presbyterian. Avocations: running, fishing, racquetball, squash. Address: 21038 W Andover Dr Mundelein IL 60060 Personal E-mail: charles.mcleskey@comcast.net.

MCLEVISH, TIMOTHY, financial professional; Various mgmt. positions Mead Corp, Dayton, Ohio, 1987-99, v.p., CFO, 1999—. Office: Mead Corp World Hdqrs Courthouse Plz NE Dayton OH 45463-0001

MCLIN, RHINE LANA, mayor, former state legislator; b. Dayton, Ohio, Oct. 3, 1948; d. C. Josef, Jr. and Bernice (Cottman) McL. BA in Sociology, Parsons Coll., 1969; MEd, Xavier U., 1972; postgrad. in law, U. Dayton, 1974-76; AA in Mortuary Sci., Cin. Coll., 1988. Lic. funeral dir. Tchr. Dayton Bd. Edn., 1970-72; divorce counselor Domestic Rels. Ct., Dayton, 1972-73; law clk. Montgomery Common Pleas Ct., Dayton, 1973-74; v.p., dir., embalmer McLin Funeral Homes, Dayton, 1972—; mem. Ohio Ho. of Reps. from 36th & 38th dists., Columbus, 1988-94, Ohio Senate from 5th dist., Columbus, 1994—2002; mem. Ways & Means Com.; controlling bd., ins. commerce comn. ranking mem.; state and local govt. com. Columbus; minority whip Ohio Senate, Columbus, 1998—2002; mayor City of Dayton, 2003—. Instr. Central State U., Wilberforce, Ohio, 1982-97; mem. Ohio Tuition Trust Authority. Mem. Dem. Nat. Com., Children's Def. Fund. Toll fellow; Paul Harris fellow; Flemming fellow; BLLD fellow; named Ohio Legislator of Yr., Ohio Social Workers Assn., 1999. Mem. Nat. Funeral Dirs. Assn., Ohio Funeral Dirs. Assn., Montgomery County Hist. Soc., NAACP (life), Nat. Coun. Negro Women (life), Delta Sigma Theta. Achievements include being first female mayor of Dayton. Office: City Hall 2nd Fl 101 W Third St Dayton OH 45402 Office Phone: 937-333-3653. Business E-Mail: Rhine.McLin@cityofDayton.org.

MCLINN, ANNA RUTH, educator; b. Magnolia, Ark., May 11, 1941; d. Willie Mae Heard and Onzelow Reed; m. Cecil Edward McLinn; children: Tiffany, David. BA in Edn., George Pepperdine U., 1963, MS in Mgmt. and Adminstrn., 1973; D (hon.), St. Sephens Coll. With L.A. Unified Sch. Dist.; prin. Marvin Ave. Sch.; prof. U. Phoenix, Calif. Adj. prof., student tchr. supr. Nat. U., Phoenix U.; spkr. in field. Numerous guest appearences on TV. Vol. House of Blues Found., 1996—, Kayne-Eras Found., fundraising com. Recipient Unsung Hero award Reliastar Life Ins. Co., L.A., 1997; Outstanding Tchr. of Yr. Theta Rho Delta Soc., 1963; Kellogg scholar, 1995. Mem. Calif. Coun. Quality and Svc. (Eureka award 1996), Associated Adminstrs. L.A., Phil-Art-Lit-Mor Club, Women on Target, Delta Sigma Theta. Democrat. Baptist. Avocations: singing, dance, painting, antique collecting. Home: 6526 W 6th St Los Angeles CA 90048

MCLOONE, EUGENE P. education educator; b. Phila., Nov. 11, 1929; married. BA, LaSalle Coll., 1951; MS in Govt. Mgmt., U. Denver, 1952; PhD, U. Ill., 1961. Carnegie fellow U. Denver, 1951-52; staff Ark. Legis. Rsch. Coun. Study on Sch. of Fin., 1952; rsch. asst. Bur. of Ednl. Rsch. U. Ill., 1952-55; Fed. Exec. fellow The Brookings Instn., 1961; specialist Sch. of Fin. U.S. Office of Edn., 1958-65; postdoctoral rsch. fellow Stanford U., 1966-67; rsch. dir. Nat. Ctr. for Edn. Stats./U.S. Dept. Edn., Washington, 1979-81; assoc. prof. U. Md. Coll. Edn., College Park, 1967-75, prof. edn. dept. edn. policy, planning and adminstrn., 1975-96, assoc. prof. dept. econs., 1967-94; sr. staff scientist George Washington U., 1966-67; postdoc. fellow Stanford U., 1967-68; assoc. dir. rsch. divsn. NEA, Washington, 1968-69, staff contact, com. for sch. fin., 1968-70; atty. gen. State of N.J., 1981-83, State of W.Va., 1981; prof. emeritus U. Md., College Park, 1996—. Cons. Addison-Wesleyan Pubs., 1992-93, Bur. of Spl. Edn., Dept. Edn., 1992, Jour. Econs. and Edn., 1989-95, Jour. Edn. Fin., 1989—, Nat. Tax Assn., 1989, Office Edn. Rsch. and Improvement, 1989, others; lectr. in field; panel mem. Statis. for Supply and Demand of Pre-Collegiate Sci. and Math. Tchrs., Nat. Rsch. Coun., NAS, 1986-90; with Heald Commn. Higher Edn. N.Y., 1960; treas. Brightright of Johnstown, 2000. Author: Pre-College Science and Mathematics Teachers: Monitoring Supply, Demand, and Quality, 1990, Report of Panel, Toward Understanding Teacher Supply and Demand: Priorities for Research and Development Interim Report, Profiles in School Support, 1969-70; co-author: Public School Finance: Profiles of the State, 1979, Documentation and Analysis of Maryland Special Services Information System, 1977; contbr. articles to profl. jours.; editor books in field. Treas. Birthright of Johnstown, 2000-02. Grantee Ford Found., 1966-68, Bur. of the Handicapped, U.S.O.E., 1977, Nat. Ctr. for Edn. Stats., 1971, 73; recipient awards in field. Mem. NEA, Am. Econ. Assn., Am. Assn. Sch. Adminstrs., Am. Edn. Fin. Assn. (pres.-elect

1995-96, pres. 1996-97, immediate past pres. 1997-98, Outstanding Svc. awsard for Contbns. to Field 2000), Phi Delta Kappa. Achievements include development of McLoone Index measure of comparative inequality in pupil expenditure.

MCLOONE, JAMES BRIAN, psychiatrist, educator; b. Phoenix, Ariz., Mar. 21, 1950; s. John Joseph and Lorraine Suzette (Hughes) McL.; m. Cathy Ebel; children: Katherine Ann, Brian Bathe. BA, U. Ariz., 1972; MD, George Washington U., 1976. Diplomate Am. Bd. Psychiatry and Neurology. Inpatient med. dir. Maricopa Med. Ctr., Phoenix, 1980-81; dir. psychiatry residency Good Samaritan Regional Med. Ctr., Phoenix, 1981—, chmn. dept. psychiatry, 1992—. Prof. clin. psychiatry U. Ariz. Coll. Medicine, Tucson, 1982—, assoc. head dept. psychiatry for acad. and clin. affairs, Phoenix campus, 1997—; chair med. edn. com. Good Samaritan Regional Med. Ctr., Phoenix, 1990—, exec. com., 1992—. Mem. Men's Art Coun. Phoenix Art Mus., 1981-87; student advisor U. Ariz. Coll. Medicine, Tucson, 1982—, Brophy Coll. Prep., Phoenix, 1982. Fellow: Am. Psychiat. Assn. (disting.); mem.: Assn. Geropsychiatrists, Am. Assn. Dirs. Psychiat. Residency Tng., Paradise Valley C.C., Alpha Omega Alpha. Roman Catholic. Avocations: golf, gardening. Office: Good Samaritan Reg Med Ctr 925 E Mcdowell Rd Phoenix AZ 85006-2579 Office Phone: 602-239-6880.

MCLUCAS, KATE, magazine editor; Exec. editor, testing dir. Infoworld, San Mateo, Calif. Office: Infoworld 155 Bovet Rd Ste 800 San Mateo CA 94402-3150

MC LURE, CHARLES E., JR., economist, consultant; b. Sierra Blanca, Tex., Apr. 14, 1940; s. Charles E. and Dessie (Evans) McL.; m. Patsy Nell Carroll, Sept. 17, 1962. BA, U. Kans., 1962; MA, Princeton U., 1964, PhD, 1966. Asst. prof. econs. Rice U., Houston, 1965-69, assoc. prof., 1969-72, prof., 1972-79, Allyn R. and Gladys M. Cline prof. econs., 1973-79; exec. dir. for research Nat. Bur. Econ. Research, Cambridge, Mass., 1977-78, v.p., 1978-81; sr. fellow Hoover Instn., Stanford U., 1981—; dep. asst. sec. Dept. Treasury, 1983-85. Sr. staff economist Coun. Econ. Advisers, Washington, 1969-70; vis. lectr. U. Wyo., 1972; vis. prof. Stanford U., 1973; cons. U.S. Treasury Dept., Labor Dept., World Bank, UN, OAS, Interam. Devel. Bank, Tax Found, Com. Econ Devel, IMF Internat Tax and Investment Ctr, govts Can., Colombia, Malaysia, Panama, Jamaica, Bolivia, Indonesia, New Zealand, Brazil, Trinidad and Tobago, Venezuela, Guatemala, Peoples Republic China, Egypt, Malawi, Mex., Bulgaria, Brazil, Russia, Ukraine, Romania, Kazakhstan, South Africa, Vietnam, Chile, Argentina. Author: Fiscal Failure: Lessons of the Sixties, 1972, (with N. Ture) Value Added Tax: Two Views, 1972, (with M. Gillis) La Reforma Tributaria Colombiana de 1974, 1977, Must Corporate Income Be Taxed Twice?, 1979, Economic Perperspectives on State Taxation of Multijurisdictional Corporations, 1986, The Value Added Tax: Key to Deficit Reduction, 1987; co-author: Taxation of Income from Business and Capital in Colombia, 1989; also numerous articles on econs., tax law and public finance. Ford Found. faculty research fellow, 1967-68 Mem. Am. Econ. Assn., Nat. Tax Assn., Beta Theta Pi. Home: 250 Yerba Santa Ave Los Altos CA 94022-1609 Office: Stanford U Hoover Instn Stanford CA 94305-6010 E-mail: mclure@hoover.stanford.edu.

MCLURE, JOHN DOUGLAS, federal official; b. Melita, Man., Can., July 10, 1942; s. Malcolm Alexander and Rachel (Simpson) McL.; m. Nicole Lafrance, Aug. 26, 1967. BSc, U. Man., Winnipeg, 1963; Ammunition Tech. Officer, Royal Mil. Coll. Sci., Wiltshire, Eng., 1964. Program analyst Treasury Bd. Secretariat, Ottawa, Ont., Can., 1975-79, group chief industry and natural resources divsn., 1979-80, dir. industry and natural resources divsn., 1980-82, asst. sec. econ. devel., 1982-84; asst. dep. min. small bus. and spl. projects Dept. Regional Indsl. Expansion, Ottawa, 1984-85, asst. dep. min. crown investments and spl. projects, 1985-86, asst. dep. min. native econ. devel., 1986-87; asst. dep. min. fin., pers., adminstrn. Dept Industry, Sci. & Tech., Ottawa, 1987-89; asst. dep. min. fin. Dept. Nat. Def., Ottawa, 1989-95, assoc. dep. min., 1995-96; dep. min. Dept. Western Econ. Diversification, Ottawa, 1996-97; sr. v.p. Hill and Knowlton Can. Ltd., Ottawa, 1997-2000; pres., CEO JDM Consulting Inc., 2000—; sr. assoc. Hill and Knowlton Can. Ltd., Ottawa, 2000—. Chmn. bd. Def. Constrn. Can., 2001—. Maj. Can. Land Forces, 1960-75. Recipient N.Am. Best Practice Recognition, Ctr. Creative Leadership, Greensboro, N.C., 1994. Mem. Assn. Profl. Execs. (Leadership award 1995), Club Link Le Fontainebleau Golf Club. Avocations: golf, alpine skiing. Home: 35 Somerset St W Ottawa ON Canada K2P OH3 Office: Hill and Knowlton Can Ltd 55 Metcalfe St Ste 1300 Ottawa ON Canada K1P 6L5 E-mail: john.mclure@hillandknowlton.ca.

MCMAHON, BRIAN, publishing executive; Pub. Car and Driver Hachette Filipacchi Mags., Inc., Ann Arbor, Mich. Office: Hachette Filipacchi Mags Inc 1499 Monrovia Ave Newport Beach CA 92663-2752 also: Car & Driver 2002 Hogback Rd Ann Arbor MI 48105-9736

MCMAHON, DONALD AYLWARD, investor, corporate director; b. N.Y.C., Feb. 20, 1931; s. William F. and Anne (Aylward) McM.; m. Nancy Lantz, Apr. 12, 1953; children: Gail, Brian, Lisa, Glenn, Ann, Carol, William, Douglas. MBA, Emory U., 1982. With Dime Savs. Bank, Bklyn., 1952; salesman Monroe Calculating Machine Co., Bklyn., 1952-55, asst. br. mgr. Pitts., 1955-56, br. mgr. Phila., 1956-63, asst. gen. sales mgr. Orange, N.J., 1963-64, Eastern regional gen. sales mgr., 1964-65, v.p. mktg., 1965-66; pres. Monroe Calculator Co. div. Litton Industries, Inc., Orange, 1966-70; v.p. Litton Industries, 1967-70; pres., chief operating officer, dir. Baker Industries, Inc., Parsippany, N.J., 1970-74; pres., chief exec. officer, dir. Royal Crown Cos., Inc., Atlanta, 1975-85. Bd. dirs. Intelligent Systems Corp., Atlanta. Bd. dirs. Boys Clubs Metro Atlanta. Mem. Sovereign Order of Knights of Malta. Home: 1665 Winterthur Close NW Atlanta GA 30328-4688

MCMAHON, EDWARD RICHARD, lawyer; b. Jersey City, June 7, 1949; s. Edward Barnawall and Jean (Sullivan) McM.; m. Ellen Mary Bosek; children: Meghan Jean, Kerry Eileen, Ryan Edward. AB, Colgate U., 1972; JD, Seton Hall U., 1975. Bar: N.J. 1975, U.S. Dist. Ct. N.J. 1975, U.S. Ct. of Appeals (3rd circ.) 1980. Law clk. to judge U.S. Dist. Ct., Newark, 1975-77; assoc. Lum, Biunno & Tompkins, Newark, 1977-83; ptnr. Lum, Danzis, Drasco, & Positan, LLC, Roseland, NJ, 1983—. Mem. Essex County Chancery Ct. Mediation Prog., 1992—, Supreme Ct. of N.J. Dist. Ethics Com., 1994—97, Supreme Ct. of N.J. Dist. Fee Arbitration Com., 2000—; founding mem. and couns. Morris & Essex Inn of Transactional Counsel, 2001—; mem. U.S. Dist. Ct. Arbitration Prog., 2001—, New Jersey Ct. Approved Mediator, 2002—. Mem. Morris County Rep. Com., N.J., 1982-94; mem. Chatham (N.J.) Boro Rep. com., 1982-94, chmn., 1986-94; bd. dirs. Madison area YMCA, 1989-95; bd. trustees Richard J. Hughes Found., 2001-; mem. N.J. State Rep. Com., 1994-. Mem.: ABA (litigation and banking sects.), Colgate U. Alumni Assn. (class rep. 1993—), 200 Club Morris County, Delbarton Sch. Alumni Assn. (class rep. 1984—), Essex County Bar Assn. (Essex County Chancery Ct. Mediation program 1992—, Supreme Ct. of N.J. dist. ethics com. 1994—97, Supreme Ct. of N.J. dist. fee arbitration com. 2000—, founding mem., counselor Morris & Essex Inn of Transactional Counsel 2001—, U.S. Dist. Ct. Arbitration program 2001—, N.J. Ct. approved mediator 2002—), Morris County Bar Assn., Am. Judicature Soc., Assn. Fed. Bar N.J., N.J. Bar Assn., Colgate (No. N.J.), Phi Alpha Delta, Delta Upsilon. Republican. Roman Catholic. Home: 150 Van Houton Ave Chatham NJ 07928-1239 Office: Lum Danzis Drasco & Positan LLC 103 Eisenhower Pky Roseland NJ 07068-1029 also: 325 Broadway New York NY 10007

MCMAHON, EILEEN MARIE, artist agent; b. Jersey City, July 15, 1953; d. William John and Marie Rita (Stringer) M. BA in Art, Jersey City State Coll., 1974; postgrad., Rutgers U., 1974-76, New Sch. for Social Research, 1976-77, Sch. of Visual Arts, 1976. Asst. curator Jersey City Mus., 1975-77; curator Ian Woodner Family Collection, N.Y.C., 1977-78; assoc. rep. Artist's Assocs., Inc., N.Y.C., 1978-81; sr. rep. Gerald and Cullen Rapp, Inc., N.Y.C., 1981-86; mktg. dir. Corey Chaloner Millen, N.Y.C., 1986-88; assoc. rep. John Locke Studios Inc., N.Y.C., 1988-97; pres. Eileen McMahon & Co., Bayonne, N.J., 1997—. Co-author, designer: mus. catalog, August Will: Scenes of Old Jersey City, 1976. Named Jersey Jour. Woman of Achievement, 1977. Office: Eileen McMahon & Co PO Box 1062 Bayonne NJ 07002-1062 Personal E-mail: eileenmcmahon@earthlink.net.

MCMAHON, GEORGE JOSEPH, academic administrator; b. N.Y.C., June 20, 1923; s. Martin Joseph and Mary (O'Connor) McM. AB, Woodstock Coll., 1946, Philosophy licentiate, 1947, MA, 1948, STL, 1954; MA, Fordham U., 1951; PhD, Laval U., 1959. Joined S.J., 1940, ordained priest Roman Cath. Ch., 1953. Instr. physics and Latin Regis H.S., N.Y.C., 1947-49; instr. philosophy St. Peter's Coll., Jersey City, 1958-60, asst. dean, dir. Sch. Bus. Adminstrn., 1961-62; instr. philosophy Loyola Sem., Shrub Oak, N.Y., 1960-61; dean Fordham Coll., Fordham U., Bronx, N.Y., 1962-74; v.p. adminstrn. Fordham U., 1974-87, v.p. Lincoln Ctr. campus, 1987-94, chaplain, 1994—. Author: The Order of Procedure in the Philosophy of Nature, 1958, The Proemium to the Physics of Aristotle, 1957. V.p. Friends of U. Laval, Que., Can.; trustee Marymount Sch. N.Y.

MCMAHON, JAMES E. lawyer; b. 1951; m. Kathy McMahon; 3 children. BS, Morningside U.; JD, U. S.D., 1977. Asst. atty. gen. S.D. Atty. Gen.'s Office, 1978—81; ptnr. Boyce, Murphy, McDowell & Greenfield, 1981—2002; pvt. practice Sioux Falls, SD, 2002—; U.S. atty. Dist. S.D., 2002—. Recipient Trial Lawyer of Yr. award, S.D. Trial Lawyers Assn., 2000. Office: PO Box 5073 4600 S Deerfield Cir Sioux Falls SD 57117

MCMAHON, JOHN ALEXANDER, law educator; b. Monongahela, Pa., July 31, 1921; s. John Hamilton and Jean (Alexander) McMahon; m. Betty Wagner, Sept. 14, 1947 (div. Mar. 1977); children: Alexander Talpey, Sarah Francis, Elizabeth Wagner, Ann Wallace; m. Anne Fountain Willets, May 1, 1977 (dec. June 1996); m. Anne Hall Davis, Apr. 18, 1999. AB magna cum laude, Duke U., 1942; student, Harvard U. Bus. Sch., 1942—43; JD, Law Sch., 1948; LLD, Wake Forest U., 1978; DSc (hon.), Georgetown U. Sch. Medicine, 1985. Bar: N.C. 1950. Prof. pub. law and govt., asst. dir. Inst. Govt. U. N.C., 1948—59; gen. counsel, sec.-treas. N.C. Assn. County Commrs., Chapel Hill, 1959—65; v.p. spl. devel. Hosp. Saving Assn., Chapel Hill, NC, 1965—67; pres. N.C. Blue Cross and Blue Shield, Inc., Chapel Hill, 1968—72, Am. Hosp. Assn., Chgo., 1972—86; chmn. dept. health adminstrn. Duke U., Durham, NC, 1986—92, exec. in residence Fuqua Sch. Bus., 1992—. Mem. Chapel Hill bd. N.C. Nat. Bank, 1967—72; bd. govs. Blue Cross Assn., 1969—72; mem. Orange County Welfare Bd., 1956—63; chmn. N.C. Comprehensive Health Planning Coun., 1968—72, Health Planning Coun. of Ctrl. N.C., 1963—69; mem. Pres.'s Com. on Health Edn., 1971—72; mem. com. health svcs. industry and health industry adv. com. Econ. Stblzn. Program, 1971—74; mem. adv. coun. Kate Bitting Reynolds Health Care Trust, 1971—95, Northwestern U., 1973—86; mem. med. adv. com. VA, 1975—85; bd. dirs. The Forest at Duke, Durham, NC, 1994—2002, Exec. Svc. Corps of Greater Triangle, 1986—99, mem. adv. bd., 2000—. Author: North Carolina County Government, 1959, The North Carolina Local Government Commission, 1960; editor: N.C. County Yearbook, 1959—64, Proceedings of the Annual National Forum on Hospital and Health Affairs, 1993—2000. Chmn. bd. trustees Duke U., 1971—83, chmn. emeritus, 1983—; bd. mgrs., mem. exec. com. Internat. Hosp. Fedn., London, 1975—85, pres., 1981—83; mem. Orange County Dem. Exec. Com., also chmn. Kings Mill Precinct, 1964—68; bd. dirs. Rsch. Triangle Found., 1971—83, 1992—, Nat. Ctr. for Health Edn., 1974—86. With USAF, 1942—46, col. Res., ret. Recipient Citation Disting. Svc. by Layman, AMA, 1978, Special award, Ill. Hosp. Assn., 1985, Dallas-Fort Worth Hosp. Coun., 1985, many others. Mem.: Inst. Medicine of NAS (Disting. Svc. award 1979), N.C. State Bar, Duke Alumni Assn. (pres. 1968—70, Silver Medal award 1986), Dunes Golf and Beach Club (Myrtle Beach), Hope Valley Country Club (Durham). Republican. Presbyterian. Home: 181 Montrose Dr Durham NC 27707-3929 Office: Duke U Fuqua Sch Bus Durham NC 27708-0120 Office Phone: 919-660-7760.

MCMAHON, JOHN E. marketing analyst; s. Robert K. and Ann L. McMahon; m. Michele M. Regnante, June 20, 1992. BA, Fordham U., 1991; MA, Clark U., Worcester, Mass., 1993; PhD, Clark U., 2004. Sr. rsch. analyst Drexel U., Phila., 1997—99, dir. of rsch., 1999—2001, asst. v.p. for devel. rsch., 2002—03; mktg. analyst The Hartford Fin. Svcs. Group, Inc., Hartford, Conn., 2004—. Dir. Assn. of Profl. Rschrs. for Advancement, Phila., 2002—03; cons. Assn. of Fundraising Profls., Phila. V.p. Cana Mission, Hancock, NH, 2001—. Recipient Grad. fellowship, Clark U., 1991—2004. Mem.: Coun. for the Advancement and Support of Edn., Assn. of Profl. Rschrs. for Advancement, Phi Alpha Theta. Home: 29 South Rd Marlborough CT 06447-1573 Office: The Hartford Fin Svcs Group Inc Hartford CT Office Phone: 860-547-6388.

MCMAHON, JOHN J., JR., metal processing company executive; Formerly pres., sec., treas., chmn. bd. dirs. McWane, Inc., Birmingham, Ala.; chmn. exec. com. McWane Corp.; also chief exec. officer Clow Corp., Birmingham. Office: McWane Inc 2030 Iverness Center Pkwy Birmingham AL 35242

MCMAHON, JOHN PATRICK, retired lawyer; b. Monroeville, Ohio, Feb. 8, 1919; s. George James and Eleanor Helene (Ruffing) McM.; m. Patricia Patterson McDanel, May 6, 1950 (dec. July 1983); children: Colleen, Kevin, Patricia, Brian, Barry, Michael; m. Mary Echard, Mar. 7, 1987. BA cum laude, Ohio State U., 1940, JD summa cum laude, 1942. Bar: Ohio 1942, U.S. Supreme Ct. 1949, U.S. Dist. Ct. Ohio 1949, U.S. Ct. Appeals (6th cir.) 1959, U.S. Ct. Appeals (D.C. cir.) 1975. Ptnr. George, Greek, King, McMahon, Columbus, Ohio, 1954-79, Baker & Hostetler, Columbus, 1979-85, ret.; with nat. coun. Ohio State U. Coll. Law, 1980—. Capt. USAAF, 1943-46, PTO. Mem. ABA, Ohio Bar Assn., Columbus Bar Assn., Transp. Lawyers Assn., Pres.' Club of Ohio State U. (Columbus), Athletic Club (Columbus), Home: 2880 Halstead Rd Columbus OH 43221-2916 Office: Baker & Hostetler 65 E State St Ste 2100 Columbus OH 43215-4260 E-mail: jmemahon@columbus.rr.com.

MCMAHON, JOSEPH EINAR, lawyer, consultant; b. Chgo., Aug. 26, 1940; s. Reynold Bernard and Dorothy Marie (Oftedahl) McM. BA cum laude, Denison U., 1962; JD, U. Mich., 1965. Bar: Mass. 1968, D.C. 1980. Asst. to Atty. Gen. and Senator Edward Brooke, Boston and Washington, 1965-67; exec. asst. Lt. Gov. Sargent of Mass., Boston, 1967-69; v.p. BedStuy D&S Corp. Restoration, Bklyn., 1969-74; dir. govt. regulations Westinghouse Electric Corp., Washington, 1974-78; v.p. corp. affairs Federated Dept. Stores, Cin., 1978-80; atty., cons. McMahon and Assocs., Washington, 1980—; v.p. pub. policy Covenant House, 2001—. Exec. dir. (part time), bd. dirs. The Get Ahead Found./USA, 1991-99. Life trustee Denison U.; visitor U. Mich. Law Sch.; 1st v.p. Boston Rep. Com., 1968-69; presdl. appointee Nat. Coun. Econ. Opportunity, 1975-76; exec. dir. Nat. Bus. for Reagan-Bush Com., 1980; dir. emeritus Luther Inst., Washington, Rodale Inst., Emmaus, Pa.; dir. Luth. Lesbian and Gay Min., San Francisco, 1994-2003; mem. outreach bd. Evang. Luth. Ch. in Am., 1995-2001. Mem. Capitol Hill Club, Phi Delta Phi, Pi Sigma Alpha, Omicron Delta Kappa. Lutheran. Office: McMahon & Assocs 2031 Q St NW Washington DC 20009 E-mail: McMahon@aol.com.

MCMAHON, LINDA E. sports association executive; b. New Bern, N.C., Oct. 4, 1948; m. Vincent K. McMahon, Aug. 6, 1966; children: Shane, Stephanie. Degree, East Carolina U. Co-founder, bd. dirs. World Wrestling Fedn. Entertainment, Inc., Stamford, Conn., 1980—, pres., 1993—, CEO, 1997—. Office: WWFE Corp Hdqs 1241 E Main St Stamford CT 06902

MCMAHON, MARIBETH LOVETTE, physicist; b. Bradford, Pa., June 8, 1949; d. James Harry and Jospehine Rose (Sylvester) Lovette; m. Frank Joseph MaMahon, Nov. 19, 1976 (div.). BS in Math., BS in Physics, Pa. State U., 1971, MS in Physics, 1974, PhD in Physics, 1976. Research asst. Pa. State U., 1971-76; advanced research and devel. engr. GTE Sylvania, Danvers, Mass., 1976-78; sr. physicist 3M Co., St. Paul, 1978-79, market devel. supr., 1979-83; market devel. mgr. Galileo Electro-Optics Corp., Sturbridge, Mass., 1983-84; product mgr. Varian Assocs., Lexington, Mass., 1984-85; mktg. dir. Bowmar, Acton, Mass., 1985-86; pres. Kilduff Inc., Peoria, Ariz., 1986—. Recipient Cert. in Appreciation of Service Pa. State U., 1971 Mem. Optical Soc. Am., Assn. Women in Sci., Assn. Physicists in Medicine, Sigma Pi Sigma, Sigma Chi Home and Office: 11327 N 82nd Dr Peoria AZ 85345-5895

MCMAHON, MARTIN JAMES, JR., law educator, consultant; b. Phila., May 3, 1949; s. Martin James and Doris (Raymond) McM.; m. Pamela Sue (Zogbaum), June 26, 1971; children: Connor Martin, Timothy James. BA, Rutgers U., 1971; JD, Boston Coll., 1974; LLM, Boston U., 1979. Bar: N.H. 1974, U.S. Dist. Ct. N.H. 1974, U.S. Tax Ct. 1978, U.S. Supreme Ct. 1978, Ky. 1981. Assoc. Hamblett & Kerrigan P.C., Nashua, NH, 1974-79; prof.-in-residence Office of Chief Counsel IRS, Washington, 1986-87; Culverhouse Scholar in Taxation U. Fla. Coll. of Law, Gainesville, 1991; Leatherman prof. of law U. Ky. Coll. of Law, Lexington, 1979-97; Clarence J. TeSelle prof. of law U. Fla. Coll. of Law, Gainesville, 1997—. Vis. assoc. prof. U. Va., Charlottesville, 1982-83; mem. IRS Ctrl. Regional Counsel Adv. Bd., Cin., 1989. Author: (text) Fundamentals of Federal Income Taxation Study Problems (with accompanying tchr.'s manual), 1985; co-author: (books) (with B. Bittker) Federal Incсome Taxation of Individuals, 1988, 2d edit. 1995, (with L. Zelenak) Federal Income Taxation of Individuals Study Problems and accompanying tchr.'s manual, 1990, 3d edit., 2002, (with others) Federal Income Taxation of Partnerships, and S Corporations, 1991, 3d edit., 1999, Federal Income Taxation of Business Organizations, 1991, 3d edit., 1999, Federal Income Taxation Cases and Materials, 1994, 4th edit., 1998, 5th edit, 2004, Federal Income Taxation of Corporations, 1997, 2d edit., 1999, (with B.B. Bittker and L. Zelenak) Federal Income Taxation of Individuals, 3d edit., 2002; editor: Bittker's Fundamentals of Federal Income Taxation Student Edition, 1982; also contbr. chpts. to books, articles to profl. jours. Fellow Am Coll. Tax Counsel; mem. ABA (tax sect.), Assn. Am. Law Schs. (chmn. tax sect. 1996), Am. Law Inst. (tax adv. group), Ky. Bar Assn., Nat. Tax Assn. Democrat. Home: 2814 NW 58th Blvd Gainesville FL 32606-6400 Office Phone: 352-846-1903.

MCMAHON, PAUL FRANCIS, finance company executive; b. Malone, N.Y., Apr. 28, 1945; s. Philip Francis and Shirley (Roy) M.; m. Sheila Ann Lester, Nov. 30, 1963; children: Michael, Marsha BS, Syracuse U., 1968. CPA, N.Y., Oreg.; cert. mgmt. acct., mgmt. cons. With Ernst & Young, Syracuse, NY, 1968—79, mgr., 1975-79, ptnr. in charge of mgmt. cons. in Europe Brussels, 1979-84, vice-chmn. Cleve., 1984-87; exec. ptnr. Ernst & Young Internat., N.Y., 1987-93; chmn. Ernst & Young Ea. Europe, 1990-93; regional dir. Asia/Pacific Ernst & Young Internat., Singapore, 1994-96; contr. Coop. Mktg. Agy., Syracuse, 1973-75; COO Amrop Internat., Brussels, 1997-2001; ptnr. Network Journey, 2002—. Treas. Chamber Music N.W.; co-chair lit. & hist. com. Arlington Club. Mem.: AICPA, Coun. Consulting Orgns. (past chmn.), Assn. Mgmt. Consulting Firms (bd. dirs.), Inst. Mgmt. Acctg., N.Y. Soc. CPAs, Oreg. Soc. CPAs. Democrat. Roman Catholic. Avocations: photography, sculpture, travel, gardening, biographies. Home: 35680 NE Wilsonville Rd Newberg OR 97132-7181 E-mail: pfmcmahon@earthlink.net.

MCMAHON, ROBERT ALBERT, JR., lawyer; b. New Orleans, July 23, 1950; s. Robert Albert and Marie Rose (Kennedy) McM.; m. Cynthia Ann Steffan, June 29, 1979; children: Angela, Jennifer, Robyn. BA cum laude, U. Southwestern La., 1972; JD, Loyola U., 1975. Bar: La. 1975, U.S. Dist. Ct. (ea. dist.) La. 1977, U.S. Ct. Appeals (5th cir.) 1978, U.S. Dist. Ct. (mid. dist.) La. 1985, U.S. Dist. Ct. (ea. dist.) Tex. 2000, U.S. Supreme Ct. 1989, U.S. Dist. Ct. (we. dist.) La. 1991. Atty. Brown & Hull, Metairie, La., 1975-76, Stewart Title La., New Orleans, 1976, Duplechin & Assocs., Gretna, La., 1977-80, Zelden & Zelden, New Orleans, 1980-81; ptnr. Bernard, Cassisa, Elliott & Davis, Metairie, La., 1982—. Vol. New Orleans Pro Bono Project, 1991—. Recipient scholarship U. New Orleans, 1968, U. Southwestern La., 1968. Mem. NRA (life), Def. Rsch. Inst., La. Assn. Def. Counsel, Jefferson Bar Assn., La. State Bar Assn.(ho. of dels. 1993—2003), Hibernians, Phi Kappa Theta. Republican. Roman Catholic. Avocations: military history, hunting, tennis, golf. Office: Bernard Cassisa Elliott & Davis 1615 Metairie Rd Metairie LA 70005-3926 Office Phone: 504-834-2612. E-mail: mcmahonr@bernard-assisa.com.

MCMAHON, ROBERT M. physician, lawyer; b. Chambersburg, Pa., Sept. 6, 1949; s. Robert James and Bernice G. (Moore) McM.; 1 child, Natalie Ann. BA, U. Calif., San Diego, 1971; JD, U. Calif., San Francisco, 1974; MD, Washington U., St. Louis, 1989. Bar: Mo., Calif., U.S. Supreme Ct.; diplomate Am. Bd. Internal Medicine, Am. Bd. Gastroenterology. Staff counsel State Bar of Calif., L.A., 1975-80; sole practice law Beverly Hills, Calif., 1980-85; physician Jewish Hosp., St. Louis, 1989-92, St. Joseph's Hosp., St. Charles, Mo., 1992-93, U. Ark., Little Rock, 1993-95; pvt. practice in gastroenterology Little Rock, 1995-97, St. Louis, 1997—. Judge pro tem Superior Ct., L.A., 1983-85. Dir. South Ctrl. Bar Assn., Compton, Calif., 1983-85. Fellow Am. Coll. Legal Medicine; mem. Am. Soc. Gastrointestinal Endoscopy, St. Louis Met. Med. Soc. (councillor 2000-03). Avocations: computer hobbyist, graphic arts, model aircraft. Office: St Louis GE Cons PC 10012 Kennerly Rd Ste 101 Saint Louis MO 63128

MCMAHON, SEAN HOWARD, social studies educator; b. Atlanta, Ga., Sept. 18, 1966; s. Howard Martin and Frances Irene McMahon; m. Tabatha Burn, May 1, 1993; children: Dylan Riley, Brendan Cullen. PhD, Fla. State U., Tallahassee, FLA, 1996; MA in History, Clemson U., Clemson, SC, 1991; BA, U. of Ga., Athens, GA, 1989. Prof. of history Lake City C.C., Lake City, Fla., 2000—. Author: (book) Social Control And Public Intellect: The Legacy Of Edward A. Ross (Pub. by Trans. Press, Rutgers, NJ, 1999). Advisor and cons. Columbia County Hist. Soc., Lake City, Fla., 2004—. Mem.: Orgn. of Am. Historians (assoc.), Fla. Conf. of Historians (life; pres. 2004—). Avocations: bicycling, jazz music. Office: Lake City Community College 149 SE Vocational Place Lake City FL 32025 E-mail: mcmahons@lakecitycc.edu.

MCMAHON, TERI LYNN, lawyer; b. Gainesville, Fla., Feb. 28, 1962; d. Edward F. and Suzann (Tope) Threadgill; m. Kevin Michael McMahon, Jan. 2, 1988; children: Kelly Marie, Rebecca Suzanne. BA, Duke U., 1984; JD, U. Mich., 1987. Bar: Ga. 1987. Assoc. Powell, Goldstein, Frazer & Murphy, Atlanta, 1987-94, Alston & Bird, Atlanta, 1994-95, ptnr., 1995—. Mem. DeKalb Med. Ctr. Found., Decatur, Ga., 1992-96, Ga. 100 Program, Atlanta, 1995; elder Decatur Presbyn. Ch., mem. class 1998, Leadership Atlanta. Mem.: ABA, Atlanta Bar Assn. (bd. mem. bus. and fin. section 2003—04), Druid Hills Golf Club. Democrat. Avocations: tennis, sporting clays. Office: Alston & Bird 1 Atlantic Center 1201 W Peachtree St Atlanta GA 30309-3424 Office Phone: 404-881-7266. Business E-Mail: tmcmahon@alston.com.

MCMAHON, TERRENCE JOHN, retired foreign service officer; b. Rockford, Ill., Aug. 7, 1936; s. Hugh Raymond McMahon and Lucile Isabelle (Hayes) Driscoll; m. Phyllis Ruth Anderson, Dec. 2, 1967; children: Kevin, Michael, Kathleen, Marianne. BS in Accountancy, U. Ill., 1958; M Internat. Pub. Policy, Johns Hopkins U., 1983. CPA, Ill. Audit supr. Coopers and Lybrand, Rockford, Ill., 1958-68; fin. analyst U.S. AID, Washington, 1968-70, dep. contr. Rio de Janeiro, 1970-73, contr. Kabul, Afghanistan, 1973-77, Amman, Jordan, 1977-79, dep. contr. Washington, 1979-83, contr. Cairo, 1983-86, dir. Office of Procurement Washington, 1986-92, dir. Kiev, Ukraine, 1993-95. Recipient Presdl. Meritorious Svc. award for fgn. svc. Pres. of U.S., 1985, 92. Roman Catholic. Avocations: fishing, boating, travel. Home: 430 Marine Dr Sequim WA 98382-8037

MCMAHON, THOMAS JOHN, law educator; b. Syracuse, NY, June 17, 1929; s. Thomas Denis and Margaret (Ryan) McMahon; m. Alcida Rose Levesque, June 2, 1956; children: Sharon Rose, Alcida Marie, Michelle Ann, Thomas Paul. AB magna cum laude, Holy Cross Coll., 1951; JD, Georgetown U., 1957. Bar: DC 57, NY 57, Conn. 60, Pa. 64, Mass. 71, U.S. Supreme Ct. 63, U.S. Claims Ct. 82, U.S. Ct. Mil. Appeals, U.S. Tax Ct., U.S. Ct. Appeals (1st, 2d, 3d, DC and fed. cirs.), U.S. Dist. Ct. Mass. 71, U.S. Dist. Ct. Conn., U.S. Dist. Ct. (ea., no., we., so. dists.) NY, U.S. Dist. Ct. (we. dist.) Pa., U.S. Dist. Ct. DC, U.S. Ct. Internat. Trade 64, U.S. Temp. Ct. Emergency Appeals 85. Assoc. Shearman & Sterling, N.Y.C., 1957—59, Keogh & Candee, Norwalk, Conn., 1959—60; atty. Am. Cyanamid Co., Stamford, Conn., 1960—63, Gulf Oil Corp., Pitts., 1963—69, Gillette Co., Boston, 1969—74;

prof. Suffolk U. Law Sch., Boston, 1974—96, prof. emeritus, 1996—. Lt. (j.g.) USNR, 1951—54, capt. JAGC USNR. Mem.: Boston Patent Law Assn. (past chmn. copyright com. 1980—85). Republican. Roman Catholic. Home: PO Box 28 Walpole MA 02081-0028 Office: Suffolk U Law Sch 120 Tremont St Boston MA 02108

MCMAHON, THOMAS MICHAEL, lawyer; b. Evanston, Ill., May 11, 1941; s. Robert C. and Kathryn D. McM.; m. Ann Kaufman, July 11, 1964; children— Michael, Patrick. Student, U. Notre Dame, 1959-61; BA, Marquette U., 1963; JD magna cum laude, Northwestern U., 1970. Bar: Ill. 1970. Mgr. legal adv. sect. Ill. EPA, Springfield, 1970-72; assoc. Sidley & Austin, Chgo., 1972-75, ptnr., founder nat. environ. group, 1975-2000, sr. counsel, 2001—. Lectr. in field; mem. City of Evanston Environ. Control Bd., 1981-83. Author: The Superfund Handbook, 1989, International Environmental Law and Regulation, 1992, Legal Guide to Working with Environmental Consultants, 1992, The Environmental Manual, 1992. Lt. USN, 1963-67. Decorated Republic of Vietnam Campaign medal. Mem. ABA (chmn. environ. disclosures com., vice-chmn. alternative dispute resolution com., past vice-chmn. environ. quality com., environ. aspects of bus. trans. com., internat. environ. law com., lectr. confs., teleconfs. and satellite seminars), Order of Coif. Office: Sidley Austin Brown & Wood Bank One Plz Chicago IL 60603-2000 E-mail: tmcmahon@sidley.com.

MCMAHON, WILLIAM EDWARD, philosophy educator; b. Chgo., Sept. 25, 1937; s. Daniel Patrick McMahon and Mary Lois Hurley; m. Mary Louise Owens, Dec. 29, 1962; children: Elizabeth Maura, Coleman William. AB, U. Notre Dame, 1959, PhD, 1970; AM, Brown U., 1961. Instr. St. Vincent Coll., Latrobe, Pa., 1961-64; asst. prof. John Carroll U., Cleve., 1967-69, U. Akron, 1969-77, assoc. prof. to prof., 1977-99, dept. chair, 1985-96, prof. emeritus, 1999—. Fellow Pullman Found., 1955-59, Brown U., 1960-61; grantee for Inst. in Medieval Philosophy, NEH, 1980. Mem. Internat. Naval Rsch. Orgn., Soc. for Am. Baseball Rsch., N.Am. Assn. for History of Lang. Scis., Am. Philos. Assn., Soc. for Medieval and Renaissance Philosophy, Ohio Philos. Assn. (v.p. 1985-91), Henry Sweet Soc. Democrat. Roman Catholic. Avocations: baseball and naval history, stamp collecting/philately. Home: 606 Nome Ave Akron OH 44320-1681 Office: U Akron Philosophy Dept 302 Olin Hl Akron OH 44325-0001 E-mail: mcmahon@uakron.edu.

MCMAINS, SARA A. engineering educator; AB, Harvard Coll., 1991; MS, U. Calif., Berkeley, 1995, PhD, 2000. Tchg. fellow Harvard Coll., Cambridge, Mass., 1990—91; software engr. GCC Techs., Bedford, Mass., 1991—93, ICEM CFD, Berkeley, 1998; grad. student rschr. U. Calif., Berkeley, 1994—2000, postdoctoral rschr., 2000—01, asst. prof., 2001—. Contbr. articles to profl. jours. Jour. Computing and Info. Sci. Engring., Jour. Engring. Manufacture, CIRP Jour. Mfg. Sys. Grad. fellow, NSF, 1993. Mem.: ASME, Assn. Computing Machinery Siggraph. Office: U Calif Berkeley 5145 Etcheverry Hall #1740 Berkeley CA 94720-1740

MCMANAMAN, KENNETH CHARLES, lawyer; b. Fairfield, Calif., Jan. 25, 1950; s. Charles James and Frances J. (Holys) McM.; m. Carol Ann Wilson, Apr. 15, 1972; children; Evan John, Kinsey Bridget, Klerin Rose. BA cum laude, S.E. Mo. State U., 1972; JD, U. Mo., Kansas City, 1974; grad., Naval Justice Sch., Newport, RI, 1975; MS in Bus. Mgmt. summa cum laude, Troy State U., Montgomery, Ala., 1978; LLM in Advanced Litigation, Nottingham-Trent U., 2004. Bar: Mo. 1975, US Dist. Ct. (we. dist.) Mo. 1975, Fla. 1976, US Dist. Ct. (No. and mid. dists.) Fla. 1976, US Dist. Ct. Mil. Appeals 1977, US Ct. Appeals (5th and 8th cirs.) 1977, US Dist. Ct. (ea. dist.) Mo. 1978, US Supreme Ct. 1978, D.C. 1991; cert. mil. judge spl. and gen. ct. martials; diplomate Am. Bd. Forensic Examiners; cert. Homeland Security, Level III, Am. Coll. Forensic Examiners Internat. Prof. bus. law Troy (Ala.) State U., 1976-78; pvt. practice; ptnr. O'Loughlin, O'Loughlin & McManaman, Cape Girardeau, Mo., 1978—2002, Kenneth C. McManaman, Esq., 2002—; prof. bus. law S.E. Mo. State U., Cape Girardeau, 1978-84, prof. criminal justice, 1998—; prof. leadership Sch. Law William Woods U., 1998—; prof. bus. mgmt. Sch. Law Nat. Inst. Trial Advocacy. Mem. Cape Girardeau County Coun. on Child Abuse, 1980—89; membership dir. S.E. Mo. scouting coun. Boy Scouts Am., 1980—82; mem. Cape Girardeau County Mental Health Assn., 1982—92; sponsor drug edn./prevention program in schs.; sec., pres. Jackson Area Soccer Assn., 1987—93; mem. Jackson R-2 Alt. Sch. ADv. Bd., 1999—; mem. dept. acctg. and fin. adv. bd. S.E. Mo. State U., 2001—03; active local and state Dem. Party, del. Dem. Nat. Conv., San Francisco, 1984; chmn. County Dem. Com., 1984—96; mem. 8th Congl. Dist. Dem. Com., 1984—86, 27th State Dem. Senatorial Com., 1980—90; ward committeeman Dem. Party, 1984—96; bd. dirs. Area-wide Task Force on Drug and Alcohol Abuse, 1984—87, Cape County chpt. Nat. Kidney Found., 1988—93. Capt. JAGC USNR, 1994—2003, GCM qualified mil. judge. Recipient Robert Chilton award City of Jackson for Leadership, Integrity and Responsibility, 1995-97; named One of Outstanding Young Men Am., 1981, 82, 84, 85, Outstanding Pub. Svc. award Cape Girardeau Police Dept. Mem. ABA (Mo. del. young lawyers divsn. 1982-83), Mo. Bar Assn. (chmn. trial advocacy task force 1983), Mo. Bar (young lawyers sect. coun. rep. dist. 13 1980-85), Fla. Bar Assn., Kansas City Bar Assn., Assn. Trial Lawyers Am., Fed. Bar Assn., Nat. Coll. Dist. Attys., Cape Girardeau County Bar Assn. (founder, pres. young lawyers sect. 1981-82), Cape County Bar Assn. (sec. 1999, treas. 2000, v.p. 2001), Naval Res. Assn. (v.p. Southeast Mo/So. Ill. chpt. 1980-85, 2001—), Grand Praetor So. Mo. Province, Order of Constantine, S.E. Mo. State Alumni Coun., Sigma Chi (numerous awards), Sigma Tau Delta, Pi Delta Epsilon. Roman Catholic. Home: 1162 Trail Ridge Dr Jackson MO 63755-3507 Office: Blattner Bldg Ste One 1028A N Kings Hwy Cape Girardeau MO 63701 Office Phone: 573-335-8522. E-mail: kenmcm@sbcglobal.net., kmcmanaman@charter.net.

MCMANIGAL, SHIRLEY ANN, university educator, dean emerita; b. Deering, Mo., May 4, 1938; d. Jadie C. and Willie B. (Groves) Naile. BS, Ark. State U., 1971; MS, U. Okla., 1976, PhD, 1979. Med. technologist, 1958-75; chair dept. med. tech. U. So. Miss., Hattiesburg, 1979-83, Tex. Tech U. Health Scis. Ctr., Lubbock, 1983-87, dean Sch. Allied Health, 1987-97. Gov.'s appointee to statewide health coord. coun., 1994-97. Leadership Tex., 1992; Lt. Alumnae Regl. dir., 1994-97. Recipient Citation, State of Tex., 1988; named Woman of Yr., AAUW, Tex. div., 1990, Woman of Excellence in Edn. YWCA, Lubbock, 1990. Mem.: AAUW (Tex. bd. dirs. 1990—94, mem. edn. found. internat. fellows panel 1994—98, chair 1998—2001), Tex. Soc. Med. Tech. (Educator of Yr. 1990), Tex. Soc. Allied Health Professions (pres. 1990—91), So. Assn. Allied Health Deans at Acad. Health Ctrs., Nat. Assn. Women in Edn., Am. Soc. Med. Tech., Clin. Lab. Mgmt. Assn. (chair edn. com. 1989, 1991), Phi Beta Delta, Alpha Eta. Home: 24633 Ivory Cane Dr 103 Bonita Springs FL 34134 E-mail: smcmnigal@comcast.net.

MCMANIS, JAMES, lawyer; b. Haverhill, Mass., May 28, 1943; s. Charles and Yvonne (Zinn) McM.; m. Sara Wigh, Mar. 30, 1968. BA, Stanford U., Palo Alto, Calif., 1964; JD, U. Calif., Berkeley, 1967. Bar: Calif. 1967, U.S. Dist. Ct. (no. dist.) Calif. 1967, U.S. Ct. Appeals (9th cir.) 1967, U.S. Supreme Ct. 1971. Dep. dist. atty. Santa Clara County Dist. Atty., 1968-71; mem. McManis, Faulkner & Morgan, San Jose, Calif., 1971—. Spl. master tech. equities litig., 1987-98; spl. examiner State Bar Calif., 1995-98; prof. law Lincoln U. Law Sch., San Jose, 1972-82; lectr. Calif. Continuing Edn. of Bar, 1989-90; instr. U. Calif. Law Sch., 1992-96, Stanford U. Sch. Law, 1994-99. Pres. Santa Clara County Bar Assn. Law Found., 1994-96, dir., 1987—. Fellow Am. Coll. Trial Lawyers, Internat. Acad. Trial Lawyers; mem. ABA, State Bar Calif., Calif. Trial Lawyers Assn., Santa Clara County Bar Assn., Boalt Hall Alumni Assn. Avocations: history, books, travel, running. Office: McManis Faulkner & Morgan 50 W San Fernando St 10th flr San Jose CA 95113 Fax: 408-279-3244. E-mail: jmcmanis@mfmlaw.com.

MCMANMON, THOMAS ARTHUR, JR., oil industry executive; b. Boston, Sept. 10, 1943; s. T. Arthur and Maura (Sullivan) M.; m. Suzanne Cole, Nov. 17, 1973; children: Katherine, Suzanne, Thomas III. BA in History, U. Notre Dame, 1966; MBA, Dartmouth Coll., 1968. V.p. N.E. Merchants Bank, Boston, 1968-77; sr. v.p. Entwistle Corp., Hudson, Mass., 1977-78, Global Petroleum Corp., Waltham, Mass., 1978—, CFO, sr. v.p. Dir. Griffith Consumers Corp., Cheverly, Md., 1985—, Atlantic Petroleum Corp., Chelsea, Mass., 1989, Montello Oil Corp., Waltham, Mass., 1980, Carl King, Dover-,Del., 1985, Nimrod Nat. Gas, Tulsa. Dir. New England Fuel Inst., Watertown, Mass., 1980—. Mem. Marion-Beverly Yacht Club, Sippican Tennis Club, Boston Algonquin Club, Brookline Country Club. Office: 800 South St Waltham MA 02453-1478

MCMANN, EDITH BROZAK, dancer, artist; b. Totowa, NJ, Mar. 26, 1929; d. Henry and Lena (Ulmer) Brozek; m. Frank Richard McMann, May 26, 1957; children: Robert, Stephen. Dance student, Sch. Am. Ballet, N.Y.C., 1945-57; art student, Westchester Art Workshop, Art Students League, N.Y.C., 1976-84; B in Profl. Studies in Dance and Visual Arts, SUNY, 1984; MS in Studio Art, Coll. of New Rochelle, 1989. Performing artist Alicia Alonso's Nat. Ballet Cuba tours, 1948-50, George Balanchine's N.Y.C. Ballet, 1950-57; visual artist N.Y.C., 1970—; intern Silvermine Coll. Art, 1989. Exhibitions include Depicting Dance in Art, Gutman Gallery, White Plains, 1990, Xavier Gallery, New Rochelle, NY, 1989—94, Mamaroneck Artist Guild Gallery, Larchmont, NY, 1990—, Beaux Arts Exhibits, 1991—94, Manhattanville Coll., Purchase, NY, 1991, Town Ctr. Gallery, Mamaroneck, 1993—, NYC Ballet, 1993—, Westbeth Gallery, NYC, 1994, Hammond Mus., Salem, NY, 1994, Town House Gallery, Stamford, Conn., 2000—, Tower Perrins, Stamford, 2000—02, Represented in permanent collections; represented in archives Libr. of Performing Arts, NYC, NYC Ballet Archives, Nat. Mus. for Women in Arts, Washington; dancer (ballets) Alicia Alonso's Nat. Ballet Cuba, Mex., Ctrl. Am., South Am., 1948—50, Apollo, Sleeping Beauty, Pas de Quatre, Ensayo Symphonica, George Balachine's NYC Ballet, 1950—57, U.S., Can., Europe, Swan Lake, Symphony C, Con Amore, Nutcracker. Recipient numerous awards for sculpture, painting and graphics including Cert. of Merit U.S. Senator-N. Spano, 1989, U.S. State Assemblyman-R. Brodsky, 1989, Letter of Appreciation U.S. Senator Pat Moynihan, 1989, Letter of Congratulations U.S. Congressman -B. Gilman, 1989. Mem. Allied Artist of Am., Hudson River Contemporary Arists, Nat. Mus. for Women in Art, Silvermine Guild of Artists, Scarsdale Art Soc., Stamford Art Assn., Mamaroneck Artists Guild (bd. dirs. assoc. rep. 1990-91, receiving com. 1992). Home: 10 Burkewood Rd Hartsdale NY 10530-2933 Personal E-mail: emcmann200@aol.com.

MCMANUS, DECLAN PATRICK See COSTELLO, ELVIS

MC MANUS, EDWARD JOSEPH, federal judge; b. Keokuk, Iowa, Feb. 9, 1920; s. Edward W. and Kathleen (O'Connor) McM.; m. Sally A. Hassett, June 30, 1948 (dec.); children: David P., Edward W., John N., Thomas J., Dennis Q.; m. Esther Y. Kanealy, Sept. 15, 1987. Student, St. Ambrose Coll., 1936-38; BA, U. Iowa, 1940, JD, 1942. Bar: Iowa 1941. Gen. practice of law, Keokuk, 1946-62; city atty., 1946-55; mem. Iowa Senate, 1955-59; lt. gov. Iowa, 1959-61; chief U.S. judge No. Dist. Iowa, 1962-85, sr. U.S. judge, 1985—. Del Democratic Nat. Conv., 1956, 60. Served as lt. AC USNR, 1942-46. Office: US Dist Ct 329 US Courthouse 101 1st St SE Cedar Rapids IA 52401-1202

MCMANUS, JAMES WILLIAM, lawyer; b. Kansas City, Mo., Aug. 1, 1945; s. Gerald B. and Mary M. McManus. BA, Rockhurst Coll., 1967; JD, St. Louis U., 1971. Bar: Mo. 1971, U.S. Dist. Ct. (we. dist.) Mo. 1972, U.S. Ct. Appeals (8th cir.) 1974, U.S. Supreme Ct. 1979, U.S. Ct. Appeals (10th cir.) 1984, U.S. Dist. Ct. Kans., 1995. Law clk. to presiding justice U.S. Dist. Ct. (we. dist.) Mo., 1971-73; assoc. Shughart, Thomson & Kilroy, P.C., Kansas City, 1973-76, dir., 1977-94; counsel Dysart, Taylor, Lay, Cotter & McMonigle, P.C., Kansas City, 1994—2002, DeWitt & Zeldin, L.L.C., Kansas City, 2002—. Course lectr. med. jurisprudence U. Health Scis., Coll. Osteo. Medicine, Kansas City, 1994. Mem. adv. coun. St. Joseph Health Ctr., 1989-2002. Named to "Best of the Bar", Appeals and Trials, Kans. City Bus. Jour., 2003; recipient Congenial Counselor award, Kansas City Metro Bar Assn., 2003, Exceptional Trial and Appellate atty. award, Mo. Ho. Reps., 2003. Mem. ABA, ATLA (membership com. 2003-), Mo. Bar Assn., Kansas City Lawyers Assn., Kansas City Met. Bar Assn. (chmn. alternate dispute resolution com. 1996-97, vice chmn. 1994-95, chmn. med. malpractice com. 1989, Congenial Counselor award 2003), Mo. Assn. Trial Attys., Nat. Lawyers Assn., St. Louis Alumni Assn. (pres. 1984-92), St. Louis U. Law Sch. Alumni Assn. Home: 6824 Valley Rd Kansas City MO 64113-1929 Office: DeWitt & Zeldin LLC Harzfeld Bldg Ste 700 Town Pavilion 1111 Main St Kansas City MO 64105 Office Phone: 816-474-3000. E-mail: jamesmcmanus@justice.com.

MCMANUS, JASON DONALD, retired editor; b. Mission, Kans., Mar. 3, 1934; s. John Alan and Stella Frances (Gosney) McM.; m. Patricia Ann Paulson, Oct. 18, 1958 (div. Feb. 1966); 1 child, John Alan; m. Deborah Hall Murphy, Dec. 2, 1973; children: Sophie Eleanor, Mage Caroline. BA, Davidson Coll., 1956, LittD. (hon.), 1979; M.P.A., Princeton U., 1958; postgrad., Oxford U., 1958-59; LittD (hon.), Monmouth Coll., 1988, U. N.C., 1991, Loyola U., Balt., 1992. Common Market bur. chief Time Mag., Paris, 1962-64, assoc. editor N.Y.C., 1964-68, sr. editor, 1968-75, asst. mng. editor, 1975-78, exec. editor, 1978-83, mng. editor, 1985-87; corp. editor Time Inc., N.Y.C., 1983-85; editor-in-chief Time Warner Inc., N.Y.C., 1987-95; ret. Author: short stories Introduction, 1960. Mem. presdl. adv. commn. Internat. Edn. Exchange, 1982-83. Rhodes scholar, 1958-59 Mem.: Century Assn. (N.Y.C.).

MCMANUS, JOHN FRANCIS, association executive, writer; b. Bklyn., Jan. 24, 1935; s. V. Paul and Dorothy F. (Devenport) McM.; m. Mary Helen O'Reilly, Oct. 19, 1957; children: John G., Margaret A. Strauss, Paul J., Mary Anne Power. BS in Physics, Holy Cross Coll., 1957. Elec. engr. Transitron Corp., Wakefield, Mass., 1960-66; field coord. The John Birch Soc., Belmont, Mass., 1966-68, projects mgr., 1968-73, dir. pub. rels., 1973-91, pres. Appleton, Wis., 1991—. Author: An Overview of Our World, 1971, The Insiders: Architects of the New World Order, 1992, 4th edit., 1995, Financial Terrorism: Hijacking America Under the Threat of Bankruptcy, 1993, Changing Commands: The Betrayal of America's Military, 1995; author weekly column, 1973-96. Lt. USMC, 1957-60, capt., USMCR, 1960-68. Avocations: reading, outdoor sports, family. Home: PO Box 3076 Wakefield MA 01880-0772 Office: John Birch Society PO Box 8040 Appleton WI 54912-8040 E-mail: jfm@jbs.org.

MCMANUS, PATRICK FRANCIS, educator, writer; b. Sandpoint, Idaho, Aug. 25, 1933; s. Francis Edward McManus and Mabel Delana (Klaus) DeMers; m. Darlene Madge Keough, Feb. 3, 1954; children: Kelly C., Shannon M., Peggy F., Erin B. BA in English, Wash. State U., 1956, MA in English, 1962, postgrad., 1965-67. News reporter Daily Olympian, Olympia, Wash., 1956; editor Wash. State U., Pullman, 1956-59; with Ea. Wash. U., Cheney, 1959—; ret., 1983; news reporter Sta. KREM-TV, 1960-62; assoc. prof. Ea. Wash. U., Cheney, 1971-74, prof., 1974-83, prof. emeritus, 1983—. Author: A Fine and Pleasant Misery, 1978, Kid Camping from Aaaaiii! to Zip, 1979, They Shoot Canoes, Don't They?, 1981, Never Sniff a Gift Fish, 1983, The Grasshopper Trap, 1985, Rubber Legs & White Tail-Hairs, 1987, The Night The Bear Ate Goombaw, 1989, Whatchagot Stew, 1989, Real Ponies Don't Go Oink!, 1991, The Good Samaritan Strikes Again, 1992, How I Got This Way, 1994, Never Cry "Arp!" and Other Great Adventures, 1996, Into the Twilight, Endlessly Grousing, 1997, The Deer on a Bicycle, Excursions Into the Writing of Humor, 2000, The Bear in the Attic, 2002, (stage play) A Fine and Pleasant Misery: The Humor of Patrick F. McManus, 1994, Misery II: McManus In Love, 1995, Pat McManus, Endlessly Grousing, 1997, Pott's Luck, 1999; assoc. editor Field & Stream mag., 1977-81; editor-at-large Outdoor Life, 1981—. Recipient Booksellers award P.N.W. Booksellers, 1983, Trustees medal EWU, 1984, Gov.'s award Wash. State Libr., 1985, Excellence in Craft award OWAA, 1986, Disting. Achievement award WSU, 1994, Founder's Day award EWU, 1994, Circle of Honor award The Outdoor Channel, 2004; named to Idaho's Hall of Fame, 1995. Mem.: Outdoor Writers Am. (bd. dirs. 1981—84, Excellence award 1986), Authors Guild. Roman Catholic. Avocations: outdoor sports, woodworking, travel. Office: PO Box 28216 Spokane WA 99228-8216

MCMANUS, PATRICK J. mayor, lawyer, accountant; b. Lynn, Mass., July 20, 1954; s. Robert A. and Kathryn M. (Gainey) McM. BA in Govt., Bowdoin Coll., 1976; MBA, Suffolk U., 1981; JD, Boston Coll., 1985. CPA, Mass.; cert. managerial acct., Mass. Tchr. Lynn Pub. H.S.; assoc. prof. bus. and fin. Salem (Mass.) State Coll.; lawyer pvt. practice Lynn; councillor at large City of Lynn, 1986-91, mayor, 1992—. Mem., trustee U.S. Conf. of Mayors, Washington, Brownsfield Task Force, Washington, Urban and Econ. Policy, Washington, Arts, Culture and Recreation, Washington; co-chair Urban Water Coun. Mem. KC, Ancient Order of Hibernians. Democrat. Roman Catholic. Office: Mayor's Office 3 City Hall Sq Lynn MA 01901-1093

MCMANUS, RICHARD PHILIP, lawyer, agricultural products company executive; b. Keokuk, Iowa, Oct. 20, 1929; s. Edward William and Kathleen (O'Connor) M.; m. Marjorie Theresa Mullaney, Nov. 5, 1955; children: Michael L., Mark J., Matthew A. BA, St. Ambrose U., Davenport, Iowa, 1949; JD, U. Mich., 1952; MBA, Roosevelt U., Chgo., 1965. Bar: Calif. 1982, Ill. 1958, Iowa 1952. Ptnr. McManus & McManus, Keokuk, 1953-63; div. counsel USN Facility Engring. Command, Great Lakes, Ill., 1963-66; v.p., dir. law Household Fin. Corp., Chgo., 1966-81; exec. v.p., sec. Security Pacific Fin. Svcs., Inc., San Diego, 1981-91, gen. counsel, 1981—91; exec. v.p./sec. Bank Am. Fin. Svcs., San Diego, 1991-92, gen. counsel, 1991—92; pres., chmn. bd. dirs. Mosamac Co., Inc., 1992. Mem. gen. com. Conf. Consumer Fin. Law, Chgo., 1975-92. Contbr. articles to profl. jours. Bd. dirs., treas., atty. Tijuana/San Diego Habitat for Humanity, Inc., 1992-95; trustee Village of Lake Bluff, Ill., 1974-78. Recipient of the San Diego Vol. Lawyer Disting. Svc. award, 1995-2004, Pres. Calif. Bar Pro Bono Svs., award, 1998. Mem. Calif. Bar Assn., San Diego Bar Assn., Calif. Fin. Svcs. Assn. (chmn. law com. 1981-92), Am. Fin. Svcs. Assn. (chmn. law forum 1980-81, Disting. Svc. award 1990), Lions, Elks, KC, Beta Gamma Sigma. Democrat. Roman Catholic. Avocations: golf, flying, sailing, woodworking. E-mail: mcman1000@peoplepc.com.

MCMANUS, WALTER LEONARD, investment executive; b. N.Y.C., Apr. 27, 1918; s. Charles E. and Eva M. (Olt) McM.; m. Lillian Ziegler, June 21, 1941; children: Walter Leonard, Peter David, Susan. Student, Harvard Bus. Sch.; BS in Fin. Sci., Georgetown U., 1940. With Crown Cork & Seal Co., Inc., Balt., 1940-60, became sec., 1945, v.p., 1949, sec.-treas., 1958-60. Pres., dir. Cem Securities Corp.; assoc. Castlewood Realty Co.; dir. Hospice of Martin County, Fla. Mem. Halifax River Yacht Club, Lighthouse Point Yacht Club, Cocoanut Point Yacht Club, Internat. Order of Blue Gavel. Home: 1766 NW Harbor Pl North River Shores Stuart FL 34994 Office: 204 E Joppa Rd Towson MD 21286-3183 E-mail: crealtycom@aol.com.

MCMASTER, ART, beauty pageant organization executive; m. Theresa McMaster; children: Natalie, Stephanie, Katie. BSBA, Rockhurst U.; postgrad., U. Mich. Field adminstrn. mgr. Raytheon Engrs., Phila., 1985—88; controller Day and Zimmerman, 1988—91; sr. planner, asst. to v.p. Saudi Arabian Oil Co., Dhahran, 1992—99; controller Miss Am. Orgn., Atlantic City, 1999—2000, v.p. fin., 2000—02, v.p., 2002—04, acting pres., CEO, 2004—; overseer scholar programs, scholarship devel., exec. prodr. Miss Am. Paegent Show. Eucharistic min. Holy Family Parish. Mem.: KC. Office: The Miss Am Orgn 2 Miss Am Way Ste 1000 Atlantic City NJ 08401*

MCMASTER, BELLE MILLER, religious organization administrator; b. Atlanta, May 24, 1932; d. Patrick Dwight and Lila (Bonner) Miller; m. George R. McMaster, June 19, 1953; children: Lisa McMaster Stork, George Neel, Patrick Miller. BA, Agnes Scott Coll., 1953; MA, U. Louisville, 1970, PhD, 1974. Assoc. corp. witness Presbyn. Ch. USA, Atlanta, 1974-77, dir. corp. witness, 1977-81, dir. div. corp. and social mission, 1981-87, dir. social justice and peacemaking unit Louisville, 1987-93; acting dir. program women in theology and ministry Candler Sch. Theology Emory U., 1993-96, dir. advanced studies Candler Sch. Theology, 1995—2003. Vice-moderator chs. commn. internat. affairs World Coun. Chs., 1984-91, mem. justice, peace and creation commn., 1991-99; chair commn. internat. affairs Nat. Coun. Chs., NYC, 1986-89, v.p., 1990-95, exec. bd., 1986-2003, chair ch. world svc. and witness unit com., 1990-2003; chair fin. com. Ch. World Svc. and Witness Unit Com., NC, 1997-99, bd. dirs., 1995-2003. Author: Witnessing to the Kingdom, 1982, book columnist "What I Have Been Reading" in Church and Society Magazine, 1993-2001; contbr. articles to profl. jours. Pres. League of Women Voters, Greenville, S.C., 1963-64; bd. dirs. Interfaith Housing, Atlanta, 1975-81. Danforth fellow, 1969-74. Mem.: MLA, Soc. for Values in Higher Edn., Acad. Am. Religion, Phi Beta Kappa. Presbyterian. E-mail: bmcmast@emory.edu.

MCMASTER, BRIAN JOHN, artistic director; b. May 9, 1943; With internat. artists dept. EMI, 1968-73; contr. opera planning English Nat. Opera, 1973-76; mng. dir. Welsh Nat. Opera, Cardiff, 1976-91; dir. Edinburgh (Scotland) Internat. Festival, 1991—; artistic dir. Vancouver (B.C.) Opera, Can., 1983-89. Office: Edinburgh Internat Festival The Hub Castlehill Edinburgh EH1 2NE Scotland

MCMASTER, HENRY DARGAN, state attorney general; b. Columbia, S.C., May 27, 1947; s. John Gregg and Ida Bacot (Dargan) McM.; m. Peggy Jean McAbee, Mar. 18, 1978 BA, U. S.C., 1969, JD, 1973. Bar: S.C., U.S. Dist. Ct. S.C., U.S. Ct. Claims, U.S. Ct. Appeals (4th cir.), U.S. Supreme Ct. Atty., legis. asst. U.S. Senator Strom Thurmond, Washington, 1973-74; ptnr. Tompkins & McMaster, Columbia, SC, 1974—81; U.S. atty. Dist. S.C., Columbia, 1981-85; atty. gen. State of SC, 2003—. Mem. U.S. Atty. Gen.'s adv. com. of U.S. Attys., Washington, 1981-83; chmn. Com. on Ct. Rules and Legislation, Washington, 1983-85. Contbr. articles to legal publs. Mem. region IV youth adv. bd. EPA, Atlanta, 1972; mem. S.C. Commn. on Higher Edcn., 1991-94; chmn. S.C. Rep. Party, 1993-2002; bd. dirs. S.C. Policy Coun., 1991-2003; atty. gen. S.C., 2003-. Mem. Richland County Bar Assn. (program com. 1978), S.C. Bar, ABA, Nat. Assn. R.R. Trial Counsel, Def. Rsch. Inst., Forest Lake Club, Centurian Soc., Caroliniana Ball Club, St. Andrew's Soc. (Columbia), Phi Delta Phi, Blue Key, Kappa Alpha (dep. province comdr. 1974-75, province comdr. 1975-91). Republican. Presbyterian. Office: 1731 Senate St Columbia SC 29201 also: Rembert C Dennis Office Bldg PO Box 11549 Columbia SC 29211

MCMASTER, JULIET SYLVIA, English language educator; b. Kisumu, Kenya, Aug. 2, 1937; emigrated to Can., 1961, naturalized, 1976; d. Sydney Herbert and Sylvia (Hook) Fazan; m. Rowland McMaster, May 10, 1968; children: Rawdon, Lindsey. BA with honors, Oxford U., 1959; MA, U. Alta., 1963, PhD, 1965. Asst. prof. English U. Alta., Edmonton, Can., 1965-70, assoc. prof., 1970-76, prof. English, 1976-86, Univ. prof., 1986—2000, prof. emeritus, 2000—. Author: Thackeray: The Major Novels, 1971, Jane Austen on Love, 1978, Trollope's Palliser Novels, 1978, (with R.D. McMaster) The Novel from Sterne to James, 1981, Dickens the Designer, 1987, Jane Austen the Novelist, 1995, Reading the Body in the Eighteenth-Century Novel, 2004; co-editor: Jane Austen's Business, 1996, Cambridge Companion to Jane Austen, 1997; gen. editor Juvenilia Press, 1993-2002; illustrator/editor children's picture book: (by Jane Austen) The Beautifull Cassandra, 1993; contbr. articles to profl. jours. Fellow Can. Coun., 1969-70, Guggenheim Found., 1976-77, Killam Found., 1987-89; recipient Molson prize in Humanities for Outstanding Contbn. to Canadian Culture, 1994. Fellow Royal Soc. Can.; mem. Victorian Studies Assn. Western Can. (founding pres. 1972), Assn. Can. Univ. Tchrs. English (pres. 1976-78), MLA, Jane Austen Soc. N.Am. (dir. 1980-91). E-mail: juliet.mcmaster@ualberta.ca.

MCMASTER, LEE P. chemicals executive; BSChemE, U. Del; PhD in Chem. Engring., MIT. Engr., project scientist chems. and plastics divsn. Union Carbide, Bound Brook, NJ, 1969—77, various bus. and mktg. positions, 1977—82, v.p., gen. mgr. specialty polymers and composites divsn., 1982—86, v.p., gen. mgr. polyolefins divsn., 1989—90, v.p., gen. mgr. unipol sys. dept., 1990—92, pres. indsl. chems. divsn., 1992—93, corp. v.p., gen. mgr. ethylene/oxide glycol, 1993—98, corp. v.p., gen. mgr. specialty polymers and porducts, 1998—2000; v.p., gen. mgr. performance products bus. Amoco Chem., 1986—87, v.p. corp. planning and devel., 1987—89; bus. group pres.

chems. bus. group Dow Chem. Co., Midland, Mich., 2000—. Mem.: Chlorine Chemistry Coun. (chmn. bd. dirs.), World Chlorine Coun. (vice chmn. bd. dirs.). Office: Dow Chem Co 47 Building Midland MI 48067

MCMASTER, MICHELE, communications educator; b. Chgo. d. Robert B. and Dorothy McM. BA, Knox Coll., 1971; MA in Counseling, Governors State U., 1975, MA in Comm., 1989; PhD in Comm. and Consciousness, Union Inst., 1999. Educator Tinley Park (Ill.) Mental Health Ctr., 1971-78; coord. out-patient psychiat. svcs. Olympia Fields (Ill.) Osteo. Med. Ctr., 1979-80; pvt. practice Park Forest, Ill., 1980-96; coord. women's svcs. South Suburban YWCA, Park Forest, Ill., 1982-84; prof. Governors State U., University Park, Ill., 1992—. Bd. mgrs. South Suburban YWCA, Park Forest, 1978-81. Office: Governors State U Coll Arts and Scis University Park IL 60466-0975

MCMASTERS, PAUL KENNETH, foundation executive; b. Dade County, Mo., Jan. 18, 1942; s. James Harvey and Evelyn Gail McMasters; m. Priscilla Jean Thomas, Feb. 19, 1967; 1 child, Amy Elaine. BA, SW Mo. State U., 1965, MA, 1973. From gen. assignment reporter to asst. mng. editor The Daily News, Springfield, Mo., 1960-79; mng. editor Coffeyville (Kans.) Jour., 1979-82; states editor USA Today, Arlington, Va., 1982-83, ops. dir. editorial dept., 1983-87, dep. editorial dir., 1987-91, assoc. editor editorial page, 1991-92; v.p. The Freedom Forum, Arlington, 1992-95; exec. dir. The Freedom Forum 1st Amendment Ctr., Nashville, 1992-95; first amendment ombudsman The Freedom Forum, Arlington, Va., 1995—. Speaker in field. Mem. editorial bd. Newspaper Rsch. Jour.; contbr. articles to profl. jours. Bd. dirs. The Media Inst., Va. Coalition for Open Govt. Recipient Inglehart First Amendment award Coll. Media Advisors, 1992, Human Rights Leadership award Freedom Mag., 1993, John Peter and Anna Catherine Zenger award, 1999, Wells Meml. Key award, 1992. Mem. Soc. Profl. Journalists (pres. 1993-94, past chmn. freedom of info., past sec.-treas.), Am. Soc. Newspaper Editors (freedom of info. com.), Assn. Educators in Journalism and Mass Comm. (newspaper divsn.). Office: The Freedom Forum First Amendment Ombudsman 1101 Wilson Blvd Arlington VA 22209-2265

MCMEEKIN, DOROTHY, botany, plant pathology educator; b. Boston, Feb. 21, 1932; d. Thomas LeRoy and Vera (Crockett) McM. BA, Wilson Coll., 1953; MA, Wellesley Coll., 1955; PhD, Cornell U., 1959. Asst. prof. Upsala Coll., East Orange, N.J., 1959-64, Bowling Green State U., Ohio, 1964-66; prof. natural sci. Mich. State U., East Lansing, 1966-89, prof. botany, plant pathology, 1989—. Author: Diego Rivera: Science and Creativity, 1985; contbr. articles to profl. jours. Mem. Am. Phytopath. Soc., Mycol. Soc. Am., Soc. Econ. Bot., Mich. Bot. Soc. (former bd. dirs.), Mich. Women's Studies Assn., Sigma Xi, Phi Kappa Phi. Avocations: gardening, sewing, travel, drawing. Home: 1055 Marigold Ave East Lansing MI 48823-5128 Office: Mich State U Dept Botany-Plant Pathology 100 N Kedzie Hall East Lansing MI 48824-1031 E-mail: mcmeekin@msu.edu.

MCMEEKIN, THOMAS OWEN, dermatologist; b. Shelby, Nebr., Apr. 17, 1945; s. Wallace Walton and Evajane (Taber) McM.; m. Dale Goodwin, 1999; children: Michele, Sean. BA with distinction, Stanford U., 1967; MD with honors, U. Rochester, 1971. Intern Beth Israel Hosp., Boston, 1971-72; resident U. Rochester (N.Y.), 1974-76, Mass. Gen. Hosp., Boston, 1976-78; clin. prof. depts. medicine, pediatrics, dermatology U. Rochester Sch. Medicine, 1978—; dermatologist pvt. practice, Rochester, 1978—; clin. asst. prof. SUNY, Buffalo, 1997—. Pres. Geneese Valley Laser Ctr., Rochester, 1990—. Capt. USPHS, 1972-74. Kohn fellow U. Rochester, 1980-81; recipient Doren J. Stephens Alumni award U. Rochester, 1971, Brian Flanagan Teaching Svc. award, 1995. Fellow Am. Acad. Dermatology (Svc. award 1993), Am. Bd. Internal Medicine, Am. Soc. LAser MEdicine (co-chmn. 1993-94), Am. Soc. Dermatologic Surgery (edn. com. 1983—); mem. N.Y. State Dermatological Soc. (v.p. 1993, treas. 1992), Buffalo Rochester Dermatological Soc. (pres. 1990), Rochester Dermatological Soc. (pres. 1980-89), Alpha Omega Alpha. Avocations: golf, tennis, computers. Office: 300 White Spruce Blvd Rochester NY 14623-1606 Personal E-mail: 041745@msn.com.

MC MEEL, JOHN PAUL, newspaper syndicate and publishing executive; b. South Bend, Ind., Jan. 26, 1936; s. James E. and Naomi R. (Reilly) McM.; m. Susan S. Sykes, Apr. 16, 1966; children: Maureen, Suzanne, Bridget. BS, U. Notre Dame, 1957. Sales dir. Hall Syndicate, 1960-67; asst. gen. mgr., sales dir. Publishers-Hall Syndicate, 1968-70; co-founder Universal Press Syndicate, Kansas City, Mo., 1970; pres. Andrews McMeel Universal, 1970—. Chmn. bd. Andrews McMeel Pub., 1973—; mem. arts and letters U. Notre Dame. Co-founder Christmas in October, Kansas City, 1984—, James F. Andrews fellowship program, U. Notre Dame, 1981, adv. com. program in journalism; bd. dirs. The Civic Coun. Greater Kansas City. Mem. Fed. Assn. USA, Sovereign Mil. Order Malta, Internat. Press Inst. (chmn. Am. com., mem. internat. bd. dirs.). Home: Three Sunset Pl 5300 Sunset Dr Kansas City MO 64112-2358 Office: Andrews McMeel Universal 4520 Main St Kansas City MO 64111-1816

MCMEEN, ELMER ELLSWORTH, III, retired lawyer, guitarist; b. Lewistown, Pa., June 3, 1947; s. Elmer Ellsworth II and Frances Josephine McM.; m. Sheila Ann Taenzler, July 31, 1971; children: Jonathan Ellsworth, Daniel Biddle, James Cunningham and Mary Josephine (twins). BA cum laude, Harvard U., 1969; JD cum laude, U. Pa., 1972. Bar: 1973, U.S. Ct. Appeals (2nd cir.) 1973, U.S. Dist. Ct. (so.and ea. dists.) NY 1975. Assoc. Cravath, Swaine & Moore, N.Y.C., 1972-75, LeBoeuf, Lamb, Greene & MacRae, LLP, N.Y.C., 1975-78, ptnr., 1979-99, of counsel, 2000, retired, 2001. Lectr. Editor U. Pa. Law Rev., 1970-72. Author: numerous guitar books; contbr. articles to legal jours.; musician numerous solo guitar recordings, (solo instrnl. audio and video lessons and performance videos) Stefan Grossman's Guitar Workshop and Rounder Records. Chmn. N.Y.C. regional com. U. Pa. Law Sch., 1984-86; class sec. Northfield Mt. Hermon Sch. Class of 1965, Mass., 1984-91. Named Internat. Musician of Yr., Internat. Biography Ctr., Cambridge, Eng., 2003. Mem.: Rockaway River Country Club. Office: 34 Angelo Dr Sparta NJ 07871 E-mail: elmcmeen@yahoo.com.

MC MENIMEN, KATHLEEN BRENNAN, secondary school educator, consultant; b. June 15, 1944; d. John Joseph and Catherine (Healy) Brennan; m. Joseph Paul McMenimen, Aug. 22, 1970; children: Meghan, Joseph Paul. BS in Edn., Boston Coll., 1966, MEd, 1974. Tchr. Boston pub. schs., 1966—2002; pvt. ednl. cons. McMenimen Assocs., 2002—. Tchr. Operation Head Start, Charlestown, Mass., summers 1966-68; ednl. dir. John F. Kennedy Family Service Center, Charlestown, 1969; seminar leader Worcester (Mass.) State Coll., 1974. Author: A Curriculum Guide for Operation Head Start, 1970; prodr.: (cable) Tick-Talk. Bd. dirs. John F. Kennedy Family Svc. Ctr., 1970-71; mem. Waltham Dem. City Com., 1975—; commr. Waltham Housing Authority, 1982-86; mem. Waltham City Coun., 1986—; elected to Waltham City Coun., 1986-87, re-elected, 1988—, v.p., 1988, chair fin. com., 1990; ward councillor City of Waltham, 1976-78, councillor-at-large, 1986-99, 2002-04; candidate for mayor City of Waltham, Mass., 1999; candidate for state rep., 2004. Recipient Commendation for cmty. svc. Waltham City Coun., 1978, Disting. Svc. award Waltham Jaycees, 1978, Disting. Dem. award, 1996. Mem. Boston Coll. Alumni Assn. (bd. dirs. 1972-74, sec. 1987, treas. 1988, v.p. 1989, pres. 1990), Boston Tchrs. Union. Home: 147 Trapelo Rd Waltham MA 02452-6305

MC MENNAMIN, GEORGE BARRY, advertising agency executive; b. N.Y.C., May 23, 1922; s. Harold G. and Hazel F. (Stanbridge) McM.; m. Marilynn L. Simon, Sept. 9, 1946; children: Marilynn Breeze, Karen Foster. BS, Harvard U., 1945. With Doremus & Co., N.Y.C., 1946-88, exec. v.p., 1967-73, pres., 1973-84, vice chmn., 1984-88, also mem. exec. com.; pub. Worldpaper, Boston, 1988. Served to lt. (j.g.) USNR, 1944-46. Mem. Fin. Advt. and Mktg. Assn. Met. N.Y. (pres. 1967), Down Town Assn., Hasty Pudding Inst. 1770, Harvard Coll. Speakers Club, Harvard Club, New Canaan Country Club, Pilgrims Club of U.S. Republican. Episcopalian. Home: 28 Cross Ridge Rd New Canaan CT 06840-0523

MCMENNAMIN, MICHAEL J. savings and loan executive, investment banker; b. Berlin, N.H., June 27, 1945; s. John Lester and Ruth Ellen (Donaldson) McM.; children: Kelly, Tricia. AB in Econs., Ohio U., 1967; MBA in Banking and Fin., Case Western Res. U., 1972. Exec. v.p. Nat. City Bank, Nat. City Corp., Cleve., 1968-81; vice chmn. Bank One Columbus (Ohio), NA, 1981-85; chief investment officer Banc One Corp., Columbus, 1981-85; ptnr., v.p. Meuse Rinker Chapman Endres & Brooks, Columbus, 1985-88; chmn. Midwest Savs. Bank, Degraff, Ohio, 1986-87; chmn., chief exec. officer Buckeye Fed. Savs. & Loan, Buckeye Fin. Corp., Columbus, 1988-90, Bank One, Columbus, 1990-95; exec. v.p. finance Banc One Corp., Columbus, 1995—. Lectr. Grad. Sch. Banking, U. Wis., Madison, 1975-80; mem. treasury and fed. agy. com. Pub. Securities Assn., 1977-81, 85; mem. exec. com. funds mgmt. div. Am. Bankers Assn., 1977-79. Author articles in field. Mem. The Golf Club (Columbus), The Capital Club (Columbus), The Athletic Club (Columbus), Wedgewood Country Club (Columbus), Pinehurst (N.C.) Nat. Golf Club, Pinehurst Country Club. Republican. Roman Catholic. Avocations: golf, squash, tennis, reading. Office: Bank One Corp 100 E Broad St Ste 1 Columbus OH 43215-3607

MCMENNAMY, ROGER NEAL, automotive executive; b. Amarillo, Tex., Oct. 9, 1942; s. Wilson Foch and Mildred Evelyn (Freudiger) McMennamy; m. Marilyn Kay Gibbons, Jan. 1, 1967; children: Timothy Neal, Traci Nicole. Student, Abilene Christian U., 1961-62; BBA in Mgmt. cum laude, U. Tex., Arlington, 1970; MBA in Fin., U. Tex., Austin, 1971. CPA Tex. Contr., treas. E. N. Wolcott Corp., Houston, 1971-73; mem. corp. staff ELPAC, Inc., Houston, 1973-74; gen. mgr. BS&B Mfg., Houston, 1974-75; gen. mgr. adminstrn. Gulf Interstate Co., Houston, 1975-77; exec. v.p., CFO NWS Supply Group, Houston, 1977-83; v.p., CFO Newpark Resources, Inc., Metairie, La., 1983-86; sr. v.p., CFO Gemcraft, Inc., 1986-88; exec. v.p., CFO Cooper Cmtys., Inc., Bella Vista, Ark., 1988-90, pres., CEO, 1990-97; pres., CEO, gen. mgr. Daryl Hickman Chevrolet, Inc., Siloam Springs, Ark., 1998—; pres., CEO Guaranteed Auto Fin., Inc., 2003—, SHAC, Inc., 2003—. With USMC, 1962—66, Vietnam. Mem.: Rotary (pres. Siloam Springs 2003—). Avocations: travel, golf, waterfowl hunting. Office: Daryl Hickman Chevrolet Inc PO Box 399 Siloam Springs AR 72761-0399

MCMICHAEL, DONALD EARL, lawyer; b. Denver, Aug. 8, 1931, s. Earl L. and Charlotte F. McM.; m. Zeta Hammond, July 6, 1955; children: Lauren A. McMichael Burnett, Thomas D., Susan E. McMichael Markle. AB, Dartmouth Coll., 1953; LLB, U. Colo., 1956. Bar: Colo. 1956, U.S. Dist. Ct. Colo. 1956, U.S. Ct. Appeals (10th cir.) 1956. Assoc. Holme Roberts & Owen, 1956-58; pres. Corp. Ins. Assocs., 1958-70; dir. trust devel. Ctrl. Bank Denver, 1970-72; ptnr. Brenman, Sobol & Baum, Denver, 1972-74, McMichael, Benedict, Multz & Lipton, Denver, 1974—99; of counsel Schmidt & Horen, Denver, 2000—02; pvt. practice, 2002—. Chmn. Denver Ctrl. YMCA, 1971-73. Capt. USAR, 1956-64. Named Layman of Yr. Denver Ctrl. YMCA, 1973, named to Denver Metro YMCA Hall of Fame, 1989. Mem. Colo. Bar Assn., Denver Bar Assn., Denver Estate Planning Coun. (sec. 1971-73). Republican. Methodist. Office: 6325 W Mansfield Ave Unit 234 Denver CO 80235-3015 Office Phone: 303-716-8406. E-mail: dmcmic@aol.com.

MCMICHAEL, GUY H., III, federal official; b. South Bend, Ind., Dec. 26, 1939; m. Nancy Moore. AB, Harvard U., 1962; JD, U. Mich., 1967. Pvt. practice, 1967—71; dept. prosecuting atty. State of Ind., 1967—71; gen. counsel com. vet. affairs U.S. Senate, Washington, 1971—77; gen. coun. Dept. Vet. Affairs (formerly VA), 1977—81; adminstrv. judge bd. contract appeals Dept. Vet. Affairs, 1981—90, chmn., chief adminstrv. judge, 1990—, acting chief staff, 2000—01, acting chief info. officer, 2001, acting under sec. benefits, 2000—02. With U.S. Army, 1962-64. Mem. ABA, Bds. Contract Appeals Judges Assn. (pres. 1989-90), Ind. Bar Assn., D.C. Bar Assn. Office: Dept Vet Affairs Bd Contract Appeals 810 Vermont Ave NW # 09 Washington DC 20420-0001

MCMICHAEL, LAWRENCE GROVER, lawyer; b. West Orange, NJ, Aug. 18, 1953; s. Robert Gerard McMichael and Mary C. (Bragg) Lewis; children: Elizabeth Joan, David Stern; m. Virginia Lee Hinrichs, Nov. 12, 1994; children: John Lawrence, Mary Christine. AB, Duke U., 1975, JD, 1978. Bar: Pa. 1978, U.S. Ct. Appeals (3d cir.) 1979, U.S. Dist. Ct. (ea. dist.) Pa. 1980, U.S. Supreme Ct. 1984. Ptnr. Dilworth Paxson LLP, Phila., 1978—. Bd. Dir. Wynnewood Civic. Assn., 1986-88. Mem. ABA, Pa. Bar Assn., Phila. Bar Assn., Pa. Bar Inst. (mem. faculty, 1984—). Office: Dilworth Paxson LLP 3200 The Mellon Bank Ctr 1735 Market St Philadelphia PA 19103-7501 Office Phone: 215-575-7268. Business E-Mail: lmcmichael@dilworthlaw.com.

MCMILLAN, C. STEVEN, consumer packaged goods company executive; b. Tyler, Tex., Dec. 10, 1945; s. Charles and Faye (Mills) McMillan; children: Mandy, Megan. BS, Auburn U., 1968; MBA, Harvard U., 1973. Mgmt. cons. McKinsey & Co., Chgo., 1973—76; pres., CEO Aqualux Water Processing Co., Ft. Lauderdale, Fla., 1976—79; pres. Electrolux Corp., Toronto, Canada, 1979—82, CEO, 1982—86; sr. v.p. strategy devel. Sara Lee Corp., Chgo., 1986—90; sr. v.p., CEO Sara Lee Bakery-Worldwide, Chgo., 1990—97; pres., COO Sara Lee Corp., 1997—2000, chmn., pres., CEO, 2001—. Bd. dirs. Sara Lee/DE, Pharmacia, Monsanto, Bank of Am. Active Joffrey Ballet, Chgo., Chgo. Symphony Orch., Chgo.; mem. adv. bd. Stedman Nutrition Ctr. Duke U. Med. Sch., J.L. Kellogg Grad. Sch. Mgmt. Mem.: Grocery Mfrs. Assn., Harvard Bus. Sch. Club of Chgo. (v.p.). Office: Sara Lee Corp 3 First National Plz Chicago IL 60602*

MCMILLAN, CAMPBELL WHITE, pediatric hematologist; b. Soochow, China, Jan. 10, 1927; s. Henry Hudson and Leila McNeill (Memory) McM.; m. Florence Jean MacKenzie, June 11, 1955; children: Ian Johnson, Sally Hudson, Donna Jean, Andrew Duncan, Bridget White, Wendy McNeill. BS summa cum laude, Wake Forest Coll., 1948; MD, Bowman Gray Sch. Medicine, 1952. Diplomate Am. Bd. Pediatrics, Pediatric Hematology-Oncology. Intern Harvard Med. Service, Boston City Hosp., 1952-53; resident in pediatrics Children's Hosp. Med. Center, Boston, 1953-55; registrar in pediatrics St. Mary's Hosp., London, 1955; pediatrician Nemazee Hosp., Shiraz, Iran, 1956-58; fellow in pediatric hematology Harvard U., 1958-60; instr. pediatrics, 1960-61; gen. practice pediatrics, 1961-63; asst. prof. pediatrics U. N.C., Chapel Hill, 1963-68, asso. prof., 1968-72, prof., 1972-92, chief div. pediatric hematology, 1963-83, prof. emeritus, 1992—. Asso. dir. Clin. Research Center, U. N.C., 1966-78 Assoc. editor: Blood Diseases of Infancy and Childhood, 1978, 84; contbr. articles profl. jours., chpts. in books. Served with USNR, 1945-46. Recipient Lederle Med. Faculty award, 1964, Disting. Alumnus award Bowman Gray Sch. Medicine, 1972, Outstanding Career Achievement award Nat. Hemophilia Found., 1998. Fellow Am. Acad. Pediatrics; mem. Soc. Pediatric Rsch., Am. Pediatric Soc., Phi Beta Kappa, Alpha Omega Alpha. Democrat. Episcopalian. Home: 408 Ridgecrest Dr Chapel Hill NC 27514-2103 *It was my extremely good fortune to live and to work in a time of the most explosive growth medical knowledge had ever undergone.*

MCMILLAN, CARY D. food products executive; Grad. Coll. Commerce and Bus. Adminstrn., U. Ill., 1980. Mgr. Arthur Andersen, Chgo., 1985—92, mng. ptnr., 1992—2000; exec. v.p., CFO Sara Lee Corp., Chgo., 2000—, CEO, branded apparel div., 2001—. Office: Sara Lee Corp 3 1st Nat Plz Chicago IL 60602-4260

MCMILLAN, CHARLES WILLIAM, consulting company executive; b. Ft. Collins, Colo., Feb. 9, 1926; s. Charles and Margaret (Jennings) McM.; m. Jardell Hollier, Feb. 12, 1951; children: Brett W., Kurt C., Scott P. BS, Colo. State U., 1948. Asst. 4-H agt., Denver, 1948; county agrl. agt. LaJara, Colo., 1949-50, Julesburg, 1950-53; faculty Colo. State U., 1954; div. head, agrl. research dept. Swift & Co., Chgo., 1954-59; exec. v.p. Am. Nat. Cattlemen's Assn., 1959-77; v.p. Nat. Cattlemen's Assn., 1977-81; asst. sec. for mktg. and inspection services USDA, Washington, 1981-85; pres. McMillan and Farrell Assocs., Inc., Washington, 1985-94, C.W. McMillan Co., Alexandria, Va., 1994—. Served to lt. (j.g.) USNR, World War II. Mem. Sigma Alpha Epsilon. Home: 4003 Pine Brook Rd Alexandria VA 22310-2144 Office: PO Box 10009 Alexandria VA 22310-0009

MC MILLAN, GEORGE DUNCAN HASTIE, JR., lawyer, former state official; b. Greenville, Ala., Oct. 11, 1943; s. George Duncan Hastie and Jean (Autrey) McM.; m. Ann Louise Dial, Nov. 20, 1971; children: George Duncan Hastie, III, Ann Dial. BA magna cum laude, Auburn U., 1966; LL.B. (Southeastern Regional scholar), U. Va., 1969. Bar: Ala. bar 1969. Research asst. dept. agronomy Auburn U., summers 1963-65; law clk. firm Lange, Simpson, Robinson & Somerville, Birmingham, Ala., summers 1967-68; law clk. to judge U.S. Dist. Ct. No. Dist. Ala., 1969-70; instr. U. Ala. Law Sch., 1969-70; individual practice law Birmingham, 1970-71; ptnr. firm McMillan & Spratling, Birmingham, 1971-86; of counsel Haskell, Slaughter, Young and Lewis, 1986; ptnr. McMillan, Jones and Assocs., 1987-90; pres. McMillan Assocs., 1990—; mem. Ala. Ho. of Reps., 1973, Ala. Senate, 1974-78; lt. gov. Ala., 1979-83. Vice-chmn. Nat. Conf. Lt. Govs., 1980-82; mem. Permanent Study Commn. on Ala.'s Jud. System, 1975-79 Chmn. Ala. Film Commn., 1976-83; mem. Arts Task Force, Nat. Conf. State Legislatures, 1978-80, Multi-State Transp. Adv. Bd., 1974-79; mem. exec. com. So. Growth Policies Bd., 1974-83, vice chmn., 1981-83; bd. dirs. Campfire, Inc., 1975-82, Met. YMCA, Birmingham, Boys and Girls Ranches, Ala., Positive Maturity, 1997—; chmn. bd., pres. Birmingham Cultural and Heritage Found., 1988—; pres., bd. dirs. Birmingham Repertory Theatre, 1989—; exec. prodr. City Stages, 2003—; vice chairperson Black Belt Cmty. Found. Served to lt. USAR, 1969. Recipient award Ala. Nurses Assn., 1975; named Legislator of Yr. Ala. Forestry Assn., 1978; Hardest Working Senator Capitol Press Corps, 1976; 1 of 4 Outstanding Young Men Ala. Jaycees, 1977; 1 of 10 Most Outstanding State Legislators Assn. Govtl. Employees, 1978; award Birmingham Emancipation Assn., 1977; award Ala. Hist. Commn., 1978; James Tingle award, 1979, Citizen of Yr. award City of Birmingham, 1990. Mem. Birmingham Bar Assn., Ala. Bar Assn., Am. Bar Assn., Birmingham Jaycees, Ala. Jaycees (dir. 1970-72), Birmingham Urban League, United Negro Coll. Fund. Democrat. Mem. Ch. of Christ. Club: Rotary (Birmingham). Office: Mc Millan Assocs Ste 900 1929 3rd Ave N Birmingham AL 35203 Office Phone: 205 321 6881.

MCMILLAN, JOHN HOWARD, industrial designer, consultant; b. Banda, Democratic Republic of Congo, Oct. 18, 1951; arrived in US, 1971; s. John Hector and Ione (Reed) McMillan. AA in Indsl. Design Tech., Art Inst. Seattle, 1992. Exec. coord., v.p. Sea Catch, Inc., Kenai, Alaska, 1971—80; design and project supr. Arctic Pipe Inspection, Kenai, 1980—83; pres., designer, inventor McMillan design, Inc., Gig Harbor, Wash., 1983—. Contbr. chapters to books. Com. mem. Maritime Pier Com., Gig Harbor, 2002—03, Skansie Park Hist., Gig Harbor, 2002—03; steering com. Shenandoah Hist., Gig Harbor, 2003. Achievements include patents for mechanical quick release to use toggle linkage; patents in field. Avocations: birdwatching, hiking, gardening. Office: McMillan Design Inc 9816 Jacobsen Ln Gig Harbor WA 98332 E-mail: seacatch7@cs.com.

MCMILLAN, JULIA A. pediatrician; b. Pinehurst, N.C., July 10, 1946; MD, SUNY, Syracuse, 1976. Intern SUNY Upstate Med. Ctr., Syracuse, 1976-77, resident in pediatrics, 1977-78, 79-80, fellow in infectious diseases, 1979-81; mem. staff Johns Hopkins U. Hosp., Balt.; assoc. prof. Johns Hopkins U., Balt., dep. dir., residency program dir., prof., vice-chair med. edn., 1996—; chair. Am. Bd. of Pediatrics, Chapel Hill. Author: Oski's Pediatrics: Principles and Practice, 3d edit., 1999, The Best of the Whole Pediatrician Catalogs, I-III, 1984, The Whole Pediatrician Catalog: A Compendium of Clues to Diagnosis and Management, 1977. Mem. ASM, IDSA, Am. Acad. Pediatrics. Office: Johns Hopkins Hosp Dept Pediatrics 600 N Wolfe St Dept Baltimore MD 21287-0005*

MCMILLAN, L. LONDELL, lawyer; b. Bklyn. BS with honors, Cornell U., 1987; JD, NYU, 1990. Bar: N.Y. 1991, Conn. 1992. Sports agt. Athletes and Artists, Inc.; atty. LeBoeuf, Lamb, Greene & MacRea, LLP; entertainment lawyer Gold, Farrelll & Marks; pres, CEO L. Londell McMillan, PC, N.Y.C., 1997—, NorthStar Business Enterprises, Inc., N.Y.C., 1997—. Contbr. articles to profl. jours. Gen. counsel, co-founder Artist Empowerment Coalition; alumni counsel bd. trustee Cornell U. Recipient Haywood W. Burns Lawyer of the Yr. award, MBBA, 2001. Mem.: ABA, Assn. Bar City of N.Y. Office: L Londell Mcmillan PC 156 W 56th St Fl 10th Fl New York NY 10019-3877

MCMILLAN, LARRY DONALD, engineering executive; b. Trout Lake, Mich., June 10, 1936; s. Ira Duncan and Lilly Bell (Reed) McM.; m. Theresa Ann Mayer, June 25, 1955 (div. July 1975); children: Aaron, Keith, Curt, Adam, Kent, Craig, Andrea; m. Victoria Jeanne Cronin, Nov. 5, 1977. BSEE, Aquinas Coll., Grand Rapids, Mich., 1965; MSEE, Ariz. State U., 1972; postgrad., U. Colo., Colorado Springs, 1990-97. Elec. engring. mgr. Motorola, Inc., Phoenix, 1966-76; mgr. process engring. Am. Microsys., Inc., Santa Clara, Calif., 1976-77; dir. engring. Nat. Cash Register Corp., Colorado Springs, 1977-79; v.p., gen. mgr. microtech. ops. Storage Tech. Corp., Louisville, Colo., 1979-80; v.p. Stephenson Western, Inc., Aurora, Colo., 1980-82; engring. mgr. Honeywell, Inc., Colorado Springs, 1982-84; v.p. rsch. and devel., corp. founder Ramtron Corp., Colorado Springs, 1984-88; CEO, pres., corp. founder Symetrix Corp., Colorado Springs, 1988—. Adj. prof. Mich. Technol. U., Houghton, 1986-88. Co-author: (chpt.) Ferroelectric Ceramics, 1993; contbr. articles to Integrated Ferroelectrics, Nature, Jour. Integrated Ferroelectrics, Condensed Matter News, Nikkei Electronics, Ferroelectrics, Jour. Applied Physics, Applied Physics Letters. Achievements include patents for Method of Making Barium Strontium Titanate, Integrated Circuit Capacitors and Process for Making the Same, Process for Making Metal Oxides, Metal Polyoxyalkylated Precursor Solutions in an Octane Solvent and Method of Making the Same, Ferroelectric Integrated Circuit, Precursors and Processes for Making Metal Oxides, Memory with Ferroelectric Capacitor Connectable to Transistor Gate, Ferroelectric Memory and Non-Volatile Memory Cell for Same, Misted Deposition Apparatus for Fabrication an Integrated Circuit, Non-Volatile Memory, Ferroelectric Dielectric Memory Cell can Switch at Least GIG Cycles and has Low Fatigue, ABO3 Structured Solid Solutions Mixed and Average Perovskites for High Dielectric Constant DRAMs and Capacitors, Precursors and Processes for Making Metal Oxides, Low Temperature Process for Fabricating Layered Superlattice Materials and Making Electronic Devices Including Same, others. Home: 3005 Blodgett Dr Colorado Springs CO 80919-4510 Office: Symetrix Corp 5055 Mark Dabling Blvd Colorado Springs CO 80918-3834

MCMILLAN, LEE RICHARDS, II, lawyer; b. New Orleans, Aug. 26, 1947; s. John H. and Phoebe (Skillman) McM.; m. Lynne Clark Potthast, June 27, 1970; children: Leslie Clark, Hillary Anne, Lee Richards III. BS in Commerce, Washington and Lee U., 1969; JD, Tulane U., 1972; LLM in Taxation, NYU, 1976. Bar: La. 1972. Assoc. Jones, Walker, Waechter, Poitevent, Carrere & Denegre, New Orleans, 1976-79, ptnr., 1979—, sect. head, corp. and securities sect., 1987—90, 1994—2002, exec. com., 1990—94, 1996—99, 2001—02, chmn. exec. com., 1991—94, 1996—98, 2001—02. Vice-chmn. Mech. Equipment Co., Inc., New Orleans, 1980-86, chmn. bd., 1986—, pres. 1989-99; mem. The Bus. Coun. Greater New Orleans, 1998—, exec. com., 1999—; bd. dirs. The Chamber/New Orleans and the River Region, 1996-98; bd. trustees Alton Ochsner Med. Found., 1995-2003. Trustee New Orleans Mus. Art., 1989-95; bd. dirs. Bur. Govt. Rsch. New Orleans, 1987-93, Louise S. McGehee Sch., New Orleans, 1982-88, co-chmn. capital fund dr., 1984-86, pres. bd. dirs., 1986-88; bd. govs. Isidore Newman Sch., New Orleans, 1991-95. Lt. JACG USNR, 1972-75. Mem. ABA (com. on negotiated acquisitions 1986-94), La. State Bar Assn. (chmn. corp. and bus. law sect. 1985-86, mem. com. on bar admissions 1986-87), Young Pres. Orgn., Washington and Lee U. Alumni Assn. (bd. dirs. 1995-99). Republican. Episcopalian. Avocation: sailing. Office: Jones Walker Waechter Poitevent Carrere & Denegre 201 Saint Charles Ave Ste 5100 New Orleans LA 70170-5101

MCMILLAN, M. SEAN, lawyer; Diploma, U. Munich, 1963; cert., Internat. Sch., Copenhagen, Denmark, 1962; SB, U. So. Calif., 1967; JD, Harvard U., 1970. Bar: Calif. 1971. Spl. projects dir. Mass. Gen. Hosp., Boston, 1967-70; ptnr. Keatinge, Libbott, Bates & Loo, Los Angeles, 1970-74, Loo, Merideth & McMillan, Los Angeles, 1974-85, Bryan Cave LLP, Los Angeles/Santa Monica, 1986—2001, Greenberg Traurig LLP, L.A., 2001—. Editor: Harvard Internat. Law Jour., 1968-70. Mem. Assn. Computing Machinery, ABA, Am. Soc. Internat. Law. Office: Greenberg Traurig LLP 2450 Colorado Ave Ste 400E Santa Monica CA 90404 E-mail: mcmillan@gtlaw.com.

MCMILLAN, MARY BIGELOW, retired minister, volunteer; b. St. Paul, July 30, 1919; d. Charles Henry and Allison (McKibbin) Bigelow; m. Richard McMillan, June 26, 1943; children: Richard Jr., Charles B., Douglas D., M. Allison, Anne E. BA, Vassar Coll., 1941; MDiv, United Theol. Sem. Twin Cities, 1978, DDiv (hon.), 1989. Ordained to ministry Presbyn. Ch., 1978. Asst. min. House of Hope Presbyn. Ch., St. Paul, 1978-82; interim pres. United Theol. Sem. Twin Cities, New Brighton, Minn., 1982-83, ret., 1987. Contb. author: The Good Steward, 1983. Regional dir. Assn. Jr. Leagues, N.Y.C., 1959—61, pres. St. Paul chpt., 1957—59; vice chair Ramsey County Welfare Bd., St. Paul, 1962—66, St. Paul Health and Welfare Planning Coun., 1964—70, F.R. Bigelow Found., St. Paul, 1988—95, also 1st vice chair; 1st vice chair, trustee Wilder Found., 1973—89; active Presbyn. Homes Found., 1996—; trustee Minn. Ch. Found., Mpls., 1984—99, United Theol. Sem. Twin Cities, 1977—89, also chmn. bd. trustees; bd. dirs. Inst. for Ecumenical and Cultural Rsch., Collegeville, Minn., 1982—2003. Recipient award for community planning United Way, 1965, also for yr. round leadership, 1973, Leadership in Community Svc. award YWCA, 1980, Sisterhood award NCCJ, Mpls., 1989; named Disting Alumna award St. Paul Acad. and Summit Sch., 1988 Mem.: Univ. Club, New Century Club. Avocations: golf, knitting, reading. Home: 2925 Lincoln Dr #713 Roseville MN 55113

MCMILLAN, PAUL JEFFREY, application developer; s. Jennie May and Rufus R McMillan; m. Kimberly Taylor, Sept. 21, 1985; 1 child, Paul Jeffrey II. Grad., Western Hills H.S., Cinc., 1981. Cert. solution developer Microsoft Corp., 2001. Sr. software engr. Ednl. Mgmt. Software Solutions, Cin., 2001—03; R&D lead S&S Healthcare Strategies, Ltd., Cin., 2003—. Sr. solutions cons., Cin., 1979—2004. Achievements include development of Transcript Recording And Attendance Keeping System; Medical Software: Patient Drug-to-drug Interaction Component; Medical Software: Patient Drug Dosage Checking Component; TRAAKS District/School/Student Record Keeping System; Transcript Recording And Attendance Keeping System. Office Phone: 513-612-6400 7116. Personal E-mail: pmcmillan1@cinci.rr.com.

MC MILLAN, R(OBERT) BRUCE, museum executive, anthropologist; b. Springfield, Mo., Dec. 3, 1937; s. George Glassey and Winnie Mae (Booth) McM.; m. Virginia Kay Moore, Sept. 30, 1961; children: Robert Gregory, Michael David, Lynn Kathryn. BS in Edn, S.W. Mo. State U., 1950; MA in Anthropology, U. Mo., 1963; PhD in Anthropology, U. Colo., 1971. Rsch. assoc. in archaeology U. Mo., 1963-65, 68-69; assoc. curator anthropology Ill. State Mus., Springfield, 1969-72, curator anthropology, 1972-73, asst. mus. dir., 1973-76, mus. dir., 1977—; exec. sec. Ill. State Mus. Soc., 1977—. Lectr. anthropology Northwestern U., 1973. Editor: (with W. Raymond Wood) Prehistoric Man and His Environments, 1976. Mem. Ill. Spl. Events Commn., 1977-79, program chmn., 1977-78; commr. Ill. and Mich. Canal Nat. Heritage Corridor Commn., 1988—; bd. dirs. Found. Ill. Archaeology, 1978-83. Grantee NSF, 1971-72, 80, NEH, 1978. Fellow AAAS, Am. Anthrop. Assn.; mem. Am. Assn. Mus. (coun. 1982-86), Midwest Mus. Conf. (pres.), Soc. Am. Archaeology, Current Anthropology (assoc.), Am. Quaternary Assn., Sigma Xi. Office: Ill State Mus 502 S Spring St Springfield IL 62706-5000 also: Dickson Mounds Museum Lewistown IL 61542 Office Phone: 217-782-7011. E-mail: rbm@museum.state.il.us.

MCMILLAN, ROBERT RALPH, lawyer; b. N.Y.C., May 21, 1932; s. Harry and Vivian (Beatty) McM.; m. Phoebe Parker Bunn, Nov. 2, 1996; children: Robin, Karen, Kenneth. Student, Adelphi U., 1951-52, 55-56; JD, Bklyn. Law Sch., 1960. Bar: N.Y. 1960. Spl. asst. staff of Richard M. Nixon, N.Y., Washington, 1960, 64-65; counsel Senator Kenneth B. Keating, Washington, 1960-62; govt. rels. advisor Mobil Oil Co., N.Y.C., 1962-63, 65-68; v.p. Avon Products, N.Y.C., 1973-78, 79-85; sr. v.p. A&S Dept. Stores, N.Y.C., 1978-79; counsel Rivkin, Radler, Bayh, Hart & Kremer, Uniondale, N.Y., 1986-91; ptnr. McMillan, Rather, Bennett & Farinoci, P.C., Melville, NY, 1991—2003, Fischbein Badillo Wagner Harding, Melville, 2003—. Bd. dirs. WellChoice, Inc., Panama Canal Commn., 1989-94, chmn., 1993-94; mem. nat. adv. coun. FannieMae, 1998-2000, co-hosts Face-Off, PBS, NY. News commentator Sta. WLIW-TV, 1993—; columnist, Anton Community Newspapers, Long Island; occasional columnist for Newsday. Trustee Adelphi U., 1984-89; bd. dirs. L.I. (N.Y.) Assn.; chmn. L.I. Housing Parntership, 1988-2002. 1st lt. U.S. Army, 1952-54. Decorated Bronze Star; recipient Excellence in Leadership award, Helen Keller Services for the Blind, Humanitarian award, Alzheimer's Assn. Mem.: AMA (bd. trustees 2002—), Suffolk County Bar Assn., Nassau County Bar Assn. Republican. Avocations: golf, fishing. Office: 909 3RD Ave New York NY 10022-4731 E-mail: mcmillanr@aol.com.*

MCMILLAN, TERRY L. writer, educator; b. Port Huron, Mich., Oct. 18, 1951; d. Edward McMillan and Madeline Washington Tillman; 1 child, Solomon Welch. BA in Journalism, U. Calif., Berkeley, 1979; postgrad., Columbia Univ., N.Y.C., 1979. Instr. U. Wyoming, Laramie, 1987-88; prof. U. Ariz., Tucson, 1988-91. Author: Mama, 1987, Disappearing Acts, 1989, Waiting to Exhale, 1992, How Stella Got Her Groove Back, 1996, A Day Late & A Dollar Short, 2001; editor: Breaking Ice: An Anthropology of Contemporary African-American Fiction, 1990; screenwriter (with Ron Bass) (movies) Waiting to Exhale, 1995, How Stella Got Her Groove Back, 1998. Recipient National Endowment for the Arts fellowship, 1988.

MCMILLAN, WENDELL MARLIN, economist; b. Dallastown, Pa., June 14, 1923; s. John Walter and Alice Mary (McCormick) McMillan; m. Eleanor Unser, July 14, 1946; children: Susan, Barbara, Douglas. Grad., York (Pa.) Jr. Coll., 1943; BS, Juniata Coll., 1948; MS, Pa. State U., 1950, PhD, 1954. Rsch. & extension asst. Pa. State U., 1950-54; agrl. economist, asst. dir. U.S. Dept. Agriculture, Washington, 1955-64; project mgr., mktg. advisor Food and Agriculture Orgn. of UN, Jordan, Saudi Arabia and Afghanistan, 1964-72; agrl. economist The World Bank, Caribbean, Sudan, 1972-76; agrl. and policy economist U.S. Dept. Agr./USAID, Syria, Indonesia, Lesotho, Liberia, 1977-80; agrl. economist Africa Bur. USAID, Washington, 1980-89. Mem. mktg. subcom. Nat. Commn. Cooperative Devel., Washington, 1964; adj. prof. York (Pa.) Coll., 1990. Author: tech./policy publs. agr. Dist. chmn. Campfire Girls No. Va., 1959—61; chmn. bd. dirs. Am. Cmty. Sch., Amman, Jordan, 1966—67, UN Staff Assn., Kabul, Afghanistan, 1969—70; bd. dirs. Hist. York, Inc., 1987—97, pres., 1995—97; mem. Hist. Soc. York County, 1987—, mem. libr. com., 1990—; trustee York County Acad., 1991—. Recipient Merit cert., USDA, 1960, 1984, Hall of Fame award, William Penn Sr. HS, 1999; Fulbright grantee, U. Copenhagen, 1954—55. Mem.: Soc. Internat. Devel., Am. Agrl. Econs. Assn., Alumni Assn. Juniata Coll. (Nat. Alumni Achievement award 1984), Alumni Assn. York Coll. (bd. dirs. 1986—91, Svc. award 1991, Disting. Alumnus 1982, Dir. Emeritus award 1997), Pi Gamma Mu. Democrat. Avocations: stamp collecting/philately, nature study, opera. Home and Office: 1775 Powder Mill Rd York PA 17403-4955

MCMILLEN, ABBIE, environmental manager; b. N.Y.C., Oct. 10, 1942; d. Albert Edward and Beatrice Cuthbert (Collingwood) Miller; m. David S. Page, Sept. 30, 1964; children: David C., Vivian W.; m. Michael A. McMillen, Feb. 14, 1980. BS in Chemistry, Brown U., 1964; MS, Purdue U., 1969. Registered Maine guide, 1997—. Mem. Maine gov.'s cabinet, dir. Maine Office Energy Resources, Augusta, 1975-77; project dir. Roy F. Weston, Inc., Burlington, Mass., 1981-92; pres. McMillen Environ. Inc., Concord, Mass., 1992-93. Exec. dir. Island Heritage Trust, 1993-95. founder, organizer Lafayette (Ind.) Environ. Action Fedn., 1969; mem., chmn. Poland (Maine) Planning Bd., 1971-73; mem. exec. com., chmn. solid waste com., Poland rep. Androscoggin Valley Regional Planning Commn., 1971-73; chmn. New Eng. steering com. for ERDA pub. meeting, 1975; mem. New Eng. Congl. Caucus Energy Congress, 1979, New Eng. Power Plant siting task force, 1980. Contbr. articles to profl. jours. Treas., Concord Art Assn., 1987-89; through-hiker Long Trail, 1989; bd. dirs. Solid Waste Composing Coun., 1991-93; pres., Castine Conservation Trust, 1994-97. David Ross fellow Purdue U., 1965. Mem. ASME (tech. papers chmn. solid waste divsn. 1991-93), Maine Organic Farmers and Gardeners Assn. (organizer, v.p. 1970-72), Mainiac Swing Dance Soc. (founder, treas. 2002—), Friends of Brooksville Libr. (v.p. 1997—), Brooksville Hist. Soc. (treas. 2000—), Mensa. Avocations: swing dancer, website manager.

MCMILLEN, ELIZABETH CASHIN, artist; b. Chgo. d. James Blaine and Hortense (Fears) Cashin; m. John Stephen Jerabek; 1 child, Michael N. Student, Western Coll. for Women, 1961-63; BA, Bard Coll., 1965. Coord. com. and juror Spectra I, sponsor state exhbn. women artists Westbrook Coll., Portland, Maine, 1979; dir. Hancock County Auditorium Art Gallery, Ellsworth, Maine, 1984, 85. Exhibited at Frick Gallery, Belfast, Maine, 1993, 94, Maine Coast Artists Juried Show, Rockport, 1994, Portland Children's Mus., 1995, Lakes Gallery, Sebago, Maine, 1995—, Maine Coast Artists, Rockport, 1998, Portland Mus. Art, 1998, 2001, American Embassy Santiago Chili, 1998—, Maine Art Gallery, Wiscasset, 2001, Payson Gallery, Portland, 2002, June Fitzpatrick at MECA, Portland, 2003; one-person shows include Area Gallery, Portland, 1994, Frick Gallery, Belfast, Maine, 1995, Lakes Gallery, Sebago, Maine, 1997, June Fitzpatrick Alternative, Portland, 1999, 2001, June Fitzpatrick Gallery, Portland, 2001; two persons show Maine Coast Artists, Rockport, 1996. Dem. chair Town of Lamoine, Maine, 1984-85, 86-87, 88-89; legislation coord. Amnesty Internat., Ellsworth, 1991-97. Democrat. Episcopalian. Avocations: writing, politics, teaching, African-Am. history.

MCMILLEN, ROBERT STEWART, lawyer; b. Yonkers, N.Y., Feb. 25, 1943; s. David Harry and Blodwyn Elizabeth (Evans) McM; m. Dorothea Anne Murray, July 2, 1966; children: Elissa London (Mrs. Elliott Aten), Tara Evans. BS, U. Rochester, 1964; JD cum laude, Albany Law Sch. Union U., 1969. Bar: N.Y. 1969, U.S. Dist. Ct. (no. dist.) N.Y. 1969. Assoc. Clark, Bartlett & Caffry, Glens Falls, N.Y., 1969-73; ptnr. Caffry, Pontiff, Stewart, Rhodes & Judge, Glens Falls, 1974-80; prin. Bartlett, Pontiff, Stewart & Rhodes, P.C., Glens Falls, 1981—. Sr. law examiner N.Y. State Bd. Law Examiners, Albany, 1986-2001, bd. mem. 2001—; bd. dirs. Cmty. Title Agy., Inc., Glens Falls, 1984—, pres., 1984-99, v.p., sec., 1999—. Editor-in-chief Albany Law Rev., 1968-69. Bd. dirs., officer Voluntary Action Ctr. of Glens Falls Area, Inc., 1970-97; bd. dirs., treas. Arts and Crafts Ctr. of Warren County, Inc., Glens Falls, 1984-94; mem. Warren County Rep. Com., Queensbury, N.Y., 1979-2001; alt. or del. Rep. Jud. Nomination Com. 4th Jud. Dist. N.Y., 1977—. Recipient Disting. Svc. award Voluntary Action Ctr. of Glens Falls Area, Inc., 1990. Mem. ABA, Nat. Conf. Bar Examiners (mem. multistate performance test com. 2001—), N.Y. State Bar Assn. (mem. com. profl. ethics 1990-99, 2000—), Warren County Bar Assn. (bd. dirs. 1979-82, treas. 2001—), Adirondack Regional C. of C. (bd. dirs. 1997-2000, vice chmn. 1999-2000, counsel 2000—), Rotary. Avocations: travel, downhill skiing, boating. Home: 147 Assembly Point Rd Lake George NY 12845-5201 Office: 1 Washington St Glens Falls NY 12801-2963 Office Phone: 518-792-2117. Business E-Mail: rsm@bpsrlaw.com.

MCMILLIAN, THEODORE, federal judge; b. St. Louis, Jan. 28, 1919; m. Minnie E. Foster, Dec. 8, 1941. BS, Lincoln U., 1941, HHD (hon.), 1981; LL.B., St. Louis U., 1949; HHD (hon.), U. Mo., St. Louis, 1978. Bar: Mo. Mem. firm Lynch & McMillian, St. Louis, 1949-53; asst. circuit atty. City of St. Louis, 1953-56; judge U.S. Ct. Appeals (8th cir.), 1987—2003, sr. judge, 2003—. Judge Circuit Ct. for City St. Louis, 1956-72, Mo. Ct. Appeals eastern div., 1972-78; asso. prof. adminstrn. justice U. Mo., St. Louis, 1970—; asso. prof. Webster Coll. Grad. Program, 1977; mem. faculty Nat. Coll. Juvenile Justice, U. Nev., 1972— Served to 1st lt. Signal Corps U.S. Army, 1942-46. Recipient Alumni Merit award St. Louis U., 1965, ACLU Civil Liberties award, 1995, Disting. Lawyer award Bar Assn. Met. St. Louis, 1996, Salute to Excellence Civil Rights award St. Louis Am., 1997, Spirit of Excellence award ABA, 2003; named Disting. Non-Alumnus U. Mo.-Columbia Law Sch., 1999. Mem. Am. Judicature Soc., Am. Bd. Trial Advs. (hon. diplomate), Lawyers Assn. Mo., Mound City Bar Assn., Phi Beta Kappa, Alpha Sigma Nu. Office: Thomas F Eagleton Court House Ste 25 162 111 S 10th St Saint Louis MO 63102

MCMILLIN, DAVID ROBERT, chemistry professor; b. East St. Louis, Ill., Jan. 1, 1948; s. Robert Cecil and Clara Rose McMillin; m. Nicole Wilson, Nov. 3, 1974; children: Robert Stephen, Andrew Wilson. BA, Knox Coll., 1969; PhD, U. Ill., 1973. Postdoctoral fellow Calif. Inst. Tech., Pasadena, 1974; asst. prof. chemistry Purdue U., West Lafayette, Ind., 1975-80, assoc. prof., 1980-85, prof., 1985—. Contbr. articles to profl. jours. Recipient F.D. Martin Teaching award Purdue U., 1975. Mem. Am. Chem. Soc., Inter-Am. Photochem. Soc. (sec. 1986-90, v.p. 1994-96, pres. 1996-98), Phi Beta Kappa, Sigma Xi. Presbyterian. Avocations: sports, reading. Office: Purdue U Dept Chemistry 560 Oval Dr West Lafayette IN 47907-2084 Business E-Mail: mcmillin@purdue.edu.

MCMILLIN, JOAN AUSTIN, social worker; b. Hartford, Conn., July 4, 1941; d. John Francis and Charlotte (Kilmer) Austin; m. J. Michael McMillin, May 9, 1970 (div. June 2002); children: John Andrew, Christy. BA, U. Conn., 1963; MSW, Boston Coll., 1966. Cert. social worker, Ill., S.D. Social worker, student suor. Hamm Psychiat. Clinic, St. Paul, 1970-74; social worker Mass. Gen. Hosp., Boston, 1966-70, VA Hosp., Sioux Falls, S.D., 1980—; clin. social worker Charter Counseling Ctr., Sioux Falls, 1991-96; dir. social svcs. Great Plains Psychol. Svcs., Sioux Falls, 1996—99; sec. govt. affairs com. AARP of S.D., 2000—. Parent trainer S.D. Parent Connection, Sioux Falls, 1986-88; bd. dirs. Community Disabilities, 1990—. Bd. dirs. Coun. for Disability Rights, Chgo., 1988-89; del. United Cerebral Palsy Assn., N.Y.C., 1987, bd. dirs., pres. S.D. chpt., Sioux Falls, 1980-87; sec., bd. dirs. Vis. Nurses Assn., Sioux Falls, 1984-88. U.S. Dept. Vocat. Rehab. grantee, 1964-66; recipient T. Brown Community Svc. award Sioux Falls Masons, 1986. Mem. Nat. Assn. Social Workers (exec. dir. S.D. chpt., 2003), Am. Bd. Examiners in Clin. Social Work, Phi Beta Kappa, Phi Kappa Phi. Home: 4409 Yellowstone Ln Sioux Falls SD 57105-6756

MCMILLIN, SCOTT, language educator; b. Pitts., June 29, 1934; s. Harvey Scott and Elizabeth (Bradley) McM.; m. Sally Ann Hyde, May 11, 1957; children: David, Paul, Andrew. BA, Princeton U., 1956; MA, George Washington U., 1960; PhD, Stanford U., 1965. Prof. English Cornell U., Ithaca, NY, 1964—. Author: Sir Thomas More and the Elizabethan Theatre, 1987, Shakespeare in Performance: Henry IV, Part One, 1991, The Queen's Men and Their Plays, 1998, The First Quarto of Othello, 2001; editor Restoration and 18th Century Comedy, 1972; contbr. articles to profl. jours. Lt. USN, 1957-60. Lt. USN, 1957—60. Fellow Am. Philosoph. Soc., Washington, 1972-73; grantee NEH, Washington, 1968, 87, fellow, 1992-93. Mem.: MLA, Am. Soc. for Theatre Rsch. (Shakespeare com.), Shakespeare Assn. Am. (trustee 1988—91). Avocation: music. Home: 507 N Tioga St Ithaca NY 14850 Office: English Dept Cornell Univ Ithaca NY 14853

MCMILLION, JOHN MACON, retired newspaper publisher; b. Coffeyville, Kans., Dec. 25, 1929; s. John Dibrell and Mattie Anna (Macon) McM.; m. Melanie Ann McMillion; children: John Thomas, Johanna, Jennifer, Amanda Student, Vanderbilt U., 1947-49; BS in Journalism, U. Kans., 1956. Police reporter Amarillo (Tex.) Globe-News, 1956; sports editor, telegraph editor Grand Junction (Colo.) Daily Sentinel, 1956-58; mng. editor Alliance (Nebr.) Times-Herald, 1958-59, Clovis (N.Mex.) Jour., 1959-62; gen. mgr. Pasadena (Tex.) Citizen, 1962; bur. mgr. UPI, 1962-66; exec. editor Albuquerque Jour., 1966-69; bus. mgr. Albuquerque Pub. Co., 1971-75; pub. Herald and News-Tribune, Duluth, Minn., 1975-86, Akron (Ohio) Beacon Jour., 1986-90, ret. Campaign mgr. gubernatorial campaign, 1969-71 Served with USN, 1950-54. Address: 302 Knife Island Rd Two Harbors MN 55616-4030

MCMILLON, DOUG, retail executive; Degree in Acctg., U. Ark.; MBA in Fin., U. Tulsa. Buyer and merchandise mgr. various cos.; buyer trainee in sporting goods Wal-Mart Stores, Inc., 1984—91, v.p. and gen. merchandise mgr. Sam's Club Internat., sr. v.p. and gen. merchandise mgr., 1999—2002, exec. v.p. merchandising Sam's Club div., 2002—. Office: Wal-Mart Stores Inc 702 SW Eighth St Bentonville AR 72716

MCMINDES, ROY JAMES, aggregate company executive; b. Essex, Md., July 12, 1923; s. Roy Preston and Edith S. (Sh) McMindes; m. Prudence Atsinger, June 8, 1946; children: Gail Karen, Joan Susan, James Lee. BS, U. Md., 1948. Pres. Sheridan Corp., Lebanon, Pa., 1951—, Grays Ferry Brick Co., Lebanon, 1971—2001, Waylite Co., Lebanon, 1976-88. Chmn. bd. Peoples Nat. Bank, Lebanon, 1984—92, dir., 1965—92. Bd. dirs. Lebanon YMCA, 1968—86, Good Samaritan Hosp., Lebanon, 1970—93. With A.C. USN, 1943—46, with USNR, 1946—52. Recipient Founders Day award, Lebanon Valley Coll., 1987. Mem.: Lebanon Valley C. of C. (pres. 1973), Lebanon Country Club, Jesters, Shriners. Republican. Presbyterian. Office: 1212 W Maple St Lebanon PA 17046-2701

MCMINN, J. B. retired philosophy educator, composer; b. Pt. Neches, Tex., Nov. 12, 1922; s. Joe Byron and Mary Thelma (Odom) McMinn; m. Dorothy Louise Smith, Aug. 31, 1944 (div. May 15, 1969); children: Jan Branton, Robert Errol. BA in English and Religious Studies, La. Coll., 1943; ThM in Hellenistic Greek, So. Sem., 1946; postgrad., La. State U., 1948; PhD in Hellenistic Greek, So. Sem., 1951; MA in Classical Greek and Philosophy, Tulane U., 1960, postgrad., 1968, U. Athens, 1970, spl. study in modern Greek and postdoctoral rsch., 1979. Asst. prof. English La. Coll., 1948—51; tchg. asst. in classics Newcomb Coll., 1951—52, Tulane U., 1952—54, asst. prof. classics, 1953—58; from asst. prof. philosophy to assoc. prof. to prof. philosophy U. Ala., 1960—87. Vis. prof. philosophy Miles Coll., 1990; vis. assoc. prof. philosophy and classics Tulane U., 1960, 61; spkr., lectr., presenter in field. Contbr. articles to profl. jours.; composer piano and vocal pieces; contbr. spirit song for Million Dollar Band of U. Ala. Fight On to Victory, 1987, poetry to anthologies; author: (book of poetry and songs) Une Petite Ménagerie, 1997, (plays) Waiting for Gotdough, 1995, (book) "Mythtaken": Le Mot de L' Énigme, 2002. Rep. commr., New Orleans, 1956—60; mem. So. Soc. Christian Leadership Conf., New Orleans, 1954—60. Cadet officer USNR, 1941—42. Recipient Merit award, U. Ala. Band Assn., 1991, VIP award, Internat. Soc. Poets, 1996, grad. scholarship in classical langs., Tulane U., 1951—54, tchg. assistantship in classical langs., 1951, Fulbright Adj. Lectr. award., 1972, West Germany Lectr. award, 1973, tchg. and rsch. grants in field, Internat. Poet of Merit award, 1996. Mem.: ASCAP, Poetry Soc. Am., Acad. Am. Poets, Nat. Acad. Popular Music-Songwriters Hall of Fame, Internat. Soc. Poets (life), Eta Sigma Phi. Office: Rembrant Music Properties PO Drawer H Rusk TX 75785 Office Phone: 800-439-2149 ext 22.

MCMORRIS, JERRY, transportation company executive, sports team executive; Past CEO NW Transport Svc, Denver; chair, pres., CEO Colorado Rockies, Denver, 1995—. Office: 4765 Oakland St Denver CO 80239-2717

MCMORROW, MARY ANN G. state supreme court chief justice; b. Chgo., Jan. 16, 1930; m. Emmett J. McMorrow, May 5, 1962; 1 dau., Mary Ann. Attened, Rosary Coll., 1948-50; JD, Loyola U., 1953. Bar: Ill. 1953, U.S. Dist. Ct. (7th dist.) Ill. 1960, U.S. Supreme Ct. 1976. Atty. Riordan & Linklater Law Offices, Chgo., 1954—56; asst. state's atty. Cook County, Chgo., 1956-63; sole practice Chgo., 1963-76; judge Cir. Ct. Cook County, 1976-85, Ill. Appellate Ct., 1985-92, Supreme Ct. Ill., 1992—. Faculty adv. Nat. Jud. Coll., U. Nev., 1984. Contbr. articles to profl. jours. Mem. Chgo. Bar Assn., Ill. State Bar Assn., Women's Bar Assn. of Ill. (pres. 1975-76, bd. dirs. 1970-78), Am. Judicature Soc., Northwestern U. Assocs., Ill. Judges Assn., Nat. Assn. Women Judges, Advocates Soc., Northwest Suburban Bar Assn., West Suburban Bar Assn., Loyola Law Alumni Assn. (bd. govs. 1985—), Ill. Judges Assn. (bd. dirs.), Cath. Lawyers Guild (v.p.), The Law Club of the City of Chgo., Inns of Ct. Office: Supreme Ct of Ill 160 N La Salle St Chicago IL 60601-3103

MCMORROW, WILLIAM J. finance company executive; b. LA; BA, MBA, U. So. Calif. Sr. v.p. Fidelity Bank, Pa.; exec. v.p., chmn. Credit Policy Com. Imperial Bank; chmn. Kennedy Wilson, Beverly Hills, Calif., 1988—, CEO, 1988—. Bd. dirs. Lusk Sch. Bus. U. So. Calif. Founder Donald F. Kennedy Youth Found., 1997—. Office: Kennedy Wilson 9601 Wilshire Blvd Ste 220 Beverly Hills CA 90210*

MCMULKIN, FRANCIS JOHN, retired steel company executive; b. Sault Ste. Marie, Ont., Can., Dec. 7, 1915; s. George Alexander and Leanor Augusta (Zryd) McM.; m. Margaret Lilian Winch, Sept. 21, 1946; children: John Bruce, Mary Diane. BS in Metallurgy, Mich. Coll. Mining and Tech., 1937; ME, Mich. Tech. U., 1945, DEngring (hon.), 1972. Formerly metallurgist Algoma Steel Corp., Sault Ste. Marie, 1937-42; rsch. fellow Ont. Rsch. Found., Mississauga, 1942-47; R&D engr. Dominion Foundries & Steel Ltd., Hamilton, Ont., Can., 1947—, dir. rsch., until 1964, v.p. rsch., 1964-85; ret. Contbr. articles to profl. publs. Recipient Disting. Alumnus award Mich. Tech. U., 1976 Fellow Am. Soc. Metals (life, William Hunt Eisenman award 1968), Engring. Inst. Can.(life, John Galbraith prize 1945, elected fellow 1981); mem. Can. Inst. Mining and Metallurgy (H.T. Airey Meml. Ann. Conf. lectr. award), AIME (Basic Oxygen Steel award 1963), Iron and Steel Soc. (charter, Disting. mem.), Metall. Soc. (elected 1997, Howe Meml. lectr. 1973), Mich. Tech. U. Metall. and Materials Acad. (charter mem. 1996), Iron and Steel Inst. (U.K.), Royal Over-Seas League (London), Hamilton Club, Hamilton Golf and Country Club, Mid Ocean Club (Bermuda). Mem. United Ch. of Canada. Home: 270 Roseland Crescent Burlington ON Canada L7N 1S3

MCMULLAN, WILLIAM PATRICK, III, investment banker; b. Newton, Miss., Dec. 29, 1952; s. William Patrick Jr. and Rosemary (Lyons) McM.; m. Rachel Smylie McPherson, Oct. 16, 1982. BA, Vanderbilt U., 1974; MBA, U. Pa., 1976. V.p. Lehman Bros. Kuhn Loeb, N.Y.C., 1976-82; assoc. dir. Prudential-Bache Securities, N.Y.C., 1982-85; mng. dir. Donaldson, Lufkin & Jenrette Securities Corp., N.Y.C., 1985-2000; mng. dir., chmn. global health care Credit Suisse First Boston, N.Y.C., 2000—03; sr. mng. dir., co-head global healthcare Bear, Stearns & Co., NYC, 2003—. Bd. dirs. Lar Lubovitch Dance Co., Project Reach Youth, The Consolidated Corp. Fund, Lincoln Ctr., The Good Dog Found. Mem. Met. Club, Mashomack Fish and Game Club, Confrerie des Chevaliers du Tastevin. Home: 607 6th St Brooklyn NY 11215-3701 Office: Bear Stearns & Co 383 Madison Ave New York NY 10179 Office Phone: 212-272-2392. Personal E-mail: pmcmullan@bear.com.

MCMULLEN, CURTIS T. mathematics professor; b. May 21, 1958; BA, Williams Coll., 1980; PhD, Harvard U., 1985. Faculty MIT, Cambridge, Mass., 1985, MSRI, 1986, Inst. Advanced Study, Princeton, NJ, 1986—87, Princeton U., NJ, 1987—90; prof. U. Calif., Berkeley, 1990—97, Harvard U., Cambridge, Mass., 1997—. Author: Logic Minimization Algorithms for VLSI Synthesis, 1984, Complex Dynamics and Renormalization, 1994, Renormalization and 3-Manifolds which Fiber over the Circle, 1996, (course notes) Riemann surfaces, dynamics and geometry, 1998, Hyperbolic manifolds, discrete groups and ergodic theory, 1996, Complex Manifolds, 1996, Complex Analysis, 1993, 1995, Theichmuller Theory, 1993; contbr. articles to profl. jours. Recipient Fields medal, 1998. Mem.: AAAS. Office: Mathematics Dept Harvard U One Oxford St Cambridge MA 02138-2901

MCMULLEN, DONALD A., JR., bank executive; BS, MBA, U. Pitts. CFA. Pres. Am. Capital Mgmt. Rsch., Houston; head capital mgmt. group Wachovia Corp., 1995—, exec. v.p., 1999, vice chmn., 1999—2001, sr. exec. v.p., 2001—; pres. adminstrn. Van Kampen/Am. Capital Mgmt. Cos., 1994. Office: Wachovia Corp Ste 400 301 S College St Charlotte NC 28288

MCMULLEN, G. ARTHUR, physician, cardiologist; b. Greeneville, Tenn., May 28, 1954; s. Raymon Wesley and Zora Jean (Spear) McM.; m. Shelley Speelman; children: Geremy, Heather, Dustin, Phillip, David. BS, Pacific Union Coll., Angwin, Calif., 1976; MD, Loma Linda U., 1979. Diplomate in internal medicine and cardiovascular diseases Am. Bd. Internal Medicine. Intern Kettering Meml. Hosp., Dayton, Ohio, 1980-81, resident, fellow,

1981-83, 84-87; cons. and practicing cardiologist and internal medicine specialist, Pt. Charlotte/Punta Gorda, Fla., 1987—. Fellow ACP, Am. Coll. Cardiology; mem. AMA, Alpha Omega Alpha. Avocations: tennis, skiing, boating, travel, computers, golf. Office: Cardiology Cons Charlotte 1655 Tamiami Trl Port Charlotte FL 33948-1042

MCMULLEN, JOHN HENRY, JR., manufacturing company executive, educator; b. Phila., Sept. 9, 1944; s. John Henry and Clara (Johnson) McM.; m. Evelyn Corrine Lawson, July 19, 1964; children: Yolanda, John III, Yvette, Yvonne. BS, Tuskegee U., Ala., 1969; MBA, Anna Maria Coll., 1984; postgrad., New Enb. Sch. Law. Cert. purchasing mgr. Asst. program planner Ingall's Shipbldg., Pascagoula, Miss., 1969-71; indsl. engr. supr. Luken's, Coatesville, Pa., 1971-76; mgr. mfg. engring. Newport News (Va.) Shipbldg., 1976-78; gen. supr. Polaroid Corp., Cambridge, Mass., 1978-85; mfg. mgr. Keene Corp., East Providence, Mass., 1985-86; master scheduler Prime Computer, Natick, Mass., 1987-89; small bus. and small disadvantaged bus. liaison officer GTE Govt. Systems Corp. (now Gen. Dynamics), Needham Heights, Mass., 1989—; mng. small bus. programs Gen. Dynamics, CA Sys., Taunton, Mass., 1999—. Instr. Anna Maria Coll., Paxton, Mass., 1983-86; adv. bd. Purchasing Ctr. Ct.-apptd. spl. advocate Suffolk County Juvenile Ct., Boston, 1983; bd. dirs. Mattapan (Mass.) Cmty. Health Ctr., 1983-93, treas. 1984-86, pres. 1987-91; treas. ADAPT, Inc., Roxbury, Mass., 1986-88, v.p., 1988-89; active Urban League Ea. Mass., 1987-91; pres., founder Alpha Phi Alpha Edn. Found, 1983-87; bd. dirs. Dr. William Price unit Am. Cancer Soc. Mem. Nat. Assn. Purchasing Mgmt. (minority bus. devel. group 1991—, contbr. Purchasing Today mag., Charles J. McDonald Minority Bus. Advocacy of Yr. award 1997), Purchasing Mgmt. Assn. Boston (treas. 1996-97), Inst. Indsl. Engrs., Exec. MBA Assn. Anna Maria Coll. (bd. dirs. 1983 86), Nat. Black MBA Assn. (co-founder, treas. Boston chpt. 1985-87), Afro-Am. Cultural Assn. Sharon (founder), Polaroid Found., Tuskegee Alumni Club (chpt. fin. sec. 1985-96, pres. 1992-93, asst. reginal fin. sec. 1988-90, asst. regional dir. 1985-91, regional dir. 1993-97, Outstanding Alumni award 1988), Tuskegee Nat. Alumni Assn. (bd. dirs.), Elks, Shriners, Alpha Phi Alpha (chpt. pres. 1981-86, Alpha Man of Yr. 1986). Avocations: bowling, racquetball, jogging, chess, motorcycling. Home: 8 Pine St Sharon MA 02067-1616 Office: 400 John Quincy Adams Rd Taunton MA 02780-1069 E-mail: tuskegee@alumnidirector.com., john.mcmullen@gdcas.com.

MCMULLEN, JOHN J. former professional hockey team executive, management consultant; m. Jacqueline McMullen; children: Peter, Catherine, John Jr. BSEE, U.S. Naval Acad., 1940; DMechE, Swiss Fed. Tech. Inst.; M in Naval Architecture and Marine Engring., MIT. Commd. ensign USN, 1940, advanced through grades to comdr., resigned, 1954; chief ship constrn. and repair U.S. Maritime Adminstrn. Office, Washington, 1954-57; chmn. John J. McMullen Assocs., Inc., 1957—98; ltd. ptnr. N.Y. Yankees Baseball Team, 1974; chmn. Houston Astros Baseball Team, 1979-92, N.J. Devils Hockey Team, East Rutherford, NJ, 1982—2000. Office: Mcmullen Consultants Inc 1 Boland Dr #302 West Orange NJ 07052-3683

MCMULLEN, SHARON JOY ABEL, life coach, marriage and family therapist; b. Peoria, Ill., June 21, 1933; d. Richard Glen Abel and Harriet Bernice Copland; m. David Winston McMullen, Dec. 27, 1956; children: David Paul, Jeniffer Joy. BA, UCLA, 1955; MA in Marriage and Family Therapy, St. Joseph Coll., 1996. Lic. marriage and family therapist, Conn.; life cert. tchr. Calif. Counselor First Ch. of Christ, Wethersfield, Conn., 1996—2003, Stafford Family Svcs., Stafford Springs, Conn., 1996—2003. Vol. staff asst. Master Therapists Workshop Series, U. Conn. Health Ctr., 1996—2003. Chair counseling task force 1st Ch. of Christ, Wethersfield, 1997-98, co-founder, team tchr. couples ministry, co-facilitator pre-marital workshops, 1997-2002. Mem. Am. Assn. of Marriage and Family Therapists (advocacy com. 1997-98), Calif. Assn. of Marriage and Family Therapists, Am. Assn. of Pastoral Counselors, Am. Assn. of Christian Counselors. Democrat. Avocations: reading, genealogy, gardening, walking. Home: 1755 Vallecito Dr San Pedro CA 90732 Office Phone: 310-833-2014. E-mail: sm@dmcma.com.

MCMULLEN, SUSAN TAYLOR, librarian; b. Oneida, N.Y., Mar. 7, 1956; d. Bert L. and Doris A. Taylor; m. John G. McMullen, June 4, 1977; children: Allison, Benjamin. BA, SUNY, Geneseo, 1977, MLS, 1978; MSc, Syracuse U., 2002. Head reference libr. Pawtucket (R.I.) Pub. Libr., 1979—87; sr. reference/electronic info. libr. Seekonk (Mass.) Pub. Libr., 1987—95; info. resources libr. Roger Williams U., Bristol, RI, 1995—. Presenter in field. Contbr. articles to profl. jours. Mem.: NEA, ALA, Assn. Coll. and Rsch. Libr. Democrat. Episcopalian. Avocations: gardening, reading, weaving. Home: 10 Musket Rd Swansea MA 02777 Office: Roger Williams Univ One Old Ferry Rd Bristol RI 02809

MC MULLIAN, AMOS RYALS, food company executive; b. Jackson County, Fla., Aug. 28, 1937; s. Andrew Jackson and Willie Ross (Ryals) McMullian; m. Jackie Williams, Aug. 27, 1960; children: Amos Ryals, Britton Jackelyn. BS, Fla. State U., 1962. Successively asst. controller, data processing coordinator, adminstrv. asst. to gen. mgr., asst. plant mgr., plant mgr. Flowers Baking Co., Thomasville, Ga., 1963—70, pres. Atlanta Baking Co. div., 1970—72, regional v.p. parent co., 1972—74, pres., COO bakery divsn., 1974—76, COO industry, 1976—81, pres., 1976—83, dir., 1981—, CEO, 1983—, co-chmn. exec. com., 1983—85, vice chmn. industry and chmn. exec. com., 1984—85, chmn. bd., CEO, chmn. exec. com., 1985—. Bd. trustees Ga. Rsch. Reliance; former chmn., bd. trustees SEL; bd. dirs. Keebler, Worldwide Lanier. Mem. adv. bd. Pres.'s Club, Fla. State U.; past chmn., dir. Southeastern Legal Found.; mem. charter group GOPAC; vestryman, sr. warden Episcopal Ch. Served USMC, 1958—61. Named Outstanding Bus. Alumnus, Fla. State U. Mem.: Gridiron Soc. U. Ga., Atlanta Commerce Club. Office: Flowers Industries Inc 1919 Flowers Cir Thomasville GA 31757-1137 E-mail: amcumllian@flocorp.com.

MCMULLIN, PAUL WAYNE, structural engineer; b. Bountiful, Utah, Feb. 18, 1973; s. Phillip Wayne McMullin and Joy Anne Cahoon; m. Kari Lin Johnson, Dec. 27, 1997; 1 child, Ruth Lorraine. BS in Mech. Engring., U. Utah, 1993, MS in Civil Engring., 2000, PhD in Civil Engring., 2003. Registered profl. engr., Utah. Prin, owner Pfeifferhorn Steel Detailing, Salt Lake City, 1996—2000; rsch. asst. U. Utah, Salt Lake City, 1998—2002; prin. engr. ABS Cons., Salt Lake City, 2002—04; pres. Pfeifferhorn Sturctural Engring., Salt Lake City, 2004—. Contbr. articles to profl. jours. Mem.: ASCE, Am. Soc. Testing Materials. Democrat. Mem. LDS Ch. Avocations: hiking, backpacking, gardening. Home: 1259 N Village Hill Cir Salt Lake City UT 84116 Office: ABS Consulting 310 S Main St Ste 300 Salt Lake City UT 84101-2142 Office Phone: 801-573-5182.

MCMULLIN, RUTH RONEY, publishing executive, trustee, management fellow; b. N.Y.C., Feb. 9, 1942; d. Richard Thomas and Virginia (Goodwin) Roney; m. Thomas Ryan McMullin, Apr. 27, 1968; 1 child, David Patrick. BA, Conn. Coll., 1963; M Pub. and Pvt. Mgmt., Yale U., 1979. Market rschr. Aviation Week Mag., McGraw-Hill Co., N.Y.C., 1962-64; assoc. editor, bus. mgr. Doubleday & Co., N.Y.C., 1964-66; mgr. Natural History Press, 1967-70; v.p., treas. Weston (Conn.) Woods, Inc., 1970-71; staff assoc. GE, Fairfield, Conn., 1979-82; mng. fin. analyst GECC Transp., Stamford, Conn., 1982—84; credit analyst corp. fin. dept. GECC, Stamford, Conn., 1984-85; sr. v.p. GECC Capital Markets Group, Inc., N.Y.C., 1985-87; exec. v.p., COO, CEO, John Wiley & Sons, N.Y.C., 1987—90, pres., CEO; CEO Harvard Bus. Sch. Pub. Corp., Boston, 1991-94; mem. chmn.'s com., acting CEO UNR Industries Inc., Chgo., 1991-92, also bd. dirs.; mgmt. fellow, vis. prof. Sch. Mgmt. Yale U., New Haven, 1994-95; chairperson trustees Eagle-Picher Personal Injury Settlement Trust, 1996—; chairperson Claims Procesing Facility, Inc., 1998—. Bd. dirs. Bausch & Lomb, Rochester, N.Y.; vis. prof. Sch. Mgmt., Yale U., New Haven, 1994-95. Mem. dean's adv. bd. Sch. Mgmt. Yale U., 1985—92; bd. dirs. Yale U. Alumni fund, 1986—92, Yale U. Press, 1988—99, Math. Scis. Edn. Bd., 1990—93; bd. dirs., treas. Mighty Eighth Air Force Heritage Mus., 2000—03; chmn. Mighty Eighth Found., 2003—; bd. dirs. Savannah Symphony, 1999—2003, The Landings Club, 2002—. Mem. N.Y. Yacht Club, Stamford Yacht Club, Yale Club. Avocations: sailing, skiing, golf, tennis. Home: 8 Breckenridge Ln Savannah GA 31411-1701 Office: Eagle Picher Trust P O box 206 652 Main St Cincinnati OH 45202-2542 Office Phone: 912-598-7197. E-mail: rrmcmullin@aya.yale.edu., rrmcmullin@direcway.com.

MCMURPHY, MICHAEL ALLEN, energy company executive, lawyer; b. Dothan, Ala., Oct. 1, 1947; s. Allen L. and Mary Emily (Jacobs) McM.; m. Maureen Daly, Aug. 8, 1970; children: Matthew, Kevin, Patrick. BS, USAF Acad., 1969; MA, St. Mary's U., San Antonio, 1972; JD, U. Tex., 1975. Bar: Tex. 1975, U.S. Supreme Ct. 1977, U.S. Ct. Mil. Appeals, D.C. 1978, U.S. Ct. Appeals (fed. cir.) 1982. Commd. 2d lt. USAF, 1969, advanced through grades to capt.; instr. Air U., Ala., 1975-79; resigned USAF, 1979; atty., advisor Oak Ridge (Tenn.) ops. U.S. Dept. Energy, 1979-83; gen. counsel COGEMA, Inc., Washington, 1983-87, v.p., 1987-88, pres., chief exec. officer Bethesda, Md., 1988—. Pres., CEO Va. Fuels, Inc., Lynchburg, 1987-92; co-CEO AREVA Enterprises, Inc., Washington, DC, 2002-03, vice chmn., pres., 2003—; bd. dirs. Nuclear Energy Inst., Washington, Soc. Gen. Techs. Nouvelles, S.A., St. Quentin, France, Transnuclear, Inc., Hawthorne, N.Y., Canberra Industries, Meriden, Conn., Cogema Resources, Inc, Casper, Wyo., Cogema Engring. Co., Richland, Wash., Numatec Hanford Co., Wash., Framatome-ANP, Inc., Lynchburg, Va. and Richland, Wash.; bd. govs. Duke Cogema Stone & Webster, LLC, Charlotte, N.C., 1998—; pres. Uranium Producers Am., 1991-92. Mem. editorial bd. Air Force Law Rev., 1977-79. Lt. col. USAFR ret., 1992. Decorated chevalier Nat. Order of Merit (France). Avocation: skiing. Office: COGEMA Inc 1 Bethesda Ctr 4800 Hampden Ln Ste 1100 Bethesda MD 20814 Business E-Mail: mcmurphy@cogema-inc.com.

MCMURRAY, JAMIE, race car driver; Race car driver Brewco Motorsports, Central, Ky. Named Champion, Lebanon I-44 Speedway, 1997. Office: c/o Brewco Motorsports PO Box 37 106 Brewer Dr Central City KY 42330

MCMURRY, IDANELLE SAM, educational consultant; b. Morganfield, Ky., Dec. 6, 1924; d. Sam Anderson and Aurelia Marie (Robertson) McM. BA, Vanderbilt U., 1945, MA, 1946. Tchr. English Abbot Acad., Andover, Mass., 1946-50, Hockaday Sch., Dallas, 1951-54, San Jacinto High Sch., Houston, 1954-55; dean of girls Kinkaid Sch., Houston, 1955-63; headmistress Harpeth Hall Sch., Nashville, 1963-79, Hockaday Sch., Dallas, 1979-89; ret.; now pvt. sch. cons. The Edn. Group, Dallas. Bd. dirs. Ednl. Records Bur., 1979-85, trustee, 1980-85. Bd. dirs. Tex. council Girl Scouts U.S., 1980-82, Town North YMCA; trustee Winston Sch., 1979-85, Spl. Care Sch., 1979-81, Asheville Sch., Manzano Day Sch. Mem. Nat. Study Sch. Evaluation (bd. dirs. 1979-83), Headmasters Assn., Nat. Assn. Ind. Schs. (bd. dirs. 1974-84, acad. com. 1974-79, sec. 1978-80, chmn. 1980-84), So. Assn. Ind. Schs. (pres. 1974-75), Tenn. Assn. Ind. Schs. (pres. 1967-68), Mid-South Assn. Ind. Schs. (pres. 1972-73), Ind. Schs. Assn. S.W. (v.p. 1967—), Nat. Assn. Prins. Schs. for Girls (sec. 1970-72, pres. 1975-77, coun. 1970-79), Nat. Assn. Secondary Sch. Prins., Country Day Sch. Headmasters Assn. (exe. com. 1984-87, v.p. 1988-89), So. Assn. Colls. and Schs. (adminstrv. coun. 1974-77, ctrl. reviewing com. 1972-77, vice chmn. secondary commn. 1975-76, chmn. 1976-77, bd. dirs. 1976-81), Ladies Hermitage Assn., Vanderilt Aid Soc. (sec. 1971-73, pres. 1994-96), Ind. Edn. Svcs. (trustee 1980-88, chmn. 1986-88), Susan Komen Found. (adv. bd.), Belle Meade Club, Centennial Club, Phi Beta Kappa, Pi Beta Phi. Democrat. Presbyterian. Office: 5 Strawberry Hill Nashville TN 37215-4118

MCMURRY, JOHN EDWARD, chemistry professor; b. N.Y.C., July 27, 1942; s. Edward and Marguerite Ann McMurry; m. Susan Elizabeth Sobuta, Sept. 4, 1964; children: Peter Michael, David Andrew, Paul Matthew. BA, Harvard U., 1964; MA, Columbia U., 1965, PhD, 1967. Prof. chemistry U. Calif., Santa Cruz, 1967-80, Cornell U., Ithaca, N.Y., 1980—. Author: textbooks; assoc. editor: Accounts of Chem. Rsch., 1975—95. Recipient Humboldt Sr. Sci. award, 1987; Sloan Found. fellow, 1969-71; Career awardee NIH, 1975-80. Fellow AAAS; mem. Am. Chem. Soc. Home: 625 Highland Rd Ithaca NY 14850-1411 Office: Cornell Univ Dept Chemistry Baker Lab Ithaca NY 14853 Office Phone: 607-255-4819. E-mail: jem24@cornell.edu.

MC MURTRY, JAMES GILMER, III, neurosurgeon; b. Houston, June 11, 1932; s. James Gilmer and Alberta Elizabeth (Matteson) McMurtry. Student, Rice U., Houston, 1950—53; MD cum laude, Baylor U., Houston, 1957. Intern Hosp. U. Pa., Phila., 1957—58; resident gen. surgery Baylor U. Affiliated Hosps., Houston, 1958—59; asst. neurol. surgery Coll. Physicians and Surgeons, Columbia U., N.Y.C., 1959—60; asst. resident neurol. surgery and neurology Neurol. Inst. N.Y., Columbia Presbyn. Med. Ctr., N.Y.C., 1960—62, chief resident neurol. surgery, 1963—65, assoc., 1965—68, asst. prof. clin. neurol. surgery, 1968—73, assoc. prof., 1973—89, prof., 1989—, Herbert and Linda Gallen prof. neurol. surgery, 2003—. Asst. attending neurol. surgeon Neurol. Inst. N.Y., N.Y.C., 1964—73, assoc. attending neurol. surgeon, 1973—89, attending neurol. surgeon, 1989—; chief neurol. surgery clinic Vanderbilt Clinic, Columbia Presbyn. Med. Ctr., N.Y.C., 1964—68; attending-in-charge neurosurgery Lenox Hill Hosp., N.Y.C., 1970—91; assoc. cons. neurol. surgery Englewood (N.J.) Hosp., 1964—; asst. cons. neurol. surgery Harlem Hosp., N.Y.C., 1964—; cons. neurol. surgery Bronx (N.Y.) VA Hosp., 1964—65; mem. NIH Parkinson Rsch. Group, Columbia U., 1965—; mem. med. adv. bd. N.Y. State Athletic Commn. Author: Medical Examination Review Book-Neurological Surgery, 1970, rev. edit., 1975, Neurological Surgery Case Histories, 1975; contbr. articles to profl. jours. Trustee Glimmerglass Opera, Morris-Jumel, Opera Manhattan. Fellow Allen fellow dept. neurol. surgery, Columbia U., 1964—65; scholar Jesse H. Jones scholar, Baylor U. Coll. Medicine, 1953—57. Fellow: ACS, Linnean Soc. (London); mem.: AMA, AAAS, AAUP, The Med. Soc. of London, Med. Strollers, Baylor U. Coll. Medicine Alumni Assn., Osler Soc., N.Y. County Med. Soc., Med. Soc. State N.Y., N.Y. Neurosurg. Soc., N.Y. Acad. Sci., N.Y. State Neurosurgery Soc., N.Y. State Soc. Surgeons, Pan Am. Med. Assn., Am. Soc. Stereotaxic Surgeons, European Congress Pediatric Neurosurgery, Am. Assn. Neurol. Surgeons, The Harveian Soc., Norfolk Yacht and Country, Met. Opera (N.Y.C., dir. and v.p. 2002), The Garrick Club (London), The Union Club, The Atheneum (London), Alpha Omega Alpha. Home: 1 Cobb Ln Tarrytown NY 10591-3003 Office: 710 W 168th St New York NY 10032-2603

MCMURTRY, LARRY JEFF, author; b. Wichita Falls, Tex., June 3, 1936; s. William Jefferson and Hazel Ruth (McIver) McM.; m. Josephine Ballard, July 15, 1959 (div. 1966); 1 child, James. BA, N. Tex. State Coll., 1958; MA, Rice U., 1960. Instr. Tex. Christian U., Ft. Worth, 1961-62; lectr. in English and creative writing Rice U., Houston, 1963-69; co-owner Booked Up Book Store, Washington, from 1970. Vis. prof. George Mason Coll., 1970, Am. Univ., 1970-71. Author: (novels) Horseman, Pass By, 1961 (Jesse H. Jones award Texas Inst. of Letters 1962), Leaving Cheyenne, 1963, The Last Picture Show, 1966, Moving On, 1970, All My Friends Are Going to be Strangers, 1972, Terms of Endearment, 1975, Somebody's Darling, 1978, Cadillac Jack, 1982, The Desert Rose, 1983, Lonesome Dove, 1985 (Pulitzer prize for fiction 1986), Texasville, 1987, Anything for Billy, 1988, Some Can Whistle, 1989, Buffalo Girls, 1990, The Evening Star, 1992, Streets of Laredo, 1993, (with Diana Ossana) Pretty Boy Floyd, 1994, The Late Child, 1995, Dead Man's Walk, 1995 (with Diana Ossana) Zeke and Ned, 1997, Commanche Moon, 1997, Duane's Depressed, 1999, Boone's Lick, 2000; (non-fiction) Walker Benjamin at Dairy Queen, 1999, Roads: Driving America's Great Highways, 2000, Paradise, 2000, Sacagawea's Nickname: Essays on the American West, 2001; (essays) In a Narrow Grave: Essays on Texas, 1968, It's Always We Rambled: An Essay on Rodeo, 1974, Film Flam: Essays on Hollywood, 1987; screenwriter: (with Peter Bogdanovich) The Last Picture Show, 1971 (Academy award nomination best adapted screenplay 1971), Texasville, 1990, Montana, 1990, Falling From Grace, 1992, (with Cybill Shepard) Memphis, 1992; also articles, essays, book revs. in N.Y. Times, Saturday Rev., Washington Post, Am. Film, others. Wallace Stegner fellow, 1960, Guggenheim fellow, 1964; recipient Barbara McCombs/Lon Tinkle award Texas Inst. of Letters, 1986. Mem. Tex. Inst. Letters (Jesse H. Jones award 1962). Office: Simon & Schuster 1230 Avenue of the Americas New York NY 10020-1586 also: care Saria Co Inc 2509 N Campbell Ave # 95 Tucson AZ 85719-3304

MCMURTRY, R. ROY, chief justice; b. Toronto, Ont., Can., May 31, 1932; s. Roland Roy and Doris Elizabeth (Belcher) McM.; m. Ria Jean Macrae, Apr. 18, 1957; children: Janet, James, Harry, Jeannie, Erin, Michael. BA with honors, U. Toronto, 1954; LLB, Osgoode Hall Law Sch., 1958; LLD (hon.), U. Ottawa, 1983, Leeds U., U.K., 1988, York U., 1991, U. Toronto, 1998. Bar: Called to bar 1958, created Queen's counsel 1970. Partner firm Benson, McMurtry, Percival and Brown; mem. Provincial Parliament for Eglinton, 1975-85; atty. gen. for Ont., 1975-85; solicitor gen. for Ont., 1978-82; high commnr. for Can. to Gt. Brit. and No. Ireland, 1985-88; ptnr. Blaney, McMurtry Stapells, Toronto, 1988-91; chmn. Can. Football League, 1989-91; assoc. chief justice Ont. Ct. Justice, Toronto, 1991-94, chief justice, 1994-96; chief justice of Ont. Ont. Ct. of Appeal, Toronto, 1996—. Freeman of City of London, 1986. Mem. United Ch. of Can. Office: Ont Ct of Appeal 130 Queen St W Toronto ON Canada M5H 2N5 E-mail: cath.lanni@jus.gov.on.ca.

MCNAB, SUSAN ELIZABETH, human resources executive; b. Nov. 4, 1949; d. James Orville and Betty Edith (Westlake) McN. BA, Purdue U., 1971; MA, U. Md., 1977; MBA, U. Puget Sound, 1984. SHRM lic. Assoc. buyer Procter & Gamble, Cin., 1971-72; counselor U. Md., College Park, 1972-73; pers. cons. Girl Scouts U.S., Burlingame, Calif., 1973-76; pers. and safety supt. Monsanto Corp., Seattle, 1976-80; mgr. pers. St. Louis, 1980-82; dir. pers. Lanoga Corp., Seattle, 1982-85, v.p., 1986-87; sr. v.p. human resources Ernst Home and Nursery, 1987-90; mgr. human resources Komo TV, 1996; sr. v.p. retail ops. Wizards of the Coast, 1997—2001; v.p. people svcs. Seattle Coffee Co., 2001—04. Lectr. in field. Contbg. author: Strike Preparation Manual, 1982; contbr. articles to profl. jours. Pres. Totem coun. Girl Scouts U.S., Seattle, 1986-90; bd. dirs. Seattle Seafair Orgn., 1980, Gov.'s Com. for Handicapped, St. Louis, 1980-82, Intiman Theater, 1998—; pres.Widbey Inst., 1986-90, bd. dir., 1999—, Grace Found., 1996—; bd. dirs. Ethnic Heritage Coun., 1997—, pres., 1998—2001; mem. U. Wash. Vis. Com., Sch. Social Work, 1999—. Named Time Mag. Newsmaker of Tomorrow, 1978, Outstanding Sr. Woman, Purdue U., 1971; recipient Cmty. Action award Girl Scouts U.S., 1980. Mem. Soc. for Human Resources Mgmt. (nat. com. employee and labor rels.), Internat. Tng. in Comm. (v.p. chpt. 1986-87, winner Internat. Speech Contest 1986, Toastmistress), Pacific N.W. Pers. Mgmt. Assn. (pres. 1998-99), Rotary (chair cmty. svc. com. Seattle club 1988-90, 97—, bd. dirs. 1999—2002), Jr. League Seattle, Wash. Athletic Club, Seattle Yacht Club. Roman Catholic. Home: 252 Lake Dell Ave Seattle WA 98122-6311

MCNABB, DAVID E. business educator, writer; b. L.A., Nov. 29, 1932; s. Jay B. McNabb and Josephine P. Recagno; m. Janet C. Lagerquist, June 12, 1962; children: Meghan, Michael, Sara. BA, Calif. State Coll., Fullerton, 1965; MA, U. Wash., 1968; PhD, Oreg. State U., 1979. Prof. Pacific Luth. U., Tacoma, 1979—98; vis. prof. UMUC-Europe, Heidelberg, Germany, 1998—99, The Evergreen State Coll., Olympia, Wash., 1999—2000, Stockholm Sch. Econs., Riga, Latvia, 2000—03. Vis. scholar Thunderbird Internat. U., Phoenix, 1990. Author: Research Methods for Public Administration, 2002, Research Methods for Political Science, 2004. Served with USN, 1952—56. Mem.: ASPA, Am. Water Works Assn., Acad. Polit. Sci., Acad. Mgmt., Rotary. Home: 605 E Barbary Rd Shelton WA 98584 Office Phone: 253-535-7245.

MCNABB, DONOVAN, professional football player; b. Chgo., Nov. 25, 1976; s. Samuel and Wilma McNabb; m. Raquel Nurse, 2003. Degree in Speech Comm., Syracuse U., 1998. Backup guard Syracuse U. basketball team, 1995—96, 1996—97; profl. football player Phila. Eagles, 1999—. Co-host (with Beasley Reece) The Donovan McNabb Show. Established own scholarship found.; mem. Life as a Rookie panel Rookie Symposium, 2000. Named NFL Player of Yr., CBS Radio, 2000; named to All Madden Team, 2000, Nat. Football Conf. Pro Bowl Team, 2000—03. Office: Phila Eagles NovaCare Way Philadelphia PA 19145*

MCNAIR, JOHN FRANKLIN, III, banker; b. Laurinburg, N.C., Apr. 12, 1927; s. John Franklin and Martha (Fairley) McN.; m. Martha Fowler, June 16, 1951; children: John Franklin IV, Elizabeth Fowler. BS, Davidson Coll., 1949; postgrad., U. N.C., 1954-56. Pres. McNair Automotive Co., Inc., Laurinburg, 1949-66, The State Bank, Laurinburg, 1966-68; sr. v.p. Wachovia Bank & Trust, Laurinburg, 1968-70, Raleigh, N.C., 1970-72, exec. v.p. Winston-Salem, N.C., 1972-77, vice chmn., 1977-85, The Wachovia Corp., Winston-Salem, N.C., 1977-87, pres., chief exec. officer, 1987-90, Wachovia Bank & Trust Co, 1987-90, also dir.; exec. v.p. First Wachovia Corp., 1986-90. Bd. dirs., pres. N.C. R.R. Co., 1993-97. Mem. N.C. State Hwy. Commn., Raleigh, 1965-69, Commn. on future N.C., Raleigh, 1981-83; chmn. N.C. Bd. Econ. Devel., 1979-85, N.C. Coun. Econ. Edn., Greensboro, 1980-82, Ind. Coll. Fund N.C., 1989-91, N.C. Citizens for Bus. and Industry, 1988-89; trustee Peace Coll., Raleigh, 1980-89, Davidson Coll., 1985-93, St. Andrews Presbyn. Coll., Laurinburg, N.C., 1968-75; trustee Old Salem, Inc., 1985-98, 99—, treas., 1990-97, chmn., 1997-98; trustee Winston-Salem Found., 1983-91, chmn., 1989-91; co-chmn. gov.'s adv. com. Superconducting Supercollider Project, 1988; trustee, 1986-2003, trustee emeritus, 2003—, mem. exec. com. Rsch. Triangle Found., 1986-99, vice chmn., 1990-93, chmn., 1992-2000; trustee exec. com. Winston-Salem Bus., Inc., 1986-02, chmn., 1990-95, mem. adv. coun., 2002—; mem. govt. performance com. State of N.C., 1991-93; bd. dirs. N.C. Enterprise Corp., 1988-93; bd. dirs. Sr. Svcs., Inc., 1994-2003, exec. com., 1998-2002, chmn., 1999-2000; chmn. Sr. Svcs. Found., 2002-; chmn. Qual Choice N.C. Inc., 1994-99, bd. dirs., 1994-2002; bd. dirs. N.C. Stroke Assn., 1998-2003, Save Our State, 1998-2003. With USN, 1945-46. Recipient Young Man of Yr. award, Laurinburg Jaycees, 1962, Silver Beaver award, Boy Scouts Am., 1967, Disting. Alumni award, Davidson Coll., 1994, citation for disting. citizenship, N.C. Citizens for Bus. and Industry, 2003. Mem. Am. Bankers Assn. (state v.p. 1980-81), Res. City Bankers Assn., N.C. Bankers Assn. (pres. 1976-77), Old Town Club, Piedmont Club, St. Andrews Soc., Rotary. Democrat. Presbyterian. Home: 1244 Arbor Rd Box 236 Winston Salem NC 27104 Office: Wachovia Bank NA 420 W 4th St Ste 100 Winston Salem NC 27101-2837

MCNAIR, JOHN WILLIAM, JR., civil engineer; b. Asheville, N.C., June 17, 1926; s. John William and Annie (Woody) McN.; m. June Clemens Kratz; childrn: Jeffry, Marsha, Cathy. BS in Forestry, Pa. State U., 1950; BSCE, Va. Poly Inst. State U., 1955; postgrad. in engring., U. Va., 1957—2004. Registered profl. engr., Va. Forester U.S. Forest Svc., Flagstaff, Ariz., 1950, U.S. Gypsum Co., Altavista, Va., 1951; mem. engring. faculty U. Va., Charlottesville, 1955-58; prin. John McNair & Assocs., Waynesboro, Va., 1958—; owner Brucheum Group, Waynesboro, 1983—; chmn., CEO Info. Systems Support, Inc., 1998—. With Va. Bd. Architects, Profl. Engrs. and Land Surveyors, 1969-79, v.p., 1977-78, pres., 1978-79. Author numerous engring. and land mgmt. study reports. Mem. Waynesboro City Coun., 1968-72, vice mayor, 1970-72; chmn. Waynesboro Indsl. Devel. Authority, 1984-2000. Capt. AUS, 1944-46, 51-53, France, Okinawa. Recipient Disting. Svc. cert. Va. Soc. Profl. Engrs., 1971. Fellow ASCE; mem. Acad. Environ. Engrs. (diplomate), Rotary, Rappahannock River Yacht Club (founding mem.). Republican. Presbyterian. Business E-Mail: jmcnair@brucheum.com.

MCNAIR, NIMROD, JR., foundation executive, consultant; b. Tuscaloosa, Ala., Nov. 2, 1923; s. Nimrod and Salemma (Flowers) McN.; m. Amy Ernestine Phillips, Apr. 27, 1943; children: Janice Lee McNair Bradd, John Rodney. BSChemE, U. Ala., 1949; MS in Aerospace Engring., Air Force Inst. Tech., 1961. Cert. mgmt. cons. Sales engr. Hunt Oil Co., Tuscaloosa, 1949-51; commd. officer USAF, 1950, advanced through grades to lt. col., 1966; prof. N.C. State U., Raleigh, 1951-55; command pilot SAC, 1955-59; grad. student USAF Inst. Tech.; dir. space planning Space Div., L.A., 1961-65; dir. mgmt. rsch. and devel. USAF, Dayton, 1969-72, staff officer, Pentagon Washington, 1965-68, reconnaissance pilot, 1968-69; ret., 1972; pres. Exec. Leadership, Inc., Chgo., 1973-80, Exec. Ministries, Inc., Atlanta, 1981-86; chmn., chief exec. officer, bd. dirs. Environ. Control Atlanta, Inc., Atlanta, 1973—, McNair Assocs., Inc., Atlanta, 1980—, Exec. Leadership Found., Inc., Atlanta, 1986—. Bd. dirs. ADA Metals, Inc., Lincolnwood, Ill.; developer, instr. bus. ethics program, U.S., Can., South Am., West Europe, East Europe, U.S.S.R. Author; Mega Values--Ten Principles for Business Success, Ten Principles for a Successful Marriage. Trustee Rep. Presl. Task Force; Rep. cand. for Gov., Ga., 1994. Decorated DFC, medal (Vietnam); recipient Gov.'s award State of

Ky., State of Ark., Commendation award for bus. ethics program U.S. Pres., Chief Exec. Officer of Fortune 500 Corps., numerous awards for speaking. Mem. Am. Mgmt. Assn. President's Assn., Ret. Officers Assn., Christian Businessmen's Com. U.S.A., Inst. for Absolute Ethics (assoc., bd. dirs.), Air Force Assn., Internat. Platform Assn., Nat. Speakers Assn., Nat. Honor Soc., Tau Beta Pi, Phi Eta Sigma. Anglican. Avocations: flying, travel, reading. Office: Exec Leadership Found 1210 Springhouse Cir Stone Mountain GA 30087 Office Phone: 678-684-3115. E-mail: mcnairn@parkspringscommunities.com.

MCNAIR, RUSSELL ARTHUR, JR., lawyer; b. Detroit, Dec. 2, 1934; s. Russell Arthur and Virla (Standish) McN.; m. Rosemary M. Chesbrough, Apr. 6, 1957; children: Julie McNair Schwerin, Russell Arthur III, Douglas S. AB in Econs. cum laude, Princeton U., 1956; JD with distinction, U. Mich., 1960. Bar: Mich. 1960, Fla. 2001. Assoc. Dickinson, Wright, Moon, Van Dusen & Freeman (now Dickinson Wright PLLC), Detroit, 1960-67, ptnr., 1968-98, chmn., 1994-98. Cons. Evans & Luptak, Boca Raton, 2000-; adj. prof. U. Detroit Sch. Law, 1968-72; mem. adv. bd. Fin. Transactions Inst., 1984-94; adj. prof. Wayne State U. Law Sch., 1994-96; spkr. in field. Trustee Children's Home, Detroit, 1975-95, pres. 1986-87, hon. trustee 1995—; mem. community leaders coun., United Way, 1994-98; dir. Mich. Jobs Commn., 1995-98. Mem.: Am. Coll. Real Estate Lawyers, Am. Law Inst., Fla. Law Assn., Mich. Law Assn. Republican. Presbyterian. Avocations: golf, tennis, platform tennis. Home: 4383 Gleneagles Dr Boynton Beach FL 33436-4802 Office: Evans & Luptak 4th Fl 4700 NW Boca Raton Blvd Boca Raton FL 33431 Office Phone: 561-443-4343. Personal E-mail: ramcnair@aol.com. Business E-Mail: ramcnair@bellsouth.net.

MCNAIR, STEVE LATREAL, professional football player; b. Mount Olive, Miss., Feb. 14, 1973; m. Mechelle McNair; 1 child, Tyler. Student, Mt. Olive H.S. Quarterback Tenn. Oilers (now called Tenn. Titans), 1995—. Named NFL Co-MVP, 2003; named to AFC Pro-Bowl Team, 2003. Office: Tennessee Titans 460 Great Circle Rd Nashville TN 37228-1404

MCNAIRY, KATE, humanities educator; d. John Egbert McNairy and Elizabeth Farr. BA, SUNY, Albany, 1976, MA, 1978. Adj. prof. Adirondack C.C., Queensbury, NY, 1987—91, Empire State Coll., Sarasota Springs, NY, 1994—2002; adminstrv. asst. NY State, Albany, 1994—2002. Contbr. poetry to lit. mags. Vol. Saratoga Arts Ctr. Mem.: Poets and Writers, Acad. Am. Poets. Avocations: drumming, photography, walking. Home: 161 Regent St # 20 Saratoga Springs NY 12866

MCNALL, SCOTT GRANT, sociologist, educator, academic administrator; b. New Ulm, Minn., Jan. 16, 1941; s. Everett Herman and Dorothy Grant (Brown) McNall; m. Sally Anne Allen, Oct. 31, 1960; children: Miles Allen, Amy Ellen. BA, Portland State U., 1962; PhD, U. Oreg., 1965. Instr. sociology U. Oreg., Eugene, 1964-65; asst. prof. U. Minn., Mpls., 1965-70; from assoc. prof. to prof. Ariz. State U., Tempe, 1970-76; prof., chmn. dept. sociology U. Kans., Lawrence, 1976-89, prof, chmn. dept. Am. studies, 1989-90; dean Coll. Arts and Scis. U. Toledo, 1990-94; provost Calif. State U., Chico, 1994—, interim pres., 2003—. Fulbright lectr., Greece, 1968—69; vis. lectr. Mid-Am. State U. Assn., 1982—83. Author: (book) The Sociological Experience, 1969, 3d edit., 1974, The Greek Peasant, 1974, Social Problems Today, 1975, Career of a Radical Rightist, 1975; author: (with Sally A. McNall) Plains Families: Exploring Sociology Through Social History, 1983, The Road to Rebellion, 1988; editor: The Sociological Perspective, 1968, 4th edit., 1977, Theoretical Perspectives in Sociology, 1979, Current Perspectives in Social Theory, 1980, 6th edit., 1985, Political Economy: A Critique of American Society, 1981; editor: (with others) Studies in Historical Social Change, 1986—, The Road to Rebellion: Class Formation and Kansas Populism, 1865-1900, 1988; editor: (with Rhonda Levine) Bringing Class Back in, 1991; editor: (with Sally A. McNall) Sociology, 1992; editor: Current Perspectives in Social Theory, 1980—87; adv. editor: Sociol. Quar., 1969—72, assoc. editor: Am. Sociologist, 1975—78, Jour. Polit. and Mil. Sociology, 1982—; contbr. articles to profl. jours. East-West Ctr. Vis. fellow, 1978, Fulbright grantee, 1983. Mem.: Pacific Sociol. Soc., Am. Sociol. Assn. (chair Marxist sect. 1989—90), Midwest Sociol. Soc. (pres. 1982—83). Democrat. Congregationalist. Home: 520 Crestwood Dr Paradise CA 95969-3825 Office: Calif State U VPAA Office Chico CA 95929 Office Phone: 530-898-6101.

MCNALLY, ALAN G. bank executive; b. Quebec, Can., Nov. 3, 1945; m. Ruth; 2 children. BSc., M Eng., Cornell U., 1967; Internat. MBA, York U., Can. With Aluminum Co. of Can.; vice chmn. personal and commercial fin. svcs. Bank of Montreal Group, 1975-93; CEO, vice chmn. Harris Bank and Haris Bankcorp Inc., 1993-1995, chmn. bd., CEO, 1995—. Trustee DePaul U., adv. bd. mem. Northwestern U. J.L. Kellogg Grad. Sch. Mgmt., bd. mem. Evenston Northwestern Healthcare, mem. bd. govs. York U., dir. Canadian Coun. for Aboriginal Bus. Gen. chair United Way/Crusade of Mercy fundraising campaign, 1996, dir. Chgo. Youth Ctrs., treas. Queen Elizabeth Hosp. Found., dir. Kid's Help Phone. Recipient Americanism award Anti-Defamation League, Community Builder award Christian Insudtrial League, Outstanding Exec. Leadership award York U. Schulich Sch. Bus., Toronto, Prime Movers award. Bd. dirs. Econ. Club Chgo., Chgo. Club, civic com. Commercial Club Chgo., Executive's Club Chgo., Glen View Club. Office: Harris Bank 111 W Monroe St Chicago IL 60603-4096

MCNALLY, ANDREW, IV, publishing executive, director; b. Chgo., Nov. 11, 1939; s. Andrew and Margaret C. (MacMillin) McN.; m. Jeanine Sanchez, July 3, 1966; children: Andrew, Carrie, Ward. BA, U. N.C., 1963; MBA, U. Chgo., 1969. Bus. mgr. edn. divsn. Rand McNally & Co., Chgo., 1967-70, exec. v.p., sec., 1970-74, pres., 1974-97, CEO, 1978-97, also chmn. bd. dirs., 1993-97; prin. Hammond Kennedy Whitney, Chgo., 1998—; chmn. Triple Tree Capital, 1998—. Bd. dir. Hubbell Inc.; bd. dirs. Reinhold Industries, Seneca Inc., Effox, Boyt Harness, Qualis. Trustee Newberry Libr.; bd. dirs. Children's Meml. Hosp.; active vis. com. of libr. U. Chgo. With Air Force N.G., 1963-69. Mem. Chgo. Club, Saddle and Cycle Club, Commonwealth Club, Racquet Club, Links (N.Y.C.). Office: Triple Tree Capital Ste 2200 333 N Michigan Ave Chicago IL 60601-4104

MCNALLY, CONNIE BENSON, magazine editor, publisher, antiques dealer; b. Chgo. d. Peter D. and Joanna Agriostathes; m. Dick Benson, Nov. 19, 1955 (div. mar. 1961); 1 child, Douglas; m. William C. McNally, July 27, 1975. Student, Univ. Wis., 1954-55; BA, Baylor, 1962. Midwest supr. Slenderella Internat., Chgo., 1955-59; dir. John Roberts Powers Sch., Dallas, 1960-62; backgammon tchr., profl. Racquet Club, Palm Springs, Calif., 1969-75, La Costa (Calif.) Resort, 1973-75; antique dealer Palm Springs, 1975—; ptnr. Carriage Trade Antiques, 1975-78; owner, mgr. McNally Co. Antiques, 1978—; editor, pub. Silver Mag., Inc., Rancho Santa Fe, Calif, 1993—. Mem. Am. Assn. Antique Dealers, Antique Dealers Assn. Calif., Country Firends (vol. chair 1985-87, area dir. 1988-89, publicity chair 1990-91, program chair 1992-93, corr. sec. 1994-95, bd. dirs.), Social Svc. League La Jolla, Soc. Am. Silversmiths, Rancho Santa Fe Rep. Women's Club. Avocations: equestrian, gourmet cook.

MCNALLY, DAVID D. federal agency administrator; b. Washington, Sept. 28, 1944; BA in Govt., Wesleyan U., 1966; MPA, Princeton (N.J.) U., 1968. Sr. staff Inst. Pub. Adminstrn., N.Y.C., 1968-71; dir. Office Urban Affairs Princeton U., 1971-74; asst. dir. fin. Mass. Dept. Pub. Welfare, 1975-77, asst. commr. adminstrn., 1977-79; dir. divsn. fin. mgmt. Health Care Financing Adminstrn. HHS, Balt., 1979-87, dir. Office of Medicaid Mgmt. Medicaid Bur., 1987-95, dir. Office Fin. Svcs. Medicaid Bur., 1995-97, dep. dir. quality and performance mgmt. group, 1997—2002, tech. dir. fin., sys. and quality group, 2002—. Mem. Phi Beta Kappa. Avocations: ancient coins, piano, guitar, tennis, squash. Office: Ctr Medicaid and State Ops Ctrs for Medicare & Medicaid Svcs HHS 7500 Security Blvd Baltimore MD 21244-1849

MCNALLY, JAMES HENRY, physicist, defense consultant; b. Orange, N.J., Dec. 18, 1936; s. James Osborne and Edith Maude (Jones) McN.; m. Nancy Lee Eudaley, July 4, 1976. B. in Engring. Physics, Cornell U., 1959; PhD in Physics, Calif. Inst. Tech., 1966. Staff mem. program mgr. Los Alamos (N.Mex.) Nat. Lab., 1965-74; asst. dir for laser and isotope separation tech. AEC/ERDA, Washington, 1974-75; assoc. div. leader, dep. for inertial fusion, asst. for nat. sec. issues Los Alamos Nat. Lab., 1975-86; dep. asst. dir. Arms Control and Disarmament Agy., Washington, 1986-88; dir. office staff Los Alamos Nat. Lab., 1988-90, Washington Inst., 1990-94; cons., 1990—. U.S. del. Geneva Conf. on Disarmament, 1969, 73, 74, Threshold Test Ban Treaty, Moscow, 1974, Nuclear Testing Talks, Geneva, 1986-88. Bd. dirs. Wilson Mesa Met. Water Dist., 1976-88; mem., v.p., pres. Mountain Canine Corps, 1994-98. Recipient Meritorious Honor award Arms Control and Disarmament Agy., 1988. Mem. AAAS, Am. Phys. Soc., Internat. Inst. Strategic Studies. Home and Office: 41 Bowen Rd Kittery ME 03904-1355

MCNALLY, JAMES RAND (RANDY MCNALLY), pharmacist, state legislator; BS, Memphis State U., 1967; postgrad., U. Tenn., 1969. Hosp. pharmacist Meth. Med. Ctr., Oak Ridge, Tenn., 1978—; mem. Tenn. Ho. of Reps. 91st-94th Gen. Assemblies, Tenn. Senate 95th-103d Gen. Assemblies, former vice chmn. fin., ways and means com., chmn. edn. com., Republican floor leader. Recipient Bill Bates award United Tenn. League, 1994, MADD Outstanding Legislator, Disting. Svc. award Am. Coun. on Alcohol Problems, 1994, Common Cause Bird Dog award, 1994; named Rep. Legislator of the Yr., 1990, Sertoma Man of the Yr., 1991; Paul Harris fellow Rotary Internat., 1996. Republican. E-mail: sen.randy. Office: 302 War Memorial Bldg Nashville TN 37243 Fax: (615) 253-0285. E-mail: mcnally@legislature.state.tn.us.

MCNALLY, JOHN JOSEPH, retired lawyer; b. N.Y.C., July 1, 1927; s. Edward E. and Virginia L. (O'Brien) McNally; m. Sally Vose Greeley, Jan. 25, 1958; children: Martha, Sarah, Elizabeth, Julie, Thomas. AB, Coll. Holy Cross, 1950; LLB, Harvard U., 1953. Bar: N.Y. 1953. Assoc. White & Case, N.Y.C., 1953-63, ptnr., 1964-94; ret., 1994. Bd. dirs. Mohawk Paper Mills, Inc. Pres. Lavelle Fund for the Blind, 1999—; bd. govs. Lawrence Hosp., Bronxville, NY, 1990—95; trustee Caedmon Sch., N.Y.C., 1968—, Lavelle Sch. for Blind, N.Y.C., 1997—99, All Hallows Found., 2000—, All Hallows H.S., N.Y.C., 2001. Fellow: Am. Bar Found.; mem.: Assn. Bar of City of N.Y., N.Y. County Lawyers Assn., N.Y. State Bar Assn. Home: 58 Avon Rd Bronxville NY 10708-1723 Office: White & Case 1155 Ave of Americas New York NY 10036-2711

MCNALLY, MICHAEL JAMES, electric power industry executive; BS in Applied Math., U. Nebr., Omaho. Pres. Houston Pipe Line Co.; mng. dir. Enron Capital and Trade Resources; prin. Enron Devel. Corp.; pres. transmisson divsn. TXU, Dallas; exec. v.p., CFO, TXU Corp., Dallas; pres. TXU Bus. Svcs., Dallas. Office: TXU Corp Energy Plz 1601 Bryan St Dallas TX 75201-3401

MCNALLY, SEAN PATRICK, prosecutor; b. Scranton, Pa., Aug. 5, 1953; s. John Patrick and Elizabeth Jane McNally; m. Diane Maureen Campanaro, June 29, 1985; 1 child, Brigid S. AA, Citrus Coll., 1973; BA, UCLA, 1975; JD, Western State U., 1979; postgrad., U. So. Calif., 1981, 82. Bar: U.S. Tax Ct. 1980, U.S. Dist. Ct. (ctrl. dist.) Calif. 1980, U.S. Dist. Ct. (so. dist.) Calif. 1981, U.S. Ct. Appeals (9th cir.) 1981. Law libr. Orange County Law Libr., Santa Ana, Calif., 1975-80; intern Orange County Dist. Atty., Santa Ana, 1978; assoc. Law Offices of Leon Najman, Costa Mesa, Calif., 1980-81; dep. dist. atty. San Bernardino County, Calif., 1981—. Mem. ABA, Calif. Trial Lawyers Assn., Assn. of Trial Lawyers of Am., Calif. Dist. Atty. Assn., L.A. Police Dept. Emerald Soc., L.A. Trial Lawyers Assn., Riverside County Bar Assn., San Bernardino County Bar Assn., Celtic Bar Assn., LA County Bar Assn., Orange County Bar Assn., Western State U. Alumni Assn., Calif. Narcotics Officers Assn., B.P.O.Elks, Delta Tau Delta, Delta Theta Phi. Republican. Roman Catholic. Avocations: boating, running, collegiate sporting events. Home: 6007 E Brighton Ln Anaheim CA 92807-4702 Office: 316 N Mountain View Ave San Bernardino CA 92415-1016 Office Phone: 909-387-8309.

MCNALLY, TERRENCE, playwright; b. St. Petersburg, Fla., Nov. 3, 1939; s. Hubert Arthur and Dorothy Katharine (Rapp) McNally. BA, Columbia U., 1960. Stage mgr. Actors Studio, N.Y.C., 1961, tutor, 1961-62; film critic The Seventh Art, 1963-65; asst. editor Columbia Coll. Today, N.Y.C., 1965-66. Author: (plays) The Lady of the Camellias, 1963, And Things That Go Bump in the Night, 1964, Apple Pie and Last Gasps, 1966, Sweet Eros, Witness, Tour, Cuba Si!, Noon, 1968, Next, 1969, Where Has Tommy Flowers Gone?, Botticelli, Bringing It All Back Home, 1971, Bad Habits, 1971 (Obie award, 1971), Whiskey, 1973, The Tubs, 1974, The Ritz, 1975 (Obie award best play, 1974), The Golden Age, 1975, Broadway, Broadway, 1979, The Five Forty-Eight, 1979, It's Only a Play, 1982, The Rink, 1984, Frankie and Johnny in the Clair de Lune, 1988, The Lisbon Traviata, 1989, Up in Saratoga, 1990, Kiss of the Spider Woman, 1990 (Tony award best book of a musical, 1993), Andre's Mother, 1990 (Emmy award), Preludes, Fuges & Rifts, Lips Together, Teeth Apart, 1991, (screenplay) Frankie and Johnny, 1991, A Perfect Ganesh, 1993 (Pulitzer prize for drama nomination, 1994), Kiss of the Spiderwoman, 1993, Love! Valour! Compassion!, 1994 (Outer Critics' Circle award best Broadway play, 1995, N.Y. Drama Critics Best Am. play, Tony award for Best Play), Master Class, 1994, Ragtime, 1997 (Tony award Best Book of a Musical Corpus Christi, 1998), The Full Monty, 2000, The Visit, 2001. Recipient Dramatists Guild Hull-Warriner award, 1973, 1988, 1990; Guggenheim fellow, 1966—69. Mem.: Am. Acad. Arts and Letters, Dramatists Guild (v.p. 1981—98). Office: care Peter Franklin William Morris Agy 1325 Avenue Of The Americas New York NY 10019-6026

MCNALLY, VINCENT JOSEPH, historian, educator; b. Philadelphia, PA, Feb. 6, 1943; s. Joseph Edward and Dorothy Elizabeth (Connor) McNally. PhD, Univ. of Dublin, Trinity College, Dublin, Ireland, 1971—77. Prof. ch. history Sacred Heart Sch. of Theology, Hales Corners, Wis., 1992—; asst. prof. history Simon Fraser U., Burnaby, Canada, 1987—92. Author: (Book) Education Facsimiles 241-260: Catholic Emancipation, 1793-1829, 1976, A History of the Roman Catholic Diocese of Victoria, B.C., 1990, Reform, Revolution and Reaction: Archbishop John Thomas Troy and the Catholic Church in Ireland, 1787-1817, 1995, The Lord's Distant Vineyard: A History of the Oblates and the Catholic Community in British Columbia, 2000, "Hope for the Future: the Church's Challenges of the New Millennium", 2000, (book) Christianity and Native Cultures: Christian and Native Spiritualities in British Columbia: The Historic Struggle to Respect Diversity and Ambiguity, 2004, (Journal: Historical Studies) Challenging the Status Quo: An Examination of the History of Catholic Education in British Columbia, 1999, (Journal: Western Oblate Studies) "Fighting for a Foundation: Oblate Beginnings in Far Western Canada, 1847-1864, 1996, (Journal: Canadian Church Historical Soci) "Fighting City Hall: The Church Tax Exemption Battle Between the City and Roman Catholic Diocese of Victoria", 1992, (Journal of Church and State) "Church-State Relations and American Influence in British Columbia before Confederation", 1992, (Catholic Historical Review) "Archbishop John Thomas Troy and the Establishment of St. Patrick's, Maynooth, 1791-1795", 1981, (Research Project) Practicing What We Preach: Testing and Publishing a Guide for Implementing a Pastoral Theology of Acceptance and Reconciliation in Northern Ireland", 2001 (Assoc. of Theological Schools in US and Canada: Lilly Research Award, 2001), (Research Project:) "Challenging Prejudice: Creating a Theology of Acceptance and Reconciliation in the Schools of Northern Ireland, 2000 (Pew Charitable Trusts, 2000), (Research Award) Researching, Writing and Publishing of a survey history: Irish Catholics: The Catholic Church in Ireland from the Reformation to the Present, 1999 (Eli Lilly Fellowship, 1999), Developing Healthy Theological Imaginations, 1998 (Lilly Endowment Fellowship for Teaching and Learning in Theology and Religion, 1998), Challenging Ourselves: A Practical Guide for Moving Beyond Prejudice in the Schools of Northern Ireland, 2004. Recipient Nat. Endowment for the Humanities Rsch. award, 2004.: American Catholic Historical Society (Peter Guilday Prize 1981). Avocations: drawing, harpsichord, painting, travel. Office: Sacred Heart School of Theology PO Box 429 Hales Corners WI 53130 Office Phone: 414-425-8300 7181. Office Fax: 414-529-6999. Personal E-mail: vmcnally@shst.edu. Business E-Mail: vmcnally@shst.edu.

MCNAMARA, AIDA SHAHID, insurance executive; b. Tehran, Iran, May 25, 1959; came to U.S., 1981; d. Labib and Esmat (Meshkat) S.; children: Hamed Meshki, Brendan McNamara, Dylan McNamara. M Econs., Farah Pahavi U., Tehran, 1981. CLU. Office mgr. Barnes Ins. Svc., Santa Monica, Calif., 1981-82; asst. to life specialist E.F. Hutton, Santa Monica, 1982-84; salesperson Mut. Omaha, Burbank, Calif., 1984-86; ins. agt. Met. Life Ins. Co., Woodland Hills, Calif., 1986-88; ind. ins. agt., security rep. Woodland Hills, 1988—; dist. sales mgr. Mut. Omaha, L.A., 1991-98, Encino, Calif., 1998—, gen. mgr., 2002—. Mem. Nat. Assn. Life Underwriters (Nat. Quality Award), Nat. Assn. Securities Dealers, Am. Soc. CLUs and ChFCs, Million Dollar Round Table (chmn. coun.). Office: Mut Omaha 11845 W Olympic Blvd # 800 Los Angeles CA 90064 Fax: 310-268-0776. E-mail: aidaminla@aol.com.

MCNAMARA, ANN DOWD, medical technologist; b. Detroit, Oct. 17, 1924; d. Frank Raymond and Frances Mae (Ayling) Sullivan; m. Thomas Stephen Dowd, Apr. 23, 1949 (dec. 1980); children: Cynthia Dowd Restuccia, Kevin Thomas Dowd; m. Robert A. McNamara, June 15, 1985. BS, Wayne State U., 1947. Med. technologist Woman's Hosp. (now Hutzel Hosp.), Detroit, 1946-52, St. James Clin. Lab., Detroit, 1960-62; supr. histo-pathology lab. Hutzel Hosp., Detroit, 1962-72, Mt. Carmel Mercy Hosp., 1972-87, ret., 1987. Docent Domino's Ctr. Architecture & Design, Ann Arbor, Mich. 1988. Mem. Am. Soc. Clin. Pathologists, Am. Soc. Med. Technology, Mich. Soc. Med. Technology, Nat. Soc. Histotechnology, Mich. Soc. Histotechnologists, Wayne State U. Alumni Assn., Smithsonian Assos., Detroit Inst. Arts Founders Soc. Home: 2488 Signature Dr Pinckney MI 48169

MCNAMARA, ANNE H. lawyer, corporate executive; b. Shanghai, Republic of China, Oct. 18, 1947; came to U.S., 1949; d. John M. and Marion P. (Murphy) H. AB, Vassar Coll., 1969; JD, Cornell U., 1973. Bar: N.Y. 1973, Tex. 1981. Assoc. Shea, Gould, Climenko & Casey, N.Y.C., 1972-76; from asst. corp. sec. to corp. sec. Am. Airlines, Inc., Dallas, 1976-88, v.p. pers. resources, 1988; sr. v.p., gen. counsel Am. Airlines (AMR Corp.), Dallas, 1988—. Bd. dirs. Louisville Gas & Electric Co., LG&E Energy Corp., Sabre Group Holdings, Inc. Office: Am Airlines Inc Dallas/Fort Worth Airport PO Box 619616 Dallas TX 75261-9616

MCNAMARA, BRENDA NORMA, secondary school educator; b. Blackpool, Lancashire, Eng., Aug. 8, 1945; arrived in U.S., 1946; d. Milford Hampson and Nola (Welsby) Jones; m. Michael James McNamara, July 19, 1969. BA in History, Calif. State U., Long Beach, 1967; postgrad., Calif. State U., various campuses, 1967—. Cert. secondary tchr. and lang. devel. specialist Calif. Tchr. history West HS, Torrance, Calif., 1968—, dept. chair, 1989-99, 2000—. Cons. Golden State Exam. in History Calif. State Dept. Edn., 1998; state del. NEA Annual Meeting, 2000, 02, local del., 03; cons. in field. Co-author: (book) World History, 1988. Western Internat. Studies Consortium grantee, 1988. Mem.: NEA, Am. Hist. Assn., Nat. Coun. Social Studies, So. Calif. Coun. Social Studies, Torrance Tchrs. Assn. (bd. dirs. 1992—), Calif. Coun. Social Studies, Calif. Tchrs. Assn. Avocations: travel, theater, mystery reading, gourmet cooking. Office: West H S 20401 Victor St Torrance CA 90503-2255

MCNAMARA, DAVID JOSEPH, financial and tax planning executive; b. Osceola, Iowa, Feb. 6, 1951; s. Loras Emmett and Nadine Evelyn (DeLancey) McN.; m. Ruth Ellen Hanken, Oct. 4,1974; children: Benjamin, Shawna, Heather. BGS, U. Iowa, 1974. Cert. fin. planner Coll. Fin. Planning, 1985; registered prin. Nat. Assn. Securities Dealers. Pres. The Planners Adv. Svcs., Inc., 1985; ptnr. VF Realty Ptnrs., West Desmoines, Iowa, 1987—. Mem.: Fin. Planning Assn. (bd. dirs. Iowa chpt. 1984—85). Republican. Office: The Planners Adv Svcs Inc 1012 Grand Ave West Des Moines IA 50265-3255

MCNAMARA, FRANCIS JOSEPH, JR., retired foundation executive, lawyer; b. Boston, Nov. 30, 1927; s. Francis Joseph and Louise (English) McN.; m. Noreen E. O'Connor, June 18, 1953 (dec. Feb. 1984); children: Francis Joseph III, Moira Patricia (Mrs. Lance F. James), John Allen, Kathleen Louise (Mrs. Robert J. Hugin), Martha Jeanne (Mrs. James R. Bordewick), Mark Jeffrey; m. Lois L. Magner, Jan. 17, 1986. AB, Georgetown U., 1949, LLB, 1951; LLD, Fairfield U., 1983. Bar: Conn. 1952. Assoc. firm Pullman, Comley, Bradley & Reeves, 1953; asst. U.S. Atty., dist. Conn., 1953-57; assoc. firm Cummings & Lockwood, Stamford, Conn., 1957-59, ptnr., 1959-91. Guest lectr. Salzburg (Austria) Seminar, 1981; chmn. grievance com. U.S. Dist. Ct. Conn., 1983-89; mem. panel comml. arbitrators Am. Arbitration Assn., Ctr. Dispute Resolution. Trustee Fairfield (Conn.) U., 1968-80, trustee emeritus, 1980—; trustee Charles E. Culpeper Trust, 1968-2001; chmn. bd. Charles E. Culpeper Found., 1968-99, pres., 1991-99. With USNR, 1946, 51-53. Fellow Am. Bar Found., Am. Coll. Trial Lawyers (state com. 1985-91, state chmn. 1989-90); mem. U.S. Supreme Ct. Hist. Soc. (Conn. state chmn. 1989-91, trustee 1992-2000), Navy League U.S., Knight of Holy Sepulchre, Knight of Malta, Knight of St. Gregory the Great, Wee Burn Country Club (Darien, Conn.), Orchid Island Golf and Beach Club (Vero Beach, Fla.). Republican. Roman Catholic. Home: 75 Bank St New Canaan CT 06840-6203 also: 10 Lost Beach Ln Vero Beach FL 32963-5000 Office: 75 Bank St New Canaan CT 06840-6203

MCNAMARA, JOHN D. food products executive; Student, Ryerson U., Toronto. Various mgmt. positions Procter & Gamble Can.; dir. Maple Leaf Monarch Co.; merchandising mgr. Arthur Daniels Midlands Co., 1985-92, pres. ADM Agri-Industries (Canadian subs.), 1992-97, group v.p., prs. N.Am. Oilseed Processing Divsn., 1997, pres. Mem. Nat. Oilseed Processors Assn., Canadian Oilseed Processors Assn. (chmn.), Canola Coun. Can. (bd. dirs.), Can. Inst. Edible Oils (bd. dirs.). Office: 4666 E Faries Pkwy Decatur IL 62526-5666

MCNAMARA, J(OHN) DONALD, retired lawyer, business executive; b. Bridgeport, Conn., Feb. 28, 1924; s. John T. and Agnes (Keating) McN.; m. Shirley Addison Holdridge, Nov. 5, 1960. BA, Dartmouth Coll., 1945; MA in Govt., Harvard U., 1947, LLB, 1950. Bar: N.Y. 1951, Conn. 1951. Assoc. Hall, Haywood, Patterson & Taylor, N.Y.C., 1951-53, 55-56; asst. U.S. Atty. U.S. Dist. Ct. (so. dist.) N.Y., 1953-55; assoc. Wickes, Riddell, Bloomer, Jacobi & McGuire, N.Y.C., 1956-57; assoc., then ptnr. Nottingham & McEniry (and successor), N.Y.C., 1957-59; sec., gen. counsel Interpub. Group of Cos., Inc., N.Y.C., 1960-79, dir., 1965-85, sr. v.p., 1966-73, exec. v.p., 1973-79, pres., 1980-85, mem. exec. com., 1967-85, mem. fin. com., 1980-85. Chmn. U.S. Nat. Tennis Championships, 1965. Served to lt. (j.g.) USNR, 1943-46. Mem. Am. Ceramic Cir., River Club, Univ. Club, Met. Opera Club (bd. dirs. 1999—, pres. 2004—), Ekwanok Country Club (bd. govs. Manchester, Vt. 1991-95), Dorset (Vt.) Field Club (bd. govs. 1996-99, pres. 1997-98), West Side Tennis Club (pres. Forest Hills, N.Y. 1964-66, 79-80). Home: 350 E 57th St New York NY 10022-2953 also: River Rd Manchester VT 05254

MCNAMARA, JOHN J(OSEPH), advertising executive, writer; b. Yonkers, N.Y., Mar. 7, 1934; m. Patricia A. Widmann, Sept. 14, 1963; children: Mary, John. BS, Yale U., 1956; MBA, NYU, 1963. Pres. Young & Rubicam Inc., from 1982; later pres. McCann Erickson Worldwide, ret., 1990. Writer, cons., bd. dirs. in field. Author: Advertising Agency Management, 1989; columnist: Gulf Stream mags. Pres. Pelham United Way, NY; chmn. Pelham Manor Planning Bd.; trustee Village of Pelham Manor, mayor, 1989—90; pres. Boys and Girls Club, Indian River County, Fla.; pres., bd. dirs. John's Island Property Owners Assn. Mem.: John's Island Club (bd. dirs.), Winged Foot Club, Pelham Country Club (pres.). Office: PO Box 8204 Vero Beach FL 32963-8204

MC NAMARA, JOSEPH DONALD, researcher, retired police chief, novelist; b. N.Y.C., Dec. 16, 1934; s. Michael and Eleanor (Shepherd) McN.; divorced; children: Donald, Laura, Karen. BS, John Jay Coll., 1968; fellow, Harvard Law Sch., 1970; DPA (Littauer fellow), Harvard U., 1973. Served to dep. insp. Police Dept., N.Y.C., 1956-73; police chief Kansas City, Mo., 1973-76, San Jose, Calif., 1976-91; rsch. fellow Hoover Instn., Stanford U., 1991—. Adj. instr. Northeastern U., 1972, John Jay Coll., 1973, Rockhurst Coll., 1975-76, San Jose State U., 1980; cons. U.S. Civil Rights Commn., 1978; lectr., appearances on nat. TV; apptd. nat. adv. bd. U.S. Bur. Justice Stats., 1980, U.S. Drug Control Policy Office, 1993; commentator Pub. Broadcasting Radio. Author: (non-fiction) Safe and Sane, 1984, (novel) The

First Directive Crown, 1985, Fatal Command, 1987, The Blue Mirage, 1990, Code 211 Blue, 1996; contbr. articles to profl. publs. Bd. dirs. Drug Policy Found., Washington; active NCCJ. Served with U.S. Army, 1958-60. Named one of 200 Young Am. Leaders Time mag., 1975; recipient disting. alumni award John Jay Coll., 1979, Pres.'s award Western Soc. Criminology1979, Morrison Gitchoff award Western Soc. Criminology, 1992, H.B. Spear award Drug Policy Found., 1992; Kansas City police named Best in Country by Nat. Newspaper Enterprises, 1974, San Jose Police Dept. named Nat. Model U.S. Civil Rights Commn., 1980; named Law Enforcement Officer of Yr., Calif. Trial Lawyers Assn., 1991. Mem. Internat. Assn. Chiefs of Police, Calif. Police Chiefs Assn., Calif. Peace Officers Assn., Major Cities Police Chiefs Assn., Police Exec. Research Forum (dir.) Office: Hoover Instn Stanford CA 94305 Office Phone: 650-723-1475. *In our country, social mobility is possible for people from even the most humble backgrounds. Despite problems, our nation has provided more liberty and dignity for the common individual than any other civilization in history. Continuation of our free society depends upon how successful we are in teaching each new generation an appreciation of our precious freedoms and the patience to achieve progress within our democratic process.*

MCNAMARA, JULIA MARY, academic administrator, foreign language educator; b. N.Y.C., Dec. 13, 1941; d. John P. and Julia (Dowd) McNamara. BA in History and French, Ohio Dominican Coll., 1965; MA in French, Middlebury Coll., 1972; MPhil, Yale U., PhD in French Lang. and Lit., 1980; DHL (hon.), Sacred Heart U., Hamden, Conn., 1984. Mem. faculty St. William Sch., Pitts., 1963-64, Holy Spirit Sch., Columbus, Ohio, 1964-65, Newark (Ohio) Cath. High Sch., 1965-66, Northwest Cath. High Sch., West Hartford, Conn., 1966-69, St. Vincent Ferrer High Sch., N.Y.C., 1969-70, St. Mary's High Sch., New Haven, 1971-74; lectr. french Albertus Magnus Coll., New Haven, 1976-80, dean of students, 1980-82, acting pres., 1982-83, pres., 1983—. Prof. French Albertus Magnus Coll., 1981—; mem. Conn. Health and Edn. Facilities Authority, Hartford, 1983—; chair Conn. Conf. Ind. Colls., Hartford, 1990-92, sec.-treas. 1986—, chmn., 1990-92; lectr. in field; assoc. fellow Yale U., Morse Coll.; bd. dirs. New Haven Savs. Bank. Chairperson United Way Greater New Haven, 1987; bd. dirs. St. Mary's High Sch., New Haven, 1982-91, ARC, New Haven Savs. Bank, 1990—; trustee Yale-New Haven Hosp., 1981— (chair med. com., 1989-91 vice chair bd., 1991—), chair, Yale-New Haven Health Sys.; adv. bd. Bank of Boston-Conn., 1983-87; adv. com. Jr. League Greater New Haven, 1985; trustee Hartford Sem., 1985-91. Fulbright fellow, Paris, 1977-78; Yale U. fellow, 1974-78, Am. Council on Edn. fellow, 1981; recipient Disting. Woman in Leadership award New Haven YWCA, 1984, Veritas award Providence Coll., 1987, Greater New Haven Jr. Achievement Ann. award, 1990. Mem. Fulbright Alumni Assn., New Haven C. of C. (bd. dirs. 1984-90), New England Assn. Schs. and Colls. (appeals bd. 1986-88). Roman Catholic. Office: Albertus Magnus Coll Office of the President 700 Prospect St New Haven CT 06511-1224

MCNAMARA, KEVIN JOHN, museum administrator; b. Abington, Pa., Oct. 6, 1957; s. John Kerwin and Dolores Ann (Auchinleck) McN; m. Juliane Cary Roebuck, July 17, 1982; children: Hilary Megan, Whitney Morgan. BA, Temple U., 1989; cert., U. Pa., 1994; MA, Temple U., 1995; cert., U. Va., 2000. Journalist Calkins Newspapers Inc., Doylestown, Pa., 1981-85; congl. aide U.S. Rep. R. Lawrence Coughlin, Washington, 1985-88; asst. dir. Fgn. Policy Rsch. Inst., Phila., 1988-93, rapporteur, 1990-93, adj. scholar, 1994—; dir. devel. Intercollegiate Studies Inst., Phila., 1994-98; assoc. v.p. Drexel U., Phila., 1998—2004; v.p. Independence Seaport Mus., Phila., 2004—. Author: The Presidency, 2000; contbg. editor Directors and Boards, 1989-90, Orbis: A Jour. of World Affairs, 1990-93; contbr. articles to profl. jours. Vol. Sam Katz for Gov., 1994, Craig Snyder for Congress, 1992, George Bush for Pres. Com., 1987-88, Snyder for State Ho. Com., 1990; cons. Coughlin for Congress Com., 1986; bd. dirs. Abington Free Libr., 1992-93. Grantee, Tawani Found., 2004; Earhart Found. fellow, 2003—04. Mem. Am. Polit. Sci. Assn., Phila. Com. Fgn. Rels., Acad. Polit. Sci., Assn. of Fundraising Profls. Republican. Avocations: reading, writing, gardening. Office: 211 S Columbus Blvd and Walnut St Philadelphia PA 19106-3199

MCNAMARA, KEVIN MICHAEL, floorcovering company executive; b. Webster, Mass., June 28, 1957; s. Bernard Francis and Genevieve Anastasia (Ostrokolowicz) McN. AD in Bus. Adminstrn., Quinsigamond C.C., Worcester, Mass., 1982; BS/BA cum laude, Clark U., Worcester, 1985. Personalized svc. rep. Norton Co., Worcester, 1976-83; sys. sales engr. Wells Fargo Alarm Svcs., Chelsea, Mass., 1983-84; dist. sales mgr. Sherwin-Williams Co., San Diego, 1984-96; sr. account exec. Solar Contract Carpet, San Diego, 1996—2001, Criterion Custom Floors, 2001—03, sr. mktg. mgr., 2003—, Bonded Carpet, San Diego, 2003—, 2003—04; sales mgr. Miramar Volkswagen/AUDI, San Diego, 2004—. Named Salesman of Yr., Painting and Decorating Contractors Am., State of Conn., 1985, 86. Mem. San Diego C. of C., San Diego Apt. Assn., Friendly Sons of St. Patrick, Elks, Sons of the Am. Legion, Hon. Deputy Sheriff's Assn. Democrat. Roman Catholic. Avocations: golf, skiing, tennis, water sports, travel, food. Home: 4905 Refugio Ave Carlsbad CA 92008-3730 Office: Miramar Volkswagen Audi 9010 Miramar Rd San Diego CA 92126

MC NAMARA, LAWRENCE J. bishop; b. Chgo., Aug. 5, 1928; s. Lawrence and Margaret (Knusman) McN. BA, St. Paul Sem., 1949; STL, Cath. U. Am., 1953. Ordained priest Roman Cath. Ch., 1953. Parish priest, tchr. Kansas City-St. Joseph Diocese, 1953—57; dir. diocesan Refugee Resettlement, 1957—60; chaplain Jackson County Jail, 1957—64; exec. dir. Campaign for Human Devel., 1973—77; bishop of Grand Island Nebr., 1978—. Roman Catholic. Office: Chancery Office PO Box 1531 Grand Island NE 68802-1531

MCNAMARA, MARGARET M. pediatrician; MD, U. Conn., 1990. Diplomate Am. Bd. Pediatrics. Resident in pediatrics U. Calif., San Francisco; chief of pediatrics U. Calif. San Francisco/Mount Zion Pediatric Practice, San Francisco. Office: UCSF Mount Zion Pediat Practice 2330 Post St Ste 320 San Francisco CA 94115-3466

MCNAMARA, MARY E. nonprofit executive, asset manager, minister; b. Mpls., Dec. 18, 1943; d. Edward Emmanuel and Gladys Theresa (Mattson) Bjorklund; m. Peter Alexander McNamara II (div.); children: Peter Alexander III, Nathaniel Paul. BA, Carleton Coll., 1965; MDiv, Harvard U., 1968. Cert. fin. planner. Program dir. St. Peter's Ch., N.Y.C., 1968-72, program dir., dep. exec., 1977-80; program dir. Ctr. Ch. on-the-Green, N.Y.C., 1972-74; program developer Westminster Presbyn. Ch., Springfield, Ill., 1974-77; assoc. Gen. Assembly Coun. Presbyn. Ch. (USA), N.Y.C., 1980—86; dir. not-for-profit sector City of N.Y., 1986—90; pres., exec. dir. Interchurch Ctr., N.Y.C., 1990-99; exec. v.p. Union Theol. Sem., N.Y.C., 1999—. V.p. Pathways for Youth, Bronx, NY, 1987—96; pres. Morningside Area Alliance, N.Y.C., 1991—98; parish assoc. Fifth Ave. Presbyn. Ch., 1998—2002. Moderator Presbyn. N.Y.C., 1995—96, chair com. on ministry, 1992—95, chair implementation task force, 1996—98; chmn. bd. dirs. exec. com. Presbyn. Conf. Ctr., Stony Point, NY, 1996—2002; bd. dirs. Union Theol. Sem., 1996—99, Blanton/Peale Inst. on Religion and Health, 1994—2001, Wartburg Adult Care Cmty., 1999—, chair elect, 2001—03, chair, 2003—, chmn. pers. com., exec. com., 2001—03. Home: 99 Claremont Ave Apt 621 New York NY 10027-5711 Office: Union Theol Sem 3041 Broadway New York NY 10027-5710

MCNAMARA, ROBERT M., JR., federal agency administrator, lawyer; b. Ohio; m. Patti Devenney; children: Brendan, Caitlin. BA, Mt. Carmel Coll., 1967; AB, John Carroll U., 1968; JD, Georgetown U., 1973. Law clk. to Hon. George C. Edwards, Jr. U.S. Ct. Appeals (6th cir.), Cin.; dep. dir. enforcement Commodity Futures Trading Commn.; gen. counsel Peace Corps.; legis. counsel U.S. Senate Judiciary com.; asst. U.S. atty. U.S. Senate Watergate Com., asst. majority counsel; asst. gen. counsel enforcement Dept. Treasury; gen. counsel CIA, Washington, 1997—. Adj. prof. law Georgetown U. Law Ctr. Symposium editor: Am. Criminal Law Rev. Office: CIA Office of Gen Counsel Washington DC 20505-0001

MCNAMARA, ROBERT STRANGE, former banking executive, former Secretary of Defense; b. San Francisco, June 9, 1916; s. Robert James and Clara Nell (Strange) McN.; m. Margaret Craig, Aug. 13, 1940 (dec.1981); children: Margaret Elizabeth, Kathleen, Robert Craig; m. Diana Masieri Byfield, 2004. AB, U. Calif., 1937, LLD (hon.); MBA, Harvard U., 1939, LLD (hon.), U. Mich., Columbia U., George Washington U., Princeton U., Amherst Coll., Williams Coll., U. Ala., Ohio State U., NYU, U. Notre Dame, U. Pa., U. St. Andrews, U. Philippines, Aberdeen U., Oxford U., U. So. Calif. Asst. prof. bus. adminstrn. Harvard U., 1940-43; exec. Ford Motor Co., 1946-61, pres., 1960-61, dir., 1957-61; sec. U.S. Dept. Def., 1961-68; pres. World Bank, 1968-81; ret., 1981. Mem., trustee pub. and pvt. instns. including Overseas Devel. Coun., Urban Inst., Enterprise Found., Brookings Inst., Royal Dutch Petroleum, Bank of Am., Washington Post Corp.; spl. cons. War Dept., 1942. Author: The Essence of Security, 1968, One Hundred Countries-Two Billion People, 1973, The McNamara Years at the World Bank, 1981, Blundering Into Disaster, 1986, Out of the Cold, 1989, In Retrospect, 1995, Argument Without End, 1999, Wilson's Ghost, 2001. Served as lt. col. USAAF, 1943-46. Decorated Legion of Merit, D.S.M.; recipient Presdl. Medal of Freedom with distinction, 1968, Christian A. Herter Meml. award, Albert Pick Jr. award U. Chgo., 1979, Franklin D. Roosevelt Freedom from Want medal, 1983, Onassis Athinai prize, 1988. Mem. Phi Beta Kappa. Office: 1350 I St NW Washington DC 20005-3305

MCNAMARA, STEPHEN, newspaper executive; b. Chgo., July 9, 1934; s. Robert Charles McNamara Jr. and Susan (Deuel) Shattuck; m. Hanne Mogensen Petterson, Feb. 21, 1960 (div. Aug. 1970); children: Lise, Natalie, Kevin; m. Kay Copeland, June 10, 1978; children: Christopher, Morgan. AB in Am. History, Princeton U., 1955. Reporter Winston-Salem (N.C.) Jour., 1955-57; sports writer Miami Herald, 1957-59; contbg. European editor Car & Driver, N.Y.C., 1960; asst. news editor, exec. sports editor, Sunday editor San Francisco Examiner, 1961—66; CEO, editor, pub. Pacific Sun, Mill Valley, Calif., 1966—; co-pub. The Ark, Tiburon, Calif., 1987-99; pres. Marin Sun Printing Co., Mill Valley, 1967-93; mng. gen. ptnr. Sunlight Investment Co., Mill Valley, 1980—. Vis. lectr. San Francisco State U., 1967; mem. innovation and planning commn. Calif. Dept. Edn., Sacramento, 1980; co-founder, pres. Marin Solar Village Corp., Mill Valley, 1976—, Marin Cmty. Video, Mill Valley, 1973-78. Mem. Soc. Profl. Journalists, Nat. Assn. Alternative Newsweeklies (pres. 1978-81), Calif. Assn. Alternative Newsweeklies (pres. 1990-92), Calif. Soc. Newspaper Editors (pres. 1985-86, bd. dirs. 1983-93), Calif. Newspaper Pubs. Assn. (bd. dirs. 1989-93), San Francisco Press Club (1st place newspaper writing award 1967, 3-2d place awards), Cap and Gown Club (Princeton U.). Democrat. Home: 2 Bradford Way Mill Valley CA 94941-1111 Office: Pacific Sun Pub 21 Corte Madera Ave Mill Valley CA 94941-1800 Personal E-mail: smcnamara@aol.com. Business E-Mail: steve.mcnamara@pacificsun.com.

MCNAMARA, TOM, scientific consulting corporation executive; b. Battle Creek, Mich., May 23, 1944; s. George P. (Stepfather) and Mildred E. Lunt; m. Ellen K. LaRue, Sept. 24, 1977; 1 child, George Lunt. Grad. in Chemistry, Boston U., 1966; MBA, Northeastern U., 1970. With corp. planning dept. Reynolds Aluminum, Richmond, Va., 1970—72; sr. cons. Technomic Cons., Chgo., 1972—74; founder, pres. NUVENTURES Cons., Chgo. and San Diego, 1975—97. Spkr. trade convs. and confs. worldwise; rfrequent guest TV and radio talk shows; on water advisor Am.'s Cup, 1988, 91, 94. Author: Henry Lunt and The Ranger, 1991, Henry Lunt and The Spymaster, 1994; co-author: America's Changing Workforce, 1990; editor: George and The Pitching Machine, 1994; contbr. articles to profl. publs. Mem. various coms. United Fund and Chgo. Assn. Commerce and Industry, 1975—79; spokesman 200th Anniversary U.S. Bill of Rights tour, 1991; Rep. nominee Ill. Gen. Assembly, 1974, 1976. Recipient Presdl. Commendation for heroism, 1974, Commendation award, Chgo. Police Dept., 1974, Pulitzer Prize nomination, 1991. Mem.: Acadia, Bath and Racquet Club Sarasota, San Diego Tennis and Racquet Club, Bahia Corinthian Yacht Club.

MCNAMARA, WILLIAM P. retail executive; b. Newton, Mass. m. Patricia Ann McCole; 2 children. BS, Boston Coll. From exec. trainee to sr. v.p., gen. merch. mgr. Filene's divsn. May Dept. Stores Co., St. Louis, 1972—95, sr. v.p., gen. merch. mgr. May merchandising divsn., 1995—97, pres., CEO Famous-Barr divsn., 1997—98, pres. May merchandising divsn., 1998—2000, vice-chmn., CEO, 2000—. Office: May Dept Stores Co 611 Olive St Saint Louis MO 63101

MCNAMARA-RINGEWALD, MARY ANN THÉRÈSE, artist, educator; b. Hempstead, N.Y., Apr. 11, 1935; d. William George Schlichtig and Alice Agnes Rakeman; m. Raymond Anthony McNamara, Apr. 22, 1957 (div. Sept. 1975); children: Thomas William, Raymond Gerard, William Daniel, Peter Joseph, James Francis Jude; m. John Drew Ringewald, Feb. 17, 1984. BS, Fordham U., 1957, Barbizon Sch., NYC, 1953; M in Studio Arts, Adelphi U., 1972; postgrad., Parsons Sch. Design, 1973-75; student, Art Students League, N.Y.C., 1973-74; postgrad., Goddard Coll., Calif., 1986-87; student, Progoff Intensive Jour. Program, N.Y.C., 1999—, Cape Cod Sch., 1993. Cert. elem. edn. and art N.Y. Elem. sch. art tchr. Dept. Edn., Freeport, N.Y., 1957-58, Farmingdale, NY, 1967; jr. and h.s. art tchr. Massapequa (N.Y.) Sch. Dist., 1970-90; owner, pres. South Shore Creative Arts Ctr., Massapequa, 1975; pvt. art tchr. various locations, 1970-90. Illustrator Doubleday, Inc., N.Y.C.; art advisory bd. Chesapeake Coll, Wye Mills, Md., 1995— (lectr., 1998, 99, 2000), Snow Princess, Fordham U., 1954; symposium coord. Hofstra U., N.Y.; lectr. Naples Philharm., 1992; judge, lectr. in field; architectural designer, M.E, 1977, M.D., 1988-, F.L., 1990. One-woman shows include Fordham U., 1954, Andonia Gallery, Massepequa, N.Y., 1974, Isis Gallery, Islip, N.Y., 1974, For the Birds, Salisbury, Conn., 1978, Harguen Gallery, Pt. Jefferson, N.Y., 1979, Adelphi U., Garden City, N.Y., 1992, Wohlfarth Gallery, Washington, 1994-95, SpanBauer Gallery Naples, Fla., 1996, Naples Philharmonic, Naples, Fla., 1992, Gallery 44, Millbrook, N.Y., 1997-98; groups shows: Acad. of Arts, Easton, Md., 1993. works exhibited at Kennedy Gallery, Key West, Fla., 1997-99, Chesapeake Coll., Md., 1998-99; represented in pvt. collections General Motors, The Benedictines, Prudential Life, St. Michael's Maritime Mus., Yupo Corp., Japan; illustrator: From a Lighthouse Window, Chesapeake Bay Maritime Mus., 1992 (Best of Balt. Book award 1993, Book award Tabasco N.Y.C. 1994); original poetry published. Pres. AAUW, L.I., 1969-71; bd. dirs. L.I. (N.Y.) Art Tchrs. Assn., 1973-76; docent U.S. Fish and Wildlife Svc., Washington, 1994-95; mem. Am. Farmland Trust; vol. Delmarva Chpt., ARC, 2001-. Recipient Nat. Middle Sch. Art Tchrs. award, Nassau County Middle Sch. Art Tchrs. Assn., 1988, Very Spl. Arts Festival for Handicapped, 1977, Festival of Creation, Diocese of RVC, 1975, Catalyst, 1975; named to Outstanding Young Women of Am., 1969; works featured in Nat. Anthology of Poetry, 1953. Mem. Internat. Welcome Fla. Assn. Series (lectr. 1994—), Nat. League Am. Pen Women (founder, pres. Naples, Fla. br. 1995—), Nat. Gallery Art (copyist 1993—), Order of the Benedictines (oblate 1990—), Working Artists Forum (Easton, Md.), NY State Art Tchrs. Assn. (bd. mem. 1972-80). Roman Catholic. Avocations: horticulture, travel, illuminations, music, poetry. Address: Marafour 5493 Anderby Dr Royal Oak MD 21662 Office: Marafour Studio 27098 Del Ln Bonita Springs FL 34135-4409

MCNAMEE, SISTER CATHERINE, theology studies educator; b. Troy, N.Y., Nov. 13, 1931; d. Thomas Ignatius McNamee and Kathryn McNamee Marois. BA, Coll. of St. Rose, 1953, DHL (hon.), 1975; MEd, Boston Coll., 1955, MA, 1958; PhD, U. Madrid, 1967. Grad. asst. Boston Coll., 1954-55; asst. registrar Boston Coll. (Grad. Sch.), 1955-57; mem. faculty Coll. St. Rose, Albany, N.Y., 1960-65, acad. v.p., 1968-75; dir. liberal arts Thomas Edison Coll., Trenton, 1975-76; pres. Trinity Coll., Burlington, Vt., 1976-79, Coll. St. Catherine, St. Paul, 1979-84; dean Dexter Hanley Coll., U. Scranton, Pa., 1984-86; pres. Nat. Cath. Ednl. Assn., Washington, 1986-96; sr. scholar Ctr. for Cath. Studies, U. St. Thomas, St. Paul, Minn., 1996-2000; prof. U. Catolica, Talca, Chile, 2000—. Bd. dirs. Am. Forum for Global Edn. Trustee assoc. Boston Coll. Spanish Govt. grantee, 1965-67; OAS grantee, 1967-68; Fulbright grantee, 1972-73 Mem. Inter-Am. Confedn. Cath. Edn., Internat. Orgn. Cath. Edn., Nat. Cath. Ednl. Assn., Internat. Fedn. Cath. Univs., Delta Epsilon Sigma. Roman Catholic. Home: Casilla 712 Talca Chile E-mail: cmncsj@chilesat.net.

MCNAMEE, JAMES M. lab administrator; With Hooper Holmes, Inc., Basking Ridge, NJ, 1968—79, officer, 1979—84, pres., CEO, 1984—, chmn., bd. dirs., 1996—. Mem., exec. com. and nom. com. Hooper Holmes, Inc., Basking Ridge, NJ. Office: Hooper Holmes Inc 170 Mt Airy Rd Basking Ridge NJ 07920*

MCNAMEE, MARK, academic administrator; BS in Chemistry, MIT, 1968; PhD, Stanford U., 1973. Postdoctoral assoc. Columbia U. Coll., 1973—75; asst. prof. U. Calif., Davis, 1975—85, prof., 1985, chair dept. biochemistry and biophysics, 1990—93, dean divsn. biol. scis., 1993—2001; provost, v.p. Va. Tech., Blacksburg, 2001—. Office: Va Tech Univ Provost and VP for Acad Affairs 210 Burruss Hall Blacksburg VA 24061*

MC NAMEE, MAURICE BASIL, English language educator; b. Montello, Wis., June 5, 1909; s. James Patrick and Ida (Griffith) McN. AB, St. Louis U., 1933, A.M., 1934, S.T.L., 1941, PhD, 1945. Joined S.J., 1927, ordained priest Roman Cath. Ch., 1940. Tchr. Creighton U. H.S., 1936-37; mem. faculty St. Louis U., 1944—, prof. English, 1960—, dir. dept., 1956-70, dir. honors program, 1950-61. Lectr. fgn. workshops, 1957-60 Author: Literary Decorum in Francis Bacon, 1950, Reading for Understanding, 1958, 68, Honor and the Epic Hero, 1960, (with J. Cronin, J. Rogers) Literary Types and Themes, 1960, 70, Essays by the Masters, 1968, Essays in Exposition, 1969, Bacon's Inductive Method and Humanistic Grammar, 1971, The Origin of the Vested Angel as a Eucharistic Symbol in Flemish Painting, 1972, The Structure of the Ignatian Meditation Pattern in Some of the Poetry of Gerard Manley Hopkins, 1990, Vested Angels: A Study of the Eucharistic Symbolism in Early Netherlandish Painting, 1999, Recollections in Tranquility, 2002. Mem. Cath. Commn. Intellectual and Cultural Affairs, 1971—; exec. dir. Samuel Cupples House Found., 1974; mem. Mayor's Council Cultural Affairs, 1979; mem. Commn. Art Archdiocese of St. Louis. Recipient Nancy McNeir Ring Outstanding Faculty award, 1973; Fleur de Lis medal St. Louis U.; Research grantee St. Louis U., 1955; Ford Found. Jesuit Faculty Fund St. Louis U., 1966; Fulbright research follow Belgium, 1966; research grantee in humanities Am. Philos. Soc., 1966, 78, Research Grant from the Beaumont Fund, St. Louis University, 1983; Research Grant from the Mellon Fund, St. Louis University and from the National Arts and Educational Foundation, 1985, Mellon Fund of St. Louis U. research grant, 1985, 87, 90, NEH research grant, 1985. Mem. Modern Lang. Assn., Soc. Art Historians (pres. 1962-64), Coll. Art Assn., Phi Beta Kappa. Democrat. Home and Office: 3601 Lindell Blvd Saint Louis MO 63108-3301

MCNAMEE, STEPHEN M. federal judge; b. 1942; BA, U. Cinn., 1964; MA, U. Ariz., 1967, JD, 1969. U.S. atty. Dist. of Ariz., Phoenix, 1985-90; U.S. Dist. judge, 1990—99; chief judge U.S. Dist. Ct. Ariz., Phoenix, 1999—. Office: US Dist Judge Sandra Day O'Connor US Ct 401 W Washington St SPC 60 Phoenix AZ 85003-2158

MCNAUGHTON, KENNETH JOHN, publisher; b. Melbourne, Australia, July 22, 1940; arrived in U.S., 1970; s. Charles Dudley and Lilian May (Besant) McN.; m. Victoria Ann Yocum, Oct. 28, 1972 (div. Oct. 1982); children: Aurelius John, Candace Ann. B chem. engr., Univ. Melbourne, 1961; M in engr. sci., Monash Univ., Clayton, Australia, 1964. Dir. comm. network Found. Faith, N.Y.C., 1966-77; asst. editor Chemical Engring., N.Y.C., 1978-81, assoc. editor, 1981-86; editor-in-chief Industrial Chemist, N.Y.C., 1986-89; dir. new publs. divsn. sci. and tech. Warren Gorham & Lamont, N.Y.C., 1989-90; mng. editor Physics Today, N.Y.C., 1991-94; assoc. pub. The Industrial Physicist, College Park, Md., 1995—. Pres. McNaughton Communications, N.Y.C., 1978—. Contbr. over 100 articles to profl. jours. Mem. Friends of Benjamin Banneker Hist. Park, Oella, Md., 1996—; founder Campaign to Save the Trees, Roosevelt Island, N.Y., 1991; pres. PTA H.S. for the Humanities, N.Y., 1990-91; pres. bd. dirs. Greystone Condominiums, 2002-2003; mem. Romnet Newsgroup, 1997-99. Recipient Broadcast awards Coun. of Chs., 1976, 78, 79, Golden Mike awards Am. Legion, 1978, 79. Mem. Port Philip Pioneers Group, Univ. Melbourne Alumni Assn. (founding pres. Northeastern Am. br. 1988-90, pres. 1992-94), Australia Soc. Phila. Avocations: music, dance, film, swimming, walking, travel. Home: 3778 College Ave Ellicott City MD 21043-4662 Office: Am Inst Physics One Physics Ellipse College Park MD 20740-3842 Personal E-mail: kmcnaugh@aip.org.

MCNAUGHTON, WILLIAM FRANK, translator, educator; b. Westboro, Mo., May 21, 1933; s. Frank McNaughton and Ruth Ellen (Flanders) Francis; m. Margaret Orminski, Apr. 4, 1956 (div. 1971); children: John Ferenc, Dorothy Ellen; m. Li Ying, Apr. 8, 1990; 1 child, Andrea. Student, U. Mo., 1951-53; studied poetry and translation with, Ezra Pound, 1953-56; student, Georgetown U., 1953-54; BA, Bklyn. Coll., 1961; PhD, Yale U., 1965. Asst. prof. Oberlin (Ohio) Coll., 1965-70; lectr. Exptl. Coll., Oberlin, 1970-71; vis. lectr. Bowling Green (Ohio) State U., 1972-74, Denison U., Granville, Ohio, 1972-78; prof. Program for Afloat Coll. Edn. (PACE) USN, Norfolk, Va., 1978-84; vis. prof. King Saud U., Abha, Saudi Arabia, 1984-85; sr. lectr. English, translation City Poly. Hong Kong, 1986-89, prin. lectr. translation, 1989-94; univ. sr. lectr. City U., Hong Kong, 1994-95, assoc. prof., 1995-98; retired, 1998. Guest lectr., U. degli Studii, Venice, Italy, 1975; coord. Tri-Coll. Chinese program, Gt. Lakes Colls. Assn., Ann Arbor, 1965-68; cons., Asian Lit. program, Asia Soc., N.Y.C., 1967-80, Nat. Translation Ctr., Austin, Tex., 1965-68, Ballantine Books, N.Y.C., 1985, Princeton U. Press, 1965; presenter papers at lit. confs. Author: Reading and Writing Chinese, 1979, rev. edit., 1999, Pound's Usura and the Islamic Concept of Riba, 1996; co-translator: Poem Without a Hero and Selected Poems of Anna Akhmatova, 1989, As Though Dreaming: The Tz'u...of Li Ch'ing-chao, 1977, A Gold Orchid: The Love Poems of Tzu Yeh, 1972; editor, translator: Light from the East, 1978, The Confucian Vision, 1974, The Book of Songs, 1971, The Taoist Vision, 1971, Guerilla War, 1971; contbr. articles to profl. publs., translations to various lit. mags.; editor-in-chief: City Univ. Bull., 1995-98; mem. editl. bd. City Univ. Press, 1996-98. Woodrow Wilson Found. fellow, 1961-62; modern fgn. lang. fellow, NDEA, 1962-65; grantee, Nat. Translation Ctr., Austin, 1967, Gt. Lakes Colls. Assn., Ann Arbor, 1965, 67-68, Asia Soc., N.Y.C., 1971-72, 74; Fulbright fellow, 1968-69. Avocations: sailing, music, venetian culture and history. Home and Office: Flat 20C Block 26 Baguio Villa 555 Victoria Pokfulam Hong Kong Office Phone: 852 2776 1426.

MCNAUGHTON, WILLIAM JOHN, retired bishop; b. Lawrence, Mass., Dec. 7, 1926; s. William John Sr. and Ruth Irene (Howe) McN. BA, U. of State of N.Y., Ossining, 1948, B of Sacred Theology, 1953; M in Religious Edn., Maryknoll Sem., Ossining, 1953. Ordained Maryknoll priest, 1953; cert. in Korean Lang. Studies, Yale U., 1954. Pastor Pouk Moun Ro Cath. Ch., Chong Ju Diocese, Korea, 1955-57, Nae Duk Dong Cath. Ch., Chong Ju Diocese, Korea, 1957-60; consultor Chong Ju Diocese, 1958-59, vicar gen., 1959-60; consecrated bishop Inchon (Korea) Diocese, 1961—2002, ret., 2002. Roman Catholic. Address: 39 Woodburn Dr Methuen MA 01844-2812

MCNAY, JOHN T. humanities educator; b. Butte, Mont., June 6, 1957; s. Mary McEachern and John T. McNay. BA in Journalism, U. Mont., 1980, MA in History, 1991; PhD in History, Temple U., 1997. Editor Livingston (Mont.) Enterprise, Livingston, 1980—81, Anaconda (Mont.) Leader, 1981—82; night editor Idaho Falls (Idaho) Post-Register, 1982; reporter Mont. Std., Butte, 1982—90; vis. asst. prof. history Cheyney U., Phila., 1997—98, Shippensburg (Pa.) U., 1998—2000; asst. prof. history U. Cin. Raymond Walters Coll., 2000—. Author: Acheson and Empire: The British Accent in American Foreign Policy. Mem.: Soc. Historians Am. Fgn. Rels., Am. Hist. Assn. Roman Catholic. Avocation: travel. Home: 6248 Cortelyou Ave Apt 4 Cincinnati OH 45213 Office: Univ Cin 9555 Plainfield Rd Cincinnati OH 45236 Business E-Mail: john.mcnay@uc.edu.

MCNEAL, BETTY JEAN, librarian, writer; b. Houston, Pa., July 31, 1932; d. Eugene and Lyda Harper Dent; m. James W McNeal, Apr. 12, 1982; m. Coleman Lewis, June 5, 1958 (div.); 1 child, John Elliott Lewis. BS in Edn., Cheyney State Tchrs. Coll., 1955; MLS, We. Mich. U., 1976; JD, Cleve. State U., 1966. Bar: Ohio 1967. Tchr. Youngstown Pub. Schs., Ohio, 1955—58, Cleve. Pub. Schs., 1958—61; libr. Wash. State U., Pullman, 1976—84; dir. pub. svcs. Gonzaga U. Law Libr., Spokane, Wash., 1984—86; dir. Nev. State

Data Ctr., Carson City, 1988—94; dir. info. svcs. Internat. Gaming Inst. U. Nev., Las Vegas, 1997—. Author: Amazing Plan for Total Success, 2000. Trustee East Cleve. Pub. Libr., 1970—71. Recipient Excellence in Jurisprudence, Lawyers Coop. Pub. Co.; Thurgood Marshall fellow, We. Mich. U., 1975—76. Mem.: Thoreau Soc. Achievements include design of Truth/Character/Wealth Power Plan for life renewal. Office: University of Nevada Las Vegas 4505 Maryland Parkway Las Vegas NV 89154

MCNEAL, DALE WILLIAM, JR., biological sciences educator; b. Kansas City, Kans., Nov. 23, 1939; s. Dale William and Geraldine Estelle (Reed) McNeal; m. Arlene Joyce Purvis, Feb. 26, 1966. BA, Colo. Coll., 1962; MS, SUNY Coll. Environ. Sci. and Forestry, Syracuse, 1964; PhD, Wash. State U., 1969. Asst. prof. dept. biol. scis. U. Pacific, Stockton, Calif., 1969-74, assoc. prof., 1974-79, prof., 1979—2002, chmn. dept., 1978-84, prof. emeritus, 2002—. Contbr. articles to profl. jours. Served with U.S. Army, 1964—66. Mem.: Calif. Acad. Scis., Internat. Soc. Plant Taxonomy, Am. Soc. Plant Taxonomists, Calif. Bot. Soc. (pres. 1987—88), Am. Bot. Soc., Sigma Xi. Republican. Episcopalian. Office: U Pacific Dept Biol Scis Stockton CA 95211-0001 Office Phone: 209-946-3019. Business E-Mail: dmcneal@pacific.edu.

MCNEAL, LYLE GLEN, science educator, rancher, consultant; b. Glendale, Calif., May 16, 1942; s. Darrell Glenn and Elizabeth Bessie McNeal; m. Nancy Coles Wilkie, Aug. 10, 1962; children: Tamara A., Sean E., Joshua M., Travis G., Susannah R., Jenny L., Ian B., Ilene L. BS in Animal Husbandry, Cal Poly Coll., 1964; MS in Animal Breeding, U. Nev., 1966; PhD in Reproductive Physiology, Utah State U., 1978. Shepherd Cal Poly Coll., Pomona, 1962—64; prof. animal sci. Cal Poly State U., San Luis Obispo, Calif., 1969—79; grad. rsch. asst. U. Nev., Reno, 1964—66, extension agt. Minden, 1966—69; rsch. scientist U.S. Sheep Experiment Sta., Dubois, Idaho, 1972—77; founder, exec. dir. Navajo Sheep Project, Logan, Utah, 1977—2002; prof. animal sci. Utah State U., Logan, 1979—. Ranch hand Bar Lazy B Ranch, Ronan, Mont., 1959—61; asst. ranch mgr. Hidden Trails Ranch, Agoura, Calif., 1960—61; Arabian horse showman Kellogg Arabian Horse Ranch, Pomona. Author: Small Ruminant Production Medicine, 2002; contbr. chapters to books. 1st lt. USAF, 1959—61, Norton AFB. Named Tchr. of Yr, U.S.D.A., 1969—94; recipient award, NHL, 1994, Nat. Camptender award, Am. Sheep Industry Assn. Mem.: Am. Livestock Breeds Conservancy (Conservation Breeder of Yr. 1996), Soc. Range Mgmt., Am. Soc. Animal Sci. (mem. tchg. com. 1972—77, Nat. Tchr. of Yr. 1996), Am. Sheep Ctr. (mem. founding bd. 1999—), Navajo-Churro Sheep Assn. (life; hon. 1986—), Dine' be'iina (life; hon. 1991—). Achievements include rescued from extinction the first domestic sheep brought to North America by the Spanish conquistadores; saved and bred back this famous Navajo-Churro sheep for the benefit of Navajo and Hispanic cultures, 1977-2002. Avocations: horseback riding, fly fishing, piloting aircraft, history, reading. Home: 85 Quarter Circle Dr Nibley UT 84321 Office: Animal & Vet Dept Utah State U 4815 Old Main Hill Logan UT 84322-4815 E-mail: sheepman@cc.usu.edu.

MCNEALEY, J. JEFFREY, lawyer, corporate executive; b. Cin., Feb. 8, 1944; s. J. Lawrence and Louise McNealey; m. Sara Wilson, Sept. 24, 1988; children: Anne Elizabeth, John Alexander. BA, Cornell U., 1966; JD, Ohio State U., 1969. Ptnr. Porter, Wright, Morris & Arthur, Columbus, Ohio, 1969—. Bd. dirs. TRC Cos., Windsor, Conn., 1985—; sec., bd. dirs. The Smoot Corp., Columbus, 1972—. Trustee Columbus Cancer Clinic, 1972—, past pres.; trustee German Village Soc., Columbus, 1986—, past pres.; bd. dirs. Columbus chpt. ARC, 1983-86, Columbus Urban League, 1984-90; active Union League Chgo., 1981—, Columbus/Dresden Sister City, Inc., 1996—; mem. vestry Trinity Episcopal Ch., 2000—. Mem. ABA, Ohio State Bar Assn. (past chmn. environ. com. 1978-84), Columbus Bar Assn., Columbus Country Club, Capital Club of Columbus, Cornell Club of Ctrl. Ohio (trustee 1978—, past pres.). Episcopalian. Avocations: flying, racquet sports, wood working, flyfishing. Office: Porter Wright Morris & Arthur 41 S High St Ste 30 Columbus OH 43215-6101

MCNEALY, SCOTT G. computer company executive; b. 1954; BA, Harvard U., 1976; MBA, Stanford U., 1980. With Rockwell Internat. Corp., Troy, Mich., 1976-78, sales engr.; staff engr. FMC Corp., Chgo., 1980-81; dir. ops. Onyx Systems, San Jose, Calif., 1981-82; co-founder Sun Microsystems Inc., Santa Clara, Calif., 1982, chmn. bd., pres., CEO, 1984—, also bd. dirs., 1985. Avocation: ameteur hockey player. Office: Sun Microsystems Inc 4150 Network Cir Santa Clara CA 95054*

MCNEELY, CAROL J. dentist; b. Chgo., July 17, 1954; d. Lewis W. and Jessie O. (Woodfin) McN.; divorced; 1 child, Matthew. Student, U. Chgo., 1972-74; DDS, U. Ill., Chgo., 1979; cert. in cosmetic dentistry, Case Western Res. U.; M of Mgmt., Northwestern U., 1995. Cert. cosmetic dentistry, 1993. Pvt. practice, Chgo., 1979—; pres. HealthS.M.A.R.T. Strategies, 1995—. Ptnr. Provident Dental Assocs., Chgo., 1983-85; owner Soulful Expressions, Chgo., 1987—; dental cons. Dental Network Am., Oakbrook Terrace, Ill., 1988-92. Mem. assoc. bd. dirs. Chgo. Child Care Soc., 1982-85; mem. scholarship fund com. Chgo. Urban League, 1989. Recipient Ptnrs. in Community award Nat. Bar Assn., 1985. Mem. ADA (task force on women and minorities 1992-93), Acad. Cosmetic Dentistry, Am. Assn. Dental Cons., Nat. Dental Assn., Chgo. Assn. Black Women Dentists (pres. 1992-94), U. Chgo. Alumni Assn. (minority mentor program). E-mail: there4Vcoach@aol.com.

MCNEELY, JAMES LEE, lawyer; b. Shelbyville, Ind., May 4, 1940; s. Carl R. and Elizabeth J. (Orebaugh) McN.; m. Rose M. Wisker, Sept. 5, 1977; children: Angela, Susan, Meg, Matt. AB, Wabash Coll., 1962; JD, Ind. U., 1965. Bar: Ind. 1965, U.S. Dist. Ct. (so. dist.) Ind. 1965, U.S. Ct. Appeals (7th cir.) 1970. Assoc. Pell & Matchett, Shelbyville, 1965-70; ptnr. Matchett & McNeely, Shelbyville, 1970-74; sole practice Shelbyville, 1974-76; sr. ptnr. McNeely & Sanders, Shelbyville, 1976-86, McNeely, Sanders & Stephenson, Shelbyville, 1986-89, McNeely, Sanders, Stephenson & Thopy, Shelbyville, 1989-96, McNeely, Stephenson, Thopy & Harrold, Shelbyville, 1997—. Guest lectr. Franklin Coll., Ind., 1965-72; judge Shelbyville City Ct., 1967-71. Chmn. Shelbyville County Rep. Cen. Com., 1968-88; bd. dirs. Ind. Lung Assn., 1972-75, Crossroads Council Boy Scouts Am., 1982; bd. dirs., pres. Shelbyville Girls Club. Named Sagamore of the Wabash, Gov. Ed Whitcomb, 1971, Gov. Otis Bowen, 1977, Gov. Robert Orr, 1986, 88, Gov. Evan Bayh, 1996, Gov. Frank O'Bannon, 1999. Fellow Ind. Bar Found. (patron, sec. 1999-2000, chair elect 2000-01, chmn. 2002-03); mem. ABA, Ind. Bar Assn. (sec. 1985-87, bd. dirs. 1976-78, chair-elect Ho. Dels. 1994-95, chair 1995-96, v.p. 1996-97, pres.-elect 1997-98, pres. 1998-99), Shelby County Bar Assn. (pres. 1975), Ind. Lawyers Commn. (pres., dir.), Fed. Merit Selection Commn. (adv. mem. 1988-92, chmn. 2001—), Shelbyville Jaycees (Distinguished Service award 1969, Good Govt. award 1970), Wabash Coll. Nat. Assn. Wabash Men (dir. 1983-89, sec. 1989-91, v.p. 1991-93, pres. 1993-95, Man of Yr. 1995), Kappa Sigma Alpha Pi chpt. (Hall of Fame 1995). Lodges: Lions, Elks, Eagles. Methodist. Avocations: golf, travel. Home: 1902 E Old Rushville Rd Shelbyville IN 46176-9569

MCNEELY, JOHN J. lawyer; b. Mpls., Oct. 8, 1931; s. John J. Sr. and Mae (Carlin) McN.; children: Mary Ann, John J. Jr., Michael F., Patricia C., David C. BS, Georgetown U., 1955, JD, 1958. Bar: Minn. 1958. Law clk. Minn. Supreme Ct., St. Paul, 1958-59; ptnr. Briggs & Morgan, St. Paul, 1959—. Sgt. USMC, 1950-52. Fellow Am. Coll. Trust and Estate Counsel; mem. ABA, Minn. State Bar Assn., Ramsey County Bar Assn., Mendakota Country Club. Home: 1183 Ivy Hill Dr Saint Paul MN 55118-1827 Office Phone: 651-808-6576.

MCNEELY, MARK, marketing professional, journalist; Grad. in journalism, U. Tenn., 1970. Reporter The Knoxville Jour., The Commerical Appeal, The Knoxville Jour., Knoxille News-Sentinel; pvt. practice as sr. ptnr., 1987—. Served in key staff and and campaign roles U.S. Senator Al Gore, Jr., former U.S. Senator Jim Sasser, and former Nashville Mayor Richard Fulton, Tenn. Supreme Ct. Office: 611 Commerce St Ste 2800 Nashville TN 37203 Business E-Mail: mmcneely@mpf.com.

MCNEIL, BARBARA JOYCE, radiologist, educator; b. Cambridge, Mass., Feb. 11, 1941; d. Archibald Pius and Katherine (Joyce) McNeil. AB, Emmanuel Coll., 1962; MD, Harvard U., 1966, PhD, 1972. Diplomate Am. Bd. Nuc. Medicine. Intern Mass. Gen. Hosp., Boston, 1966—67, resident in nuclear medicine, 1971—73; prof. radiology and clin. epidemiology Harvard Med. Sch. and Brigham & Women's Hosp., Boston, 1983—, dir. ctr. for cost effective care, 1980—93; chmn. dept., Ridley Watts prof. health care policy Harvard Med. Sch., 1988—. Chmn. Blue Cross-Mass. Hosp. Assn. Fund for Coop. Innovation, 1981—87; mem. Prospective Payment Assessment Commn., 1983—91; mem. nat. adv. coun. Agy. for Health Care Policy, Rsch. and Evaluation, 1991—96. Editor: Critical Issues in Medical Technology, 1982; contbr. articles to profl. jours. Fellow: AAAS, Am. Coll. Nuc. Physicians (Presdl. award 1995); mem.: Soc. Nuc. Medicine, Am. Coll. Radiology, Inst. Medicine (coun. 1991—), Am. Acad. Arts and Scis. Office: Harvard Med Sch Dept Health Care Policy 180 Longwood Ave Rm 202-A Boston MA 02115-5821

MCNEIL, EDWARD WARREN, real estate company executive; b. Alhambra, Calif., Jan. 5, 1942; s. Murray Charles and Helen Katherine (Curtis) McN.; m. Jutta Bocking, Apr. 1, 1941; children: Anja Britt, Bradley Stuart. Student, U. Calif., Berkeley, 1960-63. Structures engr. Peter Kiewit Sons Co., various cities, Calif., 1961-63; project engr. Huntington Harbour, Sunset Beach, Calif., 1963-64; project supt. Coordinated Realty, Inc., Anaheim, Calif., 1964-65; field ops. mgr. Lear Siegler, Saigon, Vietnam, 1965-67; project engr. Constructora Emkay, Rio Blanco, Chile, 1968-69; ptnr. The Pyramid Cos., Syracuse, N.Y., 1969-75, The Pioneer Group, Syracuse, 1975-95, ret., 1995. Past chmn., bd. dirs. Crouse Irving Meml. Hosp. Found., Syracuse, 1986—; trustee, past vice-chmn. Everson Mus. Art, Syracuse, 1981—94; past chmn., vice-chmn., bd. dirs. Syracuse Stage, 1981—93; chmn. Adirondack chpt. Nature Conservancy, 1994—2001, trustee, 2002—, trustee N.Y. state bd., 1998—; trustee Adirondack Land Trust, 1990—2002, chmn., 1994—2001; trustee Manlius Pebble Hill Sch., 1984—86, 1994—99, emeritus, 1999—; vol. pilot Nature Conservancy, No. Wings. Recipient award for svc. to the arts, Cultural Resource Coun., Syracuse, 1987. Mem. Seaplane Pilots Assn., Slocum Soc., Lake Amphibian Flyers Club, Warbirds of Am., No. Lake Flyers Club. Avocations: ocean sailing, canoeing, fly fishing, seaplane flying, aerobatics. Home: PO Box 845 Eagle Lake FL 33839-0845

MCNEIL, HELEN JO CONNOLLY, nursing educator, public health administrator; b. Olympia, Wash., June 15, 1925; d. James Ambrose and Corinne Marie (Bordeaux) Connolly; m. Robert Phillip McNeil, Aug. 16, 1947; children: Sheryl Ann Andrews, Robert John, Maureen Connolly McNeil, Kevin Charles. BSN, Seattle Coll., 1947; MSN, U. Wash., 1961, postgrad., 1974-80. RN Wash., S.C., Tex., Va., cert. pub. health nurse, 1962. Clinic nurse Schutt Clinic, Bremerton, Wash., 1947-49; staff nurse Providence Hosp., Seattle, 1950-60, Overlake Hosp., Bellevue, Wash., 1961-62; pub. health nurse Seattle King County Health Dept. and Vis. Nurse Svc., 1962-64, pub. health nurse supr., 1964-65, assoc. dir. pub. health nursing and vis. nurse svc., 1965-70, health planning and evaluation specialist, 1970-73, adminstr. S.E. dist., 1973-78, adminstr. Ctrl. dist., 1979-81, adminstr. N. dist., 1981-84, dir. nursing rsch., 1984-85; lectr. Sch. Nursing U. Wash., Seattle, 1985-87; mem. faculty S. Puget Sound C.C., Olympia, 1987-88; vis. faculty Sch. Nursing Clemson (S.C.) U., 1988; instr. coll. nursing allied health U. Tex., El Paso, 1988-90; dir. pub. health nursing Commonwealth Va., Richmond, 1990-93; lectr. Sch. Nursing Seattle U., 1995; cons. Seattle, Seaview, Wash., 1995—. Mem. panel in nursing edn. Am. Assn. Colls. of Nursing, 1985—87; adj. assoc. prof. Sch. Pub. Health U. N.C., Chapel Hill, 1980—92; adj. asst. prof. U. Wash. Sch. Nursing, 1965—85; rev. com. nursing census USPHS, 1970—72; health care cons., 1976; lectr. Congress on Nutrition, Rio de Janeiro, 1978. Author: Feasting on a Moveable Island, 1980, Reaching Out, 1998; contbr. articles to profl. jours., chpts. to books. Mem. task force Seattle Health Policy, 1981, Seattle 2000 Commn., 1973; lectr. Internat. Congress Social Psychiatry, Athens, 1974; with Project Hope Internat. Approaches in Health Care of Elderly, Milwood, Va., 1983, 84; co-project dir. occupl. health con. edn. for cmty. nurses divsn. nursing U. Wash., 1983-86; mem. ARC Disater Team, Seattle, 1995-97, Parent and Home Health Bd., Richmond, Va., 1990-93; vol. Red Cross, 1994-97. With U.S. cadet nursing corps USPHS, 1943-47. Stress Rsch. grantee Heath Resources Adminstrn., 1974; W. K. Kellog Found. grantee U. Tex., El Paso, 1990, grantee U. Wash., 1983-86; recipient Nursing Adminstrn. recognition award Jour. Nursing Adminstrn., 1993. Fellow: APHA (nursing sect. pres. 1992—93, Ruth B. Freeman Disting. Career award 1998); mem.: Assn. State and Territorial Dirs. Nursing (emeritus 1990—), Seattle Mgmt. Assn. (pres. 1976, Disting. Adminstrv. Svc. award City of Seattle 1976), Wash. State Pub. Health Assn. (pres. 1976—77, Adminstrv. Svc. award 1975), Assn. Cmty. Health Nurse Educators (founder, pres. 1985), Seattle U. Alumni (mem. nursing adv. bd. 1993—96, Cmty. Svc. Alumni award 1992), Alpha Tau Delta, Sigma Theta Tau (internat. rsch. conf. Seoul, South Korea 1984). Avocations: gardening, travel, writing, cooking, paddocks for six houses. Home and Office: PO Box 173 Seaview WA 98644-0173 Office Phone: 360-642-4958.

MCNEIL, LORI MICHELLE, professional tennis player; b. San Diego, Dec. 18, 1963; d. Charlie and Dorothy Mc. Student, Okla. State U., 1981-83. 9th ranked woman USTA, 1988, ranked 101st, 1999; winner mixed doubles (with Jorge Lozano) French Open, 1988. Achievements include Pro Tour Singles titles such as Colorado Classic, 1992, Japan Open, 1992; DFS Classic Internat. Singles Title, 1993, 94; DFS Classic Internat. Doubles Title, (with Rennae Stubbs), 1992, (with Martina Navratilova), 1993. Office: US Tennis Assn 70 W Red Oak Ln White Plains NY 10604-3602*

MCNEIL, PAUL JOSEPH, JR., employment security interviewer; b. Winthrop, Mass., Oct. 11, 1941; s. Paul Joseph Sr. and Helen Margaret (Carr) McN. Cert. in ins., U. R.I., 1965; cert. in travel agts., Travel Sch. of Am., 1968; cert., Labor Sch. of Boston, 1976, Labor Studies Inst., 1989. Field investigator R.I. Food Stamp Unit, Providence, 1965-68; cmty. rels. Coordinator Ecology Action for Rhode Island, 1970-71; sec. and rsch. asst. R.I. Worker Assn., 1973-74; enumerator R.I. Polk & Co., Providence, 1970-83; sr. employment security interviewer R.I. Dept. Employment Tng., Providence, 1984-96; sr. employment & tng. interviewer R.I. Dept. Labor & Tng., Providence, 1996—. Rec. sec. Local 189 New Eng. chpt., Boston, 1973-76, treas., 1989—; mem. bd. dirs. of R.I. Workers Assn., 1973-74, 75-76, census enumerator U.S. Census Bur., Providence, 1990; mail handler U.S. Post Office, Providence, 1980; claims interviewer R.I. Dept. Employment Security, Providence, 1979-84; rec. sec. R.I. Employment Security Alliance, Providence, 1980-90; v.p. Community Econs. Edn. Ctr., Providence, 1988-91. Exec. com. R.I. State Employees Assn., 1966-68, Community Labor Organizing Com., Providence, 1983-89, Sane Freeze, Washington, 1989-90; shop steward Local 401 SEIU, Providence, 1990-92, 1st v.p., 1992-96; rec. sec. R.I. Sane Freeze, Providence, 1988-94; mem. Nat. Com. Peace Action, 1993—; v.p. Peace Action R.I., 1994-95, pres., 1995—; coord. R.I. Nation Readers Group, 1995—; state committeeman Amvets Dept. R.I., 1965-69, 96—, adj. posts, 1965-68, trustee post 6, 1995-96; v.p. Labor Party R.I., 1994-97, treas., 1997—, pres., 1999, chmn., 1999; exec. bd. R.I. Coalition for Consumer Justice, 1997—; bd. dirs. Injured Workers R.I., 1996—, Warwick Cmty. Action, 1967-69, R.I. Legal Svcs., 1967-69; founder East Greenwich Dem. Youth Club, 1959; co-chmn. Human Rights Action Coun., Warwick, 1968-70; del. R.I. Dem. State Conv., 1976, 78; mem. R.I. Dem. State Com., 1980-86, bd. dirs., 1985-87; mem. Dem. Study Group R.I., 1986-88; organizer United Farm Workers, 1968-71; mem. Fox Point Neighborhood Housing Corp. Dirs., 1980-87, pres., 1981-83, sec., 1983-87. With U.S. Army, 1960-63, ETO. Mem. Internat. Assn. Pers. in Employment Security (R.I. chpt. bd. dirs. 1989-93, sec. 1991-93), Greater R.I. Indsl. Rels. Rsch. Assn., R.I. ACLU (bd. dirs. 1974-80, bd. sec. 1975-77, exec. com. 1979-80), Union of Peace Profls. (exec. bd. 1988-90), Nat. Writers Union, R.I. Cen. Am. Network, Cath. Peace Fellowship, Pax ChristiAncient Order, Order of Hibernians (rec. sec. Providence chpt. 1990-91, 97-98, v.p., 1998—, pres. 1991-92, state sec. 1993-96, pres. 1996—), K. of C., Sierra Club, Newport Mus. Irish History, Am. Irish Hist. Soc., R.I. Hist. Soc., R.I. Labor History Soc., Gaspee Days Com., Americans for Dem. Action, Debs Found., Edward Bellamy Meml. Assn., R.I. Irish Famine Meml. Com., Am. Legion, Indsl. Rels. Rsch. Assn., Assn. Can.-Am., Am. French Geneal. Soc., Irish Nat. Caucus, Am. Irish Polit. Edn. Com., Friendly Sons of St. Patrick (East Greenwich, R.I.). Democrat. Avocation: writing. Home: PO Box 945 Providence RI 02901-0945

MCNEIL, RAMSEY ENGLISH, religious studies educator; b. Franklin County, Va., Sept. 28, 1937; d. George Wilson and Eva Woody English; m. Carl Nixon McNeil, June 2, 1967; 1 child, Carl Nixon. BS in Edn., Radford Coll., Va., 1958; MS in Edn., Radford U., Va., 1968. Sch. tchr. Franklin County Pub. Sch., Rocky Mount, Va., 1958—59, Danville City Pub. Sch., Danville, Va., 1959—63, Roanoke (Va.) City Sch., 1963—67, Mongomery County Sch., Christiansburg, Va., 1967—70; tchr. adult Sunday sch. local chs., Va., 1966—2003, tchr. Bible quiz, 1978—89, tchr. Wed. A.M. women's Bible study, 1998—. Den mother Boy Scouts Am., Christiansburg, 1978—80; sec. bd. dirs. Montgomery Mus., Christiansburg, Va., 1995—2003; sch. vol. Mongomery County, Va., 1976—91; foster parent, 1976—86. Mem.: United Daus. Confederacy (pres. 1974—99, 1st dist. chair 1997—99, v.p. 1999—2003, 1st dist. chair 2003—, org. new chptrs. chair 1999—2003), Ea. Star (pianist 1989—96, chaplain 1998—2003). Republican. Baptist. Avocations: reading, antiques, flowers, travel. Home: 5234 Old Pagelyn Rd Radford VA 24141-6518

MCNEIL, ROBERT G. biotechnology company executive; PhD in Molecular Biology, Biochemistry and Genetics, U. Calif., Irvine. Gen. ptnr. Sanderling Venture Ptnrs., 1979—; dir. ISTA Pharms., Inc., Irvine, Calif., 1993—, chmn. bd., 1995—. Mailing: ISTA Pharmaceuticals 15279 Alton Pkwy Bldg 100 Irvine CA 92618-1

MCNEIL, ROBERT L., JR., marketing professional; b. Chgo., Oct. 3, 1969; s. Robert L. Sr. and Yvonne McNeil; m. Stacey R. McNeil. Founder, pres. Images USA, Atlanta, 1989—. Mem. Am. Mktg. Assn., Atlanta Ad Club, Ga. Minority Supplier Devel. Coun. Office: Images USA 914 Howell Mill Rd NW #300 Atlanta GA 30316-5546

MCNEILL, CORBIN ASAHEL, JR., utilities executive; b. Santa Fe, July 6, 1939; s. Corbin Asahel and Madeline (Thielen) McN.; m. Dorice Schiller, June 16, 1962; children: Michele, Corbin IV, Kevin, Alicia, Timothy. BS in Marine Engrng., U.S. Naval Acad., 1962; postgrad., Naval Nuclear Power Sch., Mare Island, Md., 1962-63, U. Calif., Berkeley, 1975-76, Syracuse U., 1983-84. Commd. ensign USN, 1962, advanced through grades to comdr., 1981, ret., 1981; sr. v.p. nuclear generation N.Y. Power Authority, White Plains, 1981-85, Pub. Service Electric & Gas Co., Hancocks Bridge, N.J., 1985-88; exec. v.p. nuclear div. PECO Energy Co., 1988-90; pres., COO Phila. Electric Co., 1990-95, pres., CEO, 1995—, also chmn., 1997—. Pres. Adwin Equipment Co., Phila., 1990—. Trustee The Meml. Hosp. of Salem County (N.J.) Inc., 1986; chmn. TeamWalk March of Dimes, Salem, 1986; bd. dirs. Oswego (N.Y.) C. of C., 1982-83. Mem. Am. Nuclear Soc., Nuclear Utility Mgmt. and Resources Com. Avocations: skiing, reading. Office: PECO Energy Co PO Box 8699 2301 Market St Philadelphia PA 19101

MCNEILL, DAN K. military career officer; b. N.C., July 23, 1946; m. Maureen McNeill; 1 child, Dan. BS in Agr. and Forestry, NC State U., 1968; grad., US Army War Coll., 1989; attended, Inf. Officer Basic and Advanced Cources, US Army Command and Gen. Staff Coll.; degree (hon.), NC State U., 2003. Commd. 2nd lt. US Army, 1968, sr. aide-de-camp to commdg. gen., 1st Inf. Divsn. (mechanized), 1971—72, fixed wing avaitor, later asst. ops. officer, later ops. officer, 55th Aviation Co., 52d Aviation Bn., Korea, 1972—73, asst. S-3 (ops.) (air), 2d Bn. (airborne), 505th Inf., 82 Airborne Divsn., 1974, commdr., combat support co., 2d Bn. (airborne), 505th Inf., 82 Airborne Divsn., 1974—76, commdr., E Co., 2d Bn. (Airborne) 505th Inf., 82d Airborne Divsn., 1977—78, sec. to gen. staff, US Army So, European Vicenza, Italy, 1984—85, exec. officer, 1st Bn., 509th Inf., later renamed 4th Bn., 325th Inf., 1982—84, commdr.,1st Bn., 325th Inf., 82d Airborne Divsn. Fort Bragg, NC, 1986—88, asst. chief of staff, G-3 (Ops.), 82d Airborne Divsn., Operation Just Cause, Panama and Operation Desert Shield/Storm, Saudi Arabia, 1989—91, commdr., 3d Brigade, 82d Airborne Corps, 1991—93, asst. S-3 (Ops.), later S-3 (Ops.), 3d Brigade, 82d Airborne Divsn., 1976—77, asst. chief of state, G-3 (Ops.), XVIII Airboboure Coprs., 1993—95, asst. divsn. commdr., 2d Inf. Divsn. Korea, 1995—96, chief of staff, XVIII Airborne Corp., 1996—97, dep. commdg. gen., I Corps and Fort Lewis, commdg. gen. 82d Airborne Divsn., 1998—2000, commdg. gen., combined joint task force-180, 2000—, commdg. gen., XVIII Airborne Corps and Fort Bragg, NC, 2000—; dep. commdg. gen., chief of staff US Army Forces Command, Fort McPherson, Ga. Asst. prof. mil. sci., first reserve officer tng. corps region Ga. Mil. Coll., Milledgeville, Ga., 1978—80; doctrine author, dept. tactics US Army Command and Gen. Staff Coll., Fort Leavenworth, Kans., 1981—82. Decorated Defense Superior Svc. medal, Legion of Merit wirh 2 Oak clusters, Bronze Star medal with 2 oak leaf clusters, Meritorious Svc. medal with 3 Oak Clusters, Army Commendation medal with 2 Oak Leaf Clusters, Army Achievement medal, Expert Infantryman badge, Army Avaitor badge, Master Parachutist badge with Bronze star, Spl. Forces Tab. Office: 82nd Airborne Divsn Fort Bragg NC 28307*

MCNEILL, DANIEL RICHARD, writer; b. San Francisco, June 1, 1947; s. Daniel Harry and Maureen Evangeline (Sherriff) McN.; m. Rosalind Deborah Gold, Dec. 20, 1984. AB, U. Calif., Berkeley, 1975; JD, Harvard U., 1982. Author: Fuzzy Logic, 1993 (L.A. Times Book prize in sci. and tech. 1993), The Face, 1998. Mem. Authors Guild. Avocations: photography, bodybuilding. Home and Office: 8110 Redlands St #306 Playa Del Rey CA 90293

MCNEILL, FELITA GALE, nurse, military officer; b. Tampa, Fla., Aug. 4, 1956; d. Claude and Violet Branton; m. Charles McNeill (div. June 1996); children: Malikah Dawkins Daffin, Kahlilah L Dawkins, Rashad Dawkins. BSN, U. of So. Fla., 1990; M in edn., 2000; EdS, U. Sarasota, 2002; student, Argosy U. Reistered nurse Manatee County Health Dept., Bradenton, Fla., 1991—94; sch. nurse Pinellas County Health Dept., St. Petersburg, 1992—94; LPN instr. Pinellas County Sch. Bd., St. Petersburg, 1994—2001, CNA instr., 1994—2001, sci. tchr., 1994—2001; faculty/rsch. instr. U. of So. Fla., Tampa, 2002—; capt./instr. U.S. Army Res., Jacksonville, Fla., 1990—. Major USAR, 1990—, St. Petersburg. Office: Felita Gale McNeill Fine Arts Studio 1600 4th St S Saint Petersburg FL 33712 Home: 3285 40th Way S Apt C Saint Petersburg FL 33711-3993

MCNEILL, G. DAVID, psycholinguist, educator; b. Santa Rosa, Calif., Dec. 21, 1931; s. Glenn H. and Ethel G. (Little) McN.; m. Nobuko Baba, Dec. 17, 1957; children: Cheryl, Randall L.B. AB, U. Calif. at Berkeley, 1953, PhD, 1962. Research fellow Harvard U., 1962-65; asst. prof. psychology U. Mich., 1965-66, assoc. prof., 1966-68; prof. psychology and linguistics U. Chgo., 1969—2001, chmn. dept. psychology, 1991-97, prof. emeritus, 2001—. Vis. fellow Ctr. for Humanities, Wesleyan U., Middletown, Conn., 1970; mem. Inst. Advanced Study, Princeton, 1973-75; fellow Netherlands Inst. for Advanced Studies, 1983-84; visitor Max Planck Inst. for Psycholinguistics, Nijmegen, Germany, 1998-99. Author: The Acquisition of Language, 1970, The Conceptual Basis of Language, 1979, Psycholinguistics: A New Approach, 1987, Gengo Shinrigaku, 1991, Hand and Mind: What Gestures Reveal about Thought, 1992; editor: Language and Gesture, 2000. Recipient Faculty Achievement award, 1991, Ann. Excellence in Pub. award Assn. Am. Pubs., Gordon G. Laing prize U. Chgo. Press, 1995; Guggenheim fellow, 1973-74; grantee NSF, 1983-89, 97—, Spencer Found., 1979-82, 89-92, 95-99, NIDCD, 1992-96, Advanced Rsch. and Devel. Agy., 2003—. Fellow AAAS, Am. Psychol. Soc.; mem. Internat. Soc. Gesture Studies (v.p. 2002—), Cognitive Sci. Soc., Linguistic Soc. Am., Violoncello Soc., Phi Beta Kappa, Sigma Xi. Office: U Chgo Dept Psychology 5848 S University Ave Chicago IL 60637-1515 E-mail: dmcneill@uchicago.edu.

MCNEILL, HOLLY MARY, theater educator, scriptwriter; b. Chgo., Nov. 29, 1961; d. Marlin Hendrick and Dorothy Lou Brown; m. Mark Allen McNeill, Dec. 30, 1984; 1 child, Mary Brown. BA in Speech and Theatre, Rowan U., 1985; MA in Curriculum and Edn., Concordia U., 1998. Substitute tchr. Highland & Sterling H.S., Lindenwold, NJ, 1988—89; youth choir dir.

Somerdale (N.J.) Presbyn. Ch., 1988—90; theatre tchr., dir. Larkin H.S., Elgin, Ill., 1998—2004. Singer, dancer: Kaliedosope, 1981—83; singer, actress: Rass Malazz, 1983; actor: Guys & Dolls, 1983, La Cageaux Folles, 1988; dir.: The Music Man, 2001—03, Bye, Bye Birdie, 2001—03, You're A Good Man, Charlie Brown, 2004. Fellow: Am. Fed. Tchrs. TV and Radio, Nat. Edn. Assn., Actor's Equity Assn. Methodist. Avocations: music, theater. Office: Larkin High Sch 1475 Larkin Ave Elgin IL 60123 Office Fax: 847-888-6996. Personal E-mail: hmcneill@aol.com.

MCNEILL, JOHN HUGH, pharmaceutical sciences educator; b. Chgo., Dec. 5, 1938; s. John and Agnes Margaret (McLean) McN.; m. Sharon Keneffly, July 27, 1963; children: Sandra, Laurie. BS, U. Alta., Can., 1960, MS, 1962; PhD, U. Mich., 1967. Lectr. pharmacy Dalhousie U., 1962-63, U. Alta., 1963; research assoc. U. Mich., Ann Arbor, 1963-65, teaching fellow, 1965-66; asst. instr. Mich. State U., East Lansing, 1966-67, asst. prof., 1967-71; assoc. prof. U. B.C., 1971-72, assoc. prof., chmn. div. pharmacology and toxicology, 1972-75, dir. rsch. and grad. studies Faculty Pharm. Scis., 1977-78, prof. Faculty Pharm. Scis., 1975—2004, dean Faculty Pharm. Scis., 1985-96, asst. dean, 1978-81, Med. Rsch. Coun. rsch. prof., 1981-82, prof., assoc. dean rsch. and grad. studies, 1982-84, prof. and dean emeritus, 2004—. Contbr. more than 800 tech. articles to profl. jours. Fellow Royal Soc. Can., Internat. Acad. Cardiovasc. Scis.; mem. Pharm. Soc. Can. (various coms. 1974-88, coun. 1977-83, v.p. 1979, pres. 1980-81), Am. Soc. for Pharm. and Therapeutics (J.J. Abel award com. 1981, Upjohn award com., 1978-80, chmn. mem. com. 1983-86), Western Pharm. Soc. (coun. 1977-81, pres. 1979-80, past pres. 1980-81), N.Y. Acad. Scis., Internat. Soc. for Heart Rsch. (coun. 1986-95), AAAS, B.C. Coll. Pharms. (coun. 1985-96), Internat. Union Pharmacologists (Can. rep. 1982-88), Am. Pharm. Assn. Office: Univ BC Fac Pharm Scis 2146 East Mall Vancouver BC Canada V6T 1Z3 Office Phone: 604-822-9373. E-mail: jmcneill@interchange.ubc.ca.

MCNEILL, PAUL DEANE, lawyer; b. Little Rock, Aug. 31, 1954; s. Charles Adrian and Erma (Rife) McN.; 1 child, Hallie Susanne. BBA, U. Ark., 1976; JD with high honors, 1979. Bar: Ark. 1979, U.S. Dist. Ct. (ea. dist.) Ark. 1979, U.S. Ct. Appeals (8th cir.) 1987, Fed. cir., 2001. Ptnr. Barrett, Wheatley, Smith & Deacon, Jonesboro, Ark., 1979-92, Womack, Landis, Phelps, McNeill & McDaniel, Jonesboro, 1992—. Bd. dirs. N.E. Ark. Legal Svcs. Bd. dirs. United Way Jonesboro, 1986-90, Jonesboro Area Softball Assn., 1987-90, Ark. State U. Sigma Chi House Corp., 1986—; telethon v.i.p. United Cerebral Palsy, Jonesboro, 1986-90; deacon First Bapt. Ch. Named one of Best Lawyers in Am., Outstanding Lawyers in Am., Best Lawyers in Ark. Mem. ABA (litigation sect.), Am. Bd. Trial Advocates (pres. Ark. chpt. 2001), Am. Coll. Trial Lawyers, Def. Rsch. Inst., Fedn. Ins. Corp. Counsel, Million Dollar Advocates Forum, Ark. Bar Assn. (exec. coun., ho. of dels., civil procedure com. 1997-2000, chmn. legal aid com.), Ark. Def. Lawyers Assn. (program chmn. 1994, pres. 1997-98), Craighead County Bar Assn. (sec. 1984-85, pres. 2001, 1st jud. trial practice com.), Sigma Chi (life), Best Lawyers In Am., Outstanding Lawyers of Am., Coll of Masters Advocates and Barristers, Million Dollar Adovates Forum. Baptist. Avocations: golf, softball, skiing. Office: Womack Landis Phelps McNeill & McDaniel Century Ctr Madison at Washington Jonesboro AR 72401 Office Phone: 870-932-0900.

MCNEILL, ROBERT PATRICK, investment counselor; b. Chgo., Mar. 17, 1941; s. Donald Thomas and Katherine (Bennett) McN.; m. Martha Stephan, Sept. 12, 1964; children— Jennifer, Donald, Victoria, Stephan, Elizabeth BA summa cum laude (valedictorian), U. Notre Dame, 1963; M.Letters, Oxford U., 1967. Chartered investment counselor. Assoc. Stein Roe & Farnham, Chgo., 1967-72, gen. ptnr., 1972-77, sr. ptnr., 1977-86, exec. v.p., 1986-89; pres., mng. dir. Stein Roe Internat., Chgo., 1989—. Underwriting mem. Lloyds of London, 1980—; dir. Comml. Chgo. Corp.; vice chmn. bd. Hill Internat. Prodn. Co., Houston, 1982—; dir., adv. bd. Touche Remnant Investment Counselors, London, 1983—; dir. TR Worldwide Strategy Fund, Luxembourg, Konrad Adenauer Fund for European Policy Studies, Fed. Republic Germany. Voting mem., sec Ill. Rhodes Scholarship Selection Com.; voting mem. Ill. rep. Great Lakes Dist. Rhodes Scholarship Selection Com.; bd. dirs. Kennedy Sch. for Retarded Children, Palos Park, Ill., 1972—, Winnetka United Way, Ill., 1984—, Division St. YMCA, Chgo., 1972—; assoc. Rush-Presbyterian-St. Lukes Med. Ctr., Chgo., 1975—; mem. leadership com. Rush Alzheimer's Disease Ctr. Rhodes scholar, 1963 Fellow Fin. Analysts Fedn.; mem. Chgo. Council on Fgn. Relations (bd. dirs., treas. 1975—), Inst. European Studies (bd. govs., vice-chmn. 1981—), Investment Analysts Soc. Chgo. (chgo. com., com. on fgn. affairs, com. on internat. and domestic issues), Assn. for Investment Mgmt. and Rsch., Chgo. Soc. Clubs, Econ. Club of Chgo, Sunset Ridge Country (bd. dirs. Northfield, Ill., 1983—). Avocations: coin collecting; bridge; golf; skiing; art. Office Phone: 312-368-7684.

MCNEILL, THOMAS B. director, retired lawyer; b. Chgo., Oct. 28, 1934; s. Donald T. and Katherine M. (Bennett) McN.; m. Ingrid Sieder, May 11, 1963; children: Christine, Thomas, Stephanie. BA, U. Notre Dame, 1956, JD, 1958. Ptnr. Mayer, Brown, Rowe & Maw, Chgo., 1962—99. Dir. Deltona Corp., Ocala, Fla. Served to capt. JAGC USAF, 1959-62. Fellow Am. Coll. Trial Lawyers; mem. Chgo. Bar Assn., Chgo. Council Lawyers, The Lawyers Club (Chgo. chpt.). Clubs: Indian Hill (Winnetka, Ill.). Home: 2418 Iroquois Rd Wilmette IL 60091-1335 E-mail: tomingrid@aol.com.

MCNEILL, THOMAS RAY, lawyer; b. Pitts., June 2, 1952; s. Thomas William McNeill and Mary (Shiveley) Hiss; m. Patsy Lynch, June 25, 1977; children: Elizabeth, Kathleen, Thomas. BSBA, U. Fla., 1974; JD, Emory U., 1977. Bar: Ga. 1977, U.S. Dist. Ct. (no. dist.) Ga. 1977. Assoc. Powell, Goldstein, Frazer & Murphy, LLP, Atlanta, 1977-84, ptnr., 1984—, mgr. corp. dept., 1993-95, bd. ptnrs., 1998—2004, co-leader Bus. Transactions Group, 2003—. Mem. Ga. Bar Assn. (exec. com. bus. law sect., 2001—), Emory U. Alumni Assn. (pres. exec. com. 1988-89, Law Sch. coun. 1990-2000, 2003—), Soc. of Internat. Bus. Fellows, Beta Gamma Sigma. Office: Powell Goldstein Frazer & Murphy 191 Peachtree St NE Ste 1600 Atlanta GA 30303-1700 Office Phone: 404-572-6681. E-mail: tmcneill@pgfm.com.

MCNEILL, WILLIAM, environmental scientist; b. Evanston, Ill., Jan. 1, 1930; s. John and Ebba Katrina (Hansen) McN.; m. Caryl Mook, June 15, 1951 (dec. 1969); children: Elizabeth Marie, Charles Craig, Margaret Ruth; m. Caecilia Cinquanto, Oct. 10, 1970. BA, Colgate U., 1951; MA, Temple U., 1955, PhD, 1961. Chief phys. chemistry br. Frankford Arsenal U.S. Army, Phila., 1959-70, dir. applied sci., 1970-75, chief scientist, environ. mgr. Rocky Mountain Arsenal Denver, 1975-80, dir. tech. ops., 1980-85; gen. mgr. Battelle Denver Ops., 1985-88; sr. tech. adviser Sci. Applications Internat. Corp., Golden, Colo., 1989-92, dir. tech. devel. Oak Ridge, Tenn., 1992-93. Mem. materials adv. bd. ceramics NAS/Nat. Rsch. Coun., Washington, 1966; mem. Gov.'s Task Group on Rocky Mountain Arsenal, 1976, Colo. Pollution Prevention Adv. Bd., Denver, 1991-99. Contbr. articles to Jour. Chem. Physics, Applied Physics Letters, more than 50 additional profl. publs. Mem. Am. Chem. Soc., Hazardous Material Control Rsch. Inst., Air and Waste Mgmt. Assn. Achievements include 11 patents for electrochemical processes, inorganic materials synthesis, electro-optical devices; demonstration and use of narrow-band optical absorbers for laser protection; leader in development of Army environmental programs; preparation of reports of expert testimony in cases involving solvent usage and disposal on military installations and industrial properties. Home: 319 Cliffrose Ct Lafayette CO 80026-9391 Office Phone: 303-604-1035. Personal E-mail: wzmcn@indra.com.

MCNEILL, WILLIAM HARDY, retired history educator, writer; b. Vancouver, BC, Can., Oct. 31, 1917; s. John Thomas and Netta (Hardy) McN.; m. Elizabeth Darbishire, Sept. 7, 1946; children: Ruth Netta, Deborah Joan, John Robert, Andrew Duncan. BA, U. Chgo., 1938, MA, 1939; PhD, Cornell U., 1947; 20 hon. degrees. Faculty U. Chgo., 1947-87, prof. history, 1957-87, Robert A. Millikan Disting. Svc. prof., 1969-87, prof. emeritus, 1987—, chmn. dept., 1961-67; pres. Demos Fund, 1968-80; chmn. bd. Demos Found., 1980-86. George Eastman vis. prof. Oxford (Eng.) U., 1980-81 Author: Greek Dilemma, War and Aftermath, 1947, Report on the Greeks, 1948, History Handbook of Western Civilization, 1948, rev. and enlarged 6th edit., 1986, America, Britain and Russia, Their Cooperation and Conflict, 1941-46, 1953, Past and Future, 1954, Greece: American Aid in Action, 1947-56, 1957, Rise of the West: A History of the Human Community, 1963, 9th edit., 1991 (Nat. Book award, Gordon J. Laing prize), Europe's Steppe Frontier, 1500-1800, 1964, A World History, 1967, 4th edit., 1998, The Contemporary World, 1967, 2d edit., 1975, The Ecumene: Story of Humanity, 1973, Venice, the Hinge of Europe, 1081-1797, 1974, The Shape of European History, 1974, Plagues and Peoples, 1976, revised edit., 1998, Metamorphosis of Greece since World War II, 1978, The Human Condition, An Ecological and Historical View, 1980, Pursuit of Power, 1982, The Great Frontier, 1983, Mythistory and other Essays, 1986, A History of the Human Community, 1986, 6th edit., 1998, Polyethnicity and National Unity in World History, 1987, Arnold J. Toynbee: A Life, 1989, Population and Politics Since 1750, 1990, Hutchins' University: A Memoir of the University of Chicago 1929-50, 1991, The Global Tradition: Conquerors, Catastrophies and Community, 1992, Keeping Together in Time: Dance & Drill in Human History, 1995, Colebrook: An Historical Sketch, 1996, De excentriciteit van het wiel en audere wereld-historische essays, 1996, The Disruption of Traditional Forms of Nurture, 1998; (with J.R. McNeill) The Human Web: A Birdseye View of World History, 2003; editor: Lord Acton, Essays in the Liberal Interpretation of History, 1967, (with others) Readings in World History, Vols. I-X, 1968-73, Human Migration, 1978, Jour. Modern History, 1971-79, Jour. Modern Greek Studies, 1983-85; mem. editl. bd. Ency. Brit., 1981-98; contbr. articles to profl. jours., chpts. to books. Trustee Athens Coll., 1970-68; vice chmn. Christopher Columbus Quincentenary Jubilee Commn., 1985-93; co-chair curriculum task force Nat. Commn. on Social Studies, 1987-89; mem. Bradley Commn. on the Teaching of History, 1986-89; vice chmn. Nat. Coun. for History Edn., 1990-94, Nat. Coun. for History Standards, 1992-94. Recipient Erasmus prize, 1996; Fulbright Research scholar Royal Inst. Internat. Affairs, Eng., 1950-51; Rockefeller grantee, 1951-52; Ford Faculty fellow, 1954-55, Carnegie grantee, 1957-62, 63-64; Guggenheim fellow, 1971-72, 86-87; Josiah H. Macy grantee, 1973-74; Rockefeller grantee, 1976 Fellow Am. Philos. Soc., Am. Acad. Arts and Scis., Brit. Acad. Arts and Scis. (corr.), Royal Hist. Soc. (corr.); mem. Am. Hist. Assn. (council, del. Am. Council Learned Socs., pres. 1985) Office: PO Box 45 Colebrook CT 06021-0045

MCNEILLY, KATHY EDEN, librarian, library director; b. St. Louis, Mo., Oct. 24, 1948; d. Edwin Winfield and Florence Sybil (Day) Eden; m. Gregory Scott McNeilly, Jan. 13, 1968; 1 child, Meghan Scott. BS, Fla. State U., Tallahassee, 1966—69; MSc of Libr. Sci., U. Tenn., Knoxville, 1973—74. Libr. asst. Oak Ridge Pub. Libr., Tenn., 1971—76, libr., cataloger, 1976—87, libr., reference, 1987—89, asst. dir., 1989—98, libr. dir., 1998—. Mem.: ALA, Tenn. Libr. Assn., East Tenn. Libr. Assn. (pres. 2002—03), DAR, Clinch Bend Chpt., Oak Ridge Breakfast Rotary (literacy chair 2002—03), Beta Phi Mu. Office: Oak Ridge Pub Libr 1401 Oak Ridge Turnpike Oak Ridge TN 37830

MCNELLEY, JUDY ANNE, small business owner; b. Commerce, Ga., Oct. 19, 1956; d. Marvin Ellis and Florence Evelyn Duncan; m. Harold Michael McNelley, Aug. 14, 1977; children: Jeremy Michael, James Todd, Joshua Duncan. Student, Young Harris Coll., 1976-77. Co-owner M & J Vending, Tunnel Hill, Ga., 1988—. Columnist Banks County News, 1992. Chmn. Whitfield County Rep. Party, 1995—, precinct capt., 1991-93, 1st vice chmn. 1993-95, conv. del., 1988—; cons. Dalton State Coll. Reps., 1998—; exec. com. 9th Congl. Dist. Ga. Rep. Party, 1995—, conv. del., 1989—; 2d v.p. Rep. Women N.W. Ga., 1993-97; mem. sex. edn. adv. com. Whitfield County Schs., Dalton, Ga., 1991-98, mem. sys. level media adv. bd., 1995-96; Sunday sch. tchr. Tunnel Hill United Meth. Ch., 1986-97; charter mem. Coun. Women Advisors to Congress, Washington, 1995. Named Hon. Life Mem. Ga. PTA, 1991, Rep. Woman of Yr., Rep. Women N.W. Ga., 1995, Cmty. Hero Torchbearer, Atlanta Com. Olympic Games, 1996; recipient Ronald Reagan award 9th Congl. Dist. Ga. Rep. Party, 1997, Vol. of Yr. award Tunnel Hill Elem. Sch., 1991. Republican. Christian. Avocations: volunteer work, collecting autographed memorabilia, reading, concerts. Home: 306 Scenic Dr Tunnel Hill GA 30755-9712

MC NELLY, FREDERICK WRIGHT, JR., psychologist; b. Bangor, Maine, Apr. 14, 1947; s. Frederick Wright and E. Frances (Cutter) McNelly; 1 adopted child, Roger McNelly foster children: Joseph, Ronald, Michael, Jeffrey. BA magna cum laude, U. Minn., 1969; MA, U. Mich., 1971, PhD, 1973. Registered clin. psychologist Ill., cert. profl. qualification, state and provincial bds. of psychology, early intervention program provider Ill. Rsch. coord. NSF project U. Minn., Morris, 1968-69, lab. instr., 1969, trainee USPHS, 1969-70, 72; teaching fellow psychology U. Mich., Ann Arbor, 1970-72; ednl. examiner Ann Arbor Pub. Schs., 1971; dir. psychol. svcs. Children Devel. Ctr., Rockford, Ill., 1972-82, program dir., 1982-86; cons. psychologist, 1986—. Lectr. Rock Valley Coll., Rockford, 1974—75; part-time pvt. practice psychology, Rockford and Belvidere, Ill., 1980—86, Beloit, Wis., 1985—86; full time, 1986—; mental health cons. Rockford Head Start, 1982—, United Cerebral Palsy, Blackhawk Region, 1986—, Access Svcs., Mendota, Ill., 1992—; mem. health svcs. adv. com. human resources dept. City of Rockford, 1985—; presenter state and regional workshops and confs. Contbr. articles to profl. jours. Active Boy Scouts Am., 1978—83, Big Bros./Big Sisters; chmn. spl. edn. regional adv. com. Bi-County Office Edn., Rockford, 1976—78; mem. Nat. and Ill. Com. Child Abuse, 1975—85; co-chmn. Winnebago County Child Protection Assn., 1980; elder Willow Creek United Presbyn. Ch., Rockford, 1980—83; mem. stronghold renovation session com. Presbytery Blackhawk, Oregon, Ill., 1985. Named U.S. Jaycees Outstanding Young Man of 1977. Mem.: Ill. Assn. Infant Mental Health, No. Ill. Alliance Mentally Ill, Nat. Assn. Mentally Ill, Nat. Assn. Disability Examiners, State Provincial Bds. Psychology, Nat. Register Health Svc. Providers Psychology, Coun. Exception Children, No. Ill. Pvt. Practice Mental Health Assn. (v.p. 1993, pres. 1994—95), No. Ill. Psychol. Assn., Ill. Psychol. Assn. Home: 11591 Beverly Ln Belvidere IL 61008-8708

MCNELLY, JOHN TAYLOR, retired journalist, educator; b. Lancaster, Wis., Oct. 2, 1923; s. Stephen Sumner and Caroline Hurd (Taylor) McN.; m. Pamela Edith Thompson, Dec. 20, 1952; children: Barbara, Duncan. BA, U. Wis., 1946, MA, 1957; PhD, Mich. State U., 1961. Reporter AP, Milw., 1948-52, Reuters, London, 1952-53; news editor U. Wis. News Service, Madison, 1957; instr., then assoc. prof. Mich. State U., East Lansing, 1957-66; assoc. prof., then prof. U. Wis., Madison, 1966-82, Evjue-Bascom prof., 1982-88, prof. emeritus, 1988—. Asst. dir. Inter-Am. Mass Communications Program, San Jose, Costa Rica, 1961-62; vis. prof. Berlin Inst. Mass. Communication in Developing Nations, W.Ger., 1965, Agrarian U., Lima, Peru, 1968-69; communication cons. UNESCO, Latin Am., 1970-75; lectr. USIA, Latin Am., 1968, 74, 80 Co-author: Communication and Social Change in Latin America, 1968; assoc. editor: Journalism Quar., 1975-77; contbr. monographs and articles to communication publs. Served with USAF, 1942-43. Fulbright-Hays Faculty fellow Lima, Peru, 1968-69 Home: 134 Larkin St Madison WI 53705-5116 E-mail: dtmcnelly@facstaff.wisc.edu.

MC NERNEY, WALTER JAMES, health policy educator, consultant; b. New Haven, June 8, 1925; s. Robert Francis and Anna Gertrude (Shanley) McN.; m. Shirley Ann Hamilton, June 26, 1948; children: Walter James, Peter Hamilton, Jennifer Allison, Daniel Martin, Richard Hamilton. BS, Yale U., 1947; M.H.A., U. Minn., 1950. Research asst. Labor-Mgmt. Center, Yale U., 1947; instr. advanced math. Hopkins Prep. Sch., New Haven, 1947-48; adminstrv. resident R.I. Hosp., Providence, 1949-50; asst. to coordinator Hosp. and Clinics of Med. Center, U. Pitts., 1950-53; also instr., then asst. prof. hosp. adminstrn. at univ. Grad. Sch. Pub. Health, U. Pitts., 1953-55; assoc. prof., dir. program hosp. adminstrn. Sch. Bus. Adminstrn., U. Mich., 1955-58; prof., dir. Bur. Hosp. Adminstrn., 1958-61; pres. Blue Cross Assn., Chgo., 1961-77; pres., chief exec. officer Blue Cross and Blue Shield Assns., Chgo., 1977-81; Herman Smith prof. health policy Grad. Sch. Mgmt., Northwestern U., 1982—; cons. in field, 1982—. Mem. Nat. Coun. on Health Planning and Devel., HEW, 1976-82; mem. bd. dirs. Nat. Health Coun., 1963-77, pres., 1972-73; mem. nat. commn. on cost of med. care AMA, 1977, mem. com. on pvt. philanthropy, 1977-78; past pres. Internat. Fedn. Vol. Health Svc. Funds; mem. devel. com. Yale U.; trustee Nat. Exec. Svc. Corps; chmn. task force on Medicaid and related progrsm HEW, 1969-70; charter mem. Inst. Medicine-NAS, chmn. bd. on health care svcs., chmn. bd. on spl. initiatives; mem. physician payment rev. commn. U.S. Congress, Dept. Vets.' Affairs; mem. Commn. on the Future Structure of Vets. Health Care; mem. coal commn. U.S. Dept. Labor; mem. coun. on performance measurement Joint Commn. on Accreditation of Healthcare Orgns.; mem. nat. adv. coun. for health care policy, rsch. and evaluation HHS; bd. dirs. Stanley Works, Medicus, Value Health Inc., Nellcor Inc., Ostel Tech., Ventritex, Inc., Hanger Orthopedics Group Inc.; chmn. bd. McNerney Heintz, Inc., Am. Health Properties Inc.; adv. coun. to dean Yale U. Med. Sci.; vis. com. U. Mich. Med. Ctr., adv. coun. chmn. Agy. for Health Care Policy and Rsch., chmn., bd. trustees Med. Outcomes Trust. Author: Hospital and Medical Economics, 1962, Regionalization and Rural Health Care, 1962; contbr. articles to profl. jours. Mem. Pres.' Com. on Health Edn., 1972-73; trustee Hosp. Research and Ednl. Trust, Inst. for Future; vis. com. Harvard Med. and Dental Schs. Served to lt. (j.g.) USNR, 1943-46. Nuffield Provincial Hosps. Trust-Kings Fund (Eng.) fellow, 1970; recipient Justin Ford Kimball award Am. Hosp. Assn., 1967; Outstanding Achievement award U. Minn., 1970, sec.'s unit citation HEW, 1970, Yale medal, 1979, award for merotorious svc. AMA, 1981, award of honor Am. Hosp. Assn., 1982, C. Rufus Rorem Health Svc. award, 1995; named 1 of 100 most important young men and women in U.S. by Life Mag., 1962; inducted into Healthcare Hall of Fame, Modern Mag., 1996. Mem.: Commonwealth, Yale (N.Y.C.). Office: Northwestern U Grad Sch Mgmt 2001 Sheridan Rd Evanston IL 60208-0814

MCNERNEY, WALTER JAMES (JIM MCNERNEY), manufacturing executive; b. Providence, R.I., Aug. 22, 1949; m. Haity McNerney, 1987; 3 children. BA in American Studies, Yale U., 1971; MBA, Harvard U., 1975. Brand mgr. Proctor & Gamble, 1975—78; sr. mgr. McKinsey & Co., 1978—82; gen. mgr., GE Mobile Communications GE Co., 1982—86; pres. GE Info. Svcs., Rockville, Md., 1988—89; exec. v.p. GE Fin. Services and Capital, Stamford, Conn., 1989—91, pres., CEO GE Elec. Distribution and Control, Plainville, Conn., 1991—92, GE Lighting, Cleveland, Ohio, 1995—97; pres. GE Asia-Pacific, Hong Kong, 1993—95; pres., CEO GE Aircraft Engines, Cin., 1997—2000; chmn., CEO 3M Co, St. Paul, 2001—. Bd. dirs. Boeing, 2001—. Office: 3M Co 3M Ctr Saint Paul MN 55144*

MCNEW, BENNIE BANKS, retired finance educator; b. Greenbrier, Ark., Nov. 12, 1931; s. Roland H. and Stella (Avery) McNew; m. Bonnie Lou Stone, Mar. 31, 1956; children: Bonnie Banks, Mary Kathleen, William Michael. BS, Ark. State Tchrs. Coll., 1953; MBA, U. Ark., 1954; PhD, U. Tex., 1961. Asst. nat. bank examiner, 1954-56; indsl. specialist Indsl. Rsch. and Ext. Ctr. U. Ark., 1956-59; lectr. finance U. Tex., 1959-61; prof. banking U. Miss., University, 1961-65, dean Sch. Bus. Adminstrn., 1965-79; dean Sch. Bus. Mid. Tenn. State U., Murfreesboro, 1980-88; prof. econs. and fin. U. Ctrl. Ark., Conway, 1988-98; ret., 1998. Asst. dir., v.p. Grad. Sch. Banking La. State U., 1966—97. Author (with Charles L. Prather): (book) Fraud Control for Commercial Banks, 1962; co-author: Money and Banking Casebook, 1966, The Bankers Handbook, 1966, A History of Mississippi, 1973. Pres. Faulkner County Singing Conv., Ark., 2002—. With U.S. Army, 1950—51. Named Disting. Undergraduate Alumnus, Sch. Bus. Adminstrn., U. Ctrl. Ark., 2002. Mem.: Ward Family Singers and Gospel Music. Soc. (pres. 2002—03), Lions (pres. Oxford, Miss. 1964—65, Edward Dalstrom Disting. Svc. award 2002, Melvin Jones fellow 2003). Home: 12 Bainbridge Dr Conway AR 72034-7217

MCNICHOLAS, EDWARD, lawyer; b. St. Louis, Jan. 27, 1969; s. Robert and Helen McNicholas; m. Andrea, Aug. 10, 1996. AB, Princeton U., 1991; JD, Harvard U., 1996. Bar: D.C. 1996, Md. 1996. Law clk. to Hon. P. Niemeyer U.S. Ct. Appeal (4th Cir.), Balt., 1996—97; assoc. counsel to Pres. The White Ho., Washington, 2000—01. Author several law rev. pieces Harvard Law Rev., 1995; editor Harvard Law Rev., Cambridge, Mass., 1994-96. Roman Catholic. Office: Sidley Austin Brown and Wood 1501 K St NW Washington DC 20005 E-mail: emcnicho@sidley.com.

MCNICHOLS, GERALD ROBERT, consulting company executive; b. Cleve., Nov. 21, 1943; s. Charles Wellington and June Beatrice (Kalal) McN.; m. Paula Kay Austin, Dec. 26, 1964; children: G. Robert Jr., Katherine Lynn Loftis, Melissa Sue Cardon. BS with honors, Case-Western Res. U., 1965; MS, U. Pa., 1966; ScD, George Washington U., 1976. Cert. cost estimator/analyst. Sr. ops. analyst Office of Sec., Dept. of Def., Washington, 1970-76; v.p. GenTech, Inc., Bethesda, Md., 1976-77, J. Watson Noah, Inc., Falls Church, Va., 1977-78; pres., chief exec. officer Mgmt. Cons. and Rsch., Inc., McLean, Va., 1978-99; sr. v.p. GRC Internat. (acquired Mgmt. Cons. and Rsch., Inc.), 1999-2000, also bd. dirs.; CEO McNichols & McNichols, Inc., Middleburg, Va., 2000—. Pres. McNichols Family Found., 2000—; chmn. bd. Metier, Ltd.; bd. dirs. Magicsoft Corp., Project Performance Corp. Co-author: Operations Research for Decision Making, 1975; contbg. author: Software Reliability, 1986, Software System Design Methods, 1986, Electronic Systems Effectiveness and Life Cycle Costing, 1983; editor Cost Analysis, 1984; contbr. articles to profl. jours. Pres. Rondelay Civic Assn., Fairfax Sta., Va., 1985-87; bd. dirs. Kennedy Ctr. Cir., 1995-2000. Capt. USAF, 1966-70. Recipient Meritorious Achievement award, Case Western Res U., 1995, Engr. Alumni Achievement award, George Washington U., 1989. Mem. Inst. Cost Analysis (pres. 1985-88), Internat. Soc. Parametric Analysts (bd. dirs. 1982-84, Frieman Lifetime Achievement award 1990), Ops. Rsch. Soc. Am. (chmn. mil. applications sect.), Assn. for Small Rsch., Engring., and Tech. Svcs. Cos. (pres.), Mil. Ops. Rsch. Soc. (sec., treas. 1986-87, v.p. adminstrn. 1987-88, bd. dirs. 1985-88, 92-96), Soc. Cost Estimating and Analysis (bd. dirs. 1990-93, Lifetime Achievement award 2000), Century Club George Mason Univ. (bd. dirs. 1997-2000). Home: 23349 Parsons Rd Middleburg VA 20117-2817 Office: McNichols & McNichols Inc PO Box 2226 Middleburg VA 20118-2226 Business E-Mail: drmcnichols@mcnichols.org.

MCNICOL, DAVID LEON, retired federal official, consultant; b. South Gate, Calif., May 18, 1944; s. Charles D. and Mary W. (Heisel) McN.; m. Lore Anne Long, Mar. 25, 1967; children: Katharine Anne, Elizabeth Mary. BA magna cum laude, Harvard U., 1966; MS, MIT, 1968, PhD, 1973. Asst. prof. econs. U. Pa., Phila., 1971-75; sr. staff economist Pres.'s Coun. of Econ. Advisors, Washington, 1976; vis. assoc. prof. econs. Calif. Inst. Tech., Pasadena, 1976-77; sr. economist Office of the Sec., U.S. Dept. of Treasury, Washington, 1977-79; dir. Office of Econ. Analysis U.S. Dept. Energy, Washington, 1980-81, dep. asst. adminstr. Office of Applied Analysis, 1981-82; dir. Econ. Analysis and Resource Planning Divsn. Office of Sec. of Def., Office of Program Analysis and Evaluation, Washington, 1982-88, dep. asst. sec., dep. dir., 1988—2002, chmn. cost analysis improvement group, 1988—2002; sr. fellow Inst. for Def. Analyses, Alexandria, Va., 2002—. Author over 20 publs. on commodity markets, regulatory econs., energy issues and econ. aspects of the U.S. def. program. Recipient Spl. Svc. award Dept. Energy, 1981, Presdl. Rank award U.S. Govt., 1988, 93, 96, 2001, Disting./Meritorius Civilian Svc. medal Dept. Def., 1988, 91, 93, 96, 97, 2001, 2002. Home: 6901 Pineway University Park MD 20782-1163 Office: Inst for Defense Analyses 4850 Mark Center Dr Alexandria VA 22311-1882 Office Phone: 703-845-4369. E-mail: dmcnicol@ida.org.

MC NITT, WILLARD CHARLES, business executive; b. Chgo., June 6, 1920; s. Willard C. and Louise (Richardson) McN.; m. Charlotte D. Boyd, Sept. 14, 1946; children: Willard Charles, James D., Peter B. McNitt. BA, Amherst Coll., 1942; A.M., Harvard Grad. Sch. Bus. Adminstrn., 1942; student, Northwestern Grad. Sch. Bus. Adminstrn., U. Chgo. Sch. Bus. Adminstrn., 1947. Asst. market planning and research Foote, Cone & Belding Co., Chgo., 1946-47; asst. sales promotion and advt. Bell & Gosset Co., Morton Grove, Ill., 1947-48; v.p. sales and mktg. Bowes Industries, Inc., Chgo., 1948-54; gen. mgr. sales and mktg. Clayton Mark & Co., Evanston, Ill., 1954-58; pres., dir. Bowey's, Inc., Chgo., 1958-62; pres., dir., mem. exec. com. H.M. Byllesby Co., Chgo., 1962-63; group v.p., dir. Consol. Foods Corp., Chgo., 1963-67; exec. v.p. consumer products group W.R. Grace & Co., N.Y.C., 1967-72; exec. v.p., dir., mem. exec. com. Ward Foods, Inc., Wilmette, Ill., 1972-73, chief operating officer, pres., dir., mem. exec. com., 1973-76; pres., chief exec. officer, dir. Westgate-Calif. Corp., and Sun Harbor Industries, San Diego, 1977-80; pres., chief exec. officer Nalley's Fine Foods, Tacoma, 1980-83; chmn., dir. Joseph Magnin Inc., 1982-85; chmn. Blue Moon Cheese Co., Thorpe, Wis., 1983—; operating ptnr. Wallner & Co., La Jolla, Calif.; vice chmn., pres., chief exec. officer, dir., mem. exec. com. Foremost Dairies, Inc., San Francisco, 1983-85. Chmn. Epcom. Bd. dirs. ATI, NCIC, Blue Moon Cheese, Del. Lightweight. Troop head local Boy Scouts Am., 1957-67. Served

to lt. (s.g.) USNR, 1942-46. Mem. Execs. Club (Chgo.), Amherst Club, Harvard Bus. Sch. Club (Chgo., N.Y.C.), Indian Hill Country Club (Winnetka), Dairymen's Club (Boulder Junction, Wis.), Chi Psi. Republican. Congregationalist. Address: 1512 Primrose Ln Glenview IL 60025-7772

MCNOWN, CADE, professional football player; b. Oreg., Jan. 12, 1977; Student, UCLA. Football player Chgo. Bears, 1999—2000, Miami Dolphins, 2001, San Francisco 49ers, 2002. Office: San Francisco 49ers 4949 Centennial Blvd Santa Clara CA 95054

MCNOWN, EDYTHE S. music educator; b. Torrington, Wyo., Oct. 18, 1925; d. Charles Mead Sandercock and Ada Mary Guy; m. Myron L. McNown, Dec. 27, 1954; children: Cynthia Ruth Harrington, Douglas Edward, Gregory Bruce. MusB in Piano, U. Wyo., 1948; MA, Kansas City U., Mo., 1951; postgrad., U. Wyo., 1949, U. Mo., 1950—51, Aspen Sch. Music, Colo., 1953. Tchr. Laramie Pub. Schs., Wyo., 1948—49, Sunset Hill Girl's Sch., Kansas City, 1952—55, 1965—69; pvt. piano tchr. Fairway, Kans., 1954—. Freelance profl. accompanist, 1950—; organist, choir dir. 3d Presbyn. Ch., Kansas City, Mo., 1951—52; dir. Jr. Boys Choir 2d Presbyn. Ch., Kansas City, Mo., 1966—71; pianist Sigma Alpha Iota Singers, Greater Kansas City, 1976—82, Cmty. Opera Co., Greater Kansas City, 1981—83; music dir. Civic Opera Theater of Kansas City, 1984—90, pianist, 1984—92. Co-founder Civic Opera Theater of Kansas City, 1984, bd. dirs., 1985—2002; vol. performer various area clubs, orgns., schs., chs.; vol. Shawnee Mission Sch. System, Kans., 1966—77; mem. Friends of Art Nelson-Atkins Mus. Art, Kansas City, 1988—. Recipient citation, Kans. Fedn. Music Clubs, 1989, Regional Winner, Nat. Fedn. of Music Club Contest, 1947; U. Kansas City fellow, 1949—50. Mem.: Music Tchrs. Nat. Assn., Musical Arts Club, Kansas City Music Club (membership chmn. 1997—99), Mus. Arts Club of Kansas City (sec. 1994—96, pres. 1980—2000, Jack Henry Pyramid of Arts, Vol. of Yr. award 1994), Phi Kappa Phi, Phi Sigma Iota, Sigma Alpha Iota (pres. 1979—81, 1st v.p. 1987—88, Cert. of Merit 1980, Rose of Honor 1981, Rose of Dedication 1992, Sword of Honor 1976, nominee for Nat. Alumni Leadership award, Diamond Sword of Honor 2004). Avocations: needlecrafts, gardening, cooking.

MCNULTY, CARRELL STEWART, JR., retired manufacturing company executive, architect; b. Newark, Dec. 4, 1924; s. Carrell Stewart and Marjorie (Yaegerlehner) McN.; m. Barbara Brokaw, June 21, 1952; children: Peter Carrell, Susan Abigail. Student, Emory U., 1941-43, U. N.C., 1943-44; BArch, Columbia U., 1950, MS in Urban Planning, 1963. Registered architect, Conn. Assoc. SMS Architects, Stamford, Conn., 1950-58, gen. ptnr., 1958-73; pvt. practice architecture Weston, Conn., 1973-76; pres. CMW Co., Weston, 1975-77, NB Products, Inc., Horsham, Pa., 1976-94, NB Instruments, Inc., Horsham, 1979-93, Environ. Svcs. and Products, Inc., Horsham, 1994-96; ret. Mem. Conn. Soc. Architects, 1963-73, sec., 1964-67, pres., 1969-70. Chair S.W. Regional Planning Agy., Norwalk, Conn., 1967-71; mem. Gov.'s Com. on Environment, New Haven, 1970, chair Gov.'s Task Force on Housing, Norwalk, 1972; bd. dirs., sec. Habitat for Humanity of Greater Bucks, Doylestown, Pa., 1990-97; pres. Ctrl. Bucks Crossroads, 1995-96. Lt. (j.g.) USNR, 1943-46; PTO. Recipient citation Am. Assn. Sch. Adminstrs., 1960, 6th Biennial Design award HUD, 1973; grantee HUD, Housing Rsch., 1970. Fellow AIA (mem. urban design com. 1963-73, chmn. 1971); mem. Bucks County Choral Soc., Sigma Nu. Democrat. Mem. United Ch. of Christ (deacon 1965-71, elder 1989-92). Avocations: computers, watercoloring, choral music. Home: 14179 SE 88th Ct Summerfield FL 34491 E-mail: llerracm@aol.com.

MCNULTY, JAMES F. engineering, construction company executive; m. Judy McNulty; children: Darby, Anne, Brigid. BS in Engring., US Mil. Acad., 1964; MS in Nuc. Physics, Ohio State U., 1970; MS in Mgmt., MIT, 1985. Rsch. assoc. Lawrence Livermore Nat. Lab., 1972—74; asst. dir. Office Mil. Applications US Dept. Energy, 1978—80; officer nuc. weapon requirements Ops. and Plans Office Dept US Army, 1980—82, sys. mgr. Pershing II Missle Sys., 1982—84, program mgr. ground based laser sys., 1985—88; dir. bus. devel. Parsons Corp., 1988—89, v.p., 1991—92, sr. v.p., mgr. sys. divsn. Pasadena, 1992—95, pres. infrastructure and tech. group, 1996, pres., CEO, 1996—, chmn., 1998—. Fellow Alfred P. Sloan, MIT. Avocations: hiking, walking, golf, reading. Office: Parsons Corp 100 W Walnut St Pasadena CA 91124-0001 Office Phone: 626-440-2000. Office Fax: 626-440-2630.*

MCNULTY, JAMES FRANCIS, JR., lawyer, consultant; s. James Francis, Sr. McNulty and Anna Mae Fiorenza; m. Be Thi Tu, Dec. 19, 1986; 1 child, Thomas Vi. *Son Thomas, mechanical prodigy, I.Q. 141, was granted a patent for improvement to stun gun invented at age 11, improved stun gun manufactured. A high school senior, Thomas is winner of a California Governor's Scholarship and has letters in football and wrestling. Father James Sr. is a retired radio engineer and electronics manufacturing company executive, who patented improvements to the x-ray machine and ultrasonic testing equipment. Mother Anna Mae is a homemaker. Wife Be is a former production supervisor, who studied in electronics documentation curriculum at RCC and is named co-inventor on patent.* BA in Sociology, Calif. State U., Fullerton, 1990; JD, Glendale U., Calif., 1991; MA in Mgmt., Claremont Grad. U., Calif., 2002; student in design, Art Ctr. Calif., 2001. Bar: Calif. 1993. Assoc. quality engr. Allen Bradley - West, Fullerton, Calif., 1981—83; plant ops. mgr. Taser Industries, Inc., Monrovia, Calif., 1983—86; CEO E.I.D. Labs, Sierra Madre, Calif., 1986—90; v.p. mktg. and product devel. Tasertron, Newport Beach, Calif., 1990—91; atty. pvt. practice, Calimesa, Calif., 1993—2004; atty., mkt. rsch. Def. Tech. Corp., 2004—; mgmt., design, and legal cons. Armor Holdings, Inc., 2004—. *Educated for a career in marketing, studied social behavior, social research methods, statistics, law, management and design. At Claremont Colleges, studied under both economist and organizational theorist Peter Ferdinand Drucker and psychologist Mihaly Csikszentmihalyi. An astute product manager recognized for his own novel designs for products responsive to researched markets, James Jr. is named inventor of 13 patents granted for mechanical and electro-mechanical products. One is with co-inventors Timothy Whelan, Singapore based management consultant and artist, and electrician Kenneth Nickey. James Jr. maintains a primarily transactional legal practice, 2.1 million dollar federal arbitration decision obtained for clients.* Contbr. articles to profl. jours. Mem.: Mensa, Phi Theta Kappa, Alpha Gamma Sigma, Alpha Kappa Delta Internat. Sociology, Delta Theta Phi Law. Republican. Achievements include patents in field. Avocations: bicycling, forensic science, opera. Home and Office: 1290 Third St Calimesa CA 92320 Office Phone: 909-795-8935. Business E-Mail: macslaw2000@yahoo.com.

MCNULTY, JOHN KENT, lawyer, educator; b. Buffalo, Oct. 13, 1934; s. Robert William and Margaret Ellen (Duthie) McN.; m. Linda Conner, Aug. 20, 1955 (div. Feb. 1977); children: Martha Jane, Jennifer, John K. Jr.; m. Babette B. Barton, Mar. 23, 1978 (div. May 1988). AB with high honors, Swarthmore Coll., 1956; LL.B., Yale U., 1959. Bar: Ohio 1961, U.S. Supreme Ct. 1964. Law clk. Justice Hugo L. Black, U.S. Supreme Ct., Washington, 1959-60; vis. prof. Sch. Law U. Tex., summer 1960; assoc. Jones, Day, Cockley & Reavis, Cleve., 1960-64; prof. law U. Calif., Berkeley, 1964-91, Roger J. Traynor prof. law, 1991—2002, Roger J. Traynor prof. emeritus, 2002—. Of counsel Baker and McKenzie, San Francisco, 1974-75; acad. visitor London Sch. Econs., 1985, Cambridge U., 1994, U. Edinburgh, 1994; vis. fellow Wolfson Coll., Cambridge, 1994, U. Innsbruck, 1996, Trinity Coll., Dublin, 1997; vis. prof. Yale U., U. Tex., U. Leiden, U. Tilburg, U. Tokyo, U. San Diego, others; lectr. univs. Cologne, Hamburg, Hitotsubashi, Kansei, Keio, Kyoto, London, Munich, Seoul, Tokyo, Tilburg, Amsterdam, Rotterdam, Vienna Econ., Tohoku, Tübingen, Waseda, Toronto, Queens, Jefferson, European Tax Coll., others; mem. adv. bd. Tax Mgmt. Author: Federal Income Taxation of Individuals, (with Lathrope) 7th edit., 2004, Federal Estate and Gift Taxation, (with McCouch) 6th edit., 2003, Federal Income Taxation of S Corporations, 1992; (with Westin & Beck) Federal Income Taxation of Business Enterprises, 1995, 2d edit., 1999; mem. bd. overseers Berkeley Jour. Internat. Law. Guggenheim fellow, 1977 Mem. ABA, Am. Law Inst. (life), Internat. Fiscal Assn. (coun. U.S. br.), Order of Coif, Phi Beta Kappa. Home: 1176 Grizzly Peak Blvd Berkeley CA 94708-1741 Office: U Calif Sch Law 422 Boalt Hl Berkeley CA 94720-7200 Office Phone: 510-642-1928. Business E-Mail: mcnultyj@law.berkeley.edu.

MCNULTY, KATHLEEN ANNE, clinical social worker, psychotherapist, business consultant; b. Hackensack, N.J., Oct. 6, 1958; d. Alfred Edward and Gertrude Natalie (Currie) McN.; m. Henry Stanislaw Kowal, Sept. 16, 1988. BA, Rutgers U., 1980; MSW, Smith Coll., 1984; postgrad., Fielding Grad. Inst., 2001—. Lic. marriage and family therapist. Mental health aide Belleville (N.J.) Mental Health Clinic, 1980-82; clin. social worker Albert Einstein Coll. Medicine, Bronx, N.Y., 1984-86, Family Guidance Bergen, Hackensack, 1986-87, Cliffwood Mental Health Ctr., Englewood, N.J., 1986-87; pvt. practice Rutherford, N.J., 1987-99, Ridgewood, N.J., 1999—. Cons. Meadowlands Weight Control, Rutherford, 1988—, St. Lukes-Roosevelt Hosp. Ctr., N.Y.C., 1988. Contbr. articles to profl. jours. Mem. Am. Orthopsychiat. Assn., Acad. Cert. Social Workers (cert.), Nat. Assn. Social Workers. Avocations: painting, singing, sports, poetry. Office Phone: 201-444-4010.

MCNULTY, MICHAEL ROBERT, congressman; b. Troy, N.Y., Sept. 16, 1947; s. John J. and Madelon McN; m. Nancy Ann Lazzaro; children: Michele, Angela, Nancy, Maria. Grad., St. Joseph's Inst., Barrytown, N.Y., 1965, Loyola U. Rome Ctr., 1968, Hill Sch. Ins., N.Y.C., 1970; BA in Polit. Sci., Coll. Holy Cross, 1969; LHD honoris causa, Coll. St. Rose, 1991; LLD honoris causa, Siena Coll., 1993, Rensselaer Polytech. Inst., 1995, Excelsior Coll., 2000. Town supr. Town of Green Island, N.Y., 1969-77, mayor, 1977-81; mem. N.Y. State Assembly, 1982-88, chmn. subcom. on town and village elections, mem. legis. commn. on rural resources, 1983-88, asst. dir. adminstrv. regulations rev. commn., 1977-82, mem. adminstrv. regulations rev. com., 1983-88; past chmn. planning com. Capital Dist. Transp. Com.; mem. 101st-102d Congresses from 23rd N.Y. dist., 1989-92, 103d-108th Congresses from 21st N.Y. dist., 1993—; mem. ways and means com.; ranking mem. subcom. on select revenue measures. Past chmn. task force for constrn. Troy-Green Island Bridge; chmn. United Way campaign, 1982 Mem. staff com. on edn. N.Y. State Constl. Conv., 1967; campaign mgr. John J. McNulty Jr. for Sheriff of Albany County, N.Y., 1973; participant 1974 polit. campaign mgmt. inst. Kent State U., Ohio; past mem. Albany County Dem. Com.; past chmn. Green Island Dem. Com.; past mem. N.Y. State Dem. Com. Democrat. Office: US Ho of Reps 2210 Rayburn Hob Washington DC 20515-0001

MCNULTY, PAUL J. prosecutor; BA, Grove City Coll.; JD, Capital U. Counsel U.S. House Com. on Standards of Official Conduct, Washington, 1983—85; dir. legal svcs. Legal Svcs. Corp., Washington, 1985—87; minority counsel House Judiciary Subcom. Crime, 1987—90; dep. dir. Office Policy Devel., dir. Office Policy and Comms. U.S. Dept. Justice, Washington, 1990—93; counsel Shaw, Pittman, Potts and Trowbridge, 1993—95, U.S. Ho. Reps. Com. on Judiciary, Washington, 1995—99; prin. assoc. dep. atty. gen. U.S. Dept Justice, 2001; chief counsel, dir. legis. ops. Office of Majority Leader U.S. Ho. Reps., Washington, 1999—2001; U.S. atty. ea. dist. U.S. Dept. Justice, Va., 2001—. Office: 2100 Jamieson Ave Alexandria VA 22314

MCNUTT, JACK WRAY, oil company executive; b. Norphlet, Ark., Sept. 7, 1934; s. Fay D. and Mattie E. (Garner) McN.; m. Jordine Chesshir, Aug. 19, 1955; 1 child, Marsha. BS, Harding Coll., 1956; MS, Columbia U., 1957. Acct. Murphy Oil Corp., El Dorado, Ark., 1957-68, exec. mgmt. asst., 1968-69, exec. v.p., 1981-88, chief operating officer, 1986-88, pres., chief exec. officer, 1988-94; ret., 1994; v.p. planning Murphy Ea. Oil Co., London, 1969-72, pres., 1972-81. Bd. dirs. First United Bancshares, El Dorado, Ark. Mem. Am. Petroleum Inst. (dir.), 25 Yr. Club. of Petroleum Industry. Home: 1705 W Cedar St El Dorado AR 71730-5309 Office: 101 W Main St Ste 509 El Dorado AR 71730-5641

MCNUTT, RICHARD HUNT, manufacturing executive; b. Princeton, N.J., Mar. 11, 1943; s. John and Dorothy Elizabeth (Hunt) McN. Student, Delaware Vly. Coll. Sci./Agr., 1965-68, Temple U., 1978-81; BS in Indsl. Engring., Shelbourn U., 1986. Cert. in vocat. edn.; cert. mfg. engr. Diemaker Custom Tool Co., 1964-67; toolmaker Penn Engring., 1967-69; machine shop mgr., R&D engr. Inertial Motors Corp., 1969-73; machinery design engr. Phila. Rivet Co., Doylestown, Pa., 1973-76; R&D mgr. PHL, Inc., Doylestown, 1976-82; asst. chief engr. PHL Inc./Levr/Air Inc., Prefco Products Inc., 1982-85, chief engr., 1985-86, v.p. ops., 1986-89, dir. engring., 1993—2003; owner Sunrise Solar Heat Co.; cons. Pipersville, Pa.; ptnr. Mediation Assocs., 1990—; R&D engr. fire/smoke divsn. Perfect Air Control, Inc., Pipersville, 2003—04; engring. dir. PHL, Inc., 2004—. Exec. v.p. Del. Water Study Citizens Group for Sound Resource Mgmt.; councillor Probational Vol. Svcs.; founding bd. dirs. Del-Aware Unltd., Inc., Del-Art Inc., Ctr. for Performing Arts, Bucks County, Pa., Del. River Greenway Partnership, Inc.; mem. Environ. Polit. Action Com.; founder AWARE, Montgomery County, 1985—, STAND, Bucks County, 1986—, Holicong CSA; mem. exec. bd. Earth Day, 1990, Earth Days Alliance, Bucks County Conservation Dist., 1993—, Del. River Greenway, 1994-96, vice chmn., 1995-96, chmn., 1996-98; v.p. Del. River Greenway Partnership Inc., 1998-99, pres., 1999-2004; mem. econ. devel. com. Del. River Wild and Scenic Study Commn., Dept. Interior Nat. Park Svc., 1994-96; founder Solebury Forum, Bucks County, Environ. Party Com.; mem. Plumstead Twp. Parks and Recreation Commn., sec., 1992-97, vice chmn., 1997-98, chmn., 1998—2004; vice chmn. Plumstead Twp. Shade Tree Commn., 1992—; planning commn. tech. adv. com. Cape May County, 2001—04; founding ptnr. Rising Nation, Native Am. Cultural Heritage Project, 2000—; Indian Coun. mem. Lenape Nation of Pa., 2003—; founder Tidewaters Gateway Partnership, 2004-. Served with USMC, 1960-64. Mem. ASHRAE, NRA (life), VFW, Soc Mfg. Engrs., Bucks County Assn. Corrections and Rehab., Am. Legion (life), Vietnam Vets. Am. (life), Ctrl. Bucks County C. of C. (environ. and govt. com. 1986—), Internat. Air Movement and Control Assn. (mem. code rev. com., fire-smoke engring. com.), Nat. Fire Protection Assn., Underwriters Lab. (standards com.). Republican. Zen Buddhist. Office: PHL Inc 5556 Stump Rd Pipersville PA 18947-1090 E-mail: phltech@pil.net.

MCPARLAND, ROBERT PATRICK, English educator, writer; b. Mar. 7, 1958; BA, Fordham U.; MA, St. John's U., 1996, Montclair State U., 1997; postgrad., Drew U., 1999—. Asst. prof. English Felician Coll., Lodi/Rutherford, NJ, 1997—. Author: The Speech of Angels, 2003; author: (fiction) In the Nick of Time, 2004. Home: 39 Rosedale Ave Elmwood Park NJ 07407-3033 Office: Dept English 262 S Main St Lodi NJ 07644 Office Phone: 201-559-6105. Business E-Mail: mcparlandr@inet.felician.edu.

MCPARTLAND, JAMES MICHAEL, university official; b. N.Y.C., Sept. 26, 1939; s. James J. and Helen M. (Leddy) McP. BS, Cornell U., 1961, MS, 1963; PhD, Johns Hopkins U., 1968. Rschr. U.S. Office Edn., Washington, 1965-67, U.S. Commn. Civil Rights, Washington, 1967-68; asst. dir. Ctr. Social Orgn. Schs., Johns Hopkins U., Balt., 1968-75, co-dir., 1976-94; dir., 1994—. Co-author: Equality of Educational Opportunity, 1966, Encyclopedia of Educational Research, 1992, Review of Research in Education, 1993; co-editor: Violence in Schools, 1977, Comprehensive Urban School Reform, 2002. Mem. Am. Edni. Rsch. Assn., Am. Sociol. Assn., Am. Statis. Assn. Democrat. Roman Catholic. Avocation: music. Home: 1102 S Streeper St Baltimore MD 21224-4873 Office: Johns Hopkins U CSOS 3003 N Charles St Ste 200 Baltimore MD 21218-3888 E-mail: jmcpartland@csos.jhu.edu.

MCPARTLAND, MARIAN, pianist, composer; b. Slough, England, Mar. 20, 1920; came to U.S., 1946; d. Frank and Janet Payne Turner; m. Jimmy McPartland, Feb. 3, 1945 (div.). Student, Guildhall Sch. Music, London. Toured English vaudeville theaters as pianist with Milly Mayerl, 1941; toured with Brit. ENSA in Europe, 1943, with USO camp shows, France, 1944; formed group with husband, played with Billie Holiday; formed own group, 1951; toured U.S. nightclubs; played Hickory House, N.Y.C., 1952-60; performed with Benny Goodman, 1963; now leads group in nightclub and sch. appearances; founded Halcyon Records, 1969; toured S.Am. with Earl Hines and Teddy Wilson, 1974; composer Twilight World, Ambience; albums include Ambience, Fine Romance, Now's the Time, Solo Concert at Haverford, From This Moment On, 1978, Live at the Carlyle, 1979, Personal Choice, 1982. Office: care Manhattan Sch Music 120 Claremont Ave New York NY 10027-4631

MCPARTLAND, PATRICIA ANN, health educator and administrator; b. Passaic, NJ; d. Daniel and Josephine McP. BA, U. Mo., 1971; MCRP, MS in Preventive Medicine, Ohio State U., 1975; EdD in Higher and Adult Edn., Columbia U., 1988; cert. distance edn., Tex. A&M U., 2000, cert. distance edn. web pub. cert., 2001. Cert. health edn. specialist, distance edn. web pub., grants specialist; workforce devel. profl. Sr. health planner Merrimack Valley HSA, Lawrence, Mass., 1977—79; planning cons., adminstr. Children's Hosp., Boston, 1979—80; exec. dir. Assn. for Workforce Alternatives, Rsch. & Devel., Inc., Marion, Mass., 1980—. V.p., cons. New Bedford (Mass.) Cmty. Health Ctr, 1993—94; chmn. edn. and tng. com. Health and Human Svc. Coalition, 1988—89; mem. project expert panel Office of Minority Health, 1997—2003; mem. New Eng. Regional Minority Health Conf. Com., 1997—99; vis. lectr. Bridgewater State Coll.; lectr. in field; project expert panel Office Minority Health's Culturally and Linguistically Appropriate Svcs.; mem. New Eng. Regional Minority Health Conf. Com., 2001—03. Mem. editl. bd. Jour. Healthcare Edn. and Tng., 1989-93; author: Promoting Health in the Workplace, 1991; reviewer Qualitative Health Rsch. Jour.; contbr. articles to profl. jours. Vol. spkr. March of Dimes Found., Wareham, Mass., 1992-93; coll.-wide vocat. Cape Cod C.C., Hyannis, Mass., 1989—; planning adv. 2nd Internat. Symposium, Pasco, Wash., 1992; v.p. New Bedford chpt. Am. Cancer Soc., 1985-90. Recipient award Excellence in Continuing Edn. Nat. AHEC Ctr. Dirs. Assn., 1994, 95, 96, 97, Sec.'s awards for Outstanding Progam in Community Health, Nat. Cancer Inst., Washington, 1990. Mem.: APHA, Nat. Assn. Workforce Devel. Profls. (bd. dirs.), Nat. Planning Conf. (mem. com. 1984—87), Southeastern Mass. Health Planning (bd. dirs., sec. 1982—87), Inst. for Disease Prevention (steering com. 1982—). Avocations: writing, acting, dance, theater, travel. Home: PO Box 1116 Marion MA 02738-0020 Office: Assn for Workforce Alternatives Rsch & Devel Inc PO Box 69 2 Spring St Marion MA 02738-1519 Office Phone: 508-748-0837. E-mail: pmcpartland@comcast.net., smahec@tiac.net.

MCPEAK, ALLAN, career services director, educator, lawyer, consultant; b. Hot Springs, Ark., Oct. 1, 1938; s. Kenneth L. and Dorothy (Whiteman) McPeak; m. Judith L. Mathison, Oct. 26, 1973. BA, U. Fla., 1960, JD, 1965; MS, Nova U., 1984; PhD, Fla. State U., 1987, MS in Instrnl. Sys., 1994. Bar: Fla. 1965, U.S. Supreme Ct. 1980. Sole practice, Naples, Fla., 1965—85; asst. dir. The Career Ctr. Fla. State U., 1987, assoc. dir. The Career Ctr., 1989; dir. career svcs. U. South Ala., Mobile, 1994—. Cons. in human rels., orgnl. devel. and career devel., Tallahassee, 1984—94, Mobile, 1994—; pres. Lawyers Abstract Svc., Naples, 1978—80; organizer Marine Savs. and Loan, Naples, 1980—81. Contbr. articles to profl. jours. With U.S. Army, 1960—63. Mem.: Fla. Bar Assn., Ala. Assn. Colls. and Employers, So. Assn. Colls. and Employers, Nat. Assn. Colls. and Employers, Blue Key, Pi Sigma Alpha.

MCPEAK, MERRILL ANTHONY, business executive, consultant, retired officer; b. Santa Rosa, Calif., Jan. 9, 1936; s. Merrill Addison McPeak and Winifred Alice (Stewart) McPeak Bendall; m. Elynor Fay Moskowitz, Nov. 10, 1956; children— Mark Allen, Brian David AB, San Diego State Coll., Calif., 1957; MS, George Washington U., Washington, 1974. Commd. 2d lt. USAF, 1957, advanced through grades to gen., 1988; pilot USAF Thunderbirds, Nellis AFB, Nev., 1966-68; comdr. Misty Forward Air Controllers, Phu Cat, Republic of Vietnam, 1969, 20th Tactical Fighter Wing RAF, Upper Heyford, England, 1980-81, 12th Air Force, Bergstrom AFB, Tex., 1987-88; comdr.-in-chief Pacific Air Forces, Hickam AFB, Hawaii, 1988-90; chief of staff USAF, Washington, 1990-94; co. dir., cons., 1994—. Chmn. ECC Internat., 1997-2003, Ethicspoint, 2003—. Decorated DSM, Silver Star, Legion of Merit, DFC. Mem. Air Force Assn., Coun. Fgn. Rels., Daedalians, Sigma Chi. Home: 17360 Grandview Ct Lake Oswego OR 97034-6362 E-mail: tmcpeak@earthlink.net.

MCPETERS, SHARON JENISE, artist, writer; b. San Bernardino, Calif., Oct. 17, 1951; d. Cecil L. and Mary I. (Tanner) McP.; 1 child, Angela M. Benders. BA in Journalism and English, U. So. Calif., 1981. Proofreader Ventura (Calif.) Coll., 1979. Prin. works include My Professors, 1993, Interpretations, 1994, The Thoughts of Socrates, 1995, Self Portrait, 1995, Happiness, 1996, My True Self, 1998, Czechoslovakia 1923, 1999, Liszt, 1999, Portrait of Ten Artists, 2000; author: (autobiography) A Human Mind, 1997, (novels) Domestic Symphonies, 1986, The Broken Heart of the World, 1999, An Illuminated Manuscript, 1994, (short stories) The Library of Heaven, 2000, A Girl Without A Name, 2001, A Sanctified Heart, Selected Poems, 1974-2002, 2003, An Intellect's Goodness, 2004. Avocation: philosophical reading.

MCPHEE, GEORGE, professional sports team executive; BA in Bus., Bowling Green State U., 1982; JD, Rutgers U., 1992. Hockey player Guelph (Can.) Platers, 1978, Bowling Green State U., 1978—82, N.Y. Rangers, 1982, N.J. Devils; v.p., dir. hockey ops. Vancouver (Can.) Canucks, 1992—97, alt. gov., 1992—; gen. mgr. Washington Capitals, 1997—, v.p., 1997—. Recipient Hobey Baker Meml. award, 1982. Office: 401 9th St NW Ste 750 Washington DC 20004*

MC PHEE, HENRY ROEMER, lawyer; b. Ames, Iowa, Jan. 11, 1925; s. Harry Roemer and Mary (Ziegler) McP.; m. Joanne Lambert, May 19, 1956 (div. Dec. 1991); children: Henry Roemer III, Joanne, Larkin, Charles; m. Selby Fleming, Jan. 27, 1999. AB cum laude, Princeton U., 1947; LLB, Harvard U., 1950. Bar: N.J. 1951, Ill. 1961, D.C. 1966. Exec. asst. to gov. State of N.J., Trenton, 1950-52; assoc. R.E. & A.D. Watson, New Brunswick, N.J., 1952-54; asst. to gen. counsel FTC, Washington, 1954; exec. asst. White House, Washington, 1954-57; asst. spl. counsel Pres. U.S., Washington, 1957-58, assoc. spl. counsel, pres., 1958-61; ptnr. Hamel & Park, Washington, 1961-88, mem. mgmt. com., 1975-85, mng. ptnr., 1980-83; ptnr. Hopkins & Sutter, 1988-93, of counsel, 1994—2002, Foley & Lardner, 2002—. Sec. N.J. Commn. on Interstate Cooperation, 1952-54; gen. counsel Rep. Nat. Fin. Com., 1968-73, Rep. Nat. Com., Washington, 1968. Chmn. bldg. com. Potomac (Md.) Presbyn. Ch., 1965-67; v.p. Rep. Club, Princeton, 1952-54; bd. dirs. Eisenhower Inst., 1983—, treas., 1991-93, mem. exec. com., 1991—. Mem. ABA, D.C. Bar Assn., N.J. Bar Assn., Lincoln's Inn Soc. Harvard Law Sch. Clubs: Tower (Princeton U.); Princeton (Washington) (pres. 1970-72), Metropolitan (Washington), Capitol Hill (Washington). Republican. Presbyterian. Avocation: tennis. Office: Hopkins & Sutter 888 16th St NW Ste 600 Washington DC 20006-4105 Address: 915 15th St NW Washington DC 20005 Office: Foley & Lardner 3000 K St NW Ste 500 Washington DC 20007

MCPHEE, JOHN ANGUS, writer; b. Princeton, N.J., Mar. 8, 1931; s. Harry Roemer and Mary (Ziegler) McP.; m. Pryde Brown, Mar. 16, 1957; children: Laura, Sarah, Jenny, Martha; m. Yolanda Whitman, Mar. 8, 1972; stepchildren: Cole Harrop, Andrew Harrop, Katherine Ryan, Vanessa Speir. AB, Princeton U., 1953; postgrad., Magdalene Coll., Cambridge (Eng.) U., 1953-54; LittD (hon.), Bates Coll., 1978, Colby Coll., 1978, Williams Coll., 1979, U. Alaska, 1980, Coll. William and Mary, 1988, Rutgers U., 1988; ScD, Maine Maritime Acad., 1992. TV playwright for Robert Montgomery Presents, N.Y.C., 1955-56; contbg. editor, assoc. editor Time mag., 1957-64; staff writer The New Yorker mag., 1965—; Ferris prof. journalism Princeton U., 1975—. Author: A Sense of Where You Are, 1965, The Headmaster, 1966, Oranges, 1967, The Pine Barrens, 1968, A Roomful of Hovings, 1968, Levels of the Game, 1969, The Crofter and the Laird, 1970, Encounters with the Archdruid, 1971, The Deltoid Pumpkin Seed, 1973, The Curve of Binding Energy, 1974, Pieces of the Frame, 1975, The Survival of the Bark Canoe, 1975, The John McPhee Reader, 1976, Coming into the Country, 1977, Giving Good Weight, 1979, Basin and Range, 1981, In Suspect Terrain, 1983, La Place de la Concorde Suisse, 1984, Table of Contents, 1985, Rising from the Plains, 1986, The Control of Nature, 1989, Looking for a Ship, 1990, Assembling California, 1993, The Ransom of Russian Art, 1994, The Second John McPhee Reader, 1996, Irons in the Fire, 1997, Annals of the Former World, 1998, The Founding Fish, 2002. Recipient award in lit., Am. Acad. and Inst. Arts and Letters, 1977, Woodrow Wilson award, Princeton U., 1982, Journalism award, Am. Assn. of Petroleum Geologists, 1982, 1987, John Wesley Powell award, U.S. Geol. Survey, 1988, John Burroughs medal, 1990, Walter Sullivan award, Am. Geophys. Union, 1993, James H. Shea award, Nat. Assn. Geology Tchrs., 1995, award for Outstanding Achievement, Am. Inst. Petroleum Geologists, 1997, award of merit, Field Mus. Natural History, 1998, Pulitzer Prize for Gen.

Non-Fiction, Annals of the Former World, 1999, Pres.'s award for disting. tchg., Princeton U., 1999, Pub. Svc. award, Geol. Soc. Am., 2002. Fellow Geol. Soc. Am.; mem. Am. Acad. Arts and Letters.

MCPHEE, JONATHAN, music director, conductor, composer, interim artistic coordinator; LRAM, Royal Acad. Music; BM, MM, Juilliard Sch. Music dir., prin. condr. Boston Ballet, 1988—; mus. dir. Symphony by the Sea, Boston, 2001—. Condr.: dance cos. The Joffrey Ballet, The Martha Graham Dance Co., The Dance Theatre of Harlem, Am. Ballet Theatre, N.Y.C. Ballet, The Royal Ballet, Covent Garden, Nat. Ballet of Can., orchs. including Buffalo Philharm., Joffrey Ballet Orch., Rochester Philharm, Opera Orch., BBC Scottish Symphony, Hague Philharm., Boston Pops, Syracuse Symphony, San Diego Symphony, San Francisco Symphony, Orchestre Colonne, The Nat. Philharm. Orch., Danish Radio Symphony Orch; rec. (films) Martha Graham works, Cave of the Heart, Errand Into the Maze, El Penintent, Michael Gandolfi's Caution to the Wind; author: (rev.) version Stravinsky's Rite of Spring; arrangements pub.: by Boosey & Hawkes. Office: Boston Ballet 19 Clarendon St Boston MA 02116-6100 also: P O Box 1425 Marblehead MA 01945

MCPHEE, MARK STEVEN, medical educator, physician, gastroenterologist; b. Kansas City, Mo., Nov. 8, 1951; s. William Robert and Mary Kay (Paige) McP.; m. Christina Marie Luebke, July 14, 1974; children: Molly Amanda, Ian Andrew. BA magna cum laude, Pomona Coll., Claremont, Calif., 1973; MD summa cum laude, U. Kans., Kansas City, 1976. Diplomate Nat. Bd. Med. Examiners; diplomate in internal medicine and gastroenterology Am. Bd. Internal Medicine. Intern, resident, fellow Harvard U. Med. Sch., Boston, 1976-80; dir. gastrointestinal endoscopy unit Kans. U. Med. Ctr., Kansas City, 1980-85; chief sect. gastroenterology St. Luke's Hosp., Kansas City, Mo., 1988-93, chair dept. medicine, 1992-97, assoc. dir. med. edn., 1995-97, dir. med. edn., 1997—; assoc. dean U. Mo.-Kansas City Med. Sch., 1997—. Asst. prof. medicine U. Kans., KansasCity, 1980-85, assoc. prof., 1985; clin. prof. medicine U. Mo., Kansas City, 1970-97, prof. medicine, 1997—. Author: Annotated Key References in Gastroenterology, 1982; contbr. chpts. to textbook, articles to profl. jours. Bd. dirs. St. Luke's Hosp., Kansas City,Mo., 1993—, Am. Digestive Health Found., Bethesda, Md., 1996—. Fellow ACP, Am. Coll. Gastroenterology; mem. Am. Gastroent. Assn. (mem. governing bd., treas.), St. Lukes Hosp. Physicians Assn. (bd. dirs.), HealthNet Physician Ptnrs. (bd. dirs.), Alpha Omega Alpha. Episcopalian. Avocations: poetry, hiking/camping, golf, tennis, sporting clay target shooting. Office: St Lukes Hosp Dept Med Edn 44th and Wornall Rd Kansas City MO 64111

MCPHEE, MARTHA, literature educator; BA magna cum laude, Bowdoin Coll., 1987; MFA, Columbia U., 1994. Fiction tchr. Gotham Writer's Workshop, N.Y.C., 1993—97; adj. prof. creative writing Columbia U., 1997—99; writer, asst. prof. creative writing Hofstra U., 2002—. Author: (novels) Bright Angel Time, 1998, Gorgeous Lies, 2002, (nonfiction) Girls: Ordinary Girls and Their Extraordinary Pursuits, 2000; translator: Crossing the Threshold of Hope, 1994, author short stories; contbr. articles to publs. Fellow, John Simon Guggenheim Meml. Found., 2003. Office: Hofstra Univ Hempstead NY 11549-1000

MC PHEETERS, EDWIN KEITH, architect, educator; b. Stillwater, Okla., Mar. 26, 1924; s. William Henry and Eva Winona (Mitchell) McP.; m. Patricia Ann Foster, Jan. 29, 1950 (div. 1981); children: Marc Foster, Kevin Mitchell, Michael Hunter; m. Mary Louise Marvin, July 21, 1984. BArch, Okla. State U., 1949; MFA, Princeton U., 1956. Instr. architecture U. Fla., 1949-51; asst. prof. Ala. Poly. Inst., Auburn (Ala.) U., 1951-54; fellow Princeton U., 1955, 81; from asst. prof. to prof. U. Ark., 1956-66; prof. Rensselaer Poly. Inst., 1966-69, dean, 1966-69; prof. Auburn U., 1969-89, dean Sch. Architecture and Fine Arts, 1969-88, dean, prof. emeritus, 1989—. Mem. Ala. Bd. Registration for Archs., 1978-87; profl. adviser South Ctrl. Bell Tel. Co., 1977-79, So. Co., 1979-81, Ala. Power Co., 1979-81, Okla. State U., 1983, Ala. Sch. Fine Arts, 1985-86; cons. Taliesin Archs., 1988-92, adj. prof. Frank Lloyd Wright Sch. of Architecture, 1992-94. Served to 2d lt. USAAC, 1943-45; capt. USAFR 1945-57. Recipient Disting. Arch. award Ala. Archtl. Found., 2001. Fellow AIA (pres. Ala. coun. 1978, Merit award 1976, East Ala. Design awards 1986, 87, 90, 92); mem. Assn. Collegiate Schs. Arch. (bd. dirs. 1970-77, Disting. Prof. 1989), Blue Key, Kappa Sigma, Omicron Delta Kappa, Kappa Kappa Psi, Tau Sigma Delta, Rotary, Watercolor Soc. Ala. (pres. 2000—). Episcopalian. Office Phone: 334-887-8779.

MCPHEETERS, F. LYNN, manufacturing executive; BS in Acctg., So. Ill. U.; grad., Duke U. Adv. Mgmt. Program, Stanford U. Adv. Fin. Mgmt. Trainee in acctg. Caterpillar, 1964, exec. v.p. fin. svcs. corp., 1990-96, corp. treas., 1996-98, v.p. corp. services div., CFO, 1998—. Office: Caterpillar Inc 100 NE Adams St Peoria IL 61629

MCPHERSON, ALAN L. history professor; b. Berkeley, Calif., Oct. 18, 1970; BA in History, U. Montreal, 1994; MA in History, San Francisco State U., 1996; PhD in History, U. N.C., 2001. Asst. prof. Howard U., Washington, 2001—. Author: Yankee No!, 2003. Office: Howard U History Dept 316 Douglass Hall 2441 6th St NW Washington DC 20059 Office Phone: 202-806-6815. Office Fax: 202-806-4471. Business E-Mail: almcpherson@howard.edu.

MCPHERSON, ALICE RUTH, ophthalmologist, educator; b. Regina, Sask., Can., June 30, 1926; came to U.S., 1938, naturalized, 1958; d. Gordon and Viola (Hoover) McP. BS, U. Wis., 1948, MD, 1951, DSc (hon.), 1997. Diplomate Am. Bd. Ophthalmology. Intern Santa Barbara (Calif.) Cottage Hosp., 1951-52; resident anesthesiology Hartford (Conn.) Hosp., 1952; resident ophthalmology Chgo. Eye, Ear, Nose and Throat Hosp., 1953, U. Wis. Hosps., 1953-55; ophthalmologist Davis and Duehr Eye Clinic, Madison, Wis., 1956-57; clin. instr. U. Wis., 1956-57; fellow retina svc. Mass. Eye and Ear Infirmary, 1957-58; ophthalmologist Scott and White Clinic, Temple, Tex., 1958-60; practice medicine specializing in ophthalmology and retinal diseases Houston, 1960—. Staff Meth., St. Luke's, Tex. Children's Hosps., Harris County Hosp. Dist., Houston; clin. asst. prof. Baylor Coll. Medicine, Houston, 1959-61, asst. prof. opthalmology, 1961-69, clin. assoc. prof., 1969-75, clin. prof., 1975-98, prof., 1998—; cons. retinal diseases VA Hosp., Houston, 1960—, Ben Taub Hosp., Houston, 1960—; mem. adv. com. for active staff appt. sect. ophthalmology Meth. Hosp., 1986-91, mem equipment com., 1993-95, mem. grievance panel, 1997; vol. clin. faculty appts. and promotions com., 1993; bd. dirs. Highlights of Ophthalmology; v.p. N.Am. Highlights of Ophthalmology Internat. Editor: New and Controversial Aspects of Retinal Detachment, 1968, New and Controversial Aspects of Vitreoretinal Surgery, 1977, Retinopathy of Prematurity: Current Concepts and Controversies, 1986. Amb. Houston Ballet, mem. Houston Ballet Found.; mem. pres.'s coun. Houston Grand Opera; condrs. cir. Houston Symphony, mem. Houston Symphony Soc.; mem. campaign for 80s Baylor Coll. Medicine; mem. Assn. for Cmty. TV, BBB, Physicians' Benevolent Fund, South Tex. Diabetes Assn. Inc., Jr. League Houston; bd. dirs. U. Wis. Found., Madison. Recipient Award of appreciation KT Eye Found., 1978, Woodlands Medal for Outstanding Contbn. to the Econ. Devel. of Cmty., 1988, spl. recognition award Assn. for Rsch. in Vision in Ophthalmology, Crystal award Recognizing Generous Support-Ptnrs. with an Eye for Vision Found. Am. Acad. Ophthalmology, 2000, Benjamin Boyd Humanitarian award Pan Am. Assn. Ophthalmology, 2001, Philip Corboy Meml. award Disting. Svc. Ophthalmology, 2002, Women of Vision Houston Delta Gamma Found., 2002; Alice R. Mc Pherson Lab. for Retina Rsch. dedicated Baylor Ctr. for Biotech., 1988; Alice R. Mc Pherson Day proclaimed in her honor Mayor of City of Houston, Mar. 12, 1988. Fellow: ACS (credentials and Tex. credentials com., com. on applications), Am. Acad. Ophthalmology (2nd v.p. 1979, vice chmn. program devel. found. bd. trustees 1993—, com. for pub. and profl. rels., bd. dirs. opthalmology edni. trust fund found., honor award 1956, sr. honor award 1986, guest of honor 1998 meeting); mem.: AMA, Highlights Ophthal. Internat., Schepens Internat. Soc. (sec. 1986—93, v.p. 1993—95, pres. 1995—97), U. Wis. Ophthal. Alumni Assn. (founding pres. 1990—93, founded Alice R. McPherson lectureship 1994), Assn. Rsch. Surgeons, Pan Am. Assn. Ophthalmology Found., Tex. Ophthal. Assn., So. Med. Soc., Rsch. to Prevent Blindness, Pan Am. Assn. Opthalmology (v.p. 1991—92, pres. elect 1992—95, AJO lectr. 1993, pres. 1995—97, pres. found. 1997, bd. dirs., membership com., Benjamin Boyd Humanitarian award 2001), Macula Soc. (credentialing com. 1992—), Internat. Soc. Eye Rsch. (credentials com. 1992—), Houston Ophthal. Soc. (pres. 1990—91, credentials com.), Harris County Med. Soc., Am. Bd. Laser Surgery, Am. Soc. Contemporary Ophthalmology (Charles Schepens Hon. award), Internat. Coll. Ocular Surgeons (vice regent 1991), Retina Soc. (v.p. 1976—77, pres. 1978—79, credentials com.), Am. Med. Women's Assn., Internat. Coll. Surgeons (vice regent 1991—), Tex. Med. Assn., Vitreous Soc., Jules Gonin Club. Achievements include research in vision and ophthalmology. Office: Tex Med Ctr 6560 Fannin St Ste 2200 Houston TX 77030-2715

MCPHERSON, DAVID, music company executive; BA, William Patterson U. V.p. Jive Records, 1994—98; exec. v.p. Epic Records divsn. Sony, 1998—2003, Sony Urban Music, Sony, U.S., 2003—. Office: Sony Music 550 Madison Ave 22d Fl New York NY 10022

MCPHERSON, DONALD PAXTON, III, lawyer; b. Balt., Aug. 9, 1941; s. Donald Paxton Jr. and Janet Lewis Russell McPherson; m. Anna Mary Teaff; children: David Russell, Cynthia Quandt. AB, Princeton U., 1963; LLB, Columbia U., 1966. Bar: Md. 1966, U.S. Dist. Ct. Md. 1967, U.S. Ct. Appeals (4th cir.) 1967. Assoc. Piper & Marbury, Balt., 1966-74, ptnr., 1974-98, head real estate dept., 1980-94, of counsel, 1998—. Mem. ABA, Md. Bar Assn. Democrat. Presbyterian. Avocations: swimming, bicycling, hiking. Office: Piper Rudnick LLP 6225 Smith Ave Baltimore MD 21209-3600

MCPHERSON, DONALD SCOTT, labor and employment arbitrator/mediator; b. Sharon, Pa., June 11, 1947; s. Donald McMillan and Lily (Smith) McP.; m. Linda Jo Leighty, Aug. 16, 1969; 1 child, Kimra Leigh. BA, Indiana U. of Pa., 1969, MA, 1971; PhD, U. Pitts., 1977. Dir. residence life Indiana U. of Pa., 1969-77, prof. employment rels., 1977-93, chmn. dept., 1977-87, disting. univ. prof., 1993—2004. Pres. Assn. Pa. State Coll. and Univ. Faculty, Indiana U. Pa. chpt., 1980. Author: Resolving Grievances, 1983; contbr. articles to profl. jours. Elder Calvary Presbyn. Ch., 1983—; sec. St. Andrew's Soc. of Indiana, 1991-94. Recipient disting. faculty award for svc., Commonwealth of Pa., 1983, Outstanding Alumni award, Indiana U. of Pa., 1983. Mem. Nat. Acad. Arbitrators, Am. Arbitration Assn., Assn. for Conflict Resolution, Indsl. Rels. Rsch. Assn. (exec. dir. Western Pa. chpt. 1982-89), Found. for Indiana U. of Pa. (bd. dir. 1977-82), Indiana Coun. on the Arts, Indiana U. of Pa. Alumni Assn. (pres. 1975-79), Clan MacPherson Assn. (life), Phi Kappa Phi. Democrat. Presbyterian.

MCPHERSON, EDWARD RUSSELL, federal agency administrator; b. Balt., Sept. 18, 1945; s. Donald Payton and Janet (Russell) McP.; m. Sally Thompson, May 12, 1969; children: Beth, Edward. BA, Williams Coll., Williamstown, Mass., 1967; MS, George Washington U., 1971. Mgmt. cons. Klein & Saks Inc., Washington, 1968, Booz Allen & Hamilton, Washington, 1971-73; v.p. corp. planning and investor relations Republic Bank Dallas, 1973-76; sr. v.p. corp. planning and investor relations RepublicBank Corp., Dallas, 1978-83, sr. v.p., chief fin. officer, 1983-84, exec. v.p., chief fin. officer, 1984-87, First RepublicBank Corp., Dallas, 1987—2001; chief fin. officer USDA, Washington, 2001—. Bd. dirs. Republic Venture Group, Dallas. Trustee Hockaday Sch., Dallas, 1987, Dallas Fiscal Affairs Com., 1983-87. Served to lt. USN, 1968-71. Office: USDA 1400 Independence Ave SW Washington DC 20250

MC PHERSON, HARRY CUMMINGS, JR., lawyer; b. Tyler, Tex., Aug. 22, 1929; s. Harry Cummings and Nan (Hight) McP.; m. Clayton Read, Aug. 30, 1952 (div.); children: Courtenay, Peter B.; m. Mary Patricia DeGroot, Oct. 17, 1981; 1 child, Sam B. BA, U. South, 1949, DCL, 1965; student, Columbia U., 1949-50; LLB, U. Tex., 1956. Bar: Tex. 1955, D.C. 1969. Asst. gen. counsel Democratic policy com. U.S. Senate, 1956-59, assoc. counsel, 1959-61, gen. counsel, 1961-63; dep. under sec. internat. affairs Dept. Army, 1963-64; asst. sec. ednl. and cultural affairs Dept. State, 1964-65; spl. asst. and counsel to Pres. Johnson, 1965-66, spl. counsel, 1966-69; pvt. practice law Washington, 1969—. Chmn. task force on domestic policy Dem. Adv. Coun. Elected Ofcls., 1974-76; mem. Pres.'s Commn. on Accident at Three Mile Island, 1979; vice chmn. John F. Kennedy Ctr. for Performing Arts, 1969-76, gen. counsel, 1977-91; bd. dirs. Woodrow Wilson Internat. Ctr. for Scholars, 1969-74; pres. Fed. City Coun., 1983-88; apptd. vice chmn. U.S. Internat. Cultural and Trade Ctr. Commn., 1988-93. Author: A Political Education, 1972, 88, 95. Mem. U.S. Base Closure and Realignment Commn., 1993. 2d lt. USAF, 1950-53. Recipient Disting. Civilian Svc. award Dept. Army, 1964, Arthur S. Flemming award, 1968, Judge Learned Hand Human Rels. award Am. Jewish Com., 1994. Mem. D.C. Bar Assn., N.Y. Council on Fgn. Relations (dir. 1974-77), Econ. Club. of Washington (pres. 1992-99). Democrat. Episcopalian. Home: 10213 Montgomery Ave Kensington MD 20895-3325 Office: Piper Rudnick 1200 19th St NW Washington DC 20036 Office Phone: 202-861-6464. E-mail: harry.mcpherson@piperrudnick.com.

MCPHERSON, JAMES ALAN, writer, educator; b. Savannah, Ga., Sept. 16, 1943; s. James and Mable (Smalls) McP.; 1 dau., Rachel Alice. BA, Morris Brown Coll., 1965; LLB, Harvard, 1968; MFA, U. Iowa, 1971. Asst. prof. lit. U. Calif., Santa Cruz, 1969-71, Morgan State U., 1975-76; assoc. prof. English U. Va., Charlottesville, 1976-81; prof. English U. Iowa, 1981—. Mem. lit. panel Nat. Endowment for Arts, 1977-80; lectr., Japan, 1989-90; vis. scholar Yale Law Sch., 1978-79. Author: Hue and Cry, 1969, Railroad, 1976, Elbow Room, 1977 (Pultizer prize 1978), A World Unsuspected, 1987, The Prevailing South, 1988, Confronting Racial Differences, 1990, Lure and Loathing, 1993, Crossings, 1993, Crab Cakes, 1998, Fathering Daughters, 1998, The View From Exile, 2000; editor Double Take Mag., 1995—; contbr. editor Atlantic Monthly, Boston, 1969. Atlantic grantee, 1968; Guggenheim fellow, 1972-73, Ctr. Behavioral Studies fellow, Stanford, Calif., 1997-98, 2002-03; Recipient award in lit. Nat. Inst. Arts and Letters, 1970, MacArthur Found. award, 1981, Excellence in Tchg. award U. Iowa, 1991, Green Eyeshades award Soc. So. Journalists, 1994; stories selected for O'Henry Collection and Best American Short Stories, 1969, 73, Best Am. Short Stories of the 20th Century, Best Am. Essays various Norton Anthologies, 1990, 93, 94, 95, Pushcart prize, 1995, 96, award Cannon Found., 2002. Mem. ACLU, NAACP, P.E.N., Am. Acad. Arts and Scis. (elected mem. 1995), Authors League.

MCPHERSON, JAMES ALDEN, publishing executive; b. Barry County, MD, June 29, 1942; s. William Daniel and Lola Agnes McPherson; m. Elizabeth Trimbe, Oct. 24, 1976; children: Sarah Elizabeth, Samuel James; m. Elizabeth Ellen Clay, Aug. 22, 1964 (div. Feb. 1976); 1 child, Andrew Clay. AA, Sch. of the Ozarks, 1962; BA, Drary Coll., 1964. Asst. to senator Stuart Symington U.S. Senate, Washington, 1969—77; exec. v.p. Mo-Ark Assn., Kansas City, Mo., 1977—84; pub. The Western Chronicle, Weston, Mo., 1984—, Buchanan County News, St. Joseph, Mo., 1995—. Trustee Mid-Continent Pub. Libr., Independence, Mo., 1989—; regional v.p. Am. Libr. Trustee Assn., Chgo., 1997—2001. Capt. USAF, 1964—69, Alexandria, Va. Office: The Western Chronicle 18275 Hwy 45 No Weston MO 64098 Business E-Mail: wcnews@mindspring.com. E-mail: mcpnews@mindspring.com.

MC PHERSON, JAMES MUNRO, history professor; b. Valley City, N.D., Oct. 11, 1936; s. James Munro and Miriam (Osborn) McPherson; m. Patricia Rasche, Dec. 28, 1957; 1 child, Joanna Erika. BA, Gustavus Adolphus Coll., 1958; PhD, Johns Hopkins U., 1963. From mem. faculty to prof. Princeton U., 1962—91, George Henry Davis '86 prof. Am. history, 1991—2004, prof. emeritus, 2004—. Jefferson lectr., 2000. Author: Struggle for Equality, 1964 (Ainsfield-Wolf award race rels., 1965), The Negro's Civil War, 1965, Marching Toward Freedom: The Negro in the Civil War, 1968, Blacks in America: Bibliographical Essays, 1971, The Abolitionist Legacy: From Reconstruction to the NAACP, 1975, Ordeal by Fire: The Civil War and Reconstruction, 1981, 1992, Battle Cry of Freedom: The Civil War Era, 1988 (Pulitzer prize for history, 1989), Abraham Lincoln and the Second American Revolution, 1991, Images of the Civil War, 1992, What They Fought For 1861-1865, 1994, The Atlas of the Civil War, 1994, Drawn With the Sword: Reflections on the American Civil War, 1996, For Cause and Comrades: Why Men Fought in the Civil War, 1997 (Lincoln prize, 1998), Lamson of the Gettysburg: The Civil War Letters of Lt. Roswell H. Lamson, U.S. Navy, 1997 (Theodore and Franklin D. Roosevelt prize in naval history, 1998), Is Blood Thicker than Water? Crisis of Nationalism in the Modern World, 1998, Writing the Civil War: The Quest to Understand, 1998, To the Best of My Ability, 2000, The American Presidents, 2000, Days of Destiny, 2001, Crossroads of Freedom: Antietam, 2002, Hallowed Ground: A Walk at Gettysburg, 2003, Illustrated Battle Cry of Freedom, 2003. Fellow, Huntington-Nat. Endowment for Humanities, 1977—78, Behavioral Scis. Ctr., Stanford U., 1982—83, Huntington-Seaver Inst., 1987—88; Danforth fellow, 1958—62, Guggenheim fellow, 1967—68. Mem.: Orgn. Am. Historians, So. Hist. Assn., Am. Hist. Assn. (pres. 2003—04), Am. Philos. Soc., Phi Beta Kappa (Jefferson lectr. 2000). Home: 15 Randall Rd Princeton NJ 08540-3609 Office Phone: 609-258-4173.

MCPHERSON, LARRY E(UGENE), photographer, educator; b. Newark, Ohio, May 1, 1943; s. Eugene Edward and Ethel Grace (Lehman) McP. BA, Columbia Coll., Chgo., 1976; MA, No. Ill. U., 1978. Instr. Columbia Coll., 1971-76; assoc. prof. photography U. Memphis, 1978—. Instr. Sch. of Art Inst. Chgo., spring 1972; workshop instr. Ohio State U., Columbus, summer 1980, VSW Summer Inst., Rochester, N.Y., summer 1988. One-man shows include Art Inst. Chgo., 1969, 78, 81, Dayton Art Inst., 1992; exhibited in group shows at Mus. Modern Art, N.Y.C., 1978, Corcoran Gallery Art, Washington, 1982, George Eastman House, Rochester, N.Y., 1982, New Orleans Mus. Art, 1992, Milw. Art Mus., 1996, Birmingham Mus. Art, 1996, Art Inst. Chgo., 1997; represented in permanent collections Mus. Modern Art, Art Inst. Chgo., George Eastman House, New Orleans Mus. Art, Mus. Fine Arts, Houston, Memphis Brooks Mus. Art, The Dayton Art Inst., Birmingham Mus. Art, Milw. Mus. Art, Ogden Mus. So. Art; author: "Memphis", Santa Fe, NM: Center for American Places, 2002. Faculty Devel. grantee U. Memphis, 1983, 92, 99; grantee-fellow Nat. Endowment for Arts, 1975, 79; Guggenheim fellow, 1980. Mem. Soc. Photog. Edn. Home: 7725 Shadow Bend Ln Arlington TN 38002-8051 Office: U Memphis Dept Art Memphis TN 38152-0001 Business E-Mail: lmcphrsn@memphis.edu.

MCPHERSON, MARY PATTERSON, charitable foundation executive; b. Abington, Pa., May 14, 1935; d. John B. and Marjorie Hoffman (Higgins) McP. AB, Smith Coll., 1957, LLD, 1981; MA, U. Del., 1960; PhD, Bryn Mawr Coll., 1969; LLD (hon.), Juniata Coll., 1975, Smith Coll., 1981, Princeton U., 1984, U. Rochester, 1984, U. Pa., 1985; LittD (hon.), Haverford Coll., 1980; L.H.D. (hon.), Lafayette Coll., 1982; LHD (hon.), U. Pa., 1985, Med. Coll. Pa., 1985. Instr. philosophy U. Del., 1959-61; asst., fellow and lectr. dept. philosophy Bryn Mawr Coll., 1961-63, asst. dean, 1964-69, assoc. dean, 1969-70; dean Bryn Mawr Coll. (Undergrad. Coll.), 1970-78, assoc. prof., from 1970; acting pres. Bryn Mawr Coll., 1976-77, pres., 1978-97, pres. emeritus, 1997—; v.p. The Andrew W. Mellon Found., 1997—. Bd. dirs. Agnes Irwin Sch., 1972-90, Shipley Sch., 1972-90, Phillips Exeter Acad., 1973-76, Wilson Coll., 1976-79, Greater Phila. Movement, 1973-77, Internat. House of Phila., 1974-76, Josiah Macy, Jr. Found., 1977—, Carnegie Found. for Advancement Teaching, 1978-86, Univ. Mus., Phila., 1977-79, University City Sci. Center, 1979-85, Brookings Inst., 1984-90, Phila. Contributionship, 1985—, Carnegie Corp. N.Y., 1985-94, Nat. Humanities Ctr., 1986-91, Amherst Coll., 1986-98, Humanity in Action, Inc., 1997—, Goldman Sachs Asset Mgmt., 1997—, The Spencer Found., 1993—, Am. Sch. Classical Studies, 1996—, Bank St. Coll., 1998—, Smith Coll., 1998—. Mem. Am. Philos. Soc., Am. Acad. of Arts and Scis., Cosmopolitan Club. Office: The Andrew W Mellon Found 140 E 62nd St New York NY 10021-8124 Office Phone: 212-838-8400.

MCPHERSON, MICHAEL, entertainer, theater producer; b. New Orleans, Feb. 20, 1968; s. Jacqueline and James McPherson. BA, Tulane U., New Orleans, 1989. Prodr. Poet Prodns., LLC, Pompano Beach, Fla., 1995—; entertainer Cirque du Soleil, Montreal, Canada, 1993—95. Prodr.(headline entertainer): (live theatrical prod.) Luminaire - The Spectrum of Light as seen through Magic, Music and Motion, (headliner) Michael McPherson's Physical Magic; dir.(entertainer): Cirque Ingenieux, Cirque 98 (Best Show of the Yr. Atlantic City 1996, 1997, 1998). Office: Poet Prodns 2521 NW 16th Ln Studio C Pompano Beach FL 33064 Office Phone: 954-956-7681. Home Fax: 954-956-7682; Office Fax: 954-956-7682. Personal E-mail: michael@poetproductions.com. E-mail: michael@poetproductions.com.

MCPHERSON, MICHAEL STEVEN, former academic administrator, economist; b. June 6, 1947; married; 2 children. BA Math., U. Chgo., 1967, MA Econs., 1970, PhD Econs., 1974. Instr. econs. dept. U. Ill., Chgo., 1971—74; asst. prof. econs. Williams Coll., 1974—81, assoc. prof. econs., 1981—84, prof. econs., 1984—96, chmn. econs. dept., then dean of faculty, 1986—91; pres. Macalester Coll., St. Paul, 1996—2003, Spencer Found., Chgo., 2003—. Cons. Data Resources, Inc., 1979, Nat. Rsch. Coun. Commn. Human Resources, 1979, Modern Lang. Assn., 1980, Nat. Acad. Edn., 1980, Smith Coll., 1982, The Coll. Bd., 1983, Rand Corp., 1985—86, U.S. Dept. Edn. Ctr. Statis., 1986. Co-author (with M.O. Shapiro): Keeping College Affordable: Government and Educational Opportunity, 1991, The Student Aid Game: Meeting Need and Rewarding Talent in American Higher Education, 1998; co-author: (with D. Hausman) Economic Analysis and Moral Philosophy, 1996; editor: The Demand for the New Faculty in Science and Engineering, 1980, Democract Development and the Art of Trespassing: Essays in Honor of Albert O. Hirschman, 1986; contbr. articles to profl. jours. Trustee Coll. Bd., 1997—. Fellow Study fellow, Am. Coun. Learned Socs., 1977—78, vis. fellow, Princeton U., 1977—78, sr. fellow, Brookings Inst., 1984—86; grantee, Ford Found., 1981—83, Mellon Found., 1984—86. Home: 1750 Summit Ave Saint Paul MN 55105-1834 Office: The Spencer Found 875 N Michigan Ave Ste 3930 Chicago IL 60611-1803

MCPHERSON, MILTON MONROE, history professor; b. Beatrice, Ala., Oct. 19, 1928; s. Laurence Milton and Annie Mae (Bell) McP.; m. Carolyn Elizabeth Coley, Dec. 16, 1955; children: Milton Jr., Herbert L., Gretchen M. BA, U. Ala., 1950, MA, 1959, PhD in Am. History, 1970. Asst. prof. history Miss. Coll., Clinton, 1959-60, Mercer U., Macon, Ga., 1960-61, Ala. Coll., Montevallo, 1961-62, Pensacola (Fla.) Jr. Coll., 1962-68; assoc. prof. history Troy (Ala.) State U., 1968-87, prof. history, 1987-89; prof. history emeritus, 1989—. Author: The Ninety-Day Wonders: OCS and the Modern American Army, 2001; editor: Memories That Lingered: The Life and Times of Laurence Milton McPherson, 1993, Timeless Moments: Essays in American History, 1995. 1st lt. US Army, 1950-53. Mem. NEA, Ala. Hist. Assn., So. Hist. Assn. Avocations: writing, reading, photography, walking, travel. Home: 206 Sherwood Ave Troy AL 36081-4534

MC PHERSON, PETER, academic administrator; b. Grand Rapids, Mich., Oct. 27, 1940; s. Donald and Ellura E. (Frost) McP.; m. Joanne McPherson; 4 children. BA in Polit. Sci., Mich. State U., 1963; MBA, Western Mich. U., 1967; JD, Am. U., 1969; LHD (hon.), Va. State U., 1964, Mt. St. Mary;s Coll., 1996; LLD (hon.), Mich. State U., 1984. Tax law specialist IRS, 1969—75; spl. asst. to Pres. Ford, deputy dir. presdl. personnel The White House, Washington, 1975—77; ptnr. Vorys, Sater, Swymour & Pease, Washington, 1977—80; adminstr. Agy. Internat. Devel., 1981—87; deputy sec. Treasury Dept., Washington, 1987—89; group exec. v.p. Bank Am., 1989—93; pres. Mich. State U., East Lansing, 1993—. Chmn. bd. Overseas Pvt. Investment Corp., 1981—87; dir. econ. policy, CPA, Iraq, 2003. Vol. Peace Corps, Peru, 1964—65; gen. counsel Reagan-Bush Transition, 1980—81. Recipient Humanitarian of Yr. award, Am. Lebanese League, 1983, UNICEF award. Mem. D.C. Bar Assn., Mich. Bar Assn. Republican. Methodist.

MC PHERSON, ROLF KENNEDY, clergyman, religious organization administrator; b. Providence, Mar. 23, 1913; s. Harold S. and Aimee (Semple) McP.; m. Lorna De Smith, July 21, 1931 (dec.); children— Marlene (dec.), Kay; m. Evangeline Carmichael, Jan. 31, 1997. Grad., So. Cal. Radio Inst., 1933; D.D. (hon.), L.I.F.E. Bible Coll., 1944; LLD (hon.), L.I.F.E. Bible Coll., Los Angeles, 1988. Ordained to ministry Internat. Ch. Foursquare Gospel, 1940. Pres. Internat. Ch. Foursquare Gospel, L.A., 1944-88, dir., 1944-92; pres. emeritus, 1988—; pres., dir. L.I.F.E. Bible Coll., Inc., L.A., 1944-88.

Mem. Echo Park Evangelistic Assn. (pres. 1944—). Mem. Internat. Ch. Foursquare Gospel. Office: Internat Ch Foursquare Gospel 1910 W Sunset Blvd Ste 200 Los Angeles CA 90026-3295 E-mail: drrolfe@pacbell.net.

MCPHERSON, STEPHEN, broadcast executive; b. Pitts., Oct. 28, 1967; BA in polit. sci., Cornell U., 1986. Fgn. exchange trader Commodities Corp., NYC, 1986—91; dir. devel. Witt-Thomas Prodns., LA, 1991—93; dir. current programming Fox Broadcasting Co., LA, 1993—94; sr. v.p. creative affairs ABC Prodns., Burbank, Calif., 1994—95; v.p. Primetime Series NBC, Burbank, 1995—98; exec. v.p. Buena Vista Prodns. Walt Disney Co., 1998—2000, pres. Touchstone TV, 2000—04, pres. ABC Primetime TV, 2004—. Office: ABC Entertainment 500 S Buena Vista St Burbank CA 91521*

MCPHERSON, VANZETTA PENN, magistrate judge; b. Montgomery, Ala., May 26, 1947; d. Luther Lincoln and Sadie Lee (Gardner) P.; m. Winston D. Durant, Aug. 17, 1968 (div. Apr. 1979); 1 child, Raegan Winston; m. Thomas McPherson Jr., Nov. 16, 1985. BS in Speech Pathology, Howard U., Washington, 1969; MA in Speech Pathology, Columbia U., 1971, JD, 1974. Bar: N.Y. 1975, Ala. 1976, U.S. Dist. Ct. (so. dist.) N.Y. 1975, U.S. Dist. Ct. (mid. dist.) Ala. 1980, U.S. Ct. Appeals (2d cir.) 1975, U.S. Ct. Appeals (11th cir.) 1981, U.S. Supreme Ct. Assoc. Hughes, Hubbard & Reed, N.Y.C., 1974-75; asst. atty. gen. Ala. Atty. Gen. Office, Montgomery, 1975-78; pvt. practice Montgomery, 1978-92; magistrate judge U.S. Dist. Ct. (mid. dist.) Ala., Montgomery, 1992—. Former co-owner Roots & Wings, A Cultural Bookplace, Montgomery, 1989—2000. Dir. Ala. Shakespeare Festival, Montgomery, 1987—, Montgomery Symphony Orch., 1995-98; chmn. trustees Dexter Ave. King Meml. Bapt. Ch., Montgomery, 1988; chmn. Leadership Montgomery; bd. mem. Lighthouse Counseling Ctr., Montgomery, 1981-84, Montgomery County Pub. Libr., 1989-90; v.p. Lanier H.S. Parent Tchr. Student Assn., Montgomery, 1990-91, Metro-Montgomery YMCA, 2000—, Ala. Arts Coun., 2001-. Recipient cert. Ala. Jud. Coll.; named Woman of Achievement Montgomery Advertiser, 1989, Boss of Yr. Montgomery Assn. Legal Secs., 1992. Mem. ABA (law office design award 1985), FBA (pres. Montgomery chpt.), Nat. Bar Assn., Ala. State Bar Assn. (chmn. family law sect. 1989-90), N.Y. State Bar Assn., Montgomery Inn of Cts. (master bencher 1992—), Ala. Black Lawyers Assn. (pres. 1979-80). Office: US Dist Ct Mid Dist Ala PO Box 1629 One Church St Montgomery AL 36104

MCQUADE, ANDREW JOHN, journalist; b. Phila., Jan. 24, 1951; s. Andrew John and Alice Kathryn McQuade; m. Denise Mary Hall, Dec. 18, 1972; 1 child, Daniel Hall. BA in Journalism, Penn State U., State College, 1972. Phila. Eagles beat writer, sports layout chief Bucks County Courier Times, Levittown, Pa., 1973—85; copy editor, layout man Phila. Daily News, 1989—2001, sports desk chief, 2001—. Recipient Of God and Youth award, Nat. Fedn. of Cath. Youth Ministry, 2000, numerous Keystone Press awards, nat. pro footballwriters award, heatline writing awards. Mem.: Soc. of Profl. Journalists, Phila. CYO (area a track treas. 2002—04). Office: Philadelphia Daily News 400 North Broad St Philadelphia PA 19101

MC QUADE, LAWRENCE CARROLL, lawyer, investment company executive; b. Yonkers, N.Y., Aug. 12, 1927; s. Edward A. and Thelma (Keefe) McQuade; m. Morrissey de Rosset Parker, Aug. 3, 1968 (dec. Oct. 1978); 1 child, Andrew Parker McQuade; m. Margaret Osmer, Mar. 15, 1980. BA with distinction, Yale U., 1950; BA, Oxford (Eng.) U., 1952, MA, 1956; LLB cum laude, Harvard U., 1954; MA (hon.), Colby Coll., 1981. Bar: N.Y. 1955, DC 1968. Assoc. Sullivan & Cromwell, N.Y.C., 1954-60; spl. asst. to asst. sec. internat. security affairs U.S. Dept. Def., Washington, 1961-63; dep. asst. sec. U.S. Dept. Commerce, Washington, 1963-64, asst. to sec., 1965-67, asst. sec., 1967-69; pres. Procon Inc., Des Plaines, Ill., 1969-75, CEO, dir., 1969-75; v.p. Universal Oil Products Co., 1972-75, W.R. Grace & Co., N.Y.C., 1975-78, sr. v.p., 1978-83, exec. v.p., 1983-87, also bd. dirs.; vice chmn. Prudential Mut. Fund Mgmt., N.Y.C., 1988-95; mng. dir. Prudential Securities Inc., 1988-92; chmn. Qualitas Internat., 1994—. Chmn., CEO Universal Money Ctrs., 1987—88; co-chmn. River Capital Internat., 1997—; expert advisor commn. on transnat. corps. UN, 1989—93; bd. dirs. Quixote Corp., Oxford Analytica, Laredo Nat. Bancshares. Author (with others): The Ghana Report, 1959; contbr. articles to profl. jours. Dir. Paul and Daisy Soros Fellowships New Ams., 1998—; bd. dirs. Fgn. Bondholders Protective Coun., N.Y.C., 1978—, Am. Forum, 1985—96, Am. Coun. on Germany, 1985—94; trustee Colby Coll., 1981—89, trustee emeritus, 1989—; dir. Czech and Slovak Am. Enterprise Funds, 1994—96, chmn., 1995—96. Rhodes scholar, Oxford U., 1952. Mem.: Pres.'s Cir. NAS, Overseas Devel. Coun. (bd. dirs. 1974—87), Mgmt. and Devel. Inst. (bd. dirs. 1970—99), Atlantic Coun. U.S. (bd. dirs. 1969—99), Nat. Fgn. Trade Coun. (bd. dirs. 1979—87), Chgo. Coun. Fgn. Rels. (bd. dirs. 1969—75), Coun. Fgn. Rels., N.Y., Met. Club (Washington), Century Club, Harvard Club, Phi Beta Kappa. Office Phone: 212-973-9800. E-mail: lmcquade@rivercapital.com.

MCQUAID, KIM, historian, educator, writer; b. Norwalk, Conn., Nov. 2, 1947; s. Francis Walter McQuaid and Margaret Fitzgerald Phelan. BA, Antioch Coll., Yellow Springs, Ohio, 1970; MA, Northwestern U., Evanston, Ill., 1973, PhD, 1975. Asst. prof. dept. history Lake Erie Coll., Painesville, Ohio, 1977—83, assoc. prof., 1983—89, prof., 1989—. Mary Ball Washington vis. prof. U.S. History U. Coll. Dublin, 1985—86; Fulbright lectr. U. Sci. Malaysia, 1995—96. Co-author: (book) Creating the Welfare State, 1980, 1994; author: Big Business and Presidential Power, 1982, The Anxious Years: America in the Vietnam-Watergate Era, 1989, Uneasy Partners: Big Business in American Politics, 1945-1990, 1994. Woodrow Wilson fellow, 1970. Green Party. Avocations: wilderness hiking, art. Home: Apt 208 686 E Erie St Painesville OH 44077 Office: Lake Erie Coll 391 W Washington St Painesville OH 44077 Office Phone: 440-375-7177. E-mail: mcquaid@lec.com.

MCQUARRIE, CLAUDE MONROE, III, lawyer; b. Ft. Benning, Ga., Oct. 15, 1950; s. Claude Monroe Jr. and Rosanne (Sprinkle) McQ.; children: Kevin Andrew, Ryan Christopher, Erin Elizabeth. BS, U.S. Mil. Acad., 1972; JD with distinction, St. Mary's U., San Antonio, 1978. Bar: Tex. 1978, U.S. Dist. Ct. (so. dist.) Tex. 1982, U.S. Ct. Mil. Appeals 1979. Commd. 2d lt. U.S. Army, 1972, advanced through grades to capt., 1976, resigned, 1982; assoc. Fulbright & Jaworski, Houston, 1982-89, ptnr., 1989—. Editor Law Rev., 1977-78. Mem. ABA, Houston Bar Assn., John M. Harlan Soc., Phi Delta Phi. Avocations: golf, skiing. Home: 5610 Orchard Valley Ct Kingwood TX 77345-1920 Office: Fulbright & JaworskiLLP 1301 Mckinney St Ste 5100 Houston TX 77010-3031 Office Phone: 713-651-5416. E-mail: cmcquarrie@fulbright.com.

MCQUARRIE, DONALD GRAY, surgeon, educator; b. Richfield, Utah, Apr. 17, 1931; s. John Gray and LoRetta (Smith) McQ.; m. Dolores Jean Dietrich, July 16, 1956; children— William Gray, Michelle Dolores Colton. BS, U. Utah, 1952, MD, 1956; PhD, U. Minn., 1964. Diplomate Am. Bd. Surgery, Am. Bd. Thoracic and Cardiovascular Surgery. Intern U. Minn. Hosps., 1956—57; resident in surgery U. Minn., Mpls., 1957—59, resident, 1961—65, asst. prof. surgery, 1964—68, assoc. prof. surgery, 1968—72, prof. surgery, 1972—2001, prof. emeritus, 2002—, vice chmn. dept. surgery, 1993—99; mem. surg. staff Mpls. VA Hosp., 1964—99, chief surg. svc., 1993—99, resident in thoracic surgery, 1965—66, dir. surg. rsch. lab., 1964—78. Vis. prof. U. Tex.-San Antonio, 1974, U. Ind. and Indpls. VA, 1977, affiliated program U. Ariz., Phoenix, 1982, Case Western Res. U., 1986. Editor, contbg. author: Head and Neck Cancer, 1986, Reoperations in General Surgery, 1991, 2d edit., 1996; contbr. articles on surg. and basic med. scis. to profl. pubs., 1955— Served to lt. M.C., USN, 1959-61 USPHS postdoctoral fellow, 1962-65 Fellow ACS (commn. on cancer 1980-89, exec. council commn. on operating room environ. 1985-91, pres. Minn. chpt. 1983-84, liaison to Assn. Oper. Rm. Nurses 1985-97, gov. 1990-96); mem. Minn. Surg. Soc. (pres. 1980-81), Assn. Acad. Surgery, Mpls. Surg. Soc. (pres. 1978-79), Soc. Head and Neck Surgeons, Central Surg. Assn., Western Surg. Soc., Soc. Univ. Surgeons, Société Internationale de Chirurgie, Am. Surg. Assn., Royal Soc. Medicine, Assn. VA Surgeons (pres. 1987), Soc. Surg. Oncology, Hennepin County Med. Soc., Minn. Med. Assn., Am. Soc. Clin. Oncology, Phi Beta Kappa, Phi Kappa Phi Clubs: Minneapolis, Interlachen Country (Mpls.). Avocations: computer applications to medicine, jewelry design, lapidary work. Home: 6625 Mohawk Trl Minneapolis MN 55439-1029

MCQUARRIE, IRVINE GRAY, neurosurgeon, educator; b. Ogden, Utah, June 27, 1939; s. Irwin Bruce and Ruby Loretta (Epperson) McQuarrie; m. Katharine Gamble Rogers, Mar. 11, 1967 (div.); children: Michael Gray, Mollie; m. Maryann Kaminski, Aug. 14, 1980 (div.); children: Morgan Elizabeth, Gray Luke. BS in Biology, U. Utah, 1961; MD, Cornell U., 1965, PhD, 1977. Diplomate Am. Bd. Neurol. Surgery. Intern, asst. surgeon, surgeon N.Y. Hosp., N.Y.C., 1965—71, 1972—73; rsch. fellow dept. physiology Cornell U. Med. Coll., N.Y.C., 1971—72, 1974—76, asst. prof. depts. physiology and surgery, 1976—81; vis. asst. prof. dept. anatomy Case Western Res. U., Cleve., 1979—81, form asst. prof. neurosurgery, 1981—87, assoc. prof., 1987—, asst. prof. devel. genetics and anatomy, 1981—85, assoc. prof., 1985—88, assoc. prof. neuroscience, 1988—. Staff neurosurgeon VA Med. Ctr., Cleve., 1981—, clin. investigator, 1981—84, med. investigator neurosurgery, 1984—90; asst. neurosurgeon Univ. Hosps. Cleve., 1981—2003; mem. adv. bd. VA Office Regeneration Rsch. Programs, 1986—88, chmn., 1988—89; Elizabeth Crosby lectr. U. Mich., 1989. Contbr. articles to profl. jours. Comdr. M.C. USNR, 1973—74. Decorated Legion of Merit U.S. Marine Corps; recipient Andrew W. Mellon Tchr.-Scientist award, 1977—79; NIH fellow, 1971—72, 1974—76, VA Individual Rsch. grantee, 1981—2002, Paralyzed Vets. Am. grantee, 1979—82, NIH grantee, 1982—89, Spinal Cord Soc. grantee, 1986—88. Mem.: AAAS, Am. Assn. Neurol. Surgeons, Am. Soc. Cell Biology. Achievements include research in mechanism of axonal regeneration in central nervous system; biochemical investigations on maintenance and replacement of nerve cell processes (called axons and dendrites) by complex intraneuronal transport mechanisms. Home: 12955 Larchmere Blvd Shaker Heights OH 44120 Office: Medical Research Office 151W 10701 East Blvd Cleveland OH 44106 Business E-Mail: irvine.mcquarrie@med.va.gov.

MCQUARY, MICHAEL S. Internet company executive; BA in Psychology, U. Va.; MBA, Pepperdine U. Territory mgr. Lily Tulip Inc., 1981-84; various mgmt. positions including sales mgr., mgr. of ops. Mobil Chem. Co., 1984-95; exec. v.p. sales and mktg., then COO Mindspring Enterprises, Atlanta, 1995, pres., COO, 1995—, also bd. dirs. Office: Mindspring Enterprises 1430 W Peachtree St NW Ste 400 Atlanta GA 30309-2935

MCQUARY, VAUGHN, management company executive; BA, U. Ark., 1978. Asst. mgr. Little Rock Airport, 1996-98; v.p. Rector Phillips Morse Mgmt. Co., Little Rock, 1980—. Chmn. Ark. State Dem. Party. Mem. Assn. State Dem. Chairs (chmn. 1997—).

MCQUEARY, CHARLES E. federal official; MS in Mech. Engring., U. Tex., PhD in Engring. Mechanics, 1966. Dir. Undersea Systems Devel. Lab. Bell Labs., 1971—87; v.p. Fed. Systems Advanced Technology Divsn. AT&T, 1987—93; pres., v.p. bus. units AT&T, Lucent Techs., 1994—97; pres. Gen. Dynamics Advanced Tech. Sys., Greensboro, NC, 1997—2002; under sec. for sci. and tech. Dept. Homeland Security, Washington, 2003—. Chair bd. dirs., campaign chair United Way, Greensboro; trustee N.C. Agrl. and Tech. State U.; mem. pres. CEO adv. com. Guilford Tech. C.C.; bd. mem. World Trade Ctr. N.C.; chair Action Greensboro Pub. Edn. Initiative; bd. mem. Guilford County Edn. Network. Named Disting. Engring. Grad., U. Tex., 1997. Office: Dept Homeland Security 3801 Nebraska Ave NW Washington DC 20016

MCQUEEN, DAVID VINCENT, research scientist; b. Oelwein, Iowa, Sept. 8, 1940; s. Charles Webster and Lana Mae McQueen; m. Birgit Marlies Ebel, Feb. 1, 1971. BA, Antioch Coll., 1963; MA, Johns Hopkins U., 1966, ScD, 1972. Assoc. prof. Johns Hopkins U., Balt., 1979—83; dir. and prof. rsch. unit in health and behavioral change U. of Edinburgh, Scotland, 1983—92; chief behavioral surveillance br. Ctrs. for Disease Control and Prevention, Atlanta, 1992—95, sr. biomed. rsch. scientist, 1996—, dir. divsn. of adult and cmty. health, 1996—98, assoc. dir. for global health promotion, 1998—. Fellow, Alexander von Humboldt Found., 1980—81. Mem.: Internat. Union for Health Promotion and Edn. (v.p. for sci. 2001). Home: 2418 Midvale Ct Tucker GA 30084 Office: Ctrs Disease Control 4770 Buford Hwy NE Atlanta GA 30341-3717 Office Phone: 770-488-5403. Business E-Mail: dvmcqueen@cdc.gov.

MCQUEEN, JUSTICE ELLIS (L. Q. JONES), actor, director; b. Beaumont, Tex., Aug. 19, 1927; s. Justice Ellis and Pat (Stephens) McQ.; m. Sue Helen Lewis, Oct. 10, 1950 (dec.); children: Marlin Randolph, Marilyn Helen, Steven Lewis. Student, Lamar Jr. Coll., 1944, Lon Morris Coll., 1949, U. Tex., 1950-51. Actor, writer, dir.: motion picture films including A Boy and His Dog, 1975 (recipient Hugo award, Sci. Fiction achievement award for dramatic presentation, Golden Boot award, Internat. Star award); actor White Line Fever, 1975, Mother, Jugs & Speed, 1976, Winterhawk, 1976, Fast Charlie, The Moonbeam Rider, 1979, Timerider: The Adventures of Lyle Swann, 1982, The Beast Within, 1982, Sacred Ground, 1983, Lone Wolf McQuade, 1983, Bulletproof, 1988, River of Death, 1989, The Legend of Grizzly Adams, 1990, Lightning Jack, 1994, The Friends of Harry, 1995, Casino, 1995, Ben Johnson: Third Cowboy on the Right, 1996, The Edge, 1997, The Patriot, 1998, The Mask of Zorro, 1998, Route 666, 2001, numerous others; tv movies include The Sacketts, 1979, Tornado!, 1996, In Cold Blood, 1996, The Jack Bull, 1999, numerous others; appeared in tv series including Gunsmoke, 1955, Alias Smith and Jones, 1971, Cannon, 1971, Cade's County, 1971, Kung Fu, 1972, Matt Helm, 1975, Charlie's Angels, 1976, Columbo: The Conspirators, 1978, The Dukes of Hazzard, 1979, The Fall Guy, 1981, The Yellow Rose, 1983, The A-Team, 1983, Walker, Texas Ranger, 1993, numerous others; producer The Big Thickett, Come In, Children, The Witchmaker; author, prodr.: The Brotherhood of Satan, 1971; dir., prodr. The Devil's Bedroom, 1964, (tv series) The Incredible Hulk, 1978. Served with USNR, 1945-46. Nominee 4 Emmy awards. Mem. Screen Actors Guild. Republican. Methodist. Home and Office: 2144 1/2 N Cahuenga Blvd Los Angeles CA 90068-2708 Office Phone: 323-463-4426. *Contribute to a space that no one can or will fill.*

MCQUEEN, MICHAEL ANTHONY, journalism educator; b. Jacksonville, Fla., Nov. 3, 1956; s. Otto John and Carolyn Irene (Cubanks) McQ.; m. Glenda Kay Wright; children: Michael Jr., Otto Sinclair. BA, Fla. State U., 1982; MA, Fla. Atlantic U. Reporter Tallahassee (Fla.) Democrat, 1977-79, Fla. Times-Union, Jacksonville, Fla., 1979-80; writer AP, Tallahassee, 1980-84; reporter, editor Miami (Fla.) Herald, 1984-94; reporter USA Today, Arlington, Va., 1989; instr. to chmn. and assoc. prof. dept. journalism and broadcasting Fla. Internat. U., Miami, 1995—2004; mng. editor Macon Telegraph, Ga., 2004—. Mem. South Fla. Vision 2020, Fort Lauderdale, Fla., 1994-95; workshop dir. Dow Jones Newspaper Fund, Princeton, N.J., 1996, 97. Author: (poetry) Apalachee Quar., 1977. Recipient Pulitzer prize (given to staff) Pulitzer Prize Bd., 1994. Nat. Assn. Black Journalists (bd. dirs. 1985-86, conv. chmn. 1986), Suth Fla. Black Journalist Assn., Soc. Profl. Journalists (bd. dirs. 1995—), Assn. for Edn. in Journalism/Mass. Comm. (newsletter editor 1997). Roman Catholic. Office: Macon Telegraph 120 Broadway PO Box 4167 Macon GA 31208-4167

MCQUEEN, PATRICK M. bank executive; BBA, U. Mich., Dearborn; MBA, Mich. State U. Commr. Mich. Fin. Instns. Bur., 1993—; acting commr. Mich. Ins. Bur., 1995; pres., CEO Bank of Bloomfield Hills, Mich., 1999—. Mem. Conf. State Bank Suprs. (bd. dirs., legis. svcs. coun., internat. task force, strategic planning coun.). Avocations: hunting, fishing. Office: Bank of Bloomfield Hills 38505 Woodward Ave Bloomfield Hills MI 48304

MCQUEEN, REGENIA, writer; b. Summerville, SC, Oct. 29, 1945; d. William McQueen and Mary Stoutamire-McQueen; m. John Ray Sanders Teasley, Oct. 11, 1961; children: John Ray Sanders Teasley, Tonya Teasley, Ieishia Teasley, Nairobi Teasley, Rhodesia Teasley, Donnish Lindsey Teasley, DeJong Lindsey Teasley. A, Cin. Tech. Coll., 1985; cert., Blackstone Sch. of Law, Dallas, 2000. Clk. Western-So. Life Ins., Cin., 1967-72, IRS, Covington, Ky., 1985-87. Author: Regenia McQueen: Born to Search, 2000, Nairobi Teasley: 1-1/2 Hour Defenseless Lamb, 2001, Witnesses to the Impossible Dreams, 2002, Regenia McQueen Life Stolen, Name, Land, Oil, Government and History, Theft in South Carolina, 2003, Regina McQueen Documents in Theft in South Carolina, 2004, Nairobi Teasley: Unlawfully Made Guilty until Lawfully Proven Innocent, 2004. V.p. 13th St Tenant Assn., 1979-85; trustee Owning the Realty, 1983-85; Rosa Parks co-chmn. Wall of Tolerance award Nat. Campaign for Tolerance, 2002. Recipient Achievement award, Ho. of Reps., Ohio, 2000. Avocations: researching, writing. Mailing: PO Box 15311 Covington KY 41015

MC QUEEN, ROBERT CHARLES, retired insurance executive; b. Santiago, Chile, Jan. 23, 1921; s. Charles Alfred and Grace Juanita (Abrecht) McQ.; m. Donna Marie Ikeler, Oct. 6, 1945; children: Scott, Jerry, Monte, Donald. AB, Dartmouth Coll., 1942. Mathematician, Equitable Life Assurance Soc., N.Y.C., 1945-49; group actuary Union Central Life Ins. Co., Cin., 1949-57; with Mut. Benefit Life Ins. Co., Newark, 1957-85, exec. v.p., 1969-71, sr. exec. v.p., chief adminstrv. officer, 1971-85, dir., 1978-85. Bd. dirs. St. Barnabas Corp. (formerly Trimark Corp.). Pres. Millburn Twp. (N.J.) Bd. Edn., 1969-71, Naples (Fla.) Bridge Ctr., 1994-96; chmn. BBB Met. N.Y., 1978-80; chmn. bd. trustees St. Barnabas Hosp., Livingston, N.J., 1983-91, trustee, 1991—. With OSS, 1943-45. Fellow Soc. Actuaries; mem. Am. Acad. Actuaries, Internat. Actuarial Assn., Canoe Brook Country Club, Quail Creek Club. Republican. Episcopalian. Home: 11408 Oakmont Ct Fort Myers FL 33908 Personal E-mail: coach1921@yahoo.com.

MCQUEEN, SCOTT ROBERT, broadcasting company executive; b. Peekskill, N.Y., June 30, 1946; s. Robert Charles and Donna Marie (Ikeler) McQ.; children: Geoffrey Scott, Mallory Morgan, Brian Daniel; 1 child, by previous marriage, Tasha Lea. BA, Dartmouth Coll., 1968. Founder Sconnix Radio Ent., Inc., Laconia, N.H., 1968, Sconnix Radio Ent., Inc. (became Sconnix Group Broadcasting, Inc.), 1971, pres., 1971—; chmn. Bluewater Broadcasting Co., 2003—. Pres. Charisma Ventures, Ltd., 1995—. Chmn. bd. advisors Pine Crest Sch., Boca Raton, Fla., 2000-02, chmn. bd. trustees, 2003—. With N.H. N.G., 1968-69. Mem. Nat. Assn. Broadcasters, Nat. Radio Broadcsters Assn., Lakes Region C. of C. (dir. 1977-81),Royal Palm Yacht and Country Club. Home: 431 E Coconut Palm Rd Boca Raton FL 33432-7915

MCQUEENEY, HENRY MARTIN, SR., publisher; b. N.Y.C., Oct. 29, 1938; s. John Henry and Catherine Mary (Quigg) McQ.; m. Elizabeth Bernino, May 14, 1960; children: Mary E., Henry M. Jr., John P., Matthew S. BBA, St. Johns U., 1961; postgrad., U. Rochester, 1965-67. Advt. sales Curtis Circulation div. Curtis Pub. Co., 1960-62, asst. mgr., 1962-63, field mgr. Rochester, NY, 1964-67, dept. mgr., account exec. Phila., 1968-74; v.p. sales, exec. v.p. mktg. Manor Books, Inc., N.Y.C., 1974-79; pres. Scott Mag. Dist. Corp., N.Y.C., 1979—93, Kearny Pub., Inc., N.Y.C., 1993-96, Princeton Pub., Inc., N.Y.C., 1996-98; CEO, DMI Worldwide, N.Y.C., 1998—; v.p. Irish Connections Mag., N.Y.C., 2000—, Iron Cross, Ltd., N.Y.C., 1998—, Koolhouse Pub. Inc., 2003—. Rep. Western N.Y. Pubs.; cons. Bipad Ednl. Program. Pres. parish bd. Roman Cath. Ch., 1965, editor newspaper, Spencerport, N.Y., 1965, diocesan leader, mem. lay bd., Rochester, 1964-67; certified as tchr. Confraternity Christian Doctrine, Diocese of Rochester, 1964. Served with USAFR, 1956-64. Mem. Am. Legion, Ancient Order of Hibernians. Home: 12 Blenheim Ln Centerport NY 11721-1704 Office: DMI Worldwide PO Box 603 Centerport NY 11721-0603 Fax: 631-261-6532. Office Phone: 631-261-6273. E-mail: dmi33@aol.com.

MCQUIGG, JOHN DOLPH, retired lawyer; b. Abilene, Tex., Oct. 19, 1931; s. John Lyman and Dorothy Elinor (King) McQ.; m. Sandra Elainea Duke, Oct. 18, 1969 (div. 1989); 1 child, John Revel. BA, Denison U., 1953; LLB, U. Tex., 1962. Bar: Fla. 1962, U.S. Supreme Ct. 1971. Account exec. San Antonio Light, 1957-59; assoc. Shackleford, Farrior, Stallings & Evans, 1962-66, ptnr., 1966-73; pres. John McQuigg, P.A., Tampa, 1973-80; shareholder Fowler, White, Gillen, Boggs, Villareal & Banker, P.A., Tampa, 1980-92; of counsel Stephen Rosen, P.A., Tampa, 1993; pvt. practice Tampa, 1994-2000; ret., 2000. Arbitrator U.S. Dist. Ct., 1990—. Judge Compensation Claims pro hac vice, 1993; bd. dirs. Fla. Gulf Coast R.R. Mus., Inc., Am. Assn. Pvt. Railroad Car Owners; pres. Fla. Coalition R.R. Passengers, 1990-99. 1st lt. USAF, 1953-57. Mem. ABA, Fla. Bar, Tampa Club. Episcopalian.

MCQUIGG, MICHELE BERGER, state legislator; b. Bay Shore, N.Y., Sept. 2, 1947; m. F. Clancy McQuigg; children: Heather Lukes, Katie Schneider. BS, Mary Washington Coll., 1968; MS, Va. Polytech. Inst. & State U., 1978. Mem. Va. State Legis., 1998—, mem. cts. of justice com., mem. counties cities & towns com., mem. labor & commerce com., cts. justice labor, commerce gen.laws counties, cities, town, 1998—. Republican. Episcopalian. Office: Gen Assembly Bldg PO Box 406 Richmond VA 23218-0406 E-mail: del-mcquigg@house.state.va.us., michele@mcquigg.com.

MCQUIGGAN, MARK C. urologist; b. Detroit, May 15, 1933; s. Mark Ronald and Catherine Charlotte (Corbeille) McQ.; m. Carolyn Ann Brunk, Mar. 25, 1961. BS, U. Mich., 1954, MD, 1958. Diplomate Am. Bd. Urology. Resident in surgery and urology U. Mich., 1959-64; group practice Urology Assocs., Detroit, 1964-67; dir. med. edn. Providence Hosp., Southfield, Mich., 1967-69; clin. instr. urology U. Mich., 1969-70; pvt. practice Southfield and Farmington Hills, 1969—. Pres. med. staff North Detroit Gen. Hosp., 1983-84, pres. Providence med. staff, 1995, 96; chmn. credentialling com. Providence Hosp., 1997, 98. Named Providence Physician of Yr., Providence Hosp. Found., 2001. Fellow ACS; mem. AMA, Am. Urological Assn., Mich. Urological Assn. (exec. com. 1987-94, pres. 1992-93). Republican. Methodist. Home: 29653 Club House Ln Farmington Hills MI 48334-2015 Office: 30055 Northwestern Hwy Ste 210 Farmington Hills MI 48334-3234 Office Phone: 248-538-1571. E-mail: markmcquiggan@aol.com.

MCQUILKIN, JOHN ROBERTSON, religion educator, academic administrator, writer; b. Columbia, SC, Sept. 7, 1927; s. Robert C. and Marguerite (Lambie) McQ.; m. Muriel Elaine Webendorfer, Aug. 24, 1948 (dec. Sept. 2003); children: Helen Marguerite, Robert Paul (dec.), David John, Virginia Anne, Amy Lambie, Douglas Kent. BA, Columbia Internat. U., 1947; M.Div., Fuller Theol. Sem., 1950. Prof. Greek, religious edn. and theology Columbia (S.C.) Internat. U., 1950-52; pres. Internat. U., 1968-90. Headmaster Ben Lippen Sch., Asheville, N.C., 1952-55; missionary The Evang. Alliance Mission, Japan, 1956-68; acting pres. Tokyo Christian U., 1963-65. Author: Measuring the Church Growth Movement, 1974, Understanding and Applying the Bible, 1992, The Great Omission, 1984, An Introduction to Biblical Ethics, 1995, Life in the Spirit, 1997, A Promise Kept, 1998, Living the Life, 2000; contbr. articles to profl. jours. Mem. Evangel. Missiological Soc. (gen. dir. 1994-97). Personal E-mail: robertsonmcquilkin@earthlink.net.

MCQUILLEN, JAMES FRANCIS, electronics executive; b. Beijing, Apr. 4, 1940; arrived in U.S., 1940; s. Francis J. and Alice D. (McWilliams) McQuillen; m. Jeanne T. Perrin, Sept. 12, 1964; children: David, Michael. BS in Gen. Engring., U.S. Mil. Acad., 1962. Sales engr. BMC Industries, San Jose, Calif., 1973-74, internat. devel. mgr. St. Paul, 1974-76, gen. mgr. Elk Grove Village, Ill., 1976-80, 1982-83, group gen. mgr., 1982—86; product mgr. Nat. Semiconductor, Santa Clara, Calif., 1980—82; v.p. Jade Corp. subs. Hanson Industries Inc.; gen. mgr. Jade Techs., Inc., Elk Grove Village, 1986—92; gen. mgr. connector products Methode Electronics, Chgo., 1993—95, v.p., gen. mgr., 1995—2000, pres., exec. v.p. interconnect products group, 2001—. Vice chmn. Cupertino (Calif.) Pks. Dept., 1972. Served to maj. U.S. Army, 1962—69, Vietnam. Decorated Bronze Star for Valor with oak leaf cluster, Air medal, Combat Infatryman's badge. Republican. Roman Catholic. Office: 7401 W Wilson Ave Chicago IL 60706-4548

MCQUILLEN, JEREMIAH JOSEPH, distribution executive; b. Buffalo, Jan. 7, 1941; s. Joseph Bernard and Marca Rita (Ammerman) McQ.; m. Maureen Elaine Brett; children: Michael, Karen, Kathleen. BS, Canisius Coll., 1962. Nat. sales mgr. Birge Wallcoverings, Buffalo, 1973-74, v.p., gen. mgr., 1976-79; v.p. mktg. Reed Decorative Products, Toronto, 1974-76; exec. v.p. Atlanta, 1979-81, Northeastern Wallcoverings, Boston, 1981-88, pres., 1989-91; pres. comml. wallcoverings Forbo Wallcoverings Inc., 1991-92; exec. v.p. Hytex Industries, Randolph, Mass., 1992-98, pres., CEO, 1998—. Served to 1st lt., U.S. Army, 1962-64. Mem. Wallcovering Distbrs. Assn. (sec., treas. 1987—, v.p. 1988, pres. 1989-90), Wallcovering Info. Bur. (pres. 1980),

Wallcovering Mfg. Assn. (v.p. 1980), Di Gamma (life). Republican. Roman Catholic. Avocations: tennis, racquetball. Home: 3 Nauset St Medfield MA 02052-3006 Office Phone: 781-963-4400. Personal E-mail: jjmhytex@aol.com.

MCQUILLEN, MICHAEL PAUL, neurologist, educator, clinical ethicist; b. N.Y.C., Sept. 9, 1932; s. Paul and Dorothy Marian (Moore) McQ.; m. Louise Devlin; children: Daniel, Thomas, Patrick, Kathleen. BA cum laude, Georgetown U., 1953, MD, 1957; MA, U. Va., 1994. Diplomate Am. Bd. Psychiatry and Neurology (bd. dirs. 1991-95, exec. com. 1995), added qualification in clin. neurophysiology. Rotating intern Royal Victoria Hosp., Montreal, Que., Can., 1957-58; resident in neurology Georgetown U. Med. Center, 1958-60; fellow in physiology Johns Hopkins U. Med. Sch. and Hosp., 1960-62, instr. medicine, 1962-65; mem. faculty U. Ky. Med. Center, 1965-74, prof. neurology, 1972-74, prof., chmn. neurology, 1987-93; prof. neurology, chmn. dept. Med. Coll. Wis., Milw., 1974-87; clin. faculty mem. dept. neurology U. Va. Health Sci. Ctr., Charlottesville, 1993-94; prof. neurology U. Rochester, N.Y., 1995—. Vis. sci. Inst. Neurophysiology U. Copenhagen, 1971-72; vis. prof. U. Ky. Med. Ctr., 1978, Royal Coll. Surgeons, Ireland, 1983. Author articles, papers in field. Mem. Cath. Commn. on Intellectual Affairs. Recipient Neurology medal Georgetown U. Med. Sch., 1957; Clin. Teaching award Med. Coll. Wis., 1976; Disting. Service award N.Y. Med. Coll., 1983; named to Johns Hopkins Soc. Scholars, 1981 Fellow Am. Acad. Neurology; mem. AMA, Royal Acad. Medicine Ireland, Nat. Myasthenia Gravis Found. (chmn. 1981-83), Am. Neurol. Assn., Am. Assn. Electromyography and Electrodiagnosis, Wis. Neurol. Assn. (pres. 81-82), Rochester Acad. Medicine, Alpha Omega Alpha. Home: 4 Bragdon Dr Rochester NY 14618-3755 Office: 919 Westfall Rd Bldg C Rochester NY 14618-2633 Office Phone: 585-240-5479. Business E-Mail: michael_mcquillen@urmc.rochester.edu.

MCQUILLIN, RICHARD ROSS, management consultant; b. Elyria, Ohio, Oct. 15, 1956; s. Wayne Rupp and Frana Rose (Romp) McQuillin; m. Riko Koga; children: Richard K., Sean K. BS, Ohio State U., 1979; MS, U. So. Calif., L.A., 1983; MBA, UCLA, 1990. Sr. staff mem. TRW Inc., Redondo Beach, Calif., 1979-88; sr. cons. Deloitte & Touche, L.A., 1990-91; cons. mgr. NetBase Computing, El Segundo, Calif., 1993-2000; chief tech. officer When2Click.com, El Segundo, Calif., 2000—. Treas., contr. Patio Creek Homeowners Assn., Torrance, Calif., 1986—91, pres., 1991—, TRW Investment Club, Redondo Beach, 1984—87. UCLA fellow, 1989. Mem.. IEEE, Beta Gamma Sigma. Home: 1281 Tennyson St Manhattan Beach CA 90266-6956 Office: NetBase Computing Inc 2101 Rosecrans Ave Ste 5250 El Segundo CA 90245-4771

MCQUISTON, ROBERT EARL, lawyer; b. Pitts., Feb. 4, 1936; s. Theodore O. and Bertha L. (Kegley) McQ.; m. Mary Hope Missimer, June 30, 1962; children: Mary Hope, Elizabeth Ann. BA magna cum laude, Yale U., 1958; JD cum laude, Harvard U., 1961. Bar: Pa. 1962. Assoc. Ballard, Spahr, Andrews & Ingersoll, LLP, Phila., Balt., Denver, Washington, Salt Lake City, 1962—69, ptnr., 1969—2001, sr. counsel, 2001—. Mem. nat. adv. group to Commr. IRS, Washington, 1985-87; lectr. in law Temple U., 1968-69, also various tax insts.; bd. dirs. Macromedia Inc., Hackensack, N.J., Gateway Communications, Inc., Binghamton, N.Y. Contbr. articles to profl. jours. Mem. Rep. Fin. Com., Harrisburg, Pa., 1983-86; trustee Am. Soc. Hypertension, 1992-98. Mem. ABA (active numerous coms. sect. taxation 1969—, including coun. mem. 1979-85, vice chmn., sec. 1982-85), Phila. Bar Assn. (bd. govs. 1978-80, mem. coun. 1969-84, sec. treas sect. on taxation 1973-75, vice chmn. 1976-78, chmn. 1978-80), Am. Coll. Tax Counsel (charter, regent 1990-98, vice chmn. 1993-94, chmn. 1994-96), Am. Tax Policy Inst. (trustee 1996-2003, pres. 2001-03), Nat. Conf. Lawyers and CPAs, Merion Cricket Club, Yale Club N.Y.C. Episcopalian. Home: 1218 Round Hill Rd Bryn Mawr PA 19010-1938 Office: Ballard Spahr Andrews et al 1735 Market St Ste 5100 Philadelphia PA 19103-7599 E-mail: mcquiston@ballardspahr.com.

MCQUOWN, JUDITH HERSHKOWITZ, author, financial advisor; b. N.Y.C., Apr. 8, 1941; d. Frederick Ephraim and Pearl (Rosenberg) H.; m. Michael L. McQuown, Jan. 13, 1969 (div. 1980); m. Harrison Roth, Dec. 8, 1985 (dec. 1997). AB, Hunter Coll., 1963; postgrad., N.Y. Inst. Fin., N.Y.C., 1965-67. Chief underwriting div. mcpl. securities City of N.Y., 1972-73; CEO Judith H. McQuown & Co., Inc., N.Y.C., 1973—. Author: Inc. Yourself: How to Profit by Setting Up Your Own Corporation, 10th edit., 2002, Tax Shelters That Work for Everyone, 1979, The Fashion Survival Manual, 1981, Playing the Takeover Market, 1982, How to Profit After You Inc. Yourself, 1985, Keep One Suitcase Empty: The Bargain Shopper's Guide to the Finest Factory Outlets in the British Isles, 1987, Keep One Suitcase Empty: The Bargain Shopper's Guide to the Finest Factory Outlets in Europe, 1988, Use Your Own Corporation to Get Rich, 1991; contbg. editor: Boardroom Reports, Physician's Fin. News, Physician's Guide to Money Mgmt.; contbr. seminars The Learning Annex, seminars The Discovery Ctr., seminars Boston Ctr. for Adult Edn., seminars First Class, seminars Learning Connection, seminars Knowledge Network. Mem. Am. Soc. Journalists and Authors. Home and Office: One Gracie Ter Apt 9C New York NY 10028

MCQUOWN, MARK, scriptwriter; b. Santa Rosa, Calif., Dec. 29, 1945; s. Robert Nicholas and Betty Jean McQuown; m. Patricia Marti McQuown; children: Megan, Gaylen; m. Lynn Helen Durqom, July 6, 1990; children: Ian Durqom, Erin Lindsey. BS in Theatre, Calif. State Poly. U., 1971; MFA in Directing, UCLA, 1974. Head of acting U. Colo., Boulder, 1977—80; artistic dir. Sirius Theatre Co., Boulder, 1980—88; theatre staff Calif. Inst. Arts, Valencie, 1993—95, faculty, 1995—97; faculty theatre Hong Kong Acad. for the Performing Arts, Wan Chai, 1997—98, Pasadena (Calif.) City Coll., 2001—03; tech. dir. Boston Ct. Theatre, 2003—. Author: (plays) P.J., 1980 (First pl. Colo. Playwright's Festival, 84, Best New Play, Denver Theatre Critics, 84), (films) The Rocking Horse Christmas, 1997 (First pl. Santa Clarita Internat. Film Festival, 97), Dot Gone, 2002 (Telluride Ind. Film Festival winner, 02). With U.S. Army, 1967—69, Germany. Mem.: SAG, NY Dramatist Guild, Actors Equity Assn. Avocations: skiing, movies, theater. Home: 25933 Sandalia Dr Valencia CA 91355 Personal E-mail: markmcquown@forevermail.com.

MCRAE, CHARLES R. (CHUCK MCCRAE), state supreme court justice; BA, Marietta Coll., 1962; JD cum laude, Miss. Coll. Sch. Law, 1970. Trial atty., Pascagoula, Miss., 1970—90; spl. chancellor, cir. ct. judge Jackson, Forrest and Lincoln Counties, Miss., 1990; justice Miss. Supreme Ct, Jackson, 1991—. Mem.: ABA, Magnolia Bar Assn., Fed. Bar Assn., Am. Judicature Soc., ATLA, Miss. Trial Lawyer's Assn. (life). Office: Supreme Court Gartin Bldg PO Box 249 Jackson MS 39205

MCRAE, HAMILTON EUGENE, III, lawyer; b. Midland, Tex., Oct. 29, 1937; s. Hamilton Eugene and Adrian (Hagaman) McR.; m. Betty Hawkins, Aug. 27, 1960; children: Elizabeth Ann, Stephanie Adrian, Scott Hawkins BSEE, U. Ariz., 1961; student, USAF Electronics Sch., 1961-62; postgrad., U. Redlands, Calif., 1962-63; JD with honors and distinction, U. Ariz., 1967; LHD (hon.), Sterling Coll., 1992; vis. fellow, Darwin Coll. and Martin Ctr., Cambridge (Eng.) U., 1996-97. Bar: Ariz. 1967, U.S. Supreme Ct. 1979; cert. real estate specialist, Ariz. Elec. engr. Salt River Project, Phoenix, 1961; assoc. Jennings, Strouss & Salmon, Phoenix, 1967-71, ptnr., 1971-85, chmn. real estate dept., 1980-85, mem. policy com., 1982-85, mem. fin. com., 1981-85, chmn. bus. devel. com., 1982-85; ptnr. and co-founder Stuckey & McRae, Phoenix, 1985—; co-founder, chmn. bd. Republic Cos., Phoenix, 1985—. Magistrate Paradise Valley, Ariz., 1983-85; juvenile referee Superior Ct., 1983-85; pres., dir. Phoenix Realty & Trust Co., 1970—; officer Indsl. Devel. Corp. Maricopa County, 1972-86; instr. and lectr. in real estate; officer, bd. dirs. other corps.; adj. prof. Frank Lloyd Wright Sch. Architecture, Scottsdale, Ariz., 1989—; instr. Ariz. State U. Coll. Architecture and Environ. Design; lead instr. ten-state-bar seminar on Advanced Real Estate Transactions, 1992; evaluation com. for cert. real estate specialist Ariz. Bar, 1994-96; mem. real estate adv. commn. Ariz. Bar, 1996—. Author: Development in Third World Countries, 2002; exec. prodr. film documentary on relief and devel. in Africa, 1990; contbr. articles to profl. jours. Elder Valley Presbyn. Ch., Scottsdale, Ariz., 1973-75, 82-85, 96-98, chair evangelism com. 1973-74, corp. pres., 1974-75, 84-85, trustee, 1973-75, 82-85, chmn. exec. com., 1984, mem. mission com. 1993—, chmn. 1998; trustee Upward Found., Phoenix, 1977-80, trustee, Valley Presbyn. Found., 1982-83, Ariz. Acad., 1971—; trustee, mem. exec. com. Phi Gamma Delta Ednl. Found., Washington, 1974-84; trustee Phi Gamma Delta Internat., 1984-86; bd. dirs. Archon, 1986-87, Hall of Fame Ariz., 1999; founder, trustee, pres. McRae Found., 1980—; bd. dirs. Food for Hungry Inc. (Internat. Relief), 1985-95, exec. com., 1986-95, chmn. bd. dirs., 1987-92; chmn. bd. dirs. Food for Hungry Internat., 1993-95, pres. adv. coun., 1995—, mem. building com., 1999—; trustee, mem. exec. com. Ariz. Mus. Sci. and Tech., 1984—, 1st v.p., 1985-86, pres., 1986-88, chmn. bd. dirs., 1988-90, exec. com. 1984-90, exhibits com. 1990—, strategic planning com., 1999—, svc. recognition 1999; Lambda Alpha Internat. Hon. Land Econs. Soc, 1988-98; sec.-treas. Ariz. State U. Coun. for Design Excellence, 1989-90, bd. dirs. 1988-99, pres. 1990-91, trustee 1999—; mem. Crisis Nursery Office of the Chair, 1988-89, Maricopa Community Colls. Found., 1988—, sec. 1990-91, 2d v.p. 1993-94, 1st v.p. and pres. elect 1994-95, pres. 1995-96, mem. Elsner scholarship com., 1999—, web site com., 1999, capital campaign cabinet, 1995-96, 98-99, mem. of chair, 1998-99, mem. nominating com., 1997—, deferred gifts com., 1999—, strategic planning com., 2000—, mem. adv. bd., 2002--; mem. Phoenix Cmty. Alliance, 1988-90, Interchurch Ctr. Corp., 1987-90, Western Art Assocs., bd. dirs., 1989-91, Phoenix Com. on Fgn. Rels., 1988-99, U. Ariz. Pres.'s Club, 1984—, chmn., 1991-92; bd. dirs. Econ. Club of Phoenix, 1987—, sec.-treas., 1991-92, v.p., 1992-93, pres. 1993-94; bd. dirs. Ctrl. Ariz. Shelter Svcs., 1995—, bd. dir., Ariz. Community Found., 1996—, invest. com., 1996—, chair, 2000-, exec. com. 1997—, treas. 1997—, chair nominating com. 1997-98, vice chair bd. dirs., 1999—, chair devel. com., 1999—, advancement com., 1999-2000, chair, 1999—, fin. and adminstrn. com. 1999—; founding mem. Alliance linking poverty and homelessness, 1996-98, bd. dirs., 1996-98, mem. exec. com., 1996-98, co-chair long range planning com., 1997-98; mem. adv. bd. Help Wanted USA, 1990-92; vol. fund raiser YMCA, Salvation Army, others; bd. dirs. Frank Lloyd Wright Found., 1992—, chair fin. com. 1997-98, chmn. bd. dirs., 1998—; mem. Taliesin Coun., 1985—; bd. dirs. Taliesin Arch., 1992-98, Taliesin Conservation Com. (Wis.), 1992—; founding mem. Frank Lloyd Wright Soc., 1993—; mem. fin. com. Kyl for Congress, 1985-92, bd. dir. campaign bd. Kyl for U.S. Senate, 1993-94, 99—; Senator Kyl Council, 1995-98; campaign com. Symington for Gov. '90, 1989-90, mem. gubernatorial adv. bd., 1990-91; mem. Gov.'s Selection Com. for State Revenue Dir., 1993; mem. bond com. City of Phoenix, 1987-88; mem. Ariz. State U. Coun. of 100, 1985-89, investment com., 1985-89; bd. govs. Twelve Who Care Hon Kachina, 1991; mem. adv. coun. Maricopa County Sports Authority, 1989-93; mem. Ariz. Coalition for Tomorrow, 1990-92; founding mem., bd. dirs. Waste Not Inc., 1990-94, pres., 1990-92, chmn., 1992-94, adv. bd. 1996—; bd. dirs. Garden Homes at Teton Pines Home Owners Assn., 1996—; selected as bearer for the Olympic Torch Relay Team, 1996; adv. bd. KAET TV PBS (Channel 8) 1999-2000. 1st lt. USAF, 1961-64. Recipient various mil. awards; 1st place award Ariz. Bar exam, 1967; named to Ariz. Hall of Fame, 1999. Mem. ABA, AIEE, AIME, Ariz. Bar Assn., Maricopa County Bar Assn., U. Ariz. Alumni Assn., Nat. Soc. Fund Raising Execs. (Philanthropy award Ariz. chpt. 1991, 97), Clan McRae Soc. N.Am. Phoenix Exec. Club, Internat. Platform Assn., Am. Friends of the U. Cambridge (Eng.), Jackson Hole Racquet Club, Teton Pines Country Club, Tau Beta Pi. Republican. Address: Republic Cos 11811 N Tatum Blvd Ste 1005 Phoenix AZ 85028-1617 E-mail: repcos@aol.com.

MCRAE, JOHN LEONIDAS, civil engineer, consultant; b. Sept. 16, 1917; s. James Wright and Lota (O'Bryant) McR.; m. Thelma Lucile Nabors, Mar. 23, 1940; children: John Malcolm, Virginia Margaret McRae Murphree Pugh. BSCE and Geotech. Engring., Northwestern U., 1948. Chief bituminous and chemistry lab. U.S. Army Engring. Waterways Exptl. Sta., Vicksburg, Miss., 1950-61, rsch. engr. mobility and environ. divsn., 1961-72; CEO Engring. Devel. Co. Inc., 1960—. Cons. on soil mechanics and bituminous pavements. Contbr. numerous tech. papers to profl. lit.; patentee in field. Fellow ASCE; mem. NSPE, ASTM, Assn. Asphalt Paving Technologists, Nat. Asphalt Paving Assn., Am. Road and Transp. Builders Assn. Baptist. Home: 416 Groome Dr Vicksburg MS 39180-5108 Office: PO Box 1109 Vicksburg MS 39181-1109 E-mail: jlmcrae@edco-gtm.com.

MCRAE, KAREN K. state legislator; b. Detroit, Feb. 19, 1944; m. Gossett W. McRae; 2 children. BSL, Georgetown U., 1965. Mem. N.H. Ho. of Reps.; vice chmn. sci., tech. and energy com. Active Goffstown Conservation Com., 1972—, chmn., 1975-79. Mem. Georgetown U. Alumni Assn. (class rep. 1975—). Avocations: skiing, gardening, gourmet cooking, baking, reading. Home: 469 Black Brook Rd Goffstown NH 03045-2931 Office: NH Ho of Reps 107 N Main St Rm 105 Concord NH 03301-4993

MCRAE, ROBERT MALCOLM, JR., federal judge; b. Memphis, Dec. 31, 1921; s. Robert Malcolm and Irene (Pontius) McR.; m. Louise Howry, July 31, 1943; children: Susan Campbell, Robert Malcolm III, Duncan Farquhar, Thomas Alexander Todd. BA, Vanderbilt U., 1943; LLB, U. Va., 1948. Bar: Tenn. 1948. Practice in, Memphis, 1948-64; judge Tenn. Circuit Ct., 1964-66, U.S. Dist. Ct. (we. dist.) Tenn., Memphis, 1966-94, chief judge, 1979-86, sr. judge, 1987-94, inactive sr. judge, 1995—; mem. Jud. Council 6th Cir., 1982-85, Jud. Conf. Commn. Adminstrn. Criminal Law, 1979-86, Jud. Conf. U.S., 1984-87; ret. (sr. status), 2001—. Pub.: Oral History of the Desegregation of the Memphis City Schools (1954-74), 1997. Pres. Episcopal Ch. men of Tenn., 1964-65. Mem. Dist. Judges Assn. 6th Circuit (pres.).

MCRAITH, JOHN JEREMIAH, bishop; b. Hutchinson, Minn., Dec. 6, 1934; s. Arthur Luke and Marie (Hanley) McR. BA, Loras Coll., Dubuque, Iowa, 1956. Ordained priest Roman Cath. Ch., 1960. Assoc. pastor St. Mary's Ch., Sleepy Eye, Minn., 1960—64, 1968—71; pastor St. Michael's Ch., Milroy, Minn., 1964—67, St. Leo's Ch., St. Leo, Minn., 1967—68; dir. Nat. Cath. Rural Life, Des Moines, 1971—78; vicar gen. Diocese of New Ulm, Minn., 1978—82; bishop Owensboro, Ky., 1982—. Roman Catholic. Home: 501 W 5th St Owensboro KY 42301-0765 Office: 600 Locust St Owensboro KY 42301-2130

MCRANEY, JOAN KATHERINE, artist; b. Magee, Miss., Mar. 21, 1936; d. Harold Bryce and Ruth Katherine (Graves) McRaney; m. William Cummings Hollis, Mar. 14, 1966 (div. June 1970); m. Richard Felder, 1997. BFA, Inst. Allende, San Miguel de Allende, Mex., 1975; postgrad., U. So. Miss., 1990—; pvt. study, Miss. sculptor Dan Askew, 1999-2000. Profl. portrait artist and contemporary sculptor, McComb, Hattiesburg, Miss., 1979—. Lectr. Lauren Rogers Mus. Art, Laurel, Miss., 1996. Exhibitions include Inst. Allende Gallery, 1973, Bellas Artes Gallery, San Miguel de Allende, 1974, Gulf South Gallery, McComb, 1982—84, Images '84, Miss Pavilion, New Orleans World Fair, 1984, Cottonlandia Mus., Greenwood, Miss., 1985—86, Woods Gallery So. Artists Invitational, U. So. Miss., 1990, Saenger Gallery, Hattiesburg, 1990, Woods and Locke Gallery, U. So. Miss., 1992—96, Lucille Parker Gallery, William Carey Coll., 1993, Miss. Collegiate Art Competition, Lauren Rogers Mus. Art, Laurel, Miss., 1996, Meridian (Miss.) Mus. Arts, 1997, USM Mus. Art, 1998, Lauren Rogers Mus., 1999, Meridian Mus. Art, 1999, Exit Gallery, Hattiesburg Downtown Gallery Walk, 1999, 2000, Impressions Gallery, 2000, 2001, McComb Pub. Libr., 2000, Southwest C.C., 2002, one-woman shows include Gulf South Gallery, MaComb, Miss., 2003, Meridian Mus. Art, 2004, Impressions Gallery, 2004. Recipient Louie B. Holmes Meml. award, McComb, 1980, 81, hon. mention Nat. Portrait Seminar, Houston, 1981, 1st pl. Pastel award South Miss. Art Assn. Cloverleaf Show, 1992, 1st pl. Drawing award, 1992, Dean's Outstanding Creativity award, 1993, 94, 1st pl. Painting award Umpteenth Ann. Student Show, Woods Gallery, 1995, Fred A. Waits Endowment, 1995, 1st pl. Drawing award, 1995, Best of Show award (mixed media sculpture), Miss. Collegiate Art Competition, 1997, Best of Sculpture award Best of Show (mixed media sculpture) Dept. Art Annual Student Exhbn., 1998, honored by Hattiesburg Arts Coun., 1998; winner juried competition Laurel Arts League, 1999, Meridian Mus. Art, 1999. Mem.: Golden Key Soc., Kappa Delta. Avocations: canoeing, photography, yoga, meditation, cooking. Home: 308 2nd Ave Hattiesburg MS 39401-3879 E-mail: refelder@netdoor.com.

MCREE, CELIA, composer, singer, actress, writer, producer; b. Memphis; d. John Louis and Leta Gwendolyn (Phillips) McR. Student, Phila. Coll. Art (U. of Arts), 1976-77, Herbert Berghof Studio, 1989, Playwrights Horizon Theater, 1989; cert. with distinction, Nat. Acad. Paralegal Studies, Christian Bros. U., 1992. Pres. Mother Records, Memphis, 1984—, You Should Meet My Mother (Publishing), Memphis, 1984—, Wild Thing Music, Memphis, 1987-99, Mother Prodns., Memphis, 1986—; producer, host Indian Talk, WEVL-FM90, Memphis, 1992-95; ptnr. The Cinema Group, N.Y.C., 1997—. Artist, group and solo exhbns. including Eads Gallery, Grover Cleveland Arts Inst., Phila. Mus. Natural History; screenwriter, film scoring; singer, writer (nat. album) including Celia McRee/Back From Under, 1985 (ASCAP Spl. Pop award 1985-86, 86-87), Archives of Modern Music NY., Celia McRee/Passion, 1994; composer, arranger, producer, pub. background and feature music ABC Network, Cable TV and Radio; signature model for KeTukla, 1st Native Am. fashion designer; co-writer Circle of Love, 1999. Entertainer Vets. Bedside Network, N.Y.C., 1981. Recipient cert. of scholarly distinction Nat. Acad. for Paralegal Studies, 1992, cert. of appreciation United Music Heritage, 1990, spl. pop award ASCAP, 1982-84, 87-93, 95-96, 96-97, 97-98, 98-99, 99-2000, 2000-01, Henrietta Hickman Morgan writing award DAR; named Female Pop Songwriter and Female Pop Vocalist of Yr., Entertainer Indi-Assn., 1994, Female Vocalist and Female Entertainer of Yr., 1995; named Most Popular Female Entertainer, Entertainer Indi-Assn., 1996, Female/Artist/Entertainer, 1996, 97, Eia's Female Entertainer/Writer, 1997. Mem. AFTRA, ASCAP, NARAS, Nat. Mus. of the Am. Indian (charter), Animal Legal Def. Fund, N.Y. Acad. Sci., Humane Soc. U.S., Mensa, Memphis Kennel Club. Office: Mother Prodns 5159 Wheelis Dr # 110 Memphis TN 38117-4519

MCREYNOLDS, MARY ARMILDA, lawyer; b. Carthage, Mo., Sept. 2, 1946; d. Allen and Virginia Madeliene (Hensley) McR. BA, Mt. Holyoke Coll., 1968; JD, Georgetown U., 1971; LLM, Harvard U., 1973. Bar: D.C. 1971, U.S. Ct. Appeals (D.C. cir.) 1971, U.S. Ct. Appeals (2d cir.) 1975, U.S. Ct. Appeals (4th cir.) 1979, U.S. Ct. Appeals (1st, 5th, 6th, 9th 10th cirs.) 1980, U.S. Supreme Ct. 1980, U.S. Ct. Appeals (11th cir.) 1981, U.S. Ct. Appeals (3rd, 7th, 8th cirs.) 1983, U.S. Ct. Appeals (fed. cir.) 1988. Law clk. U.S. Ct. Appeals for D.C. cir., 1971-72; assoc. Wilmer, Cutler & Pickering, Washington, 1973-77; sr. trial atty. civil divsn. fed. program br. U.S. Dept. Justice, 1977-79, mem. appellate staff, 1979-81; ptnr. McReynolds & Mutterperl, Washington, 1981-83, Wilner & Scheiner, Washington, 1983-89, Haley, Bader & Potts, 1989-92; pvt. practice Washington, 1992—. Gen. counsel Anchor Ednl. Found., 2002-; bd. dirs., gen. counsel Washington Bach Consort, 1977-81, 1985-92, pres. 1981-82, 89-90; pres. bd. dirs., ArtsAm., 1993—. Contbr. articles to profl. jours. Mem. ABA, Kenwood Club, City Tavern Club. Episcopalian. Home: 2101 Connecticut Ave NW Apt 26 Washington DC 20008-1754 Office: Ste 300 1701 Pennsylvania Ave NW Washington DC 20006 Office Phone: 202-879-2695. E-mail: marymcreynolds@aol.com.

MCREYNOLDS, MARY MAUREEN, small business owner; b. Tacoma, July 15, 1940; d. Andrew Harley and Mary Leone (McGuire) Sims; m. Gerald Aaron McReynolds, Dec. 10, 1964. BA, U. Oreg., 1961; PhD, U. Chgo., 1966; postgrad., San Diego State U., 1973-75. NIH postdoct. fellow U. Tex., Austin, 1966-68, mem. adj. faculty, 1980-82, mem. biosafety com., 1981—2003; rsch. assoc. Stanford U., Calif., 1968-71; chemist assoc. Syva Co., Palo Alto, Calif., 1972; environ. splst. County of San Diego, Calif., 1973-75; dept. head City of Austin, 1976-84; chief environ. officer, 1984-85; utility environ. mgr., 1985-92; mgr. environ. and regulatory svcs., 1992—2003; prin., owner McReynolds Winery, 1998—. Dir. Ctr. Environ. Rsch., 1992-2003; part-time mem. faculty Austin C.C., 1993-98; cons. enologist Mirassou Vineyards, San Jose, Calif., 1969-72; lectr. Wright Inst., Berkeley, Calif., 1971-72; instr. San Diego State U., 1974-75. Editor: Dist. 56 newsletter, 1989-90; contbr. articles to profl. jours. Mem. Austin-Saltillo Sister City Assn., 1980-99; U.S.-Mex. Sister Cities del., 1983-85; sponsor, chaperone Tex.-SouthAustralia Youth Exch., 1986; active Leadership Austin, 1987-88; mem. Austin-Adelaide Sister City Com., 1986—, chmn., 1989-91, sec., 1992-96; bd. dirs. Internat. Hospitality Coun. Austin, 1989-96; mem. steering com. Colo. River Clean Rivers; mem. adv. panel Lake Austin. USPHS tng. grantee U. Chgo., 1961-66. Mem.: Tex. Assn. Met. Sewage Agys. (sec. 1994, v.p. 1995, pres. 1996), Am. Inst. Cert. Planners (cert.), Am. Planning Assn., Water Environment Fedn. (v.p. local chpt. 1988—89, pres. 1990—91, sect. rep. 1991—94), Tex. Hill Country Winery Assn. (bd. dirs. 2003—), Sweet Adelines (bd. dirs. Tex. Star chpt. 1998—2001), Toastmasters Internat. (club pres. 1981, area gov. 1981—82, div. lt. gov. 1982—83, Able Toastmaster 1983, Dist. 56 Table Topics award 1986, Disting. Toastmaster award 1987, club pres. 1988, Able Toastmaster Bronze award 1990, Able Toastmaster Silver award 1993, club pres. 2000—01, Competent Leader award 2001, Outstanding Toastmaster Dist. 56), Soroptimists (dir. Soroptimist Manor 1978—80, 1983—85, pres. chpt. 1985—87, rep. youth citizenship award com. 1986—88, chpt. dir. 1987—88, chmn. south central region UN com. 1988—90, rep. youth forum com. 1990—92, chpt. corr. sec. 1999—2001), Zeta Tau Alpha. Avocations: gourmet food and wine, barbershop singing. Office: McReynolds Winery 706 Shovel Mountain Rd Round Mountain TX 78663

MCREYNOLDS, NEIL LAWRENCE, management consultant; b. Seattle, July 27, 1934; s. Dorr E. and Margaret (Gillies) McR.; m. Nancy Joyce Drew, June 21, 1957; children: Christopher, Bonnie. BA in Journalism, U. Wash., 1956, postgrad. bus. and fin., 1973-76. Assoc. editor Bellevue (Wash.) Am., 1956-60, editor, 1960-67; press sec. to Gov. Dan Evans State of Wash., Olympia, 1967-73; N.W. regional mgr. for pub. rels. and pub. affairs ITT Corp., Seattle, 1973-80; v.p. corp. rels. Puget Sound Power & Light, Bellevue, 1980-87, sr. v.p., 1987-95; prin. McReynolds Assocs., Seattle, 1995-97; v.p. external affairs Kaiser/Group Health, Seattle, 1997-99; pres. McReynolds Assocs., Inc. (Donworth/McReynolds), Seattle, 1999—; strategic dir. Buerk Craig Victor, Seattle, 2002—. Bd. dirs. HomeStreet Bank, Seattle, Adinfonitum, Inc., Seattle, Horizon House, Seattle, Eastern Wash. U., Cheney; bd. chair Wash. Dental Svcs., Seattle, 2004—; chmn. exec. adv. com. Edison Electric Inst., 1984—88; rsch. adv. coun. Electric Power Rsch. Inst., 1989—90; adj. prof. Grad. Sch. Bus. U. Wash., 2002—. Nat. pres. Electric Info. Coun., 1988; bd. dirs. Seattle Symphony, 1980—89, Ind. Colls. of Wash., 1984—95, Mus. of History and Industry, 1995—, Corp. Coun. for Arts, 1985—94, Wash. Nat. Pks. Fund, 1995—2000, Seattle Repertory Theatre, 1996—2002, United Way of King County, 2002—; bd. chmn. Eastside Bus. Roundtable, Bellevue, 2003—04; chmn. bd. dirs. Fred Hutchinson Cancer Rsch. Ctr., 1993—95, Leadership Tomorrow, Seattle, 1987, Seattle-King County Econ. Devel. Coun., 1994; pres. Seattle Ctr. Found., 1979—80; chair U. Wash. Bus. and Econ. Devel. Program, 1996—98; chmn. bd. trustees Bellevue C.C., 1976—77; state chmn. Nature Conservancy, 1988—90; mem. Wash. State Commn. on Trial Cts., 1990; chmn. King County 2000, 1988—90. Named Citizen of Yr., Bellevue, One of Wash. State's Three Outstanding Young Men; recipient Pres. medal Pacific Luth. U. Mem. Pub. Rels. Soc. Am. (accredited, lifetime achievement award, 2003), N.W. Elec. Light and Power Assn. (pres. 1982-83), Greater Seattle C. of C. (officer 1979-81), Soc. Profl. Journalists, Rainier Club (trustee 1995-01, v.p. 1997-98, pres. 1999-2000), Overlake Golf and Country Club (trustee 1993-96), Rotary (pres. Downtown Seattle Club 1991-92). Republican. Episcopalian. Avocations: golf, hiking, skiing, photography, mountain climbing. Home: 14315 SE 45th St Bellevue WA 98006 Office: McReynolds Assocs Inc 1200 5th Ave Ste 1800 Seattle WA 98101 E-mail: nmcreyolds@seanet.com.

MCREYNOLDS, ROSALEE, librarian; b. Fukuoka, Japan, Sept. 17, 1950; arrived in U.S., 1952; d. Donald Samuel McReynolds and Lois June Schaefer; m. Eric Christopher Sands, May 29, 1982. BA in English, U. Colo., 1972; MLS, Simmons Coll., 1977; M in Liberal Arts, Boston U., 1980. Head serials Main Libr. Loyola U., New Orleans, 1980—98, libr. spl. collections, 1998—. Contbr. articles to profl. jours. Founder Carrollton, Riverbend Neighborhood Assn., New Orleans, 1990. Recipient Preservation Hero award, Preservation Resource Ctr., 1998, Justin Winsor award, Libr. History Roundtable, 1987. Home: 938 Dante St New Orleans LA 70118

MCREYNOLDS, STEPHEN PAUL, lawyer; b. Sacramento, Oct. 16, 1938; s. Leslie N. and Mary C. McR.; m. Chodi D. Greeno, Sept. 29, 1970. AB, U. Calif., Davis, 1969; JD, U. Calif., 1972. Bar: Calif. 1972. Sole practice, Sunnyvale, Calif., 1972—. Served with U.S. Navy, 1956-62. Mem. Mensa Internat. Office: 1111 W El Camino Real # 329 Sunnyvale CA 94087-1056

MCROBBIE, MICHAEL ALEXANDER, computer scientist, researcher, academic administrator; b. Melbourne, Australia, Oct. 11, 1950; s. Alexander Hewitt and Joyce Victoria (Gair) McRobbie; m. Andrea Shirley Gibson, Dec. 22, 1973; children: Josephine Elizabeth Joyce, Lucien Richard Vernon, Arabella Diana Grace. BA with honors I, U. Queensland, 1974; PhD, Australian Nat. U., 1979. Rsch. fellow La Trobe U., Melbourne, 1979-81, U. Melbourne, 1981-83, Australian Nat. U., Canberra, 1983-87; head Automated Reasoning Project, 1985-91; reader, exec. dir. Ctr. for Info. Sci. Rsch., 1987-90; prof., exec. dir. Ctr. for Info. sci. Rsch., 1990-96; CEO CRC for Advanced Computational Systems, 1992-96; v.p. info. tech., chief info. officer Ind. U., Bloomington, 1997—, prof. computer sci., prof. philosophy, prof. computer tech., 1997—. Vis. prof. U. Kaiserlautern, Germany, 1987; Fulbright sr. fellow Argonne Nat. Lab., 1988. Co-author: (book) Automated Theorem Proving in Non-Classical Logics, 1986; author, co-author, editor: over 100 papers, articles, reports and books. Mem.: IEEE, Assn. Computer Machinery, Assn. Automated Reasoning, Columiba Club (Indpls.), Commonwealth Club (Canberra), Univ. Ho. (Australian Nat. U.). Avocations: art, book collecting, weightlifting, cricket. Office: Ind U 601 E Kirkwood Ave Franklin Hall 116 Bloomington IN 47405 E-mail: vpit@indiana.edu.

MCROBERTS, TERRY ALLAN, music educator; b. Richmond, Ind., May 11, 1954; s. Roy and Vera McRoberts. BS, Manchester Coll., 1977; MusM, Youngstown State U., 1979; DA, Ball State U., 1984. Assoc. prof. music Blue Mountain (Miss.) Coll., 1983—92; prof. music Union U., Jackson, Tenn., 1992—. Organist/choir dir. First United Meth. Ch., Ripley, Miss., 1985—92, Forest Heights United Meth. Ch., Jackson, Tenn., 1992—2001. Organist First United Meth. Ch., Jackson, Tenn., 2003—. Mem.: Soc. for Am. Music (membership com. mem.), Coll. Music Soc. (bd. mem. so. chpt. 2002), Music Tchrs. Nat. Assn. (nat. cert. tchr. music), Nat. Guild Piano Tchrs. (chair Jackson Ctr.), Am. Matthay Assn. (editor Matthay News 2002), West Tenn. Music Tchrs. Assn. (pres. 1995—97), Tenn. Music Tchrs. Assn. (pres.-elect 2001—03, pres. 2003—, Tchr. of Yr. 2002). Avocations: reading, walking. Home: 319 Parker Dr Jackson TN 38305 Office: Union Univ 1050 Union University Dr Jackson TN 38305 Office Phone: 731-661-5232. Business E-Mail: tmcrober@uu.edu.

MCRORIE, WILLIAM EDWARD, lawyer, retired life insurance company executive; b. Rutherfordton, N.C., Apr. 8, 1940; s. Cyrus Brown and Rosalie (Thompson) McR.; m. Hope Evangeline Foster, Sept. 9, 1962; children: Mark Edward, Jennifer Lynn. LLB, U. N.C., 1964. CLU; Bar: N.C., Va. State mgr. Sturdivant Life Ins. Co., Lynchburg, Va., 1965-68; sr. v.p., gen. counsel First Colony, Lynchburg, 1969-2000. Sec. Jamestown Life Ins. Co., Lynchburg, 1981-2000. Councilman City of Lynchburg. Mem. Va. Bar Assn., Assn. Life Ins. Counsel, John Lynch Soc. (sec. 1970—). Home: 2600 Link Rd Lynchburg VA 24503-3012 E-mail: wem@ntelos.net.

MC ROSTIE, CLAIR NEIL, economics professor; b. Owatonna, Minn., Dec. 16, 1930; s. Neil Hale and Myrtle Julia (Peterson) McR.; m. Ursula Anne Schwieger, Aug. 29, 1968. BSBA cum laude, Gustavus Adolphus Coll., 1952; MA in Mktg., Mich. State U., 1953; PhD in Fin., U. Wis., 1963; postgrad., U. Minn., 1971-72, Am. Grad. Sch. Internat. Mgmt., 1980-81; cert., Coll. for Fin. Planning, 1990. Cert. fin. planner. Faculty Gustavus Adolphus Coll., St. Peter, Minn., 1958-96; emeritus prof., 1996—; chmn. dept. econs. and bus. Gustavus Adolphus Coll., 1967-83, chmn., mem. various coms., 1971-96; teaching asst. Sch. Commerce, U. Wis., 1960-62. Lectr. European div. U. Md., 1966-67; vis. prof. Am. Grad. Sch. Internat. Mgmt., 1980-81; pres. Minn. World Trade Week, Inc., 1987; bd. arbitrators NASD Dispute Resolutions Inc. Editor: Global Resources: Perspectives and Alternatives, 1978, The Future of the Market Economy, 1979. Congregation pres. First Luth. Ch., St. Peter, Minn., 1972-73, 93, chmn. pastoral call com., 1968-69, chmn. staffing com., 1975, mem. ch. council, 1968-74, 89-93; chmn. social ministry com. Minn. Synod, Luth. Ch. Am., 1975, mem. long range planning com. Southwestern Minn. Synod; chmn. Rep. council arts professions, scis., Minn., 1968-70, co-chmn. state task force on Vietnam, 1968; mem. adv. commn. Minn. Dept. Manpower Services, 1967-71; mem. North Central Regional Manpower Adv. Com.; bd. dirs. Midwest China Resource Study Center; del. White House Conf. Aging, 1971. Served with U.S. Army, 1954-56. Recipient Leavey Found. award Freedoms Found., Valley Forge, Pa.; rsch. fellow Fed. Res. Bank Chgo., 1962-63. Mem. Fin. Execs. Inst., Fin. Planners Assn., Minn. Econs. Assn. (bd. dirs. 1974-75, 79-80), Masons (master, Royal Arch chpt., Zuhrah Shrine Temple, Scottish Rite), Royal Order Scotland, Alpha Kappa Psi, Iota Delta Gamma, Sigma Epsilon. Lutheran. Avocations: bird watching, backpacking, fitness and health. Home: 1208 Pine Pointe Curv Saint Peter MN 56082-1344

MCRUER, DUANE TORRANCE, aerospace engineering executive; b. Bakersfield, Calif., Oct. 25, 1925; s. John Torrance and Ruth Inez (Bartlett) McR.; m. Betty June Mechura, Oct. 5, 1955; 1 child, Lara McRuer; 1 stepson, Stephen Harsey. BS in Engring., Calif. Inst. Tech., 1945, MEE, 1948. Registered profl. engr., Calif. Tech. chief, flight controls Northrop Aircraft Inc., Hawthorne, Calif., 1948-54; pres. Controls Specialists Inc., Inglewood, Calif., 1954-57; pres., tech. dir. Sys. Tech. Inc., Hawthorne, Calif., 1957-92, chmn., 1992—. Regents lectr. U. Calif., Santa Barbara, 1976; Hunsaker prof. MIT, 1992-93; mem. NRC Aero. and Space Engring. Bd., Washington, 1978-85, NASA Adv. Coun., 1990—, NASA Aero. Adv. Com., Washington, 1978-88, Am. Automatic Control Coun. (pres. 1969-73). Author: Analysis of Nonlinear Control Systems, 1961, Aircraft Dynamics and Automatic Control, 1974; author more than 150 tech. papers, 1948—; patentee in field. Lt. (j.g.) USNR, 1943-53. Recipient Louis Levy medal Franklin Inst., Phila., 1960, Disting. Alumnus award Calif. Inst. Tech., 1983. Fellow AIAA (Mechanics and Control of Flight award 1970), IEEE, AAAS, NAE, Soc. Automotive Engrs., Human Factors and Ergonomics Soc. (A.W. Williams award 1976), Caltech Assocs., Am. Alpine Club (N.Y.C.), Sierra Club. Episcopalian. Avocation: mountain climbing. Office: Systems Tech Inc 13766 Hawthorne Blvd Hawthorne CA 90250-7083

MCSHAN, CLYDE GRIFFIN, II, financial executive; b. New Orleans, Feb. 8, 1945; s. Clyde G. and Ursula C. (Mumme) McS.; m. Deborah A. Lark, Oct. 16, 1971; children: Madylin, Kristy, Suzanne. BA, Southeastern La. U., 1966. Cert. internal auditor, cert. govt. fin. mgr., cert. office automation profl. Auditor Office of the Inspector Gen., New Orleans, 1965-72; audit br. chief Cen. Voucher Payment Ctr., New Orleans, 1972-73; evaluation staff chief Nat. Fin. Ctr., New Orleans, 1973-74, processing br. chief, 1974, ops. div. chief, 1974-78, acctg. div. chief, 1978-79, ops. div. chief, 1979-80, dep. dir., 1980-81, dir., 1981-93; dep. chief fin. officer, dir. fin. mgmt. U.S. Dept. Commerce, 1993-97; v.p. Affiliated Computer Svcs., Inc., New Orleans, 1997-2001, sr. v.p. affiliated computer svcs., 2001—03; with Lockheed Martin, 2003—04, Savantage Solutions, Inc., 2004—. Contbr. articles to profl. jours. Chmn. CASU Tenant Bd. Dirs., New Orleans, 1989-93, policy com. Fed. Exec. Bd., New Orleans, 1990-93, chmn., 1989-90, 92-93; chmn. unit I United Way of Greater New Orleans, 1989-90, chair mktg. and comm., 1991, vice chmn. cmty. resources divsn. 1991, chair 1992-93, trustee, 1990-94, 98—, chmn. unit VII, 1990, chmn. CFC, 1989, chair cmty.-wide campaign, 2001-02; mem. Tulane U. pub. adv. com. for computer info. sys., 1987—2003; acctg. dept. advt. bd. U. New Orleans, 1991-93; pres. acctg. bd. U. New Orleans, 1992-93, bd. dirs. La. Tech. Coun., Ctr. for Non-profit Resources, 1997-2002; bd. dirs. YMCA Greater New Orleans, 1990-93, 1997—, chmn. bd., 2002—04. With U.S. Army, 1965-71. Recipient Leadership award United Way, 1989, Communication and Leadership award Toastmasters, 1991, award New Orleans chpt. Federally Employed Women, 1990, 91, Presdl. Meritorious Rank award, 1989, 95, New Orleans Fed. Exec. Bd. award for outstanding leadership, 1989, Spl. award Office of the Comptroller Gen., 1989, Disting. Exec. Svc. award Sr. Exec. Assn. USDA, 1989, Elmer Staats Disting. Leadership award, 1993, Donald L. Scantlebury Meml. award for Disting. Leadership in Fin. Mgmt., 1995, Robert W. King Meml. award for disting. career accomplishments, 1997; named one of Outstanding 1990 Campaign Vols. of Yr., United Way, 1991, Fed. 100 Info. Systems Mgrs., Fed. Computer Wk., 1990, 96, to Info. Tech. Hall of Fame, 1997. Mem. Assn. Govt. Accts. (New Orleans chpt. pres. 1972-73, dir. 1970-71, 73-74, 74-75, 76-77, S.W. region v.p. 1975-76, South Ctrl. region v.p. 1981-82, mem. nat. exec. com. 1983-84, 93-96, chmn. fin. mgmt. enhancement bd. 1988-89, chmn. emerging issues 1990-91, chmn. tech. program com. 1991-93, nat. pres.-elect 1993-94, nat. pres. 1994-95), Inst. Internal Auditors, Sr. Exec. Assn., Fed. Exec. Inst. Alumni Assn. Republican. Roman Catholic. Avocation: gardening. Home: V50 5500 Toby Ln Kenner LA 70065 E-mail: cmcshanii@aol.com.

MCSHANE, IAN, actor; b. Blackburn, Lancashire, Eng., Sept. 29, 1942; m. Gwen Humble. Actor: (films) The Pleasure Girls, 1965, Sky West and Crooked, 1966, If It's Tuesday, This Must Be Belgium, 1969, Battle of Britain, 1969, Pussycat, Pussycat, I Love You, 1970, Tam Lin, 1970, Villain, 1971, Freelance, 1971, Sitting Target, 1972, Left Hand of Gemini, 1972, The Last of Sheila, 1973, Ransom, 1975, Journey Into Fear, 1975, The Fifth Musketeer, 1979, Yesterday's Hero, 1979, The Great Riviera Bank Robbery, 1979, Cheaper to Keep Her, 1980, Exposed, 1983, Torchlight, 1984, Ordeal by Innocence, 1984, Too Scared to Scream, 1985, Grand Larceny, 1987, Con Man, 1992, Sexy Beast, 2000, Bollywood Queen, 2002, Agent Cody Banks, 2003, Nemesis Game, 2003; (TV series) You Can't Win, 1966, Wuthering Heights, 1967, Bare Essence, 1983, Lovejoy, 1986, Dallas, 1989, Madson, 1996, Deadwood, 2004—; (TV miniseries) Roots, 1977, Jesus of Nazareth, 1977, Life of Shakespeare, 1978, Disraeli, 1979, Marco Polo, 1982, Evergreen, 1985, A.D., 1985, War and Remembrance, 1988, Trust, 2003; (TV films) The Wild and the Willing, 1962, Funny Noises with Their Mouths, 1963, Funeral Games, 1968, Whose Life Is It Anyway?, 1972, The Lives of Jenny Dolan, 1975, Code Name: Diamond Head, 1977, The Pirate, 1978, High Tide, 1980, The Letter, 1982, Grace Kelly, 1983, Braker, 1985, Rocket to the Moon, 1986, The Murders in the Rue Morgue, 1986, The Great Escape II: The Untold Story, 1988, Young Charlie Chaplin, 1989, Dick Francis: Twice Shy, 1989, Dick Francis: In the Frame, 1989, Dick Francis: Blood Sport, 1989, Perry Mason: The Case of the Desperate Deception, 1990, Columbo: Rest in Peace, Mrs. Columbo, 1990, White Goods, 1994, Soul Survivors, 1995, Babylon 5: The River of Souls, 1998, D.R.E.A.M. Team, 1999, Man and Boy, 2002. Office: c/o ICM 8942 Wilshire Blvd Beverly Hills CA 90211*

MCSHANE, JOSEPH MICHAEL, academic administrator, priest; b. N.Y.C., June 19, 1949; s. Owen Patrick and Catherine Veronica (Shelley) McS. AB, AM, Boston Coll., 1972; MDiv, STM, Jesuit Sch. Theology, Berkeley, Calif., 1977; PhD, U. Chgo., 1981. Ordained priest Roman Cath. Ch., 1977. English tchr. Canisius H.S., Buffalo, 1972-74; asst. prof. religious studies LeMoyne Coll., Syracuse, NY, 1982-87, assoc. prof. religious studies, 1987-91, prof., 1991-92, chairperson, 1991-92; dean Fordham Coll., Bronx, NY, 1992-98, prof. theology, 1992-98; pres. Fordham U., Bronx, NY, 2003—; pres., prof. theology U. Scranton, 1998—2003. Vis. prof. history Loyola House, Berkley, Mich., 1986—87. Author: Sufficiently Radical: Catholicism, Progressivism and the Bishops' Program of 1919, 1986; author chpt. to book; creator video: The Pilgrimage of the People of God: An Introduction to the Study of Church History, 1991; contbr. articles to profl. jours. Bd. dirs. U. Scranton, Pa., Scranton Prep. Sch., Pa., Fordham U., N.Y.C., Fordham Prep. Sch., Bronx, NY, Regis H.S., N.Y.C., Canisius Coll., Buffalo, St. Joseph's Prep. Sch., Phila. Recipient First prize Cath. Press Assn., 1992. Mem. Am. Cath. Hist. Assn., Am. Soc. Ch. History, Phi Beta Kappa. Democrat. Roman Catholic. Office: Office of Pres Fordham U Bronx NY 10458 Office Phone: 718-817-3000. E-mail: jmcshane@fordham.edu.

MCSHANE, MICHAEL JOHN, lobbyist; b. N.Y.C., Jan. 8, 1944; s. James Joseph Patrick and Theresa Elizabeth (Curtis) McS. BS, East Carolina U., 1966; cert. bus. adminstrn., Georgetown U., 1986. Pres. sec., legis asst. Congressman John J. Rooney, 1973-75; fgn svc. officer, mem. Sec. of State Henry Kissinger's staff U.S. Fgn. Svc., Jerusalem, 1975-76; v.p. Nat. Energy Rsch. Orgn., 1979-82; chmn. govt. rels. com. Am. Electronics Assn., 1982-86; sr. adv., polit. strategist Am. Embassy and Govt. of Taiwan, Taipei, 1986—; lobbyist, dir. govt. rels. TRW, Inc., Arlington, Va., 1991—. Guest lectr. Am. politics Am. U. Ctr. Congl. and Presdl. Studies, Grad. Sch. Pub. Policy Georgetown U., Notre Dame U., Randolph-Macon Coll., Univ. prof.'s lecture series Boston U., East Carolina U.; mem., team capt. 1996 local elections Official US Delegation to Albania, 1996; mem. advance team, traveling party Pres. Carter's State Visit to France, 1978, v.p. Mondale's Official Visit to The Philippines and New Zealand, 1978; founder, chair Coalition to Preserve Health Benefits, 1994; chair Dem. Leadership Coun. domestic cluster 1996 Clinton/Gore transition team, chair Chgo. Convention Com., 1996, inaugural com., 1997, bd. dirs.; adv., polit. strategist Clinton/Gore Reelection Campaign, to Sandy Thurman asst. to President for AIDS rsch., to Lanny Davis spl. counsel to President, the White House. Author: Lobbying: An Academic vs. Practical Comparison, 1997; commentator C-SPAN. Mem. staff Carter-Mondale Campaign, 1976-79; vice chair to former astronaut Sally Ride 1992 Clinton-Gore Transition Sci., Space and Tech. Cluster; mem. faculty Bryce Harlow Found. Capt. USAF, 1966-72, Vietnam. Recipient People to People Internat. award 1990, named Diplomat of Yr., 1996; recipient Torch of Birmingham Internat. Acad. for Leadership in Bus. and Adminstrn., 1995, Alumni of Yr. award East Carolina U., 1998. Mem. Am. Electronics Assn. (Outstanding Lobbyist of Yr. award 1986, chair govt. rels. com.), Coun. Fgn. Affairs. Episcopalian. Avocations: travel, teaching. Office: TRW 1001 19th St N Ste 800 Arlington VA 22209-1749 Home: 3205 Circle Hill Rd Alexandria VA 22305-1609

MCSHANE, ROSEMARY, lawyer; b. Tucson, May 4, 1950; d. John B. and Jean Ann Jacobson McShane; m. James Allen Dator, Sept. 4, 1981; 1 child, McShane Allen Dator. BA, U. Hawaii, 1973; JD, William S. Richardson Sch. Law, 1981. Pvt. practice, Honolulu, 1981-82; lawyer corp. counsel, family support divsn. City and County of Honolulu, 1983-89; lawyer dept. atty. gen., social svcs. divsn. State of Hawaii, Honolulu, 1989-93; adminstr., head hearings officer dept. atty. gen. Office Child Support Hearings, State of Hawaii, Honolulu, 1993-95; atty., divsn. head dept. corp. counsel, family support div. City and County of Honolulu, 1995—. Contbg. author: (book) Our Rights, Our Lives, 3d edit., 1996, (manual) Hawaii Divorce Manual, 3d edit., 1996. Mem. Hawaii Women Lawyers (bd. dirs. 1995-97, 99—, v.p. 1997-98, pres. 1998-99), Hawaii State Bar Assn., William S. Richardson Sch. Law Alumni Assn. Office: Dept Corp Counsel Family Support Divsn # 703 204 Makee Rd Honolulu HI 96815-3978

MCSHEFFERTY, JOHN, retired research company executive, consultant; b. Akron, Ohio, Mar. 14, 1929; s. John and Jean McS.; m. Glenna Gloria Childs, Apr. 18, 1959; children: John III, Amy Childs. BSc, U. Glasgow, 1953, PhD, 1957. Various rsch. positions Sterling Winthrop Rsch. Inst., Rensselaer, N.Y., 1957-62; dir. pharm. devel. Ortho Pharm. Corp. divsn. Johnson and Johnson, Raritan, NJ, 1962-75; dir. rsch. Janssen R & D, Inc. divsn. Johnson & Johnson, Piscataway, NJ, 1975-77; v.p. R & D family products Internat. Playtex, Paramus, N.J., 1977-79; pres. Gillette Rsch. Inst., Gaithersburg, Md., 1979-97; ret., 1997. Cons. in field. Fellow Royal Pharm. Soc. of Gt. Britain; mem. Indsl. Rsch. Inst. (bd. dirs. 1988-92, emeritt com. 1998—), Am. Acad. Dermatology, Am. Mgmt. Assn. (bd. dirs. 1994-97), Am. Chem. Soc., Am. Pharm. Assn., N.Y. Acad. Scis., Soc. Cosmetic Chemists, Dirs. Indsl. Rsch., Assn. Rsch. Dirs., Rotary, Sigma Xi. Personal E-mail: jmcs2@comcast.net.

MCSHERRY, WILLIAM JOHN, JR., lawyer, consultant; b. N.Y.C., Oct. 28, 1947; s. William John Sr. and Mary Elizabeth (Dunphy) McS.; m. Elizabeth Ann Crosby, June 8, 1974; children: Brendan, Sean, Rory. AB cum laude, Fordham U., 1969; JD cum laude, Harvard U., 1973. Bar: N.Y. 1974, U.S. Dist. Ct. (so. dist.) N.Y. 1975, U.S. Ct. Appeals (2d cir.) 1977. Assoc. Spengler, Carlson, Gubar, Brodsky & Frischling, N.Y.C., 1973-78, ptnr., 1979-88, Bryan, Cave, McPheeters & McRoberts, N.Y.C., 1989-91, Battle Fowler LLP, N.Y.C., 1991—. Exec. dir. U.S. Football League, N.Y.C., 1985-86; chmn. litigation dept. Battle Fowler, 1992-96; pres., bd. dirs. Playtex Mktg. Corp.; bd. dirs. Questron Tech., Inc. Author: (with others) Tender Offer Regulation: The Federal SEC's Challenge and New York State's Response. Derivatives Risk and Responsibility, 1996, Attorney Client Privilege in tge Second Circuit, 1998. Mem. Zoning Bd. Appeals, Village of Larchmont, N.Y., 1988-91, dep. mayor, 1992-98, bd. trustees, 1991-98. Served with USAR, 1970-75. Mem. ABA (litigation, antitrust, entertainment and sports, corp. banking and bus. law sects., subcom. litigation 1940 Act; vice-chair com. alt. dispute resolution), Assn. of Bar of City of N.Y. (mem. 1979-82 com. state cts. superior jurisdiction, 1987-90, com. arbitration and alternative dispute resolution, mem. sports law com. 1998—), Fed. Bar Council, Council N.Y. Law Assocs. (bd. dirs., treas. 1975), Phi Beta Kappa. Roman Catholic. Avocations: community involvement, sports, writing. Home: 2 Summit Ave Larchmont NY 10538-2930 Address: 75 E 55th St New York NY 10022-3205

MC SHINE, KYNASTON LEIGH, curator; b. Port of Spain, Trinidad, Feb. 20, 1935; s. Austen H. Mc S. AB, Dartmouth Coll., 1958; postgrad., U. Mich., 1958-59, Inst. Fine Arts, N.Y. U., 1960-64. Asst. prof. art history Hunter Coll., 1968-69; lectr. in art history Sch. Visual Arts, NYC, 1969-76; curator of painting and sculpture Jewish Museum, NYC, 1965-68, acting dir. mus., 1967-68; assoc. curator painting and sculpture Mus. Modern Art, NYC, 1968-71, curator painting and sculpture, 1971-80, sr. curator painting and sculpture, 1980—2001, acting chief curator painting and sculpture, 2001—03, chief curator at large, 2003—. Mem. visual arts com. N.Y.C. Cultural Council, N.Y. State Council on Arts; mem. adv. com. Skowhegan Sch. Painting and Sculpture. Author: catalogs: Josef Albers: Homage to the Square, 1964, Primary Structures, 1966, Information, 1970; editor, contbg. author catalogs: Marcel Duchamp, 1973, The Natural Paradise: Painting in America 1800-1950, 1976, Jackie Winsor, 1979, Joseph Cornell, 1980; editor (catalog): An Internat. Survey of Recent Painting and Sculpture, 1984. Mem. Internat. Assn. Art Critics, Coll. Art Assn., Am. Assn. Museums., Internat. Council Mus. (mem. internat. com. for mus. and collections of modern art) Office: 11 W 53rd St New York NY 10019-5401

MCSLARROW, KYLE E. federal agency administrator; b. Va. m. Allison McSlarrow. Bachelor's, Cornell U.; law degree, U. Va. Asst. to gen. counsel of U.S. Army office sec. U.S. Army, 1985; assoc. Hunton & Williams, Washington; dep. chief of staff, chief counsel to sen. majority leaders Bob Dole and Trent Lott, 1995—97; chief of staff to late U.S. Sen. Paul Coverdell; nat. chmn. Quayle 2000 Presdl. Campaign, 1998—2000; v.p. polit. and govt. affairs, lead Washington office Grassroots.com; chief of staff to energy sec. Spencer Abraham Dept. Energy, 2001—02, dep. sec., 2002—. Mem. Arlington County, Va. Planning Commn. Democrat. Office: Dept Energy Office of Sec 1000 Independence Ave SW Washington DC 20585-0001

MCSPADDEN, DAVID LARRY, music educator; b. Little Rock, Aug. 12, 1940; s. David Emmitt and Euna E. McSpadden; m. Anda Zirnitis, May 6, 1989; children: David, Ryan. BME, Henderson State U., Ark., 1962; MEd, U. Mo., 1970. Cert. lifetime tchg. Ark. and Mo. Dir. vocal music Gideon (Mo.) HS, 1962—65, Farmington (Mo.) HS, 1965—70; dir. music Meml. United Meth. Ch., Farmington, Mo., 1966—70; dir. choral activities Culver-Stockton Coll., Canton, Mo., 1970—; dir. music Immanuel Meth. Ch., Canton, Mo., 1974—77; choir master St. John's Episcopal Ch., Quincy, Ill., 1977—97; coord. music Culver-Stockton Coll., Canton, Mo., 1981—2004, chair, divsn. fine arts, 2004. Vocal v.p. Southeast Mo. Music Educators, 1968—70, Mo. Music Educators Assn., 1972—74; dist. dir. Am. Choral Dirs. Assn., 1977—79. Recipient Outstanding Young Educator, Jaycees, 1970, Excellenc award, Mo. Gov., 1998. Mem.: Coll. Music Soc., Am. Choral Dirs. Assn., Am. Educators Nat. Conf. Home: 604 Grant St Canton MO 63435 Office: Culver-Stockton Coll One Coll Hill Canton MO 63435 Office Phone: 217-288-6357. Office Fax: 217-231-6617. E-mail: lmcspadden@culver.edu.

MCSPADDEN, LETTIE, political science educator; b. Battle Creek, Mich., Apr. 9, 1937; d. John Dean and Isma Doolie (Sullivan) McSpadden; m. Manfred Wilhelm Wenner, Apr. 3, 1962; children: Eric Alexis, Adrian Edward. AB, U. Chgo., 1959; MA, U. Calif., Berkeley, 1962; PhD, U. Wis., 1972. Fgn. svc. officer Dept. State, Washington, 1961-63; rsch. assoc. Dept. HEW, Washington, 1965-67; asst. prof. polit. sci. U. Ill., Chgo., 1972-79, assoc. prof. polit. sci., 1979-88; prof. and chair dept. polit. sci. No. Ill. U., De Kalb, 1988-94, prof. dept. polit. sci., 1994—. Author: One Environment Under Law, 1976, The Environmental Decade in Court, 1982, United States Energy and Environmental Interest Groups, 1990. Mem. Am. Polit. Sci. Assn., Midwest Polit. Sci. Assn., Law and Society Assn., Pub. Policy Assn., Audubon Soc., Sierra Club. Democrat. Office: No Ill U Dept Polit Sci Dekalb IL 60115 Home: Apt 328 500 S Clinton Chicago IL 60607-4089

MCSPADDEN, PETER FORD, retired advertising agency executive; b. Montclair, N.J., Oct. 2, 1930; s. Chester F. and Janet (Chase) McS.; m. Barbara Dodds, June 30, 1956; children— Douglas Dodds, David Ford, Peter Chase. AB, Dartmouth, 1952. Account exec. McCann-Erickson, Inc., N.Y.C., 1956-59; with Dancer-Fitzgerald-Sample, Inc., N.Y.C., from 1959, v.p., account supr., 1965-68, sr. v.p., mgmt. supr., 1968-72, exec. v.p., 1972-74, pres., chief operating officer, from 1974; chmn. bd., chief operating officer Saatchi & Saatchi DFS Inc., N.Y.C., 1986-88, also bd. dirs., ret., 1988. Pres., bd. dirs. DFS/Dorland Worldwide; bd. dirs. Am. Advt. Fedn., Am. Assn. Advt. Agys., TriState U.; mem. Nat. Advt. Rev. Bd.; bd. trustees Bradford Coll; vice chmn. Broadstreet TV Inc, 1989—. Chmn. bd. visitors Rockefeller Ctr., Dartmouth Coll., 1989-97; pres. Greenwich (Conn.) Young Republican Club, 1966-67; bd. dirs. United Way of Tri-State, 1995 Spl. Olympic Games; campaign mgr. Congressman Lowell P. Weicker, 1968, Senator Weicker, 1970, 76, 82, 88; mem. Rep. Town Com., Greenwich, 1965-68; trustee, mem. exec. com. Greenwich Hosp.; trustee Farnsworth Mus., Rockland, Maine. Served to lt. (j.g.) USNR, 1952-55. Mem. Am. Assn. Advt. Agys. (dir.) Clubs: Riverside (Conn.) Yacht, Greenwich Country, Megunticook Golf. Home: 46 Carriglea Dr Riverside CT 06878-2402

MC SWAIN, ANGUS STEWART, JR., retired law educator; b. Bryan, Tex., Nov. 26, 1923; s. Angus Stewart and Lois (Pipkin) McS.; m. Betty Ann McCartney, June 3, 1956; 1 child, Angus Earl. BS in Civil Engring., Tex. A. and M. U., 1947; LLB, Baylor U., 1949; LL.M., U. Mich., 1951. Bar: Tex. 1949. Mem. faculty Baylor U. Law Sch., 1949—, prof. law, 1956—, dean, 1965-84, ret., 1994. Mem. panel arbitrators Fe. Mediation and Conciliation Service. Author: (with Wendorf) Cases and Materials on Texas Trusts and Probate, 1965, Supplementary Cases and Materials on Property, 1965, 78, (with Norvell and Simpkins) Cases and Materials for Texas Land Practice, 1968. Served to 1st lt., C.E. AUS, 1943-46. Mem. ABA, Tex.Bar Assn. (chmn. family law sect. 1967-69, chmn. com. on standards of admission 1972-73, 77-79), Tau Beta Pi, Phi Alpha Delta Home: 4600 Kenny Ln Waco TX 76710-2059

MCSWAIN, BYRDIE ENGLE, laboratory scientist, immunohematologist; b. Ethel, Ark., Oct. 13, 1939; d. James Marvin and Katherine Engle (Martin) McSwain. BS, U. Ark., 1968; BS in Med. Tech., U. Ark. Sch. Medicine, 1969; MS, U. Ctrl. Ark., 1973; Specialist in Blood Banking, U. Ark. Med. Scis., 1976. Cert. in regulatory affairs (RAPS). Supr. blood bank Univ. Ark. Med. Scis., Little Rock, clin. instr.; dir. tech. svcs., dir. product mgmt. ARC Blood Svcs., dir. transplantation svcs., dir. regulatory affairs, South Ctrl. area dir. tech. and regulatory svcs., acting area dir. quality assurance. Contbr. 13 articles to profl. jours. Grad. scholar Am. Soc. Med. Tech.; recipient Omicron Sigma award, Am. Soc. for Med. Tech., Outstanding Svc. award, Disting. Alumni award U. Ark. for Med. Scis. Mem. Ark. Soc. Clin. Lab. Scientists (Med. Technologist of Yr.), Am. Assn. Blood Banks, South Ctrl. Assn. Blood Banks (pres., author, editor), Am. Soc. Clin. Lab. Scientists, Clin. Lab. Mgmt. Assn. (pres. Ark. chpt.), Am. Soc. Clin. Pathologists, Regulatory Affairs Profl. Soc., Am. Soc. Quality Assurance, Phi Beta Kappa. Address: 2619 Fair Park Blvd Little Rock AR 72204-5149

MCSWAIN, RON, textiles executive; MBA, U. Mich. Pres., owner McSwain's Carpets, 1968-99; chmn. The Maxim Group, Inc., Kennesaw, Ga., 1999—. Bd. dirs. Johnson Investment Mut. Trust, Jobs Plus, Inc.; gen. ptnr. P&R Realty, Inc. Office: The Maxim Group Inc 210 Townpark Dr NW Kennesaw GA 30144-5514

MCSWAN, ANGUS, news agency executive; Bur. chief Miami Reutires Am., Inc., Miami, 1999—. Office: Reuters Am Inc 777 Brickell Ave Ste 700 Miami FL 33131-2866

MCSWEENEY, FRANCES KAYE, psychology educator; b. Rochester, N.Y., Feb. 6, 1948; d. Edward William and Elsie Winifred (Kingston) McSweeney. BA, Smith Coll., 1969; MA, Harvard U., 1972, PhD, 1974. Lectr. McMaster U., Hamilton, Canada, 1973-74; asst. prof. Wash. State U.,

Pullman, 1974-79, assoc. prof., 1979-83, prof. psychology, 1983—2004, chmn. dept. psychology, 1986-94, vice provost for faculty affairs, 2003—, prof. psychology, 2004—. Cons. in field. Contbr. articles to profl. jours. Woodrow Wilson fellow, Sloan fellow, 1968—69, NIMH fellow, 1973, Fellow: APA, Am. Psychol. Soc.; mem.: Assn. Behavior Analysis (pres.-elect), Psychonomic Soc., Phi Kappa Phi, Sigma Xi, Phi Beta Kappa. Home: 860 SW Alcora Dr Pullman WA 99163-2053 Office: Wash State U Dept Psychology Pullman WA 99164-4820 Office Phone: 509-335-3508. Business E-Mail: fkmcs@mail.wsu.edu.

MCSWEENEY, MAURICE J. (MARC MCSWEENEY), lawyer; b. Chgo., July 3, 1938; s. Thomas J. and Margaret F. (Ahern) McS.; m. Sandra A. Panosh, Sept. 30, 1967; children: Erin, Sean. BS, DePaul U., 1960; JD, U. Chgo., 1963. Ptnr. Foley and Lardner, Milw., 1963—. Bd. dirs. Harambee Elem. Sch., Internat. Clown Hall of Fame. Bd. dirs. Milw. Pub. Schs., 1973-79, Milw. chpt. ARC, 1979-85, Alverno Coll., Milw., 1984—, Health Edn. Ctr. of Wis., 1987-96. Fellow Am. Coll. Trial Lawyers; mem. ABA, Wis. Bar Assn., Milw. Bar Assn., Am. Judicature Soc. (bd. dirs. 1988-93), Milw. Area Tech. Coll. Found., Rotary (bd. dirs. Milw. 1986-88). Avocations: skiing, tennis, Karate. Office: Foley & Lardner 777 E Wisconsin Ave Ste 3800 Milwaukee WI 53202-5367

MCSWEENEY, WILLIAM LINCOLN, JR., retired publishing executive; b. Nov. 9, 1930; s. William Lincoln and Ruth Patricia (Desmond) McS.; m. Anne Cornelia Bulman, Aug. 18, 1956; children: Anne C., William L., Siobhan White, Arthur J., Sean B. BS, Boston Coll., 1953; MLA, So. Meth. U., 1980; LHD, Rockhurst Coll., 1997. Tchr. English Killingly (Conn.) H.S., 1956-57; with Hallmark Cards, Inc., Kansas City, Mo., 1957-86, area pers. mgr., 1968, sales tng. mgr., 1969-86, dir. corp. tng. and devel., 1970-86; pub. Nat. Cath. Reporter Co., 1986-96. Bd. dirs. Cath. Social Svcs., Kansas City Archdiocese, 1975-88, pres., 1980-84; bd. dirs. United Cmty. Svcs. Kansas City, 1978-84, mem. exec. com., 1978-84; bd. dirs. Kansas City Amigos De Las Americas, 1977-80, pres., 1979; bd. dirs. Johnson City YMCA, 1978-79, Jesuit Vol. Corps, Midwest, 1989-95, Mex. Am. Cultural Ctr., San Antonio, 1990—, Minority Mus., 1994-2000; bd. dirs. Pan Ednl. Inst., 1979-83, pres., 1980-81; mem. Boston Coll. Alumni Admissions Coun., 1976-96; mem. chancellor's adv. bd. Met. Cmty. Colls., 1979-80; mem. Dem. Com., Johnson County, Kans., 1980-86; bd. advisors Sch. Social Welfare U. Kans., 1983-2000, chair, 1983-91, 93-94, Avila Col., 1991-2000; chair Mayor's UN Day Dinner, Kansas City, Mo., 1990, Mayor's Breakfast, 1994—; trustee NCCJ, 1991-95, co-chmn., 1995—. With U.S. Army, 1953-56. Recipient Kansas City World Citizen of Yr. award, 1995, William V. McKenney award Boston Coll., 2000. Mem. Internat. Rels. Coun. of Kansas City (bd. dirs. 1989-2000), Cath. Press Assn., Assoc. Ch. Press, Internat. Press Inst. (bd. dirs. Am. Com. 1999—), UN Assn., Boston Coll. Alumni Assn. (past bd. dirs.), Boston Coll. Club (Kansas City), Knights of Malta. Roman Catholic. Office: 115 E Armour Blvd PO Box 419281 Kansas City MO 64141-6281

MCSWEENY, WILLIAM FRANCIS, petroleum company executive, author; b. Haverhill, Mass., Mar. 31, 1929; s. William Francis and Mary Florence (Doyle) McS.; m. Dorothy Pierce, Jan. 20, 1969; children: William Francis III, Cathy Ann, Ethan Madden Maverick, Terrell Pierce. Reporter, columnist, fgn. corr. Hearst Newspapers, 1943-67; dep. chmn., dir. pub. affairs Dem. Nat. Com., 1967-68; spl. asst. to White House Chief of Staff, 1968-69; sr. exec. v.p., bd. dirs. Occidental Internat. Corp., Washington, 1969-76, pres., 1976-91; exec. v.p. Occidental Petroleum Corp., Washington, 1984-91, cons. to chmn., 1991-95; dir. Fin. Gen. Bankshares Co., Washington, 1978-82, Chevy Chase FSB, 1985—. Mem. Lloyd's of London; pres.'s rep. to USSR, 1979; mem. Pres.'s Inaugural Com., 1980, 84, 92; Presdl. spl. rep. to Oman, 1980, Bolivia, 1982; Pres.'s com. Korean War Meml., 1987; Pres.'s commr. Exec. Exch., 1976-81; Pres.'s trustee The Kennedy Ctr., 1995—, Pres.'s rep. to Korea, 2000; mem. N.E. White Ho. Fellows Bd.; mem. U.S. Com. UNESCO; co-chair NATO 50th Summit; spl. counsel spkr. of Ho. of Reps., 1971-72; chmn. Maverick-McSweeny Cattle Co. Author: Go Up for Glory, 1965, Violence Every Sunday, 1966, The Impossible Dream, 1967; contbr. articles to profl. jours. Bd. overseers Fletcher Sch. Law and Diplomacy, Tufts U.; bd. advisors Karl F. Landegger Program Internat. Bus. Diplomacy, Sch. Fgn. Svc., Georgetown U.; trustee, pres. Holton Arms; chmn. Washington Episc. Sch.; chmn. Meridian House Internat., life trustee; mem. World Affairs Coun.; bd. dirs. The Atlantic Coun., Overseer Exec. Coun. Fgn. Diplomats, Dept. of State, The Brookings Instn. Coun., 1991-98; vice chmn. Sec. of State Fine Arts Commn.; chmn. Ford's Theatre, 1988-95, life trustee; bd. dirs. Very Spl. Arts, Arena Stage, Corcoran Gallery Art, Africare, Fed. City Coun., Washington Opera, Folger Shakespeare Theater, Cities in Schs. Nat. Learning Ctr., USO, Arms Control Assn., Nat. Assn. So. Poor, Duke Ellington Sch., Washington Ednl. TV, 1989-95; v.p. Ct. of Mary Rose, Portsmouth, Eng.; pres. Commn. to Preserve U.S. Cultural Heritage Abroad; co-chmn. State Dept. diplomatic rooms endowment; chmn. Lombardi Cancer Ctr. Coun., Georgetown U. Med. Ctr.; pres. Ams. Internat. Insts. for Advanced Studies; vice-chmn. Kennedy Ctr. Cmty. Bd., 1991-92; trustee V.P. Residence Found., Lyndon Baines Johnson Sch. Pub. Affairs, U. Tex.; juror The Heinz Found., 1995-2000; chmn. Chevy Chase for Cmty. Com., Coun. Ct. Excellence, 1996-99. Maj. inf. U.S. Army, 1950-53. Decorated Combat Inf. badge; recipient Outstanding Young Man award, Boston Jaycees, 1961, U.S. Disting. Svc. award, 1969, Outstanding Svc. spl. award, 1969, DC Disting. Citizen award, 1981, Paul Hill award, Kennedy Ctr., 1983, DC Cultural award, 1983, Armenian Earthquake Hero medal, 1989, Lincoln medal, 1991, Helen Hayes award, 1991, Washingtonian of Yr. award, 1995, Golden Plate award, Am. Acad. Achievement, 1999, Cultural Alliance award, 2000, Torch of Liberty award, Anti Defamation League, 2001, awards for domestic reports and reporting from Vietnam and Mid. East, including Best U.S. Reporting award, 1964, Angel of Arts award, Cathedral Choral Soc., 2004. Mem. Smithsonian Instn. (nat. adv. com. Kellogg Project), Mus. of Native Ams. (dir.), Alfalfa Club, Cosmos Club, 1925 F St. Club (trustee), Internat. Club (trustee). Office Phone: 240-497-7374.

MCSWINEY, CHARLES RONALD, lawyer; b. Nashville, Apr. 23, 1943; s. James W. and Jewell (Bellar) Mc.; m. Jane Detrick McSwiney, Jan. 2, 1970. BA, Kenyon Coll., Gambier, Ohio, 1965; JD, U. Cin., 1968. Assoc. Smith & Schnacke, Dayton, Ohio, 1968-72, ptnr., 1972-89, pres. and mng. ptnr., 1984-89; sr. v.p., gen. counsel The Danis Cos., Dayton, 1989-92, 99-2000; vice chmn. Carillon Capital, Inc., Dayton, 1992-99; dir. devel. Youth Haven, Inc., 2002—. Chmn., CEO Crysteco, Inc., Wilmington, Ohio, 1995-99; pres. interchange exec. Presdl. Commn. on Pers. Interchange, Washington, 1972-73. Chmn., pres. bd. trustees Dayton Ballet Assn., 1985-88; trustee Columbus (Ohio) Symphony Orch., 1981-84; chmn. Dayton Performing Arts Fund, 1989-92, Dayton Devel. Coun., 1987-90, Wright State U. Found., Dayton, 1988-94, Miami Valley Sch., Dayton, 1988-94, Arts Ctr. Found., 1986-2000; mem. bd. advisors Wright State U. Coll. Bus. Adminstrn., 1988-98; bd. vis. U. Cin. Coll. Law, 1987-89; mem. pres.'s coun. Internat. Coll. Recipient Bronze Medal for Performance U.S. EPA, 1973. Mem. Dayton Area C. of C. (trustee 1987-90). Republican. United Ch. Of Christ. Home: 1872 Timarron Way Naples FL 34109 E-mail: ronmcswiney@comcast.net.

MC SWINEY, JAMES WILMER, retired pulp and paper manufacturing company executive; b. McEwen, Tenn., Nov. 13, 1915; s. James S. and Delia (Conroy) McS.; m. Jewel Bellar, 1940; children: Charles Ronald, Margaret Ann. Grad., Harvard Advanced Mgmt. Program, 1954. Lab. technician, shipping clk. Nashville div. The Mead Corp., 1934-39; asst. office mgr. Harriman div., 1939; plant mgr. Rockport, Ind., 1940; asst. office mgr. Kingsport (Tenn.) div.), 1941-44; exec. asst. to pres. Dayton, Ohio, 1954-57; v.p. devel., 1957-59; adminstrv v.p. Harriman div. (Kingsport (Tenn.) div.), 1959; group v.p., gen. mgr. Mead Bd. div., 1961-63, exec. v.p. corp., 1963-67, pres., chief exec. officer, 1968-71, chmn. bd., chief exec. officer, 1971-78, chmn. bd., 1978-82; ret., 1982. Acct., office mgr., asst. sec.-treas. Brunswick Pulp & Paper Co., Ga., 1944-45; bd. dirs. Ultra-Met, Gosiger, Inc., Sea Island Co. Trustee Com. for Econ. Devel. Aviation cadet USAAF, 1942-44. Home: PO Box 30604 401 Ocean Rd Sea Island GA 31561

MCTAGUE, JOHN PAUL, materials scientist, educator, chemist, researcher; b. Jersey City, Nov. 28, 1938; s. James Aloysius and Teresa Eugenia (Hanley) McT.; m. Carole Frances Reilly, Dec. 30, 1961 (dec. Jan. 1997); children: Kevin W., Catherine E., Margaret A., Maureen E. BS in Chemistry, Georgetown U., 1960; PhD, Brown U., 1965, DSc (hon.), 1997. Mem. tech. staff N.Am. Rockwell Sci. Ctr., Thousand Oaks, Calif., 1964—70; prof. chemistry, mem. Inst. Geophysics and Planetary Physics UCLA, 1970—82; dep. dir. Office Sci. and Tech. Policy, Exec. Office of Pres., Washington, 1983—86, acting sci. advisor to Pres. Reagan, 1986; v.p. rsch. Ford Motor Co., Dearborn, Mich., 1986—90, v.p. tech. affairs, 1990—99; v.p. lab. mgmt., Office of Pres. U. Calif., Oakland, 2001—, prof. materials Santa Barbara, 2001—. Adj. prof. chemistry Columbia, U., 1982-83. Mem. Pres.'s Coun. Advisors on Sci. and Tech., 1990-93; mem. adv. bd. Sec. Energy, 1990—; chmn. bd. overseers Fermilab, 1994-99. Alfred P. Sloan Research fellow, 1971-73; NATO sr. fellow, 1973; John Simon Guggenheim Meml. fellow, 1975-76. Fellow AAAS, Am. Phys. Soc. (George E. Pake prize 1998); mem. Am. Chem. Soc. (Calif. sect. award 1975), Nat. Acad. Engring., Sigma Xi. E-mail: jmctague1@aol.com.

MCTEE, CINDY, classical musician, educator; b. 1953; BM, Pacific Luth. U., 1976, studied with David Robbins; MM, Yale U., 1978, studied with Krzysztof Pendereckl, Jacob Druckman, and Bruce MacCombie; PhD, U. Iowa, 1981, studied with Richard Hervig; studied with Penderecki, Marek Stachowski, and Krystyna Moszumanska-Nazar, Higher Sch. Music, Cracow, Poland. Tchr. Pacific Luth. U., Tacoma, Wash., 1981-84; assoc. to full prof. music composition U. North Tex., Denton, 1985—. Fulbright-Hayes Sr. Lectr. fellow in computer music Acad. Music, Cracow, 1990. Recipient comms. from Nat. Symphony Orch., Big Eight Band Dirs. Assn., Voices of Change, Barlow Endowment for Music Composition, Am. Guild Organists, Coll. Band Dirs. Nat. Assn., Phi Kappa Lambda Bd. Regents; works performed by Am. Symphony Orch., Nat. Repertory Orch., St. Louis Symphony, Memphis Symphony, Honolulu Symphony, Pitts. New Music Ensemble, Nat. Symphony Orch., Nippon Housou Kyoukai (NHK) Symphony Orch., Philharm. Orch., London. Recipient BMI award, Guggenheim Fellowship, 2001; grantee Wash. State Arts Commn.; Composers fellow NEA, Goddard Lieberson fellow AAAL; Acad. award in Music, AAAL, 2002. Home: 1217 Piping Rock St Denton TX 76205-8126 Office: U of North Tex Coll of Music Denton TX 76203

MCTEER, ROBERT D., JR., banker; married; 2 children. Joined Fed. Reserve Bank Richmond, 1968; sr. v.p. Baltimore branch Fed. Reserve Bank of Richmond, 1980—91; pres., CEO, Fed. Res. Bank Dallas, Tex., 1991—. Office: Fed Res Bank Dallas 2200 N Pearl St Dallas TX 75201-2272 E-mail: Bob.McTeer@dal.frb.org.

MCTIER, CHARLES HARVEY, foundation administrator; b. Columbus, Ga., Jan. 28, 1939; s. Roy and Julia (Harvey) McT.; m. Margaret Lucy Ruyl, Aug. 23, 1962; children: Margaret Marie, Charles Harvey Jr. BBA, Emory U., 1961. Administrv. asst. hosp. Emory U., Atlanta, 1961-63, bus. mgr. dept. psychiat. Sch. Med., 1963-66, assoc. dir. personnel, 1966-69, asst. to pres., bd. trustees, 1969-71; sec. Robert W. Woodruff Found., Joseph B. Whitehead Found., Lettie Pate Evans Found., Inc., Lettie Pate Whitehead Found., Inc., Atlanta, 1971-77, sec., treas., 1977-87, v.p., sec., treas., 1987-88, pres., 1988—. Chmn. Atlanta Founds. Forum, 1985-86; trustee Southeastern Coun. Founds., Atlanta, 1985-92, chmn. membership com., 1986-89, chmn. program com., 1989, chmn. bd. trustees, 1989-90; vice chmn. Coun. on Founds., Washington, 1995-97, program com., 1985-87, nominating com., 1987-88, chmn. audit and fin. com., 1990-95, chmn. mgmt. com., 1996-97; chmn. bd. trustees Found. Ctr. N.Y.C., 1994-2000, fin. and audit com., 1991-2000, exec. com., 1992-93, chmn. nominating com.; former pub. mem. Joint Commn. on Accreditation of Health Care Orgns., 1994-2003; dir. SunTrust Bank of Ga., SunTrust Bank Atlanta, 1995—, Coca-Cola FEMSA. Trustee, North Ga. United Meth. Found., 1985—; trustee, treas. Meth. Found. Ret. Mins., 1980; chmn. new ch. devel. com. North Ga. United Meth. Conf., 1980-85; mem. bd. vis. Emory U., 1985-87. Mem. Assn. Emory Alumni (bd. govs. 1987-91), Pres.'s Cir. of NAS/Inst. of Medicine, Commerce Club (bd. dirs.), Peachtree Golf Club, Piedmont Driving Club. Avocations: golf, travel. Office: Robert W Woodruff Found Inc 50 Hurt Plz SE Ste 1200 Atlanta GA 30303-2951

MCTIERNAN, CHARLES E., JR., lawyer; b. 1944; BA, Coll. St. Thomas; JD, Bklyn. Law Sch. Bar: N.Y. 1972, (U.S. Dist. Ct.) 1972, N.Y. (Ea., So. Dist.) 1972, (U.S. Ct. Appeals, Sec. Cir.) 1972, (U.S. Ct. Appeals, Fourth Cir.) 1990. Mng. editor Bklyn. Law rev.; law clk. Hon. Charles D. Breital, NY, 1970—72; assoc. Wickes Riddell Blomer Jacobi & McGuire, 1972—76; assoc. gen. counsel Kelley Drye & Warren, 1976—82, Con Edison, NY, 1985—2002, gen. counsel, 2003—. Office: Con Edison Co N Y Law Dept 4 Irving Pl Rm 1810-S New York NY 10003

MC TIERNAN, JOHN, film director; b. Albany, N.Y., Jan. 8, 1951; Dir., screenwriter Nomads, 1985; dir. Predator, 1987, Die Hard, 1988, The Hunt For Red October, 1990, Medicine Man, 1992, The Last Action Hero, 1993, Die Hard with a Vengeance, 1995, The Thomas Crown Affair, 1999, The 13th Warrior, 1999.

MCTIQUE, MAURICE P. director; Cabinet min., mem. parliament, New Zealand, 1985—97; dir. govt. accountability project Mencatus Ctr., George Mason U., Arlington, Va. Spkr. in field. Recipient Queen's Svc. Order, Queen Elizabeth II, 1999; scholar disting. vis. scholar, George Mason U. Office: 3301 N Fairfax Dr Arlington VA 22201-4433

MCTURNAN, LEE BOWES, lawyer; b. N.Y.C., Sept. 13, 1937; s. Lee M. and Alice (Light) McT.; m. Susan Cassady, Aug. 2, 1969; children: John M., Sarah D. AB magna cum laude, Harvard U., 1959; diploma in law, Oxford (Eng.) U., 1961; JD, U. Chgo., 1963. Bar: Ill. 1965, U.S. Dist. Ct. (no. dist.) Ill. 1965, U.S. Ct. Appeals (7th cir.) 1966, U.S. Supreme Ct. 1969, Ind. 1978, U.S. Dist. Ct. (so. dist.) Ind. 1978, U.S. Dist. Ct. (no. dist.) Ind. 1987. Law clk. to hon. justice U.S. Supreme Ct., Washington, 1963-64; assoc. Sidley & Austin, Chgo., 1964-69, ptnr., 1970-78, Hackman, McClarnon & McTurnan, Indpls., 1978-88, McTurnan & Turner, Indpls., 1989—. Assoc. spl. counsel procs. on chief justice R.I. Commn. Jud. Tenure and Discipline, Providence, 1985; mem. Local Rules Adv. Com. for So. Dist. Ind., 1995-2000. Adminstrv. bd. Meridian St. United Meth. Ch., 1987-90. Mem. ABA, Ind. Bar Assn., Ill. Bar Assn., Indpls. Bar Assn., 7th Cir. Bar Assn., Law Club of Indpls. (pres. 1988-90), Indpls. Am. Inn of Ct. (Master 1997-), Legal Club of Chgo., Columbia Club, Woodstock Club, Lit. Club, Rotary. Republican. Avocations: running, reading, gardening. Home: 9907 Summerlakes Dr Carmel IN 46032 Office: McTurnan & Turner 2400 Market Tower 10 W Market St Indianapolis IN 46204-2954

MCTYEIRE, ROBERT ADAMS, sound company executive; b. Birmingham, Ala., July 21, 1949; s. William Walter Jr. and Katherine Elizabeth (Meadow) McT.; m. Pamela Ann Huffstutler, Apr. 18, 1978. BS in Commerce and Bus. Adminstrn., U. Ala., 1972. Ind. sound engr., Tuscaloosa, 1972-73; owner, chief engr. Ram Sound, Tuscaloosa, 1973-89, Mary Esther, Fla., 1989—. Charter mem. nominating com. Ala. Music Hall of Fame, Muscle Shoals; cons. Klipsch and Assocs., Inc., Hope, Ark., 1984—; bd. dirs. Navarre Beach Land Co., Iron Art, Inc., The Krewe Bowlegs, Navarre Land Enterprises. Sound engr. for numerous entertainers including Tony Bennett, Dave Brubeck, Ray Charles, Ry Cooder, Fats Domino, Roy Orbison, Bob Hope, Tom Jones, B.B. King, Wynton Marsalis, Dolly Parton, Bonnie Raitt, Ray Stevens, Ramsey Lewis, George Jones, B.J. Thomas. Mem. Tuscaloosa Arts Coun. With U.S. Air N.G., 1969-71. Mem. Muscle Shoals Music Assn. Republican. Avocations: boating, cruising, fishing, music. Home and Office: Ram Sound 369 W Miracle Strip Pky Mary Esther FL 32569-1833

MCVANEY, C. EDWARD, computer software executive; b. 1940; Ptnr. Alexander, Grant & Co.; co-founder, chmn. bd. dirs., CEO J.D. Edwards & Co., 1977—. Office: JD Edwards & Co One Technology Way Denver CO 80257

MCVAY, BARBARA CHAVES, mathematics educator; b. Dallas, July 6, 1950; d. Joe M. and Dorothy May (Nock) Chaves; m. David Clyde McVay, Dec. 23, 1968; 1 child, Kathryn McVay Hearn. BS in Math., U. Tex., Arlington, 1971, MS in Math., 1999. Cert. secondary tchr. math., English, Tex. Tchr. math. C.W. Nimitz H.S. Irving (Tex.) Ind. Sch. Dist., 1972—. Bldg. rep. Dallas Tchrs. Credit Union, 1982—; part time instr. North Lake/Dallas County C.C., Irving, 1988—. Tchr. Sunday sch. North Dallas Bapt. Ch., 1971-80; ch. tng. leader 1st Bapt. Ch., Irving, 1981-85. Mem. NEA, Tex. State Tchrs. Assn., Irving Edn. Assn. (rep. 1980—), Nat. Coun. Tchrs. Math., Tex. Coun. Tchrs. Math., Greater Dallas Coun. Tchrs. Math., Math. Assn. Am., Delta Kappa Gamma. Republican. Avocations: crafts, sewing, needlecrafts. Office: CW Nimitz High Sch 100 W Oakdale Rd Irving TX 75060-6833 Office Phone: 972-273-8600. Personal E-mail: bjcmcvay@yahoo.com. Business E-Mail: bmcvay@irvingisd.net.

MCVEIGH-PETTIGREW, SHARON CHRISTINE, communications consultant; b. San Francisco, Feb. 6, 1949; d. Martin Allen and Frances (Roddy) McVeigh; m. John Wallace Pettigrew, Mar. 27, 1971; children: Benjamin Thomas Pettigrew, Margaret Mary Pettigrew. BA with honors, U. Calif.-Berkeley, 1971; diploma of edn., Monash U., Australia, 1975; MBA, Golden Gate U., 1985. Tchr., adminstr. Victorian Edn. Dept., Victoria, Australia, 1972—79; supr. Network Control Ctr. GTE Sprint Comms., Burlingame, Calif., 1979—81, mgr. customer assistance, 1981—84, mgr. state legis. ops., 1984—85, dir. revenue programs, 1986—87; comm. cons. Flores, Pettigrew & Co., San Mateo, Calif., 1987—89; telemktg. Apple Computer Inc., Cupertino, Calif., 1989—94; prin. The Call Ctr. Group, San Mateo, Calif., 1995—. Telecomm. cons. PPG Svcs., 1994—; telecomm. spkr. Dept. Consumer Affairs, Sacramento, 1984. Panelist Wash. Gov.'s Citizens Coun., 1984; founding mem. Maroondah Women's Shelter, Victoria, 1978; organizer nat. conf. Bus. Women and the Polit. Process, New Orleans, 1986; mem. sch. bd. Boronia Tech. Sch., Victoria, 1979. Recipient Tchr. Spl. Responsibilities award, Victoria Edn. Dept., 1979. Mem.: Women's Econ. Action League, Am. Telemktg. Assn. (bd. dirs. 1992), Peninsula Profl. Women's Network, Am. Mgmt. Assn., Women in Telecom. (panel moderator San Francisco 1984). Democrat. Roman Catholic. Office Phone: 650-579-1298.

MCVEY, FRANCIS DANIEL, mechanical engineer, software developer, educator; b. St. Louis, Jan. 19, 1929; s. Martin Patrick and Marguy Josephine (Boeckler) McV.; m. Anna Elizabeth Moss, Nov. 26, 1958 (dec. Dec. 1990); children: Mark Andrew, Marguy Denise, Michael Sean. BS in Mech. Engring., Washington U., St. Louis, 1952, MS, 1954. Inst. mech. engring. Washington U., St. Louis, 1954-55; group project engr., missiles engring. divsn. McDonnell Aircraft Co., St. Louis, 1955-58, assoc. scientist rsch. divsn., 1961-64, br. mgr. engring. tech. divsn., 1964-74, prin. staff engr., 1974-83; chief aerodynamicist Cleve. Pneumatic Co., Washington, 1959-61; engring. fellow McDonnell Douglas, 1983-86, sr. fellow, 1986-97, dir. CAD/CAM, 1986-97; sr. tech. fellow Boeing Co., St. Louis, 1997—, staff engring. dir., 1997-99; retired, 1999. Lectr. St. Louis U., 1964—70, 2000—, U. Mo.-Rolla extension, 1971; adj. prof. aero. and mech. engring. dept. St. Louis U., 2000—; engring. and automotive cons. Mem. exec. adv. com. on engring. St. Louis U., 1998—2004. Served with AUS, 1946—48. Recipient Lloyd R. Koenig prize in engring. Washington U., 1952. Fellow: AIAA (assoc.; chmn. St. Louis sect. 1963—66, mem. mgmt. com. 1998—2002); mem.: Am. Rocket Soc. (chmn. St. Louis sect.), Sigma Xi. Roman Catholic. Avocation: reading. Home: 7030 Delmar Blvd University City MO 63130-4301 Personal E-mail: fmcveyd@aol.com.

MCVEY, HENRY HANNA, III, retired lawyer; b. Richmond, Va., Aug. 12, 1935; s. Henry Hanna Jr. and Eva Lawson (Jennings) McVey; m. Reba Jean Robinson, Dec. 12, 1964; children: Margaret Anne McVey Singleton, Lewis Lawson, Ian Douglas. BS, BA magna cum laude, Hampden-Sydney Coll., 1957; LLB, U. Va., 1960. Bar: Va. 1960, U.S. Dist. Ct. (ea. dist.) Va. 1960, U.S. Ct. Appeals (4th cir.) 1965, U.S. Supreme Ct. 1970. Assoc. Battle, Neal, Harris, Minor & Williams, Richmond, 1960-66; ptnr. McGuireWoods LLP and predecessor firms, Richmond, 1966-99; ret., 1999. Mem. adv. group under Civil Justice Reform Act of 1990 U.S. Dist. Ct. (ea. dist.) Va. Trustee Hampden-Sydney Coll., 1989—94, 1995—, vice chair, 2001—03, chair bd. trustees, 2003—; mem. Commn. on Archtl. Rev. City of Richmond, 1985—95; mem. Planning Commn. Gloucester County, 2001—; bd. dirs. Richmond Symphony, 1977—86, 1987—99, v.p., 1979—81, exec. v.p., 1981—83, pres., 1983—85, chmn. bd. dirs., 1985—87, pres. Symphony Coun., 1999—2001; bd. dirs. Carpenter Ctr. for Performing Arts, 1982—89, Rosewell Found., 1999—2004, pres., 2001—02, v.p., 2002—03. Recipient Algernon Sydney Sullivan medallion for svc. to coll., Hampden Sydney Coll., 2001, Alumni Citation for loyal svc. to the coll., Hampden-Sydney Coll., 2002. Fellow: Am. Bar Found., Am. Coll. Trial Lawyers; mem.: Va. Bar Assn., Bar Assn. City of Richmond, Fedn. Defense and Corp. Counsel, Def. Rsch. and Trial Lawyers Assn. (past state chmn., regional v.p. 1985—87, bd. dirs. 1987—90), Va. Assn. Def. Attys. (v.p. 1981—83, treas. 1983—84, pres.-elect 1984—85, pres. 1985—86), Ware River Yacht Club (bd. dirs. 2000—). Presbyterian. Home: PO Box 43 Schley VA 23154-0043 Personal E-mail: mcvey@rivnet.net.

MCVEY, LARRY, household cleaner manufacturing executive; V.p. fin. Orange Glo Internat., Englewood, Calif. Office: Orange Glo Internatl 8200 E Maplewood Ave Greenwood Village CO 80111-4822

MCVICKER, JESSE JAY, artist, educator; b. Vici, Okla., Oct. 18, 1911; s. Jesse Allen and Clara Mae (Hendrick) McV.; m. Laura Beth Paul, Aug. 20, 1938. BA, Okla. State U., 1940, MA, 1941. Faculty Okla. State U., Stillwater, 1941—, prof. art, 1959-77, prof. emeritus, 1977—, head dept., 1959-77. Exhbns. include Med. Mus. Art, Mus. Non-Objective Painting, Chgo, Art Inst., N.A.D., Library of Congress, San Francisco Mus. Art, Denver Art Mus., Pa. Acad. Fine Arts, Carnegie Inst., Print Club Phila., Salon Des Realities Nouvelles, Paris, France, Dallas, Mus. Fine Arts, Galleria Origine, Rome, Italy, Whitney Mus. Am. Art; represented in permanent collections Library of Congress, Seattle Art Mus., Dallas Mus. Fine Arts, Met. Mus. Art, Joslyn Meml. Art Mus.; bibliography Graphic Works by J. Jay McVicker, 1986. Served with USNR, 1943-46. Mem. Soc. Am. Graphic Artists, Audubon Artists (John Taylor Arms award 1990), Print Club Phila., Pi Kappa Alpha.

MC VIE, CHRISTINE PERFECT, musician; b. Eng., July 12, 1943; m. John McVie (div.); m. Eddy Quintela. Student art sch., pvt. student sculpture. Singer, keyboardist, Fleetwood Mac, from 1970; albums with Fleetwood Mac include: Fleetwood Mac, 1968, Fleetwood Mac in Chicago, 1969, Then Play On, 1969, English Rose, 1969, Kiln House, 1970, Future Games, 1971, Bare Trees, 1972, Penguin, Mystery To Me, 1973, Heroes Are Hard to Find, 1974, Fleetwood Mac, 1975, Rumours, 1977, Tusk, 1979, Fleetwood Mac Live, 1980, Mirage, 1982, Jumping at Shadows, 1985, Tango in the Night, 1987, Greatest Hits, 1988, Behind the Mask, 1990, The Dance, 1997; solo albums include Christine Perfect, 1969, Christine McVie, 1984; composer: songs including Spare Me a Little of Your Love, Don't Stop, You Make Loving Fun, Over and Over, Hold Me, Songbird, Got a Hold on Me, Heroes Are Hard to Find, Little Lies, As Long as You Follow, Save Me, Skies the Limit. Office: care Warner Bros Records 3300 Warner Blvd Burbank CA 91505-4632

MCVIE, JOHN, musician; b. London, Eng., Nov. 26, 1945;, naturalized, U.S., 1986; s. Reg and Dorothy McVie; m. Christine Anne Perfect, Aug. 1968 (div.); m. Julie Anne Rubens, 1978; 1 child, Molly Elizabeth. Band mem. John Mayall & the Bluesbreakers, Fleetwood Mac, 1967—. Musician (bassist): (albums) (solo) John McVie's Gotta Band with Lola Thomas, 1991, (with John Mayall & the Bluesbreakers) John Mayall Plays John Mayall, 1965, Bluesbreakers with Eric Clapton, 1966, Crusade, 1967, Hard Road, 1967, So Many Roads, 1969, As It All Began: The Best of John Mayall & the Bluesbreakers, 1998, Bluesbreakers with Eric Clapton, 2002, (with John Mayall) Looking Back, 1969, Thru the Years, 1971, Banquet in Blues, 1976, John Mayall and the Bluesbreakers (London), 1988, London Blues (1964-1969), 1992, John Mayall and the Bluesbreakers (One Way), 1994, Drivin' On: The ABC Years (1975-1982), 1998, Notice to Appear/A Banquet in Blues, 2000, (with John Mayall & Friends) Along for the Ride, 2001, (with Eric Clapton) History of Eric Clapton, 1972, Crossroads, 1988, Martin Scorcese Presents the Blues: Eric Clapton, 2003, (with Fleetwood Mac) Mr. Wonderful, 1968, Blues Jam in Chicago, Vol. 1 (with Otis Spann), English Rose, 1969, Pious Bird of Good Omen, 1969, Then Play On, 1969, Blues Jam in Chicago (with Otis Span), 1970, Kiln House, 1970, Black Magic Woman, 1971, bassist: (albums) Future

Games, 1971, Bare Trees, 1972, Myster to Me, 1973, Penguin, 1973, Heroes Are Hard to Find, 1974, Fleetwood Mac in Chicago, 1975, Fleetwood Mac, 1975, Vintage Years, 1975, Alabatross (Half Christine Perfect), 1977, Original Fleetwood Mac, 1977, Rumours, 1977 (Grammy award for Album of the Yr., 1977), Best of Fleetwood Mac, 1978, Man of the World, 1978, Tusk, 1979, Fleetwood Mac Live, 1980, Mirage, 1982, Rumours/Fleetwood Mac, 1984, Cerulean, 1985, Live in Boston, 1985, London Live '68, 1986, Rattlesnake Shake, 1986, Collection, 1987, Tango in the Night, 1987, Greatest Hits Live, 1988, Live Fleetwood Mac, 1988, Blues Collection, 1989, Interview Disc, 1989, Behind the Mask, 1990, Live at the BBC, 1995, Flletwood Mac/Mr. Wonderful/Pious Bird of Good Omen, 1998, Live at the Boston Tea Party, Pt. 1: 1968 to 1970, 1998; musician: (bassist also vocals) Complete Blue Horizon Sessions: 1967-1969, 1999; musician: (bassist) Shrine '69, 1999, Show-Biz Blues: 1968 to 1970, Vol. 2, 2001, Jumping at Shadows: The Blues Years, 2002, Very Best of Fleetwood Mac, 2002, Say You Will, 2003, (others) Eddie Boyd & His Blues Band, Eddie Boyd, 1967, 7936 South Rhodes, Eddie Boyd, 1968, Long Overdue, Gordon Smith, 1968, Biggest Thing Since Colossus, Otis Spann, Christine Perfect, Christine McVie, 1970, Jeremy Spencer, Jeremy Spencer, 1970, Legendary Christine Perfect, Christine McVie, 1976, Excitable Boy, Warren Zevon, 1978, Night Eyes, Danny Douma, 1979, Perfect Stranger, Robert Fleischman, 1979, Uprooted, Rob Grill, 1979, Quiet Normal Life: The Best of Warren Zevon, 1986, Rock, Rhythm & Blues, Various Artists, 1989, Over, Under, Sideways, Down, The Yardbirds, 1990, Rock of the 70's, Vol. 2, Various Artists, 1992, I'll Sleep When I'm Dead, Warren Zevon, 1996, Under Wheels of Confusion: 1970-1987, Black Sabbath, 1996, Home of the Blues, Various Artists, 1999, Rock: Train Kept a Rollin', 1999, Genius: The Best of Warren Zevon, Warren Zevon, 2002, 20th Century Masters-The Millenium Collection: The Best of Blues Guitar, 2003, Best of British Blues, Vol. 1, 2003, Best of British Blues, Vol. 2, 2003. Named to Rock and Roll Hall of Fame, 1998. Office: Warner Bros Records Inc 3300 Warner Blvd Burbank CA 91505*

MCVISK, WILLIAM KILBURN, lawyer; b. Chgo., Oct. 8, 1953; s. Felix Kilburn and June (DePear) Visk; m. Marlaine Joyce McDonough, June 20, 1975. BA, U. Ill, 1974; JD, Northwestern U., 1977. Bar: Ill. 1977, Ind. 1999, U.S. Dist. Ct. (no. dist.) Ill. 1977, U.S. Ct. Appeals (7th cir.) 1978, U.S. Dist. Ct. (no. and so. dists.) Ind. 1999, U.S. Ct. Appeals (10th cir.) 2001. Assoc. Jerome H. Torshen, Ltd., Chgo., 1977-80, Silets & Martin, Chgo., 1980-81, Peterson & Ross, Chgo., 1981-85, ptnr., 1985-95, Johnson & Bell Ltd., Chgo., 1995—. Contbr. articles to profl. jours. Mem.: Ill. Assn. Def. Trial Lawyers (chmn. ins. coverage com. 1999—2003), Ill. Assn. Hosp. Attys. (bd. dirs. 1997—2003, pres. 2002), Am. Health Lawyers Assn., Def. Rsch. Inst. Office: Johnson & Bell 55 E Monroe St Fl 41 Chicago IL 60603-5713 Office Phone: 312-984-0229. Business E-Mail: mcviskw@jbltd.com.

MCWANE, JOYCE HOBBS, title company executive; b. Lynchburg, Va., May 4, 1947; d. Earle Benjamin Sr. and Marie (Goode) Hobbs; m. Hudson, Nov. 26, 1966 (div. 1978); m. Lawrence Henry McWane, Jr., April 5, 1986; children: Kevin, Rodney, Meghan. Student, Radford U., 1965-66; grad. in mortgage banking, Northwestern U., 1986; mgmt. cert., U. Va., 1990. V.p. Ctrl. Fidelity Bank/Wachovia Bank, Lynchburg, 1973-98; pres. Home Buyer Solutions, Inc., Nellysford, Va., 1998—. Adv. bd. GreenPoint Credit, LLC, Roanoke, Va., 1999; cons. Yates Home Sales, Blairs, Va., 1998-99. Frequent contbr. Manufactured Housing Mag. Treas. Area 8 Spl. Olympics, Roanoke, 1988-90; chair, coord. Ptnrship. Habitat for Humanity and Va. Manufactured Housing, Lynchburg, 1997. Paul Harris fellow Rotary Internat., Hardy, 1991. Mem. Fin. Women Internat. (sec. 1997-98, membership chair 1998-99), Va. Manufactured Housing Assn. (treas. 1996-98, sec. 1998-2000, bd. mem. of yr. 1998, chmn. 2000-02), Rotary (charter pres. Hardy, Va. 1990-92, Paul Harris fellow 1991), Manufactured Housing Inst. (mem. fin. com. 2001-). Avocations: golf, reading. Home: RR 1 Box 814 Roseland VA 22967-9215 Office: Home Buyer Solutions Inc PO Box 586 12 Rockfish Valley Hwy Nellysford VA 22958-3001 Fax: 434-361-2227. E-mail: jmcwane@hbsus.com.

MCWATERS, JEFFREY L. healthcare executive; b. Paducah, Ky. m. Cynthia Lamb McWaters; 2 children. B in Acctg., U. Ky., 1978. With Ernst and Young, Nashville, 1978—79, Hosp. Affiliates, 1979—93; founder, pres., CEO Options Mental Health (now Value Options), 1990—94; founder Amerigroup Corp., 1994—. Bd. dirs. Am. Assn. Health Plans, Man in the Mirror; mem. adv. bd. Monarch Bank, Envest Entrepreneurial Investments. Chmn. Amerigroup Found., 2000—. Named Entrepreneur of Yr., Ernst and Young, 1999; named to Hall of Fame, Gatton Coll. Bus. and Econs., U. Ky., 2003. Office: AMERIGROUP Corp 4425 Corporation Ln Virginia Beach VA 23462

MCWETHY, JOHN FLEETWOOD, journalist; b. Aurora, Ill., Feb. 28, 1947; s. John Adams and Mary Helen (Bell) McW.; m. Laurie Duncan, June 25, 1971; children: Adam Duncan, James Ian. BA, DePauw U., 1969; MS, Columbia U., 1970; Doctorate in Journalism (hon.), DePauw U., 2002. Def. writer Congl. Quar., Washington, 1970-72; sci. editor U.S. News & World Report, Washington, 1972-77, chief White House corr., 1977-79; chief Pentagon corr. ABC News, Washington, 1979-84; chief corr. ABC News Nat. Security and Sr. State Dept., Washington, 1984—2003; spl. corr. ABC News, 2003—. Contbg. author: Power of the Pentagon, 1972. Recipient DuPont award Columbia U. Sch. Journalism, 1984, 2002; 5 Emmy awards, 1984, 91, 92, 99, 2002, Overseas Press Club award for Inside the Other Side, 1987, Peabody award for coverage of Sept. 11, 2001. Home: 5028 30th St N Arlington VA 22207-2717

MCWETHY, PATRICIA JOAN, educational association administrator; b. Chgo., Feb. 27, 1946; d. Frank E. and Emma (Kuehne) McW.; m. H. Frank Eden; children: Kristin Beth, Justin Nicholas. BA, Northwestern U., 1968; MA, U. Minn., 1970; MBA, George Washington U., 1981. Geog. analyst CIA, McLean, Va., 1970-71; rsch. asst. NSF, Washington, 1972-74, spl. asst. to dir., 1975, assoc. program dir. human geography and regional sci. program, 1976-79; exec. dir. Assn. Am. Geographers, Washington., 1979-84, Nat. Assn. Biology Tchrs., Reston, Va., 1984-95, Nat. Sci. Edn. Leadership Assn., Arlington, Va., 1995-97; edn. dir. Nat. Alliance for Mentally Ill, Arlington, 1998-99. Prin. investigator grant on biotech. equipment ednl. resource partnership NSF, 1989-93, NSF funded internat. symposium on Basic Biol. Concepts: What Should the World's Children Know?, 1992-94; co-prin. investigator NSF grant, 1995-97; mem. chmn.'s adv. com. Nat. Com. Sci. Stds. and Assessment, 1992-95; mem. Commn. for Biology Edn., Internat. Union Biol. Sci., 1988-97; mem. exec. com. Alliance for Environ. Edn., 1987-90, chmn. program com., 1990; condr. seminars in field; lectr. in field. Author monograph and papers in field; editor handbook. NSF grantee, 1989-93, 95-97; NSF fellow, 1968-69; recipient Outstanding Performance award, NSF, 1973. Mem. Phi Beta Kappa.

MCWHINEY, GRADY, history educator; b. Sherveport, La., July 15, 1928; s. Henry Grady and Mayme (Holland) McW.; m. Sue B. Baca, Nov. 20, 1947. BS, Centenary Coll. of La., 1950; MA, La. State U., 1951; PhD, Columbia U., 1960. Asst. prof. Troy State U., Ala., 1952-54, Millsaps Coll., Jackson, Miss., 1956-59, Northwestern U., Evanston, Ill., 1960-65; assoc. prof. to prof. U.B. C., Vancouver, Can., 1965-70; vis. prof. U. Calif. - Berkeley, 1959-60, 67-68; prof. Wayne State U., Detroit, 1970-75; vis. prof. Tulane U., New Orleans, summer 1970, U. Mich., Ann Arbor, 1972-73; prof. history, dir. and disting. sr. fellow ctr. for study of so. history and culture U. Ala. University, 1975-83; Lyndon Baines Johnson prof. Am. history Tex. Christian U., Ft. Worth, 1983-96, emeritus, 1996—; disting. historian in residence U. So. Miss., Hattiesburg, 1996-97. Mem. NEH Selection Com., 1973, Jefferson Davis Award Com., 1970-72, 75-77; James Murfin Meml. lectr., 1990, Marian Alexander Blake lectr., 1991; Conf. Meml. speaker, 1991; vis. disting. prof. McMurry U., Abilene, Tex., 1997-98; pres. McWhiney Rsch. Found., 1997—. Author: Braxton Bragg and Confederate Defeat, Vol. 1, 1969, Southerners and Other Americans, 1973; (with Perry D. Jamieson) Attack and Die: Civil War Military Tactics and the Southern Heritage, 1982, Cracker Culture: Celtic Ways in the Old South, 1988, An American Civil War Primer, 1992, Battle in the Wilderness: Grant Meets Lee, 1994, 2d edit., 1998; editor: (with Sue McWhiney) To Mexico with Taylor and Scott, 1845-1847, 1969, Grant, Lee, Lincoln and the Radicals, 1964; (with Robert Weibe) Historical Vistas, 2 vols., 1963-64, Reconstruction and the Freedmen, 1963, (with Douglas Southall Freeman) Robert E. Lee's Dispatches to Jefferson Davis, 1957, 2d edit., 1994, Confederate Crackers and Cavaliers, 2001 (Fletcher Pratt prize for best Civil War book 2002). With USMC, 1945—47. Recipient Earl A. Davis award, 1974, Frank E. Vandiver award Houston Civil War Round Table, 1993, Charles L. "Pie" Dufour award New Orleans Civil War Round Table, 1994, Outstanding Scholar award U. Ala., 1980, Gallant Svc. award Chgo. Civil War Round Table, 1979, Harry S. Truman award, 1970, Pacific Br. award Am. Hist. Assn., 1969; Huntington Libr. fellow, 1984; recipient Jefferson Davis medal United Daus. of the Confederacy, 1992, Honor award Sons Confederate Vets Tex. Divsn., 1993; rsch. fellow Mosher Inst. Def. Studies, 1988—, 1st recipient Grady McWhiney award, 1998. Fellow St. George Tucker Soc.; mem. Ala. Hist. Assn. (pres. 1978-79), So. Hist. Assn. (exec. council 1976-79), Civil War Round Table U.K. (hon.), Phi Beta Kappa (Disting. Scholar). Home: PO Box 637 Abilene TX 79697-0001

MCWHINNEY, DEBORAH, finance company executive; BA, U. Mont.; grad., Pacific Coast Banking Sch. With consumer electronic banking divsn. Bank Am. Corp. 17 yrs.; exec. v.p. bus. planning and strategy Visa Internat., 1995—99; group pres. Engage Media Svc., 1999—2001; pres., exec. com. mem. Schwab Instl., Schwab & Co., Inc., 2001—. Exec. advisor to bd. and exec. team Hitachi Data Sys. and Hitachi Ltd., 2003; chair bd. trustees U. Mont. Found.; former bd. chair Electronic Funds Tranfer Assn.; bd. dirs. Novadigm, Inc., PLUS Sys., Touch Am. Holdings, Inc.; past fin. chair Women's Mus.; founding investor, former dir. First Bank Idaho. Named one of 100 Most Influential Women in Bay Area Bus., San Francisco Bus. Times, 2002, 2003, 2004, 25 Most Influential People in Planning Profession, Investment Advisor List, 2004; recipient Movers & Shakers award Fin. Planning, 2004. Achievements include apptd. by Pres. Bush to Securities Investor Protection Corp. (SIPC), 2002. Office: 101 Montgomery St San Francisco CA 94104 Office Phone: 800-854-3322.

MCWHINNEY, EDWARD WATSON, Canadian government legislator; b. Sydney, Australia, May 19, 1924; s. Matthew and Evelyn Annie (Watson) McW.; m. Emily Ingalore Sabatzky, June 27, 1951. LLB, U. Sydney, 1949; LLM, Yale U., 1951, D Juridical Sci., 1953; diploma, Acad. de Droit Internat., The Hague, 1950; LLD, U. Thessaloniki, Greece, 1998. Bar: called to Australian bar 1949, apptd. Queen's counsel, Can 1967. Crown prosecutor, Sydney, 1949-50; lectr., then asst. prof. Law Sch. and Grad. Sch., Yale U., 1951-55; prof. law, mem. Centre Russian Studies, U. Toronto, Ont., Can., 1955-66; prof. law, dir. Inst. Air and Space Law, McGill U., Montreal, Que., Can., 1966-71; prof. law, dir. internat. and comparative legal studies U. Ind., Indpls., 1971-74; disting. prof. Simon Fraser U., Burnaby, B.C., 1974-93; mem. Permanent Ct. Arbitration, The Hague, 1985-91; Paul Martin prof. U. Windsor, Can., 1986; prof. emeritus, 1992; M.P. Ho. of Commons, Ottawa, Ont., Can., 1993-2000; co-chmn. joint standing com. Senate and Ho. of Commons, Ottawa, Ont., Can., 1993-95, parliamentary sec. (fisheries and oceans), 1996-97, parliamentary sec. (fgn. affairs), 1997-2000; fed. govt. rep. nat. unity commn. Govt. of B.C., 1997-98. Vis. prof. Ecole Libre des Hautes Etudes, 1952, Heidelberg and Max-Planck-Inst., 1960-61, 90, NYU, 1954, Faculté Internat. de Droit Comparé, Luxembourg, 1959-60, U. San Antonio, 1963, U. Laval, Que., 1967, U. Paris, 1968, U. Madrid, 1968, U. Aix-Marseille, 1969, U. Nacional Autónoma de México, 1965, Inst. Univ. Luxembourg, 1972, 74, 76, Acad. Internat. Law, The Hague, 1973, 90, 2002, Aristotelian U., Thessaloniki, Greece, 1974, 78, 85, 96, 2003, U. Nice, 1976-77, Jagellonian U., Cracow, Poland, 1976, U. Paris I (Sorbonne), 1982, 85, Coll. de France, Paris, 1983, Meiji U., Tokyo, 1987, Inst. Internat. Relations, Bejing, 1987, 92, Sch. Internat. Rels., Tehran, 2003; legal cons. UN, 1953-54; cons. Japanese Commn. Constn., mem. prime minister Ont. Adv. Com. Confedn., 1964-71; cons. U.S. Naval War Coll., 1961-68; legal cons. Ministère de la Justice, Que., 1969-70; 74-75; constl. adviser to prime minister of Que., 1974-75; royal commr. Commn. Lang. Rights. Que., 1968-72; cons. U.S. Senate select com. presdl. campaign activities, 1973; spl. commr. inquiry Legislature B.C., 1974-75; chief adv. Fed. Govt.'s Task Force on Nat. Unity, 1978; commr. of enquiry, City of Vancouver, 1979; constl. adv. Fedn. Can. Municipalities, 1978-82; spl. advisor Can. del. UN Gen. Assembly, ann. sessions, 1981, 82, 83, 96; constl. adviser Indian Nations (Treaties 6-9), Can., 1980-82; mem. Assoc. de l'Inst. de Droit Internat., 1967, membre titulaire, 1975, pres. 1999-2001; mem. Assoc. de l'Acad. Internat. de Droit Comparé, Paris, 1986, mem. titulaire, 2002--; mem. Deutsche Gesellschaft für Völkerrecht, 1992. Author: Judicial Review, 4th edit, 1969, Canadian Jurisprudence, 1958, Föderalismus und Bundesverfassungsrecht, 1961, Constitutionalism in Germany, 1962, Comparative Federalism, 2d edit, 1965, Peaceful Coexistence and Soviet-Western International Law, 1964, Law Foreign Policy and the East-West Détente, 1964, Federal Constitution- Making for a Multi-National World, 1966, International Law and World Revolution, 1967, Conflit idéologique et ordre public mondial, 1970, (with M.A. Bradley) The Freedom of the Air, 1968, New Frontiers in Space Law, 1969, The International Law of Communications, 1970, Aerial Piracy and International Law, 1971, (with Pierre Pescatore) Federalism and Supreme Courts and the Integration of Legal Systems, 1973, Parliament and Parliamentary Power Today, 1976, The Executive and Executive Power Today, 1977, (with J-D Gendron and others) La situation de la lanque français au Québec (3 vols.), 1973, The Illegal Diversion of Aircraft and International Law, 1974, Parliamentary Privilege and the Broadcasting of Parliamentary Debates, 1975, The International Law of Detente, 1978, The World Court and the Contemporary International Law-making Process, 1979, Quebec and the Constitution, 1979, Municipal Government in a New Canadian Federal System, 1980, Conflict and Compromise: International Law and World Order in a Revolutionary Age, 1981, Constitution-Making: Principles, Process, Practice, 1981, Canada and the Constitution, 1982, United Nations Law Making, 1984, Supreme Courts and Judicial Law-Making, 1986, Les Nations-Unies et la Formation du Droit, 1986, Aerial Piracy and International Terrorism, 1987, The International Court of Justice and the Western Tradition of International Law, 1987, (with Nagendra Singh) Nuclear Weapons and Contemporary International Law, 1988, Judicial Settlement of International Disputes, 1990, (with G.I. Tunkin and V.S. Vereshchetin) From Coexistence to Cooperation: International Law and Organisation in the Post-Cold War Era, 1991, (with J. Zaslove and W. Wolf) Federalism-in-the-Making, Contemporary Canadian and German Constitutionalism, National and Trans-national, 1992, Judge Shigeru Oda and the Progressive Development of International Law, 1992, Judge Manfred Lachs and Judicial Law-Making, 1994, The United Nations and a New World Order for a New Millennium, 2000, (with N. Ando and R. Wolfrum) Liber Amicorum Judge Shigeru Oda, 2002, Self-Determination of Peoples and Plural-Ethinic States. Secession and State Succession and the Alternative, Federal Option, 2003, Chretien and Canadian Federalism, Politics and the Constitution, 1993-2003, 2003, The September 11 Terrorist Attacks and Invasion of Iraq in Contemporary International Law, 2004; bd. editors Australian Quar., 1949-50, Can. Yearbook of Internat. Law, 1963—, Jour. Media Law and Practice, 1980-85, Annuaire International de Justice Constitutionnelle, 1987—; editl. adv. com. Ency. Brit., 1985—; mem. bd. advisors Chinese Jour. Internat. Law, 2002—; contbr. to Ency. Brit. Served as officer Australian Air Force, 1943-45. Fellow Carnegie Endowment, 1951; Fulbright fellow, 1950-51; Sterling fellow Yale, 1950-51; Rockefeller fellow, 1960-61, 66-68; Can. Council fellow, 1960-61; fellow Am. Soc. Internat. Law, 1962-63. Mem. Australian Inst. Polit. Sci. (dir.), Internat. Law Assn. (pres. Toronto br. 1964-66, pres. Montreal br. 1970-71, chmn. exec. com. Canadian br. 1972-75), Canadian Bar Assn. (council Ont. 1956-58), Yale Law Sch. Assn. (pres. Can. 1964-69), Canadian Civil Liberties Assn. (v.p. 1965-67), Am. Soc. Internat. Law (coun. 1965-68, patron 2002—), Am. Fgn. Law Assn., Inst. interamericano de Estudios Juridicos Internacionales (dir. 1965—), Inst. Grand-Ducal de Luxembourg, Internat. Commn. Jurists (mem. coun. Can. br. 1988—), Deutsche Gesellschaft für Völkerrecht (hon. mem.), Knights of Mark Twain (U.S.) (hon., Aristotle Medal 1997). Home: 1949 Beach Ave Ste 402 Vancouver BC Canada V6G 1Z2

MCWHINNEY, IAN RENWICK, physician, educator; b. Burnley, Eng., Oct. 11, 1926; arrived in Can., 1968, naturalized, 1981; s. Archibald Renwick and Mary (Freeland) McWhinney; m. Betty Heap, Aug. 30; children: Heather, Julie. MB, BChir, Cambridge (Eng.) U., 1949, MD; MD (hon.), U. Oslo, 1991; DSc (hon.), U. Western Ont., 2000. Intern St. Bartholomews Hosp., London, 1949—50; resident Warwick (Eng.) Hosp., 1953—54; pvt. practice medicine Stratford-on-Avon, England, 1954—68; prof. family medicine U. Western Ont., London, Canada, 1968—92, prof. emeritus, 1992—; med. dir. palliative care unit Parkwood Hosp., London, Canada, 1986—91. Author: The Early Signs of Illness, 1964, Introduction to Family Medicine, 1981, A Textbook of Family Medicine, 1989, 1997. Capt. M.C. Royal Army, 1951—53. Recipient Excellence cert., Soc. Tchrs. Family Medicine, 1979, Curtis G. Hames Rsch. award, 1989, Hippocrates medal, Euro World Orgn. Nat. Colls. and Acads. of Gen. Practice, 2000. Fellow: Royal Coll. Physicians, Royal Coll. Gen. Practitioners, Coll. Family Physicians (Victor Johnston orator 1980); mem.: Inst. Medicine-NAS (fgn. assoc.), Order of Can. (officer 1998—). Office: U Western Ont Dept Family Medicine London ON Canada N6A 5C1 E-mail: irmcwhin@uwo.ca.

MCWHINNEY, MADELINE H. (MRS. JOHN DENNY DALE), economist, director; b. Denver, Mar. 11, 1922; d. Leroy and Alice (Houston) McW.; m. John D. Dale, June 23, 1961; 1 child, Thomas Denny. BA, Smith Coll., 1943; MBA, NYU, 1947. Economist Fed. Res. Bank, NYC, 1943-73, chief fin. trade statis. divsn., 1955-59, mgr. market stats. dept., 1960-65, asst. v.p., 1965-73; pres. First Women's Bank, NYC, 1974-76, Dale, Elliott & Co., Inc., Red Bank, NJ, 1977-97. Trustee Retirement System Fed. Res. Bank, 1955-58; vis. lectr. NYU Grad. Sch. Bus., 1976-77; mem. NJ Casino Control Commn., 1980-82, Women's Econ. Round Table, 1978-89, chmn. 1987-88; bd. govs. Am. Stock Exch., 1977-81; trustee Monmouth Mus., 1995—, Vis. Nurse Assn. Ctrl. Jersey, 1995-2004, Planned Parenthood Ctrl. Jersey, 1995-2003, Carnegie Corp. NY, 1974-82, Central Savs. Bank NY, 1980-82, Monmouth Conservatory Music, 2002-; trustee Charles F. Kettering Found., 1975-93, chmn. 1987-91; trustee Inst. Internat. Edn., 1975-, Investor Responsibility Rsch. Ctr., Inc., 1974-81; asst. dir. Whitney Mus. Am. Art, 1983-86; dir. Atlantic Energy Co., 1983-93; trustee Mgrs. Funds, 1983-2004; mem. adv. com. profl. ethics NJ Supreme Ct., 1983-98. Recipient Smith Coll. medal, 1971, Alumni Achievement award NYU Grad. Sch. Bus. Adminstrn. Alumni Assn., 1971, NYU Crystal award, 1982. Mem. Am. Fin. Assn. (past dir.), Money Marketeers (v.p. 1960, pres. 1961-62), Alumni Assn. Grad. Sch. Bus. Adminstrn. NYU (dir. 1951-63, pres. 1957-59), Soc. Meml. Ctr., NJ Com. Humanities, Phi Beta Kappa Fellows (v.p. 1979-87). Office: PO Box 458 Red Bank NJ 07701-0458 Home: 192 Heritage Court Little Silver NJ 07739

MCWHIRTER, BRUCE J. retired lawyer; b. Chgo., Sept. 11, 1931; s. Sydney and Martha McWhirter; m. Judith Hallett, Apr. 14, 1960; children: Cameron, Andrew. BS, Northwestern U., 1952; LLB, Harvard U., 1955. Bar: DC 1955, Ill 1955, US Ct Appeals (7th cir) 1963, US Supreme Ct. Assoc. Lord, Bissell & Brook, Chgo., 1958-62; from assoc. to sr. ptnr. Ross & Hardies, Chgo., 1962-95, of counsel, 1996—2003. Editor: Donnelley SEC Handbook, 1972—87; contbr. articles to profl jours. With U.S. Army, 1955—57. Mem.: ABA, Harvard Law Soc Ill., Chgo. Bar Assn., Harvard Club (N.Y.C.), Lawyers Club Chgo., Phi Beta Kappa. Democrat. Home: 111 Sheridan Rd Winnetka IL 60093-4223 Personal E-mail: jbmcw@aol.com.

MCWHIRTER, GLENNA SUZANNE (NICKIE MCWHIRTER), retired newspaper columnist; b. Peoria, Ill., June 28, 1929; d. Alfred Leon and Garnet Lorene (Short) Sotier; m. Edward Ford McWhirter (div.); children: Suzanne McWhirter Orlicki, Charles Edward, James Richard. BS in English Lang. and Lit., U. Mich., postgrad., 1960-63. Editl. asst. McGraw-Hill Pub. Co., Detroit, 1951-54; staff writer Detroit Free Press, Inc., Detroit, 1963-70, asst. city editor, 1971-77, columnist, 1977-88, Detroit News Inc., Detroit, 1988-97; advt. copy writer Campbell-Ewald Co., Detroit, 1967-68; ret., 1997. Author: Pea Soup, 1984 Winner 1st Place Commentary award UPI, Mich., 1979; 1st Place Columns AP, Mich., 1978, 81; 1st Place Columns Detroit Press Club Found., Mich., 1978; Disting. Service award State of Mich., 1985 Mem. Women in Comm. (Headliner award 1978), Alpha Gamma Delta. Avocations: flower gardening, interior design. Home: 495 Lake Shore Ln Grosse Pointe Woods MI 48236

MCWHORTER, DIANE, writer; b. Birmingham, Ala. Postgrad., Wellesley Coll. Writer, N.Y.C. Contbr. The N.Y. Times, USA Today, Harpers, The Nation, The New Republic, Newsday, People, Talk, The Wall Street Journal, The Washington Post, others (Pulitzer prize for gen. nonfiction, 2002); author: Carry Me Home. Recipient Pulitzer prize for Gen. Non-Fiction, 2002. Office: Simon and Schuster 1230 Ave of the Americas New York NY 10020

MCWHORTER, HOBART AMORY, JR., lawyer; b. Birmingham, Ala., Dec. 24, 1931; s. Hobart Amory and Marjorie (Westgate) McW.; remarried Feb. 1, 1997; children: Margaret G., Marjorie W. BA, Yale U., 1953; LLB, U. Va., 1958. Bar: Ala. 1958. Ptnr. Bradley Arant Rose & White, Birmingham, 1958—. 1st lt. U.S. Army, 1953-55. Fellow Am. Coll. Trial Lawyers; mem. Internat. Assn. Ins. Counsel, Nat. Assn. r.R. Counsel. Republican. Presbyterian. Office: Bradley Arant Rose & White One Federal Pl 1819 Fifth Ave N Birmingham AL 35203-2104 Office Phone: 205-521-8241.

MCWHORTER, KATHLEEN, orthodontist; b. Houston, May 29, 1953; d. Archer and Lucile (Taft) McW. BA summa cum laude, U. Houston, 1986; DDS with honors, Baylor Coll., 1990. Mgr. Am. Internat. Rent-A-Car, Houston, 1974-79; mktg. researcher Concoco Oil Co., Houston, 1979-83; orthodontist Baylor Coll. Dentistry, Dallas, 1990—. Presenter Am. Assn. Dental Rsch., Montreal, Que., Can., 1988, Cin., 1990; rsch. fellow Baylor Coll. Dentistry, Dallas, 1987, 88, 89. Contbr. articles to profl. jours. Mem. ADA, Am. Assn. Orthodontists, Am. Assn. Women Dentists, Am. Assn. Dentistry for Children, Internat. Assn. Dental Rsch., Am. Assn. Dental Rsch., Tex. Dental Assn., Dallas County Dental Soc., The Crescent Club. Avocations: tennis, walking, music, water-skiing. Office: Baylor U Coll Dentistry Dept Orthodontics 3302 Gaston Ave Dallas TX 75246-2027

MCWHORTER, SHARON LOUISE, business executive, inventor, consultant; b. Feb. 22, 1951; d. Leroy Byron Harris Jr. and Josiebell (Richards) Harris Aaron; m. Abner McWhorter II, Mar. 15, 1969 (div. Aug. 1974); 1 child, Abner III. BA, Wayne State U., 1988; cert., SBA, Detroit, 1978; cert. in sound engrng., Detroit Rec. Inst., Warren, Mich., 1982. Directory asst. Mich. Bell Telephone Co., Detroit, 1969; quality control clk. Chevrolet Gear & Axle, Detroit, 1971-74; circulation clk. Wayne County C.C., Detroit, 1977-85, mem. libr. standing com. and open house com., 1983-84; pres. Galactic Concepts & Designs, Detroit, 1977-88, cons., 1983—. Gen. ptnr., mgr. S.M.J. Corridor Devel., Detroit, 1982—, hist. rschr., 1982; del. Small Bus. Conf., 1981; ad hoc mem. Minority Tech. Coun., 1981-82; elected alt. Mich. del. White House Conf. on Small Bus., Washington, 1985-86; lectr., cons. Author, editor: Creative Dilemma newsletter, 1985—; co-patentee cup holding apparatus. Vol. counselor Barat House/March of Dimes, Detroit, 1977; active Concerned Citizens Cass Corridor, Detroit, 1982-87, Cass Corridor Citizen's Patrol, Detroit, 1983-84, Empowerment Zone Devel. Corp., Detroit, 1996—, bd. dirs., corp. chair, 1997—; pres. Wayne County chpt. MADD, Mich., 1987-88; apptd. citizen rev. com, 1988—; mem. adv. bd. Neighborhood Family Initiative, Southeastern Cmty. Found.; pres. Am. Res. Tng. Sys., Inc., 1990—. Recipient Hist. Landmark award Dept. Interior, 1983, cert. appreciation Tri-County Substance Abuse Awareness Com., 1984. Mem. Inventors Coun. Mich. (bd. dirs. 1985-88), Black Women in Bus. (sec. 1984-85), Greater Detroit C. of C., South Cass Bus. Assn. (v.p. 1987-88, pres. 1988-89), Detroit Econ. Club. Democrat. Methodist. Avocations: inventing, photography, video production. Office: SMJ Corridor Devel Co 453 Myrtle St Ste 102 Detroit MI 48201-2311

MCWHORTER, STANLEY BRUCE, English educator, researcher; b. Osco, Ky., June 17, 1930; s. Stanley Vergil and Myrtie Alice (Stearns) M. BA, Transylvania Univ., Lexington, 1954; MA, U. Ky., 1961, PhD, 1963. Life Cert. Edn. Ky., 1950. Instr. English Southwestern Coll., Winfield, Kans., 1959-60, Morehead State Univ., Ky., 1960-61, Ea. Ky. State Univ., Richmond, 1961-63; asst. prof. English W. Va. Wesleyan Coll., Buckhannon, 1963-67; assoc. prof. English Univ. S. C., Florence, 1967-70; prof. English Xavier Univ., Cincinnati, 1972-75, Univ. Dayton, Ohio, 1975-95; ret., 1995—. Ednl. coord. Natl. Folk Festival Assoc. Am., Wash. D.C., 1963-67. Author: Annotated Bibliography of William Wordsworth's Writings and Ana from 1935-1941, 1961, The Annual Anthology of College Poetry and Literature, 1965, The Idea of Religious Struggle in Four Seventeenth Century English Poets,

1967, The Use of the Folk Ballad in the English Class, 1971, Superstitions of Appalachia, 1975. Dir. civic activities Lions Clubs, Jamestown, Ky., 1953-55. Grantee continued study in chosen field, 1965; recipient Southwestern grant for Tchg. Excellence, 1959-60, Cmty. Leadership award, Lions Club Am., 1961-63, Wesleyan plaque Internat. Rels., 1963-67 Wesleyan grant for study Brit. Am. Balladry, 1963-67. Life mem. MLA Am. (edtl. supervisor, 1963-67, scholarship advanced studies, 1963), Nat. Coun. Tchrs. English, Nat. Edn. Assn. Am., Coll. Assn. English Tchrs., Am. Assn. Univ. Profs. D-Conservative. United Methodist. Avocations: running, swimming, travel. Office: Univ Dayton 300 Coll Park Ave Dayton OH 45469 Home: P O Box 3455 Dayton OH 45401 E-mail: mcwhrca@aol.com.

MCWHORTER, SUSAN CAROL, English language educator; b. Elkhart, Ind., Apr. 24, 1947; d. Benjamin E. and Anna M. (Pontious) Kirts; m. John R. McWhorter, June 20, 1970 (div. 1984); 1 child, Carole. BA in Speech, Drama and English, Butler U., 1969; MS in English Edn., Troy State U., 1974; EdS in English Edn., Fla. State U., 1985. Tchr. speech and drama Elkhart (Ind.) H.S., 1969-70; tchr. English Ben Davis H.S., Indpls., 1970-72; GED instr. Ala. Tech. Inst., Ft. Rucker, 1972-74; adminstr., coord. Vincennes U., Ft. Benjamin Harrison, Ind., 1974-75; tchr. English Jinks Jr. High, Panama City, Fla., 1975-76; adj. instr. English Gulf Coast C.C., Panama City, 1977—; tchr. Bay High School, Panama City, 1982-98; resource tchr. Bay Dist. Schs., Panama City, 1998—. Mem. Bay Arts Alliance, Panama City, 1985—, Friends of the Libr., Panama City, 1980-90; mem., mentor Orch. of St. Andrew Bay, 1997—. Recipient Golden Apple award News Channel 13, 1989. Mem. Nat. Coun. Tchrs. English, Fla. Coun. Tchrs. of English (cons. 1983—), Bay Lang. Arts Coun. (pres. 1982—), Bay County Reading Coun., Assn. Bay City Educators, Bay Edn. Found. Avocations: playing flute, ballet dancing, swimming. Home: 1880 W 24th Ct Panama City FL 32405-2228 Office: Bay Dist Schs 1311 Balboa Ave Panama City FL 32401-2080 Fax: (850) 873-7128.

MCWILLIAM, JOANNE ELIZABETH, retired religion educator; b. Toronto, Ont., Can., Dec. 10, 1928; d. Cecil Edward and Edna Viola (Archer) McW.; children, Leslie Mary Giroday, Elizabeth Dewart, Sean Dewart, Colin Dewart; m. C. Peter Slater, June 6, 1987. BA, U. Toronto, 1951, MA, 1953, U. St. Michael's, Toronto, 1966, PhD, 1968; DD honoris causa, Queen's U., Kingston, Ont., 2003. Asst. prof. religious studies U. Toronto, 1968-74, assoc. prof., 1974-87, prof., 1987, chairperson dept. religious studies, 1990-92, 93-94; Mary Crooke Hoffman prof. of Dogmatic Theology The Gen. Theol. Sem., N.Y.C, 1994-99; ret., 1999. Author: The Theology of Grace of Theodore of Mopsuestia, 1971, Death and Resurrection in the Fathers, 1986; editor: Augustine: Rhetor to Theologian, 1991, Toronto Jour. Theology. Mem. Can. Soc. for Patristic Studies (pres. 1987-90), Conf. Anglican Theologians (pres. 1990-91), Can. Soc. for the Study of Religion, Can. Theol. Soc., Am. Theol. Soc., Am. Acad. Religion. Anglican. Home: 59 Duggan Ave Toronto ON Canada M4V 1Y1 E-mail: joanne.mcwilliam@utoronto.ca.

MCWILLIAMS, C. PAUL, JR., engineering executive; b. Louisville, June 4, 1931; s. Cleo Paul and Audrey Dora (Hale) McW.; m. Barbara Ann Sparks, Feb. 22, 1950 (div. 1962); children: Bruce Kevin, Craig Tinsley; m. Barbara Ann Heintz, Apr. 25, 1980; 1 stepchild, Kimberly Jean Moorhouse Beaumont. B Chem. Engring., U. Louisville, 1954, M Engring., 1972. Lic. profl. engr., N.Y., N.C., Pa. Sr. process devel. engr. Olin Mathieson Chem. Corp., Brandenburg, Ky., 1958-66, Rochester, N.Y., 1956-66; sr. chem. engr. GTE Sylvania, Seneca Falls, N.Y., 1966-74, Eastman Kodak Co., Rochester, 1974-81; prin., treas. Flint & Sherburne Assocs., P.C., Rochester, 1981-89; project engr. Roy F. Weston, Inc., Rochester, 1989-92; engring. mgr. ECCO, Inc. (Environ. Cons. Co., Inc.), Buffalo, 1992-94; pres. ECCO Engring., Buffalo, 1993-94; staff engr. Environ. Products & Svcs., Inc., Rochester, N.Y., 1994-96; pvt. cons. engr. Webster, N.Y., 1996—. Cons. water tech. Water Tech. Corp., Tonawanda, N.Y., 1973-76; product rsch. panel Chem. Engring. Mag., 1982-83. Author: Waste Disposal Manual, 1976. Life mem. Rep. Presdl. Task Force, Webster, N.Y., 1986—; mem. Rep. Nat. Com., Webster, 1991-92. 1st lt. USAF, 1954-58, ret. lt. col. USAF, 1982. Decorated Meritorious Svc. medal. Mem. NSPE, AIChE, Soc. Am. Mil. Engrs., Res. Officers Assn. (life), Monroe Profl. Engrs. Soc. (environ. com. 1972-75, chmn. 1973-75, bd. dirs. 1982-84, program chmn. 1984), Cons. Engrs. Coun. N.Y. State (program chmn. Rochester chpt. 1986-87, sec. 1987-88, treas. 1989). Episcopalian. Achievements include replacing boiler feedwater regulators, related instrumentation and control systems and blowdown at a N.Y. State U. facility; system design for dry fabric dust collectors to remove fly ash from coal-fired boilers' flue gas. Home: 1132 Woodbridge Ln Webster NY 14580-8709 Office: C Paul McWilliams PE Cons Engr 1132 Woodbridge Ln Webster NY 14580-8709 Office Phone: 585-872-0505.

MCWILLIAMS, CAREY SCOTT, small business owner, writer; b. Fargo, ND, July 5, 1973; s. Dallas Ora and Jan Marie McWilliams. B of U. Studies, N.D. State U., 1991—97, MA in Mass Comm., 1998—2001. Campus planner Coll. of the Atlantic, Bar Harbor, Maine, 1994; owner C.O.O.P. d' Paw Inc., Fargo, ND, 2002—. Mem. cadet adv. coun. CAP, Fargo, 1987—90. Recipient Comdr.''s Award, CAP, 1988, Lucretia Kuntz Meml. Award, 1989, Billy Mitchell Award, 1989, Braille Flag Award, DAR, 1990. Mem.: NRA, Nat. Honor Soc. (Golden Key Honor Soc. 1996—). Avocations: gun collecting, target shooting, scuba diving, skydiving. Home: 4566 Domingo Rd Fargo ND 58103 Office: COOP d Paw Inc 805 S 15 St Fargo ND 58103 E-mail: books4pets@coopdpaw.com.

MCWILLIAMS, EDWIN JOSEPH, banker; b. Spokane, Washington, Aug. 11, 1919; s. Frank S. and Alice (Conlan) McW.; m. Betty J. Galbreath, Aug. 15, 1944; children: Lawrence, Barbara Anne, Marijoan, Peter. Student, U. Notre Dame, 1937-38, Marquette U., 1938-40; BS in Bus. Adminstrn, Gonzaga U., 1943. With Fidelity Mutual Savings Bank, Spokane, 1940-82, exec. v.p., 1955-58, pres., 1958-82, Fidelity Service Corp., 1983-87. Mem. adv. council Wash. State Dept. Commerce and Econ. Devel., 1977-80; U.S. del. Internat. Savs. Bank Inst., 1975, 76, 79; vice chair, dir. NW Edn. Loan Assn Pres. United Crusade Spokane County, 1966; pres., mem. exec. bd. Inland Empire coun., region 11 exec. com. Boy Scouts Am.; pres. Spokane Unltd.; mem. adv. coun. Sch. Bus., Gonzaga U.; bd. dirs., mem. exec. com. Expo '74 World's Fair, 1973-74; mem. bd. regents Ft. Wright Coll., Spokane; bd. dirs. Sacred Heart Med. Ctr., 1961-70; bd. regents Wash. State U., 1979-92; bd. dirs. Fairmont Meml. Assn. Served to lt. (j.g.) USNR, 1943-45. Mem. Nat. Assn. Mut. Savs. Banks (chmn. 1976-77), Mut. Savs. Banks Assn. State of Wash. (pres. 1980), Am. Savs. and Loan Inst. (past gov. dist. XI), Spokane C. of C. (pres. 1974-75) Clubs: Rotary of Spokane, K.C. Roman Catholic. Home: 2408 E Deerwood Ct Spokane WA 99223

MCWILLIAMS, JOHN LAWRENCE, III, lawyer; b. Phila., Dec. 21, 1943; s. John Lawrence Jr. and Elizabeth Dolores (Chevalier) McW.; m. Paula Ann Root, July 19, 1969 (dec.); children: John Lawrence, IV, Robert Root, Anne Elizabeth, David Stanford, Peter Farrell; m. Kathleen Nolan Pradella, Apr./ 3, 1993. BS, St. Joseph's U., 1965; JD, Seton Hall U., 1969. Bar: N.J. 1969, N.Y. 1975, U.S. Supreme Ct. 1975, Fla. 1977. Trial atty., regional office SEC, N.Y.C., 1969-72; assoc. Mudge Rose Guthrie & Alexander, N.Y.C., 1972-77; mem. Freeman, Richardson, Watson & Kelly, P.A., Jacksonville, Fla., 1977-89, chmn., pres., 1984-89; ptnr. Squire, Sanders & Dempsey, Jacksonville, 1989-98, Livermore, Freeman & McWilliams, P.A., Jacksonville, 1998—. Trustee Mcpl. Svc. Dist. Ponte Vedra Beach, 1981-85, chmn. bd. trustees, 1984-85; treas. Ponte Vedra Cmty. Assn., 1980-82; mem. Leadership Jacksonville, 1981, steering com., 1982; dir. Jacksonville Country Day Sch., 1985-87; pres. Jacksonville Beaches Ponte Vedra Unit Am. Cancer Soc., 1988-90; bd. dirs. Sawgrass Property Owners Assn., Inc., 2000-02. Fellow Am. Coll. Bond Counsel; mem. Nat. Assn. Bond Lawyers, The Fla. Bar, Jacksonville C. of C., Jacksonville Cmty. Coun. Inc., Univ. Club, Ponte Vedra Club, Sawgrass Club, River Club. Republican. Roman Catholic. Home: 3040 Timberlake Pt Ponte Vedra Beach FL 32082-3726 Office: Livermore Freeman & McWilliams PA 1301 Riverplace Blvd Ste 1825 Jacksonville FL 32207-9029 Office Phone: 904-399-0500. E-mail: jmcwill@lkfm.com.

MCWILLIAMS, JOHN MICHAEL, lawyer; b. Annapolis, Md., Aug. 17, 1939; s. William J. and Helen (Disharon) McW.; m. Frances Edelen McCabe, May 30, 1970; children: M. Edelen, J. Michael Jr., James McC. BS, Georgetown U., 1964; LL.B., U. Md., 1967; LLD (hon.), U. Balt., 1993. Bar: Md. 1967, U.S. Supreme Ct. 1970, U.S. Ct. Internat. Trade 1991, U.S. Ct. Mil. Appeals 1992; cert. mediator NASD. Law clk. Chief Judge Roszel C. Thomsen, U.S. Dist. Ct. Md., 1967-68; assoc. Piper and Marbury, Balt., 1968-69; asst. atty. gen. State of Md., 1969-76; gen. counsel Md. Dept. Transp., 1971-76; sr. ptnr. Tydings and Rosenberg, Balt., 1977-97; pres. McWilliams Dispute Resolution, Balt., 1997—. Permanent mem. 4th Jud. Conf.; mem. panel of disting. neutrals CPR Inst. for Dispute Resolution, 1994—2001; mem. Md. Alt. Dispute Resolution Commn., 1994—2002. Asst. editor Law Rev., U. Md., 1967; mem. nat. bd. advisors Ohio State Jour. Dispute Resolution. Chmn. Md. adv. coun. to Nat. Legal Svcs. Corp., 1975-78; mem. Gov.'s Commn. to Revise Annotated Code of Md., 1973-78; transition dir. Md. Gov.-Elect Harry Hughes, 1978-79; mem. Md. Indsl. Devel. Financing Authority, 1980; mem. Greater Balt. Com., 1979-94; mem. exec. com. Econ. Devel. Coun. Greater Balt., 1979-83; vice chmn. bd. Washington/Balt. Regional Assn., 1980-83; mem. Md. Econ. and Cmty. Devel. Adv. Commn., 1983-87; chmn. bd. Md. Econ. Devel. Corp., 1984-89. Served to 1st lt. U.S. Army, 1958-60. Fellow Am. Bar Found. (bd. dirs. 1986-88, 91-93), Internat. Acad. Mediators (v.p. 1998—), Coll. Comml. Arbitrators (pres.-elect), Md. Bar Found. (dir. 1980-82); mem. ABA (pres. 1992-93, mem. ho. of dels. 1976—, chmn. 1986-88, chmn. Md. del. 1976-86, bd. editors jour. 1986-88, 91-93) Md. Bar Assn. (pres. 1981-82), Nat. Conf. Bar Pres. (exec. coun. 1982-85), Bar Assn. Balt. City, Am. Law Inst., Am. Judicature Soc. (dir. 1974-81, exec. com. 1975-77), Am. Acad. Judicature Edn. (dir. 1977), Md. Law Rev. (trustee 1980-83), Md. Inst. Continuing Edn. Lawyers (trustee 1980-83), Inst. Internat. Bus. Law and Practice (corr.), Md. Club, Rule Day Club. Democrat. Roman Catholic. Home: 3 Merryman Ct Baltimore MD 21210-2815 Office: 1106 N Charles St Ste 300 Baltimore MD 21201 Office Phone: 410-244-8124.

MCWILLIAMS, MARGARET ANN, home economics educator, author; b. Osage, Iowa, May 26, 1929; d. Alvin Randall and Mildred Irene (Lane) Edgar; children: Roger, Kathleen. BS, Iowa State U., 1951, MS, 1953; PhD, Oreg. State U., 1968. Registered dietitian. Asst. prof. home econs. Calif. State U., L.A., 1961-66, assoc. prof., 1966-68, prof., 1968-92, prof. emeritus, 1992—, chmn. dept., 1968-76; pres. Plycon Press, 1978—. Author: Food Fundamentals, 1966, 7th edit., 1998, Nutrition for the Growing Years, 1967, 6th edit., 1999, Experimental Foods Laboratory Manual, 1977, 5th edit., 2000, Lifelong Nutrition, 2001, (with L. Kotschevar) Understanding Food, 1969, Illustrated Guide to Food Preparation, 1970, 8th edit., 1998, (with L. Davis) Food for You, 1971, 2d edit., 1976, The Meatless Cookbook, 1973, (with F. Stare) Living Nutrition, 1973, 4th edit., 1984, Nutrition for Good Health, 1974, 2d edit., 1982, (with H. Paine) Modern Food Preservation, Fundamentals of Meal Management, 1978, 4th edit., 2005, (with H. Heller) The World of Nutrition, 1984, Foods: Experimental Perspectives, 1989, 4th edit., 2000, Food Around the World: A Cultural Perspective, 2003. Chmn. bd. Beach Cities Symphony, 1991-94. Recipient Alumni Centennial award Iowa State U., 1971, Profl. Achievement award, 1977; Phi Upsilon Omicron Nat. Founders fellow, 1964; Home Economist in Bus. Nat. Found. fellow, 1967; Outstanding Prof. award Calif. State U., 1976. Mem. Am. Dietetic Assn., Inst. Food Technologists, Phi Kappa Phi, Phi Upsilon Omicron, Omicron Nu, Iota Sigma Pi, Sigma Delta Epsilon, Sigma Alpha Iota. Home: PO Box 220 Redondo Beach CA 90277-0220

MCWILLIAMS, MICHAEL, writer, publisher; b. Detroit, Aug. 28, 1952; s. Henry and Mary (Toarmina) McW. BA, Wayne State U., 1975; MFA, Columbia U., 1978. Free-lance writer Monthly Detroit mag., 1979-82, Village Voice, Rolling Stone, TV Guide, Advt. Age, N.Y. Daily News, L.A. Herald Examiner, N.Y.C., 1982-87; TV critic, 1988—2001; pub. MaryBooks, 2002—. Author: TV Sirens, 1987, (with others) The Premiere Guide to Movies on Video, 1991. Recipient Assn. of Sunday and Feature Editors award, 1st pl. Arts Criticism, 1992. Mem. Phi Beta Kappa. Avocations: television, movies, theater, music.

MCWILLIAMS, MIKE C. lawyer; b. Dallas, Nov. 10, 1948; s. Earl Dewitt and Mary Louise (Campbell) McW.; m. Sally Swatzell, Sept. 1, 1973; children: Michael, Matthew. BBA in Fin., U. Tex., 1969, JD, 1973. Bar: Tex. 1973. Assoc. Elliott, Meer, Vetter, Denton & Bates, Dallas, 1973-78; ptnr. Denton & Generis, Dallas, 1978-80, Moore & Peterson, P.C., Dallas, 1980-89, Winstead, Sechrest & Minick, Dallas, 1989—. Editor: Texas International Law Journal, 1972-73. Mem. Tex. State Bar Assn., Dallas Bar Assn., Phi Delta Phi, Beta Gamma Sigma. Office: Winstead Sechrest & Minick 5400 Renaissance Tower 1201 Elm St Ste 5400 Dallas TX 75270-2199 Office Phone: 214-745-5631.

MCWILLIAMS, ROBERT HUGH, federal judge; b. Salina, Kans., Apr. 27, 1916; s. Robert Hugh and Laura (Nicholson) McW.; m. Catherine Ann Cooper, Nov. 4, 1942 (dec.); 1 son, Edward Cooper; m. Joan Harcourt, Mar. 8, 1986. AB, U. Denver, 1938, LL.B., 1941. Bar: Colo. bar 1941. Dep. dist. atty. Denver, Co, 1941—42; special agent U.S. Office of Naval Intelligence, 1942—45; sgt. U.S. Army, Office of Strategic Services, 1945—46; dist. atty. Denver, Co., 1946—49; private practice Denver, Co, 1949—52; judge municipal ct., Denver, 1949—52, dist., city, and county, Denver, 1952—61, supreme ct. of Co., 1967—70; instructor U. of Denver, 1954—60; judge U.S. ct. of appeals (10th cir.), Denver, 1970—84; sr. judge, 1984—. Served with AUS, World War II. Mem. Phi Beta Kappa, Omicron Delta Kappa, Phi Delta Phi, Kappa Sigma. Republican. Episcopalian. Home: 137 Jersey St Denver CO 80220-5918 Office: Byron White US Courthouse 1823 Stout St Rm 216 Denver CO 80257-1823

MCWILLIAMS, SAMUEL ROBERT, secondary school educator; b. Wilkensburg, Pa., May 4, 1948; s. Paul Wigle and Elizabeth (Witman) McW.; m. Rita Mary Nock, July 31, 1983; 1 chld, Karla Marie. BA in Edn./Sci., W.Va. Wesleyan U., 1971; MA in Edn./Curriculum, Pa. State U., 1974; Ms in Microcomputers, U. Pitts., 1984. Cert. tchr., Pa.; cert. computer instr., Pa. Tchr. sci. and math. Penn-Trafford Schs., Harrison City, Pa., 1971—. Self-employed master of ceremonies and disc jockey, Level Green, Pa., 1967—. Mem. NEA (life), Alpha Psi Omega Nat. Dramatics Honorary (life), Penn-Trafford Edn. Assn., Pa. Edn. Assn., Pa. Sci. Tchrs. Assn., Bushy Run Lions Club, Psi Omega. Democrat. Presbyterian. Avocations: classic/antique autos, environmental issues, botany/gardening, discography. Home: 348 Meadowbrook Rd Level Green PA 15085-9712 Office: Penn-Trafford Sch Dist Mill St Harrison City PA 15636

MEACHAM, CHARLES HARDING, government official; b. Newman, Calif., Sept. 21, 1925; s. Vernon A. and Sara (Paulsen) M.; m. June Lorraine Yunker, June 22, 1946; children— Charles Paulsen, Bruce Herbert. BS, Utah State U., 1950. Biologist Calif. Dept. Fish and Game, 1950-56, Alaska Dept. Fisheries, 1956-59; regional supr. regions II and III Alaska Dept. Fish and Game, 1959-68; dir. internat. fisheries Office Gov. Alaska, 1968-69; commr. U.S. Fish and Wildlife Service, Dept. Interior, 1969-70, dep. asst. sec. for fish and wildlife, pks. and marine resources, commr. Internat. North Pacific Fisheries Commn. and Gt. Lakes Fishery Commn., 1969-70, commr. Internat. Pacific Salmon Fisheries Commn., 1969-70, commr. Great Lakes Fishery Commn., 1969-70, spl. asst. to area dir., 1971-74; dir. internat. affairs Office of Gov., Juneau, Alaska, 1975-80; pres. Meacham & Assocs., Anchorage, 1980—. Dep. commr. U.S. North Pacific Fur Seal Commn.; mem. Pacific and North Pacific Fisheries Mgmt. Councils, 1976-81; chmn. nat. park system adv. bd. U.S. Dept. Interior. Bd. dir. Resource Devel. Coun. for Alaska. With USMCR, 1943-46. Mem. Am. Fisheries Soc., Wildlife Soc., Pacific Fisheries Biologists, Internat. Assn. Game, Fish and Conservation Commrs., Ducks Unlimited, Alaska Miners Assn., Am. Legion, U.S.M. Raiders Assn. (pres. 2003—). Clubs: Elks. Address: PO Box 428 Sequim WA 98382-0428

MEACHAM, MARGARET MARKS, writer, educator; b. Pitts., Feb. 15, 1952; d. James Grier Marks and Rachel Miller Reed; m. John Bulkley Meacham, June 17, 1973; children: Peter, Jennifer, Katharine. BA, Trinity Coll., Hartford, Conn., 1974; MLS, U. Md., College Park, 1975. Instr. Goucher Coll., 1992—99, Towson U., Md., 1999—. Author: Secret of Huron Creek, 1995, Call Me Cathy, 1996, Oyster Moon, 1997, Quiet, You're Invisible!, 2001, A Mid-Semester Night's Dream, 2004. Mem.: Soc. Children's Book Authors and Instrs., Children's Book Guild of Washington, DC. Episcopalian. Avocations: hiking, skiing, cooking.

MEACHIN, DAVID JAMES PERCY, investment banker; b. Teignmouth, Devon, Eng., Jan. 1, 1941; arrived in U.S., 1969; s. James Alfred and Ena Annie Meachin; m. Barbara Marshall Maxwell, Sept. 25, 1971; children: Jonathan J.M., Philip D.M. BS in Phys. Sci., U. Natal, South Africa, 1960; BSChemE, U. Cape Town, South Africa, 1963; MS in Petroleum Engring., French Petroleum Inst., Paris, 1965; diploma in Indsl. Mgmt., Cambridge (Eng.) U., 1966; MBA with distinction, Harvard U., 1971. Project engr. Humphreys and Glasgow Ltd., London, 1966-69; 2nd v.p. investment banking Smith Barney and Co. Inc., N.Y.C. and Tokyo, 1971-75; v.p., gen. mgr. internat. corp. fin. Salomon Bros., N.Y.C. and London, 1975-81; mng. dir. investment banking divsn. Merrill Lynch Capital Markets, N.Y.C., 1981-91; chmn., CEO Cross Border Enterprises L.L.C., 1991—. Bd. dirs. Millennium Chems. Inc.; mem. adv. bd. Gow & Ptnrs., 2003—. Past chmn. Brit. Am. Ednl. Found.; elder Brick Presbyn. Ch., N.Y.C., 1988—; bd. dirs., vice-chmn. U. Cape Town Fund, N.Y.C., 1985—. Mem. Misquamicut Club (bd. govs.), United Oxford and Cambridge Club (U.K.), Harvard Club, Union Club, Sky Club, Kelvin Grove Club (South Africa). Avocations: sailing, golf, tennis, squash. Home: 351 E 84th St New York NY 10028 Office: Cross Border Enterprises LLC 441 Lexington Ave New York NY 10017-3910 Office Phone: 212-682-7400 ext. 230. Business E-Mail: dmeachin@crossborderent.com.

MEAD, CARL DAVID, retired educator; b. Cadiz, Ohio, May 4, 1913; s. Carl David and Neva Eloine (Walker) M.; m. Lillian Martha Felton, Apr. 15, 1938; children: Susan, Nancy. Student, Washington and Jefferson Coll., 1932-34; BS, Ohio State U., 1936, MA, 1938, PhD, 1947. Instr. English Denison U., 1938-39, Ohio State U., 1946-47; faculty Mich. State U., 1948-81, prof. English, 1957-81, head dept., 1959-66; Fulbright lectr. Philippines, 1964. Cons., chief univ. adv. group to U. Ryukyus, Okinawa, 1955-57 Author: Yankee Eloquence in the Middle West, 1951, (with others) Prentice-Hall Handbook for Writers, 1951, The American Scholar Today, 1970; Adv. editor: Dodd, Mead & Co, 1963-75; editor: Centennial Review, 1966-82. Served with AUS, 1943-46. Decorated Legion of Merit. Mem. MLA, Am. Studies Assn. Home: 2530 Marfitt Rd Apt 216 East Lansing MI 48823-6300 E-mail: meadtwo@yahoo.com.

MEAD, CHRISTINA DYKSTRA, church administrator; BA, U. Wis., Madison; MS in Pub. Adminstrn., NYU. Exec. asst. to chief exec. for fin. N.Y.C. Health and Hosps. Corp.; exec. McKinsey & Co. Internat. Cons.; v.p., CFO Reading is Fundamental; CFO Washington Nat. Cathedral, 2000—. Trustee Shipley Sch., Bryn Mawr, Pa., Campaign for Wis.; House of Ruth Washington, DC. Office: Washington Nat Cathedral Massachusetts & Wisconsin Aves NW Washington DC 20016-5098

MEAD, ELIZABETH, artist; BFA, Phila. Coll. of Art, 1985; MFA, So. Meth. U., 1989—91. Exhibitions include Pulse, Gallery Korea, N.Y.C., Influenced, PDX Gallery, Portland, Oreg., Slowness, The Art Gym, Marylhurst U., Oreg., Tachikawa Internat. Arts Festival, Japan, Stillness: Solids and Voids, NoName Exhibitions, The Soap Factory, Mpls., Minn.; artist, curator (exhibitions) Provisional Self: James W. Sullivan, Sculptures and Drawings, Meadows Mus., Dallas; exhibitions include The Anecdote of the Cylinder, Manuel Izquierdo Gallery, Portland, Oreg. Recipient Vis. Artist, Burren Coll. of Art, Co. Clare, Ireland, 1995, Artist in Residence, The Slade Sch. of Art, U. Coll., London, Eng., 2002; grantee Japan/U.S. Creative Artist Exch. Fellowship, Japan Friendship Commn. and the Nat. Endowment of the Arts, 2002-03.

MEAD, FRANK WALDRETH, taxonomic entomologist; b. Columbus, Ohio, June 11, 1922; s. Arlington Alfred and Edith May (Harrison) M.; widowed; children: David Harrison, Gregory Scott. BS, Ohio State U., 1947, MS, 1949; PhD, N.C. State U., 1968. Rsch. asst. dept. physiology Ohio State U., Woods Hole, Mass., summer 1941, rsch. asst. dept. entomology Columbus, 1948-50; Japanese beetle scout bur. entomology and plant quar. USDA, Columbus, summer 1948, biol. aid bur. entomology and plant quar., 1950-53; entomologist div. plant industry Fla. Dept. Agr., Gainesville, 1953-58, 60, biologist IV, 1983-95, emeritus, 1995—; rsch. asst. N.C. State U., Raleigh, 1958-60; state survey entomologist Fed.-State Coop. Survey, Gainesville, 1969-80. Courtesy assoc. prof. dept. entomology U. Fla., Gainesville, 1973-95, emeritus, 1995—, Fla. A&M U., Tallahassee, 1977-95, emeritus, 1995—. Co-editor Tri-ology Technical Report; contbr. articles to profl. jours. Bd. dirs., treas. Alachua Audubon Soc., Gainesville, 1968-75, 77-82; bd. dirs. Alachua County Hist. Soc. (hon. lifetime mem. 1998), Gainesville, 1980-82; former mem. steering com. Civitan Regional Blood Bank, Gainesville, 1977-79; vol. photographer P.K. Yonge Devel. Rsch. Sch. U. Fla., Gainesville, 1978—; vol. Project Graduation, U. Fla., 1994-2002; mem. Alachua Conservation Trust, 2003—. Nominee Cmty. Svc. award, Gainesville Sun, 2002; named to Registry of Remembrances, Nat. World War II Meml.; recipient award, P.K. Yonge Devel. Rsch. Sch., 2001; fellow, Ohio Acad. Sci., 1966. Mem. VFW, Internat. Order of Merit, Cambridge, Entomol. Soc. Am. (bd. dirs. S.E. br. 1978-79), Ga. Entomol. Soc., Fla. Entomol. Soc. (hon., sec. 1968-82, Cert. of Appreciation 1975, 82, 91, Cert. of Merit 1986), Fla. Mosquito Control Assn., Entomol. Soc. Washington, Soc. Systematic Biologists, SAR (Benjamin Franklin chpt. Columbus, Ohio), The Am. Legion (life), Sierra Club, Fla. Track Club, Military Book Club. Avocations: photography, history, birding. Home: 2035 NE 6th Ter Gainesville FL 32609-3758 Office: Fla Dept Agr and Cons Svcs Divsn Plant Industry PO Box 147100 Gainesville FL 32614-7100

MEAD, JAMES MATTHEW, insurance company executive; b. Erie, Pa., June 10, 1945; s. James Leonard and Olga (Richter) M.; m. Rhoda Ginsburg, Sept. 2, 1967 (div. 1971); m. Elaine Margaret Lytle, Mar. 8, 1975. BS, Pa. State U., 1967, MA, 1970. Instr. bus. Pa. State U., Middletown, 1968-71; asst. to ins. commr. Commonwealth of Pa., Harrisburg, 1971-74; asst. to pres. Capital Blue Cross, Harrisburg, 1974-78, sr. v.p., 1978-84, pres., CEO, 1984—2004, vice chmn., 2004—; mng. dir. JM Mead, LLC, 2004—. Bd. dirs. Blue Cross & Blue Shield Assn., Chgo., BCS Fin., Chgo., Greater Harrisburg Found.; bd. dirs. Fed. Res. Bank Phila., chmn. 1994-95; trustee Plan Investment Fund; bd. trustees, Lebanon Valley Coll., Annville, Pa. Contbr. articles on health care to profl. pubs. Mem. bd. advisors Pa. State U., 1985-93; chmn. savs. bond campaign for Ctrl. Pa., U.S. Treasury Dept., Harrisburg, 1986-87; bd. dirs. United Way Capital Region, 1994-98, campaign chair, 1994; bd. dirs. Harrisburg Symphony Assn., 2000-. Paul Harris fellow Rotary Internat., 1988, Alumni fellow Pa. State U., 1986. Mem. Capital Region C. of C. (bd. dirs., treas. 1987-90), Country Club of Harrisburg, Blue Ridge Country Club. Home: 1752 Conway Heath Camp Hill PA 17011 Office Phone: 717-763-1678. Personal E-mail: jamesmmead@aol.com.

MEAD, JOHN STANLEY, university administrator; b. Indpls., Dec. 9, 1953; s. Judson and Jane Mead; m. Virginia Potter, Aug. 11, 1979; children: Christopher, Carolyn. BA, Ind. U., 1976; JD, U. Ill., 1979. Bar: Ill. Staff atty. Ill. Energy Resources Commn., Springfield, 1979-82, staff dir., 1982-85; mgr. coal rsch. Ill. Dept. Energy Natural Resources, Springfield, 1985-87, dir. office of coal devel. and mktg., 1987-89; dir. coal rsch. ctr. So. Ill. U., Carbondale, 1989—, assoc. dean Grad. Sch., 1996—. Bd. dirs. Mid-West Univ. Energy Consortium Inc., Chgo.; mem., past chair Ill. Clean Coal Inst., 1986—. Mem. Ill. Bd. Natural Resources and Conservation, 1997—, sec., 2000—; mem. dist. com., scoutmaster Boy Scouts Am. Recipient gold medal Tech. Univ. Ostrava, Czech Republic, 1992, Georgius Agricola medal, 1994. Mem. Am. Radio Relay League, Ill. State Bar Assn., Carbondale Rotary Breakfast (pres. 2000-2001). Lutheran. Home: 78 Magnolia Ln Carbondale IL 62901-7665 Office: So Ill U Coal Rsch Ctr Mail Code 4623 Carbondale IL 62901 E-mail: jmead@siu.edu.

MEAD, KENNETH MINOR, federal agency administrator; b. May 14, 1947; m. Elizabeth Guerry; children: Jennifer, Hillary. Baccalaureate Degree, So. Conn. U., 1970; JD, U. S.C., 1975; John F. Kennedy Sch. Sr. Mgrs. in Govt., Harvard U., 1991. Sr. atty. Office Gen. Counsel U.S. Gen. Acctg. Office, Washington, 1975-82, asst. dir. Office Quality Assurance, 1982-86, assoc., asst. dir. transp., dir. transp. & telecom. issues, 1986-96, dep. asst. comptr. gen.

for policy, 1996-97; inspector gen. U.S. Dept. Transp., Washington, 1997—. Mem. Pres. Coun. on Integrity and Efficiency, 1997—, Comptr. Gen.'s U.S. Domestic Accountability Bd., 2001—. With USN, 1970-72. Mem. Am. Numismatic Assn., D.C. Bar Assn. Office: Dept Transp 400 7th St SW Washington DC 20590-0003

MEAD, LAWRENCE MYERS, JR., retired aerospace executive; b. Plainfield, N.J., May 11, 1918; s. Lawrence Myers and Eleanor Whitman (Machado) M.; m. Janet Chase, Feb. 21, 1942; children— Lawrence Myers, Kirtland Chase, Jonathan Taylor, Bradford Machado. BSE., Princeton U., 1940, C.E., 1941; postgrad. mgmt., Harvard Bus. Sch., 1964. With Grumman Corp., Bethpage, N.Y., 1941-93; v.p. tech. ops. Grumman Aerospace Corp., Bethpage, N.Y., 1972-75, sr. v.p. dept. ops., 1975-81, sr. v.p. tech. ops., 1981-83; sr. mgmt. cons., 1983-93. Patentee in field. Trustee, police commr., dep. mayor Village of Huntington Bay, N.Y., 1975-80; trustee N.Y.C. Hall of Sci. Fellow Poly. U., 1981. Fellow AIAA; mem. NAE, L.I. Forum on Tech. (bd. dirs., past chmn. bd.), Soc. Logistic Engrs., Soc. Advancement Materials and Process Engring., Princeton U. Alumni Assn. Democrat. Achievements include designing A6A Intruder Navy All Weather Bomber, Gulfstream III Exec. Jet Transport. Home: 88 Notch Hill Rd Apt 253 North Branford CT 06471-1851 E-mail: lmmead@aol.com.

MEAD, MATTHEW HANSEN, prosecutor; Graduate, Trinity U., U. Wyo. Sch. Law. Deputy Co. Atty. Cambell Co. Atty Office, Wyo., 1987—90; Asst. US Atty. and Special Asst. US Atty. Dist. of Wyo., 1991—95; ind. practice, 1995—97; ptnr. Mead and Phillips, 1997—2001; US Atty. Dist. of Wyo., 2001—. Office: US Attorney 2120 Capitol Rm 4002 Cheyenne WY 82001

MEAD, PHILIP BARTLETT, healthcare administrator, obstetrician, educator; b. Poughkeepsie, N.Y., June 23, 1937; s. Ralph Allen and Altina (Gervin) Mead; m. Ann Elaine Smith, June 27, 1964; children: Ralph Allen II, David Smith. BA, Hamilton Coll., 1959; MD, Cornell U., 1963. Diplomate Nat. Bd. Med. Examiners, Am. Bd. Ob-gyn. Intern in medicine Bellevue Hosp., N.Y.C., 1963-64; resident in ob-gyn. N.Y. Hosp./Cornell Med. Ctr., N.Y.C., 1964-69; asst. prof. U. Vt. Coll. Medicine, Burlington, 1971-76, assoc. prof., 1976-81, prof., 1981—2001, prof. emeritus, 2001—; hosp. epidemiologist Med. Ctr. Hosp. of Vt., Burlington, 1984-93; dir. clin. sys. Vt. Acad. Med. Ctr., Burlington, 1993-95; sr. v.p., med. dir. Fletcher Allen Health Care, Burlington, 1995-97; prof., chmn. ob-gyn. U. Vt. Coll. Medicine, 1997—2001, prof. and chmn. emeritus, 2001—; physician leader women's health care svcs. Fletcher Allen Health Care, Burlington, 1997—2001. Lt. comdr. M.C. USN, 1969—71. Fellow: ACOG, Infectious Disease Soc. Am.; mem.: Soc. Hosp. Epidemiologists, Infectious Disease Soc. Ob-Gyn. (pres. 1987—88), Phi Beta Kappa, Alpha Omega Alpha. Home: 203 Pinehurst Dr Shelburne VT 05482-6882 Office: Fletcher Allen Health Care 111 Colchester Ave Burlington VT 05401-1416 E-mail: PBMeadMD@aol.com.

MEAD, PHILOMENA, mental health nurse; b. Yonkers, N.Y., June 23, 1934; d. Alfonso F. and Jennie (Saltarelli) D'Amato; m. Kenneth Mead, Nov. 10, 1956; children: Scott Kenneth, Jeanne Bette. RN, St. Vincents Hosp., Bridgeport, Conn., 1955; BS in Psychology, Sacred Heart U., 1980; cert. in nursing mgmt., Fairfield U., 1988. Cert. psychiat. mental health nurse, nursing specialist, nat. chem. dependency nurse, CPR. Day supr.-relief, night supr. Hall Brooke Hosp., Westport, Conn., 1956-58, day supr., asst. dir. nurses, 1958-66, evening supr.-relief, 1967-68, team nurse, 1974-83, coord. nursing care, 1983-86, adminstrv. coord., 1986-87, nursing care coord. substance abuse treatment unit, 1987-91; charge evening nurse Carolton Hosp., Fairfield, Conn., 1971-73; nurse psychiat. emergency rm. and brief treatment unit West Haven (Conn.) VA, 1991—, mem. staff psychiat. emergency rm., 1995-97, ret., 1997. Roman Catholic. Avocation: genealogy. Home: 67 Adams Rd Fairfield CT 06430-3018

MEAD, PRISCILLA, state legislator; b. Columbus, OH, Feb. 7, 1944; m. John L. Mead; children: John, Willian, Neel, Sarah. Student, Ohio State U. Councilwoman, Upper Arlington, Ohio, 1982-90; mayor, 1986-90; mem. Ohio Ho. of Reps. from 28th dist., Columbus, 1992-2000, Ohio Senate from 16th dist., Columbus, 2001—. Mem. Franklin County Child Abuse and Neglect Found., Coun. for Ethics and Econs. Recipient Svc. award Northwest Kiwanis, Woman of Yr. award Upper Arlington Rotary, Citizen of Yr. award U.S. C. of C. Mem. LWV, Upper Arlington Edn. Found., Jr. League Columbus, Upper Arlington C. of C., Delta Gamma. Republican. Home: 2281 Brixton Rd Columbus OH 43221-3117 Office: Ohio Ho of Reps State House Columbus OH 43215

MEAD, WILLIAM CHARLES, physicist; b. Hazleton, Pa., Dec. 6, 1946; s. Norman Joseph and Ruth Crawford Mead; m. Carol Edna Jerome, May 24, 1969; 1 child, Bennett R. BS, Syracuse U., Syracuse, NY, 1968; MA, Princeton U., Princeton, NJ, 1970, PhD, 1974. Physicist Lawrence Livermore Nat. Lab., 1973—83; physicist, mgr. Los Alamos Nat. Lab., 1983—94; pres., chief scientist Adaptive Network Solutions Rsch. Inc., 1995—. Cons. Lawrence Livermore Nat. Lab., Livermore, Calif., 1995—99, Whistlesoft, Inc., Los Alamos, N.Mex., 1996—98, Ctr. for Adaptive Sys. Applications, Inc., Los Alamos, N.Mex., 1999, Complexica, Inc., Santa Fe, 1999—, Impulse Devices Inc., Grass Valley, Calif., 1999—2003, Los Alamos (N.Mex.) Nat. Lab., 2000—03, Gen. Fusion, Inc., 2003, Environ. Safety Svcs., 2004—. Contbr. articles to profl. jours. Second lt. USAF, 1973—73. Fellow: Am. Phys. Soc. (fellowship 1987); mem.: Internat. Neural Network Soc. Achievements include design of lead for Cairn 50X Intermediate density target, the first laser-driven target to achieve compression of DT to 10 g/cc and a major milestone of the Inertial Confinement Fusion Program; designed and developed C++ engine for Agent-Based Crisis Simulator; development of the Connectionist Hyperprism Classification network to perform task of automated ion mobility spectrum analysis; Adaptive Teaching and Learning Lab. and an Adaptive Tutor for teaching basic arithmetic facts; research in theoretical and computational effort to explore feasibility of Sonic-Cavitation-Driven Fusion; numerical simulations extending knowledge in areas such as the behavior of fluid instabilities in high-gain ICF pellets and the scaling of laser-driven ablation; testing and extending the understanding of ICF physics, providing ideas, simulations and guidance for laser-plasma coupling experiments. Avocations: classical music, photography. Office: Adaptive Network Solutions Research 10 Bonito Pl Los Alamos NM 87544 E-mail: wcmead@ansr.com.

MEADE, KENNETH ALBERT, retired minister; b. Sweet Valley, Pa., June 14, 1935; s. Delbert H. and Dorothea I. (Myers) M.; m. Jeanette H. Quigley, Dec. 18, 1954; children: Jane M. Meade Ulm, Mark K. Ministerial cert., Ea. Christian Inst., East Orange, N.J., 1955; DD (hon.), Milligan Coll., Tenn., 1986, Ea. Christian Coll., Bel Air, Md., 1986. Ordained to ministry Ch. of Christ, 1955. Student min. Ch. of Christ, Bklyn. and Greenpoint, N.Y., 1952-53; mem. Meade-Bennett Evangelistic Team, East Orange, 1953-55; sr. min. Ch. of Christ at Manor Woods, Rockville, Md., 1956—2001; amb. for Christ, Ch. of Christ at Mann Woods, 2001—. Pres. N.Am. Christian Conv., Cin., 1986, Ea. Christian Conv., Rockville, 1969, 74, 82; mem. Chaplaincy Endorsement Commn.; sec. Polish Christian Ministries, Bel Air, Md. Contbr. numerous articles to religion mags. Recipient Award of Honor, Am. Legion, 1952, Highest Comml. award Lehman High Sch. Alumni Assn., 1952. Mem. Ch. Of Christ.

MEADER, JOHN DANIEL, judge; b. Ballston Spa, N.Y., Oct. 22, 1931; s. Jerome Clement and Doris Luella (Conner) M.; m. Joyce Margaret Cowin, Mar. 2, 1963; children: John Daniel Jr., Julia Rae, Keith Alan. BA, Yale U., 1954; JD, Cornell U., 1962. Bar: N.Y. 1963, U.S. Dist. Ct. (no. dist.) N.Y. 1963, U.S. Ct. Appeals (2d cir.) 1966, U.S. Supreme Ct. 1967, U.S. Ct. Mil. Appeals 1973, Ohio 1978, U.S. Dist. Ct. (no. dist.) Ohio 1979, Fla. 1983, U.S. Ct. Appeals (4th cir.) 1992, U.S. Ct. Appeals (fed. cir.) 1993. Sales engr. Albany (N.Y.) Internat. Corp., 1954-59; asst. track coach Cornell U., 1959-62; asst. sec., asst. to pres. Albany Internat. Corp., 1962-65; asst. atty. gen. State of N.Y., Albany, 1965-68; ops. counsel, attesting sec. GE, Schenectady, 1968-77; gen. counsel, asst. sec. Glidden div. SCM Corp., Cleve., 1977-81; chmn. bd., pres. Applied Power Tech. Co., Fernandina Beach, Fla., 1981-84; pres. Applied Energy, Inc., Ballston Spa, 1984-88; judge N.Y. State Workers Compensation Bd., Albany, 1988—. Dir. Saratoga Mut. Fire Ins. Co. Author: Labor Law Manual, 1972, Contract Law Manual, 1974, Patent Law Manual, 1978. Candidate U.S. Ho. of Reps., 29th Dist. N.Y., 1964, N.Y. Supreme Ct., 1975, 87, 93. Col. JAGC, USAR, 1968-1984, dep. staff judge adv. 3d U.S. Army & Ctrl. Command, 1984, brig. gen. JAGC and Fin. Corps, N.Y. Guard, 1984-2002, state staff judge adv. and state comptr. Nat. AAU High Sch. 1000 Yard Indoor Track Champion, 1949, Nat. AAU Prep. Sch. 440 and 880 Yard Indoor Track Champion, 1950, Nat. AAU Outstanding Performer award, Melrose Games Assn., 1950, Heptagonal Track 880-Yard Champion 1954. Mem. ABA, N.Y. State Bar Assn., Fla. Bar, Amelia Island Plantation Club, Cyprus Temple Club, Yale Club Jacksonville (pres.), Masons. Republican. Presbyterian. Home: 271 Round Lake Rd Ballston Lake NY 12019-1714 Office: NY State Workers Compensation Bd 100 Broadway Albany NY 12241-0001 Office Phone: 518-474-6662. E-mail: john.meader@wcb.state.ny.us.

MEADLOCK, JAMES W. computer graphics company executive; b. 1933; married. BSEE, N.C. State U., 1956. Dept. mgr. IBM, 1956-69; pres. Intergraph Corp., Huntsville, Ala., 1969—, also chmn. bd. dirs., chief exec. officer, 1989—. Office: Intergraph Corp 1 Madison Industrial Pk Huntsville AL 35894-0001

MEADOR, CHARLES LAWRENCE, management and systems consultant, educator; b. Dallas, Oct. 7, 1946; s. Charles Leon and Dorothy Margaret (Brown), m. Diane E. Collins, May 18, 1985. BSME with honors, U. Tex., 1970; MSME, MS in Mgmt., MIT, 1972. Engring. staff Union Carbide Corp., Houston, 1967-68; instr. Alfred P. Sloan Sch. Mgmt. MIT, Cambridge, 1972-75, asst. dir. Ctr. Info. Systems Rsch., 1976-78, lectr. Sch. Engring., co-dir. Macro-Engring. Rsch. Group, 1978-99. Founder, pres. Decision Support Tech., Inc., 1974-92; co-founder, vice-chmn., dir. Software Productivity Rsch., Inc., 1985-87; pres., dir. The Softbridge Group, 1989-92; founder, CEO, Mgmt. Support Tech. Corp., 1992-99; sr. v.p., chief info. officer CIGNA Property and Casualty, 1995-98; vice-chmn., dir. Condor Tech. Solutions, Inc., 1998-2000; co-founder, chmn., dir. Clinician Support Tech., Inc., 1999-2001; commr. Nat. Imagery and Mapping Agy., 2000-01; mem. Def. Sci. Bd. Task Force, 2001. Editor: How Big and Still Beautiful? Macro-Engineering Revisited, 1980, Macro-Engineering: The Rich Potential, 1981, Macro-Engineering and the Future: A Management Perspective, 1982, Macro-Engineering: Global Infrastructure Solutions, 1992, Macro-Engineering: MIT Brunel Lectures on Global Infrastructure, 1997; mem. editorial bd. Computer Comm., 1979-91; contbr. articles to profl. jours. NSF trainee, 1970; MIT Wilfred Lewis fellow, 1971, Draper Lab. fellow, 1974. Mem. Computer Soc. IEEE (vice-chmn. Ea. Hemisphere and Latin Am. Area Com. 1977-83), Am. Soc. for Macro-Engring. (bd. dirs. 1992-96), Cosmos Club, Sigma Xi, Tau Beta Pi, Pi Tau Sigma. Office: Clinician Support Tech Inc One Wells Ave Ste 201 Newton MA 02459-3226

MEADOR, DANIEL JOHN, law educator; b. Selma, Ala., Dec. 7, 1926; s. Daniel John and Mabel (Kirkpatrick) M.; m. Janet Caroline Heilmann, Nov. 19, 1955; children: Janet Barrie, Anna Kirkpatrick, Daniel John. BS, Auburn U., 1949; JD, U. Ala., 1951; LLM, Harvard U., 1954; LLD (hon.), U. S.C., 1998. Bar: Ala. 1951, Va. 1961. Law clk. to Justice Hugo L. Black U.S. Supreme Ct., 1954-55; assoc. firm Lange, Simpson, Robinson & Somerville, Birmingham, Ala., 1955-57; faculty U. Va. Law Sch., Charlottesville, 1957-66, prof. law, 1961-66; prof., dean U. Ala. Law Sch., 1966-70; James Monroe prof. law U. Va., Charlottesville, 1970-94, prof. emeritus, 1994—; asst. atty. gen. U.S., 1977-79; dir. grad. program for judges, 1979-95. Fulbright lectr., U.K., 1965-66; vis. prof. U.S. Mil. Acad., 1984; chmn. Southeastern Conf. Assn. Am. Law Schs., 1964-65; chmn. Cts. Task Force Nat. Adv. Commn. on Criminal Justice, 1971-72; dir. appellate justice project Nat. Ctr. for State Cts., 1972-74; mem. Adv. Coun. on Appellate Justice, 1971-75, Coun. on Role of Cts., 1978-84; bd. dirs. State Justice Inst., 1986-92; exec. dir. commn. on structural alternatives Fed. Ct. Appeals, 1998-99. Author: Preludes to Gideon, 1967, Criminal Appeals-English Practices and American Reforms, 1973, Mr. Justice Black and His Books, 1974, Appellate Courts: Staff and Process in the Crisis of Volume, 1974, (with Carrington and Rosenberg) Justice on Appeal, 1976, Impressions of Law in East Germany, 1986, American Courts, 1991, 2000 (with J. Bernstein) Appellate Courts in the United States, 1994, His Father's House, 1994, Unforgotten, 1999, (with Rosenberg and Carrington) Appellate Courts: Structures, Functions, Processes, and Personnel, 1994; editor: Hardy Cross Dillard: Writings and Speeches, 1995; editor Va. Bar News, 1962-65; contbr. articles to profl. jours. 1st lt. U.S. Army, 1951-53; col. JAGC, USAR ret. Decorated Bronze Star.; IREX fellow German Dem. Republic, 1983 Mem. ABA (chmn. standing com. on fed. jud. improvements 1987-90), Ala. Bar Assn., Va. Bar Assn. (exec. com. 1983-86), Am. Law Inst., Am. Judicature Soc. (bd. dirs. 1975-77, 80-83), Soc. Pub. Tchrs. Law, Am. Soc. Legal History (bd. dirs. 1968-71), Order of Coif, Raven Soc., Phi Delta Phi, Omicron Delta Kappa, Kappa Alpha. Presbyterian. Office: U Va Sch Law 580 Massie Rd Charlottesville VA 22903-1738

MEADOR, JO GUASASCO, writer, retired information technology manager; d. James Andrew Guasasco and Dorothy Marie McCarthy; m. Edward Jackson Meador, May 19, 1984; m. Gary Daniel Croom, June 24, 1967 (div. May 0, 1982); 1 child, Kathryn Marie Croom. AA in Music, Coll. San Mateo, 1965; BA in Eng., Calif. State U., 1970. Cert. tchr. Calif., 1971. Secondary sch. tchr., Atwater and San Francisco, 1971—74; sr. systems analyst Bank of Am., San Francisco, 1975—78; data base, data adminstr. Fed. Home Loan Bank, San Francisco, 1978—83; data adminstr. Seattle First Nat. Bank, 1983—84; cons. McRoberts, Meador & Assoc., Issaquah, Wash., 1984—86; info. sys. arch. and analyst US West, Denver, 1986—89; mgr. data resource Boeing Co., Seattle, 1989—2001; ret.; free lance writer, 2001—. Dep. project mgr., info. resource mgmt. SHARE, IBM User's Group, Poughkeepsie, NY; instr. U. Calif., San Francisco, 1980—82; cons. nat. focus Info. Sys. Architecture, 1984—98; dep. project mgr., data adminstration SHARE User's Group, IBM Internat., Poughkeepsie, NY, 1986—93; instr. data resource mgmt. program U. Wash., Seattle, 1990—2000; task force mem. SHARE Internat. Task Force Application Devel. Mgmt., San Jose, Calif., 1990—92; spkr. Zachman Info. Sys.Architecture Forum, Washington, 1991; workshop leader Pac N.W. Writers Conf., 2002, Edmonds Writing Conf., 2003—04. Musician (french hornist): Symphonic; co-author: Handbook of Systems Management, 1989, 1993; editor, prin. author: book 1990 Boeing DRM Action Plan (Honors Award, Boeing Tech. Services, 1991); author: (novel) The Fool, 2002, The Parachute, 2004; contbr. poetry to poetry books, articles to profl. jours. and newsletters. Classroom instr. Jr. Achievement, Seattle, 1995. Recipient Individual Achievement award, Data Adminstrn. Mangement Assn. Internat., 1991, Vol. of the Yr., Issaquah C. Of C., 1993. Mem.: Seattle Free Lancers, Sisters In Crime, Pacific N.W. Writer's Assn. (bd. assoc. contests 1999—). Achievements include first to design and development methods for technology that enabled the transformation of business from local paper processes to global interactive systems; development of definition and development of career paths related to information resources management, including establishment of an international association, a journal, and a university level program; first to definition, design and application of Zachman Framework for information systems. Avocations: literature, art, theater, history, genealogy. Home: 4919 Harbor Hills Dr Freeland WA 98249 Personal E-mail: jo@meadornet.us.

MEADOR, JOHN MILWARD, JR., university dean; b. Louisville, Nov. 4, 1946; s. John Milward and Ruth Inez (Miller) M.; m. Judith Ann Hay, Dec. 22, 1969; children: John Milward III, Elise Kathleen. BA, U. Louisville, 1968; MA, U. Tex., 1972, MLS, 1973; cert. in pub. adminstrn., U. Utah, 1982. Cert. tchr., Ky., Tex. Stacks supr. U. Louisville Librs., 1965-68; English bibliographer M.D. Anderson Libr. U. Houston, 1973-74, head reference dept. social scis. and humanities, 1974-77, head gen. reference dept., 1977-80; asst. dir. pub. svcs. Marriott Libr. U. Utah, Salt Lake City, 1980-84; dean libr. svcs. S.W. Mo. State U., Springfield, 1984-93; dean librs. U. Miss., Univeristy, 1993—2003; dir. librs. SUNY, Binghamton, 2003—. Bd. dirs. Mo. Libr. Network Corp., 1984-90, St. Louis, S.W. Mo. Libr. Network, Springfield; cons. Dayco Corp., Springfield, 1984-86; chmn. Mo. Northwestern Online Total Integrated Systems (NOTIS) Users Group, 1988-89. Co-author: The Robinson Jeffers Collection at the University of Houston, 1975; contbr. articles to profl. jours. Sponsor Community Alternative Svc. Program, Springfield and St. Louis, 1985-93; mem. governing bd. Mo. Rsch. and Edn. Network, MOREnet, 1991-93; With U.S. Army, 1969-71, Vietnam. Recipient Nat. Essay award Propeller Club of U.S., 1964; named to Honorable Order of Ky. Colonels, Gov. Ky., 1978; summer scholar English-Speaking Union, Edinburgh, Scotland, 1968; Apple Computer's Higher Edn. Acad. Devel. Donation Program grantee, 1990. Mem. ALA, Am. Assn. for Higher Edn., Assn. Coll. Rsch. Librs., Bibliog. Soc. Am., Libr. Adminstrn. and Mgmt. Assn., other profl. orgns., English-Speaking Union Club, Rotary (chmn. students guests com. Springfield chpt. 1986-89, chmn. scholarships com. 1989-90, bd. dirs. 1990-91, bd. dirs. Oxford chpt. 1995-96), Phi Kappa Phi. Avocations: raising pure bred airedale terriers, fishing, book collecting. Home: PO Box 223 Binghamton NY 13902-0223 Office: Binghamton Univ SUNY Bartle Library Binghamton NY 13902-6012 E-mail: jmeador@binghamton.edu.

MEADOR, RON, newspaper editor, writer; b. Buffalo, N.Y., Nov. 24, 1952; s. Meril E. and Evelyn (Lyons) M.; divorced; 1 child, Benjamin Brian. BA, Ind. U., 1975. Copy editor The Courier-Journal, Louisville, 1975-78, The New York Times, 1978-80; reporter, state editor, city editor, asst. mng. editor Star Tribune, Mpls., Minn., 1980-96, mem. editl. bd., editl. writer, 1996—. Mem. Investigative Reporters and Editors, Inc., Nat. Conf. Editl. Writers, Soc. Environ. Journalists, Insts. for Journalism and Natural Resources (mem. adv. bd.). Office: Star Tribune 425 Portland Ave Minneapolis MN 55488-0002

MEADORS, ALLEN COATS, health administrator, educator; b. Van Buren, Ark., May 17, 1947; s. Hal Barron and Allene Coats (Means) M. AA, Saddleback Coll., 1981; BBA, U. Ctrl. Arki., 1969; MBA, U. No. Colo., 1974; MPA, U. Kans., 1975; MA in Psychology, Webster U., 1979, MA in Health Svcs. Mgmt., 1980; PhD in Adminstrn., So. Ill. U., 1981. Assoc. adminstr. Forbes Hosp., Topeka, 1971-73; asst. dir. health svcs. devel. Blue Cross Blue Shield of Kans., Topeka, 1973-76; asst. dir. Kansas City Health Dept. (Mo.), 1976-77; program dir., asst. prof. So. Ill. U., Carbondale, 1978-82, Webster U., St. Louis, 1978-82; assoc. prof., dir. divsn. health adminstrn. U. Tex., Galveston, 1982-84; exec. dir. N.W. Ark. Radiation Therapy Inst., Springdale, Ark., 1984-87; prof., chmn. dept. health adminstrn. U. Okla., Oklahoma City, 1989-90, dean Coll. Pub. Health, 1989-90; mem. faculty Calif. State U., Long Beach, 1977-81; mem. grad. faculty Sch. Bus. Adminstrn. U. Ark., Fayetteville, 1984-87; prof., chmn. dept. health adminstrn. U. Okla., 1987-90; dean Coll. Health, Social and Pub. Svcs. Ea. Wash. U., Cheney, 1990-94; CEO, dean Pa. State U., Altoona, 1994-99; chancellor U. N.C., Pembroke, 1999—. Cons. Surgeon Gen. Office and Air Force Sys. Contbr. articles to profl. jours. Command bd. dirs. Blair County Hall of Fame, Blair County Hist. Soc., Martin Luther King Hosp., Health Care Svcs. Adv. Bd.; bd. dirs., mem. exec. com. Altoona Symphony Orch.; bd. dirs. Southwestern Regional Med. Ctr., Home Health Agy. With Med. Svc. Corps, USAF, 1969-73. Fellow Am. Coll. Healthcare Execs.; mem. Am. Hosp. Assn., C. of C. (v.p.). Home: PO Box 1520 Pembroke NC 28372 Office: U NC at Pembroke Chancellors Office PO Box 1510 Pembroke NC 28372-1510 Office Phone: 910-521-6201. Business E-Mail: acm@uncp.edu.

MEADORS, HOWARD CLARENCE, JR., electrical engineer; b. Chgo., July 31, 1938; s. Howard Clarence and Eileen May (Baker) M.; m. Phyllis Anne Rennebaum, July 18, 1964; children: Henry Charles, William Howard, Laura Phyllis, Pamela Susan. SB, MIT, 1960, SM, 1962, Profl. Degree in Elec. Engring., 1964; PhD, Poly. Inst. NY., 1976. Mem. tech. staff Bell Tel. Labs., Inc., Holmdel, NJ, 1966—82; disting. mem. tech. staff AT&T Info. Systems Labs., Holmdel, 1983—85, supr. product devel., 1985—86; supr. adv. data communications AT&T Bell Labs., Middletown, NJ, 1986—91; Disting. mem. tech. staff AT&T Bus. Communications Systems, Holmdel, NJ, 1991—91; disting. mem. tech. staff AT&T Network Systems, Holmdel, NJ, 1994—96, Lucent Technologies, Holmdel, NJ, 1996—2001. Ednl. counselor MIT, 1973-2003, regional vice chmn., 1983-96, ctrl. NJ chmn., 1996-2003. Inventor in field. With Signal Corps, U.S. Army, 1964-66. Mem. IEEE (sr. mem. 1987), Sigma Xi, Eta Kappa Nu.

MEADORS, MARYNELL, former professional basketball coach, sports team executive; B.Health, Phys. Edn. and Recreation, Mid. Tenn. State U., 1965, M. Physiology of Exercise, 1966. Basketball coach Tenn. Tech., 1970-86, Fla. State U., 1986-96; head coach, gen. mgr. Charlotte Sting, 1997-99; dir. scouting Miami Sol, 1999—. Named Ohio Valley Conf. Coach of the Yr., 1978, 83, Metro Conf. Coach of Yr., 1990, Conf. Co-Coach of the Yr., 1991; inductee Tenn. Tech. Hall of Fame, 1992, Ohio Valley Conf. Hall of Fame, 1992. Achievements include appearing in NCAA record book in all-time coaching longevity records section (ranks third in most games coached, 786, fifth in most seasons, 26 and seventh in victories, 495). Office: Miami Sol SunTrust Internat Ctr One SE 3rd Ave Ste 2300 Miami FL 33131 Fax: 786-777-1629. E-mail: mmeadors@heat.com.

MEADOW, CHARLES, information scientist, consultant; b. Paterson, NJ, Dec. 16, 1929; s. Abraham and Florence (Troub) M.; m. Harriet Reiss, Sept. 9, 1956 (div.); children: Debra Lynne, Sandra Lee; m. Mary Louise Shinskey, June 24, 1972; children: Alison Maria, Benjamin Niland. BA, U. Rochester, 1951; MS, Rutgers U., 1954. Mathematician David Taylor Model Basin USN, Washington, 1954-55; asst. mathematician RAND Corp., Lexington, Mass., 1955-56; unit mgr. GE Co., Bethesda, Md., 1956-60; sr. sys. analyst IBM Corp., Gaithersburg, Md., 1960-68; chief sys. devel. divsn. US Nat. Bur. Stds., Gaithersburg, Md., 1968-71; tech. asst. Office of Sci. and Tech. Exec. Office of the Pres., Washington, 1970-71; asst. dir. divsn. mgmt. info. and telecom. sys. US AEC, Washington, 1971-74; prof. Drexel U., Phila., 1974-82; project mgr. Dialog Info. Svcs., Inc., Palo Alto, Calif., 1982-84; prof. faculty info. studies U. Toronto, 1984—94, assoc. dean, 1990—94, prof. emeritus, 1994—. Vis. prof. U. Sheffield, 1980-81, U. West Indies, 1990-91, U. Wash., 1993, U. NC, 1995; mem. bd. visitors Coll. Communication and Info., U. Tenn., 2002-. Author: The Analysis of Information Systems, 1967, 2nd edit., 1973, Man-Machine Communication, 1970, The Story of Computers, 1970, Sounds and Signals: How We Communicate, 1975, Applied Data Management, 1976, Text Information Retrieval Systems, 1992, 2nd. edit, 1999; co-author: (with Pauline A. Cochrane) Basics of Online Searching, 1981, (with Albert S. Tedesco) Telecommunications for Management, 1985, (with Bert R. Boyce and Donald H. Kraft) Measurement in Information Science, 1994, Ink Into Bits: A Web of Converging Media, 1998, Making Connections: Communications Through the Ages, 2002; editor Jour. Am. Soc. for Info. Sci., 1976-84, Can. Jour. Info. Sci., 1986-87. 1st Lt. USMC, 1951-53. Mem. Am. Soc. Info. Sci. and Tech. (disting. lectr. award NJ chpt. 1986, ann. rsch. award 1995, info. sci. book of yr. award 2000), Can. Assn. Info. Sci. (pres. 1994), NY Acad. Sci. (honorable mention children's sci. book awards 1975), Ret. Academics and Librs. U. Toronto (exec. com. 2000-02, coms. dir. 2001-02), Sigma Xi. Avocation: photography. Home: 1443 Hamley St Victoria BC V8S 1M9 Canada V85 1M9 E-mail: ct.meadow@shaw.ca.

MEADOW, LYNNE (CAROLYN MEADOW), theater producer; b. New Haven, Nov. 12, 1946; d. Frank and Virginia R. Meadow BA cum laude, Bryn Mawr Coll., 1968; postgrad., Yale U., 1968-70. Dir. Theatre Communications Group, 1978-80. Adj. prof. SUNY, Stony Brook, 1975-76, Yale U., Circle in the Sq., 1977-78, 89-91, NYU, 1977-80; theatre and music/theatre panelist Nat. Endowment for Arts, 1977-88; artistic advisor Fund for New Am. Plays, 1988-90. Artistic dir. Manhattan Theatre Club, N.Y.C., 1972—; guest dir. Nat. Playwrights Conf., Eugene O'Neill Theatre Ctr., 1975-77, Phoenix Theatre, 1976; dir. Ashes for Manhattan Theatre Club and N.Y. Shakespeare Festival, 1977; prodr. off-Broadway shows Ain't Misbehavin', 1978, Crimes of the Heart, 1981, Miss Firecracker Contest, 1984, Frankie and Johnny, 1987, Eastern Standard, 1988, Lisbon Traviata, 1989, Lips Together, Teeth Apart, 1991, Four Dogs and a Bone, 1993, Love! Valour! Compassion!, 1994; dir. Principia Scritoriae, 1986, Woman in Mind, 1988 (Drama Desk award), Eleemosynary, 1989, Absent Friends, 1991; dir. Broadway prodn. A Small Family Business, 1992, The Loman Family Picnic, 1993, Nine Armenians, 1996(Drama Desk nominee), Captains Courageous: The Musical, 1999, The Tale of the Allergist's Wife, 2000; (dir. Broadway prodn. and nat. tour) The Tale of the Allergist's Wife, 2000, Last Dance, 2003, Rose's Dilemma, 2003;

co-prodr. off-Broadway and Broadway show Mass Appeal, 1981. Recipient Citation of Merit Nat. Coun. Women, 1976, Outer Circle Critics award 1977, Drama Desk award, 1977, Obie award for Ashes, 1977, Margo Jones award for Continued Encouragement New Playwrights, 1981, Critics Circle award Outstanding Revival on or off Broadway for Loot, 1986, Lucille Lortel award for Outstanding Achievement, 1987, Spl. Drama Desk award, 1989, N.Y. Drama Critics Circle award Best Fgn. Play for Aristocrats, 1989, Torch of Hope award, 1989, Manhattan Mag. award, 1994, Lee Reynolds award League Profl. Theatre Women, 1994; named Northwood Inst. Disting. Woman of Yr., 1990, Person of Yr., Nat. Theatre Conf., 1992, SDCF "Mr. Abbott" award, 2003. Office: Manhattan Theatre Club 311 W 43rd St Fl 8 New York NY 10036-6413

MEADOW, WILLIAM LEE, medical educator; b. N.Y.C., N.Y., Oct. 28, 1948; s. Charles and Reine Meadow; m. Susan Goldin, June 20, 1971; children: Alexander Goldin, Nathaniel Goldin, Jacqueline Mollie Goldin. BA, Amherst Coll., 1969; MD, U. Pa., 1974, PhD, 1976. Pediat. Ill., 1981, Soc.Pediat.Rsch. Tex., 1986, Am.Pediat.Soc. Tex., 2001. Prof. pediat. U. Chgo., Chgo., 1981—. Asst. dir. MacLean Ctr. Clin. Med. Ethics, Chgo., 1994—. Office: U Chgo Dept Pediat 5841 South Maryland Ave - MC 6060 Chicago IL 60637 Office Phone: 773-702-6210. E-mail: wlm1@uchicago.edu.

MEADOWS, DENIS JOHN, writer, director; b. Pitts., Oct. 9, 1944; s. Robert Aiden Meadows and Mayme Ann Zaiden; m. Ellen Jo Anne Krug, June 7, 1980; children: Kieran, Kyla. BA, Fordham U., 1968; MA, George Washington U., 1970. Playwright-in-residence The Acting Group, N.Y.C., 1990—92; with The N.Y. Times, N.Y.C., 1976—. Author: (plays) Cafe Gruere, 1997, Di Dodi Die, 2002, Jesuit Love, 2003, (screenplays) The Kiss, More or Less, Play Reader Young Playwright's Festival, N.Y.C., 1986—88; dir. St. Francis Soccer, Bklyn., 1994—97; corr. sec. Stuyvesant HS Parents Assn., N.Y.C., 2002—03. Mem.: The Theatre Comm. Guild, The Dramatists Guild of Am. Home: 297 Sixth Ave Brooklyn NY 11215 Office: The New York Times 229 W 43 St New York NY 10036

MEADOWS, JAMES STEVEN, forester; b. Fort Knox, Ky., Aug. 23, 1954; s. James Samuel and Lillie Hurley Meadows; m. Rebecca Ann Lemann, May 23, 1976; children: Rebekah Ker, Emily Warren, Elizabeth Percy. BS in Forestry, La. State U., 1979, MS, 1981; PhD, Miss. State U., 1988. Rsch. assoc. Miss. State U., Starkville, 1985—88, postdoctoral asst., 1988—89; rsch. forester USDA Forest Svc., Stoneville, Miss., 1989—. Forestry short-course instr. Miss. State U., Starkville, Miss., 1990—; adj. prof. La. State U., Baton Rouge, 2001—, Miss. State U., 2003—; lectr. in field. Contbr. articles to profl. jours., chapters to books. Vol. (public-address announcer at athletic events) St. Joseph H.S., Greenville, Miss., 1997—2004. Recipient David M. Moehring Meml. award, Miss. State U., 1986, USDA Cert. of Merit, USDA Forest Svc., 1992, 1996, 1997, 2003; fellow Weyerhaeuser Predoctoral fellow, Miss. State U., 1982; scholar Woods and Waters scholar, La. State U., 1979. Mem.: So. Hardwood Forestry Group (secretary-treasurer 1990—2004), Gamma Sigma Delta, Xi Sigma Pi (forest ranger, nu chpt. 1980—81). Roman Catholic. Office: USDA Forest Service PO Box 227 Stoneville MS 38776 Office Phone: 662-686-3168.

MEADOWS, JOHN FREDERICK, lawyer; b. Manila, Mar. 7, 1926; s. Grover Cleveland and Millie M.; m. Karen Lee Morris, Nov. 17, 1962; children: Ian Joseph, Marie Irene. AA, U. Mich., 1944; BA (Freshman Alumni Scholar, 1943), U. Calif., Berkeley, 1948; LLB, Boalt Hall, 1951. Bar: Calif 1952, U.S. Dist. Ct. (no. dist.) Calif. 1952, U.S. Ct. Apls. (9th cir.) 1952, U.S. Sup. Ct. 1958. Assoc. Wallace, Garrison, Norton & Ray, San Francisco, 1952-56; atty. advisor Maritime Adminstrn, U.S. Dept. Commerce, Washington, 1956; trial atty., Admiralty and Shipping Sect. U.S. Dept Justice, West Coast Office, San Francisco, 1956-64, atty. in charge, 1964-72; sr. resident ptnr. Acret & Perrochet, San Francisco, 1972-76; sr. ptnr. Meadows, Smith, Lenker, Sterling & Davis, San Francisco, 1976-93, Long Beach, Calif., 1976-93, Seattle, 1976-93; mng. ptnr. west coast Kirlin, Campbell, Meadows & Keating, N.Y.C., 1993; ptnr. Jedeikin Meadows & Schneider, San Francisco, 1994. Cons. maritime law, UN; lectr. seminar Taipei, Taiwan, 1968. Author: Preparing a Ship Collision Case for Trial, 1970, Ship Collision Cases: Technical and Legal Aspects; Investigation and Preparation for Suit, 1997, contbr. articles to legal publs.; assoc. editor: Am. Maritime Cases. Lt. M.I. AUS, 1944-46. Mem. ABA, Maritime Law Assn., San Francisco Bar Assn. Republican. Roman Catholic. Home: 205 The Uplands Berkeley CA 94705-2818 Office: 333 Pine St 5th Floor San Francisco CA 94104-1958 Fax: 415-421-5658. Office Phone: 415-477-8826. E-mail: jmeadows@jmslex.com.

MEADOWS, JOYCE KATHERINE, nurse; b. Detroit, Mich., Aug. 12, 1944; d. Jesse O. and Katherine Rita Meadows; 1 child from previous marriage, Katherine Cherine. Diploma LAC USC Sch. Nursing, 1977, Enterostomal Therapy Cert., 1979. RN. RN, cons., educator, Calif., 1968—97; nurse Jerry Pettis Meml. Vets. Hosp., Loma Linda, Calif., 1978—81; educator, specialist, Vis. Nurse Assn., Inland County, Riverside, Calif., 1981—84; educator, specialist Vis. Nurse Assn., Sacramento, 1984—86, Vis. Nurse Assn., Orange County, Tustin, Calif., 1986—90; wound, ostomy specialist, educator Vis. Nurse Assn., Inland County, Riverside, Calif., 1997—. Chair nursing subcom. Dept. of Aging, Sacrament0, Calif., 1991; cons. to FHP model for govt. HMO system, Fountain Valley, Calif., 1990—96; spkr. in field. Contbr. articles to profl. publs. Educator, cons. Ostomy Assn., Riverside, Calif., 1981—84. Recipient Hands and Heart award with commendation, Max Cleland VA Adminstrn., Washington, D.C., 1980. Avocation: candlemaking, writing poetry and stories. Office: Vis Nurse of Inland County PO Box 1649 Riverside CA 92502 Home: 5505 Van Buren Blvd Riverside CA 92503-2066

MEADOWS, JUDITH ADAMS, law librarian, educator; b. Spartanburg, SC, June 5, 1945; d. Thomas Taylor and Virginia (Dayton) Adams; m. Bruce R. Meadows; children: Beth Ann Blackwood, Ted Adams Meadows. BA, Am. U., 1967; MLS, U. Md., 1979. Law libr. Aspen Sys. Corp., Gaithersburg, Md., 1979-81; dir. Fairfax (Va.) Law Libr., 1981-84, State Law Libr., Helena, Mont., 1984—. Vis. prof. U. Wash., Seattle, 1994; adj. prof. U. Great Falls, Mont., 1989-96; presiding ofcl. Gov.'s Conf. on Libr. Info. Svc., Helena, Mont., 1991. Author: (book chpts.) From Yellow Pads to Computers, 1991, Law Librarianship, 1994; contbr. articles to profl. jours. Bd. dirs. Helena Presents, 1986-92, Holter Mus. Art, 1995-2002, Mont. Supreme Ct. Commn. on Tech., Mont. Supreme Ct. Commn. on Self-Represented Litigants, Mont. Equal Justice Task Force, 2001—, Helena Edn. Found., v.p., 2003. Recipient Disting. Svc. award State Bar of Mont., 1991. Mem. Am. Assn. Law Librs. (treas. 1992-95, v.p. 1996—, pres. 1997-98, past pres. 1998—), N.W. Consortium of Law Librs. (pres.), Mont. Libr. Assn. (sec. 1986-88). Avocations: gourmet cooking, cross country skiing, reading. Office: State Law Libr Mont PO Box 203004 Helena MT 59620-3004

MEADOWS, LOIS ANNETTE, elementary school educator; b. Harrisville, W.Va., Jan. 12, 1948; d. Orvle Adam and Una Pauline (Slocum) Ingram; m. David Alan Meadows, June 15, 1969; children: Lynecia Ann, Eric Justin. BA, Glenville State Coll., 1969; MA, W.Va. U., 1980. Cert. music, elem. edn., reading, computer tech. edn., W.Va.; nat. cert. elem. tchr. Tchr. grade six Acad. Park-Portsmouth (Va.) City Schs., 1969-73; elem. substitute Wood County Schs., Parkersburg, W.Va., 1973-77; real estate agt. Nestor Realty, Parkersburg, 1974-77; tchr. grade five/music Emerson Elem. Wood County Schs., Parkersburg, W.Va., 1977-78, tchr. grade three, 1978—; edn. cons. World Book, Parkersburg, 1986—. Mentor tchr.-trainer Wood County Schs., parkersburg, 1990—; W.Va. S.T.E.P. Test com./trainer W.Va. Dept. Edn., Charleston, 1994—, mem. pool of talented educators, presenter sessions goals and objectives Ctr. Profl. Devel. Gov.'s Inst.; grant writer and spkr. in field; mem. W.Va. Dept. Edn. State Writing Manual Com., 1996-2001; coord. W.Va.-Ohio-Ky. Nat. Read-In.; presenter Gov's Summer Insts. for Ctr. for Profl. Devel., 1994—; mem. standards com. 4th grade writing assessment W.Va. Dept. Edn., 1994—. Author: (reading projects) Operation Blackout, 1986-94 (grant 1994), The Reading Room, 1988 (grant 1990), Storytime at the Mall, 1986— (grant 1994, 95); contbg. author W.V. Math Workbook, 1998, 99. Life mem. Emerson PTA, Parkersburg, 1977—; Sunday Sch. tchr. North Parkersburg Bapt. Ch., 1976-98, children's choir dir., 1976-88; fund raiser local charities, Parkersburg. Women of Excellence and Leadership Timely Honored award, W. Va. State Reading Tchr. of Yr., 1988, Finalist W. Va. State Tchr. of Yr., W.Va. Dept. Edn., 1993, Wood County Tchr. of Yr., 1993, Ashland Oil Golden Apple Achiever award, 1995, Ashland Oil Tchr. Achievement Award Winner (1 0f 10 for WV), 1998, Wood Co. PTA Outstanding Educator of Yr. award, 1995-96, award for ann. contbrs. and project work Emerson PTA, Wealth award Women of Excellence and Leadership Timely Honored, 1993, 2001; Nat. writing fellow W.Va. Writing Project, 1999. Mem. W.Va. Reading Assn. (pres. 1993-94, mem. chmn. 1994—, Spl. Svc. award 1997), Internat. Reading Assn., Wood County Reading Coun. (past pres. 1986-88, 90-92), Am. Fedn. Tchrs., Delta Kappa Gamma. Republican. Avocations: children's literature, collecting autographed books, bridge, basket weaving, family times. Home: 142 Jomar Dr Parkersburg WV 26104-9169 Office: Wood County Schs Emerson Elem 1605 36th St Parkersburg WV 26104-1939

MEADOWS, VICKERS B. federal agency administrator; Grad., Green Mountain Coll. Procuremen, dir. presdl. gifts White House, Washington, 1989—89, spl. asst. to the v.p. for adminstrn., 1985—89; dep. dir., dir. exec. svc. Dept. Transp., Washington, 1989—93; dir. adminstrn. Gov. Bush, 1995—2000; spl. asst., dir. White House Mgmt. White House, Washington, dir. adminstrn. Bush-Cheney Transition; asst. sec. for adminstrn. office, CIO, Dept. HUD, Washington, 2002—. Republican. Office: Dept HUD Adminstrn Office 451 7th St SW Washington DC 20410-1047

MEADS, DONALD EDWARD, management services company executive; b. Salem, Mass., Sept. 23, 1920; s. Laurence G. and Gertrude F. Meads; m. Jane Lightner, June 15, 1943; children: Edward G., Robert C., Laurence G., Judith C. Antrim, Suzanne M. O'Neil, Clifford L., Nancy Chapin. AB in Pre-Law, Dartmouth Coll., 1942, MBA in Fin., Harvard U., 1947. V.p., vice chmn. investment com. N.Y. Life Ins Co., N.Y.C., 1947-61; v.p. fin., chmn. investment com. Investors Diversified Svcs. Inc., Mpls., 1961-65; pres., CEO Internat. Basic Economy Corp., N.Y.C., 1965-67, chmn., CEO, 1967-71; exec. v.p., dir., CFO, chmn. investment com. INA Corp., Phila., 1971-74; chmn. bd., CEO CertainTeed Corp., Valley Forge, Pa., 1974-78, dir., 1973-78; chmn. Mateer-Burt Co., Inc., Plymouth Meeting, Pa., 1984-87, Phila. First Group Inc., 1982-90, Carver Assocs., Inc., West Conshohocken, Pa., 1978—. Hon. life trustee Valley Forge Mil. Acad. and Coll., Wayne, Pa.; hon. dir. Marine Corps Scholarship Found., Princeton, N.J.; adv. bd. World Affairs Coun. Phila. Capt. USMC, 1942-45. Decorated DFC, Air medals (6). Mem. Harvard Club N.Y.C., Union League (Phila.). E-mail: demeads@aol.com.

MEADS, MINDY, merchandising and design executive; BS, U. Ill. With Denver Dry Goods, 1974—78; sr. v.p., v.p., merchandising administr., v.p., store mgr., jeans collection buyer R.H. Macy and Company Inc., 1978—89; operating exec. The Limited, 1989—90; v.p., gen. merchandising mgr. Lands End, 1991—94, sr. v.p. merchandising and design, 1994—96; sr. v.p., gen. merchandising mgr., merchandising design planning and allocation Gymboree Corp., 1996—98; exec. v.p. merchandising and design Lands End, 1998—2003; gen. mgr. apparel Sears Roebuck and Co., 2003—04, exec. v.p., 2003—; pres. Lands End, 2003—, CEO, 2004—. Office: Sears Roebuck and Co 3333 Beverly Rd Hoffman Estates IL 60179*

MEADS, WALTER FREDERICK, communications executive, consultant, writer; b. Ft. Wayne, Ind., Mar. 11, 1923; s. Frederick C. and Minnie E. (Stephenson) M.; m. Mary E. Smith, Mar. 21, 1975; children by previous marriage: Kenneth W., Catherine L. BS, Kent State U., 1948; MA, Fairfield U. With Norman Malone & Assos., Akron, Ohio, 1946-48, Griswold-Eshleman Co., Cleve., 1949-53, Fuller, Smith & Ross, Cleve., 1953-55; sr. v.p., head of creative svc., mem. mgmt. com., vice chmn. plans and rev. bds. J. Walter Thompson Co., N.Y.C., 1955-72; pres. Meads & Assocs., 1972—. With USAAF, 1943-45. Recipient numerous nat. and local advt. industry awards. Home: 6761 Trail Ridge Dr Lakeland FL 33813-1844 Office: 6761 Trail Ridge Dr Lakeland FL 33813 *Creative freedom is probably the core concept at the heart of my life— not only for myself but for others. Life is never static; it either deteriorates or grows. All growth, to me, springs from the creative doers of the world. The rest of humanity goes along for the ride. And creative growth, in any field or endeavor, demands an attitude of freedom to shake off the shackles of habit and find new and better ways of doing things.*

MEAGHER, GEORGE VINCENT, mechanical engineer; b. Halifax, N.S., Can., Apr. 23, 1919; s. John Nicholas and Blanche Margaret (Seals) M.; m. Evelyn Margaret Hamm, June 2, 1945; children: Maureen, Lindsey, Lise, Shelagh. BSc, Dalhousie U., Halifax, 1940; B of Engring., McGill U., 1942. Engring. and mgmt. positions in industry, 1942-56; with Dilworth, Secord, Meagher & Assocs. Ltd., Toronto, 1957-92, chmn., 1988-92; pres. Tatacan Ltd., 1985-96; chmn., CEO Power Products, Ltd., 1970—80; vice chmn. Tata-DSMA, Bombay, 1970-93; pres., CEO DSMA Internat., Inc., 1980—88; dir. State Bank India, Can. Ltd., Toronto, 1984-94; founding dir., past chmn. Can.-India Bus. Coun.; pres. George V. Meagher Inc. Fellow: Engring. Inst. Can.; mem.: Profl. Engrs. Ont. Home: 500 Avenue Rd Apt 1402 Toronto ON Canada M4V 2J6 Office Phone: 416-929-8286. E-mail: meaghergv@sympatico.ca.

MEAGHER, JAMES PROCTOR, editor; b. Rock Island, Ill., June 2, 1935; s. Edmund Joseph and Pauline Marie (Proctor) M.; m. Marie Therese Lyman, Sept. 12, 1959; children: Kathleen Ann Raffa, Christopher James. BA, U. Notre Dame, 1957. Copy editor Chgo. Tribune Co., 1959-61; staff writer Nat. Observer, Washington, 1961-62, news editor Silver Spring, Md., 1962-65, sr. editor, 1965-76, asst. mng. editor, 1976-77; assoc. editor Barron's Bus. and Fin. Weekly, N.Y.C., 1977-78, news editor, 1978-82, asst. mng. editor, 1982-86, dep. editor, 1986-92, mng. editor, 1992-93, editor, 1993-95; exec. editor Dow Jones Mag. Group, N.Y.C., 1995—2002; ind. editl. cons., 2002—. Served to 1st lt. U.S. Army, 1957-59. Mem. Soc. Profl. Journalists, Sigma Delta Chi. Roman Catholic. Home: 25 Hedges Ave Chatham NJ 07928-2503 Personal E-mail: meagherj@optonline.net.

MEAKEM, CAROLYN SOLIDAY, investment executive, financial planner, money manager, consultant; b. Columbus, Ohio, Jan. 11, 1936; d. Junius Dean and Mary Elizabeth (Thomas) Soliday: m. Thomas James Meakem, Aug. 26, 1956; children: Thomas James III, Timothy Dean, Traci Lynn. BS, West Liberty Coll., 1959; MEd., U. Md., 1970. cert. fin. planner, cert. trust specialist. Tchr. Westchester Elem. Sch., Ellicott City, Md., 1956-59, Riverdale (Md.) Elem. Sch., 1959-60, Buckingham Elem. Sch., Willingboro, N.J., 1962-64, Beacon Heights Elem Sch., Riverdale, 1964-68; dir. Christian edn. Forest Lake Presbyn. Ch., Columbia, S.C., 1961-62; supr. student tchrs U. Md., College Park, 1968-69; tchr. Norwood Sch., Bethesda, Md., 1975-77; with Ferris and Co. Inc., Bethesda, 1978-88, v.p., 1984-86, sr. v.p., mem. pres.'s coun., chrmn.'s coun., 1986-88, also bd. dirs.; sr. v.p. Legg Mason, Inc., Bethesda, 1988—. Guest lectr. George Washington U., 1982-83; trustee, tchr. Wharton Sch. Security Industry Inst., Phila., 1986-95, tchr., speaker Bus. Inst. for Educators, Bethesda, 1987-95. Author: Teachers Activity Guide for Dental Health Education, 1973. Trustee, bd. dirs. Holton-Arms Sch., Bethesda, 1985-94; trustee Nat. Econ. Edn. Found., Security Industry Assn., continuing edn. com., chair ethics edn. sub-com.; founding bd. dirs., treas. Leadership Montgomery, Montgomery County, Md.; hon. bd. dirs. Found. for Boys and Girls Homes Md.; bd. dirs. Child Care Connection; trustee, governing bd. Coun. on Econ. Edn. Md. Mem. LWV (corp. bd. Montgomery County), Nat. Adv. Coun., Security Industry Assn. (regional coord. econ. edn., Best Dist. award 1992), Internat. Assn. Fin. Planners. Presbyterian. Avocations: snow and water skiing, sailing, reading, rose gardening. Home: 10215 Gainsborough Rd Potomac MD 20854-4039 Office: Legg Mason Wood Walker 6701 Democracy Blvd Ste 100 Bethesda MD 20817-1573

MEAKER, MARIJANE AGNES, author; b. Auburn, N.Y., May 27, 1927; d. Ellis R. and Ida T. M. BA, U. Mo., 1949; PhD (hon.), Southampton Coll., 1996. Author: novels (under own name) Sudden Endings, 1965, Hometown, 1967, Game of Survival, 1969, Don't Rely on Gemini, 1971, Shockproof Sydney Skate, 1972, 2d edit., 1990; (under pseudonym M.E. Kerr), Dinky Hocker Shoots Smack, 1972, Gentlehands, 1978, If I Love You, Am I Trapped Forever, 1973, I'll Love You When You're More Like Me, 1977, Is That You, Miss Blue?, 1975, Love is a Missing Person, 1975, The Son of Someone Famous, 1975, Little Little, 1981 (Soc. Children's Books Writers award 1982), What I Really Think of You, 1982, Me Me Me Me Me: Not a Novel (Best Books for Young Adults ALA), 1983, Him She Loves?, 1984, I Stay Near You (Best Books for Young Adults ALA), 1985, Night Kites, 1986, Fell, 1987, Fell Back, 1989, Fell Down, 1990; (under pseudonym Mary James) Shoebag, 1990, The Shuteyes, 1993, Frankenlouse, 1994, Shoebag Returns, 1996, (M.E. Kerr) Linger, 1993, Deliver Us from Evie, 1994, Hello, I Lied, 1997, Blood on the Forehead, 1998, What Became of Her, 2000, Slap Your Sides, 2001, Highsmith, 2003, (M.E. Kerr) Snakes Don't Miss Their Mothers, 2003. Recipient Notable Children's Book award ALA, 1972, Book of Yr. award Sch. Library Jour., 1972, 77, 78, Christopher award, 1978, Night Kites award ALA, 1986, Margaret A. Edwards award ALA, 1993, Lifetime Achievement award, The Publishing Triangle, 1998, Lifetime Achievement award The Knickerbocker, 1999, Lifetime Achievement award ALAN, 2000. E-mail: mekerr13@aol.com.

MEAKIN, FAITH ANNE, medical library director; b. Phila., Oct. 15, 1943; d. John Blanchard and Dorothy Aileen (Deane) M.; m. Edward J. Frederick, March 23, 2000. Student, Coe Coll., 1961-63; BA, Syracuse U., 1965, MLS, 1966. Intern in med. libr. sci. Biomed. Libr., U. Calif., L.A., 1966-67; head, reference dept. Biomed. Libr., U. Calif. San Diego, La Jolla, 1967-78, head, pub. svcs., 1979-83; mgmt. fellow Biomed. Libr., U. Minn., Mpls., 1978-79; head reference and readers svcs. WHO, Geneva, 1983-88; exec. dir. Southeastern/Atlantic regional med. libr. svcs. U. Md. Health Scis Libr., Balt., 1989—94; dir. Health Sci. Ctr. Librs., U. Fla., 1994—. Cons. Netherlands Leprosy Relief Assn., Amsterdam, 1988, Aga Khan U., Karachi, Pakistan, 1987—. Author. (bibliography) Spec Kit 82 Document Delivery, 1982, contbr. articles to profl. jours. USPHS intern, med. libr., L.A., 1966 67; mem. NLM Woods Hole Med. Informatics Course, Consortum of 1997. Fellow Council on Libr. Resources/Nat. Libr. Med. Health Scis. Libr. Mgmt. Intern Program, 1978-79. Mem.: Acad. of Health Info. Profl. (disting.), Assn. Acad. Health Dir., Consortium of Biomedical Librs. of the South (chair med. sch. librs. section), Libr. Assn., Beta Phi Mu. Avocations: herbalism, sci. fiction and fantasy works written by women. Home: 4015 NW 69th St Gainesville FL 32606-4215 Office: Health Scis Ctr Librs U Fla PO Box 100206 Gainesville FL 32610-0206 E-mail: faith@library.health.ufl.edu., fmeakin@cox.net.

MEAKIN, JOHN DAVID, retired university research executive, educator; b. Nottingham, Eng., Feb. 11, 1934; came to U.S., 1958, naturalized, 1972; s. Claude Edwin and Hilda May (Storer) M.; m. Katharine Sadie Glover, July 21, 1956; children: Robert Nicholas, David Harry, Ian James, William Edwin, Andrew John. BSc in Metallurgy, Leeds (Eng.) U., 1955, PhD, 1957. Vis. assoc. Franklin Inst., Phila., 1958-59; rsch. fellow U. Durham, Eng., 1960-62; sr. rsch. scientist Franklin Inst., 1962-65, prin. scientist, 1965-70, mgr. lab., 1970-74; prof. mech. engring. U. Del., 1974-98, chmn. mech. engring. dept., 1987-93, sr. scientist Inst. Energy Conversion, 1974-98, prof. emeritus, 1999—. Vis. prof. U. Del., 1967, U. Murdoch, 1983, Auckland U., 1997. Contbr. articles to profl. jours. Yorkshire Copper Works (Eng.) Research scholar, 1955; Dept. Sci. and Indsl. Research scholar, 1956-57; Imperial Chem. Industries sr. research fellow, 1961, 62 Mem. IEEE (sr.) Home: 1910 Quaker Village Rd Middlebury VT 05753-9643 Office Phone: 302-831-2421. Business E-Mail: meakin@me.udel.edu. E-mail: meakin@sover.net.

MEAL, LARIE, chemistry educator, researcher, consultant; b. Cin., June 15, 1939; d. George Lawrence Meal and Dorothy Louise (Heileman) Fitzpatrick. BS in Chemistry, U. Cin., 1961, PhD in Chemistry, 1966. Rsch. chemist U.S. Indsl. Chems., Cin., 1966-67; instr. chemistry U. Cin., 1968-69, asst. prof., 1969-75, assoc. prof., 1975-90, prof., 1990—, rschr., 1980—. Cons. in field. Contbr. articles to profl. jours. Mem. AAAS, N.Y. Acad. Scis., Am. Chem. Soc., NOW, Planned Parenthood, Iota Sigma Pi. Democrat. Avocations: gardening, yard work. Home: 2231 Slane Ave Norwood OH 45212-3615 Office: U Cin 2220 Victory Pky Cincinnati OH 45206-2822 Office Phone: 513-556-4364. Business E-Mail: meall@uc.edu.

MEALEY, BRIAN L. periodontist, military officer; b. Houston, Sept. 20, 1959; D.D.S., Univ of Tex. Health Sci. Ctr, 1979—83, M.S., 1987—90. Diplomate Am. Bd. of Periodontology, 1992. Dir. of rsch. Dept. of Periodontics, Wilford Hall Med. Ctr., Lackland AFB, Tex., 1990—94, dir. of resident edn. & tng., 1994—96, chair and grad. program dir., 2000—04; clin. asst. prof. U. Tex. Health Sci. Ctr., San Antonio, 1992—2004; adj. assoc. prof. Baylor Coll. of Dentistry TAMU, Dallas, 2000—; assoc. prof. dept. periodontics U. Tex. Health Sci. Ctr., San Antonio, 2004—. Bd. of trustees Am. Acad. of Periodontology, Chicago, 1999—2002. Author: (textbook) Periodontal Medicine, 2000; co-editor: Priodontal Medicine, 2000; mem. editl. bd. Jour. Periodontology, 2000—; contbr. articles to profl. jours.; author, co-editor: Periodontics: Medicine, Surgery, and Implants, 2004. Col. USAF, 1983—2004, Lackland AFB, Tex. Decorated Legion of Merit Meritorious Svc. medal (Two Oak Leaf Clusters) USAF, USAF Commendation medal; recipient USAF Jr. Dental Officer of the Yr., 1993, Balint Orban Meml. Rsch. award, Am. Acad. of Periodontology, 1989, R. Earl Robinson Periodontal Regeneration award, 1998. Mem.: ADA, SW Soc. of Periodontists, Air Force Assn., Am. Acad. of Periodontology (bd. of trustees 1999—2002), Omicron Kappa Upsilon. Roman Catholic. Avocations: children's activities, reading. Office: Univ Tex Health Sci Ctr Dept Periodontics 7703 Floyd Curl Dr San Antonio TX 78229

MEALEY, GRACE ELEANOR, music educator; b. Allentown, Pa., Feb. 10, 1927; d. William Jacob Mealey and Ruth May (Knittle) mealey. Attended, Homer Nearing Sch. of Music, 1946—50; studies under, Wilbur Hollman, Cedar Crest Coll., 1950—54, Dr. Ludwig Lenel, Muhlenberg Coll., 1954—58. Pvt. piano, organ tchr., Allentown, Pa., 1948—2004; organist, choir dir. Bethany Evang. Congl. Ch., Allentown, 1948—63; min. of music Emmanuel Evang. Congl. Ch., Bethlehem, Pa., 1963—97; organist, choir dir. Blvd. Evang. Congl. Ch., Allentown, 1997—2002, St. Matthew's Evang. Congl. Ch., Emmaus, Pa., 2002—. Mem.: Am. Guild of Organists, Nat. Guild of Piano Tchrs., Music Tchrs. Nat. Assn., Pa. Music Tchrs. Assn. Home and Office: 1015 N Arch St Allentown PA 18104

MEALIE, CARL A. physician, educator; b. Astoria, N.Y., Jan. 26, 1948; s. Patrick and Natalie (Previti) M.; m. Maureen Frances Maybury, Apr. 24, 1993; children: David, Ian, Daniel. BA, NYU, 1969; MD, N.Y. Med. Coll., 1974. CCRN. Chmn. Dept. Emergency Medicine St. Mary's Hosp., Roswell, N.Mex., 1975-83; emergency dept. attending physician Guadalupe Med. Ctr., Carlsbad, N.Mex., 1979-83, L.I. Jewish Med. Ctr., New Hyde Park, N.Y., 1993—, chmn. disaster preparation com., 1991—, asst. chief emergency dept., 1989-95, chief clin. ops., 1995; asst. prof. emergency medicine Albert Einstein Coll. Medicine, N.Y.C., 1995. Mem. ambulance adv. bd. Chavez County Med. Soc., Roswell, 1980-83, ambulance bd., 1981-87. Mem. City Roswell EMS Bd., 1981-93. Fellow Am. Coll. Emergency Physicians (key contact 1987—), N.Y. Acad. Medicine; me,. AMA, Am. Acad. Emergency Medicine, N.Y. State Med. Soc., Soc. Acad. Emergency Medicine. Roman Catholic. Avocations: skiing, sailing, hunting, golf. Home: 33 Heights Rd Northport NY 11768-2629 Office: LI Jewish Med Ctr Lakeville New Hyde Park NY 11040 E-mail: carl_mealie@msn.com.

MEALMAN, GLENN, corporate marketing executive; b. Prescott, Kans., June 10, 1934; s. Edgar R. and Mary E. (Holstein) M.; m. Gloria Gail Proch, June 12, 1955; children: Michael Edward, Cathy Gail. BS in Bus., Kans. State Coll., Emporia, 1957; postgrad., Harvard U., 1970. With Fleming Co., Topeka, 1957—, sr. v.p. mktg., 1981-82, exec. v.p. mktg., 1982-86, exec. v.p. Mid-Am. region, 1986-93, exec. v.p. nat. accts., 1994-96; mng. ptnr. Bus. Solutions Assocs. Dir. PBI-Gordon Co., Furrs Supermarkets. Pres. bd. Topeka YMCA, 1981; trustee Ottawa U., Kans., 1980. Served with USNR, 1954-56. Mem. Kans. State C. of C. and Industry (bd. dirs. 1991—), Blue Hills Country Club, Gainey Ranch Country Club, Rotary, Sigma Phi Epsilon (Kans. chpt.). Presbyterian. Office: PO Box 7448 Shawnee Mission KS 66207-0448

MEALS, PAMELA F. publishing executive; b. Ill. 1 child, Laura. Student, We. Oreg. State Coll. With advtsg. The Oreg. Statesman and Capital Jour., Salem; advtsg. mgr. The Idaho Statesman, Boise, 1979, pres., publ., 1994-99;

publ. Coffeyville (Kans.) Jour., 1979-82, The Palladium-Item, Richmond, Ind., 1982-85, The Olympian, Olympia, Wash., 1985-94, Bellingham Herald, Bellingham, Wash., 1999—. Bd. dirs. Boise Pub. Schs. Edn. Found., Idaho Shakespeare Festival, Albertson Coll. Annual Fund, FUNDSY, William Allen White Found. Mem. Boise Area C. of C. (bd. dirs.), Rotary Club, Idaho Bus. Coun., Pacific N.W. Newspaper Assn. (bd. dirs.), Newspaper Assn. Am. Office: The Bellingham Herald 1155 N State St Ste 1 Bellingham WA 98225-5086

MEAMBER, LAURIE ANN, marketing educator; b. Sacramento, Calif., Aug. 20, 1966; d. Ernest and Holly Meamber. BA, U. Calif., Davis, 1988; MBA, U. Calif., Riverside, 1991; PhD in Mgmt., U. Calif., Irvine, 1997. Mktg. educator George Mason U., Fairfax, Va. Contbr. chapters to books Ethnoconsumerist Methodology for Cultural and Cross-Cultural Research, Art as Life - Life as Art: The Embeddedness of Art in Life and Life in Art in Postmodernity, Cyberspace as the Next Marketing Frontier (?) - Questions and Issues. Fellow Regent's fellow, U. Calif., Irvine, 1991—95, Grad. Sch. Mgmt., U. Calif., Irvine, 1995—96, U. Calif., 1997; Rsch. grant, Sch. Mgmt., George Mason U., 1999—2001, 2003. Mem.: Aesthetics Acad. Network, Assn. Consumer Rsch. (conf. program com. 2000—00), Am. Mktg. Assn. (collegiate chpt. advisor 1999—2004), Beta Gamma Sigma. Avocation: performing arts. Office: George Mason Univ 4400 University Dr Fairfax VA 22030-4444

MEANS, ANTHONY ROSS, pharmacology educator; PhD, U. Tex., 1967. Nanaline H. Duke prof., chmn. pharmacology & cancer biology Duke U. Med. Ctr., Durham, N.C. Contbr. articles to profl. publs. Mem. Endocrine Soc. (Fred Conrad Koch award 1998). Office: Duke U Med Ctr PO Box 3813 Durham NC 27710-0001 E-mail: means001@mc.duke.edu.

MEANS, DAVID HAMMOND, retired advertising executive; b. Lebanon, Pa., Dec. 15, 1928; s. W. Horace and June (Zimmerman) M.; m. Nancy N. Downes, June 21, 1952; children: Elizabeth N., Susan Z., Emily M., David H. BA, Amherst Coll., 1950. With CIA, 1950-53, N.W. Ayer Inc., 1953-89, exec. v.p., 1976-89; ret., also bd. dirs. Mng. dir. Ayer U.S.A. and Ayer Enterprises, Inc. Bd. dirs. Waveny Care Ctr., New Canaan Nature Ctr., Schoolhouse Apts., Get About Inc. 1st lt. USAF, 1953. Mem. Bus. Profl. Advt. Assn., Merion (Pa.) Golf Club, Amherst Club (N.Y.C.), Country Club New Canaan (Conn.), Gridiron Club (New Canaan), Sr. Men's Club (New Canaan, bd. dirs.), Psi Upsilon. Episcopalian. Home: Wahackme Ln New Canaan CT 06840 E-mail: davenan28@aol.com.

MEANS, JAMES ANDREW, engineer; b. Heavener, Okla., Oct. 11, 1937; s. Edward Andrew and Lorena (Nobles) M.; Therese Louise Zimmermann, Feb. 21, 1959; children: James A. Jr., William R., Charles E., Vicky M. Locken. BSEE, U. Ariz., 1962, MSEE, 1966; PhD, U. Calif., Santa Barbara, 1972; MS in Computer Sci., Chapman U., Orange, Calif., 1988. Engr. Pacific Missile Test Ctr., Pt Mugu, Calif., 1962-72, engr. mgr., 1972-79; tech. dir. Space and Missile Test Orgn., Vandenberg AFB, Calif., 1979-89; sr. tech. advisor SRI Internat., Menlo Park, Calif., 1990—. Cons. Agri-Craft, Camarillo, Calif., 1968-70, Astro-Geo-Marine, Ventura, Calif., 1972-74. Patentee in field. Mem. Internat. Found. for Telemetering (pres. 1989-95), Internat. Test and Evaluation Assn. (Allen R. Mattews Award, 1991). Democrat. Baptist. Avocations: water-skiing, fishing, hunting, old cars. Home and Office: 284 St Andrews Way Lompoc CA 93436-1355 E-mail: jim.means@sri.com.

MEANS, JOHN BARKLEY, foreign language educator, association executive; b. Cin., Jan. 2, 1939; s. Walker Wilson and Rosetta Miller (Barkley) Means. BA, U. Ill., 1960, MA, 1963, PhD, 1968. U.S. govt. intelligence rsch. analyst on Brazil CIA, Washington, 1962-64; assoc. prof. Spanish and Portugese Temple U., Phila., 1972-82, prof. Portuguese and critical langs., 1982—2003, prof. emeritus, 2003—, co-chmn. dept. Spanish and Portuguese, 1971-75, dir. Center for Critical Langs., 1975—2003, dir. Inst. for Langs. and Internat. Studies, 1987—2003, chmn. dept. Germanic and Slavic Langs. and lit., 1992-94, chair univ. core programs, 1995-97. Cons. on Brazilian-Portuguese and second lang. acquisition and self instrnl. programs for less commonly taught langs., 1968—2003; cons. editor for langs. Norton Pubs., 1979—95; cons. in field. Editor: Essays on Brazilian Literature, 1971; author (with others): Language in Education: Theory and Practice, 1988—; co-dir. CD-ROM Critical Language Series, 1999—; contbr. articles to profl. jours. Trustee Bristol Riverside Theatre, Pa., 1990—2002; mng. trustee Means Charitable Trust, 1993—. 1st lt. U.S. Army, 1960—62. Fellow, U. Ill., 1967; grantee, U.S. Dept. Edn., 1979—83, Japan Found., 1980, 1982, 1989—91, ARCO Chem. Found., 1991, 1993; NDEA fellow, 1962, 1964. Mem.: MLA, Joint Nat. Com. for Langs. (bd. dirs.), Nat. Assn. State Univs. and Lang Grant Colls. (commn. on internat. affairs), Nat. Coun. Orgns. Less Commonly Taught Langs. (exec. sec.-treas. 1990—2001), Am. Coun. on Tchg. Fgn. Lang., Nat. Assn. Self-Instrnl. Lang. Programs (exec. dir. 1977—98, editor jour. 1978—94, exec. dir. emeritus 1999—), Nat. Coun. on Langs. and Internat. Studies (bd. dirs.), Sigma Delta Pi, Phi Lambda Beta, Pi Kappa Phi. Home: PO Box 829 Washington Crossing PA 18977-0829 Office: Temple U Ctr for Critical Langs Anderson Hall 1114 W Berks St Philadelphia PA 19122-6090 E-mail: means@temple.edu.

MEANS, MARIANNE, political columnist; b. Sioux City, Iowa, June 13, 1934; d. Ernest Maynard and Else Marie Johanne (Andersen) Hansen; m. Warren Weaver, Jr. (dec.); m. James J. Kilpatrick. BA, U. Nebr., 1956; JD, George Washington U., 1977. Copy editor Lincoln (Nebr.) Jour., 1955-57; woman's editor No. Va. Sun, Arlington, 1957-59; Washington bur. corr. Hearst Newspapers, 1959-61, White House corr., 1961-65; polit. columnist Hearst Newspapers and King Features Syndicate, 1965—, N.Y. Times News Svc., 1994—; commentator Spectrum CBS radio, Mut. Broadcasting Network, Voice of Am., U.S.I.A. World Network, Post Newsweek Stas., Nat. Pub. Radio. Author: The Woman in the White House, 1963. Recipient Front Page award N.Y. Newspaper Women, 1962; Tex. Headliners award, 1976, Hall of Fame-Sigma Delta Chi, 1988. Mem.: Internat. Women's Media Found. (bd. dirs.), Nat. Press Found. (chmn.), White House Corrs. Assn., Nat. Press Club, Cosmos Club, Gridiron Club (pres.), Sigma Delta Chi (Hall of Fame), Phi Beta Kappa, Delta Delta Delta. Home: The Westbridge #902 2555 Pennsylvania Ave NW Washington DC 20037-1613 Office: 1850 K St NW Washington DC 20006

MEANS, MICHAEL DAVID, hospital administrator; b. Lakeland, Fla., Jan. 19, 1950; married. B, U. Fla., 1971, MHA, 1974. Adminstrv. resident Manatee Meml. Hosp., Bradenton, Fla., 1974, adminstrv. asst., 1974-78; asst. dir. Orlando (Fla.) Regional Med. Ctr., 1978-80, assoc. exec. dir., 1980-81, exec. v.p., chief oper. officer, 1981-88; pres., chief exec. officer Holmes Regional Healthcare System, Melbourne, Fla., 1988—, Health First, Melbourne, Fla. Mem. Fla. Hosp. Assn. Office: Health First 6450 US Highway 1 Rockledge FL 32955-5747

MEANS, NATRONE JERMAINE, professional football player; b. Apr. 26, 1972; Student, U. N.C. Running back San Diego Chargers, 1991-96, 98—, Jacksonville Jaguars, 1996-97, San Diego Chargers, 1998-99, Carolina Panthers, 2000—. Selected to Pro Bowl, 1994. Achievements include being a mem. San Diego Chargers AFC Champions, 1994. Office: Carolina Panthers Ericsson Stadium 800 S Mint St Ste 2 Charlotte NC 28202-1502

MEANS, ROBERT TAYLOR, JR., hematologist, educator; b. Midland, Tex., July 14, 1957; s. Robert Taylor and Anna Therese (Cassidy) M.; m. Stacey W. McKenzie, May 23, 1992; children: Anna, Robert III, Patrick. BA in Biochemistry, Rice U., 1979; MD, Vanderbilt U., 1983. Diplomate Am. Bd. Internal Medicine; cert. in hematology. Resident Baylor Coll. Medicine, Houston, 1983-86; fellow in hematology Vanderbilt U., Nashville, 1986-88, instr. medicine, 1988-90, asst. prof. medicine, 1990-92; assoc. investigator VA Med. Ctr., Nashville, 1988-91, asst. chief hematology/oncology Cin., 1992-98; assoc. prof. med. U. Cin., 1992-98; prof. med., head hematology, assoc. divsn. chief Med. U. S.C., 1998-2000, dir. divsn. hematology-oncology, 2000—04; chief hematology/oncology VA Med. Ctr., Charleston, SC, 1998—2004; prof. internal medicine Va. Med. Ctr., 2004—; vice chair for rsch., dept. internal medicine U. Ky., 2004—; chief, med. svc. Va. Med. Ctr., Lexington, Ky., 2004—. Contbr. chpts. to books, articles to profl. jours. Recipient Career Devel. award Dept. Veterans Affairs., 1988, Henry Christian award Am. Fedn. Clin. Rsch., 1991. Mem. Am. Soc. Hematology, Internat. Soc. Exptl. Hematology, Phi Beta Kappa. Achievements include being first to report response of anemia of chronic disease to erythropoietin; first description of erythropoietin receptor in polycythemia. Home: 2204 Abbeywood Rd Lexington KY 40515 Office Phone: 859-281-4919. E-mail: robert.means2@med.va.gov.

MEANS, ROSALINE, business executive, business educator; b. Manila; came to U.S., 1952; d. Cheng Peng and Lu Chong (Siy) Limtiuco; m. Cyril Chestnut Means, Jr., Nov. 8, 1958 (dec. Oct., 1992); children: Elizabeth Rose Thayer Means, Annette Thayer Means, Cyril III. AA in Pre-law, U. Santo Tomas, Manila, The Philippines, 1949; BS in Comm. Edn., U. East, Manila, 1951; MA in Edn., U. Iowa, 1953; postgrad., CUNY, 1956-58. Tchr. Chinese Rep. Sch., Manila, 1947-52; corp. dir. and officer various cos. and corps., 1950-70; edn. specialist U. Hosp. Sch., Iowa City, 1952-53; lectr. SUNY Urban Ctr., Bklyn., 1967-73; adj. lectr. cmty. coll. CUNY, 1969-72, various positions, 1973-84; adj. prof. L.I. U., Bklyn., 1978; lectr. Ednl. Opportunity Ctr., Bklyn., 1973-95. Author: First Steps in Conversation, 1954; stage performances include Two for the Seesaw, The Defender, Stage Door. Mem. Legis Adv. Com. N.Y. State Senate, 11th. Dist., 1990; treas. PSC/CUNY. Recipient Cmty. Leaders and Noteworthy Ams. award, 1975-76, formal recognition Bus. and Profl. Women of Cape Ann, 1996; named Goddess of Arts-Beauty Queen, 1954, Miss Fashion Model of Yr., 1954; finalist Mrs. N.Y. Am. Beauty Pageant, 1990. Mem. Liedenkranz of City of N.Y. (music libr. and treas.). Avocations: classical music, fishing, boating. Home: 13 Salt Island Rd Gloucester MA 01930-1972

MEANS, TERRY ROBERT, federal judge; b. Roswell, N.Mex., July 3, 1948; s. Lewis Prude and Doris Emaree (Hightower) M.; m. JoAnn Huffman Harris, June 2, 1973; children: Robert, MaryAnn, Emily. BA, So. Meth. U., 1971, JD, 1974. Bar: Tex. 1974, U.S. Dist. Ct. (no. dist.) Tex. 1976, U.S. Ct. Appeals (5th cir.) 1978, U.S. Dist. Ct. (we. dist., ea. dist.) Tex. 1991. Ptnr. Means & Means, Corsicana, Tex., 1974-88; Presdl. elector, 1980; justice 10th Ct. Appeals, Waco, Tex., 1989-90; judge U.S. Dist. Ct. (no. dist.) Tex., Ft. Worth, 1991—. Chmn. Navarro County Rep. Party, Corsicana, 1976-88; pres. YMCA, Corsicana, 1984, Ft. Worth Youth Soccer Assn., 1996-97. Mem. State Bar Tex., Tarrant County Bar Assn., McLennan County Bar Assn. Baptist. Avocations: coaching soccer, racquetball. Office: 201 US Courthouse 501 W 10th St Fort Worth TX 76102-3637

MEANS, THOMAS CORNELL, lawyer; b. Charleston, S.C., Oct. 3, 1947; s. Thomas Lucas and Dean (Cornell) M.; m. Judith Faye Perlmutter, Sept. 10, 1977; children: Benjamin, Samuel. AB, Dartmouth Coll., 1969; postgrad., Princeton Theol. Sem., 1970-71; M of Pub. Adminstrn., U. Colo., 1975; JD, George Washington U., 1978. Bar: D.C. 1978, U.S. dist. Ct. (D.C. dist.), U.S. Ct. Appeals (4th and D.C. cirs.) 1979, U.S. Ct. Appeals (10th cir.) 1983, U.S. Ct. Appeals (6th and 11th cirs.) 1989, U.S. Ct. Appeals (9th cir.) 1992, U.S. Ct. Appeals (8th cir.) 1993, U.S. Ct. Appeals (5th cir.) 1996. Social worker Vinyard Childcare, Ann Arbor, Mich., 1969-70; rsch. analyst, registered lobbyist Colo. Counties, Inc., Denver, 1972-75; assoc. Jones, Day, Reavis and Pogue, Washington, 1978-79; assoc. then ptnr. Crowell & Moring LLP, Washington, 1979—. Mem. state adv. coun. on pub. Pers. Mgmt., Colo. State Govt., Denver, 1974-75; lectr. mining law; chmn. coal com. Energy and Mineral Law Found., 1988-89, chmn. spl. insts., ass. sec., 1989-91, sec., 1991-92, v.p., 1992-93, pres., 1993-94, exec. com., 1989-96, trustee, 1989—, mem. bd. editors, 1994—; bd. advisors Nat. Law Ctr., 1993-94, adv. bd. W. Va. Law Review on Nat. Coal Issues, 2001—. Contbr. articles to profl. jours. Recipient Pres.' award, Energy and Mineral Law Found., 2002. Mem. George Washington Law Alumni Assn. (bd. dirs. 1986-96, exec. com. 1987-96, treas. 1987-88, sec. 1988-90, pres. 1992-94), Order of Coif, Cosmos Club (Washington), Phi Beta Kappa. Home: 6411 Dahlonega Rd Bethesda MD 20816-2101 Office: Crowell & Moring LLP 1001 Pennsylvania Ave NW Fl 10 Washington DC 20004-2595 Office Phone: 202-624-2735.

MEANS, TINA, police officer, consultant; b. L.A., June 9, 1961; d. Melvin Julian and Theresa Alberta Means; m. Marvin Alton Hatchett, July 7, 1995; children: Ciyani, Taliya, Naleya. AA in Liberal Arts, Santa Monica Coll., 1982; BSBA, Calif. State U.-Dominguez Hill, Carson, 1984; MPA, City U., Bellevue, Wash., 1996; postgrad., Capella U. Basic, intermediate and advance certs., Calif. Commn. on Peace Officers and Tng.; cert. cons. Police officer trainee, police officer City of Pasadena, Calif., 1990-91; police officer sch. police dept. Pasadena Unified Sch. Dist., 1991—. Cons. Pasadena Prep. Sch., 1999—, Internat. Outreach Ministry, Inc., Pasadena, 1999—. Bd. dirs. Pasadena Family Ctr. Mem. ASPA, ASTD, Justice Rsch. and Stats. Assn. Avocations: reading, cooking, singing, planning training seminars. Office: Pasadena Unified Sch Dist Sch Police Dept 351 S Hudson Ave Pasadena CA 91101-3599 Home: 1291 N Vallejo Way Upland CA 91786-3052 E-mail: tlm.fifthdegree@verizon.net.

MEANS COLEMAN, ROBIN RENEE, communications educator; b. Pitts., Feb. 26, 1969; d. Marcel Theodore Sr. and Patricia (Lloyd) M.; m. Randy Tyrone Coleman, July 28, 1996. BA in Comm., Chatham Coll., 1991; MA in Comm., U. Mo., Columbia, 1993; PhD in Mass Comm., Bowling Green State U., 1996; postgrad., U. Pitts., 1996-98. Adminstrv. asst. Bethesda Adult Literacy Program, Pitts., 1990; tchg. fellow U. Mo., 1991-93; tchg.-adminstrv. fellow Bowling Green State U., 1993-96; rsch. assoc. U. Pitts., 1996-98; asst. prof. media ecology NYU, 1998—. Project cons. Ctr. Family Excellence, Pitts., 1996—. Author: African American Viewers and the Black Situation Comedy: Situating Racial Humor, 1998; contbr. profl. articles to The Bulletin, 1996. Ballot counter Boone County, Columbia, 1992; vol. voter registration Urban League, Pitts., 1988. Postdoctoral fellow U. Pitts., 1996. Mem. Internat. Comm. Assn., Speech Comm. Assn. Democrat. Baptist. Avocations: cinema, African-Am. literature, travel, 5K walk races, concerts. Office: NYU Dept Culture and Comm 239 Greene St # 735 New York NY 10003-6674 Home: 10 Allegheny Ctr Apt 105 Pittsburgh PA 15212-5222

MEANS-WILLIS, EMILY W. secondary school educator, writer; b. Paducah, Ky. d. Emory L. and Catherine M. Means; children: Carl, Derrick, Pamela. BS, Tenn. State U., 1961; MA, Gov. State U., 1974, post grad work, 1975—95. Instr. Sch. Dist. 206, Chgo. Heights, Ill., 1967—99; editing/bus. mgr. 3 B Inc., Olympia Fields, Ill., 2001—03; owner We, Us and Co., Internat. Pub. Co., Olympia Fields, 2003—. Lit. reviewer readincolor.com, anutwestaflavah.com. Author: (book) Looking for that Silver Spoon, 2003. Named in her honor is the Trail African Am. Soc. Collegiate scholarship. Mem.: Alpha Kappa Alpha. Avocations: travel, reading, bowling. Office: We Us And Co Internat P O Box 201 Olympia Fields IL 60461-0201 Office Phone: 708-769-4116.

MEANY, PHILIP AUGUSTUS, library director; b. Oakland, Calif., Oct. 20, 1938; s. John Philip and Mary Gertrude (Deasy) M. BA, St. Mary's Coll., Moraga, Calif., 1960; M Librarianship, U. Wash., 1963. Asst. libr. Centralia (Wash.) Coll., 1963-68, media svcs. and tech. processes libr., 1969-88, libr. dir., 1988—. Mem. Wash. State Bicycling Adv. Com., Olympia, 1990-99; pres. Destination Centralia Mktg. Assn., 1999-2001. Recipient Platinum Pedal, N.W. Bicycle Fedn., 1997. Mem. Coll. Librs. and Media Specialists Wash. State (pres. 1987-88), N.W. Mgmt. Ednl. Tech. Assn. Avocation: bicycling. Office: Centralia Coll Libr 600 W Locust St Centralia WA 98531

MEAR, CHARLES EUGENE, geologist, consultant; b. Dec. 2, 1926; s. Charles Russell Mear and Alice Inez Porche; m. Tonie Margaret Kubesch, Sept. 1, 1951; children: Diane, Charles E. Jr., David R., John P., Mark E., Kathryn, Caroline, Steven. BA in Geology, U. Tex., 1951, MA in Geology, 1953. Cert. petroleum geologist, profl. geoscientist geology Tex., 2003. Petroleum exploration geologist numerous oil cos., Midland, Tex., 1952—67; geologist hard minerals La. Land Exploration Co., Midland, 1967—76, Denver, 1967—76; dist. geologist mgr. Southland Royalty Co., Midland, 1976—82, v.p. geology and geophysics Ft. Worth, 1982—86; v.p. exploration Cross Timbers Oil Co., Ft. Worth, 1986—93; rsch. fellow Tex. Archeol. Lab., Austin, Tex., 1993—96; cons. geologist Austin, 1996—2003. Editor: Petroleum Geology of Mississippian Carbonates in North Central Texas, 1989; contbr. articles to profl. jours. Paratrooper 11th airborne divsn. Pacific Theater U.S. Army. Recipient Monroe G. Cheney Sci. award, W. Tex. Geol. Soc., 1991. Mem.: Soc. Sedimentary Geology (hon. life. mem. Permian Basin sect.), Am. Assn. Petroleum Geologists (sec. DPA 1997—99). Home: 7912 Taranto Dr Austin TX 78729-7441

MEARA, ANNE, actress, playwright, writer; b. Bklyn., Sept. 20; d. Edward Joseph and Mary (Dempsey) M.; m. Gerald Stiller, Sept. 14, 1954; children: Amy, Benjamin. Student, Herbert Berghoff Studio, 1953-54. Apprentice in summer stock, Southold, L.I. and Woodstock, N.Y., 1950-53; off-Broadway appearances include A Month in the Country, 1954, Maedchen in Uniform, 1955 (Show Bus. off-Broadway award), Ulysses in Nightown, 1958, The House of Blue Leaves, 1970, Bosoms and Neglect, 1986, After-Play, 1996; Shakespeare Co., Two Gentlemen of Verona, Ctrl. Park, N.Y.C., 1957, Romeo and Juliet, 1988; Broadway plays: Spookhouse, 1982, Eastern Standard, 1989, Anna Christie, 1993 (Tony nomination Best Supporting Actress); film appearances include The Out-of-Towners, 1968, Lovers and Other Strangers, 1969, The Boys From Brazil, 1978, Fame, 1979, Nasty Habits (with husband Jerry Stiller), 1976, An Open Window, 1990, Mia, 1990, Awakenings, 1991, Reality Bites, 1994, Daytrippers, 1997, The Fish in the Bathtub, 1998, Southie, 1999, The Independent, 2001, Like Mike, 2002, comedy act, 1963—; appearances Happy Medium and Medium Rare, Chgo., 1960-61, Village Gate, Phase Two and Blue Angel, N.Y.C., 1963, The Establishment, London, 1963, QE II, 1990; syndicated TV series Take Five with Stiller and Meara, 1977-78; numerous appearances on TV game and talk shows, also spls. and variety shows; rec. numerous commls. for TV and radio (co-recipient Voice of Imagery award Advt. Bur. N.Y.); star TV series Kate McShane, 1975, Archie Bunker's Place, 1979, Alf, 1986-88; other TV appearances The Sunset Gang, 1990, Avenue Z Afternoon, 1991, Murphy Brown, 1994, Homicide, 1996 (Emmy nomination), Will and Grace, 2002, Sex in the City, 2002-04, The King of Queens, 2003-04, Good Morning Miami, 2003; (TV movie) Jitters, 1997, All My Children, 1994-99, (TV movie) What Makes a Family, 2001; writer, actress TV movie The Other Woman, 1983 (co-recipient Writer's Guild Outstanding Achievement award 1983), Alf, To Make Up to Break Up, The Stiller and Meara pilot; author, actor (play) After-Play, 1996; author (play) Down the Garden Paths, 2000; video host (with Jerry Stiller) So You Want to Be an Actor? Recipient Outer Critic's Cir. Playwriting award for After-Play, 1995, 4th ann. Alan King award in Jewish Humor, 2003, Productive Aging award Jewish Coun. Aging, 2004.

MEARA, JAMES F. oil industry executive; b. Fairlawn, NJ; B in Acctg., U. Ky., 1980; MBA, Bowling Green State U., 1987. Mgr. tax audit systems and planning Marathon Oil Corp., Houston, 1988—95, tax mgr., 1997—2000, contr., 2000—02; comml. dir. Sakhalin Energy, Moscow, 1995—97; v.p. tax Marathon Oil Corp., 2002—. Mem.: Am. Inst. CPAs. Office: Marathon Oil Corp Corp Headquarters 5555 San Felipe Rd Houston TX 77056-2723

MEARDY, WILLIAM HERMAN, retired educational association administrator; b. Peoria, Ill., Feb. 28, 1925; s. Herman and Madeleine (McReynolds) Meardy; m. Joyce Dorothy Horn, Mar. 28, 1946; children: William Wesley, Karen Lynn. Student, Bradley U., 1948—51; BA, Calif. State U., LA, 1952, MA, 1958; postgrad., UCLA, 1964. Tchr. La Puente (Calif.) Union HS, 1953-56; acad., personal and job placement counselor Mt. San Antonio Coll., Walnut, Calif., 1956-63; dean student pers. svcs. Rio Hondo Coll., Whittier, Calif., 1963-67; dean student services and activities Shasta Coll., Redding, Calif., 1967-70; exec. sec. Coun. Cmty. Coll. Bds., Evanston, Ill., 1970-72; founding exec. dir. Assn. Cmty. Coll. Trustees, Washington, 1972-88, ret. Contbr. articles to profl. jours. Chmn. West Covina (Calif.) coun. Boy Scouts Am., 1960—61; vol. driver Presbyn. Hosp., Whittier, Calif.; bd. dirs. Nat. Coun. Responsible Pub. Interest Groups. With USN, 1943—46, 1st lt. USAFR, 1952. Mem.: Shriners, Masons. Home and Office: 13675 Sycamore Dr Whittier CA 90601-3848 E-mail: wmeardy2001@yahoo.com. *As I have made my way along life's road, I am often reminded of those who cared enough to help me over the rough spots. They gave me encouragement, support and love during those times I was in most need. My wife, my parents, my children, my teachers and my friends were my support team. From them I drew the strength that made me what I am today. Without them there would have been no bright tomorrow.*

MEARS, FRANCES R. communications media executive; Bur. chief Balt. AP, 1998—. Office: The Associated Press 218 Charles St #330 Baltimore MD 21201-4018

MEARS, PATRICK EDWARD, lawyer; b. Oct. 3, 1951; s. Edward Patrick and Estelle Veronica (Milsk) M.; m. Geraldine O'Connor, July 18, 1981. BA, U. Mich., 1973, JD, 1976. Bar: N.Y. 1977, Ill. 1996, Ind. 1997, U.S. Dist Ct. (so. and ea. dists) N.Y. 1977, Mich. 1980, U.S. Dist. Ct. (we. and ea. dists.) Mich. 1980, U.S. Ct. Appeals (6th cir.) 1983, Ill. 1996, Ind. 1997, U.S. Dist. Ct. (no. dist.) Ill. 1998. Assoc. Milbank, Tweed, Hadley & McCloy, N.Y.C., 1976-79; ptnr. Warner, Norcross & Judd, Grand Rapids, Mich., 1980-91; sr. mem. Dykema Gossett PLLC, Grand Rapids, 1991—2002; equity mem. Dickinson Wright, PLLC, Grand Rapids, 2002—04; equity ptnr. Baines and Thornburgh, LLP, 2004—. Adj. prof. Grand Valley State U., Allendale, Mich., 1981-84; dir. Children's Law Ctr., 1994, Grand Rapids Ballet, 1994-99, East Grand Rapids Pub. Sch. Found., 1994-98. Author: Michigan Collection Law, 1981, 2d edit., 1983, Basic Bankruptcy Law, 1986, Bankruptcy Law and Practice in Michigan, 1987, 1995, Revised Article 9 of the UCC in Michigan, 2001; co-author: Strategies for Secured Creditors in workouts and Foreclosures, 2004; contbg. author Collier Bankruptcy Practice Guide; contbr. articles to profl. jours.; editor: Jour. of the Hist. Soc. of the U.S. Dist. Ct. for the Western Dist. of Mich., 2003—. Chmn. legis. com. East Grand Rapids PTA, 1992—94; bd. dirs., sec. Grand Rapids Sister Cities Internat., 2004—. Fellow: Mich. State Bar Found. (sec. coun. real property sect. 1993—97, chair Uniform Comml. Code com. bus. law sect. 2000—), Am. Coll. Bankruptcy; mem.: ABA (chmn. workouts, bankruptcy and foreclosures 2002—04, vice chair real estate financing group 2004—), Fed. Bar Assn. (chmn. bankruptcy sect. We. Mich. chpt. 1992—94, newsletter editor 1998—2002, pres. 2001—02), Am. Law Inst., Am. Bankruptcy Inst., Mich. State Bar Assn., East Hills Athletic Club. Office: Barnes & Thrnburg LLP 99 Monroe Ave NW Ste 601 Grand Rapids MI 49503 Office Phone: 616-742-2926. E-mail: pmears@btlaw.com.

MEARS, WALTER ROBERT, journalist; b. Lynn, Mass., Jan. 11, 1935; s. Edward Lewis and Edythe Emily (Campbell) M.; m. Sally Danton, Dec. 28, 1956 (dec. Dec. 1962); children: Pamela (dec.), Walter Robert Jr. (dec.); m. Joyce Marie Lund, Aug. 4, 1963 (div. 1983); children: Stephanie Joy, Susan Marie; m. Carroll Ann Rambo, Mar. 1, 1986 (div. 1995); m. Frances R. Richarson, July 5, 1997. BA, Middlebury Coll., 1956, LittD (hon.), 1977. Newsman AP, Boston, 1956, corr. Montpelier, Vt., 1956-60, state house corr. Boston, 1960-61, newsman Washington, 1961-69, chief polit. writer, 1969-72, asst. chief Washington bur., 1973-74, spl. corr., 1975, chief, 1977-83, v.p., 1978-2001, exec. editor, 1984-88, v.p., columnist, 1989-2001. Author: (with John Chancellor) The News Business, 1983, The New News Business, 1995, Deadlines Past, 2003. Trustee Middlebury Coll., 1980-84. Recipient ann. award AP Mng. Editors Assn., 1973; Pulitzer prize for Nat. Reporting, 1977. Mem. Phi Beta Kappa, Delta Kappa Epsilon, Gridiron Club, Burning Tree Club.

MEASELLE, RICHARD LELAND, accountant; b. Detroit, Sept. 29, 1938; s. Leland Stanford and Jean Therese (Saydak) M; children: Jeffrey, Laura, Susana, Millicent, Stephen; m. Alison Price, Dec. 2, 1995. BS in Bus., Miami U., Oxford, Ohio, 1961. Office mng. ptnr. Arthur Andersen, Barcelona, Spain, 1970-72, Detroit, 1975-87, ptnr. acctg. and audit worldwide, 1987-89, worldwide mng. ptnr., 1989—; mng. ptnr. Andersen Worldwide, Mich., Ohio, Ky. and Wis., 1985-87, mng. ptnr. 1997. Mem., bd. ptnrs., mem. exec. com. Arthur Andersen Worldwide Orgn. Co-author: Helping Public Schools Succeed, 1989. Chmn. bd. trustees U. Detroit, 1985; trustee Detroit Econ. Growth Corp., 1975-87; chmn. United Negro Coll. Fund, Detroit, 1982; hon. Spanish consul to Mich.; mem. vis. com. U. Mich. Sch. Bus. Adminstrn., Tax Found.'s Policy Coun, 1990; mem. com. Chgo. Coun. Fgn. Rels., 1991; mem.

Brit. N.Am. Com.; bd. dirs. Field Mus. Natural History. With USMC, 1958-64, Res. Named Hon. Alumnus of Yr. U. Detroit, 1984, Acct. of Yr. Beta Alpha Psi-Miami U., 1989; recipient Pres.'s Cabinet award U. Detroit, 1989. Mem. AICPA, The Econ. Club of N.Y. Avocations: skiing, tennis.

MEAUX, ALAN DOUGLAS, retired facilities technician, sculptor; b. Joliet, Ill., Sept. 10, 1951; s. Berry Lee and Luella Ann (Ferguson) M.; m. Letta Sue Nygaard, Sept. 15, 1984; children: Ashley Nicole, Lacey Marie. Student, Joliet Jr. Coll., 1969-71, Bradley U., 1971-72, U.S. Dept. Agr. Grad. Sch., 1972, Skagit Valley Coll., 1983-85. Cert. specialist water distbn. Wash. state, 2002, Wash. state, 2003. Photographer J.J.C. Blazer, Joliet Herald News, Joliet, 1969-71; auto mechanic Pohanka Olds and Fiat, Hillcrest Heights, Md., 1972-74, Hoffman Olds and Rolls Royce, Hartford, Conn., 1974-75; carpenter Klappenbach Constrn. Co., Moscow, Idaho, 1975-79; property mgr. Olympic Builders, Oak Harbor, Wash., 1979-86; maintenance technician Troubleshooters Inc., Oak Harbor, 1986-87; facilities technician Island County Govt., Coupeville, Wash., 1987—. Chmn. safety com. Island County Govt., 1997, 98, 99, 2000, 03; bronze sculptor Ronin Art Prodns., Oak Harbor, 1979—; appraiser class A Mid-Am. Appraisers Assn., Springfield, Mo., 1986—; bd. dirs. North West Token Kai, U. Wash., Seattle, 1989—, lectr., 1985; contbr. Nanka Token Kai, L.A., 1985-. Author: Japanese Samurai Weapons, 1989; prin. works exhibited at Mini Guild Children's Orthopedic Show, Ballard, Wash., 1986, Worldfest/Ethnic Heritage Coun., Seattle, 1988, 89, 90, Stanwood (Wash.) Invitational Art Show, 1988. Asst. coach Whidbey Islanders Soccer League, 1997-99; safety com. chmn. Island County Govt., 1998-2003. Mem. NRA (life), Law Enforcement Alliance Am. (life), Japanese Sword Soc. U.S. (life), N.W. Token Kai (charter, bd. dirs. 1989-91), Western Mus. Conf., Wash. Mus. Assn., Ethnic Heritage Coun., Nanka Token Kai, Japan Soc., Wash. Arms Collectors Assn., North Whidbey Sportmen's Assn. (chmn. range com., trustee), Leisure Acres Water Assn. (pres. 1998-2000), Internat. Defensive Pistol Assn., Ctrl. Whidbey Sportmen's Club, Whidbey Islanders Futbol Club (asst. coach for girls under 12, 1997-99). Avocations: hunting, fishing, woodworking, reading, collecting japanese antiques. Office: Ronin Art Prodns 1287 E Hideaway Ln Oak Harbor WA 98277

MEBANE, BARBARA MARGOT, artistic director, choreographer; b. Sylacauga, Ala., July 21, 1947; d. Audrey Dixon and Mary Ellen (Yaikow) Baxley; m. James Lewis Mebane, Dec. 31, 1971; 1 child, Cieson Brooke. Grad., Brookhaven Coll., Dallas. Line performer J. Taylor Dance Co., Miami, Fla., 1964-65; sales mgr. Dixie Readers Svc., Jackson, Miss., 1965-67; regional sales mgr. Robertson Products Co., Texarkana, Tex., 1967-75; owner, pres. Telco Sales, Svc. and Supply, Dallas, 1976-90; dir. The Dance Factory performing co., Lewisville, Tex.; owner, artistic dir. Dancers Workshop Studios, Inc., Lewisville. Mgr., choreographer music videos for pay/cable TV, 1985—; prodr. theatrical/musical shows to profl. theatre, coll. dists. and high schs; pub. spkr. in field of positive thinking for women. Author: Paper on Positive Thinking, 1983. Sponsor Cancer Rsch. Ctr., Dallas, Flower Mound Bus. Womens Group; hon. chmn. Rep. State Com., Tex.; founder arts devel. and outreach Dancers Workshop Studies Inc. for underpriveledged children. Named Bus. Woman of the Yr., Gov. Anne Richards, Tex., 1994. Mem. Nat. Fedn. Ind. Businesses, Internat. Register of Profiles Cambridge, Eng., Female and Minority Owned Bus. League, PDTA (Dallas Dance Coun.), Old Town Bus. Assn. (Pres.'s adv. com. 2003-04). Avocations: working with children, teaching dance, writing. Office: Dancers Workshop 705 S Mill Lewisville TX 75057 Office Phone: 972-420-1314.

MEBANE, DAVID CUMMINS, lawyer; b. Toledo, Dec. 18, 1933; s. Donald Cummins and Frances (Malm) M.; children: Margery, Suezanne. BBA, Ariz. State U., 1957; LLD, U. Wis., 1960. Bar: Wis. 1960. Atty., trust officer First Wis. Nat. Bank, Oshkosh, 1963-67; assoc. Hayes Law Offices, Ripon, Wis., 1967; dep. dist. atty., Madison, 1967-70; asst. atty gen. Wis. Dept. Justice, Madison, 1971-73, dep. atty. gen., 1973-75; U.S. atty. U.S. Dept. Justice, Madison, 1975-77; corp. atty. Madison Gas and Electric Co., 1977-79, gen. counsel, 1979-85, v.p., 1985-87, sr. v.p., gen. counsel, dir., 1987-91, pres. and COO, 1993, pres., COO, CEO, 1994, chmn. pres. CEO, 1994—; bd. dirs. Mad. Gas and Electric, 1st Fed. Savs. Bank, Madison, 1st Capital Investment Corp., Madison, 1st Fed. Capital Corp., La Crosse. Mem. Rep. Nat. Com., Washington; chmn. Wis. Racing Commn. Served with JAGC, USAF, 1960-63. Mem. ABA, State Bar Wis., Dane County Bar Assn., Exchange Club (Madison). Home: 1122 Sunridge Dr Madison WI 53711-3365 Office: Madison Gas and Electric Co PO Box 1231 Madison WI 53701-1231

MEBANE, JULIE SHAFFER, lawyer; b. San Antonio, Mar. 13, 1957; d. John Cummins and Mildred (Hill) Mebane; m. Kenneth Jerome Stipanov, Jan. 21, 1984; children: Thomas Kenneth Stipanov, Kristen Hill Stipanov. BA in Polit. Sci., UCLA, 1978, JD, 1981. Bar: Calif. 1981, U.S. Dist. Ct. (so. dist.) Calif. 1981. Assoc. Gray, Cary, Ames & Frye, San Diego, 1981-85, Sheppard, Mullin, Richter & Hampton, San Diego, 1986-90, Scalone, Stipanov, Yaffa & Mebane, San Diego, 1990-94, Stipanov & Mebane, San Diego, 1994—. Panelist Calif. Continuing Edn. Bar, 2000—01. Bd. dirs. Episcopal Diocese San Diego, 1992—95. Mem.: ABA, San Diego Lawyers Club, Nat. Assn. Women Bus. Owners (bd. dirs. San Diego chpt. 1996—97), San Diego County Bar Assn., UCLA Alumni Assn. (gen. counsel, bd. dirs. 1992—96), Phi Beta Kappa, Kappa Alpha Theta. Democrat. Avocations: sports, travel. Office: Stipanov & Mebane 501 W Broadway Ste 520 San Diego CA 92101-3544 Office Phone: 619-235-2689. Business E-Mail: mebane@stipmeb.com.

MEBANE, WILLIAM BLACK, controller, financial consultant; b. Vernon, Tex., Dec. 15, 1927; s. David Mitchell and Ida Virginia (Black) M.; m. Joan Hebbard Dumper, Nov. 24, 1956; children— David Alexander, Virginia Ann. BBA, Tex. A&M U., 1952; MBA, Harvard U., 1954. Mem. treas.'s office staff Gen. Motors Corp., N.Y.C., 1954-70; sec.-treas. Alfred P. Sloan Found., N.Y.C., 1971-78; dir. fin. and adminstrn. Am. Diabetes Assn., N.Y.C., 1979-80, dir. planning, 1981; v.p., comptroller NCCJ, Inc., N.Y.C., 1981-86, v.p. for fiscal affairs, 1987-88; fin. cons. Internat. House, N.Y.C., 1989-90; ind. fin. cons., 1990-91; contr. Better Bus. Bur., N.Y.C., 1991-99. Vol. Essex Council Boy Scouts Am., 1967— . Served with USAAF, 1946-49. Recipient Silver Beaver award Boy Scouts Am., 1982 Mem.: Harvard Bus. Sch. (N.Y.C.); Short Hills (N.J.). Republican. Episcopalian. Home: 36 Haddonfield Rd Short Hills NJ 07078-3402

MEBUST, WINSTON KEITH, surgeon, educator; b. Malta, Mont., July 2, 1933; s. Hans G. and Anna C. (Leiseth) M.; m. Lora June Peterson, Sept. 15, 1955; children— Leanne, Kevin, Kreg, Kari. Student, U. Wash., 1951-54, MD, 1958. Diplomate: Am. Bd. Urology (trustee 1983-89, pres. 1988-89). Intern King County Hosp., Seattle, 1958-59; resident Virginia Mason Hosp., Seattle, 1959-63, Kans. U. Med. Center, 1963-66; practice medicine, specializing in urology, 1966—; instr. surgery and urology U. Kans. Med. Center, Kansas City, 1966-69, asst. prof., 1969-72, asso. prof., 1972-76, chmn. urology sect., 1974—, prof., 1977—; chief urology service VA Hosp., Kansas City, Mo., 1966-75. Contbr. articles, chpts. to med. jours. and texts. Served with U.S. Army, 1961-63. Mem. ACS, Am. Cancer Soc., Am. Bd. Surgery, Kansas City Urol. Assn., Assn. for Acad. Surgery, Am. Urol. Assn. (pres. S. Ctrl. sect. 1983, exec. com. 1992—, treas. 1996—, pres. elect 2001-02, pres., 2002-03), Wyandotte Med. Soc., Kans. Med. Assn., Soc. Univ. Urologists, Am. Assn. Genitourinary Surgeons, Sigma Xi, Alpha Omega Alpha. Republican. Home: 422 Lansbrook Dr Venice FL 34292-4620 Office: 39th and Rainbow Blvd Kansas City MO 66103 E-mail: wmebust@comcast.net.

MECH, TERRENCE FRANCIS, library director; b. Birdorup Park, Wiltshire, Eng., Feb. 24, 1953; s. Emil Paul and Madelyn Mech. BS, U. Wis., Stevens Point, 1975; MS, Ill. State U., 1978; MLS, Clarion U., 1979; EdD, Pa. State U., 1994. Pub. svcs. libr. Tusculum Coll., Greensville, Tenn., 1979-80; libr. dir. Coll. of the Ozarks, Clarksville, Ark., 1980-82, King's Coll., Wilkes-Barre, Pa., 1982—, dir. libr., 1982—, v.p. for info. and instrnl. techs., 1994—2001. Bd. dirs. Northeastern Pa. Bibliographic Ctr., 1982—; mem., officer Coun. Pa. Libr. Networks, 1984-89, chair, 1987-89. Contbr. chpts. to books and articles to profl. jours. Mem. ALA, Pa. Libr. Assn. (bd. dirs. 1986-87, various coms. 1985—). Office: Kings Coll 133 N River St Wilkes Barre PA 18711-0801

MECHAM, GLENN JEFFERSON, lawyer, mayor; b. Logan, Utah, Dec. 11, 1935; s. Everett H. and Lillie (Dunford) M.; m. Mae Parson, June 5, 1957; children: Jeff B., Scott R., Marcia, Suzanne. BS, Utah State U., 1957; JD, U. Utah, 1961; grad., Air Command and Staff Coll., 1984, Air War Coll., 1984. Bar: Utah 1961, Supreme Ct. U.S., U.S. Ct. Appeals (10th cir.), U.S. Dist. Ct. Utah, U.S. Ct. Claims. Gen. practice law, 1961-65; atty. Duchesne County, Utah, 1962, City of Duchesne, 1962; city judge Roy City, Utah, 1963-66; judge City of Ogden, Utah, 1966-69, mayor, 1992-2000. Lectr. law and govt. Stevens-Henager Coll., Ogden, 1963-75; asst. U.S. atty., 1969-72; ptnr. Mecham & Richards, Ogden, Utah, 1972-82; pres. Penn Mountain Mining Co., South Pacific Internat. Bank, Ltd.; mem. Bur. Justice Stats. Adv. Bd., U.S. Dept. Justice, U.S. Conf. Mayors; chmn. Marina Capital Inc. Chmn. Ogden City Housing Authority; chmn. bd. trustees Utah State U., Space Dynamics Lab; mem. adv. coun. Fed. Home Loan Bank; pres. Utah League Cities and Towns, 1981—82; vice chmn. Wasatch Front Reg. Coun. Col. USAF, 1957; No. Utah liaison U.S. Sen. Robert F. Bennett. Recipient Disting. Svcs. award Utah State U., Weber State U. Mem ABA, Weber County Bar Assn. (pres. 1966-68), Utah Bar Assn., Am. Judicature Soc., Weber County Bar Legal Svcs. (chmn. bd. trustees 1966-69), Utah Assn. Mcpl. Judges (sec.), Ogden-Weber C. of C. (Order of the Big Hat), Sigma Chi, Phi Alpha Delta. Home: 1715 Darling St Ogden UT 84403-0556 Office Phone: 801-725-6666.

MECHAM, STEVEN RAY, school system administrator; b. Salt Lake City, Oct. 10, 1938; s. Milton Claudius and Marjorie (White) M.; m. Donna Jean Johnson, Jan. 22, 1943; children: Brian Paul, Allan LeRoy. AS, Weber State Coll., 1958; BS, U. Utah, 1963; MA, Tchrs. Coll., Columbia U., 1965; postgrad., McGill U.; PhD, U. Calif., Santa Barbara, 1981. Prin. Montreal Oral Sch., 1966-70; state dir. hearing impaired Conn. Dept. Edn., 1970-71; dir. guidance Lexington Sch. for Deaf, N.Y.C., 1971-72; supt. Exton Elem., Ana Frank Jr. and sr. H.S., Mexico City, 1972-77; coord. spl. edn. Weber Sch. Dist., Ogden, Utah, 1977-78; prin. Roosevelt Elem. Sch., Ogden, 1978-82; asst. supt. Weber County Schs., Ogden, 1982-87; assoc. supt. Utah Schs., 1990-93; supt. Weber Sch. Dist., 1993-98, dir. Odyssey Sch., 1998—2003. Instr. U. Utah, 1965-66, St. Joseph Coll., Hartford, Conn., 1970-71; pres. Finnish Mission-LDS Russia and Baltic States, 1987-90; adj. prof. McGill U.; instr. Tchrs. Coll., Columbia U., 1968-70; acting chmn. dept. edn. U. Americas, Mexico City, 1976-77; cons. Far West Labs., San Francisco. Contbr. articles to profl. jours. Bd. dirs. Instituto Mexicano Norte Americano de Relaciones Culturales, Mexico City, 1975-76; bishop, stake pres. Ch. Jesus Christ of Latter-day Saints, pres. Finnish Mission; bd. dirs. Am. Cancer Soc. Weber County. Mem. Am. Orgn. Educators Hearing Impaired (pres.), Can. Hearing Soc. (dir.), Utah Assn. Elem. Sch. Prins., Nat. Assn. Elem. Sch. Prins., Internat. Reading Assn., Am. Assn. Sch. Adminstrs., Utah Supt. Assoc., Alexander Graham Bell Assn., PTA, Rotary.

MECHANIC, DAVID, social sciences educator; b. NYC, Feb. 21, 1936; s. Louis and Tillie (Penn) Mechanic; m. Kathleen Mars Wiltshire; children: Robert Edmund, Michael Alexander. BA, CCNY, 1956; MA, Stanford U., 1957, PhD, 1959. Faculty U. Wis., Madison, 1960—79, prof. sociology, 1965—73, John Bascom prof., 1973—79; dir. U. Wis. (Center for Med. Sociology and Health Services Research), 1971—79, chmn. dept. sociology, 1968—70; prof. social work and sociology Rutgers U., New Brunswick, NJ, 1979—, acting dean faculty arts and scis., 1980—81, Univ. prof., dean faculty arts and scis., 1981—84, Univ. prof. and Rene Dubos prof. behavioral scis., 1984—, dir. Inst. for Health, Health Care Policy and Aging Research, 1985—. Commn. on med. edn. Robert Wood Johnson Found., 1990—92, nat. dir. investigators awards in health policy rsch. program, 2000—, tech. adv. com. scholars in health policy rsch. program, 2001—, nat. adv. com. scholars in health policy rsch. program, 2002—; panelist on health svcs. rsch. Pres.'s Sci. Adv. Com., 1971—72; treatment com. on reduction of cancer mortality Nat. Cancer Inst., 1984; vice-chmn. com. pain, disability and chronic illness behavior Inst. Medicine-NAS, 1985—86, panel on prevention of disability, 1989—90, panel on new data for an aging world, 1999—2000; com. on capitalizing on social sci. and behavioral rsch. to improve the pubs. health Inst. Medicine, 1999; mem. Nat. Adv. Coun. Aging, NIH, 1982—86, Com. on Prevention of Mental Disorder, 1992—94; coord. panel Pres.'s Commn. Mental Health, 1977—78; expert adv. panel on mental health WHO, 1984—89; health adv. bd. GAO, 1987—95; panel on tech., ins. and health care sys. Office of Tech. U.S. Congress, 1992—95; nat. com. on vital and health stats. HHS, 1988—92; commn. on behavioral and social scis. and edn. NRC, 1992—95; adv. com. Picker/Commonwealth Scholars Program, 1992—99; panel on rethinking disability policy Nat. Acad. Social Ins., 1993—96; vis. scholar Kings Fund Inst., London, 1994—95; professionalism adv. com. Am. Bd. Internal Med. Found., 2002—; bd. dirs. Acad. Health. Author: Students Under Stress, 1962, Students Under Stress, 2d edit., 1978, Medical Sociology, 1968, Medical Sociology, rev. edit., 1978, Mental Health and Social Policy, 1969, Mental Health and Social Policy, rev. edit., 1980, 1989, 1999, Public Expectations and Health Care, 1972, Politics, Medicine and Social Science, 1974; author: (with Charles E. Lewis and Rashi Fein) A Right to Health, 1976; author: Growth of Bureaucratic Medicine, 1976, Future Problems in Health Care, 1979, From Advocacy to Allocation: The Evolving American Health Care System, 1986, Painful Choices: Research and Essays on Health Care, 1989, Inescapable Decisions: The Imperatives of Health Reform, 1994; author, editor: Symptoms, Illness Behavior and Help-Seeking, 1982; editor: Handbook of Health, Health Care and the Health Professions, 1983, Improving Mental Health Services: What the Social Sciences Can Tell Us, 1987, General Hospital Impatient Psychiatry, 1997, Managed Behavioral Health Care: Current Realities and Future Potential, 1998; co-editor (with Robert Hauser, Archibald Haller and Tess Hauser): Social Structure and Personality, 1982; co-editor: (with Linda Aiken) Applications of Social Science to Clinical Medicine and Social Policy, 1986; co-editor: Paying for Services: Promises and Pitfalls of Capitation, 1989; co-editor: (with Marian Osterweis and Arthur Kleinman) Pain and Disability: Clinical Behavior and Public Policy Perspectives, 1987; co-editor: (with Carl Taube and Ann Hohmann) The Future of Mental Health Services Research, 1989. Recipient Ward medal, CCNY, 1956, Med. Sociologists award, Am. Sociol. Assn., 1983, Carl Taube award, APHA, 1990, Disting. Investigator award, Assn. for Health Svcs. Rsch., 1991, Disting. Contbn. award mental health sect., Soc. for Study of Social Problems, 1991, Emily Mumford medal, Columbia U., 1991, Investigator award in health policy rsch., Robert Wood Johnson Found., 1995—99, Health Svcs. Rsch. prize, Assn. of U. Programs in Health Adminstrn. and the Baxter Allegiance Found., 1997; fellow Ford Behavioral Sci. fellow, 1956—57, NIMH rsch. fellow, 1965—66, Ctr. for Advanced Study in Behavioral Scis., 1974—75, Guggenheim fellow, 1977—78, Disting. fellow, Assn. Health Svcs. Rsch., 1996. Fellow: AAAS (chmn. sect. social, econ. and polit. scis. 1985), Assn. Health Svcs. Rsch. (disting. 1996); mem.: NAS, Nat. Acad. Sciences, Hogg Found. Mental Health (nat. adv. coun. 1987), Nat. Acad. Social Ins. (founding), Am. Acad. Arts and Scis., Inst. Medicine-NAS (governing coun. 1972—74), Sociol. Rsch. Assn. (pres. 1991—92), Am. Sociol. Assn. (chmn. med. sociol. sect. 1969—70, governing coun. 1977—78, chmn. publs. com. 1989—91, chmn. mental health sect. 1992—93, Disting. Med. Sociologist award 1983, Lifetime Achievement award mental health sect. 1994, Disting. Career award 2001), Phi Beta Kappa. Office: Rutgers U Inst Health Policy Aging Rsch 30 College Ave New Brunswick NJ 08901-1283 Home: 5 Overbrook Dr Princeton NJ 08540-3924 E-mail: mechanic@rci.rutgers.edu.

MECHEM, CHARLES STANLEY, JR., former broadcasting executive, former golf association executive; b. Nelsonville, Ohio, Sept. 12, 1930; s. Charles Stanley and Helen (Hall) Mechem; m. Marilyn Brown, Aug. 31, 1952; children: Melissa, Daniel, Allison. AB, Miami U., Oxford, Ohio, 1952; LLB, Yale U., 1955. Bar: Ohio 1955. Practice in, Cin., 1955—67; ptnr. Taft, Stettinius & Hollister, 1965—67; chmn. bd. Taft Broadcasting Co., Cin., 1967—90; commr. LPGA, Daytona Beach, Fla., 1990—95, commr. emeritus, 1995—; chmn. U.S. Shoe, 1993—95; chmn. Cin. Bell, Inc., 1996—98, Convergys Corp., 1998—2000; cons. Arnold Palmer Enterprises, Cin., 1996—. Bd. dirs. Myers Y. Cooper Co., J.M. Smucker Co., Royal Precision, Inc., Messer Constrn., Inc. Capt. JAGC U.S. Army, 1956—59. Mem.: Cin. C. of C. (pres. 1977), Comml. Club. Office: Taft Stettinius & Hollister LLP 425 Walnut St Ste 1800 Cincinnati OH 45202-4122

MECIK, Z. RICHARD, communications executive; b. Poland; came to U.S., 1980. MS, Pace U., 1986; BBA, Maritime Acad., Gdynia, Poland, 1976. Chief adminstrn. officer Polish Ocean Lines, Gdansk, Poland, 1976-81; investment acct. Columbia U., N.Y.C., 1981-84; tax cons. Mecik & Co., N.Y.C., 1984-86; sr. auditor Leshkowitz & Co., N.Y.C., 1986-89; fin. contr. Goodrich & Sherwood, N.Y.C., 1989-90; CFO Fada Industries, N.Y.C., 1990-92; COO Basic Am. Foods, San Francisco, Calif., 1992-95; dir. fin. Sprint Internat./Global One, Reston, Va., 1995—.

MECIMORE, CHARLES DOUGLAS, retired accounting educator; b. Belmont, N.C., Aug. 20, 1934; s. John Edgar and Hattie (Bolick) M.; m. Barbara Jean Chiddie, June 7, 1959; children: Laura Jean, Charles D. Jr., John Amos. BS, Pfeiffer Coll., 1958; MS, U. N.C., 1962; PhD, U. Ala., 1966. CPA, N.C.; CMA. Asst. prof. U. Ala., Tuscaloosa, 1966-67; assoc. prof. U. Ga., Athens, 1967-71; prof. U. Cin., 1971-79; prof. acctg. Sch. Bus. and Econs., U. N.C., Greensboro, 1980-98; ret., 1998. Head dept. U. N.C. Sch. Bus. and Econs., 1980-89, 96-98. Served with USAF, 1951-55. Univ. scholar, 1963-66; Haskins and Sells fellow, 1962-64; Beyer bronze medal, 1974. Mem. AICPAs, N.C. Assn. CPAs (Outstanding Educator 1985), Inst. Mgmt. Acctg. Home: 430 Marshall View Ct Winston Salem NC 27101-5285 E-mail: MecimoreC@CS.com.

MECKE, WILLIAM MOYN, public affairs consultant; b. Detroit, May 7, 1957; s. Theodore Hart McCalla Jr. and Mary Eleanor (Flaherty) M.; m. Katherine E. Bauer. BA, Georgetown U., 1979; MA, Am. U., 1982; postgrad., Oxford U., 1982, U. N.C., 1982-85. Asst. dir. Found. Study Presdl. and Congrl. Terms, Washington, 1979-82; acct. exec. Hill and Knowlton, Inc., Chgo., 1985-86; tchr. The Bolles Sch., Jacksonville, Fla., 1986-88, St. Andrew's Sch., Savannah, 1988-91, Joseph Walker Sch., Marietta, Ga., 1991-92; polit. cons. various Democratic candidates, 1992-95; tech. writer Total Sys. Svcs. Inc., Columbus, Ga., 1995; dir. mktg. Habitat for Humanity Internat., Americus, Ga., 1995-2000, media svcs. mgr., 2000-2001; mgr. comms. Ga. Regional Transp. Authority, 2001—. Co-author, editor: Presidential and Congressional Term Limitation: The Issue That Stays Alive, 1981. Asst. dir. Found. Study Presd. and Congl. Terms, Washington, 1979-82. Mem. Pub. Rels. Soc. Am. Office: Ga Regional Transp Authority Ste 900 245 Peachtree Ctr Ave NE Atlanta GA 30303 E-mail: wmecke@grta.org.

MECKEL, PETER TIMOTHY, arts administrator, educator; b. Yankton, S.D., Nov. 28, 1941; s. Myron Eugene and Cynthia Ann (Turnblom) Meckel; m. Louise Gloria Mudge, Sept. 8, 1962; children: Christina Louise, Christopher Mark; m. Adrienne Dawn Maravich, Dec. 30, 1972; children: Moya Ann, Jon-Peter. Ed., Rockford Coll., Occidental Coll. Founder, gen. dir. Hidden Valley Music Seminars, Carmel Valley, Calif., 1963—; dir. Hidden Valley Opera Ensemble, Masters Festival of Chamber Music, Master Class Series. Cons. in field. Mem. Music Educators Nat. Conf. Congregationalist. Office: Hidden Valley Opera Ensemble PO Box 116 Carmel Valley CA 93924-0116 E-mail: hvms@aol.com.

MECKLENBURG, GARY ALAN, hospital executive; m. Lynn Kraemer; children: John, Sarah. BA, Northwestern U., 1968; MBA, U. Chgo., 1970. Adminstrv. resident Presbyn.-St. Luke's Hosp., Chgo., 1969-70, adminstrv. asst., 1970-71, asst. supt., 1971-76, assoc. supt., 1976-77, U. Wis. Hosps., Madison, 1977-80; adminstr. Stanford U. Hosp. Clinics, Calif.; pres., CEO St. Joseph's Hosp., Milw., 1980-85; pres., dir. Franciscan Health Care Inc., Milw., 1985; pres., CEO Northwestern Meml. Hosp., Chgo., 1985—2001, Northwestern Meml. HealthCare, Chgo., 2001—. Preceptor, guest lectr., mem. adv. bd. Kellogg Sch. Mgmt., chgo., 1986—; pres., chief exec. officer, dir. Northwestern Healthcare Network, 1990-92. Recipient Todd Scout award Boy Scouts Am., 1998, Chgo. Bus. Hall of Fame award Jr. Achievement, 2000, GSB Disting. Pub. Svc./Pub. Sector Alumnus award U. Chgo., 2000. Mem. Am. Hosp. Assn. (sect. met. hosps., governing coun. 1984-92, chmn. 1991, 2001, trustee 1996-2002, exec. com. 1997-2002, chmn., 2001, mem. regional policy bd., #5 1984, 87-89, 91-93, 95-99, chmn. 1996-99, 2001, mem. ho. dels. 1984, 87-89, 91—, mem. com. on med. edn. 1976-80), Ill. Hosp. Assn. (bd. dirs. 1988-95, chmn. 1994, mem. adv. panel coun. tchg. hosps. 1997—), U. Chgo. Hosp. Adminstrn. Alumni Assn. (pres. 1985-86), Econ. Club Chgo., Comml. Club Chgo. Office: Northwestern Meml Hosp 251 E Huron St Ste 3-708 Chicago IL 60611-2908

MECKLER, MARY MCSTROUL, mortgage company executive, writer; b. Buffalo, Mar. 4, 1947; d. Eugene and Elizabeth Almira (Heath) McStroul; m. Matrin Herbert Meckler, Nov. 5, 1967; children: Andrew Eugene, Todd Alan, Erin Kendra Carraway. AA, San Joaquin Delta Coll., 1997; BA magna cum laude in Sociology, Calif. State U., Turlock, 1999. Lic. real estate agent Calif. Substitute tchr. Manteca (Calif.) Unified Sch., 1999—2002; home loan specialist Manteca Lending & Mortgage, 2002—. Pres. Purple Plume Press, Manteca, 2003. Author: (children's book) The Magic of Tobias Twissle, 2003, Isaac Found a Star, 2004. Mem.: Phi Kappa Phi. Avocation: travel. Office: Purple Plume Press 5980 Peach Ave Manteca CA 95337 Office Phone: 209-825-7602. E-mail: lodybesy@cs.com.

MECKLER, MICHAEL LOUIS, historian, journalist; b. Columbus, Ohio, Mar. 31, 1965; s. Lowell Courtenay and Marcia (Lipson) M. AB, Princeton U., 1987; AM, U. Chgo., 1988; PhD, U. Mich., 1994. Editorial asst. Princeton (N.J.) Archtl. Press, 1984-87; Javits fellow U. Chgo., 1987-88, U. Mich., Ann Arbor, 1988-91; producer, reporter Sta. WWJ (CBS Radio), Southfield, Mich., 1991-94; asst. editor Jour. Roman Archaeology, Ann Arbor, 1992-93; vis. asst. prof. U. Mich., 1995; lectr. Yale U., 1995—97; reporter sta. WATR, Waterbury, Conn., 1996—97; lectr. U. Conn., 1997; creator, pub., newswriting radio website (newscript.com), 1996—; vis. asst. prof. Union Coll., NY, 1997—98, Ohio State Univ., 1998—2003; columnist Columbus Dispatch, 1998—; fellow ctr. epigraphical and paleographical studies Ohio State Univ., 2003—. Contbr. articles to profl. jours. Grantee Group for the Study of Late Antiquity, 1986. Mem. Am. Hist. Assn., Am. Philol. Assn., Soc. for the Promotion of Roman Studies, Medieval Acad. Am., Celtic Studies Assn. N.Am., Radio TV News Dir. Assn. Office: Ohio State U Ctr Epigraphical and Palaeographical Studies 190 Pressey Hall 1070 Carmack Rd Columbus OH 43210-1002

MECKNA, MICHAEL, musicologist, educator; b. Long Beach, Calif., Feb. 13, 1945; m. Eva Kartinen, Feb. 18, 1976. BA, Calif. State U., Long Beach, 1967; PhD, U. Calif., Santa Barbara, 1984. C.C. instr. credential Calif., 1978. Assoc. prof. Ball State U., Muncie, Ind., 1984—90; prof. Tex. Christian U., Fort Worth, 1990—. Cons. NEH, Washington, 1987—. Author: Virgil Thomson, 1986 (Choice Outstanding Academic Book, 1987); editor: The Collected Works of Alfred B. Sedgwick, 1994; author: (encyclopedia) Twentieth-Century Brass Soloists, 1994, Satchmo: The Louis Armstrong Encyclopedia, 2004. Recipient Choice Outstanding Academic Book, ALA, 1987; fellow, NEH, 1985, 1987; Aspen fellow, Music Critics Assn., 1980. Mem.: Coll. Music Soc., Soc. for Am. Music, Am. Musicol. Soc., Pi Kappa Lambda. Avocation: ballroom dancing. Office: Texas Christian Univ School of Music Fort Worth TX 76129-0001 Office Phone: 817-257-6634. E-mail: m.meckna@tcu.edu.

MEDAK, PETER, film director; b. Budapest, Hungary; arrived in Eng., 1956; came to U.S., 1979; s. Gyula and Elisabeth (Diamonstein) M.; m. Julia Migenes, July 31, 1989 (div.); children: Christopher, Karen, Joshua, Cornelia, Martina, Jessica. Dir. (films) Negatives, 1968, A Day in the Death of Joe Egg, 1970, The Ruling Class, 1971, Ghost in a Nonnday's Sun, 1973, The Odd Job, 1977, The Changling, 1979, Zorro the Gay Blade, 1980, The Men's Club, 1986, The Krays, 1989, La Voix Humane, 1990, Let Him Have It, 1991, Romeo is Bleeding, 1992, Pontiac Moon, 1994, Hunchback of Notre Dame, 1996, Species 2, 1997, David Copperfield, 1998-99, Feast of All Saints, 2000, (stage) Miss Julie, 1977 (opera) Salome, 1988, La Voix Humane, and others. Mem. Dir.'s Guild of Am., Dir.'s Guild of U.K., Assn. of Cinematographers, Allied Technicians, Dir.'s Guild of Can. Jewish. Office: Scott J Feinstein 16255 Ventura Blvd Ste 625 Encino CA 91436-2307 also: Armstrong and Hirsch 1888 Century Park E Ste 1888 Century City CA 90067-1702 Home: 1355 North Laurel Avenue #9 West Hollywood CA 90046

MEDAK, WALTER HANS, lawyer; b. Vienna, May 10, 1915; came to U.S., 1938; s. Hugo and Grete (Figdor) M.; m. Edith Rhodes, 1944 (div. 1957); 1 child, Ronald Harvard; m. Renée Rasens, 1996. Grad., Acad. of Commerce, Vienna, 1934, U. Vienna, 1938; postgrad., U. Ga., 1939-40; MA in Econs., U. Calif., Berkeley, 1949; JD, Harvard U., 1948. Prodn. mgr. Mabs, Inc., L.A., 1942-43; prodn. engr. Kaiser Co., Richmond, Calif., 1943-45; atty. Belli & Medak, Walnut Creek, Calif., 1957-59; pvt. practice law Walnut Creek and Moraga, Calif., 1950—. Bd. dirs. Snyder/Newell, Inc., San Francisco; bd. dirs. Carnelian Woods, Carnelian Bay, Calif., pres., 1974-80. Mem. ABA, Calif. County Bar Assn., Assn. Trial Lawyers Am., Calif. Trial Lawyers Assn., Harvard Club (chmn. admissions and scholarship com. San Francisco chpt. 1973-74). Avocations: skiing, swimming, music, travel, French and German. Home: 2833 Ptarmigan Dr Apt 3 Walnut Creek CA 94595-3135 Office Phone: 925-938-8241. E-mail: medak-rasens@earthlink.net.

MEDALIE, JACK HARVEY, physician; b. Buhl, Minn., Jan. 8, 1922; married; 3 children. BSc, Witwatersrand U., Johannesburg, 1941, MD, BChir, 1945; MPH cum laude, Harvard U., 1958. Instr. dept. anatomy U. Witwatersrand, 1942—43; resident Johannesburg, 1945—47; rural family physician, 1948—53; sr. lectr. dept. social medicine Hebrew U., Hadassah, Jerusalem, 1962—66; from assoc. prof. to prof., chmn. dept. family medicine Tel Aviv U., 1966—74; chmn. dept. family medicine Case Western Res. U., 1975—87, prof. cmty. health, 1976—87, prof. family medicine, 1976—, prof. med. and pediat., 1978—87, prof. emeritus, 1992—; med. dir. Family and Cmty. Health Ctr., Jerusalem, 1953—62. Prin. investigator Israel Ischemic Heart Disease Study, 1962—75; co-prin. investigator congenital abnormality study NIH, 1972—74; Robert Wood Johnson Found. fellowship program Case Western Res. U., 1978—88; vis. prof. family medicine and epidemiology U. N.C., Chapel Hill, 1973—74; vis. sr. rsch. scientist Nat. Heart, Blood and Lung Inst., Bethesda, Md., 1974, Bethesda, 1990—91; med. coun. U. Hosps., Cleve., 1975—87; com. impaired physicians U. Hosps., Cleve., 1980—87; med. edn. com. Case Western Res. U., 1980—85, chmn. ambulatory and primary care clerkship com., 1981—83; task force health consequences bereavement NAS, 1982—85, membership com., 1984—88; dir. dept. family practice U. Hosps., Cleve., 1982—87; rsch. cons. Mt. Sinai Med. Ctr., Cleve., 1991—99. Contbr. articles to profl. jours. With U.S. Army, 1942—45, active Israel Def. Force, 1948—49. Recipient Lifetime Achievement award in medicine, Golden Age Ctrs., 1997. Fellow: Royal Soc. Med. Found., Am. Heart Assn., Am. Acad. Family Physicians; mem.: Soc. Behavioral Medicine, Soc. Tchrs. Family Medicine (chmn. task force 1985—87, Curtis Hames Career Rsch. award 1988, Cert. Excellence 1988, Maurice Saltzman award 1988), Inst. Medicine-NAS. Office: Case Western Res Univ Dept Family Medicine 10900 Euclid Ave Cleveland OH 44106-4901

MEDALIE, RICHARD JAMES, lawyer; b. Duluth, Minn., July 21, 1929; s. William Louis and Mona (Kolad) M.; m. Susan Diane Abrams, June 5, 1960; children: Samuel David, Daniel Alexander. BA summa cum laude, U. Minn., 1952; cert., U. London, 1953; A.M., Harvard U., 1955, JD cum laude, 1958. Bar: DC 1958, NY 1963. Law clk. to Hon. George T. Washington U.S. Ct. Appeals, Washington, 1958-59; asst. solicitor gen. U.S., 1960-62; assoc. Kaye, Scholer, Fierman, Hays & Handler, N.Y.C., 1962-65; dep. dir. Ford Found. Inst. Criminal Law and Procedure, Georgetown U. Law Ctr., 1965-68; ptnr. Friedman & Medalie and predecessors, Washington, 1968-98; pres. Pegasus Internat., Washington, 1970—; exec. dir. The Appleseed Found., Washington, 1993-94, chmn. bd., 1993—2002, chmn. emeritus, 2003—, pres., 1995-98; of counsel Brock Ptnrs. LLC, N.Y.C., 1995—; pvt. practice Washington, 1998—. Adj. prof. adminstrv. and criminal law Georgetown U. Law Center, 1967—70; mem. D.C. Law Revision Commn., 1975—87; chmn. Criminal Law Task Force, exec. com., 1978—82; panel comml. arbitrators Am. Arbitration Assn., 1964; vice chmn. Harvard Law Sch. Fund, 1981—84, chmn. nat. maj. gifts, 1984—86, dep. chmn., 1986—87, chmn., 1987—89; v.p., bd. dirs. Trial Lawyers for Pub. Justice, Washington, 1998—. Author: From Escobedo to Miranda: The Anatomy of a Supreme Court Decision, 1966; co-author: Federal Consumer Safety Legislation, 1970; co-author, editor: Commercial Arbitration for the 1990s, 1991; co-editor: Crime: A Community Responds, 1967; staff: Harvard Law Rev., 1956-58; case editor, 1957-58; contbr. articles to legal jours. Bd. dirs. alumni assn. Expt. in Internat. Living, Brattleboro, Vt., 1961-64, pres., 1962-63. Fulbright scholar, 1952-53; Ford fellow, 1954-55. Mem. ABA (program chair 1984, 90, chair legis. subcom. 1986-89, ADR/arbitration com., rep. on adv. com. nat. conf. Emerging ADR Issues in State and Fed. Cts. 1991, vice-chmn. 1991-94, arbitration com. litigation sect., co-chair nat. conf. Critical Issues in Arbitration 1993), D.C. Unified Bar, Assn. Bar City of N.Y., D.C. Estate Planning Coun.; fellow Am. Bar Found., Harvard Law Sch. Assn. D.C. (pres. 1976-77, nat. v.p. 1977-78), Harvard Alumni Assn. (law sch. dir. 1991-95), life mem. Am. Law Inst. (consultative group, model penal code sentencing), Cosmos Club, Harvard Club of Washington, Phi Beta Kappa, Phi Alpha Theta. Home: 3113 Macomb St NW Washington DC 20008-3325 Office: 1750 K St NW Ste 1200 Washington DC 20006-2303 Office Phone: 202-659-0880. E-mail: rmedalie@att.net.

MEDALIE, SUSAN DIANE, lawyer, management consultant; b. Boston, Oct. 7, 1941; d. Samuel and Matilda (Bortman) Abrams; m. Richard James Medalie, June 5, 1960; children: Samuel David, Daniel Alexander. BA, Sarah Lawrence Coll., 1960; MA, George Washington U., 1962, cert. pubs. spec., 1977; JD, Am. U., 1986. Bar: Pa. 1987, DC 1987. Pres. Medalie Cons., Washington, 1980—; dep. dir. U.S. Holocaust Meml. Coun., Washington, 1980—82; assoc. pub. Campaigns & Elections, Washington, 1983—84; legis. analyst Subcom./House Energy and Commerce, Washington, 1985; ea. regional dir. Josephson Found. for Adv. Ethics, L.A., 1986—88; asst. dean for external affairs George Washington U. Nat. Law Ctr., Washington, 1988—90; exec. dir. Internat. Soc. Global Health Policy, Washington and Paris, 1990—93; pvt. practice Washington, 1993—2000; exec. dir. Women's Campaign Fund, Washington, 2000—04. Corp. liaison First Hosp. Corp., Norfolk, Va., 1986—88. Editor, pub.: Getting There mag., 1977—80, sr. editor: Am. U. Law Rev., 1984—86; assoc. prodr., cons. (TV series) Prof. Arthur Miller's "Headlines on Trial", 1987—91. Exec. bd., DC Bar rep. Coalition Against Drugs and Violence, 1997—2000; nat. dep. fin. dir. Edward M. Kennedy for Pres. Com., Washington, 1979—80; del. DC Ward 3 Dem. Ctrl. Com., 1996—2000; bd. dirs., exec. com. Women's Campaign Fund, 1999—2000. Mem.: ABA, DC Unified Bar. Office: 1750 K St NW Washington DC 20006 E-mail: susanmedalie@att.net.

MEDAVOY, MIKE, motion picture company executive; b. Shanghai, Jan. 21, 1941; arrived in U.S., 1957, naturalized, 1962; s. Michael and Dora Medavoy; m. Irena Medavoy; children: Nicholas, Brian. BA, UCLA, 1963. With Casting dept. Universal Studios, 1963; agt. Bill Robinson Assocs., Los Angeles, 1963-64; v.p. motion picture dept. GAC/CMA Co., 1965-71, IFA Co., 1971-74; sr. v.p. United Artists Corp., 1974-78; one of founders, exec. v.p. Orion Pictures Co., Burbank, Calif., 1978-82; exec. v.p. Orion Pictures Corp. (formerly Orion Pictures Co.), Century City, Calif., 1982-90; chmn. Tri-Star Pictures, Inc., Culver City, Calif., 1990—, Phoenix Picture Corp., 1995—. Jury chmn. Tokyo Film Festival 1994; hon. co-chair St. Petersburg (Russia) Film Festival, 1992; adv. bd. Shanghai Film Conf.; co-chmn. Am. Cinematheque, 1997-2004, chmn. emeritus, 2004—; bd. dir. UCLA Found. Author: You're Only as Good as Your Next One, 2002. Chmn. Ctr. Internat. Rels.; co-founder Sundance Film Inst.; bd. govs. Sundance Inst., 1980-86; bd. dirs. Calif. Mus. Sci. and Industry, 1984-87; commr. L.A. Bd. Parks and Recreation, 2001; exec. adv. bd. Calif. Anti-Terrorism Info. Ctr., 2002; bd. dirs. U. Tel-Aviv., bd. advs. Harvard's Kennedy Sch. Gov., co-chair UCLA Burkle Ctr. Internat. Rels. Recipient Acad. award (mem. of team that green lit), One Flew Over the Cuckoo's Nest, Rocky, Annie Hall, Amadeus, Platoon, Dances with Wolves, Silence of the Lambs, Motion Picture Pioneer award, 1992, Career Achievement award, UCLA Alumni, 1997, Prodrs. award, Cannes Film Festival, 1998, Neil H. Jacoby award, 1999, Fred Zinneman award, Anti-Defamation League, 2001. Mem. Acad. Motion Picture Arts and Scis. (gov. 1977-81), UCLA Found., UCLA Chancellors Assocs.

MEDDING, WALTER SHERMAN, retired environmental engineer; b. St. Louis, Mar. 4, 1922; s. Walter Lyman and Elizabeth Steele (Sherman) M.; m. Mary Agnes Patty Johnson, Apr. 22, 1944; children: Jean, Walter, Mauri. BSCE, Va. Poly. Inst., 1947, MS in Sanitary Engring., 1970. Registered profl. engr., Va., N.C., Kans. Various positions U.S. Army, 1942-64; student officer advanced course The Engr. Sch., Ft. Belvoir, Va., 1952—54, head fixed bridges sect., 1954—55; asst. engr. Asmara Eritrea, chief design br. Mediterranean Divsn., Gulf Dist., Tehran, Iran, 1955-57; asst. divsn. engr. 9th Infantry Divsn., Ft. Carson, Colo., 1957-59; resident engr. USACAG, chief constrn. ops. U.S. Army Engring. Command Europe, Frankfurt, Germany, 1959-72; chief contract adminstrn. U.S. Army Engring. Divsn. Europe, Frankfurt, Germany, 1972-75; chief environ. engring. Office, Chief of Engrs., U.S. Army, Washington, 1975-86; sr. engr. Romem Aqua Sys. Co., Woodbridge, Va., 1986-97. Cons. U.S. army Ctr. for Pub. Works, Ft. Belvoir, Va., 1997-98; music tchr. Co-author: (textbook) Non-standard Military Fixed Bridges, 1954, (with E. Farago) Which Musical Instrument Shall I Play?, 1985; editor, pub. Letter to Lyman, 1978; contbr. articles to profl. jours. Mem. ASCE, Am. Waterworks Assn., Water Environ. Fedn., Conf. of Fed. Environ. Engrs. Republican. Episcopalian. Achievements include development of mil. bridge classification procedures for load carrying and rapid field design. Home: 204 Brooke Dr Fredericksburg VA 22408-2004 Personal E-mail: wsmedding@aol.com.

MEDEARIS, KENNETH ROBERT, medical products manufacturing company executive. b. Woodside, N.Y., Apr. 30, 1939; s. Kenneth Calvin and Elizabeth Marie (Stacy) M.; BSBA, Fairleigh Dickinson U., 1973; m. Ida Jane Hunter, Apr. 4, 1964. Mgr. quality assurance engring. Lockheed Electronics Co., Plainfield, N.J., 1971-74; dir. quality assurance/regulatory affairs instrument div. Baxter-Travenol, Silver Spring, Md., 1974-76, dir. mfg. ops., 1976-78; v.p. ops. Corometrics Med. Systems, Inc., Wallingford, Conn., 1978-89; pres., chief exec. officer Kontron Instruments, Inc., Everett, Mass., 1989-90, pres., CEO prin., Pinnacle Mmgt. Ltd., Madison, Conn., 1990-94, v.p., gen. mgr. Monaghan Med. Corp., Plattsburgh, N.Y., 1994—. Served with USN, 1957-61. Mem. Assn. Advancement Med. Instrumentation, Am. Mgmt. Assn., Am Soc. Quality Control, Barnes Indsl. Park Assn. Republican. Office: 5 Latour Ave Plattsburgh NY 12901-7207 Home: PO Box 1050 Clarksville VA 23927-1050

MEDEARIS, MILLER, lawyer; b. Liberty, Mo., Jan. 19, 1921; s. Thomas Whittier and Mara (Miller) Medearis; children: Christy Croshet, Kellee Reed. LLB, Cumberland U., 1948; JD, Stamford U., 1969. Bar: Okla. 1948, Calif. 1957. Claims adjustor Transit Casualty Co., LA, 1950-56, atty., trial counsel, 1956-58; ptnr. Hagenbaugh, Murphy & Medearis, LA, 1958-69, Medearis and Grimm, LA, 1969—. Sec., bd. dirs. Med. Quality Assurance, Sacramento, 1979—84, v.p., 1984—86; commr. LA Bd. Transp., 1986—92; mem. Dem. Bus. Coun., L.A., 1980; bd. dirs. Pico Rivera Cmty. Hosp., 1975—85. With USN, 1945—46. Mem.: ABA, Okla. Bar Assn., Calif. Trial Lawyers Assn., State Bar Calif., Lawyers Club LA. Democrat. Baptist. Avocations: boating, water-skiing, downhill skiing. Home: 2175 Ridge Dr Los Angeles CA 90049-1153 Office: Medearis and Grimm 1331 W Sunset Blvd Los Angeles CA 90026-4499 Office Phone: 213-250-3747.

MEDEIROS, M. JOYCE, community health educator; b. Boston, Feb. 17, 1954; d. Raymond A. and D. Jean (Russell) Harrington; m. Joseph A. Medeiros, June 26, 1977; children: Jessica A., Jo Ellen. Grad., Youville Hosp. Sch. Practical Nursing, 1973; BS in Cmty. Health Edn., U. Maine, Farmington, 1992. Lic. social worker. Staff nurse Goddard Meml. Hosp., Stoughton, Mass., 1973-87; dist. dir. Somerset Family YMCA, 1988-90; ITV aide Skowhegan (Maine) H.S., 1990-91; intern Somerset Residential Care Ctr., 1991-92, WARNACO, 1992; dir. edn. Sebasticook Valley Hosp., 1992-96; spl. needs edn. tech. transition III MSAD # 59 Madison (Maine) H.S., 1996-99; children's case mgr. Youth & Family Svcs., 1999—2003. Camp nurse, dir. 4-H Camp Farley, 1982-87, Camp at Eastward Starks, Maine, 1990. Selectman Town of Starks, 1995. Completed 2000 Honolulu Marathon, Leukemia, Lymphoma Soc. Mem.: Phi Sigma Pi, Eta Sigma Gamma. Avocations: camping, bowling, photography, ceramics, collecting music boxes. Home: 241 Dill Rd Starks ME 04911

MEDEL, REBECCA ROSALIE, artist; b. Denver, Mar. 26, 1947; d. Natividad and Josefa (Apodaca) M. BFA, Ariz. State U., 1970; MFA, UCLA, 1982. Asst. prof. fibers dept. head Tenn. Technol. U., Smithville, 1983-88; lectr. Dept. of Design, UCLA, 1989-91; studio artist, 1991—; assoc. prof. Tyler Sch. Art Temple U., 1995—. Lectr. N.C. State U., Raleigh, San Diego State U., SUNY, Purchase, 1992, Penland Sch. Asheville, N.C., Textile Study Group, N.Y.C., Calif. Coll. of Arts & Crafts, Oakland, Calif., San Jose State U., Am. Ctr., Kyoto, Japan, City Ctr., Sapporo, Japan, 1986; vis. artist U. N.D., 1985. One-woman shows include Thirteen Moons Gallery, Santa Fe, 2003, Brown Grotta Gallery, Wilton, Conn., 1996, Neuberger Mus. of Art, Purchase, N.Y., 1992-93, Bellas Artes Gallery, N.Y.C., 1991, N.D. Mus. Art, Grand Forks, 1985, Maya Behn Galerie, Zurich, 1984, UCLA, 1982, Thirteen Moons Gallery, Santa Fe, 2003; two-person exhbns. include Heath Gallery, Atlanta, 1987, Maya Behn Gallerie, 1986; group shows include Bellas Artes Gallery, Santa Fe, N.Mex., 1992, N.C. State U. Gallery, 1992, Portland Art Mus., 1995, Madison (Wis.) Art Ctr., 1995, Santa Monica (Calif.) Art Gallery, 1995, Maya Behn Gallerie, 1991, Mus. Van Bommel-Van Dam, Venlo, Netherlands, 1990, Palo Alto Cultural Ctr., 1990, Barbican Ctr. Concourse Gallery, London, 1998, Montclair (N.J.) State U. Gallery, 1998, Art Inst. Chgo., 1999, Yokohama (Japan) Mus. Art, 1999, Biennial 2000, Del. Art Mus., Wilmington, L.A. Mus. Art, 2000, Soc. Contemporary Crafts, Pitts., 2001, Westport Arts Ctr., Conn.,, 2003, many others. Recipient bronze medal Triennial of Tapestry, 1985; visual artist fellow Nat. Endowment for Arts, 1986, 88, fellow for emerging visual artists So. Arts Fedn. NEA, 1985; Pew fellow in the arts, 1999, 2003, fellow Pa. Coun. on Arts, 2001, 03; scholar to Arcosanti, Nat. Endowment for Arts, 1986, 88. Home: 2920 Meyer Ave Glenside PA 19038-1920 Office Phone: 215-782-2728.

MEDENICA, GORDON, publication executive; b. Darmstadt, Germany, Oct. 26, 1951; came to U.S., 1952; s. Walter Vojislav and Heidi Hedwig (Knoerzer) M.; m. Ann Margaret Connolly, Jan. 2, 1982; children: Madeline, Candice. AB, Harvard U., 1973, MBA, 1979. Staff acct. Meahl, McNamara & Co., Boston, 1973-74; exec. dir. BMW Car Club Am., Cambridge, Mass., 1974-77; analyst corp. planning Marriott Corp., Washington, 1979-80, sr. analyst hotel planning, 1981-82; sr. analyst strategic planning N.Y. Times Co., N.Y.C., 1982-83, project mgr. strategic planning, 1984, mgr. strategic planning and corp. devel., 1984-86, dir. planning, 1986-90; v.p. corp. planning, 1990-93; v.p. ops. and planning, 1993-96; sr. v.p., group pub. NYT Mag. Group, N.Y.C., 1996-98; pres., CEO Dorna USA, N.Y.C., 1999—. Office: Dorna USA 800 3rd Ave 28th Fl New York NY 10022-7604

MEDEROS, CAROLINA LUISA, public policy consultant; b. Rochester, Minn., July 1, 1947; d. Luis O. and Carolina (del Valle) Mederos. BA, Vanderbilt U., 1969; MA, U. Chgo., 1971. Adminstrv. asst. Lt. Gov. of Ill., Chgo., 1972; sr. research assoc. U. Chgo., 1972; project mgr., cons. Urban Dynamics, Inner City Fund and Community Programs Inc., Chgo., 1972-73; legis. asst. to Senate pres. Ill. State Senate, Chgo. and Springfield, 1973-76; program analyst Dept. Transp., Washington, 1976-79, chief, trans. assistance programs div., 1979-81, dir. programs and evaluation, 1981-88, chairwoman, sec.'s safety rev. task force, 1985-88, deputy asst. sec. for safety, 1988-89; cons. Patton Boggs LLP, Washington, 1990—. Recipient award for Meritorious Achievement, Sec. Transp. 1980, Superior Achievement award U.S. Dept. Transp., 1981, Sec.'s Gold Medal award for Outstanding Achievement, 1986, Presdl. Rank award, 1987. Home: 2723 O St NW Washington DC 20007-3128 Office: Patton Boggs LLP 2550 M St NW Washington DC 20037-1350 Office Phone: 202-457-5653. E-mail: cmederos@pattonboggs.com.

MEDFORD, RUSSELL MARSHALL, physician; b. Bklyn., Jan. 8, 1955; s. Jerome L. and Doris P. (Pinchuk) M.; m. Margaret K. Offermann, May 31, 1986; children: Arielle, Rochelle. BA, Cornell U., 1976; MS, Albert Einstein Coll. Medicine, 1980, PhD in Cell and Molecular Biology, 1982, MD, 1983. Diplomate Am. Bd. Internal Medicine. Instr. dept. medicine Harvard Med. Sch., Boston, 1986-89; assoc. physician cardiology Brigham and Women's Hosp., Boston, 1986-89; asst. prof. medicine Emory U., Atlanta, 1989-94, assoc. prof. medicine, 1994—; dir. molecular cardiology rsch. ctr., 1994—; founding scientist Athero Genics, Inc., Atlanta, 1994—, exec. v.p., 1994—; pres., CEO, 1995—. Bd. dirs. Ga. Biomed. Partnership, Atlanta; mem. site vis. rev. com. Nat. Heart, Lung and Blood Inst., 1992—, NIH, 1993—; scientific rev. Am. Jour. Physiology, Jour. Clin. Investigation, Jour. Biol. Chemistry. Contbr. articles to profl. jours. Grantee NIH, 1993, 94, 95, Am. Heart Assn., 1993, 95. Mem. Am. Fedn. Clin. Rsch., Am. Heart Assn., Am. Soc. Microbiology. Achievements include patent for treatment of atherosclerosis and other inflammatory diseases; studies on the molecular biology of cardiovascular disease and gene-directed therapy. Office: Emory U Sch of Medicine Divsn Cardiology 1639 Pierce Dr WMB 319/LL Atlanta GA 30345

MEDH, JHEEM D. medical educator, biochemist, researcher; BS in Chemistry and Biochemistry, U. Bombay, India, 1982; MS in Biochemistry, U. Bombay, 1984; PhD in Biochemistry, U. Tex. Med. Br., Galveston, 1990. Jr. rsch. fellow, dept. physiology L.T.M. Med. Coll., Bombay, 1984-86; rsch. asst., dept. human biol. chemistry and genetics U. Tex. Med. Br., 1986-90; postgrad. rsch. biochemist, dept. medicine U. Calif., San Diego, 1991-93; asst. rsch. scientist, adj. asst. prof., dept. medicine U. Iowa Coll. Medicine, Iowa City, 1993—. Presenter in field of role of LDL receptor-related protein, receptor-associated protein and lipoprotein lipase on the regulation of lipoprotein metabolism. Juvenile Diabetes Internat. Found. fellow 1992-93; recipient nat. grand-in-aid award Am. Heart Assn., 1995-98; recipient Gip Hudson award Nat. Student Rsch. Forum, 1989, Stephen C. Silverthorne award Grad. Sch. Biomed. Scis., U. Tex. Med. Br. Mem. Am. Heart Assn. (coun. for basic science), Am. Soc. Cell Biology, Juvenile Diabetes Found. Internat. Office: U Iowa Coll Med 200 CMAB Iowa City IA 52242

MEDHKOUR, AZEDINE, neurosurgeon, educator; b. Constantine, Algeria, Mar. 15, 1951; s. Kaddour and Zohra Medhkour; m. Dinia Ouniche, July 3, 1986; children: Yacine, Yousra, Miriam. MD, U. Algiers, Algeria, 1977. Bd. cert. in neurosurgery Inst. Med. Scis. of Algiers. Vice chief dept. neurosurgery, Hopital Ben Badis U. Constantine, Algeria, 1989—92; neurosurg. oncology fellow Meml. Sloan Cancer Ctr., N.Y.C., 1992—93; neurosurgery fellow in spine U. Thomas Jefferson, Phila., 1994—96; tng. in neurosurgery and skull base surgery U. Ark. Med. Scis., 1996—2000; asst. prof. neurosurgery Med. Coll. Ohio, Toledo, 2000—02, chief neurosurgery, 2002—. Editor cmty. news jour. Majid Saad Found., Toledo, 2002. Fellow Brain Tumor rsch., Mass. Gen. Hosp., 1988. Mem.: Congress Neurol. Surgeons (assoc.; internat. mem. 1993). Achievements include development of animal model for the growth of benign brain tumors; research in growth of human meningioma in the subrenal capsule of the nude mouse. Office: Med Coll Ohio 3000 Arlington Ave Toledo OH 43614 Office Phone: 419-383-3547. Personal E-mail: medhkour1@yahoo.com.

MEDICUS, HEINRICH ADOLF, physicist, researcher; b. Zurich, Switzerland, Dec. 24, 1918; came to U.S., 1950; naturalized, 1995; s. Friedrich Georg and Clara Anna (Frey) M.; m. Hildegard Julie Schmelz, June 15, 1961. Diploma, Swiss Fed. Inst. Tech., Zurich, 1943, DSc, 1949. Rsch. assoc. Swiss Fed. Inst. Tech., Zurich, 1943-50; visitor Lawrence Berkeley (Calif.) Lab., 1950-51, MIT, Cambridge, Mass., 1951-52, instr., vis. asst. prof., 1952-55; from assoc. prof. to prof. exptl. nuc. physics and history of modern physics Rensselaer Poly. Inst., Troy, NY, 1955-87, prof. emeritus, 1987—. Vis. scientist Atomic Energy Research Establishment Harwell, Eng., 1967-68, Swiss Inst. Nuclear Research, Villigen, 1974-75. Co-author: Fields and Particles, 1973; contbr. articles to profl. jours. With Swiss Army, 1937-50. Fellow Swiss Found., 1950-52 Mem. Am. Phys. Soc., Swiss Phys. Soc., Hist. of Sci. Soc., Swiss Am. Hist. Soc., Soc. Wine Educators, Hudson-Mohawk Swiss Soc. (pres. 1974—), Soc. Vignerons, Delta Tau Delta (pres. house corp. of Upsilon chpt. 1984-91, faculty adv. 1991-95), Swiss Alpine Club. Presbyterian. Avocation: wine education. Home: 1 The Knoll East Acres Troy NY 12180 Office: Rensselaer Poly Inst Dept Physics Troy NY 12180 Business E-Mail: medich@rpi.edu.

MEDIN, A. LOUIS, computer company executive; b. Balt., Oct. 2, 1925; s. Nathan and Bessie (Zell) Medin; m. Julia A. Levin, Dec. 24, 1950; children: Douglas, David, Thomas, Linda. BSChemE, Johns Hopkins U., 1948; PhD-ChemE, Ohio State U., 1951. Registered profl. engr., Md. Chem. engr. AEC, Wilmington, Del., 1951-53; rsch. engr. Ford Motor Co., Dearborn, Mich., 1953-55; chief chem. nuclear reactor tech. ALCO Products, Schenectady, 1955-58; head nuclear rsch. engr. U.S. Steel, Monroeville, Pa., 1958-63; project mgr. missile design AVCO Corp., Wilmington, Mass., 1963-65; mgr. sci. applications IBM, Manassas, Va., 1965-72, mgr. advanced applications, 1975-87; exec. dir. Inst. for Simulation and Tng., Orlando, Fla., 1987-2000; sr. assoc. Mgmt. and Ednl. Tech. Assocs., 2000—. Chmn. sci. and engring. tech. divsn. Nat. Def. Indsl. Assn.; dir. environment and life scis. Dept. Def., 1972—74; lectr. in field. Contbr. articles to profl. and tech. jours. Mem. Monroeville Parks and Recreation Commn., 1960; chmn. Monroeville Mental Health Assn., 1961; mem. Monroeville Zoning and Planning Commn., 1961; chmn. sci. and engring. tech. divsn. Nat. Def. Indsl. Assn., 1999—; dep. precinct chmn. Montgomery County Rep. Com., 1982. With USN, 1944—46, PTO. Recipient award, Am. Chem. Soc., 1957. Fellow: Am. Inst. Chemists; mem.: Am. Metall. Soc., Am. Def. Preparedness Assn. (chmn. sci. and engring. tech. divsn. 1981—, ednl. advisor Def. Jour., Am. Def. award 1984, Gold medal 1990), Am. Inst. Chem. Engrs., Nat. Security Indsl. Assn., Ohio State U. Alumni Assn., Johns Hopkins U. Alumni Assn. Home: 11401 Ridge Mist Ter Potomac MD 20854-7002 E-mail: lmedin@comcast.net.

MEDIN, ALICE LOUISE, librarian; b. Eau Claire, Wis., July 17, 1935; d. Ongle Ever and Esther Bianca (Rasmussen) Moholt; m. Myron James Medin, May 14, 1955; children: John, Kären, Anne. BA in Edn., Ea. Wash. U., 1957; MA in Libr. Sci., U. Wis., Madison, 1977. Libr. asst. U. Wis. Fond du Lac Ctr., 1979; reference libr. Plaza br. Kansas City (Mo.) Pub. Libr., 1984-86, describer old and rare books main libr., 1985; dir. Rogers (Ark.) Pub. Libr., 1987—2000. Mem. N.W. Ark. C.C. Found. Bd., Rogers, 1987-95. Bd. dirs. Bella Vista Pub. Libr., 2002—03. Recipient Intellectual Freedom Fighter award, ALA/Freedom to Read Found., 1999. Mem. AAUW (pres. Fond du Lac br. 1973-75), Ark. Libr. Assn. (mem. intellectual freedom com. 1993-2000), N.W. Ark. Libr. Assn. (v.p. 1988-89), Round Table Lectr. Club (v.p. 1979). Lutheran. Avocations: reading, knitting, theater. Home: 1 Audley Cir Bella Vista AR 72714-5645

MEDIN, JULIA ADELE, mathematics educator, researcher; b. Dayton, Ohio, Jan. 16, 1929; d. Caroline (Feinberg) Levitt; m. A. Louis Medin, Dec. 24, 1950; children: Douglas, David, Thomas, Linda. BS in Maths. Edn., Ohio State U., 1951; MA in Higher Edn., George Washington U., 1977; PhD in Counseling and Edn., Am. U., 1985. Cert. tchr., Fla., Md. Rsch. engr. Sun Oil Co., Marcus Hook, Pa., 1951-53; tchr. maths. Montgomery County Pub. Schs., Rockville, Md., 1973-88; asst. prof. maths. U. Ctrl. Fla., Orlando, 1988-90, sr. ednl. technologist Inst. for Simulation and Tng., 1990-99; sr. assoc. Mgmt. and Ednl. Tech. Assocs., 1999—. Adv. steering com. U.S. Dept. Edn. Title II, Washington, 1985-89; sr. math. educator, rschr. Inst. for Simulation and Tng., Orlando, 1988-90; judge, co-chair GII Nar. Awards; co-acad. advisor I/ITSEC Conf.; condr. nationwide rsch. project on effective use of technology in the classroom; spkr. in field. Author: Loc. of Cont. and Test Anxiety of Mar. Math. Studies, 1985; contbg. author: Math for 14 & 17 Yr. Olds, 1987; editor: Simulation and Computer-Based Technology for Education; contbr. articles to profl. jours. Dem. committeewoman Town of Monroeville, Pa., 1962; religious sch. dir. Beth Tikva Religious Sch., Rockville, 1971; cons. Monroeville Mental Health, 1960. Mem. Nat. Coun. Tchrs. Math., Math. Assn. Am. (task force on minorities in math.), Women in Math. in Edn., Nat. Coalition for Tech. in Edn. and Tng., Phi Delta Kappa, Kappa Delta Pi. Home and Office: 11401 Ridge Mist Ter Potomac MD 20854-7002 Personal E-mail: jmedin@comcast.net.

MEDIN, LOWELL ANSGARD, management executive; b. Shafer Twp., Minn., Aug. 28, 1932; s. Ansgaard Phillip Magnus and Adelaide Marie Christine (Grandstrand) M.; m. Frances Irene Knutson, Sept. 13, 1958; children: Kimberly June, James Lowell. AS in Liberal Arts, U. Minn., 1957, BBA, 1959. Dairy farmer Medin Farm, Franconia Twp., 1951-53; silo builder Lindstrom Silo, 1956-58; employment mgr. John Wood Co., St. Paul, 1959; salesperson Diversey Co., LaCrosse, Wis., 1959-60; rebuyer, inventory mgr. Montgomery Ward, St. Paul, 1960-67, rebuyer, rebuyer mgr. Chgo., 1967-85; with sales dept. J.T. Gen. Store, Palatine, Ill., 1986; rebuying mgr. Sportsmen's

Guide, Golden Valley, Minn., 1987; inventory mgr. Donald Bruce and Co., Chgo., 1988-91; supr. Pinkerton Security Ops., 1992-96. Pics coord. Hickory Farms, Itasca, Ill., 1995-98. Author: (with others) Shafer Swamp to Village, 1978, The Pioneers of Chicago County 1838-1870, 1992, The Knutson/Stavenau Family Roots, 1994. Candidate for polit. office, Mpls., 1967; del. Minn. State Dem.-Farm Labor Conv., 1956, 58; chmn. cancer drive Village of Palatine, 1968, mem. dist. 6 adv. coun., 1989-97; mem. Homeowners Coun., Palatine, 1976-77; mem. coun. Christ Luth. Ch., Palatine, 1981-86; officer Chicago County DFL Party, 1956-60; del. Chicago County DFL Conv., 1956, 58; pres. Palonis Park Homeowners Assn., Palatine, 1976-82. Cpl. U.S. Army, 1953-55, ETO. Mem. No. Ill. Civil War Roundtable (chartered officer 1983-86, trustee, sec., 2d v.p.), VFW (life, post 981, Arlington Hts.), Am. Legion (life, post 690, Palatine), Alpha Phi Omega. Republican. Lutheran. Avocations: genealogy, gardening, American history, Civil War. Home: 121 S Linden Ave Palatine IL 60074-6342

MEDIN, MYRON JAMES, JR., city manager; b. Ladysmith, Wis., July 8, 1931; s. Myron James and Mildred Clara (Johnson) M.; m. Alice Louise Moholt, May 14, 1955; children: John, Karen, Anne. BA, St. Olaf Coll., 1954; MPA, U. Mich., 1959. Adminstrv. asst. to city mgr. City of Fond du Lac, Wis., 1959-64, city mgr., 1967-83, City of New Ulm, Minn., 1964-67; city adminstr. City of Kansas City, Kans., 1983-85; pres., gen. mgr. Bella Vista Village Property Owners Assn., Ark., 1986-92. Mem. com. human devel. Nat. League of Cities, Washington, 1974-80, com. on govtl. relations, 1971-73; chmn. City Plan Commn., Fond du Lac, Wis., 1967-83 Bd. dirs. United Way, Kansas City, Kans., 1984-85, YMCA, 1984-85, Kansas City C.C. Found., 1984-85; mem. Gov.'s Regionalism Task Force Adv. Com., Madison, Wis., 1968-70; trustee Phillips Pro-Celebrity Golf Tennis Charity Classic, 1991-92, vol. historic house mus. and gardens. Lt. USAF, 1955-57. Recipient Community Service award Fond du Lac Assn. of Commerce, 1978 Mem. Internat. City Mgmt. Assn., Wis. City Mgmt. Assn. (pres. 1975-76), Wis. League of Municipalities (bd. dirs. 1978-80), Wis. Alliance of Cities (v.p. 1972-73), Am. Soc. Pub. Adminstrn. (bd. dirs. 1984-85, Pub. Adminstr. of Yr. award 1985), Bella Vista-Bentonville C. of C. (bd. dirs. 1987-91), Nat. Trust for Hist. Preservation, Benton County Hist. Soc. Lutheran. Avocations: swimming, reading, tennis, gardening, genealogy. Home: 1 Audley Cir Bella Vista AR 72714-5645

MEDINA, HAROLD RAYMOND, III, marketing executive; b. N.Y.C., May 25, 1938; s. Harold Raymond, Jr. and Janet Brevoort (Williams) M.; m. Pamela Carter Huck, Feb. 20, 1965; 1 child: Scott Arthur. AB, Princeton U., 1960. Various direct mktg. positions Time-Life Books, N.Y.C., 1962-69; mng. dir. Time-Life Books U.K., London, 1969-73; pres. Wine of Month, Redwood City, Calif., 1973-75; direct mktg. positions Franklin Mint, Franklin Center, Pa., 1975-83, gen. mgr. catalog group, 1983-84; sr. v.p. Nat. Liberty Ins. Corp., Valley Forge, Pa., 1984-92; pres. Medina Assocs., 1992—. Dir. mktg. cons. Medina Assocs., 1974-75, assoc. dir. mktg. cons., 1992—; guest lectr. direct mkgt. NYU, 1983. Membership chmn. Rose Valley Folk Pa.; chmn., bd. dirs. Hedgerow Theatre, Rose Valley; regional fund raising chmn. Exeter Acad., N.H., 1977-78; mem. fund raising com. Children's Aid Soc., N.Y.C., 1967-69. Served to 1st lt. U.S. Army, 1960-62. Mem. Am. Soc. Aging (exec. com., bus. forum on aging), Nat. Assn. Sr. Living Industries (bd. dirs. 1987-87), Direct Mktg. Assn. (chmn. ethics com. 1998-2003, seminar faculty 1994—), Direct Mktg. Idea Exch., Westhampton Country Club (N.Y., bd. dirs. 1967-69). Republican. Presbyterian. Home and Office: 12 Hilltop Rd Wallingford PA 19086-6243 E-mail: kurtmedina@aol.com.

MEDINA, J. MICHAEL, lawyer, educator; b. N.Y.C., June 28, 1950; s. Abel and Renee Medina. BA summa cum laude, Southwestern Coll., Winfield, Kan., 1972; JD with special distinction, U. Okla., 1975. Bar: Okla. 1975, U.S. Ct. Appeals (10th cir.) 1977, U.S. Ct. Appeals (5th cir.) 1978, U.S. Ct. Appeals (fed. cir.) 1982, U.S. Ct. Appeals (2d cir.) 1990, U.S. Ct. Appeals (D.C. cir.) 1994, U.S. Ct. Appeals (7th and 8th cirs.) 2002, U.S. Supreme Ct. 1979. Assoc. Holiman, Langhoz, Runnels & Dorwart, Tulsa, 1975-80, ptnr., 1980-86, shareholder, 1986-94; pvt. practice Tulsa, 1994—. Judge Okla. Ct. Appeals Temporary Divsn. # 14, 1992-93; adj. prof. law U. Tulsa Law Sch., 1988, 92-2004; mem. Supreme Ct. Appellate Rules Revision Com. Contbr. articles to profl. jours.; editor U. Okla. Law Review, 1973-75. Mem. Am. Acad. Appellate Lawyers, Order of the Coif (sec.), Assn. Bar U.S. Ct. Appeals Tenth Cir. Republican. Roman Catholic. Avocations: bridge, reading, travel. Office: 124 E 4th St Ste 100 Tulsa OK 74103-5005 Office Phone: 918-583-9947.

MEDINA, JANET GAIL, school psychologist, educator; b. NYC, Apr. 15, 1954; d. Victor Emmanuel and Barbara Florence Medina; m. Brian Eugene Gray, Sept. 10, 1977; children: Elizabeth Jessyn Medina-Gray, Jennifer Sharyn Medina-Gray. BA in Anthropology, U. of Mont., 1977; MSc in Edn. in Reading, St. Bonaventure (N.Y.) U., 1987; MA in Sch. Psychology, Alfred (N.Y.) U., 1997, cert. in Psychology, 1998, PsychD in Sch. Psychology, 1999. Cert. elem., secondary, social studies, reading and spl. edn. tchr. NY, sch. psychologist NY. Spl. edn. tchr. Andover (N.Y.) Ctrl. Sch., 1984—85, Wellsville (N.Y.) HS, 1986—88; coord. of spl. svcs. Jamestown C.C., Olean, NY, 1988—92; opportunity programs counselor Alfred (N.Y.) U., 1995—97; coord. of disabled student svcs. St. Bonaventure (N.Y.) U., 1992—95; coord. of learning support svcs. Harford C.C., Belair, Md., 1997—2000; asst. prof. of edn. McDaniel Coll., Westminster, Md., 2000—. Cons. in field; presenter in field. Contbr.: Identifying Specific Learning Disabilities: Maryland's Technical Assistance Guide, 2001, A Guide To Disability Services in Higher Education in Maryland: Transitioning for Students With Disabilites; contbr. articles to profl. jours. Bd. dir. Harford County Commn. on Disabilities, Belair, Md., 1997—2000; mem. of adv. bd. N.E. Tech. Assistance Ctr. of the Nat. Tech. Inst. of the Deaf, Catonsville, Md., 1999—. Fellow, Alfred U., 1995—97; grantee, N.Y. Devel. Disabilities Planning Coun., 1992—93, Jesse Ball Dupont Found., 2001. Mem.: Md. Assn. for Bilingual Edn. (co-founder, v.p.), Nat. Assn. for Bilingual Edn. (assoc.), So. Poverty Law Ctr. Tchg. Tolerance (assoc.), Nat. Tutoring Assn. (assoc.), Assn.on Higher Edn. and Disability (assoc.; internat. conf. co-chmn. 2001—02). Avocations: reading, hiking, canoeing, handspinning, weaving. Office: McDaniel College 2 College Hill Westminster MD 21157 Office Phone: 410-857-2417. E-mail: jmedina@mcdaniel.edu.

MEDINA, JESSE JAMES, protective services official, educator; b. Roma, Tex., May 18, 1956; s. Benigno and Celia Gonzalez M.; m. Dina Pena, May 25, 1979; children: Gerardo J., Rebecca A. AAS, Laredo (Tex.) Jr. Coll., 1977; BS, St. John's U., Springfield, Mo., 2000. Dep. sheriff Starr County, Rio Grande City, Tex., 1975-78; police officer City of Pharr, Tex., 1978-79, detective sgt., 1984-99, lt., 1984-90, capt., 1990-92, asst. chief police, 1992-96, chief police, 1996—. Sgt.-at-arms Rio Grande Valley Chief Assn., 1998. Editor State Mag. Chmn., 1983. V.p. Self Sufficiency Counsel, 1999; sec. treas. team plan com. Traffic Problem, 2000; mem. Internat. Bridge Traffic Adv. Coun., 2002--. Recipient Leadership award, Mexican Govt., 1999. Fellow Tex. Atty. Gens. Office (Excellence award 1989). Republican. Menonite. Avocations: hunting, fishing, camping. Home: 810 Tarrant Cir Pharr TX 78577-3942 Office: Pharr Police Dept 202 E Clark Ave Pharr TX 78577-3942 E-mail: jmedina@pharrpd.net.

MEDINA, KATHRYN BACH, book editor; b. Plainfield, N.J. d. F. Earl and Elizabeth E. Bach; 1 child from previous marriage. BA, Smith Coll.; MA, NYU. With Doubleday Pub. Co., Inc., N.Y.C., 1965-85; exec. editor, sr. v.p. Random House, N.Y.C., 1985—. Assoc. fellow Jonathan Edwards Coll., Yale U., New Haven, 1982—; fellow Bunting Inst., 1994—95; cons., 1995—96, Coun. Fgn. Rels. Editor books by James Atlas, Peter Benchley, Amy Bloom, Tom Brokaw, Anita Brookner, Ethan Canin, Michael Chabon, Robert Coles, Agnes deMille, E.L. Doctorow, Jane Fonda, Max Frankel, Henry Louis Gates, Jr., Carol Gilligan, Mary Gordon, David Halberstam, Kathryn Harrison, John Irving, Tracy Kidder, Wynton Marsalis, Bobbie Ann Mason, James A. Michener, Sandra Day O'Connor, Jane Pauley, Anna Quindlen, Nancy Reagan, James Reston, William Safire, Maggie Scarf, Gloria Steinem, Christopher Tilghman, Alice Walker, Daniel Yergin, Wynton Marsalis, others.

MEDINA, LUIS SANTIAGO, radiologist, researcher; b. Medellin, Colombia, Jan. 4, 1964; married. MD, CES U., 1987; MPH, Harvard U., 1997. Cert. Am. Bd. Radiology, 1994. Physician Miami Children's Hosp., 1987—. Author: Children With Headache: Clinical Predictors of Brain Lesions and the Role of Neuroimaging, Study Design and Analysis in Neuroradiology. A Practical Approach, Newborns with Suspected Occult Spinal Dysraphism. A Cost-Effectiveness Analysis of Diagnostic Strategies, False Lateralization of language cortex on functional MRI after a cluster of focal seizures., Study Design and Analysis in Neuroradiology. A Practical Approach. Recipient Sci. Exhibit Cum Laude award, RSNA, 1993, Computer Assisted Exhibit Cum Laude award, Am. Soc. Neuroradiology, 1999; fellow Roentgen Rsch. fellow, RSNA Rsch. and Edn. Fund, 1996. Office: Miami Children's Hosp 3100 SW 62 Ave Miami FL 33155

MEDINA, SANDRA, social worker, educator; b. Tulsa, Oct. 4, 1947; d. James and Erleen (Austin) Meeks; m. Michael Sellman, 1966 (div. 1979); children: Rhainnie, Morgan; m. Ernest Medina, Aug. 21, 1985; 1 child, Brendyn. Cert., Community Coll. of Denver, 1975; BS summa cum laude, Met. State Coll., Denver, 1981; MSW, U. Denver, 1983, postgrad. Lic. clin. social worker, Colo. Dir. Lafayette (Colo.) Presch./Playtime, 1973-75, Bennett (Colo.) Non-Denominational Presch., 1975-76; intern. in clin. social work Brighton (Colo.) Schs., 1981-82; adminstrv. social work intern Jefferson County (Colo.) Schs., 1982-83; med. social worker Las Animas County Health Dept., Trinidad, Colo., 1985-85; psychiat. social worker Colo. State Hosp., Pueblo, 1985-89; clin. social worker PsychCare, Greeley, 1990-92; counselor high sch. U. Northern Colo. Lab. Sch. Instr. Trinidad State Jr. Coll., 1984-85; field instr. N.Mex. Highlands U., Las Vegas, 1986-87, U. So. Colo., Pueblo, 1988-89; adj. prof. social work U. Denver, 1996-97; asst. prof. social work, practicum coord. Chadron State Coll., 1997-99. Mem. exec. com. Gov.'s Task Force on Child Abuse, Denver, 1985; bd. dirs. Adams County Rep. Advs. for Children Today, Denver, 1978-79; chairperson membership com. Met. Child Protection Coun., Denver, 1982-83. Mem. NASW. Democrat. Presbyterian. E-mail: bestmedfam@netscape.net.

MEDINA-SALINAS, ELIZABETH, publishing executive, writer; b. Brooklyn, NY, Feb. 18, 1967; d. Heriberto Medina and Gloria Morales-Cook; m. Andrew J. Salinas, July 31, 1989; 1 child, Omar J. Salinas. Real estate agent Gold Coast Sch. of Real Estate, Fla., 2001. Pres. EMS Graphic Source, Margate, Fla., 1996—99, Uzful Corp., Coral Springs, Fla., 1999—; various positions as editor, graphic designer, translator, printing broker. Book cover, El Santuario; author: Beauty Secrets, 2003. Achievements include patents pending for vehicle wiper (utility patent); parcel; necklace; vehicle wiper design. Avocations: writing, inventing, reading, travel, piano. Office: Uzful Corporation 7667 W Sample Road 210 Coral Springs FL 33065

MEDINGER, C. WYNN, design and branding consultant; b. Chestnut Hill, Pa., June 30, 1950; s. Charles W. and Margaret (Wynn) M.; m. Betsy S. Medinger; children: Christopher Wynn, Jill Barbara. BFA, Univ. of the Arts, 1972. Designer Gottschalk & Ash, Montreal, Que., Can., 1972-76; sr. designer Anspach, Grossman, Portugal, N.Y.C., 1977-98; pres. JMK Corp, Ridgefield, Conn., 1977-2000; CEO BrandLogic Corp. (merger), Wilton, Conn., 2000—, JMK, Context and Navistream Corps. Involved n corp. identity programs for GE, Texaco, IBM, Wyeth, others. Recipient numerous awards in field, including Am. Inst. of Graphic Arts, Art Dirs. Club of Chgo., Art Dirs. Club of N.Y., Can. Pub. Rels. Soc., Gold Ink awards, IBM design awards, others.

MEDLAND, MAURICE BLUE, writer; b. Centerville, Iowa, Sept. 29, 1936; s. William C. and Avis N. (Blue) M.; m. Karen A. McFarland, Aug. 7, 1965; children: Melissa A., Steven W. BS, Truman State U., 1961; MBA, Pepperdine U., 1977. Mgmt. sys. analyst Rockwell Internat. Corp., Downey, Calif., 1961-70; dir. Fluor Corp., Irvine, Calif., 1970-85; v.p. PacifiCare Health Sys., Cypress, Calif., 1985-87; novelist Calif., 1987—; instr. U. Calif., Irvine, 1998—. Adv. Calif. State U. Fullerton Writer's Program, 1998—. Author: Point of Honor, 1997. With USN, 1954-57. Recipient Apollo Achievement award NASA, 1969. Mem. The Authors Guild. Home: 19842 Villager Cir Yorba Linda CA 92886-4454 Fax: 714 779-9831. E-mail: mauricemedland@msn.com.

MEDLAND, WILLIAM JAMES, university president; b. Logansport, Ind., Jan. 1, 1944; s. Thomas Gallagher and Mary Elizabeth (Hassett) M.; m. Donna Lee Bahnaman, Mar. 12, 1977; children: Bridget Marie, Mark David, Jeanne Nicole. BA, U. Notre Dame, 1966; student, St. Louis U., 1972-74; MA in History, Ball State U., 1967, MA in Edn., 1979, PhD in History, 1980; postgrad., Inst. for Mgmt. Lifelong Edn., Harvard U., 1985, Ctr. Internat. Cooperation and Security Studies, U. Wis., 1988, Ctr. Internat. Studies, MIT, 1989, Freie Universitat, Berlin, 1991. Instr. history and philosophy Donnelly coll., Kansas City, Kans., 1967-70; curricular advisor Ball State U., Muncie, Ind., 1970-71, teaching fellow, 1977-80; asst. dean St. Louis (Mo.) U., 1971-75; employee supr. Wilson, Inc., Logansport, 1975-76; ops. mgr. Watson-Jenkins, Inc., Indpls., 1976-77; dean of coll., asst. prof. history Springfield (Ill.) Coll., 1980-81; acad. dean, assoc. prof. history and edn. Marymount Coll., Salina, Kans., 1981-86; exec. v.p., provost, prof. history St. Mary's U., Winona, Minn., 1986-91; pres., prof. history Viterbo U., LaCrosse, Wis., 1991—, also bd. dirs., CEO, 1991—. Edn. cons. Am. Inst. Banking, Springfield, 1980-81; advisor Adv. Com. to Sch. Bd., Salina, 1984, Salina Diocesan Bd. Edn., 1981-83; evaluator North Ctrl. Assn., Chgo., 1987-2000. Author: Cuban Missile Crisis of 1962-Needless or Necessary?, 1988, reprint, 1990, A Guide to Writing College Research Papers, 1989, The Catholic School: A Bibliographical Resource Guide, 1990; editor: Ind. Acad. Social Scis. jour., 1979, Perspectives: A Liberal Arts Exchange (faculty jour.), 1988. Coll. solicitor United Way, St. Louis, 1973; coord. Coll./Cmty. Artist Series, Salina, 1981—84; mem. Franciscan-Skemp Healthcare Cmty. Bd., 2002—; bd. dirs. Immaculate Heart of Mary Sem., Winona, 1987—91, La Crosse Med. Health Sci. Consortium, 1993—, Wis. Found. for Ind. Colls., 1994—98, Assn. Franciscan Colls. and Univs., 1999—; chair La Crosse Diocesan Edn. Commn., 1994—2001. Named LaCrosse Tribune Person of the Yr./ Iverson-Freking Ecumenical award, 2003; fellow Ctr. Internat. Studies, MIT/Harvard U., 1989. Mem.: KC, Wis. Assn. Ind. Colls. and Univs. (bd. dirs. 1991—), Am. Assn. Ind. Coll. Pres., Coun. Coll. Pres., Am. Assn. Higher Edn., La Crosse C. of C. (bd. dirs. 2000—, exec. com. 2001—), Rotary, Phi Delta Kappa, Phi Alpha Theta (rsch. award Ball State U. 1979). Roman Catholic. Avocations: reading, research. Home: 119 Calla Ct Onalaska WI 54650-8317 Office: Viterbo Univ Office of Pres 900 Viterbo Dr La Crosse WI 54601-4777 E-mail: wjmedland@viterbo.edu.

MEDLAR, DEBORAH STARKEY, history and political science educator; b. Devils Lake, N.D., Sept. 13, 1952; d. Harold Lee and Ruth Adele (Swan) Starkey; m. Richard Lee Medlar, July 21, 1978; children: Noah, Ira. BA cum laude, Jamestown Coll., N.D., 1976. Tchr. Egeland H.S., ND, 1976—77, Dickinson H.S., ND, 1977—79, Trinity H.S., Dickinson, ND, 1988—; adj. lectr. Dickinson State U., ND, 2001—. Tchr. cons. Nat. Geog. Soc. Mem.: APA, N.D. Geog. Alliance, Nat. Coun. for Social Studies. Office: Dickinson State Univ 291 Campus Dr Dickinson ND 58601 Business E-Mail: deborah.s.medlar@dsu.nodak.edu.

MEDLER, MARY ANN L. federal judge; JD, St. Louis U., 1983. Atty. Thompson Coburn, St. Louis, 1983-85; asst. cir. atty. Office of Cir. Atty. of City of St. Louis, 1985-92; atty. Union Pacific R.R., St. Louis, 1992-93; magistrate judge U.S. Dist. Ct. (ea. dist.) Mo., St. Louis. Office: 111 S 10th St Rm 13S Saint Louis MO 63102 E-mail: Mary_Ann_Medler@moed.uscourts.gov.

MEDLEY, ALEX ROY, executive minister; b. Columbus, Ga., Aug. 4, 1948; s. Howard and Clois Mildred (Chumney) M.; m. Patricia Stauffer, May 10, 1975; children: James Ethan, Christopher Jordan. BA magna cum laude, U. Chattanooga, 1970; cert., Grad. Sch. Ecumenical Studies, Celigny, Switzerland, 1973; MDiv, Princeton Sem., 1974. Ordained to ministry Bapt. Ch., 1975. Assoc. pastor First Bapt. Ch. Trenton, N.J., 1974-77; adminstrv. intern Nat. Ministries Am. Bapt. Chs. U.S.A., Valley Forge, Pa., 1977, nat. dir. Christian ctr., 1978-85; min. of world mission support, area min. Am. Bapt. Chs. N.J., East Orange, 1986-92, exec. min., 1992—2001; gen. sec. Am Bap. Chs. in the USA, 2002—. Intern World Coun. Chs., Geneva, Switzerland, 1973; rep. N.Am. Bapt. Fellowship, Washington, 1975-77; mem. domestic hunger/poverty working group Nat. Coun. Chs. of Christ, 1978-85, mem. gen. assembly; conf. speaker Am. Bapt. Chs., 1979; Am. Bapt. Ch. U.S.A. del. to Nat. Coun. Chs. of Christ. Editor (newsletter) Social Edn. for Action Newsletter, 1978-79. Bd. dirs. Ch. World Svc./CROP, N.J., 1975-77, Occupational Tng. Ctr., Burlington, N.J., 1992-99; sec. Key Inmate Edn. Project, Trenton, 1986; participant Nat. Religious Leadership Program, 1997-99, Bapt. World Alliance Commn. on Freedom and Justice, 2000—. Mem. Am. Bapt. Regional Exec. Mins. Coun. Baptist. Avocations: reading, fishing, hiking. Office: American Baptist Churches PO Box 851 Valley Forge PA 19482

MEDLEY, DONALD MATTHIAS, education educator, consultant; b. Faulkton, S.D., Feb. 18, 1917; s. Thomas Arnot and Cecilia Agnes (Kellen) M.; m. Betty Ann Robertsen, Aug. 23, 1948; 1 child, Timothy Laurence. BS, Coll. of St. Thomas, St. Paul, 1938; MA, U. Minn., 1950, PhD, 1954. Tchr. Am. Sch. Guadalajara, Mex., 1941-42, Floodwood (Minn.) Pub. Schs., 1946-48; instr. English, Coll. of St. Thomas, 1948-50; asst. prof. CUNY, 1954-59, assoc. prof., 1959-64, prof., 1964-65; sr. rsch. psychologist Ednl. Testing Svc., Princeton, N.J., 1965-70; disting. prof. U. Va., Charlottesville, 1970-87, prof. emeritus, 1987—. Mem. exec. bd. Consortium for the Improvement of Tchr. Evaluation, Atlanta, 1985-87. Author: (with others) Measurement-Based Evaluation of Teacher Performance, 1984, Handbook of Research on Teaching, 1963, The Teather's Handbook, 1971, Research on Teaching, Concepts, Findings, and Implications, 1979, Ency. of Educational Research, 5th edit., 1982, 6th edit., 1992, Developing Skills for Instructional Supervision, 1984, Measurement-Based Evaluation of Teacher Performance, 1984, Advances in Teacher Education, 1984, International Ency. of Education: Research and Studies, 1984, 2d edit., 1994, Assessment of Teaching: Purposes, Practices, and Implications for the Profession, 1999; contbr. articles to profl. jours. Staff Sgt. U.S. Army, 1942-46. Fellow APA; mem. Am. Ednl. Rsch. Assn. (divsn. sec. 1962), Nat. Coun. on Measurement in Edn., Assn. Tchr. Educators. Democrat. Roman Catholic. Avocation: travel. E-mail: dm4c@aol.com.

MEDLIN, JOHN GRIMES, JR., banker, director; b. Benson, N.C., Nov. 23, 1933; s. John Grimes and Mabel (Stephenson) M. BS in Bus. Adminstrn., U. N.C., 1956; grad., The Exec. Program, U. Va., 1965. With Wachovia Bank & Trust Co., Winston-Salem, N.C., 1959-93, pres., 1974; pres., CEO Wachovia Bank and Wachovia Corp., Winston-Salem, N.C., 1977-93; chmn. bd. Wachovia Corp., Winston-Salem, N.C., 1987-98, chmn. emeritus, 1998—. Trustee Nat. Humanities Ctr., Wake Forest U., The Duke Endowment, The Rsch. Triangle Found., Kenan Inst. for Ethics; mem. State Jud. Coun. N.C., 2000—; active numerous civic and svc. orgns. With USNR, 1956-59. Mem. Phi Delta Theta. Office: Wachovia Corp PO Box 3099 100 N Main St Winston Salem NC 27101-4047 Office Phone: 336-732-5000.

MEDLOCK, DONALD LARSON, lawyer; b. Port Chester, N.Y., Mar. 8, 1927; s. J. Harold and Emma Adelaide (MacLennan) M.; m. Katharine Smedes Nicholson, May 21, 1955; children: Katharine Baird, Margaret MacLennan, William Nicholson. BA with honors, Yale U., 1947, LLB, 1950. Bar: N.Y. 1950, U.S. Dist. Ct. (so. dist.) N.Y. 1951, U.S. Dist. Ct. (ea. dist.) N.Y. 1952, U.S. Tax Ct. 1952, U.S. Ct. Custom and Patent Appeals, U.S. Ct. Appeals (2d cir.) 1951. Assoc. Putnam & Roberts, N.Y.C., 1950-56, ptnr., 1957-94, sr. counsel, 1995—. Bd. dirs. Bancard Sys. of N.Y. Inc., Port Washington. Editor Yale Law Jour., New Haven, 1948-50. Sec., bd. dirs. Port Washington Community Chest, 1959-61; bd. dirs. Port Washington Estates Assn., 1958-61; mem. ann. fund parents com. Taft Sch., 1979-81; bd. mgrs., exec. com. William Sloane Ho. YMCA of Greater N.Y., 1979-84; chmn. univ. coun. com. on Law Sch. Yale U., 1979-86; chmn. Yale Alumni Fund, 1984-86, bd. dirs., 1955—, exec. com., 1980-88; chmn. Yale Law Sch. Fund, 1974-76; mem. devel. bd. Yale U., 1984-88, exec. com., 1984-86; exec. com. Yale Law Sch., 1975-79, hon., 1979—; bd. dirs. Assn. Yale Alumni, 1984-86, rep.-at-large, 1979-82, com. on undergrad. admisssions, 1979-82, com. on Yale medal, 1981; exec. com. Assn. Families U. Denver, 1982-84. Recipient citation Yale Law Sch., 1977, Yale Alumni Fund Chmn.'s award, 1979, 87, Yale medal, 1994. Mem. Fed. Power Bar Assn., Assn. of Bar of City of N.Y. (com. on profl. ethics 1958-61), Corbey Ct. Yale Law Sch., Tuscarora Club (Margaretville, N.Y., bd. dirs. 1963-95, sec. 1970-86, v.p. 1984-86), Country Club of Landfall, Manhasset Bay Yacht Club, Mory's Assn., India House, Scroll and Key Soc., Yale Club N.Y.C., Phi Beta Kappa, Phi Delta Phi. Avocations: trout fishing, tennis, reading, crossword puzzles, golf. Home: Landfall 800 Oyster Lndg Wilmington NC 28405-5292

MEDNEY, TANIA LEVY, advertising agency executive; b. Rio de Janeiro, June 19, 1955; d. Samuel and Paulette (Schinazi) L.; children: Matthew Levy, Samantha Jennifer. BA cum laude, SUNY, Albany, 1977. Sec. Benton & Bowles, Inc., N.Y.C., 1977-78, network coord., 1978-79, sr. media planner, 1979-81, Young & Rubicam, N.Y.C., 1981-82, media supr., 1982-87, media dir. Young & Rubicam Bravo, N.Y.C., 1987-88; sr. media supr. Young & Rubicam, N.Y.C., 1987-89, tng. specialist, 1983-89, mktg. and media cons., tng. specialist, 1989—; media supr. Foote, Cone & Belding, N.Y.C., 1998-99; assoc. media dir. Bates USA, N.Y.C., 1999—2001; media and mktg. cons., 2001—. Song specialist, dance and guitar instr. Author: Supervisory Skills Manual, 1984. Democrat. Avocations: dance, playing guitar, travel, photography, skiing. E-mail: tlmrio@aol.com.

MEDNICK, ROBERT, accountant; b. Chgo., Apr. 1, 1940; s. Harry and Nettie (Brenner) M.; m. Susan Lee Levinson, Oct. 28, 1962; children: Michael Jon, Julie Eden, Adam Charles. BSBA, Roosevelt U., Chgo., 1962. CPA Ill. Staff asst. Arthur Andersen, Chgo., 1962-63, sr. acct., 1963-66, mgr., 1966-71, ptnr., 1971-98, mng. dir. SEC policies, 1973-76, mng. dir. auditing procedures, 1976-79. Vice chmn. com. on profl. stds. Andersen Worldwide, 1979-82, chmn. com., 1982-98, mng. ptnr. profl. and regulatory matters, 1993-98; mem. faculty Northwestern U. Kellogg Grad. Sch. Mgmt., 1999; mem. CPR panel disting. neutrals in banking, acctg. and fin. svcs. CPR Inst. for Dispute Resolution, 2003—. Contbr. articles to profl. jours. Bd. dirs. Roosevelt U., Chgo., 1977—, vice chmn., 1986-94, sr. vice chmn., 1994—, life trustee, 1999—; bd. dirs. Auditorium Theatre Coun., 1990-96, Lake Shore Drive Synagogue, 1992—; co-chmn. adv. coun. Chgo. Action for Soviet Jewry, Highland Park, Ill., 1983-87; bd. dirs., mem. exec. com. Am. Judicature Soc., 1990-95, vice chmn., 1993-95; bd. overseers Rand Corp. Inst. Civil Justice, 1994-98; bd. dirs. Nat. Bur. of Econ. Rsch., 1998—, treas., 1999—; acccountability adv. coun. to the Comptr. Gen. of the U.S., 2000—. Sgt. USAFR, 1965-69. Recipient Silver medal Ill. CPA Soc., 1962; named One of Ten Outstanding Young Men in Chgo., Chgo. Jr. C. of C., 1973-74; recipient Rolf A. Weil Disting. Service award, Roosevelt U., Chgo., 1983; Max Block award N.Y. State C.P.A. Soc., 1984; Ann. Literary award Jour. Accountancy, 1986, 88; Andrew D. Bradin award for distinctive contbns. to discipline of accountancy Case Western Res. U., Cleve., 1996; Disting. Alumni award Roosevelt U. Walter E. Heller Coll. Bus. Adminstrn., 1997; Disting. Vis. scholar Hebrew U., Jerusalem, 1999, 2000. Mem. AICPA (bd. dirs. 1986-87, 92-94, 95-98, vice chmn. 1995-96, chmn. 1996-97, numerous coms., Elijah Watt Sells award 1962, Gold Medal for Disting. Svc. 1998), Ill. CPA Soc. (acctg. prins. com. 1973, legal liability com. 1986-89, mgmt. of acctg. practice com. 1991-94, regulation and legis. com. 1998—), Internat. Fedn. Accts. (chmn. compliance adv. panel 2003—). Jewish. Avocations: collecting art, travel. Office Phone: 312-642-0571. E-mail: bobmednick@aol.com.

MEDOFF, MARK HOWARD, playwright, screenwriter, novelist; b. Mt. Carmel, Ill., Mar. 18, 1940; s. Lawrence Ray and Thelma Irene (Butt) M.; m. Stephanie Thorne, June 24, 1972; children: Debra, Rachel, Jessica. BA, U. Miami, 1962; MA, Stanford U., 1966; DHL, Gallaudet Coll., 1981. Instr. English and drama N.Mex. State U., 1966-79, dramatist-in-residence, 1974—, head dept. drama, 1978-87, prof. drama, 1979-93, artistic dir., 1982-87, Am. S.W. Theatre Co., 1984-87. Author: (plays) When You Comin' Back, Red Ryder?, 1974, The Wager, 1975, The Kramer, 1975, The Halloween Bandit, 1978, The Conversion of Aaron Weiss, 1978, Firekeeper, 1978, The Last Chance Saloon, 1979, Children of a Lesser God, 1980 (Soc. West Theatres best play award 1982), The Majestic Kid, 1981, The Hands of Its Enemy, 1984, Kringle's Window, 1985, The Heart Outright, 1986, Road to a Revolution, 2001, Prymate, 2004, The Same Live Over, 2004, (novel) Dreams of Long Lasting: (films) When You Comin' Back, Red Ryder?, 1979, Off Beat,

1986, Apology, 1986, Children of a Lesser God, 1986, Good Guys Wear Black, 1978, Clara's Heart, 1988, The Majestic Kid, 1988, City of Joy, 1992, Homage, 1995, Santa Fe, 1997, Who Fly On Angel's Wings, 2000, Clukkin On Their Birthdays, 2002; works appear in Best Plays, 1973-74, 75-75, 79-80, Best Short Plays, 1975, The Homage that Follows, 1987; plays Stumps, 1989, Stefanie Hero, 1990, Showdown On Rio Road, 1995, Gila, 1995, A Christmas Carousel, 1996, Crunch Time, 1996, Gunfighters, A Gulf War Chronicle, 1997, A Christmas Carousel, 1998, Tommy J and Sally, 2000; dir. (film) Children on Their Birthdays. Guggenheim fellow, 1974-75; recipient Obie award, Drama Desk award, Outer Critics Circle award, Media award Pres.'s Com. Employment Handicapped, Tony award; Oscar award nominee for Best Screenplay for Children of A Lesser God, 1987; Reynolds Eminent scholar Fla. State U., 2003—. Mem. SAG, Coll. Fellows Am. Theater, Dramatists Guild, Writers Guild Am., Actors Equity Assn., PEN, Coll. Fellows of the Am. Theatre. Office: PO Box 3072 Las Cruces NM 88003-3072

MEDOFF, RICHARD BRAD, speech educator; b. NYC, June 17, 1952; s. Gilbert and Elaine Medoff. PhD, CUNY, 1993. Asst. prof. LaGuardia CC, New York, NY, 1993—98; assoc. prof. Mercy Coll., Dobbs Ferry, NY, 1999—. Editor: Soviet and East Europe Performance; author: (plays) No Change, Autopsy, the Enemy. Recipient Excellence in Tchg., Mercy College-Bronx campus, 2000. Mem.: ATHE. Home: 23 West 73rd Street New York NY 10023 Office: Mercy College 555 Broadway Dobbs Ferry NY 10522 Office Phone: 914-674-7273. Personal E-mail: rmedoff@mercy.edu.

MEDVECKY, ROBERT STEPHEN, lawyer; b. Bridgeport, Conn., Feb. 12, 1931; s. Stephen and Elizabeth (Petro) M.; m. Ellen R. Munt, Nov. 11, 1966; children— Allison L., Beth A., Craig R. AB, Dartmouth, 1952; JD, Harvard, 1955. Bar: Ill. bar 1955, Conn. bar 1958, D.C. bar 1972, Fla. bar 1989. Asso. firm Lord, Bissell & Brook, Chgo., 1955-57; gen. atty. So. New Eng. Telephone Co., New Haven, 1957-71; v.p., gen. counsel, sec. Amtrak, Washington, 1971-75; partner firm Lord, Bissell & Brook, Washington, 1975-78, Reid & Priest, N.Y.C., 1978-87. Clubs: Harvard (N.Y.C.), Fiddlesticks Country (Ft. Meyers, Fla.), Saphire Valley Country (Cashlers, N.C.). Home: 15491 Kilbirnie Dr Fort Myers FL 33912-2424 also: 457 Round Hill Rd Sapphire NC 28774-7608 E-mail: bmedvecky@yahoo.com.

MEDVECKY, THOMAS EDWARD, lawyer; b. Bridgeport, Conn., Apr. 22, 1937; s. Stephen and Elizabeth P. Medvecky; m. Patricia Conneally, Aug. 25, 1967; 1 son, Thomas Edward, II. A.B., Bowdoin Coll., 1959; LL.B., St. John's U., 1962. Bar: Conn. 1962. Assoc., Louis Katz, Danbury, Conn., 1963-68; sole practice, Bethel, Conn., 1968—; asst. town counsel Town of Bethel, 1963-67; assoc. dir. State Nat. Bank Conn. Mem. budget com. Danbury (Conn.) Community Chest, 1966-68. Served with USAR, 1962-68. Recipient Am. Jurisprudence award 1962. Mem. ABA, Conn. Bar Assn., Danbury Bar Assn. Democrat. Lutheran. Office: 99 Greenwood Ave PO Box 272 Bethel CT 06801-0272

MEDVED, MICHAEL, film critic, author, talk show host; b. Phila., Oct. 3, 1948; s. David Bernard and Renate Rosa (Hirsch) M.; m. Nancy Harris Herman, Aug. 5, 1972 (div. 1983); m. Diane Elvenstar, Jan. 27, 1985; children: Sarah Julia, Shayna Elana, Daniel Joshua. BA, Yale U., 1969; MFA, Calif. State U., San Francisco, 1974. Speech writer, polit. cons. various campaigns and politicians, Conn., Calif., D.C., 1970-73; advt. creative dir. Anrick Inc., Oakland, Calif., 1973-74; freelance writer L.A., 1974—; on-air film critic People Now, Cable News Network, L.A., 1980-83; on-air film critic, co-host Sneak Previews PBS, 1985-96; chief film critic N.Y. Post, 1993-98; Hollywood corr. The Sunday Times of London; nationally syndicated radio talk show host Salem Radio Network, Seattle, 1998—. Radio talk show host KVI AM, Seattle, 1996—98; critic The Worst of Hollywood Channel 4, England, 1982. Author: What Really Happened to the Class of '65?, 1976, The Shadow Presidents, 1979, Hospital, 1983, Hollywood vs. America, 1992; co-author: (with Harry Medved) The 50 Worst Films of All Time, 1978, The Golden Turkey Awards, 1980, The Hollywood Hall of Shame, 1984, Son of Golden Turkey Awards, 1986, (with Diane Medved) Saving Childhood, 1998. Co-founder, pres. Pacific Jewish Ctr., Venice, Calif., 1977-94; pres. Emanuel Streisand Sch., Venice, 1980-85. Mem. Writers Guild Am., AFTRA. Avocation: classical music. Office: 509 Olive Way Ste 852 Seattle WA 98101

MEDVED, ROBERT ALLEN, lawyer; b. Cleve., July 22, 1945; s. Joseph Jack and Mary (Blasko) Medved. BBA, Kent State U., 1968; JD cum laude, Seattle U., 1975. Bar: Wash. 1976, U. S. Ct. Appeals (9th cir.) 1976, U.S. Dist. Ct. (we. dist.) Wash. 1976, U.S. Dist. Ct. (ea. dist.) Wash. 1979, U.S. Supreme Ct. 1981, U.S. Ct. Appeals (D.C. cir.) 1989. Fin. analyst Ford Motor Co., Sandusky, Ohio, 1972; rsch. asst. Seattle U., 1973—75; law clk Judge U.S. Ct. Appeals (9th cir.), 1974; asst. to labor arbitrator Tacoma, 1975; law clk. to Judge U. S. Dist. Ct. (ctrl. dist.) Calif., 1976; assoc. Graham & Dunn, Seattle, 1976—82, ptnr., 1982—83, Drake and Whiteley, Bellevue, Wash., 1983—86, Foster, Pepper & Shefelman, Seattle, 1986—97; owner Law Offices of Robert A. Medved, Bellvue, 1997—. Spl. dist. counsel 8th Congl. Dist., W.Va., 1983—86. Editor-in-chief: Seattle U. Law Rev. Bd. dirs. Bellevue C.C. found., 1986—98. Lt. USN, 1968—71. Seattle U. scholar, 1974. Mem.: ABA, Wash. State Bar Assn. Roman Catholic. Office: 212 108th Ave SE Bellevue WA 98004-6209 E-mail: bob@ramedved.com.

MEDVEDOW, JILL, museum director; BA, Colgate U., 1976; M of Art History, Inst. Fine Arts N.Y., 1978. With Met. Mus. Art, N.Y.C., Franklin Furnace; founder Contemporary Art Ctr., Seattle; program mgr. New Eng. Found. Arts, Boston; dep. dir. contemproary art Isabella Stewart Gardner Mus., Boston, 1991-97; dir. Inst. Contemporary Art, Boston, 1998—. Cons., founder VitaBrevis. Office: Inst Contemporary Art 955 Boylston St Boston MA 02115-3194 E-mail: info@icaboston.org.*

MEDVIN, ALAN YORK, lawyer; b. NYC, Sept. 13, 1947; s. Murray and Leona (Alpert) Medvin; m. Harriet A. Kass, July 11, 1976; children: Michelle K., Michael J., Emily S. AB, Colgate U., 1969; JD, Rutgers U., 1972. Bar: NJ 1972, US Dist. Ct. NJ 1972, US Supreme Ct. 1981. Assoc. Horowitz, Bross & Sinins, Newark, 1972—75; ptnr. Horowitz, Bross, Sinins, Imperial & Medvin, 1976—83, Medvin & Elberg, Newark, 1983—. Adj. prof. law Rutgers U., 1987. Fellow: Roscoe Pound Found.; mem.: ATLA (state del. 1980, pres. NJ affiliate, bd. govs.), Mercer County Bar Assn., Essex County Bar Assn., NJ State Bar Assn. (Outstanding Profl. Achievement award 1982), Am. Arbitration Assn. Democrat. Jewish. Home: 165 Bertrand Dr Princeton NJ 08540-2949 Office: Medvin & Elberg 1 Gateway Ctr Newark NJ 07102-5315

MEDWEDEFF, FRED MARSHALL, dentist; b. Flint, Mich, Nov. 20, 1926; s. Marshall Herbert and Elsie Ella (Miller) M.; m. Joan Lenore Kampmeier, June 17, 1950 (div. 1973); children: Carol Medwedeff Grosvenor, Linda Medwedeff Mello, John Davis; m. Carolyn Adams Payne Gothard, Dec. 30, 1977; 1 child, Carol Lynn Gothard. BS, U. Mich., 1949; DDS, Emory U., 1954. Diplomate Am. Bd. Oral and Maxillo-Facial Radiology. Gen. practice dentistry, Nashville, 1955—; instr., then asst. prof. Vanderbilt U. Sch. Medicine, Nashville, 1955-83; staff mem. Vanderbilt U. Hosp., 1955-83; asst. prof. Meharry Med. Coll., 1970. Founder, pres. Precision X-Ray Co., Nashville, 1964-74; cons. The Masel Co.; lectr. tour on x-rays to dentists, Japan, 1973. Contbr. articles to profl. jour.; patentee in field. Served with USAAF, 1945. Mem. ADA, Tenn. Dental Assn., Nashville Dental Soc., Am. Acad. Oral and Maxillo Facial Radiology, Mid. Tenn. Acad. Implant Dentistry (founding), Pierre Fauchard Acad. (life), Psi Omega. Achievements include first to The rectang. collimation of the X-ray beam to fit the film has been recommended by the Nat. Council of Radiation Protection and should be in the legal codes of most states within a year. Home: 9646 New Hwy 96 W Franklin TN 37064-4782 Office: 21st Plaza Bldg 121 21st Ave N Nashville TN 37203-5213 Office Phone: 615-327-4246.

MEE, MICHAEL F. retired pharmaceutical executive; married; three children. Grad., Bentley Coll., 1966; MBA, U. Minn., 1968; postgrad., MIT, 1984. Various positions including contr. Hamtramck Assembly Plant Chrysler Corp., 1968-76; v.p., contr., CFO Monsanto Co., 1976-85; CFO Norton Co., 1985-90; chmn. Eastman Christensen Oil Field Svcs. subsidiary Norton Co.; CFO, chmn. bd. dirs. Wang Labs., 1990—93; sr. v.p., CFO Bristol-Myers Squibb Co., 1994—2001. Mem. bd. overseers U. Minn. Carlson Sch. Mgmt. Mem.: bd. of dir., Lincoln Nat. Corp., 2001-, Econ. Club N.Y., Conf. Bds. Counc. Fin. Execs. Office: Lincoln Nat Corp Centre Square West Tower 1500 Market St Ste 3900 Philadelphia PA 19102-2112

MEECE, ROGER A. ambassador; b. Indpls., Ind., Oct. 1949; BS, Mich. State U., 1971. Former dep. chief of mission Am. Embassy, Brazzaville, Republic of the Congo; consul gen. Halifax, Canada; dep. chief of mission Am. Embassy, Kinshasa, Democratic Republic of Congo, 1995—98; dir., Ctrl. African affairs US Dept. State, Washington, 1998—2000, U.S. amb. to Malawi Lilongwe, 2000—03; charge d' affaires Am. Embassy, Abuja, Nigeria, 2003—04; US amb. to Democratic Republic of Congo US Dept. State, Kinsasha, 2004—. Numerous staff and vol. assignments Peace Corps, Sierra Leone. Office: 2220 Kinsasha Pl Washington DC 20521-2220

MEEHAN, JEAN MARIE ROSS, human resources, occupational health and safety management consultant; b. Chgo., Mar. 16, 1954; d. A. Ronald Gonzalez and Barbara Marx Shipley; m. John J. Meehan, 1993; 1 child, Jenna A.; 1 child from previous marriage, Justin L. Ross. Diploma in Nursing, St. Mary of Nazareth Hosp., Chgo., 1974; BS in Health Arts with high honors, U. St. Francis, 1988; MPA with honors, Roosevelt U., 2000. Cert. occupl. health nurse specialist, cert. pharmacy technician (CPhT). Staff nurse St. Mary of Nazareth Hosp., Chgo., 1973-75; head nurse ambulatory care Edgebrook Med. Diagnostic Ctr., Chgo., 1975-76; occupl. health nurse Williams Electronics, Inc., Chgo., 1976-84; adminstr. safety and benefits Reliable Power Products, Franklin Park, Ill., 1984-90; corp. human resources dir. MacLean-Fogg Co., Mundelein, Ill., 1990—; pres., cons. Auriel Mgmt. Sys., Island Lake, Ill., 1992—; pres. Claim Masters LLC, 1998-99. Gov., apptd. mem. Ill. Pollution Prevention Adv. Coun., Springfield, Ill., 1993-98, mem. coun., 1993-98; adv. bd. dirs. Gt. Lakes Health Care Alliance, 1996-97; spkr. in workshops. Poetry included in Visions of Beauty, 1999 (Editor's Choice award 1999), Tides of Memory, 2000, America at the Millennium—The Best Poems and Poets of the 20th Century, 2000. Guest spkr. local schs. and environ. groups, also I.E.P.A. and U.S. E.P.A. workshops; mem. Lake County Employer Coun. Bus./Govt. Partnership, 1996-99; faculty Am. Occupl. Health Conf., 2003-04. Recipient Leadership Civic citation United Way Charities of Lake County, 1993, 94. Mem. Am. Assn. Occupl. Health Nurses, Ill. Assn. Occupl. Health Nurses, Ill. Lakeland Occupl. Health Nurses (sec.), Soc. for Human Resources Mgmt., Lake County Violence Intervention and Prevention, Lake County Employer Coun. Avocations: parenting, interior design, reading, entertaining. Office: MacLean-Fogg Co 1000 Allanson Rd Mundelein IL 60060-3804 Office Phone: 847-970-4619. E-mail: j.rossmeehan@worldnet.att.net.

MEEHAN, JOHN JOSEPH, JR., hospital administrator; b. Boston, Jan. 29, 1946; s. John Joseph and Marjorie Louise (Hill) M.; m. Pamela Marshall, Mar. 25, 1973; children— Seth, Andrew, Sean BA, Dartmouth Coll., Hanover, N.H., 1968; M.H.A., U. Minn., Mpls., 1974. Unit mgr. Boston Hosp. Women, 1971-72; adminstrv. resident Hennepin County Gen. Hosp., Mpls., 1973-74; v.p. Putnam Meml. Hosp., Bennington, Vt., 1974-79; asst. dir. Hartford Hosp., Conn., 1979-81, assoc. exec. dir., 1981-85, exec. v.p., 1985-87, pres., chief operating officer, 1987-89; pres., chief exec. officer, 1989—. Faculty Hartford Grad. Ctr., 1979-81; preceptor U. Minn., 1981—, Yale U., New Haven, 1981—; mem. New Eng. Health Care Assembly, 1975—, officer, 1982-92; pres., CEO Hartford Health Care Corp., 1989—, Conn. Health Sys., Inc., 1996—; bd. dirs. MedSpan. Active Bennington Lion's Club, 1975-79, Conn. Hosp. Assn., Urban League Greater Hartford, 1979—, Greater Hartford C. of C., 1979—, also bd. dirs., 1994-97, Hartford Downtown Coun., 1997—; chmn. ARC, Bennington, 1978-79; bd. dirs. St. Joseph Coll., ConnectiCare IPA/HMO, 1990-95, Mech. Savs. Bank, 1993—; corporator St. Francis Hosp., 1988—, Inst. Living, 1993—, New Britain Gen. Hosp., 2000—; fellow Am. Leadership Forum, 1993—. Lt. USNR, 1968-70. Decorated Naval medals and ribbons, 1968-70; recipient Disting. Naval Grad. award, 1968, Stuart Thompson M.D. award U. Minn., 1974 Mem. Am. Hosp. Assn. (regional policy bd. 1995—), Conn. Hosp. Assn. (bd. dirs. chmn. 1996—, T. Stewart Hamilton M.D. Leadership award 1999-2000), Capital Area Health Consortium.

MEEHAN, LIL EUPHRASIA THERESE, poet; b. Boston, Nov. 14, 1942; d. George Leo Meehan and Elizabeth Catherine Dalton Meehan; m. Daniel Charles McGrath, Dec. 19, 1964 (div. Aug. 1968); 1 child, Christopher. Prodn. staff U.S. Mint, San Francisco, 1980—85; freelance author, 1985—. Author (song poems): The True American, 1986, The Robe, 2000, Eyes, 2000, Emblem of Your Character, 2000, Peace Be With You, 2000, That's Our Baby Tim, 2000, Ten Years Ago That Day, 2000, So Beautiful and Rare, 2000, Even Though, 2001, Don't Let Go, 2001, Bubbles, 2001, The Best Present, 2001, You Have Arisen, 2001, Heartfelt Love in USA, 2001, Winds of Winter, 2001, Mother of Mercy, 2002; author: Reflections, 2004. With Nat. Guard U.S. Army, 1976. Democrat. Roman Catholic. Avocations: reading, writing, swimming, basketball. Home: #503 120 N Broadway Santa Maria CA 93454 Office Phone: 805-346-6554.

MEEHAN, MARTIN THOMAS, congressman, lawyer; b. Dec. 30, 1956; s. Martin T. and Alice (Britton) M.; m. Ellen T. Murphy. BA in Polit. Sci., Edn. cum laude, U. Mass., Lowell, 1978; MPA, Suffolk U., 1981, JD, 1986; student, Harvard U., 1987-88. Adminstrv. asst. to mayor City of Lowell, Mass., 1978-79; press asst. Congressman James M. Shannon, Mass., 1979-81; del. Dem. Nat. Conv., 1980, 84, 88; head rsch. analyst Joint Com. on Elec. Laws Mass. State Senate, 1981-84; dir. pub. affairs Govt. of Mass., 1985-86, dep. sec. state, 1986-90; 1st asst. dist. atty. Middlesex County, Mass., 1991-92; mem. U.S. Congress from 5th Mass. dist., 1993—, mem. armed svcs. com., judiciary com. Former teacher, adj. instr. U. Lowell, Mass.; lawyer 1986—. Named Student of Yr. Lowell Exchange Club, 1975. Mem. ABA, Mass. Bar Assn., U. Lowell Alumni Assn., The Newspaper Guild, Internat. Fedn. Journalists. Democrat. Roman Catholic. Office: US Ho of Reps 2229 Rayburn House Office Bldg Washington DC 20515-0001

MEEHAN, MICHAEL JOSEPH, lawyer; b. St. Louis, Aug. 28, 1942; s. Joseph Michael and Frances (Taylor) M.; m. Sharon Kay McHenry (div. 1988); m. Patricia Ann Shive, July 8, 1989 (dec. 1999); m. Shelley Fujiko Lee, 2002. BS in Engring., U.S. Coast Guard Acad., 1964; JD with high distinction, U. Ariz., 1971. Bar: Ariz. 1971, U.S. Ct. Appeals (6th, 8th, 9th and 10th cirs.), U.S. Supreme Ct. 1975. Law clk. Assoc. Justice William H. Rehnquist, U.S. Supreme Ct., 1972; assoc. Molloy, Jones & Donahue, P.C., Tucson, 1971-75, shareholder, 1975-93; chmn. exec. com., head trial dept., 1986-93; founder Meehan & Assocs., Tucson, 1993-2001; ptnr. Quarles & Brady/Striech Long, Tucson, 2001—03; pvt. practice Tucson, 2003—. Mem. fed. appellate rules adv. com. Jud. Conf. U.S., 1994-99. Author chpt. on appellate advocacy: State Bar of Arizona Appellate Practice Handbook. Fellow Am. Acad. Appellate Lawyers (past pres.); mem. Ariz. Bar Assn. (past chair appellate practice sect. 1999-2000). Lutheran. Avocation: golf. Office: 127 W Franklin St Tucson AZ 85701 Office Phone: 520-662-8855. E-mail: mmeehan@injurylaw.com.

MEEHAN, PATRICK JOHN, public health officer; b. Tulsa, Dec. 30, 1956; married; 2 children. BA in Chemistry, U. Calif., Santa Cruz, 1978; MD, Washington U., St. Louis, 1982. Diplomate Am. Bd. Family Practice; lic. physician, Ga. Resident in family practice Navidad Med. Ctr./U. Calif., Salinas, 1982-85; with Epidemic Intelligence Svc. CDC and Prevention, Ctr. Environ. Health and Injury Control, Atlanta, 1988-89, preventive medicine resident, 1989-91; family practice physician Su Clinica Familiar, Harlingen, Tex., 1985-87; med. dir. prenatal and family planning Region 8 Tex. Dept. Pub. Health, Harlingen, 1986-87; acting health officer, cons. in communicable disease Santa Cruz (Calif.) County Health Dept., 1987-88; dir. N.H. divsn. Pub. Health Svc., 1991-94; dir. Ga. divns. pub. health Dept. Human Resources, Atlanta, 1994-98; dir. dist. health Gwinnette County Health Dept., Lawrenceville, Ga., 1997—. Family practice physician Locum Tenens, Raymondville, Tex., 1987, Salud Para La Gente, Watsonville, Calif., 1987-88; adj. asst. prof. Emory U., Atlanta; clin. assoc. prof. Morehouse Sch. Medicine; lectr. in field. Contbr. numerous articles to profl. jours. Mem. APHA, Med. Assn. Ga., Am. Acad. Family Physicians, Ga. Pub. Health Assn., Assn. of State and Territorial Health Ofcls. (chair com. on injury control, com. on tobacco or health). Office: Gwinnette County Health Dept PO Box 897 Lawrenceville GA 30046-0897

MEEHAN, PATRICK L. prosecutor; BA, Bowdoin Coll., 1978; JD, Temple U., 1986. Assoc. Dilworth, Paxon, Kalish and Kauffman; sr. counsel, exec. dir. U.S. Sen. Arlen Specter; dist. atty. Delaware County, Pa., 1986—2001; U.S. atty. Ea. Dist. Pa. U.S. Dept. Justice, 2001—. Office: 615 Chestnut St Philadelphia PA 19106

MEEHAN, ROBERT HENRY, human resources executive, electronics company executive, business educator; b. Hackensack, N.J., June 19, 1946; s. Horace Miles and Pauline Jeannette (Pente) M.; m. Ruth Ann Auletta, Sept. 28, 1969; children: Robert Michael, Brian John. BA, Montclair State U., 1968; MA magna cum laude, Fairleigh Dickinson U., 1972; D in Profl. Studies, Pace U., 1997. Cert. secondary sch. tchr. of social studies, N.J., compensation and benefits profl. Job analyst Citicorp, N.Y.C., 1969-70, sr. job analyst, 1970-72, ofcl. asst., 1972, project specialist human resources practices/policy rev., 1973, project specialist attitude surveys, 1973-75, human resources officer nat. banking group, 1975-76; asst. dir. human resources N.Y. Power Authority, White Plains, 1976-84, dir. compensation, 1984-93, dir. compensation and human resources info. sys., 1993-94, dir. compensation and benefits strategy and devel., 1994-95, dir. compensation and benefits, 1995-98; dir. compensation Philips Electronics N.Am., 1998-2000; mng. dir. R.H. Meehan Assocs., Human Capital Cons., Maywood, NJ, 2000—01; dir. compensation, benefits and HRIS, ASML, Tempe, Ariz., 2001—. Instr. World at Work, Scottsdale, Ariz., 1986—, course coord., 1992-94, mem. cert. and currency com., 1988-89, direct compensation com. 1990-91, chmn. 1992-93, bd. dirs. 1993; adj. assoc. prof. Lubin Grad. Sch. Bus., Pace U., 1995-2001; mem. N.Y. Power Pool Salary com., 1990-98, chair, 1998; spkr. at profl. confs. Sr. author: Managing a Direct Pay Program, Cert. Course 4A, 1991, Determining Compensation Costs: An Approach to Estimating and Analyzing Expense, 1991; editor books; mem. exec. adv. panel Acad. Mgmt. Exec., 1993—; contbr. articles to profl. jours. Scoutmaster, Boy Scouts Am., Ridgefield Park, N.J., 1968; also scouting coord., Maywood, N.J., 1982-83; vestryman, sr. warden St. Martin's Episcopal Ch., Maywood, 1977-84. Mem. Soc. for Human Resource Mgmt. (mem. compensation and benefits com. 1998-2001), Metro Phoenix Human Resource Assocs., 2002—, Human Resources Assn. N.Y. (compensation com. 1998-2001), Acad. Mgmt. (exec. adv. panel jour. The Exec.), N.Y. Compensation Assn., 2000-01, Order DeMolay (master councilor 1963, 65, scribe, adv. bd. 1965-68, Meritorious Svcs. award 1965), Psi, Delta Mu Delta, Beta Gamma Sigma. Episcopalian. Avocations: golf, sailing, furniture making. Office: ASML 8555 S River Pkwy Tempe AZ 85284 Office Phone: 480-383-4043. Business E-Mail: Robert.Meehan@asml.com.

MEEHAN, SANDRA GOTHAM, corporate financial executive, consultant; b. Tokyo, June 9, 1948; d. Fred C. and Evelyn (Dirr) Gotham; m. James P. Jenkins, June 15, 1970 (div.); m. Dayton T. Carr, Dec. 27, 1986 (div. 1989), m. Michael J. Meehan, Jan. 16, 1992. Student, Stanford-in-France, Tours, 1968-69; BA, Stanford U., 1970, MA, 1971. Acct. exec. Young & Rubicam Inc., N.Y.C., 1972-78, acct. supr., 1978-80; pres. Gotham Prodns., N.Y.C., 1980-82; v.p., mgmt. supr. Ogilvy & Mather, N.Y.C., 1982-85; v.p. Steuben Glass, N.Y.C., 1985-88; sr. v.p. Siegel & Gale, N.Y.C., 1988-92; prin., mng. ptnr. Gotham Meeham Ptnrs., N.Y.C., 1992—. Sr. v.p., dir. corp. comm. Bionutrics, Inc., 1997-98; cons. Congl. coms., FDA, FTC for exec. program Am. Assn. Advt. Agys., Washington, 1978-80; cons. Ctr. Arctic Studies Sorbonne, Paris, in U.S. and Can., 1980-82; seminar dir. N.Y. chpt. Women in Bus., N.Y.C., 1983-84. Author, editor: TV documentary Inuit! The Universal Cry of the Eskimo People, 1981. Trustee, bd. dirs. Rensselaerville (N.Y.) Inst.; trustee Checkerboard Film Found.; dirs. coun. Paris Rev. of Books; N.Y.C. Mayor's rep. to Bd. of Bot. Gardens, 2001—04. Mem.: Young Profls. Group Fgn. Policy Assn. (organizing chair 1980—81), Writers Guild Am. Home: 220 E 73rd St New York NY 10021-4319 Office: Gotham Meehan Ptnrs 220 E 73rd St Ste 5G New York NY 10021-4319 Fax: 212-628-6747. Office Phone: 212-628-6810.

MEEK, CARRIE P. former congresswoman; b. Tallahassee, Fla., Apr. 29, 1926; 3 children. BS, Fla. A&M U., 1946; MS, U. Mich., 1948. Mem. Fla. Ho. of Reps., Tallahassee, 1979-82, Fla. Senate, Tallahassee, 1982—93, U.S. Congress from 17th Fla. dist., 1993—2002; mem. appropriations com.; mem. subcommittee on Treasury, Postal Svc. and Gen. Gov., subcommittee on VA, HUD, and Ind. Agencies. Recipient Benjamin Franklin award for outstanding pub. svc., Suncoast Tiger Bay Club, 2004. Democrat.

MEEK, FORREST BURNS, retired trading company executive; b. Tustin, Mich., June 11, 1928; s. Robert B. and Electa I. (Gallup) M.; m. Jean R. Grimes, June 26, 1953; children: Sally, Thomas, Nancy, Charles. AA, Spring Arbor Coll., 1950; AB, Mich. State U., 1953; postgrad., U. Ga., 1965; MA, Cen. Mich. U., 1967. Exec. sec., chmn. bd. Edgewood Press, Clare, 1971—; gen. mgr. Blue Water Imports, 1985; dir. Ctr. for Chinese-Am. Scholarly Exchs., Inc., 1989-97; gen. mgr. Blue-Water Internat. Trading Co., Inc., ret., 1998. Vis. prof. Wuhan U., China, 1986—87; dist. office mgr. Fed. Decennial Census, 1990; instr. phys. geology and astronomy Mid Mich. C.C., 2002, instr. astronomy, 2001—03; mem., chmn. Red team East Ctrl. Mich. Planning and Devel. Regional Commn.; bd. sec. ITC Shanghai Maglev, Inc., 2003. Author: Michigan Timber Battleground, 1976, Michigan Heartland, 1979, One Year in China, 1988, Michigan Logging Railroad Era, 1850-1963, 1989, Railways and Tramways, 1990, Lumbering in Eastern Canada, 1991, Pearl Harbor Remembered, 1991, Heroes of The Twentieth Century, 2000. Coordinator Clare County Bicentennial Com., 1975-76; Rep. fin. chmn., Clare County, 1966-71, asst. treas. 10th dist. Mich, 1967-69; trustee local sch. bd., 1992-96; chmn. local county jury bd., 1991-98; mem. bd. commrs. Clare County (Mich.) Dist. 4 Commn., 1998-2000, 2003—. Mem. Am. Entrepreneur Assn., Mich. Sci. Tchrs. Assn., Mich. Hist. Soc., Heartland Mich. Geneal. Soc., White Pine Hist. Soc. (exec. sec.). Republican. Avocations: astronomy, silviculture. E-mail: edgewoodpress@usa.com.

MEEK, KENDRICK B. congressman; b. Miami, Sept. 6, 1966; m. Leslie Meek; 2 children. BS, Fla. A&M U., 1989. Devel. rep. Wackenhut Corp.; mem. Fla. Ho. of Reps., Tallahassee, 1994-98; mem. for dist. 36 Fla. State Senate, Tallahassee, 1998—2002; mem. U.S. Ho. of Reps. from 17th dist., 2003—. Vice chair Com. on Criminal Justice Appropriations Fiscal Responsibility Coun., 1996-97; mem. Com. on Crime and Punishment Justice Coun., 1996-97. Mem. Fla. Young Dems., 1985—, Gtr. Miami Svc. Corp Bd., All Peoples Dem. Club, South Fla. Food Recovery Bd., North Shore Med. Ctr. Bd., IMPACT Miami, Met. Dade County Urban Revitalization Task Force; capt. Fla. Hwy Patrol, 1989-94; founder, mem. Men Against Drugs, Defending Against Drugs and Social Disorder (MAD DADS); founder Positive African-Am. Role Models Lillie C. Evans Elem. Sch., 1990; mem. adv. bd. Dems. 2000 Elected Officials; bd. dirs. Metro-Dade Cmty. Action Agy. Flemming fellow Ctr. for Policy Alternatives, 1996-97; recipient Outstanding Svc. award MADD, 1990, Positive African-Am. Role Models award Lillie C. Evans Elem. Sch., 1991, #1 award Scott-Carver Pack, 1991, award Dade Ptnrs. for Safe Neighborhoods, 1995, Legis. award MADD, 1995, Cmty. Svc. award Fla. Meml. Coll., 1995, award IMPACT Miami, 1996, Stellar Cmty. Svc. award South Fla. Assn. Black Journalists, 1996, Legis. Achievement honor Fla. Divsn. Emergency Mgmt., 1996; named St. Joseph Delaney Hurricane Hero Metro Dade County Commn., 1995, one of 50 Leaders of Tomorrow Ebony Mag., 1995, Up and Comers finalist Price Waterhouse, 1996 Quality Floridian Fla. League of Cities, 1996. Mem. NAACP (life, chmn. Miami-Dade br. Oper. Voter Registration 1995-96, v.p., Adams-Powell Civil Rights award 1996, Gwen Sawyer Cherry Meml. award Fla. Conf. NAACP brs. 1997), North Ctrl. Dade Cmty. Assn. (chmn. pub. safety com.), Fla. Agr. and Mech. U. Alumni Assn., Disabled Police Officers Assn. (adv. bd.), Omega Psi Phi. Democrat. Office: 1039 Longworth Ho Office Bldg Washington DC 20515-0917 E-mail: meek.kendrick@leg.state.fl.us.

MEEK, LINDA DUKE (LINDA BULLION MEEK), elementary school educator, writer; b. Charleston, Miss., Oct. 31, 1951; d. Charles Lester and Dell Crosthwait Bullion; m. W. E. Meek, Jr., Dec. 23, 2000; 1 child from

previous marriage, Rodney C. Duke. BS in elem. edn., U. Miss., Oxford, 1973. Cert. reading specialist Caohoma Coll., 1976. Tchr. grades 1-3 West Tallahatchie Sch., Webb, Miss., 1973—75; tchr. grade 2 Clarksdale Sch. Dist., 1975—80; tchr. grade 3 Harlingen City Ind. Sch. Dist., Tex., 1980—2000; tchr. grade 6 East Tallahatchie Sch., Charleston, Miss., 2001, tchr. grade 2, 2001—03, reading resource tchr., 2003—. Author: The Long Winding Road, 2004; composer: (recordings) Songs from the Heart, 1999, (songs) A Second Chance, 2003; contbr. articles to mag. Spkr. to groups on breast cancer awareness.

MEEK, MARK ALAN, investment executive; b. Wichita, Kans., Sept. 16, 1949; s. Elmo L. and Margaret Dorothy (Craig) M.; 1 child: Holly Marie. BS in Economics, U. Ctrl. Fla., Orlando, 1996; MA in Applied Economics, U. Ctrl. Fla., 1998. Dir. asset mgmt. Sweetser Cos., Oklahoma City, 1981-83; divsn. mgr. C.B.S. Property Svcs., Inc., Albuquerque, N.M., 1983-85; dist. mktg. mgr. Turner Devel. Corp., Tampa, Fla., 1985-87; pres. Turner Real Estate Mgmt., Inc., Tampa, 1987-89; gen. mgr. Collier Enterprises, Orlando, 1989-93; principal Litigation Cons., Orlando, 1993-98; asst. v.p. AmTrust Bank, Tampa, 1998-99; v.p. Colonial Bank, Tampa, 1999—. Author: (book) Currency Valuation & Structural Models: Lessons from the Asian Experience, 1998. Lay leader, Hyde Park United Meth. Ch., Tampa, 1999. Mem. Nat. Assn. Bus. Economists, Real Estate Investment Coun., Nat. Assn. Home Builders, Golden Key Nat. Honor Soc. Republican. Meth. Avocations: sailing, skiing, travel. Office: Colonial Bank 400 N Tampa St Ste 2500 Tampa FL 33602-4708 Home: Apt 2212 1000 S Harbour Island Blvd Tampa FL 33602-5717 E-mail: mameek@gte.net.

MEEK, PAUL DERALD, oil and chemical company executive; b. McAllen, Tex., Aug. 15, 1930; s. William Van and Martha Mary (Sharp) M.; m. Betty Catherine Robertson, Apr. 18, 1954; children: Paula Marie Meek Burford, Kathy Diane Meek Hasemann, Carol Ann Meek Miller, Linda Rae Meek. BS in Chem. Engring, U. Tex., Austin, 1953. Mem. tech. dept. Humble Oil & Refining Co., Baytown, Tex., 1953-55; with Cosden Oil & Chem. Co., 1955-76, pres., 1968-76; dir. Fina, Inc. (formerly Am. Petrofina, Inc.), Dallas, 1968—, v.p. parent co., 1968-76, pres., chief operating officer, 1976-83, pres., chief exec. officer, 1983-86, chmn. bd., pres., chief exec. officer, 1984-86, chmn. bd., 1986—. Apptd. by Gov. Wm. P. Clements, Jr. chmn. Pub. Uitilites Commn. of Tex., 1989-92. Contbg. author: Advances in Petroleum Chemistry and Refining, 1957. Chmn. chem. engring. vis. com. U. Tex., 1975-76; mem. adv. coun. Coll. Engring. Found., U. Tex., Austin, 1979—, U. Tex. Longhorn Found., 1989—, Coll. of NaturalScis. Found., 1989—; life mem.-at-large, bd. visitors McDonald Observatory dept. astonomy U. Tex.; co-chmn. indsl. divsn. United Way of Met. Dallas, 1981-82. Named Disting. Engring. Grad. U. Tex., Austin, 1969. Mem. Am. Petroleum Inst. (bd. dirs.), 25 Yr. Club of the Petroleum Industry, Founders Club of the Petrochem. Industry, Dallas Wildcat Com. (chmn. exec. com. 1987-88).

MEEK, SUSAN BIEBER, lawyer, physician, mediator, consultant; b. Chgo., Nov. 15, 1951; d. Martin S. and Anita (Felsenthal) Bieber; m. Charles Capps Meek, Jan. 16, 1977; children: Ryan, Kevin, Katy, Ann. BS, U. Ill., 1973; JD, No. Ill. U., 1976; MD, Chgo. Med. Sch., 1980. Bar: Ill. 1984, U.S. Dist. Ct. (no. dist.) Ill. 1984, Tex. 1988, U.S. Dist. Ct. (so. dist.) Tex. 1988. Intern Mayo Clinic, Rochester, Minn., 1980-81; resident in ophthalmology U. Ariz.; Corneal Rsch. fellow La. State U.; ptnr. M. Bieber and Assocs., Chgo. Med. legal cons. to numerous firms, Houston; cons. Dept HHS Office of Hearings and Appeals. Contbr. articles to profl. jours. Mem. Gov.'s Task Force on Aging. Mem. AMA, ABA (litigation, corp., health law and adminstrv. law sects.), Tex. Bar Assn. (med. malpractice com. 1991), Houston Bar Assn., Ill. Bar Assn., Chgo. Bar Assn., Health Care Lawyers Group, Am. Soc. Law and Medicine, Assn. Am. Trial Lawyers, Tex. Trial Lawyers Assn., Women Trial Lawyers Assn., Am. Judicature Soc., Am. Acad. Ophthalmology, Am. Coll. Eye Surgeons, Pan Am. Ophthalmology Soc., Contact Lens Assn., Tex. Med. Assn., Harris County Med. Soc., Sigma Xi, others. Home: 2929 Buffalo Speedway Houston TX 77098-1707 Office Phone: 713-877-1113.

MEEK, VIOLET IMHOF, retired dean; b. Geneva, Ill., June 12, 1939; d. John and Violet (Krepel) Imhof; m. Devon W. Meek, Aug. 21, 1965 (dec. 1988); children: Brian, Karen; m. Don M. Dell, Jan. 4, 1992. BA summa cum laude, St. Olaf Coll., 1960; MS, U. Ill., 1962, PhD in Chemistry, 1964. Instr. chemistry Mount Holyoke Coll., South Hadley, Mass., 1964-65; asst. prof. to prof. Ohio Wesleyan U., Delaware, Ohio, 1965-84, dean for ednl. svcs., 1980-84; dir. annual programs Coun. Ind. Colls., Washington, 1984-86; assoc. dir. sponsored programs devel. Rsch. Found. Ohio State U., Columbus, 1986-91, dean, dir. Lima, 1992—2003; ret., 2003. Vis. dean U. Calif., Berkeley, 1982, Stanford U., Palo Alto, Calif., 1982, reviewer GTE Sci. and Tech. Program, Princeton, N.J., 1986-92, Goldwater Nat. Fellowships, Princeton, 1990-98. Co-author: Experimental General Chemistry, 1984; contbr. articles to profl. jours. Bd. dirs. Luth. Campus Ministries, Columbus, 1988-91, Luth. Social Svcs., 1988-91, Americom Bank, Lima, 1992-98, Art Space, Lima, 1993—, Allen Lima Leadership, 1993—, Am. House, 1992—, Lima Vets. Meml. Civic Ctr. Found., 1992—; chmn. synodical cons. Evang. Luth. Ch. Am., Columbus, 1982; bd. trustees Trinity Luth. Sem., Columbus, 1996—; chmn. Allen County C. of C., 1995—, chair bd. dirs., 1999; bd. dirs. Lima Syphomy Orch., 1993—, pres. bd. dirs., 1997— Recipient Woodrow Wilson Fellowship, 1960. Mem. Nat. Coun. Rsch. Adminstrs. (named Outstanding New Profl. midwest region 1990), Am. Assn. Higher Edn., Phi Beta Kappa. Avocations: music, skiing, woodworking, civil war history, travel. Home: 209 W Beechwold Blvd Columbus OH 43214-2012 Office: Ohio State U 4240 Campus Dr Lima OH 45804-3576

MEEKER, DAVID ANTHONY, public relations executive; b. Akron, Ohio, June 1, 1939; s. Charles Anthony and Lucia Pauline (Schweikert) M.; m. Anita Marie De Jacimo, June 24, 1961; children: Christine Marie, Elizabeth Ann, Eileen Louise, David Edgerton. BS in Indsl. Journalism, Kent State U., 1961, postgrad., 1963-64; MS in Comms. Mgmt., Syracuse U., 1998. Editor Recordak Record, Eastman Kodak Co., N.Y.C., 1961-62; journalist Akron Beacon Jour., 1962-66, St. Louis Post-Dispatch, 1966-69; exec. sec. to mayor City of St. Louis, 1969-71; asst. dir. Ohio Dept. Natural Resources, Columbus, 1971-73; exec. dir. Ohio Dem. Party, Columbus, 1973-74; pres. Urbanistics, Inc., 1974-76; ptnr. Meeker-Mayer Pub. Rels., 1976-84; pres. David A. Meeker & Assocs., Inc., Akron, 1984-89; sr. counselor Edward Howard & Co., Akron, 1989—; also bd. dirs. Bd. dirs. Akron Regional Devel.; Dem. candidate for mayor City of Akron, 1987; mem. regional environ. priorities project pub. com. Kent State U. Sch. Journalism, 1996-97, mem. adv. bd.; chmn. Summit County Charter Commn., 1995; chmn. bd. dirs. Uilbje St. Edward. Recipient Con Lee Kelliher award Kent State U., 1966, Disting. Alumnus award Sch. Journalism, 1983, Lighthouse award Cleve. Pub. Rels. Soc. Am., 2001. Fellow Pub. Rels. Soc. Am. (nat. honors and awards com. 1981-83, chmn. 1983, nat. membership com. 1980-81, chmn. 1984, past del.-at-large nat. assembly, chmn. Counselors Acad. spring conf. 1987, pres. Akron chpt. 1982, immediate past chmn. and dir. environ. sects., past chmn. Coll. of Fellows); mem. SAR, Internat. Pub. Rels. Assn., Soc. Profl. Journalists (past pres. Buckeye chpt., John S. Knight award 1999), N.E. Ohio Regional Alliance (pres.). Roman Catholic. Avocations: tennis, fishing, antiques. Home: 269 S Rose Blvd Akron OH 44313-7843 Office: One Cascade Pla 19th Fl Akron OH 44308

MEEKER, GUY BENTLEY, banker; b. Calcutta, India, Nov. 4, 1945; (parents Am. citizens); s. Lincoln Voght and Fortune Helen (Bentley) M.; m. Lavenia Yale Nelson, Apr. 27, 1967 (div. 1979); children: G. Bentley Jr., Melissa Anne; m. Marcia Lee Zink, Nov. 4, 1984 (div. 1993). BSBA, Georgetown U., 1967; MBA, George Washington U., 1970. Cons. OAS, Washington, 1971-73; v.p. The Deltec Banking Corp., Nassau, Bahamas & N.Y.C., 1973-78, Comml. Credit Internat. Banking Corp., Balt., 1978-82; sr. v.p., gen. mgr. Union Planters Internat. Bank, N.Y.C., 1982-84; exec. v.p., gen. mgr. Worthen Bank Internat., N.Y.C., 1984-86; exec. v.p. and chief exec. officer N.Am. Bank Cen. Asia, N.Y.C., 1984-95; supervisory dir. BCA Bank Europe N.V., Amsterdam, The Netherlands, 1993-95; pres. G.B. Meeker & Co., N.Y.C., 1996—. Author articles and monographs in field. Mem. Bankers Assn. Fgn. Trade (internat. adv. coun. 1992-95, vice chmn. IAC 1994-95), Inst. Internat. Bankers (legis. and regulatory com. 1992-94, bd. trustees 1994-95), Asia Soc. (corp. coun. 1987-95), River Club, Dutch Treat Club. Roman Catholic.

MEEKER, MARY, stock brokerage executive; BA, DePauw U.; MBA, Cornell U. Tech. rsch. analyst Salomon Bros., Cowen & Co.; mng. dir. Internet, new media and PC software equity rsch. Morgan Stanley, Dean Witter, Discover & Co. (now Morgan Stanley), N.Y.C., 1991—. Office: Morgan Stanley 1585 Broadway New York NY 10036-8200 Fax: 212-761-0472. E-mail: mmeeker@ms.com.*

MEEKER, MILTON SHY, manufacturing executive; b. Nov. 9, 1933; s. David and Helen Elizabeth (Kendrick) M.; m. Nancy Orbison, Nov. 27, 1976 (dec.); 1 child, Sherwin Kendrick. BA, U. Calif., Berkeley, 1955, BS, 1959; MBA, U. Mich., 1963. With Ford Motor Co., 1959-68; dir. purchasing, mtg., rsch. mgr. Paccar, Inc., Seattle and Newark, Calif., 1968-71; commr. fed. supply svc., commr. automated data & telecomms., assoc. dep. adminstr. GSA, Washington, 1972-75; dir. purchasing chem. group FMC Corp., Phila., 1975-77, dir. purchasing planning and adminstrn. Chgo., 1977-79; gen. sales mgr. Peterbilt Motors Co. divsn. Paccar, Newark, 1979-80; mktg. mgr. Peterbilt Motors Co., Newark, 1980—89; dir. dealer devel. Paccar, Inc., Bellevue, Wash., 1989-91, exec. asst. to vice chmn., 1991-99. Chmn. Pres.'s Com. for Purchase of Products from Blind, 1973-74; bd. dirs. Nat. Industries for the Blind, 1976-86. With U.S. Army, 1957-58. Republican. Home: 7900 NE 32nd St Medina WA 98039-1030

MEEKER, ROBERT ELDON, retired manufacturing company executive; b. Moline, Ill., Sept. 6, 1930; s. Paul Edwin and Esther (Carlson) M.; m. Dorothy Elaine Nelson, Dec. 23, 1951; children: Julie Lynn Meeker Gratton, Laurie Allison Meeker Gamel, Bradford Nelson (dec.). BS in Chemistry, Ill. Wesleyan U., 1952; PhD in Phys. Chemistry, Northwestern U., 1955. Chemist, supr. Shell Devel. Co., Emeryville, Calif., 1955-64; mgr.-dir. synthetic rubber tech. ctr. Shell Chem. Co., Torrance, Calif., 1964-66, mgr. new projects N.Y.C., 1966-69; dir. exploratory sci., exploration and prodn. rsch. ctr. Shell Devel. Co., Houston, 1969-71; gen. mgr., head new enterprises divsn. Royal Dutch-Shell Co., London, 1971-72; v.p. comml., gen. mgr. Billiton Aluminum B.V. Billiton Internat. Metals subs. Shell Co., The Hague, Netherlands, 1972-74, pres. Roxana Shale Oil Co. subs. Shell Co., Houston, 1974-76; v.p., gen. mgr. energy systems mgmt. divsn. TRW, Inc., Redondo Beach, Calif., 1976-80, v.p., gen. mgr. maj. programs, 1980-86; pvt. practice cons., real estate developer Tucson, 1986-94. Patentee in field. Trustee Ill. Wesleyan U., Bloomington, 1982-94, trustee emeritus, 1994—; v.p., bd. dirs. Cobblestone Homeowners Assn., 1991-92, pres. bd. dirs., 1992-94, security chmn., 1994-97. Recipient Disting. Alumnus award Ill. Wesleyan U., 1981. Mem. Am. Parkinson Disease Assn. Inc. (pres. Ariz. chpt. 1996-2000, nat. bd. dirs. 1996—), Mercedes Benz Club Am. (pres. Chaparral sect. 1992-94). Republican. Lutheran. Avocations: photography, swimming, travel. Home and Office: 7240 N Star Fury Pl Tucson AZ 85718-1345 Office Phone: 520-577-2760. E-mail: remeeker@theriver.com.

MEEKERS, DOMINIQUE ARMAND, health and demographics researcher; b. Diepenbeek, Belgium, June 23, 1962; came to U.S., 1987; BA magna cum laude, Free U. Brussels, 1985; MA, U. Pa., 1988, PhD, 1990. Rschr. Free U. Brussels, 1985-87; rsch. assoc. NAS, Washington, 1990-91; asst. prof., rsch. assoc. Pa. State U., University Park, 1992-96; assoc. Johns Hopkins U., Balt., 1996-2001; rsch. dir. Population Svcs. Internat., Washington, 1996—2001; prof. dept. internat. health and devel. Tulane U., New Orleans, 2001—. Cons. John Snow, Arlington, Va., 1992—93, Demographic and Health Surveys, Macro Internat., Calverton, Md., 1993—97, Population Svcs. Internat., 2001—, Hewlett Found., 2003—; invited mem. Com. Reproductive Health, 2000—03, Internat. Union Sci. Study Population; adj. assoc. prof. dept. internat. health and devel. Tulane U., New Orleans, 2000—01. Contbr. articles to profl. publs. Rsch. grantee Spencer Found., 1995, U. Md., 1996, UNICEF, Bucharest, Romania, 1997, UNAIDS, 1997, Deloitte Touche Tohmatsu, 2002, UNICEF, 2002, USAID/Health Comm. Partnership, 2002-2007. Mem. APHA, Population Assn. Am., Internat. Union for Sci. Study of Population. Office: Tulane U Dept Internat Health and Devel 1440 Canal St Ste 2200 New Orleans LA 70112 Home: 5633 Durham Dr New Orleans LA 70131 Office Phone: 504-584-3655. E-mail: dmeekers@tulane.edu.

MEEKISON, MARYFRAN, writer; b. Napoleon, Ohio, Apr. 9, 1919; d. Frank J. and Elizabeth (Keyes) Shaff; m. David Meekison, June 17, 1939; children: Maureen Meekison Houppert, David Francis, Beth Ann. Student, St. Mary's Coll., Notre Dame, Ind., 1936-39. Hist. writer, photographer, Napoleon, 1963—, St. Augustine Ch., 1983—. Author: (photographer) Canal Days to Modern Ways Revisited, 1984, History of St. Augustine's 1882-1982, History of St. Augustine Ch., 1983, centennial edit.; (brochure) Canal Days to Modern Ways, 1963; mem. editorial adv. bd. Courier mag., 1989-91; contbr. articles to numerous mags. Steering com. Napoleon Susquicentennial, 1984; trustee Napoleon Pub. Lib., 1976-01. Recipient Spl. citation Courier Alumnae mag., also numerous photography and writing awards, Pres.'s medal, St. Mary's Coll., Notre Dame, Ind., 1991; named Citizen of Yr., Napoleain Area C. of C., 1990; named to St. Mary's Coll. Athletic Hall of Fame Notre Dame, 2001. Mem. Alumnae Assn. St. Mary's Coll. (bd. dirs. 1985-91), Literary Club. Democrat. Roman Catholic. Avocations: tennis, sailing. Home: PO Box 253 Napoleon OH 43545-0253

MEEKS, GREGORY WELDON, congressman; b. N.Y.C., Sept. 25, 1953; s. James Weldon and Mary (McNeal) M.; m. Simone-Marie Meeks; children: Ebony Renee, Aja J., Nia-Aiyana. BA, Adelphi U., 1975; JD, Howard U., 1978. Asst. dist. atty. Queens Dist. Atty.'s Office, 1978-81; asst. spl. narcotics prosecutor Office of Spl. Narcotics Prosecutor, 1981-83; asst. counsel State Commn. of Investigation, 1983-84; hearing officer N.Y. Family Ct., 1984-85; judge N.Y. Workers' Compensation Bd., 1985-87, supervising judge, 1987-93; mem. N.Y. State Assembly, 1993-98, 108th Congress from NY 6th dist., 1998—; mem. com. on banking and fin.svcs., 1999—; mem. com. on internat. rels., 1999—. Bd. dirs. Peninsula Gen. Hosp.; chmn. bd. Joseph P. Addabbo Family Health Care Ctr., 1990-92. Recipient Outstanding Vol. Mentor award N.Y. Mentoring, 1990, Cmty. Leader award Boy Scouts Am., 1992. Mem. Macon B. Allen Black Bar Assn. (v.p.), Queens County Bar Assn., Far Rockaway NAACP (Polit. Leadership award 1989). Democrat. Address: 660 Grassmere Ter Far Rockaway NY 11691-2556 Office: Ho of Reps 1710 Longworth Hob Washington DC 20515-0001 E-mail: congmeeks@mail.house.gov.

MEEKS, JAMES T. state senator; b. Chgo., Ill., Aug. 4, 1956; married; children: Jamie, Janet, James Jr., Jasmine. BA Philosophy, BA religion. State Senator US Senate, Dist. 15, 2003. Author: (book) Get Out of Debt & Into Praise, Life Changing Relationships: Bad Boys, Bad Girls. State Gov.; Agr. and Conservation; Appropriations II; Ed. Independent. Baptist. Office: Capitol M-121 Capitol Bldg Springfield IL 62706 also: Dist 2050 E 159th St Calumet City IL 11604 Home: 11824 S Indiana Chicago IL 60628

MEEKS, KENNETH W. civil engineer, educator; b. Union Point, Ga., Sept. 28, 1942; s. William and Iris Meeks; m. Lynn Chapman, June 15, 1968; 1 child, Michael. BS, U.S. Naval Acad., Annapolis, Md., 1965; BCE, Ga. Inst. Tech., Atlanta, 1968; MS in Civil Engring., Ga. Inst. Tech., 1969; ScD, George Washington U., Washington, 1997. Registered profl. engr., Va., La. Commd. at ensign USN, 1965—94, advanced through grades to capt., 1985; dep. head design divsn. Naval Facilities Engring. Command, Alexandria, Va., 1982—84; head facilities office Naval Sea Sys. Command, Washington, 1984—85; resident officer-in-chg. Officer in Chg. of Constrn., Diego Garcia, 1985—86; exec. officer Naval Facilities Engring. Command, Charleston, SC, 1986—89; commdg. officer Navy Pub. Works Ctr., Great Lakes, Ill., 1989—91; dir. tech. sec. Dept. Energy, Washington, 1991—94; prof. dept. civil engring. Tri-State U., Angola, Ind., 1997—. Decorated Legion of Merit; recipient Disting. Svc. award, Dept. Energy, 2000. Fellow: Soc. Am. Mil. Engrs.; mem.: ASCE, Am. Soc. Engring. Edn. Republican. Baptist. Office: Tri-State Univ Dept Civil/Environ Engring 1 University Ave Angola IN 46703

MEEKS, WAYNE A. religious studies educator; b. Aliceville, Ala., Jan. 8, 1932; s. Benjamin L. and Winnie (Gavin) M.; m. Martha Evelina Fowler, June 10, 1954 (dec. May 29, 1996); children: Suzanne, Edith, Ellen; m. Judith Colton, Mar. 18, 2000. BS, U. Ala.-Tuscaloosa, 1953; BD, Austin Presbyn. Theol. Sem., 1956; MA, Yale U., 1964, PhD, 1965; Doctor Theologiae honoris causa, U. Uppsala, Sweden, 1990. Instr. religion Dartmouth Coll., Hanover, N.H., 1964-65; asst. prof. religious studies Ind. U., Bloomington, 1966-68, assoc. prof., 1968-69; assoc. prof. religious studies Yale U., New Haven, 1969-73, prof. religious studies, 1973-84, Woolsey prof. Bibl. studies, 1984—, emeritus, 1999—, dir. divsn. Humanities, 1988-91. Author: Go From Your Father's House, 1964, The Prophet-King, 1967, Moral World of the First Christians, 1986, First Urban Christians, 1983, Origins of Christian Morality, 1993, In Search of the Early Christians, 2002; contbr. articles to profl. jours. Fulbright fellow, 1956-57; Kent fellow, 1962-64; NEH fellow, 1975-76; Guggenheim fellow, 1979-80. Fellow Brit. Acad.; mem. Soc. Bibl. Lit. (pres. 1985), Am. Acad. Religion (bd. dirs. 1974-77), Studiorum Novi Testamenti Societas (editl. bd. 1979-82, pres. 2004). Democrat. Presbyterian. Avocations: cabinet-making, hiking. Office: Yale U Dept Religious Studies PO Box 208287 New Haven CT 06520-8287 E-mail: wayne.meeks@yale.edu.

MEEKS, WILLIAM HERMAN, III, lawyer; b. Ft. Lauderdale, Fla., Dec. 30, 1939; s. Walter Herman Jr. and Elise Walker (McGuire) M.; m. Patricia Ann Rayburn, July 30, 1965; 1 son, William Herman IV; m. 2d, Miriam Andrea Bedsole, Dec. 28, 1971; 1 child, Julie Marie. AB, Princeton U., 1961; LLB, U. Fla., 1964; LLM in Tax, NYU, 1965. Bar: Fla 1964, U.S. Dist. Ct. (so. dist.) Fla. 1965, U.S. Tax Ct. 1966, U.S. Ct. Appeals (11th cir.) 1981, U.S. Supreme Ct. 1985. Ptnr. McCune, Hiaasen, Crum, Ferris & Gardner, Ft. Lauderdale, 1964-89, Fleming, O'Bryan & Fleming, Ft. Lauderdale, 1990-95, Dobbins, Meeks, Raleigh & Dover, Ft. Lauderdale, 1995—. Dir. Attys. Title Svcs., Inc., 1978-79, Attys. Title Svcs. of Broward County, Inc., 1971—, chmn., 1976-77; mem. Attys. Real Estate Coun. Broward County. Mem. ABA, Fla. Bar Assn., Broward County Bar Assn., Attys. Title Ins. Fund, Ft. Lauderdale Hist. Soc., Ft. Lauderdale Mus., Kiwanis, Lauderdale Yacht Club, Tower Club (Ft. Lauderdale), Phi Delta Phi. Democrat. Presbyterian. Office: Dobbins Meeks Raleigh & Dover 4th Fl 2601 E Oakland Park Blvd Fl 4 Fort Lauderdale FL 33306-1606 Office Phone: 954-565-2200. E-mail: whmeeks@ndmrd.com.

MEELDIJK, VICTOR ANTHONY, engineering professional; b. N.Y.C., May 17, 1953; s. Anthony and Freda M. BEE, CCNY, 1975. Safety and design engr. Ward Leonard Electric Co., Inc., Mt. Vernon, N.Y., 1975-77, New Brunswick Sci. Co., Inc., Edison, N.J., 1977-78; mgr. reliability and maintainability engring. DRS Technologies (formerly Diagnostic/Retrieval Sys.), Oakland, N.J., 1978-98; mgr. components engr. Dialogic Corp. (Divsn. of Intel), 1998—. Author: Electronic Components: Selection and Application Guidelines, 1994, updale, 1996, Component Identifier and Sourcebook, 1996, rev. 1998; cons. editor mag. Electronic Servicing and Tech., 1986; contbr. The Electronics Handbook, 1996, Semiconductor Devices And Circuits, 1999, MicroElectronics Handbook, 1999, Electronic Packaging Handbook, 2000, REA FE/EIT PM Electrical Exam, 2000; contbr. articles to profl. jours. Mem. IEEE, Inst. Environ. Scis., Electrostatic Overstress/Electrostatic Discharge Assn., The Authors Guild. Home: 1343 Valley Rd Apt E Wayne NJ 07470-8011 E-mail: v.meeldijk@dialogic.com.

MEEM, JAMES LAWRENCE, JR., nuclear scientist; b. N.Y., Dec. 24, 1915; s. James Lawrence and Phyllis (Deaderick) M.; m. Buena Vista Speake, Sept. 5, 1940; children: James, John. BS, Va. Mil. Inst., 1939; MS, Ind. U., 1947, PhD, 1949. Aero. research sci. NACA, 1940-46; dir. bulk shielding reactor Oak Ridge Nat. Lab., 1950-53, in charge nuclear operation aircraft reactor expt., 1954-55; chief reactor sci. Alco Products, Inc., 1955-57; in charge startup and initial testing Army Package Power Reactor, 1957; prof. nuclear engring. U. Va., Charlottesville, 1957-81, dept. chmn., dir. reactor facility, 1957-77, prof. emeritus, 1981—; cons. U.S. Army Fgn. Sci. and Tech. Ctr., 1981-90. Vis. cons. nuclear fuel cycle programs Sandia Labs., Albuquerque, 1977-78; vis. staff mem. Los Alamos Sci. Lab., 1967-68; mem. U.S.-Japan Seminar Optimization of Nuclear Engring. Edn., Tokai-mura, 1973 Author: Two Group Reactor Theory, 1964. Fellow Am. Nuclear Soc. (sec. reactor ops. div. 1966-68, vice chmn. 1968-70, chmn. 1970-71, Exceptional Service award 1980); mem. Am. Phys. Soc., Am. Soc. Engring. Edn., SAR Home: University Village # 1201 500 Crestwood Dr Charlottesville VA 22903-4890 E-mail: lmeem@earthlink.net.

MEENAN, ROBERT FRANCIS, rheumatologist, researcher, academician; b. Cambridge, Mass., Apr. 5, 1947; s. Paul Leo and Anna Bernadine (Curtin) M.; m. Lynda Jane Fortman, Apr. 29, 1972(div. April 1999); children: Molly, Mark. BA, Harvard U., 1968; MD, Boston U., 1972; MPH, U. Calif., Berkeley, 1977; MBA, Boston U., 1989. Diplomate Am. Bd. Internal Medicine and Rheumatology. Asst. prof. Sch. of Medicine Boston U., 1977-82, assoc. prof. Sch. of Medicine, 1982-88, prof. Sch. of Medicine, 1988—, assoc. dir. Arthritis Ctr., 1977-88, chief arthritis sect. Sch. of Medicine, 1988-92, dir. Arthritis Ctr., 1988-92, dean and prof. Sch. Pub. Health, 1992—. Nat. arthritis adv. bd. NIH, Washington, 1988-92; Svartz Meml. lectr. Swedish Med. Soc., 1989; nat. adv. coun. Agy. for Healthcare Rsch. and Quality, Washington, 2000—. Contbr. Jour. Arthritis Impact Measurement Scales, Jour. Social Security Disability, Jour. Dictionary of Rheumatic Disease, Outcome Assessmentation Clin. Moles; contbr. over 75 articles to profl. jours. Trustee Arthritis Found., 1989—, sec., 1999-2000. Internat. League Against Rheumatism fellow, 1981; recipient Nat. Svc. award Arthritis Found., 1989. Fellow ACP, Am. Coll. Rheumatology (pres. 1990-91); mem. Am. Soc. for Clin. Investigation. Achievements include development of arthritis impact measurement scales. Office: Boston U Sch Pub Health 715 Albany St Boston MA 02118-2526

MEENDSEN, FRED CHARLES, retired food company executive; b. Garden City, N.Y., Oct. 28, 1933; s. Frederick Herman and Charlotte Mabel (Reiss) M.; m. Nancy Lou Gross, Nov. 16, 1957; children: Fred Charles, Martha Anne. BA, Colgate U., 1954; MBA, Harvard U., 1956. Mem. mktg. and sales mgmt. dept. Velsicol Chem. Corp., Chgo., 1957-63; with Bestfoods Internat., Englewood Cliffs, N.J., 1963-96; pres. subs. Peterson/Puritan, Inc., Danville, Ill., 1977-83, Can. Starch Co., 1983-84, v.p. parent co., 1983-96, pres. N.Am. region corn wet milling divsn., 1984-88, v.p. corp. affairs, 1988-93, v.p. govt. affairs, 1994-96. Dir. Can. Starch Co., 1983-88; chmn. Casco Co., 1983-85; mem. U.S. C. of C. Can. Rels. Com., 1986-96, Food and Agr. Com., 1988-96; sec. Agr. Adv. Comm. on Trade, 1987-92. Author: Atomic Energy and Business Strategy, 1956. Pres. Colgate U. Alumni Corp., 1991-93, bd. dirs., 1988—; trustee Colgate U., 1993-99, trustee emeritus, 1999—; gov. Chesapeake Bay Maritime Mus., 1997—, vice chmn. 2004-; dir. Meml. Hosp., Easton, Md., 1997-1999. 1st lt. U.S. Army, 1956-59. Recipient Disting. Alumnus award Colgate U., 1999. Home: 24472 Trice Field Ct Saint Michaels MD 21663-2618

MEENGS, WILLIAM LLOYD, cardiologist; b. Zeeland, Mich., Dec. 23, 1942; s. Lloyd Stanley and Gertrude (Wyngarden) M.; m. Helen Delores Van Dyke, June 10, 1964; children: Michelle Rene, William Lloyd, Lisa Ann. AB, Hope Coll., 1964; MD, U. Mich., 1968. Diplomate Am. Bd. Cardiology, Am. Bd. Interventional Cardiology, Am. Bd. Nuc. Cardiology. Intern in internal medicine U. Hosp., Ann Arbor, Mich., 1968-69, resident in internal medicine, 1971-73, fellow in cardiology, 1973-75; practice medicine specializing in cardiology, interventional cardiology and nuc. cardiology Petoskey, Mich., 1975—. Cardiologist Burns Clinic Med. Center, Petoskey, 1975-99, chmn. dept. cardiology and cardiac surgery, 1978-89; med. dir. No. Mich. Heart Center, 1989-95; pres. Petoskey Cardiology, P.C., 1999—; chief sect. cardiology No. Mich. Hosps., 2000—; cardiologist Little Traverse Hosp., Petoskey, 1975—, dir. coronary care unit, 1986-89; dir. cardiac catheterization lab. No. Mich. Hosps., Petoskey, 1985-87, 92—, adult spl. care units, 1986-89; vice chmn. bd. dirs. Burns Clinic Med. Ctr., 1989-92. Contbr. med. articles to profl. jours. Trustee Mich. Heart Assn., 1979-83. Served as surgeon USPHS, 1969-71. Named one of Best Drs. in Am., 2001—02, 2003—04. Fellow: Soc. Cardiovasc. Angiography and Interventions, Am. Coll. Cardiology; mem.:

Am. Heart Assn. (fellow Coun. on Clin. Cardiology), Alpha Omega Alpha. Home: 1224 Autumn Ln Petoskey MI 49770-9019 Office: Petoskey Cardiology 560 W Mitchell St Ste 400 Petoskey MI 49770-2274

MEERSCHAERT, JOSEPH RICHARD, physician; b. Detroit, Mar. 4, 1941; s. Hector Achiel and Marie Terese (Campbell) M.; m. Jeanette Marie Ancerewicz, Sept. 14, 1963; children: Eric, Amy, Adam. BA, Wayne State U., 1965, MD, 1967. Diplomate Am. Bd. Phys. Medicine and Rehab., Am. Bd. Pain Medicine. Intern Harper Hosp., Detroit, 1967-68; resident in phys. medicine and rehab. Wayne State U. Rehab. Inst., Detroit, 1968-71; chief divsn. phys. medicine Naval Hosp., Chelsea, Mass., 1971-73; attending physician William Beaumont Hosp., Royal Oak, Mich., 1973—, med. dir. rehab. unit, 1979-87; pvt. practice medicine specializing in phys. medicine and rehab. Royal Oak, 1973—; pvt. practice specializing in pain medicine, 1990—. Mem. med. adv. bd. Nat. Wheelchair Athletic Assn., 1973—, U.S. team physician VII World Wheelchair Games, Stoke Mandeville, Eng.; clin. instr. Wayne State U., 1973-83, clin. asst. prof. phys. medicine and rehab., 1983—; mem. Mich. Dept. Licensing and Regulation State Bd. Phys. Therapy, 1978-81. Contbr. articles to profl. jours. With M.C. USN, 1971-73. Recipient John Hussey award Mich. Wheelchair Athletic Assn., 1981. Fellow Am. Coll. Pain Medicine; mem. Am. Acad. Phys. Medicine and Rehab. (reviewer, presenter) Am. Congress Rehab. Medicine, Mich. Phys. Medicine and Rehab. Soc., Am. Geriatrics Soc., Am. Assn. Electromyography and Electrodiagnosis, Mich. Rheumatism Soc., Mich. Acad. Phys. Medicine and REhab. (pres. 1986-87, chmn. program com. 1977-78, trustee 1980—, pres. bd. dirs. 1994-97), Oakland County Med. Soc. (bd. dirs. 1991, 97), Alpha Omega Alpha. Roman Catholic. Office: 44199 Dequindre Rd Troy MI 48085-1128

MEERSON, FELIX ZALMANOVICH, cardiologist; b. Moscow, Aug. 5, 1926; came to U.S., 1993; s. Zalman Moshevich and Minna Iyruhemonna (Ezra) M.; m. Lia Victorovna Shohova, 1953 (div. 1973); children: Nataly, Elena; m. Elena Vorontsova, Oct. 16, 1982; 1 child, Dmitry. MD, Moscow Med. Inst., 1949, PhD, 1952; DSc, Ctrl. Inst. Improving, Moscow, 1958. Sr. rsch. assoc. Inst. Phys. Methods Therapy, Yalta, 1954-55; sr. rsch. assoc. Inst. High Nervous Functioning USSR Acad. Sci., Moscow, 1955-56; assoc. prof. clin. physiology Ctrl. Inst. Improving Physician's Qualifications, 1956-57, prof., 1957-59; prof., head Lab. Exptl. Cardiology Inst. Gen. Pathophysiology Russian Acad. Med. Scis., Moscow, 1960-89, prof., dir. Ctr. Adaptive Medicine, 1990-93, mem. doctorate bd., 1960-93, mem. sci. coun., 1960-93. Sci. cons. Hypoxia Med., Ltd., Moscow, 1990-93, med. insts., Orenburg, Omsk, Irkutsk, Chelyabinsk, Russia, 1970-93; sci. head high mountain expdns. Russian Acad. Med. Scis., Caucasus, Tien Shan, 1980-93. Author: The Myocardium in Hyperfunction, Hypertrophy and Heart Failure, 1969, General Mechanisms of Adaption and Prophylactics, 1973, The Failing Heart: Adaption and Deadaptation, 1983, Adaption, Stress and Prophlaxis, 1984, Physiology of Adaptive Processes, 1986, Adaption to Stressful Situation and Physical Loads, 1988, Adaption to Hypoxia in Therapy and Prophylactics, 1989, Adaptive Protection of the Heart: Protecting Against Stress and Ischemic Damage, 1990, Protective Effects of Adaptation and Prospects of the Development of Adaptive Medicine, 1990, Protective Cross-Effects of Adaptation, 1993, Essentials of Adaptive Medicine: Protective Effects of Adaptation: A Manual, 1994; mem. editl. bd. CV World Report, 1985—, Clin. Cardiology, 1985—, Kardiology, 1985—; contbr. articles to profl. jours. Recipient medal Budapest U., Hungary, 1979, Jan Purkinie medal Prague U., Czechoslavakia, 1970, Laureate of State award USSR Govt., 1978, Hon. Scientist of Russia, Russian Govt., 1988, Gold medal USSR State Exbhn., 1989. Me. Internat. Soc. Adaptive Medicine (pres. 1990-95, founder, life pres. 1995—). Achievements include research in adaption to repeated moderate action of any environmental factor may protect animals and humans from damages impacts of other factors (cross-protective effect of adaptation); develpment of theory of long-term adaptation, a selective increase in expression of certain genes and accumulation of certain structures is the material basis of adaptation; formulation of new discipline Adaptive Medicine which is directed to study fundamental mechanisms of adaptation and use of adaptation for the treatment of diseases. Address: 2875 Cowley Way Apt 510 San Diego CA 92110-1010

MEESE, CELIA EDWARDS, pharmaceutical company executive; b. San Diego, May 10; d. Roy Clifford Edwards and Bessie Lucille (Lang) Hill; m. Jed D. Meese; 1 child, Scott Edwards Meese. BA, U. Wis.; BA (hon.), U. Taiwan. Pres. Vitaline Corp., Ashland, Oreg., 1972—; v.p. RenalChem, Inc., San Jose, Calif., 1982-90, Formulations Tech., Inc., Oakdale, Calif., 1982—; dir., trustee Oreg. Shakespeare Festival Endowment, Pacific Retirement Svcs., Medford, Oreg. Mem. Pharm. Mfrs. Assn., Mensa. Home: 88 Granite St Ashland OR 97520-2711

MEEZAN, ELIAS, pharmacologist, educator; b. N.Y.C., Mar. 5, 1942; s. Maurice and Rachel (Epstein) M.; m. Elisabeth Gascard, May 14, 1967; children: David, Nathan, Joshua. BS in Chemistry, CCNY, 1962; PhD in Biochemistry, Duke U., 1966. Asst. prof. physiology and pharmacology Duke U., Durham, NC, 1969-70; asst. prof. pharmacology U. Ariz., Tucson, 1970-75, assoc. prof., 1975-79; prof., chmn. dept. pharmacology U. Ala., Birmingham, 1979-89, prof., dir. Metabolic Diseases Rsch. Lab., 1989-93, prof. dept. pharmacology, 1993—. Assoc. editor: Life Sci., 1973-79. Helen Hay Whitney postdoctoral fellow, 1966-69; recipient NIH Rsch. Career Devel. award, 1977-79. Mem. Am. Soc. Pharmacology and Exptl. Therapeutics, Am. Soc. Biol. Chemistry, AAUP, AAAS, N.Y. Acad. Sci., Assn. Med. Sch. Pharmacology. Democrat. Jewish. Achievements include isolation of retinal microvasculature; development of method for isolating ultrastructurally and chemically intact basement membranes. Home: 1202 Cheval Ln Birmingham AL 35216-2037 Office: U Ala Dept Pharmacology Birmingham AL 35294-0001 Office Phone: 205-934-4577. Business E-Mail: Elias.Meezan@ccc.uab.edu.

MEEZAN, WILLIAM ALAN, social work educator, consultant; b. NYC, Mar. 10, 1947; s. Joseph and Beatrice (Rauch) M. BA in Psychology, U. Vt., 1967; MSW, Fla. State U., 1969; cert. in advanced social welfare, Columbia U., 1973, DSW, 1978. Social worker The Children's Village, Dobbs Ferry, N.Y., 1969-70; rsch. asst. child welfare rsch. program Sch. of Social Work Columbia U., N.Y.C., 1970-72, part-time rsch. asst. child welfare rsch. program, 1972-73; rsch. assoc. Ctr. for N.Y.C. Affairs New Sch. for Social Rsch., N.Y.C., 1973-75; study dir. Child Welfare League of Am., N.Y.C., 1975-77; cons. Children's Bur., Adminstrn. for Children, Youth and Families, Office Human Devel. Svcs. HEW, Washington, 1978; asst. prof. Jane Addams Coll. of Social Work U. Ill., Chgo., 1978-81, assoc. prof. Jane Addams Coll. of Social Work, 1981-86, chair PhD program, prof. Jane Addams Coll. of Social Work, 1986-88; John Milner prof. child welfare Sch. Social Wk., U. So. Calif., L.A., 1988—99, chair PhD program, 1989—94; Marion Elizabeth Blue prof. children and families U. Mich. Sch. Social Work, 1999—. Part-time instr. Ctr. of Social Work and Social Rsch., Fairleigh Dickinson U., Teneck, N.J., 1974-75, Adelphi U. Grad. Sch. of Social Work, Garden City, N.Y., 1978; adj. asst. prof. NYU Sch. of Social Work, N.Y.C., 1975-78; spl. asst. to exec. dir. Jewish Children's Bur., Chgo., 1986-88, steering com., sec. Group for Advancement Doctoral Edn., 1990-94; sec. Soc. For Social Work and Rsch., 2002—; bd. dirs. The Guidance Ctr., 2002—. Author: Adoption Without Angencies: A Study of Independent Adoptions, 1978, Care and Commitment: Foster Parent Adoption Decisions, 1985, Evaluating Family Based Services, 1995, Family Preservation and Family Functioning, 1997, (monographs) The Impact of Welfare on Family Stability, 1975, Foster Care Needs and Alternatives to Placement: A Projection for 1975-85, 1975, Adoptions Services in the States, 1980, Evaluation of the Wayne County Foster Care Pilot Project, 2003; editor: Child Welfare: Current Dilemas-Future Decisions, 1983, Rationing Child Protection, 1995, Research Methods with Gay, Lesbian, Bisexual and Transgender Populations, 2003; mem. editl. bd. Social Work Rsch., Child Welfare, Children and Youth Svcs. Rev., Jour. Social Svc. Rsch., others; contbr. chpts. to books, articles to jour HEW fellow, 1967-68, NIMH fellow, 1972-73, AAAS Congl. Sci. fellow, 1984-85; HEW scholar, 1975-77, U.S. Dept. Health and Human Svcs. scholar, 1980-83, 2000—; Stuart Found. scholar, 1989-95, Fulbright scholar, 1994-95, State of Calif., 1996-99, Kellogg Found., 2000—, State of Mich., 2000-02, Aspen Inst., 2000-03, Skillman Found., 2003—, Mich. Nonprofit Rsch. Program, 2003—. Mem. NASW, Am. Orthopsychiat. Assn., Acad. Cert. Social Workers, Coun. on Social Work Edn., Soc. Social Work and Rsch. (nat. sec.). Home: 3132 Birchwood Dr Ann Arbor MI 48105-9266 Office: Univ Mich 1080 S University Ann Arbor MI 48109 Office Phone: 734-763-3428.

MEFFERT, ROLAND MATTHEW, periodontist, educator; b. Cross Plains, Wis., June 30, 1932; s. John Michael and Lorraine Catherine (Garfoot) Meffert; m. Marcella Ann Czarnecki, June 12, 1954; children: Jeffrey, Lisa, Sarah, Gregory, Douglas. DDS, Marquette U., 1955; cert. in periodontics, U. Tex., Houston, 1961; cert. in periodontics, Wilford Hall USAF Med. Ctr., 1962. Commd. 1st lt. USAF, 1954, advanced through grades to col., 1970, ret., 1974; prof. dept. periodontics U. Tex. Health Sci. Ctr., San Antonio, 1974—84, 1992—2003, cons. continuing dental edn., 2003—; assoc. prof. dept. prosthodontics U. Tex. Med. Ctr., San Antonio, 2003—; prof., chmn. dept. periodontics La. State Med. Ctr., New Orleans, 1984—92. Cons. continuing dental edn. U. Tex. Health Sci. Ctr., 2003—. Contbr. chapters to books, articles to profl. jours.; co-editor: Implant Dentistry; editor emeritus: Practical Periodontics and Aesthetic Dentistry. Recipient Spl. Citation award, Am. Acad. Periodontology, 1993, 1997, Meffert-Mutlu Implant Inst. named in honor, Ankara, Turkey, 1997. Master: Am. Acad. Implant Prosthodontics; fellow: Internat. Colll. Dentists, Am. Coll. Dentists; mem.: Am. Soc. Osseointegration (diplomate, pres. 1992, Oral Implantologist of Yr. 1988), Internat. Congress Oral Implantology (diplomate, pres. 1990, Internat. Edn. award 1992, 1994), Am. Bd. Periodontology (diplomate, dir., chmn. 1990—96).

MEGAHED, MOHAMED SALAH, neurologist, educator; b. Aug. 18, 1928; MB, BChir, Cairo U., 1951, MD, 1960. Diplomate Am. Bd. Psychiatry and Neurology. Physician Royal Palace of King Saud, 1954-60; clin. clk. Inst. Nervous Diseases Nat. Hosp. Queen Square, London, 1961-64; resident in neurology SUNY, Buffalo, 1964-67, fellow in neurology, cons. attending neurologist, 1967-69; pvt. practice North Tonawanda, N.Y., 1973; chief EEG and neurology depts. Niagara Falls (N.Y.) Meml. Med. Ctr., Mt. St. Mary's Hosp., Lewiston, N.Y. Clin. assoc. prof. U. Rochester (N.Y.)-Strong Meml. Hosp., until 1996, clin. prof., 1996—. Fellow ACP, Royal Coll. Physicians (Edinburgh), Am. Acad. Neurology; mem. AMA, N.Y. State Med. Soc. Office: 1089 Kinkead Ave North Tonawanda NY 14120-2840

MEGAN, THOMAS IGNATIUS, retired judge; b. Chgo., Dec. 24, 1913; s. Charles P. and May M. (Magan) M.; m. Lucyanne Flaherty, Apr. 17, 1948; children: Anne, Thomas, Jane, Sarah, William, Molly. AB, U. Ill., 1935; JD, U. Chgo., 1938. Bar: Ill. 1939, N.Y. 1941. Mem. firm Pruitt & Grealis, Chgo., 1939-40, Pruitt, Hale & MacIntyre, N.Y.C., 1941; atty. U.S. Ordnance Dept., Chgo., 1941-42, Chgo., Rock Island and Pacific R.R. Co., Chgo., 1945-70, v.p., gen. counsel, 1970-74, v.p. law, 1974-75; adminstrv. law judge ICC, Washington, 1975-81, HHS, Washington, 1981, FERC, Washington, 1981-96; ret., 1996. Served to maj. AUS, 1942-45. Mem. ABA, Soc. Trial Lawyers Chgo., Chgo. Law Club, Phi Kappa Tau, Phi Delta Phi. Clubs: Union League (Chgo.). Home: 11108 Waycroft Way Rockville MD 20852-3217

MEGAY-NESPOLI, KAREN PATRICIA, elementary school educator; b. N.Y.C., May 4, 1954; d. Charles A. and Audrey J. (Duddy) Megay; m. Michael A. Nespoli, Oct. 13, 1979; children: Lauren Brynn, Caitlin Bree. BA, CUNY, 1976, MS, 1978; profl. diploma in adminstrn. & supr., St. John's U., 1986; EdD, Columbia U., 1998. Tchr. 3d grade Our Lady of the Miraculous Medal Sch., Queens, NY, 1977-84, adminstrv. asst. to prin., 1980-84, primary coord., 1981-84; tchr. 4th grade P.S. 87, 1984—86. Adj. asst. prof. CW Post campus L.I. U. Author: The First Year for Elementary School Teachers, 1983; contbr. articles to profl. jours. Mem. AAUW, ASCD, Internat. Reading Coun., Nat. Assn. Gifted Children, Nat. Coun. Math. Tchrs., Nassau Reading Coun., Phi Delta Kappa, Kappa Delta Pi. Office: LI U CW Post Campus Dept Curriculum and Instrn 720 Northern Blvd Greenvale NY 11548

MEGGERS, BETTY JANE, anthropologist, researcher; b. Washington, Dec. 5, 1921; d. William Frederick and Edith (Raddant) M.; m. Clifford Evans, Sept. 13, 1946. AB, U. Pa., 1943; MA, U. Mich., 1944; PhD, Columbia U., 1952; D (hon.), U. de Guayaquil, Ecuador, 1987, U. Fed. Rio de Janeiro, Brazil, 1994, U. Nat. La Plata, Argentina, 1997, U. Católica de Goiás, Brazil, 1999. Instr. anthropology Am. U., Washington, 1950-51; rsch. assoc. Smithsonian Instn., 1954—, expert, 1981—; founder, pres. Taraxacum Inc., 1977—. Hon. prof. U. de Azuay, Ecuador, 1991. Author: Environmental Limitation on the Development of Culture, 1954, Ecuador, 1966, Amazonia, 1971, 2d edit., 1996, Prehistoric America, 1972, Evolucion y Difusion Cultural, 1998, Ecologia y Biogeografia de la Amazonia, 1999, (with Clifford Evans) Archeological Investigations at the Mouth of the Amazon, 1957, Archeological Investigations in British Guiana, 1960, (with Clifford Evans and Emilio Estrada) Early Formative Period of Coastal Ecuador, 1965, (with Clifford Evans) Archeological Investigations on the Rio Napo, Eastern Ecuador, 1968; editor: Prehistoria Sudamericana, 1992. Recipient award for sci. achievement Washington Acad. Sci., 1956; gold medal 37th Internat. Congress of Americanists, 1966; Order Al Merito Govt. Ecuador, 1966; Order Bernardo O'Higgins Govt. Chile, 1985; Sec.'s Gold medal for exceptional service Smithsonian Instn., 1986; Order Andres Bello Govt. Venezuela, 1988; Order Al Mérito por Servicios Distinguidos Govt. Peru, 1989. Fellow: AAAS, Assn. Tropical Biology (hon.; councilor 1976—78, pres.-elect 1982, pres. 1983); mem.: Ecol. Soc. Am., New Eng. Antiquities Rsch. Assn., Academia Nacional Historia Ecuador (corr.), Am. Anthrop. Assn. (exec. sec. 1959—61), Museo Antropológico de la Cultura Andina (hon.), Soc. Am. Archeology (exec. bd. 1962—64), Am. Ethnol. Soc., Anthrop. Soc. Wash. (treas. 1955—60, v.p. 1965—66, pres. 1966—68), Phi Beta Kappa, Sigma Xi. Home: 1227 30th St NW Washington DC 20007-3410 Office: Smithsonian Instn Washington DC 20560-0001

MEGGS, WILLIAM JOEL, toxicologist, allergist, emergency physician, educator; b. Newberry, S.C., May 30, 1942; s. Wallace Nat and Elizabeth (Pruitt) M.; m. Susan Nancy Spring, June 11, 1966 (div. June 1998); m. Susan Krause Martin, Apr. 21, 2001; children: Jason Nathaniel, Benjamin Maffey, Thomas Clute. BS, Clemson U., 1964; PhD, Syracuse U., 1969; MD, U. Miami, 1979. Diplomate Am. Bd. Internal Medicine, Am. Bd. Allergy and Immunology, Am. Bd. Emergency Medicine, Am. Bd. Med. Toxicology. Resident in internal medicine Rochester (N.Y.) Gen. Hosp., 1979-82; staff fellow in allergy and clin. immunology Nat. Inst. Allergy and Infectious Diseases, Bethesda, Md., 1982-85; asst. dir. med. edn. emergency dept. Washington Hosp. Ctr., 1985-88; from asst. prof. allergy, immunology to sr. vice chmn. Sch. Medicine E. Carolina U., Greenville, NC, 1988—2004, sr. vice chmn. Sch. Medicine, 2004—; chmn., dir. emergency dept. Lenoir Meml. Hosp., Kinston, NC, 1990-91. Mem. Emergency Svcs. Com. Lenoir Meml. Hosp., Kinston, 1988-92; mem workshop on immune testing, Agy. for Toxic Substances and Diseases Registry, 1992, workshop on equity in environ. health, U.S. EPA, 1992, workshop on multiple chem. sensitivity syndrome, NRC, 1991; mem. rsch. adv. com. on Gulf War illnesses Dept. VA, 2002-; fellow med. toxicology NYU, 1992-96. Author: The Inflammation Cure, 2003; co-author: The Inflammation Cure, 2003; co-editor: Health and Safety in Agriculture, 1997; contbr. numerous articles and abstracts to profl. jours. Vol. physician Indigent Clinic E. Carolina U., Pitt County Med. Soc., 1988—, Pitt County Shelter, 1989—; advanced cardiac life support instr. E. Carolina U. Sch. of Medicine, 1988-2000, advanced trauma life support instr., 1991-2002; mem. Pitt County Traffic Injury Prevention Program, 1989-92; bd. dirs. Rachael Carson Coun., 1988—; mem. adv. bd. Pamplico Tar River Found., 1990—. Named Woodrow Wilson Hon. fellow, 1964, NSF post-doctoral fellow, 1969; grantee N.C. United Way, 1988-89, Greer Labs., 1989-90, Am. Lung Assn. N.C., 1992-93. Fellow Am. Coll. Emergency Physicians, Am. Coll. Med. Toxicology; mem. AMA, Am. Acad. Allergy and Immuniology, Am. Acad. Clin. Toxicology, Pitt County Med. Soc., N.C. State Med. Soc., Soc. for Acad. Emergency Medicine, N.C. Thoracic Soc. (physicians' sect.). Achievements include first to creator of the biological homing theory of the origins of life. Office: E Carolina U Sch Medicine Dept Emergency Medicine Brody Bldg 4-W54 600 Moye Blvd Greenville NC 27858-4300 Office Phone: 252-744-2954. Business E-Mail: meggsw@mail.ecu.edu.

MEGHREBLIAN, ROBERT VARTAN, manufacturing executive, physicist; b. Cairo, Sept. 6, 1922; arrived in U.S., 1923, naturalized, 1929; s. Vahan V. and Mary (Kurkjian) M.; m. Mary J. Walton, 1955 (div. 1977); Children: David V., Susan M.; Margaret M. Gordon, 1987. B in Engring. (Gotshall-Powell scholar), Rensselaer Poly. Inst., 1943; MS (Guggenheim fellow), Calif. Inst. Tech., 1950, PhD magna cum laude (Guggenheim fellow), 1953. Lectr. Oak Ridge Nat. Lab., 1952-55, assoc. project mgr., 1955-58; chief sect. Physics Jet Propulsion Lab., Calif. Inst. Tech., 1958-60, mgr. space scis. divsn., 1960-68, dep. asst. lab. dir., 1968-71, assoc. prof. applied mechanics, 1960-61; v.p. rsch. and engring. Cabot Corp., Boston, 1971-79, v.p., 1971-87; pres. Distrigas Corp., 1979-85; gen. mgr. Cabot Crystals Bus. Unit, 1985-86, dir. corp. planning and devel., 1986-87. Author: Reactor Analysis, 1960. Served to lt. (j.g.) USN, 1941-46, PTO, ATO. Fellow AIAA (assoc.), Am. Nuc. Soc.; mem. Tennis Club Santa Barbara, Santa Barbara Club, Montecito Assn. (bd. dirs. 1992-98, v.p. 1994, pres. 1995, 96, chair archtl. rev. com. 1993-95, Montecito Citizen of Yr. 2002, vice chair Montecito planning comm. 2003, chair 2004), Sigma Xi. Home: 440 Woodley Rd Montecito CA 93108-2006

MEGILL, ALLAN D. historian; b. Regina, Sask., Can., Apr. 20, 1947; came to U.S., 1980; s. Ralph Peter and Jean Tudhope (Dickson) M.; divorced; children: Jason Robert, Jessica Susan, Jonathan David; life ptnr. Rita Felski; 1 child, Maria Megill Felski. BA, U. Sask., 1969; MA, U. Toronto, 1970; PhD, Columbia U., 1975. From instr. to prof. history U. Iowa, Iowa City, 1974-90; prof. history U. Va., Charlottesville, 1990—. Rsch. fellow in history of ideas Australian Nat. U., Canberra, 1977—79, temp. lectr. modern European studies, 1979; dir. d'études invité École des Hautes Études en Scis. Sociales, Paris, 1997; v.p. Jour. of the History of Ideas, Inc., 2004—. Author: Prophets of Extremity, 1985, Karl Marx: The Burden of Reason, 2002; editor: Rethinking Objectivity, 1994; co-editor: The Rhetoric of the Human Sciences, 1987; cons. editor: Jour. of History of Ideas, 1986—89, mem. editl. bd.:, 1990—, Rethinking History, 1996—, U. Press of Va., 1991—94; contbr. articles to profl. jours. Chmn. Page-Barbour and Richard Lectures com. U. Va., 1994-96. Mem. Am. Hist. Assn. Office: U Va Corcoran Dept of History PO Box 400180 Charlottesville VA 22904 Business E-Mail: megill@virginia.edu.

MEGNA, STEVE ALLAN, secondary school educator; Secondary tchr. Vernon (NJ) H.S. Recipient Tech. Excellence award Internat. Tech. Edn. Assn. and Tech. Edn. Assn. N.J., 1992, Tech. Program of Yr. award Tech. Edn. Assn. N.J., 1989. Office: Vernon HS Rte 565 Vernon NJ 07462

MEGUID, MICHAEL M. medical educator, researcher; b. Cairo, May 14, 1944; s. Amin and Margrate Meguid; m. Victoria Perfect Meguid, Dec. 12, 1968; children: Bonnie M., Robert A. MBBS, U. Coll. Hosp. Med. Sch., 1968; PhD, Mass. Inst. Tech., 1981; certificate in molecular biology, Smith Coll., Northampton, Mass., 1998. Cert. Mass. Bd. Registration, Calif. Bd. Med. Quality Assurance, NY State Dept. Edn., Am. Bd. Surgery, 1980, Am. Bd. Surgery, 1990, Am. Bd. Nutrition, 1983, Am. Bd. Physician Nutrition Specialists, 2001. Surgical and med. intern U. Coll. Hosp. and Bethnal Green Hosp., U. London, England, 1968—69; anatomy demonstrator, dept. anatomy U. College, U. London, 1969—70; resident, dept. surgery Harvard Med. Sch. at Peter Brent Brigham Hosp., Children's Hosp. Med. Ctr., Boston U. Med. Ctr., 1970—76; resident fellow Surgical Metabolism Lab., Harvard Med. Sch. at Peter Brent Brigham Hosp., Boston, 1972—74; with Boston U. Med. Ctr., 1974—79, chief resident, 1974—76, asst. prof., dir. nutrition support team, 1976—79; resident physician Clinical Rsch. Ctr., MIT, Cambridge, Mass., 1978—81; rsch. asst., dept. nutrition and food sci. MIT, 1979—81; asst. surgeon, gen. and oncologic surgery City of Hope Nat. Med. Ctr., Duarte, Calif., 1979—82, dir., dept. nutrition, 1979—84, dir. nutrition support team, 1979—84, assoc. surgeon, gen. and oncologic surgery, 1982—84; asst. clinical prof. surgery UCLA Sch. Medicine, 1979—84; attending physician, surgical svc. Wadsworth V.A. Hosp., LA, 1979—84; prof. surgery, dept. surgery U. Hosp., SUNY Upstate Med. U., and Vet. Adminstrn., Syracuse, 1984—; assoc. dir. Breast Care Program, Syracuse, 1984—2000; dir. neuroscience program Surgical Metabolism and Nutrition Lab., 1984—; dir. surgical nutrition svc. U. Hosp., 1984—, dir. combined surgical rsch. lab., dept. surgery, 1997—. Chmn. abstract selection com. Am. Soc. Parenteral Enteral Nutrition (ASPEN), 1976—79, mem. program com., 3rd clin. congress, 1978—79, chmn. program com., 5th clinical congress, 1980—81, councilor-at-large, policy papers, 6th clinical congress, 1981—82; mem. nutrition com. Mass. Med. Soc., 1978—79; mem. Instl. Review Bd., 1985—94; examiner Am. Bd. Nutrition, Inc., 1985—89, regent, 1989—95, bd. dirs., 1990—95; chmn. Am. Inst. Nutrition-Am. Soc. Clinical Nutrition Joint Publ. Mgmt. com., 1986—92; assoc. examiner Am. Bd. Surgery, 1989, 98; panel Nat. Inst. Health Consensus, 1995—96; reviewer, cons. European Commn., Brussels, 2003—08; vis. prof. numerous coll.; rschr. and investigator in field; spkr. in field. Editor: (jour.) Nutrition: Internat. Jour. Applied and Basic Nutritional Sci., 1985—; co-editor: Current Opinions in Clinical Nutrition, 2002—; editl. reviewer (numerous jour.), 1980—; contbr. articles to jour., chapters to books. Recipient Joseph B. Goldberger award in clinical nutrition, AMA, 1997; elected fellow, Internat. Behavioral Neuroscience Soc., 1997. Fellow: N. Am. Assn. Study Obesity, Internat. Behavioral Neuroscience Soc.; mem.: ACS (candidate mem. 1975—82, fellow 1982), AAAS, Am. Soc. Bariatric Surgery, Cent. NY Surgical NY Soc., Assn. V.A. Surgeons, Cent. Surgical Assn., Am. Surgical Assn., Soc. U. Surgeons, Soc. Surgery Alimentary Tract, Soc. Surgical Oncology, Am. Soc. Clinical Nutrition (mem. Lederle award com. 1985—87, mem. long range planning com. 1986—88, chmn. Lederle award com. 1987—88, mem. com. on clinical issues in health and disease 1987—90), Coun. Biology Editors, Am. Soc. Nutritional Sci., NY Acad. Sci., Soc. Study Ingestive Behavior, Am. Psychological Soc., Soc. Neuroscience, Cent. NY Surgical Assn., Brigham Surgical Alumni, Harvard Med. Sch. Alumni, Surgical Biology Club II. Achievements include patents for gastric procedure for weight loss, 2003; common imultaneoud gene expressions in normal weight, obesity and after weight loss in hypothalamus and in subcutaneoue fat revelant to metabolic syndrome, 2004. Office: SUNY Upstate Med Univ 750 E Adams St Syracuse NY 13210 Office Fax: 315-464-6237.

MEGUID, TERRY F, investment company executive; Deputy Head of Investment Banking Division, Morgan Stanley, 1997—2000, global head, worldwide investment banking, 2001—. Office: Morgan Stanley 1585 Broadway New York NY 10036

MEHAFFEY, JOHN ALLEN, marketing, newspaper management and advertising executive; b. Brainerd, Minn. m. Mary Jean Mehaffey; children: Mark, Scott, Chris. Student, Minn. Sch. Bus. With Mehaffey Internat., Naples, Fla., 1954—. Bd. govs. Verified Audit Circulations. Ga . Nat. Newspaper Assn., Newspaper Assn. Am., Nat. Press Club (Washington), Ill. Press Assn., Assn. Free Cmty. Papers, Ind. Free Papers Assn., Fla. Free Papers Assn., Am. Mktg. Assn., Inland Press Assn., Fla. Press Assn., Soc. Profl. Journalists, Chgo. Headline Club, Internat. Platform Assn., Am. Telemktg. Assn., Naples Area C. of C., Suburban Newspaper Assn., Ctrl. States Circulating Mgrs. Assn., Inland Press Assn., Southeastern Advt. Pubs. Assn., Brainerd Lakes Area C. of C., St. Joseph's Med. Ctr. Found. (charter), Nat. Alliance for Mentally Ill., Greater Chgo. and AIll. Alliance for Mentally Ill, Motion Picture and TV Assn., Marine Habitat Found. (founding), Naples Aquarium (founding), Founding One Thousand, Naples Philharm. Ctr. for Performing Arts, Naples Conservancy, Northland Arboretum, Paul Bunyan Nature Learning Ctr. (life), Nat. Rails-to-Trails Conservancy, Internat. Press Club (Chgo.), Naples Press Club, Elks, Moose, Sigma Delta Chi. Avocation: boating. Home and Office: Mehaffey Internat PO Box 2956 Naples FL 34106-2956

MEHAFFEY, SCOTT ALAN, landscape architect; b. Princeton, Ill., Mar. 1, 1965; s. John Paul and Barbara Jean (Schaefer) M. B Landscape Architecture, U. Ill., 1987; MS in Orgnl. Leadership, Dominican U., 2003. Registered landscape architect, Ill. Landscape architect Scott Byron & Co., Inc., Lake Bluff, Ill., 1988-89, Jacobs/Ryan Assocs., Chgo., 1989-93, Morton Arboretum, Lisle, Ill., 1993—. Coun. mem. Garfield Park Conservatory Alliance, 1996-98. Mem. Preservation Fund com. Landmarks Preservation Coun. of Ill., 2000-02, Ragdale Found. Landscape Com., 2001—. Yamagami-Hope fellow Landscape Architecture Found., 1991; Student Rsch. grant U. Ill. Bd. Trustees, Champaign-Urbana, 1988; Merit award Am. Hort. Soc., Chgo. Flower and Garden Show, 1996-97. Mem. Am. Soc. Landscape Architects (continuing

edn. chmn. Ill. chpt. 1991-93, pres.-elect Ill. chpt. 1997-98, pres. Ill. chpt. 1998-99, chmn. historic preservation open com. 1995-96, ann. meeting com. 1995-99), Am. Assn. Bot. Gardens and Arboreta (historic landscapes com. 1994-99, grounds mgmt. com. 1999—, chmn. ann. conf. steering com. 2004—), Am. Assn. Museums (mus. mgmt. com. 2002—). Avocations: gardening, bicycling, travel, writing, community service. Office: The Morton Arboretum 4100 Illinois Route 53 Lisle IL 60532-1293 Business E-Mail: mehaffey@mortonarb.org.

MEHALCHIN, JOHN JOSEPH, entrepreneur, finance executive; b. Hazleton, Pa., Aug. 8, 1937; s. Charles and Susan (Korba) M.; divorced; 1 child, Martin. BS with honors (1st in class), Temple U., 1964; MBA, U. Calif., Berkeley, 1965; postgrad., U. Chgo., 1964; LHD (hon.), U. Colo., 2002. Supr. costs Winchester-Western, New Haven, 1965-67; mgmt. cons. Booz-Allen & Hamilton, N.Y.C., 1967-68; mgr. planning TWA, N.Y.C., 1968-69; officer Smith Barney, N.Y.C. and Paris, 1970-74; pres. Storage Tech. Corp., Louisville, 1974-79; sr. v.p. Heizer Corp., 1979; pres., founder Highline Fin. Svcs., Inc. and fgn. subs., Boulder, Colo., 1979—; also London, Paris and Frankfurt, Germany. Mem. strategic planning com. Coll. and Grad. Sch. Bus., U. Colo., Denver; bd. advisors U. Colo. Ctr. Entrepreneurship, U. Colo. Bus. Sch., Wolf Ventures. With AUS, 1958—61. Recipient Mack Easton award for Excellence, 1998, U. medal, U. Colo., 2002; fellow Scholarship, U. Chgo., 1964, U. Calif., Berkeley, 1964, 1965. Mem. Fin. Execs. Inst., Equipment Leasing Assn., Beta Gamma Sigma, Omicron Delta Epsilon. Home and Office: Highline Fin Svcs Inc 2930 Center Green Ct Ste 200 Boulder CO 80301-5419

MEHAN, GEORGE TRACEY, III, federal agency administrator; Grad., St. Louis U. Dir. Mo. Dept. Natural Resources, 1989—91; assoc. deputy adminstr. EPA, 1992—93; dir. Office of Great Lakes, Mich. Dept. Environ. Quality; asst. adminstr. water EPA, Washington, 2001—. Office: EPA 1200 Pennsylvania Ae NW MC 4101 Washington DC 20460

MEHIEL, DENNIS, paper and packaging company executive; Co-founder Four M, Balt., 1966, Valhalla, N.Y., 1970; Box USA (formerly Four M), Valhalla, N.Y., CEO; chmn., CEO SF Holdings Group, NY, NY, 1998—.

MEHL, DONALD EDWARD, retired marketing professional; b. Omaha, Jan. 28, 1923; s. Arthur Julius and Cecilia Mehl; m. Alice Mae Toland, Apr. 15, 1950 (dec. 1997); children: David(dec.), Kathleen Chadwick, Janice Rossi, Arthur, Therese Sellers. Student, U. Omaha, 1942, U. Minn., 1943—44; BS, Creighton U., 1949. Engring. mgr. Inland Broadcasting Co., 1942—52; telecomm. mktg. mgr. Graybar Electric, Kansas City, Mo., 1952—59; v.p., editor, pub. Tech. Publs., Inc., Kansas City, Mo., 1959—61; advt. and mktg. profl. Collins Radio, Richardson, Tex., 1961—73; mktg. dir. Rockwell Internat., Kansas City, Mo., 1973—87. Author, pub.: Sigsaly - The Green Hornet, 1997, Top Secret Communications of World War II, 2002, founder, editor, pub.: Broadcast Engring. Jour. 1st lt. signal corps U.S. Army, 1943—46. Mem.: Am. Radio Relay League. Avocation: amateur radio. Home: 1327 W Jenkins Blvd Raymore MO 64083

MEHLENBACHER, DOHN HARLOW, civil engineer, consultant; b. Huntington Park, Calif., Nov. 18, 1931; s. Virgil Claude and Helga (Sigfridson) M.; m. Nancy Moss; children: Dohn Scott, Kimberly Ruth, Mark James, Matthew Lincoln. BSCE, U. Ill., 1953; MS in City and Regional Planning, Ill. Inst. Tech., 1961; MBA, U. Chgo., 1972. Registered profl. engr., Ill.; lic. structural engr., Ill. Structural engr., draftsman Swift & Co., Chgo., 1953-54, 56-57, DeLeuw-Cather Co., Chgo., 1957-59; project engr. Quaker Oats Co., Chgo., 1959-61, mgr. constrn., 1964-70, mgr. real property, 1970-71, mgr. engring. and maintenance L.A., 1961-64; chief facilities engr. Bell & Howell Co., Chgo., 1972-73; v.p. design Globe Engring. Co., Chgo., 1973-76; project mgr. I.C. Harbour Constrn. Co., Oak Brook, Ill., 1976-78; dir. estimating George A. Fuller Co., Oak Brook, 1978; pres. Food-Tech. Co., Willowbrook, Ill., 1979-80; dir. phys. resources Ill. Inst. Tech., Chgo., 1980-92; cons. Exec. Svc. Corp., Chgo., 1994—. Arbitrator Am. Arbitration Assn. With USAF, 1954-56. Fellow ASCE. Home and Office: 436 Leitch Ave La Grange IL 60525-6126 Office Phone: 708-354-7131.

MEHLING, EMILY, artist; b. Plainfield, N.J., Aug. 28, 1932; d. Hugh and Corlyss Gibson Thompson; m. Harold Mehling, Oct. 8, 1974; children: Daniel Rodriguez, Joshua Rodriguez, Adam Rodriguez. BS, Columbia U., 1962; postgrad., Hunter Coll., 1966—68, Parsons Sch. Design, N.Y.C., 1994—96. Tchr. N.Y.C. Bd. Edn., 1967—71; art dir. Park Row Pubs., N.Y.C., 1972—80; freelance painter and sculptor N.Y.C., 1980—. Mem.: Nat. League Am. PEN Women, Found. for Modern Painters and Sculptors, Am. Soc. Contemporary Artists (treas. 2000—02), Contemporary Artist Guild, Nat. Assn. Women Artists (pres. 2002—04, organizer exhbns.), Amnesty Internat. Avocations: theater, opera. Home Fax: 212-924-7214. Personal E-mail: mehlinghe@earthlink.net.

MEHLING, ROBERT R. artist; b. Bklyn., Oct. 10, 1954; s. Robert G. Mehling and Gloria M. Theiling. AS, Suffolk County C.C., 1995—97; BFA summa cum laude, Southampton Coll., LIU, 1998—2002. Prin. works include The Teacher, 2002 (First Pl., Arts Coun. E. Islip Pub. Libr., 2003, Cert. Merit, Salmagundi Club, 2003, inclusion in Parrish Museum's 38th Juried Exhbn., 2003), Self Portrait with Attitude, 2001 (Best in Show, East End Arts Coun., 2002), Table Setting with Pitcher, 2001 (First Pl., Riverhead Free Libr., 2002), Shed Wall, 2002 (Hon. Mention, East End Arts Coun., 2003, inclusion in Parrish Museum's 38th Juried Exhbn., 2003), one-man shows include, Riverhead Free Libr., 1998, Southampton Town Hall, 1999, Avram Gallery, Southampton Coll., 2002, Port Washington Pub. Libr., 2004, exhibited in group shows, Elaine Benson Gallery, 2002, Grenning Gallery, 2003, Blue Door Gallery, 2003, Phoenix Gallery, 2003, Parrish Mus., 2003. Grantee Spl. Opportunity Stipend, NY Found. Arts, 2003. Mem.: Southampton Artists Assn. (assoc.; second v.p. 2002). Liberal. Cath. Avocations: gardening, music. Home: 410-1661 Old Country Rd Riverhead NY 11901 Office Phone: 631-208-1370. Personal E-mail: ramehshu@earthlink.net.

MEHLINGER, HOWARD DEAN, education educator; b. Hillsboro, Kans., Aug. 22, 1931; s. Alex and Alice Hilda (Skibbee) M.; m. Carolee Ann Case, Dec. 28, 1952; children: Bradley Case, Barbara Ann, Susan Kay. BA, McPherson (Kans.) Coll., 1953; MS in Edn, U. Kans., 1959, PhD, 1964. Co-dir. social studies project Pitts. pub. schs., 1963-64; asst. dir. fgn. relations project North Central Assn. Schs. and Colls., Chgo., 1964-65; mem. faculty Ind. U., Bloomington, 1965-97, prof. history and edn., 1974-97, dean Sch. Edn., 1981-90, dir. Ctr. for Excellence in Edn., 1990-99. Social studies adviser Houghton Mifflin Pub. Co.; cons. U.S. Office Edn. Co-author: American Political Behavior, 2d edit., 1977, Count Witte and the Tsarist Government in the 1905 Revolution, 1972, Toward Effective Instruction in the Social Studies, 1974, School Reform in the Information Age, 1995, Technology and Teacher Education: A Guide for Educators and Policymakers, 2002; editl. bd. Education and Society, history tchr.; editor: UNESCO Handbook on the Teaching of Social Studies, 1981; co-editor: Yearbook on the Social Studies, 1981. STAG grantee Dept. State, 1975 Mem. NEA, Nat. Council Social Studies, Am. Edn. Research Assn., Am. Hist. Assn., Am. Assn. for Advancement Slavic Studies, Phi Beta Kappa, Phi Alpha Theta, Pi Sigma Alpha, Phi Delta Kappa. Home: 3271 N Ramble Rd E Bloomington IN 47408-1094

MEHLIS, DAVID LEE, publishing executive; m. Marjie Bauman; children: Michelle, Stephen. BA in History, Wheaton Coll., 1965; postgrad., Trinity Evang. Sem., 1965-67. Various positions in mktg., then v.p. and gen. mgr. David C. Cook Pub. Co., Elgin, Ill., 1967—; now pres., CEO Cook Comm. Ministries., Colorado Springs, Colo. Bd. dirs. Scripture Press Ministries, Kids Around the World, Kingsway Publ. Ltd.; trustee Judson Coll., Elgin, 1991. Mem. Christian Booksellers Assn., Evang. Christian Pub. Assn. (bd. dirs.). Office: Cook Comm Ministries 4050 Lee Vance Vw Colorado Springs CO 80918-7102

MEHLMAN, BRUCE P. federal agency administrator; Grad., Princeton U., U. Va. Gen. counsel Nat. Rep. Congl. Com., 1996—99; gen. counsel, policy dir. House Rep. Conf.; telecom. policy counsel Cisco Sys., 1999—2001; asst. sec. for tech. policy Dept. Commerce, Washington, 2001—. Republican. Office: Dept Commerce Tech Policy 14th & Constitution Ave NW Washington DC 20230

MEHLMAN, DAVID JOEL, cardiologist, educator; b. Chgo., 1948; AB, Princeton U., 1969; MD, Johns Hopkins U., 1973. Diplomate Am. Bd. Internal Medicine, Am. Bd. Cariology, Nat. Bd. Echocardiography with subspecialty in adult comprehensive echocardiography. Intern Johns Hopkins Hosp., Balt., 1973-74, resident in medicine, 1974-76; fellow cardiology U. Chgo. Hosps., 1976-78; asst. prof. medicine U. Chgo. Med. Sch., 1978-80, Northwestern U. Med. Sch., Chgo., 1980-86, assoc. prof. medicine, 1986—; dir. adult cardiovasc. disease tng. program McGaw Med. Ctr. Northwestern U., Chgo., 1988-95, assoc. dir., 1995—. Assoc. dir. echocardiography lab. Northwestern Meml. Hosp., Chgo., 1980-95, co-dir. echocardiography lab., 1995— Fellow Am. Coll. Cardiology, ACP, AHA, Am. Soc. Echocardiography. Office: Northwestern U Med Sch Galter 8-203A 251 E Huron Chicago IL 60611-2914

MEHLMAN, EDWIN STEPHEN, endodontist; b. Hartford, Conn., Nov. 30, 1935; s. Sol Abraham and Rose (Slitt) M.; m. Lesley Judith Lunin, June 13, 1959; children: Jeffrey Cole, Brian Scott, Erik Van. BA, Wesleyan U., 1957; DDS, U. Pa., 1961; cert. endodontics, Boston U., 1965. Diplomate Am. Bd. Endodontists. Instr. oral medicine Sch. Dental Medicine Harvard U., Boston, 1965-67; clin. instr. endodontics Sch. Dental Medicine Tufts U., Boston, 1968-70, lectr. endodontics Sch. Dental Medicine, Harvard U., Boston, 1970-72, asst. clin. prof. endodontics, 1972—; staff assoc. Forsyth Dental Ctr., Boston, 1965—; asst. prof. endodontics Boston U. Sch. Dental Medicine, 1995—; pvt. practice Providence, 1965—. Vis. lectr. dental hygiene U. R.I., Kingston, 1965-71, Community Coll. R.I., Lincoln, 1990—; cons. com. on accreditation of Dentists and Dental Aux. Edn. Programs, 1974-78. Contbr. articles to profl. jours. Pres. Temple Habonim, Barrington, R.I., 1968-70, Bur. Jewish Edn. of R.I., 1980-84; area v.p. Jewish Fedn. R.I., 1975-78; mem. R.I. Legis. Commn. to Study Malpractice Crisis, 1985-86; chmn. R.I. Dental Polit. Action Com., 1987-90. Capt. USAF, 1961-63. Recipient Etherington award Six N.E. Dental Assns. for Outstanding Contbns. to Dentistry. Fellow Am. Coll. Dentists (Vol. of Yr. 2004), Internat. Coll. Dentists (dep. regent 1994-98), Pierre Fauchard Acad. (Merit award); mem. ADA (coun. on govt. affairs and fed. dental svcs. 1988-92, vice-chmn. 1991-92, 1st v.p. 1994-95, 1st dist. trustee 1999-2003), Am. Assn. Endodontists (dir. 1988-91), R.I. Dental Assn. (pres. 1986-87), N.E. Dental Assns. (Outstanding N.E. Dentist 1995, Disting. Practitioner 2000). Jewish. Avocations: reading, civic activities. Home: 3 Hanley Farm Rd Warren RI 02885-4376 Office: 130 Waterman St Providence RI 02906-2010 also: 1090 New London Ave Cranston RI 02920-3035

MEHLMAN, LON DOUGLAS, information technology specialist, investment banker, venture capitalist; b. Los Angeles, Apr. 29, 1959; s. Anton and Diane Mehlman. BA, UCLA, 1981; MBA, Pepperdine U., 1983. Cert. project mgmt. profl. Project Mgmt. Inst., 2002. Software developer Ticom Systems Inc., Century City, Calif., 1979—81; systems analyst NCR Corp., Century City, 1981—82; sr. systems analyst Tandem Computers Inc., L.A., 1982—91; sr. computer scientist Computer Scis. Corp., El Segundo, Calif., 1991-97; CIO, dir. info. tech. Globe Cast Corp., Culver City, Calif., 1997-2000; chief tech. officer, v.p. engring. MediaConnex, Inc., Hollywood, Calif., 2000-01; v.p., program mgr. info. tech. Micro Gen. Corp., Santa Ana, Calif., 2001—03; mng. dir. ITF Global Ptnrs., LLC, N.Y.C., 2003—. Author: Establishing an Enterprise Information Systems Infrastructure, 1995, Implementing TQM, 1995, Lessons Learned from the Navstar GPS Engineering Management System Project, 1997. Mem. Am. Mgmt. Assn., Project Mgmt. Inst., Armed Forces Comms. and Electronics Assn., LA Venture Assn., Assn. for Corp. Growth, Sierra Club, Phi Delta Theta. Avocations: golf, tennis, sailing, skiing, world travel. Office: ITF Global Ptnrs 291 7th Ave Penhouse New York NY 10001 E-mail: lonmx@worldnet.att.net.

MEHLMAN, MARK FRANKLIN, lawyer; b. L.A., Dec. 18, 1947; s. Jack and Elaine Pearl (Lopater) M.; m. Barbara Ann Novak, Aug. 20, 1972; children: David, Jennifer, Ilyse. BA, U. Ill., 1969; LLB, U. Mich., 1973. Bar: Ill. 1973; U.S. Dist. Ct. (no. dist.) Ill. 1973. Assoc. Sonnenschein, Nath & Rosenthal LLP, Chgo., 1973-80, mem. policy and planning com., 1989—. Trustee Groveland Health Svcs., Highland Park (Ill.) Hosp., 1991-97; trustee, treas., exec. com. Spertus Inst. Jewish Studies, Chgo., 1992-97, vice chmn. bd. trustees, 1996—; vice-chmn. regional bd. Anti-Defamation League, 1987-89, hon. life mem. nat. commn., 1993—. Fellow Am. Bar Found.; mem. ABA (chmn. mortgages and other debt financing subcom. 1991-95, supervisory coun. 1997—, sec. RPPT sect., 2004-), Am. Coll. Real Estate Lawyers (exec. com. bd. govs. 2000—, sec. 2003-, chmn. MDP com. 2000—, chmn. mem. selection com. 2000-01), Anglo-Am. Real Property Inst., Legal Club of Chgo., Lake Shore Country Club, Standard Club, Exec. Club of Chgo. Office: Sonnenschein Nath & Rosenthal LLP 233 S Wacker Dr Ste 8000 Chicago IL 60606-6491

MEHLMAN, MAXWELL JONATHAN, law educator; b. Washington, Nov. 4, 1948; s. Jacob and Betty (Hoffman) M.; m. Cheryl A. Stone, Sept. 15, 1979; children: Aurora, Gabriel. BA, Reed Coll., 1970, Oxford U., England, 1972; JD, Yale U., 1975. Bar: D.C. 1976, Ohio 1988. Assoc. Arnold & Porter, Washington, 1975-84; asst. prof. Case Western Res. U., Cleve., 1984-87, assoc. prof., 1987-90, prof. law, 1990-96, Arthur E. Petersilge prof., 1996—, prof. biomed. ethics, 1998—. Spl. counsel N.Y. State Bar, N.Y.C., 1988-94, Nat. Kidney Found., 1991; cons. Am. Assn. Ret. Persons, Washington, 1992. Editor: High Tech Home Care, 1991, (with T. Murray) Encyclopedia of Ethical, Legal and Policy Issues in Biotechnology; author: (with J. Botkin) Access to the Genome: The Challenge to Equality, 1998, (with Andrews and Rothstein) Genetics: Ethics, Law and Policy, 2002, Wondergenes: Genetic Enhancement and the Future of Society, 2003; contbr. articles to profl. jours. Active steering com. AIDS Commn. Greater Cleve., 1986-90. Rhodes scholar, 1970; Rsch. grantee NIH, 1992-94, 97—. Mem. Am. Assn. Law Schs. (chmn. sect. on law, medicine and health care 1990), Phi Beta Kappa. Avocations: skiing, choral music, sea kayaking. Office: Case Western Reserve U Sch Law-Law Medicine Ctr Gund Hall 11075 E Blvd Cleveland OH 44106

MEHNE, PAUL RANDOLPH, associate dean, medical educator; b. Wilmington, Deleware, May 27, 1948; s. Paul Herbert and Doris Ruth (Longfritz) M.; m. Carol Ann (Starner), June 12, 1971; children: Meredith Lynn, and Amy Elizabeth. BS in Environ. sci., SUNY, Syracuse, 1970; PhD, SUNY, 1976, Syracuse Univ., 1976. Asst. prof. East Carolina U. Allied Health, Greenville, NC, 1975-76; assoc. dir. East Carolina U. Ctr. Edn., Devel., and Evaluation, Greenville, NC, 1976-79; coord. of curriculum East Carolina U., Greenville, NC, 1979-81, asst. dean, 1981-85, assoc. dean, 1985-89, assoc. prof., 1988-89, dir. Ctr. Health Sci., Edn., and Info., 1988-89; assoc. dean U. Pa., Phila., 1989—91; assoc. dean acad. and student affairs, assoc. prof. environ. and occupl. medicine, family medicine Robert Wood Johnson Med. Sch., Piscataway, NJ, 1992—; chair U. wide tele medicine video com distance learning com. Univ. Medicine and Dentistry N.J., 1995-2000, chmn. acad. info. tech. adv. com., 1996-98. Chmn. exec. bd. dir. MEDCOMP Super computer Consortium, Athens, Ga., 1986—89; vis. prof. U. N.C., Chapel Hill, 1986, Tulane U., New Orleans, 1988. Contbr. articles to profl. jour. Chmn. Cmty. Appearance Commn., Greenville, NC, 1980—85; ex officio trustee Cooper Hosp. Univ. Med. Ctr., 2001—. Recipient Interactive Video Instrn. Award Digital Equipment Corp., 1985; Med. Edn. Cost Containment Award Kate B. Reynolds Health Care Trust, 1985-88; Telemedicine and Med. Informatics Award, 1996-99; U.S. Dept. Commerce NTIA/TIIAP Award for tele-medicine, 1996-98. Mem. IEEE, APHA, AAHE, NASPA, Am. Med. Informatics Assn., Am. Edn. Rsch. Assn., Assn. Am. Med. Coll. (chair consortium on student and profl. well being 1993-94, steering com. Clin. Campus Deans 2000—, chair-elect AAMC Group on Regional Med. Campuses, 2004—), Soc. of Teachers of Family Medicine, Am. Med. Informatics Assn. Office Phone: 856-757-7905. E-mail: mehne@umdnj.edu., mehne@mindspring.com.

MEHR, DAVID RALPH, geriatrician, researcher; b. San Jose, Calif., Dec. 31, 1949; s. Edwin Bernard and Helen Margulies Mehr; m. Ann Elizabeth Mehr. BA, U. of Calif., Santa Cruz, 1972; MD, U. of Calif., San Francisco, 1976; MS, U. of Mich., 1989. Lic. Mo., 1977, Mich., 1988, diplomate Am. Bd. of Family Practice, Am. Bd. Geriat. Medicine. Pvt. practice, Columbia, Mo., 1979—88; instr. family practice U. of Mich. Sch. of Medicine, Ann Arbor, 1990—92; asst. prof. family and cmty. medicine U. of Mo., Columbia Sch. of Medicine, 1992—98, assoc. prof. family and cmty. medicine, 1998—. Mem. snem-4 rev. group Ctr. for Sci. Rev., NIH, 2000—02. Recipient Physician of Yr., Boone County Med. Soc., 1988; grantee Generalist Physician Faculty Scholars award, Robert Wood Johnson Found., 1995—99, Rsch. Grant, Nat. Inst. of Aging, 2000—03;, Agy. for Healthcare Rsch. and Quality, 1996—2000. Home: 8101 E New Haven Rd Columbia MO 65201 Office: U of Mo Columbia 1 Hospital Dr Columbia MO 65212 Office Phone: 573-882-1584. Business E-Mail: mehrd@health.missouri.edu.

MEHRA, JAGDISH, economics professor; b. Amritsar, Punjab, India, Nov. 12, 1934; came to U.S., 1962; s. Manmohan and Savitri (Devi) M.; m. Sneh L. Mehra, May 19, 1949; children: Reena, Benu. BA, Birla Inst. Tech., Pilani, Rajasthan, 1955, MA, 1957; PhD, SUNY, Buffalo, 1970. Asst. prof. econs. Banasthali U., Rajasthan, 1959-60; rschr. Nat. Coun. Applied Econ. Rsch., New Delhi, 1960-61; asst. prof. Econs. Birla Inst. Tech., Pilani, 1961-62; grad. asst., econs. instr. SUNY, Buffalo, 1962-65; asst. prof. econs. Youngstown (Ohio) U., 1965-71, assoc. prof. econs., 1971-81, prof. econs., 1981—2003, prof. emeritus, 2003—; sr. rsch. fellow Am. Inst. Econ. Rsch., Great Barrington, Mass., 1982-83. Contbr. articles to profl. jours. Avocations: reading, tennis. Home: 4892 Westchester Dr Apt 2 Youngstown OH 44515-6515 Office: Youngstown State U Dept Econs Youngstown OH 44555 Office Phone: 330-941-1681. E-mail: JCmehra@cc.ysu.edu.

MEHRA, RAMAN KUMAR, aerospace and defense technology executive, automation and control engineering researcher; b. Lahore, Punjab, India, Feb. 10, 1943; came to U.S., 1964; s. Madan Mohan and Vidya Vati (Khanna) M.; m. Anjoo Talwar; children: Archana, Mandira, Kunal. BEE, Punjab Engring. Coll., 1964; MS in Engring., Harvard U., 1965, PhD, 1968. Assoc. prof. Harvard U., Cambridge, Mass., 1972-76; pres., chief exec. officer Sci. Systems, Co., Inc., Woburn, Mass., 1976—. Author: System Identification, 1976, also tech. papers on model algorithmic control (Best Paper award Internat. Fedn. Automatic Control, 1983). Recipient Eckman award Am. Automatic Control Coun., St. Louis, 1971. Fellow IEEE. Avocations: hiking, golf, tennis. Home: 5 Angier Rd Lexington MA 02420-1608 Office: Sci Systems Co Inc 500 W Cummings Park Woburn MA 01801-6503 Office Phone: 781-933-5355. E-mail: rkm@ssci.com.

MEHRBERG, RANDALL ERIC, lawyer; b. Bklyn., Dec. 29, 1955; s. Julius and June (Shapiro) M.; m. Michele Schara, Oct. 20, 1984. BS in Econs., U. Pa., 1977; JD, U. Mich., 1980. Bar: Ill. 1980, U.S. Dist. Ct. (no. dist.) Ill. 1980, U.S. Ct. Appeals (7th cir.) 1981, U.S. Supreme Ct. 1987. Ptnr. Jenner & Block, Chgo., 1980—2000; sr. v.p., gen. counsel Exelon Corp., 2000—. Asst. sec. Chgo. Pacific Corp., 1984-85; dir. Giordano Dance Co., Chgo., 1987—. Recipient Hope for the People award, HOPE Fair Housing, Ill., 1982; commendation for work for the poor, Cath. Charities, 1986, award for def. of civil liberties, ACLU, 1987. Mem. ABA, Chgo. Bar Assn. (exec. coun. young lawyers sect., David C. Hilliard award), Chgo. Counsel Lawyers. Avocations: tennis, ice hockey, skiing, children. Office: Exelon Corp 37th Floor, 10 S Dearborn St PO Box A-3005 Chicago IL 60690-3005

MEHRING, TERESA ANN, dean, education educator; b. Helena, Mont., Apr. 30, 1952; d. Donald V. and Patricia M. BS, BME, BM, St. Mary Coll., 1974; MS, Southwest Mo. State U., 1975; MSEd, U. Kans., 1979, PhD, 1981. Psychologist Mont. Spl. Edn. Regional Svcs., Glendive, 1975-78; core rschr. U. Kans, Inst. Learning Disabilites, Lawrence, 1978-81; dean, faculty mem. Emporia State U., Kans., 1981—, interim pres., 2002—. Bd. dirs. Nat. Tchr. Hall of Fame, Emporia, 1995—, interim pres., 2001—; cons. Nat. Coun. Accreditation Tchr. Edn., 1995—, United Arab Emirates U., 2001; adv. bd. Olathe Dist. Schs., Kans, 1995—. Author: (novels) Crisis Intervention for General and Special Education, 1997, Project AIM: Assessment Activities and Rubrics for Mathematics, 1993; contbr. articles to profl. jours. Mem. Guardian Angels Ch., Kansas City, 1978—. Named Adminstr. of Yr. Assn. Health Phys. Edn., Recreation and Dance Profls., 2000-2001, Kans. Educator of Yr. U. Kans. Alumni Assn., 1995, Dist. Profl. of Yr. Internat. Coun. Learning Disabilities, 1994. Mem.: Emporia C. of C., Renaissance Group (bd. dirs. 1997—2001, exec. com.), Tchr. Edn. Coun. StateColl. and Univs. (exec. com., pres. 2001—03), Am. Assn. Coll. Tchr. Edn. (nat. bd. dirs. 1998—2001). Roman Catholic. Avocations: reading, hiking, travel, music performance. Office: The Tchrs Coll Emporia State Univ 1200 Commercial Emporia KS 66801-5087 Office Phone: 620-341-5367. E-mail: mehringt@emporia.edu.

MEHRINGER, CHARLES MARK, medical educator; b. Dickinson, N.D., Nov. 21, 1945; m. Ruth Herrman; 1 child, Sydney. BS in Biology, Lamar U., 1966; MD, U. Tex., 1970. Diplomate Am. Bd. Radiology, Am. Bd. Neuroradiology. Intern UCLA Hosp., 1970-71; resident in diagnostic radiology Harbor-UCLA Med. Ctr., Torrance, Calif., 1971-74, fellow in neuroradiology, 1976-77; asst. prof. dept. radiology UCLA Sch. Medicine, 1977-80, dir. spl. procedures, 1980-94, assoc. prof. dept. radiology, 1986-96, prof. dept. radiology, 1996—, acting chmn. radiology, 1996—. Vice-chmn. dept. radiological scis. UCLA Sch. Medicine, Torrance, 1992—, acting chmn. dept. radiology, 1992—, chief diagnostic radiology, 1983-92; chief radiological svcs., cons. U.S. Air Force for Japan and Korea, 1974-76; cons. U. Calif./Irvine (Calif.) Med. Ctr., 1988—, St. Marys Med. Ctr., Long Beach, Calif., 1986—, Long Beach VA Hosp., 1979—, L.A. County Dept. Chief Med. Examiner-Coroner, 1977—; bd. dirs. Rsch. and Ednl. Inst.; presenter in field. Co-author: (with others) Neurological Surgery of the Ear and Skull Base, 1982, Vascular Surgery, 1984, 2d edit., 1994, Youman's Neurological Surgery, 1990, Common Problems in Infertility and Impotence, 1990, Intraluminal Imaging of Vascular and Tubular Organs: Diagnostic and Therapeutic Applications, 1993, Neuroradiology, A Study Guide, 1995; contbr. articles to profl. jours. Bd. dirs., exec. com. Med. Found. Harbor-UCLA Med. Ctr., 1992—. Recipient numerous grants for rsch., 1977—. Mem. Am. Coll. Radiology, Am. Soc. Neuroradiology (sr. mem.), Western Neuroradiologic Soc., L.A. Radiologic Soc. Office: Harbor UCLA Med Ctr Box 27 1000 W Carson St Torrance CA 90502-2004

MEHRMANN, CRAIGANN, nurse practitioner; b. Hershey, Pa., Jan. 6, 1953; d. Charles Craig and Martha Alene (Shepler) M. BS, Bloomsburg State Coll., 1974; AA in Nursing, Harrisburg Area C.C., 1979; BSN, Pa. State U., 1985; MSN in Nursing, U. Pa., 1986. RN, Pa.; cert. legal nurse cons. Substitute tchr. Derry Twp., Ctrl. Dauphin, and Middletown Area Sch. Dists., 1974-77; nursing asst. Milton Hershey Med. Ctr., 1978; staff nurse Holy Spirit Hosp., Camp Hill, Pa., 1979, Milton Hershey Med. Ctr., 1979-80; clin. coord. Hillcrest Women's Med. Ctr., Harrisburg, Pa., 1980-85; nurse practitioner Tri County Planned Parenthood, 1986-89, Orndorf, Raschid and Assocs., 1989-2001, Women's Health Profls. Chambersburg, 2001—; cert. legal nurse cons., 2003—. Nurse lectr. Pa. State U., 1986, Messiah Coll., 1987-89, U. Pa., 1990—. Vol. Am. Cancer Soc., ARC. Mem. AAUW, Assn. Women's Health, Obstetric and Neonatal Nurses, Am. Acad. Nurse Practitioners, Natl. Assn. Nurse Practitioners Women's Health, Harrisburg Area C.C. Alumni Assn., U. Pa. Sch. Nursing Alumni Assn., Bloomsburg State Coll. Alumni Assn., Messiah Coll. Nursing Honor Soc., Sigma Theta Tau. Methodist. Office: 757 Norland Ave Ste 210 Chambersburg PA 17201 Office Phone: 717-217-6990.

MEHROTRA, CHANDRA, psychology professor, dean; b. Laharpur, U.P., India, June 15, 1933; arrived in US, 1965; s. Kashi N. and Munni D. Mehrotra; m. Indra Rani Mehrotra, Dec. 9, 1963; children: Vijay, Gita. PhD, Ohio State U., 1968. Lic. psychologist Minn. Assoc. rsch. psychologist Ednl. Testing Svc., Evanston, Ill., 1968—70; prof. of psychology Coll. of St. Scholastica, Duluth, Minn., 1970—, dean of grad. studies, 1990—99, dean of spl. projects, 1999—. Evaluation cons. Bush Found., St. Paul, 1996—; consulting editor Tchg. of Psychology Jour., 1999—2002; editl. bd. mem. Ednl. Gerontology Jour., 1997—. Editor: (book) Teaching and Aging., 1984; co-author: Aging and Diversity, 1998, Distance Learning, 2001, Measuring Up: Assessment

Challenges & Practices for Psychology, 2004. Recipient Pub. Svc. aAward, Minn. chpt. Am. Coll. of Health Care Adminstrs., 1989. Fellow: APA (Mentor award 2003), Gerontol. Soc. of Am. Avocations: skiing, poetry, mentoring. Office: Coll of St Scholastica 1200 Kenwood Ave Duluth MN 55811 Office Phone: 218-723-6161. Personal E-mail: cmehrotr@css.edu. E-mail: cmehrotr@css.edu.

MEHROTRA, RAJNISH, nephrologist, researcher, medical educator; arrived in U.S., 1993; s. Trijugi Nath and Kamini Mehrotra; m. Kushi Tandon, Oct. 22, 1993; children: Kunaal, Ria. MB, BChir, All India Inst. Med. Scis., New Delhi, 1984—89. Diplomate Internal Medicine Am. Bd. Internal Medicine, 1998, Nephrology Am. Bd. Internal Medicine, 1999, cert. MD All India Inst. Med. Scis., 1992. Clin. instr. MCP Hanheman Sch. Medicine, Phila., 1998—99; asst. prof. medicine David Geffen Sch. Medicine, UCLA, 1999—, Harbor-UCLA Med. Ctr., Torrance, 1999—, dir., peritoneal dialysis, 1999—. Dep. editor Hemodialysis Internat., Los Angeles, 2004—. Recipient Alpha Omega Alpha, Honor Med. Soc., 1999. Fellow: ACP; mem.: Internat. Soc. Peritoneal Dialysis, Internat. Soc. Hemodialysis, Nat. Kidney Found., Am. Soc. Nephrology. Achievements include research in Defining the determinants of vascular calcification among non-dialyzed patients with diabetic nephropathy; Defined the role of patient and physician education in the utilization of peritoneal dialysis; Defining the goal arterial pH among patients undergoing peritoneal dialysis. Office: Harbor-UCLA Med Ctr 1124 W Carson St Torrance CA 90502 Office Phone: 310-222-3891. Business E-Mail: rmehrotra@rei.edu.

MEHROTRA, SUDHIR C. engineering company executive; b. 1945; BS, India Inst. Tech., Kanpur, India, 1968; PhD (hon.), U. Kan., 1979. Instr., prof. U. Kan., 1968-79; pres., treas. Vigyan, Inc., Hampton, Va., 1979—. Office: Vigyan Inc 30 Research Dr Hampton VA 23666-1325

MEHTA, A. SONNY, publishing company executive; b. India, 1943; Student, Cambridge U. Worked in paperback pub., England; formerly with Pan and Picador Pubs., England; pub., pres. Alfred A. Knopf divsn. of Random House, N.Y.C., 1987—, now pres., editor-in-chief; pres., editor-in-chief Knopf Pub. Group, N.Y.C. Office: Knopt Pub 1745 Broadway #B1 New York NY 10019-4305

MEHTA, ASHOK VALLAVDAS, pediatric cardiologist; b. Bakor, India, Jan. 16, 1951; arrived in U.S., 1975; s. Vallavdas H. and Sushila V. (Doshi) M.; m. Pragna Sheth, Apr. 2, 1978; 1 child. B of Surgery, B of Medicine, Baroda (India) Med. Coll., 1974. Diplomate Am. Bd. Pediatrics, Am. Bd. Pediatric Cardiology. Intern dept. of pediatrics Baroda Med. Coll., 1975; resident dept. of pediatrics Misericordia-Lincoln-Fordham Hosp., Bronx, N.Y., 1976-78; postdoctoral fellowship divsn. of pediatric cardiology U. Miami Sch. Medicine, 1978-80, spl. rsch. fellowship in cardiac electrophysiology, 1980-81; asst. prof. pediatrics Temple U. Sch. of Medicine, Phila., 1981-86, St. Christopher's Hosp. for Children, Phila., 1981-86; chief divsn. of pediatric cardiology James H. Quillen COM, East Tenn. State U., Johnson City, 1986-97, assoc. prof. pediatrics, 1986-93, prof. pediatrics, 1993; pvt. practice, 1997—. Vis. prof. divsn. pediatric cardiology U. W.Va. Sch. Medicine, 1985; lectr. in field; dir. pediatric preceptor program, family practice resident, Kingsport, 1986-90; dir. pediatric CME program Holston Valley Hosp. Med. Ctr., Kingsport, 1987-91; dir. Tri-Cities Children's heart Ctr., Kingsport, 1986—; cons. pediatric cardiology Holston Valley Hosp. and Med. Ctr., Johnson City Hosp. and Med. Ctr., Bristol (Tenn.) Meml. Hosp., Indian Path Hosp., Kingsport, Crippled Children's Svc. State of Tenn., Sycamore Shoals Hosp., Elizabethton, Tenn.; dir. pediatric cardiac electro-physiology and pacing fellowship, assoc. pediatric cardiologist St. Christopher's Hosp. Children, Phila., 1981-86; cons. pediatric cardiology Med. Coll. Pa., Phila., 1981-86. Referee reviewer Pediatric Cardiology, Am. Jour. of Diseases of Children; contbr. numerous articles to profl. jours. Fellow Am. Coll. Cardiology, Am. Acad. Pediatrics; mem. AMA (Physician's recognition award 1979—), Am. Heart Assn. (Southeastern Pa. chpt. 1981-86, coun. cardiovascular disease in the young 1992—, bd. dirs. Greater Kingsport chpt. 1990-92, Washington County chpt. 1992—, Young Investigator award Pa. chpt. 1982-84), Cardiac Electrophysiology Soc., Pediatric Cardiac Electrophysiology Soc., S.E. Pediatric Cardiology Soc., Tenn. Pediatric Cardiology Assn., Tenn. Pediatric Soc. (Tenn. chpt. AAP). Republican. Hindu. Avocations: stamp and coin collecting, travel, tennis. Home: 1903 Round Tree Dr Johnson City TN 37604-4104 Office: Tri-City Pediat Cardiology 4540 W Stone Dr Ste E Kingsport TN 37660-8494

MEHTA, EILEEN ROSE, lawyer; b. Colver, Pa., Apr. 1, 1953; d. Richard Glenn and Helen (Wahna) Ball; m. Abdul Rashid Mehta, Aug. 31, 1973. Student, Miami U., 1971-73; BA with distinction, Fla. Internat. U., 1974; JD cum laude, U. Miami, 1977. Bar: Fla. 1977, U.S. Dist. Ct. (so. dist.) Fla. 1977, U.S. Ct. Appeals (11th cir.) 1981. Law clk. to presiding judge U.S. Dist. Ct. (so. dist.) Fla., Miami, 1977-79; asst. atty. County of Dade, Miami, 1979-89; shareholder Fine Jacobson Schwartz Nash Block & England, Miami, Fla., 1989-94; ptnr. Eckert Seamans Cherin & Mellott, Miami, 1994-98, Bilzin Sumberg Baena Price & Axelrod, Miami, 1998—. Lectr. in field; v.p., bd. dirs. Mehtatron Enterprises, Inc., Miami, Shalimar Homes Inc., Anderson, S.C. Miami U. scholar, 1971-73. Mem. Fla. Bar Assn., Dade County Bar Assn. Office: Bilzin Sumberg Baena Price & Axelrod 2500 Wachovia Fin Ctr Miami FL 33131 Office Phone: 305-350-2380. E-mail: emehta@bilzin.com.

MEHTA, JAWAHAR LAL, cardiologist; b. India, Aug. 10, 1946; s. Mohan L. and Ishwar D. (Valecha) M.; m. Paulette Smedresman, Oct. 20, 1977; children: Asha, Jason. MD, GN Med. Coll. U. Amritsar, 1968; PhD, U. Uppsala (Sweden). Diplomate Am. Bd. Internal Medicine, Am. Bd. Cardiovascular Diseases. Intern N.Y. Med. Coll., Valhalla, NY, 1970, resident in pediat., 1971; resident in internal medicine Mt. Sinai-Beth Israel Hosp., N.Y.C., 1971-73; fellow in cardiology SUNY, NY, 1973-75; from asst. prof. to prof. medicine & physiology U. Fla. Coll. Medicine, Gainesville, 1976-2000; dir. cardiovasc. medicine, Stebbins chair in cardiology U. Ark. for Med. Sci., Little Rock, 2000—. Rsch. fellow, instr. in medicine U. Minn., Mpls., 1975—76; staff physician VA Med. Ctr., Gainesville, 1976—2000, clin. investigator, 1980—85; dir. cardiology svcs. Ctrl. Ark. Vets. Healthcare Sys., 2000—. Fellow: ACP, Am. Heart Assn., Am. Coll. Cardiology; mem.: Assn. Univ. Cardiologists, Assn. Am. Physicians, Am. Soc. Clin. Investigation. Office: U Ark for Med Scis Slot 532 Little Rock AR 72205-7199 Office Phone: 501-296-1401. Business E-Mail: mehtajl@uams.edu.

MEHTA, JAY, financial executive; b. Varanasi, India, Aug. 16, 1943; came to U.S., 1970; m. Vineeta Mehta, Feb. 20, 1969; children: Nina, Vineet. MBA in Fin., Rutgers U., 1974; MBA in Taxation, Fairleigh Dickenson U., 1983. CPA, N.J.; cert. mgmt. acct. Contract estimator NE region Otis Elevator Co. Subs. United Techs. Inc., Montvale, N.J., 1970-73, sr. contract estimator NE region, 1974-75, corp. staff acct. N.Y.C., 1976-77, sr. corp. acct., 1978; div. contr. OKI Electric Overseas Corp., Hackensack, N.J., 1979-84; corp. contr. OKI Am. Inc., Hackensack, 1984—, sr. dir. fin., treas., 1990, v.p. fin., treas., 1994-99; personal fin. advisor Am. Express, Hackensack, 2000—. Trustee OKI Am. Savs. Plan, 1981-99; ofcl. grader Inst. Mgmt. Acctg., Montvale, N.J., 1986—. Mem. AICPA, Am. Mgmt. Assn., N.J. Soc. CPAs. Republican. Avocations: reading, golf, computers. Office: OKI Am Inc Mack-Cali Ctr IV 3 University Plz Ste 612 Hackensack NJ 07601-6232 also: Am Express Mack Cali Ctr IV Paramus Rd Paramus NJ 07052

MEHTA, KAMAL DEEP, biochemistry educator, molecular biology educator; b. Delhi, India, May 1, 1956; s. Gur and Kamlesh Mehta; m. Madhu Mehta, Sept. 16, 1986; children: Sonya, Devina, Neil. MS, U. Delhi, 1978, MPhil, 1980; PhD, McMaster U., 1985. Med. rschr. U. B.C., Vancouver, 1985-87; instr. U. Tex. Southwest Med. Ctr., Dallas, 1987-92; assoc. prof. U. Ark. Coll. Medicine, Little Rock, 1992—2001; prof. Ohio State U. Coll. Medicine, 2001—. Athor: Purine and Pyrimidine Metabolism, 1986; inventor hypercholesterolemia treatment program, 2000. Mem. AAAS, Am. Assn. Biochemistry and Molecular Biology. Avocations: reading, voluntarism, cricket. Office: Ohio State U Coll Medicine 1645 Neil Ave Columbus OH 43210 Business E-Mail: mehta.80@osu.edu.

MEHTA, NARINDER KUMAR, marketing executive; b. Lahore, Punjab, India, Feb. 18, 1938; came to U.S., 1959; s. Puran Chand and Raj Rani Mehta; m. Narayanaswamy Sampath; children: Kiren, Ravi. B of Commerce, U. Delhi, India, 1958; MA, U. Minn., 1961. Program dir. All India Mgmt. Assn., New Delhi, 1963—67; with Am. Express Co., Chgo., 1968—82, dir. nat. sales N.Y.C., 1975—80, v.p. sales, 1980—82; sr. v.p. Shearson Lehman/Am. Express, Boston, 1982—85; sr. v.p. mktg. & sales Capital Credit Corp., Fairfield, NJ, 1985—94; sr. v.p. internat. mktg. Outsourcing Solutions, Inc., 1994—97; pres. Mehta Cons. Group, Dover, Mass., 1997—. Sr. v.p. Temporary Investment Funds, 1982-85, Trust for Short Term Fed. Securities, 1982-85, Mcpl. Fund for Calif. Investors, 1983-85; conducted seminars for profl. assns., colls. and univs. Contbr. articles to profl. jours. Nat. v.p. Muscular Dystrophy Assn., N.Y.C., 1984-86; student body pres. U. Delhi, India, 1958-59. Recipient 1st prize inter-coll. debate, 1958. Mem. Am. Mgmt. Assn., Tau Kappa Epsilon. Avocations: running, swimming, travel, reading. Office: Mehta Cons Group PO Box 547 4 Bryant Ln Dover MA 02030-0547 Personal E-mail: nkmehta@aol.com.

MEHTA, RAJEEV, neonatologist, researcher; arrived in U.S., 1989; s. Krishan Chand and Vimla Mehta; divorced; children: Meghan, Serena. MD, U. Coll. Med. Sci., New Delhi, India, 1979; diploma in tropical medicine and hygiene, U. Liverpool, 1984. Diplomate Am. Bd. Pediatrics, Am. Bd. Neonatal-Perinatal Medicine. Attending neonatologist Maimonides Med. Ctr., Bklyn., 1993—97, assoc. dir. neonatology, 1997—99; dir. neonatology Flushing Hosp. Med. Ctr., Queens, NY, 1999—2000; attending neonatologist St. Peter's U. Hosp., New Brunswick, NJ, 2000—; assoc. dir. neonatology Bristol-Myers Squibb Children's Hosp., Robert Johnson U. Hosp., New Brunswick, 2003—. Co-dir. applied rsch. Bristol-Myers Squibb Children's Hosp., Robert Wood Johnson U. Hosp., New Brunswick, NJ, 2003—. Contbr. articles to profl. jours. Fellow: Am. Acad. Pediat., Royal Coll. Physicians Glasgow, Royal Coll. Physicians Ireland; mem.: Royal Coll. Physicians U.K., Royal Coll. Physicians Eng., Royal Coll. Physicians London, Rotary (sgt. at arms Plainsboro, N.J. chpt.). Office: RWJMS-Univ Medicine Dentistry NJ 1 RWJ Pl MEB 348 New Brunswick NJ 08903

MEHTA, RAJENDRA H, cardiologist, researcher; s. Hasmukhrai N and Nila H Mehta. MD, U. of Bombay, 1977—86; MS, U. of Mich., 1999—2001. Clin. assoc. Cleve. Clinic Found., Cleve., 1995—96; clin. asst. prof. U. of Mich., 1996—. Assoc. editor (current jour. review). Co-investigator U. of Mich., 1996. Recipient Travel award, Bristol Myers Squibb, 1998, Proctor Harvey Young Tchr. award, Am. Coll. of Cardiology, 2002. Fellow: Am. Heart Assn. (licentiate), Am. Coll. of Cardiology (life). D-Liberal. Hindu. Achievements include research in clinical outcomes. Avocations: jogging, swimming, travel, music. Office: U of Mich 2215 Fuller Rd 7A 111E Ann Arbor MI 48105 E-mail: rmehta@umich.edu.

MEHTA, SHAILESH J. banker; b. Bombay, Maharashtra, India, Apr. 22, 1949; came to U.S., 1971; s. Jayantilal B. and Manjula J. Mehta; m. Kalpa S. Doshi, Dec. 19, 1973; children: Sameet, Sheetal BS in Mech. Engring., Indian Inst. Tech., 1971; MS in Ops. Research, Case Western Res. U., 1973, PhD in Ops. Research and Computer Sci., 1975. Sr. ops. analyst Cleve. Trust Co., 1973-75, ops. officer, 1975-76, asst. v.p. card ops., 1976-77, v.p. corp. ops. adminstrn., 1979, v.p. advanced systems planning, 1977-78, v.p. info. systems, 1979-82; exec. v.p. banking services AmeriTrust, Cleve., 1974-86; exec. v.p., COO First Deposit Corp., San Francisco, 1986-88, pres., CEO, 1988—; chmn. bd. First Deposit Nat. Bank, Tilton, N.H., 1986—; pres., chief exec. officer, chmn. bd. First Deposit Savs. Bank, Redding, Calif., 1986-90; CEO, chmn. bd. First Deposit Nat. Credit Card Bank, Concord, N.H., 1990-93; exec. v.p. Providian Corp., San Francisco, 1993-94, pres., COO, 1994-97, chmn., CEO, 1998—. Pres., dir. A.T. Venture Capital Group, Cleve., 1982-86. Mem. community adv. coun. U. Calif., Berkeley, 1991—. Mem. Am. Bankers Assn. (telecommunications group 1984—), Ohio Venture Assn., Calif. Commn. for Econ. Devel's. Adv. Coun. on Asia. Office: Providian Corp 201 Mission St San Francisco CA 94105-1831

MEHTA, SIDDARTH N. credit services company executive; b. 1958; BS, London Sch. Econs.; MS, U. Chgo. V.p. Info. Bus. Divsn. Citicorp; sr. v.p. Boston Cons. Group, L.A.; joined Household Internat. Inc., 1996—, group exec. domestic MC/Visa bus., 1998—. Office: Household Internat Inc 1441 Schilling Pl Salinas CA 93901-4543

MEHTA, ZARIN, performing company executive; b. Bombay, Oct. 28, 1938; came to Can., 1962, naturalized, 1969; s. Mehli and Tehmina Mehta; m. Carmen Lasky, July 1, 1966; children: Rohanna, Rustom. Chartered acct., London, 1957. Acct. Frederic B. Smart & Co., London, 1957-62, Coopers & Lybrand, Montreal, Que., Can., 1962-81; mng. dir. Orchestre Symphonique de Montreal, 1981-90; exec. dir., COO Ravinia Festival, 1990-2000; exec. dir. NY Philharm., 2000-. Fellow Inst. Chartered Accts. in Eng. and Wales; mem. Ordre des Comptables Agrees du Que. Office: NY Philharm Avery Fisher Hall 10 Lincoln Center Plaza New York NY 10023-6990 Business E-Mail: mehtaz@nyphil.org.*

MEHURON, WILLIAM OTTO, retired government official, consultant; b. Hammond, Ind., Nov. 20, 1937; s. Arthur and Margaret Irene (Soroka) M.; m. Charlotte Anne Nyheim, Aug. 26, 1982; children: Kimberly Anne, Kristine Lynn, Susan, Geoffrey. BSEE, Purdue U., 1959; MSEE, U. Pa., 1962, PhD, 1966. Tech. dir. naval intelligence Dept. Navy, Washington, 1974-81; dir. rsch. and engring. Nat. Security Agy., Ft. Meade, Md., 1981-85; v.p., gen. mgr. data systems div. Ampex Corp. subs. Allied-Signal Co., Redwood City, Calif., 1985-86; sr. v.p. product ops. Daisy Systems Corp., Mountain View, Calif., 1986-88; v.p., gen. mgr. Networks and Info. Security div. Unisys Def. Systems, McLean, Va., 1988-91; pres. Mehuron Assocs. Inc., 1991-95; dir. sys. acquisition office NOAA, USG, Washington, 1995-99; dir. Info. Tech. Lab., Nat. Inst. Stds. and Tech., Gaithersburg, Md., 1999—2002; pres. Mehuron Assocs., Inc., 2002—. Avocations: amateur radio (w4xm), golf, cooking, antiques. Home: 23650 Via Veneto #304 Bonita Springs FL 34134-2902 Office Phone: 239-948-9427. Personal E-mail: wmehuron@msn.com.

MEI, BETTY MUICHI, director; b. Hong Kong, 1960; arrived in U.S., 1979; d. Wai Chung Chan and Yue Mui Wong; m. Joseph Shing Mei, May 25, 1985; children: Joshua, Isaac. BA, SUNY, Plattsburgh, 1982; MA, W.Va. U., 1984, EdD, 1988. Asst. prof. Salem-Teokyo U., W.Va., 1990—93; acad. dir. W.Va. Jr. Coll., Morgantown, 1998—2000; asst. dir. W.Va. U., 2000—. Named one of Top 100 Most Influential People in Morgantown, 2003. Mem.: W.Va. Assn. Ednl. Opportunity Program Personnel, Mid-Ea. Assn. Ednl. Opportunity Programs Personnel, Ea. Comm. Assn. Avocations: reading, music, photography. Office: WVa U PO Box 6212 Student Svcs Ctr Morgantown WV 26506 Office Phone: 304-293-4316. E-mail: betty.mei@mail.wvu.edu.

MEI, TOM Y. K. lawyer; b. Kuantan, Malaysia, July 24, 1940; came to U.S., 1958. s. Hung Po and Hannah (Chung) M.; m. Margene Suzuki Mei, Sept. 1964; children: Rodney, Todd. BA in econ., Calif. State U. at L.A., 1963; JD, Western State U. Coll. Law, 1975. Bar: Calif. 1976. Claim rep. CNA Ins., L.A., 1964-66, claim supr. San Diego, 1966-76; assoc. attorney Murchison & Cumming, Santa Ana, 1976-88, ptnr., 1988—. Pres. San Diego Claims Mgr. Council, 1973. Mem. Am. Bd. Trial Advocates (bd. dirs.), Defense Rsch. Inst., Orange County Bar Assoc. Avocations: skiing, travel. Office: Murchison & Cumming 200 W Santa Ana Blvd Ste 801 Santa Ana CA 92701-4134 Office Phone: 714-972-9977.

MEIBURG, CHARLES OWEN, business administration educator; b. Seneca, S.C., Dec. 17, 1931; s. Albert and Gladys Katherine (Burley) M.; m. Elizabeth Rhodes Glenn, June 11, 1955; children: Charles O. Jr., Howard Glenn, Elizabeth Rhodes. BS in Arts and Scis., Clemson U., 1953; MA in Econs., U. Va., 1958, PhD in Econs., 1960. Assoc. prof. U. Va., Charlottesville, 1964-69, prof., 1969-82, J. Harvie Wilkinson, Jr. prof. bus. adminstrn., 1982-99, prof. emeritus, 1999—. Dir. Taylor Murphy Inst. U. Va., 1967-83; assoc. dean Darden Sch. U. Va., 1983-89. Co-author: Cases on Financial Institutions, 1979, Cases in Bank Management, 1986; editor (with others) Loan Officers Handbook, 1986. 1st lt. U.S. Army, 1953-55. Mem. Am. Econ. Assn., Fin. Mgmt. Assn., Assn. for U. Bus. and Econ. Rsch. (pres. 1971). Home: 3345 Kirkwood Ct Keswick VA 22947-9138 Office: U Va Darden Sch PO Box 6550 Charlottesville VA 22906-6550 E-mail: com@virginia.edu.

MEIDL, KEVIN, secondary school educator; b. Manitowoc, Wis., Dec. 10, 1960; s. Kenneth John LeRoy and Bernita Ann (Pritzl) M. MusB, Lawrence U., 1983; MusM in Music Edn. summa cum laude, Northwestern U., 1991; PhD in Edn. summa cum laude, LaSalle U., 1995. Tchr. music Einstein Jr. H.S., Appleton, Wis., 1983-85, Appleton (Wis.) H.S. West, 1985—. Conductor, Fox Valley Symphony Chorus, Appleton, 1983-88, St. Edward's Ch. Choir, Mackville, Wis., 1983-88, Appleton Boy Choir, 1983—; bd. dirs. A Better Chance, Appleton, 1985-91. Named Secondary Educator of Yr., Mielke Found., 1994-95. Mem. Am. Choral Dirs. Assn. (mem. state bd. 1980—), Internat. Fedn. Choral Music, Music Educators Nat. Conf., Soc. Acad. Achievement, Wis. Choral Dir. Assn. (pres.-elect 1992, pres. 1995-97), Mortar Bd., Pi Kappa Lambda, Phi Mu Alpha (pres. 1982-83). Roman Catholic. Home: 916 S Park Ave Neenah WI 54956-4259 Office: Appleton High Sch West 610 N Badger Ave Appleton WI 54914-3448 E-mail: kevinmeidl@myexcel.com.

MEIER, ARLENE, retail executive; CFO, exec. v.p.,& sec Kohl's Corp., Menomonee Falls, Wis., 1994—. Office: Kohls Corp N56 W 17000 Ridgewood Dr Menomonee Falls WI 53051

MEIER, DEBORAH, principal; M in History, U. Chgo.; degree (hon.), Harvard U., Yale U., Brown U., Columbia Tchrs. Coll. Co-founder, prin. N.Y. Ctrl. Park East Elem. and Secondary Sch.; co-prin. Mission Hill Elem. Sch., Roxbury, 1997—. Bd. mem. Nat. Acad. Edn., Ctr. for Collaborative Edn., Boston, Panasonic Found., Fairtest. Author: The Power of Their Ideas: Lessons to America from a Small School in Harlem, 1995, Will Standards Save Public Education, 2000, In Schools We Trust, 2002, Creating Communities of Learning in an Era of Testing and Standardization; mem. editl. bd.: The Nation, Dissent and the Harvard Education Letter; contbr. articles to profl. jours. Trustee Ednl. Alliance and Educators for Social Responsiblity. Recipient MacArthur award; Sr. Annenberg fellow, 1994—97. Mem.: Coalition of Essential Scis., Nat. Bd. for Profl. Tchg. Stds. (founding mem.), Carnegie Found. for Advancement in Edn. (bd. mem., vice chair). Office: Mission Hill Elem Sch 67 Alleghany St Boston MA 02120

MEIER, JOHN F. consumer products company executive; With Libbey Inc., Toledo, 1970-90, gen. mgr., 1990-93, CEO, 1993—, also chmn. bd. dirs.; pres. Owens-Ill., Inc., 1990. Bd. dirs. Tire & Rubber Co. Office: Libbey Inc 300 Madison Ave Fl 4 Toledo OH 43604-2634

MEIER, KENNETH JOHN, political scientist; b. Aberdeen, S.D., Mar. 3, 1950; s. John and Elizabeth (Malsam) M.; m. Diane Jones Meier, Dec. 31, 1972. BA, U. S.D., 1972; PhD, Syracuse U., 1975. Prof. polit. sci. Rice U., Houston, 1975-78, U. Okla., 1978-85, U. Wis., Madison, 1985-89, Milw., 1989-97; Charles Puryear prof. liberal arts Tex. A&M U., College Station, 1998—, Sara Lindsey prof. govt., 2001—. Fellow com. for hispanic pub. policy issues Inter Univ. Program Social Sci. Rsch. Coun., 1991-92; dir. Ctr. for Presdl. Studies, Policy and Governance, 2001-02. Author: Race, Class and Education, 1989, The Politics of Hispanic Education, 1991, Politics and the Bureaucracy, 1993, The Politics of Sin, 1994, The Case Against School Choice, 1995, Regulation and Consumer Protection, 1995, Applied Statistics for Public Administration, 1997, What Works: A New Approach to Program and Policy Analysis, 2000, The Politics of Fertility Control, 2001, Politics, Policy and Organizations, 2003; editor Am. Jour. Polit. Sci., 1994-98; assoc. editor Jour. Pub. Adminstrn. Rsch. and Theory. Recipient Clarence A. Kulp award, 1990, Gustavus Myers award, 1991, 93, Herbert Kaufman award, 1992, 2002, Herbert A. Simon award, 1999, award Acad. Mgmt., 2000, disting. rsch. award, Nat. Assn. Schs. Pub. Affairs and Adminstrn./ASPA, 2003; Big XII Faculty fellow, 2003. Mem. APHA, ASPA, Am. Polit. Sci. Assn., S.W. Polit. Sci. Assn. (pres.-elect 1998-99, pres. 1999-2000), Nat. Pub. Mgmt. Rsch. Assn. (pres. 2003-05), MW Polit. Sci. Assn. (pres.-elect 2004—). Office: Tex A&M U Dept Polit Sci TAMUS 4384 College Station TX 77843-0001 Office Phone: 979-845-4232. Business E-Mail: kmeier@polisci.tamu.edu.

MEIER, MARK FREDERICK, research scientist, glaciologist, educator; b. Iowa City, Dec. 19, 1925; s. Norman C. and Clea (Grimes) M.; m. Barbara McKinley, Sept. 16, 1955; children: Lauren G., Mark S., Gretchen A. BSEE, U. Iowa, 1949, MS in Geology, 1951; PhD in Geology and Applied Mechanics, Calif. Inst. Tech., 1957. Instr. Occidental Coll., L.A., 1952-55; chief glaciology project office U.S. Geol. Survey, Tacoma, 1956-85; dir. Inst. Arctic and Alpine Rsch. U. Colo., Boulder, 1985-94. Vis. prof. Dartmouth Coll., Hanover, N.H., 1964; rsch. prof. U. Wash., Seattle, 1964-86; prof. geol. scis. U. Colo., 1985-96, prof. emeritus, 1997—; pres. Internat. Comn. on Snow and Ice, 1967-71; pres. Internat. Assn. Hydrol. Scis., 1979-83; Mendenhall lectr. U.S. Geol. Survey, 1982, Walter Orr Roberts Disting. lectr. Aspen Global Change Inst., 1992. Contbr. articles to profl. jours. With USN, 1945—46. Named Meier Valley (Antarctica) in his honor; recipient 3 medals, Acad. Scis., Moscow, 1970—85, Disting. Svc. award (Gold medal), U.S. Dept. Interior, 1968, Internat. Hydrology prize, Internat. Assn. Hydrol. Scis./World Meteor. Orgn./UNESCO, 1999, Goldthwait Polar medal, Ohio State U., 2002. Fellow: AAAS (John Wesley Powell Meml. lectr. 1994), Am. Geophys. Union (com. chmn., Robert E. Horton medal 1996); mem.: Arctic Inst. N.Am. (gov. 1987—93), Internat. Glaciol. Soc. (v.p., coun., Seligman Crystal 1985), Geol. Soc. Am. (com. mem.). Office: U Colo Inst Arctic Alpine Rsch 1560 30th St Boulder CO 80309-0450 E-mail: mark.meier@colorado.edu.

MEIER, SAMUEL ARTHUR, III, historian, educator; b. Tucson, Sept. 10, 1952; s. Samuel Arthur Meier II and Charlotte Lou Meier; m. Patricia Eileen Cornell, May 6, 1978; children: Eris, Sammy. BA, UCLA, 1974; postgrad., Hebrew U., Jerusalem, 1976—77; ThM, Dallas Theol. Sem., 1978; PhD, Harvard U., 1987. Asst. pastor Paul's Union Ch., La Marque, Tex., 1978; instr. Asian Theol. Sem., Manila, Philippines, 1978—82; tchg. fellow Harvard Divinity Sch., Cambridge, Mass., 1985—86; asst. prof. Hebrew Ohio State U., Columbus, 1986—92, assoc. prof. Hebrew, 1992—, adj. prof. history, 1995—. Editor Hebrew Ann. Rev., 1986—94; bd. dirs. Melton Ctr. Jewish Studies, Columbus, 1986—, Light of the World Ministries, Indpls., 1992—; vis. scholar Rockefeller Ctr., Bellagio, Italy, 0996; Edwards lectr. in philosophy and religion Saginaw (Mich.) State U., 2000. Author: The Messenger in the Ancient Semitic World, 1988, Speaking of Speaking, 1992. Literacy work with Indians Summer Inst. Linguistics, Guatemala, 1973. Mem.: Soc. Bibl. Lit. Office: Ohio State U 203 Jennings Hall 1735 Neil Ave Columbus OH 43210 E-mail: meier.3@osu.edu.

MEIER, STEPHEN CHARLES, foundation executive; b. L.A., Apr. 22, 1950; s. Erwin William Henry and Betsy R. Meier; m. Carol Williams Meier, Apr. 20, 1974; children: Charles, Marilyn. BA, Occidental Col., 1972; MBA, Harvard U., 1977. Budget analyst Calif. Legis., Sacramento, 1973—75; various exec. positions Times Mirror, L.A., 1977—89, v.p. adminstrn. and cmty. affairs, 1989—96, v.p. pub. and govt. affairs, corp. sec., 1996—2000; bd. dirs. Pfaffinger Found., L.A., 1993—, chmn., CEO, 1997—. Tchr. BSF Internat. Bd. dirs. YMCA of Met. L.A., Tomas Rivera Policy Inst., LA, Cmty. Ptnrs.,Constl. Rights Found., L.A., 1988-2003. Fellow Thomas Watson Found., 1972-73. Mem. The Calif. Club. Congregationalist. Office: Pfaffinger Found 316 W 2d St Ste PH-C Los Angeles CA 90012

MEIER, SUE A. marriage and family therapist, director; b. Pasadena, Calif., June 21, 1948; d. Don W. and Francys P. Abbott; children: Don Page, Aaron Michael, Thomas James, Jonathan Eric. BA, Calif. State U., Northridge, 1983, MA (with distinction) in Ednl. Psychology, Counseling & Guidance, 1986, MA (with distinction) in Pub. Admin., 2001. Lic. marriage & family therapist Calif. Bd. of Behavioral Sci., 1989. Dir. Child Help USA, Nat. Child Abuse Hotline, Los Angeles, 1992—95; grant rev. U.S. Dept. Health & Human Svcs., Washington, 1996; cons. CSUN Helpline & Calif. Office Child Abuse Prevention, Los Angeles, 1996—; pvt. practice Los Angeles, 1989—; adj. faculty Antioch U., Los Angeles, 1999—, Los Angeles Cmty. Coll., Los

Angeles, 1996—; exec. dir., founder Internat. Child Abuse Network, Los Angeles, 1996—. Recipient Nat. Disting. Svc. Registry for Counseling & Devel., Nat. Svc. Registry, 1990, OUtstanding Vol. of Yr. award, San Fernando Valley Child Abuse Coun., 2003. Mem.: LA County Cmty. Coord. Project (treas. 1990—), San Fernando Valley Child Abuse Counsel (pres. 1990—), Alliance of Info. Referral Sys. (bd. dirs. 1993—98). Achievements include development of 1st facilitator training for chatroom support groups; founded Internat. Child Abuse Prevention program. Avocations: crocheting, children & grand children, mystery novels. Office: Internat Child Abuse Network Inc 7657 Winnetka 155 Canoga Park CA 91306-2677 Office Phone: 818-716-8491. E-mail: yesican@yesican.org.

MEIER, THOMAS JOSEPH, museum director, author; b. Denver, June 23, 1939; s. Henry Joseph and Helen Miriam (Croke) M.; m. Beverly Joyce Loeffler, June 8, 1963; children: Thomas, John. BS in Edn., U. Colo., 1964. Cert. tchr., Colo. Space mgmt. dir. U. Colo., Boulder, 1966-69; owner Sturtz & Copeland, Boulder, 1969-77; historian and writer Mesa Press, Boulder, 1977-90; dir. Boulder Mus. History, 1990—. Author: The Pictureman, 1994, (booklet) The Early History of Boulder 1993, contbr. articles to profl. jours. Mem. mass transit com. City of Boulder, 1973; mem. City Planning Bd., Boulder, 1974-75, City Landmark Bd., Boulder, 1974-75. Served with USMC, 1957-60. Mem. Boulder Hist. Soc. (pres. 1985), Colo. Hist. Soc. Home: 2850 Vassar Dr Boulder CO 80305-5737 Office: Boulder Mus of History 1206 Euclid Ave Boulder CO 80302-7224

MEIER, THOMAS KEITH, college president, English educator; b. Houston, Apr. 12, 1940; s. Herbert H. and Madeleine (Keith) M.; m. Mila Hillard, June 30, 1962; children: John Hillard, Keith Reilly. BA, U. Tex., 1962; AM, Columbia U., 1963, PhD, 1969; MBA, Harvard U., 1967. Fin. mgr., employee rels. mgr. Exxon Co., U.S.A. and Exxon Rsch. Engring. Co., Houston, Florham Park, NJ, 1969-79; pres. Castleton (Vt.) State Coll., 1979-87; pres., Simeon Benjamin prof. English lit. Elmira (N.Y.) Coll., 1987—. Regent Lee Coll., Baytown, Tex., 1972-73; pres. Vt. Higher Edn. Coun., 1981-82; mem. Johnson Found. (Troutbeck) Leadership Seminar, 1991—; mem. adv. coun. The Pres.'s Found. for Support of Higher Edn.; bd. dirs. Chemung Canal Trust Co., Coll. Consortium Finger Lakes, N.Y., Ind. Coll. Fund of N.Y., Coun. Ind. Colls. and Univs., Christopher Isnerwood Found. Author: Defoe and the Defense of Commerce, 1907, contbr. articles to profl. jours. Bd. dirs. Union County Urban League, Elizabeth, N.J., 1973-76, Rutland Region C. of C., 1982-86, Arnot Art Mus., 1987-99, So. Tier Econ. Growth, 1987—, N.E.-Midwest Congl. Leadership Coun., 1988—; bd. dirs. Chemung County United Way, 1990-93, chmn. 1992-93; mem. exec. coun. Five Rivers Coun. Boy Scouts Am., 1998—, mem. exec. bd. N.E. region, 2004—; corp. bd. dirs. Rutland Hosp., 1980-87; bd. dirs. Ind. Coll. Fund, 1995-97. Lt. U.S. Army, 1963-65. Recipient Outstanding Periodical Essay award Tex. Books Rev., 1979, medal of merit Elmira Coll. Alumni Assn., 1991, Medallon Presidencial Univ. InterAm. de Panama, 2002; Weaver fellow, 1968. Mem. Pico Ski Club (Vt.), Elmira Country Club, Elmira City Club, Univ. Club of N.Y.C., Harvard Club of N.Y.C., Phi Beta Kappa, Phi Eta Sigma, Phi Alpha Theta, Omciron Delta Kappa, Theta Xi, Alpha Sigma Lambda, Sigma Beta Delta, Ambda Iota Tau. Episcopalian. Home: The President's Home 855 College Ave Elmira NY 14901-2001 Office: Elmira Coll Office of Pres Elmira NY 14901

MEIER, WILBUR LEROY, JR., industrial engineer, educator, former university chancellor; b. Elgin, Tex., Jan. 3, 1939; s. Wilbur Leroy and Ruby (Hall) M.; m. Judy Lee Longbotham, Aug. 30, 1958; children: Melynn, Marla, Melissa. BS, U. Tex., 1962, MS, 1964, PhD, 1967. Planning engr. Tex. Water Devel. Bd., Austin, 1962-66, cons., 1967-72; research engr. U. Tex., Austin, 1966; asst. prof. indsl. engring. Tex. A&M U., College Station, 1967-68, assoc prof., 1968-70, prof., 1970-73, asst. head dept. indsl. engring., 1972-73; prof., chmn. dept. indsl. engring. Iowa State U., Ames, 1973-74; prof., head sch. of indsl. engring. Purdue U., West Lafayette, Ind., 1974-81; dean Coll. Engring., Pa. State U., University Park, 1981-87; chancellor U. Houston System, 1987-89; prof. indsl. engring. Pa. State U., University Park, 1989-91; dir. div. engring. infrastructure devel. NSF, Washington, 1989-91; dean Coll. Engring. N.C. State U., 1991-93, prof. indsl. engring., 1991—; program mgr. ABB Electric Systems Tech. Inst., Raleigh, N.C., 2000—. Mem. bd. visitors Air Force Inst. Technology; cons. Ohio Bd. Regents, 1990, U. Arizona, 1989, Indsl. Rsch. Inst., St. Louis, 1979, Environments for Tomorrow, Inc., Washington, 1970-81, Water Resources Engrs., Inc., Walnut Creek, Calif., 1969-70, Computer Graphics, Inc., Bryan, Tex., 1969-70, Kaiser Engrs., Oakland, Calif., 1971, Tracor, Inc., Austin, 1966-68, div. planning coordination Tex. Gov.'s Office, 1969, Office of Tech. Assessment, 1982-86, Southeast Ctr. for Elec. Engring. Edn., 1978—; mem. rev. team Naval Rsch. Adv. Com. Editor: Marcel Dekker Pub. Co., 1978—; Contbr. articles to profl. jours. Recipient Bliss medal Soc. Am. Mil. Engrs., 1986, Am. Spirit award USAF, 1984; named Outstanding Young Engr. of Yr. Tex. Soc. Profl. Engrs., 1966, Disting. Grad. Coll. Engring., U. Tex. at Austin, 1987; USPHS fellow, 1966. Fellow AAAS, Am. Soc. Engring. Edn. (chmn. indsl. engring. divsn. 1978-83), Inst. Indsl. Engrs. (dir. ops. rsch. div. 1975, pres. Ind. chpt. 1976, program chmn. 1973-75, editorial bd. Trans., publ. chmn., newsletter editor engring. economy div. 1972-73, v.p. region VIII 1977-79, exec. v.p. chpt. ops. 1981-83, pres. 1985-86), Soc. Mfg. Engrs. (Internat. Edn. award 2000), World Acad. Productivity Sci.; mem. ASCE (sec.-treas. Austin br. 1965-66, chmn. rsch. com., tech. coun. water resources planning and mgmt. 1972-74), Am. Assn. Engring. Socs. (bd. govs. 1984-86), Nat. Assn. State Univ. and Land Grant Colls. (mem. engring. legis. task force 1983-87), Assn. Engring. Colls. Pa. (pres. 1985-86, treas. 1981-87), Air Force Assn. (advisor sci. and tech. com. 1984-87), Nat. Soc. Profl. Engrs., Profl. Engrs. in Edn. (vice chmn. N.E. region 1985-87, bd. govs. 1983-85), Sigma Xi, Tau Beta Pi, Alpha Pi Mu (asso. editor Cogwheel 1970-75, regional dir. 1976-77, exec. v.p. 1977-80, pres. 1980-82), Phi Kappa Phi, Chi Epsilon. Lodges: Rotary. Home: 7504 Grist Mill Rd Raleigh NC 27615-5411

MEIERAN, EUGENE STUART, material scientist; b. Dec. 23, 1937; s. Elias and Rae (Linetsky) M.; m. Rosalind Berson, Mar. 25, 1962; children: Sharon Elizabeth, Andrew Marc. BS in Metallurgy, MIT, 1961, ScD in Material Sci., 1963; Doctorate (hon.), Purdue U., 2004. Mem. tech. staff Fairchild R&D, Palo Alto, Calif., 1963-73; engring. mgr. Intel Corp., Santa Clara, Calif., 1973-77, sr. mgr. quality assurance, 1977-84, Intel fellow, 1984—, mgr. applications lab., 1989—, Intel sr. fellow, 2003. Dir. rsch. LFM program MIT, 1993—; vis. lectr. Technion, Haifa, Israel, 1970-71, H.H. Wills Physics Lab., Bristol, Eng., 1970-71; mem. adv. bd. Lawrence Berkeley Lab., 1984—. Contbr. articles to profl. jours. AEC fellow, 1960; recipient Internat. Reliability awards, 1970, 79, 85, Carnegie medal, 2004; named Disting. Engring. Alumnus Purdue U., 1988, Perdue Band Alumni, 2000. Mem. AIME (chmn. electronic material symposium 1973—), NAE, Electron Microscope Soc. U.S.A., Tau Beta Pi, Phi Lambda Upsilon. Democrat. Jewish. Home: 5421 E Camello Rd Phoenix AZ 85018-1910 Office: Intel Corp 5000 W Chandler Blvd Chandler AZ 85226-3699 Business E-Mail: gene.s.meieran@intel.com.

MEIERHENRY, JUDITH KNITTEL, judge, lawyer; b. Burke, SD, Jan. 20, 1944; d. Adolph John and Anna Elizabeth (Voos) Knittel; m. Mark Vernon Meierhenry, May 14, 1961; children: Todd, Mary. BA in English, U. S.D., 1966, MA, 1968, JD, 1977. Bar: S.D. 1977. H.S. tchr. English Plattsmouth (Nebr.) Pub. Schs., 1966-67; instr. U. S.D., 1968-70, Hiram Scott Coll., Scottbluff, Nebr., 1970; tchr. Todd County Pub. Schs., Mission, S.D., 1971-74; ptnr. Meierhenry, DeVaney, Krueger & Meierhenry, Vermillion, S.D., 1977-79; cabinet sec. S.D. Dept. Labor, Pierre, 1980-84; cabinet sec. edn. and cultural affairs State S.D., 1983-84; sr. mgr., asst. gen. counsel Citibank S.D., 1985-88; cir. ct. judge State S.D., 1988—2002; justice S.Dak. Supreme Ct., 2002—. Mem.: Nat. Assn. Women Judges, SD Bar Assn. Office: South Dakota Supreme Ct 425 N Dakota Ave Sioux Falls SD 57104-2400 E-mail: jmeierh@aol.com.

MEIERHOFF, GAYLE PATRICE, lawyer, accountant; b. Washington, Dec. 21, 1956; d. Charles Stanton Dailey and Mary Loretta Nesline; m. Daryl William Meierhoff, Mar. 9, 1977; 1 child, Kristen Caroline. BS in Bus., Emporia State U., 1983; JD, Washburn U., 1989—91. CPA State of Kans., 1983; bar: State of Kans. 1991. Atty. Emporia (Kans.) State U., 1997—. Home: 714 West 12th Ave Emporia KS 66801 Office: Emporia State U 1200 Commercial St Emporia KS 66801 Office Phone: 620-341-5444. Personal E-mail: gmeierhoff@cableone.net. Business E-Mail: meierhof@emporia.edu.

MEIGHER, S. CHRISTOPHER, III, communications and media executive, publisher; b. N.Y.C., Sept. 23, 1946; s. Stephen Christopher and Denise (Connor) Todd; m. Grace Tebbutt, Aug. 8, 1970; children: Elizabeth, Amanda Powers. BA, Dartmouth Coll., 1968; grad. program mgmt. devel., Harvard U., 1974. Dir. circulation Fortune mag., N.Y.C., 1972-74, Sports Illustrated mag., N.Y.C., 1974-76, Time mag., N.Y.C., 1976-79; v.p. circulation Time, Inc., N.Y.C., 1981-83; pres. Time Distbn. Svc., N.Y.C., 1979-81; pub. People mag., N.Y.C., 1983-85, exec. v.p., group pub., 1985-90; pres. Time Inc. Mags. N.Y., N.Y.C., 1990-92; gen. ptnr., CEO, chmn. Meigher Comm., L.P., N.Y.C., 1993—; CEO Questmedia LLC, 2000—. Bd. dirs. Individual Investor Group, 1998—; bd. vis. Rockefeller Ctr. at Dartmouth Coll., 1997—; delegate U.S. State Dept. USA-USSR, 1988; mem. Bilateral Info. Talks, Moscow. Pub. Saveur mag., Garden Design mag., Quest mag., Smarth Health mag., Friends mag., 1992-2000. Trustee Boys Club N.Y.C., 1979—, Internat. Ho., 1985—92, Am. Ballet Theatre, 1993—, South St. Seaport, 1987—97, St. Paul's Sch., 1997—2002; mem. dream team Meml. Sloan Kettering, 1990—; mem. comm. com. St. James Episcopal Ch., 1989—95. Recipient Disting. Service award Brandeis U., 1983 Mem.: Mag. Publs. Assn. (bd. dirs. 1988—92, 1997—2002), Am. Pubs. Assn. (bd. dirs. 1988—92), Everglades Club (Palm Beach), Saratoga Reading Room, Clove Valley Rod and Gun Club, Lake George Club (trustee 1995—2002), N.Y. Yacht Club (trustee 1987—92), Racquet & Tennis Club (N.Y.), Brook Club, Bath & Tennis Club (Palm Beach), River Club. Office: Meigher Comm LP 920 Third Ave New York NY 10022 Office Phone: 646-840-3402. E-mail: scmiii@aol.com.

MEIGS, JAMES B. editor-in-chief; Editl. dir. Video Review; sr. editor Entertainment Weekly, 1989—93; editor US Mag., 1993—95; editor-in-chief Premiere Mag., 1996—2000, v.p., 1998—2000; dep. editor features Nat. Geographic Adventure, 2001—03, exec. editor, 2003—04; editor-in-chief Popular Mechanics, 2004—. Freelance writer Rolling Stone, Details, Outside, O: The Oprah Mag., Family Life, Popular Mechanics, others. Office: Popular Mechanics 810 7th Ave New York NY 10019*

MEIGS, JOHN FORSYTH, lawyer; b. Boston, Dec. 4, 1941; s. Charles H. Meigs and Florence S. Truitt; m. Carolyn J. Adams, Aug. 11, 2002; children: Amy, Perry, John. BA, Yale U., 1964; LLB, U. Pa., 1969. Bar: Pa. 1969, U.S. Supreme Ct. 1977. Assoc. Saul, Ewing, Remick & Saul (now Saul Ewing LLP), Phila., 1969-76, ptnr., 1976—. Co-chair estates and trusts Saul Ewing LLP, 1997—2003; chair personal wealth svcs. Group Saul Ewing LLP, 2000—. Contbr. articles to profl. jours. Trustee Independence Seaport Mus., 1978—, Woodmere Art Mus., 1987—2003. Mem.: ABA, Phila. Bar Assn., Pa. Bar Assn. Episcopalian. Home: 6 Norman Ln Philadelphia PA 19118-3617 Office: Saul Ewing LLP 3800 Centre Sq W Philadelphia PA 19102 Office Phone: 215-972-7812. E-mail: jmeigs@saul.com.

MEIGS, MONTGOMERY CUNNINGHAM, JR., retired military officer, educator; b. Annapolis, Md., Jan. 11, 1945; s. Montgomery Cunningham and Elizabeth Shoemaker (Griggs) M.; m. Mary Ann Mellenbruch, July 6, 1968; children: William Bradford, Matthew Montgomery. BS, U.S. Mil. Acad., West Point, N.Y., 1967; MA in History, U. Wis., 1977, PhD in History, 1982. Commd. 2d lt. U.S. Army, 1967, advanced through grades to gen.; internat. affairs fellow Coun. Fgn. Rels., N.Y.C., 1981-82; exec. officer 2d Armored Cavalry Regiment, Nurnberg, Germany, 1982-84; comdr. 1st Squadron, 1st Cavalry, 1st AD, Schwabach, Germany, 1984-86; rsch. fellow Nat. Def. U., Washington, 1986-87; chief strategic applications br. J-5 Joint Staff, Washington, 1987-90; comdr. 2d Bde 1st Armored Divsn., Desert Storm, Erlangen, Germany, 1990-91; comdg. gen. 7th Army Tng. Command, Grafenwoehr, Germany, 1991-93; chief of staff V U.S. Corps, Frankfurt, Germany, 1993-94; dep. chief of staff Ops. HQ USAREUR & 7th Army, Heidelberg, Germany, 1994; comdg. gen. 3d Infantry Divsn., 1995-96, 1st infantry Divsn., Wurzburg, Germany, 1996-97, COMEAGLE, Bosnia-Herzegovina, 1996-97, Combined Arms Ctr., Ft. Leavenworth, Kans., 1997-98; commdg. gen. U.S. Army, COMSFOR, Herzegovina, Bosnia, 1998-99; comdg. gen. U.S. Army Europe and 7th Army, 1998—2002. Tom Slick vis. prof. LBJ Sch., U. Tex., Austin, 2003—. Author: Slide Rules and Submarines, 1990; contbr. articles to profl. jours. Decorated Legion of Merit with oak leaf cluster, Bronze Star medal with V device and 2 oak leaf clusters, Purple Heart, officer French Legion of Honor, German Nat. Svc. Order with star, Bavarian Svc. Order, Dev. DSM, Army Disting. Svc. medal with oak leaf cluster. Avocations: history, hunting. Home: 106 W 32nd St Austin TX 78705-2302

MEIJER, DOUGLAS, retail company executive; b. 1954; With Meijer Inc., 1967—, co-chmn., 1990—. Office: Meijer Inc 2929 Walker Ave NW Grand Rapids MI 49544-9428

MEIJER, HANK, retail company executive; b. 1951; BA, U. Michigan, 1973. Asst. advt. dir. Meijer, Grand Rapids, Mich., mktg. dir., vice chmn. bd. dirs., co-chmn. bd. dirs., CEO, 2002—. Office: 2929 Walker Ave NW Grand Rapids MI 49544

MEIJER, MARK, retail executive; With Bud's Ambulance Svc., Grand Rapids, Mich., 1977-79; pres. Life EMS Inc., Grand Rapids, Mich., 1979—; bd. dirs. Meijer Cos. Ltd., Grand Rapids, Mich. Office: Meijer Companies LTD 2929 Walker Ave NW Grand Rapids MI 49544-9428

MEIJER, MIRIAM CLAUDE, information technology executive, historian; d. Paul Herman Ernst and Marianne Schwarz Meijer. BA, The Cath. U. of Am., Washington, 1974, MA, 1980; PhD, UCLA, 1991. Tchg. assoc. UCLA, 1983—85; adj. prof. George Washington U., Washington, 1992—93; asst. prof. U. of Ctrl. Ark., Conway, 1993—96; web content editor Insuractive.com, Alexandria, Va., 2000—01; IT staff Montgomery Coll., Takoma Park, Md., 2001—. Vol. translator Musee de l'homme, Paris, 1976—77; excavator Hebrew Union Coll., Tel Gezer, Israel, 1973; participant Operation Crossroads Africa, Togo, 1972. Author: (book) Race and Aesthetics in the Anthropology of Petrus Camper (1722-1789); contbr. articles to profl. jours. Historian Washington Ethical Soc., Washington, 1997—2000; archivist Mus. Edn. Roundtable, Washington, 1992, Nat. Anthrop. Archives, Smithsonian Inst., Washington, 1992. Fellow, Institut fuer Europaeische Geschichte fellow, Mainz, Germany, 1987; scholar Fulbright scholar, Fulbright Found., Netherlands, 1985—86. Mem.: Am. Hist. Assn., Am. Soc. for Eighteenth-Century Studies. Democrat. Achievements include research in Eighteenth-century Anthropology. Avocations: art, computers, computer graphics and animations. Office: Montgomery College 7600 Takoma Ave Takoma Park MD 20912 E-mail: miriam.meijer@montgomerycollege.edu.

MEIJER, PAUL HERMAN ERNST, educator, physicist; b. The Hague, Netherlands, Nov. 14, 1921; came to U.S., 1953, naturalized, 1959; s. Herman Willem and Elisabet (Kossmann) M.; m. Marianne Schwarz, Feb. 17, 1949; children: Onko Frans (dec.), Miriam, Daniel, Mark, Corinne. PhD, U. Leiden, Netherlands, 1951. Research assoc. U. Leiden, 1952-53, Duke U., 1954-55; vis. lectr. Case Inst. Tech., 1953-54; asst. prof. U. Del., 1955-56; asso. prof. Cath. U., Washington, 1956-60, prof. physics, 1960-92, prof. emeritus, 1992—, chmn. dept., 1980-83. Vis. prof. U. Paris, 1964-65, 72, 78, U. Nancy, 1984, 88; part-time appointment Nat. Bur. Standards; short time appointments at Naval Ordnance Lab., Livermore Radiation Lab., Naval Research Lab., Night Vision Lab., Ft. Belvoir. Author: (with E. Bauer) Group Theory, 1962, (with P. Papon, J. Leblond) The Physics of Phase Transitions, 2002; editor: Group Theory and Solid State Physics, 1964. Fulbright grantee, 1953-55, 77-78; Guggenheim grantee, 1964-65; Fulbright sr. fellow, 1978 Fellow Am. Phys. Socs.; mem. European Phys. Soc., Phys. Soc. Netherlands, Fedn. Am. Scientists, Fulbright Alumni Assn., Sigma Xi. Research, publs. statis. mechanics solids and liquids, group theory and other fields. Home: 1438 Geranium St NW Washington DC 20012-1518 Office: Cath U Am Dept Physics Hannan Hall Washington DC 20064 also: Nat Inst Standards and Tech 100 Bureau Dr Stop 8380 Gaithersburg MD 20899-8380 Office Phone: 202-319-5324. Business E-Mail: meijer@cua.edu.

MEIKLE, KAREN L. music educator, musician; b. Calif., July 31, 1956; d. T. Gordon and D. Lillian Meikle. MusB in Violin Performance, Calif. State U., Fullerton, 1979. Cert. music K-12 tchr. Calif., 1992, tchr. Ill., 1993. Tchr. asst. beginning string classes and non-music maj. theory classes Calif. State U., Fullerton, 1975—79; pvt. string instr. Fullerton, Calif., 1975—92; string ensemble contractor, 1977—92; freelance violinist L.A. County, Orange County, 1979—92; string coach Temple City H.S., Calif., 1985—87; student tchr. Arcadia Unified Sch. Dist., Calif., 1991—92; string coach Arcadia H.S. Music Camp, Calif., 1992—92; substitute tchr. Arcadia Unified Sch. Dist., Calif., 1992—93; orch. tchr. grades 4-12 DeKalb Cmty. Unit Sch. Dist. #428, Ill., 1993—. Violinist Pacific Chamber Orch., Fullerton, Calif., 1978—81; violininst Rio Hondo Symphony, Calif., 1978—91; violinist Santa Monica Symphony, Calif., 1979—81, Orquesta Sinfonica del Valle, Cali, Colombia, 1982—82, Bay Area Women's Philharm., Berkley, Calif., 1983—85, Pasadena Cmty. Orch., Calif., 1983—92, C.O.T.A. Symphony, L.A., 1984—89, Santa Maria Symphony, Calif., 1985—90, Beach Cities Symphony, Redondo Beach, Calif., 1989—90, Britt Festival Orch., Jacksonville, Oreg., 1990—, Rockford Symphony Orch., Ill., 1993—; tchr. trainee Suzuki Violin Pedagogy, Van Nuys, Calif., 1990—90. Com. chair Britt Festival Orch., Jacksonville, Oreg., 1996—2002; strategic plan team chairperson DeKalb H.S. Strategic Planning Team, Ill., 1995—96; orch. chairperson Ill. Music Educators Assn. Dist. Festival, DeKalb, 1999—2003. Mem.: Suzuki Assn. of the Americas (corr.), Music Educators Nat. Conf. (corr.), Am. String Tchrs./Nat. Sch. Orchestras Assn. (corr.). Avocations: travel, swimming. Home: 1814 Raintree Ct Sycamore IL 60178 Office: Cmty Unit Sch Dist #428 901 S 4th St Dekalb IL 60115 Personal E-mail: klmeeks@aol.com. Business E-Mail: kmeikle@dist428.org.

MEIKLE, PHILIP G. engineer, retired government agency executive; b. Glendale, W.Va., Dec. 5, 1937; s. Philip and Caroline Elizabeth (Stephens) M.; m. Linda Kay Price, July 14, 1961 (div. Aug. 1976); children: Philip Kevin, Melissa Kay BS in Mining Engring., W.Va. U., 1961, MS in Mining Engring., 1965; M.Engring. Adminstrn., George Washington U., 1980. Registered profl. engr. Mining engr. Duquesne Light Co., Pitts., 1961-63; research engr. W.Va. U., Morgantown, 1963-66; materials engr. Mobay Chem. Co., New Martinsville, W.Va., 1966-68; asst. dir. Nat. Ash Assn., Washington, 1968-72; staff mining engr. U.S. Bur. Mines, Washington, 1972-82, divsn. chief, 1982-95; ret., 1995. Mem. U.S. Nat. Com. for Tunneling Tech., Nat. Acad. Scis., Washington, 1985-90, chmn., 1988-89; adj. prof. George Washington U., 1985—; pres. Clan Lamont Soc. N.Am., 1998-2002. Contbr. articles to profl. jours., chpts. to books Recipient Superior Svc. award Dept. Interior, 1980, Meritorious Svc. award, 1986, Disting. Svc. award, 1991, Presdl. Rank award, 1991. Mem. Nat. Assn. Ret. Fed. Employees (life), Sr. Execs. Assn. (life), Coun. Former Fed. Execs. (bd. dirs., 2004-), Sigma Xi, Tau Beta Pi, Sigma Gamma Epsilon, Masons, Shriners. Republican. Baptist. Home: 6819 Brian Michael Ct Springfield VA 22153-1004

MEIKLEJOHN, ALVIN J., JR., state legislator, lawyer, accountant; b. Omaha, June 18, 1923; m. Lorraine J. Meiklejohn; children; Pamela Ann, Shelley Lou, Bruce Ian, Scott Alvin. BS, U. Denver, JD, 1951; LLD (hon.), U. No. Colo., 2000. Mem. Colo. state Senate from 19th Dist., 1976-96, chmn. com. edn.; mem. Edn. Commn. of States, 1981-96; chmn. Colo. Commn. on Ach. in Edn., 1995, mem., 1993-96, Jefferson Sch. Dist. No. R-1 Bd. Edn., 1971-77, pres., 1973-77; commr. Commn. on Uniform State Laws, 1988-96. Dir. Red Rocks C.C. Found., Aviation and Space Ctr. of the Rockies. Capt. U.S. Army, 1940—46, maj. USAF, 1947—51. Mem. Arvada C. of C., Masons, Shriners, Transp. Lawyers Assn. (pres. 1972-73). Republican. Home: 7540 Kline Dr Arvada CO 80005-3732 Office: Jones & Keller PC 1625 Broadway Ste 1600 Denver CO 80202-4727 Office Phone: 303-573-1600. E-mail: ajmeiklejohn@joneskeller.com.

MEIKLEJOHN, MINDY JUNE (LORRAINE MEIKLEJOHN), political organizer, realtor; b. Staunton, Colo., June 9, 1929; d. Edward H. and Erna E. (Schwabe) Mindrup; m. Alvin J. Meiklejohn, Apr. 25, 1953; children: Pamela, Shelley, Bruce, Scott. Student, Ill. Bus. Coll., 1948, Red Rocks C.C., 1980-81. Pvt. sec. Ill. Liquor Commn., 1948-51, David M. Wilson, Ill. Sec. of State's Office, 1951-52; flight attendant Continental Airlines, 1952-53, pvt. sec. to mgr. flight svcs. office, 1953-54; orgnl. dir. Colo. Rep. Party, Denver, 1981-85, mem. Ctrl. Com., 1987—. Campaign coord. Hank Brown's Exploratory Campaign for Gov., 1985, mgr. Hank Brown for Congress, 1985-86; dep. campaign dir. Steve Schuck for Gov., 1985-86; vice chmn. 2d Congl. Ctrl. Com. Colo.; active campaigns; del., alt. to various county, state, dist. and nat. assemblies and convs.; Colo. chmn. Citizens for Am., 1987-96; realtor, sales assoc. Metro Brokers, Inc.; mem. polit. action com. Jefferson County Bd. Realtors; bd. dirs. Humphrey Meml. Park and Mus., 1996—, Sci. and Cultural Facilities Dist., 1989-94, Jefferson County chpt. Am. Cancer Soc., 1987-91, Jefferson Found., 1991-97; apptd. trustee Harry S. Truman scholarship Found., 1991; mem. Jefferson County Hist. Commn., Colo., 1974-82, pres., 1979; vol. Jefferson County Legal Aid Soc., 1970-74; vice chmn. Jefferson County Rep. Party, 1977-81, exec. com., 1987; vice chmn. Colo. State Rep. Party, 1981-85; chmn. Rep. Nat. Pilot Project on Volunteerism, 1981; mem. adv. coun. Peace Corps, 1982-84; sect. chmn. Jefferson County United Way Fund Drive; mem. exec. bd. Colo. Fedn. Rep. Women; pres. Operation Shelter, Inc., 1983-99; chair bd. dirs. Rocky Mountain Butterfly Consortium, 1996—; state chair Citizens for Am., 1987-96. Mem. Jefferson County Women's Rep. (edn. chmn. 1987-91). Home: 7540 Kline Dr Arvada CO 80005-3732

MEIKSIN, ZVI H. electrical engineering educator; b. 1926; BSEE, Israel Inst. Tech., Haifa, 1950, Dipl. Ing., 1951; MSEE, Carnegie Mellon U., 1953; PhDEE, U. Pitts., 1959. Registered profl. engr., Pa. Design engr. McGraw Edison, Cannonsburg, Pa., 1953-54; sr. project engr. Westinghouse Electric Corp., Pitts., 1956-59; prof. dept. elec. engring. U. Pitts., 1959-91, prof. emeritus, 1991—; pres. Transtek, Inc., Pitts., 1995—2004. Cons. entr. 33 orgns. in U.S., Europe, 1959—; expert witness in field, 1991-95. Author: Thin & Thick Films, 1976, Active Filter Design, 1990; co-author: Electronic Design, 1980, 84, Microprocessor Based Design, 1986; jour. referee profl. publs., 1970—; contbr. articles to profl. jours.; inventor, holder 7 patents in field. Fellow IEEE (award coms.); mem. Eta Kappa Nu, Sigma Xi. E-mail: meiksin@pitt.edu.

MEILAN, CELIA, food products executive; b. Bklyn., Jan. 21, 1920; d. Ventura Lorenzo and Susana (Prego) Meilan. Student, CCNY, 1943—46. Codes and ciphers translator security divsn. U.S. Censorship Office, N.Y.C., 1942-46; sec., treas. Albumina Supply Co., N.Y.C., 1946-55; co-founder, co-owner, sec., treas., fin. officer Internat. Proteins Corp. (now AnimalFeeds Internat. Corp.), Clark, NJ, 1955-86, exec. v.p., 1986-92, pres., 1992-94, chair emeritus, bd. dirs., 1994—, v.p., co-owner, 1998—. Bd. dirs. Pesquera Taboquilla, Panama City, Panama, Inversiones Pesqueras S.A., British Virgin Islands; v.p., bd. dirs. Atlantic Shipers of Tex. Inc., Port Arthur, 1989; bd. dirs. Atlantic Shippers Inc., Morehead City, NC, Empacadora Nacional S.A., Panama City; v.p., dir. AnimalFeeds, Internat., Santiago, Chile. Named One of Top 50 Women Bus. Owners, Working Woman Mag./Nat. Found. Women Bus. Owners, 1994, 1995. Mem.: Nat. Found. Women Bus. Owners, Spanish Benevolent Soc. (bd. dirs. 1955—62). Avocation: Avocations: travel, hand crafts, backgammon, puzzles. Fax: 732-827-0188.

MEILLER, JAMES R. music educator; b. Rochester, NY, May 23, 1956; m. Brook Meiller; children: Stephen, Andrew. MusB, SUNY, Potsdam, 1978; MusM, U. Okla., 1980. Standard Teaching Certificate Okla., 1981, Teaching Certificate NY, 1986. Dir. band Lexington (Okla.) H.S., 1980—83, Whittier Middle Sch., Norman, 1983—87; dir. band, orch. West Mid H.S., Norman, 1988—97; dir. instrumental music Norman (Okla.) H.S., 1997—. Grad. tchg. asst. U. Okla., Norman, 1978—80. Mem.: NEA, Nat. Assn. for Music Edn., Okla. Educators Assn., Am. Fedn. Musicians, Phi Mu Alpha Sinfonia. Office: Norman High School 911 W Main Norman OK 73069 Office Phone: 405-366-5812.

MEILMAN, EDWARD, physician; b. Boston, Apr. 6, 1915; s. Harry and Jennie (Sholofsky) M.; m. Rhoeda Berman, Mar. 6, 1946. AB, Harvard U., 1936, MD, 1940. Intern Mt. Sinai Hosp., N.Y.C., 1940-42; resident Beth Israel Hosp., Boston, 1946-48, assoc. in med. and med. research, 1948-53; chmn.

dept. medicine L.I. Jewish-Hillside Med. Center, New Hyde Park, N.Y., 1953-82, chmn. emeritus dept. medicine, 1982—. Prof. medicine SUNY, Stony Brook, 1971— Contbr. articles to profl. jours. Served with USAAF, 1942-46. Fellow N.Y. Acad. Medicine, N.Y. Acad. Scis.; mem. Am. Heart Assn. (fellow council clin. cardiology, council arteriosclerosis), Am. Fedn. Clin. Research, Harvey Soc., Am. Rheumatism Assn., Phi Beta Kappa, Alpha Omega Alpha. Clubs: Harvard (N.Y.C.); Harvard (L.I.). Democrat. Jewish. E-mail: emeilman@mindspring.com.

MEIMA, RALPH CHESTER, JR., retired diplomat, real estate company executive; b. Chgo., Mar. 29, 1927; s. Ralph Chester and Grace Georgine (Larson) Meima; m. Elizabeth B. Frazier, 1994; children from previous marriage: Ralph Chester III, Stephen H. BA, U. Ams., Mexico City, 1952; MBA, Am. U., 1964. With Carborundum Co., Perth Amboy, 1952-53, Johns-Manville Corp., N.Y.C., 1953-58, Security Storage Co., Washington, 1958-61, Dept. of Commerce, 1961-68; joined U.S. Fgn. Svc., 1968; consul gen. Marseille, France, 1977-80; on loan export devel. cons. State of Md., 1980-82; pres. Atlantic Eastern Corp., 1982-87, Phoenix Internat. Mktg. Corp., 1987-89; pres., chief exec. officer FTI Inc., Annapolis, Md., 1989-95; pres. DERCO, Inc., Balt., 1995—2002. In govt. rels. iJET Travel Risk Mgmt., Inc. With USN, 1945—46. Office: Champion Realty Commercial Inc 541 B Baltimore Annapolis Blvd Severna Park MD 21146 Personal E-mail: r.meima@worldnet.att.net.

MEINDL, JAMES DONALD, electrical engineering educator, administrator; b. Pitts., Apr. 20, 1933; s. Louis M. and Elizabeth F. (Steinhauser) M.; m. Frederica Ziegler, May 21, 1961; children: Peter James, Candace Ann. BS, Carnegie Mellon U., 1955, MS, 1956, PhD, 1958. Engr. Autonetics Co., Downey, Calif., 1957, Westinghouse Co., Pitts., 1958-59; head sect. microelectronics U.S. Army Electronics Command, Ft. Monmouth, N.J., 1959-62, chief br. semicondr. and microelectronics, 1962-65, dir. div. integrated electronics, 1965-67; assoc. prof. elec. engring. Stanford U., 1967-70, prof., 1970-84, John M. Fluke prof. elec. engring., 1984-86, assoc. dean research, 1984-86, dir. integrated circuits lab., 1969-84; co-founder Telesensory Systems Inc., 1971-84; dir. Electronics Labs., Stanford U., 1972-86, dir. Ctr. Integrated Systems, 1981-86; v.p. acad. affairs, provost Rensselaer Poly. Inst., Troy, N.Y., 1986-88, prof. sci. and engring., 1986-93, sr. v.p. acad. affairs, provost, 1988-93; Joseph M. Pettit Chair prof. microelectronics Ga. Inst. Tech., Atlanta, 1993—, dir. Microelectronics Rsch. Ctr., 1997—. Cons. to govt., industry. Author: Micropower Circuits, 1969; editor: Brief Lessons in High Technology, 1989; patentee integrated cir. field; contbr. numerous articles to profl. publs. Served to 1st lt. AUS, 1959-61. Recipient Arthur S. Flemming Commn. award Washington Jr. C. of C., 1967; J.J. Ebers award IEEE Electron Devices Soc., 1980, Univ. Rsch. award Semiconductor Industries Assn., 1999. Fellow IEEE (Solid State Circuits Coun. editor jour. 1966-71, Internat. Outstanding Paper ann. awards 1970, 75-78, Beatrice K. Winner award Internat. conf. 1988, solid State Circuits medal, 1989, Edn. medal 1990, Third Millenium medal 2000), AAAS, Am. Acad. Arts and Scis.; mem. AAUP, NAE, Am. Soc. Engr. Edn. (Benjamin Garver Lamme edal 1991), Electrochem. Soc., Biomed. Engring. Soc. (co-editor Annals of Biomed. Engring. 1976-80), Sigma Xi, Tau Beta Pi, Eta Kappa Nu, Phi Kappa Phi. Office: Ga Inst Tech Microelectronics Rsch Ctr 791 Atlantic Dr Atlanta GA 30332-0001

MEINDL, ROBERT JAMES, English language educator, poet; b. Wausau, Wis., Sept. 17, 1936; s. George Martin and Adeline Emilie (Goetsch) M.; m. Victoria Lynn Chavez; children: Karin Rose, George Andrew, Damian Kurt, Erika Wittmer, Christopher Smith, Gabrielle Remelia. BS, U. Wis., 1958; MA, U. Conn., 1960; PhD, Tulane U., 1965; postdoctoral studies, U. Calif., Berkeley, 1967—68, Goethe Inst., Liblar, Germany, 1970, U. Cologne, Germany, 1970. Teaching asst. U. Conn., Storrs, 1958—60; teaching fellow Tulane U., 1960—62; lectr. U. Wis., Green Bay, 1963—65; asst. prof. to full prof. English Calif. State U., Sacramento, 1965—2002, prof. emeritus English, 2002—. Translator: Studies in John Gower, 1981; book rev. editor Studia Mystica Jour., 1984-89; contbr. numerous articles to profl. jours. With USNR, 1953-61, 79-96. Nat. Endowment for the Humanities fellow Stanford U., 1982. Mem. MLA (life), Medieval Acad. Am. (life), Medieval Assn. of Pacific, Early English Text Soc., John Gower Soc., New Chaucer Soc. Home: 2301 Pennland Dr Sacramento CA 95825-0329 Office: Calif State U 6000 J St Sacramento CA 95819-2605 Office Phone: 916-278-7704.

MEINEL, ADEN BAKER, optics scientist; b. Pasadena, Calif., Nov. 25, 1922; s. John G. and Gertrude (Baker) M.; m. Marjorie Steele Pettit, Sept. 5, 1944; children: Carolyn, Walter, Barbara, Elaine, Edward, Mary, David. AB, U. Calif., Berkeley, 1947, PhD, 1949; DSc (hon.), U. Ariz., 1990. Assoc. prof. Yerkes Obs., U. Chgo., Williams Bay, Wis., 1950-58; dir. Kitt Peak Nat. Obs., Tucson, 1958-61; prof. U. Ariz., Tucson, 1961-85; dir. Steward Obs., Tucson, 1962-66, Optical Scis. Ctr., Tucson, 1966-73; Disting. scientist Jet Propulsion Lab., Pasadena, 1985-92; ret., 1993. Regent Calif. Luth. Coll., 1961-71; cons. USAF Spl. Projects Office, 1965-80. Co-author: Applied Solar Energy, 1976, Sunsets, Twilights and Evening Skies, 1983. Recipient Warner prize Am. Astron. Soc., 1954, Van Blesbroeck award Astron. Soc. Pacific, 1990, NASA Exceptional Scientific Achievement medal, 1993; Meinel bldg. U. Ariz., dedicated 1993 Fellow Am. Acad Arts and Scis., Optical Soc. Am. (pres. 1972-73, Adolph Lomb medal 1952, Ives medal 1980), Internat. Optical Engring. Soc. (Goddard award 1984, Kingslake medal, 1993, 2000, Gold medal 1997). Home: 1600 Shoreline Dr Santa Barbara CA 93109-2024 E-mail: ameinel@earthlink.net.

MEINERT, JOHN RAYMOND, investment banker, clothing manufacturing and retailing executive; b. White Cloud, Mich., Aug. 11, 1927; m. Joyce Macdonell, Nov. 5, 1955; children: Elizabeth Tinsman, Pamela Martin. Student, U. Mich., 1944-45; BS, Northwestern U., 1949. C.P.A., Ill., 1952. With Hart Schaffner & Marx/Hartmarx Corp., Chgo., 1950-90, exec. v.p., 1975-80, vice chmn., 1981-85, sr. vice chmn., 1985-86, chmn., 1987-90, chmn. emeritus, 1990—, also bd. dirs.; prin. investment banking J.H. Chapman Group, LLC, Rosemont, Ill., 1990—, chmn., 1995—. Bd. dirs. County Seat Stores, Inc., N.Y.C., 1998-99, The John Evans Club, BBB, Chgo. C.of C.; trustee Amalgamated Ins. Fund, 1980-90, Rotary Internat. Retirement Fund, 2000-02; dir. Evanston Hosp., 1988-94, Clothing Mfrs. Assn., pres., 1982-87, chmn. 1987-90; instr. acctg. Northwestern U., 1949; faculty Lake Forest Grad. Sch. Mgmt., 1994-95; arbitrator Am. Arbitration Assn., 1993—. Chmn. bus. adv. coun. U. Ill., 1989-90; mem. Fin. Acctg. Stds. Adv. Coun., 1989-92, Chgo. Coun. Fgn. Rels., Sisters City Com.; mem. adv. coun. Northwestern U. Kellogg Grad. Sch. Recipient Alumni Merit award Northwestern U. Kellogg Grad. Sch., 1989; named Humanitarian of Yr., Five Hosp. Found., 1995. Mem. AICPA (v.p. 1985-86, bd. dirs. 1975-78, coun. 1971-93, trustee benevolent fund 1992-95, gold medal 1987), Ill. CPA Soc. (pub. svc. award 1996, pres. 1982-83, bd. dirs. 1966-68, 81-84, hon. award), Chicagoland C. of C. (bd. dirs.), Rotary (pres. Chgo. 1989-90, trustee found. 1991-95, asst. dist. gov. 1997-2000), Univ. Club, Execs. Club, Rolling Green Country Club. Presbyterian (elder). Home: 634 N Ironwood Dr Arlington Heights IL 60004-5818 Office: J H Chapman Group LLC 9700 W Higgins Rd Rosemont IL 60018-4796 Office Phone: 773-693-4800.

MEINHARDT, VICKI R. communications executive, consultant; b. Topeka, Kans., Dec. 12, 1959; d. Sidney M. Meinhardt and Mary V. Moyer; m. Dylan W. Johnson, Sept. 20, 1986; children: Cameron, Connor, Callie. BA in Journalism and Mass Comm., BA in Polit. Sci. and Pub. Adminstrn., Kans. State U., 1984. Assoc. news dir. Sta. KMAN, Manhattan, Kans., 1984-86; reporter Sta. KFAB, Omaha, 1987-89; sr. staff aid Mayor City of Omaha, 1989-94; v.p. First Data Corp., Atlanta, 1994-99; owner Meinhardt Comms., Omaha, 1999—. Session mem. Presbyn. Ch. of the Master, Omaha, 1998-2001 bd. dirs. Planned Parenthood, Omaha, 1991. Recipient Silver Platter award Kans. chpt. Nat. Edn. Assn., 1985, 86, Spot News award AP, 1985, Crystal award The Communicator, 1997. Mem. Internat. Assn. Bus. Communicators (silver quill award 1996). Republican. Avocations: woodworking, my family, church, scrapbooking.

MEINHOLD, CHARLES BOYD, health physicist; b. Boston, Nov. 1, 1934; s. Russell and Jane (Boyd) M.; m. Anne Elizabeth DuVally, Oct. 20, 1956; children: Anne Frances, Patricia Marie, Michael John, Peter Russell, Catherine Louise. BS in Physics, Providence Coll., 1956; postgrad., U. Rochester, 1956-57. Staff scientist health physics div. Brookhaven Nat. Lab., Upton, NY, 1957-72, head, sr. health physicist safety and environ. div., 1972-88, sr.scientist, div. head, 1988-91, sr. scientist radiol. sci. divsn. Dept. Advanced Tech., 1991-2001; guest scientist Dept. of Non-Proliferation and Nat. Security, 2001—. Mem. Internat. Commn. on Radiol. Protection, 1978-2001, vice chmn., 1992-2001, emeritus mem., 2002-; mem. Nat. Coun. on Radiol. Protection and Measurement, 1977-2001, pres., 1991-2002, pres. emeritus, 2002—. Pres. South Haven Bd. Edn., Brookhaven, N.Y., 1965-87. Named Hon. Prof., China Inst. Atomic Energy, 1995, China Inst. Radiation Protection, 1997. Fellow Health Physics Soc. (pres. 1980-81); mem. Internat. Radiation Protection Assn. (v.p. 1988-92, pres. 1992-96). Roman Catholic. Avocations: woodworking, sailing. Home: 41 Old South Country Rd Brookhaven NY 11719-9526 Office: Brookhaven Nat Lab Bldg 197D Upton NY 11973-5000 E-mail: cbmeinhold@optonline.net.

MEINIG, DONALD WILLIAM, geography educator; b. Palouse, Wash., Nov. 1, 1924; s William August and Annie (Malsed) M.; m. Lee McAuliffe, June 29, 1946; children: Laurel, Kristin, Lee. BS, Georgetown U., 1948; MA, U. Wash., 1950, PhD, 1953; DHL (hon.), Syracuse U., 1994. From asst. prof. to assoc. prof. U. Utah, Salt Lake City, 1950-59; assoc. prof. geography Syracuse U., N.Y., 1959-73, Maxwell prof. geography, 1973-89, Maxwell rsch. prof., 1990—. Lectr. St. Andrews U., Scotland, 1973, Charles Homer Haskins lectr. ACLS, 1992; vis. prof. Hebrew U., Jerusalem, 1974; adv. editor Wadsworth Pub. Co., 1957-61, Harper & Row, N.Y.C., 1965-83; chief editl. cons. Nat. Geog. Soc., Washington, 1982-88; councilor Am. Geog. Soc., 1993-96. Author: On the Margins of the Good Earth, 1962, The Great Columbia Plain, 1968, Imperial Texas, 1969, Southwest, 1971, The Shaping of America, Vol. 1: Atlantic America 1492-1800, 1986, Vol. 2: Continental America 1800-1867, 1993, Vol. 3: Transcontinental America 1850-1915, 1998; editor: The Interpretation of Ordinary Landscapes, 1979. Mem. N.Y. Council for Humanities, 1979-86. Served to 2d lt. U.S. Army, 1943-46. Recipient Emil and Kathleen Sick award in Western History, 1968, award of Merit Seattle Hist. Soc., 1968, award of Merit Am. Assn. State and Local History, 1969, Summerfield G. Roberts award Sons Republic of Tex., 1969, Faculty Enrichment award Can Embassy, 1980, Master Tchr. award Nat. Coun. for Geog. Edn., 1986, Charles P. Daly medal Am. Geog. Soc., 1986; Fulbright rsch. scholar U. Adelaide, 1958; Guggenheim fellow, 1966-67, NEH fellow, 1987-88. Fellow Brit. Acad. (corr.); mem. Assn. Am. Geographers (councilor 1965-67, Meritorious Contbn. award), Am. Antiquarian Soc. Office: Syracuse U Dept Geography Syracuse NY 13244-0001

MEININGER, STEVEN ROBERT, music educator; b. Ft. Benning, Ga., July 20, 1945; s. Robert Alexander and Marie Angela Meininger; m. Lynn Marie Smith, Apr. 19, 1980; children: Michael, Heidi, Katherine, Whitney. BA, U. No. Colo., 1967, MA, 1971. Tchr. Golden Jr. HS, Colo., 1968, Manning Jr. HS, 1968—73, Green Mountain HS, Lakewood, Colo., 1973—99; assoc. dir. Colo. Chorale, 1971—. Mem.: Colo. Music Educators Assn. (pres. 2004—), Nat. Assn. for Music Edn., Am. Choral Dirs. Assn. Home: 8195 W 20th Ave Denver CO 80214

MEINTSMA, PETER EVANS, history and political science educator; b. Maple Lake, Minn., Apr. 1, 1928; s. Peter and Hazel Irene (Davis) M.; m. Senora LaRea Strouse, Dec. 10, 1955; children: Kevin Jon, Kurt Robert. MA, U. Minn., 1964. Instr. Northwestern Coll., Mpls., 1958-62, 64-66, U. Wis., Superior, 1963-64; prof. Anoka Ramsey C.C., Coon Rapids, Minn., 1966—2001. Mayor City of Crystal, Minn., 1974-84, 91—; chmn. Met. Waste Control Commn., St. Paul, 1984-88; bd. mem. Assn. Met. Municipalities, 1999—; mem. steering com. cmty. and econ. devel. Nat. League of Cities. Recipient Cert. for Reflective Leadership Humphrey Inst., 1980; named Outstanding Educator of Am., 1971. Avocations: gardening, biking, music.

MEIS, NANCY RUTH, marketing executive; b. Iowa City, Aug. 6, 1952; d. Donald J. and Theresa (Dee) M.; m. Paul L. Wenske, Oct. 14, 1978; children: Alexis Wenske Burdick, Christopher Meis Wenske. BA, Clarke Coll., 1974; MBA, U. Okla., 1981. Cultural program supr. City of Dubuque, Iowa, 1974—76; from cmty. svc. dir. to program dir. State Arts Coun. of Okla. City, 1976—79; mgr. Cimarron Circuit Opera Co., Norman, Okla., 1979—82; accout exec. Bell System, Kansas City, Mo., 1980; mgr. spl. svc. Children Internat., Kansas City, Mo., 1983—86, dir. mktg. and fund raising, 1986—87, dir. devel., 1987—88, v.p. devel., 1988—90; dir. mktg., consulting svc. uni-media divsn. Universal Press Syndicate, Kansas City, Mo., 1990—95; dir. mktg. universal new media divsn. Andrews McMeel Universal, 1996—2000; v.p. content and licensing Active Buddy, Inc., N.Y.C., 2000—01; pres., co-founder Electric Prairie, LLC, 2001—. Pres. Electric Idea Cons.; cons., spkr. in field. Co-founder Girls to Women. Office Phone: 913-383-0982.

MEIS, PAUL JEAN, obstetrics and gynecology educator; b. Sioux City, Iowa, Oct. 29, 1934; s. Lee Francis and Dorothy (Trexlar) M.; m. Marcia Rose Donsker, June 28, 1958; children: Steven James, Douglas John. BS, U. Iowa, 1956, MD, 1959. Diplomate Am. Bd. Ob-Gyn., Am. Bd. Maternal-Fetal Medicine. Intern Martin Army Hosp., Ft. Benning, Ga., 1959-60; resident ob/gyn. SUNY Upstate Med. Ctr., Syracuse, 1962-65; pvt. practice, La Crosse, Wis., 1965-75; fellow Harbor Gen. Hosp., Torrance, Calif., 1975-77; asst. prof. dept. ob-gyn. Bowman Gray Sch. Medicine Wake Forest U., Winston-Salem, N.C., 1977-80, assoc. prof., 1980-85; prof. Bowman Gray Sch. Medicine Wake Forest U. Sch. Medicine, Winston-Salem, N.C., 1985—. Capt. M.C., U.S. Army, 1959-62. Office: Wake Forest U Sch Medicine Dept Ob-Gyn Medical Center Blvd Winston Salem NC 27157-0001 E-mail: pmeis@wfubmc.edu.

MEISEL, ALAN, law educator; b. Newark, Dec. 24, 1946; s. Stanley and Beatrice (Katz) M.; m. Linda S. Serody, Mar. 6, 1982; children: Matthew, Julia. BA, Yale U., 1968, JD, 1972. Bar: Conn. 1972, Pa. 1973, U.S. Dist. Ct. Conn. 1972, U.S. Dist. Ct. (we. dist.) Pa. 1973, U.S. Ct. Appeals (3d cir.) 1985. Prof. psychiatry U. Pitts., 1973—, prof. law, 1976—, Dickie, McCamey Chilcote prof. bioethics/law and psychiatry, 1995—, dir. Ctr. for Bioethics and Health Law, 1986—. Asst. dir. for legal studies Pres.'s Commn. for Study of Ethical Problems in Medicine and Biomed. and Behavioral Rsch., Washington, 1982; mem. ethics working group Presdl. Task Force on Healthcare Reform, 1993; mem. adv. coun. NHLBI, 1998—. Author: The Right to Die, 1989, 2d edit., 1995, 3d edit. 2004; co-author: Informed Consent: A Study of Decision Making in Psychiatry, 1984, Informed Consent: Legal Theory and Clinical Practice, 1987; contbr. articles to legal and med. jours. Grantee NIMH, grantee Pres.'s Commn. for Study of Ethical Problems in Medicine and Biomed. and Behavioral Rsch., 1981-82, Founds. Fund for Rsch. in Psychiatry grantee, 1979-82, Legal Svcs. Corp. grantee, 1985-87; fellow Hastings Ctr.; award for The Right to Die Am. Assn. Publs., 1989. Office: U Pitts Sch Law Pittsburgh PA 15260

MEISEL, DAN, chemist; b. Tel Aviv, July 4, 1943; s. Arie and Mariasha Miriam (Ribak) M.; m. Osnat Meisel, Dec. 30, 1965; children: Einat, Omer. BSc, Hebrew U., 1967, MSc, 1969, PhD, 1974. Prof. chemistry U. Notre Dame, Ind., 1998—, dir. Radiation Lab., 1998—2004. Adv. bd.: Jour. Phys. Chem., 1993—2002; editor: Photochem. Energy Conversion, 1989, Semiconductors Nanoclusters, 1997. Mem. AAAS, Am. Chem. Soc., Am. Nuclear Soc. Office: U Notre Dame Radiation Lab Notre Dame IN 46556-0579 E-mail: dani@nd.edu.

MEISEL, GEORGE VINCENT, lawyer; b. St. Louis, Sept. 24, 1933; s. Leo Otto and Margaret (Duggan) M.; m. Joy C. Cassin, May 18, 1963 BS summa cum laude, St. Louis U., 1956, JD cum laude, 1958. Bar: Mo. 1958. Assoc. Grand Peper & Martin, St. Louis, 1961-64, ptnr., 1965; jr. ptnr. Bryan Cave McPheeters & McRoberts, St. Louis, 1966-69; ptnr. Bryan Cave, LLP, St. Louis, 1970-2000, of counsel, 2000—. Served to 1st lt. USAF, 1958-61 Mem. ABA, Bar Assn. Met. St. Louis, Mo. Bar Assn. Clubs: Saint Louis, Mo. Athletic (St. Louis). Roman Catholic. Home: 2029 S Warson Rd Saint Louis MO 63124-1151 Office Phone: 314-259-2268. E-mail: gvmeisel@bryancavellp.com.

MEISEL, JOHN, political scientist; b. Vienna, Oct. 23, 1923; s. Fryda and Ann M. BA, U. Toronto, 1948, MA, 1950; PhD in Polit. Sci., London Sch. Econs., 1959; LLD, Brock U., 1983, U. Guelph, 1985, Carleton U., 1990, U. Toronto, 1993, Queen's U., 1996, U. Regina, 1999, U. Calgary, 2000; DU (hon.), U. Ottawa, 1983; D of Social Scis. (hon.), Laval U., 1988; LittD (hon.), U. Waterloo, 1998. Head dept. polit. studies Queen's U., Kingston, Ont., Can., 1963-67, Hardy prof. polit. sci., 1963-80, Sir Edward Peacock prof. polit. sci., 1983-93, prof. emeritus. Former chmn. Can. Radio-TV and Telecomms. Commn.; moderator symposia on finding common grounds for polit. issues confronting Yugoslavia, UN, Vienna, 1995. Author: The Canadian General Election of 1957, 1962, Papers on the 1962 Election, 1964, Ethnic Relations in Canadian Voluntary Associations, 1972, Working Papers on Canadian Politics, 1975; editor: Internat. Polit. Sci. Rev., 1979-95, (with Jean Laponce) Debating the Constitution/Débat sur la constitution, 1994. Decorated companion Order of Can.; recipient Killam award Can Coun., 1968-73. Fellow Royal Soc. Can. (pres. 1992-95); mem. Univ. Club (Toronto). Home: Colimaison Tichborne ON Canada K0H 2V0 Office: Queen's U Kingston ON Canada K7L 3N6 Office Phone: 613-533-6227. E-mail: meiselj@post.queensu.ca.

MEISEL, MARTIN, English and comparative literature educator; b. NYC, Mar. 22, 1931; s. Joseph and Sally (Rössler) Mörsel; m. Martha Sarah Winkley, Dec. 22, 1957; children: Maude Frances, Andrew Avram, Joseph Stoddard AB, Queens Coll., 1952; MA, Princeton U., 1957, PhD, 1960; postgrad., U. Rome, 1959. Instr. English Rutgers U., New Brunswick, N.J., 1957-58; instr., asst. prof., assoc. prof. Dartmouth Coll., Hanover, N.H., 1959-65; prof. English U. Wis., Madison, 1965-68; prof. English and comparative lit. Columbia U., N.Y.C., 1968—, Brander Matthews prof. dramatic lit., 1987—, chmn. dept., 1980-83, 99-01, acting v.p. arts and scis., 1986-87, v.p. arts and scis., 1989-93, prof. emeritus, 2004—. Trustee Columbia U. Press, 1990-94. Author: Shaw and the 19th Century Theater, 1963, Realizations: Narrative, Pictorial, and Theatrical Arts in 19th Century England (George Freedley Meml. award Theater Libr. Assn. 1984, Barnard Hewitt award Am. Theatre Assn. 1984), 1983; mem. editorial and adv. bds. Jour. Victorian Studies, PMLA, Jour. Contemporary Lit., Bull. Rsch. in the Humanities, 19th Century Contexts. Served with U.S. Army, 1954-56 Fellow Guggenheim Found., 1963-64, 1987-88, Am. Council of Learned Socs., 1970-71, Inst. for Advanced Studies in the Humanities, Edinburgh, 1977, Huntington Library and Art Gallery, 1978, 80, 83, Nat. Humanities Ctr., 1983-84, Wilson Ctr., Smithsonian Instn., 1987-88. Mem. MLA, Am. Soc. Theatre Rsch., North Am. Victorian Studies Assn., Assn. of Historians of 19 Century Art, Century Assn., Internat. Shaw Soc. Home: 18 Bacon Hill Rd Pleasantville NY 10570-3502 Office: Columbia U 611 Philosophy Hall New York NY 10027 Business E-Mail: mm28@columbia.edu.

MEISEL, PERRY, English educator; b. Shreveport, La., Jan. 26, 1949; s. I.S. and Rebecca (Abramson) M. BA, Yale U., 1970, MPhil, 1973, PhD, 1975. Asst. prof. English NYU, N.Y.C., 1975-81, assoc. prof. English, 1981-87, prof. English, 1987—. Author: Thomas Hardy, 1972, The Absent Father, 1980, The Myth of the Modern, 1987, The Cowboy and the Dandy, 1998; co-editor: Bloomsbury/Freud, 1985; editor: Freud, 1981. Mem. MLA, AAUP, PEN. Office: NYU Dept English 19 University Pl New York NY 10003-4556

MEISELS, GERHARD GEORGE, academic administrator, chemist, educator; b. Vienna, May 11, 1931; came to U.S., 1951, naturalized, 1961; s. Leo and Adele Josefa Maria (Seehofer) M.; m. Sylvia Claire Knopsnider, June 28, 1958; 1 dau., Laura Germaine. Student, U. Vienna, 1949-51, 52-53; MS, U. Notre Dame, Ind., 1952, PhD, 1956. Postdoctoral rsch. assoc. U. Notre Dame, 1955-56; chemist Gulf Oil Corp., Pitts., 1956-59; part-time instr. Carnegie Inst. Tech., Pitts., 1956-58; chemist nuclear divsn. Union Carbide Corp., Tuxedo, N.Y., 1959-63, asst. group leader, 1964-65; assoc. prof. U. Houston, 1965-70, prof., 1970-75, dept. chmn., 1973-75; prof., chmn. dept. chemistry U. Nebr., Lincoln, 1975-81, dean Coll. Arts and Scis., 1981-88; provost, COO U. South Fla., Tampa, 1988-94; dir. Coalition Sci. Literacy, 1994—, Suncoast Area Ctr. for Edn. Enhancement (SACEE), 1996-99. Cons. Union Carbide Corp., Gearhart-Owen Industries. Editor (spl. issue) Jour. Radiation Physics and Chemistry, 1980; contbr. writings in field to profl. publs. Sec., pres. Ramsey (N.J.) Jr. C. of C., 1959-64; active rsch. bd. All Children's Hosp.; chmn. Fla. Coalition for Improving Math. and Sci. Edn., 1998—, chmn. interim exec. dir. Fulbright fellow, Smith-Mundt fellow, 1951-52; sr. fellow Sci. Rsch. Coun., Eng., 1976. Mem. Am. Chem. Soc. (com. chmn.), Am. Soc. for Mass Spectrometry (charter, com. chmn., v.p. 1984-86, pres. 1986-88, bd. dirs. 1988-90), Fla. Acad. Scis., AAAS, Am. Phys. Soc., Coun. Sci. Soc. Pres. (exec. bd. 1989-92, chmn. elect 1990, chmn. 1991, chmn. com. on sci. priorities), Nat. Alliance State Sci. and Math. Coalitions (bd. dirs. 1999—), Coun. for Chem. Rsch. (bd. dirs. 1982-85), Conformation Judges Assn. Fla. (pres. 1996—), Fla. Higher Edn. Consortium Math. and Sci. (ctrl. steering com. 1995—, chmn. 1998-2000), Houston Kennel Club (bd. dirs. 1968-70), Cornhusker Kennel Club (pres., bd. dirs., del. to Am. Kennel Club 1976-81), St. Petersburg Dog Fanciers Assn. (sec. 1996-98, 2000—, del. to Am. Kennel Club 1998—), Sigma Xi. Home: PO Box 1347 Thonotosassa FL 33592-1347 Office: U South Fla 4202 E Fowler Ave/HMS 456 Tampa FL 33620 Office Phone: 813-974-7183. Business E-Mail: meisels@csl.usf.edu.

MEISELS, JUDITH A. piano instructor, classical pianist; b. Budapest, Hungary, July 23, 1938; came to U.S., 1957; d. Stephan and Margaret Benjamin; m. Irving M. Meisels, May 30, 1964; children: Jason D. Meisels, Adrienne C. Meisels. Diploma in piano performance, Buda Acad. Music and Budapest Conservatory of Music, Budapest, Hungary, 1950-54; student, Franz Liszt Acad. Music, Budapest, 1954-56; Matura diploma in Humanities and Natural Scis., Veres Palne Women's Gymnaziun & Coll., Budapest, 1956; student, Bklyn. Coll., N.Y.C., 1958-61; Piano pedagogy cert., New Sch. Music Studies, Princeton, NJ, 1977; postgrad., Westminster Choir Coll., Princeton, 1984—90. Cert. profl. tchr. music, N.J. Music Tchrs. Assn., nat. cert. profl. tchr. music Music Tchrs. Nat. Assn. Mem. exec. bd. rsch., planning and selecting internat. artists series, Spectrum Com., Monmouth County Arts Coun., 1980-85; cultural com., exec. bd. internat. concert and lecture series Monmouth County "Y", 1971-93; spkr., lectr. in field; panelist, conductor master classes Piano Tchrs.' Groups, N.Y.C., 1976-99; adjudicator high level prestigious piano auditions and competitions. Piano performances: classical solo and ensemble Radio Budapest, Hungary, Ministerium of Fgn. Affairs, 1948-49, Franz Liszt Acad., Budapest, 1948-56, solo performances Hungary, Austria, U.S.A., 1954-56, 73-80. Grantee Franz Liszt Acad., 1956-57. Mem. Music Tchrs. Nat. Assn., N.J. Music Tchrs. Assn., Leschetizky Assn. N.Y., Piano Tchrs. Cong. N.Y., Nat. Guild Piano Tchrs., Shore Music Educators Assn.(exec. bd., publicity chair 1976-80, recording sec. 1987-93), Cecilian Music Club of Freehold, N.J. Avocations: power walking, swimming, reading, music, arts. Studio: Ocean Twp Area 14 Joanna Ct Deal Park NJ 07723-1534

MEISELS, MARLENE, literacy and special education educator, editor; b. Chgo., July 4, 1952; d. Martin and Miriam G. Meisels. BA, Univ. Ill., Chgo., 1974, MEd, 1980; PhD, Univ. N.C., Chapel Hill, N.C., 1997. Asst. prof. Nat. Louis Univ., Chgo., 1989—94, dir. NLU lang. program, 1994—95; dir. tchg. learning ctr. Elgn (Ill.) CC, 1995—96; literacy instr. Durham Tech. CC, Durham, NC, 1992—96; sr. literacy & leadership devel. advisor Designs for Change, Chgo., 1992—2001; prin. ednl. mgr. A Word to the Wise, Chgo., 1996—; formal edn. programs mgr. Lincoln Pk. Zoo, Chgo., 2003—. Bd. dirs. Cmty. Counselling Ctrs. of Chgo., 2003—, Life Learners Inc., Highland Pk., Ill., 2003—. Editor: Schooling in America: Cases, Studies and Comment, 2000; editor: (mng.) (jour.) The High School Jour., 1994—96; contbr. articles pub. to profl. jour. Editl. rev. bd. Internat. Reading Assn., Newark, Del., 2002—; aux. fund raising com. Cmty. Counselling Ctrs. of Chgo., 2004; inclusion adv. com. Lincoln Pk. Zoo, Chgo., 2003—. Mem.: Nat. Coun. of Tchrs. of English, Internat. Reading Assn. Avocations: swimming, animal ethics, ornithology. Office: A Word to the Wise 4343 N Clarendon Ste 2504 Chicago IL 60613 Office Phone: 773-710-3867.

MEISEN, AXEL, chemical engineering educator, university dean; b. Hamburg, Germany, Oct. 17, 1943; came to Can., 1966; s. Paul and Emmi (Schaaf) M.; children: Nadine Ramona, Kai Noel. B.Sc., Imperial Coll., 1965; M.Sc., Calif. Inst. Tech., 1966; PhD, McGill U., 1970. Registered profl. engr., B.C. Asst. prof. chem. engring. U. B.C., Vancouver, 1969-74, assoc. prof., 1975-79, assoc. dean, 1976-85, prof., 1979-99, dean, 1985-97; environ. engr. Imperial Oil Enterprise Ltd., Sarnia, Ont., 1974-75; pres., vice chancellor Meml. U. Newfoundland, St. John's, 1999—. Environ. engr. Imperial Oil Enterprise, Ltd., Sarnia, Ont, 1974-75. Contbr. articles to profl. jours. Chmn. Can. Engring. Accreditation Bd., 1989-90. Fellow Chem. Inst. Can., Instn. Engrs. Ireland, Can. Acad. Engring.; mem. Can. Soc. Chem. Engrs. (pres. 1994), Assn. Profl. Engrs. B.C., Vancouver Club. Office: Meml Univ Press Off Saint John's NF Canada A1C 5S7 E-mail: president@mun.ca.

MEISENHEIMER, SHARON LEE, nurse; b. Princeton, Ill., Apr. 15, 1937; d. Lester Harry and Dorothy Marie Carlson; m. Lester Lee Meisenheimer, June 22, 1958; children: Timothy, Connie, Joel, LuAnn. Nursing diploma, Ft. Wayne Luth. Sch. of Nursing, 1957; studied at, Ft. Wayne Bible Coll., 1957—58, Summer Inst. of Linguistics, 1959. Fl. nurse/newborn nursery Paradise Valley Hosp., Nat. City, Calif., 1958—59; missionary nurse Missionary Ch., World Ptnrs., Cayapas River, Ecuador, 1959—96; night supr./staff nurse Colonial Hall Ctr. Nursing Home, Princeton, Ill., 1997—2004. Missionary nurse/ch. planting Missionary Ch. World, 1959—97; running jungle dispensary/govt. health projects Ptnrs. in Ecuador, S.A. Contbr. articles. Recipient five awards for svc. to children, young people and the cmty., Missionary Ch. of Ecuador. Missionary Ch. Avocations: gardening, music, reading, sewing, cooking. Home: 14702 2400 N Ave Walnut IL 61376

MEISENHELDER, ROBERT JOHN, II, pharmaceutical company executive; b. 1943; BS, U.S. Air Force Acad.; JD, Harvard U. Bar: Mich., 1975. V.p., assoc. gen. coun. Pharmacia & Upjohn, Inc., Kalamazoo. Office: Pharmacia & Upjohn Inc 7000 Portage Rd Kalamazoo MI 49001-0102

MEISINGER, LOUIS M. lawyer; b. NYC, Dec. 12, 1942; BA, UCLA, 1964, JD, 1967. Bar: Calif. 1968. Atty. Hill Wynne Troop & Meisinger, LA; exec. v.p., gen. coun. Walt Disney Co., Burbank, Calif., 1997—2003; sr. advisor Sheppard, Mullin, Richter & Hampton, LLP, Los Angeles, Calif., 2003—. Editor: UCLA Law Rev., 1965-67. Recipient Entertainment Lawyer of the Yr., Beverly Hills Bar Assoc./ Calif., 1999. Mem. State Bar Calif., L.A. County Bar Assn., Century City Bar Assn., Order of Coif, Phi Beta Kappa, Sigma Delta Pi, Phi Delta Phi. Office: Sheppard Mullin Richter & Hampton 333 S Hope St Los Angeles CA 90071

MEISLIN, HARVEY WARREN, emergency healthcare physician, professional society administrator; b. Rochester, NY, June 19, 1946; s. Milton M. and Celia (Weiner) M.; m. Loretta Marie Bielski, Apr. 30, 1977; children: Justin, Jonathan, Megan. BS in Chemistry, Purdue U., 1968; MD, Ind. U., 1972. Diplomate Am. Bd. Emergency Medicine, Am. Bd. Med. Spltys. (del. 1990, fin. com. 1992, exec. com. 1994); cert. cardiac life support, ACLS instr., advanced trauma life support instr. Intern U. Chgo. Hosps. and Clinics, 1973-75, resident, 1975-77, dir. div. emergency medicine, 1975-77; asst. prof. internal and emergency medicine UCLA Emergency Med. Ctr., 1977-80, resident dir. emergency medicine, 1977-80, assoc. dir., 1977-80; assoc. prof. dept. surgery emergency medicine Coll. Medicine, U. Ariz., Tucson, 1980-83, assoc. prof., 1983-85; assoc. head, dept. surgery U. Ariz., Tucson, 1995—; prof. Coll. Medicine, U. Ariz., Tucson, 1985—; chief emergency medicine U. Ariz., Tucson, 1980—; chief sect. emergency medicine dept. surgery Ariz. Health Scis. Ctr., Tuscon, 1980—, dir. emergency svcs. Univ. Med. Ctr., 1980—, dir. Ariz. Emergency Med. Rsch. Ctr., 1990—; med. dir. MEDTRAN-Aeromed. Ambulance Corp., 1985-88. Mem. emergency med. svc. com. Mid-South Health Planning Orgn., Chgo., 1974; coord. Mid-South Disaster Plan, Chgo., 1974; mem. com. revision of Disaster Plan Billings Hosp., 1974-76; mem. faculty Am. Hosp. Assn. Inst. Disaster Preparedness, 1975; vis. prof. dept. emergency medicine Denver Gen. Hosp., 1977; bd. trustees Emergency Med. Found., 1978-81; mem. med. adv. com. L.A. City Fire Dept., 1979-80; chmn.-elect Tuscon Met. EMS Coun., 1983-84, chmn., 1984-85; chmn. Tuscon Pre-Hosp. Care Coun., 1981; mem. trauma steering com. So. Ariz. Regional Trauma Ctr., 1986-88; mem. ETHICON emergency physicians adv. panel Johnson & Johnson Co., 1987-92; presenter and lectr. in field. Editor: Purdue Rivet, 1971-72, abstract sect. Annals Emergency Medicine, 1982-90, EMS sect., 1989-90; guest editor: Topics in Emergency Medicine, 1979; sci. editor: Drug Therapy, 1984—; mem. editorial bd.: Annals Emergency Medicine, 1977-90, Emergency Dept. News, 1979-87, Emergency Dept. and Ambulatory Care News, 1987-90, Digest of Emergency Medicine Care, 1981-87; contbr. articles and revs. to profl. jours. Mem. select med. adv. com. City of Tucson, 1981, med. dir. emergency med. svcs., 1982-83, 84-85; bd. dirs. so. Ariz. divsn. Am. Heart Assn., 1985-90; mem. emergency cardiac care com. so. divsn. Ariz. Heart Assn., 1986-88; mem. med. dirs. commn., dept. health svcs. State of Ariz., 1992—, also mem. Mex. border commn., 1991—; mem. med. direction commn. State of Ariz. (appointed by gov.), 1993—. Recipient Pres. gavel and plaque Am. Bd. Emergency Medicine. Fellow Am. Coll. Emergency Physicians (State of Ill. chpt.): mem. sci. adv. com. 1975, mem. sci. edn. com. 1975-76, mem. grad./undergrad. edn. com. 1976-79, mem. ethics com. 1976-77, mem. surgery/trauma task force bd. cert. exam. 1976-77, bd. dirs. 1976-77, chmn. edn. com. 1976-77; State of Calif. chpt.: mem. hosp. and contract com. 1978-79, mem. EMS and legis. com. 1978-79, mem. spl. task force on emergency dept. distbn. 1979-80, mem. membership com. 1979-80, mem. legis. com. 1979-80, mem. sci. assembly planning com. 1980-81, bd. dirs. 1979-81, mem. rsch. com. 1981; State of Ariz. chpt.: bd. dirs. 1982-92, 92—, chmn. pub. rels. com. 1982-83, v.p. and sec. 1983-84, counselor 1984-87, mem. credentials com. 1986-91, chmn. 1987-90, mem. test com. 1986-87, mem. ad hoc com. for combined tng. 1987-88, chmn. task force on emergency medicine 1987-89, mem. exec. com. 1988—, mem. fin. com. 1988—, sec./treas. 1989-90, mem. EMS com. 1990—, pres.-elect 1990-91, pres. 1991-92, chair stds. com., mem. faculty Nat. Sci. Assembly 1974-76, Cert. Appreciation award 1990); mem. APHA, Am. Coll. Physician Execs., Am. Trauma Soc., Am. Bd. Med. Specialties (mem. fin. com. 1992, mem. exec. com. 1995—, pres., 2004), Ariz. Med. Assn., Pima County Med. Soc. (bd. dirs. 1991—), Phi Rho Sigma. Avocations: racquetball, golf, skiing, automobiles. Office: U Ariz Med Ctr Sect Emergency Med 1501 N Campbell Ave Tucson AZ 85724-0001

MEISNER, MARY JO, editor; b. Chgo., Dec. 24, 1951; d. Robert Joseph and Mary Elizabeth (Casey) M.; 1 child, Thomas Joseph Gradel. BS in Journalism, U. Ill., 1974, MS in Journalism, 1976. Copy editor Wilmington (Del.) News Jour., 1975-76, labor and bus. reporter, 1976-79; labor and gen. assignment reporter Phila. Daily News, 1979, city editor, 1979-83, met. editor, 1983-85; PM city editor San Jose (Calif.) Mercury News, 1985-86, met. editor, 1986-87; city editor The Washington Post, 1987-90; mng. editor The Ft. Worth Star-Telegram, 1991-93; editor and v.p. The Milw. Jour., 1993-95; editor, sr. v.p The Milw. Jour. Sentinel, 1995-97; editor, vice chmn. Cmty. Newspaper Co., 1997—. Mem. AP Mng. Editors (bd. dirs. 1992-95), Am. Soc. Newspaper Editors, Internat. Press Inst. (bd. dirs. 1994-2000, Pulitzer prize juror 1994, 96), Mass. Newspaper Pubs. Assn. (bd. dirs. 1997—). Office: Cmty Newspaper Co 254 2nd Ave Needham MA 02494-2811

MEISSNER, EDWIN BENJAMIN, JR., retired real estate broker; b. St. Louis, Dec. 27, 1918; s. Edwin B. and Edna (Rice) Meissner; m. Nina Renard, Dec. 17, 1946; children: Edwin Benjamin III, Wallace, Robert; 1 child, Donald. BS, U. Pa., 1940. Joined St. Louis Car Co., 1934, asst. to pres., v.p., exec. v.p., 1950-56, pres., gen. mgr., 1956-61; pres. St. Louis Car div. Gen. Steel Industries, Inc., 1961-67; sr. v.p., dir. Gen. Steel Industries, Inc., 1968-74; v.p. Bakewell Corp., 1974-85; real estate broker, v.p. Hilliker Corp., St. Louis, 1985-96. Mem. pres.' coun. St. Louis U.; bd. dirs. Washington U. Med. Ctr. Redevel. Corp., Barnard Free Skin and Cancer Hosp.; past bd. dirs. James S. McDonnell USO; overseer St. Louis Symphony Soc.; hon. dir. Humane Soc. Mo.; v.p. Gateway Ctr. Met. St. Louis; chmn. Ladue (Mo.) Police and Fire Commn.; mem. Jefferson Nat. Expansion Meml. Commn.; mil. affairs com. Regional Commerce. Mem. Am. Ordnance Assn. (life), Internat. Assn. Chiefs of Police (assoc.), Mo. Assn. Chiefs of Police, Mo. Athletics Club, Westwood Country Club, Bridlespur Hunt Club, St. Louis Club, Beta Gamma Sigma. Office: 509 Olive St Ste 608 Saint Louis MO 63101-1855

MEISSNER, KATHERINE GONG, city official; b. Stockton, Calif., 1955; BA, U. Phoenix, Stockton, Calif., 1999. Mem. comty. planning dept. staff City of Stockton, Calif., 1982-85, exec. asst. city clk., 1985-96, city clk., 1996—. Office: City Stockton Office City Clk 425 N El Dorado St Stockton CA 95202-1997

MEISTAS, MARY THERESE, endocrinologist, diabetes researcher; b. Grand Rapids, Mich., July 22, 1949; d. Frank Peter and Anne Therese (Karsokas) M. MD, U. Mich., 1975. Diplomate Am. Bd. Internal Medicine, Am. Bd. Endocrinology. Intern, then resident in internal medicine Cleve. Clinic Hosp., 1975-78, endocrinology fellow, 1978-79; fellow in pediatric endocrinology Johns Hopkins Hosp., Balt., 1979-81; diabetes researcher Joslin Diabetes Ctr., Boston, 1981-86; assoc. in medicine Brigham and Women's Hosp., Boston, 1981-86; asst. in medicine, diabetes researcher Mass. Gen. Hosp., Boston, 1986-92; staff endocrinologist Emerson Hosp., Concord, Mass., 1989-2000; pvt. practice Boston, 2000—. Mem. ACP, Am. Diabetes Assn., Am. Fedn. Clin. Research, Endocrine Soc. Office: Emerson Hosp 747 Main St Ste 111 Concord MA 01742-3325

MEISTER, BERNARD JOHN, chemical engineer; b. Maynard, Mass., Feb. 27, 1941; s. Benjamin C. and Gertrude M. Meister; m. Janet M. White, Dec. 31, 1971; children: Mark, Martin, Kay Ellen. BSChemE, Worcester Poly. Inst., 1962; PhD in Chem. Engring., Cornell U., 1966. Engring. rschr. Dow Chem. Co., Midland, Mich., 1966—, sr. rsch. specialist, 1978-81, assoc. scientist, 1981-85, sr. assoc. scientist, 1985-92, rsch. scientist, 1992—. Contbr. articles to profl. jours. Mem.: AIChE, Soc. Rheology, Soc. Plastic Engrs., Am. Chem. Soc., Sigma Xi. Methodist. Home: 2925 Chippewa Ln Midland MI 48640-4181 Office: Dow Chem Co 438 Bldg Midland MI 48667-0001 *Free the mind of things you can't change, and let it focus on things you can accomplish.*

MEISTER, KAREN OLIVIA, secondary school educator; b. Newark, May 19, 1944; d. Bernice Hendricks Huebner; children: Christin, Brian, Erin. BA, Kean Coll., 1980, MA, 1987. Tchr. Union (N.J.) Bd. Edn., 1970-74; instr. Roselle (N.J.) Bd. Edn., 1982—; adj. prof. Union County Coll., 1987—92, Raritan Valley Cmty. Coll., Somerset, 1992—; Ind. Cons. Mary Kay Inc. Trainer Lit. Vol. Am., 1989-91. Mem. NEA, N.J. Edn. Assn., Internat. Reading Assn., N.J. Reading Assn., Suburban Reading Coun. Avocation: antiques. Office: Harrison Sch 310 Harrison Ave Roselle NJ 07203-1495

MEISTER, MARK JAY, museum director, professional society administrator; b. Balt., June 26, 1953; s. Michael Aaron and Yetta (Haransky) M.; m. Carla Steiger, Aug. 7, 1977; children: Rachel, Kaitlin. AB, Washington U., St. Louis, 1974; MA, U. Minn., 1976; cert. mus. mgmt., U. Calif., Berkeley, 1983. Asst. lectr. St. Louis Art Mus., 1974; asst. coord. young people's program Mpls. Inst. Arts, 1975-76, coord. mobile program, 1976, coord. tchrs. resource svcs., 1976-77; dir. Mus. Art and History, Port Huron, Mich., 1978-79, Midwest Mus. Am. Art, Elkhart, Ind., 1979-81; exec. dir. Children's Mus., St. Paul, 1981-86; dir. Mus. Art, Sci. and Industry, Bridgeport, Conn., 1986-89; exec. dir. Archaeol. Inst. of Am., Boston, 1989-99; exec. dir. Archl. Inst. Am. Inst. Archeologique d'Amerique, Boston and Toronto, 1994-99; exec. dir. Dayton Soc. Natural History, 2000—. Adj. lectr. museology Kenyon Coll., Gambier, Ohio, 1977; adj. lectr. art history Ind. U., South Bend, 1980—81; regional reviewer Inst. Mus. Svcs., Washington, 1985—86, Washington, 1989; treas., vice chmn. Minn. Assn. Mus., St. Paul, 1983—86; ex-officio trustee U.S. com. Internat. Coun. on Monuments and Sites, 1995—99. Bd. dirs. Seaway Arts Coun., St. Clair County, Mich., 1978-79, Dayton Sister Cities Com., 2000—, chair, 2003—, Dayton Peace Accords Project, 2000—, vice chair, 2003, Glen Helen Ecology Inst., 2003; mem. Mayor's Arts Adv. Com., Elkhart, 1981; mem. projects with industry bus. adv. coun. Goodwill Industries of Southwestern Conn., 1988-89; mem. exec. com., Conf. Adminstrv. Officers, Am. Coun. Learned Socs., 1994-97; pres. Asian Arts Ctr., Dayton, 2002. NEH museology fellow, Mpls. Inst. Arts, 1976-77, Kress fellow U. Minn. 1977-78, Bush leadership summer fellow, Bush Found., St. Paul, 1983; named One of Outstanding Young Men Am., 1981. Mem.: Assn. Children's Mus., Ohio Mus. Assn., Assn. Sci. and Tech. Ctrs., Am. Zoo and Aquarium Assn., Assn. Sci. Mus. Dirs., Archeol. Inst. Am., Am. Assn. Mus. Office: Dayton Soc Natural History 2600 Deweese Pkwy Dayton OH 45414-5499 E-mail: mmeister@boonshoftmuseum.org.

MEISTER, PAUL M. medical products executive; BA, U. Mich.; MBA, Northwestern U. Mng. dir. Henley, 1986—92; sr. v.p. Abex, Inc., 1992—95; exec. v.p., CFO Fisher Sci., Hampton, NH, 1998—. Vice-chmn. bd. Gen. Chem. Group, Inc.; bd. dirs. M & F Worldwide Corp., Minerals Tech., Inc., Nat. Waterworks, Inc. Office: Fisher Sci Internat Liberty Ln Hampton NH 03842

MEITZLER, ALLEN HENRY, electrical engineering educator, automotive scientist; b. Allentown, Pa., Dec. 16, 1928; s. Herbert Henry and Estella Irene (Wagner) M.; m. Joan Catherine Egan, June 13, 1953; children: Thomas Joseph, Peter Michael, David Christopher. BS, Muhlenberg Coll., Allentown, Pa., 1951; MS, Lehigh U., 1953, PhD, 1955. Mem. tech. staff Bell Labs., Whippany and Murray Hill, N.J., 1955-72; prin. research scientist, research staff Ford Motor Co., Dearborn, Mich., 1972-96, elec. engring. educator, 1996—. Adj. prof. U. Mich.-Dearborn. Patentee ultrasonic and ferroelectric devices, automotive electronic devices and systems. Prof. Wackernagel scholar, 1947-51; Hood grad. fellow, 1954-55 Fellow IEEE, Acoustical Soc. Am.; mem. Am. Phys. Soc. Republican. Home: 3055 Foxcroft St Ann Arbor MI 48104-2827

MEITZLER, LELAND KEITH, publishing executive; b. Enumclaw, Wash., Apr. 13, 1950; s. Theodore Canfield and Virginia Francis Cornett-Feller; m. Patty Sue Daffern, Sept. 1, 1968; children: Leland Neal, Dale Ralph. AA with honors, Green River CC, Auburn, Wash., 1983. Mgr. Meitzler's Greenhouse & Nursery, Puyallup, Wash., 1970-72; sales mgr. Meitzler's Wholesale Greenhouses, Orting, Wash., 1972-75; terminal mgr. Green Thumb Products Corp., Apopka, Fla., 1975-76; owner, mgr. Northwest Tropicals, South Prairie, Wash., 1976-82; pres. Meico Assocs., South Prairie, Wash., 1982-84; co-founder, pres. Heritage Quest Mag., Orting, 1985-92, mng. editor Bountiful, Utah, 1992-95, exec. editor, 1996—, touring editor, 1993-2000; v.p. print publs. and acquisitions Heritage Quest, North Salt Lake, Utah, 2000—02; owner Heritage Creations, 2003—; pub. Heritage Quest Mag. and Genealogy Bull., 2003—. Mem.: South Prairie Hist. Soc. (pres. 1982—85), Tacoma-Pierce County Geneal. Soc. (corr. sec. 1982—83, pres. 1983—85), Assn. Profl. Genealogists. Republican. Avocations: country music, genealogy, collecting political and national recovery act memorabilia. Office: Heritage Creations 425 N 400 W Ste 1A North Salt Lake UT 84054 Address: PO Box 540193 North Salt Lake UT 84054-0193 E-mail: leland@heritagecreations.com.

MEJIA, JOSE A. telecommunications industry executive; b. Venezuela; married; 2 children. BS in Indsl. and Ops. Engring., U. Mich.; MBA in Fin. and Ops. Rsch., Duke U. With IBM, Ford Motor Co.; v.p. supplier mgmt. Bay Networks, Inc., Calif., 1996—98; v.p. external mfg. strategy Nortel Networks (formerly Bay Networks), 1999; joined Lucent Techs., Murray Hill, NJ, 1999, chief procurement officer, 1999—2000, v.p. and chief supply chain officer, 2000—01, pres. supply chain networks, 2001—. Named Engr. of Yr., Hispanic Engr. Nat. Achievement Awards Corp., 2003; named one of Top 25 Execs. That Made A Difference, Electronic Buyer News, 1997. Office: Lucent Techs 600 Mountain Ave Murray Hill NJ 07974*

MEKALANOS, JOHN J. microbiology educator; PhD, UCLA, 1978. Prof., chmn. dept. microbiology and molecular genetics Harvard Med. Sch., Boston. Invited spkr. Centenary Symposium of the Pasteur Inst., 1987; mem. vaccines and related biol. products adv. com. FDA, 1988. Recipient Eli Lilly & Co. Microbiology and Immunology Rsch. award Am. Soc. Microbiology, 1991, Milton Fund award, 1981, Am. Cancer Soc. Faculty Rsch. award 1986, NIH Merit award, 1989, AAAS Newcomb Cleve. prize, 1994, City of Medicine prize Durham, N.C., 1997, Ledlie prize Harvard U., 1997. Office: Harvard Med Sch 200 Longwood Ave Boston MA 02115-5701

MEKEEL, ROBERT K. lawyer; b. Ossining, N.Y., Mar. 21, 1950; s. Ira III and Carmen E. (Munson) M.; m. Martha J. Keller, Sept. 29, 1979; 1 child, Meryl Fox. BA, Wesleyan U., Middletown, Conn., 1972; JD, U. Puget Sound, 1978. Bar: N.H. 1978, N.Y. 1979, U.S. Dist. Ct. (so. dist.) N.Y. 1980, U.S. Ct. Appeals (2d cir.) 1981, U.S. Dist. Ct. N.H. 1983, U.S. Ct. Appeals (1st cir.) 1983. Asst. dist. atty. Westchester County N.Y. Dist. Atty., White Plains, N.Y., 1979-82; assoc. Craig Wenners & McDowell, Manchester, N.H., 1983-84; clk. ct. Coos County Superior Ct., Lancaster, N.H., 1985; ptnr. McKible & Mekeel, P.A., Concord, N.H., 1986-89, Cullity Kelley & McDowell, Manchester, 1989-93, McDowell & Mekeel P.A., Manchester, 1994-96; prin. Robert K. Mekeel, P.A., Concord, 1996—. Mem. mentor program Franklin Pierce Law Sch., Concord, 1992; lectr. Nat. Bus. Inst., Eau Claire, Wis., 1993-95; mem. Million Dollar Advocates forum; mediator N.H. Superior Cts.; pvt. mediator, arbitrator disputes involving personal injury claims, pvt. mediation svcs. Coach Hopkinton (N.H.) Lacrosse Club, 2002—03. Fellow N.H. Bar Found.; mem. ATLA (N.H. rep.), N.H. Trial Lawyers Assn. (amicus com. 1994-96), N.H. Bar Assn. (com. on cooperation with cts., lectr. evidence seminar 1994). Democrat. Avocations: running, biking, swimming, drawing, wood working. Home and Office: 73 Main St Hopkinton NH 03229-2628 Office Phone: 603-746-6655. E-mail: mekeelaw@comcast.net.

MELADY, THOMAS PATRICK, academic administrator, ambassador, author, public policy expert, educator; b. Norwich, Conn., Mar. 4, 1927; m. Margaret Judith Badum; children: Christina, Monica. BA, Duquesne U., 1950; MA, Cath. U. Am., 1952, PhD, 1954. Former mem. faculties Fordham and St. John's Univs.; founder Inst. African Affairs Duquesne U., 1957; cons. to founds., govts., corps., 1959-67; hon. doctorates from 28 univs. Africa Service Inst.; prof. Afro-Asian affairs, chmn. dept. Asian studies and NonWestern civilization Seton Hall U., South Orange, N.J., 1967-69, regent, 1987-90; prof. Afro-Asian affairs, dir. Office of Internat. Studies, 1973-74; exec. v.p., prof. politics St. Joseph's U., Phila., 1974-76; pres. Sacred Heart U., Fairfield, Conn., 1976-86, prof. polit. sci., 1976-86, pres. emeritus, 1986—; asst. sec. for postsecondary edn. U.S. Dept. Edn., Washington, 1981-82; amb. to Burundi, 1969-72; amb. to Uganda, 1972-73; sr. adviser to U.S. del. to 25 UN Gen. Assembly, 1970; chmn. Conn. Conf. Ind. Colls., 1979-81; pres., chief exec. officer Conn. Pub. Expenditures Coun., 1986-89; U.S. amb. to The Holy See, Vatican City, 1989-93, 94-95; exec. dir. Cath. Network of Vol. Svcs., 1993-94; v.p. Capital Formation Counselors, 1993—. Disting. vis. prof. George Washington U. and St. John's U., 1993—94; vis. prof. Rome Grad. Ctr., 1998—99, Pontifical Gregorian U., 2001; chmn. nat. com. Cath. Campaign for Am., 1994—99; counsel to govts. and bus.; prof., sr. diplomat in residence Inst. of World Politics, 2001—. Author: Ambassadors Story: The United States and The Vatican in World Affairs, 1994, (memoirs) Faith Family Friends, 2003, and 16 other books. Knighted by Pope Paul VI, 1968 and by Pope John Paul II, 1983, 91; honored by 6 countries; recipient Native Son award, Grand Cross, Order of Malta, 1993. Mem.: Soc. of The Cincinnati, The Sacred Mil. Constantinian Order of St. George, Order of Malta. E-mail: ambmelady@aol.com.

MELAMED, ARTHUR DOUGLAS, lawyer; b. Mpls., Dec. 3, 1945; s. Arthur Charles and Helen Beatrix (Rosenberg) M.; m. Carol Drescher Weisman, May 26, 1983; children: Kathryn Henrie, Elizabeth Allyn. BA, Yale U., 1967; JD, Harvard U., 1970. Bar: D.C. 1970, U.S. Ct. Internat. Trade 1985, U.S. Ct. Appeals (9th cir.) 1971, U.S. Ct. Appeals (2d cir.) 1975, U.S. Ct. Appeals (D.C. cir.) 1978, U.S. Ct. Appeals (8th cir.) 1981, U.S. Ct. Appeals (fed. cir.) 1985, U.S. Ct. Appeals (4th cir.) 1989, U.S. Ct. Appeals (10th cir.) 1993, U.S. Supreme Ct. 1981. Law clk. U.S. Ct. Appeals for 9th Circuit, 1970-71; assoc. Wilmer, Cutler, Pickering, Hale & Dorr, Washington, 1971-77, ptnr., 1978-96, 2001—; prin. dep. asst. atty. gen. U.S. Dept. Justice, 1996-2000, acting asst. atty. gen. antitrust divsn., 2000-2001. Vis. prof. Georgetown U. Law Ctr., 1992-93, adj. prof., 1993-94. Contbr. articles to profl. jours. D.C. area chair Yale campaign, 1993-97; mem. social scis. coun. com. Yale U., 1989-94; trustee Nat. Child Rsch. Ctr., 1990-93, Sidwell Friends Sch., 2000—. Mem. ABA, Am. Law Inst., Yale Club (N.Y.C.), Kenwood Country Club. Home: 6405 Shadow Rd Bethesda MD 20815-6613 Office: Wilmer Cutler Pickering Hale & Dorr 2445 M St NW Washington DC 20037 Office Phone: 202-663-6090. Business E-Mail: doug.melamed@wilmer.com.

MELAMED, CAROL DRESCHER, lawyer; b. N.Y.C., July 12, 1946; d. Raymond A. and Ruth W. (Schwartz) Drescher; m. Arthur Douglas Melamed, May 26, 1983; children: Kathryn, Elizabeth; children from previous marriage: Stephanie Weisman, D. Wynne Brown. AB, Brown U., 1967; MAT, Harvard U., 1969; JD, Cath. U. Am., 1974. Bar: Md. 1974, D.C. 1975, U.S. Ct. Appeals (D.C. cir.) 1975, U.S. Dist. Ct. D.C. 1981, U.S. Supreme Ct. 1982. Tchr. English Wellesley (Mass.) H.S., 1968-69; law clk. U.S. Ct. Appeals (D.C. cir.), Washington, 1974-75; assoc. Wilmer, Cutler & Pickering, Washington, 1975-79; assoc. counsel The Washington Post, 1979-95, v.p. govt. affairs, 1995—. Mem. Phi Beta Kappa. Office: The Washington Post 1150 15th St NW Washington DC 20071-0002

MELAMED, LEO, global consulting firm executive; b. Bialystok, Poland, Mar. 20, 1932; came to U.S., 1941, naturalized, 1950. s. Isaac M. and Fayga (Barakin) M.; m. Betty Sattler, Dec. 26, 1953; children: Idelle Sharon, Jordan Norman, David Jeffrey. Student, U. Ill., 1950-52; JD, John Marshall Law Sch., Chgo., 1955. Bar: Ill. 1955. Sr. ptnr. Melamed, Kravitz & Verson, Chgo., 1956-66; chmn., CEO Dellsher Investment Co., 1965—93, Sakura Dellsher, Inc., Chgo., 1993—2000, Melamed & Assoc., Inc., Chgo., 1993—. Mem. Chgo. Merc. Exch., 1953—, mem. bd. govs., 1967—91, chmn. emeritus, 1991—, chmn. bd., 1969—71, 1975—77, chmn. exec. com., 1985—91, also spl. counsel, apptd. sr. policy advisor, 1997—; chmn. bd. Internat. Monetary Market, 1972—75, spl. counsel, 1976—91; mem. Chgo. Bd. Trade, 1969—; mem. corp. adv. bd. U. Ill., Chgo., 1991—; mayor Chgo. Coun. Manpower and Econ. Advisors, 1972; adv. coun. mem. Grad. Sch. Bus. U. Chgo., 1980—. Author: (sci. fiction novel) The Tenth Planet, 1987, Leo Melamed on the Markets, 1993, Escape to the Futures, 1996; editor: The Merits of Flexible Exchange Rates, 1989. Trustee Trustee John Marshall Law Sch., 1991—; coun. mem. U.S. Holocaust Meml. Mus., 1992—, dir. Named Man of Yr., Israel Bonds, 1975; recipient Am. Jewish Com. Human Rights medallion, 1991. Fellow: Internat. Assn. Fin. Engrs. (sr.); mem.: ABA, Chgo. Bar Assn., Ill. Bar Assn., Am. Judicature Soc., Nat. Futures Assn. (chmn. 1982—89, spl. advisor 1989—), Am. Contract Bridge League (life master), Standard Club, Union League Club, Econs. Club Chgo. Avocations: writing, jogging, bridge. Office: Melamed & Assocs Inc 10 S Wacker Dr Ste 3275 Chicago IL 60606-7442 E-mail: lm@sdinet.com.

MELANCON, BARRY C. professional society adminstrator; b. Houma, La., Apr. 19, 1958; s. Dudley Paul Sr. and Ethel Park M.; m. Patricia Gaudet, Aug. 4, 1979; 1 child, Connor. BS, Nicholls State U., 1978, MBA, 1984. CPA. Ptnr. Bergeron & Co. CPAs, Houma, 1979-87; exec. dir. Soc. La. CPAs, Kenner, 1987-95; pres., CEO AICPA, N.Y.C., 1995—. Dir. Ground Pat'i, Inc., Lafayette, La., 1994—. Active Independence Stds. Bd., N.Y.C., 1998-99. Mem. ASAE, N.Y. State CPAs, La. CPAs, N.J. Soc. CPAs. Avocations: golf, sports. Office: AICPA 1211 Ave of Ams New York NY 10036*

MELAND, N. BRADLY, plastic surgeon; b. Northwood, N.D., May 19, 1953; s. Noren M. and Audrey M. Meland; m. Sue Jean Revier, Aug. 19, 1978; children: Angela, Shaina, Jessica, Tessa. BS in Natural Scis., U. N.D., 1975, MS in Medicine, 1977, MD, 1979; postgrad., U. Minn., 1977-78. Diplomate Am. Bd. Surgery, Am. Bd. Plastic Surgery. Gen. surgery resident Mich. State U., Saginaw (Mich.) Coop. Hosp., 1979-84; plastic surgery fellow Mayo Grad. Sch., Rochester, Mich., 1984-86, ortho micro surg. fellow, 1986; hand fellow U. Fla., Tampa, 1987; cons. plastic surgery, cons. orthopedic hand surgery Mayo Clinic, Rochester, 1987-93, cons. plastic surgery Scottsdale, Ariz., 1993-98, chief sect. hand surgery, 1994-98; med. dir. S.W. Plastic Surgeons, Paradise Valley, Ariz., 1998—. Staff St. Mary's Hosp., Rochester, 1987-98, Meth. Hosp., Rochester, 1987-98, Maricopa County Hosp., Phoenix, 1993—, St. Lukes Hosp., Jacksonville, Fla., 1993—, Scottsdale Healthcare Shea,

1993—, Scottsdale Healthcare Osborn, 1998—; co-dir. microsurg. tchg. lab. Med. Scis. Bldg., Rochester, 1987-93; annual faculty flap dissection workshop East Va. Med. Sch., Norfolk, 1988—; co-dir., annual faculty European Flap Workshop, Hanover, Germany, 1989, 93; residency program dir. plastic surgery program Mayo Grad. Sch., Rochester, 1989-93; edn. chmn., fellowship preceptor divsn. plastic surgery Mayo Clinic Scottsdale, 1993-98; asst. prof. plastic surgery, orthopedic surgery Mayo Grad. Sch. Medicine, Rochester, 1987-90, assoc. prof. plastic surgery, orthopedic surgery, 1990-98; oral examiner Am. Bd. Plastic Surgeons, 1997—; vis. prof., lectr., presenter in field. Assoc. editor Plastic Surgery Outlook Quarterly, 1994-96, Jour. Plastic Surg. Techniques, 1994-96, European Jour. Plastic Surgery, 1994-98; assoc. contbg. editor Yearbook of Hand Surgery, 1987-98; ad-hoc reviewer Plastic Reconstructive Surgery, 1994—, Annals Plastic Surgery, 1995—; contbr. chpts. to books and articles to profl. jours. 8th grade Sunday sch. tchr. Christ Ch. Luth., 1995-97, chmn. sch. bd., 1995-97. Fellow ACS; mem. AMA, Internat. Soc. Reconstructive Microsurgery, Internat. Coll. Surgeons, Am. Assn. Plastic Surgeons (program com. 1998), Am. Soc. Plastic and Reconstructive Surgery (socioeconomic com. 1994-97, coding com. 1994-96, practice and devel. com. 1998, chmn. sci. meeting evaluation com. 1998, program chmn. annual meeting 1999, others), Am. Assn. Hand Surgery (bylaws com. 1990, program com. 1993, tech. exhibits chair 1993-96, bd. dirs. 1995-97, membership chair 1998—, others), Am. Soc. Surgery of the Hand, Am. Soc. Reconstructive Microsurgery (audit fin. com. 1989-91, tech. exhibits com. 1989-91, program com. 1991, edn. com. 1992), Am. Assn. Clin. Anatomists, Assn. Acad. Chmn. Plastic Surgery, Midwestern Assn. Plastic Surgeons (bd. dirs. 1991-92, program chmn. 1992), Maricopa County Med. Soc., Maricopa County Plastic Surg. Soc., Rocky Mountain Assn. Plastic and Reconstructive Surgeons, Priestley Surg. Soc., Sigma Xi. Avocations: skiing, golf, fishing, camping, sailing. Office: Meland Plastic Surgery Clinic 7032 Cochise St Ste A200 Scottsdale AZ 86351

MELANI, KENNETH R. insurance company executive; MD, Bowman Gray Sch. of Med., NC, 1979. Pres., CEO West Penn Cares Inc.; pres. Keystone Health Plan West; with Highmark Inc., Pittsburgh, 1989—, exec. v.p. strategic bus. devel. and health services, pres., CEO, 2003—. Mem.: Am. Coll. of Physician Executives, Am. Soc. of Internal Med., Penn. Soc. of Internal Med., Am. Med. Assn., Penn. Med. Soc., Allegheny County Med. Soc. Office: Highmark Inc 120 5th Ave Pittsburgh PA 15222-3099 Office Phone: 412-544-7000.*

MELANSON, DOROTHY, political organization administrator; b. Boston, Mass, Sept. 21, 1953; AS, Westbrook Coll., Maine, 1980. Com. woman Maine Dem. Nat., Maine, 1996; chairwoman Dem. Com., Cumberland County, Maine, 1996—2002; com. woman Maine Dem. Nat., Maine, 2000; Presdl. Elector Maine, 2000; com. woman Maine Dem. Nat., 2001—03; chairwoman Maine Dem. Party, 2003—; registered nurse Maine Med. Ctr., Maine. A longtime dem. party activist. Office: Maine Dem Party Chair PO Box 5258 12 Spruce St Augusta ME 04332

MELANSON, RICHARD ALLEN, political science educator; b. Perth Amboy, N.J., Nov. 4, 1944; s. Melvin Joseph and Helen (Hurley) Ml; m. Jane Louise Maxim, Feb. 14, 1983 (dec. Oct. 11, 2002). BA, Rutgers U., 1966; postgrad., Harvard U., 1966-67; PhD, Johns Hopkins U., 1974. Lectr. polit. sci. UCLA, 1972-74; prof. polit. sci. Kenyon Coll., Gambier, Ohio, 1974-90; dir. internat. studies Brown U., Providence, R.I., 1990-92; prof. nat. security policy Nat. War Coll., Washington, 1992—. Author: Writing History and Making Policy, 1983, Reconstructing Consensus, 1991, U.S. Foreign Policy Since Vietnam, 2000, 4th edit., 2005; co-editor: Reevaluating Eisenhower, 1987 (Choice award, 1987); mem. bd. evs.: Mershon Rev. Internat. Studies. NEH fellow, 1981. Mem. Am. Polit. Assn., Soc. Historians of Am. Fgn. Rels., Internat. Studies Assn. Avocations: crossword puzzles, lieder, bicycling. Office: Nat War Coll 4th St SW Washington DC 20319-0001 E-mail: melansonr@ndu.edu.

MELAS-KYRIAZI, THEO, electronics executive; BA in Econs., MBA, Harvard U. Former corp. fin. mgr. Bourgeois Fils & Co., NH; asst. treas. Thermo Electron, Waltham, Mass., 1986—88, treas., 1988—94, pres., CEO ThermoSpectra Corp. subs., 1994—97, chmn. ThermoSpectra, v.p. corp. strategy Thermo Electron, 1997—99, v.p., CFO, 1999—. Bd. dirs. Thoratec. Office: Thermo Electron 81 Wyman St Waltham MA 02454*

MELBOURNE, ROBERT ERNEST, civil engineer; b. Oceanside, Calif., July 17, 1929; s. Thomas Powell and Helen Millicent (Plausse) M.; m. Jeanne Edith Kuhn, Apr. 8, 1961; children: Ann Teresa Farley, Maria Helen Hayes, Steven Thomas, Louise Clare Vance. BSCE, U. So. Calif., 1951, PhD in History, 1996; MSCE, Stanford U., 1955; MA in History, U. San Diego, 1990. Registered civil engr., Calif. Engr. Morrison-Knudsen Co., Boise, Noxon, Mont., 1955-57, J.E. Haddock Ltd., Pasadena, Calif., 1957-58; pres. R.E. Melbourne Co. Inc., San Luis Rey, Calif., 1958-66; engr. constrn. and design, chief engr. San Diego County Water Authority, San Diego, 1966-90; mil. historian in pvt. practice, 1990—. Mem. adv. bd. Colorado River Bd., L.A., 1967-83. Commr. Oceanside Historic Preservation, 1997—. Lt. USN, 1951-54, PTO. Fellow ASCE; mem. U.S. Naval Inst., Soc. Am. Mil. Engrs. Soc. Mil. History, Navy League of U.S., Marine Corps Heritage Found. Republican. Roman Catholic. Home: PO Box 9 San Luis Rey CA 92068-0009

MELBY, EDWARD CARLOS, JR., veterinarian; b. Burlington, Vt., Aug. 10, 1929; s. Edward C. and Dorothy H. (Folsom) M.; m. Jean Day File, Aug. 15, 1953; children: Scott E., Susan J., Jeffrey T., Richard A. Student, U. Pa., 1948—50; DVM, Cornell U., 1954. Diplomate Am. Coll. Lab. Animal Medicine. Practice vet. medicine, Middlebury, Vt., 1954-62; instr. lab. animal medicine Johns Hopkins U. Sch. Medicine, Balt., 1962-64, asst. prof., 1964-66, assoc. prof., 1966-71, prof., dir. div. comparative medicine, 1971-74; prof. medicine, dean Coll. Vet. Medicine, Cornell U., Ithaca, NY, 1974-84; v.p. R & D SmithKline Beecham Animal Health, 1985-90, v.p. sci. and tech. assessment, 1990-91; ind. cons., 1992—. Cons. VA, NRC, NIH. Author: Handbook of Laboratory Animal Science, Vols. I, II, III, 1974-76. Served with USMC, 1946-48. Mem. Am., N.Y. State, Md., Pa. Vet. Med. Assns., Am. Assn. Lab. Animal Sci., Am. Coll. Lab. Animal Medicine, AAAS, Phi Zeta. Home: PO Box 248 Charlotte VT 05445-0248 Office: 736 Lime Kiln Rd Charlotte VT 05445-9141 E-mail: ecmelby@aol.com.

MELBY, JOHN B. composer, educator; b. Whitehall, Wis., Oct. 3, 1941; s. John B. Sr. and Margaret (Edmundson) M.; m. Carol A. Wurtz, July 7, 1961 (div. 1977); 1 child, John; m. Jane H. Thompson, June 15, 1978; children: Kirsten, Charles. MusB, Curtis Inst., 1966; MA, U. Pa., 1967; MFA, Princeton U., 1971, PhD, 1972. Assoc. prof. West Chester (Pa.) U., 1971-73; prof. music U. Ill., Urbana, 1973-97, prof. emeritus, 1997—. Assoc. U. Ill. Ctr. for Advanced Studies, 1989-90. Composer numerous mus. works for live performers, computer-synthesized tape, vocal, chamber, choral and orchestral works including 2 symph., works pub. by Associated Music Pubs., Merion Music, Inc.; recs. on Composers Recs., Inc., New World Records, Advance Records, Centaur Records, Zuma Records. Recipient 1st prize 7th Internat. Electroacoustic Music Awards, Bourges, France, 1979, Am. Acad./Inst. Arts and Letters award, 1984; Guggenheim fellow, 1983. Mem.: ACLU, Am. Composers Alliance, Am. Music Ctr., Broadcast Music Inc., Herpetologists' League, Am. Atheists. Green Party. Avocations: railroading, cooking, herpetology. Home: 5 Walter St Salem MA 01970-2518 E-mail: jbmelby@johnmelby.com.

MELCHER, JAMES PATRICK, political scientist, educator; b. Madison, Wis., Feb. 3, 1963; s. John William and Beatrice Hagensick Melcher; m. Nancy Patricia Finnegan, Jan. 2, 1999. BA, U. Wis., 1985; PhD, U. Minn., 1995. Asst. dept. rsch. Minn. Ho. of Reps., St. Paul, 1989—92; vis. asst. prof. St. John's U., Collegeville, Minn., 1995, Coll. St. Benedict, St. Joseph, Minn., 1995, U. Wis., Eau Claire, 1996; vis. term prof. Cleve. State U., 1996—99; asst. prof. U. Maine, Farmington, 1999—2004, assoc. prof., 2004—. Contbr. articles to profl. jours.; assoc. editor: website Electnet, 1996—2001. Del. Maine Dem. Conv., 2000, 2002; vestry mem. St. Mark's Episc. Ch., Augusta, Maine, 2000—. Recipient Disting. Faculty award, Cleve. State U. Student Alumni Assn., 1999. Mem.: Am. Polit. Sci. Assn. Episcopalian. Avocations: collecting postcards, fantasy football, fantasy baseball, hiking. Home: 27 Meadow Rd #204 Augusta ME 04330 Office: U Maine Farmington Dept Social Scis and Bus Farmington ME 04938 Business E-Mail: jim.melcher@maine.edu.

MELCHER, MARGARET LOUISA, editor, publishing executive; b. North Platte, Nebr., Jan. 31, 1933; d. Ralph Stanley Saul and Margaret Pearl Priest; m. Daniel Melcher, Oct. 3, 1967 (dec. 1985). BA, Hastings Coll., Nebr., 1954. Cert. pub. procedures Radcliff Coll., Mass., 1955. Tchr. Omaha Pub. Schools, Omaha, 1954—55; editor sch. libr. jour. R. R. Bowker Co., N.Y.C., 1955—61, R & D, 1961—63; freelance mktg. cons. N.Y.C., 1963—72; farmer Glen Echo Farm, Charlottesville, Va., 1973—87; owner/pub. Libros en Venta en Hispanoamérica y España, San Juan, PR, 1985—96; adv. editor Nat. Info. Svcs. Co., Balt., 1996—. Co-author (with Daniel Melcher): Melcher on Acquisition, 1971. Bd. mem. and pres. Jefferson Madison Regional Libr., Charlottesville, Va., 1979—86; mem. and v.p. LWV, Charlottesville, 1975—85. Recipient Journalism prize, Inter Am. Group of the Internat. Union of Editors, 1986. Home: Apt 602 250 W Main St Charlottesville VA 22902 Personal E-mail: melcher1933@earthlink.net.

MELCHER, SANDRA J. artist; b. Lakewood, Ohio, May 24, 1932; d. William Anthony Vago and Elizabeth Charlotte Jarabek; m. Frank T. Melcher, Jan. 12, 1951; 1 child, Renee Janine Singer. BFA, Cleve. Inst. of Art, 1954. V.p. Women's Caucus for Art, Sarasota, Fla., 1990—91, statewide exhbn. com., 1991; regional coord. Fla. Printmakers Soc., Sarasota, 1988; exhbn. chairperson Digital Fine Artists Assn., Sarasota, 1998—99; pres. Women's Caucus for Art, Sarasota, 1991—92; chairperson Riverfront Arts Adv. Com., Bradenton, Fla., 1997—98; founder, pres. Digital Fine Artists Assn., Sarasota, 1995—; faculty mem. Longboat Key (Fla.) Adult Edn. Ctr., 1998. Alumnus Cleve. Inst. of Art, Cleveland, Ohio, 1964—; mem. Nat. Assn. of Women Artists, New York City, NY, 1964—, Nat. League of Am. Pen Women, Sarasota, Fla., 1997—99, Fla. Atrtists Group, Sarasota, Fla., 1996—2000, Modern Artists Guild, Paramus, NJ, 1963—74, Art League of Manatee County, Bradenton, Fla., 1985—; bd. of directors Digital Fine Artists Assn., Sarasota, Fla., 1995—. Etching, East 12th and Prospect, Cleve. (scholarship Cleve. Inst. of Art, 1950), exhibitions include Carnegie Mellon U. (1st prize, 1949), etching, Playing An Instrument from Another Universe (Nat. Traveling Exhbn., 1971); contbr. prose poetry to anthologies (Poetry Competition winner, Am. Poetry Assn., 1987); prose poetry to anthologies, God's Touch' (Poetry Competition winner, Internat. Libr. of Poets, 2003), book of poetry, The Journey, Poetry, Art and Life. Bd. mem. Arts Coun. of Manatee County, Bradenton, 1996—98. Mem.: Bradenton Yacht Club, Mentor Harbor Yacht Club (pres. Wet Hens 1979—85), Chagrin Lagoons Yacht Club (pres.Gallery Maids 1977). Avocations: poetry, jewelry, lecturer, metaphysics, raising plants. Home: 2107 41st St W Bradenton FL 34205-1352 Office: SJM Designs 2107 41st St W Bradenton FL 34205-1352 Personal E-mail: san-j-art@mindspring.com. E-mail: san-j-art@mindspring.com.

MELCHER, ULRICH KARL, biochemistry educator; b. London, July 7, 1945; came to U.S., 1952; s. Ernst Otto and Lotte Kaethe (Findorff) M.; m. Karen Joy Sandstedt, July 13, 1968; children: Sonya Elizabeth, Katherine Ann. BS in Biochemistry, U. Chgo., 1965; PhD in Biochemistry, Mich. State U., 1970. Postdoctoral fellow dept. molecular biology U. Aarhus, Denmark, 1970-71; rsch. assoc. dept. medicine NYU Med. Sch., N.Y.C., 1971-72; rsch. assoc. dept. microbiology U. Tex. Southwestern Med. Sch., Dallas, 1972-74, asst. prof., 1974-75; asst. prof. dept. biochemistry Okla. State U., Stillwater, 1975-78, assoc. prof., 1978-83, prof., 1983—. Fulbright scholar Lab. Plant Virology, Inst. Cellular and Molecular Biology, Strasbourg, France, 1983. Contbr. articles to profl. jours. NATO postdoctoral fellow, 1970-71, NIH postdoctoral fellow, 1973-74. Mem.: AAUP, AAAS, Okla. Acad. Scis., Am. Soc. Microbiology, Am. Phytopath. Soc., Am. Soc. Plant Biologists, Am. Soc. Virology, Am. Soc. Biochemistry and Molecular Biology, Internat. Soc. Plant Molecular Biology, Phi Kappa Phi, Sigma Xi. Democrat. Office: Okla State U Dept Biochemistry & Molecular Biology 246 NRC Stillwater OK 74078-3035 Office Phone: 405-744-6210.

MELCHIOR, IB JORGEN, author, television and motion picture writer, director; b. Copenhagen, Sept. 17, 1917; arrived in U.S., 1938; s. Lauritz Lebrecht Hommel and Inger Thora (Nathansen) M.; m. Harriet Hathaway Kale, Mar. 15, 1942 (div. 1960); 1 child, Leif; m. Cleo Baldon-Chute, Jan. 18, 1964; stepchild, Dirk Arin. Postgrad., U. Copenhagen, 1937. Actor, stage mgr., co-dir. English Players, Paris, 1937—39; stage mgr. Radio City Music Hall, Ctr. Theater, N.Y.C., 1941—42; actor, writer N.Y.C., 1946—49; assoc. dir. CBS-TV, N.Y.C., 1949—50; dir. Perry Como Show, N.Y.C., 1951—54; assoc. prodr. G-L Enterprises, N.Y.C., 1952—53; screenwriter, dir., novelist, 1957—. Author: (novels) Order of Battle, 1973, Sleeper Agent, 1975, The Haigerloch Project, 1977, The Watchdogs of Abaddon, 1979, The Marcus Device, 1980, The Tombstone Cipher, 1983, Eva, 1984, V-3, 1985, Code Name: Grand Guignol, 1987, (biography) Quest, 1990, Order of Battle: Hitler's Werewolves, 1991, (autobiography) Case by Case, 1993; author: (with Cleo Baldon) Steps & Stairways, 1989, Reflections on the Pool, 1997, Lauritz Melchior: The Golden Years of Bayreuth, 2003; screenwriter Live Fast, Die Young, 1957, The Angry Red Planet, 1959, Reptilicus, 1962, Journey to the 7th Planet, 1962, Ambush Bay, 1965, Robinson Crusoe on Mars, 1964, The Time Travelers, 1964, others; dir. Angry Red Planet, The Time Travelers; translator, narrator (tapes) Hans Christian Andersen Fairy Tales, 1986; creator Space Family Robinson (spl. advisor Lost in Space, 1997-98); subject of biography: (by Robert Skotak) Ib Melchior: Man of Imagination, 2000. Mem. adv. bd. Mayor's Narcotics Info. Clinic, L.A., 1972-73; adv. coun. Danish Immigrant Mus., Elk Horn, Iowa, 1985—. With U.S. Army Mil. Intelligence, 1943-46. Decorated Bronze Star, Knight Commander Cross, Militant Order of St. Brigitte of Sweden, 1965; recipient King Christian X Erindringsmedalje, 1948, Medal of Merit Old Guard, 1965, Golden Scroll award Best Writing Acad. Sci. Fiction, 1976, Hamlet award Best Legitimate Play Shakespeare Soc. Am., 1982; named Scandinavian of Yr. Am. Scandanavian Found. L.A., 1995, Mem. Writers Guild Am. West, Dirs. Guild Am., Acad. Sci. Fiction (hon.), Manuscript Soc., Authors Guild Inc., Royal Danish Guard Assn., Danish Luncheon Club (L.A.), Adventures Club (L.A.). Home and Office: 8228 Marmont Ln Hollywood CA 90069-1624 Office Phone: 323-654-6679. Personal E-mail: ijmelchior@aol.com.

MELCONIAN, JERRY OHANES, engineering executive; b. Cairo, Jan. 22, 1934; arrived in U.S., 1967; s. Melik Melconian and Zarouca Papazian; m. Veronique Kocifay, June 12, 1998; 1 child, Terran Kirk. BSc, U. London, 1957. Sect. leader Otis Elevator Co., London, 1957-61, Rolls Royce Ltd., Derby, England, 1961-66; program coord. Textron Lycoming, Stratford, Conn., 1967-74; mgr. TF34 design to cost GE, Lynn, Mass., 1974-77; mgr. mktg. No. Rsch. and Engring. Co., Woburn, Mass., 1977-82; pres. SOL-3 Resources Inc., Reading, Mass., 1982—. Editor: Design and Development of Gas Turbine Combustors, 1980. Mem.: AIAA. Achievements include patents in field. Office: SOL-3 Resources Inc 5204 Whispering Leaf Valrico FL 33594 Office Phone: 813-643-9279.

MELCONIAN, LINDA JEAN, state legislator, lawyer; b. Springfield, Mass. d. George and Virginia Elaine (Noble) Melconian. BA, Mt. Holyoke Coll.; MA, George Washington U.; JD, George Mason U. Asst. counsel to Spkr. Thomas P. O'Neill, Jr. U.S. Ho. of Reps., Washington, 1111; pros. atty. Hampden County Dist. Atty., Springfield, Mass.; state senator Mass. Gen. Ct., Boston, 1983—, former majority leader Mass. State Senate. Instr. Mt. Holyoke Coll.; Our Lady of the Elms Coll., Baypath Coll.; incorporator Springfield Coll. Ex Officio trustee Ella T. Grasso Found., Conn.; active Dem. State Com., Mass. Home: 465 Dwight Rd Springfield MA 01108 Office: Mass State Senate Rm 511B Boston MA 02133 Business E-Mail: lmelconi@senate.state.ma.us.

MELCZEK, DALE J. bishop; b. Nov. 9, 1938; AB, St. Mary Coll., Orchard Lake, Mich.; MDiv, St. John Sem., Plymouth, Mich.; MA in Edn., U. Detroit; postgrad., U. Notre Dame. Ordained priest Roman Cath. Ch., 1964, apptd. aux. bishop Roman Cath. Ch., 1982. Assoc. pastor St. Sylvester Ch., Warren, Mich., 1964—70, co-pastor, 1970—72; pastor St. Christine Ch., Detroit, 1972—75; vicar West Detroit Vicariate, 1973—75; asst. vicar for parishes Archdiocese of Detroit, 1975—77, sec. to archbishop and vicar gen., 1977—82, archdiocesan consultor, 1972—83, aux. bishop, titular bishop of Trau, 1982—95; regional bishop Detroit N.W. Region, 1983—92; apostolic adminstr. Diocese of Gary, 1992—95, coadjutor Bishop of Gary, 1995—96, bishop of Gary, 1996—. Roman Catholic.

MELDMAN, ROBERT EDWARD, lawyer; b. Milw., Aug. 5, 1937; s. Louis Leo and Lillian (Gollusch) M.; m. Sandra Jane Setlick, July 24, 1960; children: Saree Beth, Richard Samuel. BS, U. Wis., 1959; LL.B., Marquette U., 1962; LL.M. in Taxation, NYU, 1963. Bar: Wis. 1962, Fla. 1987, Colo. 1990, U.S. Ct. Fed. Claims, U.S. Tax Ct. 1963, U.S. Supreme Ct. 1970. Practice tax law, Milw., 1963—; pres. Meldman, Case & Weine, Ltd., Milw., 1975-85; dir. tax div. Mulcahy & Wherry, S.C., Milw., 1985-90; shareholder Reinhart, Boerner, Van Deuren, S.C., 1991—. Adj. prof. taxation U. Wis., Milw., 1970—2000, mem. tax adv. coun., 1978—2000; adj. prof. Marquette U. Sch. Law, Milw., 2001—02, The U. of Queensland T.C. Beirne Sch. Law, 2002; vice chmn. Internat. Revenue Svc. Taxpayer Adv. Panel, 2003—04; sec. Profl. Inst. Tax Study, Inc., 1978—; bd. dirs. Wis. Bar Found., 1988—94; exec. in residence Deloitte & Touche Ctr. for Multistate Taxation, U. Wis., Milw., 1996—2000. Co-author: Federal Taxation Practice and Procedure, 1983, 1986, 1988, 1992, 1998, 2004, Practical Tactics for Dealing with the IRS, 1994, A Practical Guide to U.S. Taxation of International Transactions, 1996, 1997, 2004, Federal Taxation Practice and Procedure Study Guide/Quizzes, 1998; editor: Jour. Property Taxation, 1996—2002; mem. editl. bd.: Tax Litigation Alert, 1995—2000; contbr. articles to legal jours. Recipient Adj. Taxation Faculty award UWM Tax Assn., 1987; named Outstanding Tax Profl. 1992 Corp. Reports Wis. Mag. and UWM Tax Assn. Fellow Am. Coll. Tax Coun.; mem. ABA, Fed. Bar Assn. (pres. Milw. chpt. 1966-67), Milw. Bar Assn. (chmn. tax sect. 1970-71), Wis. Bar Assn. (bd. dirs. tax sect. 1964-78, chmn. 1973-74), Internat. Bar Assn., The Law Assn. for Asia and the Pacific (chair tax sect. 2000—, dep. chair bus. law sect.), Friends of Gold Meir Libr. (bd. dirs.), Marquette U. Law Alumni Assn. (bd. dirs. 1972-77), Milw. Athletic Club, Wis. Club (bd. dirs. 2003—), B'nai B'rith (trustee, Ralph Harris Meml. award Century Lodge 1969-70), Phi Delta Phi, Tau Epsilon Rho (chancellor Milw. chpt. 1969-71, supreme nat. chancellor 1975-76, v.p. Wis. chpt., tech. 1992-2000). Jewish (trustee congregation 1972-77). Home: 7455 N Skyline Ln Milwaukee WI 53217-3327 Office: 1000 N Water St Ste 2100 Milwaukee WI 53202-3197 Office Phone: 414-298-1000. E-mail: rmeldman@reinhartlaw.com.

MELDRUM, PETER DURKEE, venture capitalist, biotechnology company executive; b. Salt Lake City, June 26, 1947; s. Benjamin Nibley and Grace Natalie (Durkee) M.; m. Catherine Roper, June 16, 1970; children: Christopher Shawn. BSChemE, U. Utah, 1970, MBA, 1974. Asst. to pres. Terra Tek, Inc., Salt Lake City, 1974-78; pres., CEO Resource Enterprises, Inc., Salt Lake City, 1978-81, AgriDyne Techs., Salt Lake City, 1981-91, Founder's Fund Inc., 1991—93, Myriad Genetics Inc., Salt Lake City, 1993—. Bd. dirs. Dairy Equipment Co. Utah, Salt Lake City, Myriad Genetics, Amedica Bd. dirs., vice chmn. ARC Golden Spike, Salt Lake City, 1980-90; mem. State of Utah Council Sci. and Tech., 1984-89; mem. adv. bd. Coll. of Sci. U. Ut., Engr. Adv. Bd, U. Ut., adv. bd. High Tech Mktg. Rev., Austin, Tex., 1986-88; mem. Gov.'s Task Force on Entrepreneurship; Gov.'s Com. on Biomed. Industry, 1988-91; bd. arbitrators NASD, 1991-98; bd. dirs. Ballet West. 1st lt. USAR, 1970-72, bd. trustees, Pioneer Theatre Co. Named Entrepreneur of Yr., 2001. Mem. Utah Life Scis. Assn. (bd. dirs. 1995—), Tau Beta Pi, Phi Kappa Phi, Beta Gamma Sigma. Republican. Presbyterian. Avocations: skiing, backpacking, basketball, photography. Home: 1808 Mohawk Way Salt Lake City UT 84108-3363 Office: Myriad Genetics 320 Wakara Way Salt Lake City UT 84108-1214

MELE, ALFRED R. philosophy educator; b. Detroit, May 22, 1951; s. Alfred Emil and Rosemary (Pardo) M.; children: Al, Nick, Angela. BA, Wayne State U., 1973; PhD, U. Mich., 1979. Asst. prof. Philosophy Davidson (N.C.) Coll., 1979-85, assoc. prof., 1985-91, prof., 1991-95, Vail prof., 1995-2000; William H. and Lucyle T. Werkmeister prof. Fla. state U., Tallahassee, 2000—. Author: Irrationality, 1987, Springs of Action, 1992, Autonomous Agents, 1995, Self-Deception Unmasked, 2001, Motivation and Agency, 2003; contbr. articles to profl. jours. Fellow NEH, 1985-86, 92-93, 99-2000, Nat. Humanities Ctr., Rsch. Triangle Park, NC, 1992-93, Australian Nat. U., 1999. Mem. Am. Philos. Assn., So. Assn. Philosophy and Psychology, Internat. Soc. for Rsch. on Emotion. Avocations: racquetball, tennis. Office: Dept Philosophy Fla State Univ Tallahassee FL 32306-1500

MELEIS, AFAF IBRAHIM, nurse sociologist, educator, clinician, researcher; b. Alexandria, Egypt, Mar. 19, 1942; d. Abdel Baki Ibrahim and Soad Hussein Hassan; m. Mahmoud Meleis, Aug. 21, 1964; children: Waleed, Sherief. BS magna cum laude, U. Alexandria, 1961; MS, UCLA, 1964, MA, 1966, PhD, 1968; D of Pub. Svc. (hon.), U. Portland, 1989. Instr. U. Alexandria, 1961-62; acting instr. UCLA, 1966-68, asst. prof. nursing, then assoc. prof., 1968-75; assoc. prof., dean Health Inst., Kuwait, 1975-77; prof. nursing U. Calif., San Francisco, 1977—2001, also dir. Study Immigrant Health and Adjustment; dean Univ. of Penn. Sch. of Nursing, 2002—. Vis. prof. colls. in Sweden, Brazil, Japan, Saudi Arabia, Kuwait, Egypt; 1st Centennial prof. Columbia U., N.Y.C., 1992-94; cons., speaker in field. Author: theoretical Nursing: Development & Progress, 1985 (Book of Yr., am. Jour. Nursing, 1985), 2d edit., 1991, 3d edit., 1997; contbr. articles to rsch. and profl. jours. Recipient Helen Hahm award U. Calif. Sch. Nursing, San Francisco, 1981, Teaching awards U. Calif., San Francisco, 1981, 85, Pres. Hosni Mubarak medal of Excellence, 1990; Kellogg Internat. fellow, 1986-89. Fellow Am. Acad. Nursing; mem. Coun. Nurse Researchers, Western Soc. Research in Nursing, Am. Nurses Assn. Avocations: jogging, symphony, reading, international affairs, women's issues. Office: Univ Penn Sch Nursing 420 Guardian Dr Rm 465 NEB Philadelphia PA 19104-6096*

MELÉNDEZ, ENRIQUE, chemist, educator; b. Humacao, P.R., June 18, 1960; s. Manuel Meléndez and Olga Martínez; children: Gustavo Enrique, Mariana, Gabriel Enrique. PhD, U. Utah, Salt Lake City, 1988. Postdoctoral fellowship Bristol-Myers Squibb Co., Humacao, PR, 1988—91; asst. prof. InterAm. U. P.R., Rio Piedras, 1991—96; assoc. prof. U. P.R., Mayaguez, 1997—2002, prof., 2002—. Sci. mem. INDUNIV, Rio Piedras, PR, 1991—96. Editor: (journal) Metal Complexes in Medicine and Biology. Leader Boy Scouts Am., Rio Piedras, PR. Recipient Sci. and Math award, U. P.R., 1979; Grad. Profl. Opportunity Program (GPOP) fellowship, U. Utah, 1983-86. Mem.: Am. Chem. Soc. (pres.), Sigma Xi Sci. Soc. (hon.). Achievements include research in Development of titanium and molybdenum antitumor agents. Home: Complejo Deportivo del Oeste Cabo Rojo PR 00623 Office: Univ Puerto Rico Mayaguez Campus PO Box 9019 Mayaguez PR 00681-9019 Personal E-mail: enrique_melendez@hotmail.com. E-mail: emelendez@uprm.edu.

MELENDEZ, RODRIGO CUAUHTEMOC, dentist, read admiral US Navy; b. L.A., Oct. 23, 1943; s. Jose Chauhtemoc and Helen Antionette (Huhn) M.; m. Winifred Yoshiye Hanoaka. BS, U. So. Calif., 1966, DDS, 1968; MS, George Washington U., 1975;. cert. prosthodontics Nat. Naval Dental Sch., 1976; lic. dentist, Calif. Commd. ensign USN Dental Corps., 1965, advanced through grades to rear adm., 1998; asst. chief edn., tng. and personnel Bur. Medicine and Surgery, Washington, 1971-72; asst. dental officer USS Sanctuary, Mayport, Fla., 1972-74; resident prosthodontics Nat. Naval Dental Ctr., Bethesda, Md., 1974-76; head prosthodontic dept. Naval Sta., Rota, Spain, 1974-80, Br. Dental Clin., NTC, San Diego, 1980-81, Br. Dental Clin., Miramar, San Diego, 1981-82, 82-84, Naval Dental Clin., Camp Pendleton, Calif., 1984-86, exec. officer, 1986-89, comdg. officer Yokosuka, Japan, 1989-92, San Diego, 1995-98. Guest lectr., cons. Naval Dental Clinic, San Diego, 1980-88, Naval Hosp., Camp Pendleton, 1984-88. Fellow Am. Coll. Dentistry, Internat. Coll. Dentistry; mem. ADA, Am. Coll. Prosthodontics. Office: USN 2300 E St NW Washington DC 20372-5300 E-mail: rcmelendez@usmed.navy.mil.

MELENDEZ, ROSA MARIA, protective services official; b. Salt Lake City, Oct. 24, 1952; Diploma, Wash. State Criminal Justice, 1978. U.S. marshall We. dist. U.S. Marshall Svc., Wash., 1994—. Office: 300 US Courthouse 1010 5th Ave Seattle WA 98104-1195

MELENDY, DAVID RUSSELL, broadcast journalist; b. Corpus Christi, Tex., Oct. 19, 1948; s. Harold Orville and Marguerite Doris (Waller) M.; m. Lorna Sandra Katz, Mar. 19, 1972; children: Seth Howard, Andrew Scott. Student, George Washington U., 1966-70; BA magna cum laude, U. Hartford, 1972. News dir. Sta. WINY, Putnam, Conn., 1971-77; news anchor, reporter Sta. WPOP, Hartford, Conn., 1977-80; news dir. Sta. WNVR, Waterbury, Conn., 1980-81; news anchor, reporter St. WDRC, Hartford, Conn., 1980—81; news anchor Sta. WCBS-FM, N.Y.C., 1981; prodr., assignment editor, anchor, reporter AP Broadcast Svcs., Washington, 1981—. Instr. journalism Briarwood Coll., Southington, Conn., 1977-81; mem. broadcast adv. com. Briarwood Coll., Southington, 1978-81. Prodr., writer, reporter (audio spl. report series) Star Wars: Strategic Defense Initiative, 1985, (daily audio feature) Flashback, 1986—. Publicity chmn. Woodstock (Conn.) Players Cmty. Theater, 1972—77, Quinebaug Valley C.C. Found., Danielson, Conn., 1973—75, fundraising chmn., 1976; neighborhood coord. Am. Heart Assn., Washington, 1994, 1999, 2001; troop com. mem. Boy Scout Troop 500, 1998—99; pack com. chmn. Cub Scout Pack 230, 2000—01; asst. scoutmaster Boy Scout Troop 500, 2001—, advancement chair, 2003—. Mem.: Nat. Press Club, Com. Concerned Journalists, News Media Guild/TNG-CWA, Radio and TV News Dirs. Assn., Ho. and Senate Radio-TV Corr. Assn., Elks. Avocations: personal computers, photography, hiking, swimming. Office: AP Broadcast Svcs 1825 K St NW Washington DC 20006-1202 E-mail: david@melendy.us., dmelendy@ap.org.

MELGREN, ERIC FRANKLIN, lawyer; b. Minneola, Kans., Dec. 16, 1956; s. Carl James and Louise C. (Loechnor) M.; m. Denise Melgren, June 16, 1979; children: David W., Susan C., Peter J., Abigail J. B, Wichita State U., 1979; JD, Washburn U., Topeka, 1985. Bar: Kans. 1985, U.S. Dist. Ct. Kans. 1985, U.S. Ct. Appeals (10th cir.) 1987, U.S. Tax Ct. 1988, U.S. Supreme Ct. 1995. Law clk. U.S. Dist. Ct. Kans., Wichita, 1985-87; assoc. Foulston, Siefkin, Powers & Eberhardt, Wichita, 1987-92; ptnr. Foulston & Siefkin, Wichita, 1992—2002; US atty. U.S. Dept. of Justice, Kans., 2002—. Trustee Leadership Wichita, 1994—. Mem. Christian Legal Soc. (state dir. 1989-94), Wichita State Alumni Assn. (exec. com. 1993—), West Wichita Rotary Club. Republican. Office: 1200 Epic Ctr 301 N Main Wichita KS 67202 Office Phone: 316-269-6481.

MELIA, KEVIN, manufacturing executive; CEO Manufacturers' Svcs., Concord, Mass. Office: Manufacturers Svcs 300 Baker Ave Ste 106 Concord MA 01742-2131

MELICH, DORIS S. public service worker; b. Salt Lake City, Apr. 8, 1913; d. Edward Harrison and Marie Cushing Snyder; m. Mitchell Melich, June 3, 1935; children: Tanya Marie Melich Silverman, Michael E., Nancy Lynne, Robert Allen. BA in Western History, U. Utah, 1934. Mem. Nat. Commn. Arthritis and Related Musculoskeltal Diseases, 1974-76, Nat. Arthritis Adv. Bd., 1977-84, 86-90; Utah del. Nat. Ho. of Dels. Arthritis Found., 1982-87; pres. Utah Arthritis Found. Bd., 1975-78, v.p., 1968-69, 73-74; Utah rep. Arthritis Found. Govt. Affairs, 1983—. Leader, founder 1st Girl Scouts Lone Troop U.S., Moab, Utah, 1947, regional selections com., 1958-67; active Utah Ballet Guild, Salt Lake Art Ctr., Utah Arts Coun., 1988—, Utah State Rep. Women, YWCA; trustee emeritus Arthritus Found. Recipient Pyramid award Nat. Arthritis Found., 1986, Utah Girl Scouts Regional award, 1987, Thanks Badge, 1963, Merit Honor award U. Utah Emeritus Club, 1978, Minute Man award Utah N.G., 1985; named to Nat. Women's Wall of Fame, Seneca Falls, N.Y., 1993. Mem. AAUW, Nat. Assistance League of Salt Lake City (charter mem.), Utah Women's Forum, Order Ea. Star, Alpha Delta Pi, Beta Sigma Phi (sponsor). Home: 900 Donner Way Apt 708 Salt Lake City UT 84108-2112

MELICHER, RONALD WILLIAM, finance educator; b. St. Louis, July 4, 1941; s. William and Lorraine Norma (Mohart) M.; m. Sharon Ann Schlarmann, Aug. 19, 1967; children: Michelle Joy, Thor William, Sean Richard. BSBA, Washington U., St. Louis, 1963, MBA, 1965, DBA, 1968. Asst. prof. fin. U. Colo., Boulder, 1969-71, assoc. prof., 1971-76, prof. fin., 1976—, chmn. fin. divsn., 1978-86, 90, chmn. fin. and econ. divsn., 1993-2000, MBA/MS programs dir., 1990-93, chmn. fin. divsn., 2003—. Assoc. dir. space law bus. and policy ctr. U. Colo., 1986-87; rsch. cons. FPC, Washington, 1975-76, GAO, Washington, 1981, RCG/Hagler, Bailly, Inc., 1985—, Ariz. Corp. Commn., 1986-87, Conn. Dept. Pub. Utility Control, 1989, US SEC, 1992-95; cons. tech. edn. IBM Corp., 1985-91; dir. ann. Exch. Program for Gas Industry, 1975-94; instr. ann. program Nat. Assn. Regulatory Utility Commrs., Mich. State U., 1981-94. Co-author: Real Estate Finance, 1978, 3d edit., 1989, Financial Management, 5th edit., 1982; Finance: Introduction to Markets, Institutions and Management, 1980, 84, 88, 92, Finance: Introduction to Institutions, Investments, and Management, 9th edit., 1997, 10th edit., 2000, 11th edit., 2003, Entrepreneurial Finance, 2003; assoc. editor Fin. Mgmt. Jour., 1975-80, The Fin. Rev., 1988-91. Recipient News Ctr. 4 TV Tchg. award, 1987, MBA/MS Assn. Tchg. award, 1988, Boulder Faculty Assembly Tchg. award, 1988, Grad. Bus. Students Tchg. award, 1995, 98; grantee NSF, 1974, NASA, 1986, 87; scholar W.H. Baughn Disting., 1989-2000, U. Colo. Pres.'s Tchg., 1989—. Mem. Fin. Mgmt. Assn. (mem. com. 1974-76, regional dir. 1975-77, v.p. ann. mtg. 1985, v.p. program 1987, pres. 1991-92, exec. com. 1991-93, bd. trustees 1992-99, chmn. 25th Anniversary com. 1994-95, mem. search com. for editor of Fin. Mgmt. Jour., 1995-96, chmn. search com. editor of Fin. Practice and Edn. Jour. 1996, mem. search com. for sec./treas. 1999, 2001), Am. Fin. Assn. Western Fin. Assn. (bd. dirs. 1974-76), Fin. Execs. Inst. (acad. mem. 1975—), Ea. Fin. Assn., Southwestern Fin. Assn., Midwest Fin. Assn. (bd. dirs. 1978-80), Alpha Kappa Psi, Beta Gamma Sigma. Office: U Colo Coll Bus PO Box 419 Boulder CO 80303 Office Phone: 303-492-3182. Business E-Mail: Ronald.Melicher@colorado.edu.

MELICK, CLIFFORD FRANCIS, sociologist, researcher; b. Albany, NY, Sept. 6, 1947; s. Francis Joseph Melick, Marion Dorothy Campbell; m. Evelyn Louise Mazo, Feb. 24, 2004. BA, Siena Coll., Loudonville, N.Y., 1971; MA, SUNY, Albany, 1973, PhD, 1979. Rsch. scientist N.Y. State Divsn. for Youth, Albany, 1980—83, dir. revenue and reporting svcs., 1983—86, chief program analysis and rsch., 1986—90; dir. rsch. Greater Balt. Med. Ctr., 1990—2002, dir. clin. info. and rsch., 2002—. Mem. editl adv. bd. Rsch. in Healthcare Fin. Mgmt., Balt., 2000—; prin. advisor NEMA Rsch., Inc., N.Y.C., 1997—; mem. Greater Balt. Med. Ctr. Instnl. Rev. Bd., Balt., 1990—; bd. dirs. Analytica, Ltd., Albany, NY. Contbr. book Chronic Wound Care, 2nd edit., 1997, Chronic Wound Care, 3d edit., 2001, Current Surgical Therapy, 4th edit., 1992, Current Surgical Therapy, 5th edit., 1995, articles to profl. jours. Mem.: APHA, Soc. of Clin. Rsh. Assoc., Am. Urogynecologic Soc., Acad. Health, Soc. for the Art and Sci. Wound Mgmt., Internat. Soc. for Rschs. in Healthcare Fin. Mgmt., Free State Corvette Club. Avocation: sports cars. Home: 8207 Spring Bottom Way Baltimore MD 21208 Office: Greater Baltimore Medical Center 6569 N Charles St Se 701 Baltimore MD 21204 Personal E-mail: cmelick@comcast.net. Business E-Mail: cmelick@gbmc.org.

MELIGNANO, CARMINE (EMANUEL MELIGNANO), video engineer; b. N.Y.C., Dec. 19, 1936; s. Salvatore and Lita (Poggialli) M.; m. Eileen Kinzie; children: Lori Ann, Robert, Michael. BS in Elec. Engring., Stevens Inst. Tech., Hoboken, N.J., 1959; postgrad., William Paterson Coll., 1978, Pace U., 1979. Registered profl. engr., N.J. Quality contr. Isomet Corp., Palisades Park, N.J., 1959-63; sales engr. RCA Service Corp., Camden, N.J., 1963-73; video engr. N.J. Sports and Expn. Authority, East Rutherford, 1974-77; chief engr. Price Waterhouse, N.Y.C., 1978—. Engring. cons. Passaic County Vocat. Edn. High Sch., Wayne, N.J., 1971-77, Meadowlands Racetrack, East Rutherford, 1973-77, Royal Sound, Eatontown, N.J., 1984-86. Bd. trustees N.Y.C. chpt. Leukemia Soc., 1981-86, pres., 1987-90, nat. bd. trustees, 1990—. Recipient Emmy award NATAS, 1985, Outstanding Svc. award Leukemia Soc. Nat. Bd., 1986, Vincent T. Lombardi Humanitarian award, 1990, Pres.' award Leukemia Soc. Am., 1991, People's award, 1991, Outstanding Svc. award in New Orleans, 1994, Disting. Am. award Nat. Football Found. and Coll. Hall of Fame, 1999. Mem. Soc. Motion Picture and TV Engrs. (sec., treas. elect N.Y.C. chpt. 1984-86), Nat. Sports Com., Nat. Performing Arts Com. (vice chmn. 1985—), Friar's Club Internat. (N.Y.C., profl. mem., mem.-elect). Lodges: KC. Republican. Roman Catholic. Avocations: sports, chess, organ and piano. Office: CarMel Prodns 10 Dell Glen Ave Lodi NJ 07644-1758 Home: 421 Farnham Ave Lodi NJ 07644-1204

MELILLO, JOSEPH VINCENT, producer, performing arts; b. New Haven, Nov. 15, 1946; s. Vincent and Viola (Fucci) M. BA, Sacred Heart U., 1968; MFA, Cath. U. Am., 1972. Adminstr. City Ctr. Music and Drama, N.Y.C., 1972-75; mktg. dir. The Walnut St. Theatre, Phila., 1975-76; dir. FEDAPT, N.Y.C., 1976-80; gen. mgr. New World Festival of Arts, Miami, Fla., 1982; dir. Next Wave Festival, N.Y.C., 1983-89; artistic dir. N.Y. Internat. Festival, N.Y.C., 1990-91, exec. prodr., 1999—; producing dir. Bklyn. Acad. Music, 1991—, exec. prodr., 1999—. Trustee EnGarde Arts, N.Y.C., 1991-96; v.p., bd. dirs. Assn. Performing Arts Presenters, Washington, 1991-93; cons.-specialist Opera Am. Washington, 1991-93; cons. The Japan Found. "Performing Arts Japan", The Bush Found., St. Paul, Arts Internat., N.Y.C.; adj. prof. Theater Dept. Bklyn. Coll.; co-chair Internat. Presenters Forum; mem. cultural challenge panel N.Y.C. Dept. Cultural Affairs; bd. advisors Etantdonnes, 2000, 2001, 2002. Editor: Market the Arts, 1980. Mem. adv. bd. materials for the arts Africa Exch.: 651 program com. N.J. Performing Arts Ctr., Newark, 1199—; mem. New Haven Festival of the Arts and Ideas; advisor Rolex Mentor and Protege Program, 2002—03; program adv. panel Pew Fellowships in the Arts, 2003, chmn. multidisciplinary panel, 2003. Decorated chevalier Order of Arts and Letters; Recipient Documents of Dance award, Dance Library of Israel, 2003. Mem.: Century Assn., L'ordre des Arts et des Lettres (officer 2004). Democrat. Avocations: reading, travel. Business E-Mail: programming@bam.org.

MELIN, ROBERT ARTHUR, lawyer; b. Milw., Sept. 13, 1940; s. Arthur John and Frances Magdalena (Lanser) M.; m. Mary Magdalen Melin, July 8, 1967; children: Arthur Walden, Robert Dismas, Nicholas O'Brien, Madalyn Mary. BA summa cum laude, Marquette U., 1962, JD, 1967. Bar: Wis. 1966, U.S. Dist. Ct. (ea. dist.) Wis. 1966, U.S. Ct. Appeals (7th cir.) 1966, U.S. Ct. Mil. Appeals 1967, U.S. Supreme Ct. 1975. Law clk. U.S. Dist. Ct. (ea. dist.), Wis., 1966; instr. bus. law U. Ga., Hinesville, 1968; lectr. bus. law U. Md., Asmara, 1970; lectr. law Haile Salassie I. U. Law Faculty, Addis Ababa, Ethiopia, 1971-72; with Walther & Halling, Milw., 1973-74, Schroeder, Gedlen, Riester & Moerke, Milw., 1974-82; ptnr. Schroeder, Gedlen, Riester & Melin, Milw., 1982-84, Schroeder, Riester, Melin & Smith, Milw., 1984—. Author: Evidence in Ethiopia, 1972; contbg. author Ann. Survey African Law, 1974; contbr. numerous articles to legal jours. Rep. Class of 2000, West Point Parent Assn. Wis., 1996-99, 99—, exec. bd., 1997-98, 98—; lectr. charitable solicitations and contracts Philanthropy Monthly 9th Ann. Policy Conf., NYC, 1985; chmn. Milw. Young Dems., 1963-64. Capt. JAGC, AUS, 1967-70. Mem. ABA, Wis. Acad. Trial Lawyers, Wis. Bar Assn., Milw. Bar Assn., Am. Legion, Friends Ethiopia, Delta Theta Phi, Phi Alpha Theta, Pi Gamma Mu. Roman Catholic. Home: 8108 N Whitney Rd Milwaukee WI 53217-2752 Office: 135 W Wells St Milwaukee WI 53203-1807 Office Phone: 414-351-0539.

MELISSINOS, ADRIAN CONSTANTIN, physicist, researcher; b. Thessaloniki, Greece, July 28, 1929; came to U.S., 1955, naturalized, 1970; s. Constantin John and Olympia (Abbott) M.; m. Mary Joyce Mitchell, June 7, 1960; children: Constantin John, Andrew William. Student, Royal Naval Acad., Greece, 1945-48; MS, Mass. Inst. Tech., 1956, PhD, 1958. Naval cadet Greek Navy, 1945-48, commd. ensign, 1948, advanced through grades to lt., 1951; ret., 1954; teaching and research asst. Mass. Inst. Tech., 1955-58; instr. U. Rochester, N.Y., 1958-60, asst. prof. physics, 1960-63, assoc. prof., 1963-67, prof., 1967—, chmn. dept. physics and astronomy, 1974-77. Vis. scientist CERN European Center for Nuclear Research, 1968-69, 77-78, 89-90; cons. Brookhaven Nat. Lab., 1970-72, 75-79; vis. prof. U. Athens, 1996; vis. scientist Deutsches Electronen Synchrotron, 1997; cons. Stanford Linear Accelerator Ctr., 1995-98. Author: Experiments in Modern Physics, 1966, (with J. Napolitano) 2d edit., 2003, (with F. Lobkowicz) Physics for Scientists and Engineers, 1975; (with A. Das) Quantum Mechanics, 1985, Principles of Modern Technology, 1990. Decorated Swedish Order of Sword. Fellow Am. Phys. Soc.; mem. Greek Nat. Acad. (corr.) Achievements include experimentation with elementary particles at most major high energy accelerators in the U.S. and Europe, experimentation with high power lasers, searches for dark matter. Home: 177 Whitewood Ln Rochester NY 14618-3223 Office: U Rochester Dept Physics Rochester NY 14627 Office Phone: 585-275-2707. Business E-Mail: meliss@pas.rochester.edu.

MELITO, THOMAS, music educator, musician; b. Rochester, N.Y., Aug. 31, 1956; s. Christopher and Ann Melito. MusB, State U. of Potsdam (N.Y.), 1978. Performers cert. percussion Potsdam U., 1978. Adj. prof. music Ctrl. Conn. U., New Britain, 1999—; jazz drummer various artists, N.Y.C., NY. Clinician U. P.R., San Juan, 2003. Musician: (recording (cd) The Bopra House; musician: (drummer) (video, CD) Ken Peplowski Quintet Live at the Ambassador Theater, (CD) Michael Moore The History Of Jazz, vol. 1 (4 Star Rev., Downbeat Mag., 2003), Michael Moore The History of Jazz, vol. 2 (One of Best Jazz Albums of 2002, New Yorker Mag., 2003), Dave Santoro/ The New Standard, Dave Santoro Standards Band, Ken Peplowski Quintet /The Natural Touch, Jerry Bergonzi:Thesaurus of Intervallic Melodies. Personal E-mail: thomasm555@yahoo.com.

MELL, PATRICIA, dean; b. Cleve., Dec. 15, 1953; d. Julian Cooper and Thelma (Webb) M.; m. Michael Ragland. AB with honors, Wellesley Coll., 1975; JD, Case Western Res. U., 1978. Bar: Ohio 1979, Pa. 1988, U.S. Dist. Ct. (so. and no. dists.) Ohio 1979. Asst. atty. gen. State of Ohio, Columbus, 1978-82, sec. of state corps. counsel, 1982-84; vis. asst. prof. Capital U. Law Sch., Columbus, 1984-85, U. Toledo Law Sch., 1985-86; asst. prof. law Widener U. (formerly Delaware Law Sch.), Wilmington, 1986—88; prof. law Mich. State U. Detroit Coll. of Law, East Lansing, Mich., 1992—2003, assoc. dean for academic affairs, 2000—02; dean John Marshall Law Sch., Chicago, Ill., 2003—. Mediator night prosecutor's program, Columbus, 1984-85. Mem. scholarship screening com. Black Am. Law Student Assn. U. Toledo Law Sch., 1985-86, governing bd. Case Western Res. U. Law Sch., Cleve., 1985-88, Alliance of Black Women, Columbus, 1983-85, Capers for Judge com., Cleve., 1980-86, century club Ohio Dems., 1985-86; chmn. law student com. Young Black Dems., Columbus, 1982-84; coordinator minority affiliations subcom. Citizens for Brown for Gov., Columbus, 1981-82; mem. Nat. Beach MBA, 1986—. Recipient award Internat. Assn. Corps. Adminstrs., 1983; named one of Chicago's 100 Most Influential Women, Crain's Chicago Business, 2004. Mem. ABA, Nat. Bar Assn., Nat. Conf. Black Lawyers, Am. Arbitration Assn. (comml. arbitrator 1986—), Nat. Black MBA's, 1986-91. Lutheran. Avocations: modern languages, stained glass work, fencing, tennis, piano. Office: John Marshall Law Sch 315 S Plymouth Court Chicago IL 60604*

MELL, WILLIAM ERIC, mathematician; s. Eric William and Janice Elizabeth Mell; m. Phyllis Holly Kuna. BS in geophysics, U. Minn., 1981; MS in applied math., U. Wash., 1987, PhD in applied math., 1994. Field geophysicist Dow Chem., Crystal Falls, Mich., 1983—85; nrc post doctoral assoc. Nat. Inst. Stds. and Tech., Gaithersburg, Md., 1994—96, rsch. scientist, 1996—2000; rsch. prof. U. Utah, 2000—04; rsch. scientist Nat. Inst. Stds. Tech., 2004—. Author several sci. papers. Recipient Bigglestone award, Fire Rsch. Found. Nat. Fire Protection Assn., 2001, Presdl. Early Career award, Exec. Office of Pres., 2001. Mem.: Sigma XI. Avocations: hockey, hiking, backpacking. E-mail: ruddy@nist.gov.

MELLBERG, JAMES RICHARD, dental research chemist; b. Manitowoc, Wis., June 3, 1932; s. Millard Filmore Mellberg and Marion Eleanor (Elmer) Zimmerman; m. Gail Maureen Loehning, Sept. 26, 1956; children: Eric, Diane, Laura. BS, Wis. State U., Oshkosh, 1955; MS, Loyola U., Chgo., 1960. Head dental rsch. dept. Kendall Co., Barrington, Ill., 1958-75; assoc. dir. dental rsch. Colgate-Palmolive Co., Piscataway, N.J., 1975-94. Cons. Naval Dental Rsch. Inst., Great Lakes, Ill., 1972-94. Author: Fluoride in Preventive Dentistry, 1983; patentee in field; contbr. over 100 articles in field to sci. publs. Recipient 20 sci. exhibit awards ADA, 1964-87. Mem. Internat. Assn. Dental Rsch. (Disting. Scientist award). Avocations: bicycling, woodworking. Home: 675 Ridge Top Rd Tryon NC 28782 Personal E-mail: mellberg1@alltel.net.

MELLEMA, DONALD EUGENE, retired radio news reporter and anchor; b. Chgo., Mar. 30, 1937; s. Raymond Cornelius and Dorothy Sofia (Miller) M.; m. Freda Dieterlen Mellema, Sept. 23, 1961; children: Darryl Emerson, Duane Edward. BA in Speech, Beloit (Wis.) Coll., 1959. News dir. WGEZ Radio, Beloit, 1959; evening host, newsman WOSH Radio, Oshkosh, Wis., 1959-63; morning host, newsman WANE Radio, Ft. Wayne, Ind., 1963-65; news dir. WATI Radio, Indpls., 1965-67; news writer WGN Radio, Chgo., 1967-69; news reporter, anchor WBBM Radio, Chgo., 1969-96; ret., 1996. Mem. publs. adv. bd., pres's adv. coun., cons. Beloit Coll., 1996-2000, also profl.-in-residence; Lewis and Clark lectr. Taft H.S., 2002--. Speaker, motivator Chgo. Pub. Sch. Youth Motivation Program, 1993-96; advisor, cons. media rels. to various police and civic orgns.; commr., unit leader Boy Scouts Am., 1971-81; ch. deacon Park Ridge (Ill.) Presbyn. Ch., 1980-83. Recipient regional award Radio TV News Dirs. Assn., 1994, Newsfinder award AP, 1995, career recognition award Chgo. Police Dept., 1997, Mark Twain award Ill. AP, 1997; named to Taft H.S. Hall of Fame, 1995. Mem. Ill. News Broadcasters Assn. (Silver Dome 1st Place award 1994), Soc. Profl. Journalists (Peter Lisagor award 1991, 96, Lewis and Clark lectr. 2002—), Am. Legion. Republican. Avocations: woodworking, reading, photography, birding, travel. Personal E-mail: donmellema@netscape.net.

MELLEN, FRANCIS JOSEPH, JR., lawyer; b. Williamsport, Pa., Dec. 19, 1945; s. Francis Joseph and Mary Emma (Oberst) M.; m. Mary Wilder Davison, Aug. 2, 1975 (div. 1987); m. Beverly Joan Glascock, Sept. 2, 2000; children: Elizabeth, Catherine, Robert, Christine. BA, U. Ky., 1967, MA, 1971; JD, Harvard U., 1973. Bar: N.Y. 1974, Ky. 1975, U.S. Dist. Ct. (so. dist.) N.Y. 1974, U.S. Dist. Ct. (ea. dist.) Ky. 1977, U.S. Dist. Ct. (we. dist.) Ky. 1978, U.S. Ct. Appeals (2d cir.) 1975, U.S. Ct. Appeals (6th cir.) 1982. Assoc. atty. Rogers & Wells, N.Y.C., 1973-75, Wyatt, Grafton & Sloss, Louisville, 1975-80; ptnr. Wyatt, Tarrant & Combs, Louisville, 1980—. Co-author: Kentucky Mineral Law, 1986, Kentucky Forms and Transactions, 1991; contbr. articles to profl. jours. Mem. spl. study com. for Uniform Comml. Code, Ky. Legis. Rsch. Commn., Frankfort, 1984-91; bd. dirs. Leadership Louisville Found., 1995-2002, counsel, 1996-98, 2000-02; bd. dirs. Stage One: The Louisville Children's Theatre, 1995-2001, v.p., 1997-98, pres., 1998-2000; bd. dirs. Louisville-Jefferson County A.W.A.R.E. Coalition, 1994-98. Mem. ABA, Am. Arbitration Assn. (panel), Nat. Arbitration Forum (panel), CPR Inst for Dispute Resolution (panel), Ky. Bar Assn. (ho. dels. 1986-92), Louisville Bar Assn. (chmn. com. profl. responsibility 1992-94), Jefferson Club, Filson Club, Am. Mensa, Hon. Order of Ky. Cols. Republican. Home: 2944 Lexington Rd Louisville KY 40206-2934 Office: Wyatt Tarrant & Combs LLP 2800 PNC Plz Louisville KY 40202 Office Phone: 502-562-7290. E-mail: fmellen@wyattfirm.com.

MELLENCAMP, JOHN (JOHN COUGAR), singer, songwriter; b. Seymour, Ind., Oct. 7, 1951; m. Vicky C. (div.); children: Michelle, Teddy Joe, Justice; m. Elaine Irwin, Sept. 5, 1992. Student, Vincennes U., Ind. Albums include Chestnut Street Incident, 1977, Biography, 1978, Johnny Cougar, 1979, Nothing Matters and What If It Did, 1980, Night Dancin, 1980, American Fool, 1982, Uh-huh, 1983, Scarecrow, 1985, The Lonesome Jubilee, 1988, Big Daddy, 1989, Whenever We Wanted, 1991, Human Wheels, 1993, Dance Naked, 1994, Mr. Happy Go Lucky, 1996, The Best That I Could Do...1997, John Mellencamp, 1998, Rough Harvest, 1999; performed one song for Folkways: A Vision Shared (A Tribute to Woody Guthrie and Leadbelly), 1988; film actor, dir., soundtrack performer: Falling From Grace, 1992, Seeing in the Dark, 2000; TV appearance Bob Dylan: The 30th Anniversary Concert Celebration, 1993, Farm Aid '96, 1996. Office: Mercury Records 825 8th Ave New York NY 10019-7416

MELLER, ROBERT LOUIS, JR., lawyer; b. Mpls., Apr. 24, 1950; s. Robert Louis and June Louise (Grenacher) M. BA, Carleton Coll., 1972; JD, Cornell U., 1975. Bar: Minn., 1975, U.S. Dist. Ct. (no. dist.), 1975. Atty. Best & Flanagan, Mpls., 1977—, ptnr., 1982—. Mem. ABA, Minn. State Bar Assn., Mpls. Club, Phi Beta Kappa, Sigma Xi. Republican. Episcopalian. Home: 1800 Major Dr N Minneapolis MN 55422-4153 Office: Best and Flanagan 225 So 6th St Ste 4000 Minneapolis MN 55402-4303 E-mail: rmeller@bestlaw.com.

MELLETT, EDWIN R. soft drink executive; b. N.Y.C., Feb. 4, 1939; s. Edwin and Agnes M.; m. Frances L., Dec. 30, 1961; children: Edwin J., Kathleen A., Andrew G., Christopher R. BA, Fordham Coll., 1960; MBA in Fin., U. Pa., 1961. V.p. ea. div. Pepsi Cola Co., N.Y.C., 1975-78, pres. food svc. div., 1978-84; exec. v.p. Coca-Cola USA, Atlanta, 1984-86, pres., 1986; sr. v.p. The Coca-Cola Co., Atlanta, 1986-92; vice chmn., co-CEO, AHL Svcs. Inc., Atlanta, 1994—. Pres. N.Am. soft drink bus. sector. Coca-Cola No. Europe. Mem. Cherokee Club, Peachtree Golf Club, Buckhead Club, Windsor Club (Vero Beach, Fla.), Redstick Club (Vero Beach), Manchester Country Club (Vt.). Roman Catholic. Avocations: golf, skiing. Office: AHL Svcs Inc 3353 Peachtree Rd NE Ste 1120 Atlanta GA 30326-1053

MELLETTE, JULIAN RAMSEY, JR., dermatologist, dermatologic surgeon; b. Florence, SC, June 27, 1939; s. Julian Ramsey and Mary (Brown) Mellette; m. Elizabeth Odom, May 22, 1945; children: Elizabeth Ritland, Julian Ramsey III, Bradford. AB, Wofford Coll., 1961; MD, Med. U. S.C., 1969. Spl. agt. in charge Atlanta field office Mil. Intelligence, 1962—64; chief aerospace medicine Lyster Army Hosp., Fort Rucker, Ariz., 1971—73; chief dermatology Fitzsimmons Army Med. Ctr., Aurora, Colo., 1982—90; prof. dermatology U. Colo. Health Sci. Ctr., 1990—2003, Mohs fellowship dir., 1995—2003. Brig. gen. Joint Svc. Detachment, State of SC, 2003. Contbr. chapters to books, articles to profl. jours. Col. U.S. Army, 1961—90. Mem.: Colo. Dermatology Surg. Soc. (pres. 1989—), Internat. Soc. Dermatology Surgeons (bd. dirs. 1999—2001), Am. Coll. Mohs Surgery and Cutaneous Oncology (bd. dirs. 1993—96). Avocations: skiing, golf, scuba diving, flying. Office: Dept Dermatology PO Box 6510 Campus Stop F703 Aurora CO 80010-0510 E-mail: b.mellette@comcast.net.

MELLEY, STEVEN MICHAEL, lawyer; b. Rhinebeck, N.Y., Jan. 3, 1950; s. James Christopher and Virginia (Madonna) M.; children: Aliza, Steven Jonathan, Olivia, Bennett; m. Phoebe Kirwood. BA in Russian Studies with honors, Colgate U., 1972; JD, Tulane U., 1975. Bar: N.Y. 1976, U.S. Dist. Ct. 1976, U.S. Supreme Ct. 1980. Law clk. to hon. Matthew Braniff Criminal Dist. Judge, Orleans Parish, New Orleans; assoc. Woody N. Klose Law Offices, Red Hook, N.Y., 1975-78; ptnr. Klose & Melley, Rhinebeck, 1978-83; pvt. practice Rhinebeck, 1983—. Atty. Village of Tivoli, N.Y., 1977-78. Contbg. editor: New York Motor Vehicle Accidents, 1999; assoc. editor Tulane Forum, 1974-75. Mem. ABA, ATLA (sustaining), N.Y. State Bar Assn. (past com. mem. on specialization), Dutchess County Bar Assn. (sustaining), N.Y. State Trial Lawyers Assn., Million Dollar Advocates Forum, Phi Alpha Delta, Kappa Delta Rho. Office: 24 Closs Dr Rhinebeck NY 12572 Fax: (914) 876-5745. E-mail: melleyinjurylaw@aol.com.

MELLI, MARYGOLD SHIRE, law educator; b. Rhinelander, Wis., Feb. 8, 1926; d. Osborne and May (Bonnie) Shire; m. Joseph Alexander Melli, Apr. 8, 1950; children: Joseph, Sarah Bonnie, Sylvia Anne, James Alexander. BA, U. Wis., 1947, LLB, 1950. Bar: Wis. 1950. Dir. children's code revision Wis. Legis. Coun., Madison, 1950-53; exec. dir. Wis. Jud. Coun., Madison, 1955-59; asst. prof. law U. Wis., Madison, 1959-66, assoc. prof., 1966-67, prof., 1967-84, Voss-Bascom prof., 1985-93, emerita, 1993—. Assoc. dean U. Wis., 1970-72, rsch. affiliate Inst. for Rsch. on Poverty, 1980—; mem. spl. rev. bd. Dept. Health and Social Svcs., State of Wis., Madison, 1973—2002. Author: (pamphlet) The Legal Status of Women in Wisconsin, 1977, (book) Wisconsin Juvenile Court Practice, 1978, rev. edit., 1983, (with others) Child Support & Alimony, 1988, The Case for Transracial Adoption, 1994; co-editor: Child Support: The Next Frontier, 1999; contbr. articles to profl. jours. Bd. dirs. Am. Humane Assn., 1985-95, Frank Lloyd Wright - Wis., 2004; chair A Fund for Women, Madison, Wis., 2002, 2003. Named one of five Outstanding

Young Women in Wis., Jaycees, 1961; rsch. grantee NSF, 1983; recipient Belle Case LaFollette award for outstanding svc. to the profession, 1994, award for Outstanding Contbn. to Advancement of Women in Higher Edn., 1991, award for Lifelong Contbn. to Advancement of Women in the Legal Prof., 1994, Rotary Sr. Svc. award, Madison, Wis., 2002. Fellow Am. Acad. Matrimonial Lawyers (exec. editor jour. 1985-90); mem. Am. Law Inst. (cons. project on law of family dissolution), Internat. Soc. Family Law (v.p. 1994-2000, 02—), Wis. State Bar Assn. (reporter family law sect.), Nat. Conf. Bar Examiners (chmn. bd. mgrs. 1989, editl. adv. com.). Democrat. Roman Catholic. Avocations: walking, swimming, collecting art. Home: 2904 Waunona Way Madison WI 53713-2238 Office: U Wis Law Sch Madison WI 53706 Office Phone: 608-262-1610.

MELLING, JACK, biotechnologist, director; b. Aspull, Lancashire, Eng., Feb. 8, 1940; s. John and Mary (Marsden) M.; m. Susan Ewart, May 27, 1967. BSc, Manchester U., Eng., 1963, MSc, 1965; PhD, Bath U., Eng., 1968. Rsch. asst. Bath U., Eng., 1965-68; lectr. Heriot-Watt U., Scotland, 1968-69; sr. sci. officer Ministry of Def., Eng., 1969-73, prin. sci. officer, 1973-79; dir. vaccine rsch. and product lab. Pub. Health Lab. Svc., Eng., 1979-87; head biologics divsn. and dep. dir. Ctr. for Applied Microbiology & Rsch., Porton Down, Salisbury, England, 1987-92, dir. Porton Down, Salisbury, Eng., 1992-96, Salk Inst., Swiftwater, Pa., 1996-2000, Karl Landsteiner Inst., Vienna, 2000—03; sr. project mgr. Battelle Meml. Inst., Columbus, Ohio, 2001—. Vis. prof. Rutgers U. 1979-84, Aston U., 1981-96, Westminster U., 1995—, Zurich U., 1999—; mem. MRC Vaccine Com., 1979-96; sec. Brit. Coord. Com. for Biotech., London, 1981-85; mem. Com. Safety of Medicines, Biologic, London, 1982-99, Ministry of Agr. Toxicants in Foods com., London, 1982-94; mem. rsch. adv. com. on Gulf War vets. illnesses U.S. Dept. Vets. Affairs, 2002--; counsellor, tutor Open U., Salisbury, 1971-74; sr. sci. advisor Internat. AIDS Initiative, N.Y.C., 1999—; cons. U.S. GAO, 1998-, cons. U.S. Gen. Accounting Office, 1998-. Editor: Microbial Adhesion, 1980; editor Chem. Tech. and Biotech. Jour., 1985—; contbr. over 100 articles to profl. jours. Active Swiss Disaster Relief Orgn. Fellow Royal Pharm. Soc. G.B., Inst. of Biology. Fellow Royal Soc. Medicine, Royal Coll. Pathologists; mem. Soc. Chem. Industry (coun. mem. 1975-83, 98-2001, sec. 1975-81, chmn. biotech. group 1981-83, chmn. publs. com. 1999-2004, hon. treas. 2004—). Avocations: skiing, walking. Office: Baltelle Meml Inst 505 King Ave Columbus OH 43201-2693 Business E-Mail: jmelling@prd.net.

MELLINGER, BARRY LEE, community college president, vocational educator; b. Colorado Springs, Colo., Dec. 19, 1939; s. Paul Diffenbach and Edna R. (Detwiller) M.; m. Dorothy Bugg, June 20, 1964; children: Mim Hatten, Debbie (dec.), Sharon Sanders, Jay, Christa. AS, Perkinston (Miss.) Jr. Coll., 1960; BS, Miss. State U., 1962, MEd, 1963; PhD, Purdue U., 1973. Asst. dir. vocat.-tech. edn. Miss. Gulf Coast C.C., Perkinston, 1963-65, dir. vocat-tech. edn., 1965-67; instr. Purdue U., West Lafayette, Ind., 1967-68; asst. exec. sec. Commn. on Colls., So. Assn. Colls. and Schs., Atlanta, 1968-72, assoc. exec. sec., 1972-77; dir. vocat-tech. sch., dean occupl. edn. Dekalb C.C., Clarkston, Ga., 1977-79; v.p. instnl. affairs Miss. Gulf Coast C.C., 1979-85, pres., 1986-98; ret., 1998. Cons. Nunez C.C., Chalmette, La., 1993, Northwestern State U., Natchitoches, La., 1993. Mem. Miss. Higher Edn. Assistance Corp., Jackson, 1984-97; bd. dirs. Kids Voting Miss., 1996, 97; mem. exec. bd. Miss. Pub. Edn. Forum, 1993—; mem. Harrison County Devel. Commn., Econ. Devel. Network, 1988-89; mem. info. resource coun., Miss. Dept. Info. Tech. Svcs., 1996, 97. Recipient CEO award Assn. C.C. Trustees, 1994. Mem. Am. Assn. Cmty. and Jr. Colls. (bd. dirs. 1987-90), Nat. Alliance Cmty. and Tech. Colls. (pres. 1985-86), So. Assn. Colls. and Schs. (mem. exec. coun. 1994-96, commn. on colls. 1994-96, criteria rev. com. 1994, chmn.'s corps; chmn. reaffirmation com. to Patrick Henry C.C., Martinsville, Va. 1997, Delgado C.C., New Orleans 1996, Tex. State Tech. Coll., Amarillo 1995, Daytona Beach C.C. 1993, Santa Fe C.C., Gainesville, Fla. 1993), Miss. Assn. Colls. (mem. audit com. 1992, pres. 1990), Miss. C.C. and Jr. Coll. Assn. (chmn. 1996—), So. Assn. Cmty., Jr., and Tech. Colls. (v.p. 1988), Rotary Club (Wiggins, Miss.), Phi Delta Kappa, Iota Lambda Sigma. Avocations: woodworking, antique cars. Home: 66 Bluff Creek Rd Wiggins MS 39577-9714 Office: Miss Gulf Coast Cmty Coll PO Box 67 Perkinston MS 39573-0002

MELLINGER, LOUIS PHILIP, lawyer; b. Newark, Sept. 12, 1950; s. Leonard and Clarice Helen Mellinger; m. Rebecca Ann Thompson, Nov. 17; children: William Leonard, Robert Jon. BS with high honors, U. Md., 1972; JD, Widener U., Wilmington, Del., 1976; Cert. in Internat. Law, Institut Catholique, Paris, 1974. Bar: N.J. 1976, U.S. Dist. Ct. N.J. 1976, U.S. Supreme Ct. 1997. Sr. ptnr. Mellinger Sanders & Kartzman, LLC, Morris Plains, NJ, 1977—. Asst. city atty. City of Orange, NJ, 1978—80; exec. v.p. Anthem World Transport, Jersey City, 1987—; mcpl. ct. judge Allamuchy Twp., NJ, 1990—, Raritan Twp., NJ, 1997—; adv. counsel mem. Fleet Bank N.J., 1994—. Committeeman Rep. Party Warren County, NJ, 1989; chmn. com. for formation and implementation of cmty. dispute resolution program for Warren County Adminstrv. Offices of the Ct., 1993. Nominee Humanitarian of the Yr., Martial Arts Hall of Fame, Orlando, Fla., 2002; named to Cir. of Masters, Inst. of Sci. Martial Arts Angelic System, Hillside, N.J., 1996; recipient Disting. Svc. award in recognition of outstanding contbns. and dedicated svc. to Italian Am. Cmty., Consul Gen. on Behalf of the Italian Govt., 1996, Honor for dedicated svcs. to children of Allamuchy Elem. Sch., Allamuchy Bd. of Edn., 2002. Mem.: ATLA, ABA, Soc. of Children's Book Writers and Illustrators, Order of Ky. Cols., Kappa Tau Alpha. Avocations: running, writing children's stories, golf, martial arts, coaching youth basketball. Office: Mellinger Sanders & Kartzman LLC 101 Gibraltar Dr Ste 2F Morris Plains NJ 07950

MELLINKOFF, SHERMAN MUSSOFF, medical educator; b. McKeesport, Pa., Mar. 23, 1920; s. Albert and Helen Mussoff Mellinkoff; m. June Bernice O'Connell, Nov. 18, 1944; children: Sherrill, Albert. BA, Stanford U., 1941, MD, 1944; LHD (hon.), Wake Forest U., 1984, Hebrew Union Coll., L.A., 1988. Diplomate Am. Bd. Internal Medicine, Am. Bd. Gastroenterology, Am. Bd. Nutrition. Intern asst. resident Stanford U. Hosp., San Francisco, 1944—45; asst. resident Johns Hopkins Hosp., Balt., 1947—49, chief resident, 1950—51, instr. in medicine, 1951—53; fellow in gastroenterology Hosp. of U. Pa., Phila., 1949—50; from asst. prof. to prof. medicine UCLA Sch. of Medicine, L.A., 1962—86; dean UCLA Sch. Medicine, L.A., 1962—86, emeritus prof. of medicine, 1990—; disting. physician of VA Wadsworth VA Medical Ctr., L.A., 1990-93. Mem. sci. adv. panel Rsch. to Prevent Blindness, Inc., N.Y.C., 1975—93; mem. program devel. com. Nat. Med. Fellowships, Inc., N.Y.C., 1984—. Editl. bd.: The Pharos, 1986; contbr. articles to profl. jours. Apptd. by Gov. of Calif. to McCone Com., 1965. Capt. U.S. Army, 1945—57. Recipient Abraham Flexner award, Assn. Am. Med. Colls., 1981, J.E. Wallace Sterling Disting. Alumnus award, Stanford U. Sch. of Medicine, 1987. Master: ACP; fellow: Royal Coll. of Physicians; mem.: The Johns Hopkins Soc. of Scholars, Am. Acad. of Arts and Scis., Inst. of Medicine of NAS, Assn. Am. Physicians, Am. Gastroenterol. Assn. Assn. Avocations: reading, hiking. Office: UCLA Dept Medicine 44 138 Chs Los Angeles CA 90095-0001

MELLINS, HARRY ZACHARY, radiologist, educator; b. N.Y.C., May 23, 1921; s. David J. and Ray (Hoffman) M.; m. Judith Alice Weiss, Dec. 26, 1950; children— Elizabeth, William, Thomas. AB, Columbia Coll., 1941; MD, L.I. Coll. Medicine, 1944; MS in Radiology, U. Minn., 1951; AM (hon.), Harvard U., 1970. Intern Jewish Hosp., Bklyn., 1944-45, asst. resident in radiology, 1945-46; resident in radiology U. Minn., Mpls., 1948-50, instr. radiology, 1950-52, asst. prof., 1952-53; clin. asst. prof. radiology Wayne State U., Detroit, 1953-56; dir. radiology Sinai Hosp., Detroit, 1953-56; prof., chmn. dept. radiology SUNY, Coll. Medicine, N.Y.C., 1956-69; chief radiology Kings County Hosp. Center, Bklyn., 1956-69; radiologist-in-chief State Univ. Hosp., Bklyn., 1966-69; prof. radiology Harvard Med. Sch., Boston, 1969—87, prof. radiology emeritus, 1991—; dir. diagnostic radiology Peter Bent Brigham Hosp., 1969-79, Brigham and Women's Hosp., 1980-87, dir. edn. and tng., dept. radiology, 1987-94; co-dir. edn. and tng. dept. radiology, 1994-97; chief of radiology Harvard U. Health Svc., 1988-97; radiologist Brigham and Women's Hosp., 1998-99. Nat. cons. in radiology to surgeon gen. U.S. Air Force, 1968-79; mem. radiation study sect. NIH, 1967-71; mem. subcom. for written exam. in diagnostic radiology Am. Bd. Radiology, 1970-75; mem. radiology tng. com. research tng. grants br. Nat. Inst. Gen. Med. Scis.; mem. diagnostic research adv. group div. cancer biology and diagnosis Nat. Cancer Inst., 1975-79; guest examiner Am. Bd. Radiology. Served to capt. M.C. USAAF, 1946-48. Mem. Bklyn. Radiol. Soc. (pres. 1965-66), N.Y. Roentgen Soc. (pres 1966-67), Assn. Univ. Radiologists (pres. 1969-70, Gold medal 1986), Soc. Uroradiology (pres. 1975-76, Gold medal 2000), Am. Roentgen Ray Soc. (pres. 1977-79, Gold medal 1989), Radiol. Soc. N.Am., New Eng. Roentgen Ray Soc. (pres. 1986-87), Soc. Gastrointestinal Radiology, Alpha Omega Alpha (alumnus).

MELLINS, ROBERT B. pediatrician, educator; b. NYC, Mar. 6, 1928; s. David J. and Ray H. (Hoffman) M.; m. Sue Mendelsohn, Apr. 19, 1959; children: Claude Ann, David Rustin. AB, Columbia U., 1948; MD, Johns Hopkins U., 1952. Intern Johns Hopkins Hosp., 1952-53; mem. epidemic intelligence svc, founder poison control program Ctr. Disease Control, Chgo., 1953-55; resident in pediatrics NY Hosp., 1955-56; resident in pediat. Presbyn. Hosp., NYC, 1956-57, dir. pediatric ICU, 1970-75; assoc. prof. pediat. Columbia U., NYC, 1970-75, prof. pediat., 1975—, dir. Cystic Fibrosis Ctr., 1978-91, dir. pediatric pulmonary divsn., 1972-97. Christmas Seal prof. Can. Lung Assn., 1979-80; 1st Deans Disting. lectr. in clin. scis. Columbia U. Coll. P&S, 1982; mem. Am. Bd. Pediat., founding mem. sub-bd. on pediatric pulmonology; bd. dirs. A.P. Gold Fedn. to promote humanisim in medicine. Mem. editl. bd. Am. Rev. Respiratory Diseases, 1974-81, assoc. editor, 1984-90; contbr. articles to med. jours. V.p. Am. Lung Assn., 1987—89; chmn. steering com. multi-ctr. study heart and lung complications of HIV infection in children NIH, 1989—2003; bd. dir. Am. Lung Assn., 1981—83, LA Jonas Found., 1970—78, 1990—, Symphony of UN, 1990—; bd. dirs. Am. Lung Assn. City of N.Y., 2001—. Recipient Career Devel. award NIH, 1966-71, Career Scientist award Health Rsch. Coun. NYC Health Rsch. Coun., 1975, Stevens Triennial award for rsch. Columbia U., 1980, Health Edn. Rsch. award Nat. Asthma Edn. Program, 1992, Will Ross medal Am. Lung Assn., 1996, 2001 Life & Breath award Am. Lung Assn. NY. Mem.: Keynote Address Sixth Ann. Congress Pediatric Pulmonology, Lisbon 2004, Am. Acad. Allergy and Immunology, Soc. Critical Care Medicine, Am. Thoracic Soc. (bd. dir. 1975, 1981—84, nat. pres. 1982—83, v.p., Disting. Achievement award 1996), Am. Acad. Pediat. (Med. Edn. Lay Edn. award 1995, Kendig award as outstanding pulmonologist 2003), Am. Soc. Pharmacology and Exptl. Therapeutics, Am. Physiol. Soc., Soc. Pediatric Rsch., Am. Pediatric Soc., Fleischner Soc. (pres. 1995—), Alpha Omega Alpha. Home: 2 W 67th St New York NY 10023-6241 Office: Childrens Hosp NY-Presbyn 3959 Broadway CHC 746 New York NY 10032 Office Phone: 212-305-8430. E-mail: rbm3@columbia.edu.

MELLMAN, LEONARD, real estate investor and advisor; b. Mar. 23, 1924; s. Morris and Luba (Levin) M. BA, Temple U., 1949. Prin., owner L. Mellman Co., Phila., 1949-84, retired, 1984; prin., owner Mellman Investments, Phila., 1960—; ptnr. Mellman, Blume Co., Phila., 1979—, Cunniff, Mellman Co., Phila., 1982—. Gen. ptnr. Diamond Acres, Phila., 1981-86, Van Pelt Ct. Ltd. pres., 1985-91; pres. MLC Bd. Settlement Music Sch., Phila., 1985-91, sec. ctrl. bd., 1985-91, v.p. ctrl. bd., 1997—. Pres. arts and sci. alumni bd. Temple U., Phila., 1976-78; bd. dirs. Art Growth 2000, 1998—. With U.S. Army, 1943-46. Mem. Credit Mchts. Assn. (pres. 1970-72, man of yr. award 1970), Phila. Bd. Realtors, Temple U. Gen. Alumni Assn. (pres. 1992-94, disting. alumni award 1985), Singing City Choir (bd. dirs., pres. 1988-90), Phila. Opera Guild (bd. dirs. 1995—, pres. 1997-99, chmn. of bd. 1999-2003, hon. chmn. 2003—), Opera Vols. Internat. (treas. 1999-2003), Union League Phila. (chair, bd. trustees Scholarship Found.), Opera Vols. Internat. Democrat. Jewish. Home and Office: 220 W Rittenhouse Sq Apt 22C Philadelphia PA 19103 Personal E-mail: oprabuf@aol.com.

MELLO, CRAIG C. molecular medicine educator, researcher; B in Biochemistry, Brown U.; PhD, Harvard U. Rsch. fellow Fred Hutchinson Cancer Rsch. Ctr.; prof. molecular medicine U. Mass. Med. Sch., Worcester. Asst. investigator Howard Hughes Med. Inst., 2000—. Recipient award in molecular biology, NAS, 2003; Pew scholar, U. Calif., San Francisco, 1995. Office: Univ Mass Med Sch B2-213 Ste 219 373 Plantation St Worcester MA 01605 also: Howard Hughes Inst Medicine 4000 Jones Bridge Rd Chevy Chase MD 20815-6789

MELLO, DAWN, retail executive; b. Lynn, Mass. Student, Modern Sch. Fashion and Design, Boston. Model; asst. to fashion dir. B. Altman & Co., N.Y.C., fashion dir., 1971—75; from corp. buying officer to v.p. and gen. merchandise mgr. May Dept. Stores Co.; v.p., fashion dir. to exec. v.p., dir. fashion merchandising Bergdorf Goodman, N.Y.C., 1975—84, pres., 1984—89, 1994—99; creative dir. Gucci, 1989—94; cons. Dawn Mello and Assocs., N.Y.C., 1999—. Office: Dawn Mello and Assocs Inc 12 W 57th St # 802 New York NY 10019

MELLOAN, GEORGE RICHARD, editor, columnist, writer; b. Greenwood, Ind., Nov. 10, 1927; s. James and Sara Ollie (Merideth) M.; m. Joan Minner, July 1, 1951; children: James, Melissa, Maryanne. BS, Butler U., 1950. Reporter Logansport (Ind.) Press, 1950, Muncie (Ind.) Press, 1951, Wall Street Jour., Chgo. and Detroit, 1952-59, bur. mgr. Cleve. and Atlanta, 1959-61, page one writer N.Y.C., 1961-66, fgn. correspondent London, 1966-70, editl. writer N.Y.C., 1970—, dep. editor, internat., 1973—, op-ed columnist, 1987—. Co-author: The Carter Economy, 1978. Sgt. U.S. Army, 1946-47. Recipient Gerald Loeb award G&R Loeb Found., 1981, Daily Gleaner awards Inter-Am. Press Assn., 1983, 87. Mem. Coun. on Fgn. Rels., Dutch Treat Club, Echo Lake Country Club. Avocations: travel, golf, hiking, photography. Office: Wall Street Jour 200 Liberty St New York NY 10281-1003

MELLON, SEWARD PROSSER, investment executive; b. Chgo., July 28, 1942; s. Richard King and Constance Mary (Prosser) Mellon Burrell; m. Karen Leigh Boyd, Sept. 10, 1966 (div. 1974); children— Catharine Leigh, Constance Elizabeth; m. Sandra Springer Stout, 1975. Grad., Choate Sch., 1960; BA, Susquehanna U., 1965, DH, 1993. With Mellon Nat. Corp., Pitts., 1965-69; with T. Mellon & Sons, Pitts., 1969-71; pres. Richard K. Mellon & Sons, Ligonier, 1971—. Bd. dirs. Mellon Bank N.A., Mellon Fin. Corp. Trustee Richard King Mellon Family Found.; trustee, pres. Richard King Mellon Found.; chmn. real estate com., chmn. bd. mem. fin. and exec. com. Valley Sch. Ligonier. Mem. Western Pa. Conservancy (life), LoyalHanna Assn. (pres.), Vintage Club (Palm Springs, Calif.), Duquesne Club (Pitts.), Laurel Valley Golf Club (Ligonier), Rolling Rock Club, Rolling Rock Hunt, Phi Mu Delta. Republican. Home: Huntland Downs Box K Ligonier PA 15658 Office: PO Box Rkm Ligonier PA 15658-0780 Office Phone: 724-238-6671.

MELLON, TIMOTHY, transportation executive; s. Paul Mellon (dec.). B., Yale Univ, 1964, M., 1966. CEO, chmn. bd. dris. Guilford Transp. Industries, North Billerica, Mass. Trustee Andrew W. Mellon Found. Office: Guilford Transp Industries High St Iron Horse Pk North Billerica MA 01862 also: Guilford Transp Industries Pease Internatl Tradeport 14 Aviation Ave Portsmouth NH 03801*

MELLOR, JOHN WILLIAMS, economist, policy consultant firm executive; b. Paris, Dec. 28, 1928; came to U.S., 1929; s. Desmond W. and Katherine (Beardsley) M.; m. Arlene Patton, June 15, 1950 (div. Sept. 1972); children: Michael, Brian, Mark (dec.); m. Uma Lele, Feb. 17, 1973 (div. Apr. 1992); m. Zarmina Said, Oct. 16, 1997. BS, Cornell U., 1950, MS, 1951, PhD, 1954; Diploma, Oxford (Eng.) U., 1952. Prof. Cornell U., Ithaca, N.Y., 1953-75; chief economist USAID, Washington, 1975-77; dir. Internat. Food Policy Rsch. Inst., Washington, 1977-91; pres. John W. Mellor Assocs., Inc., Washington, 1991-98; v.p. Abt Assocs., Inc., Washington, 1998—. Mem. bd. on agrl. NAS, 1989-92; mem. Agrl. Credit Commn., Res. Bank India, 1986-88. Author: Economics of Agricultural Development, 1966 (Am. Agrl. Econs. Assn. award 1978), Accelerating Food Production Growth in Sub-Saharan Africa, 1987, Agricultural Price Policy for Developing Countries, 1988 (hon. mention Am. Agrl. Econs. Assn. 1989), Agriculture on the Road to Industrialization, 1992. Mem. Internat. Commn. on Food and Peace, 1988—. Recipient Wihuri Internat. prize Wihuri Found., Helsinki, 1985, Presdl. End Hunger award The White House, 1987, Outstanding Alumni award Cornell U., 1987. Fellow AAAS, Am. Acad. Arts and Scis., Am. Agrl. Econs. Assn. (Best Pub. Rsch. award 1967). Avocations: sailing, skiing. Office: John Mellor Assocs Inc Ste PH18 801 Pennsylvania Ave NW Washington DC 20004-2668 Office Phone: 202-347-8802. E-mail: puanaturally@aol.com., john_mellor@abtassoc.com.

MELLOR, KAREN SUSANN, entomologist; d. Douglas Robert and Brigitte Anna Nepstad. MS, U. Heidelberg, Germany, 1993. Vector control technician Dept. of Health Services/Calif., 1998. Field and lab. technician Kommunale Aktionsgemeinschaft zur Bekaempfung der Schnakenplage, Waldsee, Germany, 1988—94; biologist Millioud Beratende Ingenieure, Karlsruhe, Germany, 1994—95; sales rep. Zanus Corp., Salt Lake City, 1996—97; lab. asst. NW Mosquito & Vector Control Dist., Corona, Calif., 1997—98; entomologist Antelope Valley Mosquito & Vector Control Dist., Lancaster, Calif., 1998—. Contbr. articles to profl. jours. Mem.: Entomol. Soc. of Am. (assoc.), Soc. of Vector Ecology (assoc.), Am. Mosquito Control Assn. (assoc.). Office: AV Mosquito & Vector Control District 42624 6th St East Lancaster CA 93535 Office Fax: 661-940-6367. E-mail: karen@avmosquito.org.

MELLOR, KATHY, National Teacher of the Year 2004, ESL educator; b. Providence; BS in Elem. Edn., RI Coll., 1970, MEd, 1977; MA in Teaching, with ESL and Cross Cultural Studies, Brown U., 1989. Substitute tchr. Cranston, RI Sch. Dept., 1970—74; ESL tchr. Internat. Inst. RI, 1980—85; continuing edn. tchr., english dept. RI Coll., 1985—86; cons. for ESL North Kingstown Sch. Dept., RI, 1985; ESL tchr. Hamilton Elem. Sch., North Kingstown, RI, Davisville Mid. Sch., North Kingstown, RI, 1985—. Nat. and internat. spokesperson for education, 2004—. Named Nat. Teacher of Yr., Coun. of Chief State Sch. Officers, 2004. Achievements include redesigning her school's ESL program, which provides each student with one to three periods per day in classes for English learners. The amount of instruction given depends on their skill level; providing help to students and their families by forming a local parents group called the "Ladybugs" for speakers of other languages. This improved their ability to help their children; has instructed students from virtually every part of the globe (Laos, Korea, Bolivia, Brazil, Puerto Rico, the Philippines and the Dominican Republic); hosts an International Picnic where her students and their families gather to celebrate their achievements during the school year. Office: Davisville Mid Sch 200 School St North Kingstown RI 02852 Office Phone: 401-541-6300.

MELLOR, RONALD JOHN, history professor; b. Bklyn., Sept. 30, 1940; s. Ronald Green and Eleanor Teresa (Walsh) M.; m. Anne Tidaback Kostelanetz, June 7, 1969; 1 child, Ronald Blake. AB, Fordham Coll., 1962; cert., U. Louvain, Belgium, 1961; AM, Princeton U., 1964, PhD in Classics, 1968. Asst. prof. Classics Stanford (Calif.) U., 1965-75; assoc. prof. history UCLA, 1976-82, prof. history, 1982—. Vice-chmn. history UCLA, 1985-86, 1991-92, 1998-99, chmn. history, 1992-97; visitor Princeton Inst. Advanced Studies, 1997-98. Author: Thea Rhome, 1975, Tacitus, 1993, Tacitus and the Classical Tradition, 1995, The Roman Historians, 1999, The Ancient Roman World, 2004; editor: From Augustus to Nero: The First Dynasty of Imperial Rome, 1990, The Historians of Ancient Rome, 1997, Text and Tradition: Studies in Greek History and Historiography in Honor of Mortimer Chambers, 1999. Fellow NEH, 1969, Am. Coun. Learned Socs., 1972, Humanities Rsch. Ctr. Australian Nat. U., Canberra, Australia, 1990; hon. fellow U. Coll. London, Eng., 1969, 72, 83-85. Mem. Am. Hist. Assn., Am. Philol. Assn., Assn. Ancient Historians, Soc. for the Promotion of Roman Studies. Democrat. Avocations: opera, travel, theater, tennis. Home: 2620 Mandeville Canyon Rd Los Angeles CA 90049-1004 Office: UCLA Dept History 405 Hilgard Ave Los Angeles CA 90095-1473 E-mail: mellor@history.ucla.edu.

MELLORS, ROBERT CHARLES, physician, scientist, educator; b. Dayton, Ohio, 1916; s. Bert S. and Clementine (Steinmetz) M.; m. Jane K. Winternitz, Mar. 25, 1944; children: Alice J., Robert C., William K., John W. PhD, Western Res. U., 1940; MD, Johns Hopkins, 1944. Diplomate Am. Bd. Pathology. Intern Nat. Naval Med. Ctr., Bethesda, Md., 1944-45; rsch. fellow medicine Meml. Center Cancer and Allied Diseases, N.Y.C., 1946-50; rsch. fellow pathology Meml. Ctr. Cancer and Allied Diseases, 1950-53, asst. attending pathologist, 1953-57, assoc. attending pathologist, 1957-58. Sr. fellow Am. Cancer Soc., 1947-50; sr. clin. rsch. fellow Damon Runyon Meml. Fund, 1950-53; asst. attending pathologist Meml. Hosp., N.Y.C., 1953-57, assoc. attending pathologist, 1957-58; asst. attending pathologist Ewing Hosp., N.Y.C., 1953-57, assoc. attending pathologist, 1957-58; instr. biochemistry Western Res. U., 1940-42; rsch. assoc. Poliomyelitis Rsch. Ctr. and Dept. Epidemiology Johns Hopkins U. Sch. Hygiene, 1942-44; asst. prof. biology Meml. Ctr. Cancer and Allied Diseases, N.Y.C., 1952-53; asst. prof. pathology Sloan Kettering div. Cornell U., 1953-57, assoc. prof., 1957-58; prof. pathology Cornell U. Med. Coll., 1961-90, prof. emeritus, 1990—; adj. prof. pathology N.Y. Med. Coll., 1997—; assoc. attending pathologist N.Y. Hosp., 1961-72, attending pathologist, 1972-86; pathologist-in-chief, dir. labs., 1958-84, emeritus, 1984-85, hon. staff, 1986—; assoc. dir. rsch. Hosp. for Spl. Surgery, N.Y.C., 1958-69, dir. rsch., 1969-84, emeritus, 1984-85, scientist emeritus, 1986—; mem. rsch. adv. com. NIH, 1962-66; adv. com. Nat. Inst. Environ. Health Sci., 1966-69; com. nomenclature and classification of disease Coll. Am. Pathologists, 1960-64. Author: Analytical Cytology, 1955, 2d edit., 1959, Analytical Pathology, 1957, also 5 med. sch. tchg. documents online. Served as lt. (j.g.), M.C. USNR, 1944-46. Recipient Kappa Delta award Am. Acad. of Orthopedic Surgeons, 1962 Fellow Royal Coll. Pathologists, Molecular Medicine Soc., Am. Soc. Clin. Pathology; mem. Internat. Soc. for Optical Engring., Am. Assn. Pathologists, Am. Assn. Immunologists, Am. Soc. Biochemistry and Molecular Biology, Am. Coll. Rheumatology, Am. Orthopedic Assn. (hon.). Home: 3 Hardscrabble Cir Armonk NY 10504-2222 E-mail: rmellors@ix.netcom.com.

MELLOTT, GEORGE KENNETH, retired music educator; b. Cleve., Aug. 18, 1932; s. Samuel Wesley and Julia Ann Maria (Hottel) Mellott; m. Elecive Blair Mellott, May 21, 1960; children: Catherine Suzanne, Stephen George. BS in Edn., Ea. Ill. U., 1953, MS in Edn., 1954; MFA, U. Iowa, 1962, PhD, 1964. Band dir. Ramsey (Ill.) Cmty. Schs., 1954—55; asst. prof. music Cumberland Coll., Williamsburg, Ky., 1963—64; from asst. to full prof. So. Ill. U., Edwardsville, 1964—94, prof. emeritus, 1994. Prin. clarinet St. Louis Philharm. Orch., 1964—97. Composer various musical works. Lt. USAF, 1955—60, lt. col. Air Nat. Guard, 1960—78. Named Disting. Alumni Performer, Ea. Ill. U. Dept. Music, 1978. Mem.: SAR. Republican. Episcopalian. Avocations: fly fishing, skiing, hiking. Home: 136 Antelope Loop Walsenburg CO 81089-9590

MELLOTT, ROBERT VERNON, retired advertising executive; b. Dixon, Ill., Jan. 1, 1928; s. Edwin Vernon and Frances Rhoda (Miller) M.; m. Sarah Carolyn Frink, June 11, 1960; children: Lynn Mellott Finzer, Susan Mellott Dodge, David Robert. BA, DePauw U., 1950; postgrad., Ind. U., 1950-51, 59-61, MA, 1983. TV prodr., dir. Jefferson Std. Broadcasting Co., Charlotte, N.C., 1951-59; asst. dist. mgr. GM, Chgo., Flint, Mich., 1961-62; TV and radio comml. supr. NW Ayer & Son, Chgo., 1962-65; TV and radio prodr. Foote, Cone & Belding Advt. Inc., Chgo., 1965-67, mgr. midwest prodn., 1967-69, mgr. comml. coordination, 1969-74, v.p., mgr. comml. svcs., 1974-93; ret. Cons. speech and broadcasting comm. mem. media adv. com. Coll. of Dupage, Glen Ellyn, Ill., 1971-82; chmn. Cub Scout Com., Wheaton, Ill., 1978-79; bd. dirs. Chgo. Unltd., 1969-71. Trustee Evang. Christian Ch. Mem.: World Comm. Assn., Am. Assn. Advt. Agys. (broadcast adminstrn. policy com., broadcast talent union rels. ANA-AAAA joint policy com. 1984—93), Ind. U. Alumni Assn., DePauw U. Alumni Assn., Alpha Tau Omega, Phi Delta Phi. Republican. Mem. Evang. Christian Ch. Home: 26w130 Tomahawk Dr Wheaton IL 60187-7823

MELLOY, MICHAEL J. federal judge; b. Dubuque, IA, 1948; m. Jane Anne Melloy; children: Jennifer, Katherine, Bridget. BA, Loras Coll., 1970; JD, U. Iowa, 1974. With O'Conner & Thomas P.C. (formerly O'Conner, Thomas, Wright, Hammer, Bertsch & Norby, Dubuque, Iowa, 1974-86; judge U.S. Bankruptcy Ct. (no. dist.) Iowa, 1986-92, U.S. Dist. Ct. (no. dist.) Iowa, Cedar Rapids, 1992—2002; chief judge, 1992—99; judge U.S. Ct. Appeals (8th Cir.), 2002—. With U.S. Army, 1970-72, USAR, 1972-76. Mem. ABA,

Comml. Law League Am., Nat. Conf. Bankruptcy Judges, Eighth Cir. Judicial Coun. (bankruptcy judge rep., bankruptcy com.), Iowa State Bar Assn. (coun. mem. bankruptcy and comml. law sect.), Ill. State Bar Assn., Dubuque County Bar Assn., Linn County Bar Assn., Mason L. Ladd Inn of Ct., Rotary. Office: US Ct Appeals 8th Cir 304 Fed Bldg 101 First St Cedar Rapids IA 52401

MELLSTIG, SÖREN, lab administrator; b. 1951; Pres., CEO, dir. Gambro Inc., 2000—, bd. dirs., 2001—. Bd. dirs. Munters, MacGregor Internat., XCounter. Office: Gambro Inc 225 Union Blvd Ste 600 Lakewood CO 00228-1805*

MELLUM, GALE ROBERT, lawyer; b. Duluth, Minn., July 5, 1942; s. Lester Andrew and Doris Esther (Smith) M.; m. Julie Murdoch Swanstrom, July 23, 1966; children: Eric Scott, Wendy Jane. BA summa cum laude, U. Minn., 1964, JD magna cum laude, 1968. Bar: Minn. 1968. Assoc. Faegre & Benson, Mpls., 1968-75, ptnr., 1976—, mem. mgmt. com., 1986-98. Mem. planning com. Garret Corp. and Securities Law Inst., Northwestern U. Law Sch., 1984—; bd. dirs., mem. adv. bd. Quali Tech Inc., Chaska, Minn., 1985-98; corp. sec. Excelsior-Henderson Motorcycle Mfg. Co., Belle Plaine, Minn., 1997-2000. Hockey chmn. LARC Bd., Mpls., 1980—85. Mem. ABA (fed. securities regulation com.), Minn. Bar Assn., Hennepin County Bar Assn. (securities regulation com.). Republican. Lutheran. Avocations: tennis, golf, snow and water skiing, handball, boating. Home: 3833 Thomas Ave S Minneapolis MN 55410 Office: Faegre & Benson 2200 Wells Fargo Ctr 90 S 7th St Ste 2200 Minneapolis MN 55402-3901 E-mail: gmellum@faegre.com.

MELMAN, CYNTHIA SUE, special education educator; b. Pottsville, Pa., Nov. 13, 1946; d. Earl J. and Lillian (Zubroff) M. BA in English, Lebanon Valley Coll., 1969; MEd, Western Md. Coll., 1978. Advanced profl. cert. Md. State Dept. Edn. English tchr. Susquehanna Twp. Sch. Dist., Harrisburg, Pa., 1969-70; tchr. of the deaf Am. Sch. for the Deaf, West Hartford, Conn., 1978-80; sign lang. interpreter for the deaf Montgomery County Pub. Schs., Rockville, Md., 1980-81, tchr. of the deaf/hard of hearing, 1981—. In-svc. program masters plus 30, Montgomery County Pub. Schs., Rockville, 1982-96, base sch. rep. for energy saving and recycling program, 1994-95. Co-author: (one workbook in a series) Writing Sentences, 1981. Mem.: NEA, Montgomery County Assn. for Hearing Impaired Children. Avocations: theater, movies, music, reading, walking.

MELNICK, ALICE JEAN (AJ MELNICK), counselor; b. St. Louis, Dec. 25, 1931; d. Nathan and Henrietta (Hausfater) Fisher; m. Harold Melnick, May 24, 1953; children: Susan, Vikki, Patrice. BJ, U. Tex., Austin, 1952; MEd, U. North Tex., 1974. Lic. profl. counselor. Reporter San Antonio Light, 1952-53; instr. journalism project Upward Bound So. Meth. U., Dallas, 1967-71. Instr. writing El Centro Dallas County C.C., Dallas, part time 1972-74; instr. human devel. Richland C.C., Dallas, part-time 1974-79; tchr. English, journalism and psychology Dallas Ind. Sch. Dist., 1969-81; counselor Ursuline Acad., 1981-94; part-time instr. human devel. Sante Fe C.C.; freelance documentary photographer. Mem. Dallas Sports Car Club, N.Mex. Jewish Hist. Soc., Temple Beth Shalom. Jewish. Home: 101 Monte Alto Rd Santa Fe NM 87508-8865 E-mail: aj@melnick.net.

MELNICK, JANE FISHER, journalist, educator, photographer, literature educator; b. Boston, Sept. 26, 1939; d. Richard T. and Mary (Holcombe) Fisher; m. Burton A. Melnick, Dec. 1962 (div. 1969); 1 child, Benjamin A.; life ptnr. Eileen Willenborg, 1978—. BA cum laude, Radcliffe Coll., 1962; MA, NYU, 1985, PhD in Am. Studies, 1991. News writer, photographer, freelance editor, 1962—75; editor/writer In These Times, Chgo., 1976-78, Seven Days, N.Y.C., 1978-81; instr. writing, Am. lit. NYU, 1981-86, Loyola U., Chgo., 1988-91; asst. prof. Elmhurst (Ill.) Coll., 1991-96; writer, coll. prep. tutor Chgo., 1997—2003. Contbr. revs., photos, articles on culture and news to various publs. Recipient Phi Beta Kappa award for best creative work by an undergrad. Radcliffe Coll., 1959; Mademoiselle mag. fiction contest award, 1962, NEA grantee, 1973, dean's dissertation fellow NYU, 1987. Mem. MLA, Mid-Am. Am. Studies Assn. (exec. bd., chair essay judging com. 1995-96). Avocations: home renovation, travel. Home: 5000 N Marine Dr Apt 15A Chicago IL 60640-3226

MELNICK, JODI, dancer; Mem. Twyla Tharp Dance Co., 1991—; tchr. dance, choreographer, collaborator. Performer with Sara Rudner, with Dennis O'Connor, with Vicky Shick, with Yoshiko Chuma, with Susan Rethorst.

MELNICK, MICHAEL, geneticist, educator; b. N.Y.C., Sept. 24, 1944; s. Lester and Evelyn (Rosenberg) M.; m. Anita Goldberger, June 19, 1966; children: Cliff, Lynn. BA in Biology, NYU, 1966, DDS, 1970; PhD in Genetics, Ind. U., 1978. Instr. oral medicine Ind. U., Indpls., 1973-74, fellow in med. genetics, 1974-77, asst. prof. med. genetics, 1977-78; rsch. assoc. prof. U. So. Calif., L.A., 1978-85, assoc. prof., 1985-89, prof. genetics, 1989—. Cons. in human genetics NIH, Bethesda, Md., 1977-88, grant reviewer, 1978—; manuscript referee Am. Jour. Human Genetics, Chgo., 1980—, Am. Jour. Med. Genetics, Helena, Mont., 1980—; MRC vis. prof. McGill U., Montreal, que., 1990. Author, editor 5 books on human genetics; editor-in-chief Jour. Craniofacial Genetics, 1980-2000; contbr. more than 100 articles to profl. jours. Mem. nat. bd. Com. of Concerned Scientists, N.Y.C., 1983—; vice chmn. Youth Towns of Israel, L.A., 1986—. Capt. M.C. U.S. Army, 1970-73. Recipient Ind. U. Disting. Alumnus award, 1984; Warwick James fellow U. London/Guy's Hosp., 1992. Fellow AAAS; mem. Soc. Craniofacial Genetics (pres. 1978-79), Soc. for Developmental Biology, Am. Soc. Human Genetics, Sigma Xi. Achievements include research in delineated major gene causation of cleft lip and palate; delineated insulin-like growth factor, type 2, receptor control of fetal lung, salvary gland and palate development; application of probability neural networks to multi-gene analysis. Avocations: art, philosophy, chess. Office: Univ So California Den 4266 Mc 0641 Los Angeles CA 90089-0641 E-mail: mmelnick@usc.edu.

MELNYK, EUGENE N. private investigator; Founder, pres., CEO Trimel, 1983—91; chmn. bd. dirs. BCI, 1991—94; chmn., CEO Biovail Corp., Mississauga, Canada, 1994—. Office: Biovail Corp 2488 Dunwin Dr Mississauga ON Canada L5L 1J9

MELO, WELTON, professional soccer player; b. Rio de Janeiro, Apr. 17, 1975; Forward Brazilian Club Am., 1995, New Eng. Revolution, 1996, L.A. Galaxy, 1997—98, Miami Fusion, 1999—. Named Maj. League Soccer All-Star, 1996. Office: c/o Miami Fusion 2200 W Commercial Blvd Ste 104 Fort Lauderdale FL 33309-3058

MELODY, MICHAEL EDWARD, publishing company executive; b. Streator, Ill., Dec. 22, 1943; s. Giles Lambert and Rose Mary (Moreschi) M.; m. Carol Ann Weir, June 8, 1968 (div.); 1 dau., Alison Anne; m. Bonnie Kaye Binkert, Mar. 26, 1983. BA, Ala. Coll., 1966. Exec. editor, asst. v.p. Prentice-Hall, Inc., Englewood Cliff, NJ, 1974-79; v.p., editor-in-chief coll. divsn. Macmillan Pub. Co., N.Y.C., 1979-80, sr. v.p., pres. coll. divsn., 1980-87, pres. sch. divsn., 1987—88; v.p. higher edn. group Simon & Schuster, N.Y.C., 1988-90; sr. v.p. Houghton Mifflin Co., Boston, 1990-91, exec. v.p., 1991-95; prin. Michael E. Melody Cons., Boston, 1995-96; v.p., gen. mgr. info. prodn. Inso Corp., Boston, 1996-99; pres, CEO Sage Pubs., Inc., Thousand Oaks, Calif., 1999—, also bd. dirs. Chmn. bd. dirs. Appleton & Lange, N.Y.C., 1989-90; bd. dirs. Sage Publs., Ltd., London. Bd. overseers Huntington Theatre Co., Boston, 1993-96; bd. advisors Boston U. Sch. for the Arts, 1997-2000; bd. dirs. Judge Baker Ctr. for Children, Harvard U. Med. Sch., 1997-99, mem. exec. com.; pres. adv. coun. Calif. Luth. U., 2001—; mem. bd. trustees New West Symphony, 2003-, So. N.H. U., 2003-. Mem. Assn. Am. Pubs. (vice chmn. coll. divsn. 1981-83, chmn. coll. divsn. 1983-86, exec. com. sch. divsn. 1987-88, exec. com. higher edn. divsn. 1990—), Nat. Assn. Coll. Stores (trustee 1986-89, 94-95).

MELONE, JOSEPH JAMES, retired insurance company executive; b. Pittston, Pa., July 27, 1931; s. Dominick William and Beatrice Marie (Pignone) M.; m. Marie Jane DeGeorge, Jan. 23, 1960; children: Lisa, Carol. BS, U. Pa., 1953, MBA, 1954, PhD in Econs., 1961. CPCU, 1964, ChFC, 1984. Assoc. prof. ins. U. Pa., 1959-66, mem. pension rsch. coun., 1961-66; rsch. dir. Am. Coll. Life Underwriters, 1966-68; v.p. Prudential Ins. Co., Boston, 1969-76, sr. v.p. Newark, 1976-81, exec. v.p., 1981-84, pres., 1984-90; pres., COO, bd. dirs. The Equitable Life Assurance Soc. U.S., 1990-94; pres., COO The Equitable Cos., Inc., 1992-96, now bd. dirs., pres., CEO, 1996-98; chmn. The Equitable Life Assurance Soc. U.S., NYC, 1994-98. Chmn., CEO Equitable Variable Life Ins. Co.; bd. dirs. Foster Wheeler Corp., bd. dirs. BISYS, Inc., chmn. Horace-Mann Educators Corp.; chmn. emeritus The Equitable Cos. Author: Collectively Bargained Multi-Employer Pension Plans, 1961; co-author: Risk and Insurance, 1963, Pension Planning, 1966. Trustee Newark Mus.; chmn. ins. divsn. Cardinal's Commn. Laity NY Archdiocese; bd. overseers Wharton Sch. U. Pa.; bd. dirs. Greater NY couns. Boy Scouts Am. Morris County Country Club, Lost Tree Golf Club, Baltusrol Golf Club, Alpha Tau Omega. Home: Gen Delivery New Vernon NJ 07976-9999 Office: Equitable Cos Inc 1290 Ave of Americas New York NY 10104 Office Phone: 212-314-2060. Business E-Mail: joseph.melone@axom-financial.com.

MELOY, SYBIL PISKUR, retired lawyer; b. Chgo., Dec. 1, 1939; d. Michael M. and Laura (Stevenson) Piskur; children: William S., Bradley M. BS with honors, U. Ill., 1961; JD, Chgo. Kent Coll. Law, 1965. Bar: Ill. 1965, Fla. 1985, D.C. 1995, U.S. Dist. Ct. (no. dist.) Ill. 1965, U.S. Supreme Ct. 1972, U.S. Ct. Appeals (fed. cir.) 1983, U.S. Dist. Ct. (so. dist.) Fla. 1985, D.C. 1995. Patent chemist, patent atty., sr. atty., internat. counsel G.D. Searle & Co., Skokie, Ill., 1961-72; regional counsel Abbott Labs., North Chicago, Ill., 1972-78; pvt. practice Arlington Heights, Ill., 1978-79; asst. gen. counsel Alberto Culver Co., Melrose Park, Ill., 1979 83; corp. counsel Key Pharms., Inc., Miami, Fla., 1983-86; assoc. Ruden, Barnett, McCloskey, Smith, Schuster and Russell, Pa., 1987-89, ptnr., 1990-91, Foley & Lardner, Miami, Washington, 1991—2001. Adj. prof. Univ. of Miami Sch. of Law, 1986-92. Contbr. article on fertility control and abortion laws, book rev. on arbitration to law revs. Recipient Abbott Presdl. award, 1977; Bur. Nat. Affairs prize, 1965; Law Rev. prize for best article. Mem. ABA, Chgo. Bar Assn. (chmn.-elect and vice chmn. internat. and fgn. law com.), Am. Patent Law Assn., Am. Chem. Soc., Licencing Execs. Soc., Phi Beta Kappa, Phi Kappa Phi. Patentee oral contraceptive, 1965. also: 1676 32d St NW Washington DC 20007-2960 E-mail: smeloy@aol.com.

MELROSE, BARRY JAMES, sportscaster, former professional hockey team coach; b. Kelvington, Sask., Can., July 15, 1956; Player various minor league teams, 1973-77, 82-83, 83-86, 86-87; player Cin. Stingers, 1976-79, Winnipeg Jets, 1979-81, Toronto Maple Leafs, 1981-82, 82-83, Detroit Red Wings, 1983-84, 85-86; former gen. mgr., head coach Adirondack Red Wings; now head coach L.A. Kings, 1992-94; sportscaster ESPN, 1995—. Office: care ESPN Inc 935 Middle St Bristol CT 06010-1001

MELROY, PAMELA ANN, astronaut; b. Palo Alto, Calif., Sept. 17, 1961; d. David and Helen M.; m. Christopher Wallace. BS in Physics and Astronomy, Wellesley Coll., 1983; MSc in Earth and Planetary Scis., MIT, 1984. Commd. 2nd lt. USAF, 1983, advanced through grades to lt. col.; co-pilot KC-10, aircraft comdr., instr. pilot Barksdale AFB, Bossier City, La.; test pilot C-17 Combined Test Force; shuttle pilot NASA, Houston, pilot STS-92. Decorated Air Force Meritorious Svc. medal with oak leaf cluster, Air medal with oak leaf cluster, Aerial Achievement medal with oak leaf cluster, Expeditionary medal with oak leaf cluster. Mem. Soc. Exptl. Test Pilots, Order of Daedalians, 99s. Avocations: theater, tap and jazz dancing, reading, cooking, flying. Office: Astronaut Office/CB NASA Lyndon B Johnson Space Ctr Houston TX 77058

MELSHEIMER, HAROLD, obstetrician, gynecologist; b. Legenfeld, Germany, June 11, 1927; came to U.S., 1955; naturalized, 1960; s. Louis and Hella Leonie (Schwehr) Peterman; m. Norma Sykes Sabrina, Nov. 27, 1967; children: Laura, Linda. BS, Marburg U., West Germany, 1951, MD, 1954. Diplomate Am. Bd. Ob-Gyn. Intern Baden County Hosp., West Germany, 1954-55, St. Mary's Hosp. Med. Ctr., Long Beach, Calif., 1955-56; resident Queens Hosp. Med. Ctr., Honolulu, 1956-57, Calif. Hosp. Med. Ctr., L.A., 1957-59; pvt. practice ob-gyn. Encino, Calif., 1959-87; ret. Former dept. chief, now hon. staff mem. Am. Med. Internat. Med. Ctr., Tarzana, Calif., Encino Hosp.; founder Technion Inst. of Tech. Contbr. articles to profl. jours. Operational mem. USCG Aux., 1971. Recipient cert. of honor Wisdom Soc.; named Hon. Citizen, Rep. of Korea, 1966. Fellow ACS (life), Am. Coll. Ob-Gyn., Internat. Coll. Surgeons; mem. AMA, Calif. Med. Assn., L.A. County Med. Assn., Am. Physicians Fellowship for Israel Med. Assn., N.Y. Acad. Scis., Braemar Country Club. Avocations: travel, art, history, sailing. Home: 25660 Deertrail Dr Tehachapi CA 93561-9140 E-mail: hm4611@aol.com.

MELSHEIMER, MEL P(OWELL), venture capital and consumer products executive; b. L.A., July 9, 1939; s. Oscar Merrill M.; m. Sara Sturdevant, Sept. 1, 1962; children: Heidi, Erich, Douglas. AB, Occidental Coll., 1961; MBA, U. So. Calif., 1965. With United Calif. Bank, Los Angeles, 1962-66; sr. fin. analyst Ford Motor Co., Newport Beach, Calif., 1966-67; v.p., chief fin. officer Pepsi Cola Co. Pepsico, Inc., Purchase, N.Y., 1968-75; exec. v.p., chief operating officer AZL Resources, Inc., 1975-84; chmn. bd., chief exec. officer PHX Pacific, Inc., 1984-89; pres., chief exec. officer MPM Capital Corp., 1987-89; exec. v.p. Finevest Foods, Inc., Greenwich, Conn., 1989-92; pres., CEO Land-O-Sun Dairies Inc., 1991-92, Atlanta Dairies, Inc., 1991-92; exec. v.p., sec., chief oper. officer Dairy Holdings, Inc., Johnson City, Tenn., 1992-94; exec. v.p., COO, CFO Sonex Internat. Corp., Brewster, N.Y., 1994; pres., CEO M.P. Melsheimer & Co., Ridgefield, Conn., 1994-97; pres. NFX, 1995-96; pres., COO/CFO Harris & Harris Group, Inc., N.Y.C., 1997—. Served with U.S. Army, 1961-62. Office: Harris & Harris Group Inc 111 W 57th St Ste 1100 New York NY 10019 Office Phone: 212-582-0900. E-mail: admin@tinytechvc.com.

MELSON, MARVIN E. finance company executive; Pres. Nat. Bancshares Corp. of Tex., San Antonio, 1999—. Office: 12400 Hwy 281 North San Antonio TX 78216

MELSOP, JAMES WILLIAM, architect; b. Columbus, Ohio, June 2, 1939; s. James Brendan and Juanita Kathryn (Van Scoy) M.; m. Sandra Lee Minnich, Sept. 21, 1957; children: Deborah Lee, Susan Elizabeth, Kathryn Anne. BArch, Ohio State U., 1964; MArch, Harvard U., 1965; MBA, U. Chgo., 1975. Reg. architect, profl. engr. Architect The Austin Co., Chgo., 1967-69, mgr. bus. devel., 1969-74, asst. dist. mgr., 1974-75; pres., mng. dir. Austin Brasil, Sao Paulo, 1975-78; asst. dist. mgr. The Austin Co., Roselle, N.J., 1978-80, dist. mgr. Detroit, 1980-81, v.p., dist. mgr. Cleve., 1986, group v.p., dir., 1986—, exec. v.p. chief oper. officer, 1992, pres., CEO, 1992—, also chmn., bd. dirs.; founder, prin. owner Austin Holdings, Inc., 1997—. Named E&Y Entrepreneur of Yr., 1999. Mem. Am. Inst. Architects., Harvard Club N.Y.C., Presidents' Club, Ohio State U. (Disting. Alumnus award 1989). Home: 3165 Trillium Trail Cleveland OH 44124-5205 Office: Austin Co 3650 Mayfield Rd Cleveland OH 44121-1791

MELTON, ARTHUR RICHARD, healthcare executive; b. Ysleta, Tex., Apr. 28, 1943; s. Francis Charles and Jean (Graham) M.; m. Frances Bay, Aug. 19, 1965; children: David Bay, Amy Elizabeth. BS, U. Utah, 1969; MPH, U. N.C., 1974, D in Pub. Health, 1976. Dir. labs. S.D. Dept. Health, Pierre, 1976-87; microbiologist Utah Dept. Health, Salt Lake City, 1970-73, dir. divsn. lab. svcs., 1987-92, dep. dir., 1992-96, 98—. Mem.: Assn. State and Territorial Health Ofcls. (pres. elect 1999—2000, pres. 2000—01), S.D. Pub. Health Assn. (pres. 1980—81), Am. Pub. Health Assn. (governing coun. 1980—83). Mem. Lds Ch. Home: 6835 Heather Way West Jordan UT 84084-2304 Office: PO Box 142802 Salt Lake City UT 84114-2802 Office Phone: 801-538-6111. Personal E-mail: armelton@qwest.net. Business E-Mail: dmelton@dho.state.ut.us.

MELTON, CHARLES ESTEL, retired physicist, educator; b. Fancy Gap, Va., May 18, 1924; s. Charlie Glenn and Ella (Ayers) M.; m. Una Faye Hull, Dec. 7, 1946; 1 child, Wayne. BA, Emory and Henry Coll., 1952, D.Sc., 1967; MS, Vanderbilt U., 1954; PhD, U. Notre Dame, 1964. Physicist Oak Ridge Nat. Lab., 1954-67; prof. chemistry U. Ga., Athens, 1967-97, head dept., 1972-77; now ret. Author: Principles of Mass Spectrometry and Negative Ions, 1970, Ancient Diamond Time Capsules, Secrets of Life and the World, 1985, Primordial Petroleum, 1989; contbr. articles to profl. jours. Served with USNR, 1943-46. Recipient DeFriece medal Emory and Henry Coll., 1959; nominated Nobel Prize; recipient numerous research grants. Fellow AAAS; mem. Am. Phys. Soc., Am. Chem. Soc., Ga. Acad. Sci. Achievements include constructing equipment to crush diamonds and identify trapped material; showing natural gas and petroleum may have diffused from Earth as evidenced by petroleum deposits found near faults in Earth; calculating the temperature of the Earth at formation and the origin of the atmosphere and oceans; showing that entropy and gravity are equal and opposite forces; showing the origin of the Earth's magnetic field is caused by friction from the moon, explaining the flipping field; showing the theory of organic evolution contradicts physical laws. Home: 817 Glenn Carrie Rd Hull GA 30646-4265

MELTON, DAVID REUBEN, lawyer; b. Milw., Apr. 4, 1952; s. Howard and Evelyn M.; m. Nancy Hillary Segal, May 22, 1981; children: Michelle, Hannah. BA, U. Wis., 1974; JD, U. Chgo., 1977. Bar: Ill. 1977, U.S. Dist. Ct. (no. dist.) Ill. 1977, U.S. Ct. Appeals (7th cir.) 1981, U.S. Supreme Ct. 1982, U.S. Fed. Cir. Ct. Appeals, 1991. Assoc. Karon, Morrison & Savikas, Ltd., Chgo., 1977-83; ptnr. Karon, Morrison & Saviskas, Ltd., Chgo., 1983-87, Karon, Savikas & Horn, Ltd., Chgo., 1987-88, Keck, Mahin & Cate, Chgo., 1988-96; counsel Mayer, Brown & Platt, Chgo., 1996-99, ptnr., 2000—. Office: Mayer Brown Rowe & Maw 190 S Lasalle St Ste 3900 Chicago IL 60603-3410 E-mail: dmelton@mayerbrownrowe.com.

MELTON, DOUGLAS A. molecular and cell biology educator; BS Honors Biology, U. Illinois, Champaign-Urbana, 1971—75; BA History, Phil. of Sci., Cambridge U., 1975—77; PhD Molecular Biology, Trinity Coll. & MRC Lab. Molecular Biology, Cambridge U., Eng., 1980. Asst. prof, dept. bio chem. and molecular biology Harvard U., 1981—84, assoc. prof., 1984—87, J.L. Loeb assoc. prof. nat. sci., 1987, prof. dept. molecular and cellular biology, 1988—; biologist (med.) Mass. Gen. Hosp., Boston; assoc. mem. Children's Hosp., Boston, 1994—; investigator Howard Hughes Med. Inst., 1994—; Thomas Dudley Cabot prof. Natural Sci. Harvard U., Cambridge, Mass., 1999—. Recipient Richard Lounsbery award NAS, 1995. Mem.: Inst. Medicine. Office: Harvard Univ Dept Molecular & Cellular Bio 7 Divinity Ave Cambridge MA 02138

MELTON, EMORY LEON, lawyer, state legislator, publisher; b. McDowell, Mo., June 20, 1923; s. Columbus Right and Pearly Susan (Wise) M; m. Jean Sanders, June 19, 1949; children: Stanley Emory, John Russell. Student, Monett Jr. Coll., 1940-41, S.W. Mo. State U., 1941-42; LLB, U. Mo., 1945. Bar: Mo. 1944. Pvt. practice, Cassville, Mo., 1947—; pres. Melton Publs., Inc., 1959—; pros. atty. Barry County (Mo.), 1947-51; mem. Mo. Senate, 1973-97. Chmn. Barry County republican Com., 1964-68. Served with AUS, 1945-46. Recipient Meritorious Pub. Svc. award St. Lousi Globe-Democrat, 1976. Mem. Mo. Bar Assn., Lions, Masons. Office: PO Box 488 Cassville MO 65625-0488

MELTON, G. KEMP, former mayor; b. Charleston, W.Va., Nov. 19, 1929; m. Corena Mae Melton; 4 children. BS in Bus., W.Va. U. Sheriff, treas. Kanawha County, W.Va., 1965-68, 73-80, assessor, 1981-95; mayor City of Charleston, W.Va., 1995-99. 1st lt. U.S. Army, 1953-55, Korea. Presbyterian. Office: 5107 Carlton Dr Charleston WV 25304-2811

MELTON, GARY BENTLEY, psychology and law educator; b. Salisbury, NC, June 4, 1952; s. Harold Sumner Jr. and Marion Adair (Reeves) M.; m. Robin Jo Kimbrough, Aug. 7, 1999; children by previous marriage: Jennifer Lynn, Stephany Beth. BA, U. Va., 1973; MA, Boston U., 1975, PhD, 1978. Asst. prof. psychology Morehead (Ky.) State U., 1978-79, U. Va., Charlottesville, 1979-81; from asst. prof. to full prof. psychology and law U. Nebr., Lincoln, 1981-87, Carl A. Happold prof. psychology and law, 1987-94; dir. Consortium on Children, Families and the Law, 1987—; prof. neuropsychiatry U. S.C., Columbia, 1994-99, adj. prof. law, pediat. and psychology, 1994-99, dir. Inst. Families in Soc., 1994-99; prof. psychology Clemson U., 1999—. Dir. Inst. Family and Neighborhood Life, Clemson U., 1999—. Author: Child Advocacy: Psychological Issues and Interventions, 1993; co-author: Community Mental Health Centers and the Courts: An Evaluation of Community-Based Forensic Services, 1985, Psychological Evaluations for the Courts: A Handbook for Mental Health Professionals and Lawyers, 1987, 2d edit., 1997, Pediatric and Adolescent AIDS: Research Findings from the Social Sciences, 1992, Ethical and Legal Issues in AIDS Research, 1995, No Place to Go: Civil Commitment of Minors, 1998; editor numerous books. Mem. U.S. Adv. Bd. on Child Abuse and Neglect, 1989-93, vice-chair, 1991-93. Recipient Frederick Howell Lewis award Psi Chi, 1993, Lynn Stuart Weiss award Am. Psychol. Found., 2000. Fellow APA (chmn. various coms., Cert. of Recognition for psychology in pub. interest 1981, Disting. Contbn. to Psychology in Pub. Interest award 1985, Nicholas Hobbs award 1992, Harold Hildreth award 1992, Disting. Contbn. to Pub. Svc. award 1999); mem. Am. Psychology-Law Soc. (pres. 1990-91), Am. Orthopsychiat. Assn. (pres. 2003-), Prevent Child Abuse Am. (Donna Stone award 1992). Democrat. Mem. Unitarian Ch. Office: Clemson U Inst Family and Neighborhood Life 158 Poole Agrl Ctr Clemson SC 29634-0132 Office Phone: 864-656-6271. Business E-Mail: gmelton@clemson.edu.

MELTON, HOWELL WEBSTER, SR., federal judge; b. Atlanta, Dec. 15, 1923; s. Holmes and Alma (Combee) M.; m. Margaret Catherine Wolfe, Mar. 4, 1950; children— Howell Webster, Carol Anne. JD, U. Fla., 1948. Bar: Fla. 1948. With Upchurch, Melton & Upchurch, St. Augustine, 1948-61; judge 7th Jud. Circuit of Fla., St. Augustine, 1961-77, U.S. Dist. Ct. (mid. dist.) Fla., Jacksonville, 1977-91, sr. judge, 1991—. Past chmn. Fla. Conf. Cir. Judges, 1974; past chmn. coun. bar pres.'s Fla. Bar. Trustee Flagler Coll., St. Augustine. Served with U.S. Army, 1943-46. Recipient Disting. Service award St. Augustine Jaycees, 1953 Mem. ABA, St. Johns County Bar Assn., Jacksonville Bar Assn., Fed. Bar Assn., Fla. Blue Key, Officers Club, Masons, Phi Delta Theta, Phi Delta Phi. Methodist. Office: US Dist Ct 300 N Hogan St Ste 11-300 Jacksonville FL 32202

MELTON, WAYNE CHARLES, real estate executive; b. Oak Ridge, Tenn., Aug. 30, 1954; s. Charles Estel and Una Faye (Hull) M.; m. Maria Tobar-Conde; children: Bonnie Elizabeth, Ingrid Tatiana. AB in European Intellectual History, U. Ga., 1975; MS in Real Estate, Shepperton U., 2001, PhD in Real Estate, 2003. Br. rep. Household Internat. Consumer Fin. Co., Athens, Ga., 1975-76; asst. mgr. Athens and Hickory, N.C., Doraville, Ga., 1976-77; pres., ceo Impact Realty-Melton & Assocs. Inc., Athens, 1987—. Cons. Ga. Furniture, Charlotte (N.C.) Realty, 1987—. Trustee Mu, Inc., Page, Ga. Ho. of Reps., 1968; chmn. Madison County Reps., 1973-74; mem. Congl. Bus. Coun., 2002. Mem. Pheonix Club, Pres. Club, Zeta Beta Tau. Office: 855 Sunset Dr Bldg Ste 11 Athens GA 30606-7718

MELTZ, DAVID BARRY, law educator; b. Bklyn., Mar. 12, 1945; s. Joseph and Claire Meltz; m. Sandra Jacqueline Rosenberg, July 3, 1968; children: Anne Robin, Robert Alan, Rachel. BA cum laude, Bklyn. Coll., 1965; PhD in Polit. Sci., U. Rochester, 1970; JD, Woodrow Wilson Law Sch., 1977. Asst. prof. polit. sci. Mich. State U., Lansing, 1969-73; assoc. prof. econs. and pub. policy Ga. Inst. Tech., Atlanta, 1973-78; atty. Levine & Meltz, PC, Atlanta, 1977-91; acad. dean, prof. law John Marshall Law Sch., Atlanta, 1991-98, Disting. prof. law, 1999—. Jewish. Office: John Marshall Law Sch 1422 W Peachtree St NW Atlanta GA 30309-2947 Home: 1149 Pinehurst Rd Grayson GA 30017-1130 E-mail: conprof@aol.com.

MELTZER, ALLAN H. economist, educator; b. Boston, Feb. 6, 1928; s. George B. and Minerva I. (Simons) M.; m. Marilyn Ginsburg, Aug. 27, 1950; children: Bruce Michael, Eric Charles, Beth Denise. AB, Duke U., 1948; MA, UCLA, 1955, PhD, 1958. Lectr. econs. U. Pa., Phila., 1956-57; faculty Carnegie Mellon U. Grad. Sch. Indsl. Adminstrn., Pitts., 1957-64, prof. econs., 1964—, Maurice Falk prof. econs. and social sci., 1970-80, John M. Olin univ. prof. polit. economy and pub. policy, 1980-91, Univ. prof. polit. economy and

pub. policy, 1991-97, Allan H. Meltzer Univ. prof. polit. economy, 1997—. Vis. prof. U. Chgo., 1964-65, Fundacao Getulio Vargas, Rio de Janeiro, 1976-79, City U., London, 1979-2001; vis. fellow Hoover Instn., 1977-78; vis. scholar Am. Enterprise Inst., Washington, 1989—; co-chmn. Shadow Open Market Com., 1974-89, chmn., 1989-2000; cons. US Treasury, joint econ. com. US Congress, 1960; com. on banking and currency US Ho. of Reps., 1963-64; mem. Pres.'s Econ. Policy Adv. Bd., 1988-90; acting mem. Coun. Econ. Advisors, 1988-89; panel econ. advisors Congl. Budget Office, 1995—; cons., bd. gov. FRS, FDIC; dir. Cooper Tire & Rubber Co., 1983-98, chmn. audit and compensation com., 1996-98; hon. advisor Inst. Monetary and Econ. Studies Bank of Japan, 1987-2003; bd. dir. Sarah Scaife Found., Commonwealth Found.; dir. Stillhalter Vision AG, Zurich, 1994-2002, Advanced Materials Group, 1994-2001; chmn. Internat. Fin. Instn. adv. com. to US Congress, 1999-2000. Author: Monetary Economics, 1989, Keynes's Monetary Theory: A Different Interpretation, 1988; (with Karl Brunner) Money and the Economy: Issues in Monetary Analysis, 1993; (with Alex Cukierman and Scott Richard) Political Economy, 1991, Report of the International Financial Institution Advisory Commission, 2000, A History of the Federal Reserve, vol. 1, 2003; editor: (with Karl Brunner) Carnegie-Rochester Conf. Series, 1976-89; (with Charles Plosser), 1989-97; contbr. articles to profl. jours. Recipient Outstanding Achievement award UCLA, 1983, Money Marketeers, 1997, Educator of Yr. award Pittsburg Hist. Ctr., 2003, Irving Kristol award Am. Enterprise Inst., 2003; Social Sci. Rsch. Coun. fellow, 1955-56, Ford Found. fellow, 1962-63; named Man of Yr. in Fin., Pitts., 1995-96. Fellow: Nat. Assn. Bus. Economists (Adam Smith award 2003); mem.: Am. Fin. Assn., Western Econ. Assn. (pres. 1985—86), Internat. Atlantic Econ. Assn. (pres. 1999—2000), Am. Econ. Assn. (v.p. 1990, Disting. fellow 2002), Phila. Soc. (v.p. 1981—83), Cosmos Club. Avocations: research in macroeconomics, money, political economy, monetary history. Office: Carnegie Mellon U Dept Econs Pittsburgh PA 15213 E-mail: am05@andrew.cmu.edu.

MELTZER, BERNARD DAVID, law educator; b. Phila., Nov. 21, 1914; s. Julius and Rose (Welkov) M.; m. Jean Sulzberger, Jan. 17, 1947; children: Joan, Daniel, Susan. AB, U. Chgo., 1935, JD, 1937; LL.M., Harvard U., 1938. Bar: Ill. 1938. Atty., spl. asst. to chmn. SEC, 1938-40; assoc. firm Mayer, Meyer, Austrian & Platt, Chgo., 1940; spl. asst. to asst. sec. state, also acting chief fgn. funds control div. State, 1941—43; asst. trial counsel U.S. prosecution Internat. Nuremberg War Trials, 1945-46; from professorial lectr. to disting. svc. prof. law emeritus U. Chgo. Law Sch., 1946—; counsel Vedder, Price, Kaufman & Kammholz, Chgo., 1954-55, Sidley and Austin, Chgo., 1987-89. Hearing commr. NPA, 1952-53; labor arbitrator; spl. master U.S. Ct. Appeals for D.C., 1963-64; bd. publs. U. Chgo., 1965-67, chmn., 1967-68; mem. Gov. Ill. Adv. Commn. Labor-Mgmt. Policy for Pub. Employees in Ill., 1966-67, Ill. Civil Service Commn., 1968-69; cons. U.S. Dept. Labor, 1969-70 Author: Supplementary Materials on International Organizations, 1948, (with W.G. Katz) Cases and Materials on Business Corporations, 1949, Labor Law Cases, Materials and Problems, 1970, supplement, 1972, 75, 2d edit., 1977, supplements, 1980, 82 (with S. Henderson), 3d edit. (with S. Henderson), 1985, supplement, 1988; also articles. Bd. dirs. Hyde Park Community Conf., 1954-56, S.E. Chgo. Commn., 1956-57. Served to lt. (j.g.) USNR, 1943-46. Mem. ABA (co-chmn. com. devel. law under NLRA 1959-60, mem. spl. com. transp. strikes), Ill. Bar Assn., Chgo. Bar Assn. (bd. mgrs. 1972-73), Am. Law Inst., Coll. Labor and Employment Lawyers, Am. Acad. Arts and Scis., Order of Coif, Phi Beta Kappa Home: 1219 E 50th St Chicago IL 60615-2908 Office: U Chgo Law Sch 1111 E 60th St Chicago IL 60637-2776 Office Phone: 773-702-9585. Business E-Mail: bernard_meltzer@law.uchicago.edu.

MELTZER, CAROLYN CIDIS, neuroradiology educator; b. New Hyde Park, N.Y., Feb. 14, 1961; d. Demetrios and Xantheppe (Anadollis) Cidis; m. Kenneth Harrison Meltzer, Nov. 29, 1987. BS in Neurobiology with honors, Cornell U., 1983; MD, Johns Hopkins U., 1987. Diplomate Am. Bd. Nuclear Medicine; lic. physician, Md. Intern in internal medicine Greater Balt. Med. Ctr., Towson, Md., 1987-88; PET Rsch. fellow divsn. nuclear medicine Sch. Medicine Johns Hopkins U., Balt., 1988-89, resident in diagnostoc radiology, 1989-93, instr. radiology, 1990-94, fellow in nuclear medicine, 1992, fellow in neuroradiology, 1992-94; asst. prof. neuroradiology Med. Ctr. U. Pitts., 1994—. Mem. Johns Hopkins House Staff Coun., 1988-90; speaker and presenter in field. Reviewer Radiology; contbr. 26 artcles to med. jours., chpt. to book. Student Rsch. fellow Johns Hopkins U., 1986 Mem. AMA, Am. Soc. Neuroradiology (sr.), Am. Roentgen Ray Soc., Radiology Soc. N. Am., Soc. Nuclear Medicine, N.Y. Acad. Scis., Women in Medicine (pres. 1981-82, treas. 1982-83), Cornell Alumni Admissions Network. Office: Presbyn U Hosp Dept Radiology Divsn Neuroradiology 200 Lothrop St Pittsburgh PA 15213-2546

MELTZER, DAVID, author, musician, educator; b. Rochester, NY, Feb. 17, 1937; s. Louis and Roseamunde (Lovelace) M.; m. Christina Meyer, Apr. 1, 1958; children— Jennifer, Margaret, Amanda, Adam Benjamin ben David. Student, Los Angeles City Coll., 1955-56, U. Calif. at Los Angeles, 1956-57. Mem. cons. bd. Coordinating Coun. of Lit. Mags.; instr. M.A. program in poetics New Coll., San Francisco, 1980—, coord. writing and lit. program in undergrad. humanites program, 1987—. Author: (poetry) Tens, Selected Poems, 1973, Six, 1976, Two-way Mirror: Notebook on Poetry, 1977, The Art, The Veil, 1981, The Name, Selected Poetry, 1973-1983, 1983; editor: The San Francisco Poets, 1971, Birth, 1973, The Secret Garden: Anthology of the Classic Kabbalah, 1977, rev. edit., 1998, Birth: An Anthology of Ancient Texts, Songs, Prayers and Stories, 1981, Death: An Anthology of Ancient Texts, Songs, Prayers and Stories, 1983, The Book Within the Book: Approaching the Kabbalah, 1990, Arrows: Selected Poetry; 1952-92, 1994, Reading Jazz, 1993, Writing Jazz, 1999, No Eyes: Lester Young, 2000, San Francisco Beat: Talking with the Poets, 2001, Beat Thing, 2004, David's Copy: Selected Poems, 2005; editor, pub. The Agency, 1968, The Agency Trilogy, 1994, Under, 1995, also Tree Books, songwriter, musician, vocalist Serpent Power, 1968, Poet Song, 1970, Green Morning, 1999, soundtrack Chance, 1978. Bd. dirs. Before Columbus Found., 1977—. Coordinating Coun. of Lit. Mags. grantee, 1973-74, 81, Nat. Endowment of Arts grantee for creative writing, 1974, for pub., 1975, Calif. Arts Coun. grantee, 1979; recipient Tombstone award for poetry John Ryan Morris Meml. Found., 1992. Office: PO Box 9005 Berkeley CA 94709-0005 E-mail: dmelt@earthlink.net.

MELTZER, DONALD RICHARD, treasurer; b. Boston, Sept. 1, 1932; s. Leo N. and Betty (Flesher) M.; m. Mary Douglas Seelye, Dec. 7, 1963; children: Kimberly, Christopher. AB, Dartmouth Coll., 1954, MBA, 1955. Mgr. Peat, Marwick, Mitchell & Co., Boston, 1955-67; asst. controller United Fruit Corp., Boston, 1968-69, controller, 1969-70, v.p., controller, 1970-73; v.p., chief acctg. office United Brands Co., N.Y.C., 1973-74, v.p. fin. and adminstrn., 1974-76; v.p. fin., treas. Instron Corp., Canton, Mass., 1976-88; v.p. fin. and adminstrn., treas., chief fin. officer Dialogue, Inc., Braintree, Mass., 1988-90. Corp. fin. cons., Sudbury, Mass., 1988-96. Overseer Children's Hosp. Med. Ctr., Boston, 1980-94; fin. com. Town of Sudbury, Mass., 1967; chmn. bd. trustees First Parish Ch., Sudbury, 1970-71, treas., 1991-93; pres. Mass. Parents Assn. for Deaf and Hard of Hearing, Boston, 1976-77, bd. dirs., 1973-86. Mem. AICPA, Mass. Soc. CPAs, Fin. Execs. Inst., Am. Assn. Indsl. Mgmt. (bd. dirs. 1980-85), Walk 'N Mass Volkssport Club (co-pres. 1993-95). Avocations: postal history, stamp collecting/philately. Home: 341 Old Lancaster Rd Sudbury MA 01776-2035 E-mail: meltzwalk@aol.com.

MELTZER, E. ALYNE, elementary school educator, social worker, volunteer; b. Jersey City, May 16, 1934; d. Abraham Samuel and Fannie Ruth (Nydick) Meltzer. BA, Mich. State U., 1956. Acctg. clk. Louis Marx Co. Inc., N.Y.C., 1957-60; tchr. social studies Haverstraw HS, NY, 1960-61; tchr. Sachem Ctrl. Sch. Dist., Farmingville, NY, 1961-63, East Paterson Sch. Dist., NJ, 1964-65; case worker dept. social svc. Human Resource Adminstrn., N.Y.C., 1966-89. Mem. Yorkville Civic Coun., 1988—93; policy advisor Senator Roy Goodman Adv. Com., Albany, 1987—90; mem. Temple Shaaray Tefila. Recipient Sabra Soc. Plaque award, State of Israel New Leadership Divsn., N.Y.C., 1979, Prime Min. Club Plaque award, State of Israel Bonds, 1986—87, 1996, Pin award, 1986—87, 1990, 1994—96, others. Mem.: AAUW, Jewish Genealogy Soc., Assn. Ref. Zionists Am., Am. Jewish Com., Internat. Coun. Jewish Women (participant Jerusalem seminar 1991), Nat. Coun. Jewish Women (life; participant nat. conv. 1987, Albany Inst. 1987, Washington Inst. 1987, N.E. dist. conv. 1988, Albany Inst. 1988, Israel Summit V 1988, Washington Inst. 1989, sec. sect. pub. affairs com. 1990—93, mem. state and sec. pub. affairs com. 1990—, Albany Inst. 1991, Washington Mission 1991, co-chair Hunger Program Sunday Family Soup Kitchen 1991—93, nat. Israel affairs com. 1991—96, bd. dirs. N.Y. sect. 1991—, Jewish/Israel affairs com. sect. 1991—, Washington Inst. 1992, participant nat. conv. 1993, Albany Inst. 1993, chair Roosevelt Island Svcs. 1993—2003, participant nat. conv. 1996, Israel Roundtable 1996—99, co-chair fundraising jour. 1998—2000, co-chair sec. Yad B'Yad (Hand in Hand with Israel) cmty. svc. project 1999—, film festival com. Eleanor Leff Jewish Women's Resource Ctr. 2001—02, co-chair sec. Jewish/Israel Affairs com. 2001—04, life mem. N.Y. and Rockland County sects., advisor sec. Jewish Israeli Affairs com. 2004—, Outstanding Vol. award 1973—74, 1990—91, Donor award 1987—93, 1996), Jewish Hist. Soc. N.Y., Mich. State U. Alumni Orgn. (life; sec. N.Y. chpt. 1959—60), Mothers and Others, Rockland County Jewish Home for the Aged (life), Women's League for Israel (life), Hadassah (life), Sierra Club.

MELTZER, HAROLD, performing company executive, composer; Grad. summa cum laude, Amherst Coll.; music degree, Yale U., King's Coll., Cambridge; degree, Columbia Law Sch. Artistic dir., composer, co-founder Sequitur Music Ensemble; resident Meet the Composer, 2001. Composer: (recs.) Trapset, The Heaven of Animals. Recipient Guggenheim fellowship, 2003. Office: Sequitur Apt 3 16 E 11 St New York NY 10003

MELTZER, JAY H. lawyer, retail executive; b. Bklyn., Mar. 30, 1944; s. Solomon G. and Ethel L. (Kraft) M.; m. Bonnie R. Rosenberg, June 27, 1965; children: Wendy, Elizabeth, Jonathan. AB, Dartmouth Coll., 1964; JD, Harvard U., 1967. Bar: N.Y. 1968, Mass. 1978, U.S. Dist. Ct. Mass. 1979. Law clk. to U.S. dist. judge, 1967-68; assoc. firm Shearman & Sterling, N.Y.C., 1968-72; with Damon Corp., Needham Heights, Mass., 1972-84, gen. counsel, sec., 1973-84, v.p., 1979-84; v.p., corp. counsel The TJX Cos., Inc., Framingham, Mass., 1984-87, v.p., gen. counsel, sec., 1987-89, sr. v.p., gen. counsel, sec., 1989—. Dir. coun. Better Bus. Bur., 1990-93. Mem. ABA, Am. Soc. Corp. Secs., Am. Corp. Counsel Assn. (bd. dirs. N.E. chpt. 1991-2000), Retailers Assn. Mass. (bd. dirs., exec. com., sec.), New Eng. Corp. Counsel Assn. (bd. dirs. 1979-2003). Office: TJX Cos Inc 770 Cochituate Rd Framingham MA 01701-4672 E-mail: jay_meltzer@tjx.com.

MELTZER, MILTON, author; b. Worcester, Mass., May 8, 1915; s. Benjamin and Mary (Richter) M.; m. Hilda Balinky, June 22, 1941; children: Jane, Amy. Student, Columbia, 1932-36. Adj. prof. history U. Mass., Amherst, 1977-80. Author: more than 100 books including Mark Twain Himself, 1960; author: (with Walter Harding) A Thoreau Profile, 1962; author: Langston Hughes: A Biography, 1968, Bread and Roses, 1967, Never to Forget: The Jews of the Holocaust, 1976, Dorothea Lange: A Photographer's Life, 1978; editor (with Langston Hughes, C. Eric Lincoln, Jon Michael Spencer): A Pictorial Hisotry of African-Americans, 1994; co-editor: Lydia Maria Child: Selected Letters, 1817-1880, 1982, The Black Americans, 1984, Mark Twain: A Writer's Life, 1985, George WAshington and the Birth of Our Nation, 1986, The American Revolutionaries, 1987, Benjamin Franklin: The New American, 1988, Rescue: The Story of How Gentiles Saved Jews in the Holocaust, 1988, Starting From Home: A Writer's Beginnings, 1988, Voices From the Civil War, 1989, Columbus and the World Around Him, 1990, The Bill of Rights: How We Got It and What It Means, 1990, Thomas Jefferson: Revolutionary Aristocrat, 1991, The Amazing Potato, 1992, Slavery: A World History, 1993, Lincoln: In His Own Words, 1993, Andrew Jackson and His America, 1993, Gold, 1993, Cheap Raw Material: How Our Youngest Workers Are Exploited and Abused, 1994, Theodore Roosevelt, 1994, Weapons and Warfare, 1996, Tom Paine, 1996, The Many Lives of Andrew Carnegie, 1997, Ten Queens: Portraits of Women of Power, 1998, Food, 1998, Carl Sandburg, 1999, Witches and Witch Hunts, 1999, Driven from the Land, 2000, They Came in Chains, 2000, Ten Kings, 2001, Ain't Gonna Study War No More, 2002, The Day the Sky Fell, 2002, Great Inventions: The Cotton Gin, 2003, Great Inventions: The Printing Press, 2003, Herman Melville, 2003, Edgar Allan Poe, 2003, Hour of Freedom: American History in Poetry, 2003. Served with USAAF, 1942-46. Recipient Laura Ingalls Wilder award, Am. Libr. Assn., 2001, Regina medal, Cath. Libr. Assn., 2000. Mem. Orgn. Am. Historians, Authors Guild, P.E.N. Address: 263 W End Ave New York NY 10023-2612

MELTZER, ROBERT CRAIG, lawyer, educator; b. Chgo., July 31, 1958; s. Franklyn Richard and Zelma (Cohen) M. BA, U. Colo., 1980; cert., Inst. de Internat., Strasbourg, France, 1984; JD, No. Ill. U., DeKalb, 1985; postgrad., U. Salzburg, Austria, 1985. Bar: Ill. 1985, U.S. Dist. Ct. (no. dist.) Ill. 1985, U.S. Ct. Appeals (7th cir.) 1988, U.S. Supreme Ct. 1989. Law clk. Hurwitz & Abramson, Washington, 1980, Mayer, Brown & Platt, Chgo., 1983; lawyer UN WHO, Geneva, Switzerland, 1985; assoc. Robert C. Meltzer & Assocs., Chgo., 1986-91, Katz, Randall & Weinberg, Chgo., 1991-93, Arnstein & Lehr, Chgo., 1993-98, Grotefeld & Denenberg, Chgo., 1998-99; pres. Visanow-.com, Inc., Chgo., 1999—. Adj. prof. internat. law Ill. Inst. Tech/Chgo.-Kent Coll. Law, 1994-98; creator online immigration processing. Contbr. articles to profl. jours.; editor The Globe, Springfield, Ill., 1984-99. Pro bono lawyer Fed. Bar Assn., Chgo., 1985-98. Recipient Medal of Appreciation, Ministry of Justice, Beijing, 1996. Mem. Ill. State Bar Assn. (internat. and immigration law sect. 1985-2000, chair internat. law sect. 1990-91, Editor's award 1989, 94, 99), Am. Immigration Law Assn. Avocations: history, bread baking, golf, arts, music. Home: 71 E Division St Chicago IL 60610 Office: Visanow.com Inc 350 N La Salle St 1400 Chicago IL 60610 E-mail: meltzer@visanow.com.

MELTZER, YALE LEON, economist, educator; b. NYC, Nov. 3, 1931; s. Benjamin and Ada (Ludwin) M.; m. Annette Schoenberg, Aug. 7, 1960; children: Benjamin Robert, Philippe David. BA, Columbia U., 1954, postgrad. Sch. Law, 1954-55; MBA, NYU, 1966. Asst. to chief patent atty., prodn. mgr. Beaunit Mills, Inc., Elizabethton, Tenn., 1955—58, prodn. mgr., 1956—58; rsch. chemist N.Y. Med. Coll., N.Y.C., 1958-59, H. Kohnstamm & Co., Inc., N.Y.C., 1959-66, mgr. comml. devel., market rsch., patents and trademarks, 1966-68; sr. security analyst Harris, Upham & Co., Inc., 1968-70; instr. dept. econs. NYU, N.Y.C., 1972-79; adj. prof. dept. econs., fin. and mgmt. Pace U., N.Y.C., 1974-80, adj. assoc. prof., 1980-84; lectr. dept. polit. sci., econs. and philosophy Coll. S.I., CUNY, N.Y.C., 1977-82, asst. prof. dept. polit. sci., econs. and philosophy, 1983—. Lectr. bus., fin., econs., sci. and tech.; presenter papers confs. Author: Soviet Chemical Industry, 1966; Chemical Trade with the Soviet Union and Eastern European Countries, 1967; Chemical Guide to GATT, The Kennedy Round and International Trade, 1968; Phthalocyanine Technology, 1970; Hormonal and Attractant Pesticide Technology, 1971; Urethane Foams: Technology and Applications, 1971; Water-Soluble Polymers: Technology and Applications, 1972; Encyclopedia of Enzyme Technology, 1973; Economics, 1974; Foamed Plastics: Recent Developments, 1976; Water-Soluble Resins and Polymers: Technology and Applications, 1976; Putting Money to Work: An Investment Primer, 1976; (with W.C.F. Hartley) Cash Management: Planning, Forecasting, and Control, 1979; Water-Soluble Polymers: Recent Developments, 1979; Putting Money to Work: An Investment Primer for the '80s, 1981, updated edit., 1984; Water-Soluble Polymers: Developments since 1978, 1981; Expanded Plastics and Related Products: Developments Since 1978, 1983; contbr. articles to profl. publs.; translator Russian, French and German tech. lit. Mem. AAAS, Am. Econ. Assn. Home: 14110 82nd Dr Apt 537 Jamaica NY 11435-1106 Office: Coll Staten Island 2800 Victory Blvd Staten Island NY 10314-6609

MELUCCI, RICHARD CHARLES, research institute administrator; b. Oceanside, N.Y., July 17, 1946; s. Richard Joseph and Marcia Jane (Lockwood) M.; m. Rosanne Alice Kessel, Dec. 15, 1968; children: Christine Ann, Donna Marie, Richard Paul, Robert Joseph, John Charles. BS, Adelphi U., 1968, MBA, 1971. Planning engr. Sperry Gyroscope Co., Great Neck, NY, 1967-70; planning adminstr. PRD Elecs., Inc., Syosset, NY, 1970-73, program adminstr., 1973-74; sr. staff asst. dept. physics Brookhaven Nat. Lab., Union, NY, 1974-79, adminstr. dept. applied sci., 1979-95, lab. budget officer, 1995—. Adj. assoc. prof. computer info. systems Dowling Coll., Oakdale, N.Y., 1978—; vis. prof. SUNY at Oswego, 1982—. Recipient Cert. Inst. Certification of Computer Profls. Office: Brookhaven Nat Lab Bldg 460 Upton NY 11973 Office Phone: 516-344-2911. Business E-Mail: melucci@bnl.gov.

MELUSKY, JOSEPH ANTHONY, political science professor, department chairman; b. Pottsville, Pa., June 2, 1952; s. George John and Eleanor Elizabeth (Parulis) Melusky; m. Marie Ann Belecanech, Mar. 28, 1976; children: Michael Joseph, Jessica Marie. BA, West Chester State Coll., 1974; MA, U. Del., 1978, PhD, 1983. Lectr. U. Del., Newark, 1979-80; prof. polit. sci., chmn. dept. St. Francis U., Loretto, Pa., 1980—, dean gen. edn., 1993—94. Pres. faculty senate St. Francis U., Loretto, 1985—87, v.p. faculty senate, 1984—85, Loretto, 1990—92. Author: The Constitution: Our Written Legacy, 1991; co-author: To Preserve These Rights: The Bill of Rights 1791-1991, 1991, Bill of Rights: Our Written Legacy, 1993, The American Political System: An Owner's Manual, 2000, Cruel and Unusual Punishment: Rights and Liberties Under the Law, 2003. Judge oratorical contests on U.S. Constn. Am. Legion HS, 1991—92, 1995, 1997, 2000; judge We Are the People: The Citizen and the Constitution Pa. State Finals, 2001—04; mem. Blair County Dem. Com., 1985—90; election judge Blair Twp., East Hollidaysburg 9 Dist., 1997—. Mem.: Northeastern Polit. Sci. Assn. (dir. employment svcs. 1985—, exec. dir. 1993—97, 3d v.p. 2003—04), Pa. Polit. Sci. Assn. (v.p. 1994—96, 2002—04, pres. 1997—99). Office: St Francis U Dept History and Polit Sci Loretto PA 15940 Office Phone: 814-472-3060. Business E-Mail: jmelusky@francis.edu.

MELVILL, MICHAEL W. aircraft company executive, experimental test pilot; b. 1941; arrived in US, 1970; m. Sally Melvill; 1 child. FAA coml. cert., cert. ASEL, AMEL, instrument airplane, Rotorcraft-helicopter and Glider. V.p., gen. mgr., test pilot Scaled Co., Inc., Mojave, Calif., 1985—. Recipient Ivan C. Kincheloe trophy for work on devel. high altitude flight testing of model 281 Proteus, 1999. Mem.: Experimental Aircraft Assn., Aircraft Owners' and Pilots' Assn., Soc. Experimental Test Pilots (assoc. fellow). Achievements include participated in flight testing for Beech Starship prototype (NGBA), Fairchild's Next Generation Trainer for US Air Force (NGT), ARES, Pond Racer; built and flight tested Model 27 Variviggen; built, tested and flew around world in 1997 with Dick Rutan Model 61 Long-EZ; first flight of Model 72 GRIZZLY prototype, Model 77 SOLITAIRE prototype, Model 81 CATBIRD prototype, Model 120 PREDATOR prototype, Model 144 UAV prototype, Model 202 BOOMERANG, Model 226 RAPTOR; first flight of Model 281 PROTEUS, Model 316 SPACESHIPONE; first flight firing of GAU-12/U25mm cannon in Model 151 ARES jet fighter; only person to have flown Voyager Aircraft besides Dick Rutan and Jeana Yeager; holds 4 World and Nat. speed and altitude records in Catbird and Proteus Aircraft; first private manned mission to space, first civilian to fly a spaceship out of the atmosphere, first private pilot to earn astronaut wings, June 21, 2004; Guinness Book of World Records dubbed rocket launch "first ever privately funded manned spaceflight". Office: Scaled Composites Inc 1624 Flight Line Mojave CA 93501 Office Phone: 661-824-4541. Office Fax: 661-824-4174.

MELVILLE, MARGUERITA W. advertising executive; b. Liverpool, Eng., June 14, 1942; came to U.S., 1963; d. William and Ada Lillian Melville. Grad., Ellergreen Coll., Liverpool, 1960; diploma, Liverpool Sch. Journalism, 1962. Cert. state gen. contractor, real estate salesperson, Fla. Editl. asst. Nat. Assn. Elec. Distbn., N.Y.C., 1963-65; asst. editor Nassau (Bahamas) Guardian, 1965-68; exec. sec. Ft. Lauderdale (Fla.) News, 1969-73, sales exec., 1973-78; suburban sales mgr. West, Lauderhill, Fla., 1978-80; retail advt. mgr. Sun Sentinel, Pompano Beach, Fla., 1980-83; retail sales mgr. Ft. Lauderdale News/Sun Sentinel, 1983-90; nat. travel sales mgr. Sun Sentinel Co., Ft. Lauderdale, 1990-96, diversity trainer, 1995-99; sr. sales mgr. Leisure Group, 1997-2000; travel cons., 2001—. Bd. dirs. Sentinel Graphics FCU, 2003—. Mem. leadership in giving United Way, Broward County, 1996-99. Mem. Newspaper Advt. Sales Assn. (sec., bd. dirs. 1993-99), Fla. Hotel Motel Assn., Bon Vivants, Am. Bus. Women's Assn. (pres. 1985, Woman of Yr. award 1986), Internat. Soc. Poets. Avocations: writing, golf, collectibles, travel.

MELVILLE, ROBERT SEAMAN, chemist; b. Worcester, Mass., Nov. 20, 1913; s. Carey Eyster and Maud Tesmer (Seaman) M.; m. Eleanor Elisabeth Vogel, Mar. 6, 1942; children: Robert Andrew, John Frederick, Margaret Ellen, Emily Jean, Martin Carroll. AB in Chemistry, Clark U., 1937; PhD in Biochemistry, State U. Iowa, 1950. Chief chemist St. Luke's Hosp., Chgo., 1950-54; chief biochemist VA Hosp., Iowa City, 1954-63; chief biochemist, lab. requirement specialist VA Cen. Office, Washington, 1963-65; health sci. adminstr. Nat. Inst. Gen. Med. Scis., NIH, Bethesda, Md., 1965-67, chief automated clin. lab. program, 1967-77, spl. asst. to dir. of biomed. engring., 1977-81; dir. In Vitro Diagnostic Device Standards div. Bur. Med. Devices, FDA, Silver Spring, Md., 1981-82; cons. in clin. scis., 1983—. Clin. prof. pathology George Washington U. Med. Ctr., Washington, 1977—; pres. Trans-Tech. Biomed., 1983—. Contbr. articles on clin. lab. automation to profl. publs. With U.S. Army, 1942-46. Fellow AAAS, Am. Chem. Soc., Am. Assn. Clin. Chemistry (Joseph H. Rowe award 1972, Nat. Fisher award 1976, pres. 1969-70), Instrument Soc. Am., Assn. for Advancement of Med. Instrumentation; mem. Am. Bd. Clin. Chemists (pres. bd. dirs. 1978-81), Am. Inst. Chemists (chmn. cert. commn. in chem. engring. and chemistry 1981-84, 87-91, cert. chemist 1989—), Alpha Chi Sigma (Profl. Chemist award 1990), Lambda Chi Alpha. Clubs: Cosmos. Lodges: Masons. Unitarian Universalist. Home and Office: 11112 Kenilworth Ave PO Box 56 Garrett Park MD 20896-0056 E-mail: rsmel@starpower.net.

MELVIN, BILLY ALFRED, clergyman; b. Macon, Ga., Nov. 25, 1929; s. Daniel Henry and Leola Dale (Seidell) Melvin; m. Marcia Darlene Eby, Oct. 26, 1952; children: Deborah Ruth, Daniel Henry II. Student, Free Will Baptist Bible Coll., Nashville, 1947—49; BA, Taylor U., Upland, Ind., 1951, LLD (hon.), 1984; postgrad., Asbury Theol. Sem., Wilmore, Ky., 1951—53; BD, Union Theol. Sem., Richmond, Va., 1956; DD, Azusa (Calif.) Coll., 1968, Huntington Coll., 1995. Ordained to ministry Free Will Baptist Ch., 1951; pastor First Free Will Baptist Chs., Newport, Tenn., 1951—53, Richmond, Va., 1953—57, Bethany Ch., Norfolk, 1957—59. Exec. sec. Nat. Assn. Free Will Baptists, 1959—67; exec. dir. Nat. assn. Evangelicals, 1967—95. Baptist.

MELVIN, CHARLES ALFRED, III, superintendent of schools; b. Milw., May 19, 1950; s. Charles A. Jr. and Audry M. (Dart) M.; m. Almira M. Tiedke, Aug. 1985; children: Sean Charles, Katherin Almira. Ba, U. Wis., 1972, MA, 1975, PhD, 1979. Supr. U. Wis., Madison, 1975; prin. Sch. Dist. Beloit (Wis.) Turner, 1980, dir. instr., 1982, supt., 1986—. Recipient sch. improvement grant, Carnegie Found., Beloit Found.; named one of Top 100 Exec. Educators, NSBA. Mem. ASCD, Am. Assn. Sch. Adminstrs., Nat. Assn. Secondary Sch. Prins. Home: 1911 Vail Ter Beloit WI 53511-3148

MELVIN, CHARLES EDWARD, JR., lawyer; b. Greensboro, N.C., July 13, 1929; s. Charles Edward and Mary Ruth (Plunkett) M.; m. Jacklyn McDaniel, Mar. 1, 1958; 1 child, Dana W. BS, U. N.C., 1951, JD with honors, 1956. Bar: N.C. 1956. Of counsel Smith Moore LLP, Greensboro, 1958—. Capt. U.S. Army, 1952-54. Mem. N.C. Bar Assn. (chmn. real property sect. 1981), Am. Coll. Real Estate Lawyers, Greensboro C. of C. (pres. 1978). Office: Smith Moore LLP PO Box 21927 Greensboro NC 27420-1927 Office Phone: 336-378-5204. E-mail: charlie.melvin@smithmoorelaw.com.

MELVIN, NORMAN CECIL, lawyer; b. Balt., Aug. 21, 1916; s. Norman Cecil and Anna H. (Holzworth) M.; m. Louise A. Gillen, Feb. 10, 1945 (dec. Oct. 1958); children: Leigh G., Norman Cecil III; m. Virginia Brown Lester, Nov. 2, 1959; 1 dau., Susan A. AB, Johns Hopkins U., 1939; LL.B., Harvard U., 1942. Bar: Md. 1942. Practice law, Balt., 1946—; mem. firm Brown & Brune, 1946-52; gen. atty. Western Md. Ry. Co., Balt., 1952-66, gen. solicitor, 1966-68, v.p., gen. counsel, 1968-75, dir., 1970-75. Asst. peoples counsel Pub. Service Commn. Md., 1951-52; instr. U. Balt., 1957-66 Served to capt. AUS, 1942-46. Recipient Erskine M. Ross essay award ABA, 1950 Mem. ABA, Md. Bar Assn., Balt. Bar Assn., Soc. Colonial Wars (coun. 1966-69), SAR, Johns Hopkins Alumni Assn. (pres. 1968-70, Disting. Alumni award 1970, Heritage award 1980), Harvard Club, Johns Hopkins Club. Home: 4202 Wickford Rd Baltimore MD 21210-2930

MELVIN, PATRICIA E. artist; b. N.Y.C., Dec. 13, 1950; d. William Oscar and Eileen Monks Melvin. BA, NYU, 1973; studied, Art Students League, 1979—81; independent study, NY, Paris, Amsterdam, 1977—90. Artist-in-

residence Sight and Insight, Mill Valley, 1993—95. Painting tchr. Bronx River Art Ctr., NYC, 1998—2003. One-woman shows include Beaux Arts Gallery, Southbury, Conn., 1989, 2001, Chuck Levitan Gallery, N.Y.C., 1997, Schoolhouse Gallery, Croton, N.Y., 1997, exhibitions include Circle Work Visions Gallery, N.Y.C., 1986 87, Ten Worlds Gallery, 1988, Cassandra Kersting Gallery, Sausalito, Calif., 1993—94, G.W. Einstein, N.Y.C., 1995, Cork Gallery, Lincoln Ctr., 1999, 2000, Main St. Gallery, Dobbs Ferry, N.Y., 2002, Bronx River Art Ctr., 1997—2002, Blue Mountain Gallery, N.Y.C., 1997—2003, Audubon Artists, 2004, featured in profl. publs. and Web sites, pub. collections, NYU, N.Y.C., The New Sch., Webster Hall, Noble Maritime Collection, S.I., N.Y., Hales & Co., N.Y.C. and Calif. Bd. mem. Cooper Sq. Cmty. Devel. Com., NYC, 2002—04, mem., 1985—2004. Artist's Fellowship, NY Found. Arts, 2002. Avocations: music, tai chi.

MELVIN, PETER JOSEPH, astrophysicist, educator; b. Seattle, Mar. 12, 1944; s. William Leopold and Virginia (Stevens) M.; m. Bernice Stenman, June 6, 1967 (div. July 1974); m. Alice Sue Pfiester, May 25, 1975 (dec. 1994); children: Robert Dennis, Chloe Anne. BA, Western Wash. State Coll., 1965; MS, U. Ill., 1966, PhD, 1970. NASA trainee U. Ill., Urbana, 1966-68, instr. phys. sci., 1970-72, asst. prof., 1972-77; sr. engr. Martin-Marietta Aerospace Co., Denver, 1977-80, staff engr., 1980-83; sr. specialist engr. engring. tech. applications divsn. Boeing Computer Svcs., Seattle, 1983-86; astrophysicist U.S. Naval Rsch. Lab., Washington, 1986-99, ret., 1999; pres. B-Gravity, Inc., Waldorf, Md., 1999—. Vis. faculty applied math. divsn. Nat. Bur. Stds. Boulder (Colo.) Labs., 1977. Contbr. articles to sci. jours.; patentee in field. Mem. AIAA, Am. Math. Soc., Soc. Indsl. and Applied Math., Am. Geophys. Uion, Am. Astronautical Soc. E-mail: melvin@nrl.navy.mil, pjmelvin@comcast.net.

MELVIN, RONALD MCKNIGHT, retired museum director; b. Regina, Sask., Can., Oct. 25, 1927; came to U.S., 1953; s. M. Gordon and Mary Gillespie (McKnight) M.; m. Gwen Ellis, Apr. 30, 1955; children: Mary Fleming, Catharine Melvin. Student, U. B.C., 1945-49. Various positions Powell River Co. Ltd., Vancouver, B.C., Can., 1947-56; asst. to pres. Trans Union Corp., Chgo., 1956-58; mng. dir. Procor Ltd. subs. Trans Union Corp., Toronto, Ont., Can., 1958-64; ptnr. Blunt Ellis & Simmons, Chgo., 1964-71, pres., 1971-78; vice chmn. Blunt Ellis & Loew, Chgo., 1978-80; founding dir. Terra Mus. Am. Art, Evanston, Ill., 1980-84. Dir. Chef Pierre, Traverse City, Mich., 1972-77, Lawter Internat., Chgo., 1977-84. Author, organizer: (art exhbns.) Important Western Art from Chicago Collections, 1980 Five American Masters of Watercolor, 1981, American Naive Paintings From National Gallery of Art, 1982, Solitude--Inner Visions in American Art, 1982, Woman, 1984. Avocation: collecting worcester porcelain. Home: 585 Norfolk Rd PO Box 278 Southfield MA 01259-0278

MELVIN, RUSSELL JOHNSTON (JAY MELVIN), magazine publishing consultant; b. New Castle, Pa., Nov. 16, 1925; s. Russell Conwell and Anna Katharine (Johnston) M.; m. Helen Margaret Connery, Aug. 6, 1949; children: Thomas Kirk, Meredith. BA, U. Pa., 1949. Reporter Phila. Inquirer, 1949; copywriter, then asst. to circulation mgr. Time mag., 1949-53; with Newsweek mag., 1953-86, dir. Pacific edits., 1960-64, mng. dir. internat. edits., 1964-68, mng. editor internat. editorial service, 1969-86; cons. internat. affairs and profl. edn. Mag. Pubs. Am. (formerly Mag. Pubs. Assn.), N.Y.C., 1986—2003. V.p. Newsweek, Inc., 1965-85; founding editor The Journal, Tokyo, 1963; founding dir. Newsweek Feature Service, 1968; mem. UN Communications Adv. Coun. Served with USNR, 1942-46. Mem. Internat. Advt. Assn. (chmn., CEO 1980-85, exec. dir. Chgos. Corp. 1985-86, bd. dirs. 1988-91, mem. world coun. 1990—), Internat. Fedn. Periodical Press (vice chmn. 1990-94, mgmt. bd.), Univ. Club, Chappaqua Tennis Club, The Century Assn. Home: 153 Douglas Rd Chappaqua NY 10514-3104

MELVIN, STEWART WAYNE, engineering educator; BS in Agrl. Engring., Iowa State U., 1964, MS in Agrl. Engring., 1967, PhD, 1970. Registered agrl. engr., Iowa. With Soil Conservation Svc., USDA, 1963—67; asst. prof. Colo. State U., 1969-70, Iowa State U., Ames, 1970-74, assoc. prof. agrl. engring., 1974-79, prof. agrl. engring., 1979—, head agrl. engring., 1994—2001; project mgr. Curry-Wille and Assocs., 2002—. Vis. prof. Silsoe Coll., Eng., 1985-86. Contbr. numerous articles to profl. jours. Fellow Am. Soc. Agrl. Engrs.; mem. Internat. Soil and Tillage Rsch. Orgn., Soil and Water Conservation Soc. Am., Am. Soc. Engring. Edn., Phi Kappa Phi, Tau Beta Pi, Gamma Sigma Delta, Sigma Xi, Epsilon Sigma Phi, Alpha Epsilon. Office: Iowa State U Agrl-Biosys Engring Dept 3204 NSRIC Ames IA 50011-3310 Fax: (515) 294-4250. E-mail: swmelvin@iastate.edu.

MELVIN, VINCENT P. information technology executive; BS in Physics, Trinity Coll.; MA in Indsl Adminstrn., Carnegie Mellon U. Various mgmt. positions IBM; dir. info. tech. ea. region Solectron, Inc.; chief info. officer Sanmina-SCI Corp., San Jose, Calif., 2000—. Office: Sanmina-SCI Corp 2700 N First St San Jose CA 95134

MELZACK, RONALD, psychology educator; b. Montreal, Que., Can., July 19, 1929; s. Joseph and Annie (Mandel) M.; m. Lucy Birch, Aug. 7, 1960; children: Lauren, Joel. BSc, McGill U., Montreal, 1950, MSc, 1951, PhD, 1954; DLitt (hon.), U. Waterloo, 1992; DLaws (hon.), Dalhousie U., 2004. Lectr. Univ. Coll., London, 1957-58; assoc. prof. MIT, 1959-63; lectr. psychology McGill U., 1953-54, prof., 1963—, E.P. Taylor prof., 1986. Author: The Day Tuk Became a Hunter, and Other Eskimo Stories, 1967, Raven, Creator of the World, 1970, The Puzzle of Pain, 1973, Why the Man in the Moon is Happy, and Other Eskimo Creation Stories, 1977; author: (with P.D. Wall) The Challenge of Pain, 1982, 2d edit., 1988; author: Pain Measurement and Assessment, 1983; author: (with P.D. Wall) Textbook of Pain, 1984, 4th edit., 1999; author: (with D.C. Turk) Handbook of Pain Assessment, 1999, 2d edit., 2001; author: (with P.D. Wall) Handbook of Pain Management, 2003. Decorated Officer, Order of Can., 1995, Order of Quebec, 2000; recipient Molson prize Can. Coun., 1985, Gaston Labat award Am. Soc. Regional Anesthesia, 1989, J.J. Bonica award VI World Congress on Pain, 1990, Prix du Que. Marie-Victorin, 1994; recipient Disting. Contbn. award Can. Pain Soc., 1995, Rsch. Recognition award Canadian Anesthesiology Soc., 1997, Janet Travell award Am. Acad. Pain Mgmt., 1997, Killam prize, 2001. Fellow APA, AAAS, Royal Soc. Can., Can. Psychol. Assn. (Disting. Contbns. to Psychol. Sci. award 1986, hon. pres. 1988-89, gold medal award 2002); mem. Internat. Assn. Study of Pain (hon., past pres.). Home: 6111 Du Boisé Apt 5C Montreal QC Canada H3S 2V8 Office Phone: 514-398-6084. E-mail: rmelzack@hebb.psyche.mcgill.ca.

MEMEGER, WESLEY, JR., retired chemist, painter; b. Riverdale, Fla., Sept. 21, 1939; s. Wesley and Lucile (Reddick) Memeger; m. Harriet Bryant, Sept. 20, 1940; children: Zane David, Kim. BS, Clark Atlantic U., 1961; PhD, Adelphi U., 1966. From rsch. chemist to sr. rsch. assoc. Exptl. Sta. DuPont Co., Wilmington, Del., 1965—91, rsch. fellow Exptl. Sta., 1991—97, cons., 1997—99; ret., 1999. Contbr. articles to profl. jours.; exhibitions include Carolynn Roberts Gallery, Yorklyn, Del., 2002, 2001, Blue Streak Gallery, Wilmington, 2000. Bd. dirs. Del. Symphony Assn., 1994—2001, Mass for Homeless, Inc., 1997—2002; chmn. music com. Del. Symphony Assn., 1995—98; gallery com. mem. Del. Ctr. Contemporary Art. Mem.: N.Y. Acad. Scis., Am. Chem. Soc. Achievements include patents in field. Home: 711 Coverly Rd Wilmington DE 19802

MEMMI, ALBERT, sociologist, educator; b. Tunis, Tunisia, Dec. 15, 1920; arrived in France, 1956; s. François and Marguerite (Sarfati) M.; m. Marie-Germaine Dubach; children: Daniel, Dominique, Nicolas. PhD(hon.), U. de Beer Schéba. Prof. Lycee Carnot a Tunis, 1953; dir. Ctr. de Psycho-Pedagogie de Tunis, 1953—57; conf. head Ecole Pratique des hautes Etudes, 1958; prof. Ecole des Hautes Etudes Commerciales, 1958—64, U. Nanterre, 1990, U. Paris, 1970—. Author: Pillar of Salt, 1953, Strangers, 1955, Portrait du Colonise, 1957, Scorpion, 1969, Le Désert, 1977, Le Pharaon, The Dependency, Dictionnaire a l'usage des incrédules, 2001, Bonheurs, 1999, The Racism, Colorized and Coloriser, Dominated Man, Portrait of a Jew, Portrait du decolonise, 2003. Decorated officier de la Légion d'Honneur, officier des Palmes Acads., officier des Arts et des Lettres, officier de l'Ordre de la République Tunisienne, officier dan Varde de la culture du Burkira-Faso. Mem. Academie des Scienes d'Outre Mer, Conseil a l'Universíté de Princeton. Address: 5 rue Saint Merri, 75004 Paris France

MEMORY, JASPER DURHAM, academic administrator, physics educator; b. Raleigh, N.C., Dec. 10, 1936; s. Jasper Livingston and Margaret Moore (Durham) M.; m. Carolyn Hofler, June 4, 1961; children— Margaret Carolyn, Jasper William BS summa cum laude, Wake Forest U., 1956; PhD, U. N.C., 1960. Successively asst. prof., assoc. prof. physics U. S.C., Columbia, 1960-64; assoc. prof. N.C. State U., Raleigh, 1964-67, assoc. dean, physics and math. scis., 1973-82, prof. physics, 1967—98, vice-provost, grad. dean, 1982—86, dir. corp. and govtl. affairs, 1998-99; v.p. for research U. N.C. System, 1986—98, prof. emeritus, 1998—. Bd. govs. Research Triangle Inst., Research Triangle Park, N.C., 1983-84, Triangle Area rsch. dir., 1981-98; cons. NASA Langley, Hampton, Va., 1970-74, Ohio Bd. Regents, 1993-95, Ark. Bd. Regents, 1987, Mass. Bd. Regents, 1998; N.C. State U. rep. Oak Ridge Associated Univs., 1982-85, Grad. Record Exam. Bd., 1985-90, chair, 1989, Policy Coun., Test of English as a Fgn. Lang., 1987-88, chair, 1988. Author: Quantum Theory of Magnetic Resonance Parameters, 1968; (with others) NMR of Aromatic Compounds, 1982, High Resolution NMR in the Solid State: Fundamentals of CP/MAS, 1994. Recipient Outstanding Tchr. award N.C. State U., 1967, Disting. Alumni Service award Wake Forest U., 1981 Fellow Am. Phys. Soc.; mem. Am. Assn. Physics Tchrs., Phi Beta Kappa, Sigma Xi. Democrat. Presbyterian. Home: 4815 Rembert Dr Raleigh NC 27612-6237 E-mail: jmemory@nc.rr.com.

MENAKER, DANIEL, publishing executive; s. Robert Owen Menaker; m. Katherine Bouton; 2 children. B in English, Swarthmore Coll., 1963; M in English, Johns Hopkins U. H.S. tchr.; joined as a fact checker The New Yorker, 1969, copy editor, sr. editor; v.p., sr. literary editor Random House, Inc., N.Y.C., 1994—2001, sr. v.p., editor-in-chief Random House Imprint, 2003—; exec. editor Harper Collins, 2001—03. Author: (novels) The Treatment, 1998, (collection of short stories) Friends and Relations, 1976, Old Left and other stories, 1987. Office: Random House Inc 1745 Broadway New York NY 10019*

MENAKER, FRANK H., JR., lawyer; b. Harrisburg, Pa., Aug. 23, 1940; s. Frank H. and Romaine (Sadler) M.; m. Sharon Ann Lynch, Feb. 21, 1981; children: Denise L., Jamie E.; children by previous marriage: David C., Michelle R. BA, Wilkes Coll., 1962; JD, Am. U., 1965. Bar: D.C. 1966, Md. 1975, U.S. Supreme Ct. 1975. Formerly staff counsel Office Gen. Counsel, GAO, Washington; v.p., gen. counsel Martin Marietta Corp., 1981-95, Lockheed Martin, 1995-96, sr. v.p., gen. counsel, 1996—. Spl. counsel U.S. Commn. on Govt. Procurement, 1971. Mem. ABA (mem. sect. pub. contract law, former chair), Md. Bar Assn., Wash. Met. Corp. Counsel Assn. (bd. dirs. 1988-95). Office: Lockheed Martin 6801 Rockledge Dr Bethesda MD 20817-1877

MENAKER, MICHAEL, biology professor, department chairman; b. Vienna, May 19, 1934; came to U.S., 1934; s. William and Esther (Astin) M.; m. Shirley Ann Lasch, June 4, 1955; children: Ellen Margaret, Nicholas. BA in Biology, Swarthmore Coll., 1955; PhD in Biology, Princeton U., 1960. Asst. instr. Princeton (N.J.) U., 1955-57; postdoctoral fellow Harvard U., Cambridge, Mass., 1960-62; asst. prof. zoology U. Tex.-Austin, 1962-68, assoc. prof., 1968-72, prof., 1972-79; prof. biology U. Oreg., Eugene, 1979-86, dir. interdisciplinary program for neuroscis., 1979-81, dir. Inst. Neurosci., 1981-85; Commonwealth prof. biology U. Va., Charlottesville, 1987—, chmn. dept., 1987-93; dir. Howard Hughes Undergrad. Rsch. Program in Biol. Sci., Charlottesville, 1989-94; core investigator Sci. and Tech. Ctr. in Biol. Timing U. Va., Charlottesville, 1991—. Benjamin Meaker vis. prof. U. Bristol, Eng., 1986. Assoc. editor Behavioral Neurosci., Jour. Biol. Rhythms; contbr. articles to profl. jours. Recipient Lifetime Achievement award Am. Soc. for Photobiology, 2002, Life Achievement in Sci. award Va.'s Outstanding Scientists and Industrialists, 2003; NSF fellow, 1958-59, 60-62; NIH fellow, 1960-62; Guggenheim Found. fellow, 1971-72. Fellow AAAS, Am. Acad. Arts and Scis., Japan Soc. Promotion of Scis. (sr.); mem. Soc. Neurosci., Am. Physiol. Soc., Soc. Rsch. Biol. Rhythms. Avocations: literature, music, sailing. Office: U Va Dept Biology Gilmer Hall PO Box 400328 Charlottesville VA 22903-4328

MENAKER, RONALD HERBERT, retired bank executive; b. N.Y.C., Dec. 17, 1944; s. Harold L. Menaker and Gladys (Bleiberg) Ross; m. Kathleen Sager Thomas, Sept. 11, 1966; children: Meredith E., Kyri D. Student, Queen's Coll., 1965—66. Mng. dir. J.P. Morgan & Co., Inc., N.Y.C., 1966—2000. Bd. dirs. Reckson Assocs. Realty Corp., 2002—. Trustee NYU Med. Ctr. and Health Sys., N.Y.C., 1991, The Am. Kennel Club Mus. of the Dog, St. Louis, 1989—; bd. dirs., chmn. Am. Kennel Club, N.Y.C. 2002; trustee, vice chmn, past chmn. NYU Downtown Hosp., 1991—; bd. overseers U. Pa. Vet. Sch., 2000—. Mem.: Westminster Kennel Club. Avocations: sporting art, judging dogs. Business E-Mail: rhm@akc.org.

MENAKER, SHIRLEY ANN LASCH, psychology educator, academic administrator; b. Jersey City, July 22, 1935; d. Frederick Carl and Mary Elizabeth (Thrall) Lasch; m. Michael Menaker, June 4, 1955; children: Ellen Margaret, Nicholas. BA in English Lit., Swarthmore Coll., 1956; MA, Boston U., 1961; PhD in Clin. Psychology, 1965. Adminstrv. asst. N.J. State Fedn. Dist. Bds. Edn., Trenton, 1956-59; trainee clin. psychology Mass. Mental Health Ctr., Boston, 1960-61; intern clin. psychology Thom Guidance Clinic for Children, Boston, 1961-62; research assoc. ednl. psychology U. Tex.-Austin, 1964-67, asst. prof. ednl. psychology, 1967-70, assoc. prof., 1970-79, assoc. dean grad. sch., 1975-77; psychology cons. Research and Devel. Ctr. for Tchr. Edn., 1965-67, faculty investigator, 1967-74; assoc. prof. counseling psychology U. Oreg., Eugene, 1979-85, prof., 1985-87, assoc. dean grad. sch., 1979-84, acting dean grad. sch., 1980-81, 82-83, dean grad. sch., 1984-87; assoc. provost for acad. support and classroom mgmt., prof. U. Va., Charlottesville, 1987—2004, prof. emeritus, 2004—. Contbr. articles to profl. jours. Bd. dirs. Nat. Grad. Record Exam Bd. and Policy Council-Test of English as Fgn. Lang., Ednl. Testing Services, 1984-88. NIMH fellow, 1963-64.

MENAND, LOUIS, literature educator; Disting. prof. English Grad. Ctr. CUNY; prof. English Princeton U., Columbia U., U. Va. Sch. Law. Contbg. editor: N.Y. Rev. of Books, 1994—; author: Discovering Modernism: T.S. Eliot and His Context, 1987—; editor: The Metaphysical Club, 2001—; editor: (with A.W. Litz and L. Rainey) The Cambridge History of Literary Criticism, Vol. 7: Modernism and the New Criticism, 2000—; editor: The Future of Academic Freedom, 1998—, Pragmatism: A Reader, 1997—; editor: (with L. Berlowitz and D. Donoghue) America in Theory, 1988—. Office: CUNY Grad Ctr 365 Fifth Ave New York NY 10016-4309

MENARD, JOAN M. state legislator; BS, Bridgewater State Coll., 1967; MEd, Boston U., 1971; postgrad., Boston Coll., 1997—. Mem. Mass. Senate, Boston, 1979—; majority whip Mass. Ho. of Reps., Boston, 1984, 92-96, asst. majority whip, 1991, mem. house rules and joint rules coms., house vice chairperson election laws; elem. tchr. Somerset (Mass.) Pub. Schs., 1966-70, spl. edn. tchr., 1970-74, adminstr. spl. needs, 1974-78. Bd. dirs. Fall River Five Cents Savs. Bank, Steppinstone. Mem. adv. bd. Southeastern Mass. Labor Ctr.; chair Dem. State Com., 1993-95, del., 1980; chairwoman Mass. Dem. Party, 1997—2001, State Senator, Mass. Rep. Party, Somerset, Mass., 2000-. Mem. LWV, NOW, Women's Polit. Caucus, Somerset Cath. Womens Club, Bus. and Profl. Women's Club. Democrat. Office: 85 Merrimac St Boston MA 02114-4728

MENARD, JOHN R., JR., home improvement retail executive; b. 1940; Founder, pres., CEO Menard Inc., Eau Claire, Wis., 1960—; owner Menard Racing, 1979—. Bd. dirs. Polaris Industries. Office: Menard Inc 4777 Menard Dr Eau Claire WI 54703-9625

MENCER, C. SUZANNE, federal agency administrator; m. John Mencer; children: Jessie, Alex. BA in Spanish, Ohio State U. Tchr. Spanish, 1968—78; spl. agt. FBI, 1978—85, supervisory spl. agt., 1985—90, supr., 1990—98; pvt. cons. Anti-Terrorism Tng., Denver; exec. dir. dept. pub. safety State of Colo., Denver, 2000—03. Office: Naval Security Sta Nebraska and Massachusetts Avenues NW Washington DC 20393

MENCER, GLENN EVERELL, federal judge; b. Smethport, Pa., May 18, 1925; s. Glenn Hezekiah and Ruth Leona (Rice) M.; m. Hannah Jane Freyer, June 24, 1950; children— Ruth Ann, Cora Jane, Glenn John BBA, U. Mich., 1949, JD, 1952. Bar: Pa. 1953, U.S. Dist. Ct. (we. dist.) Pa. 1953, U.S. Supreme Ct. 1958. Sole practice, Eldred, Pa., 1953-64; dist. atty. McKean County, Pa., 1956-64; judge 48th Jud. Dist. Ct., Smethport, 1964-70, Commonwealth Ct. of Pa., Harrisburg, 1970-82, U.S. Dist. Ct., Erie, Pa., 1982—. Served with U.S. Army, 1943-45, ETO Mem. Fed. Judges Assn., Pa. Bar Assn., McKean County Bar Assn. Lodges: Masons (33 degree). Republican. Methodist. Home: 30 W Willow St Smethport PA 16749-1524 Office: US Dist Ct Fed Courthouse PO Box 1820 Erie PA 16507-0820

MENCER, JETTA, lawyer; b. Coshocton, Ohio, Apr. 7, 1959; d. William J. and Virginia M. (Fry) M. BS, Ohio State U., 1980, JD, 1983. Bar: Ohio, U.S. Dist. Ct. (so. dist.) Ohio. Assoc. Berry, Owens & Manning, Coshocton, 1983-86; asst. pros. atty. Coshocton County, 1983-86, Licking County, Newark, Ohio, 1986-88, asst. atty. gen., 1988-95; pvt. practice Coshocton, 1995-96; prosecuting atty. Coshocton County (Ohio) Prosecutor's Office, 1997-2001; atty. Lee Smith & Assocs., Columbus, Ohio, 2001—03; pvt. practice Columbus, 2003—. Treas. Coshocton County Dem. Cen. & Exec. Coms., 1984-86; chmn., 1986-88; sec., bd. dirs. Heart Ohio Girl Scout Council, Inc., Zanesville, Ohio, 1985-87; fin. chmn., bd. dirs. YMCA, Coshocton, 1985-87. Mem. Ohio State Bar Assn., Coshocton County Bar Assn., Lions Club. Democrat. Methodist. Office: 967 Delaware Ave Columbus OH 43201 Office Phone: 740-622-1051. E-mail: jmencer@columbus.rr.com.

MENCH, FRED CHARLES, classics educator; b. Phila., Dec. 22, 1937; s. Fred Charles and Violet M.; m. Martha Duvall, June 2, 1962 (dec. Feb. 1996); childre: Edward Harold, Sarah Elizabeth; m. Mary Jo Swindle, Mar. 13, 1999. BA, Kenyon Coll., 1959; MA, Yale U., 1960, PhD, 1968. Asst. prof. classics U. Tex., Austin, 1964-71; assoc. prof. classics Stockton Coll., Pomona, N.J., 1971-85, prof. classics, 1985—. Bd. dirs. Fictional Rome website; exec. dir. Interdisciplinary Ctr. Hellenic Studies. Book rev. editor: Classical World, 1983-98; contbr. articles to profl. jours. Woodrow Wilson fellow, 1959-62, Fulbright fellow, 1962-63. Mem. Am. Philological Assn., Classical Assn. Atlantic States (pres. 1980-81), Classical Humanities Soc. South Jersey (pres. 1972-98, 2000--). Home: 104 Iona Ave Linwood NJ 08221-2116 Office: Richard Stockton Coll NJ Jimmie Leeds Rd Pomona NJ 08240 Office Phone: 609-652-4495.

MENCH, JOHN WILLIAM, retail store executive, electrical engineer; b. N.Y.C., Feb. 27, 1943; s. John William and Edna (Ilgen) M.; m. Rose Irene Miller, Aug. 12, 1962 (dec. Jan. 1997); 1 child, William Ilgen; m. Ann Ward Frentress, Mar. 7, 1998. BSEE, U. S.C., 1969; MBA, Ohio U., 1983; PhD, Calif. Coast U., 1994. Registered profl. engr., Ohio, Ga.; cert. in heating, ventilating and air conditioning. Elec. engr. Uniroyal, Shelbyville, Tenn., 1969-74; facility engr. Kroger, Nashville, 1974-77, asst. mgr. facility engring. Atlanta, 1977-79, Kroger mktg. area mgr. facility engring. Columbus, Ohio, 1979-85; divsn. mgr. facility engring., v.p. Safeway Stores, Inc., Oakland, Calif., 1985-86; v.p. constrn., engring. Big V Supermarkets, Inc., Florida, N.Y., 1986-95; pres. Mench & Assocs. Inc., 1994-98. Assoc. prof. Pa. Coll. Tech., 1996-99; lectr. So. Poly. State U., 1999—; prof. Am. Contr. Exch., 1999-2003. Author (tech. manuals) Comments on Commercial Refrigeration, 1998, Comments on Commercial Air Conditioning, 1998, Plan Review, 1995, others. Trustee Meth. Ch., 1987-93; bd. dirs. Goshen Day Care Ctr., 1988-95; past v.p. Tri State V.W. Assn.; exec. adv. bd. Ohio U. Coll. Bus. Adminstrn., 1992-97, life mem.; bd. dirs. Elec. Distbn. Systems, 1993-94. Mem. ASHRAE, IEEE (sr.), Assn. Energy Engrs. (sr.). Republican. Methodist. Personal E-mail: johnmench@bellsouth.net.

MENCHACA, FRANK, editorial director; b. Huntington Station, N.Y., Aug. 5, 1961; s. Antonio and Anna (Lopez) M.; m. Deirdre Sullivan, Sept. 16, 1988; children: Gabriel, Aidan, William. BA, NYU, 1983; MA, Yale U., 1986. Jr. editor John Wiley & Sons, N.Y.C., 1983-85; assoc. editor Chelsea Hare Pubs., N.Y.C., 1985-88; lit. editor George Braziller, N.Y.C., 1988-90; assoc. editor Weekly Reader Corp., Middletown, Conn., 1990-92; acquisitions editor Millbrook Press, Brookfield, Conn., 1992-94; edit. dir. Gale Group, Woodbridge, Conn., 1994—. Book reviewer Pubs. Weekly, N.Y.C., 1990-93, participant seminar for acquisition of Latin Am. Libr. materials. Author: (books) Nicolo G and the Days of November, 1991 (VLS award 1991), AL, 1998. Instr. World Prison Poetry Ctr., New Haven, Conn., 1985-88. Mem. MLA, Am. Soc. for 18th Century Studies, Phi Beta Kappa. Democrat. Avocations: writing, publishing. Office: Primary Source Media 12 Lunar Dr Woodbridge CT 06525-2322 Home: 14 Sterling St Fairfield CT 06432-7437

MENCHER, BRUCE STEPHAN, judge; b. Washington, May 21, 1935; s. Emanuel and Bertha Miriam (Robbin) M.; m. Janet Patricia Whitfield, Nov. 24, 1974; children by previous marriage: Sean Robbin, Marc Nadzo. BA, George Washington U., 1957, JD with honors, 1960. Bar: D.C. 1960, U.S. Supreme Ct. 1964. Gen. atty. Office Gen. Counsel, Dept. Agr., 1960-61; asst. corp. counsel for D.C., 1961-67; atty.-adviser Office Gen. Counsel, Bur. for Africa, AID, 1967-69; ptnr. Wilkes & Artis, Washington, 1969-75; assoc. judge Superior Ct. D.C., 1975-91; sr. judge, 1991—; presiding judge Family div. Superior Ct. D.C., 1988-90. Professorial lectr. law George Washington U. Nat. Law Ctr., 1982-83; lectr. criminal justice Nat. Cathedral Sch./St. Albans Sch., 1985; faculty advisor Nat. Jud. Coll., 1995. Asst. rsch. editor George Washington Law Rev., 1959-60; contbr. articles to law revs. Mem. gen. alumni gov. bd. George Washington U., 1972-80; bd. dirs. Nat. Child Support Enforcement Assn., 1994-97, The Washington Savoyards Ltd., 1991-96, Trinity Chamber Orch., 2001--. Recipient Alumni Svc. award, 1975, Judge of Yr. award Assn. Plaintiffs Trial Attys., 1983, Samuel Green award for disting. svc. to Washington legal comty. and Phi Delta Phi, 1985, Disting. Alumni Achievement award George Washington U., 1987, also various appreciation and recognition awards local bar assns., D.C. and fed. govts. for work in area of family law and child support enforcement. Mem. ABA, Bar Assn. D.C., D.C. Bar, George Washington Law Assn. (exec. com. 1972-77), The Barristers (exec. com. 1981), George Washington Am. Inn of Ct. (pres. 1999—2000, Phi Delta Phi (pres. Barrister Inn 1974-75) Office: Superior Ct DC 500 Indiana Ave NW Rm 5520 Washington DC 20001-2131 Office Phone: 202-879-1358. *While it may sound old-fashioned, I attribute my appointment to the bench, in large part, to hard work, dedication, a love of the law and respect for my fellow man. One should maintain his sense of balance, always try to understand the other person's position and, at all costs, maintain a sense of humor throughout.*

MENCHER, MELVIN, journalist, retired educator; b. Bklyn., Jan. 25, 1927; s. Peter and Theresa (Sherman) M.; m. Helen Chamberlain, Aug. 27, 1947; children: Thomas, Marianne, Nicholas. Student, U. N.Mex., 1943-44; BA, U. Colo., 1947; postgrad. (Nieman fellow), Harvard, 1952-53. Reporter UP, 1947-50; state polit. corr. Albuquerque Jour., 1951-54; reporter Fresno (Calif.) Bee, 1954-58; asst. prof. journalism U. Kans., Lawrence, 1958-62; asst. prof. Columbia U., N.Y.C., 1962-65, assoc. prof., 1965-75, prof., 1975-90, assoc. dir. summer program for journalism edn. of minorities, 1971, prof. emeritus, 1990—. Contbg. author: Evaluating the Press, 1973; author: News Reporting and Writing, 1977, Basic Media Writing, 1983; editor: The FNMA Guide to Buying, Financing and Selling Your Home, 1973; contbr. articles to profl. jours. Mem. Soc. Profl. Journalists, Nat. Council Coll. Pubs. Advisers, Kappa Tau Alpha. Home: 450 Riverside Dr New York NY 10027-6801

MENCHER, STUART ALAN, sales and marketing executive; b. N.Y.C., Apr. 25, 1939; s. Meyer H. and Mildred B. Mencher; m. Judith Leslie Schneider; children: Jane Lizabeth, Tracy Ellen. B in Mgmt. Engring., Rensselaer Poly. Inst., 1960; MBA, NYU, 1965. Sales rep. Sperry Rand

Univac, Albany, N.Y., 1960-62; various sales and mktg. mgmt. positions IBM Corp., White Plains, N.Y., 1965-78, br. mgr. data processing div. Harrison, N.Y., 1978-81; dr. mktg. ops. planning, bus. mktg. dept. AT&T, Basking Ridge, N.J., 1981-83; dir. market planning, sales and mktg. div. AT&T Info. Systems, Morristown, N.J., 1983, dir. data systems mktg., 1983-84, v.p. mktg., large bus. systems div., 1985-87; sr. v.p. sales and mktg. MCI Communications Corp., Washington, 1987-90; sr. v.p., gen. mgr. U.S. distbn. div. Motorola/Codex Corp., Mansfield, Mass., 1990-91; sr. v.p., gen. mgr. Teleport Communications, N.Y.C., 1992-93, sr. v.p. nat. sales and mktg., 1994-98; v.p. strategic planning AT&T Bus. Svcs., Bridgewater, N.J., 1998-99; mng. ptnr. The Mencher Group LLC, East Hampton, NY, 1999—. Bd. dirs. Broadview Networks, N.Y.C. Pres. Westfield Men's Coll. Scholarship Club, NJ, 1977; coach Westfield Young Soccer Assn., 1976—81; mem. budget rev. com. United Fund, Westfield, 1983—85; mem. adv. bd. N.Y.C. Tech. Coll., 1993; mem. Mayor's Telecomms. Mutual Aid and Restoration Com., N.Y.C., 1992—93; v.p., bd. dirs. Ctr. Children and Families/Safespace, N.Y.C., 1999—; chmn. mktg. adv. com. YMCA Greater N.Y., N.Y.C., 1999—. Lt. USCGR, 1962—65. Avocations: golf, travel, theater, arts. Office: PO Box 5134 East Hampton NY 11937-6165

MENCHETTI, DAVID BARRY, lawyer; b. Chgo., Dec. 13, 1959; s. Leo and Diane M.; m. Lorraine C. Dorff, June 2, 1984; children, Cecilia, Quinn. BA, Stanford U., 1981; JD, Loyola U., Chgo., 1984. Bar: Ill. 1984. Staff atty. Ill. State Senate, Sprinfield, 1984-86; ptnr. Cullen, Haskins, Nicholson & Menchetti P.C., Chgo., 1986—. Author: (notebook) Penalties in Workers' Compensation Illinois Trial Lawyers WC Notebook, 1990—. Mem. Ill. State Bar Assn. (chair workers compensation com. 1996-97), Chgo. Bar Assn. (chair workers' compensation com., 1993-94), Workers Compensation Lawyers Assn. (pres. Chgo. 1999, bd. dirs. 1997—), Workplace Injury Litigation Group. Democrat. Roman Catholic. Office: Cullen Haskins Nicholson & Menchetti 35 E Wacker Dr Ste 1760 Chicago IL 60601-2271 Office Phone: 312-332-2545.

MENCHIK, PAUL LEONARD, economist, educator; b. NYC, Sept. 16, 1947; s. Irving and Elinor (Swedlow) M.; m. Bettie Ann Landauer, May 28, 1972; children: Daniel Aron, Jeremy Matthew. BA, SUNY, Binghamton, 1969; AM, U. Pa., 1971, PhD, 1976. Lectr. Rutgers Coll., New Brunswick, NJ, 1974-76; rsch. assoc. Inst. for Rsch. on Poverty, U. Wis., Madison, 1976-79; prof. dept. econs. Mich. State U., East Lansing, Mich., 1979—, chairperson dept. econs., 1992-96; sr. economist, econ. policy Office Mgmt. & Budget, Washington, 1990-91. Acad. visitor Stanford (Calif.) U., 1980, London Sch. Econ., 1987-88; vis. assoc. prof. U. Pa., Phila., 1982-83; vis. scholar Congrl. Budget Office, 1997-98; cons., advisor in field. Mem. editl. bd. Jour. Income Distbn., Amsterdam, 1992—; contbr. articles to profl. jour.; Hon. Rsch. Fellow, Univ. Coll., London, 2003. Grantee NSF, Social Security Adminstrn., U.S. Dept. Health and Human Svcs.; recipient Best Article of Yr. award Econ. Inquiry, 1987. Mem. Am. Econ. Assn., Nat. Tax Assn., Nat. Bur. Econ. Rsch. Conf. on Income & Wealth. Avocations: bowling, racquetball, golf, travel, camping. Office: Mich State U 101 Marshall Hall E Circle Dr East Lansing MI 48824 Office Phone: 517-355-4553.

MENDE, HOWARD SHIGEHARU, mechanical engineer; b. Hilo, Hawaii, Nov. 19, 1947; s. Tsutomu and Harue (Kubomitsu) M. BS in Mech. Engrng., U. Hawaii, 1969; MS in Mech. Engrng., U. So. Calif., 1975. Registered profl. engr., Calif. Mem. tech. staff I Rockwell Internat., Anaheim, Calif., 1970-71, LA, 1971-73, mem. tech. staff II, 1973-77, mem. tech. staff IV, 1984-86; devel. engr. AiRsch. Mfg. Co., Torrance, Calif., 1977-83; mech. engr. Def. Contracts Mgmt. Dist. West, Santa Ana, Calif., 1987-94, electronics engr., 1994—. Lectr. Pacific States U., LA, 1974-75. Mem. ASME. Democrat. Buddhist. Home: 1946 W 180th Pl Torrance CA 90504-4417 Office: Def Contracts Mgmt 2525 W 190th St Torrance CA 90504-6002 Business E-Mail: howard.mende@dcma.mil.

MENDE, ROBERT GRAHAM, retired engineering association executive; b. Newark, Dec. 4, 1926; s. Herman Ernest and Etta (Hillenbrand) M.; m. Joan B. Tamlyn, Apr. 12, 1958; children: Lisa Anne, Robert Graham Jr. Student, Mass. Inst. Tech., 1944-45; degree, N.Y. State Maritime Acad., 1947; BS, Webb Inst. Naval Architecture, 1951. Project engr. Foster Wheeler Corp., N.Y.C., 1953-56; dist. mgr., naval architect Bird-Johnson Co., N.Y.C., 1956-62; sr. naval architect J.J. Henry Co., Inc., N.Y.C., 1962-69; exec. dir. Soc. Naval Architects and Marine Engrs., 1969-91. Mem. marine engrng. coun. Underwriters Labs., Inc., 1969-91; ad hoc vis. com. Engrs. Coun. for Profl. Devel., 1970-72. Bd. dirs. Friends of World Maritime U., 1987-91; trustee Webb Inst. Naval Architecture, 1987-91. Lt. USNR, 1951-53. Fellow Royal Inst. Naval Architects, Soc. Naval Architect and Marine Engrs. (hon. life v.p., chmn. N.Y. sect. 1968-69, Vice Admiral E.S. Jerry Land medal 1991, Robert G. Mende Bldg. hdqrs. bldg. named in his honor); mem. ASME, Am. Soc. Naval Engrs., Am. Soc. Assn. Execs., Coun. Engrng. and Sci. Soc. Execs. (bd. dirs. 1988-91), Maritime Coll. Assn., N.E. Coast Inst. Engrs. and Shipbuilders, Webb Alumni Assn. (pres. 1970-72). *Hard work, perseverance, humility and a dash of deprivation almost always insure success. It also doesn't hurt to be in the right place at the right time.*

MENDEL, DENNIS D. lawyer; b. Chgo., Apr. 2, 1940; s. Curt W. and Herta (Sherman) M.; m. Janet Mendel; children— Lisa, Lara, Eden. B.A., U. Chgo., 1961; M.A., U. Mich., 1962; J.D., UCLA, 1965. Bar: Calif. Atty., Beneficial Standard Corp. and subs., 1966-75; v.p., sec., gen. counsel, 1975— . Mem. ABA, Calif. State Bar, Los Angeles County Bar Assn. Office: 16160 Anoka Dr Pacific Palisades CA 90272-2461

MENDEL, JERRY MARC, electrical engineering educator; b. N.Y.C., May 14, 1938; s. Alfred and Eleanor (Deutch) M.; m. Letty Susan Grossman, June 26, 1960; children: Jonathan, Aileen. BMechE cum laude, Poly. U., 1959, MEE, 1960, PhD in Elec. Engrng., 1963. Registered profl. engr., Calif. Instr. elec. engring. Poly. Inst. Bklyn., 1960-63; engrng. scientist and sect. chief McDonnell-Douglas Astronautics Co., Huntington Beach, Calif., 1963-74; prof. dept. elec. engrng. systems U. So. Calif., L.A., 1974—, chmn. dept., 1984-91, dir. Signal and Image Processing Inst., 1991-94, assoc. dir. edn. Integrated Media Sys. Ctr., 1996—. Pres., founder MENTECH, Culver City, Calif., 1983—; pres. United Signals and Systems, Inc., 1989-2001. Author: Discrete Techniques of Parameter Estimation: The Equation Error Formulation, 1973, Optimal Seismic Deconvolution: An Estimation Based Approach, 1983 (Phi Kappa Phi award 1984), Lessons in Digital Estimation Theory, 1987, Maximum-Likelihood Deconvolution, 1990, Lessons in Estimation Theory for Signal Processing, Communications and Control, 1995; editor: Prelude to Neural Networks: Adaptive and Learning Systems, 1994, Uncertain Rule-Based Fuzzy Logic Systems: Introduction and New Directions, 2001; co-editor: Adaptive Learning and Pattern Recognition Systems, 1970. Fellow IEEE (Centennial medal 1984Third Millennium medal 2000); mem. IEEE Control Systems Soc. (Disting. mem.; pres. 1986). Office: U So Calif Dept Elec Engring Sys Eeb 400 Los Angeles CA 90089-2564 Office Phone: 213-740-4445. Business E-Mail: mendel@sipi.usc.edu.

MENDEL, MARK J. venture capitalist; b. Phila., Mar. 15, 1961; s. Max Mendel III and Joan S. Mendel; m. Amelia Gallitano, May 27, 1995; children: Giacomo Martin, Malachi Jeremy. BSME, Cornell U., 1984; MS, U. Pa., 1990, PhD, 1995. EIT Del. Tech. asst. Brookhaven Nat. Lab., Upton, NY, 1983; prodn. engr. Polaroid Corp., Waltham, Mass., 1984—86; mech. engr. Analytix Med., Cambridge, Mass., 1986—88; laser engr. Mass. Gen. Hosp., Boston, 1988; rsch. fellow Scheie Eye Inst & U. Pa., Phila., 1988—95; v.p. Arch Venture Ptnrs., Chgo., N.Y.C., 1995—99; co-founder, mgr. dir. RiverVest Ventures Ptnrs., St. Louis, 2000—. Bd. dirs. Cydex Inc., Orland Park, Kans., 2000—; chmn. bd., co-founder Auxeris Therapeutics Inc, St. Louis, 2002—. Contbr. articles to profl. jours. Adv. bd. Cornell Outdoor Edn., Ithaca, NY, 2004—. Kauffman fellow, Kauffman Found., Kansas City, 1995—97. Mem.: Assn. Rsch. in Vision and Ophthalmology, Nat. Venture Capital Assn. Avocations: skiing, mountain climbing. Office: RiverVest Venture Ptnr 7733 Forsyth Blvd Ste 1650 Saint Louis MO 63130

MENDELL, MARK, architect; Grad., RISD. Pres. Camon Design, Grand Island, NY, 1992—. Cons. task force Erie County Convention Ctr. Contbr. articles to profl. jours. Bd. dirs. Am. Motorcycle Heritage Found.; bd. dirs. Albright-Knox Art Gallery. Fellow: AIA. Office: 2170 Whitehaven Rd Grand Island NY 14072

MENDELOW, CLIVE G. real estate company executive; b. 1946; V.p. Binswanger Mgmt. Corp., pres.; COO, exec. v.p. Binswanger Co., 1991; vice chmn., COO Chesterton Blumenauer Binswanger, Phila., 1997—. Eminent Profl. fellow, Royal Instn. Chartered Surveyors, London, 2002. Office: Chesterton Blumenauer Binswanger Two Logan Sq Philadelphia PA 19103*

MENDELOWITZ, ALLAN IRWIN, federal agency administrator; b. Middletown, Conn, May 1, 1943; s. Madeline Sylvia (Shlien) M.; m. Shereen Lee Lawall, June 18, 1967; children: Eitan G., Rina Y. AB, Columbia U., 1966; MA, Northwestern U., 1969, PhD, 1971. Asst. prof. econs. Rutgers U., New Brunswick, NJ, 1970-75; econ. policy fellow Brookings Inst., Washington, 1975-76; asst. dir. US GAO, Washington, 1976-80, assoc. dir., 1980-88, dir., 1988-93; mng. dir. US GA, Washington, 1993-95; exec. v.p. Export-Import Bank of the US, Washington, 1996—98; dir. Fed. Housing Finance Bd., Washington, 2001—. Contbr. articles to profl. jour. Mem. Am. Econ. Assn. Jewish. Avocations: swimming, skiing. Office: Fed Housing Finance Bd mem of the bd of dir 1777 F St NW Washington DC 20006

MENDELS, JOSEPH, psychiatrist, educator; b. Cape Town, South Africa, Oct. 29, 1937; came to U.S., 1964; s. Max and Lily (Turecki) M.; m. Ora Kark, Jan. 22, 1960; children: Gilla Avril, Charles Alan, David Ralph. MB, BChir, U. Cape Town, 1960; MD, U. Witwatersrand, Johannesburg, South Africa, 1965. Asst. prof., assoc. prof. psychiatry and pharmacology U. Pa., Phila., 1967-73; prof. U. Pa. and VA Hosp., Phila., 1973-80; med. dir. Fairmount Inst., Phila., 1980-81; hon. prof. psychiatry and human behavior Thomas Jefferson Med. Ctr., 1985—; med. dir. Med. Inst., Phila., 1981-95, Therapeutics PC, Phila., 1981-98. Cons. NIMH, NIH, numerous pharm. cos., 1968—; lectr. to univs. and hosps. worldwide, 1968—. Author, editor: Concepts of Depression, 1971, Biological Psychiatry, 1973, Psychobiology of Affective Disorders, 1981; contbr. over 200 articles to med. jours. V.p., mem. bd. govs. Am. Jewish Com.; nat. bd. dirs. Project Interchange. Fellow Internat. Coll. Neuropsychopharmacology, Am. Coll. Neuropsychopharmacology. Personal E-mail: jos@DCA.net.

MENDELSOHN, CAROL S. television producer; Student, Smith Coll., Cornell U. Writer CSI and CSI: Miami CBS, LA; with Securities and Exchange Commn.; atty. Washington; writer Fame NBC, LA; with Stephen J. Cannell; exec. prodr. Melrose Pl. NBC, 1990—99; exec. prodr. CSI CBS, LA, 2000—. Author: (TV series) Clifford the Big Red Dog, CSI (nominated Emmy Outstanding Drama Series award, 2002, 2003, nominated TV Prodr. of Yr. award, 2003, 2004), CSI: Miami, Gabriel's Fire, Hardcastle & McCormick, J.J. Starbuck, Melrose Place, Providence, Stingray, Teenage Mutant Ninja Turtles, Wiseguy, (films) To Brave Alaska.

MENDELSOHN, JOHN, oncologist, hematologist, educator, health facility executive; b. Cin., Aug. 31, 1936; s. Joe and Sarah (Feibel) M.; m. Anne Charles, June 23, 1962; children: John Andrew, Jeffrey Charles, Eric Robert. BA in Biochemical Sciences, Harvard U., 1958, MD, 1963. Diplomate Am. Bd. Internal Medicine, Am. Bd. Hematology, Am. Bd. Med. Oncology. Intern, resident Peter Bent Brigham Hosp., Boston, 1963-65, 67-68; fellow in hematology Washington U. Sch. Medicine, St. Louis, 1968-70; asst. prof. to prof. medicine U. Calif., San Diego, 1970-85, Am. Cancer Soc. prof. clin. oncology La Jolla, 1982-85, dir. Cancer Ctr., 1977-85; prof. medicine, vice-chmn. Cornell U. Med. Coll., NYC, 1985-96; Winthrop Rockefeller chmn. dept. medical oncology, co-head, molecular pharmacology and therapeutics program Meml. Sloan Kettering Cancer Ctr., NYC, 1985-96; pres., prof. medicine U. Tex. M.D. Anderson Cancer Ctr., Houston, 1996—; vice chmn. BioHouston, 2001—. Bd. sci. counselors Nat. Cancer Inst., 1986—90, 1996—2001; cons., mem. sci. adv. bd. Progenics Pharms.; founder, 1st dir. U. Calif. San Diego Cancer Ctr.; mem. Nat. Dialogue on Cancer, 1999, Team on Cancer Rsch., 2001, U. Calif. San Diego External Adv. Com., 2000, Gov.'s Biotech. Panel, Ctr. for Houston's Future; mem. external adv. bd. John Hopkins Oncology Ctr., 1993—; faculty U. Tex. Graduate Sch. Biomedical Sciences. Editor-in-chief: (textbook) The Molecular Basis of Cancer; mem. editl. bd. Growth Factors, Jour. Biol. Response Modifiers, Expert Rev. Anticancer Therapy; editor-in-chief Clin. Cancer Rsch.; founding editor Clin. Cancer Rsch.; contbr. articles to profl. jours. Mem. Gov.'s Cancer Coun., Calif., 1981—85; bd. dirs. Am. Cancer Soc., San Diego, 1981—85, Houston Grand Opera, BioHouston, Ctr. for Houston's Future, Houston Forum; bd. dirs., mem. healthcare task force Greater Houston Partnership, 1997; bd. dirs., mem. exec. com. Houston Tech. Ctr., 1998—, nat. cancer policy bd., 1999—; mem. bd. overseers Harvard Med. Sch.; trustee Houston Grand Opera. Named Headliner of Yr. in Medicine, San Diego, 1985; recipient Bourgine award for excellence in cancer rch., Svc. d'Oncologie Med. Pitie-Saltpetriere, 1997, Jill Rose award for oustanding breast cancer rsch., Breast Cancer Rsch. Found., 1999, Gold medal of Paris, 1997, Cancer Rsch. award, Bristol-Myers Squibb, 1997, Joseph H. Burchenal Clin. Rsch. award, Am. Assn. for Cancer Rsch., 1999, Simon Shubitz prize, Univ. Chgo., 2002, David A. Karnofsky award, Am. Soc. of Clin. Oncology, 2002; Fulbright scholar, U. Glasgow, Scotland, 1958—59. Mem.: ACP, AAAS (electorate nominating com. sect. on med. scis. 2001), Am. Clin. and Climatol. Assn., Harvard Overseers' Com., Royal Netherlands Acad. Arts and Scis., Inst. Medicine U.S. NAS, Century Assn., Am. Soc. Hematology, Am. Assn. Cancer Rsch. (4th Joseph H. Burchenal award 1999), Am. Soc. Clin. Oncology (lectr., David A. Karnofsky award 2002), Am. Soc. Clin. Investigation, Assn. Am. Physicians, Phi Beta Kappa. Achievements include rsch. in establishing inhibition of tumor growth by antibodies against growth factor receptors. Office: U Tex MD Anderson Cancer Ctr 1515 Holcombe Blvd # 91 Houston TX 77030-4009 E-mail: jmendelsohn@mdanderson.org.

MENDELSOHN, LOUIS BENJAMIN, financial analyst; b. Providence, R.I., Mar. 26, 1948; s. Alvin Harold and Frances (Leitner) M.; m. Illyce Deborah Greenspan, Aug. 29, 1976; children: Lane Jeffrey, Ean Graham, Forrest Lee. BS, Carnegie Mellon U., 1969; MSW, SUNY, Buffalo, 1973; MBA with hons., Boston U., 1977. Rsch. asst. Mass. Gen. Hosp., Boston, 1969-71; regional health planner Comprehensive Health Planning Coun., Buffalo, 1973-74; adminstv. resident New Eng. Hosp., Boston, 1976; mgmt. specialist Humana Hosp. Bennett, Ft. Lauderdale, Fla., 1977-78; asst. exec. dir. Humana Women's Hosp., Tampa, Fla., 1978-80; pres., CEO Market Technologies Corp., Wesley Chapel, Fla., 1979—; CEO Market Technologies LLC, 2004—, Predictive Techs. Group LLC, 2004—. Author: Trend Forecasting with Techinal Analysis: Unleashing the Hidden Power of Intermarket Analysis to Beat the Market, 2000; contbg. rschr.: The Encyclopedia of Technical Market Indicators, 1988; contbg. author: High Performance Futures Trading, 1990, Virtual Trading, 1995, Artificial Intelligence in the Capital Markets, 1995, Trade Your Way to Financial Freedom, 1999, Trading Chicago Style, 1999; contbg. writer Tech. Analysis of Stocks and Commodities Mag.; editor newsletter Neural-Financial News, 1991; developer investment software ProfitTaker, 1979—, VantagePoint, 1988—. USPHS fellow, 1975-77. Mem. Market Technicians Assn., Colleague Internat. Fedn. of Tech. Analysts, Beta Gamma Sigma. Achievements include pioneering strategy back-testing and optimization in technical analysis software for microcomputers, 1983; introduction of first commercial strategy testing trading software in financial industry for microcomputers and first intermarket analysis software in fin. industry for microcomputers. Office: Mkt Techs Corp 25941 Apple Blossom Ln Wesley Chapel FL 33544-5108 Office Phone: 813-973-0496. E-mail: lbm@tradertech.com.

MENDELSOHN, MARTIN, lawyer; b. Bkyln., Sept. 6, 1942; s. Hyman and Gertrude M.; m. Syma Barbara Rossman, Aug. 15, 1964; children: Alice S., James D. BA, Bklyn. Coll., 1963; LLB, George Washington U., 1966. Bar DC 1967, Ill., 1973, N.Y., 2003, U.S. Ct. Appeals (D.C. cir.) 1967, U.S. Supreme Ct. 1970, U.S. Ct. Appeals (3d cir.) 1971, U.S. Ct. Appeals (7th cir.) 1973, Ill. 1973, U.S. Ct. Appeals (9th cir.) 1987, U.S. Tax Ct. 1988, U.S. Ct. Appeals (2d cir.) 1988, U.S. Ct. of Appeals (5th cir.) 2000, U.S. Ct. Appeals (4th cir.) 2002. With Gen. Counsel's Office, HEW, Washington, 1966—67; legal svcs. Washington, 1967—70, 1971—72, 1973—75; counsel Legal Svcs. Corp., Washington, 1976; adminstrv. asst. U.S. Congress, Washington, 1977; chief spl. litigation U.S. Dept. Justice, Washington, 1977—79, dep. dir. office spl. investigations, 1979—80; counsel House Judiciary Com., 1980; pvt. practice Washington, 1980—88; ptnr. Dilworth, Paxon, Kalish & Kauffman, 1989—91, Verner, Liipfert, Bernhard, McPherson & Hand, 1991—2002, Schnader, Harrison, Segal and Lewis, Washington, 2002—. Author: (with Aaron Freiwald) The Last Nazi, 1994. Named officer, Order of Merit, Poland, 2000; recipient Grand Decoration of High Honor, Austria, 2002. Mem.: ABA, D.C. Bar Assn., Cosmos Club. Jewish. Home: 5705 Mckinley St Bethesda MD 20817-3638 Office: 2001 Pennsylvania Ave NW Ste 300 Washington DC 20006 Office Phone: 202-419-4220. Business E-Mail: mmendelsohn@schnader.com.

MENDELSON, ALAN CHARLES, lawyer; b. San Francisco, Mar. 27, 1948; s. Samuel Mendelson and Rita Rosalie (Spindel) Brown; children: Jonathan Daniel, David Gary; m. Agnès Marie Barbariol. BA with great distinction, U. Calif., Berkeley, 1969; JD cum laude, Harvard U., 1973. Bar: Calif. 1973. Assoc. Cooley Godward LLP, San Francisco, 1973-80, ptnr. Palo Alto, 1980-2000, mng. ptnr. Palo Alto office, 1990-95, 96-97; sec. acting gen. counsel Amgen Inc., Thousand Oaks, Calif., 1990-91; acting gen. counsel Cadence Design Sys., Inc., San Jose, Calif., 1995-96; sr. ptnr. Latham & Watkins LLP, Menlo Park, Calif., 2000—. Bd. dirs. Valentis Inc., QLT Inc.; co-chair venture & tech. group Latham & Watkins; mem. bd. advisors Santa Clara Computer and High Tech. Law Jour.; mem. emerging cos. sect. governing body Biotech. Industry Orgn., 2004—. Chmn. Piedmont (Calif.) Civil Svc. Commn., 1978-80; den leader Boy Scouts Am., Menlo Park, Calif.; fundraiser Crystal Springs Upland Sch., Hillsborough, Calif., Harvard Law Sch. Fund, U. Calif. Berkeley Health Svcs. Initiative, Lucille Packard Children's Hosp.; coach Menlo Park Little League, 1982-86; pres., mem. exec. com., bd. dirs. No. Calif. chpt. Nat. Kidney Found., 1986-98. With USAR, 1969-75. Recipient Disting. Svc. award Nat. Kidney Found., 1992; named U. Calif. Berkeley Alumni scholar, 1966, Scaife Found. scholar, 1966, One of 100 Most Influential Attys. in U.S. Nat. Law Jour., 1994, 97, 2000. Mem. Bohemian Club, Phi Beta Kappa. Jewish. Home: 76 De Bell Dr Atherton CA 94027-2253 Office: Latham & Watkins LLP 135 Commonwealth Dr Menlo Park CA 94025 Office Phone: 650-463-4693. E-mail: alan.mendelson@lw.com.

MENDELSON, ELLEN B. radiologist, educator; MD, Northwestern U. Feinberg Sch. Medicine, 1980. Cert. diagnostic radiology 1984. Intern to resident, diagnostic radiology NW U. Meml. Hosp., Chgo., 1981—84, fellowship, 1984—85; radiologist Western Penn Hosp., Pitts.; bd. mem. Monongahela Valley Hosp., Pa.; assoc. prof., radiology U. Pitts. Sch. Medicine; prof. radiology NW U., Feinberg Sch. Medicine, Chgo.; dir. breast imaging NW Meml. Hosp. Office: NW U Feinberg Sch Medicine 675 N St Clair Galter 13th Fl Chicago IL 60611 Address: NW Meml Hosp 251 E Huron St Chicago IL 60611

MENDELSON, ELLIOTT, mathematician, educator; b. N.Y.C., May 24, 1931; s. Joseph and Helen (Bienstock) M.; m. Arlene Zimmerman, Jan. 25, 1959; children: Julia, Hilary, Peter. AB, Columbia U., 1952; MA, Cornell U., 1954, PhD, 1955. Instr. U. Chgo., 1955-56; jr. fellow Soc. Fellows, Harvard U., 1956-58; Ritt instr. Columbia U., 1958-61; mem. faculty Queens Coll., CUNY, 1961—, prof. math., 1965—. Dir., instr. NSF math. program for high sch. students, 1964-71; researcher axiomatic set theory and math. logic, especially ind. various important propositions of axiomatic set theory, axiom of choice, axiom of restriction; participant NSF Time 2000 Project for future secondary sch. math. tchrs., 1998—. Author: Introduction to Mathematical Logic, 1997, Boolean Algebra and Switching Circuits, 1970, Number Systems, 1973, Beginning Calculus, 1997, 3000 Solved Problems in Calculus, 1988, Differential and Integral Calculus, 1997, Quick Calculus, 1999, Introducing Game Theory and Its Applications, 2004; contbr. articles to profl. jours. Mem. Am. Math. Soc., Math. Assn. Am., Assn. for Symbolic Logic, Phi Beta Kappa. Home: 10 Pinewood Rd Roslyn NY 11576-2420 Office: Queens Coll Dept Math Flushing NY 11367 Office Phone: 516-621-0313. E-mail: emenqc@msn.com.

MENDELSON, HAIM, artist, educator, art gallery director; b. Siemiatycze, Bielsk, Poland, Oct. 15, 1923; s. David Cemach and Frieda (Konopiati) M.; m. Lita Joan Gordon, Mar. 30, 1955 (div. June 1966); children: Paul, Jan. Student, Am. Artists Sch., 1938-41, Saul Baizerman Sch. Art, 1940-43, Ednl. Alliance Art Sch., 1946. Tchr. Ednl. Alliance, N.Y.C., 1956-61; instr. CCNY, 1961-64; tchr. Columbia Grammar Sch., 1963-64, City and Country Sch., N.Y.C., 1964-91. Dir. Hudson Guild Art Gallery, N.Y.C., 1971-94. One-man shows include Creative Galleries, N.Y.C., 1954, Caravan Gallery, N.Y.C., 1957, Chase Gallery, N.Y.C., 1960, Hudson Guild Art Gallery, N.Y.C., 1961, 76, 79, 82, 94, Yellow Poui Art Gallery, Grenada, W.I., 1973, 76, 79, 82, Ednl. Alliance, N.Y.C., 1976, Berkshire Artisans Gallery, Pittsfield, Mass., 1987, Hudson Guild, 1994. 2003; group shows include Mus. Modern Art, N.Y.C., 1940-41, Pa. Acad. Fine Arts, 1965, Butler Inst. Am. Art, Ohio, 1965, 67, St. Paul Art Ctr., 1961, 66, NAD, N.Y.C., 1965, 68, 75, 77, 90, Bronx Mus. Arts, 1976, Prints U.S.A., 1982, Gallery Assn. N.Y. State, 1975-78, Internat. Art Biennale, Malta, 1995, Glass Gallery, N.Y.C., 1995, 96, Susan Teller Gallery, 1999, 2000, 02, 03; represented in permanent collections N.Y. Pub. Libr., Minn. Mus. Art, Edward Ulrich Mus., Wichita, Kans., St. Vincent Coll., Latrobe, Pa., Griffiths Art Ctr., Canton, N.Y., Manhattan Coll., Riverdale, N.Y., Flint (Mich.) Inst. Fine Arts, The Joe and Emily Lowe Found.; portfolio drypoint engravings Grass, 1963, The Artist and His Dead, 1975. Recipient numerous awards including Spl. Distinction award Graphics Internat. Art Biennial Malta, 1995, N.Y. Ctrl. graphics award Audubon Artists, 1996; Florsheim Art Fund grantee, 1999. Mem. Fedn. Modern Painters and Sculptors, Audubon Artists, Print Consortium, Am. Soc. Contemporary Artists (Graphics award 2003). Home: 234 W 21st St # 63 New York NY 10011-3451 *Art is the avenue in which I express the significant experiences of my life. Out of feelings of expressive need, new forms and techniques spontaneously arise. The forms of the future are in life itself.*

MENDELSON, LAURANS ADAM, accountant; b. N.Y.C., July 7, 1938; s. Samuel and Blanche (Lederer) M.; m. Arlene Hope Lobel, Sept. 18, 1962; children: Eric Arthur, Victor Howard. BA, Columbia Coll., 1960; MBA, Columbia U., 1961. CPA, N.Y., Fla. Chmn., pres., CEO HEICO Corp., Hollywood, Fla., 1989—. Bd. dirs., chmn. audit com. Hawker Pacific Aerospace; co-chmn., prin. dir. HEICO Corp.; panelist ethics in Am. seminar Columbia U. Bd. dirs. Greater Miami Opera Assn., Miami; mem. bd. vis. Columbia Col., N.Y.C.; bd. govs. Philharm. Orch. Fla., Standard Club; alumni adv. bd. to bd. trustees Columbia U.; mem. citizens bd. U. Miami. Recipient Ernst & Young Entrepreneur of Yr. award, 1999. Mem. AICPA, Fla. Inst. CPAs, Greater Miami C. of C. (trustee), Aerospace Industries Assn. (bd. govs.). Jewish. Office: HEICO Corp 3000 Taft St Hollywood FL 33021-4441

MENDELSON, LEE M. film company executive, writer, producer, director; b. San Francisco, Mar. 24, 1933; s. Palmer C. and Jeanette D. (Wise) M.; children: Glenn, Linda, Jason, Sean. BA, Stanford U., 1954. With Sta. KPIX-TV, 1961-63; chmn. bd., pres. Lee Mendelson Film Prodns. Inc., Los Angeles and Burlingame, Calif., 1963—. Guest instr. in communications Stanford U. Exec. producer, co-writer (miniseries) This Is America, Charlie Brown; producer: Charlie Brown, Cathy, Betty Boop, (TV spls.) John Steinbeck's Travels with Charley, American and Americans, The Fantastic Funnies, You Asked for It, Here Comes Garfield, (animated films) A Boy Named Charlie Brown, Snoopy Come Home, Race for Your Life Charlie Brown, Peanuts, Bon Voyage Charlie Brown (And Don't Come Back), Garfield and Friends, Mother Goose and Grim. Served to 1st lt. USAF, 1954-57. Recipient 7 Emmy awards, 3 Peabody awards. Mem. Writers Guild Am., Dirs. Guild Am. Office: Lee Mendelson Film Prodn Inc 330 Primrose Rd Ste 310 Burlingame CA 94010-4028

MENDELSON, LOTTIE M. retired pediatric nurse practitioner, writer; b. Portland, Oreg., June 4, 1937; d. Esther Layton-Murphy, James A. Murphy; m. Robert Mendelson, June 22, 1958; children: David, Tamara Mendelson-

Hefetz, Mark, Michelle Rosenbloom. BS, U. Portland, 1958; MS, Oreg. Health Scis. U., 1972, Pediat. Nurse Practitioner, 1978. RN 1958, cert. pediat. nurse practitioner, 1978. Pediat. nurse practitioner Pediat. Assocs., Portland, Oreg., 1980—98; ret., 1998. Co-author: Raising Your Baby and Young Child, The New Parent's Question and Answer Book, 1992, editor (founder) Pediat. newsletter, 1984-97. Bd. dirs. Jewish Family and Child Svc., Portland, 1993—98. Mem.: Woman's Divsn. Oreg. Israel Bonds (chairperson 1981—85). Avocations: tennis, travel. Home: 5455 SW 87th Ave Portland OR 97225-1713 Personal E-mail: bbxmnr@aol.com.

MENDELSON, RICHARD DONALD, former communications company executive; b. N.Y.C., Dec. 2, 1933; s. George and Martha (Goodman) M.; m. Marilyn Miller, July 28, 1956; children: Sandra, Kenneth. BS, Wharton Sch. U. Pa., 1955; JD, NYU, 1959. Bar: N.Y., 1960; CPA, N.Y. Asst. atty. gen. N.Y. State Dept. Law, N.Y.C., 1959-70; v.p., treas. Petry TV, N.Y.C., 1971-75; v.p., dir. corp. devel. Katz Communications, Inc., N.Y.C., 1975-77, sr. v.p. ops., 1977-79, sr. v.p., chief fin. officer, 1979-81, exec. v.p., chief operating officer, 1981-82, pres., chief oper. officer, 1982-89; free-lance writer, 1989—. Mem. Employee Stock Ownership Assn. Am. (pres. 1987-88, bd. dirs.). Home and Office: 71 Saint George Pl Palm Beach Gardens FL 33418-4024

MENDELSON, ROBERT ALLEN, polymer scientist, rheologist; b. Cleve., 1930; s. Julius and Theodora Anne M.; m. Lura Lauzon, 1971 (dec. 1999); children: John A. Blackstone, Marie L. Taylor. BS in Indsl. Chemistry, Case Inst. Tech., 1952, PhD in Phys. Chemistry, 1956. From sr. rsch. chemist to sci. fellow rsch. dept. Monsanto Co., Texas City, Tex., 1956-71, sci. fellow Springfield, Mass., 1972-89, sr. sci. fellow, 1989-91; rheology focus area leader Baytown (Tex.) Polymers Ctr. Exxon Chem., 1991-94, rheology prin. investigator, 1995-99; ret., 1999. Mem. com. for pub. policy Am. Inst. Physics, 1985-89; collaborator Univ. Rsch. Programs, Cornell U., 1989-91. Mem. editorial bd. Journal of Rheology, 1986-99; contbr. articles to profl. jours.; patentee in field. Mem. AAAS, Soc. Rheology (pres. 1989-91, v.p. 1987-89, sec. 1974-78), Am. Chem. Soc. (Arthur Doolittle award div. organic coatings and plastics 1982). Home: 5001 Woodway Dr Unit 1803 Houston TX 77056-1701 Personal E-mail: robertamendelson@aol.com.

MENDELSON, SOL, physical science educator, consultant; b. Checonovska, Poland, Oct. 10, 1926; came to U.S., 1927; s. David C. and Frieda (Cohen) M. BME, CCNY, 1955; MS, Columbia U., 1957, PhD, 1961. Prof. engring. CCNY, 1955-58; sr. scientist Sprague Electric Co., North Adams, Mass., 1962-64, Airborne Instruments Lab., Melville, N.Y., 1964-65; phys. metallurgist Bendix Rsch. Lab., Southfield, Mich., 1966-67; cons., rschr., writer, N.Y.C. and Troy, Mich., 1968-72; adj. prof. phys. sci. CUNY, 1972-87. Contbr. numerous articles to sci. jours. Mem. Am. Phys. Soc., Fedn. Am. Scientists, Sigma Xi, Tau Beta Pi, Pi Tau Sigma. Achievements include rsch. on theory and mechanisms of Martensitic transformations; rsch. on degeneracy in phase transitions and its universal nature which shows that revolutions in sci. are still possible. *We have to keep reminding each other that data proclaims theory, but theory does not proclaim anything if it is not physical and addresses crucial data. Ambiguous data or unrealistic models have brought prominence to some theories, but those who succeed are based on crucial data and physical models. Such theories give insight into related problems, and to theories of many things and everything.*

MENDENHALL, CANDICE, former finance company executive; Sr. v.p. human resources Fed. Home Loan Mortgage Corp., McLean, Va. Home: 616 W Fulton St Apt 619 Chicago IL 60661-1141 Fax: 703-903-2447.

MENDENHALL, HARLAN VINCENT, research surgeon; b. Gulfport, Miss., Oct. 21, 1944; s. Harlan Harry Mendenhall and Catherine Rose (Cunningham) Cowell; m. Diann Marie Frederick, Aug. 15, 1992; children: Tai Justin, Tiffany. DVM, Colo. State U., 1968, PhD, 1981. Staff surgeon Rangitaiki Plains Dairy Co., Edgecume, New Zealand, 1968-71; grad. student exptl. surgery Colo. State U., Fort Collins, 1971-75; surg. rsch. specialist 3M, St. Paul, Minn., 1975-91; owner/operator Veterinary Surg. Specialists, Stillwater, Minn., 1977-93; sr. rsch. surgeon Primedica Corp., Worcester, Mass., 1993—. Cons. biomed. surg. rsch., Stillwater, 1992-93; lectr. surg. anatomy Colo. State U., 1973; animal care cons. St. Paul Ramsey Hosp., 1980-85; working group mem. Health Industry Mfrs. Assn./Orthopedic Surg. Mfrs. Assn. FDA panel, 1987. Author: Anterior Cruciate, 1987; author, editor: Handbook Biomaterials, 1986, 2d edit., 1998; contbr. articles to Jour. Am. Vet. Med. Assn., Clin. Orthopedic Related Rsch. Mem. Soc. for Biomaterials (PhD students award 1982), Acad. Surg. Rsch. (mem. bd. 1996-2003). Achievements in orthopedics include development of the concept of isometricity in ACL replacement surgery; achievements in ophthalmics include development of the importance of posteriorly convex lenses and haptics; achievements in microsurgery include development of the microvascular anastomotic system for small vessel anastomosis; leading research in chronic laboratory animal access. Home: 26 Grover Rd Ashland MA 01721-2510 Office: Charles River Corp 57 Union St Worcester MA 01608-1182 E-mail: vince.mendenhall@ddscriver.com.

MENDENHALL, HARRY BARTON, lawyer; b. Oct. 31, 1946; BA, Colo. Coll., 1968; JD, U. Colo., 1971. Bar: Colo. 1971. Ptnr. Mendenhall & Malouff, R.L.L.P., Rocky Ford, Colo., 1971—. Mem. nominating com. Colo. Supreme Ct., Denver, 1986-91; pres. Colo. Lawyer Trust Account Found., Denver, 1995-97. Mem. Colo. Bar Assn. (pres. 1999-2000). Office: Mendenhall & Malouff 805 Chestnut Ave Rocky Ford CO 81067-1224 E-mail: bmendenhall@centurytel.net.

MENDENHALL, JOHN RYAN, retired lawyer, transportation executive; b. Des Moines, Jan. 17, 1928; s. Merritt Blake and Elizabeth M. (Ryan) M.; m. Joan Lois Schafer, June 20, 1953; children: Thomas, James, Jane, Julie, Robert, Jennifer. BS, U. Notre Dame, 1950; JD, Harvard U., 1953. Bar: Iowa 1953, U.S. Tax Ct. 1954, D.C. 1975, U.S. Ct. Claims 1975. Mem. tax staff Arthur Andersen & Co., Cleve., 1953-63, ptnr., 1963-66, dir. taxes Chgo., 1966-70, ptnr. Washington, 1970-74, Williams, Connolly & Califano, Washington, 1974-76; gen. tax counsel Union Pacific Corp., N.Y.C., 1977-80, v.p. taxes, 1980-93. Bd. dirs. Empire Steel Castings, Reading, Pa. Co-author: Reforming the Tax Structure, 1973; contbr. articles on taxes to various jours. Bd. dirs. Cook County Hosp., Chgo., 1968-71, Inst. Rsch. on Econs. of Taxation, Washington, 1977-93, Burnside Plantation Inc., Bethlehem, Pa., 1989-93; trustee Convent of Sacred Heart, Greenwich, Conn., 1976-80; bd. govs. Bethlehem Area Found., 1989-93, chmn. 1991-92; pres. Greenwich Br. of English Spkg. Union, 1994-2000. With U.S. Army, 1946-47, Japan. Mem. ABA (tax sect., chmn. indexing com. 1985-86), Am. Coun. Capital Formation (bd. dirs. 1972-88), Bus. Roundtable (tax adv. group 1977-92), C. of C. U.S. (mem. tax com. 1972-92), Am. Law Inst. (tax adv. group 1974-88), Nat. Tax Assn. (pres. 1981-82), Nat. Chamber Found. (chmn. tax com. 1984-93), Chevy Chase (Md.) Club, Harvard Club (N.Y.C.), Belle Haven Club. Republican. Roman Catholic. Home: 47 Lafayette Pl Apt 6H Greenwich CT 06830-5402

MENDENHALL, ROBERT W. education technology executive; b. Pasadena, Calif., Nov. 18, 1954; s. Winton L. and Margaret E. (Kerr) Mendenhall; m. Kathleen A. White, 1978; children: Jamie, Robert, Christina, Virginia, Kathleen, Lori, Emily. BS in Univ. Studies, Brigham Young Univ., 1977; PhD in Instrnl. Psychology and Tech., Brigham Young U., 2003. Gen. mgr. Wicat Inst., Orem, Utah, 1977-80; pres., dir. Wicat Systems Inc., Orem, Utah, 1980—92; exec. v.p., dir. Jostens Learning Corp., San Diego, 1992—94; gen. mgr. IBM K-12 Edn., Atlanta, 1994—96, exec. cons., 1997—98; pres. Western Govs. U., Salt Lake City, 1999—. Mem. bd. for bus. and econ. devel. State of Utah, 1997—2001; mem. Commn. Tech. and Adult Learning, 1999—2000; adv. bd. Partnership for 21st Century Skills, 2003—. Missionary, bishop LDS Ch.; bd. dirs. Oquirrh Inst., 2002—; bd. dirs., chair Gina Bachauer Internat. Piano Found. Office: Western Gov U Ste 700 4001 South 700 East Salt Lake City UT 84107 Office Phone: 801-274-3280. E-mail: rwm@wgu.edu.

MENDES, SAM (SAMUEL ALEXANDER MENDES), film director, theater director; b. Reading, Eng., Aug. 1, 1965; s. James Peter and Valerie Helene Mendes; m. Kate Winslet, May 2003; 1 child. Student, U. Cambridge, Eng. Dir. film American Beauty, 1999 (Outstanding Directorial Achievement in Feature Film Dirs. Guild Am. 1999, Golden Globe for best dir. 1999, Best Dir. award Dallas-Ft. Worth Film Critics Assn. 1999, Best Dir. award Online Film Critics Soc. 1999, Best Dir. award Broadcast Film Critics Assn. 1999, Best Dir. award L.A. Film Critics Assn. 1999, Oscar for best dir. 2000, Dir. of the Yr. London Film Critics Cir. 2000, Hamburg Shakespeare prize 2000), dir. prodr. Road to Perdition, 2002; artistic dir. The Rise and Fall of Little Voice (RNT, Aldwych, Olivier and Evening Standard awards), 1992, Cabaret (Tony award), 1998, The Blue Room, 1998; dir. plays London Assurance, 1989, Cherry Orchard, 1989, Kean, 1990, Plough & the Stars, 1991, Troillis & Cressida, 1991, The Alchemist, 1991, The Sea, 1991, Richard III, 1992, The Tempest, 1993, The Birthday Party, 1994, Othello, 1997, Assasins, Translations, Glengarry Glen Ross, Glass Managerie, Company, Habelis Corpus, Front Page, To the Green Fields Beyond, Call at Donmar Warehouse. Office: Scamp Film & Theatre 26-28 Neal St London WC 2H 9QQ England E-mail: mleigh@scampltd.com.

MENDEZ, ALBERT ORLANDO, industrialist, financier; b. Bogota, Colombia, Sept. 7, 1935; came to U.S., 1960; naturalized, 1968; s. Angelino Benjamin and Ana Isabel (Gutierre de Cetina) M.; children: Nicole C., Eric A. BS in Nuclear Physics, N.C. State U., 1961, MS in Nuclear Engring., 1963; MBA, U. Hartford, 1970. Physicist, mgr. mfg. Combustion Engring. Co., Windsor, Conn., 1963-67; mgr. corp. devel. and planning Gulf Oil Corp., Pitts., 1967-71; v.p. mktg., controller for Latin Am. Xerox Corp., Stamford, Conn., 1971-76; exec. v.p., COO, chmn. ops. com., bd. dirs. Ogden Corp., N.Y.C., 1976-84; chmn., chief exec. officer, prin. shareholder Am. Indstl. Corp., Stamford, 1984—, Argo-Tech Corp., Aerospace, Cleve., 1986-89. Bd. dirs. Catalyst Energy Co., N.Y.C., 1st Prin. Corp., N.Y.C., Demag, AG, Hamburg, Germany; gen. ptnr. Agnem Holdings Ltd. Partnership, New Canaan, Conn., 1984—; pres., CEO, bd. dirs., prin. shareholder Agnem Investment Co., New Canaan, 1983—; pres., CEO, prin. shareholder AM World Trade Corp., West Palm Beach, Fla.; chmn., CEO, prin. shareholder Arden Petroleum Corp., Palm Beach, Fla., 2000—; mem. Pres.'s Adv. Com. on Def. Preparedness and Intelligence, 1986-92. Contbr. articles to profl. jours. Mem. Internat. Platform Assn., Am. mgmt. Assn., Assn. of Corp. Dirs., The Conf. Bd., Am. Nuclear Soc., Palm Beach (Fla.) Polo Club, Mar-A-Lago Club (Palm Beach). Home: 500 E 77th St Apt 1017 New York NY 10162-0004

MENDEZ, CELESTINO GALO, mathematics professor; b. Havana, Cuba, Oct. 16, 1944; came to the U.S., 1962; naturalized, 1970. s. Celestino Andres and Georgina (Fernandez) M.; m. Mary Ann Koplau, Aug. 21, 1971; children: Mark Michael, Matthew Maximilian. BA, Benedictine Coll., 1965; MA, U. Colo., 1968, PhD, 1974, MBA, 1979. Asst. prof. maths. scis. Met. State Coll., Denver, 1971-77, assoc. prof., 1977-82, prof., 1982—2002, chmn. dept. math. scis., 1980-82, adminstrv. intern office v.p. for acad. affairs, 1989-90; vis. assoc. prof. of math. U. Mich., Ann Arbor, 2002—. Assoc. editor Denver Met. Jour. Math. and Computer Sci., 1993—; contbr. articles to profl. jours. including Am. Math. Monthly, Procs. Am. Math. Soc., Jour. Personalized Instrn., Denver Met. Jour. Math. and Computer Sci. and newspapers. Mem. advt. rev. bd. Met. Denver, 1973-79; parish outreach rep. S.E. deanery, Denver Cath. Cmty. Svcs., 1976-78; mem. social ministries com. St. Thomas More Cath. Ch., Denver, 1976-78, vice-chmn., 1977-78, mem. parish coun., 1977-78; del. Adams County Rep. Conv., 1972, 74, 94, Colo. 4th Congl. Dist. Conv., 1974, Colo. Rep. Conv., 1982, 88, 90, 92, 96, 98, 2000, Douglas County Rep. Conv., 1980, 82, 84, 88, 90, 92, 94, 96, 98, 2000; alt. del. Colo. Rep. Conv., 1974, 76, 84, 2000, 5th Congl. dist. conv., 1976, mem. rules com., 1978, 80, precinct committeeman Douglas County Rep. Com., 1976-78, 89-92, mem. ctrl. com., 1976-78, 89-92; dist. 29 Rep. party candidate Colo. State Senate, 1990; mem. Colo. Rep. Leadership Program, 1989-90, bd. dirs., 1990-98; Douglas county chmn. Rep. Nat. Hispanic Assembly, 1989—; bd. dirs. Rocky Mountain Better Bus. Bur., 1975-79, Rowley Downs Homeowners Assn., 1976-78; trustee Hispanic U. Am., 1975-78; councilman Town of Parker, Colo., 1981-84, chmn. budget and fin. com., 1981-84; chmn. joint budget com. Town of Parker-Parker Water and Sanitation Dist. Bds., 1982-84; commr. Douglas County Planning Commn., 1993-97; dir. Mile High Young Scholars Program, 1995-98. Recipient Excellence in Tchg. award U. Colo. Grad. Sch., 1965-67; grantee Benedictine Coll., 1964-65, Math. Assn. Am. SUMMA grantee Carnegie Found. N.Y., 1994; program dir., grantee NSF, 1995-98; nominated candidate for first v.p Math. Assn. Am., 1999, for 2d v.p., 2001. Mem. Math. Assn. Am. (referee rsch. notes sect. Am. Math. Monthly 1981-82, gov. Rocky Mountain sect. 1993-96, investment com. 1996-02, devel. com. 1995-01, task force on reps. 1994-96, sci. policy com. 2000—, bd. govs. 1993-96, 2002—), Am. Math. Soc., Nat. Coun. Tchrs. Math., Colo. Coun. Tchrs. Math. (bd. dirs. 1994-96), Colo. Internat. Edn. Assn., Assoc. Faculties of State Insts. Higher Edn. in Colo. (v.p. 1971-73). Republican. Roman Catholic. Home: 39 Hummingbird Dr Castle Rock CO 80104-9047 Office: PO Box 173362 Denver CO 80217-3362

MENDEZ, HERMANN ARMANDO, pediatrician, educator; b. Guatemala, Apr. 26, 1949; came to U.S., 1980; citizen of El Salvador; s. Hermann and Martha (Abularach) Mendez Fortun; m. Maria Elena Ortiz, Feb. 23, 1971; children: Natalia, Amalia. MD, U. El Salvador, 1977. Diplomate Am. Bd. Pediatrics, Am. Bd. Pediatric Infectious Diseases. Asst. prof. pediats. Health Sci. Ctr. SUNY, Bklyn., 1988-91, assoc. prof. pediat. medicine, 1991—2001, assoc. prof. medicine, 1999—2001; chief dept. pediat. Lincoln Hosp., South Bronx, NY, 2000—; prof. clin. pediat. Weill Coll. Medicine, Cornell U., 2001—. Recipient Asst. Sec. for Health award USPHS, 1990, United U. Professions Excellence award Health Sci. Ctr., Bklyn., 1991, recognition award Bklyn. AIDS Task Force, 1997-98, Humanism in Medicine award Newark Beth Israel Healthcare Found., 1998, Attending of the Yr. award Children's Med. Ctr. of Bklyn., 1998, Gifts for Spl. Children award N.Y.C. Tech. Coll., 1998, N.Y. State Dept. Health Outstanding Svc. award, 1999, cert. of merit State of NY Exec. Chamber, 2002; named Physician of Yr. Salvadorean C. of C., NY, 2002. Fellow Am. Acad. Pediatrics, Infectious Disease Soc. Am. Achievements include clinical research in perinatal transmission of HIV, AIDS in children, adolescents and their families; development of systems of care for these populations and children in general, training of medical students and physicians. Office: Lincoln Med & Mental Health Ctr Dept Pediatrics 234 E 149th Bronx NY 10451-5504 Fax: 718-579-4700. Office Phone: 718-579-5800. E-mail: HAMENDEZ@aol.com.

MENDEZ, JOHN, minister; b. N.Y.C., Jan. 7, 1948; m. Sarah Lee Howard; children: Sekou, Jamila. Student, United Theol. Sem., Dayton, Postgrad. Ctr. Mental Health, N.Y.C., Southeastern Theol. Sem., Wake Forest, N.C., Shaw U., Raleigh, N.C., DD (hon.), 1991. Instr. Winston-Salem (N.C.) State U., Shaw U., Raleigh; sr. pastor Emmanuel Bapt. Ch., Winston-Salem, 1983—. Pres. Ministerial Alliance of Winston-Salem, 2003; bd. dirs. Nat. Coun. Chs.; com. mem. World Coun. Chs.; organizer Progressive Nat. Bapt. Conv. and Bapt. Ch. Movement, London and Wolverhampton, England; mentor candidates for D of Ministry degree United Theol. Sem., Dayton. Adv. com. Forsyth Tech. Coll. Sch. Nursing, Winston-Salem; cons. Urban League, Winston-Salem; founder, chairperson Citizens United for Justice, Winston-Salem; bd. dirs. N.C. Psychology Bd. Office: Emmanuel Bapt Ch 1075 Shalimar Dr Winston Salem NC 27107

MENDEZ, LUIS EDUARDO, medical educator, researcher; b. Salisbury, Md., Mar. 1, 1968; s. Luis N. and Alicia M. Mendez; m. Nahzaya M. Perez, Nov. 4, 2000. MD, U. Miami, 1993. Diplomate. Fellow Jackson Meml. Hosp., Miami, Fla., 1993—97, Emory U., Atlanta, 1997—98; assoc. prof. divsn. gynecol. oncology U. Miami, 2001—. Office: 3661 S Miami Ave Mercy Profl Bldg #308 Miami FL 33133 Office Phone: 305-243-2233. Personal E-mail: lemendez@comcast.net.

MENDEZ, OLGA A. state legislator; b. Mayaguez, P.R. BA, U. P.R.; MEd, Columbia U., 1960; PhD in Ednl. Psychology, Yeshiva U., N.Y.C., 1975. Previously assoc. prof. SUNY-Stony Brook, research psychologist Albert Einstein Coll. Med., N.Y.C., dep. commr. N.Y.C. Agy. for Child Devel.; mem. from dist. 28 N.Y. Senate, Albany, 1978—. Del. Dem. Nat. Conv., 1980, leadership position, 1984—, sec. minority conf., 1992—, chairperson conf. Home: 87 E 116th St New York NY 10029-1103 Office: N Y State Senate State Capitol 420 State Capitol Bldg Albany NY 12247

MENDEZ, RUBEN POLICARPIO, diplomat, educator, economist; b. Manila, Philippines, June 28, 1933; came to U.S., 1948; s. Mauro and Paz Policarpio M.; m. Matilda Currier McEwen, Apr. 8, 1961; children: Katherine McEwen, Tomas Currier. BA cum laude, Harvard U., 1953; MA, Columbia U., 1959; PhD, NYU, 1984. Economist Merrill Lynch, Pierce, Fenner & Smith, N.Y.C., 1959-63; econ. adviser to chmn. Nat. Econ. Coun., Manila, 1964-66; project officer UN Spl. Fund, N.Y.C., 1963-65; various positions UN Devel. Program, N.Y.C., Africa, Asia, 1966-93; chief econ. advisor UN Environ. Program, Nairobi, Kenya, 1977-81; prin. officer, historian UN Devel. Program, N.Y.C., 1993—. Adj. prof., fellow, vis. lectr. NYU, 1991—, Columbia U., 1992, Yale U., 1994—; cons. Oxford U. Press, N.Y., 1999-2000. Author: International Public Finance: A New Perspective on Global Relations, 1992; contbr. articles to profl. jours., chpts. to books. Yale rep. Acad. Coun. on UN Sys., 1997-98. Grantee Carnegie Corp., N.Y.C., 1995-98, Internat. Devel. Rsch. Ctr., Ottawa, Can., 1994-97. Mem. Am. Econ. Assn., N.Y. Acad. Scis., Soc. Internat. Devel., Harvard Club (N.Y.C.), Harvard Faculty Club, Riverdale Yacht Club, United Kenya Club (Nairobi). Avocations: history, philosophy, classical music, sailing, personal computers. Home: 313 W 263d St Bronx NY 10471 E-mail: rpmendez@post.harvard.edu.

MENDEZ, WILLIAM HUMBERT, family medicine physician; b. Mancos, Ancash, Peru, May 15, 1929; came to U.S., 1958; s. Humberto and Livia (De Los Angeles) M.; m. Ella Patricia Woltering, June 22, 1968; children: Bill, John, Michael, Angela. MD, U. San Marcos, Lima, Peru, 1958. Rotating intern Mercy Hosp., Oshkosh, Wis., 1958-59; resident in pathology St. Joseph Hosp., Marshfield, Wis., 1959-60; resident in surgery and pathology St. Joseph's Hosp., Milw., 1960-64; resident in surgery St. Luke's Hosp., Denver, 1964-66; pvt. practice Highland Med. Ctr., Denver, 1971—; asst. clin. prof. U. Colo. Med. Sch., Denver, 1995. Mem. prevention task force against drugs and violence Jeffco Bldg. Generation, Lakewood, Colo., 1985—; mem. Denver Met. YMCA, 1978—, St. Anthony Ctrs. and Luth. Med. Ctr. Fellow: Am. Acad. Family Practice; mem.: AMA (life), Am. Acad. Antiaging Medicine, Colo. Med. Soc., Am. Acad. Family Physicians (life), Peruvian Am. Med. Soc., Interam. Coll. Physicians and Surgeons. Republican. Roman Catholic. Avocation: music. Office: Highland Med Ctr 3120 W 29th Ave Denver CO 80211-3704 E-mail: WHM-Highland@juno.com.

MENDICINO, ANTHONY J. gas company executive; married; 2 children. BS in Civil Engring., Lehigh U.; MBA, U. Pa. Various positions UGI Corp., King of Prussia, Pa., treas., CFO, v.p. fin., 2000—; v.p., CFO UTI Energy Corp.; pres., COO Eastwind Group, Inc., Phila. Office: UGI Corp 460 N Gulph Rd King Of Prussia PA 19406

MENDIETA, RAQUELIN MARIA DE LA CONCEPCION, artist; b. Havana, Cuba, Aug. 4, 1946; came to the U.S., 1961; d. Ignacio Alberto and Raquel de San José (Oti) M.; m. Donald Raymond Holmes, Aug. 26, 1967 (div. Dec. 1973); m. James William Auman, Aug. 9, 1975 (div. July 1977); m. Thomas Joseph Harrington, May 17, 1978 (div. 2002); children: Raquel Cecilia, Paulette Ana, Shambhavi Elvira, Neel Miguel, Vitthal Pablo. Student, Mt. Mercy Coll., 1963-65; BA in Studio Art, U. Iowa, 1970, postgrad., 1970-72, MA in Edn., 1977. Pvt. practice exhbns. cons., 1987—. Cons. The Mus. Contemporary Art, N.Y.C., 1987, Galerie Lelong, N.Y.C., 1991—. Arts Alliance of Haverstraw, N.Y., 1992, Carla Stellweg Fine Arts, N.Y.C., 1993; humanities adv. bd. Fondo del Sol Visual Arts Ctr., Washington, 1990-93, co-chair exhbns., 1993-97; ednl. coord. Fondo del Sol, Washington, 1991; adj. prof. L.Am. studies Jersey City State Coll., 1991; trustee Arts Alliance Haverstraw, 1992-94; ednl. program specialist The Bronx (N.Y.) Mus. Arts, 1995-96; art dir., music cons. Corazon Prodns., Inc., Miami, Fla., 1996-98; lectr. in field. One woman shows include Rockland C.C., 1990, 96, Café Teatro Julia de Burgos, N.Y.C., 1993, Visceglia Arts Ctr., Caldwell, N.J., 1993, Ludwig Found. Galleries, Ltd., Havana, 2000; permanent collections Bronx Mus. Arts, Mus. of the Art Inst., Chgo. Trustee, liaison to univ. adminstrn., rep. to daycare coalition U. Parents Care Collective, Iowa City, 1971-75; vocat. advisor, arts supr. Bedford Hills (N.Y.) Correctional Facility for Women, 1985; mem. Hispanic Heritage Com., Rockland C.C., 1990-93, Hispanic Coalition Rockland County, N.Y., 1991-94. Recipient Cert. of Merit, Town of Ramapo, County of Rockland, 1992, Cert. of Recognition for developing arts programs Hispanic Coun. Rockland County, Haverstraw, 1992, Cert. of Merit, The Assembly of N.Y. State, 1993, award for contbns. to Am. art in sculpture Fondo del Sol Visual Arts Ctr., Washington, 1993. Mem. Arts Alliance of Haverstraw (hon., bd. dirs. 1993-94, trustee 1995—), Coast to Coast Nat. Women Artists of Color. Democrat. Siddha Yoga. Avocations: writing, music, personal computing, meditation, chanting. Home: 11615 SW 135th Pl Miami FL 33186-4429

MENDINI, DOUGLAS A. publishing company executive, writer; b. New Brunswick, N.J., June 13, 1953; s. T.F. Mendini and Helen Victoria Jones Mendini Renninger. BA, Seton Hall U., 1975. Sr. sales mgr. Kensington Pub. Corp., N.Y.C., 1990—. Author: What Was Hot, 1994, others; contbr. articles to numerous mags. Founder Block Assn., Manhattan, NY, 1990; bd. dirs. Cmty. Bd., Manhattan, 1990-93, bd. sec., 1993. Recipient Young Writers award Coordinating Coun. Lit. Mags., 1988. Democrat. Roman Catholic. Avocations: presidential history, furniture refinishing, american film history. Home: 403 W 54th St Apt 1D New York NY 10019-4469

MENDIUS, PATRICIA DODD WINTER, editor, educator, writer; b. Davenport, Iowa, July 9, 1924; d. Otho Edward and Helen Rose (Dodd) Winter; m. John Richard Mendius, June 19, 1947; children: Richard, Catherine M. Graber, Louise, Karen M. Chooljian. BA cum laude, UCLA, 1946; MA cum laude, U. N.Mex., 1966. Cert. secondary edn. tchr., Calif., N.Mex. English tchg. asst. UCLA, 1946-47; English tchr. Marlborough Sch. for Girls, LA, 1947-50, Aztec (N.Mex.) HS, 1953-55, Farmington (N.Mex.) HS, 1955-63; chair English dept. Los Alamos (N.Mex.) HS, 1963-86; sr. technical writer, editor Los Alamos Nat. Lab., 1987—. Adj. prof. English, U. N.Mex., Los Alamos, 1970-72, Albuquerque, 1982-85; English cons. S.W. Regional Coll. Bd., Austin, Tex., 1975—; writer, editor, cons. advanced placement English test devel. com. Nat. Coll. Bd., 1982-86, reader, 1982-86, project equality cons., 1985-88; book selection cons. Scholastic mag., 1980-82. Author: Preparing for the Advanced Placement English Exams, 1975; editor Los Alamos Arts Coun. bull., 1986-91. Chair Los Alamos Art Pub. Places Bd., 1987-92; chair adv. bd. trustees U. N.Mex., Los Alamos, 1987-93; pres. Los Alamos Concert Assn., 1972-73, 95-98, 2000-04, pres., 2003-04; chair Los Alamos Mesa Pub. Libr. Bd., 1990-94, chair endowment com., 1995-99. Mem. Soc. Tech. Communicators, AAUW (pres. 1961-63, state bd. dirs. 1959-63, Los Alamos coordinating coun. 1992-93, pres. 1993-94, 2002-04, sec. 2001-04), DAR, Order Ea. Star, Mortar Bd., Phi Beta Kappa (pres. Los Alamos chpt. 1969-72, 99, v.p. 1996-99, pres. 2000-01, dir. 2002-04), Phi Kappa Phi, Delta Kappa Gamma, Gamma Phi Beta. Avocations: swimming, reading, hiking, astronomy, singing. Home: 124 Rover Blvd Los Alamos NM 87544-3634 Office: Los Alamos Nat Lab Diamond Dr Los Alamos NM 87544 E-mail: mendius@qwest.net, pmendius@lanl.gov., pmendius@cybermesa.com.

MENDLIN, RONALD C. employment specialist, writer; b. San Francisco, Jan. 8, 1936; s. Joseph and Freda Mendlin; m. Lorraine F. Mendlin, Feb. 15, 1964; children: Andrew Scott, Susan Debra. Student, U. San Francisco, San Francisco State U.; degree, San Francisco Coll., 1958. Vocat edn. tchg. credential Calif. With City and County of San Francisco, 1962-92; employment specialist No. Calif. Svc. League, San Francisco, 1993—; part-time employment specialist San Mateo, Calif. Job developer San Mateo Employment and Tng. Ctr., Advanced Career Tech., Peninsula Placement Agy.; placement counselor Scofield Employment Agy., San Francisco; lectr. in field. Author (with Marc Polonsky): Putting the Bars Behind You, 5 vols., 2000; author: The Double You, Being Job-Ready, Job Search Tools, Networking and Interviewing for Jobs, Keeping Your Job. With N.G. USAR, 1954—63. Recipient numerous accolades, Mayor's Office. Mem.: Fiesta Gardens Home Owners Assn. (v.p.). Achievements include credited by California Department of Corrections and California State University's Sacramento Foundation for placing and assisting over 750 ex-felons from state prisons into jobs; obtained

jobs for residents in work furlough programs; obtained jobs for residents who had 6 hours to 3 days to obtain a job or be sent back to prison; saved the San Francisco Mcpl. R.R. from fin. embrassement 1974, verbally noted.

MENDONCA DE AMORIM, VALDIVIA VÂNIA SIQUEIRA, translator; b. Recife, Brazil, June 17, 1944; d. Francisco Targino and Angelica (Lucas) De Siqueira; m. Jimmie Willis Beauchamp (div. 1970); 1 child, Angélica R. Beauchamp-Ringeisen; m. João Mendonca de Amorim Filho, 2002. BS in Journalism, CEUB, 1978; MA in Portuguese and Spanish Lit., NYU, 1992. Registered profl. journalist. Social comm. sec. Office of Brazilian Presidency, Brasilia, Brazil, 1984-90; Portuguese translator Family Court, N.Y.C., 1993; translator, broker asst. Josephthal Lion & Ross, N.Y.C., 1995, U.S. Securities and Futures, N.Y.C., 1999—; in flight translator Am. Airlines. Reporter, corr., founder, tchr. Lang. Sch. Multi Lingua, Brazil, 1984—; tchr. Portuguese and Spanish, Sigma Delta Pi, Purdue U., Ind., 1982-84, NYU, 1990-92. Author: Stigma, Saga for a New World, 2003. Founder literary hour NYU; liberal artist Lafayette Art Mus., 1982-84. Mem. NYU Alumni, C. of C. of the Rockways (exec. dir. 1998). Presbyterian. Avocations: painting, piano, horseback riding, boating/fishing, golf. E-mail: vamorim8@msn.com.

MENDOZA, GEORGE, poet, author; b. N.Y.C., June 2, 1934; s. George and Elizabeth Mendoza; m. Ruth Sekora, 1967; children: Ashley, Ryan. BA, State Maritime Coll., 1953; postgrad., Columbia U., 1954-56. Author over 100 books for children and adults published worldwide; many included in Boston U.'s George Mendoza Collection, established 1984; children's books on display at the Centre Nat. d'Art et de Culture Georges Pompidou. Works include: And Amedeo Asked, How Does One Become a Man?, (illustrated by Ati Forberg), 1959, The Puma and the Pearl, 1962, The Hawk Is Humming: A Novel, 1964, A Piece of String, Astor-Honor, 1965, Gwot! Horribly Funny Hairticklers (illustrated by Steven Kellog), 1967, The Crack in the Wall and Other Terribly Weird Tales (illustrated by Mercer Mayer), 1968, Flowers and Grasses and Weeds (illustrated by Joseph Low), 1968, The Practical Man (illustrated by Imero Gobbato), 1968, Hunting Sketches (illustrated by Ronald Stein), 1968, A Beastly Alphabet (illustrated by J. Low), 1969, The Digger Wasp (illustrated by Jean Zallinger), 1969, Herman's Hat (illustrated by Frank Bozzo), 1969, The Starfish Trilogy (illustrated by Ati Forberg), 1969, (compiler) The World From My Window: Poems and Drawings (children's writings), 1969, Are You My Friend? (illustrated by F. Bozzo), 1970, The Marcel Marceau Alphabet Book, 1970, The Thumbtown Toad (illustrated by Monika Beisner), 1970, The Inspector, 1970, The Good Luck Spider & other bad luck stories, 1970, The Fearsome Brat (illustrated by F. Bozzo), 1971, Fish in the Sky (illustrated by Milton Glaser), 1971, Moonfish and owl scratchings, 1971, Moonstring, 1971, The Hunter, the Tick and the Gumberoo, 1971, The Marcel Marceau Counting Book, 1971, The Scarecrow Clock (illustrated by Eric Carle), 1971, Big Frog, Little Pond, 1971, The Scribbler, 1971, The Christmas Tree Alphabet Book, 1971, Shadowplay, 1974, Lord, Suffer me to Catch a Fish, 1974, Fishing the Morning Lonely, 1974, (with Carol Burnett) What I Want to Be When I Grow Up, 1975, (with Zero Mostel) The Sesame Street Book of Opposites, 1975, Norman Rockwell's Americana ABC (illustrated by N. Rockwell), 1975, Doug Henning's Magic Book, 1975, Lost Pony, 1976, Norman Rockwell's Boys and Girls at Play, 1976, Secret Places of a Trout Fisherman, 1977, Norman Rockwell's Diary for a Young Girl (illustrated by N. Rockwell), 1978, Magic Tricks, 1978, Mon livre de magic (French edit. of My Book of Magic), Norman Rockwell's Scrapbook for a Young Boy (illustrated by N. Rockwell), 1979, (with Andres Segovia) Segovia, My Book of the Guitar, 1979, Need a House? Call Ms. Mouse! (illustrated by Doris Susan Smith), 1981, Alphabet Sheep (illustrated by K. Reidy), 1982, The Sheepish Book of Opposites, 1982, Silly Sheep and other sheepish rhymes, 1982, Norman Rockwell's Four Seasons, 1982, Norman Rockwell's Happy Holidays, 1983, Henri Mouse (illustrated by Joelle Boucher), 1985, Henri La Souris, 1987, Norman Rockwell's Patriotic Times, 1986, (with Ivan Lendl) Hitting Hot, 1986, (with Sam Snead) Slammin' Sam, 1986, Norman Rockwell's Love and Remembrance, 1986, Top Tennis, 1987, L'Album des Noeuds, 1988, Norman Rockwell's Old Fashioned American Cookbook, 1988, Hairticklers (illustrated by Gahan Wilson), 1989, The Hunter I Might Have Been, reprint 1989, Were You a Wild Duck, Where Would You Go? (illustrated by Jane Osborn-Smith), 1990, Traffic Jam (illustrated by David Stoltz), 1990; also author screenplays for Petals from a Poem Flower, You Show Me Yours and I'll Show You Mine and scripts for Sesame Street; numerous others; over 15 books of poetry including The Hunter I Might Have Been (Lewis Carroll Shelf award 1968), The Mist Men, Goodbye, River, Goodbye; also dozens of articles in The N.Y. Times, Herald Tribune, Stern, Vogue, Harper's Bazaar, Ms., Esquire, Town & Country, Sports Afield, Men's Journal, Philadelphia Inquirer; special travel corr. Toronto Globe & Mail, 1991-94. Cited by Pres. Reagan for Norman Rockwell's Patriotic Times. Avocations: trout and salmon fishing. Worldwide fishing expeditions recorded for TV spls. *I believe we are living in a world where people no longer see each other as individuals. We have become invisible. It is necessary to save our souls. Go out to a field and pick up a fallen leaf. Look at the veins that river the leaf. Follow them until nothing else matters except for the leaf in your hand. Then you will become visible. You will see others and others will see you.*

MENDOZA, JESSICA, Olympic athlete; b. Nov. 11, 1980; BA in Am. Studies, MA in Social Sciences Ed., Stanford U. Mem. U.S. Nat. Softball Team, 2002—, U.S. Women's Softball Team, Athens Olympic Games, 2004. Named Stanford Female Conference Athlete of the Yr., 1999, Best Batter, Japan Cup, 2002, MVP, Speedline Invitational, 2002, NFCA First Team All-Am., 1999—2002; named to All-WCWS Tournament Team, 2001. Achievements include mem. Gold medal U.S. Red team, U.S. Cup, 2001; mem. Gold medal U.S. Nat. Team, ISF World Championships, 2003; mem. Gold medal U.S. Nat. Team, Pan-American Games, 2003. Office: USA Softball Complex 4845 S Shields Blvd Oklahoma City OK 73129*

MENDOZA, LAURIE PARKER, social worker; b. Bangor, Maine, Apr. 12, 1960; d. William H. Parker III and Joan C. Parker; m. Rodolfo Mendoza, Dec. 28, 1985; children: Matthew, Emma, Amalia, Isabel. AB in Psychology, Smith Coll., 1982; MA in Sch. Psychology, U. Detroit, 1983. Cert. advanced grad. study in sch. psychology Northeastern U., 1990. Page U.S. Ho. Reps., Washington, 1976—77; corrections officer, case worker Middlesex County Jail, Cambridge, Mass., 1983—88; child & family therapist Health & Edn. Svcs., Salem, 1992—99; social worker elem. sch. Salem Pub. Sch., 1999—. Columnist: various newspapers. Mem. Merrimac Old Home Days Com., 2002—03; tchr. 1st Congrl. Ch., Reading, Mass., 1991—, mem. ch. commn., 2003. Mem.: Mass. Assn. Sch. Adjustment Counselors, Psi Chi, Sigma Xi. Avocation: creative writing. Office: Carlton Elem Sch 10 Skerry St Salem MA 01970

MENDOZA, LOUIS G. literature educator, researcher; b. Houston, Aug. 25, 1960; s. Joe and Mary C. Mendoza. PhD, U. Tex., 1994. Asst. prof. English U. Houston, 1994—95; assoc. prof. U. Tex., San Antonio, 1996—. Vis. prof. Brown U., Providence, 1995—96. Author: (critical study) Historia: The Literary Making of Chicana/o History; editor: (anthology) Crossing Into America: The New Literature of Immigration. Chmn. bd. dirs. San Antonio Cultural Arts, 1997—2003. Grantee, NEH, 1999, 2001, 2003. Mem.: Nat. Assn. for Chicana and Chicano Studies (assoc.; gen. coord. 1999—2000). Office: Univ Tex San Antonio 501 W Durango Blvd San Antonio TX 78207 Home: 1202 W Russell Pl San Antonio TX 78201-5721 E-mail: lmendoza@utsa.edu.

MENDOZA, LYDIA, vocalist; Mem. El Cuarteto Carta Blanca. Recordings include: Mal Hombre, 1934; performances include Smithsonian Bicentennial Festival of Am. Folklife, Carter Presdl. Inauguration; author (compiled by Chris Strachwitz and James Nicolopulos): Lydia Mendoza: A Family Autobiography, 1993; author: (with Y. Broyles-Gonzales) Lydia Mendoza: My Life and Music, 2001. Named a Nat. Treasure, Smithsonian Instn.; named Nat. Heritage fellow, Nat. Endowment for the Arts, 1982; named to Tex. Hall of Fame; recipient Nat. Medal of Arts, Nat. Assn. for Chicana and Chicano Studies Lifetime Achievement Cmty. award, 1999, Nat. Medal of Arts, Am. Heritage award. Office: c/o Arhoolie Records 10341 San Pablo Ave El Cerrito CA 94530-3123 E-mail: chris@arhoolie.com.

MENDOZA, MARTHA, reporter; b. L.A., Calif., 1969; BA, U. Calif. Santa Cruz, 1988. Reporter Madera Tribune, Bay City News Svc., Santa Cruz County Sentinel; nat. investigative reporter Associated Press, San Jose, Calif., 1995—. Co-author: The Bridge at No Gun RI: A Hidden Nightmare from the Korean War, 2001. Recipient Pulitzer prize, 2000, Alumni Achievment award, U. Calif. Santa Cruz, 2002; John S. Knight fellow, Stanford U., 2001. Office: Associated Press 675 N 1st St San Jose CA 95112

MENDOZA, ROBERTO G., JR., banker; b. Cuba, 1945; BA, Yale U., 1967; MBA, Harvard U., 1974. With Morgan Guaranty Trust Co., N.Y.C., 1967—, formerly mng. dir.; vice chmn. J.P. Morgan & Co., N.Y.C., 1990—, former dir. for global mergers and acquisitions. Office: J P Morgan & Co 60 Wall St New York NY 10260-0001

MENDOZA, RUBEN G. anthropologist, educator, archaeologist; b. French-camp, Calif., June 18, 1956; s. Jose and Josephine Mendoza; m. Linda Marie James, June 2, 1990; children: Natalie Dawn Marie, Maya Nicole. BA, Calif. State U., Bakersfield, 1978; MA, U. Ariz., 1980, PhD, 1992. Rsch. asst. SW Mission Rsch. Ctr., Tucson, 1978—79; instr. Pima Coll., Tucson, 1979—91, Bakersfield (Calif.) Coll., 1982—86; curatorial asst. Photographic Collections, Ariz. State Mus., Tucson, 1988—90; asst. prof. U. Colo., Denver, 1991—95; assoc. prof. Calif. State U., Monterey Bay, Seaside, 1995—2001, planning faculty, 1995—97, dir. Inst. Archaeology, 1995—, prof., 2001—. Literacy pl. mentor Scholastic, Inc., N.Y.C., 1996—; contract archaeologist Ruben G. Mendoza, Archaeological Cons., Salinas, Calif., 2000—; multimedia prodr./content specialist Prentice Hall, Inc., N.Y.C., 2002—; bd. dirs. Calif. Missions Found., San Francisco; prin. investigator wireless tech. in archaeology demonstration project, Seaside, Calif. Photographer, featured archaeologist: 3d grade science text Science, 2000, 3d grade science text, video, CD-ROM Time Detectives, editl. cons.: children's book Mission Santa Cruz, Mission San Carlos Borromeo del Rio Carmelo, Mission San Juan Bautista; contbr. chapters to books, articles to profl. jours.; photographer (exhibitions) Loveland Gallery, Colo., Mexican Consulate, Denver, Colo., 1994—95, Mex. Heritage Plaza, 2000. Curatorial rep., old mission San Juan Bautista, Calif. Calif. Mission Curators and Dirs. Conf., Santa Barbara, 1997—2004; mem. grants rev. com. Calif. Missions Found., San Francisco, 2000—04. Recipient wireless tech. in tchg. and learning award, Congl. Appropriation, 2002—03; Dissertation fellow, Ford Found., NRC, Washington, 1990—91, Ford Found. fellow, 1990—91, scholar, Nat. Hispanic Scholarship Fund, 1981, 1982, 1987. Mem.: Register of Profl. Archaeologists, Am. Anthrop. Assn. (mem. sect. assembly 1998—2000, pres. Assn. Latina and Latino Anthropologists 1997—2000). Achievements include principal investigator Crescent Rockshelter Archaeological Site, Colorado; principal investigator Old Mission San Juan Bautista, California; principal investigator Mission San CArlos Borromeo del Rio Carmelo, California. Avocations: photography, multimedia development, writing, videography, gardening. Office: California State Univ Monterey Bay 100 Campus Center Seaside CA 93955-8001

MENDOZA, STANLEY ATRAN, pediatric nephrologist, educator; b. Pitts., May 7, 1940; s. Joseph William and Marian Ruth (Atran) M.; m. Carole Ann Klein, June 23, 1963; children: Daniel, Joseph. Student, Harvard U., 1957—59; BA, Johns Hopkins U., 1961, MD, 1964. Diplomate Am. Bd. Pediat. Intern Johns Hopkins Hosp., Balt., 1964-65; jr. asst. resident dept. medicine Children's Hosp. Med. Ctr., Boston, 1965-66; asst. attending physician, dir. renal rsch. labs. Children's Meml. Hosp., Chgo., 1969-71; asst. prof. pediat. U. Calif. Sch. Medicine, San Diego, 1971—73, assoc. prof., 1973—79, prof. pediat. dept. pediat. divsn. pediatric nephrology, 1979—, vice chmn. dept. pediat., 1986—87, chmn. dept. pediat., 1992—2000. Contbr. article in field to profl. publ. Served With USPHS, 1966-69. Fogarty Sr. Internat. fellow, 1978-79; Alan J. Wurtzburger rsch. scholar, 1964; recipient Johns Hopkins Med. Soc. award, 1964, hon. mention Borden Undergrad. rsch. award in medicine, 1964; Eleanor Roosevelt internat. fellow Internat. Union Against Cancer, 1984-85. Mem. Am. Fedn. Clin. Rsch., Am. Pediatric Soc., Am. Physiol. Soc., Am. Soc. Nephrology, Am. Soc. Pediatric Nephrology, Internat. Soc. Nephrology. Office: U Calif San Diego Dept Pediat 9500 Gilman Dr # 0696 La Jolla CA 92093-5004 Office Phone: 858-822-4514. E-mail: samendoza@ucsd.edu.

MENDOZA DE ARCE, DANIEL LEONEL, retired humanities educator; b. Montevideo, Uruguay, Dec. 24, 1940; arrived in U.S., 1972; s. Leonel Felix Mendoza Meggett and Thesbit Jacinta De Arce Sarlangue; m. Vreni Sophie Zentner, May 21, 1942 (div. Apr. 2000). D in Law and Social Sci., U. Uruguay, 1967, postgrad., 1968—70. Adj. prof. U. Uruguay, Montevideo, Uruguay, 1970—71; asst. prof. sociology and anthropology William Paterson Coll., Paterson, NJ, 1973—75; prof. Hispanic culture Gov.'s State U., University Pk., Ill., 1976—95; ret., 1995. Vis. prof. U. P.R., Rio Piedras, 1989, Rio Piedras, 1993—94. Author: Sociologia del Folkore Musical Uruguayo, 1972, Music in Ibero-America, 1492-1850, 2001. Rsch. fellow, Govs. State U., 1988. Mem.: Am. Musicological Soc. Home: 13261 SW 17th Ln #7 Miami FL 33175

MENDOZA-LONDONO, ROBERTO, geneticist, pediatrician; b. Bogota, Colombia, Mar. 12, 1971; s. Cesar Mendoza-Posada and Graciela Londono de Mendoza. MD, Pontificia Universidad Javeriana, Bogota, Colombia, 1994. Diplomate Am. Acad. of Pediat., 2001. Rsch. assoc. Pontificia Universidad Javeriana, Bogota, 1994—95, trainee in clin. genetics &msc, 1996—98; resident in pediat. SUNY Downstate, Bklyn., 1998—2001; postdoctoral fellow in genetics Baylor Coll. of Medicine, Houston, 2001—. Recipient Rhone-Poulenc-Rorer award for excellence in rsch., VII-Nat. Acad. Medicine, 1998, Peter J. Karl Meml. award, 2001. Mem.: Am. Soc. of Human Genetics, AAAS, Am. Acad. of Pediat. D-Liberal. Christian. Achievements include research in Role of E-selectin ligand 1 in cartilage development. Avocations: photography, travel. Home: 7777 Greenbriar 3079 Houston TX 77030 Office: Baylor College of Medicine One Baylor Plaza Rm 633E Houston TX 77030 Office Phone: 713-798-3548. Personal E-mail: rmendozal@hotmail.com. E-mail: mendozal@bcm.tmc.edu.

MENEAR, CRAIG, retail executive; b. Flint, Mich. m. Dawn Menear; children: Courtney, Danielle. BA in Bus., Mich. State U., 1979. With IKEA Wholesale, Inc., Builders Emporium, Grace Home Ctrs., Montgomery Ward; divsn. mdse. mgr. Home Depot, Inc., Atlanta, merchandising v.p. S.W. divsn., merchandising v.p. hardware, sr. v.p. merchandising hardlines, 2003—. Office: Home Depot Inc 2455 Paces Ferry Rd NW Atlanta GA 30339-4024

MENEELEY, EDWARD STERLING, artist; b. Wilkes-Barre, Pa., Dec. 18, 1927; s. Edward Sterling and Louina Halter M. Student, Murray Art Sch., Wilkes-Barre, 1947-50, Sch. Visual Arts, N.Y.C., 1952-53. Vis. lectr. Belleville Coll., St. Louis, Art Students League, N.Y.C.; lectr. Lehigh Valley Sch. System, 1987, Rogers College, Istanbul, Turkey, 1991, Lafayette Coll., 1998; pres. ESM Documentations, N.Y.C.; fine arts cons. Arts Initiatives, Inc., N.Y.C.; founder Portable Gallery Press, 1957-67. One-man exhbs. include, Donovan Gallery, Phila., 1952, Parma Gallery, N.Y.C., 1962, Teuscher Gallery, N.Y.C., 1966, 68, Inst. Contemporary Arts, London, 1971, Victoria and Albert Mus., London, 1972, U. Sussex, Eng., 1972, Whitechapel Art Gallery, London, 1973, Demos Gallery, Athens, Greece, 1976, Frank Marino Gallery, N.Y.C., 1978, 79, 80, 81, 82, Sordoni Gallery, Wilkes (Pa.) Coll., 1981, Ericson Gallery, N.Y.C., 1980, Portfolio Gallery, Atlanta, 1983, Angela Flowers Gallery, London, 1985, J.T. Gallery, Jim Thorpe, Pa, 1987, 55 Mercer St., N.Y.C., 1987, Anita Shapolsky Gallery, N.Y.C., 1988, Bucknell U. Gallery Art, Lewisburg, 1988, Recent Painting & Sculptute, Coll. Misericordia, Dallas, Pa., 1989, Mixed Media, Craft Alliance Gallery, St. Louis, 1990, Provincetown (Mass.) Art Mus., 1993, De Arte Magick Gallery, Easton, Pa., 1997, New Works, N.Y.C., 1998, 181 Hudson St. N.Y.C., 1998, 70th St. Gallery Collages, 2001, Soho Creative, N.Y.C., 2002, 03, 04, MCI Gallery, 2003, 2004. Served with USNR, 1945-47, 50-52. Nat. Endowment Arts grantee; Pollock-Krasner Found. grantee, 1986, 90, 2002. Mem. Artist Club N.Y.C., Inst. Contemporary Arts London, Josiah White Soc., Weissport, Pa.

MENEFEE, FREDERICK LEWIS, advertising executive; b. Arkansas City, Kans., Oct. 22, 1932; s. Arthur LeRoy and Vera Mae (Rather) M.; m. Margot Leuze, Sept. 16, 1955; children: Gregory S., Christina Menefee-Anderson. AA, Arkansas City Jr. Coll., 1952; BA, U. Wichita, 1958. Sports editor, bus. mgr. Ark. Light and Tiger Tales, 1949-52; sports reporter Arkansas City Daily Traveler, 1949—52; advt. mgr. Derby Star, Haysville Herald and Sedgwick County News, 1956-57; v.p., account exec. Associated Advt. Agy., 1958-64; with McCormick-Armstrong Adv. Agy. (now Menefee and Ptnrs., Inc.), Wichita, 1964—, agy. mgr., 1964—, account. supr., 1965—, gen. mgr., 1972—, pres., CEO, 1979—, chmn. bd., 1986—2003. Vol. Wichita River Festival, 1974-98; pub. rels. chmn. Wichita Centennial Nat. Art Show and Exhibit, 1969-70. With AUS, 1953-55. Named Advt. Man of Yr., Advt. Club of Wichita, 1964, Advt. Man of Yr., 9th Dist. Am. Advt. Fedn. Colo., Nebr., Iowa, Mo., Kans., 1965, Adm. Windwagon Smith III Wichita Festivals Inc., 1976. Mem. Am. Advt. Fedn. (nat. bd. dirs. 1969-70, dist. gov. 1968-69, chmn. nat. coun. govs. 1969-70), Wichita Wagonmasters (founding mem., capt. 1974-75, dir., charter, founder, commodore 1999), Wichita Advt. Club (bd. dirs. 1958-68), v.p. awards 1961-62, v.p. membership 1962, v.p. programs 1963, pres. 1964-65), PAWS Inc. (founder, 1st pres. 1978-86), Alpha Delta Sigma (pres. 1957-58, Outstanding Svc. award 1958), Quill & Scroll, 1949-50. Home: 2235 Red Bud Ln Wichita KS 67204-5346

MENEFEE, JOHN WILLIAM, III, cinematographer, producer; b. Washington, Dec. 19, 1944; s. John William Menefee Jr. and Mary Claudia (Tudor) Upchurch. Student, U. Va., 1964-66, Columbia Sch. for Motion Pictures and TV, L.A., 1992. Tour guide Universal Studios, University City, Calif., 1970-75, studio transp. driver, 1976; camera asst., trainee Dino d'Laurentis Orgn., Beverly Hills, Calif., 1976, Panavision (formerly Gen. Camera), N.Y.C., 1978; camera person Paramount Pictures, L.A., 1980, 20th Century Fox Film Corp., L.A., 1987, 96, Sony Pictures Corp., Culver City, Calif., 1992, 97, Paramount Pictures, L.A., 2000. Mem. film and TV action com. Bring Hollywood Home, L.A., 1999—; contbr., supporter World Wildlife Fund, Washington, Lambda Legal Def. Fund, N.Y.C., Cato Inst., Washington. Mem. Internat. Cinematographers Guild (cert.), Jamestown Soc. Episcopalian. Avocations: genealogy, vedic astrology, tennis, acting. Home: 1020 San Rafael Ln Pasadena CA 91105-1531 Personal E-mail: mflea3@aol.com.

MENEFEE, LINNEA-NORMA, antique dealer; b. Mpls., Mar. 5, 1924; d. Arthur Wesley and Elsie Ida Buck; m. Edward Curial Menefee, June 15, 1946 (dec. 1980); children: Edward, Joan, Barbara, Judith. Student, U. Minn., Mpls., U. Minn., Duluth, McPhail Sch. Music, Mpls. Founder Albert Lea (Minn.) Art Ctr., 1959; county chairwoman Goldwater for Pres., Albert Lea. Mem. AAUW, Am. Med. Assn. Alliance, Nat. Fedn. Rep. Women, Nat. Women of the Arts, Nat. Am. Legion Aux., Nat. VFW Aux., Nat. Assn. Family and Cmty. Edn., Order of Ea. Star, Gillette Blue Blades, Kiwanis Internat., Zeta Phi Eta, Omega Upsilon, Zeta Beta Chi. Episcopalian. Avocations: writing, reading, painting, walking.

MENEFEE, SAMUEL PYEATT, lawyer, anthropologist; b. Denver, June 8, 1950; s. George Hardiman and Martha Elizabeth (Pyeatt) M. BA in Anthropology and Scholar of Ho. summa cum laude, Yale U., 1972; diploma in Social Anthropology, Oxford (Eng.) U., 1973, BLitt, 1975; JD, Harvard U., 1981; LLM in Oceans, U. Va., 1982, SJD, 1993; MPhil in Internat. Rels., U. Cambridge, Eng., 1995. Bar: Ga. 1981, U.S. Ct. Appeals (11th cir.) 1982, Va. 1983, La. 1983, U.S. Ct. Mil. Appeals 1983, U.S. Ct. Internat. Trade 1983, U.S. Ct. Claims 1983, U.S. Ct. Appeals (10th cir.) 1983, U.S. Ct. Appeals (fed., 1st, 3d, 4th, 5th, 6th, 7th, 8th and 9th cirs.) 1984, D.C. 1985, Nebr. 1985, Fla. 1985, U.S. Supreme Ct. 1985, U.S. Ct. Appeals (D.C. cir.) 1986, Maine 1986, Pa. 1986. Assoc. Phelps, Dunbar, Marks, Claverie & Sims, New Orleans, 1983-85; of counsel Barham & Churchill PC, New Orleans, 1985-88; sr. assoc. Ctr. for Nat. Security Law U. Va. Sch. Law, 1985—, fellow Ctr. for Oceans Law and Policy, 1982-83, sr. fellow, 1985-89, Maury fellow, 1989—, adv. bd., 1997—. Vis. lectr. U. Cape Town, 1987; vis. asst. prof. U. Mo.-Kansas City, 1990; law clk. Hon. Pasco M. Bowman, U.S. Ct. Appeals (8th cir.), 1994-95; vis. prof. Regent U., 1996-97, scholar-at-large, 1997—, prof., 1998—; adv. The Am. Maritime Forum/The Mariners' Mus., 1997-98; lectr. various nat. and internat. orgns.; mem. ICC Consultative Task Force on Comml. Crime, 1996—. Author: Wives for Sale: An Ethnographic Study of British Popular Divorce, 1981, Contemporary Piracy and International Law, 1995, Trends in Maritime Violence, 1996; co-editor: Materials on Ocean Law, 1982; contbr. numerous articles to profl. jours. Recipient Katharine Briggs prize Folklore Soc., 1992; Bates traveling fellow Yale U., 1971, Rhodes scholar, 1972; Cosmos fellow Sch. Scottish Studies U. Edinburgh, 1991-92, IMB fellow, ICC Internat. Maritime Bur., 1991—, Piracy Reporting Ctr. fellow, Kuala Lampur, 1993—, Huntington fellow The Mariners Mus., 1997. Fellow Royal Anthrop. Inst., Am. Anthrop. Assn., Royal Asiatic Soc., Royal Soc. Antiquaries of Ireland, Soc. Antiquaries (Scotland), Royal Geog. Soc., Soc. Antiquaries; mem. ABA (vice-chmn. marine resources com. 1987-90, chmn. law of the sea com. subcom. naval warfare, maritime terrorism and piracy 1989—, mem. law of the sea com. steering com. 1996—, mem. working group on terrorism), Southeastern Admiralty Law Inst. (com. mem.), Maritime Law Assn. (proctor, com. mem., chmn. subcom. law of the sea 1988-91, vice chmn. com. internat. law of the sea 1991—, chair working group piracy 1992—, UNESCO study group, 1998—), Marine Tech. Soc. (co-chmn. marine security com. 1991—), Selden Soc., Am. Soc. Internat. Law, Internat. Law Assn. (com. mem., rapporteur Am. br. com. EEZ 1988-90, rapporteur Am. br. com. Maritime Neutrality 1992, observer UN conv. on Law of the Sea meeting of States Parties 1996, chmn. Am. br. com. on Law of the Sea 1996—), rapporteur joint internat. working group on uniformity of the law of piracy 1998—, (Com. Maritime Internat.), Am. Soc. Indsl. Security (com. mem.), U.S. Naval Inst., USN League, Folklore Soc., Royal Celtic Soc., Internat. Studies Assn., Royal Scottish Geog. Soc., Royal African Soc., Egypt Exploration Soc., Arctic Inst. N.Am., Internat. Studies Assn., Am. Hist. Soc., Internat. Assn. Rsch. on Peasant Diaries (nat. editor 1996—), Nat. Eagle Scout Assn., Raven Soc., Jefferson Soc., Fence Club, Mory's Assn., Elizabethan Club, Yale Polit. Union, Leander Club, Cambridge Union, United Oxford and Cambridge Univ. Club, Yale Club (N.Y.C.), Paul Morphy Chess Club, Pendennis Club, Round Table Club (New Orleans), Phi Beta Kappa, Omicron Delta Kappa. Republican. Episcopalian. Avocations: anthropology, archaeology, social history, crew, hill walking. Office: U Va Ctr Nat Sec Law 580 Massie Rd Charlottesville VA 22903-1738

MENENDEZ, ADOLFO, engineering company executive; m. Silvia Perez; children: José Adolfo, Mercedes Silvia. BSME, Manhattan Coll.; postgrad., Golden Gate U. Registered profl. engr. D.C., Va., Miss. Project mgr. internat. ops. Bechtel Power Corp.; pres., COO K & M Engring. & Cons, Corp., Washington, 1999; chmn., CEO Global Mgmt. Ptnrs., LLC, Washington, 1999—. Bd. dirs. KMR Power Corp.; cons. Wold Bank, Internat. Fin. Corp., European Bank for Reconstruction and Devel., USAID, others. Mem. Georgetown Club, U. Club, Lakewood Country Club. Office: Global Mgmt Ptnrs LLC Ste 535 1700 Rockville Pike Rockville MD 20852 E-mail: GMPLLC@worldnet.att.net.

MENENDEZ, BELINDA, broadcast executive; Student, St. Andrews U., Scotland. With internat. TV sales Televisa, 1986—95; mgr. TV sales Cisneros; internat. tv distbn. ops. mgr. Michael Solomon's S.I.E.; exec. v.p. sales Studio Canal (formerly Canal Plus DA); co-pres. Universal TV Distbn., Universal City, Calif., 2001—. Office: Universal TV Distbn USA Bldg 1440/3030 100 Universal City Plaza Universal City CA 91608-1002

MENENDEZ, MARCELINO EULOGIO (MARC MENENDEZ), marketing professional; b. Mexico City, Mex., June 1974; s. Marcelino and Sharon M. Menendez; m. Susan P. Gildo. BA, Columbia U., N.Y.C., 1996. Analyst Bayerish Vereinsbank, N.Y.C., 1993—95; mng. analyst Forest Labs., N.Y.C., 1996—97, assoc. product mgr., 1997—98; dir. of pharms. SMG Mktg. Group, Inc., N.Y.C., 1998—99; nat. sales dir. health svcs. SMG Mktg. Group, Inc./Quintiles Transnat. Corp, Chgo., 1999—2001; v.p. sales and mktg. Affiliated Network Services, LLC, Chgo., 2001—. Mng. ptnr. Roshamar, Inc., Mex. City, 1999—; prin. Guilmen Cons., Naperville, Ill., 1999—. Treas. Tallgrass Homeowners Assn.; vol. Rep. Party, Chgo., 1997—2003. Recipient Fgn. Langs. award, Bank of Am., 1992. Mem.: Acad. of Managed Care

Pharmacy, Nat. Assn. of Dental Plans, Nat. Dental EDI Coun. Orgn. (vice chiar, mktg.), Columbia U. Alumni Assn., Am. Mgmt. Assn., Med. Mktg. Assn. Avocations: exercise, technology/computers, culinary arts. Home: 3703 Mistflower Ln Naperville IL 60564 Office: Affiliated Network Svcs LLC 211 W Wacker Dr Ste 1100 Chicago IL 60606 Personal E-mail: marquis@elative.com.

MENENDEZ, ROBERT, congressman, lawyer; b. N.Y.C., Jan. 1, 1954; s. Mario and Evangelina (Lopez) M.; m. Jane Jacobsen, June 5; children: Alicia, Robert. BA, St. Peter's Coll., 1976; JD, Rutgers U., 1979. Bar: N.J. 1980. Pvt. practice, Union City, N.J., 1980-92; mem. U.S. Congress from 13th N.J. dist., 1993—; mem. transp & infrastructure com., internat. rels. com; Dem. whip at large. Mem. Congl. Arts Caucus; mem. western hemisphere ranking Dem., Africa subcom; surface transp., water resources & environment coms.; chief dep. whip 105th Congress. Mayor of Union City, 1986-92; sec. Union City Bd. Edn., 1978-82, trustee, 1974-78; pres. Alliance civic Orgn., 1982-92; mem. Gov.'s Hispanic Adv. Com., Trenton, N.J., 1984—; mem. Gov.'s Ethnic Adv. Com., Washignton, 1985—. Recipient Cmty. Svc. award Gran Logia del Norte, 1981, Outstanding Svc. award Hispanic Law Enforcement, 1981, Outstanding Cmty. Svc. Revista Actualidades, 1982, Disting. Citizen award U. Medicine and Dentistry N.J., 1994, Man of Yr. award Kiwanis, 1994. Mem. N.J. Hispanic Elected and Apptd Ofcls. (chair), Hoboken Elks Club. Democrat. Roman Catholic. Avocations: chess, racquetball. Office: Ho of Reps 2238 Rayburn Ho Office Bldg Washington DC 20515 also: 911 Bergen Ave Jersey City NJ 07306-4301

MENES, PAUL IRA, lawyer; b. Chgo., Jan. 10, 1955; s. Herbert and Leona (Lustig) M.; m. Sheryl Renee Jakofsky, Mar. 19, 1988. Student, Calif. State U., Northridge, 1973-74; AB, UCLA, 1976; JD, Southwestern U., 1980. Bar: Calif. 1981, U.S. Dist. Ct. (cen. dist.) Calif. 1981. Assoc. Menes & Turtle, L.A., 1981-82; assoc. Barry A. Menes & Assoc., P.C., L.A., 1982—; ptnr. Menes Law Corp., L.A., 1982—. Judge pro tem Mcpl. Ct., L.A. Jud. Dist., 1986—; spkr., lectr. South by Southwest Music Conf., North by Northwest Music Conf., Founds. Forum, Showbiz Expo, Calif. Lawyers for the Arts, others. Mem. ABA, Century City Bar Assn. (spl. award 1987), Assn. Trial Lawyers Am., Calif. Lawyers for the Arts, Nat. Acad. Rec. Arts and Scis. Office: 1801 Century Park E Ste 1560 Los Angeles CA 90067-2317 E-mail: paulm@meneslaw.com.

MENG, M. KATHRYN, lawyer; JD, Fordham U. Former dist. ct. bur. chief criminal divsn. Legal Aid Soc. Nassau County; ptnr. Cianciulli & Meng, P.C., Uniondale, NY. Dean Nassau Acad. Law; adj. prof. Nassau C.C. Columnist Nassau Lawyer. Bd. dirs. Sara's Ctr.; mem. outreach adv. com. St. Brigid's Ch., Westbury, eucharistic ministr. Mem.: ABA (del.), Nassau Legal Aid Soc. (former pres., former bd. dirs.), Attys. to the Bar (com. character and fitnss for admission 1983—), Criminal Cts. Bar Assn. (former pres., former bd. dirs.), N.Y. State Bar Assn. (del.), Nassau County Bar Assn. (pres., chair civil rights com., former chair lawyers assistance com., former mem. judiciary com.). Office: Cianciulli & Meng PC 773 Hampstead Tpke PO Box 246 Uniondale NY 11553-0246 Office Phone: 516-463-6036. E-mail: kmeng@cmlawgroup.net.

MENG, RU-LING, research scientist; children: Meng Huang, He Huang. BA, Ctrl. So. U. of Tech. Mining and Metallurgy Coll., Hunan, China, 1958. Instr. Ctr. So. U. of Tech. (Mining and Metallurgy Coll.), Hunan, China, 1958—59; rsch. asst. Acad. of Sci., Inst. of Mining and Metallurgy, Beijing, 1959—73; rsch. assoc. Chinese Acad. of Sci., Inst. of Physics, Beijing, 1973—79, U. of Houston, Dept. of Physics, 1979—81; vis. scholar U. of Konstanz, Dept. of Physics, Germany, 1981; rsch. assoc. Acad. of Sci., Inst. of Physics, Beijing, 1982—84, U. of Houston, Dept. of Physics, 1984—; sr. rsch. scientist Tex. Ctr. for Superconductivity at the U. of Houston, Dept. of Physics, 1987—. Sr. cons. Chan-Sha Rsch. Inst. of Mining and Metallurgy, China, 1992. Named one of the most worlds most cited authors, Inst. for Sci. Info. Current Contents, 2000; recipient ranked 25th out of the 1000 most cited physicists, Inst. for Sci. Info., 1981—97, Hon. professorship, Zhong-Shan U. (Sun Yat-Sen U.), 1992, Ctr. So. U. of Tech., 1992, Beijing Polytechnic U., 1998. Mem.: Chinese Assn. of Professionals in Sci. and Tech. (founder/1st pres.), Materials Rsch. Soc., Phi Beta Delta Internat. Assn. Achievements include discovery of high temperature superconducting Y-Ba-Cu-O system; first to succeed in fabricating texturing Y-Ba-Cu-O bar, obtained first record trapped field of 8T at 4.2k by 20 mmx6 mm YBCO discs, first to grow C60 (or carbon 60) single crystal with no defect; development of and the patent for processing techniques for highest transition superconducting temperature Hg-Ba-Ca-Cu-O and co-developed the first Hg-1212 film; first to succeed in fabricating Hg-1223 tape; first to succeed in fabricating Bi-sr-ca-cu-o on a low cost ni metal substrate. Office: Texas Ctr for Superconductivity U of Houston High Pressure Low Temperature Lab Houston TX 77204 E-mail: rmeng@uh.edu.

MENG, XIAO-LI, statistician; b. Shanghai, Jan. 24, 1963; PhD, Harvard U., 1990. From asst. to assoc. to prof. stats. U. Chgo., Chicago, 1991—2001; prof. stats. Harvard U., Cambridge, Mass., 2001—, chmn., 2004—. Assoc. editor: Annals of Stats., 1997—. Jour. Am. Statis. Assn., 1996—2002, Biometrika, 2002—. Statistica Sinica, 1992—97. Recipient 2001 COPSS award for outstanding statistician under age of 40, Com. of Pres. of Statis. Assn., 2001. Fellow: Royal Statis. Soc. (U.K.), Am. Statis. Assn. (program chair 2004 joint statis. meetings 2002—04), Inst. Math. Stats. (program chair 1999—2000); mem.: Internat. Soc. for Bayesian Analysis, Internat. Chinese Statis. Assn. (life; bd. dirs. 1996—99), Bernoulli Soc. for Math. Stats. and Probability, Biometric Soc. (regional adv. bd. 1995—97). Office: Harvard U Dept Stats Sci Ctr Oxford St Cambridge MA 02138 Business E-Mail: meng@stat.harvard.edu.

MENGDEN, JOSEPH MICHAEL, retired investment banker; b. Houston, Sept. 28, 1924; s. Hippolyt Frederick and Amalia (Dittlinger) M.; m. Suzanne Miner, Sept. 30, 1950 (dec. July 1990); children: Anne Elise Mengden Giliberto, Amanda Mary, Michael Joseph, Charles Louis, Melissa Mary Mengden Bunker, Mary Miner Mengden Fitch; m. Dorothy Duggan, July 27, 1991. Ph.B., U. Notre Dame, 1949. V.p. Nat. Bank of Detroit, 1950-67; exec. v.p. First of Mich. Capital Corp., Detroit, 1967-90, sr. cons., 1990-95. Served to 1st lt. USAAF, World War II. Decorated Air medal with 2 oak leaf clusters. Home: 321 Rivard Blvd Grosse Pointe MI 48230-1625 Personal E-mail: men@comcast.net.

MENGEDOTH, DONALD ROY, commercial banker; b. Naperville, Ill., Aug. 10, 1944; s. Orville Gustav and Bernice Lydia (Fries) M.; m. Stacy K. Halverson; children: Paul Bernard, Daniel Lawrence, Mary Bernice. BS, Marquette U., 1968, MBA, 1973. Ops. officer 1st Bank, N.A.-Milw., 1968-69, asst. v.p., 1969-71, v.p., 1971-73, sr. v.p., 1973-79; v.p. 1st Bank System, Inc., Mpls., 1979-82, sr. v.p., 1983-87, pres., CEO, 1987—2000; chmn. Cmty. First Bankshares Inc., Fargo, ND, 1987—. Bd. dirs. Treasure Enterprises, Inc., Vail Banks Inc. Adv. bd. United Way Cass-Clay Campaign, Fargo, 1988-89; chmn. Cmty. 1st Polit. Action Com., Fargo, 1988-89; bd. dirs. Fargo Cath. Schs. Network Found., 1989-92; bd. dirs., vice chmn. Red River Zool. Soc., 1993-96; chmn. Diocesan God's Gift Appeals, Fargo, 1989. Mem. Am. Bankers Assn. (govt. rels. coun., pres. 2000-2001), Am. Mgmt. Assn., N.D. Bankers Assn., S.D. Bankers Assn., Greater N.D. Assn., Fargo Country Club. Avocations: tennis, golf, hunting, reading. Office: Cmty 1st Bankshares 520 Main Ave Fargo ND 58124-0001 E-mail: don_mengedoth@cfbx.com.

MENGEL, CHARLES EDMUND, physician, medical educator; b. Balt., Nov. 29, 1931; s. Charles LeRoy and Anna (Apgar) M.; m. Paula Padgett, June 5, 1978; children: Cheryl Lynn, Charles Edmund, Gregory John, Scott Alan, Carol Ann, Michael Daniel. AB in Chemistry, Lafayette Coll., 1953; MD, Johns Hopkins U., 1957. Intern Johns Hopkins Hosp., 1957-58; resident Duke Hosp., 1958-59, 61-62; clin. assoc. NIH, 1959-61; mem. faculty Duke U. Med. Sch., 1961-65; Doan prof., dir. hematology and oncology Ohio State U., 1965-69; prof. medicine U. Mo., Columbia, 1969-82, chmn. dept., 1969-81; pvt. practive gen. medicine Moberly, Mo., 1982-88; prof. medicine Kans. U. Med. Ctr., Kansas City, 1988-98; CEO MEC Enterprises, 1999—. Author textbook; contbr. articles to med. publs. With USPHS, 1959-61. Markle scholar acad. medicine, 1963 Mem. ACP, Am. Fedn. Clin. Rsch., Am. Soc. Hematology, Am. Soc. Clin. Investigation

MENGEL, CHRISTOPHER EMILE, lawyer, educator; b. Holyoke, Mass., Sept. 11, 1952; s. Emile Oscar and Rose Ann (O'Donnell) M.; m. Ellen Christine Creager, Dec. 6, 1991; children: Meredith Anne, Celia Claire; step-children: Cara Elizabeth Creager, Kristen Michele Creager. Student, U. Notre Dame, 1970-71; BA, Holy Cross Coll., 1974; JD, Detroit Coll. Law, 1979. Bar: Mich. 1979, U.S. Dist. Ct. (ea. dist.) Mich. 1989, U.S. Ct. Appeals (6th cir.) 1990. Tchr. Holyoke Pub. Schs., 1974-76; assoc. Fried & Sniokaitis P.C., Detroit, 1980-82; prof. Detroit Coll. Law, 1982-85; pvt. practice Detroit, 1982-91; mng. ptnr. Berkley, Mengel & Vining, PC, 1992—. Mem. coun. St. Ambrose Parish, Grosse Pointe Park, Mich., 1985-88, pres. 1986-87. Matthew J. Ryan scholar, 1970; recipient Disting. Brief award Thomas M. Cooley Law Rev., 1996. Mem. ABA, Mich. Bar Assn., Detroit Bar Assn. Democrat. Roman Catholic. Avocations: baseball, sailing, photography. Home: 1281 N Oxford Rd Grosse Pointe MI 48236-1857 Office: Berkley Mengel & Vining PC 3100 Penobscot Bldg Detroit MI 48226 Office Phone: 313-961-0220. Business E-Mail: cmengel@bmvpc.com.

MENGEL, DAVID BRUCE, agronomy and soil science educator; b. East Chicago, Ind., May 1, 1948; s. Bill M. and Thelma Lee (Miller) M.; m. Susan Kay Haverstock, Aug. 30, 1968; children: David, Erin. BS in Agricultural Edn., Purdue U., 1970, MS in Agronomy, 1972; PhD in Soil Sci., N.C. State U., 1975. Cert. profl. agronomist, soil scientist. Asst. prof. agronomy La. State U., Crowley, 1975-79, Purdue U., West Lafayette, Ind., 1979-82, assoc. prof., 1982-86, prof. agronomy, 1986-98; prof., head agronomy Kans. State U., Manhattan, Kans., 1998—. Mem. Am Soc. Agronomy, Soil Sci. Soc. Am., Internat. Soil Sci. Soc., Sigma Xi, Gamma Sigma Delta, Epsilon Sigma Phi, Delta Tau Delta. Avocations: fishing, woodworking. Office: Plant Sci Ctr Dept Agronomy Kans State U 2004 Throckmorton Manhattan KS 66506-5501 E-mail: dmengel@ksu.edu.

MENGELING, WILLIAM LLOYD, retired veterinarian, virologist; b. Elgin, Ill., Apr. 1, 1933; s. William Paul and Blanche Joyce (Wormwood) M.; m. Barbara Ann Kethcart, Aug. 23, 1958; children: Michelle, Michael. BS, Kans. State U., 1958, DVM, 1960; MS, Iowa State U., 1966, PhD, 1969. Diplomate M. Coll. Vet. Microbiologists (chmn. 1977-78, bd. dirs. 1975-77). Vet. clinician St. Francis Animal Hosp., Albuquerque, 1960-61; vet. med. officer Nat. Animal Disease Ctr., Ames, Iowa, 1961-69, rsch. leader, 1969—2001, U.S. Sr. Exec. Svc., 1991—; ret., 2001. Cons. numerous state, fed., pvt. U.S. and fgn. agys.; collaborative prof., mem. grad. faculty Iowa State U. Co-editor: Diseases of Swine, 5th, 6th, 7th, 8th editions; contbr. articles to jours., chpts. to books. With U.S. Army, 1953-55. Recipient cert. appreciation USDA, 1978, George Fleming award Brit. Vet. Jour., 1978, Disting. Svc. award USDA, 1984, Gov.'s medal sci. State of Iowa, 1985, Vet. Med. Rsch. award Am. Feed Industry Assn., 1989, Leadership Merit awards USDA, 1989, 90, 91, 93, Alumnus award Kans. State U. Coll. Vet. Medicine and Vet. Med. Alumni Assn., 1999, William P. Switzer award Iowa State U. Coll. Met. Medicine, 2000, Howard Dunne Meml. award, Am. Assn. Swine Vets., 2001; elected to Agrl. Rsch. Svc. Hall of Fame, 2001. Mem. AVMA (Vet. Med. Rsch. award 1989), U.S. Animal Health Assn., Conf. Rsch. Workers in Animal Disease (pres. 1987-88, coun. 1981-86), Kiwanis (pres. 1975-76). Methodist. Avocations: wilderness survival, canoeing, camping, fishing. Home: 4220 Phoenix St Ames IA 50014-3922 E-mail: bbmengeling@aol.com.

MENGLER, THOMAS M. dean; b. May 18, 1953; BA in Philosophy magna cum laude, Carleton Coll., 1975; MA in Philosophy, U. Tex., 1977, JD, 1981. Bar: Ill., Tex., D.C., U.S. Ct. Appeals (5th, 7th and 10th cirs.), U.S. Dist. Ct. (we. dist.) Tex. Law clk. to Hon. James K. Logan U.S. Ct. Appeals for 10thCir., Olathe, Kans., 1980-81; assoc. atty. Arnold & Porter, Washington, 1982-83; asst. atty. gen. Office of Atty. Gen. of Tex., Austin, 1983-85; asst. prof. law U. Ill. Coll. Law, Champaign, 1985-89, assoc. prof., 1989-91, prof. law, 1991—, assoc. dean for acad. affairs, 1992-93, dean, 1993—2002; dean, prof. law U. St. Thomas Sch. Law, Mpls., 2002—. Contbr. numerous articles to profl. jours. Mem. ABA, Ill. State Bar Assn., Order of Coif, Phi Beta Kappa. Office: Univ St Thomas Sch Law Mail TMH 440 1000 LaSalle Ave Minneapolis MN 55403-2005

MENHALL, DALTON WINN, lawyer, insurance executive, professional association administrator; b. Edgerton, Wis., Aug. 1, 1939; s. Joseph Laurence and Mary Winn (Dalton) M.; m. Lilian Marilyn Christie, Oct. 19, 1968; children: Dalton Winn II, Rebecca Lynn, Katherine Elizabeth BA, Ill. Coll., 1962; JD, Vanderbilt U., 1965. Bar: Wis. 1965; cert. assn. exec. Staff asst. State Bar of Wis., Madison, 1965-72, dir., 1972-76, legis. counsel, dir. continuing legal edn., 1972-76; exec. dir. N.J. State Bar Assn., Trenton, 1976-86; nat. programs dir. Herbert L. Jamison & Co., 1987-91; v.p. Edward Poll & Assocs., 1995; exec. dir. San Diego County Bar Assn., 1995—. Trustee St. Patricks' Day Sch., 1994-96. Exec. v.p. Phi Alpha Delta Pub. Svc. Ctr., Washington, 1991-94; exec. dir. Phi Alpha Delta Law Frat. Internat., Granada Hills, Calif., 1992-94; bd. dirs. San Diego unit Am. Cancer Soc., 1996-98, sec.-treas., 1998, pres.-elect, 1998-99, pres., 1999-2000, bd. dirs. Calif. divsn., 1999—; mem. vestry St. John's Episcopal Ch., 1997, sr. warden, 1998-99. Fellow Am. Bar Found.; mem. ABA (cons., youth edn. and citizenship com 1993-97), Nat. Assn. Bar Execs. (pres. 1985-86), N.J. State Bar Assn., State Bar Wis., Am. Soc. Assn. Execs., Am. Judicature Soc., Nat. Assn. Bar Execs. (hon.), So. Calif. Soc. Assn. Execs., San Diego Soc. Assn. Execs. (bd. dirs. 1997-98, sec. 1998-99).

MENIL, VIOLETA CRUZ, mathematician, educator, consultant; BSE in Math. magna cum laude, U. San Carlos, Cebu, Philippines, 1965; MS in Applied Math & Stats., SUNY, Stony Brook, 1983; MA in Math. Edn., De la Salle U., Manila, 1976; PhD in Math. and Stats., NYU, 1988. Lectr. math. Baruch Coll. CUNY, N.Y.C., 1983—88, instr. stats., 1988—89; assoc. prof. De la Salle U., Manila, 1989—94, rsch. dir., 1990—93; asst. prof. Hostos C.C. CUNY, Bronx, 1994—95, CUNY, Bronx, 2000—; audit statistician N.Y.C. Comptroller's Office, 1995—98. Treas. Corner View Assn., Inc., Bklyn., 2001. Recipient Rotary Outstanding Surigaonon award (ROSA), Rotary Internat., Surigao City Chpt., 1998, Most Outstanding Nicolanian award (MONICA), San Nicolas Colege, Surigao City, 1995; Fulbright Hays scholar, Inst. Internat. Edn., 1981-1984. Mem.: Asian Am. Higher Edn. Coun. (nyc 2001—02), Am. Statis. Assn. (va., alexandria 1989—2002). Home: 4407 4th Avenue Apt B4 Brooklyn NY 11220 Personal E-mail: menilv2@aol.com.

MENINGALL, EVELYN L. educational media specialist; b. Dothan, Ala., July 22, 1935; d. Earl and Luella Koonce; m. A. Richard Meningall, Jan. 17, 1958; children: Dawn, Tracy, Richard. BS in Edn., Wayne State U., 1975; MLS, Rutgers U., 1979. Cert. ednl. media specialist Dept. Edn. State N.J., elem. sch. dept. Dept. Edn. State N.J., profl. librs. cert. Dept. Edn. State N.J. Tchr. Detroit Bd. Edn., 1975—76; libr. East Brunswick (N.J.) Pub. Libr., 1978—80; ednl. media specialist Piscataway (N.J.) Bd. Edn., 1980—98; ret., 1998. Author poetry. Active New Detroit, Inc., Delta Sigma Theta Sorority Ctrl. Jersey; vol. tutor/reader pub. schs.; vol. to holisitic score English tests Plainfield (N.J.) H.S.; recording sec. Scholarship Fund of St. Paul AME Ch. Mem.: ALA, Ednl. Media Assn., Nat. Sorority Phi Delta Kappa, Inc. (life; basileus 1987—89, exec. advisor 1989—91). Ame Church. Avocations: poetry, reading, fishing. Home: 23 Vauxhall Rd East Brunswick NJ 08816-1719

MENINO, THOMAS M. mayor; b. Dec. 27, 1942; m. Angela Faletra; children: Susan, Thomas Michael, Jr. Degree in Community Planning, U. Mass., 1988; cert. in State and Local Govt. Program, Harvard U. Mem. City Coun., Boston, 1985—, pres., 1993; mayor City of Boston, 1993—. Sr. rsch. asst. Joint Com. Urban Affairs, 1978-83; pres. U.S. Conf. Mayors, 2003. Contbr. articles to historic preservation jours. Regional chmn. Nat. Trust Historic Preservation; bd. dirs. Nat. League Cities, 1985—, mem. various coms. Office: Office of Mayor 1 City Hall Plz Fl 5 Boston MA 02201-1001

MENIUS, ESPIE FLYNN, JR., electrical engineer; b. New Bern, N.C., Mar. 5, 1923; s. Espie Flynn and Sudie Grey (Lyerly) M.; adopted children: James Benfield, Ruben Hughes, James Sechler, Steve Walden. BEE, N.C. State U., 1947; MBA, U. S.C., 1973. Registered profl. engr., N.C., S.C., Tenn., Ga., Fla. With Carolina Power & Light Co., 1947-63, asst. to dist. mgr., 1947-50, Sumter, SC, 1947-50, elec. engr. Asheville, Southern Pines and Dunn, NC, 1950-52, dist. engr. Hartsville, SC, 1952-63; sr. elec. engr. Sonoco Products Co., 1963-74, engring. group leader, 1974-89, sr. profl. engr., 1989-91; profl. cons. and elec. engr., 1991—. Instr. Florence-Darlington Tech. Ednl. Ctr. Author: Adoption of Older Children; contbr. articles to profl. jours. Active Hartsville Vol. Fire Dept., 1958-94; Fire dept. and Law Enforcement Chaplain 1985—; Eagle Scout Boy Scouts Am., 1938, scout troop leader New Bern, 1940-41, Raleigh, 1941-47, Henderson, 1948-49, Sumter, 1949-50, Asheville, N.C., 1950, Southern Pines, N.C., 1951-52, Hartsville, 1952-64; bd. mgrs. Nazareth Children's Home, Rockwell, N.C., 1980—; chmn. bd. examiners City of Hartsville, 1980-90; advocate Thornwell Children's Home, Clinton, S.C., 1990—; bd. dir. Darlington (S.C.) County Youth Home, 1992—; active Hartsville Leadership Coun., 1993—; deacon, elder, trustee, tchr. men's Bible class First Presbyn. Ch., Hartsville. Served with US Army, 1943-46. Recipient Citizenship award S.C. State Firemen's Assn., 1993; named Hartsville Citizen of Yr., Rotary, 1960; named to S.C. Fire Fighters Hall of Fame, 1995. Mem. IEEE, AAAS, VFW, Nat. Assn. Engrs., Am. Legion, Knight of St. Patrick, Scabbard and Blade, Eta Kappa Nu, Pine Burr, Phi Eta Sigma, Theta Tau, Beta Gamma Sigma. Presbyn. Home and Office: 423 W Richardson Cir Hartsville SC 29550-5437 Office Phone: 843-332-8502.

MENK, CARL WILLIAM, executive search company executive; b. Newark, Oct. 19, 1921; s. Carl William and Catherine Regina (Murray) M.; m. Elizabeth Cullum, May 31, 1947; children: Carl, Elizabeth (dec.), Mary, Paul. BSBA, Seton Hall U., 1943; MA, Columbia U., 1950. Sr. v.p. P. Ballantine & Sons, Newark, 1946-69; pres. Boyden Assocs., Inc., N.Y.C., 1969-84; chmn. Canny, Bowen, Inc., N.Y.C., 1984-98, chmn. emeritus, 1998—. Trustee Howard Savs. Bank, 1980—91. 2d lt. pilot USAAF, 1943—46. Mem. Union League NY, Spring Lake Golf Club, John's Island Club, Internat. Exec. Svc. Corps. Republican. Roman Catholic. Home: 950 Beach Rd Apt 193 Johns Island Vero Beach FL 32963

MENKE, ALLEN CARL, industrial corporation executive; b. Huntingburg, Ind., Feb. 16, 1922; s. William Ernest and Clara (Moenkhaus) M.; m. Virginia Lee MacDonald, Apr. 14, 1944; children: Janet, William, Sarah. BS in Mech. Engring, Purdue U., 1943, MS, 1948. Instr. Purdue U., 1946-48; with Trane Co., 1948-68, v.p. sales, 1963-64, exec. v.p. sales, mfg. and engring., 1964-68; v.p. Borg-Warner Corp., Chgo., 1969-76; chmn., pres., CEO Artesian Industries, Northbrook, Ill., 1976-88. Bd. dirs. Trane Co., SPS Techs., Hoover Co., Consolidated Papers Corp., York Corp., Am. Air Filter. Pres. Met. Housing Devel. Corp.; founder, pres. Winnetka Interch. Coun.; bd. dirs., past chmn. Presbyn. Home; past chmn. dean's adv. coun. Krannert Sch. Mgmt. Purdue U.; bd. dirs. McCormick Sem., U. Chgo.; trustee Kenilworth Union Ch. Served to 1st lt. AUS, 1944-46. Named Disting. Alumnus, Purdue U., 1965, Outstanding Engr. Grad., 1991, mem. Purdue Hall of Fame, Ind. Basketball Hall of Fame, 1999. Mem. Sigma Chi (Significant Order Constantine awards). Presbyterian (elder). Lodge: Mason. Home: 2 Arbor Ln #208 Evanston IL 60201

MENKEL-MEADOW, CARRIE JOAN, law educator; b. N.Y.C., Dec. 24, 1949; d. Gary G. and Margot (Sinn) Menkel; m. Robert Gary Meadow, Aug. 22, 1971. AB magna cum laude, Columbia U., 1971; JD cum laude, U. Pa., 1974; LLD (hon.), Quinnipiac Coll. Law, 1995. Bar: Pa. 1974, U.S. Ct. Appeals (3d cir.) 1975, Calif. 1979, D.C., 1997. Dir. legal writing U. Pa. Law Sch., Phila., 1974-75, clin. supt., lectr., 1976-79; staff atty. Cmty. Legal Svcs., Phila., 1975-77; prof. UCLA, 1979—, prof. law, 1979-99, Georgetown Law Ctr., Washington, 1996—; holder Phyllis Beck chair Temple U. Law Sch., Phila., 1999. Vis. prof. law Harvard Law Sch., 2001; panel mem. NAS, Washington, 1986—87, NSF, Washington, 1987—90; cons. ABA, Chgo., 1979—84; dir. UCLA Ctr. for Conflict Resolution, 1994—99, Georgetown-Hewlett Program on Conflict Resolution and Problem Solving, 2001—. Author: Mediation: Theory, Practice and Policy, 2000, Dispute Processing: Theory, Practice and Policy, 2003, What's Fair: Ethics for Negotiators, 2004, Dispute Resolution: Beyond the Adversarial Model, 2004; editor-in-chief Jour. Legal Edn., 2003—; contbr. articles to profl. jours. Chairperson Ctr. for Study of Women, UCLA; bd. dirs. Western Ctr. on Law and Poverty, L.A., 1980-86; chair CPR Commn. on Ethics and ADR. Recipient William Rutter Found. for Tchg. award, 1992, 1st prize for Acad. Scholarship on Alternative Dispute Resolution Ctr. for Pub. Resources, 1983, 91, 98. Mem.: Acad. Civil Trial Mediators, Am. Law Inst., Am. Bar Found. (bd. dir., sec., exec. com. 1994—), Law and Soc. Assn. (trustee), Ctr. for Law and Human Values (bd. dir.), Assn. Am. Law Schs. (alt. dispute resolution sect., law and social sci. sect., women in law sect., accreditation com. 1987—90, editor-in-chief Jour. of Legal Edn. 2004—), Soc. Am. Law Tchrs. (trustee), Phi Beta Kappa. Democrat. Office: Georgetown Law Ctr 600 New Jersey Ave NW Washington DC 20001-2075 E-mail: meadow@law.georgetown.edu.

MENKEN, ALAN, composer; b. New Rochelle, N.Y., July 22, 1949; Student, NYU. Composer, lyricist, performer Lehman Engel Mus. Theatre Workshop at BMI; ptnr. with Howard Ashman. Works include: (theatre) Off-Broadway debut God Bless You, Mr. Rosewater, (with Howard Ashman) Little Shop of Horrors, Kicks, The Apprenticeship of Duddy Kravitz, Diamonds, Personals, Let Freedom Sing, Weird Romance, Beauty and the Beast, A Christmas Carol; (films) Little Shop of Horrors, 1986 (Acad. award nominee for best original score 1986), The Little Mermaid, 1988 (Acad. award for best original score 1989, Acad. award for best original song 1989), Beauty and the Beast, 1990 (Acad. award for best original score 1991, Acad. award for best original song 1991), Newsies, 1992, Aladdin, 1992, (Acad. award for best original score 1993, Acad. award best original song 1993, 3 Grammy awards 1994), Lincoln, 1992, Life With Mikey, 1993; (with Stephen Schwartz) Pocahontas, 1995 (Golden Globe award 1996, Acad. award for best original score 1996, Acad. award for best original song 1996). Office: The Shukat Co 340 W 55th St Apt 1A New York NY 10019-3744

MENKEN, JANE AVA, demographer, educator; b. Phila., Nov. 29, 1939; d. Isaac Nathan and Rose Ida (Sarvetnick) Golubitsky; m. Matthew Menken, 1960 (div. 1985); children: Kenneth Lloyd, Kathryn Lee; m. Richard Jessor, Nov. 13, 1992. AB, U. Pa., 1960; MS, Harvard U., 1962; PhD, Princeton (N.J.) U., 1975. Asst. in biostats. Harvard U. Sch. Pub. Health, Boston, 1962-64; math. statistician NIMH, Bethesda, Md., 1964-66; rsch. assoc. dept. biostats. Columbia U., N.Y.C., 1966-69; mem. rsch. staff Office of Population Rsch. Princeton U., 1969-71, 75-87, asst. dir., 1978-86, assoc. dir., 1986-87, prof. sociology, 1980-82, prof. sociology and pub. affairs, 1982-87; prof. sociology and demography U. Pa., Phila., 1987-97, UPS Found. prof. social scis., 1987-97, dir. Population Studies Ctr., 1989-95; prof. sociology U. Colo., Boulder, 1997—, faculty assoc. Population Program, Inst. Behavioral Sci., 1997—; dir. Population Aging Ctr., 2000—, Inst. Behavioral Sci., 2001—, disting. prof., 2002—. Mem. social scis. and population study sect., NIH, Bethesda, 1978-82, chmn., 1980-82, population adv. com. Rockefeller Found., N.Y.C., 1981-93, com. on population and demography, NAS, Washington, 1978-83, com. on population, 1983-85, 1996-2002, chair 1998-2002, com. nat. stats., 1983-89, com. on AIDS rsch., 1987-93, chair 1990-93; co-chair panel data and rsch. priorities for arresting AIDS in sub-Saharan Africa, 1994-96, Com. on Behavioral and Social Scis. and Edn., 1991-97, sci. adv. com., Demographic and Health Surveys, Columbia, Md., 1985-90, Nat. Adv. Child Health and Human Devel. Coun., 1988-91; dir. adv. com. NIH, 1995-2000, adv. coun. Fogarty Internat. Ctr., 2000-02, cons. Internat. Centre for Diarrhoeal Disease Rsch., Bangladesh, Dhaka, 1984—. Author: (with Mindel C. Sheps) Mathematical Models of Conception and Birth, 1973; editor: (with Henri Leridon) Natural Fertility, 1979, (with Frank Furstenberg, Jr. and Richard Lincoln) Teenage Sexuality, Pregnancy and Childbearing, 1981, World Population and U.S. Policy: The Choices Ahead, 1986; contbr. articles to profl. jours. Bd. dirs. Alan Guttmacher Inst., N.Y.C., 1981-90, 93-2000, African Population and Health Rsch. Ctr., Nairobi, Kenya, 2000—. Nat. Merit scholar, 1957; John Simon Guggenheim Found. fellow, 1992-93, Ctr. for Advanced Study in Behavioral Scis. fellow, 1995-96. Fellow AAAS, Am. Statis. Assn.; mem. NAS, Inst. of Medicine, Am. Acad. Arts and Scis.,

Population Assn. Am. (pres. 1985, Mindel Sheps award 1982), Am. Pub. Health Assn. (Mortimer Spiegelman award 1975), Am. Sociol. Assn., Soc. for Study of Social Biology, Internat. Union for Sci. Study of Population (coun. 1989-97), Sociol. Rsch. Assn. (exec. com. 1991-96, pres. 1996). Office: U Colo IBS#1 483 UCB Boulder CO 80309-0483 Office Phone: 303-492-8148. Business E-Mail: menken@colorado.edu.

MENKES, JOHN HANS, pediatric neurologist; b. Vienna, Dec. 20, 1928; came to U.S., 1940; s. Karl and Valerie (Tupler) M.; m. Miriam Trief, Apr. 14, 1957 (div. Feb. 1978); m. Joan Simon Feld, Sept. 28, 1980 (dec. Nov. 2000); children: Simon, Tamara, Rafael C.; m. Myrna Fox (July 1, 2004). AB, U. So. Calif., 1947, MS, 1951; MD, Johns Hopkins U., 1952. Diplomate Am. Bd. Pediat., Am. Bd. Psychiatry and Neurology. Intern, jr. asst. resident Children's Med. Ctr., Boston, 1952-54; asst. resident pediat. Bellevue Hosp., N.Y.C., 1956-57; resident neurology, trainee pediatric neurology Columbia-Presbyn. Med. Ctr., Neurol. Inst. N.Y., N.Y.C., 1957-60; asst. prof. pediat. Johns Hopkins U., Balt., 1960-63, assoc. prof., 1963-66, asst. prof. neurology, 1964-66, chief pediatric neurology divsn., 1964-66; prof. pediat. and neurology UCLA, 1966-74, chief pediatric neurology divsn., 1966-70, prof. psychiatry, 1970-74; chief Neurology-Neurochem. Lab. Brentwood (Calif.) VA Hosp., 1970-74; clin. prof. psychiatry, neurology and pediat. UCLA, 1974-77, clin. prof. pediat. and neurology, 1977-84, prof. pediat. and neurology, 1985-89, prof. emeritus pediat. and neurology, 1989—. Dir. pediatric neurology Cedars-Sinai Med. Ctr., 1997-99, dir. emeritus pediat. neurology, 1999—; mem. metabolism study sect. NIH, 1968-70, project com., 1969-70; mem. adv. com. Nat. Inst. Child Health and Human Devel., 1985-87; mem. Dept. Health Svcs., Calif., 1980-87; mem. vaccine safety commn. Nat. Inst. Medicine, 1995—; mem. Coun. Child Neurology Soc., Dysautonomia Found., med. adv. bd. Nat. Orgn. Rare Diseases, Nat. Wilson's Disease Found.; trustee Dystonia Med. Rsch. Found., Vancouver, Can., 1985—. Author: Textbook of Child Neurology, 6th edit., 2000; (play) The Last Inquisitor, 1985 (Drama-Logue Critics award 1985), The Salvation of Miguel Toruna, 1987; (screen play) Miguel, Open Ward, 1989, The Countess of Sligo, 1992, The White Darkness, 1996, Lady Macbeth Gets a Divorce, 2001, Native Born, 2003; (novels) The Secret Diary of Alice in Wonderland, 1998, The Angry Puppet Syndrome, 1999, After the Tempest, 2003, The Waiting Game, 2000, A View of Fuji, 2000; contbr. numerous articles to profl. jours. Served with USAF, 1954-56. Mem. Am. Acad. Neurology, Am. Acad. Pediatrics, Am. Chem. Soc., Soc. for Pediatric Rsch., Sociedad Peruana de Neuro-Psiquiatria (hon.), Am. Neurochem. Soc., Am. Neurol. Assn., Am. Pediatric Soc., Child Neurology Soc. (Hower award 1980), Dramatist Guild, PEN. Jewish. Home: 10375 Wilshire Blvd Apt 11H Los Angeles CA 90024-4749 Office: 9320 Wilshire Blvd Beverly Hills CA 90212-3216 Office Phone: 310-246-6582. E-mail: jmenkes@ucla.edu., jhansmenk@aol.com.

MENN, JULIUS JOEL, scientist; b. Danzig, Free City (now Poland), Feb. 20, 1929; came to the U.S., 1950, naturalized, 1959; s. David Gregory and Regina (Ajzenstadt) M.; m. Alma R. Zito, Aug. 31, 1952 (div. 1981); children: Leslie, David (dec.), Diana (dec.); m. Dianne R. Sagner, Apr. 17, 1992. BS, U. Calif., Berkeley, 1953, MS, 1954, PhD, 1958. Dir. biochem. and insecticide rsch. Stauffer Chem. Co., Mountain View, Calif., 1957-79; dir. agrichem. rsch. Zoecon Corp., Palo Alto, Calif., 1979-85; nat. program leader crop protection Agrl. Rsch. Svc., USDA, Beltsville, Md., 1985-88; assoc. dep. area dir. Beltsville Agrl. Rsch. Ctr., 1988-94; ret., 1994; sr. agrl. policy adviser USDA/FAS, 1999—. Internat. cons. crop protection and agr. biotechnology, 1994-; chmn. Gordon Rsch. Conf., 1989; adj. prof. environ. toxicology San Jose State U., Calif., 1979-84; adj. prof. entomology U. Md., College Park, 1986-95; vis. prof. Pa. State U., 1999-2002; mem. U.S./USSR Team on Environ. Pollution, 1974-85; tech. expert UNIDO, UNDCP, 1995—. The World Bank, 1998. Editor: Insect Juvenile Hormones, 1972, Insect Neuropeptides, 1991, 12 other tech. books; contbr. over 125 articles to profl. jours. Recipient Bussart Meml. award Ea. Br. Entomol. Soc. Am., 1990, Ciba-Geigy Recognition award Ea. Br. Entomol. Soc. Am., 1991, 92. Mem. Am. Chem. Soc. (fellow pesticide chem. divsn. 1973, chmn. 1976, councilor 1981-89, adv. bd. books dept. 1991-94, Agrochem. Divsn. Internat. award for rsch. in pesticide chem. 1979), Internat. Soc. Study Xenobiotics (councilor 1983-86). Achievements include pioneered pesticide metabolism studies and research on selective insect control agents including juvenile hormones and neuropeptides; patentee in field. E-mail: menn03@comcast.net.

MENN, LISE, linguistics educator; b. Phila., Dec. 28, 1941; d. David K. and Olga (Cohen) Waldman; m. Michael D. Menn, Dec. 8, 1962 (div. Mar. 1974); children: Stephen Philip, (Daniel) Joseph; m. William Oliver Bright, Nov. 28, 1986. BA, Swarthmore Coll., 1962; MA, Brandeis U., 1964, U. Ill., 1974, PhD, 1975. Rsch. asst. Boston U. Sch. Medicine, 1977-82, rsch. asst. prof. dept. neurology, 1982-86; assoc. prof. U. Colo., Boulder, 1986-94, prof., 1994—, chair dept. linguistics, 1991-95, 96-99, 2003—04. Linguistics panel NSF, 1983-86; mem. comm. disorders rev. group NIH, 1992-95; adj. prof. Hunan U., 2001—, guest prof., 2004—. Co-author: Nonfluent Aphasia in a Multilingual World, 1995; co-editor: Exceptional Language Linguistics, 1982, Agrammatic Aphasia, 1990, Phonological Development, 1992, Methods for Study of Language Production, 2000; assoc. editor Aphasiology. Mem. AAAS (sect. linguistics), Linguistic Soc. Am. (exec. com. 1994-97), Acad. Aphasia (sec. bd. govs. 1989-92, bd. govs. 2000-03). Office: U Colo Linguistics Dept PO Box 295 Boulder CO 80309-0295 Business E-Mail: lise.menn@colorado.edu.

MENN, STEPHEN EDWARD, lawyer; b. Houston, July 30, 1956; s. Richard Max and Joyce Pearl Menn. BS in Polit. Sci., BA in Econ., U. Houston, 1979; JD, Tex. Tech U., Lubbock, 1983. Bar: Tex. 1983. Proprietor Law Office of Stephen Menn, Houston, 1991—. Author: Cold Hard Truth About Golf, 2000. Mason Tex. Freemasons, Houston. Mem.: Harris County Bar Assn. (treas. 1998—). Republican. Methodist. Avocation: golf. Office: Law Office of Stephen E Menn PO Box 572774 Houston TX 77257 E-mail: stephen_menn@sbcglobal.net.

MENNING, DALEENE YVONNE, artist, art educator, sculptor; b. Palo Alto, Calif., Aug. 7, 1938; d. Dallas Alma Tueller and Essie Maxine Anderson Tueller; m. Curtis Boyd Menning, Mar. 30, 1961; children: Lee Curtis, Meta Elizabeth. BS in Design, U. Mich., 1964, MFA, 1970. Prof. art Grand Valley State U., Allendale, Mich., 1973—2004. Lectr. Loosemore Auditorium, 2001. Prin. works include mural, Grand Rapids Spectrum Heart Hosp., 2004, Henry Hall, Grand Valley State U.; contbr. articles to periodical featured in Studio Potter and Ceramic Monthly; exhibitions include Juried Festival Exhbn., 1989 (Festival award, 1st prize, 1989), Detroit Inst. Art, 1993 (Purchase prize, 1993), Muskegon Mus. Art, 1995 (2nd prize, 1995). Mem.: Mich. Ceramic Artists Soc. Democrat. Mem. Lds Ch. Avocation: gardening. Home: 6009 W Leonard Rd Coopersville MI 49404

MENNINGER, ROY WRIGHT, medical foundation executive, psychiatrist; b. Topeka, Oct. 27, 1926; s. William Claire and Catharine (Wright) M.; m. Beverly Joan Miller, Mar. 4, 1973; children: Heather, Ariel, Bonar, Eric, Brent, Frederick, Elizabeth. AB, Swarthmore (Pa.) Coll., 1947; MD, Cornell U., 1951; DHL, Ottawa (Kans.) U., 1977; LittD, William Jewell Coll., Liberty Mo., 1985. Diplomate Am. Bd. Psychiatry and Neurology, 1959. Intern N.Y. Hosp., 1951-52; resident in psychiatry Boston State Hosp., 1952-53, Boston Psychopathic Hosp., 1953-56; from resident psychiatrist to assoc. med. psychiatrist Peter Bent Brigham Hosp., Boston, 1956-61; teaching and rsch. fellow Harvard U. Med. Sch., Boston, 1956-61; staff psychiatrist Menninger Found., Topeka, 1961-63, dir. dept. preventive psychiatry, 1963-67, pres., CEO, 1967-93, chmn. trustees, 1991—. Bd. dirs. Bank IV Topeka N.A., CML Corp., The New Eng., U.S. Behavioral Health; mem. Karl Menninger Sch. Psychiatry, Topeka, 1972—, Ind. Sector, 1990—; clin. prof. psychiatry U. Kans. Med. Ctr., Wichita, 1977—; cons. Colmery-O'Neil VA Med. Ctr., Topeka, 1979—. Author: Trends in American Psychiatry: Implication for Psychiatry in Japan; co-author: The Medical Marriage, 1988, The Psychology of Postponement in the Medical Marriage; cons. editor Jour. Medical Aspects Human Sexuality, 1967-90; editor adv. bd. Parents mag., 1966-80, Clin. Psychiatry News, 1973—; reviewer Am. Jour. Psychiatry, 1980—. Mem. sponsoring com. Inst. Am. Democracy, 1967-70; mem. adv. group Horizons '76 Am. Revolution Bicentennial Commn.; adv. bd., steering com. Topeka Inst. Urban Affairs, 1967-70; adv. bd. Highland Park-Pierce Neighborhood House, Topeka, 1967-70; bd. dirs. Shawnee council Campfire Girls, Topeka, 1962-69, A.K. Rice Inst., Washington, Sex Info. and Edn. Council U.S., 1972-73, mem. edn. com., long range planning com., 1972-73; bd. dirs. Goals for Topeka, Topeka Inst. Urban Affairs, 1969-74, v.p., 1973; med. adv. com. VA Hosp., 1972-78; mem. Gov.'s Com. on Criminal Adminstrn., 1971-74; trustee People-to-People, Kansas City, Mo., 1967-69, Baker U., 1968-72, Midwest Research Inst., 1967-1986, 86—, mem. exec. com., 1970-86; vis. lectr. Fgn. Service Inst., State Dept., 1963-66; chmn. social issues com. Group Advancement Psychiatry, 1972-82; community adv. bd. Kans. Health Workers Union, 1968-70; adv. com. to bd. dirs. New Eng. Mut. Life Ins. Co., 1968-70. With U.S. Army, 1953-55. Recipient Disting. Svs. citation U. Kans., 1985; Pacific Rim Coll. Psychiatry fellow. Fellow Am. Psychiat. Assn. (life), Joint Info. Svc. (exec. com.), Am. Coll. Psychiatry, Am. Orthopsychiat. Assn., Am. Coll. Mental Health Adminstrs.; mem. AAAS, Northeastern Group Psychotherapy (hon.), Physicians Social Responsibility, Kans. Psychiat. Soc., Greater Topeka C. of C. (dir.). Episcopalian. Avocations: stamp collecting/philately, chamber music, microcomputers. Office: Menningers PO Box 809045 Houston TX 77280

MENNINGER, WILLIAM WALTER, psychiatrist; b. Topeka, Oct. 23, 1931; s. William Claire and Catharine Louisa (Wright) Menninger; m. Constance Arnold Libbey, June 15, 1953; children: Frederick Prince, John Alexander, Eliza Wright, Marian Stuart, William Libbey, David Henry. AB, Stanford U., 1953; MD, Cornell U., 1957; LittD (hon.), Middlebury Coll., 1982; DSc (hon.), Washburn U., 1982; LHD (hon.), Ottawa U., 1986; LLD (hon.), Heidelberg Coll., 1993. Diplomate Am. Bd. Psychiatry and Neurology, Am. Bd. Forensic Psychiatry. Intern Harvard Med. Svc., Boston City Hosp., 1957-58; resident in psychiatry Menninger Sch. Psychiatry, 1958-61; chief med. officer, psychiatrist Fed. Reformatory, El Reno, Okla., 1961-63; assoc. psychiatrist Peace Corps, 1963-64; staff psychiatrist Menninger Found., Topeka, 1965—, coordinator for devel., 1967-69, dir. law and psychiatry, 1981-85, dir. dept. edn., dean Karl Menninger Sch. Psychiatry and Mental Health Scis., 1984-90, exec. v.p., chief staff, 1984-93, CEO, 1993—2001, pres., 1993—96, 1999—2001, chmn. bd. trustees, 2001—; clin. supr. Topeka State Hosp., 1969-70, sect. dir., 1970-72, asst. supt., clin., dir. residency tng., 1972-81; pres. Menninger Clinic, Topeka, 1991-96; staff Stormont-Vail Hosp., Topeka, 1984-94, assoc., 1994—2002. Adj. prof. Washburn U.; mem. Fed. Prision Facilities Planning Coun., 1970—73; mem. adv. bd. Nat. Inst. Corrections, 1975—88, chmn., 1980—84; cons. U.S. Bur. Prisons; mem. adv. bd. US Bank, Topeka, 1999—. Syndicated columnist: In-Sights, 1975—83; author: (book) Happiness Without Sex and Other Things Too Good to Miss, 1976, Caution: Living May Be Hazardous, 1978, Behavioral Science and the Secret Service, 1981, Chronic Mental Patient II, 1987; editor: Psychiatry Digest, 1971—74, Bull. of Menninger Clinic, 2001—; contbr. articles to profl. jours., chpts. to books. Mem. health and safety com. Boy Scouts Am., 1970—, chmn., 1980—85, mem. nat. exec. bd., 1980—90, mem. nat. health and safety com., 1990—; bd. dirs. Nat. Com. Prevention Child Abuse, 1975—83; mem. nat. adv. health coun. HEW, 1967—71; mem. Nat. Commn. Causes and Prevention Violence, 1968—69; rsch. adv. com. U.S. Secret Svc., 1990—; pres. Jayhawk coun. Boy Scouts Am., 1998—2001; mem. Kans. Gov.'s Adv. Commn. Mental Health, Mental Retardation an dCmty. Mental Health Svcs., 1983—90, Kans. Gov.'s Penal Planning Coun., 1970; chmn. Kans. Gov.'s Criminal Justice Coun., 1970; active Kans. Gov.'s Commn. on Crime Reduction and Prevention/Koch Commn., 1994—98; ruling elder 1st Presbyn. Ch., Topeka, 1992—95; trustee Kenworthy-Swift Found., 1980—; bd. dirs. Police Found., Washington, 1996—, Koch Crime Inst., 1998—2000; trustee Midwest Rsch. Inst., Kansas City, Mo., 1996—. With USPHS, 1959—64. Fellow: ACP, Am. Coll. Psychiatrists, Am. Psychiat. Assn. (chmn. com. chronically mentally ill 1984—86, chmn. Guttmacher award bd. 1990—96); mem.: AMA, AAAS, Am. Acad. Psychiatry and Law, Am. Psychoanalytic Assn. (chmn. com. psychoanalysis, cmty. and soc. 1984—93), Inst. Medicine NAS, Group Advancement Psychiatry (chmn. com. mental health svcs. 1974—77, 1991—2002), Stanford Assocs. Office: PO Box 4406 Topeka KS 66604-0406 Office Phone: 785-235-3400.

MENNIS, EDMUND ADDI, investment management consultant; b. Allentown, Pa., Aug. 12, 1919; s. William Henry and Grace (Addi) M.; m. Selma Adinoff, Sept. 25, 1945; children: Ardith Grace, Daniel Liam. BA, CCNY, 1941; MA, Columbia U., 1946; PhD, NYU, 1961. Security analyst Eastman, Dillon & Co., N.Y.C., 1945-46; sr. rsch. asst. Am. Inst. Econ. Rsch., Great Barrington, Mass., 1946-50; security analyst Wellington Mgmt. Co., Phila., 1950-61, dir. rsch., 1958-61, v.p., mem. investment com., 1958-66, economist, 1953-66; sr. v.p., chmn. trust investment com. Republic Nat. Bank, Dallas, 1966-72; sr. v.p., chmn. investment policy com. Security Pacific Nat. Bank, L.A., 1973-81; pres., dir. Bunker Hill Income Securities, Inc., 1973-81; chmn. bd. Security Pacific Investment Mgrs., Inc., 1977-81; ind. cons. to investment mgmt. orgns., 1982—. Tech. cons. Bus. Coun., Washington, 1962-66, 72-77, 79-81; econ. adviser sec. commerce, 1967-68; mem. investment adv. panel Pension Benefit Guaranty Corp., 1981-83. Author: How the Economy Works, 1991, 2d edit., 1999, Chinese edit., 2000; assoc. editor Fin. Analysts Jour., 1960-88; editor: C.F.A. Digest, 1971-86, Bus. Econs., 1985-99, editor emeritus, 2000—; editor: Banker's Econ. & Investment Alert, 1993—; author or editor books, chpts., numerous articles in field of econs. and investments. Trustee Fin. Analysts Rsch. Found., 1981-86. 1st lt. USAAF, 1942-45; capt. USAF, 1951-53. Fellow Nat. Assn. Bus. Economists (coun. 1967-69, David L. Williams Lifetime Achievement award 1996); mem. Fin. Analysts Fedn. (dir. 1970-72, Graham and Dodd award 1972, Molodovsky award 1972), Am. Econ. Assn., Am. Fin. Assn., L.A. Soc. Fin. Analysts, Conf. Bus. Econ. (vice chmn. 1977, chmn. 1978), Inst. CFAs (pres. 1970-72, trustee 1968-74, C. Stewart Sheppard award 1978). Home: 721 Paseo Del Mar Palos Verdes Estates CA 90274-1222 Office: PO Box 1146 Palos Verdes Estates CA 90274-7946 Office Phone: 310-373-3270. Personal E-mail: eamennis@cox.net.

MENO, JOHN PETER, chorepiscopus; b. Carlinville, Ill., Aug. 22, 1942; s. John Victor and Margaret Mary (Cena) M.; m. Rolanda A. Abyad, Sept. 14, 1968; 1 child, Peter James. MA, Am. U. Beirut, 1969; STM, Union Theol. Sem., 1972. Ordained priest Syrian Orthodox Ch. of Antioch, 1972, elevated to chorepiscopus, 1983. Gen. sec. Archdiocese of Syrian Orthodox Ch. in the U.S. and Can., Lodi, NJ, 1972—95; cathedral dean St. Mark's Syrian Orthodox Cathedral, Teaneck, NJ, 1975—; gen. sec. Archdiocese of the Syrian Orthodox Ch. for the Ea. U.S., Teaneck, 1996—. Co-sec. Standing Conf. of Oriental Orthodox Chs. in Am., N.Y.C., 1973—; co-chmn. U.S. Roman Cath.-Oriental Orthodox Cons., 1989—. Editor: Hymns of the Syrian Orthodox Church of Antioch, 1976; contbr. The Oriental Orthodox Chs. in the U.S., 1986, Dictionary of Christianity in America, 1990, Oriental Orthodox-Roman Catholic Interchurch Marriages and Other Pastoral Relationships, 1995, Nelson's New Christian Dictionary, 2001, The Encyclopedia of Christianity, 2003. Recipient Golden Cross of the Archdiocese of the Syrian Orthodox Ch. in U.S., and Can., 1992. Syrian Orthodox. Home: 263 Elm Ave Teaneck NJ 07666-2323 Office: St Mark's Syrian Orthodox Cathedral 260 Elm Ave Teaneck NJ 07666-2318 Office Phone: 201-907-0122.

MENOTTI, GIAN CARLO, composer; b. Cadegliano, Italy, July 7, 1911; came to U.S., 1928; s. Alfonso and Ines (Pellini) M. Grad. in composition, Curtis Inst. Music, 1933, Mus.B. (hon.), 1945. Tchr. Curtis Inst. Music, 1941-45. Writer chamber music, songs and operas; composer: (operas) Amelia al ballo, 1936, The Old Maid and the Thief, 1939, The Island God, 1942, The Medium, 1945 (Pulitzer Prize for music 1950), The Telephone, 1947, The Consul, 1949; Amahl and the Night Visitors, 1951, The Saint of Bleecker Street, 1954 (Pulitzer Prize for music 1955, Drama Critics' Circle Award 1955, New York Music Critics' Award 1955), Maria Golovin, 1958, The Last Savage, 1963, Labyrinth, 1963, Martin's Lie, 1964, Help, Help, the Globolinks, 1968, The Most Important Man, 1971, Arrival, 1973, Tamu-Tamu, 1973, The Egg, 1976, The Hero, 1976, The Trial of the Gypsy, 1978, Chip and His Dog, 1979, La loca, 1979, The Mad Woman, 1979, St. Teresa, 1982, A Bride from Pluto, 1982, The Boy Who Grew Too Fast, 1982, Goya, 1986, Giorino di Nozze, 1988; (symphonies/orchestral) Pastorale and Dance, 1934, (from Amelia al ballo) Prelude, 1937, (from The Old Maid and the Thief) Prelude, 1939, (from The Island God) Two Interludes, 1942, Piano Concert in F, 1945, Sebastian, 1945, Apocalypse, 1951, Introduction, March Shepherds' Dance, 1951, Violin Concerto, 1952, Triple Concerto a tre, 1970, Fantasia, 1975, Symphony No. 1: The Halcyon, 1976, Double Bass Concerto, 1983; (chamber/instrumental) Variations on a Theme of Schumann, 1931, Six Compositions, 1934, Four Pieces, 1936, Trio for a House-Warming Party, 1936, Poemetti per Maria Rosa, 1937, Ricercare e toccata, 1949, Suite, 1973, Cantilena scherzo, 1977; (vocal/choral) Baba's Aria, 1946, The Black Swan, 1946, Monica's Waltz, 1946, Lucy's Aria, 1947, Magda's Aria, 1950, Shepherd's Chorus, 1951, The Hero, 1952, The Death of the Bishop of Brindisi, 1963, Canti della lontananza, 1967, Landscapes and Remembrances, 1976, Missa o pulchritudo, 1979, Four Songs, 1981, Notturno, 1982, Muero porque no muero, 1982; (ballets) Sebastian, 1944, Errand in the Maze, 1947, The Unicorn, the Gorgon and the Manticore, or The Three Sundays of a Poet, 1956; writer own libretti.; Founder: Festival of Two Worlds, Spoleto, Italy, 1958; composer, artistic dir. Spoleto Festival USA, Charleston, S.C., 1988—. Recipient Guggenheim award, 1946, 47; Honorary associate, Nat'l Inst. for Arts and Letters, 1953, Kennedy Ctr. award, 1984, N.Y.C. Mayor's Liberty award, 1986; George Peabody Medal, Johns Hopkins Univ., 1987; named Musician of Yr., Musical Am., 1991. Mem. ASCAP.*

MENOUTIS, JAMES VASSILLIOS, research scientist; b. Hollis, N.Y., Oct. 3, 1954; s. Vassillios Dimitrios and Evangelia Eliadis M.; m. Angela Irene Parisi, July 3, 1976; children: William, Mary, Stephen, Jonathan. BS in Chemistry, N.J. City U., 1977; MA in Chemistry, Upsala Coll., 1979; PhD in Chemistry, Am. Western U., 1981. Cert. profl. chemist. Toxicology technician U.S. Testing Co., Hoboken, N.J., 1974-75; lab. supr. MetPath/Quest Clin. Labs., Teterboro, N.J., 1981-82; sr. scientist Givaudan Corp., Clifton, N.J., 1983-85; dir. R&D Intech BioLabs., East Brunswick, N.J., 1985-86; founder, CEO Analab, Inc., Edison, N.J., 1987-92; mng. dir. Lab. Tech. Venture Ptnrs. LLC, Princeton, N.J., 1992-95; CEO, sr. prin. scientist Quantex Labs., Edison, N.J., 1995—. Tech. cons. Witco Chem. Co., Perth Amboy, N.J., 1980-82; dir. CCS LLC, Cooper City, Fla., 2000—. Author: Dioxin: A Current Overview of the Occurance, Toxicity and Disposal of 2,3,7,8-Tetrachlorodibenzo-p-dioxin, 1984; editor: Cons. Guide Tech. Rev. Series Jour., 1990; contbr. articles to profl. jours. Fellow Am. Inst. Chemists; mem. Am. Chem. Soc., Nat. Assn. Rocketry. Office: Quantex Labs 22 Distribution Blvd Edison NJ 08817

MENOYO, ERIC FELIX, lawyer; b. N.Y.C., May 9, 1944; s. Enrique and Frances (Villela) M.; m. Deirdre Caitlin Ryan, Aug. 12, 1967; children: Eric Edward, Sarah Micela Holch. AB in English, Georgetown U., 1966, JD, 1969; LLM in Taxation, NYU, 1975. Bar: N.Y. 1969, Mass. 1976, U.S. Dist. Ct. (ea. dist.) Mass. 1976, U.S. Ct. Appeals (1st cir.) 1976. Assoc. Barrett Smith Schapiro & Simon, N.Y.C., 1969-76, Palmer & Dodge, Boston, 1976-77, ptnr., 1978—. Lectr. law Northeastern U., 1986-87, Mass. Continuing Legal Edn., Boston, 1978—; trustee Cora du Bois Charitable Trust, 1995-. Trustee Nashoba-Brooks Sch. Concord (Mass.), Inc., 1984-90, 1st Parish Sudbury, 1979-82, Sudbury Valley Trustees, Inc., 1991—, pres., 1994-96. Fellow Am. Coll. Trust and Estate Counsel; mem. ABA, Boston Bar Assn., Am. Law Inst., Larchmont Yacht Club. Unitarian Universalist. Avocations: sailing, hiking. Home: 388 Willis Rd Sudbury MA 01776-1332 Office: Palmer & Dodge LLP 111 Huntington Ave Boston MA 02199-7613 Office Phone: 617-239-0128. E-mail: emenoyo@palmerdodge.com.

MENSAH, GEORGE A. medical association administrator, educator; b. Ghana; Grad. in Biology with honors, Harvard U.; MD, Washington U. Bd. cert. internal medicine and subspecialty of cardiovasc. diseases. Ho. officer internal medicine, clin. and rsch. fellow N.Y. Hosp.-Cornell Med. Ctr.; asst. prof. medicine, assoc. dir. Lab. Echocardiology Vanderbilt U.; assoc. prof. medicine/cardiology, dir. hypertension unite Med. Coll. Ga.; assoc. dir. echocardiology, dir. med. specialties practice MCG Hosp. and Clinic Ambulatory Care Ctr. Recipient Searle Disting. Rsch. award Internat. Soc. on Hypertension in Blacks, 1995, 5-yr. Minority Supplement award NIH, 1996. Fellow ACP, Am. Coll. Cardiology; mem. Pan-African Soc. Cardiology (chair subcom. on ultrasound), Assn. Black Cardiologists (exec. bd., v.p.). Achievements include research in the application of echocardiography to hypertension, cardiovascular disease and general population resarch.

MENSCHEL, RICHARD LEE, investment banker; b. N.Y.C., Jan. 6, 1934; s. Benjamin and Helen (Goldsmith) M.; m. Ronay Arlt, Aug. 21, 1974; children: Charis, Sabina, Celene. BS, Syracuse U., 1955; MBA, Harvard U., 1959. Assoc. securities sales adminstr. Goldman, Sachs & Co., N.Y.C., 1959-67; v.p. Goldman, Sachs & Co., N.Y.C., 1967-69; ptnr. securities sales Goldman, Sachs & Co., N.Y.C., 1969-88, mgmt. com., 1980-88, ltd. ptnr., sr. dir., 1988—. Bd. dirs. T. Rowe Price Co-chmn. City of N.Y. Transitional Gov. Search Panel, 1977; pres., bd. dirs. Joffrey Ballet Found., 1977-79; bd. dirs. Nat. Corp. Fund for Dance, 1977-79; trustee Fed. Protestant Welfare Agys., 1978-81, The Hastings Ctr., 1995-97, Nightingale Bamford Sch., 1989-96, The Jewish Mus., 1987-2000, Nantucket Conservation Found., Storm King Art Ctr., Conn. Coll., 2001—; mng. dir. Horace W. Goldsmith Found., 1980—; bd. dirs. Mcpl. Art Soc., 1980-92; trustee, mem. exec. com. George Eastman House, Rochester, N.Y., 1980-94, Vera Inst. Justice, 1989—, Pierpont Morgan Libr., 1994—; trustee, treas., mem. exec. com. N.Y. Acad. Medicine, 1992-99; mem. vis. com. Harvard Grad. Sch. Bus. Adminstrn., 1985-91; dean's coun. Harvard Sch. Pub. Health; mem. exec. com. on univ. resources, co-chair Harvard U. campaign; mem. adv. bd. Mus. Modern Art, Oxford, 1987—; chmn., trustee Hosp. for Spl. Surgery, 1990—. 2d lt. USAF, 1955-56. Mem.: India House, Harvard. Home: 660 Park Ave New York NY 10021-5963 Office: Goldman Sachs & Co 85 Broad St New York NY 10004-2456

MENSCHEL, ROBERT BENJAMIN, investment banker; b. N.Y.C., July 2, 1929; s. Benjamin and Helen (Goldsmith) M.; m. Joyce Virginia Frank, Dec. 5, 1968; children: David F., Lauren E. BS, Syracuse U., 1951, LLD (hon.), 1991; postgrad., NYU, 1951-53. Mem. N.Y. Stock Exchange, N.Y.C., 1950-51; specialist HW Goldsmith and Co., N.Y.C., 1951-54; with Goldman, Sachs & Co., N.Y.C., 1954-66, gen. ptnr. instl. sales, 1966-78, ltd. ptnr., 1979-2000, sr. dir., 2000—. Mem. Pres. Clinton's com. on the arts and the humanities; pres., trustee, exec. and fin. com., mem. investment com., co-chmn. photography com. Mus. Modern Art; trustee Inst. Advanced Study, Princeton, Chess in the Schs., N.Y.C.; trustee, mem. exec. com. Syracuse U.; former trustee, mem. exec. com. Montefiore Hosp.; trustee, mem. exec. com. Guild Hall, East Hampton, NY, past chmn. bd.; pres. bd. trustees, mem. exec. com. Dalton Sch., N.Y.C.; past bd. advs. Grad. Sch. Inst. Internat. Bus. Pace U.; mem. exec. bd. N.Y. chpt. Am. Jewish Com., NY; bd. dirs., mem. fin. and exec. com. N.Y. Pub. Libr., N.Y.C.; bd. dirs. Parks Coun.; trustee Human Rights Watch; mng. dir. Horace W. Goldsmith Found.; bd. dirs. associated YM-YWHA; v.p. bd. trustees, mem. fin. and exec. com. Temple Emanu-El, NY; trustee N.Y. Presbyn. Hosp. Recipient George Arents medal Syracuse U., 1984. Mem.: Dunes Racquet Club (East Hampton), City Athletic Club (N.Y.C.), India Ho. Home: 920 5th Ave New York NY 10021-4160 also: Further Amagansett NY 11930 Office: Goldman Sachs & Co 85 Broad St New York NY 10004-2456 E-mail: robert.menschel@gs.com.

MENSCHER, BARNET GARY, steel company executive; b. Laurelton, N.Y., Sept. 5, 1940; s. Samuel and Louise (Zaimont) M.; m. Diane Elaine Gachman, June 12, 1966; children: Melissa Denise, Corey Lane, Scott Jay. Student, Centenary Coll., 1958-59; BBA, U. Tex., 1963. Vice pres. mktg. Ella Gant Mfg., Shreveport, La., 1964-66; warehouse mgr., dir. material control Gachman Steel Co., Fort Worth, 1966-68, gen. mgr. Houston, 1968-70; v.p. sales Gachman Metal Co., Houston, 1971-76; pres. Menko Steel Service, Inc., Houston, 1979—; CEO NEXTLEVEL, Houston, 1998—. Investment cons. D & L Enterprises, 1966—. Mem. solicitation com. United Fund, 1969-76; mem. Nat. Alliance of Businessmen Jobs Program, 1969—. Served with AUS, 1963-65. Mem. Tex. Assn. Steel Importers, Purchasing Agts. Assn. Houston, Credit Assn. Houston, Am. Mgmt. Assn., Assn. Steel Distbrs., Nat. Assn. Elevator Contractors, Phi Sigma Delta, Alpha Phi Omega. Home: 1200 Post Oak Blvd Apt 1007 Houston TX 77056-3181

MENSE, ALLAN TATE, research and development engineering executive; b. Kansas City, Mo., Nov. 29, 1945; s. Martin Conrad Mense and Nancy (Tate) Johnson; m. Kim Eisele; children from previous marriage: Melanie Georgia, Eileen Mense Hartzell. BS, U. Ariz., 1968, MS, 1970; PhD, U. Wis., 1977; MS

in Indsl. Engring., Ariz. State U., 1999. Registered profl. indsl. engr., ASQ cert. reliability engring. Scientist Oak Ridge (Tenn.) Nat. Lab, 1976-79; sr. staff sci. and tech. comm. U.S. Ho. Reps., Washington, 1979-81; sr. scientist McDonnell Douglas Astro. Co., St. Louis, 1981-85; from dep. chief scientist to chief scientist Dept. Def. Strategic Def. Initiative Orgn., Washington, 1985-88; v.p. rsch. Fla. Inst. Tech., Melbourne, 1988-92; pres. Advanced Tech. Mgmt., Inc., Tempe, Ariz., 1992-97; lead sys. engr. Motorola Space Sys. Tech. Group, Chandler, Ariz., 1998—2001; chief engr., sr. engring. fellow Raytheon Missile Sys., 2002—. Vis. scholar Sloan Sch., MIT, 1995-96. Contbr. over 60 articles to profl. jours. Ariz. State U. scholar, 1996-97. Mem. AIAA (sr. mem.), IEEE (chmn. energy com. 1985—, sr. mem.), Nat. Def. Industries Assn., Am. Phys. Soc., Am. Nuclear Soc., Inst. Indsl. Engrs., Fla. Com. Nat. Space Club (charter), Sigma Xi, Theta Tau, Pi Mu Alpha. Episcopalian. Office: 1151 E Hermans Rd B840/MS8 Tucson AZ 85706 Home: 1052 E Baldy Spring Pl Green Valley AZ 85614 Office Phone: 520-794-4720. Business E-Mail: allan_t_mense@raytheon.com.

MENSES, JAN, artist, draftsman, etcher, lithographer, muralist; b. Rotterdam, Netherlands, Apr. 28, 1933; emigrated to Can., 1960, naturalized, 1965; s. Jan and Elisabeth Wilhelmina (Schwarz) M.; m. Rachel Régine Kadoch, Dec. 7, 1958; children: Salomon, Hnina Sarah, Nechamah Elisabeth Halo. Student, Acad. Fine Arts, Rotterdam, Officers Acad. Royal Dutch Air Force, 1953-55. Cert. Royal Can. Academician, Academician of Nations, Academician of Europe, Academician of Italy. Lectr. in fine arts Concordia U., Montreal, 1973-76, others. One-man shows include Montreal Mus. Fine Arts, 1961, 65, 76, Isaacs Gallery, Toronto, Ont., Can., 1964, Delta Gallery, Rotterdam, 1965, Galerie Godard Lefort, Montreal, 1966, Gallery Moos, Toronto, 1967, Rotterdam Art Found., 1974, Galerie Mira Godard, Toronto, 1977, Montreal, 1978, Seasons Galleries, The Hague, 1980, U. B.C. Fine Arts Gallery, Vancouver, 1981, Galerie Don Stewart, Montreal, 1981, Mead Art Mus., Amherst, Mass., 1983, Agnes Etherington Art Mus., 1984, Blom and Dorn Gallery, N.Y.C., 1985, 86-93, Marywood Coll. Mus., Scranton, Pa., 1985, Saraya-Wolfson Ctr., Safed, Israel, 1987, Mayanot Gallery, Jerusalem, 1987-88, Esperanza Gallery, Montreal, 1988, 89, Gallery Hamaayan Haradum, Safed, Israel, 1989-2000, Blom and Dorn Gallery, Hartford, Conn., 1995, Nora Gallery, Jerusalem, 1995, 96, 97, Artist's Colony, Safed, Israel; over 300 group shows include Montreal World Exhbn., 1967, Salon Internat. Art, Basel, Switzerland, 1972, 74, Can. Nat. Exhbn., 1972, Centennial Exhbn., Royal Can. Acad., Toronto, 1980, Que. Biennale I, II, III, Montreal, 1977, 79, 81, Foire Internat. D'Art Contemporain Paris and Internat. Fair Koln Germany, 1986, Migdal Ha-Emek, Israel, 1988, Group of 8 Israel, Toronto, 1990, Royal Can. Acad. Show, Toronto, 1991; represented in permanent exhbn. Gallery Hamaayan Haradum, Safed, Profl. Artists' Assn., Artists Colony, Safed; represented in permanent collections U. Coll. Cape Breton Art Gallery, Sydney, N.S., Canada, Museo Ciani di Villa Caccia, Lugano, Switzerland, The Art Gallery of Hamilton, Ont.,Can., David Giles Carter Collection, New Haven, Gallery of Nova Scotia-Halifax, Can, Jewish Public Libr. Collection, Montreal, Can., Cadillac Fairview Collection, Toronto, Can, Museum Modern Art, N.Y.C., Phila. Mus. Art, Solomon R. Guggenheim Mus., N.Y.C., Yivo Inst., N.Y.C., Bklyn. Mus., Art Inst. Chgo., Cleve. Mus. Art, Detroit Inst. Arts, Yale U., U. Montreal, Queens U., Kingston, Mead Art Mus., Amherst Coll., Jonathan Edwards Coll., New Haven, Victoria & Albert Mus., London, Vatican Mus., Rome, Quebec Art Bank, Concordia U., Montreal, Haifa Mus. Modern Art, Hebrew U., Jerusalem, Govt. of Que., Yad Vashem Holocaust Meml., Jerusalem, Mus. Boymans-van Beuningen, Rotterdam, Stedelijk Mus., Amsterdam, Rijksmuseum, Amsterdam, Nat. Gallery Can., Ottawa, Gallery Stratford, Montreal Mus. Fine Arts, Musée d'Art Contemporain, Montreal, Que. Provincial Mus., Que. Art Bank, Art Bank of the Can. Coun., Ottawa, Ariz. State Mus., Tucson, Hebrew U., Jerusalem, City of Safed-Israel, Holocaust Mus., Majdeanek, Poland, Holocaust Meml. Ctr., Toronto, Lavalin Mus. Coll, Montreal, Oshawa Mus., Ont., Dept. External Affairs Govt. Can., Ottawa, Can. Jewish Congress Mus., Montreal, Israel Mus., Jerusalem, Holocaust Mus., Majdanek, Poland, McGill U., Montreal, Olympia & York Collection, Toronto, CBC Collection, Montreal, Kingston (Ont.) U. Mus. Collection, N.Y. Pub. Libr., Worcester (Mass.) Art Mus., Currier Gallery Art, Manchester, N.H., Art Gallery of U. N.H., Durham, Mus. Art. RISD, Providence, Olympia & York Collection, Toronto, Collection Rishon Le'Zion, Jerusalem, Rose Art Mus., Brandeis U., Waltham, Mass., C.I.L. Collection Montreal, Tel Aviv U., McGill U. Coll., Montreal, Can. Jewish Congress Mus., Montreal, Young Israel of Montreal (Coll.), Can., Confedn. Art Ctr., Charlottetown-Prince Edward Island, Can., Thomas More Inst., Montreal; paintings include Klippoth Series, 1963-78, Kaddish Series, 1964-80, Hechaloth Series, 1973—, Tikkun Series, 1978—; mural for, Montreal Holocaust Meml. Center. Mem. Pres.'s Coun. of U. N.H. Served with Royal Dutch Air Force Res., 1953-55. Recipient 5 1st prizes Nat. Art Exhbn., Quebec, Que., 1960-65; Grand prize Concours Artistiques de la Province de Que., 1965; prize X and XI Winnipeg (Man., Can.) Shows, 1966, 68; prize IX Internat. Exhbn. Drawings and Prints, Lugano, 1966; prize Ofcl. Centennial Art Competition, Toronto; 1st prize Hadassah, 1969, 71, 82; Recipient Imago award U. Montreal, 1971; award Reeves of Can., 1969; Tigert award Ont. Soc. Arts, 1970; Loomis and Toles award, 1972; J. I. Segal award J. I. Segal Fund Jewish Culture, 1975; Gold medal Accademia Italia Delle Arte, Italy, 1980; Gold medal Internat. Parliament U.S.A., 1982; Gran Premio delle Nazioni, Italy, 1983, European Banner of Arts with Gold medal, 1984, Oscar d' Italia, 1985, 1st prize III Que. Biennale, 1981, OSA award of merit, Toronto, 1981, 82; World Culture prize Italy, 1984; Golden Flame of World Parliament (U.S.A.) award, 1986; Ish Shalom award Jerusalem, 1993; numerous others; Can. Council sr. arts fellow, 1969-70, 71-72, 81-82; grantee, 1966-67, 67-68; travel grantee, 1968, 73 Mem. Royal Can. Acad. Arts, Acad. Italia Arte e del Lavoro, Acad. Nazioni, Maestro Accademico-Accademia Bedriacense (Italy), Jewish Am. Acad. Arts and Scis., Israeli Art Assn. (Telaviv), Israel Assn. Profl. Artists Safed, Acad. Europa, Academician Italy, Israel Assn. Visual Art (Jerusalem). Jewish. Address: PO Box 43150 HAR NOF Jerusalem 91400 Israel *My works have dealt with death, the eclipse of faith, exile, the Galut. They are shaped by my childhood experiences, real and imagined, in Nazi-occupied Europe; influenced by and rooted in my principles and standards of conduct as an Orthodox Jew in the post-holocaust/pre-Messianic era. They are an attempt to translate these experiences into visual contemporary terms (imagery conflicts and reconciliations of conflicts) in order to ascend from the personal/specific to the universal/general. They are a lament, an elegy, a denial and confirmation, an expression of the attitude of the soul in its debasement and dignity towards its Creator; a striving towards serenity in anticipation of the Redemption: a form of prayer.*

MENTE, RONALD F. consulting company executive; b. Chgo., Sept. 17, 1941; s. Fred Vincent and Edna Frances Mente; m. Alexandra Georgine Wojtas, Nov. 7, 1969 (div. July 1976). BA, Mont. State U., 1964; MS, DePaul U., 1975; MA, Northeastern Ill. U., 1979; PhD, Vrije U., 1999. Chemist Cities Svc. Oil Co., Cicero, Ill., 1964-67; chief chemist No. Petrochem Mineral Divsn., Lemont, Ill., 1967-69; chemist, chief corp. rsch. chemistry Culligan, Inc., Northbrook, Ill., 1969; rsch. chemist Ctrl. Soya Corp., Chgo., 1970-76; pres. Ronald F. Mente, Cons., St. Petersburg, Fla., 1976—. Contbr. articles to profl. jours. Mem. N.Y. Acad. Scis., Pi Gamma Mu, Delta Upsilon Sigma, Gamma Theta Upsilon, Sigma Psi. Roman Catholic. Achievements include conducting study documenting radioecology of pines in nature. Home: 939 45th St N St Petersburg FL 33713-6255 Office: Premack & Assocs Pinellas Co Inc Ste 10 8130 66th St North Pinellas Park FL 33781 E-mail: ronmente@hotmail.com.

MENTEER, DAVID HILTON, producer, production manager; b. L.A., Apr. 7, 1939; s. Hilton Greene and Virginia Rose (Kershner) Menteer; m. JoAnne Letty Bagwell, Dec. 30, 1960 (div. June 1986); children: Jon-David, Kevin James; m. Kathryn Jan Severson, May 30, 1987. BS, U. Miami, 1964. Tv cameraman WTVJ, Miami, Fla., 1962-65; tv engr. ABC Network, L.A., 1965-66, stage mgr., assoc. dir., 1966-68; freelance stage mgr., assoc. dir. L.A., 1968-73; asst. dir., second unit dir., prodn. mgr. Universal Studios, L.A., 1973-79; freelance producer, prodn. mgr. L.A., 1979—. With USN, 1957-61, PTO. Mem. Dirs. Guild Am. Avocations: profl. diver, comml. pilot. Office: Dolphin Cay Prodns 4515 Park Serena Calabasas CA 91302-1775

MENTON, TANYA LIA, lawyer, educator; b. Chgo., Sept. 13, 1964; d. Joseph Bernard and Rosalind Marie (Macey) M. BA magna cum laude, Northwestern U., 1986, JD, 1989. Bar: Calif. 1989, N.Y. 1993. V.p. litigation and employment practices ABC, Inc., L.A., 1989—91; counsel Townley and Updike, N.Y.C., 1991—96; v.p. ABC, Inc., N.Y.C., 1993—96. Adj. prof. Mercy Coll., Dobbs Ferry, N.Y., 1993-2000; lectr. on sexual harassment, discrimination and mgmt. tng. various orgns. Editor: (legal publ.) California Employment Law Letter, 1989-91. Nat. Harry S. Truman scholar, 1982-86. Mem. ABA, Calif. Bar Assn. (labor and employment sect.), N.Y. State Bar Assn. (labor and employment sect.). Democrat. Avocations: horseback riding, softball, cooking. Home: # 17P 301 E 79th St Apt 17P New York NY 10021-0940 Office: ABC Inc 77 W 66th St New York NY 10023-6201

MENTZ, BARBARA ANTONELLO, lawyer; b. Kansas City, Mo., July 4, 1944; d. John Francis and Eleanor Barbara (Vagnino) Antonello; m. Lawrence Mentz, Nov. 10, 1973; children: Kathleen Elizabeth, Lawrence Goodwin. BA in Econs., U. Kans., 1965; JD magna cum laude, U. Notre Dame, 1973. Bar: N.Y. 1974, U.S. Dist. Ct. (so. and ea. dists.) N.Y. 1974, U.S. Ct. Appeals (2d cir.) 1974, U.S. Supreme Ct. 1977, U.S. Ct. Appeals (9th cir.) 1981, U.S. Ct. Appeals (3d cir.) 1983, N.J. 1985, U.S. Dist. Ct. N.J. 1986. Various positions with ins. cos., Chgo., 1965—68, Kansas City, Mo., 1968—70; assoc. Sullivan & Cromwell, N.Y.C., 1973—77, Forsyth, Decker, Murray and Hubbard, N.Y.C., 1977-79; ptnr. Hall, McNicol, Hamilton & Clark, N.Y.C., 1979-86; sr. litig. counsel CBS, 1986-88; assoc. gen. counsel, prin. Deloitte & Touche USA LLP, N.Y.C., 1988—. Contbr. articles to profl. jours., chpt. to supplements, publs. Mem. ABA (antitrust sect. 1979-90), Nat. Futures Assn. (panel of arbitrators 1985—), Assn. Bar City of N.Y. (prof. discipline com. 1983-86, antitrust and trade regulation com. 1988-91). Home: 140 W 86th St Apt 2B New York NY 10024-4067 Office: Deloitte & Touche USA LLP 1633 Broadway New York NY 10019-6708 E-mail: bmentz@deloitte.com.

MENTZ, HENRY A., III, plastic surgeon; b. New Orleans, Apr. 9, 1958; s. Henry A. Jr. and Ann (Lamantia) M.; m. Paula Comiskey, May 20, 1989; children: Henry A. IV, James August. BS, La. State U., 1980, MD, 1984. Diplomate Am. Bd. Facial Plastic Surgery, Otolaryngology, Plastic Surgery. Intern otolaryngology Tulane U., New Orleans, 1984-89; resident plastic surgery St. Joseph's Hosp., Houston, 1989-91; founder, ptnr. Aesthetic Ctr. for Plastic Surgeons, Houston, 1991—. Clin. assoc. prof. Baylor U., Houston, 1992—, St. Joseph U., Houston, 1992—; chief surgery Sharpstown Gen. Hosp., Houston, 1994—, chief plastic surgery, 1994—; pres., Houston Soc. of Plastic Surgeons, 2000-01. Fellow ACS, Internat. Coll. Surgeons, Am. Acad. Otolaryngology; mem. Am. Soc. Plastic and Reconstructive Surgeons, N.Am. Liposuction Soc. Republican. Episcopalian. Office: Aesthetic Ctr for Plastic Surgery Kimberly Profl Bldg 12727 Kimberley Ste 300 Houston TX 77024

MENTZ, HENRY ALVAN, JR., federal judge; b. New Orleans, Nov. 10, 1920; s. Henry Alvan and Lulla (Bridewell) M.; m. Ann Lamantia, June 23, 1956; children: Ann, Carli, Hal, Frederick, George BA, Tulane U., 1941; JD, La. State U., 1943. Bar: La. 1943, U.S. Dist. Ct. (ea. dist.) La. 1944. With legal dept. Shell Oil, New Orleans, 1947-48; pvt. practice Hammond, 1948-82; judge U.S. Dist. Ct. (ea. dist.) La., New Orleans, 1982—, sr. judge, 1992—. Editor: Combined Gospels, 1976 Pres. La. Soc. Music and Performing Arts, 1994-97, L.A. Civil Svc. League, 1979-81; bd. dirs. Southea. La. U. Found., Salvation Army; chmn. Tulane U. 50th Anniversary Reunion for 1991. Decorated 2 Battle Stars, Bronze Star; recipient Disting. Svc. award AMVETS, 1950. Mem. SAR, Royal Soc. St. George (pres.), Boston Club New Orleans, Delta Tau Delta. Republican. Episcopalian. Home: 2105 State St New Orleans LA 70118-6255 Office: US Dist Ct C-114 US Courthouse 500 Camp St New Orleans LA 70130-3313

MENTZ, LAWRENCE, lawyer; b. N.Y.C., Nov. 5, 1946; s. Joseph Walter and Audrey Cecilia (Armstrong) M.; m. Barbara Antonello, Nov. 10, 1973; children: Kathleen Elizabeth, Lawrence Goodwin. BS in Physics, Rensselaer Poly. Inst., 1968; JD, U. Notre Dame, 1973. Bar: N.Y. 1973, DC 1974. Assoc. Condon & Forsyth, N.Y.C., 1973-80, ptnr., 1981-89, Biedermann, Hoenig, Massamillo & Ruff, N.Y.C., 1990—; counsellor at law. Speaker Worldwide Airlines Customer Rels. Assn. Conf., Singapore, 1983, 2d Cir. Speakers Bur., Com. on BiCentennial of U.S. Constn., 1987; arbitrator U.S. Dist. Ct. (ea. dist.) Bklyn., 1986—; bd. dirs. Black Mountain Mgmt. Inc. With USNR, 1969-70. Mem. ABA, Fed. Bar Coun., N.Y. State Bar Assn. (exec. com. sect. on comml. and fed. litigation, fed. judiciary com., 1993, com. Supreme Cts.), Assn. of Bar of City of N.Y. (com. on aeronautics law, task force on N.Y. Constl. Conv., com. on state legis.), Wings Club. Roman Catholic. Avocations: swimming, running, stamp collecting/philately. Office: Biedermann Hoenig Massamillo & Ruff 90 Park Ave New York NY 10016-1301 E-mail: lmentz@bhmr.com.

MENTZ, STEVEN ROGER, language educator; b. N.Y.C., Nov. 3, 1966; s. John Roger and Marilyn Knerr Mentz; m. Alinor Clemens Sterling, July 6, 1996; children: Ian Wallace, Olivia Clemans. AB, Princeton U., 1989; MA, MPhil, Yale U., 1998, PhD in English, 2000. Asst. prof. English Iona Coll., New Rochelle, NY, 2000—03, St. John's U., Jamaica, NY, 2003—. Co-editor: Rogues and Early Modern English Culture, 2004. Office: St John's U 800 Utopia Pkwy Jamaica NY 11439 Office Phone: 718-990-6690. E-mail: mentzs@stjohns.edu.

MENTZER, JOHN RAYMOND, electrical engineer, educator; b. Arch Spring, Pa., June 16, 1916; s. Walter Ray and Katheryn Henderson (Barr) M.; m. Bernice Roslyn Simon, Feb. 17, 1945; children— Jacqueline Ferne, Richard Alan. BS, Pa. State U., 1942, MS, 1948; PhD, Ohio State U., 1952. Engr. Westinghouse Electric Corp., Balt., 1942-46, Ordnance Research Lab., 1946-48; research asso. Ohio State U., 1948-52; mem. staff Lincoln Lab., M.I.T., 1952-54; mem. faculty Pa. State U., 1954—, prof. engring. scis., 1956—, head dept. engring. sci. and mechanics, 1974-81, prof. emeritus engring. scis., 1981—. Author: Scattering and Diffraction of Radio Waves, 1955. Recipient Service award Pa. State U., 1979 Sr. mem. IEEE; mem. Am. Soc. Engring. Edn., AAAS, Sigma Xi. Home: 557 Clarence Ave State College PA 16803-3456 Office: 117 Hammond Bldg University Park PA 16802-1401

MENTZER, RAYMOND ALBERT, religious history educator; b. Pitts., Sept. 20, 1945; s. Raymond A. and Anna M. (Snyder) M.; m. Elizabeth J. Palmer, Sept. 14, 1968; children: Sarah, John. BA, Fordham U., 1967; MA, U. Wis., 1970, PhD, 1973. Prof. history Mont. State U., Bozeman, 1973-2001; Krumm Family Prof. in Reformation Studies U. Iowa, Iowa City, 2001—. Author: Heresy Proceedings, 1984, Blood and Belief, 1994; editor: Sin and the Calvinists, 1994; co-editor: Society and Culture in the Huguenot World, 2002; gen. editor Sixteenth Century Essays and Studies. Mem. Sixteenth Century Studies (pres. 1996-97), Phi Beta Kappa. Office: U of Iowa 314 Gilmore Hall Iowa City IA 52242 E-mail: raymond-mentzer@uiowa.edu.

MENTZER, ROBERT MELVIN, JR., surgeon; b. Omaha, Jan. 30, 1945; m. Monika Mentzer, Nov. 29, 1968; children: Markus, Stefan. BS, Coll. William & Mary, 1967; MD, U. Md., 1971. Resident U. Va. Med. Ctr., Charlottesville, 1980; thoracic surgeon Frankfurt Army Regional Med. Ctr., Frankfurt, Germany, 1980—82; asst. prof. physiology, dir. carotid-peripheral vascular U. Va. Med. Ctr., Charlottesville, 1982—86, asst. prof. surgery, 1982—85, assoc. prof. surgery divsn. thoracic and cardiovasc. surgery, 1985—86; prof. dept. surgery and dept. physiology SUNY, Buffalo, 1987—91, vice chmn. dept. surgery, chief divsn. cardiothoracic surgery, 1987—91, head dept. surgery, dir. 2d heart transplant program in N.Y., 1987—91, interim chmn. dept. surgery, pres. u. surg. assn. dept. surg, 1990—91; prof., chmn. divsn. cardiothoracic surgery U. Wis. Sch. Medicine, Madison, 1991—97, dir. cardiopulmonary transplant program, 1991—97; Frank C. Spencer prof., chmn. dept of surgery, prof. physiology U. Ky. Coll. Medicine, Lexington, 1997—, dir. transplant ctr., 1997—. Pres., chmn., bd. dirs. Ky. Med. Svcs. Found., Lexington, 1998—; cons. surg. care VA Med. Ctr., Lexington, 1997—. Grantee NIH, 1994—. Mem. ACS, Soc. Thoracic Surgery (v.p. CCCETS), Assn. for Acad. Surgery, Am. Surg. Assn., Am. Soc. Transplant Surgeons, So. Surg. Assn., Am. Coll. Cardiology, Soc. Univ. Surgeons, Am. Heart Assn., Am. Assn. Thoracic Surgery, Assn. for Surg. Edn., Internat. Soc Heart Rsch., Halsted Soc. Office: U Ky Dept Surgery 800 Rose St Mn 264 Lexington KY 40536-0298 Office Phone: 859-323-6013. E-mail: mentzer@email.uky.edu.

MENUTIS, JAMIE, training services executive, writer; b. Houston, June 4, 1964; d. James P. Menutis and Ruth Ann Pellerin-Menutis; 1 child, Ana Sofia Rosales. BA, cert. refugee studies program, Webster U., Vienna, Austria, 1988; MA, Georgetown U., 1990. Cert. French lang. proficiency, Spanish lang. proficiency. Campaign asst. Campaign Calif., L.A., 1986—87; rsch. asst. refugee status adv. com. Govt. Can., Ottawa, Canada, 1986—87; rsch. asst. UN Ctr. for Social Devel. and Humanitarian Affairs, Vienna, 1988, U.S. Cath. Conf.-Migration and Refugee Services, Washington, 1989—90; resettlement program officer Internat. Rescue Com., Freetown, Sierra Leone, 1991—92, liaison officer Nairobi, Kenya, 1992; edn. program mgr.-emergency ops. Trocaire, Somalia, 1993; tng. dir. NEU, Inc., New Orleans, 1993—2001; dir. R & M R&D, New Orleans, 1993—. Cons. Ctr. for Effective Non-Profit Mgmt., New Orleans, 1993; fast track trainer U. New Orleans-Small Bus. Devel. Ctr., 1996; staff www.Gal.net, 2002—. Author: (book) Where the Natives Feast in New Orleans...A Secret Guide to Local Restaurants, 2002, (government reference) Ten Year Country Profile Reports on Chile, El Salvador and Nicaragua, 1987, (reference) United Nations Center for Social Development and Humanitarian Affairs Bulletin, 1988, (testimonial address for Congress) United States Policy towards Central American and Eastern Europeans Refugees, 1989; contbr. political newsletter Campaign California, 1986; photographic exhbn., portraits of African and Indian Children, 1988; author: (tng. manual) Customer Service Training "Understanding the Customer", 2001, Cultural Orientation Training-International Rescue Committee, Sierra Leone, 1992; contbr. curriculum Somalia-Primary School Materials Development, 1993, articles to profl. jours. Mem. Ladies Philoptochos Soc., New Orleans, 2002; supporter March of Dimes, New Orleans, 1999, Habitat for Humanity, New Orleans, 1998, Amnesty Internat., Washington, 1984. Recipient Medal of Honor for Svc., Internat. Rescue Com., 1992. Mem.: Fgn. Rels. Assn. New Orleans, Georgetown U. Alumni Assn., Pi Sigma. Avocations: photography, travel, yoga, gourmet cooking. Office: Ste 200 108 Royal St New Orleans LA 70130 Personal E-mail: jmenutis@mindspring.com. Business E-Mail: jamie@nativesfeast.com.

MENY, ROBERT GEORGE, former medical research administrator, physician; b. Hackensack, N.J., Jan. 7, 1945; m. Janet McHugh, Apr. 28, 1990; children: Danielle, Ellen, Gus. BS, Tulane U., 1966; MD, Columbia U., 1971. Intern and resident in pediat. N.Y. Hosp., N.Y.C., 1971—73; fellow in neonatology U. Md. Hosp., Balt., 1975—77; mem. staff neonatal ctr. Rutgers Med. Sch., New Brunswick, NJ, 1977—80; dir. Hurley Neonatal Ctr., Flint, Mich., 1980—83; dir. Sudden Infant Death Syndrome Inst. U. Md., Balt., 1983—99; pvt. practice Towson, Md., 1999—. Capt. USAF. Mem.: Am. Assn. Sudden Infant Death Prevention Physicians (pres.-elect 1995, chmn. bd. 1998). Office: O'Dea Bldg #409 7505 Osler Dr Towson MD 21204

MENZA, CLAUDIA MARCELLA, literary agent; b. N.Y.C., June 11, 1947; d. John Gaetano and Antonina (di Lorenzo) M.; m. James R. Forker, May 29, 1971 (div. 1980); m. Charles Anthony Frye, Dec. 16, 1989 (dec. Oct. 1994). BA, Oberlin Coll., 1969. Asst. editor Evergreen Rev., N.Y.C., 1969-73; gen. editor, prodn. mgr. Grove Press, Inc., N.Y.C., 1973-83; sr. editor Art Dir. News, N.Y.C., 1983-85; pres. Claudia Menza Lit. Agy., N.Y.C., 1983—. Cons. Riverrun Press, N.Y.C., 1983-96; guest lectr. Tex. A&M U., Prairie View, Tex., 1986, NYU, N.Y.C., 1986-87; cons., panelist Nat. Civil Rights Mus. Conf. The Power of the Word, Memphis, 1995; panelist NYU, 1998, The New Sch., N.Y.C., 2000, The Lost State Writers Conf., Greeneville, Tenn., 2000, Harlem Book Fair, 2001; panelist African Am. Lit. Conf., Raleigh, NC, 2003. Author: Cage of Wild Cries, 1990, The Lunatics Ball, 1994, (plays), 2002; co-author: The Dream Book: An Anthology of Writing by Italian-American Women, 1985 (Am. Book award, 1985); actor: Damned Pub. Riverside Studios, 1999. Working mem. Congress of Racial Equality, Hempstead, N.Y., 1961, Student Nonviolent Coord. Com., Oberlin, Ohio, 1965, Students for Dem. Soc., Oberlin, 1965, The West Village Com., N.Y.C., 1980. Mem. PEN, Internat. Platform Assn., Acad. Am. Poets, Italian-Am. Writers Assn., Assn. Authors Reps. Avocations: reading, music, theater. Office: Claudia Menza Lit Agy 1170 Broadway Ste 807 New York NY 10001-7507

MENZA, MATTHEW A. psychiatrist; b. Sept. 11, 1950; BA, U. Va., 1973; MD, Temple U., 1980; postgrad., Harvard U., 1985. Intern NYU Med. Sch. Bellvue Hosp., N.Y.C., 1980—81, resident, 1981—84; chief divsn. clin. psychopharmacology Robert Wood Johnson Med. Sch., Piscataway, NJ, 1996—, acting chmn. dept. psychiatry, 2003—. Contbr. over 60 articles to profl. jours. Bd. govs. Univ. Med. Group, New Brunswick, N.J., 1999—. Office: Robert Wood Johnson Med Sch Dept Psychiatry 675 Hoes Ln Piscataway NJ 08854-5627 Office Phone: 732-235-4440. Business E-Mail: menza@umdnj.edu.

MENZEL, IDINA, actress, singer; b. May 30, 1971; d. Stuart and Helene Mentzel; m. Taye Diggs, 2003. BFA in drama, Tisch Sch. Arts, NYU. Actor: (Broadway plays) RENT, 1995—97 (Tony award nominee), Aida, 2001, Funny Girl, 2002, Wicked, 2003— (Tony award best actress in a musical, 2004); (plays) The Wild Party, 1999, Summer of '42, 2000, Hair, 2001, The Vagina Monologues, 2002; singer: (albums) Still I Can't Be Still, 1998, Here, 2004; actor: (films) Kissing Jessica Stein, 2001, Just a Kiss, 2002, The Tollbooth, 2004; composer: (songs) Follow If You Lead for film "The Other Sister", 1999. Office: Gershwin Theater 222 W 51st St New York NY 10019

MENZEL, MARYBELLE PROCTOR, volunteer; b. Milledgeville, Ga., Feb. 5, 1940; d. Ennis Hall Proctor and Sara (Evans) McCarthy; m. Robert John Menzel, Sept. 1, 1961; children: Blake, John, Craig. BA cum laude, Wesleyan Coll., Macon, Ga., 1962; MA with highest distinction, U. Ctrl. Fla., 1986. Cert. highest level tchr. Fla. Tchr. Spaulding Jr. H.S., Griffin, Ga., 1962, East Syracuse (N.Y.) Minoa H.S., 1964—65, Coral Gables (Fla.) H.S., 1965—66; dir. Gerber Child Care Ctr., Indialantic, Fla., 1981, Brevard C.C. Coop Presch., Melbourne, Fla., 1982—85; adj. instr. English and Humanities Brevard C.C., Cocoa, Fla., 1985. Mem.: AAUW (Nat. award Fundraising AAUW Ednl. Found. 2001, Garden of Victories award 1993), Colo. AAUW (dir. ednl. found. 2000—01, pres. elect 2001—02, pres. 2002—, state exec. bd., mem. women's lobby), Wesleyan Coll. Million Dollar Women, Nat. Mus. Women in the Arts (friend), Nat. Mus. Women's History (charter), Nat. Trust for Historic Preservation, Phi Kappa Phi. Democrat. Methodist.

MENZEL, WILLIAM CLARENCE, JR., nuclear quality engineer; b. Chgo., July 12, 1942; s. William Clarence and Iris Johnston M.; m. Margaret Ann Lagle, Apr. 3, 1964 (div. June 1977); children: Kimberly Menzel Bramlett, William Edward, Timothy Ian; m. Constance Ellen Carter, Mar. 27, 1992. BS in Math., U. Montevallo, 1965. Sr. field engr. reliability & quality assurance Bendix Launch Support Divsn., Kennedy Space Ctr., Fla., 1967-77; engr. quality assurance Rockwell Internat., Kennedy Space Ctr., Fla., 1977; mgr. supplier evaluation program Tenn. Valley Authority, Knoxville, TN, 1977-80, Chattanooga, 1981-94; supr. vendor audits Brown & Root, Houston, 1980-81; cons. nuclear engr., 1994—. Vol. fireman Bellwood (Fla.) Vol. Fire Dept., 1972-73, vol. fire chief, 1973-74; coach Shirley Temple Softball, Titusville, Fla., 1975. With U.S. Army Rserve, 1961-67. Baptist. Avocations: reading, water sports. Home and Office: 2613 Hills Chapel Rd Dandridge TN 37725-6809

MENZER, JOHN, department store executive; Pres., CEO Wal-Mart Stores Inc., Bentonville, Ariz., 1999—. Office: Wal-Mart Stores Inc 702 SW 8th St Bentonville AR 72716-6299

MENZER, ROBERT EVERETT, toxicologist, educator; b. Washington, Dec. 21, 1938; s. Russell Ernest and Ora Taylor (Oates) M.; m. Sara Lee Gribbon, Dec. 29, 1962; children: R. Eric, Paul D., Joan Coleraine. BS in Chemistry, U. Pa., 1960; MS, U. Md., 1962; PhD, U. Wis., 1964. Instr. U. Wis., Madison, 1964; mem. faculty U. Md., 1964-89, asst. prof. entomology, 1964-69, assoc. prof., 1969-73, prof., 1973-89, assoc. dean grad. studies and research, 1974-77, acting dean, 1977-80, chmn. grad. program marine-

estuarine-environ. scis., 1978-89, dir. Water Resources Research Ctr., 1981-89; dir. environ. rsch. lab. EPA, Gulf Breeze, Fla., 1989-95, sr. sci. advisor Nat. Ctr. for Environ. Rsch. Washington, 1995—2001. Prof. emeritus U. Md., 1990—; chmn. hazardous substances data bank rev. panel Nat. Library Medicine, 1973-97. Contbr. articles to profl. jours. Recipient U. Md. Alumni award, 1974 Fellow Washington Acad. Scis.; mem. AAAS, Am. Chem. Soc., Soc. Toxicology, Estuarine Rsch. Fedn., Sigma Xi, Phi Kappa Phi. Clubs: Cosmos (Washington). Republican. Episcopalian. Home: 90 Highpoint Dr Gulf Breeze FL 32561-4014 Personal E-mail: remenzer@att.net.

MENZIA, KATHRYN MARIE, educational consultant; b. Ipswich, S.D., Sept. 5, 1956; d. Gabriel Francis and Mary Menzia; children from previous marriage: Natasha Nicole Walker, Joshua Paul Walker. AA in Speech Therapy, Moorhead (Minn.) State Coll., 1978; BS in Psychology, S.D. State U., 1980; MS in Rehab. Counseling, Ea. Mont. Coll., 1990. Cert. Commn. on Rehab. Parent-tchr. alt. Yellowstone Boys' Ranch, Billings, Mont., 1980—81; semi-ind. living instr. Snowy Mountain Industries, Lewistown, Mont., 1982—83; trainer Residential Support Svc., Billings, 1984—85; rehab. counselor Med. Mgmt. Inc., N.W., Kalispell, Mont., 1991—92, Crawford & Co., Missoula, Mont., 2000; vocat. counselor Concentra Integrated Svc., Lewistown, 2001—03, Clark Fork Vocat. Rehab. Svc., Lolo, Mont., 2003—. Contbr. poetry to anthologies. Vice chair, chair Protection and Advocacy for Individuals with Mental Illness, Helena, Mont., 1999—2000; mem. choir John XXIII Cath. Ch.; bd. dirs. Mont. Advocacy Program, Helena, 1999—2000. Avocations: reading, dance, wood restoration projects, poetry, piano.

MENZIES, CARL STEPHEN, agricultural research administrator, ruminant nutritionist; b. Menard, Tex., Mar. 6, 1932; s. Alex L. and Marguerite (Watson) M.; m. Shirley W. Martin, Sept. 2, 1952; children: John S., Linda D. BS, Tex. Tech Coll., 1954; MS, Kans. State U., 1956; PhD, U. Ky., 1965. Instr. animal sci. Kans. State U., Manhattan, 1955-58, asst. prof., 1958-65, assoc. prof., 1965-69; rsch. asst. animal sci. U. Ky., Lexington, 1961-62; head animal sci. dept., prof. S.D. State U., Brookings, 1969-71; resident dir. of rsch., prof. animal sci. Tex. Agrl. Experiment Sta., San Angelo, 1971-96; prof. emeritus Tex. A&M U., 1997. Cons. Pakistan project King Ranch, Kingsville, Tex., 1975; bd. dirs. sml. ruminant Cooperative Rsch. Support Program project U.S. AID, Davis, Calif.; mem. adv. com. sheep rsch. sta. USDA Agrl. Rsch. Sta., Dubois, Idaho, 1985—; mem. adv. bd. agrl. program Angelo State U., 1986—; mem. fiber adv. com. Tex. Dept. Agr., 1999—. Contbr. articles to profl. jours. Chmn. livestock com. Goals for San Angelo, 1988-90. Named to Manard Sch. Hall of Fame; recipient Appreciation for Svc. award Kansas. Purebred Sheep Breeders Assn., 1968, Silver Ram award Am. Sheep Prodrs. Coun., 1988, Tex. A&M U. Dep. Chancellor for Agr. Award for Disting. Performance in Adminstrn., 1983, Disting. Alumnus, Coll. of Agr. Tex. Tech. U., 1993. Fellow Am. Soc. Animal Sci.; mem. Coun. Agrl. Sci. and Tech., San Angelo C. of C. (bd. dirs. 1990-93), Rotary, Tex. Sheep and Goat Raisers Assn. (past pres.), Sigma Xi, Gamma Sigma Delta, Phi Kappa Phi, Alpha Zeta. Avocations: ranching, producing registered sheep, outdoor activities.

MENZIES, HENRY HARDINGE, architect; b. Hickory, N.C., Apr. 20, 1928; s. Henry Hardinge and Hallie (Lloyd) M. AB in Lit., U. N.C., 1948; postgrad., U. So. Calif., 1948-49; BArch, N.C. State U., 1958. Founder, ptnr. The Architects Group, Boston, 1962-63; individual practice architecture Boston, 1964-78; ptnr. Menzies and LeMieux, N.Y.C., 1978-82; pvt. practice architecture New Rochelle, N.Y., 1983—. Lectr. in field. Works include coll. and seminary, Natick, Mass., 1964, Heights Sch., Washington, 1965, St. Marie's Ch., Lowell, Mass., 1966, Central Cath. H.S., Lawrence, Mass., 1971, Walker Sch., Needham, Mass., 1972, Baird Residence, Sherborn, Mass., 1972, Layton Cultural Ctr., Brookfield, Wis., 1974, Shellbourne Conf. Ctr., Valparaiso, Ind., 1974, Wespine Study Ctr., Pembroke, Mass, 1982, alterations to residences in Greenwich, Conn., 1984, Garwood Bldg. at Arnold Hall, 1986, Midtown Ctr., Chgo., 1986, Student Ctr., Houston, 1986, Windmoor Ctr., South Bend, Ind., 1986, alterations to student residences in Milw. and Providence, 1989-91, renovation of interior St. Aloysius Ch., New Canaan, Conn., 1993-96, chapel at Warwick House, Pitts., 1993, chapel at Westfield Residence, L.A., 1994, chapel at Allview Ctr., Columbia, Md., 1994, chapel at St. John Fisher Residence, Stamford, Conn., 1994, master plan, crypt chapel St. Mary of the Angels Ch., Chgo., 1996—, Shrine at Conf. Ctr., Schulenberg, Tex., chapel Lincoln Green student residence, Urbana, Ill., 1997—, new facade of St. Aloysius Ch., New Canaan, 1997—, Willows Acad., Chgo., 1997—, Cath. Info. Ctr. Washington, 1999-2000, St. Michael's Ch., Gastonia, N.C., 2000—, Cathedral St. Augustine, Bridgeport, Conn., 2003, Paducah, Ky., 2003, H.S. Charlotte, 2003, Salisbury, N.C., 2003, Norhal, Ill., 2003; contbr. articles to profl. jours. Served to 1st lt. USNR, 1951-55. Mem. AIA (N.Y. chpt. 1978-84, Westchester/Mid-Hudson chpt. 1985—). Roman Catholic. Office: 99 Overlook Cir New Rochelle NY 10804-4501 Office Phone: 914-637-9597. E-mail: hmenzies@aol.com.

MENZIES, IAN STUART, newspaper editor; b. Glasgow, Scotland, Mar. 11, 1920; came to U.S., 1944, naturalized, 1948; s. John S. and Gertrude (Mephius) M.; m. Barbara Edith Newton, June 16, 1945; children: Marla Ann, Gillian Jean, Alexa Stuart, Deborah Newton. Student, Royal Tech. Coll., 1937-39; Nieman fellow, Harvard U., 1961-62; L.H.D., Salem State Coll., 1978. Reporter Boston Globe, 1948-57, sci. editor, 1957-63, fin. editor, 1963-65, mng. editor, 1965-70, assoc. editor, 1970-85; sr. fellow John McCormack Inst. Pub. Affairs, U. Mass., Boston, 1985—. Vis. assoc. Joint Ctr. for Urban Studies, Mass. Inst. Tech.-Harvard, 1970-71. Mem. Hingham (Mass.) Sch. Com., 1962-68. Served to lt. Royal Naval Vol. Res., 1939-46. Decorated D.S.C.; recipient Pub. Service award Nat. Edn. Writers, 1961, Pub. Service award AAAS, 1963, Heywood Broun award, 1961, Sevellon Brown award, 1959, Rudolph Elie award, 1959, A.P. Big City award, 1958, U.P.I. award, 1959. Mem. Harvard Club, Hingham Yacht Club, Brit. Officers Club New Eng. Home and Office: 2201 Hockley Dr Hingham MA 02043-4705 Office: U Mass McCormack Inst Boston MA 02125

MENZNER, DONALD, food products executive; CEO Marathon (Wis.) Cheese. Office: Marathon Cheese 304 East St Marathon WI 54448

MENZNER, JOHN B. retail executive; BBA, Loyola U., 1972, MBA, 1980. CPA. Sr. v.p. Ben Franklin Retail Stores, Inc., Carol Stream, Ill., 1985—88, exec. v.p., 1988—91, COO, CFO, 1991—93, pres., 1993—95; exec. v.p. and CFO Wal-Mart Stores, Inc., 1995—99, pres. and CEO Wal-Mart Internat., 1999—. Bd. dirs. Wal-Mart de Mex., Seiyu Ltd., Japan, Emerson Electric, U.S.-China Bus. Coun., Guangdong Province Gov.'s Econ. Advisors in China. Mem.: AICPA, CIES The Food Bus. Forum (bd. dirs.), Fin. Execs. Inst. Office: Wal-Mart Stores Inc 702 SW Eighth St Bentonville AR 72716

MEO, DIANE SUE, artist, writer; d. Harold Joseph and Blanche Celia Schaeffer; m. Louis F. Meo, Sept. 26, 1965; children: Jeni-Lou, Louis Vincent. Student, U. Albany, 1976—77. Staff artist Rubin Donnelly, Albany, NY, 1964—66; staff artist illus. dept. Albany Med. Ctr., 1967—68; owner In Honor of the Native Am. Spirit, Albany. Adv. bd. Brattelboro Retreat Alternatives, Albany, 1995—96. Exhibitions include Mandela. Pres. Concerned Parents for the Handicapped, Albany, 1973—74. Recipient 1st pl., Guilderland League Arts, N.Y., 1978, 2d pl., 1979. Avocations: photography, interior decorating, gardening, woodworking. Home: 4 Dewberry Ct Albany NY 12203-5904 Office: In Honor of the Native Am Spirit 4 Dewberry Ct Albany NY 12203-5904

MEOLA, JANICE GRACE, lawyer; b. Newark, Jan. 10, 1966; d. William Frank and Rose Marie Meola. BS in Fin., Pa. State U., 1988; JD, U. N.C., Chapel Hill, 1991. Bar: N.J., D.C., U.S. Dist. Ct. N.J. Jud. clk. Superior Ct. of N.J., Jersey City, 1991-92; litigation assoc. Bumgardner, Hardin & Ellis, Springfield, N.J., 1992-94; environ. counsel CNA Ins. Cos., Cranbury, N.J., 1994-96; assoc. counsel Suburban Propane, L.P., Whippany, N.J., 1996-98, counsel, 1998-99, gen. counsel, sec., 1999—. Mem. ABA, Am. Corp. Counsel Assn., N.J. Corp. Counsel Assn. (bd. dirs.), Am. Soc. Corp. Secs., Propane Gas Def. Assn. Office: Suburban Propane LP PO Box 206 240 Route 10 Whippany NJ 07981-0206 Home: 17 Wilton Terr Verona NJ 07044-2534

MEOLA, MARC, librarian; b. NJ, 1968; s. Anthony and Angelina M.; m. Christine Brisson, July 15, 1995; 1 child, Miles. BA in Philosophy, Rutgers Coll., New Brunswick, NJ, 1990; MA in Philosophy, Johns Hopkins U., Balt., 1995; MLS, Rutgers U., New Brunswick, 1997. Reference libr. Temple U., Phila., 1997—2000; humanities libr. Coll. of N.J., Ewing, NJ. Author: Starting and Operating Live Virtual Reference Services, 2002; contbr. articles. Bd. dirs. Logan Sq. Neighborhood Assn., Philadelphia, Pa., 2003; bd. adv. com. Raritan Valley C.C., North Branch, NJ, 2001—. Nat. Leadership grant, Inst. Mus. and Libr. Scis., 2000. Mem.: ALA (com. profl. ethics 2000—03), Assn. Coll. and Rsch. Librs. (ALA conf. program coord. team 2003—), Rutgers Club (bd. dirs. 2003, Phila.), Beta Phi Mu, Phi Beta Kappa. Democrat. Avocations: bicycling, chess. Home: Philadelphia PA Office: Coll NJ Roscoe L West Libr PO Box 7718 Ewing NJ 08628

MEOLA, TONY, professional soccer player, actor; b. Belleville, N.J., Feb. 21, 1969; s. Vincent and Maria Meola; m. Colleen Meola; 1 child, Jonathan. Student, U. Va., 1986—89. Goalkeeper CONCACAF World Cup Qualifying Games, 1989, U.S. World Cup Team, 1990, Brighton Football Club, England, 1990, Fort Lauderdale Strikers, Am. Profl. Soccer League, 1991, U.S. Nat. Team, 1992—94, Long Island Roughriders, 1994—95, U.S. World Cup Team, 1994, NY-NJ MetroStars, Secaucus, 1996—98, Kansas City (Mo.) Wizards, 1998—. Actor: (plays) Tony N' Tina's Wedding, 1995. Named Hermann Trophy winner, MVP, U.S. Cup, 1993; recipient Mo. Athletic Club Player of Yr., 1989. Achievements include drafted ctr. fielder N.Y. Yankees; tried out as placekicker for N.Y. Jets, 1994; mem. N.J. State H.S. Soccer Champions, 1986; NCAA Division I Co-Champions, 1989. Office: care Kansas City Wizards Two Arrowhead Dr Kansas City MO 64129

MERANUS, LEONARD STANLEY, lawyer; b. Newark, Jan. 7, 1928; s. Norman and Ada (Binstock) M.; m. Jane B. Holzman, Sept. 20, 1989; children: Norman, James M., David. LittB, Rutgers U., 1948; LLB, Harvard U., 1954. Bar: Ohio 1954. Assoc. Paxton & Seasongood, cin., 1954-59, ptnr., 1959-85, pres., 1985-89; ptnr. Thompson, Hine and Flory, 1989-96, ptnr.-in-charge Cin. office, 1989-91, mem. firm mgmt. com., 1991-93, of counsel, 1998—; adj. prof. law U. Cin. Coll. Law, 1998-2000. Bd. dirs. Jewish Hosp., 1976-86, chmn. of the bd., 1983-86; trustee Andrew Jergens Found., 1962-97. Mem. ABA, Ohio Bar Assn., Cin. Bar Assn., Am. Arbitration Assn. (chmn. comml. arbitration adv. com., Ohio panel large, complex arbitration cases). Office: Thompson Hine LLP 312 Walnut St Ste 14 Cincinnati OH 45202-4089

MERBLER, CANDACE ANNE, librarian; b. Bklyn., July 14, 1956; d. Patricia Anne M. Daly and Charles Fuoco; m. Richard Albert Merbler, Feb. 14, 1987 (div. Mar. 5, 2003). BA, U. Albany, 1979, MLS, 1999. Ref. support assoc. U. Albany, 1979—. Pres. United Univ. Profls., Albany, 2001—. Mem. Town of Greenfield UDAG Com., Greenfield Center, NY, 1996—. Recipient Excellence award, United U. Professions, N.Y., 1991, Initiatives for Women award, U. Albany, 2002; fellow RASS Dewey fellow, N.Y. Libr. Assn., 1999; scholar Alice-Hastings Murphy scholar, U. Albany Libraries, 1991, Inst. Info. Lit. scholar, Assn. Coll. & Rsch. Libraries, 2002. Mem.: ALA (assoc.), SUNY Librs. Assn. (assoc.), Hudson-Mohawk Libr. Assn. (assoc.), Ea. N.Y. Assn. of Coll. & Rsch. Librs. (assoc.), N.Y. Libr. Assn. (assoc.). Avocations: gardening, crafts, crocheting. Home: 788 Coy Rd Greenfield Center NY 12833 Office: U Albany 1400 Washington Ave Albany NY 12222 Office Phone: 518-442-3564. E-mail: cmerbler@uamail.albany.edu.

MERCADO, LILLIAN AMENSINA, counselor; b. Newark, Dec. 29, 1965; d. Cecil Antonio Davis and Ines Mercedes Serrano; m. Jose Altagricia Mercado, July 30, 1983; children: Celia Mercedes, Matthew Samuel. Data entry installation dept. Sears Roebuck, Wayne, NJ, 1988—93; office mgr. J. Mercado Contracting, Newark, 1992—; cons. asst. Consumers, Montclair, NJ, 1993—94; collector Popular Club Plan, Garfield, NJ, 1994; telemarketer Americana Portraits, West Orange, NJ, 1997—99, customer svc. rep., 1999—2001; bilingual adherence counselor North Jersey Cmty. Rsch. Initiative, Newark, 2001—. Notary pub. Mercado Agy., Newark, 1992—; staff writer Cisco's Artistic Prodn., Jessup, Md., 1995—. Mem. Nat. Black HIV/AIDS Awareness Day, 2003, 2004. Roman Catholic. Avocations: reading, writing, meditation. Home: 474 Summer Ave Newark NJ 07104 Office: North Jersey Cmty Rsch Inst 393 Ctrl Ave Newark NJ 07103 Office Phone: 973-483-3444. Home Fax: 973-482-7142. E-mail: ladyamensina@aol.com.

MERCADO, MARY GONZALES, cardiologist; b. Houston, July 9, 1959; d. Frank Reyes and Joyce (Byrd) Gonzales; m. Antonio Gonzalez Mercado, May 25, 1985. BS magna cum laude, U. Tex., San Antonio, 1987; MD with honors, Baylor Coll. of Medicine, 1992. Diplomate Am. Bd. Internal Medicine, Am. Bd. Cardiovasc. Diseases, Am. Bd. Nuclear Cardiology. Intern U. Tex. Affiliated Hosps., San Antonio, 1992-93, resident, 1993-95, chief resident, 1995-96, fellow in cardiology, 1996-99; pvt. practice, Ozark, Ala. Presenter confs. and symposiums. Contbr. articles to med. publs. Mem. AMA, Am. Soc. Echocardiography, Am. Coll. Cardiology, Am. Soc. Nuc. Cardiology, Tex. Med. Assn., Ala. Med. Assn., Bexar County Med. Soc., Dale County Med. Soc. E-mail: mgmercado@charter.net.

MERCADO, NANCY, writer, educator; b. Atlantic City, N.J., Dec. 12, 1959; d. Salomon and Maria Mercado. BA, Rutgers U., 1982; MA, NYU, 1989; PhD, Binghamton U. SUNY, 2004. Artistic dir. The Young Life Theatre Group P.R.O.C.E.E.D., Inc., 1987—97, founding dir. The Lola Rodríguez de Tió Cultural Inst., 1995—97; faculty mem. Boricua Coll., N.Y.C., 1997—. Presenter in field. Author: It Concerns the Madness, 2000; contbr. poems to mags. and books; prodr.(writer, dir.): (plays) Palm Trees In the Snow, 1989, (writer) Chillin', 1990, (writer, dir.) Forever Earth, 1991, It Is I: Stay Alive, 1992, Planet Earth, 1993, Alicia in Projectland, 1994, (dir.) Let There Be Children, 1995, (writer, dir.) Away, 1996; contbr. articles to profl. publs. Recipient Clifford D. Clark Spl. Rsch. award, Binghamton U., 2003; grantee, N.J. State Coun. Arts, 1989—97; Clifford D. Clark fellow, Binghamton U., 2001—. Home: 953 Amsterdam Ave #3D New York NY 10025

MERCADO-RAMOS, FERDINAND, former secretary of state; b. Lares, P.R., June 18, 1957; m. Michelle Waters Munoz; children: Ferdinand Giovanni, Andres Fernando. BS in Psychology, U. P.R., 1978; JD, Inter-Am. U. P.R., 1981; postgrad., Universidad Computense Madrid. Sec. of state, San Juan, PR, 2000—03. Author: Grito a la Intimidad, 1976, Un Pensamiento en Viaje, 1990.

MERCADO-VALDES, FRANK, broadcast executive; b. 1965; Student, U. Miami. Founder, CEO Heritage Network (formerly African Heritage Network), N.Y.C., 1993—. Exec. prodr. A Tribute to Alex Haley, 1994. With USMC. Named one of Most Influential People in Art, Culture and Media, City New Pub., 1998. Office: Heritage Network 50 Broadway New York NY 10004

MERCANTI, JOHN M. sculptor, engraver; b. Phila., Apr. 27, 1943; married; 2 children. Student, Pa. Acad. Fine Arts, Phila. Coll. Art, Fleisher Art Meml. Sch. Sculptor, engraver US Mint, 1974—. With Pa. Army Nat. Guard. Recipient Sculptor of Yr., Am. Numismatic Assn., 2001. Office: 801 9th St NW Washington DC 20220

MERCER, CHRISTINA MARIE, writer, artist; b. Erie, Pa., Jan. 12, 1959; d. Robert Leroy McGill and Norma Jean Tinti; m. Michael Dennis Mercer, July 26, 2002; children: Ryan David Gray, Miranda. BFA, Am. Continental U., 2004. Vocat. trainer Barber Nat. Inst., Erie, 1989—2003. Author: A Legacy of Love, 2001; contbr. articles to newspapers. Vol. Barber Nat. Inst., 1989—2004. Office: Barber Nat Inst 136 East Ave Erie PA 16507 Personal E-mail: phel783@ma.rr.com.

MERCER, EARNEST BRANT, retired finance educator; b. Gordon, Ala., Dec. 2, 1932; s. Ernest Harmon and Burma Mae Mercer; m. Mary Kate Griffin, Dec. 21, 1935; children: Harry Brant, Deborah Kate Olivier. B in profl. studies, MBA, Pace U. of NY, 1982—84; D of business adminstrn. (hon.), Webber Internat. U., 1998—2003. Mid. mgr. IBM Corp., Armonk, NY, 1958—87; owner/mgr. Human Resource Mgmt. Cons., Auburndale, Fla., 1987—; adj. prof. Webber Internat. U., Babson Pk., Fla., 1999—2004. Cons. Human Resource Mgmt., Auburndale, Fla., 1987—. Author: (novels) A Cabin on the Mountain, (book) The Time of My Life: The Adventures of a Farm Boy. Mem. Auburnale H.S. Bus. Adv. Com., Auburndale, Fla., 1998—2000, Webber Internat. U. Bus. Adv. Coun., Babson Pk., Fla.; ruling elder First Presbyn. Ch., Cranbury, NJ, 1971—74; mem. Media Solutions Internat., Atlanta, 1998—2002. Petty officer second class, naval intelligence NAVY, 1950—53, Japan. Recipient Cmty. Svc., Auburndale City Commn., 1994, Life Mem. Auburndale C. of C., Auburndale C. of C., 1994. Mem.: Auburndale Rotary Club (licentiate; mem. 1988—2004), Lions Club (licentiate; v.p. 1974—75). R-Consevative. Prostestant. Avocations: tennis, woodworking, writing, international travel. Home: 594 Somerset Dr Auburndale FL 33823 Personal E-mail: emercer2@tampabay.rr.com.

MERCER, EDWIN WAYNE, lawyer; b. Kingsport, Tenn., July 19, 1940; s. Ernest LaFayette and Geneva (Frye) M. BBA, Tex. Tech U., 1963; JD, S. Tex. Coll. Law, 1971. Bar: Tex. 1971, U.S. Dist. Ct. (no. dist.) Tex 1975, U.S. Supreme Ct. 1976, U.S. Ct. Appeals (5th Cir.) 1979. Pvt. practice, Houston, 1971-73; gen. counsel, corp. sec. Alcon Labs., Inc., Ft. Worth, 1973-81; ptnr. Gandy Michener Swindle Whitaker Pratt & Mercer, Ft. Worth, 1981-84; v.p., gen. counsel, corp. sec. Pengo Industries, Inc., Ft. Worth, 1984-90, also bd. dirs.; pvt. law practice, 1990—. Bd. dirs. Soc. for Prevention Blindness, 1979—. Mem. ABA, State Bar Tex., Coll. State Bar Tex., South Tex. Coll. Law Alumni Assn., Tex. Tech U. Ex-Assn., Ft. Worth Club, Delta Theta Phi, Phi Delta Theta. Methodist. Office Phone: 817-731-1959.

MERCER, EVELYN LOIS, retired guidance counselor; b. Ellensboro, N.C., Apr. 25, 1934; d. Milton Bernadine Robinson Sr. and Lois Lenora Robinson; m. Theodore Roosevelt Mercer Sr. (div. June 1978); children: Theodore Roosevelt Jr., Brian Vincent, David Lemuel. BS in Math., Livingstone Coll., 1957; MEd in Guidance and Counseling, U. Cin., 1972; student, U. Akron, 1973, Miami U., Ohio, 1973—75, U. Akron, 1974. Cert. math tchr. Ohio, 1963, guidance counselor Ohio, 1972, lic. profl. counselor Ohio Counselor & Social Worker Bd., 1984. Math tchr. Jackson County Pub. Schs., Gumberry, NC, 1957—60, Cin. Pub. Schs., Cin., 1963—72, guidance counselor, 1972—73, Winton Woods City Sch. Dist., Cin., 1973—94, ret., 1994. Mem. adv. com. conselor edn. U. Cin., Cin., 1975—76; admissions adv. bd. Cin. Tech. Coll., Cin., 1975—81, The Ohio State U., Columbus, Ohio, 1982—85; nursing sch. adv. bd. Deaconess Hosp. Sch. Nursing, Cin., 1983—88; dir. Sch. Counseling Cons. Svc., Cin., 1994—, Charlotte, NC, 1994—. Docent Mint Mus., Charlotte; mem. housing commn. City of Forest Park, Cin., 1974—76; Dem. precinct exec. Hamilton County Bd. Elections, Cin., 1974—96. Named Outstanding Counselor of Yr., Inroads of Cin., 1984. Mem.: NEA, AAUW (pres. Charlotte br. 2001—03), Am. Assn Coll. Admissions Counselors, Ohio Assn. Coll. Admissions Counselors, Ohio Sch. Counselors Assn., Ohio Edn. Assn., Livingstone Coll. Alumni Assn., U. Cin. Alumni Assn., Nat. Assn. Advancement for Colored People, Les Birdies Golf Club Charlotte (founder 1999, pres. 1999—2001), Order of Eastern Star, Zeta Phi Beta. Democrat. Methodist. Avocations: golf, travel, bridge, volunteering, gardening. Home and Office: 4101 Rye Mill Ct Charlotte NC 28277

MERCER, FRANCES DECOURCY, artist, educator; b. Centreville, Miss., June 14, 1944; d. John Homer Jr. and Patricia Powers (Given) Mercer. BA in English Lit., U. Miami, 1969, MA in History of Art, 1971; MFA in Painting, San Francisco Art Inst., 1974. Cert. tchr. Fla. Instr. South Fla. Art Inst., Hollywood, Fla., 1979—81; tchg. asst. San Francisco Art Inst., 1974; instr. Broward C.C., Ft. Lauderdale, Fla., 1979—83; owner 17th St. Galleries, Ft. Lauderdale, 1984—91; tchr. Broward County Sch. Bd., 1980—82; adj. prof. Fla. Atlantic U., 1979—80. Exhibited in group shows at Grove Art Gallery, Coconut Grove, Fla., 1973, Emanuel Walter Gallery, San Francisco, 1975, The Lucian LaBaudt Gallery, 1976, The Both Up Gallery, Berkeley, Calif., 1976, Discover Ctr., Ft. Lauderdale, 1980, Nova U. Artoberfest, Art and Culture Ctr. Hollywood, 1981, Indian Hammock Hunt and Riding Club, Okeechobee, Fla., 1998, A.E. Backus Gallery and Mus., Ft. Pierce, Fla., 2000, pvt. collections. Scholar Tuition scholar, San Francisco Art Inst., 1972, 1973, 1974. Avocations: photography, trail hiking, kayaking, golf, sailing. Home: #200 Blue Heron Ln 32801 Hwy 441 Okeechobee FL 34972 E-mail: fmercer@floridawatercolors.com.

MERCER, JAMES LEE, management consultant; b. Sayre, Okla., Nov. 7, 1936; s. Fred Elmo and Ora Lee (Davidson) M.; m. Karolyn Lois Prince, Nov. 16, 1962; children: Tara Lee, James Lee. BS, U. Nev., 1964, MBA, 1966; postgrad. exec. devel. program, Cornell U., 1979. Cert. in mcpl. adminstrn. U. N.C., 1971, lifetime Jr. coll. tchng. credential Calif., cert. mgmt. cons. Methods and results supr. Pacific Tel. & Tel., Sacramento, 1965-66; prodn. control supr. Gen. Dynamics, Pomona, Calif., 1966-67; nuclear submarine project mgr. Litton Industries, Pascagoula, Miss., 1967-70; asst. city mgr. City of Raleigh, N.C., 1970-73; nat. program dir. Pub. Tech., Inc., Washington, 1973-76; gen. mgr. Battelle So. Ops., Atlanta, 1976-79; v.p. Korn/Ferry Internat., Atlanta, 1979-81; pres. James Mercer & Assocs. Inc.; mgmt. cons. Atlanta, 1981-86; chief Indsl. Ext. Divsn., Ga. Inst. of Tech., Atlanta, 1981-83; dir. govtl. cons. svc. Coopers & Lybrand, 1983-84; regional v.p. Wolfe & Assocs., Inc., 1984-86; pres., CEO, chmn. Mercer, Slavin & Nevins, Inc., 1986-90, The Mercer Group, Inc., 1990—. Ad hoc prof. N.C. State U., 1972-73; bd. dirs. Taratec Corp., Columbus; lectr., spkr. in field. Author: Public Management Systems, 1978, Public Technology, 1981, Managing Urban Government Services, 1981, Strategic Planning for Public Managers, 1990, Public Management in Lean Years, 1992; contbr. numerous articles to profl. jours. Chmn. Raleigh Mayor's Civic Ctr. Authority Study Commn., 1971; founding bd. dirs. Mordecai Sq. Hist. Soc., Nat. Civic League; founding mem. U. S.C. Master of Pub. Adminstrn. adv. bd., 1987-97; founding mem. Calif. Poly. State U., adv. coun. Coll. Bus. Adminstrn., San Luis Obispo, 1980-95; founding mem., bd. trustees U. Nev. Found., Reno, 1985-91, trustee emeritus, 1991—. With USN, 1955-59. Mem.: NC League of Municipalities (George C. Franklin award 1971), Instit. Mgmt. Cons. (Atlanta Chpt. (v.p. membership 1991—97, bd. dirs. 1991—97), Contract Svcs. Assn. Am. (bd. dirs. 1994—), Ga. Indsl. Devel. Assn., Tech. Transfer Soc. (dir. 1978—87, treas. 1985—86), Internat. Pers. Mgmt. Assn., Govtl. Fin. Officers Assn., Inst. Indsl. Engrs. (chpt. pres. 1969—70, past pres.'s award 1970), Am. Soc. Pub. Adminstrn., Internat. City-County Mgmt. Assn., Raleigh Forward Leadership Orgn., U. Nev. Alumni Assn. (exec. com. 1969—79, Oustanding Alumnus), Shriners, Rotary, Atlanta C. of C., Masons, Beta Gamma Sigma. Home: 28 Sierra del Sol Santa Fe NM 87508-2136 Office: 551 W Cordova Rd Ste 726 Santa Fe NM 87505-1825 Office Phone: 505-466-9500. E-mail: mercer@mindspring.com.

MERCER, JOHN A. former state legislator; b. Missoula, Mont., Jan. 21, 1957; m. Tine Mercer; children: Thomas, Michael. BA in Bus., U. Mont., 1979; JD, Northwestern U., 1982. Pvt. practice, Polson, Mont., 1982; mem. Mont. Ho. of Reps., 1984—, minority whip, 1989-90, minority leader, 1991-92, house spkr., 1993—2000, mem. rules com., mem. legis. adminstrv. com.; gov. bd. mem. Mont. St. U. Office: Montana St U MT Higher Education Complex 2500 Broadway Helena MT 59620 E-mail: john@polsonlaw.com.

MERCER, LARRY, retail executive; Pres. northeast divsn. The Home Depot, Inc., South Plainfield, N.J., 1991-96, exec. v.p. ops., group pres. Atlanta, 1996—. Office: The Home Depot Inc 2455 Paces Ferry Rd SE Atlanta GA 30339-4024

MERCER, MELVIN RAY, electrical engineer, educator; b. Lubbock, Tex., Sept. 5, 1946; s. Dixie Melvin and Ollie Faye (Sheppard) M.; m. Sharry Billene Cannon, Sept. 9, 1967; children: Rebecca Raylene, Elizabeth Anne. BSEE, Tex. Tech U., 1968; MSEE, Stanford U., 1971; PhD in Elec. Engring., U. Tex., 1980. Registered profl. engr., Tex. Rsch. and devel. engr. GTE Sylvania, Mountain View, Calif., 1968-73; mem. tech. staff Hewlett-Packard Labs., Palo Alto, Calif., 1973-77; lectr. U. Tex., San Antonio, 1977-80; mem. tech. staff Bell Labs., Murray Hill, N.J., 1980-83; asst. prof. elec. and computer engring. U. Tex., Austin, 1983-87, assoc. prof., 1987-91, prof., 1991-95; prof. computer engring. dept. elec. engring. Tex. A&M U., College Station, 1995—, computer engring. chair elec. engring., 1995—. Lectr. Kilgore (Tex.) Jr. Coll., 1977; cons. Rothe Devel. Co., San Antonio, 1979, Lockheed Missiles and Space Co., Austin, 1983, IBM, Austin, 1984, 88-90,

Harris Semicondr., Dallas, 1983-86, 99-2000, State of Tex., Austin, 1984-85, CBS, N.Y.C., 1985-86, Teltech Resource Network, Mpls., 1986-93, Motorola Semicondr., Austin, 1987-88, 91, 99, TSSI, Beaverton, Oreg., 1988-94, MCC, Austin, 1989, Cimflex Teknowledge, Pitts., 1989-90, Rockwell, Newport Bch., Calif., 1991, 95, Integra Test, L.I., N.Y., 1993, Teradyne, 1993 94, Sematech, 1994, AT&T, Oklahoma City, 1995-97, Sanke & Luck, Houston, 1997-98, Taylor & Dunham, 1995, 97, 99-2000, Fulbright & Jaworski, 1997, 99-2002, Hale & Dorr, 2001, 03, Akin, Gump, Strauss, Haner & Feld, 2000, Harris Corp, Melbourne, Fla., 1999-2002, Sigma Tel, Austin, 1999-2000, others; advisor NSF, Washington, 1987-88, mem. engring. initiation awards evaluation panel, 1987, 1993; mem. program com. 1st MCC-Univ. Rsch. Symposium, 1987; lectr. in field. Contbr. articles to profl. jours.; patentee in field. Recipient Presdl. Young Investigator award NSF, 1986, rsch. award Office Naval Rsch., 1986-95, Advanced Projects Rsch. Adminstrn., 1992-95; Werner W. Dornberger Centennial tchg. fellow U. Tex., 1984-90, Engring. Found. endowed faculty fellow, 1990-91, Temple Found. endowed prof. engring., 1991-95; grantee Univ. Rsch. Inst., 1983, Bur. Engring. Rsch., 1984, AT&T Info. Sys., 1985-88, Microelectronics and Computer Tech. Corp., 1985-90, Internat. Test Found., 1986-89, Semicondr. Rsch. Corp., 1989-95, 2000—, IBM, 1989-92, 2001–, Tex. Advanced Tech. Program, 1990-92, 98-2000, 02–, Motorola, 1991-98. Fellow IEEE (editor Design and Test of Computers mag. 1985-88, mem. program com. design for testability workshop Vail, Colo. 1989-95); mem. Computer Soc. of IEEE (vice chmn. Ctrl. Tex. chpt. 1983-85, chmn. 1985-86), Internat. Test Conf. (program com. 1986-89, program vice chmn. 1988, program chmn. 1989, steering com. 1988-93, mktg. vice chmn. 1990, planning chmn. 1992-93, best paper award 1982, hon. mention 1988), Internat. Conf. on CAD (program com. 1987), Design Automation Conf. (best paper award 1991, best paper award Very Large Scale Integrated Cir. Test Symposium 1999), Austin C. of C. (recruitment resource 1983-87), Tau Beta Pi, Eta Kappa Nu, Phi Kappa Phi, Phi Eta Sigma. Avocations: racquetball, swimming, scuba. Office: Tex A&M U Dept Elec Engring 214 Zachry Bldg College Station TX 77843-3259 Office Phone: 979-862-3360. Business E-Mail: mercer@ee.tamu.edu.

MERCER, RICHARD JAMES, lawyer; b. New London, Conn., Oct. 2, 1950; s. James Wilson and Marianne (Wieczorek) M.; m. Ann Holly Gutting, Oct. 9, 1970 (div. 1977); m. Harriet Allston Jopson, May 1, 1982; 1 child, James. BBA, Old Dominion U., 1972; JD, Coll. William and Mary, 1975; LLM in Taxation, Boston U., 1977, LLM in Banking, 1986. Assoc. Epstein & Epstein, Norfolk, Va., 1975, Bernard A. Kaplan, Boston, 1975-76; sole practice, 1976-78, 1979-80; ptnr. Shagory & Shagory, Boston, 1978-79, Alpert, Thurman & Mercer, Boston, 1980-82; assoc. counsel First Nat. Bank Boston, 1983-85, asst. v.p., assoc. counsel, 1985-86, sr. counsel, 1986—. Town coordinator George Bush Presdl. Campaign, Weston, 1980. Mem. ABA, Boston Bar Assn., Am. Arbitration Assn. (arbitrator 1978), Mass. Bar Assn., Va. Bar Assn. Republican. Episcopalian. Office: First Nat Bank Boston 100 Federal St Boston MA 02110-1802

MERCER, RICHARD JOSEPH, retired advertising executive, freelance writer; b. Elizabeth, NJ, Mar. 29, 1924; s. George Washington and Margaret Elizabeth (Walsh) M.; m. Muriel Davis, June 24, 1945 (dec. Mar. 1999); children: Richard George, Karen, James Davis, Lesley Ann; m. Joan Youmans Cozens, Apr. 2, 2001. L.B. in Journalism, Rutgers U., 1949. Announcer, copywriter, news reporter Sta. WCTC, New Brunswick, N.J., 1946-49; asso. creative dir., then v.p., dir. BBDO, Inc., N.Y.C., 1949-76; sr. v.p., creative exec. SSC&B, Inc., N.Y.C., 1977-83, exec. v.p. creative, 1983-85; sr. v.p., assoc. creative dir. McCann-Erickson, Inc., N.Y.C., 1985-87. Lectr. Rutgers U. Sch. Bus., New Brunswick, NJ, 1988-89; spkr. in field. Chmn. Roselle (N.J.) Police Raise Referendum Com., 1958; promotion chmn. Cranford (N.J.) United Fund, 1960; publicity dir. Friends of Mendham (N.J.) Libr., 1974-75; bd. dirs. Friends of Nantucket Atheneum, 1991-2000, pres., 1996-98; trustee Atheneum, 1993-98; mem. Nantucket Airport Commn., 1999-2002. With A.C. USNR, 1943-45. Decorated Air medal.; Recipient 10 Clio awards, 2 Effie awards, also Silver Key award Advt. Writers Assn. N.Y.C. Mem. NATAS, Air Force Assn. (life), Nat. Assn. Scholars, Col. Henry Rutgers Soc., Am. Fedn. Musicians, Broadcasters Found. Roman Catholic. Office Phone: 508-228-4394.

MERCER, RON, professional basketball player; b. May 18, 1976; Student, U. Ky. Guard Boston Celtics, 1997-99, Denver Nuggets, 1999-00, Orlando Magic, 2000, Chgo. Bulls, 2000—. Named SEC Player of the Yr., 1997. Office: c/o Chgo Bulls United Ctr 1901 W Madison St Chicago IL 60612-2459

MERCER, WILLIAM W. prosecutor; BA, U. Mont.; MPA, Harvard U.; JD, George Mason U. Counselor to asst. atty. gen., sr. policy analyst Office of Policy Devel. U.S. Dept. Justice, 1989—94, asst. U.S. atty. Dist. Mont., 1994—2001, U.S. atty., 2001—. Office: PO Box 1478 Billings MT 59103

MERCHANT, ISMAIL NOORMOHAMED, film producer, film director; b. Bombay, Dec. 25, 1936; arrived in U.S., 1958; s. Noormohamed and Hazrabi (Memon) Rehman. BA, St. Xavier's Coll., Bombay, 1958; MBA, NYU, 1960. V.p. Merchant Ivory Prodns. Inc., N.Y.C., 1962—. Prodr.: (films) The Householder, 1963, Shakespeare Wallah, 1965, The Guru, 1969, Bombay Talkie, 1970, Adventures of a Brown Man in Search of Civilization, 1971, Savages, 1972, Helen, Queen of the Nautch Girls, 1973, Autobiography of a Princess, 1975, The Wild Party, 1975, Sweet Sounds, 1976; prodr., prodr.: (films) Roseland, 1977, Hullabaloo Over Georgie and Bonnie's Pictures, 1978, The Europeans, 1979, The Five-Forty-Eight, 1979, Jane Austen in Manhattan, 1980, Quartet, 1981, Heat and Dust, 1983, The Bostonians, 1984, A Room With a View, 1986, The Deceivers, 1988, Slaves of New York, 1988, The Perfect Murder, 1988, Mr. and Mrs. Bridge, 1990, The Ballad of the Sad Cafe, 1991, Howards End, 1992, The Remains of the Day, 1993, Jefferson in Paris, 1995, Feast of July, 1995, Surviving Picasso, 1996, A Soldier's Daughter Never Cries, 1998, The Golden Bowl, 2000, Le Divorce, 2003, Heights, 2004; dir.: Creation of Woman, 1960, Mahatma and the Mad Boy, 1973, The Courtesans of Bombay, 1982, In Custody, 1993, The Proprietor, 1996, Cotton Mary, 1999, The Mystic Masseur, 2001; author: Ismail Merchant's Indian Cuisine, 1986, The Making of the Deceivers, 1988, Ismail Merchant's Vegetarian Cuisine, 1991, Ismail Merchant's Florence, 1994, Once Upon a Time...The Proprietor, 1996, Ismail Merchant's Paris: Filming and Feasting in France, 1999, Ismail Merchant's Passionate Meals: The New Indian Cuisine for Fearless Cooks and Adventurous Eaters, 2d edit., 2001, (autobiography) My Passage from India–A Film Makers Journey from Bombay to Hollywood and Beyond, 2003; prodr.: Heights, 2004. Decorated comdr. des Arts and Lettres France, Padma Bhushan India. Fellow: Brit. Acad. Film and TV Arts (hon.). Home: 400 E 52nd St New York NY 10022-6404 Office: 250 W 57th St Ste 1825 New York NY 10107-1899 E-mail: imerchant@merchantivory.com.

MERCHANT, JAMES A. medical educator; MD, U. Iowa; PhD in Epidemiology, U. N.C. Resident Cleve. Metro. Gen. Hosp.; fellow Duke U.; Trudeau fellow Brompton Hosp., London; mem. faculty U. N.C., 1973-75; adj. prof. W.Va. U., 1985-81; mem. faculty Coll. Medicine U. Iowa, 1981—. Contbr. articles to profl. jours. Mem. APHA, Am. Coll. Radiology, Am. Lung Assn., Am. Occupl. Medicine Assn., Am. Thoracic Soc., Internat. Assn. Occupl. Health, Nat. Inst. Occupl. Safety and Health (mem. bd. sci. counselors), Alpha Omega Alpha. Office: U Iowa Coll Medicine 2707 Steindler Building Iowa City IA 52242-1008

MERCHANT, MYLON EUGENE, physicist, engineer; b. Springfield, Mass., May 6, 1913; s. Mylon Dickinson and Rebecca Chase (Currier) M.; m. Helen Silver Bennett, Aug. 4, 1937; children: Mylon David (dec.), Leslie Ann Merchant Alexander(dec.), Frances Sue Merchant Jacobson. BS magna cum laude, U. Vt., 1936, DSc (hon.), 1973; DSc, U. Cinn., 1941; DSc (hon.), U. Salford, Eng., 1980; D of Engring (hon.), Kettering U., 1994. Rsch. physicist Milacron, Inc., 1940-48, sr. rsch. physicist, 1948-51, asst. dir. rsch., 1951-57, dir. phys. rsch., 1957-63, dir. sci. rsch., 1963-69, dir. rsch. planning, 1969-81, prin. scientist, mfg. rsch., 1981-83; dir. advanced mfg. rsch. Metcut Rsch. Assocs., Inc., 1983-90; sr. cons. TechSolve, Cin., 1990—. Adj. prof. mech. engring. U. Cin., 1964-69, mfg. engring., 2001-; vis. prof. mech. engring. U. Salford, Eng., 1973—; hon. prof. U. Hong Kong, 1995—. Bd. dirs. Dan Beard coun. Boy Scouts Am., 1967-80, pres.'s coun., 1980— . Recipient Georg Schlesinger prize City of Berlin, 1980; Otto Benedikt prize Hungarian Acad. Scis., 1981, 1st Japan Soc. Precision Engring. prize, 1997; named to Automation Hall of Fame, 1995. Fellow Soc. Tribologists and Lubrication Engrs. (pres. 1952-53), Am. Soc. Metals Internat., Ohio Acad. Sci., Soc. Mfg. Engrs. (hon. mem., pres. 1976-77); mem. NAE, ASME (hon., mfg. medal 1988), Internat. Instn. Prodn. Engring. Rsch. (hon., pres. 1968-69), Engrs. and Scientists of Cin. (pres. 1961-62), Fedn. Materials Socs. (pres. 1974), Phi Beta Kappa, Sigma Xi, Tau Beta Pi. Achievements include research on machining process and systems approach to manufacturing. Home: 3939 Erie Ave Apt 105 Cincinnati OH 45208-1913 Office: TechSolve 6705 Steger Dr Cincinnati OH 45237-3097 Office Phone: 513-948-2067. E-mail: merchant@techsolve.org., gmerchant@fuse.net.

MERCHANT, NATALIE ANNE, musician, singer; b. Jamestown, N.Y., Oct. 26, 1963; d. Tony and Ann Merchant; 1 child. Lead singer band 10,000 Maniacs, 1981-1993; solo artist, 1993—; founder Myth Amer. Records LLC, 2003—. Albums with 10,000 Maniacs include Human Conflict Number Five, 1982, Secrets of the I Ching, 1983, The Wishing Chair, 1986, In My Tribe, 1987, Blind Man's Zoo, 1989, Hope Chest, 1990, Our Time in Eden, 1992, 10,000 Maniacs MTV Unplugged, 1993; solo album Tigerlily, 1995, Ophelia, 1998, Live In Concert, 1999, Motherland, 2001, Natalie Merchant, 2001, Motherland, 2001, The House Carpenter's Daughter, 2003; composer soundtracks: Felicity, 1998, Earthlings, 2003. Office: Myth Amer Records 660 Madison Ave 10th Fl New York NY 10021

MERCHANT, P. GLENN, military officer, physician; b. Quonset Point, RI, Jan. 6, 1953; s. Paul Glenn and Mary Joan Merchant; m. Debra Colleene Brown, Nov. 25, 1951; children: Nicholas Ryan, Kaitlin Elizabeth, Joshua Daniel. BS in Biology, The Citadel, 1980—83; MD, Med. U. of SC., 1983—87; BA in Polit. Sci., The Citadel, 1971—75; Masters in Pub. Health and Tropical Medicine, Tulane U. Sch. of Pub. Health & Tropical Medicine, 1991—92. Diplomate Am. Bd. of Preventive Medicine, 1994. Marine aviator VMA-542, Cherry Point, NC, 1977—80; sr. med. officer USS John C. Stennis (CVN 74), Norfolk, 1994—97; asst. prof. Uniformed Services U., Bethesda, 1997—; dir. DOD Ctr. for Edn. & Rsch. in Patient Safety, Bethesda, 2002—. Capt. USN, 1987—2003. Recipient Delta Omega Scholastic Honor Soc., Tulane U. Sch. of Pub. Health, 1992, Phi Kappa Phi Honor Soc., The Citadel, 1983. Fellow: Am. Coll. of Preventive Medicine (chair 2003—), Aerospace Med. Assn. (v.p. 2001—03). Methodist. Office: Uniformed Services U 4301 Jones Bridge Rd Bethesda MD 20814-4799 Office Phone: 301-295-1493. Business E-Mail: gmerchant@usuhs.mil.

MERCHANT, ROLAND SAMUEL, SR., health facility administrator, educator; b. N.Y.C., Apr. 18, 1929; s. Samuel and Eleta (McLymont) M.; m. Audrey Bartley, June 6, 1970; children: Orelia Eleta, Roland Samuel, Huey Bartley. BA, NYU, 1957, MA, 1960; MS, Columbia U., 1963, MSHA, 1974. Asst. statistician N.Y.C. Dept. Health, 1957-60, statistician, 1960-63, N.Y. Tb and Health Assn., N.Y.C., 1963-65; biostatistician, adminstrv. coord. Inst. Surg. Studies, Montefiore Hosp., Bronx, N.Y., 1965-72; resident in adminstrn. Roosevelt Hosp., N.Y.C., 1973-74; dir. health and hosp. mgmt. Dept. Health, City of N.Y., 1974-76; from asst. adminstr. to adminstr. West Adams Cmty. Hosp., L.A., 1976; spl. asst. to assoc. v.p. for med. affairs Stanford U. Hosp., Calif., 1977-82, dir. office mgmt. and strategic planning, 1982-85, dir. mgmt. planning, 1986-90; v.p. strategic planning Cedars-Sinai Med. Ctr., L.A., 1990-94; cons. Roland Merchant & Assocs., L.A., 1994—. Clin. assoc. prof. dept. family, cmty. and preventive medicine Stanford U., 1986—88; dept. health rsch. and policy Stanford U. Med. Sch., 1988—90. With U.S. Army, 1951—53. Fellow, USPHS. Fellow: APHA, Am. Coll. Healthcare Execs.; mem.: N.Y. Acad. Scis. Home: 27335 Park Vista Rd Agoura Hills CA 91301-3639 Office Phone: 818-879-8732.

MERCHANT, SHARON J. state legislator; b. West Palm Beach, Fla., Aug. 30, 1963; BS in Internat. Affairs, Fla. State U., 1986. Exec. v.p. Equipment Rental Svc.; mem. Fla. Ho. of Reps., Tallahassee, 1992—; vice chair Palm Beach Legis. Del., 1993-94, chair, 1994-95. Chair Com. on Transp. and Econ. Devel. Appropriation Fiscal Responsibility Coun., 1996-97; mem. Com. on Utilities and Comms. Econ. Impact Coun., 1996-97, Com. on Water and Resource Mgmt. Govtl. Responsibility Coun., 1996-97. Mem. small bus. adv. bd. Fla. Atlantic U.; mem. Fla. Def. Conversion and Transition Commn., Transp. Task Force, Seminole Boosters, Big Bros./Big Sisters, Young Reps. Palm Beaches, Palm Beach County Republican Exec. Com. Recipient Roll Call Fla. C. of C., 1993, 94, 95, 96, 97, Champion for Econ. Devel. award Rep. Caucus, 1994; named Legis. of Yr. Assn. Retarded Citizens, 1995. Mem. Am. Legis. Exch. Coun., Nat. Assn. Women Bus. Owners, Nat. Assn. Women in Constrn., Northside Rep. Club, Rep. Club Palm Beaches. Episcopalian. Avocations: softball, golf, gym, walking. Home: 824 US Highway 1 North Palm Beach FL 33408-3873 Office: Fla Capitol 401 S Monroe St Rm 221 Tallahassee FL 32301-2034

MERCIER, EILEEN ANN, corporate financial executive; b. Toronto, Ont., Can., July 7, 1947; d. Thomas Sidley and Frances Katherine (Boone) Falconer; m. Ernest Cochrane Mercier, Feb. 8, 1980; children: Jenny, Sheelagh, Peter, Michael, Stuart. BA with honors, Wilfred Luth. U., 1968; MA, U. Alta., Can., 1969; fellow, Instn. Can. Bankers, 1975; MBA, York U., 1977. Mgr. corp. fin. Toronto-Dominion Bank, 1972-78, portfolio mgr. TD capital; dir., U.S. comm. ops. Canwest Capital Corp., Toronto, 1978-81; mgr. fin. strategy & planning Gulf Can. Ltd., Toronto, 1981-86, mgr. corp. fin.; v.p. The Pagurian Corp., Toronto, 1986-87; v.p., treas. Abitibi-Price, Inc., Toronto, 1987-88, v.p. corp. devel., 1989-90, sr. v.p., CFO, 1990-95. Bd. dirs. Hydro One, Inc., TeeKay Shipping Corp., The CGI Group Inc., Winpak Ltd., ING Bank Can., Quebecor World, Inc., Shermag Ltd. Past chmn., mem. bd. govs. Wilfrid Laurier U., Waterloo, Ont., York U., U. Health Network. Recipient Outstanding Bus. Leader award Sch. Bus. and Econs., Wilfrid Laurier U., 1991, Award for Outstanding Contbn. Schulich Sch. of Bus. York U., 1997. Office: 199 Cranbrooke Ave Toronto ON Canada M5N 1M6

MERCIER, RITA, mayor; Mem. Lowell (Mass.) City Coun., 1996—2002; mayor State of Mass., Mass., 2002—. Com. organizer Com. to Elect Senator Henry Jackson for Pres., Bklyn., Senator Edward Kennedy Re-election Com., Com. to Protect Jobs, The Use of Convenient Containers (The Bottle Bill); bd. dir. Friends Coun. Aging. Mem.: East End Club (mem. ladies auxilliary), Greek Am. Legion, Post 662 VFW (mem. honor guard). Office: 375 Merrimack St Lowell MA 01852

MERCKER, MARY ALICE, aviation school administrator; b. Kansas City, Mo., June 29, 1932; d. Kenneth Foster Rhees and Catherine Mary (Tellman) Henel; m. Reid Martin, Nov. 23, 1950 (div. Nov. 1969); children: Reid J., Kenneth C., Mark T., Mary M., Theodore H., Sylvia R., Ben X., Teresa I. Student, Phoenix Coll., 1949-50; AA, Pima Coll., 1990-93; student, U. Ariz., 1994. Fed. aviation adminstr.; comml. pilot; cert. flight instr. Instr. Ariz. Sch. Aviation, Tucson, 1979, Tucson Cmdr., 1980, AVRA Flt. Ctr., Marana, Ariz., 1976-78; pres., founder Alpha Air, Inc., Tucson, 1980—; sec., treas. Manasco Inc., Tucson, 1987—. Aviation cons., Tucson, 1987—; adj. profl aviation Pima C.C., Tucson, 1988-94, curriculum cons., 1988-93. Author: Northumberland Dreaming, 1998, also numerous poems. Recipient 2nd Place Sparrowgrass Poetry Forum, 1996, 1st Place Sparrowgrass Chapbook award, 2001. Mem. Ariz. Pilots Assn., Aircraft Owners and Pilots Assn., 99's (life). Home: 6220 W Belmont Rd Tucson AZ 85743-9212 Office: Alpha Air Inc HC 2 Box 282 Tucson AZ 85735-9709 E-mail: alphair@msn.com.

MERCURI, JOAN B. museum administrator; b. N.Y.C. BA, Va. Commonwealth U., 1984. Mgmt. positions various corps., Ill., 1986-96; exec. dir. Frank Lloyd Wright Home and Studio Found., Oak Park, Ill., 1996—; pres., CEO Frank Lloyd Wright Preservation Trust, Oak Park, 2000—. Mem. Am. Assn. Museums, Nat. Trust for Hist. Preservation, Frank Lloyd Wright Bldg. Conservancy, Am. Soc. Assn. Execs., Assn. Fundraising Profls., Board Source.

MERCURIO, MIA LYNN, education educator; b. Bridgeport, Conn., June 9, 1971; d. Jon Peter and Anne Marie Mercurio; m. Charles Richard Allan, Oct. 5, 2003. BA, Manhattan Coll., 1993; MA, Columbia U., 1994; diploma, Harvard U., 1996; EdM, Columbia U., 1995, EdD, 2002. Reading tchr. Pear Tree Point Sch., Darien, Conn., 1996—97; reading specialist Flood Mid. Sch., Stratford, Conn., 1997—98; reading instr. Am. U., Wash., DC, 1998—99; asst. prof. edn. Salisbury (MD) State U., 1999—2000, Lehman Coll., City U. of NY, Bronx, 2000—. Asst. and grad. prof. adv. N.Y.C. Tchg. Fellows, Bronx, 2003. Contbr. articles various profl. jours. Mem.: CHADD, Nat. Counc. of Tchrs. of English, Internat. Reading Assn., Theta Alpha Kappa, Epsilon Sigma Pi, Kappa Delta Pi. Catholic. Home: 198 Hill Farm Rd Fairfield CT 06824 Office: Lehman Coll 250 Bedford Pk Blvd W Bronx NY E-mail: kmmerc@aol.com.

MERCURIO, RENARD MICHAEL, real estate corporation executive; b. N.Y.C., June 22, 1947; s. Pasquale J. and Ann F. Mercurio; m. Abbie Gonzalez, June 29, 1968; children— Kristin, Allison. BA, Queens Coll., N.Y.C., 1968; MBA, U. Rochester, 1969. CPA, N.Y.; lic. real estate broker, Calif. Sr. accountant Peat, Marwick & Mitchell, N.Y.C., 1969-73; mgr. Gulf & Western Industries, Inc., N.Y.C., 1973-78; v.p., treas. Famous Players Ltd., Toronto, Ont., Can., 1978-81; exec. v.p. Famous Players Realty Ltd., Toronto, 1981-84; pres. Design Twenty-Seven Ltd., Toronto, 1984—, Renric Holdings, Ltd., 1987—; CFO Schickedanz Real Estate, Palm Beach Gardens, Fla., 1999—2003. Mem. AICPA, N.Y. State Soc. CPAs.

MERDEK, ANDREW AUSTIN, publishing/media executive, lawyer; b. Portland, Maine, Oct. 11, 1950; s. Philip and Eleanor (Weiss) M.; m. Jeanne Mullen, July 22, 1983; children: David, Jonathan. AB, Middlebury Coll., 1972; JD, U. Va., 1978. Bar: D.C. 1978, U.S. Dist. Ct. D.C. 1979, U.S. Ct. Appeals (D.C. cir.) 1979, U.S. Supreme Ct. 1982. Reporter, editor Portland Press Herald, 1973-75; assoc. Dow, Lohnes & Albertson, Washington, 1978-86, ptnr., 1986-87; v.p., gen. mgr. Atlanta Constitution and Journal, 1987-92; v.p. legal affairs Cox Enterprises, Inc., Atlanta, 1993—, gen. counsel, 1993—, corp. sec., 1993—. Mem. Newspaper Assn. of Am. (chmn. legal affairs com.), Order of Coif, Phi Beta Kappa. Home: 445 Mount Vernon Hwy NW Atlanta GA 30327-4313 Office: Cox Enterprises Inc 6205 Peachtree Dunwoody Rd Atlanta GA 30328- E-mail: andy.merdek@cox.com.

MERDINGER, CHARLES JOHN, civil engineer, naval officer, academic administrator; b. Chgo., Apr. 20, 1918; s. Walter F. and Catherine (Phelan) M.; m. Mary McKelleget, Oct. 21, 1944; children: Anne, Joan, Susan, Jane. Student, Marquette U., 1935-37; BS, U.S. Naval Acad., 1941; BCE, Rensselaer Poly. Inst., 1945, MCE, 1946; DPhil (Rhodes scholar), Brasenose Coll., Oxford U., Eng., 1949; LHD (hon.), Sierra Nev. Coll., 1987; DLitt (hon.), U. Nev., Reno, 1994. Registered profl. engr., Wis. Commd. ensign USN, 1941, advanced through grades to capt. Civil Engr. Corps, 1959; served aboard USS Nevada, USS Alabama Atlantic and Pacific, 1941-44; design, constrn. pub. works Washington, others, Panama, 1946-47, Washington, Bremerton, Wash., Adak, Alaska and Miramar, Calif., 1949-56; comdg. officer, dir. U.S. Naval Civil Engring. Lab., Port Hueneme, Calif., 1956-59; pub. works officer U.S. Fleet activities, Yokosuka, Japan, 1959-62; head English, history and govt. dept. U.S. Naval Acad., Annapolis, Md., 1962-65; asst. comdr. ops. & maintenance Naval Facilities Engring. Command, Navy Dept., 1965-67; pub. works officer Seabees (NSA), DaNang, Vietnam, 1967-68; comdg. officer Western div. Naval Facilities Engring. Command, San Bruno, Calif., 1968-70; pres. Washington Coll., Chestertown, Md., 1970-73; v.p. Aspen (Colo.) Inst. Humanistic Studies, 1973-74; dep. dir. Scripps Instn. Oceanography, La Jolla, Calif., 1974-80; dir. Avco, 1978—. Author: Civil Engineering Through the Ages, 1963; contbr.: articles to Ency. Britannica; others. Mem. Md., Calif., Oreg. and Nev. Selection Coms. for Rhodes Scholars, sec. Nev. Com., 1982-89; exec. vol. Boy Scouts Am.; sec., mem. exec. com. Md. Ind. Coll. and Univ. Assn., 1971-72; mem. So. Regional Edn. Bd, 1971-73, Nat. Com. History and Heritage of Am. Civil Engring., 1965-72; Alumni trustee U.S. Naval Acad., 1971-74; mem. coun. Rensselaer Poly. Inst., 1972—; trustee Found. for Ocean Rsch., 1976-80, Desert Rsch. Inst. Found., Nev., 1983-92, U. Nev. Reno Found., 1986-93; chmn. bd. trustees Sierra Nev. Coll., 1980-87, chmn. bd. emeritus, 1987; commr. N.W. Assn. Commn. on Colls., 1988-93. Pfc Wis. Nat. Guard, 1935—37. Decorated Legion of Merit with combat V; named All-Am. in lacrosse, 1945, Papal Knight Grand Cross Equestrian Order of Holy Sepulchre of Jerusalem, 1992; inducted into Rensselaer Athletic Hall of Fame, 1983; recipient Disting. Eagle Scout award, 1984. Fellow ASCE (Nat. History and Heritage award 1972), Explorers Club, Soc. Am. Mil. Engrs. (Toulmin medal 1952, 57, 61); mem. NSPE, Soc. History Tech., Am. Soc. Engring. Edn., Brasenose Soc., Pearl Harbor Survivors Assn., Nat. Eagle Scout Assn. (regent), Phalanx, Sigma Xi, Tau Beta Pi, Chi Epsilon. Clubs: Vincent's, Oxford. Roman Catholic. Home: 726 Tyner Way PO Box 7249 Incline Village NV 89452-7249 also: 5538 Caminito Consuelo La Jolla CA 92037-7217

MEREDITH, DALE DEAN, civil engineering educator; b. Centralia, Ill., Mar. 24, 1940; s. Leslie Edward Meredith and Beulah Marie (McClelland) Nattier; m. Linda Jean Hutson, July 3, 1965; children: Sarah Elizabeth, Laura Jane. AA, Centralia Twp. Jr. Coll., 1961; BS, U. Ill., 1963, MS, 1964, PhD, 1968. Registered profl. engr., N.Y., Ill. Asst. prof. U. Ill., Urbana, 1968-73; assoc. prof. civil engring. SUNY, Buffalo, 1973-79, prof., 1979-2000, chmn. dept. civil engring., 1987-96, prof. emeritus, 2000—. Co-author: Design and Planning Engineering Systems, 1973, 2d edit., 1985; also over 50 articles. Vice pres. Baptist Conv. N.Y., Syracuse, 1982-84, 94-95, chmn. exec. bd., 1987. Grantee U.S. Office Water Research and Tech., 1966-73, 75-78, U.S. Dept. Interior, 1968-79, U.S. Dept. Commerce, 1976-79, various pvt. cos., 1979—, N.Y. State Agys., 1980-2000. Fellow ASCE (chmn. exec. com. Water Resources Planning and Mgmt. div., 1988, editor jour. Water Resources Planning and Mgmt. 1982-84); mem. Am. Geophys. Union, Am. Soc. Engring. Edn., Am. Water Resources Assn. (editor Water Resources Bull. 1990-91). Office: SUNY Dept Civil Engring Buffalo NY 14260-4300 E-mail: ciedale@eng.buffalo.edu.

MEREDITH, GARY S. physician; b. NYC, Apr. 13, 1954; s. Sidney and Ann M.; m. Michelle Rose Pantirer, Jan. 8, 1984; children: Joshua, David. BA, Boston U., 1976; MD, N.Y. U., 1981. Diplomate Am. Bd. Internal Medicine, Am. Bd. Rheumatology. Intern Bellevue Hosp., N.Y.C., 1981-82, resident, 1982-84; fellow NYU Med. Ctr., 1984-86, chief fellow rheumatology, 1985-86; chief divsn. rheumatology dept. internal medicine Franklin Hosp. Med. Ctr., Valley Stream, N.Y., 1990—; pvt. practice, Rockville Centre, N.Y., 1986—. Physician NYU Med. Ctr., Franklin Hosp. Med. Ctr., Mercy Med. Ctr., South Nassau Cmtys. Hosp.; clin. asst. prof. medicine Sch. Medicine NYU. Contbr. articles to profl. jours. Fellow ACP, Am. Coll. Rheumatology. Office: 242 Merrick Rd Rockville Centre NY 11570-5254 Office Phone: 516-536-9424.

MEREDITH, OWEN NICHOLS, public relations executive, genealogist; b. Etowah, Tenn., Mar. 27, 1924; s. Owen Habner and Ora (Nichols) M.; m. Mary Virginia Wright, July 19, 1980. BA, U. Va., 1946; MA, Syracuse U., 1952. Sub-features editor Together mag.-Meth. Pub. House, Nashville and Chgo., 1953-57; pub. info. dir. Nashville-Davidson County ARC, 1957-70; exec. dir. Tenn. State Mus., Nashville, 1970-72; owner, mgr. Gazetteer Typesetters, Nashville, 1973-74; pub. relations dir. Tenn. ARC, Nashville, 1974-89; pvt. practice Nashville, 1989—. Author: The Parish Activities Handbook, 1996, (with R. McBride) The Hedden Family of North Georgia, 1957, The Nichols Family of North Georgia, 1960, (with Lee Seitz) A History of the American Red Cross in Nashville, Tennessee, 1982, (with Mary Virginia Meredith and Susan Wright Lyons) One Cup Love and a Pinch of Catnip, 1998; editor: (with McBride and M. Rothrock) Eastin Morris' 1834 Tennessee Gazetteer, 2d edit., 1971; contbr. articles, photographs and book revs. to hist. jours. Mem. ARC Disaster Res., 1989—; vol. archivist Diocese of Nashville, 1992—. Mem. Pub. Rels. Soc. Am. (cert.), Tenn. Soc. Health Care Pub. Rels., Internat. Assn. Bus. Communicators, Confederate Meml. Lit. Soc. (Tenn regent 1972-80), Tenn. Exec. Residence Preservation Found., 1971—), Conf. for Pastoral Planning and Coun. Devel. Office: 410 Lancaster Ave Nashville TN 37212-4013 E-mail: meredithm@k12tn.net.

MEREDITH, THOMAS C. academic administrator; Vice chancellor exec. affairs U. Miss., until 1988; pres. Western Ky. U., Bowling Green, 1988-97; chancellor U. Ala. Sys., Tuscaloosa, 1997—2002. Office: Chancellor Univ Sys Ga 270 Washington St SW Atlanta GA 30334-9007 E-mail: chancellor@usg.edu.

MEREDITH, THOMAS J. civic leader, philanthropist, former computer company executive; B.Polit. Sci., St. Francis Coll., Loretto, Pa., 1972; JD, Duquesne U., 1975; LLM in Taxation, Georgetown U., 1977. Bar: Calif., D.C., Pa. Dir. tax rsch. and planning Castle & Cooke, Inc.; sr. tax cons. Arthur Young & Co.; co-founder, gen. mgr. Amdahl Capital Corp.; v.p., treas. Sun Microsys., Inc.; sr. v.p., CFO Dell Computer Corp., Round Rock, Tex., 1992—2001; mng. dir. Dell Ventures, 2000—01; CEO MFI Capital. Dir. Freemarkets, Inc., Tipping Point; adj. prof., McCombs Sch. Business Univ. Texas; adv. bd. Wharton Sch., Univ. Penn., Univ. Texas. Chair, pres. Meredith Private Found., 1998—; founding investor & chair Austin Idea Network. Mem. Fin. Execs. Inst. Office: Austin Idea Network PO Box 2570 Austin TX 78768

MERENDINO, K. ALVIN, surgical educator; b. Clarksburg, W.Va., Dec. 3, 1914; s. Biagio and Cira (Bivona) M.; m. Shirley Emma Jane Hill, July 6, 1943; children: Cira Anne Watts, Nancy Jane Napuunoa, Susan Hill Mitchell, Nina Merendino-Sarich, Maria King Merendino-Stillwell. BA, Ohio U., 1936, LLD (hon.), 1967; MD, Yale U., 1940; PhD, U. Minn., 1946. Diplomate Am. Bd. Surgery, Am. Bd. Thoracic Surgery. Intern Cin. Gen. Hosp., 1940-41; resident U. Minn. Hosp., Mpls., 1941-45; rsch. asst. Dr. Owen H. Wangensteen, 1942-43; trainee Nat. Cancer Inst., 1943-45; dir. program in postgrad. med. edn. in surgery Ancker Hosp., St. Paul, 1946-48; instr. dept. surgery U. Minn., Mpls., 1944-45, asst. prof. dept. surgery, 1945-48; assoc. prof. dept. surgery U. Wash., Seattle, 1949-55, dir. exptl. surgery labs., dept. surgery, 1950-72, prof. dept. surgery, 1955-81, prof. emeritus, 1981—, prof. and adminstrv. officer dept. surgery, 1957-64, prof., chmn., 1964-72; chmn. dept. surgery King Faisal Specialist and Rsch. Ctgr., Riyadh, Saudi Arabia, 1976, dir. med. affairs, 1976-79, dir. Cancer Therapy Inst., spl. cons. to Coun., supr. for exec. mgmt., assoc. dir. med. affairs, 1981-82; dir. ops. King Faisal Med. City, Riyadh, 1981-85. Mem. adv. com. for med. rsch., Boeing Airplane Co., 1959-67, chmn., 1962l cons. Children's Orthopedic Hosp., Seattle, 1972-82; mem. adv. com. on heart disease and surgery for crippled children's svc., Wash. State Dept. Health and Div. Vocational Rehab., 1961; mem. surgery study sect. NIH, 1958-62, subcom. on prosthetic valves for cardiac surgery, chm. 1st Nat. Conf., 1960, mem. adv. com. 2d Nat. Conf. on Prosthetic Heart Valves, 1969, Surgery A study sect. chmn., 1970-72, Nat. Heart and Lung Inst. Tng. Com., 1965-69; cons. VA, Seattle, 1949-59, 65-81; mem. adv. com. on hosps. and clinics, USPHS, 1963-66; mem. surgery test com. Nat. Bd. Med. Examiners, 1963-67; mem. surgery resident rev. com., Conf. Com. on Grad. Edn. in Surgery, 1963-73, vice-chmn., 1972-73; chmn. 2d Saudi Arabian Med. Conf., Riyadh, 1978; mem. com. on postgrad. med. edn., Kingdom of Saudi Arabia Ministry of Health, 1978-79. Editor in chief: Prosthetic Valves for Cardiac Surgery, 1961; assoc. editor: Prosthetic Heart Valves, 1969; mem. editorial bd. Am. Jour. Surgery,. 1958-83, Jour. Surg. Rsch., 1961-69, Pacific Medicine and Surgery, 1964-68, King Faisal Hosp. Medicine Jour. (renamed Annals of Saudi Medicine), 1981-85; contbr. articles to profl. jours., chpts. to books; producer movies on surgery. Recipient cert. of merit Ohio U. Alumni Assn., 1957, Outstanding W.Va. Italian-Am. award W.Va. Italian Heritage Festival Inc., Clarksburg, W.Va., 1984, Spirit of Freedom award A. James Mancin, Sec. State W.Va., 1984, Disting. W. Virginian award State of W.Va., 1984, John Baird Thomas Meml. award Ohio U.; named Surgery Alumnus of Yr., U. Minn., 1981, Disting. Citizen Wash. State, Lt. Gov. John Cherberg, 1981, K. Alvin Merendino Day Seattle, Mayor Charles Royer, 1981; NIH grantee, 1951-76; Verdi scholar Yale U. Fellow ACS (numerous coms., bds.), Soc. of Univ. Surgeons (councilman at large 3 yrs.), Internat. Soc. Surgery; mem. Am. Surg. Assn. (adv. mem. com. 1959-64, v.p. 1972-73), Am. Assn. for Thoracic Surgery, Halsted Soc., Henry N. Harkins Surg. Soc., N. Pacific Coast Surg. Assn., Seattle Surg. Soc. (honored special tribute annual meeting 1997), So. Surg. Soc. (Arthur H. Shipley award 1972), Am. Bd. Surgery 1958-64 (vice chmn. 1962-63, chmn. 1963-64, emeritus 1964—); University Club, Seattle Golf Club, Phi Beta Kappa, Sigma Xi, Beta Theta Pi (sec., pres.), Phi Beta Pi (hon.). Republican. Episcopalian. Avocations: golf, fly fishing, bird hunting, gardening. Home: The Highlands Shoreline WA 98177

MERENSTEIN, JOEL HARVEY, physician, researcher; b. Pitts., Nov. 9, 1934; s. Morris Merenstein and Sarah Shrinsky; m. Nancy W. Weintraub, June 16, 1957; children: Gary, Bruce, Daniel, Beth. BS, Univ. Pitts., Pitts., 1956, MD, 1960. Diplomate Am. Bd. Family Practice, lic. Pa. Clin. instr. Univ. Pitts. Sch. of Medicine, Pitts., 1969—70, clin. asst. prof., 1970—72; med. dir. Russellton Med. Group, New Kensington, Pa., 1972—74; clin. assoc. prof. Univ. Pitts. Sch. of Medicine, Pitts., 1977—80, chief divsn. of family medicine, 1979—80; dir. of rsch. and fellowships Univ. Pitts. Sch. of Medicine, St. Margaret Family Practice Residency program, Pitts., 1981—; clin. assoc. prof. Univ. Pitts. Sch. of Medicine, Pitts., 1989—2000; pvt. practice Penn Plum Family Medicine, Pitts., 1995—. Clin. prof. of family medicine Univ. Pitts. Sch. of Medicine, Pitts., 2000—; project dir. area health edn. ctr. Univ. Pitts., 1979—80; vis. prof. Haifi Univ., Israel, 1992; reveiwer and cons. Thomas Jefferson Univ., 1994; cons. Univ. Wash., Seattle, 1996. Contbr. articles to numerous prol. jour. Com. mem. Pitts. Regional Health Care, Pitts., 2001—. Capt. USAF, 1961—63, USAF Hosp., Dover, De. Named one of Best Drs. in Am., 2002—; recipient Excellence in Edn. award, Soc. of Tchr. of Family medicine, 1994, Award of Merit, Am. Bd. of Family Practice, 1995. Mem.: AAFP GAP, AAFP, STFM (editl. bd. 1992—2000, chair comm. com. 1996—2000, bd. dirs. 1996—2000). Avocations: writing, hiking, reading, tennis, family activites. Home: 5600 Munhall Rd Pittsburgh PA 15217 Office: UPMC St Margaret 3937 Butler St Pittsburgh PA 15201 Office Phone: 412-622-7343 ext. 317. Business E-Mail: joelm@pitt.edu.

MERESCHAK, VOLMAR A. retired obstetrician-gynecologist; b. Ansonia, Conn., 1921; MD, U. Pa., 1945. Diplomate Am. Bd. Ob-Gyn. Intern Grace-New Haven Cmty. Hosp., 1945-46; resident in ob-gyn. Kings County Hosp., Bklyn., 1948-49, Lincoln Hosp., N.Y.C., 1950-51; staff Warren Hosp., Phillipsburg, N.J.; ret. Fellow ACS; mem. ACOG, AMA, Am. Soc. Colposcopy and Cervical Pathology.

MERFELD, AUDRA L. language educator; b. Dubuque, Iowa, Aug. 30, 1974; d. Linda M. and David J. Merfeld. BA in French and English, Clarke Coll., 1996; MA in French, Penn State U., 2002. Tchg. asst. French U. Iowa, Iowa City, 1998—99, Pa. State U., University Park, 1999—; instr. English lang. Universite Lumiere Lyon II, Lyon, France, 2000—01. Pres. French Grad. Orgn. Pa. State, University Park, Pa., 2003—04, v.p., 2002—03; French lang. program coord. Summer Intensive Lang. Inst. Pa. State, 2003—04; grad. student del. Grad. Student Assn. Pa. State, 1999—2000; instr. French Summer Intensive Lang. Inst. Pa. State, 2002—04. Recipient John and Catherine O'Malley award French, Clarke Coll., 1994, John and Catherine O'Malley award Spanish, 1996, Socrates Award, 1995; Sr. Mary St. Clara Sullivan scholar, 1994, Presdl. scholar, 1992—96, All Am. scholar, 1996. Mem.: Am. Assn. Teachers French, Am. Coun. Tchg. Fgn. Langs., French Hist. Studies, World Tang Soo Do Assn., Phi Sigma Iota, Kappa Gamma Pi. Achievements include research in Presentation of research paper at 56th Annual Kentucky Foreign Language Conference (2003); Presentation of research paper at Winthrop-King Institute for French Studies conference in Tallahassee, Florida (2003); co-created a collaborative language class linking a college class with a high school class in France; co-created a new college course called Exploring the City of Light: Parisian Spaces and Places. Avocations: travel, martial arts, reading, writing, movies. Business E-Mail: alm334@psu.edu.

MERFELD, GERALD LYDON, artist; b. Des Moines, Feb. 19, 1936; m. Carol L. Fiser; 1 child, Elizabeth Ann. Studied with William Mosby, Chgo. Studio asst. Dean Cornwell; combat artist USN. Group exhbns. include Mass. Mus. of Fine Arts, Springfield, Smithsonian Inst., Audubon Artists, N.Y.C., Nat. Acad. of Western Art, others; represented in permanent collections Marietta Coll., USN Archives, John J. McDonough Collection of Am. Art, John Deere & Co. Bd. dirs. Frontier Pathway Scenic Byway, Colo., 1995-98. Recipient Gold Medal of Honor, Am. Artist Profl. League, 1989, Am. Artists Mag. award Knickerbocker Artists, 1989, 2 Gold medals Washington Sq. Exhibit, N.Y.S., Painting award Okal. Mus. of Art, 1975, Mainstreams Juror's award of Merit, Marietta Coll., 1976, Mainstreams award of Distinction, 1977, First prize Hope Show, 1980, First prize Butler Inst. of Am. Art. Office: Brookwood Gallery 2302 Muddy Rd Westcliffe CO 81252 E-mail: gmerfeld@earthlink.net.

MERGLER, H. KENT, investment counselor; b. Cin., July 1, 1940; s. Wilton Henry and Mildred Amelia (Pulliam) M.; m. Judith Anne Metgzer, Aug. 17, 1963; children: Stephen Kent, Timothy Alan, Kristin Lee. BBA with honors, U. Cin., 1963, MBA, 1964. CFA, C.I.C. Portfolio mgr. Scudder, Stevens & Clark, Cin., 1964-68, exec. v.p. Chgo., 1970-73; v.p. Gibralter Rsch. & Mgmt., Ft. Lauderdale, Fla., 1968-70; ptnr. Stein Roe & Farnham, Ft. Lauderdale, 1973-84; ptnr., pres., dir., prin. Stein Roe & Farnham, Inc., Chgo., 1984-91, also mem. exec. com.; pres. Stein Roe Investment Trust; mng. ptnr., chief investment officer Loomis, Sayles & Co., L.P., Palm Beach Gardens, Fla., 1992-2000; chmn., pres., CEO Northstar Capital Mgmt., Inc., 2000—. Arbitrator Nat. Assn. Security Dealers, Inc., 1976-82. Chmn. adminstrv. bd. Christ United Meth. Ch., Ft. Lauderdale, 1981-83; mem. fin. com. Kenilworth Union Ch., 1989-92, bd. dirs., 1994-99; chmn. investment com. Broward Cmty. Found., 1992-2001; mem. Martin County Econ. Coun., 1992-2000; bd. dirs. Pine Crest Prep. Sch., 1982-84, bd. advisors, 1984-87; corp. adv. bd. U. Cin. Coll. Bus. Adminstrn., 1991-94; bd. dirs. Hibiscus House Children's Found., 1993-99, 2001—, chmn. investment com., 1994-99, 2001--; bd. dirs. Coral Ridge Little League, 1976-84, pres., 1980-81; elder, chmn. fin. com., chmn. stewardship com. First Presbyn. Ch., Stuart, 2001—. Mem. Fin. Analysts Soc. So. Fla. (bd. dirs. 1974-78, pres. 1975), Bond Club Ft. Lauderdale (bd. dirs. 1978-82), Willoughby Golf Club, Cullasaja Club (Highlands, N.C.), City Club Palm Beach, Beta Gamma Sigma, Beta Theta Pi. Republican. Home: 3980 SE Old Saint Lucie Blvd Stuart FL 34996-5119 Office: 4400 PGA Blvd Ste 600 Palm Beach Gardens FL 33410-6559

MERGLER, HARRY WINSTON, retired engineering educator; b. Chillicothe, Ohio, June 1, 1924; s. Harry Franklin and Letitia (Walburn) M.; m. Irmgard Erna Steudel, June 22, 1948; children— Myra A. L., Marcia B. E., Harry F. BS, MIT, 1948; MS, Case Inst. Tech., 1950, PhD, 1956. Aero. research scientist NACA, 1948-56; faculty Case Inst. Tech., 1957—, prof. engrng., 1962—, Leonard Case prof. elec. engrng. emeritus, 1988—; dir. Digital Systems Lab., 1959—. Vis. scientist, USSR, 1958; vis. prof. Norwegian Tech. U., 1962; cons. to industry, 1957—; editor Control Engrng. mag., 1956—; pres. Digital/Gen. Corp., 1968-72; cons. Exploratory Research div. NSF. Author: Digital Systems Engineering, 1961, also articles, chpts. in books. Served with AUS, 1942-45. Recipient Case gold medal for sci. achievement Case Inst. Tech., 1980. Fellow IEEE (bd. dirs. 1987-89, v.p. 1989, Lamme medal 1978, Centennial medal 1984, 3d Millennium medal 2000); mem. NAE, Indsl. Electronic Soc. (pres. 1977-79), Cleve. Engrng. Soc., N.Y. Acad. Scis., Blue Key, Sigma Xi, Tau Beta Pi, Theta Tau, Pi Delta Epsilon, Zeta Psi. Home: 9658 Halyards Ct Fort Myers FL 33919-4492 Personal E-mail: hwmergler@aol.com.

MERGLER, NANCY L. academic administrator; BA in Psychology, Syracuse U., 1972, MA in Developmental Psychology, 1975, PhD in Developmental Psychology, 1977. Tchg. asst. dept. psychology Syracuse U., 1973—75; asst. prof. dept. psychology Washington Coll., 1976—83, assoc. prof., 1984—94; prof. dept. psychology U. Okla., 1995—, sr. v.p., provost, 1995—. Contbr. articles to profl. jours. Mem.: APA, Okla. Psychol. Assn., Southwestern Psychol. Assn., Ea. Psychol. Assn., Gerontol. Soc. Office: Provosts Office 104 Evans Hall Univ Okla Norman OK 73019-0390*

MERGUERIAN, ARSHAG, architect; b. Gaza, Sept. 25, 1926; came to U.S., 1956; s. Merguer and Coharig (Hagopian) M.; m. Barbara-Joyce Nahigian, Aug. 13, 1961; children: Gayané-Karen, Tamara-Elaine. BA, Am. U. Beirut, 1950, BSc in Civil Engrng., 1952; MArch, Harvard U., 1960. Registered architect, Mass. Civil engr. Motherwell Bridge, Qatar, 1952-55, 1955—56; self-employed arch. Cambridge and Wellesley, Mass., 1966—. Author book revs. and articles on arch.; commd. projects, Saudi Arabia, 1977-80. Vice chair Wellesley Design Rev. Bd., 1980-90, mem., 1990—; chair Am. Gen. Benevolent Union Am., Watertown, Mass., 1962-64; mem. Wellesley Hist. Dist. Commn., 1980—. Mem. AIA. Armenian Apostolic. Avocations: skiing, tennis, swimming. Home: 21 Pine Tree Rd Wellesley MA 02482-4711

MERHIGE, ROBERT REYNOLD, JR., lawyer; b. NYC, Feb. 5, 1919; s. Robert Reynold and Eleanor (Donovan) Merhige; m. Shirley Galleher, Apr. 24, 1957; children: Robert Reynold III, Mark Reynold. LLB, U. Richmond, 1942, LLD (hon.), 1976; LLM, U. Va., 1982; LLD (hon.), Washington and Lee U., 1990, Wake Forest U., 1994. Bar: Va. 1942. Ptnr. Bremner Merhige Montgomery & Baber, Richmond, 1945-67; judge U.S. Dist. Ct., Richmond, 1967—; resigned, 1998; counsel Hunton & Williams, Richmond, 1998—. Guest lectr. trial tactics Law Sch. U. Va., Edwald Disting. prof. law, 1987—88; adj. prof. Law Sch. U. Richmond, 1973—87; appeal agt. Henrico County Draft Bd., 1954—67; mem. NCAA spl. com. discipline rules; profl.-in-residence, Zambia, 1994. Co-author: Virginia Jury Instructions. Mem. Richmond Citizens Assn. With USAF, World War II. Decorated Air medal with four oak leaf clusters; named Citizen of the Yr., 3d Dist. Omega Psi Phi, 1972, Richmond Urban League, 1977, Style Mag., 1986, Richmonder of the Yr., 1984, 1987; named one of 100 Most Influential Richmonders of Last Century, Style Mag. and Valentine Mus., 2000; recipient Amara Civic Club award, 1968, Spl. award, City of Richmond, 1967, Disting. Alumni award, U. Richmond, 1979, Disting. Svc. award, Nat. Alumni Coun. U. Richmond, 1979, Herbert T. Harley award, Am. Judicature Soc., 1982, Athenian Citizen medal, 1979, Torch of Liberty award, Anti-Defamation League of B'nai B'rith, 1982, T.C. Williams Sch. of Law Disting. Svc. award, 1983, Pres.'s award, Old Dominion Bar Assn., 1986, William J. Brennan award, 1986, Merit Citation award, NCCJ, 1987, William B. Green award for professionalism, U. Richmond, 1989, Marshal-Wythe medallion (William & Mary Faculty award), 1989, Lewis F. Powell, Jr. award, Am. Inns of Ct., 1999. Fellow: Va. Law Found.; mem.: Nat. Arbitration Forum (arbitrator), Nat. Patents Bd. (cert. panelist), FedNet (dispute resolution), John Marshall Inns of Ct. (founding mem.), Jud. Conf. U.S., Va. Trial Lawyers Assn. (chmn. membership com. 1964—65, Disting. Svc. award 1977), Am. Law Inst. (faculty), Richmond Bar Assn. (pres. 1963—64, multi-dist. lit. panel 1990—, Hill-Tucker award 1991), Va. Bar Assn., Omicron Delta Kappa (Hunter W. Martin Profl. award 1998). Office: Hunton & Williams Riverfront Plz East Tower 951 E Byrd St Richmond VA 23219-4074 Office Phone: 804-788-8711. E-mail: r.merhige@hunton.com.

MERIDEN, TERRY, physician; b. Damascus, Syria, Oct. 12, 1946; arrived in U.S., 1975; s. Izzat and Omayma (Aidi) Meriden; m. Lena Kahal, Nov. 17, 1975; children: Zina, Lana. BS, Sch. Sci., Damascus, 1968; MD, Sch. Medicine, Damascus, 1972, doctorate cum laude, 1973. Diplomate Am. Bd. Internal Medicine. Resident in infectious diseases Rush Green Hosp., Romford, Eng., 1973; house officer in internal medicine and cardiology Ashford (Eng.) Group Univ. Hosps., 1973-74; sr. house officer in internal medicine and neurology Grimsby (Eng.) Group Univ. Hosps., 1974; registrar in internal medicine and rheumatology St. Annes Hosp., London, 1974-75; jr. resident in internal medicine Shadyside Hosp., Pitts., 1975-76, sr. resident in internal medicine, 1976-77; fellow in endocrinology and metabolism Shadyside Hosp. and Grad. Inst., Pitts., 1976-77; clin. asst. prof. U. Ill., Peoria, 1979; pres. Am. Diabetes Assn., Peoria, 1982-84; dir. Proctor Diabetes Unit, Peoria, 1984—, 1984—. Adviser Gov. of Ill. on diabetes. Mem. editl. bd. Diabetes Forecast mag., Clin. Diabetes, 1990; contbr. articles to profl. jours. Fellow: ACP, Am. Coll. Endocrinology; mem.: ADA (chmn. profl. edn. and rsch. 1980—, mem. editl. bd., mem. Spanish lit. bd., nat. bd. dirs. 1986—, vice chmn. nat. com. on diabetes edn. and affiliate svcs. 1986—, Outstanding Svc. award 1984, Outstanding Diabetes Educator award 1986), AMA (Recognition award 1985), Am. Coll. Endocrinology, Am. Assn. Clin. Endocrinology (founding), Am. Cancer Soc. (Life Line award 1983), Obesity Found. (Century award 1984, Recognition award 1985). Home: 115 E Coventry Ln Peoria IL 61614-2103 Office: 900 Main St Ste 300 Peoria IL 61602-1049 Office Phone: 309-673-1717. E-mail: tmeriden@aol.com.

MERIDETH, SUSAN CAROL, business administration educator; b. St. Louis, May 25, 1956; d. George Getzel Brody and Jacquie Jean Lammers; m. John Wolf Merideth, July 28, 1979; children: Laura, Michelle. AAS, St. Louis C.C., 1977; BS, Fontbonne U., 1979; Master of Bus. Adminstrn., Maryville U., 1994. Presch. tchr. various instns., San Diego, 1979—82, Greater San Diego Health Plan, San Diego, 1985—87; supr. Cmty. Care Network, San Diego, 1987—90; mgr. St. John's Mercy Med. Ctr., St. Louis, 1990—95; contracts mgr. Nashua Eye Assocs., Nashua, 1996—98; practice mgr. Found. Med. Ptnrs., Nashua, 1998—99; assoc. prof. bus. adminstrn. Hesser Coll., Manchester, NH, 2000—. Mem.: AAUP, Nat. Bus. Edn. Assn., New England Regional Adv. Bd., Phi Theta Kappa (faculty advisor Alpha Nu Upsilon chpt. 2002—, mem. Pi Kappa chpt.). Office: Hesser Coll 3 Sundial Ave Manchester NH 03103 Office Phone: 603-668-6660.

MERIGAN, THOMAS CHARLES, JR., internist, medical researcher, educator; b. San Francisco, Jan. 18, 1934; s. Thomas C. and Helen M. (Greeley) Merigan; m. Joan Mary Freeborn, Oct. 3, 1959; 1 child, Thomas Charles III. BA with honors, U. Calif., Berkeley, 1955; MD, U. Calif., San Francisco, 1958. Diplomate Am. Bd. Internal Medicine. Intern 2d and 4th Harvard med. services Boston City Hosp., 1958—59, asst. resident medicine, 1959—60; clin. assoc. Nat. Heart Inst., NIH, Bethesda, Md., 1960—62; assoc. Lab. Molecular Biology, Nat. Inst. Arthritis and Metabolic Diseases, NIH, 1962—63; practice medicine specializing in internal medicine and infectious diseases Stanford, Calif., 1963—; asst. prof. medicine Stanford U. Sch. Medicine, 1963—67, assoc. prof. medicine, 1967—72, head div. infectious diseases, 1966—92, prof. medicine, 1972—, George E. and Lucy Becker prof. medicine, 1980—. Dir. Diagnostic Microbiology Lab. Univ. Hosp., 1966—72, dir. Diagnostic Virology Lab., 1969—99; dir. Ctr. AIDS Rsch. Stanford U., 1988—; hosp. epidemiologist, 1966—88; mem. microbiology rsch. tng. grants com. NIH, 1969—73, virology study sect., 1974—78; cons. antiviral substances program Nat. Inst. Allergy and Infectious Diseases, 1970—94, mem. AIDS clin. drug devel. commn., 1986—94; mem. Virology Task Force, 1976—78, bd. sci. counselors, 1980—85; mem. U.S. Hepatitis panel U.S. and Japan Coop. Med. Sci. Program, 1979—90; mem. AIDS subcom. Nat. Adv. Allergy and Infectious Diseases Coun., 1988—89; co-chmn. interferon evaluation group Am. Cancer Soc., 1978—81; vaccines and related biol. products adv. com. Ctr. for Drugs and Biols., FDA, 1984—88; internat. adv. com. on biol. sci. Sci. Coun., Singapore, 1985—88; adv. com. J.A. Hartford Found., 1979—84; mem. Albert Lasker awards jury, 1981—84; peer rev. panel U.S. Army Med. R&D Com., 1986—88; nat. com. to rev. current procedures for approval New Drugs for Cancer and AIDS, 1989—90; mem. Com. to Study Use of Coms. within FDA, 1991—92. Contbr. articles on infectious diseases, virology and immunology to jours.; editor: Antivirals with Clinical Potential, 1976, Antivirals and Virus Diseases of Man, 1979, Antivirals and Virus Diseases of Man, 4th edit., 1997, Regulatory Functions of Interferon, 1980, Interferons, 1982, Interferons as Cell Growth Inhibitors, 1986; assoc. editor: Virology, 1975—78, Cancer Rsch., 1987—91; co-editor: (monograph series) Current Topics in Infectious Diseases, 1975—92, Cytomeglovirus Infect and Ganciclovir, 1988, Focus on Didanosine (ddI), 1990, Practical Diagnosis of Viral Infection, Textbook of AIDS Medicine, 1994, Practical Diagnosis of Viral Infection, Textbook of AIDS Medicine, 2d edit., 1999, Surrogate Markers for HIV Infection, 1995, Antimicrobial Therapy in Vaccines, 1999; mem. editl. bd.: Archives Internal Medicine, 1971—81, Jour. Gen. Virology, 1972—77, Infection and Immunity, 1978—81, Intervirology, 1973—85, Proc. Soc. Exptl. Biology and Medicine, 1978—87, Revs. of Infectious Diseases, 1979—89, Jour. Interferon Rsch., 1980—89, Antiviral Rsch., 1980—86, Jour. Antimicrobial Chemotherapy, 1981—91, Molecular and Cellular Biochemistry, 1982—89, AIDS Rsch. and Human Retroviruses, 1983—, Jour. Virology, 1984—89, Biotechnology Therapeutics, 1988—98, Jour. Infectious Diseases, 1989—94, Clin. Drug Investigation, 1989—, HIV: Advances in Rsch. and Therapy, 1999—2000, Internat. Jour. Antimicrobial Agts., 1990—99, The AIDS Reader, 1991—, AIDS, 1993—, Clin. Immunotherapeutics, 1994—, Antiviral Therapy, 1996—99. Recipient Borden award for Outstanding Rsch., Am. Assn. Med. Colls., 1973, Merit award, Nat. Inst. Allergy and Infectious Diseases, 1988, Maxwell Finland Lectureship award, Infectious Diseases Soc. Am., 1988; fellow Guggenheim Meml. fellow, 1972. Fellow: AAAS (counsilor); mem.: AMA, Royal Soc. Medicine, Calif. Acad. Medicine, Santa Clara County Med. Soc., Calif. Med. Assn., Internat. Soc. Interferon Rsch. (coun. 1983—89), Pan Am. Group for Rapid Viral Diagnosis, Inst. Medicine, Am. Soc. Virology, Infectious Diseases Soc. Am., Soc. Exptl. Biology and Medicine (publ. com. 1985—89), Western Soc. Clin. Rsch., Am. Fedn. Clin. Rsch., Am. Assn. Immunologists, Am. Soc. Clin. Investigation (coun. 1977—80), Am. Soc. Microbiology, Western Assn. Physicians, Assn. Am. Physicians, Alpha Omega Alpha. Home: 148 Goya Rd Portola Valley CA 94028-7307 Office: Stanford U Sch Medicine Divsn Infectious Diseases Stanford CA 94305

MERILAN, MICHAEL PRESTON, astrophysicist, educator, dean; b. Columbia, Mo., Jan. 5, 1956; s. Charles Preston and Phyllis Pauline (Laughlin) M.; m. Karene Anne Yanuklis, Sept. 2, 1995. BS summa cum laude in Physics, U. Mo., Columbia, 1978, MS, 1980; PhD in Astronomy, Ohio State U., 1985. Grad. tchg. asst. U. Mo., Columbia, 1978-80; grad. tchg. assoc., instr. dept. astronomy Ohio State U., Columbus, 1980-85; asst. prof. dept. physics and astronomy SUNY, Oneonta, 1985-91, assoc. prof., 1991—, chmn. dept. physics and astronomy, 1990-93, acting dean divsn. sci. and social sci., 1993-96, dean, 1996—. Astron. cons. Ohio Dept. Natural Resources, 1982-83; Oneonta smart node advisor Cornell Nat. Supercomputer Facility, Oneonta, 1987-92. Contbr. articles to profl. jours. O.M. Stewart fellow U. Mo., 1979; U. Mo. Curators scholar, 1974-78; Mahan Writing award U. Mo., 1975. Mem. AAAS, Am. Astron. Soc., Astron. Soc. Pacific, Internat. Amateur Profl. Photoelectric Photometry Assn., Sigma Xi, Phi Eta Sigma, Phi Kappa Phi, Phi Beta Kappa, Pi Mu Epsilon, Sigma Pi Sigma, Omicron Delta Kappa. Achievements include analytic and numeric investigation of protostellar hydrodynamics; determination of the properties of static and slowly rotating partially degenerate relativistic stellar structures. Office: Dean Sci and Social Sci SUNY-Oneonta 336 Netzer Bldg Oneonta NY 13820 Business E-Mail: merilamp@oneonta.edu.

MERIN, MITCHELL M, corporate financial executive; Grad., Trinity Coll., 1975. Pres., dir. Morgan Stanley Investment Advisors, Inc., 1997—98; pres., COO, investment mgmt. Morgan Stanely, 1998—; CEO Morgan Stanley Investment Advisors, Inc., 1998—, pres. for various companies of, 1999—, CEO for various companies of, 2002—. Office: Morgan Stanley 1585 Broadway New York NY 10036

MERINI, RAFIKA, foreign language, cultures and literatures educator; b. Morocco; d. Mohamed M. and Fatima Merini. BA in English cum laude, U. Utah, 1978, MA in Romance Langs. and Lits., 1981; postgrad., U. Wash., 1980-82; cert. in translation, SUNY, Binghamton, 1988, PhD in Comparative Lit., 1992. Tchg. asst. U. Utah, Salt Lake City, 1978-80, U. Wash., Seattle, 1980-82; adminstrv. asst., tchr. French, interpreter The Lang. Sch., Seattle, 1982-83; lectr. Pacific Luth. U., Tacoma, spring 1983; instr. French and Spanish Ft. Steilacoom C.C. (now Pierce C.C.), 1983—85; tchg. asst. dept. romance langs. SUNY, Binghamton, 1985-87, tchg. asst. women's studies dept., summer 1988, tchg. asst. comparative lit. dept., 1986-88; vis. instr. humanities and French Union Coll., Schenectady, NY, 1988—89; vis. instr. dept. fgn. langs. and lits. Skidmore Coll., Saratoga Springs, N.Y., 1989-90; asst. prof. dept. modern and classical langs. State U. Coll., Buffalo, 1990—96, assoc. prof. dept. modern and classical langs., 1996—. Coord. Buffalo State Coll. women's studies interdisciplinary unit State U. Coll., Buffalo, 1993-99, adviser French Club, 1990-93; founder, dir. Trois-Pistoles French Immersion Program, U. Western Ont.-Buffalo State Coll., London, 1994, 95; presenter, spkr., conf. organizer in field. Author: Two Major Francophone Women Writers, Assia Djébar and Leïla Sebbar: A Thematic Study of Their Works, 1999, 2d printing, paperback edit., 2001; mem. editl. bd. Jour. Middle Eastern and North African Intellectual and Cultural Studies; contbr. articles to profl. jours. Grantee Nat. Defense Student award U. Utah, 1974; also numerous other grants and awards. Mem. MLA, Am. Assn. Tchrs. French, Women in French, Conseil Internat. d'Etudes Francophones, Pi Delta Phi, Soc. Hon.

Française, Kappa Theta (hon.). Home: PO Box 1063 Buffalo NY 14213-1063 Office: State Univ Coll-Buffalo Modern & Classical Langs 1300 Elmwood Ave Buffalo NY 14222-1095 E-mail: merinir@buffalostate.edu.

MERINO, AKINDOTUN, small business owner, consultant; arrived in U.S., 1988; d. Timothy and Omotola Akinyemi; divorced; 1 child, Lon Ogunduyile; m. Kevin Anthony Merino, July 17, 1999; 1 child, Abrianna. BA in Edn., U. Lagos, 1987; MA in Edn., Pepperdine U., 1993; postgrad., Capella U., 2004. Cert. tchr. Calif. Writer Resume Svc., Torrance, Calif., 1989—90; asst. store mgr. Thrifty Corp., L.A., 1990—93; educator West Angles Christian Acad., LA, 1993—95, San Bernardino (Calif.) Unified Sch., 1995—2003; pres., family cons. Jars Edn. Inst., Rancho Cucamonga, Calif., 2003—; pres. Living Desires Network. Coord. Avid, San Bernardino, 1999—2003; spkr. in field. Author: Academic Success, 2003, Bathtub Therapy, 2004, (manual) Living Desires, 2003. Mem.: Am. Cons. League, Am. Psychol. Assn., Indep. Edn. Cons. Assn., Calif. Tchr. Assn. Office: Jars Edn Inst 9333 Baseline Rd Ste 120 Rancho Cucamonga CA 91730 Office Phone: 909-476-2323. E-mail: webmaster@jarsinstitute.com.

MERINOFF, HERMAN I. vintager, wine company executive; Chmn., pres., CEO Sonoma Vineyards, Healdsburg, Calif.; CEO Charmer Industries Inc., Queens, N.Y. Vintager, wine and spirits executive. Chmn., pres., chief exec. officer Sonoma Vineyards, Healdsburg, Calif; chief exec. officer, Charmer Industries Inc., Queens, New York. Office: Sonoma Vineyards 11455 Old Redwood Hwy Healdsburg CA 95448-9523

MERINOFF, SPENCER, food products executive, CEO Sunbelt Beverage, Balt. Office: Sunbelt Beverage Corporation 226 Dover Rd Glen Burnie MD 21060-6414 Fax: 410-832-7730.

MERIWETHER, HEATH J. newspaper consultant, retired newspaper publisher; b. Columbia, Mo., Jan. 20, 1944; s. Nelson Heath and Mary Agnes (Immele) Meriwether; m. Patricia Hughes, May 4, 1979; children: Graham, Elizabeth. BA in History, BJ, U. Mo., 1966; MAT, Harvard U., 1967; Advanced Exec. Program, Northwestern U. Journalism fellow Stanford U.; reporter Miami (Fla.) Herald, 1970—72, editor Broward and Palm Beach burs., 1972—77, exec. city editor, 1977—79, asst. mgr. editor news, 1979—80, mng. editor, 1981—83, exec. editor, 1983—87, Detroit Free Press, 1987—95, pub., 1996—2004; newspaper cons., 2004—. Chmn. Ready to Succeed Partnership, 2002—04; bd. dirs. Rails to Trails Conservancy, Detroit Symphony Orch., 1996—. Lt. USNR, 1967—70. Roman Catholic. Avocation: tennis. Office: 217 River Rd GrandView-on-Hudson NY 10960 E-mail: hmeriwether@knightridder.com.

MERK, BRADLEY ROBERT, orthopedic surgeon; s. Richard and Bonnie Merk; m. Kristin L Todaro, Aug. 30, 1997; children: Abigail, Emma, Katherine. MD, U. of Ill., 1994—99. Diplomate Am. Bd. of Orthop. Surgery, 2002. Asst. prof. of orthop. surgery Northwestern U., Chgo., 2001—; dir. of orthop. trauma Northwestern Meml. Hosp., Chgo., 2002—. Office: Northwestern Medical Faculty Foundation 675 North St Claire Ste 17-100 Chicago IL 60611

MERK, ELIZABETH THOLE, investment company executive; b. Salt Lake City, July 29, 1950; d. John Bernard and Emily Josephine (Knotek) Thole; m. J. Eliot Merk, July 26, 1996 (div.); 1 child from previous marriage, William Lance Ulich. BA, U. Hawaii, Hilo, 1984, paralegal cert. cum laude, 1989; postgrad.in bus. administrn., U. Hawaii, Manoa, 1985-86. Lic. gen. agt. Hawaii, Tex.; registered investment advisor, stock broker Hawaii, Tex., Calif., Utah. Regional archtl. rep. Lightolier, Inc., Salt Lake City, 1978-80; group sales rep. FHP/Utah, Salt Lake City, 1980-81; health net rep. Blue Cross Corp., L.A., 1981-82; v.p. fin. Bus. Support Systems, Hilo, 1983-89; rep. Prudential Ins. and Fin. Svcs., Honolulu, 1989-97; registered rep. Pruco Securities Corp. subs. Prudential Ins. & Fin. Svcs., 1989-97; acct. exec. Dean Witter Reynolds, 1997-98; adv. assoc., registered prin. Mutual Svc. Corp., 1998—2001; adv. assoc., registered rep. Centaurus Fin. Inc., 2001—. Docent Lyman House, 1984-85, L.A. County Mus. of Art, 1980-81, S.L.C. Art Mus., 1970-80; bd. dirs. YWCA, Hawaii Island, 1980-91, 1st v.p., 1988. Named YWCA Vol. of Yr., 1991, Top 25 Women owned Firms in Hawaii, Pacific Bus. News, 2001, 2002, 2003, Women Who Mean Bus. in Hawaii, Pacific Bus. News, 2001, 2002, 2003; named to Ct. of the Table Million Dollar Round Table, 2000; recipient Nat. Quality award 1991, 92, 93, 94, Nat. Sales Achievement award NAIFA, 1992, 93; Paul Harris fellow Rotary Internat., 1997. Fellow: Life Underwriters Tng. Coun.; mem.: AAUW (bd. dirs. Hilo chpt. 1987—89, fundraiser chmn. Kona chpt. 1992, Steven Bufton grantee 1985), Securities Industry Assn., Million Dollar Round Table (mem. ct. of the table 2000, mem. Top of the Table 2001—04), Nat. Assn. Ins. and Fin. Advisors (charter mem.), Nat. Assn. Life Underwriters (legis. rep. West Hawaii chpt. 1995—97), Am. Bus. Women's Assn. (pres. Nani O Hilo chpt. 1995—96, membership chmn. 1996—97, inner circle 1997—), Outdoor Circle, Soroptimists. Roman Catholic. Office: 118 Kamehameha Ave Hilo HI 96720 Office Fax: 808-883-8399.

MERK, FREDERICK BANNISTER, biomedical educator, medical researcher; b. Cambridge, Mass., Feb. 21, 1936; s. Frederick and Lois Alberta (Bannister) M.; m. Linda Jean Poole, Oct. 22, 1966 (dec. Dec. 1994); children: John F., R. Daniel; m. Laura Ann Bradford, July 11, 1998; 1 stepchild, Letty A. Bradford. AB, Harvard Coll., 1958; PhD, Boston U., 1971. Asst. prof. pathology Boston U. Sch. Medicine, 1972-73; assoc. prof. dept. pathology Tufts U. Sch. Medicine, Boston, 1973—2002, assoc. prof. dept. anatomy, 1973—2002, emeritus prof. pathology and anatomy, 2002—, part time tchr. anatomy, 2002—, dir. electron microscopy facility, 1975-85. Cons. electron microscopy Mass. Gen. Hosp., Boston, 1964-85; cons. toxicol. testing Transgenic Scis., Worcester, Mass., 1988-91, U.S. Army, 1998-2001. Contbr. more than 60 articles to profl. jours. Trustee Broadway United Meth. Ch., Lynn, Mass., chmn. 1994-2000; lay rep. of Ch. to ann. New Eng. Conf., 2000—. Recipient Distng. Career in Tchr. award, 2002; grantee, NIH, 1994—98. Mem. Am. Soc. Cell Biology, Fedn. Am. Soc. Exptl. Biology, Am. Assn. Anatomists, Microscopy Soc. Am., Boston Cancer Rsch. Assn., Sigma Xi. Achievements include research on biology of cells in target organs responding to hormones with emphasis on benign prostatic hypertrophy (enlargement) and prostate cancer. Home: 28 Warwick Rd Melrose MA 02176 Office: Tufts Univ Sch Medicine Dept Anatomy 136 Harrison Ave Boston MA 02111-1800 E-mail: fmerk@hotmail.com.

MERKEL-MORAN, CHRISTA ILSE, investor, linguist, educator; b. Leipzig, Saxony, Germany, Jan. 5, 1946; arrived in U.S., 1968; d. Erich Harry and Ilse Dora (Waehnert) Merkel; m. William Joseph Moran, May 5, 1967 (dec. Mar. 4, 1979); children: Leslie Paige, Linda Christa. BA, U. Tuebingen, 1968; postgrad., U. Alaska, 1968—69. German linguistics. Clk. Anchorage Westward Hotel, 1969—71; sales mgr. Windsor Park Hotel, Washington, 1971—75; linguist, instr. Def. Lang. Inst., Dept. Def., Washington, 1975—79; investor in real estate, sports cars Atlanta, 1979—. Cons. Dept. Def., 1976-79; real estate agt., Northside Realty Co., Atlanta, 1992—. Author: Die Millie Miglia, 1969; Der Nuerburgring, 1975; German Culture, 1977. Chairperson for a United Germany Com., Washington, Atlanta, Leipzig chpt.; fundraiser UNICEF. Named Sportswriter of Yr., ADAC of Germany, 1977. Democrat. Home: PO Box 34165 Pensacola FL 32507-4165 Office: Buckhead Brokers 5395 Roswell Rd NE Atlanta GA 30342-1976

MERKER, STEVEN JOSEPH, lawyer; b. Cleve., Feb. 21, 1947; s. Steven Joseph and Laverne (Zamenik) Merker; m. Janet L. Whyatt; children: Steven, Rena, Ashley, Matthew. BS, Case Inst. Tech., 1968; MS, U. Fla., 1973; JD, George Washington U., 1976. Bar: Ohio 1976, U.S. Dist. Ct. (no. dist.) Ohio 1976, U.S. Dist. Ct. Colo. 1979, U.S. Ct. Appeals (10th cir.) 1979, U.S. Supreme Ct. 1989. Assoc. Jones, Day, Reavis & Pogue, Cleve., 1976-78, Davis, Graham & Stubbs, Denver, 1978-82, ptnr., 1983-96, chmn. labor and employment group, 1989-96; chmn. litig., labor and employment groups Merrick, Calvin & Merker, LLP, 1996-97; ptnr. Dorsey & Whitney LLP, Denver, 1997—, mng. ptnr. Denver office, 2000—. Mem. Tenth Cir. Adv. Com., 1997—2000. Bd. dirs. Very Spl. Arts, Colo., 1994—, Am. Liver Found., 2002—; legal counsel Coloradans for Lamm-Dick campaign, Denver, 1982, Nancy Dick for U.S. Senate Com., Denver, 1984, Cantrell for Dist. Atty., Jefferson County, Colo., 1984. Capt. USAF, 1969—72. Mem.: ABA, Denver Bar Assn., Colo. Bar Assn. Office: Dorsey & Whitney LLP 370 17th St Ste 4700 Denver CO 80202-5644 Office Phone: 303-629-3400. E-mail: merker.steve@dorseylaw.com.

MERKERSON, S. EPATHA, actress; b. Saginaw, Mich., Nov. 28, 1952; BFA, Wayne State U. Broadway and Off-Broadway productions include The Piano Lesson, I'm Not Stupid (Obie award 1992); appeared in films including Terminator II, Jacob's Ladder, Navy Seals, Loose Cannons, Random Hearts, 1999, The Rising Place, 2001, Radio, 2003, Jersey Girl, 2004; television guest appearances include The Cosby Show, Equal Justice, Elysian Fields, Moe's World; television series roles include Pee Wee's Playhouse, Mann & Machine, Here & Now, Law & Order; A Place for Annie, 1994, A Mother's Prayer, 1995, Breaking Through, 1996, An Unexpected Life, 1998, Exiled, 1998. Nominated for Tony award, 1990, Drama Desk award, 1990, Helen Hayes award, 1990, L.A. Theater Critics award, 1990. Office: Law & Order c/o Universal Television 100 Universal City Plz Universal City CA 91608-1002*

MERKIN, ALBERT CHARLES, pediatrician, allergist; b. Chgo., Sept. 4, 1924; s. Harry A. and Goldie (Lamasky) M.; m. Eunice Aprill, Aug. 22, 1948; children: Audrey, Ellen, Joseph. Student, U. Ill., 1942-44; MD, U. Ill., Chgo., 1949. Diplomate Am. Bd. Allergy and Immunology, Am. Bd. Pediatrics. Intern, resident Cook County Hosp., Chgo.; resident Children's Meml. Hosp., Chgo.; with Valley Pediatric and Allergy Clinic, Las Vegas, Nev. Capt. USAF, 1950-53. Fellow Am. Acad. Pediatrics (state chmn. Nev. 1961-64, sect. allergy and immunology), Am. Coll. Allergy; mem. Am. Acad. Allergy, Allergy Subsplty. Group of Acad. Pediatrics (cert. pediatric allergist). Avocations: reading, travel. Office: Valley Pediat & Allergy Clinic 222 S Rainbow Blvd Ste 119 Las Vegas NV 89145-5343 Office Phone: 702-341-8695.

MERKIN, WILLIAM LESLIE, retired lawyer; b. NYC, Apr. 30, 1929; s. Jules Leo Merkin and Rae (Levine) Lesser; children: Monica Jo, Lance Jeffrey, Tiffany Dawn. BA, U. Tex., Austin, 1950; JD, St. Mary's U., San Antonio, 1953. Bar: Tex. 1953, U.S. Ct. Mil. Appeals 1954, U.S. Dist. Ct. (we. dist.) Tex. 1957, U.S. Ct. Appeals (5th cir.) 1969, U.S. Supreme Ct. 1970. Pvt. practice, El Paso, Tex., 1956-71; sr. ptnr. Merkin & Gibson, El Paso, Tex., 1972-78, Merkin, Hines & Pasqualone, El Paso, Tex., 1978-90; ret. Lectr. U. Tex.-El Paso, 1978—; cons. in field. Served to capt. JAGC, U.S. Army, 1953-56. Mem. Tex. State Bar Assn., Soc. Profls. in Dispute Resolution, Am. Trial Lawyers Assn., Tex. Trial Lawyers Assn., Common Cause, Internat. Wine and Food Soc. (pres. 1979-80), Am. Arbitration Assn. (part-time arbitrator), Nat. Assn. Securities Dealers (part-time arbitrator), Del Norte Club (El Paso), B'nai B'rith (pres. 1961-62), Phi Delta Phi. Home: 1442 Seacoast Dr Imperial Beach CA 91932-3183 Office Phone: 619-423-1718.

MERLINO, ANTHONY FRANK, orthopedist; b. Providence, Jan. 21, 1930; s. Anthony Frank and C. Mildred (Campagna) Merlino; m. Dolores Mary Aucello, Nov. 22, 1956; children: Christa Marianne, Paula Nicole. BS, Providence Coll., 1951; MS, U. Conn., 1952; MD, Jefferson Med. Coll., 1956. Diplomate Am. Bd. Ortho. Surgery. Intern St. Joseph Hosp., Providence, 1956—57; resident orthop. surgery VA Hosp., Phila., 1959—63; orthop. surgeon Phila., 1963—68, Providence, 1968—. Attending orthop. surgeon, pres. med. staff St. Joseph Hosp., Providence, 1974—75, trustee, 1973—76, med. staff, trustee joint conf. com., 1982; attending orthop. surgeon Our Lady of Fatima Hosp., North Providence, RI; vis. orthop. surgeon R.I. State Hosp., Howard, 1968—75; asst. orthop. surgeon Hahnemann Med. Coll., Phila., 1965—69; pediat. orthop. surg. cons. Crippled Children's Program of R.I., 1968—86; cons. orthop. surgeon Roger Williams Gen. Hosp., Providence, 1969—89; v.p. R.I. Orthop. Group, Inc., Providence, 1969—83, pres., 1983—; team physician hockey and basketball teams Providence Coll., 1968—87; mem. R.I. Gov.'s Med. Malpractice Commn., 1975—77, R.I. Bd. Examiners in Chiropractic, 1977—80; mem. study commn. R.I. Med. Rev. Bd., 1977—85; mem. corp. Blue Cross/Blue Shield R.I., 1976—87; physician, adv. R.I. Assn. Med. Assts., 1979—84; mem. R.I. Worker's Compensation Adv. Panel, 1978—88; mem. adv. bd. Cath. Social Svcs., 1981—84; police surgeon Am. Law Enforcement Officers' Assn., 1980; cons. orthop. surgery Am. Assn. Medicolegal Cons., 1980—90. Contbr. articles to profl. jours. Pres. Hindle Bldg. Assocs., 1983—; mem. med. splty. adv. bd. Med. Malpractice Prevention, 1985—90. Capt. med. corp. USAF, 1957—59. Recipient Dr. William McDonnell award, Providence Coll. Alumni Assn., 1981. Fellow: ACS (pres. R.I. chpt. 1982—84), Latin Am. Soc. Orthop. and Traumatology, Internat. Coll. Surgeons, Am. Acad. Orthop. Surgeons; mem.: AMA, Providence Med. Soc., Jefferson Orthop. Soc., R.I. Med. Soc. (commr. profl. rels. 1976, ho. of dels. 1976—82, commr. internal affairs 1982), R.I. Orthop. Soc. (sec.-treas. 1978—80, v.p. 1980—82, pres. 1982—84), Ea. Orthop. Soc., New Eng. Orthop. Assn., Am. Soc. Law and Medicine, Internat. Soc. Rsch. in Orthop. and Trauma, Internat. Soc. Orthop. and Traumatology, Am. Med. Photography Assn., Am. Orthop. Soc. for Sports Medicine, Am. Coll. Sports Medicine, Am. Acad. Compensation Medicine, Am. Profl. Practice Assn., Pan-Pacific Surg. Assn., Am. Fracture Assn., Am. Coll. Legal Medicine, Orthop. Rsch. and Edn. Found. (life), Thomistic Inst. Drs. Guild, R.I. Hist. Soc., 100 of R.I. Club, Mal Brown Club, Boston Orthop. Club. Roman Catholic. Home: 2 Countryside Dr North Providence RI 02904-3419 Office: 655 Broad St Providence RI 02907-1444

MERLIS, GEORGE, television producer; b. Bklyn., Feb. 7, 1940; s. Martin Richard and Ethel (Pollack) M.; m. Susan Haviland Crane, Nov. 21, 1963; children: James Duncan, Andrew Richard. BA, U. Pa., 1960, MA, 1961. Sports editor Rome (Italy) Daily Am., 1961; reporter N.Y. World-Telegram and Sun, N.Y.C., 1962-65, asst. city editor, 1965-67; day city editor World Jour. Tribune, N.Y.C., 1967; supr. editorial tng. program N.Y. News, N.Y.C., 1967-68; dir. pub. relations ABC News, N.Y.C., 1967-72; field producer Reasoner Report, 1972-75; exec. producer Good Morning America, 1975-81, CBS Morning News, 1981-83, Entertainment Tonight, 1983-84, Dick Cavett, USA, 1985, Great Weekend, 1987-88; supervising producer ABC-TV's Home Show, 1988-91; exec. producer Willard Scott's Home and Garden Almanac, 1994—97, Kitty Bartholomew You're Home, 1994-98, The Urban Gardener with Mesach Taylor, 1996; exec. producer, writer, dir. Harlem Hellfighters, 1997, Better Homes and Gardens, 1998-99. Dir. Closer to Truth, 1999; prodr., writer, dir. Secrets of San Simeon with Patricia Hearst, 2000; exec. prodr., dir. Flea Market Finds with the Kovels, 1999-2003. Author: V.P. a Novel of Vice Presidential Politics, 1971, (with Al Ubell) Al Ubell's Energy-Saving Guide for Homeowners, 1980, (with Al Ubell) Save Energy, Save Money, 2001, How to Make the Most of Every Media Appearance, 2003; contbr. articles to TV Guide. Recipient Emmy award as exec. prodr. Better Homes and Gardens, 1999. Mem. Nat. TV Acad. Arts and Scis., Dirs. Guild of Am. Office: Mezzanine 4801 Wilshire Blvd Los Angeles CA 90010-3811

MERLO, LARRY J. retail executive; Sr. v.p. stores CVS Pharmacy, Inc., Woonsocket, RI, 1994—98, exec. v.p. stores, 1998—2000, CVS Corp., Woonsocket, 2000—. Office: CVS Corp Corp Hdqrs 1 CVS Dr Woonsocket RI 02895

MERLO, MICHAEL J. investment banker; b. Bklyn., Mar. 12, 1948; s. Michael Merlo and Vera Colletti; m. Geraldine Dielia Monahan, Aug. 21, 1988; children: Michael, Allison, Christopher. BS, C.W. Post Coll., LI, NY, 1971; MBA, Adelphi U., LI, NY, 1976. Sr. v.p. middle market group head Fleet Bank, NYC, 1994—2000; sr. v.p., chief credit officer Signature Bank, NYC, 2000—. Bd. dir. NY Inst. Coll. Tech., LI, NY. Bd. dirs. Boy Scouts Nassau County. Recipient Man of Yr., March of Dimes, 2000, Ellis Island Medal of Honor, Nat. Ethnic Coalition Originators, 2004. Mem.: Garden City Country Club. Office: Signature Bank 565 Fifth Ave New York NY 10017-2496

MERLY, MIRIAM NAVEIRA, state supreme court justice; b. Santurce, P.R., July 28, 1934; married; 2 children. BA, Mount St. Vincent Coll., N.Y., 1956; JD, U. P.R. Law Sch., 1960; LLM, Columbia U., 1969; postgrad., Leiden U., Holland, 1971-72; LLD, U. Georgetown Sch. Law, 1990. Law clerk P.R. Supreme Ct., 1963-71, asst. atty. gen. Dept. Justice, 1966-73, asst. solicitor gen. Dept. Justice, 1973-76, assoc. justice, 1985—, pres. judicial commn. on gender bias, 1992—; tchr. Law Sch. U. P.R., 1971-72; atty. pvt. practice, 1976-85; prof. Sch. Law Inter Am. U. Office: Supreme Ct PO Box 2392 San Juan PR 00902-2392

MERMANN, ALAN CAMERON, retired pediatrics educator, chaplain; b. Bklyn., June 23, 1923; s. William Joseph and Ada Fischer (McCree) M.; m. Constance Barnes, Sept. 4, 1948 (div. Mar. 1988); children: Edith, Constance, Sarah, Elizabeth; m. Cecily Allen Reynolds, Apr. 15, 1989. BA, Lehigh U., 1943; MD, Johns Hopkins U., 1947; MDiv, Yale U., 1979, MST, 1988, MA, 1999. Diplomate Am. Bd. Pediatrics; med. license, Conn.; ordained to Christian ministry, United Ch. of Christ, 1979. Intern pediatrics Bellevue Hosp., N.Y.C., 1947-48, Johns Hopkins Hosp., Balt., 1948-49; sr. asst. resident pediatrician N.Y. Hosp., N.Y.C., 1949-50; resident pediatrician Meml. Hosp., N.Y.C., 1950-51; rsch. fellow Sloane-Kettering Inst., N.Y.C., 1953-54; pvt. practice pediatrics Guilford, Conn., 1954-82; clin. instr. pediatrics Yale Sch. Medicine, 1954-59, asst. clin. prof. pediatrics, 1959-71, assoc. clin. prof. pediatrics, 1971-79, clin. prof. pediatrics, 1979—. Trustee New Eng. Coll., Henniker, N.H., 1969-91; fellow Branford Coll., Yale U., 1979-00; mem. instnl. rev. bd. Union Carbide Corp., Danbury, Conn., 1991—; lectr. pastoral theology Yale Divinity Sch., 1979-82; asst. pastor First Congregational Ch., Guilford, 1979-82; assoc. pastor Ch. of Christ Congl., United Ch. of Christ, Norfolk, Conn., 1995—; chaplain Yale Sch. Medicine, 1982-00, human investigation com., 1983-91, med. ctr. bioethics com., chair pediatrics ethics com., sch. medicine admissions com., com. on well-being of students. Author: Some Chose to Stay: Faith and Ethics in a Time of Plague, 1997, To Do No Harm: Learning to Care for The Seriously Ill, 1999; contbr. articles to profl. jours. Lt. USNR, 1951-53. Fellow Am. Acad. Pediatrics. Democrat. Avocations: dixieland, jazz, dance, gardening. Home: 185 Ashpohtag Rd Norfolk CT 06058

MERMELSTEIN, JULES JOSHUA, lawyer, township commissioner; b. Phila., Apr. 25, 1955; s. Harry and Ellen Jane (Greenberg) M.; m. Ruth Susan Applebaum, Aug. 18, 1974; children: Hannah Leona, Benjamin Isaac. BA, Temple U., 1977; JD, Am. U., 1979; MEd, Beaver Coll., 1994. Bar: Pa. 1980, U.S. Dist. Ct. (ea. dist.) Pa. 1980, U.S. Ct. Appeals (3d cir.) 1982, U.S. Supreme Ct. 1982. Ptnr. Mermelstein & Light, Norristown and Hatboro, Pa., 1980-83; v.p., gen. counsel Am. Ins. Cons., Feasterville, Pa., 1983; staff atty. Hyatt Legal Svcs., Phila., 1983-84, mng. atty., 1984-85; pvt. practice Phila./Montgomery County, 1985-93; tchr., social studies coord. The Bridge, 1997-99; atty. Levin & Assocs., Wyncote, Pa., 1998—2001, mng. atty., 2002—03; title agt. Forward Abstract, LLC, Glenside, Pa., 2002—. Prof. law St. Matthew Sch. Law, Phila., 1985—87; adj. prof. criminal justice Glassboro State U., NJ, 1988; faculty polit. sci. dept. Temple U., 1989; ednl. cons. Interim Ho., 1998—2000. Editor: The Montco Democrat, 1990-92. Vol. atty. ACLU, Phila., 1980-93; chmn. Tikkun Olam (Repair the World) Com., 1989-92, 98-2000; area rep. Montgomery County Dem. Exec. Com., 1982-85, 88-94; treas., 1994-98, candidate coord., 1982, nominee for dist. atty., 1983, committeeman, 1973-77, 82-85, 88-92, campaign mgr. Talbot for state legis., 1988; Upper Dublin chmn. Dukakis-Bentsen, 1988, chair Upper Dublin Dem. Com., 1990-91, commr. Upper Dublin Twp., 1992—; Dem. candidate Pa. State Legis., 2000; bd. dirs. Reconstructionist Congregation Or Hadash, Ft. Washington, Pa., 1988-92, 96-2000, 2001-2003, confirmation tchr., 1994—. Jewish. Home: 18 Northview Dr Glenside PA 19038-1318 E-mail: JulesMermelstein@hotmail.com.

MERMIN, N. DAVID, physicist, researcher, writer; b. New Haven, Mar. 30, 1935; s. John and Eva M.; m. Dorothy E. Milman, June 9, 1957; children: Jonathan George, Elizabeth Ruth AB summa cum laude, Harvard U., 1956, A.M., 1957, PhD, 1961. NSF postdoctoral fellow U. Birmingham, Eng., 1961-63; postdoctoral fellow U. Calif., San Diego, 1963-64; asst. prof. physics Cornell U., Ithaca, N.Y., 1964-67, assoc. prof. physics, 1967-72, prof. physics, 1972-90, Horace White prof. physics, 1990—, dir. Lab. Atomic and Solid State Physics, 1984-90. Loeb lectr. Harvard U., Cambridge, 1980, Emil Warburg prof. U. Bayreuth, Germany, 1981, Walker Ames prof. U. Washington, Seattle, 1984; Wunsch lectr. Technion, Haifa, Israel, 1992; Japan Soc. for Promotion of Sci. fellow Nagoya U., 1982; Lorentz prof. U. Leiden, 1995. Author: Space and Time in Special Relativity, 1968, Solid State Physics, 1976, Boojums All the Way Through, 1990; contbr. articles to profl. jours. Sloan Found. fellow, 1966-68; Guggenheim Found. fellow, 1970-71 Fellow AAAS, Am. Acad. Arts and Scis., Am. Phys. Soc. (Julius Edgar Lilienfield prize 1989); mem. NAS. Avocation: piano. Home: 75 Hickory Rd Ithaca NY 14850-9606 Office: Cornell U Lab Atomic and Solid State Phys Clark Hall Ithaca NY 14853-2501

MERNA, GERALD FRANCIS, advertising executive, retired military officer; b. N.Y.C., Apr. 1, 1930; s. George F. Merna and Geraldine (Byers) Kraus; m. Dorothy May Sedlack, Feb. 10, 1951; children: Linda Carol Figura, Gerald Thomas. BS, George Washington U., 1973, MS, 1977; postgrad., U. So. Calif., 1975, U. Va., 1983. Enlisted USMC, 1947, advanced through grades to master gunnery sgt., 1966, commd. 2d lt., 1966, promoted to 1st lt. in Vietnam, 1967, with 1952-53, Vietnam, 1966-67; ret. USMC, 1968; various positions U.S. Postal Svc., Washington, 1968-82, exec. asst. to Postmaster Gen., 1978-82, sectional ctr. mgr., 1982-87; ret., 1987; advt. dir. Signal mag.-Jour. Armed Forces Communications and Electronics Assn., Fairfax, Va., 1987-93; assoc. pub. Nat. Def. Mag., Arlington, Va., 1993-98; v.p. Nat. Def. Indsl., Arlington, 1993-98; pres. Merna and Assocs., 2002—. V.p. ops. Va. Hills Civic Assn., Alexandria, 1971-72; mem. covenants com. Cascades Comm. Assn., 1998-00, chair 2000—. Mem. The Ret. Officers Assn. (life), Marine Corps League, Marine Corps Res. Officers Assn. (life), 1st Marine Divsn. Assn. (life), 3rd Marine Divsn. Assn. (life), Nat. Def. Indsl. Assn. (life), Am. Legion (lfie), USMC Mustang Assn., VFW (life), Armed Forces Comms. and Electronics Assn., Nat. League Postmasters U.S. (v.p. 1989-92). Home and Office: The Cascades 46386 Bluestem Ct Potomac Falls VA 20165-6461 E-mail: gmerna@erols.com.

MEROLLA, CAROL ANN, writer, consultant; b. Providence, R.I., Aug. 8, 1945; d. Ralph Thomas and Lena Marie Biccicco; m. Anthony Joseph Merolla, May 30, 1964; children: Anthony, Kevin, Kimberly. Diploma, St. Joseph Sch. Nursing, R.I., 1981, U. R.I., 1991, Sch. Children's Lit., 2002. Office mgr. Fabro, Inc., Providence, 1964—80; nurse Cherry Hill Manor, Johnston, RI, 1981—82; pvt. duty nurse self-employed, North Scituate, RI, 1983—86; therapy asst. Providence Phys. Therapy, Warwick, RI, 1987—88; therapy asst., office mgr. Garden City Phys. Therapy, Cranston, RI, 1989—94; office mgr. AFD, Inc., Providence, 1995—; freelance writer self-employed, Johnston, RI, 1994—. Author: (book of poetry) Quiet Reflections, 1999, The Time of Christmas, 2000, The Power of the Pen, 2001, Walk Beside Me, 2002, Scenes of Nature, 2004, (preschool fiction) Two Kittens for Kim, 2002, Sammy and Mouse, 2002, (preteen non-ficiton) Letters to God, 2003, (preschool fiction) Bird in the Bush, 2004. Instr. exercise pool program Duscidphy C.C., RI, 1980—81; capt. Am. Cancer oc., N.Y.C., 1962—64, 1980—83; vol. Salvation Army, North Providence, RI, 1997—; catechist tchr. St. Robert Bellarmine Parish, Johnston, 2004—. Mem.: Soc. Children's Book Writers & Illustrators (assoc. writer 2001—), Internet Soc. Poets (poet laureate 1998—, Poetic award 2002, 2003), Nat. Authors Registry (life Pres. award of lit. excellence for poems 2000, 2002). Republican. Roman Catholic. Avocations: walking, photography, swimming, illustration, recreational programs for seniors. Home and Office: 682 Greenville Ave Johnston RI 02919 Office Phone: 401-231-5083. Office Fax: 401-946-8036. E-mail: afd10@cox.net.

MEROLLA, MICHELE EDWARD, chiropractor, broadcaster; b. Providence, Feb. 20, 1940; s. Joseph and Viola (Horne) M.; m. Ednamarie G.; children: Michele Edward II, Matthew Joseph, Samantha Joan, Alexandra Marie. BS, Bryant Coll., 1961; DC, Chiropractic Inst. N.Y., 1965; LHD, Logan Chiropractic Coll., St. Louis, 1973. Owner chiropractic clinics chiropractic clinics, New Bedford, Taunton, Somerset, Seekonk, Attleboro, others, Mass., 1965—. Daily Network radio talk show hoset Holistic Hotline; owner radio sta. WJYT-AM, Attleboro, Mass. Editor: New Eng. Jour. Chiropractic. Mem. New Bedford City Coun., 1969-73, Airport Commn., 1972-75, Sch. Com., 1978-86, Recreation Commn., 1983-89, Fairhaven (Mass.) Sch. Com.,

2000—; pres. New Bedford Aid Ctr., 1977; bd. dir. Your Theatre Inc. Recipient Svc. award New Eng. Chiropractic Coun., 1973. Mem. Am. Chiropractic Assn., Nat. Assn. Broadcasters, Mass. Assn. Broadcasters, Southeastern Mass. Chiropractic Soc. (bd. dir.), Mass. Chiropractic Soc., NY Acad. Sci., Fla. Chiropractic Soc., New Bedford Preservation Soc. (bd. dir.). Home: 62 Manhattan Ave Fairhaven MA 02719-1825 Office: 73 Alden Rd Fairhaven MA 02719: Lighthouse Point FL E-mail: DRMEROLLA@AOL.COM.

MERON, THEODOR, judge, law educator, researcher; b. Kalisz, Poland, Apr. 28, 1930; came to U.S., 1978, naturalized, 1984; s. Yhiel and Bluma (Lipschitz) Znamirowski; m. Monique Jonquet, Mar. 13, 1981; children: Daniel, Amos. M.J., Hebrew U., 1954; LL.M., Harvard U., 1955, S.JD, 1957; diploma in Pub. Internat. Law, Cambridge U., Eng., 1957. Bar: Israel 1971, N.Y. 1984. Legal advisor to Fgn. Ministry of Israel, 1967-71; Israeli ambassador to Can., 1971-75; permanent rep. U.N., Geneva, 1977; prof. law Sch. Law, NYU, N.Y.C., 1978—. Carnegie lectr. Hague Acad. Internat. Law, 1980; Sir Hersch Lauterpacht Meml. lectr.; vis. fellow All Souls Coll., Oxford U., England, Max-Planck Inst., Heidelberg, Germany; vis. prof. Grad. Inst. Internat. Studies, Geneva, prof. law, 1991—95; pub. mem. U.S. Del. Conf. on Human Dimension Conf. on Security and Coop. in Europe, Copenhagen, 1998; mem. U.S. del. Rome Diplomatic Conf. on the Establishment of an Internat. Criminal Ct.; vis. prof. law Harvard U., Berkeley Law Sch.; counselor on internat. law U.S. Dept. State, 2000—01; judge appeals chamber Internat. Criminal Tribunal for former Yugoslavia, 2001—. Author: Investment Insurance in International Law, 1976, The United Nations Secretariat, 1977, Human Rights Law-Making in the United Nations, 1986, Human Rights in Internal Strife: Their International Protection, 1987, Human Rights and Humanitarian Norms as Customary Law, 1989, Henry's Wars and Shakespeare's Laws, 1993, Bloody Constraint: War and Chivalry in Shakespeare, 1998, International Law in the Age of Human Rights, 2004; editor: Human Rights in International Law, 1984; editor in chief: Am. Jour. Internat. Law, 1983-88; contbr. articles to profl. publs. Rockefeller Found. fellow, 1975-76; Humanitarian Trust student Cambridge U., 1956-57. Mem.: Inst. of Internat. Law, Internat. Law Assn., Coun. on Fgn. Rels., Inst. of Internat. Humanitarian Law, French Inst. Internat. Law, Am. Soc. Internat. Law (Cert. Merit 1987), UN Assn. of U.S. (hon.). Office: NYU Law Sch 40 Washington Sq S New York NY 10012-1099

MEROW, JAMES F. federal judge; AB, George Washington U., 1953, JD, 1956. Bar: Va., 1956, D.C., 1958. Trial atty., br. dir., civil divsn. U.S. Dept. Justice, Washington, 1959-78; trial judge U.S. Ct. Claims, Washington, 1978-82; judge U.S. Ct. Fed. Claims, Washington, 1982—. With JAGC, U.S. Army, 1956-59. Mem. ABA, Fed. Bar Assn., Va. State Bar. Office: US Ct Fed Claims 717 Madison Pl NW Washington DC 20005

MEROW, JOHN, lawyer; b. Little Valley, N.Y., Dec. 20, 1929; s. Luin George and Mildred Elizabeth Merow; m. Mary Alyce Smith, June 19, 1957; 1 child, Alison. Student, UCLA, 1947—48; BS in Engring., U. Mich., 1952; JD, Harvard U., 1958. Bar: N.Y. 1958, U.S. Supreme Ct. 1971. Assoc. Sullivan & Cromwell, N.Y.C., 1958-64, ptnr., 1965-96, vice chmn., 1986-87, chmn., sr. ptnr., 1987-94, sr. counsel, 1997—. Bd. dirs. Seligman Group Investment Cos., Commonwealth Industries, Inc.; trustee, vice chmn. N.Y. Presbyn. Healthcare Sys., Inc.; trustee N.Y. Presbyn. Hosp.; trustee Friends of the Archbishop of Canterbury's Anglican Communion Fund. Chmn. bd. dirs. Am.-Australian Assn., 1986—99; bd. dirs. Mcpl. Art Soc. N.Y.; mem. exec. com., sec. U.S. Coun. Internat. Bus.; bd. dirs., sec. Met. Opera Club, 1986—94; trustee Anglican Investment Agy. Trust. Lt. USN, 1952—55. Named hon. officer Order of Australia. Mem. Am. Law Inst. (advisor corp. governance project 1978-92), Coun. on Fgn. Rels., Soc. Mayflower Desc., Links Club, Pilgrims, Piping Rock Club, Down Town Assn., Union Club, Griffis Faculty Club, River Club. Home: 435 E 52d St New York NY 10022 also: 51 Fruitledge Rd Glen Head NY 11545-3316 Office: Sullivan & Cromwell LLP 125 Broad St New York NY 10004-2498 Office Phone: 212-558-3616. E-mail: merowj@sullcrom.com.

MERRELL, JAMES HART, history educator; b. Mpls., Oct. 19, 1953; s. David John and Jessie (Clark) M.; m. Linda Keiko Yamane, Jan. 7, 1978; children: David Yamane, John Nemoto, Wilson Nemoto. B.A., Lawrence U., Appleton, Wis., 1975; B.A., Oxford U., 1977; M.A., Johns Hopkins U., 1979, Ph.D., 1982. Asst. prof. history Coll. William and Mary, Williamsburg, Va., 1982-84; asst. prof. Vassar Coll., 1984-89, assoc. prof., 1989-91, prof., 1991—. Author: The Indians' New World: Catawbas and Their Neighbors from European Contact Through the Era of Removal, 1989 (Bancroft prize, Frederick Jackson Turner award, Merle Curti award, 1990), Into the American Woods: Negotiators on the Pennsylvania Frontier, 1999, (Bancroft prize, finalist Pulitzer prize, 2000); Editor: (with D.K. Richter) Beyond the Covenant Chain: The Iroquos and their Neighbors in Indian North America, 1600-1800, 1987 (with P.C. Mancall) American Encounters: Natives and Newcomers From European Contact to Indian Removal, 1500-1850, 1999 (with P.C. Mancall and F. Hoxie) American Nations: Encounters in Indian Country, 1850 to Present, 2001; contbr. articles to profl. jours. Rhodes scholar, 1975; fellow Danforth Found., 1975, Newberry Library, 1981, Inst. Early Am. History, 1982, Nat. Endowment Humanities, 1990, 92, Guggenheim Found., 1991, Am. Coun. Learned Socs., 1991. Mem. Orgn. Am. Historians, Soc. Am. Historians. Avocations: squash; tennis. Home: 34 Coachlight Dr Poughkeepsie NY 12603

MERRELL, JAMES LEE, religious editor, clergyman; b. Indpls., Oct. 24, 1930; s. Mark W. and Pauline F. (Tucker) M.; m. Barbara Jean Burch, Dec. 23, 1951; children: Deborah Lea Merrell Griffin, Cynthia Lynn Archer, Stuart Allen. AB, Ind. U., 1952; MDiv, Christian Theol. Sem., 1956; LittD, Culver-Stockton Coll., 1972. Ordained to ministry Christian Ch., 1955; asso. editor World Call, Indpls., 1956-66, editor, 1971-73; pastor Crestview Christian Ch., Indpls., 1966-71; editor The Disciple, St. Louis, 1974-89; sr. v.p. Christian Bd. Publ., 1976-89; sr. minister Affton Christian Ch., St. Louis, 1989-94; interim chaplain Culver-Stockton Coll., Canton, Mo., 1995; interim sr. pastor Friedens United Ch. of Christ, Warrenton, Mo., 1995-98, St. Johns United Ch. of Christ, Mehlville, Mo., 1998—2002, Hamilton Christian Ch., Creve Coeur, 2002—03, Redeemer Evang. Ch., St. Louis, 2003—. Bd. dirs. Horizons mag., 1995-98. Author: They Live Their Faith, 1965, The Power of One, 1976, Discover the Word in Print, 1979, Finding Faith in the Headlines, 1985, We Claim Our Heritage, 1992. Chmn. bd. Kennedy Meml. Christian Home, Martinsville, Ind., 1971-73; trustee Christian Theol. Sem., 1978-81. Recipient Faith and Freedom award Religious Heritage of Am., 1983; lifetime achievement award Mo. State Sen., 2000. Mem. Associated Ch. Press (award 1973, 79, 80, 81, 82, dir. 1974-75, 78-81, 1st v.p. 1983-85), Christian Theol. Sem. Alumni Assn. (pres. 1966-68), Religious Pub. Rels. Coun. (awards 1979, 80, 84, 87, 90, pres. St. Louis chpt. 1985-86), Sigma Delta Chi (award 1952), Theta Phi. Home: 248 Greycliff Bluff Dr Saint Louis MO 63129-5081 E-mail: JLeeMer@aol.com. *As a religious communicator and as a pastor, I have always believed in applying the same standards in the sacred realm as in the secular. I have tried to pursue the truth, to keep my constituency informed, to celebrate the noble in life, to fight against those who would lie, distort and hide God's truth in the name of some supposed good.*

MERRELL, JESSE HOWARD, writer; b. Shelby, Ala., Dec. 9, 1938; s. James Walton and Emma Thelma (Davis) M.; m. Betsy Lee Davis, Jan. 11, 1964 (div. 1979); children: Sandra, Mark, Brad, Carolyn, Gwen. Grad., Shelby High Sch., Columbiana, Ala., 1957. Pitcher Cin. Redlegs, 1958-62; reporter, news dir. WHAP Radio, Hopewell, Va., 1963; writer/editor Hopewell News, 1963-65; state editor Daily Progress, Charlottesville, Va., 1965-68; assoc. editor Transport Topics, Washington, 1968-75; spl. asst. to pres. Am. Trucking Assn., Washington, 1975-76; editor Transport Topics, Washington, 1976-77; pres. Merrell Ent., Washington, 1977—. Pub. rels. com. Am. Movers Conf., Washington, 1969-72; instr. Dale Carnegie courses, Washington, 1974-81, 1st pres., 1980-81; cons. Mid. Atlantic Conf., Riverdale, Md., 1981-82, Contract Carrier Conf., 1977-82; speechwriter ICC, Washington, 1982. Author: (novel) A Christmas Gift, 1979; syndicated columnist Religion and the Times, Washington Welter, (genealogy) The Merrells of Alabama, 1995, My Name is America! I Was Born at Jamestown!, 2002. Mem. Nat. Trust for Hist. Preservation, Assn. Preservation Va. Antiquities. With U.S. Army, 1960-62. Recipient George Washington Honor award Freedoms Found., 2002, Liberty award Congress of Freedom, Jackson, Miss., 1970, 71, Honor Cert., Freedoms Found., 1972, 1st place editorial writing Va. Press Assn., 1965, 1st place news writing, 1966. Mem. Nat. Press Club, Assn. Preservation Va. Antiquities, Gen. Washington's Coun. of the 1607 Soc. (charter mem.), Regent's Circle of Mt. Vernon, Jamestown 2007 Spkrs. Bur., Jamestown-Yorktown Found., Colonial Williamsburg Raleigh Tavern Soc. Avocation: photography. Office: Merrell Ent 2610 Garfield St NW Washington DC 20008-4104

MERRELL, RONALD CLIFTON, surgeon, educator; b. Birmingham, Ala., June 18, 1946; s. Greene Lawrence and Florence (Jones) M.; m. Marsha Karen Cox, Dec. 24, 1966; children: Alexandria, Alison, R. Clifton. BS in Chemistry, U. Ala., 1967, MD, 1970. Diplomate Am. Bd. Surgery. Resident and fellow in surgery Wash. U., St. Louis, 1970-77; asst. prof. surgery Stanford (Calif.) U., 1979-84; assoc. prof. surgery U. Tex. Med. Sch., Houston, 1984-88, prof. surgery, 1988-94, M.D. Anderson Cancer Ctr., Houston, 1988-94; assoc. dean clin. affairs U. Tex. Med. Sch., Houston, 1988-92, vice dean, 1992-93; prof. surgery, chmn. dept. surgery Yale U., 1993—99; Stuart McGuire prof. surgery, chmn. dept. surgery Va. Commonwealth U., Richmond, 1999—2003, prof. surgery, 2003—; dir. Med. Informatics Tech. App Consortium. Author 3 books; contbr. over 200 articles to profl jours., 30 chpts. to books. Maj. U.S. Army, 1977-79. Recipient Basil O'Connor award March of Dimes, 1979, Rsch. Career Devel. award NIH, 1979-84, Henry J. Kaiser award Stanford U., 1982, 83, John P. McGovern Outstanding Tchr. award U. Tex. Med. Sch., 1988, Dean's Teaching Excellence award, 1983-89, Pub. Svc. award NASA, 1998, Disting. medal as Friend of Democritus, U. Greece, 1998; grantee NASA. Fellow ACS, Soc. Univ. Surgeons; mem. Am. Assn. Endocrine Surgery, Am. Coll. Surgeons, Alpha Omega Alpha. Democrat. Episcopalian. Achievements include research in the transplantation of telemedicine and islets of Langerhans. Office: PO Box 980519 Richmond VA 23298-0519 E-mail: ronald.merrell@vcu.edu.

MERRELL, W. M. advertising executive; Grad., Fla. State U. Copywriter Liller, Neal, Battle & Lindsey; with Howard, McKinney & Silver, Raleigh, N.C.; pres., CEO Howard, Merrell & Ptnrs., Raleigh, 1976—. Office: Howard Merrell & Ptrns Ste 500 8521 Six Forks Rd Raleigh NC 27615

MERRIAM, ALLEN HAYES, speech communication educator; b. Orange, NJ, July 28, 1942; s. Rutherford Douglas and Virginia (Johnson) M.; m. Sharan Ballard, Sept. 5, 1964 (div. 1981); children: Paul, Laura; m. Linda Kay Thompson, May 25, 1992. BA, Drew U., 1964; MA, Ohio U., 1970, PhD, 1972. Asst. prof. speech comm. Coll. N.J., 1972-77; asst. prof. U. Va., Charlottesville, 1977-78, Va. Tech. U., Blacksburg, 1978-82; assoc. prof. Mo. So. State U., Joplin, 1982-88, prof., 1988—. Author: Gandhi vs. Jinnah, 1980, People of the Millennium, 2000, America in Person, 2001; contbr. articles to profl. jours. Vol. Peace Corps, Kabul, Afghanistan, 1965-67. Mem. NAACP, Ctrl. States Comm. Assn. Home: 1419 Marzelle Ct Joplin MO 64801-8263 Office: Mo So State U Dept Communication Joplin MO 64801 Office Phone: 417-625-9654. Business E-Mail: merriam-a@mssu.edu.

MERRIAM, DANIEL F(RANCIS), geologist; b. Omaha, Feb. 9, 1927; s. Faye Mills and Amanda Frances (Wood) M. m. Annie Laura Young, Feb. 12, 1946; children: Beth Ann, John Francis, Anita Pauline, James Daniel, Judith Diane. BS in Geology, U. Kans., 1949, MS, 1953, PhD, 1961; MSc in Geology, Leicester U., England, 1969; DSc, Leicester U., 1975. Geologist Union Oil Co. Calif., 1949-51, 52; asst. instr. U. Kans., 1951-53, instr., 1954, rsch. assoc., 1963-71; geologist Kans. Geol. Survey, 1953-58, head divsn. basic geology, 1958-63, chief geol. rsch., 1963-71; Jessie Page Heroy prof. geology dept. geology Syracuse U., 1971-81, chmn. dept. geology, 1971-80; Endowment Assn. Disting. prof. natural scis. dept. geology Wichita State U., 1981-93, chmn. dept. geology, 1981-87; sr. rsch. scientist Kans. Geol. Survey, U. Kans., 1993-97, emeritus, 1997—. Vis. rsch. scientist Stanford U., 1963; dir. Internat. Field Inst. to Japan, Am. Geol. Inst., 1967; vis. prof. geology Wichita State U., 1968-70; vis. geol. scientist Am. Geol. Inst., 1969; cons. nat. gas survey Fed. Power Commn., 1972-75, 78, chmn. supply tech. adv. com., 1975-77; ad hoc panel earth resources survey NAS/NRC, 1972-73, chmn. U.S. Nat. Com. for Internat. Geol. Correlation program, 1976-79, ex-officio, 1979-80, 81-83, U.S. Nat. Com. on History of Geology, 1989—; Esso Disting. lectr. U. Sydney, Australia, 1979; mem. U.S. Nat. Commn. for UNESCO, U.S. Dept. State, 1979-85; vis. prof. Centre d'Informatique Geologique, Ecole des Mines de Paris, Fontainebleau, 1980; vis. sr. scientist Kans. Geol. Survey, 1990-93; vis. scientist GeoForschungsZentrum, Potsdam, Germany, 1992; adj. prof. Emporia State U., Kans., 1993—. Author: The Geologic History of Kansas: Kansas Geological Survey, 1963, (with J.W. Harbaugh) Computer Applications in Stratigraphic Analysis, 1968, Computer Fundamentals for Geologists: COMPUTe, 1975, Bibliography of Computer Applications in the Earth Sciences, 1988; founder, editor-in-chief Jour. Math. Geology, 1968-76, 94-97, Computers & Geosciences, 1975-95; founder, editor Kansas Geological Survey, Computer Contributions, 1966-71, Syracuse University Geological Contributions, 1973-81; editor (series) Computer Applications in the Earth Sciences, 1969—, Computers and Geology, 1976-90, Computer Methods in the Geosciences, 1982—, (books and vols.) Mathematical Models of Sedimentary Processes, 1972, The Impact of Quantification on Geology, 1974, Random Processes in Geology, 1976, Geomathematics: Past, Present, and Prospects, 1978, Down-to-Earth Statistics: Solutions Looking for Geological Problems, 1981, Current Trends in Geomathematics, 1988, (colloquium) Geostatistics, 1970; translation editor Statistics for Geoscientists, 1987; co-editor Pacific Geology, 1971-83; editl. cons. Geosystems, 1971-83; mem. editl. rev. bd. Colo. Sch. Mines Quarterly, 1974-90; mem. editl. adv. bd. Geophysical Computer Programs, 1975-76, Applied Geochemistry, 1985-93; mem. editl. bd. History of Earth Science Soc., 1982-2000; reviewer for nat. and internat. jours.; contbr. notes, articles to numerous jours. Bd. dirs. Kans Geol. Found., 1989-92. Fullbright-Hayes Sr. Rsch. fellow, U.K., 1964-65. Fellow AAAS (sr., electorate nomination com. 1977-80, chairperson sect. E 1983-84, Sci. software adv. panel 1986-91, SWARM 64th local arrangement com. chmn. 1988), Geol. Soc. Am. (sr., com. on publs. 1973-76, chmn. com. geology dept. 1975-78), Geol. Soc. London (William Smith medal 1992), Sigma Xi (sec. Kansas chpt. 1994-96, pres. 1997-98); mem. Am. Assn. Petroleum Geologists (hon., chmn. 1954, 57, ednl. exhibits com., rsch. com., 1964-67, assoc. editor bulletin 1969-75, Geobyte 1985-92, computer applications in geology com. 1971-81, 86—, N.Y. Dist. rep. 1974-76, Kans. Dist. rep. 1956-57, 1985-91, chmn. 1989-91, Kans. rep. Midcontinent sect. 1988-92, Disting. Svc. award 1987, Cert. of Merit 1987, 93), Soc. Econ. Paleontologists and Mineralogists (hon., chmn. organizer rsch. group in computer tech. 1970-75, 82-82, 89-90, publs. com. 1980-83, chmn. publs. 1981-82, chmn. Pa. Stratigraphy working group Midcontinent sect. 1986—, ad. hoc. com. databases 1985-88, chmn databases 1986-88, organizer computer applications com. 1988—, chmn. computer applications 1988-92, procedures com. 1989-2001, chmn. 1993-94, spl. advisor headquarters and bus. com. 1988-91, chmn. 1991-98), Nat. Assn. Geology Tchrs. (v.p. Kans.-Okla. sect. 1986, pres. 1987-89, sec. 1994—), Geosci. Info. Soc. (program com 1980-81), Internat. Union Geol. Scis., Internat. Geol. Correlations Program (U.S. del. 1969, sci. com. 1975-79, 76-77, chmn. ad hoc com. publs. 1980, adv. bd. publs. 1980-89, chmn. 1980-84), Internat. Geol. Congress (alternate U.S. del. VII ordinary sessions coun. 1984, U.S. del. VIII ordinary sessions coun. 1989), Internat. Assn. Math. Geology (mem. coun. 1968—, sec.-gen. 1972-76, pres. 1976-80, interim archivist 1989-92, archivist 1992—, William Christian Krumbein medal 1981, pubs. com. 1997—, organizing com. 8th ann. meeting 2001), Leicester Geol. Soc. (hon. life 1965), Sylvester-Bradley Geol. Soc. (hon. v.p. 1978-79), Classification Soc. (chmn. mem. com., bd. dirs. 1968-71), N.Y. State Geol. Assn. (exec. sec. 1972-77, pres. 1977-78, bd. dirs. 1987-83), Kans. Geol. Soc. (hon., bd. dirs., dir. many confs., presdl. citation 1989), Kans. Acad. Sci. (mem. coun. at large 1983-86, v.p. 1987, pres.-elect 1988, pres. 1989, chmn. com. for 2001, 1989-92, assoc. editor Transactions 1990-92, editor, 1992—, strategic planning com. 2000—, gen. chmn. 119th Ann. Meeting 1987, 131st Ann. Meeting 2001), History of Earth Sci. Soc. (Earth Science History editl. bd. 1982—), Sigma Gamma Epsilon (pres. Alpha chpt. 1952-53, nat. coun. 1983-95, nat. pres. 1990-95, nat. editor The Compass, 1983-92, hon.), Phi Kappa Phi, Sigma Xi (Kans. chpt. sec. 1994-96, pres. 1997-98). Office: U Ks Kansas Geol Survey Lawrence KS 66047

MERRIAM, DWIGHT HAINES, lawyer, land use planner; b. Norwood, Mass., Apr. 20, 1946; s. Austin Luther and Lillian Diana (Olsen) M.; m. Cynthia Ann Hayes, May 21, 1966 (div. June 1992); children: Sarah Ann Leilani, Jonathan Hayes; m. Susan Manning Standish, May 6, 1995; children: Alexander Harlan, Lucy Caroline. BA cum laude, U. Mass., 1968; M in Regional Planning, U. N.C., 1974; JD, Yale U., 1978. Bar: Conn. 1978, Mass. 1980, U.S. Dist. Ct. Conn. 1981, U.S. Dist. Ct. Hawaii 1984, U.S. Supreme Ct. 1990, U.S. Ct. Appeals (4th cir.) 1993. Land use planner Charles E. Downe, Newton, Mass., 1968; assoc. Byrne, Buck & Steiner, Farmington, Conn., 1978, Robinson, Robinson & Cole, Hartford, Conn., 1979-83; ptnr. Robinson & Cole LLP, Hartford, 1984—. Adj. prof. law Western New Eng. Coll., 1978-86, U. Conn., 1982, 84-87, Vt. Law Sch., 1994—; instr. planning U. Bridgeport, 1981-83, U. Conn., 1986-92; mem. faculty Nat. Coll. Dist. Attys., 1983-87, Nat. Jud. Coll., 1994; mem. faculty Am. Law Inst.-ABA Land Use Inst., 1988—; instr. city and regional planning Memphis State U., 1989, 94; spkr. in field. Author: The Complete Guide to Zoning, 2004; co-author: The Takings Issue, 1999; co-editor: Inclusionary Zoning Moves Downtown, 1985; contbr. more than 175 articles and book revs. to profl. jours. Bd. dirs. Conn. chpt. Appleseed Found., 1997-2000, Am. Boat Builders and Repairers Assn., 1995-1999, Growth Mgmt. Inst., Washington, 1992—, Housing Edn. Resource Ctr., 1984-88, Housing Coalition for Capitol Region, Inc., 1984-86; bd. dirs. Conn. Fund for Environment, 1981-85, legal adv. com., 1985-88, legal adv. bd., 1978-81; mem. Environment 2000 environ. plan adv. bd. Conn. Dept. Environ. Protection, 1987-91; assoc. Environ. Law Inst., 1987—; mem. housing task force Conn. Dept. on Aging, 1981; mem. Gov.'s Housing Task Force, Conn., 1980-81. With USN, 1968-75, Vietnam; capt. USNR, 1975-99. Fellow: Am. Inst. Cert. Planners (pres. 1988—90); mem.: ABA (coun. state and local govt. sect. 2000—), Am. Coll. Real Estate Lawyers, Assn. State Floodplain Mgrs., Internat. Mcpl. Law Assn. (chmn. sect. on zoning, planning and land devel. 1988—89, chmn. Conn. 1999—2003), Am. Planning Assn. (chmn. legis. com. Conn. chpt. 1978—80, exec. com. planning and law divsn. 1978—88, chmn. planning and law divsn. 1984—86, editl. adv. bd. 1984—92, bd. dirs. 1988—90), Conn. Bar Assn. (exec. com. zoning and planning sect. 1985—87, 1991—). Democrat. Unitarian Universalist. Avocations: sailing, skiing. Home: 80 Latimer Ln Weatogue CT 06089 Office: Robinson & Cole LLP 280 Trumbull St Hartford CT 06103-3597 Office Phone: 860-275-8228. Business E-Mail: dmerriam@rc.com.

MERRIAM, JOHN GOODWIN, political scientist, educator; b. Lausanne, Switzerland, Mar. 27, 1933; parents U.S. citizens; s. Gordon Phelps and Eunice Wilbur (Brandt) M.; m. Kathleen Howard, June 20, 1961 (div. 1989); children: Heather S., Christopher H., Jennifer S. Truax; m. Nancy J. Fox, Nov. 27, 1993. BA, Hamilton Coll., 1955; postgrad., Harvard U., 1961; MA, Boston U., 1962; PhD, Ind. U., 1970. Instr. Ricker Coll., Houlton, Maine, 1960-61, 64; teaching fellow Am. U. in Cairo, Egypt, 1964-66, asst. prof., 1966-67; instr., asst. prof., assoc. prof. polit. sci. Bowling Green (Ohio) State U., 1967-93, assoc. prof. emeritus, 1993—. Part-time prof. Lourdes Coll., 1993—; bd. dirs. Alliance Francaise de Toledo, 1986-93, Ohio Middle East Policy Coun., 1987—. With U.S. Army, 1955-58. Grantee Ind. U., Bloomington, 1961-62; Ford Found fellow, 1962-64. Mem. Middle East Inst., Middle East Policy Coun., Pi Sigma Alpha, Delta Tau Kappa. Democrat. Episcopalian. Avocation: walking. Home: 3033 Hopewell Pl Toledo OH 43606-3105 Office: Bowling Green State U Dept Polit Sci Bowling Green OH 43403-0001

MERRIAM, ROBERT W. engineering executive, educator; b. Providence, July 18, 1923; s. Paul Adams and Marian Lewis M.; m. Nancy Ann Allen, Dec. 21, 1954; children: Susan Allen Jones, Paul Adams, II. BS in Engring. Sci. and Applied Physics, Harvard Coll., 1949; MS in Engring. Sci. and Applied Physics, Harvard Engring. Sch., 1950. Reg. profl. engr., R.I. Instr. elec. engring. Swarthmore (Pa.) Coll., 1950-52; engr. Metals & Controls Corp., Attleboro, Mass., 1953-55; pres. Merriam Instruments, East Greenwich, R.I., 1955-99. Assoc. prof. U. R.I., Kingston, 1969-79. Editor: History of Wireless Communication in the U.S., 1989; patentee in field; contbr. articles to popular publications. Pres., dir. N.E. Wireless and Steam Mus., East Greenwich, 1964—; chmn. Planning Bd., East Greenwich, 1970s; hon. trustee Heritage Trust of R.I. With U.S. Army Signal Corp., 1942-46, ETO. Recipient Antoinette Downing award State of R.I., 1998; named Engr. of Yr., Nat. Assn. of Power Engrs., 1998, award Soc. Indsl. Archeology Gen. Tools, 2001. Fellow Radio Club Am. (Batcher award 1979); mem. IEEE (life), Am. Radio Relay League (life), Nat. Marine Electronic Assn. (hon., dir. 1957), Nat. Assn. Power Engrs. (hon.), Vet. Wireless Assn. (Marconi Gold medal 1995), 20:00 Club (Meritorious Amateur Seamanship award 1955), Rhode Soc. Profl. Engrs. (Engr. of Yr. 1999), Hope Club, Harvard Club (Boston). Personal E-mail: newsm@ids.net.

MERRICK, GEORGE BOESCH, aerospace company executive; b. Burlington, Iowa, Mar. 9, 1928; s. Dale McKeen and Marjorie May (Boesch) M.; m. Eleanor Gamble Moore, Sept. 1, 1951; children: Charles, Ellen, Elizabeth. BS, U. Minn., 1949. With N.Am. Aviation (name changed to Rockwell Internat.), 1949; dir. Apollo Command and Service Module, Space div., 1966-72; v.p., program mgr. Apollo Program, 1972-74, v.p., program mgr. Space Shuttle Orbiter Program, 1974-76; pres. space div. Rockwell Internat., Downey, Calif., 1976-78, pres. space systems group, 1978-80, corp. v.p., 1980-91, ret., 1991. Recipient Pub. Svc. award, NASA. Fellow Am. Astron. Soc., AIAA.

MERRICK, JANNA CAROL, political scientist, educator; b. Lafayette, Ind., Apr. 11, 1949; d. W. Leslie and Sadie Alice Lowrey; 1 child, Christopher. PhD, U. of Wash., 1974. Prof. of polit. sci. St. Cloud (Minn.) State U., 1977—93; assoc. dean for acad. affairs U. of South Fla., Sarasota, 1993—2000, prof. of govt. and internat. affairs Tampa, 1993—. Vis. scholar Ctr. for Biomed. Ethics, U. of Minn., Mpls., 1992—93, The Hastings Ctr., Briarcliff Manor, NY, 1990; vis. lectr. U. of Toulouse, France, 1990; acad. adminstr. edn. Harvard U., Boston, 1987. Co-editor: (book) Encyclopedia of Biomedical Policy, 1996; author: Reproductive Issues in America, 2003; contbr. articles to profl. jours. Citizen mem. Fla. Bar Assn. Grievance Com., Sarasota, 1995—98; ethics com. mem. All Children's Hosp., St. Petersburg, Fla., 1993—96; bd. dirs. Area Health Edn. Ctr., Sarasota, 1998—2002. Mem.: Am. Polit. Sci. Assn. (mem. com. on profl. ethics, rights, and freedoms 1994—97), Assn. for Politics and the Life Sci. (coun. mem. 1991—2000), Politics and the Life Scis. (editl. adv. bd. 2001—02). Methodist. Avocations: swimming, bicycling, photography. Office: U South Fla 4202 E Fowler Ave Bradenton FL 34202 Office Phone: 813-974-2384. Personal E-mail: jannamerrick@hotmail.com. E-mail: merrick@cas.usf.edu.

MERRICK, PHILLIP, technology company executive; BS in Computer Sci., U. Melbourne. Dir. devel. Magna Software Corp.; v.p. engring. Open Software Assocs.; founder webMethods Inc.; founder, pres., CEO Web Methods Inc., Fairfax, Va. Spkr. in field. Office: webMethods Inc 3930 Pender Dr Fairfax VA 22030-6076

MERRICK, RAYMOND F. state representative; b. Smith, Alberta, Can., Oct. 18, 1939; m. Phyllis Merrick; children: Michael, Matthew. BBA, Washburn U., 1965. Mgr. sales Folger's Coffee; gen. mgr. Treat Am., sr. v.p., Myron Green Cafeterias Co., gen. mgr.; owner MSM Mgmt.; mem. Kans. Ho. of Reps., 2000—, asst. majority leader. Pres. booster club Blue Valley H.S., 1995—98; pres. Blue Valley Riding Home Assn. Republican. Lutheran. Office: 180-W State Capitol 300 SW 10th Ave Topeka KS 66612 Address: 6874 W 164th Terr Stilwell KS 66085

MERRIER, HELEN, actress, writer; b. Chgo., Mar. 10, 1932; d. Miner Thompson and Helen (Hembree) Coburn; m. Tim Meier, Dec. 23, 1954; 1 child, William Frank. BA, Mills Coll., 1954; BS, Northwestern U., 1955. Radio roles include Ma Perkins, One Man's Family, Standard School House of the Air, 1934-52; stage roles include Finian's Rainbow, 1952, The Happy Time, 1952, The Night of January 16th, 1952, No Exit, 1953, Tiger at the Gates, 1953, Caeser and Cleopatra, 1953, The Cocktail Party, 1953, Streetcar Named Desire, 1953, Misalliance, 1956, Cry the Beloved Country, 1956, Cat in a Tin Roof, 1963, Take Me Along, 1966, Caucasian Chalk Circle, 1967, The Devils, 1968, Electra, 1969, Jean Harlow and Billy the Kid, 1969, Three-Penny Opera, 1969, A Shot in the Dark, 1970, Private Lives, 1970, The

Importance of Being Earnest, 1971, Forty Carats, 1972, Paris is Out!, 1972, A Christmas Carol, 1973, The Sea Gull, 1975, Something more than Ordinary, 1976, Three Dollar Bill, 1976, Maid to Marry, 1977, Scrooge, the musical, 1984, Prisoner of Second Avenue, 1985, Tom Sawyer, 1986, Comedy of Errors, 1987, Juno and the Paycock, 1987, Woman of the Year, 1989, Time and the Conways, 1991, Cinderella, 1991, Sweeney Todd, 1991, The Birds, 1993, Dreams of Defiance (rev.), 1994, Lady Lucinda's Scrapbook (solo play), 1996-98, As You Like It hike, 1998-99, A Midsummer Night's Dream hike, 1999, 2001, Vieux Carre, 1999, Woman Talk (cabaret), 1999—, Healthy-Minded Little Old Lady Songs (solo cabaret), 2000—, William Inge Festival, 2000, Robin Hood hike, 2000-01, Rip van Winkle hike, 2001, Stephen Foster in Song and Story (solo cabaret), 2001—, Eleemosynary, 2002. Recipient The Spirit of Theater award, 2000, Disting. Svc. award The Salvation Army, 2000. Mem. Victory Svcs. Club (London), Arts Club Chgo. Home: 915 Linden Ave Wilmette IL 60091-2712 Personal E-mail: hmerrier@@worldnet.att.net .

MERRIFIELD, DONALD PAUL, hispanic ministries coordinator; b. Los Angeles, Nov. 14, 1928; s. Arthur S. and Elizabeth (Baker) M. BS in Physics, Calif. Inst. Tech., 1950; MS, U. Notre Dame, 1951; A.M., Ph.L. in Philosophy, St. Louis U., 1957; PhD, MIT, 1962; S.T.M., U. Santa Clara, Calif., 1966; S.T.D. (hon.), U. So. Calif., 1969; D.H.L. (hon.), U. Judaism, 1984, Hebrew Union Coll.-Jewish Inst. Religion, 1986. Joined Soc. of Jesus, 1951; ordained priest Roman Cath. Ch., 1965; instr. physics Loyola U., Los Angeles, 1961-62; lectr. Engring. Sch., Santa Clara, 1965; cons. theoretical chemistry Jet Propulsion Lab., Calif. Inst. Tech., 1962-69; asst. prof. physics U. San Francisco, 1967-69; pres. Loyola Marymount U., Los Angeles, 1969-84, chancellor, 1984—2002; Hispanic pastoral ministry, regent, sr. rsch. fellow Chaminade U., Honolulu, 2002—. Mem. Sigma Xi. Office: 2727 Pamoa Rd Honolulu HI 96822-1838 Office Phone: 808-721-3541. Business E-Mail: dmerrifi@chaminade.edu. E-mail: dmerrifield@calprov.org. *In today's world, we all stand in need of that pragmatic hope which allows us to see the possibilities for building a more just society and meeting the challenges before us. Without such hope we are paralyzed before our difficulties. With a less realistic hope, too idealistic, we are continually overwhelmed by failures. But with an openness to possibilities, we can move ahead with determination.*

MERRIFIELD, DUDLEY BRUCE, business educator, former government official; b. Chgo., June 13, 1921; s. Fred and Anna (Marshall) M.; m. Paula Sorensen, June 8, 1949; children: Bruce, Robert, Marshall. AB in Chemistry, Princeton U., 1942; MS in Chemistry, U. Chgo., 1948, PhD in Chemistry, 1950. Disting. vis. prof. Georgetown U. Bus. Sch., Washington. Sr. rsch. chemist Monsanto, St. Louis, 1950-56; mgr. polymer rsch. Tex.-U.S. Chem. Co., Parsippany, N.J., 1956-63; dir. R & D Petrolite Corp., St. Louis, 1963-68; v.p. tech. and ventures Occidental Petroleum Co., Houston, 1968-77; v.p. tech. and venture mgmt. Continental Group, Stamford, Conn., 1977-82; asst. sec. for productivity, tech. and innovation Dept. Commerce, Washington, 1982-89; undersec. econ. affairs, 1986-87; Walter Bladstrom prof., emeritus Wharton Bus. Sch., U Pa., Phila., 1989-94; pres., CEO Pinnacle Rsch. Inst. Devel. Co., 1991—. Adv. bd. Binat R & D Found., U.S., Israel, France, India, 1979—; disting. vis. prof. mgmt., Georgetown U., Washington. Contbr. articles to profl. jours.; patentee in field. Exec. coun. Episcopal Ch., 1973-79; chmn. Princeton Alumni Coun., 1968-72. With USMC, 1943-46. Fellow AAAS, Inst. for Chemists; mem. Am. Chem. Soc., Indsl. Rsch. Inst. (dir., pres.-elect 1977-82 M. Holland award), Am. Mgmt. Assn. Hall of Fame (trustee, chmn. rsch. coun.), Dirs. Rsch., Sigma Xi Republican. Episcopalian. Office: Pridco Mgmt Corp Ste 604 1316 New Hampshire NW Washington DC 20036 E-mail: prioco@verizon.net.

MERRIFIELD, ROBERT BRUCE, biochemist, educator; b. Ft. Worth, Tex., July 15, 1921; s. George E. and Lorene (Lucas) Merrifield; m. Elizabeth Furlong, June 20, 1949; children: Nancy, James, Betsy, Cathy, Laurie, Sally. BA, UCLA, 1943, PhD, 1949, U. Colo., 1969, Uppsala U., 1970, Yale U., 1971, Newark Coll. Engring., 1972, Med. Coll. Ohio, 1977, Boston Coll., 1984, Fairleigh Dickinson U., 1985, N.J. U. Medicine & Dentistry, 1985, U. Barcelona, 1986, Adelphi U., 1987, U. Montpellier, 1988, Delaware Valley Coll., 1991, Scripps Rsch. Inst., 1998, Rockefeller U., 1998. Chemist Park Research Found., 1943—44; research asst. Med. Sch., UCLA, 1948—49; asst. Rockefeller Inst. for Med. Research, 1949—53, assoc., 1953—57; asst. prof. Rockefeller U., 1957—58, assoc. prof., 1958—66, prof., 1966—92, John D. Rockefeller prof., 1984—92, emeritus prof., 1992—. Assoc. editor: Internat. Jour. Peptide and Protein Research; contbr. Named one of Top 75 Contbrs. to Chem. Enterprise during past 75 yrs., Chem. & Engring. News, 1998; recipient Lasker award biomed. rsch., 1969, Gairdner award, 1970, Intra-Sci. award, 1970, Nichols medal, 1973, Alan E. Pierce award, Am. Peptide Symposium, 1979, Nobel prize in chemistry, 1984, UCLA Disting. Svc. medal, 1986, Royal Soc. Chemistry medal, 1987, Rudinger award, European Peptide Soc., 1990, Chem. Pioneer award, Am. Inst. Chemists, 1993, Glenn T. Seaborg medal, 1993, UCLA Alumnus of Yr. award, 1997, award, Assn. Biomolecular Resource Facilities, 1998. Mem.: NAS USA, Am. Soc. Biol. Chemists, Am. Chem. Soc. (award creative work synthetic organic chemistry 1972, Hirschmann award in peptide chemistry 1990, Glenn T. Seaborg award 1993), Alpha Chi Sigma, Phi Lambda Upsilon, Sigma Xi. Achievements include discovery of solid phase peptide synthesis; completed (with B. Gutte) 1st total synthesis of an enzyme, 69. Office: Rockefeller Univ Dept Chemistry 1230 York Ave New York NY 10021-6307

MERRILL, ABEL JAY, lawyer; b. Balt., Mar. 25, 1938; s. Yale and Evelyn (Cordish) M.; m. Susan Stein, June 15, 1963; children: Adam L., Julie F. BA, Colgate U., 1959; LLB, U. Md., 1964. Bar: Md. 1964. Law clk. U.S. Ct. Appeals, Balt., 1964-65; assoc. Gordon, Feinblatt & Rothman, Balt., 1965-70; atty. pvt. practice, Annapolis, Md., 1970-78, 83—; prin. Blumenthal, May, Downs & Merrill, Annapolis, 1979-83; mem. firm Merrill & Cruttenden, P.A. Mem. inquiry com. Atty. Grievance Commn. Md., 1975-85, character com. Ct. of Appeals, 1987-88; mem. pension oversight bd. Anne Arundel County, Md., 2000-03. Co-author: (software) Maryland Wills and Trusts. Fellow Am. Coll. Probate Counsel; mem. ABA, Md. Bar Assn., Anne Arundel County Bar Assn. Office Phone: 410-268-0006. E-mail: abelj@merillaw.com.

MERRILL, ARTHUR ALEXANDER, financial analyst; b. Honolulu, June 17, 1906; s. Arthur Merton and Grace Graydon (Dickey) M.; m. Elsie Louise Breed, Aug. 17, 1929; 1 child, Anne Louise Merrill Breiling. BS in Elec. Engring, U. Calif., 1927; MBA, Harvard U., 1929. Mem. engring., statistics, and mgmt. depts. Gen. Electric Co., Schenectady, also N.Y.C., 1927-61; fin. writer and analyst, pres. Merrill Analysis Inc., Haverford, Pa., 1961—. Author: How Do You Use a Slide Rule, 1961, Chess Openings Simplified, 1974, Behavior of Prices on Wall Street, 1985, Battle of White Plains, 1975, Seasonal Tendencies in Stock Prices, 1975, Filtered Waves, Basic Theory, 1977, Bias in Hourly, Daily and Weekly Wave Patterns, 1979, Remembering Names, 1985; editor: Tech. Trends, 1961-88. Mem. Market Technicians Assn. (chartered, Ann. award 1977), Fin. Analysts Fedn., N.Y. Soc. Security Analysts, Mensa, Intertel, Soc. Preservation and Encouragement Barber Shop Quartet Singing Am., Sigma Xi, Theta Chi, Tau Beta Pi, Eta Kappa Nu. Republican. Congregationalist. Home and Office: 3300 Darby Rd Apt 3325 Haverford PA 19041-1071

MERRILL, ARTHUR LEWIS, retired theology educator; b. Tura, Assam, India, Sept. 14, 1930; s. Alfred Francis and Ida (Walker) M.; m. Barbara Jean Mayer, Aug. 18, 1951 (dec. June 1978); children: Margaret Jean, Katherine Merrill Nelson, Robert L.; m. Margaret Z. Morris, Sept. 11, 1985. BA, Coll. of Wooster, 1951; BD with distinction, Berkeley Bapt. Div. Sch., 1954; PhD, U. Chgo., 1962. Ordained to ministry United Ch. of Christ, 1954. Asst. prof. Bapt. Missionary Tng. Sch., Chgo., 1957-58; assoc. prof. Mission House Theol. Sem., Plymouth, Wis., 1958-62, United Theol. Sem. Twin Cities, New Brighton, Minn., 1962-67, prof., 1967-95, prof. emeritus, 1995—. Author: United Theological Seminary of the Twin Cities: An Ecumenical Venture, 1993; co-author: Biblical Witness and the World, 1967; co-editor: Scripture in History and Theology, 1977; contbr. articles to profl. publs. ATS-Lilly postdoctoral fellow, 1966-67. Mem. Soc. Bibl. Lit., Am. Schs. Oriental Rsch., Israel Exploration Soc., Minn. Theol. Libr. Assn. (pres. 1994-95). Home: 36177 Wabana Rd Grand Rapids MN 55744-6446 E-mail: artgaro@paulbunyan.net.

MERRILL, CHARLES EUGENE, lawyer; b. San Antonio, Aug. 26, 1952; s. Charles Perry and Florence Elizabeth Merrill; m. Carol Ann Rutter, Apr. 28, 1984; children: Elizabeth C., Charles C. AB, Stanford U., 1974; JD, U. Calif., Berkeley, 1977. Bar: Mo. 1977, Calif. 1983, Ill. 1993. Mem. Husch & Eppenberger, LLC, St. Louis, 1977—. Mem. ABA, Bar Assn. of Met. St. Louis. Office: Husch & Eppenberger LLC 190 Carondelet Plz Ste 600 Saint Louis MO 63105-3441 E-mail: charlie.merrill@husch.com.

MERRILL, DEANE WHITNEY, JR., secondary school educator, consultant; b. Orange, New Jersey, May 9, 1938; s. Deane Whitney Merrill Sr. and Harriet Mary (Ray); m. Anna Christine Morben, July 2, 1995. PhD, U. of Calif., Berkeley, 1960—67. Scientist Lawrence Berkeley Lab., Berkeley, 1960—98; tchr. Mohawk Trail Regional H.S., Buckland, Mass., 2001—04. Cons. 22 Mechanic St., Shelburne Falls, Mass., 1998—. Author: (numerous scientific publications in) Physics, Demography, Pub. Health, Bio-stats., Epidemiol. Achievements include development of density equalizing map projections (cartograms). Home: 22 Mechanic St Shelburne Falls MA 01370 Personal E-mail: merrill@crocker.com.

MERRILL, DENISE, state legislator; b. Calif. BA, U. Conn., 1988; JD, San Francisco Law Sch. Bar: Calif. 1978. Tchr. Vershire Sch., 1979-81; exec. dir. Consortium Law-Related Edn., 1983-92; cons. State Dept. Edn., Conn., 1984-91; mem. Dist. 54 Conn. State Ho. of Reps., 1993-99, dep. majority leader, 1999—. Mem. Mansfield Bd. Edn., 1991-93. Office: PO Box 804 Storrs Mansfield CT 06268-0804

MERRILL, EDWARD WILSON, chemical engineering educator; b. New Bedford, Mass., Aug. 31, 1923; s. Edward Clifton and Gertrude (Wilson) M.; m. Genevieve de Bidart, Aug. 19, 1948; children: Anne de Bidart, Francis de Bidart. AB, Harvard U., 1945; DSc, MIT, 1947. Research engr. Dewey & Almy div. W.R. Grace & Co., 1947-50; mem. faculty MIT, 1950-98, prof. chem. engring., 1964-98, Carbon P. Dubbs prof., 1973-96, emeritus, 1998—. Cons. in biochem. engring. Harvard U. Health Svcs., 1982-94; cons. in field. Contbr. articles to profl. jours. on polymers, rheology, med. engring.; patentee chem. and rheological instruments. Pres. bd. trustees Buckingham Sch., Cambridge, 1969-74; trustee Browne and Nichols Sch., Cambridge, 1972-74, hon. trustee, 1974—. Fellow Am. Inst. for Med. and Biol. Engring., Am. Acad. Arts and Scis.; mem. AIChE (Alpha Chi Sigma award 1981, Charles M.A. Stine award 1993, Founders award 2000), Am. Chem. Soc., Soc. for Biomaterials (Clemson U. Award 1990, Founders award 2003). Home: 90 Somerset St Belmont MA 02478-2010 Office Phone: 617-253-4593. Office Fax: 617-489-2165. Business E-Mail: emerrill@mit.edu.

MERRILL, FRANK HARRISON, data processing executive, consultant; b. Pitts., June 20, 1953; s. Edgar Frank and Harriet Margaret (Gallagher) M.; m. Rita Alice Mae Murray, May 27, 1977; 1 child, Laura Margaret. BSMetE, Colo. Sch. Mines., 1971-76; M of Computer Info. Systems, U. Denver, 1988. Cert. sys. profl., computer programmer; cert. PICK profl.; cert. computer profl.; A+ cert., MCSE. Metall. engr. Inspiration Copper Co., Miami, Ariz., 1979-80, Cominco Am., Inc., Bixby, Mo., 1980-81; programmer, analyst M.L. Foss, Inc., Denver, 1981-83, Titsch & Assocs., Denver, 1983; data processing mgr. PBI/BAXA, Inc., Denver, 1983-86; owner (systems cons.) Dynamic Solutions, Denver, 1986—; dir. software devel. Drycreek Assocs. Corp., 2004—. Cons. in field, Denver, 1985—; instr. continuing edn. User's Group, Denver, 1985—2001; instr. computer info. sys. U. Denver, 1990-97; mem. grad. computer info. sys. faculty Colo. campus, U. Phoenix, 1991-94; bd. dirs. Inst. for Cert. of Computer Profls. 1993-96, Drycreek Assocs. Corp., 2004-. Adult leader Boy Scouts Am., Denver and Globe, Ariz., 1973-86, Denver, 1996—; mem. Marriage Encounter Interfaith Bd., Denver, 1985-89, chair, 1988-89; mem. coun. Rocky Mountain Aldersgate Marriage Encounter, 1986-94, exec. couple, 1990-94; mem. Volksmarch Steering Com. Lakewood on Parade, 1990-95; mem. St. Andrew's Soc. Colo.; nominating com. Free Meth. Ch., 1989-92, ch. bd. property and fin., 1992-94. 2d lt. U.S. Army, 1977-79. Named to PICK Industry Accreditation Coun., 1990; recipient God and Svc. award Free Meth. Ch., 1984. Mem. IEEE, SAR, Assn. Sys. Mgmt. (profl. pres. Mile-Hi chpt. 1992-93, mem. internat. cert. adv. com. 1993-95, chmn. 1994-95, mem. divsn. 17 coun. 1994-96, vice chmn. 1995-96, Distinguished Service award 1996), Colo. Pick Users' Group (edn. chmn. 1984—2001), Info. Sys. Security Assn., Scottish-Am. Mil. Soc. (charter, post contr. Post 100 Colo. 1991-95), Falcon Wanderers Club, Cheyenne High Plains Wanderers Club, A.C. Gilbert Heritage Soc. (Rocky Mtn. Regnl. pres. 1994-2000, mem. nat. exec. bd. 1995—2002), Nat. Soc. Magna Charta Dames & Barons. Republican. Mem. Free Methodist Ch. Avocations: model railroading, model rocketry, hiking, camping, mountain climbing.

MERRILL, GEORGE VANDERNETH, lawyer, investment executive; b. NYC, July 2, 1947; s. James Edward and Claire (Leness) M.; m. Janice Anne Humes, May 11, 1985; children: Claire Georgina, Anne Stewart. Student, Phillips Exeter Acad., 1960—64; AB magna cum laude, Harvard U., 1968, JD, 1972; MBA, Columbia U., 1973. Bar: NY 1973, U.S. Dist. Ct. (so. and ea. dists.) NY 1974, U.S. Ct. Appeals (2d cir.) 1974. Assoc. Cleary, Gottlieb, Steen & Hamilton, NYC, 1974-77, Hawkins, Delafield & Wood, NYC, 1977-79; v.p. Irving Trust Co., NYC, 1980-82, Listowel, Inc., NYC, 1982-84, bd. dirs., exec. v.p., 1984-93; v.p. instl. portfolio mgmt. Shawmut Investment Advisors, 1993-95; also co-mgr. Shawmut Growth & Income Equity Mut. Fund; v.p. instl. portfolio mgmt. Fleet Investment Advisors, 1995-96, also co-mgr. Galaxy Growth & Income Equity Mut. Fund.; v.p. trust and instl. portfolio mgmt., mem. Fla. equity com. No. Trust Corp., Chgo., 1996-2000; v.p., sr. personal investment officer, sector head Bank of NY, NYC, 2000—, mem. investment policy com., 2004—. Bd. dirs. Pres. Arell Found., NYC, 1985-93, also bd. dirs., pres. Northfield Charitable Corp., NYC, 1986-93; v.p., sec. Brougham Prodn. Co., NYC, 1986-89, bd. dirs., sr. v.p., sec., 1990-93; v.p., sec. Marinetics Inc., NYC, 1988-90, sr. v.p., sec., 1991-93, also bd. dirs., 1989-93; v.p. Sci. Design and Engring. Co., Inc., NYC, 1987-88, bd. dirs., exec. v.p., 1989-93. John Harvard scholar; recipient Detur award Harvard U., 1968. Mem. ABA, Am. Mgmt. Assn., Nat. Cum Laude Soc., The Brook, Union Club (NYC), Down Town Assn., Racquet and Tennis Club, Somerset Club (Boston), Signet Soc. (Cambridge), Pilgrims of U.S. Home: 2 Pierce Rd Riverside CT 06878 Office: The Bank of NY 5th Fl 1290 Ave of the Americas New York NY 10104 Business E-Mail: gmerrill@bankofny.com.

MERRILL, HARVIE MARTIN, manufacturing executive, director; b. Detroit, Apr. 26, 1921; s. Harvie and Helen (Nelson) M.; m. Mardelle Merrill; children— Susan, Linda. BS in Chem. Engring, Purdue U., 1942. Devel. engr. Sinclair Refining Co., 1946-47; research and gen. mgr. 3M Co., St. Paul, 1947-65; v.p. fabricated products Plastics div. Stauffer Chem. Co., N.Y.C., 1965-69; with Hexcel Corp., San Francisco, 1969-86, pres., chief exec. officer, 1969-86, chmn. bd., 1976-88. With USAF, 1942-46. Mem. Pacific-Union Club, Bohemian Club San Francisco, Villa Taverna (San Francisco), Burlingame Country Club. Home: 1170 Sacramento St San Francisco CA 94108-1943

MERRILL, JEAN FAIRBANKS, writer; b. Rochester, NY, Jan. 27, 1923; d. Earl Dwight and Elsie (Fairbanks) M. BA, Allegheny Coll., 1944; MA, Wellesley Coll., 1945. Feature editor Scholastic Mags., 1947-50; editor Lit. Cavalcade, 1956-57; publs. div. Bank St. Coll. Edn., 1964-65. Children's books include Henry, the Hand-Painted Mouse, 1951, The Woover, 1952, Boxes, 1953, The Tree House of Jimmy Domino, 1955, The Travels of Marco, 1956, A Song for Gar, 1957, The Very Nice Things, 1959, Blue's Broken Heart, 1960, Shan's Lucky Knife (Jr. Lit. Guild selection), Emily Emerson's Moon, 1960 (Jr. Lit. Guild selection), The Superlative Horse (Jr. Lit. Guild selection), 1961 (Lewis Carroll Shelf award 1963), Tell About the Cowbarn, Daddy, 1963, The Pushcart War (Lewis Carroll Shelf award), 1964 (Boys Club Am. Jr. Book award), High, Wide & Handsome, 1964 (Jr. Lit. Guild selection), The Elephant Who Liked to Smash Small Cars, 1967, Red Riding, 1968, The Black Sheep, 1969, Here I Come-Ready or Not!, 1970, Mary, Come Running, 1970, How Many Kids are Hiding on My Block?, 1970, Please, Don't Eat My Cabin, 1971, The Toothpaste Millionaire (Dorothy Canfield Fisher Meml. award 1975-76), 1972 (Sequoyah award 1977), The Second Greatest Clown in the World, 1972, The Jackpot, 1972, The Bumper Sticker Book, 1973, Maria's House, 1974, The Girl Who Loved Caterpillars, 1992; poetry books edited include A Few Flies and I, 1969; libretto for chamber opera Mary Come Running, 1983. Fulbright fellow India, 1952-53 Mem. Authors League, Vt. Arts. Coun., Vt. Inst. Natural Sci., Vt. Nat. Resources Coun., Fulbright Assn., Women's Internat. League Peace and Justice, Sierra Club, Audobon Soc., Women's Internat. League Peace and Justice, Phi Beta Kappa. Office Phone: 802-728-9549. *My interest in writing children's books may have derived from the impact certain books had on me as a child, and a wish to recreate the quality of that experience. As to my general motivation as a writer, I would say that it is to celebrate those aspects of the human experience that affirm the creative and life-reverencing instinct in man. I always hope that my stories may be essentially liberating, opening the reader to emotional, as well as intellectual experience, and that they may be entertaining, encouraging the capacity for joy by evoking the free play of a reader's curiosity, humor and inventiveness.*

MERRILL, JOSEPH MELTON, medical educator; b. Andalusia, Ala., Dec. 8, 1923; s. Walter C. and Mary T. (McLaney) M.; m. Gudrun Wallgren, Sept. 15, 1960; children: Maria, Caroline. MD, Harvard Med. Sch., 1948. Diplomate Am. Bd. Internal Medicine. With VA Med. Ctr., Nashville, 1960-64; chief Gen. Clin. Rsch. Ctrs. NIH, Bethesda, 1964-67; dean sci. affairs Baylor Coll. Medicine, Houston, 1967-77, prof., 1967—. Capt. USAF, 1951-53. Office: Baylor Coll Medicine One Baylor Plz Scurlock Ste 1406 Houston TX 77030

MERRILL, MARTHA, library media educator; b. Anniston, Ala., Apr. 21, 1946; d. Walter James and Polly (McCarty) M. BA, Birmingham-So. Coll., 1968; MS, Jacksonville (Ala.) State U., 1974; PhD, U. Pitts., 1979. Social worker Tuscaloosa (Ala.) County Dept. Human Resources, 1968-71, Calhoun County Dept. Human Resources, Anniston, 1971-73, social scis./bus. libr. Jacksonville State U., 1974-86, prof. instrnl. media, 1987—. Editor: Reference Services and Media, 1999; co-author: Dictionary for School Library Media Specialists, 2001. Mem. Friends of Libr. bd. Anniston-Calhoun County Pub. Libr., 1984—. Recipient Ala./SIRS Intellectual Freedom award, Intellectual Freedom Com., Ala. Libr. Assn., 1992, Ala. Beta Phi Mu chpt. Libr. of Yr. award, 1997. Mem. ALA (exec. bd., Intellectual Freedom Round Table 1987-93), Ala. Libr. Assn. (pres. 1990-91, Disting. Svc. award 1995 Outstanding Publ. award, 2004), Ala. Assn. Coll. and Spcl. Librs. (pres. 1989-90), Southeastern Libr. Assn. (chair intellectual freedom com. 1986-88, chair resolutions com. 1990-92). Office: Jacksonville State U Coll Edn Dept Ednl Resources Jacksonville AL 36265 Office Phone: 256-782-5011. E-mail: mmerrill@jsucc.jsu.edu.

MERRILL, RICHARD AUSTIN, lawyer; b. Logan, Utah, May 20, 1937; s. Milton Rees and Bessie (Austin) M.; m. Elizabeth Duvall, Aug. 26, 1961; children— Patricia, John. AB, Columbia U., 1959, LLB, 1964; BA (Rhodes scholar), Oxford (Eng.) U., 1961, MA, 1965. Bar: N.Y. 1964, D.C. 1965, Va. 1980. Law clk. to Hon. Carl McGowan, U.S. Ct. Appeals for D.C., 1964-65, Va. bar, 1980; assoc. firm Covington & Burling, Washington, 1965-69, spl. counsel, 1991—; assoc. prof. law U. Va., 1969-72, prof., 1972-75, Daniel Caplin prof. law, 1977—, Arnold Leon prof., 1985-88, dean sch. law, 1980-88, Albert C. Tate Jr. rsch. prof., 1989-91. Gen. counsel FDA, Washington, 1975-77; cons. in field. Mem. Inst. Medicine (council) 1985-88, Nat. Acad. Scis., 1977—, Bd. on Toxicology and Environ. Health Hazards, 1979-85; bd. dirs. Immunex Corp. Author: (with Jerry L. Mashaw and Peter Shane) American Administrative Law, 2d edit., 1985, (with Peter B. Hutt) Food and Drug Law, 1980. Bd. trustees Thomas Jefferson Meml. Found. Mem. Am. Bar Found., Va. Bar Found., Am. Law Inst., Food and Drug Inst. (trustee). Office: U Va Sch Law 580 Massie Rd Charlottesville VA 22903-1738

MERRILL, ROBERT, baritone; b. Bklyn., June 4, 1919; s. Abraham and Lillian (Balaban) Miller; m. Marion Machno, May 30, 1954; children: David Robert, Lizanne. MusD(hon.), Gustavus Adolphus Coll., 1970; MusD (hon.), CUNY, 1996. Ind. baritone, N.Y.C. and on tour, 1945—. Baritone in concert, opera and on radio and TV; singer: (Operas) debut, 1945, Escamillo in Carmen, Germont in La Traviata, Valentine in Faust, Amonasro in Alda, Marcello in La Boheme, Don Carlo in La Forza del Destino, Sir Henry Ashton in Lucia de Lammermoor, sang in La Traviata condr. Arturo Toscanini over NBC network, with NBC, 1946—, opened Met. Opera season Rodrigo in Don Carlo, 1950, appeared in Toscanini's final opera performance and rec. as Renato in Un Ballo in Maschera, opened Met. season as Valentine in Faust, 1953, as Figaro in Barber of Seville, 1954, Rigoletto in Rigoletto, Barnaba in Giocanda, Scarpia in Tosca, Renato in Un Ballo in Maschera, Iago in Otello, Count di Luna in Il Trovatore, Tonio in Pagliacci, Gerard in Andrea Chenier, 1962, Sir Henry in Lucia, 1964, Valentine in Faust, 1965, Germont in La Traviata, 1967, Amonasro in Aida, 1969, also opened Met. Opera season, 1971, opened Royal Opera House-Covent Garden season as Germont in La Traviata, 1967, Met. Opera visit to Japan, Tokyo, 1975, appeared in concerts, 1975, (rec. artist) RCA-Victor, Angel, London, Columbia labels; author: (novels) The Divas, 1978, (autobiography) Once More From the Beginning, 1965, Between Acts, 1976. Mem. Nat. Coun. of the Arts, 1968—74. Named winner, Met. Auditions of the Air, 1945, Father of Yr. in Music, 1980; recipient Music Ann. award for rec. Ah, QDite Alla Giovine, 1946, Harriet Cohen Internat. Music award, 1961, best opera rec. award, NARAS, 1962, 1964, Handel medal, City of N.Y., 1970, medal, Westchester C.C. Found., 1981, Nat. Medal of Arts, 1993, Internat. Dor L'Dor award, B'nai B'rith, 1994, Lawrence Tibbett award, Am. Guild Mus. Artists Relief Fund, 1996, medal of honor for music, Nat. Arts Club, 1998, medal of honor, Ellis Island, 1999, NY Yankees Lifetime Achievement Award, 2003. Mem.: SAG, AGVA, AFTRA, Am. Guild Mus. Artists, Actors Equity Assn., Opera Guild, Friars Club (monk 1968—). Achievements include 1st American opera singer to give 500 performances at Metropolitan Opera, N.Y.C., 1973; official singer New York Yankees, 1967; performer for Pres. Roosevelt, Truman, Eisenhower, Kennedy, Johnson, Nixon, Ford, Carter, Reagan; only singer to perform for both houses of Congress at Roosevelt Meml. Avocations: golf, baseball, fine art. *If you honestly feel that you are doing your best, it makes good criticism even sweeter and bad criticism less painful.*

MERRILL, STEPHEN, lawyer, consultant, former governor; Student, U. N.H., Georgetown U. Former personal counsel to Sec. Air Force, Pentagon; atty. gen. State of NH, Concord, 1985—89, gov., 1993—97; of counsel Choate, Hall and Stewart, Boston, 1997—99; pres. Bingham Consulting Group Bingham Dana LLP, Boston, 1999—, ptnr., 1999—. Mem. NH task force on Child Abuse and Neglect, former pres., legal counsel. Served to capt. USAF. Recipient AG Profl. award. Fellow: ABA; mem.: Nat. Attys. Gen. Emeritus (co-chmn.), Nat. Gov.'s Assn. Emeritus, Ea. Assn. Attys. Gen. (chmn.), Phi Beta Kappa (Ford Found. scholar). Office: Bingham Dana LLP 150 Federal St Boston MA 02110-1713

MERRILL, STEVEN WILLIAM, research and development executive; b. Oakland, Calif., Aug. 6, 1944; s. David Howard and Etha Nadine (Wright) M. BA in Chemistry, Calif. State U., Hayward, 2004. Lic. pyrotechnic, Calif. Apprentice Borgman Sales Co., San Leandro, Calif., 1960—64; assembler Calif. Fireworks Display, Rialto, Calif., 1970; pyrotechnician Hand Chem. Industries, Milton, Canada, 1972—74; dir. R&D Pyrospectaculars, Rialto, 1988—92; pyrotechnic cons., 1993—; owner, dir. Merrill Prodns. Ordnance, Crestline. Experimenter in field, 1958—; chief chemist Baron Blakesly Solvents, Newark, Calif., 1987-88; court expert San Francisco Superior Ct., 1971, Victorville (Calif.) Superior Ct. Counselor Xanthos, Inc., Alameda, Calif., 1970. Mem. AAAS, Am. Chem. Soc., Am. Stats. Assn., Am. Bd. Forensic Examiners, Internat. Platform Assn. Avocations: wood carving, sculpture, photography, electronics, automobile restoration. Home and Office: Merrill Prodns Ordnance PO Box 676 Crestline CA 92325-0676 Office Phone: 909-338-2913. E-mail: birdscare@aol.com.

MERRILL, THOMAS WENDELL, lawyer, educator; b. Bartlesville, Okla., May 3, 1949; s. William McGill and Dorothy (Glasener) Merrill; m. Kimberly Ann Evans, Sept. 18, 1973; children: Jessica, Margaret, Elizabeth. BA, Grinnell Coll., 1971, Oxford U., 1973; JD, U. Chgo., 1977. Bar: Ill. 1980, U.S. Dist. Ct. (no. dist.) Ill. 1980, U.S. Ct. Appeals (5th cir.) 1982, U.S. Ct. Appeals (7th cir.) 1983, U.S. Ct. Appeals (9th and DC cirs.) 1984, U.S. Supreme Ct. 1985. Clk. U.S. Ct. Appeals (DC cir.), Washington, 1977-78, U.S. Supreme Ct., Washington, 1978-79; assoc. Sidley & Austin, Chgo., 1979-81, counsel,

1981-87, 90—; dep. solicitor gen. U.S. Dept. Justice, 1987-90; prof. law Northwestern U., Chgo., 1981—2003, John Paul Stevens prof., 1993—2003; prof. law Columbia U., 2003—. Co-author: (book) Property: Takings, 2002; contbr. articles to profl. jours. Rhodes scholar, Oxford U., 1971, Danforth fellow, 1971. Home: 2828 Broadway Apt 7C New York NY 10025 Address: 435 W 116th St New York NY 10027

MERRILL, VINCENT NICHOLS, retired landscape architect; b. Reading, Mass., Apr. 28, 1912; s. Charles Clarkson and Bessie Louise (Nichols) M.; m. Anna Victoria Swanson, Jan. 20, 1943 (dec. Feb. 1996); m. Natalie Ames Prentice, Aug. 16, 1997 (dec. Jan. 2003). AB, Dartmouth Coll., 1933; M in Landscape Architecture, Harvard U., 1937. Office asst. Shurcliff & Shurcliff, Boston, 1937-42, 47-54, ptnr., 1954-58, Shurcliff & Merrill and predecessors Shurcliff, Shurcliff & Merrill, Boston, Mass., 1958-81; prin. Shurcliff & Merrill, Cambridge, Mass., 1981-89; retired, 1998. Founder, bd. dirs., pres. Charles River Watershed Assn., Auburndale, Mass., 1963-75; bd. dirs. Charles Basin Adv. Com., Boston, 1979-82; pres. Hubbard Ednl. Trust, Cambridge, 1981-89, bd. dirs., 1989-95. Capt. U.S. Army, 1942-46, ETO. Recipient Gold medal Mass. Hort. Soc., 1988. Fellow Am. Soc. Landscape Architects; mem. Boston Soc. Landscape Architects (pres. 1961-63), Hort. Club of Boston (hon. mem., pres. 1992-94). Avocation: home landscaping. Home and Office: #B-205 97 Warren Ave Plymouth MA 02360-2425

MERRILL, WENDY JANE, insurance company executive; b. Waterbury, Conn., Dec. 4, 1961; d. David Kenneth and Jane Joy (Nevius) Merrill; m. Aidan T. Harrison (div. Nov. 1998); children: Christopher Harrison, Charlotte Harrison, Ryan Harrison; m. Michael G. Kelly, Oct. 2, 1999. BA in Journalism, George Washington U., Washington, 1981; MBA in mgmt., Cornell U., 1992. Intern in edn. HEW, Washington, summer 1978, writer, summer 1979; rsch. asst. dep. health svcs. adminstrn. George Washington U., Washington, 1979-81; sec. Nat. Assn. Beverage Importers, Washington, 1981; account exec. Staff Design, Washington, 1982; adminstrv. aide Internat. Food Policy Rsch. Inst., Washington, 1983-86; program assoc. Acad. for Ednl. Devel., Washington, 1986-87; pvt. practice cons. Washington, 1987-88; adminstrv. mgr. food and nutrition policy program Cornell U., Ithaca, 1988-92; cons. in mgmt. of med. practices Med. Bus. Mgmt., Ithaca, 1994-95; realtor Century 21 Alpha, 1995-97; compensation mgr. Santa Clara (Calif.) U., 1996-98; sr. compensation analyst Stanford (Calif.) U., 1998-99; human resources cons. Siemens Info. and Comm. Networks, 2000; compensation and benefits mgr. Kana Comms., 2000-2001; U.S. compensation mgr. KLA-Tencor, 2001—02; pres. The Benefits Source Ins. Svcs. Inc., Calif., 2003—. Cons., editor George Washington U., 1986; cons., rapporteur Internat. Food Policy Restaurant Inst., Washington and Copenhagen, Denmark, 1987; cons., adminstr. Hansell & Post, Washington, 1987-88, Cornell U., Washington and Ithaca, 1988; pvt. practice cons., 2001—. Sponsor Worldvision, Tanzania, 1988-91. George Washington U. scholar, 1979-81. Mem. AMA, Soc. for Human Resources Mgmt., Sigma Delta Xi (scholar 1980). Democrat. Episcopalian. Avocations: piano, hiking, swimming. Home: 745 S Mary Ave Sunnyvale CA 94087 E-mail: wendy@benefits-source.org.

MERRILL, WILLIAM DEAN, retired architect, medical facility planning consultant; b. Portland, Oreg., June 1, 1915; s. Charles O. and Grace (Ruhl) M.; m. Bernice E. Wickham, Apr. 19, 1943 (dec. Sept. 1996); 1 child, Sue Ann Merrill Boardman; m. Irene Moe, July 30, 2001. Student in Fine Arts and Forestry, Oreg. State U., 1936-38; student in Architecture, U. Oreg., 1939-42. Registered architect, Oreg., Calif., NCARB Prin. W.D. Merrill, Architect, Portland, 1956-64; architect, ptnr. Bissell & Merrill, Architects, Stockton, Calif., 1964-68; architect, Kaiser Engrs., Kaiser Found. Hosps. design and constrn., 1968-81; pvt. practice hosp. design and constrn., residential design and constrn., Bay Area, 1981-91; hosp. and sch. constrn. insp. Office of State Health Planning and Devel., State of Calif., 1984-93; ret. 1996. Served as lt. (j.g.) USNR, 1942-44, PTO. Mem. AIA (emeritus). Republican. Home: 25411 E Cedar Glen Loop Welches OR 97067

MERRILL, WILLIAM H., JR., lawyer, corporate professional; b. Indpls., Apr. 11, 1942; s. William H. and Jane (Robinson) M.; m. Winifred Jane Baur, July 25, 1964; children: Michele Jane, Betsy Diane. BS, Butler U., 1965; JD, Ind. U., 1967. Bar: Ind. 1967. Trust officer Mchts. Nat. Bank, Indpls., 1965—69; gen. counsel Everett I. Brown Co., Indpls., 1969—85; v.p., gen. counsel Landeco, Inc., Indpls., 1970—85; pres. Bash Seed Co., Indpls., 1975—97; gen. ptnr. Meta Ptnrs., 1984—90. Pres. Meta Investment Co., 1988-90, Meta Mgmt. Co., 1988-90, Northwest Develop. Corp., 1975—, Scotts Garden Ctr., Inc., 1977-97; bd. dirs. Custom Molded Products, Inc. Mem. Carmel (Ind.) City Plan Commn., 1975-85, pres. 1982-85. Mem. ABA, Ind. Bar Assn., Indpls. Bar Assn., Crooked Stick Golf Club. Home: 3725 W 106th St Carmel IN 46032-7719 Office: 3205 W 71st St Indianapolis IN 46268-2244

MERRIM, LOUISE MEYEROWITZ, artist, actress; b. N.Y.C. d. Leo and Jeanette (Harris) Meyerowitz; m. Lewis Jay Merrim, June 27, 1948; children: Stephanie, Andrea Merrim Goff (dec.). BFA, Pratt Inst., 1947; MFA, Columbia U., 1951; postgrad., Post Coll., 1971-72, New Sch., 1977-78. Art tchr. pub. schs., N.Y.C., 1947-51, Port Washington, N.Y., 1970-83. One-woman shows include Plandome Gallery, L.I., Isis Gallery, N.Y., San Diego art Inst., Pan Pacific Hotel, San Diego; exhibited in group shows at Nassau County Fine Arts Mus. (Bronze award), Heckscher Mus. (Nora Mirmont award), Nat. Acad., Nat. Assn. Women Artists (Medal of Honor, Charlotte Whinston award), Audubon Artists (Stephen Hirsch Meml. award), Cork Gallery, Warner Comm. Gallery, L.I. Art Tchrs. (two awards of excellence), L.I. Art Tchrs. Award Winners Show, Pt. Washington Libr. Invitational, Glen Cove (2nd prize), Manhasset Art Assn. (best in show, five 1st prizes), San Diego Art Inst., San Diego Mus. Art (Gold award), Oceanside Mus. Art, Hank Baum Gallery, San Francisco, Tarbox Gallery, Clark Gallery, Knowles Gallery, San Diego, Golden Pacific Arts Gallery, San Diego, Henry Chastain Gallery, Scottsdale, Boehm Gallery/Palomar Coll., Hyde Gallery/Grossmont Coll., Timmons Gallery, Rancho Santa Fe, Calif.; included in permanent collection of San Diego Mus. Art; appeared in numerous theatrical prodns. including Fiddler on the Roof, Barefoot in the Park, N.Y., Anything Goes, The Musical Comedy Murders of 1940, Anastasia (Drama award), Fiddler on the Roof, The Music Man, What's Wrong With this Picture?, Marvin's Room, San Diego, The Foreigner; dir. Under Milkwood; dir., appeared in Spoon River Anthology. Mem. Nat. Assn. Women Artists, N.Y. Soc. of Women Artists, Contemporary Artists Guild of N.Y., Audubon Artist (N.Y.), San Diego Art Inst., Artists Guild of San Diego Art Mus. (pres. 1993), Artists Equity, Actors Alliance. Avocations: tennis, poetry, travel. Home: 3330 Caminito Vasto La Jolla CA 92037-2929 E-mail: louisemer@hotmail.com.

MERRIMAN, CHRISANN, marketing professional; d. Daniel Patrick (Stepfather) and Diane Marie Hogan; m. Kelly John Merriman, Nov. 7, 1998; 1 child, Owen Tiernan. BS in mktg., Rivier Coll., 1993—96; MBA, NH. Coll., 1997—99; MS in bus. edn., So. NH. Univeristy, 2000—01. Cert. profl. marketer Am. Mktg. Assn. Mktg. specialist MediaOne Group, Andover, Mass., 1998—2000; industry mktg. mgr. Enterasys Networks, Inc., Andover, Mass., 2000—04; mktg. mgr. VIEO, Inc., Austin, Tex., 2004—. Educator U. of Phoenix Online, 2001—. Mem.: Nat. Assn. of Bus. Educators, Am. Mktg. Assn., Acad. of Mgmt. Home: 1112 Laurel Glen Blvd Leander TX 78641 Office Phone: 512-677-0788.

MERRIN, SEYMOUR, computer marketing company executive; b. Bklyn., Aug. 13, 1931; s. Joseph and Esther Bella (Manelis) M.; m. Elaine Cohen, Sept. 4, 1960 (dec. May 1962); m. Elizabeth Jenifer Slack, Oct. 12, 1963 (dec. Mar. 1995); children: Charles Seymour, Marianne Jenifer Weights; m. Helene Claire Singer, Sept. 1, 2001. BS, Tufts Coll., 1952; MS, U. Ariz., 1954; PhD, Pa. State U., 1962. Geologist Magma Copper Co., Superior, Ariz., 1954, U.S. Geol. Survey, 1956-58; chemist IBM, Poughkeepsie, NY, 1962-64; mgr. package devel., mgr. reliability and failure analysis Sperry Semiconductor divsn. Sperry Rand, Norwalk, Conn., 1965-68; cons. materials tech. Fairfield, Conn., 1967-69; v.p., dir. Innotech Corp., Norwalk, 1969-74; divsn. mgr. Emdex divsn. Exxon Enterprises, Milford, Conn., 1974-78; chmn., dir. Computerworks, Westport, Conn., 1978-85; v.p., dir. personal computing svc. Gartner Group, Inc., Stamford, Conn., 1984-87; pres. Merrin Resources, Southport, Conn., 1987-89, Merrin Info. Svcs., Inc., Santa Fe, 1987—. Bd. dirs. Micrografx Corp., Allen, Tex.; mem. adv. panel Apple Computer Co., Cupertino, Calif., 1982-83; mem. adv. bd. Compaq Computer Corp., Houston, 1984-85, Computer and Software News, N.Y.C., 1984-89; mem. program adv. bd. Comdex, Boston, 1985—; lectr. in field. Contbr. numerous articles to profl. publs.; patentee in field. Served with U.S. Army, 1954-56. Fellow Geol. Soc. Am., Am. Inst. Chemists; Computing Tech. Industry Assn. (founder, pres. 1981-83, bd. dirs. 1981-84). Home and Office: 840 Camino de las Trampas Santa Fe NM 87501 E-mail: smerrin@aol.com.

MERRING, ROBERT ALAN, lawyer, arbitrator, mediator; b. Middletown, N.Y., Oct. 5, 1951; s. Merton Joseph and Mabel Ruth M.; m. Lynn S. Connor, Mar. 16, 1996. Student, Ohio Wesleyan U., 1969—70; AB, Stanford U., 1973; JD in Internat. and Fgn. Law with honors, Columbia U., 1977; cert. Pepperdine Sch. Law, Inst. for Dispute Resolution, 1996. Bar: Calif. 1977, U.S. Dist. Ct. (cen. dist.) Calif. 1978, U.S. Dist. Ct. (so. and ea. dists.) Calif. 1980, U.S. Ct. Appeals (9th cir.) 1980, U.S. Dist. Ct. (no. dist.) Calif. 1983, U.S. Supreme Ct. 1987, Colo. 1989. Assoc. Pacht, Ross, Warne, Bernhard & Sears, Inc., L.A., 1977-79, Donovan Leisure Newton & Irvine, L.A., 1979-81, Cutler and Cutler, L.A., 1983-88, Friedemann & Hart, Irvine, 1988-89; pvt. practice Newport Beach and Irvine, Calif., 1989—. Mem. San Diego-Orange County Am. Arbitration Assn. panel comml. arbitrators, 1993—, panel mediators, 2002-; civil arbitrator, judge pro tem Orange County Superior Ct., 1993—; mediator U.S. Bankruptcy Ct. (ctrl. dist.) Calif., 1996—; mediator Orange County Superior Ct., 1998-2002; clin. prof. Loyola U. Law Sch., Los Angeles, 1981-82. Editor Columbia Jour. Transnat. Law, 1976-77. Columbia U. Internat. fellow, 1975—76. Mem. ABA, Orange County Bar Assn. (chair intellectual property and tech. law sect. 2000-01), Assn. Bus. Trial Lawyers, Am. Arbitration Assn., State Bar of Calif. (del. 1998—). E-mail: clawyer@attglobal.net.

MERRION, ARTHUR BENJAMIN, mathematics professor, tree farmer; b. Williamstown, NJ, Oct. 25, 1938; s. Anthony Robert and Eva May Merrion; m. Martha Jane Banse, Dec. 26, 1965 (div. May 1977); children: Benjamin Thomas, Elizabeth Jane. Attended, Rutgers U., 1957, Drexel Inst. Tech., 1961; fellowship, Appalachian State U., 1965; AB in Math., Pfeiffer Coll. (now Univ.), 1965; MS in Numerical Sci., Johns Hopkins U., 1976. Navigations scientist Oceanographic Office, Suitland, Md., 1966—72, Def. Mapping Agy. Hydrographic Ctr., 1972—78; fellow ops. rsch. analysis Sec. Army Pentagon, Washington, 1978-80; ops. rsch. analyst Asst. Sec. Army, Washington, 1980-86; tree farmer Huntingtown, Md., 1986-98. Instr. math. and stats. Embry-Riddle Aeronautical U., 1993-94; math. instr. Charles County C.C., 1990-91; tutor Literary Coun., navigation scientist Silas Bent Naval Oceanographic Vessel, 1966. Author: A Short Story By Edgar Allen Pooh. With U.S. Army, 1957-58. Mem. Md. Soc. SAR, Nat. Soc SAR. Achievements include research in in applying mathematical chaos theory to weather modification. Avocations: chess, violin, Judo, wrestling, ice skating. Home: PO Box 1639 West Jefferson NC 28694-1639 *The Bible says many different things to many different people. To Thomas Alva Edison it was a "Chemist's Handbook". To me it is the source of all man's creativity, directly from the greatest Creator of all. It is a source of inspiration, a solace for periods of depression, and a prescription when I'm in error.*

MERRIS, RUSSELL L. mathematician, educator; b. Mar. 1943; s. Russell H. Merris and Joan D. Seiss, Barbara Merris (Stepmother); m. Karen D. Merris, Dec. 1964; children: Kimberly L., Rhian M. PhD, U. Calif., Santa Barbara, 1969. Prof. Calif. State U., Hayward, Calif., 1971—. Fulbright lectr. in Parkistan Calif. State U., Hayward, 1973; vis. prof. Inst. of Physics and Math., Lisbon, Portugal, 1973—74; invited prof. U. Laval, Quebec, Canada, 1977; NAS exch. scientist, Czech Republic, 79; SERC vis. fellow U. Edinburgh, Scotland, 1993. Author: (textbooks) Intro. to Computer Math., 1985 (Soc. for Tech. Comm. award of merit, 1986), Multilinear Algebra, 1997, Graph Theory, 2001, Combinatorics, 2d edit., 2003; editor: (profl. jours.) Linear and Multilinear Algebra, Math. Inequalities and Applications; contbr. articles to profl. jours. Trustee Hayward Unified Sch. Dist., Hayward, Calif., 1987—91, Hayward Shoreline Planning Agy., Hayward, Calif., 1987—91. Postdoctoral rsch. associateship, NAS/NRC, 1969—71. Mem.: Internat. Lunear Algebra Soc., Assn. Women in Math., Soc. Indsl. & Applied Math. (editor, SIAM Jour. on Matrix Analysis and Applications), Math. Assn. of Am. (editor, Spectrum series). Office: Dept of Math & Comp Sci Calif State U Hayward CA 94542 Office Phone: 510-885-3244. E-mail: merris@csuhayward.edu.

MERRISS, PHILIP RAMSAY, JR., banker; b. NYC, June 7, 1948; s. Philip Ramsay and Elisabeth (Paine) M.; m. Janet Henry Hylan, Oct. 27, 1973. AB in Econs. magna cum laude, Lafayette Coll., 1970; MBA with high distinction, Dartmouth Coll., 1972. Assoc. corp. fin. dept. A.G. Becker and Co. Inc., N.Y.C., 1972-73; fin. analyst corp. banking dept. Chase Manhattan Bank, 1973, asst. treas. N.Y.C. dist., 1974-75, 2d v.p. mining and metals div., 1976-78, 2d v.p. petroleum div., 1979-86, client exec., v.p. pub. utilities component, 1987-89, credit supv. officer, div. exec., v.p. U.S. pvt. banking, 1989-94; credit exec. J.P. Morgan Pvt. Bank, N.Y.C., 1994-97, mng. dir. and credit exec., 1997—. Capt. U.S. Army, 1978. Tuck scholar Dartmouth Coll., 1972. Mem. Am. Econ. Assn., Aircraft Owners and Pilots Assn., Weston Gun Club, Yale Club, Fairfield County Hunt Club, Fairfield County Fish and Game Club, Phi Beta Kappa. Republican. Episcopalian. Home: 100 Hills Point Rd Westport CT 06880-5111 Office: JP Morgan Chase & Co 345 Park Ave New York NY 10154-1002

MERRITT, BRUCE GORDON, lawyer; b. Iowa City, Oct. 4, 1946; s. William Olney and Gretchen Louise (Kuever) M.; m. Valerie Sue Jorgensen, Dec. 28, 1969; children: Benjamin Carlyle, Alicia Marie. AB magna cum laude, Occidental Coll., 1968; JD magna cum laude, Harvard U., 1972. Bar: Calif. 1973, D.C., 1996, N.Y. 1996. Assoc. Markbys, London, 1972-73, Nossman, Krueger & Marsh, L.A., 1973-79, ptnr., 1979-81; asst. U.S. Atty., L.A., 1981-85; ptnr. Hennigan & Mercer, L.A., 1986-88, Debevoise & Plimpton, L.A., 1989-95, N.Y.C., 1996—2001. Adj. prof. law Loyola Law Sch., L.A., 2003—. Fellow Am. Coll. Trial Lawyers; mem. Calif. State Bar Assn. (exec. com. litig. sect. 1992-95), L.A. County Bar Assn. (del. state bar conf. 1984-86), Phi Beta Kappa, Harvard Club (N.Y.C.). Office Phone: 818-521-1812. Personal E-mail: Brucegmerritt@aol.com.

MERRITT, CAROLYN, government agency administrator; Diploma, Radford U. Mngr. of solid and hazardous waste and environmental health and safety Champion Intl. Corp., 1988—94; sr. project mngr. RMT/Jones and Neuse, Inc., Houston, 1994; sr. v.p. for Environment, Health and Safety IMC Global Inc., Northbrook, Ill.; chmn, CEO U.S. Chemical Safety and Hazard Investigation Board, 2002—. Office: 2175 K Street NW Ste 400 Washington DC 20037 Office Phone: 702-261-7600.

MERRITT, DEBORAH FOOTE, state legislator, vocational coordinator; b. Peterborough, N.H., June 19, 1961; d. William Lewis and Mary Elizabeth (Moore) Foote. BA in Sociology, Bowdoin Coll., 1983; MPA, U. N.H., 1994. Tchr. math. Buckley Sch., Sherman Oaks, Calif., 1983-84, Chaminade Coll. Prep. Sch., Canoga Park, Calif., 1984-85; saleswoman Smith Barney, L.A., 1985-87, B.R. Stickle & Co., Chgo., 1987; trader Harris Trust, Chgo., 1988-90; bus. mgr. Merritt Chiropractic, Durham, N.H., 1990-94; state rep. N.H. Gen. Ct., Concord, 1993—; marketer Devel. Svcs. of Stafford County, Dover, 1994; residential counselor Our House, Dover, 1994; vocat. coord. Riverbend Cmty. Mental Health, Concord, N.H., 1995-98; dir. programs and ops. Divsn. Elderly and Adult Svcs., Concord, 1998—. Bd. dirs. Our House, 1993-94, counselor, 1994-95; adv. bd. health & human svcs. dist. coun. Inst. Disability. Mem. NOW, N.H. Women's Lobby, Gt. Concord C. of C., Planned Parenthood No. New Eng., Women's Legis. Lobby (vice chair Strafford County del. 1994-95, chmn. 1996—), N.H. Assn. for the Blind (bd. dirs.). Democrat. Office: Divsn Elderly & Adult Svcs 129 Pleasant St Concord NH 03301-3852 Home: PO Box 1091 Wolfeboro Falls NH 03896-1091

MERRITT, ELEANOR LYNETTE, artist, educator; b. N.Y.C., Aug. 17, 1933; d. Wilbert Alexander and Lynette Hyacinth Lipsett; m. Lorenzo Merritt, June 26, 1954 (div. Oct. 1975); m. W.H. Chris Darlington, July 26, 1980; children: Lori Ellen, Lisa Ann. BA, Bklyn. Coll., 1955, MA, 1958. Cert. secondary art tchr. N.Y.C. Art tchr. N.Y.C. Sch. Sys., 1955-59; secondary sch. art tchr. Westbury Schs., L.I., N.Y., 1960-70, dist. chairperson, 1971-82. Lectr. C.W. Post Coll., N.Y., 1978-82, Nassau C.C., N.Y., 1978-82, Art League Manatee County, Bradenton, Fla., 1997—; lectr., docent Ringling Mus. Art, Sarasota, Fla., 1989—. One-woman shows include Nassau County Cultural Mus., Hempstead, N.Y., 1974, Am. Internat. Coll., Springfield, Mass., 1975, 81, The Craftery Gallery, Hartford, Conn., 1976, Women's Resource Ctr., Sarasota, 1987, 92, Shrine of the Black Madonna, Cultural Ctr., Houston, 1988, U. Fla., St. Petersburg, 1988, Manatee C.C., Venice, 1988, Ctrl. Nat. Bank, Sarasota, 1991, Zora Neale Hurston Mus., Eatonville, Fla., 1993, Fine Arts Gallery Ctrl. Libr., Tampa, 1994, Barrier Island Group for the Arts, Sanibel, Fla., 1995, Unit Gallery, Sarasota, 1995, Hillsborough C.C., Tampa, 1997, Palm Harbor, Sarasota, 1998; exhibited in group shows at Salt Creek Art Works, St. Petersburg, Carver Cultural Ctr., San Antonio, Fla. State Capital Gallery, Tallahassee, Hillsborough C.C. Libr., Tampa, Artists Unlimited: The Channel Dist., Tampa, Women's Caucus for Art, Miami, Michael Gold Gallery, N.Y.C., Daytona (Fla.) Beach C.C., City U., Shimonoseki, Japan, 1996, Steinbaum Gallery, N.Y.C., 1997, Self Gallery, Hilton Head, S.C., 1998, Jacksonville Mus. Contemporary Art, 1998, Diverse Origins, Colo., 1998, African Am. Mus., Tampa, 1997, Venice Biennel, 1999, many others; exhibited in corp. exhbns. Atlanta Life Ins. Co., Isphording, Payne, Korp., Inc., Venice, Holiday Inn Crown Plaza, Tampa, Fla., Automatic Data Processing Corp., Roseland, N.J. V.p. Sarasota Arts Coun. Bd., 1996—; chairperson Sarasota County Commn. Art in Pub. Places, 1997—; pres. Venice (Fla.) Art Ctr. Bd., 1998—. Recipient Woman of Impact award County Commn. on the Status of Women, Sarasota, 1997; named Sarasota Artist of the Yr., Sarasota Visual Arts Ctr., 1994. Mem. Women's Mus. Art (charter), Women's Caucus for Art (pres. Sarasota chpt. 1988-93, v.p. nat. orgn. 1990-96, Nat. Pres. award 1996), Pen Women Am. (Sarasota chpt.), Fla. Artist Group (area III), Petticoat Painters. Avocations: gardening, travel, lecturing.

MERRITT, GILBERT STROUD, federal judge; b. Nashville, Tenn., Jan. 17, 1936; s. Gilbert Stroud and Angie Fields (Cantrell) M.; m. Louise Clark Fort, July 10, 1964 (dec.); children: Stroud, Louise Clark, Eli. BA, Yale U., 1957; LLB, Vanderbilt U., 1960; LLM, Harvard U., 1962. Bar: Tenn. 1960. Asst. dean Vanderbilt U. Law Sch., 1960-61, lectr., 1963-69, 71-75, assoc. prof. law, 1969-70; assoc. Boult Hunt Cummings & Conners, Nashville, 1962-63; asst. metro. atty. City of Nashville, 1963-66; U.S. Dist. atty. for (mid. dist.) Tenn., 1966-69; ptnr. Gullett, Steele, Sanford, Robinson & Merritt, Nashville, 1970-77; judge U.S. Ct. Appeals (6th cir.), Nashville, 1977-2001, chief judge, 1989—96, sr. judge., 2001—. Exec. sec. Tenn. Code Commn., 1977. Mng. editor: Vanderbilt Law Rev, 1959-60; contbr. articles to law jours. Del. Tenn. Constl. Conv., 1965; chmn. bd. trustees Vanderbilt Inst. Pub. Policy Studies. Mem. ABA, Fed. Bar Assn., Tenn. Bar Assn., Nashville Bar Assn., Vanderbilt Law Alumni Assn. (pres. 1979-80), Am. Law Inst., Order of Coif. Episcopalian. Office: US Ct Appeals Customs Ho 701 Broadway Ste 303 Nashville TN 37203-3967 also: 532 Potter Stewart US Courthouse 100 E Fifth St Cincinnati OH 45202-3988

MERRITT, HOWARD SUTERMEISTER, retired art educator; b. Ithaca, N.Y., June 12, 1915; s. Ernest and Bertha (Sutermeister) M.; m. Florence Sederquest Hill, June 27, 1941; children— Jessica, Stephen, Jonathan, James. BA, Oberlin Coll., 1936; M.F.A., Princeton U., 1942, PhD, 1958. Mem. faculty U. Rochester, N.Y., 1946-80, prof. emeritus, 1980—. Cons. 19th Century Am. Painting, 1960— Contbr. exhbn. catalogues and articles to various publs. Served with AUS, 1942-45. Decorated Bronze Star; Nat. Endowment for Humanities summer grantee, 1966-68 Mem. Coll. Art Assn. Home: 85 Bellevue Dr Rochester NY 14620-2703 Office: Dept of Fine Arts University Rochester Rochester NY 14627

MERRITT, JAMES W., JR., state legislator, real estate developer; b. Indpls., July 28, 1959; s. James Warner and Marion Jane (Brown) M.; m. Kelley A. McCloskey, May 10, 1985. BS in Arts & Sci., Ind. State U., 1981. Candidate asst. Merchert for Congress, Indpls., 1981-82; campaign mgr. Hillis for Congress, Kokomo, 1982-83; dist. asst. U.S. Rep. Bud Hillis, Kokomo, 1983; property mgr. Circle Fin. Corp., Indpls.; mem. Ind. Senate from 31st dist., Indianapolis, 1990—. Mem. ward chmn. Marion County Rep. Party Lawrence Twp. 1987—. Mem. Jr. Achievement, Toastmasters. Republican. Office: Circle Fin Corp 9102 N Meridian St Indianapolis IN 46260-1860 Address: Ind Senate Dist 31 200 W Washington St Indianapolis IN 46204-2728

MERRITT, JEAN, consulting firm executive, psychotherapist; b. N.Y.C., Oct. 29, 1952; d. Harry and Ruth (Happel) Packman; m. Richard L. Kashinsky, Aug. 2, 1976 (div.); m. Richard L. Merritt, May 5, 1985 (div. June 2002); children: Courtney Morgan, Melissa Morgan Grad. high sch., Bayside, N.Y. From contr. to v.p., sec., treas. Kaswol Corp., Richmond Hill, NY, 1973—85; corp. exec. Federated Cons. Svc., Inc., Bayside, NY, CFO Jupiter, Fla., 1985—2002, psychotherapist, 2004—. Coach Queens Spl. Olympics, 1985. Mem. Nat. Trust for Hist. Preservation, Nat. Fedn. Wildlife, Ctr. for Environ. Edn., Defenders of Wildlife, Nat. Resource Def. Coun., Humane Soc. of U.S., Sierra Club, Amnesty Internat. Presbyterian. Avocations: flying, art collecting, painting, interior design, gourmet cooking. Home: Apt 2K 520 W 43 St New York NY 10036 E-mail: jeanie22m@aol.com.

MERRITT, JERALYN E. lawyer; b. N.Y.C., N.Y., Sept. 28, 1949; BA, Case Western Res. U., 1971; JD, U. Denver, 1973. Bar: Colo. 1974, (U.S. Dist. Ct. Colo.), U.S. Ct. Appeals (10th cir.) 1981, (N.Y.) 1990, U.S. Supreme Ct. 1990, (Ariz.) 1999, U.S. Ct. Appeals (9th cir.). Mem. legal adv. bd. Martindale-Hubbell LexisNexis, 1996—; mem. editl. bd. Matthew Bender Criminal Publs., 1999—; lectr. law U. Denver Coll. Law, 2001—. Fellow: Am. Bd. Criminal Lawyers (mem. bd. govs. 1994—); mem.: ABA (criminal justice sect. coun. 2000—), Colo. Criminal Def. Bar, Denver Bar Assn., Colo. Bar Assn., Nat. Assn. Criminal Def. Lawyers (bd. dirs. 1995—2001, sec. 2002—, co-chair/vice-chair legis., Internet, and innocence project coms. 1995—, 1st Ann. Marshall Stern award for outstanding legis. achievement 1995). Office: Ste 1700 950 17th St Denver CO 80202

MERRITT, JOE FRANK, industrial supply executive; b. Paris, Tex., Dec. 9, 1947; s. Henry Grady and Margaret Leon (Murrell) M.; m. Barbara Jean Sands (div. May 1973); 1 child, Daniel Joe; m. Bonnie Louise McLure, Feb. 1, 1975; 1 stepchild, David Wright Dwyer. BA in Govt., U. Tex., Arlington, 1970; student, All-Inclusive Sch., 1999. Cert. contractor Dept. Def. U.S.A. and Can. With purchasing A.F. Holman Boiler Works Inc., Dallas, 1970-77; supply salesman Stanco Indsl. Supply, Dallas, 1977-79, Tool Splty. Indsl. Supply, Dallas, 1979-80, Briggs-Weaver Indsl. Supply, Dallas, 1980-81; owner, pres. Joe F. Merritt & Co., Inc., Carrollton, Tex., 1981; v.p., gen. mgr. Abrasives & Buffs Co., Dallas, 1981-83; owner, pres. Buff, Polish & Grind Indsl. Supply Co., Inc., Argyle, Tex., 1984—. Cons. The Broadway Collection, Olathe, Kans., 1990, Offenhauser Co., Houston, 1993-94, 1998, Innovation Industries, Russellville, Ark., 1994; instr. buff, polish and grind methods quality control dept. Rsch. Facility, Peterbilt Motors Co., 1994; trainer Peterbilt Madison-Tenn. plant, 1997, DBC Indsl., Garland, Tex., 1999, Am. Ironhorse Motorcycle Co., Ft. Worth, 2000, Chgo. Iron and Bridge, Tex., 2000, Verdin Co., Cin., 2002, Nike Golf, Ft. Worth, 2003, Midwest Motorcycle Supply, Mo. and Mex., 2004. Creator State of the Art Rsch. and Tchg. Facility, 1984, 100% Virgin Lambswool Buffing Belt, 1987 CB & I USAF Meml. at Pentagon, Washington, 2004, spl. extra wide spindle buffers; contbr. articles to profl. jour. Recipient Cert. of Appreciation, City of Carrollton, 1981. Republican. Methodist. Avocations: travel, animals, landrover-4 wheel drive vehicle. Office: Buff Polish & Grind Indsl Supply 1907 E FM407 Argyle TX 76226-9447 Fax: 940-455-7385. Office Phone: 940-455-2269. E-mail: joe@buffpolishgrind.com.

MERRITT, JOHN HOWARD, secondary school educator; b. Salisbury, Md., May 19, 1948; s. Robert Wilson and Iris Amy (Horsey) M.; m. Carole A. Tramontana; children: Robert W. II, John H. Jr.; 1 stepchild, Stephen A. Capelli Jr. BS, Salisbury State Coll., 1971; MEd, Salisbury State U., 1990. Cert. secondary tchr., Md. Propr. constrn. bus., Salisbury, 1977-86; high sch. math. tchr. Wicomico Count Schs., Salisbury, 1986—. Instr. math. NROTC

Prep Sch., San Diego, 1988-91. Capt. USNR, 1970—2003. Mem.: Kappa Delta Pi. Republican. Methodist. Avocations: swimming, gardening, residential real estate investments, commodity futures trading, ocean and river kayaking.

MERRITT, LAVERE BARRUS, engineering educator, civil engineer; b. Afton, Wyo., Mar. 11, 1936; s. Joseph M. and Lera (Barrus) M.; m. Jackie Call, Jan. 5, 1956 (dec. Sept. 1999); m. Diane Mainord, July 14, 2001; children: Teri, Lynn, Rachel, Shaun; stepchildren: Julia, Aaron, Benjamin, Annie. BSCE, U. Utah, 1963, MSCE, 1966; PhD, U. Wash., 1970. Registered profl. engr., Utah, Ariz. Prof. civil and environ. engring. Brigham Young U., Provo, Utah, 1970—, chmn. dept. civil engring., 1986-92; co-chmn. faculty senate, 1996-97. Cons. engring. firms, 1970—. Chmn. Provo Met. Water Bd., Utah, 1978-87. Named Utah Engring. Educator of Yr., Utah Joint Engring. Coun., 1987, Educator of Yr., Am. Water Resources Assn., Utah, 2004. Mem. ASCE (nat. dir. 1982-85), Am. Acad. Environ. Engrs., Water Environment Fedn. (nat. dir. 1981-84, Bedell award), Am. Water Works Assn., Am. Soc. Engring. Edn., Sigma Xi. Republican. Mem. Lds Ch. Home: 562 E 3050 N Provo UT 84604-4264 Office: Brigham Young U 370 CB Provo UT 84602-4067 Office Phone: 801-422-6333. Business E-Mail: MerrittL@byu.edu.

MERRITT, LORETTA GAETANA, principal, primary education educator; b. Passaic, N.J., Dec. 21, 1944; d. James A. and Rosalia (Ricci) Domino; m. Robert V. Merritt, Apr. 29, 1973. BA in Elem. Edn., William Paterson, 1966; MA in Edn. Adminstrn., Kean Coll. N.J., 1987; postgrad., various colls., 1984-90. Cert. early childhood/nursery sch. tchr., prin., supr. First grade, kindergarten and pre-kindergarten tchr. Roosevelt Sch. #10, Passaic, N.J., 1966-97, acting asst. prin., 1993; tchr. elem. math, reading Martin Luther King Sch. #6, Passaic, 1997-2000; prin. early childhood Passaic Pub Sch. #16, Passaic, 2000—. Adv. mem. pupil assistance coun. #10 Sch., Passaic, 1986—, chairperson site-based coun., 1992-94, mem.-advisor devel. kindergarten full-day curriculum com., 1992, mem.-advisor for devel. basic skills checklist test com., 1992, mem. dist. steering com., 1993-94, chairperson Passaic Early Childhood Adv. Coun., 2003-. Recipient Gov.'s Convocation on Excellence in Tchg., N.J. State Dept. Edn., Trenton, 1987, Passaic County Tchr. of the Year, 1987-88. Mem. NEA, Nat. Assn. Edn. Young Children, N.J. Edn. Assn., Edn. Assn. Passaic (rep. 1993-95), N.J. Assn. Elem. Sch. Prins., N.J. Prins. and Supts. Assn., Passaic Assn. Supts. and Prins., Kindergarten Tchrs. Assn., PTO Dist. #10 (cons. 1994), Kappa Delta Phi. Avocations: arts and crafts, gardening, travel. E-mail: loleka21@aol.com.

MERRITT, NANCY-JO, lawyer; b. Phoenix, Sept. 24, 1942; d. Robert Nelson Meeker and Violet Adele Gibson; children: Sidney Kathryn, Kurt, Douglas. BA, Ariz. State U., 1964, MA, 1974, JD, 1978. Bar: Ariz. 1978, U.S. Dist. Ct. Ariz. 1978, U.S. Ct. Appeals (9th cir.) 1984. Shareholder Fennemore Craig, P.C., Phoenix. Author: Understanding Immigration Law, 1993; sr. editor: Immigration and National Law Handbook, 1993—; contbr. articles to profl. jours. Chair bd. dirs. TERROS, 1995-97. Fellow Ariz. Bar Found.; mem. ABA, Am. Immigration Lawyers Assn. (chairperson Ariz. chpt. 1985-87, several coms., Pro Bono award), Ariz. Bar Assn. (immigration sect.), Nucleus Club. Democrat. Avocations: modern literature, south american literature, hiking, gardening. Office: Fennemore Craig PC 3003 N Central Ave Ste 2600 Phoenix AZ 85012 Office Phone: 602-916-5000. E-mail: njmerritt@fclaw.com.

MERRITT, ROBERT S. food products executive; V.p. fin. and acctg., CFO Vie de France Corp., 1981—85; v.p. fin. Job's, 1985—88; exec. v.p. adminstr., CFO JB's Restaurants, Inc., 1988—89; v.p., CFO Outback Steakhouse, Inc., Tampa, Fla., 1990—91, sr. v.p. fin., CFO, treas., sec., 1991—. Office: Outback Steakhouse Inc 2202 N West Shore Blvd 5th Fl Tampa FL 33607*

MERRITT, THOMAS BUTLER, lawyer; b. Toledo, Apr. 3, 1939; s. George Robert and Bernice (Gerwin) M.; m. Mary Jane Bothfeld, July 23, 1966; children— Thomas Butler, Haidee Soule, Theodore Bothfeld AB magna cum laude, Harvard U., 1961, LLB cum laude, 1966. Bar: Mass. 1966, U.S. Supreme Ct. 1974, N.H. 1994. With N.Y. State Dept. Civil Svc., Albany, 1961-62; intern Office of Legal Advisr U.S. Dept. State, Washington, 1965; law clk. to assoc. justice Arthur E. Whittemore Supreme Jud. Ct. Mass., Boston, 1966-67; assoc. Nutter, McClennen & Fish, Boston, 1967-69, Palmer & Dodge, Boston, 1969-73; asst. counsel to Gov. Mass., 1973; reporter of decisions Supreme Jud. Ct. Mass., Boston, 1974-94; pvt. practice NH, 1994—. Contbr. articles to profl. jours. Mem. Conservation Commn. Town of Sherborn, Mass., 1969-74, chmn., 1972-74; mem. corp. Tenacre Country Day Sch., Wellesley, Mass., 1972-84, trustee, 1973-78; planning bd. Town of Hollis, N.H., 1995-98. 1st lt. U.S. Army, 1962-63, capt. USAR, 1963-69. Mem.: Assn. Reporters of Jud. Decisions (pres. 1983—84), Internat. Law Assn. (Am. br.), Am. Soc. Internat. Law, Fed. Bar Assn., N.H. Bar Assn., Mass. Bar Assn., Am. Law Inst. (life), Harvard Faculty Club (Cambridge), Harvard Club of Boston, Union Club. Episcopalian. Office: PO Box 324 Litchfield NH 03561-0324

MERRITT, WILLIAM ALFRED, JR., retired lawyer, real estate company executive; b. N.Y.C., Aug. 7, 1936; s. William Alfred and Florence Anne (O'Connor) M.; m. Christine Marie Cartnick, Sept. 27, 1969; children— William Tyler, Brian Edward, Elizabeth Cody BA in Econs., Holy Cross Coll., Worcester, Mass., 1958; LLB, Harvard U., 1964. Bar: N.Y. 1965. Assoc. Olwine, Connelly, Chase, O'Donnell & Weyher, N.Y.C., 1964-68; v.p. ops. and controls Bunge Corp., N.Y.C., 1968-81; exec. v.p. TIE/Communications Inc., Seymour, Conn., 1981-90; pres. Wiltel Communications Systems Inc, Rolling Meadows, Ill., 1991-92; gen. counsel Carolina Barnes Capital Inc., Stamford, Conn., 1992—; ptnr. Seaboard Equities Inc., Stamford, Conn., 1992—, KM Group, Stamford, Conn. Served to capt. USNR, 1958-80. Mem. Wee Burn Club, Harvard Club (N.Y.). Avocations: skiing, boating, golf. Home: 83 Brookside Rd Darien CT 06820-3505 Office: Ste 602 One Dock St Stamford CT 06902 Personal E-mail: w59merr@aol.com.

MERRY, ROBERT WILLIAM, publishing executive; b. Tacoma, Wash., Mar. 5, 1946; s. Robert Ellsworth and Carol Beatrice (Rasmussen) M.; m. Susan Diane Pennington, Sept. 20, 1969; children: Robert Ellsworth II, Johanna Lynn, Stephanie Ann. BA in Comms., U. Wash., 1968; MS in Journalism, Columbia U., 1972. Legis. reporter, gen. assignment reporter, copy editor Denver Post, 1972-74; reporter Nat. Observer Dow Jones & Co., Inc., 1974-77, reporter Wall St. Jour., 1977-86; exec. editor Roll Call, Newspaper of Capitol Hill, 1986-87; mng. editor Congl. Quar., Inc., Washington, 1987-89, exec. editor, 1990-97; also bd. dirs. Congl. Quar., Inc. and Times Publishing Co., Washington; pres., publisher Congl. Quar., Inc., Washington, 1997—. Bd. dirs. Times Publ. Co., St. Petersburg, Fla.; appeared on CBS Face the Nation, NBC Meet the Press, ABC Good Morning Am., CNN Newsmakers, and Take Two, C-SPAN, numerous other local and Can. programs. Author: Taking On the World: Joseph and Stewart Alsop-Guardians of the American Century, 1996; contbr. chpts. to books. Juror Pulitzer prize. With U.S. Army, 1968-71. Avocations: jogging, biking, hiking, biography, movies. Office: Congl Quarterly Inc 1255 22nd St NW Washington DC 20037-1001 E-mail: rmerry@cq.com.

MERRYMAN, GEORGE, automotive executive; CFO Jordan Motors Inc., Mishawaka, Ind. Office: Jordan Motors Inc 609 E Jefferson Blvd Mishawaka IN 46545-6524

MERSEL, MARJORIE KATHRYN PEDERSEN, lawyer; b. Manila, Utah, June 17, 1923; d. Leo Henry and Kathryn Anna (Reed) Pedersen; m. Jules Mersel, Apr. 12, 1950; 1 child, Jonathan. AB, U. Calif., 1948; LLB, U. San Francisco, 1948. Bar: D.C. 1952, Calif. 1955. Pvt. practice, Beverly Hills, Calif., 1961—71, L.A., 1997—; staff counsel Dept. Real Estate State of Calif., L.A., 1971—97. Pub. counsel, 2000—02. Active L.A.-Guangzhou Sister City. Mem.: ABA, Current Affairs Forum, World Affairs Coun., So. Calif. Women Lawyers Assn. (treas. 1962—63), Trial Lawyers Assn., L.A. County Bar Assn., Beverly Hills Bar Assn., Beverly Hills C. of C., L.A.-Guanghou Sister City Assn., Sierra Club, L.A. Athletic Club. Home: 13007 Hartsook St Sherman Oaks CA 91423-1616 Office: Dept Real Estate 107 S Broadway Ste 8107 Los Angeles CA 90012-4402

MERSEREAU, HIRAM STIPE, wood products company consultant; b. Portland, Oreg., Aug. 4, 1917; s. E.W. and Ruth (Stipe) M.; m. Margaret Daggett, Dec. 25, 1937; children: Hiram Stipe, John Bradford, Timothy Daggett. Student, George Washington U., 1936-37, Harvard U., 1959. With Weyerhauser Timber Co., Klamath Falls, Oreg., 1937-38, Alexander-Yawkey Lumber Co., Prineville, Oreg., 1938-52; gen. mgr. lumber div. Crossett Co., Ark., 1954-62; corp. sr. v.p., gen. mgr. So. div. Ga.-Pacific Corp., 1963-82, cons., 1982—. Past dir. Citizens & So. Nat. Bank, Augusta, Appalachian Hardwood Mfrs. Inc., Merry Cos., Inc., Augusta. Past bd. dirs. Young Life, Ga. Conservancy, Jr. Achievement Augusta; bd. dirs. Augusta br. Boys Clubs Am., Augusta Cancer Fund; trustee Paine Coll., Augusta. Mem. Nat. Forest Products Assn. (exec. com., dir.) Republican. Presbyterian (elder). Home: 6 Turnberry Ln Sea Pines Plantation Hilton Head Island SC 29928

MERSEREAU, JOHN, JR., Slavic languages and literatures educator; b. San Jose, Calif., Apr. 16, 1925; s. John Joshua and Winona Beth (Roberts) M.; m. Nanine Landell, July 11, 1953; children: Daryl Landell, John Coates. AB, U. Calif., 1945, MA, 1950, PhD, 1957. Teaching fellow, Slavic dept. U. Calif., Berkeley, 1950-52, research asst., 1953-54; instr. Slavic dept. U. Mich., Ann Arbor, 1956-59, asst. prof., 1959-61, assoc. prof., 1961-63, prof., 1963—, chmn. dept., 1961-71, 85-89, prof. emeritus, 1990—, dir. Residential Coll., 1977-85. Mem. Joint Com. Eastern Europe of Am. Council Learned Socs./Social Sci. Research Council, 1971-74, chmn., 1973-74. Author: Mikhail Lermontov, 1962, Baron Delvig's Literary Almanac: Northern Flowers, 1967, Translating Russian, 1968, Russian Romantic Fiction, 1983, Orest Somov, 1989, How to Grill a Gourmet, 2000, Overdue at Immokalee, A Tale of Preemptive Assassination, 2003; assoc. editor Mich. Slavic Pubs., 1962—; contbr. articles to profl. jours. Served to lt. (j.g.) USNR, 1943-46, PTO. Calmerton Slavic scholar U. Calif., Berkeley, 1954-55; Ford Found. fellow, London and Paris, 1955-56, Guggenheim fellow, 1972-73; recipient Disting. Service award U. Mich., Ann Arbor, 1961. Mem. Am. Assn. Advancement Slavic Studies, U. Mich. Research Club. Clubs: Waterloo Hunt (Grass Lake, Mich., sec. 1970-80); Commanderie de Bordeaux (Detroit). Avocations: flying, gourmet cuisine, raising horses. Office: U of Mich Slavic Dept Ann Arbor MI 48109 E-mail: merserea@umich.edu.

MERSEREAU, STEPHEN CROCKER, electronic commerce executive; b. Miami, Fla., Sept. 10, 1950; s. Holland Crocker and Joanne (Stoptaugh) M., m. Karen Marie Hosbein (div. 1990); children: Gage, Catherine; m. Lauren Melinda Tyler, May 3, 1992; children: Anson, Lena. BS with highest distinction, Ind. U., 1977; MBA, Harvard U., 1988. CPA, N.Y. Mgr. Price Waterhouse, N.Y.C., 1977-85; exec. v.p. ops. and fin. Am. Natural Beverage Corp., N.Y.C., 1985-89; pres. Centerline Rehab Group, N.Y.C., 1989-92; CEO INFINICOM, 1992-99, Connecity.Com, 1999-2000, Motoworld Network, 2000—. Bd. dirs. Best Practices Benchmarking & Cons., Inc. Mem. exec. com., treas. N.Y. Vietnam Vets. Memorial Comm. Office of the Mayor, 1983-*; spl. advisor N.Y. Cmty. Trust. Ssgt. USAF, 1971-75. Recipient Pres. Citation Campaign medal USAF, 1973; named Outstanding Young Man of Am., Jaycees, 1979. Mem. AICPA, DAV, N.Y. New Media Assn., Electronic Retailing Assn., Harvard Club N.Y.C., Ind. U. Alumni Assn., Beta Gamma Sigma, Beta Alpha Psi. Avocations: travel, skiing, flying. Home: 914 Rock Rimmon Rd Stamford CT 06903-1220

MERSEREAU, SUSAN, information systems company executive; b. Portland, Oreg., Sept. 5, 1946; d. Roland William Mersereau and Barbara Munro; m. Robert Stier, June 19, 1968; 1 child, Arran Elizabeth; m. Philip White, Nov. 17, 1989; children: Richard, Brandon. BA in History, Scripps, 1968; MAT in Edn. History, U. Chgo., 1971; MA in Whole Systems Design, Antioch, 1990. Tchr. South Shore High Sch., Chgo., 1969-70; adminstrv. asst. U. Ill., Chgo., 1970; rsch. analyst U. Wash., Seattle, 1971-72; dir. planning rsch. and evaluation Seattle Sch. Dist., 1972-80; program mgr. Weyerhauser Co., Tacoma, 1980-81, mgr. advanced tech., 1981-83, dir. telecom., 1983-88; gen. mgr., v.p. Weyerhauser Info. Systems, Tacoma, 1988-92, v.p. total quality region adminstrv. svcs. and aviation, 1992—98; v.p. organizational effectiveness Weyerhauser Co., 1998—2003, sr. v.p. information technology, CIO, 2003—. Bd. dirs. King County Jr. Achievemen, King County United Way. Avocations: skiing, art, hiking, tennis, fishing. Office: Weyerhaeuser Company Ch1b25 Tacoma WA 98477-0001

MERSKY, ROY MARTIN, law educator, librarian; b. N.Y.C., Sept. 1, 1925; s. Irving and Rose (Mendelson) Mirsky; m. Rosemary Bunnage; children: Deborah, Lisa, Ruth. BS, U. Wis., 1948, JD, 1952, MALS, 1953. Bar: Wis. 1952, U.S. Supreme Ct. 1970, Tex. 1972, U.S. Ct. Appeals (5th cir.) 1981, N.Y. 1983. Cataloger U.S. govt. documents U. Wis. Law Libr., 1951—52; reference asst. Madison Free Libr., Wis., 1952; pvt. practice law Wis., 1952—54; readers adv., reference and catalog libr., mcpl. reference libr. at City Hall, Milw. Pub. Libr., 1953—54; chief readers and reference svc. Yale Law Libr., 1954—59; dir. Wash. State Law Libr., 1959—63; exec. sec. Jud. Coun. Commn. Wash. Court Report, State of Wash., 1959—63; prof. law, law libr. U. Colo., Boulder, 1963—65; prof. law, dir. rsch. U. Tex., Austin, 1965—, William Stamps Farish Centennial prof. law, 1996—2001, Harry M. Reasoner Regents chair in law, 2001—, prof. Grad. Sch. Libr. and Info. Sci., 2003—. Vis. prof. law, dir. law libr. N.Y. Law Sch., N.Y.C., 1982-84; M.D. Anderson Found. vis. prof. law Queen Mary and Westfield Coll., U. London, 1994; interim dir. Jewish Nat. and Univ. Libr., Hebrew U., 1972-73; vis. fellow Australian Nat. U. Fac. of Law, Canberra, 1999; cons. to legal pubs. and law schs.; panelist various confs.; lectr. in field. Author: A Treasure in Jerusalem, 1974, (with J. Myron Jacobstein) Fundamentals of Legal Research, 7th edit., 1998, 8th, edit., 2002, (with Dunn) Legal Research Illustrated, An Abridgement of Fundamentals of Legal Research, 8th edit., 2002, (with Albert P. Blaustein) The First One Hundred Justices: Statistical Studies on the Supreme Court of the United States, 1978, (with W. Bader) The First One Hundred Eight Justices, 2004, (with Gary R. Hartman, Suzanne F. Young, Jill Duffy and Jake Liehert) A Documentary History of the Legal Aspects of Abortion in the United States, 1990, 96, 2001 (with Jacobstein Hartman and Bonnie Koneski-White) Reports on Successful and Unsuccessful Nominations, 1992, 95, 96, (with Gary Hartman and Cindy L. Tate) Landmark Supreme Court Cases, 2004; contbr. articles to profl. jours., chpts. to books; editor numerous books in field. Bd. dirs. Ctrl. Tex. chpt. ACLU, pres., 1968; bd. dirs. Human Rights Documentation Exch., 1997-2001; mem. bd. advisors Anti-Defamation League, Austin, 1974-78, Tex. Book Festival, 2001—; bd. dirs. Hillel Found., 1980-83; bd. dirs. Tex. Com. for Humanities, 1978-80, chair, 1980-82, conf. facilitator, 1982. With U.S. Army, 1944-46, ETO. Decorated Bronze Star. Fellow Am. Bar Found. (life), Coll. Law Practice Mgmt., Tex. Bar Found.; mem. ABA (various coms.), AAUP (chmn. nominating com. 1979-80), Am. Law Inst., Assn. Am. Law Schs. (various coms.), Internat. Assn. Lawyers and Jurists (bd. govs. Am. sect. 1980-95), Nat. Bar Assn., Am. Assn. Law Librs. (chair various coms.), Am. Soc. Info. Sci. (pres. Tex./Okla. chpt. 1992-94), Scribes (bd. dirs. 1974-94, book awards com. 1978-96, pres. 1991-93, chair Scribes Law Review Competition award com. 1993—), Soc. Am. Law Tchrs. (bd. govs. 1979-88, nominations com. 1984), ALA (rsch. librs. group 1987, libr. edn. divsn.), Am. Soc. Indexers, Internat. Assn. Law Librs. (U.S. adv. coun.), Internat. Fedn. Libr. Assns., Nat. Librs. Assn. (pres. 1980-81), Spl. Libr. Assn., State Bar Tex. (mem. edit. bd. jour.), State Bar Wis. (bd. mem. nonresident lawyers divsn. 1992-98, 2003-2004), Nat. Assn. Coll. and Univ. Attys., Tex. Assn. Coll. Tchrs., Tex. Humanities Alliance (bd. dirs. 1986-88), Tex. Supreme Ct. Hist. Soc. (bd. trustees 1988-94, exec. bd. 2002—), Order of Coif (mem. triennial book award com.). Home: 6412 Cascada Dr Austin TX 78750-8157 Office: U Tex Sch Law Tarlton Law Libr 727 E Dean Keeton St Austin TX 78705-3224 Office Phone: 512-471-7735. Business E-Mail: rmersky@mail.law.utexas.edu.

MERTEN, ALAN GILBERT, academic administrator; b. Milw., Dec. 27, 1941; s. Gilbert Ervin and Ruth Anna (Ristow) M.; m. Sally Louise Otto; children: Eric, Melissa. BS, U. Wis., 1963; MS, Stanford U., 1964; PhD, U. Wis., 1970. Asst. prof. U. Mich., Ann Arbor, 1970-74, assoc. prof., 1974-81, prof., 1981-86, assoc. dean, 1983-86; dean U. Fla., Gainesville, 1986-89; dean Johnson Grad. Sch. of Mgmt. Cornell U., Ithaca, N.Y., 1989-96; pres. George Mason U., Fairfax, Va., 1996—. Bd. dirs. Comshare, Inc., Ann Arbor, Citigroup Mut. Funds, Digital Net, Brainbench; mem. Fla. Gov.'s Select Com. on Workforce 2000, 1988-89. Author: Internal Control in U.S. Corporations, 1980, Senior Management Control of Computer-Based Information Systems, 1983. Mem. Airport Authority, Gainesville, Fla., 1986-89. Served to capt. USAF, 1963-67. Lutheran. Home: 11020 Popes Head Rd Fairfax VA 22030-4608 Office: George Mason U Office of Pres Fairfax VA 22030-4444 E-mail: amerten@gmu.edu.

MERTENS, JOAN R. museum curator, art historian; b. N.Y.C., Oct. 10, 1946; d. Otto R. and Helen H. M. BA, Radcliffe Coll., 1967; PhD, Harvard U., 1972. Curatorial asst. Met. Mus. Art, N.Y.C., 1972-73, asst. curator, 1973-76, assoc. curator, 1976-81, curator Greek and Roman dept., 1981—, curator, adminstr., 1983-90, mem. editorial bd. Mus. Jour., 1976—; adj. prof. NYU, Inst. Fine Arts, 1992—. Author: Attic White-Ground*Its Development, 1977, Greek Bronzes in the Metropolitan Museum of Art, 1985, (with others) Ancient Art from Cyprus: The Cesnola Collection in the Metropolitan Museum of Art, 2000, (with others) The Cesuola Collection: Terracottas, 2004. Mem. Archaeol. Inst. Am., German Archael. Inst. (corr. mem.) Home: 124 E 84th St New York NY 10028-0915 Office: Met Mus Art Fifth Ave at 82nd St New York NY 10028

MERTENS, LYNNE G. retail executive; CEO, pres. Waller, The Graphics Resource, San Francisco, Calif. Office: Waller 339 Harbor Way South San Francisco CA 94080-6919 Fax: 650-589-0578.

MERTENS, THOMAS ROBERT, biology professor; b. Fort Wayne, Ind., May 22, 1930; s. Herbert F. and Hulda (Burg) M.; m. Beatrice Janet Abair, Apr. 1, 1953; children: Julia Ann, David Gerhard BS, Ball State U., 1952; MS, Purdue U., 1954, PhD, 1956. Research assoc. dept. genetics U. Wis.-Madison, 1956-57, asst. prof. biology Ball State U., Muncie, Ind., 1957-62, assoc. prof., 1962-66, prof., 1966-93, dir. doctoral programs in biology, 1974-93, disting. prof. biology edn., 1988-93, prof. emeritus, 1993—. Author: (with A. M. Winchester) Human Genetics, 1983 (with R.L. Hammersmith) Genetics Laboratory Investigations, 9th edit., 1991, 12th edit., 2001 (co-recipient William Holmes McGuffey Longevity award Text and Acad. Authors Assn. 1998); contbr. numerous articles to profl. jours. Co-recipient Gustav Ohaus award for innovative coll. sci. tchg. NSTA, 1986, recipient Disting. Svc. to Sci. Edn. citation, 1987; fellow NSF, 1963-64, Ind. Acad. Scis., 1969. Fellow AAAS; mem. Nat. Assn. Biology Tchrs. (pres. 1985, hon. mem. 1988), Am. Genetic Assn., Genetics Soc. Am. Episcopalian. Home: 1501 N Wheeling 9B-4 Muncie IN 47304-1277 Office: Ball State U Dept Biology Muncie IN 47306-0001 Office Phone: 765-285-8820.

MERTINS, DETLEF, architect, educator; BArch, U. Toronto, 1980; PhD in Architecture, Princeton U., 1996. Instr. U. Toronto, 1991—2003, Can. Rsch. chair in architecture, 2001—03; prof., chair dept. architecture U. Pa. Sch. Design, 2003—. Vis. prof. Columbia U., Harvard U., Princeton U., Rice U. Author: The Presence of Mies, 1994, The Victory of Building a Style, 2000, others. Recipient Konrad Adenauer Rsch. prize, Alexander von Humboldt Found. and Royal Can. Soc., 2003; vis. scholar fellow, Can. Ctr. for Architecture, 1998. Office: Univ Pa 207 Meyerson Hall Philadelphia PA 19104-6311

MERTINS, JAMES WALTER, entomologist; b. Milw., Feb. 18, 1943; s. Walter Edwin and Harriet Ellen (Sockett) M.; m. Marilee Eloise Joeckel, Dec. 8, 1979. BS in Zoology, U. Wis., Milw., 1965; MS in Entomology, U. Wis., 1967, PhD in Entomology, 1971. Project assoc. dept. entomology U. Wis., Madison, 1971-75, rsch. assoc. dept. entomology, 1975-77; asst. prof. dept. entomology Iowa State U., Ames, 1977-84; entomol. cons. Ames, 1984-89; entomologist Nat. Vet. Svcs. Labs. USDA Animal and Plant Health Inspection Svc., Ames, 1989—. Co-author: (textbook) Biological Insect Pest Suppression, 1977, Russian edit., 1980, Chinese edit., 1988; contbr. articles to profl. jours. NSF Grad. fellow, 1970. Mem. Entomol. Soc. Am. (Insect Photography award 1984, 86, 2003), Entomol. Soc. Can., Mich. Entomol. Soc., Wis. Entomol. Soc. (pres., sec., treas., bd. dirs.), Cyclone Corvettes, Inc. (co-founder, pres. 1978, 79, sec., treas., bd. dirs., Mem. of Yr. 1982), Am. Mensa. Avocations: insect photography, Corvette automobile activities, gardening, movies, insect collecting. Office: USDA Animal and Plant Health Inspection Svc PO Box 844 Ames IA 50010-0844 Business E-Mail: James.W.Mertins@aphis.usda.gov.

MERTON, ROBERT C. economist, educator; b. N.Y.C., July 31, 1944; s. Robert K. and Suzanne (Carhart) M. BS in Engring. Math., Columbia U., 1966; MS in Applied Math., Calif. Inst. Tech., 1967; PhD in Econs., MIT, 1970; MA (hon.), Harvard U., 1989; LLD (hon.), U. Chgo., 1991; Prof. honoris causa degree, HEC Sch. Mgmt., Paris, 1995; D Econ. Sci. (hon.), U. Lausanne, Switzerland, 1996; Dr honoris causa, U. Paris Dauphine, 1997, Universidad Nacional Mayor de San Marcos, Lima, Peru, 2004; D of Mgmt. Sci. (hon.), Nat. Sun Yat-sen U., Kaoshiung, Taiwan, 1998; DS (hon.), Athens U. Econs. and Bus., 2003. Instr. econs. MIT, Cambridge, 1969-70; asst. prof. fin. Alfred P. Sloan Sch. Mgmt., 1970-73, assoc. prof., 1973-74, prof., 1974-80, J.C. Penney prof. mgmt., 1980-88; vis. prof. fin. Harvard U., Boston, 1987-88, George Fisher Baker prof. bus. adminstrn., 1988-98, John and Natty McArthur University prof., 1998—. Rsch. assoc. Nat. Bur. Econ. Rsch., 1979—; mem. internat. bd. sci. advisors Tinbergen Inst.; co-founder Long-Term Capital Mgmt., L.P., Greenwich, Conn., 1993—99; mem. adv. bd. nuServe, 2001—, AlphaSimplex Group, 2001—; acad. adv. bd. Real Option Group, 1999—; bd. dirs. Vical Inc., MF Risk, Inc., Dimensional Funds, Cmty. First Fin. Group, Peninsula Banking Group; co-founder, chief sci. officer, mem. bd. dirs. Integrated Fin. Ltd., 2002—; mem. competitive markets adv. coun. Chgo. Merc. Exch., 2004—. Author: Continuous-Time Finance, 1990, rev. edit., 1992; co-author: Casebook in Financial Engineering: Applied Studies of Financial Innovation, 1995, The Global Financial System: A Functional Perspective, 1995, Finance, 2000, Transparency, Risk Management and International Financial Fragility, 2003; editor: The Collected Scientific Papers of Paul A. Samuelson, vol. III, 1972; mem. editl. bd. Internat. Econ. Rev., 1972-77, Jour. Fin., 1973-77, Jour. Money, Credit and Banking, 1974-79, Jour. Fin. Econs., 1974-83, Jour. Banking and Fin., 1977-79, 92-2003, Fin. India, 1988—, Geneva Papers on Risk and Ins., 1989-96, Jour. Fixed Income, 1991—, Fin. Rev., 1992-97, Jour. Fin. Edn., 1995—, European Fin. Rev. (now Rev. Fin.), 1997—; mem. adv. bd. The New Palgrave Dictionary of Money and Finance, Math. Fin., Rev. Derivatives Rsch., Nihon Finance Gakkai, The Brookings-Wharton Papers on Financial Policy, Internat. Jour. Theoretical and Applied Finance, Jour. Investment Mgmt., North Holland Series of Handbooks in Finance, Jour. Banking and Fin., 2003—, Annals of Fin., 2004—, Jour. Fin. Lit., 2004—; mem. adv. coun. Fin. Analyst Jour., 2003—; contbr. articles to profl. jours. Mem. hon. bd. Internat. Raoul Wallenberg Found., 2003—, Angelo Roncalli Internat. Com., 2003—. Recipient Leo Melamed prize U. Chgo. Sch. Bus., 1983, Roger Murray prize Inst. for Quantitative Rsch. in Fin., 1985, 86, Disting. Scholar award Ea. Fin. Assn., 1989, Internat. INA-Nat. Acad. Lincei prize Nat. Acad. Lincei, Rome, 1993, FORCE award for fin. innovation Fuqua Sch. Bus., Duke U., 1993, Fin. Engr. of Yr. award Internat. Assn. Fin. Engrs., 1993, Alfred Nobel Meml. Prize in Econ. Scis., 1997, Heroes Among Us award Boston Celtics, 1997, Michael Pupin medal Columbia U., 1998, Disting. Alumni award Calif. Inst. of Tech., 1999, MFD Lifetime Achievement award Boston U., 1999, Lifetime Achievement award Risk Mag., 2003, Nicholas Molodovsky award Assn. Investment Mgmt. Rsch., 2003; inducted Derivatives Hall of Fame, 1998, named Risk Hall of Fame, Risk Mag., 2002. Fellow Internat. Assn. Fin. Engrs. (sr.), Econometric Soc., Am. Acad. Arts and Scis., Inst. Quantitative Rsch., Fin. Mgmt. Assn., Am. Fin. Assn. (dir. 1982-84, pres. 1986, fellow 2000—); mem. NAS, Bachelier Fin. Soc., Soc. for Fin. Studies (v.p. 1993), Hon. Order Ky. Cols., Tau Beta Pi, Sigma Xi. Office: Harvard U Grad Sch Bus Adminstrn Morgan 397 Soldiers Field Rd Boston MA 02163 Business E-Mail: rmerton@hbs.edu.

MERTZ, DOLORES MARY, farmer, state legislator; b. Bancroft, Iowa, May 30, 1928; d. John Francis and Gertrude (Erickson) Shay; m. H. Peter Mertz (dec. 1983), Dec. 27, 1951; children: Peter, Mary Simpson, David, Ann Cornicelli, Helen Powell, Janice, Carol. AA, Briar Cliff Coll., 1948. Pres. Coun. Cath. Women, Sioux City, Iowa, 1986-88; state regent Cath. Daus. Am., Iowa, 1988-94; county supr. Kossuth County, Iowa, 1983-89; mem. Iowa Ho. of Reps., Des Moines, 1989—. Dem. precinct com. person, Kossuth County, Iowa, sec. 1975—. Recipient Womens Leadership award Iowa Lakes Com-

munity Coll., 1988; named Woman of Yr. Beta Sigma Phi Internat., West Bend, Iowa, 1989; recipient Iowa Lakes Community Coll. Disting. Svc. award, 1992, Guardian of Small Businsess award. Mem. Soroptomist Internat. (Woman of Distinction award 1987), Drama Club (pres. 1970's). Liberal. Roman Catholic. Office: Iowa Ho of Reps State Capitol Des Moines IA 50319-0001 Home: 607 110th St Ottosen IA 50570-8504

MERTZ, FRANCIS JAMES, university president; b. Newark, Sept. 24, 1937; s. Frank E. and Marian E. (Brady) M.; m. Gail Williams, Apr. 11, 1964; children: Lynn, Christopher, Suzanne, David, Amy, Jonathan. BA, St. Peter's Coll., 1958; JD, NYU, 1961; LLD (hon.), Felician Coll., 1984, Stevens Inst. Tech., Hoboken, N.J., 1988, Fairleigh Dickinson U., 1999, Kunghnam Univ., 1999, Coll. St. Elizabeth, 2002. Bar: N.J. 1967. Exec. v.p. St. Peter's Coll., Jersey City, 1972-78; v.p., CFO N.Y. Med. Coll., Valhalla, 1978-79; dir. adminstrn. Sage Gray Todd and Sims, N.Y.C., 1979-81; pres. Ind. Coll. Fund N.J., Summit, 1981-90, Assn. Ind. Colls. and Univs. N.J., Summit, 1982-90, Fairleigh Dickinson U., Teaneck, N.J., 1990-99, pres. emeritus. Bd. dirs., chmn. St. Joseph's Home for the Blind, 1998—; chmn. bd. regents Seton Hall U., 2002-04; mem. N.J. Commn. on Higher Edn., 2004—, N.J. Higher Edn. Student Assistance Authority. Home: 54 Woodcrest Dr Morristown NJ 07960-4541 Office: Fairleigh Dickinson U 285 Madison Ave Madison NJ 07940-1099 Office Phone: 973-267-1506. Business E-Mail: mertz@fdu.edu.

MERTZ, WALTER, retired government research executive; b. Mainz, Germany, May 4, 1923; s. Oskar and Anne (Gabelmann) M.; m. Marianne C. Maret, Aug. 8, 1953. MD, U. Mainz, 1951. Intern County Hosp., Hersfeld, Germany, 1952-53; resident Univ. Hosp., Frankfurt, Germany, 1953; vis. scientist NIH, Bethesda, Md., 1953-61; chief dept. biol. chemistry Walter Reed Army Inst. Research, Washington, 1961-69; mem. staff Nutrition Inst., Agrl. Research Service, Dept. Agrl., Beltsville, Md., 1969-72, chmn. inst., 1972-92; ret. Dir. Human Nutrition Research Ctr.; lectr. George Washington U. Med. Sch., 1963-73 Served with German Army, 1941-46. Recipient Osborne and Mendel award Am. Inst. Nutrition, 1971, Superior Performance award Dept. Agr., 1972, Lederle award in Human Nutrition, 1982, Internat. prize for Modern Nutrition, 1987, award for Disting. Svc., Dept. Agr., 1988. Mem. Am. Inst. Nutrition, Am. Soc. Biol. Chemists, Am. Soc. Clin. Nutrition Home: 12401 Saint James Rd Rockville MD 20850-3744 E-mail: wmcmertz@aol.com.

MERULLO-BOAZ, LISA HELEN, marketing and fundraising executive; b. N.Y.C., Oct. 25, 1953; d. Irving and Hazel (Jacob) Siegel; m. Edward J. Merullo, Oct. 4, 1975 (div.); children: Aaron E., Jenny L.; m. Jeffrey A. Boaz, July 4, 1993. BA, Northeastern U., 1975. Prodn. and adminstrv. asst. Gennard Andreozzi Inc., N.Y.C., 1978; adminstrv. asst. WNET/13, N.Y.C., 1978-79; prodn. sec. MacNeil/Lehrer Report, N.Y.C., 1979-81, prodn. asst., 1981-82; membership, mktg. and fundraising adminstr. Leventhal-Sidman Jewish Cmty. Ctr., Newton, Mass., 1988-97; devel. assoc. Ben-Gurion U., Newton office, 1997-98; devel. mgr. AIDS Action Com., Boston, 1998—. Exec. prodr. (cable TV show) JCC-TV, 1994-97. Jewish. Avocations: cooking, camping, physical fitness. Office: AIDS Action Com 131 Claredon St Boston MA 02116-1443

MERVILLE, LAWRENCE JOSEPH, finance educator; b. Nashville, Apr. 7, 1943; s. Lawrence Augustus Merville and Emma June (Collier) Park; m. Sheryl Wolff, Aug. 9, 1968; 1 child, Lauren Anne. BA, Vanderbilt U., 1965; MBA, U. Tex., 1968, PhD, 1971. Fin. analyst Tex. Instruments, Dallas, 1968-70; asst. prof. fin. Ind. U., Bloomington, 1971-73; prof. fin. U. Tex., Dallas, 1973—. Pres. Merville & Assocs., Dallas; cons. Tex. Pub. Utility Com., Austin, 1983-85. Author: Economics and Finance, 1990; contbr. articles to profl. jours. Dir. Pub. Utility Programs, Dallas, 1978-82, Pub. Utility Ctr., Dallas, 1981-87. NSF fellow U. Tex., Austin, 1965. Mem. Am. Fin. Assn., Fin. Mgmt. Assn. (program com.), Western Fin. Assn. (program com.), Soc. for China Studies, Dallas Economist Club (membership com.), Phi Beta Kappa. Republican. Avocations: travel, jogging, fishing, theater. Office: Univ Tex Dallas 2601 N Floyd Rd Richardson TX 75080-1407

MERWIN, DAVIS UNDERWOOD, newspaper executive; b. Chgo., June 22, 1928; s. Davis and Josephine (Underwood) M.; m. Nancy Snowden Smith Tailer, Nov. 14, 1958 (dec. Feb. 1995); children: Davis Fell, Laura Howell; m. Sharon Adkins Todd, May 12, 1998. AB, Harvard U., 1950; LLD (hon.), Ill. Wesleyan U., 1991. Pres. Evergreen Comm., Inc., Bloomington, Ill., 1969-80; pub. Daily Pantagraph, 1968-80; pres. Wood Canyon Corp., Tucson, 1989-93; vice-chmn. Bloomington Broadcasting Corp., 1993-99. Dir. State Farm Growth, Balanced Mcpl. Bond and Interim Funds, State Farm Variable Products Funds. Trustee emeritus Ill. Wesleyan U.; trustee Ill. Nature Conservancy. Recipient Disting. Svc. award U.S. Jaycees, 1959 Mem. Am. Newspaper Pubs. Assn., Inland Daily Press Assn. (pres. 1977, chmn. bd. dirs. 1978), Harvard Club (Chgo.), Phoenix-SK Club, Hasty Pudding Club, Bloomington Country Club, Ristigouche Salmon Club. Republican. Unitarian Universalist. Office: 2422 E Washington St Bloomington IL 61704-4478 Mailing: PO Box 1665 Bloomington IL 61702-1665 E-mail: DUMerwin@aol.com.

MERWIN, EDWIN PRESTON, healthcare educator, consultant; b. Revere, Mass., Oct. 13, 1927; s. George Preston and Edith Charlotte (Miller) Merwin; m. Marylynn Joy Bicknell, Nov. 3, 1979; stepchildren: Charles John Burns, Patrick Edward Burns, Stephen Allen Burns, John David Light, Robert Allen Light, Frederick John Light; 1 child from previous marriage, Ralph Edwin. BS, U. So. Calif., 1955, postgrad., 1957, San Fernando Valley State Coll, 1965—66; MPH (USPHS fellow), U. Calif., Berkeley, 1970; PhD, Brantridge Forest, Eng., 1971. Tng. office Camarillo (Calif.) State Hosp., 1961—66; asst. coord. mental retardation programs State of Calif., Sacramento, 1966—67; project dir. Calif. Coun. Retarded Children, Sacramento, 1967—69; asst. dir. Golden Empire Comprehensive Health Coun., Sacramento, 1970—76, health care cons., 1976—77; gen. ptnr. EDRA Assocs., 1976—. Tchr. Ventura (Calif.) Coll., 1962—66, Merritt Coll., Oakland, Calif., 1969; cons. Calif. Dept. Health, 1977—78, Calif. Office Statewide Health Planning and Devel., 1978—79, chief health pers. info. and analysis sect., 1981—82, asst. chief divsn. health professions devel., 1981—84, asst. dep. dir., 1984—85; chief health professions career opportunity program State of Calif., Sacramento, 1979—81; project dir. Alzheimer Disease Insts., Calif., 1986—87; chief demonstration project sect. divsn. Health Projects and Analysis, 1987—89, chief policy analysis and professions devel. sect., 1989—93; sr. adj. prof. Golden Gate U., 1976, mem. adv. com. health faculty, 1995—; lectr. continuing edn. program U. Calif., Berkeley; instr. Los Rios CC Dist., 1982—; mem. Task Force New Health Care Sys. Macedonia; cons. NIMH, HEW, Calif. Assn. Health Facilities; founder, cons. Internat. U. Am., 1995—. Author (with Fred Heck): (book) Written Case Analysis, 1982; author: (with Carl Brooks) Health Algorythm - circa 2030, 1999; editor: T. patrick Heck Meml. Case Series, 1982; contbr. articles to profl. jours. Mem. health adv. coun. San Juan Sch. Dist., 1972—73; treas. Calif. Camping and Recreation Coun., 1972—73; bd. dirs. Sacramento Rehab. Facility, 1970—76, v.p., 1973—76; bd. dirs. Sacramento Vocat. Svcs., 1986—93; founder, life mem. S.O.T.S., 1989—. Recipient Pres.'s award, Golden Gate U., 1982. Mem.: AAAS, DAV (life), Calif. State Sheriffs Assn., Nat. Assn. Retarded Children (dir., Svc. award 1984), Sacramento Mental Health Assn., Calif. Pub. Health Assn., Am. Assn. Mental Deficiency, Sacramento Assn. Retarded (life), Miles Merwin Assn., SCAPA Praetors U. So. Calif., Marines Meml. Assn. (life), Am. Legion, Phi Kappa Tau. Home: 8008 Archer Ave Fair Oaks CA 95628-5907 Office: Golden Gate U 3620 Northgate Blvd Ste 100 Sacramento CA 95834-1619

MERWIN, JOHN DAVID, retired lawyer, former governor; b. Frederiksted, St. Croix, V.I., Sept. 26, 1921; s. Miles and Marguerite Louise (Fleming) M.; m. Marjorie Davis Spaulding, Feb. 18, 1993. Student, U. Lausanne, Switzerland, 1938-39, U. P.R., 1939-40; BSc, Yale U., 1943; JD, George Washington U., 1948. Bar: Conn., V.I. 1949. Practice law, St. Croix, V.I., 1949-50, 1953-57, 67-85; gen. counsel, v.p. Rob't L. Merwin & Co., Inc., 1953-57; senator-at-large V.I. Legislature, 1955-57; govt. sec. for V.I., 1957-58; gov. V.I., 1958-61; rep. Chase Manhattan Bank, Nassau, Bahamas, 1961-65; exec. v.p. Equity Pub. Corp. Orford, N.H., 1965-67. Chmn. V.I. Port Authority, 1972-75; Rep. candidate for Pres. N.H. Primary Election, 1992; pres. The Nason Found., Cleve., 1981-2002. Capt. F.A. AUS, 1942-46, 50-53. Decorated Bronze Star; Croix de Guerre with silver star. Mem. Conn., N.H., V.I. bar assns., Phi Delta Phi. Clubs: Tennis of St. Croix (V.I.), Yale (N.Y.C.)., Cosmos (Washington). Episcopalian. Home and Office: PO Box 2213 New London NH 03257-2213 E-mail: jdmerwin@hotmail.com.

MERZ, JAMES LOGAN, electrical engineering and materials educator, researcher; b. Jersey City, Apr. 14, 1936; s. Albert Joseph and Anne Elizabeth (Farrell) M.; m. Rose-Marie Weibel, June 30, 1962; children: Kathleen, James, Michael, Kimarie. BS in Physics, U. Notre Dame, 1959; postgrad., U. Göttingen, Fed. Republic Germany, 1959-60; MA, Harvard U., 1961, PhD in Applied Physics, 1967; PhD (hon.), Linköping U., Sweden, 1993. Mem. tech. staff Bell Labs., Murray Hill, N.J., 1966-78; prof. elec. engrng. U. Calif., Santa Barbara, 1978-94, prof. materials, 1986-94, chmn. dept. elec. and computer engrng., 1982-84, assoc. dean for rsch. devel. Coll. Engrng., 1984-86, acting assoc. vice chancellor, 1988, dir. semiconductor rsch. corp. core program on GaAs digital ICs, 1984-89, dir. Compound Semiconductor Rsch. Labs., 1986-92, dir. NSF Ctr. for Quantized Electronic Structures, 1989-94; Freimann prof. elec. engrng. U. Notre Dame (Ind.), 1994—, v.p. for grad. studies and rsch., dean Grad. Sch., 1996-2001. Mem. exec. com. Calif. Microelectronics Innovation and Computer Rsch. Opportunities Program, 1986-92; mem. NRC com. on Japan, NAS/NAE, 1988-90; mem. internat. adv. com. Internat. Symposium on Physics of Semiconductors and Applications, Seoul, Republic of Korea, 1990, Conf. on Superlattices and Microstructures, Xi'an, China, 1992; participant, mem. coms. other profl. confs. and meetings. Contbr. over 400 articles to profl. jours.; patentee in field. Fulbright fellow, Danforth Found. fellow, Woodrow Wilson Found. fellow; Alexander von Humboldt rsch. awardee, 2002. Fellow IEEE, Am. Phys. Soc.; mem. IEEE Lasers and Electro-Optics Soc. (program com. annual mtg. 1980), IEEE Electron Device Soc. (sec. 1994, 95), Am. Vacuum Soc. (exec. com. electronic materials and processing divsn. 1988-89), Materials Rsch. Soc. (editl. bd. jour. 1984-87), Soc. for Values in Higher Edn., Inst. Electronics, Info. and Comm. Engrs. (overseas adv. com.), Sigma Xi, Eta Kappa Nu. Achievements include research in field of optoelectronic materials and devices: semiconductors and ionic materials; optical and electrical properties of implanted ions, rapid annealing; semiconductor lasers, detectors, solar cells, other optoelectronic devices; low-dimensional quantum structures, nanostructures. Office: U Notre Dame Dept Elec Engrng 203B Cushing Hall Notre Dame IN 46556-5637 E-mail: jmerz@nd.edu.

MERZBACHER, EUGEN, physicist, researcher; b. Berlin, Apr. 9, 1921; came to U.S., 1947, naturalized, 1953; s. Siegfried and Lilli (Wilmersdoerffer) M.; m. Ann Townsend Reid, July 11, 1952; children: Celia, Charles, Matthew, Mary. Licentiate, U. Istanbul, 1943; AM, Harvard U., 1948, PhD, 1950; DSc (hon.), U. N.C., Chapel Hill, 1993. High sch. tchr., Ankara, Turkey, 1943—47; mem. Inst. Advanced Study, Princeton, NJ, 1950—51; vis. asst. prof. Duke U., Durham, NC, 1951—52; from mem. faculty to Kenan prof. physics U. N.C., Chapel Hill, 1952—91, Kenan prof. emeritus, 1991—. Vis. prof. U. Wash., 1967-68, U. Edinburgh, Scotland, 1986; Arnold Bernhard vis. prof. physics Williams Coll., 1993; chair Internat. Conf. on Physics of Electronic and Atomic Collisions, 1987-89; sr. advisor APS, 1998-99. Author: Quantum Mechanics, 3d edit., 1998; also articles. NSF Sci. Faculty fellow U. Copenhagen, Denmark, 1959-60; recipient Thomas Jefferson award U. N.C., 1972; Humboldt sr. scientist award U. Frankfurt, Germany, 1976-77. Fellow AAAS, Am. Phys. Soc. (pres. 1990); mem. Am. Assn. Physics Tchrs. (Oersted medal 1992), Sigma Xi. Achievements include research on applications of quantum mechanics to study atoms and nuclei. Home: 1396 Halifax Rd Chapel Hill NC 27514-2724 E-mail: merzbach@physics.unc.edu.

MESA, NILDA, artist; b. Havana, Cuba; d. Roland J. and Zoila Mesa; m. Robert Seyffert; children: Marina, Amalie. JD, Harvard Law Sch., Cambridge, 1985—88; BA, Northwestern U., Evanston, Ill., 1977—81; Post Baccalaureate, Md. Inst., Coll. of Art, Balt., 1996—98. Bar assn.: DC, Bar assn. (inactive): Calif. Gen. mgr. El Sol del Bronx (newspaper), New Rochelle, NY, 2004—; founder and artistic dir. Unity Canvas, New York, 2001—; asst. dep. for environment US Air Force, Washington, 1994—98; asst. dir. White Ho. Coun. on Environ. Quality, 1996—97; counsel, NAFTA task force US EPA, Washington, 1993—94; dep. atty. gen. Calif. Atty. Gen., 1989—91; legislative aide, fgn. policy & def. US Senator Alan Cranston, Washington, 1982—84; editl. asst. Fgn. Policy mag., Washington, 1981—82. Bd. mem. Williamsburg Art & Hist. Ctr., Bklyn., 2003—. Founder and artistic director (exhibition 9/11 artists' response) Unity Canvas (NY Found. for the Arts, New Yorker of the Week, 2002); author: (What Does War Have To Do... essay) KnitLit Too; exhibition, (LaGuardia CC). Mem. ABA -Steering Com. on Environ. Law, Washington, 1997—99, Williamsburg Art & Hist. Ctr., Bklyn., 2003; vol. arts tchr. PS 75, NY, 2003—04. Recipient Profl., US EPA, 1994, USAF, 1998. Mem.: NY Artists Cir., DC Bar Assn. Achievements include being an abstract painter, sculptor, and designer, maintaining studios in NY and France; serving as gen. mgr. of a weekly Spanish-lang. newspaper. Home: 100 St Nicholas Ave New York NY 10026

MESAK, HANI IBRAHIM, finance educator; b. Cairo, Feb. 21, 1944; s. Ibrahim M. Wassif and Mary K. Ghobrial; m. Eugenie Milad Habib, Aug. 23, 1977; 1 child, Irene Ann. BSc, Cairo U., 1965, Grad. Diploma, 1969; PhD, U. Pa., 1974. Engr. Orgn. Small Scale Industries, Cairo; mgmt. rsch. analyst Wharton Sch. U. Pa., Philad., 1970—73; project leader Data Analysis Ctr., NJ, 1974—75; assoc. prof. U. La., Monroe, 1987—89; prof. La. Tech U., Ruston, 1989—. Asst. prof. Kuwait U., 1975—87. Contbr. articles to profl. jours. (Irwin McGraw-Hill Disting. Paper award SW Fedn. Adminstrv. Disciplines, 99, Best Theoretical/Empirical Paper award Decision Scis. Inst., 02). Mem.: Decision Sciences Inst. (assoc. editor Decision Scis. jour. 1999, named to Hall of Fame). Democrat. Eastern Orthodox. Avocations: travel, ping pong/table tennis. Home: 904 Monterey Dr Ruston LA 71270 Office: La Tech U PO Box 10318 Ruston LA 71272 Office Phone: 318-257-3506. E-mail: mesak@cab.latech.edu.

MESA-LAGO, CARMELO, economist, educator; b. Havana, Cuba, Aug. 11, 1934; s. Rogelio M. and Ana Maria (Lago); m. Elena Mesa-Gross, Sept. 3, 1966; children: Elizabeth, Ingrid, Helena. LLB, U. Havana, 1956; LLD, U. Madrid, 1958; MA in Econs., U. Miami, 1965; PhD, Cornell U., 1968. Asst. prof. Cath U. Villanueva, Havana, Cuba, 1956-57, 59-61; rsch. assoc. U. Miami, Fla., 1962-65; asst. prof. U. Pitts., 1968-71, assoc. prof., 1971-76, prof., 1976-81, disting. prof. econs. and L.Am. affairs, 1981-99, disting. prof. emeritus, 1999—; dir. Ctr. L.Am. Studies, 1974-86; prof. Fla. Internat. U., 1999—2002. Vis. prof. Oxford U., 1977, Mellon vis. prof. Fla. Internat. U., 1995, vis. prof. Inst. Univ. Ortega y Gasset, 1990-91, 2003; Bacardi chair U. Miami, 1994; regional advisor Econ. Commn. Latin Am., Santiago, Chile, 1983-84; rsch. assoc. Max-Planck-Inst., Munich, 1991-92, 2002, Free U. Berlin, 1997; cons. in field. Author: Cuba in the 1970's, 1974, 2nd edit. 1978, Social Security in Latin America, 1978, The Economy of Socialist Cuba, 1981 (A.P. Whitaker 1982), The Crisis of Social Security and Health Care: Latin American Experiences and Lessons, 1985, Ascent to Bankruptcy: Financing Social Security in Latin America, 1989, Health Care for the Poor in Latin America and the Caribbean, 1992, Cuba After the Cold War, 1993, Changing Social Security in Latin America, 1994 (Outstanding Book Choice award 1995), Are Economic Reforms Propelling Cuba To the Market?, 1994, Do Options Exist? The Reform of Pensions and Health Care in Latin America, 1999, Market, Socialist and Mixed Economies: Comparative Policy and Performance, 2000, (paperback, 2003); former editor: Yearbook Cuban Studies. Recipient numerous rsch. grants, 1986—; Fulbright scholar, 1998, 2003; recipient Alexander von Humboldt sr. rsch. prize, 1990-91, 96-97, 2001 Mem. Latin Am. Studies Assn. (pres. 1980), Caribbean Studies Assn. (eec. coun. 1973-74), Am. Econ. Assn., Assn. Comparative Econs., Internat. Assn. Labor Law and Social Security, Coun. on Fgn. Rels. and the Nat. Acad. of Social Ins. Democrat.

MESCHER, WILLIAM CLARENCE, state legislator, management consultant; b. Belknap, Ill., Sept. 5, 1927; s. Clarence H. and Jane (Richards) M.; m. Sallie Kitty Stanley, Feb. 15, 1986; children: Barbara, Kathy, Reed, Karen. BSEE, U. Ill., 1953; MBA, Northwestern U., 1966. Registered profl. engr., Ill., S.C. Past pres. and CEO, Santee Cooper, PSA; pres. William Mescher & Assocs. Mgmt. Cons., Monks Corner, SC, 1976—89; mem. S.C. Senate, Columbia, 1993—. Chmn. gen. com., mem. edn. com., judiciary com., labor, commerce and industry com.; chmn. Demand Reduction Sys. S.C.; adj. prof. U.S.C.; bd. dirs. S.C. Nat. Bank, Moncks Corner; former mem. Utility Tech. Mgmt. Del. to China, S.C. Gov.'s S.W.-Korea Internat. Trad Commn., U.S.-Japan Internat. Commn., World Energy Conf. Bird bander U.S. Dept. Interior; chmn. Berkeley County Mus.; past mem. bd. dirs. Coastal Carolina coun. Boy Scouts Am.; mem. S.C. Coun. on Econ. Edn., Charleston-Trident Devel. Bd.; bd. dirs. Charleston Symphony Orch. Staff sgt. U.S. Army, Korea. Recipient Silver Beaver award Boy Scouts Am. Mem. ASME (adv. bd.), Am. Pub. Power Assn. (past pres.), Tri-County C. of C. (bd. dirs.), Charleston-Trident C. of C., VFW (life), Am. Legion, Greater U. S.C. Alumni Assn. (life), Tau Beta Pi. Republican. Methodist. Office: 303 Gressette Bldg Columbia SC 29202 E-mail: wmescher@homexpresswam.net.

MESCHUTT, DAVID RANDOLPH, historian, curator; b. N.Y.C., May 29, 1955; s. Philip Frederick and Mary Evelyn (Mahanes) M.; m. Sarah Caroline Bevan, July 14, 1990. BA in Journalism, Washington and Lee U., 1977; MA in History Mus. Studies, SUNY, Cooperstown, 1988; postgrad., Attingham Summer Sch., Gt. Britain, 1988, 98, postgrad., 2004, Royal Collection Studies Programme, 2000. Rschr. Thomas Jefferson Meml. Found., Charlottesville, Va., 1977-78, Frick Art Reference Libr., N.Y.C., 1980-86; curator art West Point (N.Y.) Mus./U.S. Mil. Acad., 1988-98; consulting curator N.Y. State Office of Pks., Recreation and Hist. Preservation, Waterford, N.Y., 1999—. Guest curator N.Y. State Hist. Assn., Cooperstown, 1986-87, Brandywine River Mus., Chadds Ford, Pa., 1992, Va. Hist. Soc., Richmond, 1999; cons. Curatorial Office, U.S. Dept. Treasury, Washington, 1988, Albany (N.Y.) Inst. History and Art, 1988. Author: A Bold Experiment: John Henri Isaac Browere's Life Masks of Prominent Americans, 1988; co-author: The Portraits and History Paintings of Alonzo Chappel, 1992; assoc. editor Am. Nat. Biography, Oxford U. Press, 1994-99, contbr., 1994—; contbr. articles to profl. jours. Nourse Found. fellow, 1986-87, Nat. Endowment for Arts fellow, 1987, Soc. Colonial Wars fellow, 1988, Andrew W. Mellon fellow Va. Hist. Soc., 1992, Anne S.K. Brown fellow Brown U., 1993, Mayers fellow Huntington Libr. and Art Gallery, 1997. Mem.: Walpole Soc., N.Y. State Hist. Assn., Va. Hist. Soc., Ralph Vaughan Williams Soc., Herbert Howells Soc., Historians Brit. Art, Assn. Historians Am. Art. Methodist. Avocation: music. Office: c/o Glen Burnie Mus 530 Amherst St Winchester VA 22601-3802

MESELSON, MATTHEW STANLEY, biochemist, educator; b. Denver, Col., May 24, 1930; s. Hymen Avram and Ann (Swedlow) M.; m. Jeanne Guillemin, 1986; children: Zoe, Amy Valor. Ph.B., U. Chgo., 1951, D.Sc. (hon.), 1975; PhD, Calif. Inst. Tech., 1957; Sc.D. (hon.), Oakland Coll., 1964, Columbia, 1971, Yale U., 1987, Princeton U., 1988. From research fellow to sr. research fellow Calif. Inst. Tech., 1957-60; asso. prof. biology Harvard U., 1960—, prof. biology, 1964-76, Thomas Dudley Cabot prof. natural scis., 1976—. Recipient Eli Lilly award microbiology and immunology, 1964, Alumni medal U. Chgo., 1971; Lehman award 1975, Presidential award 1983, N.Y. Acad. Scis., 1975; Alumni Disting. Svc. award Calif. Inst. Tech., 1975; Leo Szilard award Am. Phys. Soc., 1978; MacArthur fellow, 1984-89. Fellow AAAS (Sci. Freedom and Responsibility award, 1990); mem. NAS (Molecular Biology prize 1963), Inst. Medicine, Am. Acad. Arts and Scis., Fedn. Am. Scientists (chmn. 1986-88, Pub. Svc. award 1972), Coun. Fgn. Rels., Accademia Santa Chiara, Am. Philos. Soc., Royal Society (London), Académie des Sciences (Paris), Genetics Soc. Am. (Thomas Hunt Morgan medal 1995). Office: Harvard U Fairchild Biochem Bldg 7 Divinity Ave Cambridge MA 02138-2019

MESERVE, MOLLIE ANN, publisher; b. Dallas, Dec. 9, 1944; d. Ralph and Emly (Stewart) Lacey; m. Walter Joseph Meserve, June 18, 1981. BA, U. Tex., Dallas, 1976; MFA, Ind. U., 1981. Pres. Feedback Theatrebooks, 1983—, Prospero Press, Maine, 1992—. Dir. FS Drama award, 1985—87. Author (designer): Format Guidelines & Sample, 2001; co-author, designer, illustrator A Chronological Outline of World Theatre, 1992, The Theatre Lover's Cookbook, 1992, The Musical Theatre Cookbook, 1993, Prospero's Almanac, Vol. I, 1997, co-editor, designer When Conscience Trod the Stage: American Plays of Social Awareness, 1998, Fateful Lightning: America's Civil War Plays, 2000, Americana Series, Pre-World War I American Plays: The Poor of New York, 2001, Nick of the Woods, 2001, The Great Divide, 2001, The Girl with the Green Eyes, 2001, Three Short Plays by William Dean Howells: The Garroters, The Mousetrap, The Unexpected Guests, 2001, The Candidates, 2004, Aria da Capo, 2004, co-editor, designer, illustrator Witchcraft, 2001, Superstition, 2001, A Texas Steer, 2002, co-editor, illustrator Americana Series Plays: The Contrast, 1996, He and She, 2001; co-author: Aspirations, Challenges, and Accomplishments: America's Literary Dramatists of the 1850s, Jour. of Am. Drama and Theatre, 2001; editor: The Playwright's Companion: A Practical Guide to Script Opportunities in the U.S.A., 1985—99. Recipient Open Cir. Playwright award Goucher Coll., 1977, Biennial Promising Playwright award Colonial Players, 1977, Playwright Contest award Country Playhouse, 1984, Winning Work-in-Progress award Nat. Playwrights Showcase, 1988. Avocations: reading, writing, gardening, cooking, home design. Office: Feedback Theatrebooks PO Box 174 Brooklin ME 04616

MESERVE, RICHARD ANDREW, lawyer; b. Medford, Mass., Nov. 20, 1944; s. Robert William and Gladys Evangeline (Swenson) M.; m. Martha Ann Richards, Sept. 20, 1966; children: Amy, Lauren. BA, Tufts U., 1966; JD, Harvard U., 1975; PhD in Applied Physics, Stanford U., 1976. Bar: Mass. 1975, D.C. 1980, U.S. Supreme Ct. 1982. Law clk. Mass. Supreme Jud. Ct., Boston, 1975-76; law clk. to presiding justice U.S. Supreme Ct., Washington, 1976-77; legal counsel Pres. Sci. Adviser, Washington, 1977-81; ptnr. Covington & Burling, Washington, 1981-99, sr. of counsel, 2004—; chmn. U.S. Nuc. Regulatory Commn., Washington, 1999—2003; pres. Carnegie Instn. Washington, 2003—, also bd. dirs. Chmn. com. to assess safety and tech. issues at Dept. Energy reactors, NAS, 1987-88, chmn. com. on fuel economy of automobiles and light trucks, 1991-92, chmn. com. on declassification of info. for Dept. Energy's environ. programs, 1994-95, chmn. bd. on radioactive waste mgmt., 2004-; co-chmn. AAAS-ABA Nat. Conf. Lawyers and Scientists, 1988-94; mem. adv. bd. Sec. Energy, 1996-99; mem. bd. overseers for arts and scis. Tufts U., 1994-2002; chmn. internat. nuc. safety group IAEA, 2003-. Fellow: AAAS, Am. Acad. Arts and Scis., Am. Phys. Soc.; mem.: NAE, Am. Philos. Soc., Sigma Xi, Phi Beta Kappa. Democrat. Home: 708 Berry St Falls Church VA 22042-2402 Office Phone: 202-387-6404.

MESERVE, WALTER JOSEPH, drama studies writer, publisher; b. Portland, Maine, Mar. 10, 1923; s. Walter Joseph and Bessie Adelia (Bailey) M.; m. Mollie Ann Lacey, June 18, 1981; children by previous marriage— Gayle Ellen, Peter Haynes, Jo Alison, David Bryan Student, Portland Jr. Coll., 1941-42; AB, Bates Coll., Lewiston, Maine, 1947; MA, Boston U., 1948; PhD, U. Wash., 1952. From instr. to prof. U. Kans., Lawrence, 1951-68; prof. dramatic lit. and theory Ind. U., Bloomington, 1968-88, assoc. dean rsch. and grad. devel., 1980-83, dir. Inst. for Am. Theatre Studies, 1983-88; disting. prof. grad. ctr. CUNY, N.Y.C., 1988-93, disting. prof. emeritus, 1993—. V.p. Feedback Svcs., N.Y.C., 1983— Author: An Outline History of American Drama, 1965, rev. edit., 1994, Robert Sherwood, 1970, An Emerging Entertainment, 1977, Heralds of Promise, 1986, A Chronological Outline of World Theatre, 1992; co-author: The Revels History of Drama in English, Vol. VIII, 1977; editor: Plays of WD Howells, 1960, On Stage, America! A Selection of Distinctly American Plays, 1996; co-editor: The Poor of New York, 2001, Nick of the Woods, 2001, Three Short Plays by William Dean Howells, 2001, He and She, 2001, The Girls with the Green Eyes, 2002, A Texas Steer, 2002, The Octroon, 2002; editor-in-chief Feedback Theatrebooks, 1985—; co-editor: Modern Literature from China, 1974, Modern Drama from Communist China, 1970, American Sateric Comedies, 1969, When Conscience Trod the Stage, 1998, Fateful Lightning, 2000, Americana Series--Pre World War I American Plays, 1995—; co-founder, co-editor: Jour. Am. Drama and Theatre, 1989-93; compiler: Studies in Death of a Salesman, 1972, American Drama to 1900, 1980; co-compiler: Who's Where in the American Theatre, 1990, 3d edit., 1992; co-author: Musical Theatre Cookbook, 1993, Playhouse America!, 1991, The Theatre Lover's Cookbook, 1992, Prospero's Almanac, Vol. I,

1994; adv. bd. College Literature, 1990-95. Reader Guggenheim Found., 1988-2000. With AC, U.S. Army, 1943-46 Fellow NEH, 1974-75, 83-84, 88-89, Rockefeller Found., 1979, Guggenheim Found., 1984-85 Mem.: Cosmos Club.

MESERVE, WILLIAM GEORGE, lawyer; b. Medford, Mass., June 14, 1940; s. Robert William and Gladys Evangeline (Swenson) M.; m. Susan Mary Rycroft, Oct. 21, 1967; children: Daniel Scott, Susan Elizabeth, Jonathan Robert. BA, Tufts U., 1962; LLB, Harvard U., 1965; MSc, London Sch. Econs., 1966. Bar: Mass. 1966, U.S. Dist. Ct. Mass. 1970, U.S. Ct. Appeals (1st cir.) 1973. Legal asst. to commr. FTC, Washington, 1966-67; staff counsel com. on commerce U.S. Senate, Washington, 1967-69; assoc. Ropes & Gray, Boston, 1970-76, ptnr., 1976—2002, sr. counsel, 2002—. Geology field asst. McMurdo Sound, Antarctica, 1959-60, Inglefield Land, Greenland, summer 1965. Trustee Tufts U., Medford, 1979—97, AFS Intercultural Programs Inc., N.Y.C., 1979—92, 1993—96, New Eng. Med. Ctr., Inc., Boston, 1988—97, Lifespan of Mass., Inc., 1997—2002; bd. visitors Fletcher Sch. Law and Diplomacy Tufts U., Medford, 1971—; bd. dirs. United South End Settlements, Boston, 1979—, Earthwatch Expdns., Inc., The Ctr. for Field Rsch., Maynard, 1996—, AFS-USA, N.Y.C., 1999—, Conservation Edn. and Rsch. Trust, Oxford, England, 2004—; bd. govs. New Eng. Med. Ctr. Hosps., Boston, 1982—94, 1995—97, 2004—. Fellow Am. Coll. Trial Lawyers; mem. ABA, Boston Bar Assn., Phi Beta Kappa. Clubs: Appalachian Mountain (Boston) (rec. sec. 1977-78). Democrat. Office: Ropes & Gray 1 International Pl Fl 41 Boston MA 02110-2624 Business E-Mail: wmeserve@ropesgray.com.

MESHACH, JOSEPH ROBERT, music educator; b. Newton, N.J., Oct. 28, 1962; s. Robert Franklin and Ruth Gertrude Meshach; m. Cathy Smith; 1 child, Jennifer Grace. B in Music Edn., Newberry Coll., 1985. Band dir. Barnwell (S.C.) HS, 1985—92, Walterboro (S.C.) HS, 1992—2003, Colleton County (S.C.) High Sch., 2003—. Choir dir. Bethel Presbyn. Ch., Walterboro, 1994—. Named to All-Am. Hall of Fame Band Honors, Purdue U., 1980; recipient Dist. Achievement award, Am. Legion, 1981. Mem.: S.C. Band Dir.'s Assn. (All-State band chmn. 2001—, so. region band chmn. 1994—98, State 4A Marching Band champions 1992, Outstanding Performance award 1992—2002, Lower State Marching Band Champions 1992—2001, State 4A Marching Band champions 1993, 1995, 1997), S.C. Music Educators Assn., Music Educators Nat. Conf., Phi Beta Mu, Phi Mu Alpha Sinfonia (Acad. Achievement award 1984). Home: 301 Canal St Walterboro SC 29488 Office: Colleton County High Sch 1379 Mighty Cougar Dr Walterboro SC 29488 Office Phone: 843-538-2907. Office Fax: 843-538-8151. Personal E-mail: joejoe@lowcountry.com.

MESHBESHER, RONALD I. lawyer; b. Mpls., May 18, 1933; s. Nathan J. and Esther J. (Balman) M.; m. Sandra F. Siegel, June 17, 1956 (div. 1978); children: Betsy F., Wendy S., Stacy J.; m. Kimberly L. Garnaas, May 23, 1988; 1 child, Jolie M. BS in Law, U. Minn., 1955, JD, 1957. Bar: Minn. 1957, U.S. Supreme Ct. 1966. Prosecuting atty. Hennepin County, Mpls., 1958-61; pres. Meshbesher and Spence Ltd., Mpls., 1961—. Lectr. numerous legal and profl. orgns.; mem. adv. com. on rules of criminal procedure Minn. Supreme Ct., 1971-91; cons. on recodification of criminal procedure code Czech Republic Ministry of Justice, 1994. Author: Trial Handbook for Minnesota Lawyers, 1992; mem. bd. editors Criminal Law Advocacy Reporter; mem. adv. bd. Bur. Nat. Affairs Criminal Practice Manual; contbr. numerous articles to profl. jours. Mem.: ABA, ATLA (bd. govs. 1968—71), Attys. for Criminal Justice, Trial Lawyers for Pub. Justice, Minn. Assn. Criminal Def. Lawyers (pres. 1991—92, Disting. Svc. award 2001), Minn. Trial Lawyers Assn. (pres. 1973—74, Lifetime Achievement award 2001), Nat. Assn. Criminal Def. Lawyers (pres. 1984—85), Am. Acad. Forensic Scis., Am. Bd. Criminal Lawyers (v.p. 1983), Am. Bd. Trial Advs., Am. Coll. Trial Lawyers, Internat. Acad. Trial Lawyers, Minn. Bar Assn. Avocations: bicycling, photography, travel, flying, theater. Home: 2010 Sugarwood Dr Orono MN 55356-9339 Office: Meshbesher & Spence 1616 Park Ave Minneapolis MN 55404-1695 Office Phone: 612-339-9121. E-mail: rmeshbesher@meshbesher.com.

MESHEL, HARRY, former state senator, political party official; b. Youngstown, Ohio, June 13, 1924; s. Angelo and Rubena (Markakis) Michelakis; children: Barry, Melanie. BSBA, Youngstown Coll., 1949; MS, Columbia U., 1950; LLD (hon.), Ohio U., Youngstown State U., Ohio Coll. Podiatric Medicine; LHD (hon.), Youngstown State U. Exec. asst. to mayor City of Youngstown, Ohio, 1964-68, urban renewal dir., 1969; mem. 33d district Ohio Senate, Columbus, 1971-93, Dem. minority leader, 1981-82, 85-90, pres. and majority leader, 1983-84, com. mem. econ. develop., sci. & tech., state & local govt., ways & means, commerce & labor, controlling bd., state employment compensation bd., fin. chmn., 1974-81, rules chmn., 1983-84, com. mem. rules, reference & oversight, 1985-90; state chair Ohio Dem. Party, 1993-95. Real estate broker; adj. prof. polit. sci. Ohio U.; faculty mem. (limited svc.) Youngstown State U.; div. mgr. investment firm; Ohio Senate special com. mem. Task Force on Drug Strategies, Ohio Acad. Sci. Centennial Celebration Commn., Motor Vehicle Inspection & Maintenance Program, Legis. Oversight Com., Ohio Boxing Commn., Correctional Inst. Inspection Com., Ohio Small Bus. & Entrepreneurship Coun., Gov.'s Adv. Coun. Travel & Tourism, Legis. Svc. Commn., Capital Sq. Rev. & Adv. Bd., others. Past pres., past lt. gov. Am. Hellenic Ednl. Prog. Assn. (AHEPA); precinct committeeman Mahoning County Dem. Party, ward captain, mem. exec. com.; campaign mgr. local candidates, county campaign mgr. presdl. candidates; del. Dem. Mid-Term Conv., 1981; founder Great Lakes/N.E. Legis. Coalition; chmn., founder Nat. Dem. State Legis. Leaders Assn.; dir. State Legis. Leaders Found.; state/fed. assembly, mem. communications com. Nat. Conf. State Legis., legis. mgmt. com., govt. opers. com.; chair fiscal affairs com. Midwest Conf. Coun. State Govts., task force on econs. & fiscal affairs; del., exec. com. Dem. Nat. Com.; mem. Dem. Leadership Coun., State Dem. Exec. Com.; exec. com. Assn. State Dem. Chairs; bd. trustees Nat. Hall of Fame for Persons with Disabilities; mem. St. Nicholas Greek Orthodox Ch.; mem. Mill Creek Metro Park Bd. Commrs. With USN, 1943-46. Decorated two Bronze Battle Stars; recipient Dist. Svc. award Office of Pres., Top Legislator award Ohio Union Patrolmen Assn., Dist. Citizen award Med. Coll. Ohio, City of Hope Leadership award, 1993, Legis. Leadership award Ohio Coalition for Edn. of Handicapped Children, Phillips Medal of Pub. Svc., Ohio U., John E. Fogarty award Gov.'s Com. of Employment of Handicapped, Gov.'s award, 1992, U. Cin. Award for Excellence, Lamp of Learning award Ohio Edn. Assn., Black Cultural Soc. award East Liverpool, Mahoning Valley Man of Yr. award, Mahoning Valley Econ. Devel. Corp., Office Holder of Yr. award Truman-Johnson Dem. Women, Best Interest of Children award Fathers of Equal Rights, Founders Day award Circle of Friends Found., Helping Hand award Easter Seal Soc., Honorary Riverboat Captain award Mahoning County Dem. Party, Community Svc. and Special Svcs. awards Eastern Orthodox Men's Soc., Periclean award AHEPA, Academy of Achievement award Nat. AHEPA Ednl. Found., Nat. Svc. Dem. award AHEPA, 1994, Disting. Citizen award Youngstown State U. Alumni Assn., numerous appreciation and recognition awards; recipient Outstanding Legislator awards Ohio Acad. Trial Lawyers, Ohio Assn. Pub. Sch. Employees, Ohio Rehab. Assn., League Ohio Sportsmen; recipient Dist. Svc. awards Youngstown State U., Ohio Edn. Assn., Ohio Union Patrolmen Assn., Ohio Disabled Vets., AFL-CIO Ohio Barbers Union, AFL-CIO Nat. Assn. of Theatre Owners of Ohio; named Guardian of the Menorah, Youngstown B'nai B'rith, Outstanding Dem., Fairfield Dem. Club, 1993; named to Ohio Vets. Hall of Fame. Mem. (life) NAACP, ACLU, AMVETS (Legislator of Yr. 1993), VFW, Am. Legion, Cath. War Vets (Dist. Legislator award), Vet. Boxers Assn. Mercer County, Pa., Trumbull County Boxers' Legends of Leather (Man of Yr. award Hall of Fame), William Holmes McGuffey Hist. Soc., Buckeye Elks Lodge (hon.); mem. Kiwanis Internat., Urban League, Alliance C. of C., Southern Community Jaycees (hon.), Soc. for Preservation of Greek Heritage, Greek Am. Progressive Assn., Pan Cretan Assn., Arms Hist. Mus. Soc., Eagles, Moose, The Stambaugh Pillars.

MESHII, MASAHIRO, materials science educator; b. Amagasaki, Japan, Oct. 6, 1931; arrived in US, 1956; s. Masataro and Kazuyo M.; m. Eiko Kumagai, May 21, 1959; children: Alisa, Erica. BS, Osaka (Japan) U., 1954, MS, 1956; PhD, Northwestern U., 1959. Lectr., rsch. assoc. dept. materials sci. and engring. Northwestern U., Evanston, Ill., 1959-60, asst. prof., assoc. prof., then prof., 1960-88, chmn. dept. materials sci. and engring., 1978-82, John Evans prof., 1988—2003, John Evans prof. emeritus, 2003—. Vis. scientist Nat. Rsch. Inst. Metals, Tokyo, 1970-71; NSF faculty rsch. participant Argonne (Ill.) Nat. Lab., 1975; guest prof. Osaka U., 1985; Acta/Scripta Metallurgica lectr., 1993-95. Co-editor: Lattice Defects in Quenched Metals, 1965, Martensitic Transformation, 1978, Science of Advanced Materials, 1990; editor: Fatigue and Microstructures, 1979, Mechanical Properties of BCC Metals, 1982; contbr. over 245 articles to tech. publs. and internat. jours. Recipient Founders award Midwest Soc. Electron Microscopists, 1987, Meritorious award for best paper Iron and Steel Soc., 1993; named Best Tchr. of Yr., Engring. Students of Northwestern U., 1978; Fulbright grantee, 1956; Japan fellow, 1957. Fellow ASM (Henry Marion Howe medal 1968, Best Acad. Paper award 1994), Japan Soc. Promotion of Sci.; mem. AIME, Metallurgical Soc., Japan Inst. Metals (hon., Achievement award 1972). Home: 3051 Centennial Ln Highland Park IL 60035-1017 Office: Northwestern U Dept Materials Sci Eng Evanston IL 60208-3108 Office Phone: 847-491-3213. Business E-Mail: m-meshii@northwestern.edu.

MESHKE, GEORGE LEWIS, drama and humanities educator; b. Yakima, Wash., Oct. 7, 1930; s. George Joseph and Marye Elizabeth (Lopas) M. BA, U. Wash., 1953, MA, 1959, PhD in Drama, 1972. Cert. tchr., Wash. Tchr. English and drama Zillah High Sch., Wash., 1955-58, high sch., Bellevue, Wash., 1958-60, Federal Way, Wash., 1960-70; dir., actor Old Brewery Theatre, Helena, Mont., 1962-66; prof. drama Yakima Valley C.C., Yakima, 1970-2000, part-time instr., 2001—. Casting dir., dir. summer seminar Laughing Horse Summer Theatre, Ellensburg, Wash., 1989-96, Children's Lit. Inst., 2000; adj. prof. grad. studies Ctrl. Wash. U., Tchr. Exch., London, 1995, People-to People Exch., China, 2000, Mongolia, Manchuria, 2001; lectr. Inquiring Mind series Wash. State Humanities, 1989-91; regional dir. Am. Coll. Theatre Festival, Washington, 1980-86; arts dialogue J.F. Kennedy Ctr., Washington, 1987—; casting dir., actor Hollywood Ind. Prodns.; adv. coun. Kennedy Ctr. Author, producer Towers of Tomorrow, 1985, The Halls of Yesterday-Yakima Hist. drama; appeared in Yakima, Washington, 1998. Regional bd. dirs. Common Cause, Yakima, 1971-73; active Nat. Hist. Soc., Nat. Wilderness Soc., Roosevelt Meml. Found., Wash. State Commn. Humanities, Drama League, People to People Tours, Clinton Libr. With U.S. Army, 1953-55, Austria. Recipient Gold medal Kennedy Ctr., 1985, Wash. State Humanities medal, 1983, NISAD medal, 1989, Wash. State Drama award, 1999. Mem. ACLU, VFW, Wash. Edn. Assn., N.W. Drama Assn., Am. Edn. Theatre Assn., Am. Fedn. Tchrs., Kennedy Libr., Amnesty Internat. Carter Libr., Libr. Congress (assoc.), Phi Delta Kappa. Democrat. Avocations: travel, mountain climbing, skiing, reading. Home: 5 N 42nd Ave Yakima WA 98908-3214 Office: Yakima Valley CC 16th And Nob Hill Blvd Yakima WA 98907 Office Phone: 509-574-4839.

MESIA, AUGUSTO FAJARDO, pathologist; b. Naga City, Philippines, June 6, 1956; MD, U. of the East, Philippines, 1981. Diplomate Am. Bd. Pathology, Philippine Bd. Pathology. Internist Armed Forces of the Philippines, Philippines, 1981-82; res. to chief res. anatomic and clin. pathology U. Philippines Gen. Hosp., 1983-87; res. anatomic and clin. pathology SUNY Bklyn., 1991-95; fellowship NYU Med. Ctr., 1995-96; attending pathologist Bellevue Hosp. NYU Med. Ctr., N.Y.C., 1996—. Mem. AMA, Internat. Soc. Gynecologic Pathologists, Internat. Acad. Pathologists, Coll. Am. Pathologists. Office: NYU MC 560 1st Ave New York NY 10016-6402

MESKILL, THOMAS J. federal judge; b. New Britain, Conn., Jan. 30, 1928; s. Thomas J.M. Meskill; m. Mary T. Grady; children: Maureen Meskill Heneghan, John Peter, Eileen Meskill Gallupe, Thomas. BS, Trinity Coll., Hartford, Conn., 1950, LL.D., 1972; JD, U. Conn., 1956; postgrad., Sch. Law, NYU; LL.D., U. Bridgeport, 1971, U. New Haven, 1974. Bar: Conn. 1956, Fla. 1957, D.C. 1957, U.S. Ct. Appeals (2d cir.) 1975, U.S. Supreme Ct. 1971. Former mem. firm Meskill, Dorsey, Sledzik and Walsh, New Britain; mem. 90th-91st Congresses 6th Conn. Dist.; gov. Conn., 1971-75; judge U.S. Ct. Appeals (2d cir.), New Britain, Conn., 1975—, chief judge, 1992-93, sr. judge, 1993—. Pres. New Britain Council Social Agys.; Asst. corp. council City of New Britain, 1960-62, mayor, 1962-64, corp. counsel, 1965-67; mem. Constl. Conv., Hartford, 1965. Served to 1st lt. USAF, 1950-53. Recipient Disting. Svc. award Jr. C. of C., 1964, Jud. Achievement award ATLA, 1983, Learned Hand medal for Excellence in Fed. Juridprudence, Fed. Bar Coun., 1994. Mem. Fla. Bar Assn., Con. Bar Assn. (Henry J. Naruk Jud. award 1994), Hartford County Bar Assn., New Britain Bar Assn., KC. Republican. Office: US Ct Appeals 114 W Main St New Britain CT 06051-4223

MESKILL, VICTOR P. academic administrator, educator; b. Albertson, N.Y., May 9, 1935; s. James Joseph and Ida May (Pfalzer) M.; m. Gail King Heidinger, 1986; children by previous marriage— Susan Ann, Janet Louise, Gary James, Glenn Thomas, Kenneth John, Matthew Adam. BA, Hofstra U., 1961, MA (grad. scholar), 1962; PhD, St. John's U., 1967; postgrad. insts., Ohio State U., 1968; postgrad., Harvard U., 1972, NYU, 1973; DSc (hon.), Samara State Aerospace U., Russia, 1993; LHD (hon.), St. John's U., 1995; DCL (hon.), Moscow Internat. U., Russia, 1996; DCL (hon.), D Ecology/Biosphere (hon.), Coll. Puschino State U., Moscow, 1996; D of Pedagogy (PdD) (hon.), Dowling Coll., 1997; D of Econs. (hon.), U. Istanbul, Turkey, 1997; D of Sci., Yanshan U., Peoples' Republic of China, 1998. Lab. asst., instr. biology Hofstra U., 1960-62; N.Y. State teaching fellow St. John's U., 1962-63; instr. biology Nassau (N.Y.) C.C., 1963-64; tchr. sci. Central H.S. Dist. 2, Floral Park, N.Y., 1963-64; lectr. biology C.W. Post Coll., Greenvale, N.Y., 1963-64, instr. biology, 1964-67, asst. prof., 1967-68, assoc. prof., 1968-74, assoc. dir. Inst. for Student Problems, supr. student tchrs., 1967-68, asst. dean Coll., dean summer sch., coordinator Admissions Office, coordinator adult and continuing edn. programs, 1968-69; dean adminstrn. C.W. Post Ctr. of L.I. U., 1969-70, v.p. adminstrn., 1970-77, prof. biology, 1975-77; pres. Dowling Coll., Oakdale, L.I., 1977-2000, pres. emeritus, 2000—. Cons. in edn. and biology; chem. technician, detective Tech. Rsch. Bur., Nassau County Police Dept., 1958-63, mem. sci. adv. com., 1970; mem. adv. coun. Aerospace Edn. Coun. Inc., 1968; trustee, mem. state legis. com. Commn. Ind. Colls. and Univs.; mem. evaluation teams Mid. States Assn., 1971—; mem. higher edn. adv. com. N.Y. State Senate; mem. Nassau-Suffolk Comprehensive Health Planning Coun.; chmn. Internat. and Mediterranean Studies Group Conf. Contbr. articles to profl. jours. Founding mem., vice-chmn. bd. trustees Nassau Higher Edn. Consortium; bd. dirs. Suffolk County coun. Boy Scouts Am.; mem. N.Y. State Energy Rsch. and Devel. Authority, Town of Islip Devel. Commn.; chmn. bd. trustees L.I. Regional Adv. Coun. Higher Edn.; chmn. L.I. Mid Suffolk Bus. Action; bd. dirs. Southside Hosp., N.Y.; v.p. L.I. Forum for Tech.; former commr. Suffolk County Vanderbilt Mus.; mem. Bus. Coun. N.Y.; hon. mem. U. Pau and Pays de l'Adour, Pau, France, 1994; hon. prof. Minjiang U., Fuzhou, Peoples Republic of China, 1994; active mem. Universal Life Keeping Problems Acad., Dept. Justice Russian Fedn., Moscow. Decorated commendatore dell'Ordine al Merito (Italy); NSF rsch. grantee, 1967-69; Named Tchr. of Year, Aesculapius Med. Arts Soc., C.W. Post Coll. of L.I. U., 1967; Disting. Faculty Mem. of Year, C.W. Post Ctr. L.I. U., 1977, Educator of Yr. WLIW Channel 21, 1996, Officier dans l'ordre des Palmes Académiques, 2001; recipient George M. Estabrook award Hofstra U., 1978, Higher Edn. Leadership award Corning Glass Works, 1987, Disting. Leadership award L.I., 1989, Diploma Merito, Garibaldi Inst., Rome, Diploma of Honor, Rsch. Ctr. for Islamic History, Art and Culture, Istanbul, Turkey, Advancement for Commerce and Industry Disting. Svc. award in field of edn., 1997. Mem. AAAS, Coun. Advancement and Support of Edn., Am. Assn. Collegiate Registrars and Admissions Officers, Am. Assn. Higher Edn., Am. Inst. Biol. Scis., Am. Soc. Zoologists, Am. Assn. U. Adminstrs., Commn. on Ind. Colls. and Univs. (trustee), Nat. Assn. Biology Tchrs., Nat. Sci. Tchrs. Assn., Soc. Protozoologists, N.Y. Acad. Scis., Camilo Josè Cela Found. (hon.), Met. Assn. Coll. and Univ. Biologists (founder, mem. steering com.), Bus. Coun. N.Y., Oakdale C. of C. (founding mem., dir.), Russian Soc. Plant Physiologists (corr.), Universal Life Keeping Problems Acad. Moscow, Tsiolkovski Space Acad. Moscow (fgn.), Univ. Club (N.Y.C.), Wings Club (N.Y.C.), Nat. Arts Club (N.Y.C.), L.I. Coun. Fgn. Rels., L.I. Assn. Commerce and Industry (v.p. edn., dir.), Alpha Chi, Kappa Delta Pi, Phi Delta Kappa, Sigma Xi, Beta Beta Beta, Alpha Eta Rho, Delta Mu Delta, Kappa Delta Rho. E-mail: vpmphd@aol.com.

MESNIAEFF, GREGORY, economist, securities analyst; b. N.Y.C., Jan. 13, 1958; s. Peter G. and Maria A. (Voropajeff) M.; m. Elizabeth Burke, June 18, 1989. BBA Baruch Sch. Bus., CUNY, N.Y.C., 1986; MA in Econs., Trinity Coll., Hartford, 1989. Market rschr. Blair TV, N.Y.C., 1989-90; industry analyst telecomms. Northern Bus. Info./McGraw Hill, N.Y.C., 1990-94; assoc. v.p. equity rsch. Wheat First Butcher & Singer, Richmond, Va., 1994-96; sr. v.p. equity rsch. Robinson-Humphrey Co., Atlanta, 1996—2002; mng. dir. PT Capital LLC, N.Y.C., 2002—. Fellow Trinity Coll. Bd. Fellows, Hartford, 1994-96. Recipient All-Star Analyst Telecom. Equipment Wall St. Jour., 1998. Mem. Nat. Assn. Bus. Econs., N.Y. Soc. of Security Analysts (mem. Investment Strategy Com.) Athletic Club, Russian Nobility Assn. Am., Royal Economic Soc., N.Y. Yacht Club, City Island Yacht Club, N.Y. Athletic Club, Russian Nobilty Assn. Am., Soc. for the Preservation of New England Antiquities. Republican. Russian Orthodox. Avocations: skiing, sailing, bicycling, historic preservation. Home: PO Box 1021 Sharon CT 06069

MESNIKOFF, ALVIN MURRAY, psychiatry educator; b. Asbury Park, N.J., Dec. 25, 1925; s. Nathan and Rachel (Feinberg) M.; m. Wendy Savin, June 15, 1952; children: Nathaniel, Rachel, Joel, Ann. AB, Rutgers U., 1948; postgrad., Yale U., 1948-49, Stanford U., 1949-50; MD, U. Chgo., 1954; cert. Psychoanalytic medicine, Columbia U., 1962. Diplomate: Am. Bd. Psychiatry and Neurology. Pvt. practice, 1958—; collaborating psychoanalyst Columbia U. Psychoanalytic Ctr. for Tng. and Rsch., N.Y.C., 1962—; dir. Washington Heights Cmty., N.Y. State Psychiat. Inst., N.Y.C., 1965—68; assoc. clin. prof. psychiatry Columbia U. Coll. Physicians and Surgeons, 1958—68; prof. psychiatry SUNY, Bklyn., 1968—81; dir. South Beach Psychiat. Ctr., S.I., NY, 1968—75; regional dir. N.Y. State Dept. Mental Health, N.Y.C., 1975—78, dep. commr. rsch., 1978—81; Marion E. Kenworthy prof. Psychiatry Columbia U. Sch. Social Work, 1981—89; lectr. Union Theol. Sem., N.Y.C., 1989—90. Cons. St. Vincent's Hosp., S.I., 1970-76; attending psychiatrist S.I. Hosp., 1972-76; sr. attending psychiatrist St. Luke's/Roosevelt Hosp. Ctr., N.Y., 1987—; cons. Ford Found., N.Y.C., 1980-81 Contbr. chpts. to books, articles to profl. jours. Bd. dirs. Reality House, 1967-74; mem. task force med. sch. enrollment and physician manpower N.Y. State Bd. Regents, 1973-75, mem. task force on gen. and splty. hosp. care N.Y. State Health Planning Commn., 1973-74. Served with U.S. Army, 1943-45. Grantee Ford Found., 1982 Fellow Am. Psychiat. Assn. (life); mem. Am. Psychoanalytic Assn., Assn. Psychoanalytic Medicine, Am. Friends Tel Aviv U. (chmn. 1974-75), Phi Beta Kappa. Jewish. Office: 300 Central Park W New York NY 10025-6541 Office Phone: 212-663-5701.

MESROBIAN, ARPENA SACHAKLIAN, publisher, editor, consultant; b. Boston; d. Aaron H. and Eliza Sachaklian; m. William J. Mesrobian, June 22, 1940 (dec.); children: William S.(dec.), Marian Elizabeth (Mrs. Bruce MacCurdy). Student, Armenian Coll. of Beirut, Lebanon, 1937-38; AA, Univ. Coll., Syracuse (N.Y.) U., 1959, BA magna cum laude, 1971; MSsc, Syracuse U., 1973. Editor Syracuse U. Press, 1955-58, exec. editor, 1958-61, asst. dir., 1961-65, acting dir., 1965-66, editor, 1968-85, assoc. dir., 1968-75, dir., 1975-85, 87-88, dir. emeritus, 1985. Dir. workshop on univ. press. pub. U. Malaysia, Kuala Lumpur, 1985; cons. Empire State Coll. Book rev. editor: Armenian Rev., 1967-75; author: (book) Like One Family: The Armenians of Syracuse, 2000; mem. publs. bd. Courier, 1970-94; mem. adv. bd. Armenian Rev., 1981-83; contbr. numerous articles, revs. to profl. jours. Pres. Syracuse chpt. Armenian Relief Soc., 1972-74; sponsor Armenian Assembly, Washington, 1975; mem. mktg. task force Office of Spl. Edn., Dept. Edn., 1979-84, Adminstrn. of Developmental Disabilities, HHS; mem. publs. panel Nat. Endowment for Humanities, Washington; bd. dirs. Syracuse Girls Club, 1982-87; pres. trustees St. John the Bapt. Armenian Apostolic Ch. and Cmty. Ctr., 1991-95. Named Post-Standard Woman of Achievement, 1980; recipient Chancellor's award for disting. service Syracuse U., 1985; Nat. award U.S. sect. World Edn. Fellowship, 1986; N.Y. State Humanities scholar. Mem. Women in Communications, Soc. Armenian Studies (adminstrv. council 1976-78, 85-87, sec. 1978, 85-87), Syracuse U. Library Assocs. (v.p. 1983-88), Am. Univ. Press Services (dir. 1976-77), Armenian Lit. Soc., Armenian Community Center, Assn. Am. Univ. Presses (v.p. 1976-77), UN Assn. (bd. dirs. 1983-88, v.p. 1985), Phi Kappa Phi, Alpha Sigma Lambda. Mem. Armenian Apostolic Ch. (past trustee). Club: Zonta of Syracuse (pres. 1979-80, 1st v.p. 1985-86, dist. historian Dist. 2 Zonta Internat. 1993-96).

MESSA, CHARLES ANGELO, III, plastic surgeon; b. Phila., Feb. 8, 1963; s. Charles Angelo Jr. and Roberta Elizabeth (Price) M.; m. Linda Mary Schultz, Aug. 13, 1988; children: Charles Angelo IV, William Joseph. BA magna cum laude, LaSalle U., 1985; MD, Pa. State U., 1989. Diplomate Am. Bd. Surgery. Intern U. Mass. Sch. Medicine, 1989-90; resident in surgery U. Mass. Sch. Medicine Ctr., Worcester, 1990-94; resident in plastic and reconstructive surgery U. Pa. Med. Ctr., Phila., 1994-96; surgeon Cosmetic Surgery Ctr., Weston, Fla. Presenter in field. Contbr. articles to profl. jours. Fellow ACS (assoc.), Am. Soc. Laser Med. and Surg.; mem. AMA, Pa. Med. Soc., Fla. Med. Assn., Mass. Med. Soc. Republican. Roman Catholic. Office: Weston Cosmetic Surgery Ctr Ste 1 & 2 17180 Arvida Pkwy Weston FL 33326 E-mail: drmessa@westoncosmeticsurgery.com.

MESSA, JOSEPH LOUIS, JR., lawyer; b. Phila., Mar. 24, 1962; s. Joseph Louis and Virginia (Ciaffoni) M. BS, Tulane U., 1984; JD, Temple U., 1988. Bar: Pa. 1988, N.J. 1988, U.S. Dist. Ct. N.J. 1988, U.S. Dist. Ct. (eastern dist.) Pa. 1998, U.S. Ct. Appeals (3d cir.) 1996. Assoc. Duane Morris & Heckscher, Phila., 1988-90; ptnr. Ominsky & Messa, Phila., 1990-2000, Messa & Assocs., P.C., Phila., 2001—. Ward leader Rep. Party, Phila. 1985—, city com., 1985—, exec. com., 1985—. Mem. ATLA, ABA, Pa. Trial Lawyers (cons., seminar presenter, liability com.), Phila. Trial Lawyers, N.J. Trial Lawyers, Pa. Bar Assn., N.J. Bar Assn., Phila. Bar Assn., Burlington County Bar Assn., Camden County Bar Assn., Million Dollar Advocates Forum. Roman Catholic. Avocations: physical fitness, bodybuilding, waterskiing, boating, travel. Office: Messa & Assoc PC 123 S 22nd St Philadelphia PA 19103 E-mail: jlmessajr@aol.com.

MESSAC, ACHILLE, mechanical engineer, aerospace engineer; b. Haiti; m. Paula Messac. BS, MS, PhD in Aerospace Eng., Mass. Inst. Tech., 1986. Assoc. prof. Rensselaer Polytechnic Inst., Troy, NY, 2000—, Northeastern U., Boston, 1994—2000. Assoc. editor AIAA Jour., Wash., DC, 1999—2002. Recipient CAREER award, NSF, 1997-2002. Office: Rensselaer Polytechnic Inst JEC 2049 110 8th St -- Mech Eng Dept Troy NY 12180

MESSEMER, GLENN MATTHEW, lawyer; b. Hartford, Conn., Jan. 7, 1947; s. Joseph M. and Mary S. Messemer. BSBA, Georgetown U., 1968; JD, U. Conn., 1971. Bar: Conn. 1972. Staff atty. Kaman Corp., Bloomfield, Conn., 1972-74; asst. sec., 1974-79; asst. v.p., 1979-81; v.p., gen. counsel, 1981—. Prof. bus. law Sch. Bus. Adminstrn., U. Hartford (Conn., 1974-80; legal counsel Am. Helicopter Soc.; arbitrator Am. Arbitration Assn., 1978-82. Bd. dirs., trustee, regent U. hartford, 1993—. Served with M.I., U.S. Army, 1969-75. Mem. ABA, Conn. Bar Assn. (founding; exec. com., sec.), Hartford County Bar Assn. Clubs: Hartford Golf, Hartford, Masons. Office: Kaman Corp 1332 Blue Hills Ave Bloomfield CT 06002

MESSENGER, GEORGE CLEMENT, engineering executive, consultant; b. Bellows Falls, Vt., July 20, 1930; s. Clement George and Ethel Mildred (Farrar) M.; m. Priscilla Betty Norris, June 19, 1954; children: Michael Todd, Steven Barry, Bonnie Lynn. BS in Physics, Worcester Poly U., 1951; MSEE, U. Pa., 1957; PhD in Engring., Calif. Coast U., 1986. Rsch. scientist Philco Corp., Phila., 1951-59; engring. mgr. Hughes Semicondr., Newport Beach, Calif., 1959-61; divsn. mgr. Transitron Corp., Wakefield, Mass., 1961-63; staff scientist Northrop Corp., Hawthorne, Calif., 1963-68; cons. engr. Las Vegas, Nev., 1968—. Lectr. UCLA, 1969-75; v.p., dir. Am. Inst. Fin., Grafton, Mass., 1970-78; gen. ptnr. Dargon Fund, Anaheim, Calif., 1983—; v.p., tech. dir. Messenger and Assoc., 1987—, registered investment adviser, 1989—. Co-author: The Effects of Radiation on Electronic Systems, 1986, Single Event Phenomena, 1997; contbg. author: Fundamentals of Nuclear Hardening, 1972, Nonvolatile Semiconductor Memory Technology, 1998; contbr. articles to profl. jours.; patentee microwave diode, hardened semicondrs. Recipient Naval Rsch. Lab. Alan Berman award, 1982, Best Paper award HEART Conf., 1983, Spl. Merit award, 1983, Pete Haas award, 1992, Goddard award for

outstanding profl. achievement Worcester Poly. Inst., 1996. Fellow IEEE (Merit award 1986); mem. Rsch. Soc. Am., Am. Phys. Soc. Congregationalist. Home and Office: 3111 Bel Air Dr Apt 7F Las Vegas NV 89109-1510 E-mail: gpmessenger@cox.net.

MESSENKOPF, EUGENE JOHN, real estate developer and hotel executive; b. N.Y.C., Jan. 26, 1928; s. John Philip and Helen Bessie (Holden) M.; m. Martha Ann Crane, Jan. 29, 1955; children: Diane, Nancy, Eugene John, Susan. BBA, Iona Coll., 1950; MBA, NYU, 1956. CPA, N.Y. Sec.-treas. KLM Process Co., N.Y.C., 1952-54; acct. Am. Tobacco Co., N.Y.C., 1954-56; staff acct. Peat, Marwick & Mitchell, N.Y.C., 1956-60; exec. v.p. Donaldson, Lufkin & Jenrette, Inc., N.Y.C., 1960-84, pres., chief exec. officer real estate div., 1977-84; pres., chief exec. officer Meridian Investing and Devel. Corp., 1977-84; pvt. practice cons., 1984—. Mem. adv. bd. NYU Real Estate Inst., 1981-85; mem. exec. coun. small scale devel. Urban Land Inst., 1983-90; chmn. Wall St. Tax Com., N.Y.C., 1965-68; bd. dirs. SIA Acctg. Div., N.Y.C., 1965-79. Trustee, chmn. fin. com. Mt. Vernon Hosp., 1982-87. Served as sgt. AUS, 1950-52, Korea. Recipient Brother Loftus award Iona Coll., 1976. Mem. AICPA, N.Y. State Soc. CPAs, Fin. Execs. Inst. Republican. Roman Catholic. Achievements include walking 2000 mile Appalachian Trail, 1987.

MESSER, DONALD EDWARD, theological school president, theology educator; b. Kimball, SD, Mar. 5, 1941; s. George Marcus and Grace E. (Foltz) M.; m. Bonnie Jeanne Nagel, Aug. 30, 1964; children: Christine Marie, Kent Donald. BA cum laude, Dakota Wesleyan U., 1963, LHD (hon.), 1977; MDiv magna cum laude, Boston U., 1966, PhD, 1969. Asst. to commr. Mass. Commn. Against Discrimination, Boston, 1968-69; asst. prof. Augustana Coll., Sioux Falls, SD, 1969-71; assoc. pastor 1st United Meth. Ch., Sioux Falls, 1969-71; pres. Dakota Wesleyan U., Mitchell, SD, 1971-81, Iliff Sch. Theology, Denver, 1981-2000, pres. emeritus and prof. practical theology, 2000—. Author: Christian Ethics and Political Action, 1984, Contemporary Images of Christian Ministry, 1989, Send Me? The Intinerancy in Crisis, 1991, The Conspiracy of Goodness, 1992, Caught in the Crossfire: Helping Christians Debate Homosexuality, 1994, Calling Church and Seminary Into the 21st Century, 1995, Unity, Liberty, and Charity: Building Bridges Under Icy Waters, 1996, How Shall We Die? Helping Christians Debate Assisted Suicide, 1997, The Befuddled Stork: Helping Persons of Faith Debate Beginning of life Issues, 2000, Breaking the Conspiracy of Silence: Christian Churches and the Global AIDS Crisis, 2004; contbr. articles to Face to Face, The Christian Century, The Christian Ministry. Active Edn. Commn. of U.S., 1973-79; co-chmn. Citizens Commn. Corrections, 1975-76; vice chmn. SD Commn. on Humanities, 1979-81. Dempster fellow, 1967-68; Rockefeller fellow, 1968-69. Mem. Soc. Christian Ethics, Am. Acad. Religion, Assn. United Meth. Theol. Schs. (v.p. 1986-91, pres. 1991-92). Democrat. Office: Iliff Sch Theology 2201 S University Blvd Denver CO 80210-4798

MESSER, THOMAS MARIA, museum director; b. Bratislava, Czechoslovakia, Feb. 9, 1920; came to U.S., 1939, naturalized, 1944; s. Richard and Agatha (Albrecht) M.; m. Remedios García Villa, Jan. 10, 1948. Exch. student, Inst. Internat. Edn., 1939; student, Thiel Coll., Greenville, Pa., 1939-41; BA, Boston U., 1942; degree, U. Sorbonne, Paris, 1947; MA, Harvard U., 1951; DFA (hon.), U. Mass., 1962, U. of Arts, Phila., 1988. Dir. Roswell (N.Mex.) Mus., 1949-52, Am. Fedn. Arts, N.Y.C., 1952-56; hon. prof. Johann Wolfgang Goethe U., Frankfurt, 1997—. Dir. Inst. Contemporary Art, Boston, 1957-61, Solomon R. Guggenheim Mus., N.Y.C., 1961-88, Peggy Guggenheim Collection, Venice, Italy, 1980-88, Solomon R. Guggenheim Found., N.Y.C., trustee, 1980-90, dir. emeritus, 1990—; chief curator Schirn Kunsthalle, Frankfurt, 1994-99; adj. prof. Harvard U., 1960, Barnard Coll., 1966, 71; prof. Hochschule für Angewandte Kunst, Vienna, Austria, 1984; pres. Assn. Art Mus. Dirs., 1974-75, hon. mem., 1988—; pres. Icom's internat. com. Modern Art Mus., 1976-80, hon. mem., 2000—; trustee Inst. Internat. Edn., 1990-98, hon. mem., 1998—; founding mem. Am. Arts Alliance, Washington, 1978-81; pres. The MacDowell Colony Inc., 1977-78; mem. adv. bd. Palazzo Grassi, Venice, 1986-97; trustee Fontana Found., Milan, 1996—2003, The Isamu Noguchi Found., N.Y.C. & Tokyo, 1988—; sr. cultural advisor, trustee Am.'s Soc., 1988—; sr. advisor visual arts Caixa Found., 1991-96; adv. com. Nat. Gallery, Czech Republic, 1994-99. Author: Edvard Munch, 1973, Vasily Kandinsky, 1997; contbr. to mus. catalogues, art jours. Decorated chevalier Legion d'Honneur, France, 1980, Officier Legion d'Honneur, France, 1989; recipient Goethe medal Fed. Republic Germany; spl. fellow for study in Brussels Belgian-Am. Ednl. Found., 1953; sr. fellow Ctr. Advanced Studies, Wesleyan U., 1966. Mem. Internat. com. for Mus. and Collections Modern Art, Century Assn. (N.Y.C.). Home: 35 Sutton Pl New York NY 10022-2464 E-mail: tmmesser@aol.com.

MESSERLE, JUDITH ROSE, medical librarian, public relations director; b. Litchfield, Ill., Jan. 16, 1943; d. Richard Douglas and Nelrose B. Wilcox; m. Darrell Wayne Messerle, Apr. 26, 1968; children: Kurt Norman, Katherine Lynn. BA in Zoology, So. Ill. U., 1966; MLS, U. Ill., 1967. Cert. med. libr. Libr. St. Joseph's Sch. Nursing, Alton, Ill., 1967-71, dir. med. info. ctr., 1971-76, dir. info. svcs., 1976-79; dir. ednl. resources and cmty. rels. St. Joseph's Hosp., 1979-84; dir. Med. Ctr. Libr. St. Louis U., 1985-88; libr. Francis A. Countway Libr. Harvard Med. Sch. and Boston Med. Libr., 1989—. Cons., 1973—; instr. Lewis and Clark Coll., 1975. Med. Libr. Assn. Bd. dirs. Family Svcs. and Vis. Nurses Assn., Alton, 1976-79. Fellow AAAS, Med. Libr. Assn. (search com. for exec. dir. 1979, dir. 1981-84, pres. 1986-87, legis. task force 1986-90, task force for knowledge and skills 1988-92, nominating com. 1996); mem. OCLC (spl. libr. adv. com. 1994-98), AMA (com. on allied health edn. and accreditation 1991-94), Assn. Acad. Health Sci. Libr. Dirs. (editl. bd. for ann. stats. 1989-94, Region 8 adv. bd. 1992-93, joint legis. task force 1992—, pres. 1993, charting the future task force 2001-03, scholarly communication task force 2003-), Am. Med. Informatics Assn. (planning com. 1990, publs. com. 1994-96, ann. mtg. com. 1996-98), Ill. State Libr. Adv. Com., Midwest Health Sci. Libr. Network (divsn. health sci. coun.), St. Louis Med. Librs., Hosp. Pub. Rels. Soc. St. Louis, Nat. Libr. Medicine (biomed. libr. rev. com. 1988-92). Office: Countway Libr Medicine 10 Shattuck St Boston MA 02115-6011

MESSERLE, KENNETH C. state senator; b. Coos Bay, Oreg., May 8, 1940; m. Lola Messerle; children: Anthony, Blaine, Molly. BS, Oreg. State U., 1962. Owner, mgr. Messerle and Sons, Cattle and Timber, 1962-96; dir. Security Bank Holding Co., 1992—, Lincoln Security Bank, 1997—; Rep. rep. dist. 48 Oreg. Ho. of Reps., 1996-2000; Rep. senator dist. 24 Oreg. State Senate, 2000—. Mem. full ways and means com. Oreg. Ho. of Reps., mem. Pacific fisheries legis. task force, 1997—, natural resources ways and means subcom., 1999, interim task force on children and families, gen. govt. ways and means subcom., 1999, environ. and land use transp. task force, 1999—, co-chair salmon recovery and stream restoration. Chmn. Port of Bandon Relending Corp.; commr. Port of Bandon; dir. Coquille Sch. Bd.; mem. Coos County Water Resources Com.; dir. Coos Soil and Water Dist. Mem. Oreg. Coastal Zone Mgmt. Assn. Roman Catholic. Office: 94271 Coos Sumner Ln Coos Bay OR 97420 also: Oreg State Senate H-381 State Capitol Salem OR 97310 Fax: 541 269-2510; 503 986-1336. E-mail: repMessLola@harborside.com., messerle.rep@state.or.us.

MESSERLI, DOUGLAS, writer, publisher; b. Waterloo, Iowa, May 30, 1947; s. John H. and Lorna (Caspers) M.; companion Howard N. Fox. BA in English, U. Md., 1972, MA in English, 1974, PhD in English, 1979. Admissions coord. U. Wis., Madison, 1967-69; asst. head protocol Columbia U., N.Y.C., 1969-70; grad. asst., tchr., coord. interns U. Md., 1973-77; pub. Sun & Moon Press, L.A., 1976—2003; prof. dept. English Temple U., Phila., 1979-84; dir. The Contemporary Arts Ednl. Project, Inc., 1983—; pub. Green Integer, 1998—. Part-time faculty mem. Calif. Inst. Tech., Pasadena, 1987-89, Otis Coll. Art and Sesign, L.A., 1989-2004; pub. Green Integer, 1998—. Author: (poetry) Dinner on the Lawn, 1979, Some Distance, 1982, River to Rivet: A Manifesto, 1985, River to Rivet: A Poetic Trilogy, 1985, Maxims from My Mother's Milk/Hymns to Him: A Dialogue, 1988, An Apple, A Day, 1993, After, 1998, primerias palavras, 1999, (drama) Silence All Round Marked: An Historical Play in Hysteria Writ, 1992, (as Kier Peters) The Confirmation, 1993, also A Dog Tries to Kiss the Sky: Six Short Plays, 2003, (fiction/film/poetry) Along Without: A Fiction in Film for Poetry, 1993, The Walls Come True: An Opera for Spoken Voices, 1996, (fiction as Joshua Haigh) Letters from Hanusse, 2000, (poetry) Primeiras palavras, 1999, (poetry) Bow Down, 2002, (poetry) First Words, 2004; editor: From the Other Side of the Century: A New American Poetry 1960-1990, 1994, The Sun & Moon Guide to Eating Through Literature and Art, 1994, 50: A Celebration of Sun & Moon Classics, 1995, From the Other Side of the Century II: A New American Drama 1960-95, 1998, The PIP Anthology of World Poetry of the 20th Century. Decorated chevalier des Arts et Lettres (France); recipient Carey-Thomas award Pubs. Weekly, 1987, Harry Ford Editor's award, 1994, Am. Book award, 1998; Found. for Contemporary Performance Arts grantee, 2002. Mem. MLA, Am. Booksellers Assn. Office: Green Integer 6022 Wilshire Blvd Los Angeles CA 90036-3607 E-mail: lilycat@sbcglobal.net.

MESSERSCHMIDT, WILLIAM HARCLERODE, retired army noncommissioned officer, musician; b. Lebanon, Pa., Apr. 30, 1947; s. Harry Edgar and Sylva (Harclerode) M.; m. Janice Andersen, Dec. 28, 1971; children: William F., Ann K., Dorothy R., Edward D. MusB with distinction, Eastman Sch. Music, 1969; postgrad., Cath. U. Am., 1983, Va. Theol. Sem., 1992-96. Enlisted man U.S. Army, 1969, advanced through grades to sgt. maj., 1994; percussionist U.S. Army Field Band, Ft. George G. Meade, Md., 1969-74, U.S. Army Band (Pershing's Own), Ft. Myer, Va., 1974-85, asst. sect. leader, 1985-89, leader percussion sect., 1989-94, leader percussion group, 1994—2002; ret., 2002. Pvt. tchr. percussion, Springfield and Woodbridge, Va., 1975—; adj. instr. percussion No. Va. C.C., Woodbridge, 1983—; percussionist Prince William Symphony Orch., Lake Ridge, Va., 1989-93, The Fifes and Drums of Prince William, III, Woodbridge, 2003—; timpanist, percussionist orchs. with Nt. Christian Choir, Gaithersburg, Md., 1990—. Choir dir. Grace Ref. Presbyn. Ch., Woodbridge, 1985-93. Mem. Percussive Arts Soc., Am. Fedn. Musicians, Smithsonian Assocs., Kappa Delta Pi. Avocations: reading literature, philosophy and art history, tennis, German. Home: 5400 Staples Ln Woodbridge VA 22193-3562

MESSICK, EDWARD BURTON, elementary school educator, secondary school educator; b. Millsboro, Del., June 19, 1943; s. Clifford Uyle and Dorothy (Wisteria) Messick; m. Barbara Tanner, Nov. 22, 1975. BSc, U. of Del., 1976—79; MSc, McDaniel Coll., 1997—98. Math tchr. Sussex Ctrl. Mid. Sch., Millsboro, Del., 1979—2001, Garrett Mid. Sch., Boulder, Nev., 2001—03, Gt. Falls Pub. Sch., Mont., 2003—. Mem./adv. Kiwanis Club, 1996—2000; co-sponsor Key Club (Kiwanis). E-4 U.S. Army, 1965—71. Mem.: Math. Assn. of Am., Nat. Coun. Teachers of Math., Nat. Edn. Assn., Am. Legion. Meth. Avocations: jogging, scuba diving, travel, reading, skiing. Home: 1210 5t St So Great Falls MT 59405 Office: Gt Falls Pub Schools 1900 2nd Ave So Great Falls MT 59405

MESSIER, IRENE M. state legislator; b. Manchester, N.H., May 9, 1923; m. Armand Messier; 3 children. Student, N.H. Sch. Acctg. and Fin. Mem. from dist. 50 N.H. State Ho. of Reps., mem. environ. and agr. com. Del. Constnl. Conv., 1984; mem. Manchester Rep. City Com., ward 10 Rep. chmn. and ballot inspector; mem. Hillsborough County Exec. Com.; mem. Mayor's Liaison Commn.; active ARC. Mem. LWV, Manchester Cmty. Concerts Assn. (bd. dirs., officer), Greater Manchester Rep. Women's Club. Home: 40 New Gate Cir Manchester NH 03102-5147 Office: NH State Senate State Capital Concord NH 03301

MESSIER, MARK DOUGLAS, professional hockey player; b. Edmonton, Alta., Can., Jan. 18, 1961; With Indpls. Racers, 1978, Cin. Stingers, 1979, Edmonton Oilers, Canada, 1979—91, team capt., 1988—91; with N.Y. Rangers, 1991—97; center Vancouver Canucks, Vancouver, 1997—2000; with NY Rangers, NY, 2000—. Player NHL All-Star Game, 1982—84, 1986, 1988—92, 1994, Stanley Cup Championship Game, 1984, 85, 87, 88, 90, 94. Named NHL Player of Yr., 1989, 1990, 1991—92; named to Sporting News All-Star Team, 1981—82, 1982—83, 1989—90, 1991—92; recipient Conn Smythe Trophy, 1984, Lester B. Pearson award, 1989—90, 1991—92, Hart Trophy, 1990, 1992. Office: New York Rangers 2 Penn Plaza New York NY 10121

MESSIER, MICHAEL C. television director, actor, writer; b. Arlington, Va., Dec. 5, 1973; s. Maurice and Phyllis Clark Messier. BA, RI Coll., Providence, 1998. Direct sales Trinity Rep. Co., 1998—2003; actor Murder on Us Dinner Theatre, 2001—02; TV show prodr. & host The Mike Messier Show, Providence, 2002—. HBO reality show semi-finalist "Candidate 2012", Los Angeles, Calif., 2002; actor, dir. Daydream Theatre, RI, 2003—. Site mgr. RI Children's Crusade, 1999. Independent. Christian. Avocations: chess, reading, films, theater, acting. E-mail: messierfilm@yahoo.com.

MESSIER, PIERRE, lawyer, manufacturing executive; b. Montreal, Que., Can., Mar. 3, 1945; s. Lionel and Anita (Caron) M.; m. Ginette Piche, July 11, 1970; 1 child, Mathieu. BA, Coll. St. Viateur, Outremont, Que., 1964; Lic. in Law, U. Montreal, 1968; diploma in adminstrv. scis., Ecole Hautes Etudes Commerciales, Montreal, 1973. Bar: Que. 1969. Assoc. Lemay & Messier, Montreal, 1969-75; v.p., sec. gen. counsel Can. Cement Lafarge, Ltd., Montreal, 1975-84; v.p., sec. Lafarge Corp., 1983-84; v.p. bus. devel., legal affairs Norsk Hydro Can. Inc., Montreal, 1989-98; lawyer Leduc LeBlanc, Montreal, 1998-2000; pvt. practice, cons., 2000—02, 2003—; sr. legal counsel Bombardier, Inc., Montreal, 2002—03. V.p. Que. Bar Svc. Corp. Pres. Centre Pedagogique Lucien-Guilbault Inc.; v.p. Coll. Jean de Brebeuf, 1991-97; pres. Greenfield Park Bd. Revision, 1973-74; bd. dirs. Societe Progres Rive Sud, Longueuil, Que., 1974-75. Mem. Can. Bar Assn. (pres. young lawyers sect. 1976, nat. exec. 1977-78), Montreal Jr. Bar (treas. 1972), Que. Mfrs. and Exporters Alliance (bd. dirs. 1996-98), St. Denis Club (Montreal), Que. Secs. and Gen. Counsel Assn. (sec. 1998). E-mail: pichemessier@sympatico.ca., pierre.messier@nftc.com., pierre.messier@L-3com.com.

MESSIN, MARLENE ANN, plastics company executive; b. St. Paul, Oct. 6, 1935; d. Edgar Leander and Luella Johanna (Rahn) Johnson; m. Eugene Carlson (div. 1972); children: Rick, Debora, Ronald, Lori; m. Willard Smith (dec. 1975); m. Frank Messin, Sept. 24, 1982; 5 stepchildren. Bookkeeper Jeans Implement Co., Forest Lake, Minn., 1952-53, 1953—57, Great Plains Supply, St. Paul, 1960-62, Plastic Products Co., Inc., Lindstrom, Minn., 1962-75, pres., 1975—; co-owner, treas. Gustaf's Fine Gifts, Lindstrom, 1985—. Bookkeeper Trinity Luth. Ch., Lindstrom, 1976-81. Recipient award, Diversity 2000/Woman-Owned Bus. in Minn. Mem. Soc. Plastic Engrs., Swedish Inst., Soc. Plastic Industry, Minn. State Hist. Soc., Chgo. County Hist. Soc. Home: 28968 Olinda Trl Lindstrom MN 55045-9429 Office: 30355 Akerson St Lindstrom MN 55045-9456

MESSINA, BONNIE LYNN, lawyer; b. Lima, Ohio, Mar. 17, 1961; m. Dominick Messina. BA, We. Md. Coll., 1983; JD magna cum laude, U. Balt., 1991. Bar: Md. 1991. Claim adjuster The Hartford, Hunt Valley, Md., 1983-86, claim supr., 1986-88; assoc. Venable, Baetjer & Howard, Balt., 1991-94; sr. counsel U.S. Fidelity & Guaranty Co., Balt., 1994-98, St. Paul Fire & Marine Ins. Co., Balt., 1999, group claims counsel, 1999—. Assoc. editor U. Balt. Law Rev., 1990-91. Mem. jud. selection com. Women's Law Ctr., Balt., 1993-2000; mentor U. Balt. Sch. of law, Balt., 1993-97. Recipient Am. Jurisprudence award Balt., 1989, 90 (2). Mem. ABA, Md. State Bar Assn., Balt. County Bar Assn., Md. Assn. Def. Trial Counsel, Def. Rsch. Inst., Inc. Office: St Paul Fire & Marine Ins Co Ins Co 5801 Smith Ave Baltimore MD 21209-3652

MESSINA, DANIEL S. insurance company executive; CFO Aetna, Inc., Hartford, Conn.; now pres., COO, Magellan Health Svcs., Inc., Columbia, Md. Office: Magellan Health Svcs Inc 6950 Columbia Gateway Dr Columbia MD 21046

MESSINA, LOUIS MICHAEL, vascular surgeon, educator; b. Bklyn., July 27, 1951; s. John Louis and Elizabeth Ann (Ross) M.; m. Katie Ragland, June 17, 1978; children: Julia Antoinette, Peter Louis, Katharine Elizabeth. BA, Fordham U., 1973; MD summa cum laude, SUNY Downstate Med. Ctr., Bklyn., 1978. Diplomate Nat. Bd. Med. Examiners, Am. Bd. Surgery with subspecialty in vascular surgery, Am. Bd. Critical Care. Intern U. Calif., San Francisco, 1978-79, resident, 1980-85, postdoctoral fellow, 1981-83, vascular surgery fellow, 1985-86, instr. dept. surgery, 1985-86, prof., 1995—, chief vascular surgery, 1995—; asst. prof. U. Mich., Ann Arbor, 1986-93, assoc. prof., 1993-95. Vis. prof. Pacific Vascular Rsch. Found.; E.J. Wylie Endowed chair in vascular surgery, vice chair dept. surgery; physician dir. UCSF Heart and Vascular Ctr. Engel scholar, 1975. Roman Catholic. Achievements include research on regeneration of microcirculation, gene therapy for limb ischemia. Office: U Calif San Francisco # A581 400 Parnassus Ave San Francisco CA 94122-0222 Office Phone: 415-353-4366. Business E-Mail: messina@surgery.ucsf.edu.

MESSINA, PAUL FRANCIS, education consultant; b. Newport, R.I., Aug. 31, 1962; s. Nunzio Francis and Ilse Ingeborg (Maibaum) M. BS, SUNY, Albany, 1988; MS, Tex. A&M, Texarkana, 1992. Cert. tchr., Tex., La. Instr. math and physics St. Mary's High Sch., Natcitoches, La., 1989-91, Liberty-Eylau High Sch., Texarkana, Tex., 1991-93, chm. dept. sci., 1992-93; preventive medicine officer U.S. Army, 1993-98; edn. cons. Hewlett-Packard Co., Irving, Tex., 1998—. Adj. instr. physics Northwestern State U., Natchitoches, 1989-91; adj. instr. math. Texarkana Coll., 1991-93; mem. Merrill Pub. Physics Adv. Coun., 1990-93; adj. instr. physics Ga. Mil. Coll., 1993-95. With U.S. Army, 1988-89, USAR. Tandy Tech. scholar Tandy Corp., 1992; grantee Eisenhower mini-grant, Liberty-Eylau Ind. Sch. Dist., Texarkana, 1992. Mem. NEA, Tex. State Tchrs. Assn. (bldg. rep.), Am. Assn. Physics Tchrs., Tex. Acad. Sci., Sci. Tchrs. Assn. Tex., Cen. La. Astronomy Soc., U.S. Profl. Tennis Registry, Nat. Tennis Acad. Roman Catholic. Avocations: tennis, computing, music. Office: U Tex San Antonio 6900 N Loop 1604 W San Antonio TX 78249 Home: 117 1st St Boerne TX 78006-2910

MESSING, DEBRA, actress; b. Bklyn., Aug. 15, 1968; m. Daniel Zelman; 1 child. Actor: (films) Walk in the Clouds, 1995, McHale's Navy, 1997, Prey, 1997, Celebrity, 1998, Mothman Prophecies, 2002, Hollywood Ending, 2002, Along Came Polly, 2004; (TV series) Ned and Stacey, 1995, Prey, 1998, Will & Grace, 1998— (Emmy award best actress in a comedy, 2003), numerous TV guest appearances, including Seinfeld, Partners, NYPD Blue. Office: c/o Gersh Agy 232 N Canon Dr Beverly Hills CA 90210

MESSING, EDWARD M. urologic surgeon; b. Bklyn., Feb. 5, 1947; s. Mortimer M. and Sylvia Anne (Eisenberg) M.; m. Susan P. Gitlin, Aug. 18, 1968; children: Ross B., James Adam. AB in Biology, U. Chgo., 1968; MD, NYU, 1972. Resident NYU-Bellevue Hosp., N.Y.C., 1972-74, Stanford (Calif.) U., 1974-78; from asst. prof. to prof. urology & oncology U. Wis., Madison, 1982-95; prof., chair dept. urology U. Rochester (N.Y.), 1995—. Interim dir. cancer ctr. U. Rochester, 1996—; co-chair genitourinary com. Ea. Coop. Oncology Group, 1987—. With USPHS, 1978-80. Tumor Biology & Immunology fellow UCLA Sch. Medicine, L.A., 1980-82. Fellow Am. Coll. Surgeons; mem. Wis. Urological Soc. (pres. 1991-92). Achievements include demonstration that screening for bladder cancer with chemical reagent strips is feasible, cost effective and saves lives; elucidated role of epidermal growth factor in the development of bladder cancer; demonstrated that early hormonal therapy of prostate cancer prolonged life compared with delayed therapy. Office: U Rochester 601 Elmwood Ave # 656 Rochester NY 14642-0001

MESSING, JOACHIM WILHELM, molecular biology educator; b. Duisburg, Germany, Sept. 10, 1946; came to U.S., 1978; s. Heinrich and Martha (Pfeifer) M.; m. Rita C. Stremmer, Sept. 25, 1975; 1 child, Simon. MS, Free U., Berlin, 1971; Dr.Rer.Nat., LM U., Munich, 1975. Rsch. assoc. U. Calif., Davis, 1978-80; asst. prof. biochemistry U. Minn., St. Paul, 1980-82, assoc. prof., 1982-84, prof., 1984-85; univ. prof. molecular biology Waksman Inst. Rutgers U., Piscataway, N.J., 1985—, dir. rsch. Waksman Inst., 1985-88, dir. Waksman Inst., 1988—. Mem. sci. adv. bd. Am. Cyanamid Co., Princeton, N.J., 1985-89, Metrigen, Inc., Piscataway, 1988-90; bd. dirs. Pharmacia Biotech., Inc., Piscataway. Co-author: An Introduction to Recombinant DNA Techniques: Basic Experiments in Gene Manipulation, 1988; co-editor: Molecular Biology of Plants: A Laboratory Course Manual, 1985; contbr. articles to profl. jours. Trustee Rutgers Preparatory Sch., Somerset, N.J., 1992—. Ranked first among sci. leaders of the decade as most cited U.S. scientist under 45 yrs. old The Scientist, 1990. Mem. AAAS, Am. Soc. Biol. Chemistry, Am. Soc. Microbiology, Internat. Soc. Plant Molecular Biology. Achievements include development of DNA purification techniques using genetic rather than physical methods; analysis of gene structure and organization, transposition and somatic recombination on the DNA sequence level in plants; discovery of high methionine maize; research on post-transcriptional regulation of gene expression and genomic imprinting. Office: Rutgers U Waksman Inst 190 Frelinghuysen Rd Piscataway NJ 08854-8020

MESSING, KAREN, occupational health researcher; b. Springfield, Mass., Feb. 2, 1943; BA, Harvard U., 1963; MSc, McGill U., 1970, PhD in Biology, 1975. Rsch. asst. biochemistry Jewish Gen. Hosp., Montreal, Can., 1970-71; NIH fellow genetics Boyce Thompson Inst. Plant Rsch., 1975-76; prof. ergonomics U. Quebec, Montreal, 1976—, dir. Ctr. Study Biol. Interactions & Environ. Health, 1990—95, 2000—03, dir. grad. ergonomics program, 1999-2000. Disting. fellow Que. Coun. for Social Rsch., 1995-97, Can. Inst. Health Rsch., 2001—; invited rschr. Inst. Cancer Montreal, 1983-95, Sweden Nat. Inst. Working Life, 1997-98; mem. bd. dirs. Quebec Sci. & Tech. Mus., 1984-86, Quebec Coun. Social Affairs, 1984-90. Author: One-Eyed Science: Occupational Health and Working Women, 1998, Integrating Gender in Ergonomic Analysis, 1999; editor: Women and Health, Policy and Practice in Health and Safety, Internat. Jour. Health Svcs., Recherches Feministes Salud y Trabajo, Policy and Practice in Health and Safety; co-editor: Women's Health at Work, 1998. Mem. Am. Pub. Health Assn., Assn. Can. Ergonomists. Office: Univ Que at Montreal CP 8888 succursale Centre-ville Montreal QC Canada H3C 3P8 E-mail: messing.karen@uqam.ca.

MESSING, SARA VIRGINIA DRICK, lawyer; b. Williamsport, Pa., June 8, 1941; d. Jacob Ralph and Sara Belva (Bitting) Drick; m. Aaron I. Messing, Oct. 30, 1966; children: Benjamin, Jacob. BA, Ohio Wesleyan U., 1963; LLB, Albany Law Sch., 1966. Bar: N.J. 1967, U.S. Ct. Appeals (3d cir.) 1967, U.S. Supreme Ct. 1975; cert. civil trial atty., N.J. Sr. trial atty. Doreen M. Ryan, Esquire, Cranford, NJ, 1966—. Charter mem. Garden State Theatre Organ Soc., Inc., 1973—. Mem. Morris County Bar Assn., Order of Ea. Star, Alpha Xi Delta. Home: 37 Birch St West Orange NJ 07052-4533 Office: Law Offices of Doreen M Ryan 65 Jackson Dr Cranford NJ 07016-3516 Personal E-mail: nghy@msn.com. Business E-Mail: vmess@allstate.com.

MESSINGER, DONALD HATHAWAY, lawyer; b. Lyons, N.Y., July 1, 1943; s. Donald H. and Thelma (Hubbard) M.; m. Sara L. Stock, June 3, 1967; children— Michael David, Robert Stephen, Daniel Mark BA, Colgate U., 1965; JD, Duke U., 1968. Bar: Ohio 1968. Assoc. Thompson Hine LLP, Cleve., 1968-76, ptnr., 1976—, vice chair corp. practice group, 1989-92, ptnr.-in-charge Cleve. office, 1991-96, mem. exec. com., 1996-2000. Sec., bd. dirs. Am. Steel and Wire Corp., 1986-93; bd. dirs. Cedar Fair Mgmt. Co., 1993-2002. Trustee Community Info.-Vol. Action Ctr., 1981-88, pres. 1981-84; trustee Free Med. Clinic Greater Cleve., 1970—, sec., 1970-82, v.p. 1982-86, 96-2002, pres. 2002-; trustee Cleve. Hearing and Speech Ctr., 1980—, v.p. 1984-86, 92-93, pres., 1986-88, 98-2000; trustee U. for Young Ams., 1982-95, sec., 1982-86, pres., 1986-88, chmn. 1991-95; mem. exec. bd. Boy Scouts Am., 1983-88; Leadership Cleve., 1984—; trustee, sec. Bus. Vols. Unltd., 1992—; sec. Buckeye Area Devel. Corp., 1970-90; mem. adv. bd. Greater Cleve. New Stadium. Recipient Community Svc. award Fedn. for Community Planning, 1981-82; named one of Outstanding Young Citizens of Greater Cleve., 1971-75. Mem. ABA, Ohio Bar Assn., Cleve. Bar Assn. (trustee 1975-79, chmn. securities law inst. 1983), Nat. Assn. Bond Lawyers Home: 21550 Shelburne Rd Shaker Heights OH 44122

MESSINGER, SHELDON L(EOPOLD), law educator; b. Chgo., Aug. 26, 1925; s. Leopold J. and Cornelia (Eichel) M.; m. Mildred Handler, June 30, 1947; children— Adam J., Eli B. PhD in Sociology, UCLA, 1969. Assoc. rsch. sociologist Ctr. Study Law and Soc. U. Calif., Berkeley, 1961-69, rsch. sociologist, 1969-70, prof. criminology, 1970-77, prof. law jurisprudence and social policy program, 1977-88, Elizabeth J. Boalt prof. law, 1988-91, prof.

law emeritus, 1991—, prof. grad. sch., 1995-97, vice chmn., 1961-69, acting dean criminology, 1970-71, dean criminology, 1971-75, chmn. program, 1983-87. Author, co-author numerous books, articles. Mem. Coun. U. Calif. Emeriti Assns. (chair-elect 1999-2000, chair 2000-01). Home: 860 Indian Rock Ave Berkeley CA 94707 2051 Office: U Calif Sch Law Boalt Hall Berkeley CA 94720 E-mail: slm@uclink.berkeley.edu.

MESSITTE, PETER JO, judge; b. Washington, July 17, 1941; s. Jesse B. and Edith (Wechsler) M.; m. Susan P. Messitte, Sept. 5, 1965: children: Zachariah, Abigail. BA cum laude, Amherst Coll., 1963; JD, U. Chgo., 1966. Bar: Md. 1969, DC 1969, U.S. Ct. Appeals (4th cir.) 1977, U.S. Supreme Ct. 1973, U.S. Ct. Appeals (DC cir.) 1982, U.S. Ct. Appeals (5th cir.) 1983. Assoc. Zuckert, Scoutt & Rasenberger, Washington, 1968-71; solo practice Chevy Chase, Md., 1971-75; mem. Messitte & Rosenberg, P.A., Chevy Chase, 1975-81; prin. Peter J. Messitte, P.A., Chevy Chase, 1981-85; assoc. judge Cir. Ct. for Montgomery County Rockville, Md., 1985-93; judge U.S. Dist. Ct. Md., Greenbelt, 1993—. Mem. Internat. Jud. Rels. Com. Jud. Conf. U.S., 1997-2003. Bd. dirs. Cmty. Psychiat. Clinic, Montgomery County, Md., 1974-85, v.p. 1980-85; Peace Corps vol., Sao Paulo, Brazil, 1966-68; Md. del. Dem. Nat. Conv., N.Y.C., 1980. Recipient tchg. citations Fed. Deposit Ins. Corp. Bank Exam. Sch., 1975, 79, Am. Inst. Banking, 1978, Elizabeth Scull award for Outstanding Svc. to Montgomery County, Md., 1993, Spl. citation Divorce Roundtable Montgomery County, 1993, Gran Cruz da Ordem São José Operário-Brazilian Labor Tribunal, Mato Grosso, 2001, Medalha de Mérito Académico, Academia Paulista de Magistrados, 2002, Contbr. Mental Health Cmty. Psychiat. Clinic, 1986, Leadership in Law award, Md. Daily Record, 2002. Fellow: Md. Bar Found. (H. Vernon Eney award for contbn. to adminstrn. of justice 2001); mem.: ABA, Jud. Inst. Md. (bd. dirs. 1989—93), Charles Fahy Inn of Ct. (master 1987 88), Fed. Judges Assn. (4th jud. cir.), Am. Law Inst., Montgomery County Bar Assn. (Century of Svc. award 1999), Instituto Paulista de Advogados (hon.), Md. Bar Assn., D.C. Bar Assn., Inter-Am. Bar Assn., Fed. Bar Assn., Montgomery County Inn of Ct. (pres. 1988—90, Leadership in Law award 2002). Jewish. Office: US Courthouse 6500 Cherrywood Ln Greenbelt MD 20770-1249

MESSMAN, JACK L. oil executive; b. Clarksburg, W.Va., Mar. 13, 1940; s. Marvin C. and Betty L. (Jones) M.; m. Maggie Saran, Apr. 18, 1997; children: Valerie Lynne, Kyle Andrew. B in Chem. Engring., U. Del., 1962; MBA, Harvard U., 1968. Ptnr. Butcher & Singer, Phila., 1971 73; pres. Norcross, Inc., West Chester, Pa., 1973-80; v.p. corp. devel. UGI Corp., Valley Forge, Pa., 1980-81; exec. v.p. Safeguard Scientifics, King of Prussia, Pa., 1981-83; pres., CEO Novell Data Sys., Inc., Orem, Utah, 1981-83; exec. v.p., CFO Warner Amex, N.Y.C., 1983-86; chmn., CEO Somerset House Corp., Houston, 1986-88; CEO, bd. dirs. USPCI, Inc., Oklahoma City, 1988-91; chmn., CEO Union Pacific Resources, Inc., Ft. Worth, 1991-99; pres., CEO Cambridge (Mass.) Tech. Ptnrs., 1999—. Bd. dirs. Wawa, Inc. (Pa.), Novell Inc., Utah, Safeguard Scientifics, Inc., Cambridge Technology Ptnrs., Tandy Corp., U.S. Data. Served to 1st lt. U.S. Army, 1963-65. Mem. River Crest Country Club (Ft. Worth), Mira Vista Club (Ft. Worth). Republican. Episcopalian. Office: Cambridge Technology Partners PO Box 9269 Waltham MA 02454-9269

MESSMER, DONALD JOSEPH, business management educator, marketing consultant; b. St. Louis, July 30, 1936; s. Edgar Louis and Lucille Louise (Straub) Messmer; m. Charlotte Jean Fox; 1 child, Angeline Charlotte. BSBA with honors, Washington U., St. Louis, 1969, PhD, 1974. Asst. mgr. M.A. Bell Co., St. Louis, 1956-61; dist. sales exec. U. S. Gypsum Co., St. Louis, 1962-65; br. sales exec. Victor Comptometer Corp., St. Louis, 1965-68; asst. prof. Coll. William and Mary, Williamsburg, Va., 1973-76, assoc. prof., 1976-81, prof., 1981—, J.S. Mack prof., 1982—, dir. exec. MBA program, 1988-91, coord. MBA field studies program, 1998—; pres. The Wessex Group, Ltd., Williamsburg, 1979—. Bd dirs Williamsburg Winery, Ltd, Chateau Hotels Ltd; co-founder Sr Execs Resource Corps. Editor (assoc ed): Decision Scis Jour, 1985—88; contbr. articles to profl jours. Bd dirs, treas Community Action Agency, Williamsburg, 1984—91, United Way Greater Williamsburg, 1985—91, pres, 1989. Recipient Pres.'s cmty. svc. award, Coll. William and Mary, 1999. Mem.: Southeastern Decision Scis Inst (pres 1985—86), Am Mkt Asn (Dissertation Award 1974), Decision Scis Inst (mkt coord 1985—86), Rotary (bd. dirs. 1990—92, program chair 2003, bd. dirs. 2003—, pres. 2004, pres.-elect 2003—04), Beta Gamma Sigma, Alpha Mu Alpha. Republican. Avocations: fishing, golf. Office: Coll William and Mary Grad Sch Bus Williamsburg VA 23185-8795 Office Phone: 757-221-2911. Personal E-mail: don.messmer@wessexgroup.com. Business E-mail: don.messmer@business.wm.edu.

MESSMER, HAROLD MAXIMILIAN, JR., (MAX MESSMER), financial services executive; b. Jackson, Miss., Feb. 20, 1946; s. Harold Maximilian and Margaret (Dee) M.; m. Marcia Elizabeth Nesmith, Apr. 5, 1973; children: Michael Christopher, Matthew Gordon. AB summa cum laude, Loyola U., 1967; JD cum laude, NYU, 1970. Ptnr. corp. law and securities O'Melveny & Myers, Los Angeles, 1970-81; sr. v.p., gen. counsel Pacific Holding Corp., Los Angeles, 1981-82, pres., chief operating officer, 1982-85; pres., dir., chief operating officer Cannon Mills Co. (subs.), Kannapolis, N.C., 1982-85; chmn., dir. Castle & Cook Inc., San Francisco, 1985; chmn., pres., chief exec. officer Robert Half Internat. Inc., San Francisco, 1985—; dir. Nat. Bank N.C., Charlotte. Adj. prof. Claremont Grad. Sch. Bus.(exec. mgmt. program), 1979-82; bd. dirs. Health Care Property Investors, Los Angeles, BF Enterprises Inc., N.C. Nat. Bank, Charlotte. Trustee Davidson (N.C.) Coll., 1984—; appointee Pres. Reagan's Adv. Com. on Trade Negotiations, 1985-87. Served with USAR, 1971-75. Mem. ABA, Los Angeles County Bar Assn., Calif. Bar Assn. Served with USAR, 1971-75. Office: Robert Half Internat Inc 2884 Sand Hill Rd Ste 200 Menlo Park CA 94025-7059

MESSMORE, DAVID WILLIAM, construction executive, former psychologist; b. Indpls. s. Max J. and Betty G. (Miller) M.; m. Sondra Renée Bastian, Aug. 22, 1981; children: Kristen Nicole, Eric Christian William David. AB in Social Sci., Calif. State Coll., Long Beach, 1968; PhD in Student Devel., Counseling and Clin. Psychology, Mich. State U., 1972. Lic. class A gen. contractor, Tex., Va.; lic. psychologist, Calif., Mich.; lic. sch. psychologist, Calif.; cert. mediator Supreme Ct. Va. Counselor Okemas (Mich.) Pub. Sch., 1970-72; psychologist Frederick Ctr. Day Hosp., Grand Rapids, Mich., 1972-73, Newport-Mesa Schs., Newport Beach, Calif., 1973-80; commr. Bd. Med. Quality Assurance, State of Calif. Psychol. com., Sacramento, 1980-82; pres. and CEO Bridgewater Constrn., Inc., Chesapeake, Va., 1987-2001. Psychol. counselor Camp Highfields Residential Sch., Onondago, Mich., 1971; cons. The Open Door, Lansing, Mich., 1971-72, Juv. and Domestic Rels. Ct. the Family Ct., State of Va., Chesapeake, 1989-91; pres. Bridgewater Consultation Svcs., Chesapeake, 1989-91; intern Counseling Ctr., Calif. State U., Long Beach, asst. prof. ednl. psychology, 1981; instr. Golden West Coll., Huntington Beach, Calif., 1977-78; advisor, counselor dean of students Mich. State U., 1969-71; pres., CEO Hampton Rds. Multimedia, 1996-98; founding mem., pres. Va. Challenge Inc. (wrestling), 1999—. Author: (manual) The Impact of Divorce on Families, 1989, Personal Revelation- A Message and Prophecy from God, 2003; designer sch. crest Long Beach City Coll., 1965. Active Gt. Bridge Conf. Com., Chesapeake, 1987-91; treas. Paint Your Heart Out, Chesapeake, 1993, Hampton Rds. Rep. Alliance, 1996-97; coach parks and recreation, commr. transp. and safety City of Chesapeake, 1994-96, vice-chmn., 1995-96; fin. com. city com. Rep. Party of Chesapeake, vice-chmn., 1996-97, acting chmn., 1997; treas. Citizens for a Better Chesapeake, 1996-97; v.p. Virginia Challenge Wrestling, Inc., 1999—, 1st v.p., 2001-03, also founding mem.; pres., founder Found. of the Holy Cross, 2003—. Recipient Cert. of Appreciation Chesapeake Vols. in Youth Svcs., Inc., 1989, Outstanding Svc. award, 1990, Gov.'s award State of Va., 1990. Mem. Nat. Mid. Sch. Sch. Wrestling Champaionship (founding mem., v.p. 2001—), Rotary Internat. (bd. dirs. Chesapeake club 1990-94, Disting. Svc. award 1990) 1988-98, Nat. Youth Sports Coaches Assn., Delta Tau Delta. Avocations: tennis, reading, investments.

MESSNER, HOWARD MYRON, professional association executive; b. Newark, June 10, 1937; s. Elias and Freda (Trachtenberg) M.; m. Aletha Bragg, 1960 (div. 1980); children: Jennifer, Linda, David; m. Melba June Meador, June 22, 1986. BA, Antioch Coll., 1960; MA, U. Mass., 1962. Mgmt. analyst Office Gov., Mass., 1960-61; staff asst. to adminstr. NASA, Washington, 1962-65; mgmt. analyst Bur. Budget, Washington, 1965-71; dir. adminstrn. EPA, Washington, 1971-75, asst. adminstr. for adminstrn., 1983-87; asst. dir. Congl. Budget Office, Washington, 1975-77, Office Mgmt. and Budget, Washington, 1977 83; contr. Dept. Energy, Washington, 1983; exec. v.p. Am. Cons. Engr. Coun., 1987—99; pres. Nat. Acad. Pub. Adminstrn. Recipient William A. Jump Meml. award, 1971, Presdl. Disting. Exec. award, 1986, Outstanding Pub. Service award Nat. Capital chpt. Am. Soc. Pub. Adminstrn., 1986, Chancellor's medal U. Mass., 1988. Mem. Nat. Acad. Pub. Adminstrn. (trustee), Cosmos Club. Democrat. Jewish. Home: 1683 Justin Dr Gambrills MD 21054-2012

MESSNER, JAMES W. advertising executive; b. 1939; Attended, 1959-61. With Sta. WCSM, Celina, Ohio, 1961-63, Sta. WTOD, Toledo, 1961-63, Detroit Advt. Agy., 1965-68, Norman, Navan, Moore & Bard, 1968-77; chmn., CEO J.W. Messner Inc., Grand Rapids, Mich., 1977—. Office: JW Messner Inc 161 Ottawa Ave NW Ste 403 Grand Rapids MI 49503-2760*

MESSNER, MICHAEL A. sociologist, educator; b. Salinas, Calif., July 1, 1952; s. Russell J., Jr. and Anita C. Messner; m. Pierrette M. Hondagneu-Sotelo, June 13, 1987; children: Miles Hondagneu-Messner, Sasha P. Hondagneu-Messner. PhD, U.Calif., Berkeley, 1985. Prof. of sociology USC, Los Angeles, Calif. Author: (book) Power at Play: Sports and the Problem of Masculinity (Book of the Yr.: North Am. Soc. for the Sociology of Sport, 1993), Sex, Violence and Power in Sports, Politics of Masculinities: Men in Movements, Taking the Field: Women, Men, and Sports. Mem.: N. Am. Soc. for Sociology of Sport (pres. 1995—96, Book of Yr. 1993). Home: Univ Southern Calif Los Angeles CA 90089-2539 Office: Univ Southern Calif Dept Sociology Los Angeles CA 90089-2539

MESSNER, TERRY BONACCOLTA, communications consultant; b. N.Y.C., Nov. 1, 1950; d. Peter Bonaccolta and Concetta Livoti; m. Thomas Gerard Messner, Nov. 28, 1971; 1 child, Zachary. Grad., Valley Stream South, 1968. Acct. supr. Doyle Dane Bernbach, N.Y.C., 1970-80; exec. v.p. Levine Huntley Schmidt, N.Y.C., 1981-91; pres. Bonaccolta Cons., N.Y.C., 1992—; co-founder Rep. Advt. Inc., 1999. New bus. cons. for advt. agys. Vol. fundraiser Graham-Windham, N.Y.C., 1994, Einstein Hosp., N.Y.C., 1997, Lawrenceville Sch., N.Y.C., 1999; bd. dirs. Cath. Big Sisters. Named one of 100 Leading Women, Advt. Age, 1986, one of 50 Best and Brightest, Advt. Age, 1987; recipient Agy. of Yr. award Adweek, 1990. Roman Catholic.

MESSNER, THOMAS G. advertising executive, copywriter; b. N.Y.C., Jan. 26, 1944; s. Malcolm V. Messner and Virginia M. Burkard; m. Terry Carol Bonaccolta, Nov. 28, 1971; 1 child, Zachary. Letter carrier U.S. Post Office, N.Y.C., 1965-67; copywriter Occidental Life Calif., L.A., 1967-68; mail boy D'Arcy Advt., N.Y.C., 1968; copywriter BBDO, N.Y.C., 1968-69, Doyle Dane Bernbach, N.Y.C., 1969-72; creative dir. Ally and Gargano, N.Y.C., 1972-86; founder, ptnr. Messner Vetere Berger Carey Schmetterer, N.Y.C., 1986-92; ptnr. Messner Vetere Berger McNamee Schmetterer Euro RSCG, N.Y.C., 1992—; founder Grand Old Website Co., 1999. Former prof. Sch. Visual Arts, N.Y.C.; copywriter MCI; bd. dirs., US. bd., internat. bd. Eurol RSCG; founder, pres. The Grand Old Website Co., Rep. Advt. Inc. Copywriter Ronald Reagan 1984 Presdl. campaign Repub. Nat. Com., NY, 1984; copywriter George Bush 1988 presdl. campaign, 1988, Bob Franks Senatorial Campaign, 2000, Andrew O'Rourke for Gov., NY, 1986. Named CLIO Hall of Fame. Mem. Mortons Group, E-Media Investment Group, Fenway Club. Roman Catholic. Office: Messner Vetere Berger McNamee Schmetterer Euro RSCG 350 Hudson St Fl 7 New York NY 10014-4509 E-mail: tom.messner@mvbms.com.

MESTECHKIN, MIKHAIL MARKOVICH, math physicist; b. Kiev, USSR, June 2, 1932; s. Mark Mikhailovich and Bella Grigorjevna (Greben') M.; m. Liya Semenovna Gutyrya, Apr. 23, 1955; 1 child, Tanya. MS, Odessa State U., 1955; PhD in Math./Physics, Leningrad State U., 1961, ScD in Math./Physics, 1970. Tchr. high and mid. sch. Railway Sta., Yasinovataja, Ukraine, 1955-57; asst. prof. Mordovian State U., Saransk, 1960-65; head theoretical chemistry dept., prof. Inst. Phys. Organic and Coal Chemistry, Donetsk, Ukraine, 1965-96; ret. Author: Density Matrix Method in theory of Molecules, 1977, Spin-Extended Hartree-Fock Method, 1983 (Bronze medal of Soviet Ind. Exhbn. 1990), Hartree-Fock Instability Theory and Molecular Stability, 1986; contbg. author: Density Matrices and density Functionals, 1987, Fullerene Science and Technology, 1997; contbr. 250 articles to profl. jours., including Jour. Phys. Chemistry Ref. Data, others. Mem. World Assn. Theoretical Organic Chemists (diploma Soviet Union br.). Home: Unit 33 12773 Seabreeze Farms Dr San Diego CA 92130-3752 E-mail: mmm3ls@ixpres.com.

MESTON, CINDY M(AY), psychologist, educator; b. Abbotsford, B.C., Can., Nov. 6, 1960; arrived in U.S., 1995; d. Joseph Orvil and Mary Elizabeth Meston. BA in Psychology, U. B.C., Vancouver, 1991, MA in Clin. Psychology, 1993; PhD in Clin. Psychology, U. B.C., 1995. Clin. intern. U. Wash. Sch. Medicine, Seattle, 1994—95, sr. post doctoral fellow reproductive and sexual medicine clinic, 1995—96; rsch. fellow Social Sci. Rsch. Coun., Ford Found., 1996—97; acting asst. prof. dept. psychiatry and behavioral scis. U. Wash. Sch. Medicine, Seattle, 1997—98; asst. prof. dept. psychology U. Tex., Austin, 1998—2001, assoc. prof., 2002—. Trainee juvenile svcs. to ct. Willingdon Detention Ctr., Burnaby, B.C., 1990—91; trainee psychology outpatient clinic U. B.C., Vancouver, 1991—94; extern psychiatry outpatient ctr. U. Wash. Med. Ctr., Seattle, 1993, extern Madison Clinic for AIDS, 93, intern Pain Svc., 94, intern dept. rehab. medicine, 95, intern psychiatry outpatient ctr., 95, fellow reproductive and sexual medicine clinic, 1995—96, fellow dept. urology, 1995—96, fellow dept. ob-gyn., 1995—96, psychologist reproductive and sexual medicine clinic, 1997—98; intern dept. neuropsychiatry Harborview Med. Ctr., Seattle, 1994—95; spkr. in field. Mem. editl. bd. Archives Sexual Behavior, 2001—, Jour. Sex and Marital Therapy, 2001—, Internat. Jour. Impotence Rsch., 2002—, jour. reviewer numerous jours. in field; contbr. numerous articles to profl. jours., chapters to books; interview subject KXAN-TV, Austin, 1999, NBC Nat. News, 2000, featured in article Wall St. Jour., 1998, NY Times, 1999, Newsweek, 2000. Grantee, Rsch. Coun. Can., 1996—98, Social Sci. Rsch. Coun., Ford Found., 1996—98, Eli Lilly and Co., 1999—2001, Target Health, Inc., 1999—2001, NitroMed, Inc., 1999—2002, Lilly ICOS LLC, 2000—02, Athena Inst. for Women's Wellness, 2000—03, NIH, 2001—; scholar, U. B.C., 1989—94. Mem.: APA, Internat. Soc. for Study Women's Sexual Health (sci. program com. ann. meeting 2002, pres. 2003), Soc. Sci. Study Sex, Can. Psychol. Assn., Internat. Acad. Sex Rsch. (sci. program com. ann. meeting 1999, chair poster session 1999, 2000, sci. program com. ann. meeting 2001). Office: U Tex 108 E Dean Keeton Austin TX 78712

MESTRALLET, GÉRARD, utilities executive, professional society administrator; b. Paris, Apr. 1, 1949; arrived in Belgium, 1991; s. Georges Julien Marie and Paule Andrée Augustine (Besnard) M.; m. Joëlle Emilienne Renée Arcens, Sept. 7, 1974; children: Stephanie, Caroline, Bastien. Grad., Ecole Polytech., Paris, 1968, Ecole Aviation Civile, 1971, Inst. for Study of Politics, Toulouse, France, 1973; postgrad., Ecole Nat. d'Adminstrn., Paris, 1978. Counsellor Minister Transp., Econs., Fins., & Budget, Paris, 1973-84; chargé de mission Suez, Paris, 1984-86, dél. adjoint indsl. affairs, 1986-91, dir. gen. adjoint, 1991—; CEO Soc. Gen. de Belgique, Brussels, 1991; chmn., CEO Compagnie de Suez, Paris, 1995-97; CEO, pres. exec. bd. Suez Lyonnaise des Eaux, Paris, 1997—. Chmn. bd. Tractebel; mem. chief exec. Hong Kong's Coun. Advisors; mem. European Round Table of Industrialists. Dir. bd. Saint-Gobain, Ecole Polytechnique; mem. supr. bd. AXA, Casino, Crédit Agricole Indosuez, Soc. du Louvre; advisor to Mayor of Shanghai, China. Office: Suez 16 rue de la Ville lEveque 75008 Paris France

MESTRES, JEAN L. See SULC, JEAN LUENA

MESTRES, RICARDO A., III, motion picture company executive; b. N.Y.C., Jan. 23, 1958; s. Ricardo Angelo Jr. and Ann (Farnsworth) M.; m. Tracy Stewart; children: Alexander Carson, Carrie Ann. AB, Harvard U., 1980. Creative exec. Paramount Pictures, L.A., 1981-82, exec. dir. prodn., 1982-84, v.p. prodn., 1984-85, Walt Disney Pictures, Burbank, Calif., 1985-86, sr. v.p. prodn., 1986-88; pres. prodn. Touchstone Pictures, Burbank, Calif., 1988-89; pres. Hollywood Pictures, Burbank, Calif., 1989-94; co-founder Great Oaks Entertainment, Burbank, Calif., 1995-97; prin. Ricardo Mestres Prodns., Disney Studios, Burbank, Calif., 1997—. Prodr: Jack, 101 Dalmations, Flubber, Home Alone 3, The Visitors, The Hunted. Mem. Acad. Motion Picture Arts and Scis. Office: Ricardo Mestres Prodns 115 Barrington Walk Los Angeles CA 90049

MESTRES, RICARDO ANGELO, JR., lawyer; b. NYC, Aug. 12, 1933; s. Ricardo Angelo and Anita (Gwynne) M.; m. Ann Farnsworth, June 18, 1955; children: Laura, Ricardo III, Lynn, Anthony. AB, Princeton U., 1955; LLB, Harvard U., 1961. Bar: N.Y. 1962, U.S. Supreme Ct. 1970. Assoc. Sullivan & Cromwell, N.Y.C., 1961-67, ptnr., 1968-2000, chmn., sr. ptnr., 1995-2000, sr. counsel, 2001—. Trustee Unitarian Ch. All Souls, N.Y.C., 1973-79, 84-87; trustee Phillips Exeter Acad., 1989-99, pres. bd. trustees, 1993-99. Served to lt. USN, 1955-58. Mem.: ABA, Coun. Fgn. Rels., Am. Law Inst., Assn. Bar City N.Y. (corp. law, securities regulation law and state legis. coms.), N.Y. State Bar Assn., Mill Reef Club (Antigua), Links Club, Phi Beta Kappa. Office: Sullivan & Cromwell 125 Broad St Fl 32 New York NY 10004-2498

MESZAROS, PEGGY S. academic administrator; BS, Austin Peay State U.; MS, U. Ky.; PhD, U. Md. Dept. head Hood Coll.; dean human environ. scis. U. Ky.; assoc. dean, dir. acad. affairs Okla. State U.; dean Coll. Human Resources, prof. family and child devel. Va. Tech.; sr. v.p., provost Va. Poly. Inst. and State U., Blacksburg, 1995-2000, William E. Lavery prof. human devel., 2000—. Mem. Nat. Higher Edn. Com., Nat. Ext. Com. Mem. Am. Assn. Family and Consumer Scis., Kappa Omicron Pi. Office: Va Poly Inst and State U Blacksburg VA 24061-0202

MÉSZAROS, PETER ISTVAN, astrophysicist, researcher, astronomy educator; b. Budapest, Hungary, July 15, 1943; came to U.S., 1968; m. Deborah Ann Runde, Nov. 2, 1974; 1 child, Andor Istvan. MS in Physics, U. Buenos Aires, 1967; PhD, U. Calif., Berkeley, 1972. Rsch. assoc. Princeton (N.J.) U. Obs., 1972-73; rsch. fellow Inst. of Astronomy Cambridge (Eng.) U., 1973-75; staff scientist Max Planck Inst. for Astrophysics, Garching, Fed. Republic of Germany, 1975-83; assoc. prof. Pa. State U., University Park, 1983-87, prof., 1987—, head dept. astronomy and astrophysics, 1993—. Vis. scientist Inst. Theoret. Physics U. Calif., Santa Barbara, 1995, cons.; vis. scientist NASA-Goddard Space Flight Ctr., Greenbelt, Md., 1980-82, Harvard-Smithsonian Ctr. for Astrophysics, Cambridge, 1982-83, 90; cons. Max Planck Inst. for Astrophysics, Garching, 1983-87, NASA, 1987—, Tokyo Met. U., 1990, Cambridge U., 1991. Author: (monograph) High Energy Radiation From Magnetized Neutron Stars; contbr. articles to Astrophys. Jour., Phys. Rev., Astron & Astrophysics; contbr. over 130 articles to profl. jours. U. Calif. fellow, 1970-72, Irex fellow NRC, 1986, Smithsonian Inst. fellow, 1982, 83, 90, Royal Soc. Guest Rsch. fellow, 1991; recipient First prize Gravity Rsch. Found., 1976. Fellow Am. Phys. Soc.; mem. Am. Astron. Soc. (exec. com. 1987-89), Internat. Astron. Union. Achievements include discovery of growth rate of cold matter perturbations in radiation dominated cosmological models; development of radiative cross sections for cyclotron radiation in neutron stars; research in spherical accretion on black holes, the development of models of accreting pulsars and neutron stars, and development of models for cosmological gamma-ray burst sources. Office: Pa State U Dept Astron & Astrophysics 525 Davey University Park PA 16802

MESZNIK, JOEL R. investment banker; b. Oct. 3, 1945; m. Lynne Gladstein, Mar. 25, 1979; children: Daniel, Jared, Kara. BS, CCNY, 1967; MBA, Columbia U., 1970. Engr. Ebasco Svcs., N.Y.C., 1967-70; banker Citibank, N.Y.C., 1970-71, Newhouse Capital, N.Y.C., 1971-72, Matthews & Wright, N.Y.C., 1972-76; mng. dir. Drexel Burnham Lambert, N.Y.C., 1976-89; pres. Mesco Ltd., 1990—. Bd. dirs. RAIT, Incentive Capital Group, Pharma/wHealth, Greenfield Online, USA Data, NetByTel. Office: 470 Main St Ste 315 Ridgefield CT 06877-4516

METALLO, FRANCES ROSEBELL, mathematics professor; b. Jersey City, N.J. d. Vincenzo James and Lucille (Frank) M. BA in Math., Jersey City State Coll., 1985, MA in Math. Edn., 1987. Math. tchr. Emerson High Sch., Union City, N.J., 1990-92; math tchr. gifted/talented program Jefferson Annex Woodrow Wilson Sch. Dist. Union City, 1992-95; math tchr. Woodrow Wilson Sch., Dist. Union City, 1995—. Adj. tchr. math. Hudson County C.C., 1987—, Jersey City State Coll., 1986—, tutor, 1983-86; reviewer for Nat. Coun. Tchrs. Math mag., A Plus for Kids Tchr. Network, 1994, grantee 1993, 96 Contbr. articles to profl. publs.; author, History of the Abacus and Study of Sorubah, The Abaacus: It's History and Application Module 17, A concise Dictionary of Math and Symbols, Smile, Basic Algebra is Fun. Nominee Pres. award for sci. and math tchg. Mem. Nat. Coun. Tchrs. Math., Assn. Math. Tchrs. of N.J., Alumni Assn. Jersey City State Coll., Math. Assn. Am., Am. Soc. Prevention of Cruelty to Animals, Assn. of Women in Math., Am. Math. Soc., Dozenal Soc., Kappa Delta Pi, Phi Delta Kappa. Avocations: developing classroom math. materials, crochet, embroidery, piano. Office: 80 Hauxhurst Ave Weehawken NJ 07086-6837

METCALF, CINDY W. political organization administrator; Former chair Vt. Dem. Party, Montpelier; chief of staff Office of the Lt. Gov., Montpelier, Vt., 2001—. Office: 115 State St Drawer 33 Montpelier VT 05633

METCALF, DAVID ROY, retired pediatrician; b. N.Y.C., Oct. 6, 1920; s. Oscar and Celia (Halpern) Siegel; m. Sheila Trimble Metcalf; children: Evan, Conard, MetcalfcELIA. BS, Antioch Coll., 1943; MD, U. Rochester Med. Sch., 1946. Intership U. Colo. Sch. of Medicine, 1950—52, pediat. residency, 1952—55, psychiat. residency, 1956—60; psychoanalytic tng. Denver Inst. of Psychoanalysis, 1965. Contbr. articles various profl. jours. Past mem. Denver Psychoanalytic Assn.; emeritus Am. Psychoanalytic Assn. Achievements include research in devel. in humas of the electroencephalogram ie; electrical brain-devel. in rel. to psychological devel. Avocations: leading reading groups of classical lit., supr. psychotherapists. Home: PO Box 830 Philipsburg MT Office: 13 Cusabo Rd Fripp Island SC 29920 Office Phone: 406-543-2355. E-mail: drm1272000@yahoo.com.

METCALF, DONALD, biomedical researcher; BSc, U Sydney, Sydney, Australia; MB, BS, U Sydney; MD, U. Sydney. Carden fellow, cancer rsch. Walter & Eliza Hall Inst. Med. Rsch., Victoria, Australia, 1954—, head, cancer rsch. unit, asst. dir., 1965-96; rsch. prof., cancer biology U. Melbourne, Australia, 1986-96; emeritus prof. Walter & Eliza Hall Inst. Med. Rsch., Royal Melbourne Hosp., 1996—. Visiting prof., Australia, Britain, Canada, France, the Netherlands, New Zealand, Switzerland, and U.S. Author of over 600 articles in acad. journals. Recipient Armand Hammer Prize for Cancer Rsch., 1988, Sloan Prize, General Motors Cancer Rsch. Foundation, Albert Lasker Clinical Rsch. Award, 1993, Louisa Gross Horwitz Prize, Columbia U., 1993, Jessie Stevenson Kovalenko Medal Nat. Acad. of Sciences 1994, Gairdner Foundation Internat. Award, 1994. Mem., Royal Soc., 1983— (Wellcome Prize, 1986); foreign assoc. mem., Nat. Acad. Sciences, 1987—; hon. foreign mem., Assn. Amer. Physicians, 1988—. Achievements include being an important contributor to the clinical use of molecules called colony-simulating factors (CSFs), which control the growth and development of blood cells. Office: Walter and Eliza Hall Inst Med Rsch 1G Royal Parade Parkville VIC 3050 Australia E-mail: Metcalf@wehi.edu.au.

METCALF, ERIC QUINN, professional football player; b. Seattle, Jan. 23, 1968; Degree in liberal arts, U. Tex., 1990. With Cleve. Browns, 1989—94; wide receiver, kick returner, running back Atlanta Falcons, 1995—96; kick returner, wide receiver San Diego Chargers, 1997—98; wide receiver Arizona Cardinals, 1998—99, Carolina Panthers, 1999—. Named to Sporting News Coll. All-Am. 2d team, 1987, Sporting News NFL All-Pro Team, 1993—94, Pro Bowl, 1993—94. Office: Carolina Panthers 800 S Mint St Charlotte NC 28202-1502

METCALF, HOWARD, military officer; b. New Orleans; Student, U. Md. Enlisted U.S. Army, 1969—71, infrantryman 90th Replacement Bn. and 321st Transp. Co., 1970—71, enlisted as legal specialist, 1977, bn. legal NCO 1st Bn., 44th Air Def. Artillery, NCOIC of claims; lawyer's asst., NCOIC of adminstrn. sect. and pre-trial sect. 21st Support Command, Germany, instr./developer Co. C, 1st Bn., Troop Brigade; sr. legal NCO Combined Field Army Korea; 71 D br. mgr. U.S. Army, Falls Church, Va., 1st sgr. Co. A, 369th AG Bn. Ft. Jackson, SC; chief legal NCO 8th US Army, Republic of Korea; sgt. mgr. Judge Advocate Gen.'s Corps, U.S., Washington, 1998—. Decorated Def. Meritorious Svc. medal, Meritorious Svc. medal with 4 oak leaf clusters, Army Commendation medal with 1 oak leaf cluster, Army Achievement medal with 1 oak leaf cluster, Vietnam Svc. medal, Republic of Vietnam Campaign medal. Office: Office of Judge Advocate General US Army Pentagon Washington DC 20310-1500

METCALF, JACK, former congressman, retired state senator; b. Marysville, Wash., Nov. 30, 1927; s. John Read and Eunice (Grannis) M.; m. Norma Jean Grant, Oct. 3, 1948; children: Marta Jean, Gayle Marie, Lea Lynn, Beverlee Ann. Student, U. Wash., 1944-45; BA, BEd, Pacific Luth. U., 1951. Tchr. Elma (Wash.) pub. schs., 1951-52, Everett (Wash.) pub. schs., 1952-81; mem. Wash. Ho. of Reps., 1960-64, Wash. Senate, 1966-75, 80-92, U.S. Ho. of Reps. from 2d Wash. dist., 1995-2001. Chmn. environment and natural resources com., 1988-92; mem. domestic & internat. monetary policy, fin. instns. & consumer credit, aviation, surface transp. coms. Hon. chmn. Innocent Property Owners Protection Initiative. Mem. Coun. State Govts., Wash. Edn. Assn. (bd. dirs.), Wash. Assn. Profl. Educators (state v.p. 1979-81, state pres. 1977-79), Nat. Conf. State Legislatures, Western States Recycling Coalition, South Whidbey Kiwanis. Republican. Home: 4693 E Saratoga Rd Langley WA 98260-9694

METCALF, KAREN, retired foundation executive; b. Reading, Mass., Dec. 12, 1936; d. Albion Edmund and Natalie Viola (Ives) M. AB, Vassar Coll., 1958; MBA, Harvard U., 1968. CFA. Sec. Radio Liberty Com., N.Y.C., 1958-60; rsch. asst. Air Inc., Cambridge, Mass., 1960-64; sys. analyst Keydata Corp., Watertown, Mass., 1964-66; customer edn. cons. Interactive Data Corp., N.Y.C., 1968; portfolio mgr. Scudder, Stevens & Clark, N.Y.C., 1969-81; v.p. fin. and adminstrn. N.Y. Cmty. Trust, N.Y.C., 1981—2002. Episcopalian. Avocations: travel, opera.

METCALF, ROBERT JOHN ELMER, industrial consultant; b. Glen Ellyn, Ill., June 27, 1919; s. Elmer Simpson and Vida Marie Metcalf; B.S.M.E., U. Pitts., 1947; m. Rosemarie Rusch, Sept. 11, 1947; children: Kathleen, Karen, Patti, Pamela. Asst. staff supr. Westinghouse Electric Co., Buffalo, 1949-52, assoc. engr., 1952-54; assoc. Gemar Assocs., Inc., Greenwich, Conn., 1954-66. v.p., 1966-83; cons., 1983-92 . Served with U.S. Army, 1943-46. Mem. Inst. Mgmt. Cons. (founding). Roman Catholic. Home and Office: Apt 331 444 Paula Dr N Dunedin FL 34698-1820

METCALF, WAYNE C., III, insurance commissioner; m. Shirley Imada Metcalf. BA in Polit. Sci., U. Hawaii, 1975; JD, 1978; student, Tufts U., 1992-93. Atty. pvt. practice, 1979—; spl. cons. UN, 1994; ins. commr. Dept. Commerce and Consumer Affairs State Hawaii, 1994-97, 99—. Staff Senate Jud. Com., 1973-75; staff dir. Senate Pres.'s Office, 1975-78; vice-chmn. House Com. on Jud., 1984-86; chmn. House Com. on Jud., 1986-92; mem. house coms. Comsuner Protection and Commerce, 1984-92, Land Use and Hawaiian Affairs Plannong, 1984-86, Labor and Pub. Employment Transp., 1985-88, Housing, Health Humand Svcs, 1988-90, Housing, Health, 1990-92. Recipient Disting. Alumni award U. hawaii, 1988, Disting. Legislator award, Nat. Dem. State LEgis. Leaders Assn., 1988; named one of Hawaii's five best legislators by polit. columnist Dan Boylan, 1990, 92. Office: Ins Divsn Dept Commerce Consumer Affairs PO Box 3614 Honolulu HI 96811-3614

METCALF, WILLIAM EDWARDS, educator, museum curator; b. East Grand Rapids, Mich., Dec. 16, 1947; s. George Ellington and Ruthanne (Schnitzler) M.; m. Margaret Mary Finn, May 21, 1972 (annulled 1984); 1 son, Daniel F.; m. Jane Salinger, Oct. 26, 1991; 1 child, Lydia Qiao Salinger. BA, U. Mich., 1969, MA, 1970, PhD in Classical Studies (Horace H. Rackham prize fellow), 1973. Asst. curator Roman and Byzantine coins Am. Numismatic Soc., N.Y.C., 1973-75, assoc. curator, 1975-78, curator, dep. chief curator, 1978-79, chief curator, 1979-2000, hon. curator, 2000—; prof. classics Yale U., 2002—. Adj. prof. art history and archaeology Columbia U., 1978—, adj. prof. classics, 1998; adj. prof. history, 1993; adj. prof. classics NYU, 1996, 2000-01, Princeton U., 1999, Bryn Mawr U., 2000; curator coins and medals Yale U. Art Gallery, 2002—; vis. prof. classics NYU, 2001-02. Author: The Cistophori of Hadrian, 1980, The Silver Coinage of Cappadocia, Vespasian-Commodus, 1995; editor: Studies in Early Byzantine Gold Coinage, 1988, America's Gold Coinage, 1990, Mnemata: Papers in Memory of Nancy M. Waggoner, 1991; adv. com. Lexicon Iconographicum Mythologiae Classicae, 1979—; adv. bd. Am. Jour. Archaeology, 1980-97; editor book revs. Am. Jour. Numismatics, 1989-2000; mem. editl. bd. Revue Suisse de Numismatique, 2002—contbr. articles on Roman and Byzantine coinage to profl. jours. NEA fellow for mus. profls., 1978; mem. Inst. for Advanced Study, 1988-89 Fellow Am. Numismatic Soc. (life); mem. Royal Numismatic Soc., Am. Philol. Assn. (subcom. on classical bibliography 1979-89), Archaeol. Inst. Am. (exec. com. NY 1976-80, chmn. numismatics com. 2000--), Columbia U. Seminar on Classical Civilization, Internat. Numismatic Commn. (1st v.p. 1997-2003), Soc. Antiquaries London. E-mail: william.metcalfe@yale.edu.

METCALFE, DEAN DARREL, medical research physician; b. Medford, Oreg., June 27, 1944; s. Darrell S. and Lucille E. (Moore) Metcalfe; m. Joan I. Peterson, Dec. 21, 1977; children: Justin, Jonathan, Elisabet. BS, No. Ariz. U., 1966; MS in Microbiology, U. Mich., 1968; MD, U. Tenn., 1972. Medicine residency Univ. Mich. Hosps., Ann Arbor, 1972—74; clin. assoc. NIH, Bethesda, Md., 1974—77; Rheum fellow Harvard Med. Sch. and Hosp., Boston, 1977—79; clin. investigator NIH, Bethesda, 1979—85; head mast cell physiology sect. lab. of clin. investigation Nat. Inst. of Allergy and Infectious Diseases, Bethesda, 1985—93, head allergic diseases sect., 1994—95; chief lab. allergic diseases Nat. Inst. of Allergy and Infectious Diseases NIH, Bethesda, 1995—. Co-dir. Allergy-Immunology Tng. Program NIAID/NIH, Bethesda, 1979—; dir. Am. Bd. Allergy-Immunology, Phila., 1990—. Capt. USPHS, 1979—. Recipient Commendation medal, USPHS, 1985, Outstanding Svc. medal, 1991. Fellow: Am. Rheumatism Assn., Am. Acad. Allergy and Immunology (bd. dirs.); mem.: Assn. Am. Physicians, Am. Soc. for Clin. Investigation, Am. Fedn. Clin. Rsch. Office: NIH NI AID Dir 10 Center Dr Msc 1881 Bldg 10 Bethesda MD 20892-0001*

METCALFE, ROBERT DAVIS, III, lawyer; b. Bridgeport, Conn., July 2, 1956; s. Robert Davis Jr. and Barbara Ann (Peaslee) M. BA summa cum laude, U. Conn., 1978, JD, 1981; MA, Trinity Coll., 1982, Am. Mil. U., 1997. Bar: Conn. 1981, U.S. Supreme Ct. 1986, D.C. 1990, Md. 1991. Judge adv. USN, Norfolk, Va., 1982-85; spl. asst. U.S. atty. U.S. Dept. Justice, Norfolk, 1985, trial atty. Washington, 1985—. Instr. ARC, Hartford, Conn., 1976-80; legis. asst. Conn. Gen. Assembly, Hartford, 1977. Served to lt. USN, 1982-85. Mem. Fed. Bar Assn., Conn. Bar Assn., Judge Adv. Assn., Mensa, Phi Beta Kappa. Republican. Roman Catholic. Avocations: martial arts, reading, sailing, trap and skeet shooting, stamp collecting/philately.

METCALFE, ROBERT M. communications executive; b. Bklyn., 1946; BEE, B in Mgmt., Mass. Inst. Tech., 1969; M in Applied Math., Harvard U., 1970, PhD in Computer Sci., 1973. With computer sci. lab. Xerox Palo Alto Rsch. Ctr., 1973-79; founder 3Com Corp., Santa Clara, Calif., 1979-90; v.p. tech. Internat. Data Group, Boston, 1990—; pub. Info World Pub. Co., San Mateo, Calif., 1992-94, columnist, exec. corr., 1994—. Vis. fellow U. Cambridge, Eng., 1991-92. Inventor Ethernet and Local Area Networking. Bd. trustees MIT. Recipient Grace Murray Hepper award, 1980, Alexander Graham Bell medal, 1988, Pub. Understanding of Sci. award, 1995. Mem. AAAS, Nat. Acad. Engring. Office: Internat Data Group 410 Beacon St Boston MA 02115-1103

METCALFE, WALTER LEE, JR., lawyer; b. St. Louis, Dec. 19, 1938; s. Walter Lee and Carol Metcalfe; m. Cynthia Williamson, Aug. 26, 1965; children: Carol, Edward. AB, Washington U., St. Louis, 1960; JD, U. Va., 1964. Bar: Mo. 1964. Ptnr. Armstrong, Teasdale, Kramer & Vaughan, St. Louis, 1964—81; sr. ptnr. Bryan Cave LLP, St. Louis, 1982—, now chmn. From dep. chmn. to chmn. Fed. Res. Bd., St. Louis. Bd. dirs. Washington U., St. Louis, Danforth Found., St. Louis RCGA, Pulitzer Found. Arts, St. Louis Children's Hosp. Mem.: ABA, St. Louis Bar Assn., Mo. Bar Assn., Noonday Club, Bogey Club. Episcopalian. Home: 26 Upper Ladue Rd Saint Louis MO 63124-1675 Office: Bryan Cave 211 N Broadway 1 Metropolitan Sq Ste 3600 Saint Louis MO 63102-2750

METERSKY, MARK L. physician; m. Karen Metersky. MD, NYU Sch. of Medicine, 1985. Bd. Cert. Internal Medicine, Pulmonary Medicine, Critical Care Am. Bd. of Internal Medicine, 1993. Assoc. prof. medicine U. of Conn. Sch. of Medicine, Farmington, 1993—. Dir. of pulmonary and critical care fellowship. Author rsch. pubs. on pneumonia. Fellow: Am. Coll. of Chest Physicians. Office: Univ of Conn Sch of Med 263 Farmington Ave Farmington CT 06030

METHENY, PATRICK BRUCE, musician; b. Lee's Summit, Mo., Aug. 12, 1954; Student, U. Miami, Fla. Instr. dept. music U. Miami; mem. faculty Nat. Stage Band Camps, Fla., Berklee Coll. Music, Boston. Guitarist with Gary Burton Quintet, 3 yrs, mus. dir. and guitarist Pat Metheny Group, 1978—; performer (tours in): U.S., Europe, Can., Japan, USSR, S.Am.; rec. artist ECM Records, currently Geffen Records; composer (for guitar and band): (records) Bright Size Life, 1976, Watercolors, 1977, Pat Metheny Group, 1978, New Chautauqua, 1979, American Garage, 1980, 80/81, 1980, As Falls Wichita, So Falls Wichita Falls, 1981, Offramp, 1982, Travels, Rejoicing, 1983, Works, First Circle, 1984, Still Life (Talking), 1987, Works II, 1988, Letter From Home, 1989, (with Roy Haynes and Dave Holland) Question and Answer, 1990 (Grammy award Best Jazz Composition, 1990), Secret Story, 1992, The Road to You, 1993 (Jazz Instrumental Grammy award, 1994), (with Ornette Coleman) Song X, 1986 (Best Jazz Album award Downbeat mag. Readers' Poll, 1986, Downbeat Readers Poll Jazz Album of Yr., Guitarist of Yr., 1989, Best Jazz Colloboration Album award Cashbox mag., 1986, John Pareles Top Albums of 1986 award N.Y. Times); composer: (films) (scores with David Bowie) The Falcon and the Snowman, 1984, Twice in a Lifetime, 1985. Nominee Grammy award, 1980, 1981; named Best Jazz Musician Jazziz Readers' Poll, 1986, Best Jazz Guitarist, Downbeat mag., 1986; recipient 7 Grammy awards, Outstanding Jazz Album award Boston Music Awards, 1986, Guitar Player mag. Gallery of Greats, 1982—86, Outstanding Guitarist Boston Music Awards, 1986, Outstanding Jazz Fusion Group Boston Music Awards, 1986. Office: Geffen Records 10900 Wilshire Blvd Ste 1000 Los Angeles CA 90024-6501

METKA, PHILLIP EDWARD, comptroller; b. Harrisburg, Pa., Dec. 30, 1938; s. Joseph Ambrose and Louise Cecile (Bokan) M.; m. Nancy Lee Cougnet. Feb. 17, 1962; children: Stacey Ann, Daniel Joseph. Student, Pa. State U., 1956-58, Northwestern U., 1967-71; BS in Acctg., No. Ill. U., 1977. CPA, Ill. Field auditor direct mktg. div. Jewel Cos., Inc., Harrisburg and Pitts., Pa., 1960—66, mgr. gen. acctg. Barrington, Ill., 1966—75, mgr. internal and tax audit, 1975—80; cfo & treas., v.p., sec. B.F. Shaw Printing Co., Dixon, Ill., 1980—. Pres. Rotary, 1993—94, treas., 1995—; bd. dirs. Dixon High Sch. Athletic Booster Club, 1985—91, Dixon Area C. of C., 2000—, treas., 2003—; bd. dirs. Dixon Petunia Festival Corp., 1989—, pres., 1994—95; bd. dirs. Casa-Lee & Carroll Counties, 2004—. Mem.: Fin. Execs. Internat., Internat. Newspaper Fin. Execs., Am. Inst. CPA's, Dixon Elks, Rotary. Republican. Roman Catholic. Home: 1126 N Jefferson Ave Dixon IL 61021-1244 Office: BF Shaw Printing Co 444 Pine Hill Dr PO Box 487 Dixon IL 61021 Office Phone: 815-284-4000 223.

METRESS, SEAMUS P. anthropology educator, Irish studies researcher; b. Southampton, N.Y., Sept. 25, 1933; s. James Francis and Hilda Irene Metress; m. Eileen Katherine Ryan, Oct. 1974. BS, U. Notre Dame, 1955; MS, Columbia U., 1957; PhD with honors, Ind. U., 1971. Tchr. various schs., N.Y., 1955-64; prof. anthropology Clarion (Pa.) State Coll., 1966-69, U. Toledo, 1969-71, master tchr., 1991-93, Doermann Presdl. lectr., 1997. Participant profl. meetings. Author: (with C. Kart) Nutrition and Aging: A Review of the Literature, 1979, Nutrition, the Aged, and Society, 1984, (with S. Rogers) Guide to the Use of Library Information Sources in Anthropology, Sociology and the Applied Health Scis., 1979; Listen Irish People, 1979, The Irish-American Experience: A Guide to the Literature, 1981, The Hunger Strike and the Final Struggle, 1983, A Regional Guide to Informational Sources on the Irish in the United States and Canada, 1986, Human Osteology for the Archaeologist, 1989, Dying Colonialism and Irish Nationalism in Conflict, 1992, Outlines in Irish History, 1995, The American Irish and Irish Nationalism: Sociohistorical Introduction, 1995, The Irish in Canada, 1998, The American Irish and the Growth of Development of the Catholic Church, 1998, (with Kart and E. Metress) Aging, Health and Society, 1986, Human Aging and Chronic Disease, 1992, (with K. Annable) The Irish in the Great Lakes Region: A Bibliographic Survey, 1990, (with R. Rajner) The Great Starvation: An Irish Holocaust, 1996, (with D. Johnston) The Irish in America: A Regional Bibliography, 1999, The Long Struggle: An Irish Legacy, 2000, (with E. Metress) The Irish in Michigan, 2004; contbr. articles to profl. jours., including Am. Gael, Linkages, Ohio Jour. Chiropractry, Internat. Affairs, Internat. Jour. Health Svcs., Sociol. Abstracts, Quar. Rev. Ideology, Jour. Am. Ethnic History, Nat. Jour. Sociology, Irish People. Pres. Clan Na Gael, Toledo, 1979—. Recipient Irish Freedom award Irish No. Aid. Mem. Am. Anthrop. Assn., Am. Cath. Hist. Soc., Am. Conf. on Irish Studies, Celtic League Internat., Can. Assn. for Irish Studies, Ctr. for Study Am. Catholicism, Cath. Hist. Soc., Immigration History Soc., Cath. Hist. Soc. Phila. Mem. Green Party. Latin Rite Catholic. Avocations: hiking, nature study. Office: U Toledo Bancroft St Toledo OH 43606

METREY, GEORGE DAVID, social work educator, academic administrator; b. Milw., July 23, 1939; s. Richard Joseph and Catherine (Evans) M.; m. Cheryl Ann Mosca, June 21, 1969 (dec. May 7, 2000); 1 child, Mary Beth. AB, Marquette U., 1961; MSW, Fordham U., 1963; PhD, NYU, 1970. Lic. ind. clin. social worker, R.I., N.J. Social worker N.J. Diagnostic Ctr., Edison, 1963-64, asst. social work supr., 1964-66, dir. psychiat. social work, 1966-70; coordinator undergrad. social work program Kean Coll., N.J., 1970-73, assoc. prof. social work, 1970-74, prof., 1974-79, chmn. dept. sociology, anthropology and social work, 1973-77, dir. social work program, acting assoc. dean Sch. Arts and Sci., 1977-79; dean Sch. Social Work, prof. R.I. Coll., Providence, 1979—, ast. v.p. acad. affairs, 2000—02; ret., 2004. Field instr. Fordham U. Sch. Social Service, 1966-70, adj. prof., 1969-77; adj. assoc. prof. Rutgers U. Grad. Sch. Social Work, 1972-73 Mem. program com. R.I. affiliate Am. Heart Assn., 1980-90, bd. dirs., 1983-89, chmn. program com., 1985-87, exec. com., 1985-87; sec. bd. dirs. Adoption R.I., 1987-89, pres. bd. dirs., 1989-92. Recipient Fordham U. Grad. Sch. Social Svc. Outstanding Alumni, 1984, Spl. Disting. Svc. award R.I. Coll. Alumni Assn., 1996. Mem. NASW (N.J. Social Worker of Yr. 1977, pres. 1978-80, parliamentarian R.I. 1981—, treas. R.I. chpt. 1986-87, nat. competence cert. commn. 1989-91, nat. 2d v.p. 1978-80, chair nat. program com. 1981-83), Coun. on Social Work Edn. (bd. dirs. 1979-82, commn. on accreditation 1996-2002, commn. on ednl. policy, 2002—), Acad. Cert. Social Workers, Nat. Assn. Deans and Dirs. Schs. Social Work (nominating com. 1993-96, program com. 1993-96), Alpha Phi Omega, Gamma Pi Mu, Alpha Delta Mu (regional v.p.). Roman Catholic. Home: PO Box 206 Wyckoff NJ 07481-0206 Office: RI Coll Sch Social Work Providence RI 02908 Office Phone: 401-456-8042. Business E-Mail: gmetrey@aol.com.

METROS, MARY TERESA, librarian; b. Denver, Nov. 10, 1951; d. James and Wilma Frances (Hanson) Metros. BA in English, Colo. Women's Coll., 1973; MA in Librarianship, U. Denver, 1974. Adult svcs. libr. Englewood Pub. Libr., Colo., 1975—81, mgr. adult svcs., 1983—84; sys. cons. Dataphase Sys., Kansas City, Mo., 1981—82; circulation libr. Westminster Pub. Libr., Colo., 1983; supr. pub. svcs. Tempe Pub. Libr., Ariz., 1984—90, libr. dir., 1990—. Mem.: ALA, Mt. Plains Libr. Assn., Libr. Adminstrn. and Mgmt. Assn., Ariz. Libr. Assn., Pub. Libr. Assn. Democrat. Office: Tempe Pub Libr 3500 S Rural Rd Tempe AZ 85282-5405 Office Phone: 480-350-5551. E-mail: teri_metros@tempe.gov.

METTE, JOSEPH P. museum director and park facilities superintendent; Dir. California State Capitol Mus., Sacramento, Calif.; dist. supt. pks. and recreation dist. office San Luis Obispo (Calif.) Coast Dist., 1998—. Office: Ca Dept of Parks and Rec 1416 Ninth St PO Box 942896 Sacramento CA 94296*

METTEE-MCCUTCHON, ILA, municipal official, retired career army officer; b. Mobile, Ala., May 1, 1945; d. John Martin and Anna Ruth (Cleveland) Mettee; m. John Robert McCutchon, Oct. 13, 1974; 1 child, Erin Tempest. BS, Auburn (Ala.) U., 1967, MS, 1969; grad., various army schs. Rsch. psychologist VA Hosp., Tuskegee, Ala., 1967-69; clin. psychologist U. Ala. Med. Ctr., Birmingham, 1969-71; commd. 1st lt. U.S. Army, 1971, advanced through grades to col., 1992. Officer in charge Alcohol and Drug Abuse Rehab. Ctr., Presidio, San Francisco, 1971-73; strategic intelligence officer 8th Psychol. Bn., 1973-75; tactical intelligence officer, ops. officer, co. comdr. 525th MI Brigade (Airborne), Ft. Bragg, N.C., 1976-79; project officer Command, Control, Comms. and Intelligence Directorate, Combined Arms Combat Devel. Activity, Ft. Leavenworth, Kans., 1979-82; student Command and Gen. Staff Coll., 1982-83; ops. officer Army Spl. Security Group, Washington, 1983-86; Def. Lang. Inst. Presidio of Monterey, 1986-87; chief U.S. So. command Joint Intelligence Ctr., Republic of Panama, 1987-89; comdr. 741st M.I. Bn., Ft. Meade, Md., 1989-91; U.S. Army War Coll., 1991-92; strategic intelligence officer Internat. Mil. Staff NATO, Brussels, 1992-94; comdr. Presidio of Monterey and Ft. Ord, Calif., 1994-96, chief base realignment and closure/environ. mgmt., 1996-97, ret. with honors, 1997. Elected to Marina City Coun., 1998, Rep. ctrl. com. Monterey County, 2000, Mayor City of Marina, 2002-; apptd. housing cmty. and econ. devel. policy com. League Calif. Cities', 1999-. Decorated Army Commendation medal (3), Meritorious Svc. medal (4), Def. Meritorious Svc. medal, Army Achievement award (2), Legion of Merit (2), Def. Superior Svc. medal; named Woman of Yr. Marina, 2001, Philanthropist of Yr., 2001. Mem. NAFE, Nat. Assn. Univ. Women, Nat. Women's Polit. Caucus, VFW, Assn. U.S. Army, Alumni Assn. U.S. Army War Coll., WAC Found., Women in NATO, Am. Legion (post 694), Ft. Ord Alumni Assn. (adv. bd.), Girl Scouts of Monterey Bay (bd. dirs.), Cmty. Human Svcs. (bd. dirs.), Rotary Internat. (local chpt.), Monterey Rep. Women, Marina C. of C., Marina Bus. Assn., Marina Larger Libr. Com. Home: 3181 DeForest Rd Marina CA 93933 Office: City Hall City of Marina 211 Hillcrest Ave Marina CA 93933-3534 Office Phone: 831-884-1278.

METTERS, SAMUEL, engineering executive; b. Tex., Nov. 12, 1934; Grad., U.S. Army Comd. Gen. Staff Coll., U.S. Army Air Def. Missile Ctr., Indsl. Coll. Armed Forces; BS in Arch. Engring., A&M U.; BA in Arch., Urban Planning, U. Calif., Berkeley; MS in Sys. Mgmt., MS in Pub. Adminstrn., D in Pub. Adminstrn., U. So. Calif.; grad. owner/pres. mgmt. program, Harvard U. Lic. profl. engr. Commd. U.S. Army, 1958, various assignments, 1962-65, stationed at, 1968, Fort Bliss, Tex., 1969-72, various assignments Vietnam, 1972-74, stationed at Washington, 1977-79, ret., 1979; program mgr., mgmt. info. sys. coord. HBH Co., Rosslyn, Va. Bd. dirs. U.S. Black Engrs. Pubs., Inc.; bd. advisors Riggs Nat. Bank, Va. Commerce Bank. Bd. dirs. Granville Acad., United Black Coll. Fund, U.S. Black Engr. of Yr. Awards Program, No. Va. Urban League, A&M U. Found., Univ. Louisville; trustee Fairfax Bus. Partnership; mem. dean's adv. com. coun. George Mason U.; treas., pres. Nat. Capital Coun. Boy Scouts Am. Mem. Nat. Purple Heart Assn., Nat. Aeronautics Space Adminstrn. Adv. Coun., Armed Forces Comm. Electronic Assn., Profl. Svc. Coun., U. So. Calif. Alumni Assn. (life), A&M Nat. Alumni Assn. (pres.). Office: Metters Industries Inc 8200 Greensboro Dr Mc Lean VA 22102-3803

METTERS, THOMAS WADDELL, sports writer; b. Columbus, Ohio, Apr. 17, 1939; s. Thomas Hammond and Charlotte Ann (Waddell) M. BS in Journalism, Ohio U., 1965. Sports editor The Traveller, Ft. Lee, Va., 1960-62; sports writer The Athens (Ohio) Messenger, 1965—. Asst. to officials Legion Baseball, Athens, 1962—. Contbr.: Ohio Interscholastic Athletic Media Guide, 1985. Bd. dirs. Athens H.S. Booster Club, 1975—, Athens H.S. Athletic Hall of Fame, 2000; ofcl. scorekeeper Am. Legion World Series, Millington, Tenn., 1989. With U.S. Army, 1959-62. Named to Ohio H.S. Basketball Coaches Assn. Hall of Fame, 1993; recipient Contributor award Ohio H.S. Track & Field Coaches Assn., 1995, Ohio H.S. Athletic Assn. Media Svc. award, 1998. Mem. Soc. Profl. Journalists (Recognition plaque 1973), Ohio Associated Press Sports Writers Assn. (pres. 1984), Green & White Club (sec. 1983-2004, historian 2004—, Jonesy Sams award 1987), Ohio Prep Sports Writers Assn. (Hall of Fame 1990), Ky. Colonels, Am. Legion. Republican. Avocation: bowling. Home: 71 Sunnyside Dr Athens OH 45701-1921 Office: The Athens Messenger 9300 Johnson Rd Athens OH 45701 Office Phone: 740-592-6612 221.

METTETAL, H. NOLAN, state legislator, pharmacist; b. Baton Rouge, Nov. 9, 1945; m. Kay Ford. Student, NW Miss. C.C., U. Miss. Senate State of Miss., 1996-97, 97—. Vice chmn. econ. devel., tourism and parks com.; mem. coms. of appropriations, edn., ins., juvenile justice, public health and welfare, and pub. property. Mem. Miss. Pharmacist Assn., Alumni Assn. of N.W. C.C., Alumni Assn. U. Miss. Methodist. Office: State Capitol Bldg PO Box 1018 Jackson MS 39215-1018 E-mail: nmettetal@mail.senate.state.ms.us.

METTINGER, KARL LENNART, pharmaceutical executive; b. Helsingborg, Sweden, Nov. 1, 1943; came to the U.S., 1989; s. Nils Allan and Anna Katarina (Hallberg) M.; m. Chesne Maree Ryman, 1979; m. Miki Ilaw, 1998. MD, U. Lund, 1973; PhD, Karolinska Inst., 1982. Intern Stockholm Hosps., 1973-74; resident Karolinska Hosp., Stockholm, 1974-77, clin. neurologist, 1977-85; med. dir. Kabi Hematology, Stockholm, 1985-87; dep. gen. mgr. Kabi Cardiovascular, Stockholm, 1987-89; med. dir. Ivax/Baker Norton Pharms., Miami, Fla., 1989-93, sr. clin. dir., 1993-98, exec. dir., clin. rschr., 1998-2000; sr. v.p. chief med. officer SuperGen, San Ramon, 2000—. Assoc. prof. Karolinska Inst., Stockholm, 1983-91; cons. neurologist Odenplan Med. Ctr., Stockholm, 1984-89. Author: Cerebral Thromboembolism, 1982, Refaat--Myths and Billions in Biotech, 1987; editor: Coronary Thrombolysis: Current Answers to Critical Questions, 1988, Controversies in Coronary Thrombolysis, 1989. Bd. dirs. Bass Mus. Arts, 1999-2001; v.p. Friends of Music, U. Miami, 2000-2001; bd. dirs. Oakland East Bay Symphony, 2002—. Lt. Swedish Army, 1979. Recipient Silver award Spanish Health Ministry, 1989, Classical Langs. award King Gustav V Found., 1963. Mem. Swedish Stroke Soc. (bd. dirs. 1979-89, pres. 1984-86), Swedish Med. Soc., Swedish Christian Med. Soc. (bd. dirs. 1972-88, pres. 1983-88), Am. Heart Assn., Internat. Assn. Christian Physicians (exec. com. 1975-86). Home: 1367 La Loma Ave Berkeley CA 94708 Office: SuperGen 4140 Dublin Blvd Ste 200 Dublin CA 94568

METTY, THERESA M. communications executive; Degree in Bus., Harvard U. Leader Associated Spring Divsn. Barnes Group, Inc., 1975—95; with IBM, 1995—98; v.p. global procurement IBM, 1998—2000; from sr. v.p. and gen. mgr. supply chain Personal Comms. Sector Motorola Inc., Schaumberg, Ill., 2000—03, sr. v.p. and chief procurement officer, 2003—. Active purchasing coun. Mfrs. Alliance Productivity and Innovation; bd. dirs. The Inst. Supply Mgmt., Nat. Minority Supplier Devel. Coun., Women's Bus. Enterprise Nat. Coun.; spkr. in field. Office: Motorola Inc 1303 E Algonquin Rd Schaumburg IL 60196

METZ, ADAM S. real estate executive; BA, Cornell U.; MMgmt, Northwestern U. Corp. lending officer 1st Nat. Bank Chgo., 1983-87; v.p. Capital Markets Group, JMB Realty, 1987-93; treas., CFO, exec. v.p, dir. acquisitions Urban Shopping Ctrs., Inc., 1993-2000, pres., 2000—01; co-founding ptnr. Polaris Capital LLC, Northbrook, Ill., 2003—. Trustee Amli Residential Properties, 2003—, Ctr. for Urban Land Econs. Rsch., U. Wis., 1997—. Mem. Internat. Coun. Shopping Ctrs. Office: Polaris Capital LLC 1033 Skokie Blvd Ste 660 Northbrook IL 60062 Office Phone: 847-480-9180. E-mail: metza@comcast.net.

METZ, ANTHONY J., III, federal judge; Bankruptcy judge U.S. Dist. Ct. (so. dist.) Ind., Indpls., 1997—. Office: 317 US Courthouse 46 E Ohio St Indianapolis IN 46204-1903 E-mail: anthony_metz@insb.uscourts.gov.

METZ, CHARLES EDGAR, radiology educator; b. Bayshore, N.Y., Sept. 11, 1942; s. Clinton Edgar and Grace Muriel (Schienke) M.; m. Maryanne Theresa Bahr, July, 1967 (div. 1988); children: Rebecca, Molly. BA, Bowdoin Coll., 1964; MS, U. Pa., 1966, PhD, 1969. Instr. radiology U. Chgo., 1969-71, asst. prof., 1971-75, assoc. prof., 1976-80, dir. grad. programs in med. physics, 1979-85, prof., 1980—, prof. structural biology, 1984-86, prof. med. physics, 2003—. Mem. diagnostic rsch. adv. group Nat. Cancer Inst., 1980-81; mem. sci. com. Nat. Coun. on Radiation Protection and Measurements, 1982-95, Internat. Commn. on Radiation Units and Measurements, 1988-96, chmn. sci. com., 1992-99; cons. and lectr. in field. Assoc. editor: Radiology Jour., 1986—91, Med. Physics Jour., 1992—95, mem. editl. bd.: Med. Decision Making Jour., 1980—84; contbr. over 200 articles to sci. jours. and chpts. to books. Fellow Am. Assn. Physicists in Medicine; mem. Radiol. Soc. N.Am., Am. Assn. Physicists in Medicine, Soc. Med. Decision Making, Assn. Univ. Radiologists, Soc. for Health Svcs. Rsch. in Radiology, Phi Beta Kappa, Sigma Xi. Achievements include development of software analysis for ROC used in more than 7000 labs worldwide. Office: U Chgo Dept Radiology MC2026 5841 S Maryland Ave Chicago IL 60637-1463 E-mail: c-metz@uchicago.edu.

METZ, CRAIG HUSEMAN, business executive; b. Columbia, S.C., Aug. 26, 1955; s. Leonard Huseman and Annette (Worthington) M.; m. Karen Angela McCleary, Aug. 11, 1984; 1 child, Preston Worthington. BA, U. Tenn., 1977; JD, U. Memphis, 1986; cert., U.S. Ho. of Reps. Rep. Leadership Parliamentary Law Sch., 1987. Bar: S.C., D.C., U.S. Ct. Claims, U.S. Supreme Ct., U.S. Ct. Appeals (4th cir.). Canvass coord., liaison Campaign to Re-elect Congressman Floyd Spence, 1978; del., chmn. Shelby County Del. to 1983 Tenn. Young Rep. Fedn. Conv.; vice chmn. Shelby County Young Reps., 1983-84, chmn., 1984-85; Shelby County adminstr., asst. to Tenn. state exec. dir. Reagan-Bush Campaign, 1984; field rep. Campaign to Re-elect Congressman Floyd Spence, 1986; spl. asst. to Congressman Floyd Spence, 1986-88; counsel com. on labor and human resources U.S. Senate, 1988-90; commr.'s counsel U.S. Occupl. Safety and Health Rev. Commn., Washington, 1990-91; spl. asst. to asst. sec. for legis. and congl. affairs, dep. asst. sec. for congl. liaison US Dept. Edn., 1991—93; asst. dir. Divsn. Congl. Affairs AMA, Washington, 1993; chief of staff Congressman Floyd Spence, Washington, 1993—2001; adminstr. Office of the Second Congl. Dist. of S.C., U.S. Ho. of Reps., Washington, 2001; govt. rels. mgr. EMC Corp., Arlington, Va., 2001—. Judge nat. writing competition U.S. Constn. Bicentennial, S.C. 1987-88; mem. Ch. of the Ascension and Saint Agnes, Washington, The Palmetto Conservation Found. Recipient award of merit Rep. Party of Shelby County, 1985, Outstanding Leadership award Shelby County Young Reps., 1985, Meritorious Svc. medal Mil. Dept. S.C., Legis. award Res. Officers Assn. U.S., Order of the Palmetto, Palmetto Patriot award, Pres.'s award of N.G. Assn. S.C.; Hon. Washington fellow U. S.C. Washington Fellows Program. Mem. Rep. Nat. Lawyers Assn. (state chmn. S.C. chpt. 1987-90), Freedoms Found. Valley Forge, Va. Hist. Soc., Assn. for Preservation Va. Antiquities, Land Trust of Va., Preservation Alliance of Va., Va. Geneal. Soc., U. South Caroliniana Soc., Palmetto Trust for Historic Preservation, Palmetto Conservation Found., Lowcountry Heritage Soc., Orangeburg County (S.C.) Hist. Soc., Savannah River Valley Geneal. Soc., The Oyster Bay Hist. Soc., Hist. Soc. of Washington County, Va., Randolph County Genealogical Soc., Fairfax Genealogical Soc., Nat. Trust for Hist. Preservation (assoc. Capital region), SAR, St. David's Soc., St. Andrew's Soc. Washington, Royal Soc. St. George/St. George's Soc. Balt., Mil. Soc. War of 1812, Vet. Corps Arty. State of N.Y., Gen. Soc. War of 1812, Mil. Order Loyal Legion of U.S., Order of St. John (Hospitaller), SCV, Mil. Order Stars and Bars, Sons and Daus. Colonial and Antebellum Bench and Bar 1565-1861, Sons of the Revolution, Soc. King Charles the Martyr, Clan Lockhart, Am. Clan Lockhart Soc., Newcomer Soc. U.S., English Speaking Union, The Churchill Ctr., German Soc. Md., Propeller Club Wash., Randolph County Geneal. Soc., Fairfax Geneal. Soc., Friend of Scouting, Boy Scouts of Am., Ky. Col., Nat. Cathedral Assn., Washington D.C. Area Alumni Assn. of Sigma Alpha Epsilon Fraternity, U. Tenn. Nat. Alumni Assn., Sigma Alpha Epsilon, Phi Alpha Delta (v.p. McKellar chpt., Outstanding Svc. award 1983). Republican. Episcopalian. Home: 8505 Westown Way Vienna VA 22182-2513 Office: Crystal Park One Ste 907 2011 Crystal Dr Arlington VA 22202

METZ, EMMANUEL MICHAEL, investment company executive, lawyer; b. Pitts., Sept. 19, 1928; s. Solomon and Gertrude (Krieger) M.; m. Janine Spaner, Apr. 3, 1964. BA, Dartmouth Coll., 1949; LLB, Harvard U., 1952; LLM, NYU, 1958. Bar: N.Y. 1952. Atty. ABC, N.Y.C., 1956-58; security analyst Standard & Poor's, N.Y.C., 1958-68; mng. dir. CIBC Oppenheimer Corp., N.Y.C., 1968—. Author: Street Fighting at Wall and Broad, 1982. Lt. USN, 1952-56. Home: 150 E 56th St New York NY 10022-3631 Office: 200 Park Ave New York NY 10166 Office Phone: 212-667-5430. Business E-Mail: michael.metz@opco.com.

METZ, FERDINAND, chef, educator, academic administrator; b. Munich; BS, U. Pitts., 1973, MBA, 1975; apprenticeship, Sch. for Hotel and Restaurant Adminstrn., Cooking Trade Coll., Munich, Germany. Cert. master chef, Am. Culinary, Fedn., 1982. European apprentice in cooking and baking, 1956—62; commis tounant Hotel Deutscher Kaiser, Munich; saucier, garde manger, decorateur, sous chef Preakness Hills Country Club, Wayne, NJ; poissonier, garde manger, entremetier Le Pavillon, NYC, 1961—64; banquet chef Plaza Hotel, NYC, 1964—65; with Heinz, U.S.A., Pitts., 1965—80, sr. mgr., new product develop., mgr., new product develop., chief, product develop., exptl. chef; pres. Culinary Inst. Am., Hyde Park, NY, 1980—2001, pres. emeritus Beacon, NY, 2001—. Team mem., capt., team mgr., chmn. US Culinary Olympic Team, 1968-1988 (30 gold medals in internat. competition); mgr. Am. Team (Culinary World Cup, Luxemburg, 1986); head, cons., Ferdinand Metz Culinary Innovations, LLC and Master Chefs' Assocs.; lectr. German Hotel and Restaurant Industry; owner Café Cappuccino, Pitts., Gourmet Cooking Sch. for Food Enthusiasts, Pitts.; Internat. Culinary judge representing U.S.A., 1980-. Author: The Culinary Olympics Cookbook, 1976, 1980, 1984, 1988. Trustee St. Francis Hosp., Poughkeepsie, 1981-90. Co-recipient World Championship, hot foods divsn. Internat. Kockkunst Ausstellung, Internat. Culinary Competition, Germany, 1988; recipient Who is Who in Cooking, 1985, Lifetime Achievement award, James Beard Found. 1999, Medal of French Republic, 1967, Gold Plate award Internat. Foodservice Mfrs. Assn., 1983, Hotel Olympia Gold Medal of the British Chef's Soc., Centennial medal, Soc. Culinaire Philanthropique, Grand prize for Culinary Arts, German Govt., Leadership award, Restaurant Bus. Mag., 1985, Team Grand prize, Culinary World Cup Competition, Luxembourg, 1986, Courvoisier "Order of Napoleon", 1986, Caterina de Medici Edu. award, 1987, Corning Higher Edu. award, Commn. Independent Coll. & U., 1990, Silver Spoon award, Food Arts Magazine, 1995, Lifetime Achievement award, Tastemaster, 1992 & 1999, Ty award, NY Restaurant Assn., 1999, Coll. Diplomates, Nat. Restaurant Assn., Diploma and Medal Hon., Maires Cuisiniers de France, 2001, Hon. Gold medal, Masters Chefs of Frame, 2003; inducted into the Am. Acad. of Chefs Hall of Fame, 2003; named Maitre D'Honneur, La Chaine des Rotisseurs, 1997, Man Yr., Innovator Yr. award, MUFSO, 1998, Top 25 Movers and Shakers, Self Magazine, 1998, Escoffier Soc., 2002. Mem. Am. Culinary Fedn. (pres. 1979-83, chmn., mem. honor soc. 1971-, nat. chmn., culinary and master chef cert. com., 1976-85, named Nat. Chef Yr., 1968, Nat. Culinarian Yr., 1985, Educator Yr., 1998), Internat. Foodsvc. Mfrs. Assn., World Assn. of Cooks Societies (hon. mem., v.p. 1981-85, pres. 2004-), Am. Acad. Chefs.; tres. Nat. Restaurant Assn. Edu. Found., 2003-, Societe Culinaire Philanthropique, Vatel Club, Les Amis D'Escoffier Soc., James Beard Found., La Chaine des Rotisseurs; hon. mem. Canadian Chefs de Cuisine, German Chefs' Assn., Am. Dietetic Assn., Internat. Chefs' Assn.; trustee Coun. of Independent Colls. & U. NY, 1983-92, Centre Internat. de Glion, Switzerland, 1987-97, Culinary Inst. Am. 1975-80 (Outstanding Chef Yr., 1975), Nat. Restaurant Assn. Edu. Inst., 1994-. Office: Culinary Inst Am 5 Slocum Rd Beacon NY 12508 Office Phone: 845-838-5448. Office Fax: 845-838-5449. Business E-Mail: F_Metz@msn.com.*

METZ, MARY SEAWELL, foundation administrator, retired academic administrator; b. Rockhill, S.C., May 7, 1937; d. Columbus Jackson and Mary (Dunlap) Seawell; m. F. Eugene Metz, Dec. 21, 1957; 1 dau., Mary Eugena. BA summa cum laude in French and English, Furman U., 1958; postgrad., Institut Phonetique, Paris, 1962-63, Sorbonne, 1962-63; PhD magna cum laude in French, La. State U., 1966; HHD (hon.), Furman U., 1984; LLD (hon.), Chapman Coll., 1985; DLT (hon.), Converse Coll., 1988. Instr. French La. State U., 1965-66, asst. prof., 1966-67, 1968-72, assoc. prof., 1972-76, dir. elem. and intermediate French programs, 1966-74, spl. asst. to chancellor, 1974-75, asst. to chancellor, 1975-76; prof. French Hood Coll., Frederick, Md., 1976-81, provost, dean acad. affairs, 1976-81; pres. Mills Coll., Oakland, Calif., 1981-90; dean of extension U. Calif., Berkeley, 1991-98; pres. S.H. Cowell Found., San Fransisco, 1999—. Vis. asst. prof. U. Calif.-Berkeley, 1967-68; mem. commn. on leadership devel. Am. Coun. on Edn., 1981-90, adv. coun. Stanford Rsch. Inst., 1985-90, adv. coun. Grad. Sch. Bus., Stanford U.; bd. dirs. PG&E, SBC Comms., Inc., Union Bank, Longs Drug Stores, S.H. Cowell Found. Author: Reflets du monde francais, 1971, 78, Cahier d'exercices: Reflets du monde francais, 1972, 78, (with Helstrom) Le Francais a decouvrir, 1972, 78, Le Francais a vivre, 1972, 78, Cahier d'exercices: Le Francais a vivre, 1972, 78; standardized tests; mem. editorial bd. Liberal Edn., 1982— . Trustee Am. Conservatory Theater. NDEA fellow, 1960-62, 1963-64; Fulbright fellow, 1962-63; Am. Council Edn. fellow, 1974-75 Mem. Western Coll. Assn. (v.p. 1982-84, pres. 1984-86), Assn. Ind. Calif. Colls. and Univs. (exec. com. 1982-90), Nat. Assn. Ind. Colls. and Univs. (govt. rels. adv. coun. 1982-85), So. Conf. Lang. Teaching (chmn. 1976-77), World Affairs Coun. No. Calif. (bd. dirs. 1984-93), Bus.-Higher Edn. Forum, Women's Forum West, Women's Coll. Coalition (exec. com. 1984-88), Phi Kappa Phi, Phi Beta Kappa. Address: PO Box 686 Stinson Beach CA 94970-0686 also: 9 Regulus Ct Alameda CA 94501-1015 Office: SH Cowell Found 120 Montgomery St San Francisco CA 94104-4303

METZ, ROBERT ROY, publisher, editor; b. Richmond Hill, N.Y., Mar. 23, 1929; s. Robert Roy, Sr. and Mary (Kissel) M.; m. Susan Lee Blair, 1984; children: Robert Sumner, Christopher Roy. BA, Wesleyan U., Middletown Conn., 1950. Copyboy N.Y. Times, 1951, asst. fgn. news desk, 1952; rewriteman cable desk I.N.S., 1953, overnight cable editor, 1954-56, asst. feature editor, 1956-58; asst. news editor Newspaper Enterprise Assn., 1958, news editor, 1959-63, mng. editor, 1963-66, exec. editor, 1966-68, v.p., 1967-71, editorial dir., 1968-71, pres., editor, dir., 1972-94; dir. Berkeley-Small Inc., 1974-77; chmn. Berkley-Small Inc., 1976-77; v.p., dir. United Feature Syndicate, 1976-77, pres., editor, 1978; pres., editor, dir. United Media, 1978-93, chmn., 1993-94; media cons., 1994—. Pres. Peter Pan Children's Fund, 1997—. Mem.: Union League (N.Y.C.). Lutheran. Home: 193 Swamp Rd East Hampton NY 11937

METZ, ROBIN O. writer, educator, poet; b. Pittsburgh, Pa., Jan. 4, 1942; s. Robert Frederick and Isabell Metz; m. Elizabeth Carlin, Dec. 20, 1995; m. Elizabeth Jahnke, Aug. 29, 1992 (dec. Feb. 20, 1993); m. Lynn Hellerstedt Harlan (div.); children: Lisa Metz-Belzer, Ronnah. BA, Princeton U., Princeton, New Jersey, 1964; MFA, U. of Iowa, Iowa City, Iowa, 1967. Phillip sidney post prof. of english Knox Coll., Galesburg, Ill., 1967—, dir., program in creative writing, 1984—; dir., london florence program Associated Colleges of the Midwest, Chicago, Ill., 1993—94, faculty fellow, chgo. urban studies program, 1989—90, faculty fellow, chgo. arts program, 1991—92, 1998—99. Mem. adv. coun Ctr. for Excellence in the Arts and Humanities, Iowa State U.; non-resident fellow Ctr. for Am. Progress, Washington. Author: (book) Unbidden Angel (Rainer Maria Rilke Internat. Poetry Prize, 1999), poetry, fiction, poetry, River Stories (Miss. Valley Internat. Poetry Prize, 1989), poetry/fiction/nonfiction, poetry, . Recipient Syndicated Fiction Prize(s), Nat. Endowment for the Arts/PEN USA, Marshall Frankel Am. Fiction Prize, Other Voices, Roll of Honor Citation(s), The Best Am. Short Stories, Phillip Greene Wright Award for Disting. Tchg., Knox Coll., Caterpillar Corp. Award for Exceptional Achievement, Environ. Award(s) for Wildlife Habitat and Forestry, State of Wis. (Crawford County); fellow Individual Writer's Fellowship, Ill. Arts Coun. Mem.: Poetry Soc. of Am., Am. Acad. of Poets, Associated Writing Programs, PEN Internat./USA-West. Home: 695 North Broad Street Galesburg IL 61401 Office: Knox College K-50 Galesburg IL 61401 Personal E-mail: rmetz@knox.edu. E-mail: rmetz@knox.edu.

METZ, STEVEN KENT, federal agency administrator, writer; b. Charleston, W.Va., June 30, 1956; s. David N. and Carolyn Ann (Powell) M.; m. Jayne Godwin Nelson, Aug. 14, 1977; children: Rachel Elizabeth, Stephanie Eleanor. BA, U. S.C., 1977, MA, 1981; PhD, Johns Hopkins U., 1985. Vis. prof. polit. sci. Va. Tech, Blacksburg, Va., 1984-87; prof. internat. rels. U.S. Army Command and Gen. Staff Coll., Ft. Leavenworth, Kans., 1987-91; prof. low intensity conflict and Third World studies Air War Coll., Maxwell AFB, Ala., 1991-93; rsch. prof. nat. security affairs Strategic Studies Inst. U.S. Army War Coll., Carlisle Barracks, Pa., 1993-2000, Henry L. Stimson prof. mil. studies, 1993-95, dir. rsch., chmn. regional strategy and planning dept., 2001—. Lectr., cons. in field. Contbr. articles to profl. jours., chpts. to books. Republican. Home: 5 Countryside Dr Carlisle PA 17013-9036 Office: Strategic Studies Inst US Army War Coll Carlisle Barracks PA 17013 E-mail: steven.metz@carlisle.army.mil.

METZ, STEVEN WILLIAM, small business owner; b. Inglewood, Calif., Nov. 30, 1946; s. Glenn Ludwig and Kathleen Martha (Peterson) M.; m. Michelle Marie McArthur, Aug. 11, 1989; 1 child, Glenn Christian. Student, Fullerton Coll., Calif. Supt. Oahu Interiors, Honolulu, 1969-71, Hackel Bros., Miami, Fla., 1971-73; exec. v.p. Tru-Cut Inc., Brea, Calif., 1974-82; gen. mgr. The Louvre', Grass Valley, Calif., 1983-85; mfg. engring. mgr. Rexnord Aerospace, Torrance, Calif., 1986-87; pres., founder Metz/Calcoa Inc., Torrance, Calif., 1987—. Mfg. rep. consul Orange County Spring, Anaheim, 1987—, TALSCO, 1994—, Precision Resources, 1994—, GEMTECH, 1994—; mfg. rep. consul Alard Machine Products, Gardena, Calif., 1988—, v.p. spl. projects, 1997—. Charter mem. Rep. Presdl. Task Force, 1991—; mem. L.A. Coun. on World Affairs, 1991-92. With U.S. Army, 1966-68. Recipient Appreciation awards DAV, 1968, Soc. Mfg. Engrs., 1991. Fellow Soc. Carbide Engrs.; mem. Soc. Carbide and Tool Engrs. (chpt. pres. 1980-82, Appreciation award 1981), Rep. Presdl. Legion of Merit. Avocations: golf, swimming, riding, boating.

METZ, T(HEODORE) JOHN, librarian, educator; b. Erie, Pa., Nov. 5, 1932; s. Theodore John and Dorothy Pearl (Schutte) M.; m. Dorothy Page Neff, June 11, 1955; 1 child, Margaret Elizabeth MusB, Heidelberg Coll., 1954; MA in Music, Miami U., Oxford, Ohio, 1955; MLS, U. Mich., 1959. Libr. II U. Wis., Madison, 1959-61; asst. libr. Lawrence U., Appleton, Wis., 1961-67; dir. librs. U. Wis.-Green Bay, 1967-75; exec. dir. Midwest Region Library Network, Evanston, Ill., 1975-79; coll. libr., assoc. prof. Carleton Coll., Northfield, Minn., 1979-97, coll. libr. emeritus, 1998—. Speaker, participant, coord. numerous confs. and insts., 1969—; chmn. several state libr. groups, 1971-76; mem. several nat. libr. adv. coms., 1974-80; bldg. cons. Carleton Coll., others, 1978—; mem. Citizen Amb. Rsch. Librs. del. to Ea. Europe, 1992. Author: MIDLNET Symposium Report, 1976 Chmn. Green Bay Symphony, 1971-76; mem. various bds. coms., relating to mus. activities; performer Green Bay and other orchs., 1955— Library Service scholar U. Mich., 1957; Library Service fellow U. Mich., 1958 Mem. ALA, Assn. Coll. Rsch. Librs., Internat. Fedn. Libr. Assns. Avocations: musical activities; hunting; fishing; gardening. E-mail: tmetz@carleton.edu.

METZ, THOMAS FREDRIC, career military officer; b. Elkin, N.C., Sept. 21, 1948; m. Pamela Redmond; children: Elizabeth, Cade, Patrick. BS, U.S. Mil. Acad., 1971; M in Mech. Engring., N.C. State U., 1980; grad., Command and Gen. Staff Coll., Army War Coll. Registered profl. engr., Va. Enlisted U.S. Army, 1966, commd. 2nd lt. inf., 1971, advanced through grades to lt. gen., 2002, various positions, 1972-76, aide-de-camp for Comdr., Readiness Region VI, 1976, comdr. C Co., 4th Bn., 54th Inf., 194th Armor Brigade, 1977-78; asst. prof. mech. engring. dept. U.S. Mil. Acad., West Point, N.Y., 1981-84; S-3/XO 3d Bn., 7th Inf., S-3 197th Separate Inf. Brigade Ft. Benning, Ga.; divsn. chief Inf. Sch. Combat Devel. Directorate, 1984-87; comdr. 4th Bn., 15th Inf., 194th Armor Brigade Ft. Knox, 1987-89; G-3, 2d Inf. Divsn., 1990-92; comdr. 2d Brigade, 1st Inf. Divsn., 1992-94; chief of staff Ft. Riley, 1994-95; dir. exptl. force coordination cell, 4th Inf. Divsn. U.S. Army, Fort Hood, 1995-97; asst. divsn. comdr. for support 4th Inf. Divsn., 1997-98; dep. dir. Joint Warfighting Capability Assessment, J8 The Joint Staff, Washington, 1998-2000, vice dir., force structure, resources, & assessment, J-8, 2000—01; comdr., 24th Infantry Divsn. (Mechanized) U.S. Army, Fort Riley, Kans., 2001—03; chief of staff US Centl. Command, Operation Enduring Freedom, 2002—03; comdr., III US Corps U.S. Army, Fort Hood, Tex., 2003—; comdr. Multi-Nat. Corps. Iraq, 2004—. Decorated Legion of Merit with two oak leaf clusters, Meritorious Svc. medal with three oak leaf clusters, Army Commendation medal with two oak leaf clusters, Good Conduct medal. Office: 6791 Patton Dr Fort Hood TX 76544-1343 E-mail: metztf@js.pentagon.mil.*

METZ, WERNER ADAM, physicist; b. Savannah, Ga., May 18, 1953; s. Werner Adam, Sr. and Ricarda Rodriguez Metz; m. Cheryl Metz, Aug. 27, 1977. BA in Physics, U. of Chgo., 1975; MS in Physics, Ga. Tech, 1977, PhD in Physics, 1982. Sr. engr. NCR Microelectronics, Ft. Collins, Colo., 1981—86; prin. scientist Digital Imaging, Polaroid Corp, Cambridge, 1986—92, tech. bus. mgr., 1992—96; sr. mgr., sr. staff arch. Digital Imaging and Video Divsn., Intel Corp, Chandler, Ariz., 1996—2001; chief tech. officer, digital capture operation New Bus. Group, Intel Corp., Chandler, Ariz., 2001—. Chair pcmcia subcom. on memory cards for imagings PCMCIA, Santa Clara, Calif., 1991—95. Author: (28 technical papers) J. Applied Physics, Applied Phys. Letters, Electron Device Letters, IEEE Trans on Consum Electronics. Chair for removable memory std. ISO TC42/WG 18 Digital Photography, Geneva, Switzerland, 1993—2002. Recipient Excellence award in Low power CMOS process, NCR Corp., 1985, Excellence award in std. cell arch., Intel Corp., 1986, Intel award for Arch. of dual mode CMOS based camera, 1996, Intel award for devel. of next generation conf. camera, 1999. Mem.: AAAS, Internat. Soc. for Optical Engring/Soc. for Imaging Sci. and Tech., IEEE, Am. Phys. Soc., Sigma Pi Sigma. Achievements include patents for 16 patents in medicine, Physics, microelectronics, digital imaging products and sci; first to Digital still cameras, CMOS image sensors, digital processing algorithms; discovery of Semiconductor processing for selective tungsten and refractory metals; patents pending for 7 Patents Pending; discovery of Semiconductor processes: selective tungsten deposition; development of Dual mode video/still camera, scanners, digital printers; invention of co-inventor of MXP5X00 image processor arch. E-mail: werner.metz@ieee.org.

METZEL, ALAN BARRY, manufacturing engineer; b. Hagerstown, Md., Sept. 25, 1944; s. Richard Cavanaugh (Stepfather) and Honora Irene McCoppin; m. Sheila Eileen Shobe, July 28, 1967; children: Michael Alan, Amanda Eileen. AS in Engring. Tech., Hagerstown Jr. Coll., 1965; BS in Mech. Engring., Univ. Tenn., Knoxville, 1969. Tooling supr. Ea. Products Corp., Hagerstown, Md., 1969—73; mfg. engr. Mack Trucks Powertrain Divsn., Hagerstown, Md., 1973—91; mfg. liaison United Def., York, Pa., 1998—99; quality engr. Northrop Grumman Electronic Sector, Linthicum, Md., 2000—. Past pres., past v.p., past exec. comm. mem. Hagerstown Jr. Coll. Alumni Assn., 1970. Mem.: Coordinate Measurement Sys. Com., Am. Soc. Quality, Soc. Mfg. Engrs. Home: 12637 Bradbury Ave Smithsburg MD 21783-1417 Office: Northrop-Grumman 7323 Aviation Blvd Linthicum MD 21090 Office Phone: 410-765-2090. Personal E-mail: almetzel@aol.com.

METZEN, JAMES P. state legislator, bank executive; b. Oct. 1943; m. Sandie Metzen; two children. Student, U. Minn. Banker; mem. Minn. Ho. of Reps., St. Paul, 1975-86, Minn. Senate from 39th dist., St. Paul, 1986—, pres., 2002—. Chmn. govt. op. and vets. com.; mem. jobs, energy and cmty. devel., state govt. fin. divsn. commerce and consumer protection, rules and adminstrn. Minn. State Senate. Office: 312 Deerwood Ct South Saint Paul MN 55075-2102 also: State Senate State Capital Building Saint Paul MN 55155-0001

METZENBAUM, HOWARD MORTON, former senator, consumer organization official; b. Cleve., June 4, 1917; s. Charles I. and Anna (Klafter) M.; m. Shirley Turoff, Aug. 8, 1946; children: Barbara Jo, Susan Lynn Hyatt, Shelley Hope, Amy Beth. BA, Ohio State U., 1939, LLD, 1941. Chmn. bd. Airport Parking Co. Am., 1958-66, ITT Consumer Services Corp., 1966-68, Com-Corp, 1969-74; U.S. senator State of Ohio, 1974, 1977-94; chmn. Consumer Fedn. Am., Washington, 1994—. Mem. War Labor Panel, 1942-45, Ohio Bur. Code Rev., 1949-50, Cleve. Met. Housing Authority, 1968-70, Lake Erie Regional Transit Authority, 1972-73, Ohio Ho. of Reps., 1943-46, Ohio Senate, 1947-50; chmn. anti-trust sub-com., labor sub-com. U.S. Senate; mem. intell com., budget com., environ. and pub. works com., judiciary com., labor and human resources, energy and natural resources, dem. policy com.; bd. mem., pub. citizen, D.C. Pub. Libr. Bd. Trustee Mt. Sinai Hosp., Cleve., 1961—73, treas., 1966—73; nat. co-chmn. Nat. Citizen's Com. Conquest Cancer; former vice chmn. fellows Brandeis U.; chmn. Am. Friend Rabin Ctr., Tel Aviv; past bd. dirs. Coun. Human Rels., United Cerebral Palsy Assn., Nat. Coun. Hunger and Malnutrition, Karamu House, St. Vincent Charity Hosp., Cleve., St. Jude Rsch. Hosp., Memphis. Mem. Order of Coif, Phi Eta Sigma, Tau Epsilon Rho. Home: 5610 Wisconsin Ave Bethesda MD 20815-4415

METZENBAUM, SHELLEY H. educational consultant, government agency administrator, consultant; d. Howard Morton and Shirley Metzenbaum; m. Steven Kelman, July 6, 1980; children: Jody Kelman, Leora Kelman. BA, Stanford U., 1974; M in Pub. Policy, Harvard U., 1978, PhD in Pub. Policy, 1992. Econ. devel. specialist State of Ark., Washington, 1980—81; dir. Wash. office City of Boston, Washington, 1981—82; dir. capital budgeting Commonwealth Mass., Boston, 1987—90; undersecretary Mass. Exec. Office Environ. Affairs, Boston, 1990—91; assoc. adminstr. U.S. Environ. Protection Agency, Washington, 1993—97; cons. Concord, Mass., 1997—; vis. prof. U. Md. Sch. Pub. Affairs, College Park, 1997—. Exec. dir. performance mgmt. project Kennedy Sch., Cambridge, Mass., 1998—2001; sr. cons. Facility Reporting Project, Boston, 2002—; exec. dir. Environ. Compliance Consortium, Washington, 1997—; cons. in field of govt. mgmt.; rschr., writer on govt. mgmt. Grantee, The Joyce Found., Chgo., Pew Charitable Trust, Phila. Fellow: Nat. Acad. Pub. Adminstrn. (elected 2002—); mem.: Coun. Excellence in Govt. (prin. 1998—).

METZGER, PATRICIA ANN, lawyer; b. Phila., Mar. 10, 1941; d. Freeman Weeks and Evelyn (Heap) M.; m. Karl Hormann, June 30, 1980. BA with distinction, U. Pa., 1963, LLB cum laude, 1966. Bar: Mass. 1966, D.C. 1972, U.S. Tax Ct. 1988. Assoc., then ptnr. Mintz, Levin, Cohn, Glovsky and Popeo, Boston, 1966—75; assoc. tax legis. counsel U.S. Treasury Dept., Washington, 1975-78; shareholder, dir. Goulston & Storrs, P.C., Boston, 1978-98; stockholder Hutchins, Wheeler & Dittmar, P.C., Boston, 1998—2002; of counsel Vacovec, Mayotte & Singer LLP, Newton, Mass., 2003—. Lectr. program continuing legal edn. Boston Coll. Law Sch., Chestnut Hill, Mass., spring, 1974; lectr. grad. tax program Boston U. Law Sch., 2001—03; mem. adv. com. NYU Inst. Fed. Taxation, N.Y.C., 1981—87; mem. practitioner liaison com. Mass. Dept. Revenue, 1985—90; spkr. in field. Author: Federal Income Taxation of Individuals, 1984; mem. adv. bd. Corp. Tax and Bus. Planning Rev., 1996—; mem. authors' panel Jour. Passthrough Entities, 2003—; mem. editl. bd. Am. Jour. Tax Policy, 1995-98; contbr. articles to profl. jours., chpts. to books. Bd. mgrs. Barrington Ct. Condominium, Cambridge, Mass., 1985-86; bd. dirs. University Road Parking Assn., Cambridge, 1988—; trustee Social Law Libr., Boston, 1989-93. Mem. ABA (tax sect., vice-chair publs. 2000-02, mem. coun. 1996-99, chmn. subcom. allocations and distbns. partnership com. 1978-82, vice chmn. legis. 1991-93, chmn. 1993-95, com. govt. submissions, vice liaison 1993-94, liaison 1994-95, North Atlantic region, co-liaison 1995-96, N.E. region, regional liaison meetings com.), FBA (coun. on taxation, chmn. corp. taxation com. 1977-81, chmn. com. partnership taxation 1981-87), Mass. Bar Assn. (coun. tax sect. 2001-2004), Boston Bar Assn. (coun. 1987-89, chmn. tax sect. 1989-91), Am. Coll. Tax Counsel (bd. regents 1999-2004), Boston Estate Planning Coun. (exec. com. 1975, 79-82). Avocation: vocal performances (as soloist and with choral groups). Office: Vacovec Mayotte & Singer LLP Two Newton Pl Ste 340 255 Washington St Newton MA 02458-1634 Office Phone: 617-964-0500.

METZGER, BRUCE MANNING, clergyman, educator; b. Middletown, Pa., Feb. 9, 1914; s. Maurice Rutt and Anna Mary (Manning) M.; m. Isobel E. Mackay, July 7, 1944; children: John Mackay, James Bruce. AB, Lebanon

Valley Coll., 1935, DD, 1951; ThB, Princeton Theol. Sem., 1938, ThM, 1939; AM, Princeton U., 1940, PhD, 1942; LHD (hon.), Findlay U., 1962; DD (hon.), St. Andrews U., Scotland, 1964; DTheol (hon.), Münster U., Fed. Republic Germany, 1970; DLitt (hon.), Potchefstroom U., South Africa, 1985. Ordained to ministry Presbyn. Ch. USA, 1939. Teaching fellow N.T. Princeton Theol. Sem., 1938-40, mem. faculty, 1940—, prof. N.T. lang. and lit., 1954-64, George L. Collord prof. N.T. lang. and lit., 1964-84, emeritus, 1984—. Vis. lectr. Presbyn. Theol. Sem. South, Campinas, Brazil, 1952, Presbyn. Theol. Sem. North, Recife, Brazil, 1952; mem. Inst. for Advanced Study, Princeton, 1964-65, 73-74; scholar-in-residence Tyndale House, Cambridge, 1969; vis. fellow Clare Hall, Cambridge, 1974, Wolfson Coll., Oxford U., 1979, Macquarie U., Sydney, Australia, 1982, Caribbean Grad. Sch. of Theology, Jamaica, 1990, Seminario Internacional Teológico Bautista, Buenos Aires, 1991, Griffith Thomas Lectrs., Dallas Theol. Sem., 1992; mem. mng. com. Am. Sch. Classical Studies, Athens, Greece; mem. Standard Bible com. Nat. Coun. Chs., 1952—, chmn., 1975—; mem. seminar N.T. studies Columbia U., 1959-80; mem. Kuratorium of Vetus-Latina Inst., Beuron, Germany, 1959—; adv. com. Inst. N.T. Text Rsch., U. Münster, 1961—, Thesaurus Linguae Graecae, 1972-80; Collected Works of Erasmus, 1977—; chmn. Am. com. versions Internat. Greek N.T., 1950-88; participant internat. congresses scholars, Aarhus, Aberdeen, Bangor, Basel, Bonn, Brussels, Budapest, Cairo, Cambridge, Copenhagen, Dublin, Exeter, Frankfurt, Heidelberg, London, Louvain, Manchester, Milan, Munich, Münster, Newcastle, Nottingham, Oxford, Prague, Rome, St. Andrews, Stockholm, Strasbourg, Toronto, Trondheim, Tübingen; mem. Presbytery, N.B. Author: The Saturday and Sunday Lessons from Luke in the Greek Gospel Lectionary, 1944, Lexical Aids for Students of New Testament Greek, 1946, enlarged edit., 1955, A Guide to the Preparation of a Thesis, 1950, An Introduction to the Apocrypha, 1957, Chapters in the History of New Testament Textual Criticism, 1963, The Text of the New Testament, Its Transmission, Corruption, and Restoration, 1964, 3rd with B.D. Ehrman 4th enlarged edit., 2004, (with H.G. May) The Oxford Annotated Bible with the Apocrypha, 1965, The New Testament, Its Background, Growth, and Content, 1965, 3d edit., 2003, Index to Periodical Literature on Christ and the Gospels, 1966, Historical and Literary Studies, Pagan, Jewish, and Christian, 1968, Index to Periodical Literature on the Apostle Paul, 1960, 2nd edit., 1970, A Textual Commentary on the Greek New Testament, 1971, 2d edit., 1994, The Early Versions of the New Testament, 1977, New Testament Studies, 1980, Manuscripts of the Greek Bible, 1981, The Canon of the New Testament, 1987, (with Roland Murphy) The New Oxford Annotated Bible with the Apocrypha, 1991, (with M.D. Coogan) The Oxford Companion to the Bible, 1993, Breaking the Code-Understanding the Book of Revelation, 1993, Reminiscences of an Octogenarian, 1997, (with Coogan) The Oxford Guide to People & Places of the Bible, 2001, (with Coogan) The Oxford Guide to Ideas and Issues of the Bible, 2001, The Bible in Translation, Ancient and English Versions, 2001; mem. editorial com.: Critical Greek New Testament, 1956-84; chmn. Am. com., Internat. Greek New Testament Project, 1970-88; sec. com. translators: Apocrypha (rev. standard version); editor: New Testament Tools and Studies, 30 vols, 1960-2000, Oxford Annotated Apocrypha, 1965, enlarged edit., 1977; Reader's Digest Condensed Bible, 1982; co-editor: United Bible Societies Greek New Testament, 1966, 4th edit., 1993; compiler: Index of Articles on the New Testament and the Early Church Published in Festschriften, 1951, supplement, 1955, Lists of Words Occurring Frequently in the Coptic New Testament (Sahidic Dialect), 1961, Annotated Bibliography of the Textual Criticism of the New Testament, 1955, (with Isobel M. Metzger) Oxford Concise Concordance to the Holy Bible, 1962, (with R.C. Dentan and W. Harrelson), The Making of the New Revised Standard Version of the Bible, 1991; contbr. articles to jours. Chmn. standard bible com. Nat. Coun. Chs., 1977-2000. Recipient cert. Disting. Svc. Nat. Coun. Chs., 1957, Disting. Alumnus award Lebanon Valley Coll. Alumni Assn., 1961, citation of appreciation Laymen's Nat. Bible Assn., 1986, Disting. Alumnus award Princeton Theol. Sem., 1989, lit. competition prize Christian Rsch. Found., 1955, 62, 63, E.T. Thompson award, 1991. Mem. Am. Philos. Soc., Soc. Bibl. Lit. (pres. 1970-71, past del. Am. Coun. Learned Socs.), Am. Bible Soc. (bd. mgrs. 1948—, chmn. com. transls. 1964-70), Am. Philol. Assn., Studiorum Novi Testamenti Societas (pres. 1971-72), Cath. Bibl. Assn., N.Am. Patristic Soc. (pres. 1972), Soc. Textual Scholarship (pres. 1995), Am. Soc. Papyrologists; hon. fellow, corr. mem. Higher Inst. Coptic Studies, Cairo; corr. fellow Brit. Acad. (Burkitt medal in Bibl. studies 1994). Republican. Home: 20 Cleveland Ln Princeton NJ 08540-3050 Office: Princeton Theol Sem 64 Mercer St Princeton NJ 08542-0803 Office Phone: 609-921-8300. E-mail: denise.schwalb@ptsem.edu.

METZGER, DELORES VIRGINIA, social services professional; b. Albert, Feb. 25, 1952; d. Arthur Willard and Delores Fredricka Maxwell; m. Albert Timothy Metzger, Apr. 15, 1972; children: Brian Timothy, Damien Phillip. AA degrees, Dundalk C.C., 1975, 89; BA, U. Balt., 1992; MSW, U. Md., 1994. Lic. social worker. Child support enforcement agt. Dept. Human Resources, Balt., 1983-85, adminstrv. reviewer Family Investment Adminstrn., 1985-87, asst. field supr., 1987-90, field supr., 1990-95, program mgr., 1995-96, mgmt. analyst, 1997-99, program analyst Social Svcs. Adminstrn., 1999—. Chair hospitality com. PTA High Point Elem. Sch., 1980-90; ch. vol. Our Daily Bread, Balt. Mem. Loyal Order of the Moose. Avocations: reading, bowling, contestant on wheel of fortune. Office: Dept Human Resources 311 W Saratoga St Baltimore MD 21201-3500

METZGER, ERIKA ALMA, education educator; b. Berlin, Apr. 8, 1933; arrived in U.S., 1958; Staatsexamen, Free Univ. Berlin, Germany, 1958; MA, Cornell U., 1961; PhD, SUNY, Buffalo, 1967. Tchg. asst. Cornell Univ., Ithaca, NY, 1958—61; instr. U. Ill., 1961—63; asst. and assoc. prof. SUNY, Buffalo, 1963—79, full prof. emeritus, 1979—. Dir. undergrad. and grad. studies SUNY, 1977—87. Author (and editor): Herrn von Hoffmanswaldau, 1970—90, Companion to the Works of Rainer Maria Rilke, 2001. Grantee publ. grants, German Rsch Found., 1974—91. Office: SUNY DRL 910 Clemens Hall Buffalo NY 14260

METZGER, ERNEST HUGH, aerospace engineer, research scientist; b. Nurnberg, Germany, Oct. 22, 1923; came to U.S., 1939, naturalized, 1943; s. Paul Arthur and Charlotte Babette (Kann) M.; m. Sarah Temple Grinnell, Nov. 19, 1956; children: Lisa Metzger Dunning, Charlotte Bennett (dec.), George Grinnell. BS, CCNY, 1949; MS, Harvard U., 1950. Automatic control engr. Bell Aerospace Co. div. Textron, Buffalo, 1950-54, tech. dir. inertial nav. systems, 1954-60, chief engr., inertial instruments, 1960-70, chief engr., gravity gradiometer systems, 1970-83, dir. gravity sensor systems, 1983-86, exec. dir. engring., 1986-89, cons., 1989-95, Bell Geospace Inc., Buffalo, 1995—. Mem. panel future navigation systems Nat. Acad. Sci., com. on geodesy NRC, 1988-89, accelerator criteria com. NASA, tech. com. navigation guidance and control, AIAA, 1989—; vis. lectr. dept. aernautics and astronautics Stanford U., 1990 Contbr. articles to profl. jours.; patentee in field Served with AUS, 1943-46 Recipient Aerospace Pioneer award Niagara Frontier sect. AIAA, 1977; named to Niagara Frontier Aviation Hall of Fame, 1992. Mem. IEEE, Inst. Navigation (Thurlow award for outstanding contbn. to sci. navigation 1983), AAAS, Air Force Assn., N.Y. Acad. Scis., Explorers Club, Sigma Xi, Tau Beta Pi, Eta Kappa Nu Clubs: Harvard, Buffalo Ski. Home: 90 High Park Blvd Buffalo NY 14226-4209 E-mail: semetz@ix.netcom.com.

METZGER, HENRY, federal research institution administrator; b. Mainz, Germany, Mar. 23, 1932; came to U.S., 1938; naturalized, 1945; s. Paul Alfred and Anne (Daniel) M.; m. Deborah Stashower, June 16, 1957; children: Eran D., Renée V., Carl E. MD, Columbia U., 1957. Chief chem. immunology sect. Nat. Inst. Arthritis & Musculoskeletal & Skin Disease/NIH, Bethesda, Md., 1973—2002; br. chief USPHS, Bethesda, 1983-94, sci. dir., 1987-98, med. officer grade VI, 1975-98; scientist Sr. Biomed. Rsch. Svc., 1999—2002, scientist emeritus, 2002—. Carl Prausnitz Meml. lectr., 1982; Ecker Meml. lectr. Case Western Res. U., Cleve., 1984; Harvey Soc. lectr., 1984; Eli Nadel Meml. lectr. St. Louis U., 1987; Rodney Porter Meml. lectr., 1993; Burroughs-Wellcome lectr., 1994; R.E. Dyer lectr., 1995; mem. health rsch. coun. BMFT, German Govt., 1994-97. Editor: Fc Receptors & the Action of Antibodies, 1990; assoc. editor Ann. Rev. Immunology, 1982-96; contbr. numerous articles to profl. jours.; mem. editl. bd. numerous sci. jours. Recipient Meritorious Svc. award USPHS, 1978, Disting. Svc. award, 1985, 97, Joseph Mather Smith prize Columbia U., 1984. Fellow AAAS, Am. Acad. Allergy and Immunology; mem. NAS, Am. Assn. Immunologists (pres. 1991-92), Am. Soc. Biol. Chem. Molecular Biology, Am. Soc. Cell Biology, Internat. Union Immunol. Soc. (pres. 1992-95), Found. for Advanced Edn. in the Scis. (pres. 1990-92), Alpha Omega Alpha. Home: 3410 Taylor St Chevy Chase MD 20815-4024 Office: NIH Rm 9n228 10 Center Dr 9000 Rockville Pike Bethesda MD 20892-1820 E-mail: metzgerh@exchange.nih.gov.

METZGER, JAMES W. military officer; s. Mr. and Mrs. George Metzger; m. Mary Jane Bachmann; children: Jennifer, Amy. Grad. with distinction, U.S. Naval Acad., 1971; MEE, Mich. State U.; ed., Nuc. Power Sch., Bainbridge, Md. Commd. ensign USN, advanced through grades to rear adm.; elec. officer, main propulsion asst. USS George Bancroft; engring. officer USS Indpls., 1977-81; mem. nuc. propulsion examining bd. U.S. Pacific Fleet; exec. officer USS Tautog, Pearl Harbor, Hawaii, 1983-86; comdr. USS Mpls.-St. Paul, 1987-90; dir. Submarine Prospective Comdg. Oficer Sch., 1991; exec. asst. to comdr. in chief U.S. Atlantic Fleet, Norfolk, Va., 1991-93; comdr. Submarine Devel. Squadron 12, 1993; exec. asst. Vice Chief of Naval Ops.; exec. asst., naval aide Sec. of Navy; dep. dir. for strategy and policy USN, Washington, 1997-98, commr. of subm. group 8, 1998—2001; assist. to chmn. Joint Chiefs of Staff, Washington, 2002—. Decorated Legion of Merit with five gold stars. Office: OCJCS Pub Affairs 9999 Joint Staff Rm 2D844 Washington DC 20318-9999

METZGER, JEFFREY PAUL, lawyer; b. Oct. 13, 1950; s. John E. and Ellen J. M; m. Stephanie Ann Stahr, Dec. 27, 1977. BA magna cum laude, Amherst Coll., 1973; JD, Georgetown U., 1976. Bar: D.C. 1977. Legis. asst. U.S. Senator Joseph Biden, Jr., Del., 1973; assoc. Collier, Shannon, Rill and Scott, Washington, 1976-79, Cole and Groner PC, Washington, 1979-82; trial atty. comml. litigation br. civil divsn. U.S. Dept. Justice, Washington, 1982-85; mem. prof. staff Pres.'s Blue Ribbon Commn. on Def. Mgmt., Washington, 1985-86; asst. gen. counsel Unisys Corp., McLean, Va., 1986-88, v.p., assoc. gen. counsel, 1989—. Mem. ABA. Office Phone: 703-439-5609. Personal E-mail: Jeffrey.Metzger@unisys.com.

METZGER, PAUL THOMAS, lawyer; b. Trenton, Mich., May 26, 1950; s. Roland Arthur and A. Doreen (Bloomer) M.; children: Timothy, Andrew, Christopher. AB, Harvard U., 1971, JD, 1976. Bar: Ill. 1976, U.S. Tax. Ct. 1977. Assoc. Bell, Boyd & Lloyd, Chgo., 1976-83, ptnr., 1984—, chmn. tax dept., 1988—. Spkr. Am. Mgmt. Assn., Chgo., 1987-95. Bd. dirs. Assn. House, Chgo., 1984—, treas., 1986-88, pres., 1990-92; bd. dirs. Ounce of Prevention Fund, Chgo., 1983—, chmn., 1995-98; mem. adv. bd. Cabrini Green Legal Aid Clinic, Chgo., 1985-96. Recipient Vol award Assn. House Chgo., 1986, Leadership citation United Way Crusade of Mercy, 1987. Mem. ABA (cert. appreciation Young Lawyers sect. Chgo. 1986-87), Chgo. Coun. Lawyers, Chgo. Fed. Tax Forum, Mid-Day Club. Democrat. Home: 2258 N Lincoln Park West Chicago IL 60614 Office: 70 W Madison St Ste 3200 Chicago IL 60602-4244 Office Phone: 312-807-4333. Business E-Mail: pmetzger@bellboyd.com.

METZGER, ROBERT STREICHER, lawyer; b. St. Louis, Sept. 27, 1950; s. Robert Stanley and Jean Harriet (Streicher) M.; m. Stephanie Joy Morgan, Nov. 16, 1980; children: Michael, Kristen, Marisa. BA, Middlebury Coll., 1974; JD, Georgetown U., 1977. Bar: Calif. 1978, D.C. 1978. Legis. aide U.S. Rep. Robert F. Drinan, Washington, 1972-73; legis. asst. U.S. Rep. Michael J. Harrington, Washington, 1973-75; rsch. fellow Ctr. for Sci. and Internat. Affairs Harvard U., Cambridge, Mass., 1977-78; assoc. Latham & Watkins, LA, 1978-84, ptnr., 1984-90, Kirkland & Ellis, LA, 1990-93, Troop, Meisinger, Steuber & Pasich and predecessor, LA, 1993-97, Gibson, Dunn & Crutcher LLP, LA, 1997—. Chmn. Aerospace and Govt. Practice Group, 1997—, Telecom. Practice Group, 2000-; cons. Congl. Rsch. Svc., Washington, 1977-78. Contbr. articles to profl. jours. Mem. ABA (litig. pub. contracts sect.), Fed. Comm. Bar Assn., Internat. Inst. for Strategic Studies, Pacific Coun. on Internat. Policy, Jonathan Club. Office: Gibson Dunn & Crutcher LLP 333 S Grand Ave Los Angeles CA 90071-3197 Office Phone: 213-229-7000. Business E-Mail: rmetzger@gibsondunn.com.

METZGER, SIDNEY, retired communications engineer; b. N.Y., Feb. 1, 1917; m. Miriam Lipstein; children: David, Sally, Philip. BSEE, N.Y. Univ., 1937; MEE, Polytech. Inst. Bklyn., 1950. Engr. U.S. Signal Corps. Lab., NJ, 1939—45; head radio relay divsn. Fed. Telecommunications Labs. Internat. Tel. & Tel. Corp., 1945—54; mgr. communications engring. Astro Elect. Prod. Divsn. RCA, 1954—63; mgr. engring. divsn. Communications Satellite Corp., 1963-67, asst. v.p. and chief engr., 1968-72, asst. v.p. and chief scientist, 1972-80, v.p. and chief scientist, 1980-82; cons. engr., 1982—93; ret., 1993. Recipient Aerospace award Aerospace & Elec. Systems Soc., 1975, Internat. Communication award IEEE, 1976, Koji Kobayashi Computers & Communication award, 1985, Aerospace Communication award Am. Inst. Aeronaut. & Astronaut., 1984. Fellow IEEE, AIAA; mem. Nat. Acad. Engring, Sigma Xi. Address: 700 John Ringling Blvd Apt N-206 Sarasota FL 34236-1500 E-mail: mimsid7@comcast.net.

METZGER, VERNON ARTHUR, management educator, consultant; b. Baldwin Park, Calif., Aug. 13, 1918; s. Vernon and Nellie C. (Ross) Metzger; m. Beth Alrene Metzger, Feb. 19, 1955; children: Susan, Linda, David. BS, U. Calif., Berkeley, 1947, MBA, 1948. Estimating engr. C.F. Braun & Co., 1949; prof. mgmt. Calif. State U., Long Beach, 1949-89, prof. emeritus, 1989—, founder Sch. of Bus. Mgmt. cons. Mem. Fire Commn., Fountain Valley, Calif., 1959—60; mem. mgmt. task force to promote modern mgmt. in Yugoslavia, U.S. State Dept., 1977; mem. State of Calif. Fair Polit. Practices Commn., Orange County Transit Com.; pres. Orange County Dem. League, 1967—68. With USNR, 1942—45. Recipient Outstanding Citizen award, Orange County. Fellow: Soc. Advancement Mgmt. (life; dir.); mem.: Orange County Indsl. Rels. Rsch. Assn. (v.p.), Acad. Mgmt., Tau Kappa Upsilon, Alpha Kappa Psi, Beta gamma Sigma. Home: 1938 Balearic Dr Costa Mesa CA 92626-3513 Office Phone: 714-557-6415.

METZGER, YALE HYDER, lawyer, educator; b. Adrian, Mich., Oct. 20, 1959; s. John Andrew and Shirley Jane Metzger; m. Susan E. Richmond, May 19, 1995. BA in Justice, U. Alaska, 1987; JD cum laude, Gonzaga U., 1995. Bar: Alaska 1995, U.S. Dist. Ct. Alaska 1996. Law clk. to magistrate judge U.S. Dist. Ct., 1995-96; atty. in pvt. practice Anchorage, 1995—. Mem. paralegal edn. adv. com. U. Alaska, Anchorage, 1989—; adj. prof. U. Alaska, Anchorage, 1996—. With USAF, 1982-85. Mem.: ATLA, Whittier Boat Owners' Assn., S.Am. Explorers Club, Anchorage Inn of Ct. (sec. 1999—2000, treas. 2000—02). Avocations: exploration of amazon rainforest in ecuador, sailing in prince william sound, scuba diving, hunting big game in alaska and africa. Office: 425 G St Ste 510 Anchorage AK 99501-2160

METZL, JORDAN D, sports medicine physician, director; b. Kansas City, Mo., June 25, 1966; MD, U. Mo., 1993. Cert. pediat. 1998, sports med. 2001. Residency Tufts U.; fellowship Harvard Med. Sch.; fellowship in pediat. sports and dance med. Children's Hosp., Boston; asst. attending physician Hosp. for Special Surgery, N.Y.C., co-founder, med. dir., Sports Med. Inst. for Young Athletes, 2001—, founder, dir., Sports Med. for the Athletic Child. Mem. U.S. Com. Med. Adv. Bd., 1998; lectr. in field; asst. prof. dept. pediat. Cornell Med. Coll.; med. corr. CBC Saturday Early Show; team physician Fieldston HS, Trinity HS, Riverdale Sch., Spence Sch.; med. cons. Fred's Team, Sloan-Kettering Cancer Ctr., Iona Coll., St. John's U. Author: The Young Athlete, A Sports Doctor's Complete Guide for Parents, 2002; contbr. monthly column to Child Magazine, articles to profl. pubs.; mem. editl. adv. bd.: Pediatric Annals, Pediatric Emergency Care, Sports Medicine in Primary Care. Achievements include appearing regularly on local and national radio and television programs including CBS and NBC News and in the A&E documentary, Playing to Extremes; appearances in the NY Times; doctor for Broadway shows Cabaret, Rocky Horror Picture Show, and the Radio City Rockettes. Avocations: marathon running, triathlete. Office: Hosp Special Surgery 535 E 70th St New York NY 10021 also: 523 E 72nd St 4th flr New York NY 10021 Address: 519 E 72nd St Ste 206 New York NY 10021

METZLER, JERRY DON, retired nursing administrator; b. Mishawaka, Ind., Mar. 6, 1935; s. Gerald Donald and Cleota Christabell (Dowell) M.; m. Dorothy J. Masters, Aug. 18, 1962. BS, Ariz. State U., 1962, MEd, 1967; BSN, San Diego State U., 1973; MS, U. Ariz., Tucson, 1980. Tchr. sci. Washington Sch., Sanger, Calif., 1963-68; tchr. biology San Jacinto (Calif.) H.S., 1968-70; staff nurse Maricopa County Hosp., Phoenix, 1973-76, St. Luke's Hosp., Phoenix, 1976-77; instr. nursing, dept. head Gila Pueblo Coll., Globe, Ariz., 1977-78; nurse educator, asst. dir. nursing USPHS Indian Hosp., Tuba City, Ariz., 1980-84; asst. nursing svc. mgr. Phoenix Indian Med. Ctr., 1984-85, pub. health educator, 1985-88; dir. nursing USPHS Indian Hosp., Owyhee, Nev., 1988-90; sr. project officer USPHS, Dallas, 1990-97; ret., 1997. With USN, 1956-60, USPHS, 1980-97. Mem. ANA, Res. Officers Assn., Commd. Officers Assn. USPHS, Masons, Sigma Theta Tau. Republican. Methodist. Home: 3413 N 44th Pl Phoenix AZ 85018-6025 Office Phone: 602-955-6720. Personal E-mail: jdmetzler@juno.com.

METZLER, PAUL RAYMOND, electrical engineer, consultant; b. St. Louis, Sept. 19, 1949; s. Raymond Herman and Rita Fanny (Morton) M.; m. Barbara Mary Dolan, May 18, 1974 (div. Dec. 1985); children: Tammi Marie, Julie Lynn, Brian Keith; m. Roxy Susan Clark, Dec. 20, 1987. BSEE, U. Mo., Rolla, 1973. Registered profl. engr., Tenn., Nev., Mo., Ill. Elec. engr. Titanium Pigment div. NL Industries, St. Louis, 1974-76, Reynolds Elec. & Engring. Co., Inc., Las Vegas, Nev., 1983-88; sr. elec. engr. Carborundum Environ. Systems div. Kennecott Corp., Knoxville, Tenn., 1976-81; instrument and control project engr. Chem. Separations Corp., Knoxville, 1981-82; cons. engr. PM Engring. Assocs., Knoxville, 1982-84; quality control engr. C.R. Fedrick, Inc., Kaneohe, Hawaii, 1988-89; cons. PM Engring. Assocs., Pearl City, Hawaii, 1989-92, Lawton, Okla., 1992-94; v.p. Pacific Rim Cons. & Inspection Corp., Aiea, Hawaii, 1991-92; elec. inspector Sverdrup-CRSS Jacob Facilities, Inc., St. Louis, 1996-2000; cons. engr. Criterium-McMahon Engrs., St. Louis, 2000—; office mgr., elec. engr. Selective Site Cons., Inc., Creve Coeur, Mo., 2001—. Mem. vestry Grace Episcopal Ch., Kirkwood, Mo., 1999-2001, jr. warden, 2001. Fellow: Internat. Biog. Assn. (life); mem. NSPE, Illuminating Engring. Soc. N.Am. (assoc.), Silver State Computer Users Group (v.p. 1984-86, libr. 1986-88), Instrument Soc. Am., Nat. Fire Protection Assn., Brotherhood of St. Andrew Inc. (life), Mo. Soc. Profl. Engrs., Order of Engr. (charter), Nat. Model R.R. Assn. (editor Rail Post Office 1997-2001), Big Bend R.R. Club (pres. 2001—), Kirkwood R.R. Assn. (pres. 1997—). Home: 5404 Medalton Way Saint Louis MO 63128-3531 Office: 13503 Coliseum Dr Chesterfield MO 63017 E-mail: pmetzler@swbell.net.

METZLER, ROBERT J., II, lawyer; b. Allentown, Pa., Feb. 5, 1948; s. Robert J. and Jean (Rockey) M.; m. Deborah Anne Tamoney, Aug. 21, 1976; children: Melissa, Robert III, Margot, Matthew. BA, Princeton U., 1970; JD, U. Conn., 1973. Bar: N.Y. 1974, Conn. 1976, U.S. Dist. Ct. (so. and ea. dists.) N.Y. 1974, U.S. Ct. Appeals (2d cir.) 1976. Atty. N.Y.C. Law Dept., 1973-75; law clk. to Hon. Thomas J. Meskill U.S. Ct. Appeals (2d cir.), N.Y.C. and New Britain, Conn., 1975-76; assoc. atty. Tyler, Cooper & Alcorn, LLP, New Haven, Conn., 1976-81, ptnr. New Haven and Hartford, Conn., 1982—. Dir. Common Ground Youth Leadership Forum, Hartford, 1987-98, W. Hartford Youth Hockey Assn., 1988-93, United Way Capital Region, Hartford, 1989—; dir. United Way Conn., 1997—, chmn., 2003—. Fellow Am. Coll. Investment Counsel; mem. Nat. Assn. Stock Plan Profls., Conn. Bar Assn. (chmn. pub. utility law sect. 1982-84). Office: Tyler Cooper & Alcorn City Pl Fl 35 185 Asylum St Hartford CT 06103 E-mail: metzler@tylercooper.com.

METZLER, RUTH HORTON, genealogical educator; b. Eden, New York, Aug. 4, 1927; d. John Morris and Bernice Louise (Horton); m. Henry George Metzler, Sept. 4, 1948; children: Kathleen, Ronald, Janice, Margaret. Attended, Wheaton Coll., 1945-48; BA (hon.), Wilmington Coll., 1956; MLS, State Univ. of N.Y., Geneseo, 1962. Cert. tchr., libr. media splty., N.Y. Cataloging typist Peoria Pub. Libr., Ill., 1949-52; cataloging asst. Wilmington Coll. Libr., Ohio, 1953-56; sch. libr. K-12 Nunda Ctrl. Sch., NY, 1956-65; head libr. media ctr. Irondequoit H.S., Rochester, NY, 1965-84; pres. Rochester Geneal. Soc., NY, 1989-93; instr., lectr. Rochester Mus. and Sci. Ctr., NY, 1990—. Author of several family histories. Organizing instr. Genealogy workshops, Rochester Mus. and Sci. Ctr; contbg. lectr. Nat. Geneal. Conf., Rochester, 1990; others. Mem. N.Y. Libr. Assn.,;N.Y. State Tchr. Retirement Sys.; New Eng. Hist. and Geneal. Soc.; Kodak Geneal. Soc., N.Y.; State Coun. of Geneal.; Genealogy Round Table of Monroe County (del. 1996—); Rochester Geneal. Soc.; Geneal. Educators (organizing mem. 1996). Republican. Baptist. Avocations: family history photography, genealogy, writing.

METZNER, BARBARA STONE, university counselor; b. St. Louis, June 9, 1940; d. Wendell Phillips and Lois Custer (Rake) Metzner. AB, Ind. U., 1962, MS, 1964, EdD, 1983; BA, Purdue U., 1979. Asst. dean students U. Ill., Urbana, 1964-68; undergrad. advisor UCLA, 1968-69; asst. dean students Ohio State U., 1969-72; student affairs officer San Diego State U., 1972-76; sr. counselor Ind. U. - Purdue U., Indpls., 1976—. Supr. Ednl. Testing Svc., Indpls., 1980-90; cons. editl. bd. Nat. Acad. Advising Assn., Manhattan, Kans., 1987-93; adj. prof. Ind. U., 1987—; mgr. Info. Svcs. Univ. divsn. Ind. U.-Purdue U., Indpls., Ind., 1989-91. Contbr. articles to profl. jours., chpts. to books. Mem. Marion County Precinct Election Bd., 1980-92; mem. exec. com. Ind. Allied Health Assn., 1983-84; VIP escort Pan Am. Games, 1987. Spencer Found. grantee, 1985. Mem. AAAS, APA, Am. Edn. Rsch. Assn., Assn. Instl. Rsch., Kappa Alpha Theta (vol. charity benefits 1980-90), Phi Beta Kappa. Avocations: tennis, chinese cooking, fine arts. Office: IUPUI 815 W Michigan St Indianapolis IN 46202-5199

METZNER, CHARLES MILLER, federal judge; b. N.Y.C., Mar. 13, 1912; s. Emanuel and Gertrude (Miller) M.; m. Jeanne Gottlieb, Oct. 6, 1966. AB, Columbia U., 1931, LL.B., 1933. Bar: N.Y. 1933. Pvt. practice, 1934; mem. Jud. Council State N.Y., 1935-41; law clk. to N.Y. supreme ct. justice, 1942-52; exec. asst. to U.S. atty. Gen. Herbert Brownell, Jr., 1953-54; mem. firm Chapman, Walsh & O'Connell, 1954-59; judge U.S. Dist Ct. (so. dist.) N.Y., 1959—. Mem. Law Revision Commn. N.Y. State, 1959; chmn. com. adminstrn. magistrates system U.S. Jud. Conf., 1970-81; chmn. Columbia Coll. Coun., 1965-66. Pres. N.Y. Young Republican Club, 1941; Trustee Columbia U., 1972-84, trustee emeritus, 1984—; bd. dirs. N.Y.C. Ctr. Music and Drama, 1969-74. Recipient Lawyer Div. of Joint Def. Appeal award, 1961, Columbia U. Alumni medal, 1966, Founders award Nat. Coun. U.S. Magistrates, 1989. Mem. ABA, Am. Law Inst., Fed. Bar Coun. (cert. Disting. Jud. Svc. 1989).

METZNER, RICHARD, advertising executive; Grad., Harvard U. Fin. analyst Am. Airlines; co-founder TMSI, 1985; sr. v.p. strategy Brierly & Ptnrs., Dallas, 1990-95, pres., 2000—; v.p., mktg Continental Airlines, 1995-2000. Named Marketer of Yr. Brandweek, Marketing 100 Advt. Age. Office: Brierley & Ptnrs Ste 1000 8401 N Central Expy Dallas TX 75225

METZNER, RICHARD JOEL, psychiatrist, psychopharmacologist, educator; b. L.A., Feb. 15, 1942; s. Robert Gerson and Esther Rebecca (Groper) M.; children: Jeffrey Anthony, David Jonathan; m. Leila Kirkley, June 26, 1993. BA, Stanford U., 1963; MD, Johns Hopkins U., 1967. Diplomate Am. Bd. Psychiatry and Neurology. Intern Roosevelt Hosp., N.Y.C., 1967-68; resident in psychiatry Stanford U. Med. Ctr., 1968-71; staff psychiatrist divsn. manpower and tng. NIMH-St. Elizabeths Hosp., Washington, 1971-73; chief audiovisual edn. sys. VA Med. Ctr. Brentwood, L.A., 1973-79; from asst. prof. psychiatry to assoc. clin. prof. UCLA Neuropsychiat. Inst., 1980-96, clin. prof., 1996—. Lectr. Sch. Social Welfare, 1975-84; pvt. practice medicine specializing in psychiatry, Bethesda, Md., 1972-73, L.A., 1973—, Sedona, Ariz., 1997—; dir. Western Inst. Psychiatry, L.A., 1977—; pres. Psychiat. Resource Network, Inc., 1984-90. Contbr. articles to profl. jours.; prodr., writer numerous films and videotapes. With USPHS, 1968-71. Recipient 6 awards for film and videotape prodns., 1976-80. Fellow: Am. Psychiat. Assn. (life Disting.); mem.: UCLA Psychiat. Clin. Faculty Assn. (pres. 2001—02), Mental Health Careerists Assn. (chmn. 1972—73), So. Calif. Psychiat. Soc., Phi Beta Kappa. Democrat. Jewish. Office: 25 Cindercone Cir Sedona AZ 86336 Office Phone: 928-204-5850. E-mail: rmetzner@ucla.edu., rmetzner@earthlink.net.

MEUNIER, MONIQUE, dancer; b. L.A. Studied with Irena Komoskova, studied with Yvonne Mounsey; student, Sch. Am. Ballet, 1988. Mem. corps de ballet N.Y.C. Ballet, 1990—97, soloist, 1997—98, prin., 1998—2002; soloist Am Ballet Theatre, NYC, 2002—. Dancer (ballets) Agon, Apollo, Harlequinade, The Nutcracker, Swan Lake, Tschaikovsky Piano Concerto No. 2, Vienna Waltzes, The Sleeping Beauty, Ash, Delight of the Muses, A Schubert Sonata, Slavonic Dances. Office: Am Ballet Theatre 890 Broadway New York NY 10003

MEUNIER, ROBERT RAYMOND, research electrical engineer, optical engineer; b. Hollywood, Calif., Mar. 27, 1957; s. Raymond Robert and Anna Marie (Rapp) M; m. Janet E. Bost. ASD in Laser Electro-Optics, Pasadena (Calif.) City Coll., 1984; BS in Mgmt., Pepperdine U., 1993. Lab. asst. Jet Propulsion Lab., Pasadena, Calif., 1984-85; rsch. engr. satellite sys. Rockwell Internat., Seal Beach, Calif., 1985-89; electro-optical engr. Cymbolic Scis. Internat., Irvine, Calif., 1989-90; project engr. OCA Applied Optics, Garden Grove, Calif., 1990-92; owner, program mgr. Integrated Scientific, Mission Viejo, Calif., 1992-96; sr. sys. test engr. Rocketdyne Corp., Granada Hills, Calif., 1994-96; prog. mgr. Newport Corp., Irvine, Calif., 1996—. Mem. Laser Inst. Am., Soc. Photo-optical Instrumentation Engrs., L.A. Collegiate Coun. (alumnus), Inter Orgnl. Coun. (founder, chmn. 1981-82), Nat. Mgmt. Assn., Internat. Platform Assn., Lions Club, Inventors Forum, Sigma Pi. Republican. Four Square Evangelical Protestant.

MEUNIER, VINCENT, physicist; BS in Physics, Namur U., Belgium, 1996, MS in Physics, 1998, PhD in Physics, 1999. R&d staff mem. Oak Ridge Nat. Lab., Oak Ridge, Tenn., 2004—; rsch. assoc. Oak Ridge Associated U., Oak Ridge, Tenn., 2002—04, NC State U., Raleigh, NC, 2000—02. Rschr. Oak Ridge Nat. Lab., Oak Ridge, Tenn., 2002—. Contbr. articles to sci. jours. Grantee Rsch. Assoc., Nat. Funds for Sci. Rsch. of Belgium, 2000-2004; scholar Rsch. Asst., Funds for Sci. Rsch. of Belgium, 1996-1999. Mem.: Materials Rsch. Soc., Am. Phys. Soc. E-mail: vm2@ornl.gov.

MEURLIN, KEITH W. airport manager; BA, Univ. of Vermont, 1972; MS, Univ. of Southern California, 1977. Served in U.S. Air Force and Nat. Guard, 1972—; now gen. mgr. Washington Dulles Internat. Airport; mobilization asst. Langley AFB, Va. Recipient Meritorious Service Medal, Air Force Outstanding Unit Award, National Defense Srvc. Medal. Office: Hdq Air Reserve Personnel Cntr Office of Public Affairs Denver CO 80280 also: 1 Saarinen Center MA-210 Dulles VA 20166

MEVERS, FRANK CLEMENT, state archivist, historian; b. New Orleans, Oct. 10, 1942; s. Lloyd F. and Mary Ashley (Collins) M.; m. Kathryn Ann Hayes, Dec. 23, 1967; children: John F., Lauren K. BA in History, La. State U., 1965; PhD in Am. History, U. N.C., 1972; MA, La. State U., 1967. Editor Papers of James Madison, Charlottesville, Va., 1972-74, Papers of Josiah Bartlett, Concord, N.H., 1974-77, Papers of William Plumer, Concord, 1977-79; state archivist State of N.H., Concord, 1979—. Editor, author: New Hampshire: State That Made US a Nation, 1989. Mem. Pub. Libr. Bd. Trustees, Concord, 1979-99. With U.S. Army, 1967-69, Korea. Episcopalian. Avocation: stamp collecting/philately. Home: 29 Bradley St Concord NH 03301-6432 Office: NH State Archives 71 S Fruit St Concord NH 03301-2410 Office Phone: 603-271-2236. Personal E-mail: eatright@comcast.net. Business E-Mail: fmevers@sos.state.nh.us.

MEW, CALVIN MARSHALL, advertising executive; b. Oakland, Calif., Oct. 27, 1947; s. Thomas Bing and May (Jan) m. Mary Farnham Crawford, Oct. 20, 2001. BA, Yale U., 1969; MDiv, Union Theol Sem., 1973; postgrad., Columbia U., 1973-79, Harvard U., 1984. Tutor Union Theol. Sem., 1973-77; adj. lectr. Hunter Coll., 1977-79; market analyst Kenyon & Eckhart Advt., Inc., N.Y.C., 1979-82, v.p. market plans, 1982-83, rev. v.p. strategic plan, 1983-85, v.p. strategic mktg. svcs., 1985-88, sr.v.p. strategic and forward planning, 1988-90; sr. v.p., mng. dir. Bozell, Inc., 1990-93, exec. v.p., mng. dir., 1993—. Gen. mgr. Bozell Austria, 1994; exec. v.p., regional dir. L.Am. Bozell Worldwide, Inc., 1996; dir. Capritauro Investments, Ltd., 2002. Contbr. articles to profl. jours. Bd. dirs. Union Theol. Sem., 1984—, vice chmn., 1992—. Recipient Cogswell award Yale U., 1969; Columbia U. fellow, Rockefeller Bros. Fund fellow. Mem. Am. Acad. Religion, Soc. Bibl. Lit. Presbyterian. Home: 895 W End Ave New York NY 10025-3500 Office: Bozell Inc 40 W 23rd St New York NY 10010-5215

MEW, THOMAS JOSEPH, III, (TOMMY MEW), artist, educator; b. Miami, Fla., Aug. 15, 1942; s. Thomas Joseph and Maude Edith (Perry) M.; m. Mary Ann Kelley, June 17, 1966; 1 son, Thomas Joseph IV. BS, Fla. State U., 1962, MA, 1964; PhD, NYU, 1966. Grad. instr. Fla. State U., 1963; asst. prof. art Troy State U., 1966-68, Jacksonville U., 1968-70; prof., chmn. dept. art Berry Coll., 1970—, Dana prof. art. Juror art shows: vis. artist; lectr. in field, cons. art; dir. Fluxus West/Southeast; dir. Moon Gallery. Exhibited in one-man shows Parkway Gallery, Miami, 1962-63, 319 Gallery, N.Y.C., 1968, Meridian (Miss.) Mus., 1976, C.D.O. Gallery, Parma, Italy, 1978, Calif. State U., Sacramento, 1979, Miss. Mus. Art, Jackson, 1979, Art Inst. for Permian Basin, ITex, Arte Studio, Bergamo, Italy, Queen Street Gallery, Belfast, No. Ireland; group shows include High Mus., Atlanta, 1971, 72, 74, New Reform Gallery, Aalst, Belgium, 1975, U. Guelph, Ont., Can., 1975, Neuberger Mus., Purchase, N.Y., 1978, Arte Fiera, Bologna, Italy, 1979; represented in permanent collections, Kansas City Art Inst., Mildura Art Centre, Australia, Wichita Art Mus., Jacksonville (Fla.) Art Mus., Macon Mus. Art, AT&T, Harn Mus., U. Iowa; host: Cable TV show Art: The Mew View, 1978—; Filmmaker, 1966-69; contbr. articles to profl. jours. Bd. dirs. Rome Arts Council, 1984—; bd. dirs. Interface. Recipient Gellhorn award N.Y. U., 1966; Cowperthwaite grantee, 1972; Lilly Found. grantee, 1975; Gulf Life grantee, 1977. Mem. Southeastern Coll. Art Conf., Coll. Art Assn. Am., Am. Fedn. Arts, Nat. Art Edn. Assn., Am. Assn. Art Dealers, Omicron Delta Kappa, Phi Kappa Phi. Home: PO Box 495028 Mount Berry GA 30149-5028 Office: Berry Coll Art Dept PO Box 580 Mount Berry GA 30149 Office Phone: 706-236-2219. E-mail: tmew@berry.edu. *I've always moved in the direction of my dreams . . . always tried to make the great dream a reality.*

MEYBURG, ARNIM HANS, transportation engineer, educator, consultant; b. Bremerhaven, W. Ger., Aug. 25, 1939; came to U.S., 1965; s. Friedel and Auguste (Kleeberg) M.; m. Ruth Meyburg; 1 child, Jennifer Susan. Student, U. Hamburg, 1960-62, Free U. Berlin, 1962-65; MS (Fulbright travel grantee), Northwestern U., 1968, PhD, 1971. Research assoc. Transp. Center, Northwestern U., 1968-69; asst. prof. transp. engring. Cornell U., 1969-75, assoc. prof., 1975-78, prof., 1978—, acting chmn. dept., 1977-78, chmn. dept., 1980-85, dir. Sch. Civil and Environ. Engring., 1988-98, chmn. bd. Univ. Transp. Rsch. Ctr., 1992-95; dir. Transp. Infrastructure Rsch. Consortium, 1995—. Vis. mem. faculties U. Calif., Irvine, Tech. U. Munich, Germany, (Fulbright lectr.) U. Sao Paulo, Brazil, 1984, Tech. U. Brunswick, W. Ger., 1985-86; Humboldt Found. research fellow, 1978-79; prin. investigator projects Dept. Transp., NSF, Nat. Coop. Hwy. Research Program, N.Y. State Dept. Transp., U.S. Dept. Transp. Author: (with others) Urban Transportation Modeling and Planning, 1975, Transportation Systems Evaluation, 1976, Survey Sampling and Multivariate Analysis for Social Scientists and Engineers, 1979, Survey Methods for Transport Planning, 1995; co-editor: (with others) Behavioral Travel-Demand Models, 1976, New Horizons in Travel-Behavior Research, 1981, Selected Readings in Transport Survey Methodology, 1992; contbr. articles to profl. jours., chpts. to books. NSF Research Initiation grantee, 1973; recipient Humboldt U.S. Sr. Scientist award, 1984, Fulbright sr. lectr. award, 1984. Mem. ASCE, AAUP, Transp. Rsch. Bd., Transp. Rsch. Forum, Sigma Xi, Chi Epsilon. Office: Cornell U 220 Hollister Hall Ithaca NY 14853-3501 E-mail: ahm2@cornell.edu.

MEYE, ROBERT PAUL, retired seminary educator, administrator, writer; b. Apr. 1, 1929; s. Robert and Eva (Pfau) Meye; m. Mary Cover, June 18, 1954; children: Marianne Meye Thompson, Douglas, John. BA in English Lit., Stanford U., 1951; BD, Fuller Theol. Sem., 1957; ThM in N.T., 1959; DTheol magna cum laude, U. Basel, Switzerland, 1962; DD, Eastern Bapt. Theol. Sem., 1990. Prof. No. Bapt. Theol. Sem., Lombard, Ill., 1962-77, dean, 1971-77, Sch. Theology, Fuller Theol. Sem., Pasadena, Calif., 1977-90, dean emeritus, 1992—. Assoc. provost for Ch. Rels. and Christian Community, 1990-92, prof.N.T. interpretation, 1977-92, prof. emeritus, 92—. Author: Jesus and the Twelve, 1968; co-editor: Studies in Old Testament Theology, 1992; contbr. articles to profl. jours., dictionaries, and encys. Served to lt. (j.g.) USN, 1946-47, 51-54, Korea. Mem.: Inst. Bible Rsch., Soc. Bibl. Lit., Chgo. Soc. Bibl. Rsch., Studiorum Novi Testamenti Societas, Nat. Assn. Bapt. Profs. Religion. Republican. Home: 1170 Rubio St Altadena CA 91001-2027 Office: Fuller Theol Sem 135 N Oakland Ave Pasadena CA 91182-0001 E-mail: rmeye@aol.com.

MEYER, ALAN DOWNING, management educator; b. L.A., Mar. 12, 1946; s. William Claire and Helen Maegan Meyer; m. Nancy Drach, Oct. 4, 1976; children: Lauren Drach, Andrew Downing. BA in Econ., U. Wash., 1968, MBA, 1970; PhD, U. Calif., Berkeley, 1978. Asst. prof. U. Wis., Milw., 1978—84; Lundquist prof. mgmt. U. Oreg., Eugene, 1984—. Fellow Acad. Mgmt., bd. govs., 1998—2001; vis. assoc. prof. Cornell U., Ithaca, NY, 1991—92; vis. prof. Hong Kong U. Sci. and Tech., 1997—98. Assoc. editor-in-chief Orgn. Sci., sr. editor, consulting editor Acad. Mgmt. Jour. Grantee, NSF, 1985—87, 2002—, U.S. Army Rsch. Inst., 1986—91. Office: U Oreg Lundquist Coll Bus Eugene OR 97403

MEYER, ALBERT JAMES, educational researcher; b. Cleve., Sept. 24, 1929; s. Jacob Conrad and Esther Agnes (Steiner) M.; m. Mary Ellen Yoder, Aug. 21, 1954; children: Richard, Anne, Kathryn, Barbara, Elaine. BA, Goshen Coll., 1950; MA, Princeton U., 1952, PhD, 1954. Asst. in teaching and rsch. Princeton (N.J.) U., 1950-53; fellow U. Basel, Switzerland, 1953-54, rsch. assoc., 1956-57; dir. for France, rep. European peace sect. Mennonite Ctrl. Com., 1954-57; asst. prof. physics Goshen (Ind.) Coll., 1958-61, prof., rsch. prof., 1967-89, adj. rsch. prof., 1989—; acad. dean, prof. Bethel Coll., North Newton, Kans., 1961-66, Menno Simons lectr., 1993; exec. sec., pres. Mennonite Bd. Edn., Elkhart, Ind., 1967-95; vis. fellow Princeton (N.J.) U., 1995-96. Exec. for secretariat Puidoux Theol. Confs., 1955-57; former mem. staff Mennonite Student Svcs. Com.; former coord. com. on liberal arts edn. North Ctrl. Assn. Colls. and Secondary Schs.; vis. rsch. scientist U. Paris, 1974-75; vis. rschr. New Coll. Berkeley, 1986-87; presenter in field; former cons. Conrad Grebel Coll., U. Waterloo, Ont., Can.; mem. peace and social concerns com. Mennonite Ch., 1959-71; former mem. Continuation Com. of Hist. Peace Chs.; mem. interch. rels. staff Mennonite Ch. U.S.A., 1997. Contbr. articles to denominational periodicals and sci. jours. Princeton U. exch. fellow and Charles Foster Kent fellow Nat. Coun. for Religion in Higher Edn., 1953-54. Mem. Denominational Execs. for Ch.-Related Higher Edn. (chmn. 1984-86), Am. Assn. for Higher Edn., Am. Assn. Physics Tchrs. Avocations: tennis, hockey, hiking. Home: 708 Emerson St Goshen IN 46526-3904

MEYER, ALDEN MERRILL, environmental association executive; b. Buffalo, Mar. 21, 1952; s. Arthur Merrill Meyer and Susan (Rogers) Meyer Markle BA, Yale U., 1975; MS, Am. U., 1990. Energy policy analyst Conn. Citizen Action Group, Hartford, 1975-78, Environ. Action Found., Washington, 1979-82; exec. dir. Environ. Action, Inc., 1983-85, League Conservation Voters, Washington, 1985-88; dir. climate change and energy policy Union of Concerned Scientists, Washington, 1989-92, legis. dir., 1992-95, dir. govt. rels., 1995—2003, dir. strategy and policy, 2003—. Bd. dirs. Ams. for Environment, Washington, 1983-87, chmn., 1985-87; bd. dirs. Urban Environment Conf., Washington, 1984-87, Zero Population Growth, 1989-98; pres. bd. dirs. Safe Energy Comm. Coun., Washington, 1980-85; chmn. U.S. Climate Action Network, 1990-2000; mem. state and local adv. bd. U.S. Dept. Energy, 1994-2000, mem. elec. syss. reliability task force, 1997-99; mem. Sec. Energy Adv. Bd., 1999-2002. Chmn. bd. dirs. Washington Waldorf Sch., 2002—. Democrat. Avocations: hiking, camping, skiing, singing. Home: 15 Montgomery Ave Takoma Park MD 20912-4614 Office: Union of Concerned Scientists 1707 H St NW # 600 Washington DC 20006-3919 Office Phone: 202-223-6133. E-mail: ameyer@ucsusa.org.

MEYER, ALICE VIRGINIA, state official; b. N.Y.C., Mar. 15, 1921; d. Martin G. and Marguerite Helene (Houzë) Kliemand; m. Theodore Harry Meyer, June 28, 1947; children: Robert Charles, John Edward. BA, Barnard Coll., 1941; MA, Columbia U., 1942. Tchr. pub. schs., Elmont, N.Y., 1942-43; tchr. Fairlawn (N.J.) High Sch., 1943-47; office mgr., sales rep. N.Y.C., 1948-55; substitute tchr. Pub. Schs., Easton, Conn., 1965-72; state rep., asst. minority leader Conn. State Legislature, Hartford, 1976-93. Mem. Ct. Bd. of Govs. for Higher Edn., 1993—, vice-chair, chair. bd. govs. for higher edn. Mem. Edn. Commn. of the States, 1985—87; life trustee Discovery Mus., 1980—; trustee United Way Regional Youth Substance Abuse Project, Bridgeport, 1983—93; vice chmn. Easton Rep. Town Com., 1970—78; mem. strategic planning com. Town of Easton, 1993—; vice chmn. ct. adv. coun. on intergovtl. rels., 1988—; mem. Conn. Commn. on Quality Edn., 1992—93; supporter Conn. Small Towns, 1988; mem. Conn. Humanities Coun., 1974—76, Conn. Film Commn., 1985—88; co-chair Com. on State Plan of Conservation and Devel., 1985—87; mem. Lt. Gov.'s Commn. on Mandate Reduction, 1995; sec. Easton Free Sch. Scholarship Fund, 1980—; pres. Barnard Class of 1941, 1996—; justice of the peace, 2001—; ct. adv. coun. career and vocat. edn., 1980—88; bd. dirs. 3030 Park, 1993—; Fairfield County Lit. Coalition Bridgeport, 1988—94. Named Legislator of Yr. Conn. Libr. Assn., 1985; Guardian Small Bus. grantee Nat. Fedn. Ind. Bus., 1987; honoree Fairfield YWCA Salute to Women, 1988, Conn. Assn. Small Towns, 1990; named grant to AAUW Fellowship Fund, Bridgeport Br., 1970, Conn. State AAUW, 1974; recipient Conn. Friends of Libr. Hon. award, 1984, Disting. Svc. award Conn. State Coun. on Voc/Tech. Edn., 1986, Sacred Heart U. Ctr. for Policy Issues award, 1988, citation Conn. Bd. for Acad. Affairs, 1992, citation Charter Oak Coll., 1993, Spl. Day Recognition, Town of Weston, 1993, Cert. of Recognition, Town of Westport, 1993, Citation for Fostering Open Access to Higher Edn., AAUW, 1994, Disting. Rep. award Easton Rep. Town Com., 2000, Pub. Svc. award Conn. Sec. of State, 2003, others. Mem.: LWV, AAUW (local pres. 1976, bd. dirs. 1982), Nat. Order Women Legislators (regional dir. 1987—, past pres. Conn. chpt.), Conn. Assn. Sch. Adminstrs. (hon.), Bus. and Profl. Women. Congregationalist. Avocations: swimming, sailing, bridge. Home: 18 Lantern Hill Rd Easton CT 06612-2218

MEYER, ANDREA PEROUTKA, small business owner; b. Prague, Czechoslovakia, Nov. 29, 1963; came to U.S. 1970; d. George and Alena Peroutka; m. Dana Charles Meyer, Oct. 16, 1983. BA in Liberal Arts, U. Tex., 1985, M in Libr. of Info. Sci., 1986. Libr. IBM, Austin, Tex., 1985-86; rsch. specialist Career Track Seminars, Boulder, Colo., 1986-88; founder, pres. Working Knowledge, Boulder, 1988—. Project mgr. Interesting Orgns. Database for MIT, 1995—; cons. The Tom Peters Group, Palo Alto, Calif., 1989-95. Author: (workbooks) Stress Management Strategies, 1987, How to Give Presentations, 1988; co-author: (audio tape) How to Set Up a Corporate Library, 1989; co-editor Briefing Book for Inventing the Organizations of the 21st Century, 1995-96; assoc. editor Inside Decisions, 1995-96; contbr. chpts. to 3 books. Recipient Ray C. Janeway scholarship, Tex. Libr. Assn., 1985, Philip Morris scholarship, 1981-85. Mem. Planning Forum (v.p. comm., bd. dirs. Denver chpt.), Product Devel. and Mgmt. Assn. (newsletter editor), Toastmasters, Mensa (chmn. scholarship com.), Pres.'s Assn., European Consortium of Info. Cons., Phi Beta Kappa. Avocations: reading, hiking, writing, travel. Home and Office: 515 Forest Ave Boulder CO 80304-2550 E-mail: dcmeyer@knewbiquity.com.

MEYER, ANDREW W. retired publishing executive; b. Phila., July 29, 1941; s. John O. and Katherine (Wachter) M.; m. Helen Hope Hogan, Nov. 1963; children: Kelly Ann, Michael, Melissa, Suzanne, Jennifer. BS in Accounting, St. Joseph's U., Phila., 1963; MBA in Finance, U. Conn., 1973. CPA. Sr. accountant Jenkins Fetterolf, Phila., 1963-67; asst. treas. PA & S Small Co., York, 1967-71; v.p. finance Xerox Pub. Group, Greenwich, Conn., 1971-82, R.R. Bowker, N.Y.C., 1982-94; COO Reed Reference Pub., New Providence, N.J., 1995-96; v.p. admin. pub. Bus. Info. Svcs. Grp. Lexis-Nexis, New Providence, 1996-97; v.p. admin. Martindale-Hubbell, New Providence, 1997—2000, CEO and pres., 2000—01.

MEYER, ANN JANE, human development educator; b. N.Y.C., Mar. 11, 1942; d. Louis John and Theresa Meyer. BA, U. Mich., 1964; MA, U. Calif., Berkeley, 1967, PhD, 1971. Asst. prof. dept. human devel. Calif. State U., Hayward, 1972-77, assoc. prof., 1977-84, prof., 1984—. Mem. APA. Office: Calif State U Dept Human Devel Hayward CA 94542 Office Phone: 500-885-3076. Business E-Mail: ameyer@csuhayward.edu.

MEYER, ARMIN HENRY, retired diplomat, author, educator; b. Ft. Wayne, Ind., Jan. 19, 1914; s. Armin Paul and Leona (Buss) M.; m. Alice James, Apr. 23, 1949; 1 dau., Kathleen Alice. Student, Lincoln (Ill.) Coll., 1931-33; AB, Capital U., 1935, LL.D., 1957; MA, Ohio State U., 1941, LL.D., 1972, Wartburg Coll., S.D. Sch. Mines and Tech., 1972. Faculty Capital U., Columbus, Ohio, 1935-41; staff OWI, Egypt, Iraq, 1942-46; U.S. pub. affairs officer Baghdad, Iraq, 1946-48; pub. affairs adviser U.S. Dept. State, 1948-52; sec. Am. Embassy, Beirut, 1952—55, dep. chief mission Kabul, Afghanistan, 1955—57; dep. dir. Office South Asian Affairs Dept. State, 1957-58, dep. dir. Office Near Eastern Affairs, 1958-59, dir. Office Nr. Ea. Affairs, 1959-61, dep. asst. sec. of state for Nr. Ea. and South Asian Affairs, 1961, amb. to Lebanon, 1961—65, amb. to Iran, 1965—69, amb. to Japan, 1969—72; spl. asst. to sec. state, chmn. Cabinet Com. to Combat Terrorism, 1972-73. Vis. prof. Am. U., 1974-75; dir. Ferdowsi project Georgetown U., 1975-79, adj. prof. diplomacy, 1975-86; Woodrow Wilson vis. fellow, 1974—; cons. internat. bus. and environment, 1975—. Author: Assignment Tokyo: An Ambassador's Journal, 1974, Quiet Diplomacy, Fro Cairo to Tokyo in the Twilight of Imperialism, 2003; co-author: Education in Diplomacy, 1987. Hon. mem. Lincoln Sesquicentennial Commn., 1959; bd. dirs. Washington Inst. Fgn. Affairs, 1979—, pres., 1988-98. Recipient Meritorious Svc. award Dept. State, 1958, Superior Honor award, 1973; decorated Order of Rising Sun, 1st class (Japan), 1982; inducted into Hall of Excellence Ohio Fedn. Ind. Colls., 1989. Mem. Sigma Psi. Lutheran. Home: 4610 Reno Rd NW Washington DC 20008-2941 Home Fax: 202-237-7721. Personal E-mail: 70117.2165@compuserve.com. *Faith in God; where there is a will there is a way; if a job is worth doing it is worth doing well; and the Golden Rule.*

MEYER, AUGUST CHRISTOPHER, JR., broadcasting company executive, lawyer; b. Champaign, Ill., Aug. 14, 1937; s. August C. and Clara (Rocke) M.; m. Karen Haugh Hassett, Dec. 28, 1960; children: August Christopher F., Elisabeth Hassett. BA cum laude, Harvard U., 1959, LLB, 1962. Bar: Ill. 1962. Founding ptr. Meyer-Capel, Champaign, Ill., 1962-77, of counsel, 1977—2003; owner, dir., officer Midwest TV, Inc., Sta. KFMB-TV-AM-FM, San Diego, Sta. WCIA-TV, Champaign, Ill., Sta. WMBD-TV-AM, WMXP, Peoria, Ill., 1968—, pres., 1976—. Bd. dirs. BankIll., Main St. Trust Inc.; spl. asst. atty. gen. State of Ill., 1968-76. Chmn. bd. trustees Carle Found. Hosp., Urbana, Ill. Mem. Ill. Bar Assn., Champaign County Bar Assn. Clubs: Champaign Country. Home: 1408 S Prospect Ave Champaign IL 61820-6837 Office: Midwest TV Inc PO Box 197 100 W University Ave # 401 Champaign IL 61824-0197 also: Sta KFMB PO Box 85888 7677 Engineer Rd San Diego CA 92111-1515

MEYER, B. FRED, small business executive, home designer and builder, product designer; b. LI, NY, Jan. 6, 1918; s. Barthold Fred and Edna May (Clark) M.; m. Mary E. Carman, July 18, 1951; children: Patricia Meyer Sauer, Susan Meyer Sachs. Student, Pratt Inst., 1935-39, Johns Hopkins U., 1946-48, Wayne State U., 1954-55. Registered builder, Fla. Project engr. Lear, Inc., Grand Rapids, Mich., 1948-51; engring. exec. GM Corp., Warren, Mich., 1951-75; pres. BFM Assocs., Inc. (name Fred Meyer, Inc. 1990), Sarasota, Fla., 1975—. Capt. USAAF, 1942-46, ETO. Achievements include patents for pendulum type seat belt retractor, power window switch, power window actuator, 6-way seat switch, 6-way seat actuator, rear trunk pull-down mechanism. Avocations: golf, computers, travel. Home and Office: 4753 Antler Trail Sarasota FL 34238 Office Phone: 941-586-4131. Personal E-mail: bfredm@hotmail.com.

MEYER, BARBARA JEAN, science educator; d. Chester L. and Theresa I. Meyer; m. Thomas W. Cline, Sept. 7, 1986. BA, Stanford U., 1971; PhD, Harvard U., 1979. Asst. and assoc. prof. MIT, Cambridge, Mass., 1982—90; HHMI investigator, prof. genetics U. Calif., Berkeley, 1990—, head divsn. genetics, 1995—98, mem. pres.' coun. on nat. labs., 1998—. Mem. nat. adv. rsch. resources coun. NIH, Bethesda, Md., 1993—97; sci. adv. coun. Helen Hay Whitney Found., N.Y.C., 2000—; mem. sci. adv. bd. Max Planck Inst., Berlin, 2001—; lectr. Harvey Soc., 2000; investigator Howard Hughes Med. Inst., 1997—. Contbr. articles to profl. jours. Recipient Woman's Faculty award, NSF, 1989—90, Merit award, NIH, 1995—. Fellow: Am. Acad. Arts and Scis.; mem.: NAS, Genetics Soc. (bd. dirs. 1993—96). Office: HHMI / U Calif 16 Barker Hall Berkeley CA 94720-3204

MEYER, BARRY MICHAEL, motion picture executive; b. N.Y.C., Nov. 28, 1943; s. Perry and Lillian Helen (Katz) M.; m. Barbara Patricia, June 12, 1966; children: Matthew, Elizabeth. BA, U. Rochester, 1964; JD, Case Western Res. U., 1967. Bar: NY. Legal counsel ABC, NYC, 1968-70, dir. bus. affairs LA, 1970-71, Warner Bros. TV, LA, 1971-73, v.p. bus. affairs, 1973-77, exec. v.p., 1977-84, Warner Bros. Inc., LA, 1984—99, chmn., CEO, 1999—. Contbr. articles to profl. jours. Bd. dirs. San Fernando Valley Child Guidance Clinic, Calif. Mem. Hollywood Radio and TV Soc. (bd. dirs.), Nat. Acad. TV Arts and Scis. (bd. dirs.), Am. Mgmt. Assn. Office: Warner Bros Inc 4000 Warner Blvd Burbank CA 91522-0002*

MEYER, BERNARD STERN, lawyer, former judge; b. Balt., June 7, 1916; s. Benjamin and Josephine Meyer; m. Elaine Strass, June 25, 1939 (div.); children: Patricia, Susan; m. Edythe Birnbaum, Apr. 18, 1975; m. Hortense Fox, Oct. 29, 1991. BS, Johns Hopkins U., 1936; LLB, U. Md., 1938; LLD, Hofstra U., 1980, Western State U., 1982, Union U., 1984. Bar: Md. 1938, D.C., N.Y. 1947. Assoc. Fisher & Fisher, Balt., 1938-41; with Office Gen. Counsel Treasury Dept., Washington, 1941-43; pvt. practice N.Y.C., 1948-54; ptnr. Meyer, Fink, Weinberger & Levin, N.Y.C., 1954-58; justice N.Y. State Supreme Ct., 1959-72; of counsel Fink, Weinberger, Fredman & Charney, PC, N.Y.C., 1973-79; ptnr. Meyer, English & Cianciulli, PC, Mineola, N.Y., 1975-79; assoc. judge N.Y. Ct. Appeals, Albany, 1979-86; dep. atty. gen. in charge spl. Attica investigation State of N.Y., 1975; ptnr. Meyer, Suozzi, English & Klein PC, Mineola, 1987—. Assoc. spl. counsel Moreland Commn. To Study Workmen's Compensation Adminstrn. and Costs, 1955-57; mem. com. on govt. integrity State of N.Y., 1987-90; mem. Com. for Modern Cts., 1987—. Author: Judicial Retirement Laws of the Fifty States and the District of Columbia, 1999; contbr. articles to profl. jours. Founder United Fund L.I.; past adv. bd. Commn. Law and Social Action, Am. Jewish Congress; chmn. Task Force on Permanency Planning for Foster Children, 1986-91; past pres., bd. dirs. Health and Welfare Coun. Nassau County; past bd. dirs. Nassau-Suffolk region NCCJ, Nassau County coun. Boy Scouts Am., Nat. Ctr. for State Cts.; mem. Coalition for Effective Govt., 1991—. Lt. USNR, WWII. Recipient Disting. Svc. award L.I. Press, Presdl. medal Hofstra U., Disting. Svc. award Legal Aid Soc. Nassau County, N.Y., Johns Hopkins U. Disting. Alumnus award. Mem. ABA (adv. com. on fair trial free press, vice chmn. sr. lawyers divsn. judiciary com.), Am. Bar Found., Am. Coll. Trial Lawyers, Am. Law Inst., N.Y. Bar Assn. (chmn. jud. sect., com. on legis. policy), N.Y. Bar Found., Bar of City of N.Y. (chmn. libr., matrimonial, election law com.), Nassau County Bar Assn. (Disting. Svc. medallion 1982), Nat. Conf. State trial Judges (exec. com., past chmn.), Nat. Coll. State Jud. (bd. dirs.), Assn. Supreme Ct. Judges (past pres., chmn. pattern jury instrn. com. 1962-79), Supreme Ct. Hist. Soc., Com. Modern Cts., Nassau County Lawyers Assn. (award), Scribes, Order of Coif, Omicron Delta Kappa. Office: Meyer Suozzi English & Klein PC 1505 Kellum Pl Mineola NY 11501-4824 Office Phone: 516-741-6565. Business E-Mail: bmeyer@msek.com.

MEYER, BETTY JANE, former librarian; b. Indpls., July 20, 1918; d. Herbert and Gertrude (Sanders) Meyer. BA, Ball State Tchrs. Coll., 1940; BS in Library Sci., Western Res. U., 1945. Student asst. Muncie (Ind.) Pub. Libr., 1936—40; libr. asst. Ohio State U. Libr., Columbus, 1940—42, cataloger, 1945—46, asst. circulation librarian, 1946—51, acting circulation librarian, 1951—52, adminstrv. asst. to dir. librs., 1952—57, acting assoc. reference librarian, 1957—58, serials cataloger, 1958—65, head serial divsn. catalog dept., 1965—68, head acquisition dept., 1968—71, asst. dir. librs., tech. svcs.,

1971—76, acting dir. libr s., 1976—77, asst. dir. librs., tech. svcs., 1977—83; libr. asst. Grandview Heights Pub. Libr., Columbus, 1942—44; student asst. Case Inst. Tech., Cleve., 1944—45. Instr. library adminstrn. Ohio State U. Libr., 1958—63, asst. prof., 1963—67, assoc. prof., 1967—75, prof., 1975—83, prof. emeritus, 1983—; mem. Ohio Coll. Libr. Ctr. Adv. Com. on Cataloging, 1971—76, mem. adv. com. on serials, 1971—76; mem. Inter-Univ. Libr. Coun., Tech. Svcs. Group, 1971—83; mem. bd. trustees Columbua Area Libr. and Info. Coun. Ohio, 1980—83. Grantee Ohio State U., 1975—76. Mem.: PEO, AAUP, ALA, Acad. Libr. Assn., Franklin County Libr. Assn., No. Ohio Tech. Svcs. Librarians, Ohio Valley Group Tech. Svcs. Librarians, Ohioana Libr. Assn., Ohio Libr. Assn., Assn. Coll. and Rsch. Librs., Assn. Faculty and Profl. Women Ohio State U., Delta Kappa Gamma, Beta Phi Mu. Home: Apt B138 6000 Riverside Dr Dublin OH 43017

MEYER, BILL, publishing executive, editor; b. Pratt, Kans., Aug. 6, 1925; s. Otto William and Ruth Clarinda (Jones) Meyer; m. Joan Aileen Wight, Sept. 11, 1949; 1 child, Eric Kent. BS in Journalism, U. Kans., 1948. News editor Marion County Record, Hoch Pub. Co., Inc., Marion, Kans., 1948—67, editor, pub., 1967—; owner Cottonwood Valley Agy., Marion, 1990-98, Hoch Pub. Co., Inc., Marion, 1998—. Polit. interviewer Sta. KPTS-TV, Wichita, 1983—98; lectr. media law Wichita (Kans.) State U., 1985; mil. cons., travel agt. Battlefield Tours, Slidell, La., 1990—; bd. dirs. Ctrl. Nat. Bank. Past pres. Marion Sch. Dist. Bd. Edn., Marion County Hosp. Dist.; bd. dirs. Marion Manor Nursing Home, Kans. Hist. Soc., 1985—; trustee, past pres. William Allen White Found., Lawrence, Kans. With U.S. Army, 1943—45, ETO. Named Kans. Master Editor, Kans. Leader of the Yr., 2003, Hon. Col., Kans. Cavalry, 1987, Hon. Ky. Col., Kans. Newspaper Hall of Fame, 2004; recipient commendation, Kans. Ho. of Reps., 1982, 99th Inf. Divsn. Assn., 1986, 1989, Clyde Reed Kans. Master Editor award, Kans. Newspaper Found., 1997, Cervi award, Internat. Soc. Weekly Newspaper Editors. Mem.: Soc. Profl. Journalists, Kans. Press Assn. (pres. 1982—83, Boyd Cmty. Svc. award 1979, Outstanding Mentor award 1999), Nat. Newspaper Assn., 99th Inf. Divsn. Assn. (editor 1971—, pres. 1998—99), Marion C. of C. (past bd. dirs.), Kiwanis (pres. Marion 1957), Shriners, Masons. Republican. Methodist. Avocation: military history. Home: 425 Locust St Marion KS 66861-1429 Office: Hoch Pub Co Inc 117 S 3rd St Marion KS 66861-1621 Personal E-mail: bill@marionkansas.com. E-mail: editor@marionrecord.com.

MEYER, BRECKIN, actor; b. Mpls., May 7, 1974; m. Dorothy Kaplan, Oct. 14, 2001; 1 child, Caitlin Willow. Actor: (films) Freddy's Dead: The Final Nightmare, 1991, Payback, 1995, Clueless, 1995, The Craft, 1996, Escape from L.A., 1996, Prefontaine, 1997, Touch, 1997, Dancer, Texas Pop. 81, 1998, 54, 1998, Go, 1999, The Insider, 1999, Tail Lights Fade, 1999, Road Trip, 2000, Rat Race, 2001, Kate & Leopold, 2001, (voice) Pinocchio, 2002, Garfield: The Movie, 2004; (TV films) Camp Cucamonga, 1990, Betrayed: A Story of Three Women, 1995, Rock Times, 2000; (TV series) Child's Play, 1982, Potato Head Kids, 1985, The Jackie Thomas Show, 1992, The Home Court, 1995, (voice) King of the Hill, 1997, The Near Future, 2000, Inside Schwartz, 2001, Married to the Kellys, 2003. Office: c/o the Gersh Agy PO Box 5617 Beverly Hills CA 90210*

MEYER, BRUD RICHARD, retired pharmaceutical company executive; b. Waukegan, Ill., Feb. 22, 1926; s. Charles Lewis and Mamie Olive (Broom) M.; m. Betty Louise Stine (dec. 1970); children: Linda (Mrs. Gary Stillabower), Louise (Mrs. Donald Knochel), Janet (Mrs. Gerald Cockrell), Jeff, Karen, Blake, Amy; m. Barbara Ann Hamilton, Nov. 26, 1970. BS, Purdue U., 1949. With Eli Lilly & Co., Indpls., 1949-87, indsl. engr., 1949-56, supr. indsl. engr., 1956-59, sr. personnel rep., 1960-64, personnel mgr. Lafayette, Ind., 1964-67, asst. dir., 1967-69, dir. adminstrn., 1969-79, dir. personnel and public relations, 1980-87, ret., 1987. Bd. dirs. Lafayette Home Hosp., 1977—. Hanna Community Ctr., 1983—, Tippecanoe Hist. Corp., 1985—; bd. dirs. United Way Tippecanoe County, 1970-76, pres., 1974; bd. dirs. Legal Aid Soc. Tippecanoe County, 1973—. Jr. Achievement, pres., 1979; bd. dirs. Lilly Credit Union, 1969-75, pres., 1973-74; mem. Citizen's Com. on Alcoholism, 1966-72; bd. dirs. Greater Lafayette Cmty. Ctrs., 1975-79, pres., 1977-78; bd. dirs. Tippecanoe County Child Care, 1990—, pres., 1998-99; mem., mng. dir. Battle Tippecanoe Outdoor Drama Bd. With USAAF, 1943-45. Mem. Pi Tau Sigma, Lambda Chi Alpha, C. of C. Greater Lafayette (bd. dirs., v.p. 1969-73), Battleground Hist. Soc. Methodist. Home: 4217 Trees Hill Dr Lafayette IN 47909-3451 Office: Eli Lilly & Co PO Box 7685 Lafayette IN 47903-7685

MEYER, C. RICHARD, architect; BArch, U. Calif., Berkeley, 1968. Registered architect, Wash. With The Callison Partnership, Seattle, 1977—, dir. quality assurance. Mem. adv. bd. cert. program project mgmt. U. Wash.; contracts rev. panelist Soc. Archtl. Adminstrs.; mem. faculty Pacific real estate symposium N.W. Real Estate Inst.; guest lectr. Archtl. Registration Exam. Seminar; guest lectr. coll. architecture and urban planning U. Wash.; guest panelist Internat. Conf. of Bldg. Ofcls. Nat. Conf., 1991. Mem. AIA (treas. Seattle chpt., mem. steering com. Pacific NW regional conf., vice-chair nat. risk mgmt. com., mem. steering com. nat. practice com., liaison to Am. Arbitration Assn.), Nat. Inst. Bldg. Scis. Office: The Callison Partnership Ltd 1420 5th Ave Ste 2400 Seattle WA 98101-2343

MEYER, CHESTER F. language educator, writer; s. Chester F. Meyer; m. Eleanor June Blonk, July 15, 1979. BA, Middlebury Coll., 1964; MS, C. W. Post Coll., 1972. Cert. Secondary Sch. English Tchr. N.Y. State & N.J. State. Tchr. English Commack Twp. H.S., NY, 1966—69; tchr., edn. supr.,edn. dir. Several N.Y. Agy., N.Y.C., 1969—75; script writer, filmmaker PanFilms, New York, 1975—77; mng. editor, writer Common Cents Mag., New York, 1977—79; tchr. English Pequannock Twp. H.S., Pompton Plains, NJ, 1979—. Co-author (and composer with John Arthur Long): (children's book with cds of text & songs) The Tooth Fairy Legend: The Touch of Kindness. 1st lt. Mil. Police Corps U.S. Army, 1964—66, France. Mem.: NEA, Pequannock Township Edn. Assn., N.J. Edn. Assn., Nat. Coun. Tchrs. English, Dramatists Guild of Am., Inc. Office: Pequannock Township High School 85 Sunset Road Pompton Plains NJ 07444

MEYER, CHRISTOPHER HAWKINS, lawyer; b. Springfield, Mo., Sept. 29, 1952; s. Richard DeWitt and Nancy (Hawkins) M.; m. Karen Anne Adams, Aug. 8, 1987; 1 child, C. Andrew Meyer. BA in Econs. magna cum laude, U. Mich., 1977, JD cum laude, 1981. Bar: D.C. 1981, U.S. Ct. Appeals (D.C. cir.) 1982, U.S. Ct. Appeals (9th cir.) 1983, Colo. 1985, U.S. Ct. Appeals (10th cir.) 1985, Idaho, U.S. Ct. Appeals (8th cir.). Counsel water resources program Nat. Wildlife Fedn., Washington, 1981-84, assoc. prof. adjoint, counsel Rocky Mountain Natural Resources Clinic Boulder, Colo., 1984-91; ptnr. Givens Pursley, Boise, 1991—. Contbr. articles to profl. publs. Mem. steering com. Idaho Environ. Forum. Recipient Lawyer of Yr. award Environ. Policy Inst., 1984, Water Conservationist of Yr. Nebr. Wildlife Fedn., 1989. Mem. Phi Beta Kappa. Home: 3443 S Millspur Way Boise ID 83716-8648 Office: Givens Pursley LLP 601 W Bannock St Boise ID 83702-7720 Office Phone: 208-388-1236. E-mail: chrismeyer@greenspursley.com.

MEYER, SIR CHRISTOPHER J.R. former diplomat; b. Beaconsfield, Eng., Feb. 22, 1944; m. Catherine Laylle; 2 sons, 2 stepsons. Student, Lancing Coll., Eng., Peterhouse, Cambridge, Eng., Paul Nitze Sch., Bologna, Italy, Lycee Henri IV, Paris; MA in History, Cambridge U., 1965. Joined Diplomatic Svc., London, 1966-68, with Moscow, 1968-70, Madrid, 1970-73; head Soviet sect. East European and Soviet dept. Fgn. and Commonwealth Office, London, 1973-76; speech-writer to fgn. sec. policy planning staff Diplomatic Svc., London, 1976-78; mem. UK rep. to European Comtys., Brussels, 1978-82; polit. counselor British Embassy, Moscow, 1982-84; fgn. office spokesman, press sec. to fgn. sec. Fgn. and Commonwealth Office, London, 1984-88, min. Washington, 1989-92; min., dep. head mission British Embassy, 1992—93, govt. spokesman, press sec. to prime min., 1994-97, Brit. amb. to Fed. Rep. Germany, 1997; Brit. amb. to U.S. Washington, 1997—2003; chmn. U.K. Press Complaints Commn., 2003—. Vis. fellow Harvard U. Ctr. for Internat. Affairs, 1988-89; hon. fellow Peterhouse, Cambridge U., 2001—. Named Knight Comdr. of the Order of St. Michael and St. George, 1998. Avocations: tennis, watching soccer, listening to jazz music. Office: 1 Salisbury Sq London EC4Y 8JB England Fax: 011 44 207 353 8355.

MEYER, CHRISTOPHER RICHARD, lawyer; b. Springfield, Ohio, June 18, 1952; s. Eugene Francis and Marilyn Crawford (Hopping) M.; m. Sharman Elizabeth, Sept. 8, 1973; children: Elizabeth Ann, Emily McClead, Timothy Joseph. BA summa cum laude, Ohio State U., 1974, JD, 1977. Bar: Ohio, U.S. Dist. Ct. (so. and no. dists.) Ohio, U.S. Ct. Appeals (6th cir.), U.S. Supreme Ct. Ptnr. Reese, Pyle, Drake & Meyer, Newark, Ohio, 1977—. Legal counsel Licking Meml. Hosp., Newark Ohio, 1983—, State Farm Ins. Co., Bloomington, Ill., 1977—, St. Paul Ins. Co., Columbus, Ohio, 1977—, spl. coun. Ctrl. Ohio Tech. Coll. Mem. Ohio State Bar Assn. (negligence com., litigation sect.), Ohio Assn. Civil Trial Attys., Soc. Ohio Hosp. Attys., Phi Beta Kappa. Home: 976 Briarhill Dr Newark OH 43055-2249 Office: Reese Pyle Drake & Meyer 36 N 2d St PO Box 919 Newark OH 43058-0919 E-mail: cmeyer@rpdm.com.

MEYER, DALE ROBERT, ophthalmologist; b. Balt., Nov. 7, 1957; m. Joy Marie Leuchten, Sept. 30, 1986; children: Eric James, Elena Elizabeth. BA, U. Va., 1979; MD, U. Md., 1984. Diplomate Am. Bd. Ophthalmology, Nat. Bd. Med. Examiners. Intern Greater Balt. Med. Ctr., 1980-84; resident in ophthalmology Greater Balt. Med. Ctr.-Johns Hopkins U., 1985-88; fellow in oculoplastic & orbital surgery W.Va. U., Morgantown, 1988-89, Ore. Health Scis. U., Portland, 1989-90; asst. prof. ophthalmology Albany (N.Y.) Med. Coll., 1990-95, assoc. prof., 1995—2000, prof., 2000—. Staff eye pathology svc. The Wilmer Inst. Johns Hopkins U., 1983, 86, orbital and ocular oncology svc. dept. ophthalmology U. Br. Columbia, Vancouver, 1990; instr. dept. ophthalmology Ore. Health Scis. U., 1989, W.Va. U. Med. Ctr., 1988-89; dir. oculoplastic and orbital surgery svc., Albany Med. Coll., 1990—, dir. med. student ophthalmology edn., 1990—, chairperson Continuing Med. Edn. Coun., 1991—, student promotions com., 1990—, faculty senate rep., 1990—, edn. coun., 1990—, acad. governing coun., 1990—. Reviewer Archives of Ophthalmology, Am. Jour. Ophthalmology. Cons. oculoplastic and orbital surgery Project ORBIS, 1991. Sight Conservation Rsch. Soc. grantee, 1990-91, NIH grantee, 1991, others. Mem. AMA, Am. Acad. Ophthalmology, Am. Coll. Surgeons, Am. Soc. Ophthalmic Plastic and Reconstructive Surgery, Assn. Rsch. Vision & Ophthalmology, Rsch. to Prevent Blindness, Inc., Christian Med. & Dental Soc., N.Y. Ophthalmol. Soc., Eastern N.Y. Eye/ENT Soc. (program chairperson 1991—, v.p. 1992-93, pres. 1993-94). Home: 74 Westview Rd Voorheesville NY 12186-4942 Office: Albany Med Coll Lions Eye Inst 35 Hackett Blvd Albany NY 12208

MEYER, DANIEL JOSEPH, machinery company executive; b. Flint, Mich., May 31, 1936; s. John Michael and Margaret (Meehan) M.; m. Bonnie Harrison, June 22, 1963; children: Daniel P., Jennifer. BS, Purdue U., 1958; MBA, Ind. U., 1963. CPA, N.Y. Mgr. Touche, Ross & Co., Detroit, 1964-69; contr. Cin. Milacron, Inc., 1969-77, v.p. fin., treas., 1977-83, exec. v.p. fin. and adminstrn., 1983-86, pres., COO, 1987-90, pres., CEO, 1990-91, chmn., CEO, 1991-92, also bd. dirs. Bd. dirs. E.W. Scripps Inc., Hubbell Inc., Cin. Bell Inc., AK Steel. With U.S. Army, 1959. Mem. Am. Inst. CPAs, Kenwood Country Club (Cin.). Clubs: Kenwood Country (Cin.). Home: 8 Grandin Ln Cincinnati OH 45208-3304 Office: 2090 Florence Ave Cincinnati OH 45206-2425

MEYER, DANIEL KRAMER, real estate executive; b. Denver, July 15, 1957; s. Milton Edward and Mary (Kramer) M. Student, Met. State Coll., Denver, 1977-78, U. Colo., 1978-80. Ptnr., developer RM & M II (Ltd. Partnership), Englewood, Colo., 1981-87; pres. Centennial Mortgage and Investment, Ltd., Englewood, Colo., 1984-87; prin. Capriole Properties, Greenwood Village, Colo., 1983—. Alumni mem. bd. trustees Kent Denver Country Day Sch., 1981-83; sec. dist. 37 ctrl. and vacancy com. Colo. Ho. of Reps., 1991-92. Recipient Pamela Davis Beardsley devel. award Kent Denver Sch., 1995. Mem.: Greenwood Athletic Club. Republican. Avocations: climbing, rollerblading, political economy, 20th century English lit., metaphysics.

MEYER, DENNIS IRWIN, lawyer; b. Dayton, Ohio, Oct. 20, 1935; s. Luther Edward and Mary (McGee) M.; m. Rita Murray, June 23, 1962; children: Matthew, Michael, Rita Catherine, Peter, Denise, Abigail. BS, U. Dayton, 1957; LLB, Georgetown U., 1960, LLM, 1962. Bar: Ohio 1960, D.C. 1962. Atty.-advisor U.S. Tax Ct., Washington, 1960—62; sr. counsel Baker & McKenzie, Washington, 1965—. Bd. dirs. United Fin. Banking Cos., Vienna, Va. Mem. ABA, Internat. Fiscal Assn., Met. Club, Belle Haven Country Club, Avenel Golf Club, Robert Trent Jones Golf Club. Roman Catholic. Office: Baker & McKenzie 815 Connecticut Ave NW Washington DC 20006-4004 Office Phone: 202-452-7008. E-mail: dennis.i.meyer@bakernet.com.

MEYER, DERRICK R. information technology executive; BS in Computer Engring., U. Ill.; MBA, Boston U. With Intel Corp., 1983—86, Digital Equipment Corp., 1986—96; dir. engring. Athlon Advanced Micro Devices, Austin, Tex., 1996—99, v.p. engring. computation products group Sunnyvale, Calif., 1999—2001, group v.p. computation products group, 2001—02, exec. v.p. computation products group, 2002—. Office: Advanced Micro Devices One AMD Pl PO Box 3453 Sunnyvale CA 94088-3453*

MEYER, DIANE CHRISTINE, social worker; b. Meadowbrook, Pa., May 9, 1963; d. Robert Francis and Carole Ann Meyer; children: Stephen Francis, Alexander Gerard, Robert Nathaniel. BA in Psychology, LaSalle U., Phila., 1989. Childcare supr. St. Mary's Villa, Ambler, Pa., 1989—91; caseworker Bucks County Children & Youth, Doylestown, Pa., 1991—2001, casework supr., 2001—. Democrat. Roman Catholic. Avocation: reading. Home: 4218 Miladies Ln Doylestown PA 18901 Office: Bucks County Children and Youth 4259 W Swamp Rd Doylestown PA 18901

MEYER, DONALD ROBERT, state agency administrator, banker, lawyer; b. Phoenix, June 4, 1942; s. Donald and Eleanor M.; m. Virginia Whitesel, Sept. 3, 1966; 2 children. BA, U. Calif., Berkeley, 1964, JD, 1967; postgrad., Harvard U., 1968. Bar: Calif. 1972, U.S. Peace Corps. Lectr. Seoul Nat. Univ., Korea, 1969-70; assoc. Graham & James, San Francisco, 1971-76; asst. sec. Calif. First Bank (name now Union Bank), San Francisco, 1973-76, v.p., 1976-78, gen. counsel, 1976-96, sr. v.p., 1978-96; corp. sec., exec. v.p. gen. counsel UnionBanCal Corp., 1996—98; commr. Fin. Institutions, Calif., 2000—. Contbr.: Intro to the Law & Legal System of Korea, 1983. Mem. Habitat for Humanity Internat., Sierra Club; co-chmn. San Francisco/Seoul Sister City Com., 1980-90; trustee Asian Art Found. of San Francisco, 1985-92, 97—; commr. Asian Art Mus., San Francisco, 1985-91. Recipient Key to Seoul, Korea, 1984. Mem. ABA, San Francisco Bar Assn., Am. Bankers Assn. (v.p. Calif. State 1982-83), Calif. Bankers Assn. (chmn. legal affairs com. 1982-84, svc. award 1989), Korean-Am. C. of C. (dir. San Francisco sec., bd. dirs. 1974-93, pres. 1996-98, chmn. 1998-2002), Soc. Calif. Pioneers, Bohemian Club. Republican. Episcopalian. Personal E-mail: dmeyerberk@cs.com. Business E-Mail: dmeyer@dgi.ca.gov.

MEYER, EDGAR, musician, composer; BMus, Ind. U., 1984. Bassist Strength in Numbers, 1986—92. Vis. prof. double bass Royal Acad. Music London; adj. assoc. prof. double bass Vanderbilt U. Musician: (albums) Appalachian Journey, 1999 (Grammy award, 1999), Perpetual Motion, 2002 (Grammy award, 2002), Bach: Unaccompanied Cello Suites Performed on Double Bass, Schubert: Trout Quintet: Arpeggione Sonata, 1996, Appalachia Waltz, 1996, Uncommon Ritual, 1997, At the Octoroon Balls, Short Trip Home, 1999, Listen to the Storyteller, 1999, Appalachian Journey Live in Concert, 2000, Barber, Meyer: Violin Concertos, 2000, Appalachian Journey, 2000, Heartland: An Appalachian Anthology, 2001, Classical Hits, 2001, Classic Yo-Yo, 2001, The Americian Seasons, 2001, Silk Road Journeys: When Strangers Meet, 2002, Edgar Meyer, 2002. Recipient Avery Fisher prize, 2000; fellow MacArthur Found. fellow, 2002; grantee Avery Fisher Career grantee, 1994. Mem.: Chamber Music Soc. Lincoln Ctr. Office: c/o IMG 825 Seventh Ave New York NY 10019

MEYER, EDMOND GERALD, energy and natural resources educator, resources scientist, entrepreneur, former chemistry educator, university administrator; b. Albuquerque, Nov. 2, 1919; s. Leopold and Beatrice (Ilfeld) M.; m. Betty F. Knobloch, July 4, 1941; children: Lee Gordon, Terry Gene, David Gary. BS in Chemistry, Carnegie Mellon U., 1940, MS, 1942; PhD, U. N.Mex., 1950. Chemist Harbison Walker Refractories Co., 1940-41; instr. Carnegie Mellon U., 1941-42; asst. phys. chemist Bur. Mines, 1942-44; chemist research div. N.Mex. Inst. Mining and Tech., 1946-48; head dept. sci. U. Albuquerque, 1950-52; head dept. chemistry N.Mex. Highlands U., 1952-59; dir. Inst. Sci. Rsch., dean Grad. Sch. U. Wyo., 1957—63, dean Coll. Arts and Sci., 1963-75, v.p. rsch., 1974-80, prof. energy and natural resources, 1981-89, prof. and dean emeritus, 1989—. Exec. cons. Diamond Shamrock Corp., 1980; sci. adviser Gov. of Wyo., 1964-90; pres. Coal Tech. Corp., 1981—; cons. Los Alamos Nat. Lab., NFS, HHS, GAO, TVA, Wyo. Bancorp; contractor investigator Rsch. Corp., Dept. Interior, AEC, NIH, NSF, Dept. Energy, Dept. Edn.; Fulbright exch. prof. U. Concepcion, Chile, 1959. Co-author: Chemistry-Survey of Principles, 1963, Legal Rights of Chemists and Engineers, 1977, Industrial Research & Development Management, 1982; contbr. articles to profl. jours.; patentee in field. Mem. Laramie Regional Airport Bd., 1989-93, treas., 1994-97, chair; active Laramie City Coun., 1997-2001, vice mayor, 1998-2001. Lt. comdr. USNR, 1944-46, ret. Recipient Disting. Svc. award Jaycees; rsch. fellow U. N.Mex., 1948-50. Fellow AAAS, Am. Inst. Chemists (hon. fellow; pres. 1992-93, chmn. 1994-95); mem. AIChE (sr.), Assoc. Western Univs. (chmn. 1972-74), Am. Chem. Soc. (councilor 1962-90, chmn. Wyo. sect. 1997, 2002), Biophys. Soc., Coun. Coll. Arts and Scis. (pres. 1971, sec.-treas. 1972-75), dir. Washington office 1973), Laramie C. of C. (pres. 1984), Sigma Xi. Home: 1058 Colina Dr Laramie WY 82072-5015 Office: U Wyo Coll Arts Scis Laramie WY 82073-0966 Office Phone: 307-766-5445. Business E-Mail: egmeyer@uwyo.edu.

MEYER, EDWARD HENRY, advertising agency executive; b. N.Y.C., Jan. 8, 1927; s. I.H. and Mildred (Driesen) M.; m. Sandra Raabin, Apr. 26, 1957; children: Margaret Ann, Anthony Edward. BA with honors in Econs, Cornell U., 1949. With Bloomingdale's div. Federated Dept Stores, 1949-51, Biow Co. (agy.), 1951-56; with Grey Advt., Inc., N.Y.C., 1956—, exec. v.p., 1963-68, pres., chief exec. officer, 1968—, chmn. bd., 1970—. Bd. dirs. Ethan Allan Interiors Inc., Harman Internat. Industries, Inc., JIm Pattison Group, Inc. Trustee Am. Mus. Natural History, Guggenheim Mus., NYU Med. Ctr., Film Soc. of Lincoln Ctr. With USCGR, 1945-47. Mem. Econ. Club (N.Y.C.), Univ. Club (N.Y.C.), Harmonie Club (N.Y.C.), Century Country Club, Atlantic Golf Club. Office: Grey Global Group Inc 777 3rd Ave New York NY 10017-1401

MEYER, ELLEN L. academic administrator; BA and MS Geo Wash U. Vp for mktg and exten, dean of cont studies and dir of exten prog and summer sch Minneapolis College of Art and Design; dir of cont ed and spec prog RI Sch of Design; pres. Atlanta Coll. Art, 1992—. Mem.: National Black Arts Festival Bd of Dir, Metro Atlanta Arts Fund Adv Bd, vice chair, bd of dir, Atl Reg Consortium for Higher Ed. Achievements include 1992-93 graduate, Midtown Leadership Program, Atlanta; 1994 graduate, Leadership-Atlanta. Office: Atlanta Coll Art President 1280 Peachtree St NE Atlanta GA 30309-3502

MEYER, EUGENE CARLTON, retired editor; b. McGregor, Iowa, Dec. 10, 1923; s. Gilbert Nelson and Christine Winnifred (Henkes) M.; m. Maxine Beth Mallory, June 1, 1947; children— Bruce, Mary Lynn, John BS, Iowa State U., 1946. Farm news editor Sta. WHO, Des Moines, 1947-48; assoc. editor Hoard's Dairyman, Fort Atkinson, Wis., 1948-72, mng. editor, 1972-88. Trustee Fort Atkinson Meml. Hosp., 1966-81, pres. bd. trustees, 1976-81. Navigator, USAAF, WWII. Recipient Disting. Service award Am. Dairy Sci. Assn., 1980, Disting. Grad. award Iowa State Dairy Sci. Club, Iowa State U., 1981, Agrl. Leadership award Alpha Gamma Rho, 1982, Award of Distinction U. Wis.-Madison, 1982, Disting. Citizen of Agr. Nat. Milk Producers, 1988, Henry A. Wallace award Iowa State U., 1989, Richard E. Lyng award, 1989, Econ. Contribution award Ft. Atkinson C. of C., 1982, Nat. Assn. Animal Breeders Disting. Svc. award, 1988, Disting. Svc. award for Cmty. Svc. Ft. Atkinson Lions Club, 1995; named Industry Person of Yr. World Dairy Expo, 1988. Mem. Nat. Dairy Shrine (pres. 1980, Guest of Hon. 1986) Republican. Methodist. Home: 524 Jackson St Fort Atkinson WI 53538-1356

MEYER, F. WELLER, bank executive; b. Washington, Dec. 15, 1942; s. Martin William and Sallie Rita (Weller) M.; m. Brenda Burton, Sept. 27, 1972; children: F. Weller Jr., Brandon Michael. BS, U. Md., 1977. V.p. W.S. Steed Mortgage Co., Wheaton, Md., 1970-73; asst. dir. Mortgage Bankers Assn. Am., Washington, 1973-77; mng. dir. Mortgage Systems Corp., Bethesda, Md., 1977-83; pres., CEO Westmark Mortgage Corp., Rockville, Md., 1983-87, Acacia Fed. Savs. Bank, Falls Church, Va., 1987—. Bd. dirs. Acacia Fed. Svcs. Bank, Calvert Group Ltd.; 2d vice chmn. Am.'s Cmty. Bankers; former pres. Thrift Instns. Adv. Coun. to the Fed. Res.; mem. nat. adv. coun. Fed. Nat. Mortgage Assn.; mem. Nat. Assn. Homebuilders Mortgage Roundtable. Co-author: Residential Mortgage Underwriting, 1981, Consturction Lending—Residential, 1981, Construction Lending—Residential Income Property, 1981, Income Property Underwriting, 1981. Dir. Make-A-Wish Found. of the Mid-Atlantic, 1991-97, No. Va. Comty. Found., Fairfax, Va., 1989; mem. Citizen's Housing Adv. Com., Montgomery County, Md., 1988-90. 1st lt. U.S. Army, 1967-70, Vietnam. Mem. Optimists (pres. Washington 1978-79), Old Guard Assn. Republican. Roman Catholic. Avocations: golf, hunting, jogging. Home: 9809 Kendale Rd Rockville MD 20854-4246

MEYER, FERDINAND CHARLES, JR., lawyer; b. San Antonio, Sept. 30, 1939; Student, Tulane U.; BBA, U. Tex., 1961, LLB, 1964. Bar: Tex. 1966, U.S. Dist. Ct. (we. dist.) Tex. 1969, U.S. Ct. Appeals (5th cir.) 1971, U.S. Supreme Ct. 1975, U.S. Ct. Appeals (11th cir.) 1979, D.C. 1986. V.p., gen. counsel CSW Svcs.; ptnr. Matthews & Branscomb, San Antonio; v.p. asst. gen. counsel CSW Corp., 1986-88; v.p., gen. counsel Ctrl. & S.W. Corp., 1988-90, sr. v.p., gen. counsel, 1990-98, gen. counsel, 1990-2000, exec. v.p., gen. counsel, 1998-2000. Instr. trial advocacy St. Mary's Sch. Law, 1980-86. Capt. USAR. Fellow Am. Coll. Trial Lawyers, Tex. Bar Found.; mem. ABA, Am. Bd. Trial Advs. (adv.), State Bar Tex., Dallas Bar Assn., San Antonio Bar Assn., Internat. Assn. Def. Counsel, Phi Alpha Delta. Office: PO Box 7616 Dallas TX 75209-7616

MEYER, FRANCES MARGARET ANTHONY, elementary and secondary school educator, health education specialist; b. Stella, Va., Nov. 15, 1947; d. Arthur Abner Jr. and Emmie Adeline (Murray) Anthony; m. Stephen Leroy Meyer, Aug. 2, 1975. BS, Longwood Coll., 1970; MS, Va. Commonwealth U., 1982, PhD, 1996. Cert. tchr., Va. Health, phys. edn., and dance tchr. Fredericksburg (Va.) City Pub. Schs., 1970-89; AIDS edn. coord. Va. Dept. Edn., Richmond, 1989-90, health edn. specialist, 1990-94, comprehensive sch. health program specialist, 1994—2003; ednl. cons. Fredericksburg, Va., 2003—. Mem. rev. bd. Nat. Commn. for Health Edn. and Credentialing, Inc., conf. and profl. devel. rev., 1996-2000. Author (with others): Elementary Physical Education: Growing through Movement-A Curriculum Guide, 1982; contbr. articles to profl. jours. Dir. Va. Children's Dance Festival, 1981—96, 1997—; vol. ARC, Fredericksburg, 1976—84, 1997—2001, Va. affiliate AHA, 1982—93, 1999—2001; mem. ctrl. steering com. Health, Mental Health and Safety in Schs. Nat. Guidelines Project, Am. Acad. Pediat., 2000—02; Va. Affiliate Am. Cancer Soc. Richmond, Va.; mem. Public Health Edn.Coun., Comprehensive Sch. Health Edn. Team, Va. Alliance Adolescents and Sch. Health, 1990—; bd. dirs. Va. HIV/AIDS Network ARC, 1997—2001. Recipient gov.'s medal for substance abuse and prevention edn. State of Va., 1997, Alumni Cmty. Svc. award Va. Commonwealth U., 1998, Youth Edn. award for Leadership in the healthy devel. of children Am. Cancer Soc., 2002, Disting. Leadership in Phys. Edn. award Nat. Assn. Sport and Phys. Edn., 2004. Fellow: North Am. (honor) Soc. Health, Phys. Edn., Recreation, Sport and Dance; mem.: AAPHERD (chmn. divsn. 1970—, chmn. so. dist. applied strategic planning com. 2002—04, past v.p., nominating com., social justice com., pres.-elect so. dist., strategic planning com., So. Dist. honor award 1995, pres.'s recognition award 1997, svc. award 1997, So. Dist. honor award 1999, nat. honor award 1999), ASCD, AAUW (com. 1989—90, 1995—), NEA, Dance Edn. Orgn. (charter mem.), Va. Assn. for Health, Phys. Edn., Recreation and Dance (various coms. 1970—, health edn. editor Va. Jour. 1994—2003, past pres., Tchr. of Yr. 1983, Va. Honor award 1988, Va. Pioneer award 2003), Va. Alliance for Arts Edn. (adv. bd. 1980—83, 1989—90, 1994—96), Am. Coll. Health Assn. (curriculum and tng. rev. panel 1992—94), Soc. State Dirs. Health, Phys. Edn. and Recreation (legis. affairs com. 1994—98, mem. applied strategic planning com. 1994—2001, pres.-elect 1997, pres. 1998, past pres. 1999, think tank chair 2000—02, Healthis acad. rev. com. 2001—03,

applied policy & legis. com. 2002—, Presdl. award 1996, Presdl. Recognition award 1997, 2000, Simon A. McNeely Honor award 2000, Julian B. Smith award 2004), Va. Health Promotion and Edn. Coun. (bd. dirs. 1990—96), Internat. Coun. for Health, Phys. Edn., Recreation, Sport and Dance (internat. commns. for health edn. and commn. for dance and dance edn., mem. jour. articles rev. com.), Va. Mid. Sch. Assn., Va. Edn. Assn., Nat. Mid. Sch. Assn., Nat. Dance Assn. (bd. dirs. 1996—, pres. 2001—03, Presdl. citation 1998, svc. award 1998, 2000, Pres.'s Merit award 2001), Nat. Network for Youth Svcs. (adv. bd. 1994—98, rev. panel), Longwood Coll. Alumni Coun. (bd. dirs. 1987—90), Delta Kappa Gamma (pres. Beta Eta chpt. 1988—90). Baptist. Avocations: travel, dance, swimming, reading, theatrical performances.

MEYER, FRED ALBERT, JR., political science educator; b. Milw., Oct. 7, 1942; s. Fred Albert and Rose Henrietta (Hafemann) M. BA, U. Wis., 1964; MA, U. Wis., Milw., 1966; PhD, Wayne State U., 1974. Instr. Carroll Coll., Waukesha, Wis., 1970-71; prof. Polit. Sci. Ball State U., Muncie, Ind., 1971—. Editor Ind. Jour. Polit. Sci. Co-editor: Determinants of Law Enforcement Policies, 1979, Evaluating Alternative Law Enforcement Policies, 1979; co-author: The Criminal Justice Game, 1980; co-editor: State Policy Problems, 1993. Chair adv. com. on sex discrimination Ind. Civil Rights Commn., 1983-84; chair Ind. Sexual Harassment Task Force, 1989-92; chair Gender Fairness Coalition of Ind., Indpls., 1988-93, sec., 1994-97, chair 1998—; chair Ind. Found. on Gender-Based Edn., Indpls., 1988-93, 1998-2001, Gender Fairness Found. Ind., 2002—; chmn., Perham com. task force on women coll. scis. and humanities Ball State U., 1998-; sec. Healthy Mothers Healthy Babies of Delaware County, 1995-96, vice chair, 1996—; mem. coun. Policy Studies Orgn., 1994-98, bd. dirs. LWV Ind., 1998-2000, Ind. Pro-Choice Action League, 1984-90; chair Perham com. task force status of woman Coll. Scis. & Humanities, 1997—. Recipient grant to produce videotape on access to prenatal care in Delaware County, Ind. Hoosier Heartland chpt. March of Dimes, Muncie, 1990; Ford Found. Legis. fellow Mich. Senate, 1965-66. Mem. Am. Polit. Sci. Assn., Policy Studies Orgn., Midwest Polit. Sci. Assn., Western Polit. Sci. Assn., So. Polit. Sci. Assn., Audubon Soc., Sierra Club, Environ. Defense Fund, World Wildlife Fund, Earth Justice. Avocations: reading, art history, listening to music, animal welfare. Office: Polit Sci Dept Ball State U Muncie IN 47306-0001

MEYER, FRED JOSEF, financial executive; b. Zurich, Switzerland, Jan. 1, 1931; came to U.S., 1959; s. Josef and Claire (Lehmann) M.; m. Beverly Ruth Carter, Apr. 9, 1961 (div. Feb. 1975); children: Fred Jay, Marcus Clinton, Michael Josef; m. Marie-Noelle Vigneron, Oct. 30, 1975. MS, Fed. Inst. Tech., Zurich, 1956; MBA, Harvard U., 1961; LLD (hon.), Sacred Heart U., 1981. V.p. planning & adminstrn. Sandoz, Inc., Hanover, N.J., 1971-73, exec. v.p., chief fin. officer, 1973-78; pres., CEO Sandoz U.S., Inc., Greenwich, Conn., 1978-81; mng. dir., CEO Wander Ltd., Berne, Switzerland, 1981-82; sr. v.p., chief fin. officer CBS, Inc., N.Y.C., 1982-88; chief fin. officer Omnicom Group, Inc., N.Y.C., 1988-98, vice chmn., 1998-99, spl. advisor exec. office, 2000—03. Bd. dirs. Zurich Life Ins. Co. N.Y., N.Y.C., Actelion Ltd., Basle, Novartis Corp., N.Y.C., Ptnrs. Group USA Inc., NYC Mem. Fin. Execs. Inst., Econ. Club, Harvard Club (N.Y.C.), Greenwich Country Club. Republican. Congregationalist. Office: Omnicom Group Inc 437 Madison Ave New York NY 10022-7001

MEYER, FRED WILLIAM, JR., memorial parks executive; b. Fair Haven, Mich., Jan. 7, 1924; s. Fred W. and Gladys (Marshall) M.; m. Jean Hope, Aug. 5, 1946; children— Frederick, Thomas, James, Nancy. AB, Mich. State Coll., 1946. Salesman Chapel Hill Meml. Gardens, Lansing, Mich., 1946-47; mgr. Roselawn Meml. Gardens, Saginaw, Mich., 1947-49; dist. mgr. Sunset Meml. Gardens, Evansville, Ind., 1949-53; pres., dir. Memory Gardens Mgmt. Corp., Indpls., Covington Meml. Gardens, Ft. Wayne, Ind., Chapel Hill Meml. Gardens, Grand Rapids, Mich., Forest Lawn Memory Gardens, Indpls., Lincoln Memory Gardens, Indpls., Chapel Hill Meml. Gardens, South Bend, Ind., Mercury Devel. Corp., Indpls., Quality Marble Imports, Indpls., Quality Printers, Indpls., Am. Bronze Craft, Inc., Judsonia, Ark. Mem. C. of C., A.I.M., Am. Cemetery Assn., Sigma Chi, Phi Kappa Delta. Clubs: Columbia, Meridian Hills Country, Woodland Country. Home: 110 E 111th St Indianapolis IN 46280-1051 Office: 3733 N Meridian St Indianapolis IN 46208-4305

MEYER, G. CHRISTOPHER, lawyer; b. Fremont, Nebr., Mar. 27, 1948; s. Gerald William and Mildred Ruth (Clausen) M.; children: Kate, Stacy, Jon, Robert. Student, Grinnell (Iowa) Coll., 1966-69; BA, U. Kans., 1970; JD, U. Pa., 1973. Bar: Ohio 1973, U.S. Dist. Ct. (no. dist.) Ohio 1975, U.S. Ct. Appeals (6th cir.) 1982. Assoc. Squire, Sanders & Dempsey, L.L.P., Cleve., 1973-82, ptnr., 1982—. Mem. ABA, Greater Cleve. Bar Assn., Am. Coll. Bankruptcy. Office: Squire Sanders & Dempsey LLP 4900 Key Tower 127 Public Sq Cleveland OH 44114-1304 Office Phone: 216-479-8692. E-mail: cmeyer@ssd.com.

MEYER, GEORGE HERBERT, lawyer; b. Detroit, Feb. 19, 1928; s. Herbert M. and Agnes F. (Eaton) M.; m. Carol Ann Jones, 1958 (div. 1981) children: Karen Ann, George Herbert Jr.; m. Katherine Palmer White, Nov. 12, 1988. BA, U. Mich., 1949; JD, Harvard U., 1952; cert., Oxford (Eng.) U., 1955; LLM in Taxation and Labor Law, Wayne U., 1962. Bar: D.C. 1952, Mich. 1953. Assoc. firm Fischer, Franklin & Ford, Detroit, 1956-63, mem. firm, 1963-74; established firm George H. Meyer, 1974-78; sr. mem. firm Meyer and Kirk, 1978-85; sr. mem. Meyer, Kirk, Snyder & Safford PLLC, Bloomfield Hills and Detroit, Mich., 1985-99; mng. mem. Meyer, Kirk, Snyder & Lynch PLLC, Bloomfield Hills, Mich., 2000—. Curator Step Lively exhibit Mus. Am. Folk Art, N.Y.C., 1992; lectr. Am. Folk Art. Author: Equalization in Michigan and Its Effect on Local Assessments, 1963, Folk Artists Biographical Index, 1986, American Folk Art Canes: Personal Sculpture, 1992. Chmn. Birmingham (Mich.) Bd. Housing Appeals, 1964-68; vice chmn. Birmingham Bd. Zoning Appeals, 1966-69; mem. Birmingham Planning Bd., 1968-70; trustee, Bloomfield Village, Mich., 1976-80, pres., 1979-80; trustee Am. Mus. Folk Art, N.Y.C., 1987—; mem. exec. bd. Detroit Area coun. Boy Scouts Am., 1976—, counsel, 1986-95,v.p., 1996—; mem. nat. adv. bd. Folk Art Soc. Am., 1994—; trustee Detroit Sci. Ctr., 1985-99. 1st lt. JAG, USAF, 1952-55, maj. Res. ret. Recipient Silver Beaver award Detroit Area coun. Boy Scouts Am., 1989. Mem. ABA, Detroit Bar Assn., Oakland County Bar Assn., State Bar Mich., Harvard Law Sch. Assn. Mich. (dir. 1959—, pres. 1970-78), Detroit Sci. Mus. Soc. (pres. 1961-74, chmn. 1974-76), Am. Folk Art Soc. (pres. 2000—), Cranbrook Writers Guild (pres. 2000—), Prismatic Club,(pres. 2002—), Scarab Club, Harvard Club (N.Y.C.), Detroit Athletic Club, Masons, Rotary, Phi Beta Kappa, Alpha Phi Omega, Pi Sigma Alpha. Republican. Unitarian. Office: Meyer Kirk Snyder & Lynch PLLC 100 W Long Lake Rd Ste 100 Bloomfield Hills MI 48304-2773 E-mail: gmeyer@meyerkirk.com.

MEYER, GREG CHARLES, psychiatrist; b. Bismarck, N.D., Aug. 17, 1935; s. Oscar Clarence and Agnes Josephine (Pearson) M. Degree in profl. engring., Colo. Sch. Mines, 1958, Alexander Hamilton Bus. Inst., 1960; MME, U. So. Calif., 1965; MD, Marquette U., 1970. Diplomate Am. Bd. Psychiatry and Neurology, Am. Bd. Forensic Medicine, Am. Bd. Disability Analysts, Am. Bd. Forensic Examiners. Engr. Minuteman-Thiokol, Brigham City, Utah, 1958-61; sr. engr. Saturn S-II N.Am. Aviation, Downey, Calif., 1962-65; design specialist Titan-Martin, Denver, 1965-66; rotating intern Weld Country Gen. Hosp., Greenly, Colo., 1970-71; psychiatric resident Ariz. State Hosp., Phoenix, 1971-74, psychiatrist, 1974-76; pvt. practice Mesa-Tempe, Ariz., 1975-94; psychiatrist Ariz. Ctrl. Med. Ctr., 1995-99; med. dir. Ctrl. Ariz. Med. Ctr., 1997-99. Chmn. psychiatry Desert Samaritan Hosp., Mesa, 1982-86, 90-94, chmn. joint mental health, 1981-83, mem. edn. com., 1979-82, quality assurance com., 1979; exec. com. Desert Vista Hosp., Mesa, 1988-94, chief of staff, 1989; chmn. psychiatry Mesa Luth. Hosp., 1984-85, exec. com., 1984-85; mng. ptnr. Desert Samaritan Med. Bldg. II, Mesa, 1985-86; rsch., edn. com. East Valley Camel Back Hosp., 1989-90, quality assurance com., 1985; med. dir. Ctrl. Ariz. Med. Ctr., 1997-99. Co-discoverer Larson-Meyer Transform. Coach Pop Warner Football, 1974. With USMCR, 1953-59. Fellow Am. Bd. Disability Analysts; mem. AMA, Am. Psychiat. Assn., Ariz. Med. Assn., Ariz. Psychiat. Assn., Phoenix Psychiat. Coun., Maricopa County Med. Assn., Christian Med./Dental Assn., Triple Nine Soc., SCV, Wingfield Family Soc. Republican. Lutheran. Avocations: multi engine instrument pilot, sailing, computers, canoeing, photography.

MEYER, HARRY MARTIN, JR., retired health science facility administrator; b. Palestine Tex., Nov. 25, 1928. s. Harry Martin and Marjory Isabel (Griffin) M.; m. Mary Jane Martin, Aug. 19, 1949 (div. 1966); children: Harry, Mary, David; m. Barbara Story Chalfant, Nov. 21, 1966. BS Hendrix Coll., 1949, MD U. Ark., 1953; Diplomate Am. Bd. Pediatics, 1960. instr. biology Little Rock Coll., 1949, intern. Walter Reed Army Hosp., Washington, 1953-54, med. officer dep. virus and rickettsial diseases, Walter Reed Army Inst. Rsch., 1954-57, asst. resident dep. pediatrics, N.C. Meml. Hosp., Chapel Hill, 1957-59, head virology sect. div. biologics standards, NIH, Bethesda, Md., 1959-64, chief lab. of viral immunol., div. biologics standards, NIH, 1964-72, dir. bur. biologics FDA, Bethesda, 1972-82, dir. Ctr. for Drugs & Biologics FDA, Rockville, Md., 1982-86, pres. med. research div. Am. Cyanamid Co., Pearl River, N.Y., 1986-93; retired 1993. Served to rear admiral USPHS, 1959-86, capt. U.S. Army, 1953-57. Mem. AMA, Am. Epidemiol. Soc., Am. Acad. Pediatrics, Am. Pediatric Soc. Protestant. Avocations: sailing, scuba diving, skiing, back packing. Contbr. articles to profl. jours.; patentee in field. E-mail: hanksji@interislend.net

MEYER, HELEN BERNADINE, financial services company executive; b. Ireton, Iowa, Mar. 2, 1929; d. Adolph J. and Haldora J. (Barnes) Opdahl; m. W. Thomas Logan, Nov. 19, 1955 (div. Mar. 1961); 1 stepchild, Thomas C. Logan; m. William James Meyer, Oct. 19, 1968 (dec. Aug. 1993); 1 adopted child, H.B. Kris. Student, Sch. Mpls. Inst. Art, 1946-49. NASD registered rep., Iowa, Minn. Advt. artist, writer, mgr. Lawton Co., Cinn., 1949-51; illustrator, acct. exec. Simons Advt., N.Y.C., 1951—53; asst. advt. mgr. Max Wiesen & Sons, Inc., N.Y.C., 1953-54, Mays Dept. Store, Bklyn., 1954-55; advt. and pub. rels. dir. Dayton's-Fantle's, Sioux Falls, S.D., 1955-66; comml. illustrator Meyer Advt., Worthington, Minn., 1967-69, comml. and continuity writer electronic media, 1970-76; regional promotions dir. shopping mall devel. Developers Diversified, Cleve., 1977-79; fin. svcs. exec. Meyer Ins. and Investment, Worthington, 1980—. Charter mem. Advt. Artist Guild, 1960-66, dir., 1963-64. Charter treas. pres. Zonta Internat. Sioux Falls, 1957-66; pub. rels., promotions staff Am. Cancer Soc., Worthington, 1972-77. Lutheran. Achievements include patent for surgical support. Home: 29744 290 St Worthington MN 56187 Office Phone: 888-526-2482.

MEYER, HELEN M. judge; BSW, U. Minn.; JD, William Mitchell Coll. Law. Cert.: Nat. Bd. Trial Advocacy (civil trial specialist). Ptnr. Pritzker & Meyer, 1987—96, Meyer and Assocs., 1996—2002; assoc. justice Minn. Supreme Ct., St. Paul, 2002—. Mem. Jud. Merit Selection Commn., Minn. Mem.: Acad. Cert. Trial Lawyers, Minn. Trial Lawyers Assn. (bd. dirs.), Minn. State Bd. Legal Cert. (bd. dirs.), Minn. State Bar Assn. (cert. civil trial specialist). Office: Minn Jud Ctr 25 Reverend Dr Martin Luther King Jr Blv Saint Paul MN 55155

MEYER, HORST, physics educator; b. Berlin, Mar. 1, 1926; BS, U. Geneva, 1949; PhD in physics, U. Zurich, 1953. Fellow Swiss Assn. Rsch. Physics and Math. Studies, Oxford, Eng., 1953-55; Nuffield fellow Clarendon Lab. U. Oxford, 1955-57; lectr., rsch. assoc. dept. engring. and applied physics Harvard U., Cambridge, Mass., 1957-59; from asst. prof. to prof. Duke U., Durham, N.C., 1959-84, Fritz London prof. physics, 1984—. Vis. prof. Technische Hochschule, Federal Republic of Germany, 1965, Tokyo U., 1980, 81, 83; traveling fellow Japanese Soc. for Promotion Sci., 1971, vis. scientist, 1979; guest scientist Inst. Laue-Langevin, France, 1974, 75; Yamada Found. fellow, Japan, 1986; guest scientist USSR Acad. Sci., 1988; guest prof. Toyota Inst. Tech., Nagoya, Japan, Oct. 1998; chmn. Gordon Conf. on Solid H2, 1990; western chmn. conf. quantum crystals, Almaty, Kazakhstan, 1995. Editor Jour. Low Temperature Physics, 1992—, mem. editorial bd., 1988-92; contbr. articles to profl. jours. Alfred P. Sloan fellow, 1961-65. Fellow Am. Phys. Soc. (Jesse Beams prize, 1982, Fritz London prize 1993). Achievements include exptl. rsch. on the properties of liquid and solid helium, critical phenomena in fluids, solid hydrogen and deuterium, magnetic insulators, critical phenomena. Office: Duke U Dept Physics PO Box 90305 Durham NC 27708-0305 Office Phone: 919-660-2520.

MEYER, IRWIN STEPHAN, lawyer, accountant; b. Monticello, NY, Nov. 14, 1941; s. Ralph and Janice (Cohen) M.; children: Kimberly B., Joshua A. BS, Rider Coll., 1963; JD, Cornell U., 1966. CPA NJ; bar: NY 1966. Tax mgr. Lybrand Ross Bros. & Montgomery, NYC, 1966—71; mem. Ehrenkranz, Ehrenkranz & Schultz, NYC, 1971—74; prin. Irwin S. Meyer, 1974—77, 1982—97; mem. Levine, Honig, Eisenberg & Meyer, 1977—78, Eisenberg, Honig & Meyer, 1978—81, Eisenberg, Honig, Meyer & Fogler, 1981—82, Janow & Meyer, LLC., 1997—2004; prin. Irwin S. Meyer, LLC, Pearl River, NY, 2004—. With U.S. Army, 1966—71. Mem. ABA, NY Bar Assn., Am. Assn. Atty.-CPA, NY Assn. Atty.-CPAs, NJ Soc. CPAs. Office: 1 Blue Hill Plz Ste 1006 Pearl River NY 10965-3100 Office Phone: 845-735-9400. Business E-Mail: irwin@mytaxplanner.com.

MEYER, J. THEODORE, lawyer; b. Chgo., Apr. 13, 1936; s. Joseph Theodore and Mary Elizabeth (McHugh) M.; m. Marilu Bartholomew, Aug. 16, 1961; children: Jean, Joseph. BS, John Carroll U., 1958; postgrad., U. Chgo.; JD, DePaul U., 1962. Bar: Ill. 1962. Ptnr. Bartholomew & Meyer, Chgo., 1963-83; mem. Ill. Gen. Assembly, Ho. of Reps. 28th Legis. Dist., 1966-72, 74-82. Chmn. House environ. study com., 1968; chmn. energy environ. com. and natural resources com.; mem. appropriations and exec. com.; chmn. Joint House/Senate com. to review state air and water plans, 1968; mem. Fed. State Task Force on Energy; chmn., founder Midwest Legis. Coun. on Environ., 1971; mem. Joint Legis. Com. on Hazardous Waste in Lake Calumet Area, 1987; chmn. Gov.'s adv. com. to streamline the Ill. environ. protection act, 1999-2001, Ill. Regulatory Revision Commn., 1999-2001; mem. Ill. Pollution Control Bd., Chgo., 1983-98, Ill. EPA, 1998-99; lectr. in field. Recipient Appreciation award Ill. Wildlife Fedn., 1972, Environ. Quality award Region V, EPA, 1974, Pro Bono Publico award Self-Help Action Ctr., 1975, Merit award Dept. Ill. VFW, 1977, Environ. Legislator of Yr. award Ill. Environ. Coun., 1978-79; named Disting. Lawyer Legislator of Yr., Hon. Tex. Citizen, hon. lt. aide-de-camp Ala. State Militia. Fellow Chgo. Bar Found.; mem. ABA, Ill. Bar Assn., Chgo. Bar Assn., Nat. Rep. Legis. Assn., Nat. Trust Hist. Preservation, Nat. Wildlife Fedn., Ill. Hist. Soc. Republican. Roman Catholic.

MEYER, JACK EDWARD, radiologist, educator; b. Davenport, Iowa, Oct. 21, 1939; s. Russell and Ellen Meyer; m. Mary Jean Meyer, Jan. 9, 1966; children: Heather, Hilary. BA, Grinnell (Iowa) Coll., 1961; MD, Cornell U., 1965; MS (hon.), Harvard U., 1991. Diplomate Am. Bd. Radiology; lic. physician, Mass., Calif., Mich. Intern San Francisco Gen. Hosp., 1965-66; resident in radiology U. Mich., Ann Arbor, 1968-69, Mass. Gen. Hosp., Boston, 1969-71, asst. radiation medicine, 1971-72, head oncologic diagnostic radiology, 1979-85; chief diagnostic radiology Pondville Hosp., Walpole, Mass., 1972-78, chief radiology, chief staff, 1978-79; prof., chmn. dept. radiology U. Louisville, Ky., 1985-87; acting dir. diagnostic radiology Brigham and Women's Hosp., Boston, 1987-88, dir. diagnostic radiology, 1989-99; dir. breast imaging Dana-Farber Cancer Inst., Boston, 2001—. Asst. prof. radiology Boston U., 1972-74, assoc. clin. prof., 1974-79; asst. prof. U. Mass., Boston, 1976-77, assoc. prof. radiology, 1977-79; asst. prof. radiology Harvard Med. Sch., Boston, 1979-82, assoc. prof. radiology, 1982-85, 87-91, prof. radiology, 1991—; dir. diagnostic oncoradiology Dana-Farber Cancer Inst., Boston, 1991-99; dir. breast imaging, Brigham and Womens Hosp, Boston, 1999—2002. Author: (with others) Interventional Radiology, 1981, Cancer: A Manual for Practitioners, 6th edit., 1982, Lymphatic Imaging, 2d edit., 1985; cons. to editorial bd. jours.; contbr. numerous articles and abstracts to profl. jours. Examiner Am. Bd. Radiology, 1992—. Capt. USAF, 1966-68. Fellow: Am. Coll. Radiology; mem.: Radiol. Soc. N. Am., Mass. Radiol. Soc., Mass. Med. Soc. Office: Brigham and Womens Hosp Dept Diagnostic Radiology 75 Francis St Boston MA 02115-6106 E-mail: jmeyer@partners.org.

MEYER, JAROLD ALAN, oil company research executive; b. Phoenix, July 28, 1938; s. Lester M. and Anita (Walker) M.; m. Diane Louise Wheeler; children: Ronald Alan, Sharon Lynne. BSChemE, Calif. Inst. Tech., 1960, MS, 1961. Mgr. process devel. Chevron Rsch., Richmond, Calif., 1978-82; tech. mgr. Chevron U.S.A., El Segundo, Calif., 1982-84; v.p. process rsch. Chevron Rsch., Richmond, 1984-86, pres., 1986—; sr. v.p. Chevron Rsch. and Tech., Richmond, 1990-93; ret., 1993; prin. J.A. Meyer Assocs., Martinez, Calif., 1993—. Bd. dirs. Solvent Refined Coal Internat., Inc., San Francisco; mem. adv. bd. Surface Sci. and Catalysis Program Ctr. for Advanced Materials, Lawrence Berkeley Lab., 1988-91; mem. adv. coun. Lawrence Hall Sci., 1989-94; indsl. advisor Accreditation bd. for Engring. and Tech. Inventor petroleum catalysts; contbr. articles to profl. jours. Bd. visitors U. Calif., Davis, 1986-93, trustee found., 1989—. Mem. Nat. Acad. Engring., Am. Chem. Soc., Nat. Petroleum Refining Assn., Indsl. Rsch. Inst., Conf. Bd. Internat. Rsch. Mgmt. Coun., Accreditation Bd. for Engring. and Tech. Indsl. Advisor, Sigma Xi, Tau Beta Pi. Avocations: electronics design and constrn., photography. Home and Office: 849 Corte Briones Martinez CA 94553-5950

MEYER, JEROME J. diversified technology company executive; b. Caledonia, Minn., Feb. 18, 1938; s. Herbert J. and Edna (Staggemeyer) M.; m. Sandra Ann Beaudoin, June 18, 1960; children— Randall Lee, Lisa Ann, Michelle Lynn Student, Hamline U., 1956-58; BA, U. Minn., 1960. Devel. engr. Firestone Tire & Rubber Co., Akron, Ohio, 1960-61; v.p., gen. mgr. Sperry Univac, St. Paul, 1961-79; group v.p. Honeywell, Inc., Mpls., 1979-84; pres., chief operating officer Varian Assocs., Palo Alto, Calif., 1984-86, also bd. dirs.; pres., chief exec. officer Honeywell Inc., 1986-90; from pres. to chmn., CEO Tektronix Inc., Beaverton, Oreg., 1990-99, chmn., 1999—. Bd. dirs. Oreg. Pub. Broadcasting, Esterline Tech., Oregon Bus. Coun., AMP, Std. Ins. Co. Trustee Oreg. Grad. Inst., Willamette U., Oreg. Children's Found. Mem. Oregon Golf Club. Avocation: golf. Office: Tektronix Inc PO Box 500 14200 SW Karl Braun Dr Beaverton OR 97077-0001

MEYER, JOHN ALBERT, lawyer; b. Sioux Falls, S.D., Dec. 6, 1946; s. John Richard Meyer and Beryl Geneva (Birkland) Ritz; m. Donna Rae Finch, Jan. 21, 1983; 1 child, Elizabeth Ann. BS, Iowa State U., 1969; JD, U. Iowa, 1972. Bar: Iowa 1972, Ill. 1972, U.S. Dist. Ct. (no. dist.) Ill. 1972, U.S. Supreme Ct. 1977, U.S. Tax Ct. 1981. Asst. U.S. atty. U.S. Atty's Office U.S. Dist. Ct. (no. dist.) Ill., Chgo., 1972-77; ptnr. Johnson & Colmar, Chgo., 1977-83, Bortman, Meyer & Barasa, Chgo., 1983—. Recipient Disting. Svc. award FBI, 1975. Mem. Chgo. Bar Assn., Ill. State Bar Assn., ABA. Office: 20 S Clark St Ste 2210 Chicago IL 60603-1805 Office Phone: 312-346-9000. E-mail: chgolegal@aol.com.

MEYER, JOHN EDWARD, nuclear engineering educator; b. Pitts., Dec. 17, 1931; s. Albert Edward and Thelma Elizabeth (Brethauer) M.; m. Gracyann Lenz, June 13, 1953; children: Susan Meyer Heydon, Karl, Karen Meyer Gleasman, Thomas. BS, MS, Carnegie Inst. Tech., 1953, PhD (ASME Student award 1955), 1955. Engring. and mgmt. positions Westinghouse Bettis Atomic Power Lab., West Mifflin, Pa., 1955-75; vis. lectr. U. Calif., Berkeley, 1968-69; prof. nuclear engring. MIT, 1975-98, ret., 1998. Cons. in field. Author papers in field. Recipient Bettis Disting. Service award, 1962, Outstanding Tchr. award nuclear engring. M.I.T., 1979, Alumni Merit award Carnegie Mellon U., 1987. Fellow Am. Nuclear Soc.; mem. ASME, Sigma Xi.

MEYER, JOHN FREDERICK, engineering educator; b. Grand Rapids, Mich., July 26, 1934; s. Frederick Albert and Harriet (Stibbs) M.; m. Nancy Shaw Briggs, July 4, 1959; children: John, Patricia, James. BS, U. Mich., 1957; MS, Stanford U., 1958; PhD, U. Mich., 1967. Data systems engr. Douglas Aircraft Corp., Santa Monica, Calif., 1957; research engr. Caltech, Jet Propulsion Lab., Pasadena, Calif., 1958-67; asst. prof. U. Mich., Ann Arbor, 1968-71, assoc. prof., 1971-76, prof. elec. engring. and computer sci., 1976—2002, dir. Computing Research Lab., 1984-89, prof. emeritus elec. engring. and computer sci., 2002—. Cons. Calif. Inst. Tech. Jet Propulsion Lab., 1979—91, Indsl. Tech. Inst., Ann Arbor, 1985-92, CIMSA, Paris, 1992, Bendix Advanced Tech. Ctr., Columbia, Md., 1977-85, Thomson CSF, Paris, 1975, Italtel, Milan, 1990—99, Applied Scis. Corp., Reading, Mass., 1993, U. Ill., 2002—. Patentee Time Division Multiplexer, 1963 (NASA Inventions award 1964). Precinct chmn. 3d ward Democratic Party, Ann Arbor, 1971-74. Recipient Disting. Service Award U. Mich., 1964, Silver Core award IFIP, 1995, Golden Core award 1996; IBM fellow, 1957 Fellow IEEE; mem. AAAS, IEEE Computer Soc. (Cert. of Appreciation 1981, 95, Meritorious Svc. award 1985). Home: 1946 Ridge Ave Ann Arbor MI 48104-6306 Office: U Mich 4111 EECS Bldg Ann Arbor MI 48109-2122 Business E-Mail: jfm@eecs.umich.edu.

MEYER, JOHN P. communications executive; BA in Acctg., U. No. Iowa; grad. Program for Mgmt. Devel., Harvard Bus. Sch. CPA. Auditor Deloitte & Touche, 1973—82; various pos. Centel, Chgo., 1982—86, corp. controller, 1986—93, v.p., 1986—93; sr. v.p., controller Sprint Corp., Overland Park, Kans., 1993—. Dir. Kansas City Minority Supplier Coun. Mem.: Conf. Bd. Controllers Coun., Am. Inst. CPA's. Office: Sprint Corp 6200 Sprint Pkwy Overland Park KS 66251

MEYER, JOHN ROBERT, economist, educator; b. Pasco, Wash., Dec. 6, 1927; s. Philip Conrad and Cora (Kempter) M.; m. Lee Stowell, Dec. 17, 1949; children: Leslie Karen, Ann Elizabeth, Robert Conrad. Student, Pacific U., 1945-46; BA, U. Wash., 1950; PhD (David A. Wells prize), Harvard U., 1955. Jr. fellow Harvard U., 1953-55, asst. prof., 1955-58, assoc. prof., 1958-59, prof. econs., 1959-68, found. prof. transp. and logistics, 1973-83; prof. Yale U., 1968-73; Harpel prof. capital formation and econ. growth Harvard U., 1983-96, prof. emeritus, 1997—. Vice chmn. Union Pacific Corp., 1982-83, dir., 1978-99; trustee Pacific U. Author (with Edwin Kuh): The Investment Decision-An Empirical Inquiry, 1957; author: (with others) Competition in the Transportation Industry, 1959, The Urban Transportation Problem, 1965, Techniques of Transport Planning, 1970, Economics of Competition in the Telecommunications Industry, 1980, Autos, Transit and Cities, 1981, Deregulation and the Future of Intercity Passenger Travel, 1987, Going Private: The International Experience with 'Transport Privatization, 1993, Moving to Market: Restructuring Transport in the Former Soviet Union, 1996, Chile: Political Economy of Urban Development, 2002, other books; contbr. articles. Mem. Presdl. Task Forces on Transp., 1964, 80, Presdl. Commn. on Population Growth and Am. Future, 1970-72; pres. Nat. Bur. Econ. Research, 1967-77. Served with USNR, 1946-48. Recipient Roy W. Crum award, transp. rsch. bd. Nat. Acad. Scis. and Nat. Acad. Engring., 2002; Guggenheim fellow, 1958. Fellow: Econometric Soc., Am. Acad. Arts and Scis.; mem.: Econ. History Assn., Coun. Fgn. Rels., Am. Econ. Assn. (mem. exec. com. 1971—73). Home: 572 Kinzie Island Ct Sanibel FL 33957-5021 Office: Harvard U Jt Ctr Housing Studies 1033 Massachussetts Ave 5th Fl Cambridge MA 02138-5801 Personal E-mail: jrobtmeyer@aol.com.

MEYER, JOHN STIRLING, neurologist, educator; b. London, Feb. 24, 1924; came to U.S., 1940; s. William Charles and Alice Elizabeth (Stirling) M.; m. Wendy Haskell, July 20, 1947 (dec. 1986); children: Jane, Anne, Elizabeth, Helen, Margaret; m. Katharine Sumner, Aug. 2, 1987; m. Cora Bess Parks, Apr. 6, 1996. BSc, Trinity Coll., Hartford, Conn., 1944; MD, CM, McGill U., Montreal, Que., 1948, MSc, 1949. Diplomate Am. Bd. Neurology and Psychiatry. Intern Yale-New Haven Hosp., 1948-49, resident neurology, 1949-50, Boston City Hosp., 1950-52, resident neurophysiology, 1952-53, fellow neurophysiology, 1954-55; instr. rsch. assoc. Harvard Med. Sch., Boston, 1955-57, resident neurophysiology, 1952-53; prof., chair dept. Wayne State U., Detroit, 1957-69, Baylor Coll. Medicine, Houston, 1969-75, prof. neurology, 1976—; demonstrator neuropathology and teaching fellow neurology Harvard U. Med. Sch., 1950-52; sr. rsch. fellow USPHS, 1952-54; instr. medicine Harvard U. Med. Sch., 1954-56; assoc. vis. physician neurology Boston City Hosp., 1956-57; cons. and lectr. neurology U.S. Naval Hosp., Chelsea, Mass., 1957; prof. neurology and chmn. dept. sch. medicine Wayne State U., 1957-69, chmn. dept., 1969-76; prof. neurology, dir. stroke lab. Baylor Coll. Medicine, Houston, 1976—; with VA Med. Ctr., Houston. Chair stroke panel Pres.' Commn. on Heart Disease Cancer & Stroke, Washington, 1964-65; mem. nat. adv. coun. Nat. Inst. Neurol. Diseases & Stroke, Bethesda, Md., 1965-69. Author 29 books; contbr. over 879 articles to profl. jours. Mem.

jury Albert Lasker Med. Rsch. Awards, N.Y.C., 1965-69. Lt. (s.g.) Med. Corps USN, 1953-55, Korea. Recipient Harold G. Woff award, Am. Assn. for Study of Headache, 1977, 78, 79, Baylor Coll. Medicine award, Houston, 1980, 85, 90, 95, 2000, Mihara award Mihara Found., Tokyo, 1987, Bertha Lecture award Salzburg Conf., Washington, 1992. Mem. Am. Heart Assn. (bd. dirs. 1968-70, chair coun. on stroke 1968-70). Republican. Episcopalian. Achievements include development of xenon contrast method for measuring cerebral blood flow using computerized tomography; research in importance of mild cognitive impairment as treatable prodrome of dementia in the elderly. Office: VA Med Ctr Rm 225 2002 Holcombe Blvd Bldg 110 Houston TX 77030-4211 Fax: 713-794-7583. E-mail: jmeyer@bcm.tsu.edu.

MEYER, JON HOWARD, utility executive, consultant; b. Islip, N.Y., Jan. 5, 1962; s. Howard Charles and Betty Alice Meyer; m. Janet Hope Kinder, Jan. 14, 1984; children: Benjamin, Derek. Constrn. laborer Gulf Constructors, Sarasota, Fla., 1981-82; wastewater plant operator City of Ft. Meade, Fla., 1982-84; asst. chief operator Polk County Utlilties, Bartow, Fla., 1984-96; mgr. wastewater Severn Trent-Avatar Utility Svcs., Fort Myers, 1996-2001; project mgr. Fla. Water Svcs., Marco Island, Fla., 2001—. Recipient Ops. of Excellence award Fla. Dept. Environ. Protection, 1996, 97, 98, Lakeside Outstanding Plant award Lakeside Equipment, 1999, Leroy Henry Scott award Fla. Water Environ. Fedn., 1999, Earle B. Phelps award 2000, William D. Hatfield award, 2001. Mem. Fla. Water & Pollution Control Operators Assn. (sec., treas. 1998-99),. Fla. Water Environment Assn. (ops. rsch. com. 1996-2001). Office: Fla Water Svcs 960 Collier Blvd Marco Island FL 34145 Home: 1025 Mayfair Pl Kissimmee FL 34758-2906 E-mail: dodoguru@yahoo.com.

MEYER, JON KEITH, psychiatrist, psychoanalyst, educator; b. Springfield, Ill., May 6, 1938; m. Eleanor Fumie Yamashita, June 6, 1964; children: David Christopher, Laura Tamiko. AB summa cum laude, Dartmouth Coll., 1960; MD, Johns Hopkins U., 1964; grad., Washington Psychoanalytic Inst, 1980. Intern internal medicine Johns Hopkins Hosp., Balt., 1964-65, resident in psychiatry, 1965-67, 69, St. Elizabeth's Hosp., Washington, 1968; spl. asst. to dir. NIMH, Bethesda, Md., 1969-71; asst. prof. psychiatry Johns Hopkins Med. Sch., Balt., 1971-76, assoc. prof., 1976-83; prof. psychiatry Med. Coll. Wis., Milw., 1983—2003, prof. psychoanalysis, 1996—2003, prof. family medicine, 1990—2003, prof. psychiatry and psychoanalysis emeritus, 2003—; tng. and supervising analyst Chgo. Inst. for Psychoanalysis, 1987—2002; vice chmn. Dept. of Psychiatry, 1993—2003; chief psychiatry Froedtert Meml. Luth. Hosp., Milw., 1994-97; tng. and supervising analyst Wis. Psychoanaltic Inst., Milw., 2001—, Washington Psychoanalytic Inst., 2004—. Med. dir. Wis., Psychoanalytic Found., Milw., 1987-91, sec. bd. dirs., 1988-91. Author books; editl. bd. Jour. Am. Psychoanalytic Assn., 1991-94; nat. editor: The American Psychoanalyst, 1997-2001; contbr. chpts. to books, numerous articles to profl. jours. Comdr. USPHS, 1967—71. Recipient Dennison Rsch. prize, Johns Hopkins Med. Sch., 1964; Sr. fellow, Dartmouth Coll., 1959—60, Daniel Webster Nat. scholar, 1956—60, Rufus Choate scholar, Erik Erikson scholar, Austen Riggs Ctr., Stockbridge, Mass., 1991—92, Ctr. Advanced Psychoanalytic Studies, 1998—. Fellow: Am. Coll. Psychoanalysts, Am. Psychiat. Assn.; mem.: Washington Psychoanalytic Soc., Balt.-Washington Psychoanalytic Soc., Wis. Psychoanalytic Soc. (pres. 1989—91), Assn. for Child Psychoanalysis (candidate councilor 2001—03), Am. Psychoanalytic Assn. (exec. councilor 1993—97, chmn. com. on exec. coun. structure and function 1995—98, sec. 1997—2001, chmn. com. on cmty. clinics 1997—2002, exec. com. 1997—2002, adminstrv. bd. Jour. Am. Psychoanalytic Assn. 1997—2002, com. on insts. 1998—2002, com. on bylaws 2001—02, adminstrv. bd. Jour. Am. Psychoanalytic Assn. 2002—, exec. com. 2002—, pres.-elect 2002—04, pres. 2004—, Edith Sabshin Tchg. award 1999), Internat. Psychoanalytic Assn. (com. on constn. and by-laws 1997—2001, com. on procedural codes 1997—2001, task force on structure and mission 1997—2001, ho. dels. 1998—2001, chair ho. of dels. 1999—2000). Avocations: photography, hiking, kayaking. Office: 2210 Dalewood Rd Lutherville MD 21093

MEYER, JOSEPH B. Secretary of State, former academic administrator; b. Casper, Wyo., 1941; m. Mary Orr; children: Vincent, Warren. Student, Colo. Sch. Mines; BA, U. Wyo., 1964, JD, 1967; postgrad., Northwestern U., 1968. Dep. county atty. Fremont County, Wyo., 1967-69; assoc. Smith and Meyer, 1968-71; asst. dir. legis. svc. office State of Wyo., Cheyenne, 1971-87, atty. gen., 1987-95; spl. asst. to pres. Univ. Wyo., Laramie, 1995-98; sec. of state State of Wyoming, 1999—. Condr. numerous govt. studies on state codes including Wyo. probate, criminal, state adminstrn., banking, domestic rels., game and fish, state instn.; employment security, worker's compensation, motor vehicle, others; condr. legis. rev. of adminstrv. rules; negotiator with Office of Surface Mining for Wyo. state preemption; instr. Wyo. Coll. Law, fall, 1986; lectr. Rocky Mountain Mineral Law Found., 1977; chmn. Conf. Western Atty. Gen., 1992—93; mem. exec. com. Nat. Assn. Attys. Gen.; mem. Bush-Cheney Transition Team, 2000—01. Bd. dirs. Cheyenne Jr. League, 1982—85; mem. Cheyenne Bd. of Health, 1999—; instr. Boy Scouts Am. Mem. Rotary. Republican. Congregationalist. Avocations: golf, tennis, gardening, wood carving, rock hunting. Office: State Capital Bldg Cheyenne WY 82002-0001 E-mail: jmeyer3@state.wy.us.

MEYER, JUDY L. science educator, director; BS in Zoology, U. Mich.; MS in Zoology, U. Hawaii; PhD in Ecology, Cornell U. Co-dir. River Basin Sci. and Policy Ctr., Athens, Ga.; Disting. Rsch. prof. Inst. Ecology U. Ga. Mem. com. Nat. Acad. Scis./NRC; mem. Improving Nat. Water Quality Assessment Program USGS; elected U.S. nat. rep. Internat. Assn. Theoretical and Applied Limnology; chair sci. and tech. adv. com., bd. dirs. Am. Rivers; chair edn. and sci. adv. com., bd. dirs. Upper Chattahoochee Riverkeeper; bd. dirs. Ga. Land Trust Svc. Ctr. Recipient Creative Rsch. medal, U. Ga. Rsch. Foun.; grantee, NSF, EPA, U.S. Dept. Agr., U.S. Dept. Energy, U.S. Forest Svc., U.S. Geol. Survey, U.S. Fish and Wildlife Svc., Ga. Dept. Natural Resources, Turner Found. Fellow: AAAS; mem.: Nat. Coun. Sci. Soc. Pres. (exec. com.), Ecol. Soc. Am. (v.p., pres.). Office: River Basin Sci and Policy Ctr 201 N Milledge Ave Athens GA 30602-5482

MEYER, KARL ERNEST, journalist; b. Madison, Wis., May 22, 1928; s. Ernest Louis and Dorothy (Narefsky) M.; m. Sarah Nielsen Peck, Aug. 12, 1959 (div. 1972); children: Ernest, Heather, Jonathan; m. Shareen Blair Brysac, Jan. 6, 1989. BA, U. Wis., 1951; MPA, Princeton (N.J.) U., 1953, PhD, 1956. Reporter N.Y. Times, N.Y.C., 1952, mem. editl. bd., 1979-98; editl. writer Washington Post, 1956-65, chief London Bur., 1965-70, N.Y.C. corr., 1970-71; Washington corr. New Statesman, 1961-65; sr. editor, TV critic Saturday Rev., N.Y.C., 1975-79; corr. in residence Fletcher Sch. Law and Diplomacy, Tufts U., 1979; editor World Policy Jour., N.Y.C., 2000—. Vis. journalist fellow Duke U., Durham, NC, 1988; vis. prof. Yale U., New Haven, 1983, New Haven, 90; McGraw prof. in writing Princeton U., 1993—94; vis. prof. Bard Coll., NY, 2002. Author: The New America, 1961, (with Tad Szulc) The Cuban Invasion, 1962, Fulbright of Arkansas, 1963, The Pleasures of Archaeology, 1971, The Plundered Past, 1973, Teotihuacán, 1975, The Art Museum: Power, Money, Ethics, 1979, Pundits, Poets and Wits: An Omnibus of American Newspaper Columns, 1990, (with Shareen Brysac) Tournament of Shadows: The Great Game and Race for Empire in Central Asia, 1999, The Dust of Empire, 2003. Recipient citation for excellence Overseas Press Club, 1961, Bronze medal for editl. writing Sigma Delta; George Foster Peabody Broadcasting award 1983, Disting. Achievement award Sch. Journalism, U. Wis., 1985; Davenport Coll. of Yale U. fellow; Wisenschaftskolleg Inst. Adv. Studies (Berlin) fellow, 1994-95, Reuter fellow Oxford (Eng.) U., 1996-97. Mem. PEN Club Internat., Coun. on Fgn. Rels., NYU Soc. Fellows, Century Assn., Authors League Am. Home: 50 W 96th St New York NY 10025-6526 Office: World Policy Jour 66 5 Th Ave Ste 900 New York NY 10011 Office Phone: 212-229-5808 104. Business E-Mail: meyerk@newschool.edu.

MEYER, KARL WILLIAM, retired university president; b. Ft. Wayne, Ind., May 8, 1925; s. K.W. and L. (Hofacker) M.; m. Margery R. Hamman, Apr. 15, 1950; children— Mary, William, Frederick, Ann, Jean. AB, Valpariaso U., 1948; M.F.S., U. Md., 1949; PhD, U. Wis., 1953; postgrad., U. Basel, Switzerland, 1948-49; postdoctoral fellow, U. Mich., 1958-59. Faculty Valparaiso U., 1952-53, Augustana Coll., 1953-55, Wis. State U., 1955-58; dean instrn., dir. grad. studies Wayne State Coll., 1959-63; asst. dir. bd. regents Wis. State Colls., Madison, 1963-64; pres. U. Wis.-Superior, 1964-87. Author: Karl Liebknecht: Man Without a Country, 1957; Contbr. articles to profl. jours. Served with USAAF, 1943-46, ETO. Home: W7861 Homestead Ct Holmen WI 54636-9440 E-mail: meyk25@aol.com.

MEYER, LAURENCE HARVEY, former federal official; b. Bronx, N.Y., Mar. 8, 1944; BA magna cum laude, Yale U., 1965; PhD in Econs., MIT, 1970. Co-founder, pres. Laurence H. Meyer and Assocs., St. Louis, 1982-96; bd. govs. Fed. Res. Sys., Washington, 1996—2002. Prof. econs. Washington U., St. Louis, 1969-96, rsch. assoc. Ctr. for Study of Am. Bus., former chmn. econs. dept.; economist Fed. Res Bank, N.Y.; vis. scholar Fed. Res. Bank, St. Louis, disting. scholar, Ctr. for Strategic and Internat. Studies Author textbook on macroeconomic modeling; contbr. numerous articles to profl. jours. Named Top Forecaster for Yr., Bus. Week mag., 1986; recipient Ann. Forecast award, 1993, 96. Office: CSIS 1800 K St NW Ste 400 Washington DC 20006

MEYER, LAWRENCE GEORGE, lawyer; b. East Grand Rapids, Mich., Oct. 2, 1940; s. George and Evangeline (Boerma) M.; children from previous marriage: David Lawrence, Jenifer Lynne; m. Linda Elizabeth Buck, May 31, 1980; children: Elizabeth Tilden, Travis Henley. BA with honors, Mich. State U., 1961; JD with distinction, U. Mich., 1964. Bar: Wis., 1965, Ill. 1965, U.S. Supreme Ct. 1968, D.C. 1972. Assoc. Whyte, Hirschboeck, Minahan, Hardin & Harland, Milw., 1964-66; atty. antitrust div. U.S. Dept. Justice, Washington, 1966-68; legal counsel U.S. Senator Robert P. Griffin, Mich., 1968-70; dir. policy planning FTC, 1970-72; ptnr. Patton, Boggs & Blow, Washington, 1972-85, Arent, Fox, Kintner, Plotkin & Kahn, Washington, 1985-96, Gadsby & Hannah, 1996-2001; pvt. practice Washington, 2001—. Contbr. articles on antitrust and trial practice to law jours.; asst. editor. U. Mich. Law Rev., 1960-61. Bd. dirs. Hockey Hall of Fame, Toronto, 1993-99, Woodrow Wilson House, 1997—. Recipient Disting. Svc. award FTC, 1972. Mem. ABA, D.C. Bar Assn., Wis. Bar Assn., Ill. Bar Assn., US Senate Ex S.O.B.s Club, City Tavern Club, Sulgrave Club, Congl. Country Club. Home: 8777 Belmart Rd Potomac MD 20854-1610 Office Phone: 202-661-3910. E-mail: larry@lawlgm.com.

MEYER, LISA MARIE, elementary school educator; b. Livonia, Mich., Nov. 15, 1961; d. James Theo and Dolores Lola Bishop; m. John Melville Meyer, May 22, 1982; children: Jessica Ellen, Brittany Allyssa. AA, Henry Ford C.C., Dearborn, Mich., 1981; B in Music Edn., Ea. Mich. U., 1987; M in Elem. Edn., Wayne State U., 1991. Cert. tchr. music edn., elem. edn. Mich. Elem. music tchr. Detroit Pub. Schs., 1987—89; music tchr. Dearborn Pub. Schs., 1989—95, music resource tchr., 1995—. Adj. instr. William Tyndale Coll., Farmington Hills, Mich., 1986—; cons. Ideas, LLC, West Norwalk, Conn., 2000—; mem. adv. bd. Ward Pre-Sch., Northville, Mich., 1987—90. Named one of Best 100 for Music Edn. in Am., Music Tchr. Nat. Assn., 2001; recipient Named one of Best of 100 for Music Edn. in Am., 2002. Mem.: Mich. Music Educator Assn. (Outstanding Adminstr. award 2001, 2002), Am. Orff Schulwerk Assn., Nat. Assn. Music Edn. Avocations: singing, camping, hiking. Home: 43069 Devon Ln Canton MI 48187 Office: Dearborn Pub Schs 18700 Audette Dearborn MI 48124 E-mail: meyerl@dearborn.k12.mi.us.

MEYER, LYNN NIX, lawyer; b. Vinita, Okla., Aug. 10, 1948; d. William Armour and Joan Ross Nix; children: Veronica, Victoria, David. BA, Baldwin Wallace Coll., 1978; JD, Case Western Res. U., 1981. Bar: Ky. 1982, Colo. 1984. Paralegal Texaco Devel., Austin, Tex., 1976-77; legal asst. Alcan Aluminum, Cleve., 1977-79; assoc. Wyatt, Tarrant & Combs, Lexington, Ky., 1982-83; ptnr. Meyer, Meyer & Assocs., P.C., Denver, 1984-85; gen. counsel Carbon Fuels Corp., 1985-95; in pvt. practice Denver, 1996-97; asst. gen. counsel products Gambro, Inc., Lakewood, Colo., 1997—. Mem. ABA, Colo. Bar Assn., Ky. Bar Assn., Arapahoe County Bar Assn. Home: 10487 E Ida Ave Englewood CO 80111-3746 Office: 10810 W Collins Ave Lakewood CO 80215-4439 E-mail: lynn.meyer@gambrobct.com.

MEYER, MARA ELLICE, special education consultant, principal; b. Chgo., Oct. 28, 1952; d. David and Harriett (Lazar) Einhorn; m. Leonard X. Meyer, July 20, 1986; children: Hayley Rebecca, David Joseph. BS in Speech and Hearing Sci., U. Ill., 1974, MS in Speech and Lang. Pathology, 1975, postgrad. in pub. policy PhD program, 1990—. Cert. speech and lang. pathologist, spl. edn. tchr., reading tchr. Speech and lang. pathologist Macon-Piatt Spl. Edn. Dist., Decatur, Ill., 1975-76; speech and lang. pathologist, reading specialist, learning disabilities coord. Community Consolidated Sch. Dist. # 59, Arlington Heights, Ill., 1976-87; test cons. Psychol. Corp., San Antonio, 1987-89; adj. prof. Nat.-Louis U., Evanston, Ill., 1985-87, 2003—; ednl. cons. The Psychol. Corp., 1987-89, Am. Guidance Svc., Circle Pines, Minn., 1989-94; pvt. practice ednl. cons. Deerfield, Ill., 1994—. Project dir. Riverside Pub. Co., Chgo., 1993-94; mem. adv. coun. to Headstart, Dept. Human Svsc., City of Chgo., 1990-99; cons. Spl. Edn. Dist. of Lake County, 1995—, Waukegan (Ill.) Pub. Schs., 1997; cons. Lake Zurich Pub. Schs., 1996-98; asst. prin., inclusion coord. Mundelein (Ill.) Sch. Dist., 1999-2001; spl. edn. adminstr. Wilmette Schs., 2001-2003; spl. cons. Avoca Sch. Dist. 37, Wilmette, Ill., 2003—. Area coord. Dem. Party, Lake County, Ill., 1978—; pres. Park West Condo Assn., Lake County, 1983-88. Mem. NEA, ASCD, Nat. Assn. Elem. Prins., Nat. Family Partnership Network, Am. Speech-Lang. and Hearing Assn., Ill. Speech-Lang. and Hearing Assn., Ill. Prins. Assn., Internat. Reading Assn., Coun. on Exceptional Children. Avocations: swimming official, leisure reading, technical reading. Home: 1540 Central Ave Deerfield IL 60015-3963 Personal E-mail: maraemeyer@comcast.net. Business E-Mail: Mara.Meyer@nl.edu.

MEYER, MARGARET ELEANOR, microbiologist, educator; b. Westwood, Calif., Feb. 8, 1923; d. Herman Henry and Eleanor (Dobson) M. BS, U. Calif., Berkeley, 1945; PhD, U. Calif., Davis, 1961. Pub. health analyst USPHS, Bethesda, Md., 1945-46; swine Brucellosis control agt. Dept. Agr., Davis, 1946-47; bacteriologist U. Calif., Davis, 1947-61; research microbiologist U. Calif. (Sch. Vet. Medicine), 1961-77, prof. vet. pub. health and microbiologist exptl. sta., 1977—; research microbiologist U. Calif. Med. Sch., Los Angeles, 1961-77; supr. Brucella identifications lab. WHO, U. Calif.-Davis, 1964—, prof. vet. pub. health, 1973—; also dir. M.A. program in preventive vet. medicine. Cons. subcom. on Brucella Internat. Com. Bacterial Taxonomy, 1962—, mem., 1966—; mem. 5th Pan Am. Congress Veterinary Medicine, Venezuela, 1966; mem. Internat. Congress Microbiology, Moscow, 1966, Mexico City, 1970, Munich, Ger., 1978, mem., officer, Eng., 1986; mem. Internat. Conf. Culture Collections, Tokyo, 1968; mem. adv. com. to Bergey's Manual Determative Bacteriology, 1967; cons. in resident Pan Am. Health Orgn., Zoonoses Lab., Buenos Aires, 1968; mem. brucellosis tech. adv. com. U.S. Animal Health Assn., 1977; FAO cons. on brucellosis control in dairy animals, Tripoli, Libya, 1981, mem. 3d internat. brucellosis symposium, Algiers, 1983; cons. Alaska Dept. Fish and Game, 1976, FAO, Libya, 1981, Bering Straits Reindeer Herders Assn., Nome, Alaska, 1981; invited speaker Internat. Symposium on Advances in Brucellosis Rsch., Tex. A&M U., 1989, Internat. Bison Conf.; resident cons. on brucellosis control in sheep and goats Am. Near East Refugee Aid, East Jerusalem, 1989; cons. on brucellosis in Yellowstone Nat. Pk., Nat. Pk. Svc., 1991—; invited mem. nat. symposium on brucellosis in the Greater Yellowstone Area, Jackson Hole, Wyo., 1994; cons. on brucellosis control in livestock for Armenia, 1994—. Contbr. articles to profl. jours. Bd. dirs. Carmichael Park and Recreation Dist., Calif., 1975; mem. Sacramento County Grand Jury, 1999-2000. Recipient Research Career Devel. award USPHS-NIH, 1963 Fellow Am. Pub. Health Assn., Am. Acad. Microbiology; mem. Soc. Am. Microbiologists, N.Am. Conf. Animal Disease Research Workers, Am. Coll. Vet. Microbiologists (hon. affiliate), U.S. Animal Health Assn. (chmn. brucellosis tech. advisory com. 1978-79), Internat. Assn. Microbiol. Socs. (mem. 1st intersect. congress 1974), AAUW, No. Calif. Women's Golf Assn., U. Calif. Alumni Assn., Sigma Xi. Clubs: U. Calif. Faculty (Davis); El Dorado Royal Country (Shingle Springs, Calif.); Reno Women's Golf. Home: 5611 Fair Oaks Blvd Carmichael CA 95608-5503 Office: U Calif Sch Vet Medicine Dept Epidemiology & Preventive Medicine Davis CA 95616

MEYER, MARJORIE JEAN, real estate manager; b. Hagerstown, Md., Feb. 11, 1949; d. Jerome Benjamin Meyer and Franceska Robin Finberg; m. Allan Brian Korsakov, Nov. 30, 1942; 1 child, Elissa Korsakov. BA, Fla. State U., 1971. Cert. mgr. cmty. assns. Profl. Cmty. Assn. Mgrs. Owner, pres., CEO Prime Site, Inc. AAMC, Houston, 1980—2001, chmn. bd., 2001—; v.p., nat. dir. edn. and cert. Associa, Dallas and Houston, 2001—. Adv. bd. Houston Ind. Bank, 1995—98; tchg. faculty Cmty. Assns. Inst.; host weekly talk show KSEV AM 700 Cmty. Spotlight. Contbr. articles various profl. jours. Mem. Tex. Legis. Action Com., Houston, 2001—, chair, 1993—2001; chmn. Cmty. Assn. Inst. Presidents Club. Named Vol. of Yr. award, Cmty Assn. Inst., 2002; named to Hall of Honors, 1989. Mem.: Cmty. Assns. Inst. (treas. 2003—04, v.p. 2001—02, Award of Exellence in Pub. Affairs 1994, 1998), Phi Beta Kappa. Office: Associa 8955 Katy Fwy Ste 301 Houston TX 77024-1627 Office Phone: 713-932-6111. E-mail: mmeyer@associaonline.com.

MEYER, MARSHALL WARNER, management and sociology educator; b. Washington, June 24, 1942; s. Richard Sol and Mildred (Warner) M.; m. Judith Pinsof, Mar. 20, 1966; children: Joshua Micah, Gabriel Sol. BA, Columbia U., 1964; MA, U. Chgo., 1965, PhD, 1967; MA, U. Pa., 1987. Instr., lectr. Harvard U., Cambridge, Mass., 1967-69; asst. prof. Cornell U., Ithaca, N.Y., 1969-73; assoc. prof. U. Calif., Riverside, 1973-75, prof. sociology, 1975-87; vis. prof. UCLA, 1985-86; vis. prof. mgmt. Yale U. Sch. Mgmt., New Haven, 1986-87; prof. mgmt. and sociology Wharton Sch., U. Pa., Phila., 1988—, Richard A. Sapp prof., 2002—. Vis. scholar Russell Sage Found., N.Y.C., 1993-94; vis. prof. mgmt. Hong Kong U. Sci. and Tech., 1996, Tsinghua U., 1999, Chinese U., Hong Kong, 2001. Author: Bureaucracy in Modern Society, 1972, 87, Permanently Failing Organizations, 1989, Rethinking Performance Measurement, 2002; assoc. editor Adminstrv. Sci. Quar., 1987—. Cons. L.A. Police Commn., 1979-80; dir. Chamber Orch. Phila., 2000—; chief exec. Leadership Inst., 1996—. Mem. Acad. of Mgmt., Am. Sociol. Assn. Avocations: computers, music, bicycling, skiing. Office: U Pa Wharton Sch Dept Mgmt Philadelphia PA 19104

MEYER, MAX EARL, lawyer; b. Hampton, Va., Oct. 31, 1918; s. Earl Luther and Winifred Katherine (Spacht) M.; m. Betty Maxwell Dodds, Sept. 22, 1945; children: Scott Maxwell, Ann Culliford. AB, U. Nebr., 1940, JD, 1942. Bar: Nebr. 1942, Ill. 1946. Assoc. firm Lord, Bissell & Brook, Chgo., 1945-53, ptnr., 1953-85; chmn. Chgo. Fed. Tax Forum, 1965, U. Chgo. Ann. Fed. Tax Conf., 1972; mem. Adv. Group to Commr. of IRS, 1967. Lectr. in field. Bd. dirs. Music Acad. of the West, chmn. 1993-94. Mem.: ABA (coun. tax sect. 1969—72), Am. Coll. Tax Counsel, Chgo. Bar Assn. (chmn. taxation com. 1959—61), Nebr. Bar Assn., Ill. Bar Assn. (coun. tax sect. 1973—76), Birnam Wood Golf Club, Valley Club of Montecito, Law Club (Chgo.), Legal Club, Masons. Republican. Presbyterian.

MEYER, MICHAEL EDWIN, lawyer; b. Chgo., Oct. 23, 1942; s. Leon S. and Janet (Gorden) M.; m. Catherine Dieffenbach, Nov. 21, 1982; children: Linda, Mollie, Patrick, Kellie. BS, U. Wis., 1964; JD, U. Chgo., 1967. Bar: Calif. 1968, U.S. Supreme Ct. 1973. Assoc. Lillick & McHose, L.A., 1967-73, ptnr., 1974-90, mng. ptnr., 1986-87; ptnr. Pillsbury Madison Sutro, 1990—, mem. mgmt. com., 1990-92; mng. ptnr. Pillsbury Winthrop, L.A., 1999—2003, Piper Rudnick LLP, 2004—. Judge pro tem Beverly Hills Mcpl. Ct., Calif., 1976-79, Los Angeles Mcpl. Ct., 1980-86; lectr. in field. Bd. dirs. Bldg. Owners and Mgrs. Assn. Greater L.A., L.A. coun. Boy Scouts Am., L.A. Sports and Entertainment Commn., L.A. Econ. Devel. Corp.; pub. counsel United Way Greater L.A., Los Angeles County Bar Found., trustee, 1997—, Reviving Baseball in Inner Cities; mem. L.A. County Sheriff Youth Found. Recipient Good Scout award L.A. coun. Boy Scouts Am., 1992, Man of Yr. award United Way, 1996, NACORE Real Estate Profl. of the Yr., 2002. Mem. ABA, Am. Arbitration Assn. (arbitrator), Calif. Bar Assn., Los Angeles County Bar Assn. (trustee 1997—), L.A. Bar Assn., Am. Coll. of Real Estate Lawyers, U. Chgo. Alumni Assn. So. Calif. (pres. 1980-82), Calif. Club, U. L.A. Club (dir. 1979-85, pres. 1984-85), L.A. Country Club. Jewish. Home: 759 31st St Manhattan Beach CA 90266-3456 Office: Piper Rudnigh LLP 550 S Hope St Los Angeles CA 90071 Office Phone: 213-330-7777. Business E-Mail: michael.meyer@piperrudnick.com.

MEYER, MIKE, management consultant; CEO CAP Gemini Am., N.Y.C. Office: CAP Gemini America 29th Fl 1114 Ave of the Americas New York NY 10036

MEYER, MILTON EDWARD, JR., lawyer, artist; b. St. Louis, Nov. 26, 1922; s. Milton Edward and Jessie Marie (Hurley) M.; m. Mary C. Kramer, Nov. 5, 1949 (dec. Dec. 1999); children: Milton E. III, Melanie M. Meyer Francis, Daniel K., Gregory N.; m. Mildred R. Emrick, Nov. 18, 2003. BS in Bus. Adminstrn, Washington U., 1943; LL.B., St. Louis, U., 1950; LL.M., N.Y. U., 1953. Bar: Mo. 1950, Colo. 1956. Trust adminstr. Mississippi Valley Trust Co., St. Louis, 1946-50; asso. firm Burnett, Stern & Liberman, St. Louis, 1953-56; founding partner firm Hindry & Meyer, Denver, 1956-79, chmn. bd., 1970-79; spl. counsel Schmidt, Elrod & Wills, and predecessors, 1979-83, pres., 1980-82; sec. C.A. Norgren Co., Littleton, Colo., 1960-78, dir., 1971-78. Contbr. articles to profl. jours. Chmn. Denver Rotary's Artists of Am. Exhbn., 1990—92; bd. dirs. Nat. Club Assn., 1971—91, pres., 1976—78; bd. dirs. Denver Cmty. Concert Assn., 1960—64, Sewall Rehab. Ctr., Denver, 1965—68, Carl A. Norgren Found., 1960—70; Denver Leadership Found., 1983—93, Found. Colo. Women's Coll., 1982—86, chmn., bd. dirs., 1984—86; bd. dirs. Conf. Pvt. Orgns., 1982—89, chmn., bd. dirs., 1984—88. Officer, U.S. Airborne Infantry U.S. Army, 1943—46, World War II, officer, U.S. Airborne Infantry U.S. Army, 1950—52, Korean War. Recipient Wisdom Soc. award of honor. Mem. ABA, Colo. Bar Assn., Denver Bar Assn., Greater Denver Tax Counsels Assn. (founder, chmn. 1957, Denver Estate Planning Coun. (founder, pres. 1958), Am. Coll. Probate Counsel, Knickerbocker Artists, Pastel Soc. Am., Pastel Soc. West Coast (Disting. Pastellist award), Internat. Assn. Pastel Socs. (founder, dir. 1994—), Salmagundi Club, Cherry Hills Country Club, Pinehurst Country Club (pres. 1979-80), Denver Execs. Club, Hundred Club Denver, Rotary (bd. dirs. 1991-93), Phi Eta Sigma, Beta Gamma Sigma, Omicron Delta Kappa, Beta Theta Pi. Republican. Roman Catholic. Home: 7123 W Belmont Dr Littleton CO 80123 E-mail: miltonmeyer@comcast.net.

MEYER, PAUL REIMS, JR., orthopedic surgeon; b. Port Arthur, Tex. s. Paul Reims and Evelyn (Miller) M.; m. Lesa W. Meyer; children: Kristin Lynn, Holly Dee, Paul Reims III, Stewart Blair. BA, Va. Mil. Inst., 1954; MD, Tulane U., 1958; MA of Mgmt., J.L. Kellogg Grad. Sch. of Mgmt. (Northwestern U.), 1992. Dir. Spine Injury Ctr. Northwestern U., Chgo., 1972—, prof. orthopaedic surgery, 1981—. Cons. Nat. Inst. Disability and Rehab. Rsch. VA, Washington, 1978-2000; clin. prof. surgery Dept. Surgery, USUHS; mem. adv. com. World Rehab. Fund, 1990—; mem. bd. councilors Am. Acad. Orthopaedic Surgeons, 1993-96. Author: Surgery of Spine Trauma, 1988; patentee cervical orthosis. Col. M.C., USAR. Fellow ACS, Am. Acad. Orthop. Surgeons; mem. Sociéé Internationale de Chirurgie Orthopédique et de Traumatologie, Internat. Med. Soc. Paraplegia, Am. Trauma Soc. (bd. dirs. 1988—), Am. Orthop. Assn., Am. Spinal Injury Assn. (past pres.), Soc. Med. Cons. to Armed Forces, Mid-Am. Orthop. Assn. Roman Catholic. Avocations: photography, fishing, amateur radio, aviation, boating. Office: Northwestern Meml Hosp 250 E Superior St Ste 619 Chicago IL 60611-2950 also: Northwestern Meml Hosp Ste 11-245 201 E Huron Chicago IL 60611 E-mail: Interspace@nwu.edu.

MEYER, PAUL WILLIAM, arboretum director, horticulturist; b. Cin., Aug. 30, 1952; s. Edward F. and Dorothy (Schroeder) M.; m. Debra L. Rodgers, May 16, 1990. BSc, Ohio State U., 1973; MSc, U. Del., 1976; diploma, U. Edinburgh, 1988. Curator Morris Arboretum U. Pa., Phila., 1976-91, dir., 1991—. Bd. dirs. The Henry Found., 1992-2000; chair Springfield Twp. planning com., Montgomery County, Pa., 1993. Mem. Am. Assn. Bot. Gardens and Arboreta (bd. dirs. Montgomery County Land Trust, Montgomery County Open Space). Avocations: bicycling, swimming, backpacking, rowing, gardening. Office: Morris Arboretum of Univ Pa 9414 Meadowbrook Ave Philadelphia PA 19118-2697

MEYER, PEARL, executive compensation consultant; b. N.Y.C. d. Allen Charles and Rose Weissman; m. Ira A. Meyer. BA cum laude, postgrad., NYU. Statis. specialist, exec. comp. div. Gen. Foods Corp., White Plains, NY; exec. v.p. and cons. Handy Assocs., Inc., N.Y.C., NY; founder, chair Pearl Meyer & Ptnrs., N.Y.C., NY, 1989—. Lectr. exec. compensation confs. and seminars. Contbr. articles to profl. jours. Recipient Entrepreneurial Woman award, Women Bus. Owners N.Y. Mem.: Pers. Accreditation Inst., Women's Econ. Roundtable, Soc. Human Resources Mgmt. (cert. accredited pers. diplomate), WorldatWork, Am. Mgmt. Assn., Women's Forum, Sky Club, Sedgewood Club, Phi Beta Kappa, Beta Gamma Sigma, Pi Mu Epsilon. Office: Pearl Meyer & Ptnrs 445 Park Ave New York NY 10022-2606

MEYER, PHILIP GILBERT, lawyer; b. Louisville, June 26, 1945; s. Henry Gilbert and Adele (Gutermuth) M.; m. Jackie Darlene Watson, Jan. 30, 1971 (div. Apr. 1976); m. Sylvia Saunders, Oct. 9, 1976. BBA, U. Mich., 1967; JD, U. Tex., 1970. Bar: Tex. 1970, Mich. 1971, U.S. Tax Ct. 1972, U.S. Dist. Ct. (ea. dist.) Mich. 1971, U.S. Ct. Appeals (6th cir.), 1972, U.S. Dist. Ct. (no. dist.) Ohio 1976, U.S. Dist. Ct. (we. dist.) Mich. 1993, U.S. Dist. Ct. (no. dist.) Ill. 1998. Law clk. Wayne County Cir. Ct., Detroit, 1970-72; atty. Leonard C. Jaques, Detroit, 1972; assoc. Christy & Robbins, Dearborn, Mich., 1972-73; ptnr. Foster, Meadows & Ballard, Detroit, 1973-79; of counsel Christy, Rogers & Gantz, Dearborn, 1979-81, Rogers & Gantz, Dearborn, 1981-86; prin. Philip G. Meyer and Assocs., Farmington Hills, 1986—. Adj. prof. U. Detroit Sch. Law, 1979. Mem. ABA (com. vice chmn. rules and procedure 1982-88), Maritime Law Assn. U.S., Mich. Bar Assn. (vice chmn. admiralty sect. 1978), Tex. Bar Assn., Detroit Bar Assn. (vice chmn. admiralty com. 1991-93, chmn. admiralty sect. 1993-95), Propeller Port of Detroit Club (pres. 1984-85). Republican. Home: 5905 Independence Ln West Bloomfield MI 48322-1854 Office: Ste 113 30300 Northwestern Hwy Farmington Hills MI 48334-3212 Office Phone: 248-737-0700.

MEYER, PRISCILLA ANN, Russian language and literature educator; b. Aug. 26, 1942; d. Herbert Edward and Marjorie Rose (Wolff) M.; m. William L. Trousdale, Sept. 15, 1974; 1 dau., Rachel V. BA, U. Calif., Berkeley, 1964; MA, Princeton U., 1966; PhD, 1971. Lectr. in Russian lang. and lit. Wesleyan U., Middletown, Conn., 1968-71, asst. prof., 1971-75, assoc. prof., 1975-88, prof., 1988—. Vis. asst. prof. Yale U., 1973, adv. coun. dept. Slavic lang. and lit. Princeton U., 1998-2002. Co-editor: Dostoevsky and Gogol, 1979; editor: Life in Windy Weather (by Andrei Bitov), 1986, author: Find What the Sailor Has Hidden: Vladimir Nabokov's Pale Fire, 1988; co-editor: Essays on Gogol: Logos and the Russian Word, 1992; co-editor: Nabokov's World, 2001; translator stories; mem. editl. bd. Slavic and East European Jour., 1999—; contbr. articles to profl. jours. Scholar Internat. Rsch. and Exch. Bd., 1973; grantee Ford Found., 1964-68, 70; hon. vis. fellow Sch. Slavonic and East European Studies London U., 1997, 2001. Mem. Am. Coun. Tchrs. Russian (dir. 1983-86), Am. Assn. Tchrs. Slavic and East European Studies, Internat. Vladimir Nabokov Soc. (v.p. 1983-85, 2002-04, pres. 1985-87, 2004-), Tolstoi Soc., Dostoevsky Soc., Conn. Acad. Arts and Scis. Office: Russian Dept Wesleyan U Middletown CT 06459-0001 Office Phone: 860-685-3127. E-mail: pmeyer@wesleyan.edu.

MEYER, PUCCI, newspaper editor; b. N.Y.C., Sept. 1, 1944; d. Charles Albert and Lollo (Offer) M.; m. Michael V. McGill, Oct. 28, 2001. BA, U. Wis., 1966. Asst. editor Look mag., N.Y.C., 1970-71, editorial asst. Paris, 1967-69; reporter Newsday, Garden City, L.I., N.Y., 1971-73; style editor N.Y. Daily News Sunday Mag., N.Y.C., 1974-76, assoc. editor, 1977-82, editor, 1983-86; sr. editor Prodigy, White Plains, N.Y., 1987; spl. projects editor N.Y. Post, N.Y.C., 1988-89, style editor, 1990-92, food editor, 1992-93, assoc. features editor, 1993—94, travel editor, 1994—2004. Contbr. articles to various nat. mags. Recipient Pulitzer prize as mem. Newsday investigative team that wrote articles and book The Heroin Trail, 1973.

MEYER, RACHEL ABIJAH, foundation director, artist, theorist, poet; b. Job's Corners, Pa., Aug. 18, 1963; d. Jacob Owen and Velma Ruth (Foreman) M.; children: Andrew Carson, Peter Franklin. Student, Lebanon Valley Coll. Restaurant owner Purcy's Place, Ono, Pa.; restaurant mgr. King's Table Buffet, Citrus Heights, Calif.; product finalizer TransWorld Enterprises, Blaine, Wash.; dir., support svcs. adminstr. Tacticar Found., Sacramento, 1991—; tchr. Tacticar Inst., 1995; chair Coniferms, Sacramento, 1996—. Author: Year of the Unicorn, 1994. Avocations: researching, writing, painting.

MEYER, RAYMOND GEORGE, II, lawyer; b. Racine, Wis., Dec. 12, 1947; s. Raymond George and Marie Johanna (Heusdens) M.; m. Elaine Ann Pulvermacher, Aug. 18, 1973; children: Raymond George III, Amaliya R. BA, U. Wis., 1969, JD, 1974. Bar: Wis. 1974, U.S. Dist. Ct. (ea. and we. dists.) Wis. 1974. Assoc. Koenen Law Office, Port Washington, Wis., 1974-77; ptnr. Koenen & Meyer, Port Washington, 1978—. Contbr. articles to Railroad Model Craftsman, Railmodel Jour, Am. Jour. of Family Law, Wis. Jour. of Family Law, Wis. Opinions. With USMC, 1969-71. Recipient legal svcs. grant Wis. Trust Account Found., Madison, 1987, 89, 91. Mem.ABA, Wis. Bar Assn., Ozaukee County Bar Assn. (pres. 1986-87), Saukville C. of C. (pres. 1980-82), Port Washington C. of C., Port Washington-Saukville Jaycees (pres. 1977-78) (senator 1983). Avocations: bicycling, model shipbuilding, model trains. Home: 616 S Garfield Ave Port Washington WI 53074-2317 Office: Koenen & Meyer 110 E Main St Port Washington WI 53074-1914 Office Phone: 414-284-5566. E-mail: ray2@execpc.com.

MEYER, RAYMOND JOSEPH, former college basketball coach; b. Chgo., Dec. 18, 1913; s. Joseph E. and Barbara (Hummel) M.; m. Margaret Mary Delaney, May 27, 1939 (dec. 1985); children— Barbara (Mrs. Gerald Starzyk), Raymond Thomas, Patricia (Mrs. Thomas Butterfield), Merianne (Mrs. James McGowan; dec. 1997), Joseph, Robert. AB, U. Notre Dame, 1938. Asst. coach U. Notre Dame, 1941-42; basketball coach DePaul U., Chgo., 1942—. Author: How To Play Winning Basketball, 1960, Basketball as Coached by Ray Meyer, 1967, Ray Meyer, 1 Coach, 1980, Coach, 1987. Named Coach of Yr. Chgo. Basketball Writers, 1943, 44, 48, 52, Coach of Yr. Nat. Assn. Basketball Coaches, 1978-79, Sportwriters Coach of Yr., 1978, Salvation Man of Yr., 1990; recipient Marine Corps Sportsman of Yr. award, 1979, Bunn award, 1981, Victor award, 1981, Lincoln Acad. award, 1988, Nat. Basketball Coach's Golden Jubilee award, Notre Dame Lifetime Achievement award 1998; inducted into Basketball Hall of Fame, 1979, Basketball Hall of Fame Chgo., 1981, Basketball Hall of Fame Ill., Golden Anniversary award Nat. Basketball Coaches, 1992, Naismith Found. Good Sportsman's award, 1998. Mem. Nat. Basketball Coaches Assn. Roman Catholic. Home: 2518 W Cedar Glen Dr Arlington Heights IL 60005-4336 Office: 100 Turner Ave Elk Grove Village IL 60007-3933 Office Phone: 847-439-0738.

MEYER, RICHARD CHARLES, microbiologist, educator; b. Cleve., May 2, 1930; s. Frederick Albert and Tekla Charlotte (Schrade) M.; m. Carolyn Yvonne Patton, Apr. 6, 1963; children: Frederick Gustav, Carl Anselm. B.Sc., Baldwin-Wallace Coll., 1952; M.Sc., Ohio State U., 1957, PhD, 1961. Teaching and research asst. Ohio State U., 1956-61, research assoc., 1961-62; microbiologist Nat. Cancer Inst., NIH, Bethesda, Md., 1962-64; asst. prof. vet. pathology and hygiene and microbiology U. Ill., Urbana-Champaign, 1965-68, assoc. prof., 1968-73, prof., 1973-89, prof. emeritus, 1989—. Served with C.E. U.S. Army, 1952-54. Mem. Am. Acad. Microbiology, AAAS, Am. Inst. Biol. Sci., Am. Soc. Microbiology, Sigma Xi, Gamma Sigma Delta, Phi Zeta. Republican. Lutheran. Home: 1504 S Buckthorn Ln Mahomet IL 61853-3632 Office: Dept Vet Pathobiology U Ill at Urbana-Champaign Urbana IL 61801

MEYER, RICHARD W. school librarian; b. St. Louis, Jan. 22, 1943; s. Norman K. Meyer and Melba R. Reisel; m. Clare S. Siesennop, Apr. 12, 1944; children: Sharyn C. Moore, Karyn A. BS in Chemistry, U. Mo., 1967; BA Libr. Sci., U. of Mo., Columbia, MO, 1962—67; MS Libr. Sci., U. of Ill., Champaign, IL, 1969—70; MA Economics, Clemson U., Clemson, SC, 1982—86. Asst. libr. E.I. duPont de Nemours, Aiken, SC, 1967—69; dir. libr. tech services Ind. State U., Terre Haute, Ind., 1976—79; asst. dir. libr. U. Tex. at Dallas, Richardson, 1970—76; assoc. dir. libraries Clemson U., Clemson, 1979—91; dir. libr. Trinity U., San Antonio, 1991—2000; dean and dir. libraries Ga. Inst. Tech., Atlanta, 2000—. Cons. Harris Corp., Melbourne, Fla., 1985—86, Chemists Club N.Y., N.Y.C., 1991—92, Mackenzie U., Sao Paulo, Brazil, 1998—99. Contbr. articles to profl. jours. Field svc. rev. team mem. United Way of San Antonio, 1998—2000. Recipient G.K. Saur Best Article award, Coll. and Rsch. Libraries, 1999, ALCTS/Blackwells Scholarship award, 2002; grantee, Andrew W. Mellon Found., 1995—2000. Mem.: So. Assn. Colls. and Schs. (mem. reaffirmation rev. teams 1999—2002), ALA. Conservative. Home: 2433 Mill Ridge Walk Atlanta GA 30345 Office: Georgia Institute of Technology 704 Cherry St Atlanta GA 30332-0900 Business E-Mail: richard.meyer@library.gatech.edu.

MEYER, ROBERT ALAN, consultant; b. N.Y.C., Mar. 20, 1946; s. Leonard and Mildred M.; m. Gail Rein, Oct. 29, 1967; children: Jonathan, Caroline. BA in Econs., Am. Internat. Coll., 1967; MBA, NYU, 1973. 2nd v.p., mgr. mcpl. bond research Smith Barney Harris Upham and Co., Inc., N.Y.C., 1973-76; 1st v.p., dir. mcpl. bond research E.F. Hutton and Co. Inc., N.Y.C., 1976-82; v.p., mgr. mcpl. bond research Merrill Lynch Pierce Fenner and Smith Inc., N.Y.C., 1982-84; pres. Bond Investors Guaranty Ins. Co., N.Y.C., 1984-90; pres., chief exec. officer Greig Fester Fin. Guaranty Brokers, Inc., N.Y.C., 1991-94; prin. Meyer Cons. Group Inc., Holmdel, N.J., 1994-98; chmn., pres., CEO RAM Reinsurance Co. Ltd., Hamilton, Bermuda, 1998-2001; prin. Meyer Cons. Group Inc., Holmdel, N.J., 2001—. Mem. India House. Office: 20 Stoney Brook Rd Holmdel NJ 07733 E-mail: mcgramgm@msn.com.

MEYER, ROBERT ALLEN, human resource management educator; b. Wisconsin Rapids, Wis., May 31, 1943; s. Charles Harold and Viola Bertha (Stoeckmann) M.; 1 child, Timothy Charles. BA, Valparaiso (Ind.) U., 1966; MA, Mich. State U., 1967, PhD, 1972, postgrad., 1981. Asst. prof. Muskingum Area Tech. Coll., Zanesville, Ohio, 1972-74, adj. prof. U. Fla., Gainesville, 1974-80; dean acad. affairs Santa Fe Community Coll., Gainesville, 1974-80; asst. prof. Purdue U., W. Lafayette, Ind., 1982-84, Ga. State U., Atlanta, 1985-89; assoc. prof., program coord. U. N. Tex., Denton, 1989-91; Fulbright profl. scholar, Bangkok, 1991-92; coord. travel, tourism, hotel, restaurant mgmt. program U. Hawaii Manoa Campus, Honolulu, 1992-97; dir. distance edn., dir. travel, hotel and restaurant mgmt. SPC, St. Petersburg, Fla., 1997—; 21573325. Investor, asst. mgr. LaSiene Restaurant, Ann Arbor, Mich., 1970-72; investor, cons. Cafe Brittany St. Thomas, U.S. V.I., 1974-80, owner, operator, Houston, 1980; pres. RTM Cons., Honolulu, Hawaii, 1989—; educator World Tourism Orgn., 1993—; mem. vis. ind. coun. C. of C., 1993—; club mgr. Assn. Am., 1994—; dir. edn. Am. Assoc. Real Estate License Law Officials. Contbr. articles to profl. jours. Founding mem. Fla. Distance Learning Consortium, 1998—; bd. dirs., founder Fla. Virtual Campus, 1998—, dir. hospitality program, 1998—. Recipient White House Commendation for Partnerships with Industry and Higher Edn.,1984, George Washington Medal of Honor for innovations in higher edn., Freedoms Found., 1985, 86, Achievement award in hospitality edn. Coun. of Hotel, Restaurant & Instl. Edn., 1987. Mem. Assn. Real Estate Lic. Law Ofcls. (distance edn. coun. bd. mem. 1999—), Tarrant County Hotel and Motel Assn., Dallas Hotel Assn., Am. Soc. Tng. and Devel., Travel Ind. Assn. Tex., Hotel Sales & Mktg. Assn. (bd. dirs. 1985-89), Coun. of Hotel, Restaurant and Instl. Edn. (grad. com. 1989-90). Office: St Petersburg Coll PO Box 13489 Saint Petersburg FL 33733-3489 Home: 13108 Angler St Spring Hill FL 34609-5907 Office Phone: 727-394-6165. E-mail: rmeyer1@tampabay.rr.com.

MEYER, ROBERTA, mediator, communication consultant; b. San Francisco, July 27, 1936; d. Theodore Robert and Virginia (Organ) Meyer; m. G. William Sheldon; children: Megan McDougall Radeski, Deborah Ann Guerra. Student, U. Utah, 1974. Cert. mediator. Founder, pres., exec. dir. Roberta Meyer Communication Cons., Inc., San Francisco, 1977—. Presenter numerous workshops in alcoholism and communication; nat. spkr. Nat. Found. Alcoholism Comm.; keynote spkr. Calif. Women's Comm. Alcoholism, 1981; mem. adv. bd. Soviet Am. Alliance Alcoholism and Other Addictions; founder Youth Dance Experience, 1999. Author: (book) Facts About Booze and Other Drugs, 1980, The Parent Connection: How to Communicate with Your Child about Alcohol and Other Drugs, 1984, Listen to the Heart, 1989, (screenplays) Understanding Addition, 1988, Better Relationships Through Effective Communication, 1991; numerous radio and TV appearances; dir.: Meyer Method Dance Program for ballroom dancers, One Meyer Method Dance Training Video, 1998. Mem. adv. bd. Marin Svcs. Women, 1980; vol. Calif. Pacific Med. Ctr., San Francisco Ballet Aux.; mem. N.Y.C. and San Francisco Ballet Cos., 1950—56, San Francisco Ballet Sch., 1956—65; founder, dir. Ballet Arts San Francisco, 1965—78, San Francisco Ballroom Dance Theatre and the accelerated dance programs, 1994—. Named 56th Point of Light, Pres. Bush, 1990; recipient award, Optimists Club. Mem.: Childrens Theatre Assn., Nat. Coun. Alcoholism and Drug Dependence Calif. (pres. 1988—91), San Francisco Womens Rehab. Assn. (pres. 1975—76, dir., founder Youth Dance Project 1999), Nat. Coun. Alcoholism (co-chmn. pub. info. com. 1985—, v.p. Bay area 1988—, bd. dirs. Teen Kick Off 1987—, Alcoholism and Drug Rsch. Comm. Ctr. 1990—, pres. 1988—, creator, cons. youth aware program 1974—), Nat. Collaborative Planning and Cmty. Svc. (cert.), San Francisco C. of C. Address: 158 Rainbow Dr #5897 Livingston TX 77399

MEYER, ROGER ALBERT, surgeon; b. Hoquiam, Wash., June 23, 1937; m. Shelby Jean Phillips, Dec. 28, 1963 (dec.); children: Kirsten, Jennifer, Darin; m. Sheila Mary Hanley, Sept. 29, 1996. DDS, U. Wash., 1961, MS, 1967; MD, Creighton U., 1975. Diplomate Am. Bd. Oral and Maxillofacial Surgery. Dental intern USPHS Hosp., Norfolk, Va., 1961-62; dental surgeon and clin. investigaor NIDR/NIH, Bethesda, Md., 1962-63; resident oral and maxillofacial surgery U. Wash. Affiliated Hosps., Seattle, 1963-67; resident gen. surgery U. Vt. Med. Ctr., Burlington, 1975-76; clin. assoc. prof. dept. surgery Oreg. Health Scis. U., Portland, 1976-79; assoc. prof., chmn. oral and maxillofacial surgery Emory U. Sch. Dentistry, Atlanta, 1979-86; clin. asst. prof. plastic surgery Emory U. Sch. Medicine, Atlanta, 1981—. Cons. cleft lip, palate and craniomaxillofacial surgery State of Ga. Dept. Human Resources, Atlanta, 1981—. Author numerous chpts. in surg. textbooks and articles in profl. jours. Fellow Am. Coll. Surgeons, Am. Coll. Dentists; mem. AMA, ADA, Am. Assn. Oral and Maxillofacial Surgeons, Am. Soc. Maxillofacial Surgeons, Am. Cleft Palate-Craniofacial Assn., Alpha Omega Alpha. Avocations: music (piano), tennis, skiing, running, white water kayaking. Office: East Cobb Surg Ctr Bldg H 1000 Johnson Ferry Rd Marietta GA 30068-5420

MEYER, ROGER ARNOLD, management consultant, writer; b. Jacksonville, Ill., Jan. 23, 1943; s. Arnold Henry Meyer and Hazel Elizabeth; m. Elizabeth Lynn, Mar. 22, 1969; children: Roger Matthew, Erin Elizabeth. BA, Milligan Coll., 1966; MA, La. State U., 1972, PhD, 1974. mgmt. cons. Clin. intern in psychology Southwestern Med. Sch., Dallas, 1973-74; Clay County dir. Smoky Mountain Mental Health Ctr., Marble, 1974-76, clin. dir. inpatient unit Franklin, N.C., 1976-78; clin. psychologist Valley Psychiat. Hosp., Chattanooga, 1979-80; clin. dir. Hiwassee Mental Health Ctr., Cleveland, Tenn., 1980-84; clin. psychologist Brainerd Psychol Svcs., Chattanooga, 1980-95; dir. counseling svc. Chattanooga Bible Inst., 1982-95; mgmt. cons. Brainerd Cons. Svcs., Chattanooga, 1996—. Cons. clin. hypnosis Am. Soc. Clin. Hypnosis, 1994. Contbr. articles to profl. jours. Program chmn. Brainerd Kiwanis Club, Chattanooga, 1982-95; bd. dirs. T-Cap, Nashville, 1992-94. Lt. USN, 1966-69. Mem. ASTD (program chair), Chattanooga Human Resources Assn., Chattanooga C. of C. (br. bd. dirs., v.p. 1999—), Chattanooga Assn. for Clin. Pastoral Care (pres. 1984-85, treas. 1988), Inst. for Mgmt. Cons. Democrat. Presbyterian. Avocations: woodworking, wood carving, gardening, hiking, canoeing. Office: Brainerd Cons Svcs 6074 E Brainerd Rd Chattanooga TN 37421-3908

MEYER, RON, film company executive; b. 1944; m. Kelly Chapman; children, Jennifer, Sarah, Carson, Eli. With Paul Kohner Agency, 1964-1970; agent William Morris Agency, Beverly Hills, CA, 1970-1975; co-founder, pres. Creative Artists Agency, Inc., Beverly Hills, CA, 1975-95; pres., COO Universal Studios Inc., Universal City, 1995—; pres./COO Vivendi Universal Entertainment. Served with USMC. Office: Universal Studios Inc 100 Universal City Plz Universal City CA 91608 E-mail: susan.fleishman@unistudios.com.

MEYER, RUSSELL WILLIAM, JR., aircraft company executive; b. Davenport, Iowa, July 19, 1932; s. Russell William and Ellen Marie (Matthews) M.; m. Helen Scott Vaughn, Aug. 20, 1960; children: Russell William, III, Elizabeth Ellen, Jeffrey Vaughn, Christopher Matthews, Carolyn Louise. BA, Yale U., 1954; LLB, Harvard U., 1961. Bar: Ohio 1961. Mem. firm Arter & Hadden, Cleve., 1961-66; pres., chief exec. officer Grumman Am. Aviation Corp., Cleve., 1966-74; exec. v.p. Cessna Aircraft Co., Wichita, Kans., 1974-75, chmn. bd., chief exec. officer, 1975-2000, chmn., 2000—. Bd. dirs. Nations Bank, Pub. Broadcasting Svc., Welfare to Work Partnership; presdl. appointee Aviation Safety Commn., 1987—; mem. Pres.' Airline Commn., 1993; dir. Pub. Broadcasting Sys. Chmn. bd. trustees 1st Bapt. Ch., Cleve., 1972-74; bd. dirs. United Way, Wichita and Sedgwick County; trustee Wesley Hosp. Endowment Assn., Wake Forest Univ.; bd. govs. United Way Am., 1993—. With USAF, 1955-58. Recipient Collier trophy Nat. Aeronautic Assn., 1986, George S. Dively award Harvard U., 1992, Wright Bros. Meml. trophy, 1995, Disting. Svc. Citation U. Kans., 2000; named Kansan of the Yr., 1998. Mem. ABA, Ohio Bar Assn., Kans. Bar Assn., Cleve. Bar Assn., Gen. Aviation Mfrs. Assn. (chmn. bd. dirs. 1973-74, 81-82, 93-94), Wichita C. of C. (chmn. 1988—, bd. dirs.), Wichita Club, Wichita Country Club, Pine Valley Club, Cypress Point Club, Double Eagle Country Club, Flint Hills Nat. Club, Latrobe Country Club. Home: 600 N Tara Ct Wichita KS 67206-1830 Office: Cessna Aircraft PO Box 7704 1 Cessna Blvd Wichita KS 67215-1424 Office Phone: 316-517-8000.

MEYER, SCOTT D. public relations firm executive; b. Mpls., Oct. 7, 1949; BA in Journalism, U. Minn., 1972; postgrad., N.Y. Inst. of Fin. Asst. v.p., corp. rels. Piper, Jaffray & Hopwood, 1976-77, mgr. investor rels. Internat. Multifoods, 1977-79; dir. pub. rels. First Nat. Bank of Mpls., 1979-80; gen. mgr. pub. rels. Control Data Corp., 1980-84; exec. v.p. Dorn Pub. Rels., 1984-85, pres., from 1985; chmn., chief operating officer Mona, Meyer & McGrath, Mpls.; now vice chmn. Mona, Meyer, McGrath & Gavin, Inc., Mpls. Address: Shandwick Intl 387 Park Ave S Fl 4 New York NY 10016-8810

MEYER, SHELDON, publisher; b. Chgo., June 8, 1926; s. Arthur Christof and Hester Truslow (Sheldon) M.; m. Margaret Mary Kirk, July 29, 1964; children: Arabella Christina, Andrew Kirk. AB summa cum laude, Princeton U., 1949; MA (hon.), U. Oxford, 1993. With Funk & Wagnalls Co., 1951—55; assoc. editor Grosset & Dunlap, 1955-56; with Oxford Univ. Press, N.Y.C., 1956-96, editor, 1956-70; exec. editor Trade Books, 1970-82, v.p., 1974-79, sr. v.p., 1982-96, consulting editor, 1997—. Recipient The Lawrenceville medal. Mem. Am. Assn. Univ. Presses (bd. dirs. 1969-71, 79-82, v.p. 1979-80), Am. Hist. Assn., Orgn. Am. Historians, Inst. Early Am. History and Culture (bd. dirs. 1985-87), Nat. Bd. Rev. Motion Pictures, Century Assn., Phi Beta Kappa. Home: 180 Riverside Dr New York NY 10024-1021

MEYER, SHELDON ELLIOTT, music educator; b. Albert Lea, Minn., Aug. 31, 1954; s. Orlando Warren and Evangelene Marie Meyer; m. Holly Jean Brase, Sept. 1, 1984; children: Bethany B., Erin B. BS, U. Minn., St. Paul, 1977; MusB, Minn. State U., Mankato, Minn., 1999. Tchr. agr. Howard Lake Schs., Howard Lake, Minn., 1977—79; farmer Kiester, Minn., 1979—96; piano tchr., organist, 1979—96; dir. bands I.S.P. #640, Wabasso, Minn., 1999—2004. Counselor MSU-M Band Camp, Mankato, Minn., 1999; activities dir. Upper Midwest String Camp, Mankato, Minn., 2002—04. Arranger: instrumental; composer: Eine Dankett Gott, 2003. Bd. dirs., v.p. Redwood Civic Music, Redwood Falls, Minn., 2002—03. Mem.: Music Educators Nat. Conf., Minn. Band Dirs. Assn. Office: Wabasso Pub Schs 1333 Mary St Wabasso MN 56293

MEYER, SUSAN M. lawyer; b. 1943; BA in Philosophy and Psychology, Marquette U.; JD, Fordham U. Officer, investigator Washington Met. Police Dept.; gen. counsel Beatrice Consumer Durables, Northbrook, Ill., G.D. Searle & Co., Skokie, Ill.; sr. counsel Beatrice Cos., Inc., Chgo., 1986-91; v.p., sec., dep. counsel Gen. Instrument Corp., Chgo., 1991-98; v.p., sec., gen. counsel United Stationers Inc., Des Plaines, Ill., 1998—. Office: 2200 E Golf Rd Des Plaines IL 60016-1246

MEYER, SUSAN MOON, speech language pathologist, educator; b. Hazleton, Pa., Mar. 8, 1949; d. Robert A. and Jane W. (Walters) Moon; m. John C. Meyer Jr., Feb. 16, 1989; children: Chris, Scott. BS, Pa. State U., 1971, MS, 1972; PhD, Temple U., 1983. Cert. tchr., Pa. Speech-lang. pathologist, instr. Elmira (N.Y.) Coll., 1973-74; speech-lang. pathologist Arnot-Ogden Hosp., Elmira, 1973-74; supr. Sacred Heart Hosp. Speech and Hearing Ctr., Allentown, Pa., 1974-75; speech-lang. pathology instr. Kutztown (Pa.) U., 1975-78, asst. prof., 1978-82, assoc. prof., 1982-85, prof., 1985—. Owner Speech and Lang. Svcs., Allentown, 1975-87; cons. Vis. Nurses Assn., Allentown, 1975-85, Home Care, Allentown, 1975-85. Author: Survival Guide for the Beginning Speech-Language Clinician, 1998. Mem. Am. Speech-Lang.-Hearing Assn. (cert., councilor 1986-89, numerous Continuing Edn. awards), Pa. Speech-Lang.-Hearing Assn. (cert., v.p. profl. preparation 1985-89, Appreciation award 1987-89, 2001), Northea. Speech and Hearing Assn. Pa. (pres. 1984-86, Outstanding Dedication award 1985, Honors of the Assn. award 1999), Coun. Suprs. Speech-Lang. Pathology and Audiology. Avocations: family activities, cross-country skiing, British sports cars, reading. Bus. Office: Kutztown U Dept Speech-Lang Kutztown PA 19530 Business E-Mail: smeyer@kutztown.edu.

MEYER-BAHLBURG, HEINO F.L. psychology educator; b. Hamburg, Germany, Feb. 26, 1940; came to U.S., 1969; s. Wilhelm and Marie Luise Meyer-B. Vordiplom in Psychology, U. Hamburg, 1963, Diplom Psychology, 1966; D in Natural Scis., U. Düsseldorf, Germany, 1970. Sci. asst. U. Düsseldorf, 1970; rsch. asst., then rsch. assoc. prof. psychiatry and pediat. SUNY Med. Sch., Buffalo, 1970-77; rsch. scientist N.Y. State Psychiat. Inst., N.Y.C., 1977—; from assoc. clin. prof. med. psychology to prof. clin. psychology in psychiatry Columbia U. Coll. Physicians and Surgeons, 1978—; pediat. behavioral endocrinologist Presbyn. Hosp., N.Y.C., 1978-90, prof. psychologist in psychiat. svc., 1990—. Contbr. numerous articles to profl. publs. Recipient Disting. Sci. Achievement award Soc. for Sci. Study of Sex, 1993; grantee NIMH, NICHD. Mem. AAAS, APA, Soc. Pediat. Psychology, Internat. Acad. Sex Rsch., German Sexual Rsch. Soc., Internat. Soc. Psychoneuroendocrinology, Soc. Sci. Study Sex, Soc. Rsch. Child Devel., Soc. Sexual Therapy and Rsch., Lawson Wilkins Pediat. Endocrine Soc., Harry Benjamin Internat. Gender Dysphoria Assn. Office: Columbia U Dept Psychiatry 1051 Riverside Dr Unit 15 New York NY 10032-2695 Business E-Mail: meyerb@childpsych.columbia.edu.

MEYERHOFF, ERICH, librarian, administrator; b. Braunschweig, Germany, Nov. 24, 1919; came to US, 1935; s. Karl and Irma Meyerhoff; m. Inge Zuber; children: Tina, C. Michael BS, CCNY, 1943; MS, NY Sch. Social Work, 1949; MSLS, Columbia U., 1951, cert. advanced librarianship, 1974. Social worker various orgns., to 1951; reference librarian Columbia U. Med. Library, NYC, 1951-57; librarian, asst. prof. Downstate Med. Ctr., SUNY, Bklyn., 1957-61; dir. Med. Library Ctr. NY, NYC, 1961-67; librarian Health Scis. Library, SUNY-Buffalo, 1967-70, Cornell U. Med. Coll., NYC, 1970-86, asst. dean, 1977-86; chief library svc. VA Med. Ctr., NYC, 1986-88; archives librarian NYU Med. Ctr., 1980-91; asst. curator Ehrman Med. Libr.-Archives, NYU Sch. Medicine, 1991—. Adj. instr. biomed. comms. Columbia U., 1976-81; cons. U. Mich., Ann Arbor, 1968, NY Met. Reference Rsch. Libr. Agy., 1968-69, Coll. Physicians Phila., 1969-70. Fellow AAAS, Med. Library Assn. (cert., bd. dirs. 1972-76, chmn. various coms. 1968-72, 78-81, Inst. for Sci. Info. award 1981-82, Janet Doe lectr. 1977, Marcia C. Noyes award 1997), NY Acad. Medicine; mem. AAUP, Spl. Libraries Assn., Archons Colophon, Am. Assn. History Medicine, Am. Printing History Assn., Met. NY Archivists Roundtable. Avocation: travel. Home: 90 La Salle St New York NY 10027-4719 Office: NYU Med Ctr Archives 550 1st Ave New York NY 10016-6402 Office Phone: 212-263-8280. E-mail: meyere01@library.med.nyu.edu.

MEYERHOFF, JACK FULTON, financial executive; b. Joliet, Ill, May 15, 1926; s. Charles F. and Helen (Ferguson) M.; m. Mary Margaret Williams, Jan. 2, 1949; children— Keith F., Greg H., Deborah S., Todd C. BS, Miami U.,

Oxford, Ohio, 1947; postgrad., Ohio Wesleyan U., 1944-45; grad. Advanced Mgmt. Program, Harvard U., 1968. C.P.A., Ohio, Ill. Mgr. Arthur Andersen & Co., Chgo., Cin., Cleve., 1947-59; treas. MacGregor Sports, Cin., 1959-63; v.p., corp. controller Brunswick Corp., Chgo., 1963-77, chief fin. officer, 1972-77, v.p. corp. affairs, 1977-80, v.p. human resources, 1980-81; chmn., chief exec. officer MarJac Assocs., Nokomis, Fla., 1981—; pres., dir. Charles Oxford Corp., Nokomis, 1984—. Bd. dir. Sherwood Med. Industries, Inc., Old Orchard Bank & Trust Co., Tech: Time Inc., Nokomis; organizer, vice chmn. bd. trustees Caldwell Trust Co. and Trust Cos. Am., Venice, Fla., 1993—. Treas., bd. dir. Cove Sch.; bd. dir., pres. Skokie Valley Cmty. Hosp., No. Ill. Indsl. Assn.; v.p., bd. dir. Jr. Achievement; bd. dir. Chgo. Responsibility Growth, Gulf Area Med. Properties; chmn. bd. Bon Secours-Venice Hosp., Venice Hosp. Found.; bd. dir. J. Clifford MacDonald Handicapped Ctr. of Tampa, Sarasota Com. of 100, Triangle Econ. Devel. Coun. (bd. dir., treas.), Manatee C.C. Found., Boys and Girls Club of Venice, Pillar Cmty., Venice, Fla.; mem. adv. coun. Miami U., Georgetown U., U. So. Fla. With USNR, 1944-46. Mem. Am. Inst. C.P.A.s, Ohio Soc. C.P.A.s, Ill. Soc. C.P.A.s, Fin. Exec. Inst., Nat. Assn. Acct., Harvard Bus. Sch. Alumni Assn., Miami U. Exec. Alumni Council (bd. dir., treas.), Venice Area C. of C. (bd. dir., treas.), Sigma Alpha Epsilon, Delta Sigma Pi, Beta Alpha Psi, Beta Gamma Sigma Clubs: Venice Yacht, Mid America, Econ., Misty Creek Country. Lodges: Masons, Rotary. Methodist. Home: 20 Inlets Blvd Nokomis FL 34275-4108 Office: MW Assoc PO Box 1326 Nokomis FL 34274-1326 E-mail: meyerhoffjm@comcast.net.

MEYERINK, VICTORIA PAIGE, film producer, actress; b. Santa Barbara, Calif., Dec. 27, 1960; d. William Joseph Meyerink and Jeanne Baird; m. Lawrence David Foldes, Apr. 24, 1983. Student, U. So. Calif., 1978-80. Actress, 1962—; v.p. Star Cinema Prodn. Group, Inc., 1981-85; pres. Star Entertainment Group, Inc., L.A., 1985—. Mem. faculty Internat. Film & TV Workshops, 1991—; lectr. colls. & film festivals. Prodr. (motion pictures) The Great Skycopter Rescue, 1982, Young Warriors, 1984, Night Force, 1987, Prima Donnas, 1996, Finding Home, 2004; actress (TV series) The Danny Kaye Show, Green Acres, My Three Sons, Family Affair, The FBI, Adam 12, (motion pictures) Speedway, Night of The Grizzly, Seconds, Brainstorm, The Littlest Hobo, (TV spl.) It Isn't Easy Being a Teenage Millionairess, numerous comml s. Recipient Mayoral Proclamation for Outstanding Achievement, City of L.A., Cert. of Recognition for 25 Yrs. Outstanding Contbns. to the Entertainment Industry, City of L.A., Outstanding Achievement award Acad. Family Films & TV. Mem. Acad. Motion Picture Arts & Scis. (exec. com. Student Acad. Awards 1996—), L.A. Film Tchrs. Assn. Avocations: languages, travel, music, scuba diving, gourmet cooking.

MEYEROVITZ, FAYONA BRENDA, psychologist, consultant; d. Michael and Sarah Esta (Silpert) Siew; m. David Charles Meyerovitz, Apr. 26, 1995. BA, U. of the Witwatersrand, Johannesburg, South Africa, 1991—93, Honours (Indsl. Psychology), 1994—94; MA (Indsl. Psychology), U. of the Witwatersrand, Johannesburg, 1995—95. Cert. professional psychology South African Med. and Dental Coun., 1997. Lectr. Mt. Scopus Campus, Johannesburg, 1995—96; head of human resources and lectr. Boston City Campus, Johannesburg, 1997—97; indsl. psychologist Pvt. Practice, Johannesburg, 1998—99; prin. (co-founder) Select Strategy, Boston, 2000—. Mem.: Human Factors and Ergonomics Soc., Chpt. Activation Sub-Committee of Chpt. Affairs Com. (nat. chair 2004), Health Professions Coun. of South Africa, Internat. Assn. of Applied Psychology, Orgnl. Psychology Divsn., Human Factors and Ergonomics Soc., Human Factors and Ergonomics Soc., New Eng. Chpt. (pres. 2003), Human Factors and Ergonomics Soc., New Eng. Chpt. (pres. 2002). Achievements include reviving New England Chpt. of the Human Factors and Ergonomics Soc. from inactivity and building a thriving profl. cmty. with structures to support profl. edn. and outreach.

MEYEROWITZ, ELLIOT MARTIN, biologist, educator; b. Washington, May 22, 1951; s. Irving and Freda (Goldberg) M.; m. Joan Agnes Kobori, June 17, 1984; 2 children. AB, Columbia U., 1973; MPhil, Yale U., 1975, PhD, 1977. Rsch. fellow Stanford U., Calif., 1977-79; asst. prof. biology Calif. Inst. Tech., Pasadena, 1980-85, assoc. prof., 1985-89, prof., 1989—, George W. Beadle prof. biology, 2002—, chair, 2000—. Mem. editl. bd. Trends in Genetics, Current Biology, Cell, Devel., Genome Biology; contbr. articles to profl. jours. Recipient LVMH Sci. pour l'Art Sci. prize, 1996, Internat. prize for biology, Japan, 1997, Mendel medal, U.K., 1997, Wilbur Cross medal Yale U., 2001; Jane Coffin Childs Meml. fund fellow, 1977-79, Sloan Found. fellow, 1980-82. Fellow: AAAS; mem.: NAS (Lounsbery award 1999), Academie des Scis. (fgn. mem./France), Internat. Soc. for Plant Molecular Biology (pres. 1995—97), Genetics Soc. Am. (pres. 1999, medal 1996), Bot. Soc. Am. (Pelton award 1994), Am. Soc. Plant Biologists (Gibbs medal 1995), Am. Acad. Arts and Scis., Am. Philos. Soc. Office: Calif Inst Tech Divsn Biology 156 29 Pasadena CA 91125-0001 Office Phone: 626-395-6889. Business E-Mail: meyerow@caltech.edu.

MEYERROSE, DALE WILLIAM, career officer; BS in Econs., USAF Acad., 1975; MBA, U. Utah, 1978. Commd. 2d lt. USAF, 1975, advanced through grades to brig. gen., 1998; maintenance officer 4th Combat Comms. Group, Altus AFB, Okla., 1976-77; aide-de-camp, asst. exec. officer to the comdr. European Comms. Divsn., Kapuan Air Sta., West Germany, 1977-79; aide-de-camp to the comdr. Air Force Comms. Command, Scott AFB, Ill., 1979-80; chief of maintenance 1974th Comms. Group, Scott AFB, 1980-82; mem., air staff tng. program officer Sec. of the Air Pers. Coun., The Pentagon, Washington, 1982-83; various assignments Hdqrs. USAF, The Pentagon, Washington, 1983-85; chief future concepts, dep. chief of staff, 1990-91; comdr. 2048th Comms. Squadron, Carswell AFB, 1985-87; comms. support officer Nat. Mil. Command Ctr. the Joint Staff, the Pentagon, Washington, 1987-90; comdr. 3rd Combat Comms. Group, Tinker AFB, Okla., 1992-94; dir. comms. Operation Southern Watch, Riyadh, Saudi Arabia, 1993; dir. comms. and info. Hdqrs. USAF in Europe, Ramstein AB, Germany, 1994-96, Hdqrs. Air Combat Command, Langley AFB, Va., 1996—. Brig. gen., U.S. Base Command, Peterson AFB, Colorado Springs. Decorated Legion of Merit. Office: US Base Command J6 250 S Peterson Blvd # J6 Colorado Springs CO 80914-3285

MEYERS, ABBEY S. foundation administrator; b. Bklyn., Apr. 11, 1944; m. Jerrold B. Meyers, Oct. 23, 1966; children: David, Adam, Laura. AAS, N.Y.C. Community Coll., 1962; LHD (hon.), Alfred U., 1994. Comml. artist various advt. agys., N.Y.C., 1962-65; dir. patient svcs. Tourette Syndrome Assn., Bayside, N.Y., 1980-85; exec. dir., founder Nat. Org. for Rare Disorders, Danbury, Conn., 1985—, pres. U.S. commr. Nat. Commn. on Orphan Diseases, Washington, 1986-89; mem. subcom. Human Gene Therapy NIH, Bethesda, Md., 1989-92; mem. recombinant DNA adv. com. NIH, 1992-96; mem. Health Care Payor Adv. Commn. on Conn. Commn. on Hosps. and Health Care, 1992-94; mem. FDA Biol. Response Modifiers Com., 1995-99; mem. DHHS Nat. Human Rsch. Protection Adv. Com., 2000-2002. Author: (with others) Orphan Drugs and Orphan Diseases: Clinical Reality and Public Policy, 1983, (with others) Cooperative Approaches to Research and Development of Orphan Drugs, 1985, (with others) Tourette Syndrome: Clinical Understanding and Treatment, 1988, (with others) Physicians Guide to Rare Diseases, 1992. Bd. dirs. Nat. Orphan Drug and Device Found., N.Y.C., 1982-85; leader Coalition to Pass Orphan Drug Act of 1983, 1979-82. Recipient Pub. Health Svc. award HHS, 1985, Commr.'s Spl. citation FDA, 1988. Mem. Nat. Health Coun. (bd. dirs. 1989-94), Alliance of Genetic Support Groups (bd. dirs. 1987-89), European Orgn. for Rare Disorders (hon. pres. 1997—). Avocations: reading, horseback riding. Office: Nat Orgn for Rare Disorders PO Box 1968 Danbury CT 06813-1968 E-mail: orphan@rarediseases.org.

MEYERS, ALBERT IRVING, emeritus chemistry educator; b. N.Y.C., Nov. 22, 1932; s. Hyman and Sylvia (Greenberg) M.; m. Joan Shepard, Aug. 10, 1957; children: Harold, Jill, Lisa BS, NYU, 1954, PhD, 1957. Rsch. chemist Cities Svc. Oil Co., Cranbury, N.J., 1957-58; asst., assoc. prof., prof. La. State U., New Orleans, 1958-70, Boyd prof., 1969; prof. Wayne State U., Detroit, 1970-72, Colo. State U., Fort Collins, 1972—2003, disting. prof., 1986—2003, John K. Stille prof. chemistry, 1993—2003, prof. emeritus chemistry, 2003—. Spl. postdoctoral fellow Harvard U., Cambridge, 1965-66; cons. G.D. Searle Co., Skokie, Ill., 1972-84, Mid-West Rsch. Inst., Kansas City, Mo., 1974-77, NIH, Bethesda, Md., 1977-79, 85-89, Bristol-Myers Squibb Co., 1983-95, Roche Colo., 1989—, GlaxoSmithKline Co., 1994-2001; mem. sci. adv. bd. La Jolla, Calif., Avanir Bioscis., La Jolla. Editor Jour. Am. Chem. Soc., 1979-85; mem. editl. adv. bd. Jour. Organic Chemistry, 1990-95, Tetrahedron, 1990-2003, Jour. Chem. Soc. Perkin, 1993, Jour. Chem. Soc. Chem. Commn., 1996, Heterocycles, 1974—; contbr. over 500 articles to profl. jours. Recipient Alexander von Humboldt award Fed. Republic of Germany, 1984, Disting. Alumni award NYU, 1990, award in synthetic chemistry Am. Chem. Soc., 1985, A.C. Cope Scholar award, 1987, Yamada prize, Japan, 1996, award Internat. Soc. Heterocyclic Chemistry, 1997; named Man of Yr., New Orleans Jaycees, 1968, Boyd Prof. La. State U., 1969; recipient pioneer award Am. Insts. Chemists, 1998. Fellow AAAS, Nat. Acad. Sci.; mem. Royal Soc. Chemistry (silver medalist 1982), Phila. Organic Chemistry Soc. (Allan Day award 1987). Home: 1500 Hepplewhite Ct Fort Collins CO 80526-3822 Office: Colo State Univ Dept Chemistry Fort Collins CO 80523-0001 E-mail: aimeyers@lamar.colostate.edu.

MEYERS, ALBERT THOMAS MARIE, academic counsellor; b. Luxembourg, Luxembourg, May 31, 1946; s. Hubert and Annelise (Jansen) M.; m. Angela Maria Delahaye, June 5, 1971; children: Annette, Christiane, Philippe, Catherine. Mech. Engring. Diploma, Tech. Coll. Aachen, Germany, 1970; Dr.Ing., U. Bochum, Germany, 1976. Sci. employee U. Bochum, 1970-76, acad. counsellor, 1976-77, sr. acad. counsellor, 1977—. Guest lectr. Tongji U., Shanghai, 1983; lectr. U. Bremen, Germany, 1987-89. Reviewer Applied Mechanics Revs., 1983-85; contbr. articles to profl. jours. Mem. GAMM. Avocations: classical music, church organ. Home: Maischützenstr 1 D-44805 Bochum Germany Office: Univ of Bochum Universitaetsstr 150 D-44780 Bochum Germany E-mail: meyers@web.de., meyers@tm.bi.ruhr.uni-bochum.de.

MEYERS, AMY, museum director; m. Jack Meyers; 1 child, Rachel. BA, U. Chgo.; PhD in Am. Studies, Yale U. Rschr. Dumbarton Oaks; rschr. Ctr. for Advanced Study in Visual Arts, Nat. Gallery; curator Am. Art, Henry E. Huntington Libr., Art Collections and Bot. Gardens, San Marino, Calif.; dir. Yale Ctr. for Brit. Art; prof. art Yale U. Adj. faculty Calif. Inst. Tech.; vice chair, Huntington rep. Assn. Rsch. Insts. in History of Art, 1995—2000. Co-editor (with Margaret Pritchard): Empire's Nature: Mark Catesby's New World Vision; co-editor: (with Alan Trachtenberg and Neil Gray Jr.) Classic Essays on Photography. Office: Yale Ctr for Brit Art PO Box 208280 1080 Chapel St New Haven CT 06520-8280

MEYERS, ANN ELIZABETH, sports broadcaster; b. San Diego, Mar. 26, 1955; d. Robert Eugene and Patricia Ann (Burke); m. Donald Scott Drysdale, Nov. 1, 1986; children: Donald Scott Jr., Darren John, Drew Ann. Grad., UCLA, 1978. Profl. basketball player N.J. Gems, 1979-80; profl. basketball player Ind. Pacers NBA, 1979; sports broadcaster Ind. Pacers, 1979-80; sportscaster men's basketball U. Hawaii, Honolulu, 1981-82; sportscaster men's and women's basketball UCLA, 1982-84, 89—; sportscaster volleyball, basketball, softball, tennis ESPN, 1981—; sportscaster Olympic Games ABC, L.A., 1984; sportscaster volleyball, softball, tennis, basketball, soccer Sportsvision, 1985-87; sportscaster volleyball, basketball, softball Prime Ticket, 1985-97; sportscaster CBS-TV, 1991—, ESPN Women's Basketball, Fox Women's Basketball, WNBA-NBC World Championships; sportscaster Olympic Games NBC, Sydney, Australia, 2000. Sportscaster Goodwill Games, WTBS, 1986, 90; sportscaster basketball NBC and ESPN, 1996-97, WNBA, NBA, ESPN, 1996—. Winner Silver medal Montreal Olympics, 1976, Gold medal Pan Am. Games, 1975, Silver medal, 1979, All-Am. UCLA, 1975, 76, 77, 78; 1st woman named to Hall of Fame UCLA, 1987; named to Women's Sports Hall of Fame, 1987, Orange County Sports Hall of Fame, 1985, Calif. H.S. Hall of Fame, 1990, Basketball Hall of Fame, 1993, Nat. H.S. Hall of Fame, 1995, NBC Hoop It Up, 1995, 96, 97, Cath. Youth Orgn. Hall of Fame, 1996, Women's Basketball Hall of Fame, 1999. Office: c/o Lampros and Roberts 16615 Lark Ave Ste 101 Los Gatos CA 95032-7645

MEYERS, ARCHIE L., JR., risk management consultant; Various mgmt. positions Crawford & Co., Atlanta, 1959, br. mgr., 1976, pres., claims svc. bus. unit, 1995-98, pres., chief oper. officer, 1998, chair, CEO, 1999—. Office: Crawford & Co 5620 Glenridge Dr NE PO Box 5047 Atlanta GA 30302

MEYERS, CAROL LYONS, religion, history and archaeology educator; b. Wilkes Barre, Pa., Nov. 26, 1942; d. Harry J. and Irene R. (Winkler) Lyons; m. Eric Mark Meyers, June 25, 1964; children: Julie Kaete, Dina Elisa. AB with honors, Wellesley Coll., 1964; MA in Near Ea. and Judaic Studies, Brandeis U., 1966, PhD, 1975. Area supr. Joint Expdn. to Tell Gezer, Israel, 1964—67; editorial asst., asst. to registrar Ashdod Excavation Project, Israel, 1963—65; quadrangle dir. Brandeis U., Waltham, Mass., 1965—67; teaching asst. Boston Area Seminar Internat. Students, 1965; area supr., lect. Joint Expdn. to Khirbet Shema, Israel, 1970—71, area supr., 1971, field supr., 1972; assoc. dir. Joint Expdn. to Meiron, Israel, 1978; co-dir. Joint Sepphoris Project, Israel, 1985—, Sepphoris Regional Project, Israel, 1993—; instr. Bible Acad. Jewish Studies without Walls, N.Y.C., 1974—78; instr. Ctr. Continuing Edn., Duke U., Durham., NC, 1978—79; asst. prof. religion Duke U., Durham., NC, 1977—84, assoc. prof., 1984—90, assoc. dir. women's studies, 1985—, prof., 1990—, acting dir. women's studies, 1992, Mary Grace Wilson prof., 2002—, acting dir., Judaic studies, 2004. Internat. corr. fellow Rennert Ctr. for Jerusalem Studies, Bar Ilan Univ., 1998—. Author: The Tabernacle Menorah, 1976; Excavations at Ancient Meiron, Upper Galilee, Israel, 1971—72; Excavations at Ancient Meiron, Upper Galilee, Israel, 1974—75; Excavations at Ancient Meiron, Upper Galilee, Israel, 1977; author: The Word of the Lord Shall Go Forth, 1983, Haggai, Zechariah 1-8, 1987, Discovering Eve: Ancient Israelite Women in Context, 1988, Sepphoris, 1991, Zechariah 9-14, 1993, Ethics and Politics in the Hebrew Bible, 1995, Community, Identity and Ideology: Social Science Approaches to the Hebrew Bible, 1996, Sepphoris in Galilee: Cross-Currents of Culture, 1996, Families in Ancient Israel, 1997, Women in Scripture: A Dictionary of Named and Unnamed Women in the Hebrew Bible, The Apocryphal/Deuterocanonig Books, and the New Testament, 2000; contbr. articles to profl. jours. Bd. dirs. Bethel Community, Durham, 1980. Recipient Wellesley Coll. Alumnae Achievement award, 1999, Edn. Endowment award, Women's Inst. for Continuing Jewish Edn., 2001; grantee Ednl. Found. Girls, 1963, 1964, Brandeis U., 1996, Undergrad. Tchg. Coun. Duke U., 1978—79, Coop. Program in Judaic Studies, 1981; Wellesley Coll. scholar, 1962—64, Brandies U. fellow, 1967—69, Thayer fellow, Albright Inst. Archaeol. Rsch., Jerusalem, 1975—76, NEH fellow, 1982—83, 1990—91, Oxford Ctr. for Postgrad. Hebrew Studies fellow, 1982—83, Queen Elizabeth House fellow, Oxford U., 1982—83, Howard Found. fellow, 1984—85, Ctr. Theol. Inquiry fellow, 1990—91, rsch. assoc., Fachbereich Evangelische Universität, U. Frankfort, 1995, Duke Rsch. Coun., 1983—84, 1984—85, 1987—88, 1990—91, 1992—93, 1993—94. Mem.: N.C. Mus. Art (Judaica com. 2003—), Hadassah (edn. chmn. 1970—71), Soc. for Values Higher Edn., Nat. Women's Studies Assn., Soc. Bibl. Lit. (chmn. seminar 1981, steering com. seminar on monarchy 1982, program com. 2000—), Israel Exploration Soc., Albright Inst. Archaeol. Rsch. (fellowship com. 1979—82, v.p. 1982—94, trustee 1994—, chair, Dever prize com. 2001—), Cath. Bibl. Assn., Brit. Sch. Archaeology Jerusalem, Assn. Jewish Studies, Archaeol. Inst. Am. (v.p. 1976, sec. treas. 1984—85), Am. Sch. Oriental Rsch. (com. on archaeol. policy 1976—81, com. on pubs. 1977—92, editl. com. 1978—, com. on archaeol. policy 1997—2003, 2003—), Am. Acad. Religion, Jewish Fedn. Mem. Jewish Reconstructionist Ch. Home: 3202 Waterbury Dr Durham NC 27707-2416 Office: Duke U Dept Religion PO Box 90964 Durham NC 27708-0964 Office Phone: 919-660-3514.

MEYERS, CHRISTINE LAINE, marketing and media executive, consultant; b. Detroit, Mar. 7, 1946; d. Ernest Robert and Eva Elizabeth (Laine) M.; 1 child, Kathryn Laine; m. Oliver S. Moore III, May 12, 1990. BA, U. Mich., 1968. Editor indsl. rels. diesel divsn. Gen. Motors Corp., Detroit, 1968; nat. advt. mgr. J.L. Hudson Co., Detroit, 1969-76, mgr. internal sales promotion, 1972-73, dir. pub., 1973-76; nat. advt. mgr. Pontiac Motor divsn., Mich., 1976-78; pres., owner Laine Meyers Mktg. Cos., Inc., Troy, Mich., 1978—; founder, owner CORP! Mag., 1998—. Dir. Internat. Inst. Met. Detroit, Inc. Contbr. articles to profl. publs. Bus. adv. coun. Ctrl. Mich. U., 1977-79; pub. adv. com. on jud. candidates Oakland County Bar Assn.; adv. bd. Birmingham Cmty. Hosp., Bank of Am., 1999-2001; bd. dirs. YMCA, Mich., 1992-98, Haven, 1997—, Automation Alley, Oakland County, 1999—. Named Mich. Ad Woman of Yr., 1976, one of Top 10 Working Women, Glamour mag., 1978, one of 100 Best and Brightest Advt. Age, 1987, one of Mich.'s top 25 female bus. owners Nat. Assn. Women Bus. Owners, One of Top 10 Women Owned Bus., Mich., 1994; recipient Vanguard award Women in Comm., 1986, Lifetime Achievement award Northwood U., 2002. Mem. Internat. Assn. Bus. Communicators, Adcraft Club, Women's Advt. Club (1st v.p. 1975), Women's Econ. Club (pres. 1976-77), Internat. Women's Forum Mich. (founding pres. 1986-97), Internat. Inst. Detroit (bd. dirs. 1986-89), Detroit C. of C., Troy C. of C., Mortar Bd., Quill and Scroll, Pub. Rels. Com. Women for United Found., Founders Soc. Detroit Inst. Arts, Fashion Group, Pub. Rels. Soc. Am., First Soc. Detroit (exec. com. 1970-71), Kappa Tau Alpha. Home: 5165 Longmeadow Rd Bloomfield Hills MI 48304-3657 Office: Laine Meyers Mktg Cos Inc 3645 Crooks Rd Troy MI 48084-1642 Office Phone: 248-458-2677 x301. Business E-Mail: cmyers@corpmagazine.com.

MEYERS, DANIEL MICHAEL, music educator, researcher; b. Manistee, Mich., Sept. 14, 1960; s. Robert F. Sr. and Elaine F. Meyers; m. Melissa Dawn Guertin. BMus Edn., U. Mich., 1983. Freelance profl. musician trumpet, 1983—; dir. of bands Grand Traverse Area Cath. Schools, Traverse City, Mich., 1983—86; music instr. West Shore C.C., Scottville, Mich., 1990—99, prof. music and humanities, 1999—; music dir. St. Johns Luth. Ch., Ludington, Mich., 1991—. Bd. dirs. Manistee Symphony Orch. and Chorus, 1999—2001, White Pine Music Com., Ludington, 1998—2002; mem. adv. bd. LudingtonCity Band Shell, 1997. Mem.: Mich. Sch. Band and Orch. Assoc., Coll. Band Directors Nat. Assoc. Roman Catholic. Avocations: golf, hunting, music composition, skiing, boating. Home: 1507 Moody St Whitehall MI 49461 Office: West Shore CC 3000 N Stiles Rd Scottville MI 49454 Personal E-mail: dmeyers@westshore.edu. E-mail: dmeyers@westshore.edu.

MEYERS, DAVID GEORGE, internist, cardiologist, educator; b. Muscatine, Iowa, Oct. 5, 1950; BS, Loras Coll., 1972; MD, U. Iowa, 1976; MPH, Med. Coll. Wis., 1998. Intern Creighton U., 1976-77, resident medicine, 1977-79; fellow cardiology Med. Coll. Va., 1979-81; from asst. prof. internal medicine to assoc. prof. Neb. U. Med. Ctr., Omaha, 1981-93; mem. faculty U. Kans. Med. Ctr., Kansas City, 1994, prof. internal medicine and preventive medicine, 1994—, dir. of preventive Cardiology, 1994—. Fellow ACP, Am. Coll. Cardiology, Am. Coll. Chest Physicians, Am. Heart Assn., Am. Coll. Preventive Medicine; mem. Am. Coll. Epidemiology, Am. Soc. Preventive Cardiology. Office: U Kans Med Ctr 3901 Rainbow Blvd Kansas City KS 66160-0001 Business E-Mail: dmeyers@kumc.edu.

MEYERS, DAVID L. food products executive; CFO Del Monte Foods, San Francisco. Office: Del Monte Foods PO Box 193575 San Francisco CA 94119-3575

MEYERS, ERIC MARK, religion educator; b. Norwich, Conn., June 5, 1940; s. Karl D. and Shirlee M. (Meyer) M.; m. Carol Lyons, June 25, 1964; children: Julie Kaete, Dina Elisa. AB, Dartmouth Coll., 1962; MA, Brandeis U., 1964; PhD, Harvard U., 1969. Lerner prof. religion, archeol., bibl. study, ancient hist. Duke U., Durham, N.C., 1969—, dir. grad. program in religion, 1979-86, 2001—; dir. Annenberg Inst., Phila., 1991-92. Pres. Am. Schs. of Oriental Rsch., Balt., 1990—96; commentator on biblical archaeology; dir. 8 digs Israel, Italy, 1970—2000; co-dir. seminar Duke U., 2004. Author: 10 books; co-author: The Cambridge Companiion to the Bible, 1997; editor (in chief): The Oxford Encyclopedia of Archaeology in the Near East, 5 vols., 1997; contbr. articles more than 350 to profl. jours.; frequent guest (TV series) A&E channel, Discovery channel; frequent guest: History Channel. Jewish. Avocations: singing (baritone), golf, the arts, travel. Home: 3202 Waterbury Dr Durham NC 27707-2416 Office: Duke U 118 Gray Bldg PO Box 90964 Bldg Durham NC 27708-0964 E-mail: emc@duke.edu.

MEYERS, GEOFFREY GROMAN, financial executive; b. rochester, Minn., Apr. 5, 1944; s. Ward Carl and Ruth (Groman) M.; m. Molly Ann Murtagh, July 31, 1982. BA, Northwestern U., 1966; MBA, Ohio State U., 1969. With Owens-Ill. Inc., 1970—, mgr. strategic planning glass container div., 1980-82, dir. ops. control, 1984-86, dir. fin., asst. treas., 1986-88; exec. v.p. fin./adminstrn. Health Care and Retirement Corp. (subs. Owens-Ill. Inc.), Toledo, 1988—; asst. to chmn. Gerresheimer Glas, Deusseldorf, Fed. Rep. Germany, 1982-84. Mem. Inverness Club. Avocations: family, sports. Office: Health Care and Retirement Corp 1 Seagate Toledo OH 43604-1558

MEYERS, GERALD A. metal products executive; With Logan Aluminum Inc., Bowling Green, Ky., Alcan & Logan, U.S. and Canada; pres., coo Ravenswood Aluminum Corp., W.Va., pres & CEO, Century Aluminum Corp., Monteray, Calif., 1992—. Office: Century Aluminum Corp 2511 Garden Rd Monterey CA 93940

MEYERS, GERALD CARL, finance educator, writer, expert witness, consultant; b. Buffalo, Dec. 5, 1928; s. Meyer and Berenice (Meyers) M.; m. Barbara Jacob, Nov. 2, 1958. BS, Carnegie Inst. Tech., 1950, MS with distinction, 1954. With Ford Motor Co., Detroit, 1950-51, Chrysler Corp., Detroit and Geneva, 1954-62; with Am. Motors Corp., Detroit, 1962-84, v.p., 1967-72, group v.p. product, 1972-75, exec. v.p., 1975-77, pres., 1977-84, COO, 1977, chmn., CEO, 1977-82, ret., 1984; Ford disting. prof. Grad. Sch. Indsl. Adminstrn. Carnegie Mellon U., Pitts., 1985-96; prof. U. Mich. Bus. Sch., Ann Arbor, 1995—. Pres. Gerald C. Meyers Assocs., Inc., West Bloomfield, Mich.; adj. prof. Sch. Bus. U. Mich., Ann Arbor. Author: When It Hits the Fan, Managing the Nine Crises of Business; co-author: Dealers, Healers, Brutes and Saliors; bus. commentator Nat. Pub. Radio, Fox News Cable TV, CNBC TN Network; contbr. articles to N.Y. Times, Wall St. Jour., L.A. Times. 1st lt. USAF, 1951-53. Decorated Legion of Honor (France). Mem. Econ. Club Detroit, Tau Beta Pi, Phi Kappa Phi, Omicron Delta Kappa. Address: U Mich Bus Sch D 3246 701 Tappan Ave Ann Arbor MI 48109-1217 Office: 5600 W Maple Rd Ste B216 West Bloomfield MI 48322-3787

MEYERS, HOWARD L. lawyer; b. Dec. 22, 1948; BS, U. Del., 1970; JD, U. Va., 1973. Bar: Pa. 1973. Sr. ptnr. in bus. and fin. sect., mng. ptnr. Phila. office Morgan, Lewis & Bockius. Mem. ABA, Phila. Bar Assn., Greater Phila. C. of C. (mem. exec. com., bd. dirs., gen. counsel). Office: Morgan Lewis & Bockius 1701 Market St Philadelphia PA 19103-2903

MEYERS, JAMES B. secondary school educator; Social studies tchr. Farmington (N.H.) High Sch. Named N.H. State Social Studies Tchr. of Yr., 1993. Office: Farmington High Sch 1 Thayer Dr Farmington NH 03835

MEYERS, JAMES FRANK, electronics engineer; b. Binghamton, N.Y., Sept. 9, 1946; s. Edwin Fox and Louise (Okrepkie) M. BEE, U. Louisville, 1969, ME, 1972; postgrad., George Washington U. Instr. elec. engring. lab. U. Louisville, 1968-69; engring. coop. technician Langley Research Ctr., NASA, Hampton, Va., 1966-69, aerospace technologist, 1969—. Contbr. articles to profl. jours.; patentee in field. Mem. IEEE (sect. chmn. 1975), Turnberry Two Owners Assn. (pres., dir. 1979-82), Sports Car Club Am. (div. rallye exec. 1982-86), Eta Kappa Nu, Tau Beta Pi, Sigma Tau. Office: NASA Langley Rsch Ctr Mail Stop 493 Hampton VA 23681-0001 Business E-Mail: James.F.Meyers@nasa.gov.

MEYERS, JAN, retired congresswoman; b. Lincoln, Nebr., July 20, 1928; m. Louis Meyers; children: Valerie, Philip AA in Fine Arts cum laude, William Woods Coll., 1948; BA in Communications (hon.), U. Nebr.-Lincoln, 1951; LittD, William Woods Coll., 1986; LLD (hon.), Baker U., 1993. Mem. Overland Park (Kans.) City Coun., 1967-72; pres. Overland Park City Council; mem. Kans. Senate, 1972-84, chmn. pub. health and welfare com., local govt. com.; mem. 99th-103rd Congresses from 3rd Kans. Dist., 1985-97, mem. com. internat. rels., chmn. sml. bus. com., mem. com. on econ. and ednl. opportunities. Chmn. pub. health and welfare com., chmn. local govt. com., vice chmn. transp. com., vice chmn. utilities com. Kans. Senate. 3rd Dist. co-chmn. Bob Dole for U.S. Senate, 1968; chmn. Johnson County Bob

Bennett For Gov., 1974; mem. Johnson County Cmty. Coll. Found.; bd. dirs. Johnson County Mental Health Assn.; mem. fundraising com. Johnson County Am. Cancer Soc.; mem. com. for Ctr. for Aging, Kans. U. Med. Ctr.; bd. dirs. Johnson County Libr. Assn. Recipient Outstanding Elected Ofcl. of Yr. award Assn. Cmty. Mental Health Ctrs. Kans., Woman of Achievement Matrix award Women in Communications, Disting. Service award Bus. and Profl. Women Kansas City, William Woods Alumna award of distinction, Cmty. Svc. award Jr. League Kansas City, 1st Disting. Legislator award Kans. Assn. C.C.s, Outstanding Svc. award Kans. Library Assn., United Community Services, Kans. Pub. Health Assn., award Gov.'s Conf. Child Abuse and Neglect, Outstanding Legislator award Kans. Action for Children, Friend award Nat. Assn. County Park and Recreation Ofcls., 1987, Disting. Alumna award, 1991, Spirit of Enterprise award U.S. C. of C., Guardian of Small Bus. award Nat. Fedn. Ind. Bus. Mem. LWV (past pres. Shawnee Mission) Methodist.

MEYERS, JOHN ALLEN, magazine publisher; b. Winnetka, Ill., Feb. 21, 1929; s. Fred W. and Ruth B. (Burras) M.; m. Jane Bowers, Sept. 18, 1954; children: Jennifer, Katherine, John. BA, Mich. State U., 1951, Litt.D. (hon.), 1978; postgrad., Columbia U., 1965. Mgr. Cleve. Time mag., 1960-63, mgr. Chgo., 1963-65, mgr., 1965-68, worldwide advt. sales dir., 1968-72; v.p. Time, Inc., publisher Sports Illustrated mag., 1972-78; pub. Time mag., 1978-85; chmn. Time Inc. Mag. Co., 1985-88; chmn. emeritus Time Inc., 1988—. Appointed presdl. bd. adv. on Pvt. Sector Initiatives; chmn. J.A.M. Enterprises. Editor-in-chief Constitution mag. Bd. dirs, pres., Found. for the U.S. Constn. Served with USMC, 1951-53. Decorated Purple Heart. Office: Time & Life Bldg 1221 Avenue Of The Americas New York NY 10020-1001

MEYERS, JOSEPH MICHAEL, biologist, researcher; b. York, Pa., Nov. 20, 1948; s. James Harry and Jane Rojahn Meyers; m. June Rose Wagner; children: Christy, Alita Sara, Annie Jane. BS, Lebanon Valley Coll., 1970; MS in Forest Resources, U. Ga., 1978, PhD, 1982. Postdoc. rsch. assoc. Savannah River Ecology Lab., Aiken, SC, 1983—84; state program coord. nongame wildlife Ala. Dept. Conservation, Montgomery, Ala., 1984—90; rsch. wildlife biologist US Geol. Svc. Patuxent Wildlife Rsch. Ctr., Athens, Ga., 1990—. Consulting biologist Dames & Moore, Cranford, NJ, 1973—75. Editor (guest editor): Southea. Naturalist, 2001—; contbr. Our Living Resources, articles to profl. jours. Recipient Wildlife Conservationist of Yr., Dixie Zool. Soc., 1984. Mem.: Assn. Tropical Biology, Wilson Ornithol. Soc., Am. Ornithologists' Union, Cooper Ornithol. Soc., Neotropical Ornithol. Soc. (treas. 1999—2003), Brit. Ornithologists' Union, Am. Inst. Biol. Sci., Wildife Soc. (newsletter editor 1999—2002, Svc. Award 2001), Sigma Xi. Achievements include development of method to radio-mark parrots for 1 year; restoration of bald eagle to SE US. Avocations: fishing, canoeing, oceanography, music, coin collecting/numismatics. Office: USGS Patuxent Wildlife RschCenter U Ga Warnell Sch Forest Res Athens GA 30602-2152 E-mail: jmeyers@smokey.forestry.uga.edu.

MEYERS, KAREN DIANE, lawyer, educator, corporate officer; b. Cin., July 8, 1950; d. Willard Paul and Camille Jeannette (Schutte) M.; m. William J. Jones, Mar. 27, 1978. BA summa cum laude, Thomas More Coll., 1974; MBA, MEd, Xavier U., 1978; JD, U. Ky., Covington, 1978. Bar: Ohio 1978, Ky. 1978; CLU; CPCU; cert. structured settlement cons. Clk. to mgr. Baldwin Co., Cin., 1970-78; adj. prof. bus. Thomas More Coll., Crestview Hill, Ky., 1978—, CSSC-U. Notre Dame, 1994, CSSC, 1994; asst. sec., asst. v.p., sr. counsel The Ohio Life Ins. Co., Hamilton, 1978-91; prin. KD Meyers & Assocs., 1991; v.p. Benefit Designs, Inc., 1991-96, Little, Meyers, Garretson & Assocs., Ltd., Cin., 1996—; adj. prof. Miami U., 1998—. Bd. dirs. ARC, Hamilton, 1978-83, vol., 1978—; bd. dirs. YWCA, Hamilton, 1985-91. Gardner Found. fellow, 1968-71; recipient Ind. Progress award Bus. & Profl. Women, 1990. Fellow Life Mgmt. Inst. Atlanta; mem. ABA, Soc. Chartered Property Casualty Underwriters (instr. 1987—), Cin. Bar Assn., Butler County Bar Assn., Ohio Bar Assn., Ky. Bar Assn. Roman Catholic. Avocations: aerobics, jogging, crafts. Home: 7903 Hickory Hill Ln Cincinnati OH 45241-1363

MEYERS, LAWRENCE EDWARD, state judge; m. Barbara Meyers; children: Kelli Kelli, Clay. BA in History and Chemistry, So. Meth. U., 1970; JD, U. Kans., 1973; postgrad., U. Tex., Arlington, Tex. Wesleyan U. Asst. dist. atty. Montgomery County, Kans., 1973—75; pvt. practice Ft. Worth, 1975—88; assoc. justice U.S. Ct. Appeals (2nd cir.), Ft. Worth, 1988—92; judge Ct. Criminal Appeals, Ft. Worth, 1992—. Instr. Tex. Christian U., Ft. Worth. Mem. parish coun. St. Mary's of Assumption, Ft. Worth. Mem.: Tarrant County Bar Assn., State Bar Kans., State Bar Tex. Republican. Office: Court of Criminal Appeals Supreme Ct Bldg 201 W 14th St Austin TX 78701-1614 also: PO Box 12308 Austin TX 78711-2308

MEYERS, LINDA DEE, federal agency administrator; b. Chgo., Dec. 31, 1945; m. L. Richard Meyers; 2 children. BA in Phys. Edn. & Health with honors, Goshen Coll., 1968; MS in Nutrition, Colo. State U., 1974; PhD in Human Nutrition, Cornell U., 1978. Tchr. Swaneng Hill Secondary Sch., 1968-71; staff Bioteko Rural Coop., Serowe, Botswana, 1972; rsch. asst. dept. food sci. and nutrition Colo. State U., 1973-74; scientist Nat. Ctr. Health Statistics HHS, Washington, 1976-78, sr. nutrition advisor, 1986—, dep. dir. & team leader nutrn., environ. hlth. & sci. coord., 1996—; exec. dir., food & nutrition bd. Inst. of Med. of the Nat. Academies, Washington, 2003—. Contbr. articles to profl. jours. Mem. APHA, Am. Soc. Nutritional Scientists, Am. Soc. Clin. Nutrition, Am. Soc. Nutritional Scis., Omicron Nu, Phi Kappa Phi. Office: Inst of Med 500 Fifth St NW Washington DC 20001

MEYERS, MARLENE O. retired health facility administrator; m. Eugene Meyers; children: Lori, Lisa, Dean. BSN, U. Sask., 1962; postgrad., U. Oslo, Norway, 1973; MSc, U. Calgary, Alta., Can., 1976; continuing edn., Harvard U., 1980, Banff Sch. Mgmt., 1985, U. Western Ont., Can., 1993; EMT-B, Scottsdale C.C., 2000. RN, Ariz. Various nursing positions, Alta. and B.C., Can., 1962-69; instr., chair Mount Royal Coll. Allied Health, Calgary, 1969-82; asst. exec. dir. Rockyview Hosp., Calgary, 1982-85; v.p. patient svcs. Calgary Gen. Hosp., 1985-91, pres., CEO, 1991-95, Meyers and Assocs. Health Care Mgmt. Cons., Calgary, 1995—98; clin. nurse Scottsdale Behavioral Health Ctr., 1999—. Surveyor Can. Coun. on Health Facilities Accreditation, 1986-97; mem. adv. com. for South Caucasus Health info. project, Can. Adv. Com. Named Calgary Woman of Yr. in field of Health, 1982; recipient Heritage of Svc. award, 1992. Mem. Alta. Assn. RNs (hon.), Can. Coll. Health Svcs. Orgn., Can. Exec. Svcs. Orgn., Can. Soc. for Internat. Health (bd. dirs. 1997-2001, South Caucasus adv. com. 2001—), Rotary Internat. Home and Office: 244 Osprey Cir Hope ID 83836-9664 also: 10464 E Cannon Dr Scottsdale AZ 85258-4929

MEYERS, MARY ANN, foundation administrator, writer, consultant; b. Sodus, N.Y., Sept. 30, 1937; d. Harold Galpin and Clarice Mildred (Daniel) Dye; m. John Matthew Meyers, Aug. 22, 1959; children: Andrew Christopher, Anne Kathryn. BA magna cum laude, Syracuse U., 1959; MA, U. Pa., 1965, PhD, 1976. Editorial asst. Ladies' Home Jour., Phila., 1959-62; editor, asst. dir. news bur. U. Pa., Phila., 1962-65, asst. to pres., 1973-75, univ. sec., lectr. Am. civilization, 1980-90; contbg. writer The Pennsylvania Gazette, Phila., 1965—97; dir. coll. rels., editor Haverford Horizons, lectr. in religion Haverford (Pa.) Coll., 1977-80; pres. The Annenberg Found., St. Davids, Pa., 1990-92; v.p. for external affairs Moore Coll. Art and Design, Phila., 1995-97; sr. fellow The John Templeton Found., Radnor, Pa., 1997—. Vis. com. dept. biology U. Pa., 1996—2002; mem. bd. advisors The Peter Gruber Found., St. Thomas, U.S. V.I., 2001—. Author: A New World Jerusalem, 1983, Art, Education and African American Culture: Albert Barnes and the Science of Philanthropy, 2004; contbg. author: Death in America, 1975, Gladly Learn, Gladly Teach, 1978, Coping with Serious Illness, 1980, Religion in American Life, 1987; contbr. articles to profl. jours. Judge recognition program Coun. for Advancement and Support Edn., Washington, 1977—78, chair creative editing and writing workshop, 1978; mem. Picker Found. Program on Human Qualities in Medicine, N.Y.C., Phila., 1980—83; del. Phila.-Leningrad Sister Cities Project, 1986; trustee U. Pa. Press., 1985—; vice chmn. U. Pa. 250th Anniversary Commn., 1987—90; mem. steering com. of bd. trustees U. Pa., Annenberg Sch. for Comm., 1990—92; mem. adv. bd. U. Pa., Annenberg Ctr. for the Performing Arts, 1990—98; mem. bd. overseers U. Pa., Sch. Arts and Scis., 1990—97; mem. steering com. of bd. trustees Annenberg Ctr. for Comm., U. So. Calif., L.A., 1990—92, The Annenberg Washington Program in Comm. Policy Studies of Northwestern U., Washington, 1990—92; dir., sec. Am. Acad. Polit. and Social Sci., 1992—, World Affairs Coun. Phila., 1990—95; dir. Diagnostic and Rehab. Ctr., Phila., 1993—2002. Recipient Excellence award Women in Communications, Inc., 1973-74, award for pub. affairs reporting Newsweek/Coun. for Advancement and Support Edn., 1977, Silver medal Coun. for Advancement and Support Edn., 1986. Mem. Am. Acad. Polit. and Social Sci. (sec. and dir. 1992-), Cosmopolitan Club, Sunday Breakfast Club, Phi Beta Kappa (mem. steering com. Delaware Valley chpt. 1995-97). Roman Catholic. Home: 217 Gypsy Ln Wynnewood PA 19096-1112

MEYERS, MICHAEL E. venture capitalist; Biotechnology, med. device rsch. assoc. Hambrecht & Quist, N.Y.C.; spl. asst. to CEO St. Barnabas Comm. Enterprises, N.Y.C.; v.p., health care investment banking., head pharm. & drug delivery focus group Cowen & Co., N.Y.C.; dir., biotechnology and pharm. investment banking Merrill Lynch & Co., N.Y.C.; ptnr., mng. dir. Global Biomedical Partners, 2000—02; mng. mem. Trivium Capital Mgmt., N.Y.C., 2002—. Bd. dirs. Triad Therapeutics, Devax, Clearant, and Vision Technologies. Office: Trivium Capital Mgmt 540 Madison Ave New York NY 10022-3213

MEYERS, MORTON ALLEN, physician, radiology educator; b. Troy, N.Y., Oct. 1, 1933; s. David and Jeanne Sarah (Dunn) M.; m. Beatrice Applebaum, June 1, 1963; children— Richard, Amy. MD, SUNY, Upstate Med. Coll., 1959. Diplomate Am. Bd. Radiology. Intern Bellevue Hosp., N.Y.C., 1959-60; resident in radiology Columbia-Presbyn. Med. Ctr., N.Y.C., 1960-63; fellow Am. Cancer Soc., 1961-63; prof. dept. radiology and medicine Cornell U. Med. Ctr., N.Y.C., 1973-78; prof., chmn. dept. radiology SUNY Sch. Medicine, Stony Brook, 1978-91, prof. dept. radiology, 1991-98, disting. univ. prof., 1998—. Vis. investigator St. Mark's Hosp., London, 1976; spkr. Radiol. Soc. N.Am., 1986. Author: Diseases of the Adrenal Glands: Radiologic Diagnosis, 1963, Dynamic Radiology of the Abdomen: Normal and Pathologic Anatomy, 1976, 5th edit., 2000, Iatrogenic Gastrointestinal Complications, 1981; series editor: Radiology of Iatrogenic Disorders, 1981-86; editor: Computed Tomography of the Gastrointestnal Tract: Including the Peritoneal Cavity and Mesentery, 1986, Neoplasms of the Digestive Tract: Imaging, Staging, and Management, 1998; founding editor in chief Abdominal Imaging, 1976—; mem. editl. bd. Iatrogenics, Surg. and Radiol. Anatomy; contbr. chpts. to med. textbooks, articles to profl. jours.; speaker in field. Served to capt. M.C. U.S. Army, 1963-65. Fellow Am. Coll. Radiology, Am. Coll. Gastroenterology; mem. Radiol. Soc. N.Am., Am. Roentgen Ray Soc., Am. Gastroenterol. Assn., Soc. Uroradiology, Soc. Gastrointestinal Radiologists, Assn. Univ. Radiologists, N.Y. Roentgen Ray Soc., N.Y. Acad. Gastroenterology, European Soc. Gastrointestinal and Abdominal Radiology (hon.), European Assn. Radiology (hon.), Alpha Omega Alpha. Home: 14 Wainscott Ln East Setauket NY 11733-3816 Office: SUNY Health Scis Ctr Sch Medicine Dept Radiology Stony Brook NY 11794-0001

MEYERS, NANCY JANE, screenwriter, producer, director; b. Phila., Dec. 8, 1949; d. Irving H. and Patricia (Lemisch) M. BA, Am. U., Washington, 1971. Dir.: (films) The Parent Trap, 1998, What Women Want, 2000, Somethings Gotta Give, 2003; prodr.: (films) Private Benjamin (Acad. award nominee, Writers Guild award 1980), Baby Boom, 1987, Father of the Bride, 1991, A Place to be Loved (assoc. prodr.), 1991, I Love Trouble, 1994, Father of the Bride Part II, 1995, Ted Hawkins: Amazing Grace (co-prodr.), 1996, What Women Want, 2000, The Affair of the Necklace, 2001, Something's Gotta Give, 2003; wrote.: (films) Private Benjamin, 1980, Irreconcilable Differences, 1984, Protocol, 1985, Baby Boom, 1987, Father of the Bride, 1991, Once Upon A Crime..., 1992, I Love Trouble, 1994, Father of the Bride Part II, 1995, The Parent Trap, 1998, Something's Gotta Give, 2003. Mem. ASCAP, Acad. Motion Picture Arts and Scis., Writers Guild Am. West. Office: Creative Artists Agy 9830 Wilshire Blvd Beverly Hills CA 90212-1825

MEYERS, PAMELA SUE, lawyer; b. Lakewood, N.J., June 13, 1951; d. Morris Leon and Isabel (Leibowitz) M.; m. Gerald Stephen Greenberg, Aug. 24, 1975; children: David Stuart Greenberg, Allison Brooke Greenberg. AB with distinction, Cornell U., 1973; JD cum laude, Harvard U., 1976. Bar: N.Y. 1977, Ohio 1990. Assoc. Stroock & Stroock & Lavan, N.Y.C., 1976-80; staff v.p., asst. gen. counsel Am. Premier Underwriters, Inc., Cin., 1980-96; legal counsel Citizens Fed. Bank, Dayton, Ohio, 1997-98; gen. counsel, sec. Mosler Inc., Hamilton, Ohio, 1998—2001. Bd. dirs. Hamilton County Alcohol and Drug Addiction Svc. Bd., 1996-2000, Adath Israel Synagogue, 1999—. Mem. Cin. Bar Assn., Harvard Club of Cin. (pres. 1998-99, bd. dirs. 1993-2000), Phi Beta Kappa. Jewish. Avocations: piano, reading, tennis. Home: 3633 Carpenters Creek Dr Cincinnati OH 45241-3824 Personal E-mail: psmeyers@fuse.net.

MEYERS, RICHARD JAMES, landscape architect; b. Columbus, Ohio, Jan. 25, 1940; s. Ralph Joseph and Margaret Mary (Kruse) M.; m. Mary Igoe, Jan. 12, 1963; children: Gregory James, Helen Marie, Andrew James. B.Landscape Arch., Ohio State U., 1961. Registered landscape architect, Ohio, Mich., Fla., Ind.; cert. Council Landscape Archtl. Registration Bds. Jr. planner Columbus Planning Commn. (Ohio), 1960-62; landscape architect Behnke-Nes & Assocs., Cleve., 1962-65, Arthur Hills & Assocs., Toledo, 1965-67; ptnr. Mortensen-Meyers Assocs., Toledo, 1967-69; prin. MMSS Inc., Toledo, 1969-71, The Collaborative, Inc., Toledo, 1973-99; bd. dirs., past pres. Council Landscape Archtl. Registration Bd., Syracuse, N.Y., 1978-86, Ohio Bd. Landscape Architect Examiners, 1975-83. Adv. bd. Ohio State U. Land Architecture, 1999—, Toledo Mcpl. Cemetery Commn., 1999—; bd. dirs. Toledo Botanical Gardens, 2000—; trustee adv. coun. Schedel Arboretum & Gardens, 2000-; mem. Scenic Ohio adv. bd., 1998-; mem. Natural Resources Assistance Coun., State of Ohio, 2001-; mem. USGA course-rating com., Toledo Dist., 2002-. Mem. St. Vincent Hosp. and Med. Ctr. Assocs., Toledo, 1978—83; com. mem. Downtown Toledo Vision, Inc., 1988—99; chmn. Toledo Lucas County Plan Commn., 1989—99, Toledo Adminstrv. Bd. Zoning Appeals, 1994—99; chmn. campaign divsn. United Way, 1991; bd. dirs. Family Svcs. Grater Toledo, 1977—82, Toledo Ctrl. City Neighborhood, 2001—; com. mem. Toledo Met. Area Coun. of Govt., 1972—79, 1987—89, Toledo Bot. Gardens Design Rev. Bd., 1988—90; chmn. Met. Parks Com. of 25, 1991, 1997, 2002; mem. adv. bd. U. Toledo-Stranahan Arboretum, 1994—. Dumbarton Oaks Jr. summer scholar, 1960; recipient First Honor Design award Am. Assn. Nurserymen, 1974; named Disting. Alumnus, Ohio State Univ. Coll. Engring., 1996. Fellow Am. Soc. Landscape Architects (merit design award Ohio chpt. 1975, 81, 83, 85, Outstanding Svc. to Profession award 1983, Ohio Chpt. medal 1984); mem. AIA, Ohio Chpt. of Am. Soc. Landscape Architects (v.p. 1974-76), Urban Land Inst., Soc. for Coll. and Univ. Planning, Am. Forestry Assn., Am. Planning Assn., Rails to Trails Conservancy, Ohio Pks. and Recreation Assn., Heatherdowns Country Club (bd. dirs. 1983). E-mail: rjmeyers@buckeye-express.com. *I am fortunate to be part of a profession dedicated to improving and beautifying our physical environment through the preservation and protection of our natural resources and by the sensitive blending of economic and social needs with these natural systems. Landscape architecture provides me with a great deal of personal satisfaction.*

MEYERS, ROBERT ALLEN, chemist, publisher; b. LA, May 15, 1936; s. Jack B. Meyers and Pearl (Cassell) Thorpe; m. Roberta Lee Hart, June 24, 1961 (div. 1976); children: Tamara, Robert Jr.; m. Ilene Braun, Feb. 27, 1977; children: Jenifer, Jacalyn. BA, San Diego State U., 1959; PhD, UCLA, 1963. Postdoctoral fellow, mem. faculty Calif. Inst. Tech., Pasadena, 1963-64; rsch. scientist Bell & Howell Rsch. Ctr., Sierra Madre, Calif., 1965; project mgr. TRW Def. & Space, Redondo Beach, Calif., 1966-81; bus. area mgr. TRW Energy Group, Redondo Beach, 1981-86; mgr. process devel. TRW Def. & Space, Redondo Beach, 1986-88, mgr. new projects devel., 1988-95; pres. Ramtech Ltd., Mill Valley, Calif., 1995—. Del. U.S.-USSR Working Group, Washington and Moscow, 1973-80; chmn. adv. bd. Guide to Nuclear Power Tech., NYC, 1982-84; adv. coun. chemistry dept. UCLA, 1991—. Author: Coal Desulfurization, 1977; editor: Coal Handbook, 1981, Coal Structure, 1982; editor: Handbook of Petroleum Refining Processes, 1986, 3rd edit., 2003, Handbook of Synfuels Technology, 1984, Handbook of Energy Technology and Economics, 1983, Handbook of Chemicals Production Processes, 1986, 2d edit., 2004, others; editor-in-chief Ency. Phys. Sci. and Tech., 1987, 92, 2001, Ency. of Modern Physics, 1990, Ency. Lasers and Optics, 1991, Ency. Telecom., 1989, Molecular Biology and Biotech., 1995, Ency. Molecular Biology and Molecular Medicine, 1995, Ency. Environ. Analysis and Remediation, 1998, Ency. Environ. Pollution and Control, 1999, Ency. of Analytical Chemistry, 2000, Ency. Molecular Cell Biology and Molecular Medicine, 2004. Mem.: Am. Soc. Cell Biology, Am. Inst. Chem. Engrs., Am. Chem. Soc. Avocations: swimming, bicycling, tennis, golf. Office: Ramtech Ltd 7 Harbor Point Dr Mill Valley CA 94941 Personal E-mail: robertmeyers101@comcast.net.

MEYERS, SHARON MAY, sales executive; b. Whittier, Calif., Feb. 8, 1946; d. Hubert Miller and Garnet May (Prater) Jones; m. Gary Lee Klink, June 18, 1966 (div.); children: Robert Douglas, Jeffrey Loren; m. Carl Eugene Meyers, Dec. 16, 1989. Student, Pasadena Coll. (scholar), 1963-65; AA, Rio Hondo Coll., 1978; student, Calif. State U., Fullerton, 1978; BSBA, U. Redlands, 1982. Sec. Armorlite Lens Co., Pasadena, 1963-64, James, Pond & Clark, Pasadena, 1964-65; sales sec. Fiberboard Paper, Commerce, Calif., 1965-67; instr. aide East Whittier Sch. Dist., Calif., 1974-78; sales rep. Gen. Can Co., Montebello, Calif., 1978-86, Brouse-Whited Creative Packaging, Marina del Rey, Calif., 1986; br. mgr. Gen. Can Inc., Hayward, Calif., 1986-88; bus. banking mgr. Wells Fargo Bank NA, San Jose, Calif., 1988-89; sales rep. Moore Bus. Products, Colorado Springs, Colo., 1990-93, Assoc. Bus. Products, Santa Rosa, Calif., 1993-94, Advantage Bus. Forms, Oreg., 1994-96, Tekprinting Svcs., Inc., Medford, Oreg., 1996—. Sec. ch. bd. Ch. of the Nazarene, 1973-76, childrens dir., 1965-69; youth dir. Womens Christian Temperance Union, 1965-69; treas. PTA, 1977-79; bd. dirs. Bay ARea Crisis Nursery, Concord, Calif.; vol. Valley Meml. Nosp. Emergency Rm., Livermore, Calif., vol. lunch buddy program Washington Elem. Sch., 1999—. Named Sales Rep of Yr. Moore Bus. Products, 1991. Republican. Avocations: writing, cooking. Home: PO Box 1413 Shady Cove OR 97539-1413 E-mail: mckeymse1989@aol.com., sharon@tek-printing.com.

MEYERS, STUART IRWIN, real estate developer; b. N.Y.C., Aug. 7, 1941; s. Herman and Helen Noah Meyeroff; m. Carol Ann Goldstein, Sept. 26, 1964 (div. Apr. 1970); m. Arlene Merryl Meyers, June 20, 1976 (div. Sept. 1998); children: Wendy Jill Meyers-Crabb, Jeffrey Brian. BS in Econ., U. Pa., 1963; MBA in Acctg., Columbia U., 1964. CPA N.Y., Fla. Sr. auditor Price Waterhouse & Co., NYC, 1964-68; dir. corp. devel. mergers and acquisitions ITT Corp., NYC, 1969-73; staff v.p. mergers and acquisitions RCA Corp., NYC, 1973—75; v.p. contr./CFO trucks equipment div. Hertz Corp., 1975—76; v.p. mergers and acquisitions Kraft Inc., Glenview, Ill., 1976-81; sr. v.p. mergers and acquisitions United Brands Corp., 1981-84; sr. v.p. devel. The Related Co., Miami, Fla., 1985-93; chmn., founder, prin. The Cornerstone Group, Coral Gables, Fla., 1993—; chmn. Cornerstone Strats., LLC, St. Thomas. Bd. dirs. Affordable Housing Tax Credit Coalition, Washington; bd. dirs., founder Affordable Housing Providers, Tallahassee; bd. dirs., trustee Nat. Assn. Home Builders Multifamily Coun., Chgo., 1997. Named Pillars of the Industry - Freddie Mac "Builder of the Yr.", 2003; recipient Builder of the Yr. Award, Multifamily Exec. Mag., 2003. Mem.: AICPA, N.Y. State CPA Soc., Fla. CPA Soc., St. Thomas Yacht Club, LaGorce Country Club (founder), Penn Club, Dade Alumni Club U. Pa. (bd. dirs.), Wharton Sch. Club S. Fla. (bd. dirs.). Jewish. Avocations: piano, golf, ranching, skiing, yachting. Office: Cornerstone Strategies LP 6100 Red Hook Quarters Ste B2-5 Saint Thomas VI 00802 Home: Elysian Beach Resort Unit # 349 Saint Thomas VI 00802 Office Phone: 340-715-6099.

MEYERS, TEDSON JAY, lawyer; b. Bayonne, N.J., May 6, 1928; s. Irving and Norma Miriam (Anson) M.; m. Patricia Elizabeth Sullivan, Apr. 10, 1965 (div. Apr. 1978); children: Mary, John, Katherine; m. Lynn Scholz, Aug. 6, 1978 (div. Oct. 1992); m. Arden Schell, Dec. 27, 2000. Student, Ohio State U., 1945-47; BA, NYU, 1949, MA, 1950; JD, Harvard U., 1953. Bar: D.C. 1953, N.Y. 1957, U.S. Supreme Ct. 1971. Asst. counsel Office Gen. Counsel, Dept. Navy, Washington, 1955-56; assoc. Liebman, Eulau & Robinson, N.Y.C., 1956-58; staff counsel for govt. regulations ABC, N.Y.C., 1958-61; adminstrv. asst. to chmn. FCC, Washington, 1961-62; asst. to dir., dir. overseas ednl. TV projects Peace Corps, Washington, 1962-68; pvt. practice Washington, 1968-70; ptnr. Sullivan Beauregard Meyers & Clarkson, Washington, 1970-74, Peabody Lambert & Meyers, Washington, 1974—84, Reid & Priest, Washington, 1984-96, Coudert Brothers, Washington, 1996—2003. Adj. prof. comm. San Diego State U., 1993—; founding pres. Harvard Legis. Rsch. Bur., 1952—53; mem. White House Task Force on Ednl. TV Overseas, 1966—68; trustee Global Legal Info. Network Found., 2001—; mem. adv. panel on internat. telecomm. law U.S. State Dept., 1987—; bd. govs. Internat. Coun. for Computer Comm., 1986—, pres., 2000—02; bd. dirs. Cyber Century Forum. Contbr. conf. papers and articles to profl. publs. Mem. City Coun. Washington, 1972-75; bd. govs. Met. Washington Coun. Govts., 1973-75; chmn. Bicycle Fedn. of Am., 1977—; bd. dirs. U.S. Coun. for World Comm. Yr. 83, 1982-84; dir. The Arthur C. Clarke Found. of the U.S. Inc., 1987—, chmn., 2003—; bd. dirs. Friends of Law Libr. Congress, 2001-, pres., 2003-. Lt. USMC, 1953-55, Korea. Recipient Sec. of Army Pub. Svc. medal; rsch. fellow Carnegie Found., 1949. Fellow: Am. Bar Found.; mem.: ABA (sect. sci. and tech. 1982—85, coun. mem. sect. sci. and tech. 1983—87, chmn. standing com. law libr. congress 2000, co-founder and chmn. internat. telecomm. com.), Internat. Telecomm. Acad. Russia (hon. academician 2002—), Soc. Satellite Profls., Pacific Telecomm. Coun., Royal TV Soc., Internat. Inst. Comm., Fed. Comm. Bar Assn., Cosmos Club Found. (trustee, chmn. 1985—88, 1990—), Cosmos Club (pres. 1988—90), Alpha Epsilon Pi. Avocations: bicycling, motorcycling, computers, sculling, military music. Office: Ste 1200 1627 I St NW Washington DC 20006-4007 E-mail: tmeyers@tedson.com.

MEYERS, WAYNE MARVIN, microbiologist; b. Huntingdon County, Pa., Aug. 28, 1924; s. John William and Carrie Venca (Weaver) Meyers; m. Esther Louise Kleinschmidt, Aug. 26, 1953; children: Amy, George, Daniel, Sara. BS in Chemistry, Juniata Coll., 1947, DSc (hon.), 1986; diploma, Moody Bible Inst., 1950; MS in Med. Microbiology, U. Wis., 1953, PhD in Med. Microbiology, 1955; MD, Baylor Coll. Medicine, 1959. Instr. Baylor Coll. Medicine, 1955-59; intern Conemaugh Valley Meml. Hosp., Johnstown, Pa., 1959-60; staff physician Berrien Gen. Hosp., Berrien Center, Mich., 1960-61; missionary physician Am. Leprosy Missions, Congo/Zaire, Burundi, 1961-73; prof. pathology Sch. Medicine U. Hawaii, Honolulu, 1973-75; chief microbiology divsn. Armed Forces Inst. Pathology, Washington, 1975-89, chief mycobacteriology, 1989—, registrar leprosy registry, 1975—; mem. leprosy panel U.S.-Japan Coop. Med. Sci. Program, 1976-83; mem. sci. adv. bd. Leonard Wood Meml., 1981-85, sci. cons. dir., 1985-87, sci. dir., 1987-90; cons., 1990—; rsch. affiliate Tulane U., 1981—. Bd. dirs. Gorgas Meml. Inst. Tropical and Preventive Medicine, Inc. Bd. dirs. Jour. Leprosy, 1978—93; contbr. chapters to books, articles to profl. jours. Adv. bd. Damien-Dutton Soc. Leprosy Aid, Inc., 1983—96, corp. bd. dirs., 1996—; adv. bd. Am. Leprosy Missions, Inc., 1979—88, chmn. bd. dirs., 1985—88, program cons. to bd. dirs., mem. bd. references, 1988—; mem. Hansen's Disease rsch. adv. com. Gillis W. Long Hansen's Disease Ctr., Carville, La., 1985—92, chmn., 1985—92; mem. Buruli Ulcer task force WHO, 1998—. With U.S. Army, 1944—46. Allergy Found. Am. fellow, 1957, 1958, WHO Rsch. grantee, 1978—87. Mem.: Internat. Soc. Travel Medicine, Binford-Dammin Soc. Infectious Disease Pathologists (sec.-treas. 1988—91, pres. 1995—96), Am. Soc. Microbiology, Am. Soc. Tropical Medicine and Hygiene, Internat. Soc. Tropical Dermatology, Internat. Acad. Pathology, Internat. Leprosy Assn. (councillor 1978—88, pres. 1988—93), Sigma Xi. Achievements include research in human and experimental leprosy, and other mycobacterial diseases. Office: Armed Forces Inst Pathology Washington DC 20306-6000 Office Phone: 202-782-1873. Personal E-mail: wmekmeyers@erols.com.

MEYERSON, ADAM, foundation administrator; b. Phila., Aug. 2, 1953; s. Martin and Margy Ellin (Lazarus) M.; m. Nina Hope Shea, Sept. 13, 1986; children: Thomas Abraham, William Ulysses, Henry Elijah. BA, Summa Cum Laude, Yale U., 1974; student, Harvard U., 1977-79. Mng. editor The Am. Spectator, Bloomington, Ind., 1974-77; editorial writer Wall St. Jour., N.Y.C., 1979-83; editor Policy Rev. The Heritage Found., Washington, 1983-98, v.p. ednl. affairs, 1993—2001; pres. Philanthropy Roundtable, Washington,

2001—. Co-editor: The Wall Street Journal on Management, 1985. Home: 3714 Ingomar St NW Washington DC 20015-1820 Office: Philanthropy Roundtable 1150 17th St NW # 503 Washington DC 20036

MEYERSON, CHRISTOPHER CORTLANDT, lawyer; b. Princeton, N.J., July 7, 1962; s. Dean and Beatrice Meyerson; m. Megumi Kawaguchi; children: Kenneth, David. BA in Govt. magna cum laude, cert. in L.Am. studies, MA in History, Harvard U., 1985; MPhil in Polit. Sci., Columbia U., 1993; LLM, Kyoto (Japan) U., 1994; JD, Columbia U., 2001. Bar: D.C. 2001. Intern Bur. Inter-Am. Affairs, Office Policy Planning/Coord. U.S. State Dept., Washington, summer 1982; rsch. asst. Harvard U., 1982-83; intern, rschr. macro econ. rsch. dept. Banco Itau, São Paulo, 1983-84; human rights intern Coalition for Homeless, N.Y.C., summer 1988; legal intern gen. counsel Mus. Modern Art, N.Y.C., summer 1989; law clk. Office of Chief Counsel for Internat. Commerce U.S. Commerce Dept., Washington, summer 1991; editl. asst. Kyoto Comparative Law Ctr., summer 1994, 95; vis. scholar Associated Kyoto Program, 1996. Summer assoc. Venable, Baetjer, Howard & Civiletti, Washington, 1998; law clk. Office of Chief Counsel for Import Adminstrn., U.S. Commerce Dept., Washington, 1999-2000. Author various publs. on internat. trade. Recipient scholarship, Japanese Govt., 1991—97, Jr. Scholar award, Internat. Studies Assn. Internat. Polit. Economy, 2000. Mem. ABA. Episcopalian. Home: 7306 Summit Ave Chevy Chase MD 20815-4030

MEYERSON, IVAN D. lawyer, holding company executive; AB, U. Calif., Berkeley, 1966; JD, Stanford U., 1969. Bar: Calif. 1970. Assoc. Herzstein & Maier, San Francisco, 1970-75, ptnr., 1976-78; atty. SEC, 1975-76; assoc. gen. counsel McKesson Corp, San Francisco, 1984-87; v.p., gen. counsel McKesson Corp., San Francisco, 1987-98; sr. v.p., gen. counsel McKesson - HBOC Inc., San Francisco, 1998—. Office: McKesson Corp 1 Post St Ste 3275 San Francisco CA 94104-5292

MEYERSON, LAWRENCE BERNARD, physician; b. Columbus, Ohio, Feb. 4, 1941; s. Joseph Randall and Minnie (Lemel) M.; m. Harriet Seldon, June 14, 1964; children: Michael, Jeffery, Daniel. BA, Ohio State U., 1962, MD, 1965. Diplomate Am. Bd. Dermatology. Intern Tripler Gen. Hosp., Honolulu, 1965-66; resident Brooke Gen. Hosp., San Antonio, 1966-69; chief of dermatology Walson Army Hosp., Ft. Dix, N.J., 1969-71; pres. Dermatology Ctr. PA, Irving, Tex., 1971—. Asst. clin. prof. U. Tex. S.W. Med. Sch., Dallas, 1971—. Contbr. articles to profl. jours. Maj. U.S. Army, 1965-71. Fellow Acad. Dermatology, Soc. of Laser Medicine and Surgery, Soc. Dermatol. Surgery; mem. Dallas County Med. Soc., Tex. Dermatologic Soc., Dallas Dermatologic Soc. (past pres.), Alpha Omega Alpha. Avocations: photography, skiing, boating. Office: Dermatology Ctr PA 2015 W Park Dr Irving TX 75061-2113

MEYERSON, MARGY ELLIN, urbanist, civic volunteer; b. Washington, Feb. 25, 1923; d. Arthur and Frieda (Langer) Lazarus; m. Martin Meyerson, Dec. 31, 1945; children: Adam, Laura (dec.), Matthew. BA, U. Chgo., 1943; postgrad., Harvard U., 1947-48, U. Pa., 1953-56; MA, Bryn Mawr Coll., 1953, U. Pa., 1993. Asst. to gen. counsel Pa. Postwar Planning Commn., 1944-45; assoc. Phila. Housing Assn. and Citizens Council on City Planning, 1945; mgmt. staff Chgo. Housing Authority, 1946. Cons. Ill. Postwar Planning Commn., 1948; assoc. Com. on Nat. Policy, Yale U., 1948-49; lectr. social scis. Drexel U., 1956-57, city and regional planning U. Calif., Berkeley, 1965-66; bd. dirs., exec. com. Phila. Regional Housing Assn., 1952-57; v.p., treas. Community Devel Co., Inc., 1957-63; bd. dirs., exec. com. Niagara Frontier Housing Devel., 1967-70; co-chmn. Cathedral Pk. Devel., Buffalo, 1968-70; commr. Phila. City Planning Commn., 1971-81; bd. dirs. Tensiodyne, Inc., Girard Bank Co-editor: Urban Housing, 1966, Japanese translation 1975; co-editor abstracts sect. Jour. Am. Inst. Planners, 1952-60. Trustee Oakland (Calif.) Mus., 1965-66; trustee Rosenbach Found., Rosenbach Mus. and Library, 1975—, chmn. 1979-92; trustee Presby.-U. Pa. Med. Ctr., 1983-95, exec. com. 1985-95; trustee Lewis Stevens Community Trust, 197785, v.p. 197985; mem. Pa. Humanities Council, 1981-86; adv. council Hampshire Coll., 1981—; bd. dirs. World Affairs Council, Am. Coll. in Paris Found., 1982-87; trustee Presbyn. Found. Phila., 1995-, New Courtland Elder Svcs., 1985-; overseer U. Pa. Libr., 1990-, co-chmn. Friends of the Libr., 1990-. Recipient Susan B. Anthony prize Bryn Mawr Coll., 1953, ann. award for best paper Nat. Hwy Rsch. Bd., 1953; named Disting. Dau. of Pa., 1982; Martin and Margy Meyerson Professorship named in their honor U. Pa., 1995, Martin and Margy Meyerson chair fgn. affairs named in their honor Philippine Women's U., Manila. Mem. Prytanean Soc., Martin Margy Meyerson Conf. Ctr., Cosmopolitan Club (Phila.). Address: 2016 Spruce St Philadelphia PA 19103-6524

MEYERSON, MARTIN, university educator, urban and regional planner; b. N.Y.C., Nov. 14, 1922; s. Samuel and Etta (Berger) M.; m. Margy Ellin Lazarus, Dec. 31, 1945; children: Adam, Laura (dec.), Matthew. BA, Columbia U., 1942; MCP, Harvard U., 1949; LLD, U. Pa., 1970, Queen's U., Can., 1968, Shiraz U., Iran, 1973, U. Edinburgh, 1976; PhD honoris causa, Hebrew U., 1987; also 18 other hon. doctorates including ScD, LHD, LittD, DFA, DHum, 1967-98. Mem. staff Michael Reese Hosp., Chgo., 1945-47; asst. prof. coll. and grad. social scis. U. Chgo., 1948-52; assoc. prof., dept. chair city and regional planning U. Pa., 1952-56, prof., 1956-57, pres., 1970-81, pres. emeritus, 1981—, chmn. U. Pa. Press, chmn. adv. bd. Inst. Rsch. Higher Edn., Fels Ctr. Govt., 1981—, bd dirs. Lauder Inst. Mgmt. and Internat. Studies, co-chmn. Commn. for U. Pa. 250th Anniversary, 1987-90, Univ. prof., 1977—; exec. dir. action Am. Coun. to Improve Our Neighborhoods, 1955-56, trustee, 1956-66; Frank Backus Williams prof. city planning and urban rsch. Harvard U., 1957-63, acting dean Grad. Sch. Design, 1963; founding dir. Joint Ctr. for Urban Studies, MIT and Harvard U., 1958-63; dean, prof. urban devel. Coll. Environ. Design, U. Calif., Berkeley, 1963-66; interim chancellor U. Calif., Berkeley, 1965; pres., prof. public policy SUNY, Buffalo, 1966-70; prof. Inst. Urban Rsch. U. Pa.; dir. visitor Inst. for Advanced Study, Princeton, N.J., 1983-84; pres. U. Pa., 1986-99. Dir. Real Estate Rsch. Corp., 1961-67, Marine Midland Bank, 1966-70, 1st Fidelity Bancorp. (now First Union), Scott Paper Co., Penn Mut. Life, Saint Gobain Corp., Certain Teed, Norton, Avatar, Universal Health Svcs.; cons. to govts., pvt. firms U.S. and abroad, UN missions, urban/econ. devel. to, Japan, Indonesia and South Asia, Yugoslavia, 1958-65; sr. advisor urban and regional pub. and pvt. devel. Arthur D. Little, Inc., 1958-66; cons. Sears Roebuck Found., 1958-69; chmn. bd. Western N.Y. Nuclear Rsch. Ctr., 1966-70; adv. coun. NASA, 1960-65; White House presdl. task forces, urban policy, 1960-69; mem. coun. Electric Power Rsch. Inst., 1973-77; mem. U.S. del. UN Conf. on Sci. and Tech. for Less Developed Areas, 1963. Author: (with E. C. Banfield) Politics, Planning and the Public Interest, 1955, Housing, People and Cities, 1962, Face of the Metropolis, 1963, Boston, 1966, Gladly Learn and Gladly Teach, 1978; editor: Conscience of the City, 1970, McGraw-Hill Series on Cmty. Devel.; mem. editorial bd. Ency. Britannica, 1980-98, Daedalus, 1972-90. Mem. Air Conservation Commn., 1962-66; mem. Bay Area Conservation and Devel. Commn., 1965-66; chmn. Assembly Univ. Goals and Governance, 1969-74; commr. N.Y. State Commn. on Post-Secondary Sch. Edn., 1976-77; hon. prof. Nat. U. Asuncion, 1969—, Beijing U., 1996—; bd. dirs. Phila. Bicentennial Corp., 1970-76, Greater Phila. Partnership, 1973-81, Afro-Am. Film Found., 1966-70, Niagara U., 1968-70, Center for Community Change, 1968-72, Acad. Religion and Mental Health, 1970-78, Center for Ednl. Devel., 1967-70, Phila. Mus. Art, 1974—, Nat. Urban Coalition, 1969-78; trustee, Niagara U., 1968-70, Am. Coll., 1982-92, Curtis Inst. Music, 1987-94, United World Coll.N. Mex., 1984—, Am. Schs. Oriental Rsch., 1985—, Tel Aviv U., Coll. Bd., 1986-92, Hebrew U., Internat. House Ctr., Monell Chem. Senses Ctr., chmn., 1993—, Fgn. Policy Rsch. Inst., 1981—, Panasonic Found., 1982—, Ctr. for Visual History, U.S. Com. on the Constl. System; founding dir. Internat. Centre for Study East Asian Devel. Japan; Inst. for Internat. Edn., 1971—, chmn., 1981-85; bd. dirs. Internat. Council Ednl. Devel., 1971-94, Am. Council Financial Aid to Edn., 1975-81, Open Univ. Found., U.K., 1979-82; chmn. council pres. Nat. Accelerator Lab., 1972-73; co-chmn. Images (French TV), 1976-79, Salzburg Seminar Bd., 1978—, sr. fellow, 1997—; co-chmn. Marconi Internat. Fellowship Found., chair exec. com., 1978-96, chmn. bd. dirs., 1996—; Internat. gov. Center Environ. Studies, London, 1966-84; mem. sr. exec. council Conf. Bd., 1970-77; trustee Aspen Inst., 1976-96; chair coun. UN Centre for Regional Devel., Nagoya, Japan, 1983-93; chair internat. selection commn. Phila. Liberty Medal, 1988—; bd. overseers Koc Univ., Bosphorus, Turkey, 1994—; bd. dirs. Internat. Literacy Inst., 1995—. Decorated commendatore Knight-Commdr. (Italy); chevalier de l'Ordre Nat. de Mérite (France); Order of the Rising Sun Emperor of Japan; recipient Einstein medal Am. Technion Soc., 1976, Disting. Achievement award U. Calif. Berkeley, 1984, John Jay award Columbia U., 1982, Disting. Educator award Assn. Collegiate Schs. of Planning, 1996; overseas fellow Churchill Coll. Urban Planning, Cambridge U., 1983; hon. fellow Soc. for Tech. Communication, 1988; Wheelwright fellow Harvard U.; Meyerson Hall named in his honor U. Pa. Grad. Sch. Fine Arts; Martin and Margy Meyerson Professorship named in honor U. Pa., 1995, Philippine Women's U., Manila. Fellow Am. Acad. Arts and Scis., Royal Soc. Arts (Franklin fellow), Buckminster Fuller Inst. of Design Scis. (founder), Am. Philos. Soc. (exec. com.), Nat. Acad. Edn.; mem. Am. Soc. Planning Ofcls. (past dir., aide to exec. dir.), Am. Inst. Planners (past gov., spl. award winner), Internat. Assn. Univs. Paris (Am. dir. 1975—, head 1982-85, hon. pres. 1985—), Coun. Fgn. Rels., European Acad. Arts, Scis. and Letters (academician), Phi Beta Kappa. Clubs: Philadelphia, Century (N.Y.C.), Cosmos (Washington), U. Pa. (N.Y.C.). Office: Univ Pa 225 Van Pelt Library Philadelphia PA 19104

MEYERSON, SEYMOUR, retired chemist; b. Chgo., Dec. 4, 1916; s. Joseph and Rena (Margulies) M.; m. Lotte Strauss, May 22, 1943; children: Sheella, Elana. SB, U. Chgo., 1938, postgrad., 1938-39, 47-48, George Williams Coll., 1939-40; DSc (hon.), Valparaiso Univ., Ind., 1995. Inspector powder & explosives Kankakee Ordnance Works, Joliet, Ill., 1942; chemist Deavitt Labs., Chgo., 1941-42; from chemist to rsch. cons. Standard Oil Co. (Ind.) Rsch. Dept. (now BP Corp.), Whiting, Ind.-Naperville, Ill., 1946—84. Mem. indsl. adv. coun. chemistry dept. U. Okla., Norman, 1967-69; Frontiers in Chemistry lectr. Wayne State U., 1965; invited spkr. James L. Waters Symposium, Pitts. Conf., Chgo., 1995. Charter mem. editl. adv. bd. Organic Mass Spectrometry, 1968-87, Mass Spectromony Revs., 1980-87; author, co-author 190 sci. publs. 2d lt. AUS, 1943-46, ETO. Mem. Am. Chem. Soc. (Frank H. Field and Joe L. Franklin award for outstanding achievement in mass spectrometry 1993), Am. Soc. for Mass Spectrometry. Achievements include research in chemistry of gas-phase organic ions; patents in field. Home: 43 Vermont Ct Unit A1 Asheville NC 28806-3058 Personal E-mail: meyerson43@hotmail.com.

MEYERSON, STANLEY PHILLIP, lawyer; b. Apr. 13, 1916; s. Louis A. and Ella Meyerson; m. Sherry Maxwell, Nov. 30, 1996; children: Marianne Martin, Camilla, Margot Ellis, Stanley P. AB, Duke U., 1937, JD, 1939. Bar: SC 1939, NY 1940, Ga. 1945, US Supreme Ct. Ptnr. Johnson Hatcher & Meyerson, Atlanta, 1945-55, Hatcher, Meyerson, Oxford & Irvin, Atlanta, 1955-78, Westmoreland, Hall, McGee, Oxford & Meyerson, Atlanta, 1978-88, McGee & Oxford, Atlanta, 1988—. Former adj. prof. Ga. State U.; dir., officer various corps. Contbr. Co-founder West Paces Ferry Hosp., Atlanta, Annandale at Suwanee for the Handicapped; trustee Hudson Libr., Inc., Highlands, NC, MetroGroup, Atlanta; del. Moscow Conf., Law and Bilateral Econ. Rels., 1990. Lt. comdr. USNR, 1943—45. Mem.: ABA (former professionalism com.), Atlanta Bar Assn. (former sec.), Ga. Bar Assn. (former chmn. tax com.), Georgians for Nixon (chmn. 1960), Duke U. Alumni Assn. (former pres. Atlanta chpt.).

MEYER WEISGERBER, MARTHA LINDSEY, account executive; b. Summit, N.J., May 28, 1955; d. William Harold and Hattie Griffin (Ward) Meyer; m. James Curtis Weisgerber, June 22, 1991; 1 child, Emily Griffin. BA, Wake Forest U., 1977. Sales-mfrs. rep. Philip Morris Tobacco Co., Winston-Salem, 1977-82; pharm. sales rep. USV Pharm. Divsn.-Revlon Corp., Winston-Salem, 1982-84, Upjohn Pharms., N.J., 1984-89; hsop. sales rep., med. sys. rep., area account mgr. Lederle Labs. divsn. Am. Cyanamid, 1989—. Deacon, elder First Presbyn. Ch., Cranford, N.J., 1995—. Mem. Jr. League Elizabeth Plainfield (bd. mem. 1991-92). Republican. Avocations: swimming, gardening. Home: 313 N Union Ave Cranford NJ 07016-2414 Office: Wyeth Ayerst Pharm PO Box 7447 Philadelphia PA 19101-7447

MEYLER, NICHOLAS JAMES, management consultant; b. San Fernando, Calif., Dec. 31, 1959; s. James Albert and Dorothy Adele (Leifson) Meyler. AB in Philosophy, Princeton U., 1981. Asst. quality control mgr. Calif. Tech. Plating Corp., San Fernando, 1986—87; sales exec. west coast MacDermid, Inc., San Fernando, 1987—89; mng. ptnr. Wingate Dunross, Inc., Agoura Hills, Calif., 1989—. Author (inventor, rschr.): (rsch. into time-travel cryptography) The Encryptment Thesis. Scholarship, Joy Mfg. Co., 1977—81. Mem.: US Fencing Assn. (assoc.). Republican. Achievements include discovery of Strong evidence of Time-travel and Alternate Universes encrypted (and deciphered) in major artworks by Mozart, Bach, etc; invention of Encryptment Thesis: Methodologies, patterns, and systems of practical reasoning to predict and prevent catastrophes, using logic and metaphysics based upon the presumption of time-travel; Prediction/ prevention of catastrophe based on time-travel and theory of naming; research in deciphering time-travel encrypted fragments in artworks, researching predictive methods with applications to National Security, etc; invention of Iran-contra plot, which I devised out of a passage (p. 518) of James Joyce's Finnegans Wake, and submitted to the Whitehouse, in 1984. Avocations: fencing, chess, mountain climbing, hiking, weight-training. Office: Wingate Dunross Inc 30851 Agoura Rd #301 Agoura Hills CA 91301 Office Phone: 818-597-3200 ext. 211. E-mail: nickm@wingate-dunross.com.

MEYLER, WILLIAM ANTHONY, financial executive; b. Newark, Oct. 29, 1944; s. Raymond Francis and Margaret (Loveless) M.; BS, St. Joseph's Coll., 1966; MBA, Fairleigh Dickinson U., 1974; m. Dana Irene Brennan, May 3, 1975; children: Daniel, Diana. CPA, N.J. Sr. acct. Ernst & Young, Trenton, N.J., 1970; dir. acctg. Baker Industries, Inc., Parsippany, N.J., 1971-72; mgr. corp. acctg. Witco Chem. Corp., N.Y.C., 1973-75, asst. to controller, 1976-79, asst. controller world-wide ops., 1977-82, asst. controller mgmt. info. systems, 1982-84; ptnr. Letters, Meyler & Co., CPAs, 1984-91; cons., exec. v.p. Investment Techs., Inc., Edison, N.J., 1985-91, also bd. dirs.; pvt. practice, Middletown, N.J., 1991—; exec. v.p., CFO Gateways to Space, Inc., 1994-96, also bd. dirs.; adj. prof. Monmouth Coll., 1983-85. Fellow N.J. Soc. CPA's; mem. AICPA, Am. Acctg. Assn., Middletown C. of C., Rotary. Home: 30 Southview Ter S Middletown NJ 07748-2415 Office: One Arin Park 1715 Highway 35 Middletown NJ 07748-1867 Office Phone: 732-671-2244.

MEYSTEL, MICHAEL A. Internet executive; b. Moscow, Feb. 12, 1973; came to the U.S., 1978; s. Alexander M. and Marina M. (Selitsky) M.; m. Robin L. Weiss, May 25, 1997 (div.); 1 child, Jacob. Student, Drexel U., 1989—94. Sys. and network adminstr. Drexel U., Phila., 1991—94; sr. sys. analyst Bell Atlantic, Malvern, Pa., 1994—95; pres., CEO Cognisphere, Inc., West Chester, Pa., 1995—; sr. sys. analyst Decision One Corp., Malvern, 1995—96; cons., application developer Shared Med. Sys., Malvern, 1996—97, Conectiv Energy, Newark, Del., 1997—98, Anderson BDG, Inc., Allentown, Pa., 1998; cons./tech. lead The Vanguard Group, Valley Forge, Pa., 1998—; dir. info. tech. MRDS, Inc., 1999—2003, COO, 2003—. Sys. cons. ADREM, Inc., Bala, Pa., 1991-94; rsch. asst. Siemens Corp. Rsch., Princeton, N.J., 1992; pres., CEO ICSC Corp., West Chester, 1995-2000. Achievements include inventor/patentee apparatus for text structuring. Office: Cognisphere Inc PO Box 2591 West Chester PA 19380

MEZACAPA, EDNA S. music educator, elementary school educator; b. Flint, MI, Jan. 23, 1948; d. Jack E. and Vlasta A. Tremayne; m. Nicklas A. Mezacapa, July 25, 1970; children: Amy Anne, Sara Marie. MusB, Heidelberg Coll., Tiffin, Ohio, 1970. Gen. music tchr. Bellevue (Ohio) City Schs., 1969—73; youth choir dir. Findlay Episc. Ch., Findlay, Ohio, 1975—78; subs. tchr. Rochester (N.Y.) Schs., 1979—81; youth choir dir. Ch. of the Epiphany, Rochester, 1979—81; music tchr., K-8 St. Mary's Cath. Sch., Kalamazoo, 1981—82, St. Ludmila Cath. Sch., Cedar Rapids, Iowa, 1984—86; tchr. Christian edn. Calvary Episc. Ch., Rochester, Minn., 1986—87; subs. music tchr., 1-6 Rochester City Schs., Rochester, Minn., 1988—90, music tchr., 1-6, 1990—. Dir. Calvary Episc. Youth Choir, 1995—96, Suzuki Orch., 2001—03. Dir. youth choir Calvary Episcopal Ch., 1996—97; dir. Suzuki Orch., 2001—03.

MEZEI, MIHALY, chemist; b. Budapest, Hungary, June 17, 1944; came to U.S., 1973; s. Arpa and Eva (Erdély) Mezei; m. Katalin Agnes Bencsáth, July 2, 1970. Diploma, Eötvös Lorand U., Budapest, Hungary, 1966, PhD, 1972. Systems programmer Hungarian Chem. Industries, Budapest, Hungary, 1966-72, Young & Rubican Internat. Inc., N.Y.C., 1973—74; postdoctoral fellow NYU, N.Y.C., 1974—76; sr. rsch. assoc. Hunter Coll., CUNY, N.Y.C., 1976—86, adj. assoc. prof., 1976-78, 88-90; mgr. biomolecular computing N.Y.C., 1987—91; rsch. assoc. prof. Mt. Sinai Sch. Medicine, CUNY, N.Y.C., 1991—. Mem. grad. chemistry faculty CUNY, Grad. Ctr., N.Y.C., 1989—; mem. sci. adv. bd. Locus Pharms., 1991-94. Contbr. more than 130 sci. papers to profl. pubs. Bd. dirs. Westerly Tenants' Assn., N.Y.C., 1980—. Grantee CUNY, 1988-91; recipient Shannon award NIH, 1991-93. Mem. Am. Chem. Soc., N.Y. Acad. Scis., Sigma Xi. Avocations: photography, bicycle riding. Office: NYU Mt Sinai Sch of Medicine Dept Physiology & Biophysics New York NY 10029

MEZEY, ANDREW PETER, pediatrician, educator; b. Budapest, Hungary, Apr. 28, 1937; MD, NYU, 1960. Diplomate Am. Bd. Pediat. Intern then resident Bronx Mcpl. Hosp. Ctr., N.Y.C., 1960—64; mem. staff Jacobi Med. Ctr., N.Y.C., 1966—98, Montefiore Med. Ctr., NY, 1966—, North Ctrl. Bronx Hosp., NY, 1979—98; prof. Albert Einstein Coll. Medicine, Bronx, NY, 1994—, assoc. dean grad. medicine edn. and affilate, 1994—; chmn. dept. pediat. Beth Israel Med. Ctr., St. Luke's-Roosevelt Hosp. Ctr., 1998—2000; vice chmn. dept. pediat. Maimonides Med. Ctr., Bklyn., 2001—. Mem. Am. Acad. Pediat. Office: Maimonides Med Ctr Dept Pediatrics 1301 57th St Brooklyn NY 11219 Office Phone: 718-283-3650. E-mail: amezey@maimonidesmed.org.

MEZEY, ROBERT, poet; b. Phila., Feb. 28, 1935; s. Ralph and Clara (Mandel) M.; m. Olivia Simpson (div.); children: Naomi, Judah, Eve. Student, Kenyon Coll., 1951-53; BA, U. Iowa, 1959; postgrad., Stanford U., 1960-61. Lectr. Western Res. U., Cleve., 1963-64, Franklin & Marshall Coll., Lancaster, Pa., 1965-66; asst. prof. Fresno (Calif.) State U., 1967-68, U. Utah, Salt Lake City, 1973-76; prof., poet-in-residence Pomona Coll., Claremont, Calif., 1976-99; ret., 1999. Author: (poems) The Lovemaker, 1960 (Lamont award), White Blossoms, 1965, The Door Standing Open, 1970, Selected Translations, 1981, Evening Wind, 1988 (Bassine citation, PEN prize 1989), Collected Poems 1952-1999, 2000 (Poets prize 2002); editor Naked Poetry, 1968, Poems from the Hebrew, 1973, Collected Poems of Henri Coulette, 1990, Selected Poems of Thomas Hardy, 1998, The Poetry of E.A. Robinson, 1999, Poems of the American West, 2002; translator: Tungsten (César Vallejo), 1987. With U.S. Army, 1953—55. Fellow Ingram Merrill, 1973, 89, Guggenheim Found., 1977, Stanford U., 1960, NEA, 1987; recipient Poetry prize Am. Acad. Arts and Letters, 1982. Avocations: tennis, chess. Home: 960 E Bonita Ave # 28 Pomona CA 91767 E-mail: mezteadancer@aol.com.

MEZIANE, MOULAY AHMED, physician; b. Taza, Morocco, Aug. 28, 1952; came to U.S., 1979; s. Abdelmadjid and Khedoudja (Senouci) M.; m. Anissa Venessa Schweiger, Dec. 13, 1990; children: Brahim, Tarik, Malik, Amina, Nabil. BS, Lycee El-Mokrani, Algiers, Algeria, 1972; MD, U. Algiers, 1979. Intern Algiers U. Hosp., 1978-79; resident in diagnostic radiology Johns Hopkins HOsp., Balt., 1980-84; mem. staff Johns Hopkins Hosp., Balt., 1984-87; mem. staff, co-head thoracic imaging Cleve. Clin. Found., 1987-90, mem. staff, head thoracic imaging, 1990—. Author: High Resolution CT of the Lung, 1986 (gold medal); contbr. articles to profl. jours. Avocations: competitive running, painting, photography. Office: Cleve Clin Found 5500 Euclid Ave Cleveland OH 44195-0001

MEZNAR, JOAN ELLEN, historian, educator; b. Phila., June 12, 1956; d. Leonard Marvin and Dona Ruth Meznar; m. Kenneth Veld Gouwens, May 10, 1996. BA, Bryan Coll., Dayton, Tenn., 1976—78; MA, Ohio State U., Columbus, 1978—80; PhD, U. Tex., Austin, 1980—86. Asst. prof., latin am. studies Mt. Holyoke Coll., South Hadley, Mass., 1986—89; asst. prof., history U. S.C., Columbia, 1989—95; assoc. prof., history Westmont Coll., Santa Barbara, Calif., 1995—99; asst. prof., history Ea. Conn. State U., Willimantic, 1999—2001, assoc. prof., history, 2001—. Contbr. articles to profl. jours.; contbg. editor: (handbook) Handbook of Latin Am. Studies, Libr. Congress, 1994—. Recipient Excellence in Tchg., Mortar Bd. Soc., 1991, 1992; fellow, Ctr. for Latin Am. Studies, U. Chgo., 1999, Nat. Endowment for Humanities, 2003; Fulbright scholar, 1993. Mem.: Assn. Confraternity Studies, New Eng. Coun. on Latin Am. Studies, Southeastern Coun. on Latin Am. Studies, Am. Hist. Assn., Renaissance Soc. Am. Office: Eastern Conn State Univ 83 Windham St Willimantic CT 06226 E-mail: meznarj@easternct.edu.

MEZVINSKY, EDWARD M. lawyer; b. Ames, Iowa, Jan. 17, 1937; m. Marjorie Margolies; 11 children. BA, U. Iowa, 1960; MA in Polit. Sci., U. Calif., Berkeley, 1963, JD, 1965. State rep. Iowa State Legislature, 1969-70; U.S. congressman 1st Dist., Iowa, 1973-77; U.S. rep. UN Commn. on Human Rights, 1977-79; chmn. Pa. Dem. State Com., 1981-86. Author: A Term to Remember; contbr. articles to law jours. Mem. Pa. Bar Assn., Bar of the Supreme Ct. of U.S., Omicron Delta Kappa. Office: 9 Elliott Ave Bryn Mawr PA 19010-3407

MEZYK, STEPHEN, chemist, educator; b. Melbourne, Victoria, Australia, June 18, 1960; PhD, U. Melbourne, Australia, 1989. Rsch. scientist Atomic Energy of Can. Ltd, Deep River, Canada, 1992—2000; prof. Calif. State U., Long Beach, 2000—. Cons., Long Beach, Calif., 2000—. Grantee Grant, NSF, 1998-2000. Mem.: Am. Chem. Soc. (student affiliate advisor 2001—03). Office: California State Univ 1250 Bellflower Blvd Long Beach CA 92660 E-mail: smezyk@csulb.edu.

MEZZULLO, LOUIS ALBERT, lawyer; b. Balt., Sept. 20, 1944; m. Judith Scales, Jan. 2, 1970. BA, U. Md., 1967, MA, 1976; JD, T.C. Williams Law Sch., 1976. Bar: Va. 1976. Sales rep. Humble Oil (name now Exxon), Richmond, Va., 1970-72; acctg. Marcoin, Inc., Richmond, 1972-73; pvt. practice bookkeeping, tax preparation, Richmond, 1973-76; assoc. McGuire, Woods, Battle and Boothe, Richmond, 1976-79; dir. Mezzullo & McCandlish, Richmond, 1979-2000; mem. Mezzullo & Guare, PLC, Richmond, 2000—03. Contbr. articles to profl. jours. Former bd. dirs. Richmond Symphony; bd. dirs. Va. Mus. Fine Arts Found.; former pres. Southampton Citizens Assn., Richmond, 1986. Served with USAR, 1969-75. Mem. ABA (tax sect.), Internat. Acad. Estate and Trust Law, Am. Coll. Trust and Estate Counsel, Am. Coll. Tax Counsel (chair), Va. State Bar (tax sect.), Am. Coll. Employee Benefit Counsel, Va. Bar Assn., Am. Bar Found., Va. Law Found., Estate Planning Coun. Richmond, Trust Adminstrs. Coun., Am. Coll. Employee Benefits Counsel, Willow Oaks Country Club. Home: 2961 Westchester Rd Richmond VA 23225-1842 Office: McGuireWoods LLP One James Ctr 901 E Cary St Richmond VA 23219 Office Phone: 804-775-4312. E-mail: lmezzullo@mcguirewoods.com.

MFUME, KWEISI, civil rights advocate, former congressman; b. Balt., Oct. 24, 1948; divorced; children: Donald, Kevin, Keith, Ronald, Michael, Christopher. BS, Morgan State U., 1976; MA, Johns Hopkins U., 1984. Mem. Balt. City Council, 1979-87, 100th-104th Congresses from 7th Md. dist., 1987-96, former chmn. congl. black caucus, ranking minority mem., mem. banking and fin. svcs. subcom. on gen. oversight and investigations; mem. small bus. com., mem. joint econ. com.; pres., CEO NAACP, 1996—. Former adj. prof. polit. sci. Morgan State U., Balt. Baptist. Office: NAACP 4805 Mount Hope Dr Baltimore MD 21215-3297

MHATRA, NAGESH, health products executive; PhD in Biochemistry/Microbiology, Rutgers U. Pres. Beckton Dickinson Europe Diagnostics, Grenoble, France; mng. dir. Miles-Yeda, Rehavet, Israel; dir., pres. and corp. v.p. Immunocytometry System divsn. Beckton Dickinson; with Miles Labs. (Bayer, AG); chmn. bd. Guava Technologies, Inc., Burlingame, Calif. Office: Guava Technolgies Inc 863C Mitten Rd Burlingame CA 94010

MIAN, GUO, electrical engineer; b. Shanghai, Feb. 6, 1957; came to U.S., 1987; s. Wenseng Mian and Guorong Sun; m. Ann Wang, Nov. 1, 1989; children, Lucy and Steve. BS in Physics, Shanghai U. Sci. & Tech., 1982; MS

in Physics, Western Ill. U., 1989; DSc in Elec. Engring., Washington U., 1992. Mgr. Rec. Media Lab. Magnetic Rec. Ctr., Shanghai (China) Ctrl. Chem. Ltd., 1982-85; vis. scientist materials sci. lab. Keio U., Yokohama, Japan, 1985-87; sr. rsch. elec. engring. Quantum Corp., Milpitas, Calif., 1992-93, Conner Peripherals, San Jose, Calif., 1993-95; sr. mgr. HDD R&D Ctr. Samsung Info. Sys. Am., San Jose, Calif., 1995—. Contbr. articles to Jour. Materials Sci., IEEE Trans. Magnetics, Jour. Magnetism & Magnetic Materials, Jour. Applied Physics, Japanese Jour. Applied Physics, Jour. Japanese Magnetic Soc. Recipient C & C Promotion award Found. for C & C Promotion, Tokyo, 1986. Mem. IEEE, IEEE Magnetics Soc., IEEE Computer Soc., Am. Phys. Soc. Achievements include discovery of transverse correlation length in magnetic thin film media, a linear relationship between correlation function of media noise and an off track displacement of a recording head, an algorithm to determine an autocorrelation signal to noise ratio for an arbitrary data sequence in time domain, an algorithm to determine a nonlinear bit shift in high density magnetic storage by a time domain correlation analysis which has been implemented in Lecory 7200 and 9350 digital scopes, an in-situ measurement of exchange coupling of magnetic thin film, mechanism of residual stress forming and releasing in electronic ceramics processing; inventor in field. Home: PMB 18 43494 Ellsworth St Fremont CA 94539-5819

MIAN, LAL SHAH, entomologist, educator; b. Pakistan, Mar. 4, 1945; s. Mohammad Shah M.; m. Judith Anne Conatser, Dec. 26, 1983; children: David Shah and Adam Shah. BSc in Agrl. with honors, U. Peshawar, 1967, MSc in Agrl. with honors, 1972; MS in Agrl., Am. U., Beirut, Lebanon, 1974; PhD in Entomology, U. Calif., Riverside, 1982. Registered Environ. Health Specialist. Tech. asst. forest entomology Forest Rsch. Inst., Peshawar, 1967-68; instr. entomology U. Peshawar, 1969-72, lectr. entomology, 1974-77; vector ecologist San Bernardino (Calif.) County Vector Control Program Pub. Health Dept., 1986-99; adj. lectr. dept. health sci. and human ecology Calif. State U., San Bernardino, 1993, 95, 98, asst. prof., 1999—2003, coord. environ. health sci. program, 2001—, assoc. prof., 2003—. Mem. San Bernardino County Africanized Honey Bee Task Force, Africanized Honey Bee Steering Com.; coord.environ. health sci program Calif. State U., San Bernardino, 2001—; faculty coun. Water Resources Inst., 2002—. Author (with others): Distribution, Transport and Fate of the Insecticides Malathion and Parathion in the Environ., 1981, Interagency Guidelines for the Surveillance and Control of Selected Vector-borne Pathogens in California, 1995, Inland Empire Environ. Quality Paradigm, 2000; reviewer Environ. Entomology, jour. Econ. Entomology, annals. Entomological Soc. Am., 1980—85, jour. Am. Mosquito Control Assn., 2000, assoc. edt. Bull. Soc. Vector Ecology, 1991—92, editl. bd. Wing Beats, 1992—94, jour. Bull./Soc. Vector Ecology, 1992—; contbr. articles over 70 articles to profl. jours., numerous interviews to newsmedia. Elected mem. U. Senate Lectrs. Constituency, 1976-77, U. Syndicate 23-mem Governing Body, 1976-77; mem. Curriculum Com. Faculty Agrl., 1975-76, Resident Dir. Tchr. Student Ctr., 1975-77, Chancellor's Search Com. for Dean Coll. Natural and Agrl. Scis. U. Calif., 1981, Grad. Student Coun. U. Calif., 1981, Student Mini-Grant Adv. Com. U. Calif. Coop. Ext., 1981-82. Postdoctoral fellow in mosquito rsch. U. Calif., 1982-86; assistantship in mosquito rsch. U. Calif., 1981-82; Dawood Found. scholar U. Peshawar, 1962-63, Directorate of Edn. scholar U. Peshawar, 1962-67, Dept. Agrl. scholar U. Peshawar, 1964-67, U.S. Aid scholar Am. U., 1972-74, Ctrl. Overseas scholar U. Calif., 1977-82; Cmty. Univ. Partnership fellow Calif. State U., 2000-01, summer rsch. faculty fellow, 2000, mini-grant award fellow, 2000-02. Mem.: AAAS, Big Bear Valley (coordinated resource mgmt. plan group 1993—94, mem. univ. diversity com. 2000—, cmty.-univ. partnershis forum 2001), Soc. Vector Ecology (local arrangements com. 1993, program com. endl. programs in vector control com. 1993, pubs. com. 1998, 2000—), Entomol. Assn. So. Calif., Nat. Environ. Health Assn., Calif. Environ. Health Assn., Mosquito and Vector Control Assn. Calif. (disease control subcom. vector control com. 1990—93, pubs. com. 1990—94, tng. and cert. 1991—2001, chem. control com. 1993—97, Africanized honey bee ad hoc com. 1993—99, procs. 1997, 1998—2000, pub. edn. 2002—), N.Y. Acad. Scis., Entomol. soc. Am., Am. Mosquito Control Assn. (recertification and tng. com. 1992—94, recertification com. 1994—95, pub. rels., edn. com. 1998—2002), Am. Registry Profl. Entomologists, Internat. N.W. Conf. Diseases in Nature Communicable to Man, Sigma Xi. Democrat. Office: Calif State Univ Dept Health Sci/Human Ecol San Bernardino CA 92407-2397 E-mail: lmian@csusb.edu.

MIANO, LOUIS STEPHEN, arts advisor; b. N.Y.C., July 28, 1934; s. Louis Clyde and Zefira (Palombo) M. BA, Dartmouth Coll., 1955; MA, Columbia U., 1958. Writer Look Mag., N.Y.C., 1960-61; editor Show Mag., N.Y.C. and L.A., 1961-63; assoc. producer ABC-TV, N.Y.C. and L.A., 1963-66; vice-chmn., dir. creative services AC&R Advt., N.Y.C., 1966-90. Sec. EEE Theatrical Ventures, N.Y.C., 1974—; cons. in field. Co-producer plays: Design for Living, Corpse, The Seagull, Legends, Inner Voices, 1974-86 Trustee Marymount Manhattan Coll., N.Y.C., 1980-2002; cons. Home Box Office, 1991-92; bd. dirs. Nat. Bd. of Rev. of Motion Pictures, 1995—, Gotham Chamber Opera, 2000—; bd. dirs., sec. Circle-in-the Square; gen. dirs. coun. N.Y.C. Opera, 1998—. Mem. Century Assn. Home and Office: 430 E 57th St New York NY 10022-3061

MIAOULIS, IOANNIS NIKOLAOS, mechanical engineer, educator; b. Athens, Greece, July 24, 1961; came to U.S., 1980; s. Nikolaos Ioannis and Titika Photini (Kokkinopoulou) M.; m. Beth Karen, Sept. 23, 1984; children: Marina, Katrina. BSME, Tufts U., 1983, MA in Econs., 1986, PhD, 1987; SMME, MIT, 1984. Asst. prof. mech. engring. Tufts U., Medford, Mass., 1987-93, assoc. prof., 1993-97, prof., 1997—, assoc. dean engring., 1993-94; dean Tufts U. Sch. Engring., Medford, Mass., 1994—2002; interim dean Tufts U. Sch. Arts and Scis., Medford, Mass., 2001, assoc. provost, 2001—02. Pres., dir. Mus. Sci., Boston, 2003—; cons. in field. Contbr. over 100 articles to profl. jours. Elected mem. Mass. Tech./Engring. Edn. Adv. Bd., 1999—, chair 2000—; elected mem. Mass. Math. & Sci. Edn. Bd., 1995-99, Tufts Alumni Coun., Medford, 1994—; elected coun. mem. Pomposítticut Sch., Stow, Mass., 1993-98. Recipient Presdl. Young Investigator award NSF, 1991, Inventor's Assn. award, New. Eng., 1990, William P. Desmond award Citizen's Edn. Resource Ctr., Mass., 1996, Cmty. & Leadership award Toastmasters Internat., Mass., 1995, Jaycees Outstanding Young Leader award, 1999. Mem. ASME, AAAS, Am. Soc. Engring. Edn., Materials Rsch. Soc. Achievements include 2 U.S. patents; research in area of heat transfer in materials processing, microscale heat transfer, comparative biomechanics. Office: Mus Sci 1 Science Park Boston MA 02114

MICA, JOHN L. congressman; b. Binghamton, N.Y., Jan. 27, 1943; s. John and Adeline Resciniti M.; m. Patricia Szymanek, 1972; children: D'anne, Clark. AA, Miami-Dade C.C., 1965; BA, U. Fla., 1967. Pres. MK Devel. Inc., 1975—92; mem. Fla. Ho. of Reps., 1977—81, mem. appropriations com., mem. ethics com., mem. elections com., mem. cmty. affairs com.; chief of staff U.S. Senate, Washington, 1981—85; mng. gen. ptnr MD Cellular Comm., 1986—92; mem. U.S. Ho. of Reps. from 7th Fla. Dist., Washington, 1993—. Mem. transp. and infrastructure com., govt. reform and oversight com., chmn. subcom. on aviation, 1993—. Author: Factor affecting local government reorganization efforts in Florida, Urban and Environmental Issues. Formerly with Beth Johnson Mental Health Bd., PTA Bd., Zora Neale Hurston Meml. Com. Recipient Outstanding Svc. award Fla. Conservative Union, Outstanding Svc. award Fla. Cancer Soc., Outstanding Svc. award Sertoma, Outstanding Young Men of Am. award; named one of five outstanding Young Men in Fla. Mem.: Fla. Jaycees Statewide (Good Govt. award 1973), Winter Park Jaycees (Good Govt. award 1972), Tiger Bay Club, Kiwanis. Republican. Episcopalian. Office: US House of Reps 2445 Rayburn Bldg Washington DC 20515-0907 E-mail: john.mica@mail.house.gov.

MICALE, FRANK JUDE, lawyer; b. Pitts., Jan. 10, 1949; s. Frank Jacob and Catherine Anna (Wagner) M.; m. Jane Sincler Czak. BA, Duquesne U., 1971, JD, 1977. Bar: Pa. 1977, U.S. Dist. Ct. (we. dist.) Pa. 1977, U.S. Ct. Appeals (3rd cir.) 1978. U.S. Supreme Ct. 1986; cert. Nat. Bd. Trial Advocacy. Law clk. to judge U.S. Ct. Appeals (3rd cir.), 1977-78, U.S. Dist. Ct. (we. dist.) Pa., 1978-79; assoc. Egler & Reinstadtler, Pitts., 1979-80; dep. atty. gen., sr. dep. atty. gen. in charge torts litigation sect. western region Office of Atty. Gen. Commonwealth of Pa., 1980-92; pvt. practice, 1992—. Mem. ABA, Am. Arbitration Assn., Pa. Bar Assn., Allegheny County Bar Assn., Acad. Trial Lawyers Allegheny County. Home: 5521 Claybourne St Pittsburgh PA 15232-1634 Office: 11269 Perry Hwy Ste 400 Wexford PA 15090 E-mail: frankmac@msn.com.

MICALLEF, JOSEPH STEPHEN, retired lawyer; b. Malta, Oct. 19, 1933; came to U.S., 1949; s. John E. and Josephine (Brownrigg) M.; m. Jane M. Yungers, Sept. 5, 1959; children: Lisa R., Maura J. Fisk, Sara M. Hulse, Amy A., Joseph S. Jr. BA cum laude, U. St. Thomas, 1958, LLB, JD, 1962. Pres., CEO Fiduciary Counselling, Inc., St. Paul, 1961-71, dir., cons., 1971-95. Trustee Gt. No. Iron Ore Properties Trust, St. Paul, The Charles A. Lindbergh Fund, Mpls.; mem. bd. visitors U. Minn. Law Sch., Mpls. Past pres., mem. exec. com. Minn. Hist. Soc., St. Paul; bd. dirs. Minn. Air NG Hist. Found., Inc., Plymouth Music Series, Ramsey County Hist. Soc.; bd. overseers Hill Monastic Manuscript Libr.; past regent St. John's U., Collegeville, Minn.; mem. investment adv. com. Archdiocese St. Paul/Mpls.; mem. fin. coun. Cathedral of St. Paul; dir. emeritus Sci. Mus. Minn., St. Paul; trustee James Jerome Hill Ref. Libr., St. Paul. Decorated Knight of the Sovereign Mil., Order of Malta, 1981, Knight of the Equestrian Order of Holy Sepulchre of Jerusalem, Hon. Consul Gen. of Malta, St. Paul/Mpls. Mem. ABA (com. on real property, probate and trust law), Minn. Bar Assn. (subcom. on the Minn. nonprofit corp. act trust law com.), Minn. Coun. on Founds. (govt. rels. com.), Minn. Club (bd. govs.), Town & Country Club, Casino Maltese Club, The Union Club (Malta). Office: Great Northern Iron Ore Properties W 1290 First National Bank 332 Minnesota St Saint Paul MN 55101-1361

MICEK, ERNEST S. former food products executive; b. Arcadia, Wis., Feb. 18, 1936; m. Sally Micek; 4 children. BSChE, U. Wis., 1959. Mgr. Cargill, Inc., Mpls., 1959, asst. v.p., gen. mgr. corn milling dept., 1973, v.p. milling divsn., 1978, pres. corn milling divsn., 1981, pres. food sector, 1992, exec. v.p., 1993, pres., 1994-98, chmn., pres., CEO, 1995-99. Bd. dirs. Cargill, Inc., Schneider Nat.; chmn. ECAT; mem. bd. overseers, mem. internat. adv. bd. Carlson Sch. Mgmt.; mem. Pres.'s Export Coun., U.S. sect. Pacific Basin Econ. Coun. Bd. dirs. United Way Exec. Com., Mpls.; trustee U. St. Thomas, U. Wis. Alumni Rsch. Found. Named Man of Yr., Consumers for World Trade, 1999; recipient Disting. Svc. citation, U. Wis. Dept. Engring., 1991, Coya Knudson Humanitarian award, 1999. Mem.: Nat. Assn. Mfrs. (bd. dirs., exec. com.). Office: Adminstrv office Cargill Inc PO Box 5724 Minneapolis MN 55440-5724

MICELI, MARCIA P. management consultant, educator; Student, DePauw U., 1971—72; BA with distinction, Ind. U., 1974, MBA in Pers. and Indsl. Rels., 1978, DBA in Pers. and Orgnl. Behavior, 1982. Assoc. instr. Ind. U., Bloomington, 1980—81; asst. prof. Ohio State U., 1987—92, chair dept. mgmt. and human resources Coll. Bus., 1991—93, sr. assoc. dean acad. programs Max M. Fisher Coll. Bus., 1993—96, acad. dir. MBA programs, 1994—96, prof. Fisher Coll. Bus., 1992—98, Hoyt prof. mgmt., 1998; prof. McDonough Sch. Bus. Georgetown U., Washington, 1998—. Vis. disting. scholar Georgetown U., Washington, 1997. Cons. Working It Out, 1986—89, mem. editl. bd. Acad. Mgmt. Rev., 1991—93, Pers. Psychology, 1991—92, 1996—; contbr. articles to profl. jours. Grantee, U.S. Dept. Labor, 1981, Ohio State U., 1985—86; Rsch. grantee, 1983—85, Summer co-fellow, 1991, co-grantee, Inst. Internal Auditors, 1986—89, Ctr. Labor Rsch., 1991—92. Mem.: World at Work, Acad. Mgmt. (mem. exec. com. pers./human resources divsn. 1986—90), Beta Sigma Gamma, Phi Beta Kappa, Sigma Iota Epsilon. Office: Georgetown U McDonough Sch Bus 309 Old North Washington DC 20057 Business E-Mail: micelim@msb.edu.

MICELI, THOMAS JOSEPH, economist, educator; b. Hartford, Conn., Mar. 26, 1959; s. Rosario Thomas and Shirley Bennett Miceli; m. Ana Maria Verissimo, Mar. 21, 1987; children: Thomas Joseph, Nicolas Michael. PhD, Brown U., Providence, R.I., 1988. Assoc. prof. U. Conn., Storrs, 1993—98, prof. econs., 1998—. Author: Econs. of the Law. Mem.: Am. Econ. Assn. Home: 34 Webster Hill Blvd West Hartford CT 06107 Office: U Conn Dept Econ 341 Mansfield Rd Storrs CT 06269-1063 E-mail: thomas.miceli@uconn.edu.

MICELI, WILLIAM CYRIL, SR., director; b. Chgo., Jan. 9, 1949; s. Cyril Francis and Mary Elizabeth Miceli; m. Phyllis M. Michaud, Aug. 22, 1976 (div. May 1998); 1 child, William Cyril Jr. BS in Edn., No. Ill. U., 1970; MA in History, NE Ill. U., 1974. Tchr. Jones H.S. Chgo. Pub. Schs., 1971—78, asst. prin., scheduler Jones H.S., 1978—98, scheduler Jones H.S., 1998—2003, programmer, troubleshooter dept. H.S. programs, 2003—04, dir. citywide student scheduling svcs. Office of H.S. Programs, 2004—. Acting prin. Jones H.S. Chgo. Pub. Schs., 1988. Founder Mayfair Youth Orgn., 1967—, Thai Found., 1977—; bd. dirs. Old Timers Baseball Assn. Republican. Roman Catholic. Avocations: coin collecting/numismatics, coaching, political activities. Home: 5157 N Lowell Chicago IL 60630 Office: Chgo Pub Schs Dept HS Programs 125 S Clark 9th Fl Chicago IL 60603

MICHA, DAVID ALLAN, chemistry and physics educator; b. Argentina, Sept. 12, 1939; came to U.S., 1966, naturalized, 1974; s. Simon David and Catalina (Cohen) M.; m. Rebecca Stefan, 1991; children: Michael F., Anna K. MS, U. Cuyo, Bariloche, Argentina, 1962; DSc, U. Uppsala, Sweden, 1966. Rsch. assoc. Theoretical Chemistry Inst. U. Wis., Madison, 1966-67; asst. rsch. physicist Inst. Pure and Applied Sci. U. Calif., La Jolla, 1967-69; assoc. prof. chemistry and physics U. Fla., Gainesville, 1969-74, prof., 1974—, dir. Ctr. Chem. Physics, 1982-91, head phys. chem. divsn., 1999—. Vis. prof. U. Gothenburg, Sweden, 1970, Harvard U., 1972, 90, 98, 2000, 01, Max-Planck Inst., Göttingen, Germany, 1976, 96, Imperial Coll., London, 1977, U. Calif., Santa Barbara, 1982, U. Colo. and Weizmann Inst., Israel, 1983, U. Buenos Aires, 1988, 95, Supercomputer Inst., Fla. State U., 1991; mem. adv. panel div. advanced sci. computing NSF, 1990-92, Max-Planck Inst. Astrophysik, Munich, Germany, 1996, 97. Mem. editl. bd. Internat. Jour. Quantum Chemistry, 1979-88, Few-Body Systems, 1985—; editor Finite Systems and Multiparticle Dynamics, 1990—, symposium procs.; contbr. several book chpts., numerous articles to sci. jours. Recipient U.S. Sr. Scientist award A. Von Humboldt Found., 1976, Sr. Faculty Rsch. award Sigma Xi, 1985; Alfred P. Sloan Found. fellow, 1971-74; Nat. Bur. Standards JILA fellow, 1983. Fellow Am. Phys. Soc. (vice chmn. topical group on few body sys. and multi-particle dynamics 1986-88, chmn. 1988-89); mem. Am. Chem. Soc., Sigma Xi. Office: U Fla 2318 New Physics Bldg Gainesville FL 32611-8435 E-mail: micha@qtp.ufl.edu.

MICHAEL, ALFRED FREDERICK, JR., pediatric nephrology educator; b. Phila. s. Alfred Frederick and Emma Maude (Peters) M.; m. Jeanne Jones; children: Mary, Susan, Carol. MD, Temple U., 1953. Diplomate Am. Bd. Pediatrics (founding mem. sub-bd. pediatric nephrology, pres. 1977-79). Pediat. diagnostic lab. immunology and pediatric nephrology intern Phila. Gen. Hosp., 1953-54; resident Children's Hosp. and U. Cin. Coll. Medicine, 1957-60; postdoctoral fellow dept. pediatrics and biochemistry Med. Sch., U. Minn., Mpls., 1960-63, assoc. prof., 1965-68, prof. pediatrics, lab. medicine and pathology, 1968-88, dir. pediatric nephrology, 1968—86, Regents' prof., 1986—, head dept. pediatrics, 1986-97, interim dean, 1996-97, dean, 1997—2002. Established investigator Am. Heart Assn., 1963-68. Past mem. editl. bd. Internat. Yr. Book of Nephrology, Am. Jour. Nephrology, Kidney Internat., Clin. Nephrology, Am. Jour. Pathology; contbr. articles to profl. jours. Served with USAF, 1955-57. Recipient Alumni Achievement award Temple U. Sch. Medicine, 1988, Diehl award, 2003; NIH fellow, 1960-63, Guggenheim fellow, 1966-67, NIH Merit awardee, 1992-2002. Fellow AAAS; mem. AMA, Am. Soc. Clin. Investigation, Assn. Am. Physicians, Am. Pediat. Soc., Soc. for Pediat. Rsch., Am. Assn. Investigative Pathology, Am. Soc. Cell Biology, Am. Soc. Nephrology (coun., pres.-elect 1992—, pres. 1993, John Peters award), Internat. Soc. Nephrology, Soc. for Exptl. Biology and Medicine, Minn. Med. Assn. Home: 1986 Lower Saint Dennis Rd Saint Paul MN 55116-2820 Office Phone: 612-626-4949.

MICHAEL, ANN DOZIER MARINO, real estate broker; b. Durham, N.C., Apr. 22, 1944; d. Walter Joseph and Ellen G. (Cheek) Dozier; m. John Harrison Marino, Oct. 15, 1966 (div. Jan. 1981); children: John Harrison Jr., Ann Southerlyn; m. G. Revell Michael, July 4, 1998. BA, Salem Coll., 1966. Sales assoc. Rector Assocs. Realtors, Alexandria, Va., 1984-96, Pardoe and Graham, Alexandria, 1997—2002; assoc. broker McEnearney Assocs. Realtors, Alexandria, 2002—. Vol. Jr. League, Chgo., 1970-71; bd. dirs. Jr. League, Washington, 1979-95, Vol. Clearing House, Washington, Project Open Rd., Chgo., Fire and Burn Inst., Washington; mem. parents coun. Burgundy Farm Sch., 1983; mem. parish coun. St. Mary's, Alexandria, 1977-80. Recipient Rookie of Yr. award No. Va. Bd. Realtors, 1985, Lifetime Top Prodr. Club, Lifetime Million Dollar Club, No. Va. Bd. Realtors, 1985-2002. Mem.: Fairfax Hunt Club, Salem Coll. Alumnae Club (pres. Chgo. chpt. 1970—73). Republican. Roman Catholic. Office: McEnearney Assocs 109 S Pitt St Alexandria VA 22314

MICHAEL, CECIL FRANCIS, JR., pediatrician; b. Albuquerque, June 3, 1950; s. Cecil F. and Gene (Clairmont) M.; m. Karen Sara Dworkin, June 28, 1975; children: Kristen, Jonathan. BA in Chemistry, U. N.M., 1972, MD, 1976. Resident in pediats. Phoenix Affiliated Pediat. Program, 1976-79; pvt. practice Cactus Children's Clinic, Glendale, Ariz., 1979—. Chmn. pediat. dept. Thunderbird Samaritan Hosp., Glendale, 1981-83; mem. grievance com. Maricopa County Med. Soc., Phoenix, 1987. Contbr. article to profl. jour. Recipient Top Doctor Nurse's List award, Phoenix Mag. Poll, 1997, Top Doctor Doctor's Poll, 1998. Fellow Am. Acad. Pediats.; mem. AMA, Ariz. Med. Assn., Maricopa County Med. Soc. Democrat. Roman Catholic. Avocations: golf, exercise, gardening, mountain biking. Office: Cactus Childrens Clinic 5310 W Thunderbird Rd Ste 300 Glendale AZ 85306-4710

MICHAEL, CREIGHTON, artist, educator; b. Knoxville, Tenn., Jan. 12, 1949; s. James Eugene and Genetha Draughon (Duffey) M.; m. Leslie Cecil, Sept. 10, 1989; 1 child, Balin Cecil. BFA with honors, U. Tenn., Knoxville, 1971; MA in Art History, Vanderbilt U., 1976; MFA in Painting/Multi-Media, Washington U., St. Louis, 1978. Vis. prof. painting SUNY, Buffalo, 1985; vis. artist U. Alaska, Anchorage, 1986, Washington U., St. Louis, 1987, SUNY, Purchase, 1988, Muhlenberg Coll., Allentown, Pa., 1986, 91, Va. Commonwealth U., 1991, 99, Haverford (Pa.) Coll., 1993, Princeton U., 1998, 2000, 01, 03, Purchase Coll, SUNY, 2001, others; adj. faculty R.I. Sch. Design, Providence, 1986-2004; critic Pa. Acad. Fine Arts, Phila., 1995-96. Solo exhbns. include David Beitzel Gallery, N.Y.C., 1988, Haines Gallery, San Francisco, 1990, Pence Gallery, Santa Monica, Calif., 1988, 90, Ruth Siegel Gallery, N.Y.C., 1991, San Antonio Art Inst., 1992, High Mus. Art, Atlanta, 1987, Katonah Mus. Art, N.Y., 1994, Vanderbilt U., Nashville, 1996, Kim Foster Gallery, N.Y.C., 1996, 97, 99, Robischon Gallery, Denver, 1990, 92, 94, 97, 99, 2003, Birke Art Gallery, Marshall U., Huntington, W.Va., 1998, Queens Mus. Art Bulova Corp. Ctr., 1998, Galerie Trois Points, Montreal, Que., 1999, Reynolds Gallery, Richmond, Va., 1999, Elmhurst (Ill.) Art Mus., 2000, Neuberger Mus., 2001, Freedman Gallery, Albright Coll., Reading, Pa., 2001, Von Liebig Art Ctr., Naples, Fla., 2003, U. Richmond (Va.) Mus., 2003, Collaborative Concepts, Beacon, N.Y., 2003; exhibited in group shows at Muhlenberg Coll., Allentown, Pa., Rosa Esman Gallery, N.Y.C., N.J. Ctr. for Visual Arts, Summit, L.I. U., Bklyn., Mandeville Gallery/U. Calif., San Diego, Morris Mus., Morristown, N.J., Denver Art Mus., Weatherspoon Art Gallery/U. N.C., Greensboro, Ark. Arts Ctr., Little Rock, Hopper House Art Ctr., Nyack, N.Y., Kiang Gallery, Atlanta, Albright-Knox Art Gallery, Buffalo, N.J., Neuberger Mus. Art, Purchase, N.Y., Robert Kidd Gallery, Birmingham, Mich., Islip Art Mus., West Islip, N.Y., Grossman Gallery, Lafayette College, Easton, Pa., Munson-Williams-Proctor Inst. Art, Mus. Art, Utica, N.Y.; others; represented in collections at Bklyn. Mus., Denver Art Mus., High Mus. Art, NYU, Pfizer, Inc., Progressive Corp., Vanderbilt U., R.I.S.D. Mus. Art, Am. Express Neuberger Mus. Art., Weatherspoon Art Gallery, Nat. Gallery Art, Washington, others; subject of numerous articles. Edward Albee Found. fellow, 1985; Pollock-Kranser Found. grantee, 1985; N.Y. Found. for Arts fellow, 1987; Golden Found. grantee, 2000. Home: 44 Deer Knl Mount Kisco NY 10549-4706 E-mail: info@creightonmichael.com.

MICHAEL, ERNEST ARTHUR, mathematics professor; b. Zurich, Switzerland, Aug. 26, 1925; came to U.S., 1939; s. Jakob and Erna (Sondheimer) M.; m. Colette Verger Davis, 1956 (div. 1966); children: Alan, David, Gerard; m. Erika Goodman Joseph, Dec. 4, 1966; children: Hillary, Joshua. BA, Cornell U., 1947; MA, Harvard U., 1948; PhD, U. Chgo., 1951. Mem. faculty dept. math. U. Wash., Seattle, 1953—, asst. prof., 1953-56, assoc. prof., 1956-60, prof., 1960-93, prof. emeritus, 1993—. Mem. Inst. for Advanced Study, Princeton, 1951-52, 56-57, 60-61, 68, Math. Research Inst., E.T.H., Zürich, 1973-74; vis. prof. U. Stuttgart, Ger., 1978-79, U. Munich, Fed. Republic Germany, 1987, 88, 92-93. Editor: Procs. Am. Math. Soc., 1968-71, Topology and Its Applications, 1972-94, Set-Valued Analysis, 1993—; contbr. articles to profl. jours. Served with USNR, 1944-46. Grantee AEC; Grantee Office Nav. Research; Grantee NSF; Grantee Guggenheim Found.; Grantee Humboldt Found. Mem. Am. Math. Soc., Math. Assn. Am., ACLU, Amnesty Internat. Jewish. Home: 22200 Chinook Rd Woodway WA 98020-7200 Office: U Washington Dept Math Box 354350 Seattle WA 98195-4350

MICHAEL, GARY G. retired retail supermarket and drug chain executive, university administrator; b. 1940; m. Meryle Kay Michael; 3 children. BS in Bus., U. Idaho, 1962. Staff acct. Ernst & Ernst, CPA's, 1964-66; with Albertson's, Inc., Boise, Idaho, 1966—2001, acct., 1966-68, asst. controller, 1968-71, controller, 1971-72, v.p., controller, 1972-74, sr. v.p. fin., treas., 1974-76, exec. v.p., 1976-84, vice chmn., CFO, corp. devel. officer, 1984-91, chmn., CEO, 1991—2001; interim pres. U. Idaho, Moscow, Idaho, 2003—. Bd. dirs. Questar Inc., Boise Cascade, Food Mktg. Inst., Clorox, Harrah's Entertainment, Highway 12 Ventures. Served to 1st lt. U.S. Army, 1962-64. Office: Clorox 1221 Broadway Oakland CA 94612 also: U Idaho Admin Bldg, Room 105 Moscow ID 83844-3151 Business E-Mail: gmichael@uidaho.edu.

MICHAEL, GEORGE T. real estate manager; s. Lorriane Cooper; m. Terrelyn Michael, Sept. 9, 1989. AA, Bronx C.C., 1978; diploma, NYU Grad. Sch. of Bus., 1980. Mgr., owner various real estate properties, N.Y.C., 1980—. Author: (sch. newspaper) The Communicator, 1975. V.p. Adults & Youth for a Better Baisley Inc., Jamaica, 1984. Avocations: book collecting, stamp collecting/philately, track. Office Phone: 718-468-4481. Office Fax: 718-468-1512. E-mail: gtmdred@aol.com.

MICHAEL, HART E. pharmaceutical executive; Degree in Bus. Econ. & Geography, U. Calif., Santa Barbara; MBA, Calif. State U., Fresno. Various fin. positions with high technology cos.; treas., dir. fin. Avantek, Inc., 1982—90; exec. v.p., CFO Vestar, Inc., 1990—95, chmn., pres., 1994—95; v.p., CFO NeXstar Pharma., Inc., 1995—99, chmn. mgmt. com., 1998—99; CFO, sr. v.p., ops. Allos Therapeutics, Inc., Westminster, Colo., 1999—, pres., CEO, 2001—. Office: Allos Therapeutics Inc 11080 Circle Point Rd Ste 200 Westminster CO 80020

MICHAEL, HENRY N. geographer, anthropologist; b. Pitts., July 14, 1913; s. Anthony M. and Albina (Dubska) M.; m. Ida Nemez, June 18, 1943; children: Susan Shelley, Richard Carleton, Andrew Paul. BA, U. Pa., 1948, MA, 1951, PhD, 1954. Instr. geography U. Pa., 1948-54; faculty Temple U., 1958-80, prof. geography, chmn. dept., 1965-73, prof., 1965-80. Rsch. assoc. Univ. Mus., Phila., 1959-82, sr. fellow, 1982—; mem. Bi-Nat. Commn. Social Scis. Humanities, Am. Council Learned Socs./Acad. Scis. USSR, 1975—. Editor: Anthropology of the North, 1959-72; editor, author: Dating Techniques for the Archaeologist, 1971, 73, 82; translator, editor various archaeol. and ethnographic works; mem. adv. publs. com. Mus. Applied Sci. Ctr. for Archaeology, U. Pa., Anthropology and Archaeology of Eurasia-A Jour. of Transls., Alaska-Siberia Rsch. Ctr.; mem. editorial bd. Expedition-The Univ. Mus. Mag. Archaeology and Anthropology, U. Pa.; contbr. articles to profl. jours. Served to 1st lt. AUS, 1942-45. Decorated Purple Heart; recipient Dir.'s award U. Pa. Mus. Archaeology, Anthropology, 2000. Fellow Am. Anthrop. Assn., Arctic Inst. N.Am.; mem. Phila. Anthrop. Soc. (coun. 1954-90), Delaware Valley Assn. Geographers, Assn. Am. Geographers, Sigma Xi. Home: 2712 Pine Valley Ln Ardmore PA 19003-1719 Office: Univ Museum U Pa Philadelphia PA 19104

MICHAEL, JAMES HARRY, JR., federal judge; b. Charlottesville, Va., Oct. 17, 1918; s. James Harry and Reuben (Shelton) m. Barbara E. Puryear, Dec. 18, 1946 (dec. Dec. 2002); children: Jarrett Michael Stephens, Victoria von der Au. BS, U. Va., 1940, LLB, 1942. Bar: Va. 1942. Sole practice, Charlottesville; ptnr. Michael & Musselman, 1946-54, J.H. Michael, Jr., 1954-59, Michael & Dent, 1959-72, Michael, Dent & Brooks Ltd., 1972-74, Michael & Dent, Ltd., 1974-80; assoc. judge Juvenile and Domestic Rels. Ct., Charlottesville, 1954-68; judge U.S. Dist. Ct., Charlottesville, 1980-95, sr. judge, 1996—; mem. Va. Senate, 1968-80. Exec. dir. Inst. Pub. Affairs, U. Va., 1952; chmn. Coun. State Govts., 1975-76, also mem. exec. com.; chmn. So. Legis. Conf., 1974-75. Mem. Charlottesville Sch. Bd., 1951-62; bd. govs. St. Anne-Belfield Sch., 1952-76. Served with USNR, 1942-46; comdr. Res. ret. Wilton Park fellow Wilton Park Conf., Sussex, Eng., 1971 Fellow Am. Bar Found.; mem. ABA, Va. Bar Assn. (v.p. 1956-57), Charlottesville-Albermarle Bar Assn. (pres. 1966-67), Am. Judicature Soc., 4th Jud. Conf., Va. Trial Lawyers Assn. (Va. disting. svc. award 1993), Assn. Trial Lawyers Am., Raven Soc., Sigma Nu Phi, Omicron Delta Kappa. Episcopalian (lay reader). Office: US Dist Ct 255 W Main St Rm 320 Charlottesville VA 22902-5058

MICHAEL, JERROLD MARK, public health specialist, former university dean, educator; b. Richmond, Va., Aug. 3, 1927; s. Joseph Leon and Esther Leah M.; m. Lynn Y. Simon, Mar. 17, 1951; children: Scott J., Nelson L. BCE, George Washington U., 1949; MSE, Johns Hopkins U., 1950; MPH, U. Calif., Berkeley, 1957; DrPH (hon.), Mahidol U., 1983; ScD (hon.), Tulane U., 1984. Commd. ensign USPHS, 1950, advanced through grades to rear adm., asst. surgeon gen., 1966; ret., 1970; dean Sch. Pub. Health, U. Hawaii, Honolulu, 1971-92, prof. pub. health, 1971-95; emeritus prof. pub. health U. Hawaii, Honolulu, 1995—; adj. prof. global health George Washington U., 1997—. Bd. dirs. Nat. Health Coun., 1967-78, Nat. Ctr. for Health Edn., 1977-90; mem. nat. adv. coun. on health professions edn., 1978-81; chmn. bd. dirs. Kuakini Med. Ctr., Honolulu; sec., treas. Asia-Pacific Acad. Consortium Pub. Health; vis. prof. U. Adelaide, 1993, George Washington, 1994; hon. prof. Beijing Med. U., 1994; adj. prof. internat. pub. health Goerge Washington U., 1997—. Contbr. articles to profl. jours.; assoc. editor Jour. Environ. Health, 1958-80, Asia-Pacific Jour. of Pub. Health, 1986-95. Pres. Commd. Officers Found., 2000—. Served with USNR, 1944-47. Decorated Meritorious Svc. medal, comdr. Royal Order of Elephant (Thailand); recipient Walter Mangold award, 1961, J.S. Billings award for mil. medicine, 1964, Gold medal Hebrew U., Jerusalem, 1982, San Karcil Gold medal, Malaysia, 1989, Disting. Svc. award Pacific Island Health Officers Assn., 1992, USPHS awards, Commd. Officers Assn. Brutsche award, 1999, Founders award Asia-Pacific Acad. Consortium pub. health, 2003, others. Fellow Am. Public Health Assn.; mem. Am. Acad. Health Adminstrn., Am. Soc. Cert. Sanitarians, Nat. Environ. Health Assn., Am. Acad. Environ. Engrs. Clubs: Masons. Democrat. Jewish. Home: 16736 Gooseneck Ter Olney MD 20832-2456

MICHAEL, JONATHAN EDWARD, insurance company executive; b. Columbus, Ohio, Mar. 19, 1954; BA, Ohio Dominican Coll., 1977. CPA, Ohio. Acct. Coopers & Lybrand, Columbus, Ohio, 1977-82; chief acct. RLI Ins. Co., Peoria, Ill., 1982-84, controller, 1984-85, v.p. fin., CFO, 1985—, exec. v.p., 1991-94, pres., COO, 1994-2000, pres., CEO, 2001—, chmn. bd., 2002—. Mem.: Mt. Hawley Country (Peoria). Roman Catholic. Avocation: golf. Office: RLI 9025 N Lindbergh Dr Peoria IL 61615-1499

MICHAEL, M. BLANE, federal judge; b. Charleston, S.C., Feb. 17, 1943; AB, W.Va. U., 1965; JD, NYU, 1968. Bar: N.Y. 1968, U.S. Dist. Ct. (so. and ea. dists.) N.Y. 1968, W.Va. 1973, U.S. Ct. Appeals (4th cir.) 1974, U.S. Dist. Ct. (so. dist.) W.Va. 1981. Counsel to Gov. W.Va. John D. Rockefeller IV, 1977—80; atty. Jackson & Kelly, Charleston, W.Va., 1981—93; fed. judge U.S. Ct. Appeals (4th cir.), Charleston, W.Va., 1993—. Mem.: ABA, Kanawha County Bar Assn., W.Va. Bar Assn., Phi Beta Kappa. Office: US Circuit Judge Robert C Byrd US Courthouse 300 Virginia St E Rm 7404 Charleston WV 25301-2504

MICHAEL, NOREEN, commissioner, educator; Commr. of edn. Virgin Islands Dept. Edn., Charlotte, 2002—. Office: Commr of Education 44-46 Kongena Gade St Thomas VI 00802

MICHAEL, WILLIAM BURTON, psychologist, educator; b. Pasadena, Calif., Mar. 6, 1922; s. William Whipple and Helen Augusta (Schultz) M.; m. Martha Walker Hennessey, Aug. 30, 1947 (dec. 1959); m. Joan Yvonne Johnson, Aug. 26, 1966 AB, UCLA, 1943; MS in Edn., U. So. Calif., Los Angeles, 1945, MA in Psychology, 1946, PhD, 1947. Lectr. engring. math. Calif. Inst. Tech., Pasadena, 1942-45; lectr. math., psychology and edn. U. So. Calif., L.A., 1944-47; asst. prof. psychology Princeton U., N.J., 1947-50; rsch. assoc. Rand Corp., Santa Monica, Calif., 1951-52; dir. testing bur. U. So. Calif., L.A., 1952-62, prof. edn. and psychology, 1957-62, 1967—, U. Calif., Santa Barbara, 1962-67. Cons. in field. Author: Teaching for Creative Endeavor, 1967; co-author: Psychological Foundations of Learning and Teaching, 2d edit., 1974, Handbook in Research and Evaluation, 3d edit., 1995 (standardized tests) Study Attitudes and Methods Survey, Dimensions of Self-Concept; editor Ednl. and Psychol. Measurement, 1985-95; cons. editor Jour. Pers. Evaluation in Edn., Ednl. Rsch. Quar., Spanish Jour. Psychology; contbr. chpts. to books and articles to profl. jours. Mem., bd. dirs. Neuro-Psychiat. Clinic, L.A. and Pasadena, 1958—; mem. L.A. Philharm. Assn., 1965—; advisor Sch. of Comm., Arcadia, Calif., 1981—. Fellow APA; mem. Am. Ednl. Rsch. Assn. (exec. com., editor Rev. Edn. Rsch. 1962-65), Western Psychol. Assn., Northeastern Ednl. Rsch. Assn., Nat. Coun. on Measurement in Edn., Calif. Ednl. Rsch. Assn. (pres. 1965), Phi Beta Kappa, Sigma Xi, Phi Kappa Phi, Psi Chi, Phi Delta Kappa. Congregationalist. Avocations: Music; travel; reading; ice cream gourmet. Home: 325 Callita Pl San Marino CA 91108-2311 Office: U So Calif Sch Edn Los Angeles CA 90089-0031

MICHAELIDES, CONSTANTINE EVANGELOS, architect, educator; b. Athens, Greece, Jan. 26, 1930; came to U.S., 1955, naturalized, 1964; s. Evangelos George and Kalliopi Constantine (Kefallonitis) M.; m. Maria S. Canellakis, Sept. 3, 1955; children: Evangelos Constantine, Dimitri Canellakis. Diploma in Architecture, Nat. Tech. U., Athens, 1952; M.Arch., Harvard U., 1957. Practice architecture, Athens, 1954-55, St. Louis, 1963—; asso. architect Carl Koch, Jose Luis Sert, Hideo Sasaki, Cambridge, Mass., 1957-59, Doxiadis Assos., Athens and Washington, 1959-60, Hellmuth, Obata & Kassabaum, St. Louis, 1962; instr. Grad. Sch. Design Harvard U., 1957-59, Athens Inst. Tech., 1959-60; asst. prof. architecture Washington U., St. Louis, 1960-64, assoc. prof., 1964-69, prof., 1969-94, assoc. dean Sch. Architecture, 1969-73; dean Washington U., Sch. Architecture, 1973-93, dean emeritus, 1993—; Ruth and Norman Moore vis. prof. Washington U., St. Louis, 1995. Vis. prof. (Sch. Architecture), Ahmedabad, India, 1970; counselor Landmarks Assn. St. Louis., 1975-79 Author: Hydra: A Greek Island Town: Its Growth and Form, 1967, The Aegean Crucible: Tracing Vernacular Architecture in Post-Byzantine Centuries, 2003; contbr. articles to profl. jours. Mem. Mcpl. Commn. on Arts, Letters, University City, Mo., 1975-81. With Greek Army Res., 1952-54. Fellow AIA (Rsch. award 1963-64, Presdl. Citation 1992); mem. Tech. Chamber of Greece, Soc. Archtl. Historians, Modern Greek Studies Assn., Hellenic Soc. St. Louis (pres. 1991, 95, 96). Home: 735 Radcliffe Ave Saint Louis MO 63130-3139 Office: Washington U Sch Architecture 1 Brookings Dr Saint Louis MO 63130-4899

MICHAELIDES, DOROS NIKITA, internist, medical educator; b. Nicosia, Cyprus, Jan. 7, 1936; came to U.S., 1969; s. Nikita P. and Elpinike (Taliadorou) M.; m. Eutychia J. Loizides, Feb. 27, 1965; children: Nike-Elsie, Joanna-Doris. MD magna cum laude (Royal Greek Govt., Scholar) U. Athens, 1962; DTM and H (Greek State Scholarship, Found. Scholar) U. Liverpool, Eng., 1967; MSc in Clin. Biochemistry (Greek State, Scholarship Found. Scholar), U. Newcastle-upon-Tyne (Eng.), 1969. Diplomate Am. Bd. Family Practice, Am. Bd. Allergy and Immunology; qualified Am. Bd. Internal Medicine; cert. in infectious diseases and immunochemistry, Eng. Clk., intern U. Uppsala, Sweden, 1962; resident Nicosia Gen. Hosp., 1963—66; fellow U. Liverpool Hosps., 1967; fellow internal and clin. medicine Royal Infirmary U. Edinburgh, 1967—68; rsch. fellow Royal Victoria Infirmary U. Newcastle-upon-Tyne, 1968—69; resident internal medicine Bapt. Meml. Hosp., Memphis, 1969—72; fellow in chest diseases We. Okla. Chest Disease Hosp., 1970—71; chief clin. immunology/respiratory care ctr. Erie, Pa.; chief respiratory care ctr. VA Med. Ctr., Erie, 1972—84, acting chief dept. medicine, 1980—81; asst. clin. prof. medicine Hahnemann U. Sch. Medicine, Phila., 1977—, Gannon U., Erie, 1977—. Mem. staff internal medicine Hamot Med. Ctr., immunology and chest diseases Metro Health Ctr., Erie; preceptor medicine St. Vincent's Health Ctr.; affiliate staff Cleveland Clinic Found.; vol. physician Greek Nat. Guard, Cyprus, 1964. Author: The Occurrence of Proteolytic Inhibitors in Heart and Skeletal Muscle, 1969; Blood Gases, Acid-Base and Electrolytes Disturbances, 1980; Immediate Hypersensitivity: The Immunochemistry and Therapeutics of Reversible Airway Obstruction, 1980; The Equivalent Potency of Corticosteroid Preparations used in Reversible Airway Obstruction, 1981; contbr. articles to med. jours. Recipient citation for outstanding svcs. to vets. DAV, 1975, citation Adminstr. U.S. Vets. Affairs, 1978. Fellow ACP (life), Am. Assn. Cert. Allergists, Am. Coll. Allergy and Immunology (com. autoimmune diseases), Am. Assn. Clin. Immunology and Allergy (pulmonary com.), Am. Coll. Chest Physicians (life; critical care com.), Royal Soc. Medicine, Am. Coll. Angiology, N.Y. Acad. Scis., Am. Coll. Clin. Pharmacology, Am. Assn. Cert. Allergists. Greek Orthodox. Home: 4107 State St Erie PA 16508-3129 Office: Allergy Immunology & Chest Diseases 1611 Peach St Ste 220 Erie PA 16501-2121 E-mail: dnm777@pol.net.

MICHAELIDES, EFSTATHIOS EMMANUEL, mechanical engineer; b. Thessaloniki, Greece, Feb. 13, 1955; s. Emmanuel Efstathios and Eleni M.; m. Maria-Laura Garcia, July 31, 1982; children: Emmanuel Alexandros, Dimitris Nicolas, Eleni Guadalupe. BA, Oxford U., 1977, MA honoris causa, 1983; MS, Brown U., 1979, PhD, 1980. Asst. prof. U. Del., Newark, 1980-85, assoc. prof., 1985-89, acting chmn., 1985-86; head of mech. engring. Tulane U., New Orleans, 1990-92, prof., 1990—, assoc. dean, 1992—2003, dir. South-Ctrl. Regional Ctr., Nat. Inst. for Global Environ. Change, 2002—, sr. Fulbright fellow, 1997, Leo S. Weil prof. mech. engring., 1998—. Cons. DuPont, Chevron, Exxon, TASA; chair Internat. Conf. on Multiphase Flow-2001. Editor nine books, presenter more than 120 conf. papers; contbr. more than 90 articles to profl. jours.; patentee in field. Mem. ASME (Freeman Scholar award 2002), ASEE, Am. Phys. Soc. Avocation: stained glass windows/master craftsman. Office: Sch Engring Tulane Univ New Orleans LA 70118 E-mail: emichael@tulane.edu.

MICHAELIS, ELIAS K. neurochemist; b. Wad-Medani, Sudan, Oct. 3, 1944; came to U.S., 1962; married, 1967; 1 child. BS, Fairleigh Dickinson U., 1966; MD, St. Louis U. Med. Sch., 1969; PhD in Physiology and Biophysics, U. Ky., 1973. Spl. fellow rsch. dept. physiology and biophysics U. Ky., 1972-73, from asst. prof. to prof. depts. human devel. and biochemistry, 1982-87; chair pharmacology and toxicology U. Kans., Lawrence, 1988—. Dir. ctr. biomed. rsch. and Higuchi bioscis. rsch. ctr. U. Kans., 1988—. Mem. AAAS, Am. Soc. Neurochemistry, Am. Soc. Biochemistry and Molecular Biology, Internat. Soc. Biomedical Rsch. on Alcoholism, Soc. Neuroscience, N.Y. Acad. Sci. Achievements include research in characterization of L-glutamate receptors in neuronal membranes, in membrane protein isolation and chemical analysis, in characterization of membrane transport systems for amino acids, sodium, potassium, and calcium, in neuronal membrane biophysics, in molecular neurobiology.

MICHAELIS, MICHAEL, management and technical consultant; b. Berlin, June 8, 1919; s. George and Martha (Bluth) M.; m. Diana Ordway Tead, Sept. 11, 1954; children: Ordway Peter, David Tead; m. Cintra McIlwain Williams, Mar. 19, 1966 (div. Nov. 1975); m. Caroline Crutcher Bishop, Mar. 17, 1984. BSc in Engring., U. London, 1941. Rsch. asst., group leader Rsch. Labs. Gen. Electric Co., Ltd., U.K., 1935-45, staff physicist and cons., 1945-49; dir. physics divsn. Radiochem. Centre, U.K. Atomic Energy Authority, 1949-51; cons. Arthur D. Little, Inc., Cambridge, Mass., 1951-52, staff cons., 1952-61, sr. asso., 1957-61, head nuclear mgmt. cons. services, 1956-61, internat. bus. devel. services, 1959-61, policy adviser to several large corps, 1954-61, mgr. Washington ops., 1963-72, sr. cons., 1972-81; pres., CEO Partners In Enterprise, Inc., 1981—2000. Cons. to Pres.'s Spl. Asst. Sci. and Tech., The White House, 1961-63; exec. sec. The White House Panel on Civilian Tech., 1961-63; exec. dir. rsch. mgmt. adv. panel, com. on sci. and tech. U.S. Ho. of Reps., 1963-67; dep. coord. then Pres.-elect Carter's Task Force on Sci. and Tech. Policy, 1976; mem. tech. adv. bd. to U.S. Sec. Commerce, 1978-81; mem. citizens adv. coun. Congl. Caucus for Sci. and Tech., 1983-86; mem. nat. com. Am. Goals and Resources, Nat. Planning Assn., 1964-67, mem. adv. com. sci., tech. and economy, 1966-68; vice chmn. com. internat. affairs Atomic Indsl. Forum, 1958-60; assoc. with Anglo-Am. Radar Rsch. Project, World War II. Editor, project dir.: Federal Funding of Civilian Research and Development, 1976; Contbr. articles to profl. jours. Fellow AAAS (chmn. engring. sect. 1980-82, exec. dir. sr. scientists and engrs. program 1989-90); mem. IEEE (sr.), Sci. Film Assn. (founder 1943, sec. 1943-48, v.p. 1948-51), Am. Nuclear Soc., Boston Com. Fgn. Rels., Royal Inst. Physics and Phys. Soc., Soc. Internat. Devel., Royal Instn. Elec. Engrs., Assn. Hosp. Physicists, Nat. Planning Assn., World Future Soc. (dir.), U.S. C. of C. (chmn. com. on govt.-industry rels. in sci. and tech. 1963-64), Interdisciplinary Comm. Assocs. Inc. (dir. 1969-79), Am. Econ. Assn., Am. Soc. Cybernetics, Am. Soc. for Pub. Adminstrn., Atlantic Coun. U.S., Cosmos Club (Washington, sec. 1994-97, v.p. 1997-98, pres. 1998-99), Harvard Faculty Club. Home and Office: 6812 Meadow Ln Chevy Chase MD 20815-5018 Office Phone: 301-986-1950. E-mail: zmichael@verizon.net. *The Constitution of the U.S. diffuses power so as to better secure liberty. But it also intends that practice will integrate the dispersed powers into a workable government. It confers upon its branches autonomy but also reciprocity, separateness but also interdependence. It is incumbent on each of us to help make this system work, and to make it responsive to the human needs of our country and the world.*

MICHAELIS, PAUL CHARLES, engineering physicist executive; b. Bronx, N.Y., June 18, 1935; s. Paul Fredrick and Rose (Landsbury) M.; m. Geraldine A. DeCuollo, June 29, 1958; 1 son, Paul Charles. BS in Elec. Engring, Newark Coll. Engring., 1964, MS in Physics, 1967. With AT&T Bell Labs., Murray Hill and Whippany, N.J., 1953-96; assoc. mem. tech. staff Bell Telephone Labs., 1963-67, mem. tech. staff, 1967-82, tech. mgr., 1982-96, ret., 1996; founder P.C. Michaelis Tech. Cons. Inc., Watchung, N.J., 1996—. Lectr. USSR Acad. Scis., 1972 Contbr. articles to profl. jours.; patentee in optics, magnetics, mechanics and electronics. Mem. IEEE (life; Morris N. Liebmann award 1975), AAAS, Am. Phys. Soc., U.S. Naval Inst., Am. Soc. Naval Engrs., Lions (past pres. Watchung club), Raritan Yacht Club (sec.). Home: 103 High Tor Dr Watchung NJ 07069-5424 also: 151 Amherst Dr Bayville NJ 08721 Office: P C Michaelis Tech Cons Inc 103 High Tor Dr Watchung NJ 07069-5424 E-mail: paul@michaelis.com.

MICHAELS, ALAN RICHARD, sports commentator; b. Bklyn., N.Y., Nov. 12, 1944; s. Jay Leonard and Lila Ruth (Ross) Michaels; m. Linda Anne Stamaton, Aug. 27, 1966; children: Steven, Jennifer. BA, Ariz. State U., 1966. TV/radio play-by-play announcer Cin. Reds, 1971—73, San Francisco Giants, 1974—76; sports commentator ABC TV Network, N.Y.C., 1976—. Recipient Nat. Sportscaster of Yr. award, Nat. Sportscasters and Sportswriters Assn., 1980, 1983, 1986, Emmy award, 1987. Avocations: reading, tennis. Office: ABC Sports Inc 47 W 66th St New York NY 10023-6290

MICHAELS, ALEX P. film company executive; s. Sylvester Dunlap and Rosa McCastle. CEO Prelude2Cinema/Prelude Prodns., Inc., Cleve. Author: (TV movie) What Angels Fear (Emmy Award, 1999, Dramatic Scene award, 1999); dir.: (short movie) The IT girl (3 1/2 Stars Film Threat, 2003). Avocations: jazz/ blues, chess. Office: Prelude2Cinema/ Prelude Productions Inc 2847 Ambler Ave Cleveland OH 44104 Personal E-mail: showbiz@prelude2cinema.com.

MICHAELS, ELISE **See GILLEM, ELISE**

MICHAELS, HELENE, broadcast executive; m. Geoffrey De Stefano, 2000. Pres. Columbia Tristar TV, Culver City, Calif. Office: Columbia Tristar TV 9336 Washington Blvd Culver City CA 90232-2628

MICHAELS, JACK D. office furniture manufacturing executive; BSME, U. Cin. Various postions Internat. Harvester Co., sr. v.p., gen. mgr., mng. dir., worldwide pres. agrl. and constrn. equipment ops., J. I. Case Co.; pres.-internat. Hussmann Corp., pres., CEO; pres. Hon Industries, Inc., Muscatine, Iowa, 1990—, CEO, 1991—, chmn., 1996—. Office: Hon Industries Inc 414 E 3rd St PO Box 1109 Muscatine IA 52761-7109

MICHAELS, JENNIFER TONKS, foreign language educator; b. Sedgley, England, May 19, 1945; d. Frank Gordon and Dorothy (Compston) Tonks; m. Eric Michaels, 1973; children: Joseph, David, Ellen. MA, U. Edinburgh, 1967, McGill U., 1971, PhD, 1974. Teaching asst. German dept. Wesleyan U., 1967-68; instr. German dept. Bucknell (Pa.) U., 1968-69; teaching asst. German dept. McGill U., Can., 1969-72; prodn. asst. Pub. TV News and Polit. program, Schenectady, N.Y., 1974-75; from asst. prof. to assoc. prof. Grinnell (Iowa) Coll., 1975-87, prof., 1987—. Vis. cons. German dept. Hamilton Coll., 1981; cons. Modern Lang. dept. Colby Coll.; panelist NEH, 1985; spkr. in field. Author: D.H. Lawrence, The Polarity of North and South, 1976, Anarchy and Eros: Otto Gross' Impact on German Expressionist Writers, 1983, Franz Jung: Expressionist, Dadaist, Revolutionary and Outsider, 1989, Franz Werfel and the Critics, 1994; contbr. numerous articles, revs. to profl. jours. Mem. MLA, Am. Assn. Tchrs. of German, Soc. Exile Studies, German Studies Assn. (sec. treas. 1991-92, v.p. 1992-94, pres. 1995-96, numerous coms.). Democrat. Avocations: music, travel, reading. Office: Grinnell Coll German Dept PO Box 805 Grinnell IA 50112-0805 E-mail: michaels@grinnell.edu.

MICHAELS, JOHN PATRICK, JR., investment banker, media broker; b. Orlando, Fla., May 28, 1944; s. John Patrick and Mary Elizabeth (Slemons) M.; 1 child, Kimberly Lynn. Grad., Jamaica Coll., Kingston, 1961; BA magna cum laude, Tulane U., 1966; MA in Comm. (ABC fellow), U. Pa., 1968; MA (hon.), St. Leo Coll., 1981. With Times Mirror Co., 1968-72; v.p. mktg. and devel. TM Comms. Co., 1968-72; v.p. Cable Funding, NYC, 1973; founder, chmn. Comm. Equity Assoc., 1973—. Tulane scholar, 1962-66; Tulane fellow, 1963-66. Fellow Inst. Dir. (London), Royal Overseas Club (UK), RNC Regents (co-chmn.); mem. Master of Fox Hounds, Nat. Cable TV Assn., Cable TV Pioneers, Broadcast Pioneers, Phi Beta Kappa, Phi Eta Sigma, Sigma Chi (Significant SIG). Home: 5117 S Nichol St Tampa FL 33611-4132 Office: 101 E Kennedy Blvd Ste 3300 Tampa FL 33602-5151

MICHAELS, LORNE, television writer, producer; b. Toronto, Ont., Can., Nov. 17, 1944; Grad., U. Toronto, 1966. Former prodr. CBC, Toronto; writer Rowan and Martin's Laugh-In, NBC, also other TV series, L.A., 1968-75; chmn. bd., founder Broadway Video, N.Y.C. Writer, prodr. (TV series) The Hart & Lorne Terrific Hour, 1970, writer, exec. prodr. Saturday Night Live, 1975—80, 1985—; prodr.: (TV series) The New Show, 1984; exec. prodr.: Sunday Night, 1988, The Kids in the Hall, 1989—94, Late Night with Conan O'Brien, 1993—, The Vacant Lot, 1994; writer, prodr. (TV special) Lily Tomlin, 1975, The Paul Simon Special, 1977, Steve Martin's Best Show Ever, 1981, The Best of John Belushi, 1985; prodr.: (TV special) Saturday Night Live - Robbin Williams, 1986, The Best of Gilda Radner, 1989, Saturday Night Live: The Best of Eddie Murphy, 1998, Saturday Night Live: The Best of Steve Martin, 1999, Saturday Night Live: The Best of Dana Carvey, 1999, Saturday Night Live: The Best of Chris Rock, 1999, Saturday Night Live: The Best of Will Ferrell, 2002; writer, exec. prodr. (TV special) The Best of Dan Aykroyd, 1986; exec. prodr.: (TV special) Saturday Night Live: The Best of Chris Farley, 1998, Saturday Night Live: The Best of Phil Hartman, 1998, Saturday Night Live: The Best of Mike Myers, 1998, Saturday Night Live: The Best of Adam Sandler, 1999; co-exec. prodr. (TV special) Rolling Stone Presents Twenty Years of Rock & Roll, 1987; prodr.: (TV films) Things We Did Last Summer, 1977; exec. prodr.: The Rutles: All You Need Is Cash, 1978, Mr. Mike's Mondo Video, 1979, Simon and Garfunkel: The Concert in Central Park, 1982, The Rutles 2: Can't Buy Me Lunch, 2002, America's Most Terrible Things, 2002; writer, prodr. (TV films) Gilda Live, 1980, (films) Three Amigos, 1986; prodr.: (films) Coneheads, 1983, Nothing Lasts Forever, 1984, Wayne's World, 1992, Coneheads, 1993, Wayne's World II, 1993, Tommy Boy, 1995, Stuart Saves His Family, 1995, Black Sheep, 1996, Kids in the Hall: Brain Candy, 1996, A Night at the Roxbury, 1998, Superstar, 1999, The Ladies Man, 2000, Enigma, 2001. Recipient 4 awards Writers Guild Am., 8 Emmy awards NATAS; named Broadcaster of Yr. Internat. Radio and TV Soc., 1992; recipient George Foster Peabody award for Saturday Night Live, 1990; named to TV Acad. Hall of Fame, 1999; received star on Hollywood Walk of fame. Office: Broadway Video 1619 Broadway Fl 9 New York NY 10019-7463*

MICHAELS, MARION CECELIA, newswriter, editor, news syndicate executive; b. Black River Falls, Wis. d. Leonard N. and Estelle O. (Payne) Doud; m. Charles Webb (div.); children: Charles, David, Robert; m. Mark J. Michaels (div.); 1 child, Merry A. Student, MIT, 1962-64, U. Wis., 1971-76, BS in Bus. Edn., 1978, MS in Spl. Edn., 1981. Mgr., instr. bus. program Blackwell Job Corps Ctr., 1987-89; mgr. Michaels Secretarial Svc., Black River Falls, Wis., 1979-83; columnist, editor Michaels News, Black River Falls, 1983—, pres., 1989—. Hon. appt. rsch. bd. advisors Am. Biog. Inst., 1996-2001. Author: The Little Cowboy: Pursuing Dana's Dream, 1998, September's Song, 2003—, Dana's Dream, 2004; columnist Single Parenting, 1983—94, Parenting Plus, 1990—2004, editor, contbr. (column) Surviving Single, 1990—95, To Read or Not (Fiction), 1985—, To Read or Not (Non-Fiction), 1985—2004, Report From Planet Earth, 1985—2004, Travel Tidbits, 1991—95, Surviving Sane, 1995—98. Chmn. Brockway Cmty. Orgn., 1969-71; chair, counselor Brockway Youth Group, 1970-72; chmn. labor com. Dem. Platform Com., Wis., 1975-76; candidate State Assembly, 1978, 82; co-founder Franklin Delano Roosevelt Meml., 1997; mem. LWV. Named to Internat. Poetry Hall of Fame, 1997. Mem.: Assn. Rsch. and Enlightenment, Physicians for Social Responsibility, Union Concerned Scientists, Internat. Soc. Poets (Poet of Yr. nominee 1997, 1999, Internat. Poet of Merit award 1999, Poet of Yr. nominee 2000, 2001, 2002, 2003), Women's History Mus. (charter mem.), Wilson Ctr., League of Conservation Voters, Inst. for Noetic Sci., Amnesty Internat., Pub. Citizen, Am. United, Nat. Parks, Clean Wis., So. Poverty Law Ctr., Natural Resources Def. Coun., Co-op Am., Nat. Trust for Pub. Edn., Friends of the Earth, Peale Ctr. for Positive Living, Nat. Com. to Protect Soc. Security and Medicare, Common Cause, Internat. Fund for Animals, Phi Delta Kappa, Pi Omega Pi. Avocations: singing, dance, walking, swimming.

MICHAELS, RICHARD EDWARD, lawyer; b. Chgo., June 10, 1952; s. Benjamin and Lillian (Borawski) Mikolajczewski; m. Karen Lynn Belau Michaels, May 17, 1980; children: Jonathan R., Timothy R., Matthew R. BS in Commerce summa cum laude, DePaul U., 1973; JD, Northwestern U., 1977. Bar: Ill. 1977, U.S. Dist. Ct. (no. dist.) Ill. 1977, U.S. Ct. Appeals (7th cir.) 1977; CPA, Ill. Acct. Touche Ross & Co., Chgo., 1973-74; assoc. Schuyler, Roche & Zwirner and predecessor firm Hubachek & Kelly Ltd., Chgo., 1977-83; ptnr. Schuyler, Roche & Zwirner, Chgo., 1983—, pres., 1994—. Mem. adv. bd. Thrivent Fin., 2002—. Mem. Northwestern U. Law Rev., 1976-77. Mem. adv. bd. Greater Chgo. agy. Luth. Brotherhood, 1999—2002; chmn. Hawkswimming Maine South H.S., 2001—02; vice chmn. congregation St. Andrew's Luth. Ch., Park Ridge, Ill., 1990—92, chmn. congregation, 1992—94. Mem. ABA, Internat. Bar Assn., Ill. Bar Assn., Chgo. Bar Assn., DePaul U. Alumni Assn., DePaul U. Boosters, Chgo. Athletic Assn., Northwestern Club, C.A.A. Club, Beta Gamma Sigma, Pi Gamma Mu, Beta Alpha Psi. Lutheran. Avocations: photography, golf. Home: 808 Elm St Park Ridge IL 60068-3312 Office: Schuyler Roche & Zwirner 130 E Randolph St Ste 3800 Chicago IL 60601-6342 Office Phone: 312-565-8438. Business E-Mail: rmichaels@srzlaw.com.

MICHAELS, ROBERT A. real estate development company executive; BSBA, JD, U. S.D. With Gen. Growth, 1972—, gen. counsel, exec. v.p., dir. corp. leasing; pres., CEO Gen. Growth Mgmt., Inc.; pres., COO Gen. Growth Properties, Inc. Bd. dirs. Gen. Growth Properties, Inc., Gen. Growth Mgmt., Inc.; bd. dirs. Ctr. for Urban Land Econs. Rsch., Sch. of Bus. U. Wis.-Madison.; spkr. in field. Editor Law Rev., U. S.D.; contbr. articles to profl.

jours. Mem. ABA, S.D. Bar Assn., Iowa Bar Assn., Minn. Bar Assn., Internat. Coun. of Shopping Ctrs. (exec. com., bd. trustees, govt. affairs chmn. states Iowa, Nebr., S.D., state dir. Minn., S.D., N.D.). Office: 110 N Wacker Dr Chicago IL 60606-1511*

MICHAELS, WILLARD A. (BILL MICHAELS), retired broadcasting executive; b. Omaha, May 13, 1917; s. Gus M. and Bessie (Kerstine) M.; m. Helen Louise Mintel, Nov. 20, 1938 (dec. Sept. 2000); children: Marcella, Lawrence Richard, Betty Michaels Westbrook BA, Trinity U., 1940. Asst. sports editor San Antonio Express, 1937-40; sports announcer, sales mgr., gen. mgr. KABC, San Antonio, 1940-53; gen. mgr. KGBS-TV, 1954; v.p. WJBK-TV, Detroit, 1955-61; dir. Storer Broadcasting Co., Miami Beach, Fla., 1960-85, TV v.p., 1961-66, exec. v.p., 1966-67, pres., 1967-74, chmn., 1974-82, ret., 1982. Chmn. New Boston Garden Corp. (Boston Bruins), 1972-75; dir., mem. exec. com. Northeast Airlines, 1965-72, pres., 1970-72; dir. Delta Airlines, 1972-90, adv. dir., 1990—. Trustee Storer Found. Home: 154 Manchester Way Shavano Pk San Antonio TX 78249

MICHAELSON, ARTHUR M. lawyer; b. N.Y.C., May 16, 1927; s. Samuel H. and Augusta L. M.; m. Arline L. Kahn, June 30, 1957; children: Barbara L., Sarah E., David N. AB, Columbia U., 1947; LLB, Yale U., 1950. Bar: N.Y. 1950, U.S. Supreme Ct 1964. Partner Wachtel & Michaelson, N.Y.C., 1957-66; v.p. McCrory Corp., N.Y.C., 1966-68, Glen Alden Corp., N.Y.C., 1968-73; partner Miller, Singer, Michaelson & Raives, N.Y.C., 1973-84; counsel Hofheimer Gartlir & Gross, 1984—. Author: (with J. Blattmachr) Income Taxation of Estates and Trusts, 1980, 85, 89, 95, 96, 98. Bd. dirs., mem. exec. com. Amnesty Internat. of U.S.A., Inc., 1972-81, vice chmn., 1975-76. Served with USN, 1945-46. Mem. ABA, Assn. Bar City N.Y. Office: 530 5th Ave New York NY 10036-5101

MICHAELSON, BENJAMIN, JR., lawyer, director; b. Annapolis, Md., May 30, 1936; s. Benjamin and Naomi Madora (Dill) M.; m. Frances Means Blackwell, Apr. 12, 1986; children: Benjamin, Robert Wendell. BA, U. Va., 1957; JD, U. Md., 1962. Bar: Md. 1962, U.S. Dist. Ct. Md. 1976. Assoc. Goodman, Bloom & Michaelson, Annapolis, Md., 1962-63; atty. pvt. practice, Annapolis, 1963-73, 77-81; sr. ptnr. Michaelson & Christhilf, Annapolis, 1973-77; ptnr. Michaelson & Simmons, Annapolis, 1982-86, Michaelson & Newell, Annapolis, 1987-88, Michaelson, Krause & Ferris, Annapolis, 1988-91; atty. pvt. practice, Annapolis, 1991-2000; of counsel McNamee, Hosea, Jernigan & Kim, 2000—04. Pres. Michaelson Title & Escrow Co., 1993-2001; gen. counsel, dir. Annapolis Fed. Savs., 1965-94 Counsel Anne Arundel County (Md.) Bd. Edn., 1966-76; mem. vestry St. Anne's Episcopal Ch., Annapolis, 1997-2003, sr. warden, 1999-2003. Lt. U.S. Army, 1957-59. Fellow: Am. Coll. Mortgage Attys.; mem.: Anne Arundel County Bar Assn., Md. Bar Assn. (chmn. real property, planning and zoning sect. coun. 1982—84, grievances commn. inquiry panel 1976—85, vice chmn. 1983—85, grievance commn. rev. bd. 1985—88), Jaycees (Md. state legal counsel 1964—65, nat. dir. 1965—66, Outstanding Young Men Am. 1995), Rotary (pres. 1975—76, Paul Harris fellow), Sailing Club Chesapeake (commodore 1982), Delta Theta Phi. Republican. Episcopalian. Home: 1612 Winchester Rd Annapolis MD 21401 Office: 705 Melvin Ave Ste 102 Annapolis MD 21401-1534

MICHAELSON, PETER LEE, lawyer; b. N.Y.C., Aug. 29, 1952; BS in Elec. Engring. and Econs., Carnegie-Mellon U., 1974, MSEE, 1975; JD, Duquesne U., 1979; LLM in Trade Regulation, NYU, 1985; postgrad., Harvard U., 1993, 96, 97, postgrad., 96, 97, 99. Bar: Pa. 1979, N.J. 1980, (U.S. Patent and Trademark Office) 1980, (U.S. Dist. Ct. N.J.) 1980, (U.S. Ct. Claims) 1980, (U.S. Ct. Mil. Appeals) 1980, (U.S. Tax Ct.) 1980, (U.S. Ct. Appeals (3d cir.)) 1981, (U.S. Ct. Appeals (fed. cir.)) 1983, N.Y. 1986, (U.S. Supreme Ct.) 1986, Alaska 2000, cert.: Ctr. Effective Dispute Resolution (mediator), lic.: Chartered Inst. Arbitrators, Eng. (arbitrator). Electronics project engr. Control Systems Research, Inc., Pitts., 1975-76; electronics devel. engr. Aluminum Co. Am., Alcoa Tech. Ctr., Prodn. Equip. Lab., Pitts., 1976-77, Rockwell Internat. Corp., Pitts., 1977-79; corp. patent atty., mem. patent and legal staff Bell Telephone Labs., Holmdel, N.J., 1979-82; atty. Pennie & Edmonds, N.Y.C., 1982-84; prin. Michaelson & Assocs., Counsellors at Law, Red Bank, NJ, 1984—. Mem. disting. panel neutrals tech. ICANN domain names and Y2K panels CPR Inst. Dispute Resolution, N.Y.C.; accredited mediator Centre for Effective Dispute Resolution, London; approved mediator/arbitrator in intellectual property and ICANN domain name and keyword disputes World Intellectual Property Orgn., Geneva; arbitrator ICANN domain name disputes, mem. adv. com. IP panel Nat. Arbitration Forum, Mpls.; arbitrator, mediator U.S. Dist. Ct. (ea. dist.) N.Y.; arbitrator London Ct. Internat. Arbitration, N.Am. Coun., Internat. C.of C., Paris, Internat. Ct. Arbitration, U.S. Coun. for Internat. Bus., N.Y.C.; mediator N.J. Superior Ct.; mem. CPR Inst. Dispute Resolution; master Justice Marie Garibaldi Am. Inn of Ct. for Alternative Dispute Resolution; arbitrator comm. and tech. panel Am. Arbitration Assn.; mem. CEDR, London; mediator, arbitrator Intellectual Property Panel, mem. adv. com.; presenter in field US and Abroad. Contbr. articles to profl. jours. Mem. Sch. Budget Adv. Com., Rumson, NJ, 1981—85, Zoning Bd. Adjustment, Rumson, 1988—93. Fellow: Chartered Inst. Arbitrators; mem.: AIPPI, Assn. Fed. Bar N.J., Monmouth County Bar Assn., Fed. Bar Assn., Monmouth County Bar Assn., Assn. Conflict Resolution, N.J. Intellectual Property Law Assn., Am. Intellectual Property Law Assn., Am. Arbitration Assn. Home: 15 Holly Tree Ln Rumson NJ 07760-1950 Office: Michaelson & Assocs 328 Newman Springs Rd Parkway 109 Office Ctr PO Box 8489 Red Bank NJ 07701-8489 Office Phone: 732-530-6671. E-mail: pmichaelson@mandw.com.

MICHALAK, EDWARD FRANCIS, lawyer; b. Evanston, Ill., Sept. 6, 1937; s. Leo Francis Michalak and Helen Sophie (Wolinski) Krakowski. BSBA, Northwestern U., 1959; LLB, Harvard U., 1962. Bar: Ill. 1962. Assoc. McDermott, Will & Emery, Chgo., 1963-69, ptnr., 1969—. Served to sgt. USAR, 1962-68. Mem. Ill. Bar Assn., Chgo. Bar Assn., Beta Gamma Sigma, Beta Alpha Psi. Roman Catholic. Avocations: golf, opera. Home: 3455 Harrison St Evanston IL 60201-4953 Office: McDermott Will & Emery 227 W Monroe St 47th Fl Chicago IL 60606-5096 Office Phone: 312-984-7506. Business E-Mail: emichalak@mwe.com.

MICHALAK, JANET CAROL, childhood education educator, coordinator; b. Buffalo, Mar. 22, 1949; d. Theodore and Thelma Ruth (Roesch) Vukovic; m. Gerald Paul Michalak, June 19, 1971; children: Nathan, Justin. BS in Edn., SUNY Coll. at Buffalo, Buffalo, 1970; MS in Edn., SUNY, Buffalo, 1971, EdD, 1981. Cert. tchr. nursery, kindergarten, grades 1-6, reading tchr., English tchr. grades 7-12, N.Y. Reading tchr. Tonawanda (N.Y.) Sch. System, 1971-80; instr. Niagara County C.C., Sanborn, N.Y., 1980-82, asst. prof., 1982-85, assoc. prof., 1985-91, prof., 1991—, coord., prof. childhood edn. Adj. lectr. SUNY, Buffalo, 1990—91. Recipient Pres.'s award for Excellence in Teaching, Niagara County C.C., 1990, Nat. Inst. for Staff & Orgnl. Devel. Excellence award, 1991, SUNY Chancellor's award for Excellence in Teaching, 1991. Mem. Coll. Reading Assn., Internat. Reading Assn., N.Y. Coll. Learning Skills Assn., Niagara Frontier Reading Coun. (bd. dirs. 1986-88, 97—). Republican. Avocation: reading. Home: 184 Montbleu Dr Getzville NY 14068-1329 Office: Niagara County CC 3111 Saunders Settlement Rd Sanborn NY 14132-9487 E-mail: michalak2@yahoo.com., michalak@niagasacc.suny.edu.

MICHALEK, SUZANNE M. biology professor; b. Chgo., July 19, 1944; BS, Ill. State U., 1967, MS, 1968; PhD in Microbiology, U. Ala., 1976. Rsch. asst. microbiology and immunology Nat. Inst. Dental Rsch. NIH, Bethesda, Md., 1972-76, fellow microbiology and immunology, 1977-79; investigator Inst. Dental Rsch. U. Ala., Birmingham, 1980-85, scientist, 1985—, sr. investigator Rsch. Ctr. Oral Biology, 1988—. Mem. Am. Soc. Microbiology, Am. Assn. Immunologists, Internat. Assn. Dental Rsch., Am. Assn. Dental Rsch., Soc. Exptl. Biology and Medicine. Office: U Ala Rsch Ctr in Oral Biology Bbrb 258 845 S 19th St Birmingham AL 35294-0001

MICHALIK, JOHN JAMES, legal educational association executive; b. Bemidji, Minn., Aug. 1, 1945; m. Diane Marie Olson, Dec. 21, 1968; children: Matthew John, Nicole, Shane. BA, U. Minn., 1967, JD, 1970. Legal editor Lawyers Coop. Pub. Co., Rochester, NY, 1970—75; dir. continuing legal edn. Wash. State Bar Assn., Seattle, 1975—81, exec. dir., 1981—91; asst. dean devel. and cmty. rels. Sch. Law U. Wash., 1991—95; dir., CEO Assn. Legal Adminstrs., Vernon Hills, Ill., 1995—. Fellow: Coll. Law Practice Mgmt.; mem.: Nat. Trust Hist. Preservation, Am. Mgmt. Assn., Am. Soc. Assn. Execs. Lutheran. Office: Assn Legal Adminstrs 75 Tri-State Internat Ctr # 222 Lincolnshire IL 60069-4435 E-mail: jmichalik@alanet.org.

MICHALOPOULOS, GEORGE KONSTANTINE, academic administrator; b. Samos, Greece, Jan. 1, 1946; came to U.S., 1971; m. Patricia Michalopoulos. MD, Athens U. Med. Sch., Greence, 1969; PhD, U. Wis., 1977. Intern U. Wis., 1971-72, resident, 1972-77; asst. prof. pathology Duke U. Med. Ctr., Durham, N.C., 1977-83, assoc. prof. pathology, 1983-87, prof. pathology, 1987-91; prof., chmn. dept. pathology U. Pitts. Sch. Medicine, 1991—, assoc. vice chancellor health scis., interim dean, 1995-98. Rschr. in liver regeneration; lectr. in field. Mem. editl. bd. Human Pathology, Journal of Pathology, Lab. Investigation Jour. of the Nat. Cancer Inst., Jour. of Cell Physiology. Mem. AMA, Am. Soc. Investigative Pathology (coun. mem., mem. rsch. com.), U.S. and Can. Acad. Pathology, Am. Assn. Cancer Rsch., Am. Assn. Pathologists, Am. Assn. Study of Liver Disease, Am. Soc. Cell Biology, Allegheny County Med. Assn., Pitts. Pathology Soc., Cell Biology Soc., Univ. Assn. Rsch. & Edn. in Pathology (v.p. 1994-95, mem. long-range planning com.), Assn. Pathology (mem. rsch. com), Am Soc. for Investigative Pathology (coun. mem. 1994-96), Assn. of Molecular Pathology (founding mem. 1994). Office: U Pitts Sch Medicine S410 Biomed Sci Tower Dept Pathology 200 Lothrow St Pittsburgh PA 15261

MICHALS, LEE MARIE, travel agency administrator; b. Chgo., June 6, 1939; d. Harry Joseph and Anna Marie (Monaco) Perzan; children: Debora Ann, Dana Lee, Jami. BA, Wright Coll., 1959. Cert. travel specialist and cons., destination specialist. Internat. travel sec. E.F. MacDonald Travel, Palo Alto, Calif., 1963-69; pres. Travel Experience, Santa Clara, Calif., 1973-88; ptnr. Cruise Connection, Mountain View, Calif., 1983-85; travel specialist Allways Travel, Sunnyvale, Calif., 1992-98; adminstrv. asst. Ventures Extraordinaire, Inc., San Mateo, Calif., 1998—. Former stars rep. Hertz, Ritz Carlton, Marriott Hotels, various airlines and tour cos. Mem. Am. Soc. Travel Agts., Inst. Cert. Travel Agts., Bay Area Travel Assn., Pacific Area Travel Agts., San Jose Women in Travel (organizing pres. 1971, 1st v.p. 1989, del. to internat. fedn. women's travel orgn. 1997-99). Office: Sutter Travel 693 E Remington Dr #A Sunnyvale CA 94087 Office Phone: 408-481-3838.

MICHALSKI, THOMAS JOSEPH, city planner, developer; b. Waukesha, Wis., Jan. 28, 1933; s. Thomas and Anna (Benca) M. B.Arch., U. Mich., 1956, M.City Planning, 1959; postgrad., Magdalene Coll., U. Cambridge, Eng., 1988—. Urban renewal planner City of Milw., 1956-57; land planner, urban designer Baltimore County, Md., 1959-60; planning cons. City of N.Y., 1961-77; project mgr. Yanbu Indsl. Complex, Royal Comm., Saudi Arabia, 1980-83; cons. UN Ctr. for Human Settlements, Habitat Nairobi, Kenya, 1984—; bd. Community Housing Initiative Trust, 1993-98; faculty U. Mich., 1994; bd. dirs., cons. EMTEL, Inc., 2000—02. Mem. faculty NYU, 1965-66, CUNY, 1970-71, Rollins Coll., 1992—; town planning cons. new town in Iran, 1977; mem. Community Bd. 8, N.Y.C., 1972-76, chmn. landmarks com.; cons. Islamic Devel. Bank, 1989—, Fla. Solar Energy Ctr. Affordable Living Conf., 1991. Author: In Search of Purpose: Essays on Planning the Human Environment, 1961, Human Values and the Emerging City, 1967 Founding mem. Friends of Cen. park; 1000 Friends of Fla., 1987—; pres. Brevard 21 Inc., 1988—; bd. govs. Coll. Architecture and Urban Planning, U. Mich., 1984-88; bd. ACLU, 1993—. Wis. Architects Found. scholar, 1953-56; Vincent Astor Found. grantee, 1971, World Wildlife Fund Successful Communities grantee, 1991. Fellow Am. Hort. Soc.; mem. Am. Planning Assn. (charter), Am. Inst. Cert. Planners, Royal Town Planning Inst., Town and Country Planning Assn., Internat. Fedn. Housing and Planning, Nat. Trust for Historic Preservation, Wis. Soc. Archtl. Historians, Mich. Urban Planning Alumni Soc. (bd. dirs. 1984-88), Audubon Soc. Fla. (chmn. conservation com. 1987-91), Assn. for Asian Studies, Worldwatch Inst., English-Speaking Union (London), Brevard County (Fla.) Democratic exec. com., So. Poverty Law Ctr., U. Mich. Club (N.Y.C.), Sierra Club, Delta Chi (Morrey Outstanding Alumnus award 1984). Roman Catholic. Home: 1925 Greenway Dr Apt I1 Melbourne FL 32901-4446 E-mail: tjmichalski1@aol.com. *The educated person prepares mightily to do something constructive about that which is displeasing, to sustain that which is good, and to discriminate the one from the other.*

MICHAUD, GEORGES JOSEPH, astrophysics educator; b. Que., Can., Apr. 30, 1940; s. Marie-Louis and Isabelle (St. Laurent) M.; m. Denise Lemieux, June 25, 1966. BA, U. Laval, Que., 1961, BSc, 1965; PhD, Calif. Tech. Inst., Pasadena, 1970. Prof. U. Montreal, Can., 1969—; dir. Ctr. Rsch. en Calcul Appliqué, 1992-96, assoc. dean of grad. studies, 1997-2000. Recipient Steacie prize NRC, 1980, Medaille Janssen, Acad. Scis., Paris, 1982, Prix Vincent, ACFAS, 1979; Killam fellow Conseil des Arts, 1987-89. Office: Universite de Montreal Dept de Physique Montreal QC Canada H3C 3J7 E-mail: georges.michaud@umontreal.ca.

MICHAUD, MICHAEL ALAN GEORGE, diplomat, writer; b. Hollywood, Calif., Aug. 22, 1938; s. George Emile and Nathalie Adele (Neagles) M.; m. Carmen Yvonne Mitchell, Sept. 1960 (div. 1963); m. M. Grace Russo, June 5, 1965 (div. 1996); m. Sandra Arbuthnot, July 31, 1996; children: Jon C., Cassandra M., Jason M., Joshua M. BA, UCLA, 1960, MA, 1963; postgrad., Georgetown U., 1978-79. Commd. fgn. service officer Dept. State, 1963; consular officer Dacca, East Pakistan, 1963-65; analyst Bur. Intelligence and Research/Dept. State, Washington, 1965-66; staff asst. Bur. Near Eastern and South Asian Affairs Dept. State, Washington, 1966-67; polit. officer Am. Embassy, Tehran, 1967-68, econ. officer, 1968-70; info. officer USIS, Bombay, India, 1970-72, co-dir., 1971-72; country officer for Iran Dept. State, 1972-74, country officer Australia, Papua New Guinea and Solomon Islands, Bur. East Asian Affairs, 1974-76; dep. dir. Office Internat. Security Policy, Bur. Politico-Mil. Affairs, 1976-78; trainee Georgetown U., Washington, 1978-79; officer-in-charge U.K. and Bermuda Affairs, Bur. European Affairs Dept. State, 1979-80; consul gen. Am. Consulate Gen. Belfast, No. Ireland, 1980-83; Una Chapman Cox fellow Fgn. Service Inst. Dept. State, 1983-84, div. chief fgn. service counseling and assignments, 1984-85, spl. asst. for space policy, 1985-86, dir. Office Advanced Tech., 1986-89; counselor sci., tech. and environ. affairs Am. Embassy, Paris, 1989-93, minister-counselor environ. sci. and tech. Tokyo, 1993-95. Author: Reaching for the High Frontier, 1986; editor: Flotsam and Jetsam lit. ann., 1956; founding editor: Open Forum, 1974-76 (Honor award 1976); mem. editorial bd.: Fgn. Service Jour., 1977-79; contbr. numerous articles, papers, book revs., short stories to various publs. Recipient Superior Honor award Dept. State, 1966; recipient Meritorious Honor award Dept. State, 1976; Scott fellow, 1962 Fellow Brit. Interplanetary Soc.; mem. Internat. Inst. Space Law, Internat. Acad. Astronautics, AAAS, AIAA, Space Studies Inst., Nat. Space Soc., Am. Astron. Soc., Nature Conservancy. Office: 437 Cannon House Office Building Washington DC 20515 E-mail: magmichaud@hotmail.com.

MICHAUD, MICHAEL HERMAN, congressman; b. Millinocket, Maine, Jan. 18, 1955; s. James Leroy and Jean (Morrow) M. Grad., Schenck H.S., 1973; student, U. Maine, 1979. Papermaker Gt. No. Paper Co., 1973-80, mem. staff finishing dept., 1981—; mem. dist. 134 Maine Ho. of Reps., Augusta, 1980—94, mem. regional conf. task force on environment, chmn. energy and natural resources com., spkr. pro tem, chmn. appropriations and fin. affairs com., mem. legis. svc. com.; mem. Dist. 3 Maine Senate, Augusta, 1994—2002, pres. pro tem.; mem. U.S. Ho. Reps. from 2d Maine dist., 2003—. Mem. com. Eastmill Fed. Credit Union, 1979—; area coord. Merril for Gov. campaign, 1978; v.p. Maine Young Dems., 1978-80, del. state conv., 1980, 82, 84, del. nat. conv., 1979. Mem. Nat. Conf. State Legislators, Katahdin Friend of Retarded Children Assn., East Br. Snow Rovers, KC. Democrat. Office: Great Northern Paper Co Bowater, Main St East Millinocket ME 04430 also: 437 Cannon Ho Office Bldg Washington DC 20515-1902 Home: 111 Main St East Millinocket ME 04430

MICHAUDON, ANDRÉ FRANCISQUE, physicist; b. Cavaillon, Vaucluse, France, May 14, 1929; s. Maurice Louis and Jeanne Francoise (Chatal) Michaudon; children: Claire Hello, Helene Caron. Engring. degree, Ecole Supérieure Ingenieurs Arts et Métiers, Paris, 1951, Ecole Supérieure Electricite, 1953; DSc, U. Paris, 1964. Rsch. engr. Le Materiel Teléphonique, Boulogne, France, 1954-56; group leader Commissariat à Energie Atomique, Cen Saclay, France, 1956-64, 65-72, div. head Bruyeres le Chalel, France, 1972-79, dept. dept. head Limeil, France, 1979-83; theorist MIT, Cambridge, 1964-65; French co-dir. Inst. Laue Langevin, Grenoble, France, 1983-89; prof. Inst. Nat. des Scis. et Techniques Nucléaires, Saclay, Orsay, France, 1969-84; sr. sci. adv. Los Alamos (N.Mex.) Nat. Lab., 1989—. Mem. exec. coun. European Sci. Found., Strasbourg, France, 1987—90; mem. adv. coun. Census Bur. for Nuc. Measurements, European Union, Geel, Belgium, 1990—95; cons. Orgn. for Econ. Cooperation and Devel., Paris, 1989—92. Contbr. articles to profl. jours.; author (author, editor): (book) Nuclear Fission, 1981; editor (co-gen. editor): Neutron Sources, 1983, Neutron Radiative Capture, 1984, Probability & Statistics, 1991. Lt. French Navy, 1953-54. Named knight, Order of Merit, Paris, 1984; recipient written congratulations, Minister of the Navy, France, 1954, award, Acad. des Scis., Paris, 1980. Fellow: Am. Nuclear Soc., Am. Phys. Soc.; mem.: N.Y. Acad. Scis., Francaise de Physique. Avocations: music, tennis, skiing, golf, hiking. Home: 333 Otero St Unit 6 Santa Fe NM 87501-6212 Office: Los Alamos Nat Lab Sr Sci Advisor Lansce Do Ms H 845 Los Alamos NM 87545-0001 E-mail: michaudon@lanl.gov.

MICHEJDA, OSKAR, civil engineer, structural engineer, consultant; b. Trzyniec, Silesia, Czechoslovakia, May 19, 1922; arrived in U.S., 1966; s. Oskar and Paula Michejda; m. Irena Maria Michejda, Apr. 8, 1925; 1 child, John. MSCE, Polytechnic U., Wroclaw, Poland, 1950, D of Engring., 1960. Registered profl. engr., Conn., Fla., Ind., N.J., N.Y., S.C., Wash. Prof., dean faculty Mech. Engring. Dept., Czestochowa, Poland, 1951—65; sr. lectr. Engring. Dept., Khartoum, Sudan, 1965—66; assoc. prof. Cooper Union Sch. Engring., N.Y.C., 1996—98; prof. Ind. Inst. Tech., Ft. Wayne, 1968—74; stress analysis mgr. Burns & Roe, Inc., Oradell, NJ, 1974—86; engring. cons. Sarasota, Fla., 1986. Author: (textbooks) Mechanics of Materials, 1955, others; contbr. rsch. papers to periodicals. Scholar, Sheffield U., 1959, MIT, 1960. Achievements include patents in field. Office: 3663 Country Pl Blvd Sarasota FL 34233 Office Phone: 941-921-3445.

MICHEL, ANTHONY NIKOLAUS, electrical engineering educator, researcher; b. Rekasch, Romania, Nov. 17, 1935; came to U.S., 1952; s. Anton Michel and Katharina (Metz) Malsam; m. Leone Lucille Flasch, Aug. 17, 1957; children: Mary Leone, Katherine Jean, John Peter, Anthony Joseph, Patrick Thomas. BSE.E., Marquette U., 1958, MS in Math., 1964, PhD in Elec. Engring., 1968; D.Sc. in Math., Tech. U. Graz (Austria), 1973. Registered profl. engr., Wis. Engr. in tng. U.S. Army C.E., Milw., 1958-59; project engr. AC Electronics div. Gen. Motors Corp., Milw., 1959-62, sr. research engr., 1962-65; asst. prof. elec. engring. Iowa State U., Ames, 1968-69, assoc. prof., 1969-74, prof., 1974-84; prof. elec. engring. U. Notre Dame, Ind., 1984-87, chmn. dept. elec. and computer engring., 1984-88, Frank M. Freimann prof. engring., 1988—2002, dean coll. engring., 1988—98, dean emeritus, 1998—, prof. emeritus, 2002—. Cons. Houghton Mifflin Co., 1975, Acad. Press, 1983; cons. editor William C. Brown Co. Pubs., Dubuque, Iowa, 1982-83; vis. prof. Tech. U. Vienna, 1992, Ruhr U., Bochum, Germany, 1999, Johannes Kepler U., Linz, Austria, 2004. Author: (with others) Qualitative Analysis of Large Scale Dynamical Systems, 1977, Mathematical Foundations in Engineering and Science, 1981, Ordinary Differential Equations, 1982, Applied Linear Algebra and Functional Analysis, 1993, (with Derong Liu) Dynamical Systems with Saturation Nonlinearities, 1993, (with Kaining Wang) Qualitative Theory of Dynamical Systems, 1994, (with Kaining Wang) Qualitative Theory of Dynamical Systems, 2d edit., revised and expanded, 2001, (with Panos J. Antsaklis) Linear Systems, 1997, (with Derong Liu) Qualitative Analysis and Synthesis of Recurrent Neural Networks, 2002; contbr. articles to profl. jours., chpts. to books. Research grantee NSF, 1972—; research grantee Dept. Def., 1968-72; Fulbright fellow Tech. U. Vienna, Austria, 1992; recipient Alexander von Humboldt Rsch. award U.S. Sr. Scientists, 1998. Fellow IEEE (mng. editor Trans. on Cirs. and Sys. 1981-83, Best Trans. Paper award 1978, 83, 93, Centennial medal 1984, Millenium medal 2000); mem. IEEE Cirs. and Sys. Soc. (pres.s 1989, Myril B. Reed Outstanding Paper award 1993, Tech. Achievement award 1995, Golden Jubilee medal 1999), IEEE Control Sys. Soc. (Disting. Mem. award 1998), Russian Acad. Engring. (hon.), Sigma Xi, Eta Kappa Nu, Pi Mu Epsilon, Phi Kappa Phi. Home: 17001 Stonegate Ct Granger IN 46530-6948 Office: U Notre Dame Dept Elec Engring Coll Engring Notre Dame IN 46556 Office Phone: 574-631-4395. Business E-Mail: anthony.n.michel.1@nd.edu.

MICHEL, BERNARD, civil engineering educator, consultant; b. Chicoutimi, Que., Canada, May 31, 1930; s. Joseph Williams and Jeanne (Tremblay) M.; m. Mariette Boivin, Sept. 7, 1954; children: Marianne, Francois, Luc, Jacques, Charles, Christine. B.Applied Sci., Laval U., 1954; Dr. Engring., Grenoble U., 1962. Registered profl. engr., Que. Research engr. Lasalle Hydraulic Lab., Quebec, 1956-60; head dept. civil engring. Laval U., Quebec, 1960-63, prof., 1963—; chmn., CEO Cameco Corp., Saskatoon, Can. V.p. Arctec Can. Ltd., Ottawa, Ont., 1973-78; cons. Recherches Bermic, Inc., Quebec, 1978— Author: Ice Mechanics, 1978; patentee in field. Recipient Gzowski medal Engring. Inst. Can., 1963 Fellow Engring. Inst. Can., Can. Soc. Civil Engring. (Keefer medal 1977, 81, Prix Camille A. Dagenais 1983); mem. Royal Soc. Can., mem. Internat. Assn. Hydraulic Research (chmn. com. ice problems 1970-76) *The biggest challenge in research is the understanding of natural processes, particularly in the field of glaciology. Nothing is so worthwhile to mankind as to follow up with engineering applications.*

MICHEL, CLIFFORD LLOYD, lawyer, investment executive; b. N.Y.C., Aug. 9, 1939; s. Clifford William and Barbara Lloyd (Richards) M.; m. Betsy Shirley, June 6, 1964; children: Clifford Fredrick, Jason Lloyd, Katherine Beinecke. AB cum laude, Princeton U., 1961; JD, Yale U., 1964. Bar: N.Y. 1964, U.S. Dist. Ct. (so. dist.) N.Y. 1968, U.S. Ct. Appeals (2d cir.) 1967, U.S. Supreme Ct. 1972. Assoc. Cahill Gordon & Reindel, N.Y.C., 1964-67, Paris, 1967-69, N.Y.C., 1969-71, ptnr. Paris, 1972-76, N.Y.C., 1976-2001, sr. counsel, 2001—; pres., CEO, Wenonah Devel. Co., 1976—. Bd. dirs. Alliance Barnstain Mut. Funds, Placer Dome Inc. Bd. dirs. Jockey Hollow Found., HomeWinds Found., St. Mark's Sch., Morristown Meml. Hosp., Meml. Health Found. Mem. ABA, FBA, N.Y. State Bar Assn., New York County Lawyers Assn., Am. Soc. Internat. Law, Racquet and Tennis Club, River Club, The Links, Shinnecock Hills Golf Club, Somerset Hills Country Club, Essex Hunt Club, Sankaty Head Golf Club (Mass.), Golf de Morfontaine (France), Travellers Club (Paris), Loch Lomond Club (Scotland), Nantucket Golf Club, Mayacama Golf Club, Tarratine Club. Republican. Office Phone: 908-901-0007. Personal E-mail: cowpoke0007@aol.com.

MICHEL, DONALD CHARLES, editor; b. Ventura, Calif., Nov. 17, 1935; s. Charles J. and Esther Caroline (Heilert) M.; m. Loretta Perron, May 4, 1963; children: Edwin, Robert, Christopher. BA, UCLA, 1958, MS, 1959. Editor San Fernando (Calif.) Sun, 1958-60; successively reporter, weekend editor, mng. editor Valley Times Today, North Hollywood, Calif., 1960-63; feature editor Houston Chronicle, 1963-68; asst. mng. editor features Chgo. Daily News, 1968-77; exec. v.p., editor Chgo. Tribune-N.Y. News Syndicate, 1977-84; v.p. adminstrn. and editl. devel. L.A. Times Syndicate, 1984-93, dir. book devel., 1993-97; cons. LA. Times Syndicate, 1998-99; ret. Photo exhbn., Sedona, 2001; founder DLM Images, 2003. Home: 3000 Adornos Way Burbank CA 91504-1609

MICHEL, ELIZABETH CHENEY, social reform consultant; b. Pitts., Feb. 11, 1951; d. George Philip and Charlotte Elizabeth (Cowser) Cheney; m. Raymond Joseph Michel, Oct. 21, 1973 (div. June 1997); children: Keith Raymond, Grant Petersen. BA, Rollins Coll., 1973; M in Comm., U. Ctrl. Fla., 1988, PhD, 1992. Vis. prof. Univ. Ctrl. Fla., Orlando, Fla., 1989-92; assoc. prof., chair comm. program Mars Hill (N.C.) Coll., 1993-99; comms. cons., v.p. Comms. Strategies-Healthcare.com, Corp., 1999-2000; dir. change mgmt. Ga. Tech. Authority, 2001—. Pres. Kairos Commn. Strategies, Atlanta, 1998—; bd. dirs. Biltmore Inst., 1997—, cons., 1996—; bd. dirs. Commn. on Industries of the Mind, Atlanta; vice-chair 21st Century Comm., 1996—;

project coord. for joint comm. with Chinese Acad. Social Scis., China; del. to Consortium for Global Edn., China, 1998; vis. prof. comm. Kennesaw State U.; mem. internat. del. to Conf. on Environ. Sustainability, Shanghai, 2000, Implementation Strategies for SMEs, Networking 2000, Paris, 2000; v.p. Systems and Strategies; mem. bd. advisor Atlantic U. Chinese Medicine, 2000—, chair bd. dirs., 2001—. Author: 4 Simple Steps to Communications that Connect! and Kairos Community Strategies Interactive CD-ROM, 2000; chief editor: An Orchestra of Voices: Making the Argument for Press and Speech Freedom in the People's Republic of China, 2000; contbr. articles to mag. Bd. dirs. Atlanta Women's Network, 2000—01. Internat. Rsch. grant Appalachian Coll. Assn., 1994, 96, 97, Mellon Found., 1994, 95, 96, 97; Vis. Rsch. fellow Chinese Acad. Social Scis., 1996, 97. Mem.: Women's Network, Brit. Am. Bus. Group, Am. Educators Journalism and Mass Comm., Nat. Comm. Assn., Atlanta Coun. on Internat. Rels., Dem. Women's forum, Metro Atlanta C. of C., Women's Commerce Club, Ga. Exec. Women's Network, Atlanta Women's Network-Strategic Planning, Kappa Delta Phi, Phi Kappa Phi. Presbyterian. Avocations: acting. music, postmodernism, drawing.

MICHEL, HARTMUT, biochemist; b. Ludwigsburg, Germany, July 18, 1948; m. Ilona S. Leger, 1979; 2 children. Doctorate, U. Wurzburg, 1977. With Max Planck Inst. Biochemistry, Martinsried, Germany, 1979-87. Co-recipient Nobel prize for chemistry, 1988. Office: Max Planck Inst Biophysics Marie-Curie-Str 15 60439 Frankfurt Germany E-mail: hartmut.michel@mpibp-frankfurt.mpg.de.

MICHEL, MARY ANN KEDZUF, nursing educator; b. Evergreen Park, Ill., June 1, 1939; d. John Roman and Mary Kedzuf; m. Jean Paul Michel, 1974. Diploma in nursing, Little Company of Mary Hosp., Evergreen Park, 1960; BSN, Loyola U., Chgo., 1964; MS, No. Ill. U., 1968, EdD, 1971. Staff nurse Little Co. of Mary Hosp., 1960-64; instr. Little Co. of Mary Hosp. Sch. Nursing, 1964-67, No. Ill. U., DeKalb, 1968-69, asst. prof., 1969-71; chmn. dept. nursing U. Nev., Las Vegas, 1971-73, prof. nursing, 1975—, dean Coll. Health Scis., 1973-90; pres. PERC, Inc.; mgmt. cons., 1993—95. Mgmt. cons. Nev. Donor Network, 1993; mem. So. Nev. Health Manpower Task Force, 1975; mem. manpower com. Plan Devel. Commn., Clark County Health Sys. Agy., 1977-79, mem. governing body, 1981-86; mem. Nev. Health Coordinating Coun., Western Inst. Nursing, 1971-85; mem. coordinating com. assembly instnl. adminstrs. dept. allied health edn. and accreditation AMA, 1985-88; mem. bd. advisors So. Nev. Vocat. Tech. Ctr., 1976-80; sec.-treas. Nev. Donor Network, 1988-89, chmn. bd., 1988-90. Contbr. articles to profl. jours. Trustee Desert Spring Hosp., Las Vegas, 1976-85; bd. dirs. Nathan Adelson Hospice, 1982-88, Bridge Counseling Assocs., 1982, Everywoman's Ctr., 1984-86; chair Nev. Commn. on Nursing Edn., 1972-73, Nursing Articulation Com., 1972-73, Yr. of Nurse Com., 1978; moderator Invitational Conf. Continuing Edn., Am. Soc. Allied Health Professions, 1978; mgmt. cons. Nev. Donor Network, 1994-95, Donor Organ Recovery Svc., Transplant Recipient Internat. Orgn., S.W. Eye Bank, S.W. Tissue Bank. Named Outstanding Alumnus, Loyola U., 1983; NIMH fellow, 1967-68. Fellow Am. Soc. Allied Health Professions, 1991, (chair nat. resolutions com. 1981-84, treas. 1988-90, sec's. award com. 1982-83, 92-93, nat. by-laws com. 1985, conv. chair 1987); mem. AAUP, Am. Nurses Assn., Nev. Nurses Assn. (dir. 1975-77, treas. 1977-79, conv. chair 1978), So. Nev. Area Health Edn. Coun., Western Health Deans (co-organizer 1985, chair, 1988-90), Nat. League Nursing, Nev. Heart Assn., So. Nev. Mem. Hosps. (nursing recruitment com. 1981-83, mem. nursing practice com. 1983-85), Las Vegas C. of C. (named Woman of Yr. Edn.) 1988, Slovak Catholic Sokols, Phi Kappa Phi (chpt. sec. 1981-83, pres.-elect 1983, pres. 1984, v.p. Western region 1989-95, editl. bd. jour. Nat. Forum 1989-93), Alpha Beta Gamma (hon.), Sigma Theta Tau, Zeta Kappa. Office: U Nev Las Vegas 4505 S Maryland Pky Las Vegas NV 89154-9900 Office Phone: 702-895-3719. Personal E-mail: m.a.michel@worldnet.att.com.

MICHEL, PAUL REDMOND, federal judge; b. Philadelphia, Pa., Feb. 3, 1941; s. Lincoln M. and Dorothy (Kelley) Michel; m. Sally Ann Clark, 1965 (div. 1987); children: Sarah Elizabeth, Margaret Kelley; m. Elizabeth Morgan, 1989. BA, Williams Coll., 1963; JD, U. Va., 1966. Bar: Pa. 1967, U.S. Supreme Ct. 1970. Asst. dist. atty. Dist. Atty.'s Office, Phila., 1967—71, dep. dist. atty. for investigations, 1972—74; asst. spl. prosecutor Watergate investigation Dept. Justice, Washington, 1974—75, dep. chief pub. integrity sect., Criminal div. and prosecutor "Koreagate" investigation, 1976—78, assoc. dep. atty. gen., 1978—81, acting dep. atty. gen., 1979—80; asst. counsel intelligence com. U.S. Senate, 1975—76, counsel and adminstrv. asst. to Sen. Arlen Specter, 1981—88; judge U.S. Ct. Appeals (Fed. cir.), Washington, 1988—. Instr. appellate practice and procedure George Washington U. Nat. Law Ctr., 1991—97; instr. appellate advocacy John Marshall Law Sch., Chgo., 1991—. 2d lt. USAR, 1966—72. Office: US Ct Appeals Fed Cir 717 Madison Pl NW Washington DC 20439

MICHEL, SHARON LEE, systems and information technology director; b. Waterloo, Wis., Dec. 23, 1946; d. Charles Raymond and Harriet Agatha (Sheridan) M. BS, U. Wis., Stevens Point, 1969. Systems analyst Employee Trust Funds State of Wis., Madison, 1976-79, dir. systems mgmt. bur., 1979-84, chief applications devel. Natural Resources, 1984-97, IT dir., 1997—. Vice chmn. orgn. Dem. Party Dane County, Madison, 1986, co-chmn., 1987-88; mem. elections com. Dem. Party Wis., 1988-2002; elected ward committeewoman Dem. Party, 1989-2000; co-chmn. Polit. Action Com., 1989, candidate recruitment, 1990; vice chair fin. devel. Nat. Women's Polit. Caucus-Wis. State Policy Coun., 1991—, co-chair, 1992-93. Mem. NAFE, NOW, Data Processing Mgmt. Assn. (v.p., sec. so. Wis. chpt. 1983, v.p0. 1984, Individual Performance award 1985, 91, 94, exec. v.p. 1989, pres. 1990). Democrat. Roman Catholic. Avocation: photography. Home: 4849 Sheboygan Ave Apt 319 Madison WI 53705-2934 Office: Dept Natural Resources State Wis PO Box 7921 Madison WI 53707-7921

MICHEL, THOMAS MARK, internal medicine educator, scientist, physician; b. Portland, Oreg., July 14, 1955; AB in Biochem. Scis., Harvard U., 1977; PhD in Biochemistry, Duke U., 1983, MD, 1984. Diplomate Am. Bd. Internal Medicine, Am. Bd. Cardiovasc. Disease. House officer, jr. and sr. resident in medicine Brigham and Women's Hosp., Boston, 1984-87, clin. and rsch. fellow in medicine cardiovasc. div., 1987-88, assoc. physician, staff physician cardiovasc. div., 1988—; clin. fellow in medicine Harvard U. Med. Sch., Boston, 1984-87, rsch. fellow dept. genetics, 1988-90, instr. medicine, 1988-89, asst. prof., 1989-95, assoc. prof., 1995—; chief cardiology Boston VA Healthcare Sys., 1999—. Tutor in biochem. scis. Harvard Coll., Harvard U., Cambridge, Mass., 1990—; lectr. molecular mechanisms of disease Harvard Med. Sci.-MIT health scis. and tech. program, 1990—; speaker at seminars, confs. and univs.; vis. lectr. U. Alta., U. Calgary, U. Alcala, Madrid, St. Bartholomew's Hosp., London; Cecilie Greig vis. prof. Hammersmith Hosp., Royal Postgrad. Med. Sch., London; plenary lectr., Nitric Oxide Forum, Tokyo. Contbr. articles to med. jours. Recipient John J. Abel award in Pharmacology Am. Soc. for Pharmacology Therapeutics, 1995, young scholar's award Am. Soc. Hypertension, 1991; Harvard nat. scholar Harvard U., 1973-77; fellow NIH, 1977-84. Fellow Am. Coll. Cardiology; mem. ACP, Am. Fedn. for Clin. Rsch., Henry Christian award for excellence in rsch. 1992, 93), Am. Heart Assn. (Established Investigator award 1993—, Clinican-Scientist award 1988-93), Am. Soc. for Biochemistry and Molecular Biology, Mass. Med. Soc. Office: Brigham & Women's Hosp Harvard Med Sch 75 Francis St Boston MA 02115-6106

MICHELI, FRANK JAMES, lawyer; b. Zanesville, Ohio, Mar. 23, 1930; s. John and Theresa (Carlini) M.; m. Doris Joan Clum, Jan. 9, 1954; children: Michael John, James Carl, Lisa Ann, Matthew Charles. Student, John Carroll U., Cleve., 1947-48, Xavier U., Cin., 1949-50; LL.D., Ohio No. U., Ada., 1953. Bar: Ohio 1953. Since practiced in, Zanesville; partner Leasure & Micheli, 1953-65, Kincaid, Micheli, Geyer & Ormond, 1965-75, Kincaid, Cultice, Micheli & Geyer (and predecessor), 1982-92; ptnr. Micheli, Baldwin, Bopeley & Northrup, 1992—. Instr. bus. law Meredith Bus. Coll., Zanesville, 1956; lectr. on med. malpractice, hosp. and nurse liability. Dir. Public Service for, City of Zanesville, 1954. Mem. Internat. Assn. Ins. Counsel, Def. Rsch. Inst., Ohio Def. Assn., Am. Ohio bar assns., Am. Judicature Soc., Am. Arbitration Assn. (mem. nat. panel), Am. Bd. Trial Advs. (bd. dirs. Ohio chpt. 1991-95, pres. 1997). Clubs: Elk. Home: 160 E Willow Dr Zanesville OH 43701-1249 Office: PO Box 788 3808 James Ct Ste 2 Zanesville OH 43702-0788 E-mail: micheli@cyberzane.net.

MICHELINI, SYLVIA HAMILTON, auditor; b. Decatur, Ala., May 16, 1946; d. George Borum and Dorothy Rose (Swatzell) Hamilton; m. H. Stewart Michelini, June 4, 1964; children: Stewart Anthony, Cynthia Leigh. BSBA summa cum laude, U. Ala., Huntsville, 1987. CPA, Ala.; cert. govt. fin. mgr., fraud examiner. Acct. Ray McCay, CPA, Huntsville, 1987-88; auditor Def. Contract Audit Agy., Huntsville, 1989-92; auditor-office of inspector general George C. Marshall Space Flight, Center, Ala., 1992-97; contr. Hamilton Hotels, Inc., 1997-2001; ret. Exec. bd. Decatur City PTA, 1976-78; pres., v.p. Elem. Sch. PTA, Decatur, 1977-79; leader Girl Scouts U.S. and Cub Scouts, Decatur, 1972-77; active local ARC, 1973-77. Mem. AICPA, AAUW (chpt. treas. 1988-90), Nat. Assn. Accts. (dir. community svc. 1987-88, v.p. adminstrn. and fin. 1988-89, pres. 1989-90, nat. com. on ethics 1990-91), Nat. Notary Asns., Am. Soc. Women Accts. (chpt. treas. 1989-90, dir. chpt. devel. 1989-90), Assn. Govt. Accts. (sec. 1992-93, chmn. pub. rels. 1993-94), Ala. Soc. CPAs (profl. ethics com. 1993-94), Inst. Internal Auditors (dir. awards and recognition 1996-97, sec. 1999-2001, 2003—), Inst. Mgmt. Accts. (v.p. comms., dir. program book 1991-94, Dixie coun. dir. newsletters 1992-93, dir. ednl. programs 1992-93, 93-94, nat. com. ethics, 1990-97, nat. fin. com. 1997-98), Ala. Soc. CPAs (govtl. acctg. and auditing com. 1994-95), Inst. Mgmt. Accts. (nat. bd. dirs. 1994-97, nat. fin. com. 1997-98), Phi Kappa Phi. Baptist. Avocations: reading, walking, sewing, research, music. Home and Office: 2801 Sylvia Dr SE Decatur AL 35603-5643 E-mail: michelin@hiwaay.net.

MICHELIS, MICHAEL FRANK, nephrologist; b. Bklyn., Dec. 11, 1938; s. Michael and Gisella (Gammer) M.; m. Mary Ann Wolak, July 28, 1973; children: Elizabeth Ann, Katherine Clare. BA, Columbia U., 1959; MD, George Washington U., 1963. Intern, resident Lenox Hill Hosp., N.Y.C., 1963-65; resident Hosp. Med. Coll. Pa., Phila., 1965-67; fellow in renal disease, dept. medicine U. Pitts. Sch. Medicine, 1969-70, asst. prof. medicine, 1971-75; chief renal diagnostic unit VA Hosp., Pitts., 1971-75; asst. prof. clin. medicine NYU Med. Sch., 1975-93; assoc. prof. clin. medicine N.Y. Med. Coll., 1980-87, prof., 1987-92; assoc. prof. clin. medicine Cornell U. Med. Coll., 1992-93; prof. clin. medicine NYU Med. Coll., 1993—; dir. nephrology sect. Lenox Hill Hosp., N.Y.C., 1975—. Spl. lectr. Georgetown U. Med. Sch., 1973-85; lectr. Western Pa. Continuing Edn. for Physicians, 1972-75, vis. prof., 1976; mem. merit rev. bd. VA, 1973-76; cons. clin. fellowship rev. com. NIH, 1981-85; mem. exec. com. End Stage Renal Disease Network, N.Y.C., 1981-85; mem. med. adv. bd. Nat. Kidney Found. of N.Y./N.J., 1987-2001; vice-chair med. adv. bd., trustee Kidney and Urology Found. Am., 2001—. Mem. editl. bd. Clin. Nephrology, 1979-89, Geriat. Nephrology, 1986, Jour. Geriatric Nephrology and Urology, 1989—, Am. editor, 1989-98; contbr. articles to profl. jours. Served to maj. M.C., AUS, 1967-69. Decorated Army Commendation medal; Health, Rsch. and Svcs. Found. grantee, 1970, 72, 74. Mem. AMA (invited lectr. 1973-75), ACP, Am. Fedn. Clin. Rsch., Am. Soc. Nephrology, Internat. Soc. Nephrology, Internat. Soc. for Geriatric Nephrology and Urology (pres. 1999-2003), Ctrl. Soc. Clin. Rsch. Greek Orthodox. Home: 16 Woodland Park Dr Tenafly NJ 07670-3027 Office: Lenox Hill Hosp 100 E 77th St New York NY 10021-1850 Office Phone: 212-988-3506. E-mail: mfmich@ix.netcom.com.

MICHELL, AURIEL IBN, lawyer, writer; b. Miami, Fla., Apr. 8, 1948; s. Sylva Rivkah Mazoulay and Arie Stepthen Michell. DD, Hamilton State U., 1975; LLD, Southland Coll. Law, 1976; LLM, Clearwater Coll. of Law, 1979; ThD, Slidell Bapt. Sem., 1989; JD, Kensington U., 1993. Bar: Calif. Bar 1979. Tax lawyer City of Refuge, El Paso, Tex., 1994—; gen. counsel Intl Inst. for Health & Wellness, Orem, Utah, 1999—. Author: (book) Let's Talk Jewish, 1998 (religious best seller, 2000), Visions, 2000 (New Poet of the Yr. award, 2001), (poetry) From Deep Inside My Soul, 2001 (Internat.Poet of Merit award, 2002). Bd. of dirs. Tampa (Fla.) Food Bank, 1982—85. Maj. U.S. Army, 1967—73. Mem.: ABA, Fed. Bar Assn. Democrat. Jewish. Avocation: travel, writing, speaking. Office: City of Refuge c/o Rio Verde University POBox 971166 Orem UT 85097 E-mail: ctyrfugedu3@hotmail.com.

MICHELMAN, KATE, advocate; married; 3 daughters. Dir. Planned Parenthood, Harrisburg, Pa., 1980-85; pres. Nat. Abortion and Reproductive Rights Action League, Washington, 1985—. Spkr. in field. Named one of 100 Most Powerful Elites in the Nation's Capitol Washingtonian Mag., named a fellow of John F. Kennedy Sch. Govt.'s Inst. of Politics Harvard U., 1994. Office: Nat Abortion Rights Action League 1156 15th St NW Ste 700 Washington DC 20005-1744

MICHELS, DOUG, computer company executive; Grad., U. Calif., Santa Cruz. Pres., CEO SCO, Santa Cruz, Calif., 1979—; pres. UniForums, 1989-90. Office: PO Box 1900 Santa Cruz CA 95061-1900

MICHELS, FRANCES G. management company executive; Sr. v.p., supr. svcs. Morrison Mgmt. Splsts., Smyrna, Ga., 1996—. Office: Morrison Mgmt Specialists 1955 Lake Park Dr Ste 400 Smyrna GA 30080

MICHELS, ROBERT, psychiatrist, educator; b. Chgo., Jan. 21, 1936; s. Samuel and Ann (Cooper) M.; m. Verena Sterba, Dec. 23, 1962; children—Katherine, James. BA, U. Chgo., 1953; MD, Northwestern U., 1958. Intern Mt. Sinai Hosp., N.Y.C., 1958-59; resident in psychiatry Columbia Presbyn.-N.Y. State Psychiat. Inst., N.Y.C., 1959-62; mem. faculty Coll. Physicians and Surgeons, Columbia U., N.Y.C., 1964-74, assoc. prof., 1971-74; psychiatrist student health service Columbia U., 1966-74; supervising and tng. analyst Columbia U. Center for Psychoanalytic Tng. and Research, 1972—; attending psychiatrist Vanderbilt Clinic, Presbyn. Hosp., N.Y.C., 1964-74; Barklie McKee Henry prof. psychiatry Cornell U. Med. Coll., N.Y.C., 1974-93, chmn. dept. psychiatry, 1974-91, Stephen and Suzanne Weiss dean, 1991-96; provost for med. affairs Cornell U., 1991-96, Walsh McDermott U. prof. of medicine, 1996—, univ. prof. psychiatry, 1996—; psychiatrist-in-chief N.Y. Hosp., 1974-91, attending psychiatist, 1991—. Attending psychiatrist St. Luke's Hosp. Ctr., N.Y.C., 1966—. Co-author: The Psychiatric Interview in Clinical Practice, 1971; contbr. articles to profl. jours. Served with USPHS, 1962-64. Mem. Am. Psychiat. Assn., Am. Coll. Psychiatrists, N.Y. Psychiat. Soc., Royal Medico-Psychol. Assn., Psychiat. Rsch. Soc., Assn. Rsch. in Nervous and Mental Diseases, Assn. Acad. Psychiatry, Am. Psychoanalytic Assn., Internat. Psychoanalytic Assn., Ctr. Advanced Psychoanalytic Studies, N.Y. Acad. Scis., Alpha Omega Alpha. Office: Cornell U Med Coll 418 E 71st St New York NY 10021-4894 Office Phone: 212-746-6001.

MICHELSEN, CHRISTOPHER BRUCE HERMANN, surgeon; b. Boston, Aug. 18, 1940; s. Jost Joseph and Ingeborg Elizabeth (Dilthey) M.; children: Heidi Elizabeth, Matthew Christopher, Joshua Jost. BA, Bowdoin Coll., 1961; MD, Columbia U., 1969. Diplomate Am. Bd. Orthop. Surgery, Am. Bd. Forensic Medicine. Intern Columbia Presbyn. Med. Ctr., N.Y.C., 1969—70, resident, 1970—71; orthop. resident N.Y. Orthop. Hosp., N.Y.C., 1971—73, jr. Anne C. Kane fellow, 1973—74, sr. Anne C. Kane fellow and hip fellow, 1974—75, traveling fellow, 1975—76; intenrat. A-O fellow, postgrad. fellow in biomechanics Case Western Res. U., N.Y.C., 1975—76, instr. biomed. engring., 1975—76; prof. clin. orthop. surgery, orthop. surgeon Columbia Coll. Physicians and Surgeons, 1976, vice chmn. dept. orthop. surgery, 2002—; chief orthop. svc. Allen Pavillion, Columbia Presbyn. Med. Ctr., 1993—, chief orthop. spine surgery svc., 1998—. Col. USAR, ret. Fellow ACS, Am. Assn. for Surgery of Trauma, Am. Orthop. Assn., N.Am. Spine Soc., Am. Acad. Orthop. Surgeons, Internat. Coll. Surgeons, N.Y. Acad. Medicine; mem. AMA, Am. Coll. Physicians Execs., Orthop. Rsch. Soc., Am. Soc. Bone and Mineral Rsch., Royal Soc. Medicine (affiliate). Office: 5141 Broadway New York NY 10034-1159 Home: 14 Wyldwood Dr Tarrytown NY 10591-5059

MICHELSEN, W(OLFGANG) JOST, neurosurgeon, educator, retired; b. Amsterdam, Holland, Aug. 20, 1935; came to U.S., 1936; s. Jost Joseph and Ingeborg Mathilde (Dilthey) M.; m. Constance Richards, Sept. 21, 1963 (div. 1987); children: Kristina, Elizabeth, Ingrid; m. Claude Claire Grenier, Mar. 30, 1988 (div. Oct. 1992); m. Martha Reed, Sept. 21, 1996. AB magna cum laude, Harvard U., 1959; MD, Columbia U., 1963. Diplomate Am. Bd. Neurol. Surgery. Intern in surgery Case Wester Res. U. Hosps., Cleve., 1963-64; asst. resident in neurology Mass. Gen. Hosp., Boston, 1964-65; asst. resident, then chief resident neurol. surgery Columbia-Presbyn. Med. Ctr., N.Y.C., 1965-69; from instr. to assoc. prof. neurosurgery Columbia U. Coll. Physicians and Surgeons, N.Y.C., 1969-89, prof. clin. surgery, 1990—; fellow in neurosurgery Presbyn. Hosp., N.Y.C., 1969-71, dir. neuro vascular surgery, 1989-90; dir. neurosurgery St. Luke's Roosevelt Hosp. Ctr., N.Y.C., 1990—; prof. and chmn. dept. neurological surgery Albert Einstein Coll. Medicine, Bronx, N.Y., 1992-97; dir. neurosurgery Montefiore Med Ctr, Bronx, 1992-97; ret., 1997. Asst. attending in neurosurgery, St. Luke's Hosp. Ctr., 1970—; cons. neurosurgeon Nyack (N.Y.) Hosp., 1972—, Englewood (N.J.) Hosp., 1972—; vis. prof. neurosurgery Tufts U., 1975, Emery U., 1977, Presbyn.-St. Luke's Hosp. Ctr., Chgo., 1978, Yale U., 1980; guest faculty Northwestern U., 1977, 78, U. Chgo., 1977, Colby Coll., 1980; mem. numerous panels on neurosurgery. Contbr. articles to profl. publs. 1st lt. U.S. Army, 1954-57. Grantee NIH, USPHS. Fellow ACS, Am. Heart Assn.; Mem. AMA, Am. Assn. Neurol. Surgeons (mem. sect. pediatric neurosurger), Neurosurg. Soc. Am. (v.p. 1984-85, pres. 1987-88), Congress Neurol. Surgeons, N.Y. Neurosurg. Soc., Neurosurg. Soc. State N.Y., N.Y. Acad. Scis., Assn. Rsch. in Nervous and Mental Diseases, Internat. Neurosurg. Soc., Internat. Pediatric Neurosurg. Soc., N.Y. State Med. Soc., N.Y. County Med. Soc. Office: 330 Borthwick Ave Ste 108 Portsmouth NH 03801 Office Phone: 603-436-4666.

MICHELSOHN, MARIE-LOUISE, mathematician, educator; b. N.Y.C., Oct. 8, 1941; d. Marcel and Lucy Friedmann; children: Didi, Michelle. BS, U. Chgo., 1962, MS, 1963, PhD, 1974. Asst. prof. U. Calif. San Diego, La Jolla, 1974-75; lectr. U. Calif., Berkeley, 1975-77; mem. Inst. des Hautes Études Scientifiques, Bures sur Yvette, France, 1977-78; asst. prof. SUNY, Stony Brook, 1978-82, assoc. prof., 1982-88, prof., 1988—. Visitor Inst. Matematica Pura e Aplicada, Rio de Janeiro, 1980, Rsch. Inst. for Math. Scis., Kyoto, Japan, 1986, Tata Inst., Bombay, 1986-87; vis. mem. Inst. des Hautes Études Scientifiques, Bures-sur-Yvette, 1983-84, 93, 99-2000; dir. grad. program Dept. of Math SUNY, Stony Brook; rsch. prof. Math. Scis. Rsch. Inst., 1993-94. Author: Spin Geometry, 1989; contbr. articles to Am. Jour. Math., Acta Mathematica, Inventiones Mathematicae, Procs. London Math. Soc., Jour. Algebraic Geometry. Grantee NSF. Mem. Am. Math. Soc. Achievements include research in complex geometry, characterization of balanced spaces, Clifford and spinor cohomology, the geometry of spin manifolds and the Dirac operator, riemannian manifolds of positive curvature, the theory of algebraic cycles. Office: SUNY Dept Math Stony Brook NY 11794-0001

MICHELSON, GERTRUDE GERALDINE, retired retail company executive; b. Jamestown, NY, June 3, 1925; d. Thomas and Celia Rosen; m. Horace Michelson, Mar. 28, 1947 (dec. Apr. 2002); children: Martha Ann (dec.), Barbara Jane. BA, Pa. State U., 1945; LLB, Columbia U., 1947; LLD with honors, Adelphi U., 1981; DHL with honors, New Rochelle Coll., 1983; LLD with honors, Marymount Manhattan Coll., 1988; PhD in Policy Analysis, Rand Grad. Sch., 2002. Mgmt. trainee Macy's NY, 1947-48, various mgmt. positions, v.p. employee personnel, 1963-70, sr. v.p. labor consumer rels., 1970—72; sr. v.p. pers. labor consumer rels. Macy & Co., Inc., 1972-79, sr. v.p. external affairs, 1979-80, R.H. Macy & Co., Inc., 1980-92, sr. advisor, 1992-94; ret., 1995. Chmn. Helena Rubinstein Found.; bd. dirs. Markle Found.; chmn. emeritus bd. trustees Columbia U.; life trustee Spelman Coll.; past pres. bd. overseers Tchrs. Ins. Annuity Assn. Am. Coll. Retirement Equities Fund. Recipient Disting. Svc. medal Pa. State U., 1969. Mem. NYC Ptnrship. (vice chmn.), Women's Forum, Econ. Club NY Home: 70 E 10th St New York NY 10003-5102 Office: Federated Dept Stores Inc 151 W 34th St New York NY 10001-2101

MICHELSON, LILLIAN, librarian, researcher; b. N.Y.C., June 21, 1928; d. Louis and Dora (Keller) Farber; m. Harold Michelson, Dec. 14, 1947; children: Alan Bruce, Eric Neil, Dennis Paul. Vol. Goldwyn Libr., Hollywood, Calif., 1961-69; owner Former Goldwyn Rsch. Libr., Hollywood, 1969—; ind. location scout, 1973—. Mem. Motion Picture Libr. Found., 2002—, Friends L.A. Pub. Libr. Mem.: Acad. Motion Picture Arts and Scis. Office: c/o Dreamworks SKG Rsch Libr 1000 Flower St Glendale CA 91201-3007 Office Phone: 818-695-6445. E-mail: hmichelson@dreamworks.com.

MICHELSON, PAUL E. historian, educator; b. Ebolowa, Cameroon, Mar. 19, 1945; s. Edwin and Verna Michelson; m. Jean T. Michelson; children: David A., Paul-Philip E. PhD, Ind. U., Bloomington, 1967—75. Asst. prof. to prof. Huntington Coll., Ind., 1974—92, disting. prof., history, 1992—. Vis. lectr. Fgn. Svc. Inst., Va., 1988—; sci. coun. Institutul de Istorie A. D. Xenopol, Romania, 2001—; nat. sec. Conf. on Faith and History, 2004—. Contbr. articles to profl. jours.; mem. editl. bd. Revue des Etudes Sud-Est Europeenes, Romania, 1990, Balkanistica, 1995, Bibliophilos, 1999. Founding bd. mem. Ind. Region Three Libr. Svcs. Authority, Ind., 1975—77, La Fontaine Arts Coun., Huntington, Ind., 1977—78; mem., exec. leadership team Ch. of the United Brethren in Christ, 1993—, mem., gen. bd., 1993—; v.p., Ind. chpt. AAUP, 1981—82. Fellow, Ford Found., 1970—71, Internat. Rsch. and Exchanges Bd., 1973—74, Nat. Endowment for Humanities/U. Va., 1978, Nat. Endowment for Humanities/Princeton U., 1989; Richard M. Weaver fellow, Intercollegiate Studies Inst., 1968—69, Fulbright-Hays Rsch. Fellow for Romania, U.S. Dept. Edn., 1971—72, Fellow for Romania, Internat. Rsch. and Exchanges Bd., 1971—73, 1982—83, Fulbright-Hays Sr. Rsch. Fellow for Romania, Coun. for Internat. Exch. of Scholars, 1982—83, 1989—90. Mem.: United Brethren Hist. Soc., Soc. for Romanian Studies (sec.-editor 1977, Disting. Svc. Citation 1993), S.E. European Studies Assn. (mem. of nat. bd. 1991—), Conf. on Faith and History (nat. sec. 2004), Am. Assn. for the Advancement of Slavic Studies, Am. Hist. Assn., Alpha Chi Nat. Honor Soc. (mem. of nat. coun. 1986—98, Disting. Svc. Award 2001). Protestant. Avocations: books, travel, tennis, stamp collecting/philately. Home: 1632 N Jefferson Huntington IN 46750 Office: Huntington Coll 2303 College Ave Huntington IN 46750 Office Phone: 260-359-4242. E-mail: pmichelson@huntington.edu.

MICHELSON, ROBERT C. engineering educator, researcher; s. Carroll Edward and Evelyn Othea Michelson; m. Denise Susan Dodson; children: Christian, Stuart. BEE, Va. Poly. Inst. and State U., 1969—73; MEE, Ga. Inst. Tech., 1973—74. Rsch. engr. ii U.S. Naval Rsch. Lab., Washington, D.C., DC, 1972—73; prin. rsch. engr. / adj. assoc. prof. Ga. Inst. Tech., Atlanta, 1974—. Pres. Assn. Unmanned Vehicle Systems, Internat., Washington, D.C., DC, 1993—95. Contbr. articles to tech. pub. Deacon Presbyn. Ch. Am., Atlanta, 1990—. Recipient Pioneer Award, Assn. Unmanned Vehicle Systems, Internat., 1998, 2001 TOP Pirelli Award diffusion sci. culture, Internat. Jury including Nobel Lauriats, Pirelli Corp., 2001, Best Multimedia Project from any Ednl. Instn. in World, 2001. Mem.: AIAA (sr.), IEEE (sr.; editor robotic systems), Sci. Rsch. Soc. N.Am., Assn. Unmanned Vehicle Systems, Internat. (life; pres.), SE Marine Aquarium Soc. (life). Achievements include patents for Entomopter and Method for Using Same, U.S. Patent No. 6, 082, 671, July 4, 2000; Battery State of Charge Detector with Rapid Charging Capability and Method, U.S. Patent No. 6, 094, 033, July 25, 2000; Reciprocating Chemical Muscle (RCM) and Method for Using Same, U.S. Patent No. 6, 446, 909, September 10, 2002; research in Archaeological field work in Eastern Anatolia pertaining to the Durupinar formation and the lost city of Naxuan. Avocations: marine aquaria, experimental aircraft, scuba diving, archaeology, history. Office: Georgia Tech Rsch Inst GTRI-ATAS-CCRF 7220 Richardson Rd Smyrna GA 30080

MICHELSON, SONIA, music educator, author; b. L.A., Feb. 14, 1928; d. Maurice and Elizabeth (Jacobs) Saeta; m. Irving Michelson, Apr. 4, 1954 (div. Aug. 1982); children: Ann Michelson Shoham, Louis E., Hadassah Zelman, Zahava Waldman, Elisheva Levin, Eliyahu Michaeli, Yaacov. BA, U. Calif., Berkeley, 1949. Instr. in guitar Suzuki Music Acad. of Chgo., 1980-81, Music Arts Sch., Highland Park, Ill., 1973-82; dir. in classical guitar Michelson Classic Guitar Studio, Chgo., 1973-88, dir. L.A., 1988—. Cons. Music Educators Nat. Conf., Atlantic City, N.J., 1976; columnist Guitar Found. of Am., L.A., 1984—. Author: Easy Classic Guitar Solos, 1977, Classical Guitar

Study, 1982, New Dimensions in Classical Guitar for Children, 1984, Young Beginner's First Repertoire for Classical Guitar, 1996; contbr. articles to profl. jours. Mem. Am. String Tchrs. Assn. (spl. cons. 1977-85), Chgo. Classical Guitar Soc. (pres. 1978-88), Guitar Found. of Am. (mem. editorial bd. 1972), Suzuki Assn. Am., Nat. Music Tchrs. Assn., Music Tchrs. Assn. Calif. Democrat. Jewish. Avocations: Hebrew and Israeli language studies, reading, gardening, writing, music rsch. Home: 1465 Reeves St Los Angeles CA 90035-2945

MICHELSTETTER, STANLEY HUBERT, lawyer; b. Milw., July 8, 1946; s. Donald Lee and Gloria (Menke) M.; m. Joyce Bladow, Apr. 29, 1972; children: Chad S., Chris E. BA in Math., U. Wis., 1968, JD, 1972. Bar: Wis. 1972, U.S. Dist. Ct. (we. dist.) Wis. 1972. Staff atty. Wis. Employment Rels. Commn., Milw., 1972-80; pvt. practice, Milw., 1980—; adminstrv. law judge, equal rights div. adminstrn. Wis. Dept Industry, Labor and Human Rels., Milw., 1992-93. Chmn. North Shore Rep. Club, Milw., 1984-86; bd. dirs. Jewish Family Svcs., 2002—. Served to 2d lt. Wis. N.G., 1968-74; dir. Jewish Family Svcs. 2002-. Mem. Wis. Bar Assn. (chmn. 1993), Milw. Bar Assn., Nat. Acad. Arbitrators, Indsl. Rels. Rsch. Assn. (bd. dirs. 1987—), Nat. Assn. R.R. Rels., Rotary. Republican. Jewish. Home: 1500 W Green Brook Rd Milwaukee WI 53217-1515 Office: 1749 N Prospect Ave Milwaukee WI 53202-1966 also: PMB 37 5185 Broadway Gary IN 46409-2708 E-mail: stan@stamm.com.

MICHENER, JAMES LLOYD, medical educator; b. Dec. 19, 1952; m. Gwendolyn Curtis Murphy; children: Rebecca Liane, Joshua Kieran. BA, Oberlin (Ohio) Coll., 1974; MD, Harvard Med. Sch., 1978. Diplomate Am. Bd. Family Practice. Resident in family medicine Duke U. Med. Ctr., Durham, N.C., 1978-81, Kellogg fellow, 1981-82, clin. prof. dept. cmty. and family medicine, 1994—, chmn. dept. cmty. and family medicine, 1994—. V.p. Durham Health Care, Inc., 1985-86; project reviewer Ctrs. Disease Control and Prevention, 2002-. Co-author: Nutrition in Practice, 1990, 2d edit., 1992; contbr. numerous articles to med. pubs. including Academic Medicine, The Jour. of Family Practice, Medical Care, others; mem. editl. bd. Rx Nutrition, 1989-91; presenter in field. Bd. dirs. N.C. Med. Soc. Found., 1995—; STFM rep. resource com. on nutrition edn. Am. Acad. Family Practice Found., 1987-91. Grantee The Fullerton Found., Inc., The Josiah Macy, Jr. Found., U.S. Dept. Health and Human Svcs., Kate B. Reynolds Charitable Trust, N.C. Health and Wellness Trust. Mem. AMA, Assn. Am. Med. Colls. (exec. coun. 2001—), Assn. Tchrs. Preventive Medicine (chmn. coun. acad. units 2002—), Am. Acad. Family Physicians Found., Am. Heart Assn. (del. Nat. Cholesterol Edn. Program 1987), NC Acad. Family Physicians (bd. dirs. 1995—), Assn. Dept. Family Medicine (bd. dirs. 1997—, sec. 1998—), Coun. Acad. Socs. (adminstrn. bd. 2000—), World Orgn. Nat. Colls., Acads. and Academic Assn. Gen. Practitioners and Family Physicians, Assn. Am. Med. Colls., Am. Austrian Founds. Internat. Health Forum (mem. steering com.). Home: 4011 Duck Pond Trail Chapel Hill NC 27514-9758 Office: Duke U Med Ctr PO Box 2914 Durham NC 27710-0001 Office Phone: 919-681-3178. Business E-Mail: miche001@mc.duke.edu.

MICHENFELDER, ALBERT A. lawyer; b. St. Louis, July 21, 1926; s. Albert A. and Ruth Josephine (Donahue) M.; m. Lois Barbara Sullivan, Sept. 03, 1949 (div. May 2, 1967); children: Michael J., Ann C. Michenfelder Yancey, Elizabeth D. Michenfelder Brown; m. Ramona Jo Dysart, July 12, 1968 (dec. Jan. 2, 1998); 1 child, Julie D. Michenfelder Wolfe. B of Naval Sci., Marquette U., 1946; LLB, St. Louis U., 1950. Bar: Mo. 1950, U.S. Dist. Ct. (ea. dist.) Mo. 1950, U.S. Supreme Ct. 1975. Assoc. Flynn & Challis, St. Louis, 1950-54; pvt. practice St. Louis, 1954-55; of counsel Husch & Eppenberger LLC, St. Louis. Mem. 21st Cir. Jud. Commn., St. Louis, 1981-87. Contbr. articles to profl. jours. City atty. City of Webster Groves, Mo., 1966-79; mem. John Marshall Club, St. Louis. Lt. (j.g.) USNR, 1944-47. Mem. Mo. Bar Assn., Bar. Assn. Met. St. Louis, St. Louis County Bar Assn. (pres. 1966), Westborough Country Club. Republican. Avocations: golf, tennis. Office: Husch & Eppenberger LLC 190 Carondelet Plz Ste 600 Saint Louis MO 63105-3441 E-mail: al.michenfelder@husch.com.

MICHENFELDER, JOSEPH FRANCIS, public relations executive; b. Webster Groves, Mo., Mar. 30, 1929; s. Albert Aloysius and Ruth Josephine (Donahue) M.; m. Audrey Laurine Glynn, Aug. 8, 1970. BA, N.Y. State U., N.Y.C., 1951, STB, 1954, MRE, 1955; MS in Journalism, Columbia U., 1958. Projects dir. Maryknoll Headquarters, Ossining, N.Y., 1955-57, communications dir., 1958-62; dir., chief exec. officer Noticias Aliadas, S.A., Lima, Peru, 1962-69; pub. rels. dir. Pub. Affairs Analysts, Inc., N.Y.C., 1970-72, exec. v.p., 1973-89; sr. v.p. Napolitan Assocs./PAA, Inc., N.Y.C., 1989-95; pres., CEO, 1995—. Pres. IDOC/N.Am., Inc., N.Y.C., 1976—. Mng. Editor (polit. quarterly) POLITEIA, 1970-73; co-producer: TV documentary A Quiet Revolution, 1987. Trustee The Fund for Peace, 1994—, Coun. on Hemispheric Affairs, Washington, 1980—; cons. UNESCO WHO, Bogota, Lima, 1964-66; bd. dirs. Jobs for Youth, Inc., N.Y.C., 1978-84. Mem. Internat. Pub. Relations Assn., Internat. Assn. Polit. Cons., Columbia U. Journalism Alumni Fed. (pres. 1971-74), Ovrses Press Club, Columbia Club. Democrat. Avocations: theater arts, film, creative writing, ecology, third world affairs. Office: Napolitan Assocs PAA Inc 55 5th Ave New York NY 10003-4301 E-mail: pancomm@aol.com.

MICHERO, WILLIAM HENDERSON, retired retail trade executive; b. Fort Worth, June 19, 1925; s. William Alvin and Lela Belle (Henderson) M.; m. Nan Elaine Henderson, July 9, 1948; children— Jane Elaine Michero Christie, William Sherman, Thomas Edward. BS in Commerce, Tex. Christian U., 1948. Sec. Tandy Corp., Fort Worth, 1960-75, v.p., 1970-75; with Tandycrafts, Inc., Fort Worth, 1975-90, sr. v.p., sec., dir., 1979-83, chmn. bd., 1983-90, ret., 1990. Sec. B.F. Johnston Found., Fort Worth, 1962-90. Bd. dirs. David L. Tandy Found., Fort Worth, 1968-99, Oakwood Cemetery Assn., 1979-89, Panther Boys Club, 1974-78, Fort Worth Mus. Sci. and History, 1973-75, pres. 1975, United Way; chmn. Distributive Edn. Council, 1970. Served with U.S. Navy, 1943-46. Mem.: Fort Worth, Colonial Country. Home: 1600 Texas St #1417 Fort Worth TX 76109-3434

MICHIE, SARA H. pathologist, educator; b. Tulsa, Okla., Jan. 3, 1955; BS in Biology, Stephen F. Austin U., 1977; MD, U. Tex., Houston, 1981. Diplomate Am. Bd. Pathology. Resident anatomic pathology Stanford (Calif.) U. Med. Ctr., 1981—83, postdoctoral fellow immunology dept. pathology, 1983—84, 1986—87, postdoctoral fellow diagnostic immunopathology, 1984—85; resident dept. pathology U. Iowa, Iowa City, 1985—86, postdoctoral fellow, 1986; assoc. investigator lab. svc. VA Hosp., Palo Alto, Calif., 1988—89, staff physician, 1989—, assoc. investigator, 1990—91; clin. instr. pathology dept. Stanford U., 1989—92, asst. prof. pathology, 1992—. Contbr. articles to profl. jours. Recipient Rsch. award, Am. Diabetes Assn., 1996. Mem.: Bay Area Flow Cytometry Group, Soc. Investigative Pathology, Am. Soc. Investigative Pathology, Alpha Omega Alpha, Sigma Xi. Office: VA Hosp Palo Alto 3801 Miranda Ave Stop 154F Palo Alto CA 94304-1207

MICHIELLI, FRANK V. architectural firm executive; Design ptnr. East Hampton RECenter, 2000—, Davis Brody Bond, NY, NY, 2000—. Planning project, Eskind Biomedical Libr./Vanderbilt Univ. Med. Ctr. (award winning), Design and the Polytechnic Univ. Master Plan, East Hampton RECenter (AIA Award of Merit, NY State, 2000, AIA Award for Architecture, NY State, 2001). Mem.: AIA. Office: Davis Brody Bod, LLP 315 Hudson St, 9th fl New York NY 10013

MICHITSCH, JOHN F. career officer; b. Plainview, N.Y., July 9, 1943; BA, U. Dayton, 1965; MS, Case Western Res. U., 1968. Asst. S-3 Arty. Combat Leader Bn., Ft. Sill, Okla., 3d Armored Divsn. Arty., Hanau, Germany; alpha battery comdr./S-3 2d Bn., Saudi Arabia; sec. gen. staff, R&D coord. U.S. Army Tank Automotive Command, Warren, Mich.; ops. officer dept. army inspector gen. office Pentagon, Washington; chief tactical wheeled divsn., assoc. dir. Tank Automotive Command, Warren; bn. comdr. Camp Stanley, Korea; staff officer ground combat sys. divsn. Office Dep. Chief of Staff, R&D & Acquisition, Pentagon, Washington; mil. asst., exec. officer for dep. under sec. of def. Strategic and Theater Nuclear Forces; divarty comdr. 3d Armor Divsn. Arty.; chief of staff, dep. comdr. 7th Army Tng. Command, Grafenwoehr, Germany; comdr. Simulation, Tng. and Instrumentation Command, Orlando, Fla.; maj. gen., program exec. officer ground combat/support sys. Picatinny Arsenal, Dover, N.J., 1995-00. Asst. prof. mil. sci. U. Dayton. Home: PO Box 746 Baltimore MD 21203-0746

MICHNICH, MARIE E. health policy analyst, consultant, educator; M Health Svs. Adminstrn., DrPH Health Svs. Rsch., UCLA. Asst. prof. health svs. U. Washington; sr. exec. v.p. Health Policy, Am. Coll. Cardiology Clin. Practice and Sci. Svs. Divsn.; dir. Health Policy Programs and Fellowships Nat. Acad. Scis. Inst. Medicine, 2002—. Cons, spkr. in field; legis. asst. health policy Medicare, Medicaid, maternal and child health; legis. asst. U.S. Senate Majority Leader Robert Dole; mem. several nat. health policy groups. Robert Wood Johnson Health Policy fellow. Mem.: Am. Pharm. Assn. Found. (1st pub. mem. bd. dirs. 2002—), Robert Wood Johnson Health Policy Fellows Program (mem. adv. bd., dir.), Health Care Quality Alliance (former chmn.). Office: Office Health Policy Programs Fellowship 500 5th St NW Washington DC 20001

MICHOPOULOS, ARISTOTLE V. humanities educator, researcher; b. Kotylion, Arcadia, Peloponnesos, Greece, Apr. 22, 1944; s. Vassilios A. Michopoulos and Anastasia D. Papazafeiropoulos; m. Despina Dimitropoulos (div. Jan. 30, 1996). BA, U. of Athens, Athens, Greece, 1967; MA, Grad. Ctr. of C.U.N.Y., New York, NY, 1976; PhD, Fla. State U., Tallahassee, FL, 1980. Translator Greek Orthodox Archdiocese of N. & S. Am., New York, NY, 1970—71; translator and adminstr. Hellenic indsl. Devel. Corp., New York, NY, 1972—74; h.s. tchr. Bd. of Edn. of NYC, New York, NY, 1975—76; adj. instr. Fla. State U., Tallahassee, 1977—78, asst. project dir. and curriculum writer, 1978—80; asst. prof. U. of Fla., Gainesville, Fla., 1980—87; prof. of greek studies and dir. Hellenic Coll., Brookline, Mass., 1987—2002. Dean Hellenic Coll., Brookline, Mass., 1995—2002, Greek studies dept. dir., 1987—; translator, cons. Various Organizations, Many, 1980—. Rep. to u.s. dept. of edn. Greek Orthodox Archdiocese, New York, NY, 1992—98; del., com. mem. Coun. on Hellenes Abroad, Chicago, Ill., 1995—2002; nat. coord. Paideia project, Greece, 1999—2004. Recipient Fulbright award, Fulbright Program, 1977, Socratic award, U. Fla., 1999; fellow, US Dept. of H.E.W., 1976—79. Mem.: Kotylion Syllogos (cons. 1980—2003, Merit Award 2000), Am. Hellenic Edn. Assn. (AHEPA), Modern Greek Studies Assn. Avocations: tennis, swimming, backgammon, travel. Office: Hellenic College 50 Goddard Avenue Brookline MA 02445

MICKEL, EMANUEL JOHN, foreign language educator; b. Lemont, Ill., Oct. 11, 1937; s. Emanuel John and Mildred (Newton) M.; m. Kathleen Russell, May 31, 1959; children: Jennifer, Chiara, Heather. BA, La. State U., 1959; MA, U. N.C., 1961, PhD, 1965. Asst. prof. U. Nebr., Lincoln, 1965-67, assoc. prof., 1967-68, Ind. U., Bloomington, 1968-73, prof., 1973—, dir. Medieval Studies Inst., 1976-91, chmn. French and Italian, 1984-95. Cons. NEH; French advisor Soc. Rencesvals, 1995-98; adv. bd. mem. Nineteenth Century French Studies, 1995—. Author: Marie de France, 1974, Eugene Fromentin, 1982, Ganelon Treason and the Chanson de Roland, 1989, Jules Vernes Complete Twenty Thousand Leagues Under the Sea, 1992, Enfances Godefroi and Retour de Cornumarant, 1999. Capt. U.S. Army, 1963-65. Grantee NEH, Washington, 1978-84; Lilly Open fellow Lilly Found., Indpls., 1981-82; Chevalier dans l'Ordre des Palmes Academiques, 1997. Avocations: music, theater, sports, travel, ancient literature. Office: French & Italian Dept Indiana Univ 642 Ballantine Hall Bloomington IN 47401-5020 Business E-Mail: mickel@indiana.edu.

MICKELSON, CLAUDIA ANN, biosafety officer, scientist; b. Detroit, Mar. 8, 1944; d. Gordon Francis and Virginia Randall Roberts; m. Michael Jay Mickelson, Sept. 1966; 1 child, David Paul. PhD, U. Rochester, 1974. Rsch. fellow U. Glasgow, Scotland, 1979-81; sr. rsch. fellow U. Melborne, Victoria, Australia, 1981-86; mem. xenotransplantation adv. bd. FDA, Washington, 1998—. Author: (book. chpt.) Principles of Biosafety, 2000. Recipient William J. O'Brian award Tufts U., 1995. Mem. AAAS (DOSER adv. bd. 1998-2001). Avocations: hiking, gardening, travel. Office: MIT 77 Massachusetts Ave 56-255 Cambridge MA 02139-4307 Office Fax: (617) 258-5856.

MICKELSON, PHIL, professional golfer; b. San Diego, June 16, 1970; m. Amy; 3 children. Student, Ariz. State U., 1992. Profl. golfer PGA, 1992—. Founder The Phil and Amy Mickelson Charitable Fund. Recipient Fred Haskins award, 1990, 91, 92, Jack Nicklaus award, 1990, 91, 92; won NCAA Championships, 1989, 90, 92; 1st team All-Am. with Sun Devils; Espy Award for Best Male Golfer, Best Championship Performance, ESPN, 2004. Achievements include 1st left-hander to win U.S. Amateur, 1990; 1st player in PGA history to win same tournament as amateur and profl. (No. Telecom Open); winning The Masters Tournament, 2004; Presidents Cup, 1994, 1996, 1998, 2000, 2003; Ryder Cup, 1995, 1997, 1999, 2001, 2004; 23 career PGA Tour Victories. Office: care PGA Box 109601 100 Avenue Of Champions Palm Beach Gardens FL 33418*

MICKELSON, STACEY, state legislator; BA, Minot State U., 1994. Govt. rels. dir. Artspace Projects, Inc; rep. Dist. 38 N.D. Ho. of Reps., 1994-2000, mem. fin. and taxation com., vice-chmn. transp. com. Mem. interim taxation, adminstrv. rules coms. Bowhay Inst. for Legis. Leadership and Devel. fellow. Mem. Am. Coun. Young Polit. Leaders, Darden Program Emerging Polit. Leaders, Flemming Fellows. Home: 410 Groveland Ave #702 Minneapolis MN 55403

MICKENS, RONALD ELBERT, applied mathematician, physics educator; b. Petersburg, Va., Feb. 7, 1943; s. Joseph Persival and Daisy (Brown) M.; m. Maria Kelker, Aug. 13, 1977; children James Williamson, Leah Maria. BA, Fisk U., 1964; PhD, Vanderbilt U., 1968. NSF postdoctoral fellow MIT, Cambridge, 1968-70, vis. prof., 1973-74; prof. physics Fisk U., Nashville, Tenn., 1970-81, Clark Atlanta U., 1982—, Callaway prof., 1986. Vis. prof. Morehouse Coll., Atlanta, 1979-80, Joint Inst. for Lab. Astrophysics, Boulder, Colo., 1981-82; cons. adv. bd. NSF, Nat. Urban Coalition, Nat. Rsch. Coun., Am. Inst. Physics and a variety of univs. and nat. labs. Author: Nonlinear Oscillations, 1981, Difference Equations, 1987, Difference Equations: Theory and Applications, 1990, Nonstandard Finite Difference Models of Differential Equations, 1994, Oscillations in Planar Dynamical Systems, 1996; editor: Mathematics and Science, 1990, Applications of Nonstandard Finite Difference Schemes, 2000, Edward Bouchet: The First African American Doctorate, 2002, Mathematical Methods for the Natural and Engineering Sciences, 2004; contbr. numerous rev. articles, abstracts and gen. articles to publs. Fellow Woodrow Wilson Found., Danforth Found., UNCF, Joint Inst. for Lab. Astrophysics; grantee ARO, NSF, DOE, NASA, NIH, 1968—. Fellow Am. Phys. Soc. (con., adv. bd.); mem. AAAS, European Phys. Soc., Soc. Indsl. and Applied Math., Am. Math. Soc. Achievements include construction of new finite-difference schemes for numerical solution of differential equations; new perturbation techniques for nonlinear difference and differential equations; construction of global methods for nonlinear oscillatory systems; investigation of properties of rate constants for third-order chemical react. Office: Clark Atlanta U Physics Dept Atlanta GA 30314 Business E-Mail: rohrs@math.gatech.edu.

MICKIEWICZ, ELLEN PROPPER, political and social science educator; b. Hartford, Conn. d. George K. and Rebecca (Adler) Propper; m. Denis Mickiewicz; 1 son, Cyril. BA, Wellesley Coll.; MA, Yale U., PhD, 1965. Lectr. dept. polit. sci. Yale U., 1965-67; asst. prof. dept. polit. sci. Mich. State U., East Lansing, 1967-69, assoc. prof., 1969-73, prof., 1973-80; prof. dept. polit. sci. Emory U., Atlanta, 1980-88, dean Grad. Sch. Arts and Scis., 1980-85, Alben W. Barkley prof. polit. sci., 1988-93; James R. Shepley prof. pub. policy, prof. polit. sci. Duke U., Durham, N.C., 1994—, dir. DeWitt Wallace Ctr. for Comm. and Journalism Terry Sanford Inst. Pub. Policy, 1994—. Vis. prof. Kathryn W. Davis Chair Wellesley Coll., 1978; vis. com. dept. Slavic lang. and lit. Harvard U., 1978-85, vice chmn. vis. com. Russian Rsch. Ctr., Harvard U., 1986-92; mem. subcom. on comms. and society Am. Coun. Learned Socs./Soviet Acad. Scis., 1986-90; mem. com. on internat. security studies, Am. Acad. Arts and Scis., 1988-90; fellow The Carter Ctr., 1985—, dir. Commn. on Radio and TV Policy; mem. area adv. com. for Ea. Europe and USSR, Coun. for Internat. Exch. Of Scholars, 1987-90; mem. acad. adv. coun. The Kennan Inst. for Advanced Russian Studies, 1989-93; mem. bd. overseers Internat. Press Ctr., Moscow, 1995; dir., commr. Commn. Radio and TV Policy, 1990. Author: Soviet Political Schools, 1967, Media and the Russian Public, 1981, Split Signals: Television and Politics in the Soviet Union, 1988 (Electronic Book of Yr. award Nat. Assn. Broadcasters and Broadcast Edn. Assn. 1988); co-author: Television and Elections, 1992, Television/Radio News and Minorities, 1994, Changing Channels: Television and the Struggle for Power in Russia, 1997, revised and expanded edit., 1999; editor: Soviet Union Jour., 1980-90; co-editor: International Security and Arms Control, 1986, The Soviet Calculus of Nuclear War, 1986; editor, contbr.: Handbook of Soviet Social Science Data, 1973; mem. editl. bd. Jour. Politics, 1985-88, Harvard Internat. Jour. Press/Politics, 1995—, Polit. Comms., 1996—, Polit. Comm., 1995—. Founder, 1st chmn. bd. dirs. Opera Guild of Greater Lansing, Inc., 1972-74. Recipient Outstanding Svc. to Promote Dem. Media in Russia award Journalists Union of Russia, 1994; Ford Found. Fgn. Area Tng. fellow, 1962-65, Guggenheim fellow, 1973-74; Sigma Xi grantee, 1972-74, John and Mary R. Markle Found. grantee, 1984-88, 94-96, 95—, Ford Found. grantee, 1985, 88-91, 92—, Rockefeller Found. grantee, 1985-87, W. Alton Jones Found. grantee, 1987-88, Eurasia Found. grantee, 1993-94, Carnegie Corp. of N.Y. grantee, 1996—. Mem. Am. Assn. for Advancement Slavic Studies (bd. dirs. 1978-81, mem. awards com., mem. endowment com. 1984-86, pres. 1987-88), Am. Polit. Sci. Assn.,Internat. Studies Assn. (v.p. N.Am. 1983-84), Dante Soc. Am., So. Conf. Slavic Studies (exec. com. 1983-84), Counc. Fgn. Rels. Office: Duke U Sanford Inst Pub Policy PO Box 90241 Durham NC 27708-0241

MICKLE, MARLIN HOMER, electrical engineer, educator; b. Windber, Pa., July 5, 1936; s. Howard T. and Ruth Elma (Corle) M. BS, U. Pitts., 1961, MS, 1963, PhD, 1967. Jr. engr. IBM, 1962; engr. Westinghouse Co., 1964; mem. faculty U. Pitts., 1962—, assoc. prof. elec. engring., 1968-75, prof., 1975—, dir. computer engring. program, 1982-84, Nickolas A. DeCecco prof., 2001—. Program dir. system theory & applications NSF, 1974-75; cons. NSF, Batelle, Contraves-Goerz, TASC, Westinghouse, AMSCO, Tex. Instruments, Inc., Compunetics, others; pres. Mickle Computer Techs., Inc., Pitts., 1979-85; v.p., dir. Power Resources, Inc., Pitts., 1980-84; dir. Univ. Rsch. & Devel. Assocs., Inc., assoc. dir. Swanson Inst. for Product Innovation, 2001 . Author: (with T.W. Sze) Optimization in Systems Engineering, 1972; mem. editl. bd. Jour. Interdisciplinary Modeling and Simulation, 1978-80; editor-in-chief Internat. Jour. Paralle and Distributed Systems and Networks, 1997-2002; contbr. articles to profl. jours. Dist. lay leader Pitts. dist. United Meth. Ch., 1971-73; bd. dirs. Asbury Heights, Pitts., 1982—, Wesley Hills of Mt. Lebanon, Pitts., 1985-86; chmn. bd. dirs. Emory Sr. Housing, Pitts., 2000—. With USAF, 1954-58. Fellow IEEE (life). Republican. Home: 4601 5th Ave Apt 723 Pittsburgh PA 15213-3657 Office: U Pitts Dept Elec and Computer Engring Pittsburgh PA 15261-0001

MICKO, ALEXANDER S. financial executive; b. Munich, May 8, 1947; came to U.S., 1952, naturalized, 1957; s. Zygmunt and Maria (Huber) M.; m. Sharon E. Judge, June 7, 1969; 1 child, Brian A. BS, LaSalle U., 1969. CPA, N.J., Pa. Audit mgr. Price Waterhouse, Phila., 1970-77; asst. chief fin. investigations div. of Casino Gaming Enforcement, State of N.J., Trenton, 1977-79; v.p. fin. TeleScis., Inc., Mt. Laurel, N.J., 1979-87; v.p. fin., chief fin. officer, asst. sec. Dechert, Price & Rhoads, Phila., 1987-89; v.p. fin., treas., sec. NET Atlantic, Inc., Thorofare, N.J., 1989-92; v.p., contr. AAA Mid-Atlantic, Inc., Phila., 1992—. Owner AM Fin. Services, Medford, N.J., 1986—; cons. United Computer Services, Berlin. N.J., 1982—; lectr. in field. Bd. dirs. Forest Hills Civic Assn., Williamstown, N.J., 1976. With USMC, 1969-75. Recipient Michael A. DeAngelis Outstanding Profl. Achievement award, LaSalle U., Phila., 1985. Mem. AICPA, N.J. Soc. CPAs, Pa. Inst. CPAs, Fin. Execs. Inst., Nat. Assn. Accts. Roman Catholic. Avocations: skiing, golf. Home: 5 Huntington Cir Medford NJ 08055-3315 Office: AAA Mid Atlantic Inc PO Box 820884 Philadelphia PA 19182-0884 Office Phone: 215-864-7595. Personal E-mail: amicko@aol.com.

MICKUM, GEORGE BRENT, III, lawyer; b. Washington, Jan. 13, 1928; s. George Brent and Anna May (Love) M.; m. Lora Mattare, June 27, 1953; children— George Brent, Luke Anthony, Ann Elizabeth, Paul Christopher, Joseph Benedict, Mark Andrew. B.S., Georgetown U., 1949, LL.B., 1952. Bar: U.S. Dist. Ct. 1952, U.S. Ct. Appeals (D.C. cir.) 1952, U.S. Supreme Ct. 1960, U.S. Ct. Appeals (4th cir.) 1967, U.S. Ct. Appeals (2d cir.) 1975, U.S. Ct. Appeals (9th cir.) 1977, U.S. Ct. Appeals (5th and 7th cirs.) 1981. Law clk. U.S. Ct. Appeals D.C., Washington, 1952-53; law clk. to assoc. justice Stanley F. Reed, U.S. Supreme Ct., Washington, 1953-54; pvt. practice, 1954—; now mem. Steptoe & Johnson Chartered, Chevy Chase, Md.; dir. Gen. Bus. Services Inc., Rockville, Md. Served to sgt. U.S. Army, 1944-46. Mem. D.C. Bar, Bar Assn. D.C., ABA (sect. litigation). Democrat. Roman Catholic. Clubs: Internat. (Washington), Columbia Country (Chevy Chase). Office: Steptoe & Johnson Chartered 8th Floor 1250 Connecticut Ave NW Washington DC 20036

MICOZZI, MARC STEPHEN, health executive, physician, educator; b. Norfolk, Va., Oct. 27, 1953; s. Edio Dominic and Huguette (Picon) M.; m. Carole Ann O'Leary, Oct. 8, 1982; 1 child, Alicia Madeleine. Cadet, USAF Acad., 1971-72; BA, Pomona Coll., 1974; MD, U. Pa., 1979, PhD, 1986. Diplomate Am. Bd. Pathology. Rsch. fellow City of Hope Nat. Med. Ctr., Duarte, Calif., 1973; chem. engr. Gould Corp., El Monte, Calif., 1974; Luce Found. scholar Mindanao, The Philippines, 1976-77; clin. applications chemist McDonnell-Douglas Corp., Pasadena, Calif., 1978; postdoctoral fellow Allied Inst. Environ. Health, Princeton, N.J., 1979; resident in pathology Pa. Hosp., Phila., 1980-83; med. examiner Dade County Med. Examiner's Office, Miami, Fla., 1983-84; sr. investigator Nat. Cancer Inst., Bethesda, Md., 1984-86; dir. Nat. Mus. Health and Medicine, Washington, 1986-95; exec. dir. Coll. Physicians' of Phila., 1995—2002; exec. dir. Integrative Medicine Thomas Jefferson U. Hosp., Phila., 2002—. Adj. prof. Uniformed Svcs. U. Health Scis., Bethesda, 1986-95, U. Pa. Sch. Medicine, 1996—; vis. lectr. Georgetown U. Sch. Medicine, Washington, 1986—, Johns Hopkins U. Sch. Medicine, Balt., 1988—; adj. prof. dept. phys. medicine U. Pa., 1996—. Editor: Nutrition and Cancer, 1989; assoc. editor Health Care, Jour. Human Orgn., 1983-89; contbr. chpts. to books and numerous articles to profl. jours. Del. White House Conf. on Youth, Estes Park, Colo., 1971, UN Conf. on Human Environ., Stockholm, 1972, NATO Advanced Study Inst., Brussels, 1982; mem. Calif. Gov.'s Adv. Com., 1972-74. Fellow Human Biology coun., Soc. for Applied Anthropology, Am. Anthrop. Assn.; Am. Acad. Forensic Scis., Am. Pub. Health Assn., N.Y. Acad. Scis. Roman Catholic. Office: Thomas Jefferson U Hosp Ste 6215 Philadelphia PA 19107

MICZEK, KLAUS ALEXANDER, psychology educator; b. Burghausen, Bavaria, Germany, Sept. 28, 1944; came to U.S., 1967; s. Erich and Irene (Wirthl) M.; m. Christiane Baerwaldt, Aug. 8, 1970; 1 child, Nikolai A. Tchrs. cert., Paedagogische Hochschule, Berlin, 1966; PhD, U. Chgo., 1972. Asst. prof. Carnegie-Mellon U., Pitts., 1972-74, assoc. prof., 1974-79, Tufts U., Medford, Mass., 1979-83, prof., 1983-93, Moses Hunt prof. psychiatry, psychology, pharmacology and neuroscience, 1993—. Cons. Solvay-Pharma v.b., Weesp, The Netherlands, 1984-99, NIH, Rockville, Md., 1984—, Forest Labs., N.Y.C., 2003-; Boehringer Ingelheim, Germany, 2003-; Boerhaave prof. U. Leiden, The Netherlands, 1987; mem. panel on violence, NAS, 1989-92. Editor: Ethopharmacology, 1983, Ethopharmacological Aggression Research, 1984; field editor, coord. editor Behavioral Pharmacology, Jour. Psychopharmacology; contbr. articles on psychopharmacology, 1973—. Rsch. grantee Nat. Inst. Drug Abuse, 1973—, Nat. Inst. Alcoholism and Alcohol Abuse, 1981—; recipient Solvay-Duphar award APA, 1993, Bundesverdienstkreuz Cross of Merit, Fed. Republic of Germany, 1996, Gold medal Charles U., Prague, 2004. Fellow APA (program chmn. 1981, pres. div. psychopharmacology 1990-91, master lectr. 1999), Behavioral Pharmacol. Soc. (pres. 1992-94), Internat. Soc. for Rsch. on Aggression (councilor 1987); mem. Soc. Neurosci., N.Y. Acad. Scis., Internat. Primatol. Soc. Office: Tufts U Dept Psychology 530 Boston Ave Medford MA 02155-5532 Business E-Mail: klaus.miczek@tufts.edu.

MIDDAUGH, ROBERT BURTON, artist; b. Chgo., May 12, 1935; s. John Burton and Mae Knight (Crooks) M. Student, U. Chgo., 1960-64; BFA, Art Inst. Chgo., 1964. Curator art collection 1st Nat. Bank Chgo., 1971-83. Designed, executed ednl. display, Prehistoric Project at Oriental Inst. of U. Chgo., 1968; One-man shows include, Kovler Gallery, Chgo., 1965, 67, 69, Martin Schweig Gallery, St. Louis, 1970, 72, 79, 83, U. Wis., 1976, 81, 82, Fairweather Hardin Gallery, Chgo., 1977, 80, 83, 85, Rockford Art Mus., 1987, Zaks Gallery, Chgo., 1992, 93, 97; group shows, including, Art Inst. Chgo., 1964, 66, 78, 79, Evanston (Ill.) Art Center, 1966, Joslyn Art Mus., Omaha, 1968, U. Notre Dame, 1969, Va. Mus. Fine Arts, Richmond, 1966; represented in permanent collections, Art Inst. Chgo., Boston Mus. Fine Arts, Fine Art Mus. of South, Mobile, Ala., Los Angeles County Mus., Phoenix Art Mus., Worcester (Mass.) Art Mus., Ill. State Mus., Springfield. Served with U.S. Army, 1958-60. Archivist, Chgo. Park Dist., 1998—. Mem. Arts Club Chgo.

MIDDELKAMP, JOHN NEAL, pediatrician, educator; b. Kansas City, Mo., Sept. 29, 1925; s. George H. and Clara M. (Ordelheide) M.; m. Roberta Gill, Oct. 3, 1949 (div. 1970); children— Sharon Ann, Steven Neal, Susan Jean, Scott Alan; m. Lois Harper, Mar. 1, 1974 BS, U. Mo., 1946; MD, Washington U., St. Louis, 1948. Diplomate Am. Bd. Pediatrics. Intern D.C. Gen. Hosp., Washington, 1948-49; resident St. Louis Children's Hosp., 1949-50, 52-53; instr. pediatrics Washington U., 1953-57, asst. prof. pediatrics, 1957-64, assoc. prof., 1964-70, prof., 1970-98, prof. emeritus, 1998—; dir. ambulatory pediatrics St. Louis Children's Hosp., 1974-91. Author: Camp Health Manual, 1984; contbr. articles, chpts. to profl. publs. Served to comdr. M.C., USNR, 1943-66. NIH postdoctoral fellow, 1961-62 Mem. Am. Acad. Pediatrics, Am. Soc. Microbiology, Infectious Diseases Soc. Am., Am. Pediatric Soc., Ambulatory Pediatric Assn., Sigma Xi, Alpha Omega Alpha Home: 8845 Paragon Cir Saint Louis MO 63123-1114 Office: 1 Childrens Pl Saint Louis MO 63110-1002 Office Phone: 314-747-4479.

MIDDENDORF, ALICE CARTER, volunteer; b. Balt., Dec. 7, 1940; d. John William and Alice Temple (Carter) M. BA, Wellesley Coll., 1963, Oxford U., Eng., 1972. Libr. Boston Athenaeum Libr., 1963-66; editor Houghton Mifflin Co., Boston, 1966-69; bd. dirs. Balt. Zool. Soc., 1976; cons. Nat. Zoo, Washington, 1976-77, G. Ward & Assocs., Ridgefield, Conn., 1976-79; from bd. dirs. to bd. govs. Nat. Aquarium in Balt., 1976-88, sec. bd. govs., 1987-88, chmn. animal policy com., 1982-88; bd. dirs. Total Health Care (merger Constant Care and West Balt. Cmty. Health Ctrs.), Balt., 1981—; sec. bd. dirs. Total Health Care (merger Constant Care Med. Ctr. and West Balt. Constant Health Ctr.), Balt., 1990-93, 97-98; treas., 1998. Adv. bd. Nat. Aquarium in Balt., 1989-94, 99—, bd. govs., 1994-99, sec. bd. govs., 1995-99; bd. dirs. Constant Care Med. Ctr., Balt., Park Heights Street Acad., Balt., sec., 1988-90; pres. Fulmar Corp., Cayman Islands, Brit. West Indies, 1991-99; pres., chmn. bd. dirs. Lystra Hill Farms, Inc., Goleta, Calif., 1996-97. Bd. dirs. Scenic Md., 2002—. Recipient Pres.'s Citation, Pres. City Coun. Balt., 1974, 76, Award of Appreciation, Mayor of Balt., 1981. Avocations: scuba, underwater photography, marine biology, malacology, travel, reading. Home and Office: 1301 Hillside Rd Stevenson MD 21153-2019

MIDDENDORF, J. WILLIAM, II, investment banker; b. Balt., Sept. 22, 1924; m. Isabelle Paine, Mar. 7, 1953; children: Frances, Amy, John W. IV, Ralph Henry. B in Naval Sci., Holy Cross Coll., 1945; AB, Harvard U., 1947; MBA, NYU, 1954; LLD (hon.), Troy State U.; LittD (hon.), Sch. of Ozarks, Am. Christian Coll.; D. Social Scis. (hon.), Netherlands-Am. Inst. Commd. ensign USN, 1945, advanced through grades to lt. (j.g.), ret., 1946; with credit dept. Chase Manhattan Bank, 1947-52; ptnr. Wood Struthers and Co., 1958-61; sr. ptnr. Middendorf, Colgate and Co., 1962-69; ambassador to The Netherlands, 1969-73; sec. USN, 1974-77; pres., CEO Fin. Gen. Bankshares, Inc., 1977-81; ambassador to Orgn. Am. States, 1981-85, European Communities, 1985-87; chmn. Middendorf & Assocs., Inc., 1989—. Chmn. presdl. task force Project Econ. and Social Justice, 1986-90; mem. U.S. Del. to supervise elections in Suriname, 1988; treas. Internat. Rep. Inst. Composer 8 symphonies, 100 marches, (opera) King Richard, nat. independence march for Belize, other compositions for Latin Am. countries; guest condr. Boston Pops, St. Louis Symphony, Ind. U., others; contbr. articles to profl. jours. Mem. U.S. Olympic com., 1979-89, U.S. Olympic Selection com. for field hockey; judge field hockey Olympics, Rome, 1960; former mem. vis. com. dept. Am. paintings Met. Mus. Art, N.Y.C., vis. com. dept. Am. Art, Mus. Fine Arts, Boston; hon. v.p. Naval Hist. Found.; treas. Goldwater for Pres. com., 1962-64, Presdl. Transition com. 1968, Rep. Nat. Com., 1964-69; alt. del. for Gov. Reagan, 1980; del. State of Conn., 1964, 68, State of Va., 1996; co-chmn. Virginians for Reagan, 1980, fin. com. Va. GOP, 1980-81; coord. internat. econ. and naval adv. com. Reagan for Pres. campaign, 1980; chmn. Congl. Boosters com., 1978-81; chmn. CIA Transition Team, 1980-81; chmn. fin. com. Pres. Reagan's 1981 Inaugural com.; trustee Naval War Coll. Found., Heritage Found., Washington; past trustee Hoover Instn. for War Revolution and Peace, Corcoran Gallery, N.Y. Hist. Soc., Balt. Mus. Art, Greenwich Hist. Soc., Boston Symphony, Middlesex Sch., Concord, Mass., Nat. Symphony Orch., Mass. Gen. Hosp., Boys Club N.Y.; bd. electors Ins. Hall of Fame; bd. dirs. Georgetown U., John Philip Sousa Meml. Found., Newport Art Mus. and Mariners' Mus., Norfolk, Va.; chmn. bd. dirs. council statesmen Ludwig von Mises Inst.; chmn. Com. for Monetary Rsch. and Edn. Inc., Netherlands-Am. Amity Trust, Def. Forum Found., Navy League Awards com., 1977—; former mem. com. Dept. State Fine Arts Com.; founding chmn. U.S. Navy Meml. Found.; past chmn. Netherlands-Am. Inst., Wolf Trap Farm Park, John Carter Brown Library Assocs., Providence, Asian Composers Expo., European Council of Boy Scouts. Decorated Grand Master Order of Orange Nassau (Netherlands), Order of Arab (Republic Egypt), Grand Master of Order of Naval Merit (Republic Brazil); recipient Superior Honor award Dept. State, 1974, Disting. Pub. Svc. award Dept. Def., 1975, 76, Navy Disting. Pub. Svc. award, 1976, Naval Disting. Svc. medal Republic Brazil, 1976, Ludwig von Mises Free Market award, 1985, Inter-Am. Music Coun. award, 1985, Edwin Franko Goldman award Am. Bandmasters Assn., 1987, Assn. Harvard Clubs Am. award, Disting. Svc. medal Purdue Univ. Bands, Netherlands Soc. Phila. Gold medal, Good Citizenship medal Nat. Soc. SAR, Medal of Honor, Midwest Nat. Band Assn., Invest in Am. Am. Eagle award, 1988, Eugene J. Keogh Disting. Pub. Svc. award NYU, 1989, Nat. Commendation award Pres.' Coun. Phys. Fitness and Sports, 1989, Leadership award Am. Friends of Turkey, 1989, Adm. Arleigh Burke Leadership award, 1998, Arleigh Burke award 1998; named Alumnus of Yr. NYU, 1978; Nat. Masters Sculling champion, 1979, Gold medal The Holland Soc. Mem. Am. Antiquarian Soc., Harvard Alumni Assn. (permanent class com. 1947), Soc. Cin. (hon.), ASCAP, Walpole Soc., Co. Mil. Historians, Mil. Order Loyal Legion, SAR, Soc. of SAR, Field Hockey Assn. Am. (past pres., player/mgr. nat. team 1963), U.S. Naval Inst., Navy League. Clubs: Angler's, Downtown Assn., Union (N.Y.C.); Army-Navy, Capitol Hill, Met., Potomac Boat (Washington); Sakonnet Golf (Little Compton, R.I.); Somerset (Boston). Mailing: PO Box 1037 Little Compton RI 02837

MIDDENDORF, JOHN HARLAN, English literature educator; b. N.Y.C., Mar. 31, 1922; s. George Arlington and Margaret (Hofmann) M.; m. Beverly Bruner, July 14, 1943 (dec. 1983); children: Cathie Jean Middendorf Hamilton, Peggy Ruth Middendorf Brindisi; m. Maureen L. MacGrogan, Jan. 31, 1986. AB, Dartmouth Coll., 1943; AM, Columbia U., 1947, PhD, 1953. Lectr. English CCNY, 1946, Hunter Coll., 1946-49; faculty Columbia, 1947—, prof. English, 1965-89, prof. emeritus, 1990—, dir. grad. studies, 1971-74, vice-chmn., 1976-80. Chmn. English test com. Coll. Entrance Exam. Bd., 1967-69 Contbr. articles, revs. to profl. jours.; Editor: English Writers of the Eighteenth Century, 1971; asst. editor: Johnsonian News Letter, 1950-58; co-editor, 1958-78, editor, 1978-90; asso. editor: Yale edit. Works Samuel Johnson, 1962-66; gen. editor, 1966— . Served to lt. (j.g.) USNR, 1943-46. Faculty fellow Fund Advancement Edn., 1951-52; grantee Coun. Rsch. Humanities, 1958-59, Am. Philos. Soc., 1962, Am. Coun. Learned Socs., 1962, NEH, 1976-88. Mem. Johnsonians (sec.-treas. 1958-68, chmn. 1969, 79), Univ. Seminar on 18th Century European Culture (chmn. 1973-75, 85-87), Oxford Bibliog. Soc., Grolier Club, English Inst. (mem. supervisory com. 1963-66), Modern Lang. Assn., Soc. Sr. Scholars, Am. Soc. 18th Century Studies, Phi Beta Kappa. Home: 404 Riverside Dr New York NY 10025-1861 Office: Columbia U Dept English New York NY 10027

MIDDLEBROOK, DIANE WOOD, English language educator, writer; b. Pocatello, Idaho, Apr. 16, 1939; d. Thomas Isaac and Helen Loretta (Downey) Wood; m. Jonathan Middlebrook, June 15, 1963 (annulled 1976); 1 child, Leah Wood; m. Carl Djerassi, June 21, 1985. BA, U. Wash., 1961; MA, Yale U., 1962, PhD, 1968; LittD (hon.), Kenyon Coll., 1999. Asst. prof. Stanford (Calif.) U., 1966-73, assoc. prof., 1973-83, prof., 1983-2001, prof. emerita, 2002—, dir. Ctr. for Rsch. on Women, 1977-79. Author: Walt Whitman and Wallace Stevens, 1974, Worlds into Words: Understanding Modern Poems, 1980, Anne Sexton, A Biography, 1991, Suits Me: The Double Life of Billy Tipton, 1998, Her Husband: Hughes and Plath, a Marriage, 2003; editor: Coming to Light: American Women Poets in the Twentieth Century, 1985; author: (poetry) Gin Considered as a Demon, 1983. Founding trustee Djerassi Resident Artists Program, Woodside, Calif., 1980—83, chair, 1994; trustee San Francisco Art Inst, 1993. Finalist Nat. Book award, 1991; recipient Yale Prize for Poetry; fellow Ind. Study, NEH, 1982—83, Bunting Inst., Radcliffe Coll., 1982—83, Guggenheim Found., 1988—89, Rockefeller Study Ctr., 1990. Fellow: Royal Soc. Lit.; mem.: MLA, Authors Guild, Christs Coll. Cambridge (hon.), Biographers Club. Avocations: collecting art, theater. Home: 1101 Green St Apt 1501 San Francisco CA 94109-2012 Office: Agent Georges Borchardt 136 E 57th St New York NY 10022 Office Phone: 415-474-1866. E-mail: dwm@stanford.edu.

MIDDLEBROOK, JOHN G. marketing executive, advertising executive; BS in Engring., GM Inst.; M in Mktg., Mich. State U. With GM Oldsmobile Div., 1959—67, GM Pontiac Div., 1967, asst. sales mgr., 1969—70, sales analysis mgr., 1970, dir. mktg. svcs., 1977; zone mgr. GM Corp., Washington, 1977, dir. mktg. ops., 1978, mgr. product planning, devel., 1979—81; dir. passenger car planning GM Worldwide, 1981—83; dir. car distbn., sales analysis, strategic planning GM Pontiac Div., 1983, asst. gen. sales mgr., merchandising, ops., 1984—85; v.p. sales, svc, mktg. Saturn Corp., 1985—87; v.p. mktg product planning staff GM Corp., 1987—89; gen. mgr. GM Pontiac Motor Div., 1989, GM Chevrolet Div., 1996, GM Corp., 1999—2000, v.p. mktg, advt., 2000—. Pres. Boy Scouts, Detroit. Office: GM Corp 300 Renaissance Ctr PO Box 300 Detroit MI 48265-3000

MIDDLEBROOK, STEPHEN BEACH, lawyer; b. Hartford, Conn., 1937; BA, Yale U., 1958, LLB, 1961. Bar: Conn. 1961. Counsel Aetna Life and Casualty Co., Hartford, Conn., 1969-71, asst. gen. counsel, 1971-78, corp. sec., 1973-83, v.p., gen. counsel, 1981-88, sr. v.p., gen. counsel, 1988-90, sr. v.p., exec. counsel, 1990-94; spl. counsel Day, Berry & Howard, Hartford, 1995—. Vis. fellow Rand, Santa Monica, Calif., 1994. Office: Day Berry & Howard City Place I Hartford CT 06103-3499 E-mail: sbmiddlebrook@dbh.com.

MIDDLEBROOKS, DELORIS JEANETTE, nurse, educator; b. Cedar Rapids, Iowa, Apr. 9, 1931; d. Harland R. and Rosa V. (Anderson) Hickey; m. Johnnie L. Middlebrooks, Apr. 25, 1962 (dec.); children: James, Kathleen. Diploma, Evang. Hosp. Sch. Nursing, 1956; BSN, State U. Iowa, 1958; MS in Nursing, U. Calif., San Francisco, 1960; EdD, U. Nev., Las Vegas, 1985. Instr., coord. Nev. State Hosp. Sch. Practical Nursing, Sparks, 1963-66; staff nurse St. Mary's Hosp., Reno, 1966-68; instr., coord. Reno VA Sch. Practical Nursing, 1968-72; instr., coord. health occupations Wooster High Sch., 1972-73; nursing faculty Truckee Meadows C.C., 1973-94, ret., 1994; intermittent staff nurse VA Hosp., 1984-86; instr., review course Stanley Kaplan Ednl. Ctr., 1987-89; clin. nursing faculty Western Nev. C.C., Carson City, 1987, Northern Nev. C.C., Elko, 1979-93; guest assoc. prof. nursing Lewis-Clark State Coll., Lewiston, Idaho, 1989. Cons. Irish Bd. Nursing, Dublin, Ireland, 1985. Nominated Nev. Voc. Tchr. of Yr., 1975, 79, 88, 89; Recipient March of Dimes Community Leadership award, 1990. Mem.: ANA, Am. Assn. for the History of Nursing, Nev. Nurses Assn., Phi Kappa Phi, Sigma Theta Tau. Home: 1385 Ebbetts Dr Reno NV 89503-1918

MIDDLEBROOKS, EDDIE JOE, environmental engineer; b. Crawford County, Ga., Oct. 16, 1932; s. Robert Harold and Jewell LaVerne (Dixon) M.; m. Charlotte Linda Hardy, Dec. 6, 1958; 1 child, Linda Tracey. BCE, U. Fla., 1956, MS, 1960; PhD, Miss. State U., 1966. Registered profl. engr., Ariz., Miss., Utah, Wash., Colo.; registered land surveyor, Fla. Asst. san. engr. USPHS, Cin., 1956-58; field engr. T.T. Jones Constrn. Co., Atlanta, 1958-59; grad. teaching asst. U. Fla., 1959-60; research asst. U. Ariz., 1960-61; asst. prof., then assoc. prof. Miss. State U., 1962-67; research engr., asst. dir. San. Engring. Research Lab., U. Calif.-Berkeley, 1968-70; prof. Utah State U., Logan, 1970-82, dean Coll. Engring., 1974-82; Newman chair natural resources engring. Clemson U., 1982-83; provost, v.p. acad. affairs Tenn. Tech. U., 1983-88, U. Tulsa, 1988-90, prof. chem. engring., 1988-92, Trustees prof. chem. engring., 1990-92, acting pres., 1990; prof. civil engring. U. Nevada, Reno, 1992-97. Mem. nat. drinking water adv. council EPA, 1981-83; cons. EPA, UN Indsl. Devel. Orgn., Calif. Water Resources Control Bd., City and County of San Francisco, State of Colo., South Fla. Water Mgmt. Dist. (Everglades), also numerous indsl. and engring. firms. Author: Modeling the Eutrophication Process, 1974, Statistical Calculations-How to Solve Statistical Problems, 1976, Biostimulation and Nutrient Assessment, 1976, Water Supply Engineering Design, 1977, Lagoon Information Source Book, 1978, Industrial Pollution Control, Vol. 1: Agro-Industries, 1979, Wastewater Collection and Treatment: Principles and Practices, 1979, Water Reuse, 1982, Wastewater Stabiliation Lagoon Design, Performance and Upgrading, 1982, Reverse Osmosis Treatment of Drinking Water, 1986, Pollution Control in the Petrochemicals Industry, 1987, Natural Systems for Waste Management and Treatment, 1988, 2d edit., 1995, Japanese transl.; contbr. tech. articles to profl. jours. Fellow ASCE; mem. Water Environment Fedn. (dir. 1979-81, 91-92), Eddy medal 1969), Assn. Environ. Engring. Profs. (pres. 1974), Utah Water Pollution Control Assn. (pres. 1976), Internat. Assn. on Water Quality, Am. Soc. Engring. Edn., Am. Acad. Environ. Engrs. (diplomate, trustee 1992-95, v.p. 1995, pres. 1997-98), Sigma Xi, Omicron Delta Kappa, Phi Kappa Phi (Disting. mem.), Tau Beta Pi, Sigma Tau. Home and Office: 360 Blackhawk Ln Lafayette CO 80026-9392 Office Phone: 303-664-5292. Personal E-mail: Joemiddle@aol.com.

MIDDLEDITCH, LEIGH BENJAMIN, JR., lawyer, educator; b. Detroit, Sept. 30, 1929; s. Leigh Benjamin and Hope Tiffin (Noble) M.; m. Betty Lou Givens, June 27, 1953; children: Leigh III, Katherine Middleditch McDonald, Andrew B. BA, U. Va., 1951, LLB, 1957. Bar: Va. 1957. Assoc. James H. Michael, Jr., Charlottesville, Va., 1957-59; ptnr. Battle, Neal, Harris, Minor & Williams, Charlottesville, 1959-68; legal adviser U. Va., Charlottesville, 1968-72; ptnr. McGuire, Woods, Battle & Boothe (now McGuire Woods LLP), Charlottesville, 1972-99, of counsel, 2000—; v.p. McGuire Woods Cons. LLC, Charlottesville, 2001—. Lectr. Grad. Bus. Sch., U. Va., Charlottesville, 1958-94, lectr. Law Sch., 1970-90. Co-author: Virginia Civil Procedure, 1978, 2d edition, 1992; contbr. articles to profl. jours. Chmn. U. Va. Health Svcs. Found., 1988-97; bd. mgrs. U. Va. Alumni, 1994-2001, pres., 2000-01; bd. dirs., chmn. Va. Health Care Found., 1997-98; trustee Claude Moore Found., 1991—; mem. Va. Health Planning Bd., 1989—; bd. visitors U. Va., 1990-94; trustee Thomas Jefferson Meml. Found., Monticello, 1994-2002. Fellow Am. Bar Found., Va. Bar Found.; mem. ABA (bd. govs. 1999-2002), Va. State Bar (coun., chmn. bd. govs. various sects.), Charlottesville-Albemarle Bar Assn. (pres. 1979-80), U. Va. Law Sch. Alumni Assn. (pres. 1979-81), U.S. C. of C. (bd. dirs. 1998—2004), Va. C. of C. (pres. 1988-90), Omicron Delta Kappa. Episcopalian. Office: McGuire Woods LLP PO Box 1288 Charlottesville VA 22902-1288 Office Phone: 434-977-2543.

MIDDLEKAUFF, ROBERT LAWRENCE, history educator, administrator; b. Yakima, Wash., July 5, 1929; s. Harold and Katherine Ruth (Horne) M.; m. Beverly Jo Martin, July 11, 1952; children: Samuel John, Holly Ruth. BA, U. Wash., 1952; PhD, Yale U., 1961. Instr. history Yale U., New Haven, 1959-62; asst. prof. history U. Calif., Berkeley, 1962-66, assoc. prof., 1966-70, prof., 1970-80, Margaret Byrne prof. history, 1980-83, prof. history, 1988-92, emeritus prof., 2000—, Preston Hotchkis prof., 1992—; dir. Huntington Libr., Art Gallery and Bot. Gardens, San Marino, Calif., 1983-88; Harmsworth prof. history Oxford (Eng.) U., 1996-97. Mem. coun. Inst. Early Am. History and Culture, Williamsburg, Va., 1974-76, 85-88. Author: Ancients and Axioms, 1963, The Mathers, 1971, The Glorious Cause: The American Revolution, 1763-1789, 1982, Benjamin Franklin and His Enemies, 1996. Served to 1st lt. USMC, 1952-54, Korea. Recipient Bancroft prize, 1972, Commonwealth Club Gold medal, 1983; fellow Am. Coun. Learned Socs., 1965, NEH, 1973, Huntington Libr., 1977. Fellow Am. Acad. Arts and Scis.; mem. Am. Hist. Assn., Orgn. Am. Historians, Am. Philos. Soc., Soc. Am. Historians, Am. Antiquarian Soc., Assocs. Early Am. History and Culture (mem. exec. com.), Colonial Soc. Mass. (corr.). Home: 5868 Ocean View Dr Oakland CA 94618-1535 Office: Univ Calif Dept History Berkeley CA 94720-2550 E-mail: rlmiddlek@juno.com.

MIDDLETON, ANTHONY WAYNE, JR., urologist, educator; b. May 6, 1939; s. Anthony Wayne and Dolores Caravena (Lowry) M.; m. Carol Samuelson, Oct. 23, 1970; children: Anthony Wayne, Suzanne, Kathryn, Jane, Michelle. BS, U. Utah, 1963; MD, Cornell U., 1966. Intern U. Utah Hosps., Salt Lake City, 1966-67; resident in urology Mass. Gen. Hosp., Boston, 1970-74; practice urology Middleton Urol. Assocs., Salt Lake City, 1974—. Mem. staff LDS Hosp., chmn. divsn. urology, 1995—2004, Salt Lake Regional Med. Ctr., 1977—79, 1984—86; assoc. clin. prof. surgery U. Utah Med. Coll., 1977—; vice-chmn. bd. govs. Utah Med. Self-Ins. Assn., 1980—81, 1996—, chmn., 1985—87; chmn. med. adv. bd. Uroquest Co., 1996—99; med. dir. Uromed, prostate microwave co., 1999—2000, Utah divsn. Rocky Mountain Prostate, 2001—, Utah-Idaho Lithotripsy, 2001—. Editor: AACU-FAX, 1992—; assoc. editor Millenial Star Brit. LDS mag., 1960-61; contbr. articles to profl. jours. Mem. U. Utah Coll. Medicine Dean's Search Com., 1983—84; bd. dirs. Utah Symphony, 1985—2002, Primary Children's Found., 1989—96; mem. Utah Crime Reparations Bd., 2000—, chmn., 2002—; staff pres. Primary Children's Med. Ctr., 1982; vice chmn. Utah Med. Polit. Action Com., 1978—81, chmn., 1981—83, Utah Physicians for Reagan, 1983—84; del. Utah State Rep. Conv., 2000—01; bishop, later stake presidency Ch. Jesus Christ Latter-day Saints; bd. dirs. Utah chpt. Am. Cancer Soc., 1978—86, Utah Symphony and Opera, 2002—, Timpanogos Club, 1978—, 2d asst. to pres., 2002—03, 1st asst. to pres., 2003—. Capt. USAF, 1968—70. Mem.: AMA (del. to Ho. of Dels. 1998—, chmn. ref. com. I 2001, mem. governing coun. SSS 2002—, alt. del. to Ho. of Dels., 1987-88, 89-92, 94, 96-98), ACS, Am. Assn. Clin. Urologists (bd. dirs. 1989—90, nat. pres.-elect 1990—91, pres. 1991—92, nat. bd. chmn. urologic polit. action com. UROPAC 1992—98, Disting. Svc. award 2000), Salt Lake Surg. Soc. (treas. 1977—78), Utah Urol. Assn. (treas. 1977—78, pres. 1978—79), Salt Lake County Med. Assn. (sec. 1965—67, pres. liaison com. 1980—81, pres.-elect 1981—83, pres. 1984), Am. Urologic Assn. (socioecons. com. 1987—90, chmn. western sect. socioecons. com. 1989—90, chmn. western sect. health policy com. 1990—2002, pres.-elect western sect. 1999—2000, pres. 2000—01), Utah Med. Assn. (pres. 1987—88, bd. dirs. 1998—, Disting. Svc. award 1993), Beta Theta Pi (chpt. pres. Gamma Beta 1962), Alpha Omega Alpha, Phi Beta Kappa. Republican. Home: 2798 Chancellor Pl Salt Lake City UT 84108-2835 Office: 1060 East 1st South Salt Lake City UT 84102-1520 Office Phone: 801-531-9453. E-mail: awmiddleton@msn.com.

MIDDLETON, CHRISTOPHER, Germanic languages and literature educator; b. Truro, Cornwall, Eng., June 10, 1926; came to U.S., 1966; s. Hubert Stanley and Dorothy May (Miller) M. BA, U. of Oxford, Eng., 1951, PhD, 1954. Lectr. King's Coll., London, 1955-65; prof. Germanic langs. and lit. U. Tex., Austin, 1966-98. Author: Selected Writings, 1989, Andalusian Poems, 1993, The Balcony Tree, 1992, Intimate Chronicles, 1996, Twenty Tropes for Doctor Dark, 2000, The Word Pavilion and Selected Poems, 2001, Of the Mortal Fire, 2003, Jackdaw Jiving: Essays on Poetry and Translation, 1998, In the Mirror of the Eighth King, 1999, Faint Harps and Silver Voices-Selected Translations, 2000, Crypto-Topographia: Stories of Secret Places, 2002. Recipient trans. prize Schlegel-Tieck/Govt. Fed. Republic Germany, 1985, Anglo-Swiss Cultural Rels. prize Max Geilinger Stiftung, Zurich, Switzerland, 1987; Guggenheim Found. poetry fellow, 1974-75, NEH poetry fellow, 1980. Mem. Akademie der Künste Berlin. Office: U Tex Dept Of Germanic Langs Austin TX 78712

MIDDLETON, DAVID, physicist, applied mathematician, educator; b. N.Y.C., Apr. 19, 1920; s. Charles Davies Scudder and Lucile (Davidson) M.; m. Nadea Butler, May 26, 1945 (div. 1971); children: Susan Terry, Leslie Butler, David Scudder Blakeslee, George Davidson Powell; m. Joan Bartlett Reed, 1971; children: Christopher Hope, Andrew Bartlett, Henry H. Reed. Grad., Deerfield Acad., 1938; AB summa cum laude, Harvard U., 1942, AM, 1945, PhD in Physics, 1947. Tchg. fellow electronics Harvard U., Cambridge, Mass., 1942, spl. rsch. assoc. radio rsch. lab., 1942-45, NSF predoctoral fellow physics, 1945-47, rsch. fellow electronics, 1947-49, asst. prof. applied physics, 1949-54; cons. physicist Cambridge, 1954—2004, Concord, Mass., 1957-71, N.Y.C., 1971—; adj. prof. elec. engring. Columbia U., 1960-61; adj. prof. applied physics and comm. theory Rensselaer Poly. Inst., Hartford Grad. Ctr., 1961-70; adj. prof. communication theory U. R.I., 1966—; adj. prof. math. scis. Rice U., 1979-89. U.S. del. internat. conf. Internat. Radio Union, Lima, Peru, 1975; lectr. NATO Advanced Study Inst., Grenoble, France, 1964, Copenhagen, 1980, Luneburg, Germany, 1984; mem. Naval Rsch. Adv. Com., 1970-77; mem., cons. Inst. Def. Analyses; mem. sci. adv. bd. Supercomputing Rsch. Ctr., 1987-91; cons. physicist since 1946, orgns. including Johns Hopkins U., SRI Internat., Rand Corp., USAF, Cambridge Rsch. Ctr., Comm. Satellite Corp., Lincoln Lab., NASA, Raytheon, Sylvania, Sperry-Rand, Office Naval Rsch., Applied Rsch. Labs., U. Tex., GE, Honeywell Transp. Sys. Ctr. of Dept. Transp., Dept. Commerce Office of Telecom., NOAA, Office Telecom. Policy of Exec. Office Pres., Nat. Telecom. and Info. Adminstrn., Sci. Applications Inc. (SAIC), Naval Undersea Warfare Ctr., Lawrence Livermore Nat. Labs., Planning Rsch. Corp., Applied Physics Labs. U. Wash., 1992—, Kildare Corp., 1995—, Karmanos Cancer Inst., 1997-2001, others. Author: Introduction to Statistical Communication Theory, 1960, 3d edit., 1996, Russian edit. Soviet Radio Moscow, 2 vols., 1961, 62, Topics in Communication Theory, 1965, 87, Russian edit., 1966; sci. editor English edit. Statistical Methods in Sonar (V.V. Ol'shevskii), 1978; mem. editl. bd. Info. and Control, Advanced Serials in Electronics and Cybernetics, 1972-82; contbr. articles to tech. jours. Recipient award (with W.H. Huggins) Nat. Electronics Conf., 1956; Wisdom award of honor, 1970; First prize 3d Internat. Symposium on Electromagnetic Compatibility Rotterdam, Holland, 1979; awards U.S. Dept. Commerce, 1978. Fellow AAAS, IEEE (life, awards 1977, 79), Am. Phys. Soc., Explorers Club, Acoustical Soc. Am., N.Y. Acad. Scis., Electromagnetics Acad. MIT; mem. Am. Math. Soc., NAE, Author's Guild Am., Harvard Club (N.Y.C.), Cosmos Club (Washington), Dutch Treat (N.Y.C.), Phi Beta Kappa, Sigma Xi. Achievements include research in radar, telecommunications, underwater acoustics, oceanography, seismology, systems analysis, electromagnetic compatibility, communication theory; pioneering research in statistical communication theory. Home and Office: 127 E 91st St New York NY 10128-1601 Home (Summer): 13 Harbor Rd Harwich Port MA 02646

MIDDLETON, ELIZABETH MCPHEE, research scientist; d. George Edward McPhee, Jr. and Elizabeth LaFond McPhee; children: Edward Lloyd III, Christine Elizabeth. BS in Zoology, U. Md., 1967, MS in Ecology, 1976, PhD in Botany, 1993. Rsch. asst. dept. zoology U. Md., College Park, 1965—67; instr. phys. scis. Md. Pub. Sch. Sys., Prince George's County, Mount Ranier, 1967—72, Greenbelt, 1967—72; grad. tchg. asst. dept. zoology U. Md., 1974—75; analyst, programmer, project coord. Computer Sciences Corp., Silver Spring, 1975—78; project mgr., remote sensing specialist Ea. Regional Remote Sensing Applications Ctr., NASA/Goddard Space Flight Ctr., Greenbelt, 1978—83; rsch. scientist Biospheric Sciences Br., NASA/Goddard Space Flight Ctr., 1984—. Project mgr., plant fluorescence project, joint nat. aeronautics and space agy., U.S. dept. of agr. Nat. Aeronautics and Space Agy., Goddard Space Flight Ctr., Greenbelt, 2000—, dep. project mgr., the ecology component of the large scale atmosphere-biosphere study in amazonia, lba-ecology, 1996—98. Choir mem. Christ Episcopal Ch., Columbia, Md., 1988—2003; chorus mem. Columbia Pro Contare, 1984—2003. Named to Mortar Bd., Sr. Women's Hon., U. Md., 1966. Mem.: IEEE, Ecol. Soc. Am. (assoc.). R-Liberal. Christian. Achievements include research in The effect of UV-B irradiation on plants and amphibians; The spectral and bidirectional reflectance properties of vegetation canopies; The interaction of carbon and nitrogen cycles on plant physiology, spectral reflectance properties, and spectral fluorescence properties. Avoca-

tions: singing, swimming, tennis, skiing, knitting, reading, travel. Office: National Aeronautics and Space Agency Goddard Space Flight Ctr Greenbelt MD 20771 E-mail: elizabeth.m.middleton@nasa.gov.

MIDDLETON, GEORGE, JR., clinical child psychologist; b. Houston, Feb. 26, 1923; s. George and Bettie (McCrary) M.; m. Margaret MacLean, Nov. 17, 1953. BA in Psychology, Birmingham-Southern Coll., 1948; MA in Psychology, U. Ala., Tuscaloosa, 1951; PhD in Clin. Psychology, Pa. State U., 1958. Lic. psychologist, La.; diplomate Am. Coll. Forensic Examiners, Am. Bd. Psychol. Specialities. Asst. clin. psychology Med. Coll. Ala., Birmingham, 1950-52; dir. dept. psychology Bryce Hosp., Tuscaloosa, 1952-54; instr. counseling Coll. Bus. Adminstrn. Pa. State U., 1956-58; asst. prof. spl. edn. McNeese State U., 1962-65, assoc. prof. spl. edn., 1962-65; dir. La. Gov.'s Program for Gifted Children, 1963—; prof. spl. edn. McNeese State U., 1965-73, prof. psychology, 1973-74; pvt. practice clin. psychology and neuropsychology, 1974—; cons. psychologist Calcasieu Parish Sch. Bd., 1975—. Vis. scholar U. Victoria, BC, Can., 1970-71. Mem. Am. Psychol. Assn., Nat. Acad. Neuropsychology, Internat. Neuropsychol. Soc., La. Psychol. Assn. (pres. 1973-74), La. Sch. Psychol. Assn., S.W. La. Psychol. Assn. (pres. 1965, 73, 84), La. State Bd. Examiners Psychologists (chmn. 1977-78), Coun. for Exceptional Children, Am. Coll. Forensic Examiners, 1996. Assn. for the Gifted. Episcopalian. Home and Office: 2001 Southwood Dr Ste A Lake Charles LA 70605-4139

MIDDLETON, HERMAN DAVID, SR., theater educator; b. Sanford, Fla., Mar. 24, 1925; s. Arthur Herman and Ruby Elmerry (Hart) M.; m. Amelia Mary Eggart, Dec. 1, 1945; children— Herman David, Kathleen Hart. BS, Columbia U., 1948, MA, 1949; PhD, U. Fla., 1964; postgrad., N.Y. U., 1950, Northwestern U., 1951. Instr., dir. drama and speech Maryville (Tenn.) Coll., 1949-50; instr., designer, tech. dir. theatre U. Del., 1951-55; asst. prof., head dept. drama U. N.C., Greensboro, 1956-59, assoc. prof., head dept. drama and speech, 1959-65, prof., head dept., 1965-74, prof., 1974-79, Excellence Fund prof. dept. communication and theatre, 1979-90, prof. emeritus, 1990. Designer Chucky Jack, Great Smokey Mountains Hist. Soc., Gatlinburg, Tenn., 1956, designer, dir., 1957; communications cons. N.C. Nat. Bank, 1968, Jefferson Standard Life Ins. Co., Greensboro, N.C., 1969, Gilbarco, Inc., Greensboro, 1969-70, 73. Drama critic, columnist Sunday Star, Wilmington, Del., 1952; theatre editor: Players Mag, 1959-61; theatre columnist: Sunday editions Greensboro Daily News, 1959-62; contbr. articles to profl. jours. Mem. N.C. Arts Council Commn., 1964-66, Guilford County Bi-Centennial Celebration Commn., 1969-70; pres. Shanks Village Players, Orangeburg, N.Y.C., 1947-48, Univ. Drama Group, Newark, Del., 1954-55; bd. dirs. Broadway Theatre League Greensboro, 1958-60, Greensboro Community Arts Council, 1964-67, 69-72, Greensboro Community Theatre, 1983-86, Carolina Theatre Commn., 1990—; organizer-cons. The Market Players, West Market St. United Meth. Ch., 1979-82. Served with USN, 1943-46. Recipient O. Henry award Greensboro C. of C., 1966, Gold medallion Amoco Oil Co., 1973, Suzanne M. Davis award Southeastern Theatre Conf., 1975, Marian A. Smith Disting. Career award N.C. Theatre Conf., 1990. Mem. Am. Nat. Theatre and Acad. (organizer, exec. v.p. Piedmont chpt. 1957-60), Am. Theatre Assn. (chmn. bd. nominations 1971-72), Am. Coll. Theatre Festival (regional festival dir. 1973, 80, regional dir., mem. nat. com. 1978-80), Assn. for Theatre in Higher Edn. (founding mem. 1986-87), Speech Communication Assn. Am., Nat. Collegiate Players, Southeastern Theatre Conf. (bd. dirs. 1963-68, 87-92, pres. 1965, pres. pro-tem 1966), Carolina Dramatic Assn. (bd. dirs. 1958-59), N.C. Drama and Speech Assn. (pres. 1966-67), N.C. Theatre Conf. (co-organizer 1971, bd. dirs. 1984-92, pres. 1987-88), Assn. for Theater in Higher Edn., Phi Delta Kappa, Phi Kappa Phi, Theta Alpha Phi, Alpha Psi Omega. Democrat. Methodist. Home: 203 Village Ln Unit A Greensboro NC 27409-2517

MIDDLETON, JACK BAER, lawyer; b. Philadelphia, Jan. 13, 1929; s. Harry C. and Mildred Cornell (Baer) M.; m. Ann (Dodge), Aug. 22, 1953; children: Susan D., Jack B. Jr., Peter C. BA, Lafayette Coll., 1950; JD (hon.), Boston U., 1956. Bar: N.H., 1956, U.S. Dist. Ct. Vt., 1988, U.S. Ct. Appeals (1st cir.), 1957, U.S. Supreme Ct., 1972. Assoc. McLane, Graf, Raulerson, and Middleton, Manchester, NH, 1956—62; ptnr., dir. McLane, Graf, Raulerson, and Middleton, Manchester, NH, 1962—. Spl. justice Merrimack, N.H. Dist. Ct., 1964-87; bd. dir. Greater Manchester Devel. Corp., 1983-95; commr. Uniform State Laws, 1971-74; trustee New Eng. Law Inst., 1977-80. Author: (with others) Summary of New Hampshire Law, 1964, Compendium of New Hampshire Law, 1969, Trial of a Wrongful Death Action in New Hampshire, 1977; editor Boston U. Law Rev., 1954-56; contbr. articles to legal journals. Mem. Mt. Washington Commn., 1969—, Bedford, N.H. Sch. Bd., 1960-66; mem. adv. bd. Merrimack Valley Coll.; trustee, sec. Mt. Washington Obs., 1957—; chmn. bd. trustees White Mountain Sch., 1976-79; campaign chmn. United Way Greater Manchester, 1987, bd. dir., 1986-92, chmn., 1990-91; bd. dir. N.H. Pub. Radio, 1988-91; bd. gov. N.H. Pub. TV, 1994-2003, chmn., 1997-99. Sgt. USMCR, 1950-52. Fellow Am. Coll. Trial Lawyers (chmn. N.H. sect. 1988-90), Am. Bar Found. (life); mem. ABA (ho. dels. 1984—, bd. gov. 1996-2002, sec. elect 1998-99, sec. 1999-2002), New Eng. Bar Assn. (bd. dir. 1977-88, pres. 1982-83), N.H. Bar Assn. (pres. 1979-80), N.H. Bar Found. (bd. dir. 1979-92, chair 1983-90), Nat. Ctr. State Ct. (dir. 1999—), Nat. Conf. Bar Found. (trustee 1985-92, pres. 1989-90), Nat. Conf. Bar Pres. (exec. coun. 1987-95, pres. 1993-94), N.H. Bus. and Industry Assn. (bd. dir. 1988—, sec. 1990-), Manchester C. of C. (bd. dir. 1967-89, chmn. 1984-85), New Eng. Coun. (bd. dirs. 1991-2004), New Eng. Legal Found. (bd. dirs. 2001-04). Office: McLane Graf Raulerson and Middleton 900 Elm St Ste 1001 Manchester NH 03101-2029 Office Phone: 603-628-1446.

MIDDLETON, JAMES ARTHUR, oil and gas company executive; b. Tulsa, Mar. 15, 1936; s. James Arthur and Inez (Matthews) M.; m. Victoria Middleton; children: Robert Arthur, James Daniel, Angela Lynn; stepson: Andrew Davis Fitzhugh. BA, Rice U., 1958, BS in Mech. Engring., 1959. With Atlantic Richfield Co., 1959-96; design engr. Dallas, 1962-67; tech. planner, 1967-69; mgr. shale devel., 1969-72; mgr. engring. dept. Los Angeles, 1972-74; mgr. Prudhoe Bay project Pasadena, Calif., 1974-80; v.p., mgr. corp. planning Los Angeles, 1980-81; pres. ARCO Coal Co., Denver, 1981-82; sr. v.p. ARCO Oil and Gas Co., Dallas, 1982-85, pres., 1985-90, sr. v.p. parent co., 1981-87, exec. v.p. parent co., 1987-94, also bd. dirs.; chmn., CEO Crown Energy Corp., Salt Lake City, 1996-2000; pres. Jam Energy Co., 2000—. Bd. dirs. Tex. Utilities Co., Dallas., ARCO Chem. Co., Berry Petroleum Co. Corp. rep. Circle Ten coun. Boy Scouts Am.; bd. dirs. L.A. coun. Boy Scouts Am., United Way Met. Dallas, Dallas Coun. on World Affairs, Jr. Achievement So. Calif. 2d lt. C.E., AUS, 1959-60 Reicpient ASME Petroleum div. Oil Drop award. Mem. Soc. Petroleum Engrs. of AIME, Tex. Mid-Continent Oil and Gas Assn., Am. Petroleum Inst., Rocky Mountain Oil and Gas Assn., We. States Petroleum Assn. (chmn. bd. dirs.), Nat. Gas Suppliers Assn. (chmn.), L.A. C. of C. (bd. dirs.), L.A. Music Ctr. Founders, Ctr. for Strategic and Internat. Studies (CSIS)-Dallas Round Table, Am. Enterprise Forum Chief Execs. Round Table, Dallas Petroelum Club, Tower, Northwood, Calif. Club, Bel-Air Country Club, L.A. Country Club. Office: 574 Chapala Dr Pacific Palisades CA 90272-4429

MIDDLETON, LINDA JEAN GREATHOUSE, lawyer; b. Poplar Bluff, Mo., Sept. 22, 1950; d. Casper Scott and Anna Garnelle (Qualls) Greathouse; m. Roy L. Middleton, Sept. 27, 1969. BS cum laude, Ark. State U., 1972; JD, Baylor U., 1974. Bar: Tex., 1974; CPCU, CLU. Asst. v.p., asst. sec., atty. Equitable Gen. Ins. Co., Ft. Worth, 1977-81; gen. counsel, corp. sec. Chilton Corp., Dallas, 1981-83; mgr. pub. affairs Fina Oil and Chem., Dallas, 1983-85, corp. sec., sr. atty., 1983—. Sec. Parliamentarian, Dallas, 1985—. Sec. Homeowners Assn., Dallas, 1981—. Mem. Tex. Bar Assn., Dallas Bar Assn. Baptist. Avocations: painting, sewing, piano. Office: 615 Lakeshore Dr Little Elm TX 75068-5036

MIDDLETON, MICHAEL JOHN, civil engineer; b. NYC, May 14, 1953; s. Vincent Aloysius and Mary Hilda (Lehane) Middleton. BS in Civil Engring., U. Calif., Davis, 1975. Registered profl. engrl., Calif., Wash., Hawaii. From project mgr. to v.p. G.A. Fitch & Assoc., Concord, Calif., 1975—80; from project mgr. to sr. v.p. Santina & Thompson, Inc., Concord, 1980—2003; pvt. practice Concord, 2003—. Scholar, Calif. Scholarship Fedn., 1971. Roman Catholic. Home and Office: 1409A Bel Air Dr Concord CA 94521-5348 E-mail: mjmiddlcton@comcast.nct.

MIDDLETON, NORMAN GRAHAM, social worker, psychotherapist; b. Jacksonville, Fla., Jan. 21, 1935; s. Norman Graham and Betty (Quina) M.; m. Judy Stephens, Aug. 1, 1968; stepchildren: Monty Stokes, Toni Stokes. BA, U. Miami (Fla.), 1960; MSW, Fla. State U., 1962. Casework counselor Family Svc., Miami, 1962-64; psychiat. social worker assoc. firm Drs. Warson, Steele, Wiener, Sarasota, Fla., 1964-66; psychotherapist Sarasota, 1966—. Instr. Manatee Jr. Coll., Bradenton, Fla., 1973-76. Author: The Caverns of My Mind, 1985, Imaginative Healing, 1993, Spirited Imagination, 2002. Pres. Coun. on Epilepsy, Sarasota, 1969-70. Served with USAF, 1954-58. Fellow Fla. Soc. Clin. Social Work (pres. 1978-80); mem. Am. Group Psychotherapy Assn., Am. Assn. Sex Educators and Counselors (cert. sex educator). Democrat. Episcopalian. Home: 16626 Winburn Dr Sarasota FL 34240-9221 Office: 1257 S Tamiami Trail Sarasota FL 34239-2219 Office Phone: 941-366-3334. Business E-Mail: fallenpine@aol.com.

MIDDLETON, TERESA MUIR, Internet company executive, researcher; b. London; d. Francis Robert and Marjorie Banwell Muir; children: Christopher, Andrew, Claire. BSc, Syracuse U., 1978; MBA, Pepperdine U., 1982. Rschr. SRI Internat., Menlo Park, Calif., 1970—90, program mgr., 1990—94, assoc. dir., 1994—98, assoc. dir. emeritus, 1998—; CEO PatchWorx, Inc., Menlo Park, 1998—. Founding dir. Nat. Cristina Found., Greenwich, 1989—; mem. com. Nat. Conf. Tech. and Disabilities, Northridge, 1989; chmn. virtual Reality Conf., Menlo Park, 1991; rschr. in field. Editor: Virtual Worlds: Real Challenges, 1991. Dir. telecom. for the deaf Deafnet Dissemination Project, 1984. Recipient Mimi award, SRI Internat., 1997. Avocations: swimming, music, travel. Office: Patchworx Inc 333 Ravenswood Ave BS372 Menlo Park CA 94025 Personal E-mail: tmiddleton@aol.com. Business E-Mail: tmiddleton@patchworx.org.

MIDDLETON-DOWNING, LAURA, psychiatric social worker, artist, small business owner; b. Edinburg, Ind., Apr. 20, 1935; d. John Thomas Jr. and Rowene Elizabeth (Baker) Middleton; m. George Charles Downing, 1974 (div. 1986). BA in English Lit., U. Colo., 1966, MFA, 1969, BA in Psychology, 1988; MSW, U. Denver, 1992; Doctor of Clin. Hypnotherapy, Am. Inst. Hypnotherapy, 1995. Cert. clin. hypnotherapist, Calif., Colo.; cert. past life therapist, Colo., In ternat. Bd. for Regression Therapy-Level II cert. Profl. artist, Silver Plume and Boulder, Colo., 1965—; profl. photographer Silver Plume, Boulder, 1975—; art tchr. U. Colo., Boulder and Longmont, 1971-73; mem. survey crew Bur. of Land Mgmt., Empire, Colo., 1984-85; cons. social work and psychotherapy Boulder, 1992—; psychiat. and med. social worker Good Samaritan Health Agy., Boulder, 1993-97; pvt. practice clin. hypnotherapy Boulder, 1995—; pvt. practice past-life therapist, 1995—. Ind. distbr. Super Blue Green Algae, 1996—; pres. Phoenix LG, Inc., 1998—. Author, photographer Frontiers, Vol. IV, No. 1, 1979; works exhibited in 15 one-woman shows, 1969—; numerous group exhbns. including group exhbn., Colo. History Mus., Denver, 1997 98. Trustee Town of Silver Plume, Colo., 1975-84; co-founder, pres. Alma Holm Rogers Nat. Orgn. Women, Clear Creek County, 1975-82; mem. Ctrl. Mountain Coun., Clear Creek County, 1980; chairperson Mary Ellen Barnes Cmty. Ctr. Project, Silver Plume, Colo., 1983; vol. Rape Crisis Team, Boulder, 1989-90, Child & Family Advocacy Program, Boulder, 1992-97; adv. bd. mem. Good Samaritan Agy., Boulder, 1993-97; caring minister vol. First Congl. Ch., Boulder, 1995-98; founding mem. Front Range Women in the Visual Arts, Boulder, Colo., 1974. Recipient Juried Exhbn. Merit award Colo. Women in the Arts, 1979; Women's Incentive scholar U. Colo., Boulder, 1989; Grad. Sch. Social Work scholar U. Denver, 1991; Colo. Grad. grantee U. Denver, 1992. Mem. AAUW, NASW, DAR, Colo. Advs. for Responsible Mental Health Svcs., Eye Movement Desensitization Reprocessing Network, Internat. Assn. for Regression Rsch. and Therapies, Inc. (Ecocycle, Colo. block leader), Natural Resources Def. Coun., The Nature Conservancy, World Wildlife Fedn., Bus. Women's Leadership Group, Sierra Club, Defender of Wildlife, Psi Chi. Avocations: inline skating, skipping, photography, travel, volunteerism. Office: PO Box 2312 Boulder CO 80306-2312

MIDDLEWOOD, MARTIN EUGENE, technical communications specialist, writer, consultant; b. Galesburg, Ill., Mar. 21, 1947; s. Martin and Bernetta Maxine (Henderson) M.; m. Mona Marie Jarmer, Sept. 10, 1971; children: Erin, Martha, Emily, Margaret. BA, Ea. Wash. U., 1973, MA, 1980. Writer tech. manuals Tektronix, Inc., Beaverton, Oreg., 1976-77, tech. writer, 1977-79, sr. tech. writer, 1979-82, supr. pub. rels., 1982-84, mgr. pub. rels., 1984-85, mgr. mktg. communications Vancouver, Wash., 1985-86; dir. info. strategy and svcs. Waggener Edstrom, Portland, Oreg., 1986-98; pub. Cognizer Report, Portland, Oreg., 1990-94. Chmn. adv. bd. sci. and tech. writing, Clark Coll., Vancouver, 1984—; owner communications cons. firm, Vancouver, 1978-98; pres., owner Frontline Strategies, Inc., 1998—. Author: (ednl. brochure series) Oscilloscope Measurements, 1979 (award of excellence Willamette Valley chpt., Network Svcing., won Awd. of Distinction, 1980, Soc. Tech. Communication, 1980); contbr. articles to profl. jours. Served with USMC, 1967-70. Recipient cert. recognition Clark Coll., Vancouver, 1984, 86, 89, 92-99, award of excellence Pacific N.W. chpt. Internat. Assn. Bus. Communicators, 1985. Mem. Soc. Tech. Communication (sr., pres. Willamette Valley chpt. 1983-85, award of recognition 1986, chpt. pub. achievement award 1985, awards of distinction, 1980, 81). Avocations: photography, martial arts. Home and Office: 10816 NW Oxbow Ridge Dr Vancouver WA 98685 Office Phone: 360-882-1164. Personal E-mail: martinm@pacifier.com.

MIDELFORT, HANS CHRISTIAN ERIK, history professor; b. Eau Claire, Wis., Apr. 17, 1942; s. Peter Albert and Gerd (Gjems) M.; m. Corelyn Forsyth Senn, June 16, 1965 (div. Dec. 1981); children: Katarina, Kristian; m. Cassandra Clemons Hughes, May 25, 1985 (div. April 1996); 1 child, Lucy; m. Anne L. McKeithen, June 22, 1996. BA, Yale U., 1964, MPhil, 1967, PhD, 1970. Instr. Stanford (Calif.) U., 1968-70; asst. prof. U. Va., Charlottesville, 1970-72, assoc. prof., 1972-87, prof., 1987—, Charles Julian Bishko prof. history, 1996—. Vis. prof. Harvard U., Cambridge, Mass., 1985, U. Stuttgart, Germany, 1988, U. Bern, Switzerland, 1988, Wolfson Coll., Oxford U., 2002, Yale U., 2003; prin. Brown Coll., U. Va., 1996-2001; Dwight Terry lectr. Yale U., 2003. Author: Witch Hunting in Southwestern Germany, 1972 (Gustave Arlt prize 1972), Mad Princes of Renaissance Germany, 1994 (Roland H. Bainton prize 16th Century Studies Conf. 1995), A History of Madness in 16th Century Germany, 1999 (Ralph Waldo Emerson prize, Phi Beta Kappa, 1999, Roland H. Bainton prize 16th Century Studies Conf. 2000); editor: Johann Weyer, On Witchcraft, 1998; co-editor: Europe, 1450-1789. Encyclopedia of the Early Modern World, 2003; translator: Imperial Cities and the Reformation (Bernd Moeller), 1972, Revolution of 1525 (Peter Bickle), 1981, Shaman of Oberstdorf (Wolfgang Behringer), 1998. Mem. Soc. Reformation Rsch. (pres. 1992-93). Office: U Va Dept History Charlottesville VA 22903 Office Phone: 434-924-7949. E-mail: hem7e@virginia.edu.

MIDGLEY, A(LVIN) REES, JR., reproductive endocrinology educator, researcher; b. Burlington, Vt., Nov. 9, 1933; s. Alvin Rees and Maxine (Schmidt) M.; m. Carol Crossman, Sept. 4, 1955; children: Thomas, Debra, Christopher. BS cum laude, U. Vt., 1955, MD cum laude, 1958. Intern U. Pitts., 1958-59, resident dept. pathology, 1959-61, U. Mich., Ann Arbor, 1961-63, instr. pathology, 1963-64, asst. prof., 1964-67, assoc. prof., 1967-70, prof., 1970—, dir. Reproductive Scis. Program, 1968—. Chmn. BioQuant of Ann Arbor, Inc., 1985-89. Contbr. articles to med. jours. Recipient Parke-Davis award, 1970; Ayerst award Endocrine Soc., 1977; Smith Kline Bio-Sci. Labs. award, 1985; NIH grantee, 1960—; Mellon Found. grantee, 1979-91. Mem. Soc. Study Reprodn. (pres. 1983-84), Endocrine Soc., Am. Assn. Pathology, Am. Physiol. Soc. Home: 101 W Liberty St Apt 340 Ann Arbor MI 48104-1359 Office: U Mich Rm 1101 Reproductive Scis Program 300 N Ingalls Bldg Fl 11 Ann Arbor MI 48109-2007

MIDKIFF, KIMBERLY ANN, paralegal; b. Kingsport, Tenn., Nov. 27, 1958; d. Harold Douglas and Mary Lou (Carden) M. Student, U. Tenn., 1976-80, 94—. Cert. legal asst. Nat. Assn. Legal Assts. Legal sec. Gilreath & Rowland, Knoxville, Tenn., 1981-83, Tenn. State Atty. Gen.'s Office, Knoxville, 1983-84, Bond, Carpenter & O'Connor, Knoxville, 1984; paralegal Gilreath & Assocs., Knoxville, 1984-89, Lewis, King, Krieg, Waldrop & Catron, P.C., Knoxville, 1989—. Active Westminster Presbyn. Ch., Knoxville. Mem. Nat. Assn. Legal Assts., Tenn. Paralegal Assn., Knoxville Paralegal Assn., Delta Gamma Alumnae Assn., Golden Key Nat. Honor Soc., Phi Kappa Phi, Phi Alpha Theta. Democrat. Presbyterian. Avocations: vocal and piano music, horseback riding, reading, theater, hiking. Office: Lewis King Krieg Waldrop & Catron PC One Centre Square 5th Fl 620 Market St Knoxville TN 37902-2231

MIDKIFF, ROBERT RICHARDS, financial and trust company executive, consultant; b. Honolulu, Sept. 24, 1920; s. Frank Elbert and Ruth (Richards) M.; m. Evanita Sumner, July 24, 1948; children: Mary Lloyd, Robin Starr, Shelley Sumner, Robert Richards Jr., David Wilson. BA, Yale U., 1942; grad. Advanced Mgmt. Program, Harvard U., 1962; LHD, U. Hawaii, 2002. Asst. sec. Hawaiian Trust Co., 1951-56, asst. v.p., 1956-57, v.p., 1957-65; dir. Am. Factors, Ltd., 1954-65; v.p. Amfac, Inc., 1965-68; exec. v.p., dir. Am. Security Bank, Honolulu, 1968-69, pres., dir., 1969-71; pres., CEO, dir. Am. Trust Co. Hawaii, Honolulu, 1971-93; chmn. bd. dirs. Bishop Trust Co. Ltd., Honolulu, 1984-93; pres., CEO Am. Fin. Svcs. of Hawaii, 1984-93. Co-chmn. Gov.'s Archtl. Adv. Com. on State Capitol, 1960-65; co-chmn. Gov.'s Adv. Com. on Fine Arts for State Capitol, 1965-69; past chmn., bd. dirs. Hawaii Visitors Bur.; past pres., bd. dirs. Downtown Improvement Assn., Lahaina Restoration Found., Hawaii Cmty. Found.; bd. dirs., pres. Atherton Family Found.; past chmn. Profit Sharing Rsch. Found.; past bd. dirs. Coun. on Founds.; chmn., bd. dirs. Hawaii Theatre Ctr.; chmn. bd. dirs. Good Beginnings Alliance, past chmn. bd. dirs. Mem. Coun. on Founds., Profit Sharing Coun. Am. (past bd. dirs.), Small Bus. Coun. Am. (past bd. dirs.), ESOP Assn. Am. (past bd. dirs.), Pacific Club, Waialae Golf Club, Phi Beta Kappa. Episcopalian. Office: 4477 Kahala Ave Honolulu HI 96816-4924 Office Phone: 808-734-8132. Office Fax: 808-737-9007. Personal E-mail: rrmhi@aol.com.

MIDLARSKY, MANUS ISSACHAR, political scientist, educator; b. N.Y.C., Jan. 28, 1937; s. Max and Rachel (Potechin) M.; m. Elizabeth Steckel, June 25, 1961; children— Susan, Miriam, Michael. BS, CUNY, 1959; MS, Stevens Inst. Tech., 1963; PhD (Ford Found. fellow), Northwestern U., 1969. Instr. polit. sci. U. Colo., Boulder, 1967-68, asst. prof., 1968-71, assoc. prof., 1971-74, prof., 1974-89, dir. Ctr. Internat. Relations, 1983-89; Moses and Annuta Back prof. internat. peace and conflict resolution Rutgers U., New Brunswick, N.J., 1989—. Cons. USAF, 1968 Author: On War: Political Violence in the International System, 1975, The Disintegration of Political Systems: War and Revolution in Comparative Perspective, 1986, The Onset of World War, 1988, The Evolution of Inequality: War, State Survival, and Democracy in Comparative Perspective, 1999; editor: Inequality and Contemporary Revolutions, 1986, Handbook of War Studies, 1989, 93, The Internationalization of Communal Strife, 1992, (with J. Vasquez and P. Gladkov) From Rivalry to Cooperation: Russian and American Perspectives on the Post-Cold War Era, 1994, Inequality, Democracy and Economic Development, 1997, Handbook of War Studies II, 2000. Faculty fellow Richardson Inst. Conflict and Peace Research, London, 1977-78; faculty fellow Council Research and Creative Work, U. Colo., 1977-78; NSF grantee, 1973-76, 81-83, 83-85, 86-89; Nat. Endowment Humanities grantee, 1980, 83, U.S. Inst. of Peace grantee, 1997-98. Mem. Am. Polit. Sci. Assn. (pres. conflict processes sect. 1985-88) Internat. Studies Assn. (pres. West 1980-81, v.p. 1986-87), Am. Soc. Polit. and Legal Philosophy, Inter-Univ. Seminar in Armed Forces and Soc. Office: Rutgers U Dept Polit Sci 89 George St New Brunswick NJ 08901-1411

MIDLER, BETTE, singer, entertainer, actress; b. Honolulu, Dec. 1, 1945; m. Martin von Haselberg, 1984; 1 child, Sophie. Student, U. Hawaii. Debut as actress (films), Hawaii, 1965, mem. cast Fiddler on the Roof, N.Y.C, 1966—69, Salvation, 1970, Tommy, Seattle Opera Co., 1971, nightclub concert performer on tour U.S., from 1972; appearance Palace Theatre, N.Y.C., 1973, Radio City Music Hall, 1993, TV appearances include The Tonight Show, Bette Midler: Old Red Hair is Back, 1978, Gypsy, 1993 (Golden Globe award best actress in a mini-series or movie made for television, 1994, Emmy nomination, Lead Actress - Special, 1994), Seinfeld, 1996, Diva Las Vegas, 1997, Murphy Brown, 1998, appeared Clams on The Half-Shell Revue, N.Y.C., 1975, recs. include The Divine Miss M, 1972, Bette Midler, 1973, Broken Blossom, 1977, Live at Last, 1977, The Rose, Thighs and Whispers, 1979, Songs for the New Depression, 1979, Divine Madness, 1980, No Frills, 1984, Mud Will Be Flung Tonight, 1985, Beaches (soundtrack), 1989, Some People's Lives, 1990, Bette of Roses, 1995, Bathhouse Betty, 1998, Bette, 2000; actor: (films) Hawaii, 1966, The Rose, 1979 (Academy award nomination best actress, 1979), Divine Madness, 1980, Jinxed, 1982, Down and Out in Beverly Hills, 1986, Ruthless People, 1986, Outrageous Fortune, 1987, Oliver and Company (voice), 1988, Big Business, 1988, Beaches, 1988, Stella, 1990, Scenes From a Mall, 1991, For the Boys, 1991 (Academy award nomination best actress, 1991), Hocus Pocus, 1993, Get Shorty, 1995, The First Wives Club, 1996, That Old Feeling, 1997, Get Bruce, 1999, Isn't She Great, 1999, Drowning Mona, 2000, Isn't She Great, 2000, The Stepford Wives, 2004; appeared in cable TV (HBO) prodn. Bette Midler's Mondo Beyondo, 1988; author: A View From A Broad, 1980, The Saga of Baby Divine, 1983; exec. prodr., composer (TV show) Bette, 2000, exec. prodr. Some of My Best Friends, 2001, (films) Divine Secret of the Ya-Ya Sisterhood, 2002. Recipient After Dark Ruby award, 1973, Grammy awards, 1973, 1990, spl. Tony award, 1973, Emmy award for NBC Spl., Ol' Red Hair is Back, 1978, 2 Golden Globe awards for The Rose, 1979, Golden Globe award for The Boys, 1991, Emmy award The Tonight Show appearance, 1992. Office: Endeavor Entertainment care Adam Venit 9701 Wilshire Blvd Fl 10 Beverly Hills CA 90212*

MIECZKOWSKI, YANEK, history professor, writer; b. Ithaca, NY; s. Bogdan and Seiko Mieczkowski. BA, Ithaca Coll., 1987; MA, Columbia U., 1989, PhD, 1995. Writing fellow Oxford U. Press, 1995—96; prof. Dowling Coll., Oakdale, NY, 1996—. Advanced placement exam reader Ednl. Testing Svc., 2000—. Author: The Routledge Historical Atlas of Presidential Elections, 2001. Rsch. grant, Gerald R. Ford. Found., 2003. Home: 4713 Wilshire Ln Oakdale NY 11769-1450 Office: Dowling Coll History Dept Oakdale NY 11769-1999 Office Phone: 631-244-3470. Business E-Mail: mieczkoy@dowling.edu.

MIEL, JAN, humanities educator; b. Wayne, Pa., Oct. 10, 1930; s. Charles Jan and Mary (Long) M.; m. Elizabeth MacKiernan, Sept. 10, 1960; children: Persephone, Justin. AB, Harvard U., 1952; MA, Princeton U., 1960, PhD, 1965. Instr. Goucher Coll., Towson, Md., 1960-62; asst. prof. MIT, Cambridge, Mass., 1962-64, Wesleyan U., Middletown, Conn., 1964-70, assoc. prof., 1970-78, prof., 1978-99. Author: Pascal and Theology, 1970, Pascal and Theology (Japanese transl), 2000; contbr. articles to profl. jours. Mem. exec. coun. Diocese of Conn., Hartford, 1999-2002. Cpl. U.S. Army, 1953-55. Fellow Johns Hopkins U., 1968, NEH, 1976, Guggenheim Found., 1977. Mem. MLA, N.Am. Soc. for 17th Century French Lit. Anglican. Home: 29 Gordon Pl Middletown CT 06457 Office: Wesleyan U Coll Letters Middletown CT 06459

MIELE, ALFONSE RALPH, former government official; b. N.Y.C., Jan. 6, 1922; s. Angelo and Alesia (Laudadio) M.; m. Gloria I. Litrento, Nov. 22, 1942 (dec. Dec. 1977); children: Richard Lynn, Barbara Jo, Steven Arnold; m. Ann Carlino Valerio, Mar. 31, 1979 (dec. June 1988); m. Dorothy A. McGowan, July 7, 1990. AB in Litteris Gallicis with honors, Fordham U., 1942; postgrad., U. Nancy, France, 1945; MA, Columbia U., 1947, PhD, 1958. Commd. 2d lt. U.S. Army, 1942; advanced through grades to col. USAF, 1961; served in 377th Automatic Weapons Bn., 1942-45; ret., brig. gen.; instr. French and pub. speaking Fordham Prep. Sch., N.Y.C., 1946-47; asst. prof. French and Russian U.S. Naval Acad., 1949-52; exec. officer to NATO comdrs., 1953-55; teaching asst. Columbia U., 1955-58; assoc. prof. French USAF Acad., 1958-60, prof., head dept. fgn. langs., 1960-67, assoc. dean, chmn. divsn. humanities, 1967-68; exec. v.p. Loretto Heights Coll., Denver, 1968-70; pres. Coll. St. Rose, Albany, 1970-72; prof. gen. edn. Schenectady County C.C., Schenectady, N.Y., 1972-73; dep. asst. adminstr. internat. aviation affairs FAA,

Washington, 1973-75, edn. specialist, 1976—;, 1968. Asst. dir. pub. affairs U.S. Dept. Interior, Washington, 1975-76; chief negotiator civil aviation tech. agreement with USSR, 1973-75; project dir. Nat. Aviation Edn. Program for Am. Indians, 1978; asst. dir. Union County (N.J.) Coord. Agy. for Higher Edn., 1979-82; rep. Eckhart Assocs., 1983-88; relocation specialist Bradley/Wildman Co., Monument, Colo., 1989-92. Mem. Westfield (N.J.) Bd. Edn., 1985-88; bd. dirs. Pike's Peak chpt. ARC, 1990-93; pres. Colorado Springs World Affairs Coun., 1993-95; bd. dirs. and patron Tri-Lakes Ctr. for the Arts, 1998—. Decorated Bronze Star for heroism in ground combat, Legion of Merit (2) with oak leaf cluster, Belgian Fourragère; chevalier Palmes Academiques France; recipient Encaenia award Fordham Coll., 1962 Mem. Monument C. of C. (bd. dirs. 1992-94). Home: PO Box 321 Monument CO 80132-0321 *Be ever curious and willing to dare. The sweet becomes even sweeter when the bitter is overcome. Each living moment is a learning experience and adds to the anticipation of better tomorrows. The journey of life is exciting— live with that thought in mind.*

MIELE, ANGELO, engineering educator, researcher, consultant, author; b. Formia, Italy, Aug. 21, 1922; arrived in U.S., 1952, naturalized, 1985; s. Salvatore and Elena (Marino) Miele. DCivil Engring., U. Rome, Italy, 1944, DAero. Engring., 1946; DSc (hon.), Inst. Tech., Technion, Israel, 1992. Asst. prof. Poly. Inst. Bklyn., 1952- 55; prof. Purdue U., 1955-59; dir. astrodynamics Boeing Sci. Rsch. Labs., 1959-64; prof. aerospace scis., math. scis. Rice U., Houston, 1964-88, Foyt Family prof. engring., 1988-93, Foyt prof. emeritus engring., aerospace scis., math. scis., 1993—, rsch. prof., 2001—. Cons. Douglas Aircraft Co., 1956—58, U.S. Aviation Underwriters, 1987, Boeing Comml. Airplane Co., 1989, European Space Tech. Engring. Ctr., 2002; cons. Allison divsn. GM Corp., 1956—58; Breakwell Meml. lectureship Internat. Astron. Fedn., 1994; Gaspare Santangelo Meml. lectureship Italian Assn. of Aeronautics and Astronautics, 2001. Author: Flight Mechanics, 1962; editor: Theory of Optimum Aerodynamic Shapes, 1965, Applied Mathematics in Aerospace Science and Engineering, 1994; contbr. numerous articles on aerospace engring., windshear problems, hypervelocity flight, interplanetary flight, math. programming, optimal control theory and computing methods to sci. jours. Pres. Italy in Am. Assn., 1966—68. Decorated knight comdr. Order Merit Italy; recipient Levy medal, Franklin Inst. of Phila., 1974, Brouwer award, AAS, 1980, Schuck award, Am. Automatic Control Coun., 1988, Latina prize, 2002, Flight Mechanics award, AIAA, 1982, Pendray Aerospace Lit. award, 1982. Fellow: Am. Astronautical Soc., AIAA (hon. Pendray Aerospace Lit. award 1982, Mechs. and Control of Flight award 1982), Franklin Inst.; mem.: Tex. Acad. Engring., Scis. and Medicine, Nat. Acad. Engring. of Argentina (corr.), Internat. Acad. Astronautics, Acad. Scis. Turin (corr.), Russian Acad. Scis. (fgn.), NAE. Home: 3106 Kettering Dr Houston TX 77027-5504 Office: Rice Univ MS-322 Aero-Astronautics Group 6100 Main St Houston TX 77005-1827 Office Phone: 713-348-4907. Business E-Mail: miele@rice.edu.

MIELE, JOEL ARTHUR, SR., civil engineer; b. Jersey City, May 28, 1934; s. Jene Gerald Sr., and Eleanor Natalie (Bergida) M.; m. Faith Roseann Trombetta, July 21, 1952 (div. 1954); m. 2d Josephine Ann Cottone, Feb. 14, 1959; children: Joel Arthur, Jr., Vita Marie, Janet Ann. BCE, Poly. Inst. Bklyn., 1955. Lic. profl. engr. NY, NJ, Fla.; profl. planner NJ; chartered engr., U.K. Civil engr. Yudell & Miele, Queens, NY, 1955-57; chief engr. Jene G. Miele Assocs., Queens, 1960-68; prin., CEO Miele Assocs., Queens, 1968-94; commr. NYC Planning Commn., 1990-94; commr. Dept. of Bldgs. City of NY, 1994-96; commr. Dept. Environ. Protection, NYC, 1996—2002, NYC Bd. Stds. and Appeals, 2002—. Mem. NY State Bd. for Engring. and Land Surveying, 1997—. Patentee masonry wall constrn. Mem. Cmty. Bd. 10, Queens, 1971-90, chmn., 1978-90; mem. bd. visitors Creedmoor State Hosp., 1978—, pres., 1979—; trustee Queens Borough Pub. Libr., 1979—, pres., 1995-96; bd. dirs. Peninsula Hosp. Ctr., 1984—, chair, 1990—; bd. mem. Peninsula Gen. Nursing Home, 1985—, chair, 1990—; bd. mem. Queens County Overall Econ. Devel. Corp., 1989-94, pres., 1991-94; trustee Queens Pub. Comm. Corp., 1983—; exec. v.p. Queens County and mem. Nat. Coun. Boy Scouts Am., 1991—; bd. mem. Am. Parkinson Disease Assn., 1985—, mem. exec. com., 1987—, v.p., 1996—; pres. Internat. Parkinsons Found., Netherlands, 1997—; dir. Queens Libr. Found., 1997—; dir. Assn. Met Water Agys., 1997-2002, Assn. Met. Sewerage Agys., 1997-2002; mem. Nat. Coun. Examiners Engring. & Surveying, 1997—. Lt. (j.g.) USN, 1957-60; capt. USNR, 1960-88, ret., 1988; RADM LH NY Naval Militia, 1998. Named Italian-Am. of Yr. Ferrini Welfare League, Queens, 1980, Hon. Mem. of Queens Chpt. AIA, 1994, Hon. Profl. Affiliated Mem. NY Soc. Archs., 1994; recipient Outstanding Cmty. Leader award Boy Scouts Am., 1987, Pride of Queens award, 1990, Pub. Servant Extraordinaire award United Cerebral Palsy of Queens, 1994, Good Scout award Greater NY Coun. Boy Scouts Am., 1994, Nat. Silver Beaver Court of Honor award, Boy Scouts of America, 1997, United Hosp. Funds Disting. Trustee award for Extraordinary Svc., 1997, NYSSPE Outstanding PE Mgr. of Yr. award, 1997, Disting. Alumni award, Poly. U., 1998, Humanitarian of Yr. award Guide Dog Found., 2000, Spl. Recognition for Pub. Svc. award NY Bldg. Congress, 2002, Golden Eagle award Boy Scouts Am., 2002. Fellow ASCE (life), NSPE (trustee polit. action com. 1990-96); mem. NY State Soc. Profl. Engrs. (v.p. 1984-86, pres. 1988-89, nat. dir. 1987-90, Engr. of Yr. 1983), Soc. Am. Mil. Engrs., NY State Assn. of Professions (founding). Democrat. Congregationalist. Office Phone: 212-788-8661. Personal E-mail: jmiele2@nyc.rr.com.

MIELKE, CLARENCE HAROLD, JR., hematologist; b. Spokane, Wash., June 18, 1936; s. Clarence Harold and Marie Katherine (Gillespie) M.; m. Marcia Rae, July 5, 1964; children: Elisa, John, Kristina. BS, Wash. State U., 1959; MD, U. Louisville, 1963. Intern San Francisco Gen. Hosp., 1963-64; resident in medicine Portland VA Hosp., 1964-65, San Francisco Gen. Hosp., 1965-67; fellow in hematology U. So. Calif., 1967-68; tchg. fellow, asst. physician, instr. Tufts-New Eng. Med. Ctr. Hosps., Boston, 1968-71; sr. scientist Med. Rsch. Inst., San Francisco, 1971-90; chief hematology Presbyn. Hosp., San Francisco, 1971-82; asst. prof. clin. medicine U. Calif. Sch. Medicine, San Francisco, 1971-80, assoc. clin. prof., 1979-90. bd. dirs. Inst. Cancer Rsch., 1992—. Trustee, bd. dirs. Med. Rsch. Inst. San Francisco, Sacred Heart Hosp. Found., 1997-2000, Rockwood Clinic Found., 1994—; dir. emeritus Inst. Cancer Rsch.; trustee emeritus, bd. dirs. Med. Rsch. Inst., 1988—; dir. Health Rsch. and Edn. Ctr., Wash. State U., 1989—, prof. pharmacology, 1989—, prof. vet. medicine, 1989—, assoc. dean rsch., 1992-2004; dir. Spokane (Wash.) Heart Study, 1994—. Editor emeritus Jour. Clin. Aphesis, 1981; contbr. chpts. to books, articles to med. jours. Named Nat. Disting. Eagle Scout, 1998; NIH grantee, 1973-88. Fellow ACP; mem. AAAS, AMA, Internat. Acad. Clin. and Applied Thrombosis and Hemostasis, Internat. Soc. Hematology, Am. Coll. Angiology; mem. Am. Soc. Internal. Medicine, Internat. Soc. Thrombosis and Hemostasis, Am. Heart Assn., N.Y. Acad. Scis., Spokane Med. Soc., Internat. Soc. Angiology. Office: PO Box 1495 Spokane WA 99210-1495

MIELKE, JAMES EDWARD, geochemist; b. Toledo, Oct. 6, 1940; s. Herbert Edward and Naomi Hilletje (Raabe) M.; m. Laurie Beth Retter, Dec. 19, 1966; children: Erin Christine, Emily Jane. BS, MIT, 1962; MS, U. Ariz., 1965; PhD, George Washington U., 1974. Mine geologist potash exploration N.S. Rsch. Found., 1962; geologist S.W. field party Universal Engring. Corp., Boston, 1963-64; geochemist C-14 dating lab. Smithsonian Instn., Washington, 1964-73; specialist in marine and earth scis. Congl. Rsch. Svc./Libr. of Congress, Washington, 1973-2000, retired, 2000. Liaison to Nat. Materials Adv. Bd., Nat. Rsch. Coun., Washington, 1981-86. Author more than 170 publs. including articles in profl. jours., com. prints, Congl. Rsch. Svc. reports; co-author: Strategic and Critical Materials, 1985, Review of Research in Modern Problems in Geochemistry, 1979. Pres. Home Buyers, Inc., Washington, 1976-83. Smithsonian Instn. Rsch. grantee, 1966-69. Mem. AAAS, Am. Geophys. Union, Marine Tech. Soc., Internat. Marine Minerals Soc. Republican. Lutheran. Avocation: folk dancing. Home: 2803 Washington Ave Chevy Chase MD 20815-3009

MIELKE, PAUL WILLIAM, JR., statistician, consultant; b. St. Paul, Feb. 18, 1931; s. Paul William and Elsa (Yungbauer) M.; m. Roberta Roehl Robison, June 25, 1960; children: William, Emily Spear, Lynn Basila. BA, U. Minn., 1953, PhD, 1963; MA, U. Ariz., 1958. Tchg. asst. U. Ariz., Tucson, 1957-58, U. Minn., Mpls., 1958-60, statis. cons., 1960-62, lectr., 1962-63; from asst. to assoc. prof. dept. stats. Colo. State U., Fort Collins, 1963-72, prof. dept. stats., 1972—. Co-author: Permutation Methods: a Distance Function Approach; contbr. articles Am. Jour. Pub. Health, Jour. of Statis. Planning and Inference, Ednl. and Psychol. Measurement, Biometrika, Earth-Sci. Revs., Weather and Forecasting, Jour. Behavioral and Ednl. Stats. Capt. USAF, 1953-57. Fellow Am. Statis. Assn.; mem. Am. Meteorol. Soc. (Banner I. Miller award 1973, 94), Biometric Soc. Achievements include rsch. in common statistical methods (t test and analysis of variance) based on counter intuitive geometric foundations and provided alternative statistical methods which are based on appropriate foundations. Home: 736 Cherokee Dr Fort Collins CO 80525-1517 Office: Colo State U Dept Stats Fort Collins CO 80523-1877 Office Phone: 970-491-6465. Business E-Mail: paul.mielke@colostate.edu.

MIERA, LUCILLE CATHERINE MIERA, artist, retired art educator; b. Socorro, N.Mex., Nov. 25, 1931; d. Stephen Maurice and Carmen Rosela (Baca) Miera; m. Vito Modesto Miera Jr., Aug. 22, 1953; children: Stephanie Lucille Miera Mansfield, Jennifer Ann Miera Eberhart. BA, U. N.Mex., 1973, MA, 1976, Ednl. Specialist Sch. Adminstrn., 1984. Cert. tchr., adminstr., N.Mex. Apprentice land surveying and draftsmen Stephen M. Miera, Regional Land Surveyor, Albuquerque, 1946-49; typist Albuquerque Abstract & Title, 1950; typist, engring. draftsman U.S. Army Corps Engrs., Albuquerque, 1950-57; engring. draftsman U.S. Dept. Interior, Albuquerque, 1957-59; art tchr., art dept. chair Albuquerque Pub. Sch. Sys., 1973-93, reviewer curriculum devel. plan jr. high schs.; reviewer mid. schs.; ret. Prof. asst. U. N.Mex., Albuquerque, 1974; mid. sch. articulation rep. Taylor Middle Sch., Albuquerque, 1974-83; art rep. North Ctrl. Evaluation Middle Sch., Albuquerque, 1978; pres., art tchr. N.Mex Art League, Albuquerque, 1996, 97, 99; founder art program Emeritus Acad., Tech. Vocat. Inst., 1997, art. tchr., bd. dirs. 1997—. Exhibitions include Mus. Art, Toledo, Ohio, 1964, Kirtland AFB Officers Club, Albuquerque, 1967—68, U. N.Mex., 1969—76, 1999—2000, Albuquerque Pub. Schs. Adminstrn. Bldg., 1973—93, United Bank N.Mex., 1982, Albuquerque C. of C., 1999, exhibited in group shows at N.Mex. State Fair Fine Arts Gallery, N.Mex. State Fair Hispanic Art Gallery, Scottsdale Village Cir. Art Gallery, Old Town Albuquerque De Colores Soaring Eagle and La Hacienda Galleries, Coronado Airport Gallery. Mem., flyer distbr. Rep. Party, Albuquerque, 1954; poll clk. Bernalillo County, Albuquerque, 1960; leader Campfire USA, Albuquerque, 1966, 80; treas. Manzano Band, Albuquerque, 1977; pres. Glenwood Neighborhood Assn., Albuquerque, 1984-87; pres., nat. area dir. Res. Officers Assn. Ladies, Washington, 1989-91. Mem. Nat. Mus. Women's Art (charter), Nat. Hist. Soc., N.Mex. Assn. Educators Ret., N.Mex. Watercolor Soc., N.Mex. Res. Officer Ladies (pres.), N.Mex. Archdiocesan Coun. Cath. Women (pres. 1974), Epsilon Sigma Alpha. Avocations: travel, instructing and displaying art to promote art in the community. Home: 4405 Glenwood Hills Dr NE Albuquerque NM 87111-4260 E-mail: lmierart@aol.com.

MIERENFELD, GARY M. retail executive; V.p. distbn. Circuit City, Richmond, Va., 1993—99, sr. v.p. distbn. and nat. svc., 1999—2003, sr. v.p. store devel., procurement, distbn. and svc., 2003—. Office: Circuit City 9950 Mayland Dr Richmond VA 23233-1464

MIERS, HARRIET E. lawyer; b. Dallas, Aug. 10, 1945; BS, So. Meth. U., 1967, JD, 1970. Bar: Tex. 1970. Pres. Locke Purnell Rain Harrell, PC, Dallas. Chair Tex. Lottery Commn.; bd. dirs. Capstead Mortgage Corp., Coamerica Bank, Tex. Comments editor Southwestern Law Jour., 1969-70. Former mem.-at-large Dallas City Coun.; trustee Southwestern Legal Found. Named 1 of 50 Top Women Lawyers Nat. Law Jour., 1998. Fellow Am. Bar Found., Tex. Bar Found. (life); mem. ABA (jour. bd. editors, ho. dels., chair credentials and admissions com., election law com., bus. and cmty. activities), Dallas Bar Found., Dallas Bar Assn. (pres. 1985, chmn. bd. dirs. 1981), State Bar Tex. (pres. 1992-93, dir. 1986-89), Attys. Liability Assurance Soc. (bd. dirs.). Office: Locke Purnell Rain Harrell 2200 Ross Ave Ste 2200 Dallas TX 75201-6776 E-mail: hemiers@lprh.com.

MIES, RICHARD W. career officer; b. Chgo. m. Sheila McCann; children: Rachel Anne, Sara Elizabeth. BS, U.S. Naval Acad., 1967; M, Harvard U., 1982. Commd. USN, 1967, advanced through grades to adm., 1998; comdr. in chief U.S. Strategic Command. Office: 901 SAC Blvd Offutt A F B NE 68113-6000

MIFFLIN, FRED JOHN, Canadian government official; b. Bonavista, Nfld., Can., 1938; m. Gwenneth Davies; children: Cathy, Mark, Sarah. Grad., Can. Navy's Venture Tng. Program, U.S. Naval War Coll., Nat. Def. Coll., Kingston, Ont. Enlisted Can. Navy, 1954, advanced through ranks to rear admiral, 1985, head nat. def. secretariat; mem. parliament Canadian Govt., 1988-96, parliamentary sec. to min. nat. def. & vet. affairs, 1993, min. fisheries & oceans, 1996-97; min. vet. affairs and sec. of state Atlantic Can. Opportunities Agy., 1997-99. Avocations: country music, cooking. Office: Confederation Bldg, Rm 207 Ho of Commons Ottawa ON Canada K1A OA6

MIGALA, LUCYNA J. journalist, arts administrator, radio station executive; b. Krakow, Poland, May 22, 1944; came to U.S., 1947, naturalized, 1955; d. Joseph and Estelle (Suwala) M.; m. Frank A. Cizon, Oct. 9, 1998. Student, Loyola U., Chgo., 1962-63, Chgo. Conservatory of Music, 1963-70; BS in Journalism, Northwestern U., 1966. Radio announcer, prodr. Sta. WOPA, Oak Park, Ill., 1963—66; writer, reporter, prodr. NBC News, Chgo., 1966—69, 1969—71; prodr. NBC local news, Washington, 1969; prodr., coord. NBC network news, Cleve., 1971—78, field prodr. Chgo., 1978—79; v.p. Migala Comm. Corp., 1979—. Program and news dir., on-air personality Sta. WCEV, Cicero, Ill, 1979—; lectr. City Colls., Chgo., 1981, Morton Coll., 1988. Columnist Free Press, Chgo., 1984-87. Founder, artistic dir., gen. mgr. Lira Ensemble (formerly The Lira Singers), Chgo., 1965—. Artist-in-residence, Loyola U., Chgo.; mem., chmn. various cultural coms. Polish Am. Congress, 1970-80; bd. dirs. Nationalities Svcs. Ctr., Cleve., 1973-78; bd. dirs., v.p. Cicero-Berwyn Fine Arts Coun., Cicero, Ill., 1980-87; mem. City Arts I and II panels Chgo. Office of Fine Arts, 1986-89, 94; v.p. Chgo. chpt. Kosciuszko Found., 1983-86; bd. dirs. Polish Women's Alliance Am., 1983-87, Ill. Humanities Coun., 1983-89, mem. exec. com., 1986-87; bd. dirs. Ill. Arts Alliance, 1989-92; founder, gen. chmn. Midwest Chopin Piano Competition (later Chgo. Chopin Competition), 1984-86; founding mem. ethnic and folk arts panel Ill. Arts Coun., 1984-87, 92-94; mem. Polonia Census 2000 Com.; bd. dirs.Polish-Am. Leadership Initiative, Chgo., 2001—. Decorated Cavalier's Cross of Merit govt. of Poland; recipient AP Broadcasters award, 1973, Emmy award NATAS, 1974, Cultural Achievement award Am. Coun. for Polish Culture, 1990, award of merit Advocates Soc. Polish Am. Attys., 1991, Human Rels. Media award City of Chgo., 1992, Outstanding Achievement award Minister of Fgn. Affairs Rep. of Poland, 1994, Civic Achievement award Polish Am. Hist. Assn., 2000, Nat. Creative Arts award Polish Am. Hist. Soc., 2003; Washington Journalism Ctr. fellow, 1969. Mem. Soc. Profl. Journalists. Office: Sta WCEV 5356 W Belmont Ave Chicago IL 60641-4103 also: The Lira Ensemble 6525 N Sheridan Rd # Sky905 Chicago IL 60626-5344 E-mail: limgala@liraensemble.com.

MIGDOL, MARVIN JACOB, public relations and marketing executive, consultant; b. Rochester, N.Y., Jan. 11, 1937; s. Frank and Dorothy (Krieger) M.; m. Frances Scheiner, June 13, 1959 (div. June 1970); children: Helene Ellen, Steven Gary, Larry Jay; m. Grace Miron, Dec. 26 1970 (div. Aug. 1986); children: Michael Alan, Susan Renee, Honi Faith; m. Roni Habel, June 30, 1991 (div. Dec. 1992); m. Fay Herschberg, Dec. 27, 2003. BA in Sociology, U. Buffalo, 1959; postgrad., U. Miami, 1959-60; MS in Communications, Boston U., 1961. Dir. pub. rels. United Fund, Reading, Pa., 1961-63, Rensselaer Poly. Inst., Troy, NY, 1963-64, Touro Infirmary, New Orleans, 1964, Hamot Hosp., Erie, Pa., 1964-65, United Jewish Fedn., Buffalo, 1965-68; pres. Marvin J. Migdol Inc., Dallas, 1968—. Instr. Boston U., 1962—, Pa. State U., 1962—, U. Tex., 1962—, Collin County C.C., Plano, 1990-91. Author: Public Relations Handbook, 1963, Comics as a Public Relations Tool in Communications, 1971, The Migdol Manual, 1972, Success in the 1990's, 1987, Greater Virility: Overcoming Impotence, 1993; contbr. numerous articles to profl. jours. Reporter Rep. Nat. Conv., Dallas, 1964; asst. dist. commr. Boy Scouts Am., Dallas, 1980-85; exec. bd. dirs. EPCOT Resorts, Lake Buena Vista, Fla., 1992—; v.p. Am. Jewish Congress, S.W. Region, 2001--. Recipient Pub. Rels. award Coun. Jewish Welfare Funds & Fedn., N.Y.C., 1967, Am. Contract Bridge League, Memphis, 1983-87, Nat. Bus. League, West Palm Beach, Fla., 1968; Entrepreneur of the Yr. Venture mag., Dallas, 1987; Award of Merit Big Brothers & Sisters, Dallas, 1987, major league volleyball, San Jose, Calif., 1987. Mem. U.S. Profl. Mktg. Assn. (pres. 1990—), Am. Assn. Indsl. Editors (bd. dirs. 1967-70), Am. Coll. Pub. Rels. Assn. (bd. dirs. 1964-66), Inst. for Info. and Comm. (bd. dirs. 1971—), Dallas Belles (dir. mktg. and pub. rels. 1987—), Jewish Nat. Fund (area dir.), Dallas Bridge Assn. (chmn. publicity), Dallas C. of C. (mem. econ. and internat. coun.), U. Buffalo Alumni Assn. We. Pa. and Tex., 1964-65, Temple Shalom (vice chmn. bldg. fund 1971-72, mem. Brotherhood bd. 1985-86), Jewish Cmty. Ctr., Alpha Epsilon Pi (gov., 1970-79), Phi Delta Phi, (v.p. 1959-60, treas. 1960—). Jewish. Avocations: writer, lecturer, baseball and softball umpire, Boy Scout leader. Office: CAREington Internat Corp 7400 Gaylord Pkwy Frisco TX 75034 Home: 18715 Gibbons Dr Dallas TX 75287 Office Phone: 469-252-5816.

MIGEON, BARBARA RUBEN, pediatrician, geneticist; b. Rochester, N.Y., July 31, 1931; d. William Saul and Sara (Gitin) Ruben; m. Claude Jean Migeon, Apr. 2, 1960; children: Jacques Claude, Jean-Paul, Nicole. BA, Smith Coll., 1952; MD, SUNY, Buffalo, 1956. Diplomate Am. Bd. Pediatrics; cert. in med. genetics. Pediatric residency The Johns Hopkins U., Balt., 1956-59; fellow in endocrinology Harvard U. Med. Sch., Boston, 1959-60; fellow in genetics The Johns Hopkins Sch. Medicine, Balt., 1960-62, assoc. prof. pediatrics, 1970-79, joint appointment in biology, 1978—, prof., 1979—, founding dir. PhD program in human genetics, 1979-89. Mem. Genetics Study Sect., NIH, Bethesda, Md., 1975-77, Mammalian Genetics Study Sect., NIH, Bethesda, 1977-79, Human Genome Study Sect., NIH, Bethesda, 1991-93. Contbr. more than 100 rsch. papers to profl. publs. Named Prin. Investigator NIH grant, 1971—; recipient Outstanding Woman Physician award Med. Coll. Pa.; Vis. investigator Carnegie Instn. of Washington, 1975, Exch. prof. Guys Hosp., 1986. Mem. Am. Pediatric Soc., Am. Soc. Human Genetics. Office: Inst Genetic Medicine BRB 459 The Johns Hopkins U Baltimore MD 21205 Office Phone: 410-955-3049. E-mail: bmigeon@jhmi.edu.

MIGHELL, KENNETH JOHN, lawyer; b. Schenectady, N.Y., Mar. 17, 1931; s. Richard Henry and Ruth Aline (Simon) M.; m. Julia Anne Carstarphen, Aug. 24, 1961; children: Thomas Lowry, Elizabeth Anne. BBA, U. Tex., 1952, JD, 1957. Bar: Tex. 1957. Assoc. Scurry, Scurry, Pace & Wood, Dallas, 1957-61; asst. U.S. Atty. Justice Dept., Dallas, 1961-77; 1st asst. No. Dist. Tex., 1972-77; U.S. Atty. No. Dist., Tex., 1977-81; ptnr. Cowles & Thompson, Dallas, 1981-96, of counsel, 1996—. Chmn. bd. mgmt. Downtown Dallas YMCA, 1974-76; pres. Dallas Area Am. Lung Assn., 1985-87; bd. dirs. YMCA Met. Dallas, 1987—; chmn. adv. bd. Southwestern Law Enforcement Inst., 1994-98; mem. SW Legal Found., CLE adv. com. 1999-2003. With USN, 1952-54; capt. USNR, 1954-78. Mem.: FBA, Nat. Assn. Former U.S. Attys. (pres. 1995), State Bar Tex. (bd. dirs. 1994—95), Dallas Bar Found. (trustee 1994—2001, vice chmn. 1999—2000, chmn. 2001—02), Dallas Bar Assn. (bd. dirs. 1984—89, chmn. 1989, v.p. 1990—91, pres. 1993). Democrat. Methodist. Office: Cowles & Thompson 901 Main St Ste 4000 Dallas TX 75202-3793 E-mail: kmighell@cowlesthompson.com.

MIGHT, THOMAS OWEN, newspaper company executive; b. Fort Walton Beach, Fla., Apr. 22, 1951; s. Gerald William and Rosina (Bugner) M.; m. Sept. 22, 1973; children— Mathew, Daniel BS in Indsl. Engring., Ga. Tech. U., 1972; MBA, Harvard Bus. Sch., 1978. Asst. to pub. Washington Post, 1978-80, mgr. plant, 1980-81, v.p. prodn., v.p. marketing; now pres., CEO, divsn. Cable One The Washington Post Co., Phoenix, 1981—. Served to capt. U.S. Army, 1972-76 Roman Catholic.

MIGIELICZ, GERALYN, photojournalist; b. St. Louis, Feb. 15, 1958; d. Edward J. and Mary Ann (McCarthy) M. BJ, U. Mo., 1979. Photographer Emporia (Kans.) Gazette, 1979-80; chief photographer St. Joseph (Mo.) News-Press & Gazette, 1980-83; photo editor, photographer Seattle Times, 1984; picture editor Rocky Mountain News, Denver, 1985-86; graphics editor San Jose (Calif.) Mercury News, 1986-92, dir. photography, 1992—. Mem. faculty Poynter Inst., U. Mo. Workshop, Latin Am. Photojournalism Conf. Recipient Individual Editing awards Soc. Newspaper Designers, 1988-98, Editing awards, 91-98; named for Overall Excellence in Editing, Picture of Yr. Contest, U. Mo., 1993. Office: San Jose Mercury News 750 Ridder Park Dr San Jose CA 95131-2432

MIGLIARO, MARCO WILLIAM, electrical engineer; b. N.Y.C., Mar. 29, 1948; s. Marco Salvatore and Anna (Dalton) M.; children: Kristen Marie, Meredith Anne, Marie Angela, Marco Thomas; m. Jasoda Badlu, Nov. 19, 1988. BEE, Pratt Inst., 1969; postgrad., N.J. Inst. Tech., 1970-72. Registered profl. engr., N.Y., N.J., Pa., Mass., Fla. Engr. Am. Electric Power, N.Y.C., 1969-78; staff engr. Gibbs & Hill, Inc., N.Y.C., 1978-81; sr. cons. engr. Ebasco Svcs., Inc., N.Y.C., 1981-88; tech. mgr. ABB Impell Corp., Melville, NY, 1988-90; sr. staff specialist for nuc. engring. Fla. Power & Light, Juno Beach, 1990-96, chief elec./I&C engr., 1996—2003; pres. ESA Cons. Engrs., PA, Jupiter, Fla., 2003—; pres., CEO IEEE Industry Stds. and Tech. Orgn., 2003—. Developer seminar on stationary batteries, 1987. Contbg. author: Handbook of Power Calculations, 1984, 99, Standard Handbook for Electrical Engineers, 1999; also articles. Recipient Meritorious Svc. award Am. Nat. Standards Inst., 1994. Fellow IEEE (pres. 2001—, stds. assn. bd. govs. 1998—, bd. dirs. 1990-92, 2001, fin. com. 1990-92, dir. stds. 1990-91, mem. exec. com. 1992, v.p. stds. activities, 1992, 2001, Stds. medal 1986, Stds. Bd. Disting. Svc. award 1993, Charles Proteus Steinmetz award 1996, Third Millennium medal 2000); mem. IEEE Power Engring. Soc. (Disting. Svc. award 1988, 92), Industry Standards and Tech. Orgn. (bd. dirs. 2000—, chmn. 2000-03). Avocations: fishing, travel, music. Home: PO Box 9253 Jupiter FL 33468-9253 Office: ESA Cons Engrs PA PO Box 9251 Jupiter FL 33468-9251 Office Phone: 561-691-1946.

MIGLIN, MARILYN, cosmetics executive; Student, Northwestern U. Profl. ballerina; model Marshall Fields; founder, owner Marilyn Miglin Cosmetic Co., 1963—. Active Mayor Richard M. Daley's spl. com. tourism; officer Chgo. Conv. and Tourism Bur.; apptd. Gov. James Edgar Econ. Devel. Bd.; past pres. Oak St. Coun.; founder Women of Destiny (mentoring program); bd. mem. Ctr. for Craniofacial Anomalies, U. Ill., Chgo. Named in her honor Marilyn Miglin Day, Chgo., 1998; named one of Chgos. 100 Most Influential Women, Crain's Chgo. Bus., 2004. Office: 120 E Oak St Chicago IL 60611-1204*

MIGLIO, DANIEL JOSEPH, retired telecommunications company executive; b. Phila., June 23, 1940; s. Daniel Joseph and Eleanor (Zucca) M.; children: Paige Leslie, Marcus Daniel. BS in Econs., U. Pa., 1962. With So. New Eng. Telephone Co, 1962-84; acct. New Haven, Conn., 1962-67; budget coordinator, 1967-69; dist. traffic mgr. New London, Conn., 1969-72; gen. acctg. mgr. New Haven, 1972-74; div. ops. mgr. Hartford, Conn., 1974-78; gen. mgr. corp. planning New Haven, 1979-83; v.p. corp. planning and regulatory matters, 1983-84; sr. v.p. fin. and planning So. New Eng. Telecommunications Corp., New Haven, 1984—; now chmn. & ceo So. New England Telecommunications Corp.; ret. Bd. dirs. 1st Constn. Bank, New Haven. Charter mem., bd. dirs. Clinton (Conn.) Jaycees, 1967-68; chmn. allocations com., bd. dirs. United Way, New Haven, 1973-74, New Haven Symphony Orch., 1990—; bd. dirs., v.p., pres. Gateway Counseling, Essex, Conn., 1975-86; bd. govs. Old Saybrook (Conn.) Hist. Soc., 1979-80; trustee Rector's Concern, Old Saybrook, 1980-88; chmn. So. New Eng. Telephone Co. Polit. Action Com., New Haven, 1987—. Mem. U.S. Telephone Assn. (bd. dirs., exec. com. 1984—), Conn. Joint Coun. on Econ. Edn. (fin. chmn. 1988—), U. Pa. Club Greater Hartford, Univ. Club Hartford, Kappa Alpha. Republican. Episcopalian. Avocations: cross country skiing, hiking, golf, tennis. Office: So New England Telecom Corp 227 Church St Fl 15 New Haven CT 06510-1801

MIGNONE, MARIO B. Italian studies educator; came to U.S., 1960; m. Lois Mignone, June 29, 1968; children: Pamela Anne, Cristina Maria, Elizabeth Maria. BA, CCNY, 1967; MA, Rutgers U., 1969, PhD, 1972. Disting. prof. Italian lang. SUNY, Stony Brook, 1970—, dir. undergrad. studies, 1976-83, dir. grad. studies, 1983-87; founder, exec. dir. Ctr. for Italian Studies, chmn. French and Italian dept., Stony Brook, 1988—98. Author: The Theater of Eduardo De Filippo, 1974, Abnormality and Anguish in the Narrative of Dino Buzzati, 1981, Eduardo De Filippo, 1984, Pirandello in America, 1988, Columbus: Meeting of Cultures, 1993, Italy Today: A Country in Transition, 1995, Italy Today: At the Crossroads of the New Millennium, 1998; assoc. mng. editor Forum Italicum, 1986-94, editor, 1994—; contbr. articles to profl. jours. Mem. Am. Assn. Tchrs. Italian (pres. 1982-84), Assn. Italian Am. Educators (pres. 1997—). Home: 17 Salt Meadow Ln Stony Brook NY 11790-1109 Office: SUNY Dept European Langs Lits Stony Brook NY 11794-3359 Office Phone: 631-632-7444. E-mail: mmignone@notes.cc.sunysb.edu.

MIGUE, JEAN LUC, economics professor; b. Montreal, Que., Can., Apr. 13, 1933; s. Joseph Alfred and Marie Laurence (Venne) M.; m. Renee Caron, Sept. 13, 1958; children: Paule, Pascal, Nicolas. BA in Econs, U. Montreal, 1953, MA, 1956; PhD in Econs, Am. U., 1968. Researcher Bank of Can., 1957-58; prof. Laval U., 1962-70; prof. econs. Nat. Sch. Public Adminstrn., Quebec, 1970-99. Mem. staff Econ. Coun. Can., 1973-74 Author: The Price of Health, 1974, Le Prix du Transport, 1978, Nationalistic Policies of Canada, 1979, L'Economiste et La chose Publique, 1979, The Public Monopoly of Education, 1989, Federalism and Free Trade, 1993, Etatisme et Declin du quebec, 1999, Le Monopole de La Santé, 2001, Statism and Health in France, 2004. Fellow Massey Found., 1956, sr. fellow, The Fraser Inst. Fellow Royal Soc. Can.; mem. Mont Pelerin Soc. Roman Catholic. E-mail: jlmigue@videotron.ca.

MIHAL, SANDRA POWELL, systems analyst; b. Balt., Dec. 15, 1941; d. Sanford William and Mary Louise (Barry) Powell; m. James George Anderson, June 15, 1963; children: Robin Marie, James Brian, Melissa Lee, Derek Clair; m. Charles Turner Barber, Apr. 18, 1978; stepchildren: Gretchen Jayco, Katrina Hope; m. Ladislaw Paul Mihal, May 25, 1991; stepchildren: Alexander Paul, Suzie May, Natasha Elizabeth, Rudy Darius. BA, Mt. St. Agnes Coll., 1963; MA, N.Mex. State U., 1970, Purdue U., 1975; EdD, Vanderbilt U., 1990. Cert. tchr., Md. Tchr. Ridgely Dulaney Jr. H.S., Towson, Md., 1964; grad. asst. N.Mex. State U., Las Cruces, 1967—69; acad. advisor, instr. polit. sci. Purdue U., West Lafayette, Ind., 1974—78; prof., acad. sys. analyst U. So. Ind., Evansville, 1978—82; assoc. prof., chair dept. computer info. sys. Henderson (Ky.) C.C., 1982—88; prof. computer tech., divsn. chair Anne Arundel C.C., Arnold, Md., 1988—91; computer sys. analyst immigration and naturalization svc. Dept. of Justice, Washington, 1991—92, Glynco, Ga., 1995—; dep. program mgr. distributed learning Fed. Law Enforcement Training Ctr., Homeland Security, Glynco, Ga., 2002—. Bd. dirs. Ind. Polit. Sci. Assn., Muncie, 1984-88, Internat. Studies Assn.-Midwest, Chgo., 86-88; pres. Ky. Acad. Computer Users' Group, Lexington, 1985-86; mem. telecom. adv. bd. C.C. Sys., Annapolis, Md., 1990-91; computer sys. network analyst CLARC Svcs., Pt. Charlotte, Fla., 92-95; adj. prof. history and polit. sci. Edison C.C., Punta Gorda, Fla., 1993-95. Author: Learning By Doing BASIC, 1983, Computers Learning By Doing, 1984; contbr. to several profl jours. 1980-90; author, spkr. series Faculty/Staff Edison CC 94, Ednl. Tech. Nova U., 1995. Block coord. several neighborhood assns.; computer adv. bd. Henderson County Sch., 1982-88; chmn. Newburgh (Ind.) Youth Orgn., 78-86; judge Sci. Fair, Annapolis, 1988-90; nomination bd. Ky. Higher Edn. Assn., 1989-91; mem. Charlotte Chorale, Port Charlotte, 1992-94, Peace River Power Squadron, Port Charlotte, 1994-96. Coast Guard Aux., 1995-97. Md. State Tchr. Bd. Edn. scholar, 1960-63; fellow Sloan Found., 1973-75, U. Ky., 1984. Mem. Soc. Applied Learning Tech., Assn. Computing Machinery (v.p. 85—), Am. Legion, Pi Gamma Mu. Democrat. Mem. Ch. Of Christ. Avocations: sailing, singing, swimming, cooking, playing the dulcimer. Home: 112 Oak Ridge Rd Brunswick GA 31523-9741 Office Phone: 912-267-2591. Business E-Mail: sandy.mihal@dhs.gov.

MIHALAS, DIMITRI MANUEL, astrophysicist, educator; b. Los Angeles, Mar. 20, 1939; s. Emmanuel Demetrious and Jean (Christo) M.; children: Michael Demetrious, Alexaudra Genevieve. BA with highest honors, UCLA, 1959; MS, Calif. Inst. Tech., 1960, PhD, 1964. Asst. prof. astrophys. scis. Princeton U., 1964-67; asst. prof. physics U. Colo., 1967-68; asso. prof. astronomy and astrophysics U. Chgo., 1968-70, prof., 1970-71; adj. prof. astrogeophysics, also physics and astrophysics U. Colo., 1972-80; sr. scientist High Altitude Obs., Nat. Center Atmospheric Research, Boulder, Colo., 1971-79, 82-85; G.C. McVittie prof. astronomy U. Ill., 1985-98; astronomer Sacramento Peak Obs., Sunspot, N.Mex., 1979-82; staff mem. Los Alamos Nat. Lab., 1998—. Cons. Los Alamos Nat. Lab, 1981-98; vis. prof. dept. astrophysics Oxford (Eng.) U., 1977-78; sr. vis. fellow dept. physics and astronomy Univ. Coll., London, 1978; mem. astronomy adv. panel NSF, 1972-75 Author: Galactic Astronomy, 1969, 2d edit, 1981, Stellar Atmospheres, 1970, 2d edit., 1978, Theorie des Atmospheres Stellaires, 1971, Foundations of Radiation Hydrodynamics, 1984; assoc. editor Astrophys. Jour, 1970-79, Jour. Computational Physics, 1981-87, Jour. Quantitative Spectroscopy, 1984-94; mem. editorial bd. Solar Physics, 1981-89. NSF fellow, 1959-62; Van Maanen fellow, 1962-63; Eugene Higgins vis. fellow, 1963-64; Alfred P. Sloan Found. Research fellow, 1969-71; Alexander von Humboldt Stiftung sr. U.S. scientist awardee, 1984. Mem. U.S. Nat. Acad. Sci., Internat. Astron. Union (pres. commn. 36 1976-79), Am. Astron. Soc. (pub. bd. 1995-99, mem. coun. 2000—03, Helen B. Warner prize 1974), Astron. Soc. Pacific (dir. 1975-77) Home: 3202 Woodland Rd Los Alamos NM 87544-0806 Office: Los Alamos Nat Lab X-7 MS-F699 Los Alamos NM 87545-0001 E-mail: dmihalas@lanl.gov.

MIHALY, EUGENE BRAMER, corporate executive, consultant, writer, educator; b. The Hague, The Netherlands, Nov. 11, 1934; s. Eddy and Cecile (Bramer) Kahn; stepson of Eugene Mihaly; m. Stacey Beth Pulner, Apr. 21, 1996; children: Lisa Klee, Jessica; stepchildren: Stephanie Pulner, Andrew Pulner. AB magna cum laude, Harvard U., 1956; PhD, London Sch. Econs. and Polit. Sci., 1964. Aviation/space editor Hartford (Conn.) Courant, 1960-61; internat. economist AID, Washington, 1964-65; dep. dir. Peace Corps, Tanzania, 1966, dir., 1967-68, dep. dir. East Asia/Pacific bur., 1969, dir. office program devel., evaluation and rsch., 1969-70; assoc. dir. Inst. Internat. Studies, U. Calif., Berkeley, 1970-72; pres. Mihaly Internat. Corp., 1972—; chmn. bd. Mihaly Internat. Can., Ltd., 1992—; sr. lectr. Haas Sch. Bus. U. Calif., Berkeley, 1991-95. Adj. prof. Amos Tuck Sch. Dartmouth Coll., 1997-2002. Author: Foreign Aid and Politics in Nepal: A Case Study, 1965; contbr.: Political Development in Micronesia, 1974, Management of the Multinationals, 1974; also articles to various publs. Chmn. emeritus Calif.-S.E. Asia Bus. Coun.; chmn. Global R.I.; pres. Found. for Ocean State Pub. Radio; chmn. R.I. Coun. for the Humanities. Mem. Coun. on Fgn. rels., Signet Soc. Home: 4 Half Mile Rd Barrington RI 02806

MIHAN, RICHARD, retired dermatologist; b. Dec. 20, 1925; s. Arnold and Virginia Catherine (O'Reilly) M. MD, St. Louis U., 1949. Diplomate Am. Bd. Dermatology. Intern L.A. County Gen. Hosp., 1949-51, resident in dermatology, 1954-57; pvt. practice in dermatology L.A., 1957-95; prof. emeritus U. So. Calif., 1989—. Lt. Comdr. USNR, 1951-53. Fellow ACP; mem. AMA, Pacific Dermatol. Assn. (exec. bd. 1971-74), Am. Acad. Dermatol., Calif. Med. Assn. (chmn. dermatol. sect. 1973-74), L.A. Met. Dermatology Soc. (pres. 1975-76), L.A. Acad. Medicine (pres. 1988-89), Order of St. John of Jerusalem, of Rhodes, and of Malta, Order of St. Lazarus (comdr.), Calif. Club. Roman Cath. Home: 3278 Wilshire Blvd Apt 503 Los Angeles CA 90010-1431

MIHELIC, TRACEY L. lawyer; b. Lake Forest, Ill., Sept. 12, 1965; BA, Ill., 1990. With Gardner, Carton & Douglas, Chgo., 1990—2000, ptnr., 1998—2000, Baker & McKenzie, Chgo., 2000—. Mem.: ABA, Internat. Emissions Trading Assn., Emissions Mktg. Assn., Ill. State Bar Assn. Office: Baker and McKenzie One Prudential Plz 130 E Randolph Dr Chicago IL 60601

MIHM, JOHN CLIFFORD, chemical engineer; b. Austin, Tex., July 28, 1942; s. Clifford Henry and Adeline (Cleary) M.; m. Janet Eleanor Skales, May 29, 1964; 1 child, Mary Lynn, 1 granddaughter, Cassandra. AA, Frank Phillips Coll., 1962; BSChemE, Tex. Tech. U., 1964. Registered profl. engr., Tex. With Phillips Petroleum Co., 1964—, v.p. corp. engring., 1987-92, v.p. R & D, 1992-93, sr. v.p. corp. tech., 1993-99, sr. v.p. tech. and project devel., 1999—2002; engr. mgr. E & P Phillips Petroleum Co., Stavanger, Norway, 1977-82. Adv. bd. Tex. Tech. U., Lubbock, Tex., 1985—, pres. deans coun., 1996-98. Bd. dirs. Boy Scouts Am., Bartlesville, 1986—, area III pres., 1998-2002, So. region bd. dirs., 1998—. Named Disting. Engr., Tex. Tech. U., 1984; named to Okla. State U. Coll. of Engring. Arch. and Tech. Hall of Fame, 1999. Fellow ASME (ind. adv. bd. 1989-2002, found. bd. dirs. 2000—); mem. NSPE (mem. adv. bd. 1994-2002), AIChE (ECC divsn., bd. dirs. 1989-93, chmn. 1992-93), Okla. Soc. Profl. Engrs. (Outstanding Engr. in Mgmt. award 1991), Soc. Petroleum Engrs. (Disting. Mem. 2000), Okla. Engring. Found. (bd. dirs., pres. 1993-97). Republican. Roman Catholic. Office: Conoco Phillips Co 260 Rf Bartlesville OK 74004-0001 Home: Apt 114 5200 Town & Country Blvd Frisco TX 75034-6885

MIHM, MARTIN CHARLES, JR., pathologist, educator; s. Martin Charles and Cecilia Matilda (Hepp) M. AB, Duquesne U., 1955; MD, U. Pitts., 1961; MA (hon.), Harvard U., 1990. Diplomate Am. Bd. Dermatology, Am. Bd. Pathology. Intern Mt. Sinai Hosp., N.Y.C., 1961-62, resident in medicine, 1963-64; resident in dermatology Mass. Gen. Hosp., Boston, 1964-67, resident in Pathology, 1968-72, chief dermatopathology, 1973-94; asst. prof. pathology Harvard U. Med. Sch., Boston, 1972-75, assoc. prof., 1975-79, chief dermatopathology, 1982-93; prof. pathology Mass. Gen. Hosp.-Harvard U., Boston, 1980-93; prof., chief dermatopathology, dermatology Albany (N.Y.) Med. Coll., 1993—. Pathologist Malignant Melanoma Coop. Group, 1972—77; chmn. pathology com. Intergroup Melanoma Study, 1983—88; chief sr. adminstr. Wellman Labs., Mass. Gen. Hosp., 1985—93; cons. WHO, 1985—; adj. prof. pathology Vanderbilt U., 1989—; chmn. pathology standing com., 1991—; clin. prof. pathology Harvard Med. Sch., 1996—; sr. dermatopathologist and pathologist Mass. Gen. Hosp., 1996—; adj. prof. Thomas Jefferson Med. Sch., 2000—; prof. otolaryngology U. of Ark. Sch. of Med. Scis., 2002—. Author: Primer of Dermatopathology, 1984, 2d edit., 1992, Problematic Pigmented Lesions, 1990; co-author: Melanoma and Nevi, 1997, The Melanocytic Proliterations, 2001; editor: Lymphoproliferative Disorders of the Skin, 1986, Pathbiology and Recognition Malignant Melanoma, 1988; contbr. articles to med. jours.; overseer Boston Symphonic Orch., 2001-. Served to comdr. USPHS, 1967-69. Recipient Gold Humanism award, Harvard Med. Sch., 2004. Fellow: ACP, Am. Soc. Dermatopathology, Am. Acad. Dermatology; mem.: AMA (Harvard Med. Sch. rep. to med. sch. sect. 1991), Harvard Dermatology House Officer's Assn. (pres. 1982), Italian Assn. Ambulatory Dermatologists (hon.), Italian Soc. of Anatomic Pathology (hon.), Soc. of Dermatology, Mexico (hon.), Fort Orange Club, Albany, Harvard Club (Boston, N.Y.C.), Pi Gamma Mu, Alpha Omega Alpha. Independent. Roman Catholic. Home: 27 Chilton St Brookline MA 02446 Office: Mass Gen Hosp Warren Bldg 827 55 Fruit St Boston MA 02114 Office Phone: 617-724-1350. E-mail: mmihm@partners.org.

MIHM, MICHAEL MARTIN, federal judge; b. Amboy, Ill., May 18, 1943; s. Martin Clarence and Frances Johannah (Morrissey) M.; m. Judith Ann Zosky, May 6, 1967; children— Molly Elizabeth, Sarah Ann, Jacob Michael, Jennifer Leah BA, Loras Coll., 1964; JD, St. Louis U., 1967. Asst. prosecuting atty. St. Louis County, Clayton, Mo., 1967-68; asst. state's atty. Peoria County, Peoria, Ill., 1968-69; asst. city atty. City of Peoria, Ill., 1969-72; state's atty. Peoria County, Peoria, Ill., 1972-80; sole practice Peoria, Ill., 1980-82; U.S. dist. judge U.S. Govt., Peoria, Ill., 1982—; chief U.S. dist. judge U.S. Dist. Ct. (ctrl. dist.) Ill., 1991—98. Chmn. com. internat. jud. rels. U.S. Jud. Conf., 1994—96, mem. exec. com., 1995—97, mem. com. jud. br., 1987—93, mem. com. internat. jud. rels., 1998—2002; mem. Supreme Ct. Fellows Commn., 2000—; adj. prof. law John Marshall Law Sch., 1990—. Past mem. adv. bd. Big Brothers-Big Sisters, Crisis Nursery, Peoria; past bd. dirs. Salvation Army, Peoria, W.D. Boyce council Boy Scouts Am., State of Ill. Treatment Alternatives to Street Crime, Gov.'s Criminal Justice Info. Council; past vice-chmn. Ill. Dangerous Drugs Adv. Council; trustee Proctor Health Care Found., 1991-2002. Recipient Good Govt. award Peoria Jaycees, 1978, Vincent C. Immel Alumni Merit award St. Louis U. Sch. Law, 1997, Disting. Alumnus in Pub. Svc. award Loras Coll., 2000. Mem. Peoria County Bar Assn. Roman Catholic. Office: US Dist Ct 204 Federal Bldg 100 NE Monroe St Peoria IL 61602-1003

MIHRAM, GEORGE ARTHUR, mathematician; b. Norman, Okla., Sept. 21, 1939; s. Russell George and Ella Lee (Stanaland) M.; m. Danielle Redibaum, Dec. 22, 1965. BS summa cum laude, U. Okla., 1960; postgrad., Wash. State U., Pullman, 1960—61; MS, Okla. State U., 1962, PhD, 1965. Operational rschr. Ops. Rsch., Inc., Silver Spring, Md., 1965-66; systems analyst Joint Chiefs of Staff, Washington, 1966-68; asst. prof. U. Pa., Phila., 1968-74; mem. faculty U. So. Calif., University Park, 1978-79. Cons. IBM Corp., East Fishkill, NY, 1973, Acad. Natural Scis., Phila., 1970-71, Office Asst. Sec. Def., 1969, Hdqrs. USAF, 1968-69. Author: Statistical Foundations and Methodology, 1972, An Epistle to Dr. Benjamin Franklin, 1975, A Critique of World Models, 1975; co-author: Human Knowledge: Role of Models, Metaphors, and Analogy, 1974, Religion: Man's Earliest Science, 1978, Credibility: Every Computer Programme is a Simulation Model, 1985, Tele-cybernetics: Implications for the International Marketplace, 1988, Telecybernetics: Inferences from Living Systems to Both Science and Political Science, 1994, The Enhanced Electronic Postmark, 1997, Resolving Two Congressional Duties, 2000, The Scientific Method, 2003; assoc. editor: Simulation, 1973-75, Internat. Jour. Gen. Systems, 1973—, Modeling and Simulation, 1974-92; contbr. Oxford English Dictionary, 2d edit. Mem. peer rev. panels NSF, Washington, 1974, 82. Capt. U.S. Army, 1966-68. Decorated Joint Svcs. Commendation medal; recipient award Conf. Simulation of Large Systems, Bielefeld, Germany, 1980, award Conf. Systems Rsch. Cybernetics, Baden-Baden, Germany, 2003; Fulbright scholar U. Sydney, Australia, 1964-65; NSF rsch. initiation grantee, 1970-72, internat. travel grantee, 1975, NATO grantee, 1977. Mem. AAAS (fellow nominee 1974, profl. socs. ethics group 1987-95, program liaison to Am. Math. Soc. com. 1992-94), Am. Philos. Assn., Soc. Study Social Problems, Internat. Soc. Sys. Sci., Soc. Computer Simulation (chmn. tech. com. on verification and validation 1974-75), Soc. Lit. and Sci., Internat. Assc. Statis. Computing, Internat. Assn. Cybernetics, Math. Assn. Am., Am. Math. Soc., Am. Statis. Assn., Biometric Soc., Can. Math. Soc., Assn. Computing Machinery, Interface (of Computer Sci. and Stats.) Found., Ops. Rsch. Soc. Am. (ethics and profl. practice com. 1983-95), Sigma Xi, Phi Beta Kappa, Pi Mu Epsilon, Phi Eta Sigma. Avocation: mankind's search for truth mimes nature's biochemical process ensuring survival. Home and Office: PO Box 1188 Princeton NJ 08542-1188

MIHURA, JONI L. psychologist, educator; b. Stillwater, Okla., Sept. 25, 1960; PhD, Okla. State U. Lic. clin. psychologist Ohio. Assoc. prof. psychology U. Toledo, 1996—. Rschr. in field; pvt. practice psychotherapy. Predoctoral fellow, Ford Found., 1990—93. Mem.: APA (fellow 1999—2000), Soc. Psychotherapy Rsch., Soc. Personality Assessment (Samuel J. and Anne G. Beck award for outstanding early career sch. in personality assessment 2002). Office: U Toledo 2801 W Bancroft St Toledo OH 43606

MIKA, JOSEPH JOHN, program director, educator, consultant; b. McKees Rocks, Pa., Mar. 1, 1948; s. George Joseph and Sophie Ann (Stec) M.; m. Marianne Hartzell; children: Jason-Paul Joseph, Matthew Douglas, Meghan Leigh. BA in English, U. Pitts., 1969, MLS, 1971, PhD in Libr. Sci., 1980. Asst. libr., instr. Ohio State U., Mansfield, 1971-73; asst. libr., asst. prof. Johnson State Coll., Vt., 1973-75; grad. asst., tchg. fellow Sch. Libr. and Info. Sci., U. Pitts., 1975-77; asst. dean, assoc. prof. libr. svc. U. So. Miss., Hattiesburg, 1977-86; dir. libr. and info. sci. program Wayne State U., 1986—95, 2002—, prof., 1986—. Cons. to libraries; co-owner Libr. Jobs Network, Libr. Tng. Network. Editor Jour. of Edn. for Libr. and Info. Sci., 1995—2005. Col. USAR. Decorated DSM. Mem. ALA (councilor 1983-86, 98-2001, chmn. constn. and bylaws com. 1985-86), Assn. Libr. and Info. Sci. Edn. (chmn. membership com. 1982-83, chmn. nominating com. 1982, exec. bd. 1986), Miss. Libr. Assn. (pres.-elect 1985), Mich. Libr. Assn. (chair libr. edn. com. 1989), Leadership Acad. (oversight com. 1989-95), Assn. Coll. and Rsch. Librs. (chmn. 1982-83, chmn. budget com. 1982-83), Soc. Miss. Archivists (treas., exec. bd. 1981-83), Mich. Ctr. for the Book (chair 1994-2001), Kiwanis (Hattiesburg), Beta Phi Mu (pres.-elect 1987-89, pres. 1989-91), Phi Delta Kappa. Home: 222 Abbott Woods Dr East Lansing MI 48823-1995 Office: Wayne State U Libr and Info Sci Program 106 Kresge Library Detroit MI 48202 E-mail: aa2500@wayne.edu.

MIKALAUSKAS, KENNETH, communications executive; BA in Math., Swarthmore Coll.; MBA in Fin., Columbia U. With Comcast Corp., Phila., 1988—, dir. corp. fin., asst. treas., 1996—98, v.p. fin., 1998—, asst. treas. Office: Comcast 1500 Market St Philadelphia PA 19102

MIKALOW, ALFRED ALEXANDER, II, deep sea diver, marine surveyor, marine diving consultant; b. N.Y.C., Jan. 19, 1921; m. Janice Brenner, Aug. 1, 1960; children: Alfred Alexander, Jon Alfred. Student, Rutgers U., 1940; MS, U. Calif., Berkeley, 1948; MA, Rochdale U. (Can.), 1950. Owner Coastal Diving Co., Oakland, Calif., 1950—, Divers Supply, Oakland, 1952—; dir. Coastal Sch. Deep Sea Diving, Oakland, 1950—. Capt. and master rsch. vessel Coastal Researcher I; mem. Marine Inspection Bur., Oakland. marine diving contractor, cons. Mem. adv. bd. Medic Alert Found., Turlock, Calif., 1960—. Author: Fell's Guide to Sunken Treasure Ships of the World, 1972; (with H. Rieseberg) The Knight from Maine, 1974. Lt. comdr. USN, 1941-47, PTO, 1949-50, Korea. Decorated Purple Heart, Silver Star. Mem. Divers Assn. Am. (pres. 1970-74), Treasury Recovery, Inc. (pres. 1972-75), Internat. Assn. Profl. Divers, Assn. Diving Contractors, Calif. Assn. Pvt. Edn. (no. v.p. 1971-72), Authors Guild, Internat. Game Fish Assn., U.S. Navy League, U.S. Res. Officers Assn., Tailhook Assn., U.S. Submarine Vets. WWII, Explorer Club (San Francisco), Calif. Assn. Marine Surveyors (pres. 1988—), Soc. Naval Archs. and Marine Engrs. (assoc.), Masons, Leions, Am. Legion, VFW. Office: 52 Mira Loma Rd Orinda CA 94563-2332

MIKALSON, JON DENNIS, classics educator; b. Milw., Aug. 1, 1943; s. John Martin and Evelyn Kathryn (Heuser) M.; m. Mary Helen Villemonte, Aug. 28, 1966; children: Melissa, Jacquelyn. BA, U. Wis., 1965; postgrad., Am. Sch. Classical Studies, Athens, Greece, 1968-69; PhD, Harvard U., 1970. Asst. prof. classics U. Va., Charlottesville, 1970-75, assoc. prof., 1975-84, prof., 1984—, William R. Kenan Jr. prof. classics, 1999—, chmn. dept. classics, 1978-90. Dir. Echols Scholar Program, 1997-2000; vis. scholar Corpus Christi Coll., Cambridge, Eng., 1977-78, mem. Inst. for Advanced Study, Princeton, N.J., 1984-85; Whitehead prof. Am. Sch. Classical Studies, 1995-96. Author: The Sacred and Civil Calendar of the Athenian Year, 1975, Athenian Popular Religion, 1983, Honor Thy Gods: Popular Religion in Greek Tragedy, 1991, Religion in Hellenistic Athens, 1998, Herodotus and Religion in the Persian Wars, 2003, Ancient Greek Religion, 2004; contbr. articles to profl. and scholarly jours. James Rignall Wheeler fellow Am. Sch. Classical Studies, 1968-69, NEH fellow, 1977-78, Herodotus fellow Inst. for Advanced Study, 1984-85. Mem. Am. Philol. Assn., Am. Sch. Classical Studies, Archeol. Inst. of Am., Classical Assn. of Middle West and South (pres. so. sect. 1988-90), Classical Assn. of Va., Phi Beta Kappa, Phi Eta Sigma, Phi Kappa Phi, Omicron Delta Kappa. Clubs: Lions. Home: PO Box 664 Crozet VA 22932-0664 Office: U Va Dept Classics PO Box 400788 453 Cabell Hall Charlottesville VA 22904-4788 Office Phone: 434-924-3008. Business E-Mail: jdm9x@virginia.edu.

MIKAN, KATHLEEN JOYCE KEHRER, medical/surgical nurse, educator; b. Galion, Ohio; BSN cum laude, Ohio State U., Columbus, 1961; MSN, U. Colo., Denver, 1963; PhD, Mich. State U., East Lansing, 1972; postdoctoral, U. Utah, Salt Lake City, 1991. Staff nurse Ohio State U. Hosp., Columbus, 1961; asst. instr. Ohio State U., Columbus, 1961-62, instr. med.-surg. nursing, team nursing and fundamentals of nursing, 1963-65; asst. prof. Mich. State U., East Lansing, 1965-67, co-dir. multi-media project, 1967-69; asst. prof. Case Western Res. U., Cleve., 1970-72, assoc. in nursing, 1970-74, program dir. Health Sci. Communications Ctr., 1971-74, ednl. specialist primary health practitioner program, 1972-74, assoc. prof., 1972-74, adminstrv. officer, 1973-74; dir. learning resources U. Ala., Birmingham, 1974-91, prof., 1974—, mem. faculty post master fellowship program in oncology nursing edn., 1980-83, media dir., 1984-87, 1985-89, project faculty, cost mgmt. edn. for nurses contract, 1986-88, media expert, 1988-91, prof., 1974—. Nurse Camp Taconic, Pittsfield, Mass., summers, 1961, 62; mem. planning com. 5th Nat. Learning Resources Conf. U. Tex., San Antonio, 1994; SCAMC referee for paper selection Ann. Symposium on Computer Applications in Med. Care, 1985—; out of state expert rsch. proposal reviewer La. Edn. Quality Support Fund State of La. Bd. Regents, 1990; cons. expansion of learning resource capacity and computer utilization to various schs. nursing; mem. spl. project review panel divsn. of Nursing HEW, 1989—; mem. adv. bd. dirs. The Soc. Nursing Profls., 1991—; speaker, presenter in field; cons. WHO, Indonesia, 1995; sec. Univ. Ala. Birmingham Faculty Senate, 1995-97. Manuscript reviewer FOCUS, 1984—; author (with Eula Aiken) In Computer Applications in Nursing Education and Practice, 1992; contbr. articles to profl. jours. Mem. Lung Resource Ctr. Com. Ala. Lung Assn., 1980-90, community health and program support com., 1990—. Recipient Red Ribbon award Am. Film Festival Case Western Res. U., 1972, Bronze award Internat. Film and TV Festival Case Western Res. U., 1972. Fellow Am. Acad. Nursing (Svc. cert. 1990); mem. ANA (coun. on computer applications in nursing), Assn. for Ednl. Communications and Tech., Nat. League for Nursing (nat. forum on computers in health care and nursing, coun. on nursing informatics), Ala. Instrl. Media Assn., Ala. Lung Assn., Ala. State Nurses Assn., Am. Acad. of Nursing (pub. rels. com. 1987-90), Ohio State U. Nursing Alumnae Assn., U. Colo. Alumni Assn., U. Colo. Sch. of Nursing Alumni, Lambda Alpha Delta, Sigma Theta Tau (Internat. Officer award 1985-91, heritage com. 1985-91, sec. 1985-91, publ. com. 1987-91, Internat. Heritage award, chair 1991, co-chair resolutions com. biennial conv. 1991, co-chair voting com. biennial conv. 1991, libr. sci. com. 1991—, evaluation visitor 1991, installing officer 1992), Phi Kappa Phi, Am. Nurses Found. Century Club.

MIKATA, YOZO, mechanical engineer, application developer; b. Nichinan, Miyazaki, Japan, Jan. 29, 1956; arrived in U.S., 1981; s. Chotaro and Fumiko (Kato) Mikata. BSCE, U. Tokyo, 1979, MSCE, 1981; PhD in Mech. Engring., U. Del., Newark, 1984. Postdoctoral fellow Northwestern U., Evanston, Ill., 1984-87; postgrad. rsch. engr. U. Calif., San Diego, 1987-89; rsch. assoc. U. Ill., Urbana-Champaign, 1989-90; asst. prof. Old Dominion U., Norfolk, Va., 1990-96; sr. rsch. scientist ICAM, NASA Langley Rsch. Ctr., Hampton, Va., 1996-99; software engr. Bell Atlantic Network Svcs., Silver Spring, Md., 1999-2000; structural mechanics engr. Lockheed Martin Co., Schenectady, N.Y., 2000—. Contbr. articles to profl. jours. Rsch. grantee, Engring. Found., 1992, NASA Langley Rsch. Ctr., 1993, 1994. Mem.: ASME, Am. Acad. Mechanics, Soc. Indsl. and Applied Math. Achievements include research in on micromechanics of coated fiber composite materials providing analytical solutions, and thereby contributed to the understanding of local mechanical behavior of coatings; on wave propagation, fracture mechanics, dynamic phase transformation. Avocations: swimming, dance, jazz, astronomy, number theory. Office: Lockheed Martin Co PO Box 1072 Schenectady NY 12301

MIKEL, THOMAS KELLY, JR., laboratory administrator; b. Aug. 27, 1946; s. Thomas Kelly and Vrazo Anne (Katherine) M. BA, San Jose State U., 1973; MA, U. Calif., Santa Barbara, 1975. Asst. dir. Santa Barbara Underseas Found., 1975—76; marine biologist PJB Labs., Ventura, Calif., 1981—88; lab. dir. ABC Labs., Ventura, 1988—. Instr. oceanography Ventura Coll., 1980—81; chair joint task group, sect. author 20th edit. Stds. Methods Exam. Water & Wastewater APHA, 1996; biol. coord. Anacapa Underwater Natural trail U.S. Nat. Park Svc., 1976; designer ecol. restoration program of upper Newport Bay, Orange County, Calif., 78; rsch. contbr. 3d Internat. Artificial Reef Conf., Newport Beach, Calif., 1983, Ann. Conf. Am. Petroleum Inst., Houston. With U.S. Army, 1968—70. Mem.: ASTME (rsch. contbr. 10th ann. symposium 1986), Soc. Environ. Toxicology and Chemistry (bd. dirs. 2000—), Soc. Population Ecologists, Assn. Environ. Profls. Democrat.

MIKELL, FRANK LEONARD, cardiologist; b. Augusta, Ga., Apr. 26, 1947; s. Frank Leonard and Mary (Herndon) M.; three children. BA, Emory U., 1969; B in Med. Scis., Dartmouth Med. Sch., 1972; MD, Emory U. Med. Sch.,

1974. Asst. prof. medicine U. Minn., Mpls., 1979-82; interventional cardiologist Prairie Cardiovasc. Cons., Springfield, Ill., 1982—. Clin. assoc. prof. medicine So. Ill. U. Med. Sch., Springfield, 1987—. Fellow Am. Coll. Cardiology, Am. Coll. Chest Physicians, Am. Coll. Physicians, Soc. Cardiac Angiography & Intervention, Coun. Clin. Cardiology Am. Heart Assn. Avocations: golf, hunting. Office: Prairie Cardiovasc Cons PO Box 19420 Springfield IL 62794-9420

MIKELS, RICHARD ELIOT, lawyer; b. Cambridge, Mass., July 14, 1947; s. Albert Louis and Charlotte Betty (Shapiro) M.; m. Deborah Gwen Katz, Aug. 29, 1970; children: Allison Brooke, Robert Jarrett. BS in Bus. Adminstrn., Boston U., 1969, JD cum laude, 1972. Bar: Mass. 1972, U.S. Dist. Ct. Mass. 1974, U.S. Ct. Appeals (1st cir.) 1978. Legal examiner ICC, Washington, 1972-74; ptnr. Riemer & Braunstein, Boston, 1974-80; ptnr., chmn. comml. law sect. Peabody & Brown, Boston, 1980-88; mem., chmn. comml. law sect. Mintz, Levin, Cohn, Ferris, Glovsky and Popeo, P.C., Boston, 1988—. Contbr. articles to profl. jours. Tng. adv. com. Jewish Vocat. Svc., Boston, 1991, 95, 96, bd. dirs., 1995-99, vice chair microenterprise adv. com. 1997; vice-chair lawyers com. Combined Jewish Philanthropies, 1994, 95. Fellow Am. Coll. Bankruptcy; mem. ABA, Am. Bankruptcy Inst. (bd. dirs. 2000—), Assn. Comml. Fin. Attys., Comml. Law League Am., Mass. Bar Assn., Boston Bar Assn., Boston U. Law Alumni Assn. (mem. exec. com., pres. exec. com. 2000-01). Office: Mintz Levin Cohn Ferris Glovsky & Popeo PC 1 Financial Ctr Fl 39 Boston MA 02111-2657

MIKELSONS, J. GEORGE, air aerospace transportation executive; Chmn., CEO Am. Trans Air, Inc., Indpls., 1980-98, chmn., 1998—. Office: Am Trans Inc Indpls Internat Airport PO Box 51609 Indianapolis IN 46251-0609

MIKESELL, JOHN L. economics professor; b. Bloomington, Ind., Oct. 23, 1942; s. R.M. and Minnie (Shigley) M.; m. Karen Roberts, June 13, 1964; children: Elizabeth, Tom, Dan. BA in Econs., Wabash Coll., 1964; MA in Econs., U. Ill., 1965, PhD in econ., 1969. Asst. prof. econs. W.Va. U., Morgantown, W.Va., 1968-72; assoc. prof. sch. pub. and environ. affairs Ind. U., Bloomington, 1973-78, prof., 1978—. Assoc. dean acad. affairs Ind. U., 1986—92, dir. grad. profl. programs, 2001—. Author: Fiscal Administration, 2003; co-author: (with J. Due) Sales Taxation (outstanding acad. book 1984); contbr. articles to profl. jours. Mem. Phi Beta Kappa, Omicron Delta Epsilon. Home: 5930 E Lampkins Ridge Rd Bloomington IN 47401-9726 Office: Ind U 260 Sch of Pub Environ Affairs Bloomington IN 47405-1701

MIKESELL, MARVIN WRAY, geography educator; b. Kansas City, Mo., June 16, 1929; s. Loy George and Clara (Wade) M.; m. Reine-Marie de France, Apr. 1, 1957. BA, UCLA, 1952, MA, 1953; PhD, U. Calif.-Berkeley, 1959. Instr. to prof. geography U. Chgo., 1958—, chmn. dept. geography, 1969-74, 83-86. Del. U.S. Nat. Commn. for UNESCO Author: Northern Morocco, 1961; editor: Readings in Cultural Geography, 1962, Geographers Abroad, 1973, Perspectives on Environment, 1974. Fellow Am. Geog. Soc. (hon.); mem. Assn. Am. Geographers (pres. 1975-76, Disting. Career award 1995). Clubs: Quadrangle. Home: 1155 E 56th St Chicago IL 60637-1530 Office: Com Geog Studies 5828 S University Ave Chicago IL 60637-1583 E-mail: mmikesel@uchicago.edu.

MIKESELL, RAYMOND FRECH, economics professor; b. Eaton, Ohio, Feb. 13, 1913; s. Otho Francis and Josephine (Frech) M.; m. Desyl DeLauder, 1937 (div.); children: George DeLauder and Norman DeLauder (twins); m. Irene Langdoc, 1957 (dec.); m. Grace Schneiders, 1997. Student, Carnegie Inst. Tech., 1931-33; BA cum laude, MA, Ohio U., 1935, PhD, 1939. Asst. prof. econ. U. Wash., 1937-41; economist OPA, Washington, 1941-42, U.S. Treasury Dept., 1942-46, rep., 1943-44, cons., 1946-47; on Middle East affairs FOA, 1953; chief fgn. minerals div. Pres.'s Materials Policy Commn., 1951-52; mem. staff Fgn. Econ. Policy Com. (Randall Com.), 1953-54; mem. U.S. Currency Mission to Saudi Arabia, 1948; spl. U.S. rep. to Israel, summer 1952; mem. U.S. mission to Israel, Ethiopia, summer 1953; prof. econs. U. Va., 1946-57; W.E. Miner prof. econs. U. Oreg., 1957-87, emeritus prof. econ., 1987—; dir. Inst. Internat. Studies and Overseas Adminstrn., 1958-60; assoc. dir. Inst. Internat. Studies and Overseas Adminstrn. U. Oreg., 1960-68; vis. prof. Grad. Inst. Internat. Studies, Geneva, 1964. Sr. staff mem. Council Econ. Advisers, Exec. Office of Pres., 1955-56, cons. to Council Econ. Advisers, 1956-57; cons. Pan Am. Union, 1954-63, Dept. State, 1947-53, 63-67, 71-83, Ford Found., 1962, Dept. Commerce, 1962-64, ICA, 1952-53, 61-62, OAS, 1963-73, AID, 1964-71; mem. UN Econ. Commn. for Latin Am. working group on regional market, 1958; cons. Senate Fgn. Relations Com., 1962, 67, World Bank, 1968, Inter-Am. Devel. Bank, 1968-75; mem. panel advisers Sec. Treasury, 1965-69; sr. fellow Nat. Bur. Econ. Research, 1972-73 Author: U.S. Economic Policy and International Relations, 1952, Foreign Exchange in the Postwar World, 1954, The Emerging Pattern of International Payments, 1954, Foreign Investments in Latin America, 1955, Promoting United States Private Investments Abroad, 1957, Agricultural Surpluses and Export Policy, 1958, U.S. Private and Government Investment Abroad, 1962, (with M. Trued) Arabian Oil, 1949, (with H. Chenery) Postwar Bilateral Payments Agreements, 1955, (with J. Behrman) Financing Free World Trade with the Sino-Soviet Bloc, 1958, Public International Lending for Development, 1966, (with R.W. Adler) Public External Financing of Developing Banks, 1966, Public Foreign Capital for Private Enterprises in Developing Countries, 1966, The Economics of Foreign Aid, 1968, Financing World Trade, 1969, (with others) Foreign Investment in the Petroleum and Mineral Industries, 1971, (with H. Furth) Foreign Dollar Balances and the International Role of the Dollar, 1974, Foreign Investment in the Copper Industry, 1975, The World Copper Industry, 1979, New Patterns of World Mineral Development, 1979, The Economics of Foreign Aid and Self-Sustaining Development, 1983, Foreign Investment in Mining Projects, 1983, Petroleum Company Operations and Agreements in the Developing Countries, 1984, Stockpiling Strategic Materials, 1986, Nonfuel Minerals: Foreign Dependence and National Security, 1987, (with John W. Whitney) The World Mining Industry: Investment Strategy and Public Policy, 1987, The Global Copper Industry: Problems and Prospects, 1988, (with Lawrence F. Williams) International Banks and the Environment, 1992, Economic Development and the Environment, 1992, The Bretton Woods Debates, 1994, (with Richard Auty) Sustainable Development in Mineral Economies, 1998, Foreign Adventures of an Economist, 2000; mem. editl. adv. bd. Middle East Jour., 1947-58; mem. bd. editors: Am. Econ. Rev., 1953-55. Home: 2290 Spring Blvd Eugene OR 97403-1860

MIKIEWICZ, ANNA DANIELLA, marketing and international business exporter; b. Chgo., Dec. 22, 1960; d. Zdislaw and Lucy (Magnusweska) M. BS in Mktg., Elmhurst Coll., 1982; postgrad., Triton Coll. Asst. to midwestern regional mgr. Melster Pub. Co., Chgo., 1983; sales rep. First Impressions, Elk Grive, Ill., 1984; asst. to Midwestern dist. mgr. Airco Ind. Gases, Broadview, Carol Stream, Ill., 1985; customer svc. & ops. mgr. Yamazen USA, Inc., Schaumburg, Ill., 1985-88; nat. sales & mktg. coord. Kitamura Machinery U.S.A. Inc., 1988-95; mktg. mgr. Beth Lee Boutique, 1995-97; internat. bus. export control sales coord. MHI Machine Tool USA, Inc. subs. Mistubishi Heavy Industries, 1997-99; internat. bus. asst. to exec. v.p. sales America Excel, Inc., Palatine, Ill., 1999—; internat. bus. Brazil Market JST Sales Am., Inc., Palatine, 2000—. Named Chgo. Polish Queen Polish Am. Culture Club, 1983-84. Mem. NAFE. Republican. Roman Catholic.

MIKITA, JOSEPH KARL, broadcast executive; b. Va., Oct. 3, 1918; s. John and Catherine (Wargofcak) M.; m. Mary Therese Benya, Nov. 26, 1942; children: Patty-Jane Mikita McGlynn, Michael, M. Noël Mikita Garagiola. BS, Fordham U., 1939; MS, Columbia U., 1940. Treas., controller Capital Cities Broadcasting Co., Albany, N.Y., 1955-58; controller Westinghouse Broadcasting Co., Inc., N.Y.C., 1958-60, v.p. fin., 1960-64, v.p. fin. and adminstrn., 1964-65, sr. v.p., 1965-69, 1975—; also dir., exec. v.p. Westinghouse Electric Corp. for Broadcasting, Learning and Leisure Activities, N.Y.C., 1969-75. Dir. Sutro Tower, Inc. Author: (with others) The Business of Broadcasting, 1964. Bd. dirs. Fordham U. Council, Albany County Workshop, Albany County Heart Assn., Citizens For Reasonable Growth, Boca Raton; chmn. bd. Instructional TV. Served to maj. AUS, 1940-45, ETO. Recipient Order of Merit (Silver), Westinghouse Electric Corp., Disting. Service Alumni award Fordham U., 1969. Mem. AICPA, Internat. Radio and TV Soc., N.Y. Soc. CPAs, Fin. Execs. Inst. (dir., past pres. Manhattan chpt.), Inst. Broadcasting Fin. Mgmt. (past dir.), Town Club, Westchester Country Club, Boca Raton Club, M.G.A., JDM Country Club, Royal Palm Yacht and Country Club, Palm Beach County Golf Assn., Golden Harbour Yacht Club (commodore), Rotary (1st v.p. N.Y.). Home: 3125 NE 7th Dr Boca Raton FL 33431-6906 Office: 90 Park Ave New York NY 10016-1301 Personal E-mail: jkmikita@aol.com.

MIKITKA, GERALD PETER, investment banker, financial consultant; s. Michael and Helen M.; m. Nancy Lee, 1977; children: Richard, Jeffrey, Jennifer. BSBA in Fin., Roosevelt U., 1966, postgrad., 1967. Diplomate: registered investment advisor. Sr. investment exec. Shearson Hammill & Co., Chgo., 1967-73; chmn., pres. Capital Directions, Inc., Chgo., 1973—. Pres. CDI Fin. Advisors, Chgo., 1974—, CDI Properties, Chgo., 1974—, CDI Communications, Inc., Chgo., 1978—, A.B. Properties Inc., Chgo., 1986—, Am. Eagle Realty Inc., Chgo., 1988—, Grand Caribbean Properties Inc., Chgo., 1988, Cain Estates Inc., Chgo., 1988—, Caribbean Sea Properties Inc., Chgo., 1989—. Served with U.S. Army, 1967-69. Mem. Nat. Assn. Securities Dealers, Securities Investment Protection Assn., Broadcast Fin. Mgmt. Assn., Nat. Radio Broadcast Assn., Internat. Assn. Fin. Planning. Lodges: Rotary.

MIKKELSON, DEAN HAROLD, geological engineer, writer; b. Devils Lake, ND, July 25, 1922; s. John Harold and Theodora (Eklund) M.; m. Delphene (Doss), May 30, 1946; 1 child, Lynn Dee Hoffman. Attended, N.D. State Coll., 1940—41; midshipman, U.S. Naval Acad., 1942—45; BS in Geol. Engring., U. N.D., 1956. Registered engr., Okla. 2d officer U.S. Lines, Quaker Lines-States Lines, Portland, Oreg., 1945—48; ptnr. J.I. Case Farm Machinery and Packard Automobile Franchises, Devils Lake, ND, 1948—52; oil and gas lease broker Devils Lake, ND, 1952—54; geologist Sohio Petroleum Co., Okla. City, 1956—58; geol. engr. Petrobras, Belem do Para, Brazil, 1958—60; pvt. practice Okla. City, 1961—78; pres., owner Dogwatch Petroleum, Inc., Okla. City, 1978—98; owner Spindrift Press, Okla. City, 1998—. Agrl. pilot summers in N.D., Mont., Tex., N.Mex., 1952-56. Author: (as Dee Geo) Danny; contbr. articles to profl. journals. Candidate Okla. Rep. State Legislature, Oklahoma City, 1958; del. various county and state conv., N.D. and Okla., 1948-68. With N.D. Nat. Guard, 1938-40, U.S. Army Air Corps., 1942, U.S. Naval Acad., 1942-45, U.S. Maritime Svc., 1945-48. Mem. Okla. City Geol. Soc., Masons, Shriners, Jesters, Am. Legion, Sportsmans Country Club. Republican. Avocations: hunting, fishing, golf, painting, singing. Office: Spindrift Press 4725 NW 59 Ter Oklahoma City OK 73122

MIKKLESEN, EDWIN JENS, psychiatrist; b. Nebr., 1948; MD, U. Nebr., 1973. Bd. cert. psychiatry, bd. cert. child psychiatry. Intern Mayo Clinic, Rochester, 1973—74; resident psychiatry Mass. Mental Health Ctr./Harvard Med. Sch., Boston, 1974—76; resident rsch. NIMH, Bethesda, Md., 1976—78; resident child psychiatry Yale Child Study Ctr., New Haven, 1978—80; with Mass. Mental Health Ctr., Boston; assoc. prof. psychiatry Harvard Med. Sch. Author (with others): No Safe Place: Toxic Waste, Leukemia, and Community Action, 1997. Recipient Frank J. Menolascino award, Am. Psychiat. Assn., 2003.

MIKLOSHAZY, ATTILA, bishop; b. Apr. 15, 1931; Ordained priest Roman Cath. Ch., 1961, consecrated bishop Roman Cath. Ch., 1989. Priest Soc. of Jesus, 1961—89; bishop Apostolate to Hungarians, Scarborough, Canada, 1989—. Mem.: Jesuit Soc. Office: St Augustine's Sem 2661 Kingston Rd Scarborough ON Canada M1M 1M3

MIKULAS, DANA CAMERON, voice educator, music educator; b. Birmingham, Ala., Nov. 13, 1977; d. Terry Ray and Patricia Ann Wade; m. Jonathan Michael Mikulas. MusB, Dallas Bapt. U., 1998—2000. Kodaly cert. Plano ISD, Tex., 2003. Voiceteacher RMTA, Richardson, Tex., 1999—; music tchr. Plano ISD, Plano, Tex., 2000—. Performer: (opera) Hansel & Gretel; musician: (albums) The Love I Found in You. Praise & worship leader, soloist, choir mem. First Bapt. Ch., Plano, Tex., 2000—03. Recipient All-Level Music award, Dallas Bapt. U., 2000; Music scholarship, 1998—2000, grant, Plano Futures Found., 2003. Mem.: Tex. Music Educators Assn., Music Teachers Nat. Assn., Tex. Music Teachers Assn., Richardson Music Teachers Assn. (co-chairman of sacred festival, monitor chmn. for festivals 2001—03), Nat. Honors Soc., Zeta Tau Alpha (music & svc. committees 1996—98).

MIKULSKI, BARBARA ANN, senator; b. Balt., July 20, 1936; d. William and Christine (Kutz) M. BA, Mt. St. Agnes Coll., 1958; MSW, U. Md., 1965; LLD (hon.), Goucher Coll., 1973, Hood Coll., 1978, Bowie State U., 1989, Morgan State U., 1990, U. Mass., 1991; DHL (hon.), Pratt Inst., 1974. Tchr. Vista Tng. Ctr. Mount St. Mary's Sem., Balt.; social worker Balt. Dept. Social Services, 1961-63, 66-70; mem. Balt. City Council, 1971-76, 95th-99th Congresses from 3d Md. Dist., 1977-87; U.S. senator from Md., 1987—; sec. Dem. Conf. 104th-106th Congress. Adj. prof. Loyola Coll., 1972-76; mem. U.S. Senate labor and human resources com., 1987—, ranking mem. subcom. on aging, 1993—; mem. appropriations com., 1987, ranking mem. subcom. on vets., housing, and ind. agys., 1987—. Bd. visitors U.S. Naval Acad. Recipient Nat. Citizen of Yr. award Buffalo Am.-Polit. Eagle, 1973, Woman of Yr. Bus. & Profl. Women's Club Assn., 1973, Outstanding Alumnus U. Md. Sch. Social Work, 1973, Govt. Social Responsibility award, 1991. Mem. LWV. Democrat.

MIKUMO, AKIKO, lawyer; b. Kyoto, June 18, 1953; BA, U. Calif., Berkeley, 1978; JD, NYU, 1982. Assoc. Weil, Gotshal & Manges LLP, N.Y.C., 1982—90, ptnr., 1990—, head U.S. practice London, 1998—2000. Mem.: ABA (mem. com. on corp. law 1993—), Assn. of the Bar of the City of N.Y. Office: Weil Gotshal & Manges LLP 767 Fifth Ave New York NY 10153

MIKUS, ELEANORE ANN, artist; b. Detroit, July 25, 1927; d. Joseph and Bertha (Englot) M.; m. Richard Burns, July 6, 1949 (div. 1963); children: Richard, Hillary, Gabrielle. Student, Mich. State U., 1946-49, U. Mex., summer 1948; B.F.A., U. Denver, 1957, MA, 1967; postgrad., Art Students League, 1958, NYU, 1959-60. Asst. prof. Cornell U., Ithaca, N.Y., 1979-80, assoc. prof., 1980-92, prof. art, 1992-94, prof. emerita, 1994—. Asst. prof. art Monmouth Coll., West Long Branch, N.J., 1966-70, prof. Cornell, Rome, 1989; vis. lectr. painting Cooper Union, N.Y.C., 1970-72, Central Sch. Art and Design, London, 1973-77, Kensington Inst., London, 1974-77, Harrow (Eng.) Coll. Tech. and Art, 1975-76. One-woman shows at Pace Gallery, N.Y.C. (1963, 64, 65) and O.K. Harris Gallery (1971, 72, 73, 74), N.Y.C., Baskett Gallery, Cin., 1982, 84-85, Claudia Carr Gallery, 1998—, Mitchell Algus Gallery, N.Y.C., 1998, 2003, 04; represented in permanent collections including Met. Mus. Art, N.Y.C., Mus. Modern Art, N.Y.C., Whitney Mus., N.Y.C., Los Angeles County Mus., Cin. Mus., Birmingham (Ala.) Mus. Art, Norton Simon Mus., Pasadena, Bklyn. Mus., Honolulu Acad. Arts, Indpls. Mus. Art, Nat. Gallery Art, Washington, Victoria and Albert Mus., London, Libr. of Congress, Washington, Tucson Mus. of Art, Blanton Mus. U. Tex., U. Ariz. Mus. Art, Tucson, Univ. Ariz., Tucson, De Cordova Mus., Lincoln, Mass.; subject of book Eleanore Mikus, Shadows of the Real (by Robert Hobbs and Judith Bernstock), 1991. Guggenheim fellow, 1966-67; Tamarind fellow, 1968; MacDowell fellow, 1969; Xadpo fellow drawing and painting, 2004. Home: PO Box 4775 Ithaca NY 14852-4775 Office: Cornell U Dept Art Tjaden Hall Ithaca NY 14853 also: 270 Luce Rd Groton NY 13073-9747 Office Phone: 607-533-7766. E-mail: mikusart44@hotmail.com.

MIKVA, ABNER JOSEPH, lawyer, retired federal judge; b. Milw., Jan. 21, 1926; s. Henry Abraham and Ida (Fishman) M.; m. Zoe Wise, Sept. 19, 1948; children: Mary, Laurie, Rachel. JD cum laude, U. Chgo., 1951; DL (hon.), U. Ill., 1980, Am. U., 1991, Northwestern U., 1991, Tulane U., 1993, Ill. Inst. Tech., 1997, Santa Clara U., 2000, Wm. Mitchell Coll. Law, 2001; DHL (hon.), Hebrew U., 1989, U. Wis., 1995, De Paul U. Law Sch., 2002. Bar: Ill. 1951, D.C. 1978. Law clk. to Hon. Sherman Minton U.S. Supreme Ct., 1951; ptnr. Devoe, Shadur, Mikva & Plotkin, Chgo., 1952-68, D'Ancona, Pflaum, Wyatt & Riskind, 1973-74; lectr. Northwestern U. Law Sch., Chgo., 1973-75, U. Pa. Law Sch., 1983-85, Georgetown Law Sch., 1986-88, Duke U. Law Sch., Durham, NC, 1990-91, U. Chgo. Law Sch., 1992-93; mem. Ill. Gen. Assembly from 23d Dist., 1956-66, 91st-92d Congresses from 2d Dist. Ill., 94th-96th Congresses from 10th Dist. Ill., mem. ways and means com., judiciary com.; chmn. Dem. Study Group, 1979; from judge to chief judge U.S. Cir. Ct. Appeals D.C., 1979-94, chief judge, 1991-94; counsel to the Pres. The White House, Washington, 1994-96; arbitrator JAMS, Inc., 1997—. Vis. prof., Walter Schaefer chair in pub. policy U. Chgo., 1996-98; vis. prof. U. Ill. Coll. Law, 1998-2000, U. Chgo., 2000—. Author: The American Congress: The First Branch, 1983, The Legislative Process, 1995, An Introduction to Statutory Interpretation, 1997. With USAAF, WWII. Sr. fellow Inst. Govt. & Pub. Affairs U. Ill., 1998-2000; recipient Page One award Chgo. Newspaper Guild, 1964, Best Legislator award Ind. Voters Ill., 1956-66, Alumni medal U. Chgo., 1996, Paul Douglas Ethics in Govt. award, 1998; named one of Ten Outstanding Young Men in Chgo., Jr. Assn. Commerce and Industry, 1961. Fellow Am. Acad. Arts and Scis.; mem. ABA, Chgo. Bar Assn. (bd. mgrs. 1962-64), D.C. Bar Assn., Am. Law Inst., U.S. Assn. Former Mems. Congress, Order of Coif, Phi Beta Kappa. Home: Ph 6 5020 S Lake Shore Dr Chicago IL 60615-3253 Office Phone: 773-834-5852. E-mail: amikva@law.uchicago.edu.

MILAM, JOHN DANIEL, pathologist, educator; b. Kilgore, Tex., May 22, 1933; s. Ott G. and Effie (White) M.; m. Carol Jones Milam, Aug. 1, 1959; children: Kay, Beth, John Jr., Julie. BS, La. State U., 1955, MS, 1957, MD, 1960. Attending pathologist St. Luke's Episcopal Hosp., Houston, 1967—89, chief of staff, 1981—83; cons. in pathology Tex. Children's Hosp., Houston, 1979—99, emeritus, 2000—; adj. prof. lab. medicine M.D. Anderson Cancer Ctr., U. Tex., Houston, 1990—; prof. pathology and lab. medicine U. Tex. Med. Sch., Houston, 1989—2002, prof. emeritus, 2002—; cons. in pathology Hermann Hosp., Houston, 1974—88, active med. staff, 1988—, med. dir. lab. svcs., 1990—95; chief pathology Lyndon B. Johnson Gen. Hosp., Houston, 1995—2001. Trustee Am. Bd. Pathology, 1985—96, pres., 1995, life trustee, 1996—. Contbr. numerous articles to profl. jours., abstracts, chpts. to books. Bd. dirs. Greater Houston area chpt. ARC, 1978—. Recipient Disting. Physician award, Hermann Hosp., 1996. Mem.: Houston Soc. Clin. Pathologists (pres. 1975, Harlan J. Spjut award 2003), Am. Soc. Clin. Pathologists (Commn. on Continuing Edn. Disting. Svc. award 1993, Israel Davidsohn Disting. Svc. award 2001), Tex. Soc. Pathologists (pres. 1978, George T. Caldwell award 1981), Am. Assn. Blood Banks (pres. 1984, Disting. Svc. award 1988). Republican. Baptist. Home: 11927 Arbordale Ln Houston TX 77024-5001 Office: U Tex Houston Med Sch Rm 2-022 Dept Pathology 6431 Fannin St Houston TX 77030-1501 Office Phone: 713-500-5336. Business E-Mail: john.d.milam@uth.tmc.edu.

MILAM, JOSEPH WALTON, JR., judge; b. Danville, Va., June 3, 1956; s. Joseph Walton and Calvine (Pegram) M.; m. Katherine Warfield, Aug. 15, 1981; children: Joseph III, Wallis Warfield. BS, Emory U., 1978; JD, U. Richmond, 1983. Bar: Va. 1983. Prin. Woods, Rogers & Hazlegrove, PLC (and predecessor firms), Roanoke, Va., 1983—2001; cir. judge 22d Cir. Ct. Va., 2001—. Assoc. editor U. Richmond Law Rev., 1982-83. Bd. dirs., sec. Roanoke Vocat. Edn. Found., Inc., 1986-89; bd. dirs. Leadership Danville, 1990-94; bd. dirs. Goodwill Industries, Danville, 1996-2001, pres., 1999-2000; bd. dirs. Danville Mus. History and Fine Arts, 1997-2000, United Way Danville, Pittsylvania County, 1997-2000; treas. Leadership Southside, 1993-94; pres. Danville Estate Planning Coun., 1997-98. Mem. ABA, Va. State Bar Assn., Va. Bar Assn., Danville Bar Assn. (past pres.), Danville Area C. of C. (bd. dirs., vice-chmn. 1992-94, chmn. 1995). Office: Cts and Jail Bldg 401 Patton St PO Box 1401 Danville VA 24543-1401 E-mail: milamjw@ci.danville.va.u2.

MILAM, WILLIAM BRYANT, former ambassador, senior policy scholar, economist; b. Bisbee, Ariz., July 24, 1936; s. Burl Vivian and Alice Vera (Pierce) M.; step-children: Erika, Fred. AB, Stanford U., 1959; MA, U. Mich., 1970; postgrad., Am. U., 1973. Polit. officer Dept. State, Washington, 1967-69; fin. economist Dept. State and Am. Embassy, Washington and London, 1970-75; energy economist Dept. State, Washington, 1975-77, dep. office dir., 1977-80, office dir., 1980-83; dep. chief of mission Am. Embassy, Yaounde, Cameroon, 1983-85; dep. asst. sec. Dept. State, Washington, 1985-90; U.S. amb. to Bangladesh, 1990-93; spl. negotiator oceans environ. sci. Dept. State, Washington, 1993-95; chief of mission Am. Embassy, Monrovia, Liberia, 1995-98, U.S. amb. to Pakistan, Islamabad, 1998-2001; with Woodrow Wilson Internat. Ctr. for Scholars, 2002—. Calif. State scholar, 1956-59; recipient James Clement Dunn award Dept. of State, 1981, Superior Honor award, 1983, Pres.'s Meritorious Svc. award U.S. Govt., 1990, Pres. Outstanding Svc. award, 1991. Avocations: reading, golf, writing. Office: One Woodrow Wilson Plaza 1300 Pennsylvania Ave NW Washington DC 20004 Personal E-mail: milamwb@mindspring.com.

MILANDER, HENRY MARTIN, educational consultant; b. Northampton, Pa., Apr. 17, 1939; s. Martin Edward and Margaret Catherine (Makovetz) M.; children: Martin Henry, Beth Ann. BS summa cum laude, Lock Haven U., Pa., 1961; MA, Bowling Green (Ohio) State U., 1962; EdS (Future Faculty fellow 1964), U. No. Iowa, 1965; EdD, Ill. State U., Normal, 1967. Instr. Wartburg Coll., Waverly, Iowa, 1962-64; asst. prof. Ill. State U., 1966-67; dean instrn. Belleville (Ill.) Area Coll., 1967-69; v.p. acad. affairs Lorain County Community Coll., Elyria, Ohio, 1969-72; pres. Olympic Coll., Bremerton, Wash., 1972-87, Northeastern Jr. Coll., Sterling, Colo., 1988-95; ednl. cons., 1995—. Pres. Bremers, Inc., 1986-87. Contbr. articles to profl. jours. Pres. Kitsap County Comprehensive Health Planning Council, 1975-76; pres. Logan County Colo. United Way, 1992-93. Recipient Faculty Growth award Wartburg Coll., 1963, Community Service award, 1975, Chief Thunderbird award, 1985. Mem. Am. Assn. C.C., Am. Assn. Sch. Adminstrs., N.W. Assn. Cmty. and Jr. Colls., Wash. Assn. C.C. (pres. 1984-85), Wash. C.C. Computing Consortium (chmn. bd. dirs. 1985-87), Puget Sound Naval Bases Assn. (pres. 1982-86), Wash. Assn. C.C. Pres. (pres. 1984-85), Bremerton Area C. of C. (pres. 1977-78), Colo. Assn. C.C. Pres. (pres. 1993-94), Rotary (pres. Sterling Club 1992-93), Kappa Delta Pi, Phi Delta Kappa. Lutheran. Home: 709 E Pointes Dr West Shelton WA 98584-6305

MILANICH, JERALD THOMAS, archaeologist, museum curator; b. Painesville, Ohio, Oct. 13, 1945; s. John Joseph and Jean Marie (Bales) M.; m. Maxine L. Margolis, Dec. 20, 1970; 1 child, Nara Bales. BA, U. Fla., 1967, MA, 1968, PhD, 1971. Fellow Smithsonian Inst., Washington, 1971-72; asst. prof. anthropology U. Fla., Gainesville, 1972-75; asst. curator Fla. Mus. Natural History, 1975-77, assoc. curator, 1977-81, chmn. dept. anthropology, 1981-83, 91-94, curator, 1981—. Author: (with Samuel Proctor) Tacachale -- Essays on the Indians of Florida and Southeastern Georgia During the Historic Period, 1978; (with Charles Fairbanks) Florida Archaeology, 1980; McKeithen Weeden Island, 1984; Early Prehistoric Southeast, 1985; (with Susan Milbrath) First Encounters, Spanish Explorations in the Caribbean and the United States, 1492-1570, 1989; The Hernando de Soto Expedition, 1990; Earliest Hispanic-Native America Interactions in the Greater American Southwest, 1991; (with Charles Hudson) Hernando de Soto and the Indians of Florida, 1993, Archaeology of Precolumbian Florida, 1994, Florida Indians and the Invasion of Europe, 1995, The Timucua, 1996, Archaeology of Northern Florida, 1997, Florida Indians From Ancient Times to the Present, 1998, Laboring in the Fields of the Lord: Spanish Missions and Southeastern Indians, 1999, Famous Florida Sites: Mount Royal and Crystal River, 1999; mem. editl. bd.: Archaeology Mag., 1992-2002, contbg. editor, 2002--. Trustee Archeol. Inst. Am., 2004—. Recipient Ripley P. Bullen award, 1980, Rembert Patrick Book award, 1994-95, medal Fla. Acad. Sci., 2004; grantee NSF, 1970-71, 73-75, 77-82, Wentworth Found., 1976-77, 81-84, 91, NEH, 1985, 87-89, Fla. Divsn. Hist. Resources, 1981, 83-89, 91, 96-97, 2000-02, 03-04. Mem. Soc. Am. Archaeology (exec. bd. 1990-93), Soc. Profl. Archeologists (cert., pres. 1981-82), So. Anthrop. Soc., S.E. Archeol. Conf. (pres. 1986-88). Office: Fla Mus Natural History Gainesville FL 32611-7800

MILANO, ALYSSA, actress; b. N.Y.C., Dec. 19, 1972; d. Thomas M. and Lin Milano. Student, Bel Air Prep. Sch., L.A. Appeared on TV series Who's the Boss?, 1984-92, Melrose Place, 1997-98, Charmed, 1998- (also prodr.); appeared in TV movies The Canterville Ghost, 1986, Dance'Til Dawn, 1988, Conflict of Interest, 1992, Candles in the Dark, 1993, Casualties of Love: The Long Island Lolita Story, 1993, Confessions of a Sorority Girl, 1994; appeared in various TV spls.; on TV shows Body by Jake, 1988, The Arsenio Hall Show, 1989, various shows for American Treasury, 1989, To Brave Alaska, 1996;

film actress Old Enough, 1982, Commando, 1985, Speed Zone, 1989, Where the Day Takes You, 1992, Little Sister, 1992, Double Dragon, 1993, Embrace of the Vampire, 1995, At Home with the Webbers, 1993, The Surrogate, 1995, Public Enemy # 1, 1995, No Fear, 1996, Glory Daze, 1996, Jimmy Zip, 1996, Below Utopia, 1997, Hugo Pool, 1997, Buying the Cow, 2002, Kiss the Bride, 2002, Dickie Roberts: Former Child Star, 2003; stage debut in Annie, various cities, 1980-81; stage appearances include All Night Long, Second Stage Theatre Co., N.Y.C., 1984, Jane Eyre, Theatre Opera Music Inst., N.Y.C., others; TV guest appearances include The Outer Limits, 1995, Spin City, 1996, Fantasy Island, 1998; prodr. Below Utopia, 1997. Recipient Best Supporting Actress award Youth Films Awards; Silver prize Tokyo Music Festival, 1989. Mem. SAG, AFTRA, Actors' Equity Assn.*

MILANOVICH, NORMA JOANNE, training and development company executive; b. Littlefork, Minn., June 4, 1945; d. Lyle Albert and Loretta (Leona) Drake; m. Rudolph William Milanovich, Mar. 18, 1943 (dec.); 1 child, Rudolph William Jr. BS in Home Econs., U. Wis., Stout, 1968; MA in Curriculum and Instrn., U. Houston, 1973, EdD in Curriculum and Program Devel., 1982. Instr. human svcs. dept. U. Houston, 1971-75; dir. videos project U. N.Mex., Albuquerque, 1976-78, dir. vocat. edn. equity ctr., 1978-88, asst. prof. occupational edn., 1982-88, coord. occupational vocat. edn. programs, 1983-88, dir. consortium rsch. and devel. in occupational edn., 1984-88; pres. Alpha Connection Tng. Corp., Albuquerque, 1988—; exec. dir. Trinity Found., 1991—; pres. Athena Leadership Ctr., 1999—. Adj. instr. Cen. Tng. Acad., Dept. Energy, Wackenhut; mem. faculty U. Phoenix; adj. faculty So. Ill. U., Lesley Coll., Boston; lectr. in field. Author: Model Equitable Behavior in the Classroom, 1983, Handbook for Vocational Technical Certification in New Mexico, 1985, A Vision for Kansas: Systems of Measures and Standards of Performance, 1992, Workplace Skills: The Employability Factor, 1993; editor: Choosing What's Best for You, 1982, A Handbook for Handling Conflict in the Classroom, 1983, Starting Out...A Job Finding Handbook for Teen Parents, Going to Work...Job Rights for Teens; author: JTPA Strategic Marketing Plan, 1990, We, The Arcturians, 1990, Sacred Journey to Atlantis, 1991, The Light Shall Set You Free, 1996; editor: Majestic Raise newsletter, 1996—, Celestial Voices newsletter, 1991—; conf. presenter in field. Del. Youth for Understanding Internat. Program, 1985—90; mem. adv. bd. Southwestern Indian Poly. Inst., 1984—88; com. mem. Region VI Consumer Exch. Com., 1982—84; coord. various countries Worldwide Conf. for Peace on Earth, U.S., Portugal, India, Eng., Italy, Jordan, Iceland, 1999—2004; coord. Customized Leadership Programs, 2004; bd. dirs. Albuquerque Single Parent Occupational Scholarship Program, 1984—86. Grantee N.Mex. Dept. Edn., 1976-78, 78-86, 83-86, HEW, 1979, 80, 81, 83, 84, 85, 86, 87. Mem. ASTD, Am. Vocat. Assn., Vocat. Edn. Equity Coun., Nat. Coalition for Sex Equity Edn., Am. Home Econs. Assn., Inst. Noetic Scis., N.Mex. Home Econs. Assn., N.Mex. Vocat. Edn. Assn., N.Mex. Adv. Coun. on Vocat. Edn., Greater Albuquerque C. of C., NAFE, Phi Delta Kappa, Phi Upsilon Omicron, Phi Theta Kappa. Democrat. Roman Catholic. Office: Athena Leadership Ctr Scottsdale AZ 85259 E-mail: info@athenalctr.com.

MILARDO, MARGARET POWERS, language educator; b. New Haven, Conn., May 23, 1944; d. Patrick Joseph and Myra (Coad) Powers; m. Sebastian G. Milardo, July 27, 1968; children: Angela, Sebastian J. BA, Marietta Coll., Ohio, 1966; MA, U. Mass., 1967. Lang. arts tchr. Bonny Eagle Mid. Sch., West Buxton, Maine, 1986—2002; gifted coord. Massabesie H.S., Waterboro, Maine, 2002—; instr. St. Joseph's Coll., Standish, Maine, 2001—. Judge Maine Ednl. Assessments, Garham, Mass., 1998—2001; writing resident Vt. Studio Ctr., Johnson, 1999. Author: Brandi, 2002, Sign of the Seasons, 1990. State coord. Maine Nat. History Day, 1990—2002; judge Odyssey of the Mind, Maine, 2002—. Mem.: Northern New Eng. Sabre Assn., Maine Gifted/Talented Edn. Assn. Avocations: writing, skiing, bicycling. Home: 461 River Rd Hollis ME 04042-3503

MILASKI, JOHN JOSEPH, business transformation industry consultant; b. Johnson City, N.Y., Sept. 16, 1959; s. John Walter and Nellie Joan (Panaro) Milaski; m. Ann Mildred Caldwell, Jan. 22, 1994; children: Ian Alexander, Isaac Nicholas. AAS, Broome C.C., 1979; BSEE, Rochester Inst. Tech., 1984; MBA, Syracuse U., 1991. Registered engr., N.Y.; cert. bus. transformation cons. Design engr. IBM, Endicott, N.Y., 1979-84, systems engr., 1984-85, mktg. cons., 1985-91, cons. Cons. & Sys. Integration Svcs. upstate N.Y., 1992-94, cons. Worldwide Document Mgmt. Solutions Group, 1995-96, con. Worldwide Cons. Svcs., 1996-99; prin. IBM WW BT Cons. Svcs., 2000—. Ga. state advisor to Nat. Rep. Senatorial Com., 1997. Inventor. Vol. IBM Olympic Force Team 1996 Summer Olympics; trust mgr. Nat. Trust for Hist. Preservation; charter mem., life mem. Statue of Liberty-Ellis Island Found., Inc.; charter mem. Nat. WWII Meml.; founding mem. Nat. Wall of Tolerance; charter mem. Nat. D-Day Mus.; life mem. Republican Nat. Com.; mem. presdl. victory team Rep. Nat. Com. Recipient Utilities Industry Mktg. Excellence award IBM Systems Engring. Symposium, 1989, 91. Mem. IEEE (sr.), ASME (sr.), Am. Mgmt. Assn., Am. Prodn. and Inventory Control Soc. (sr.), Internat. Platform Assn., Computer and Automated Sys. Assn., N.Y. State Sheriff's Assn., Ga. State Sheriff's Assn., Ga. State Troopers Assn., U.S. Holocaust Meml. Mus. (charter mem.), IBM 100 Percent Club, U.S. C. of C., Internat. Directory of Disting. Leadership, Nat. Mus. of the Am. Indian (charter), Nat. WWII Meml. Soc. (charter), Am. Battle Monuments Commn. (charter), Libr. of Congress (charter), Nat. Trust for Historic Preservation, Centennial Olympic Pk. in Atlanta (constructing donor). Republican. Roman Catholic. Avocations: skiing, travel, boating. Home: 2315 Sagramore Pl Cape Coral FL 33914-2571

MILAVSKY, HAROLD PHILLIP, real estate executive; b. Limerick, Sask., Can., Jan. 25, 1931; s. Jack and Clara M. B in Commerce, U. Sask., Saskatoon, Can., 1953; LLD (hon.), U. Sask., 1995, U. Calgary, 1995. Chief acct., treas., controller Loram Internat. Ltd. div. Mannix Co. Ltd., Calgary, Alta., Can., 1956-65; v.p., chief fin. officer Power Corp. Devels. Ltd., Calgary, Alta., Can., 1965-69; exec. v.p., bd. dirs. Great West Internat. Equities Ltd. (name now Trizec Corp. Ltd.), Calgary, Alta., Can., 1976-94; pres. Trizec Corp. Ltd., Calgary, Alta., Can., 1976-86, bd. dirs., 1976-94, chmn., 1986-93, Quantico Capital Corp., Calgary, 1994—. Bd. dirs. Consol. Properties Ltd., Citadel Diversified Mgmt., Ltd., Calgary, ENMAX Corp., Prime West Energy Inc., Calgary, Aspen Properties, Ltd., Calgary, Torode Realty, Ltd., Calgary. Past dir. Conf. Bd. Can., Terry Fox Humanitarian Award Program; past gov. Acctg. Edn. Found. Alta.; hon. col. 14th Svc. Battalion, Calgary; bd. dirs. Tennis Can., chmn., 2001—. Recipient B'nai Brith award of merit, 1952, Commemorative medal 125th Birthday of Can., 1992. Fellow Inst. Chartered Accts. Alta.; mem. Inst. Chartered Accts. Sask., Can. Inst. Pub. Real Estate Cos. (past pres., bd. dirs.), Can. C. of C. (past chmn.), Internat. Profl. Hockey Alumni (founding dir.), Petroleum Club, Ranchmen's Club. Avocations: skiing, tennis, horseback riding. Office: Quantico Capital Corp 1920-855 Second St SW Calgary AB Canada T2P 4J7

MILBANK, JEREMIAH, foundation executive; b. N.Y.C., Mar. 24, 1920; s. Jeremiah and Katharine (Schulze) M.; m. Andrea Hunter, July 19, 1947 (dec. Oct. 1982); children: Jeremiah III, Victoria Milbank Whitney, Elizabeth Milbank Archer, Joseph H.; m. Rose Jackson Sheppard, May 4, 1991 (dec. Feb. 1998); m. Mary G. Rockefeller, Jan. 25, 1999. BA, Yale U., 1942; MBA, Harvard U., 1948; L.H.D. (hon.), Ithaca (N.Y.) Coll., 1976, Sacred Heart U., Conn.; LL.D., Manhattan Coll. With J.M. Found., N.Y.C., pres., 1971—. Pres. Turkey Hill Corp., 1972—. Author: First Century of Flight in America, 1942. Chmn. emeritus Boys and Girls Clubs Am.; hon. pres. Internat. Ctr. for the Disabled, 1991—; fin. chmn. Rep. Nat. Com., 1969-72, 75-77. Lt. USNR, 1943-46. Mem. River Club (N.Y.C.), Round Hill Club (Greenwich), Yale Club. Republican. Office: 60 E 42nd St New York NY 10165-0006

MILBOURNE, WALTER ROBERTSON, lawyer; b. Phila., Aug. 27, 1933; s. Charles Gordon and Florie Henderson (Robertson) M.; m. Georgena Sue Dyer, June 19, 1965; children: Gregory Broughton, Karen Elizabeth, Walter Robertson, Margaret Henderson. AB, Princeton U., 1955; LL.B., Harvard U., 1958. Bar: Pa. 1959. Assoc. firm Pepper, Hamilton & Sheetz, Phila., 1959-65, Obermayer, Rebmann, Maxwell & Hippel, Phila., 1965-67, ptnr., 1968-84, Saul, Ewing, Remick & Saul, 1984-2000, of counsel, 2001—. Bd. dirs. Pa. Lumbermen's Mut. Ins. Co., Phila. Reins. Corp.; co-chmn. Nat. Conf. Lawyers and Collection Agys., 1979-90; chmn. bus. litigation com. Def. Rsch. Inst., 1986-89, mem. law instsn. com., 1989-95; mem. panel of disting. neutrals CPRR Inst. Dispute Resolution, 2000—. Chmn. mental health budget sect. Phila. United Fund, 1967—70; pres. Found. Internat. Assn. Def. Counsel, 1997—2001. Fellow: Am. Coll. Trial Lawyers (mem. internat. com. 1992—96); mem.: ABA, Phila. Bar Assn., Pa. Bar Assn., Phila. Lawn Tennis Assn. (pres. 1969—70), Merion Cricket Club. Republican. Home: 689 Fernfield Cir Wayne PA 19087-2002 Office: Saul Ewing Remick & Saul 3800 Centre Sq W Philadelphia PA 19102 Office Phone: 215-972-1975. E-mail: Waltermilb@aol.com.

MILBRATH, ROBERT HENRY, retired petroleum executive; b. Apr. 17, 1912; s. Paul and Mabel (Volkman) M.; m. Margaret Ripperger, Jan. 19, 1940; children: Robert S., Constance, Susan. BS, U.S. Naval Acad., 1934. With Standard Oil Co. N.J., 1934-74; v.p., gen. mgr. Esso Sociedad Anonima Petrolera Argentina, 1938-42, 45-50; area contact East Coast South Am., mktg. coordination, 1950-52; dir. Internat. Petroleum Co., 1954—, v.p., 1956; v.p., dir. Esso Export Corp. N.Y., 1957-59, exec. v.p., dir., 1959-61; pres., dir. chmn. exec. com. Esso Internat., Inc. (formerly Esso Export Corp.), 1961-66; exec. v.p. Esso Europe, 1966-68; logistics coordinator Standard Oil Co. (N.J.) (now Exxon Corp.), 1968-69, dir., v.p., 1969-70, dir., sr. v.p., 1970-73, ret., 1974. Cons. Boys Clubs Am., 1978-84. Served to lt. comdr. USNR; asst. naval attache 1942, Buenos Aires; chief Latin Am. sect. Army-Navy Petroleum Bd. 1943-45, Washington. Mem. U.S. Naval Acad. Alumni Assn. Clubs: University (N.Y.C.), Ponte Vedra Club. Republican. Home: Apt 3221 5200 SW 25th Blvd Gainesville FL 32608

MILBRETT, TIFFENY CARLEEN, professional soccer player; b. Portland, Oreg., Oct. 23, 1972; Degree in comms. mgmt., U. Portland. Mem. U.S. Women's Nat. Soccer Team; profl. soccer player N.Y. Power, 2001—03. Mem. championship team, Montricoux, France, 1993. Named World Cup Champion, 1999; recipient Gold medal, Centennial Olympic Games, 1996, 3d place medal, 1995, Silver medal, World Univ. Games, 1993, Sydney Olympic Games, 2000. Office: c/o US Soccer Fedn 1801 S Prairie Ave # 1811 Chicago IL 60616-1319

MILBURN, RICHARD HENRY, physics educator; b. Newark, June 3, 1928; s. Richard Percy and Lucy Elizabeth (Karr) M.; m. Nancy Jeannette Stafford, Aug. 25, 1951; children— Sarah Stafford, Anne Douglas. AB, Harvard U., 1948, A.M., 1951, PhD, 1954. Instr. Harvard U., Cambridge, Mass., 1954, 56-57, asst. prof., 1957—61; assoc. prof. physics Tufts U., Medford, Mass., 1961-65, prof., 1965-98, John Wade prof., 1990-98, rsch. prof., 1998—2003, prof. emeritus, 2003. Fulbright lectr., India, 1984 Trustee Cambridge Friends Sch., 1989-95. With U.S. Army, 1954-56. Sheldon travelling fellow, 1948-49; NSF fellow, 1952-53; Guggenheim fellow, 1960 Fellow Am. Phys. Soc. (past chmn. New Eng. sect.); mem. Am. Assn. Physics Tchrs., AAAS, AAUP. Achievements include research on high energy and elementary particles physics. Home: 1 Plymouth Rd Winchester MA 01890-3620

MILBURY, MIKE, professional hockey coach; b. Boston, 1953; married; 1 child, Caitlin. Player Boston Bruins, NHL, 1976-87, coach, gen. mgr. Am. Hockey League affiliate Maine, 1987-89, head coach, asst. gen. mgr., 1989-91, asst. gen. mgr., 1991-96; gen. mgr. N.Y. Islanders, 1996-98, 99—, head coach, 1998-99. Office: New York Islanders Nassau Collisium 1255 Hempstead Tpke Uniondale NY 11553-1200

MILCHAN, ARNON, film producer; b. Britis Palestine (now Israel), Dec. 6, 1944; Prodr. (plays) Tomb, It's So Nice To Be Civilized, Amadeus (Paris prodn.), (TV) MASADA, 1981, (TV series) The Client, 1995, (films) Black Joy, 1977, The Medusa Touch, 1978, Dizengoff 99, 1979, The King of Comedy, 1983, Once Upon a Time in America (also actor), 1984, Brazil, 1985, Stripper, 1986, Legend, 1986, Man on Fire, 1987, The Adventures of Baron Munchausen, 1989, Who's Harry Crumb, 1989, The War of the Roses, 1989, Big Man on Campus, 1990, Pretty Woman, 1990, Q&A, 1990, Guilty by Suspicion, 1991, JFK, 1991, Switch, 1991, The Mambo Kings, 1992, Memoirs of an Invisible Man, 1992, The Power of One, 1992, Under Siege, 1992, Sommersby, 1993, Falling Down, 1993, Made in America, 1993, Free Willy, 1993 (exec. prodr.), The Nutcracker, 1993, That Night, 1993, Heaven and Earth, 1993, The New Age, 1993, Striking Distance, 1993, Six Degrees of Separation, 1993, Second Best, 1994, Boys on the Side, 1994, Natural Born Killers, 1994, The Client, 1994, Cobb, 1994, Bogus, 1995, Under Siege 2: Dark Territory, 1995, Free Willy 2: The Adventure Home, 1995, Empire Records, 1995, Copycat, 1995, Heat, 1995, The Sunchaser, 1996, Carpool, 1996, Bogus, 1996, A Time to Kill, 1996, The Mirror Has Two Faces, 1996, Tin Cup, 1996, L.A. Confidential, 1997, Murder at 1600, 1997, Free Willy 3: The Rescue, 1997, The Devil's Advocate, 1997, Breaking Up, 1997, The Man Who Knew Too Little, 1997, Dangerous Beauty, 1998, City of Angels, 1998, The Negotiator, 1998, A Midsummer Night's Dream, 1999, Simply Irresistable, 1999, Goodbye Lover, 1999, Fight Club (exec. prodr.), 1999, Entrapment, 1999, The Hunt for the Unicorn Killer, 1999, Big Momma's House, 2000, Tigerland, 2000, Joe Somebody (exec. prodr.), 2001, Don't Say A Word, 2001, Black Knight, 2001, Freddy Got Fingered (exec. prodr.), 2001, Joy Ride (exec. prodr.), 2001, High Crimes, 2002, Life or Something Like It, 2002, Unfaithful (exec. prodr.), 2002, Daredevil, 2003, Runaway Jury, 2003, Down with Love (exec. prodr.), 2003; (TV); exec. prodr.: Squach, 2000, Noriega: God's Favorite, 2000 (TV), Up at the Villa, 2000 Office: New Regency Enterprises 10201 W Pico Blvd Bldg 12 Los Angeles CA 90064-2606

MILCHOVICH, RAYMOND J. engineering executive; b. Oct. 8, 1949; m. Sherri Milchovich. Grad., Calif. U. Pa., 1971, Harvard U. Advanced Mgmt. Program. With Wis. Steel and Wheeling-Pittsburg Steel; chmn., pres., CEO Kaiser Aluminum, Foster Wheeler Ltd., 2001—. Office: Perryville Corp Parl PO Box 4000 Clinton NJ 08809-4000

MILDREN, JACK, bank executive, former state official; b. Kingsville, Tex., Oct. 10, 1949; s. Larry J. and Mary Glynne (Lamont) M.; m. Janis Susan Butler, Jan. 14, 1972; children: Leigh, Lauren, Drew. BBA, U. Okla., 1972. Cert. petroleum landman. Mem. Balt. Colts Football Team, 1972-73, New England Patriots Football Team, 1974; v.p. Saxon Oil Co., 1972-79; co-founder, pres. Regency Exploration Inc., 1977-88; ind. oil oper., 1988-90; lt. gov. State of Okla., Oklahoma City, 1990-95; pres., CEO Pre-Paid Legal Svcs. Inc., Ada, OK, 1995; owner LJM Fin., 1997—; vice chmn. Arvest Banks, 2003—. Bd. dirs. Children's Med. Rsch. Found., Arts Coun. Oklahoma City, Nat. Football League Players Found. and Hall of Fame, State Ctr. Com., Jim Thorpe Club; mem. Leadership Okla., Leadership Oklahoma City; mem. Com. to Devel. Biotech. Industry in Okla. Named All-Am. Football Player, 1971, Acad. All-Am., 1971, Nat. Football Found. Hall Fame, 1971, Most Valuable Player Sugar Bowl, 1972, Best QB in U. Oklahoma history, numerous other athletic awards; inducted into Okla. Sports Hall of Fame, 1998, GTE Acad. Hall of Fame, 1998. Mem. Beta Gamma Sigma, Phi Delta Theta (past pres., bd. dirs.) Meth. Home: 1701 Guilford Ln Oklahoma City OK 73120-1013 Office: PO Box 55500 Oklahoma City OK 73155 Office Phone: 405-419-3721.

MILDVAN, DONNA, infectious diseases physician; b. Phila., June 20, 1942; d. Carl David and Gertrude M.; m. Rolf Dirk Hamann; 1 child, Gabriella Kay. AB magna cum laude, Bryn Mawr Coll., 1963; MD, Johns Hopkins U., 1967. Diplomate Am. Bd. Internal Medicine and Infectious Diseases. Intern, resident Mt. Sinai Hosp., N.Y.C., 1967-70, fellow, infectious diseases, 1970-72; asst., assoc. prof. clin. medicine Mt. Sinai Sch. Medicine, N.Y.C., 1972-87; prof. clinical medicine Dept. Medicine, Mt. Sinai Sch. Medicine, N.Y.C., 1987-88, prof. medicine, 1988-94; physician-in-charge infectious diseases Beth Israel Med. Ctr., N.Y.C., 1972-79, chief, div. infectious diseases, 1980—; prof. medicine Albert Einstein Coll. of Medicine, N.Y.C., 1994—. Mem. AIDS charter rev. com., NIH/Nat. Inst. Allergy and Infectious Diseases, Bethesda, 1987—; cons. FDA, Rockville, 1987—, Ctrs. for Disease Control, Atlanta, 1985-86; among first to describe AIDS, "Pre-AIDS", AIDS Dementia, 1982, among first to study AZT, 1986; Keynote speaker, II Internat. Conf. on AIDS, Paris, 1986 and other achievements in field; Sophie Jones Meml. lectr. in infectious diseases U. Mich. Hosps., 1984. Contbr. numerous articles to profl. jours; co-editor two books, several book chpts. and abstracts on infectious diseases and AIDS. Grantee N.Y. State AIDS Inst., 1986-87; Henry Strong Denison scholar Johns Hopkins U. Sch. Medicine, 1967; recipient Woman of Achievement award AAUW, 1987; contract for antiviral therapy in AIDS, Nat. Cancer Inst./Nat. Inst. Allergy and Infectious Diseases, 1985-86, subcontract Nat. Inst. Allergy and Infectious Diseases, ACTU, 1987-99, prin. investigator, 2000—. Fellow Infectious Diseases Soc. Am.; mem. Am. Soc. Microbiology, AAAS, Harvey Soc., Internat. AIDS Soc. Democrat. Jewish. Avocation: old movies. Office: Beth Israel Med Ctr 1st Ave New York NY 10003-7903

MILENTHAL, DAVID, advertising executive; B in Journalism, Ohio State U. Mgr. comms. Ohio Blue Shield; dir., organizer Pub. Interest Ctr., Ohio Environtl. Protection Agy.; pres., CEO Milenthal Advt. Agy.; exec. v.p. Hameroff/Milenthal, Inc.; pres., CEO HMS Ptnrs., chmn. Recipient Silver medal award Advt. Fedn. of Columbus; named Man of Yr. Temple Israel, Ten Outstanding Young Citizens Jaycees, People to Watch Columbus Monthly. Office: HMS Ptnrs Ste 5 250 Civic Center Dr S Columbus OH 43215-5086

MILES, AMY E. recreational facility executive; With PricewaterhouseCoopers, LLC, 1989—98; sr. mgr. Deloitte & Touche, 1998—99; from sr. v.p. fin. to exec. v.p., CFO, treas. Regal Entertainment Group, Englewood, Colo., 1999—2000, exec. v.p., 2000—, CFO, 2000—, treas., 2000—. Office: Regal Entertainment Group 9110 East Nichols Ave Ste 200 Englewood CO 80112*

MILES, ARTHUR J. financial planner, consultant; b. N.Y.C., Sept. 2, 1920; s. Levi and Rachel Goldsworthy (Hiscock) M.; m. Pearl Cooper, Nov. 27, 1947; children: Beverly Miles Kerns, Douglas Robert. BBA, Pace U., 1958; MBA, NYU, 1963; postgrad., Dartmouth Coll., 1966, Brown U., 1970-71. Instr. Brown U., Providence, 1970-71; with Dime Savs. Bank, N.Y.C., 1938-81, exec. v.p., treas., 1975-78, sr. exec. v.p., treas., 1978-81; pres. AJM Assocs., Floral Park, N.Y., then Sarasota, Fla., 1981—. Newscaster Sta. WUSF-FM, Tampa, Fla.; bd. dirs. Cultural Instns. Retirement System, N.Y.C., 1968—89; fin. cons. Bklyn. Inst. Arts and Scis., 1972—89. Trustee, nat. treas. Alcoholics Anonymous, N.Y.C., 1970-79; tech. adviser N.Y.C. Fin. Liason Com., 1975-76. Served to sgt., inf. U.S. Army, 1942-45, Philippines. Fellow Fedn. Fin. Analysts; mem. Nat. Assn. Bus. Economists, Internat. Assn. Fin. Planners, Broadcast Pioneers, NYU Club, Marco Polo Club (N.Y.C.), Tournament Players Club. Republican. Office: AJM Assocs 8325 Shadow Pine Way Sarasota FL 34238-5624

MILES, BRIAN JOHN, urologist; b. Belfast, Ireland, Nov. 8, 1946; s. William Livingston and Kathleen (Jamison) M.; m. Renee' Gig DeBlaise, Sept. 15, 1990. BS, Mich. State U., 1967; MS in Engring., U. Mich., 1968, MD, 1974. Diplomate Am. Bd. Urology. Intern surgery Georgetown U., Washington, 1974-75; resident urology Walter Reed Army Med. Ctr., Washington, 1978-82; instr. Dept. of Urology Mich. Army Med. Ctr., Tacoma, 1982-84; instr. Dept. of Surgery U. Washington, Seattle, 1982-84; staff physician Dept. of Surgery Henry Ford Hosp., Detroit, 1984-91; assoc. prof. U. Mich., Ann Arbor, 1984-93; dir. resident edn. Henry Ford Hosp., Detroit, 1987-93, dir. urologic oncology, 1988-93; assoc. prof. Scott Dept. of Urology, Houston, 1993-2000; prof. Scott Dept. Urology, Houston, 2000—, disting. Cullen chair in Urology, 2003; chief of urology VA Med. Ctr., Houston, 1993-98, St. Luke's Episcopal Hosp., Houston, 1993—; med. dir. Tex. Cancer Inst., 1999—; dist. cullen chair in Urology Scott Dept. Urology, 2003—. Assoc. editor: (book) Comprehensive Textbook of Genitourinary Oncology, 1995. Ltc. Army Med. Corp, 1975-84. Mem. ACS, Am. Urologic Assn. (Prostate Cancer Outcomes Analysis Grant 1995, 96), Soc. Urologic Oncology, Soc. of Univ. of Urologist, Societe' Internat. d'Urologie. Avocations: history, sports, reading. Home: 3781 Farbar St Houston TX 77005-3713 Office: Scott Dept Urology 6560 Fannin St Ste 2100 Houston TX 77030-2769 Office Phone: 713-798-5137. E-mail: bmiles@bcm.tmc.edu.

MILES, CHRISTINE MARIE, museum director; b. Madison, Ind., Mar. 2, 1951; d. Leland Weber and Mary Virginia (Geyer) M. BA, Boston U., 1973; MA, George Washington U., 1982; postgrad., Mus. Mgmt. Inst., 1985. Curatorial asst. Mus. City of N.Y., 1973-75; art gallery dir. South Street Seaport Mus., N.Y.C., 1975-77; rschr. The Octagon, AIA Found., Washington, 1978-80; dir. Fraunces Tavern Mus., Washington, 1980-86, Albany (N.Y.) Inst. History and Art, 1986—. Bd. dirs. SUNY-Albany Found. Author, writer/coordinator, compiler of catalogs in field. Mem. Arts Commn. City of Albany; pres. Gallery Assn. N.Y. State, 1991-93, Mus. Assn. N.Y. State. Mem. Am. Assn. Mus. Office: Albany Inst History and Art 125 Washington Ave Albany NY 12210-2296

MILES, DAVID MICHAEL, lawyer; b. Jackson, Mich., Aug. 5, 1954; s. Richard George and Joann Marie (Stefanoff) M.; m. Noelle Suzanne McHugh, Sept. 6, 1986; children: Amy Elizabeth, Margaret Noelle, Lane McHugh. Student, U. Mich., 1972-74; BA cum laude, Clark U., 1976; JD magna cum laude, George Washington U., 1979. Bar: D.C. 1979, U.S. Ct. Appeals (4th cir.) 1980, U.S. Dist. Ct. Md. 1980, U.S. Dist. Ct. D.C. 1983, U.S. Supreme Ct. 1983, U.S. Ct. Appeals (D.C. cir.) 1981, U.S Ct. Appeals (9th cir.) 1984, U.S. Ct. Appeals (2d cir.) 1986. Law clk. to Chief Judge Edward Northrop, U.S Dist. Ct. Md., 1979-80; law clk. to Cir. Judge George MacKinnon U.S. Ct. Appeals, Washington, 1980-81; assoc. Fried, Frank, Harris, Shriver & Jacobson, Washington, 1981-86, ptnr., 1986-92, Sidley & Austin, Washington, 1992—. Co-author: The Law of Financial Services, 1988; contbr. articles to profl. jours. Home: 5229 Westpath Way Bethesda MD 20816 Office: Sidley, Austin, Brown & Wood 1501 K St NW Washington DC 20005 Office Phone: 202-736-8556. Personal E-mail: DavidM9876@aol.com. Business E-Mail: dmiles@sidley.com.

MILES, DON CLIFFORD, architect; b. Ft. Knox, Ky., Sept. 17, 1942; s. Don and Kathrine Eva (Gray) M.; m. Pamela Wait, Aug. 6, 1972; children: Katherine Wait, Lesley Gray, Nicole Conel. BArch with honors, U. Wash., 1966; MArch, M of City Planning in Urban Design, Harvard U., 1971. Registered architect, Wash. Assoc. ptnr. Zimmer, Gunsul, Frasca Partnership, Seattle. Cons., lectr. numerous orgns., cities, corps. Prin. projects include Pedestrian Corridor, Major Pub. Open Spaces, CBD Transit Ctr., Bellevue, Wash., Banfield Light Rail Project, Portland, Boise (Idaho) Downtown Major Pub. Open Space, Street Improvements and Transit Malls, Honolulu Rapid Transit Project, Revitalization of State St., Chgo., Midway Corridor Project, Mpls., High Capacity Transit Project, Seattle, Ctrl. Orange County Aerial Fixed Guideway, Mission Valley West Extension Light Rail Project, San Diego, Master Plan for Capitol of State of Wash., Seattle Union Sta. Redevel. Plan, Weyerhauser Corp. Campus, Quadrant Corp. site, Lake Union, Seattle, Whitman Coll. Bd. dirs., founder Project for Pub. Spaces, 1975—; bd. dirs. Seattle Children's Mus., 1978-82; trustee Queen Ann Community Coun., 1978-80. Fellow AIA, Inst. Urban Design. Avocations: skiing, jogging. Home: 611 W Comstock St Seattle WA 98119-3422 Office: Zimmer Gunsul Frasca 925 4th Ave 2400 Seattle WA 98104-1146

MILES, DONALD F. lawyer; b. Marysville, Calif., Apr. 11, 1949; AB with honors, Stanford U., 1971; JD, U. Calif., San Francisco, 1974. Bar: Calif. 1974, U.S. Dist. Ct. (no. dist.) Calif. 1974, U.S. Dist. Ct. (ea. dist.) Calif. 1977, U.S. Dist. Ct. (so. dist.) Calif. 1986, U.S. Supreme Ct. 1987, U.S. Dist. Ct. (ctrl. dist.) Calif. 1991. Law clk. to Hon. William P. Clark Jr. Supreme Ct. Calif., 1974-75; mem. Howard, Rice, Nemerovski, Canady, Falk & Rabkin, P.C., San Francisco. Spl. master U.S. Dist. Ct. (no. dist.) Calif.; instr., adj. faculty mem. Hastings Coll. Law U. Calif.; faculty mem., bd. dirs. Hastings Nat. Coll. Advocacy; mem. adv. com. Calif. Legis. Joint Com. Tort Liability. Author: (with others) Civil Procedure During Trial, vol. II, 1984, 95, California Liability Insurance Practice, 1991, Continuing Education of the Bar Action Guide, 1991; author, narrator: (videotape) Laying a Foundation to Introduce Evidence, 1989; contbr. articles to profl. jours. Bd. chmn. The Glenwood Sch. Found. Mem. ABA (sect. torts and ins. practice), State Bar Calif., Assn. Def. Counsel No. Calif., Bar Assn. of San Francisco, Internat. Assn. Def. Counsel, Def. Rsch. Inst., Thurston Soc., Order of Coif. Office: Howard Rice Nemerovski Canady Falk & Rabkin PC 3 Embarcadero Ctr Ste 700 San Francisco CA 94111-4074

MILES, DORIS COOPER, bank executive; b. Camp Le June, N.C., Jan. 16, 1963; d. Thomas Wayne and Linda Gene (DuVall) Cooper; 1 child, J. Brian. Sales and mktg. sec. Hawthorne at Leesburg, Fla., 1989—91; contr. to Delta Techop and Credit Union Norrell Svcs., Atlanta, 1991—93; workers compensation adminstr. Riscorp, Maitland, Fla., 1995—96; sales and leasing adminstr. Jaymark Bldrs., Clermont, Fla., 1996—98; EAS contr. to IBM Norrell Spherion, Atlanta, 1998—2000, Orlando, Fla., 2000—01; dealer fin. sec. Independent Bank, Cleveland, Tenn., 2001—. Author: (booklet) To the Policy Holder, 1994, (book) Mommy and the Masher, 1996, The Storm's Heart, 1998, Between Love and Duty, 2001. Avocations: motivational speaking, travel, photography. Home: 17837 Lake Lucy Lane Groveland FL 34736

MILES, FRANK CHARLES, retired newspaper executive; b. Detroit, Jan. 1, 1926; s. Nelson and Ethel Jane (Mennill) M.; m. Catharine Estelle Coleman, Sept. 4, 1948 (dec. Aug. 2000); children: Barbara Ann, Diana Estelle; m. Joan Ashkin, Feb. 1, 2003. Student, Westervelt Bus. Coll., 1947-48. With Thomson Newspapers Ltd., Cambridge, Ont., Can., 1950-52, 54-55; bus. mgr. Sarnia (Ont.) Obs., 1952-54; gen. mgr. Pembroke (Ont.) Obs., 1956-58, Moose Jaw (Sask.) Times-Herald, Can., 1958-62; pub. Austin (Minn.) Daily Herald, 1962-66; sr. v.p., gen. mgr. Thomson Newspapers Inc., Des Plaines, Ill., 1966-89, exec. v.p. acquisitions, 1990-91, ret., 1991, also bd. dirs.; founder Ashkin/Miles Creative Enterprises, 2003—. Vol. assignments Internat. Media Fund, Baltics, Albania, 1992-93; Knight fellowship Moscow, 1994, Ctrl. for Ind. Journalism, Bucharest, Romania, 1995, Kocise Slovakia, 1996, Internat. Rsch. & Exch. Corp., Zagreb, Croatia, Belarus, 1997, Brest, Minsk, Belarus, 1997-98. Mem. Assn. Integration of Whole Person, Sigma Delta Chi. Republican. Mem. United Ch. of Christ. Home: 3892 Bordeaux Dr Punta Gorda FL 33950

MILES, HARRY LEHMAN, lawyer, educator; b. May 4, 1944; s. Sidney and Beatrice (Lehman) M. AB, Dartmouth Coll., 1965; JD, Bklyn. Law Sch., 1969; MA in Comms., U. Mass., Amherst, 1972. Tchr. James Madison H.S., Bklyn., 1966-70; instr. U. Mass., Amherst, 1970-72; practice law Amherst, 1971-75; asst. dist. atty. Northwestern Dist., Mass., 1975-79, 1st asst. dist. atty., 1979-80; ptnr. Growhoski, Callahan & Miles, Northampton, Mass., 1980-94, Green, Miles, Lipton, & Fitz-Gibbon, Northampton, Mass., 1994—. Past adj. prof. law Western New Eng. Coll. Sch. Law; v.p., dir. Western Mass. Legal Services Corp. Mem. Shutesbury (Mass.) Bd. Health, 1972-74, Shutesbury Fin. Com., 1973-74. Fellow Am. Acad. Forensic Scis. (jurisprudence sect.), Am. Coll. Trial Lawyers, Mass. Bar Found.; mem. ABA, Mass. Bar Assn., Hampshire County Bar Assn., Mass. Assn. Criminal Defense Lawyers, Dartmouth Lawyers Assn. Democrat. Office: Green Miles Lipton Fitz-Gibbon 77 Pleasant St PO Box 210 Northampton MA 01061-0210 E-mail: harrymiles@aol.com.

MILES, JACK (JOHN RUSSIANO), journalist, educator; b. Chgo., July 30, 1942; s. John Alvin and Mary Jean (Murphy) Miles; m. Jacqueline Russiano, Aug. 23, 1980; 1 child, Kathleen. LittB, Xavier U., Cin., 1964; PhB, Pontifical Gregorian U., Rome, 1966; student, Hebrew U., Jerusalem, 1966—67; PhD, Harvard U., 1971. Asst. prof. Loyola U., Chgo., 1970—74; asst. dir. Scholars Press, Missoula, Mont., 1974—75; postdoctoral fellow U. Chgo., 1975—76; editor Doubleday & Co., N.Y.C., 1976—78; exec. editor U. Calif. Press, Berkeley, 1978—85; book editor L.A. Times, 1985—91, mem. editl. bd., 1991—95; dir. Humanities Ctr. Claremont (Calif.) Grad. U., 1995—97; Mellon vis. prof. Calif. Inst. Tech., 1997—98; sr. advisor to pres. J. Paul Getty Trust, L.A., 1999—. Contbg. editor: Atlantic Monthly, 1995—; author: Retroversion and Text Criticism, 1984, God: A Biography, 1995, Christ: A Crisis in the Life of God, 2001; contbr. learned and popular articles to various periodicals; book reviewer. Recipient Pulitzer Prize for biography, 1996; Guggenheim fellow, 1990—91, 2002—, MacArthur fellow, 2003—. Mem.: PEN, Amnesty Internat., Am. Acad. Religion, Nat. Book Critics Cir. (pres. 1990—92). Episcopalian. Office: J Paul Getty Trust 1200 Getty Center Dr Ste 1100 Los Angeles CA 90049-1688

MILES, JESSE MC LANE, retired accounting company executive; b. De Funiak Springs, Fla., June 17, 1932; s. Percy Webb and Dora (Pippin) M.; m. Catherine Rita Eugenio, July 18, 1959; children: Jesse Jr., Catherine, Teresa, John, Thomas, Robert BSBA, U. Fla., 1954. CPA NY. Mem. staff, mgr., prin. Arthur Young & Co., N.Y.C., 1954-63, ptnr., 1963-89, dep. chmn.-internat., 1985-89; chmn. Arthur Young Internat., 1985-89; ptnr. Ernst & Young, 1989-92; co-chmn. Ernst & Young Internat., 1989-92; ret., 1992. Mem. AICPA, N.Y. Inst. CPAs, Blind Brook Club (Rye Brook, N.Y.), Boca Pointe Country Club (Boca Raton, Fla.). Home: 7077 Via Mediterrania Boca Raton FL 33433

MILES, JIM, former state offical; b. Oct. 10, 1941; Prof. of law Greenville Tech. Coll., SC; Sec. of State State of S.C., 1991—2002; candidate for governor, 2002. Former councilman City of Greenville, SC. Mem. Soc. Internat. Bus. Republican.

MILES, JOANNA, actress, playwright, director; b. Nice, France, Mar. 6, 1940; came to U.S., 1941, naturalized, 1941; d. Johannes Schiefer and Jeanne Miles; m. William Burns, May 23, 1970 (div. 1977); m. Michael Brandman, Apr. 29, 1978; 1 child, Miles. Grad., Putney (Vt.) Sch., 1958. Mem. Actors Studio, Playwrites and Dirs. Workshop, N.Y.C., 1966; co-founder, mem. L.A. Classic Theatre, 1986. Founder, mem. Playwrights Group/LAWW, 1991-98, L.A. Writer's Workshop, 1996-98. Appeared in: (motion pictures) The Way We Live Now, 1969, Bug, 1975, The Ultimate Warrior, 1975, Golden Girl, 1978, Cross Creek, 1983, As Is, 1986, Blackout, 1988, Rosencrants and Guildenstern are Dead, 1991, The Rhinghart Theory, 1994, Judge Dredd, 1994, Alone, 1996; numerous television films including In What America, 1965, My Mothers House, 1963, Glass Managerie, 1974, Born Innocent, 1974, Aloha Means Goodbye, 1974, The Trial of Chaplain Jensen, 1975, Harvest Home, 1977, Fire in the Sky, 1978, Sophisticated Gents, 1979, Promise of Love, 1982, Sound of Murder, 1983, All My Sons, 1987, The Right to Die, 1987, The Habitation of Dragons, 1991, Heart of Justice, 1991, Water Engine, 1991, Cooperstown, 1992, Legionnaires, 1992, Life Lessons, 1992, Willing to Kill, 1992, The American Clock, 1993, Dark Reflections, 1993, Outcry, 1994, Everything to Gain, 1995, Small Vices, 1998, Crossfire Trail, 1999, Thin Aire, 1999, Monty Walsh, 2002; episodes in numerous TV series including: Barney Miller, Dallas, St. Elsewhere, The Hulk, Trapper John, Kaz, Cagney and Lacey, Studio 5B, 1989, Star Trek: The Next Generation, 1990, 91, Life Stories, 1991, HBO Life Stories, 1993, Total Security, 1997, Nothing Sacred, 1998, Chicago Hope, 1998-99, ER, 2000, 01, Family Law, 2000, Judging Amy, 2003; stage plays include Once in a Life Time, 1963, Cave Dwellers, 1964, Drums in the Night, 1968, Dracula, 1968, Home Free, 1964, One Night Stands of a Noisy Passenger, 1972, Dylan, 1973, Dancing for the Kaiser, 1976, Debutante Ball, 1985, Kramer, 1977, One Flew Over the Cuckoo's Nest, 1989, Growing Gracefully, 1990, Cut Flowers, 1994; performed in radio shows Sta. KCRW Once in a Lifetime, 1987, Babbit, 1987, Sta. KPFK, Grapes of Wrath, 1989, The White Plague, Sta. KCRW, 1991, Chekhov Short Stories, Sta. KCRW, 1992; playwright, v.p. Brandman Productions; author; (plays) Ethanasia, A Woman in Reconstruction, Hostages, Feathers, On the Shelf. Pres. Children Giving to Children. Recipient 2 Emmy awards, 1974, Women in Radio and TV award, 1974, Actors Studio Achievement award, 1980, Dramalogue award, 1996, Vision award 2003; nominated Golden Globe, 1974. Mem. Acad. Motion Picture Arts and Scis., Acad. TV Arts and Scis Office: Brandman Prodns 2062 Vine St Apt 5 Hollywood CA 90068-3928: Merritt Blake 1327 Ocean Ave J Santa Monica CA 90401 Office Phone: 323-463-3224., 310-899-9898. Personal E-mail: jmilesb@aol.com.

MILES, JOHN BILL, accountant, tax advisor; b. Knox County, Ky., Sept. 18, 1931; s. John Ishmael and Allie Arizona (Engle) M.; m. Mary Patricia Wilson, May 25, 1963; children: Melanie, Jennifer, Dennis. BSC, Salmon P. Chase Coll., Highland Heights, 1962; BS in Acctg., U. Cin., 1972; MBA, Lincoln Grad. Sch. Mgmt., Des Moines, 2001. CPA; accredited tax advisor; enrolled agt. Cost acct. Avco Corp., Cin., 1956—58; chief auditor Pepsi-Cola Bottling Co., Cin., 1958—64; property acct. Monsanto Co., Addyston, Ohio, 1964—66; sec.-treas. Shur-Good Biscuit Co., Inc., Cin., 1966—79; acct. Fabritec Internat. Corp., Cold Spring, Ky., 1980—98; ind. practice acctg. Cheviot, Ohio, 1999—. Lt. Col. Ohio Mil. Res. Mem.: NRA, AICPA, Ohio Assn. Ind. Accts., Nat. Soc. Accts., Ohio Soc. CPAs, State Guard Assn. U.S., Assn. U.S. Army, Am. Legion, Ohio Mil. Res. Assn., Honorable Order Ky. Cols., Fur Takers of Am., Accts. for Pub. Interest, Cheviot Rep. Club. Home: 3816 Roswell Ave Cincinnati OH 45211-3329

MILES, JOHN FREDERICK, retired manufacturing company executive; b. Fredericton, N.B., Can., Aug. 13, 1926; s . Ralph Edward and Hazel Jean (Young) M.; m. Frances Power, Oct. 2, 1950; children: John F., Robert D., Dalyce J., Leytha J. Sr. Matric, U. N.B., 1944; B.Sc. in Chem. Engring., Queen's U., Kingston, Ont., Can., 1948. Prodn. mgr. Dominion Steel & Coal Corp. Ltd., 1948-65, jr. engr., 1948-49, battery foreman coke ovens, 1949-51, gen. foreman coke ovens, 1951-56, rsch. engr. coke ovens and blast furnaces, 1956-57, asst. supt. blast furnace dept., 1957-58, asst. to gen. supt., 1958-60, asst. works mgr. Sidney Works, 1960-62, gen. mgr. Etobicoke Works, 1962-65; works mgr. Slater Steels—Hamilton Spltly. Bar Div. (div. Slater Industries), Hamilton, Ont., Can., 1965-66, 1966-71, v.p. mfg., 1971-86, div. pres., 1986-91, pres., CEO, 1991-93, bd. dirs., 1991-99. Mem. Assn. Profl. Engrs. Ont., Assn. Iron and Steel Engrs. E-mail: johnmiles73@hotmail.com.

MILES, KENNETH ONTARIO, academic program director; b. Washington; s. Lessie Olivia Walker. BA, U. Va., 1992, MEd, 1998. Tchr., coach Gonzaga Coll. High Sch., Washington, 1993-95; acad. lifeskills coord. U. Va., Charlottesville, 1995-97; coord. acad. support football Syracuse (N.Y.) U. Athletic Dept., 1997—2002; dir. student svcs. Sch. Info. Studies Syracuse (N.Y.) U., 2002—. Mem. Nat. Assn. of Student Personnel Adminstrs., Nat. Assn. of Grad. Admissions Profls., Black Coaches Assn., Nat. Assn. Advisors Athletics (chmn. ethnic concerns com. 1999-2000). Democrat. Baptist. Avocation: weight training. Office: Syracuse U Sch Info Studies 4-206 Ctr for Sci and Tech Syracuse NY 13244-4100 E-mail: komiles@syr.edu.

MILES, LAVEDA ANN, advertising executive; b. Greenville, S.C., Nov. 21, 1945; d. Grady Lewis and Edna Sylvia (Mahaffey) Bruce; m. Charles Thomas Miles, Nov. 10, 1974; 1 child, Joshua Bruce. A in Bus. Adminstrn., North Greenville Jr. Coll. Traffic mgr. WFBV-TV, Greenville, 1968-74; pub. svc. dir., traffic mgr. WTCG-TV, Atlanta, 1974-75; traffic mgr. Henderson Advt. Co., Greenville, 1975-77, broadcast coord., 1977-79, dir. broadcast bus., 1979-82, v.p., dir. broadcast bus., 1982-89, bus. mgr. creative dept., 1989-91, dir. creative svcs., 1991-93, sr. v.p., 1994-96, v.p., dir. creative svcs., 2000—; owner Altamont Mktg., 1996-99. Mem. Leadership S.C., 1994-95; bd. dirs. Boys Home of the South, 2003—. Named one of 100 Best and Brightest Women, Ad Age and Advt. Women of N.Y., 1988. Mem. Advt. Fedn. Greenville (sec. 1979-81), Greenville Ad Club (sec. 1999-2000, pres. 2000—, Silver medal awrd 2003). Republican. Baptist.

MILES, LELAND WEBER, university president; b. Balt., Jan. 18, 1924; s. Leland Weber and Marie (Fitzpatrick) M.; m. Mary Virginia Geyer, July 9, 1947; children: Christine Marie, Gregory Lynn. AB cum laude, Juniata Coll., 1946; MA, U. N.C., 1947, PhD, 1949; postgrad., Duke U., 1949; DLitt (hon.), Juniata Coll., 1969; LHD (hon.), Rosary Hill Coll., 1970; LLD (hon.), Far East U., 1979; DHC (hon.), U. Guadalajara, Mex., 1984; Order of Merit, Alfred U., 1986. Assoc. prof. English Hanover Coll., 1949-50, prof., chmn. English dept., 1950-60; assoc. prof., asst. to head English dept. U. Cin., 1960-63, prof., 1963-64, founder humanities reading program for engrs., 1961; dean Coll. Arts and Scis., U. Bridgeport, Conn., 1964-67; pres. U. Bridgeport, 1974-87; founder U. Bridgeport Sch. Law, 1977; pres. emeritus U. Bridgeport, 1987—; pres. Alfred U., 1967-74. Bd. dirs. United Illuminating, 1978-94, chmn. audit com., 1992-94, Grolier, 1984-88, Wright Managed Investment Funds, 1988—, Internat. Peace Acad., 1982-90, mem. adv. coun., 1990—; Danforth scholar Union Theol. Sem., 1956; Lilly fellow Sch. Letters Ind. U., 1959; Am. Council Learned Socs. fellow Harvard, 1963-64; Sr. Fulbright Research scholar Kings Coll. U. London, 1964, vis. scholar, 1972; seminar leader, deans and presidents insts. Am. Council on Edn., 1973-79; chmn. bd. Acad. Collective Bargaining Info. Service, Washington, 1977-79; producer, moderator Casing the Classics CBS Sta. WHAS-TV, Louisville, 1958-61; moderator Aspen (Colo.) Inst. for Humanistic Studies, 1969-70; lectr. Keedick Lecture Bur., N.Y.C., 1956-83. Author: John Colet and the Platonic Tradition, 1961; editor: St. Thomas More's Dialogue of Comfort Against Tribulation, 1965, Where Do You Stand On Linquistics?, 1964, revised, 1968; sr. editor: (with Stephen Graubard and later Stephen B. Baxter) Studies in British History and Culture, 1965-79, Provoking Thought: What Colleges Should Do For Students, 2001; contbg. editor Nat. Forum, 1983-91, editl. advisor, 1991-94; contbr. articles to learned jours., chpts. in books. Trustee Western N.Y. Nuclear Rsch. Ctr., 1967-73; chmn. bd. Coll. Ctr. Finger Lakes, 1968-71; vice-chmn. bd. Empire State Found., 1969-71, chmn., 1971-73; mem. New Eng. Bd. Higher Edn., 1985-87, Ambs. Roundtable, 1986-92, Fuld Found./Nat. League Nursing Adv. Coun. on Accreditation, 1986-88; chmn. Ettinger scholarship com. Edml. Found. Am., 1987-93; bd. dirs. Conn. Grand Opera, 1978-89, Bridgeport Bus. Coun., 1982-88; bd. dirs. Save the Children, 1988-95, chmn. adv. coun., 1990-95. 1st lt. USAAF, 1944-45; capt. USAFR. Decorated DFC with oak leaf cluster, Crown Decoration of Honor 3rd Order Iran, 1978; chevalier l'Ordre des Palmes Académique (France), 1984; recipient Rosa and Samuel Sachs prize Cin. Inst. Fine Arts, 1961, Cultural medal Republic of China, 1983, Disting. Svc. award Greater Bridgeport Bar Assn., 1986, Outstanding Civilian Svc. medal Dept. Army, 1988; Miles scholars Alfred U., 1995—. Fellow Royal Soc. Arts, Manufactures and Commerce (life); mem. Renaissance Soc. Am., English Speaking Union (bd. dirs. Greenwich, Conn. chpt. 1998—), Internat. Assn. Univ. Pres. (pres. 1981-84, pres. emeritus 1984—, chief UN mission 1988-97, World Peace award 1987, chmn. UN commn. on arms control edn. 1991-96, mem. coun. sr. advisers 1992—), Knights of Malta (order of the Orthodox Knights Hospitaller of St. John of Jerusalem, Russian orthodox br.), Phi Kappa Phi. Clubs: Univ. (N.Y.C.); Country of Fairfield (Conn.). Episcopalian. Home (Summer): 87 Field Point Dr Fairfield CT 06824-6329 Home (Winter): 2110 Ben Franklin Dr Sarasota FL 34236

MILES, RAYMOND EDWARD, former university dean, organizational behavior and industrial relations educator; b. Cleburne, Tex., Nov. 2, 1932; s. Willard Francis and Wilma Nell (Owen) M.; m. Lucile Dustin, Dec. 27, 1952; children: Laura, Grant, Kenneth. BA with highest honors, U. North Tex., 1954, MBA, 1958; PhD, Stanford U., 1963. Clk. Santa Fe R.R., Gainesville, Tex., 1950-55; instr. mgmt. Sch. Bus. U. North Tex., Denton, 1958-60; asst. prof. organizational behavior and indsl. relations Sch. Bus. Adminstrn. U. Calif.-Berkeley, 1963-68, assoc. prof., 1968-71, prof., 1971—, assoc. dean Haas Sch. of Bus., 1978-81, dean, 1983-90; dir. Inst. Indsl. Relations, 1982-83; cons. various pvt., pub. orgns. Author: Theories of Management, 1975, (with Charles C. Snow) Organization Strategy, Structure and Process, 1978, (with Charles C. Snow) Fit, Failure, and the Hall of Fame, 1994; co-author: Organizational Behavior: Research and Issues, 1976; co-editor, contbg. author: Organization by Design: Theory and Practice, 1981. Served to 1st. lt. USAF, 1955-58. Mem. Acad. Mgmt. Democrat. Unitarian Universalist. Home: 8640 Don Carol Dr El Cerrito CA 94530-2733 Office: U Calif Walter A Haas Sch Bus Berkeley CA 94720-0001 E-mail: miles@haas.berkeley.edu.

MILES, RICHARD BRYANT, mechanical and aerospace engineering educator; b. Washington, July 10, 1943; s. Thomas Kirk and Elizabeth (Bryant) M.; m. Susan McCoy, May 14, 1983; children: Thomas, Julia. BSEE, Stanford U., 1966, MSEE, 1967, PhD in Elec. Engring., 1972. Rsch. assoc. elec. engring. dept. Stanford (Calif.) U., summer 1972; asst. prof. mech. and aerospace engring. dept. Princeton (N.J.) U., 1972-78, assoc. prof., 1978-82, prof., 1982—, chmn. engring. physics program, 1980-96, acting chmn. dept. mech. and aero. engring., 2002. Lectr. Northwestern Poly. U., Xian, China, 1987; rsch. scientist CNRS; vis. prof. U. Marseilles, France, 1995. Contbr. articles to profl. publs., chpt. to book and conf. procs.; patentee in field. Bd. dirs. Fannie and John Hertz Found., Livermore, Calif., 1989—. Fannie and John Hertz Found. fellow, 1969-72. Fellow AIAA (Aerodynamic Measurement Tech. TC award 2000) Optical Soc. Am.; mem. IEEE (sr.), Am. Phys. Soc. Office: Princeton U Mech & Aerospace Engring D-414 Eng Quad Olden St Princeton NJ 08544-0001 Office Phone: 609-258-5131.

MILES, RICHARD R. writer, curator; b. Tokyo, Apr. 1, 1938; s. Robert Henri and Eleanor Alfrida Perreau-Saussine; m. Xuong-Hong Quach, Feb. 1, 1994. BA, Georgetown U., 1958, UCLA, 1960, MFA, 1980. Cert. tchr., Calif.; cert. adminstrv., Calif. Actor, L.A., 1945-60; novelist, 1965-72; pres. Burbank (Calif.) Tchrs. Assn., 1977-79; dir. Meilinki Enterprises Ltd., L.A., 1982—. Author: (novels) That Cold Day In The Park, 1965, Angel Loves Nobody, 1969, The Moon Bathers, 1972, (non-fiction) Prints of Paul Jacoulet, 1980, Watercolors of Paul Jacoulet, 1988, Elizabeth Keith-The Printed Works, 1992, Printmaker in Paradise: Charles W. Bartlett, 2001. Recipient Samuel Goldwyn award, UCLA, 1979, 80. Mem. Writers Guild Am., New England Appraisers Assn. Avocation: reading.

MILES, SARA JOAN, dean; b. Muncie, Ind., June 26, 1938; d. Raymond Earl and Norma Vivian Wasson; m. John E. Miles; children: Julia Elizabeth Robinson, Stephen John. BA, Ball State U., 1960; M in Religious Edn., Tex. Christian U., 1963; MS in Biology, U. Ill., 1970; PhD in History of Sci., U. Chgo., 1988. H.s. sci. tchr. Muncie City Sch. Sys., 1960—61; missionary sci. tchr. Disciples of Christ Chs., Bolenge via Mbandaka, Congo, 1965—68; counselor, asst. dir. gen. curriculum U. Ill., Urbana, 1969—73; faculty mem. biology/history Wheaton (Ill.) Coll., 1974—94; faculty mem. history/biology Ea. Coll., St. Davids, Pa., 1994—96, undergrad. dean, 1996—2000; v.p. instl. effectiveness Ea. U., 2000—02, founding dean Nueva Esperanza Ctr. for Higher Edn. Phila., 2002—. Contbr. articles to profl. jours. Fellow: Am. Sci. Affiliation (coun., adv. bd. 1994—); mem.: AAAS (at large, sect. l 1994—96), History of Sci. Soc. (chair various committees, Dibner lectr., rep. to AAAS Com. X 1989—), Am. Hist. Assn., Phi Alpha Theta, Sigma Xi. Presbyterian. Avocations: travel, reading. Office: Ea U 1300 Eagle Rd Saint Davids PA 19087-3696 E-mail: smiles@eastern.edu.

MILES, THOMAS CASWELL, aerospace engineer; b. Atlanta, Mar. 21, 1952; s. Franklin Caswell and Eugenia Frances (Newsom) M.; m. Linda Susan Duggleby, Aug. 10, 1980. BMET, So. Poly. State U., 1977; postgrad., Troy State U., 1978-80. Assoc. engr. aircraft design Lockheed Martin Aero. Co., Marietta, Ga., 1980-82, engr., aircraft design, 1982-85, sr. engr., aircraft design, 1985-89, group engr., 1989-90, specialist engr., 1990-98, sr. specialist engr., 1998-2001, staff engr., 2001—. Mem. SAE-A-6 Mil. Aircraft & Helicopter Panel, 1987-91, SAE-A-10 Aircraft Oxygen Equipment Com., 1996—. Mem. AIAA, (assoc. fellow), ASME, ASTM, Nat. Mgmt. Assn. (bd. dirs. 1996-2000), Soc. Automotive Engrs. (SAE co. rep., SAE Atlanta sect. vice chmn. aircraft), Oxygen Standardization Coord. Group, Assn. Fraternity Advisors (affiliate), Wick's Lake Homeowners Assn. (pres. 1995, v.p. 1996, 97), Tau Kappa Epsilon (Providence advisor 1999-2002, dist. pres. 1987-88, dist. v.p. 1984-99, chpt. advisor 1980-87, key leader 1985, 90, So. Order of Honor 1989, Edn. Found. medal of excellence 2002). Avocations: sailing, screen printing. Home: 1926 Wicks Ridge Ln Marietta GA 30062-6777 E-mail: tekezeke@aol.com.

MILES, WENDELL A. federal judge; b. Holland, Mich., Apr. 17, 1916; s. Fred T. and Dena Del (Alverson) M.; m. Mariette Bruckert, June 8, 1946; children: Lorraine Miles, Michelle Miles Kopinski, Thomas Paul. AB, Hope Coll., 1938, LLD (hon.), 1980; MA, U. Wyo., 1939; JD, U. Mich., 1942; LLD (hon.), Detroit Coll. Law, 1979. Bar: Mich. Ptnr. Miles & Miles, Holland, 1948-53, Miles, Mika, Meyers, Beckett & Jones, Grand Rapids, Mich., 1961-70; pros. atty. County of Ottawa, Mich., 1949-53; U.S. dist. atty. Western Dist. Mich., Grand Rapids, 1953-60, U.S. dist. judge, 1974—, chief judge, 1979-86, sr. judge, 1986—. Cir. judge 20th Jud. Cir. Ct. Mich., 1970-74; instr. Hope Coll., 1948-53, Am. Inst. Banking, 1953-60; adj. prof. Am. constl. history Hope Coll., Holland, Mich., 1979—; mem. Mich. Higher Edn. Commn.; apptd. Fgn. Intelligence Surveillance Count, Washington, 1989—. Pres. Holland Bd. Edn., 1952-63. Served to capt. U.S. Army, 1942-47. Recipient Liberty Bell award, 1986. Fellow Am. Bar Found.; mem. ABA, Mich. Bar Assn., Fed. Bar Assn., Ottawa County Bar Assn., Grand Rapids Bar (Inns of Ct. 1995—), Am. Judicature Soc., Torch Club, Rotary Club, Masons. Office: US Dist Ct 236 Fed Bldg 110 Michigan St NW Ste 452 Grand Rapids MI 49503-2363 Home (Winter): 16380 Kelly Cove Dr #305 Fort Myers FL 33908 Office Phone: 616-456-2314. Business E-Mail: miles@miwd.uscourts.gov.

MILES-CLARK, JEARL, olympic athlete, track and field; b. Gainesville, Fla., Sept. 4, 1966; m. J.J. Clark, Nov. 30, 1996. BA in Business, Ala. A&M, 1988. Winner N.C.A.A. Divsn. II Nats. 400m, 1985; mem. U.S.A. Olympic Team, 1992, 1996. Achievements include world Champion 400m, 1993, USA Outdoor 800m champion, 1st pl. 400 meter, Verizon Millrose Games, 400 meter USA Outdoor champ, 2002, 1st pl., Oracle Open, 2002, ranked #1 in the US at 400meter, #2 in US at 800 meter by Track and Field News, 2002. Office: c/o USA Track & Field 1 Rca Dome Ste 140 Indianapolis IN 46225-1023

MILES-LA GRANGE, VICKI, judge; b. Oklahoma City, Okla., Sept. 30, 1953; d. Charles and Mary (Greenard) Miles. BA, Vassar Coll., 1974; LLB, Howard U., 1977; cert., U. Ghana, West Africa; DHL (hon.), Oklahoma City U., 1995. Legis. aide Spkr. House Rep. Carl Albert, 1974-76; law clerk Judge Woodrow Seals U.S. Dist. Ct. (so. dist.), Tex., 1977-79; fellow, atty. criminal divsn. U.S. Dept. Justice, Washington, 1979-83; asst. dist. atty. Dist. Atty.'s Office, Oklahoma County, 1983-86; pvt. practice Oklahoma City, 1986-93; mem. Okla. Senate (Dist. 48), 1987-93; U.S. atty. U.S. Dept. Justice, Oklahoma City, Okla., 1993-94; judge U.S. Dist. Ct. (we. dist.), Oklahoma City, 1994—. Bd. trustees Vassar Coll. Mem. ABA, Nat. Bar Assn., Okla. Bar Assn., Am. Inns Ct. Democrat. Baptist. Office: US Dist Judge US Courthouse 200 NW 4th St Ste 5011 Oklahoma City OK 73102-3031

MILETICH, IVO, library and information scientist, bibliographer, educator, linguist, literature research specialist; b. Pucisca, Yugoslavia, Apr. 18, 1936; came to U.S., 1966, naturalized, 1972; s. Josip and Mandina (Bagich) M.; m. Mira Pilja, Mar. 11, 1967; children: George Edward, Marina Julie. AB, Acad. Edn., Split, Yugoslavia, 1960; AM in History, U. Skopje, Macedonia, Yugoslavia, 1966; cert. advanced study, English Inst., Chgo., 1969; MA in Libr. Sci., Rosary Coll., River Forest, Ill., 1971. Cert. libr., Va. Tchr. various schs., Yugoslavia, 1959-65; asst. bibliographer Slavic langs. and lit. Joseph Regenstein and Sam Harper Librs., U. Chgo., 1967-71; tchr. Croatian lang. co-edn. YMCA Community Coll., Chgo., 1969-71, 74—; bibliographer Old Dominion U., Norfolk, Va., 1971-74; assoc. prof. libr. sci., bibliographer Chgo. State U., 1974—. Translator, interpreter English, Latin, Croatian, Serbian, Macedonian, Bulgarian, Old Ch. Slavic, Slovene, 1969—; interpreter Berlitz Trans. Ctr. Sch. Langs.; lectr. South Slavonic langs., lit., history and culture, Balkan states culture, heritage and folk lit., transl. techniques; lectr. in field. Contbr. various confs., seminars, workshops, jours., transl. of articles, studies, work on dictionary, Berlitz Transl. Svc. transl. and interpretation. Recipient cert. of appreciation YMCA C.C., Chgo., 1976, cert. Beta Phi Mu, U. Pitts., 1972, Am. Translators Assn., 1980, Assn. Coll. and Rsch. Librs., 1986. Mem. ALA, Am. Fedn. Tchrs., Assn. Coll. and Rsch. Librs., Chgo. Acad. Libr. Coun. Libr. of Congress (assoc.), Soc. Scholarly Publishing, Beta Phi Mu. Home: 618 Exchange Ave Calumet City IL 60409-3903 Office: Chgo State U Rm Lib 203 95th St at King Dr Chicago IL 60628

MILEWSKI, BARBARA ANNE, pediatrics nurse, neonatal/perinatal nurse practitioner, critical care nurse; b. Chgo., Sept. 11, 1934; d. Anthony and LaVerne (Sepp) Witt; m. Leonard A. Milewski, Feb. 23, 1952; children: Pamela, Robert, Diane, Timothy. ADN, Harper Coll., Palatine, Ill., 1982; BS, Northern Ill. U., 1992; postgrad., North Park Coll. RN Ill., cert. CPR instr. Staff nurse N.W. Cmty. Hosp., Arlington Heights, Ill., Resurrection Hosp., Chgo.; nurse neonatal ICU Children's Meml. Hosp., Chgo.; day care cons. Cook County Dept. Pub. Health; owner, CEO Child Care Health Cons. CPR instr. Stewart Oxygen Svcs., Chgo., Harper Coll., Children's Meml. Hosp.; instr., organizer parenting and well baby classes and clinics; health coord. CEDA Head Start; mem. adv. bd. Cook County Child Care Resource and Referral; dir. Albany Park Head Start. Vol. Children's Meml. Hosp., Boy Scouts Am. Mem.: Am. Mortar Bd., Sigma Theta Tau.

MILEY, DAVID, professional baseball coach; Catcher Cin. (Ohio) Reds, 1980—87, coach, 1987—2003, mgr., 2003—. Office: 100 Main St Cincinnati OH 45202*

MILEY, GEORGE HUNTER, nuclear and electrical engineering educator; b. Shreveport, La., Aug. 6, 1933; s. George Hunter and Norma Angeline (Dowling) M.; m. Elizabeth Burroughs, Nov. 22, 1958; children: Susan Miley Hibbs, Hunter Robert. BS in Chem. Engring., Carnegie-Mellon U., 1955; MS, U. Mich., 1956, PhD in Chem. Nuclear Engring., 1959. Nuclear engr. Knolls Atomic Power Lab., Gen. Electric Co., Schenectady, 1959-61; mem. faculty U. Ill., Urbana, 1961—, prof., 1967—, chmn. nuclear engring. program, 1975-86, dir. Fusion Studies Lab., 1976—, fellow Ctr. for Advanced Study, 1985-86; dir. rsch. Rockford Tech. Assocs. Inc., 1990-94; pres., dir. rsch. NPL Assocs. Inc., 1994—; chief scientist Lattice Energy, LLC, 2001—03. Vis. prof. U. Colo., 1967, Cornell U., 1969-70, U. New South Wales, 1986, Imperial Coll. of London, 1987; mem. Ill. Radiation Protection Bd., 1988—; mem. Air Force Studies Bd., 1990-94; chmn. tech. adv. com. Ill. Low Level Radioactive Waste Site, 1990-96; chmn. com. on indsl. uses of radiation Ill. Dept. Nuclear Safety, 1989-2000. Author: Direct Conversion of Nuclear Radiation Energy, 1971, Fusion Energy Conversion, 1976; editor Jour. Fusion Tech., 1980-2001; U.S. assoc. editor Laser and Particle Beams, 1982-86, mng. editor, 1987-91, editor-in-chief, 1991-2002; U.S. editor Jour. Plasma Physics, 1995-2003. Served with C.E. AUS, 1960. Recipient Western Electric Tchg.-Rsch. award, 1977, Halliburton Engring. Edn. Leadership award, 1990, Edward Teller medal, 1995, Scientist of Yr. award Jour. New Energy, 1996, Scientist of the Yr. award Inst. for New Energy 1996, Cert. Recognition award NASA, 2003; NATO sr. sci. fellow, 1975-76, Guggenheim fellow, 1985-86, Japanese Soc. Promotion of Sci. fellow, 1994. Fellow IEEE (Fusion Tech. Achievement award, 2003), Am. Nuclear Soc. (dir. 1980-83, Disting. Svc. award 1980, Outstanding Achievement award Fusion Energy divsn. 1992), Am. Phys. Soc.; mem. Am. Soc. Engring. Edn. (chmn. energy conversion com. 1967-70, pres. U. Ill. chpt. 1973-74, chmn. nuclear divsn. 1975-76, Outstanding Tchr. award 1973), Sigma Xi, Tau Beta Pi. Presbyterian. Achievements include research on fusion, energy conversion, reactor kinetics. Office: U Ill 214 Nuclear Engring Lab 103 S Goodwin Ave Urbana IL 61801-2901 Office Phone: 217-333-3772. E-mail: georgehm@aol.com. *My professional goal has been to insure that future generations have a plentiful supply of economical, readily available energy such as offered by fusion. Not only should this insure a continued improvement in the standard of living for persons in all nations, but it should help maintain peace which is threatened by the struggle to obtain and control limited natural sources of energy.*

MILFORD, FREDERICK JOHN, retired research company executive; b. Cleve., July 1, 1926; s. Frederick Charles and Florence M.; m. Jean Irene Olson, Sept. 8, 1951; 1 child, Cheryl Lynn. BS in Physics, Case Inst. Tech., 1949; PhD in Physics, M.I.T., 1952. Instr. Case Inst. Tech., Cleve., 1952-56, asst. prof., 1956-59; div. cons. Battelle Columbus Labs., 1959-62, div. chief, 1962-64, sr. fellow, 1964-66, dir. research in phys. scis., 1966-73, scientist, 1973, dept. mgr., 1973-76, assoc. dir., 1976-85, chief scientist, 1985-87, v.p. spl. programs, 1987-89, ret., 1989. Vis. prof. physics U. Wash., 1969 Author: (with J.R. Reitz) Foundations of Electromagnetic Theory, 1960, 4th edit., 1993. Emeritus mem. adv. bd. Central Ohio Salvation Army. Served with USNR, 1945-46. George Eastman fellow, 1951-52; Focke scholar, 1948-49 Fellow Am. Phys. Soc.; mem. Masons, Kit Kat Club. Home: 1411 London Dr Columbus OH 43221-1543

MILFORD, MURRAY HUDSON, retired soil science educator; b. Honey Grove, Tex., Sept. 29, 1934; s. Murray Lane and Vivian Ione (Hudson) M.; m. Marsha Ann Rasmussen, July 21, 1961; children: Rebecca Ione, Murray Daniel. BS in Agronomy, Tex. A&M, 1955, MS in Agronomy, 1959; PhD in Soil Science, U. Wis., 1962. Cert. profl. soil scientist. Rsch. assoc. Cornell U., Ithaca, N.Y., 1962-63, asst. prof., 1963-68, assoc. prof., 1968, Tex. A&M U., College Station, 1968-74, prof., 1974-2001; ret., 2001. Author: (lab. manual) Soils and Soil Science-Lab. Exercises, 1970. 1st lt. USAR, 1955-57. Recipient so. region award for excellence in coll. and univ. tchg. in food and agrl. scis. Nat. Assn. State Univs. and Land Grant Colls., Higher Edn. Program, USDA, 1995. Fellow AAAS, Am. Soc. Agronomy (pres. Tex. chpt. 1982-83, Resident Edn. award 1978), Soil Sci. Soc. Am. (Edn. award 1988); mem. Soil and Water Conservation Soc. (pres. Tex. coun. of chpts. 1987). Democrat. Presbyterian. Home: 3606 Tanglewood Dr Bryan TX 77802-3320 E-mail: mmilford@tca.net.

MILGRAM, JEROME H. marine and ocean engineer, educator; b. Phila., Sept. 23, 1938; s. Samuel J. and Fannie M. BSEE, BS in Naval Architecture and Marine Engring., MIT, 1961, MS, 1962, PhD in Hydrodynamics, 1965. Registered profl. engr., Mass. With Scripps Inst. Oceanography, San Diego, summer 1961; project engr. Block Assocs., Cambridge, Mass., 1961-67; asst. prof. MIT, Cambridge, 1967-70, assoc. prof., 1970-77, prof. ocean engring., 1977-89, William I. Koch prof. marine tech., 1989—. Rsch. assoc. in biophysics Harvard U. Med. Sch., 1974-76; vis. prof. in naval architecture and marine engring. U. Mich., 1988-89; design dir. Am. 3 Found., 1991-95; guest investigator Woods Hole Oceanog. Instn., 1996—; vis. prof. Johns Hopkins U., 1996-97; investigator and expert witness for marine casualties. Contbr. articles to profl. jours.; patentee in field. Recipient Am. Bur. Shipping award, 1961, Alan Berman Outstanding Rsch. Publ. award U.S. Naval Rsch. Lab., 1990, AT&T Design Innovation award, 1992. Fellow Soc. Naval Archs. and Marine Engrs. (life); mem. NAE (life), Nat. Rsch. Coun. (marine bd. 1998-2001). Home: 20 Blossom Hill Rd Winchester MA 01890-3455 Office: MIT 77 Massachusetts Ave Rm 5-318 Cambridge MA 02139-4307 Office Phone: 617-253-5943. Business E-Mail: jmilgram@mit.edu.

MILGRAM, RICHARD MYRON, music school administrator; b. Moultrie, Ga. s. Bernard Byron and Libbie Elaine M.; m. Judith Lee Milgram; children: Rhonda Beth, Gary David. MusB, Berklee Coll. Music, Boston; MusM, Boston U. Cert. tchr. Mass., Conn. Tchr. Norwood (Mass.) Pub. Schs., 1969-72; asst. prof. Merrimack Coll., North Andover, Mass., 1972-75; tchr. Guilford (Conn.) Pub. Schs., 1975-77; pres., co-founder Shoreline Sch. Art and Music, Branford, Conn., 1978—. Mem. music edn. coun./student tchr. practicum com. Westfield (Mass.) State Coll., 1978-81, New Haven Arts Coun.; judge various music competitions; performance Carnegie Hall, 1997, Quick Ctr. for the Arts/Fairfield U., 1998; guest condr. Conn. Symphonic Band, 1997. Contbr. revs. to music jours. Mem. Phi Mu Alpha Sinfonia. Office: Shoreline School of Art & Music Ste 2 540 E Main St Branford CT 06405-2946

MILGRIM, DARROW A. insurance company executive; b. Chgo., Apr. 30, 1945; BA, Calif. State U., San Bernardino, 1968; postgrad., U. So. Calif., 1972. Accredited ins. advisor, cert. ins. counselor; sch. adminstr. Tchr. Rialto (Calif.) Unified Sch. Dist., 1969-70, Las Virgenes Unified Sch. Dist., Westlake Village, Calif., 1970-78; instr. Calif. State U., Northridge, 1980-84; pres. Darrow Milgrim Ins. Svcs., Inc.; ins. broker, dir. Speare Ins. Brokers, Blade Ins. Svcs., Sherman Oaks, Calif., 1984—2004; sr. v.p. Acordia Calif., Inc., Sherman Oaks, 2004—. Cons. Ronald McDonald House Charities, SC, L.A., 1986—95, ACA Legis. Task Force and Nat. Pub. Policy com.; bd. dirs. Calamigos Star C Ranch Summer Camp, Malibu, Calif., Calamigos Environ. Edn. Ctr., Malibu. Editor: Legislation and Regulations for Organized Camps, 1987. Pres. Calif. Camping Adv. Coun., Long Beach, 1985—87, 1999—2000; bd. dirs. Calif. Collaboration Youth, Sacramento, 1985—, Cmap Ronald McDonald Good Times, 1989—95; commr. dept. pks. and recreation City of Agoura Hills, Calif., 1987—93. Mem.: Agts. and Brokers State Legis. Coun., Ins. Brokers and Agts. L.A. Coun., Am. Camping Assn. (bd. dirs. So. Calif. sect., mem. nat. pub. policy com. Martinsville, Ind. 1980—98, nat. bd. dirs. 1990—95, legis. liaison, regional honor 1986). Office: Acordia Calif Inc 15303 Ventura Blvd 7th Fl Sherman Oaks CA 91403 Office Phone: 818-464-9300. Business E-Mail: darrow_milgrim@acordia.com.

MILGRIM, ROGER MICHAEL, lawyer; b. N.Y.C., Mar. 22, 1937; s. Isreal and Iola (Lash) M.; m. Patricia Conway, July 10, 1971; children: Justin. BA, U. Pa., 1958; LLB, NYU, 1961, LLM, 1962. Bar: N.Y., U.S. Supreme Ct. Assoc. Baker & McKenzie, Paris, 1963-65, Nixon Mudge et al, N.Y.C., 1965-68; mem. Milgrim Thomajan & Lee P.C., N.Y.C., 1968-92; ptnr., chmn. intellectual property group Paul, Hastings, Janofsky & Walker LLP, N.Y.C., 1992—, chmn. litigation dept., 1999-2000. Adj. prof. sch. law NYU, N.Y.C., 1974—95. Author: Milgrim on Trade Secrets, 1967, supplement, 2003, Milgrim on Licensing, 1990, supplement, 2003. Trustee Coll. Wooster, 1994-97, Bklyn. Hosp., 1982-91; bd. dirs. Fulbright Assn., 1998—, chmn. Fulbright Prize com., 1999-01; bd. dirs. Technip, 1998—; bd. advs. UniStates LLC, 2000—. Mem. Knickerbocker Club, Phila. Cricket Club. Republican. Home: 301 E 52nd St New York NY 10022-6319 Office: Paul Hastings Janofsky & Walker LLP 75 E 55th New York NY 10022-3205 E-mail. rogermilgrim@paulhastings.com.

MILGROM, FELIX, immunologist, educator; b. Rohatyn, Poland, Oct. 12, 1919; came to U.S., 1958; naturalized, 1963; s. Henryk and Ernestina (Cyryl) M.; m. Halina Miszel, Oct. 15, 1941; children: Henry, Martin Louis. Student, U. Lwow, Poland, 1937-41, U. Lublin, 1945; MD, U. Wroclaw, Poland, 1947; MD (hon.), U. Vienna, Austria, 1976, U. Lund, Sweden, 1979, U. Heidelberg, Fed. Republic Germany, 1979, U. Bergen, Norway, 1980; DSc (hon.), U. Med. Dent., N.J., 1991. Rsch. assoc., prof. dept. microbiology Sch. Medicine U. Wroclaw, 1946-54, chmn. dept., 1954; prof., head dept. microbiology Sch. Medicine, Silesian U., Zabrze, Poland, 1954-57; rsch. assoc. Svc. de Chime Microbienne, Pasteur Inst., Paris, 1957; rsch. assoc. prof. dept. bacteriology and immunology U. Buffalo Sch. Medicine, 1958-62; assoc. prof., then prof. and disting. prof. microbiology Sch. Medicine, SUNY, Buffalo, 1962—, chmn. dept., 1967-85. Author: Studies on the Structure of Antibodies, 1950; co-editor: International Convocations on Immunology, 1969, 75, 79, 85, Principles of Immunology, 1973, 2d edit., 1979, Principles of Immunological Diagnosis in Medicine, 1981, Medical Microbiology, 1982; editor in chief Internat. Archives of Allergy and Applied Immunology, 1965-91; contbg. editor Vox Sanguinis, 1965-76, Transfusion, 1966-73, Cellular Immunology, 1970-83, Transplantation, 1975-78; contbr. numerous articles to profl. jours. Recipient Alfred Jurzykowski Found. prize, 1986, Paul Ehrlich and Ludwig Darmstaedter prize, 1987. Mem. Am. Assn. Immunologists, Transplantation Soc. (v.p. 1976-78), Am. Acad. Microbiology, Coll. Internat. Allergologicum (v.p. 1970-78, pres. 1978-82, hon. mem. 1990—), Polish Acad. Arts and Scis., Sigma Xi. Achievements include research on the serology of syphillis, Tb, rheumatoid arthritis, organ and tissue specificity including blood groups, transplantation and autoimmunity. Home: 474 Getzville Rd Buffalo NY 14226-2555 Office Phone: 716-829-3816.

MILHAM, JULEE LYNN, lawyer, arbitrator, mediator; b. Chapel Hill, N.C., May 24, 1963; d. Richard Joseph and Peggy Joyce Milham. BA, Stetson U. DeLand, 1983; JD, Stetson U. St. Petersburg, 1986. Bar: Fla. 1986, Calif. 1987, D.C. 1989, U.S. Dist. Ct. (mid. dist.) Fla. 1991, U.S. Ct. Appeals (11th cir.) 1994; cert. mediator, Fla. Atty. at law sole propr., St. Petersburg, 1986—. Traffic ct. hearing officer Pinellas County Ct., Fla., 1994—, small claims hearing officer, 1997—; mediator/arbitrator, 1994—; adj. prof. entertainment law Stetson Coll. Law. Author: The Practice of Music Law in Florida, 2003. Mem. Fla. Bar (chair emeritus entertainment sect., chair small claims rules com.). Office: 505 76th Ave Saint Petersburg Beach FL 33706-1805 Fax: 727-363-1925. Office Phone: 727-363-8114. E-mail: julee@eMusiclaw.com.

MILHORAT, THOMAS HERRICK, neurosurgeon; b. N.Y.C., Apr. 5, 1936; s. Ade Thomas and Edith Caulkins (Herrick) M.; m. Edith Mostile, 1961; children: John Thomas, Robert Herrick. BA, Cornell U., 1957, MD, 1961. Intern, asst. resident in gen. surgery N.Y. Hosp.-Cornell Med. Ctr., 1961—63, asst. resident, chief resident in neurosurgery, 1965—68, asst. neurosurgeon NIH, 1968—71; clin. assoc., dept. surg. neurology Nat. Inst. Neurol. Diseases and Blindness, Bethesda, 1963—65; assoc. prof. neurol. surgery, assoc. prof. child health and devel. George Washington U. Sch. Medicine, Washington, 1971—74, prof. neurol. surgery, prof. child health and devel., 1974—81; chmn. dept. neurosurgery Children's Hosp. Nat. Med. Ctr., Washington, 1971—81; prof. neurol. surgery, dept. chmn. SUNY Health Sci. Ctr., Bklyn., 1982—2001; chmn. dept. neurosurgery North Shore/L.I. Jewish Health System, 2002—; founder, dir. Chiari Inst. North Shore Univ. Hosp., 2002—; prof. neurol. surgery N.Y.U. Sch. Medicine, 2002—. Neurosurgeon-in-chief Kings County Hosp. Ctr., 1982—2001; regional chmn. neurol. surgery L.I. Coll. Hosp., 1986—2001; program dir. Neurosurgery Rsch. Tng. Program, 1982—2001; mem. Nat. Coun. Scientists NIH, 1969—82. Author: Hydrocephalus and Cerebrospinal Fluid, 1972, Pediatric Neurosurgery, 1978, Cerebrospinal Fluid and the Brain Edemas, 1987; (with M.K. Hammock) Cranial Computed Tomography in Infancy and Childhood, 1981; mem. editl. bd. Neurosurgery, 1997—, Neurosug Focus: Syringomyelia, 2000—; contbr. more than 325 articles to profl. jours. Lt. comdr. USPHS, 1963—65. Recipient 1st prize in pathology, Cornell U. Med. Sch. Dept. Ob-Gyn., 1960, Charles L. Horn prize Cornell Med. Sch., 1961, Best Paper award ann. combined meeting N.Y. Acad. Medicine/N.Y. Neurosurg. Soc., 1965, Pudenz award for Excellence in CSF Physiology, 1994, E Jefferson Browder award for excellence in Neurosurgery, 1996, Arthur A. Kaplan award for excellence in neurosurgery, 1999; named one of N.Y.'s Best Doctors, N.Y. Mag., 1992-2004, Best Doctors in Am., 1997-2004. Mem. AAMS, Internat. Soc. Pediat. Neurosurgery, Am. Assn. Neurol. Surgery, Am. Syringomyelia Alliance Project (chmn. med. adv. bd. 1996—), Am. Acad. Pediat. (surg. sect.), Soc. Pediat. Rsch., N.Y. Acad. Medicine, N.Y. Soc. Neurosurgery (pres. 1988-90), Bklyn. Neurologic Soc. (pres. 1988-95), Soc. Neurosci., Internat. Soc. Neurosci., Soc. Neurol. Surgeons, Sigma Xi. Avocations: golf, billiards, gardening. Office: North Shore Univ Hosp Dept Neurosurgery Manhasset NY 11030 Office Phone: 516-562-3020. Business E-Mail: milhorat@nshs.edu.

MILHOUSE, PAUL WILLIAM, bishop; b. St. Francisville, Ill., Aug. 31, 1910; s. Willis Cleveland and Carrie (Pence) M.; m. Mary Frances Noblitt, June 29, 1932; children: Mary Catherine Milhouse Hauswald, Pauline Joyce Milhouse Vermillion, Paul David. AB, U. Indpls. (formerly Ind. Ctrl. U.), 1932; DD, U. Ind. (formerly Ind. Ctrl. U.), 1950; BD, Am. Theol. Sem., 1937, ThD, 1946; LHD, Westmar Coll., 1965; STD, Oklahoma City U., 1969; DD, So. Meth. U., 1969. Ordained to ministry United Brethren Ch., 1931. Pastor United Brethren Ch., Birds, Ill., 1928-29, Elliott, Ill., 1932-37, Olney, Ill., 1937-41, 1st Ch., Decatur, Ill., 1941-51; assoc. editor Telescope-Messenger, 1951-58; exec. sec. gen. coun. Evang. United Brethren Ch., 1959-60, bishop, 1960-68, United Meth. Ch., 1968—. Presiding bishop Southwestern Area, Evang. United Brethren Ch., 1960-68; presiding bishop United Meth. Ch., Okla., 1968-80; pres. Coun. United Meth. Bishops, 1977-78; bishop-in-residence Oklahoma City U., 1980-91, U. Indpls., 1992-97; mem. commn. to unite Evang. United Brethren Ch. and Meth. Ch., 1960-68; spkr. in field. Author: Enlisting and Developing Church Leaders, 1946, Come Unto Me, 1946, Lift Up Your Eyes, 1955, Doorways to Spritual Living, 1950, Except the Lord Build the House, 1949, Christian Worship in Symbol and Ritual, 1953, Laymen in the Church, 1957, At Life's Crossroads, 1959, Phillip William Otterbein, 1968, Nineteen Bishops of the Evangelical United Brethren Church, 1974, Organizing for Effective Ministry, 1980, Theological and Historical Roots of United Methodists, 1980, Detour Into Yesterday, 1984, Okla. City U., Miracle at 23d and Blackwelder, 1984, Transforming Dollars into Service, A History of Methodist Manor, 1987, St. Lukes of Oklahoma City, 1988, Franklin United Methodist Community, (a brief history), 1999; also articles; editor: Facing Frontiers, 1960. Trustee United Theol. Sem., 1959-68, hon. life trustee, 1980—, hon. chmn. capital fund campaign, 2001; trustee Westmar Coll., 1960-68, Western Home, 1960-68, So. Meth. U., 1968-80, Oklahoma City U., 1968-80, hon. life trustee, 1980-99, emeritus trustee, 1999—, Francis E. Willard Home, 1968-80, Meth. Manor, 1968-80, Boys Ranch, 1968-80, Last Frontier coun. Boy Scouts Am., 1968-80. Recipient Disting. Alumnus award Ind. Ctrl. U. (now U. Indpls.), 1978, Gene and Joanne Sease award, 2000, Disting. Friend award Oklahoma City U., 1979, Disting. Svc. award, 1980, Top Hand award Oklahoma City C. of C., 1980, Bishop Paul W. Milhouse award Oklahoma City U., 1990, Disting. Svc. award for contbns. to United Meth. history Gen. Commn. on Archives and History, 1996, Johson County Health Found. Pres. Cir. award, 2001. Mem. Mark Twain Writers Guild, Epsilon Sigma Alpha, now Alpha Chi. Mem. United Brethren Ch. *Life is a gift to be lived in harmony with the purpose of God, who holds us accountable for the way we live.*

MILIC-EMILI, JOSEPH, physiologist, educator; b. Sezana, Slovenia, May 27, 1931; arrived in Can., 1963; s. Joseph Milic-Emili and Giovanna Milic-Emili Perhavec; m. Ann Harding, Nov. 2, 1957; children: Claire, Anne-Marie, Alice, Andrew. MD, U. Milan, 1955; Dr. honoris causa, U. Louvain, Belgium, 1987, Kunming Med. Coll., China, 1987, U. Montpellier, France, 1994, U. Ferrara, Italy, 1996, U. Athens, Greece, 1998, U. Ljubljana, Slovenia. Asst. prof. physiology and exptl. medicine McGill U., Montreal, Que., Can., 1963-65, assoc. prof., 1965-69, prof., 1970-97, prof. emeritus, 1998—, dir. Meakins-Christie Labs., 1979-94. Vis. prof. Lab. de Physiologie Faculte de Medecine Saint-Antoine, Paris, Svc. de Pneumologie Hosp. Beaujon, Paris, 1978-79, 94-95, chmn. dept. physiology, 1973-78; vis. cons. medicine Royal Postgrad. Med. Sch., London, 1969-70; vis. cons. Aeronautics Imperial Coll. Tech., London, 1969-70; asst. prof. physiology U. Liege, Belgium, 1958-60; asst. prof. U. Milan, 1956-58. Mem. editl. bd. Jour. Applied Physiology, 1970-76, Rev. Française des Maladies Respiratoires, 1979-96, Rivista de Biologia, 1979-86, Am. Rev. Respiratory Disease, 1982-89, Reanimation, Soins Intensifs, Medicine d'Urgence, 1984-95. Mem. applied physiology and bioengring. study sect. NIH, 1975-78. Decorated Order of Can.; recipient Gold medal C. Forlanini U. Pavia, Italy, 1982, Am. Coll. Chest Physicians medal, 1984, 98, Harry Wunderly medal Thoracic Soc. Australia, 1988, medal Italian Sch. Mil. Medicine, 1990, medal Med. Sch. Brest, 1997, medal Med. Sch. Ferrara, 1997, medal Med. Sch. Bologna; author of one of 100-most cited articles in clin. rsch. of 1960s; named one of 1,000 most-cited contemporary scientists, 1965-78, 1998 Presdl. award European Respiratory Soc., 1998 Disting. Lectr. in Physiology Am. Coll. Chest Physicians. Fellow Royal Soc. Can., Slovenian Acad. Sci. (fgn. corr.), Soc. Med. Clin. Bononiensis Sci.; mem. Am. Physiol. Soc., Can. Physiol. Soc., Can. Thoracic Soc., Med. Rsch. Coun. (mem. grants com. 1980), Soc. Pneumologie Belge (hon.), Brazilian Physiol. Soc. (hon.), Hellenic Thoracic Soc. (hon.), Polish Pneumological Soc. (hon.), Chilean Resp. Soc. (hon.). Home: 4394 Circle Rd Montreal QC Canada H3W 1Y5 Office: McGill U Meakins-Christie Labs 3626 St Urbain St Montreal QC Canada H2X 2P2 Office Phone: 514-398-3864. Business E-Mail: joseph.milic-emili@mcgill.ca.

MILIO, LOUIS ROMOLO, retired law educator, social worker; b. Balt. s. Placido and Rose (Pirrotti) M.; m. Ellenor K. Stafford, July 8, 1978 (dec. Sept. 1990). LLB, U. Balt., 1948, LLM, 1950, JD, 1972; LLD (hon.), We. U., 1951. Cert. social worker asst., Md. Copy boy Balt. Sun, 1943; cost acct. Continental Can Co., Balt., 1945; tax bailiff City Bur. Collections, Balt., 1946-49; atty. City Bur. Recreation, Balt., 1948—, social worker/drug counselor, 1970—; staff dept. welfare City of Balt., 1964-65; case worker Hdqrs. Office, Balt., 1965-66. Instr. Italian and pub. speaking YWCA, Balt., 1944; prof. law Ea. Coll. of Commerce, Balt., 1950-51; prof. philosophy Johns Hopkins Univ., Balt.; pres. Milio Cometics Co., Internat., Lady Eleanor Beauty Soap. Author: Faith, Hope & Charity, 1949; patent pending Milio Aviation Safety Sys. Co-founder, sec. Good Neighbor League, Balt., 1948; candidate U.S. Congress, 1946, 50; candidate Mayor Balt. City, 1952, 56, 59; candidate gov. Md., 1966-74. Pvt. 1st Class Md. State Guard, 1943-94. Mem. Star Spangled Banner Flag House Assn (last living resident). Dem. Roman Cath. Avocations: swimming, walking, bowling, cooking, gardening. Home and Office: Village of Cross Keys 2 Cross Keys Rd Apt C Baltimore MD 21210-1719

MILIORA, MARIA TERESA, chemist, psychotherapist, psychoanalyst, educator; b. Somerville, Mass., June 29, 1938; d. Andrew and Maria Civita (Gallinaro) Migliorini. BA cum laude, Regis Coll., 1960; PhD, Tufts U., 1965; MSW, Boston U., 1985. Rsch. asst. Tufts U., Medford, Mass., 1960-64, rsch. assoc., 1965-66; assoc. prof. Suffolk U., Boston, 1965-68, 1968-71, prof., 1971—, chmn. dept. chemistry, 1972-84, presdl. search com., 1980, faculty rep. strategic planning com., 1992—; faculty Boston Inst. for Psychotherapy, 1992-96, Tng. and Rsch. Inst. for Self Psychology, N.Y.C., 1994—. Rsch. assoc. Bio-Research Inst., Cambridge, Mass., 1968. Author: Narcissism, the Family, and Madness, 2000, The Scorsese Psyche on Screen, 2004; contbr. articles to profl. jours. Faculty rep. to trustees Joint Coun. on Univ. Affairs, Suffolk U., 1973-77, 79-81; convenor Pres.'s Commn. on Status of Women, 1974-78, speaker ednl. policy com., 1972-73; chair cultural diversity CLAS Curriculum, 1991—. Mem. AAUP (chpt. pres. 1970), NASW, Am. Chem. Soc. (alt. councillor 1976-82, councillor 1979-82, bd. dirs. Northeastern sect. 1976-80, chmn. pub. rels. sect. 1977-79), Mass. Acad. Clin. Social Work, Nat. Assn. for Advancement Psychoanalysis, Nat. Membership Com. on Psychoanalysis, Sigma Xi (chpt. pres. 1972-73), Sigma Zeta (chpt. sect. 1970-80), Alpha Lambda Delta, Delta Epsilon Sigma. Home: 41 Irving St Newton MA 02459-1611 Office: Suffolk University Beacon Hill Boston MA 02114 Office Phone: 617-357-0223. E-mail: Theresa0369@comcast.net.

MILISSIS, NICHOLAS GEORGE, lawyer; b. Chgo., Oct. 28, 1974; s. Andrew and Aphrodite Milissis; m. Lena Memmos, Apr. 17, 2004. BA in Psychology, U. Ill., Chgo., 1997; JD, Kent Coll., 2000; PhD in Internat. Law, Fairfax U., 2001. Bar: Ill. 2002, U.S. Dist. Ct. (no. dist.) Ill. 2002. Law clk., office mgr. Legal Advocates Group, P.C., Chgo., 2000—02, sr. ptnr., 2002—. Contbr. magazine. Chmn. Athens Sister City com. Chgo. Sister Cities Internat., 2002; sustaining mem., team leader Rep. Nat. Com., Washington, 2001; parish coun. bd. dirs., sec. Annunciation Greek Orthodox Cathedral, Chgo., 2003. Recipient Knight of Royal Brotherhood of St. Michael of the Wing for services to Portuguese Crown, Dom Duarte, Duke of Braganza, 2003. Master: Hellenic Armigers Soc. (pres., founder 2003); mem.: Hellenic Bar Assn. Ill. (scholar 1998), Am. Acad. Promotion of Geneal. and Heraldic Scis. (life), Chgo. Kent Student Bar Assn., Chicago-Kent Hellenic Law Students Assn. (pres. 1997—2000), Panarcadian Fedn. Am. (pres. youth chpt. 1998—2000), Golden Key (life), Psi Chi (life). Greek Orthodox. Avocations: heraldry, genealogy, ethnic percussion. Office: Legal Advocates Group PC 6601 N Avondale Ste 203 Chicago IL 60631 E-mail: nmilissis@sbcglobal.net.

MILITA, MARTIN JOSEPH, lawyer; b. Vineland, N.J., May 14, 1953; s.Martin Joseph and Mary Elizabeth (Gavigan) M.; m. Janet D. Milita, Oct. 3, 1981; 1 child, Samantha Anne. BA, Kings Coll., 1976; JD, Temple U., 1979. Bar: Pa. 1979, N.J. 1979, U.S. Dist. Ct. N.J. 1979. Tchg. fellow Temple U., Phila., 1978; asst. dist. atty. Bucks County Dist. Atty.'s Office, Doylestown, Pa., 1979-81; asst. prosecutor Hunterdon County Prosecutor's Office, Flemington, N.J., 1981-84; dep. atty. gen. State of N.J., Trenton, 1984-90; assoc. Sills Cummis et al, Newark, 1990-94; counsel Riker, Danzig, Scherer, Hyland & Perretti, LLP, Morristown, N.J., 1994—. Contbr. articles to law jours. Mem. adv. bd. Rep. Nat. Com., Washington, 1994—. Mem. N.J. Bar Assn. Roman Catholic. Avocations: civil war history, collecting civil war art and artifacts. Office: A Fiore & Sons 1230 McCarter Hwy Newark NJ 07104-3710

MILITELLO, SAMUEL PHILIP, lawyer; b. Buffalo, Dec. 16, 1947; s. Samuel Anthony and Katherine (Pesono) M.; m. Anne Little, May 27, 1972, divorced Dec. 26, 2003; children: Matthew Samuel, Rebecca Anne, Caitlin Frances. BA, Canisius Coll., 1969; JD, SUNY, Buffalo, 1972. Bar: NY 1972, US Ct. Mil. Appeals 1973, US Army Ct. of Mil. Rev. 1976, US Ct. Claims 1977, US Supreme Ct. 1977, US Dist. Ct. (we. dist.) NY 1986, US Dist. Ct. (no. dist.) NY 1987, US Dist. Ct. (ea. dist.) NY 1994, US Ct. Appeals (2d cir.), 1990. Assoc. Williams & Katzman, Watertown, NY, 1978-79; legal counsel, mgr. of litigation Parsons Corp., Pasadena, Calif., 1979-84; gen. counsel, sec. Envirogas, Inc., Hamburg, NY, 1984-86; assoc. Bond, Schoeneck & King, Watertown, 1987-88; mng. ptnr. Samuel P. Militello, PC, 1995, Watertown, 1989-1995; counsel Parsons Gilbane, New Orleans, 1979-81; gen. counsel The Stebbins Engring. and Mfg. Co. and subs., 1986—. Capt. JAGC, US Army, 1973-78. Decorated Army Commendation medal with one oak leaf cluster, Meritorious Service medal. Mem. ABA, NY State Bar Assn., Bar Assn. of Erie County (NY), mem. of Bd. of Dir., No. Wy. Builders Exchange, 1989-1995; mem., Bd. of Dir. of Mery Hosp. of watertwon, NY; mem., of Sch. Bd. of Imaculate Heart, Ctrl. HS, 1988-2000; Knights of Columbus, 4th degree; Bar Assn. of Jefferson County (NY), Am. Legion, K.C. (adv. 1978-79). Roman Catholic. Office: 1619 Ohio St Watertown NY 13601-3032

MILIUS, JOHN FREDERICK, film writer, director; b. St. Louis, Apr. 11, 1944; s. William Styx and Elizabeth (Roe) M.; 3 children. Grad., U. So. Calif., 1967. Instr. motion pictures script analysis U. So. Calif., fall 1973, advanced motion picture script analysis, spring 1974 Films include: (screenwriter) Devil's 8, 1969, Evel Knievel, 1971, Dirty Harry (uncredited), 1971, Jeremiah Johnson, 1972 (Heritage Wrangler Award), The Life and Times of Judge Roy Bean, 1972, Magnum Force, 1973, Apocalypse Now, 1979 (with Francis Ford Coppola, Academy Award nominee Best screenplay), Extreme Prejudice, 1987, Geronimo: An American Legend, 1993, Clear and Present Danger, 1994, Mexico, 1999, (TV) Melvin Purvis: G-Man, 1974; dir., screenwriter: Dillinger, 1973, The Wind and the Lion, 1975 (National Bell Ringers ednl. award,

Writers Guild nom. for Best Orig. Screenplay), Big Wednesday, 1978, Conan the Barbarian, 1982, Red Dawn, 1984, Farewell to the King, 1989, Flight of the Intruder, 1990, The Northmen, 1999, (TV) Rough Riders, 1997; exec. prodr.: Hardcore, 1979, Used Cars, 1980, Uncommon Valor, 1983; exec. prodr., co-screenwriter: 1941, 1979; dir.: (TV) The Twilight Zone, 1985, Motorcycle Gang, 1994; actor: Deadhead Miles, 1974, Hearts of Darkness: A Filmmaker's Apocalypse, 1991, Ben Johnson: Third Cowboy on the Right, 1996, (TV) American Cinema, 1994, Frank Capra's American Dream, 1997; spiritual advisor: Lone Wolf McQuade, 1983. Recipient Nat. Student Film Festival award U. So. Calif., 1968; numerous gun shooting awards; honored by Winchester for The Wind and the Lion. Office: care Jeff Berg International Creative Mgmt 8942 Wilshire Blvd Beverly Hills CA 90211-1934

MILK, JARED MARC, real estate company executive, writer; b. Gt. Neck, NY, Dec. 24, 1969; AA in Bus., SUNY, 1990; BA in Theater & Comms., SUNY, Old Westbury, 1992. Real estate sales NY, real estate broker NY. Broker Surf Realty, 1995-96; owner Milk and Assocs., 1996—, Hamajama Wood Boxes and Bags, 1996—, Castlecove Vending Machines, 1988—, ATM Credit Card Machines, 1999—, Ads-in-Motion, 2000—, Jared's Nuts, Cedarhurst, NY, 2001—, Driving Sch., Cedarhurst, 2001—, Milk Realty, 2004—; broker Candie's, 2002; pers. asst. Health Care, 1998. Ally for Hire, 2003; Cool Kids Cook, 03. Author: Flying Feathers, 1993; co-author: (book-on-cassette) Cinderella Cockroach, 1990, A Christmas Tale, 1994, A Chanukah Tale, 1995, The Mystery of the Old Fishing Shack, 1999, Legally Raped, 1999, Confessions on the Psycho Lane, 1999. Mem.: Notary Pub. Assn., NY State Real Estate Assn., Nassau Rep. Club. Jewish. Avocations: tennis, collecting, ice-skating, golf, travel, antiques. Office: PO Box 24 Cedarhurst NY 11516 Office Phone: 516-569-1244. E-mail: milk-1224@webtv.net.

MILKEN, MICHAEL R. think-tank executive, philanthropist; b. 1946; Grad. summa cum laude, U. Calif., Berkeley; MBA, U. Pa. Securities trader Drexel Burnham Lambert, until 1990; chmn. The Milken Inst., 1991—; chair Knowledge Universe, 1996—. Author: Taste for Living Series cookbooks. Chair Assn. Cure of Cancer of the Prostate; co-founder Milken Family Found., 1982. Office: care Milken Inst 1250 Fourth St Ste 200 Santa Monica CA 90401

MILKMAN, BEVERLY L. federal agency administrator; b. Ft. Pierce, Fla., Jan. 9, 1945; d. Robert George and Annette (Leatherwood) Lyford; m. Raymond H. Milkman, Feb. 27, 1972; 1 child, Katherine. BA magna cum laude, U. Ariz., 1967; MLA with honors, Johns Hopkins U., 1972; MA, George Washington U., 1978. Rsch. analyst Peat, Marwick, Mitchell & Co., 1967-69, program analyst, 1970-72, spl. asst. to dep. sec., 1972-74, spl. asst. to asst. sec., 1974-80, dir. office tech. assistance, 1980-81, dir. office of planning, tech. assistance, rsch. and evaluation, 1981-86, dep. dir. grant programs, 1986-88; exec. dir. Com. for Purchase from People Who are Blind or Severely Disabled, 1988—. Assoc. editor Economic Development Quarterly; contbr. articles to profl. publs. Recipient Disting. and Meritorious Exec. Rank awards, 1993, 96. Office: Com Purchase from People Who Are Blind or Severely Disabled 1215 Jefferson Davis Hwy Arlington VA 22202-4302

MILKMAN, ROGER DAWSON, genetics educator, molecular evolution researcher; b. N.Y.C., Oct. 15, 1930; s. Louis Arthur and Margaret (Weinstein) M.; m. Marianne Friedenthal, Oct. 18, 1958; children: Ruth Margaret, Louise Friedenthal, Janet Dawson Milkman Lussenhop, Paul David. AB, Harvard U., 1951, A.M., 1954, PhD, 1956. Student, asst., instr., investigator Marine Biol. Lab., Woods Hole, Mass., 1952-72, 88-96; instr., asst. prof. U. Mich., Ann Arbor, 1957-60; assoc. prof., prof. Syracuse U., N.Y., 1960-68; prof. biol. scis. U. Iowa, Iowa City, 1968-2001, prof. emeritus, 2001—, chmn. univ. genetics PhD program, 1992-93. Vis. prof. biology Grinnell (Iowa) Coll., 1990; mem. genetics study sect. NIH, 1986-87; NSF panelist, 1996-99; adj. scientist Marine Biol. Lab., Woods Hole, 2002—, Josephine Bay Paul Ctr. Translator: Developmental Physiology, 1970; editor: Perspectives on Evolution, 1982, Experimental Population Genetics, 1983, Evolution jour., 1984-86; mem. editl. bd. Jour. Bacteriology, 1998-2000; contbr. articles to profl. jours. Sec. Soc. Gen. Physiologists, 1963-65, Am. Soc. Naturalists, 1980-82; alumni rep. Phillips Acad., Andover, Mass., 1980-94. NSF grantee, 1959—; USPHS grantee, 1984-87. Fellow AAAS; mem. Am. Soc. for Microbiology, Genetics Soc. Am., Corp. Marine Biol. Lab., Soc. for Gen. Microbiology (U.K.). Jewish. Avocation: mountain hiking. Home and Office: 12 Fells Rd Falmouth MA 02540-1626 Office Phone: 508-289-7390. E-mail: rmilkman@mbl.edu.

MILL, JETH, performing company executive; Exe. dir. Des Moines Symphony. Office: Des Moines Symph 221 Walnut St Des Moines IA 50309

MILLAN, ALVIN, speech pathology/audiology services professional, educator; b. San Juan, P.R., May 28, 1968; s. William Millan and Aura Fuentes; m. Norma Rodriguez, Dec. 19, 1992; children: Liz C., Kenneth X. B in Speech Therapy, U. P.R., 1990, M in Speech Lang. Pathology, 1992, cert. in early intervention devel. deficiencies, 1996. Cert. speech lang. pathologist P.R., assistive tech. cert. Prof. speech lang. and comm. disorders U. P.R. Med. Scis. Campus, San Juan, 1991—. Contbr. articles to profl. jours. Fellow: Assn. Reading Devel., Assn. Curriculum Devel.; mem.: Am. Speech and Lang. Assn. (advocacy spkrs. bur. 1999—2001), P.R. Orgn. Speech-Lang. Pathology and Audiology (pres. adv. bd. 1996—99, v.p. 1999—2000, sec. 2000—). Avocations: reading, writing, meditation, spirituality, travel. Home: Calle San Patricio aa-15 Alturas de San Pedro Fajardo PR 00738 Office: Ctr Rehab del Habla Lenguaje Ave Gen Valero 313-B Fajardo PR 00738

MILLANE, LYNN, retired town official; b. Buffalo, Oct. 14, 1928; d. Robert P. and Justine A. (Ross) Schermerhorn; m. J. Vaughan Millane, Jr., Aug. 16, 1952; children: Maureen, Michele, John, Mark, Kathleen. EdB, U. Buffalo, 1949, EdM in Health Edn., 1951. Coun. mem. Amherst (N.Y.) Town Bd., 1982—96, dep. town supr., 1990-96, supr., 1996. Founder, liaison 1st adult day svcs. adv. bd. Town of Amherst, 1988, liaison to ad hoc cable TV com., 1992—96, liaison to Amherst C. of C., 1993—96, 1st records mgmt. adv. bd., liaison ethics bd., 1994—96; legis. liaison SUNY Family Violence Clin. Sch. Law, Buffalo, 1997—98; pres. E.J. Meyer Hosp. Jr. Bd., 1962—64; commr. N.Y. State Ethics Commn., 1999—; mem. adv. bd. N.Y. State Office Aging, 1996—2004, chair adv. bd., 1997—2004; bd. dirs. Kaledia Health, 1998—2000. Pres. Aux. to Erie County Bar Assn., 1966-68, Womens Com. Buffalo Philharm. Orch., 1976-78, v.p. adminstrn., 1975-76, v.p. pub. affairs, 1974-75, chair. adv. bd., 1979-82; v.p. Buffalo Philharm. Orch. Soc., Inc., 1976-78, coun. mem., trustee, 1979-87, bd. overseers, 1987-92; dir. 8th jud. dist. N.Y. State Assn. Large Towns, 1989-91; bd. dirs. oper. bd. Millard Fillmore Suburban Hosp., 1992-98; 1st v.p. Fams for 17, 1980-82, Friends of Baird Hall SUNY, Buffalo, 1980-82; exec. bd. Womens Exec. Coun. Erie County Rep. Com., 1969-71, Longview Protestant Home for Children, 1979-85, 2d v.p., 1982-85; bd. dirs. Amherst br. ARC, 1982-91, by-laws com., 1981, 84, chair sr. concerns com., 1982-91, liaison code of ethics com., 1987-89; nat. music com. Womens Assn. for Symphony Orchs. in Am. and Can., 1977-79; coun. mem. Am. Symphony Orch. League; sec. Amherst Sr. Citizens Adv. Bd., 1980-81, liaison from Amherst Town Bd., 1982-96; liaison to the Alternate Fuel and Clean Cities Com., 1994-96; dir.-at-large cmty. adv. coun. SUNY, Buffalo, 1981-91; co-assoc. chair maj. gift divsn. capital campaign Daemen Coll., 1983-84, trustee, 1998-; chair mem. com. Daemen Coll Trustees, 2003—; co-chair Women United Against Drugs Campaign, 1970-72; founding mem. Lunch and Issues, Amherst, 1981—; edn. com., bd. dirs. Network in Aging of Western N.Y., Inc., 1982-89, housing com., 1987-89; bd. dirs. Amherst Elderly Transp. Corp., 1982-99; committeeman dist. Town of Amherst Rep. Com.; treas. Town and Country Rep. Club, 1980-81; nominating com. Fedn. Rep. Womens Clubs Erie County, 1980; del. N.Y. State Govs. Conf. on Aging, 1995, White House Conf. on Aging, 1995, named mem. aging svcs.; mem. Erie County indsl. Devel. Agy. Erie County Regional Devel. Corp., 1996-97; mem. adv. bd. Amherst Symphony Orch., 2003-; vol. life project Greater Buffalo chpt. ARC, 2002-04, mem. svc. to older adults com., 2002-04. Named Homemaker of Yr., Family Circle mag., 1969, Woman of Substance, 20th Century Rep. Women, 1983, Woman of Yr., Buffalo Philharm. Orch. Soc., Inc., 1982, Outstanding Woman in Cmty. Svc., SUNY, Buffalo, 1985; recipient Good Neighbor award, Courier Express, 1978, Merit award, Buffalo Philharm. Orch., 1978, edn. Rep. Womens Clubs Erie County award, 1982, Disting. Svc. award, Town of Amherst Sr. Ctr., 1985, Amherst Adult Day Care and Vis. Nurses Assn., 1994, Susan B. Anthony award, nterclub Coun. Western N.Y., 1991, Cmty. Svc. award, Amherst Rep. Com., 1991, D.A.R.E. award, Town of Amherst Police Dept., 1994, Amherst South Rotary Club, 1997, Outstanding Cmty. Svc. award, Amherst Sr. Citizen Found., 1997, Lynn Millane Cmty. Svc. award named in her honor, Rep. honoree, award for svc., Town of Amherst Youth Bd., 1996, award for care and assistance to sr. citizens of N.Y. State, Batavia Nursing Home, 2000, Woman of Distinction award, NY State Senate, 2003; hon. Paul Harris fellow. Mem. Amherst C. of C. (VIP dinner com. 1984), LWV, SUNY Buffalo Alumni Assn. (life, presdl. advisor 1977-79), Amherst Symphony Orch. Assn. (bd. dirs. 1981-87, roster chair 1982-84, nominating chair 1985-86, vice-chair 50th ann. com. 1994-96, adv. com. 2003-), Niagara Connect, Amherst Rep. Womens Club (bd. dirs. 1963-65, 99), Zonta (pres. Amherst chpt. 1986-88, Zontian of Yr. 1992), Pi Lambda Theta (hon.).

MILLAR, GORDON HALSTEAD, mechanical engineer, agricultural machinery manufacturing executive; b. Newark, Nov. 28, 1923; s. George Halstead and Dill E. (McMullen) M.; m. Virginia M. Jedryczka, Aug. 24, 1957; children: George B., Kathryn M., Juliet S., John G., James H. B.M.E., U. Detroit, 1949, D.Sc. (hon.), 1977; PhD, U. Wis., 1952; L.H.D., West Coast U., 1984; D.Sc. (hon.), Western Mich. U., 1986. Registered profl. engr., Fla., Ill., Iowa, Mich., Minn., Ohio. Supr. new powerplants Ford Motor Co., 1952-57; engring. mgr. Meriam Instrument Co., Cleve., 1957-59; dir. new products McCulloch Corp., Los Angeles, 1959-63; with Deere & Co., 1963-84, v.p. engring., 1972-84; exec. assoc. Southwest Research Inst., 1987. Mem. Fed. Adv. Com. Indsl. Innovation, 1979; chmn. West Ctrl. Ill. Edn. Telecom. Corp.; pres. Accreditation Bd. for Engring. and Tech., 1983-85; pres., fellow Accreditation Bd. for Engring. and Tech. Contbr. articles to profl. jours.; patentee in field. Chmn. Quad Cities chpt. United Way, 1976-77; bd. dirs.; adv. council Bradley U. Coll. Engring. and Tech.; mem. exec. com. Illowa council Boy Scouts Am., 1977-79. Served with U.S. Army, World War II. Decorated Purple Heart; recipient Alumnus of Year award U. Detroit, 1976, Comdrs. medal for pub. svc. Dept. Army, 1989 Fellow ASME (hon. life mem.), Soc. Automotive Engrs. (pres. 1984, bd. dirs. 1984-86, mem. nat. nominating com.); mem. NAE, NSPE, Engrs. Joint Coun., Indsl. Rsch. Inst., Engring. Soc. Detroit, Am. Soc. Agrl. Engrs., Ill. Soc. Profl. Engrs., Moline C. of C., Aviation Coun. Home: 1840 Wiley Post Trl Port Orange FL 32128-6756

MILLAR, JAMES F. pharmaceutical executive; Exec. v.p. No. Group Cardinal Health Inc., Dublin, Ohio, with distbn., pres. drug wholesaling opers., exec. v.p., Pharm. Distbn. and Med. Products. Office: Cardinal Health Inc 7000 Cardinal Pl Dublin OH 43017-1092

MILLAR, JAMES ROBERT, economist, educator, university official; b. San Antonio, Tex., July 7, 1936; s. James G. and Virginia M. (Harrison) M.; m. Gera Ascher, July 4, 1965; children: Leo Schaeg (dec.), Mira Gail. BA, U. Tex., 1958; PhD in Econs., Cornell U., 1965. Asst. prof. dept. econs. U. Ill., Urbana, 1965-70, assoc. prof., 1970-72, prof., 1973-89, assoc. vice chancellor for acad. affairs, 1984-89, dir. internat. programs and studies, 1984-89; prof. econs. and internat. affairs George Washington U., Washington, 1989—, dir. Inst. for European, Russian and Eurasian Studies, 1989-01, assoc. dean Elliott Sch. Internat. Affairs, 1989-95, acting dean, 1994. Mem. acad. coun. Kennan Inst. Advanced Russian Studies, 1975-84; young faculty exchangee Moscow State U., 1966; cons. to congressmen and various U.S. govt. depts., 1972—; dir. Soviet Interview Project, 1981-88; sec., bd. dirs. Midwest Univs. Consortium for Internat. Activities, 1984-88, chmn. bd., 1988-89; bd. dirs., chair fin. com. Internat. Rsch. and Exchs. Bd., 2002—. Author: The ABCs of Soviet Socialism, 1981 (non-fiction award Soc. Midland Authors, 1981), The Soviet Economic Experiment, 1990; editor, contbr. The Soviet Rural Community, 1971; editor: Slavic Rev., Am. Quar. Soviet and East European Studies, 1975-80, Problems of Post-Communism, 1996-2003; editor, contbr. Politics, Work and Daily Life, A Survey of Former Soviet Citizens, 1987; editor, contbr. Cracks in the Monolith: Party Power in the Brezhnev Era, 1992, The Social Legacy of Communism, 1994; editor-in-chief: Encyclopedia of Russian History, 4 vols., 2004; contbr. articles on studies on Soviet/Russian economy and econ. history to scholarly jours. Served with Q.M.C. U.S. Army, 1960. Ford Found. fgn. area fellow, 1961-64; sr. scholar rsch. travel grantee to USSR, 1972; Internat. Rsch. and Exchs. Bd./USSR Acad. Scis. travel exchangee, 1979; fellow Woodrow Wilson Internat. Ctr. for Scholars, 1988-89, Guggenheim fellow, 1995-96; Internat. Rsch. and Exchs. Bd. advanced rsch. grantee, 1996. Mem. AAAS, Internat. Com. Ctrl. and East European Studies (bd. dirs., v.p. 2001—), Econ. History Assn., Am. Assn. Advancement Slavic Studies (del. Am. Coun. Learned Soc. 1992-98, bd. dirs. 1995-2001, v.p. 1998-99, pres. 1999-2000, chair coun. of member insts. 1995-99), Am. Coun. Learned Soc. (treas., bd. dirs. 1996-2002, sec. 1994-96, mem. exec. com. del., chair 1992-95, mem. joint com. with Social Sci. Rsch. Coun. 1990-95), N.Y. Acad. Sci., Phi Beta Kappa (pres. Alpha chpt. 1998-01). Home: 2801 New Mexico Ave NW Apt 1215 Washington DC 20007-3942 Office: George Washington U Inst Eur Russ Eurasian Studies 1957 E St NW Ste 412 N Washington DC 20052-0001 Office Phone: 202-994-1645. Business E-Mail: millar@gwu.edu.

MILLAR, JEFFERY LYNN, writer; b. Houston, July 10, 1942; s. Daniel Lynn Millar and Betty Ruth (Shove) Coons; m. Lynne McDonald, Dec. 21, 1964 (div. Aug. 1983); m. Peggy V. Watson, Apr. 1, 1994. BA, U. Tex., 1964. Reporter Houston Chronicle, 1964-65, film critic, 1965-2000, columnist, 1972-2000. Writer, co-creator: (comic strip) Tank McNamara, Universal Press Syndicate, Kansas City, 1974—.

MILLAR, JOHN DONALD, occupational and environmental health consultant, essayist, musician; b. Newport News, Va., Feb. 27, 1934; s. John and Dorothea Virginia (Smith) M.; m. Joan M. Phillips, Aug. 17, 1957; children: John Stuart, Alison Gordon, Virginia Taylor. BS, U. Richmond, 1956; MD, Med. Coll. Va., 1959; D.T.P.H., London Sch. Hygiene and Tropical Medicine, 1966; D of Pub. Svc. (hon.), Greenville (Ill.) Coll., 1994. Cert. specialist in Gen. Preventive Medicine, 1969. Intern U. Utah Affiliated Hosps., Salt Lake City, 1959-60, asst. resident in medicine, 1960-61; chief Epidemic Intelligence Svc., Ctr. for Disease Control, USPHS, HEW, Atlanta, 1961-63, dep. chief surveillance sect. epidemiology br., 1962-63, chief smallpox unit, 1963-65, dir. smallpox eradication program, 1966-70, dir. Bur. State Svcs., 1970-78, asst. dir. Ctr. for Disease Control for Pub. Health Practice, 1979-80; dir. Nat. Ctr. Environ. Health, Atlanta, 1980-81, Nat. Inst. for Occupation Safety and Health, Atlanta, 1981-93, chmn. exec. com. Nat. Toxicology Program, 1989-93; pres. Don Millar & Assocs., Inc., Atlanta, 1993—. Adj. prof. occupational and environ. health Sch. Pub. Health Emory U., Atlanta, 1988-98; cons. on smallpox, smallpox eradication, immunization programs and occupational and environ. health WHO; mem. WHO expert adv. panel on occupational health; bd. dirs. Farm Safety 4 Just Kids, 1993-98; tech. adv. bd. Ctr. Protect Workers' Rights, 1993; disting. fellow, vice chmn. Pub. Health Policy Adv. Bd., Inc., Washington, 1998—; mem. string bass sect. DeKalb Symphony Orch., 1982—, Gainesville (Ga.) Symphony Orch., 2000—, N.E. Ga. Mountain Chamber Orch., 2001—, Truett-Macconnell Coll. Wind Symphony, 2002—. Mem. editl. bd. Am. Jour. Indsl. Medicine, 1985—, Am. Jour. Occupl. Psychology, 1993-2000, Am. Jour. Preventive Medicine, 1993—2000; contbr. articles to profl. jours. Recipient Surgeon Gen's. Commendation medal, 1965, Okeke prize London Sch. Hygiene and Tropical Medicine, 1966, Presdl. award for mgmt. improvement, 1972, W.C. Gorgas medal Assn. Mil. Surgeons U.S., 1987, Lucas lectr. Faculty Occupational Medicine Royal Coll. Physicians, London, 1987, Outstanding Med. Alumnus award Med. Coll. Va., 1988; also recipient Equal Employment Opportunity award, 1975, Medal of Excellence, 1977, Joseph W. Mountin lectr. award, 1986, Alexander D. Langmuir MD Meml. lectr. award, 2001, all from Ctrs. for Disease Control, Disting. Svc. medal USPHS, 1983, 88, Exemplary Svc. medal Surgeon Gen. U.S., 1988, Giants in Occupational Medicine lectr. U. Utah, 1989, William S. Knudsen award Am. Coll. Occupational Medicine, 1991, presdl. citation APA, 1991, William Steiger Meml. award Am. Conf. Govtl. Indsl. Hygienists, 1993, Health Watch award for outstanding contbns. toward improving health of minority populations, 1992, Award of Merit Minerva Edn. Inst., 1993, Alumni Disting. Svc. award U. Richmond, 1993, Jeff Lee Mem. Lectr. Am. Indusl. Hygiene Assoc. San Diego, Calif., 2002; named to Order Bifurcated Needle, World Health Orgn., 1978, Faculty Occupational Medicine, Royal Coll. Physicians, London, 1990; elected Safety and Health Hall of Fame Internat., Nat. Safety Coun., 1997. Mem. Am. Indsl. Hygiene Assn. (hon.), Am. Coll. Occupl. and Environ. Medicine, Am. Epidemiol. Soc., Collegium Ramazzini, Am. Assn. Pub. Health Physicians., Assn. Mil. Surgeons U.S., Pub. Health Svc. Commissioned Officers Assn., Alpha Omega Alpha.

MILLAR, MICHAEL WILLIAM, musician; b. N.Y.C., June 22, 1953; s. W. Llewellyn and Janet Josephine (Dean) M.; m. Lisa Rochelle Branch, July 30, 1983 (dec. Aug. 1987); m. Dava Grace Smart, June 25, 1989; children: Emily Ellyn, Matthew Ian. MusB in Performance, U. Colo., Boulder, 1976; MA in Music Performance, Calif. State U., L.A., 1980; D in Musical Arts, Claremont Grad. U., 1999; studied with George Roberts, Jeffrey Reynolds, Roy Main, Peter F. Drucker, Jean Lipman-Blumen, Nancy van Deusen. Trombonist Harry James Orch., 1980-85, Les Hooper Grand Band, 1983—. Mem. faculty U. Colo., Denver, 1987, Calif. State Poly. U., Pomona, 2004-, Internat. Trombone Festival, 2001; dir. Entrepreneurship Ctr. for Music, U. Colo., Boulder, 2002-03; has appeared with various brass ensembles, big bands, symphony orchs. and other mus. groups; performed in TV and radio jingles for Budweiser, Toyota, Anheuser Busch, Mountain Dew, IBM, TWA, Gt. Western Bank, Texaco, Am. Express, Honda, Delta Airlines, Qantas, Sunny Delight, Disney World, AT&T, numerous others. Albums include Blast Off, 1981, Anything Goes, 1989, Singin' With the Big Bands, 1994; appeared in films Patch Adams, Hot to Trot, Sing, For the Boys, The Doors, on TV in Hull High, Jerry Lewis MDA Telethon Orch., 1995-; performed with L.A. Philharm., Steve Allen, Ray Anthony, Tex. Beneke Orch., George Burns, Ray Charles Orch., Rosemary Clooney, Ray Conniff, Merv Griffin, Jerry Lewis, Shari Lewis, Mills Bros., Liza Minnelli, Helen O'Connell, Patti Page, Debbie Reynolds, Kenny Rogers, Artie Shaw, The Smothers Brothers, numerous others; recs. with Southwest Chamber Music, Ray Anthony, Poco, Joey DeFrancesco, Bruce Lofgren Jazz Orch., others. Mem. NARAS, Rec. Musicians Assn., Am. Fedn. Musicians, Ams. for the Arts. Home: 25430 Via Impreso Valencia CA 91355-2709 Office Phone: 818-901-6843. E-mail: millar@music.org.

MILLAR, RICHARD WILLIAM, JR., lawyer; b. LA, May 11, 1938; LLB, U. San Francisco, 1966. Bar: Calif. 1967, U.S. Dist. Ct. (cen. dist.) Calif. 1967, U.S. Dist. Ct. (no. dist.) Calif. 1969, U.S. Dist. Ct. (so. dist.) Calif. 1973, U.S. Supreme Ct. Assoc. Iverson & Hogoboom, Los Angeles, 1967-72; ptnr. Eilers, Stewart, Pangman & Millar, Newport Beach, Calif., 1973-75, Millar & Heckman, Newport Beach, 1975-77, Millar, Hodges & Bemis, Newport Beach, 1979—. Bd. trustees Western State U. Coll. Law, 2004—. Fellow: Am. Bar Found.; mem.: ABA (litigation sect. trial practice com., ho. of dels. 1990—), Orange County Bar Assn. (chmn. bus. litig. sect. 1981, chmn. judiciary com. 1988—90, sec. 1999, treas., dir. charitable fund 2000, pres.-elect 2001, pres. 2002, treas., dir. charitable fund 2003), Calif. Bar Assn. (lectr. CLE), Pacific Club, Bohemian Club (San Francisco). Home: 71 Hillsdale Newport Beach CA 92660 Office: Millar Hodges & Bemis One Newport Pl Ste # 900 Newport Beach CA 92660 E-mail: millar@mhblaw.net.

MILLARD, CHARLES WARREN, III, museum director, writer; b. Elizabeth, N.J., Dec. 20, 1932; s. Charles Warren and Constance Emily (Keppler) M. AB magna cum laude, Princeton U., 1954; MA, Harvard U., 1963, PhD, 1971. Asst. to dir. Fogg Art Mus. Harvard U., Cambridge, Mass., 1963-64; asst. to dir. Dumbarton Oaks, Washington, 1965-66; dir. Washington Gallery Modern Art, 1966-67; teaching fellow Harvard U., 1968-69; curator 19th Century European art L.A. County Mus. Art, 1971-74; chief curator Hirshhorn Mus. and Sculpture Garden Smithsonian Instn., Washington, 1974-86; adj. prof. Johns Hopkins U., Balt., 1983-86; dir. Ackland Art Mus. U. N.C., Chapel Hill, 1986-93, adj. prof., 1986-93; chmn. vis. com. to fine arts dept. Boston U., 1977-80. Chmn. nat. adv. bd. Ackland Art Mus., 2000-04. Author: The Sculpture of Edgar Degas, 1977, La Vie d'Auguste Preault, Auguste Preault Sculpteur Romantique, 1809-1879, 1997; art editor Hudson Rev., 1972-87; contbr. articles to profl. jours. With USN, 1956-59.

MILLARD, DONALD REX, financial executive; b. Atlanta, Ga., June 24, 1947; s. Rex and Martha Nell (Gilstrap_ M.; m. Fay Simmons, Mar. 15, 1968; children: Lisa, Bradley. BBA, U. Ga., 1968. CPA Ga. Audit mgr. Peat, Marwick, Main & Co., Atlanta, 1968-78; v.p. fin. Chick-fil-A Inc., Atlanta, 1978-82; pres. Dental One Inc., Atlanta, 1982-87; v.p. fin, CFO HEalthdyne Inc., Marietta, Ga., 1987—. Pub. chmn., Fin. Execs. Inst., Atlanta, 1987—. Mem. AICPA, Ga. Assn. CPA, Assn. Corp. Growth, Fin. Execs. Inst. (publicity chmn. 1987—). Avocations: racquetball, skiing.

MILLARD, ESTHER LOUND, foundation administrator, educator; b. Metaline, Wash., June 10, 1909; d. Peter S. and Emily Christine (Dahlgren) Lound; m. Homer Behne Millard, Apr. 25, 1951 (dec. May 1962). BA, U. Wis., 1933, MA, 1935. Cert. tchr., Oreg., Wis. Instr. U. Hawaii, Honolulu, 1938-43; joined USN, 1943, advanced through ranks to lt. commdr., resigned, 1952; dir. Millard Sch., Bandon, Oreg., 1954-81; pres. Millard Found., Bandon, 1984—. Trustee Falcon Found., Colorado Springs, Colo., 1986—; established scholarship fund for med. sch. students, U. Wis, Millard honors program benefitting cadets at USAF Acad. Recipient Bardeen Fellow, U. Wis. Med. Sch. Mem. Bascom Hill Soc. (U. Wis.), Women's Meml. Found. (charter), Phi Beta Kappa. Republican. Avocations: reading, music, gardening. Home: 56557 Tom Smith Rd Bandon OR 97411-6309

MILLARD, JAMES KEMPER, marketing executive; b. Lexington, Kentucky, Oct. 28, 1948; s. Lyman Clifford and Cora (Carrick) M.; m. Madelyn (Hooper), Nov. 26, 1983; children: Lyman Clifford III, Sean Duffy, James Kemper Jr., Caroline Carrick. BA, Transylvania Univ., Lexington, Ky., 1971. Writer AP, Lexington, Ky., 1970—71; asst. news. dir. Sta. WLEX-TV, FM, Lexington, Ky., 1971—76; prod. Ky. Dept. Pub. Info., Frankfort, 1973; dir. Univ. rels. Transylvania Univ., Lexington, Ky., 1973—79; acct. supr. Abbott Advt., Inc., Lexington, Ky., 1979—85; mktg. dir. Steak N' Shake, Inc., Indpls., 1985; field mktg. mgr. Blue Bell, Pa., 1985—86; field mktg. dir. Nutri Sys. Inc., Blue Bell, Pa., 1986—88, v.p. comm., 1988—90, sr. v.p. mktg., 1990—91; pres. Mktg. Comm. Overview, Inc., Exton, Pa., 1991—93, Waterwild Mktg., Lexington, Ky., 1993—94; dir. promotion and devel. Sta. WKYT-TV, Lexington, Ky., 1994—99; exec. cons. E Corp., Lexington, Ky., 1999—2000; pres. ConnectedCampus.com., 1999—2000; sr. v.p. devel. strategy Equity Technologies and Resources, Inc., Lexington, Ky., 2000—02; pres. ETCR Mergers and Acquisitions, Inc., Lexington, Ky., 2001—; pres., CEO Equity Technologies and Resources, Inc., Lexington, Ky., 2002—; COO Verified Prescription Safeguards, Inc., Lexington, Ky., 2002—; pres., CEO VPS Holding, LLC, Lexington, Ky., 2002—; dir. Waterwild Farm, LLC, Lexington, Ky., 2003—. Mem. acad. adv. com. Ea. Ky. U., Richmond, 1983-87; treas. Bluegrass Integrated Pest Mgmt., Lexington, 1983-85; case study spkr. Radio Advertisers Bur., 1989-90. Author: C and O Streamliners, 1994. Mem. Comdr. in Chief Leadership Cir., 1990—; pres. Swan Kitchen Car Co., 1990—; mem. Hon. Order Ky. Colonels, 1976—; cons. Jr. Achievement; mem. campaign cabinet United Way Bluegrass, 1995, mem. dream team, 1998—99; mem. devel. coun. Midway Coll., 1995—99; deacon Ctrl. Christian Ch., Lexington, Ky., 1984—86; bd. dir. Chesapeake and Ohio Hist. Soc., Clifton Forge, Va., 1993—98; v.p. Chesapeake and Ohio Hist. Soc., Clifton Forge, Va., 1994—97; bd. dir. Found. for Affordable Housing, 1995—, Friends of McConnell Springs, 1998—; vice chmn. Friends of Mc Connell Springs, 2001—; bd. dir. Bluegrass Trust for Hist. Preservation, 1998—2003, v.p., 1999, pres., 2000—02; trustee Lexington History Mus., Ky., 2000—; mem. bd. Lexington, Fayette Rural Land Mgmt., Ky.; mem. Am. Assn. Pvt. R.R. Car Owners, 1990—, R.R. Passenger Car Alliance, 1990—. Recipient Great Menu Award Nat. Restaurant Assn., 1982; Key Man Award Jerrico Inc., 1981; Silver and Bronze ADDY Awards Lexington Advt. Club, 1982; Gold Award Fla. Restaurant Assn., 1984; Innovative Idea Award Ky. Broadcasters Assn., 1995. Mem. Rotary Internat., Delta Sigma Phi (pres. U. Ky. corp. bd. 1994-97). Democrat. Address: Waterwild Farm PO Box 12012 Lexington KY 40579-2012 Personal E-mail: jmillard@mis.net.

MILLARD, NEAL STEVEN, lawyer, educator; b. Dallas, June 6, 1947; s. Bernard and Adele (Marks) Millard; m. Janet Keast, Mar. 12, 1994; 1 child, Kendall Layne. BA cum laude, UCLA, 1969; JD, U. Chgo., 1972. Bar: Calif. 1972, U.S. Dist. Ct. (ctrl. dist.) Calif. 1973, U.S. Tax Ct. 1973, U.S. Ct.

Appeals (9th cir.) 1987, N.Y. 1990. Assoc. Willis, Butler & Schiefly, L.A., 1972-75; ptnr. Morrison & Foerster, L.A., 1975-84, Jones, Day, Reavis & Pogue, L.A., 1984-93, White & Case, L.A., 1993—. Instr. Calif. State Coll., San Bernardino, 1975—76; lectr. Practising Law Inst., N.Y.C., NY, 1983—90, Calif. Edn. Bar, 1987—90; adj. prof. U. So. Calif. Law Ctr., L.A., 1994—. Mem. citizens adv. com. LA. Olympics, 1982—84; trustee Altadena (Calif.) Libr. Dist., 1985—86; bd. dirs. Woodcraft Rangers, L.A., 1982—90, pres., 1986—88; bd. dirs. Los Angeles County Bar Found., 1990—2000, pres., 1997—98; mem. Energy Commn. county and cities of L.A., 1995—99; mem. jud. procedures commn. Los Angeles County, 1999—, chair, 2000—02; bd. dirs. Inner City Law Ctr., 1996—99. Mem.: ABA, Am. Law Inst., Pub. Counsel (bd. dirs. 1984—87, 1990—93), Los Angeles County Bar Assn. (trustee 1985—87), N.Y. State Bar Assn., Calif. Bar Assn., U. So. Calif. Inst. Corp. Counsel (mem. adv. bd. 1998—), U. Chgo. Law Alumni Assn. (pres. 1998—2001), Beach Club, Calif. Club, Chancery Club, Phi Beta Kappa, Phi Delta Phi, Pi Gamma Mu. Office: White & Case 633 W 5th St Ste 1900 Los Angeles CA 90071-2087 Office Phone: 213-620-7773. Business E-Mail: nmillard@whitecase.com.

MILLARD, RICHARD STEVEN, lawyer; b. Pasadena, Calif., Feb. 6, 1952; s. Kenneth A. and Kathryn Mary (Paden) M.; m. Jessica Ann Edwards, May 15, 1977; children: Victoria, Elizabeth, Andrew. AB, Stanford U., 1974; JD magna cum laude, U. Mich., 1977. Bar: Calif. 1977, Ill. 1985. Assoc. Heller, Ehrman, White & McAuliff, San Francisco, 1977-81, Mayer, Brown & Platt, Chgo., 1982-83, ptnr., 1984-99, Weil, Gotshal & Manges, Redwood Shores, Calif., 1999—. Mem. ABA, Order of Coif. Office: Weil Gotshal & Manges 201 Redwood Shores Pkwy Redwood City CA 94065 E mail: richard.millard@weil.com.

MILLBERG, JOHN C. lawyer; b. New London, Conn., Jan. 4, 1956; s. Melvin Roy and Dorothy (Van Zandt) M.; m. Lori Bruce, Oct. 18, 1981; children: Kathryn Faye, Rebecca Ann, Melvin Roy III. BA, Bowling Green State U., 1977; JD, Wake Forest U., 1980. Bar: Tex. 1980, N.C. 1986, S.C. 2000, U.S. Dist. Ct. (so. dist.) Tex. 1981, U.S. Ct. Appeals (5th and 11th cirs.) 1981, U.S. Dist. Ct. (ea., mid. and we. dists.) N.C. 1986, U.S. Ct. Appeals (4th cir.) 1986, U.S. Dist. Ct. S.C. 2002. Assoc. Crain Caton James & Womble, Houston, 1981—85; assoc., dir. Maupin, Taylor, Ellis & Adams, Raleigh, NC, 1985—94; mng. ptnr. Millberg, Gordon & Stewart, PLLC, Raleigh, NC, 1994—. Mem. bar candidate com. N.C. Bd. Law Examiners, 1988-90. Scholar Wake Forest U. Sch. Law, 1977-80. Mem. N.C. Assn. Def. Attys. (exec. com., v.p. southeastern region), Nat. Assn. R.R. Trial Counsel. Office: Millberg Gordon & Stewart PLLC S 104 1101 Haynes St Raleigh NC 27604-1455

MILLEN, KEVIN S. architectural firm executive; Chief exec. officer, mng. ptnr. Gresham, Smith & Ptnrs., Birmingham, Ala. Office: Gresham Smith & Ptnrs 3595 Grandview Pkwy Ste 300 Birmingham AL 35243-1927

MILLENDER-MCDONALD, JUANITA, congresswoman, school system administration; b. Birmingham, Ala., Sept. 7, 1938; d. Shelly and Everlina (Dortch) M.; m. James McDonald III, July 26, 1955; children: Valeria, Angela, Sherryll, Michael, Roderick. BS, U. Redlands, Calif., 1980; MS in Edn., Calif. State U., L.A., 1986; postgrad., U. So. Calif. Manuscript editor Calif. State Dept. Edn., Sacramento; dir. gender equity programs L.A. Unified Sch. Dist.; mem. U.S. Congress from 37th Calif dist., Washington, 1996—; mem. small bus. com., transp. and infrastructure com.; mem. Ho. Com. on Ho. Adminstrn.; tchr., sch. adminstr., 1981—90; Carson mayor pro-tempore; mem. Calif. Assembly, 1992—96, Jt. Com. Libr., Dem. Homeland Security Task Force, New Democrat Coalition, Regional Whip. City councilwoman, Carson; bd. dirs. S.C.L.C. Pvt. Industry Coun. Policy Bd., West Basin Mcpl. Water Dist., Cities Legis. League (vice chmn.; mem. Nat. Women's Polit. Caucus; mem. adv. bd. Comparative Ethnic Tng. U. So. Calif.; founder, exec. dir. Young Advocates So. Calif. Mem. NAACP, NEA, Nat. Assn. Minority Polit. Women, NAFE, Nat. Fedn. Bus. and Profl. Women, Assn. Calif. Sch. Adminstrs., Am. Mgmt. Assn., League African Women, L.A. World Affairs Coun., Nat. Female Execs., Nat. Coun. Jewish Women, Carson C. of C., Phi Delta Kappa. Democrat. Office: US House Reps 1514 Ho Office Bldg Washington DC 20515-0537*

MILLER, ADELE ENGELBRECHT, educational administrator; b. Jersey City, July 31, 1946; d. John Fred and Dorathea Kathryn (Kamm) Engelbrecht; m. William A. Miller, Jr., Dec. 21, 1981. BS in Bus. Edn., Fairleigh Dickinson U., 1968, MBA magna cum laude, 1974; cert. in pub. sch. adminstrn. and supervision, Jersey City State Coll., 1976. Bus. tchr. Jersey City Bd. Edn., 1967-99, coord. coop. bus. edn. programs, 1973-99, acting v.p., 1985-86, prin. of summer sch., 1986, chmn. dept., 1996-99. Adj. instr. St. Peter's Coll., 1974-75; curriculum cons. Cittone Bus. Sch., 1981-82; mem. adv. coun. Dickinson H.S., 1973-99, chmn., 1978-80; organizer, bd. dirs. Frances Nadel and Cooke-Connolly-Coffey-Witt Faculty Meml. Scholarships, 1978-99; trustee Dickinson H.S. Parents Coun., 1985-88. Co-author: New Jersey Cooperative Business Education Coordinators Resource Manual, 1984; author coop. bus. edn. study course Jersey City Pub. Schs., 1980, 84. Mem. Citizens Adv. Coun. to Mayor of Jersey City, 1968—71; organizer, dir. Jersey City Youth Week, 1970—72; chmn. juv. conf. com. Hudson County Juv. Ct., 1978—; v.p., sec., trustee, chmn. dinner-musicale Jersey City Coll.-Comty. Orch., 1979—88; explorer scouting adv. bd. Hudson-Hamilton coun. bd. Scouts Am., 1985—88; trustee YWCA of Hudson County, 1988—99; dir. CREATE Charter High Sch., 2001—. Recipient Dickinson H.S. Key Club Tchr. of Yr. award 1971, Merrill-Lynch Outstanding Performance in Edn. award, 1995; named Educator of Yr. Dickinson H.S. Parents Coun., 1987-88. Mem.: AAUW (edn. chmn., sec. N.J. divsn., del. to White House briefing on edn., women's issues, arms control, dist. coord., chmn. nominations, historian), NEA, Vocat. Edn. Assn. N.J., N.J. Bus. Edn. Assn., N.J. Coop. Bus. Edn. Coords. Assn. (pres., v.p., sec., treas., Coop. Edn. Coord. of Yr.), Jersey City Edn. Assn. (bldg. dir.), N.J. Edn. Assn., Lake Hopatcong Yacht Club, Coll. Club Jersey City (pres., v.p., sec.), Jersey City Woman's Club (scholarship chmn., adviser Jr. Woman's Club), NJ Fedn. Women's Clubs, Internat. Rotary (nominating com. 2002, asst. gov. 2003, Vocational Svc. award 2001), Rotary (asst. gov. dist. 7490 2001, nominations com. 2001, Paul Harris Fellow, Walter Head Fellow, Vocat. Svc. award 2001), Phi Delta Kappa. Home: PO Box 8004 13 King Rd Jersey City NJ 07307 E-mail: millerassoc@nac.net.

MILLER, ALAN, newswriter; b. Mar. 5, 1954; BA in English, Wesleyan U., 1976; MA in Polit. Sci., U. Hawaii, 1978. Polit. reporter, state investigative reporter The Times Union, Albany, NY, 1978—81; state polit. reporter, county polit. reporter The Record, Hackensack, NJ, 1982—87; state and fed. polit. reporter valley edit. L.A. Times, 1987—89, staff writer Washington bur., 1989—94, investigative reporter Washington bur., 1994—. Recipient Pulitzer prize for nat. reporting, 2003, George Polk award, 1996, Goldsmith prize for investigative reporting, 1996, Investigative Reporters and Editors medal, 1996, Nat. Headliners award, 1st pl. for investigative reporting, 1996. Office: LA Times Washington Bur Ste 1100 1875 I St NW Washington DC 20006

MILLER, ALAN B. hospital management executive; b. N.Y.C., Aug. 17, 1937; s. Daniel and Mary (Blumenthal) M.; m. Jill K. Stein, Oct. 5, 1968; children: Marc Daniel, Marni Elizabeth, Abby Danielle. BA, Coll. William and Mary, 1958; MBA, U. Pa., 1960. V.p. Young & Rubicam, Inc., N.Y.C., 1964-69; sr. v.p. Am. Medicorp., Inc., L.A., 1970, pres., chief exec. officer Phila., 1973-77, chmn. bd., 1977, Hosp. Underwriting Group, 1977-78; founder, pres., chmn. bd. Universal Health Svcs., King of Prussia, Pa., 1978—; chmn., founder UHT-Real Estate Trust, King of Prussia, 1986—. Formerly health care adviser Fed. Mediation and Conciliation Svc.; chmn., pres. Universal Health Svcs. Real Estate Investment Trust, N.Y. Stock Exch., 1986—; bd. dirs. CDI Corp., N.Y. Stock Exch., Broadlane, Penn Mut. Life Ins.; mem. exec. bd. Wharton Sch., U. Pa. Chmn. Opera Co. of Phila.; dir. Regional Performing Arts Ctr. Capt. USAR. Mem. Phila. C. of C. (past bd. dirs.). Home: 57 Crosby Brown Rd Gladwyne PA 19035-1512 Office: Universal Health Svcs Inc 367 S Gulph Rd King Of Prussia PA 19406

MILLER, ALAN D. editor; m. Kris Miller; 3 children. Degree, Ohio U. Asst. mng. editor days The Columbus (Ohio) Dispatch, 2000—04, mng. editor news, 2004—. Office: The Columbus Dispatch 34 S Third St Columbus OH 43215*

MILLER, ALAN JAY, rare book dealer, author; b. Bklyn., July 11, 1936; s. Louis and Claire (Maltz) M.; m. Susan Ruth Morris, Oct. 29, 1961; children—Laurie Ann, Adam Louis. BA, Cornell U., 1957. Chartered fin. analyst. Pres. Analysis-in-Depth Inc., N.Y.C., 1965-67; mng. editor Value Line Investment Survey, N.Y.C., 1967-68; rsch. dir. Emanuel Deetjen & Co., N.Y.C., 1968-69; exec. v.p., dir. Intersci. Capital Mgmt. Corp., N.Y.C., 1969-71; pres., dir. ICM Equity Fund Inc., N.Y.C., 1970-71, ICM Fin. Fund Inc., N.Y.C., 1970-71; v.p., assoc. rsch. dir. Bache & Co., Inc., N.Y.C., 1972, G.H. Walker & Co., Inc., N.Y.C., 1972-73; 1st v.p., assoc. rsch. dir. Blyth Eastman Dillon & Co. Inc., N.Y.C., 1974-76; dir. rsch. E.F. Hutton & Co., Inc., N.Y.C., 1976-81, sr. v.p., 1976-80, exec. v.p., 1981-88; dir. Hutton Investment Mgmt., 1976-88; mng. dir. SLH Asset Mgmt. Shearson Lehman Hutton, Inc, N.Y.C., 1988-90; sr. v.p. Martin E. Segal Co., N.Y.C., 1990-92. Adj. assoc. prof. Columbia U. Grad. Sch. Bus., 1978-79; mem. faculty N.Y. Inst. Fin., 1977-98; adj. prof. Adelphi U. Coll., 1993-98; rare book dealer, 1998—. Author: Socially Responsible Investing: How to Invest with Your Conscience, 1991, Standard and Poor's 401(k) Planning Guide, 1995. E-mail: alan@alansbooks.com.

MILLER, ALAN M. editor, educator, writer; b. N.Y.C., July 24, 1934; s. Philip and Sylvia (Lubash) M.; children: Neil, Peter, Stephanie Cook, Douglas; m. Sharon A. Tanenbaum, Aug. 29, 1996; step-children: Holly Harouche, Becky Theodoratos. AB, Syracuse U., 1955, LLB, 1958, JD, 1968. Asst. counsel 3 joint legis. coms. N.Y. State Legislature, 1968-70; counsel to minority Nassau County Bd. Suprs., 1974-75; prin. atty. editor Thomson/West, Eagan, Minn., 1985—2004. Adj. faculty film and screenwriting Mpls. Coll., 1999—, Hofstra U., 1990-97, Discovery Ctr., 1990-94, N.Y. Inst. Tech., Old Westbury, 1987-89, Inner Hills C.C., 2004—; presenter 2nd ann. Internat. Conf. on Law and Psychiatry, Jerusalem, 1986, Sun County Airlines Scholarships CTEE, 2004. Columnist South Shore Record, Woodmere, N.Y., Another Viewpoint, 1985-99 (awards N.Y. Press Assn. 1988, 89, 94, Best column award 1992), Single-Minded, 1991-92, N.Y. Bowler, 1991-93 (Bowling Mag. awards 1990-93, Best column award 1992), Nostalgia Mag., 1990-91; writer-editor USCAdvantage, 1995-99 (Immy awards 1996, 97); editor: Beyond the Bar, West Group, 2000-02; contbr. articles to publs., including N.Y. Times, Newsday, Newsday Mag., Mpls. Star-Tribune. Assembly dist. leader N.Y. State Dem. Com., 1965-76; Commr. Village of Woodsburgh, N.Y., 1980, telecom. com. City of Eagan, Minn., 2001—, chmn., 2002, vice-chmn., 2003; citizens adv. com. Minn. Twins, 2000-02; vice-chmn. Minn. Assn. Cable TV Adminstrs., 2002-03; host and prodr. cable TV Access to Democracy, 2001—, TwinsTalk, 2003—. Recipient awards for coverage of Persian Gulf War from Israel, 1991, Nat. Coun. Jewish Women, 1991, Five Towns Sr. Couns. Mem. Screenwriters Workshop. Jewish. Home: 4316 Aries Ct Eagan MN 55123-1825 Office: 1400 Hennepin Ave Minneapolis MN 55403 Personal E-mail: alanmillermn@comcast.net.

MILLER, ALAN STANLEY, ecology center administrator, law educator; b. Detroit, Dec. 22, 1949; s. Ralph and Ruth (Leeman) M.; m. Susan O'Hara, Aug. 25, 1973; 1 child, Joanna. AB in Goverment, Cornell U., 1971; JD, M of Pub. Policy, U. Mich., 1974. Bar: Mich. 1974, D.C. 1975. Rsch. atty. Environ. Law Inst., Washington, 1974-77; atty. ABA, Washington, 1978-79, Natural Resources Def. Coun., Washington, 1979-84; assoc. World Resources Inst., Washington, 1984-86; asst. prof. law Widener U., Wilmington, Del., 1988-89; exec. dir. Ctr. Global Change, College Park, Md., 1989-96; prof. Vermont Law School, South Royal, Vt., 1991-93; exec. dir. Renewable Energy Policy Project Univ. Md., 1996-97; sr. environ. specialist GEF Secretariat, Washington, 1997—, team leader. Head EPA Transition Team for Pres. Clinton Wash. D.C. 1992, Energy Task Force State of Md. Annapolis, Md. 1991-92; bd. dirs. Environmental Exchange; adjunct prof. Maryland Law Sch. 1989—; vis. asst. prof. U. Iowa Coll. of Law 1979, Wash. Coll. of Law Am. U., Wash., D.C. 1986, Duke U. N.C. 1990, Vt. Law Sch 1991, 92; mem. adv. bd. Office Tec. Assessment, Washington, 1989. Co-author: (book) International Regulation Flourocarbons, 1980, Green Gold, 1994; monographs) Growing Power, The Sky is the Limit, 1985, Environmental Regulation, 1992. Bd. dirs. Solar Light Fund, 1988, Renewable Energy Inst., 1995—. Fulbright scholar Macquarie Univ., Australia, 1977-87, Fulbright scholar Tokyo Univ. Law Sch., Japan, 1987-87; Stratospheric Ozone Protection award U.S. EPA Washington, D.C. 1992. Mem. ABA (global climate com. 1992-93, chair 1993-94). Avocations: jogging white-water rafting, writing. Office: GEF Secretariat Rm G6-016 1818 H St NW Washington DC 20433-0001

MILLER, ALBERT J. cardiologist, internist; b. Chgo., 1922; MD, Northwestern U., 1946. Diplomate Am. Bd. Internal Medicine, Am. Bd. Cardiovascular Diseases. Intern Michael Reese Hosp., Chgo., 1945-46, resident in medicine, 1950, fellow in cardiology rsch. Cardiovascular Inst., 1948-50; resident in medicine VA Hosp., Hines, Ill., 1950-51; attending physician Northwestern Meml. Hosp., Chgo.; prof. clin. medicine, cardiology Northwestern U. Med. Sch. Author: The Lymphatics of the Heart, 1982, Diagnosis of Chest Pain, 1988; has done basic rsch. on lymphatics of the heart. Fellow ACP, Am. Coll. Cardiology, Am. Fedn. for Clin. Rsch., Ctrl. Soc. for Clin. Rsch. Office: Clin Cardiol Group Ltd 676 N Saint Clair St Ste 1930 Chicago IL 60611-2956 Office Phone: 312-642-2502. E-mail: ajmiller22@sbcglobal.net.

MILLER, ALBERT JAY, retired library director; b. Beaver Falls, Pa., Dec. 7, 1927; s. Joseph Jefferson and Alberta Fae (Shaffer) Miller. BS, Geneva Coll., 1952; MLS, Rutgers U., 1958; postgrad., U. Chgo., 1960-61, U. Pitts., 1963-68, U. Mich., 1969. Libr. West Allegheny Jr. H.S., Imperial, Pa., 1959-60, Butler (Pa.) Area Sr. H.S., 1962-67, Pa. State U., New Kensington, 1969-89, tchr.-libr. continuing edn. dept., 1970-89, ret. libr. and info. svcs. dir. emeritus, 1989, prof. emeritus. Author: A Selective Bibliography of Existentialism in Education and Related Topics, 1969, Confrontation, Conflict and Dissent, 1972, Death: A Bibliographical Guide, 1977; book and media rev. editor: Learning Today, 1978—; mem. editl. bd. Learning Today, 1979—. Tchr., judge Nat. Baton Twirling Assn., 1998; instr. water safety ARC, New Kensington, 1969—, Citizens Gen. Hosp., 1971—72; active Boy Scouts Am., 1970—; bd. dirs. Westmoreland County, Butler County mental health issues; mem. Allegheny-Kiski Human Rels. Coun., 1976—77; bd. dirs. Allegheny-Kiski Sr. Citizens Ctr., 1976—77, fund raising chmn., 1989—90, 2d v.p., 1997—98, pres., 1998—; mem., pub. rels. dir. Twirling Unlimited, Akron, Ohio; baton twirler Kensington Firemens Band; entrepreneur Al's Terrific Twirling Tricks-Catch It; book reader People's Libr., New Kensington; Sunday sch. tchr. Manchester Reformed Presbyn. Ch., 1970—, elder, clk. session, 1984—, Sabbath sch. supt., 1990; elder emeritus Eastvale Reformed Presbyn. Ch., mem. Christian edn. com., tchr. adult Sabbath sch., 2003; bd. corporators Geneva Coll., Beaver Falls, Pa., 1987—. Named Twirling champion, N.Y. State Hall of Fame, 1999. Mem.: ALA, NEA (life), U.S. Twirling Assn., Pa. Libr. Assn., Pa. Edn. Assn. (life). Democrat. Home: 160 Crosswynds Dr Beaver Falls PA 15010-1182

MILLER, ALFRED MONTAGUE, lawyer; b. Augusta, Ga., Jan. 5, 1940; s. Dessie Ford and May Belle (Power) M.; m. Lynthia Wofford, Aug. 25, 1962 (div. 1979); children— William Montague, Stephen Mathews; m. Peggy Elaine Mays, July 26, 1980. B.B.A., U. Ga., 1961, J.D., 1963. Bar: Ga. 1962, Superior Ct. Ga. 1962, U.S. Dist. Ct. (so. dist.) Ga. 1963, U.S. Ct. Appeal (11th cir.) 1981, U.S. Supreme Ct. 1978. Ptnr. Fulcher, Fulcher, Hagler, Harper and Reed, Augusta, 1963-71, Dye, Miller, Tucker and Everitt, P.A., Augusta, 1971—90, of counsel 1990-; pres. Club Car, Inc., 1990-2001; dir. First Bank of Ga., 2001-. Fellow Ga. Bar Found., Am. Coll. Trial Lawyers; mem. Am. Judicature Soc., ABA, Lawyers-Pilot Bar Assn., State Bar Ga. (bd. govs. 1977-85), Augusta Bar Assn. (pres. 1985), Internat. Assn. Def. Counsel, Beta Gamma Sigma, Chi Phi (pres. 1960-61), Phi Delta Phi. Presbyterian. Home: 4384 Deer Run Evans GA 30809-4440 Office: Tucker Everitt Long Brewton & Lanier PO Box 2426 Augusta GA 30903-2426 E-mail: mill4384@aol.com.

MILLER, ALICE, state representative; b. L.I., Mar. 3, 1939; d. Edward and Alice Miller. BA, Bennington Coll., 1960; MS, Bank St. Coll., 1964; postgrad., NYU, 1966. Adminstrv. planning mgr. Roche Diagnostics, N.J., 1989-93; state rep. Vt. Ho. Reps., 1996—. Vice-chmn. Bd. Selectman, Shaftbury, Vt., 1994—; dir. Nat. Follow Through Program, Brattleboro, Vt., 1968-77; dir. Student Affairs, Bennington Coll., 1977-88. Mem. Bennington Profl. Women, Workforce Investment Bd., Bennington Learning Inst., Vt. Film Commn., New England Bd. Higher Ed.

MILLER, ALLAN JOHN, lawyer; b. Beachwood, Ohio, Oct. 17, 1921; s. Carl Frederick and Rhoda (Warren) M.; m. Marjorie Hewitt Pirtle, Aug. 10, 1946; children: James W., Patricia Anne. BBA, Fenn Coll., 1946; LL.B., Western Res. U., 1948; D. (hon.), Dyke Coll., Cleve., 1986. Bar: Ohio 1948. With Standard Oil Co., Ohio, 1948-77, treas., 1967-77; mem. firm Kiefer, Knecht, Rees, Meyer & Miller, Cleve., 1977-81. Dir. United Screw & Bolt Corp., 1977-97. Chmn. bd. dirs. Luth. Med. Ctr., Cleve., 1967-82; pres. Luth. Med. Ctr. Med. Staff Found., 1979-85; bd. dirs. Christian Residencies Found., 1972-77, St. Luke's Hosp. Assn., 1973-84; chmn. bd. trustees Dyke Coll., Cleve., 1971-86. With AUS, 1943-46, PTO. Mem. Cleve. Treas.'s Club. Clubs: Capri Isles Golf Club (Venice, Fla.). Presbyterian. Home: Apt 531 900 Tamiami Trl S Venice FL 34285-3627

MILLER, ALLEN RICHARD, retired mathematician; b. Bklyn., 1942; BS, Bklyn. Coll., 1965; MA, U. Md., 1971. Mathematician U.S. Naval Rsch. Lab., Washington, 1968-93; prof. George Washington U., Washington, 1992-95. Reviewer: Math. Revs. With U.S. Army, 1965-67.

MILLER, ALWIN VERMAR, educational advisor, consultant; b. Dardanelle, Ark., Oct. 12, 1922; s. William Marshall and Ollie Vernice (Green) M.; m. Patricia Jane Knox, Dec. 31, 1945; children: Carol, Alwin, William, Nitiya, Thomas. AA, Ark. Poly. Inst., 1939; BS, BA with honors, UCLA, 1947, MEd, 1948, EdD, 1956; cert., Internat. Inst. Edn1. Planning, (UNESCO), 1967—68. Instr. Chico (Calif.) State Coll., 1948-49; assoc. prof. So. Oreg. Coll., Ashland, 1949-57; edn. advisor AID, Washington, 1957-75; cons. on internat. devel. Upper Marlboro, Md., 1975—. Lt. col. USAF, 1942-46. Mem. ASTD, Soc. Internat. Devel., Internat. Soc. Ednl. Planning, Res. Officers Assn. (v.p. DC dept. 1986-87, treas. 1991-97, pres.-elect 1997-98, pres. 1998-99, Reilly Meml. Scholarship com. 1999-2002, retirement com. 2002-), Am. Legion (post comdr. 1995-96, 99-2000, dept. vice comdr. 1996-97, dept. comdr. 1997-98, vice chmn. nat. security 1999-), Mil. Order World Wars (chpt. pres. 1999-2002, nat. security com. 2002-, nat. legis. com. 2002-, sr. vice comdr. Dept. of Md., 2003-04, comdr. dept. Md. 2004—), Nat. Sojourners, Mil. Order of Temple of Jerusalem, Forty and Eight (grand conducteur 2000-2001), Lions, Masons, Shriners, K.T., Phi Delta Kappa. Democrat. Office: 8107 Bird Ln Greenbelt MD 20770-2104 Office Phone: 301-441-8201. E-mail: avmiller46@cs.com.

MILLER, ANDREA LYNN, library science educator; b. Warren, Pa., Sept. 25, 1957; d. Harlan Kermit and Hazel Adeline Samuelson; m. Michael Edward Miller, oct. 16, 1953; 1 child, Lena. BS in Edn., Clarion U., 1978, MA in English, 1982, MSLS, 1991; PhD in Info. Scis., U. Pitts., 1997. English tchr. Redbank Valley Sch. Dist., New Bethlehem, Pa., 1979-86, sch. libr. media specialist, 1986-92; assoc. prof. libr. sci. Clarion (Pa.) U., 1992—, dir. Inst. for Study and Devel. of Sci. Libr. Info. Ctrs., 2000—, dept. chair and program dir. dept. libr. sci., 2002—. Distance edn. trainer Cmty. Agile Ptnrs. in Edn., Bethlehem, 1999—, Ctr. for Distance Edn., Pa. State Sys. Higher Edn., Harrisburg, 1999—. Contbg. author: Powerful Public Relations with Full-time Results, 2d edit., 2001; author profl. devel. workshop in field. Trustee Clarion Free Pub. Libr., 1993-99. Recipient Laura Braun scholarship, 1993; grantee Pa. State Sys. Higher Edn., 1999. Mem. ALA, ASCD, Assn. Libr. and Info. Sci. Edn., Pa. Assn. Ednl. Comms. and Tech., Assn. Pa. State Coll. and Univ. Facilities (chmn. nominating com. 1995-97), Assn. Libr. Svc. to Childen, Young Sch. Librarians (chmn. Highsmith rsch. grant award 1999-2001), Pa. Sch. Librarians Assn. (co-chmn. state curriculum com. 1998-2002), Internat. Assn. Sch. Librarians, Assn. Ednl. Comms. and Tech., Delta Kappa Gamma. Democrat. Baptist. Avocations: travel, golf, biking. Home: 35 Ross St Clarion PA 16214 Office: Clarion U Pa 840 Wood St Clarion PA 16214 Fax: (814) 393-2150. E-mail: amiller@clarion.edu.

MILLER, ANDREW PICKENS, lawyer; b. Fairfax, Va., Dec. 21, 1932; s. Francis Pickens and Helen (Hill) M.; m. Penelope Farthing, Nov. 18, 1990; children: Julia Lane, Andrew Pickens, Elise Givhan, Winfield Scott, Lucia Holcombe. AB magna cum laude, Princeton U., 1954; postgrad., New Coll., Oxford (Eng.) U., 1954-55; LLB, U. Va., 1960. Bar: Va. 1960, U.S. Supreme Ct. 1967, D.C. 1979. Asso. Penn, Stuart & Stuart, 1960-62; ptnr. Penn, Stuart & Miller, Abingdon, Va., 1963-69; atty. gen. State of Va., 1970-77; ptnr. Mays, Valentine, Davenport & Moore, Richmond, Va., 1977-78, Dickstein, Shapiro, Morin & Oshinsky, LLP, Washington, 1979—2002, Powell Goldstein Frazer & Murphy LLP, Washington, 2003—. Pres., Young Democratic Clubs Va., 1966-67; chmn. Washington County Dem. Com., 1967-69; Dem. nominee for U.S. Senate from Va., 1978; bd. dirs. Barter Found., 1962-69; trustee King Coll., 1966-74; mem. adv. bd. Ams. for Effective Law Enforcement, 1973-77, Center for Oceans Law and Policy, 1975-79; vice-chmn. Va. Bd. Corrections, 1983-86. Served to 1st lt. AUS, 1955-57. Fellow Am. Bar Found., ABA (ho. dels. 1971-76, action commn. to reduce ct. costs and delay 1979-84, commn. on pub. understanding about the law 1992-95); mem. So. Conf. Attys. Gen. (vice chmn. 1972-73, chmn. 1973-74), Nat. Assn. Attys. Gen. (exec. com. 1973-74, chmn. antitrust com. 1971-76, Wyman Meml. award 1976), Va. Bar Assn. (chmn. young lawyers sect. 1967-68, exec. com. 1985-88), Am. Judicature Soc. (bd. dirs. 1973-76, exec. com. 1974-76), Soc. of Cin. (Va. standing com. 1986-89, 93-96, asst. sec., 1992-95, sec. gen. 1995-98), The John Marshall Found. (pres. 1987-89), Phi Beta Kappa, Omicron Delta Kappa. Presbyterian. Home: 1503 35th St NW Washington DC 20007-2729 Office: Powell Goldstein Frazer & Murphy LLP 1001 Pennsylvania Ave 6th Fl Washington DC 20004-2582 Office Phone: 202-624-7386. E-mail: amiller@pgfm.com.

MILLER, ANNE BURKE, lawyer; b. Kansas City, Kans., Sept. 18, 1956; d. Paul and Patricia Ann (Pierson) Burke; children: Emily, Kathleen, Erin. BA in Liberal Arts, U. Kans., 1978, JD, 1981. Bar: Kans. 1981, U.S. Dist. Ct. Kans. 1981. Assoc. Miller, Ball & Miller, Manhattan, Kans., 1981-86; ptnr. Everett, Seaton, Miller and Seaton, Manhattan, 1986—; pvt. practice, 2003—. Mem. Leadership Kans., 1986; bd. dirs. United Way, Manhattan, 1987. Veta B. Lear and Watkins-Berger scholar Kans. U., 1975-78. Fellow Am. Acad. Matrimonial Lawyers, Am. Bar Found., Kans. Bar Found. (bd. dirs., sec. treas. 1999, pres. 2001); mem. ABA, Kans. Bar Assn. (chmn. domestic violence task force 1985, pres. family law sect., pres. young lawyers divsn. 1987-88, bd. govs. 1988-94, Outstanding Svc. award 1996), Riley County Bar Assn. (pres. 1988—), Kans. Judicial Coun., Family Law Adv. Com., Phi Beta Kappa, Phi Kappa Phi. Republican. Presbyterian. Avocations: skiing, travel, reading, swimming. Home: 3130 Amherst Ave Manhattan KS 66503-3008 Office: Commerce Bank Bldg Lower Lobby 727 Poyntz Ave Manhattan KS 66502 Office Phone: 785-539-6500.

MILLER, ANNETTE K. See MATEMA, ZSUN-NEE KIMBALL

MILLER, ANTHONY BERNARD, physician, medical researcher; b. Woodford, Eng., Apr. 17, 1931; married, 1952; 5 children. BA, U. Cambridge, 1952, MB, BChir, 1955. House officer Oldchurch Hosp., Romford, Eng., 1955-57; med. registrar Luton and Dunstable Hosp., Eng., 1959-62; mem. sci. staff Med. Research Council Tb and Chest Disease Unit, London, 1962-71; assoc. prof. preventive medicine and biostats. U. Toronto, 1972-76, prof., 1976-96, chmn. dept., 1992-96, dir. grad. program in epidemiology, 1986-91; dir. epidemiology unit Nat. Cancer Inst. Can., Toronto, 1971-86; dir. Nat. Breast Screening Study, 1980—, WHO Collaborating Ctr. on Evaluation of Screening for Cancer, 1991-2000; prof. emeritus, 1997—; head divsn. of clin. Epidemology German Cancer Rsch. Ctr., Heidelberg, 1999—2003. Nat. Health scientist, 1988-93; mem. working cadre Bladder Cancer Project, U.S., 1973-75; mem. epidemiology com. Breast Cancer Task Force, U.S., 1973-77, chmn., 1975-77; mem. Fed. Task Force Cervical Cytol. Screening, Can.,

1974-76, 80-81, Union Internat. Contre le Cancer com., controlled therapeutic trials, 1978-82, Multidisciplinary project breast cancer, 1978-82, chmn. project on screening, 1982-93; mem. sci. council Internat. Agy. Research Cancer, Lyon, 1981-85, chmn., 1985; mem. com. on diet, nutrition and cancer NRC of U.S., 1980-83, mem. oversight com. radioepidemiologic tables, 1983-84, com. on diet and health, 1986-89, com. on dietary guidelines implementation, 1988-91, chmn. com. on environmental epidemiology, 1990-94; chmn. Ont. Task Force on Primary Prevention of Cancer, 1994-95. Served with RAF, 1957-59. Mem. Can. Oncology Soc. (sec.-treas. 1975-79, pres. 1980-81), Soc. Epidemiology Research, Internat. Epidemiology Assn., Am. Soc. Preventive Oncology (pres. 1983-85), Am. Coll. Epidemiology (bd. dirs. 1987-89). E-mail: ab.miller@sympatico.ca.

MILLER, ANTOINETTE, publishing executive; V.p. finance USA Today, Arlington, Va. Office: USA Today 7950 Jones Branch Dr Mc Lean VA 22108-0001

MILLER, ARJAY, retired university dean; b. Shelby, Nebr., Mar. 4, 1916; s. Rawley John and Mary Gertrude (Schade) M.; m. Frances Marion Fearing, Aug. 18, 1940; children: Kenneth Fearing, Ann Elizabeth (Mrs. James Olstad). BS with highest honors, UCLA, 1937; LL.D. (hon.), 1964; postgrad., U. Calif.-Berkeley, 1938-40; LL.D. (hon.), Washington U., St. Louis; LL.D., Whitman Coll., 1965, U. Nebr., 1965, Ripon Coll., 1980. Teaching asst. U. Calif. at Berkeley, 1938-40; research technician Calif. State Planning Bd., 1941; economist Fed. Res. Bank San Francisco, 1941-43; asst. treas. Ford Motor Co., 1946-53, controller, 1953-57, v.p., controller, 1957-61, v.p. finance, 1961-62, v.p. of staff group, 1962-63, pres., 1963-68, vice chmn., 1968-69; dean Grad. Sch. Bus., Stanford U., 1969-79, emeritus, 1979—. Former chmn. Automobile Mfrs. Assn., Econ. Devel. Corp. Greater Detroit; councillor The Conf. Bd.; past chmn., life trustee Urban Inst.; mem. Public Adv. Commn. on U.S. Trade Policy, 1968-69, Pres.'s Nat. Commn. on Productivity, 1970-74. Trustee Internat. Exec. Svc. Coirps.; hon. trustee The Brookings Instn.; dir. emeritus S.R.I. Internat.; dir. Pub. Policy Inst. Calif.; former pres. Detroit Press Club Found.; former chmn. Boy Area Coun. Capt. USAAF, 1943-46. Recipient Alumnus of Year Achievement award UCLA, 1964; Distinguished Nebraskan award, 1968; Nat. Industry Leader award B'nai B'rith, 1968 Fellow Am. Acad. Arts and Scis. Clubs: Pacific Union, Bohemian. Presbyterian.

MILLER, ARNOLD, electronics executive; b. N.Y.C., May 8, 1928; s. Sam and Mina (Krutalow) M.; m. Beverly Shayne, Feb. 5, 1950; children: Debra Lynn, Marla Jo, Linda Sue BS in Chemistry, UCLA, 1948, PhD in Phys. Chemistry, 1951. Registered profl. engr., Calif. Rsch. phys. chemist Wrigley Rsch. Co., Chgo., 1951; supr. phys. chemistry Armour Rsch. Found., Chgo., 1951-54, mgr. chemistry and metals, 1954-56; chief materials sci. dept. Borg-Warner Rsch. Ctr., Des Plaines, Ill., 1956-59; dir. rsch. Rockwell Corp., Anaheim, Calif., 1959-66, dir. microelec. ops., 1967-68; group exec. materials ops. Whittaker Corp., L.A., 1968-70; pres. Theta Sensors, Orange, Calif., 1970-72; mgr. xeroradiography Xerox Corp., Pasadena, Calif., 1972-75, corp. dir. rsch. and adv. devel. Stamford, Conn., 1975-78, El Segundo, Calif., 1978-81, v.p. electronics div., 1981-84, pres. electronics div., 1984-87, corp. officer Stamford, 1984-87; pres. Tech. Strategy Group, Fullerton, Calif., 1987—. Bd. dirs. Spectro Diode Labs, San Jose, Calif., Semicondr. Rsch. Corp., Colorep Inc., Carlsbad, Calif.; bd. dirs., chair audit com. Merisel Computer Products, El Segundo, Calif., lead dir., 1989—; mem. vis. com. on materials sci. U. So. Calif., L.A., 1966-68; mem. State of Calif. Micro Bd., 1984-2000. Editorial adv. bd. Advances in Solid State Chemistry; co-editor Electronics Industry Development; contbr. numerous articles to profl. jours. and monographs; patentee in field. Mem. civilian adv. group Dept. Commerce, 1959-60; mem. 5th decade com., also adv. com. on engring. and mgmt. program UCLA, 1984-; mem. com. on scholarly commn. with People's Republic of China, Tech. Transfer Task Force, Nat. Acad. Sci., Washington, 1985; bd. dirs. Orange County Pacific Symphony, Fullerton, Calif., 1982-; mem. univ.'s adv. bd. Calif. State U.-Fullerton, 1986-, chair, 1991-; v.p., bd. dirs. Heritage Pointe Home for the Aging, 1987-97; chmn. Indsl. Assocs. sch. engring. and computer sci. Calif. State U., 1987-97, trustee continuing learning ctr., 1993-; mem. Overseas Devel. Coun., 1988-; mem. Nat. Com. U.S.-China Rels., 1990-; trustee So. Calif. Coll. of Optometry, 1996-, sec.-treas. 1997-2003; bd. mem. Cmty. Found., 1995-, v.p., 1997-. Recipient Sci. Merit award Navy Bur. Ordnance/Armour Rsch. Found., 1952, IR-100 award, 1964, 69; named hon. alumnus Calif. State U., Fullerton, 1996, Univ. medal. Inst. Gerontology Calif. State U., Fullerton, 2002. Fellow AAAS; mem. IEEE, AIME, Am. Chem. Soc., So. Calif. Coalition Edn. Mfg. Engring. (bd. dirs. 1994-98), Elec. Industry Assn. (past chmn. microelectronics), Phi Beta Kappa, Sigma Xi, Phi Lamda Upsilon Home: 505 Westchester Pl Fullerton CA 92835-2706 Office: Tech Strategy Group PO Box 5769 Fullerton CA 92838-0769 Office Phone: 714-447-8887. E-mail: amiller@fullerton.edu.

MILLER, ARTHUR, playwright, author; b. N.Y.C., Oct. 17, 1915; s. Isadore and Augusta (Barnett) Miller; m. Mary Grace Slattery, Aug. 5, 1940 (div. 1956); children: Jane Ellen, Robert; m. Marilyn Monroe, June 1956 (div. 1961); m. Ingeborg Morath, Feb. 1962; children: Rebecca Augusta, Daniel. AB, U. Mich., 1938, LHD, 1956; LittD (hon.), Oxford U., 1995, Harvard U., 1997, Brandeis U., 1998. Assoc. prof. drama U. Mich., 1973-74. Author: (plays) Honors at Dawn, 1936 (Avery Hopwood award for playwriting U. Mich), No Villain: They Too Arise, 1937 (Avery Hopwood award for playwriting U. Mich.), Man Who Had All the Luck, 1944 (Nat. prize Theatre Guild), That They May Win, 1944, All My Sons, 1947 (N.Y. Drama Critics Circle award, Tony award best play, Donaldson award), Death of a Salesman, 1949 (N.Y. Drama Critics Circle award, Tony award, Donaldson award, Pulitzer prize in drama), The Crucible, 1953 (Tony award, Donaldson award, Obie award, 1958), A View from the Bridge, 1955 (Antoinette Perry award Best Revival), A Memory of Two Mondays, 1955, After the Fall, Incident at Vichy, 1964, The Price, 1968, Fame, The Reason Why, 1970, The Creation of the World and Other Business, 1972, Up From Paradise, 1974, The Archbishop's Ceiling, 1976, The American Clock, 1980, Some Kind of Love Story, Elegy for a Lady, 1983, Playing for Time, Danger: Memory!, 1986, The Last Yankee, 1990 (BBC Best Play award, 1992), The Ride Down Mt. Morgan, 1991, Broken Glass, 1994 (Olivier award London, 1995), Mr. Peter's Connections, 1998, Finishing the Picture, Resurrection Blues; (play adaptation) Enemy of the People (Ibsen), 1950, (screenplays) The Story of G.I. Joe, 1945, The Misfits, 1961, The Hook, 1975, Everybody Wins, 1990, The Crucible, 1995, (teleplays) Death of a Salesman, 1966, The Price, 1971, Fame, 1978, Playing for Time, 1980 (George Foster Peabody award, 1981, Outstanding Writing Emmy award, 1981), All My Sons, 1987, An Enemy of the People, 1990, The American Clock, 1994, Situation Normal, 1944, Focus, 1945, Jane's Blanket, 1963, I Don't Need You Anymore, 1967, In Russia, 1969, In the Country, 1977, The Theatre Essays of Arthur Miller, 1978, Chinese Encounters, 1979, Salesman in Beijing, Timebends: A Life, The Misfits and Other Stories, 1987, (novella) Homely Girl, 1994; exec. prodr.: Death of a Salesman, 1985 (Outstanding Drama/Comedy Spl. Emmy award, 1985); author: (plays) Finishing the Picture, 2004. Recipient Bur. New Plays prize Theatre Guild, 1938, Nat. Assn. Ind. Schs. award, 1954, Gold Medal for drama Nat. Inst. Arts and Letters, 1959, Anglo-Am. award, 1966, Creative Arts award Brandeis U., 1970, Lit. Lion award, N.Y. Pub. Libr., 1983, John F. Kennedy Lifetime Achievement award, 1984, Algur Meadows award, So. Meth. U., 1991, Antoinette Perry Lifetime Achievement award, 1999, Prix Molière, 1999, Dorothy and Lillian Gish award, 1999, Praemium Imperiale award, Japan.*

MILLER, ARTHUR MADDEN, lawyer, investment banker, brokerage house executive; b. Greenville, SC, Apr. 10, 1953; s. Charles Frederick and Kathryn Irene (Madden) M.; m. Roberta Beck Connolly, Apr. 17, 1993; children: Isabella McIntyre Madden, Roberta Beck Connolly. AB in History, Princeton U., 1973; MA in History, U. NC, 1976; JD with distinction, Duke U., 1978; LLM in Taxation, NYU, 1982. Bar: N.Y. 1979, U.S. Dist. Ct. (so. dist.) N.Y. 1979. Assoc. Mudge Rose Guthrie Alexander & Ferdon, N.Y.C., 1978-85; v.p. pub. fin. Goldman, Sachs & Co., N.Y.C., 1985—. Trustee Convent of the Sacred Heart, NY, 2003—, St. Andrew's Sch., Del., 2003—; adv. bd. Mary Baldwin Coll., Staunton, Va., 1982—86; trustee Princeton U. Rowing Assn., NJ, 1980—, pres., 1986—95; trustee Rebecca Kelly Dance Co., NYC, 1984—86; steward Power Ten, 1992—95. Mem. ABA (tax sect. com. on tax exempt financing 1985—), Nat. Assn. Bond Lawyers (lectr. 1985—), Pub. Securities Assn. (cons. 1985—), Practising Law Inst. (lectr. 1980, editor/author course materials 1980—), Bond Attys. Workshop (editor/author course material 1983—, lectr. 1983—), Princeton Club. Office: Goldman Sachs & Co 85 Broad St New York NY 10004-2456

MILLER, ARTHUR RAPHAEL, law educator; b. N.Y.C., June 22, 1934; s. Murray and Mary (Schapin) Miller; m. Ellen Monica Joachim, June 8, 1958 (div. 1978); 1 child, Matthew Richard; m. Marilyn Tarmy, 1982 (div. 1988); m. Sandra L. Young, 1992 (div. 2001). AB, U. Rochester, 1955; LLB, Harvard U., 1958; student, Bklyn. Coll., 1952, 55, CCNY, 1955. Bar: N.Y. 1959, U.S. Supreme Ct. 1959, Mass. 1983. With Cleary, Gottlieb, Steen & Hamilton, N.Y.C., 1958-61; assoc. dir. Columbia Law Sch. Project Internat. Procedure, N.Y.C., 1961-62; instr. Columbia U. Law Sch., 1961-62; asso. prof. U. Minn. Law Sch., 1962-65; prof. law U. Mich. Law Sch., 1965-72; vis. prof. Harvard U. Law Sch., 1971-72, prof., 1972-86, Bruce Bromley prof., 1986—. Rsch. assoc. Mental Health Rsch. Inst., 1966-68; dir. project computer assisted instn. Am. Assn. Law Schs., 1968-75; spl. rapporteur State Dept. concerning chpt. II of Hague Conv., 1967; del. U.S.-Italian Conf. Internat. Jud. Assistance, 1961, 62; chmn. task force external affairs Interuniv. Communications Council, 1966-70; mem. law panel, com. sci. and tech. info. Fed. Council Sci. and Tech., Pres.'s Office Sci. and Tech., 1969-72; mem. adv. group Nat. Acad. Sci. Project on Computer Data Banks, 1970-78; mem. spl. adv. group to chief justice Supreme Ct. on Fed. Civil Litigation; mem. com. on automated personal data systems HEW, 1972-73; chmn. Mass. Security and Privacy Council, Mass. Commn. on Privacy; mem. U.S. Commn. New Technol. Uses Copyrighted Works, 1975-79; reporter U.S. Supreme Ct.'s Adv. Com. on Civil Rules, 1978-86, mem. 1986-91; faculty Fed. Jud. Ctr.; reporter study on complex litigation Am. Law Inst.; bd. dirs. Research Found. on Complex Litigations, 1975-80; bd. overseers Rand Inst. on Civil Justice, 1998-2002. Author: The Assault on Privacy: Computers, Data Banks, and Dossiers, 1971, Miller's Court, 1982; (with others) New York Civil Practice, 8 vols., Civil Procedure Cases and Materials, 7th edit., 1997, Federal Practice and Procedure: Civil, 34 vols., 1969—, CPLR Manual, 1967; host syndicated TV shows in Context, Miller's Law, Miller's Court, Headlines on Trial; legal expert Good Morning America. Served with AUS, 1958-59. Recipient Nat. Emmy award for The Constitution, That Delicate Balance. Mem. Am. Law Inst. Office: Harvard U Harvard Law Sch Cambridge MA 02138

MILLER, AUDREY THORNTON, retired educational administrator; b. Glassboro, N.J., June 22, 1937; d. Aubrey and Rebecca Thornton; m. Kenneth C. Miller, Sr., Nov. 20, 1967; children: Yvette A. Rudd, Kenneth C. Jr. BS, Cheyney U., 1963; MEd, Rutgers U., 1974; EdD, Nova Southeastern U., 1998. Cert. prin., supr. N.J. Tchr. Camden (N.J.) Bd. Edn., 1963-74, asst. to prin., 1974-97, vice prin. H.C. Sharp Sch., 1997-2000; ret., 2000. Advisor Theta Chi City Wide chpt. Rowan U., 1980-85, Sharp Sch. Safety Patrol, Camden, 1991-95, Network III Drug Program, Camden, 1993-96; adv. bd. Carter's Psychol. Svc., Camden County, 1995—. Author: Using the Writing Process to Enchance Elementary Students Writing Proficiency and Teachers' Instructional Strategies, 1998. V.p. Garden City Alumnae of Delta Sigma Theta Sorority, Inc., Sicklerville, N.J., 1989-91; chair Career Women's Ministry, St. Matthews Bapt. Ch. Williamstown, N.J., 1993-96, chief ednl. svcs. comty. devel. ctr. programs SMCDC, 2003. Recipient Set a Good Example award Gov. Christie Whitman, Trenton, 1994, Disting. Achievement award, Camden Bd. Edn., 1994, 96, Proclamation, Bd. Chosen Freeholders, Camden County, 2000, Cheyney U. Alumni Outstanding Service Award, 2003. Mem. NAACP, AFL-CIO, Black Women's Edn. Alliance (Educator's award 1992), Camden City Fedn. Sch. Adminstrs., N.J. Fedn. Colored Women's Club (Outstanding Svc. in Edn. award 2000), Cheyney U. Alumni Assn. (life, area rep. S. Jersey chpt., 2000-02, OUtstanding Chpt. Leadership award 2003), Nova Southeastern U. Alumni Assn., Rutgers U. Alumni, Delta Sigma Theta Sorority (life), Kappa Delta Pi. Democrat. Avocations: interior decorating, travel, tennis. Home: 4 Pierson Pl Sicklerville NJ 08081-2006 Personal E-mail: milerau@aol.com.

MILLER, BARBARA KENTON, retired librarian; b. N.Y.C., Sept. 21, 1934; d. Robert Alfred and Kathleen Hope (Levy) Kenton; m. John Arnold Miller, June 15, 1955; children: Valerie Ann Miller, Jennifer Karen Kraft. BA with distinction, Finch Coll., 1960; MLS, C.W. Post, 1976. Cert. libr., N.Y. Libr., cons. archivist Coun. Fgn. Rels., N.Y.C., 1977-2000; ret., 2000. Cons. archivist Coun. on Fgn. Rels. Mem. Spl. Librs. Assn., Beta Phi Mu. Avocations: dogs, golf. Office: Coun Fgn Rels 58 E 68 St New York NY 10021-5953 Personal E-mail: bkmiller55@aol.com.

MILLER, BARBARA STALLCUP, development consultant; b. Montague, Calif., Sept. 4, 1919; d. Joseph Nathaniel and Maybelle (Needham) Stallcup; m. Leland F. Miller, May 16, 1946; children: Paula Kay, Susan Lee, Daniel Joseph, Alison Jean. BA, U. Oreg., 1942. Women's editor Eugene Daily News, Oreg., 1941-43; law clk. J. Everett Barr, Yreka, Calif., 1943-45; mgr. Yreka C of C., 1945-46; N.W. supr. Louis Harris Assocs., Portland, Oreg., 1959-62; dir. pub. rels., fund raising Columbia River coun. Girl Scouts U.S.A., 1962-67; pvt. practice pub. rels. cons. Portland, Ohio, 1967-72; adviser, student publs., asst. prof. comms. U. Portland, 1967-72, dir. pub. rels. info., asst. prof. comms., 1972-78, dir. devel., 1978-79, exec. dir. devel., 1979-83; assoc. dir. St. Vincent Med. Found., 1983-88; dir. planned giving Good Samaritan Found., 1988-95; planned giving cons., 1995—. Contbr. articles to profl. jours. Pres. bd. dirs. Vols. of Am. of Oreg., Inc., 1980-84, pres. regional adv. bd., 1982-84; chmn. bd. dirs. S.E. mental Health Network, 1984-88; nat. bd. dirs. Vols. of Am., Inc., 1984-96; pres., bd. dirs. Vol. Bur. Greater Portland, 1991-93; mem. U. Oreg. Journalism Advancement Coun., 1991-2003. Named Oasis Sr. Role Model, 1992, Ont. Presdl. Citation, Oreg. Communicators Assns., 1973, Matrix award, 1976, 80, Miltner award U. Portland, 1977, Communicator of Achievement award Oreg. Press Women, 1992, Willamette Valley Devel. Officers award, 1992 (Barbara Stallcup Miller Profl. Achievement award 1992). Mem. Nat. Coast Trail Assn. (pres. bd. dirs. 1997-2003), Nat. Soc. Fundraising Execs., Nat. Planned Giving Coun., Women in Comm. (NW regional v.p. 1973-75, Offbeat award 1988), Nat. Fedn. Press Women, Oreg. Press Women (dist. dir.), PRSA (dir. local chpt., Marsh award 1989), Oreg. Fedn. Womens Clubs (comms. chmn. 1978-80), Alpha Xi Delta (found. trustee, editor 1988-95), Portland Zenith (pres. 1975-76, 81-82, 2002—04). Unitarian Universalist. Home and Office: 1706 Boca Ratan Dr Lake Oswego OR 97034-1624 Personal E-mail: bmiller@teleport.com.

MILLER, BARRY, research administrator, psychologist; b. N.Y.C., Dec. 25, 1942; s. Jack and Ida (Kaplan) M.; m. Susan Hallermeier; children: Eric, Arianne, Kristina, Barrie. BS in Psychology, Bklyn. Coll., 1965; MS in Psychology, Villanova U., 1967; PhD in Psychiatry, Med. Coll. Pa., 1971. Instr. psychology Villanova (Pa.) U., 1971-73; asst. dir. dept. behavioral sci., med. rsch. scientist Ea. Pa. Psychiatric Inst., Phila., 1971-73, sr. med. rsch. scientist, 1973-80; dir. Pa. Bur. Rsch. and Tng., Harrisburg, 1973-81; asst. prof. psychology U. Pa. Med. Sch., Phila., 1975-78, asst. clin. prof. psychology, 1978—; assoc. prof. psychiatry Med. Coll. Pa., Phila., 1981-90, rsch. assoc. prof. medicine, 1983-90, assoc. dean for rsch., 1981-90; dir. for rsch. devel. Albert Einstein Healthcare Network, Phila., 1990-95; dir. The Permanente Med. Group Rsch. Inst., Oakland, Calif., 1995-99; adj. assoc. prof. psychiatry Med. Coll. Pa., Phila., 1990—; rsch. assoc. prof. psychiatry Temple U. Sch. Med., Phila., 1990—; adminstrv. dir. rsch. ops. Divsn. Rsch., Oakland, Calif., 1999—. Mem. sci. and tech. task force Pa. Econ. Devel. Partnership, Harrisburg, 1987-88, adv. com. Clin. Rsch. Ctr. Psychopathology of Elderly, Phila., 1985-88; mem. cancer control prgram Pa. Dept. Health, 1994; vis. rsch. assoc. prof. Med. Coll. Pa., Phila., 1991—. Contbr. articles to profl. jours.; mem. editorial bd. Jour. Mental Health Adminstrn., 1988—, assoc. editor, 1989—. Bd. dirs. Community Mental Health Ctr. 6A, Phila., 1969-73, Northwest Jewish Youth Ctrs., Phila., 1974-75; mem. Lafayette Hill Civic Assn., 1973-86, Citizens Coun. Whitemarsh (Pa.) Twp., 1975-86; pres., bd. dirs. Golden Eagle Luxury Homeowners Assn., Pleasanton, Calif., 1995-97. Grantee HHS, NIH. Mem. AAAS, Am. Psychol. Assn., Assn. Mental Health Adminstrs., Assn. Univ. Tech. Mgrs., Soc. Rsch. Adminstrs., Calif. Psychol. Assn. Avocation: hiking. Office: Divsn Rsch 2000 Broadway Oakland CA 94612-3429 Office Phone: 510-891-3408. Business E-Mail: barry.x.miller@kp.org.

MILLER, BEBE, choreographer; b. N.Y.C., Sept. 20, 1950; BA in Fine Arts, Earlham Coll., 1971; MA in Dance, Ohio State U., 1975. Owner Bebe Miller Co., N.Y.C., 1985—; prof. dance Ohio State U., 2002—. Bd. dirs. Dance USA, Dance Theater Workshop, Danspace Project; tchr. U. Ill., Champaign/Urbana, UCLA, NYU, Mt. Holyoke Coll., Movement Rsch., N.Y.C., Sarah Lawrence Coll., U. Minn., Mills Coll., Middlebury Coll., Va. Commonwealth U., Tex. Women's U., Cal Arts and Stanford U. Choreographer (theatre) Tiny Sisters in the Enormous Land, 1995, Going to the Wall, 1998, (original works) Oreg. Ballet Theatre, Boston Ballet, Dayton Contemporary Dance Co. and others. Recipient 2 Bessie awards, award, Am. Choreographer, 1988, Young Artists Recognition award, Dewars, 1990; fellow, Creative Artists Pub. Svc., 1984, Nat. Found. for Arts, 1984, Nat. Endowment for Arts, 1985—88, John Simon Guggenheim Found., 1988. Office: Bebe Miller Co 54 W 21st St Ste 502 New York NY 10010

MILLER, BENJAMIN K. retired state supreme court justice; b. Springfield, Ill., Nov. 5, 1936; s. Clifford and Mary (Luthyens) M. BA, So. Ill. U., 1958; JD, Vanderbilt U., 1961. Bar: Ill. 1961. Ptnr. Olsen, Cantrill & Miller, Springfield, 1964-70; prin. Ben Miller-Law Office, Springfield, 1970-76; judge 7th jud. cir. Ill. Cir. Ct., Springfield, 1976-82, presiding judge Criminal div., 1977-81, chief judge, 1981-82; justice Ill. Appellate Ct., 4th Jud. Dist., 1982-84, Ill. Supreme Ct., Springfield, 1984-2001, chief justice, 1991-93, ret., 2001. Adj. prof. So. Ill. U., Springfield, 1974—; chmn. Ill. Cts. Commn., 1988-90; mem. Ill. Gov.'s Adv. Coun. on Criminal Justice Legis., 1977-84, Ad Hoc Com. on Tech. in Cts., 1985—. Mem. editorial rev. bd. Illinois Civil Practice Before Trial, Illinois Civil Trial Practice Pres. Cen. Ill. Mental Health Assn., 1969-71; bd. govs. Aid to Retarded Citizens, 1977-80; mem. Lincoln Legals Adv. Bd., 1988—. Lt. USNR, 1964-67. Mem. ABA (bar admissions com. sect. of legal edn. and admissions to bar 1992—), Ill. State Bar Assn. (bd. govs. 1970-76, treas. 1975-76), Sangamon County Bar Assn., Ctrl. Ill. Women's Bar Assn., Am. Judicature Soc. (bd. dirs. 1990-95), Abraham Lincoln Assn. (bd. dirs. 1988-98). Address: 100 E Bellevue PL Apt 29F Chicago IL 60611-5194

MILLER, BERNARD JOSEPH, JR., advertising executive; b. Louisville, July 31, 1925; s. Bernard J. Sr. and Myrtle (Herrington) M.; m. Jayne Hughes, Aug. 7, 1948 (div. Oct. 1970); children: Bernard J. III, Jeffrey, Janet Marie.; m. Brita Naujok, Nov. 24, 1970; 1 child, Brian. BS, Ind. U., 1949. Merchandising mgr. Brown-Forman Distillers, Inc., Louisville, 1949-54; v.p. Phelps Mfg. Co., Terre Haute, Ind., 1954-60; pres. Columbian Advt. Inc., Chgo., 1960-87, chmn., 1987—. 2d lt. USAF, 1943-46, PTO. Mem. Point of Purchase Advt. Inst. (dir. 1970-73), Saddle and Cycle Club (bd. dirs. 1987-90, 99—). Avocations: tennis, downhill skiing, collecting first edition autographed books. Office: Columbian Advt Inc 201 E Ohio St Chicago IL 60611-3238

MILLER, BETH MCCARTHY, television director; Dir.: (TV series) Saturday Night Live, 1975, 1995—, The Jon Stewart Show, 1993—, The Colin Quinn Show, 2002, (TV spl.) Eagles: Hell Freezes Over, 1994—, Nirvana Unplugged, 1994—, James Taylor Live, 1998—, Saturday Night Live: The Best of Adam Sandler, 1999—, Saturday Night Live Christmas, 1999—, Saturday Night Live: 25th Anniversary, 1999, America: A Tribute to Heroes, 2001, NBC 75th Anniversary Spl., 2002, Saturday Night Live: The Best of Will Ferrell, 2002, GQ Men of the Yr. Awards, 2003; dir., prodr.: MTV Video Music Awards, 2003. Nominee Outstanding Directorial Achievement in Musical/Variety award, DGA, 2000, 2004, Emmy award, 1999, 2000, 2003; recipient Outstanding Directorial Achievement in Musical/Variety award, DGA, 2001, 2002. Office: Saturday Night Live 30 Rockefeller Plaza 50th St and 6th Ave New York NY 10112

MILLER, BETTY BROWN, freelance writer; b. Altus, Ark., Dec. 21, 1926; d. Carlos William and Arlie Gertrude (Sublett) Brown; m. Robert Wiley Miller, Nov. 15, 1953; children: Janet Ruth, Stephen Wiley. BS, Okla. State U., 1949; MS, U. Tulsa, 1953; postgrad., Am. U., 1966-68. Tchr. LeFlore (Okla.) H.S., 1947-48, Osage Indian Reservation H.S., Hominy, Okla., 1948-50, Jenks (Okla.) H.S., 1950-51; instr. Sch. Bus. U. Tulsa, 1950-51; tchr. Tulsa pub. schs., 1951-54; instr. Burdette Coll., Boston, 1954-55; reporter Bethesda-Chevy Chase Tribune, Montgomery County, Md., 1970-73; freelance writer, contbr. newspapers and mags., 1973—. V.p. Kenwood Park (Md.) Citizens Assn., 1960; mem. Ft. Sumner Citizens Assn., editor newsletter, 1969; mem. Md. State PTA, editl. coord. leadership conf., 1973-74; founder, chair Montgomery County Forum Edn., 1970-75; trustee Friends Valley Forge Nat. Hist. Park; bd. dirs. Friends Curtis Inst. Music; mem. Nat. Mus. Women in the Arts, Musical Fund Soc. Phila.; trustee adv. Help the Aged. Mem.: DAR, PEO, Union League Phila. (past mem. ladies com., mem. ladies adv. com.), The Nat. Gravel Soc., Internat. Platform Assn., Montgomery County Press Assn., Nat. Soc. Arts & Letters (past editor mag., bd. dirs. pub rels., past nat. corr. sec.), Huguenot Soc. Pa. (v.p. 1989—92, pres. 1993—95, past bd. dirs., hon. v.p. 1997—), Nat. League Am. Pen Women (former budget chmn., past nat. treas.), Soc. Descendants of Washington's Army at Valley Forge (past nat. comdr. in chief, past inspector gen. Nat. Huguenot Soc., past. mem. gen. coun.), Acorn Club Phila., Sedgeley Club (pres. Phila. 1985—88), Washington Club, U.D.C., Adventures Unltd. (chmn. Washington chpt.), Capital Spkrs. Club Washington (past pres.), Melba T. Croft Music Club, Order Ea. Star (life). Republican. Address: PO Box 573 Valley Forge PA 19481-0573

MILLER, BEVERLY WHITE, former college president, educational consultant, consultant; b. Willoughby, Ohio, 1923; d. Joseph Martin and Marguerite Sarah (Storer) White; m. Lynn Martin Miller, Oct. 11, 1945 (dec. 1986); children: Michaela Ann, Craig Martin, Todd Daniel, Cass Timothy, Simone Agnes. AB, Western Res. U., 1945; MA, Mich. State U., 1957; PhD, U. Toledo, 1967; LHD (hon.), Coll. St. Benedict, St. Joseph, Minn., 1979; LLD (hon.), U. Toledo, 1988. Chem. and biol. researcher, 1945-57; tchr. schs. in Mich., also Mercy Sch. Nursing, St. Lawrence Hosp., Lansing, Mich., 1957-58; mem. chemistry and biology faculty Mary Manse Coll., Toledo, 1958-71, dean grad. div., 1968-71, exec. v.p., 1968-71; acad. dean Salve Regina Coll., Newport, R.I., 1971-74; pres. Coll. St. Benedict, St. Joseph, Minn., 1974-79, Western New Eng. Coll., Springfield, Mass., 1980-96, pres. emerita, 1996—. Higher edn. cons., 1996—; cons. U.S. Office Edn., 1980; mem. Springfield Pvt. Industry Coun./Regional Employment Bd., exec. com., 1982-94; mem. Minn. Pvt. Coll. Coun., 1974-79, sec., 1974-75, vice chmn., 1975-76, chmn., 1976-77; cons. in field. Author papers and books in field. Corporator Mercy Hosp., Springfield, Mass. Recipient President's citation St. John's U., Minn., 1979; also various service awards; named disting. alumna of yr. U. Toledo, 1998. Mem. AAAS, Am. Assn. Higher Edn., Assn. Cath. Colls. and Univs. (exec. bd.), Internat. Assn. Sci. Edn., Nat. Assn. Ind. Colls. and Univs. (govt. rels. adv. com., bd. dirs. 1990-93, exec. com. 1991-93, treas. 1992-93), Nat. Assn. Biology Tchrs., Assn. Ind. Colls. and Univs. of Mass. (exec. com. 1981-96, vice chmn. 1985-86, chmn. 1986-87), Nat. Assn. Rsch. Sci. Tchg., Springfield C. of C. (bd. dirs.), Am. Assn. Univ. Adminstrs. (bd. dirs. 1989-92), Delta Kappa Gamma, Sigma Delta Epsilon. Office: 6713 County Road M Delta OH 43515-9778

MILLER, BONNIE SEWELL, marketing professional, writer; b. Junction City, Ky., July 24, 1932; d. William Andrew and Lillian Irene (McCowan) Sewell; m. William Gustave Tournade Jr., Nov. 5, 1950 (div. 1974); children: Bonnie Sue Tournade Zaner, William Gustave III, Sharon Irene Tournade Leach; m. Bruce George Miller, Nov. 15, 1981. BA, U. South Fla., 1968, MA, 1973. Cert. tchr., Fla. Chair dept. English Tampa (Fla.) Cath. H.S., 1972-78; tchr. Clearwater (Fla.) H.S., 1978-80; mgr. prodn. svcs. Paradyne Corp., Largo, Fla., 1980-83; freelance writer, cons. Tampa, 1983-84; mgr. product documentation PPS, Inc., Largo, 1984-86, mgr. mktg. comm., 1986-87; writer Nixdorf Computer Corp., Tampa, 1988-89; mktg. dir. Suncoast Schs. Fed. Credit Union, Tampa, 1989-98; co-owner, v.p., writer, cons. Need-A-Writer, Inc., Tampa, 1998—; instr. profl. and tech. writing U. South Fla., 2004—. Instr. English, Hillsborough C.C., Tampa, 1975—87; cons. bus. writing Coronet Instrnl. Media Writing Project, Tampa, 1976, Nat. Mgmt. Assn.,

Tampa, 1981—87; adj. instr. profl. writing U. South Fla., 1993; adj. instr. tech. writing U. Tampa, 2002, English instr., 2002—. Author: Youth Financial Literacy, 1999, Effective Business Writing for Credit Unions, 2000; contbr. articles to profl. jours. Bd. dirs. SERVE, Tampa, Credit Union Mktg. Assn. Coun., Sing Parent Displaced Homemakers Group; legis. chair Tampa PTA, 1965; judge speech contest Am. Legion, Tampa, 1976; vol. North Tampa Vol. Libr., 1988. NEH fellow, 1975. Mem. NAFE, Soc. Tech. Communicators, Am. Assn. Bus. Women, Kappa Delta Pi. Democrat. Baptist. Avocations: writing, sewing, gardening, exotic birds, travel, decorating. Home and Office: 516 2d Ave SE Lutz FL 33549 E-mail: bmiller@sunstarcom.net.

MILLER, BRIAN CRAIG, historian, educator; b. Norristown, Pa., July 21, 1978; s. Craig and Linda Miller. BA, Penn State U., 2000; MA, U. of Miss., 2002; PhD in History, U. Miss., 2002—. History instr. U. Miss., U., Miss., 2000—. Author book reviews in various historical journ. Travel grant, Soc. of Mil. Historians, 2003. Mem.: U. Miss. Alumni Assn., Penn State Alumni Assn., So. Hist. Assn., Orgn. of Am. Historians, Soc. of Civil War Historians, Nat. Assn. of Eagle Scouts, Phi Alpha Theta. Independent. Avocations: college sports, musical theater, travel, reading historical works, movie buff. Office: U Miss 310 Bishop Hall University MS 38671 Office Phone: 662-915-6976.

MILLER, BRUCE, advertising executive; Pres, new bus. contact Suissa Miller Advt, L.A. Office: Suissa Miller Advertising 8687 Melrose Ave Los Angeles CA 90069-5701

MILLER, BRUCE J. performing arts educator, director; b. Phila., May 30, 1950; s. Marvin and Jeanne I. Miller; m. Amy Weiner, June 18, 1988; 1 child, Emma. MFA, Temple U., 1978. Chair theatre dept. Walnut Hill Sch., Natick, Mass., 1986—94; dir. acting programs U. Miami, Coral Gables, 1994—. Author: Head-First Acting; actor: (theatre/commercials/industrial films); dir.: (plays); contbr. articles to profl. jours.; author: The Actor as Storyteller. Recipient O'Neill Critic's Inst. Festival award, Am. Coll. Theatre Festival, 2003. Mem.: SAG (assoc.), Am. Fedn. TV and Radio Artist (assoc.), Actors' Equity Assn. (assoc.). Office: University of Miami Hecht Bldg 2nd fl Coral Gables FL 33124-4820 Personal E-mail: millbru@miami.edu. E-mail: bmiller@miami.edu.

MILLER, BUFFY, dancer; b. Atlanta; Studies with, Patricia Bromley; student, New Ballet Sch. Mem. Feld Ballet Tech. Soc., 1986—97; with Ballet Tech., 1997—. Office: 108 High St 2 Portland ME 04101-3815

MILLER, C. ARDEN, physician, educator; b. Shelby, Ohio, Sept. 19, 1924; s. Harley H. and Mary (Thuma) Miller; m. Helen Meihack, June 26, 1948; children: John Lewis, Thomas Meihack, Helen Lewis, Benjamin Lewis. Student, Oberlin Coll., 1942—44; MD cum laude, Yale, 1948. Intern, then asst. resident pediatrics Grace-New Haven Community Hosp., 1948—51; faculty U. Kans. Med. Center, 1951—66, dir. childrens rehab. unit, 1957—60, dean Med. Sch., dir., 1960—66; prof. pediatrics and maternal and child health U. N.C., Chapel Hill, 1966—98, emeritus, 1998—, vice chancellor health scis., 1966—71, chmn. dept. maternal and child health, 1977—87. Chmn. exec. com. Citizens Bd. Inquiry into Health Svcs. for Am., 1968—71. Mem. editl. bd.: Jour. Med. Edn., 1960—66; contbr. articles to profl. jours. Trustee Appalachian Regional Hosps., 1974—84, Planned Parenthood Fedn.; chmn. Alan Guttmacher Inst., 1978—84, 1986—. Recipient Robert H. Felix Disting. Svc. award, St. Louis U., 1977, Martha Mae Eliot award in pub. health, 1984, O. Max Gardner award, U. N.C., 1987; scholar Am. Markle scholar in med. scis., 1955—60. Fellow: Royal Soc. Health (hon.), Clare Hall Cambridge (Eng.) U. (life); mem.: APHA (chmn. action bd. 1972—75, pres. 1974—75, Sedgewick Meml. medal 1986), Inst. of Medicine NAS, Assn. Am. Med. Colls. (v.p. 1965—66), Soc. Pediat. Rsch., Delta Omega, Alpha Omega Alpha, Sigma Xi. Home: 350 Carolina Meadows Villa Chapel Hill NC 27517-7549 E-mail: Arden_Miller@unc.edu.

MILLER, CALLIX EDWIN, manufacturing executive, consultant; b. South Bend, Ind., Mar. 27, 1924; s. Callix Edwin and Marguerite Cash (Sweeney) M.; m. Theresa Ann Pirchio, June 25, 1949; children: Madeline, Callix, John, David, Thomas. BS in Archtl. Engring., U. Notre Dame, 1949. Mgr. engring. Internat. Mining and Chem. Corp., Chgo., 1951-61; exec. dir. Sperry Rand Corp., N.Y.C., 1961-64; v.p. Internat. Minerals & Chem. Corp., Chgo., 1964-72, Assocs. Corp. N.Am., Dallas, 1972-78; corp. v.p. tech. resources Clark Equipment Co., Buchanan, Mich., 1978-85. Consulting services covering design, planning, feasibility studies, econ. devel.; adj. prof. arch U. Notre Dame, 2000-01. Bd. dirs. Chgo. Area coun. Boy Scouts Am., 1967-70, Alexian Bros. Hosp., Chgo., 1966-68; mem. adv. coun., Holy Cross Coll., Notre Dame, Ind., 2002. Served with USNR, 1943-45. Mem. AIA, ASCE, Soc. Am. Mil. Engrs., Am. Concrete Inst., Knollwood Country Club, Northbrook, Ill. Sports Club, Faculty Club (U. Notre Dame), Elks, K.C. Republican. Roman Catholic. Home: 16174 Baywood Ln Granger IN 46530-9716

MILLER, CAMILLE, school system administrator; d. Richard Lewis and Bessie Bonner-Lewis; m. Clarence Miller, Sept. 13, 1956; children: Maria Antoinette, Kimberly Ann, Cassandra Lynn. Bus. cert., Berkeley Adult Trade Sch., 1959. Cusp. svc. rep. Am. Savings and Loan, El Cerrito, Calif., 1967—74; site supr. W. Contra Costa Sch. Dist., Richmond, Calif., 1975—82, 1996—, libr. asst., 1982—88, instrnl. asst., 1988—96. Avocations: reading, travel, board games. E-mail: cami440@aol.com.

MILLER, CANDICE S. congresswoman; b. May 7, 1954; m. Donald G. Miller; 1 child, Wendy Nicole. Student, Macomb County C.C., Northwood U. Sec., treas. D.B. Snider, Inc., 1972-79; trustee Harrison Twp., 1979-80, supr., 1980-92; treas. Macomb County, 1992-95; sec. of state State of Mich., Lansing, 1995—2003; mem. U.S. Ho. Reps. from Mich. 10th dist., 2003—. Mem. Lake St. Clair Blue Ribbon Commn. Chair John Engler for Gov. campaign, Macomb County; del. Rep. Nat. Conv., 1996; co-chair Rep. Platform Com., 1996, Dole/Kemp Presdl. Campaign, Mich., 1996, Bush/Cheney Presdl. Campaign, Mich., 2000; mem. Carehouse-Macomb County Child Adv. Ctr., Selfridge Air Nat. Guard Base Cmty. Coun., Detroit Econ. Club; mem. adminstrv. bd. Mich. State, mem. safety commn. Republican. Avocations: boating, yacht racing. Office: 508 Cannon HOB Washington DC 20515

MILLER, CARL GEORGE, automotive parts manufacturing executive; b. Milw., Oct. 3, 1942; s. Carl Conrad and Agnes Frances (Patla) M.; m. Patricia Ann Smith, Apr. 27, 1968; children: Gregory, Brian. BS, St. Louis U., 1964. CPA, Mo. Audit mgr. Ahrens & McKeon, CPAs, St. Louis, 1967-73; supr. internal audit Gen. Dynamics Corp., St. Louis, 1973-75, mgr. fin. analysis, 1975-78, dir. fin. analysis, 1978-80; v.p., contr. Quincy (Mass.) Shipbldg. div. Gen. Dynamics Corp., 1980-86; v.p. fin. Cessna Aircraft Co., Wichita, Kans., 1986-88; v.p., contr. Ft. Worth div. Gen. Dynamics Corp., Ft. Worth, 1988-90; v.p., contr. TRW, Inc., Cleve., 1990-96, exec. v.p., CFO, 1996—. Mem. adv. coun. So. U. and A&M Bus. Sch., Case Western Reserve U. Acctg. Dept. Mem. AICPA, Fin. Execs. Inst. (com. on corp. reporting), Mfr. Alliance for Productivity and Innovation (fin. coun. II), Mo. Soc. CPA, Mayfield Country Club, Delta Sigma Pi (pres. 1963-64). Republican. Lutheran. Avocations: travel, reading. Office: TRW Inc 1900 Richmond Rd Cleveland OH 44124-3760

MILLER, CAROLANN, physical therapist, educator; d. Arthur Madison and Catherine Ann Miller. BS in Phys. Therapy, Boston U., 1984; MS in Phys. Therapy, MGH Inst. Health Professions, 1994; PhD, Walden U., 2001. Assoc. prof. North Ga. Coll. & State U., Dahlonega, 1996—; phys. therapist NE Rehab. Ctr., Dahlonega, Ga. Contbr. chapters to books Prosthetic Requirements for the Older Adult, articles to profl. jours. Mem.: Ga. Consortium Phys. Therapy Educators (assoc.), Am. Phys. Therapy Assn. (assoc. cert. geriatric specialist 1996), Amputee Found. Greater Atlanta (life), Amputee Coalition Am. (life), Omicron Delta Kappa. Achievements include research in quality of life issues for elderly. Office: North Ga Coll & State Univ Natural Health Sci Bldg PT Dahlonega GA 30597 Office Phone: 706-864-1475. E-mail: camiller@ngcsu.edu.

MILLER, CAROLE ANN LYONS, editor, publisher, video producer, writer, marketing specialist; b. Newton, Mass. d. Markham Harold and Ursula Patricia (Foley) Lyons; m. David Thomas Miller, July 4, 1978. BA, Boston U., 1964; bus. cert., Hickox Sch., Boston, 1964; cert. advt. and mktg. profl., UCLA, 1973; cert. retail mgmt. profl., Ind. U., 1976. Editor Triangle Topics, Pacific Telephone, L.A.; programmer L.A. Ctrl. Area Spkrs. Bur., 1964-66; mng. editor, mktg. dir. Teen mag., L.A. and N.Y.C., 1966-76; advt. dir. L.S. Ayres & Co., Indpls., 1976-78; v.p. mktg. The Denver, 1978-79; founder, editor, pub. Clockwise mag., Ventura, Calif., 1979-85; mktg. mgr., mgr. pub. rels. and spl. events Robinson's Dept. Store, L.A., 1985-87; exec. v.p., dir. mktg. Harrison Svcs., L.A., San Francisco, 1987-93; pres. divsn. Miller & Miller MillerMania, Video Image and Mktg., Camino, Calif., 1993—. Instr. retail advt. Ind. U., 1977-78. Recipient Pres.'s award Advt. Women of N.Y., 1974, Seklemian award, 1977, Pub. Svc. Addy award, 1978, Disting. Svc. award Bay Area chpt. Assn. Image Cons., Internat., 2003. Mem. Image Cons., Internat. (1st Ever Oustanding Svc. award Bay Area chpt. 2004), Advt. Women N.Y., Retail Advt. and Mktg. Assn., Fashion Group Internat., Bay Area Integrated Mktg., San Francisco Fashion Group, UCLA Alumni Assn. (life), Media Coms. (life), Assn. Image Cons. Internat. Office Phone: 530-644-4919. E-mail: caroleann@millermania.com.

MILLER, CHARLES, business management market research consultant; b. Crowley, La., Nov. 1, 1959; s. Rufus Paul and Rose (Lacombe) M.; m. Monica Lynn Habetz, Aug. 10, 1985; children: Monique L., Paul T. BS, La. State U., 1981, MS, 1985; PhD, Ohio State U., 1989. Rsch. asst. horticulture dept. La. State U., Baton Rouge, 1977-78, La. State Soil Testing Lab., Baton Rouge, 1978-81; rsch. assoc. La. Rice Rsch. Sta., Crowley, 1982; agriculture tchr. Acadia Parish Sch. Bd., Crowley and Iota, 1982-87; rsch. assoc. Ohio State U., Columbus, 1987-89, asst. prof., 1989-92; prin., dir. relationship assessment practice S4 Cons. Inc., Powell, Ohio, 1992-98; co-founder, sr. v.p. Insight MAS, Dublin, Ohio, 1998—; co-founder, ptnr. Iota (La.) Trucking, 2000—. Co-author: (with D.C. Swaddling) Customer Power: How to Grow Sales and Profits in a Customer-Driven Marketplace, 2001. Minister, lector St. John Neumann Ch., Sunbury, Ohio, 1992—. Recipient project grant for tchr. prep. program U.S. Dept. Edn., 1990, Am. Farmer award Nat. Future Farmers Am., 1979. Mem. Am. Mktg. Assn., Am. Soc. for Quality, Omicron Tau Theta (editor 1991-92, Outstanding Svc. award 1992), Phi Delta Kappa, Gamma Sigma Delta, Alpha Zeta. Roman Catholic. Avocation: woodworking. Office: Insight MAS 4230 Tuller Rd Dublin OH 43017-5065 Business E-Mail: Cmiller@insightmas.com.

MILLER, CHARLES A. lawyer; b. Oakland, Calif., Feb. 7, 1935; s. Frank and Janice (Greene) M.; m. Jeanette Segal, Sept. 27, 1964; children: Jennifer Fay Haight, Charlotte Irene Marvin, Ira David. AB, U. Calif., Berkeley, 1955, LLB, 1958. Law clk. to assoc. justice U.S. Supreme Ct., Washington, 1958-59; assoc. Covington & Burling, Washington, 1959-67, ptnr., 1967—, chmn. mgmt. com., 1991-95. Mem. criminal justice coordinating bd., Washington, 1977-78; chmn. hearing com. Bd. on Profl. Responsibility, Washington, 1980-86. Pres. U. Calif. Alumni Club, Washington, 1962-70; mem. various coms. and adv. bds. Washington Pub. Sch. System, 1972-79; chmn. lawyers com. Washington Performing Arts Soc., 1984-86; bd. dirs. Dumbarton Concert Series, Washington, 1986—, chmn., 1990—; trustee U. Calif. Berkeley Found., 2001—, Fed. City Coun.; chair D.C. Citizens Welfare Transformation Com., 1996-97; co-chair Task Force on D.C. Governance, 1996-98; mem. Mayor's Commn. on Juvenile Justice, Washington, 2001-02. Mem. ABA, D.C. Bar Assn., U. Calif. Alumni Assn. (trustee 1989-92), Burning Tree Club (Bethesda, Md.). Democrat. Jewish. Office: Covington & Burling 1201 Pennsylvania Ave NW PO Box 7566 Washington DC 20044-7566 E-mail: cmiller@cov.com.

MILLER, CHARLES E. (CHUCK MILLER), judge; b. Washington, Sept. 26, 1944; s. Charles Edward Miller and Mary (Cox) M.; divorced; 1 child, Samantha Mcgill Cox. BA, So. Meth. U., 1971, JD, 1972. Bar: Tex. 1972. Assoc. Roseborough & Curlee, Dallas, 1972-77; judge County Criminal Ct. #7, Dallas, 1977-82, Ct. Criminal Appeals, Austin, Tex., 1983-94; state judge at large State of Tex., 1995—. Adj. prof. criminal law So. Meth. U. Law Sch., Dallas, 1980—82; arbitrator comml., employment and labor panels Am. Arbitration Assn., 1995—; labor arbitrator Fed. Mediation and Conciliation Svc., 2002—, arbitrator, labor roster, 2003—. Author and lectr. in field. Mem. nat. adv. coun. Nat. victim Ctr., NYC and Washington; mem. nat. steeringcom. Victims Constitutional Amendment Network; mem. adv. bd. victims Organized to Ensure Rights and Safety; mem. victim assistancecom. Tex. Young Lawyers Assn.; parliamentarian state exec. bd. People Against Violent Crime. With US Army, 1966-70. Named Disting. Mil. Grad., Officer Candidate Sch., Ft. Sill, Okla., 1968, Best Dallas Misdemeanor Ct. Judge, Dallas Bar Assn., 1982, Best Dallas Criminal Ct. Judge, Dallas County Criminal Bar Assn., 1982; decorated Army Commendational medal, 1970; recipient Sunny von Bulow Nat. Victim Advocacy Ctr. Appreciation cert., 1987, US Dept. Justice Victims of Crime Appreciation cert., 1992, Victims Organized to Ensure Rights and Safety Advocate for Justice award, 1993, People Against Violent Crime Appreciation cert., 1993. Mem. SAR, State Bar Tex. (chmn. criminal law sect. 1981-82, course dir. advanced criminal law course 1990, chmn. crime victim com. 1992-94, crime victim & witness, 1994, cert. specialist in criminal law), Coll. State Bar Tex., Tex. Bar Found. Republican. Home and Office: 1701 Foggy Glen Cv Ste 100 Austin TX 78733-1541 E-mail: judgechuckmiller@att.net.

MILLER, CHARLES EDMOND, retired library administrator; b. Bridgeport, Conn., Aug. 3, 1938; s. Edmond and Irene Ovelia (Boudreaux) M.; m. Alice Ann Phillips, June 2, 1962; children— Alison, Charles Edmond, Catherine, Susan. Student, U. Hawaii, 1957-58; BA, McNeese State U., 1964; MS in L.S, La. State U., 1966. Tchr. Lake Charles (La.) High Sch., 1964-65; mem. staff La. State U. Library, Baton Rouge, 1966-69; asso. dir. Tulane U. Library New Orleans, 1969-73; dir. Fla. State U. Library, Tallahassee, 1973-2000; ret., 2000. Vis. coms. So. Assn. Colls. and Schs.; bd. dirs. SOLINET, 1979-81, 85-86, corp. v.p., vice chmn., 1980-81; cons. in field; adv. com. State Libr. Fla.; bd. dirs. Ctr. for Rsch. Librs., 1976-77, 91-97, sec., 1993-96; mem. policy bd. Fla. Libr. Network; pres. Assn. Southeastern Rsch. Librs., 1982-84; mem. rsch. libr. adv. com. Online Computer Libr. Ctr., Inc., Dublin, Ohio, 1993-98. Asst. editor: La. Library Assn. Bull, 1967; contbr. articles to library sci. jours.; book revs. to Southeastern Librarian. Served with USMCR, 1956-59. Mem. ALA, Fla. Libr. Assn. (dir. 1979-81), Southeastern Libr. Assn., Assn. Coll. and Rsch. Librs., Assn. Rsch. Librs. (bd. dirs. 1985-90, v.p., pres.-elect 1987-88, pres. 1988-89), Fla. Ctr. Libr. Automation (chmn. bd. dirs. 1985-96), Rsch. Librs. Group (exec. com. 1988-90, bd. dirs. 1991-94), Phi Kappa Phi, Beta Phi Mu, Sigma Tau Delta.

MILLER, CHARLES HAMPTON, lawyer; b. Southampton, N.Y., Jan. 25, 1928; s. Abraham E. and Ethel (Simon) M.; m. Mary Fried, Aug. 26, 1956; children: Cathy Lynn, Steven Scott, Jennifer Lee. BA, Syracuse U., 1949; LLB, Columbia U., 1952. Bar: N.Y. 1952, Republic of Korea 1954, U.S. Ct. Appeals (2d cir.) 1958, U.S. Supreme Ct. 1969, U.S. Ct. Appeals (3d cir.) 1972, U.S. Ct. Appeals (7th cir.) 1973, U.S. Ct. Appeals (9th cir.) 1995; cert. mediator (so. and ea. dists.) N.Y., mediator Supreme Ct. N.Y. County; arbitrator Ea. dist. N.Y. Asst. counsel Waterfront Commn., N.Y. Harbor, 1954-56; asst. atty. U.S. Atty. for So. Dist. N.Y., 1956-58; assoc. Cole & Deitz, NYC, 1958-61, Marshall Bratter Greene Allison & Tucker, NYC, 1961-64, ptnr., 1964-82, Hess Segall Guterman Pelz Steiner & Barovick, NYC, 1982-86, Loeb & Loeb LLP, NYC, 1986-2000, counsel, 2000—. Mem. faculty Continuing Legal Edn., Columbia U. Law Sch., 1976-82. With U.S. Army, 1952-54. Fellow: Am. Bar Found.; mem.: ABA, Assn. of Bar of City of NY. Home: 171 Ralph Ave White Plains NY 10606-3813 Office: Loeb & Loeb LLP 345 Park Ave Fl 18 New York NY 10154-1895 Office Phone: 212-407-4910.

MILLER, CHARLES MAURICE, lawyer; b. L.A., Sept. 7, 1948; BA cum laude, UCLA, 1970; postgrad., U. So. Calif., L.A., 1970-71; JD, U. Akron, 1975. Bar: Ohio 1975, Calif. 1978, U.S. Dist. Ct. (cen. dist.) Calif. 1978, U.S. Ct. Appeals (9th cir.) 1978, U.S. Supreme Ct. 1981. Gen. atty. U.S. Immigration & Naturalization Svc., U.S. Dept. Justice, L.A., 1976-79; ptnr. Miller Law Offices, L.A., 1979—. Adj. prof. law U. West L.A., 1989-90. Co-editor: The Visa Processing Guide: Process and Procedures at U.S. Consulates and Embassies, 11th edit., 2004; articles editor U. Akron Law Rev., 1974-75. Mem. Calif. Bd. Legal Specialization, San Francisco, 1988-89. Mem. Bar of Calif. (chmn. immigration splty. 1988-89, commr. immigration splty. 1987-90), Am. Immigration Law Found. (bd. trustees 1995-98), Am. Immigration Lawyers Assn. (bd. dirs. 1998-2001, mem. bd. govs., chair So. Calif. chpt. 1993-94, INS headquarters liaison com. 1997-98, co-chair mentor program 1990-91, co-chair visa office liaison 1991-92, vice chair 1994-95, co-chair consular rev. task force 1993-95, Jack Wasserman Meml. award for excellence in immigration litigation 1995). Office: Miller Law Offices 12441 Ventura Blvd Studio City CA 91604-2407

MILLER, CHARLES RICKIE, thermal and fluid systems analyst, engineering manager; b. New Albany, Ind., Oct. 4, 1946; s. Marshall Christian and Thelma Virginia (Martin) M.; m. Janel Howell, Nov. 24, 1968; children: Kimberly, Brian, Audrey, Rachel. BA in Physics, DePauw U., 1969; postgrad., Rice U., 1969-70, U. Houston, 1972-76. Tech. editor ITT/Fed. Electric Corp., Houston, 1970-71, LTV/Svc. Tech. Corp., Houston, 1971; sys. safety engr. Boeing Aerospace Corp., Houston, 1971-76; thermal analyst space sys. divsn. Rockwell Internat. Corp., Houston, 1976-89; mgr. thermal and fluid sys. for space shuttle payloads Space Shuttle Program Office, NASA/L.B. Johnson Space Ctr., Houston, 1989—. Mem. editl. team Apollo 14, 15 preliminary sci. reports, 1971-72; mem. sys. integration negotiating team for Space Shuttle to Mir Space Sta. rendezvous and docking missions, 1993-98, chmn. negotiating team for Space Shuttle to Mir Space Sta. water preparation and transfer, 1994-98, space shuttle program co-chmn. for shuttle/internat. space sta. program joint tech. working groups for thermal control, environ. control and life support sys., 1996—. Bd. dirs. Space City Aquatic Team, Houston, 1990-91. Rector scholar DePauw U., 1964-68; Rice fellow Rice U., 1969-70. Mem. AIAA, ASME, Nat. Space Soc., Air Force Assn., Am. Inst. Physics, Planetary Soc., Sigma Pi Sigma. Avocations: children's sports, jogging, science fiction, military history. Home: 806 Walbrook Dr Houston TX 77062-4030 Office: NASA Mail Code MO2 LB Johnson Space Ctr Houston TX 77058 Office Phone: 281-483-1229. E-mail: cmiller@ems.jsc.nasa.gov.

MILLER, CHARLES T. lawyer; b. Winslow, Wash., June 27, 1948; s. Charles Wilbur and Pharoeba H. (Good) M.; m. Rebecca Louise Campbell, Aug. 17, 1974; children: Angela Dawn, Emily Grace, Kathryn Louise. BS in Criminal Justice, W.Va. State Coll., 1973; JD, W.Va. U., 1977. Bar: W.Va. 1977, U.S. Ct. Appeals (4th cir.) 1977. Asst. prosecuting atty., Kanawha County, W.Va., 1977-82; assoc. and ptnr. E. F. Thaxton Attys., Charleston, 1982-84; 1st asst. U.S. atty. so. dist. W.Va. Dept. Justice, Charleston, 1984-93, 94—, former U.S. atty. so. dist. W.Va. With USN, 1966-69, Vietnam; maj. W.Va. Army Nat. Guard; lt. col. W.Va. Air Nat. Guard. Decorated Navy Achievement medal, Rep. of Vietnam Svc. medal, Rep. of Vietnam Campaign ribbon, Rep. of Vietnam Cross of Gallantry, Combat Action ribbon, Presdl. Unit citation. Presbyterian. Avocation: carpentry.

MILLER, CHARLES W. state representative; b. Tompkinsville, Ky, Aug. 2, 1939; m. Carmen Miller; children: Charles, Stephanie, Caroline. MA, Western Ky. Univ., 1967, BS, 1963; AA, Lindsay Wilson Coll., 1960. State Rep. House of Rep., Dist. 28, 1998—; prin. Pleasure Ridge Pk. HS; Asst. prin. Jefferson County Ky. Pub. Sch.; tchr., coach Jefferson County Bd. of Ed. Bd. of Dir. 15th Dist. Parent Tchr. Assoc.; bd. of dir. Columbia Humana, Nortons Hosp., 1987—; Bd. of Control KASSP, KHSAA; dir. Pleasure Ridge Pk. Nat. Bank, 1999—; mem. Sr. Ctr. in the Schools Program; pres. SW Comm. Festival, 1987—98; Bd. of Control State YMCA; Bd. of Dir. Pleasure Ridge Pk. Vol. Fire Dept., 1989—97; pres. area 1 Coun., Chamber of Commerce, 1993—95. Nominee Nat. Parent Tchr. Assoc. Ed. of the Yr., 1995; recipient Outstanding Prin. of the Yr., 15th Dist. Parent Tchr. Assoc., 1993—95, 15 Dist. Parent Tchr. Assoc. Hall of Fame, 1994. caususes: mem., Job Link Adv. Comm.; chmn., LIT Comm.; Camp Mngr., Metro United Way for JCPS; comm. mem., Safe Sch. Comm.; comm. mem., SW Lib. Focus Group. Democrat. Baptist. Office: Capitol 700 Capital Ave c/o Ann Hancock Frankfort KY 40601 also: Dist 3608 Gateview Cir Louisville KY 40272

MILLER, CHARLES WALLACE, historian, environmental geologist, educator; b. Phoenix, July 7, 1946; s. Charles W. and Emabel O. Miller; m. Connie Raschke, June 3, 1972; 1 child, Geoffrey Wallace. BA, U. Md., 1969; MA, U. Tex., 1970; BS, SUNY, Albany, 1978; PhD, Union Inst., 1990. Tchr. pub. schs., San Antonio, 1971-76; instr. San Antonio Coll., 1972-78, St. Mary's Univ., San Antonio, 1976-78, Cochise Coll., Sierra Vista, Az., 1989-90, Pima C.C., Tucson, 1998—; environ. geologist U.S. Geol. Survey, Metairie, La., 1978-80; field geologist U.S. Bur. Land Mgmt., Moab, Utah, 1980-84; historian U.S. Bur. Reclamation, Salt Lake City, 1990-94; environ. scientist USAF, Tucson, 1994—. Mineral cons., Tucson, 1984-89. Author: Stake Your Claim! The Tale of America's Enduring Mining Law, 1991, The Spirit of the Pioneers Still Rules, 1997, The Automobile Gold Rushes, 1998. Vol. Christ Comty. Ch., Tucson, also various youth orgns. including Boy Scouts and one-on-one mentoring program for troubled youth; group coord. Combined Fed. Campaign. Mem. Nat. Eagle Scout Assn., Mining History Assn., James Madison Brigade for Preservation of the U.S. Constn., Mensa, Hist. Soc., Golden Key, Phi Alpha Theta, Pi Sigma Alpha. Achievements include climbed two tallest peaks in the lower 48; rim-to-rim trek across Grand Canyon. Avocations: backpacking, scuba diving, photography, lifeguarding. Home: 136 S Shadow Creek Pl Tucson AZ 85748-3278 Office: USAF 355 CES CEVA Davis Monthan AFB AZ 85707

MILLER, CHERYL DEANN, former professional basketball coach, broadcaster; b. Riverside, Calif., Jan. 3, 1964; BA in Broadcast Journalism, U. So. Calif., 1985. Basketball player Jr. Nat. Team, 1981, U.S. Nat. Team, 1982, U.S. Olympics, 1984; commentator ABC Sports; head coach women's basketball U. So. Calif., 1993-94; commentator TNT Sports, Atlanta, 1996; gen. mgr., head coach Phoenix Mercury, 1997—2000. Player JC Penney All-Am. Team Five, U. So. Calif. Women's Basketball Team, World Championship Team, 1983. Recipient Sports Illustrated Player of Yr., 1986, Naismith Player of Yr. award, Kodak All-Am. award, more than 1,140 trophies and 125 plaques including Nat. Sports Festival, 1981, Pan Am. Games, 1983, FIBA World Championship, Goodwill Games, gold medal 1984 Olympic Games; elected to Naismith Basketball Hall of Fame, 1995.*

MILLER, CHRISTINE ODELL COOK, judge; b. Oakland, Calif., Aug. 26, 1944; m. Dennis F. Miller; 2 children. BA in Polit. Sci., Stanford U., 1966; JD, U. Utah, 1969. Bar: D.C., Calif. Law clk. to Hon. David T. Lewis U.S. Ct. Appeals (10th cir.), Salt Lake City; trial atty. Dept. Justice, U.S. Ct. Claims; team leader atty. FTC; atty. Hogan & Hartson, Washington; spl. counsel Pension Benefit Guaranty Corp.; dep. gen. counsel U.S. Ry. Assn.; ptnr. Shack & Kimball, Washington; judge U.S. Ct. Fed. Claims, Washington, 1982—. Comment editor Utah law Rev. Scholar U. Utah Coll. Law. Mem. D.C. Bar Assn., Calif. State Bar, Order of Coif, Univ. Club, Cosmos Club. Avocation: geneology. Office: US Ct Fed Claims 717 Madison Pl NW Ste 716 Washington DC 20005-1011

MILLER, CLAIRE ELLEN, children's writer, editor, educator; b. Milw., July 17, 1936; d. Emil George Benjamin and Phyllis Dorothy (Rahn) Holtzen; m. Gerald Ray Miller, June 21, 1958; children: Karin, Russell. BS in Edn., Concordia U., 1961. Tchr. Grace Episcopal Day Sch., Silver Spring, Md., 1971-77, The Norwood Sch., Bethesda, Md., 1977-79; writer Media Materials, Balt., 1980; project editor Ednl. Challenges, Alexandria, Va., 1981; asst. mng. editor Ranger Rick Mag., Nat. Wildlife Fedn., Vienna, Va., 1981-87, mng. editor, 1988-2001, contbg. editor, 2002—; propr. Claire Ellen Miller, Writer and Editor, Rockville, Md., 2001—. Author numerous activity books for presch. thru mid. sch., 1979-80; project editor 6 vocabulary books, 1981; author numerous children's mag. and newspaper stories and books, 1981—. Mem. Assn. Ednl. Pubs., Md. Ornithol. Soc. Democrat. Lutheran. Avocation: birding. Home and Office: 17501 Kirk Ln Rockville MD 20853-1033 Personal E-mail: clairemiller@erols.com.

MILLER, CLIFFORD ALBERT, merchant banker, business consultant; b. Salt Lake City, Aug. 6, 1928; s. Clifford Elmer and LaVeryl (Jensen) M.; m. Judith Auten, Sept. 20, 1976; 1 child, Courtney; children by previous

marriage, Clifford, Christin, Stephanie. Student, U. Utah, 1945-50, UCLA, 1956. Pres. Braun & Co., L.A., 1955-82, chmn., 1982-87; exec. v.p. Gt. Western Fin. Corp., Beverly Hills, Calif., 1987-91; chmn. Clifford Group, Inc., bus. cons., 1992—; mng. dir. Shamrock Holdings, Inc., 1992—, Shamrock Capital Advisors, L.P., 1992—. Bd. dirs. Frontier Bank, Park City, Utah, Triad Broadcasting Co., Inc. Monterey, Calif.; cons to White House, 1969-74. Trustee Harvey Mudd Coll., Claremont, Calif., 1974—, chmn. bd. trustees, 1991-98; chmn. bd. dirs. L.A. Master Chorale, 1989-93, chmn. emeritus, 1993; mem. chmn.'s coun. Music Ctr. Unified Fund Campaign; bd. trustees Keck Grad. Inst. Applied Life Scis., Claremont, 1997—. Mem. Calif. Club, Wilshire Country Club, Park Meadows Country Club, Pi Kappa Alpha. Office: Shamrock Holdings Inc 4444 W Lakeside Dr PO Box 7774 Burbank CA 91510-7774

MILLER, CORBIN RUSSELL, investment company executive; b. Huntington, W.Va., Apr. 6, 1948; s. Corbin Russell and Ernestine (Thorne) M.; m. Kathryn Ann Anderson, Sept. 16, 1978. AB cum laude, Princeton (N.J.) U., 1971. Trainee Morgan Guaranty Trust Co., NYC, 1972-74, asst. treas., 1974-77; assoc. Wm. Sword & Co. Inc., Princeton, 1977-79; v.p. J. Henry Schroder Corp., NYC, 1979-83, J. Henry Schroder Bank & Trust, NYC, 1983-87; sr. v.p. IBJ Schroder Bank & Trust Co., NYC, 1987-90; chmn. Koala Techs. Corp., Pleasanton, Calif., 1990-91; mng. dir. Regent Ptnr. Inc., NYC and Denver, 1991-92; exec. v.p. S.N. Phelps & Co., Greenwich, Conn., 1992-95; exec. v.p., CFO, dir. Carey Internat., Inc., Washington, 1995-96; pres. Lombard North Am. Inc., San Francisco, 1997-99; sr. ptnr. Continuum Ventures LLC, NYC, 2000—. Bd. dirs. Met. Opera Guild, N.Y.C., 1994—. Mem. Am. Soc. Order St. John of Jerusalem (chancellor 1999-2002), Met. Opera Club (pres. 1992-94), Knickerbocker Club, Rockaway Hunting Club, Racquet and Tennis Club, The Brook. Republican. Episcopalian. Avocation: golf. Home: 1165 5th Ave New York NY 10029-6931 Office: Continuum Ventures LLC 300 Park Ave Fl 17 New York NY 10022-7402 E-mail: cm@corbinmiller.us.

MILLER, DAN, retired congressman; b. Mich., May 30, 1942; m. Glenda Darsey; children: Daniel, Kathryn. Grad., U. Fla., 1964; MBA, Emory U., 1965; PhD, La. State U., 1970. Ptnr. Miller Enterprises, Bradenton, Fla.; restaurant owner Twin Dolphin Marina Grille, Fla., 1977—; instr. Ga. State U., U. South Fla., Sarasota; mem. 103rd-106th Congresses from 13th Fla. Dist., 1993—2003; mem. appropriations com. Mem. govt. reform com.; chmn. subcom. on the Census. Mem. Manatee C. of C. Episcopalian. Office: US Ho of Reps 127 Cannon Hob Washington DC 20515-0001

MILLER, DANIEL RAYMOND, prosecutor; b. Evansville, Ind., Sept. 20, 1963; s. Daniel Edgar and Virginia Sue (Baumgart) M. BA magna cum laude, DePauw U., 1985; JD cum laude, Ind. U., 1989. Bar: Ind. 1989. Clk. to Hon. William I. Garrard, Ind. Ct. of Appeals, Indpls., 1989-90; dep. pros. atty. Vanderburgh County Pros.'s Office, Evansville, 1990—, dir. gun violence program, 2003—04, dir. drug law enforcement program, 2004—. Pres. Substance Abuse Coun. Vanderburgh County, 1997-98; chmn. pastoral coun. St. John Cath. Ch., Evansville, 1995-98; mem. Diocese of Evansville Pastoral Coun., 1997-2000; pres. 4-H Coun., 1999, 2003-2004, Nat. 4-H Leadership Trust, 2004-06. Meml. Ind. Bar Assn., Ind. Drug Enforcement Assn., Nat. Dist. Attys. Assn., 4-H Club Assn. (bd. dirs. 1995-2001, leader Energetics club 1991—, treas. 2000-2001, pres. Vanderburgh County 4-H Leaders 2001-02), St. Vincent DePaul Soc. (pres. 1994, 2003—, sec. conf. 1995-03) Vanderburgh County Coop. Ext. Svc. (bd. dirs. 2000—). Republican. Roman Catholic. Avocations: gardening, church choir. Home: 13521 N Green River Rd Evansville IN 47725-9769 Office: Vanderburgh Co Pros Office Rm 108 City County Adm Bldg Evansville IN 47708 Office Phone: 812-435-5118. E-mail: drmprosec@aol.com.

MILLER, DARCY M. publishing executive; b. Glen Ridge, N.J., June 17, 1953; d. Paul Richardson and Susan (Alling) Miller; m. James R. Donaldson III, Feb. 6, 1988 (div.); 1 child, Zoe Alling Donaldson; m. Richard G. Powers, Aug. 23, 2003. Co-founder, assoc. pub. Mus. Mag., N.Y.C., 1979-83; pub. Crop Protection Chems. Ref., N.Y.C., 1983-85; assoc. pub. Chief Exec. Mag., N.Y.C., 1986-87, pub., 1987-89, exec. v.p., 1989-96; pub. Stagebill, N.Y.C., 1996-97; group pub. Am. Baby Group, 1997-2000, pres., 2000—01; pres. corp. sales Primedia Inc., N.Y.C., 2001—03; sabbatical, 2003—. Mem.: ASCAP, Advt. Women of N.Y. Democrat. Episcopalian.

MILLER, DAVID ALLEN, air force officer; b. Galion, Ohio, Sept. 3, 1963; s. Richard Allen and Dorothy S. (Stoyanovich) M.; m. Regina Denise Fulkerson, Mar. 16, 1987; children: Christopher David, Alexandra Lauren. BS, Bowling Green (Ohio) U., 1985, Tex. A&M U., 1987; MS, U. Md., 1994. Commd. 2d lt. USAF, 1986, advanced through grades to lt. col., 1998, ret., 1996; comdr., dir., CFO Palehua Solar Obs., Honolulu, 1996—99; chief of weather staff officer 14th Air Force, 1999—2001; dep. dir. internat. fellows program Internat. Student Mgmt. Office, 2001—. Team chief Air Force Space Forecast Ctr., Falcon, Colo., 1994-96 Contbg. author, editor: Maryland Pilot Earth Science and Technology Education Network, 1994; author, editor: Financial Services Report, 2004. Vol. St. Andrew's Epis. Cathedral, Honolulu, 1996-99, Camp Timberline, Hawaii, 1999; earth sci. instr. Md. High Sch. Tchrs., 1993-94; clean air forecaster U. Md., College Park, 1993-94, trooper, stable mgr. cavalry, 1993; sailor Pacific Yacht Club, Hickam AFB, 1997. Decorated Commendation medal, first oak leaf, Meritorious Svc. first oak leaf medal. Mem. AAAS, Air Force Space Command Officers Club, Am. Phys. Soc. Achievements include development of technique to forecast spacecraft internal changing conditions. Home: 6528 Osprey Point Ln Alexandria VA 22315-5908 Office: Internat Fellows Program Eisenhower Hall Rm 124 408 4th Ave Fort Mcnair DC 20319

MILLER, DAVID E. state representative; b. Cleve., Sept. 23, 1962; m. Donna Miller. BS in Engring., Boston U., 1984; DDS, U. Ill., 1988. Pvt. practice, Dolton, Ill., 1988—, Chgo.; mem. Ill. Ho. of Reps., 2000—. Fellow: Leadership Greater Chgo.; mem.: Am. Dental Assn. (liaison to Congressman Jesse Jackson, Jr.), Dolton C. of C. (pres.-elect), Ill. State Dental Soc. (pres. polit. action com., William J. Greek Meml. Leadership award). Democrat. Baptist. Office: 272-S STratton Office Bldg Springfield IL 62706 Address: 1350 E Sibley Blvd Dolton IL 60419

MILLER, DAVID EDMOND, physician; b. Biscoe, N.C., June 6, 1930; s. James Herbert and Elsie Dale (McGlaughon) M.; m. Marjorie Willard Penton, June 4, 1960; children: Marjorie Dale, David Edmond. AB, Duke U., 1952, MD, 1956. Diplomate Am. Bd. Internal Medicine (subspecialty bd. cardiovascular disease). Internmed. ctr. Duke U., Durham, N.C., 1956-57, resident in internal medicine, 1957-58, 59, 60, research fellow cardiovascular disesase, 1958-59, 61, assoc. internal medicine and cardiology, 1963-79, clin. asst., prof. medicine cardiology, 1979-91; practice medicine specialising in internal medicine and cardiology Durham, 1964-2000; attending physician internal medicine div. cardiology Watts Hosp., Durham, 1964-76, chief medicine, 1975-76; attending physician cardiology divsn. internal medicine Durham Regional Hosp. (formerly Durham County Gen. Hosp.), 1976-2000, chmn. dept. internal medicine, 1976-82, pres. med. staff, 1980-81, ret., 2000. Adv. com. Duke Med. Ctr. Contbr. articles to profl. jours. Council clin. cardiology N.C. chpt. Am. Heart Assn., 1963—. Served to lt. comdr. USNR, 1961-63. Fellow ACP, Am. Coll. Cardiology, Royal Soc. Medicine, Royal Soc. Health; mem. AMA, So. Med. Assn., N.C. Med. Soc. (del. ho. of dels. 1981, 82, 83), N.C. Durham-Orange County Med. Soc., Am. Soc. Internal Medicine, N.C. Soc. Internal Medicine (exec. coun. 1984-92), Am. Fedn. Clin. Rsch. Clubs: Hope Valley Country, Carolina Yacht. Methodist. Home: 1544 Hermitage Ct Durham NC 27707-1680

MILLER, DAVID EMANUEL, physics educator, researcher; b. Bethel, Vt., Aug. 30, 1943; s. Manuel Southworth and Lucille (Shurtleff) M. BA, U. Vt., 1965; MA, SUNY, Stony Brook, 1967, PhD, 1971; Habilitation in Theoretical Physics, U. Bielefeld, Germany, 1978. Instr. physics SUNY, Stony Brook, 1970-71; Wissenschaftlicher asst. Freie U., Berlin, 1972-75; scientist U. Bielefeld, 1975-78, Heinrich-Hertz Stipendium, 1977-78; privat dozent U. Bielefeld, 1978-83, univ. prof., 1987—; asst. prof. of physics Pa. State U., Hazleton, 1983-86, assoc. prof., 1986-92, prof., 1992—. Recipient Heinrich-Hertz stipendium, 1977-78, Fulbright award U. Wroclaw, Poland, 1997, Rudjer Boskovic Inst., Croatia, 2004. Mem. Am. Phys. Soc., Am. Assn. Physics Tchrs., Fulbright Assn., Deutsche Physikalische Gesellschaft, Deutscher Hochschulverband, N.Y. Acad. Sci., Am. Math. Soc., Phi Beta Kappa, Sigma Xi. Home: PO Box 611 Conyngham PA 18219-0611 Office: Pa State U High Acres Hazleton PA 18201 E-mail: om0@psu.edu., dmiller@physik.uni-bielefeld.de.

MILLER, DAVID GROFF, insurance agent; b. Kansas City, Kans., Aug. 17, 1949; s. Vincent G. and Ruth (Whitton) M.; m. Marjorie Zwiers, 1979. BA, U. Kans., 1972. CLU. Press aide to U.S. Senator James B. Pearson, 1974-75; fed. grant adminstr. Kans. Gov. Robert Bennett, 1975-78; brokerage rep. Paul Revere Co., Overland Park, Kans., 1979-85; prin. Miller Agy., Inc., Eudora, 1985—. Rep. dist. 43 Kans. State Reps., 1981-91; chmn. Kans. State Rep. Party, 1995-98. Mem.: Ind. Ins. Agts., Omicron Delta Kappa. Methodist. Office: Miller Agy Inc PO Box 460 Eudora KS 66025-0460

MILLER, DAVID R. academic administrator; BS, U. Calif., Berkeley; PhD, Princeton U. Acting dean engring. U. Calif. San Diego, La Jolla, assoc. dean engring., assoc. vice chancellor, acting sr. vice chancellor, 2003—. Office: UCSD Office Sr Vice Chancellor Acad Affairs 9500 Gilman Dr Dept 0001 La Jolla CA 92093-0001*

MILLER, DAVID W. lawyer; b. Indpls., July 1, 1950; s. Charles Warren Miller and Katherine Louise (Beckner) Dearing; m. Mindy Miller, May 20, 1972; children: Adam David, Ashley Kay, Amanda Katherine Kupfer. BA, Ind. U., Bloomington, 1971; JD summa cum laude, Ind. U., Indpls., 1976. Bar: Ind. 1977. Investigator NLRB, Indpls., 1971-76; assoc. Roberts & Ryder, Indpls., 1977-80, ptnr., 1981-86, Baker & Daniels, Indpls., 1986—. Bd. dirs. Everybody's Oil Corp., Anderson, Ind. Bd. dirs. S. Madison Cmty. Found., Pendleton, Ind. Mem. Ind. Bar Assn. (chmn. labor law sect. 1981-82). Republican. Office: 300 N Meridian St Ste 2700 Indianapolis IN 46204-1750

MILLER, DAVID WILLIAM, historian, educator; b. Coudersport, Pa., July 9, 1940; s. Arthur Charles and Kathryn Marie (Long) M.; m. Margaret Vick Richardson, Aug. 22, 1964; 1 child, Roberta Neal. BA, Rice U., 1962; MA, U. Wis., 1963; PhD, U. Chgo., 1968. Instr. history Carnegie Mellon U., Pitts., 1967-68, asst. prof., 1968-73, assoc. prof., 1973-80, prof., 1980—. Adj. prof. religious studies U. Pitts., 1998—. Author: Church, State and Nation in Ireland, 1898-1921, 1973, Queen's Rebels: Ulster Loyalism in Historical Perspective, 1978; editor: Peep o'Day Boys and Defenders: Selected Documents on the Disturbances in County Armagh, 1784-1796, 1990; co-editor: Piety and Power in Ireland, 1760-1960, 2000; assoc. editor: New Dictionary of National Biography, 1994—, Encyclopedia of Ireland, 2001—; prin. developer: (interactive atlas) Great American History Machine, 1994. Sr. research fellow Inst. Irish Studies Queen's U., Belfast, Northern Ireland, 1975-76. Mem. Am. Hist. Assn., Am. Conf. for Irish Studies. Democrat. Presbyterian. Avocations: walking, singing. Office: Carnegie Mellon Univ Dept of History Schenley Park Pittsburgh PA 15213 E-mail: dwmiller@cmu.edu.

MILLER, DAWN L. literature educator; d. John Merritt and Cora Armenda (LaRue) Hyndman; m. Louis J. Miller, June 11, 1966; 1 child, Daniel Louis. BS, St. Mary-of-the-Woods, 1963; MS in Edn., St. Francis U., 1971; MA, Ind. U., Ft. Wayne, 1994; cert. in organ, Notre Dame U., 2000. Profl. life tchg. lic. Ind. Tchr. St. Vincent Sch., Ft. Wayne, 1964—67, St. Joseph Sch., Garrett, Ind., 1974—90, Bishop Leurs H.S., Ft. Wayne, 1990—91; adj. faculty Ivy Tech. State Coll., Ft. Wayne, 1991—96, Ind. U.-Purdue U., Ft. Wayne, 1992—. Nominee Ind. Tchr. of Yr., Diocese of Ft. Wayne-South Bend, 1990. Mem.: AAUP, Nat. Coun. Tchrs. English. Democrat. Roman Catholic. Avocations: piano, organ. Office: Ind Univ Purdue Univ 2101 Coliseum Blvd Fort Wayne IN 46805

MILLER, DEANE GUYNES, salon and cosmetic studio owner; b. El Paso, Tex., Jan. 12, 1927; d. James Tillman and Margaret (Brady) Guynes; m. Richard George Miller, Apr. 12, 1947; children: J. Michael, Marcia Deane. Degree in bus. adminstrn., U. Tex., El Paso, 1949. Owner four Merle Norman Cosmetic Studios, El Paso, 1967-96; pres. The Velvet Door, Inc., El Paso, 1967-96. Pres., bd. dirs. YWCA, 1967; v.p. sun Bowl Assn., 1970; bd. dirs. El Paso Symphony Assn.; bd. dirs., treas. El Paso Mus. Art, trustee, 1990, pres., 1990-93; chmn. bd. El Paso Internat. Airport; bd. dirs., sec. Armed Svcs. YMCA, 1987, 1st v.p., 1990; trustee Internat. Mus. of Art, 1999, pre., 2003. Named Outstanding Woman field of civic endeavor El Paso Herald Post. Mem. Women's C. of C. (pres. 1969), Pan Am. Round Table (dir., pres. 1987), Internat. Assn. for Visual Arts (v.p. 1998, 2000). Home: 1 Silent Crest Dr El Paso TX 79902-2160 Office: 1211 Montana Ave El Paso TX 79902

MILLER, DEANNA, editor, writer; b. Dc, May 11, 1971; BA in English with concentration in lang., writing, and in rhetoric, U. Md., 1993; student, Montgomery Coll., Germantown, Md. ESL tutor U. Md., Balt., 1989—91; publications asst. Group 1 Software, Lanham, Md., 1993—94; tech. writer InterCon Sys., Inc., Herndon, Va., 1994—95; live-in nanny Goshen, Md., 1995—96; copy editor Optical Soc. of Am., DC, 1997—98; jour. mng. editor Am. Inst. of Aeronautics & Astronautics, Reston, Va., 1998—99; assoc. editor Chem. & Engring. News, Washington, 1999—. Author: Time to Tell 'Em Off! A Pocket Guide to Overcoming Peer Ridicule, 2002, Sky Bounce, 2003 (field nominated for 4 ALA awards, 2003, winner Religion Communicators Council's Wilbur award in fiction book category, 2004), many songs. Recipient Award of Achievement, Soc. for Tech. Communication, 1995. Mem.: Internat. Thespian Soc. (life), Nat. Honor Soc. (life). Avocations: singing, dance, human rights activism (particularly as an abolitionist).

MILLER, DECATUR HOWARD, lawyer; b. Balt., June 29, 1932; s. Lawrence Vernon and Katherine Louise (Baum) M.; m. Sally Burnam Smith, Nov. 23, 1963; 1 dau., Clemence Mary Katherine. BA, Yale U., 1954; LL.B., Harvard U., 1959. Bar: Md. 1959. Assoc. Piper & Marbury, Balt., 1959-62, 1963-66, ptnr., 1967-94, ptnr. emeritus, 1995—, mng. ptnr., 1974-87, chmn., 1987-94; Md. Securities commr., 1962-63. Bd. dirs. Mercantile Funds. Trustee Enoch Pratt Free Libr., 1975—, v.p., 1977—85, pres., 1985—89; trustee Calvert Sch., Balt., 1976—89, pres., 1982—87; trustee Walters Art Gallery, Balt., 1987—91; bd. sponsors Sellinger Sch. Bus. and Mgmt. Loyola Coll., 1990—98; active Mayor's Bus. Adv. Coun., 1993—99; bd. vis. U. Md. Balt. County, 1994—2000; bus. sch. adv. coun. Morgan State U., 1994—96; chmn. Equal Justice Coun., 1999—2003; bd. dirs. Balt. Symphony Orch., 1970—, v.p., 1978—86, 1988—90, pres., 1990—92, life dir., 2002—; bd. dirs. United Way Ctrl. Md., 1988—91, The Leadership, 1990—93, Empower Balt. Mgmt. Corp., 1995—, Coll. Bound Found., 1990—2001, chmn., 1994—96; bd.dirs. Greater Balt. Com., 1988—96, chmn., 1992—94; bd. dirs. U. Md. Found., 2000—03. With U.S. Army, 1954—56. Mem. Md. Bar Assn., Am. Law Inst., Am. Bar Found., Md. Bar Found., Elkridge Club, Ctr. Club, Elizabethan Club, Lawyers Round Table. Home: 3704 N Charles St Apt 1305 Baltimore MD 21218

MILLER, DENNIS, comedian; b. Pitts., Nov. 3, 1953; m. Ali Espley, 1988; 2 children, Holden, Marlon. BA, Point Park Coll. Stand-up comic, cast mem. Saturday Night Live, 1985-91; prodr., writer, host Dennis Miller Show, 1992; exec. prod., writer, host Dennis Miller Live, 1994—2002; announcer Monday Night Football, 2000—02; exec. prod., host Dennis Miller, 2004—. HBO spls. include: Mr. Miller Goes to Washington, 1988, host 13th Annual Young Comedians Show, 1989, (also prodr., writer) Black & White, 1990, They Shoot HBO Specials, Don't They?, 1993, Dennis Miller: Citizen Arcane, 1996, Dennis Miller: The Millenium Special, 1999, Raw Feed, 2003; host Freedomfest: Nelson Mandela's 70th Birthday Celebration, The America's Choice Awards, 1990, 43d Annual Primetime Emmy Awards Presentation, 1991; albums include The Off-White Album, 1989; film appearances include: Disclosure, 1994, The Net, 1995, Tales From the Crypt Presents: Bordello of Blood, 1996, Murder at 1600, 1997, Joe Dirt, 2001; TV appearances include Sam Kinison: Why Did We Laugh?, 1998, Saturday Night Live: The Best of Phil Hartman, 1998, The Best of Chris Farley, 1998, Bad Boys of Saturday Night Live, 1998; (video) The Best of Mike Myers, 1998, 25th Anniversary, 1999; TV series include NewsRadio, 1995. Recipient Best Writing Emmy award for a Variety/Music Program for Dennis Miller Live, 1994, 1995, 1996, 1998. Office: Internat Creative Mgmt Inc 8942 Wilshire Blvd Beverly Hills CA 90211-1934

MILLER, DENNIS EDWARD, health medical executive; b. Detroit, Dec. 21, 1951; m. Deborah Ann Keith, Feb. 12, 1977. BS, Austin Peay State U., 1973; MBA, U. South Fla., 1981. CPA. Chief exec. officer Hosp. Corp. of Am., Bennettsville, S.C., 1976-84; div. v.p. Westworld Community Healthcare, Waco, Tex., 1984-86; group v.p. Nat. Healthcare, Inc., Dothan, Ala., 1986-87; COO Healthcare Connections, Brentwood, Tenn., 1988; cons. VHA Physician Svcs., Inc., Dallas, 1988-90; asst. adminstr., CFO Clarksville (Tenn.) Meml. Hosp., 1990; Franklin, Tenn., 1990; sr. v.p., COO Eastside Ventures, Inc., Birmingham, Ala., 1990-93; sr. v.p. Ea. Health System, Inc., Birmingham, 1993—2002; CEO Williamson Med. Ctr., Franklin, 2002—. Chmn. Minority Leadership Task Force, Ea. Health System, Inc., 1994-95. Sec. Ala. Health Svcs. Bd.; mem. Literacy Coun. Ala., Ala. Hosp. Assn. State Legis. Com., future directions com.; chmn. Birmingham Regional Healthcare Exec. Forum; chmn. friends of scouting campaign Boy Scouts Am., 1996; mem. Franklin Land Use Steering Com. subcom., Leadership Franklin, 2002, Franklin Tomorrow. Fellow Am. Coll. Healthcare Execs. (chmn diplomate credentials com., Ala. Regent's award for exec. excellence 1995), Hosp. Fin. Mgmt. Assn. (Follmer Bronze Merit award for outstanding svc.); mem. AICPA, Tenn. Soc. CPAs, Ala. Soc. CPAs (chmn. state legis. com.), Ala. Hosp. Assn. (future directions com.), Birmingham C. of C. (chmn. memberhsip com.), Birmingham East Rotary Club (pres., chmn. membership com.), Franklin Noon Rotary Club, Mensa, Shriners, Masons, Birmingham Touchdown Club, Sigma Chi. Avocations: hunting, fishing, gardening, antique collecting. Office: Williamson Med Ctr 2021 Carothers Rd Franklin TN 37067 Office Phone: 615-435-5151. Business E-Mail: dmiller@wmed.org.

MILLER, DENYCE KARLINA, tax specialist; b. Chgo., July 2, 1963; d. Sidney Miller, Vera Miller. BS in Commerce, DePaul U., 2001, M in Acctg., 2002. CPA Ill. Tax cons. Denyce Miller Tax Svc., Bellwood, Ill., 2001—; postal employee devel. tng. technician USPS, Chgo., 1985—. Mem. fin. com. Am. Postal Workers Union, Chgo., 2001—03. Author: Blind Love, 1996. Coord. hearing impaired Am. Postal Workers Union, Chgo., 1992—94, dir. clk. craft, 2001—03, coord. hearing impaired, 2001—03; combined fed. campaign key worker USPS, Chgo., 1989. Recipient Taekwondo First Dan award, Kukkiwon World Taekwondo Hdqs., 1996. Mem.: AICPA (Scholarship award 2001), Inst. Mgmt. Accts. (Scholarship award 2001), Ill. Cert. Pub. Accts. Soc. Democrat. Mem. Apostolic Ch. Avocation: Tae Kwon Do. Home: 1012 Marshall Bellwood IL 60104-2322 Office Phone: 708-268-1554. Home Fax: 708-544-8419. Personal E-mail: denyce@wans.net. E-mail: dmtaxes@hotmail.com.

MILLER, DIANE DORIS, executive search consultant; b. Sacramento, Jan. 18, 1954; d. George Campbell and Doris Lucille (Benninger) M. BA, U. Pacific, 1976, Golden Gate U., 1985, MBA, 1987. Mgr. A.G. Spanos, Sacramento, 1977-81, Lee Sammis, Sacramento, 1981-83; v.p. Consol. Capital, San Francisco, 1983-86; pres. Wilcox Miller & Nelson, Sacramento, 1986—. Bd. dirs. Umpqua Holding Co. Bd. dirs. Sacramento Symphony En Corps, 1982-84, Sacramento Ballet, 1983-84, 86-92, Sacramento Symphony Assn., 1988-92, Oakland Ballet, Calif., 1984-85, Sacramento Symphony Found., 1994-98, Sacramento Reg. Found., 1996-99, Umpqua Holdings Corp., 2004-; chmn. bd. Sacramento Met. C. of C., 1998-2002; mem. Golden Gate U., 1995-97. Named Vol. of Yr., Jr. League, 1983; recipient award, Bus. Jour., 2002, Sacramento Bus. Woman of the Yr., 2003. Mem. U. Pacific Alumni Assn. (bd. dirs. 1978-85), Sacramento Metro. C. of C. (bd. dirs., Bus. Vol. in the Arts 1989); Calif. C. of C. (bd. dirs. 2004—); Humboldt Bancorp. (bd. dirs. 2004—). Republican. E-mail: dmiller@wilcoxcareer.com.

MILLER, DIANE WILMARTH, retired human resources director; b. Clarinda, Iowa, Mar. 12, 1940; d. Donald and Floy Pauline (Madden) W.; m. Robert Nolen Miller, Aug. 21, 1965; children: Robert Wilmarth, Anne Elizabeth. *Husband Robert N. Miller, BA 1962 Cornell College, JD 1965 University of Colorado Law School, Boulder, is currently a partner in the law firm Perkins Coie in Denver. He is a past U.S. Attorney for the District of Colorado. Son Robert Wilmarth Miller, BA 1996 Hastings College, JD 1999 University of Wyoming College of Law, Laramie, is currently employed as a deputy district attorney in the DA's office in Greeley, Colorado. Daughter, Anne Elizabeth Miller, BA 1999 University of Denver, was awarded Denver University's prestigious Pioneer Award and is currently a State Farm agent in Westminster, Colorado.* AA, Colo. Women's Coll., 1960; BBA, U. Iowa, 1962; MA, U. No. Colo., 1994. Cert. tchr., Colo.; vocat. credential, Colo.; cert. sr. profl. in human resources; lic. Colo. Ins. Prodr. Sec.-counselor U. S.C. Rep., Myrtle Beach AFB, 1968-69; instr. Coastal Carolina Campus U. S.C., Conway, 1967-69; tchr. bus. Poudre Sch. Dist. R-1, Ft. Collins, Colo., 1970-71; travel cons. United Bank Travel Svc., Greeley, Colo., 1972-74; dir. human resources Aims C.C., Greeley, 1984—2001, ret., 2001. Instr. part-time Aims Cmty. Coll., 1972—89. Active 1st Congl. Ch., Greeley. Mem.: Philanthropic Ednl. Orgn. (pres. 1988—89), Women's Panhellenic Assn. (pres. 1983—84), Questers (pres. 2002—04), WTK Club, Scroll and Fan Club (pres. 1985—86). Home: 3530 Wagon Trail Pl Greeley CO 80634-3405

MILLER, DON WILSON, nuclear engineering educator; b. Westerville, Ohio, Mar. 16, 1942; s. Don Paul and Rachel (Jones) M.; m. Mary Catherine Thompson, June 25, 1966; children: Amy Beth, Stacy Catherine, Paul Wilson Thompson. BS in Physics, Miami U., Oxford, Ohio, 1964, MS in Physics, 1966; MS in Nuc. Engring., Ohio State U., 1970, PhD in Nuc. Engring., 1971. Rsch. assoc. Ohio State U., Columbus, 1966-68, univ. fellow, 1968-69, tchg. assoc., 1969-71, asst. prof. nuc. engring., 1971—74, assoc. prof., 1974-80, chmn. nuc. engring. program, 1977-97, prof., 1980—, dir. nuc. reactor lab., 1977—2002. Sec., treas. Cellar Lumber Co., Westerville, Ohio, 1972-84, 85—; cons. Monsanto Rsch. Corp., Miamisburg, Ohio, 1979, NRC, Washington, 1982-84, 99—, Scantech. Corp., Santa Fe, 1984-95, Neoprobe Corp., Columbus, 1990, Electric Power Rsch. Inst., Palo Alto, Calif., 1992-94; mem. adv. com. on reactor safeguards Nuc. Regulatory Commn., 1995-99. Patentee in field; contbr. articles to profl. jours. Mem. Westerville Bd. Edn., 1976-91, pres., 1977-78, 86-88; mem. Ohio Sch. Bd.'s Assn., Columbus, 1976-91; mem. fed. rels. com. Nat. Sch. Bd.'s Assn., Washington, 1984-86. With USAR, 1968-69. Named Tech. Person of Yr. Columbus Tech. Coun., 1979; named to All Region Bd. Ohio Sch. Bd's. Assn., 1981, 86, Westerville South H.S. Hall of Fame, 1996; recipient Achievement award Mid Ohio Chpt. Multiple Sclerosis Soc., 1988. Fellow Am. Nuc. Soc. (chmn. edn. divsn. 1986-87, bd. dirs. 1989-91, chair human factors divsn. 1993-94, v.p./pres. elect 1995-96, pres. 1996-97, Cert. Appreciation 1991); mem. IEEE (sr. mem.), Am. Soc. Engring. Edn. (chmn. nuc. engring. divsn. 1978-79, Glenn Murphy award 1989), Instrument Soc. Am. (sr. mem.), Nuc. Dept. Heads Orgn. (chmn. 1985-86), Westerville Edn. Assn. (Friend of Edn. award 1992), Rotary (Courtright Cmty. Svc. award 1989), Kiwanis, Hoover Yacht Club, Alpha Nu Sigma (chmn. 1991-93). Avocations: American history, travel, amateur radio. Home: Friendship Village 5675 Ponderosa Dr Columbus OH 43231 Office: Ohio State U Dept Mech Engring Nuc Engring Program 650 Ackerman Rd Ste 255 Columbus OH 43202 Office Phone: 614-292-7979. E-mail: miller.68@osu.edu.

MILLER, DONALD, food products executive; CFO Schwans Sales Enterprises, Marshall, Minn., v.p. fin., CEO. Office: Schwans Sales Enterprises 115 W College Dr Marshall MN 56258-1747

MILLER, DONALD EUGENE, lawyer; b. Providence, Mar. 20, 1947; s. Meyer Samuel and Beatrice (Wattman) M.; m. Deborah Neary Miller, Mar. 14, 1987. BA, Boston U., 1968; JD, U. Pa., 1972. Law clk. Assoc. Justice Alfred H. Joslin Supreme Ct., Providence, 1972-73; prin., lawyer Temkin, Merolla & Zurier, Providence, 1973-81, Temkin & Miller, Ltd., Providence, 1981-91; exec. v.p., gen. counsel, corp. sec. The Fairchild Corp., McLean, Va., 1991—. Author: (treatise) Buying and Selling a Small Business, 1987. Mem. RI Bar, Mass. Bar, DC Bar. Avocation: dog breeding and exhibiting. Home: 10704 Riverwood Dr Potomac MD 20854-1332 Office: The Fairchild Corp 1750 Tysons Blvd Mc Lean VA 22102

MILLER, DONALD KEITH, venture capitalist, asset management executive; b. Akron, Ohio, Feb. 2, 1932; s. Clinton Raymond and Hazel Elizabeth (Curl) M.; m. Barbara Dewees Duff, Sept. 25, 1971 (div. 1983); children: Prescott Clinton, Barclay St. John; m. Priscilla Corwith Barker, Sept. 17, 1988. BS, Cornell U., 1954; MBA, Harvard U., 1959. Asst. treas. Chase Manhattan Bank, N.Y.C., 1959-62; asst. to v.p. Electric Bond & Share, N.Y.C., 1962-66; gen. ptnr. G.H. Walker & Co. Inc., N.Y.C., 1966-74; sr. v.p. White Weld & Co., N.Y.C., 1974-77; mng. dir. Blyth Eastman Paine Webber Inc., N.Y.C., 1978-86; chmn. Greylock Fin., 1987-98, Christensen Boyles Corp., Salt Lake City, 1987-95; chmn., CEO, Thomson Adv. Group L.P., Stamford, Conn., 1990-93, vice chmn., 1993-94; pres., CEO, TAG Inc., 1994-97; pres. Presbar Corp., Greenwich, Conn., 1998—; chmn. Axiom Internat. Investors, LLC, Greenwich, 1999—. Bd. dirs. RPM, Inc., Medina, Ohio, chmn. audit com.; bd. dirs. Huffy Corp., Dayton, Ohio, Dallas, Layne Christensen, Mission Woods, Kans. 1st lt. U.S. Army, 1954-57. Avocations: tennis, squash. Home: 588 Round Hill Rd Greenwich CT 06831-2724 Office Phone: 203-422-8060. Business E-Mail: dmiller@axinvest.com.

MILLER, DONALD LANE, publishing executive; b. Pitts., May 14, 1918; s. Donald Edwin and Arvilla (Lane) M.; A.B., Kenyon Coll., 1940; Russian interpreter cert. U. Colo., 1946; postgrad. U. Pitts., 1947-48; m. Norma Reno, Feb. 2, 1951. Reporter, Pitts. Sun-Telegraph, 1940-42, Washington Post, 1946; with pub. rels. dept. Westinghouse Electric Corp., Pitts., 1947-51; reporter Billboard and Tide, 1953; pub. rels. dir. Nat. Agrl. Chem. Assn., Washington, 1954-58; sec. Donald Lerch & Co., Washington, 1958-61; pres. Asso. Pub. Rels. Counselors, Washington, 1961-77; chmn. Braddock Comm., Inc.; chmn. emeritus Children's Aid Internat.; exec. dir. All Am. Conf., Washington, 1962-75. Editor GOP Nationalities News, Rep. Nat. Com., 1960; pub. rels. nationalities div. Rep. Nat. Com., 1964; coord. life underwriters sect. Citizens for Nixon-Agnew, 1968; co-pub. Cmty. Forum, 1996-2002. Served from ensign to lt., USNR, 1942-46; from lt. to lt. comdr., 1951-53. Decorated Knight of Europe. Mem. English Speaking Union, SAR, Phi Beta Kappa, Delta Tau Delta. Clubs: Nat. Press. Author: Strategy for Conquest, 1966, George to George: 200 Years of Presidential Quotations, 1989, Call of the Northern Neck, 1992. Home: 450 Fleets Bay Rd Weems VA 22576 Office: PO Box 710720 Herndon VA 20171-0720

MILLER, DONALD LESESSNE, publishing executive; b. N.Y.C., Jan. 10, 1932; s. John H. and Mamie (Johnson) M.; m. Ann Davie, Aug. 12, 1951 (div. 1981); children: Lynn, Mark; m. Gail Aileen Wallace, June 27, 1981. BA, U. Md., 1967; cert., Harvard Grad. Sch. Bus. Adminstrn., 1969. Enlisted U.S. Army, 1948, advanced through grades to maj., 1966, ret., 1968; spl. asst. to pres., mgr. corp. recruitment Inmont Corp., N.Y.C., 1968-70; v.p. indsl. relations Seatrain Shipbldg. Corp., N.Y.C., 1970-71; dep. asst. sec. def. U.S. Dept. Def., Washington, 1971-73; v.p. personnel mgmt. Columbia U., N.Y.C., 1973-78; dir. personnel devel. and adminstrn. Internat. Paper, N.Y.C., 1978-79; v.p. employee relations Consol. Edison N.Y., N.Y.C., 1979-86, Dow Jones & Co., Inc., N.Y.C., 1986-95; CEO, pub. Our World News. Bd. dirs. Bank of N.Y., Bank of N.Y. Co. and Schering-Plough Corp. Author: An Album of Black Americans in the Armed Forces, 1969. Chmn. bd. emeritus Associated Black Charities, N.Y.C., 1982-94. Decorated Legion of Merit; decorated Commendation Medal; recipient Disting. Civilian Service medal Dept. Def., 1973, Disting. Alumnus award U. Md., 1977 Mem. Alpha Sigma Lambda, Pi Sigma Alpha, Phi Kappa Phi, Alpha Phi Alpha, Sigma Pi Phi.

MILLER, DONALD MUXLOW, accountant; b. Luverne, Minn., Feb. 21, 1924; s. Henry Clay and Mildred Eva (Muxlow) M.; m. Eunice Jean Gibson, Feb. 19, 1944 (dec. Feb. 17, 2004); children: SueRilla M., Donna Jean Eichten, Patsy Ann Pushee. Student, Metro State, St. Paul, 1973-84. CPA. Mgr. Hines & Paulus, CPA, Worthington, Minn., 1952-65; commandant Minn. Vets. Home, Mpls., 1965-68; prin. D.M. Miller, Acct., 1968-70, 76-78; asst. sec. Minn. State Senate, St. Paul, 1970-72; comptr. Western Oil Co., Mpls., 1972-76; commr. Dept. VA, State of Minn., St. Paul, 1978-81; pres. D.M. Miller & Assoc., Ltd., Mpls., 1981-97; chief exec. officer MARD, Inc., Mpls., 1985-95; v.p. Miller, Micketts & Assocs. Ltd., Mpls., 1993-96; pres. D.M. Miller Ltd., Worthington, 1997—2003. Trustee Heart Professorship Found., 1987-91; pres. Legionville Sch. Patrol Camp, Brainerd, Minn., 1963-64; pres. bd. govs. Big Island Vets. Camp, Mpls., 1986-88. 2d lt. USAAC, 1942—46, 1st lt. USAF, 1951—52. Recipient Volunteer of the Year award Kidney Found., 1975. Mem. VFW, Minn. Assn. Pub. Accts. (dist. dir. 2002—), Nat. Assn. State Vets. Homes (hon. life mem., reg. v.p. 1967-68), Nat. Assn. State Dirs. Vets Affairs (reg. v.p. 1978-79), Minn. Gaming Assn. (exec. sec. 1987-92), Am. Legion (hon life mem., comdr. Minn. 1962-63, nat. com. chmn. 1980-84, pres. Minn. Found. Bd. 1990-91). Presbyterian.

MILLER, DONALD ROSS, management consultant; b. Huntington, N.Y., Aug. 5, 1927; s. George Everett and Ethel May (Ross) M.; m. Constance Higgins, 1948 (div. 1955); children: Donald Ross Jr., Cynthia Lynn, Candace Lee; m. Janet Heyman Behr, Apr. 15, 1965; children: Jeffrey Lawrence, Wendy Lorraine. BS/BEA, MIT, 1950. Cert. mgmt. cons. Inst. of Mgmt. Cons. Staff engr. Stop & Shop, Inc., Boston, 1950-56; v.p., dir. Cresap, McCormick and Paget, Inc., N.Y.C., 1956-76; mng. dir. Donald R. Miller Mgmt. Cons., Palm Desert, Calif., 1977—. Pres., CEO Carl Fischer Inc., N.Y.C., 1996; bd. dirs. Nash Finch Co., Mpls., chmn. bd. dirs., 1995-2000; bd. dirs. Michael Anthony Jewelers, Inc., Mt. Vernon, N.Y., Western Horizon Resorts, Inc., Gunnison, Colo. Author: Management Practices Manual, 3 vols., 1963, (booklet) Management of Managerial Resources, 1969. Bd. dirs. Queens Mus. Art, Flushing, N.Y., 1982-93, pres., 1988-92; pres. Lexington House, Forest Hills, 1984-2001; mem. MIT Alumni Adv. Coun., Cambridge, Mass., 1955-75; bd. govs. Alumni Ctr. N.Y.C., 1965-75, chmn., 1968-72; bd. dirs. Vol. Cons. Group, N.Y., 1969-79; trustee Queens Theatre in the Park, Flushing Meadow, N.Y., 1976-82; mem. vestry St. Margaret's Episcopal Ch., Palm Desert, Calif., 2003—, sr. warden, 2004—; With U.S. Maritime Svc., 1945-46, ETO, U.S. Army, 1946-48. Mem. Nat. Assn. Corp. Dirs., Inst. Mgmt. Cons., Sky Club. Episcopal. Avocations: tennis, reading. Home and Office: 73850 Fairway Dr #10 Palm Desert CA 92260

MILLER, DONNA REED, city official; married; children: Tari McSween (dec.), Shakira. Mem. Dem. exec. com. 59th Ward, Phila., 1970-87; city councilwoman dist. 8 Phila., 1996—. Chair Parks and Recreation com., cultural com. Phila. City Coun., vice chair edn. com. Office: Room 312 City Hall Philadelphia PA 19107-3201 E-mail: donna.miller@phila.gov.

MILLER, DOROTHY ANNE SMITH, retired cytogenetics educator; b. N.Y.C., Oct. 20, 1931; d. John Philip and Anna Elizabeth (Hellberg) Smith; m. Orlando Jack Miller, July 10, 1954; children: Richard L., Cynthia K., Karen A. BA in Chemistry magna cum laude, Wilson Coll., Chambersburg, Pa., 1952; PhD in Biochemistry, Yale U., 1957. Rsch. assoc. dept. ob-gyn Columbia U., N.Y.C., 1964-72, from rsch. assoc. to asst. prof. dept. human genetics-devel., 1973-85; prof. dept. molecular biology and genetics Wayne State U., Detroit, 1985-94, prof. dept. pathology, 1985-96, prof. Ctr. for Molecular Medicine and Genetics, 1994-96. Vis. scientist clin. and population cytogenetics unit Med. Rsch. Coun., Edinburgh, Scotland, 1983-84; vis. prof. dept. genetics and molecular biology U. la Sapienza, Rome, 1988; vis. disting. fellow La Trobe U., Melbourne, Australia, 1992. Contbr. numerous articles to sci. jours. Grantee March of Dimes Birth Defects Found., 1974-93, NSF, 1983-84. Mem. Am. Soc. Human Genetics, Genetics Soc. Am., Genetics Soc. Australia, Phi Beta Kappa. Presbyterian. Home: 1915 Stonycroft Ln Bloomfield Hills MI 48304-2339

MILLER, DOUGLAS ANDREW, lawyer, educator; b. Chgo., May 10, 1959; s. Walter William and Jean (Johnson) M.; m. Birgitte Jorgensen, Aug. 4, 1984. BS, Boston Coll., 1981; JD, Ill. Inst. Tech. Chgo., 1986. Bar: Fed. Trial, Ill., U.S. Dist. Ct. (no. and centrl. dists.) Ill. Assoc. Bresnahan, Garvey, O'Halloran & Colman, Chgo., 1986-90; ptnr. Williams & Montgomery, Ltd., Chgo., 1990—2002, Haynes, Studnicka, Kahan, O'Neill & Miller, 2002—. Adj. prof. law Loyola U., Chgo., 1997—. Contbr. articles to profl. jours. Mem. Ill. State Bar Assn. (civil practice sect., torts sect.), Chgo. Bar Assn. (vice-chmn. bench and bar com.), Ill. Assn. of Def. Trial Counsel. Avocation: tennis. Office: Haynes Studnicka Kahan O'Neill & Miller 208 S LaSalle St Chicago IL 60604 Office Phone: 312-332-6644 ext. 20.

MILLER, DOUGLAS B. theology studies educator; b. Ft. Dodge, Iowa, Apr. 12, 1955; s. Wilbur W. and LeAnna M. Miller. BA, Oral Roberts U., 1977; MDiv, Associated Mennonite Bibl. Sem., 1988; PhD, Princeton Theol. Sem., 1996. Assoc. prof. bibl. and religious studies Tabor Coll., Hillsboro, Kans., 1993—. Author: (book) Symbol and Rhetoric in Ecclesiastes, An Akkadian Handbook, with R. Mark Shipp; editor: (jour.) Direction; contbr. articles to profl. jours.; editor: Believers Ch. Bible Commentary. Mem.: Cath. Bibl. Assn., Soc. Bibl. Lit. Home: 601 S Lincoln St Hillsboro KS 67063 Office: Tabor College 400 S Jefferson St Hillsboro KS 67063 Personal E-mail: dougm@tabor.edu.

MILLER, DOUGLAS L. lawyer; b. Reading, Pa., Nov. 17, 1950; BA, MA, Yale U., 1972; JD, Harvard U., 1975. Bar: Ga. 1975. Lawyer Troutman Sanders, Atlanta, 1975—99, mng. ptnr. having oversight of the Project Develop. and Fin. Practice Group Hong Kong, China, 1997—99. Miller acted as lead counsel in state regulatory rate case proceedings, as well as fuel cost recovery and demandside cost recovery riders, prudence reviews of nuclear power plant construction, nuclear power plant ops., fossil plant construction, and coal procurement practices. Mem. ABA, State Bar Ga. As a ptnr. responsible for troutman Sanders' independent power and internat. privatization practice, Miller fparticipated in independent power projects throughout the US and in numerous fgn. countries, including Mexico, China, Indonesia, Pakistan, the Philippines, and Turkey. He also participated in privatization projects in the Bahamas, Trinidad and Tobago, Argentina, Brazil, Chile, Venezuela, and Australia. Address: Troutman Sanders Corp Hdqs 1155 Perimeter Ctr W Atlanta GA 30338

MILLER, DUANE KING, health and beauty care company executive; b. N.Y.C., Mar. 1, 1931; s. Henry Charles and Helen Marion (King) M.; m. Nancy L. Longley, June 6, 1954; children: Cheryl L., Duane L. AB in Econs. and Fin., NYU, 1951. V.p. mktg. Warner-Chilcott divsn. Warner Lambert Co., Morris Plains, N.J., 1970-72, pres. divsn., 1973-77; exec. v.p. Am. Optical div., pres. Am. Optical Internat div. Warner Lambert Co., Southbridge, Mass., 1978; pres. biol. and proprietary products divsn., v.p. Revlon Health Care Group, Revlon Corp., Tuckahoe, N.Y., 1978-80, pres. ethical, proprietary and vision care divsns., 1981-82, corp. v.p. parent co., 1982, pres. Revlon Health Care Group, 1983-92, corp. exec. v.p. parent co., 1984-92, pres. Revlon Health Beauty Care and Internat. Group, 1988-92, ret., 1992; pres. DKL Properties, health care cons., Promedex Techs., 1992—. Author: (with others) Marketing Planning for Chief Executives and Planners, 1966. Mem. Rep. Nat. Com. Mem. Princeton Club N.Y., Cripple Creek (Del.) Golf Club, Masons, Shriners. Home: 8 Western Dr Colts Neck NJ 07722-1271 Office: 483 Rte 520 Marlboro NJ 07746

MILLER, DWIGHT MERRICK, archivist, historian; b. Keosauqua, Iowa, July 25, 1932; s. Leo Albert and Beryl Irene (Merrick) M.; m. Frances Florine Olney, Nov. 19, 1961 (dec. Sept. 1977); 1 child, Dianne; m. Judith Spencer, 1979 (div. 1988); m. Pauline K. Leaverton, 1999. BA, U. Iowa, Iowa City, 1959; MA, Truman State U., Kirksville, 1961; attended, The American U., Washington, 1963-64. Asst. archivist Manuscript Divsn., Library of Congress, Washington, 1961-64; sr. archivist Herbert Hoover Presdl. Libr., West Branch, 1964-99. Compiler, asst. editor: The Public Papers of the Presidents: Herbert Hoover; 1929-1933 (6 vols.), 1974-77; co-editor: Herbert Hoover and Harry S. Truman: A Documentary History, 1992, Historical Materials in the Herbert Hoover Presidential Library, 1996, Herbert Hoover and Franklin D. Roosevelt: A Documentary History, 1998; editor: Laura Ingalls Wilder and the American Frontier: Five Perspectives, 2002. Co-chmn. Iowa Sesquicentennial Commn. Cedar Cty., Tipton, 1995-97. Mem. Herbert Hoover Presdl. Libr. Assn., Friends of the Univ. of Iowa Libraries (adv. bd. 1976-81), Manuscript Soc., Ft. Ticonderoga Assn. (adv. bd. 1991—). Presbyterian. Avocations: book collecting, historical Iowa pottery. Home: 10 Rita Lyn Ct Iowa City IA 52245-3504

MILLER, DWIGHT RICHARD, professional hair care industry executive, cosmetologist, consultant; b. Johnstown, Pa., Jan. 24, 1943; Grad., Comer & Doran Sch., San Diego; DSci. (hon.), London Inst. for Applied Rsch., 1973. Cert. aromatherapist; lic. cosmetologist., instr.; Brit. Mastercraftsman. Styles dir. Marinello-Comer, Hollywood, Calif., 1965-67; expert Pivot Point Internat., Chgo., 1967-68; styles dir. Lapins, L.A., 1969; dir. Redken, L.A., 1970, Vidal Sassoon, London, 1971-74; world amb. Pivot Point, New Zealand and Australia, 1974-75, internat. artistic dir., 1975-78; internat. dir., co-founder Hair Artists Inst. & Registry, 1978-81; internat. artistic dir. Zotos Internat., Darien, Conn., 1981-87, Matrix Essentials, Inc., Solon, Ohio, 1987-92; bd. dirs., founder, v.p. creative Anasazi Exclusive Salon Products, Inc., Dubuque, Iowa, 1992-96; pres. Anasazi Salon Sys., Santa Fe, 1996-98; cons., 1998—; pres. Sahag Products, 2004—; salon owner Santa Fe, 2004—. Judge hairdressing competitions Norwegian Masters, Australian Nat. Championships, N.Am. Hairstyling Awards; pres. Intercrimpers, London, 1974-75; celebrity stylist Doris Day, Juliet Prowse, Cindy Crawford, Monica Seles; cons. in field. Author: Sculptic Cutting Pivot Point 75, Prismatics, 1983, Milady's Standard System of Salon Skills, 1998, Amos Master Cutting System, 2000; prodr.(and dir.): (documentaries, 15), (numerous tech. and industry videos); contbr. articles and photographs to popular mags.; mem. editl. bd.: Shades mag., Launchpad mag. With USMC, 1960—64. Named Artistic Dir. Yr. Am. Salon mag., Intercoiffure Educator of the Century; presented with Order of White Elephant, 1976; recipient London Gold Cup for Best Presentation London Beauty Festival, 1982, Dr. Everett G. McDonough award for Excellence in Permanent Waving, World Master award Art and Fashion Group, 1992, N.Am. Hairstylist of the Yr. award, 2000. Mem. Cercle des Arts et Techniques de la Coiffure, Intercoiffure, Haute Coiffure Franchaise, Soc. Cosmetic Chemists, Hair Artists Great Britain, Internat. Assn. Trichogists, Nat. Cosmetologists Assn. (HairAmerica, cert. instr.), Am. Soc. Phytotherapy and Aromatherapy, HairChicago (hon.), Art and Fashion Group (pres. 1993), 'Dressers MC (pres. 1990—), London's Alternative Hair Club (patron), Salon Assn., Am. Beauty Assn., Beauty and Barber Suppy Inst., Alternative Hair Club North Am. (hon. pres. 2003—). Achievements include development of several profl. product lines including Vidal Sassoon-London, Design Freedom, Bain de Terre, Ultra Bond, Vavoom!, Systeme Biolage, Anasazi, Sheer Blonde, Beach Blonde. Home and Office: 707 Don Gaspar Ave Santa Fe NM 87505-2629 E-mail: dwight@dwightmiller.com.

MILLER, EARL K. neuroscientist, educator; BA in Psychology summa cum laude, Kent State U., 1985; MA in Psychology and Neurosci., Princeton U., 1987, PhD in Psychology and Neurosci., 1990. Rsch. asst. Kent State U., Ohio, 1983-85; asst. in instr. Princeton U., NJ, 1985-89, rsch. asst., 1985-90, lectr., 1989-90; intramural rsch. fellow Lab. Neuropsychology NIMH, Bethesda, Md., 1990-95; asst. prof. neurosci. dept. brain and cognitive scis. MIT, Cambridge, Mass., 1995-99, assoc. prof. neurosci., 1999—, assoc. mem. Ctr. for Learning and Memory, 1996-99, mem. Ctr. for Learning and Memory, 1999—, investigator Clin. Rsch. Ctr., 1996—, adj. lab. head Inst. Phys. and Chem. Rsch.-Japan, 1998—, dir. grad. studies in brain and cognitive scis., 2000—. Mem. steering com. Boston Area Neurosci. Group, 1997-2000; mem. various coms., MIT; lectr. in field. Mem. editl. bd. Neuron, 2000—, Jour. Cognitive, Affective, and Behavioral Neurosci., 2000—; contbr. articles to profl. jours. Recipient Predoctoral Tng. award NIH, 1986, Troland Rsch. award NAS, 2000, Young Investigator award Soc. for Neurosci., 2000; predoctoral fellow Nat. Rsch. Svc., 1987, Alfred P. Sloan Rsch. fellow, 1996, Whitehall Found. fellow, 1996; Pew scholar, 1996, McKnight scholar, 1996, John Merck scholar, 1998. Mem. Internat. Assn. for the Study of Attention and Performance (adv. coun. 1999—), Phi Beta Kappa. Office: MIT Dept Brain & Cognitive Scis 77 Massachusetts Ave Cambridge MA 02139-4307 Fax: 617-258-7978. E-mail: ekm@ai.mit.edu.

MILLER, EDWARD BOONE, lawyer; b. Milw., Mar. 26, 1922; s. Edward A. and Myra (Munsert) M.; m. Anne Harmon Chase Phillips, Feb. 14, 1969 (dec. Dec. 2001); children by previous marriage: Barbara Miller Anderson, Ellen Miller Gerkens, Elizabeth Miller Lawhun, Thomas; stepchildren: T. Christopher Phillips, Sarah Phillips Parkhill. BA, U. Wis., 1942, LL.B., 1947; student, Harvard Bus. Sch., 1942-43. Bar: Wis. 1947, Ill. 1948. With firm Pope, Ballard, Shepard & Fowle, Chgo., 1947-51, 52-70, ptnr., 1953-70, 75-93, mng. partner, 1979-82, chmn. labor and employment law dept., 1975-76, 87-88, 90-91; of counsel Seyfarth Shaw, Chgo., 1994—2004; arbitrator and mediator Glenview, Ill., 2004—. Mem. adv. com. Ctr. for Labor Mgmt. Dispute Resolution, Stetson U., 1984—2003, Inst. Indsl. Rels., Loyola U., 1987-91, Kent Pub. Employee Labor Rels. Conf., 1988—, Ill. Ednl. Labor Rels. Bd., 1988—; exec. asst. to industry mems. Regional Wage Stblzn. Bd., Chgo., 1951-52, industry mem., 1952; chmn. NLRB, Washington, 1970-74; mem. panel of labor law experts Commerce Clearing House, 1987—; dir. Chgo. Wheel & Mfg. Co., 1965-70, 75-88, Andes Candies, Inc., 1965-68, 75-80 Mem. Gov. Ill. Commn. Labor-Mgmt. Policies for Pub. Employees, 1966-67; chmn. Midwest Pension Conf., 1960-61; mem. labor relations com. Ill. C. of C., 1953-70; bd. dirs. Am. Found. Continuing Edn., 1960-69. Served to lt. USNR, 1943-46. Mem. ABA (NLRB practice and procedures com., internat. labor law com.), Ill. Bar Assn., Wis. Bar Assn., Chgo. Assn. Commerce and Industry (chmn. labor relations com. 1980-86, bd. dirs. 1987-97), Am. Employment Law Coun. (mem. adv. bd. 1995—), Coll. Labor and Employment Lawyers (emeritus mem.), Order of Coif. Clubs: Legal (Chgo.), Law (Chgo.), Cliff Dwellers ctr. (Chgo.), 1939-03. Republican. Congregationalist. Home and Office: 632 Chatham Rd Glenview IL 60025-4402 Office Phone: 847-729-2857. E-mail: milleed@aol.com.

MILLER, EDWARD CARL WILLIAM, physician; b. Norfolk, Va., Mar. 4, 1952; s. Yale M. and Virginia (Getz) M.; m. Jayne R. Sternal, Dec. 28, 1974; children: Jamie, Sara, Joni. BA, Northwestern U., 1973; MD, U. Ill.-Chgo., 1977. Physician U. Ill. Health Svcs., Urbana, 1980-81; emergency physician Mercy Hosp., Urbana, 1981-85, St. Michael Hosp., Milw., 1985—, St. Francis Hosp., Milw., 1998—. Fellow Am. Coll. Emergency Physicians, Am. Acad. Family Physicians. Republican. Lutheran. Avocations: sailing, woodworking, computers. Home: 3926 W Le Mont Blvd Mequon WI 53092-5226 Office: St Michael Hosp 2400 W Villard Ave Milwaukee WI 53209-4999 E-mail: edm3565592@yahoo.com.

MILLER, EDWARD DANIEL, financial services executive; b. 1940; married. Grad., Pace U. With Mfrs. Hanover Trust Co., N.Y.C., 1961-91, pres., vice chmn. Chemical, 1991-95; sr. vice chmn., bd. dir. Chase Manhattan Corp., N.Y.C., 1995-97; dir., chmn, CEO Equitable Life Assurance Soc., N.Y.C., 1997—; sr. exec. v.p., mem. exec. com. AXA, N.Y.C., 1997—2001; pres., CEO AXA Financial, 1997—2001, supervisory bd., 2001—. Office: AXA Financial Inc Rm 3403 1290 Avenue Of The Americas Fl 16 New York NY 10104-0101

MILLER, EDWARD DORING, anesthesiologist; b. Rochester, N.Y., Feb. 1, 1943; s. Edward D. and Natalie (Sidam) Miller; m. Leslie Coombs, June 15, 1968 (dec. Apr. 1987); children: Sara Davenport, Katherine Coombs; m. Lynne Root, Apr. 30, 1988; children: Lawrence Root, Elizabeth Root Fusco. AB, Ohio Wesleyan U., 1964; MD, U. Rochester, 1968. Diplomate Am. Bd. Anesthesiology, Am. Coll. Anesthesiology; cert. critical care medicine. Surg. intern Univ. Hosp., Boston, 1968-69; anesthesia resident Peter Bent Brigham Hosp., Boston, 1969-71; fellow in physiology Harvard Med. Sch., Boston, 1971-73; dir. anesthesia research Brooke Army Med. Ctr., Ft. Sam Houston, Tex., 1973-75; asst. prof. anesthesiology U. Va. Med. Ctr., Charlottesville, 1975-79, assoc. prof. anesthesiology, 1979-82, prof. anesthesiology, 1982-83, prof. anesthesiology, surgery, 1983-86; E.M. Papper prof. anesthesiology, chmn. dept. Columbia U. Coll. Physicians and Surgeons, N.Y.C., 1986-94; Mark C. Rogers prof., chmn. dept. anesthesiology Johns Hopkins U., Balt., 1994—, interim dean med. faculty, v.p. medicine Sch. of Medicine, 1996-97, dean Sch. of Medicine, 1997—, CEO Sch. of Medicine, 1997—. Sr. scientist physiology, pharmacology Hosp. Necker, Paris, 1981-82; examiner Am. Bd. Anesthesiology; v.p. clin. faculty U. Va., 1983-85, pres. 1985-86. Editor Anesthesia and Analgesia, 1982-92; contbr. numerous articles to profl. jours. Pres. Barracks-Rugby-Preston Neighborhoods, Va., 1977-79; vestry Christ Episc. Ch., Va., 1985-86. Served to maj. M.C., U.S. Army, 1973-75. Recipient Research Career Devel. award Nat. Inst. Gen. Med. Scis., 1978-83; NIH grantee, 1977-87, Inst. Nat. de la Sante et de la Recherche Medicale grantee, 1981-82. Mem. Assn. U. Anesthetists (sec. 1984-87), Am. Soc. Anesthesiologists, Am. Physiol. Soc., Internat. Anesthesia Research Soc. (trustee 1988—), Soc. Critical Care Medicine, Soc. Cardiovascular Anesthesiologists, Assn. Univ. Anesthesiologists (pres. 1990-92), Found. for Anesthesia Edn. and Rsch. (bd. dirs. 1986—), Up Med. Bd. Presbyn. Hosp. Office: Johns Hopkins U Sch Med Adminstrn 733 N Broadway Ste 100 Baltimore MD 21205-2196 Office Phone: 410-955-3180.

MILLER, ELDON EARL, corporate business publications consultant, retired manufacturing company executive; b. Hutchinson, Kans., Jan. 1, 1919; s. Robert Dewalt and Martha Velva (Stauffer) M.; m. Margaret Borgsdorf, Mar. 26, 1950. BA, UCLA, 1941. Formerly newspaper editor, mag. editor, pub. relations cons., polit. writer; with Purex Industries, Inc., Lakewood, Calif., 1950-85, asst. sec., 1971-72, v.p. corp. relations, 1972-85, cons. bus. publs., corp. relations, 1985—. Republican. Presbyterian. Home and Office: 26685 Westhaven Dr Laguna Hills CA 92653-5767

MILLER, ELEANOR, English language and literature educator; b. Mill Valley, Calif. BA with honors, U. Nev., 1966, PhD in English with honors, 1970. Instr. English Valley Coll., San Bernardino, Calif., 1983-84, Crafton Hills Coll., Redlands, Calif., 1984-86, Coll. of the Desert, Palm Springs, Calif., 1986-90; prof. English Composition & Literature So. Nev. C.C., Las Vegas, 1990—. Chair teaching-learning excellence com. So. Nev. C.C., Las Vegas, 1991-94, new faculty mentor, 1995—. Author: English Placement Grading, 1991, CCSN Writing Across the Curriculum, 1994, New Faculty Mentoring, 1997, Teaching Excellence, 1998. Advisor/participant Women's Re-entry Ctr., Palm Springs/Las Vegas, 1989-94; vol. Womyn's Festival Com., U. Nev., Las Vegas, 1994—; mem. adv. bd. Collegiate Press, 1998—. Mem. AAUW, Nat. Coun. Tchrs. English, Nev. State Tchrs. English, Nev. Adult Edn. Assn., Nev. Humanities Com., Mountain Plains Adult Edn. Assn., U. Nev. Alumni Assn., Women in Comm., Phi Kappa Phi. Avocations: reading, travel. Office: So Nev CC 3200 E Cheyenne Ave North Las Vegas NV 89030-4228

MILLER, ELEANORA GENEVIEVE, freelance/self-employed poet; b. Gowrie, Iowa, Nov. 17, 1916; d. Alfred Theodore and Jennie Wilhelmina (Carlon) Liljegren; m. Chester Forest Miller, June 1, 1941; children: Carolin Miller Gibson, Loring. BA, Augustana Coll., Rock Island, Ill., 1938; MA, Drake U., 1983. Tchr. English and speech Keota (Iowa) High Sch., 1938-39, Moulton (Iowa) High Sch., 1940-41; reporter Des Moines Register, 1956—; bookkeeper Miller Ins. Ltd., Leon, Iowa, 1980—98; writer pvt. practice, Leon, 1938—. Author: (books of poetry) Poems in Iowa Annual of Lyrical Poetry, 1955, Interviewing the Ghosts, 2001, numerous poems published; winner of over 18 awards for poetry, (book) Interviewing the Ghosts, 2001; editor (newsletter) For Front, 1971-75. Vol. ARC, 1962-73; sec. South Ctrl. Iowa Theatre, Leon, 1978—; mem. Iowa Gov.'s Civil Rights Commn., 1961-65; state chmn. Iowa Citizens for Human Rights, 1965; mem. bd. ch. and society Iowa Conf., United Meth. Ch., 1985-90; lay speaker United Meth. Ch., Creston Dist., 1980—. Mem. VFW Aux. (Iowa state pres 1955-56), Nat. League of Am. Penwomen (br. pres. 1964-66, state pres. 1966-68, 1st pl. lyric poetry 1972), Iowa Poetry Assn. (state pres. 1972-74). Republican. Avocations: vocal music, book collecting. Home and Office: 208 SW Church St Leon IA 50144-1349

MILLER, ELIZABETH RODRIGUEZ, city official; b. Tucson, Feb. 22, 1954; d. Tony S. Martinez and Maria (Corral) Rodriguez; m. Marc Alan Miller, Nov. 5, 1972; children: Andrea Eve, Matthew Luke, Meredith C. BA in Spanish, U. Ariz., 1976, MLS, 1978. Unit mgr. S. Tucson Libr., 1978-80; activities coord. community cable com. City of Tucson, 1980; info./reference mgr. Tucson Pub. Libr., 1981-84, agy. mgr., 1984-85, regional mgr., 1985-87, asst. dir. pub. svcs., 1987-89; dep. exec. dir. divsn. ALA Libr. Adminstrn. & Mgmt. Assn., Chgo., 1990; dep. dir. Tucson Pima Libr., 1990-91, libr. dir., 1991-96; asst. city mgr. City of Tucson, 1996—. Co-editor: Great Library Promotion Ideas V, 1990; contbr. articles to profl. jours. Mem. adv. bd. libr. power grant Tucson Unified Sch. Dist., 1992-95; bd. dirs. Tucson area Literacy Coalition, 1992-95, YWCA, 1998—2001; active Hispanic Profl. Action Com., 1992—. Mem. ALA (mem. pres. program com. 1987, mem. nominating com. 1991-93), REFORMA (chair elections com. 1983-84, 85, chair conf. program 1987, pres. 1987-88), Libr. Adminstrn. and Mgmt. Assn. (mem. cultural diversity com. 1991-92, chair 1992-93, mem. nominating com. 1992-93), Pub.

Libr. Assn. (mem. Pub. Libr. Assn.-Libr. Adminstrn. and Mgmt. Assn. cert. com. 1991-92, chair 1992-93, chair Allie Beth Martin Award com. 1987-88, mem. 1989), Ariz. Libr. Assn. (Libr. of Yr. 1995), Ariz. State Libr. Assn. (chair svcs. to Spanish-speaking Roundtable 1980-82, pres. pub. libr. divsn. 1984-85, chair ann. conf. 1986), Internat. City/County Mgmt. Assn. (assoc., participant Comparative Performance Measurement Consortium 1994-96, U. Ariz. Hispanic Alumni Assn., Women at the Top (mem. Carondelet health network fin. com). Office: City Mgrs Office City Hall 10th Fl West PO Box 27210 Tucson AZ 85726-7210

MILLER, ELLEN, advertising executive; Pres. health care mktg. svcs. Draft Worldwide (formerly DraftDirect Worldwide), Chgo. Office: Draft Worldwide 633 N Saint Clair St Chicago IL 60611-3234

MILLER, ELLEN S. marketing communications executive; b. Indpls., June 28, 1954; d. Harold Edward and Lilian (Gantner) M. BA, DePauw U., 1976; postgrad., Sch. Visual Arts, N.Y.C., 1981-82. Editorial asst. Daisy mag., N.Y.C., 1976-77; asst. dept. mgr., Christmas hiring mgr. Bloomingdale's, N.Y.C., 1978; sales rep. Rosenthal USA Ltd., N.Y.C., 1979, mktg. asst., 1980-81, dir. mktg. comms., 1982-90; mgr. consumer mktg. Creamer Dickson Basford, Providence, 1990, v.p., 1991-94; prin. E.S. Miller Comm., Providence, 1994—. Instr. Learning Connection. Editor Community Prep. Sch. newsletter, 1993. Trustee Cmty. Prep Sch., Providence, 1993—, mem. exec. com., 1997—. Recipient Bell Ringer award New Eng. Pub. Club, 1992, 93, Iris award N.J. chpt. Internat. Assn. Bus. Communicators, 1993, Silver Quill award Dist. I, 1993, Holland award Ctrl. Mass. Advt. Club, 1997. Mem. Pub. Rels. Soc. Am., Nat. Tabletop Assn. (com. chair 1989), Internat. Tabletop Awards (bd. dirs. 1989), Rotary Club. Republican. Presbyterian. Office Phone: 401-724-3773. E-mail: ellensmiller@att.net.

MILLER, ELLIOTT CAIRNS, retired bank executive, lawyer; b. Cambridge, Mass., May 4, 1934; s. James Wilkinson and Mary Elliott (Cairns) M.; m. Mary Killion, July 2, 1960; children: Jonathan Vaill, Stephen Killion. AB, Harvard Coll., 1956; JD, U. Mich., 1961; LLM, Boston U., 1970. Bar: Conn. 1962. Assoc. Robinson & Cole, Hartford, Conn., 1961-66, ptnr., 1967-72; v.p., counsel Soc. for Savs., Hartford, Conn., 1972-73, sr. v.p., 1973-78, exec. v.p., 1978, pres., CEO, dir., 1979-90; pres., CEO Soc. for Savs. Bancorp Inc., 1987-90. Bd. dirs. nat. council Savs. Inst., Washington, 1984-88. Trustee, chmn. Kingswood-Oxford Sch., West Hartford, 1977-87; trustee Coordinating Coun. on Founds., 1987-90; bd. dirs. Downtown Coun., Hartford, 1975-90; trustee Greater Hartford Arts Coun., 1980-88; trustee Wadsworth Atheneum, 1990-99; trustee Hartford Stage Co., 1973-85, 1985—; corporator Hartford Hosp., Inst. of Living; mem. transition com. Conn. State Treas. Denise Nappier, 1998-99. With U.S. Army, 1956-58. Mem. Conn. Bar Assn., The 1892 Club (Hartford), Monday Evening Club (Hartford), Dauntless Club (Essex, Conn.), Ferrari Club Am., Bernese Mountain Dog Club. Methodist. Home: 9 Champlin Sq Essex CT 06426-1101

MILLER, EMILIE F. former state senator, consultant; b. Chgo., Aug. 11, 1936; d. Bruno C. and Etta M. (Senese) Feiza; m. Dean E. Miller; children: Desireé M., Edward C. BSBA, Drake U., 1958. Asst. buyer Jordan Marsh Co., Boston, 1958-60, Carson, Pirie, Scott & Co., Chgo., 1960-62; dept. mgr., asst. buyer Woodward & Lothrop, Washington, 1962-64; state labor coord. Robb Davis Daliles Joint Campaign; legis. aide Senator Adelard Brandt, Va., 1980-83; fin. dir. Saslaw for Congress, 1984; legis. cons. Va. Fedn. Bus. Profl. Women, 1986-87, 98-00; senator Va. Gen. Assembly, Richmond, 1988-92; cons. apptd. by Gov. Wilder to bd. dirs. Innovative Tech. Authority, 1992-94, Ctr. for Innovative Tech., 1992-94; cons., 1992—; sr. mgr. Thompson, Cobb, Bazilio & Assocs., 1998—. Bus. tng. seminars Moscow, Nizhny Novgorod, Russia, 1993, Novgorod, St. Petersburg, 1995; cons. in field. Guest editl. writer No. Va. Sun, 1981; host, prodr. weekly TV program, Channel 61. Mem. State Ctrl. Com. Dem. Party Va., Richmond, 1974—, steering com., 2000—, chair 11th congrl. dist., 2001—; mem. Fairfax County Dem. Com., 1968—, chair, 1976-80, 98-200, Presdl. Inaugural Com., 1977, 1992 Dem. Nat. Platform Com., Va., Dem. Adv. Com. Robb-Spong Commn., 1978-79; chair 11th Congrl. Dist. Dem. Com., 2001—; founder, chair Va. Assoc. Dem. County and City Chmn., 1976-80; chmn. Fairfax County Dem. Com., 1976-80, 1998-00; security supr. 1980 Dem. Nat. Conv.; v.p. Va. Fedn. Dem. Women, 1992-94; bd. dirs. Stop Child Abuse Now, 1988, Ctr. Innovative Tech., 1992-94, Ct. Apptd. Spl. Advs., 1993-96; nat. alumni bd. J.A. Achievement, BRAVO adv. com. for the first Gov.'s Awards for Arts in Va., 1979-80; lay tchr. St. Ambrose Cath. Ch., 1963-80; del. to White House Conf. on Children, 1970; chair Va. Coalition for Mentally Disturbed, 1992-94; mem. com. of 100, Va. Opera Bd., 1994-99; bd. dirs. Social Action Linking Together. Recipient Disting. Grad. award Jr. Achievement, 1973, Woman of Achievement award Fairfax (Va.) Bd. Suprs. and Fairfax County Commn. for Women, 1982, Cmty. Svc. award Friends of Victims Assistance Network, 1988, Founders award Fairfax County Coun. of Arts, 1989, Mental Health Assn. of Northern Va. Warren Stambaugh award, 1991, Ann. Svc. award Va. Assn. for Marriage and Family Therapy, 1991, Psychology Soc. of Washington Cmty. Svc. award, 1993, pacesetter award So. Women in Pub. Leadership Conf., 1996. Mem. NOW, Nat. Mus. Women in the Arts, Va. Assn. Female Execs. (mem. adv. bd., bd. dirs., v.p. 1992-99), Va. Assn. Cmty. Svc. Bds. (chmn. 1980-82), North Va. Assn. Cmty. Bds. (chmn. 1978-79, 95-98), Fairfax County Coun. Arts (v.p. 1980—, mem. exec. com. internat. children's festival, Founders award 1989), Fairfax County C. of C. (mem. legis. com.), Greater Merrifield Bus. and Profl. Assn., Mental Health Assn. No.Va. (bd. dirs.), Ctrl. Fairfax C. of C., Falls Church C. of C., Bus. and Profl. Women's Fedn. Va., Mantua Citizens Assn. (exec. bd.), Bus. and Profl. Women's Club (pres. Falls Church chpt. 1994-96, Woman of Yr. award 1990), Women's Nat. Dem. Club (past v.p., mem. bd. govs.), Downtown Club (Richmond), Va. Assn. Female Execs. (bd. dirs. 1992-99), Phi Gamma Nu. Democrat. Roman Catholic. Avocations: cubs fan, tennis, art. Home: 8701 Duvall St Fairfax VA 22031-2711 Office: 1101 15th St NW Washington DC 20005 Personal E-mail: EmilieMiller@cs.com.

MILLER, EMILY ELIZABETH, elementary school educator, editor; b. New York, NY, Nov. 7, 1919; d. Lewis Cooke and Helen Elizabeth Wechsler; m. Harry Miller, Jan. 20, 1952; children: Robert Lawrence, Roger David. BA, Hunter Coll., 1942; MA, Teacher's Coll., Columbia, 1958; MA in French Lit., Queens Coll., 1992. Cert. tchr. Calif., 1949. Tchr. San Francisco Pub. Sch., 1950—51, NY Bd. of Edn., Brooklyn, NY, 1962—87. Editor of Clarion newsletter Am. Assn. U. Women, New York, NY, 1975—2001. Del. Conv. AAUW, Ottawa, Canada, 2001—01; rep. UN, Org - Status of Women NGO, New York City, NY, 2001—02. Mem.: Columbia Club. Avocation: french conversation groups.

MILLER, ERIKA, on-air business news reporter; BA in Polit. Sci. with honors, UCLA; student, NYU. Field prodr., assignment editor Bus. News, CNBC, Ft. Lee, N.J.; prodr., reporter Nightly Bus. Report, N.Y.C.; corr. Morning Bus. Report, N.Y.C. Avocations: antiques, travel. Office: NBR 74 Trinity Pl New York NY 10006-2003

MILLER, ERNEST CHARLES, management consultant; b. Bronx, N.Y., July 14, 1925; s. Ernest Philip and Elizabeth (Hellwig) M.; m. Edith Grosvenor Porterfield, Nov. 11, 1947 (div. Oct. 3, 1963); children: Laura Lee, Marcy Rogers, Ernest Charles; m. Tung-fen Lin, Jan. 8, 1985. AB, Yale U., 1945; MA, U. Pa., 1949. Lic. psychologist, N.Y. Instr. U. Pa., 1947-51, cons., 1950-53; br. mgr., bd. dirs. Richardson, Bellows, Henry & Co., Inc., 1953-55; mgr. personnel tech. Am. Standard, Inc., 1955-59; mng. prin. Hellwig, Miller & Assos., Westport, Conn., 1959-61; sr. assoc. Cresap, McCormick & Paget, Inc., N.Y.C., 1961-63; with Am. Mgmt. Assns., N.Y.C., 1964-83, pres. AMACOM div., 1978-81, group v.p. AMA Publs. Group, 1981-83; pres. Miller, Hellwig Assocs., 1984—. Author works in strategic planning, orgn. devel., human resources, exec. compensation and mgmt. Bd. dirs. La Jolla Inst. for Allergy and Immunology; mem. Columbia U. All-Univ. Seminar, China Internat. Bus. Orgn. and Mgmt. NEH fellow, 1980 Mem. APA, Soc. Indsl. and Orgnl. Psychology. Episcopalian. Office: Miller Hellwig Assocs 150 W End Ave New York NY 10023-5713

MILLER, EUGENE, university official, business executive; b. Chgo., Oct. 6, 1925; s. Harry and Fannie (Prosterman) M.; m. Edith Sutker, Sept. 23, 1951 (div. Sept. 1965); children: Ross, Scott, June; m. Thelma Gottlieb, Dec. 22, 1965; stepchildren: Paul Gottlieb, Alan Gottlieb. BS, Ga. Inst. Tech., 1945; AB magna cum laude, Bethany Coll., 1947, LLD, 1969; diploma, Oxford (Eng.) U., 1947; MS in Journalism, Columbia U., 1948; MBA, NYU, 1959; postgrad., Pace U., 1973—. Reporter, then city editor Greensboro (N.C.) Daily News, 1948-52; S.W. bur. chief Bus. Week mag., Houston, 1952-54, assoc. mng. editor N.Y.C., 1954-60; dir. pub. affairs and communications McGraw-Hill, Inc., 1960-63, v.p., 1963-68; sr. v.p. pub. rels. and investor rels., exec. com. N.Y. Stock Exch., N.Y.C., 1968-73; sr. v.p. CNA Fin. Corp., Chgo., 1973-75; chmn. Eugene Miller & Assos., Glencoe, Ill., 1975-77; v.p. USG Corp., Chgo., 1977-82, sr. v.p., 1982-85, mem. mgmt. com., 1982-91, exec. v.p., CFO, 1985-87, elected vice chmn., CFO, 1987-91, mem. exec. com., also bd. dirs.; prof., exec.-in-residence Coll. Bus. Fla. Atlantic U., 1991—; chmn., CEO Ideon Group, Inc., Jacksonville, Fla., 1996. Adj. prof. mgmt. NYU, 1963-65; prof. bus. adminstrn. Fordham U., 1969-75; prof. fin., chmn. dept. Northeastern Ill. U., 1975-78; lectr. to bus. and edn. groups; bd. dirs. MRFI, Inc., Chgo., bd. dirs., mem. adv. bd. dirs. Nationwide Acceptance Corp., Chgo.; cons. to sec. Dept. Commerce, 1961-66; editor-in-residence U. Oreg., 1992; exec.-in-residence U. Ill., 1991, U. Wis., 1991, U. Toronto, 1992; exec.-in-residence, POHL fellow U. Wyo., 1992; mem. adv. bd. CFO mag., 1991-99; bd. dirs. RJD Holdings, Inc., Chgo.; cons. Arthur Andersen & Co., Chgo., 1992-97; bd. dirs. Niche Directories, Inc., Boca Raton, Fla.; arbitrator NYSE, 2002—. Author: Your Future in Securities, 1974, Barron's Guide to Graduate Business Schools, 1977, 13th edit., 2003; contbg. editor: Public Relations Handbook, 1988, Boardroom Reports, 1986—; writer syndicated bus. column., 1964-86; mem. editl. bd. IRQ mag., 1997—. Trustee Bethany Coll., 1970—; mem. alumni bd. Columbia U. Sch. Journalism. Comdr. USNR, World War II, ret. Recipient outstanding achievement award Bethany Coll., 1963, 50th anniversary award Sch. Journalism Columbia U., also honors award, 1963, Sch. Journalism Ohio U., 1964, disting. svc. award in investment edn. Nat. Assn. Investment Clubs, 1980, Roalman award Nat. Investor Rels. Inst., 1987. Fellow Pub. Rels. Soc. Am.; mem. Soc. Am. Bus. Editors and Writers (founder, Pres.'s award 2003), Fin. Execs. Inst., Arthur Page Soc., St. Andrew's Country Club, Sigma Delta Chi, Alpha Sigma Phi. Home: 7351 Ballantrae Ct Boca Raton FL 33496-1423 Office: Fla Atlantic U 777 Glades Rd Boca Raton FL 33431-6424 Office Phone: 561-852-1925. Personal E-mail: Gene160@aol.com.

MILLER, EUGENE ALBERT, retired bank executive; married. BBA, Detroit Inst. Tech., 1964; grad., Sch. Bank Adminstrn., Wis., 1968. With Comerica Bank-Detroit (formerly The Detroit Bank, then Detroit Bank & Trust Co.), 1955—, v.p., 1970-74, contr., 1971-74, sr. v.p., 1974-78, exec. v.p., 1978-81, pres., 1981-89, CEO, 1989—, chmn., 1990—2002; with parent co. Comerica Inc. (formerly DETROITBANK Corp.), 1973—, treas., 1973-80, pres., 1981—, CEO, 1989-92, chmn. bd., 1990-92; pres., COO Comerica Inc. (merged with Manufacturers Nat. Corp.), Detroit, 1992-2000; chmn., CEO Comerica Bank (merged with Manufacturers Nat. Corp.), Detroit, 1993—. Office: Comerica Inc Mail Code 7887 39400 Woodward Ave Ste 255 Bloomfield Hills MI 48304

MILLER, FRANCES SUZANNE, historic site curator; b. Defiance, Ohio, Apr. 17, 1950; d. Francis Bernard Johnson and Nellie Frances (Holder) Culp; m. James A. Batdorf, Aug. 7, 1970 (div. Aug. 1979); 1 child, Jennifer Christine Batdorf; m. Rodney Lyle Miller, Aug. 8, 1982 (div. Apr. 1987). BS in History/Museology, The Defiance Coll., 1990; AS in Bus. Mgmt., N.W. Tech. Coll., 1986. With accts. receivable dept. Ohio Art Co., Bryan, Ohio, 1984-87; leasing agent Williams Met. Housing Authority, Bryan, 1987-91; acting site mgr. James A. Garfield Nat. Historic Site, Mentor, Ohio, 1991—. Mem. AAUW (pres. 1993-95, treas. 1995-98), Nat. Trust Hist. Preservation, Ohio Mus. Assn., Ohio Assn. Host. Socs. and Mus., Cleve. Restoration Soc., Phi Alpha Theta. Avocations: needlecrafts, reading. Home: 8 Meadowlawn Dr Unit 19 Mentor OH 44060-6230

MILLER, FRANK LUBBOCK (CHAR), IV, historian, educator; b. St. Louis, Nov. 23, 1951; s. Frank Lubbock Miller, III and Helen Hartnett Miller; m. Judith Deborah Lipsett, June 19, 1977; children: Benjamin David Lipsett, Rebecca Shira Lipsett. BA, Pitzer Coll., 1975; MA, PhD, Johns Hopkins U., 1981. Vis. asst. prof. history dept. U. Miami, Fla., 1980—81; asst. prof. history dept. Trinity U., San Antonio, 1981—86, assoc. prof. history dept., 1986—91, prof., chair history dept., 1998—, dir. urban studies dept., 2000—, chair dept. history, 1998—2004. Sr. fellow Pinchot Inst. for Conservation, Washington, 1998—; trustee adv. bd. The Witte Mus., San Antonio, 2001—. Author: (biography) Fathers and Sons: The Bingham Family and the American Mission, Gifford Pinchot and the Making of Modern Environmentalism (2002 Ind. Publishers Assn. Biography Prize; 2002 Nat. Outdoor Book Award for History/Biography; ForeWord Magazine's Gold Award for B), (history) Deep in the Heart of San Antonio: Land and Life in South Texas, 2004; editor: (anthology) American Forests: Nature, Culture, and Politics, Out of the Woods: Essays in Environmental History, Water and the Environment since 1945: Global Perspectives, Water and the West: A High Country News Reader, Fluid Arguments: Five Centuries of Western Water Conflict, On the Border: An Environmental History of San Antonio, Urban Texas: Politics and Development, Missions and Missionaries in the Pacific, An Environmental Atlas of the United States and Canada, (documentary collection) To Raise the Lord's Banner: Selected Correspondence of Hiram Bingham, Fifty Years of the Texas Observer, 2004; author: (history) The Greatest Good: 100 Years of Forestry in America (2000 Soc. of Nat. Assn. Publications Excel Gold Award; 2000 Wash. Book Publishers Awards: First Pl. and &#82), (essay collection) Gifford Pinchot: The Evolution of an American Conservationist; contbr. chapters to books, articles to profl. jours.; assoc. editor: Environ. History, 1998—2000, mem. editl. bd.; 2000—, Pacific Hist. Rev., 2002—, Trinity Univ. Press, 2002—, contbg. writer: Tex. Observer, 1998—. Pres. Congregation Beth Am, San Antonio, 1989—91. Named Piper Prof., Minne Stevens Piper Found., 2002; recipient Hoffman Faculty Advisor Rsch. award, Phi Alpha Theta, 1993; Hon. Gilman fellow, Johns Hopkins U., 1978—79, Archie K. Davis fellow, North Carolina Soc., 1993, Dr. and Mrs. Z. T. Scott Faculty fellow, Trinity U., 1997. Mem.: Forest History Soc. (bd. dirs. 2002—, Bell fellow 1992), Western Hist. Assn., Tex. State Hist. Soc., Orgn. Am. Historians, Am. Soc. Environ. History (treas. 1999—2001), Soc. Am. Foresters (corr.). Office: Trinity Univ Dept History One Trinity Pl San Antonio TX 78212-7200 E-mail: fmiller@trinity.edu.

MILLER, FREDERICK ROBESON, banker, director; b. Oakland, Calif., Oct. 11, 1927; s. Charles Lennon and Juliet Robeson (Chamberlain) M.; m. Nancy McDaniel, July 19, 1952; children: Susan Chase Miller Clark, Stephen Robeson, Elizabeth Rockwell BA, Yale U., 1952. With J.P. Morgan & Co., Inc., 1952-54; v.p. Phila. Nat. Bank, 1954-69; pres. Waterbury Nat. Bank, Conn., 1969-71, City Nat. Bank, Bridgeport, Conn., 1971-72, Conn. Nat. Bank, Bridgeport, 1973-83, also chief exec. officer, vice chmn.; vice chmn. Hartford Nat. Corp., until 1984. Served with U.S. Army, 1946-47. Mem. Sons of the Revolution, Tubac Golf Resort, Yale Club N.Y.C. Republican. Episcopalian. Home: PO Box 1503 Tubac AZ 85646-1503 E-mail: milltubac@worldnet.att.com.

MILLER, FREDERICK STATEN, retired music educator, academic administrator; b. Lima, Ohio, Dec. 12, 1930; s. Donald Frederick and Esther Lillian (Moore) Miller; m. Florence Dorothy Mistak, June 20, 1959; children: Jennifer Leigh Greene, John Staten. B of Music Edn., Northwestern U., 1957, M in Music, 1958; D of Music Performance, U. Iowa, 1974. Mem. music faculty U. Ark., Fayetteville, 1958-64; asst. dir. bands Northwestern U., Evanston, Ill., 1964-70, assoc. dean, sch. music, 1970-76; dean, sch. music DePaul U., Chgo., 1976-95, ret., 1995. Bd. dirs., Concertante de Chgo.; accreditation evaluator North Ctrl. Assn., Boulder, Colo., 1982—91, Nat. Assn. Schs. Music, Washington, 1981—91; mem. bd. edn. New Trier H.S., 1997—2001. Composer/arranger numerous pub. works for band; editor music publs. Served with USN, 1948-52. Mem. ASCAP, Nat. Assn. Schs. Music (hon. life, regional chmn. 1982-84, instl. rep., treas. 1984-88, v.p. 1988-91, pres. 1991-94), John P. Paynter Found., Pi Kappa Lambda (bd. regents 1970-74), Phi Kappa Phi. Clubs: University (Chgo.); Sheridan Shore Yacht (Wilmette, Ill.). Roman Catholic. Avocations: sailing, cooking, jazz performance. Home: 1322 Greenwood Ave Wilmette IL 60091-1624

MILLER, FREDERICK WILLIAM, publisher, lawyer; b. Milw., Mar. 18, 1912; s. Roy W. and Kathryn (Oehlers) M.; m. Violet Jane Bagley, Mar. 31, 1939. BA, U. Wis., 1934, LLB, 1936. Bar: Wis. 1936. Assoc. Tenney & Davis, Madison, 1935-36; atty. State of Wis., Madison, 1936-77; pub. The Capital Times Co., Madison, 1979—, also dir.; dir. Madison Newspaper, Inc., 1970—, chmn. bd., 1980—; dir. Evjue Found., Inc., Madison, 1957—. Trustee Evjue Charitable Trust, Madison, 1970— . Mem. Wis. Bar Assn. Clubs: Madison Club, Univ. Club. Office: Capital Times Co PO Box 8056 1901 Fish Hatchery Rd Madison WI 53713-1248

MILLER, GAIL WOOD, literature educator, consultant; b. Staten Island, N.Y., Mar. 31, 1943; d. Roy Pearson and Frances Marie (Bush) Wood; m. Robert Greve, Feb. 7, 1964 (div. Oct. 1980); children: Paul Greve, Wendy Greve Romano, Mark Greve, Andrew Greve; m. Peter Miller, June 10, 2000; stepchildren: Juliana, Marco, Sequoia. AAS in Comm., Fashion Inst. Tech., N.Y.C., 1962; BA in English with honors, CUNY, 1983; MA in Poetics, NYU, 1990, PhD in English Edn., 1999. Placement dir., curriculum designer, adult edn. Coll. of Staten Island, NY, 1983—85, writing instr., adult edn. and children's enrichment program, 1983—95, reading & writing specialist, spl. svcs. for disadvantaged students, 1985—87, lectr., adj. assoc. prof. English, 1985—2002, dir., English learning ctr., 1987—2002, assoc. prof., edn., 2001; prof., English Berkeley Coll., West Paterson, NJ, 2002—. Cons., mentor Am. Reads Challenge, Staten Island, NY, 1997—2002. Author: (book) How to Study: Use Your Personal Learning Style, 1997; contbr. articles to profl. jours. Mem.: MLA, Nat. Coun. of Tchrs. of English, Coun. of Writing Program Adminstrs., Internat. Reading Assn., Delta Psi Omega, Kappa Delta Pi. Avocations: photography, painting, dance. Office: Berkeley Coll 44 Rifle Camp Rd West Paterson NJ 07424 Business E-Mail: gwm@berkeleycollege.edu.

MILLER, GALE TIMOTHY, lawyer; b. Kalamazoo, Sept. 15, 1946; s. Arthur H. and Eleanor (Johnson) M.; m. Janice Lindvall, June 1, 1968; children: Jeremy L., Amanda E., Timothy W. AB, Augustana Coll., 1968; JD, U. Mich., 1971. Bar: Mich. 1971, Colo. 1973, U.S. Dist. Ct. Colo. 1973, U.S. Ct. Appeals (10th cir.) 1979, U.S. Supreme Ct. 1997. Trial atty. FTC, Washington, 1971-73; assoc. Davis Graham & Stubbs LLP, Denver, 1973-77, ptnr., 1978—, chmn. exec. com., 1998—2001. Bd. dirs. Sr. Housing Options, Inc., 1980-93, Colo. Jud. Inst., 1999—; chair Colo. Lawyers Com., 1989-91, bd. dirs., 1987—, mem. exec. com., 2004—. Recipient Cmty. Svc. award Colo. Hispanic Bar Assn., 1996; named Individual Lawyer of Yr., Colo. Lawyers Com., 1994. Mem. ABA (antitrust sect. task force on model civil antitrust jury instrns. 1985-87), Colo. Bar Assn. (chair antitrust sect. 1996-98), Denver Bar Assn. Democrat. Lutheran. Office: Davis Graham & Stubbs LLP 1550 17th St Ste 500 Denver CO 80202 Office Phone: 303-892-7368.

MILLER, GARY EVAN, psychiatrist, mental health services professional; b. Cleve., Aug. 19, 1935; s. Henry M. and Mollie (Price) M.; m. Karen Ann Marie Barrett, Sept. 16, 1972; children: Anna Charis, Rebecca Elizabeth. MD, U. Tex., Galveston, 1960. Diplomate in psychiatry, addiction psychiatry, and geriatric psychiatry Am. Bd. Psychiatry and Neurology. Intern Montefiore Hosp., NYC, 1960-61; resident in psychiatry U. Hosp. Cleve., 1961-62, Austin State Hosp., Tex., 1963-65; dep. commr. mental health services Dept. Mental Health and Mental Retardation, Tex., 1967-70; dir. Rio Grande State Ctr. for Mental Health and Mental Retardation, Dept. Mental Health, Harlingen, Tex., 1966-67; asst. commr., dir. Rochester regional office State Dept. Mental Hygiene, NY, 1970-72; clin. asst. prof. psychiatry U. Rochester Sch. Medicine and Dentistry, 1970-72; asst. clin. prof. psychiatry SUNY, Buffalo, 1970-72; cons. mental health Ga. Dept. Human Resources, Atlanta, 1972, dir. div. mental health, 1972-74; clin. prof. psychiatry Emory U. Sch. Medicine, Atlanta, 1972-74; vice chmn. Ga. State Planning and Adv. Coun. for Devel. Disabilities Services and Constrn., 1972-73; cons. mental health services orgn. and adminstrn., 1974-76; dir. mental health and devel. services State of NH, 1976-82; commr. Tex. Dept. Mental Health and Mental Retardation Austin, 1982-88; clin. prof. psychiatry U. Tex. Health Sci. Ctr., Houston, adj. assoc. prof. psychiatry San Antonio, 1984-95; dir. profl. svcs. HCA Gulf Pines Hosp., Houston, 1988-94, chief of staff, 1993; clin. dir. adult psychiatry Cypress Creek Hosp., Houston, 1994-2000, med. dir., 2000—03, pres. med. staff, 1996; assoc. clin. psychiatry Post Oak Psychiatry Assoc., Houston, 1988-90; pres. Alternative Svc. Network, Houston, 1990—; chief of staff Kingwood (Tex.) Health Ctr., 2003—. Dir. state alcoholism program in South Tex. region, 1966—67; dir. state alcoholism program in Ga., 1972—74; mem. faculty U. SC Sch. Alcohol and Drug Studies, 1975; mem. quality assurance com. Aetna US Healthcare Pharmacy, 1999—2001. Contbr. articles to profl. jours. Served as capt. M.C., US Army, 1962-63. Recipient Cert. of Recognition, Ga. Psychol. Assn., 1973. Fellow Am. Psychiat. Assn. (disting. life; cert. in adminstrv. psychiatry, com. on psychiat. adminstrn. and mgmt. 1999-2002); mem. AMA, Am. Soc. Clin. Psychopharmacology (cert.), Am. Soc. Addiction Medicine (cert. alcoholism and other drug dependencies), Am. Acad. Addiction Psychiatry, NH Psychiat. Soc. (pres. 1981-82), Nat. Assn. State Mental Health Program Dir. (bd. dir. 1984-88, sec. 1986-88), NH Med. Soc., Am. Acad. Psychiatry and the Law, Am. Assn. Psychiat. Adminstr. (pres. Tex. chpt. 1986), Tex. Med. Assn., Tex. Soc. Psychiat. Physicians, Mental Health Assn. Greater Houston (bd. dir. 1989-95, v.p. advocacy 1990-95, adv. coun. 1999—), Alpha Omega Alpha. Home: 5314 Westminister Ct Houston TX 77069-3338 Office: 530 Wells Fargo Dr Ste 110 Houston TX 77090-4026 Office Phone: 281-440-6899. E-mail: gmillermd@asnwk.com.

MILLER, GARY G. congressman; b. Huntsville, Ark., 1948; m. Cathy, 1972; 4 children. Student, Mt. San Antonio C.C. Founder G. Miller Devel. Co.; mem. U.S. Congress from 42nd Calif. dist., Washington, 1999—; mem. budget com., fin. svcs. com., sci. com. Bd. dirs. Sonrise Christian Sch., 1982; appointed to Diamond Bar (Calif.) Mcpl. Adv. Coun., 1988; elected to 1st Diamond Bar City Coun., 1989; mayor, 1992; elected to Calif. State Assembly, 1995 (chmn. budget com. and banking and fin. com., vice chmn. transp. com.). With U.S. Army. Republican. Achievements include proposing 24 bills signed into law, successfully negotiated funding of 1st class size reduction program, and produced balanced budget that reduced the bus. tax. to 1973 levels while maintaing a $310 million reserve. Office: US Ho Reps 1037 Longworth Ho Office Bldg Washington DC 20515-0001

MILLER, GARY H. lawyer; b. New Orleans, Mar. 11, 1957; s. Leo Jr. and Suzanne Robinowitz (Meltzer) M.; m. Ellen Baldwin Hoffman, Oct. 18, 1986; children: Matthew Hilliard, Katherine Elise. BA magna cum laude, New Eng. Coll., 1979; JD cum laude, Tulane U., 1982. Assoc. Jones Walker, New Orleans, 1982-89, ptnr., 1990—. Mem. moot ct. bd. Tulane U. Sch. Law, 1980-82; lectr in field. Bd. dirs. Golden Retriever Club Greater New Orleans, Inc., 1980, Burtheville Cmty. Assn., Inc., 1997—; class agt. New England Coll. Mem. La. Bar Assn. (treas. consumer protection, lender liability and bankruptcy sect. 1990-91, chmn. consumer protection, lender liability and bank sect. 1991-92), Phi Tau Beta. Democrat. Jewish. Avocations: retriever and obedience training, fishing, hunting, guitar. Office: Jones Walker 201 Saint Charles Ave Ste 5200 New Orleans LA 70170-5100 E-mail: fisher31157@msn.com, gmiller@joneswalker.com.

MILLER, GARY J. political economist; b. Urbana, Ill., Jan. 2, 1949; s. Gerald J. and Doris Elaine (Miner) M.; m. Anne Colberg, Jan. 29, 1971; children: Neil, Ethan. BA, U. Ill., 1971; PhD, U. Tex., 1976. Asst. prof. Calif. Inst. Tech., Pasadena, 1976-79; assoc. prof. Mich. State U., East Lansing, 1979-86; Taylor prof. polit. economy Washington U., St. Louis, 1986-97; assoc. dean for acad. affairs Olin Sch. Bus., St. Louis, 1995-96, prof. polit. sci. Author: Cities by Contract, 1981, Reforming Bureaucracy, 1987, Managerial Dilemmas, 1992. NSF grantee, 1981, 83, 92, 03. Mem. Phi Beta Kappa, Phi Kappa Phi (Disting. Faculty award 1994). Democrat. Office: Washington U Dept Polit Sci 1 Brookings Dr Dept Polit Saint Louis MO 63130-4899 E-mail: gjmiller@artsci.wustl.edu.

MILLER, GARY L. gas company executive; CFO Enterprise Products Ptnrs. L.P., Houston, until 2000. Office: Enterprise Products Inc PO Box 4324 Houston TX 77210-4324

MILLER, GENE EDWARD, newspaper reporter and editor; b. Evansville, Ind., Sept. 16, 1928; m. Electra Sonia Yphantis, Apr. 13, 1952 (dec. May 1993); children: Janet Irene, Theresa Jean, Thomas Raphael, Roberta Lynn; m. Caroline Heck, Mar. 1, 1998. AB in Journalism, Ind. U., 1950, LL.D. (hon.), 1977; Nieman fellow, Harvard U., 1967-68. Reporter Jour.-Gazette, Ft. Wayne, Ind., 1950-51, Washington Bur. Wall St. Jour., 1953-54, Richmond (Va.) News Leader, 1954-57, Miami (Fla.) Herald, 1957—. Author: Invitation To A Lynching, 83 Hours Till Dawn. Served with AUS, 1951-53. Recipient Pulitzer prize for local reporting, 1967, 76 Office: 1 Herald Plz Miami FL 33132-1609

MILLER, GENEVIEVE, retired medical historian; b. Butler, Pa., Oct. 15, 1914; d. Charles Russell and Genevieve (Wolford) M. AB, Goucher Coll., 1935; MA, Johns Hopkins U., 1939; PhD, Cornell U., 1955. Asst. in history medicine Johns Hopkins Inst. History of Medicine, Balt., 1943—44, instr., 1945—48, rsch. assoc., 1979—94; asst. prof. history of sci. Case Western Res. U. Sch. Medicine, Cleve., 1953-67, assoc. prof., 1967-79, assoc. prof. emeritus, 1979—; rsch. assoc. med. history Clevel. Med. Libr. Assn., 1953-62; curator Howard Dittrick Mus. Hist. Medicine, 1962-67, dir., 1967-79. Corr. mem. fgn. socs. history of medicine. Author: William Beaumont's Formative Years: Two Early Notebooks 1811-1821, 1946; The Adoption of Inoculation for Smallpox in England and France, 1957 (William H. Welch medal Am. Assn. History Medicine 1962), Bibliography of the History of Medicine of the U.S. and Canada, 1939-1960, 1964, Bibliography of the Writings of Henry E. Sigerist, 1966, Letters of Edward Jenner and Other Documents Concerning the Early History of Vaccination, 1983; assoc. editor Bull. of History of Medicine, 1944-48, acting editor, 1948, mem. adv. editl. bd., 1960-92; mem. bd. editors Jour. History of Medicine & Allied Scis., 1948-65; editor Newsletter Am. Assn. History of Medicine, 1986-96; contbr. articles to profl. jours. Alumna trustee Goucher Coll., Balt., 1966-69; trustee Judson Retirement Cmty., Clevel., 1993-99, Am. Coun. Learned Socs. fellow, 1948-50, Dean Van Meter fellow, Goucher Coll., 1953-54. Fellow Cleve. Med. Libr. Assn. (hon.); mem. Am. Assn. History Medicine (pres. 1978-80, mem. coun. 1960-63, Lifetime Achievement award 1999), Am. Hist. Assn., Internat. Soc. History of Medicine, Soc. Archtl. Historians, Phi Beta Kappa. Democrat. Home and Office: Judson Manor Apt 616 1890 E 107th St Cleveland OH 44106-2251

MILLER, GEOFFREY, child neurologist; b. Manchester, Eng., Feb. 1, 1947; came to U.S., 1988; s. Erwin and Cynthia Sarah Miller; m. Patricia Sarah Craigie, June 21, 1985; children: Joanne, Sally, Alethea. BA, MB, ChB, BAO, Trinity Coll., Dublin, Ireland, 1972, MA, 1982; MD, U. Western Australia, 1985; MPhil, U. Glasgow, Scotland, 2002. Diplomate Am. Bd. Psychiatry and Neurology, Am. Bd. Child Neurology, Am. Bd. Neurodevelopmental Disabilities. Fellow Royal Postgrad. Med. Sch., London, 1982-83; devel. pediatrician Princess Margaret Hosp. for Children, Perth, Australia, 1983-85; med. dir. Sir David Brand Ctr. for Cerebral Palsy, Perth, Australia, 1983-84; assoc. prof. pediat. Pa. State U., Hershey, 1988-92; co-dir. Muscular Dystrophy Assn. Clinic, Hershey, 1988-92, clinic physician Houston, 1998—; prof. pediat. and neurology Baylor Coll. Medicine, Houston, 1992—, chief devel. pediat. sect., 2000—02; dir. Meyer Ctr. Devel. Pediat., Tex. Childrens Hosp., 2000—02. Vis. specialist West Australian Soc. for Crippled Children, Perth, 1983; investigator Neuromuscular Rsch. Inst., Perth, 1984-87. Editor: Static Encephalopathies, 1992, Cerebral Palsies, 1998; contbr. articles to jours. in field. Capt. Royal Army Med. Corps, 1970-78. Elected and inducted into Am. Neurol. Assn., 1996. Fellow Royal Coll. Physicians, Royal Coll. Australasian Physicians; mem. Royal Coll. Physicians (London), Child Neurology Soc. (membership com. 1996-97, internat. affairs com. 1997—, chmn. 2002-), Internat. Child Neurology Soc., Soc. for Devel. Pediat., Am. Acad. Cerebral Palsy and Devel. Medicine (outcomes com. 2001—). Avocations: rugby, soccer. Office: Tex Childrens Hosp 6621 Fannin St Houston TX 77030-2303 E-mail: gmiller@bcm.tmc.edu.

MILLER, GEORGE, congressman; b. Richmond, Calif., May 17, 1945; s. George and Dorothy (Rumsey) M.; m. Cynthia Caccavo, 1964; children: George, Stephen. BA, San Francisco State Coll., 1968; JD, U. Calif., Davis, 1972. Legis. counsel Calif. senate majority leader, 1969-73; mem. U.S. Congress from 7th Calif. dist., 1975—; mem. edn. and workforce resources com., chmn. dem. policy com. Chmn. subcom. on oversight and investigations, 1985—, chmn. subcom. on labor stds., 1981-84, chmn. select com. on children, youth and families, 1983-91, chmn. com. on natural resources, 1991-94; mem. com. on edn. and lab., dep. majority whip, 1989-94; vice chair Dem. Policy Com., 1995—. Mem. Calif. Bar Assn. Democrat. Office: House of Reps 2205 Rayburn Ho Office Bldg Washington DC 20515-0001

MILLER, GEORGE ARMITAGE, psychologist, educator; b. Charleston, W.Va., Feb. 3, 1920; s. George E. and Florence (Armitage) M.; m. Katherine James, Nov. 29, 1939 (dec. Jan. 1996); children: Nancy, Donnally James. BA, U. Ala., 1940, MA, 1941; AM, Harvard U., 1944, PhD, 1946; PhD (hon.), U. Louvain, 1976; D Social Sci. (hon.), Yale U., 1979; DSc (hon.), Columbia U., 1980, U. Sussex, 1984, New Sch. Social Rsch., 1993; LittD (hon.), Charleston U., 1992; DSc (hon.), New Sch. Social Rsch., 1993, Princeton U., 1996, Williams Coll., 2000; DSc (hon.), Carnegie Mellon U., 2003. Instr. psychology U. Ala., 1941-43; rsch. fellow Harvard Psycho-Acoustic Lab., 1944-48; asst. prof. psychology Harvard U., 1948-51, assoc. prof., 1955-58, prof., 1958-68, chmn. dept psychology, 1964-67, co-dir. Ctr. for Cognitive Studies, 1960-67; prof. Rockefeller U., N.Y.C., 1968-79, adj. prof., 1979-82; prof. psychology Princeton U., 1979-90, James S. McDonnell Disting. prof. psychology, 1982-90, James S. McDonnell Disting. prof. psychology emeritus, 1990—, program dir. McDonnell-Pew Program in Cognitive Neurosci., 1989-94; assoc. prof. MIT, 1951-55. Vis. Inst. for Advanced Study, Princeton, 1972-76, 82-83, mem., 1950, 70-72; vis. prof. Rockefeller U., 1967-68, MIT, 1976-79, group leader Lincoln Lab., 1953-55; fellow Ctr. Advanced Study in Behavioral Scis., Stanford U., 1958-59; Fulbright research prof. Oxford (Eng.) U., 1963-64; Sesquicentennial prof. U. Ala., 1981. Author: Language and Communication, 1951, (with Galanter and Pribram) Plans and the Structure of Behavior, 1960, Psychology, 1962, (with Johnson-Laird) Language and Perception, 1976, Spontaneous Apprentices, 1977, Language and Speech, 1981, The Science of Words, 1991; editor Psychol. Bulletin, 1981-82. Recipient Disting. Service award Am. Speech and Hearing Assn., 1976, award in behavioral scis. N.Y. Acad. Scis., 1982, Hermann von Helmholtz award Cognitive Neurosci. Inst., 1989, Nat. Medal Sci. NSF, 1991, Gold Medal Am. Psychological Found. 1990, Nat. Medal of Sci. 1991, Louis E. Levy medal Franklin Inst., 1991, John P. Govern award, Am. Assn. for Advancement of Sci., 2000; Guggenheim fellow, 1986, William James fellow Am. Psychological Soc., 1989; Fondation Fyssen Priz Internat. for cognitive sci., 1992. Fellow Brit. Psychol. Assn. (hon.); mem. NAS, AAAS (chmn. sect. J 1981, John P. McGovern award 2000), APA (pres. 1968-69, Disting. Sci. Contbn. award 1963, William James Book award divsn. gen. psychology 1993, Outstanding Lifetime Contbn. to Psychology award 2003), Eastern Psychol. Assn. (pres. 1961-62), Acoustical Soc. Am., Linguistic Soc. Am., Am. Statis. Assn., Am. Philos. Soc., Am. Physiol. Soc., Psychometric Soc., Soc. Exptl. Psychologists (Warren medal 1972), Am. Acad. Arts and Scis., Psychonomic Soc., Royal Netherlands Acad. Arts and Scis. (fgn.), Sigma Xi. Home: 16 Willow St Princeton NJ 08542-6923 Office: Princeton Univ Dept Psychology Green Hall Princeton NJ 08544

MILLER, GEORGE DAVID, retired military officer, not-for-profit executive; b. McKeesport, Pa., Apr. 5, 1930; s. George G. and Nellie G. (Cullen) M.; m. Barbara Aex; 1 child from previous marriage: George David Jr.; stepchildren: Jason Dunn, Elizabeth Dunn. BS, U.S. Naval Acad., 1953; MS in Aerospace Engring, Air Force Inst. Tech., 1966; postgrad., Nat. War Coll., 1970-71. Commd. 2d lt. U.S. Air Force, 1953, advanced through grades to lt. gen., 1981; ops. officer, comdr. 22d Spl. Ops. Squadron, Nakhon Phanom Royal Thai AFB, Thailand, 1969—70; dep. comdr. for ops., vice comdr., comdr. 55th Strategic Reconnaissance Wing, Offutt AFB, Nebr., 1971-74; comdr. 17th Air div., 307th Strategic wing, U-Tapao Airfield, Thailand, 1974-75; comdr. 57th Air Div. Minot AFB, N.D., 1975-76; asst. dep. chief staff ops. hdqrs. SAC, Offutt AFB, Nebr., 1976-77; dep. dir. single integrated operational plan Joint Strategic Target Planning Staff, Joint Chiefs of Staff, 1977-79; dir. plans USAF, Washington, 1979-80, asst. dep. chief staff ops., plans and readiness, 1980-81; vice comdr.-in-chief SAC, Offutt AFB, Nebr., 1981-84; exec. dir., sec.-gen. U.S. Olympic Com., 1984-87; pres. exec. dir. Morris Animal Found., 1987—92; pres., CEO The Nat. Fire Protection Assoc., 1992—2002; pres. Miller Assocs. Consulting. Bd. dirs. RJA Group, Inc., Target Safety Inc. Decorated Def. D.S.M., Air Force DSM, Legion of Merit, D.F.C. with 3 oak leaf clusters Air medal with 18 oak leaf clusters, others. Mem.: VFW, World Orgn. of Bldg. Ofcls. (pres. 2003—), Confedn. of Fire Protection Assns. Internat. (chmn. 1992—), Metro Fire Chiefs Assn., Nat. Fire Protection Assn. (pres. emeritus), Mil. Officers Assn. Am. (1st vice-chmn.), Air Force Assn., Daedalians, Shriners, Scottish Rite, Masons, Am. Legion. Lutheran. Home: 20 Phillips Pond Natick MA 01760-5643

MILLER, GEORGE DEWITT, JR., lawyer; b. Detroit, Aug. 20, 1928; s. George DeWitt and Eleanor Mary Miller; m. Prudence Brewster Saunders, Dec. 28, 1951; children: Margaret DeWitt, Joy Saunders. BA magna cum laude, Amherst Coll., 1950; JD with distinction, U. Mich., 1953. Bar: Mich. 1953, U.S. Dist. Ct. (so. dist.) Mich. 1953, U.S. Ct. Appeals (6th cir.) 1960, U.S. Tax Ct. 1960. Assoc. Bodman, Longley & Dahling, Detroit, 1957-61, ptnr., 1962—. Trustee, mem. Matilda R. Wilson Fund, 1993—, pres., 1998—; trustee Maplegrove Ctr./Kingswood Hosp., Henry Ford Health Sys., 1995—, Music Hall Ctr. Performing Arts, 2002—; dir. Detroit Symphony/Orch. Hall, 2001—. Capt. USAF, 1953-56. Recipient Commendation medal. Fellow Mich. State Bar Found.; mem. ABA, State Bar Mich., Detroit Bar Assn., Orchard Lake Country Club, Order of Coif, Phi Beta Kappa. Episcopalian. Avocations: yacht racing, shooting, gardening. Home: 320 Dunston Rd Bloomfield Hills MI 48304-3415 Office: Bodman Longley & Dahling 100 Renaissance Ctr Ste 34 Detroit MI 48243-1001

MILLER, GEORGE H. architectural firm executive; b. Berlin, June 7, 1949;, naturalized; BArch, Pa. State U., 1973. Registered Iowa, N.Y., Mass., Pa., Ohio, Okla., Tex., Fla., Ind., D.C. With Liu Urban Design Assocs., 1974—75, I.M. Pei & Ptnrs., 1975—89; ptnr. Pei Cobb Freed & Ptnrs., N.Y.C., 1989—. Studio critic Columbia U. Sch. Arch., 1978; tchr., lectr., guest critic Columbia U., Yale U., Pa. State U., N.Y. Inst. Tech. Contbr. articles to profl. jours. Fellow: AIA (participant N.Y.C. justice com. symposium, mem. large firm roundtable); mem.: Mcpl. Arts Soc., Soc. Archtl. Historians, Ordre des Archs., Archtl. League N.Y., Nat. Coun. Archtl. Registration Bds. Office: Pei Freed & Ptnrs LLP 88 Pine St New York NY 10005*

MILLER, G(EORGE) WILLIAM, merchant banker, business executive; b. Sapulpa, Okla., Mar. 9, 1925; s. James Dick and Hazle Deane (Orrick) M.; m. Ariadna Rogojarsky, Dec. 22, 1946. BS in Marine Engring., U.S. Coast Guard Acad., 1945; JD, U. Calif., Berkeley, 1952; hon. degree, Babson Coll, Boston U., Brown U., Bryant Coll., Fairfield U., Fla. State U., R.I. U. Bar: Calif. 1952, N.Y. 1953. Asst. sec. Textron Inc., 1956-57, v.p., 1957-60, pres., 1960-74, COO, 1960-67, CEO, 1967-78; chmn. Fed. Res. Bd., Washington, 1978-79; sec. of Treasury Washington, 1979-81; chmn. G. William Miller & Co. Inc., Washington, 1981—; chmn., CEO Federated Dept. Stores, Inc., 1990-92; chmn. bd. HomePlace of Am., Inc., 1995-2001, The H. John Heinz III Ctr. Sci., Econ., Environ., 2000—. Bd. dirs. Repligen Corp., Simon Property Group, Inc. Past chmn. adv. coun. Pres.'s Com. EEO, 1963—65; mem. coun. Nat. Found. Humanities, 1966—67; chmn. bd. dirs. Washington Opera; bd. dirs. USCG Acad. Found., 1969—78, pres., 1973—77, chmn., 1977—78. U. Calif. fellow, Berkeley. Mem. State Bar Calif., Nat. Alliance Businessmen (bd. dirs. 1968-78, chmn. 1977-78), Conf. Bd. (trustee 1972-78, chmn. 1977-78), Bus. Coun., Lyford Cay Club (Nassau), Acoaxet Club (Westport, Mass.), Brook Club (N.Y.C.), Burning Tree Club, Chevy Chase Club, Order of Coif, Phi Delta Phi. Office: 1100 Connecticut Ave NW Ste 725 Washington DC 20036-4101 Office Phone: 202-429-1780. E-mail: miller@gwmco.com.

MILLER, GERALD MILTON, II, management consultant; b. Reading, Pa., July 12, 1962; s. Gerald Milton and Diane Mae M.; m. Laurie Ann Rozzi, Nov. 24, 1984 (div. Nov. 1988); m. Gretchen Elise Bendorf, May 19, 1992; children: Calvin Thomas, Drew Alan. BA in Econs., Pa. State U., 1984; MA in Econs., George Washington U., 1987; PhD in Econs., George Mason U., 1989. Cert. integrated resource mgmt., mgmt. acct. Asst. mgr. Heister Corp., State Coll., Pa., 1981-84; mathemat. economist U.S. Dept. Commerce, Washington, 1984-86; sr. analyst Synergy, Inc., Washington, 1986-89; ptnr. Deloitte Cons., Parsippany, N.J., 1989-98, mng. dir. Munich, Germany, 1999—. Author: Antitrust and Industrial Performance, 1993. Nat. grad. fellow NSF, 1986. Mem. Am. Prodn. and Inventory Control Soc., Inst. Mgmt. Accts. (cert. mgmt. acct.), Inst. Mgmt. Accts. Republican. Avocations: canoeing, weight training, golf, hiking. Home: PO Box 820 Ten Westport Rd Wilton CT 06897-0820 Office: Deloitte Cons Isartorplatz 8 Munich 80331 Germany

MILLER, GERALDINE (TINCY), real estate company executive, educational association administrator; m. Vance Miller; 4 children. BS, So. Meth. U.; MS in Reading, Tex. A&M U. Vice chmn. Henry S. Miller Cos., 1994—. Tchr. reading lab. Tex. Scottish Rite HOsp. for Crippled Children, Highland Park Presbyn. Hillier Sch. for Dyslexia; bd. mem. Literacy Instrn. for Tex. Mem. Tex. State Bd. Edn., 1988—, pres., 2003—; chair fund-raising events United Cerebral Palsy Assn., Dallas Opera, Dallas Symphony Orch., TACA, Crystal Charity Ball; active I Have A Dream Found., Nat. Orton-Dyslexia Soc., Boy's and Girl's Club Greater Dallas, Dallas County Heritage Soc. Recipient Hall of State award for civic involvement, Dallas Hist. Soc., 1995, Tom Landry award of excellence in volunteerism, 1999. Mem.: Acad. Lang. Therapist Assn., Internat. Reading Assn., Kappa Delta Pi, Phi Delta Kappa. Republican. Address: 1100 Providence Tower West 5001 Spring Valley Rd Dallas TX 75244-3910

MILLER, G(ERSON) H(ARRY), research institute director, mathematician, computer scientist, chemist; b. Phila., Mar. 2, 1924; m. Mary Alexa Heath, Jan. 28, 1961; children: Byron, Alexandra. BA, Pomona Coll., 1949; MEd in Counseling and Pers., Temple U., 1951; PhD. in Ednl. Psychology, U. So. Calif., 1957; MS in Math., U. Ill., 1982, postgrad., 1963-65. Jr. high sch. and jr. coll. instr. math. L.A. Sch. Dist., 1953-57; assoc. prof. Western Ill. U., Macomb, 1957-60; prof. Towson State U., Balt., 1960-61; prof. math. and edn. Parsons Coll., Fairfield, Iowa, 1961-65; prof. Tenn. Technol. U., Cookeville, 1966—67; prof. math. and computer sci. Edinboro (Pa.) U., 1968-71, 81-89, asst. dir. Institutional Rsch., 1972-80, emeritus prof., 1989—; dir. Studies On Smoking, Inc. and SOS Stop Smoking Clinic, Edinboro, 1972—. Spkr. state, nat. and internat. profl. meetings; condr. seminars on smoking and health London, Fed. Republic Germany, Alaska, New Brunswick, N.J., Chgo., Costa Rica, Nice, Washington, Alexandria, Va., Boston, on asbestos exposure damage, Argentina; dir. Nat. Study Math. Requirements for Scientists and Engrs., 1966-73; condr. Nat. Symposium for Am. Inst. Biol. Scis., Am. Chem. Soc. and Am. Soc. Engring. Educators, 1970-75; dir. Math. for Industry Confs. Contbr. numerous articles to profl. jours. Pres. Edinboro YMCA, 1972-83; bd. dirs. Common Cause, Harrisburg, Pa., 1975-80; Sgt. USAAF, 1943-46, PTO. Grantee U.S. Office Edn., 1968, 70, No Other World, 1973, NAS, 1980, ITT Life Ins. Corp., 1983, Erie Comty. Found., 1987. Fellow Am. Inst. Chemists (cert. profl. chemist), AAAS; mem. APHA, Am. Assn. World Health, Am. Chem. Soc., Am. Soc. Engring. Edn., Internat. Assn. Pure and Applied Chemists, Internat. Soc. for Preventive Oncology, Math. Assn. Am., Am. Diabetes Assn., Sch. Sci. and Math. Assn., N.Y. Acad. Scis. (hon.), Acad. Sr. Profls. (hon.). Home and Office: Studies on Smoking 125 High St Edinboro PA 16412-2552 also: 25 Crescent Pl S Saint Petersburg FL 33711-5118

MILLER, GREEN RUSSELL, economist, educator; b. Kenvir, Ky., Mar. 10, 1939; s. Clifford Wesley and Lorene (Farmer) M.; m. Carolyn Sue Blackburn, Oct. 7, 1966; children: Laura Marie, Russell Wesley. BA, U. Tex., El Paso, 1969; MA, U. Oreg., 1971; PhD, U. Ky., 1985. Asst. prof. Sch. Pub. Affairs, Ky. State U., Frankfort, 1977; instr. Transylvania U., Lexington, 1973-79; prof. econs. Morehead (Ky.) State U., 1979—, dir. Ctr. for Econ. Edn., 1979—96. Bd. dirs. Ky. Council Econ. Edn., Louisville, 1979-96; cons. to various law firms, Ky., 1973—. Contbr. numerous articles to profl. jours. Coach Little League Baseball, Morehead, 1982-85, Youth Soccer League, 1985-86; bd. dirs. St. Albans Ch., Morehead, 1979-82, Gethsemane Luth. Ch., 1989-97; vol. One-on-One program Dept. of Corrections, Lexington, 1973-82, Morehead Cmty.Fed. Credit Union (treas. 1999-) Mem. Midwest Econ. Assn., Ky. Econs. Assn., Mo., Internat. Bus. and Econ. Rsch. Assn. (Best Paper award, 2003),Valley Econ. Assn. (Jerome F. Schwier merotorious svc. award 1997), So. Econ. Assn., Ky. Assn. Ednl. Opportunity Program Pers., Joint Coun. on Econ. Edn., Nat. Assn. Econ. Educators, Ky. Coun. on Econ. Edn. (bd. dirs. 1979-96, Outstanding Ctr. Dir. 1981-82), Assn. Ky. Econ. Educators (charter, mem. original bylaws com., nominating com. 1985-93), Nat. Assn. Forensic Econs. (charter, bd. dirs. 1986-87, bus. editor Jour. of Econs. 1990-97, chair acctg.-econs.-fin. 1988-2002). Democrat. Lutheran. Avocations: hiking, reading. Home: 1240 Rodburn Hollow Rd Morehead KY 40351-9092 Office: Morehead State U UPO 1280 222 Combs Morehead KY 40351

MILLER, GREGORY ALLEN, psychology educator; b. St. Louis, Dec. 28, 1952; s. H. Glen and Betty A. (Woodruff) M.; m. Margarita Ham, Aug. 22, 1981. AB magna cum laude, Harvard U., 1975; MS, U. Wis., 1978, PhD, 1982. Lic. clin. psychologist, Ill. Intern in clin. psychology Rush-Presby. St. Luke Med. Ctr., Chgo., 1981-82; asst. prof. psychology U. Ill., Champaign, 1982-87, assoc. prof., 1987-93, prof., 1993—. Editor Psychophysiology; contbr. articles to profl. jours. Mem. Soc. for Psychophysiol. Rsch. (past pres.), Soc. for Rsch. Psychopathology, Am. Psychol. Soc. Office: U Ill Dept Psychology 603 E Daniel St Champaign IL 61820-6232

MILLER, GREGORY KENT, structural engineer; b. Anaconda, Mont., July 6, 1951; s. Robert Bruce and Lois Patricia (Arvish) Miller. BS in Civil Engring./Engring. Mechanics, Mont. State U., 1973, MS in Engring. Mechanics, 1974. Project engr. U.S. Energy R&D Adminstrn., Idaho Falls, Idaho, 1974-77; structural engr. EG&G Idaho, Inc., Idaho Falls, 1977-93; supr. Lockheed Martin Idaho Technologies Co., Idaho Falls, 1994-99, BBWI, Idaho Falls, 1999—. Contbr. articles to profl jours. Mem.: ASME (comt mem boiler and pressure vessel code sect III 1995—), Phi Kappa Phi (Sr of Yr 1973), Tau Beta Pi. Achievements include research in advanced modeling and analysis methods for evaluating failure of fuel particles in high-temperature gas-cooled reactors; contributed to technology for analyzing complex material behavior in pressure vessels; advanced methods for evaluating containers bearing nuclear materials for impact loads associated with accidental drop events. Office: BBWI Technologies Co PO Box 1625 Idaho Falls ID 83415 3765 E mail: gkm@inel.gov.

MILLER, GREGORY R. lawyer; Chief asst. U.S. atty. Dept. Justice, Tallahassee, U.S. atty., 1993-98; asst. U.S. atty. Dept Justice, Tallahassee, 2000—02, U.S. atty, 2002—; assoc. Fowler, White, Gillen, Boggs, Villareal and Banker, PA, Tallahassee, 1998-2000. Office: US Atty's Office 111 N Adams St Tallahassee FL 32301 Office Phone: 850-942-8430. Business E-Mail: gregory.miller@usdoj.gov.

MILLER, H. TODD, lawyer; b. Buffalo, N.Y., Sept. 19, 1947; s. Henry Opel and Irene Teresa (Hauck) M.; m. June Diehl Lancaster, Aug. 1, 1970; children: Catharine Maclay, Todd Lancaster, Peter Hanes. BA, SUNY, Buffalo, 1969; JD, Duke U., 1971. Bar: N.C. 1971, D.C. 1973. Jud. clerk to Hon. Charles R. Simpson U.S. Tax Ct., Washington, 1971-73; assoc. atty. Hogan & Hartson LLP, Washington, 1973-78, ptnr., 1979—. Mem. Phi Beta Kappa, Order of the Coif. Episcopalian. Office: Hogan & Hartson Columbia Sq 555 13th St NW Ste 9W-312 Washington DC 20004-1161 Office Phone: 202-637-5667.

MILLER, HAROLD ARTHUR, lawyer; b. St. Marie, Ill., Aug. 18, 1922; s. Arthur E. and Luletta (Noé) M.; m. Michele H. Rogivue, Nov. 21, 1947; children: Maurice H., Jan Leland, Marc Richard. BS in Acctg., U. Ill., 1942, JD, 1950. Bar: Ill. 1950, U.S. Dist. Ct. Ill. 1950, U.S. Tax Ct. 1950. Fgn. svc. officer U.S. State Dept., Paris, France, 1945-48; ptnr. Filson, Williamson & Miller, Champaign, Ill., 1950-60, Williamson & Miller, Champaign, 1960-72, Miller & Hendren, Champaign, 1972—. Atty. Christie Clinic Found., Champaign, 1960—; atty. pub. schs. dists., Champaign & Vermilion Counties, Ill., 1960—; atty. for municipalities in Champaign County, Ill., 1970—. Author: Estate Planning for Doctors, 1961, Intervivos Trusts Alternative to Probate, 1996. Bd. dirs., officer Urbana Ill. Sch. Dist., 1957-69; chmn., trustee Parkland Coll., Champaign, 1971-91; founding bd. mem. CCDC Found., Champaign-Urbana Ednl. Found., Moore Heart Found., Christie Found.; life mem. PTA. With Spl. Svcs., U.S. Army, 1942-45, ETO. Mem. ABA, Am. Judicature Soc., Ill. and Local Bar Assns., Ill. Trial Lawyers Assn., Alpha Kappa Psi. Presbyterian. Office: Miller & Hendren Attys 30 E Main St #200 Champaign IL 61820-3629 E-mail: ham@mhlawoffice.com.

MILLER, HAROLD EDWARD, retired manufacturing conglomerate executive, consultant; b. St. Louis, Nov. 23, 1926; s. George Edward and Georgenia Elizabeth (Franklin) M.; m. Lilian Ruth Gantner, Dec. 23, 1949; children—Ellen Susan, Jeffrey Arthur. BSBA, Washington U., St. Louis, 1949. Vice pres. Fulton Iron Works Co., St. Louis, 1968-71, pres., 1971-79, chmn. bd., 1979-90; v.p. Katy Industries Inc., Elgin, Ill., 1976-77, exec. v.p., 1978-90, also dir., to 1990; pres. HM Consulting, Palatine, Ill., 1990—. Internat. cons. Vigel Spa, Italy; v.p. Vigel U.S.A. Inc., 1996—. Served with U.S. Army, 1945-46. Mem. Barrington Tennis Club, Inverness Golf Club. Presbyterian. Office Phone: 847-991-7852. E-mail: hmillercons84@sbcglobal.net.

MILLER, HARRY BRILL, scenic designer, actor, director, acting instructor, lyricist, interior designer; b. Jersey City, Jan. 26, 1924; s. Max Joseph Miller and Lillian (Hirsch) Grodjesk. BA, U. Mich., 1946; MA, Smith Coll., 1948. Set designer, asst. scenic designer various Broadway, Off Broadway and summer shows, N.Y.C., 1948-72; scenic designer NBC-TV, N.Y.C., 1950-63; art dir. MPO-Video Prodns., N.Y.C., 1962; scenic designer CBS-TV, N.Y.C., 1963-91. Indsl. show designer Norelco, Thompson CSF, Engelhard, N.Y.C., 1958-75; interior designer Interior Comml. Constrn. Assocs., Hialeah, Fla., 1969-70; dir., writer Miramar Minstrels, N.Y.C., 1979—; dir. PACT Theatres, N.Y.C., 1995-98; acting tchr. Emmanuel Midtown Young Men and Young Women's Hebrew Assn., N.Y.C., 1989-90. Set designer (TV shows) Princeton '54, '55, '56 (Peabody 1954, 55), The Price is Right, 1962-63, Jackie Gleason Show, 1969-70, CBS News and Special Events, 1986-91, (mus. show) Nashville at the Garden, 1972; art dir. (TV show) Guiding Light, 1978-86 (2 Emmys 1984, 85), The Edge of Night, 1964-69; prodn. designer TV show Captain Kangaroo, 1970-78 (various Peabody awards); set design asst. (Broadway mus.) Funny Girl, 1964, (Broadway play) Sign in Sidney Brustein's Window; actor Kaye Playhouse, N.Y.C., 1998. Sgt. U.S. Army, 1943-46. Recipient Teaching Assistanship French Govt., Paris, 1948. Mem. United Scenic Artists, Miramar Ski Club (trip chair 1991-93, v.p. 1997-98, pres. 1999-2000). Avocations: skiing, dance, swimming, painting, acting. Address: 333 W 56th St Apt 7B New York NY 10019-3770

MILLER, HARRY CHARLES, JR., physician, urologist, educator; b. Ridgewood, N.J., Sept. 22, 1928; s. Harry Charles and Ruth G (McDermott) M.; m. Kari L. Palmer, June 14, 1969; children: Harry C., Carolynn A., Barbara J., Janet E., Jennifer T., Sandra L. AB, Amherst Coll., 1950; MD, Yale U., 1954. Intern Duke U. Hosp., Durham, N.C., 1954-55; resident U. Rochester Med. Ctr., N.Y., 1959-62; pvt. practice specializing in urology Washington, 1973-95; asst. prof. urology U. Rochester Health Sci. Ctr., 1962-71; assoc. prof. U. Okla. Health Sci. Ctr., Oklahoma City, 1971-73; prof., chmn. dept. urology George Washington U. Med. Ctr., Washington, 1973-95. Served with U.S. Army, 1955-57. Mem. AMA, ACS, Am. Urol. Assn. (exec. com. 1980-86, pres. Mid-Atlantic sect. 1991-92, bd. dirs. 1992-98, sec.-treas. Mid-Atlantic sect. 1986-91), Am. Acad. Pediat., Societe Internationale d'Urologie, Soc. Pediat. Urology, Soc. Univ. Urologists, Am. Assn. Clin. Urologists (sec.-treas. 1987-91, pres.-elect., pres. 1993-94, historian 1995—), Beekeepers Assn. No. Va. (treas. 1976-79),Great Falls Grange, River Bend Golf and Country Club, Urology Polit. Action Com. (treas. 1992-96), Wash. Urologic Soc. (pres. 1985-86. Office: George Washington U Med Ctr 2150 Pennsylvania Ave NW Washington DC 20037-3201

MILLER, HARRY FREEMAN, university administrator; b. Vallejo, Calif., Aug. 27, 1946; s. Theodore Harry and Grace (Eubank) M.; 1 child, Charissa Rainie. BA, Howard U., 1969; JD, U. Calif., Davis, 1972; cert., Harvard U.,

1989, U. Chgo., 1998. Grad. legal counsel Office of Calif. Atty. Gen., San Francisco, 1972—73; assoc. gen. sec. Stanford U., Palo Alto, Calif., 1973-79; asst. dean, lectr. law Syracuse (N.Y.) U., 1979-81; dir. devel. Georgetown U. Law Ctr., Washington, 1981-83; v.p. instnl. advt. Morgan State U., Balt., 1983-91; assoc. v.p., dir. planned giving U. South Fla., Tampa, 1991-95; assoc. v.p. devel. Tex. So. U., Houston, 1996—2000; dir. devel. Tex. A&M Inst. Bioscis. and Tech., Houston, 2001—. Host Lou Rauls Telethon for United Negro Coll. Fund, Syracuse, 1981, adv. com., Tampa, 1993-95; active Nat. Sports Festival Com., Syracuse, 1981. Mem. Nat. Soc. Fund Raising Execs., Assn. Fund Raising Officers (bd. dirs. 1984-90), Am. Inst. Parliamentarians, Leadership Tampa, Tampa Urban League (bd. dirs. 1993-95), Phi Alpha Delta. Office: Texas A&M U System 2121 W Holcombe Blvd Houston TX 77030 Office Phone: 713-677-7559.

MILLER, HARRY GEORGE, education educator; b. Waukesha, Wis., Feb. 15, 1941; s. Harry Fricke and Ethel Ruth (D'Amato) M.; m. Mary Frances Shugrue, June 20, 1964; children: Alicia, Michael, Anne, Dierdre, Courtney. BA, Carroll Coll., 1963; M.Ed., U. Nebr., 1967, Ed.D., 1970. Tchr. Westside Community Schs., Omaha, 1964-67; demonstration tchr. East Edn. Complex, Lincoln (Nebr.) Pub. Schs., 1967-68; instr. curriculum research Tchrs. Coll., U. Nebr., Lincoln, 1968-70; faculty So. Ill. U., Carbondale, 1970—, asso. prof. edn., dept. secondary edn., 1972—, chmn. dept. secondary edn., 1973-75, prof., chmn. dept. ednl. leadership, 1975—; dean, prof. Coll. Tech. Careers, 1980-89; assoc. v.p. acad. affairs So. Ill. U., 1989-92; dean, prof. Ctr. Adult and Continuing Edn. The Am. U., Cairo, 1992—. Rsch. prof. Min. Edn., Thailand, 1978, vis. prof., Malaysia, 80, Republic of Korea, 85, PRC, 1991; cons. to various orgsn. and instns., 1969—74. Author: Beyond Facts: Objective Ways to Measure Thinking, 1976, Adults Teaching Adults, 1977, Responsibility Education, 1977, The Adult Educator: A Handbook for Staff Development, 1978, An Introduction to Adult and Continuing Education, 1979, The Education of Adults, 1981, The Life-long Learning Experience, 1986, Grassroots, 1992, Veiled Voices, 1993, Come, Sit Awhile, 1995, Assalaamu Aleikum, 1997, Mazmaza, 2000; also monographs; mem. editorial bd. Traning, 1976. Exec. dir. Mid. East Assn. of Nat. Schs., 1999—; mem. Ill. Migrant Coun., 1974; mem. adv. bd. Evaluation and Devel. Ctr., Rehab. inst., Carbondale, 1974—80; bd. dirs. St. Joseph's Hosp., Overseas Ednl. Svcs., 1997—, Am. Ednl. Network, 1998—, Cairo Am. Coll., 1996—. Grantee Fulbright grantee, Republic of Togo, 1982. Mem. Pub. Adult and Continuing Edn. Assn., Rural Edn. Assn., Ill. Coun. for Social Studies (hon.), Community Svcs. Assn. Cairo (bd. dirs. 1994-96), Greater Cleve. Coun. for Social Studies (hon.), Ednl. Coun. fo 100 Inc., Coll. of Cons. Clubs: K.C. Democrat. Roman Catholic. Office: Am U Ctr Adult and Cont Educ PO Box 2511 113 Sharia Kasr Aini Cairo Egypt Office Phone: (20-2) 797-6840. Office Fax: (20-2) 797-6858. E-mail: harrymlr@aucegypt.edu.

MILLER, HARVEY R. lawyer, bankruptcy reorganization specialist; b. Bklyn., Mar. 1, 1933; married Grad., Columbia U. Law Sch., 1959. Sr. ptnr. Weil Gotshal and Manges LLP, N.Y.C. Adj. prof. law NYU Law Sch.; lectr. law Columbia U. Law Sch. Office: Weil Gotshal & Manges LLP 767 5th Ave Fl 29 New York NY 10153-0023 E-mail: harvey.miller@weil.com.

MILLER, HARVEY S. SHIPLEY, foundation trustee, private investor; b. Phila., Sept. 28, 1948; s. Frank Leroy and Betty Charlotte (Elfont) M. BA, Swarthmore Coll., 1970; JD, Harvard U., 1973. Bar: N.Y. 1973. Assoc. Debevoise & Plimpton, N.Y.C., 1973-75; curator and dir. dept. collections and spl. exhbns. Franklin Inst., Phila., 1975-81; v.p. Energy Solutions, Inc., N.Y.C., 1982-84; pres., chief exec. officer, dir. Daltex Med. Scis., Inc., N.Y.C., 1983-86, dir. exec. com., 1983-94, chief operating officer, vice chmn., 1986-91, pres., chief operating officer, 1991-93; trustee The Judith Rothschild Found., N.Y.C., 1993—. Author: Milton Avery: Drawings and Paintings, 1976, It's About Time, 1979; author, editor: New Spaces: Exploring the Aesthetic Dimensions of Holography, 1979; co-author: Rapid Inactivation of Infectious Pathogens by Chlorhexidine-coated Gloves, 1992; contbr. articles to profl. jours. Mem. vis. com. on photography George Eastman House, Rochester, N.Y., 1976-78; trustee Milton and Sally Avery Arts Found., N.Y.C., 1983—, sec., 1996—; trustee The Franklin Inst., Phila., 1993-95, Phila. Mus. Art, 1985—, exec. com., 1993-96; assoc. trustee U. Pa., 1981-95; trustee Arcadia U., 2002-; bd. govs. Print Club, Phila., 1976-87; bd. overseers U. Pa. Sch. Nursing, 1981—, Edith C. Blum Art Inst. Bard Coll., 1984-87; bd. dirs., mem. corp. MacDowell Colony, N.Y.C., 1982-85; exec. bd. dirs. Fabric Workshop, Phila., 1976-86; mem. prints and drawings and photographs trustees adv. com. Phila. Mus. Art, 1974—, trustee, 1985—, investment com., 1989-95, exec., devel. and exhbn. coms., 1993-96, chair 125th ann. campaign, 1999-2002; mem. vis. com. modern art Met. Mus. Art, 1998—; bd. assocs. Swarthmore Coll. Librs., Phila., 1978-86; treas., dir. Arcadia Found., Norristown, Pa., 1981—; chmn. adv. bd. Inst. Contemporary Art U. Pa., 1982-84; trustee, vice chmn. coms. on instrn. Pa. Acad. Fine Arts, 1982-91, trustee emeritus, 1991—, chmn. collections and exhbns. com., 1985-87; trustee N.Y. Studio Sch., 1974-80, U. of the Arts, 1979-86; mem. exec. bd. Citizens for Arts in Pa., 1980; adv. bd. The Highlands Hist. Soc., 1999—; bd. dirs. Once Gallery, Inc., 1974-75, Wildlife Preservation Trust Internat., Inc., 1990-95; mem. Mayor's Cultural Adv. Coun., Phila., 1987-91; chair Mayor's Art-in-City Hall Program, Phila., 1992-94; trustees coun. Nat. Gallery Art, Washington, 1995-2000, 2001—; mem. collections com. Hist. Soc. Pa., 1991-93, councilor trustee, 1992-93; mem. vis. com. photographs Met. Mus. Art, 1996—, vis. com. modern art, 1998—; mem. trustees' com. on drawings Mus. Modern Art, 1996—, trustee, 2003—, Prints and Illustrated Books, Museum of Modern Art, 2001—; mem. photography accessions com. San Francisco Mus. of Modern Art, 1997-2002; arts adv. com. Fund for the Waterworks, 1999-2001; founding mem., bd. trustees Maltz Jupiter (Fla.)Theatre, 2001—; bd. dirs. Am. Patrons of the Tate Gallery, 2003—; charter mem. The Drawings Group, L.A. County Mus. Art, 2003—; mem. drawings com. L.A. Mus. Contemporary Art, 2003—; bd. trustees Whitney Mus. Am. Art, 2004—, chmn. com. on drawings, 2004—; bd. overseers Hammer Jus., L.A., 2004—; trustee Ursinus Coll., 2004—, Point Found., 2004—. Named 1st non-Russian recipient of Diploma of Merit, Russian Ministry of Culture, 2002. Fellow The Pierpont Morgan Libr., Coll. Physicians Phila.; mem. ABA, Assn. of Bar of City of N.Y., Athenaeum, Libr. Co. Phila., Am. Philos. Soc., Hist. Soc. Pa., Phila. Art Alliance, Union League of Phila., Harvard Club of N.Y.C., Swarthmore Club Phila., Palm Beach Yacht Club, Sunnybrook Golf Club, Phi Sigma Kappa. Republican. Home: Plumlyn 7036 Sheaff Ln Fort Washington PA 19034-2017 Office: 1110 Park Ave New York NY 10128-1201

MILLER, HEIDI G. diversified financial company executive; b. 1951; married; 2 children. BA in History, Princeton U., 1974; PhD in History, Yale U., 1979. Various positions to mng. dir. emerging markets structured finance group Chemical Bank, 1979—92; joined as v.p. and asst. to the pres. Travelers Group, 1992, CFO, 1995—98, Citigroup (merger of Citibank and Travelers Group), N.Y.C., 1998—2000; CFO, sr. exec. v.p. strategic planning and adminstrn. Priceline.com, Norwalk, Conn., 2000; vice chmn. Marsh & McLennan Co., Inc., N.Y.C., 2001—02; exec. v.p. strategy and devel., CFO Bank One Corp., 2002—. Bd. dirs. Merck & Co., Inc., General Mills Inc. Trustee Princeton U., NYU Med. Sch. Office: Bank One Corp 1 Bank One Plaza Chicago IL 60670*

MILLER, HELEN, state representative, lawyer; b. Newark, N.J., Nov. 1945; BA, Howard U.; MS, Our Lady of the Lake U.; JD, Georgetown U. Bar: (D.C.), (Iowa). Atty.; state rep. dist. 49 Iowa Ho. of Reps., 2003—; mem. econ. growth com.; mem. human resources com.; mem. transp. com.; mem. justice sys. appropriations subcom. Vol. Cmty. Sch. Improvement Adv. Bd., Webster County Crime Stoppers, Leadership Iowa; cmty. task force adv. bd. Ft. Dodge Correctional Facility; 2d vice chair Iowa Dem. Party; exec. dir., bd. dirs. Young At Art. Democrat. Office: State Capitol East 12th and Grand Des Moines IA 50319 Address: PO Box 675 Fort Dodge IA 50501

MILLER, HENRY FRANKLIN, lawyer; b. Phila., May 19, 1938; s. Lester and Bessie (Posner) M.; m. Barbara Ann Gendel, June 20, 1964; children: Andrew, Alexa. AB, Lafayette Coll., 1959; JD, U. Pa., 1964. Bar: Pa. 1965. Law clk. U.S. Dist. Ct. Del., Wilmington, 1964-65; assoc. Wolf, Block, Schorr & Solis-Cohen LLP, Phila., 1965—71, ptnr., 1971—. Pres. Soc. Hill Synagogue, Phila., 1978-79, Big Brothers/Big Sisters Assn. of Phila., 1980-81, Jewish Family & Children's Agy., Phila., 1986-88. 1st lt. U.S. Army, 1959-60. Mem. Am. Coll. Real Estate Lawyers. Avocations: swimming, hiking, bicycling, reading. Office: Wolf Block Schorr & Solis-Cohen LLP 1650 Arch St Fl 21 Philadelphia PA 19103-2029 Office Phone: 215-977-2182. Business E-Mail: hmiller@wolfblock.com.

MILLER, HERBERT DELL, petroleum engineer; b. Oklahoma City, Sept. 29, 1919; s. Merrill Dell and Susan (Green) M.; m. Rosalind Rebecca Moore, Nov. 23, 1947; children: Rebecca Miller Wheeler, Robert Rexford. Registered profl. engr., Okla., Tex. Field engr. Amerada Petroleum Corp., Houston, 1948-49, Hobbs, N.Mex., 1947-48, dist. engr. Longview, Tex., 1949-57, sr. engr. Tulsa, 1957-62; petroleum engr. Moore & Miller Oil Co., Oklahoma City, 1962-78; owner Herbert D. Miller Co., Oklahoma City, 1978—. Maj., F.A., AUS, 1941-47; ETO. Decorated Bronze Star with oak leaf cluster, Purple Heart (U.S.); Croix de Guerre (France). Mem. AIME, Oklahoma City Golf. Republican. Episcopalian (pres. Men's Club 1973). Home and Office: 1819 W Wilshire Blvd Oklahoma City OK 73116-4115

MILLER, HERBERT ELMER, accountant; b. DeWitt, Iowa, Aug. 11, 1914; s. Elmer Joseph and Marian (Briggs) M.; m. Lenore Snitkey, July 1, 1938; 1 dau., Barbara Ruth. AB, State U. Iowa, 1936, MA, 1937; PhD, U. Minn., 1944; Dr. h.c., Free U. Brussels, 1982; D.H.L. (h.c.), De Paul U., 1983. C.P.A., Iowa. Acctg. prof. U. Minn., U. Mich., Mich. State U., 1938-70; ptnr. Arthur Andersen & Co., Chgo., 1970-78; dir. Sch. Acctg., U. Ga., Athens, 1978-83. Co-author: Finney-Miller accounting series, 1950-70; editor, contbr.: C.P.A. Rev. Manual, 1951-79. Mem. AICPA (bd. dirs. 1968-70), Am. Acctg. Assn. (pres. 1965-66), Federated Schs. Acctg. (pres. 1982), Beta Gamma Sigma, Beta Alpha Psi (nat. pres. 1961-62) Home: 145 S Stratford Dr Athens GA 30605-3025

MILLER, HINDA, state senator, management consultant; b. Montreal, Can., Apr. 18, 1950; m. Joel Miller; 2 children. BA, Parson's Sch. Design, 1972; MFA, N.Y. U., 1976. Bus. cons.; senator State of Vt., 2003—. Mem. Vt. Bus. Social Responsibility; bd. trustees Champlain Coll. Commr. Burlington Internat. Airport. Mem.: Lake Champlain C. of C. Democrat. Office: 84 DeForest Heights Burlington VT 05401

MILLER, HOPE RIDINGS, author; b. Bonham, Tex. d. Alfred Lafayette and Grace (Dupree) Ridings; m. Clarence Lee Miller, Sept. 26, 1932 (dec. Jan. 1965). BA, U. Tex.; MA, Columbia; D.Litt., Austin Coll. Society editor Washington Post, 1938-45; Washington corr. Town and Country mag., 1944-46, The Argonaut mag., 1945-49; Washington columnist Promenade mag., 1945-51; syndicated column McNaught, 1945-50; asso. editor Diplomat mag., 1952-55, editor in chief, 1956-66; television prodn. staff Metromedia, Inc., 1966-70; Washington editor Antique Monthly, 1976-89. Mem. editorial adv. bd. Horizon mag., 1978-89. Author: Embassy Row: The Life and Times of Diplomatic Washington, 1969, Great Houses of Washington, 1969, Scandals In The Highest Office: Facts and Fictions in the Private Lives of Our Presidents, 1973; script for cassette tape Circling Lafayette Square, 1976. Mem. women's bd. Columbia Hosp., Friends of the Folger Library, Washington Heart Assn. Mem. Nat. Press Club, Hist. Soc. Washington, Friends of LBJ Libr., Am. News women's Club, The Circle of the Nat. Gallery of Art, Stephen F. Austin Soc., Am. Archives of Art, Smithsonian Assocs., Nat. Mus. Women in the Arts, Sulgrave Club. Home: 1868 Columbia Rd NW Washington DC 20009-5183

MILLER, HOWARD, writer, researcher; b. Queens, NY, Aug. 2, 1962; s. Richard Miller and Miller Merna. BS, Northwestern U., Evanston, Ill., 1980—84. Project mgr. British Airways, 1999—2000; writer, rsch analyst Ind. Aviation Rsch., 2001—; fin. con. Smith Barney, N.Y.C., NY, 1990—93; data base mgr., admin. asst. M Corp., N.Y.C., NY, 1995—96; production mgr. Mother Son, N.Y.C., NY, 1998—99, Consulate Gen. Israel, Office of Cultural Affairs, N.Y.C., NY, 1998—2000. Rsch cons. Terminal One GroupAssn. LP, 1999—2000; rsch analyst Lynn Edward Kenner Law Office, 1999—2000; chair Greater N.Y. Coun. of Gay and Lesbian Jewish Orgn., 1996—2000; spl. events programmer Various Rel. Orgns., 1999—2000; prodn. mgr. Office Cultural Affairs, USA Consulate General of Israel, 1998. Contbr. newsletter. Mem.: Greater N.Y. Coun. of Gay and Lesbian Jewish Orgn.

MILLER, I. GEORGE, physician, educator, researcher; b. Chgo., Apr. 18, 1937; s. Irving George and Florence (Levy) M.; m. Arlette Goldmuntz, Mar. 25, 1962; children: Lisa, John, David. AB, Harvard U., 1958, MD, 1962. Intern Univ. Hosp., Western Res. U., Cleve., 1962-63; resident Univ. Hosp., Western Res., U., Cleve., 1963-64; epidemiology intelligence oficer Communicable Disease Ctr. USPHS, Atlanta, 1964-66; research fellow in medicine Harvard U. Med. Sch., Boston, 1966-69; asst. prof. pediatrics, epidemiology, biophysics and biochemistry Yale Sch. Medicine, New Haven, 1969-72, J.F. Enders prof., 1979—. Mem. exptl. virology study sect. NIH, 1974-77; mem. sci. adv. com. Damon Runyon Fund, 1979-85, dir., 1985-94; Leukemia Soc. Am., 1976-81. Contbr. numerous articles, chpts. to profl. publs.; editl. bd. Jour. Virology, 1981-87, Virology, 1982-86. Recipient epidemic Intelligence Service Alumni Assn. prize, 1967; Macy faculty scholar, 1977, Am. Cancer Soc. scholar, 1990; Howard Hughes Med. Inst. investigatorship, 1972-80 Fellow Infectious Diseases Soc. (Squibb award 1982, Enders award 1989); mem. Am. soc. Clin. Investigation, Am. Pediatric Soc., Am. Soc. Virology, Assn. Am. Physicians, Inst. Medicine. Jewish. Office: Yale U Sch Medicine Pediatrics Infectious Diseases PO Box 208064 New Haven CT 06520-8064 Office Phone: 203-785-4758. Business E-Mail: george.miller@yale.edu.

MILLER, IRIS ANN, landscape architect, urban designer, educator; b. Pitts., Jan. 6, 1938; d. Bernard and Sadye (Topel) Ress; m. Lawrence Alan Miller, Jan. 24, 1959; children: Bradley Stuart, Richard Lyle, Stefan Ress. BS cum laude, U. Pitts., 1959, MEd in Secondary Edn., 1961; postgrad. in psychology and counseling, U. Md., 1962-68; MArch, Cath. U. Am., 1979. Tchr. various pub. and pvt. schs., Pitts., Monroeville, Pa., Montgomery County, Md., 1959-61, 63-64; free lance landscape design Washington, 1965-81; architecture design and research O'Neil and Manion Architects, Bethesda, Md., 1979, 81; architecture design and drawing Frank Schlesinger Architects/Planners, Washington, 1979-80; prin. Iris Miller Urbanism and Landscape Design, 1982—; cons. architecture design Washington, 1982—. Vis. lectr. Cath. U. Am., Washington, 1983-86, vis. asst. prof., 1987-93, adj. asst. prof., 1993-96, adj. assoc. prof., 1997—, dir. landscape, arch. studies, 1986-89, dir. landscape studies, 1990—; urban design cons. Techworld, Washington, 1984-86; devel. dir. Tech. 2000 Mus., 1985-86; dir., presenter lectr. series resident assoc. program Smithsonian Instn., Washington, 1982, 83, 85, 87, 89, 98; dir., founder 7th, 8th and 9th Sts. Group Streetscape project, Washington, 1986-89, others; founder Charrette urban design seminar, Washington, Dallas, Alexandria, Va., St. Louis and Cleve., 1982-89; initiator, participant Sarasota (Fla.) Regional Urban Design Assistance R/UDAT Team, 1983, seminar Nat. Gallery Art, Washington, 1984, Nat. Arboretum, 1988, symposia Cath. U. Am., 1987—; invited jury panel, Fulbright Travel Awards, 1997-99; Lambda Alpha Internat. Hon. Soc., 1998—;facilitator/panel North Capital St./Fruxton Circle Charette, 2001; invited panel Japan Triennial Echigo-Tsumari, 1999, 2000; spkr., team leader McMillan Reservoir Charrette, Washington, 1999; apptd. mem. D.C. Downtown Partnership Streetscape subcom., 1989-91, D.C. Interactive Downtown Task Force Streetscape and Traffic subcom., 1996; D.C. Stakeholder Signage Subcommittee, 1997—, D.C. Stakeholder Traffic Subcommittee, 1998, D.C. Stakeholder Streetscape Subcom., 1999; co-founder, co-chmn. Brookland/CUA Neighborhood Improvement Partnership, 1999—; founder, co-dir. symposium. Libr. of Congress, 1995; dir. symposium D.C. Interagy. Task Force Seminar on Streetscape and Signage, 1995; dir., mem. steering com. numerous confs. in field; invited participant Congress for New Urbanism, 1994—; program spkr. U.S. Embassy Amman, Jordan, 1992, ICOMOS, 1992, 93, U. Va., 1993, Ecole Nationale Superieure du Paysage/Versailles, France, 1993, U. Osaka, Japan, 1993, 95, 96, 97 Tokyo Inst. Tech. U., 1993, Chiba Inst. Tech., Japan, 1998, SUNY, Buffalo, 1994, U. Colo., Denver, 1994, Mayors Inst. on City Design, St. Louis, 1994, Tongji U., Shanghai, China, 1995, 97, Tsinghua U., China, 1995, 98; jury critic Cath. U. Am., 1980-99, U. Puerto Rico, U. Va., 1993, Tsinghua U., China, 1998; instr. ceramics, Bethesda, Md., 1975-76. Author, co-editor: (book) Urban Design: Visions and Reflections, 1991, Capital Visions: Reflections on a Decade of Urban Design Charrettes and a Look Ahead, 1995, (map and text) Visions of Washington: Composite Plan of Urban Interventions, 1991; author: D.C. Streetscape & Signage Resource Manual, 1996; co-author: Retrospective Catalogue: Collegiate Exhibition for Excellence in Urban Design, 1997, Washington In Maps, 2002; contbr. articles to profl. jours.; landscape design featured in major landscape archtl. jours. in US and Japan, 1998, 2000; featured nationally in Assoc. Press articles on fragrant landscapes, 1999; curator, author exhbn. and catalogue on Washington Maps Sumner Sch. Mus., 1987, 92, U. Md., 1993, Embassy of France, 1993, SUNY Buffalo, 1994, U. Calif., Berkeley, 1994, U. Toronto, Can., 1995; curator, author exhbn. ACSA Ann. Meeting, Montreal, 1994; co-curator, author exhbn. and catalogue Octagon Mus., 1987; project dir., curator Paris-Washington Exhbn., 1987—; exhibitor, installation, Tokyo, Japan, 1997; recent residential and other landscape projects include Univ. Club. Wash., 1997-98, Salle de Fete Site Plan, Francheville, France, 1993, Kahn Residence, Arlington, Va., 1993-94, Marks Residence, Silver Spring, Md., 1993, Nesse, Lewis Residence, Silver Spring, 1992, Friedman Residence, Washington, 1992, Drysdale Hershon Residence, Washington, 1991, Miller Residence, Washington, 1990—, Sexton Residence, Kenwood, Chevy Chase, Md., 1990, 95, Romano Residence, Fairfax Station, Va., 1989, Mushinski Residence, Bethesda, Md., 1989, 8th St. Mall Washington, 1987-88, Mishkin, Jennis Residence, Bethesda, 1988, Cramer Residence, Bethesda, 1988; recent home design and renovations include Sexton Residence, Chevy Chase, 1994, Miller Jayapal Residence, San Francisco, 1993, Marks Residence, Silver Spring, 1993, Miller Residence, 1991, Washington, Mishkin Jennis Residence, Bethesda, 1988. Co-chmn. stamp com. Bicentennial Washington, 1987-90; founding mem. Washington Network, 1986-89; mem. adv. panel L'Enfant Forum, Washington, 1987-90, Hist. Georgetown Found., 1989-90; trustee John J. Sexton Fund for Local Govt. Studies, Sch. Pub. Affairs, U. Md., College Park, 1983-93; dir., founder Pub.-Pvt. Partnership and Univ. Scholarship Outreach Inner-City H.S. Program, Cath. U. Am., Washington Pub. Schs., 1985—; dir., founder Intern Exch. Program Landscape Architecture France-U.S.A., Cath. U. Am., U. Va., Friends of Vieilles Maisons Francaises, 1991-98, study-travel Asia Arch./Landscape Scholarship Fund, 1998—; dir., co-founder Intern Exch. Program Landscape Architecture China-U.S.A., Cath. U. Am., Tongji U., Shanghai, 1995—, Osaka U., Japan, 1996—, Chiba Inst. Tech., Japan, 1998-99; historic landscape com. U.S./Internat. Coun. on Monuments and Sites, 1990—; active Cultural Alliance Greater Washington, Nat. Trust Historic Preservation, Ikebana Internat., His. Soc. Washington, Nat. Mus. for Bldg. Arts; alumni coun. Sch. Architecture and Planning, Cath. U. Am., 1986—; mem. com. on environment Congress for New Urbanism, 1994—. Travel rsch. grantee Cath. U. Am., 1978, 79; grantee Govt. France, 1985, NEA (2), 1982, 92; recipient Program Devel. award Cath. U. Am., 1978. Mem. AIA (assoc., nat., regional and urban design exhbn. and panel, chmn. edn. subcom. 1987-96, sec. edn. subcom. 1997—, chmn., founder data base on design edn. and urban design, chmn. edn. conf. 1983, chmn. newsletter 1993, edn. com. D.C. chpt. 1981-83, Charrette co-chmn., program devel. award 1982), Assn. Collegiate Schs. Architecture (spkr. N.E. region conf. 1989, spkr. ann. meeting 1991-92, chmn. panel 1989—, chair Collegiate Exhbn. for Excellence in Urban Design 1990—, author conf. procs. 1991-93, Citation for Urban Design 1993, 95), Am. Soc. Landscape Architects (Potomac chpt. strategic planning com. 1994-95), Am. Planning Assn., U.S.-Internat. Coun. on Monuments and Sites (program spkr. 1987, 92, 93, hist. landscapes com.), Friends Vieilles Maisons Francaises (program spkr. 1987, 92), Friends of Vieilles Maisons Francaises, Congress for New Urbanism (com. on environment 1994—), Alpha Epsilon Phi (pres. D.C. alumni 1965-67). Avocations: photography, japanese flower arranging, tennis, jogging. Home: 3820 52nd St NW Washington DC 20016-1924

MILLER, IRVING FRANKLIN, chemical engineer, educator, biomedical engineer, educator, academic administrator; b. N.Y.C., Sept. 27, 1934; s. Sol and Gertrude (Rochkind) M.; m. Baila Hannah Milner, Jan. 28, 1962; children: Eugenia Lynne, Jonathan Mark. BS in Chem. Engring., NYU, 1955; MS, Purdue U., 1956; PhD, U. Mich., 1960. Rsch. scientist United Aircraft Corp., Hartford, 1959-61; from asst. prof. to prof., head chem. engring. Poly. Inst. Bklyn., 1961-72; prof. bioengring., head bioengring. program U. Ill., Chgo., 1973-79, acting head sys. engring. dept., 1978-79, assoc. vice chancellor rsch., dean Grad. Coll., 1979-85, prof. chem. engring., head chem. engring., 1986-95, dir. Ctr. for Advanced Edn. and Rsch., 1989-90, dir. Office of Spl. Projects, 1990-92, dir. bioengring. program, 1992-95; dean Coll. Engring. U. Akron, Ohio, 1995-98, prof. biomed. engring., 1998-2000; dir. corp. ops. BioTechPlex Corp., 2002—. Cons. to industry; cons. NAS, NIH; dir. distance learning programs Ohio Aerospace Inst., 1998—2000. Editor: Electrochemical Bioscience and Bioengineering, 1973; contbr. articles profl. jours. Mem. AIChE, AAAS, Am. Chem. Soc., Biomed. Engring. Soc., N.Y. Acad Scis. Home: 1746 N Larrabee St Chicago IL 60614-5634 Office Phone: 847-437-9311. E-mail: ifmiller@uic.edu.

MILLER, JACK, publishing company executive; b. Middletown, Ohio, Sept. 11, 1931; s. John William and Helena Bernice (Pendleton) M.; m. Barbara Elaine Stutsman, Jan. 19, 1952; children: Stacy Lynn, John Dewey, Tamara Leigh, Mark Douglas, Matthew Scott, Delano Mitchell. BS in Civil Engring., Wash. State U., Pullman, 1958. Sales engr. Armco Steel Corp., Middletown, Ohio, 1958-64; v.p., dir. mktg. Mes-Tex, Houston, 1964-67, Kirby Bldg. Sys., Houston, 1967-69; pres. Group Comm., Inc., Houston, 1969-81, chmn. bd. dirs., 1981—. Lectr. in field; condr. seminars in field. Author: Selling Building Systems, 1970, Profitable Management Techniques for Contractors, 1973, A Professional Approach to Marketing for the Construction Industry, 1977, Design/Build, Build/Lease, and Financing Building Projects, 1977, Human Stress ... How to Turn It Into Success, 1978, Advanced Negotiating Skills and Strategies, 1979, The Jack Miller Reports, 1985, Rules You Should Know About Investing, 1988, 16 Opportunities in Build/Lease, 1988, Rules You Should Know About Motivation, 1988, Rules You Should Know to be a Better Manager, 1988, Rules You Should Know About Investing in Real Estate, 1988, Rules You Should Know About Time Management and Speed Reading/Speed Learning, 1988, The Important Steps that Take You to Health, Wealth and Happiness, 1992, Rules You Should Know Before You Build Your Important Project, 1993, Total Quality Management for the Construction Industry, 1993, Guide Manual for a Win/Win Negotiator, 1999. Elder Pines Presbyn. Ch., Houston, 1996—. With USAF, 1950-54. Mem. ASCE, Associated Builders and Contractors, Associated Gen. Contractors, Am. Soc. for Quality, The Jack Miller Network, Tau Beta Pi, Phi Kappa Phi. Republican. Presbyterian. Office: Group Comm 10417 Rockley Rd Houston TX 77099-3565

MILLER, JACK CONWAY, landscape artist, art gallery director, owner; b. Collegeville, Pa., Jan. 23, 1924; s. John W. and Marguerite Blanche (Conway) M.; m. Marguerite F. Martin, Feb. 10, 1948 (dec. Feb. 1978); children: Lynne, Craig, Mark (dec.), Susan; m. Carmen Aline Morin, Sept. 9, 1983. BSc, Phila. Coll. Pharmacy & Sci., 1944, MSc, 1948; PhD in Art Therapy (hon.), La. State U., 1988. Mgr. Ampul & Injection dept. McNeil Labs., Phila., 1948-52; sales mgr. Curtiss Breeding Svcs., Gary, Ill., 1952-71; co-founder Indoor Racket Complex Frog Hollow, Inc., Worcester, Pa., 1970-71; owner, operator Equity Semen Svcs., Inc., Trappe, Pa., 1970-76; co-owner, officer, operator Village Market, Inc., Boyertown, Pa., 1971-73; co-owner Equity Art Svcs., Collegeville, 1977—; creator, owner traditional Japanese moss garden Dans La Forêt, Collegeville, Pa., 1981—; owner Dans La Forêt Gardens & Nursery, Collegeville, 1981—; co-owner Morin-Miller Galleries, N.Y.C., 1985-90; prin. Japanese Gardens Landscaper, 1981—. Cons. bamboo installation Phila. Mus. Art, 2000; writer, lectr., tchr. in field. Created Japanese Zen Garden at Pagoda 100, Pagoda 10, 1999, expanded Pagoda gardens in Bala Cynwyd, 1992, Rosemont sect. Montreal, Que., Can., 1997; creator, owner Kare san-sui Dans La Forêt, Collegeville, Pa., 1981-2000 (now included in Archives of Am. Gardens, Smithsonian Instn.), brown-round granite sculpture Briar Hill Farm, Ambler, Pa.; editor Pa. Farm-O-Gram Dairy Newsletter, 1965-71; works featured in The American Gardner, Jour. Japanese Gardening. Bd. dirs. Pa. All Am. Dairy Show, Harrisburg, 1970, 71. Capt. infantry and combat engrs. U.S. Army, 1944-46, ETO & Pacific. Mem. Am. Rhododendron Soc., Pa. Horticultural Soc., Rock Garden Soc. Achievements include having works included in Archives of Am. Gardens at the Smithsonian Inst., Washington. Avocations: music, reading, travel.

MILLER, JACK DAVID R. radiologist, physician, educator; b. Johannesburg, Apr. 15, 1930; s. Harold Lewis and Inez (Behrman) M.; m. Miriam Sheckter, Dec., 1988. B.Sc., M.B., Ch.B., U. Witwatersrand, Johannesburg, 1956. Diplomate: Am. Bd. Radiology. Intern Coronation Hosp., Johannesburg, 1957-58; resident in radiology Passavant Meml. Hosp., Chgo., 1959-62, Wesley Meml. Hosp., Chgo., 1959-62; fellow in radiology Northwestern U. Med. Sch., 1962-63; chmn. dept. radiology U. Hosp., Edmonton, Alta., Can., 1971-83; radiologist, dept. radiology U. Alta Hosp., 1963—2004, head, dir. neuroradiology, 1984—92; prof. emeritus radiology U. Alta., 1997—. Clin. prof. radiology U. Alta., 1971— Fellow Royal Coll. Physicians Can., Am. Coll. Radiology. Office: U Alberta Dept Radiology Edmonton AB Canada

MILLER, JACKIE DEAN, I, genealogist, historian; b. Cleve., Sept. 6, 1959; s. Lloyd Keith Miller and Lou Eva Isaacs; m. Mary Margaret Diachar, Apr. 23, 1991; children: Sheila Florencie, Jackie Herman II. Student, Sch. Paralegal Studies-PSCDI, Atlanta, 1996—97, Union Inst. and Colls., 1998—2002. Boy's adventure corp leader/local officer The Salvation Army - Citadel/Price Hill Corp, Cin., 1986—91; treas. Hamblen County Hist. Soc., Morristown, Tenn., 1995—96. Editor/founder/owner The Country Peddler Newspaper, Cin., 1983—86; radio dj WAIF Radio 88.5 FM, Cin., 1986—88; columist Ask the Col. The Appalachian Connection Newspaper, Cin., 1999—2000; rep. S.W. Ohio State of Ohio - We Care Network, Cin. Author: (book family genealogy history) The Isaacs Family of Kentucky 1600's-1991, (book of poems) On Gossamer Wings, (book family genealogy history) The English Bates to America 1415-1994, Johnson Family of Kentucky, Martin Family of Floyd County, Kentucky, (book genealogy family history) Miller Family in Search of Pocahontas, Hugh Arbuthnot & Margaret Keith, Rev. Samuel Walker 1586-2003, James Bane & Elizabeth Clark, poems. With USN, 1977—78. Named Ky. Col., Ky. Gov. Ned McWherter, 1990; recipient Key To the City of Morristown, Tenn., Mayor John R. Johnson for the City of Morristown, Tenn., 1994, Key to the City of Johnson City, Tenn., Reece Sexton for the City of Johnson City, Tenn., 1994, Rank of Col., N.Mex Gov. Bruce King for the State of N.Mex., 1994, Proclamation declaring a day in my honor, Mayor Jean Dean for City of Huntington, W.Va., 1995, Key to the City Elsmore, Ky., Key to the City Nashville, Tenn., Proclamation honors, Bridgeport, Conn., Anaheim, Calif. Republican. Baptist. Home: 1718 Commanche Trl Elsmere KY 41018 Office: It's Genealogy Baby Inc 1718 Commanche Trl Elsmere KY 41018 Personal E-mail: hillbillie_jack@yahoo.com. E-mail: thekeithfamilyus@yahoo.com.

MILLER, JACQUELINE WINSLOW, library director; b. N.Y.C., Apr. 15, 1935; d. Lynward Roosevelt and Sarah Ellen (Grevious) W.; 1 child, Percy Scott. BA, Morgan State Coll., 1957; MLS, Pratt Inst., 1960; grad. profl. seminar, U. Md., 1973. Cert. profl. libr. With Bklyn. Pub. Libr., 1957-68; head ext. svcs. New Rochelle (N.Y.) Pub. Libr., 1969-70; br. adminstr. Grinton Will Yonkers (N.Y.) Pub. Libr., 1970-75; dir. Yonkers Pub. Libr., 1975-96. Mem. adj. faculty grad. libr. studies Queens Coll., CUNY, 1989, 90. Mem. commr.'s com. Statewide Libr. Devel., Albany, N.Y., 1980; mem. N.Y. Gov.'s Commn. on Librs., 1990, 91; bd. dirs. Cmty. Planning Coun., Yonkers, N.Y., 1987; mem. Yonkers Black Women's Polit. Caucus, 1987; pres. bd. Literacy Vols. of Westchester County, 1991-92; mem. fair campaign practices com. LWV, 1996—. Recipient Yonkers Citizen award Ch. of Our Saviour, 1980, 2d Ann. Mae Morgan Robinson award Yonkers chpt. Westchester Black Women's Polit. Caucus, 1992, 3d Ann. Equality Day award City of Yonkers, 1992, African-Am. Heritage 1st award YWCA, 1994; named Outstanding Profl. Woman Nat. Assn. Negro Bus. and Profl. Women's Clubs Inc., 1981. Mem. ALA (councilor 1987-91), N.Y. State Libr. Assn., Pub. Libr. Dirs. Assn. (exec. bd.), N.Y. State Pub. Libr. Dirs. Assn., Westchester Libr. Assn., Yonkers C. of C. (bd. dirs. 1992-95), Educate the Girls, Inc. (bd. dirs., 2003—) Rotary (Yonkers chpt.). E-mail: jacki@sprynet.com.

MILLER, JAMES CLIFFORD, III, economist; b. Atlanta, June 25, 1942; s. James Clifford and Annie (Moseley) M.; m. Demaris Humphries, Dec. 22, 1961; children: Katrina Demaris, John Felix, Sabrina Louise. BBA, U. Ga., 1964; PhD in Econs., U. Va., 1969; LLD (hon.), U. of Pacific, 1987; PhD (hon.), Kennesaw Coll., 1988. Asst. prof. Ga. State U., Atlanta, 1968-69; economist U.S. Dept. Transp., Washington, 1969-72; assoc. prof. econs. Tex. A&M U., College Station, 1972-74; economist U.S. Coun. Econ. Advs., Washington, 1974-75; asst. dir. U.S. Council Wage and Price Stability, Washington, 1975-77; resident scholar Am. Enterprise Inst., 1977-81; adminstr. Office Info. and Regulatory Affairs, Office Mgmt. and Budget and exec. dir. Presdl. Task Force on Regulatory Relief, Washington, 1981; chmn. FTC, Washington, 1981-85; dir. Office Mgmt. and Budget, Washington, 1985-88; disting. fellow, chmn., counsellor Citizens for a Sound Economy, 1988—2002; disting. fellow Ctr. for Study of Pub. Choice George Mason U., 1988—2002; sr. fellow Hoover Instn., 1988—. Pres., chmn. bd. Econ. Impact Analysts, Inc., 1978-2002; chmn. CapAnalysis Group of Howrey Simon Arnold & White, 2002-; bd. govs. US Postal Svc., 2003-. Author: Why the Draft?: The Case for a Volunteer Army, 1968, Economic Regulation of Domestic Air Transport: Theory and Policy, 1974, Perspectives on Federal Transportation Policy, 1975, Benefit-Cost Analyses of Social Regulation: Case Studies from the Council on Wage and Price Stability, 1979, Reforming Regulation, 1980, The Federal Trade Commission: The Political Economy of Regulation, 1987, The Economist as Reformer, 1989, Fix the U.S. Budget: Urgings of an "Abominable No-Man", 1994, Monopoly Politics, 1999. Candidate for Rep. nomination for U.S. Senate for Va., 1994, 96. Thomas Jefferson fellow, 1965-66, DuPont fellow, 1966-67, Ford Found. fellow, 1967-68. Mem. Am. Econ. Assn., Pub. Choice Soc., So. Econ. Assn. (exec. com. 1980-81, v.p. 1990-91), Adminstrv. Conf. U.S. (vice chmn. 1987-88). Republican. Baptist. Office: The CapAnalysis Group 1299 Pennsylvania NW Ste 300 Washington DC 20004 Office Phone: 202-383-6633. E-mail: millerjim@capanalysis.com.

MILLER, JAMES EDWARD, computer scientist, educator; b. Lafayette, La., Mar. 21, 1940; s. Edward Gustave and Orpha Marie (DeVilbiss) M.; m. Diane Moon, June 6, 1964; children: Deborah Elaine, Michael Edward. BS, U. La., 1961, PhD, 1972; MS, Auburn U., 1964. Systems engr. IBM, Birmingham, Ala., 1965-68; asst. prof. U. West Fla., Pensacola, 1968-70, chmn. systems sci., 1972-86; grad. rschr. U. La., Lafayette, 1970-72; computer systems analyst EPA, Washington, 1979; prof., chmn. computer sci. and stats. U. So. Miss., Hattiesburg, 1986-92, prof., 1992—2003; program evaluator Computer Sci. Accreditation Commn., 1986-92; prof. computer sci. and stats. U. So. Miss. Gulf Coast, Long Beach, 2003—. Cons., lectr. in field; co-dir. NASA/Am. Soc. Engring. Edn. Faculty Fellowship Program-Stennis Space Flight Ctr., 1990—. Author numerous articles for tech. publs. Mem. Assn. Computing Machinery (editor Computer Sci. Edn. spl. interest group bull. 1982-97), Data Processing Mgmt. Assn. (dir. edn. spl. interest group 1985-86), Am. Soc. for Engring. Edn. Democrat. Methodist. Office: U So Miss Gulf Park 730 E Beach Blvd Long Beach MS 39560-1000 Office Phone: 228-865-4531. Business E-Mail: jim.miller@usm.edu.

MILLER, JAMES GEGAN, research scientist, physics educator; b. St. Louis, Nov. 11, 1942; s. Francis John and Elizabeth Ann (Caul) M.; m. Judith Anne Kelvin, Apr. 23, 1966; 1 child, Douglas Ryan. AB, St. Louis U., 1964; MA, Washington U., 1966, PhD, 1969. Asst. prof. physics Washington U., St. Louis, 1970-72, assoc. prof., 1972-77, prof. physics, 1977—, dir. lab. for ultrasonics, 1987—, rsch. asst. prof. medicine, 1976-81, rsch. assoc. prof. medicine, 1981-88, rsch. prof. medicine, 1988-2000, prof. biomed. engring., 1999—, Albert Gordon Hill prof. physics, 1999—, prof. medicine, 2000—. Contbr. articles to profl. jours.; patentee in field. Recipient I-R 100 award Indsl. Research Devel. Mag., 1974, 78; NIH, NASA grantee, NIH Merit Award, 1998. Fellow IEEE (sr., gov. com. Ultrasonics, Ferroelectrics and Frequency Control Soc. 1978-80,86-88, 92-94), Am. Inst. Ultrasound in Medicine, Acoustical Soc. Am. (Silver medal 2004), Am. Inst. Med. and Biol. Engring.; mem. Am. Phys. Soc., Sigma Xi (nat. lectr. 1981-82). Office: Washington Univ St Louis Physics Dept CB 1105 One Brookings Dr Saint Louis MO 63130 Office Phone: 314-935-6229. E-mail: james.g.miller@wustl.edu.

MILLER, JAMES L. food products executive; b. 1948; Grad., Cornell U., 1972. V.p. sales, pres., gen. mgr Sysco Corp., Houston, 1972-83; v.p., gen. mgr., exec. v.p., COO no. divsn. PYA/Monarch, Inc., Balt., 1983-89; pres., COO U.S. Foodservice, Inc., Hanover, Md., 1989—. Office: U S Foodservices Inc 9755 Patuxent Woods Dr Columbia MD 21046-2286

MILLER, JAMES M. lawyer; b. Berwyn, Ill., Apr. 25, 1950; m. Luz Angela Aristizabal, July 13, 1991; children: Hillary Daniela, Maxwell James. BA magna cum laude, U. Miami, 1972; JD, U. Chgo., 1975. Bar: Fla. 1975. Shareholder Akerman, Senterfitt & Eidson P.A., Miami, Fla. Bd. dirs. Miami Mus. Sci., pres. 1989-91. Mem. ABA (litigation sect., corp., banking and bus. law sect.), Fla. Bar (vice-chmn. 11th jud. cir. grievance com. B 1982-84), Dade County Bar Assn. Office: Akerman Senterfitt SunTrust International Center One SE 3d Ave 28th Fl Miami FL 33131

MILLER, JAMES MCCALMONT, pediatrician; b. Springfield, Mass., Sept. 25, 1938; s. John Haynes and Josephine (Darrah) M.; m. Jane Rose, July 7, 1975; children: John, Charlotte, Willard. AB, Hamilton Coll., 1960; MD, Cornell U., 1964. Resident U. Colo. Med. Ctr., Denver, 1964-67; staff pediatrician Kaiser Permanente Med. Ctr., Walnut Creek, Calif., 1969-87, chief pediatrician, 1971-82, Pleasanton, Calif., 1982-87; staff pediatrician Appalachian Regional Health, Hazard, Ky., 1987-92, N.W. Pediat. Ctr., Centralia, Wash., 1992—. Clin. assoc. U. N.Mex., Albuquerque, 1967-69; instr. U. Calif., San Francisco, 1969-87, U. Ky., Lexington, 1988-92. With U.S. Army, 1967-69. Fellow Am. Acad. Pediat.; mem. Wash. State Med. Assn. Office: Northwest Pediatric Ctr 1911 Cooks Hill Rd Centralia WA 98531-9027 E-mail: jmiller@localaccess.com.

MILLER, JAMES VINCE, university president; b. Waynetown, Ind., July 16, 1920; s. J. Vince and Hazel B. (Spore) M.; m. Mildred Mae Hockersmith, June 13, 1943; children: Maryllyn Jean, Rachel Katherine. BA in Philosophy and English, U. Indpls., 1942; M.Div. in History and Lit., United Sem., Dayton, Ohio, 1945; postgrad., Earlham Coll., 1945-46; PhD in Philosophy, Boston U., 1955; LL.D. (hon.), Otterbein Coll., 1971, U. Indpls., 1979. Ordained to ministry Evang. United Brethren Ch., 1945; pastor Greensfork, Ind., 1944-46, Stow, Mass., 1946-48; faculty dept. philosophy and religion Bates Coll., Lewiston, Maine, 1950-61, prof., 1960-61, chmn. dept., 1958-61; acad. dean Otterbein Coll., Westerville, Ohio, 1964-68, v.p. for acad. affairs, acad. dean, 1968-71; pres. Pacific U., Forest Grove, Oreg., 1971-83, pres. emeritus, 1983—; pres. Nat. Coll. of Naturopathic Medicine, Portland, Oreg., 1989-93, pres. emeritus, 1993—. Adj. prof. Union Grad. Sch., 1970-78, San Francisco Theol. Sem., 1979-86; chmn. N.W. Assn. Pvt. Colls. and Univs., 1974-76; treas. Oreg. Ind. Coll. Assn., 1974-75, 76-78, chmn., 1978-79; adv. com. Oreg. Ednl. Coordinating Commn., 1976-79; chmn. council for higher edn. United Ch. Bd. Homeland Missions, 1975-76; former mem. adv. com. Gov.'s Listening Post; former mem. spl. com. on future of edn. in Oreg., Oreg. Ednl. Coordinating Commn.; mem. Oreg. Bd. Optometry, 1988-92. Mem.: Rotary. Methodist. Address: 1633 Mowry Sq Richland WA 99354-2612

MILLER, JAN DEAN, metallurgy educator; b. Dubois, Pa., Apr. 7, 1942; s. Harry Moyer and Mary Virginia (McQuown) M.; m. Patricia Ann Rossman, Sept. 14, 1963; children: Pamela Ann, Jeanette Marie, Virginia Christine. BS, Pa. State U., 1964; MS, Colo. Sch. of Mines, 1966, PhD, 1969. Rsch. engr. Anaconda Co., Mont., 1966; asst. prof. metallurgy U. Utah, Salt Lake City, 1968-72, assoc. prof., 1972-78, prof., 1978-2000, Ivor D. Thomas prof., 2000—, dept. chmn., 2002—; rsch. engr. Lawrence Livermore Lab., Calif., 1972. Cons. on processing of mineral resources to various cos. and govt. agys. Editor: Hydrometallurgy, Research, Development, and Plant Practice, 1983, others; contbr. over 400 articles to profl. jours.; 25 patents in field. Recipient Marcus A. Grossman award Am. Soc. Metals, 1974, Van Diest gold medal Colo. Sch. of Mines, 1977, Extractive and Processing Lectr. award The Minerals, Metals and Materials Soc., 1992, Disting. Achievement medal Colo. Sch. of Mines, 1994; Centennial fellow Coll. of Earth and Mineral Scis., Pa. State U., 1996, Best Paper award for fundamental rsch. 2000 TAPPI Recycling Symposium, 2000. Mem. NAE, AIME (Henry Krumb lectr. 1987, Richards award 1991, Mineral Industry Edn. award 1997, Aplan award 2003), Soc. Mining, Metallurgy and Exploration (chmn. mineral processing divsn. 1980-81, Disting. Mem. award 1992, Antoine M. Gaudin award 1992), Fine Particle Soc., Am. Chem. Soc., Soc. Mining Engrs. (bd. dirs. 1980-83, program chmn. 1982-83, Taggart award 1986, Stefanko award 1988, 2002), Metall. Soc. (Extractive Metallurgy Tech. award 1988), Salt Lake Swim and Tennis Club, U. Utah Faculty Club. Baptist. Office: U Utah Metall Engring 135 S 1460 E Rm 412 Salt Lake City UT 84112-0114 Office Phone: 801-581-5160. Business E-Mail: jdmiller@mines.utah.edu.

MILLER, JAN PAUL, lawyer; b. Md. married; 2 children. Bachelor, U. N.C., 1982; grad. cum laude, Harvard U., 1985. Adj. prof. George Washington U., Washington; asst. U.S. atty. Dist. Md., 1989—2002; U.S. atty. Ctrl. Dist. Ill., 2002—. Chief narcotics prosecution unit Dist. Md., 1992; pros. atty. So. Divsn. Dist. Md., 1995, sr. litigation counsel, 2000. Recipient numerous commendations from law enforcement agencies, including FBI, U.S. Customs Svc., Drug Enforcement Adminstrn., U.S. Secret Svc., U.S. Postal Ins. Office: Ctrl Dist Ill 600 E Monroe St Ste 312 Springfield IL 62701

MILLER, JANEL HOWELL, psychologist; b. Boone, N.C., May 18, 1947; d. John Estle and Grace Louise (Hemberger) Howell; m. C. Rick Miller, Nov. 24, 1968; children: Kimberly, Brian, Audrey, Rachel. BA, DePauw U., 1969; postgrad., Rice U., 1969; MA, U. Houston, 1972; PhD, Tex. A&M U., 1979. Lic. clin. psychologist, sch. psychologist, Tex. Assoc. sch. psychologist Houston Ind. Sch. Dist., 1971-74; rsch. psychologist VA Hosp., Houston, 1972; assoc. sch. psychologist Clear Creek (Tex.) Ind. Sch. Dist., 1974-76; instr. psychology, counseling psychology intern Tex. A&M U., 1976-77; clin. psychology intern VA Hosp., Houston, 1977-78; coord. psychol. svcs. Clear Creek Ind. Sch. Dist., 1978-81, assoc. dir. psychol. svcs., 1981-82; pvt. practice Houston, 1982—. Faculty U. Houston-Clear Lake, 1984—; adolescent suicide cons., 1984—. DePauw U. alumni scholar, 1965-69; NIMH fellow U. Houston, 1970-71. Mem. APA, Am. Assn. Marriage and Family Therapists, Soc. for Personality Assessment, Am. Coll. Forensic Examiners, Internat. Rorschach Soc., Tex. Psychol. Assn., Tex. Assn. Marriage and Family Therapists, Houston Psychol. Assn. (media rep. 1984-85), Houston Assn. Marriage and Family Therapists. Home: 806 Walbrook Dr Houston TX 77062-4030 Office: 16854 Royal Crest Dr Houston TX 77058-2529 Office Phone: 281-461-4098. Business E-Mail: shrinkskate@sbcglobal.net.

MILLER, JANICE, electronics executive; B in Polit. Sci., U. Ariz.; MBA in Fin., Ariz. State U. With McDonnell Douglas; mng. dir. strategic planning Best Western Internat.; v.p. corp. strategic planning Avnet, Phoenix, 2001—02, v.p., dir. orgnl. devel., 2002. Mem. Gov.'s Ariz.-Mex. Commn. Bd., 2003; chmn. strategic planning com. United Way; bd. dirs. Centennial Village Housing Project, Strategic Leadership Forum. Office: Avnet Inc 2211 S 47th St Phoenix AZ 85034

MILLER, JEAN PATRICIA SALMON, art educator; b. Little Falls, Minn., Sept. 28, 1920; d. Albert Michael and Wilma (Kaestner) Salmon; m. George Fricke Miller, Sept. 8, 1951 (dec. Apr. 1991); children: Victoria Jean, George Laurids. BS, St. Cloud State Tchrs. Coll., 1942; MS, U. Wis., Whitewater, 1976. Lic. cert. secondary English, art, Wis. Tchr. elem. and secondary art Pub. Schs. Sauk Center, Minn., 1943; tchr. secondary art Bd. Edn., Idaho, 1945; tchr. elem. and secondary art Elkhorn (Wis.) Area Schs., 1950-78; tchr. art adult edn. Kenosha Tech. Coll., Elkhorn, Wis., 1969; cooperating tchr., supr. art majors in edn. U. Wis., Whitewater, 1970-77. Coord. Art Train Project, Walworth County. Represented in permanent collections Irwin L. Young Auditorium, U. Wis., Whitewater. Sec. Walworth County Needs of Children and Youth, Williams Bay, Wis., 1956-57; co-chair, sponsor Senate Bill 161-art requirement for h.s. grad., 1988-89. Recipient Grand award painting Walworth County Fair, 1970, 3rd award painting Geneva Lake Art Assn., Lake Geneva, Wis., Acrylic Painting First award Badlants Art Assn., 1994. Mem. Nat. Art Edn. Assn., Wis. Women in Arts, Wis. Art Edn. Assn., Wis. Regional Artists Assn. (co-chmn. Wis. regional art program 1992, 93, corr. sec. 1992—), Walworth County Art Assn. (bd. dirs. 1979-94, pres. 1986-87), Badlands Art Assn., Kiwanis, Elks, Alpha Delta Kappa (pres. Theta chpt. Wis. 1968-70), Delta Kappa Gamma (Iota chpt.). Home and Office: PO Box 26 Taylor ND 58656-0026

MILLER, JEANNE-MARIE ANDERSON (MRS. NATHAN J. MILLER), English language educator, academic administrator; b. Washington, Feb. 18, 1937; d. William and Agnes Catherine (Johns) Anderson m. Nathan John Miller, Oct. 2, 1960. BA, Howard U., 1959, MA, 1963, PhD, 1976. Instr. dept. English Howard U., Washington, 1963-76, asst. prof., 1976-79, assoc. prof., 1979-92, prof., 1992-97, prof. emeritus, 1997—, asst. dir. Inst. Arts and Humanities, 1973-75, asst. acad. planning, office v.p. for acad. affairs, 1976-90. Cons. Am. Studies Assn., 1972-75, Silver Burdett Pub. Co., NEH, 1978—; mem. adv. bd. D.C. Libr. for Arts, 1973—. Editor, Black Theatre Bull., 1977-86; Realism to Ritual: Form and Style in Black Theatre, 1983; assoc. editor Theatre Jour., 1980-81; contbr. articles to profl. jours. and books. Mem. Washington Performing Arts Soc., 1971—, Friends of Sta. WETA-TV, 1971—, Mus. African Art, 1971—, Arena Stage Assocs., 1972—, Washington Opera Guild, 1982—, Wolf Trap Assocs., 1982—, Drama League N.Y., 1995, Shakespeare Theatre, 2001—, Met. Opera Guild, 2002—. Ford Found. fellow, 1970-72, So. Fellowships Fund fellow, 1973-74; Howard U. rsch. grant, 1975-76, 94-97, ACLS grant, 1978-79, NEH grant, 1981-84. Mem.: LWV (D.C. chpt.), MLA, ACLU, AAUP, Folger Shakespeare Libr., Acad. Am. Poets, Am. Theatre and Drama Soc., Studio Mus. Harlem, Nat. Mus. Women in Arts, Nat. Bldg. Mus., Winterthur Guild, Hist. Soc. Washington, D.C. Preservation League, Nat. Trust Historic Preservation, Zora Neale Hurston Soc., Langston Hughes Soc., Ibsen Soc., Friends of Kennedy Ctr. for Performing Arts, Am. Assn. Higher Edn., Coll. Lang. Assn., Common Cause, Am. Assn. Higher Edn., Am. Studies Assn., Coll. English Assn., Nat. Coun. Tchrs. English, Sierra Club, Pi Lambda Theta. Democrat. Episcopalian. Home: 504 24th St NE Washington DC 20002-4818

MILLER, JEFF, congressman; b. St. Petersburg, Fla., June 27, 1959; m. Griswold Vicki Miller; 2 children. BA, U. Fla., 1984. Mem. Fla. Ho. of Reps., 1998—2002, U.S. Congress from 1st Fla. Dist., 2002—. Past chmn. Escambia County Legislative Del., 1999—2000. Mem. Fla. Hist. Soc., various areas of C. of C., Elizabeth Chapel United Meth. Ch., Chumuckla; mem. bd. dirs. Santa Rose County United Way; Pregnancy Resource Ctr. Milton Milton; Gulf Coast Coun. Boy Scouts Am.; Fla. FFA Found. Mem.: Coun. Ready Infrastructure, Com. on Rules, Ethics and Elections, Com. on Gen. Govt. Appropriations, Congl. Redistricting Com., Utilities and Telecommunications Com. (chmn.), Com. on Vet. Affairs, Ho. Armed Svcs. Com. Republican. Office: Congress 331 Cannon HOB Washington DC 20515-0901

MILLER, JERRY ALLAN, JR., pediatrician; b. Abingdon, Va., May 31, 1951; MD, Med. Coll. Ga., Augusta, 1976. Diplomate Am. Bd. Pediat. Intern in family practice U. Tex. Med. Sch., Houston, 1976-77, resident in pediatrics, 1977-80; with Nat. Health Svc. Corps, Thomson, Ga., 1980-82; pvt. practice Augusta (Ga.) Pediatric Assocs., 1982—. Chmn. bd. dirs. Summer Med. Inst., Phila., Augusta, 1992-96. Fellow Am. Acad. Pediat.; mem. Phi Beta Kappa, Alpha Omega Alpha. Presbyterian. Avocations: tennis, surfing. Office: Augusta Pediatric Assocs PC 1230 Augusta West Pkwy Augusta GA 30909-1854

MILLER, JERRY HUBER, retired university chancellor; b. Salem, Ohio, June 15, 1931; s. Duber Daniel and Ida Claire (Holdereith) M.; m. Margaret A. Setter, 1958; children: Gregory, Joy, Carol, Beth, David. BA, Harvard U., 1953; MDiv., Hamma Sch. Theology, 1957; DD (hon.), Trinity Luth. Sem., 1981. Ordained to ministry Luth. Ch., 1957. Research assoc., intern Cornell U., Ithaca, N.Y., 1955-56; instr. Wittenberg U., Springfield, Ohio, 1956-57; parish pastor Ch. of Good Shepherd, Cin., 1957-62; asst. to pres. Ohio Synod Luth. Ch. Am., 1962-66; sr. campus pastor, dir. campus ministry U. Wis., Madison, 1966-69; regional dir. Nat. Luth. Campus Ministry, Madison, 1969-76, exec. dir. Chgo., 1977-81; pres. Calif. Luth. U., Thousand Oaks, 1981-92, chancellor, 1992-94, pres. emeritus, 1994—; ret. Ventura County Maritime Mus., Channel Islands Harbor, Calif., 1993-95. Chmn. Los Robles Bank, Thousand Oaks, 1987-2000; mem. exec. com. Coun. Ind. Colls., Washington, Assn. Ind. Calif. Colls. and Univs., 1981-92, Coun. Luth. Colls., Luth. Ednl. Conf. N.Am., 1977-94; vice chair bd. behavioral sci. State Calif.; bd. dirs. Santa Barbara Bank and Trust. Editor: The Higher Disciplines, 1956; contbr. articles to profl. jours. Bd. dirs. Wittenberg U., Augustana Coll., Rock Island, Ill., United Way, Thousand oaks, Ventura County chpt. ARC, Thousand Oaks, YMCA; chmn. bd. dirs. Los Robles Hosp.; vice chair Stagecoach Inn Mus. Found., 1998—; bd. trustees Ventura County Maritime Mus., 1993—. Named Man of Yr., Salem, 1975, Man of Yr. Conejo Valley, 1999; Siebert Found. fellow, 1975. Mem. Am. Assn. Higher Edn., Council Advancement and Support Edn., Harvard Alumni Assn., Western Coll. Assn. (bd. dirs.), Conejo Valley C. of C. (bd. dirs.), Conejo Symphony Orch. (bd. dirs.), Conejo Valley Hist. Soc. (bd. dirs. 1995—). Clubs: Harvard (Ill., Ohio, Wis., Calif.), YMCA (regional bd. dirs., vice chair 1996-99), Rotary. Avocations: skiing, golf, hiking, travel. E-mail: msmjhm@aol.com.

MILLER, JO CAROLYN DENDY, family and marriage counselor, educator; b. Gorman, Tex., Sept. 16, 1942; d. Leonard Lee and Vera Vertie (Robison) Dendy; m. Douglas Terry Barnes, June 1, 1963 (div. June 1975); children: Douglas Alan, Bradley Jason; m. Walton Sansom Miller, Sept. 19, 1982. BA, Tarleton State U., 1964; MEd, U. North State, 1977; PhD, Tex. Woman's U., 1993. Tchr. Mineral Wells (Tex.) H.S., 1964-65, Weatherford (Tex.) Mid. Sch., 1969-74; counselor, instr. psychology Tarrant County Jr. Coll., Hurst, Tex., 1977-82; pvt. practice family and marriage counseling Dallas, 1982—. Author: (with Velma Baker, Jeannene Ward) Becoming: A Human Relations Workbook, 1981. Mem. ACA, Tex. State Bd. Examiners Profl. Counselors, Tex. State Bd. Marriage and Family Therapists, Tex. Counseling Assn., North Ctrl. Tex. Counseling Assn., Dallas Symphony Orch. League, Nat. Coun. Family Rels., Tex. Mental Health Counselors Assn., Internat. Assn. for Marriage and Family Counselors. Methodist. Office: Jo Carolyn Dendy Miller, PhD 8222 Douglas Ave Ste 777 Dallas TX 75225-5938 Office Phone: 214-691-0400.

MILLER, JOHN DAVID, manufacturing executive; b. Utica, N.Y., Mar. 24, 1945; s. David Gordon and Eleanor Katherine (Brant) M., m. Ann Geraldine Johnston, Feb. 25, 1968; children: Shannon, Adra. BSME, Rochester Inst. Tech., 1968. Jr. engr. Pall Corp., Cortland, N.Y., 1968-70; staff engr., 1970-71; group leader Pall Corp., Cortland, N.Y., 1971-76, mgr. filter design, 1976-78, v.p., tech. dir., 1978-86, sr. v.p., dir. R&D, 1986-2000, chief tech. officer, 2000—. Patentee filter equipment. Mem. ASME. Unitarian Universalist. Avocations: song writing, sculpture, rowing, squash. Office: Pall Corp 25 Harbor Park Dr Port Washington NY 11050-4664

MILLER, JOHN EDDIE, lawyer; b. Wayne, Mich., Nov. 14, 1945; s. George Hayden and Georgia Irene (Stevenson) M.; m. Nancy Carol Sanders, Jan. 7, 1968; children: Andrea Christine, Matthew Kit. BA, Baylor U., 1967; JD, U. Memphis, 1973; LLM, U. Mo., 1980. Bar: Mo. 1974, U.S. Dist. Ct. (we. dist.) Mo. 1974, Tex. 1982. Asst. prof. Central Mo. State U., Warrensburg, 1973-74; sole practice Sedalia, Mo., 1974-79; sr. contract adminstr. Midwest Research Inst., Kansas City, Mo., 1979-81, Tracor Inc., Austin, Tex., 1981-84; contract negotiator Tex. Instruments, Austin, 1984-86; sr. contract adminstr. Tracor Aerospace Inc., Austin, 1986-87, Radian Corp., Austin, 1987-96; counsel., asst. co. sec. Radian Internat. LLC, Austin, 1996—. Corp. sec. Radian Southeast Asia Ltd., Bangkok, 1995—, dir. Radian Southeast Asia Ltd., Bangkok, 1996—; corp. sec. Radian Internat. Overseas Mgmt. Co., 1996—; instr. bus. law State Fair CC, Sedalia, 1974-79, Austin CC, 1983-84. Bd. dirs. Legal Aid Western Mo., 1977—79, Boy's Club, Sedalia, 1974—79. Served with U.S. Army, 1968—71. Mem.: U.S. Tennis Assn., Tex. Bar Assn. (intellectual property law sect., internat. law sect., computer law sect.), Mo. Bar Assn. (internat. law com., patent, trademark and copyright law com., tech. law com.), Phi Alpha Delta. Office Phone: 512-231-6062. E-mail: johnemiller@excite.com., ttjohnemiller@hotmail.com.

MILLER, JOHN GRIDER, writer; b. Annapolis, Md., Aug. 23, 1935; s. John Stanley and Ruby Corinne (Young) M.; m. Susan Bradner Bailey, Oct. 26, 1974; children: Kerry, John, Alison. BA, Yale U., 1957. Commd. 2d lt. USMC, 1957, advanced through grades to col., inf./ops. advisor Vietnamese Marine Corps., 1970-71, prin. speechwriter for Commandant, 1971-76, commd. officer Battalion Landing Team, 1977-78, asst. chief of staff ops. and plans III Amphibious Force, 1982-83, dep. dir. Marine Corps History Washington, 1983-85, ret., 1985; mng. editor Procs. and Naval History U.S. Naval Inst., Annapolis, Md., 1985-2000. Author: The Battle to Save the Houston, 1985, (Pocket Books edit., 1992, Bluejacket edit., 2000), The Bridge at Dong Ha, 1989, (Dell edit. 1990, Bluejacket edit., 1996, Audiobook edit., 1997), Punching Out: A Guide to Post-Military Transition, 1994, The Co-Vans: U.S. Marine Advisors in Vietnam, 2000; contbf. author: The Marines, 1998, Commandants of the Marine Corps, 2004. Decorated Legion of Merit with gold star, Bronze Star with combat V, Cross of Gallantry, Vietnamese Marine Corps.; recipient Author of Yr. award Naval Inst., 1990, Alfred Thayer Mahan award Navy League of U.S., 2002. Mem. Marine Corps. Hist. Found. (bd. dirs., Gen. Wallace M. Greene Jr. Book award 1989, Disting. Svc. award 1998), Mil. Order of World Wars (past chpt. comdr., chmn. nat. mag. com.), Civitan Internat. (past chpt. pres.), Washington Naval and Maritime Corrs.' Cir., New Providence Club, Annapolis Chorale. Avocations: music, piano, choral singing, boating. Home: 21 Sands Ave Annapolis MD 21403-4426 E-mail: millerjohng@comcast.net.

MILLER, JOHN LAURENCE, professional golfer; b. San Francisco, Apr. 29, 1947; s. Laurence O. and Ida (Meldrum) M.; m. Linda Strouse, Sept. 17, 1969; children: John Strouse, Kelly, Casi, Scott, Brent, Todd. Student, Brigham Young U., 1965-69. Profl. golfer, 1969—. Pres. Johnny Miller Enterprises, Inc.; golf commentator, NBC. Author: Pure Golf, 1976, Johnny Miller's Golf for Juniors, 1987. Named PGA Player of Yr., 1974; elected to Golf Hall of Fame, 1999. Achievements include major tournaments won in the Southern Open, 1971, Heritage Classic, 1972, 74, Ortago Golf Classic, New Zealand, 1972, U.S. Open at Oakmont County Club, 1973, Lancome Trophy Tournament, Paris 1973, 74, Bing Crosby Pro Am, 1974, Phoenix Open, 1974, 75, Dean Martin-Tucson Open, 1974, 75, Tournament of Champions, 1974, Westchester Classic, 1974, World Open, 1974, Dunlop Phoenix, Japan, 1974, Kaiser Internat., 1974, 75, Bob Hope Desert Classic, 1975, 76, British Open Crown, 1976, NBC Tucson Open, 1976, Jackie Gleason Inverarry Classic, 1980, Sun City, 1981, Joe Garagiola Tucson Open, 1981, Glen Campbell L.A. Open, 1981, Wickes Andy Williams San Diego Open, 1982, Honda Inverrary Classic, 1983, AT&T Pebble Beach Nat. Pro-Am, 1987, 94, World Cup individual titles, 1973, 75, Ryder Cup, 1975, 81. Office: PGA Am/Sr Tour 100 Ave of the Champions PO Box 109601 Palm Beach Gardens FL 33410-9601 also: NBC Sports 30 Rockefeller Plz Fl 2 New York NY 10112-0002

MILLER, JOHN LEED, lawyer; b. Geneva, Ill., May 7, 1949; s. John Axel and Martha Mary (Masilunis) M.; m. Roosy Yanti, Jan. 2, 2001. BA, Northwestern U., 1971; JD, U. Chgo., 1975. Bar: Ill. 1975, U.S. Dist. Ct. (no. dist.) Ill., U.S. Ct. Appeals (7th and 8th cirs.). Assoc. counsel Profl. Ind. Mass-Mktg. Adminstrs., Chgo., 1975-76; legis. counsel to minority leader Ill. Ho. of Reps., Chgo. and Springfield, Ill., 1977-80, chief legal counsel, 1980, chief counsel to spkr., 1981-83; ptnr. Shaw and Miller, Chgo., 1981-84, Theodore A. Woerthwein, Chgo., 1984-85, Woerthwein & Miller, Chgo., 1985—. Joint sec., sec. Asian Am. Coalition of Chgo., 2003—04. Statewide chmn. Ill. Young Voters for the Pres., 1972; dir. Ill. Ho. Rep. campaign com., 1976, 78, cons., 1982; pres. Newberry Pla. Condominium Assn., 1989-94. With ISNG, 1969-75. James scholar, 1970. Mem. Lawyers for the Creative Arts, Primitive Art Soc. Chgo. (treas. 1984-86, v.p. 1987, pres. 1988-89), Indonesia-Am. Assn. Ill. (bd. dirs.), Adventurers Club (participant first descent of Boh River, Borneo), Phi Eta Sigma, Phi Beta Kappa. Moslem. Office: Woerthwein & Miller PO Box A 3612 Chicago IL 60690-3612 Home: 4030 Enfield Ave Skokie IL 60076-1934

MILLER, JOHN NELSON, banker, educator; b. Youngstown, Ohio, Sept. 15, 1948; s. W. Frederic and Julia Elizabeth (Lohman) M. MusB in Cello, Westminster Coll., 1970; MBA in Fin., U. Pa., 1974. Asst. br. mgr. Mahoning Nat. Bank, Youngstown, 1970—72; asst. dir. fin. svcs. dept. Mellon Bank N.Am., Pitts., 1974—76; v.p., head cash mgmt. divsn. Md. Nat. Bank, Balt., 1976—79; v.p., mgr. corp. cash mgmt. divsn. N.Y. Bank of Am., N.Y.C., 1978—80; dir. cash mgmt., strategic planning, product mgmt. and tng. Bank of Am. S.F., 1980—81; v.p., global account officer for utilities/telecomm. Bank of Am., N.Y.C., 1981—84, team leader, CFO, corp. payment divsn. large corp. sales, 1984—87, mgr. credit preparation and analysis unit N.Am. divsn., 1987—88; v.p., ea. region mgr. cash mgmt. divsn. Wells Fargo Bank of N.Y., 1988—90, v.p., mgr. Ea., Midwestern, Rocky Mt., Pacific & nat., 1990—93; v.p. and group sales mgr. Bank of Am., NT and SA Fgn. Currency Svcs., San Francisco, 1993—94; v.p., regional sales mgr. Bank of Am. Global Payment Svcs., Bank of Am., 1994—99; sr. v.p. Global Payment Svcs. Bank of Am., 1999—2004; svc. mgr. EVP Sales NA, Concord, Calif., 2004—. Lectr. Wharton Grad. Sch., U. Pa., Am. Mgmt. Assn. cash mgmt. seminars, Bank Adminstrn. Inst.; spkr. Payment Sys. Inc., Corp. EFT Seminar, Atlanta, Nat. Conf. Treasury Mgmt. Assn.; mem. Corp. Payment Task Force, N.Y.C., Corp. EFT Cost-Benefit Task Force. Chmn. ann. giving program Wharton Grad. Sch., 1977-79; trustee San Francisco Performances, 1993-99; bd. trustees Westminster Coll., New Wilmington, Pa., 2003—; mem. exec. bd. Diablo Silverado coun. Boy Scouts Am. Mem. Wharton Grad. Sch. Alumni Assn., (pres. local club, rep., nat. dir., exec. com.), Bank Adminstrn. Inst. (subcom. interindustry commn.), Am. Nat. Stds. Inst. (subcom. interindustry optical scan stds.) Cash Mgmt. Inst. (dir.), Omicron Delta Kappa, Mchts. Club Balt., Univ. Club Pitts., Rotary. Office: CA4-706-06-01 1850 Gateway Blvd Concord CA 94520-3282

MILLER, JOHN PETER (JACK MILLER), journalist; b. Aug. 3, 1928; s. Wesley and Margaret (Baker) M.; m. Helen DeMars, July 30, 1949; children: Candice(dec.), Gregory(dec.). Student, Welland and Toronto. From sports page editor to front page editor Welland Evening Tribune, 1949—53; with Hamilton (Ont.) Spectator, 1953—71, radio and TV columnist, 1955—71; with Toronto Daily Star, 1971—91, radio and TV columnist, 1971—78, comm. editor, 1979—85, sci. columnist, 1982—85, sci. writer, 1985—89, sci. editor, 1989—91, sci. corr., 1991—95; prof. journalism NIagara Coll., 1996—99. Frequent TV and radio appearances. Contbr. stories to mags. Mem.: Can. Sci. Writers Assn. (2 writing awards 1985, writing award 1987, 2 writing awards 1988, writing award 1989). Office: 162 Martindale Rd Apt 103 Saint Catharines ON Canada L2S 3S4 E-mail: deejackmiller@yahoo.com.

MILLER, JOHN R. accountant; b. Wilkes-Barre, Pa., Nov. 28, 1946; s. John Turner and Elsie May (Johns) M.; children: Stephen, Jo-El. BS in Commerce and Fin., Wilkes U., 1968. CPA, Pa., N.Y.; cert. govt. fin. mgr. Audit exec. Com. of Pa., Harrisburg, 1971-73; sr. acct. KPMG LLP, Phila., 1968-71, mgr. Harrisburg, 1973-76, sr. mgr. N.Y.C., 1976-79, ptnr., 1979—, ptnr.-in-charge Metro N.Y. govt. practices, 1993-95, also bd. dirs., ptnr.-in-charge of nat. assurance and resource mgmt. practices, 1995-97; northeast regional ptnr.-in-charge KPMG Cons., N.Y.C., 1997; nat. mng. ptnr. pub. svcs. mgmt. com. KPMG LLP, N.Y.C., 1997-98, vice chmn. health care and public sector, 1998—; vice-chmn. KPMG N.Y. Found., 1997—; chair Global Govt. KPMG, N.Y.C. Mem. U.S. Auditing Standards Adv. Coun., Washington, 1990-93, 97-98, chair, 2001—; mem. Govtl. Acctg. Standards Adv. Coun., Norwalk, Conn., 1987-91. Bd. dirs. Rye (N.Y.) YMCA, 1988-97, Osborn Retirement Community, 1991—. Wilkes U., 1999—; mem. Nat. Civic League, Denver, 1985—95; trustee Citizens Budget Commn., N.Y.C., 1985—2002; Prin. Coun. for Excellence in Govt., Washington, 1987—; bd. advisors Chariot Capital; vestry mem. Trinity Ch.; trustee and regent Cath. of St. John, The Divine. Recipient Ellis Island medal of honor, 2002. Mem. AICPA (chmn. govt. acctg. and auditing com. 1987-90, chmn. audit quality 1991-95, chmn. govt. and nonprofit expert panel 2000—03), Pa. Inst. CPAs (Leadership award 1968), N.Y. State Soc. CPAs, Masons, Coveleigh Club, Sky Club, Assn. of Govt. Accts. (Einhorn-Gary Outstanding Contbn. award 2000, Andy Barr award for leadership excellence 2001), Soc. of Magi. Episcopalian. Avocations: travel, reading, sports. Office: KPMG LLP 345 Park Ave New York NY 10154-0004 Office Phone: 212-872-5833.

MILLER, JOHN RICHARD, interior designer; b. Washington, Feb. 11, 1927; s. John Henry and Helen (Vermillion) M.; m. Audrey Gene Owens, Nov. 6, 1946; children: Pamela Dawn, Felicity Amanda, Timothy John. Diploma in interior design, Colbert Inst., Washington, 1950. Designer Hollidge Interiors, Washington, 1950-51; pres. Miller's Interiors Inc., Temple Hills, Md., 1951—. Bd. dirs. St. Barnabas Venture, Temple Hills. Author: Training for Design Related Trades, 1976; columnist Washington Star, 1971-79. Mem. Pres.'s Com. on Employment of Handicapped, 1978-82, White House Design Com., 1969-74, Presdl. Barrier Free Design Com., 1972-80. With USN, 1944-46, PTO. Fellow Am. Soc. Interior Designers (pres. Potomac chpt. 1973-80, nat. dir. 1960-74, chmn. opportunity guidance coun. 1972-74); mem. Nat. Soc. Interior Designers (pres. Potomac chpt. 1974-76), Tantallon Country Club (Oxon Hill, Md.). Democrat. Episcopalian. Avocations: tennis, reading. Home: 13710 Piscataway Dr Fort Washington MD 20744-6634 Office: Millers Interiors Inc 13710 Piscataway Dr Fort Washington MD 20744

MILLER, JOHN RIPIN, federal agency administrator, former congressman; b. N.Y.C., May 23, 1938; m. June Marion Hamula BA, Bucknell U., 1959; MA, JD, Yale U., 1964. Bar: Wash. Asst. atty. gen. State of Wash., 1965-68; practice law, 1968-72; pres. Seattle City Council, 1972-80; adj. prof. govt. law U. Puget Sound, 1981-84; mem. 99th-102d Congresses from 1st Wash. Dist., 1985—93; dir. & sr. adv. Office to Combat Trafficking in Persons U.S. Dept. State, Wash., DC, 2002—04, dir., Office to Monitor & Combat Trafficking, 2004—. Chmn. Discovery Inst. Cascadia Project, Seattle, 1992—2003. Recipient Humanitarian award, Discovery Inst., 2004. Mem. Wash. State Bar Assn. Office: Harry S Truman Bldg 2201 C St NW Rm 7226 Washington DC 20520*

MILLER, JOHN ROBERT, oil industry executive; b. Lima, Ohio, Dec. 28, 1937; s. John O. and Mary L. (Zickafoose) M.; m. Karen A. Eier, Dec. 30, 1961; children: Robert A., Lisa A., James E. BSChE with honors, U. Cin., 1960, D.Comml. Sc. hon., 1983. With Standard Oil Co., Cleve., 1960-86, dir. fin., 1974-75, v.p. fin., 1975-78, v.p. transp., 1978-79, sr. v.p. tech. and chems., 1979-80, pres., COO, bd. dirs., 1980—86; chmn., CEO TBN Holdings, Cleve., 1986—2000, Petroleum Ptnrs., Cleve., 2000—03. Bd. dirs. Cambrex Corp., Eaton Corp., Graphic Packaging Corp.; former chmn. Fed. Res. Bank, Cleve. Mem. Pepper Pike Club, The Country Club, Chagrin Valley Hunt Club, Tau Beta Pi. Office: 29325 Chagrin Blvd Ste 301 Cleveland OH 44122 Office Phone: 216-464-4614. Business E-Mail: office@johnrmiller.com.

MILLER, JOHN RONALD, minister; b. L.A., Jan. 4, 1938; s. Clarence Raymond and Yolanda Sarah (Capenaro) M.; m. Madelon Louise Tetaz, Mar. 26, 1966; children: Sarah Louise, John Ronald. BA, Southwestern Coll., 1960; MDiv, Drew U., 1963; MA, Rutgers U., 1966. Ordained to ministry United Meth. Ch., 1965, United Ch. Christ, 1966. Pastor Burden (Kans.) Meth. Ch., 1958-60; min. Wilson Meml. Union Ch., Watchung, N.J., 1961—. Mem. Consultation on Ch. Union, Princeton, N.J., 1982—, com. on disabled United Ch. of Christ, Montclair, N.J., 1982—. Chmn. Dorthea Dix Chapel Bldg. Program; pres. Trenton Psychiat. Hosp.-State of N.J., 1985; mem. N.J. State Bd. Human Svcs., 1996—. Southwestern Coll. scholar, 1960, Tipple scholar, 1960. Mem. Nat. Coun. Chs. of Jesus Christ (governing bd. 1985—), Internat. Coun. Community Chs. (moderator ecumenical commn. 1984—, regional trustee, exec. bd. 1987, v.p. exec. bd. 1991, pres. communion 1995-97), Optimists. Mem. United Ch. Of Christ. Office: Mary E Wilson Meml Union Ch 7 Valley Rd Watchung NJ 07069-6034 Office Phone: 908-755-5020.

MILLER, JOHN T., JR., lawyer, educator; b. Waterbury, Conn., Aug. 10, 1922; s. John T. and Anna (Purdy) M.; children: Kent, Lauren, Clare, Miriam, Michael, Sheila, Lisa, Colin, Margaret. AB with high honors, Clark U., 1944; JD, Georgetown U., 1948; Docteur en Droit, U. Geneva, 1951; postgrad., U. Paris, 1951. Bar: Conn. 1949 (inactive), D.C. 1950, U.S. Ct. Appeals (2d, 3d, 5th, 10th, 11th and D.C. cirs.), U.S. Supreme Ct. 1952. With Econ. Cooperation Adminstn. Am. Embassy, London, 1950-51; assoc. Covington & Burling, 1952-53, Gallagher, Connor & Boland, 1953-62; pvt. practice Washington, 1962—. Adj. prof. law Georgetown U. Law Ctr., Washington, 1959—; mem. Panel on Future of Internat. Ct. Justice. Co-author: Regulation of Trade, 1953, Modern American Antitrust Law, 1958, Major American Antitrust Laws, 1965; author: Foreign Trade in Gas and Electricity in North America: A Legal and Historical Study, 1970, Energy Problems and the Federal Government: Cases and Material, 8th edit., 1996, Deregulated Natural Gas and Electric Power Industries Seminar: Case Material, 4th edit., 2004; contbr. articles to profl. jours. Trustee Clark U., 1970-76, De Sales Sch. of Theology, 1993-97; mem. bd. advisors Georgetown Visitation Prep. Sch., 1978-94, trustee, 1994-96, emeritus trustee, 1996—; former fin. chmn. troop 46 Nat. Capital Area coun. Boy Scouts Am.; pres. Thomas More Soc. Am., 1996-97. 1st lt. U.S. Army, 1943-46, 48-49. Decorated Bronze Star; recipient 10 yr. teaching award Nat. Jud. Coll., 1983. Mem. ABA (coun., chmn. adminstrv. law sect. 1972-73, ho. dels. 1991-93), AAUP, D.C. Bar Assn., Energy Bar Assn. (pres. 1990-91), Congl. Country Club, Army and Navy Club (bd. govs. 2000—), DACOR, Prettyman-Leventhal Am. Inn of Ct. (master 1988-99, pres. 1995-96), Sovereign Mil. Order of Malta (knight). Republican. Roman Catholic. Home: 4721 Rodman St NW Washington DC 20016-3234 Office: 1001 Connecticut Ave NW Washington DC 20036-5504 E-mail: jtmillerjr@erols.com.

MILLER, J(OHN) WESLEY, III, lawyer; b. Springfield, Mass., Oct. 3, 1941; s. John Wesley Jr. and Blanche Ethel Miller. AB, Colby Coll., 1963; AM, Harvard U., 1964, JD, 1981. Bar: Mass. 1984, U.S. Dist. Ct. Mass. 1984, U.S. Supreme Ct. 1993. Instr. English Heidelberg Coll., Tiffin, Ohio, 1964-69, U. Wis., 1969-77; real estate broker, 1977-84. Founder Miller-Wilson Family Papers, U. Vt., Madison (Wis.) People's Poster and Propaganda Collection, St. Hist. Soc. Wis. Author: History of Buckingham Junior High School, 1956, The Millers of Roxham, 1958, Symphonic Heritage, 1959, Community Guide to Madison Murals, 1977, Aunt Jennie's Poems, 1986, Blanche and John's Fernbank: A Wilbraham Camping Experience, 2001; founding editor: Hein's Poetry and the Law Series, 1985—; editor: Curiosities and Law of Wills, 1989, Lawyers Alcove, 1990, Famous Divorces, 1991, Legal Laughs, 1993, Coke in Verse, 1999, Law and Lawyers Laid Open, 2002; founding editor: Law Libr. Microform Consortium Arts Law Letters Collection, 1991—; exhibitor A Salute to Street Art, State Hist. Soc. Wis., 1974; contbr. Poems of Ambrose Philips, 1969, Oxford English Dictionary, 1995—; postcard publishing, 1999-. Recipient Cmty. Activism award Bay State Objectivist, 1993, 94, 95; fellow Wisdom Hall of Fame, 2000, Samuel Victor Constant fellow, 2001. Mem. MLA, Am. Philol. Assn., Milton Soc., New Eng. Historic Geneal. Soc., Vt. Hist. Soc., Wis. Acad. Scis., Arts and Letters, Pilgrim Soc., Ancient and Hon. Arty. Co., Mayflower Soc., Soc. Colonial Wars, Sons and Daus. of the Victims of Colonial Witch Trials, Mensa, Springfield Renaissance Group. Office: 5 Birchland Ave Springfield MA 01119-2708 *The advancement of learning is my goal. Professionalism is the standard, and nothing else will do.*

MILLER, JOHN WILLIAM, JR., bassoonist; b. Balt., Mar. 11, 1942; s. John William and Alverta Evelyn M.; m. Sibylle Weigel, July 12, 1966 (div. 2000); children: Christian Desmond, Andrea Jocelyn, Claire Evelyn. BS, M.I.T., 1964; MusM with highest honors, New Eng. Conservatory, 1967, Artist's Diploma, 1969. Instr. bassoon Boston U., 1967-71, U. Minn., 1971—; prin. bassoonist, founding mem. Boston Philharmonia Chamber Orch., 1968-71; prin. bassoonist Minn. Orch., Mpls., 1971—. Dir. Boston Baroque Ensemble, 1963-71, John Miller Bassoon Symposium, 1984—; mem. Am. Reed Trio, 1977—; faculty Sarasota Music Festival, 1986—, Affinis Seminar, Japan, 1992; vis. faculty Banff Ctr. for Arts, 1987; faculty Nordic Bassoon Symposium, 1993—. Soloist on recs. for Cambridge, Mus. Heritage Soc., Pro Arte; featured guest artist 1st Internat. Bassoon Festival, Caracas, Venezuela, 1994. Recipient U.S. Govt. Fulbright award, 1964-65, Irwin Bodky award Cambridge Soc. Early Music, 1968 Mem. Internat. Double Reed Soc., Minn. Bassoon Assn. (founder) Home: 706 Lincoln Ave Saint Paul MN 55105-3533 Office: 1111 Nicollet Mall Minneapolis MN 55403-2406

MILLER, JON PHILIP, marketing and business development professional, pharmaceutical executive; b. Moline, Ill., Mar. 30, 1944; s. Clyde Sheldon and Alice Lenora (Taes) M.; m. Shirley Ann Hymes, Aug. 21, 1965; children: Melissa, Elizabeth. AB, Augustana Coll., 1966; PhD, St. Louis U., 1970; MBA, Pepperdine U., 1983. Rsch. assoc. to sr. biochemist ICN Pharm., Inc., Irvine, Calif., 1970-72, leader molecular pharmacology group, 1972-73, head molecular pharmacology/drug metabolism dept., 1973-76, dir. biology div., 1975-76; dir. SRI-NCI liaison group SRI Internat. (formally Stanford Rsch. Inst.), Menlo Park, Calif., 1976-78, sr. bioorganic chemist, 1978-80, head medicinal biochemistry program, 1980-84, dir. biotech. rsch. dept., 1982-85, dir. biotech. and biomed. rsch. lab., 1985-92, assoc. dir. life scis. div., 1989-92; dir. bus. devel., strategic mktg. MDS Panlabs, Inc., Bothell, Wash., 1992-98; dir. pharm. mktg. Applied Biosystems, Foster City, Calif., 1998—2001; dir. bus. devel. ACLARA Bioscis., Mountain View, Calif., 2001—03; pres. Miller & Co., Foster City, 2003—. Office: Miller & Co 1147 Blythe St Foster City CA 94404

MILLER, JONATHAN F. Internet company executive; V.p., programming and NBA entertainment NBA, NYC; launched Paramount Comedy Channel, London; joined Nickelodeon, 1993; CEO, mng. dir Nickelodeon UK, 1993; mng. dir. Nickelodeon Internat.; pres., CEO USA Broadcasting, 1997—99, USA Electronic Commerce Solutions, 1999—2000, USA Info. and Services (USAIS), 2000—02; CEO AOL, 2002—. Office: AOL 22000 AOL Way Dulles VA 20166 Office Phone: 703-265-1000.

MILLER, JONATHAN WOLFE, theater and film director, physician; b. London, July 21, 1934; s. Emanuel Miller; m. Helen Rachel Collet, 1956; 3 children. Ed., St. John's Coll., Cambridge U.; MB Ch, Univ. Coll. Hosp. Med. Sch., London, 1959; DLitt (hon.), U. Leicester, 1981, Cambridge U., 1996; Dr. (hon.), Open U., 1983. Dir. Nottingham Playhouse, 1963-69; assoc. dir. nat. Theatre, 1973-75; mem. Arts Coun., 1975-76; artistic dir. Old Vic, 1988-90; lectr. Nat. Gallery, 1995, Met. Mus., N.Y.C., 1995; curator major exhbn. Nat. Gallery, London, 1998. Vis. prof. drama Westfield Coll., U. London, 1977-78; lectr. wide variety of subjects. Co-author, actor in Beyond the Fringe, 1961-64; dir. Under Plain Cover Royal Ct. Theatre, 1962, The Old Glory, N.Y.C., 1964, Prometheus Bound, Yale Drama Sch., 1967, Oxford and Cambridge Shakespeare Co. prod. of Twelfth Night, on tour in U.s., 1969; dir. for Nat. Theatre, London: The Merchant of Venice, 1970, Danton's Death, 1971, The School for Scandal, 1972, The Marriage of Figaro, 1974; other prodns. include: The Tempest, London, 1970, Prometheus Bound, London, 1971, The Taming of the Shrew, Chichester, Eng., 1972, The Seagull, Chichester, 1973, The Malcontent, Nottingham, Eng., 1973, The Family in Love, 1974, The Importance of Being Earnest, 1975, All's Well That Ends Well, Measure For Measure, Greenwich Season, 1975, Three Sisters, 1977; dir. operas Arden Must Die, 1973, Sadler's Well Theatre, 1974, The Cunning Little Vixen, Glyndebourne, 1975, 77, Marriage of Figaro, Vienna State Opera, 1991, Robert Devereux, Monte Carlo, 1992, Die Gezeichnete, Zurich, 1992, Maria Stuarda, Monte Carlo, 1993, the Secret Marriage, Opera North, 1993; dir. for English Nat. Opera: The Marriage of Figaro, 1978, The Turn of the Screw, 1979, 91, Arabella, 1980, Othello, 1981, Rigoletto, 1982, 85 (alwo at Met. Opera, N.Y.C.), Fidelio, 1982, 83, Don Giovanni, 1985, The Magic Flute, 1986, Tosca, 1986, The Mikado, 1986, 88, The Barber of Seville, 1987, Cosi fan Tutte, 1995, Carmen, 1995; dir. for Kent Opera: Cosi Fan Tutte, 1975, Rigoletto, 1975, Orfeo, 1976, Eugene Onegin, 1977, La Traviata, 1979, 96, Falstaff, 1980, 81, Fiedlio, 1982, 83, 88; dir. for La Scala Milan: La Fanciulla del West, 1991, Manon Lescaut, 1992; dir. for Maggio Musicale, Florence: Don Giovanni, 1990, Cosísi fan Tutte, 1991, 94, Marriage of Figaro, 1992, La Bohéme, 1994, La Bohéme, which transfered to La Bastille, 1995, dir., Strass Ariadne auf Naxos, 1997; dir. Met. Opera, N.Y.: Katya Kabanova, 1991, Pelléas et Mélisande, 1995; dir in co-prodn. with L.A. Music Ctr. and Houston Grand Opera House Der Rosenkavalier, 1994; dir. Broadway play Long Day's Journey Into Night, 1986, The Taming of the Shrew at Royal Shakespeare Co., Stratford, 1987, Andromache, One Way Pendulum, Bussy D'Ambois, all at Vic, 1988, The Tempest, 1988, Turn of the Screw, 1989, Kimg Lear, 1989, The Liar, 1989; films include: Take a Girl Like You, 1969; TV films include: Whistle and I'll Come to You, 1967, Alice in Wonderland, 1967, The Body in Question Series, 1978, Henry the Sixth, part I, 1983, States of Mind Series, 1983; exec. prodr. Shakespeare TV series, 1979-81; author (TV) McLuhan, 1971, The Body in Question, 1978, States of Mind, The Facts of Life, Subsequent Performances, 1986, Who Cares, Born Talking, Museums of Madness, Anthropology, Opera Works; editor: Freud: The Man, His World, His Influence, 1972, The Don Giovanni Book, 1990; actor (TV) Jonathan Miller on Reflection, 1998, (TV mini-series) The Talk Show Story, 2000. Decorated Order of Brit. Empire; named Dir. of Yr., Soc. West End Theatre Awards, 1976; recipient Silver medal Royal TV Soc., 1981; fellow Univ. Coll. London; hon. fellow St. John's Coll., Cambridge U.; rsch. fellow in history of medicine Univ. Coll., London U., 1970-73. Fellow Royal Coll. Physicians (London and Edinburgh); mem. AAAS (fgn. mem.). Office: care IMG Artists 616 Chiswick High St London W45RX England

MILLER, JOSEF M. otolaryngologist, educator; b. Phila., Nov. 29, 1937; married, 1960; 3 children. BA in Psychology, U. Calif., Berkeley, 1961; PhD in Physiology and Psychology, U. Wash., 1965; MD (hon.), U. Göteborg, Sweden, 1987; MD (h.c.), U. Turku, Finland, 1995. USPHS fellow U. Mich., 1965-67, rsch. assoc., asst. prof. dept. Psychology, 1967-68, prof., dir. rsch. dept. Otolaryngology, dir. Kresge Hearing Rsch. Inst., 1984—; asst. prof. depts. Otolaryngology, Physiology and Biophysics U. Wash., Seattle, 1968-72, rsch. affiliate Regional Primate Rsch. Ctr, 1968-84, assoc. prof., 1972-76, acting chmn. dept. Otolaryngology, 1975-76, prof., 1976-84; Lunn and Ruth Townsend prof. comm., 1996—. Mem. study sect. Nat. Inst. Neurol. and Communicative Disorders and Stroke, NIH, 1978-84, ad hoc bd. dirs. sci. counselors, 1988; sci. rev. com. Deafness Rsch. Found., 1978-83, chair, 1983—; mem. faculty Nat. Conf. Rsch. Goals and Methods in Otolaryngology, 1982; adv. com. hearing, bio-acoustics and biomechanics Commn. Behavioral and Social Scis. and Edn., Nat. Rsch. Coun., 1983—; hon. com. Orgn. Nobel Symposium 63, Cellular Mechanisms in Hearing, Karlskoga, Sweden, 1985; cons. Otitis Media Rsch. Ctr., 1985-89, Pfizer Corp., 1988; faculty opponent U. Göteborg, Sweden, 1987; rsch. adv. com. Gallaudet Coll., 1987; chair external sci. adv. com. House Ear Inst., 1988-91; author authorizing legis. Nat. Inst. Deafness and Other Comm. Disorders, NIH, 1988, co-chair adv. bd. rsch. priorities com., bd. dirs. Friends adv. coun., 1989—, chair rsch. subcom., 1990-93, treas., bd. dirs., 1996—; grant reviewer Mich. State Rsch. Fund, NSF, VA; reviewer numerous jours. including Acta Otolaryngologica, Jour. Otology, Physiology and Behavior, Science. Mem. editorial bd. Am. Jour. Otolaryngology, 1981—, AMA, Am. Physiology Soc., Annals of Otology, Rhinology and Laryngology, 1980—, Archives of Oto-Rhino-Laryngology, 1985-93, Hearing Rsch., Jour. Am. Acad. Otolaryngology-Head and Neck Surgery, 1990—. Bd. dirs. Internat. Hearing Found., 1985—. Fellow U. Wash., 1962-65, Kresge Hearing Rsch. Inst., U. Mich., 1965-67; recipient award Am. Acad. Otolaryngology; grantee Deafness Rsch. Found., U. Wash., 1969-71; rsch. grantee NIH, 1969-73. Mem. AAAS, Am. Acad. Otolaryngology and Head and Neck Surgery (com. rsch. in otolaryngology 1971-82, continuing edn. com. 1975-79, NIH liaison com. 1988—, program steering com. jour. 1990, Pres. Citation 1997), Am. Auditory Soc., Am. Otological Soc., Am. Neurotological Soc., Am. Otologic Honor Soc., Acoustical Soc. Am. (com. rsch. psychol., physiol. acoustics 1969-78), Fedn. Am. Physiol. Soc., Fedn. Am. Socs. Exptl. Biology, Soc. Neurosci., Assn. Rsch. Otolaryngology (sec.-treas. 1979-80, pres. elect 1981, pres. 1982. program dir. mtg. 1983, award of merit com. 1985, 95-96, chair 1988, program dir., pres. symposium homeostatic mech. of inner ear 1993), Finnish Acad. Otolaryngology (hon.), Sigma Xi. Office: U Mich Kresge Hearing Rsch Inst 1301 E Ann St Rm R5032 Ann Arbor MI 48109-0506

MILLER, JOSEPH A. chemicals executive; b. West Pittston, Pa., Jan. 1942; BS, Va. Mil. Inst., 1963; PhD in Chemistry, Pa. State U., 1966. Various positions in R&D, mfg., bus., and mktg. E.I. DuPont de Nemours & Co., 1966—2001, sr. v.p., 1994-96, chief tech. officer, 1996, sr. v.p. R&D, 1994—2001, sr. v.p., chief tech. officer, 2001—02; exec. v.p., chief tech. officer Corning (N.Y.) Inc., 2002—. Mem. Ctr. Sci., Math. and Engring. Edn., NRC. Mem. U. Del. Rsch. Found.; bd. trustees U. Del.; mem. adv. bd. dept. chem. engring. U. Del., Ga. Tech.; co-chair commn. to reform sci. edn. in Del. pub. schs. Capt. U.S. Army, 1967-69. Pa. State U. Alumni fellow. Fellow AAAS; mem. NAE, AIChE, Am. Chem. Soc. (Barnes award for rsch. leadership 1998, mem. adv. steering com. for chemistry in a biol. context), Indsl. Rsch. Inst., Nat. Sci. Bd., Chem. Heritage Found., Coun. for Competi-

tiveness, Nat. Sci. and Tech. Bd. Internat. Adv. Panel of Singapore, Nat. Sci. Resources Ctr. (chmn. of bd.), Del. Sci., Math. and Tech. Edn. Found., Del. Pub. Policy Inst. Office: Corning One Riverfront Plaza Corning NY 14831*

MILLER, JOSEPH ARTHUR, manufacturing engineer, consultant; b. Brattleboro, Vt., Aug. 28, 1933; s. Joseph Maynard and Marjorie Antoinette (Hammerberg) Miller; m. Ardene Hedwig Barker, Aug. 19, 1956; children: Stephanie L., Jocelyn A., Shana L., Gregory J. BS in Agrl., Andrews U., Berrien Springs, Mich., 1955; MS in Agrl. Mechs., Mich. State U., 1959; EdD in Vocat. Edn., UCLA, 1973. Constrn. engr. Thornton Bldg. & Supply, Inc., Williamston, Mich., 1959-63, C & B Silo Co., Charlotte, Mich., 1963-64; instr. and dir. retraining Lansing C.C., Mich., 1964-68; asst. prof./prog. coord./coop coord. San Jose State U., 1968-79; mfg. specialist Lockheed Martin Missiles and Space (and predecessor cos.), Sunnyvale, Calif., 1979-81, rsch. specialist, 1981-88, NASA project mgr., 1982-83, staff engr., 1988-96, rsch. staff engr., 1996-98, coord. flexible mfg. system simulation project, 1994-96, team mem. federally funded AIMS Agile Mfg. project, 1995-97, team mem. corp funded machining outsource initative project, 1995-97, coord. productivity improvement program, 1996-98; engring. and constrn. cons. Berry Creek, Calif., 1998—. Agrl. engring. cons. USDA Poultry Expt. Sta., 1960—62; computer numerical control cons. Dynamechtronics, Inc., Sunnyvale, 1987—90; machining cons. Space Sys. divsn. Lockheed, 1986—96; instr. computer numerical control DeAnza Coll., Cupertino, Calif., 1985—88, Labor Employment Tng. Corp., San Jose, Calif., 1988—93; career counselor Pacific Union Coll., Angwin, Calif., 1985—92; instr. computer-aided mfg. and non traditional machining San Jose State U., 1994—97; team leader pursuit of excellence machine tool project Lockheed Martin Missiles and Space, Sunnyvale, 1990—95, coord. safety award program, 1997—98, mem. quality awareness program screening com., 1998. Author: Student Manual for CNC Lathe, 1990; contbr. articles to profl. jours. UCLA fellow, 1969—73. Mem.: Am. Soc. Indsl. Tech. (pres. 1980—81), Calif. Assn. Indsl. Tech. (pres. 1974—75, 1984—85), Nat. Assn. Indsl. Tech. (pres. industry divsn. 1987—88, mem., chmn. accreditation visitation teams 1984—, bd. cert. 1991—92), Soc. Mfg. Engr. (sr.; chmn. edn. com. local chpt. 1984—85, career guidance counselor 1986—88). Seventh Adventist. Avocations: violin, woodcarving, gardening, designing, building and landscaping homes, feeding hummingbirds. Home: PO Box 190 Berry Creek CA 95916-0190 Personal E-mail: jodenie@cncnet.com.

MILLER, JOSEPH IRWIN, automotive manufacturing company executive; b. Columbus, Ind., May 26, 1909; s. Hugh Thomas and Nettie Irwin (Sweeney) M.; m. Xenia Ruth Simons, Feb. 5, 1943; children: Margaret Irwin, Catherine Gibbs, Elizabeth Ann Garr, Hugh Thomas, II, William Irwin. Grad., Taft Sch., 1927; AB, Yale U., 1931, MA (hon.), 1959, LHD (hon.), 1979; MA, Oxford (Eng.) U., 1933; LLD, Bethany Coll., 1956, Tex. Christian U., Ind. U., 1958, Oberlin Coll., Princeton, 1962; LL.D., Hamilton Coll., 1964, Columbia, 1968, Mich. State U., 1968, Dartmouth, 1971, U. Notre Dame, 1972, Ball State U., 1972, Lynchburg Coll., 1985; L.H.D. (hon.), Case Inst. Tech., 1966, U. Dubuque, 1977; Hum.D., Manchester U., 1973, Moravian Coll., 1976. Assoc. Cummins Engine Co., Inc., Columbus, Ind., 1934—, v.p., gen. mgr., 1934-42, exec. v.p., 1944-47, pres., 1947-51, chmn. bd., 1951-77, chmn. exec. com., 1977-95; dir., 1995-97; hon. chmn. Cummins Engine, from 1997. Pres. Irwin-Union Bank & Trust Co., 1947-54, bd. dir., 1937—, chmn., 1954-75; chmn. exec. com. Irwin Union Corp., 1976-90, hon. chmn., 1997—; bd. dirs. Irwin Fin. Corp., 1990—; mem. Commn. Money and Credit, 1958-61, Pres.'s Com. Postal Reorgn., 1968, Pres.'s Com. Urban Housing, 1968; chmn. Pres.'s Com. on Trade Rels. with Soviet Union and Eastern European Nations, 1965, Nat. Adv. Commn. on Health Manpower, 1966; vice chmn. UN Commn. on Multinat. Corps., 1974; adv. council U.S. Dept. Commerce, 1976; mem. Study Commn. on U.S. Policy Toward So. Africa, 1979-81. Pres. nat. Coun. Chs. of Christ U.S.A., 1960-63; trustee Nat. Humanities Ctr., 1978-90, Carnegie Instn., Washington, 1988-91; mem. cen. and exec. coms. World Coun. Chs., 1961-68; trustee Ford Found., 1961-79, Yale Corp., 1959-77, Urban Inst., 1966-76, Mayo Found., 1977-82; fellow Branford Coll. Recipient Rosenberger award U. Chgo., 1977, 1st MacDowell Colony award, 1981; hon. fellow Balliol Coll., Oxford (Eng.) U.; Benjamin Franklin fellow Royal Soc. Arts. Fellow Am. Acad. Arts and Scis., Royal Inst. Brit. Architects (hon.); mem. AIA (hon.), Am. Philos. Soc., Ind. Acad., Bus. Coun., Conf. Bd. (sr.), Phi Beta Kappa, Beta Gamma Sigma. Mem. Christian Ch. Home: Columbus, Ind. Died Aug. 26, 2004.

MILLER, JOSEPH MORTON, internist; b. Boston, Nov. 9, 1921; s. Benjamin and Esther (Sugar) M.; m. Betty Jean Harris, Sept. 17, 1976; children: Beth, Keith, Eric, Gregory, Coralia. AB, Harvard Coll., 1942; MD, Harvard Med. Sch., 1945; MPH, Harvard Sch. Pub. Health, 1960. Diplomate Am. Bd. Internal Medicine, Preventive Medicine. Intern Mt. Sinai Hosp., N.Y.C., 1945-46; resident Cushing VA Hosp., Framingham, Mass., 1949-50; cons. occupl. health Durham, N.H., 1980—. Cons. environ. and toxicology. Capt. U.S. Army, 1946-48. Mem. APHA, Am. Coll. Environ. and Occupl. Medicine. fellow Am. Coll. Phys. Home and Office: 13 Burnham Ave Durham NH 03824-3010

MILLER, JUDITH A. federal official; BA summa cum laude, Beloit Coll., 1972; JD, Yale U., 1975. Bar: U.S. Supreme Ct., U.S. Ct. Appeals (D.C. cir.), U.S. Ct. Appeals (armed forces cir.). Clk. to Judge Harold Leventhal, U.S. Ct. of Appeals for D.C. cir., Washington; clk. to Assoc. Justice Potter Stewart Supreme Ct. of U.S., Washington; asst. to sec., dep. sec. of def. Office of Spl. Asst., Washington, 1977-79; assoc., ptnr. Williams & Connolly, Washington, 1979-94; adv. bd. on investigative capability Dept. Def., Washington, gen. counsel, 1994—. Civil justice reform act adv. group U.S. Dist. Ct. D.C.; mem. jud. conf. D.C. Cir. Recipient Vol. Recognition award Nat. Assn. of Attys. Gens.; DOD medal for Disting. Pub. Svc., 1997, Beloit Coll. Disting. Svc. Citation, 1997. Fellow Am. Bar Found.; mem. ABA, Am. Law Inst. Office: Office of Gen Counsel 1600 Defense Pentagon Washington DC 20301-1600

MILLER, JUDITH BEINSTEIN, psychology professor; b. Phila., Sept. 10, 1942; d. Joseph Beinstein and Ruth Gilden; m. Edward J. Miller, Feb. 22, 1976; 1 child, Benjamin David. PhD, U. Pa., 1972. Prof. psychology Oberlin Coll., 1972—. Contbr. articles to profl. jours. Mem.: Soc. for Personality and Social Psychology, Internat. Assn. for Relationship Rsch., Am. Psychol. Soc. Achievements include research in Psychology of close relationships and gender. Home: 8730 Gatewood Dr North Ridgeville OH 44039 Office: Oberlin Coll 120 W Lorain St Oberlin OH 44074 E-mail: judith.miller@oberlin.edu.

MILLER, JUDITH BRAFFMAN, writer; b. St. Louis, Feb. 21, 1947; d. William and Lorraine Shirley Braffman; m. Mark Ellis Miller, June 9, 1968. BA, U. Calif., Berkeley, 1969. Freelance writer, 1978—. Mem. Amnesty Internat., N.Y.C., 2002—. Fellow: Royal Astron. Soc. Gt. Britain; mem.: AAAS, ACLU, Nat. Space Soc., Planetary Soc., Am. Inst. Physics, Brit. Astron. Assn., Am. Aston. Soc., Am. Chem. Soc., N.Y. Acad. Scis., Am. Soc. Journalists and Authors, Union Concerned Scientists. Avocations: naturalist, poetry, politics. Home and Office: 1149 Partridge Ave Saint Louis MO 63130 Office Phone: 314-725-7096.

MILLER, JUDITH WOLFE COHEN, consultant; b. Boston, Aug. 19, 1928; d. Benjamin and Charlotte Frances (Wolfe) Cohen; m. Sanford Arthur Miller, Aug. 17, 1958; children: Wallis Jo, Debra Lauren. BS, Northeastern U., 1949. Research technician Mass. Gen. Hosp., Boston, 1949-51, NE Med. Ctr., Boston, 1951-52; spl. asst. MIT, Cambridge, 1952-61; v.p., treas. S.A. Miller and Assoc., Inc., San Antonio, Washington, 1987—. Cons. 9th internat. symposium on the U.S. Constitution Smithsonian Inst., Washington, 1987. Chmn. MIT Matrons, 1972, New Eng. Consevatory Prep. Sch. Parents' Assn., Boston, 1976, First Bicentennial '87 Symposium "The Constitution", Washington, 1985; Montgomery County chmn. Nat. Symphony Orch. Womens' Com., Washington, 1979-81; boutique chmn. Decorators' Showhouse Nat. Symphony Orch., Washington, 1981, 86; docent Nat. Archives Vols., Washington, 1979—; co-chmn. Am. Newspaper Pub. Assn. Found. Colloquium, Washington, 1985; pres. Nat. Archives Vols., Washington, 1983-84; vice-chmn. Constitution Study Group at Nat. Archives, Washington, 1982-87; docent Inst. Texan Culture, San Antonio, 1988-91; program chmn. U. Tex. Health Sci. Ctr. Club, San Antonio, 1988-89; White House vol. Presdl. Student Correspondence, 1996-2001. Mem.: Welcome to Washington. Home and Office: SA Miller & Assocs Inc 5450 Whitley Park Ter Apt 704 Bethesda MD 20814-2066 Fax: 301-897-0888. Office Phone: 301-897-3796.

MILLER, JUDSON FREDERICK, lawyer, former military officer; b. Tulsa, Dec. 5, 1924; s. Herbert Frederick and Martha (Davidson) M.; m. June Hirakis, Aug. 4, 1967; children by previous marriage: Kathleen, Shelley, Douglas, Judson Frederick. BS, U. Md., 1961; postgrad., Army War Coll., 1961-62; MA, George Washington U., 1962; JD, U. Puget Sound, 1980. Bar: Wash. 1981. Commd. 2d lt. U.S. Army, 1943, advanced through grades to maj. gen., 1975; platoon leader, co. comdr. 4th Cav. Group, Europe, 1944-46, 82d Airborne Div., 1947-50; with 187th Airborne RCT and Hdqrs. 8th Army, 1950-52; instr. Armored Sch., 1953-56; bn. comdr. 14th Armored Cav., 1958-60; with Hdqrs. U.S. Strike Command, 1963-65; brigade comdr., chief of staff 4th Inf. Div., Vietnam, 1966-67; mem. gen. staff Dept. Army, 1967-68; dep. comdg. gen. Ft. Ord, Cal., 1968-69; asst. chief of staff Hdqrs. Allied Forces Central Europe, 1969-71; asst. comdr. 3d Inf. Div., Germany, 1971-73; chief of staff I Corps Group, Korea, 1973-75; dep. comdg. gen. VII Corps, Germany, 1975-77; ret., 1977; assoc. F.G. Enslow and Assocs., Tacoma, 1981—. Decorated Silver Star, Legion of Merit, Bronze Star with V device and oak leaf cluster, Joint Service Commendation medal, Air medal with 8 oak leaf clusters, Purple Heart, Vietnamese Gallantry Cross with palm; named to Okla. Mil. Acad. Hall of Fame, 1988. Mem. ABA, Assn. U.S. Army. Clubs: Tacoma Country, Lakewood Racquet. Home: 8009 75th St SW Tacoma WA 98498-4817 Office: Tacoma Mall Office Bldg 4301 S Pine St Ste 205 Tacoma WA 98409-7205

MILLER, KAREN L. dean, nursing educator; BSN, Case Western Res. U.; MSN, PhD in Nursing, U. Colo. V.p. The Children's Hosp., Denver; assoc. prof. Coll. Nursing U. Colo. Health Scis. Ctr.; dean, prof. Sch. Nursing U. Kans., 1996—, dean Sch. Allied Health, 1998—. Mem. editl. bd. IMAGE: Jour. Nursing Scholarship. Grantee NIH, 1992. Fellow Am. Acad. Nursing; mem. ANA, ANA Coun. Nurse Rschrs., Am. Orgn. Nurse Execs., Coun. on Grad. Edn. for Nursing Adminstrn., Midwest Alliance in Nursing, Midwest Nursing Rsch. Soc., Sigma Theta Tau (collateral reviewer rsch. com.). Office: U Kans Sch Nursing 390 Rainbow Blvd Kansas City KS 66160-0001

MILLER, KARL A. management counselor; b. Reading, Pa., Feb. 27, 1931; s. Harvey and Kathleen Schwartz (Bechtel) M.; m. Carol Joann Mickle, July 28, 1956; children: Dawn Alison, Kevin Bryan. BS in Indsl. Engring., Pa. State U., 1953; MS in Indsl. Mgmt., MIT, 1963. Bus. mgr. GE, Evendale, Ohio, 1953-55, Lynn, Mass., 1956-63; asst. to pres. Burns & Roe, N.Y.C., 1964-65; cons. George Armstrong Co., N.Y.C., 1966-68; sr. cons. H.B. Maynard Co., N.Y.C., 1968-70; mng. ptnr. Kamid Assocs. Mgmt. cons. to newspapers, electronic media, agribus., govt., architects, engrs., constrn., mfg. and health care delivery firms, Yonkers, N.Y., 1971—; owner David Goliath Ltd.; developer, owner joint tech. projects serving Pacific Rim Aircraft Maintenance Sta., 1990—; ptnr. Power Jets Unltd., 1992—, Pegasus Power Prodrs. Ltd., 1994—; arbitrator Better Bus. Bur. of N.Y.C., 1982-84; lectr. fin. profitability and mktg. Bucknell U., Pa., Mercy Coll., N.Y., Dominican Coll., Blauvelt, N.Y., 1981-82; speaker in field. Author: Estimating: A Management Process for SEMS at Surrey University, England, 1998, Networking in Jet Engine Retrofitting, 1963, The Farm Machinery Market, 1973; editor Jet Engine Newsletter, 1955-56; contbr. articles to profl. jours. Pres. men's brotherhood Collegiate Ch. N.Y.C., 1970-72; pres. Westchestertowne Houses Condominium, Yonkers, 1971-76, Coun. Condominiums N.Y. State, 1972-76; commr. of deeds City of Yonkers, 1976, chmn. citizens budget adv. com., 1975-76. Recipient Speak Up award Peabody (Mass.) Jr. C. of C., 1960, Minuteman citation, 1960, Henry B. Kane award MIT, 1990. Mem.: Triangle Frat., Internat. Platform Assn., Westchester Personal Computer Users Group, Chinese-Am. MIT, Nat. Mus. Naval Aviation Found. (Pensacola), Air Force Assn. (Gen. Carl A. Tooey Spaatz chpt. 251 pres. 1995—2001, N.E. region pres. 2001—, pres. N.E. region 2001—), Yonkers C. of C. (pres.'s club 1975—78), U.S. Naval Inst. (life), MIT Alumni Ctr. N.Y.C. (gov. 1970—81), U.S. Naval Meml. Found. (nat. adv. coun. 1993—), Army/Navy Club Washington, Am. Legion (life; vice-comdr. 1995, post comdr. 1996—99), Sigma Tau. Republican. Mem. Protestant Dutch Reformed Ch. Home: Unit 21 412 N Broadway Yonkers NY 10701-1938 Office: PO Box 63 Yonkers NY 10703-0063 E-mail: vze2t5zq@verizon.net.

MILLER, KEITH ALLEN, judge, lawyer; b. Jacksonville, N.C., Aug. 21, 1953; s. Paul V. Miller and Ruth E. Vanderpool; children: Esther, Gail, Joel, Jared, Isaac. BS in Phys. Scis., Pacific Union Coll., Angwin, Calif., 1978; JD, Syracuse U., 1990; postgrad., Willamette U., 1991-94. Bar: Oreg. 1992, U.S. Ct. Vet. Appeals 1992, U.S. Supreme Ct. 1999. Orchadist Miller Farms, Umqua, Oreg., 1981-85; pvt. practice atty. Sublimity, Oreg., 1992-95, Sweet Home, Oreg., 1996—; peer ct. judge Linn County Cts., Sweet Home, 1998—. Dir. guardian ad-litem program ABA, Chgo., 1983. Columnist Horse Cents, 1993. Dir. John Anderson for Pres., Douglas County, Oreg., 1980, Multiple Sclerosis Soc. Douglas County, Roseburg, Oreg., 1980; organizer, pres. Dallas Mobile Home Pk. Renters Assn., 1992-94; Dem. candidate Oreg. State Rep. Dist. 34, 1992, 94. Petty officer USN, 1979-80. Scholar Am. United Separation Ch. and State, 1985. Mem. Oreg. Criminal Def. Lawyers Assn. Democrat. Avocations: auto restoration, stamp collecting/philately, boat building. Office: 1262 Main St Sweet Home OR 97386-1608 Fax: 541-367-4209.

MILLER, KEITH LLOYD, lawyer; b. Harvey, N.D., July 27, 1951; s. Lloyd Vernie and Marian A. (Leintz) M.; m. Linda Suzanne Nelson, Aug. 7, 1971; children: Christopher Nelson, ann Elizabeth. BA, Concordia Coll., Moorhead, Minn., 1972; JD, U. N.D., 1975. Bar: Minn. 1976, U.S. Dist. Ct. Minn. 1976, U.S. Ct. Appeals (8th cir.) 1976, N.D. 1982, U.S. Dist. Ct. N.d. 1982. Assoc. Stefanson, Landberg & Alm, Moorhead, 1976-78; ptnr. Miller, Norman & Assocs., Ltd., Moorhead, 1978—. Cons. Nat. Legal Svcs. Corp., Washington, 1984-86; dir. Northwestern Minn. Legal Svcs. Corp., Moorhead, 1981-87, chmn. bd., 1983-86. Contbr. articles to profl. jours. Bd. dirs. Clay County Dem. Farm Labor Party, Moorhead, 1984-86; advisor Nat. Moot Trial Competition Team, Concordia Coll., 1986-96; mem. organizing com., 1st pres. Judge Ronald N. Davies Inn of Ct., 1996-97. Mem.: ATLA, Acad. Cert. Trial Lawyers Minn., Am. Arbitration Assn. (arbitrator 1980—), State Bar Assn. N.D., N.D. Trial Lawyers Assn., Minn. State Bar Assn. (mem. civil litigation sect. governing coun. 2002—03), Minn. Trial Lawyers Assn. (bd. govs. 1987—, treas. 1995—96, sec. 1996—97, v.p. 1997—98, pres.-elect 1998, pres. 1999—2000, contbr. to jour.). Lutheran. Office: Miller Norman & Assocs 403 Center Ave Ste 201 Moorhead MN 56560-1900 Office Phone: 218-233-2495. Business E-Mail: klmiller@mnalaw.com.

MILLER, KEN, state legislator; b. Fort Collins, Colo., Feb. 1, 1957; m. Peggy Miller. Student, Ft. Collins VoTech. Farmer; roofing and wood mfg. contractor; mem. Mont. Senate, Dist. 11, Helena, 1994—; chair bills and jour. com., vice chair local govt. com. Mont. Senate; mem. joint appropriations subcom. on edn./cultural resources Mont. State Senate, mem. natural resources com., mem. fin. and claims com.; adminstr. polit. orgn., state chmn. Ma. Republican Party, 2001—. Republican. Home: PO Box 186 Laurel MT 59044-0186 Office: 1419-B Helena Ave Helena MT 59601 E-mail: Ken@cw2.com.

MILLER, KEN LEROY, religious studies educator, consultant, writer; b. San Antonio, July 29, 1933; s. Eldridge and Paskel Dovie (Vick) M.; m. Eddie Juanell Crawford, June 14, 1953 (dec. Apr. 1981); children: Kimberly Miller Stern, Kerry, Karen Miller Davis; m. Carolyn Gayle Conatser, May 4, 1982; children: Sheila Stanley, Keith Conatser. BA, Abilene Christian U., 1958; MEd, Trinity U., 1965; EdD, Ariz. State U., 1975. Cert. tchr., Tex. Tchr. SAn Antonio Ind. Sch. Dist., 1957-58; tchr., adminstr. N.E. Ind. Sch. Dist., San Antonio, 1958-69; min. edn. MacArthur Park Ch. of Christ, San Antonio, 1960-69; prin. Ralls (Tex.) Ind. Sch. Dist., 1969-70; minister of edn. S.W. Ch. of Christ, Phoenix, 1970-74; adminstr., tchr. Lubbock (Tex.) Christian Sch./U., 1974-77; minister of edn. Sunset Ch. of Christ, Lubbock, 1977-87; prof. religious edn. Harding U., Searcy, Ark., 1987-98; tchr. ESL, Pitman Creek Ch. of Christ, Plano, Tex., 2002—03. Curriculum cons. Sweet Pub. Co., Ft. Worth, 1988-98; leader internat. and nat. religious edn. workshops and seminars. Author: Moral and Religious Stages of Development, 1975, (curriculum) Old Testament Personalities, 1980, Organization, Administration, Supervision of the Bible School, 1993, Recruiting, Training, Retaining Teachers in the Bible School, 1993, Curriculum for the Bible School, 1993; editor: Recipes for Living and Teaching, 1982, (curriculum) Growing in Knowledge, 1977-90, The MINNITH series, 1991-2003; guest editor, contbr. Christian Family 1984. With U.S. Army, 1954-56. Mem. Christian Educators, Christian Edn. Assn., Religious Edn. Assn., Assn. Secondary Schs. and Colls., Alpha Psi Omega, Sigma Tau Delta. Republican. Mem. Ch. of Christ. Avocations: fishing, hunting, reading, travel, writing, poetry readings. Home: 1417 Thames Dr Plano TX 75075-2734 E-mail: cmillerway@yahoo.com.

MILLER, KENNETH EDWARD, sociologist, educator; b. N.Y.C., June 17, 1929; s. Joseph F. and Irene (Edersheim) M.; m. Andrée Nora Barthelemy, Feb. 14, 1959 (div. Nov. 1984); children: Jennifer Andrée, Christopher Kenneth; m. Janet Sue Daniels, May 21, 1990. BA, U. Ala., 1953, MA, 1956; PhD, Duke, 1965; MS, Drake U., 1986. Asst. to pres., dir. devel. Jacksonville (Fla.) U., 1957-60; dir. Health Council, asso. dir. Community Planning Council, Birmingham, Ala., 1960-62; asst. prof. sociology Emory U., Atlanta, 1966-70, acting chmn. dept., 1969-70; prof. sociology Drake U., Des Moines, 1970-96, chmn. dept., 1970-79, 82-88, asst. to dean for grad. studies, 1991-92, prof. emeritus, 1996—. Research sociologist U. Ala., 1956-57; research asso. U.S. Civil Service Commn., summer 1968. Served with USN, 1946-48. Postdoctoral research fellow Duke, 1965-66. Mem. Midwest Sociol. Soc. Home: 2129 NW 140th St Clive IA 50325-8730

MILLER, KENNETH GREGORY, retired air force officer; b. Bryan, Tex., July 28, 1944; s. Max Richard and Catherine Mae (Sultzman) M.; m. Ann Marguerite Perpich, Nov. 25, 1966; children: Keith G., Deborah J., Craig S. BS in Aero. Engring., Purdue U., 1966; MS in Systems Mgmt., U. So. Calif., 1970; grad., Nat. War Coll., Washington, 1986; postgrad., U. Va., 1988. Commd. 2d lt. USAF, 1966, advanced through grades to brig. gen., 1995; with Office Sec. Def., Washington, 1980-81; various positions to dir. field ops. F-16 System Program Office, Wright-Patterson AFB, Ohio, 1981-86; chief engring. div. Sacramento Air Logistics Ctr., McClellan AFB, Calif., 1986-87; dir. materiel mgmt. Ogden Air Logistics Ctr., Hill AFB, Utah, 1987-89; vice comdr. Acquisition Logistics Div., Wright-Patterson AFB, 1989-90; comdr. Air Force Contract Mgmt. Divsn., Kirtland AFB, N.Mex., 1990; comdr. western dist. Def. Contract Mgmt. Command, L.A., 1990-91; dir. C-17 Program Office, Wright-Patterson AFB, 1991-93; dep. asst. sec. for acquistion USAF, Washington, 1993-94, dir. supply hdqrs., 1994-95; v.p. for gulf ops. BDM Fed., 1995-96; group v.p. for advanced tech. svcs. group RJO Enterprises, Inc., 1997; sr. v.p. Dayton ops. CACI, Inc., 1997-99; group v.p. Air Force programs Anteon Corp., 1999—. Mem. engring. bd. visitors Purdue U. Decorated Disting. Svc. medal, Legion of Merit (2), Def. Superior Svc. medal; recipient award of merit Freedom Found; named Outstanding Aerospace Engr., Purdue U., Disting. Engring. Alumnus, Purdue U., 2001; named to ROTC Hall of Fame, 2001. Mem. Nat. Contract Mgmt. Assn. (bd. advisors 1990-92), Soc. Logistics Engrs., Nat. Def. Indsl. Assn. Office: 1560 Wilson Blvd Ste 800 Arlington VA 22209 Home: 9061 Daybreaker Drive Park City UT 84098 E-mail: kmiller@anteon.com.

MILLER, KENNETH MICHAEL, electronics executive, director; b. Chgo., Nov. 20, 1921; s. Matthew and Tillie (Otto) M.; m. Dolores June Miller, Jan. 16, 1943 (dec. Dec. 1968); children: Barbara Anne Reed, Nancy Jeanne Hathaway, Kenneth Michael, Roger Allan; m. Sally J. Ballingham, June 20, 1970 (dec. Apr. 2002). Student, Ill. Inst. Tech., 1940-41, UCLA, 1961. Electronics engr. Rauland Corp., Chgo., 1941-48; gen. mgr. Lear, Inc., Santa Monica, Calif., 1948-59; v.p., gen. mgr. Motorola Aviation Electronics, Inc., Culver City, Calif., 1959-60; v.p., gen. mgr. instrument divsn. Daystrom, Inc., L.A., 1961; gen. mgr. metrics divsn. Singer Co., L.A. and Bridgeport, Conn., 1962-65; v.p., gen. mgr. Lear Jet Corp., 1965-66; pres., dir. Infonics, Inc., 1967-68; v.p., gen. mgr. Computer Industries, Inc., 1968-69; dir. ops., tech. products group Am. Std. Corp., McLean, Va., also v.p., gen. mgr. Wilcox Elec. divsn. Kansas City, Mo., 1969-71; pres. Wilcox Elec., Inc. subs. Northrop Corp., Kansas City, 1971-72; v.p., dir. World Wide Wilcox, Inc. subs., McLean, 1971-72; pres., CEO, dir. Penril Corp., Rockville, Md., 1973-86; pres. K-M Miller and Assocs., Rockville, 1986—. Dir. George Mason Bank, NA, Washington, Palmer Nat. Bank, Washington. Mem. adv. bd. Washington Bus. Jour.; contbr. articles to profl. jours. Mem. regional planning coun. Cmty. Mental Health Svcs., Bridgeport, 1964; mem. bd. Bridgeport Capital Fund Com.; trustee Park City Hosp.; vice dir. Montgomery County Arts Coun.; bd. dirs. U. Bridgeport; mem. Md. State Com. High Tech. Recipient Job Makers award Mfrs. Assn. Bridgeport, 1963. Fellow Radio Club Am. (dir., chmn grants-in-aid com.); mem. AIAA, IEEE, Aircraft Owners and Pilots Assn., Am. Mgmt. Assn., Armed Forces Comm. and Electronics Assn. (life), Electronic Industries Assn., Instrument Soc. Am. (life), Nat. Aero. Assn., Soc. Non-Destructive Testing, Soc. Automotive Engrs., Air Force Assn., Am. Radio Relay League (life), Amateur Satellite Corp. (life), Am. Def. Preparedness Assn. (life), Aero. Elec. Soc. (life), Nat. Capital DX Assn. (pres. 1987-88), Assn. Old Crows (life), Mfrs. Assn. Bridgeport (dir.), Bridgeport Engring. Inst., Bridgeport C. of C. (pres. 1964), Quarter Century Wireless Assn. (life, Disting. Svc. award 1994), Soc. Wireless Pioneers, Rolling Hills Country Club (Wichita), Algonquin Club (Bridgeport). Home and Office: 16904 George Washington Dr Rockville MD 20853-1128 Office Phone: 301-774-7709. E-mail: kmm@prodigy.net.

MILLER, KENNETH WILLIAM, II, research and development engineering executive; b. Cleve., May 11, 1951; s. Kenneth William and Margaret Mary Miller; m. Joan Ellen Pattillo, Aug. 12, 1972 (div. Oct. 1992); children: Kenneth William III, Victoria Joan, Christopher John. BSEE, MIT, 1974, MS in Mgmt. of Tech., 1983; postgrad., Am. U. Paris, 1994-95, Harvard U., 1997. From process engr. to sr. equipment engr. Corning (N.Y.) Glass Works, 1974-78, supr. process engring., 1978-80, sr. mkt. devel. analyst, 1980, sr. project engr., 1980-81; product engring. mgr. Duracell Divsn. Gillette, Lexington, N.C., 1983-85; mgr. advanced tech. Gen. Dynamics Advanced Tech., Greensboro, N.C., 1985; v.p., bd. dirs. Frey Holdings, Inc., Mansfield, 1985-89; v.p. Intellogistics, Inc., Columbus, Ohio, 1989, Zack's Investment Rsch., Chgo., 1991. Computer programmer Fed Res Bank Boston, 1972—74; lectr mgt sci Ohio State Univ, 1988. Author: International Technology Strategy, 1983, GATT, 1994 (Cetus Paribus), Our Future Welfare, 1995, Godspace 2084, 2002; contbr. articles to profl. jours. Rep. candidate state rep., Richland County, Ohio, 1988; Rep. candidate Mansfield City Coun., 1989; exec. com. Richland County Rep. Party. Mem.: SAR (Mass. bd. mgrs. 2001—02), IEEE (sr.), Ohio Acad. Sci. (life; judge), MIT Alumni Assn., Eagle Scout Assn. (life). Methodist. Avocations: camping, personal computing, international travel. Home and Office: 525 Chevy Chase Mansfield OH 44907-1548 Personal E-mail: kwmillerII@aol.com.

MILLER, KEVIN ROBERT, employee benefit consultant; b. Miller, S.D., Sept. 7, 1961; s. Robert Leo and Norma Cecelia (Pottebaum) M.; m. Ellen Susan Arends, Sept. 21, 1985; children: Collin John, Tyler Jordan, Jacob Robert. BS in Bus. Mgmt. and Mktg., No. State Coll., 1983. CLU The Am. Coll.; cert. fund specialist Inst. Cert. Fund Specialists, chartered fin. cons. The Am. Coll., chartered mutual fund counselor Coll. for Fin. Planning. Credit rep. Citibank S.D., NA, Sioux Falls, 1983-84; terr. mgr. Cosmair Inc., Mankato, Minn., 1984-86; employee benefit cons., retirement planner Arends Assocs., Inc., Albert Lea, Minn., 1986-90; employee benefits cons. Fringe Benefits Design, Eden Prairie, Minn., 1990-94, pres., CEO Bloomington, Minn., 1995—. Mem. Kiwanis. Republican. Roman Catholic. Office: Fringe Benefits Design 7900 Xerxes Ave S Ste 700 Bloomington MN 55431-1127

MILLER, KIRK EDWARD, lawyer, health foundation executive; b. San Jose, Calif., June 9, 1951; BA in Polit. Sci., U. Calif., Riverside, 1973; JD, Syracuse U., 1976. Bar: Colo. 1976, Calif. 1980, Tex. 1993. Assoc. Hughes & Dorsey, Denver, 1977-78; v.p., assoc. gen. counsel Am. Med. Internat., Inc., Dallas, 1979-88, v.p., sec., gen. counsel, 1988-91; with McGlinchey Stafford Lang, Dallas, 1991-94; sr. v.p., sec., gen. counsel Kaiser Found. Health Plan, Inc., Kaiser Found. Hosps., Inc., Oakland, Calif., 1994—2002, sr. v.p., legal svcs., 2002—. Instr. Syracuse U., 1975-76. Mem. ABA (co-vice chair com. health care fraud and abuse 1995-96). Office: Kaiser Found Health Plan 1 Kaiser Plz Oakland CA 94612-3610

MILLER, L. MARTIN, accountant, financial planning specialist; b. N.Y.C., Sept. 17, 1939; s. Harvey and Julia (Louis) M.; m. Judith Sklar, Jan. 21, 1962; children: Philip, Marjorie. BS, Wharton Sch., U. Pa., 1960; M Taxation, Villanova Law Sch., 2001. CPA; CFP; accredited fin. planning specialist. Jr. acct. Deloitte, Haskins & Sells, N.Y.C., 1960-62, sr. acct. Phila., 1962-64; mng. ptnr. Cogen, Sklar LLP, Phila., 1964—. Treas. Coronet Container Co., Inc., Phila., Val Mar Realty Corp., N.Y.C.; dir. Penn Internat. Trading Co., Phila.; mng. dir. CPA Tax Forum, 1966-69; underwriting mem. Lloyds of London, 1978-95, chmn. Mid-Atlantic region, 1991-92; mem. faculty Wharton Sch. U. Pa., 1992-2004, Villanova U., 2003; mem. MBA program faculty LaSalle U., 2003; lectr., discussion leader on fin. and taxation. Author: Accountants Guide to S.E.C. Filings, 1968, Salaries, Penn. Non-Profit Report, 1997, Worker Compensation, Practical Tax Strategies, 2000; contbr. articles to profl. jours. Mem. Phila. Rep. Com., 1963-67, treas. Daerr-Bannon for state rep. com., 1997; chmn. Lower Merion Twp. scholarship fund, 1975-78; bd. dirs. Main Line Br. ARC, 1997-2000; bd. dirs. Penn Valley Civic Assn., 1973-79, Gladwyne Civic Assn., 1992-95; mem. Lower Merion Planning Commn., 1978-82, Gov.'s Tax Study Commn.; pres. Mensa Edn. and Rsch. Found., 1984-86; mem. SEC Forum on Small Bus. Capital Formation, 1983, Pa. Impact, 1995; apptd. to Pa. State Bd. Accountancy, 1985-94, chmn., 1990-91; elected sch. bd. dir. Lower Merion Twp., 1993-97, also chmn. fin. com. Served with U.S. Army, 1961-62. Recipient Outstanding Achievement award Germantown Civic Assn., 1965. Mem. Pa. Inst. CPAs (edn. com. 1975-78, bd. dirs. 1979-81, by-laws chmn. 1980-83, mem. non-profit orgns. com. 1995-99, fin. planning com. 2002-2003), Nat. Assn. State Bds. Accountancy (edn. com. 1987, nominating com. 1989, experience com. 1990, continuing edn. com. 1995—), Am. Arbitration Assn. (mem. comml. panel, 2002—), Cert. Fin. Planner (bd. ethics 1995-97), AICPAs (nat. tax commn. 1979-82, exec. com. self regulation divsn. for CPA firms 1984-87, acctg. and rev. svcs. com. 1985-88, long range planning com., ethics divsn. 1985-88, specialization bd. 1989-90, ethics exec. com. 1990-93, mem. curriculum and acctg. edn. 1993-96, chmn. fin. assistance task force 1995, bd. dirs. Estate Planning Coun. 1998-2004, nomination com. 1999), Little 10 Acctg. Assn. (edn. chmn. 1980-84), Main Line C. of C. (govt. affairs com. 1991-99), Mensa (internat. fin. officer 1970-74), Masons (past master), Plays and Players Club (treas. 1978-79), Beta Alpha Psi. Home: 204 Dove Ln Haverford PA 19041-1902 Office: Cogen Sklar LLP 150 Monument Rd Bala Cynwyd PA 19004-1702

MILLER, LARRY H. professional sports team executive, automobile dealer; b. Salt Lake City; m. Gail Miller; 5 children. Formerly with auto parts bus., Denver and Salt Lake City; now owner auto dealerships, Salt Lake City, Albuquerque, Denver and Phoenix; part-owner Utah Jazz, NBA, Salt Lake City, 1985—86, owner, 1996—. Office: c/o Utah Jazz 301 W South Temple Salt Lake City UT 84101-1216 also: Larry H Miller Group 5650 S State St Murray UT 84107-6131

MILLER, LARRY THOMAS, accountant; b. Omaha, Oct. 24, 1940; s. Elmer Thomas and Lucile Valentine (Hammon) M. Student, U. Omaha, 1958-63. With acctg. dept. Union Pacific R.R. Co., Omaha, 1959-92, tax acct., 1969—92; prin. Doyle Distbg., Omaha, 1996—. Author: (song lyrics) for country albums America, Bad Girl Problem, Fire Fool, 1997, HillTop Country, Love is Sweet, Holman Hollow, 1998; co-author: (how-to book) Bowling Our way, 1996. Served with U.S. Army, M.P., 1965-67. Mem. Am. Acctg. Assn. Home: 2353 N 92nd Ave Omaha NE 68134-5930 Office: Doyle Distributing 2353 N 92nd Ave Apt 14 Omaha NE 68134-5930 E-mail: dyldstrb@mitec.net.

MILLER, LAURA, mayor, journalist; b. Balt., Nov. 18, 1958; m. Steven Wolens; children: Alex, Lily, Maxwell. Grad., U. Wis., Madison. Mem. Dallas City Coun., 1998—2002; mayor City of Dallas, 2002—. Columnist, investigative reporter Dallas Observer, metro columnist Dallas Times Herald, New York Daily News, The Dallas Morning News, The Miami Herald. Recipient H.L. Mencken Writing award, Balt. Sun, 1995, 6 Katie awards, Dallas Press Club, 2 Tex. Headliner awards, 2 Philbin awards, Dallas Bar Assn., cert. of merit, ABA. Office: Dallas City Hall 1500 Marilla St Rm 5EN Dallas TX 75201-6390*

MILLER, LAURA JEAN, medical center director; b. Louisville, Nov. 11, 1946; d. Arthur and Marion (Adams) M.; m. Garrett Van Koughnett; children: Michael J. Uhlik, Caroline E. Uhlik. BA, U. Mo., Columbia, 1970; MPA, U. Mo., Kansas City, 1978. Presdl. mgmt. intern U.S. Dept. Vets. Affairs, Topeka, 1978-79, Kansas City, Mo., 1979-80, asst. to chief of staff, 1980-86, regional quality assurance mgr. Grand Prairie, Tex., 1986-89, assoc. dir. trainee Dallas, 1989-90, asst. med. ctr. dir., 1990-91, assoc. med. ctr. dir. Salem, Va., 1991-94, med. ctr. dir. Pitts., 1994—. Mem. exec. planning coun. U. Pitts., Western Psychiat. Inst. and Clinic, 1995—; mem.adv. bd. Vietnam Vets. Leadership Program Western Pa., Pitts., 1995—. Mem. Am. Coll. Healthcare Execs., Health Exec. Forum of Southwestern Pa., Interagy. Healthcare Inst. Alummni. Office: VA Med Ctr 7180 Highland Dr Pittsburgh PA 15206-1206

MILLER, LENORE WOLF DANIELS, speech-language pathologist; b. N.Y.C., Mar. 9, 1937; d. Samuel D. and Sarah (Reisman) Wolf; m. Marshall Nelson Daniels, Mar. 30, 1958 (div. Jan. 1965); m. Macey I. Miller, Dec. 11, 1977; 1 child, Suzanne Hayley. BA, CUNY, 1958, MA, 1961; ScD, Boston U., 1983. Sr. speech pathologist L.I. Coll. Hosp., N.Y.C., 1959-68; supr. speech-lang. pathology Tufts-New England Med. Ctr., Boston, 1968-87, dir. speech-lang. pathology, 1987-95, co-dir dept. speech-lang. pathology, 1987-95; pvt. and cons. practice speech-lang. pathology, Newton, Mass., 1995—. Asst. prof. depts. otolaryngology and rehab. medicine Tufts U. Sch. Medicine, 1992—96, asst. prof. dept. child psychiatry, 1995—96; adj. faculty Emerson Coll., 1993, Northeastern U., 1994, Boston U., 1993—, Mass. Gen. Hosp. Inst. Health Professions, 1998, 2002; specialist in areas of cranio-facial anomalies, voice disorders, dysfluency, lang. and motor-speech disorders, pediat., adult and geriatric; presenter in field. Contbr. articles to profl. jours. Mem. Am. Fedn. Musicians, 1965—80; del. Mass. Health Coun., Boston, 1974, 1975; mem. Tanglewood Festival Chorus, 1971—75, Newton Singers, 2001—03, Newton Choral Soc., 2004—; former actor Ivy Tower Playhouse, Spring Lake, NJ, Bklyn. Heights Repertory Co. Theatre, Bklyn. Nat. Office Edn. grantee, 1980. Mem.: Boston Area Voice Interest Group, Mass. Speech-Lang.-Hearing Assn. (pres. elect 1976—77, pres. 1977—78, sr. chair govtl. affairs 1988—91, honors 1979), Am. Cleft Palate-Craniofacial Assn. (pub. rels. com. 1973—74, by-laws com. 1977—78), Am. Assn. Pvt. Practice Speech Pathology and Audiology, Am. Speech-Lang.-Hearing Assn. (legis. coun. 1973—75, chair com. spl. rules 1974—75). Avocations: singing, drama, gourmet cooking, biking, tennis.

MILLER, LEROY PAUL, JR., secondary English educator; b. Holyoke, Mass., Feb. 21, 1949; s. Leroy Paul Sr. and Rose Marie (Danehey) M. AA, Northampton (Mass.) Jr. Coll., 1972; BA, U. New Eng., Biddeford, Maine, 1974; MEd, Springfield (Mass.) Coll., 1977; postgrad., Am. Internat. Coll., Springfield. Cert. elem. tchr., English tchr., history tchr., guidance counselor Mass. Sch. adjustment counselor Holyoke Pub. Schs., 1978-79, ednl. programmer, 1979-80, tutor Chpt. I, 1980-81; tutor Amherst (Mass.) Pub. Schs., 1982-84; tchr. West Springfield (Mass.) Pub. Schs., 1985-86; tchr. English Springfield Pub. Schs., 1986—. Fundraiser M. Marcus Kiley Mid. Sch.; alumni counselor U. New Eng., 1977—. Mem. NEA, ASCD, Nat. Coun. Tchrs. English, Mass. Tchrs. Assn., Springfield Edn. Assn. (faculty rep. 1986—), U. New Eng. Alumni Assn. (v.p. 1990—), Elks, Psi Chi. Democrat. Roman Catholic. Avocations: reading, bowling. Home: 2 Gerard Way Holyoke MA 01040-1204 Office: M Marcus Kiley Mid Sch 180 Cooley St Springfield MA 01128-1108 Office Phone: 413-787-7240. Personal E-mail: lmill55169@aol.com.

MILLER, LESLIE ANNE, lawyer; b. Franklin, Ind., Nov. 4, 1951; d. G. Thomas and Anne (Gaines) Miller; m. Richard B. Worley, Feb. 14, 1987. AB cum laude, Mt. Holyoke Coll., 1973; MA in Polit. Sci., Rutgers U., 1974; JD, Dickinson Sch. Law, Carlisle, Pa., 1977; LLM with honors, Temple U., 1994; LLD (hon.), Thomas Jefferson U. Coll. Health Profls., 2002; HHD (hon.), Wilson Coll., 2001. Bar: Pa. 1977, U.S. Dist. Ct. (ea. dist.) Pa. 1977, U.S. Ct. Appeals (3d cir.) 1980, U.S. Dist. Ct. (ea. dist.) Pa. 1987. Assoc. LaBrum & Doak, Phila., 1977-81, ptnr., 1982-86, Goldfein & Joseph, Phila., 1986-95, McKissock & Hoffman, P.C., Phila., 1995—2003; gen. counsel Gov. Pa., 2003—. Bd. dirs. WHYY-TV, 1996-2003; del. Third Circuit Jud. Conf., 1981, 82, 85; mem. Jud. Inquiry and Rev. Bd., 1990-94, chair, 1993-94; mem. faculty trial advocacy program Dickinson Sch. Law, 1992, 94; mem. hearing com., disciplinary bd. Supreme Ct. Pa., 1996—; mem. faculty Acad. Advocacy Temple U., 1994—; judge pro tem Ct. of Common Pleas; interm pres. Kimmel Ctr. for the Performing Arts, 2001-02. Mem. acad. ball com. Phila. Orch., 1986-87, 89-91, 95-96, mem. acad. music com. 1998—; mem. Open Space Task Force Com., Lower Merion Twp., Pa., 1990, bd. dirs., 1990-94, mem. counsel, 1990, Lower Merion Conservancy, 1995-97, 2000—, others; bd. dirs. Med. Coll. Pa., 1985-96, sec., 1987-92, chair presdl. search com., 1993, chair presdl. inauguration, 1987, chair com. on acad. affairs, 1989-95, chair dean's search com., 1994-95, chair nomenclature com., 1996; bd. dirs. Med. Coll. Hosps., 1991-96, Allegheny Health Edn. and Rsch. Found., 1993-96, Hahnemann U. Med. Sch., 1994-96, Pa. Ballet, 1994—, St. Christopher's Hosp. for Children, 1991-94, vice chair, 1990-94; bd. dirs. Phila. Free Libr., 1997—, bd. dirs. Kimmel Ctr. for the Performing Arts, 1999—, interim pres., 2001-02, vice chair bd. dirs., 2002—; hon. chair Pa. Breast Cancer Coalition, 2003; trustee Mt. Holyoke Coll., 2000—; bd. govs. Dickinson Sch. Law, Pa. State U., 2001—. Recipient Mary Lyon award Mt. Holyoke Alumni Assn., 1985, Alumnae Medal of Honor, 1988, Hon. Alumnae award, 1989, Pres.'s award Med. Coll. Pa., 1993, Sylvia Rambo award Dickinson Sch. of Law, 1997, Star award Forum of Exec. Women, 1998, Ann Alpern award PBA Women in the Profession, 1999, Sandra Day O'Connor award Phila. Bar Assn., 1999, Outstanding Leadership in Support of Legal Svcs. award Pa. Legal Svcs., 1999, Women Making History Nat. Assn. of Women Bus. Owners, 2002, Women of Distinction award, Phila. Bus. Jour., 2001, Internat. Women's Forum "Women Who Make a Difference" award, 2003, Pink Ribbon award Pa. Breast Cancer Coalition, 2003, Woman One award Drexel U. Inst. for Women's Health and Leadership, 2004; named to Pa. Honor Roll of Women, 1996; named Disting. Dau. of Pa., Gov. of Pa., 1999. Fellow Am. Bar Found., Pa. Bar Found.; mem. ABA, Phila. Bar Assn. (mem. exec. com. divsn. young lawyers 1982-85, mem. bicentennial com 1986-87, bd. govs. 1990-93, mem. gender bias task force 1993-97, chair com. on jud. selection and retention 1987-89, vice chair 1985-87, investigative divsn. 1982-85, chair Andrew Hamilton Ball 1989, trustee Phila. Bar Found. 1990-97, co-chair century three commn. 1995-97, others), Pa. Bar Assn. (found. ho. dels. life fellow, bd. govs. 1980-83, 84-87, 91-93, chair young lawyers divsn. 1982-83, mem. long range planning com. 1985-87, mem. com. on professionalism, 1987-91, vice chmn. jud. inquiry and rev. bd. study com. 1989-91, sec. 1984-87, chair ho. dels. 1991-93, chair commn. on women in the profession 1993-95, v.p. 1996-97, pres. 1998-99, immediate past pres. 1999—, apptd. mem. ct. jud. discipline 1999), Pa. Bar Inst. (mem. faculty, course planner), Phila. Assn. Def. Counsel (mem. exec. coun. 1987-90, 94, mem. joint trial demonstration with Phila. Trial Lawyers Assn. 1993), Def. Rsch. Inst. (spkr. toxic torts seminar 1983), Phila. Bar Edn. Advocacy Women Litigators (course planner, mem. faculty 1995), Women's Assn. Women's Alternatives (bd. dirs. 1983-94, vice chair 1985-94), Phila. Forum Exec. Women, Pa. Women's Forum (pres. 2002-04), Com. of Seventy, Mt. Holyoke Alumnae Assn. (bd. dirs. 1986-89, 1999—). Democrat. Lutheran. Avocations: collecting American antiques, gardening, running. Office: Governors Office of Gen Counsel 225 Main Capitol Bldg Harrisburg PA 17120 E-mail: millesq@aol.com.

MILLER, LEWIS NELSON, JR., banker; b. 1944; BA, Washington and Lee U., 1966; postgrad., U. Va., 1972. With 1st & Mchts. Nat. Bank, 1969-70; planning mgr. Cen. Fidelity Bank N.A., Richmond, Va., 1972-73, planning officer, then asst. v.p., 1973-75, v.p., 1975-76, sr. v.p., mgr. fin. group, 1976-78, chief fin. officer, 1978-79, exec. v.p., 1979-82, exec. v.p., chief adminstrv. officer, from 1982; with Cen. Fidelity Banks Inc., Richmond, 1972-2000, sr. v.p., 1980-82, corp. exec. officer, 1982-83, exec. v.p., 1983-84, pres., later also treas., bd. dirs., from 1984; now chmn., pres., chief exec. officer Cen. Fidelity Banks, Richmond. Lt. USN, 1966-69 Office: Ctrl Fidelity Banks Inc PO Box 27602 1021 E Cary St Richmond VA 23261

MILLER, LIA VERENA REYES, management services executive; b. Pasay City, Manila, Philippines, Sept. 1, 1966; d. Rudy San Pedro and Cecilia San Pedro (Suarez) Reyes; m. Thomas Michael Miller, Oct. 3, 1998; stepchildren: Michael Bradley, Brenton Joseph. BS, Marymount Coll., 1988. Creative dir. Pacific Design, Indpls., 1989-91; v.p. ops. Park Kwik Corp. of Am., Indpls., 1988-92; self-employed parking cons. N.Y.C., 1992-95; dir. Internat. Parking Profls., Singapore, 1997—; pres. ParkAsia, Inc., Philippines, 1995—, Parking Co. Asia, Philippines, 1999—. Cons. Fort Bonifacio Devel. Corp., Manila, Philippines, 1995-99, Kerry Properties, Hong Kong, 1997-98, Metro Pacific Land Corp., Manila, Philippines, 1997, Totsuka Station, Japan, 1997. Chmn. Bus. Encouraging Students for Tomorrow, Ind., 1989-90 (recipient Leadership award 1990); vol. Kiwanis Club Indpls., 1986; counselor, leader Eli Lilly Project Leadership, Ind., 1984; mem. Women's Round Table, Ind., 1989-92, Commn. for Downtown Indpls., 1989-91. Mem. Nat. Parking Assn., Internat. Parking Inst. Avocations: scuba diving, drawing and painting, tennis, travel.

MILLER, LINDA B. political scientist; b. Manchester, NH, Aug. 7, 1937; d. Louis and Helene (Chase) M. AB cum laude, Radcliffe Coll., 1959; MA, Columbia U., 1961, PhD, 1965. Asst. prof. Barnard Coll., 1964-67; rsch. assoc. Princeton U., 1966-67, Harvard U., 1967-71, 76-81, lectr. polit. sci., 1968-69; assoc. prof. Wellesley (Mass.) Coll., 1969-75, prof. polit. sci., 1975—2004, chmn. dept., 1985-89. Vis. prof. rsch. Watson Inst., Brown U., 1997, adj. prof. internat. rels., 1998—2000, 2003—, sr. fellow, 2000—03; vis. prof. polit. sci. Brown U., 1997. Author: World Order and Local Disorder: The United Nations and Internal Conflicts, 1967, Dynamics of World Politics: Studies in the Resolution of Conflicts, 1968, Cyprus: The Law and Politics of Civil Strife, 1968; co-author, co-editor: Ideas and Ideals: Essays on Politics in Honor of Stanley Hoffmann, 1993; editor Internat. Studies Rev., 1999-2002; contbr. articles to profl. jours. Internat. Affairs fellow Coun. Fng. Rels., 1973-74, Rockefeller Found. fellow, 1976-77, Oceanographic Instn. sr. fellow, 1979-80, 82-83, NATO social sci. rsch. fellow, 1982-83. Mem. Inst. Strategic Studies, Internat. Studies Assn., Coun. Fgn. Rels., Phi Beta Kappa. Home: PO Box 415 South Wellfleet MA 02663-0415 Office: Wellesley Coll Dept Polit Sci Wellesley MA 02482 also: Watson Inst Brown U PO Box 1970 Providence RI 02912-1970 Office Phone: 401-863-1598. Business E-Mail: Linda_Miller@brown.edu.

MILLER, LINDA B. administrator; Pres. Vol. Trustees Found., Washington. Office: Vol Trustees Found 818 18th St NW Ste 900 Washington DC 20006-3513

MILLER, LINDA KAREN, retired secondary school educator, social studies educator, law educator; b. Kansas City, Jan. 22, 1948; d. Bennie Chris and Thelma Jane (Richey) M. B of Secondary Edn., U. Kans., 1970; M of Secondary Edn., U. Va., 1978, EdD, 1991. Tchr. social studies Pierson Jr. H.S., Kansas City, 1970—72; substitute tchr. Fairfax Pub. Schs., Va., 1972—73; reading aide Lake Braddock Secondary Sch., Burke, Va., 1973—74; tchr. social studies Mark Twain Intermediate Sch., Alexandria, Va., 1974—75, Herndon Intermediate Sch., Va., 1975—78, Fairfax H.S., 1978—86, 1987—2002; ret., 2002. Cons. in field; instr. Sch. Law Cmty. Coll. So. Nev., Las Vegas, 2003. Named Pre-Collegiate Tchr. of Yr., Orgn. Am. Historians, 1996, Secondary Tchr. of Yr., Nat. Coun. for Social Studies, 1996, U. Va., 1997, Outstanding Secondary Tchr., Va. Hist. Soc., 1998, Va. Geography Tchr. of Yr., 1999, Global Technet Tchr. of Yr., Nat. Peace Corps Assn., 1999, Nat. Peace Educator, 2002; recipient George Washington medal, Valley Forge Freedom Found., 1988, Excellence in Tchg. award, U. Kans. Sch. Edn., 1999, Celebrating Tchg. Excellence award, Am. Coun. Tchrs. Russian, 1998, World History Tchg. prize, World History Assn., 2002, Humanities Leadership award, Nat. Endowment Humanities, 2003; fellow, Korean Soc., 2000, 2004, Am. Revolution fellow, NY Hist. Soc., 2001. Mem. Nat. Coun. Social Studies (curriculum com. 1991-94), Am. Legal History Soc., Orgn. Am. Historians, Nev. Coun. Social Studies, U. Va. Alumni Assn. Republican. Episcopalian. Avocation: doll collecting. Personal E-mail: luckylinda0122@yahoo.com.

MILLER, LORING ERIK, insurance agent, broker; b. N.Y.C., Apr. 6, 1951; s. Martin and Frances (Kaufman) M.; m. Ilene Jane Cook, Dec. 18, 1983; children: Justin, Jennifer, Mallory. Student, L.I. U., 1968-72; diploma, GM Sch. Dealership Mdse./Mgmt., 1977. Treas. Dial Chevrolet Inc., Westbury, N.Y., 1970-77, v.p., owner, 1977-88; pres. Middle Country Brokerage Inc., Westbury, 1984-87, Loring E. Miller Agy. Inc., Mineola, N.Y., 1978—. Bd. dirs., pres. Nassau County Police Res. Assn., 1985—; chmn. bd. dirs., founder Suffolk County Police Res., 1997—; assoc. dir. N.Y.C. Police Res. Assn., 1986—, N.Y. Finest Found.; state trustee, lodge pres. N.Y. State Fraternal Order of Police.; bd. dirs., Suffolk County Crime Stoppers; scoutmaster Boy Scouts Am., 1994-97; hon. mem. Nassau County Police Dept.; dir. N.Y. Law Enforcement Found.; main bd. dirs., peace officer, dir. spl. ops. divsn. law enforcement Nassau County Soc. Prevention Cruelty to Animals. Mem.: Profl. Ins. Agts. N.Y. Office: 398 Willis Ave Mineola NY 11501-1819

MILLER, LORRAINE, business owner; BA in History, U. Utah. Lab. technician U. Utah Med. Ctr., 1972-75; pres. Cactus & Tropicals, Inc., Salt Lake City, 1975—. Mem. adv. bd. Utah Securities Commn., 1994; panelist Am. Arbitration Assn., 1991; pres., bd. dirs. Phoenix Inst., 1986-87. Vol. VISTA, 1966-69; mem. Gov.'s Task Force Entrepreneurism, 1988, Gov.'s Task Force Work Force Devel., 1994; mentor Women's Network Entrepreneurial Tng., Small Bus. Adminstrn., 1990; mem. adv. bd. Utah Dem. Health Care Task Force, 1991, Women's Bus. Devel. Office State of Utah, 1990-92; employer Supportive Employment for the Handicapped, 1990-92. Recipient Pathfinder award Salt Lake C. of C., 1986, Women of Achievement award YWCA, 1992; named Nat. Small Bus. Person of Yr. by U.S. Small Bus. Adminstrn., 1994. Mem. Nat. Assn. Women's Bus. Owners (pres. Salt Lake chpt. 1992), Utah Assn. Women's Bus. Owners (pres. 1992, 1st v.p. 1991, bd. dirs. 1985, 89-90, named Woman Bus. Owner of Yr. 1987), Wasatch Cactus & Succulent Soc. (co-founder). Office: Cactus & Tropicals 2735 S 2000 E Salt Lake City UT 84109-1749

MILLER, LOUIS E. airport terminal executive, accountant; b. Salt Lake City, Apr. 24, 1948; Student, U. Utah; grad., Stevens Henager Bus. Coll. CPA. Responsible fin. and adminstrn. Airport Authority; dep. dir. airports Salt Lake City; ptnr. pub. acctg. firm; internal auditor Salt Lake City Corp.; promoted to exec. dir., CEO Salt Lake City Airport Authority; CPA; exec. dir., CEO Tampa Internat. Airport, 1996—. Pres. Westshore alliance; mem. bd. Tampa Bay Conv. & Visitors Bur. (TBCVB); mem. bd. dirs. Tampa Bay Partnership, Met. Planning Orgn., Greater Tampa C.of C.; mem. bd. dirs. Policy Com. Com. of One Hundred. Served U.S. Army. Named to Utah Travel Coun.'s Tourism Hall of Fame; recipient Freedom of Enterprise award, Utah Assn. Cert. Pub. Accts., Svc. to Industry award, Associated Gen. Contractors of Am. Utah chpt. . Mem.: Airports Coun. Internat. (chmn. N.Am. region 1994). Office: PO Box 22287 Tampa FL 33622

MILLER, LOUIS H. lawyer; b. Lampeter, U.K., Apr. 22, 1945; m. Diane Matuszewski, Dec. 31, 1973; children: Margaret, Anthony. BA in History, Rutgers Coll., 1967; JD, Temple U., 1970. Bar: N.J. 1970, U.S. Dist. Ct. N.J. 1970, U.S. Supreme Ct. 1996. Law clk. to Judge Thomas Beetel Hunterdon County Ct., Flemington, N.J., 1970-71; law clk. to Judge Baruch Seidman Superior Ct. N.J. Chancery, Trenton, N.J., 1971-72; assoc. Jefferson, Jefferson & Vaida, Flemington, 1972-75; ptnr. Vaida & Miller, Flemington, 1975-78; pvt. practice Flemington, 1978-81, 88—; judge Superior Ct. N.J., Flemington, 1981-88; of counsel Levinson Axelrod Wheaton & Grayzel, Flemington, 1990-97. Spl. dep. atty. gen. N.J. Hunterdon County Prosecutor Office, Flemington, 1972-73; condemnation commr. Appt. Superior Ct. N.J., Flemington, 1988—, N.J. Assembly spkrs. commr.; commr. N.J. State Commn. Investigation, Trenton, 1993-97; arbitrator U.S. Fed. Dist. Ct. N.J., 1989—. Twp. committeeman Alexandria Twp. Com., R.D. Milford, N.J., 1978-81. Mem. Am. Judges Assn., Am. Judicature Soc., N.J. State Bar Assn. (mem. dist. ethics com. 1980-81, mem. mcpl. ct. practice com. 1996—), Hunterdon County Bar Assn., Consular Law Soc., Welsh Am. Geneal. Soc., Welsh North Am. C. of C. (bd. dirs.), USF Constellation Mus. (mem. bd. trustees 2003-). Republican. Avocations: paleontology, travel, hiking. Office: PO Box 850 40 Main St Flemington NJ 08822-1411 Office Phone: 908-782-1818. Personal E-mail: millerlh@earthlink.net.

MILLER, LOUIS HOWARD, biologist, researcher; b. Balt., Feb. 4, 1935; s. David and Daisy (Arenson) Miller; m. Nancy Jo Harned, Sept. 26, 1959; 1 child, Jennifer. BS, Haverford Coll., 1956; MD, Washington U., St. Louis, 1960; MS in Parasitology, Columbia U., 1964. Asst. prof. then assoc. prof. Coll. of P & S, Columbia U., N.Y.C., 1967—71; head malaria sect. NIAID, NIH, Bethesda, Md., 1971—92, chief lab. parasitic diseases, 1992—. Contbr. articles to profl. jours. Capt. U.S. Army, 1965—67. Recipient Paul Ehrlich/Ludwig Darmstaedter prize, 1989, Award for Disting. Achievement in Infectious Disease Rsch., Bristol-Myers Squibb, 1996, Commonwealth award in sci. and invention, 1999. Fellow: ACP, Queensland Inst. Med. Rsch., Royal Soc. Tropical Medicine and Hygiene; mem.: Assn. Am. Physicians, Inst. of Medicine, NAS, Am. Soc. Tropical Medicine and Hygiene (pres. 1988).

MILLER, MALCOLM HENRY, manufacturing sales executive, real estate developer; b. Elgin, Ill., Feb. 6, 1934; s. Carl Theodore and Alice Lucy (Garbisch) M. BA, U. Wis., 1957; postgrad., Am. Inst. Fgn. Trade, 1961, U. N.Mex., 1963. Sales engr. Fairbanks Morse Corp., Beloit, Wis., 1962; pvt. practice real estate Albuquerque, 1964-75; supt., v.p. Walworth Foundries, Inc., Darien, Wis., 1959-61, exec. v.p. sales, co-owner, 1975—; v.p. sales, co-owner Waukesha Specialty Co., Inc., Darien, 1975—. Treas. Fastcast, Inc., Albuquerque, 1993—. Loan advisor, developer Community Assn. for Sr. Housing, Albuquerque, 1967-70; Rep. candidate for state senator N.Mex., 1970; active fin. com. Bernalillo County Reps., N.Mex., 1970-80, Walworth County Reps., Wis., 1976-77; mem. Congressman Ryan's 1st Dist. Small Bus. Adv. Com. Served to 1st lt. US Army, 1957-59. Mem. Am. Foundrymen's Assn., Dairy Food Industries Supply Assn., Dairy Food Industries Supply Assn. (bd. dir. 1992-95), Santa Fe Opera Guild, Big Foot Country Club, Nat. "W" Club, Masons, The Madison Club, Sigma Alpha Epsilon. Republican. Episcopalian. Avocations: health activities, cinema, opera, fly fishing. Home: 223 Fremont St PO Box 37 Walworth WI 53184-0037 Office: Walworth Foundries Inc PO Box 160 Hwy 14 and I-43 Interchange Darien WI 53114

MILLER, MARCIA E. federal government official; married; 1 son. BA, Miami U., Oxford, Ohio, 1977; MA, Johns Hopkins U., 1981. With internat. trade divsn. Am. Textile Mfrs. Inst.; internat. economist Wilmer, Cutler & Pickering, 1985-87; profl. staff mem. Senate Com. on Fin., 1987-93, chief internat. trade counsellor, 1993-95, minority chief internat. trade counsellor, 1995-96; chmn. U.S. Internat. Trade Commn., Washington, 1996-98, vice chmn., 1998—, commr., 2000—. Office: US Internat Trade Commn USITC Bldg 500 E St SW Washington DC 20436

MILLER, MARGARET ALISON, education educator; b. L.A., Dec. 17, 1944; d. Richard Crump and Virginia Margaret (Dudley) M.; m. Spencer Hall, Aug. 21, 1967 (div. 1977); 1 child, Justin Robinson; m. Alan Blair Howard, Oct. 7, 1990. BA in English summa cum laude, UCLA, 1966; postgrad., Stanford U., 1966-67; PhD in English, U. Va., 1971. Instr. English U. Va., Charlottesville, 1971-72; from asst. prof. to assoc. prof. U. Mass., Dartmouth, 1972-83, prof. English, 1983-86, co-dir. women's studies program, 1981-83, asst. to dean arts and scis., 1983-85, asst. to pres., 1985-86; acad. affairs coord. State Coun. Higher Edn. for Va., Richmond, 1986-87, assoc. dir. for acad. affairs, 1987-97; pres. Am. Assn. for Higher Edn., Washington, 1997-2000; pres. emerita Am. Assn. Higher Edn., Washington, 2000—; prof. higher edn. policy U. Va., Charlottesville, 2001—. Head English sect. transitional summer program Brown U., 1976; instr. honors program Va. Commonwealth U., 1991-93; cons. Coun. Rectors, Budapest, 1993, Minn. State U. System, Mpls., 1992, U.S. Dept. Edn., Washington, 1990—, S.C. Higher Edn. Commn., 1989-90, Edn. Commn. States, Denver, 1994-2000; presenter in field; participant UNESCO World Conf. on Higher Edn., 1998; adv. commr. Edn. Commn. of the States, 1998-2000; chair steering com. Washington Higher Edn. Secretariat, 1997-2000; mem. Nat. Postsecondary Edn. Cooperative, 1997-2000; cons. Nat. Ctr. for Pub. Policy and Higher Edn., 1998—; bd. dirs. Nat. Ctr. for Edn. Mgmt. Sys., 2001—, Edn. Direct; participant Aspen Inst., 1998; exec. editor Change mag., 2000—; judge Tchrs. Ins. Annuity Assn./Coll. Retirement Equity Fund Hesburgh awards, 1999—. Contbr. articles to profl. jours. Mem. Am. Assn. Higher Edn. (leadership coun.), Am. Coun. on Edn. (exec. com. identification program in Va. 1988-97, participant nat. identifica-

tion program's 41st nat. forum for women leaders in higher edn. 1989, adv. bd. Policy Inst.), Phi Beta Kappa. Avocations: reading, gardening, travel. Home: 2176 Lindsay Rd Gordonsville VA 22942-1620 Office: Curry Sch Edn U Va 405 Emmett St S Charlottesville VA 22903 E-mail: pmiller@virginia.edu.

MILLER, MARGERY, psychologist, speech pathologist, mental health educator, administrator; b. May 7, 1951; m. Donald F. Moores; children: Kip Lee, Tige Justice. BA, Elmira Coll., 1971; MA, NYU, 1972; EdS, MS, SUNY, Albany, 1975; MA, Towson State U., 1987; PhD, Georgetown U., 1991. Lic. speech pathologist Md., lic. psychologist Md., cert. tchr. nursery-6th grades, spl. edn. NY, nationally cert. sch. psychologist. Speech and lang. pathologist Mental Retardation Inst. Flower and Fifth Ave. Hosp., NYC, 1971—72; cmty. speech/lang. pathologist, dir. speech and hearing svc. NY State Dept. Mental Hygiene, Troy, 1972—74; instr. comm. disorders dept. Coll. St. Rose, Albany, NY, 1975—77; clin. supr. U. Md., College Park, 1978; speech/lang. pathologist Md. Sch. for Deaf, Frederick, 1978—84; auditory devel. specialist Montgomery County Pub. Schs., Rockville, Md., 1984—87; coord. Family Life program Nat. Acad. Gallaudet U., Washington, 1987—88, interim dir., 1988—89; dir. Counseling & Devel. Ctr. N.W. Campus, Washington, 1989—93; prof. psychology, coord. psychology internship program Gallaudet U., Washington, 1993—; lic. practicing psychologist Bethesda, Md., 1998—. Instr. sign lang. program Frederick C.C.; dance instr. for deaf adolescents; diagnostic cons. on speech pathology. Author: It's O.K. To Be Angry, 1976; contbr. chpt. to Cognition, Education, and Deafness: Directions for Research and Instruction, 1985; mem. editl. rev. com. Gov.'s Devel. Disabilities Coun. Md., 1984; presenter at confs.; contbr. articles to profl. jours. Vol., choreographer Miss Deaf Am. Pageant, 1981. Office of Edn. Children's Bur. fellow, 1971. Mem.: Am. Assn. of Higher Edn., Am. Psychol. Assn., Nat. Assn. Sch. Psychologists, Nat. Assn. of Deaf, Am. Speech, Lang. and Hearing Assn. (cert. clin. competence in speech/lang. pathology). Office: Gallaudet U 800 Florida Ave NE Washington DC 20002-3660 E-mail: margery.miller@gallaudet.edu.

MILLER, MARIAN, professional society administrator; Grad., Ind. U. 3rd v.p., sec. Nat. Fedn. Rep. Women, Alexandria, Va., 1st v.p., mem. exec. com., also bd. dirs., pres. Chair program by-laws, sr. Am. and leadership coms., regent Nat. Fedn. Rep. Women. Advisor to Suellen Reed State Supt. Com., to Steve Goldsmith for Gov. Campaign; statewide vol. coord. for v.p. Dan Quayle's 1st U.S. Senate campaign, U.S. Senator Dan Coats, Gov. Otis Bowen, John Murtz for Gov. Campaigns; del. Rep. Nat. Convs., 1988, 92, 96; precinct committeewoman Tippecanoe County; pres. Tippecanoe County RWC; active Ind. Com. Humanities, Gov.'s Adv. Com. on Pub. Welfare, Pension Mgmt. Legis. Study Commn.; active gov. rels. com. Ind. Hosp. Assn.; bd. dirs. United Way Ind.; del. to White House Conf. on Aging; chmn. Ind. Commn. on Aging; del. to Nat. Forum on Excellence in Edn.; founder Hoosier Assocs., 1975—. Recipient Pres.'s award Ind. U. Alumni Assn., Sagamore of the Wabash award Gov. Ind. Office: Nat Fedn Rep Women 124 N Alfred St Alexandria VA 22314-3011 Fax: 703-548-9836.

MILLER, MARILEE HEBERT, arts administrator, producer, director, consultant; b. Laredo, Tex., Feb. 25, 1949; d. Minos Joseph and Eulalie (Fisher) Hebert; m. Stewart E. Slater, Dec. 3, 1972 (div. July 1978); m. Robert K. Miller, Jan. 2, 1999. BA, Baylor U., 1970, MA, 1972. Cert. secondary sch. tchr., Tex. Actress, dir., assoc. producer Everyman Players, Ky. and La., 1972-80; community rels. dir. Actors Theatre of Louisville, 1973-74, dir. children's theatre, lunchtime & cabaret theatre, 1974-76, dir., apprentice intern program, 1974-77, new play festivals coord., 1979-81, mgr. internat. touring, 1980-98, assoc. dir., 1981-98; sr. v.p. external affairs Ky. Ctr. for the Arts, 1998—. Guest dir. Louisville Children's Theatre, 1978; grants panelist Ky. Arts Coun., La. Arts Coun.; conf. lectr. Ky. Arts Coun., Va. Arts Commn., Southeastern Theatre Conf., S.W. Theatre Conf., So. Arts Fedn. Author: (play) Hey Diddle Diddle!, 1976. Pres. Ky. Citizens for Arts, 1985-86, 90-92; co-chmn. subcom. on arts Edn. Workforce, 1990-93; grad. Leadership Louisville, 1989, bd. dirs., 1992-98; vice-chmn. Focus Louisville, 1994-96; chmn. nonprofit recruitment com., chmn. Louisville Downtown Mgmt. Dist., 1996-97, Leadership Ptnrs., 1996; chmn. Farm Works Coun., 1997-99; mem. Downtown Devel. Implementation com., Louisville, 1991-93; Louisville Forum adv. coun., 1995-96; bd. dirs. Louisville Ctrl. Area, 1996-98; pres. Park IV Condo Assn., 1989-91, sec. Main St. Assn., 1992-96, v.p., 1997—; staging dir., cons. Walnut St. Bapt. Ch., 1980-99, chmn. strategic planning, 1998, co-chair Phase II Facilities 2000, 1997-2000. Bingham fellow, 1995-96; recipient Ky. Commonwealth award 1996, NACL Disting. Leadership award, 1997. Democrat. Baptist. Avocations: travel, hiking, music. Office: Ky Ctr for Arts 501 W Main St Louisville KY 40202-2989 E-mail: mmiller@kca.org.

MILLER, MARILYN LEA, library science educator; AA, Graceland Coll., 1950; BS in English, U. Kans., 1952; AMLS, U. Mich., 1959, PhD of Librarianship and Higher Edn., 1976. Bldg.-level sch. libr. Wellsville HS, Kans., 1952-54; tchr.-libr. Arthur Capper Jr. HS, Topeka, 1954-56; head libr. Topeka HS, Topeka, 1956-62; sch. libr. cons. State of Kans. Dept. of Pub. Instrn., 1962-67; from asst. to assoc. prof. Sch. Librarianship Western Mich. U., Kalamazoo, 1967-77; assoc. prof. libr. sci. U. NC, Chapel Hill, 1977-87, prof., chair dept. libr. and info. studies Greensboro, 1987-95, prof. emeritus, 1996—. Vis. faculty Kans. State Tchrs., Emporia, 1960, 63, 64, 66, U. Minn., Mpls., 1971, U. Manitoba, Winnipeg, Can., 1971; vis. prof. Appalachian State U., Boone, NC, 1987; adv. bd. sch. libr. media program Nat. Ctr. for Edn. Stats., 1989, user rev. panel, 1990; chair assoc. dean search com. Sch. Edn., 1988, coord. Piedmont young writers conf., 1989-94, 97-99, chair race and gender com., 1990-93, SACS planning and evaluation com., 1990-91, learning resources ctr. adv. com., 1991-93; hearing panel for honor code U. NC Greensboro, 1988-91, assn. women faculty and administrv. staff, 1987-95, faculty coun., 1987-95, chair, 1994-95, univ. libr. com., 1987-88, com. faculty devel. in race and gender scholarship, 1990-92; lectr. and cons. in field. Editor: Pioneers and Leaders in Library Service to Youth, 2003; mem. editl. bd. The Emergency Librarian, 1981-97, Collection Building: Studies in the Development and Effective Use of Library Resources, 1978-96; contbr. chpt. to books, articles to profl. jour. Children's libr. specialists to visit Russian sch. and pub. libr., book publs., Moscow, Leningrad, Tashkent, 1979; hon. del. White House Conf. on Libr. and Info. Svcs., Washington, 1991; head del. Romanian Summer Inst. on Librarianship in U.S., 1991; citizen amb. People to People Internat. Program, People's Republic of China, 1992, Russian and Poland, 1992, Russia, 1994, Barcelona, 1995; exec. bd. dirs. Friends of Greensboro Pub. Libr., 1996-99, chair gift shop and coffee shop adv. com., 1996-2002; chair Citizens Materials Adv. com., 1999—, Citizens Strategic Long Range Planning com., 1994-95, 2001-02, chair, 2002—, Sch. Pub. Libr. com., 2002-. Recipient Freedom Found. medal, 1962, Disting. Svc. to Sch. Librs. award Kans. Assn. Sch. Librs., 1982, Disting. Svc. award Graceland Coll., 1992, Disting. Alumnus award Sch. Libr. and Info. Studies, U. Mich., 1988, Contribution to Libr. Info. Sci. award Assn. Libr. Info. Sci., 1999; Delta Kappa Gamma scholar, 1972. Mem.: ALA (awards com. 1971—72, chair Chgo. conf. resolutions 1972, chair 1973—75, resolutions com. 1976—78, adv. com. Nat. Ctr. Ednl. Stats. 1984, standing com. libr. edn. 1987—91, yearbook adv. com. 1988—90, chair 1989—90, pres. 1992—93, exec. dir. 1994, chair rsch. com., chair search com., Disting. Svc. award Am. Assn. Sch. Librs. 1993), Friends of N.C. Pub. Librs. (bd. dirs. 2000—), So. Assn. Colls. and Schs. (accreditation team 1988), Southeastern Libr. Assn. (chair libr. educators sect. 1990—92), N.C. Assn. Sch. Librs., Assn. Libr Svc. to Children (bd. dirs. 1976—81, pres. 1979—80, rsch. com. 1982—85, chair 1984—85), Assn. Ednl. Comms. and Tech., Am. Assn. Sch. Librs. (nominating com. 1980, pub. com. 1981—82, chair search com. exec. dir. 1985, v.p., pres.-elect 1985—86, pres. 1986—87, coord. coms. nat. stds. vision and implementation 1995—98), N.C. Libr. Assn. (life; edn. libr. com. 1978—80, 1982—86, bd. dirs. 1987—99, exec. bd. status women roundtable 1989—, chmn.-elect 1995—97, chmn. 1997—99, commn. on status of sch. librs. 1999—2000).

MILLER, MARK C. waste management administrator; BS in Computer Sci., Purdue U. From mgr. to v.p. Internat. Divsn. Abbott Labs., 1976—89, v.p. Internat. Divsn., 1989—92; pres. Stericycle Inc., Lake Forest, Ill., 1992—, CEO, 1992—. Bd. dir. Ventana Med. Sys., Inc., Lake Forest Hosp. Office: Stericycle Inc 28161 North Keith Drive Lake Forest IL 60045*

MILLER, MARK KARL, journalist; b. Meadville, Pa., Aug. 5, 1953; s. Richard Karl and Ellener Louise (Zimber) M. BA in Comms. and Journalism, Shippensburg U. of Pa., 1975. Editl. asst. Broadcasting mag., Washington, 1975, staff writer, 1976—77, asst. editor, 1977—80, sr. news editor, 1980—87, asst. mng. editor, 1987—91; mng. editor Broadcasting & Cable mag., Washington, 1991—98, Digital TV mag., Washington, 1999; freelance editor, writer, photographer, rschr., 2000—. Mem. editl. adv. bd. Shippensburg U. of Pa., 1989-94, mem. profl. adv. bd. comm./journalism dept., 1994-96. Recipient Outstanding Alumnus award Shippensburg U., 1992. Mem. Soc. Profl. Journalists, Art Deco Soc. of Washington (bd. dirs., publs. chair 1986-97), Nat. Press Club. Home and Office: 2425 Valley Way Cheverly MD 20785-2956 Office Phone: 301-773-0058. E-mail: mkmiller@comcast.net.

MILLER, MARK WILLIAM, investment advisor, writer; b. Kansas City, Mo., Mar. 23, 1964; s. William Joseph and Arden (Roberts) M.; m. Kelly Lyn Macklin, Sept. 18, 1998. BS in Polit. Sci. and Econs., Kans. U., 1987. Registered investment advisor, Kans.; registered in. cons. Fin. planner IDS/Am. Express, Overland Park, Kans., 1987-89; registered rep. Stern Bros. and Co., Kansas City, 1989-91; mut. fund mgr. DST Systems, Inc., Kansas City, 1993; pres. Sensible Saver Publs., Inc., Kansas City, 1993—; CEO, cons. Miller Capital Mgmt., Inc., Overland Park, 2000—. Author: The Sensible Saver, 1996, The Complete Idiot's Guide to Being a Cheapskate, 1999. Vol. Birchwood Ch., Independence, Mo., 2000. Avocations: golf, flying. Office: Miller Capital Mgmt Inc 4650 College Blvd Ste 210 Overland Park KS 66211 Fax: (913) 327-7374. E-mail: millercapital@cs.com.

MILLER, MARLIN J., JR., pharmaceutical executive; Pres., CEO Arrow Internat., Inc., Reading, Pa. Office: Arrow Internat Inc 2400 Bernville Rd Reading PA 19605-9458

MILLER, MARSHALL LEE, lawyer; b. Chattanooga, Tenn., Oct. 18, 1942; BA, Harvard U., 1964; student, Oxford U., Eng., Heidelberg U., Germany; JD, Yale U., 1970. Bar: D.C. 1971, U.S. Supreme Ct. 1979. Spl. asst. to adminstr. U.S. EPA, 1971-73; assoc. dep. atty. gen. U.S. Dept. Justice, 1973-74; asst. sec. labor (acctg.), dep. adminstr. OSHA, 1975-76; ptnr. Baise & Miller, Washington. Bd. editors: Yale Law Jour.; Soviet Mil. editor: Armed Forces Jour., 1983-87; author books internat. and environ. topics. Bd. dirs. Bulgarian-Am. Enterprise Fund, Electronic Warfare Assocs., Am. Coun. of Internat. Living, Am. Assn. Advancement Sci. Office: Baise & Miller 1020 19th St NW Ste 400 Washington DC 20036-6101 Home: PO Box 1311 Bethany Beach DE 19930-1311

MILLER, MARTIN E. engineer, consultant; BSEE, U. Pacific. V.p. engring. Cacheon, San Francisco, 2000—02, GPware, Menlo Park, Calif., 2002—03. Mem.: IEEE, SVASE CTO Group, SDFORUM, Alpha Kappa Lambda (pres.). Achievements include patents pending for integration of personal information manager with navigation system. Personal E-mail: martin@m-vision.com.

MILLER, MARTIN EUGENE, school system consultant, negotiator, lobbyist; b. Decatur, Ill., May 14, 1945; s. Floyd Homer and Vivian LaVerne (Gould) M.; m. Sherry Kay Bandy, May 25, 1968; children: Liane, Laura. BS, U. Ill., 1968; MEd, U. North Fla., 1974. Cert. math. tchr.; cert. ednl. adminstrn. and supervision. Tchr. Decatur (Ill.) Pub. Schs., 1968, Clay County Sch. Bd., Green Cove Springs, Fla., 1970-74, coord. cert. pers., 1974-77, dir. instructional pers., 1977-78, dir. pers. svcs., 1978-81, asst. supt. for human resources and labor rels., 1981-93, dir. cmty. and govtl. rels., 1993-97; gen. dir. govtl. rels. Duval County Pub. Schs., Jacksonville, Fla., 1997—2001; pres. Miller Consulting Group, Inc.; v.p. Sch. Dist. Mgmt. Svcs., Inc. Past mem. Edn. Stds. Commn., Tallahassee, 1985-93, vice chmn., 1988-92; past mem. Blue Cross-Blue Shield Adv. Coun., Jacksonville, Fla.; past mem. Fla. Ednl. Leaders Forum. Served as staff sgt. USAF, 1968-70. Mem.: Fla. Ednl. Legis. Liaisons (past pres.), Fla. Edn. Negotiators (past pres.), Fla. Assn. Sch. Adminstrs., Am. Assn. Sch. Adminstrs., Phi Delta Kappa. Republican. Presbyterian. Avocations: home computers, music, swimming. Home: 1612 Bay Cir W Orange Park FL 32073-4746 Office: 1612 Bay Circle West Orange Park FL 32073 E-mail: martinmiller@MillerConsultingGroup.com.

MILLER, MARY HELEN, retired public administrator; b. Smiths Grove, KY, June 30, 1936; d. Walter Frank and Lottie Belle (Russell) Huddleston; m. George Ward Wilson, Sept. 12, 1958 (div. Sept. 1973); children: Ward Glenn, Amy Elizabeth Huddleston; m. Francis Guion Miller Jr., June 6, 1981. BA, Western Ky. U., 1958. Tchr. Fayette County Schs., Lexington, Ky., 1958-60, Seneca High Sch., Louisville, 1960-63, Shelby County High Sch., Shelbyville, Ky., 1963-69; rsch. analyst Legis. Rsch. Com., Frankfort, Ky., 1973-79, asst. dir., 1979-83, 90-91; chief exec. asst. Office Gov., Frankfort, 1983-87, 93-95, legis. liaison, 1991-93; cabinet sec. Natural Resources and Environ. Protection Cabinet, Frankfort, 1987-88; sales assoc. W. Wagner, Jr. Comml. Real Estate, Louisville, 1989-91; ret., 1996. Author: (constl. revision) Citizens Guide To/Perspective, 1978, (booklet) A Look at Kentucky General Assembly, 1979, A Guide to Education Reform, 1990, (handbook) Gubernatorial Transition in Kentucky, 1991. Active Leadershi Ky. Alumni, Frankfort, 1986, Waterfront Devel. Corp. Bd., Louisville, 1986—87, Greater Louis Partnership Econ. Devel., 1988—92, Shelbyville 2000 Found. Bd., 1991—92; mem., sec. Regional Airport Authority Bd., Louisville, 1986—89; pres. Shelby County Cmty. Theatre Bd., Shelbyville, 1989—90; mem. Ky. Long Term Policy Bd., 1992—99, chair, 1995; mem. Ky. Hist. Properties Commn., 1995—99; chair Shelby County Cmty. Found., 1995—2000; exec. com. Ky. Hist. Soc., 2002—; mem. Shelby Devel. Found., 2003—. Recipient Vic Hellard Jr. Pub. Svc. in Ky. award, 1999; named Shelbyville Citizen of Yr., 1998. Mem. Caryatid Book Club (pres. 1999), Women's Initiative Networking Groups (pres. 1998), Western Ky. U. Alumni Assn. (bd. dirs. 1992-95). Democrat. Episcopalian. Avocations: reading, theater, gardening, antiques. Home: 1116 Main St Shelbyville KY 40065-1420

MILLER, MARY HOTCHKISS, lay worker; b. Washington, Dec. 4, 1936; d. Neil and Esther LeMoyne (Helfer) H.; m. Ronald Homer Miller, May 20, 1961; 1 child, Timothy Ronald. BA, Western Md. Coll., 1958; MRE, Union Theol. Sem. 1960; Cert., Windham House, N.Y.C., 1960. Dir. Christian Edn. Bruton Parish ch., Williamsburg, Va., 1960-61; dir. Christian Edn. (part-time) All Saints Episcopal Ch., Bklyn., 1961-62; adminstrv. and program asst., Christian Social Rels. Dept., Exec. Coun. Episcopal Ch. U.S.A. Episcopal Ch. Ctr., N.Y.C., 1967-72; nat. treas., mem. bd., chmn. Episcopal Peace Fellowship, Washington, N.Y.C. and Chgo., 1972-88, exec. sec. Washington, 1989-2001; mem. Standing Commn. on Anglican and Internat. Peace with Justice, Epis. Ch., 2001—; ret., 2001. Bd. dirs., exec. com. Nat. Campaign for Peace Tax Fund, Washington, 1989—91; bd. dirs. Ctr. on Conscience and War/Nat. Interreligious Svc. Bd. for Conscientious Objectors, Washington, 1989—96, Washington, 2001—; coord. The Consultation. Contbr. articles to Witness mag. and jours., newsletters in field; editl. bd. ISSUES of Gen. Convs. of Episcopal Ch., 1973-91; designer ch. vestments and banners. Democrat. Episcopalian. E-mail: mary.miller@ecunet.org.

MILLER, MARY JEANNETTE, office management specialist; b. Washinton, Sept. 24, 1912; d. John William and David Evengline (Hill) Sims; children: Sylvenia Delores Doby, Ferdi A., Cecil Jr.(dec.). Student, Howard U., 1929—30, U. Ill., 1940—42; student Dept. Agrl., U. Md.Grad. Sch., 1975; Cert. in Vocat. Photography, Prince George C.C., 1986. Chief mail processing unit Bur. Reclamation, Washington, 1940—57; records supr. AID, 1957—71; office engr. Bechtel Assocs., Washington, 1976—79; records mgmt. cons. AID, 1980—84; docent Mus. African Art Smithsonian Instn., Washington, 1986—89; circulation asst. Prince George County Libr. System, Hyattsville, Md., 1987—91; ret. Real estate assoc., tchr. English as Second lang. Ministry Edn., Seoul, Korea, Saint Helena, 1960—61; cons. Ministry Fin., Laos, 1968—70, Ministry Fin. Royal Lao Govt., 1971—74, AID Missions, Yemen, Sudan, Somalia, 1982; mem. Friends of Internat. Edn. Com., 1985—92; sec., treas., bd. dirs. Miller Transitional, Inc. Author Handbooks on Office Mgmt.; contbr. articles to travel books. Mem.: AARP, NAFE, Montgomery County Bd. Realtors, Am. Mgmt. Assn., Soc. Am. Archivists, Nat. Trust Hist. Preservation, Am. Fgn. Svc. Assn., Zeta Phi Beta. Roman Catholic. Home: 5601 Seminary Rd #602-N Falls Church VA 22041-3504

MILLER, MAURICE DEAN, special education educator; b. Terre Haute, Ind., Apr. 2, 1946; s. Richard C. and Violet E. (Rhoads) M.; m. Naomi Pearl Evans, Aug. 9, 1968; children: Jennifer, Zachary. BSEd, Ill. State U., 1968; MSEd, No. Ill. U., 1971; PhD, So. Ill. U., 1976. Cert. elem., secondary and spl. edn. tchr., Ill. Tchr. Lena (Ill.)-Winslow Jr. High Sch., 1968-70; learning disabilities specialist Kendall County Spl. Edn., Yorkville, Ill., 1970-72; spl. edn. tchr. Western Ill. U., Macomb, 1972-74; instr., grad. fellow So. Ill. U., Carbondale, 1974-76; asst. prof. Tenn. Technol. U., Cookeville, 1976-78; prof. spl. edn. Ind. State U., Terre Haute, 1978—. Cons. edn. of gifted children Ind. Dept. Edn., Indpls., 1982—; cons. edn. of handicapped children Ind. Pub. Schs., Terre Haute, 1982—. Contbr. articles to ednl. jours. Mem. Nat. Assn. for Gifted, Coun. Exceptional Children, Phi Delta Kappa. Methodist. Avocations: camping, biking. Office: Ind State U Spl Edn Terre Haute IN 47809-0001

MILLER, MAYNARD MALCOLM, geologist, educator, research institute director, explorer, legislator; b. Seattle, Jan. 23, 1921; s. Joseph Anthony and Juanita Queena (Davison) M.; m. Joan Walsh, Sept. 15, 1951; children: Ross McCord, Lance Davison. BS magna cum laude, Harvard U., 1943; MA, Columbia U., 1948; PhD, St. John's Coll., Cambridge (Eng.) U., 1957; student, Naval War Coll., Air War Coll., Nat. Def. U., Oak Ridge Inst. Nuc. Sci.; DSc (hon.), U. Alaska, 1990. Registered profl. geologist, Idaho. Asst. prof. naval sci. Princeton (N.J.) U., 1946; geologist Gulf Oil Co., Cuba, 1947; rsch. assoc., coord., dir. Office Naval Rsch. Juneau Icefield Rsch. Project, Am Geog. Soc., N.Y.C., 1948-53; staff scientist Swiss Fed. Inst. for Snow and Avalanche Rsch., Davos, 1952-53; instr. dept. geography Cambridge U., 1953-54, 56; assoc. prodr., field unit dir. film Seven Wonders of the World Cinerama Corp., Europe, Asia, Africa, Mid. East, 1954-55; rsch. assoc. Lamont Geol. Obs., N.Y.C., 1955-59; sr. scientist dept. geology Columbia U., N.Y.C., 1957-59; asst. prof. geology Mich. State U., East Lansing, 1959-61, assoc. prof., 1961-63, prof., 1963-75; dean Coll. Mines and Earth Resources U. Idaho, Moscow, 1975-88, prof. geology, dir. Glaciological and Arctic Scis. Inst., 1975—; dir., state geologist Idaho Geol. Survey, 1975-88; rep. Legislature of State of Idaho, Boise, 1992-2000. Prin. investigator, geol. sci. contracts and projects for govt. agys., univs., pvt. corps., geographic socs., 1946—; geophys. cons. Nat. Park Svc., NASA, USAF, NAS; organizer, leader USAF-Harvard Mt. St. Elias Expdn., 1946; chief geologist Am. Mt. Everest Expdn., Nepal, 1963; dir. Nat. Geographic Soc. Alaskan Glacier Commemorative Project, 1964—; organizer, field leader Nat. Geographic Soc. Joint U.S. Can. Mt. Kennedy Yukon Meml. Mapping Expdn., 1965, Museo Argentino de Ciencias Naturales, Patagonian expdn. and glacier study for Inst. Geologico del Peru and Am. Geog. Soc., 1949-50, adv. missions People's Republic of China, 1981, 86, 88, 98, geol. expdns. Himalaya, Nepal, 1963, 84, 87, USAF ice survey mission to Ellesmere Land, North Pole and Polar Sea, 1951; organizer, ops. officer pioneering USN-LTA blimp geophysics flight to Ice Island T-3 and North Pole area for Office Naval Rsch., 58; prin. investigator U.S. Naval Oceanog. Office sea and pack ice Rsch. Ice Island T-3 Polar Sea, 1967-68, 70-73; dir. lunar field sta. simulation USAF-Boeing Co., 1959-60; prin. investigator Nat. Geographic Soc. 30 Yr. Remap of Lemon, Taku and Cathedral Massif Glaciers, Juneau Icefield, 1989-2002; exec. dir. Found. for Glacier and Environ. Rsch., Pacific Sci. Ctr., Seattle, 1955-95, 1997—, chmn., 1992—, pres., 1955-85, trustee, 1960—, organizer, dir. Juneau Icefield Rsch. Program (JIRP), 1946 ; cons. Dept. Hwys. State of Alaska, 1965; chmn., exec. dir. World Ctr. for Exploration Found., N.Y.C., 1968-71; dir., mem. adv. bd. Idaho Geol. Survey, 1975-88; chmn. nat. coun. JSHS program U.S. Army Rsch. Office and Acad. Applied Sci., 1982-90; sci. dir. U.S. Army Rsch. Office and DOD Nat. Sci. and Humanities Symposia program, 1991—; disting. guest prof. China U. Geoscis., Wuhan, 1981—, Changchun U. Earth Scis., People's Republic of China, 1988—; adj. prof. U. Alaska, 1986—. Author: Field Manual of Glaciological and Arctic Sciences; co-author books on Alaskan glaciers and Nepal geology; contbr. over 200 reports, sci. papers to profl. jours., ency. articles, chpts. to books, monographs; prodr., nat. lectr. films and videos. Past mem. nat. exploring com., nat. sea exploring com. Boy Scouts Am.; past mem. nat. adv. bd. Embry Riddle Aero. U.; bd. dirs. Idaho Rsch. Found.; pres. state divsn. Mich. UN Assn., 1970-73; mem. Centennial and Health Environ. Commns., Moscow, Idaho, 1987—. With USN, 1943-46, PTO. Decorated 11 campaign and battle stars; Fulbright scholar Cambridge U., 1957; named Leader of Tomorrow Seattle C. of C. and Time mag., 1953, one of Ten Outstanding Young Men U.S. Jaycees, 1954; recipient commendation for lunar environ. study USAF, 1960, Hubbard medal (co-recipient with Mt. Everest expdn. team) Nat. Geog. Soc., 1963, Elisha Kent Kane Gold medal Geog. Soc. Phila., 1964, Karo award Soc. Mil. Engrs., 1966, Franklin L. Burr award Nat. Geog. Soc., 1967, Nat. Commendation Boy Scouts Am., 1970, Disting. Svc. commendation plaque UN Assn. U.S., Disting. Svc. commendation State of Mich. Legis., 1975, Outstanding Civilian Svc. medal U.S. Army Rsch. Office, 1977, Outstanding Leadership in Minerals Edn. commendations Idaho Mining Assn., 1985, 87, Nat. Disting. Tchg. award Assn. Am. Geographers, 1996; recipient numerous grants NSF, Nat. Geog. Soc., NASA, ARO, M.J. Murdock Trust, Dept. of Interior, others, 1948—. Fellow Geol. Soc. Am., Arctic Inst. N.Am., Explorers Club; mem. AAAS (councillor, Pacific divsn. 1978-88), AIME, ASME (hon. nat. lectr.), Am. Geophys. Union, Internat. Glaciological Soc. (past councilor), Assn. Am. State Geologists (hon.), Am. Legis. Exch. Coun., Am. Assn. Amateur Oarsmen (life), Am. Alpine Club (past councilor, life), Fulbright Assn., Alpine Club (London), Appalachian Club (hon. corr.), Brit. Mountaineering Assn. (hon., past v.p.), The Mountaineers (hon.), Cambridge U. Mountaineering Club (hon.), Himalayan Club (Calcutta), English Speaking Union (nat. lectr.), Naval Res. Assn. (life), Dutch Treat Club, Circumnavigators Club (life), Adventurers Club N.Y. (medalist), Am. Legion, VFW, Harvard Club (N.Y.C. and Seattle), Sigma Xi, Phi Beta Kappa (past pres. Epsilon chpt.), Phi Kappa Phi. Republican. Methodist. Avocations: skiing, mountain climbing, photography. Home: 514 E 1st St Moscow ID 83843-2814 Office: U Idaho Coll Sci and Earth Resources Moscow ID 83844-3022 also: Found Glacier & Environ Rsch 4470 N Douglas Hwy Juneau AK 99801-9403 Office Phone: 208-882-1237. E-mail: jirp@uidaho.edu.

MILLER, MICHAEL, physician, educator; b. Queens, NY, June 19, 1957; s. Irving Maltz and Lenore (Goldstein) Miller; m. Lisa L. Miller; children: Avery Lauren, Ilana Frieda, Myles Solomon. BA, Rutgers U., 1979; MD, Robert Wood Johnson Med. Sch., 1983. Diplomate Am. Bd. Internal Medicine, Am. Bd. Cardiovascular Disease, Nat. Bd. Med. Examiners. Intern dept. medicine Med. Ctr. U. Cin., 1983-84, resident internal medicine, 1984-86; lipoprotein metabolism fellow Sch. Medicine Johns Hopkins U., Balt., 1986-89, cardiovascular disease fellow, 1988-91; dir. ctr. preventive cardiology U. Md. Med. Sys., Balt., 1991—; assoc. prof. medicine divsn. cardiology Sch. Medicine U. Md., Balt., 1991—; asst. prof. medicine divsn. cardiology Sch. Medicine Johns Hopkins U., Balt., 1991—; adj. asst. prof. dept. medicine Baylor Coll. Medicine, Houston, 1992—. Tchr. Sch. Medicine U. Md., 1994—, Johns Hopkins U., 1993—, Balt. Pub. Sch. Sys., 1991—; lectr. in field. Author: The Practice of Coronary Disease Prevention, 1996, The Cholesterol Planner, 3d edit., 2004-; contbr. chpts. to books and articles to profl. jours.; reviewer numerous jours.; featured in ednl. recordings, 1990—. Mem. Gov.'s Task Force Cardiovasc. Disease Prevention. Grantee NIH/Am. Heart Assn., 1989—, Bristol-Myers Squibb, 1991-93, Sandoz, 1992-93, Pfizer, 1992—, Merck, 1997—; recipient Robert Galbraith award, 1979, William F. Grupe award, 1983, Samuel Kaslev award, 1994. Fellow Am. Coll. Cardiology (co-author Preventive Cardiology, 1998—), Am. Heart Assn. Coun. Arteriosclerosis; mem. AAAS, Am. Soc. Preventive Cardiology (pres.), Am. Heart Assn. Coun. Epidemiology, Phi Beta Kappa. Jewish. Avocations: skiing, tennis, hiking. Home: 4301 Norwood Rd Baltimore MD 21218-1119 Office: U Md Divsn Cardiology 22 S Greene St Baltimore MD 21201-1544 Office Phone: 410-328-6299. E-mail: llmmmiller@aol.com., mmiller@medicine.umaryland.edu.

MILLER, MICHAEL JEFFREY, editor, columnist; b. Chgo., Dec. 10, 1958; s. Kenneth Maynard and Joan (Callner) Miller; m. Joan A. Slobin, Oct. 18, 1987. BS in Computer Sci., Rensselaer Poly., Troy, N.Y., 1979; MS in Journalism, Northwestern U., Evanston, Ill., 1980. Sr. editor Bldg. Design and Constrn., Chgo., 1980—83; west coast bur. chief Popular Computing, San Francisco, 1983—85; exec. editor InfoWorld, Menlo Park, Calif., 1985—89, editor, 1989—90, editor-in-chief, 1991, PC Mag., N.Y.C., 1991—; exec. v.p., editl. dir. Ziff-Davis Pub., 1997—. Mem.: Soc. Profl. Journalists, Am. Soc. Technion. Office: PC Mag 28 E 28th St New York NY 10016-7930

MILLER, MICHAEL JON, survey engineer; b. Parkers Prairie, Minn., Mar. 17, 1950; s. Buford Kenneth and Gretchen Cena (Sharp) M.; m. Terry Lynn Peck, May 20, 1972; children: Livia Mica, David Peter. BS, U. Wis., Platteville, 1972; M of Pub. Adminstrn., Ariz. State U., 1988. Cert. profl. land surveyor, Wis., Ariz., soil tester, Wis. Chief of surveys Hovelsrud Cons. Assn., Richland Ctr., Wis., 1972-78; ops. mgr. Tech. Advisors, Inc., Phoenix, 1978-82; profl. surveyor Coe and Van Loo, Inc., Phoenix, 1982-83; survey engr. City of Phoenix, 1983—. Land surveyor mem. Ariz. Bd. Tech. Registration, 1989-97, emeritus mem., 1997—, sec., 1990-91, vice chmn., 1991, chmn., 1991-92, vice chmn. 1993-94, chmn. 1994-95; mem. Enforcement Adv. Com., 1997—. Content editor The Ariz. Surveyor; contbr. articles to profl. jours. Dep. registrar Dem. Party of Ariz., Phoenix, 1983-94; clk. Phoenix Friends Meeting, 1985-86; recording clk. Intermountain Yearly Meeting of Religious Soc. of Friends, 1984-85. Fellow Am. Congress on Surveying and Mapping (membership chmn. 1987-88); mem. Nat. Soc. Profl. Surveyors (gov. for Ariz. 1985-89), Western Fedn. Land Surveyors (state del. 1988-89), Ariz. Profl. Land Surveyors (sec. 1983-84, pres. 1985-86, Outstanding award 1981, life mem. award 1996), Nat. Coun. Examiners for Engrs. and Surveyors (chmn. western zone nominating com. 1998), Am. Pub. Works Assn., Am. Soc. for Pub. Adminstrn. (bd. dirs. Ariz. chpt. 2000—, pres.-elect 2004, comm. dir. sect. for historic, artistic and reflective expression, vice chmn. 2004-), World Clown Assn., Internat. Jugglers Assn., Greater Ariz. Bicycle Assn. Democrat. Avocations: history, writing, juggling, bicycling. Home: 4026 E Campbell Ave Phoenix AZ 85018-3709 Business E-Mail: michael.miller@phoenix.gov. E-mail: mjm4449@excite.com.

MILLER, MICHAEL PATIKY, lawyer; b. Huntington, N.Y., Apr. 16, 1944; s. George J. and Alida (Patiky) Miller; m. Dorothy Denn, Dec. 25, 1966; children: Lauren M. Golubtchik, Jonathan M., Rachel Miller Lazarus. AB, Rutgers U., 1965; JD, NYU, 1968. Bar: N.J. 1968, U.S. Dist. Ct. N.J. 1968, Calif. 1975, U.S. Dist. Ct. (no. dist.) Calif. 1975, U.S. Tax Ct. 1977, U.S. Ct. Appeals (9th cir.) 1977, U.S. Ct. Appeals (fed. cir.) 1984, U.S. Dist. Ct. (cen. dist.) Calif. 1982, U.S. Supreme Ct. 1983, U.S. Claims Ct. 1986. Chief of procurement and admin. law U.S. Army, 1973—74; atty. Electric Power Research Inst., Palo Alto, Calif., 1974-77; assoc. Weinberg, Ziff & Kaye, Palo Alto, 1977-78; ptnr. Weinberg, Ziff & Miller, Palo Alto, 1978—, mng. ptnr., 1990-98; lectr. on tax and estate planning U. Calif. Extension, 1980—. Author: Creditor Rights in Proceedings Outside Estate Adminstrn., 1995, rev., 1999, Estate Planning for Foreign Nationals in Silicon Valley, 2000, Death, Debts and Taxes 2000, rev. 2004; co-author: Decedents Estate Practice, 2001, rev. 2004, Trust Administration, 2d edit., 2001—; contbg. author: California Wills and Trusts, 1991, Estate Planning for Unmarried Couples, 1998, California Trust Administration, 1999, Trust and Estate Litigation, 2004; contbr. chpts. in books and articles to profl. jours. Treas. No. Calif. region United Synagogue Am., 1985-89, pres., 1992-95. Capt. U.S. Army, 1969-74, Vietnam, Ethiopia. Recipient Lion of Judah award, 1984, Cert. Merit U. Judaism, 1992. Mem. ABA (chmn. region VI pub. contract law sect. 1975-78, commn. tax practice in small law firms, com. on taxation of trusts, estates, taxation sect. 1986—), N.J. State Bar, State Bar of Calif. (commr. tax law adv. commn. 1989-92, 93-95, chair 1994-95, mem. bd. legal specialization 1994-95, chair probate sect. 1982), Silicon Valley Bar Assn. (pres. 2000-02, trustee 2002-). Office: Weinberg Ziff & Miller 400 Cambridge Ave Palo Alto CA 94306-1507 Office Phone: 650-329-0851.

MILLER, MIKE, state legislator, small business owner; b. Fairbanks, Alaska, Aug. 7, 1951; m. Susan Miller; children: Teffonie, Carissa. Student, U. Alaska. Owner, mgr. Santa Claus House; mem. Alaska State Senate, senate pres., 1997-98, chair health edn. and social svcs. com., chair legis. coun., mem. com. on coms., rules com., transp. com. Bd. mem. Project 714 (STARS); active Drug Intervention and Prevention Program for Secondary Schs. With Alaska Air Nat. Guard. Mem. NRA, Nat. Fedn. Ind. Bus., Alaska Pvt. Home Educators Assn., North Pole C. of C. Republican. Avocations: coin and stamp collecting, sports, family activities, church activities, Alaska and U.S. history. Office: State Capitol 120 4th St Rm 119 Juneau AK 99801-1142 Fax: 907-465-3883. E-mail: senatormikemiller@legis.state.ak.us.

MILLER, MILTON ALLEN, lawyer; b. L.A., Jan. 15, 1954; s. Samuel C. and Sylvia Mary Jane (Silver) Miller; m. Mary Ann Toman, Sept. 10, 1988; 1 child, Mary Ann. AB With distinction and honors in Econs., Stanford U., 1976; JD with honors, Harvard U., 1979. Bar: Calif. 1979, U.S. Ct. Appeals 9th cir.) 1979, U.S. Supreme Ct. 1989, Calif. (U.S. Dist. Ct. (cen., no. and so. dists.)) 1981. Law clk. U.S. Ct. Appeals (9th cir.), Sacramento, 1979—80; assoc. Latham & Watkins, L.A., Calif., 1979—87, ptnr., 1987—. Chmn. ethics com. Latham & Watkins, L.A., 1986—. Author: (non fiction) Attorney Ethics, 1993; editor: (articles) Harvard Law Rev., 1978—79; contbr. articles to profl. jours. Named to The Best Lawyers in Am., 2003, So. Calif. Super Lawyers, 2004. Mem.: ATLA, ABA, L.A. County Bar Assn. (chmn. profl. responsibility and ethics com.), Calif. State Bar Assn. (mem. com. on profl. responsibility), Harvard Club (Boston and NY), Phi Beta Kappa. Office: Latham & Watkins 633 W 5th St Ste 4000 Los Angeles CA 90071-2005 Office Phone: 213-485-1234. Business E-Mail: milt.miller@lw.com. *Notable cases include Medavoy vs. Klein and Raquel Welch vs. MGM Corp.; served as trial and insurance counsel in San Juan Dupont Plaza Hotel Fire litigation.*

MILLER, MILTON HOWARD, psychiatrist; b. Indpls., Sept. 1, 1927; s. William and Helen L. (Lefkovits) M.; m. Harriet Sanders, June 27, 1948; children— Bruce, Jeffrey, Marcie. BS, Ind. U., 1946, MD, 1950; diploma in psychiatry, Menninger Sch., Topeka, 1953. Intern Indpls. Gen. Hosp., 1950-51; resident Menninger Sch. Psychiatry, Topeka, 1951-53; with dept. psychiatry Univ. Hosps., U. Wis., Madison, 1955-71, prof., 1961-71, chmn., 1962-71; dir. Wis. Psychiat. Inst., 1962-71; vis. prof. Nat. Taiwan U., Taipei, 1969-70; prof. psychiatry U. B.C., Vancouver, 1972-78, head dept. psychiatry, 1972-78; dir. WHO-U. B.C. Mental Health Tng. Centre, Vancouver, 1974-78; dep. dir coastal region Dept. of Mental Health, L.A. County, 1978-86; chmn. dept. psychiatry Harbor-UCLA Med. Ctr., Torrance, Calif., 1978—; prof., vice chmn. dept. psychiatry UCLA, 1978—; dep. med. dir. Dept. of Mental Health, L.A., 1986-96; hon. prof. Hunan (China) Med. U., 1996—. Cons. in field. Author: Psychiatry: A Personal View, 1981; Contbr. articles to profl. jours. Fellow Am. Psychiat. Assn., Royal Coll. Psychiatry; mem. Can. Psychiat. Assn., Royal Coll. Physicians and Surgeons (examiner 1973—), Can. Med. Assn., World Fedn. for Mental Health (mem. exec. bd. 1973—) Home: 1321 W Paseo Del Mar San Pedro CA 90731-6054 Office: Harbor UCLA Med Ctr Dept Psychiatry Torrance CA 90509-2910 *For many years I worked hard for my parents and myself. Later I worked hard for my wife, children, friends and self. These last years I've been including strangers and it's better.*

MILLER, MORGAN LINCOLN, textile manufacturing company executive; b. New Rochelle, N.Y., Feb. 11, 1924; s. Harry H. and Belle M.; m. Marjorie Leff, June 8, 1952; children: Betsy, Harry Robert, Amy, Cindy. BA, Lehigh U., Bethlehem, Pa., 1947. With Nat. Spinning Co., Inc., 1959—, exec. v.p., 1964—, vice chmn., 1990—; pres. Jr. Accent Dress Mfg. Co., 1956—, Coquet Bathing Suit Mfg. Co., 1954—. Vice chmn. Continum Health V.p. Westchester (N.Y.) Reform Temple, 1971, Westchester Jewish Cmty. Svcs., White Plains, NY, 1970; trustee Beth Israel Med. Ctr. With USNR, 1942—45. Named Industry Man of Year United Jewish Appeal, 1980. Mem.: Quaker Ridge Golf Club. Republican. Office: 111 W 40th St New York NY 10018-2506

MILLER, MORRIS HENRY, lawyer; b. Thomasville, Ga., June 14, 1954; s. Gibbes Ulmer and Marianne (Morris) M.; m. Anita Carol Payne, Mar. 23, 1985; children: Morris Payne, Rose Elizabeth, David Gibbes, Paul Louis Henry, John Henry. BS in Acctg. summa cum laude, Fla. State U., 1976; JD, U. Va., 1979. Bar: Fla. 1979. Assoc. Holland & Knight, Tampa, Fla., 1979-84, ptnr. Tallahassee, 1984—, chmn. health law practice, 1989—2001, knowledge mgmt. ptnr., 2001—04. Dist. fin. chmn. Gulf Ridge coun. Boy Scouts Am., 1988-89, mem. pack com., cubmaster Pack 23, Suwannee River Area coun., 1995-98, scoutmaster Troop 182, 1997-99, scoutmaster Troop 10, 2000-01, asst. scoutmaster, 2002—, dist. nominating com.; mem. Leadership Tampa, 1986, Leadership Tampa Bay, 1989; bd. dirs. John G. Riley House Mus. Ctr. for African-Am. History and Culture, 1998-99, Tallahassee YMCA, 1994-2002, chmn. long range planning com., 1997; founder, chmn. Tampa Bus. Com. for Arts, Inc., 1988-89; elder Presbyn. Ch. Mem. ABA (health law sect.), Fla. Bar (chmn., vice chmn. computer law com. 1983-89, Fla. corp. law revision com. 1986-89, health law sect.), Tallahassee Bar Assn. Office: Holland & Knight 315 S Calhoun St Ste 600 Tallahassee FL 32301-1897 Office Phone: 850-425-5655. Business E-Mail: morris.miller@hklaw.com.

MILLER, NANCY ELLEN, computer consultant; b. Detroit, Aug. 30, 1956; d. George Jacob and Charlotte M. Miller. BS in Computer and Comm. Scis. with honors, U. Mich., 1978; MS in Computer Scis., U. Wis., 1981. Product engr. Ford Motor Co., Dearborn, Mich., 1977; computer programmer Unique Bus. Sys., Inc., Southfield, Mich., 1978; tchg. asst. U. Wis., Computer Scis. Dept., Madison, 1978—82; computer scientist Lister Hill Nat. Ctr. Biomed. Commns., Nat. Libr. Medicine, NIH, Bethesda, Md., 1984—88; pvt. practice West Bloomfield, Mich., 1993—. *Nancy E. Miller's professional interests in the field of artificial intelligence include: knowledge representation, expert systems, default logic, planning, knowledge-based systems, case-based reasoning, logic programming, agents, fuzzy logic, neural networks, and genetic programming. She is also interested in object-oriented programming and design. Ms. Miller is highly skilled in the following computer languages, systems, and tools: Lisp, Prolog, C++, C, Pascal, UNIX, Windows, Framekit, HTML, etc. She has used rapid prototyping and structured programming methodologies. Ms. Miller has worked in many facets of computer science, from research and development to end-user applications, in academia, government and industry, and on all sizes of computers.* Mem. NARAL Pro-Choice Am., Wash., DC, 2004—, Nat. Women's Polit. Caucus, Washington, 1984—. Recipient Jour. of Am. Soc. for Info. Sci. Best Paper award, 1988. Mem. Assn. for Computing Machinery (sec. S.E. Mich. spl. interest group on artificial intelligence 1993-94), Am. Assn. for Artificial Intelligence, Assn. for Logic Programming, U. Wis. Alumni Assn. (life), U. Mich. Alumni Assn. (life), Am. Contract Bridge League, Pro-Choice Am., Hadassah, Jewish Fedn. Met. Detroit, Mensa, Planned Parenthood Fed. Am. NY, Bloomfield Hills, Dem. Nat. Com. Wash., Hadassah: The Women's Zionist Orgn. of Am., Inc. Home and Office: 6220 Village Park Dr Apt 104 West Bloomfield MI 48322-2146 E-mail: NancyMiller588@msn.com.

MILLER, NANCY K. literature educator; PhD, Columbia U. Disting prof of Eng and comparative lit at Grad Ctr City U. N.Y., N.Y.C. Contbr. articles to profl. jours.; author: (books) Bequest and Betrayal: Memoirs of a Parent's Death, and, But Enough about Me: Why We Read Other People's Lives. Office: CUNY Grad Ctr PhD Program in Eng 365 5th Ave New York NY 10016-4309 E-mail: nmiller@gc.cuny.edu.

MILLER, NEIL STUART, advertising executive; b. N.Y.C., July 30, 1958; s. Irving Israel Maltz and Lenore (Goldstein) M.; m. Karen Joyce Salomon, Nov. 22, 1987; children: Lindsay Alexandra, Jacqueline Olivia, Sara Allison. BS, SUNY, Buffalo, 1980; MBA, SUNY, Binghamton, 1982. CPA, N.Y. Staff auditor Peat Marwick Mitchell & Co., N.Y.C., 1982-83; ops. auditor Gulf & Western Industries, N.Y.C., 1983-84; spl. projects acct. Mickelberry Comms., N.Y.C., 1984-86; v.p. fin. Ptnrs. & Shevack Inc. (subs. Mickelberry Comms. Inc.), N.Y.C., 1986-87, sr. v.p. fin., 1987-89, exec. v.p., CFO, 1989-96, exec. v.p., COO, 1996-98; sr. v.p., fin. dir. McCann Erickson New York (subs. Interpublic Group of Cos.), N.Y.C., 1998-2000; CFO N.Am. MindShare (subs. WPP Group PLC), N.Y.C., 2000; COO TN Media (subs. True North Comm./Interpublic Group of Cos.), NYC, 2000—01; CFO N.Am. Foote, Cone & Belding (subs. Interpub. Group of Cos.), N.Y.C., 2001—. Mem. AICPA, N.Y. State Soc. CPAs (past mem. com. CFOs and advt.). Avocations: skiing, motorcycling, golf. Home: 594 W Saddle River Rd Upper Saddle River NJ 07458-1115 Office: Foote Cone & Belding 100 W 33rd St New York NY 10001-2900 Office Phone: 212-885-3755.

MILLER, NEWTON EDD, JR., communications educator; b. Houston, Mar. 13, 1920; s. Newton Edd and Anastasia (Johnston) M.; m. Edwina Whitaker, Aug. 30, 1942; children: Cathy Edwina, Kenneth Edd. BS, U. Tex., 1939, MA, 1940; PhD, U. Mich., 1952; LL.D., U. Nev., Reno., 1974. Tutor U. Tex., Austin, 1940-41, instr., 1941-45, asst. prof. speech, 1945-47; research asst. Navy Conf. Research, 1947-52; mem. faculty U. Mich., Ann Arbor, 1947-65, successively lectr., instr., asst. prof. speech, 1947-55, assoc. prof., 1955-59, prof., 1959-65, asst. dir. summer session, 1953-57, assoc. dir., 1957-63, asst. to v.p. acad. affairs, 1963-65; chancellor U. Nev., Reno, 1965-68, pres., 1968-73, U. Maine, Portland-Gorham, 1973-78; chmn. communications dept. No. Ky. U., 1978-87, emeritus, 1987—, interim gen. mgr. Sta. WNKU, 1985-86. Mem. adv. com. to commr. of edn. U.S. Office of Edn., Accreditation and Instl. Eligibility, 1976-79, acting chmn., 1977-78; mem. Judicial Edn. Study Group Am. Univ. Law Inst., 1977-78; mem. Nat. Accreditation Commn. for Agys. Serving Blind and Physically Handicapped, 1988-97, pres., 1991-92, bd. dirs., 1999—. Author: Post War World Organization, Background Studies, 1942, (with J.J. Villareal) First Course in Speech, 1945, (with W.M. Sattler) Discussion and Debate, 1951, Discussion and Conference, 2d edit., 1968, (with Stephen D. Boyd) Public Speaking: A Practical Handbook, 1985, 2d edit., 1989; co-editor: Required Arbitration of Labor Disputes, 1947. Pres. bd. dirs. Perry Nursery Sch., 1956-57, Sierra Cmty. Orch., 1989-94; mem. Ann Arbor Bd. Edn., 1959-65, Washtenaw County Bd. Edn.; sec. bd. dirs. Behringer Crawford Mus.; bd. dirs. Siera Arts Found., 1992—; pres. Reno/Sparks Theater Cmty. Coalition, 1994-96; mem. Nev. Humanities Com., 1994-2001. Recipient Gov.'s Disting. Svc. to Arts award, 2003. Mem. Mich. Assn. Sch. Bds. (dir.), N.W. Assn. Colls. and Secondary Schs. (chmn. higher commn. 1971-73), Am. Forensic Assn. (pres. Midwest sect. 1950-53), Central States Speech Assn. (pres. 1958-59), Mich. Speech Assn. (exec. sec. 1950-55), Speech Communication Assn. (chmn. fin. bd.), Assn. Western Us. (chmn. 1971-72), Coun. on Naturopathic Med. Edn., Delta Sigma Rho (nat. v.p. 1948-52), Phi Kappa Phi. Address: 1480 Ayershire Ct Reno NV 89509-5248

MILLER, NICOLE JACQUELINE, fashion designer; b. Ft. Worth, Tex., Mar. 20, 1951; d. Grier Bovey and Jacqueline (Mahieu) M. BFA, RISD, 1973; cert. de coursspeciale, École de la Chambre Syndicale de la Couture Parisienne, Paris, 1971. Opened boutique Gamine, Stockbridge, Mass., 1973—74; asst. designer Clovis Ruffin, N.Y.C., 1974; designer Raincheetahs, N.Y.C., 1974-75, P.J. Walsh, N.Y.C., 1975-82, Nicole Miller, N.Y.C., 1982—. Mem. Sports Commn. of N.Y., Commn. of Status of Women; bd. trustees R.I. Sch. of Design. Bd. dirs. Smith's Food and Drug. Recipient Dallas Fashion award, 1991, Earnie award for children's wear, Michael award for fashion. Mem. Fashion Group, Fashion Roundtable, Coun. of Fashion Designers of Am., N.Y. Athletic Club. Avocations: skiing, ice skating, waterskiing, wind surfing. Office: 525 7th Ave Fl 20 New York NY 10018-4901*

MILLER, NODINE, judge; b. Dayton, Ohio, Dec. 13, 1938; d. Joseph Frederick and Nellie Naomi (Balzer) Cook; 1 child, Jessica Inez; m. Donald Alan Antrim, Jan. 2, 1998. Student, U. Vienna, Austria, 1961, Georgetown U., 1959; BA, Miami U., 1960; JD, Capital U., 1976. Bar: Ohio 1976, U.S. Dist. Ct. (so. and ea. dists.) Ohio 1981. Legal asst. Mayer, Tingley, Hurd & Emens, Columbus, Ohio, 1971-72; law clk. Brownfield, Kosydar, Bowen, Bally & Sturtz, Columbus, Ohio, 1975; atty. assigned to commr. Divsn. Securities, Ohio Dept. Commerce, Columbus, 1976-79, atty. inspector securities, 1977-79, deputy commr. securities, 1978-81; atty. Luper, Wolinetz, Sheriff & Niedenthal, Columbus, 1981-92; judge Franklin County Mcpl. Ct., Columbus, 1982-92. Sec. bd. trustees Ohio Judicial Coll.; co-chair Jury Svc. Com. Ohio Judicial Conf.; mem. exec. com. Ohio Judicial Conf.; chmn. rules com. Franklin County Commn. Recipient George E. Tyack award for judicial excellence, Franklin County Trial Lawyers Assn. Mem. Ohio State Bar Assn., Columbus Bar Assn. Avocations: quilting, hiking, fly fishing, skiing, reading. Office: Common Pleas Ct Hall of Justice 369 S High St Fl 6B Columbus OH 43215-4516

MILLER, NORMAN CHARLES, JR., editor, reporter; b. Pitts., Oct. 2, 1934; s. Norman Charles and Elizabeth (Burns) M.; m. Mollie Rudy, June 15, 1957; children— Norman III, Mary Ellen, Teri, Scott. BA, Pa. State U., 1956. Reporter Wall Street Jour., San Francisco, 1960-63, reporter N.Y.C., 1963-64, bur. chief Detroit, 1964-66, Washington corr., 1966-72, Washington Bur. chief, 1973-83; nat. editor Los Angeles Times, 1983-97; lectr. journalism U. So. Calif., 1997—2001; ret., 2001. Author: The Great Salad Oil Swindle, 1965 Served to lt. (j.g.) USN, 1956-60. Recipient Disting. Alumnus award Pa. State U., 1978; George Polk Meml. award L.I. U., 1963; Pulitzer Prize, 1964 Mem.: Gridiron (Washington). Roman Catholic. Avocation: tennis.

MILLER, ORLANDO JACK, obstetrician, gynecologist, educator, geneticist; b. Oklahoma City, May 11, 1927; s. Arthur Leroy and Iduma Dorris (Berry) M.; m. Dorothy Anne Smith, July 10, 1954; children: Richard Lawrence, Cynthia Kathleen, Karen Ann. BS, Yale U., 1946, MD, 1950. Intern St. Anthony Hosp., Oklahoma City, 1950-51; asst. resident in obstetrics and gynecology Yale-New Haven Med. Center, 1954-57, resident, instr., 1957-58; vis. fellow dept. obstetrics and gynecology Tulane U. Service, Charity Hosp., New Orleans, 1958; hon. research asst. Galton Lab., Univ. Coll., London, 1958-60; instr. Coll. Physicians and Surgeons Columbia U., N.Y.C., 1960, asso. dept. obstetrics and gynecology, 1960-61, asst. prof., 1961-65, asso. prof., 1965-69, prof. dept. human genetics and devel., dept. obstetrics and gynecology, 1969-85; asst. attending obstetrician, gynecologist Presbyn. Hosp., N.Y.C., 1964-65, assoc., 1965-70, attending obstetrician and gynecologist, 1970-85; prof. molecular biology, genetics and ob-gyn. Wayne State U. Sch. Medicine, Detroit, 1985-94, prof. Ctr. for Molecular Medicine and Genetics, 1994-96, prof. emeritus, 1996—, chmn. dept. molecular biology and genetics, 1985-93, dir. Ctr. for Molecular Biology, 1987-90. Bd. dirs. Am. Bd. Med. Genetics, 1983-85, v.p., 1983, pres., 1984, 85. Author: (with E. Therman) Human Chromosomes, 2000; editor Cytogenetics, 1970-72; assoc. editor: Birth Defects Compendium, 1971-74, Cytogenetics and Cell Genetics, 1972-97; mem. editl. bd. Cytogenetics, 1961-69, Am. Jour. Human Genetics, 1969-74, 79-83, Gynecologic Investigation, 1970-77, Teratology, 1972-74, Cancer Genetics and Cytogenetics, 1979-84, Jour. Exptl. Zoology, 1989-92, Chromosome Rsch., 1994-99; mem. editl. bd. com. Genomics, 1987-93, assoc. editor, 1993-96; mem. adv. bd. Human Genetics, 1978-98; cons. Jour. Med. Primatology, 1977-94; consulting editor McGraw-Hill Yearbook of Sci. and Tech., 1995—, Encyclopedia of Science and Technology, 1997—; contbr. chpts. to textbooks and articles to med. and sci. jours. Mem. sci. adv. com. on rsch. Nat. Found. March of Dimes, 1967-96, mem. sci. com., 1996—; mem. sci. rec. com. Basil O'Connor starter grants, 1973-77, 86-94; mem. human embryology and devel. study sect. NIH, 1970-74, chmn., 1972-74; mem. com. for study of inborn errors of metabolism NRC, 1972-74; mem. sci. adv. com. virology and cell biology Am. Cancer Soc., 1974-78, mem. sci. adv. com. cell and devel. biology, 1986-90; mem. human genome study sect. NIH, 1991-94; U.S. rep. permanent com. Internat. Congress of Human Genetics, 1986-91. With AUS, 1951-53. James Hudson Brown Jr. fellow Yale U., 1947-48; NRC fellow, 1953-54; Population Council fellow, 1958-59; Josiah Macy Jr. fellow, 1960-61; NSF sr. postdoctoral fellow U. Oxford, 1968-69; vis. scientist U. Edinburgh, 1983-84; Disting. vis. fellow, Fogarty Internat. fellow LaTrobe U., Melbourne, Australia, 1992; recipient Pres. Disting. Scientist award Soc. for Gynecol. Investigation, 1999. Fellow AAAS; mem. AAAS, Am. Genetic Assn., Am. Soc. Human Genetics (bd. dirs. 1970-73, 86-90), Genetics Soc. Am., Genetics Soc. Australia, Acad. Scholars, Wayne State U. (life, pres. 1996-97), Sigma Xi. Home: 1915 Stonycroft Ln Bloomfield Hills MI 48304-2339 Office: 540 E Canfield St Detroit MI 48201-1928 Personal E-mail: ojmiller@comcast.net.

MILLER, OSCAR, economics professor; b. Chgo., Oct. 1, 1920; s. Meyer and Dina (Shenfeld) M.; m. Esther Bromberg, June 10, 1945; children: Lauren, Sharon, Ira. MA, U. Chgo., 1948. Instr. econs. U Ill., Chgo., 1948—, prof. econs., 1972—, dean students, assoc. vice chancellor, 1979-83. Lectr. on politics and econs. in free mkt. Mem. econ. adv. bd. U.S. Israel C. of C., Chgo., 1990—. Lt. USN, 1942-45. Recipient Pepper award Claude Pepper, 1993, Alumni award of Disting. Tchg. Coll. Bus. Adminstrn., U. Ill., Chgo., 1993. Jewish. Achievements include cited in volume eleven History of US Naval Operations in WWII. Home: 7201 N Lincoln Ave Apt 201 Lincolnwood IL 60712-1822 Office: U Ill at Chicago 601 S Morgan St # Mc144 Chicago IL 60607-7100 E-mail: oscar.miller@comcast.net.

MILLER, PAMELA GUNDERSEN, mayor; b. Cambridge, Mass., Sept. 7, 1938; d. Sven M. and Harriet Adams Gundersen; m. Ralph E. Miller, July 7, 1962; children: Alexander, Erik, Karen. AB magna cum laude, Smith Coll., 1960. Feature writer Congl. Quar., Washington, 1962-65; dir. cable TV franchising Storer Broadcasting Co., Louisville, Lexington, Ky., 1978-80, 81-82; mem. 4th dist. Lexington Fayette County Urban Coun., 1973-77; councilwoman-at-large, 1982-93; vice mayor, 1984-86, 89-93; mayor, 1993—2003. Dep. commr. Ky. Dept. Local Govt., Frankfort, 1980-81; pres. Pam Miller, Inc., 1984-94, Cmty. Ventures Corp., 1985-95. Mem. Fayette County Bd. Health, 1975—77, Downtown Devel. Commn., 1975—77; bd. dirs. YMCA, Lexington, 1975—77, 1985—90, Fund for the Arts, 1984—93, Coun. of Arts, 1978—80, Sister Cities, 1978—80; vice chmn. Prichard Com. for Acad. Excellence, 1983—; alt. del. Dem. Nat. Com., 1976; chair Fund for Arts Campaign, 2003—04. Named woman of achievement YWCA, 1984, outstanding Woman of Blue Grass AAUW, 1984. Mem. LWV (dir. 1970-73), Profl. Women's Forum. Home: 140 Cherokee Park Lexington KY 40503-1304

MILLER, PATRICIA A. training services executive; b. Pa., Jan. 7, 1949; BA, Radford Coll., 1970; JD, George Mason U., 1992; cert., Harvard U., 1994. Proprietor Patricia A. Miller Real Estate Cons., 1975—; sr. v.p. The Gussie Group, 1988—89; pvt. practice law, 1992—; proprietor Patricia A. Miller ADR Cons., 1994—; pres. Nat. Inst. for Conflict Resolution, Inc., 1994—; dispute resolution faculty in field. Nat. Ams. with Disabilities Act panelist Dept. Justice, 1996—2000; commr. Md. Alt. Dispute Resolution Commn., 1998—2000; internat. panelist World Bank Mediation Program, 2000—; cons. and spkr. in field. Founder, chmn. bd. dirs., dir. Anne Arundel County Ct., Apptd. Spl. Advs., Inc., 1994—; dir., officer Hospice of the Chesapeake Found., Inc., 1999—; active Md. Promise Steering Com., 1998. Named to Md.'s Top 100 Women, The Daily Record, 2000; recipient commendation, Chief Judge Robert Bell, 1998—2000. Mem.: Md. State Bar Assn. (mem. leadership coun. ADR sect. 2000—). Office: Nat Inst for Conflict Resolution Inc 170 West St Annapolis MD 21401

MILLER, PATRICIA A. music educator, opera and concert artist; b. Washington, June 16; d. Robert Lee and Bernice (Echols) Miller. MusB, Boston U.; MusM, New Eng. Conservatory; artist's diploma, Accademia di Santa Cecilia, Rome; postdoctoral diploma, Mozarteum, Salzburg. Artist Thea Dispeker Artist's Mgmt., Inc., N.Y.C., 1981—95; assoc. prof. Music, artist-in-residence U. Mo., Columbia, 1983—85; prof. Music, artist-in-residence George Mason U., Fairfax, Va., 1991—; prof. Voice Oberlin Coll. Conservatory, Oberlin, Ohio, 2000—01. Lectr. Smithsonian, Wash., DC, 2000—02. Opera recording, ERCOLE Amante, London, 1986, televised opera, Carmen, Bogota, Columbia, 1985, Porgy & Bess, Lyon, France, 1996; opera artist, Basel, Lyon, San Francisco, NYC, Bogota, Munich, Frankfort, Verona, Ge, Tokyo, Melbourne, Paris (Chatelet), Rome, Berlin, concert/recital artist, Vienna, Lisbon, Boston, Pittsburgh, Austin, NYC, Kennedy Ctr., Wash. DC, 2000, Kiev, 2002, Austrian Embassy, 2003, Salzburg, Austria, 2004, (solo recital) Schloss Leopoldskron Great Hall, 2004. Recipient Shining Star, Cmty Svc. award, Nat. Urban League; grantee, Am. Embassy, 2002; Fulbright scholar, Rome. Mem.: Va. Commn. Arts, NEA Panel (Nat. Endowment for the Arts) (mem. 2003), Fulbright Assn. (bd. dirs. Nat. Capitol area), Nat. Assn. Tchrs. Singing (bd. dirs., VA State), Sigma Alpha Iota (Alumni Artistry, Leadership award 2004). Methodist. Avocations: travel, walking, swimming, cooking. Office: George Mason Univ Dept Music MSN-3E3 4400 University Dr Fairfax VA 22030-4444

MILLER, PATRICIA LOUISE, state legislator, nurse; b. Bellefontaine, Ohio, July 4, 1936; d. Richard William and Rachel Orpha (Williams) M.; m. Kenneth Orlan Miller, July 3, 1960; children: Tamara Sue, Matthew Ivan. RN, Meth. Hosp. Sch. Nursing, Indpls., 1957; BS, Ind. U., 1960. Staff nurse Cmty. Hosp., Indpls., 1958, Meth. Hosp., Indpls., 1959; office nurse A.D. Dennison, MD, 1960-61; rep. State of Ind. Dist. 50, Indpls., 1982-83; senator State of Ind. Dist. 32, Indpls., 1983—, chair senate health and provider svcs. com., 1983—; mem. labor and pension com., 1983-94; mem. edn. com., 1984-90; legis. appt. and elections com., chmn. interim study com. pub. health and mental health Ind. Gen. Assembly, 1986; chair Senate Enfiron. Affairs, 1990-92; health and environ affairs, 1992—; mem. election com., 1992—; mem. budget subcom. Senate Fin. Com., 1995—. Mem. Bd. Edn. Met. Sch.

Dist., Warren Twop., 1974-82, pres., 1979-80, 80-81; mem. Warren Twp. Citizens Screening Com. for Sch. Bd. Candidates, 1972-74, 84, Met. Zoning Bd. Appeals, Divsn. I, apptd. mem. City-County Coun. on Aging, Indpls. 1977-80; mem. State Bd. Vocat. and Tech. Edn., 1978-82, sec., 1980-82, mem. gov.'s Select Adv. Commn. for Primary and Secondary Edn., 1983; precinct committeeman Rep. Party, 1968-74, ward vice-chmn., 1975-78, ward chmn., 1978-85, twp. chmn., 1985-87; vice chmn. Marion County Rep., 1986—; del. Rep. State Copnv., 1968, 74, 76, 80, 84, 86, 88, 90, 92, 94, sgt. at arms, 1982, mem. platform com., 1984, 88, 90, 92, co-chmn. Ind. Rep. Platform Com., 1992; del. Rep. Nat. Conv., 1984, alternate del., 1988, Rep. Presdl. Elector Alternate, 1992; active various polit. campaigns; bd. dirs. PTA, 1967-81; pres. Grassy Creek PTA, 1971-72; state del. Ind. PTA, 1978; mem. child car adv. com. Walker Career Ctr., 1976-80, others; bd. dirs. Ch. Fedn. Greater Indpls., 1979-82, Christian Justice Ctr., Inc., 1983-85, Gideon Internat. Aux., 1977Y; mem. United Meth. Bd. Missions Aux. Indpls., 1974-80, v.p., 1974-76, mem. nominating com., 1977; bd. dirs. Lucille Raines Residence, Inc., 1977-80; exec. com. S. Ind. Conf. United Meth. Women, 1977-80, lay del. s. Ind. Conf. United Meth. Ch., 1977—, fin. and adminstrn. com., 1979-88, planning and rsch. com., 1980-88, co-chmn. law adv. com., chmn. health and welfare, conf. coun. ministries, also mem. task force, bd. ordained ministry, also panel, chmn. com. on dist. superintendency, dist. coun. on ministries; sec. Indpls. S.E. Dist. Council on Minstries, 1977-78, pres. 1982; chmn. council on ministries Cumberland United Meth. Ch., 1969-76; chmn. stewardship com. Old Bethal United Meth. Ch., 1982-85, fin. com., 1982-85, adminstrv. bd., mem. council on ministries, 1981-85; co-chair Evangelism Com., 1994—; jurisdictional del. United Meth. Ch., 1988, 92; alternate del. United Methodist Ch. Gen. Conf., 1988, del. 1992; mem. adv. com. Warren Fine Arts Found., 1991—; mem. adv. bd. St. Francis Hosp., 1992—, mem. health and human svcs. com. Midwest Legis. Conf., 1995. Recipient Lambda Theta Honor for Outstanding contbr. in fiedl of end., 1976; named Woman of Yr. Cumberland Bus. and Profl. Women, 1979; Ind. Vocat. Assn. citation award, 1984, others. Mem. Indpls. dist. Dental Soc. Women's Aux., Ind. Dental Assn. Women's Aux., Am. Dental Assn. Women's Aux., Coun. State Govt. (intergovtl. affairs com.), Nat. Conf. State Legis. (vice chmn. health com. 1994—), Warren Twp. Rep., Franklin Rep., Lawrence Rep., Center Twp. Rep., Fall Creek Valley Rep, Marion County Coun. Rep. Women (3rd v.p. 1986-89), Ind. Women's Rep. (legis. chair 1988-89), Nat. Fedn. rep. Women, Beech Grove Rep., Perry Twp. Rep., Indpls. Women's Rep. Club (3rd v.p. 1989—), Indpls. Press Club. Office Phone: 317-232-9400. Business E-Mail: s32@in.gov.

MILLER, PATRICK DWIGHT, JR., religion educator, minister; b. Atlanta, Oct. 24, 1935; s. Patrick Dwight and Lila Morse (Bonner) M.; m. Mary Ann Sudduth, Dec. 27, 1958; children: Jonathan Sudduth, Patrick James. AB, Davidson Coll., 1956; BD, Union Theol. Sem., Va., 1959; PhD, Harvard U., 1964. Ordained to ministry Presbyn. Ch., 1963. Pastor, minister Trinity Presbyn. Ch., Traveler's Rest, S.C., 1963-65; asst. prof. Bibl. studies Union Theol. Sem., Richmond, Va., 1966-68, assoc. prof., 1968-73, prof., 1973-84, dean of faculty, 1979-83; Charles T. Haley prof. of Old Testament Theology Princeton (N.J.) Theol. Sem., 1984—. Author: The Divine Warrior in Early Israel, 1973, The Hand of the Lord, 1977, Sin and Judgment in the Prophets, 1982, Interpreting the Psalms, 1986, Deuteronomy, 1990, They Cried to the Lord, 1994, The Religion of Ancient Israel, 2000, Israelite Religion and Biblical Theology, 2000; editor: Theology Today, 1990—. Mem. Soc. of Bibl. Lit. (sec.-treas. 1987-88, pres. 1998), Rev. Std. Version Translation Com. Democrat. Presbyterian. Office: Princeton Theol Sem PO Box 821 Princeton NJ 08542-0803

MILLER, PATRICK WILLIAM, research administrator, educator; b. Toledo, Sept. 1, 1947; s. Richard William and Mary Olivia (Rinna) M.; m. Jean Ellen Thomas, Apr. 5, 1974; children: Joy, Tatum, Alex. BS in Indstrl. Edn., Bowling Green State U., 1971, MEd in Career Edn. and Tech., 1973; PhD in Indstrl. Tech. Edn., Ohio State U., 1977; Master's cert. Govt. Contract Adminstrn., George Washington U., 1995. Tchr. Montgomery Hills Jr. High Sch., Silver Spring, Md., 1971-72, Rockville (Md.) High Sch., 1973-74; asst. prof. Wayne State U., Detroit, 1977-79; assoc. prof., grad. coord. indstrl. edn. and tech. Western Carolina U., Cullowhee, N.C., 1979-81; assoc prof. U. No. Iowa, Cedar Falls, 1981-86; dir. grad. studies practical arts and vocat.-tech. edn. U. Mo., Columbia, 1986-89; devel. editor Am. Tech. Pubs., Homewood, Ill., 1989-90; proposal mgr. Nat. Opinion Rsch. Ctr. U. Chgo., 1990-96; dir. grants & contracts City Colls. Chgo., 1996-99; assoc. v.p. acad. affairs Prairie State Coll., 1999—2001, also dean workforce devel. and career edn., 1999—2001; prof. Govs. State U., University Park, Ill., 2001—. Pres. Patrick W. Miller and Assocs., Munster, Ind., 1981—; presenter, advisor and cons. in field. Author: Nonverbal Communication: Its Impact on Teaching and Learning, 1983, Teacher Written Tests: A Guide for Planning, Creating, Administering and Assessing, 1985, Nonverbal Communication: What Resarch Says to the Teacher, 1988, How To Write Tests for Students, 1990, Nonverbal Communication in the Classroom, 2000, Nonverbal Communication in the Workplace, 2000, Grant Writing: Strategies for Developing Winning Proposals, 2d edit., 2002, Test Development: Guidelines, Practical Suggestions and Examples, 2001; mem. editl. bd. Jour. Indsl. Tchr. Edn., 1981-88, Am. Vocat. Edn. Rsch. Jour., 1981-85, 94—, Tech. Tchr., 1982-84, Jour. Indsl. Tech., 1984—, Jour. Vocat. and Tech. Edn., 1987-90, Human Resource Devel. Quar., 1989—; also articles. Sec. U. No. Iowa United Faculty, Cedar Falls, 1983-84, pres., 1984-86. Lance cpl. USMC, 1966-68, Vietnam. Recipient editl. recognition award Jour. Indsl. Tchr. Edn., 1984, 86, 88; named One of Accomplished Grads. of Coll. Tech., Bowling Green State U., 1995. Mem. ASTD, Am. Ednl. Rsch. Assn., Assn. for Career and Tech. Edn., Am. Vocat. Edn. Rsch. Assn., Nat. Assn. Indsl. Tech. (chmn. rsch. grants 1982-87, pres. industry divsn. 1991-92, chmn. exec. bd. 1992-93, past pres. 1993-94, Leadership award 1992, 93), Nat. Assn. Indsl. and Tech. Tchr. Educators (pres. 1988-89, past pres. 1989-90, trustee 1990-93, Outstanding Svc. award 1988, 90), Internat. Tech. Edn. Assn., Coun. Tech. Tchr. Edn., Epsilon Pi Tau, Phi Delta Kappa.

MILLER, PAUL AUSBORN, adult education educator; b. East Liverpool, Ohio, Mar. 22, 1917; s. Harry A. and Elizabeth (Stewart) M.; m. Catherine Spiker, Dec. 9, 1939 (dec. Dec. 1964); children— Paula Kay, Thomas Ausborn; m. Francena Lounsbery Nolan, Jan. 15, 1966. BS, U. W.Va., 1939; MA, Mich. State U., 1947, PhD, 1953. County agrl. agt. in, W.Va., 1939-42; extension specialist sociology and anthropology Mich. State U., East Lansing, 1947-55, asst. prof., 1947-52, assoc. prof., 1953, prof., 1953-61, dir. coop. ext. svc., 1954-58, provost, 1959-61; pres. W.Va. U., Morgantown, 1962-66; asst. sec. for edn. HEW, Charlotte, 1966-68; disting. prof. edn., dir. univ. planning studies U. N.C., Charlotte, 1966-68; prof. adult edn. N.C. Sate U. at Raleigh, 1668-69; pres. Rochester (N.Y.) Inst. of Tech., 1969-79, pres. emeritus, 1979—, prof., 1979-83. Sr. program cons. W.K. Kellogg Found., 1979-83; adj. prof. rural sociology U. Mo.-Columbia, 1994—. Author: Community Health Action, 1953; co-author: Patterns for Lifelong Learning, 1973; contbr. to publs. in field. Mem. Colombian Commn. Higher Edn., 1960-61. Served as 1st lt. USAAF, 1942-46. Named to the Internat. Adult and Continuing Edn. Hall of Fame. Fellow Am. Sociol. Assn.; mem. Rural Sociol. Soc., Phi Kappa Phi, Epsilon Sigma Phi. Home: 1909 Walden Ct Columbia MO 65203-5407 E-mail: millerpaul@missouri.edu.

MILLER, PAUL DAVID, aerospace executive; BA, Fla. State U.; MBA, U. Ga. Commd. USN, advanced through grades to four star adm.; comdr.-in-chief U.S. Atlantic Command; supreme allied comdr.-Atlantic NATO; with Litton Marine Sys., 1995-99; pres. Sperry Marine Inc.; CEO Alliant Techsystems, Inc., Hopkins, Minn., 1999—, also chmn. bd. dirs.

MILLER, PAUL DEAN, breeding consultant, geneticist, educator; b. Cedar Falls, Iowa, Apr. 4, 1941; s. Donald Hugh and Mary (Hansen) M.; m. Nancy Pearl Huser, Aug. 23, 1965; children: Michael, Steven. BS, Iowa State U., 1963; MS, Cornell U., 1965, PhD, 1967. Asst. prof. animal breeding cornell U., Ithaca, N.Y., 1967-72; v.p. Am. Breeders Svc., De Forest, Wis., 1972-95; exec. dir. Nat. Dairy Herd Improvement Assn., 1996—2003; pres. Windsor (Wis.) Park Inc., 1985—. Adj. prof. U. Wis., Madison, 1980—, sr. scientist, 2003—; dir. Internat. Com. on Animal Recording, 1998-2003. Contbr. articles to profl. jours. Mem. Beef Improvement Fedn. (disting. svc. award 1980), Am. Soc. Animal Sci., Am. Dairy Sci. Assn., Nat. Assn. Animal Breeders (dir. 1983-92, v.p. 1986). Republican. Office: Univ Wis 446 Animal Sci Bldg 1675 Observatory Dr Madison WI 53706-1284 Home: 6301 Fox Run Sun Prairie WI 53590-9357 E-mail: pdmil@aol.com., pdmiller2@wisc.edu.

MILLER, PAUL J. lawyer; b. Boston, Mar. 27, 1929; s. Edward and Esther M.; children— Robin, Jonathan; m. Michal Davis, Sept. 1, 1965; children— Anthony, Douglas BA, Yale U., 1950; LL.B., Harvard U., 1953. Bar: Mass. 1953, Ill. 1957. Assoc. Miller & Miller, Boston, 1953-54; assoc. Sonnenschein Nath & Rosenthal, Chgo., 1957-63, ptnr., 1963—. Bd. dirs. Oil-Dri Corp. Am., Chgo. Trustee Latin Sch. of Chgo., 1985-91. 1st lt. JAGC, U.S. Army, 1954-57. Fellow Am. Bar Found.; mem. Tavern Club, Saddle and Cycle Club, Law Club, Phi Beta Kappa. Avocation: gardening. Office: Sonnenschein Nath & Rosenthal 233 S Wacker Dr Ste 8000 Chicago IL 60606-6491 E-mail: pjm@sonnenschein.com.

MILLER, PAUL MCGRATH, JR., executive search consulting company executive; b. Oct. 31, 1935; s. Paul McGrath and Lena D. (Carr) M.; m. Charlene F. Russnak, Sept. 12, 1970 (div.); children: Andrew McGrath, Christopher Paul; m. C. Sue Whitehouse, Aug. 12, 1989 (div.). BMechE, Cornell U., 1958; MBA, Harvard U., 1966. Foreman Procter & Gamble, Cin., 1958-60; market analyst United Aircraft Co., Sunnyvale, Calif., 1963-64; asst. to chmn. bd. Boise Cascade Corp. (Idaho), 1966, gen. mktg. mgr. Insulite divsn., 1966-67, nat. sales mgr. Lumber and Plywood, 1967-68, asst. to exec. v.p. Paper Group, 1968-69; group dir. mktg. Am. Std., Inc., N.Y.C., 1969-71; dir. corp. comms. Indian Head, Inc., N.Y.C., 1971-74; v.p. mktg. Ball & Socket Mfg. Co., Cheshire, Conn., 1975, Cory Coffee Svc., Chgo., 1976, v.p., gen. mgr., 1977 80; v.p., ptnr. Korn/Ferry Internat., Chgo., 1980-87; ptnr. LAI, Inc. (formerly Lamalie Assocs. Inc.), Chgo., 1987-99, TMP Exec. Search, Lexington, Va., 1999-2001, Stratford Group, Lexington, 2001; pres. Oak Hill Search, LLC, Lexington, Va., 2002—. Mem. Winnetka (Ill.) Caucus, 1980. Capt. USAF, 1960-63. Mem. Racquet Club (Chgo.), Harvard Club (N.Y.C.), Harvard Bus. Sch. Club (Chgo., dir.), Harvard U. Club (Chgo., dir.). Presbyterian.

MILLER, PAUL S(AMUEL), lawyer; b. Paterson, N.J., Apr. 8, 1939; s. Louis and Etta (Wolff) M.; m. Carol Plesser, Mar. 26, 1961; children: Nicole F., Margo H., Jason E. BA, Rutgers U., 1960, JD magna cum laude, 1962. Bar: N.Y. 1963. Assoc. Kaye, Scholer, Fierman, Hayes & Handler, N.Y.C., 1962-63, Rubin, Baum & Levin, N.Y.C., 1964; ptnr. Fishman, Miller & Zimet, N.Y.C., 1964-70; counsel Leasing Cons., Inc., Rosyln, N.Y., 1970-71; with Pfizer Inc., N.Y.C., 1971—2002, assoc. gen. counsel, v.p., gen. counsel, 1986-92, sr. v.p., gen. counsel, 1992-99, exec. v.p., gen. counsel, 1999—2002; spl. counsel Kaye Scholer LLP, N.Y.C., 2002—. Ofcl. corr. Pharm. Mfrs. Assn., mem., chmn. exec. com. law sect., 1989-90. Mem. United Jewish Appeal Com., Essex County, 1981-83, co-chmn. Livingston sect., 1982; chmn. bd. dirs. Citizens Crime Commn. of N.Y.C., Inc.; bd. dirs. Am. Israel Pub. Affairs Com., Am. Jewish Congress, Jewish Theol. Sem., U.S. C. of C., chmn. Nat. Chamber Litigation Coun.; mem. bus. adv. coun. Touro Law Sch.; mem. bd. overseers Inst. Civil Justice, RAND. Albert Einstein Coll. Medicine, Jaffee Inst. Strategic Studies at Tel Aviv U. Mem. ABA (antitrust law sect., corp. banking and bus. law sect., natural resources law sect., sci. and tech. sect., mem. health law forum com.), N.Y. State Bar Assn. (antitrust law sect., food and drug law sect.). Office: Kaye Scholer LLP 425 Park Ave New York NY 10022

MILLER, PEGGY GORDON ELLIOTT, university president; b. Matewan, W.Va., May 27, 1937; d. Herbert Hunt and Mary Ann (Renfro) Gordon; m. Robert Lawrence Miller, Nov. 23, 2001; children from previous marriage: Scott Vandling Elliott III, Anne Gordon Elliott. BA, Transylvania Coll., 1959; MA, Northwestern U., 1964; EdD, Ind. U., 1975; degree (hon.), Transylvania U., 1993, Chungnam Nat. U., Korea, 2000. Tchr. Horace Mann H.S., Gary, Ind., 1959-64; instr. English Am. Inst. Banking, Gary, 1969-70, Ind. U. N.W., Gary, 1965-69, lectr. Edn., 1973-74, asst. prof. edn., 1975-78, assoc. prof., 1978-80, supr. secondary student tchg., 1973-74, dir. student tchg., 1975-77, dir. Office Field Experiences, 1977-78, dir. prof. devel., 1978-80, spl. asst. to chancellor, 1981-83, asst. to chancellor, 1983-84, acting chancellor, 1983-84, chancellor, 1984-92; pres. U. Akron, Ohio, 1992-96, S.D. State U., 1998—. Sr. fellow Nat. Ctr. for Higher Edn., 1996-97; vis. prof. U. Ark., 1979-80, U. Alaska, 1982; bd. dirs. Lubrizol Corp., A. Schulman Corp., Commn. on Women in Higher Edn., Akron Tomorrow, Ohio Aerospace Consortium, Ohio Super Computer Com.; holder VA Harrington disting. chair in edn., 1994-96, Charles G. Herbrich chair in leadership mgmt., 1996—. Author: (with C. Smith) Reading Activities for Middle and Secondary Schools: A Handbook for Teachers, 1979, Reading Instruction for Secondary Schools, 1986, How to Improve Your Scores on Reading Competency Tests, 1981, (with C. Smith and G. Ingersoll) Trends in Educational Materials: Traditionals and the New Technologies, 1983, The Urban Campus: Educating a New Majority for a New Century, 1994, also numerous articles. Bd. dirs. Meth. Hosp., N.W. Ind. Forum, N.W. Ind. Symphony, S.D. Art Mus., Boys Club N.W. Ind., Akron Symphony, NBD Bank, John S. Knight Conv. Ctr., Inventure Pl., Akron Roundtable, Cleve. Com. Higher Edn., 4-H Found., S.D. Art Mus., S.D. Value. Recipient Disting. Alumni award Northwestern U., UA Disting. Alumni award, 1994, Dist. Alumni award, Ind. U., 2004, numerous grants; Am. Council on Edn. fellow in acad. adminstrn. Ind. U., Bloomington, 1980-81. Mem. Assn. Tchr. Educators (nat. pres. 1984-85, Disting. Mem. 1990), Ind. Assn. Tchr. Educators (past pres.), North Ctrl. Assn. (mem. commn. at large), Am. Assn. State Colls. and Univs. (acting v.p. divsn. acad. and internat. programs 1997, bd. dirs., treas., chmn. global priorities commn.), Am. Coun. Edn. (bd. dirs., exec. com.), Leadership Devel. Coun. ACE, Office Women Higher Edn., Ohio Inter Univ. Coun. (chairperson), Internat. Reading Assn., Akron Urban League (bd. dirs.), P.E.O., Cosmos Club, Phi Delta Kappa (Outstanding Young Educator award), Delta Kappa Gamma (Leadership/Mgmt. fellow 1980), Pi Lambda Theta, Pi Kappa Phi, Chi Omega. Episcopalian. Avocation: music. Home: 929 Harvey Dunn St Brookings SD 57006-1347 Office: South Dakota State Univ Office of the Pres Adminstrn Bldg 201 Brookings SD 57007-0001 Office Phone: 605-688-4111. E-mail: Peggy_Miller@sdstate.edu.

MILLER, PHILIP GRAY, artist; b. Seattle, Aug. 18, 1947; s. Robert Chester and Angnes Minto (Weston) M. Student, Whitman Coll., Walla Walla, Wash., 1965-69. Artist, musician Gallery Functional Art, Santa Monica, L.A., 1970—. Furniture maker Sonrisa Bernice Steinbaum Gallery, N.Y.C.; cons. Inner Cities Murals Project, L.A., 1992—, Met. Transp. Agy., L.A., 1993-94. Author (novella) Death Valley Girls, 1989, (screenplay) Hurt By Love, 1993, (book) Cynic's Guide to Spiritual Awakening, 1993; curator Punch Gallery, L.A., 1993; permanent exhibhibn., a Colony for AVT Nespelem, Washington, 1997—, writer, actor, film maker; works represented in permanent collections Conrado Terasas City Coun., L.A., Laguna Beach (Calif.) Mus., Venice (Calif.) Family Clinic, AIDS Project L.A.; represented in group shows Punch Gallery, 1996, Gallery Function al Art, 1997; Plates of the Vain pictorial book, 1999. Min. Universal Life Ch., Seattle, L.A., 1969—. Recipient Design 100 award Met. Home, 1989. Avocations: yoga, cats, gardening, basketball. Office: Philip Miller Design 11100 Cumpston St Ste 11 North Hollywood CA 91601-2713

MILLER, PHILIP JOHN, insurance consultant; b. Yonkers, N.Y., Apr. 28, 1945; s. Arnold Norris and Shirley Miller; m. Violet Ann Miller, Oct. 6, 1968; 1 child, Andrea Marie. BA, L.I. U., 1966; M, CCNY, 1967. Lic. property/casualty/health ins. broker. V.p. Montgomery and Montgomery, N.Y.C., 1970—77; sr. v.p. Kornreich Orgns., N.Y.C., 1977—95; pres. Creative Resources Group, Hauppauge, NY, 1995—2000, Prosulting Inc., Northport, NY, 2000—. Cons. ins. fraud FBI, 1995—; cons. U.S. Govt., Washington, 2000—. Author: Serious on Safety, 2002; co-author: Food Equipment Facts, 1988; author: Onwards and Upwards, 2003; guest appearances for various topics on insurance for Fox Five and CNBC, guest spkr. Dr. Bernard Meltzer show, 1990. Mem. Presdl. Roundtable, Washington, 2000—, Senatorial Inner Cir., Washington, 2001—, Senatorial Trust, 2001—. Capt. spl. ops. U.S. Army, 1962—67. Named Businessman of Yr., NRCC, Washington, 2003. Mem.: Associated Risk Mgrs. Avocations: martial arts, architectural landscaping, writing. Office: Prosulting Inc 111 Soundview Ter Northport NY 11768 Office Phone: 631-757-9458. Fax: 631-757-9458.

MILLER, PHILLIP EDWARD, environmental scientist; b. Waterloo, Iowa, May 29, 1935; s. Joe Monroe and Katherine Elva (Groom) Miller; m. Cathy Ann Love, Sept. 15, 1962; children: Eric Anthony, Bryan Edward, Stefan Patrick, Gregory Joseph. BA in Sci. Edn., U. No. Iowa, 1961; MA in Sci. Edn., U. Iowa, 1964; postgrad., U. Wis., 1966-68. Physics and chemistry tchr. Millersburg (Iowa) Cmty. HS, 1961-62; supervising tchr. NSF Insvc. Inst. U. Iowa, Iowa City, 1962-64; instr. biology, area coord. Office Equal Opportunity Western Ky. U., Bowling Green, 1964-66; sci. editor, journalism instr.-sci. and tech. writing Mich. State U., East Lansing, 1968-74; asst. prof. agr., forestry and home econs. U. Minn., St. Paul, 1974-77; sr. editor atomic energy div. E.I. du Pont de Nemours and Co., Aiken, SC, 1977-89; sr. scientist environ. protection dept. Westinghouse Savannah River Co., Aiken, 1989-99; pres. Agy. Book Authors, Collectors and Understanding Sci., Aiken, 1994—. Radiol. air and drinking water program owner environ./govt. group Morrison Knudsen Corp., Aiken, 1999—2000; prin. scientist Washington Group Internat., Inc., Aiken, 2000—03; panelist 26th Internat. Tech. Comm. Conf., LA, 1979; participant Dept. Energy/Westinghouse Sch. Environ. Excellence, Cin., 1991; invited contbr. to procs. 1st Tatarstan Symposium Energy, Environment and Econs., Kazan, Russia, 1992. Mem. publs. com. Ctrl. Assn. Sci. and Math. Tchrs., Iowa City, 1969—72; editor: Nat. Task Force Agrl. Energy R & D, 1976; editor, contbr.: Minn. Sci. Mag., 1974—77; contbr. articles to profl. jours. Judge speech Optimist and 4-H Club Contests, Aiken, 1985—86. Sgt. U.S. Army, 1955—58. Recipient Disting. Marksman Badge Gold medal, 1st pl. Sci. Writing, Argonne Labs. Assn., 1973, Profl. Achievement Permanent Profl. cert., Iowa State Bd. Pub. Instrn., 1974, Blue ribbon, Am. Assn. Agrl. Coll. Editors, Tex. A&M, 1976. Achievements include research in the causes and timing of pre-adolescent initial interest in science; discovery of low-zinc root environment causes delay of development and acceleration of senescence in tobacco plants.

MILLER, R. WARBURTON, psychologist, farmer; b. Bellefonte, Pa., Nov. 23, 1921; s. Joseph Frederick and Mary (Warburton) Miller; m. Joyce Larayne Miller; children: Pamela Joyce, Page Layne. AB, Pa. State U., 1942; MA, U. of the Redlands, 1951; PhD, U. So. Calif., 1957; postgrad., San Bernardino Valley Coll., Columbia U., U. Mich., U. Minn., L.A. State Coll., U. Internat., Saltillo, Coah, Mex., Inst. Mex. Cultura Internat., Guadalajara; JD, Loma Linda Coll. Law, 1985. Lic. clin. psychologist, marriage, family and child counselor, clin. speech pathologist. Capt. USN, 1942-44, 51-53; officer USNR, 1942-74; staff psychologist San Bernardino County Med. Ctr., 1968-74; forensic psychologist/clin. psychologist; pvt. practice with Dr. Joyce Miller. Mem. psychology examining com. State Bd. med. Examiners, 1970—74; dir. Mojave Valley Coordinating Coun. Family Mental Health, 1971—72; lectr. U. So. Calif., U. Redlands, Loma Linda U.; bd. dirs., v.p. E. Pioneer Mut. Water Co.; expert witness in forensic psychology; chmn. bd. dirs. AVORA Corp. Author (with Joyce Miller): Dealing with the Behavioral Problems in the Elementary School, 1968, A Layman's Handbook for Aphasic Rehabilitation, 1973; contbr. articles to profl. jours. Bd. dirs. State of Calif. Psychologists Polit Action Com.; past pres. Carriage Club, Civic Light Opera Assn., San Bernardino chpt. City of Hope Hosp. # 434, San Bernardino County Navy League; bd. dirs., past pres. Goodwill Industries Inland Counties; pres. San Bernardino Libr. Found., 1995—. Recipient George Washington medal, Freedoms Found. Valley Forge, 1970, 1972, 1973, honor cert., 1974, Disting. citizens Lifetime Achievement award, Calif. Inland Empire Coun., Boy Scouts Am., 2000. Fellow: Am. Assn. Marriage Counselors; mem.: SAR (past pres. So. Calif. chpt. Riverside, past pres. State of Calif., nat. trustee 1970—74, v.p. gen. nat. soc. western dist. 1972—74, chmn. nat. soc. Ind. Day com. 1971—73, nat. exec. com. 1973—74, sec. gen. nat. soc. 1974—76), Inland So. Calif. Soc. Clin. Psychologists, Calif. Sate Psychol. Assn., San Bernardino Area C. of C. (bd. dirs. 1990—, pres. 1999), Naval Res. Assn., Rotary (Paul Harris award), Hon. Order Ky. Cols., Masons, Kappa Sigma, Pi Delta Sigma, Tau Kappa Alpha. Avocation: travel. Home and Office: 6836 Palm Ave Highland CA 92346-2513 Office Phone: 909-881-2786. E-mail: drbob@omnivision.com.

MILLER, RACHEL L. social worker, consultant; b. Mittenwald, Germany, Jan. 9, 1948; d. James H. and Emily Rapp; m. Walter R. Miller, Sept. 18, 1965; children: Elise Miller-Hooks, Paul R. BA, L.I. U., Greenvale, N.Y., 1982; MSW, Adelphi U., 1994; cert. in psychotherapy, N.Y. Sch. Psychoanalytic Psychotherapy and Psychoanalysis, N.Y.C., 2002. LCSW. Dir. mktg. and devel. Learning Wall Inc., Roslyn, NY, 1982—86; dir. devel. Mindplay Software, Tucson, 1986—91; clin. social worker Zucker Hillside Hosp., Glen Oaks, NY, 1994—. Cons. Brisol Myers Squibb, Princeton, NJ, 2002—03; adv. bd. Schizophrenia Digest, Buffalo, 2002—. Editor: Diagnosis: Schizophrenia, 2002; contbr. articles to profl. jours. and publs. Grantee Nicholas Family Found., N.Y.C., 1999—2000. Mem.: NASW, Assn. Advancement of Social Work with Groups. Office: Zucker Hillside Hosp 75-59 263 St Glen Oaks NY 11004 Office Phone: 718-470-8081. E-mail: rmiller@lij.edu.

MILLER, RALPH BRADLEY, congressman; b. Fayetteville, N.C., May 19, 1953; s. Nathan David and Margaret Virginia (Hale) M.; m. Esther Susan Hall, Dec. 19, 1981. BA, U. N.C., 1975; MSc, London Sch. Econs., 1978; JD, Columbia U., 1979. Bar: N.C. 1979, U.S. Dist. Ct. (ea. dist.) N.C. 1980, U.S. Ct. Appeals (4th cir. 1980), U.S. Dist. Ct. (mid. dist.) N.C. 1983. Law clk. to Hon. J. Dickson Phillips Jr. U.S. Ct. Appeals (4th cir.), 1979-80; assoc. Allen, Steed & Allen, Raleigh, N.C., 1980-82, Barringer, Allen & Pinnix, Raleigh, N.C., 1982-84, LeBoeuf, Lamb, Leiby & MacRae, Raleigh, N.C., 1985-88; prin. Nichols, Miller & Sigmon, Raleigh, N.C., 1988-90; pvt. practice Raleigh, N.C., 1991—; mem. N.C. Ho. of Reps., Raleigh, 1992—96, N.C. Senate, Raleigh, 1997—2002, chmn. Sen. Jud. II Com.; mem. U.S. Ho. of Reps from 13th N.C. dist., 2003—. Chmn. Wake County Dem. Com., 1985-87; mem. state exec. com. N.C. Dem. Com., 1985-89, 91-97; mem. N.C. Environ. Rev. Commn., 1994-95, mem. sentencing and policy adv. com. Mem. ATLA, N.C. Bar Assn., Wake County Bar Assn., N.C. Acad. Trial Lawyers, Am. Judicature Soc. Democrat. Episcopalian. Office: 1505 Longworth Ho Office Bldg Washington DC 20515-3313 E-mail: rbradleymiller@mindspring.com.

MILLER, RAYMOND EDWARD, computer science educator; b. Bay City, Mich., Oct. 9, 1928; s. Martin Theophil and Elizabeth Charlotte (Zierath) M.; m. Marilyn Lueck, June 18, 1955; children: Patricia Ann, Laura Jean, Donna Lyn, Martha Eileen. BS in Mech. Engring., U. Wis., 1950; BEE, U. Ill., 1954, MS in Math., 1955, PhD in Elec. Engring., 1957. Design engr. IBM, Endicott, Poughkeepsie, NY, 1950—51, mem. rsch. staff Yorktown Heights, NY, 1957—81; dir., prof. Ga. Inst. Tech., Atlanta, 1980—89, prof. emeritus, 1989—; dir. Ctr. Excellence in Space Data and Info. Scis. NASA, Greenbelt, Md., 1988—93; prof. U. Md., College Park, 1989—2001, prof. emeritus, 2002—. Pres. Computing Scis. Accreditation Bd., 1985-87. Author: Switching Theory, Vols. I and II, 1965; editor: (with J.W. Thatcher) Complexity of Computer Computation, 1972; patentee in field. Lt. USAF, 1951-53. Fellow AAAS, IEEE; Assn. for Computing Machinery, IEEE Computer Soc. (v.p. edn. acts 1991-92). Lutheran. Avocations: tennis, fishing. Office: U Md Dept of Computer Sci A V Williams Bldg College Park MD 20742-0001 Office Phone: 301-405-2675.

MILLER, RAYMOND ELMO, speech educator; b. Stockton, Calif., July 20, 1953; s. John Franklin and Artis Miller. Student, Modesto Jr. Coll., 1972—75; MA magna cum laude, Calif. State U., 1981. Clin. rehabilitative svcs. credential Calif. Speech pathologist Stanislaus County Schools, Modesto, Calif., 1982—92, Nashville City Schools, 1992—97, Patterson Unified Sch. Dist., Patterson, Calif., 1997—. Author: (novels) Ghost Dance Insurrection, 2000, (book) Jazzman Chronicles, 2003, (Haight Ashbury lit. jour.) The Killing Spirit, 2004. Dir. of plays Modesto Civic Theatre, Modesto, Calif., 1987—92; dir. Golden Gaslight Theatre, Denair, Calif., 1990; mem. San Francisco Jazz, 2003—. Nominee Pushcart prize (Lynx Eye), 1998; recipient Calif. Jr. Colleges Gold award. Mem.: Calif. Teachers Assn., Calif. Speech, Language and Hearing Assn. Avocation: golf. Home: 541 Hunter Ave Modesto CA 95350

MILLER, RAYMOND JARVIS, agronomy educator; b. Claresholm, Alta., Can., Mar. 19, 1934; came to U.S., 1957, naturalized, 1975; s. Charles Jarvis and Wilma Macy (Anderson) M.; m. Frances Anne Davidson, Apr. 28, 1956; children: Cheryl Rae, Jeffrey John, Jay Robert. BS, U. Alta., Edmonton, 1957;

MS, Wash. State U., 1960; PhD, Purdue U., 1962; Doctorate (hon.), Moscow State Agro Engring. U., 2000. Mem. faculty N.C. State U., 1962-65, U. Ill., 1965-69; asst. dir., then assoc. dir. Ill. Agrl. Expt. Sta., 1969-73; dir. Idaho Agrl. Expt. Sta., 1973-79; dean U. Idaho Coll. Agr., 1979-85, v.p. for agr.; dean Coll. Agr. and Coll. Life Sci. U. Md., College Park, 1986-89, vice chancellor agr. and natural resources, 1989-91; pres. Md. Inst. for Agrl. and Natural Resources, 1991-93, prof. agronomy, 1986—, dir. internat. program agrl. natural resources, 1998—. Internat. expert in areas of agrl. sci. and edn. with spl. emphasis on Russia, former Soviet Union, East Europe, China, L.Am. and the Pacific Rim. Author numerous papers in field. Pres. Idaho Rsch. Found., 1980-85; bd. govs. Agrl. Rsch. Inst., 1979-80; chmn. legis. subcom. Expt. Sta. Com. on Policy, 1981-82; chmn. bd. divsn. agr. Land Grant Assn., 1985-86; co-chmn. Nat. Com. Internat. Sci. Edn. Joint Coun., USDA, 1991-94; bd. dirs. C.V. Riley Found., 1985-93; chmn. budget com. Bd. Agr., Nat. Assn. State Univs. and Land Grant Colls., 1993; mem. U.S./Russian Subcom. on Agrl. Rsch., Edn. and Ext., 1996—. Fed. Provincial grantee U. Alta., 1954-56, Dan Baker scholar U. Alta., 1954-56; grantee Internat. Congress Soil Sci., 1960, Purdue U. Rsch. Found., summers 1960, 61 Fellow AAAS, Am. Soc. Agronomy, Soil Sci. Soc. Am.; mem. Internat. Soc. Soil Sci., Clay and Clay Minerals Soc., Am. Chem. Soc., Am. Soc. Plant Physiolotists, Elks, Lions, Sigma Xi, Phi Kappa Phi, Gamma Sigma Delta, Alpha Zeta. Home: Apt 716 9348 Cherry Hill Rd College Park MD 20740 Office: Symons Hall Univ Md College Park MD 20742 Office Phone: 301-405-1316. E-mail: millerrj@umd.edu.

MILLER, REGINALD WAYNE, professional basketball player; b. Riverside, Calif., Aug. 24, 1965; Student, UCLA. Profl. basketball player Ind. Pacers, 1987—. Mem. Dream Team I, 1994, Dream Team II, 1996. Named to NBA All-Star team, 1990, 1994. Achievements include being a holder of NBA Playoff record most three-point field golas in one quarter (5), 1994; being co-holder NBA Playoff record most three point field goals in one half (6), 1994, 95; being first Pacers player to surpass 15,000 career points; being a 5 time all star. Office: c/o Indiana Pacers Market St Arena 300 E Market St Fl 1 Indianapolis IN 46204-2603

MILLER, RICHARD A. health products executive; MD summa cum laude, SUNY. Diplomate Am. Bd. Internal Medicine, Am. Bd. Med. Oncology. Pres., CEO, dir. Pharmacyclics, Inc., Sunnyvale, Calif., 1991—; co-founder IDEC Pharms. Corp., 1984—92. Clin. prof. oncology Stanford Univ. Med. Ctr., Calif. Office: Pharmacyclics Inc 995 E Arques Ave Sunnyvale CA 94086

MILLER, RICHARD ALAN, economist, educator; b. Springfield, Ohio, Feb. 25, 1931; s. Ross and Beatrice Miller; m. Joan Taylor Walton, July 7, 1956; children: Carol Elizabeth, Jean Anne, Eric Ross. BA, Oberlin Coll., 1952; MA, Yale U., 1957; MA (hon.), Wesleyan U., 1972; PhD, Yale U., 1962. Mem. faculty Wesleyan U., Middletown, Conn., 1960—, chmn. dept. econs., 1968-69, 71-73, 75-76, 92-94, Andrews prof., 1995-98, Woodhouse/Sysco prof., 2002—. Vis. lectr. Yale U., New Haven, 1961-62, vis. assoc. prof., 1967-68, vis. prof., 1973, 83, 85, 95; vis. assoc. prof. U. Calif., Berkeley, 1969-70; vis. prof. U. Adelaide, Australia, 1981; vis. lectr econs. U. Conn., Storrs, 1983; economist Econ. Policy Office, Antitrust Div., U.S. Dept. Justice, Washington, 1973-74, cons., 1974-75; cons. antitrust sect. State Conn., 1980, 82; dir. Kawanhee, Inc., Maine, 1975-81, 82-86 Contbr. articles on indsl. orgn. and antitrust econs. to profl. jours. Mem. cert. adv. coun. Dept. Edn., State Conn., 1982-86; mem. coms. Bd. for State Acad. Awards. State Conn., 1978-97; dean faculty of Cons. Examiners., 1985-87; trustee Conn. Joint Coun. Econ. Edn., 1982-85. Served to lt. (j.g.) USNR, 1952-55. Ford Found. fellow Yale U., 1958-59; NSF fellow MIT, 1964-65, Wesleyan U., 1965-69; Shelby Cullom Davis Found. grantee Wesleyan U., 1979-82; Fulbright fellow N.Z. Inst. Econ. Research, 1986, 88. Mem. Am. Econs. Assn., Indsl. Orgn. Soc. Congregationalist. Home: 83 Paterson Dr Middletown CT 06457-5138 Office: Wesleyan U Dept Econs Middletown CT 06459-0001 Office Phone: 860-685-2354. Business E-Mail: ramiller@wesleyan.edu.

MILLER, RICHARD BRUCE, electronics company executive; b. Bryn Mawr, Pa., Jan. 2, 1947; s. Robert and Kathryn (Marks) M; m. Nedra Lynn Herbert, Aug. 28, 1971; children: Sean Patrick and Ryan Cameron. BA in Polit. Sci., Shippensburg State U., 1969, MA in Polit. Sci., 1975. Asst. city mgr. City of Chambersburg, Pa., 1970-72; city mgr. City of New Cumberland, Pa., 1972-76, Montgomery Twp., N.J., 1976-78; from internal control mgr. to contr. Xerox Corp., Harrisburg, Pa., 1978-83, field adminstrn. ops. mgr. Stamford, Conn., 1983-85; ctr. mgr. N.Y., 1985-88; transition mgr. bus. ops. Stamford, Conn., 1988-89; mgr., ops. support Ea. region, 1989-90; mgr. quality/customer satisfaction Xerox Corp., Stamford, 1990-91, mgr. customer svc. ops., 1991-92, mgr. sys. products adminstrn. Rochester, N.Y., 1992-93, mgr. customized solutions adminstrn., 1993-94, market to collection, 1994-95; from infrastructure delivery mgr. to applications mgr. Office Document Products, 1995-97, applications mgr., 1997; applications framework mgr. Year 2000 Program Office Xerox Corp. Info. Mgmt., Rochester, 1997-2000; mgr. productivity office Xerox Corp., 2000-01, mgr. fin. outsourcing N.Am. info. mgmt., 2001—. Mem. All Star Club Xerox Corp., 1982-83, 85-86, 87-88, 89-90, grad. Astronaut VII, 1987, chief info. officer Leadership award, 1995. Bd. dirs. So. Conn. Child Guidance Ctr., 1988-90, Child Care Ctrs., Stamford, 1990-92; cubmaster Boy Scouts Am., Fairport, N.Y., 1994-95; youth sports coach Southeast YMCA, Pittsford, N.Y., 1993-96, Fairport Youth Lacrosse, 1994-2000; registrar Perinton Youth Hockey, 1998-2000. Republican. Roman Catholic. Avocations: tennis, boating, amateur radio, reading. Home: 60 Vineyard Hill Fairport NY 14450 Office: 100 S Clinton Ave Xerox Sq 9-9-6 Rochester NY 14644 Business E-Mail: bruce.miller@usa.xerox.com. E-mail: bmiller5@rochester.rr.com.

MILLER, RICHARD CONNELLY, publishing executive, writer; b. Cleve., Sept. 17, 1925; s. Levi Lewis and Linda Storer Connelly Miller; m. Cora Ann McCaughna, Jan. 10, 1953; children: John, Lisa, Eric, Michael, Andrew, Kate. BA, Ohio State U., 1949; cert., U. Paris, 1951; MA, Claremont U., 1956; PhD, U. Calif., Berkeley, 1961. Mcht. seaman Nat. Maritime Union, 1945—50, 1953; fgn. corr. Cleve. Plain Dealer, Paris, 1950—53; journalist, photographer various newspapers, Ohio, Calif.; instr. Golden Gate Coll., San Francisco, 1958; prof. Coll. of the San Francisco Art Inst., 1959—80; ops. mgr. Dada Found. Imprints, LLC, Monterey, Calif., 1997—. Author: 10 novels, 1 biography, 1 history book. Congl. candidate 12 Congl. Dist. Calif. Dem. Primary, 1964, 1966. Served with USMC, 1943—45. Mem.: PEN, Nat. Writers' Union. Home: 280 Grove Acre Ave Pacific Grove CA 93950 Office: Dada Found Imprints LLC PO Box 621 Monterey CA 93942 Personal E-mail: dadaklub@aol.com.

MILLER, RICHARD J. wholesale pharmaceutical distribution company executive; V.p. auditing Cardinal Health, Inc., 1994-95, v.p. contr., 1995-99, corp. v.p., 1999, exec. v.p., 1999, CFO, exec. v.p., principle acctg. officer, 1999—. Office: Cardinal Health Inc 7000 Cardinal Pl Dublin OH 43017

MILLER, RICHARD J. pharmacologist, educator; b. London, Eng., July 8, 1950; BSc with 1st class honors, U. Bristol, 1972; MA, PhD, U. Cambridge, 1976. Tutor in biochemistry and pharmacology U. Cambridge, St. John's and Trinity Colls., England, 1972—75; postdoctoral rschr. Burroughs Wellcome Labs., Research Triangle Park, NC, 1976—77; from asst. prof. to assoc. prof. U. Chgo., 1977—81, prof. dept. pharmacol. and physiol. scis., 1981—95, William Mabie prof. neurosci., 1995—2001; prof. dept. molecular pharmacology and biol. chemistry Northwestern U., Chgo., 2001—. Mem. neurosci. study sect. NIH; mem. biomed. study sect. NIH, Nat. Inst. Drug Abuse; chmn. Gordon Conf. on Opiate Action, 1985; mem. sci. adv. bd. Nova Pharms., 1985—90, Synaptic Pharms., 1990—2000, Salk Inst. Biotech./Indsl. Assocs., 1991—2000; Rainbow Meml. lectr. U. Pa., 1988; Grass lectr. Emory U., 1990; Stirling Meml. lectr. U. Minn., 1990; Grass lectr. U. Ind., 1992, U. Man., 1992; Parke-Davis Disting. Neurosci. lectr., 94; Grass lectr. U. Utah, 1994, Tex. Tech. U., 1997. Mem. editl. adv. bd.: Molecular Biology, Brit. Jour. Pharmacology, Med. Biology, others, mem. molecular sct. editl. adv. bd.: European Jour. Pharmacology. Mem.: Brit. Pharmacol. Soc., Am. Soc. for Pharmacology and Exptl. Therapeutics (John Jacob Abel award 1983), Soc. for Neurosci., Internat. Soc. for Toxicology, Sigma Xi. Achievements include research in neuronal signal transduction. Office: Northwestern U Med Sch Molecular Pharmacology & Biol Chemistry 303 E Chicago Ave Chicago IL 60611

MILLER, RICHARD KIDWELL, artist, actor, educator; b. Fairmont, W.Va., Mar. 15, 1930; s. Maurice Entler and Lillian (Reed) M.; m. Teresa Marie Robinson, Apr. 27, 1957. Student, Pa. Acad. Fine Arts, 1948-49; BA, Am. U., 1953; MFA, Columbia U., 1956. Instr. painting Scarsdale (N.Y.) Community Sch., 1970-75; asst. prof. Kansas City Art Inst., 1968-69. Participated extensively in profl. theater as actor and singer including roles in Broadway Prodn. Baker Street, Oliver, Funny Girl, Wonderful Town, Illya, Darling, Indians, Rise and Fall of the City of Mahogonny; actor stock cos. including Fiddler on the Roof; one-man art shows include Trans-Lux Gallery, Washington, 1951, Bader Gallery, Washington, 1954, Balt. Mus. Art, 1955, Graham Gallery Ltd., N.Y.C., 1960, 62, 65, Argas Gallery, Madison, N.J., 1966, Jefferson Place Gallery, Washington, 1966, Albrecht Kemper Mus. Art, St. Joseph, Mo., 1969, L.I. U., 1973, Aaron Berman Gallery N.Y.C., 1983, Westbeth Gallery, N.Y.C., 1982, John Jay Gallery, N.Y.C., 1998, 2000, JCC of Mid-Westchester, 2001, Retrospective Exhbn., U. W.Va., 2004; group shows include Corcoran Gallery Art., 1950-51, 53, Pa. Acad. Fine Arts, 1951, 64, Carnegie Internat., 1961, Salon de National, Paris, 1954, Whitney Mus., 1958, U. Nebr., 1963, Martha Jackson Gallery, N.Y.C., 1973, Nat. Acad. Design, N.Y.C., 1996, 2002, 04, Art of the Northeast, New Caanan, Conn., 1996, others; represented in permanent collections Albrecht Kemper Mus. of Art, St. Joseph, Mo., Hirshorn Mus. and Sculpture Garden, Washington, Phillips Collection, Washington, Rochester Mus. Art, U. Ariz. Mus. of Art, Tucson, Watkins Gallery Collection, Washington, U. W.Va., Morgantown, also numerous private collections; featured in Jan. edit. Am. Artist Mag., 1988, Christian Sci. Monitor, 1990, World Artists (Claude Marks), 1991. Washington Times Herald scholar, 1944, 45, 46; Gertrude Whitney scholar, 1948-53, 55-56; Fulbright fellow, 1953-54 Address: 222 W 83d St Apt 8C New York NY 10024-4913 *I have an insatiable need to express myself— I suppose I was born with it. I was given more than one talent to satisfy this need, and for that I thank God. I have endeavored to use these talents to the absolute best of my ability. I can do no more than that. Some times I have succeeded, and many times I have failed, but the real joy and meaning is in the doing. All the pain has been worth it.*

MILLER, RICHARD L. architectural executive; b. Salina, Kans., Jan. 31, 1941; s. L. William and Inez Corine (DeMars) M.; m. Sharalena Miller, June 22, 1963; children: Lora Miller Vinson, Scott Miller. Student, Kansas Wesleyan U., 1959-61; BArch, U. Kans., 1966, postgrad., 1966-67. Registered architect, 38 states and V.I. Assoc. Earl Swensson Assocs., Nashville, 1967-73, pres., 1973—. Mem. hosp. licensure task force State of Tenn. Dept. Pub. Health, 1975, Ambulatory Surg. Treatment Ctr. Act Task Force, 1976-77, SCARAB, Hon. Archtl. Frat., Nursing Home Task Force, 1977-78; participant Internat. Pub. Health Seminar, Budapest, 1984; speaker Fla. HRS seminars, 1986, 90; mem. ann. faculty health care forum on health facilities design, 1990; speaker numerous confs. in field, including World Workplace, 1995, NeoCon '95 World's Trade Fair, 1995, Health Facility Inst. Fifth Ann. Conf., 1994. Co-author: New Directions in Hospital and Healthcare Facility Design, 1995. Mem. Leadership Nashville, 1993-94. Fellow AIA (com. architecture for health 1980), Tenn. Soc. Architects (ad hoc fire com. 1975). Mem. Christian Ch. Avocations: golf, kite flying, sailing. Office: Earl Swensson Assocs 2100 W End Ave Ste 1200 Nashville TN 37203-5239

MILLER, RICHARD MARK, lawyer; b. Feb. 12, 1952; s. Abraham and Phyllis (Isaacson) M.; m. Beverly Elaine Sparks, Aug. 7, 1976 (div. 1992); m. Cathryn Alexandra Mitchell, Oct. 3, 1993; children: Jeffrey Brian, David Gregory, Scott Alan, Jenifer Marlena. BA, Bklyn. Coll., 1973; JD, SUNY, Buffalo, 1976. Bar: N.Y. 1977, N.J. 1977, U.S. Dist. Ct. (so. and ea. dists.) N.Y. 1977, U.S. Dist. Ct. N.J. 1977. Gen. counsel Amswiss Internat. Corp., Jersey City, 1976-78; assoc. gen. counsel Loeb Rhoades, Hornblower, N.Y.C., 1978-79, Shearson Loeb Rhoades, 1979-80; assoc. counsel Bausch & Lomb Inc., Rochester, N.Y., 1980-83, counsel, 1983-85; sr. atty. Cheseborough Pond's Inc., 1985-87; corp. counsel Prince Sports Group, Inc. (formerly Prince Mfg., Inc.), Princeton, N.J., 1987-90, gen. counsel, 1990-93; cons. Proskauer Rose Goetz & Mendelsohn, N.Y.C., 1993-94; counsel Stark & Stark, Princeton, 1994-96; prin. Miller & Mitchell PC, Princeton, 1996—. Chmn. Internat. Trade Network. Mem.: Rotary Club (co-chmn. vocational com.). Home: 29 Crusher Rd Hopewell NJ 08525-2201 Office: MillerMitchell PC 134 Nassau St 2d Fl Princeton NJ 08542 Office Phone: 609-921-3322. E-mail: rmiller@millermitchell.com.

MILLER, RICHARD MCDERMOTT, sculptor; b. New Philadelphia, Ohio, Apr. 30, 1922; s. J. Harry and Clela Belle (McDermott) M.; m. Audrey F. Miller, 1942; 1 dau., Sue Ann (Mrs. Kenneth Hartz); m. Gloria B. Bley, Mar. 18, 1961. Student, Cleve. Inst. Art, 1940-42, 49-51. Prof. emeritus Queens Coll., CUNY. One man shows include Peridot Gallery, N.Y.C., 1964, 66, 67, 69, Washburn Gallery, N.Y.C., 1971, 74, 75, 77, Canton (Ohio) Art Inst., 1980, 20-yr. retrospective Artists Choice Mus., N.Y.C., 1984, Springfield (Mo.) Mus. Art, 1985, Friends of Figurative Sculpture Gallery, N.Y.C., 1987-99, 2002, Philharm. Ctr., Naples, Fla., 1991, J.J. Brookings Gallery, San Francisco, 1997, Barnet Park, Spartanburg, S.C., 1999, Brookgreen Gardens, S.C., 2001, 8-foot bronze figure of Mary Cassatt, Converse (S.C.) Coll., 2004; represented in numerous pub. and pvt. collections; author: Figure Sculpture in Wax and Plaster, 1971. Served with AUS, 1942-46. Mem. NAD (pres. 1989-92), Sculptors Guild, Nat. Sculpture Soc. (pres. 1997-2000), Century Assn. Address: 53 Mercer St New York NY 10013-2617 E-mail: sohosculpt@aol.com.

MILLER, RICHARD SHERWIN, law educator; b. Boston, Dec. 11, 1930; s. Max and Mollie Miller; m. Doris Sheila Lunchick, May 24, 1956; children: Andrea Jayne Armitage, Matthew Harlan. BSBA, Boston U., 1951, JD magna cum laude, 1956; LLM, Yale U., 1959. Bar: Mass. 1956, Mich. 1961, Hawaii 1977. Pvt. practice law, Boston, 1956—58; assoc. prof. law Wayne State U., Detroit, 1959—62, prof., 1962—65; prof. law Ohio State U., Columbus, 1965—73, dir. clin. and interdisciplinary programs, 1972—73; prof. U. Hawaii, Honolulu, 1973-95, prof. emeritus, 1995—, dean, 1981-84. Vis. prof. law USIA/U. Hawaii, Hiroshima U. Affiliation Program, Japan, 1986, Victoria U., Wellington, New Zealand, 1987; del. Hawaii State Jud. Conf., 1989-92; cons. Hawaii Coalition for Health, 1997—. Author: Courts and the Law: An Introduction to our Legal System, 1980; editor: (with Roland Stanger) Essays on Expropriations, 1967; editor-in-chief: Boston U. Law Rev., 1955-56; contbr. articles to profl. jours. Mem. Hawaii Substance Abuse Task Force, 1994-95; arbitrator Hawaii Ct. Annexed Arbitration Program, 1995-99; bd. dirs. Drug Policy Forum Hawaii, 1996—; mem. Save our Star-Bulletin Com., 1999-2001, Citizens for Competitive Air Travel, 2002, Citizens Against Gasoline Price Gouging, 2003—. 1st lt. USAF, 1951-53. Sterling-Ford fellow Yale U., 1958-59; named Lawyer of Yr. Japan-Hawaii Lawyers Assn., 1990; recipient Cmty. Svc. award Hawaii Med. Assn. Alliance, 1999. Mem. ABA, Hawaii State Bar Assn., Hawaii ACLU, Am. Inn of Ct. IV (emeritus founding mem., master of the bench), Am. Law Inst., Honolulu Cmty.-Media Coun. (chair 1994-89, treas. 2000-02, vice chair 1998-2000), Yale Club of Hawaii. Office: U Hawaii Richardson Sch Law 2515 Dole St Honolulu HI 96822-2328 Business E-Mail: rmiller@aya.yale.edu.

MILLER, RICHARD STEVEN, lawyer; b. Mt. Vernon, N.Y., Dec. 5, 1951; s. Norman and Mildred (Curtis) M. BA, U. Pa., 1974; JD, NYU, 1977. Bar: N.Y. 1978, U.S. Dist. Ct. (so. and ea. dists.) N.Y. 1978, U.S. Ct. Appeals (2d cir.) 1978. Asst. dist. atty. Kings County, N.Y., 1977-79; with Hahn & Hessen, N.Y.C., 1979-82, Levin & Weintraub & Crames, N.Y.C., 1982-87; counsel, then ptnr. Rogers & Wells, N.Y.C., 1987-91; ptnr. Dewey Ballantine LLP, N.Y.C., 1991-2001; prin. shareholder Greenburg Traurig LLP, N.Y.C., 2001—, co-chmn. nat. reorgn., bankruptcy and restructuring practice, 2001—. Mem. ABA, Internat. Bar Assn., Am. Bankruptcy Inst. Office: Greenberg Traurig 200 Park Avenue 15th Fl New York NY 10166 Office Fax: 212-801-6400. E-mail: millerrs@gtlaw.com.

MILLER, RICHARDS THORN, naval architect, engineer; b. Jan. 31, 1918; s. Herman Geistweit and Helen Buckman (Thorn) M.; m. Jean Corbat Spear, Sept. 13, 1941 (dec.); children: Patricia (Mrs. Charles G. Fishburn), Linda (Mrs. John X. Carrier); m. Alice Johnson Houghton, May 19, 1984. BS in Naval Arch. and Marine Engring., Webb Inst. Naval Arch., 1940; Naval Engr., MIT, 1951. Registered profl. engr. Commd. ensign USN, 1940, advanced through grades to capt., 1960; head preliminary design br. Bur. Ships, 1960-63; dir. Mine Def. Lab., Panama City, Fla., 1963-66; dir. ship design Naval Ship Engring. Ctr., 1966-68; specialized work design oceanographic rsch. ships, mine sweepers, torpedo boats, destroyers; ret., 1968. Mgr. ocean engring. Oceanic divsn. Westinghouse Electric Corp., 1969-75, adv. engr., 1975-79; cons. naval arch. and engr., 1968—; arbitrator admiralty and ship bldg. contract cases, 1978—; mem. com. naval arch. Am. Bur. Shipping, 1960-63, mem. tech. com., 1978-92; mem. ship structure com., 1966-68. Author: (with R.G. Henry) Sailing Yacht Design, 1963, (with K.L. Kirkman) Sailing Yacht Design—A New Appreciation, 1990; also sects. in books, articles. Decorated Navy Legion of Merit; recipient William Selkirk Owen award Webb Alumni Assn., 1983. Fellow Soc. Naval Archs. and Marine Engrs. (chmn. S.E. sect. 1965-66, chmn. marine sys. com. 1970-77, chmn. tech. and rsch. steering com. 1977-78, chmn. small craft com. 1983-87, v.p. tech. and rsch. 1979-81, hon. life v.p. 1981—, mem. coun. 1976—, mem. exec. com. 1977-81, Capt. Joseph H. Linnard prize 1964, Disting. Svc. award 1988); mem. Am. Soc. Naval Engrs. (mem. coun. 1976-78), U.S. Naval Inst., Christie Soc., Md. Bd. for Profl. Engrs., N.Y. Yacht Club, Annapolis Yacht Club, Sailing Club of the Chesapeake, Sigma Xi. Home and Office: BayWoods of Annapolis 7101 Bay Front Drive Apt 316 Annapolis MD 21403-3701

MILLER, RITA, personnel consultant, diecasting company executive; b. Bklyn., Jan. 15, 1925; d. Joseph and Etta M.; BA, Bklyn. Coll., 1947; MA, Boston U., 1949; children: Erika Greenwald, Roy Barnet Glickman. Personnel officer, sec. to pres. Marine Elec. Corp., Bklyn., 1943-47; script writer Song Debut, Boston, 1949-50; dir. Writers' Workshops, interviewer pub. opinion surveys, New Rochelle, N.Y., 1962-64; mgr. employee relations Dynacast div. Coats & Clark, Inc., Yorktown Heights, 1966-89. Mem. Am. Soc. Personnel Adminstrn., Westchester Personnel Mgmt. Assn. (dir.), Personnel Council New Rochelle, Bus. and Profl. Women U.S.A., Nat. Sociology Hon. Soc. Editor: The Management Consultant (George Kenning), 1965; contbr. articles to profl. jours. Home: 16 Congress St New Rochelle NY 10801-1902

MILLER, ROBERT, advertising executive; b. N.Y.C., June 2, 1923; s. Samuel and Adele (Elswit) M.; m. Frances Fitzgerald, June 10, 1944 (dec. 1978); children: Marc Robert, William Fitzgerald, Daniel Bates, Ellen Minette (Mrs. John Meyer); m. Sandra Gold, 1980; 1 child, Richard Scott. Student, NYU, 1940-42, Syracuse U., 1943. Newsroom employee N.Y. Daily Mirror, 1942; with Miller Advt. Agy., Inc., N.Y.C., 1946—, v.p., 1948-54, chmn. bd., 1954-57, pres., 1958—, Miller Advt. Service Corp., 1956-62, Miller Advt. Agy. Ill., Inc., 1965-73, also bd. dirs. Bd. dirs. Hereford Ins. Co., Inc., 1988-94. Author: Clash of Cultures, 2003; Contbg. editor Madison Avenue mag., 1975-78. Bd. govs. Roslyn Democratic Club, 1957-61, 68-73; mem. Nassau County Dem. Com., 1958-61, 68-73; Bd. dirs. Shalom Peace Found., 1970-89. Served to 1st lt. USAAF, 1942-46. Mem.: VFW, Jewish War Vets., Am. Legion. Home: 301 E 52nd St New York NY 10022-6319 also: 17 Shelly Dr Ellenville NY 12428-1809 Office: Miller Advt Agy Inc 71 Fifth Ave New York NY 10003-3004 E-mail: bobmiller@miller.aa.com.

MILLER, ROBERT ALLEN, hotel executive; b. Chgo., Nov. 26, 1945; m. Diana Marie Hall, Dec. 29, 1967; children: David, Allison, Brian. BSBA, U. Fla., 1967. CPA, Fla. Auditor, acct. Arthur Young & Co., Tampa, Fla., 1967-72; chief fin. officer Fleetwing Corp., Lakeland, Fla., 1972-78; pres. Am. Resorts Corp., Lakeland, 1978-84; v.p. Marriott Internat., Bethesda, Md., 1984—. Office: Marriott Internat 1 Marriott Dr Washington DC 20058-0001

MILLER, ROBERT ARTHUR, former state supreme court chief justice; b. Aberdeen, S.D., Aug. 28, 1939; s. Edward Louis and Bertha Leone (Hitchcox) Miller; m. Shirlee Ann Schlim, Sept. 5, 1964; children: Catherine Sue, Scott Edward, David Alan, Gerri Elizabeth, Robert Charles. BSBA, U. S.D., 1961, JD, 1963. Asst. atty. gen. State of S.D., Pierre, 1963—65; pvt. practice law Philip, SD, 1965—71; state atty. Haakon County, Philip, 1965—71; city atty. City of Philip, 1965—71; judge State of S.D. (6th cir.), Pierre, 1971—86, presiding judge, 1975—86; justice S.D. Supreme Ct., Pierre, 1986—2001, chief justice, 1990—2001, ret., 2001—. Bd. dirs. Nat. Conf. of Chief Justices, 1996—97, State Justice Inst., 1998—, chair, 1998—; trustee S.D. Retirement Sys., Pierre, 1974—85, chmn., 1982—85; mem. faculty S.D. Law Enforcement Tng. Acad., 1975—85; bd. dirs. U. S.D. Law Sch. Found., 1990—. Mem. S.D. State Crime Commn., 1979—86; mem. adv. commn. S.D. Sch. for the Deaf, 1983—85, Comm. Svcs. to Deaf, 1990—92; cts. counselor S.D. Boy's State, 1986—, Nat. Awards Jury Freedoms Found., 1991. Mem.: S.D. Judge's Assn. (pres. 1974—75), State Bar of S.D., Elks. Roman Catholic. Avocations: golf, hunting. Office: SD Supreme Ct State Capitol Bldg 500 E Capitol Ave Pierre SD 57501-5070

MILLER, ROBERT BRANSON, JR., retired newspaper publisher; b. Battle Creek, Mich., Aug. 10, 1935; s. Robert Branson and Jean (Leonard) M.; m. Pattricia E. Miller; children: Melissa Ann, Gregory Allen, Jennifer Lynn, Jeffrey William. Grad., Hotchkiss Sch., Lakeville, Conn., 1953; BA, Mich. State U., 1959. Advt. salesman State Jour., Lansing, Mich., 1959-61, circulation sales rep., 1961-62, reporter, 1962-65, nat. advt. mgr., 1965-66; asst. to pub. Idaho Statesman, Boise, 1966-69, pub., 1969—71, Daily Olympian, Olympia, Wash., Battle Creek Enquirer, 1979-90, pub., chmn., 1980—91. Bd. dirs. Battle Creek chpt. ARC; advisor Big Bros./Big Sisters; sr. advisor United Way; trustee Miller Found., Battle Creek, 1963—. With USNR, 1956-58.

MILLER, ROBERT CARL, retired library director; b. May 9, 1936; m. Jeanne M. Larson. BS in History and Philosophy, Marquette U., 1958; MS in Am. History, U. Wis., 1962; MA in Libr. Sci., U. Chgo., 1966. Head telephone reference Library of Congress, Wash., 1959-60; reference librarian Marquette U., Milw., 1960-62, acquisition librarian, 1962-66; head tech. services/librarian Parsons Coll., Fairfield, Iowa, 1966-68; head acquisitions dept. U. of Chgo. Library, Ill., 1968-71, assoc. dir (reader services), 1971-73; assoc dir (gen. service) U. of Chgo., 1973-75; dir. of libraries U. Mo., St. Louis, 1975-78; dir of libraries U. of Notre Dame, Ind., 1978-97, ret., 1997. Vis. prof. IBIN-U. Warsaw, Poland, 1992, 93, 97, 2000, 02. Contbr. to prof. jour. Fellow Woodrow Wilson Found. (sr.), Coun. on Libr. Resources; mem. ALA, Polish Inst. of Arts and Letters of Am. Roman Catholic. Home: 27752 Woodland Dr Chisago City MN 55103 E-mail: miller.1@nd.edu.

MILLER, ROBERT CARMI, JR., microbiology educator, university administrator; b. Elgin, Ill., Aug. 10, 1942; s. Robert C. and Melba I. (Steinke) M.; m. Patricia A. Black, Aug. 29, 1964; children: Geoffrey T., Christopher J. BS in Physics, Trinity Coll., Hartford, Conn., 1964; MS in Biophysics, Pa. State U., 1965; PhD in Molecular Biology, U. Pa., 1969. USPHS trainee U. Pa., Phila., 1966-69; postdoctoral fellow U. Wis., Madison, 1969-70; rsch. assoc., Am. Cancer Soc. postdoctoral fellow MIT, Cambridge, 1970-71; asst. assoc. prof. U. B.C., Vancouver, 1971-79, prof. microbiology, 1980-96, head dept. microbiology, 1982-85, dean sci., 1985-88, v.p. rsch., 1988-95, univ. senate, 1985-88; assoc. vice provost for rsch., dir. technology transfer U. Wash., Seattle, 1995-2000, vice provost, 2000—01; vice chancellor rsch. U. Calif., Santa Cruz, 2001—. Vis. prof. Inst. Molecular Biology, U. Geneva, Switzerland, 1976; mem. grants com. on genetics Med. Rsch. Coun., 1980-82; mem. Grants Panel A Nat. Cancer Inst., 1981-85; biotech. com. B.C. Sci. Coun., 1981-87, univ./industry program grant com., 1987-92; biotech. com. Med. Rsch. Coun., 1983; assoc. com. for biotech. NRC, 1983-86; strategic grant com. biotech. NSERC, 1985-87; bd. dirs. Paprican, Discovery Found., Sci. Coun. B.C., TRIUMF. Assoc. editor: Virology, 1974—85, Jour. Virology, 1975—84, contbr. over 125 articles to profl. jours.; author rsch. papers:. Recipient gold medal Nat. Sci. Coun. B.C., 1993; grantee Natural Sci. and Engring. Rsch. Coun., 1971-96, Med. Rsch. Coun., 1981, 86-89, Nat. Cancer Inst., 1982-86. Fellow: Royal Soc. Can. Office: U Calif Santa Cruz Social Scis II Rm 261 Santa Cruz CA 95060 Business E-Mail: rcmiller@cats.ucsc.edu .

MILLER, ROBERT CHARLES, retired physicist; b. State College, Pa., Feb. 2, 1925; s. Lawrence P. Miller and Eva Mae (Gross) Wiedemann; m. Virginia Callaghan, Aug. 30, 1952; children: Robin Kingon Storey, Jeffrey Lawrence Miller, Lauren Wray Lynch. AB, Columbia U., 1948, MA, 1952, PhD, 1956. Staff mem. Johns-Manville Research Ctr., Finderne, N.J., 1948-49; teaching asst. in physics Columbia U., N.Y.C., 1949-51, lectr. in physics, 1951-53; mem. tech. staff Bell Telephone Labs., Murray Hill, N.J., 1954-63, head solid state spectroscopy research dept., 1963-67; staff mem. Inst. Defense Analyses, Arlington, Va., 1967-68; head optical elec. research dept. Bell Telephone Labs., Murray Hill, 1968-77; mem. tech. staff AT&T Bell Labs., Murray Hill, 1977-84, disting. mem. tech. staff, 1984-88, ret., 1988. Cons. Office of Sec. Def., Arlington, Va., 1968-75. Inventor (with Dr. J.A. Giordmaine) Optical Parametric Oscillator, 1965 (co-recipient R.W. Wood prize, 1986); contbr. articles to profl. jours. Served with U.S. Army, 1943-46, ETO. RCA predoctoral fellow Columbia U., 1953-54. Fellow Am. Phys. Soc.; mem. AAAS, N.Y. Acad. Scis., Sigma Xi. Avocations: sailing, sports cars, tennis. Home: 65 Eaton Ct Cotuit MA 02635-2908 E-mail: rvcmiller@prodigy.net.

MILLER, ROBERT EARL, engineering educator; b. Rockford, Ill., Oct. 4, 1932; s. Leslie D. and Marcia V. (Jones) M. BS, U. Ill., 1954, MS, 1955, PhD, 1959. Asst. prof. theoretical and applied mechanics U. Ill., Urbana, 1959-61, assoc. prof., 1961-68, prof., 1968-94, prof. emeritus, 1994—. Cons. in field to industry U.S. Army; in various positions in industry, summers, 1963-68 Contbr. articles to profl. jours. Mem. AIAA, Am. Soc. Engring. Edn. (Disting. Engring. award 1991), ASCE. Office: U Ill 216 Talbot Lab 104 S Wright St Urbana IL 61801-2935 E-mail: rem@uiuc.edu.

MILLER, ROBERT EDVIN, environmental education specialist, researcher, industrial hygienist; b. Lancaster, Pa., May 8, 1935; s. Grant Edvin and Regina (Keller) M.; m. Nancy Jean Gustafson, May 29, 1982; children: Lenore Ruth, David Robert, Robert E. Jr., Stacy JoAnn, Regina Louise. BA, U. Millersville, 1966; MS, U. Md., 1976. Tchr. pub. schs., Lancaster, Pa., 1966-68, Pottstown, Pa., 1968-70; faculty rsch. asst. U. Md., Solomons, 1970-76, environ. specialist III Cambridge, 1971-81, environ. specialist IV, 1982-90; fisheries biologist Horn Point Environ. Labs., Cambridge, 1981-83. Prof. Wor-Wic Tech. Nursing Sch., Cambridge, 1981-83; referee Fishery Bull., Cmbridge, 1982-83, Bull. of Marine Sci., Cambridge, 1983—. Narrator and cons. ednl. film Chesapeake Blues, 1974 (Golden Eagle award 1975); contbr. articles to profl. jours. Mem. ways and means com. United Fund of Dorchester County, Cambridge, 1982-85; tchr. Dorchester County Adult Edn. and Queen Anne County Adult Edn., Kent Island, Md., 1983. Grantee Power Plant Siting Program, 1979-81, Univ. Md., 1983-84, Waddell Found., 1983. Mem. Roddy Sci. Soc. (pres. 1965), Atlantic Estuarine Rsch. Soc. (membership com. 1973), Estuarine Rsch. Soc., Nat. Marine Edn. Assn., Nat. Sci. Tchrs. Assn. (comm. com., evaluation com., safety officer U. Md., 1996—, ind. hyg. IV, gov. advisery coun. for controlled hazardous substances, 1999—). Republican. Home: 5531 Whitehall Rd Cambridge MD 21613-3443 Office: Horn Point Environ Labs PO Box 775 Cambridge MD 21613-0775

MILLER, ROBERT G. drug store chain company executive; b. 1944; With Albertson's Inc., 1961-89, exec. v.p. retail ops., 1989-91; chmn. bd., pres., CEO Fred Meyer Inc., Portland, Oreg., 1991-99; COO Kroger Co., Cin., 1999; chmn. and CEO Rite Aid Corp., Camp Hill, Pa., 1999—. Office: Rite Aid Corp 30 Hunter Ln Camp Hill PA 17011-2410

MILLER, ROBERT HAROLD, otolaryngologist, educator; b. Columbia, Mo., July 2, 1947; s. Harold Oswald and Ruth Nadine (Ballew) M.; m. Martha Guillory, Apr. 18, 1981; children: Morgan Guillory, Reed Thurston. BS in Biology, Tulane U., 1969, MD, 1973; cert. in otolaryngology-head/neck surg., UCLA Med. Ctr., 1978; MBA, Tulane U., 1996. Diplomate Am. Bd. Otolaryngology. From asst. prof. to assoc. prof. otolaryngology-head and neck surgery Baylor Coll. Medicine, Houston, 1978-87; prof., chmn. otolaryngology-head and neck surgery Tulane Sch. Medicine, New Orleans, 1987-98, vice-chancellor for clin. affairs, 1997-99; dean U. Nev. Sch. Medicine, 1999—2001, prof., 1999—2002; prof. otolaryngology-head and neck surgery Tulane Sch. Medicine, New Orleans, 2002—03; exec. dir. Am. Bd. Otolaryngology, Houston, 2004—. Bd. dirs. Am. Bd. Otolaryngology; chief of staff Tulane Hosp., 1995-96. Mem. editl. bd. Archives of Otolaryngology, 1986—, Head & Neck Surgery, 1987—, Larynoscope '96. Named Outstanding Young Man, Houston C. of C., 1980; Robert Wood Johnson Health Policy fellow, 1996-97. Fellow ACS, Am. Soc. Head & Neck Surgery, Am. Acad. Oto-Head & Neck Surgery (Disting. Svc. award 1994, Honor award 1991), Triological Soc. (exec. sec. 1992-97). Avocations: tennis, computers. Office: Am Bd Otolaryngology 3050 Post Oak Blvd Ste 1700 Houston TX 77056 Home: 103 Sycamore Dr Metairie LA 70005 Office Phone: 713-850-0399. Business E-Mail: rmiller@aboto.org.

MILLER, ROBERT JAMES, educational association administrator; b. Mansfield, Ohio, Jan. 27, 1926; s. Dennis Cornelius and Mabel (Snyder) M.; m. Jerri Ann Burran, June 5, 1952; children: Robert James Jr., Dennis Burran. Student, Heidelberg Coll., 1946-47; BS, U. N.Mex., 1950, MA, 1952; postgrad., Miami U., Oxford, Ohio, 1951-55; MBA, Fla. Atlantic U., 1978. Asst. exec. sec. Phi Delta Theta Hdqrs., Oxford, 1951-54, adminstrv. sec., 1954-55, exec. v.p., 1955-91; pres. Phi Delta Theta Found., Oxford, 1984-96; bus. mgr. The Scroll, Oxford, 1955-91; cons., 1997—. Dir. Interfrat. Found., 1995—. Editor: Phikeia—The Manual of Phi Delta Theta, 1951, 19 edits., 1989, Phis Sing, 1958, Constitution and General Statutes of Phi Delta Theta, Fraternity Education Foundations, 1962, Directory of Phi Delta Theta, 1973. Chmn. United Appeal, Oxford, 1960; bd. dirs. U. N.Mex. Alumni Assn., 1961-68, Work Devel. Assn., 1999—; pres. Fedn. of Clubs, Oxford, 1964, McGuffey PTA, 1971, Miami U. Art Mus., 1993-94, McCullough-Hyde Hosp., Oxford, 1966, chmn. endowment adv. com., 1988-89; vol. leader Boy Scouts Am., Oxford, 1966-79. Recipient citizen of yr. award City of Oxford, 1968, citation Theta Chi, 1967, Order of Interfrat. Svc. Lambda Chi Alpha, 1994, interfrat. leadership award Sigma Nu, 1994, accolate for intrafraternity svc. Kappa Alpha, meritorious svc. award Boy. Scouts Am., 1977, others; Interfrat. Inst. fellow Ind. U., 1988. Mem. Nat. Intrafraternity Conf. (various coms. 1954-96, gold medal 1992), Am. Soc. Assn. Execs. (cert.), Cin. Soc. Assn. Execs., Fraternity Execs. Assn. (pres. 1962-63, disting. svc. award 1991), Edgewater Conf. (pres. 1978-79), Summit Soc., Country Club Oxford (bd. dirs.), Order of Symposiarchs, Order of Omega, Rotary (founder Oxford club 1965, pres. 1966, merit award 1974, dist. gov. S.W. Ohio 1978-79, study group exch. leader South Africa 1992), Blue Key, Phi Delta Kappa, Omicron Delta Kappa. Home: 15 Woodcrest Way Oxford OH 45056-9485 Office: Phi Delta Theta Ednl Found 2 S Campus Ave Oxford OH 45056-1801 Office Phone: 513-523-6966.

MILLER, ROBERT JOSEPH, lawyer, former governor; b. Evanston, Ill., Mar. 30, 1945; s. Ross Wendell and Coletta Jane (Doyle) Miller; m. Sandra Ann Searles, Oct. 17, 1949; children: Ross, Corrine, Megan. BA in Polit. Sci., U. Santa Clara, 1967; JD, Loyola U., 1971. First legal advisor Las Vegas (Nev.) Met. Police Dept., 1973—75; justice of the peace Las Vegas Twp., 1975—78; dep. dist. atty. Clark County, Las Vegas, 1971—73, dist. atty., 1979—86; lt. gov. State of Nev., 1987—89, gov., 1989—98; sr. ptnr. Jones Vargas, Las Vegas, 1999—. Chmn. Nev. Commn. on Econ. Devel., Carson City, 1987—91, Nev. Commn. on Tourism, Carson City, 1987—91; mem. Pres. Reagan's Task Force on Victims of Crime, 1982; chmn. Nev. divsn. Am. Cancer Soc., 1988—90. Mem.: Nev. Dist. Attys. Assn. (pres. 1979, 1983), Nat. Govs. Assn. (vice chmn. exec. com. 1995—96, chmn. 1996—97, past chmn. com. on justice and pub. safety, chmn. legal affairs com. 1992—94, lead gov. on transp. 1992—), Western Govs. Assn. (chmn. 1993—94), Nat. Dist. Attys. Assn. (pres. 1984—85). Democrat. Roman Catholic. Office: Jones Vargas 3rd Fl S 3773 Howard Hughes Pkwy Las Vegas NV 89109-0949

MILLER, ROBERT LOUIS, university dean, chemistry educator; b. Chgo., Jan. 26, 1926; s. Sam P. and Ida (Reich) M.; m. Virginia Southard, Oct. 26, 1947 (dec. Sept. 1973); children: Ruth, Stephen, Martin, Andrew; m. Bonnie Seay Berard, Nov. 28, 1975; children: Edouard, Derek. PhB, U. Chgo., 1947, BS, 1949, MS, 1951; PhD, Ill. Inst. Tech.; PhD (NSF Sci. faculty fellow), 1963. Mem. faculty U. Ill. Chgo. Circle Campus, 1953-67, asst. dean Coll. Liberal Arts and Scis., 1963-65, assoc. dean Coll. Liberal Arts and Scis., 1965-67; prof. chemistry U. N.C.-Greensboro, 1968-98, dean arts and scis., 1968-85, acting dean Grad. Sch., 1989-91, spl. asst. to the provost, 1993-94, acting assoc. provost, 1994-96, spl. asst. to provost, 1996-97, interim head dept. math. scis., 2001—03. Am. Council Edn. adminstrv. intern SUNY-Binghamton, 1967-68 Mem. exec. com. of com. environ. affairs Piedmont Council Govts., 1971-76; mem. Greensboro Task Force on Energy; chmn. residential and transp. subcom Greensboro Energy Commn.; mem. Bd. Edn., Oak Park, Ill., 1965-66; bd. dirs. Hospice at Greensboro, 1981-87, pres., 1982-84, vol. 1988-89; vol., mem. bd. dirs. Cities in Schs., 1988-92; bd. dirs. Gilbert Pearson Audubon Soc., Greensboro Civil Liberties Union, Weatherspoon Gallery, 1981-85. Served with AUS, 1944-46, ETO. Mem. AAAS, Sigma Xi (treas. chpt.). Home: 4020 Watauga Dr Greensboro NC 27410-4502 E-mail: rmill07@bellsouth.net.

MILLER, ROBERT NOLEN, lawyer; b. Monmouth, Ill., May 30, 1940; s. Robert Clinton and Doris Margaret (Nolen) M.; m. Diane Wilmarth, Aug. 21, 1965; children: Robert Wilmarth, Anne Elizabeth. BA, Cornell Coll., Mt. Vernon, Iowa, 1962; JD, U. Colo., 1965. Bar: Colo. 1965. Assoc. firm M. Quiat, Denver, 1965-66, Fischer & Beaty, Ft. Collins, Colo., 1969-70; dist. atty. Weld County Dist. Atty's. Office, Greeley, Colo., 1971-81; U.S. atty. U.S. Dept. Justice, Denver, 1981-88; chief counsel litigation and security US West Inc., Englewood, Colo., 1988-93; of counsel Patton, Boggs & Blow, Denver, 1993-94; ptnr., head litig. LeBoeuf, Lamb, Greene & Mac Crae, Denver, 1994—2003; ptnr. Perkins Coie, Denver, 2003—. Instr. bus. law Am. U., U. S.C., Myrtle Beach, 1966-69; mem. Gov.'s Commn. for Columbine and Civil Justice Reform, 1999—; mem. Supreme Ct. Nominating Commn., 1999—. Co-author: Deathroads, 1978 Bd. dirs. Boys Club, Greeley, 1974-78, 1st Congl. Ch., Greeley, 1975-78; Rep. candidate for atty. gen. Colo., 1977-78. Capt. USAF, 1966-69. Recipient Citizen of Yr. award Elks Club, Greeley. Mem. Fed. Bar Assn. (pres. Colo. chpt. 1983-84), Colo. Dist. Atty's Coun. (pres. 1976-77), Colo. Bar Assn., Weld County Bar Assn., Rotary (pres. local chpt. 1980-81). Republican. Avocations: fishing, hunting, reading. Office: Perkins Coie 1899 Wynhoop Ste 200 Denver CO 80202-1043 Office Phone: 303-291-2313. Business E-Mail: Amiller@perkinscioe.com.

MILLER, ROBERT SCOTT, mental health administrator, social worker; b. Seattle, Dec. 12, 1947; s. Bert Lester and Carol Theresa (Gustafson) M.; m. Karen Ann Staake, Nov. 12, 1977; children: Sarah, Megan, Emily. BA in Sociology cum laude, Seattle Pacific U., 1970; AM in Social Work, U. Chgo., 1972; MA in Human Resources Mgmt., Pepperdine U., 1977; diploma in life skills coaching, Stonebridge Associated Colls., U.K., 2002. LCSW. Br. supr. Wash. State Dept. Social and Health Svcs., Oak Harbor and Anacortes, 1975—78, supr. casework Everett, 1973—75; lectr., coord. rural cmty. mental health project U. Wash., Seattle, 1978—83; exec. dir. Armed Svcs. YMCA, Oak Harbor, 1984—86; area dir. United Way of Island County, Oak Harbor, 1986—88, exec. dir., 1988—92, Saratoga Cmty. Mental Health, Coupeville, Wash., 1992—93; outpatient therapist, attention-deficit/hyperactivity disorder mental health specialist Cath. Cmty. Svcs. Northwest, Oak Harbor, Wash., 1993—96; dir. Cath. Cmty. Svcs. N.W., Oak Harbor, Wash., 1996—2001, Mount Vernon, Wash., 1996 99, clin. dir. Everett, Wash., 1998 ; privacy officer Health Ins. Portability and Accountability Act (HIPAA), 2001—; pvt. practice counselor, 2001—; cons., psychiat. hosp. surveyor, quality control rev. CompTech Assocs., Balt., 2004—. Internship supr. counseling program, Seattle U., 1998-99, Bastyr U., 2000-01; instr. sociology and psychol. Chapman U. Naval Air Sta. Whidbey Island, Orange, Calif., 1988-95, 2004-; practicum instr. sch. social work Ea. Wash. U., 2003. Contbr. articles to profl. jours. Bd. dirs. Puget Sound chpt. Huntington's Disease Soc. Am., 1989-93, pres., 1991, fundraising chmn., 1989-91, v.p., 1990; adv. bd. United Ways Wash., 1991-92; chmn. Island County bd. emergency food and shelter program Fed. Emergency Mgmt. Agy.; vice chmn. Cmty. Resource Network, Oak Harbor, 1991; steering com. Greater Oak Harbor Econ. Summit, 1991; strategic planning com. Whidbey Gen. Hosp., Coupeville, 1992-93; exec. com. Mt. Baker coun. Boy Scouts Am., 1993; bd. dirs. Opportunity Coun., Bellingham, 1993-94, Concerts on the Cove, Coupeville, 1993-96, v.p., 1994-95; active Oak Harbor Citizen's Comprehensive Plan Task Force, 1994, Readiness to Learn Coupeville Cmty. Team, 1996; risk mgmt. subcom. chair Assoc. Provider Network, 1997-98; child study team Island County, 1996-99, child protective team, 1997-99; health adv. bd. Head Start, Mt. Vernon, Wash., 1999-2002. Recipient outstanding svc. award Armed Svcs. YMCA of U.S., Dallas, 1985, two program merit awards McDonald's Corp., Oak Harbor, 1986; named Alumni of a Growing Vision, Seattle Pacific U., 1991, Diplomat of Yr. Greater Oak Harbor C. of C., 1991. Mem. NASW (bd. dirs. Wash. chpt. 1982-85), Wash. Assn. Social Welfare (pres. 1975-76), Acad. Cert. Social Workers, Sunrise Rotary Club (sec. Oak Harbor chpt. 1998-99). Roman Catholic. Avocations: reading, genealogy, fishing, computers. Home: 2450 S Rocky Way Coupeville WA 98239-9610 Office: Ste B206 275 SE Cabot Dr Oak Harbor WA 98277 Office Phone: 360-240-8090. E-mail: robertmiller@onebox.com.

MILLER, ROBERT STEVEN, secondary school educator; b. Van Nuys, Calif., Aug. 9, 1963; s. Frederick Earl and Mary (Brash) M. AA, L.A. Valley Coll., 1984; BSBA, Calif. State U., 1987, MA in History, 1990. Cert. substitute tchr., 1993-96. Study group leader, study skills researcher Ednl. Opportunity Program Calif. State U., L.A., 1989-93, faculty mem. History Dept., lectr., 1990-92; sec., treas. Agate/Amethyst World, Inc., Van Nuys, Calif., 1986-91, v.p., 1992-96; with Summer Bridge Program Calif. State U., L.A., 1994-96; tchr. history Chatsworth (Calif.) H.S., 1996—. Mng. editor jour. Perspectives, 1990, editor-in-chief, 1991. Jake Gimbel scholar, 1989. Mem. Am. Historians Assn., The Soc. for Historians of Am. Fgn. Rels., Phi Alpha Theta (v.p. 1990, pres. 1991, Eta Xi chpt., Ledeboer Family scholar 1989), Pi Sigma Epsilon (v.p. 1986-87, pres. 1988 Phi chpt.), Mu Kappa Tau (pres. and founder 1989, Calif State U. LA chpt.). Democrat. Roman Catholic. Home: 13750 Runnymede St Van Nuys CA 91405-1515 Office: Chatsworth HS 10027 Lurline Ave Chatsworth CA 91311-3153

MILLER, ROBERT STEVENS, JR., finance professional; b. Portland, Oreg., Nov. 4, 1941; s. Robert Stevens and Barbara (Weston) M.; m. Margaret Rose Kyger, Nov. 9, 1966; children: Christopher John, Robert Stevens, Alexander Lamont. AB with distinction, Stanford U., 1963; LLB, Harvard U., 1966; MBA, Stanford U., 1968. Bar: Calif. bar 1966. Fin. analyst Ford Motor Co., Dearborn, Mich., 1968-71, spl. studies mgr. Mexico City, 1971-73; dir. fin. Ford Asia-Pacific, Inc., Melbourne, Australia, 1974-77, Ford Motor Co., Caracas, Venezuela, 1977-79; v.p., treas. Chrysler Corp., Detroit, 1980-81, exec. v.p. fin., 1981-90, vice chmn., 1990-92; sr. ptnr. James D. Wolfensohn, Inc., N.Y.C., 1992-93; chmn. Fed. Mogul corp., Smithfield, Mich. Chmn. bd. dirs. Morrison Knudsen Corp., 1995-96, Waste Mgmt., Inc., 1997—; bd. dirs. Fed.-Mogul, Pope & Talbot, Symantec, Morrison Knudsen; chmn. bd. Waste Mgmt. Inc., 1997—. Office: Fed Mogul Corp 26555 Northwestern Hwy Southfield MI 48034

MILLER, ROBERT W. music educator, musician; b. Iron Mountain, Mich., Dec. 25, 1950; s. Walter Harry and Caroline Louise Miller. BMus, U. Mich., 1973; MMus, Peabody Conservatory of Music, Balt., 1974; Dr.Musical Arts, Peabody Inst. of Johns Hopkins U., Balt., 1979. Disting. prof. of music, artist-in-residence East Stroudsburg U. of Pa., 1977—. Adj. prof. music Essex C.C., Balt., 1975—77; piano faculty Interlochen Ctr. of Arts, Mich., 1978—80; summer faculty Mansfield Coll./Oxford U., England, 1986—89, IFK U. of Salzburg and Cultural Studies Acad., Austria, 1991—; guest artist N.Y. Philharm. Ensembles, N.Y.C., 1998; solo and chamber music recitals Weill Recital Hall at Carnegie Hall, N.Y.C., 1998—; guist artist N.Y. Philharm. Ensembles, N.Y.C., 2002; rehearsal pianist Van Cliburn at Interlochen Ctr. for the Arts, 1975—80. Musician: (solo piano recital) Salle Cortot, 1992, 2000, Weill Recital Hall at Carnegie Hall, 1992, 2000, (piano concerto soloist) World Youth Symphony, Peabody Symphony, Montclair Chamber Ensemble, Pine Mountain Music Festival; recording artist Media Rite Prodns., Educo Records. Founder, artistic dir. Carter Chamber Music Series, East Stroudsburg, 1993—; competition judge Pa. Gov.'s Sch. of Arts, Tatamy, 1978—. Named to Outstanding Young Men of Am., 1980; recipient Disting. Prof. award, East Stroudsburg U., 2002; scholar F. Lammot Belin Arts scholar, Waverly, Pa., 1991. Mem.: Assn. of Pa. State Coll. and Univ. Faculty, Music Tchrs. Nat. Assn., Am. Liszt Soc. Avocations: swimming, scuba diving, water-skiing, hiking. Mailing: East Stroudsburg Univ Dept Music Fine Arts Bldg East Stroudsburg PA 18301 E-mail: Robert.Miller@po-box.esu.edu.

MILLER, ROBERTA BALSTAD, social scientist; b. Mpls., June 25, 1940; d. Gerhard Oliver and Laverne K. (Anderson) Balstad; m. Gary David Lange, Nov. 26, 1959 (div. 1968); m. Floyd John Miller, June 15, 1969; 1 child, Aaron Gerhard. BA, U. Minn., 1964, MA, 1970, PhD, 1973. Rsch. assoc. AIA, Washington, 1974; staff assoc. Social Sci. Rsch. Coun., Washington, 1975-81; exec. dir. Consortium Social Sci. Assns., Washington, 1981-84; divsn. dir. NSF, Washington, 1984-93; pres., CEO Consortium Internat. Earth Sci. Info. Network (CIESIN), University Center, Mich., 1993-98; adj. prof. natural resources policy behavior U. Mich., 1993-97; sr. rsch. scientist, dir. CIESIN Columbia U., NYC, 1998—. Guest scholar Woodrow Wilson Internat. Ctr. Scholars, 1994; sr. assoc. mem. St. Anthony's Coll., U. Oxford, England, 1991—92; mem. chmn. NATO adv. panel on Advanced Sci. Insts./Advanced Rsch. Workshops, Brussels, 1988—91; chmn. steering com. space applications and commercialization Nat. Rsch. Coun., 1999—2002, mem. exec. com. Space Studies Bd., 1995—2000, mem. climate rsch. com., 1997—99, mem. com. on global change rsch., 1999—2002; chmn. U.S. Nat. Com. on Sci. and Tech. Data, 2003—; mem. U.S. Nat. Com. IIASA, 1995—; chmn. adv. bd. Luxembourg Income Survey, 1987—91. Author: City and Hinterland, 1979; editor (with Harriet Zuckerman) Science Indicators: Implications for Research and Policy, 1979; contbr. articles to profl. jours.; translator poetry of Jorge Luis Borges, 1989, 90, 91, N.P. von Wyk Louw, 1998. Bd. trustees Newport Schs., Kensington, Md., 1986-91, St. Anthony's Coll. Trust, 1994—, sec., 1997-2000, chair, 2000—, bd. dirs. Open GIS Consortium 2003—; adv. trustee Environ. Rsch. Inst. Mich., 1995-98. Recipient NSF Meritorious Svc. award, 1993. Fellow: AAAS (com. mem., chmn. 1987—93), NY Acad. Scis.; mem.: Coun. Fgn. Rels., Am. Lt. Translators Assn., Internat. Social Sci. Coun. (com. 1991—95, v.p. 1992—94), US Man Biosphere Program (com., chmn. 1989—91), Cosmos Club. Lutheran. Office: CIESIN Columbia U PO Box 1000 Palisades NY 10964-8000 Home: 507 W 111th St Apt 1 New York NY 10025 Office Phone: 845-365-8988., 845-365-8950.

MILLER, ROGER ALLEN, physicist; b. Chillicothe, Ohio, June 27, 1934; s. Joseph Perrin and Mary Josephine (Sowers) M.; m. Barbara Pauline Rice, Aug. 31, 1957; children: Erich Rice, Gretchen Rice, Carl Rice. BS, Ohio U., 1956; PhD, Case Inst., 1963. Rsch. assoc. Case Inst., Cleve., 1963-64; rsch. physicist Corning (N.Y.) Inc., 1964-71, sr. rsch. physicist, 1971-79, devel. assoc., 1979-87, sr. rsch. assoc., 1987—. Spl. lectr. physics Elmira Coll., N.Y., 1966-69; mem. edit. bd. Fiber and Integrated Optics, Pasadena, Calif., 1976-86, mem. adv. bd. 1986-88. Contbr. articles to profl. jours. AART award Assn. for the Advancement Radiation Tech., 1990. Mem. Am. Phys. Soc., Optical Soc. Am., Am. Assn. Physics Tchrs., Sigma Xi, Phi Beta Kappa, Phi Kappa Phi. Achievements include contributions to the development of lead free Steuben crystal; development of optical waveguide coatings and coating applicators; design and development of the first, all dielectric, low-loss optical waveguide cable; patentee in field. Office: Corning Inc Sullivan Pk Sp Fr 03 # 1 Corning NY 14831-0001 E-mail: ramiller@localnet.com.

MILLER, ROGER L. architectural firm executive; b. Brooklandville, Md. BS, MArch, Ga. Inst. Tech. Registered Ga., Tenn., S.C., N.C., cert. NCARB. Joined Cooper Carry Inc., Atlanta, 1979, prin., 1990, v.p., 1994—. Recipient Kenneth M. Murchison award, Ga. Inst. Tech. Mem.: Nat. Assn. Office and Indsl. Pks. Office: Cooper Carry Inc Ste 200 3520 Piedmont Rd NE Atlanta GA 30305-1595*

MILLER, RONALD, writer, critic; b. Santa Cruz, Calif., Feb. 28, 1939; s. Fred Robert and Evelyn Lenora Miller; m. Darla-Jean Irene Rode, Nov. 2, 1963. AA, Monterey Peninsula Coll., 1958; BA, San Jose State U., 1961. Reporter Santa Cruz (Calif.) Sentinel, 1959-62; reporter, chief news bur. San Jose (Calif.) Mercury News, 1962-77, editor T.V., 1977-99; syndicated TV columnist Knight Ridder Syndicate, 1978-99. Commentator, critic Sta. KLOK, San Jose, 1981-83; nat. judge Cableace awards, 1987; adj. instr. Whatcom C.C., Bellingham, Wash., 2001—, Western Wash. U., 2003—. Author: (foreword) Les Brown's Encyclopedia of Television, 1992; co-author: Masterpiece Theatre, 1995, Author: Mystery! A Celebration, 1996 (Agatha, Anthony, and Macavity award nominee 1996-97); contbr. articles and short fiction to various mags.; columnist, mng. editor The Columnists.com website, 1999—; mystery columnist Alibris.com. website, 2000, PBS mystery.com website, 2001-2002. Recipient Nat. Spot News Photo award Sigma Delta Chi, 1961, Outstanding Alumnus award San Jose State U. Dept. Journalism and Mass Comm., 1985, Nat. Headline award Press Club Atlantic City, 1994. Democrat. Home and Office: 5437 Canvasback Rd Blaine WA 98230

MILLER, RONALD ALFRED, family physician; b. Orange, Calif., Sept. 27, 1943; s. Alfred Casper and Inez Geraldine (Gunderson) M.; m. Jean Ilene Andrews, June 18, 1966; children: Jon, Lauri, Bryan. BA, Pacific Luth. U., 1965; MD, U. Wash., 1969. Diplomate Am. Bd. Family Practice (bd. dirs. 1985-90, pres. bd. 1989-90). Intern in medicine Parkland Meml. Hosp., Dallas, 1969-70; gen. practice residency USPHS Gallup Indian Med. Ctr., Gallup, N.Mex., 1970-72; prin. Medical Doctor Glacier Med Assocs., Whitefish, Mont., 1972—. Clin. prof. U. Wash., Seattle, 1975—; coord. community clin. unit in family medicine, U. Wash., Whitefish, 1975—; bd. dirs. Utah Med. Ins. Assn., Salt Lake City, 1987—. Bd. dirs. Whitefish Housing Authority, 1977-82; mem. alumni bd. Pacific Luth. U., Tacoma, 1976-81, pres., 1979-80; mem. Glacier Community Chorale, Whitefish, 1984—, bd. dirs., 1990-92. Lt. comdr. USPHS, 1970-72. Mem. Am. Acad. Family Physicians (com. on continuing med. edn. 1977-81, com. on edn. 1984-89, Mead Johnson award Grad. Edn. in Family Practice 1972), Mont. Acad. Family Physicians (bd. dirs., sec./treas, v.p., pres. 1982-83, del. nat. congress 1978-84), Rotary, Alpha Omega Alpha. Republican. Lutheran. Avocations: hunting, fishing, skiing, backpacking, choral singing. Home: 1046 7th St W Whitefish MT 59937-3227 Office: 1111 Baker Ave Whitefish MT 59937-2905

MILLER, RONALD BAXTER, English language educator, writer; b. Rocky Mount, NC, Oct. 11, 1948; s. Marcellus Cornelius and Elsie (Bryant) M.; m. Jessica Garris, June 5, 1971 (div. 1998); 1 child, Akin Dasan; m. Diana L. Ranson, Sept. 3, 2000. BA magna cum laude, N.C. Ctrl. U., 1970; AM, Brown U., 1972, PhD, 1974. Asst. prof. English Haverford Coll., Haverford, Pa., 1974-76; assoc. prof. English, dir. Black lit. program U. Tenn., Knoxville, Tenn., 1977-81, prof. English, dir. Black lit. program, 1982-92, Lindsay Young prof. liberal arts and English, 1986-87; prof. English, dir. Inst. for African Am. Studies U. Ga., Athens, 1992—. Instr. summer sch. Roger Williams Coll., Bristol, R.I., 1973; lectr. SUNY, 1974; Mellon prof. Xavier Univ., New Orleans, 1988; Irvine Found. visiting scholar Univ. San Francisco, 1991. Author: (reference guide) Langston Hughes and Gwendolyn Brooks, 1978, The Art and Imagination of Langston Hughes, 1989 (Am. Book award, 1991), (monograph) Southern Trace in Black Critical Theory: Redemption of Time, 1991; editor, contbr.: Black American Literature and Humanism, 1981, Black American Poets Between Worlds, 1940-60, 1986; co-author and co-editor: Call and Response The Riverside Anthology of African American Literary Tradition, 1998, ed., "The Short Stories", Collected Works of Langston Hughes 15, 2002; mem. editl. bd. Tenn. Studies in Lit., 1991-93, Black Fiction Project (Yale-Cornell-Duke-Harvard), 1985—, U. Ga. Press, 1994-97; contbr. numerous articles and revs. to profl. jour. Recipient award Am. Coun. of Learned Soc., 1978, Golden Key Faculty award Nat. Golden Key, 1990, 95, Alpha award for disting. svc. U. Ga. Athens, 1993, Am. Book award, 1991; Lilly Sr. Tchg. fellow U. Ga. Athens, 1994, Lanston Hughes prize, 2001; Nat. Rsch. Coun. sr. fellow, 1986-87, NDEA fellow, 1970-72, Ford Found. fellow, 1972-73, NEH fellow, 1975; Nat. Fellowships Fund dissertation grant, 1973-74, others. Mem. MLA (exec. com. Afro-Am. Lit. Discussion Group 1980-83, chair 1982-83, mem. del. assembly 1984-86, 97-99, com. on langs. and lits. of Am. 1993-97, chair 1996), Langston Hughes Soc. (pres. 1984-90, exec. editor Langston Hughes Review 1993—). Office: U Ga Inst African Am Studies Athens GA 30602 E-mail: rbmiller@uga.edu., rbmiller6@charter.net.

MILLER, RONALD EUGENE, regional science educator; b. Seattle, Sept. 1, 1933; s. Eugene H. and Nellie A. (Myers) M. BA, Harvard U., 1955; MA, U. Wash., 1957; PhD, Princeton U., 1961. Asst. prof. regional sci. U. Pa.,

Phila., 1962-65, assoc. prof., 1965-71, prof., 1971-95, chmn. dept., 1981-84, prof. emeritus, 1995—. Author: Input-Output Analysis, 1985, Optimization, 2000; Dynamic Optimization and Economic Applications, 1979; also articles; editor Jour. Regional Sci., 1965— . Mem. Regional Sci. Assn. Home: 137 Elfreths Aly Philadelphia PA 19106-2005 Office: U Pa Regional Sci Program 3718 Locust Walk Philadelphia PA 19104-6209 E-mail: remiller@sas.upenn.edu.

MILLER, RONALD K. real estate broker, educator; b. Penn Yan, Ny, Apr. 8, 1948; s. Harold and Helen Miller; m. Marguerite Miller, July 16, 2001; children: Jennifer McKay, Kristoffer; m. Jane Miller, Jan. 2, 1970 (div. May 1, 2001). BA, MacMurray Coll., Jacksonville, Illinois, 1970; MA, Elmira Coll., Elmira, NY, 1975. Educator Canandaigua Schools, Canandaigua, NY, 1970—71, Dundee Schools, Dundee, NY, 1972—. Assoc. broker Keuka Shoreline Properties, Penn Yan, NY, 1992—. Choir dir. First Presbyn. Ch., Penn Yann, NY, 1970—2002. Avocations: gardening, woodworking. Office: Dundee Central School 55 Water Street Dundee NY 14837

MILLER, RONALD LYNN, director; b. Pitts., Sept. 1, 1950; s. Calvin John and Virginia (Ricca) Miller; m. Mary Eileen McCoy, Apr. 12, 1988; children: Veronica Lynn, Maria Eileen. B, Westminster Coll., 1972; M in religion, Pitts. Theological Seminary, 1975; vis. scholar, U. Oxford, 1990—92; PhD in sociology and internat. studies, U. Pitts., 1994. Prof., sociology U. Pitts., 1980—88, prof., religion, 1988—92, prof., global studies, 1992—96; founder to dir. Ctr. for Global Studies Internat. Interdisciplinary, Pitts., 1995—. Lectr. various Universities. Author: Introduction to Global Studies, 2003, Revolution in Japan and England, 1996, Individual Identity Formation, 1984. Mem.: World Hist. Assn., Am. Sociol. Assn., Am. Acad. of Religion, Am. Psycho. Soc., Am. Polit. Sci. Assn., Am. Physical Soc., Am. Philos. Assn., Internat. Neural Network Soc., Assn. for the Study of Ethnicity and Nationalism, Am. Musicological Soc., Am. Math. Soc., Math. Assn. of Am., Ling. Soc. of Am., Law and Soc. Assn., Modern Lang. Assn., Internat. Studies Assn., Info. Theory Soc., Am. Hist. Assn., Geol. Soc. of Am., Internat. Geog. Union, Assn. of Am. Geographers, Coun. for European Studies, Am. Econ. Assn., Eco. Soc. of Am., Communal Studies Assn., Internat. Soc. for the Comparative Study of Civilizations, Internat. Union of Pure and Applied Chemistry, Am. Chem. Soc., Genetics Soc. of Am., Am. Soc. for Micro., Soc. for the Study of Evolution, Soc. of Systematic Biologists, Am. Astron. Soc., Nat. Assn. of Artists' Org., Assn. for Asian Studies, Am. Assn. for Artificial Intelligence, Am. Anthrop. Assn., Am. Studies Assn., African Studies Assn. Achievements include patents pending for a module for doing global studies at the university level. Office: Ctr for Global Studies Internat Interdisciplinary 40 Beltzhoover Ave Pittsburgh PA 15210 Office Phone: 412-381-3753. E-mail: ronaldlynnmiller@centerforglobalstudies.com.

MILLER, RONALD MELLADO, education educator; b. El Paso, Texas, Nov. 3, 1970; s. Donald Hale and Corina Mellado Miller; m. Patricia Marie Addicks, Feb. 4, 1995; children: Hannah Aurora, Gideon McKay, Shiloh Marie, Eve Asenath. MS, Purdue Univ., 1997—99, PhD, 2000—03. Sci. rschr. Purdue Univ., West Lafayette, Ind., 1997—2003; prof. Brigham Young Univ., Laie, Hawaii, 2003—. Statis., human factors engrng. cons. Miller Consulting, West Lafayette, Ind., 1995; human factors engrng. cons. Purdue Univ. Human Factors in Aviation Rsch. Group, West Lafayette, Ind., 1998—; statis., human factors engrng. cons. Miller Consulting, Laie, Hawaii, 2003—. Internat. cmty. activist Purdue Univ., West Lafayette, Ind., 1998—2003, Brigham Young U., Hawaii, Laie, Hawaii, 2003. Grantee Rsch. Grant, Purdue U., 2002; scholar Mosell-Watt Bell Scholarship, Brigham Young U., 1995—97; Grad. Fellowship, Purdue Univ., 1997—2003. Mem.: APA, Psychonomic Soc., Am. Statis. Assn., Human Factors and Ergonomic Soc. Mem. Church Of Jesus Christ Latter Day Saint. Achievements include research in refuted the fundamental theoretical difference between pavlovian and instrumental conditioning; co-author of the only current theory how mental chunking operates. Avocations: travel, swimming, surfing. Office: Brigham Young Univ Hawaii 55-220 Kulanui St BYUH Box #1970 Laie HI 96762 Home: 55-457 Moana St Laie HI 96762 Office Phone: 808-293-3831. Business E-Mail: millerr@byuh.edu.

MILLER, ROSS HAYS, retired neurosurgeon; b. Ada, Okla., Jan. 30, 1923; s. Harry and Helen (Rice) M.; m. Catherine Railey, May 2, 1943; children—Terry Hays, Helen Stacy. BS, East Central State Coll., Ada, 1943; MD, U. Okla., 1946; MS in Neurosurgery, U. Minn., 1952. Diplomate: Am. Bd. Neurol. Surgery (chmn. exam. com. 1978-84). Intern St. Luke's Hosp., Cleve., 1946-47; fellow in neurosurgery Mayo Clinic, Rochester, Minn., 1950-54; instr. in neurosurgery Mayo Med. Sch., 1954-63, asst. prof. neurosurgery, 1963-73, asso. prof., 1973-75, prof., chmn. dept. neurosurgery, from 1975, now ret. Vis. prof. neurol. surgery Med. Coll. Ga., Augusta Contbr. articles to profl. jours. Trustee East Central State U. Found. Served as capt., M.C. U.S. Army, 1947-49, Korea. Named to Okla. Hall of Fame, 1977, Athletic Hall of Fame, East Central U. Okla., 1977; recipient Disting. Alumnus award East Central U. Okla., 1974, Mayo Found. Disting. Alumnus award, 1992. Mem. AMA, ACS, Am. Assn. Neurol. Surgeons (chmn. com. profl. practice 1976-79, dir. 1976-79, v.p. 1979, rep. to Council Med. Splty. Socs. 1980-84), Congress Neurol. Surgeons (exec. com. 1963-65), Minn. Soc. Neurol. Scis., Neurosurg. Soc. Am. (v.p. 1975), Soc. Neurol. Surgeons (v.p. 1983), Sigma Xi.

MILLER, ROSS M. financial services company executive; b. Greenville, S.C., Jan. 6, 1954; s. Milton Gerald Miller and Sara Stein; m. Mary M. O'Keeffe, July 20, 1979; children: Alison, Catherine. BS, Calif. Inst. Tech., 1975; AM, Harvard U., 1977, PhD, 1979. Asst. prof. U. Houston, 1979-82, Calif. Inst. Tech., Pasadena, 1981, Boston U., 1981-89; sr. staff scientist GE Corp. R&D, Schnectady, N.Y., 1989-95; sr. v.p. Natwest Markets and dir. rsch. NatWest Investment Mgmt., Boston, 1995-96; pres. Miller Risk Advisors, Niskayuna, N.Y., 1996—. Mem. program com. Internat. Conf. on Artificial Intelligence Applications on Wall St. and Internat. Workshop on Artificial Intelligence in Econs. and Mgmt.; cons. MAC Group, Cambridge, Mass., 1983-85, FTC, Washington, 1982-85, Millipore, Inc., Bedford, Mass., 1983-84, U.S. Dept. State, Washington, 1987. Author: Computer-Aided Financial Analysis, 1990; contbr. articles to profl. jours. Achievement Rewards for Coll. Scientist fellow, 1973, Grad. fellow Harvard U., 1975, Lock Soc. Hon. fellow Boston U., 1984. Mem. Am. Econs. Assn., Am. Fin. Assn., Econometric Soc., Boston Security Analysts Soc., Boston Econ. Club.

MILLER, ROY RAYMOND, optician, oculist; b. Delta, Ohio, Sept. 20, 1929; s. Roy Draton and Ethel Bernice (Shaffer) M.; m. Evelyn Frances Birsen, Jan. 16, 1954; children: Stephanie, Christopher, Neil Benjamin. Student, Burnham High Sch., Sylvania, Ohio. Lic. Optician. Optician Miller Opticians Inc., Lima, Ohio, 1961—; pres. Miller Opticians and Miller, Lima, 1961—, Artificial Eye Lab., Toledo, 1961-88; lic. ocularist Miller Artificial Eye Lab., Toledo. Appointed to Ohio Optician and Oculorist Bd., Gov. Vonivoich, 1995; pres. Ohio Optical Dispensers Bd., 2004—; bd. dir. U.S. Selective Svc. Sys. Lectr. Nat. Convention, 1978, 1987. Candidate U.S. Congress, Lima 1984, zoning appeals bd. Shawnee Twp., 1980-88, lic. bd. Ohio Optical Dispensing Bd., 1979-85, reapptd., 2000. Cpl. US Army, 1951-52. Recipient award Nat. Acad. Achievements, 1995; inducted into The Internat. Poetry Hall of Fame, 1998, Sylvania H.S. Hall of Fame, 2003. Fellow Nat. Acad. Opticianry (Contbn. to Edn. of Opticianry award 1995), Internat. Acad. Opticians; mem. Am. Soc. Ocularists, Opticians Assn. Am. (diplomate, past bd. dirs., Optician of Yr. 1995, finalist Entrepreneur of Yr. nomination 1995, Honored Fellow 2003), Guild Prescription Opticians of Am. (bd. dirs.), Optician Assn. Ohio (past pres.), Sertoma (pres. 1983-84), Kiwanis (pres. 1973-74). Republican. Roman Catholic. Avocations: marathon runner, skiing, bicycling. Office: Miller Opticians Inc 825 W Market St Ste 202 Lima OH 45805-2794

MILLER, SANDRA A. CARAMELA, gerontologist, educator; b. Painesville, Ohio, June 1, 1957; d. Paul M. and Jane E. (Zaffuto) Caramela; m. Charles S. Miller, May 3, 1985; 1 child, Shannon; stepchildren: Carrie J., Charles A. BA in Psychology, U. Akron, 1980, MA in Psychology, cert. in gerontology, U. Akron, 1991, PhD in Psychology, 1997. Instr. U. Akron, Ohio, 1989-92, fellow, adj. Inst. Life-Span Devel., 1997—, adj. faculty, 2000—; coord. dir. pediatric rsch. St. Luke's Hosp., Cleve., 1992-94; statistician, epidemiologist All Kids Count Consortium, Cleve., 1993-94; dir. forensic tng. Cuyahoga County Coroner's Office, Cleve., 1995—, rschr., project dir., 1997—. Mem. consortium Child Protection Coalition, Cuyahoga County, Ohio, 1993-96, All Kids Count, Cleve., 1993-94; mem. adv. bd. Cmty. Medicine Forum Violence, 1993-94; dir., pres. bd. dirs. Safe and Secure Home, Inc., Macedonia, Ohio, 1996-00. Mem. APA, Gerontol. Soc. Am., Assn. Death Edn. and Counseling, Inst. Trauma and Loss in Children, Soc. Psychol. Study Social Issues, Assn. Health Svcs. Rsch., Sigma Phi Omega. Home: 8375 N Boyden Rd Sagamore Hills OH 44067-1711 Office: Cuyahoga County Coroners Office 11001 Cedar Ave Cleveland OH 44106-3043

MILLER, SANFORD, car rental company executive; b. 1954; Grad., SUNY-Oswego, 1975. Licensee ops, mgr. Budget Group, Inc., Daytona Beach, Fla., from 1980, ptnr. franchises N.Y.C., owner franchises through no. Fla., from 1984; dir. mktg. and spl. accounts Budget Corp., 1989-91; v.p. Tranex Rental N.Y., Inc. operators Albany and Rochester brs., 1991-94, Capital City Leasing, Inc., operators Richond, Va. franchise, 1991-94; chmn. bd. dirs., CEO Budget Group Inc., 1994—. Mem. Travel Bus. Roundtable; chmn. licensee local market adv. bd. Budget Sys., 1989-90. Mem. Fla. Commn. Tourism, 1999—. Named Fla.'s Ernst & Young Master Entrepreneur of Yr., 1998. Mem. Travel Industry Assn. Am. (exec. com. 1999—), Am. Car Rental Assn. (pres. 1993), World Travel and Tourism Coun. Office: Budget Group Inc 125 Basin St Ste 210 Daytona Beach FL 32114-5077*

MILLER, SANFORD MARVIN, anesthesiology educator; b. Phila., Dec. 28, 1932; AB, U. Chgo.; MD, Jefferson Med. Coll., 1957. Diplomate Am. Bd. Anesthesiology. Intern Jefferson Hosp., Phila., 1957-58, resident in anesthesiology, 1958-60; fellow Westminster Hosp., London, 1960-61; attending anesthesiologist, asst. prof. NYU Med. Ctr., N.Y.C., 1975-2000, assoc. prof., 2000—; attending anesthesiologist Bellevue Hosp., N.Y.C., 1975, asst. dir. anesthesiology, 2002—. Mem. AMA, Am. Soc. Anesthesiologists, Am. Coll. Anesthesiologists. Office: NYU Med Ctr 560 1st Ave New York NY 10016-6402 E-mail: sanford.miller@med.nyu.edu.

MILLER, SARABETH, secondary school educator; b. Apr. 6, 1927; d. Clayton Everett and Margaret (Noland) Reif; m. Lloyd Melvin Miller, Dec. 2, 1944; children: Virginia, Shirley, Judith, John, Nola, Steven. BA, Valparaiso U., 1972, MA in L.S., 1977; postgrad., Purdue U., 1983, Ind. U., 1986, postgrad., 1991, Art Inst. Ft. Lauderdale, Fla., 1992, Ind. State U., 1996, postgrad., 1997, St. Joseph U., 1998. Lic. tchr. Ind., cert. data processing. Office employee Porter County Herald, Hebron, Ind., 1954—55, Little Co. of Mary Hosp. and Home, San Pierre, Ind., 1960—65, Jasper County Co-op, Tefft, Ind., 1965—69, Hannon's, Valparaiso, 1969—72; tchr. art DeMotte (Ind.) elem. sch., 1972—76, Kankakee Valley High Sch., Wheatfield, Ind., 1976—. Participant Lilly Creative Tchr.'s Workshop. Participant (art and lit. mag.) Mirage; contbr. articles and photographs to local newspapers. Leader 4-H Club, Kouts; participant North Ctrl. Regional Forum, 1991, 1992, 1993; participant archeol. dig K.V. Hist. Soc. and Notre Dame; mem., elder Kouts Presbyn. Ch.; mem. adv. com. secondary sch. showcase Valparaiso U. Recipient various prizes, Lake Ctrl. (Ind.) Fair, 1975, 1980, photography award, Ind. Dept. Tourism, 1976, Porter County Fair, 1989, 1996, 1998, 2000, 2001, 2004, Gainer Bank Calendar award, 4-H Alumni award, 2002, 4-H 45 yr. leader tenure award, 1994; grantee, Nat. Gallery of Art, 1993; Lilly Endowment fellow, Lilly Extending Tchr. Creativity Inst., 1987, 1994, 1995, 1996, 2002, 2003, 2004. Mem.: AIA, NEA, North Ctrl. Assn. Secondary Schs. (mem. evaln. team), Kankakee Valley Tchrs. Assn., Ind. Art Edn. Assn., Ind. Tchrs. Assn., Nat. Art Edn. Assn., Nat. Mus. American Indians, Smithsonian Instn., Hist. Landmarks, Kankakee Valley Hist. Soc. Presbyterian. Home: 1056 S Baums Bridge Rd Kouts IN 46347-9712 Business E-Mail: smiller@kv.k12.in.us.

MILLER, SARAH PEARL, librarian; b. Wilkensburg, Pa., Aug. 31, 1938; d. Samuel Henry and Anna Deborah (Shirley) Lyons; m. Paul Victor Miller, Apr. 15, 1989; children: Cheryl, Michael, Daniel, Lorel. BS, Indiana U. of Pa., 1960; MREM, Denver Conservative Bapt. Sem., 1965; MA, U. Denver, 1966. Libr. Denver Conservative Bapt. Sem., 1966—. Mem. Am. Theol. Libr. Assn. (bd. dirs. 1978-81, 90-91, index bd. 1983-90). Home: 15707 E Grand Ave Aurora CO 80015-1708

MILLER, SCOTT D. lawyer; b. Redondo Beach, Calif., 1961; BSE, Ariz. State U., 1982; JD, Columbia U., 1985. Bar: Calif. 1987. Assoc. Sullivan & Cromwell, London. Office: Sullivan & Cromwell 9a Ironmonger Ln St Olave's London EC2V 8EY England

MILLER, SHANNON, Olympic athlete; b. Rolla, Mo., Mar. 10, 1977; Student, Boston Coll. MBA program at Carroll Sch. Gymnist U.S. National Gymnastic Team, 1990—97. Named Female Athlete of Yr., Nat. March of Dimes Found., 1993. Christian Scientist. Achievements include most decorated gymnast in U.S. history; won a total of 58 International and 49 National competition medals; won Silver Medal, all-around and balance beam, Barcelona Olympic Games, 1992; Bronze Medal, U.S. Gymnastic Team, Barcelona Olympic Games, 1992; Bronze Medal, floor exercise, Barcelona Olympic Games, 1992; Gold Medal, uneven bars, all-around, floor exercise, World Gymnastic Championships (Great Britan), 1993; Gold Medal, all-around, balance beam, World Gymnastic Championships (Australia), 1994; Gold Medal, U.S. Gymnastic Team, Atlanta Olympic Games, 1996; Gold Medal, balance beam, Atlanta Olympic Games, 1996. Address: 8 Easy Street Edmond OK 73003

MILLER, SHEILA, state legislator; d. Vernon and Mildred M.; m. Michael Miller; 1 child, Emilie C. BS cum laude, Pa. State U., 1974. Rep. dist. 129 State of Pa., 1993—. Bd. dirs. Berks County Farmland Preservation. Mem. Nat. Cattlemens Assn., Berks Farm Bur., Berks Cattlemens Assn., Pa. Cattlemens Assn., Heidelberg Heritage Soc., Berks County Rep. Women, Phi Kappa Phi, Gamma Sigma Delta Agrl. Alumni Soc. Republican. Office: Pa Ho of Reps B13 Main Capitol Bldg PO Box 202020 Harrisburg PA 17120-2020

MILLER, SHELBY ALEXANDER, chemical engineer, educator; b. Louisville, July 9, 1914; s. George Walter and Stella Katherine (Cralle) M.; m. Jean Adele Danielson, Dec. 26, 1939 (div. May 1948); 1 son, Shelby Carlton; m. Doreen Adare Kennedy, May 29, 1952 (dec. Feb. 1971). BS, U. Louisville, 1935; PhD, U. Minn., 1943. Registered profl. engr., Del., Kans., N.Y. Asst. chemist Corhart Refractories Co., Louisville, 1935-36; teaching, rsch. asst. chem. engring. U. Minn., Mpls., 1935-39; devel. engr., rsch. chem. engr. E.I. duPont de Nemours & Co., Inc., Wilmington, Del., 1940-46; assoc. prof. chem. engring. U. Kan., Lawrence, 1946-50, prof., 1950-55; Fulbright prof. chem. engring. King's Coll. Durham U., Newcastle-upon-Tyne, Eng., 1952-53; prof., chem. engring. U. Rochester, 1955-69, chmn., 1955-68; assoc. lab. dir. Argonne (Ill.) Nat. Lab., 1969-74; dir. Ctr. Ednl. Affairs, 1969-79, sr. chem. engr., 1969-84, ret., cons., 1984—. Vis. prof. chem. engring. U. Calif., Berkeley, 1967-68; vis. prof. U. of Philippines, Quezon City, 1986; cons. in field. Editor: Chem. Engring. Edn. Quar, 1965-67; sect. editor: Perry's Chem. Engrs.' Handbook, 5th edit., 1973, 6th edit., 1984, 7th edit., 1997; contbr. to McGraw-Hill Ency. Sci. and Tech., 5th edit., 1982, 6th edit., 1987, 7th edit., 1992; contbr. articles to profl. jours. Sec. Kans. Bd. Engring. Examiners, 1954-55; mem. adv. com. on tng. Internat. Atomic Energy Agy., 1975-79; treas. Lawrence (Kans.) League for Practice Democracy, 1950-52; sec. Argonne Credit Union, 1994-97. Fellow AAAS, Am. Inst. Chemists, Am. Inst. Chem. Engrs. (past chmn. Kansas City sect.); mem. Am. Chem. Soc. (past chmn. Rochester sect.), Soc. Chem. Industry, Am. Soc. Engring. Edn. (past chmn. grad. studies div.), Am. Nuclear Soc., Filtration Soc., Triangle, Sigma Xi, Sigma Tau, Phi Lambda Upsilon, Tau Beta Pi, Alpha Chi Sigma. Presbyterian. Office: Argonne Nat Lab Chem Tech Divsn Argonne IL 60439-4837 Home: 215 55th St Unit 322 Clarendon Hills IL 60514-1590 E-mail: millers@cmt.anl.gov.

MILLER, STANFORD, retired reinsurance executive, lawyer; b. Kansas City, Mo., Nov. 15, 1913; s. Hugh and Gertrude Anna (Kraft) M.; m. Gloria Goble, July 11, 1942 (div. 1958); 1 child, Hans Hugh; m. Beverly Breuer, Apr. 19, 1962; 1 son, Bradford Channing. BA, U. Kans., 1934; JD, U. Chgo., 1938. Bar: Mo. 1938. Former chmn., CEO, Employers Reins. Corp. Lectr. in field. Author: (with Robert D. Brown) Health Insurance Underwriting, 1962; also articles. Trustee emeritus U. Mo. Kansas City; trustee emeritus Kans. chpt. Nature Conservancy. Mem. Mo. Bar Assn., Reins. Assn. Am. (past chmn.), Health Ins. Assn. Am. (former sec., dir.), Phi Alpha Delta, Alpha Tau Omega. Clubs: Rotary, Profl. Men's, Mission Hills Country. Home: 2709 Tomahawk Rd Shawnee Mission KS 66208-1827 E-mail: smiller@blitz-it.net.

MILLER, STEPHEN RALPH, lawyer; b. Chgo., Nov. 28, 1950; s. Ralph and Karin Ann (Olson) M.; children: David Williams, Lindsay Christine. m. Sheila L. Krysiak, Feb. 2, 1998. BA cum laude, Yale U., 1972; JD, Cornell U., 1975. Bar: Ill. Assoc. McDermott, Will & Emery, Chgo., 1975-80, income ptnr., 1981-85, equity ptnr., 1986—, mgmt. com. mem., 1992-95. Mem. spl. task force on post-employment benefits Fin. Acctg. Standards Bd., Norwalk, Conn., 1987—91. Contbr. articles to profl. jours. Mem. Chgo. Coun. on Fgn. Rels., 1978—, devel. com., 1997-2002, chair devel. subcom., 1999-2002, external rels. com., 2002-03; trustee police pension bd., Wilmette, Ill., 1992-98; trustee Seabury We. Theol. Sem., Evanston, Ill., 1994-2002, chancellor, 1996-97, chair trusteeship com., 2000-02. Mem.: ABA, Cornell Club Chgo., Lawyers' Club Chgo., Yale Club Chgo. Avocations: sailing, water-skiing, cross country skiing. Office: McDermott Will & Emery 227 W Monroe St Ste 4700 Chicago IL 60606-5096 Office Phone: 312-984-7634. Business E-Mail: smiller@mwe.com.

MILLER, STEPHEN WARREN, dean; b. Rockville Centre, N.Y., July 23, 1954; s. Warren Harding Miller and Carol Simon; m. Laurie Robin Hogan (div. July 1988); 1 child, James Warren. AA, Indian River C.C., 1974; BS, Fla. State U., 1977, MS, 1982. Cert. career devel. facilitator master instr. Nat. Occupl. Info. Coord. Com.; cert. instr. Zenger/Miller Tng. Corp. Sports reporter WECA/ABC, Tallahassee, Fla., 1976-77, WXLT/ABC, Sarasota, Fla., 1980-82; 7th and 8th grade sci. tchr. St. Anastasia Sch., Ft. Pierce, Fla., 1978-80; dir. student life Macon (Ga.) C.C., 1981-86; assoc. dean continuing edn. Fla. Atlantic U., Ft. Lauderdale, 1986—. Bd. dirs. Am. Coll. Testing, Iowa City, Iowa, 1995—; bd. advisors PACE Ctr. for Girls, Ft. Lauderdale, 1996—. Contbr. to book: High Technology and the 3 Rs, 1985; contbr. articles to profl. jours. Mem. Broward Rep. Leadership, Ft. Lauderdale, 1997—; bd. dirs. SAILS Found., Macon and Ft. Lauderdale, 1995—; chpt. advisor Phi Delta Kappa, Boca Raton, 1988-89; mem. career adv. bd. Broward County Sch. Bd., Ft. Lauderdale, 1991—; chmn. Broward County Americorp., 1995-96; mem. bus. devel. com. Broward Econ. Devel. Bd., 1988—, pres. A Child is Missing. Named Disting. Pres., Kiwanis Internat., 1985, Kiwanian of Yr., 1984, Outstanding Young Man of Am. U.S. Jaycees, 1983. Mem. Ft. Lauderdale C. of C. (bd. govs. 1995-97, Proclamation award). Republican. Episcopalian. Avocations: jet skiing, golf, guitar, reading. Office: Fla Atlantic U 1515 W Commercial Blvd Fort Lauderdale FL 33309-3095 Fax: (954) 351-4176.

MILLER, STEVEN, medical administrator; Grad., U. Mo., Kansas City. Hosp. staff, faculty Wash. U., 1990—, nephrology fellow, 1988, asst. prof., 1991—97, assoc. prof., 1997—, dir. hypertension clinic divsn. nephrology; med. dir. systemwide renal network Barnes-Jewish Hosp.; chief med. officer Wash. U. Sch. Medicine-Barnes Jewish Hosp., 1999—. Mem.: Internat. Soc. Nephrology, ACP.*

MILLER, STEVEN H. museum director; b. Phila., 1947; m. Jane McClure Pelson; children: Andrew Steven, Katherine Ann. BA, Bard Coll., 1970; cert. in conservation sci., Internat. Ctr. for Study of Preservation and Restoration of Cultural Property, Rome, 1978. Asst. to sr. curator Mus. of City of N.Y., N.Y.C., 1971-72, asst. curator paintings, prints and photographs, 1973-77, curator prints and photographs, 1977-79, curator, dept. head fine art collections, history and spl. collections, 1979-85, sr. curator, 1985-87; asst. dir. Maine State Mus., 1987-91; dir. of mus. Western Res. Hist. Soc., Cleve., 1991-95; exec. dir. The Bennington (Vt.) Mus., 1995—2001, Morris Mus., Morristown, NJ, 2001—; exec. v.p. Morris Mus. Found., Morristown, NJ, 2001—. Adj. prof. mus. studies Case Western Res. U., 1991—94, Seton Hall U.; lectr. NYU, 1978—87, Columbia U., N.Y.C., 1981, 82, New Sch. for Social Rsch., N.Y.C., 1978, 83, Maine State Mus., 1987—91. Author catalogs; contbr. articles to profl. jours. Charter and former mem. hist. preservation com. City of Gardiner, Maine; mem. Williamstown Art Conservation Ctr.; bd. govs. Bard-St. Stephen's Alumni Assn.; bd. trustees Hist. Deerfield, Mass.; past bd. dirs. Vt. Mus. and Gallery Alliance; former mem. landmarks preservation com. Shaker Heights, Ohio; former mem. adv. com. Blaine House Restoration, Maine; former mem., art adv. com. Gracie Mansion Conservancy, N.Y.C.; former mem. adv. coun. Mus. Moving Image, Astoria, NY. Mem.: NARAS (assoc.), Century Assn., Maine Assn. Mus. (co-founder, charter coun. mem.), Am. Assn. Mus. (mem. mus. advocacy team, mem. mus. accreditation vis. com.), Park Ave. Club (Morristown). Home: 45 Washington Ave Morristown NJ 07960-5622

MILLER, STEVEN JEFFREY, lawyer; b. Chgo., Feb. 13, 1954; s. Hadley Allan and Carol Joan (Prince) M.; m. Mona Joy Deutsch, Aug. 21, 1977. BA magna cum laude, U. Pa., 1974; JD, Stanford U., 1977. Bar: Calif. 1977, U.S. Dist. Ct. (cen. dist.) Calif. 1978, U.S. Dist. Ct. (so. dist.) Calif. 1982, U.S. Dist. Ct. (no. and ea. dists.) Calif. 1987, U.S. Dist. Ct. Ariz. 1990, U.S. Ct. Appeals (9th cir.) 1978, U.S. Ct. Appeals (10th cir.) 1981, U.S. Supreme Ct. 1982. Assoc. Lawler, Felix & Hall, L.A., 1977-84, Wyman, Bautzer, Kuchel & Silbert, L.A., 1984-86; sole practitioner Bel Air, Calif., 1987-89; assoc. gen. counsel Ernst & Young, L.A., 1989-94; v.p., dir. legal rsch. Legal Rsch. Network, L.A., 1996-99; gen. counsel, sec. InterPacket Networks, Inc., 1999-2001; atty. The Quisenberry Law Firm, 2001—02. Judge pro tem L.A. County Mcpl. Ct., 1987-89. Trustee U. Synagogue, L.A., 1984—, sec., 1985-89, pres., 1989-91, exec. com., 1985-94. Mem. ABA, Calif. Bar Assn., L.A. County Bar Assn. Democrat. Avocations: softball, racquetball, bowling, bridge, rotisserie league baseball.

MILLER, STEVEN MAX, humanities educator; b. Portland, Ind., Feb. 9, 1950; s. J. Max and Belva Kathryn (Kitty Booher) M.; m. Fran Felice Koski, May 30, 1985 (div. 1992). BA in English with high honors, Coll. of William and Mary, 1972; MA in English Lang. and Lit., Ind. U., 1975, PhD in English Lang. and Lit., 1985. Sr. libr. asst. cataloger rare books and spl. collections Lilly Libr., Bloomington, Ind., 1972-76; prof. English Millersville (Pa.) U., 1985—; dir. univ. honors program Millersville (Pa.) U., 1999-2001, dir. Honors Coll., 2001—. Cons. women writers project Brown U., Providence, 1990-95. Contbr. articles to profl. jours. Grantee NEH, 1991, 92. Mem. MLA, John Donne Soc. Am., Spenser Soc. Episcopalian. Avocation: gardening. Office: Millersville U Honors Coll PO Box 1002 Millersville PA 17551-0302

MILLER, STEVEN SCOTT, lawyer; b. N.Y.C., May 28, 1947; s. Stanley Irwin and Corinne (Mass) M.; m. Nina Catherine Augello, Apr. 24, 1983. BA cum laude, U. Pa., 1967; JD cum laude, NYU, 1970. Bar: N.Y. 1971, U.S. Dist. Ct. (so. and ea. dists.) N.Y. 1972, U.S. Ct. Appeals (2d cir.) 1974. Law clk. to judge U.S. Dist. Ct. (so. dist.) N.Y., N.Y.C., 1970-71; assoc. Proskauer Rose Goetz & Mendelsohn, N.Y.C., 1971-78, Rosenman & Colin, N.Y.C., 1978-81, ptnr., 1981-92; v.p., asst. gen. counsel J.P. Morgan Chase & Co. (formerly Chase Manhattan Bank), N.Y.C., 1992—. Editor NYU Law Rev., 1968-70. Mem.: NY State Bar Assn., NYU Law Sch. Alumni Assn. (pres. 2000—02). Home: 135 E 83rd St New York NY 10028-2408 Office: JP Morgan Chase & Co 1 Chase Manhattan Plz Fl 26 New York NY 10081-0001

MILLER, STEWART RANSOM, lawyer; b. Dallas, June 11, 1945; s. Giles Edwin and Betty Jane (Stewart) Miller; m. Alice Miller, Aug. 30, 1997; children: Rhett, Melissa, Christi, Anna, Ross. BA, Austin Coll., 1968; JD, U. Tex., 1970. Bar: Tex. 1970, U.S. Dist. Ct. (ea. dist.) Tex. 1971, U.S. Dist. Ct. (no. dist.) Tex. 1972, U.S. Dist. Ct. (so. dist.) Tex. 1989, U.S. Dist. Ct. (we. dist.) Tex. 1992, U.S. Tax Ct. 1977, U.S. Ct. Appeals (5th cir.) 1977, U.S. Ct. Appeals (9th cir.) 1995, U.S. Supreme Ct. 1977, U.S. Dist. Ct. (no. dist.) Okla. 1987; cert. consumer bankruptcy law specialist, 1993-2003; cert. comml. real estate law specialist 1983-99. Assoc. Wade & Thomas, Dallas, 1970-71; asst. gen. counsel Sammons Enterprises Inc., Dallas, 1971-78; ptnr. The Miller & Miller Firm, PLLC, Dallas, 1978-99; consumer atty. Legal Svcs. of North Tex. Inc., Dallas, 1999—2002; gen. counsel Legal Aid Soc. Tex., 2002—; ptnr.

Miller & Miller, Dallas, 2004—. Adj. law prof. SMU Poverty Law Clinic, 2000-02. Mem. Charter Commn. Town of Highland Park; bd. dirs., sec. Aberrant Behavior Ctr. Inc., Dallas, 1978-85, Behavioral Rsch. Ctr. cInc., Dallas, 1980-85. Mem. State Bar Tex. (legal svcs. to the poor com. 2002—), Dallas Bar Assn., Dallas Bus. Assn. (past pres.), Nat. Assn. Consumer Advocates. Episcopalian. Home: 9310 Esplanade Dr Dallas TX 75220-5038 Office: Ste 600 1250 W Mockingbird Ln Dallas TX 75247-6929 Office Phone: 214-267-9090. E-mail: srm@stewartmillerlaw.com.

MILLER, STUART A. real estate executive, lawyer; Grad., Harvard U.; JD, U. Miami, 1982. Various positions homebuilding divsn. Lennar Corp., Miami, Fla., pres. homebuilding divsn. and former investment divsn., 1991—97, pres., CEO, 1997—, also bd. dirs. Bd. dirs. Union Bank Fla. Office: Lennar Corp 700 NW 107th Ave Ste 400 Miami FL 33172-3154

MILLER, STUART D. surgeon; s. Philip H. and Bunny M. Miller; m. Jacqueline Miller; children: Rachel H., Emily N., Joshua H. AB, Brandeis U., 1981; MD, Georgetown U., 1988. Diplomate Am. Bd. Orthop. Surgery. Residency, dept. orthop. surgery Henry Ford Hosp., Detroit, 1988—93; mem. tchg. staff dept. orthop. surgery Union Meml. Hosp., Balt., 1993—. Cons. Biomet, Warsaw. Fellow: Am. Orthop. Foot and Ankle Soc., Am. Acad. Orthop. Surgery; mem.: Md. Orthop. Soc. Achievements include design of ankle arthrodesis nail; patents for modular bone screw with bioresorbable head; research in resection interposition arthroplasty of great toe; nerve injury and treatment in the lower extremity; bone cartilage transplant to foot and ankle. Avocations: bicycling, tennis. Office: Greater Chesapeake Orthop Assoc 3333 N Calvert St Ste 400 Baltimore MD 21218 Office Phone: 410-554-6530.

MILLER, SUSAN ANN, retired school system administrator; b. Cleve., Nov. 24, 1947; d. Earl Wilbur and Marie Coletta (Hendershot) M. BS in Edn., Kent State U., 1969; MEd, Cleve. State U., 1975; PhD, Kent State U., 1993. Cert. supt.; cert. elem. prin., cert. elem. supervisor; cert. Learning Disabled/Behavior Disabled tchr.; cert. tchr. grades 1-8; cert. sch. counselor; lic. counselor. Tchr., guidance counselor, interim prin. North Royalton City Schs., Ohio, 1969-84; dir. elem. and spl. edn., acting supt., asst. supt. Ednl. Svc. Ctr. of Cuyahoga County, Valley View, Ohio, 1984—. Contbr. articles to profl. jours. Grantee Latchkey Program, State Dept. Edn., North Coast Leadership Forum, Peer Assistance and Rev., Entry Yr. Program, Alt. II.3. Mem. ASCD, Coun. Exceptional Children, Phi Delta Kappa. Office: ESC Cuyahoga County 5700 W Canal Rd Valley View OH 44125-3326 Home: 7236 Morning Star Trail Sagamore Hills OH 44067 E-mail: susan.a.miller@lnoca.org.

MILLER, SUSAN M. telecommunications industry executive; BA in English Lit. and Art History, Dickinson Coll., 1981; JD, Cath. U. Columbus Sch. Law, 1984. Counsel telecomm. Weil, Gotshal, & Manges, N.Y.C.; counsel GTE; v.p., gen. counsel ATIS, Washington, 1988—99, pres., CEO, 1999—. Rep. ATIS FCC, Am. Nat. Stds. Inst., N.Am. Numbering Coun., Network Reliability and Interoperability Coun., Internat. Engring. Consortium Adv. Coun. Office: ATIS 1200 G St NW Ste 500 Washington DC 20005

MILLER, SUZANNE MARIE, state librarian; b. Feb. 25, 1954; d. John Gordon and Dorothy Margaret (Sabatka) M.; 1 child, Altinay Marie. BA in English, U. S.D., 1975; MA in Library Sci., U. Denver, 1976, postgrad. in law, 1984. Librarian II U. S.D. Sch. of Law, Vermillion, 1977-78; law libr. U. LaVerne, Calif., 1978-85, instr. in law, 1980-85; asst. libr. tech. svcs. McGeorge Sch. Law, Calif., 1985-99, prof. advanced legal rsch., 1994-99; state librarian S.D. State Library, Pierre, 1999—2004; state chief libr. Minn. Dept. Edn., Roseville, 2004—. Co-author (with Elizabeth J. Pokorny) U.S. Government Documents: A Practical Guide for Library Assistants in Academic and Public Libraries, 1988; contbr. chpt. to book, articles to profl. jours. Pres. Short Grass Arts Coun., 2001—03; bd. dirs. Black Hills Playhouse Bd., 1999—2004, S.D. Ctr. for the Book Bd., 2002—04. Recipient A. Jurisprudence Award Bancroft Whitney Pub. Co., 1983. Mem.: ALA, Western Coun. State Librs. (sec. 2001—02), Chief Officers of State Libr. Agys. (sec. 2002—), Western Pacific Assn. Law Librs. (sec. 1990—94, pres. elect 1994—95, pres. 1995—96, local arrangements chair 1997), No. Calif. Assn. Law Librs. (mem. program com., inst. 1988), Mt. Plains Libr. Assn. (S.D. rep. to exec. bd. 2001—04), So. Calif. Assn. Law Librs. (arrangements com. 1981—82), Am. Assn. Law Librs., S.D. Libr. Assn. Roman Catholic. Home: 448 McCarrons Blvd So Roseville MN 55113 Office: Minn Dept Edn 1500 Hwy 36 West Roseville MN 55113-4266 Office Phone: 651-582-8791. E-mail: suzanne.miller@state.mn.us.

MILLER, TAMMIE R. public relations consultant, writer; b. Bklyn., July 26, 1967; d. Earlie and Emma Bone; m. Tammie R. Bone, Feb. 25, 2000; children: Akilah Benay Oates-Miller, Naomi Salee'. AS in Polit. Sci., L.I. Univ., 1992. Cert.: Adelphi U. (para-legal) 1993. Pharmacy technician N.Y. Hotel Trades Coun., Bklyn., 1994—97, eligibility specialist N.Y.C., 1997—2001. Cons., advisor Pentecostal Ch., Bklyn., 1997—. Author: (book) Tumble-Weed Fever (Langston Hughes Award for Excellence in Creative Writing, 2003). Evangelist Apostolic Ch., Bklyn., 1980—99; woman's counselor and advisor Hebrew Israelites, Bklyn., 1999—2004. Grantee Walton Meml. Fund for Lit. Excellence, Pentecostal Chs, 2003. Personal E-mail: tmiller3527867@verizon.net.

MILLER, TED ROBERT, policy analyst; b. Sept. 17, 1947; s. Marvin Lester and Carolyn Ruth Miller; m. Valerie Sue Nelkin. BS in Engring., Case Western Res. U., 1968; MS in Ops. Rsch., U. Pa., 1971, M in City Planning, 1970, PhD in Regional Sci., 1975. Ops. rsch. analyst U.S. Dept. Commerce, Nat. Bur. Stds. and HEW, Washington, 1971-75; staff dir. task force on Nat. Blood Data Ctr. Am. Blood Commn., Rosslyn, Va., 1975-77; asst. dir. urban and econ. devel. Nat. Inst. Advanced Studies, Washington, 1977-78; v.p. Granville Corp., Washington, 1978-84; sr. rsch. assoc. Urban Inst., Washington, 1984-93; dir. Children's Safety Network Econ. and Ins. Rsch. Ctr., 1992—. V.p. Nat. Pub. Svcs. Rsch. Inst., Calverton, Md., 1993-96, pres., 1997-2002; prin. rsch. scientist Pacific Inst. Rsch. and Evaluation, Calverton, 1997—. Mem. editl. bd. Jour. Safety Rsch., 1991—, Jour. Forensic Econs., 1991-2002, Acc. Analysis and Prevention, 1993—, Inj. Prev., 2002-; contbr. articles to profl. jours. Mem. Bd. Proprs. Ea. N.J., 1974-98; pres. Adelphi Ter. Condo. Assn., 1979-81. Recipient Nationwide on Your Side Hwy. Safety award, 1996. Fellow Assn. Advt. Automotive Medicine, Am. Inst. Cert. Planners; mem. AAAS, APHA (Excellence in Sci. award injury control sect. 1999), So. Regional Sci. Assn. (exec. coun. 1990-92), Am. Econ. Assn., Pi Delta Epsilon. Democrat. Office: 11701 Beltsville Dr Ste 300 Beltsville MD 20705

MILLER, TERRY MORROW, lawyer; b. Columbus, Ohio, Mar. 11, 1947; s. Robert E. and Elizabeth Jane (Morrow) M.; m. Martha Estella Johnson, Mar. 20, 1976; 1 child, Timothy. BS, Ohio State U., 1969, JD, 1975. Bar: Ohio 1975, U.S. Ct. Appeals (6th cir.) 1979, U.S. Supreme Ct. 1980. Asst. atty. gen. State of Ohio, Columbus, 1975-77; ptnr. Miller & Noga, Columbus, 1977-81; assoc. Vorys, Sater, Seymour and Pease, Columbus, 1981-85, ptnr., 1986—. Trustee Columbus Literacy Coun., 1997—. Sgt. U.S. Army, 1969-71, Okinawa. Mem. Ohio State Bar Assn., Columbus Bar Assn., Little Turtle Country Club (mems. coun. 1997-2000, pres. 1998-2000). Avocations: golf, Ohio history. Home: 288 E North Broadway Columbus OH 43214-4114 Office: Vorys Sater Seymour et al PO Box 1008 52 E Gay St Columbus OH 43215-3108 Office Phone: 614-464-5645. E-mail: tmmiller@vssp.com.

MILLER, THERESA L. library director; b. Port Huron, Mich., Apr. 2, 1959; d. David R. Miller and Mary Louise Preininger. AA, AS, St. Clair County C.C., Port Huron, Mich., 1990; BS, Wayne State U., 1992, MLIS, 1994. Support tutor St. Clair County C.C., 1988-89, master tutor, 1989-91; circulation supr. Baker Coll. of Port Huron, 1992-95, faculty math., 1998; pub. spkr. Mich., 1988—; investigative asst. Huffmaster Cos., Port Huron, 1998-2000; libr. dir. Baker Coll. of Pt. Huron, 1995—; judge Bus. Profs. of Am., St. Clair County, 1994—2000, 2003—04. Baker coll. rep. County Tech. Adv. Com., St. Clair County, 1997—; adv. bd. mem. Baker Coll. of PH Career Svcs., 1997—2003; judge Bus. Profs. of Am., St. Clair County, 2003—04, Port Huron H.S. Writing Competition, 1997—2001. Editor: (newsletter) Baker Beacon, 1997; author: (newsletter) LUC News, 1993-96; author: (book) A Reference Librarians User Guide to the Internet, 1993. Recorder for the blind, Libr. of Mich., Lansing, 1996—; mem. gov. bd. Seaway Cmty. Freenet, St. Clair County, 1995-96; pres., founding bd. First Night of Port Huron, 2001-04, bd. dir. Mem.: ALA, Internat. Libr. Support Group (founder 1999—, chmn.), Librs. Using Computers/Mich. (chair 1994—96), Mich. Libr. Assn., Optimists (Port Huron bd. dirs. 1997—99, pres. Pt. Huron chpt. 2000—01, lt. gov. Mich. 2001—), Phi Theta Kappa (treas. 1989—90, founding alumni pres. St. Clair C.C. chpt. 1991). Avocations: profl. singing, jewelry collecting, auctions, theater, investing. Office: Baker Coll Port Huron Libr 3403 Lapeer Rd Port Huron MI 48060 Office Phone: 810-989-2122. Business E-Mail: theresa.miller@baker.edu.

MILLER, THOMAS EUGENE, lawyer, writer; b. Bryan, Tex., Jan. 4, 1929; s. Eugene Adam and Ella Lucille (Schroeder) M. BA, BS, Tex. A&M U., 1950; MA, U. Tex., 1956, JD, 1966; postgrad., U. Houston, 1956-58, U. Calif., 1983. Bar: Tex. 1966. Rsch. technician M.D. Anderson Hosp., Houston, 1956-58; claims examiner trainee Social Security Adminstrn., New Orleans, 1964; trademark examiner U.S. Patent and Trademark Office, Washington, 1966; editor Bancroft-Whitney Co., San Francisco, 1966-92. Author: (under pseudonym Millard Thomas) Home From 7-North, 1984; contbr. to numerous legal publs. Mem. Dem. Nat. Com., 1981-; mem. Celebrate Bryan Com., chmn. Bryan Med. Heritage Com. Mem. ABA, World Lit. Assn., World Inst. Achievement, United Writers Assn. India, Nat. Trust for Hist. Preservation, Tex. Bar Assn., U. Tex. Sch. of Law, Non-practicing Alumni Adv. Coun., African Wildlife Found., World Wildlife Fund, Internat. Platform Assn., Nat. Writers Assn., Scribes, Acad. Polit. Sci., Press Club, Commonwealth Club, Westerners Club, Rotary Club (Paul Harris fellow, Found. fellow), Menninger Soc., Tex. A&M U. Faculty Club, Phi Kappa Phi, Psi Chi, Phi Eta Sigma. Methodist. Home: 101 N Haswell Dr Bryan TX 77803-4848 Office Phone: 979-822-1907. *Personal philosophy: Use your experience and abilities not only to understand life and to succeed, but also to help others' journeys through life.*

MILLER, THOMAS G. career officer; b. Ft. Bragg, N.C., July 12, 1952; Brig. gen., dep. dir. for ops. J-3 U.S. Pacific Command, 1998—2000; assist. div. comndr. 10th Mountain Division at Fort Drum, NY, 2001—. Office: Public Affairs Fort Drum NY 13602-5028

MILLER, THOMAS J. state attorney general; b. Dubuque, Iowa, Aug. 11, 1944; s. Elmer John and Betty Maude (Kross) Miller; m. Linda Cottington, Jan. 10, 1981; 1 child, Matthew. BA, Loras Coll., Dubuque, 1966; JD, Harvard U., 1969. Bar: Iowa 1969. With VISTA, Balt., 1969—70; legis. asst. to U.S. rep. John C. Culver, 1970—71; legal edn. dir. Balt. Legal Aid Bur., part-time faculty U. Md. Sch. Law, 1971—73; pvt. practice McGregor, Iowa, 1973—78; city atty., 1973—79, Marquette, Iowa; atty. gen. of Iowa, 1978—90, 1994—; ptnr. Faegre & Benson, Des Moines, 1991—95. Chmn. Microsoft case exec. com.; co-chmn. Airline Competition Working Group; pres. 2d Dist. New Dem. Club, Balt., 1972. Mem.: NAAG (pres. 1989—90, chmn. consumer protection, ins., budget, and antitrust coms., Wyman award 1990), ABA, Iowa Bar Assn., Common Cause. Democrat. Roman Catholic. Office: Office of the Atty Gen Hoover State Office Bldg 1305 E Walnut St Des Moines IA 50319-0112

MILLER, THOMAS J. former ambassador; b. Chgo., 1948; m. Bonnie Miller; 2 children. BA in Polit. Sci., U. Mich., 1969, MA in Asian Studies and Polit. Sci., 1973, PhD in Polit. Sci., 1975. Various to sr. fgn. svc./min. counselor U.S. Dept. State, 1976—, analyst for Vietnam, Laos, & Cambodia, 1976—77, spl. asst. to under sec. polit. affairs, 1977—79; dep. prin. officer U.S. Consulate, Chiang Mai, Thailand, 1979—81; dep. chief of mission U.S. Embassy, Athens, 1994-97; spl. coord. for Cyprus (amb.) U.S. Dept. State, 1997-99, U.S. amb. to Bosnia and Herzegovina, 1999—2001, U.S. amb. to Greece, 2001—04. Lectr. in field; initiator Model UN programs at three Washington high schs. Recipient numerous awards in field. Avocations: speaks greek, spanish, thai, indonesian, japanese.

MILLER, THOMAS ROBBINS, lawyer, publisher; b. Chgo., Mar. 8, 1938; s. William Whipple and Helen (Robbins) M.; m. Tran Tuong Nhu, July 3, 1974; children: Toby, Teddy, Nathalie, Gabriella. BA, Yale U., 1960; LLB, Stanford U., 1965; cert., Parker Sch. Fgn. and Comparative Law, Columbia U., 1966. Bar: N.Y. 1966, Calif. 1974. Assoc. Webster & Sheffield, N.Y.C., 1965-68; sole practice N.Y.C., 1968-74, Berkeley, 1974-89; pub. Lancaster Miller Pubs., Berkeley, 1974-89; sr. ptnr. Miller & Ngo, PLC, Oakland, Calif., 1989—. Founder, pres. Internat. Children's Fund, Berkeley, 1974—; cons. Peace Corps, Washington, 1961, Ctr. for Constl. Rights, UNICEF, N.Y.C., 1973-76; dep. dir. Calif. Rural Legal Assistance, San Francisco, 1977-79; gen. counsel Global Exch.; co-founder Parwaz Afghan Women's Microlending Fund. Named 1 of 10 Outstanding Young Men in U.S., U.S. Jaycees, 1974 Democrat. Office: 725 Washington St Oakland CA 94607-3924 Office Phone: 510-891-0616. Personal E-mail: viasco@aol.com.

MILLER, THOMAS V. MIKE, JR., state legislator; b. Clinton, Md., Dec. 3, 1942; married; 5 children. BS, U. Md., 1964, JD, 1967. Mem. Ho. of Dels., 1971-75; atty.; mem. Dist. 27 Md. Senate, 1975—, pres., 1987—, co-chmn. legis. policy com., mem. rules and spending affordability com., mem. joint com. on legis. ethics, mem. adv. coun. lead poisoning, mem. Md. housing policy commn., mem. State House Trust, 1987—, mem. vet. home commn., 1987, mem. state commn. on capital city, 1987—. Mem. Md. 1992 Commn., 1989, Gov.'s Task Force on Trees and Forests, 1990—; pres. So. State Senate Leaders Conf., 1988; mem. Surratts, Brandywine, Nottingham, Ft. Washington and Upper Marlboro Dem. Clubs; pres. Senate Pres. Forum. Named Disting. Alumnus of Yr., U. Md., 1988, Outstanding Citizen, Prince George's County Bd. Trade, Outstanding Legislator, Md. Mcpl. League, Legislator of Yr. Md. Retailers Assn., 1998; recipient William P. Coliton Cmty. Svc. award Johns Hopkins U., Pub. Svc. award Local 400 AFL-CIO, Outstanding K.C. award, Bulger award for legis. excellence. Mem. ABA, Md. Bar Assn., Prince George's County Bar Assn. Democrat. Office: State House, H-107 Annapolis MD 21401-1991

MILLER, THORMUND AUBREY, lawyer; b. Pocatello, Idaho, July 14, 1919; s. Roy Edmund and Lillian (Thordarson) Miller; m. Hannah A. Flansburgh, Feb. 10, 1946 (dec. Jan. 2003); children: Karen Lynette Van Gerpen, Christine Alison Westall; m. Barbara Singelyn, May 8, 2004. BA, Reed Coll., 1941; LLB, Columbia U., 1948; grad., Advanced Mgmt. Program, Harvard Bus. Sch., 1961. Bar: Calif. 1949, D.C. 1951, U.S. Supreme Ct. 1960. Assoc. McCutchen, Thomas, Matthews, Griffiths & Greene, San Francisco, 1948-50; atty. So. Pacific Transp. Co., Washington, 1950-56, asst. gen. atty., 1956-59, gen. atty., 1959-66, sr. gen. atty., 1966-75, gen. solicitor, 1975-79, gen. commerce counsel, 1979-83, dir., mem. exec. com., 1983-87, v.p., gen. counsel, 1983-89; gen. counsel So. Pacific Communications Co., San Francisco, 1970-79, dir., 1970-81; pvt. practice law Atherton, Calif., 1989-96. Pres. Wood Acres Citizens Assn., Bethesda, Md., 1955-56; exec. com. Holbrook Palmer Recreation Park Found., 1979—, pres., 1982-84; bd. dirs. Atherton Civic Interest League, 1981—, pres., 1992-94; mem. Atherton Park and Recreation Commn., 1991-95, San Mateo Civil Grand Jury, 1997; alumni bd. Reed Coll., 1971-72, trustee, 1987-2002, campaign com., 1995-2000; joint donor Thormund A. Miller/Walter Mintz chair in econ. history; bd. dirs. Assocs. U. Calif. Press, 1994—. Lt. USNR, 1942-46. Mem.: ABA, Calif. Bar Assn. Presbyterian.

MILLER, TIMOTHY ALDEN, plastic and reconstructive surgeon; b. Inglewood, Calif., Dec. 11, 1938; s. Henry Bernard and Florence Algena (Maddock) M.; 1 child, Matthew Christopher. Student, U. Calif., Berkeley; MD, UCLA, 1963. Diplomate Am. Bd. Surgery, Am. Bd. Plastic Surgery (dir. 1991-97). Intern Vanderbilt U. Hosp., Nashville, 1963-64; resident in surgery, dept. surg. pathology UCLA, 1966-67, resident, then chief resident gen. and thoracic surgery, 1967-69, acting asst. prof., 1969-70, prof. surgery, 1981—; asst. surg. resident John Hopkins Hosp., 1967; fellow plastic and reconstructive surgery U. Pitts., 1970-72; chief plastic surgery West L.A. VA Med. Ctr., 1973—; prof., chief plastic and reconstructive surgery UCLA Sch. Medcine, 2002—. Author: (novel) Practice to Deceive, 1991; assoc. editor Jour. Plastic & Reconstructive Surgery, 1987-93, co-editor, 1994-99. Trustee Children's Inst. Internat., 1995-2000. Capt. U.S. Army, 1964-66, Vietnam. Decorated Bronze Star; recipient Thomas Symington award Pitts. Acad. Medicine, 1971. Mem. Am. Soc. for Plastic Surgery (co-editor Jour. Plastic and Reconstructive Surgery), Am. Soc. for Aesthetic Plastic Surgery (bd. dirs. 1990-95), Plastic Surgery Ednl. Found. (bd. dirs. 1991-95). Office: UCLA Med Ctr 200 Ucla Medical Plz Ste 465 Los Angeles CA 90095-8344

MILLER, TONYA ALICIA, training and development specialist, management consultant; b. Newark, Sept. 16, 1970; d. Mike Joe and Janette Miller. BA, Hampton U., 1992; MS, Old Dominion U., 1994, PhD, 1999. Assoc. mgr. AT&T, Morristown, NJ, 1996—97; prof./instr. Old Dominion U., Norfolk, Va., 1997—2000; human resources and developement specialist Gen. Electric, Atlanta, 2000—02; S.E. regional tng. and devel. specialist ADT/Tyco Fire & Security, Norcross, Ga., 2002—04; human resources mgr. Tyco Fire & Security, 2004—. Orgnl. devel. specialist Sentara Health Systems, Norfolk, 1995—96; bus. devel. specialist Gen. Electric, Richmond, Va., 1997—98; orgnl. devel. specialist City of Norfolk, 1998—2000; spkr./presenter in field. Chairperson United Way, Morristown, 1996—97; mentor Delta Sigma Theta, Norfolk, 1997—2000; big sister Big Sister Program, Norfolk, 1998—2000; campaign fellow City of Norfolk, 1999—2000. Named one of 30 leaders of the Future, Ebony Mag., 2001; Am. Doctoral Rsch. Assistantship, Old Dominion U., 1992—95, 1999, Commonwealth of Va. fellow, State of Va., 1995—97, One Yr. Dissertation fellow, So. Regional Ednl. Bd., 1998—99. Mem.: Soc. for Indsl. and Orgnl. Psychology (assoc.), Alpa Kappa Mu, Psi Chi (sec. 1991—92), Beta Kappa Chi, Delta Sigma Theta. Achievements include research in work-life role integration. Office: Tyco Fire & Security One Town Ctr Rd Boca Raton FL 33468 Personal E-mail: tam1929@aol.com.

MILLER, VALERIE CAROL, journalist; b. Chgo. d. V. Heinz and Arlene Elizabeth Miller. A in Gen. Studies, C.C. So. Nev.; BA Comms., U. Nev., 1998. Travel coord. Great Escape Travel, Las Vegas, 1996—97; staff writer, reporter U. Nev. Las Vegas Rebel Yell Students Newspaper, 1997—98; travel coord. World Travel and Accessories, Las Vegas, 1998—2000; reporter, freelance writer, intern Las Vegas Sun Newspaper, 1998—2000; broadcaster, disk jockey Sta. KLAV AM 1230, Las Vegas, 1997—; reporter, staff writer Las Vegas Bus. Press Newspaper, 2000—; staff writer Las Vegas Sr. Press. Host radio show Valerie's Music Magic. Vol. Shade Tree Shelter, Las Vegas, 2002; vol. writer Nev. Times Newspaper, Las Vegas, 1995, 1997. Nominee Journalist of Merit award, Nev. Press Assn., 2002, 2003, Small Bus. Journalist of Yr., Nev. Small Bus. Adminstrn., 2003; recipient Best Feature Story award, Nev. Press Assn., 2001, Small Bus. Journalist of Yr. award for Nev., U.S. Small Bus. Assn., 2002, Merit award for news writing, Internat. Assn. Bus. Comm., 2003, Merit award for series writing, 2003, Best Bus. Story award, Nev. Press. Assn. Fellow: Soc. for the Advanced Placement of Materials, Working in Comms., Soc. Profl. Journalists, 3rd Wave Nev., Tortois Group; mem.: Phi Lambda Eta. Avocations: travel, writing poems and song lyrics, movies. Home: 613 Mosswood Dr Henderson NV 89015-8329 Office: Las Vegas Bus Press 1385 Pama Ln Ste 111 Las Vegas NV 89119

MILLER, VELVET G. healthcare administrator; b. Reading, Pa., Aug. 16, 1945; d. Louis L. and Pattee J. Miller; m. Calvin E. Davis, Sept. 14, 1991; 1 child, Toby L. C. BSN, Wagner Coll., 1967; MEd, Temple U., 1976; MPA, Harvard U., 1984; PhD, Boston U., 1997. RN. Assoc. commr. Mass. Dept. Pub. Welfare, Boston, 1988-89, Mass. Dept. Health, Boston, 1989-91; v.p. Wagner Coll., S.I., 1991-92; Medicaid dir. N.J. Dept. Human Svcs., Trenton, 1994-96, dep. commr., 1996-98; exec. dir. Children's Futures N.J., Princeton, 1998-99; ptnr. Davis Miller Group, Trenton, 1991—; pres., CEO Horizon/Mercy, Trenton, 2001—02, My Parent's Concierge, 1999—. Mem. adv. bd. Urban Inst., Washington, 1996—2004, Finding Common Ground, Columbia U., N.Y.C., 1997—2003. Co-author: (book) Renegotiating Healthcare, 1995 (ANA CPR inst. award, 1995, 1996); contbr. articles and reports to profl. jours. Bd. dirs. Families USA, Washington, 1993—99. Recipient Pub. Svc. award, N.J. Pub. Policy Rsch. Inst., 1998, Carballo award for excellence in pub. svc., Commonwealth of Mass., 1988. Fellow: Am. Acad. Nursing; mem.: ANA, APHA. Democrat. Presbyterian. Home and Office: 219 Cornwall Ave Trenton NJ 08618-3321 E-mail: vmiller8529@comcast.net.

MILLER, VERNE WILLIAM, computer engineer, consultant; b. Chgo., Mar. 22, 1953; s. Fritz Henry and Dorothy Ruth Miller. Student in Computer Engring., DeVry U., Chgo., 2002—03. Registered: State of Ill. (Police Officer) 1983, lic.: Glock, Inc. (Glock Armorer & Instructor) 1996; cert. CPR instr. ARC, 1995, emergency first aid instr. ARC, 1995, lic. emergency rescue technician State of Ill., 1987, controlled Substance Class I and II State of Ill., 1989. Mech. engr. Sheldons Mfg. Corp., Elgin, Ill., 1973—76; law enforcement officer Chgo. Union Sta. RR Police, Chgo., 1982—87, Amtrak Police Dept., Chgo., 1987—2001; cons., rschr. LETCON, Harwood Heights, Ill., 1990—. Cons. U.S. Dept. of Justice, Office of Justice Stats., Washington, 1990—94; adv. bd. mem. Nat. Tactical Officers Assn., 1992—94; cons. and trainer Midwest Tactical Tng. Inst., Freeport, Ill., 1989—91. Author: (book) Police Identification Guide to Street Gangs; Volumes I & II; contbr. articles to profl. jours. Spkr. - anti-drug edn. Bartlett Sr. Citizens Groups, Bartlett, Ill., 1989—91. Recipient Exceptional Svc. award, Amtrak Police Dept., 1996, Life Saving award, 1997. Mem.: IEEE, Ill. State Rifle Assn., NRA (life), Law Enforcement Alliance of Am., Clan Kincaid Scottish Heritage Soc., North Am. Hunting Club, Tau Alpha Pi (Nu Delta chpt. v.p. 2003—04, Nu Delta chpt. pres. 2004—05). R-Consevative. Lutheran, Missouri Synod. Avocations: photography, writing. Home: 5654 W Gunnison St Chicago IL 6060-3216 Personal E-mail: vwmiller@earthlink.net.

MILLER, VERNON DALLACE, minister; b. McClure, Ill., Sept. 27, 1932; s. Homer Lee and Marie Kathleen (White) M.; m. Alice Elizabeth Wright, July 25, 1954; children: Ronald, Philip, Elizabeth, Annette, Douglas. Student, Moody Bible Inst., 1950-53, S.E. Mo. State, 1954, So. Ill. U., 1956-57; BA, Cedarville Coll., 1963, LittD, 1988. Ordained to min. Bapt. Ch., McClure, 1953. Pastor Camp Creek Bapt. Ch., Murphysboro, Ill., 1953-54, Bible Fellowship Bapt. Ch., Carterville, Ill., 1954-57, Faith Bapt. Ch., Mattoon, Ill., 1957-60, Immanuel Bapt. Ch., Arcanum, Ohio, 1961-63; editor, bus. mgr. Regular Bapt. Press, Chgo., 1963-70; pres. Ch. Bldg. Cons., Chgo., 1971-87; exec. editor, treas. Gen. Assn. of Regular Bapt. Chs., Schaumburg, Ill., 1987-97; min. christian edn. Berean Bapt. Ch., Portage, Mich., 1998—. Exec. bd. Awana Youth Assn., Streamwood, Ill., 1965-83, Grand Rapids (Mich.) Bapt. Coll. and Sem., 1981-91, Shepherds Bapt. Ministries, Union Grove, Wis., 1965-96. Editor: (mag.) The Baptist Bulletin, 1987-97. Del. Ill. Small Bus. Com., Springfield, Ill., 1984. Mem.: Christian Ministries Mgmt. Assn. Republican. Baptist.

MILLER, VIDA O. state representative, art gallery owner; b. Travelers Rest, S.C., July 22, 1950; d. David William and Imogene Tankersley Osteen; m. James Dores Miller, Mar. 26, 1978; stepchildren: Jimmy, Allyson. Student, N. Greenville Coll., Bob Jones U. Owner Grayman Gallery; state rep. dist. 108 S.C. Legis., 1997—, mem. edn. and pub. works com., mem. invitations and meml. resolutions com., sec. agr. natural resources and environ. affairs. com., 1996—98, mem. environ. affairs I subcom. Sec. House Dem. Caucus. Mem. Georgetown County Sch. Bd., 1988—94, sec., 1992—94; past bd. dirs., organizer Georgetown County Human Rels. Coun.; bd. dirs. Five Rivers Commn. Develop. Corp.; mem. Georgetown County League Women Voters; bd. dirs. Rice Mus. Cultural Develop.; chmn. Georgetwon County Legis. Del.; gen. assembly mem. S.C. Sch. Bds. Stratgic Planning Team; mem. S.C. Dept. Transp. Road Enhancement Com., S.C. Dept. Transp. Minority Bus. com.; bd. dirs. Waccamaw Regional Planning Commn.; vice chmn. Grand Strand Transp. Authority; mem. Gov.'s Med. Sch. Task Force, Palmetto Pride, Tourism Caucus and Arts Caucus; bd. dirs. First Steps; sec. House Dem. Caucus. Named Outstanding Legis. of Yr., S.C. Sch. Bds., 1999, 2000. Mem.: Georgetown County Bus. and Profl. Women, Georgetown County Wateroclor Soc. (bd. dirs.), S.C. Watercolor Soc. (regional dir. 1992—95), Waccamaw Arts & Craft Guild (bd. dirs. 1992—94), Pawleys Island-Litchfield Merchants Assn. (bd. dirs., organizer 1986—89), Natl. Found. Women Legislators (state co-chmn.). Democrat. Office: State Capitol 335D Blatt Bldg Columbia SC 29211 Home: PO Box 3157 Pawleys Island SC 29585 Address: 335 Westfield Dr Pawleys Island SC 29585 E-mail: VOM@scstatehouse.net.

MILLER, VINCENT PAUL, JR., geography and regional planning educator; b. Swissvale, Pa., May 11, 1932; s. Vincent Paul and May Eleanor Miller; m. Alida Field Ward, July 23, 1960; 1 child, Bradley Cleland. BS, Muskingum Coll., 1954; MS, Pa. State U., 1957; PhD, Mich. State U., 1970. Social sci. asst. Quartermaster R&D Comdt., Natick, Mass., 1957-59; instr. Coll. of Wooster, Ohio, 1959-60; asst. instr. Mich. State U., East Lansing, 1961; assoc. prof. Indiana (Pa.) U., 1962-70, prof., 1970-98, prof. emeritus, 1999—. Author: Project Ebenezer: Modeling Holistic Missions, 1981, Central Place Hierarchy & Access to Services, 1985; editor/author: The Future at the Bicentennial, 1977, Planning Issues in Marginal Areas, 1991, Technology, Landscape, and Arrested Development: Essays on the Geography of Marginality, 1997; editor: The Pa. Jr. Geographer, 1965-66, The Pa. Geographer, 1966-75. Dir. rsch. Ministries in Action, Miami, Fla., 1980—, dir. holistic curriculum devel., 1999—; bd. mem. Birthright, Indiana, United Ministry Indiana U. of Pa., pres. bd. 1997; mem. com. Diaconal Ministries Com., Kiskiminitas Presbytery, chair self-devel. of people com., 2002—; cons. Iona Study Ctr., Ministries in Action; co-founder PIMA (Planning Marginal Areas), 1979. Ctrl. Pl. Rsch. grantee, 1985, Travel grantee U. Presbyn. Ch., 1995. Mem. AAAS, Assn. Am. Geographers (bd. rural devel. splty. group 1984-88, sec. treas. 1984-86, pres. 1986-88), Assn. Pub. Justice, Pa. Geog. Soc. (pres. 1979-80), Soc. for Advancement of Scandinavian Studies, Ctrl. Ind. Model R.R. Club (pres. 2002, Sigma Xi (pres. Ind. chpt. 1977-78). Avocations: music, writing, photography, yard work, model railroading. Home: 111 View St Indiana PA 15701-1547 Office: Indiana U of Pa Dept Geography & Regional Pl Indiana PA 15705-0001

MILLER, W. KIEVIT, writer; b. Bklyn., Mar. 5, 1950; s. Walter Benedict Miller and Gladys Christina Marie Swadba; children: Cove Kievit, Brook Kievit. BA in Environ. Studies, Fla. Internat. U., Tamiami, 1984. Dist. coord. Broward Soil and Water Conservation Dist., Davie, Fla., 1985; tchr. Mus. of Discovery and Sci., Fort Lauderdale, Fla., 1984, 1993; head guide Seminole Tribe of Fla., Big Cypress Reservation, 1999; founder, CEO BIOKIND Tours, LLC, Venus, Fla., 2000—. Author: (book) BIOKIND Rhetoric for a New Paradigm, A Field Guide for the Future, 2000, BIOKIND Tracks, Traces of & Whispers for (and from) the Soul, 2003. Capt. USCG. Scholar, Audubon Soc., 1984, Art of Living Found., 1996. Office Phone: 863-531-0093. Business E-Mail: biokindtours@biokind.com.

MILLER, W. MARSHALL, II, insurance broker; b. Roanoke, Va., Feb. 3, 1953; s. Warren M. and Anne (Cooper) M. BA, Coll. William and Mary, 1975. CLU, ChFC. Spl. agt. Prudential Ins. Co., Newport News, Va., 1976—; owner and pres. Ins. Consultants of Va., Inc., Newport News, 1979—. Mem. Soc. Fin. Svc. Profls., Advanced Assn. Life Underwriters, Internat. Assn. Fin. Planners, Peninsula Estate Planning Coun., Peninsula Chartered Life Underwriters (v.p. 1982-83), Million Dollar Round Table. Lutheran. Avocations: golf, photography, travel, gardening, bridge. Office: Ins Consultants of Va Inc 825 Diligence Dr Ste 201 Newport News VA 23606-4272 E-mail: marshall@insurance-icv.com.

MILLER, WALKER DAVID, judge; m. Susanne Hauk; 3 children. LLB, U. Colo., 1963; M in Comparative Law, U. Chgo., 1965. Bar: Colo. 1963, U.S. Dist. Ct. 1965, U.S. Ct. Appeals 1971, U.S. Supreme Ct. 1970. Asst. prof. Sch. Law, U. Kans., Lawrence, 1966-69; ptnr. Miller & Ruyle, Greeley, Colo., 1969, Miller, Ruyle, Steinmark & Shade, Greeley, 1970-74; solo practice, Greeley, Colo., 1974-92; ptnr. Karowsky, Witwer, Miller and Oldenburg, Greeley, 1992-96; judge U.S. Dist. Ct. Colo., Denver, 1996—. Office: US Dist Ct Colo 901 19th St Rm A938 Denver CO 80294-1929

MILLER, WALTER JAMES, English and humanities educator, writer; b. McKee City, N.J., Jan. 16, 1918; s. Walter Theodore and Celestia Anna (Simmons) Miller; children: Naomi, Jason, Robin, Jared, Elizabeth. BA, CUNY, 1941; MA, Columbia U., 1952. Instr. English Poly. Inst. Brooklyn, N.Y., 1946-53, asst. prof., 1953-55; asst. prof. English and modern langs. Colo. State U., Ft. Collins, 1955-56; assoc. prof. English NYU, N.Y.C., 1958-66, prof. English, 1966-84, prof. emeritus, 1984—. Dir. Summer Writers Conf. Hofstra U., Hempstead, NY, 1972—79, NYU, NYC, 1983—85. Author: Engineers as Writers, 1953, Making an Angel: Poems, 1977, 1001 Ideas for English Papers, 1994, Love's Mainland: New and Selected Poems, 2001, Joseph in the Pit: A Verse Drama, 2002; author, translator: Annotated Jules Verne, 1995; editor, translator: Verne's 20,000 Leagues Under the Sea, 1993; contbg. editor Simon and Schuster, 1969-97. Recipient Spl. award, Engrs. Coun. Profl. Devel., 1966, Charles Angoff award, The Lit. Rev., 1983, Gt. Tchr. award, NYU Alumni Assn., 1980, Fisher Second Harvest award, CUNY Alumni Assn., 1997; fellow, Ruttenberg Found., 1999—2004. Office: NYU 50 W 4th St Rm 330 New York NY 10012-1165

MILLER, WALTER LUTHER, pediatrician, educator; b. Alexandria, Va., Feb. 21, 1944; s. Luther Samuel and Beryl (Rinderle) M. SB, MIT, 1965; MD, Duke U., 1970. Diplomate Am. Bd. Pediatrics. Intern, then resident Mass. Gen. Hosp., Boston, 1970-72; staff assoc. NIH, Bethesda, Md., 1972-74; sr. resident U. Calif., San Francisco, 1974-75, rsch. fellow, 1975-78, asst. prof. pediatrics, 1978-83, assoc. prof., 1983-87, prof., 1987—, dir. Child Health Rsch. Ctr., 1992—, faculty biomed. scis. grad. program, 1982—, faculty genetics grad. program, 1998—, assoc. prof. metabolic rsch. unit, 1983-87, dir. peidat. endocrinology tng. program, 1994—, chief divsn. endocrinology, 2000—. Editor DNA and Cell Biology Jour., 1983—; mem. editl. bds. numerous sci. jours.; contbr. articles to profl. jours., chpts. to books. Del. Dem. Nat. Conv., N.Y.C., 1976. Served with USPHS, 1972-74. Recipient Nat. Rsch. Svc. award NIH, 1975, Clin. Investigator award, 1978, Albion O Bernstein award N.Y. Med. Soc., 1993, Clin. Endocrinology Trust medal Brit. Endocrine Soc., 1993, Henning Andersen prize European Soc. Pediatric Endocrinology, 1993, Samuel Rosenthal Found. prize for excellence in acad. pediatrics, 1999. Fellow: AAAS, Molecular Medicine Soc.; mem.: Androgen Excess Soc. (founding mem., bd. dirs. 2002—), Am. Soc. Biochem. Molecular Biology, Lawson Wilkins Pediat. Endocrine Soc. (edn. com. 1992—96, coun. 1995—96, corp. adv. bd. 1998—2002), Am. Soc. Clin. Investigation, Am. Soc. Human Genetics, Endocrine Soc. (fin. com. 1999—2002, Edwin B. Astwood lecture award 1988), European Soc. for Paediatric Endocrinology (hon.), Japanese Soc. for Pediat. Endocrinology (hon.), We. Soc. Pediat. Rsch. (Ross Rsch. award 1982), Soc. Pediat. Rsch., Am. Pediat. Soc., Am. Acad. Pediats., Assn. Am. Physicians, Am. Soc. for Microbiology, Theta Delta Chi. Achievements include patents in field. Office: U Calif Med Ctr Dept Pediat 1466 4th Ave San Francisco CA 94143-0978

MILLER, WALTER NEAL, insurance company consultant; b. N.Y.C., Nov. 26, 1929; s. Morton and Kathryn (Gersten) M.; m. Nancy Louise Clapp, Sept. 11, 1954; children— Scott, Timothy, David, Kathryn Wallace, Amy Tully. BA, Swarthmore Coll., 1951. With N.Y. Life Ins. Co., N.Y.C., 1951-86; sr. v.p., actuary Prudential Ins. Co., Newark, 1986-93; sr. v.p., chief actuary Prudential Preferred Fin. Svcs., Liberty Corner, NJ, 1993-94; pvt. practice cons., 1994—. Author: (with others) Analysis of Actuarial Theory for Variable Life Insurance, 1969; contbr. articles to profl. jours. Mem. Soc. Actuaries (bd. dirs.), Am. Acad. Actuaries (bd. dirs., v.p.), Actuarial Stds. Bd. (chmn.), Estuary Coun. Srs. (pres. bd. dirs.). Home: 48 Eagle Ridge Dr Essex CT 06426-1370 E-mail: walterm746@aol.com.

MILLER, WALTER RICHARD, JR., banker; b. N.Y.C., Nov. 20, 1934; s. Walter Richard and Ann M. (Phelan) M.; m. Joan M. Groark; children: Kathryn A., Margaret E., Jennifer M., Walter Richard III. AB, Dartmouth Coll., 1955; MBA, Columbia U., 1957; PhD, NYU, 1965. Dir. mktg., v.p. Mellon Nat. Corp., Pitts., 1965-78; sr. v.p. First Atlanta Corp., 1979-81; exec. v.p. Norwest Corp., Mpls., 1981-86; pres., chief exec. officer First Constn. Fin. Corp., New Haven, 1987-91, also bd. dirs.; pres., CEO First Constn. Bank, New Haven, 1987-90; pres. Fin. Mktg. and Planning Co., Whitneyville, Conn., 1990—. Exec.-in-residence Quinnipiac Coll., 1990-91, prof. fin. and mktg., 1991-95; pres. CIRRUS Sys., Inc.; exec. dir. Wright Investors' Svc., Milford, Conn., 1995-2003; pres. One Am.Found., 2003—. Contbr. articles, chpts. to profl. pubs. Bd. dirs. St. Paul Chamber Orch., Minn. Pub. Radio, Sci. Mus. Minn., Quinnipiac Coll., Hamden, Conn., Quinnipiac Coun. Boy Scouts Am., The Mus. of AM. Theatre; chmn. bd. Orch. New England; pres. One America Found., 2003—. With USAF, 1958. Teaching fellow NYU, N.Y.C., 1960; Ford Found. fellow NYU, 1962 Mem. Interbank Card Assn. (internat. chmn., bd. dirs.), Am. Mktg. Assn. (contbg. editor), Bank Mktg. Assn. (bd. dirs., chmn. mktg. planning council, chmn. mktg. mgmt. council), Somerset Club, New Haven County Club, Quinnipiack Club, Lawn Club. Home and Office: 470 Whitney Ave Apt B1 New Haven CT 06511

MILLER, WARREN LLOYD, lawyer; b. Bklyn., July 18, 1944; s. Allan and Ella Miller; m. Jana Lee Morris, May 13, 1978; children: Lindsey Beth, Alan Gregory, William Brett. BA with high honor, Am. U., 1966; JD with honors, George Washington U., 1969. Bar: Va., 1969, D.C., 1969, U.S. Supreme Ct., 1981. Law clk. to Hon. Edward A. Beard Superior Ct. D.C., 1968-69; asst. U.S. atty. for D.C., 1969-74; ptnr. Stein, Miller & Brodsky, 1974-85; pres. Warren L. Miller, P.C., 1986—; of counsel Reed, Smith, Shaw & McClay, 1986-93. Lectr. Georgetown U. Law Sch., 1970-71, Am. U., 1971-72; mem. Jud. Conf. D.C. Cir., 1984—; pres. Asst. U.S. Attys. Assn. of D.C., 1983-84. Contbr. articles to profl. jours. Parliamentarian credentials and rules coms. Rep. Nat. Conv., 1984; mem. D.C. Law Revision Commn., 1987-91 (apptd. by Pres. Reagan), mem. U.S. Commn. for Preservation of Am.'s Heritage Abroad, 1992— (apptd. by Pres. Bush, reapptd. by Pres. Clinton 1996, 99), now chmn. (apptd. by Pres. Bush) 2001—; bd. dirs. Found. for Buchenwald and Mittelbau-Dora Memls., 1994—; spkr. ceremonies commemorating 50th anniversary of liberation of Buchenwald Concentration Camp, Buchenwald, Germany, 1995, Ceremony Dedicating Little Camp Meml., Buchenwald, Germany, 2002; spkr. U.S. Holocaust Meml. Mus., 1995, 2002; fundraiser for Rep. Nat. Com. and Pres. Bush, 1988-92; co-chmn. dinner for V.P. Bush, 1988; vice-chmn. Pres.'s Dinner, 1989; co-chmn. Pres.'s Club, Washington, D.C., 1990-92; chmn. fundraiser for U.S. Senator Christopher Bond, 1992, 97, 2003; chmn., fundraiser U.S. Senator John Warner, 1996; vice-chmn., fundraiser Senator Bob Dole, 1996; co-chmn., fundraiser Gov. George W. Bush Presdl. Exploratory Com., 1999, honoring Pres. George W. Bush, 2003; mem. host com., fundraiser for Gov. George W. Bush, 2000, U.S. Sen. John Warner, 2001, Gov. Jeb Bush, 2002, v.p. Dick Cheney, 2003; co-leader U.S. Del. to Internat. Conf., Warsaw, Poland, 2002 (apptd. by Sec. State Colin Powell). Recipient Comdr. Cross of the Order of Merit, Rep. Poland, Pres. Poland, 2003. Mem. Congl. Country Club (Bethesda, Md.), Phi Delta Phi, Omicron Delta Kappa, Pi Gamma Mu. Office: 2300 N St NW Washington DC 20037-1122

MILLER, WAYNE, actor, designer, producer, impresario; b. N.Y.C., Apr. 5, 1951; s. Charles E. and Agnes (Dunigan) M.; m. Donna D'Ermilio, Dec. 30, 1979. Pres. Carriage Trade, Inc., Howell, N.J., 1984-95; prin. Stage Door Theatrical, S.I., N.Y., 1991—. Scenic and lighting designer, N.Y.C., 1976—; dir. Snug Harbor Cultural Ctr., 1998—; pres. lighting designer Staten Island Shakespearean Theatre, 1996—; with Time Warner Cable, 2001—. Acting roles include (cable TV show) Walking the Dog, 1990, Cranial Crunch, 1997-2004, (TV show) Guiding Light, 1984, (classical play) Richard III, 1984, Macbeth, 1984, (mus. play) Anything Goes, 1985, Annie, 1986, La Cage Aux Folles, 1988, Showboat, 1988, Mame, 1989, Chicago, 1990, 42d St., 1990, Love Letters, 1993, Mr. Roberts, 1994, Mack and Mabel, 1994, (sage plays) All My Sons, 1995, Laughter on the 23d Floor, 1996, Sideman, 1999, Art, 2001; concert appearance with S.I. Symphony, 2002-03; scenic and lighting designer Oklahoma, 1984, On Borrowed Time, 1985, Carousel, 1986, Is There Life After High Sch., 1988, Chicago, 1995, The Miser, 1995, The Crucible, 1996, The Blue Angel, 1998, Prisoner of 2d Ave, 1999, Rumors, 2000, Misery, 2000, Dancing at Lughnasa, 2001, M Butterfly, 2001, Steel Magnolias, 2002, Wit, 2002, Annie, 2003, Sweeney Todd, 2003, Fifth of July, 2003, Night of the Iguana, 2004, also concerts and revs.; prodr. The Blue Angel, N.Y. premier, 1998. V.p. S.I. Civic Theatre, 1984-89; bd. dirs. S.I. Coun. on Arts, 1988. Mem. Snug Harbor Cultural Ctr., N.Y.C. Opera Guild. Address: Roundabout Theatre Co 208 Kissel Ave Staten Island NY 10310-1669

MILLER, WILBUR HOBART, management consultant; b. Boston, Feb. 15, 1915; s. Silas Reuben and Muriel Mae (Greene) Miller; m. Harriett I. Harmon, June 20, 1941; children: Nancy Iber Miller Harray, Warren Harmon, Donna Sewall Miller Davidge. BS, U. N.H., 1936, MS, 1938; PhD, Columbia U., 1941. Rsch. chemist Am. Cyanamid Co., Stamford, Conn., 1941—49, Washington tech. rep., 1949—53, dir. food industry devel., 1953—57, tech. dir. products for agr. Cyanamid Internat. N.Y.C., 1957—60; sr. scientist Dunlap & Assocs., Darien, Conn., 1960—63; sr. assoc. Dunlap & AssoCs., Darien, 1963—66; coord. new product devel. Celanese Corp., N.Y.C., 1966—67, mgr. comml. rsch., 1967—68, dir. corp. devel., 1969—84; bus. diversification cons., 1984—. Lectr. bus. and soc. Western Conn. State Coll., 1977—79; mem. pres.'s coun. U. N.H., 1982—; internat. fellow U. Bridgeport, 1985—88. Contbr. scientific papers to profl. jours.; patentee in field. Chmn. Stamford Forum World Affairs, 1954—87, hon. chmn., 1987—; mem. advb. bd. Ctr. Study Presidency, 1980—99; bd. dirs. Stamford mphony, Stamford Hist. Soc., 1988, v.p., 1991—92, pres., 1993—95, Coun. Continuing Edn., Stamford, 1963, bd. dirs., 1960—70, Stamford Sr. Ctr., 1997—, vice chmn., 2002—03, chmn., 2003—; elder United Presbyn. Ch., mem. nominating com., 1960—63; pres. Interfaith Coun. Stamford, 1973. Recipient Am. Design award, 1948, Outstanding Achievement award, Coll. Tech., U. N.H., 1971, Golden Rule award, J.C. Penney & Co., 1986; Univ. fellow, Columbia U., 1940—41. Fellow: AAAS, Am. Inst. Chemists (councillor N.Y. chpt. 1984—85); mem.: Am. Acad. Polit. and Social Scis., Soc. Internat. Devel., Inst. Food Tech., Société de Chimie Industrielle (v.p. fin. Am. sect. 1980—84, bd. dirs. 1984—), N.Y. Acad. Scis., Am. Chem. Soc. (news svc. adv. bd. 1948—53), Chemists Club (treas. N.Y.C. chpt. 1982—84), Sigma Xi, Phi Kappa Phi, Alpha Chi Sigma. Home: 122 Palmers Hill Rd #1111 Stamford CT 06902-2134

MILLER, WILBUR RANDOLPH, university educator and administrator; b. Elsberry, Mo., Nov. 12, 1932; s. Charles Clifton and Pauline Jean (Dryden) M. Student, SE Mo. U., 1951-53; BEd, U. Mo., 1954, MEd, 1955, EdD, 1960. Cert. secondary tchr., Mo. Tchr. indsl. arts Hazelwood Sch. Dist., St. Louis, 1955-56, U. Lab. Sch., Columbia, Mo., 1956-60; indsl. tchr. educator Purdue U., West Lafayette, Ind., 1960-63; asst. prof. U. Mo., Columbia, 1963-67, assoc. prof. and chmn. dept. coll. edn., 1967-76, prof. and assoc. dean coll. edn., 1976-86, dean coll. edn., 1986-91, prof., dean emeritus, 1992; cons. Rep. of Turkey, 1993, 94; assoc. v.p. for devel. Auburn U., 1996—. Chmn. adv. coun. Fed. Rsch. Ctr. in Vocat. Edn., Ohio State U., Columbus, 1981-84; internat. edn. cons. 1992—; edn. adv. bd. DeVry Inc., Oakwood Terrace, Ill., 1986—; mem. pvt. post-sec. tech. sch. accreditation commn. Accrediting Commn. Career Schs. and Colls. Tech., 1994-98. Author: Teaching Children Through Construction Activities, 1985, Instructors and Their Jobs, 1998, 2d edit., 2002, The Golf Primer, 1991, Handbook for College Teaching, 1997, 2d edit., 2003; editor: (series) Basic Industrial Arts, 1978; contbr. more than 40 articles to profl. jours. Pres., bd. dirs. Lenoir Inc., Columbia, 1977-84; mem. Woodhaven Sch. Bd., Columbia, 1982-83. With USNR, 1955-63. Recipient U. Mo. Faculty/Alumni award, 1985. Mem. Nat. Assn. Indsl. Tchr. Educators (pres., officer 1965-74), Am. Indsl. Arts Assn. (v.p. 1980), Mo. Vocat. Assn. (pres. 1974-75), Mo. Assn. Colls. for Tchr. Edn. (pres. 1987-90), Am. Vocat. Assn. (Outstanding Svc. award 1979), U. Mo. Faculty Club (officer 1977-82), Kiwanis. Mem. Christian Ch. (Disciples Of Christ). Avocations: golf, travel, home maintenance. Office: PO Box 2683 Auburn AL 36831-2683

MILLER, WILLIAM ALVIN, clergyman, author, lecturer; b. Pitts., Jan. 1, 1931; s. Christ William and Anna Ernestine (Wilhelm) M.; m. Marilynn Mae Miller, Aug. 8, 1953; children: Mark William, Eric Michael. BA, Capital U., 1953; MDiv, Luth. Theol. Sem., Columbus, Ohio, 1957; MST, Andover Newton Theol. Sch., Newton Centre, Mass., 1958, D of Ministry, 1974. Ordained to ministry Luth. Ch.; lic. marriage & family therapist, Minn.; cert. chaplain Assn. of Profl. Chaplains. Pastor St. James Luth. Ch., Balt., 1958—66; chaplain Fairview Hosp., Mpls., 1966—73, dir. dept. religion & health, 1973—87; instr. Fairview Sch. Nursing, Mpls., 1967—75, Luther Northwestern Theol. Sem., St. Paul, 1973—85; pres. Woodland Pub. Co., Wayzata, Minn., 1979—2000; dir. Woodland Pastoral Assocs., Mpls., 1987—96; assoc. pastor Ctrl. Luth. Ch., Mpls., 1989—94. Chair bd. dirs. Luth. Social Svcs. Md., Balt., 1963-65; adminstr. Dialogue 88, Mpls., 1987-88; marriaage & family therapist emeritus, Minn. Author: Why Do Christians Break Down?, 1973, Big Kids' Mother Goose, 1976, When Going to Pieces Holds You Together, 1976, You Count, You Really Do!, 1976, Mid Life, New Life, 1978, Conversations, 1980, Make Friends With Your Shadow, 1981, Prayers at Mid Point, 1983, The Joy of Feeling Good, 1986, Your Golden Shadow, 1989, 91, Meeting the Shadow, 1991; assoc. editor Jour. Pastoral Care, Decatur, Ga., 1984-88, editl. cons., 1988—; contbr. articles to profl. jours. Chaplain, Jr. C. of C., Randallstown, Md., 1962-64; bd. dirs. Am. Protestant Health Assn., Schaumburg, Ill., 1983-89; clin. mem. Am. Assn. Marriage & Family Therapy, 1989-96, Minn. Assn. Marriage & Family Therapy, 1989-96. Fellow Coll. Chaplains (pres. 1985-87), Assn. Mental Health Clergy (Anton T. Boisen award 1989); mem. Assn. Clin. Pastoral Edn. (supr. emeritus 2000—), Am. Assn. Marriage and Family Therapy, Minn. Assn. Marriage and Family Therapy. Avocations: cabinetmaking, publishing, construction. Home and Office: 2005 Xanthus Ln N Minneapolis MN 55447-2053

MILLER, WILLIAM CHARLES, theological librarian, educator; b. Mpls., Oct. 26, 1947; s. Robert Charles and Cleithra Mae (Johnson) M.; m. Brenda Kathleen Barnes, July 24, 1969; children: Amy Renee, Jared Charles. BA, Ind. Wesleyan U., 1968; MLS, Kent State U., 1974, PhD, 1983; postgrad., U. Kans., 1984; MA in Religious Studies, Ctrl. Bapt. Theol. Sem., 1988; MBA, MidAm. Nazarene U., Olathe, KS, 1997; STM, Nashotah House, 2001. Ordained to ministry Ch. of Nazarene, 1986. Libr. technician Kent State U., 1972-74; catalog libr. Mt. Vernon Nazarene Coll., Ohio, 1974-76, catalog and acquisitions libr., 1976-78; dir. libr. svcs., prof. theol. bibliography Nazarene Theol. Sem., Kansas City, Mo., 1978—, dean for adminstrn., 1996-98, 99—. Adj. rsch. assoc. U. Kans., 1984-85; adj. prof. MidAm. Nazarene U., Olathe, Kans., 1994-2000; bd. dirs. Small Libr. Computing Inc.; pres. Mo. Libr. Network Corp., St. Louis, Mo., 1998-2001. Author: Holiness Works: A Bibliography, 1986; editor TUG Newsletter, 1984-87, bd. dirs., 1985-88; editor Jour. Religious and Theol. Info., 1990-98. With U.S. Army, 1968-72. Mem. ALA, Am. Assn. Higher Edn., Assn. Study Higher Edn., Bibliog. Soc. Am., Bibliog. Soc. London, Kansas City Met. Libr. Network (coun. mem. 1987-89), Am. Theol. Libr. Assn. (bd. dirs. 1985-88), Kansas City Theol. Libr. Assn. (pres. 1985-89), Wesleyan Theol. Soc., Ch. Eng. Record Soc., Beta Phi Mu. Home: 18290 W 155th Ter Olathe KS 66062-6718 Office: Nazarene Theol Sem 1700 E Meyer Blvd Kansas City MO 64131-1246 Office Phone: 816-333-6254. E-mail: wcmiller@nts.edu.

MILLER, WILLIAM CHARLES, lawyer; b. Jacksonville, Fla., Aug. 6, 1937; s. Charles and Mary Elizabeth (Kiger) M.; m. Hadmut Gisela Larsen, June 10, 1961; children: Monica Lee, Charles Andreas. BA, Washington and Lee U., 1958, LLB, 1961; LLM, NYU, 1963; postgrad., Harvard U., 1978. Bar: Fla. 1961, Calif. 1984, Ind. 1987, U.S. Supreme Ct. 1968. Counsel to electrochem., elastomers and internat. depts. E.I. duPont de Nemours & Co., Wilmington, Del., 1963-66; counsel S. Am. ops. Bristol-Myers Co., N.Y.C., 1967-69; internat. counsel Xerox Corp., Stamford, Conn., 1969-79, assoc. gen. counsel, 1979-80; v.p., gen. counsel, sec. Max Factor & Co., Hollywood, Calif., 1981-85, Boehringer Mannheim Corp., Indpls., 1985-92; v.p., gen. counsel Collagen Corp., Palo Alto, Calif., 1992-95, Gen. Probe Inc., San Diego, 1995-96, Safeskin Corp., San Diego, 1996-98; exec. v.p. Lipomatrix Inc., Neuchatel, Switzerland, 1998-99; gen. counsel Turbostar Comm. Corp., 2000—02, exec. v.p., gen counsel, 2002—03; exec. v.p., dir., gen. counsel Aesthetic and Reconstructive Techs., Inc., 2002—. Bd. dirs. Southwestern Legal Found., 1975-85. Fulbright scholar, 1959-60; Ford Found. fellow, 1961-62; Hague Acad. fellow, 1963; German Govt. grantee, 1962-63; Kappa Sigma scholar, 1959. Mem. Internat. Bar Assn., ABA, Calif. Bar Assn., Fla. Bar Assn., Ind. Bar Assn., Masons, Elks, Phi Beta Kappa, Phi Delta Phi, Delta Theta Phi. Republican. Mem. Christian Ch. Home: 4521 Randag Dr Fort Myers FL 33903-4731

MILLER, WILLIAM CHARLES, architect, educator; b. San Francisco, May 11, 1945; s. Francis Leland and Ethel Lorene (Britt) M.; m. Beverly Jean McConnell, Dec. 22, 1968; children: Britt A., David A. BArch, U. Oreg., 1968; MArch, U. Ill., 1970. Registered architect, Ariz., Kans., Utah. Asst. prof. Coll. Architecture U. Ariz., Tucson, 1970—77; assoc. prof. dept. architecture Kans. State U., Manhattan, 1977-86, prof., 1986-92, head dept., 1990-92; prof. Coll. of Architecture and Planning U. Utah, Salt Lake City, 1992—, dean, 1992—2002; architect various firms. Guest lectr. in field; presenter numerous profl. socs. and orgns.; dir. west ctrl. region Assn. Collegiate Schs. Architecture, 1988-91, chair theme paper sessions ann. meeting, San Francisco, 1990, chair regional paper sessions ann. meeting, Washington, 1991, co-chair adminstrv. conf., Milw., 1995; bd. dirs. Nat. Archtl. Accrediting Bd., 1996-99; mem. Utah Architects Lic. Bd., 2000—; vis. prof. U. Ill., Urbana Champlain, Ill., 2003. Author: Alvar Aalto: An Annotated Bibliography, 1984; co-editor: The Architecture of the In-Between, 1990, Architecture: Back to Life, 1991; contbr. over 60 articles to profl. jours., chpts. to books. Bd. dirs. Assist, Inc., 1992-2002, Artspace, Inc., 1997-2002, Contemporary Arts Group, 1992-96, Salt Lake City Art Design Bd., 1995-2003. Recipient Disting. Prof. award Assn. Collegiate Schs. Architecture, 2004, Svc. awards Nat. Coun. Archtl. Registration Bds., Nat. Archtl. Accrediting Bd. Fellow AIA (pres-elect Flint Hills, treas. Utah, exec. com., treas., exec. com. Western Mountain region, elected coll. of fellows 1997); mem. Am.-Scandinavian Found., Soc. for Advancement Scandinavian Studies, Tau Sigma Delta. Office: U Utah Coll Architecture & Planning Salt Lake City UT 84112 Business E-Mail: miller@arch.utah.edu.

MILLER, WILLIAM FREDERICK, research company executive, educator, business consultant; b. Vincennes, Ind., Nov. 19, 1925; s. William and Elsie M. (Everts) M.; m. Patty J. Smith, June 19, 1949; 1 son, Rodney Wayne. Student, Vincennes U., 1946-47; BS, Purdue U., 1949, MS, 1951, PhD, 1956; DSc (hon.), 1972. Mem. staff Argonne Nat. Lab., 1955-64, assoc. physicist, 1956-59, dir. applied math. div., 1959-64; prof. computer sci. Stanford U., Palo Alto, Calif., 1965-97, Herbert Hoover prof. pub. and pvt. mgmt. emeritus, 1997—, assoc. provost for computing, 1968-70, v.p. for rsch., 1970-71, v.p., provost, 1971-78; mem. Stanford Assocs., 1972—; pres emeritus., CEO SRI Internat., Menlo Park, Calif., 1979-90; chmn. bd., CEO SRI Devel. Co., Menlo Park, David Sarnoff Rsch. Ctr., Inc., Princeton, NJ, 1987—90. Chmn. emeritus bd. dirs. Borland Software, Sentius Corp.; founder, chmn. Nanostellar, Inc.; professorial lectr. applied math. U. Chgo., 1962-64; vis. prof. math. Purdue U., 1962-63; vis. scholar Ctr. for Advanced Study in Behavioral Scis., 1976; mem. adv. coun. BHP Internat., 1990-97; computer sci. and engring bd. NAS, 1968-71; mem. Nat. Sci. Bd., 1982-88; corp. com. computers in edn. Brown UU., 1971-79; mem. policy bd. EDUCOM Planning Coun. on Computing in Edn., 1974-79, chmn., 1974-76; mem. ednl. adv. bd. Guggenheim Meml. Found., 1976-80; com. postdoctoral and doctoral rsch. staff NRC, 1977-80, computer sci. and telecom.; dir. Fund Am., 1977-91, Fireman's Fund Ins., 1977-91, Wells Fargo Bank and Co., 1996-97, Varian Assocs. Inc., 1973-96. Mem. editl. bd. Pattern Recognition Jour, 1968-72, Jour. Computational Physics, 1970-74. Served to 2d lt. F.A. AUS, 1943-46. Recipient Frederic B. Whitman award United Way Bay Area, 1982, Sarnoff Founders medal, 1997, David Packard Civic Entrepreneurship Team award, 1998, Robert K. Jaedicke Silver Apple award Stanford U. Bus. Sch. Alumni, 1998, The Dongbaeg medal Order of Civil Merit, The Rep. of Korea, 2000, The Okawa prize, The Okawa Found. for Info. and Telecoms., 2000, Most Mentor award Internat. Angel Investors, 2002; named to Silicon Valley Engring. Hall of Fame, 2001, Jr. Achievement Bus. Hall of Fame, 2002. Fellow IEEE (life), Am. Acad. Arts and Scis., AAAS; mem. Soc. Indsl. and Applied Math., Assn. Computing Machinery, Nat. Acad. Engring., Sigma Xi, Tau Beta Pi (Eminent Engr. 1989). Office: Stanford U Grad Sch Bus Stanford CA 94305

MILLER, WILLIAM GREEN, ambassador; b. N.Y.C., Aug. 15, 1931; m. Suzanne Lisle; 2 children. BA, MA, Oxford U., U.K.; postgrad., Harvard U. Tutor Winthrop House Harvard U., 1956-59; with Fgn. Svc., 1959; vice consul, polit. officer Isfahan, Iran, 1959-62; polit. officer Tehran, Iran, 1962-64; line officer, exec. secretariat Dept. of State, 1965-66; mem. Sr. Interdepartmental Group, 1966-67; spl. asst. fgn. affairs and def. Senator John Sherman Cooper, 1967-73; staff dir. Senate Select Com. Emergency Powers, 1973-75, Senate Select Com. to Study Govtl. Ops. with Respect to Intelligence Communities, 1975-76, Senate Select Com. Intelligence, 1976-81; assoc. dean, adj. prof. internat. politics Fletcher Sch. Law and Diplomacy, 1981-83, rsch. assoc., 1983-85; faculty assoc. Harvard Ctr. Middle Eastern Studies, 1983-86; pres. Am. Com. U.S.- Soviet Rels., 1986-92; U.S. amb. to Ukraine,

1993-98. Cons. D.H. Sawyer and Assocs., Ltd., N.Y.C., 1985; bd. dirs. Internat. Found., pres. 1986-92; pres. Com. Am.- Russian Rels., cons. Catherine T. MacArthur Found., 1992-93. Contbr. articles to profl. jours. Bd. mem. UN Assn., 2002—; co-chmn. bd. Myiv-Mohyla U. Found., 2002—; bd. dirs. The Andrei Sakharov Found., 1998—, Inst. Soc. Action and Renewal in Eurasia, 1998—; bd. mem. US - Ukraine Found., 2002—. Rsch. fellow Harvard Ctr. Sci. and Internat. Affairs, 1984-86, John F. Kennedy Sch. of Govt. fellow Harvard U., 1986. Fellow Rsch. Inst. of Politics; mem. Nat. Acad. Pub. Diplomacy, Nat. Acad. Pub. Adminstrn., Internat. Inst. Strategic Studies, Coun. Fgn. Rels., Children of the 21st Century, Middle East Inst., Soc. Iranian Studies, Search For Common Ground. Office: Woodrow Wilson Internat Ctr Scholars 1 Woodrow Wilson Plaza 1300 Pennsylvania Ave NW Washington DC 20004-3002 Office Phone: 202-691-4000. Business E-Mail: wmiller@igc.org.

MILLER, WILLIAM HARLOWE, JR., lawyer; b. Mineola, NY, Apr. 22, 1939; s. William Harlowe and Martha Owen (Clarke) M.; m. Jean McKenzie Piersol, Oct. 1, 1966; children: William Harlowe III, Thomas P. Grad., Phillips Exeter Acad., 1957; AB, Princeton U., 1961; JD, Syracuse U., 1966. Bar: N.Y. 1967, Conn. 1970. Assoc. Humes, Andrews, Botzow & Wagner, N.Y.C., 1966-71, ptnr., 1972-93, Walter, Conston, Alexander & Green, P.C., 1993-2000, Davidson, Dawson & Clark, LLP, N.Y.C., 2001—. Trustee Greens Farms Acad., Westport, Conn., 1983-94. Served to lt. USNR, 1961-63. Mem. ABA, Regional Bar Assn., Conn. Bar Assn., Norwalk Yacht Club (bd. dirs. 1972-91), NY Yacht Club. Home: 4 Valley Rd Wilson Point South Norwalk CT 06854 Office: Davidson Dawson & Clark LLP 330 Madison Ave New York NY 10017 also: 30 Center St Darien CT 06820-4529

MILLER, WILLIAM HUGHES, theoretical chemist, educator; b. Kosciusko, Miss., Mar. 16, 1941; s. Weldon Howard and Jewel Irene (Hughes) M.; m. Margaret Ann Westbrook, June 4, 1966; children: Alison Leslie, Emily Sinclaire. BS, Ga. Inst. Tech., 1963; AM, Harvard U., 1964, PhD, 1967. Jr. fellow Harvard U., 1967-69; NATO postdoctoral fellow Freiburg (Germany) U., 1967-68; asst. prof. chemistry U. Calif., Berkeley, 1969-72, assoc. prof., 1972-74, prof., 1974—, dept. chmn., 1989-93, chancellor's prof., 1998—, Kenneth S. Pitzer disting. prof., 1999—. Fellow Churchill Coll., Cambridge (Eng.) U., 1975-76; hon. prof. Shandong U., People's Republic of China, 1994. Alfred P. Sloan fellow, 1970-72; Camille and Henry Dreyfus fellow, 1973-78, Guggenheim fellow, 1975-76, Christensen fellow St. Catherine's Coll., Oxford, 1993; recipient Alexander von Humboldt-Stiftung U.S. Sr. Scientist award, 1981-82, Ernest Orlando Lawrence Meml. award, 1985, Hirschfelder prize in theoretical chemistry, U. Wis., 1996, Alumni Achievement award Ga. Inst. Tech., 1997, Spiers medal Faraday divsn. Royal Soc. Chemistry, London, 1998. Fellow AAAS, Am. Acad. Arts and Scis., Am. Phys. Soc. (Irving Langmuir award 1990); mem. NAS, Am. Chem. Soc. (Theoretical Chemistry award 1994, Ira Remsen award 1997, Peter Debye award 2003), Internat. Acad. Quantum Molecular Sci. (Ann. prize 1974). Office: U Calif Dept Chemistry Berkeley CA 94720-0001

MILLER, WILLIAM IRWIN, finance company executive; b. Columbus, Ind., Apr. 30, 1956; s. Joseph Irwin and Xenia Ruth (Simons) M.; m. Lynne Marie Maguire, Oct. 29, 1983; children: Katherine Maguire, Laura Marie, Emily Elizabeth. BA, Yale U., 1978; MBA, Stanford U., 1981. Sect. mgr. Cummins Engine Co., Inc., Charleston, S.C., 1978-79; assoc. Warburg Pincus Capital Corp., N.Y.C., 1981-83; pres. Irwin Mgmt. Co., Inc., Columbus, 1984-90, also bd. dirs.; chmn. Irwin Fin. Corp., Columbus, 1990—. Chmn. Irwin Mgmt. Co. and Tipton Lakes Co., Columbus, 1984—; bd. dirs. Cummins Inc., Irwin-Sweeney-Miller Found., Columbus, Tennant Co., Mpls., New Perspective Fund, L.A., New World Fund, L.A. Trustee The Taft Sch., Watertown, Conn., 1979--, Christian Theol. Sem., Indpls., 1988-94, Europacific Growth Fund, L.A., 1992—; bd. dirs. Cummins Found., Columbus, Ind., 1989—, Irwin Fin. Found., Columbus, 1991—, The Heritage Fund of Bartholomew County, Columbus, 1998—; mem. investment com. Yale U., New Haven, 1995-99, 2000—; mem. Ctrl. Ind. Corp. Partnership, Indpls., 1999—, Nat. Bldg. Mus., 2001—. Office: Irwin Fin Corp 500 Washington St PO Box 929 Columbus IN 47202-0929

MILLER, WILLIAM LEE, JR., minister; b. Mammoth Spring, Ark., Dec. 27, 1926; s. William L. and Janie Katherine (Murrell) M.; m. Marion Evelyn O'Neal, Mar. 23, 1947 (div. 1976); children: Georgia Katherine Miller Beach, William Lee III; m. Judith Ann Bell, Nov. 28, 1977 (dec. July 1997); m. Delores Bryan, Dec. 27, 1998. AB, Phillips U., 1950, LittD, 1968; postgrad., U. Ark., 1951-52, Tex. Christian U., 1958, U. Ky., 1961; BD, Lexington Theol. Sem., 1961, MDiv, 1997. Ordained to ministry Christian Ch. (Disciples of Christ), 1950. Pastor 1st Christian Ch., Rogers, Ark., 1952-59, Rogers Heights Christian Ch., Tulsa, 1961-62; v.p. Bd. Higher Edn., Indpls., 1962-68; pres. Bd. Higher Edn. Christian Ch. (Disciples of Christ), 1968-77; v.p. devel. Nat. City Christian Ch. Corp., Washington, 1977-82; upper Midwest regional min., pres. Christian Ch. (Disciples of Christ), Des Moines, 1982-93; pres. Miller Devel. Assoc. Dir. Christian Ch. Found., Indpls., 1968-77, 84-93; trustee Bethany Coll., W.Va., 1972-85, Culver Stockton Coll., 1970-77, 82-94, Tougaloo Coll., Jackson, Miss., 1970-76, Christian Theol. Sem., Indpls., 1987-94. Author: Vision with Passion, A Church history of the Christian Church (Disciples of Christ. Precinct committeeman Dem. Party, Indpls., 1968-72; mem. Reagan First Inaugural Religious Com.; bd. dris. St. Louis Christian Home, 1956-59; chmn. Coop. Coll. Registry, Washington, 1963-70; mem. Disciples of Christ Ch., Disciples Soc. for Faith & Reason; bd. dirs., exec. com. Christian Ch. D.C., N.C., 1995-98; pres. Friends of Dare County (N.C.) Librs., 1997-99; v.p. North Dare County Ministerial Assn., 1998-99. Mem. Disciples of Christ Hist. Soc., Coun. Christian Unity (exec. com. 1968-77), Nat. Evangelitic Assn. (bd. dirs. 1983-86), Am. Assn. Higher Edn., Masons, KT, NAACP, Sigma Chi, Am. Legion, Interfaith Alliance, Amnesty Internat., Sierra Club. Mem. Christian Ch. (Disciples Of Christ). Home and Office: Miller Devel Assocs 1710 W Long Blvd Raymore MO 64083-9116

MILLER, WILLIAM NAPIER CRIPPS, lawyer; b. Long Branch, N.J., June 7, 1930; adopted s. Julia (Erwin) M.; m. Carolyn Anderson, Jan. 19, 1951 (div. 1963); children: Bruce Douglass, Jennifer Erwin; m. Hannelore Steinbeck, Dec. 4, 1970 AA, Coll. Marin, 1949; student, U. Calif.-Berkeley, 1949-51, JD, 1955. Bar: N.Y., Calif. 1956, U.S. Supreme Ct. 1983. Assoc. Mudge, Stern, Baldwin & Todd, N.Y.C., 1955-58, Pillsbury, Madison & Sutro, San Francisco, 1959-65, ptnr., 1966—; staff NYU Law Sch., 1957-58; ct. adv. com. Calif. State Assembly Judiciary Com., 1979-80. Author: Long Pig, 2002. Bd. dirs. Laguna Honda Hosp., San Francisco, 1966—; bd. visitors U. Calif.-Hastings Law Sch. Served with USAF, 1951-52. Recipient Bur. Nat. Affairs award U. Calif.-Hastings, 1955; recipient Thurston Soc. award, 1953. Fellow Am. Coll. Trial Lawyers; mem. ABA, San Francisco Bar Assn., Order of Coif, St. Francis Yacht Club, Silverado Country Club. Home: 16 George Ln Sausalito CA 94965-1890 Office: Pillsbury Winthrop LLP PO Box 7880 San Francisco CA 94120-7880 Office Phone: 415-983-1464. E-mail: wmiller@pillsburywinthrop.com.

MILLER, WILLIAM RICHEY, JR., lawyer; b. Oklahoma City, Apr. 4, 1947; s. William Richey and Edna Rosalind (Nielsen) M.; m. Susan Hammond, Aug. 2, 1970; children: Brooke, Karen. BA, Pomona Coll., Claremont, Calif., 1969; MA, Claremont Grad. Sch., 1972; JD, Lewis and Clark Coll., 1975. Bar: Oreg. 1975, U.S. Dist. Ct. Oreg. 1976, U.S. Ct. Appeals (9th cir.) 1976. Staff atty. Oreg. Ct. Appeals, Salem, 1975-76; with firm Griffith, Bittner, Abbott & Roberts, Portland, Oreg., 1976-83; ptnr. Davis Wright Termaine, Portland, 1983—. Adj. prof. Lewis and Clark Law Sch., 1975-78. Bd. dirs. Portland Civic Theatre, 1988-91, Am. Lung Assn. Oreg., Portland, 1985-88, Oreg. Bus. Com. for the Arts, Portland, 1991-93. Mem. Oreg. State Bar (sect. chair 1990-91), Comml. Fin. Assn., Oreg. Bankers Assn., Lewis and Clark Alumni Assn. (bd. dirs. 1989-92). Presbyterian. Home: 843 Lakeshore Rd Lake Oswego OR 97034-3704 Office: Davis Wright Tremaine 1300 SW 5th Ave Ste 2300 Portland OR 97201-5682 Office Phone: 503-778-5304.

MILLER, WILMA HILDRUTH, education educator; b. Dixon, Ill., Mar. 8, 1936; d. William Alexander and Ruth Karin (Hanson) M. BS in Edn., No. Ill. U., DeKalb, 1958, MS in Edn., 1961; DEd, U. Ariz., 1967. Cert. reading specialist. Elem. tchr. Dist. 170, Dixon, Ill., 1958-63, Dist. 1, Tucson, Ariz., 1963-64; asst. prof. edn. Wis. State U., Whitewater, 1965-68; assoc. prof. edn. Ill. State U., Normal, 1968-72, prof., 1972-98, prof. emeritus, 1998—. Author: Diagnosing and Correcting Reading Difficulties in Children, 1988, Reading Comprehension, 1990, Complete Reading Disabilities Handbook, 1993, Alternative Assessment Techniques in Reading and Writing, 1995, Reading and Writing Remediation Kit, 1997, The Reading Teacher's Survival Kit, 2001, Reading Skills Problem Solver, 2002, Survival Reading Skills for Secondary School Students, 2003, 101 Ways for Developing Emergent Literacy, 2004, others; contbr. over 225 articles to profl. jours. Altar Guild, usher, greeter, communion asst. Our Saviour Luth. Ch., Normal, 1990—. Recipient Outstanding Contbn. to Edn. award No. Ill. U., 1998. Mem. Internat. Reading Assn. (parent and reading com. 1972-74, editl. adv. bd. 1995-98, Outstanding Dissertation award 1968), Mid-State Reading Coun. (editl. adv. bd. 1991-98), Alpha Upsilon Alpha (advisor Reading chpt. 1993-98), Pi Lambda Theta, Kappa Delta Pi, Phi Delta Kappa. Avocations: travel, writing, animals (particularly dogs), reading, antiques. Home: 302 N Coolidge St Normal IL 61761-2435 E-mail: whmille@ilstu.edu.

MILLER, YOLANDA, publisher, writer; b. Chicago Heights, Ill., Aug. 5, 1957; m. Andrew Miller, Apr. 2, 1983. BS cum laude, U. Wis., Stout, 1978; MS in Rehab. Counseling, U. Wis., Milw., 1984. Pub. Victory Publs., Racine, Wis., 1996—. Author: (poetry) Ode to Precious, Priceless and Irreplaceable African-American Men, 1996. Avocation: reading. Home: 2526 Delaware Ave Racine WI 53403-3432

MILLER, YVETTE, lawyer, publishing executive; BA, Adelphi U.; JD, St. John's U., N.Y. Litig. assoc. Weil, Gotshal & Manges; gen. atty. pub. sect. CBS; v.p., dep. gen. counsel Hachette Filipacchi; with G + J USA, N.Y.C., 1993—2000, v.p., gen. counsel, 2000—. Office: G + J USA Pub Legal Dept 375 Lexington Ave New York NY 10017-5514

MILLER, ZELL BRYAN, senator, former governor; b. Young Harris, Ga., Feb. 24, 1932; s. Stephen Grady and Birdie (Bryan) M.; m. Shirley Carver, Jan. 14, 1954; children: Murphy Carver, Matthew Stephen. Student, Young Harris Coll.; AB, MA, U. Ga. Dir. Ga. Bd. Probation, 1965-66; dep. dir. Ga. Dept. Corrections, 1967-68; exec. sec. to gov. Ga., 1968-71; mem. State Bd. Pardons and Paroles, Atlanta, 1973-75; lt. gov. State of Ga., 1975-90, gov., 1990-98; prof. polit. sci. and history U. Ga., 1999; U.S. senator from Ga., 2000—. Prof. Young Harris Coll., 1959-64, Emory U., Young Harris Coll., U. Ga.; bd. dirs. various corps., including Overseas Pvt. Investment Corp. (OPIC), Ga. Power, Gray Comms., Ezgov.com, Post Properties, Kollmann USA; keynote speaker Democratic Nat. Convention, NYC, 1992, Republican Nat. Convention, NYC, 2004. Author: The Mountains Within Me, 1985, Great Georgians, 1983, They Heard Georgia Singing, Corps Values, 1996, 2d edit., 1997, A National Party No More: The Conscience of a Conservative Democrat, 2003. Mem. Ga. Senate, 1960-64; mayor Young Harris, 1959; exec. dir. Democratic Com. Ga., 1971-72; pres. Coun. State Govts., 1991; vice chmn. So. Gov.'s Assn., 1991; bd. dirs. Towns County Hosp. Authority. Served with USMC, 1953-56. Mem. Ga. Sch. Food Services Assn. (life), Ga. Peace Officers Assn. (life), Gridiron Soc. U. Ga., Blue Key, Lions Club. Democrat. Methodist. Address: US Senate 257 Dirksen Senate Office Bldg Washington DC 20510

MILLER, ZOYA DICKINS (MRS. HILLIARD EVE MILLER JR.), civic worker; b. Washington, July 15, 1923; d. Randolph and Zoya Pavlovna (Klementinovska) Dickins; m. Hilliard Eve Miller, Jr., Dec. 6, 1943; children: Jeffrey Arnot, Hilliard Eve III. Grad., Stuart Sch. Costume Design, Washington, 1942; student, Cochran Galleries of Fine Arts, 1942, Sophie Newcomb Coll., 1944, New Eng. Conservatory Music, 1946, Colo. Coll., 1965; grad., Internat. Sch. Reading, 1969; student, Cochran Galleries of Fine Arts, 1942. Lic. pvt. pilot. Instr. Stuart Summer Sch. Costume Design, Washington, 1942; fashion coord. Julius Garfinckel, Washington, 1942-43; fashion coord., cons. Mademoiselle mag., 1942-44; star TV show Cowbelle Kitchen, 1957-58, Flair for Living, 1958-59; model mags. and comml. films, also nat. comml. recs., 1956-80; dir. rsch. devel. Webb-Waring Inst. for Cancer, Aging and Antioxidant Rsch., Denver, 1973—. Contbr. articles, lectrs. on health care sys. and fund raising. Mem. exec. com., bd. dirs. El Paso County chpt. Am. Lung Assn. Colo., 1965—84, bd. dirs., 1965—87, chmn. radio and TV coun., 1963—70, mem. med. affairs com., 1965—70, pres., 1965—66, procurer found. funds, 1965—70; developer nat. radio ednl. prodns. for internat. use Am. Lung Assn., 1963—70, coord. statewide pulmonary screening programs, other states, 1965—72; chmn. benefit fund raising El Paso County Cancer Soc., 1963; co-founder, coord. Colorado Springs Debutante Ball, 1967—; coord. Nat. Gov.'s Comprehensive Health Planning Coun., 1967—74, chmn., 1971—72, Colo. Chronic Care Com., 1969—73, chmn. fund raising, 1970—72, chmn. spl. com. conl. studies on nat. health bills, 1971—73; mem. Colo.-Wyo. Regional Med. Program Adv. Coun., 1969—73, Colo. Med. Found. Consumers Adv. Coun., 1972—78; mem. decorative arts com. Colorado Springs Fine Arts Ctr., 1972—75; founder, state coord. Nov. Noel Pediat. Benefit Am. Lung Assn., 1973—87; founder, chmn. bd. dirs. Newborn Hope, Inc., 1987—; mem. adv. bd. Wagon Wheel Girl Scouts, 1991—94; mem. cmty. adv. coun. Beth-El Nursing Sch., 1998—; bd. dirs. Episcopal Columbarium Assn., 2001, The Family Attachment Ctr., Inc. Zoya Dickins Miller Vol. of Yr. award established Am. Lung Assn. of Colo., 1979; recipient James J. Waring award Colo. Conf. on Respiratory Disease Workers, 1963, Nat. Pub. Rels. award Am. Lung Assn., 1979, Gold Double Bar Cross award, 1980, 83, Jefferson award Am. Inst. Pub. Svc., 1991, Thousand Points of Light award The White House, 1992, Recognition award So. Colo. Women's C. of C., 1994, Silver Spur Cmty. award Pikes Peak Range Riders, 1994, Silver Bell award Assistance League Colorado Springs, 1996, Svc. to Mankind award Centennial Sertoma Club, 1997, Help Can't Wait award Pikes Peak chpt. ARC, 1997, Cmty. Weaver award The Independent News, 1997, Apgar award Colo. March of Dimes, 1998; named Humanitarian of Yr., Am. Lung Assn. of Colo., 1987, One of 50 Most Influential Women in Colorado Springs by Gazette Telegraph Newspaper, 1990, One of 5 Leading Ladies Colo. Homes & Lifestyles Mag., 1991. Mem.: Nat. Soc. Fund Raising Execs., Denver Round Table for Planned Giving, Colo. Assn. Fund Raisers, Nat. Soc. Colonial Dames, The Family Attachment Ctr., Nat. Cowbell Assn. (El Paso county pres. 1954, TV chmn., chmn. nat. Father of Yr. contest Colo. 1956—57), Broadmoor Garden Club, Garden of the Gods Club, Cheyenne Mountain Country Club. Home: 74 W Cheyenne Mountain Blvd Colorado Springs CO 80906-4336

MILLERICK, JAYNE MARCUCCI, Republican party chairman; b. Boston, Mass, 1974; m. Shawn Mellerick. BA Polit. Sci., Univ. of New Hampshire, Durham, 1995. Dep. press sec. US Sen. Robert Smith; asst. sec. NH Rep. State Com. Exec. Bd., NH; intern for former Gov. Steve Merrill office State House, NH, 1995, scheduling dir.; dep. campaign mgr. Jay Lucas Rep. nominee for gov., NH, 1998; exec. dir. NH Rep. State Com., 1999—2000; ind. polit. cons. Rep. Nat. Com., 2002; chmn. New Hampshire Rep. State Com., 2003—; pres. Marcucci Consulting, 2003—. The first-ever recipient of the Ronald Reagan Young Rep. Award will be Jayne Marcucci. Office: 134 No Main St Concord NH 03301

MILLER-LANE, BARBARA See LANE, BARBARA

MILLER-LERMAN, LINDSEY, state supreme court justice; b. L.A., July 30, 1947; BA, Wellesley Coll., 1968; JD, Columbia U., 1973; LHD (hon.), Coll. of St. Mary, Omaha, 1993. Bar: N.Y. 1974, U.S. Dist. Ct. (so. dist.) N.Y. 1974, U.S. Ct. Appeals (2d cir.) 1974, Nebr. 1976, U.S. Dist. Ct. (ea. dist.) N.Y. 1975, U.S. Dist. Ct. Nebr. 1976, U.S. Ct. Appeals (8th cir.) 1979, U.S. Supreme Ct. 1982, U.S. Ct. Appeals (6th cir.) 1984, U.S. Ct. Appeals (10th cir.) 1987. Law clk. U.S. Dist. Ct., N.Y.C., 1973-75; from assoc. to ptnr. Kutak Rock, Omaha, 1975-92; judge Nebr. Ct. Appeals, Lincoln, 1992-98, chief judge, 1996-98; justice Nebr. Supreme Ct., 1998—. Contbr. articles to profl. jours. Bd. dirs. Tuesday Musical, Omaha, 1985—. Office: Nebr Supreme Ct State Capitol Rm 2222 Lincoln NE 68509

MILLER UDELL, BRONWYN, lawyer; b. Danbury, Conn., Aug. 7, 1972; BA, Barnard Coll., Columbia U., 1994; JD, U. Miami, 1997. Bar: (Fla.) 1997. Asst. state atty. State of Fla., 1997—; adj. prof. Fla. Internat. U., Miami, 2001—02. Mem. Witness Justice Adv. Bd. Mem. Cmtys. in Schs. Miami Mentoring Program, Coral Gables Sr. H.S. Parent Tchr. Assn.; co-chair Expert Corps. Vol. Mem.: League of Prosecutors, Fla. Assn. Women Lawyers, Fla. Pros. Attys. Assn., Federalist Soc. Lawyer's Divsn., Elephant Forum, Phi Delta Phi. Office: Office of the State Atty 1350 NW 12th Ave Miami FL 33136

MILLER-YOUNG, CORRIENE CALHOUN, nursing educator; b. N.Y.C., Oct. 22, 1959; d. Timothy E. Calhoun and Suzetta Franklin; children: Christopher, Jeremy, James, Aja. BSN, Rutgers U., Newark, 1982; postgrad., Memphis State U., 1992—. RN, N.J., Tenn.; cert. wound ostomy nurse; cert. wound and ostomy specialist. Staff nurse Muhlenberg Hosp., Plainfield, N.J., 1981-86, Kimberly Nurses, Union, N.J., 1986-89; health coord. Neighborhood House, Plainfield, 1989-91; staff nurse/nurse clinician Bapt. Meml. Hosp., Memphis, 1991-2000; LPN instr. Tenn. Tech. Ctr., Memphis, 1994—. Named Nurse of Month, Kimberly Nurses, 1987. Mem. ANA, Kappa Delta Pi.

MILLET, JOHN BRADFORD, retired surgeon; b. Buffalo, Aug. 8, 1916; s. John Alfred Parsons and Alice Jeannette (Murrell) M.; m. Constance Hopkins Dallas, Nov. 1974; children: John Bradford Jr., David Francis, Polly Watson. BS, Harvard U., 1938, MD, 1942. Diplomate Am. Bd. Surgery. Surg. intern Mass. Gen. Hosp., Boston, 1942-43, surg. resident, 1946-49; chief thoracic surgery, partner Slocum Dickson Clinic, Utica, N.Y., 1949-55; pvt. practice medicine specializing in surgery Utica, 1955—; sr. attending surgeon St. Luke's Meml. Hosp. Ctr., Utica, 1955-81, chief dept. surgery, 1969-70; sr. attending surgeon St. Elizabeth's Hosp., 1955—, Faxton Hosp., 1979-86; ret., 1985; asst. to pres. Mohawk Metal Products Inc., 1989-91; pres. Miltel divsn. Millwheel, Inc., 1992-94. Former cons. surgeon Herkimer Meml. Hosp., Rose Hosp., Rome, N.Y., Marcy (N.Y.) State Hosp.; former med. adv. to Vis. Nurse Assn.; former dir. Health Systems Agy. Cen. N.Y., Med. Securities Fund, 1964-65, Med. Funds Mgmt. Corp., 1964-65, Digimetrics Inc., M.V. Hockey Inc., Millwheel Inc., IEX Inc., JDC Resources, Inc., B.F.I. Telecommunications Co. Inc., Utica Disposables Inc., Input Specialists Inc., LJB Ventures Inc.; pres. White Birch Home of Utica, Inc.; adminstrv. asst. U.S. Bur. Census, 2000, H&R Block, 2001. Former med. adv. com. Planned Parenthood of Mohawk Valley; pres. Midstate Com. on Area Wide Health Planning, 1966-72; co-chmn. citizens com. on devel. of med. sch. in Utica area; co-developer Brookside Racquet Club, Wedgewood Apartments, Treadway Resort, Meadows. Maj. M.C. AUS, 1943-46. Fellow ACS, Am. Coll. Chest Physicians; mem. AMA, Am. Thoracic Soc., Coll. Angiology, Central N.Y. Surg. Soc., Mohawk Valley Surg. Soc. (pres., 1968-69), Central N.Y. Acad. Medicine, Oneida County (chmn. edn. com., 1968-69), N.Y. State Soc. Surgeons (bd. dirs. 1970-85), N.Y. State Med. Soc. (com. for homeless), Pan-Am. Med. Assn., Pan Pacific Surg. Assn., Utica Med. Club (pres. 1960-61), Med. Soc. N.Y. State (com. on homeless), Night Stick Club (chief 1965-66), Harvard Club of Mohawk Valley (pres. 1951-66), Harvard Coll. Alumni Club (Fund area chmn.), Ft. Schuyler Club, Sadaquada Golf Club, Adirondack League Club, Ideal Flying Club, Rotary, Masons, Shriners (potentate 1981-82). Republican. Episcopalian. Home: Acacia Village # 218 2160 Bleecker St Utica NY 13501-1734 E-mail: bmillet111@aol.com.

MILLET, JOHN PORATH, lawyer; b. Detroit, Feb. 3, 1943; s. John Pettigrew and Doris Frieda (Porath) M.; m. Cecelia Fay McCallister, Apr. 14, 1973; children: Karen Anne, John Christopher. BBA, N. Tex. State U., 1966; JD, So. Meth. U., 1969. Bar: Tex. 1969, U.S. Dist. Ct. (no. dist.) Tex. 1971. Fellowship prof. bus. law U. North Tex., 1969-70; examining atty. Fidelity Title Co., Dallas, 1970-72; atty., plant mgr., 1973-75; atty., plant mgr. Chgo. Title Co., Dallas, 1975-76; sr. v.p. USLIFE Title Co., San Antonio, 1976-83; v.p., chief title officer Dallas & Tex. Title Companies, Dallas, 1984-85; exec. v.p., Dallas Title Co., 1985-87, v.p. ops. Comml. Title Co./Lawyers Title of San Antonio/LandAm. Lawyers Title of San Antonio, 1987—; exec. v.p. Am. Title Co. Dallas, 1987-90. Instr. law Eastfield Coll., Dallas, 1975-76; instr. Tex. Land Title Sch. Mem. Tex Bar Assn., Early Ford V-8 Club. Republican. Methodist. Home: 13310 Serenity Ln San Antonio TX 78232-4883 Office: Landamerica Lawyers Title 12400 Network Blvd Ste 100 San Antonio TX 78249 E-mail: jmillet@landam.com.

MILLETT, KATE (KATHERINE MURRAY MILLETT), political activist, sculptor, artist, writer; b. St. Paul, Sept. 14, 1934; m. Fumio Yoshimura, 1965. BA magna cum laude, U. Minn., 1956; postgrad. with 1st class honors, St. Hilda's Coll. Oxford, Eng., 1956-58; PhD with distinction, Columbia U., 1970. Instr. English U. N.C. at Greensboro, 1958; file clk. N.Y.C.; kindergarten tchr., 1960-61; sculptor, Tokyo, 1961-63; tchr. Barnard Coll., 1964-70; tchr. English Bryn Mawr (Pa.) Coll., 1970. Disting. vis. prof. Sacramento State Coll., 1972—73; adj. prof. NYU, N.Y.C.; founder Women's Art Colony Farm, Poughkeepsie, NY; rep. as non-govtl. orgn. on behalf of human rights UN. Author: Sexual Politics, 1970, The Prostitution Papers, 1973, Flying, 1974, Sita, 1977, The Basement, 1979, Going to Iran, 1982, The Loony Bin Trip, 1990, The Politics of Cruelty, 1994, A.D., 1995, Mother Millett, 2001; co-prodr., co-dir. film Three Lives, 1970; one-woman shows Minami Gallery, Tokyo, Judson Gallery, N.Y.C., 1967, Noho Gallery, N.Y.C., 1976, 79, 80, 82, 84, 86, 93, 99, 2001, Women's Bldg., L.A., 1977; drawings Andre Wanters Gallery, Berlin, 1980, Courtland Jessup Gallery, Provincetown, Mass., 1991, 92, 93, 94, 95, 98, 99, Retrospective Exhbn., U. Md., 1997, Hunter Coll., 1998, Northampton Ctr. for the Arts, 1998, John Jay Coll., N.Y.C., 1998, Nohs Gallery, 2002. Mem. Congress of Racial Equality; chmn. edn. com. NOW, 1966; active supporter gay and women's liberation groups, also mental patients liberation and political prisoners; UN rep. for polit. prisoners. Mem. Phi Beta Kappa. Office: 20 Old Overlook Rd Poughkeepsie NY 12603-6220

MILLETT, STEPHEN MALCOLM, futurist, consultant, historian; b. N.Y.C., Feb. 22, 1947; s. John David and Catherine (Letsinger) M.; m. Sherry Richards, Sept. 2, 1989; children: Jennifer Jane, Ann E. AB, Miami U., Oxford, Ohio, 1969; MA, Ohio State U., 1970, PhD, 1972. Rschr. Battelle, Columbus, Ohio, 1979—. Mgr. tech. forecasts incl. Strategic Technologies 2005 and 2020 and Energy Innovations 2010. Author: Manager's Guide to Technology Forecasting, 1991, Scottish Settlers of America, 1996; pub. and editor U.S. Scots, 1992-97. Mem. at large Ohio Bd. Edn., 2003. Capt. USAF, 1973—79. Mem. World Futures Soc., Assn. of Profl. Futurists (founding mem.), Phi Delta Theta. Avocations: scottish history and culture, antiques. Home: 3673 Tillbury Ave Columbus OH 43220-5068 Office: Battelle 505 King Ave Columbus OH 43201-2693 E-mail: milletts@battelle.org.

MILLGATE, JANE, language professional; b. Leeds, Eng., June 8, 1937; d. Maurice and Marie Barr; m. Michael Millgate, Feb. 27, 1960. BA with honors, Leeds U., Eng., 1959, MA, 1963; PhD, U. Kent, Eng., 1970. Instr. U. Toronto, Ont., Can., 1964-65, lectr., 1965-70, asst. prof., 1970-72, assoc. prof., 1972-77, prof. English, 1977-97, prof. emeritus, 1997—, vice-dean arts and scis., 1983-87. Mem. bd. regents Victoria U., Toronto, 1981-86. Author: Macaulay, 1973, Walter Scott, 1984, 2d edit., 1987, Scott's Last Edition: A Study in Publishing History, 1987; editor: Editing 19th Century Fiction, 1978; contbr. articles to profl. jours. Doctoral fellow Can. Coun., 1968-70; rsch. fellow Can. Coun., 1972, 74-75, Social Scis. and Humanities Rsch. Coun. Can., 1980-81, 85-87, 88-90, 91-2001, Connaught Rsch. fellow, 1995-96; recipient Rose Mary Crawshay prize Brit. Acad., 1988. Fellow Royal Soc. Can., Royal Soc. Edinburgh; mem. Victorian Studies Assn. (pres. 1978-80), Assn. Can. Univ. Tchrs. English (pres. 1980-82), Can. Fedn. for Humanities (exec. 1981-83, 95-96), Assn. Scottish Lit. Studies, Soc. for History of Authorship, Reading, and Pub., Bibliog. Soc., Edinburgh Sir Walter Scott Club (pres. 2002-03). Home: 1 Balmoral Ave Apt 809 Toronto ON Canada M4V 3B9

MILLGATE, MICHAEL (MICHAEL HENRY MILLGATE), retired English educator; b. Southampton, Eng., July 19, 1929; arrived in Can., 1964; s. Stanley and Marjorie Louisa Millgate; m. Jane Barr, Feb. 27, 1960. BA, Cambridge U., 1952, MA, 1956; postgrad., U. Mich., Ann Arbor, 1956-57; PhD, U. Leeds, 1960. Tutor Workers' Ednl. Assn., Eng., 1953-56; lectr. English lit. U. Leeds, 1958-64; prof., chmn. dept. English York U., Ont., Can., 1964-67; prof. English U. Toronto, 67-94, univ. prof., 87-94, univ. prof. emeritus, 1994—. Carpenter lectr. Ohio Wesleyan U., 1978; vis. scholar Meiji U., 1985. Author: William Faulkner, 1961, American Social Fiction, 1964, The Achievement of William Faulkner, 1966, Thomas Hardy: His Career as a

Novelist, 1971, Thomas Hardy: A Biography, 1982, Testamentary Acts: Browning, Tennyson, James, Hardy, 1992, Faulkner's Place, 1997, Thomas Hardy: A Biography Revisited, 2004; editor: Tennyson: Selected Poems, 1963, Thomas Hardy: The Life and Work of Thomas Hardy, 1985, William Faulkner Manuscripts, 20 (4 vols.), 21 (2 vols.), 22 (4 vols.), 23 (2 vols.), 1986, New Essays on Light in August, 1987, Thomas Hardy: Selected Letters, 1990, Letters of Emma and Florence Hardy, 1996, Thomas Hardy's Public Voice, 2001; co-editor: Transatlantic Dialogue, 1966, Lion in the Garden, 1968, The Collected Letters of Thomas Hardy, Vol. I, 1978, Vol. II, 1980, Vol. III, 1982, Vol. IV, 1984, Vol. V, 1985, Vol. VI, 1987, Vol. VII, 1988, Thomas Hardy's Studies, Specimens, Etc. Notebook, 1994. Mem. ednl. adv. bd. John Guggenheim Meml. Found., 1994—. Can. Coun. leave fellow, 1968-69, S.W. Brooks fellow U. Queensland, 1971; Killam sr. rsch. scholar, 1974-75; John Simon Guggenheim Meml. fellow, 1977-78, Connaught sr. fellow, 1979-80; Social Sci. and Humanities Rsch. Coun. Can. leave fellow, 1981-82, grantee, 1977—; Can. Coun. grantee, 1973-77; Killam rsch. fellow, 1986-88. Fellow Royal Soc. Lit., Royal Soc. Can. (Pierre Chauveau medal 1999); mem. MLA (adv. com. Ctr. for Edit. Am. Authors 1971-74, com. on scholarly edits. 1985-89), Victorian Studies Assn. Ont. (pres. 1970-72), Thomas Hardy Soc. (v.p. 1973—), Tennyson Soc. Home: 1 Balmoral Ave Apt 809 Toronto ON Canada M4V 3B9 E-mail: michael.millgate@utoronto.ca.

MILLHAUSER, STEVEN, writer; b. N.Y.C., Aug. 3, 1943; BA, Columbia Coll., 1965; postgrad., Brown U., 1968-71. Vis. assoc. prof. English Williams Coll., 1986—88; assoc. prof. Skidmore Coll., Saratoga Springs, NY, 1988—92, prof. English, 1992—. Author: Edwin Mullhouse: The Life and Death of an American Writer, 1972, Portrait of a Romatic, 1977, In the Penny Arcade, 1985, From the Realm of Morpheus, 1986, The Barnum Museum, 1991, Little Kingdoms, 1993, Martin Dressler: The Tale of an American Dreamer, 1996, The Knife Thrower and Other Short Stories, 1998, Enchanted Night, 1999; contbr. short stories to periodicals. Recipient Pulitzer Prize for fiction, 1997. Office: Skidmore Coll Dept English 307 Palamountain Bldg Saratoga Springs NY 12866

MILLHISER, THOMAS MCNALLY, lawyer; b. Richmond, Va., Mar. 30, 1949; s. Ross Randolph and Eleanor Katherine (McGue) M.; m. Rochelle Diane DeCovny, May 19, 1971; children: Ian R., Neil McG., James McN. BS, Georgetown U., 1971; JD summa cum laude, Washington and Lee U., 1981. Bar: Va. 1981, U.S. Tax Ct. 1984, U.S. Ct. Appeals (4th cir.) 1984, U.S. Supreme Ct. 2003. Data processing mktg. rep. IBM Corp., Arlington, Va., 1971-73; v.p. Hill-n-Dale Meat Co., Downingtown, Pa., 1973-78; ptnr. Hunton & Williams, Richmond, Va., 1981—. Note and comment editor Washington and Lee U. Law Rev., 1981; contbr. articles to profl. jours. Bd. dirs. ARC, Greater Richmond chpt., 1986-92, chmn., 1991-92, Sch. of Performing Arts in Richmond Cmty., 1986-92, Washington and Lee U. La. Coun., 1990-99, pres., 1994-95, Riverside Sch., 1995—, v.p. 1997—; bd. dirs. Family and Children's Svcs., 1995-2001; trustee The Hill Sch., 2001—, Valentine Mus., Richmond History Ctr., 1999—. Mem. Va. State Bar, Am. Coll. Trust and Estate Counsel, Richmond Estate Planning Coun., Commonwealth Club, Country Club Va., The Hill Sch. Alumni Assn. (pres. 1997-2001), Order of Coif. Avocations: tennis, bridge, swimming, automobiles, wine. Home: 8703 Berwickshire Dr Richmond VA 23229-7832 Office: Hunton & Williams Riverfront Plz East Twr/951 East Byrd St Richmond VA 23219 Office Phone: 804-788-8732. Business E-Mail: tmillhiser@hunton.com.

MILLIAN, KENNETH YOUNG, public policy consultant; b. Washington, Sept. 29, 1927; s. John Curry and Myrtle (Young) M.; m. Alva Randolph Clarke, Sept. 10, 1949; children: J. Randolph, Kenneth Y. Jr., Kathleen M. Gilbert, Elizabeth M. Allen. BA, U. Md., 1951; MA in Internat. Rels., George Washington U., 1969; Diploma, Nat. War Coll., Washington, 1969; MS in Bus., Columbia U., 1980. Officer U.S. Fgn. Svc., 1951-76; corp. exec. W.R. Grace & Co., N.Y.C, 1976-93, corp. v.p., dir. govt. rels. Washington, 1982-88, corp. v.p., dir. environ. policy N.Y.C., Fla., 1988-93; ret., 1993; pres. Millian Assocs. LLC, Washington, 1993-2000; chmn. Millian Byers Assocs. LLC, 2000—. Pres. Found. for Pres. Pvt. Sector Survey on Cost Control (Grace Commn.), 1986-92. Bd. govs. Wesley Theol. Sem., Washington, 1988—, chmn., 1996-2000, chmn. investment com., 2003—; bd. govs. Nat. Dem. Club, Washington, 1998-02. Avocations: sailing, golf. Office: Millian Byers Assocs LLC 1090 Vermont Ave NW Ste 300 Washington DC 20005-4966 Office Phone: 202-842-5000. E-mail: kym@milbya.com.

MILLICAN, KIRK, architect; b. Ft. Worth, Oct. 4, 1951; s. Harold F. and Georgia N. (Williams) Millican; m. Marian McKeever, Oct. 25, 1986; 1 child, Carter. BA, Washington U., 1973, MArch, 1976. Designer Growald Architects, Ft. Worth, 1977-78; architect S.I. Morris Assocs., Houston, 1978-79; sr. v.p., prin. project designer, mgr., dir. transp. Hellmuth, Obata & Kassabaum, Dallas, 1979—. Prin. works include Cedars Sta., 1996 (Honor award Tex. Soc. Archs., 1996), Tarrant County Jail, Dallas Area Rapid Transit (Dallas Planning award, 1996, Nat. Honor award for Design, 2000), Houston Metro Light Rail (Houston AIA Design award, 2004), Art on Go Exhbn., Mus. Fine Arts, Houston, 2001, Ft. Worth Conv. Ctr. expansion (Best Real Estate Deal, 2003), exhibitions include Mus. Fine Arts, Houston, 2001, pub. art commn., City of Ft. Worth, 2002—. Founder, treas. Urban Strategies, Ft. Worth, 1991—; bd. dirs. Arts Coun. Ft. Worth, 1994—2001, James L. West Spl. Care Ctr., 1999—2004, mem. exec. com., 2004; founder, bd. dirs. Contemporary Art Ctr., Ft. Worth, 1995—99, pres., 1999; mem. urban design com. Downtown Ft. Worth, 1992—2004; mem. urban design com., vice chair City of Ft. Worth Pub. Art Commn., 2002—. Recipient Streams and Valleys, Inc. award, 1993, Leadership Arts award, Dallas Bus. Com. Arts, 1993. Mem.: AIA (exec. com. 1991—94, nat. chmn. interiors com. 1994, spkr. 1995—2002), Tex. Soc. Archs. (state chmn. interiors com. 1986—91, spkr. 2000, 2001, 2004, Honor award 1997, Dallas Planning award 1998), Colonial Country Club. Methodist. Avocations: running, skiing.

MILLICHAP, JOSEPH GORDON, neurologist, educator; b. Wellington, Eng., Dec. 18, 1918; came to U.S., 1956, naturalized, 1965; s. Joseph P. and Alice (Flello) M.; m. Mary Irene Fortey, Feb. 25, 1946 (dec. Oct. 1969); children: Martin Gordon, Paul Anthony; m. Nancy Melanie Kluczynski, Nov. 7, 1970 (dec. Apr. 1995); children: Gordon Thomas, John Joseph. M.B. with honors in Surgery, St. Bartholomew's Med. Coll., U. London, Eng., 1946, MD in Internal Medicine, 1951, diploma child health, 1948. Diplomate: Am. Bd. Pediatrics, Am. Bd. Neurology and Child Neurology, Am. Bd. Electroencephalography. Intern, resident St. Bartholomew's Hosp., 1946-49, Hosp. Sick Children, London, 1951-53, Mass. Gen. Hosp., Boston, 1958-60; pediatric neurologist NIH, 1955-56; USPHS fellow neurology Mass. Gen. Hosp., Boston, 1958-60; cons. pediatric neurology Mayo Clinic, 1960-63; pediatric neurologist Children's Meml. Hosp., Northwestern Med. Center, Chgo., 1963—; prof. neurology and pediatrics Northwestern U. Med. Sch., 1963—. Cons. surgeon gen. USPHS; mem. med. adv. bds. Ill. Epilepsy League, Muscular Dystrophy Found., Cerebral Palsy Found., 1963—; vis. prof. Gt. Ormond St. Hosp., U. London, 1986-87. Author: Febrile Convulsions, 1967, Pediatric Neurology, 1967, Learning Disabilities, 1974, The Hyperactive Child with MBD, 1975, Nutrition, Diet and Behavior, 1985, Dyslexia, 1986, Progress in Pediatric Neurology, 1991, Vol. II, 1994, Vol. III, 1997, Environmental Poisons in Our Food, 1993, A Guide to Drinking Water, Hazards and Health Risks, 1995, Attention Deficit Hyperactivity and Learning Disorders, 1998, (with G.T. Millichap) The School in a Garden, 2000; editor Jour. Pediatric Neurology Briefs; contbr. articles to profl. jours., chpts. to books. Chmn. research com. med. adv. bd. Epilepsy Found., 1965— . Served with RAF, 1949-51. Named New Citizen of Year in Met. Chgo., 1965; recipient Americanism Medal D.A.R., 1972, Brennemann award Chgo. Pediat. Soc., 1998; USPHS research grantee, 1957 Fellow Royal Coll. Physicians; mem. Am. Neurol. Assn., Am. Pediatric Soc., Am. Soc. Pediatric Research, Am. Acad. Neurology, Am. Soc. Pharmacology and Exptl. Therapeautics, Soc. Exptl. Biology and Medicine, Am. Bd. Psychiatry and Neurology (asst. examiner 1961—), A.M.A. Episcopalian. Home: PO Box 11391 Chicago IL 60611-0391 Office: Children's Meml Hosp Box 51 2300 N Childrens Plz Chicago IL 60614-3394

MILLIGAN, ARTHUR ACHILLE, retired banker; b. Oxnard, Calif., Oct. 29, 1917; s. John Leslie and Julia (Levy) M.; m. Jeanne Welch, Dec. 12, 1942; children: Michael S., Marshall C. BA, Stanford U., 1938. Pres., CEO Bank of A. Levy, Oxnard, Calif., 1955-82, chmn. bd. dirs., 1982-87, chmn. exec. com., 1988-95; dir. Oxnard Frozen Foods Corps., 1958-90; chmn. Real Estate Investment Trust of Calif., Santa Monica, 1968-87, ret. Lt. USN, 1942-45. Mem. Ind. Bankers So. Calif. (pres. 1958), Western Ind. Bankers (pres. 1961), Calif. Bankers Assn. (pres. 1964), Am. Bankers Assn. (pres. 1978), Valley Club (Montecito, bd. dirs. 1969-72, 85-87, 88—, pres. 1990-92), Elks, Rotary (pres. 1949—). Republican.

MILLIGAN, CYNTHIA HARDIN, university dean, lawyer; BA, U. Kans., 1967; JD, George Washington U., 1970. Bar: D.C. 1970, Nebr. 1977. Assoc. Arent, Fox, Kintnor, Plotkin & Kahn, Washington, 1970-77; ptnr. Rembolt, Ludtke, Milligan & Berger, Lincoln, Nebr., 1977-87; dir. Nebr. Dept. Banking and Fin., Lincoln, 1987-91; pres. CMA, Lincoln, 1991-98; dean U. Nebr. Coll. Bus. Adminstrn., Lincoln, 1998—. Bd. dirs. Wells Fargo & Co., San Francisco, Gallup Orgn., Princeton, N.J., Calvert Funds, Bethesda, Md. Trustee W.K. Kellogg Found., Battle Creek, Mich. Fellow Nebr. Bar Found.; mem. Nebr. Bar Assn. Office: U Nebr Coll Bus Adminstrn PO Box 880405 Lincoln NE 68588-0405

MILLIGAN, EDWARD C. bank executive; Chmn., pres., CEO First Sterling Bank, Marietta, Ga. Mem. Ga. Bankers' Assn. Office: PO Box 2141 Marietta GA 30061-2141

MILLIGAN, GLENN WESLEY, business educator; b. Enid, Okla., June 11, 1949; s. Donald Lee and Wanda Lee Milligan. BA, U. So. Calif., 1971; MA, Calif. State U., 1974; PhD, Ohio State U., 1978. Cert. quality engr. Prof., chair Fisher Coll. of Bus., Ohio State U., Columbus, 1978—. Dept. chair Fisher Coll. of Bus., Columbus, 1996—, undergrad. programs chair, 1994-96. Contbr. articles to profl. jours. With U.S. Army, 1971-78. Mem. Classification of N.Am. (bus. mgr. 1987-90), Am. Soc. for Quality, Am. Psychol. Assn. Democrat. Avocations: music, travel. Office: Fisher Coll of Bus Ohio State U Columbus OH 43210

MILLIGAN, JOHN DRANE, historian, educator; b. N.Y.C., Oct. 11, 1924; s. Carl Glover and Hazel Gray (Drane) M.; m. Joyce Mary Jervis, Nov. 16, 1946; children: Jacqueline M., Paula J., Mary M., Elizabeth Y. BA, U. Mich., 1952, MA, 1953, PhD, 1961. Tchg. asst. U. Mich., 1951-52, tchg. fellow, 1954-56; from asst. prof. to prof. history SUNY, Buffalo, 1962-2000, dir. grad. programs in history, 1963-68, 94-95, dir. undergrad. programs in history, 1979-86, acting dept. chmn., summers, 1977, 78-80, 88, prof. emeritus, 2000. Vis. prof. McMaster U., Hamilton, Ont., Can., summer 1964, 69-70 Author: Gunboats Down the Mississippi, 1965, From the Fresh-Water Navy, 1861-1864, 1970; also chpts. in books, articles in jours., encys. Mem. Ann Arbor chpt. NAACP, exec. bd., 1956-61; mem. ACLU, exec. bd., 1959-61; mem. campaign coms. for various candidates for local and nat. office, 1960-76; mem. Buffalo NAACP, Buffalo Housing Opportunities Made Equal, Citizens Council on Human Relations, Physicians for Social Responsibility, Common Cause, Amnesty Internat.; faculty chmn. United Fund dr., 1977; active Foster Parents Plan, 1955-70; adoptive parent Internat. Social Services; founder charitable trust for minority coll. scholarships. Served with USAAF, 1943-46, USAFR, 1946-56. James B. Angell scholar U. Mich.; grantee Research Found. SUNY; grantee U.S. Naval Inst.; Citation of Civil War Round Table; Moncado Award of Am. Mil. Inst. Mem.: Soc. Civil War Historians, Afro-Am. Hist. Soc., Buffalo and Erie County Hist. Soc., So. Hist. Assn., Assn. Am. Historians, Am. Hist. Assn., SUNY Buffalo Founders' Soc., Buffalo Coun. for Responsibility in Fgn. Policy, SUNY Buffalo Pres.'s Assocs., Civil War Round Table, Silver Wings Assn., Cambria Flying Soc., Niagara Soaring Club, Aircraft Owners and Pilots Assn., Soaring Soc. Am., Exptl. Aircraft Assn., Phi Alpha Theta, Phi Kappa Phi, Tau Sigma Delta. Home: 21 Allenhurst Rd Buffalo NY 14214-1201 *If an individual cannot influence for the better the course of humankind, one can sometimes influence for the better the life of another individual.*

MILLIGAN, SISTER MARY, theology educator, religious consultant; b. Los Angeles, Jan. 23, 1935; d. Bernard Joseph and Carolyn (Krebs) M. BA, Marymount Coll., 1956; Dr. de l'Univ., U. Paris, 1959; MA in Theology, St. Mary's Coll., Notre Dame, Ind., 1966; STD, Gregorian U., 1975; D. honoris causa, Marymount U., 1988. Tchr. Cours Marymount, Neuilly, France, 1956-59; asst. prof. Marymount Coll., Los Angeles, 1959-67; gen. councillor Religious of Sacred Heart of Mary, Rome, 1969-75, gen. superior, 1980-85; asst. prof. Loyola Marymount U., Los Angeles, 1977-78, provost, 1986-90, prof., 1990—96, dean liberal arts, 1992-97, provincial superior, 1997—2003; prof. St. John's Sem., 2003—. Pres. bd. dirs. St. John's Sem., Camarillo, Calif., 1986-89; mem. exec. com. Internat. Union Superiors Gen., Rome, 1983-85; mem. planning bd. spiritual renewal program Loyola Marymount U., Los Angeles, 1976-78. Author: That They May Have Life, 1975; compiler analytical index Ways of Peace, 1986; contbr. articles to profl. jours. Vis. scholar Grad. Theol. Union, Berkeley, 1986. Mem. Calif. Women in Higher Edn., Coll. Theology Soc., Cath. Biblical Assn. Democrat. Roman Catholic. E-mail: mmilligan@sjs-sc.org.

MILLIGAN, MICHAEL LEE, dentist; b. Kenton, Ohio, Sept. 5, 1952; s. Robert L. and Lena R. (Chiesa) M.; m. Karen S. Nice, Sept. 20, 1975; children: Kristen, Patrick, Lyndsey, Marisa. BS, U. Houston, 1975; DMD, So. Ill. U., 1978. Gen. practice dentistry, Bloomington, Ill., 1978—. Co-developer Eastland Profl. Bldg., Bloomington, 1987-88. Co-founder World Golf Tour, 1997; founder Nat. Competitive Golf Tour, 2001. Ill. Men's Golf Champion, 1974, Ill. Men's Match Play Golf Champion, 1977, Chgo. Dist. Golf. Champion, 1973, 74, 77, Butler Nat. Amateur Golf Champion, 1994. Mem. ADA, Ill. Dental Soc., McLean County Dental Soc. (pres. 1987-88). Lodges: KC. Home: 208 Grandview Dr Normal IL 61761-3135 Office: 1404 Eastland Dr Ste 101 Bloomington IL 61701-7904 E-mail: pharmike1@aol.com.

MILLIGAN, ROBERT FRANK, state agency administrator; b. Teaneck, N.J., Dec. 27, 1932; m. June; 4 children. BS in Engring., U.S. Naval Acad., 1956; MBA, U. Rochester, 1969; postgrad., U. Md. Commd. USMC, advanced through grades to lt. gen.; comdr. pre-positioning MAGTF; comdr. U.S. Forces in Caribbean; comdg. gen. Fleet Marine Forces, Pacific; ret., 1991; comptr. State of Fla., Tallahassee, 1995—. Mem. Fla. Cabinet. Republican. Office: Office of Comptr 101 E Gaines St Tallahassee FL 32399-0350

MILLIGAN, ROBERT H. state legislator, air traffic controller; b. Augusta, Maine, Aug. 31, 1927; m. Barbara E. Milligan; 2 children. BS, Md. U., 1946; postgrad., Okla. Lawton U., 1971. Ret. air traffic controller; mem. N.H. Ho. of Reps. Chmn. aviation group, mem., pub. protection com., vet. affairs com., transp. com., rules com., N.H. Ho. of Reps., 1993—; mem. exec. commn. Hills County. Mem. Wasserman (N.H.) Park Com., 1991—, Budget Com., 1991-92; bd. dirs. Merrimac (N.H.) Parks and Recreation, 1972; pres. Olom Ch. Coun. Mem. VFW (chmn. scholar com. 1992—, judge advocate #8641), Am. Legion, Elks (inner guard 1954), quarterback Club (charter mem.). Address: 42 Patten Rd Merrimack NH 03054-3064

MILLIGAN, STEVE, retail executive; BA in Acctg., The Ohio State U. CPA AICPA. Sr. mgr. Price Waterhouse; corp. asst. controller Dell Inc.; sr. v.p. Western Digital Corp., Lake Forest, Calif., 2002—, CFO, 2002—. Recipient Elijah Watt Sells award, 1985. Office: Western Digital Corp 20511 Lake Forest Dr Lake Forest CA 92630-7741*

MILLIGAN, TERENCE GILBERT, music educator; b. Austin, Tex., Apr. 21, 1945; s. Gilbert Woodrow Milligan and Selma Irma Nauert (Milligan); life ptnr. James William Schumacher, June 16, 1987; m. Susan Brantley Brantley, May 29, 1969 (div. July 14, 1986); children: Sean Michael, Julie Kathleen. MusB in Edn., West Tex. State U., 1968, MA in Music, 1971; D of Musical Arts, U. Tex., 1978. Dir. bands Canyon Jr. H.S., Tex., 1968—69; dir. bands and orchestras Bonham Jr. H.S., Amarillo, 1969—71; asst. dir. bands and orchestras Permian H.S., Odessa, 1971—75; grad. tchg. asst. U. Tex., Austin, 1975—78; dir. bands NW Mo. State U., Maryville, 1978—79; prof. music U. Cin., Coll.-Conservatory Music, 1979—. Singer, soloist May Festival Chorus, Cin., 1979—84, Vocal Arts Ensemble, 1981—94, VocalPoint!, 1992—, Cin. Men's Chorus, 1992—. Contbr. articles to profl. jours. Mem. AIDS Volunteers of Cin., Cin., 1987; past pres. Cin. Men's Chorus, 1994—98; dir. Music Bowl - Ohio, 1979—91. With U.S. Army, 1968—69. Mem.: Music Educators Nat. Converence, Coll. Band Directors Nat. Assn., Phi Delta Theta (life; past chpt. pres. 1966—67), Kappa Kappa Psi (life; chpt. sponsor 1979—93), Phi Mu Alpha Sinfonia (life; chpt. advisor 1992). Democrat-Npl. Episcopal. Avocations: french culture and cuisine, travel in france, italy, quebec (canada). Home: 3536 Handman Ave Cincinnati OH 45226 Office: College-Conservatory of Music University of Cincinnati Cincinnati OH 45221-0003 Personal E-mail: tmilligan@fuse.net. Business E-Mail: milligtg@uc.edu.

MILLIGAN, VICTOR, consulting engineer; b. Belfast, No. Ireland, Nov. 11, 1929; arrived in Can., 1956; s. Albert and Margaret (Walker) M.; m. Mary Ann Pelikan, July 20, 1955 (dec. 1988); children: Jeffrey, Michael; m. Audrey Morrow, Oct. 9, 1990 (dec. Oct 2003). BS, Queen's U., No. Ireland, 1951, MS, 1952, DSc (hon.), 1993; D Engring. (hon.), Waterloo U., Ont., Can., 1990. Registered profl. engr. Ont., Alta., Nfld. Asst. engr. James Williamson & Ptnrs., Glasgow, Scotland, 1952-54; rsch. fellow Purdue U., Lafayette, Ind., 1954-55; tech. officer Imperial Chem. Industries Ltd., Cheshire, Eng., 1955-56; from dist. to asst. chief engr. Geocon, Ltd., Toronto, Ont., Can., 1956-60; prin. Golder Assocs., Toronto, 1960-74, pres., CEO, chmn., 1974-84, sr. prin., chmn., cons., 1984-94. Mem. faculty engring. sci. adv. com. U. Western Ont., 1973-76; adj. prof. dept. geol. engring. U. Toronto, 1980-83; pres. Consulting Engrs. Ont., 1982-83; chmn. assoc. com. on geotechnical rsch. NRC, 1984-89. Co-author: Stability in Open Pit Mining, 1971, Geotechnical Practice in Open Pit Mining, 1972; founding editor Can. Geotechnical Jour., 1963-68; contbr. over 50 sci. papers. King George VI Meml. Rsch. fellow 1954-55; recipient Engring. Excellence medal Assn. Profl. Engrs. Ont., 1988, Beaubien award Assn. Consulting Engrs. Canada Outstanding Excellence, 1997; fellow Can. Acad. Engring., 1994. Fellow ASCE, Geol. Soc. Can., Engring. Inst. Can. (Julian C. Smith medal 1991), Royal Acad. Engring.; mem. Can. Geotech. Soc. (R.F. Legget award 1973), Internat. Soc. Soil Mechanics and Geotech. Engring.

MILLIKAN, CLARK HAROLD, physician; b. Freeport, Ill., Mar. 2, 1915; s. William Clarance and Louise (Chamberlain) M.; m. Gayle Margaret Gross, May 2, 1942 (div. Apr. 1966); children: Terri, Clark William, Jeffry Brent; m. Janet T. Holmes, July 21, 1966 (div. Dec. 1987); m. Nancy Futrell, Dec. 28, 1987. Student, Parsons (Kans.) Jr. Coll., 1935; MD, U. Kans., 1939. Diplomate Am. Bd. Psychiatry and Neurology. Intern St. Luke's Hosp., Clev., 1939-40, asst. resident medicine, 1940-41; from resident neurology to asst. prof. neurology State U. Iowa, Iowa City, 1941-49; staff Mayo Clinic, Rochester, Minn., 1949—, cons. neurology, 1958—; dir. Mayo Center for Clin. Rsch. in Cerebrovascular Disease; prof. neurology Mayo Sch. Medicine; physician-in-chief pro tem Cleve. Clinic, 1970; prof. neurology U. Utah Sch. Medicine, Salt Lake City, 1976-87, U. Miami (Fla.) Sch. Medicine, 1987-88; scholar in residence, dept. neurology Henry Ford Hosp., Detroit, 1988-92; prof. neurology Sch. of Medicine Creighton U., Omaha, 1992-94; clin. prof. neurology Med. Coll. Ohio, Toledo, 1994-97; dir. acad. affairs Intermountain Stroke Rsch. Found., Salt Lake City, 1997—. Asst. chmn., editor trans. 2d Princeton Conf. Cerebrovascular Disease, 1957, chmn. confs., 1961, 64; chmn. com. classification and nomenclature cerebrovascular disease USPHS, 1955-69; mem. council Nat. Inst. Neurologic Diseases and Blindness, NIH, USPHS, 1961-65, div. regional med. program, 1965-68; A.O.A. lectr. Baylor U., Waco, Tex., 1952; James Mawer Pearson Meml. lectr., Vancouver, B.C., Can., 1958; Conner Meml. lectr. Am. Heart Assn., 1961; Peter T. Bohan lectr. U. Kans., 1965, 73 Editor: Jour. Stroke, 1970-76, assoc. editor, 1976—. Recipient Outstanding Alumnus award U. Kans., 1973 Fellow ACP, Am. Acad. Neurology (founding chmn. sect. on stroke and vascular neurology 1994), Royal Soc. Medicine; mem. AMA, AAUP, AAAS, Assn. Rsch. Nervous and Mental Disease (pres. 1961), Am. Neurol. Assn. (1st v.p. 1969-70, pres. 1973-74), Minn. Med. Assn., Four County Med. Soc. South Minn., Cen. Neuropsychiat. Assn., N.Y. Acad. Sci., Am. Heart Assn. (chmn. coun. cerebrovascular disease 1967-68, Gold Heart award 1976, Spl. Merit award 1981), Nat. Stroke Assn. (pres. 1986, editor Jour. Stroke and Cerebrovascular Disease 1990—), Sigma Xi. Office Phone: 801-263-0611. E-mail: clarkmillikan@yahoo.com.

MILLIKAN, JAMES ROLENS, cleaning service executive, musician, composer, fitness consultant; b. Beaumont, Tex., Jan. 15, 1950; s. George Lee and Gertrude Louise (Mann) M.; m. Dorothy Jane Albright, Apr. 22, 1989. BFA, U. Houston, 1968; MFA, Juilliard Sch., 1971. Mgr., ptnr. Edward, Bankers & Co., Houston, 1971-73; prop. gen. Max M. Kaplan Properties, San Antonio, 1973-75; gen. bldg. mgr. Property Mgmt. Systems, Atlanta, 1975-79; dir. real estate Sun Life Group Am., Atlanta, 1979-81; prin. The Millikan Cos., Atlanta, 1981-85, J.R. & Co., Atlanta, 1985-87; sr. v.p., gen. mgr. east coast Nat. Cleaning Contractors, Inc., Atlanta, 1987-93; prin., pres. Master Bldg. Cleaners Inc., Atlanta, 1993—; owner Atlanta Kicksport. Owner ATlanta Kicksport; cons., Sun Life Group Am., 1982-84, McFaddin Ventures, Houston, 1983-84. Composer: Crystal Blue Persuasion (gold record 1969), Crimson & Clover (gold record 1969), Mony Mony (gold record 1969), I Love You More Today than Yesterday (gold record 1970), 1900 Yesterday (gold record 1971), others; instrumentalist for orchs. of Duke Ellington, Count Basie, Buddy Rich, Woody Herman and Glenn Miller, 1965-68; drummer, arranger, conductor for recording artist Petula Clark, 1968-71, leader J.R. and Co., Jazz Ensemble. Founder, pres., St. Luke's Econ. Devel. Corp., Atlanta, 1979, bd. dirs.; bd. dirs. St. Jude's House, Atlanta, 1984, Am. Suicide Found., chmn. Southeastern Divsn. Nat. Bd. Am. Found. for Suicide Prevention; mem. Home Bldg. with Habitat for Humanity. With U.S. Army, 1970-76. Mem. Bldg. Owners and Mgrs. Atlanta, Am. Mktg. Assn., Am. Suicide Found. (bd. dirs.), Bldg. Svc. Contractors Assn. Internat. Democrat. Episcopalian. Avocations: music, golf, skiing, white water rafting, running, kick boxing. Home and Office: Master Bldg Cleaners Inc 2722 Vinings Oak Dr SE Atlanta GA 30080

MILLIKAN, LARRY EDWARD, dermatologist; b. Sterling, Ill., May 12, 1936; s. Daniel Franklin and Harriet Adeline (Parmenter) M.; m. Jeanine Dorothy Johnson, Aug. 27, 1960; children: Marshall, Rebecca. BA, Monmouth Coll., 1958; MD, U. Mo., 1962. Intern Great Lakes Naval Hosp., Ill., 1962-63; housestaff in tng. U. Mich., Ann Arbor, 1967-69, chief resident, 1969-70; asst. prof. dermatology U. Mo., Columbia, 1970-74, assoc. prof., 1974-81; chmn. dept. dermatology Tulane U., New Orleans, 1981—. Cons. physician Charity Hosp., New Orleans, Tulane U. Hosp., New Orleans, Riley Hosp., Anderson Hosp., Rush Hosp., all Meridian, Miss.; mem. bd. trustees Sulzberger Inst. for Dermatological Edn., 1995-99; chmn. cont. med. edn. com. La. State Med. Soc., 1994-97. Assoc. editor Internat. Jour. Dermatology, 1980-99, Clinics in Dermatology, 1999—; mem. editl. bd. Current Concepts in Skin Disorders, Am. Jour. Med. Scis.; mem. editl. bd. Clinics in Dermatology, 1985—, assoc. editor, 1999—; contbr. articles to med. jours. Bd. dirs. Women's Dermatol. Assn., 1994-99. With USN, 1960-67. Recipient Andres Bello awrd Govt. of Venezuela, 1989, citation of merit Sch. Medicine, U. Mo., 1993, Faculty Alumnus award U. Mo., 1997; named Disting. Alumnus, Monmouth Coll., 1990; Nat. Cancer Inst. grantee, 1976-84. Fellow ACP; mem. AAAS, AMA, Am. Acad. Dermatology (bd. dirs. 1986-90), Am. Dermatol. Assn., Am. Dermatol. Soc. for Allergy and Immunology (pres., bd. dirs.), Soc. for Investigative Dermatology (past pres. South sect.), So. Med. Assn. (vice chmn. dermatology sect. 1984, chmn. 1994), Coll. Physicians Phila., Assn. Profs. Dermatology (bd. dirs. 1984-86), Orleans Parish Med. Soc., La. Med. Soc., Pan Am. Med. Assn., Internat. Soc. Dermatology (dep. sec. gen. 1989—), Mo. Allergy Assn. (past pres.), Am. Coll. Cryosurgery, Assn. Acad. Dermatol. Surgeons, Internat. Soc. Dermatol. Surgery, Internat. Acad. Cosmetic Dermatology (sec. gen. 1996-), Dermatol. Found. Leaders Soc. (state chmn. 1993-97). Office: Tulane Univ Sch Medicine Dept of Dermatology 1430 Tulane Ave TB36 New Orleans LA 70112-2699

MILLIKAN, WILLIAM, labor historian; b. Iowa City, Iowa, July 22, 1947; s. Clark and Gayle Millikan; life ptnr. Emily Gherity; children: Lenore Millibergity, DeeDee Tillitt, George Bergin, Jackson, Daniel Bergin, Lea Olsen. BA in History, U. of Minn., 1985. Author: (scholarly article) Minnesota History (Solon J. Buck award, 1986, 1989, 1994), (mag. article) Union

Advocate (2d award Best Instl. Profile Internat. Labor Comm. Assn., 1998), (nonfiction history book) A Union Against Unions: The Minneapolis Citizens Alliance and Its Fight Against Organized Labor, 1903-1947, 2001. Mem.: Ind. Scholar's Forum. Achievements include research in Revealed bus. origins of the Taft Hartley Act; Detailed complex bus. control of soc. that enables suppression of labor unions and radical polit. groups; Cooperative corruption and the founders of Minnesota. Avocations: gardening, backpacking. Personal E-mail: wmmillikanga@usfamily.net.

MILLIKEN, DOUGLAS GORDON, financial consultant, municipal official; b. Denver, June 13, 1957; s. J. Gordon and Marie (Machell) M. M in Acctg. and Fin. Mgmt., U. Denver, 1980. CPA, 1980. Ind. fin. cons., Centennial, Colo., 1990—. Mem. fin., acctg., intergovtl. rels. com. Nat. League Cities, 2002—; elected. treas. City of Centennial, 2001. Bd. mem., Colo. Legal Initiatives Project, Denver, 1993-96. Mem. Colo. Soc. CPAs, Rocky Mountain Wrestling Club (founding mem. 1994). Avocation: amateur wrestling. Home: 5315 S Nepal Way Centennial CO 80015-2143 Office: City of Centennial Ste 200 12503 E Euclid Dr Centennial CO 80111-6400 E-mail: doug@dougmilliken.com.

MILLIKEN, JEFFREY, cardiothoracic surgeon; b. Wyandotte, MI, Mar. 15, 1956; s. Francis and Nancy Milliken; m. Julie Mills, Oct. 24, 1998; children: Sarah, Amanda. Biomedical sci., U. Mich., 1974—77; med. degree, Univ. Mich. Med. Sch., 1976—80. Cert. Nat. Bd. Med. Examiners 1981, Am. Bd. Thoracic Surgery 1989, Am. Bd. Thoracic Surgery, Recertification 1998, Am. Bd. Surgery 1987. Surgery internship UCLA, L.A., Calif., 1980—81, resident in surgery, 1981—82, rsch. fellow cardiothoracic surgery, 1982—84, sr. residency surgery, 1984—85, chief resident gen. surgery, 1985—86, chief resident cardiothoracic surgery, 1986—88; sr. registrat cardiac surgery Victorian Pediat. Cardiac Surgical Unit Royal Children's Hosp., Victoria, Australia, 1988—89; asst. prof. surgery UCLA Coll. Medicine, Harbor-UCLA Med. Ctr., Torrance, Calif., 1989—95, chief div. cardiothoracic surgery, 1989—95; clin. assoc. prof. surgery UCI Coll. Medicine, UCI Med. Ctr., Orange, Calif., 1995—99, chief div. cardiothoracic surgery, 1995—, clinical prof. surgery, 1999—. Office: UCI Med Ctr Hosp 101 The City Dr Bldg 53 Rm 117 Orange CA 92868 Business E-Mail: jcmillik@uci.edu.

MILLIKEN, JOHN GORDON, research economist; b. Denver, May 12, 1927; s. William Boyd and Margaret Irene (Marsh) M.; m. Marie Violet Machell, June 13, 1953; children: Karen Marie, Douglas Gordon, David Tait, Anne Alain. BS, Yale U., 1949, BEng, 1950; MS, U. Colo., 1966, PhD, 1969. Registered profl. engr., Colo. Engr. U.S. Bur. Reclamation, Denver, 1950-55; asst. to plant mgr. Stanley Aviation Corp., Denver, 1955-56; prin. mgmt. engr., dept. mgr. Martin-Marietta Aerospace Divsn., Denver, 1956-64; mgmt. engr. Safeway Stores, Inc., Denver, 1964-66; sr. rsch. economist, prof., assoc. div. head U. Denver Rsch. Inst., 1966-86; pres. Univ. Senate, 1980-81; prin. Milliken Chapman Rsch. Group, Inc., Littleton, Colo., 1986-88, Milliken Rsch. Group, Inc., Littleton, 1988—. Vis. fellow sci. policy rsch. unit U. Sussex, Eng., 1975-76; cons. mgmt. engr. Author: Aerospace Management Techniques, 1971, Federal Incentives for Innovation, 1974, Recycling Municipal Wastewater, 1977, Water and Energy in Colorado's Future, 1981, Metropolitan Water Management, 1981, Technological Innovation and Economic Vitality, 1983, Water Management in the Denver, Colorado Urban Area, 1988, Benefits and Costs of Oxygenated Fuels in Colorado, 1990, Water Transfer Alternatives Study, 1994, Colorado Springs Water Resources Plan Alternative Assessment Study, 1995, Colorado Springs Utilities Wastewater Infrastructure Alternatives Study, 1998; contbr. articles to profl. jours. Bd. dirs. S.E. Englewood Water Dist., 1963—, South Englewood San. Dist., 1965—; bd. dirs. South Suburban Pk. and Recreation Dist., 1971-96, chmn., 1990-92; v.p. South Suburban Land and Facilities Corp., 2001—; chmn. Dem. Com. of Arapahoe County, 1969-71, 5th Congl. Dist. Colo., 1972-73, 74-75; mem. exec. com. Colo. Faculty Adv. Coun., 1981-85; mem. Garrison Diversion Unit Commn., 1984; trustee Colo. Local Govt. Liquid Asset Trust, 1986—, chmn., 1991-93; bd. dirs. Colo. Spl. Dist. Assn. Property and Liability Pool, 1989—, pres. 1997-98. With M.C., U.S. Army, 1945-46. Recipient Adlai E. Stevenson Meml. award, 1981, cert. of Appreciation for svc. to Nation, U.S. Sec. Interior, 1984, hon. title "Amicus Universitatis," U. Denver, 1994, Disting. Svc. award Spl. Dist. Assn. Colo., 1995; Milliken Park named in his honor for svcs. to Littleton Centennial Cmty., 1996. Mem. Acad. Mgmt., Nat. Assn. Bus. Economists, Yale Sci. and Engrng. Assn., Am. Water Works Assn., Sigma Xi, Tau Beta Pi, Beta Gamma Sigma, Sigma Iota Epsilon. Congregationalist. Home and Office: 6502 S Ogden St Centennial CO 80121-2561 E-mail: jgordonmil@aol.com.

MILLIKEN, MARY SUE, chef, television personality, writer; Former mem. staff Le Perroquet, Chgo., Restaurant d'Olympe, Paris; formerly chef, co-owner City Cafe, L.A.; chef, co-owner CITY, L.A., 1985—94, Border Grill, L.A., 1985—91, Santa Monica, 1990—. Co-host (TV series) Too Hot Tamales, 1995—, Tamales' World Tour, (radio show) Good Food; co-author: City Cuisine, 1989, Mesa Mexicana, 1994, Cantina, 1996, Cooking with Too Hot Tamales, 1997. Active Scleroderma Rsch. Found. Named Chef of Yr., Calif. Restaurant Writers, 1993. Mem.: Chef's Collaborative 2000, Women Chefs and Restaurateurs. Office: Border Grill 1445 4th St Santa Monica CA 90401

MILLIKEN, ROGER, textile company executive; b. N.Y.C., Oct. 24, 1915; s. Gerrish and Agnes (Gayley); m. Justine V. R. Hooper, June 5, 1948 (dec.); children: Justine, Nancy, Roger, David, Weston. Student, Groton Sch., 1929-33; AB, Yale U., 1937; LLD (hon.), Wofford Coll., Rose-Hulman Inst. Tech., Phila. Coll. Textiles and Sci., Brenau Coll., The Citadel; D. Textile Industry (hon.), Clemson U.; DHL (hon.), Converse Coll.; D. Bus. admin. (hon.), U. S.C., Spartanburg; LLD (hon.), LaGrange Coll., Furman U.; HHD (hon.), Presbyterian Coll. Bd. dirs. Milliken & Co. (formerly Deering Milliken), Spartanburg, SC, 1941—, pres., 1947-83, chmn., CEO, 1983—. Chmn. bd. Inst. Textile Tech., 1948—97, chmn. emeritus, 1997—; bd. dirs. S.C. Textile Mfrs. Assn. Chmn. Greenville-Spartanburg Airport Commn.; trustee Wofford Coll., SC. Named Businessman of the Yr., SC C. of C., 1981, Citizen of the Carolinas, NC C. of C., 1991, Leader of the Century, Textile World Mag., 1999; named to SC Bus. Hall of Fame, 1985, SC Hall of Fame, 1998, Nat. Bus. Hall of Fame, 2000; recipient Neville Holcombe Disting. Citizenship Award, Spartanburg Area C. of C., 1985, Lifetime Achievement Award, No. Textile Assn., 1999. Mem.: AIA (hon.), Bus. Council, Garden Club Am. (mem.-at-large), Yeamans Hall, Augusta Nat. Golf, Links, Union League. Office: Milliken & Co PO Box 3167 Spartanburg SC 29304

MILLIMET, ERWIN, lawyer; b. N.Y.C., Oct. 7, 1925; s. Maurice and Henrietta (Cohen) Millimet; children: Robert, James, Rachel, Sarah. BA magna cum laude, Amherst Coll., 1948; LLB cum laude, Harvard U., 1951. Bar: N.Y. 1952. Formerly sr. ptnr., chmn. exec. com. Stroock & Stroock & Lavan, N.Y.C.; ret., 1991. Mem. faculty Grad. Sch. Mgmt., U. Mass. Mem. bd. visitors U. San Diego Law Sch.; mem. Five Coll. LIR (learning in retirement), Northhampton, Mass.; active Nat. Support Group for Africa; founder Citizens for Am., Washington, 1984; mem. Rep. Presdl. Task Force. Mem. N.Y. State Bar Assn., Assn. of Bar of City of N.Y., Fed. Bar Assn., Rep. Club (N.Y.C. and Washington), Phi Beta Kappa. E-mail: emill@gis.net.

MILLIN, LAURA JEANNE, museum director; b. Elgin, Ill., June 11, 1954; d. Douglas Joseph and Patricia Ruth (Feragen) M. BA in Interdisciplinary Studies, The Evergreen State Coll., 1978. Dir. On The Boards, Seattle, 1979; art dir. City Fair Metrocenter YMCA, Seattle, 1980; dir. Ctr. on Contemporary Art, Seattle, 1981; co-owner Art in Form Bookstore, Seattle, 1981-89; co-dir. 3d internat festical of films by women dirs. Seattle Art Mus. & 911 Contemporary Arts, 1988; auction coord. Allied Arts of Seattle, 1989; dir. Missoula (Mont.) Mus. of the Arts, 1990—. Dir. Visual AIDS Missoula Mus. of the Arts, 1989; curator Radio COCA, Ctr. on Contemporary Art, Seattle, 1986, co-curator, 1981, 83; lectr. in field. Co-editor: Another (ind. feminist newspaper), Seattle, 1989, editor: (exhibition catalog) James Turrell: Four Light Installations, 1981. Bd. dirs. Internat. Festival of Films by Women Dirs., Seattle, 1987, 89, Nine One One Comtemporary Arts Ctr., Seattle, 1981-87, bd. chmn. 1981-85; bd. advisors REFLEX (art mag.), Seattle, 1988-89, Ctr. on Contemporary Art, Seattle, 1983-86; state vis. Mont. Arts. Coun., Missoula, 1991, NEA, Mpls., 1988, Chgo., 1987;; panelist Mont. Arts Coun., Helena, 1990; cons. Seattle Arts Commn., 1989, juror, 1985. Home: 1721 S 9th St W Missoula MT 59801-3432 Office: Art Mus Missoula 335 N Pattee St Missoula MT 59802 4520

MILLING, BERT WILLIAM, JR., magistrate judge; b. Mobile, Ala., Mar. 5, 1946; s. Bert William and Marjorie Ann (Smith) M.; m. Priscilla Pitman, Apr. 15, 1966; children: Brooks Pitman, Jeremy Bacon, Maran Celeste. AB in Philosophy, The Coll. of William and Mary, 1968; JD, U. Ala., 1971. Bar: Ala. 1971. Legal officer 212th Arty. Group, Fort Lewis, Wash., 1971-72; legal asst. officer Judge Advocate Gen.'s Office, Ft. Sill, Okla., 1972-74; spl. asst. atty. gen. Dist. Atty.'s Office, Mobile, 1974-75, asst. dist. atty., 1977-78; assoc. Sintz, Pike, Campbell & Duke, Mobile, 1975-77; ct. referee Juvenile Div. of Cir. Ct., Mobile, 1978-81; counsel U.S. Senate Com. on Jud., Subcom. on Security & Terrorism, Washington, 1981-83; asst. U.S. atty. Justice Dept., Mobile, 1983-86; U.S. magistrate judge U. S. Dist. Ct. So. Dist. Ala., Mobile, 1986—. Capt. U.S. Army, 1971-74; maj. N.G., USAR, 1975-87. Mem. Ala. Bar Assn., Mobile Bar Assn., Fed. Magistrate Judges Assn., Christian Legal Soc. Anglican. Avocations: photography, music, reading, exercising, family activities. Office: US Courthouse 113 Saint Joseph St Mobile AL 36602-3606

MILLING, MARCUS EUGENE, SR., geologist; b. Galveston, Tex., Oct. 8, 1938; s. Robert Richardson and Leonora Mildred (Currey) M.; m. Sandra Ann Dunlay, Sept. 11, 1959; 1 child, Marcus Eugene Jr. BS in Geology, Lamar U., 1961; MS in Geology, U. Iowa, 1964, PhD in Geology, 1968. Cert. petroleum geologist. Rsch. geologist Exxon Prodn. Rsch. Co., Houston, 1968-76; prodn. geologist Exxon Co. U.S.A., Kingsville, Tex., 1976-78, dist. explt. geologist New Orleans, 1978-80; mgr. geol. rsch. Arco Oil and Gas Co., Plano, Tex., 1980-86, chief geologist Dallas, 1986-87; assoc. dir. Bur. Econ. Geology U. Tex., Austin, 1987-92; exec. dir. Am. Geol. Inst., Alexandria, Va., 1992—. Vice-chmn. Offshore Tech. Conf., Dallas, 1984-87; dir. Geosci. Inst. for Oil and Gas Recovery Rsch., Austin, 1988-91. NSF fellow, 1966. Fellow Geol. Soc. Am. (councilor 1986-89); mem. Am. Assn. Petroleum Geologists, Soc. Petroleum Engrs., Am. Inst. Profl. Geologists (Ben H. Parker Meml. medal 1997), Blue Key, Sigma Xi. Home: 11457 Hollow Timber Ct Reston VA 20194-1980 Office: Am Geol Inst 4220 King St Alexandria VA 22302-1507 E-mail: mmilling@dgiweb.org.

MILLIS, ROBERT LOWELL, astronomer, science observatory director; b. Martinsville, Ill., Sept. 12, 1941; m. Julie Drean, 1965; children: David, Daniel. BA, Ea. Ill. U., 1963; PhD in Astronomy, U. Wis., 1968. Staff astronomer Lowell Obs., Flagstaff, Ariz., 1967—86, assoc. dir., 1986—90, acting dir., 1989—90, dir., 1990—. Mem. Am. Astron. Soc., Internat. Astronomy Union, Divsn. Planetary Sci. (sec.-treas. 1985-88, chmn. 1994-95). Achievements include discovery of the Rings of Uranus (with J.L. Elliot); research in planetary satellites and ring systems; the occultation studies of solar system objects; comet and Kuiper belt objects. Office: Lowell Observatory 1400 W Mars Hill Rd Flagstaff AZ 86001-4499 Business E-Mail: rim@lowell.edu.

MILLISOR, KENNETH RAY, lawyer; b. Belle Center, Ohio, Jan. 31, 1937; s. Darrel R. and Clara Sue (Miller) M.; m. Annette M. Seifert Ross, June 7, 1985. BA, Ohio Wesleyan U., 1959; JD, Ohio State U., 1960. Bar: Ohio 1960, U.S. Dist. Ct. (no. dist.) Ohio, 1965, U.S. Ct. Appeals (6th cir.) 1965, U.S. Ct. Appeals (D.C. cir.) 1975, U.S. Supreme Ct. 1970. Ptnr. Poetzel & Andress, Akron, Ohio, 1960-74, Millisor & Nobil, Akron and Cleve., 1975—. Past v.p. Akron Area coun. Boy Scouts Am.; active United Way. Mem. ABA, Ohio Bar Assn., Cleve. Bar Assn., Order of Coif, Shoreby Club (pres. 2000-03). Democrat. Home: 864 Beach Rd Lakewood OH 44107 Office: Millisor & Nobil Co 9150 S Hills Blvd Ste 300 Cleveland OH 44147-3599 Office Phone: 440-838-8800. E-mail: KMillisor@millisor.com.

MILLMAN, AMY J. government official; b. Bklyn., June 12, 1954; m. Aug. 3, 1984; 2 children. BA in History, Carnegie Mellon U., 1976; MPA, George Washington U., 1978. Rschr. Congl. Quar., Inc., Washington, 1976-79; analyst OSHA, Dept. Labor, Washington, 1979-81; Washington rep. The Philip Morris Cos., Inc., 1981-91; dir. legis. affairs The Am. Trucking Assn., Inc., Washington, 1991-93; exec. dir. Nat. Women's Bus. Coun., Washington, 1993—2001; pres. Springboard Enterprises, 2001—. Adj. prof. George Washington U., Sch. Bus. and Public Mgmt., 2001—; bd. advisors Enterprising Woman Magazine, 2001—. Mem. Phi Kappa Phi.

MILLMAN, BRUCE RUSSELL, lawyer; b. Bronx, N.Y., June 4, 1948; s. Meyer and Garie (Solomon) M.; m. Lorrie Jan Liss, Aug. 12, 1973; children: Noemi, Avi. AB, Princeton U., 1970; JD, Columbia U., 1973. Bar: N.Y. 1974, U.S. Dist. Ct. (ea. and so. dists.) N.Y. 1975, U.S. Ct. Appeals (2d dir.) 1978, U.S. Supreme Ct. 1978. Assoc. Rains & Pogrebin and predecessors, Mineola, NY, 1973-79, ptnr., 1980—2004; prin. Grotta, Glassman & Hoffman, P.A., N.Y.C., 2004—. Arbitrator Nassau County Dist. Ct., Mineola, 1981-83. Contbr. New York Employment Law, 1995, Labor and Employment Law for the Corporate Counselor and General Practitioner, 1994, Updating Issues in Employment Law, 1986, Public Sector Labor and Employment Law, 1988. Bd. dirs. West Side Montessori Sch., N.Y.C., 1984-90, sec., 1985-87, pres., 1987-90. Harlan Fiske Stone scholar Columbia U. Law Sch., N.Y.C., 1971, 73. Mem. ABA, N.Y. State Bar Assn. (chair labor and employment law sect. 1997-98), Nassau County Bar Assn., Indsl. Rels. Rsch. Assn. (bd. dirs. L.I. chpt. 1984—, pres. 1995-96). Home: 60 Riverside Dr New York NY 10024-6108 Office: Grotta Glassman & Hoffman PA 650 Fifth Ave New York NY 10019 also: 532 Broadhollow Rd Melville NY 11747 Office Phone: 212-261-2175. Business E-Mail: millmanb@gghlaw.com.

MILLMAN, IRVING, microbiologist, educator, retired inventor; b. N.Y.C., May 23, 1923; BS, City Coll. N.Y., 1948; MS, U. Ky., 1951; PhD, Northwestern U., 1954. Asst. prof. Northwestern U., 1954; formerly with Armour & Co., Pub. Health RSch. Inst. of N.Y.C., Merck Inst. Therapeutic Rsch.; adj. prof. Hahnemann U., Phila. Inducted Nat. Inventors Hall of Fame, 1993. Fellow Am. Acad. Microbiology; mem. N.Y. Acad. Scis., AAAS, Am. Soc. Microbiology. Achievements include development of test to identify Hepatitis B in blood samples. Office: Nat Inventors Hall Fame 221 S Broadway St Akron OH 44308-1505 also: Sch Med MCP Hahnemann U 2900 W Queen Ln Philadelphia PA 19129-1033*

MILLMAN, JOAN, state legislator; BA, Bklyn. Coll., 1962, MLS, 1974. Mem. 52nd Dist. N.Y. State Assembly, Albany, 1997—, mem. small bus. com., mem. aging com., mem. social svcs. com., mem. alcoholism and drug abuse com., mem. librs. and edn. tech. com.; elem. sch. tchr. Pub. Sch. 10, Bklyn., 1964-74, sch. libr., 1974-86. Ednl. cons. N.Y.C. Coun. Pres. Carol Bellamy and Senator Marty Connor, facilitator for comprehensive sch. devel. and planning. Mem. Ind. Neighborhood Dems., Bklyn. Heights Assn., Cadman Towers Assn.; bd. dirs. N.Y. State Bklyn. Devel. Zone; mem. South Bklyn. Enterprise Empowerment Zone, citywide adv. com. on mid. sch. initiatives; chairperson Kings County Dem. Com. Office: 341 Smith St Brooklyn NY 11231-4607

MILLMAN, JODE SUSAN, lawyer, writer; b. Poughkeepsie, N.Y., Dec. 28, 1954; d. Samuel Keith and Ellin Sadenberg (Bainder) M.; m. Michael James Harris, June 20, 1982; children: Maxwell, Benjamin. BA, Syracuse U., 1976, JD, 1979. Bar: N.Y. 1980, Mich. 2001, U.S. Dist. Ct. (so. and ea. dists.) N.Y. 1982, U.S. Supreme Ct. 1983. Asst. corp. counsel City of Poughkeepsie, 1979-81; assoc. Law Office of Lou Lewis, Poughkeepsie, 1981-85; pvt. practice Poughkeepsie, 1985—; pres. Seats Pub. Co., 2001—. Staff counsel City of Poughkeepsie Office of Property Devel., 1990—; gen. mgr. WCZX-Comms. Corp. Author: (novels) (children's books) Birthday Wishes and Rock'n Roll Dreams, The Firebird Ballet, Goldie Lox and the Three Behrs, (non-fiction) SEATS: New York (150 Seating Plans to Metro N.Y. Theatres, Concert Halls and Stadiums), SEATS: Chicago (125 Seating Plans to Metro Chgo./Millw. Theatres, Concert Halls and Sports Stadiums); contbg. author: Kaminstein Legislative History of the Copyright Law, 1979. Pres. Dutchess County (N.Y.) Vis. Bur., 1980—82; mem. assigned counsel program Dutchess County Family Ct.1985, 1985—; trustee Greater Poughkeepsie Libr. Dist., 1991—94, Poughkeepsie Day Sch., 1995—2002; bd. dirs. Poughkeepsie Ballet Theater, 1982, Jewish Cmty. Ctr., 1988. Mem.: Washtenaw County Bar Assn., Mich. Bar Assn., Dutchess County Bar Assn. (grievance com. 1994—2001), N.Y. State Bar Assn. Democrat. Jewish. Office: 3997 Preserve Dr Dexter MI 48130 E-mail: jodem54@aol.com.

MILLMAN, MARILYN ESTELLE, elementary school educator; b. Lynn, MA, Nov. 28, 1936; d. Benjamin and Dora (Goldman) Millman. BS, Boston U., 1958. Elem. tchr. Beverly (Mass.) Sch. Dist., 1958—64, Lagunitas (Calif.) Sch. Dist., 1964—65, San Rafael (Calif.) City Schs., 1965—97; founder, pres. Marilyn Millman Scholarship Found., 1997—. Vol. chair and bd. dirs. Susan G. Komen Breast Cancer Found.

MILLMAN, RICHARD GEORGE, architect, educator; b. St. Johns, Mich., Feb. 12, 1925; s. Harold Fildew and Elizabeth Hill (Van Deusen) M.; m. Mary Louise Manley, June 17, 1950; childen: John Richard, Ruth Barbara. BArch, U. Mich., 1951, MArch, 1962. Registered arch., Mich., Ohio, Ala. Job capt. Smith Hinchman & Grylls, Detroit, 1951-52; designer assoc. Eliot Robinson, AIA, Birmingham, Mich., 1952-55; designer Eero Saarinen Assocs., Bloomfield Hills, Mich., 1955-56; assoc. Chas. W. Lane Assocs. Inc., Ann Arbor, Mich., 1956-59; prin. Kainlauri, MacMullan, Millman, Ann Arbor, 1959-62; assoc. prof. Ohio U., Athens, 1962-68; prof. Auburn (Ala.) U., 1968—, head architecture dept., 1968-73, 84-85, head indsl. design dept., 1988-89. Prof. Mid. East Tech. U., Ankara, Turkey, 1966-67, King Faisal U., Dammam, Saudi Arabia, 1979-81. One man shows include Dhahran Art Group, Saudi Arabia, 1981, Peet Gallery, Auburn U., 1983, 91, Heritage Hall Mus., Talladega, Ala., 1998; author: Washtenaw Community College, 1962, Auburn U. Tour Guide, 1990. With U.S. Army, 1943-46, ETO, PTO. Decorated Bronze Star; recipient Cert. of Honor Ala. Hist. Commn., 1977; Alumni scholar U. Mich., 1961; Fulbright lectr. Exch. Com., Mid. East Tech. U., 1966. Mem. AIA (treas. Ala. coun. 1969, v.p. 1970, pres. 1972, emeritus 1990, Auburn chpt. pres. 1970, emeritus), Nat. Coun. Archtl. Registration Bd. (cert.), Auburn Arts Assn., Ga. Watercolor Soc. (signature mem.), Watercolor Soc. Ala. (signature mem.; pres. 2003), So. Watercolor Soc. (signature mem.). Avocations: painting, photography. Home: 736 Brenda Ave Auburn AL 36830-6038 E-mail: millmmm@charter.net.

MILLNER, ROBERT B. lawyer; b. N.Y.C., Apr. 20, 1950; s. Nathan and Babette E. (Leventhal) M.; m. Susan Brent, June 5, 1983; children: Jacob, Daniel, Rebecca. BA, Wesleyan U., 1971; JD, U. Chgo., 1975. Bar: Ill. 1975. Law clk. to Hon. George C. Edwards U.S. Ct. Appeals for 6th Cir., Cin., 1975-76; with Sonnenschein Nath & Rosenthal, Chgo., 1976—, ptnr., 1982—. Mem. Panel of Bankruptcy Trustees, Chgo., 1992—97, Am. Coll. of Bankruptcy, 2002—. Editorial bd. Jour. Corp. Disclosure and Confidentiality, 1989-92; contbr. articles to profl. jours. Trustee Anshe Emet Synagogue, Chgo., 1990-93; v.p. Am. Jewish Cong. midwest region, 1995—. Fellow: Am. Bar Found.; mem.: Comml. Bar Assn. (hon. overseas mem.), Chgo. Bar Assn., Am. Bankruptcy Inst., ABA (co-chair bankruptcy and insolvency com. litigation sect. 1992—95, 2001—), Wesleyan Alumni Club Chgo. (pres. 1988—90), Std. Club, Legal Club, Phi Beta Kappa. Office: Sonnenschein Nath & Rosenthal 8000 Sears Tower Chicago IL 60606

MILLOY, FRANK JOSEPH, JR., surgeon; b. Phoenix, June 26, 1924; s. Frank Joseph and Ola (McCabe) M. BS, Notre Dame U., 1946; MS, Northwestern U., 1949, MD, 1947. Diplomate Am. Bd. Surgery and Thoracic Surgery. Intern Cook County Hosp., Chgo., 1947-49, resident, 1953-57; practice medicine, specializing in surgery Lake Forest, Ill., 1958—. Hon. attending staff Presbyn.-St. Lukes Hosp.; former mem. attending staff Cook County Hosp.; mem. staff U. Ill. Rsch. Hosp.; clin. assoc. prof. surgery, U. Ill. Med. Sch.; assoc. prof. surgery Rush Med. Sch. Contbr. more than 35 articles to profl. jours., chpts. to books. Cons. West Side Vet. Hosp. Served as apprentice seaman USNR, 1943-45; lt. M.C., USNR, 1950-52; PTO. Mem.: ACS, Soc. Med. History Chgo. (pres.), Cook County Hosp. Surg. Alumni Assn., Karl Meyer Surg. Soc. (sec.), Warren Cole Surg. Soc. (past sec.), Ill. Thoracic Surg. Soc. (past pres.), Soc. Thoracic Surgeons, Am. Coll. Chest Physicians, Internat. Soc. Surgery, Chgo. Surg. Soc., Univ. Club (Chgo.), Met. Club, Knights of Malta, Phi Beta Pi. Home: 574 Jackson Ave Glencoe IL 60022-2036 Office Phone: 847-835-5578.

MILLS, AGNES EUNICE KARLIN, artist, printmaker, sculptor; b. N.Y.C., Apr. 2, 1915; d. Herman Karlin and Celia (Ducoffe) Karlin; m. Saul Mills, May 10, 1938 (dec. Nov. 1993); children: Karen, Marghe. Grad., Cooper Union Art Sch., N.Y.C., 1938; BFA, Pratt Inst., 1975; student, NYU. One-woman shows include Carus Gallery, N.Y.C., Unitarian Soc., Manhasset, N.Y., Harbor Gallery, Cold Spring Harbor, N.Y., North Truro Art Gallery, Cape Cod, Mass., Alfredo Valente Gallery, N.Y.C., Robbins Gallery, East Orange, N.J., Nuance Galleries, Tampa, Friends of Tampa Ballet, Graphic Eye Coop Gallery, Pt. Washington, N.Y., City Ctr. Gallery, N.Y.C., Lincoln Ctr. Art Gallery, N.Y.C., North Shore Cmty. Arts Ctr., Great Neck, N.Y., Delray Beach Works in Progress Gallery, Boca Raton Cmty. Ctr., Palm Beach Pub. Libr., Gramercy Park Armory, N.Y.C.; exhibited in group shows at Alfredo Valente Gallery, N.Y.C., Audubon Soc., N.Y.C., Bowdoin Coll. Mus. Art, Brunswick, Maine, Brandeis U., Waltham, Mass., Bklyn. Mus. Art, Brown U., Providence, Butler Inst. Am. Art, Youngstown, Ohio, Colgate U. Libr., Hamilton, N.Y., Cornell U., Ithaca, N.Y., East Hampton (N.Y.) Guild Artists, Gallery K, Woodstock, N.Y., Graphic Eye Coop Gallery, Port Washington, N.Y., Heckscher Mus., Huntington, N.Y., Hunterdon County Mus., Clinton, N.J., Joan Avnet Gallery, Great Neck, N.Y., Lincoln Ctr. Libr. Performing Arts, N.Y.C., Madison Gallery, N.Y.C., Boca Raton City Hall, Boca Raton Cmty. Ctr., Boca Raton Libr.; represented in permanent collections at Boca Raton Mus. Art, Nat. Women in the Arts Mus. Home: 1070 SW 22nd Ave Villa 13#3 Delray Beach FL 33445-6030

MILLS, BARRY, academic administrator, lawyer; b. Providence, Sept. 8, 1950; m. Karen Gorden Mills. BA in Biochemistry and Govt. cum laude, Bowdoin, 1972; PhD, Syracuse U., 1976; JD, Columbia U., 1979. Bar: N.Y. 1980. Mem. Debevoise & Plimpton, NYC, 1979—86, ptnr., 1986—; pres. Boudoin Coll., Brunswick, Maine, 2001—. Acad. affairs com. Bowdoin Coll., Brunswick, Maine, bd. trustees, 1994—2000, chmn. bd. student affairs com. Harlan Fiske Stone scholar, Columbia Law Sch., 1979. Mem. Assn. of Bar of City of N.Y. Office: Debevoise & Plimpton 875 3rd Ave Fl 23 New York NY 10022-6225 also: Boudoin Coll Hawthorne-Longfellow Hall 5700 College Station Brunswick ME 04011-8448

MILLS, BELEN COLLANTES, early childhood education educator; b. Philippines; d. Ricardo and Epifania (Tomines) C.; m. Ralph A. Mills; children: Belinda Mills Keiser, Roger A. BSE, Leyte Normal Coll., Tacloban, Leyte, Philippines, 1954; MS in Edn., Ind. U., 1955, EdD, 1967. Prof. emeritus early childhood edn. Fla. State U., Tallahassee, 2002. Early childhood cons. to ednl. agys. and orgns. Author books on early childhood edn., phonics-based children's books and acad. readiness computer programs; contbr. articles to profl.jours. Smith-Mundt Fulbright scholar. Mem. Nat. Assn. for Edn. of Young Children, Nat. Assn. Early Childhood Tchr. Edn., World Coun. for Curriculum and Instrn., Assn. Childhood Edn. Internat. Home: PO Box 20023 Tallahassee FL 32316-0023 E-mail: raintown@polaris.net.

MILLS, BOB, member of Canadian parliament; b. Young, Sask., Can. m. Nicole Mills; children: Ken, Kari Anne, Melinda, Rosanno, Ric, Amanda. BA in Sci. and Edn., U. Sask. Tchr. biology Lindsay Thurber Comprehensive H.S., 1965-79; founder Mills Travel, Ltd., 1979—; elected to House of Commons, Red Deer, Canada, 1993—. Parliamentary activities include mem. steering com. on fgn. affairs and internat. trade, Ofcl. Opposition Fgn. Affairs Critic, Opposition Health Critic, 2000—, mem. standing com. on health, chief environ. critic. gen., 2001—. Mem. Am. Express Network (recipient Travel Hall of Fame award 1992). Avocations: farming, gardening, photography, travel. Office: Rm 920 Confed Ottawa ON Canada K1A OA6 Office Phone: 613-995-0590. E-mail: millsb@parl.gc.ca.

MILLS, CAROL MARGARET, business consultant, public relations consultant; b. Salt Lake City, Aug. 31, 1943; d. Samuel Lawrence and Beth (Neilson) M. BS magna cum laude, U. Utah, 1965. With W.S. Hatch Co., Woods Cross, Utah, 1965-87, corp. sec., 1970-87, traffic mgr., 1969-87, dir. publicity, 1974-87, cons. various orgns., 1988—. Bd. dirs. Intermountain Tariff Bur. Inc., 1978-88, chmn., 1981-82, 1986-87; bd. dirs. Mountainwest Venture Group. Fund raiser March of Dimes, Am. Cancer Soc., Am. Heart Assn.; active senatorial campaign, 1976, gubernatorial campaign, 1984, 88, congl. campaign, 1990, 92, 94, vice chair voting dist., 1988-90, congl. campaign, 1994, chmn. 1990-92, chmn. party caucus legis. dist.; witness transp. com. Utah State Legislature, 1984, 85; apptd. by gov. to bd. trustees Utah Tech. Fin. Corp., 1986—, corp. sec., mem. exec. com., 1988—; mem. expdn. to Antaractica, 1996, Titanic '96 expdn.; mem. Iceland and Greenland expdn., 2001; mem. Pioneer Theatre Guld, 1985–. Recipient Svc. awards W.S. Hatch Co., 1971, 80; VIP chpt. Easter Seal Telethon, 1989, 90, Outstanding Vol. Svc. award Easter Seal Soc. Utah, 1989, 90. Mem. Nat. Tank Truck Carriers, Transp. Club Salt Lake City, Am. Trucking Assn. (mem. pub. rels. coun.), Utah Motor Transport Assn. (bd. dirs. 1982-88), Internat. Platform Assn., Traveler's Century Club, Titanic Internat., Beta Gamma Sigma, Phi Kappa Phi, Phi Chi Theta. Home: HC 11 Box 329 Kamiah ID 83536-9410 Office: PO Box 1495 Kamiah ID 83536-1495

MILLS, CELESTE LOUISE, dog breeder, hypnotherapist, professional magician; b. LA, May 16, 1952; d. Emery John and Helen Louise (Bradbury) W.; m. Robert Richardson Feigel, Apr. 11, 1971 (div. 1973); m. Peter Alexander Mills, June 12, 1991. (div. 1992). BBA, Western State U., Doniphan, Mo., 1987; PhD in Religion, Universal Life Ch. Univ., 1987; grad., Hypnotism Tng. Inst., Glendale, Calif., 1990. Cert. hypnotherapist. Credit mgr. accounts receivable Gensler-Lee Diamonds, Santa Barbara, Calif., 1973-74, Terry Hinge and Hardware, Van Nuys, Calif., 1975-78; credit mgr., fin. analyst Peanut Butter Fashions, Chatsworth, Calif., 1978-82; personal mgr. Charter Mgmt. Co., Beverly Hills, Calif., 1982-83; co-owner, v.p. Noreen Jenney Communicates, Beverly Hills, 1983-85; corp. credit mgr., fin. analyst Ctrl. Diagnostic Lab., Tarzana, Calif., 1985-89; credit mgr., fin. analyst Metwest Clin. Lab., Inc., Tarzana, Calif., 1989-90; pvt. practice, clin. hypnotherapist Sherman Oaks, Calif., 1990—. Cons. Results Now, Inc., Tarzana, 1986-87; profl. magician Magic Castle, Hollywood, 1989—, Prodr., host (TV) Brainstorm, 1993—, Dances with Woofs, 2003. Media spokesperson Am. Cancer Soc., 1990—. Mem. NAFE, NOW, Nat. Humane Ednl. Found., Credit Mgrs. Assn. Trade Groups (bd. govs. 1988-89), Nat. Clin. Lab. Trade Group (chmn. 1988-89), Med. and Surg. Suppliers Trade Group (vice chmn. 1988-89, chmn. 1989-90), Soc. Am. Magicians, Acad. Magical Arts, Internat. Brotherhood of Magicians, Assn. Advanced Ethical Hypnosis, Am. Coun. Hypnotist Examiners, Golden Retriever Club of Am. (bd. dirs. LA chpt. 2002—). Avocations: scuba diving, sailing. Office Phone: 818-989-7999. E-mail: qnwoof@aol.com.

MILLS, CHARLES GARDNER, lawyer; b. Griffin, Ga., Feb. 29, 1940; s. Charles G. and Marguerite (Powell) M. AB, Yale U., 1962; JD, Boston Coll., 1967; LLM, Touro Coll., 2002. Bar: N.Y. 67, U.S. Dist. Ct. (so. and ea. dists.) 72, U.S. Ct. Appeals (2d cir.) 75, U.S. Supreme Ct. 77, U.S. Ct. Fed. Claims 91, U.S. Ct. Appeals for Vets. Claims 96, U.S. Dist. Ct. (no. dist.) N.Y. 99. Assoc. Smart & McKay, N.Y.C., 1967-68, Smart & Mills, N.Y.C., 1969-71, Eaton & VanWinkle, N.Y.C., 1971-82, Payne, Wood & Littlejohn, Glen Cove and Melville, N.Y., 1982-91; pvt. practice, Glen Cove, 1991—. With U.S. Army, 1962-64, ETO. Mem. Assn. Bar City N.Y., Nassau County Bar Assn., Rotary (pres. Glen Cove Club 1989-90), Am. Legion (comdr. Locust Valley, N.Y. post 1988-90, comdr. Nassau County com. 1995-96, N.Y. Judge Advocate, 1998—), Soc. Colonial Wars, SCV, Order of the Arrow. Republican. Roman Catholic. Office: 56 School St Glen Cove NY 11542-2512

MILLS, CHARLES S. healthcare supplies and products company executive; b. Sept. 30, 1961; BS, MBA, Cornell U. With IBM; then joined Medline Industries, Mundelein, Ill., 1986, pres. textile divsn., 1991—97, CEO, 1997—.

MILLS, DALE DOUGLAS, journalist; b. Seattle, Oct. 4, 1930; d. Donald Emery and Antoinette (Kinleyside) Douglas; m. William Russell Mills, Aug. 13, 1955; children: Lida Susan, William Tad Jr., Peter Donald, Jane Douglas. BA, U. Wash., 1952. Reporter Seattle Times, 1954-55, 74-83; asst. libr. Harvard U., 1955-56; editor Puget Soundings mag., 1968-71. Author: Deliver Us From Squid Roe, 1995. Mem. com. sign control Seattle City Coun., 1970-72; rsch. dir. City Coun. campaign; bd. mgrs. King County Juvenile Ct.; trustee Allied Arts Seattle; bd. dirs. King County Coun. for Prevention of Child Abuse and Neglect. Recipient awards for excellence in reporting Wash. Press Assn., Nat. Fedn. Press Women, Allied Daily Newspapers, C.B. Blethen Meml. award for disting. investigative reporting, Excellence award Soc. Profl. Journalists/Sigma Delta Chi. Mem.: Jr. League Seattle, Seattle Times Stars, Helen T. Bush Children's Hosp Guild., Sunset Club, Seattle Yacht Club, Kappa Kappa Gamma.

MILLS, DANIEL QUINN, business educator, consultant, author; b. Houston, Nov. 24, 1941; s. Daniel Monroe and Louise (Quinn) M.; children: Lisa Ann, Leandra, Shirley Elizabeth, Eliza Day, Sargent; m. Elizabeth Moore. BA, Ohio Wesleyan U., 1963; MA, Harvard U., 1965, PhD, 1968. Prof. MIT, Cambridge, 1968-75, Harvard Bus. Sch., Boston, 1976—. Impartial umpire Plan to Settle Disputes in Constrn., 1973-79, Trans-Alaska Pipeline, 1975-78, AFL-CIO Internal Disputes Plan, 1975-82; commr. Nat. Commn. on Employment Policy, Washington, 1982-86. Author: Industrial Relations in Construction, 1971, Labor, Government and Inflation, 1975, Labor-Management Relations, 1978, 5th edit., 1993, The New Competitors, 1985, Not Like Our Parents: The Baby-Boom Generation, 1987, The IBM Lesson, 1988, The Rebirth of the Corporation, 1990, The GEM Principle, 1994, Broken Promises: What Went Wrong at IBM, 1996, e-Leadership, 2000, Buy, Lie and Sell High: How Investors Lost Out on Enron and The Internet Bubble, 2002, Wheel, Deal and Steal: Deceptive Accounting, Deceitful CEO's and Ineffective Reforms, 2003. Mem. Am. Econ. Assn., Indsl. Rels. Rsch. Assn., Phi Beta Kappa Mem. United Ch. of Christ. Office: Harvard U Harvard Bus Sch Soldiers Field Rd Allston MA 02163

MILLS, DON HARPER, pathology and psychiatry educator, lawyer; b. Peking, China, July 29, 1927; came to U.S., 1928; s. Clarence Alonzo and Edith Clarissa (Parrett) M.; m. Lillian Frances Snyder, June 11, 1949; children: Frances Jo, Jon Snyder. BS, U. Cin., 1950, MD, 1953; JD, U. So. Calif., 1958. Diplomate Am. Bd. Law in Medicine. Intern L.A. County Gen. Hosp., 1953-54, admitting physician, 1954-57, attending staff pathologist, 1959—; pathology fellow U. So. Calif., L.A., 1954-55, instr. pathology, 1958-62, asst. clin. prof., 1962-65, assoc. clin. prof., 1965-69, clin. prof., 1969—, clin. prof. psychiatry and behavioral sci., 1986—. Asst. in pathology Hosp. Good Samaritan, LA, 1956-65, cons. staff, 1962-72, affiliating staff, 1972-91; dep. med. examiner Office of LA County Med. Examiner, 1957-61; instr. legal medicine Loma Linda (Calif.) U. Sch. Medicine, 1960-66, assoc. clin. prof. humanities, 1966-95; cons. HEW, 1972-73, 75-76, Dept. of Def., 1975-80; bd. dirs. Am. Bd. Legal Medicine, Inc., Chgo.; med. dir. Profl. Risk Mgmt. Group, 1989-2001; med. dir., Octagon Risk Svcs., Inc., 2001—. Column editor Newsletter of the Long Beach Med. Assn., 1960-75, Jour. Am. Osteopathic Assn., 1965-77, Ortho Panel, 1970-78; exec. editor Trauma, 1964-88, mem. editl. bd., 1988—; mem. editl. bd. Legal Aspects of Med. Practice, 1972-90, Med. Alert Comms., 1973-75, Am. Jour. Forensic Medicine and Pathology, 1979-87, Hosp. Risk Control, 1981-96; contbr. numerous articles to profl. jours. Bd. dirs. Inst. for Med. Risk Studies, 1988—; mem. adv. bd. Pacific Ctr. for Health Policy and Ethics, 1997—, chmn., 1999—. Recipient Ritz Heerman award Calif. Hosp. Assn., 1986, Disting. fellow Am. Acad. Forensic Scis., 1993, Genesis award Pacific Ctr. for Health Policy and Ethics, 1993, Founder's award Am. Coll. Med. Quality, 1994. Fellow Am. Coll. Legal Medicine (pres. 1974-76, bd. govs. 1970-78, v.p. 1972-74, chmn. malpractice com. 1973-74, jour. editl. bd. 1984—, gold medal 1999), Am. Acad. Forensic Sci. (gen. program chmn. 1966-67, chmn. jurisprudence sect. 1966-67, 73-74, exec. com. 1971-74, 84-88, v.p. 1984-85, pres. 1986-87, ethics com. 1976-86, 91-2001, chmn. ethics com. 1994-2001, long-term planning com. 1990—, jour. editl. bd. 1965-79); mem. AMA (jour. editl. bd. 1973-77), AAAS, ABA, Am. Coll. Med. Quality (hon. life), Calif. Med. Assn., L.A. County Med. Assn., L.A. County Bar Assn., Am. Health Lawyers Assn., Calif. Soc. Hosp. Attys. Home: 700 E Ocean Blvd Unit 2606 Long Beach CA 90802-5039 Office: 5000 Airport Plaza Dr Ste 250 Long Beach CA 90815-4959 E-mail: Don.Mills@octagonrs.com.

MILLS, EDWIN SMITH, economics professor; b. Collingswood, N.J., June 25, 1928; s. Edwin Smith and Roberta (Haywood) M.; m. Barbara Jean Dressner, Sept. 2, 1950; children: Alan Stuart, Susan Dorinda; m. Margaret M. Hutchinson, Jan. 22, 1977. BA, Brown U., 1951; PhD, U. Birmingham, Eng., 1956. Asst. lectr. Univ. Coll. North Staffordshire, Eng., 1953-55; instr. MIT, 1955-57; mem. faculty Johns Hopkins, Balt., 1957-70, prof. econs., 1963-70, chmn. dept. econs., 1966-69; prof. econs. and pub. affairs, Gerald L. Phillippe prof. urban studies Princeton U., 1970-75, prof. econs., 1975-87, chmn. dept., 1975-77; Gary Rosenberg prof. real estate and fin. Kellog Sch. Mgmt. Northwestern U., Evanston, Ill., 1987—96, emeritus prof., 1996—. Vis. research fellow Cowles Found., Yale, 1961; sr. profl. staff Council Econ. Advisers, 1964-65 Author: The Burden of Government, 1986. 2d lt. U.S. Army, 1946—48. Recipient numerous rsch. grants and contracts, 1960—95. Mem. Am. Econ. Assn., Phi Beta Kappa. Home: 1 Calvin Cir Apt B105 Evanston IL 60201-1953 Office: Northwestern U Ctr Real Estate Rsch Kellogg Graduate School 2001 Sheridan Rd Evanston IL 60208-2001 Office Phone: 847-491-8340.

MILLS, ELIZABETH SHOWN, historical writer, genealogist; b. Cleve., Miss., Dec. 29, 1944; d. Floyd Finley Shown and Elizabeth Thulmar (Jeffcoat) Carver; m. Gary B. Mills, 1963; children: Clayton Bernard, Donna Rachal, Daniel Garland. BA, U. Ala., 1980. Cert. genealogist, geneal. lectr. Profl. geneal. writer, educator, 1972—; editor Nat. Geneal. Soc. Quar., Arlington, Va., 1987—2002. Faculty Samford U. Inst. of Genealogy and Hist. Rsch., Birmingham, Ala., 1980—; trustee Assn. for Promotion of Scholarship in Genealogy, N.Y., 1984-90; contract dir., cons. U. Ala., 1985-92; faculty Nat. Inst. of Geneal. Rsch., 1985-97. Author, editor, translator Cane River Creole Series, 6 vols.; author: Evidence: Citation and Analysis for the Family Historian, 1997, Professional Genealogy: A Manual for Researchers, Writers, Editors, Lecturers, and Librarians, 2001, Isle of Canes, 2004; contbr. articles to profl. jours. Trustee Nat. Bd. Certification Genealogists, 1984—, v.p., 1989-94, pres., 1994-96; trustee Assn. Profl. Genealogists, 1984-90, 92-94, regional v.p., 1988-89. Named Outstanding Young Women of Am. Jaycees, Gadsden, 1976, Outstanding Alumna award U. Ala. New Coll., Tuscaloosa, 1990. Fellow Am. Soc. Geneal. (sec. 1992-95, v.p. 1995-98, pres. 1998-2001), Nat. Geneal. Soc. (councilor 1987-92), Utah Geneal. Assn., Grady McWhiney Rsch. Found. (sr.); mem. Assn. Profl. Genealogists (Smallwood Svc. award, 1989). Republican. Roman Catholic.

MILLS, EUGENE SUMNER, academic administrator; b. West Newton, Ind., Sept. 13, 1924; s. Sumner Amos and Lela (Weatherly) M.; m. Dorothy Frances Wildman, Oct. 22, 1945; children: David Walden, Sara Anne. AB, Earlham Coll., 1948; MA, Claremont Grad. U., 1949, PhD, 1952; Spl. Postdoctoral Auditor, Harvard, 1958-59; LLD (hon.), N.H. Coll., 1979, U. N.H., 1988; LHD (hon.), Earlham Coll., 1987. From instr. to prof. psychology Whittier (Calif.) Coll., 1950—60, prof., 1960—62, chmn. dept. psychology, 1952—62; pres. Whittier (Calif.) Coll. and Whittier Coll. Sch. of Law, 1979-89; prof. psychology Whittier (Calif.) Coll., 1979-89, emeritus prof. psychology, pres. emeritus, 1989—; faculty U. NH, Durham, 1962—79, pres., 1974—79. Vis. prof. U. Victoria, B.C., 1958, 60; bd. dirs. Elderhostel, Inc., 1977-97, chmn., 1984-90, vice chmn., 1996-97; vice chmn. Fedco Inc., 1996-98; interim pres. Earlham Coll., 1996-97; mem. NH Psychol. Assn., 1962-79, pres., 1969-70, bd. dirs., 1967-70; trustee Earlham Coll., 1996-69, 96-97, hon. lifetime trustee, 1997—. Author: George Trumbull Ladd: Pioneer American Psychologist, 1969, The Story of Elderhostel, 1993; contbr. articles to profl. jours. Bd. dirs. LA County coun. Boy Scouts Am., 1981—89; bd. dirs. Fedco Charitable Found., 2001—. Danforth Found. grantee; NSF grantee. Fellow Am. Psychol. Assn.; mem. Western Psychol. Assn., Sigma Xi, Phi Kappa Phi., Omicron Delta Kappa Mem. Soc. Of Friends.

MILLS, FREDERICK VANFLEET, art educator, educator, watercolorist; b. Bremen, Ohio, June 5, 1925; s. Frederick William and Juanita Ellen (VanFleet) M.; m. Lois Jean Rademacher; children: Mark Steven (dec.), Michael Sherwood, Mollie Sue, Merre Shannon, Randal Dean, Susan Lynn, Todd Patrick, Shondra Marie. BS, Ohio State U., 1949; MS, Ind. U., 1951, EdD, 1956; postgrad., U.S. Army Staff and Command Coll., 1973-76. Tchr. art, supr. Celina (Ohio) Pub. Schs., 1949-51; instr. univ. h.s. Ind. U., 1951-55, prof. art, art edn., chmn. dept. art edn., 1959-65; vis. prof. U. Tex.-Austin, 1965; chmn. dept. related arts, crafts and interior design U. Tenn., Konxville, 1966-68; prof. art, chmn. dept. art Ill. State U., 1968-85, prof. emeritus, 1985—; dist. prof. art Lincoln Coll., Normal, 1986—. Rsch. reader humanities HEW, 1968-69; resource person arts, edn. and Ams. panel Rockefeller Report Am Coun. Arts in Edn., 1977-78; cons. Latin Am. Fulbright Scholarship Program Harvard U., 1981-82; mem. com. Ill. Fine Arts Rev. for Capital Devel. Bd., 1987—, planning com. Nat. Inst. Advanced Studies in Art and Design and Archives of Am. Art Sch., 1988—, rsch. com. Nat. Sch. Art and Design. One-man shows include McLean County Arts Ctr., Bloomington, Ill., Lincoln (Ill.) Coll., Ill. Agriculture Assn. Credit Union Art Exhbn. Series, Bloomington, Suzette Schochet Gallery, Newport, R.I.; represented in permanent collections Ill. State U. Credit Union, Normal, Ill. State U. Computer Lab., Normal, Mid-Ill. Credit Union, Bloomington, I Wonderlin Gallery, Normal, Ill., State Farm Ins. Co., Kemper Fin. Securities/Kemper Fin. Fund, First of Am. Bank, Ill., Diamond Star Motors Corp., Easter Seal Assn., City of Vladimir, Russia, City of Asahikawa, Hokkaido, Japan, County of McLean, City of Bloomington, Town of Normal; author, editor: The Status of the Visual Arts in Higher Education, 1976, New Perspectives in Visual Arts Administration, 1977, Issues in the Administration of Visual Arts, 1978, Politics and the Visual Arts, 1979, The Visual Arts in the Ninth Decade, 1980; editor Western Arts Bull., 1958-62; featured in 12 part ser. As An Artist Sees local pub. access; contbr. to profl. jours. Pres. Ill. Alliance Art Edn., 1975-77, Ill. Task Force for Arts Edn. in Gen. Edn., 1976-77; mem. Tenn. Arts Commn., 1967-68, Nat. Alliance Arts Edn./Kennedy Ctr., 1975-77; charter trustee Ill. Summer Sch. for Arts, v.p., v.p. Found. Bd., 1988-94; bd. dirs., co-founder Sugar Creek Arts Festival, Normal, 1985—; chair major gifts com. Normal Theater Restoration Project, 1992—; bd. dirs., v.p. McLean County Arts Ctr., Bloomington, 1980-90, sponsor Skilled Crafts award, 1968—. Served to maj. USAR; Col. Ill. Militia. Recipient Recognition award Alliance for Arts Edn., 1984, Outstanding Svc. award Ill. Alliance Arts Edn., 1984, 1994 Ornament of Yr./Artist of Yr. award, Ill. State U. Alumni Assn. Svc. Awd.; subject articles, TV interviews Mem. Nat. Council Art Adminstrs. (charter, sr. rsch. editor bd. dirs. 1973-81), Nat. Assn. Schs. Art (instnl. del. 1974-84, nominating com. 1977-78, rsch. com. 1976-77), Western Arts Assn. (pres. 1962-64), Coll. Art Assn., Nat. Art Edn. Assn. (dir. 1964-66), Scabbard and Blade, Phi Delta Kappa, Delta Tau Delta, Delta Phi Delta. Clubs: Rotary Internat. Home: 25306 Arrowhead Lne Hudson IL 61748-9414 *As I reflect on my life and career up to this point, I feel that consistency and humaneness are two words that come to mind. It seems extremely important to be consistent when a person relates to others, and if that is coupled with humaneness and consideration of the value of others, being aware of their strengths and weaknesses, their likes and dislikes, it becomes easier to relate to them in this most complex world of ours.*

MILLS, GEORGE MARSHALL, insurance consultant; b. Newton, N.J., May 20, 1923; s. J. Marshall and Emma (Scott) M.; m. Dorothy Lovilla Allen, Apr. 21, 1945; children: Dianne (Mrs. Thomas McKay III), Dorothy L.A. (Mrs. Edward Sphatt). BA, Rutgers U., 1943; MA, Columbia U., 1951. CLU, CPCU; chartered fin. cons.; cert. govt. fund mgr. Pres. George M. Mills Inc., North Brunswick, N.J., 1946-75; pres. CORECO, Inc., Newark, 1960-78; risk mgr. N.J. Hwy. Authority, Woodbridge, 1976-95; pres. Assoc. Risk Mgmt., North Brunswick, N.J., 1995—. Cons. Govs.'s Com. on Bus. Efficiency in Pub. Schs., 1979-80; cons. Risk Mgmt. Ins., Real Estate. Bd. dirs. Alpha Chi Rho Edni. Found., vice-chmn. 1991-95; workshop Easter Seal Soc.; mem. Gov.'s Task Force on Sound Mcpl. Govt., 1981-82; pres. Nat. Interfrat. Conf., 1979-80. With USNR, 1943-46. Mem. Congl. Bus. Adv. Coun. (chmn. 2003-), Am. Coll. Life Underwriters, Am. Coll. Property Liability Underwriters, Internat. Bridge Tunnel and Turnpike Assn. (chmn. risk mgmt. com. 1980-95, mem. bus. ins. risk mgmt. bd. 1988-95, chair Congress Bus. Adv. Coun., 2003-, Matthew J. Lenz Jr. medal 1989, Paul K. Addams award 1992), New Brunswick Hist. Soc., English Speaking Union, Rutgers Club (trustee), Alpha Chi Rho (nat. councillor 1964-70, nat. pres. 1970-73, nat. treas. 1975-78), Kappa Kappa Psi, Tau Kappa Alpha, Phi Delta Phi. Mem. Reformed Ch. Am. Home: 1054 Hoover Dr New Brunswick NJ 08902-3244

MILLS, GLORIA ADAMS, energy service consultant; b. Chgo., Mar. 1, 1940; d. Edward Charles and Olive Margaret (McCarty) Adams; m. Peter Mills, Dec. 29, 1962 (div. July 1986). BA, Rosary Coll., River Forest, Ill., 1962, MALS, 1970; MBA, U. Chgo., 1976. Lit. chemist UOP, Inc., Des Plaines, Ill., 1962-70, supr. patent libr., 1970-77, mktg. engr., 1977-81, mgr. project devel., 1981-83; v.p. mktg. Covanta Waste to Energy, Inc., Fairfield, N.J., 1983-87, sr. v.p. mktg., 1987-89, exec. v.p. mktg., 1989-94, exec. v.p. bus. devel., 1994-01, ret., 2001. Chmn. of bd. Ambiente 2000 S.r.l., 1998-01, mem. indsl. adv. bd. So. Ill. U. Coll. Engring. and Tech., Carbondale, 1985-90, 2000—; mem. cmty. sta. bd. WHTJ Charlottesville PBS, 2004—. Contbr. articles to profl. jours. Mem. ASME (solid waste processing div., medal of achievement 2001), Am. Chem. Soc. Avocations: travel, reading.

MILLS, HELENE AUDREY, education educator; b. Oct. 6, 1933; d. Paul Albert and Mabel Meister; m. Ray Mills, Apr. 17, 1954; children: Keith, Katherine (dec.), Kevin. BS in Family Life Edn., Wayne State U., 1954, MEd in Human Resources, 1965, EdD in Gen. Adminstrn., 1980. Supr., instr. Wayne State Coll. Edn., 1958-67; tchr. life studies, health edn. Seaholm H.S., Birmingham, Mich., 1967-72, 74-77, asst. to prin., 1974-77, asst. prin., 1978-79, prin., 1990-97, Derby Mid. Sch., Birmingham, 1980-90; asst. prof. Oakland U., Rochester Hills, Mich., 1997—. Adj. prof. Wayne State U., Detroit, 1989-91, Oakland U., Rochester, 1985-89, asst. prof., 1997—. Consulting editor Clearing Ho., 1985-97; contbr. articles to profl. jours. Mem. steering com. Meadowbrook Leadership Acad., 1984-87; mem. Detroit Strategic Planning Task Force, 1986-88; mem. exec. bd. Oakland County Youth Assistance, 1987-90; program chairperson women's group Northbrooke Ch., 1997-99, mem. adult minstries purpose com., 1998-99. Recipient PTSA Coun. Pres. award, 1982, Celebration of Women award Greater Detroit Coun. NA'AMAT USA, 1986, Exemplary Secondary Sch. award State Mich., 1991. Mem. NASCD, Nat. Staff Devel. Assn., Nat. Secondary Prins. Assn., Mich. Assn. Supervision and Curriculum Devel., Mich. Coun. Family Rels., Mich. Secondary Prins. Assn., Oakland County Secondary Prins. Assn. (pres. 1983-85, Prin. of the Yr. 1991), Phi Delta Kappa (chmn. mem. Oakland br. 1998—). Office: Oakland U 311 Odowd Hall Rochester Hills MI 48309-4423 E-mail: mills@oakland.edu.

MILLS, HOLLY LYNN, registered nurse; b. Canton, Ohio, Dec. 11, 1957; d. William Louis and Ruth Elinor Drumm; m. James Harold Mills, Aug. 29, 1981 (div. Sept. 1999); children: William Glenn, Sarah Elizabeth, James Harold. RN, Aultman Hosp. Sch. Nursing, 1979; BS in edn., Franciscan U., 2002, BS in nursing, 2004. Staff nurse Aultman Hosp., Canton, Ohio, 1979—81, Ohio Valley Hosp., 1982—83; student worker Franciscan U., Steubenville, 2000—02; sub. tchr. Edison Local/Indian Creek Jefferson County, Ohio, 2002—; staff nurse orthops. Aultman Hosp., 2003. Sch. vol. Edison Local Schools, Richmond, Ohio, 1991—2003. Mem.: East Sprinfield Women's Club, Sigma Tau Delta, Kappa Delta Pi. Protestant. Avocation: reading. Home: 1819 Township Hwy 219 Richmond OH 43944

MILLS, HUGH MILTON, JR., retired college president; b. Albany, Ga., Oct. 24, 1922; s. Hugh Milton Mills Sr. and Johnie Lamar West; m. Evelyn Heath, Oct. 6, 1944 (dec. Aug. 1994); children: Hugh Milton III, Ralph West, Rebecca Ann. AA, N. Ga. Coll., 1943; BS in Edn., U. Ga., 1945, MEd, 1947, EdD, 1956; LLD (hon.), Brenau Coll., 1983. Cert. profl. tchr., Ga. Tchr., coach Rockmart (Ga.) H.S., 1945-47, Albany (Ga.) H.S., 1947-48; from instr. to asst. prof. U. Ga., Athens, 1948-51, from asst. prof. to assoc. prof., 1953-65; supervising prin. Rockmart Pub. Schs., 1951-53; pres. Gainesville (Ga.) Jr. Coll., 1965-84; interim pres. Brenau Coll., Gainesville, 1985; pres. emeritus Gainesville Coll., 1985—. Cons. Ga. Dept. Vocat. Rehab., Atlanta, 1955-65. With U.S. Army Air Corp, 1942-43. Named Ga. Man of the Yr. Conservation Dist. Ga., 1986. Mem. Phi Beta Kappa, Phi Kappa Phi, Kappa Delta Pi, Phi Delta Kappa. Baptist. Avocation: woodworking. Office: Gainesville Coll PO Box 1358 Gainesville GA 30503

MILLS, JAMES, language educator; s. James and Christina Noble Rutherford (Crawford) Mills; m. Jo Anne Homer, 1968; children: Michael, Shauna, Robert, Joseph. BA in French, Brigham Young U., 1969, MA in French, 1972; PhD, U. Utah, 1980. Cert. tchr. Utah. Instr. French So. Utah State Coll., Cedar City, 1972—76, asst. prof. French, 1976—81, assoc. prof. French, 1989—91, prof. French, 1991—; asst. prof. French U. Pa., Clarion, 1987—89. Lectr., presenter in field. Contbr. articles to profl. jours. Vol. Boy Scouts Am., Enoch, Utah, 1982—87; panelist Camp Shakespeare, Cedar City, 1993. Sgt. U.S. Army, 1969—71 USAR, 1971—72. Recipient numerous Rsch. grants. Mem.: Utah Acad. Scis., Arts and Letters, Rocky Mountain MLA, So. Utah Univ. Faculty Senate. Avocations: reading, piano, walking, writing, travel. Office: So Utah Univ Dept Fgn Lang Humanities & Philosophy 531 W Center Cedar City UT 84720 Business E-Mail: mills@suu.edu.

MILLS, JAMES STEPHEN, medical supply company executive; b. Chgo., Sept. 29, 1936; s. Irving I. and Beatrice (Shane) M.; m. Victoria L. Krisch, Mar. 23, 1973; children: Charles, Donald, Margaret. BS in Bus., Northwestern U. Vice pres. sales Mills Hosp. Supply Co., Chgo., 1961-66; pres. Medline Industries Inc., Northbrook, Ill., 1966-75, co-chair, 1975—. Served with AUS, 1958-64. Jewish. Home: 500 N Green Bay Rd Lake Forest IL 60045-2146 Office: Medline Industries Inc 1 Medline Pl Mundelein IL 60060

MILLS, JERRY WOODROW, lawyer; b. Springfield, Mo., July 17, 1940; s. Woodrow Wilson and Billie Louise M.; m. Marion Cargile, Mar. 27, 1964; children: Eric E., Brendon W. BSEE, Tex. A&M U., 1963; JD, Georgetown U., 1967. Bar: Tex. 1967, U.S. Patent Office 1967. Ptnr. Richards, Harris & Hubbard, Dallas, 1970-82, Baker, Mills & Glast, Dallas, 1982-90; sr. ptnr. BakerBotts LLP, Dallas, 1990—. Adj. prof. So. Meth. U. Law Sch., 1994-97. Bd. dirs. Dallas Legal Svcs. Project, 1972-75, Dallas Theater Ctr. Fellow Tex. Bar, Dallas Bar; mem. ABA, Tex. State Jr. Bar Assn. (treas. 1975, dir.), Dallas Jr. Bar Assn. (pres. 1971, Outstanding Young Lawyer award 1975), Dallas Bar Assn. (bd. dirs. 1983-85). Methodist. Office: BakerBotts LLP 800 Trammell Crow Ctr 2001 Ross Ave Ste 900 Dallas TX 75201-2917 E-mail: jmills@bakerbotts.com.

MILLS, JOHN T. oil industry executive, corporate financial executive; b. Canton, Ohio, 1947; B Econs., Ohio U., 1969; JD, Ohio State U., 1973. Dir. taxes and energy promoted to sr. v.p. fin. and adminstrn. USX Corp., 1998; tax specialist Marathon Oil, Findlay, Ohio, 1976, chief tax counsel, 1984, sr. v.p., CFO, 2001—. Mem.: ABA, Horizon Offshore (mem. bd. dirs.), Ohio Bar Assn., Ohio State U. Coll. Law Alumni Assn. (mem. nat. coun.), Am. Petroleum Inst. (gen. com. on fin.), Fin. Execs. Inst. Office: Marathon Oil Corp Corp Hdqrs 5555 San Felipe Rd Houston TX 77056-2723 Business E-Mail: ptijerina@marathonoil.com.

MILLS, JON, dean, law educator; b. Miami, Fla., July 24, 1947; s. Herb J. and Marguerite (Sweat) M.; m. Beth Bechard; children: Marguerite, Elizabeth. BA, Stetson U., 1969, LLD, 1986; JD, U. Fla., 1972. Mem. Fla. Ho. of Reps., 1978-88, majority leader, 1986-87, speaker, 1987-88; ptnr. McGalliard, Mills, DeMontmollin, Smith, Monaco & Sieg; mem. faculty U. Fla., Gainesville, 1973—80, prof. law, 1996—, interim dean, 1999—2001, dean, 2001—03. Bar U.S. Ct Appeals (11th Cir.); mem. Fla. Constitution Revision Commn., 1997—98. Co-author: Voting Rights and Democracy, 1996; contbr. articles to profl. jours. 1st lt. USAR. Decorated Order of Coif; recipient Allen Morris award, 1979-80, 1985-86, Outstanding Legis. award Fla. Health Care Assn., 1982, Most Valuable Member award Fla. Constn. Revision Commn., 1998; named Rep. of Yr. Assn. Retarded Citizens Fla., 1981. Fellow Am. Bar Found.; mem. ABA, Fla. Bar Assn., Pi Kappa Alpha, Fla. Blue Key. Methodist. Home: 2727 NW 58th Blvd Gainesville FL 32606-8516 Office: U Fla Coll Law 230 Bruton-Geer Hall Gainesville FL 32611 also: PO Box 117625 Gainesville FL 32611

MILLS, JOSHUA REDMOND, financial executive; b. Lynn, Mass., Aug. 30, 1936; s. Joshua and Adelaide (Redmond) M.; m. Annette Aliferis Perillo, May 29, 1965; children: Carlotta, Anastasia AB, Harvard U., 1957; postgrad., NYU, 1960-65. Cert. employee benefits specialist. With Chase Manhattan Bank, N.Y.C., 1960-63; With Continental Bank Internat., N.Y.C., 1963-66; v.p. Amerconsult Corp., N.Y.C. and Peru, 1966-74; pres. Joshua Mills & Co., North Stonington, Conn., 1974—, Fin. Counsel Corp., Westerly, R.I., 1984—. Chmn. strategy com., mem. gen. council Presbytery of N.Y.C., 1976-81; rep. to Town Meeting, Greenwich, Conn., 1981-83; mem. steering com. Tri-State Urban Conf., Fairfield County 2000 Task Force (conf.) Mem. Harvard Club (N.Y.C.), Mason's Is. Yacht Club. Libertarian. Office: 183 Providence New London Tpke North Stonington CT 06359-1721

MILLS, KEVIN LEE, information technology researcher; b. Frederick, Md., Oct. 21, 1951; s. John Lee and Doris Jean (Comer) M.; m. Karen June Davis, Dec. 30, 1972; children: Colin Walter, Elizabeth Anne. BS in Polit. Sci. and Econs., Frostburg (Md.) State U., 1973; MS in Tech. Mgmt., Am. U., 1979; PhD in Info. Tech., George Mason U., 1996. Sr. computer analyst System Devel. Corp., McLean, Va., 1976-81; project mgr. Tesdata Systems Corp., McLean, 1981-82; computer scientist Nat. Bur. of Stds., Gaithersburg, Md., 1982-84, group leader, 1984-87; divsn. chief Nat. Inst. Stds. and Tech., Gaithersburg, 1987-95; program mgr. Def. Advanced Rsch. Projects Agy., Arlington, Va., 1996-98; adj. prof. George Mason U., 1996—; divsn. chief Nat. Inst. Standards & Technology, Gaithersburg, Md., 1999-2001, sr. rsch. scientist, 2001—. Cons. in field, 1980-82. Contbr. articles to jours. Capt. USMC, 1972-78. Mem. IEEE (sr.), Assn. for Computing Machinery. Avocations: hiking, writing, reading, photography. E-mail: kmills@nist.gov.

MILLS, LAUREL, writer; b. Farmington, Maine, Jan. 19, 1946; d. Lewis Bradley and Doris Elizabeth (Brown) Lothrop; m. Thomas Waman Mills, Sept. 3, 1965 (div. Mar. 1982); children: Beth, Marissa, Neil. AA in English, U. Wis., Fox Valley, 1982; BS in English, U. Wis., Oshkosh, 1984, MA in Humanities, 1989. Outreach libr. Eliza D. Smith Pub. Libr., Menasha, Wis., 1984-87; sr. lectr. in English U. Wis. - Fox Valley, Menasha, 1988—. Tchr. of writing poetry, The Clearing, Ellison Bay, Wis., 1994-2000; instr. of creative writing, U. Wis., Oshkosh, 1988—, Fox Valley, 1986-97. Editor: Fox Cry Rev., 1997—; author: (novel) Undercurrents, 2001, (poetry books) Canada Geese Coming Home, 1986 (Writers award Coun. for Wis.), The Gull Is My Divining Rod, 1985 (Outstanding Achievement Honors Wis. Libr. Assn. 1985), Troika IV: Hidden Seed, 1992 (Posner Poetry award), I Sing Back, 1997 (Pippistrelle Best of Small Press award); contbr. to literary mags., anthologies and songs. Named Outstanding Young Alumni U. Wis., Oshkosh, 1990; recipient Writers Residency, Ragdale Found., Lake Forest, Ill., 1997, 2000-02. Mem. Wis. Fellowship of Poets (sec. 1986-87). Democrat. Avocations: swimming, reading, bicycling. Office: U Wis-Fox Valley 1478 Midway Rd Menasha WI 54952-1297 Home: 1925 Dordona Dr Neenah WI 54956-1165 E-mail: lmills@uwc.edu., writemills@prodigy.net.

MILLS, LAWRENCE, lawyer, business and transportation consultant; b. Salt Lake City, Aug. 15, 1932; s. Samuel L. and Beth (Neilson) M. BS, U. Utah, 1955, JD, 1956. Bar: Utah 1956, ICC 1961, U.S. Supreme Ct. 1963. With W.S. Hatch Co. Inc., Woods Cross, Utah, 1947-89, gen. mgr., 1963-89, v.p., 1970-89, also dir. Bd. dirs. Nat. Tank Truck Carriers, Inc., Washington, 1963—, pres., 1974-75, chmn. bd., 1975-76; mem. motor carrier adv. com. Utah State Dept. Transp., 1979—; keynote speaker Rocky Mountain Safety Suprs. Conf., 1976; mem. expedition to Antartica, 1996, Titanic Expedition, 1996. Contbr. articles to legal and profl. jours. and transp. publs. Del. to County and State Convs., Utah, 1970-72; v.p. Utah Safety Coun., 1979-82, bd. dirs., 1979—, pres., 1983-84; mem. Utah Gov's Adv. Com. on Small Bus.; capt. Easter Seal Telethon, 1989, 90; state vice chmn. High Frontier, 1987—; mem. adv. com. Utah State Indsl. Commn., 1988—, chmn. com. studying health care cost containment and reporting requirements 1990—; mem. expdn. to Antarctica, 1996, Titanic '96 expedition, Iceland expedition, 2001, Greenland expedition, 2001. Recipient Safety Dir. award Nat. Tank Carriers Co., 1967, Outstanding Svc. and Contbn. award, 1995, Trophy award W.S. Hatch Co., 1975, Disting. Svc. award Utah State Indsl. Commn., 1992, Outstanding Svc. award Utah Safety Coun., 1994. Mem. Salt Lake County Bar Assn., Utah Motor Transport Assn. (dir. 1967—, pres. 1974-76, Outstanding Achievement Award 1989), Utah Hwy. Users Assn. (dir. 1981—), Indsl. Rels. Coun. (dir. 1974—), Salt Lake City C. of C., U.S. Jaycees (life Senator 1969—, ambassador 1977—, pres. Utah Senate 1979-80, Henry Giessenbier fellow 1989), Nat. Petroleum Coun., Utah Associated Gen. Contractors (assoc. 1975-77, 88—), Silver Tank Club, Hillsdale Coll. President's Club, Traveler's Century Club. Home: HC 11 Box 329 Kamiah ID 83536-9410 Office: PO Box 1495 Kamiah ID 83536-1495 *Personal philosophy: Excessive government regulation stifles individual initiative. We should learn from the downfall of communism.*

MILLS, LINDA S. public relations executive; b. San Antonio, June 26, 1951; d. Frank M. and Betty A. (Young) M. BA, St. Mary's U., 1971. Asst. dir. Paseo Del Rio Assn., San Antonio, 1971-74; mktg. officer Frost Nat. Bank, San Antonio, 1974-79; account exec. Fleishman-Hillard Inc., St. Louis, 1979-81, v.p., sr. ptnr., 1981-85, exec. v.p., sr. ptnr., 1985-97, dir. corp. planning, 1986-97; sr. exec. v.p. comm. SBC Comm. Inc., San Antonio, 1997—. Mem. adv. bd. St. John's Mercy Med. Ctr.; bd. trustees St. Mary's U. Mem. Pub. Relations Soc. Am., Noonday Club. Office: SBC Comm Inc PO Box 2933 San Antonio TX 78299-2933

MILLS, LOIS JEAN, design company executive, retired education educator, aide; b. Chgo., Oct. 20, 1939; d. Martin J. and Annabelle M. (Hrabik) Rademacher; m. Frederick V. Mills, Dec. 1, 1974; children: Todd, Susan, Randal, Merre, Mollie, Michael, Mark (dec.). BS in Edn., Ill. State U., Normal, 1962, MS in Edn., 1969. Lectr. elem. curriculum Ill. State U., 1973-90; in-svc. advisor for elem., gifted, critical thinking and study skills, coop. learning Title I State Bd. Edn., Springfield, Ill., 1969-90; elem. tchr., supr. Metcalf Lab. Sch. Ill. State U., 1962-72; legis. aide to Asst. Majority Leader Senator John Maitland, Jr., Ill. Gen. Assembly, 1990-95; pres., ptnr. Mills Design Assocs., 1996—. Mem. state rep. Dan Rutherford's house task force for statute repeal, 1995—, adv. roundtable, 1995—, legis. task force for cmty. residential svcs. deaf adults, 1995—; campaign coord. Asst. Majority Leader Senator John Maitland, Jr., 1995—; county campaign ccord. for Ill. Comptroller Loleta Didrickson, 1994-98. Contbr. articles to profl. jours. Pres. Leadership Ill., 1994—, pres.-elect, 1993-94; past pres. governing bd. Lake Bloomington Assn., v.p., 1993-94, pres., 1994-95; mem. mgmt. com. McLean County 21st Century commn., 1991-92, vice chair cmty. rels., 1991-92; commr. McLean County Regional Planning commn., vice chair 1994-95; charter bd. govs. Ill. Lincoln Excellence in Pub. Svc. Series, 1994—, charter bd. dirs., Save the Patient health edn. and resources orgn., other civic activities; mem. Ill. steering com. Beijing-UN Women's Conf. One Yr. Later, 1996; mem. gov.'s commn. on status of women, Econ. Opportunities Working Group, 1998-. State U. Annuitants Assn. and Found. Social Security Equity/Offset. Recipient Exemplary Tchr. awards Ill. State U. Student Elem. Edn. Bd., Women of Distinction award YWCA of McLean County, Ill. State Univ. Alumni Assn. Svc. Awd. Mem. NAFE, Ill. State U. Alumni Assn. (bd. dirs. 1982—, internat. pres. 1992-94, 1994—), McLean County Rep. Women's Club (v.p. 1986, pres. 1987, past pres. 1988), Ill. Rep. Committeewoman's Roundtable, Ill. Fedn. Rep. Women, Nat. Fedn. Rep. Women, Internat. Platform Assn. Home: K-162 Lake Bloomington 25306 Arrowhead Ln Hudson IL 61748-9414

MILLS, MARGARET H. language educator; b. Davenport, Iowa, Jan. 8, 1954; d. Oliver Wendell and Elizabeth Barrett Hill; m. Marcus M. Mills, May 22, 1976; children: Olivia Lauren, Hillary Barrett, Caroline Manning. BA; MA, U. Iowa; PhD in Slavic Linguistics, U. Mich., 1985; student in Pub. Health, U. Iowa, 2004—. Instr., asst. prof. Russian Ill. State U., Normal, 1984—86; asst. prof. Russian Georgetown U., Washington, 1986—89, U. Iowa, Iowa City, 1989—93; assoc. prof. Russian, 1993—2000, prof. Russian, 2000—. Author: Topics in Colloquial Russian, 1990, UI Neonatology Handbook, 1997, Slavic Gender Linguistics, 1999, Medical Issues and Health Care Reform in Russia, 1999; contbr. articles to profl. jours. Grantee, Nat. Rsch. Coun., 1997, Social Sci. Rsch. Coun., 1996—98, NIH, 2000, Eurasia Found., Washington and Moscow, 2000, Am. Coun. Internat. Edn., Moscow, 2001. Office: U Iowa Dept Russian Iowa City IA 52242 Office Phone: 319-335-2848.

MILLS, MICHAEL JAMES, architect; b. Streator, Ill., Feb. 18, 1951; s. Harry Nelson and Ruth Ludia (Piel) M.; m. Kathryn Louise Brewington, June 6, 1974 (div. Feb. 1977); m. Beverly Jane Ballard, Mar. 14, 1981; children: Kevin Charles, Jeffrey Ross, Caroline Ruth. BA, Princeton U., 1973; cert., ICCROM, 1979; MS, Columbia U., 1980. Registered architect, N.J., S.C., N.Y., D.C., Pa., Mich.; lic. profl. planner, N.J. Draftsman John Milner Assocs., West Chester, Pa., 1973-74, John Diehl & Assocs., Princeton, N.J., 1974-75; project mgr. Heritage Studies, Princeton, N.J., 1975-76; draftsman Short and Ford Architects, Princeton, N.J., 1976-78; apprentice architect The Ehrenkrantz Group, N.Y.C., 1979-80, Short & Ford & Ptnrs., Princeton, 1980-83, assoc., 1983-87; partner Short & Ford & Ptnrs. (name changed to Ford, Farewell, Mills and Gatsch Architects 1992), Princeton, 1987-92, 1992—. Cons. Burlington County Hist. Dist. Commn., Burlington, N.J., 1983-93. Contbr. articles to profl. jours. Chmn. Hopewell Planning Bd., 1985-89. Excellence in Architecture N.J. Soc. Architects, 1989, 92, 98, hon. mention, 1983. Mem. AIA, Assn. Preservtion Tech., Nat. Trust for Hist. Preservation, N.J. Soc. Architects, U.S.-Internat. Coun. on Monuments and Sites. Presbyterian. Avocations: guitar, photography, tennis. Office: Ford Farewell Mills and Gatsch Architects 864 Mapleton Rd Princeton NJ 08540-9538

MILLS, MICHAEL PAUL, judge; b. Charleston, South Carolina, Aug. 25, 1956; s. Paul H. and Shirley (Dulaney) M.; m. Mona (Robinson), Aug. 2, 1976; children: Alysson, Chip, Rebekah, Penn. AA, Itawamba Cmty. Coll., Fulton, Miss., 1976; BA, U. Miss., 1978, JD, 1980; LLM, U. Va., 2001. Bar: Miss., 1980; U.S. Ct. Appeals (Fed. Cir.), 1986; U.S. Ct. Appeals (5th cir.), 1980; U.S. Supreme Ct., 1990. Pvt. practice, Miss., 1980-95; legis. Miss. Ho. of Reps., Jackson, Miss., 1983-95; mem. Nat. Conf. Commr. on Uniform State Laws, 1993—; justice Miss. Supreme Ct., Jackson, Miss., 1995—2001; judge US Dist. Ct. (no. dist.), Miss., Oxford, 2001—. Adj. prof. law U. Miss. Office: Fed Bldg Rm 335 911 Jackson Ave Oxford MS 38655

MILLS, NICOLAUS, American studies educator, writer; b. Cleve., Dec. 2, 1938; s. Nicolaus and Muriel Mills. AB, Harvard U., 1960; PhD, Brown U., 1966. Asst. prof. English. U. Mich., Ann Arbor, 1965-70; rschr. Ctr. for Urban and Minority Studies Columbia U. Tchrs. Coll., N.Y.C., 1970-72; prof. Am. studies Sarah Lawrence Coll., Bronxville, N.Y., 1972—. Author: American and English Fiction in the Nineteenth Century, 1973, The Crowd in American Literature, 1986, Like a Holy Crusade: Mississippi 1964, 1992, The Triump of Meanness: America's War Against Its Better Self, 1997, Their Lost Battle: The Fight for the National World War II Memorial, 2004; Editor: Comparisons: A Short Story Anthology, 1972, The Great School Bus Controversy, 1973, The New Journalism, 1974, Busing USA, 1979, Culture in the Age of Money, 1990, Forty Years of Dissent, 1994, Agruing Immigraton, 1994, Debating Affirmative Action, 1994; co-editor: The New Killing fields: Massacre and the Politics of Intervention, 2002; mem. editl. bd. Dissent, 1980-; Sunday mag. columnist Cleve. Plain Dealer, 1998-99; contbr. articles to mags. and newspapers, including N.Y. Times, L.A. Times, Newsday, Chgo. Tribune, San Francisco Chronicle, Nation, New Republic, Yale Rev., Dissent, Boston Globe. Woodrow Wilson fellow, 1960, Rockefeller Found., 1980; grantee Am. Coun. Learned Socs., 1971, Hewlett-Mellon grantee Sarah Lawrence Coll., 1996; sr. scholar Woodwor Wilson Internat. Ctr., Washington, 2001-2002. Mem.: PEN. Democrat. Office: Sarah Lawrence Coll One Mead Way Bronxville NY 10708 Business E-Mail: nmills@slc.edu.

MILLS, OLAN, II, photography company executive; b. 1930; married. Grad., Princeton U., 1952. With Olan Mills, Inc., Chattanooga, 1955—, now chmn., sec., also bd. dirs. Office: Olan Mills Inc Gen Offices 4325 Amnicola Hwy Chattanooga TN 37406-1014

MILLS, P. GERALD, retail executive; b. 1929; With L.S. Ayres & Co., buyer, stores mgr., pres., CEO; chmn., CEO Dayton Hudson's, Mpls., 1978-81, Detroit, 1981-82; exec. v.p. Dayton Hudson Corp., 1982-85; chmn. bd., pres., CEO Jacobson Stores, Inc., Jackson, Mich., 1996—. Bd. dirs. Comerica Inc., Detroit, Norwest Bank, Mpls. Chmn. bd. trustees Earlham Coll., Richmond, Ind.; bd. dirs. Detroit Renaissance Found., Indpls. Symphony Orch. Office: Jacobson Stores Inc 3333 Sargent Rd Jackson MI 49201-8847 Fax: (516) 764-1479.

MILLS, REBECCA, national park administrator; BA, Swarthmore Coll., 1961; MSW, U. Calif., Berkeley, 1968. Cmty. and individual social work, 1963-69; adminstrv. analyst Statewide Pres.'s Office U. Calif., 1969-72; exec. dir. Advocates for Women Econ. Devel. Ctr., 1972-76; cons. in fundraising and tng. Stanford U., Girl Scouts USA, others, 1976-78; equal opportunity mgr., chief youth programs Western Regional Nat. Park Svc., 1978-95; supr. Gt. Basin Nat. Park, 1995—. Office: Great Basin Nat Pk Hwy 488 Baker NV 89311

MILLS, RICHARD HENRY, federal judge; b. Beardstown, Ill., July 19, 1929; s. Myron Epler and Helen Christine (Greve) M.; m. Rachel Ann Keagle, June 16, 1962; children: Jonathan K., Daniel Cass. BA, Ill. Coll., 1951; JD, Mercer U., 1957; LLM, U. Va., 1982. Bar: Ill. 1957, U.S. Dist. Ct. Ill. 1958, U.S. Ct. Appeals 1959, U.S. Ct. Mil. Appeals 1963, U.S. Supreme Ct. 1963. Legal advisor Ill. Youth Commn., 1958-60; state's atty. Cass County, Virginia, Ill., 1960-64; judge Ill. 8th Jud. Cir., Virginia, 1966-76, Ill. 4th Dist. Appellate Ct., Springfield, Ill., 1976-85, U.S. Dist. Ct. (cen. dist.) Ill., Springfield, 1985—. Adj. prof. So. Ill. U. Sch. Medicine, 1985—; mem. adv. bd. Nat. Inst. Corrections, Washington, 1984-88, Ill. Supreme Ct. Rules Com., Chgo., 1963-85. Contbr. articles to profl. jours. Pres. Abraham Lincoln coun. Boy Scouts Am., 1978-80. With U.S. Army, 1952-54, Korea, col. res.; maj. gen. Ill. Militia. Recipient George Washington Honor medal Freedoms Found., 1969, 73, 75, 82, Disting. Eagle Scout Boy Scouts Am., 1985. Fellow Am. Bar Found.; mem. ABA, Nat. Conf. Fed. Trial Judges (chmn. 1999-00), Ill. Bar Assn., Chgo. Bar Assn., Cass County Bar Assn. (pres. 1962-64, 75-76), Sangamon County Bar Assn., 7th Cir. Bar Assn., Am. Law Inst., Fed. Judges Assn., Army and Navy Club (Washington), Sangamo Club, Masons (33 degree), Lincoln-Douglas Am. Inn of Ct. 150 (founding, pres. 1991-93). Republican. Office: US Dist Ct 600 E Monroe St Ste 117 Springfield IL 62701-1659 Office Phone: 217-492-4340.

MILLS, RICHARD PAUL, school system administrator; b. Paris, Nov. 28, 1944; m. Judith Mills. BA with honors, Middlebury Coll., 1966; MA in Am. History, Columbia U., 1967, MBA, 1975, EdD, 1977. Tchr. history Dalton Sch., N.Y.C., 1967—71; creator with others Elizabeth Seeger Sch., N.Y.C., 1971—73; planning assoc. N.J. Dept. of Edn., 1975-78, dir. policy analysis, 1978-80, dep. asst. commr., 1980-82, spl. asst. to the commr., 1982-84; spl. asst. to Gov. Thomas H. Kean of N.J., 1984-88; commr. of edn. State of Vt., 1988-95, State of N.Y., 1995—; pres. Univ. of the State of N.Y., 1995—. Adj. asst. prof. Columbia Univ. Tchrs. Coll., 1977; adj. assoc. prof. Rider Coll., N.J., 1979; cons. task force to oversee fiscal reform in Newark, 1975; tchr. The Dalton Sch., N.Y.C., 1967-71, Elizabeth Seeger Sch., N.Y.C., 1971-73; mem. Carnegie Task Force on Learning in the Primary Grades; chair mgmt. group Nat. Alliance for Restructuring Edn.; bd. New Stds. Project; mem. bd. Nat. Ctr. on Edn. and the Economy. Contbr. articles to profl. jours. U.S. rep. to standing com. European Ministers of Edn., 1987. Office: NY State Edn Dept 111 Edn Bldg 89 Washington Ave Albany NY 12234-4909

MILLS, RILLA DEAN, university administrator, consultant; b. Mt. Pleasant, Iowa, Dec. 16, 1942; s. Chester Jimmie and Leora Mae (Riley) M.; m. Sue Veranne Cornick, June 6, 1965; children— Jason Cornick, Jesse Nelson Student, Talladega Coll., 1964; BA, U. Iowa, 1965; A.M., U. Mich., 1967; PhD, U. Ill., 1981. Editor The Daily Iowan, Iowa City, 1963-64; reporter The Evening Sun, Balt., 1967-69; Moscow and Washington corr. The Sun, Balt., 1969-75; instr. U. Miss., Oxford, 1976; asst. prof., lectr. U. Ill., Urbana, 1976-79; lectr., assoc. prof. Calif. State U.-Fullerton, 1979-83; dir. Sch. Journalism Pa. State U., University Park, 1983—. Cons. various newspapers Contbr. articles to popular and scholarly jours. Gannett teaching fellow, Ind. U., 1977; adminstrv. fellow Columbia U., 1985 Mem. Assn. for Edn. in Journalism and Mass Communication, Speech Communication Assn., Phi Kappa Phi Home: 640 Royal Cir State College PA 16801-6459

MILLS, ROBERT LEE, academic administrator emeritus; b. Erlanger, Ky., Nov. 13, 1916; s. John Clifford and Dixie Lee (Morris) M.; m. Mildred Sizer, June 24, 1942; children: Robert Lee, Dixie Louise, Barbara Jean. AB in Math. and Physics, U. Ky., 1938, MA in Ednl. Adminstrn, 1941, Ed.D., 1951; LLD, William Jewell Coll., 1971. Tchr. Covington (Ky.) pub. schs., 1938-41; head hydraulics br. Air Force Tech. Sch., Lincoln, Nebr., 1942-44; mem. supervisory staff electromagnetic plant Oak Ridge, Tenn., 1944-48; research asst. U. Ky., Lexington, 1948-51, dean admissions, registrar, 1954-57; dir. research, head bur. adminstrn. and finance Ky. Dept. Edn., 1951-54; chmn. dept. ednl. adminstrn. U. Tex., Austin, 1957-59; pres. Georgetown (Ky.) Coll., 1959-78, chancellor, 1978-86, pres. emeritus, 1987—. Exec. sec. Ky. Adv. Commn. Ednl. Policy, 1952-54; v.p. Ky. Assn. Colls. and Secondary Schs., 1962-63, exec. com., 1959-64, pres., 1963-64; chmn. exec. com. Ky. Ind. Coll. Found.; mem. Ky. Commn. on Higher Edn., 1967-70, Ky. Govt. Council, 1968-72; adviser Texas Assn. Sch. Bds., 1957-59 Contbr. articles to profl. jours. Cons. Pres.' Com., White House Conf. Edn., 1955; mem. Ky. Devel. Council, 1961-65, Ky. Constn. Revision Assembly, 1964-66. Recipient Distinguished Alumni award U. Ky., 1963, Centennial award, 1964 Mem. Nat., Ky. edn. assns., Newcomen Soc., So. Assn. Bapt. Colls. (pres. 1965-66), Bapt. World Alliance (mem. exec. com. 1965-70, chmn. men's dept. 1965-67), So. Assn. Colls. and Schs. (commn. on colls. 1971-77), Kappa Delta Pi, Phi Delta Kappa, Phi Kappa Tau. Lodges: Kiwanis. Democrat. Baptist.

MILLS, RUSSELL ANDREW, dean; b. St. Thomas, Ont., Can., July 14, 1944; s. Gerald Armond and Phyllis Marie (Hulse) M.; m. Judith Elizabeth Zimmerman, Mar. 25, 1967; children: Lara, Colin, Patrick. BA, U. Western Ont., London, 1967, MA, 1968. Reporter London (Ont.) Free Press, 1964-67; city editor The Oshawa (Ont.) Times, 1970; asst. city editor, night editor, asst. mng. editor The Ottawa (Ont.) Citizen, 1971-85, exec. editor, 1975-76, editor, 1977-84, gen.mgr., 1984-86, pub., 1986-89; pres. Southam Newspaper Group, Toronto, Canada, 1989-92; pres., publ. The Ottawa (Ont.) Citizen, 1992—2002; dean Sch. Media and Design Algonquin Coll., Ottawa, Canada, 2003—.

MILLS, STEPHANIE ELLEN, writer; b. Berkeley, Calif., Sept. 11, 1948; d. Robert C. and Edith (Garrison) M.; m. Philip Thiel (div. 1990). BA, Mills Coll., 1969. Campus organizer Planned Parenthood, Alameda, San Francisco, Calif., 1969-70; editor in chief Earth Times, San Francisco, 1970; story editor Earth, San Francisco, 1971; conference facilitator Mills Coll., Oakland, 1973-74; writer family planning program Emory Univ., Atlanta, 1974; dir. outings program Friends of the Earth, San Francisco, 1975-76, dir. membership devel., 1976-78; fellow Found. for Nat. Progress, San Francisco, 1978-80; from asst. editor to editor CoEvolution Quar., Sausalito, Calif., 1980-82; editor in chief, rsch. dir. Calif. Tomorrow, San Francisco, 1982-83; dir. devel. World Coll. West, San Rafael, Calif., 1983-84; freelance writer, lectr., 1984—; adj. prof. Grand Valley State Univ., Traverse City, Mich., 2002. V.p. Earth First! Found., 1986-89; pres. No. Mich. Environ. Action Coun., 1987-88; mem. planning com. Great Lakes Bioregional Congress, 1991; pres. bd. dirs. Oryana Natural Foods Coop., 1992-93; mem. adv. coun. Earth Island Inst., mem. adv. bd. Orion Soc., mem. Am. for Maine Woods, Nat. Park Adv. com., Northwoods Wilderness Recovery. Author: In Service of the Wild: Restoring and Reinhabiting Damaged Land, 1995, Whatever Happened to Ecology?, 1989, Epicurean Simplicity, 2002; editor: Turning Away from Technology: A New Vision for the Twenty-first Century, 1997 (Utne Visionary award 1996); editor, contbr. In Praise of Nature, 1990; corr. Wild Earth; editor-in-chief Not Man Apart newsletter from Friends of the Earth, 1978; editl. adv. E; contbr. to Ency. Brit. Book of Yr., 1998; contbr. articles to popular mags. Bd. dirs. Planned Parenthood Fedn. Am., 1970-76. Recipient award Mademoiselle, 1969, Friends of UN Environ. Program, 1987; grantee Point Found., 1972, IRA-HITI Found., 1992; resident Blue Mountain Ctr., 1983, 86. Avocations: swimming, cooking. Office: care Katinka Matson Brockman Inc 5 E 59th St New York NY 10022-1027

MILLS, STEPHEN, artistic director; Prin. dancer Ballet Austin, 1987, choreographer, 1988, resident choreographer, 1992, assoc. artistic dir., 1999—, artistic dir. Instr. Internat. Theatrical Inst., Cyprus; master tchr. Booker T. Washington H.S. for the Performing Arts, Dallas, Va. Sch. of the Arts, New Orleans Ctr. for Creative Arts, Stephens Coll., Mo., Point Park Coll., Pitts., Ballet Austin. Choreographed works have been shown at Ballet Builders at Lincoln Ctr., 1998, Rencontres Chorégraphiques Internat. des Seine-Saint-Denis, Paris, Cuballet, Havana, The Dayton Ballet, The Sarasota (Fla.) Ballet, Ballet Pacifica, Dallas Black Dance Theatre, Dance Kaleidoscope, Ontario Ballet Theatre, Toronto, Icelandic Ballet Co., Reykjavik0; performing mem. Harkness Ballet, Am. Dance Machine, Cin. Ballet, Indpls. Ballet Theatre, Balanchine Repertoire. Office: Ballet Austin 3002 Guadalupe St Austin TX 78705-2818

MILLS, STEVEN A. information technology executive; Sales trainee, mktg. rep. IBM, N.Y.C., 1974—80, mem. bus. planning staff divsn. data processing, 1981—82, mgr. bus. planning staff, 1982—84, adminstrv. asst. to v.p. and asst. group exec. plans and controls, 1984—85, dir. planning info. sys. and comm. group, 1985—88, dir. fin. planning, 1988—89, dir. ops. programming sys., 1989—90, asst. gen. mgr. fin. and planning, 1990—92, gen. mgr. Santa Teresa lab., 1992—95; gen. mgr. software group strategy and solutions IBM Software Group, 1995—2000, sr. v.p., group exec., 2000—. Mem. ops. com. IBM, mem. worldwide mgmt. coun., mem. corp. tech. com. Office: IBM 1133 Westchester Ave White Plains NY 10604

MILLS, STEVEN R. food products executive; b. 1955; Controller Archer Daniels Midland Co., 1994—, group v.p., 2002—. Office: Archer Daniels Midland Co 4666 Farus Pkwy Decatur IL 62526

MILLS, TEHERAN L. (TERRY MILLS), sociology educator; b. N.Y.C., Feb. 5, 1949; s. Lehman R. and Shirley Marie MIlls; m. Antonia Allen, Feb. 10, 1968; children: Brion K., Dion L. BA in Polit. Sci., L.I. U., 1974; MA in Sociology, U. So. Calif., 1995, PhD in Sociology and Gerontology, 1996. Asst. prof. U. Fla., Gainesville, 1996—. Editl. bd. Jour. Family Issues, Gainesville. Faculty advisor Alpha Kappa Delta Sociology Honor Soc., Gainesville. Avocations: hiking, golf, travel. Office: U Fla PO Box 117330 Gainesville FL 32611-7330 Fax: (352) 392-6568. E-mail: tlmills@soc.ufl.edu.

MILLS, WILLIAM HAROLD, JR., construction company executive; b. St. Petersburg, Fla., July 24, 1939; s. William Harold and Caroline (Bonfoey) M.; m. Sylvia Ludwig, Jan. 4, 1962 (div. 1975); children— William Harold III, Robert Michael, Leslie Anne; m. Kimberly Keyes, May 4, 1985 (div. 1988); m. Gigi Alice Schmidt, Aug. 1, 1990. Grad., Woodberry Forest Sch., 1954-57; BS in Civil Engring., U. Fla., 1961. Cert. Class A gen. contractor, Fla. V.P. bus. devel. Mills & Jones Constrn., St. Petersburg, Fla., 1964-68; v.p. Wellington Corp., Atlanta, 1968-71; exec. v.p. Mills & Jones Constrn., St. Petersburg, Fla., 1971-79; pres., chmn. Federal Constrn. Co., St. Petersburg, 1979-88, vice chmn., 1988—; pres., chair Univ. Housing Svcs., Inc., St. Petersburg. Mem. adv. com. St Petersburg Port, 1993—. Pres. St. Petersburg Progress, Inc., 1986-87; active mem. Suncoasters, St. Petersburg, 1974—, St. Anthony's Devel. Found., St. Petersburg, 1983-86; past chmn. Pinellas Marine Inst., St. Petersburg, Blue Ribbon Zoning Com., City of St. Petersburg; mem. Tony Janus Award Com.; former mem. Pinellas County Constrn. Licensing Bd., Tampa Bay Aviation Adv. Com., United Fund Pinellas County; former mem. U. South Fla. Campus Adv. Bd. Served with USPHS, 1962-64. Named Hon. Royal Navy Liaison officer Her Majesty's Royal Navy, 1984. Mem. ASCE, NSPE, Am. Mgmt. Assn., Mensa, St. Petersburg Area C. of C. (bd. govs. 1983-85), Fla. Sports Adv. Coun., Order of Salvador/Salvador Dali Mus., St. Petersburg Yacht Club, Dragon Club, Les Ambassadeurs Club (London), Annabel's Club (London), Useppa Island Club (past bd. govs.), Sigma Alpha

Epsilon, U.S. Croquet Assn., Univ. Fla. Pres.'s Coun. (life). Republican. Episcopalian. Home: 1260 Brightwaters Blvd NE Saint Petersburg FL 33704-3728 Office: 25 2d St N Ste 400 Saint Petersburg FL 33701 E-mail: wmillsjr@uhsi.com.

MILLS, WILLIAM HAYES, lawyer; b. Gordo, Ala., Mar. 30, 1931; s. Early S. and Bama (Cameron) M. LLB, U. Ala., 1956. Bar: Ala. 1956. Pvt. practice, Birmingham, Ala.; ptnr. Rogers, Howard, Redden & Mills, 1961—79, Redden, Mills & Clark, 1979—. Arbitrator Fed. Mediation and Conciliation Svc., Am. Arbitration Assn. Served with AUS, 1948-50, 50-51. Mem. ABA, Ala. Bar Assn., Birmingham Bar Assn., ATLA. Baptist. Home: 2105 Williamsburg Way Birmingham AL 35223-1740 Office: Redden Mills & Clark 940 Financial Ctr Birmingham AL 35203 Office Phone: 205-322-0457. E-mail: whm@rmclaw.com.

MILLS, WILLIAM R. food products executive; V.p. fin., sec. Weis Markets, Sundbury, Pa., 1992—2002, sr. v.p., 2002—, CFO, 2002—, treas., 2002—. Bd. dirs. Weis Markets. Office: Weis Markets 1000 S Second St Sunbury PA 17801*

MILLSAPS, FRED RAY, investor; b. Blue Ridge, Ga., Apr. 30, 1929; s. Samuel Hunter and Ora Lee (Bradshaw) M.; m. Audrey Margaret Hopkins, June 22, 1957; children: Judith Gail, Stephen Hunter, Walter Scott. AB, Emory U., 1951; postgrad., U. Wis. Sch. Banking, 1955-57, Harvard Bus. Sch., 1962; LLD, Fla. So. Coll., 1991. V.p. Fed. Res. Bank, Atlanta, 1958-64; fin. v.p. Fla. Power & Light Co., 1965-69; chmn., pres. Landmark Banking Corp. of Fla., Ft. Lauderdale, 1969-78. Bd. dirs. Franklin Templeton Mut. Funds, Mut. Shares Funds. Chmn. South Fla. Coordinating Coun., 1976-78, WPBT Cmty. TV Found. of South Fla., 1973-75, Fla. So. Coll., Lakeland, 1976-95, Broward Performing Arts Authority, Honda Classic, Broward Workshop, Holy Cross Health Corp.; mem. Fla. Coun. of 100. Mem. Coral Ridge Country Club. Methodist.

MILLSAPS, WILLIAM HOBART, JR., newspaper editor; b. Chattanooga, July 1, 1942; s. William Hobart and Myra Sue (Bryant) M.; m. Nancy Dickenson Hurt; children: Katherine Gail Millsaps Renick, Camerian Sue. Student, U. Tenn., 1960-66. Sports writer The Knoxville (Tenn.) Jour., 1963-66, Richmond (Va.) Times-Dispatch, 1966-71, assoc. sports editor, 1972, exec. sports editor, 1973-76, sports editor, 1977-91, mng. editor, 1992-93, exec. editor, 1994—, sr. v.p., 1996—. Pres. U.S. Basketball Writers Assn., 1986, AP Sports Editors, 1980; pres. Leadership Metro Richmond Alumni Assn., 1995. Named to, U.S. Basketball Writers Assn. Hall of Fame, media wing Va. Sports Hall of Fame; recipient 11 Va. Sports Writer of Yr. awards, Nat. Sportscasters and Sportswriters Assn. Mem. AP Mng. Editors, Am. Soc. Newspaper Editors, Willow Oaks Country Club Richmond, Downtown Club Richmond. Presbyterian. Avocations: reading, golf. E-mail: bmillsaps@timesdispatch.com.

MILLSPAUGH, MARTIN LAURENCE, real estate developer, urban development consultant; b. Columbus, Ohio, Dec. 16, 1925; s. Martin Laurence and Elisabeth (Park) M.; m. Meredith Plant, May 10, 1952; children: Elisabeth, M. Laurence, Meredith, Thomas. AB summa cum laude, Princeton U., 1949. Reporter, columnist Richmond News Leader, Va., 1949-53; urban affairs writer Balt. Evening Sun, 1953-57; asst. commr. Urban Renewal Adminstrn., Washington, 1957-60; dep. gen. mgr. Charles Ctr., Balt., 1960-65; pres., chmn., CEO Charles Ctr.-Inner Harbor Mgmt., Inc., 1965-85; exec. v.p., pres., vice chmn. Enterprise Devel. Co., Columbia, Md., 1985—, also bd. dirs.; pres. Enterprise Internat. Devel. Co., Columbia, 1988-91, vice chmn., 1991—, Enterprise Real Estate Svcs., Inc., 1996—. Cons. to pvt. developers and local pub. agys., Mass., Va., S.C., Fla., Calif., Sydney, 1981—; conducted seminars in Nagasaki and Kagoshima, Japan, 1991-92; lectr. Columbia U., Princeton U., Johns Hopkins U., U. Md., U. New Orleans, NYU, Acad. Polit. Sci., AAAS, Lambda Alpha Internat., 1991, 95, U.K. Inst. Travel and Tourism, 1993, Can. Water Resources Assn., 1991, Nat. Bldg. Mus., 1995, Internat. Property Market, Cannes, 1996, others; appeared on USIA Worldnet TV Dialogue, Montevideo, Uruguay, 1990, Recife and Rio de Janeiro, 1995. Author: (with others) The Human Side of Urban Renewal, 1958; author, editor (monograph) Baltimore's Charles Center, 1964; author (newspaper series) Design for Living (hon. mention Heywood Broun award 1957); profl. appearances include VOA, 1994, CBS Sunday News, 1994; contbr. articles to profl. jours. Trustee Enoch Pratt Free Libr., Balt., 1965-85, Gilman Sch., 1975-80, Bryn Mawr Sch. for Girls, 1978-81; bd. dirs. Planned Parenthood Assn. Md., 1962-65, Roland Park Civic League, 1962-64, sec., 1963-64, Blue Cross of Md., Inc., 1970-80, Balt. Symphony Orch. Assn., 1974-78, YMCA of Greater Balt. area, 1977-81; Md. Internat. Coun., Balt., 1992-96, mem. long range planning com., 1994-96, sec., 1995-96; mem. chair nominating com. World Trade Ctr. Inst., 1996-01; mem. task force Twentieth Century Fund, N.Y.C., 1984-85; mem. adv. coun. real estate devel. program Columbia U. Grad. Sch. Architecture and Planning, 1985-94; bd. advisors Fight-Blight Fund, Balt., 1961-62, Waterfront Ctr., Washington, 1987-90; adv. bd. Nat. Aquarium, Balt., 1988-2001, Sch. Bus. Mgmt. Morgan State U., 1993-94, Real Estate Inst., Sch. Profl. and Bus. Studies Johns Hopkins U., 1994—, chair, 2000-2002; pres.'s adv. bd. U. Md. Balt. County, 1989-94; mem. adv. bd. Ctr. for Balt. Studies/U. Balt., 2001-02; mem. adv. panel Ctr. Strategic and Internat. Studies, Washington, 1993-94; mem. Md. Transp. Real Estate Adv. Group, 1996; mem. U.S. Senate Productivity Award Selection Com. for Md., 1987. Served to sgt. USAF, 1944-46, PTO. Recipient Disting. Svc. award U.S. Housing and Home Fin. Agy., Washington, 1960, Urban Planning award The Waterfront Ctr., 1995, Awd. for Civic Accomplishment Greater Balt. Comm., 1981, Prix of Excellence Awd. Internat. Real Estate Fedn., 1997, Awd. of Excellence, 1980. Mem. Urban Land Inst. (exec. group internat. coun., 1989-97, vice chmn. internat. coun. 1995-96, chair adv. panel for city of Harrisburg, Pa., 1984, internat. com. 1987-88, Balt. dist. coord. 1987-91, vice-chmn. dist. coun. com. 1991-94, exec. com. 1992-, mem. adv. panel for Oklahoma City, 1995, hon. life coun. mem. 1995-, chair Project Analysis Chattanooga, 1999, awards com. 1995-97), Internat. Real Estate Fedn., Greater Balt. Com. (urban affairs coun. 1982-87), Coun. on Urban Econ. Devel., Internat. Downtown Assn., Internat. New Town Assn. (mem. adv. panel for waterfront devel. for City of Malmo, Sweden 1987), Phi Beta Kappa, Lambda Alpha. Clubs: Center, Balt., 14 W Hamilton St (Balt.); Ivy (Princeton, N.J.). Democrat. Episcopalian. Home and Office: 203 Ridgewood Rd Baltimore MD 21210-2538 Office: Enterprise Devel Co 10320 Little Pataxent Pkwy Columbia MD 21044 E-mail: martinmillspaugh@ereserve.com.

MILLSTEIN, DAVID J. lawyer; b. N.Y.C., Apr. 15, 1953; s. Stanley and Irma (Klein) M. AB, U. Calif., Berkeley, 1975, JD, 1979. Bar: Calif. 1979, U.S. Dist. Ct. (no. dist.) Calif. 1979, U.S. Dist. Ct. (ea. dist.) Calif. 1984. Assoc. Bostwick & Tehin, San Francisco, 1991-93; asst. dist. atty. San Francisco Dist. Atty.'s Office, 1993—; pvt. practice San Francisco, 1982-95, 97—; ptnr. Millstein & Doolittle, San Francisco, 1996-97; chief asst. dist. Atty. City and County of San Francisco, 1996; ptnr. Millstein & Assocs., San Francisco, 1997—. Judge pro tem San Francisco Mcpl. Ct., 1983—; probation monitor Calif. State Bar, 1995—; panelist Calif. Psychol. Assn.; lectr. San Francisco Gen. Hosp., Stanford U., 1994, Boalt Hall Sch. of Law, U. Calif., Berkeley, 1995-98, 2002–; adj. prof. Hastings Coll. Law, San Francisco, 1993—, co-chair advocacy sect., 1994-95; chief asst. dist. atty. City and County of San Francisco, 1996. Author supplement to How to Prepare For, Take and Use a Deposition, 1995; contbr. articles to law jours. Office: 685 Market St Fl 6 San Francisco CA 94105

MILLSTEIN, HERBERT SYDNEY, management consultant; b. Chgo., May 17, 1920; s. John and Bessie (Friedman) Millstein; m. Karen Annette Edward, Aug. 21, 1971; children: Merle, Randy, Howard stepchildren: David, Daniel, Dale, Douglas. BS, U. Ill., 1942; MBA in Exec. Program, UCLA, 1960. Tng. officer, contbg. negotiator VA, East St. Louis, Ill., 1947-48; indsl. engr. Arthur K. Meyer Co., L.A., 1948-52; radar test engr. Hughes Aircraft, L.A., 1952; chief prodn. divsn., spl. asst. ballistic missiles and space, chief ballistic missile logistics mgmt. div. USAF L.A. Air Procurement Dist., 1952-59; mem. tech. staff Intellectronics Lab., TRW, Canoga Park, Calif., 1959-60; v.p. Ops. Rsch., Inc., Santa Monica, Calif., 1960-62; v.p., co-founder Mgmt. Tech., Inc., L.A., 1962-68; pres., dir. Mktg. Scis. Corp., Washington, 1968-74; tech. dir. JFMIP; dir. nat. productivity group, acctg. and fin. mgmt. divsn. GAO, Washington, 1974-86; pres. TRM, 1986-90; pres., chmn. bd. Millins Corp., Oviedo, Fla., 1990—; pres. Chiofbrd. Co-founder Inst. Applied Pub. Fin. Am. U., adj. prof. Contbr. articles to profl. jours. Chancellor Farms Civic Assn., Springfield, Va., 1979—80. With USAAF, 1944—46. Mem.: AIAA, AAAS, Ind. Acad. Sci., Assn. Govt. Accts. (cert. govt. fin. mgr.), Inst. Mgmt. Scis., Ops. Rsch. Soc. Am. Home and Office: 3449 Sterling Lake Cir Oviedo FL 32765-5168 Office Phone: 407-977-6678. E-mail: HKMills2@aol.com.

MILLSTEIN, IRA M. lawyer, lecturer; b. N.Y.C., Nov. 8, 1926; s. Harry M. and Birdie E. (Rosenbaum) M.; m. Diane G. Greenberg, July 3, 1949; children: James Eliot, Elizabeth Jane. BS, Columbia U., 1947, LL.B., 1949. Bar: N.Y. 1949, U.S. Supreme Ct. 1973. Atty. antitrust div. Dept. Justice, Washington, 1949-51; assoc. firm Weil Gotshal & Manges LLP, N.Y.C., 1951-57, ptnr., 1957—. Fellow faculty govt. John F. Kennedy Sch. Govt., Harvard U., 1983-87; Eugene F. Williams Jr. vis. prof. in competetive enterprise and strategy Yale Sch. Mgmt., 1996—; chmn. pvt. sector adv. group on corp. Global Corp. Governance Forum sponsored by World Bank/OECD-Paris, Washington, 1999—; counsel, bd. dirs. Lower Manhattan Devel. Corp., 2002–; chmn. bd. Internat. Inst. for Corp. Governance, Yale Sch. Mgmt., 2002—. Author: (with Katsh) The Limits of Corporate Power, 1981, (with McAvoy) The Recurrent Crisis in Corporate Governance, 2003; contbr. articles to profl. jours. Mem. Nat. Commn. on Consumer Fin., 1969-72, chmn., 1971-72; chmn. exec. com. bd. overseers Albert Einstein Coll. Medicine, Yeshiva U., Bronx, N.Y., 1981—; former chmn. bd. trustees Cen. Pk. Conservancy, 1990-99; co-chair NYSE, NASD Blue Ribbon com. on improving audit coms., 1999. Decorated chevalier Nat. Order of Merit, France. Mem. Am. Acad. Arts and Scis. (elected), ABA (chmn. antitrust law sect. 1977-78), N.Y. State Bar Assn. (chmn. antitrust law sect. 1967-68), Nat. Assn. Corp. Dirs. (bd. dirs. 1994—), Met. Club, Quaker Ridge Golf Club. Home: 1240 Flagler Dr Mamaroneck NY 10543-4601 Office: Weil Gotshal & Manges LLP 767 5th Ave Ste 3201 New York NY 10153-0023 E-mail: ira.millstein@weil.com.

MILLSTEIN, LINCOLN, digital media company executive; BA in Polit. Sci., U. Conn.; postgrad., Stanford U., 1980—81. Reporter, editor The Hartford Courant, 1973—83, bus. editor, 1981—83; various editor positions The Globe, 1983—85; v.p. new media The Boston Globe, 1995—99; CEO Boston.com, 1998—99; group v.p., pub. N.Y. Times Digital, N.Y. Times Co., NY, 1999—2000, exec. v.p., 2000—. Profl. Journalism fellow, NEH, 1980—81. Achievements include development of and introduction of The Globe 100 list of the top companies in Massachusetts in 1989. Office: NY Times Digitial NY Times Co 8th Fl 500 Seventh Ave New York NY 10018*

MILLSTEIN, RICHARD ALLEN, federal agency administrator; b. N.Y.C., Jan. 21, 1945; s. Abraham and Minnie (Zahn) M.; m. Nancy Louise Karelitz, Aug. 10, 1968; children: Danna Karen, Eric Jon, Todd David. BA, NYU, 1964; JD cum laude, Boston U., 1968. Bar: N.Y. 1968. Spl. asst. to dir. NIMH, Chevy Chase, Md., 1968-70, from legal asst. to acting chief legis. svcs. br. Rockville, Md., 1970-73; chief legis. svcs. unit Alcohol, Drug Abuse and Mental Health Adminstrn., Rockville, 1973-77, 78-79, assoc. adminstr. planning, policy analysis and legis., 1979-85, assoc. adminstr. for policy coordination, 1986-87; profl. staff liaison Pres.'s Commn. on Mental Health The White House, Washington, 1977-78, sr. staff mem. Drug Abuse Policy Office, 1987-88; exec. asst. to asst. sec. for health HHS, Washington, 1985-86; dep. dir. Nat. Inst. on Drug Abuse, Rockville, 1988—92, 1994—2003, acting dir., 1992—94; acting dep. dir. John G. Fogarty Internat. Ctr. for Advanced Study in Health Scis., NIH, Bethesda, Md., 2004—. Editor Periodic Summaries of Proposed and Enacted Fed. Legis., 1971-77; columnist On the Federal Scene Adminstrn. in Mental Health, 1973-76; contbr. articles to profl. jours. Bd. dirs., chmn. youth commn., sec., v.p. Congregation Har Shalom, Potomac, Md., 1984-85, 87-89. Recipient cert. appreciation Spanish Heritage Pub. Health Svc. Workers, 1981, Equal Employment Opportunity award Parklawn Asian/Pacific Am. Community, 1985, Superior Svc. award USPHS, 1986; Meritorious Exec. Rank award Pres. of U.S., 1988, Disting. Exec. Rank award, 1991. Mem. Md. Congress Parents and Tchrs. (hon. life). Office: Fogarty Internat Ctr NIH 31 Center Dr Rm B2CO2 Bethesda MD 20892-2220

MILLSTONE, DAVID JEFFREY, lawyer; b. Morgantown, W.Va., 1946; AB, Johns Hopkins U., 1968; JD, W.Va. U., 1971. Bar: Ohio 1971. Ptnr. Squire, Sanders & Dempsey LLP, Cleve. Co-author: Wage Hour Law--How to Comply, 2001; editor: Ohio and Fed. Employment Law Manual, 2001. Chair regional bd., nat commr. Anti-Defamation League. Mem.: ABA. Office: Squire Sanders & Dempsey 4900 Key Tower 127 Public Sq Ste 4900 Cleveland OH 44114-1304 E-mail: dmillstone@ssd.com.

MILMAN, DORIS HOPE, retired pediatrics educator, psychiatrist; b. N.Y.C., Nov. 17, 1917; d. Barnet S. and Rose (Smoleroff) Milman; m. Nathan Kreeger, June 15, 1941; 1 child, Elizabeth Kreeger Goldman. BA, Barnard Coll., 1938; MD, NYU, 1942. Diplomate Am. Bd. Pediat.; lic. physician, N.Y. Intern Jewish Hosp., Bklyn., 1942-43, resident, 1944-46, fellow in pediat., 1946-47; postgrad. extern in psychiatry Bellevue Hosp., N.Y.C., 1947-49; attending pediat. psychiatrist Jewish Hosp., Bklyn., 1950-56; asst. prof. pediat. Health Sci. Ctr. at Bklyn. SUNY, 1956-67, assoc. prof., 1967-73, prof., 1973-93, prof. emeritus, 1993—, acting chmn. dept. pediat., 1973-75, 82. Pvt. practice child and adolescent psychiatry, Bklyn., 1950-90; vis. prof. Ben Gurion U. of the Negev, Beersheva, Israel, 1977. Co-editor: AAP Adolescent Newsletter, 1993—; copyeditor: Bellevue Lit. Rev., 2001—. Mem. adv. bd. N.Y. Assn. for the Learning Disabled, N.Y.C., 1975-80. Recipient Disting. Alumna award Barnard Coll., 1986, Solomon R. Berson Achievement award NYU Sch. Medicine, 1991; Grace Potter Rice fellow Barnard Coll., 1938-39. Fellow Am. Acad. Pediat. (emeritus), Am. Psychiat. Assn. (disting. life fellow); mem. AAAS, Am. Orthopsychiat. Assn. (life), Am. Pediat. Soc. (emeritus), N.Y. Pediat. Soc. (emeritus), Phi Beta Kappa, Alpha Omega Alpha. Home: 2373 Broadway Apt 2028 New York NY 10024-2842

MILME, PATRICK JOSEPH, retired lawyer; b. Oct. 2, 1939; s. Hugh A. Milmoe and Mary Francis (O'Connell) Steenken; m. Carolyn Mann, Nov. 30, 1963; children: Mary Kaye Chrysicas, Caroline Pugh, Hugh. BA, Coll. William and Mary, 1959; JD, U. Va., 1962. Bar: N.Y. 1962, Va. 1962, Fla. 1989. With Davis & Polk, N.Y.C., 1965-72; ptnr. Hunton & Williams, Richmond, Va., 1972-2001, ret., 2001—. Chmn. DARE Marina, Inc., Grafton, Va., 1992—, States Roofing Corp., Norfolk, Va., 1994—, Virginia Beach Marlin Club, Inc., Sterling Eagle, 1980—. Trustee Village of Atlantic Beach, N.Y., 1965-72; bd. dirs. St. Joseph's Villa, Richmond, Va., 1985-91, Hanover Tavern Found., 1998-2001. Capt. U.S. Army, 1963-65. Mem. Am. Coll. Real Estate Lawyers. Avocations: boating, fishing. Office: Hunton & Williams Riverfront Plz East Tower 951 E Byrd St Richmond VA 23219-4074 E-mail: pmilmoe@hunton.com.

MILMORE, JENNIFER, actress; T.V. actress. Appeared in film To Wong Foo, Thanks for Everything, Julie Newmar, 1995, North Beach, 2000; T.V. series Jesse, 1998-2000; T.V. guest appearances in 21 Jump St., 1987, Friends, 1997, Veronica's Closet, 1997, Yes, Dear, 2003-. Office: c/o Bright-Kauffman-Crane Prodns 300 S Lorimar Plz Bldg 140 Burbank CA 91522-0001*

MILNE, CHRISTOPHER MCQUISTON WILMOTH, photographer, journalist, educator; b. N.Y.C., June 6, 1934; s. C. Lee Wilmoth and Helen Milne; m. Vesta Seymour, Jan. 6, 1999; children: Bruce, Milne, Geoffrey, David, James, Kevin. BA, Geneva Coll., 1956; studied color photography, Roman Vishniak, Montreal, 1973; MA, U. Fla., 1985. Writer U.S. Steel, Pitts., 1957-61; writer, owner Interprel Corp., Pitts., 1961—; writer, corr. U.P.I., Washington, 1969-87; pub., editor Ea. Shore Echo, Halifax, 1976-77; founder Marine Gallery and Mus., Canada, 1978; instr. various colls., 1988—; publ. Safe Harbour Press, Crescent, Pa., 1989—; CEO, Milne Inst., Crescent, 1999—. Spl. investigator Scranton commn. investigating killings Kent State U., 1971; mem. speaker's bureau Ethics in Journalism. Editor: RR Stations of Pennsylvania, 1967; author: Ethics for Journalists, 2000; contbr. articles & photographs to Official Railway Guide, 1978-79; photographer traveling exhibit A Brutal Season, Northern Ireland, 1988-, When Trains Were King, 1992—; asst. editor Can. Nat. Rlwys., 1978; official photographer CPR, 1974. Mem. primetimers policy com. Christ Ch. at Grove Farm; counselor House Trailer Com. on Aging, 1970; spl. investigator Ay. for Social Concerns of United Meth. Ch., 1972. Mem. SAR, VFW, Nat. Geog. Soc. (life), Soc. Profl. Journalists, Train Collectors Assn., Profl. Photographers Am., Elks, Nat. Multiple Sclerosis Soc., N.H. Art Assn., Newburyport (Mass.) Art Assn., Pitts. History and Landmarks Found. (docent). Office: Milne Inst PO Box 331 Glenwillard PA 15046 Office Phone: 724-457-7753.

MILNE, GORDON A. construction executive, mortgage company executive; BA in Econs., Brigham Young U., 1975; MBA, U. Chgo., 1977. CPA. Various positions Kaufman and Broad Mortgage Co., 1986—91; sr. v.p., CFO Bow Valley Energy Inc., Calgary, Canada, 1991—94; v.p. Fin. Divsn. Can. Occidental Petroleum Ltd., Calgary, 1994—96; sr. v.p. fin., CFO Agrium Inc., Calgary, 1996—2000; exec. v.p. Ryland Group, Inc., Calabasas, Calif., 2000—, CFO, 2000—. Office: The Ryland Group Inc 24025 Park Sorrento Ste 400 Calabasas CA 91302

MILNE, JAMES F. former secretary of state; b. Barre, Vt., July 8, 1950; m. Judith Garigliano; 4 children. BS in Pharmacy, Mass. Coll. Pharmacy, 1974. City clk., treas. City of Barre (Vt.), 1988-94; sec. of state State of Vt., 1995-98. Pharmacist, mgr. Allan Milne Pharmacy, 1974-88. Mem. Nat. Ski Patrol, Mutuo, Inc. Mem. Nat. Assn. Secs. State, Vt. Municipal Clks. and Treas. Assn., Vt. Jaycees (pres. 1979-80), U.S. Jaycees (nat. v.p. 1980-81), Barre Elks Lodge, Barre Country Club, Barre Rotary Club (pres. 1985-86). Republican.

MILNE, JOHN N. rental company executive; Mem., corp. fin. dept. Drexel Burnham Lambert, Inc., 1987—90; various sr. exec. positions United Waste Sys., Inc., 1990—93, vice chmn., chief acquisition officer, 1993—97; pres. United Rentals Inc., Greenwich, Conn., 2001—, co-founder, CFO, 2002—. Office: United Rentals Inc 5 Greenwich Office Park Greenwich CT 06830*

MILNER, BRENDA ATKINSON LANGFORD, neuropsychologist; b. July 15, 1918; arrived in Can., 1944; d. Samuel and Leslie (Doig) Langford. BA, Cambridge (Eng.) U., 1939, MA, 1949, ScD, 1972; PhD, McGill U., 1952, DSc (hon.), 1991, U. Man., 1982, Wesleyan U., 1991, Acadia U., 1991, U. St. Andrews, 1992, U. Hartford, 1997, McMaster U., 1999, Meml. U., 2002; LLD (hon.), Queen's U., 1980, U. Lethbridge, 1986, Mt. Holyoke Coll., 1986, U. Laval, 1987, U. Toronto, 1987, Cambridge U., 2000; LHD (hon.), Mt. St. Vincent U., 1988; Doctorate (hon.), U. de Montrèal, 1988; ScD (hon.), Columbia U., 2002, U. Naples II, 2002; DU (hon.), U. Ottawa, 2004. Exptl. officer U.K. Ministry of Supply, 1941-44; prof. agrégé Inst. Psychology U. Montreal, 1944-52; rsch. assoc. psychology dept. McGill U., Montreal, 1952-3, lectr. dept. neurology and neurosurgery, 1953-60, from asst. prof. to assoc. prof. to prof. psychology, 1960-93; Dorothy J. Killam prof. Montreal Neurol. Inst., 1993—. Head neuropsychology rsch. unit Montreal Neurol. Inst., 1953-90; Clothworkers fellow Girton Coll., Cambridge, 1972-73; hon. fellow Newnham Coll., Cambridge, 1989—. Mem. editl. bd. Neuropsychologia, 1973-93, Behavioral Brain Rsch., 1980-88, Hippocampus, 1990-96. Decorated officer Order of Can., officer Nat. Order of Que., 1985; Career investigator Med. Rsch. Coun. Can., 1964-99; recipient Kathleen Stott prize Newnham Coll., 1971, Karl Spencer Lashley award Am. Philos. Soc., 1979, Izaak Walton Killam Meml. prize Can. Coun., 1983, Hermann Von Helmholtz prize Cognitive Neurosci. Inst., 1984, Penfield award Can. League Against Epilepsy, 1984, Wilder Penfield prize Province of Que., 1993, Neural Plasticity prize Found. IPSEN, Paris, Met. Life Found. award, 1996; named Gt. Montrealer, 1987; named to Can. Med. Hall of Fame, 1997; Hon. mem., European Bran and Behavior Soc., 1999; John P.M. Govern award in the Behavioral Sci., Am. Assn. to the Advancement of Sci., 2001; D.O. Hebb award, Canadian Soc. for Brain Brain Behaviour and Cognitive Sci., 2001; Micheal Saviazin award, Club de rechereches cliniques du Québec, 2002; Golden Jubilee Medal Her Majesty Queen Elizabeth II, 2002. William James fellow Am. Psychol. Soc., 1989 Fellow APA (Disting. Contbn. award 1973), AAAS, Royal Soc. London, Royal Soc. Can. (McLaughlin medal 1995), Can. Psychol. Assn.; mem. NAS (fgn. assoc.), Am. Epilepsy Soc. (William G. Lennox award 1974, 95), Am. Neurol. Assn., Association de Psychologie Scientifique de Langue Française, Brit. Soc. Exptl. Psychology, Exptl. Psychol. Soc., Psychonomic Soc., Ea. Psychol. Assn., Internat. Neuropsychology Symposium, Internat. Brain Rsch. Orgn. (exec. sec. 1993-97), Soc. Neurosci. (Ralph W. Gerard prize 1987), Am. Acad. Neurology (assoc.), Assn. Rsch. in Nervous and Mental Diseases (assoc.), Royal Soc. Medicine (affiliate), European Brain and Behavior Soc. (hon.), Sigma Xi. Office: Montreal Neurol Inst 3801 University St Montreal QC Canada H3A 2B4 Office Phone: 514-398-8503. E-mail: bmilner@bic.mni.mcgill.ca.

MILNER, CHARLES FREMONT, JR., manufacturing executive; b. Durham, NC, July 21, 1942; s. Charles Fremont and Eloyse Sargent Milner; m. Molly Franc Wakefield, Aug. 28, 1965; children: Bernadette Ann Milner Gardner, Eloyse Lee Milner Ellerman. BA, Guilford Coll., 1963; MBA, Harvard U., 1965. Asst. to comptroller Harvard U., 1965-66; instr. Northeastern U., Boston, 1965-66; with Burlington Hosiery Co. divsn. Burlington (N.C.) Industries, 1966-71, asst. v.p., 1970-71; exec. v.p. Parklane Hosiery Co., Inc., New Hyde Park, N.Y., 1971-74; pres. Rudin & Roth, Inc. divsn. NCC Industries, N.Y.C., 1974-75; v.p. apparel group M. Lowenstein and Sons, N.Y.C., 1975-76; pres., CEO BBC, Inc. and Camp Industry divsns. Genesco, Inc., 1976-80; gen. mgr. Johnston and Murphy Shoe Co. divsn., 1979—82; gen. mgr. footwear mktg. and mfg. Genesco, Inc., 1980-81, v.p., 1981-82; pres., CEO Hope Hosiery Mills and C.M. Industries, Inc., Denver, Pa., 1983—. Trustee Friends Acad., Locust Valley, N.Y., 1974-79, Guilford Coll., 1982-97, vice chmn., 1989, chmn., 1990-97; mem. class chief fund agt. Harvard Bus. Sch., 1986-91, 40th reunion co-chmn. 2005, alumni bd., 1992-2001, v.p., 1995-97, pres., 1997-99, past pres., 1999-2001. Mem. Nat. Assn. Hosiery Mfrs. (dir. 1978-82, 87—, exec. com. 1989-93, 99—, 2d vice-chmn. 1991-92, vice-chmn. 1992, chmn. 1993), Lancaster Country Club (bd. govs. 2004—), Hamilton Club, Moselem Springs Golf Club. Home: 158 Hamilton Rd Lancaster PA 17603-4734 Office: 205 Washington St Denver PA 17517 E-mail: mmilner@socksmyway.com.

MILNER, CLYDE A., II, historian; b. Durham, N.C., Oct. 19, 1948; s. Charles Fremont and Eloyse (Sargent) M.; m. Carol Ann O'Connor, Aug. 14, 1977; children: Catherine Carol, Charles Clyde. AB, U. N.C., 1971; MA, Yale U., 1973, MPhil, 1974, PhD, 1979. Admissions counselor Guilford Coll., Greensboro, N.C., 1968-70; acting instr. Yale U., New Haven, 1974-75; research fellow McNickle Ctr., Chgo., 1975-76; instr. Utah State U., Logan, 1976-79, asst. prof., 1979-82, assoc. prof., 1982-88, prof., 1988—2002; dir. Mountain West Ctr. for Regional Studies, 1997-2000; dir. PhD program in heritage studies Ark. State U., 2002—, prof., 2002—. Reader of manuscripts History Book Club, Inc., 1986—; exec. dir. Am. Studies program, Utah State U., 1997-2000. Author: With Good Intentions, 1982; editor: Major Problems in the History of the American West, 1989, co-editor 2d edit., 1997; editor: A New Significance: Re-envisioning the History of the American West, 1996; assoc. editor The Western Hist. Quar., 1984-87, co-editor, 1987-89, editor, 1990-97, exec. editor, 1998-2002; co-editor: Churchmen and the Western Indians, 1985, Trails: Toward a New Western History, 1991, Oxford History of the American West, 1994 (Western Heritage award for non-fiction Nat. Cowboy Hall of Fame 1994, Caughey Western History Assn. award for best book on history of Am. West 1995). Recipient Paladen Writing award The Montana Mag. Western History, 1987, Faculty Svc. award Associated Students Utah State U., 1987, Outstanding Social Science Researcher award Utah State U., 1983, (with Carol A. O'Connor) Charles Redd prize Utah Acad. Scis., Arts and Letters, 1996; fellowship fund established in his honor Western Hist. Quar. Utah State U., 2002. Mem. Western History Assn., Orgn. Am. Historians (Disting. lectr. 2004—), Phi Alpha Theta, Phi Beta Kappa. Mem. Soc. Of Friends. Home: 1306 E Country Club Terr Jonesboro AR 72401-4325 Office: Ark State U Heritage Studies PhD Program PO Box 69 State University AR 72467 Office Phone: 870-910-8217.

MILNER, DEBBI ELISSA, computer company executive; m. John Milner; 2 children. BA in English Lit., History, SUNY, Binghamton, 1981. Prin., owner Jade Sys. Corp., Cold Spring, NY, 1984—. Office: Jade Systems Corp 3377 Rte 9 Cold Spring NY 10516

MILNER, HAROLD WILLIAM, hotel executive; b. Salt Lake City, Nov. 11, 1934; s. Kenneth W. and Olive (Schoettlin) M.; m. Susan Emmett, June 19, 1959 (div. 1976); children— John Kenneth, Mary Sue; m. Lois Friemuth, Aug. 14, 1977; 1 dau., Jennifer Rebecca. BS, U. Utah, 1960; MBA, Harvard, 1962. Instr. Brigham Young U., Provo, Utah, 1962-64; v.p. Gen. Paper Corp., Mpls., 1964-65; dir. finance Amalgamated Sugar Co., Ogden, Utah, 1965-67; corp. treas. Marriott Corp., Washington, 1967-70; pres., chief exec. officer, trustee Hotel Investors, Kensington, Md., 1970-75; pres., chief exec. officer Americana Hotels Corp., Chgo., 1975-85, Kahler Corp., Rochester, Minn., 1985-97; pres., CEO The Kensington Co., Salt Lake City, 1997—. Trustee Baron Asset Funds, 1987—. Author: A Special Report on Contract Maintenance, 1963. Served as lt. AUS, 1960. Mem. Minn. Bus. Partnership (dir. 1991—). Mem. Lds Ch. Office: The Kensington Co 2293 Morning Star Dr Park City UT 84060-6725 Office Phone: 435-649-9130. Personal E-mail: hmilner@aol.com.

MILNER, IRVIN MYRON, lawyer; b. Cleve., Feb. 5, 1916; s. Nathan and Rose (Spector) M.; m. Zelda Winograd., Aug. 15, 1943 AB cum laude, Western Res. U. (now Case Western Res. U.), 1937, JD, 1940, LL.M., 1970. Bar: Ohio 1940, U.S. Dist. Ct. (no. dist.) Ohio 1946. Pvt. practice, Cleve., 1946—. Exec. sec., counsel Men's Apparel Club Ohio, Cleve., 1947-48; adj. instr. Sch. Law, Case Western Res. U., 1965-66; spl. counsel Ohio Office Atty. Gen., 1960-70; legal counsel Korean Am. Assn. Greater Cleve., 1973-95. Mem. Cleve. Fgn. Consular Corps., 1970 96, hon. consul Rep. of Korea for Cleve., 1970-96; bd. dirs. Internat. Human Assistance Programs, Inc., 1973-79, voting corp. mem., 1980-88; mem. Republican Nat. Com. Served with U.S. Army, 1941-45, ETO. Decorated Order Diplomatic Svc. Merit-Heung-in medal (Republic of Korea), 1975; named to Disting. Alumni Hall of Fame, Cleveland Heights (Ohio) High Sch., 1983. Fellow Internat. Consular Coll., Ohio Bar Found.; mem. ABA (small bus. com., corp. bus. law sect. 1971-74), Greater Cleve. Bar Assn., Cuyahoga County Bar Assn. (pres. 1975-76, co-chmn. jud. standards com. 1987-88, life trustee, award of Special Merit 1976, Pres.' award 1988), Ohio State Bar Assn. (coun. dels., 1976-86, com. on legal ethics and profl. conduct 1984-97), Cuyahoga County Bar Found. (sec.-treas. 1980-84, bd. dirs. 1984—), Cuyahoga County Coun. Ohio VFW (comdr. 1958, Merit award 1958), Am. Security Coun. (nat. adv. bd.), Cleve. Coun. on World Affairs, Greater Cleve. Vets. Coun. (pres. 1956), Western Res. Coll. Alumni Assn. (bd. dirs. 1982-88), Cleve. City Club, Masons (32 deg.), Tau Epsilon Rho (chancellor Cleve. Grad. chpt. 1987-88), Delta Phi Alpha. Jewish.

MILNER, JOHN, computer company executive; BA, England. Programmer analyst ICL, England, 1978; lead sys. analyst Wall St. Sys.; v.p. Jade Sys. Corp., Cold Spring, N.Y., 1984—. Office: Jade Systems Corp 203 Jaycox Rd Cold Spring NY 10516

MILNER, JOHN D. architectural firm executive, educator; Adj. prof. arch. U. of Pa., 1976—; prin. John Miller Archs., 1989—. Nat. peer arch. Nat. Endowment for the Arts, Gen. Svcs. Adminstrn.; fine arts jury Am. Acad., Rome, 1998; octagon com. Am. Arch. Found. Fellow, Am. Inst. Architecture, 2003. Office: John Miller Archs 104 Lakeview Dr Chadds Ford PA 19317

MILNER, RICHARD GERARD, physicist; b. Cork, Ireland, Dec. 2, 1956; s. William and Maura (McGrath) M.; m. Eileen Troy, June 21, 1980; children: William, Samuel, David. BS with honors, Univ. Coll. Cork, 1978, MS, 1979; PhD, Calif. Inst. Tech., 1985. Rsch. assoc. Calif. Inst. Tech., 1985-88, rsch. scientist, 1988; asst. prof. MIT, Cambridge, 1988-93, assoc. prof., 1993-98, prof., 1998—, dir. of Bates Linear Accelerator Ctr., 1998—. Recipient Presdl. Young Investigator award NSF, 1989. Office: Bates Linear Accelerator MIT 77 Massachusetts Ave Cambridge MA 02139-4301 E-mail: milner@mitlns.mit.edu.

MILNER ANDERSON, KATHERINE, broadcast executive; BA in Edn., U. Miss., 1969. Dir., exec. sec. Dept. Transp., Washington, 1981-83; assoc. dir. Offive of Cabinet, White Ho., Washington, 1983-84; dir. Corp. Pub. Broadcasting, Washington; chief fin. officer Team Washington, Inc., Alexandria, Va., 1986—. Bd. dirs. Columbia Hosp. Women Found. Chair Am. Cancer Soc. Ball; sponsor Spl. Olympics, Barbados. Office: Corp Pub Broadcasting 901 E St NW Ste 300 Washington DC 20004-2012

MILNES, ARTHUR GEORGE, electrical engineer, educator; b. Heswall, Eng., July 30, 1922; came to U.S., 1957, naturalized, 1964; s. George and Marion (Teasdale) M.; m. Mary Laverne Wertz, Dec. 4, 1955; children: Sheila Rae, Brian George, John Teasdale. BSc, U. Bristol, Eng., 1943, MSc, 1947, DSc, 1956. With Royal Aircraft Establishment, 1943-57, prin. sci. officer, 1952-57; mem. faculty Carnegie-Mellon U., Pitts., 1957-87, prof. elec. engring., 1960-87, assoc. head dept., 1966-69, Buhl prof., 1973-87, prof. emeritus, 1987—. Cons. to industry on semiconductor devices, 1957 Author: Transductors and Magnetic Amplifiers, 1957, (with D.L. Feucht) Heterojunctions and Metal-Semiconductor Junctions, 1972, Deep Impurities in Semiconductors, 1973, Semiconductor Devices and Integrated Electronics, 1979; contbr. articles to profl. jours. FOA rsch. fellow NAS-Royal Soc. London, 1954. Fellow IEEE (J.J. Ebers award 1982, van der Ziel award 1993), Am. Phys. Soc., Instn. Elec. Engrs. (London). Home: 1417 Inverness St Pittsburgh PA 15217-1157 Office Phone: 412-683-7965.

MILNES, SHERRILL E. baritone; b. Downers Grove, Ill., Jan. 10, 1935; s. James Knowlton and Thelma (Roe) M.; m. Maria Zouves, Dec. 19, 1996; children by previous marriage— Eric, Erin, Shawn. Student, North Central Coll., Ill.; B in Music Edn., Drake U., 1957, M in Music Edn., 1958; postgrad., Northwestern U., 1958-61; studied with Boris Goldovsky, Rosa Ponselle, Andrew White, Hermanes Baer; postgrad. hon. degree, Ripon Coll., Drake U., Coe Coll., Westminster Choir Coll., SUNY, Potsdam. Disting. prof. Yale U. Sch. Music. Operatic debut Goldovsky Opera Co., N.Y.C., 1960; leading baritone N.Y.C. Opera Co., Met. Opera Co., 1965—; European debut in Macbeth, Vienna, 1970; appearances major world opera cos. including Covent Garden, London, L'Opera, Paris, Staasoper, Vienna, Austria, Teatro Colon, Argentina, La Scala, Milan, Hamburg, Munich, Salzburg, Frankfurt, Berlin, Zurich, as well as continued appearances in the U.S. in San Antonio, Cin., Miami, Houston, Pitts., Chgo., Balt.; numerous TV, concerts, recitals, recordings (RCA, Deutsche Grammophon, Angel/EMI, London, Decca, Philips, CBS). Decorated Order of Merit (Italy); chevalier of French Republic; Ford Found. awardee, 1962. Mem. Tucker Found. (v.p.), Phi Mu Alfa Sinfonia (life). Office: care Herbert Barrett 1776 Broadway Ste 1610 New York NY 10019-2002

MILNIKEL, ROBERT SAXON, lawyer; b. Chgo., Aug. 17, 1926; s. Gustav and Emma Hazel (Saxon) M.; m. Virginia Lee Wylie, July 26, 1969; children: Robert Saxon Jr., Elizabeth Wylie. AB, U. Chgo., 1950, JD, 1953. Bar: Ill. 1953, U.S. Dist. Ct. 1954. Assoc. Traeger, Bolger & Traeger, Chgo., 1953-57, Heineke, Conklin & Schrader, Chgo., 1958-66; ptnr. Peterson & Ross, Chgo., 1966—2003. With USN, 1944-46, PTO. Mem. Beta Theta Pi (pres. chpt. and alumni assn.), Cliffdwellers Club (bd. dirs. Arts Found.) Republican. Lutheran. Home: 601 Ridge Rd Kenilworth IL 60043-1042 E-mail: milnikel@enteract.com.

MILNOR, HAZEL, nurse; b. Marble, Ark., Apr. 2, 1921; d. Andrew Jackson and Laura Jane (Davis) Spencer; m. John Champion Milnor, June 21, 1951 (dec. Aug. 1989); children: Mary Christine, Jean Ann Laura. RN, Calif., Hawaii. Nurse pvt. duty, Calif., 1942—; surg. nurse Queen's Hosp., Hawaii, 1944-46; flight attendant United Airlines, San Francisco, 1946-51. Author: Entertaining in Hawaii, 1977, (poetry) As Angels Watch, 1997. Founding pres. Spl. Angels Ministry, Hawaii; chair develop. com. Spl. Angels. Inducted Internat. Poetry Hall of Fame. Mem. Assn. Retarded Citizens, Clipped Wings (mem.-at-large, mem. coms.), Internat. Soc. Poets (disting.), Oahu Country Club. Republican. Episcopalian. Avocations: collecting angels, travel.

MILNOR, JOHN WILLARD, mathematician; b. Orange, N.J., Feb. 20, 1931; AB, U. Princeton, 1951, PhD, 1954; DSc (hon.), Syracuse U., 1965, U. Chgo., 1967. Mem. faculty Princeton U., 1953—62, prof., 1960—62, Henry Putman chair, 1962; prof. math., dir. Inst. Math. Scis. SUNY, Stony Brook, NY, 1988—. Recipient Fields medal, Internat. Congress Math. in Stockholm, 1962, Nat. medal of Sci., 1967, Leroy P. Steele prize, 1982, Wolf prize, Israel, 1989, Steele prize, 2004; fellow Alfred P. Sloan fellow, 1955—59. Mem.: NAS, Russian Acad. Scis. (fgn. mem.), Am. Math. Soc., Am. Philos. Soc., Am. Acad. Arts and Sci. Achievements include proof that a 7-dimensional sphere can have several differential structures; research in holomorphic dynamics. Office: SUNY Inst Math Sci Math Bldg 5D 148 Stony Brook NY 11794-3660

MILNOR, WILLIAM ROBERT, physician; b. Wilmington, Del., May 4, 1920; s. William Robert and Virginia (Sterling) Milnor; m. Gabriella Mahaffy, Aug. 19, 1944; children: Katherine Alexander, William Henry. AB, Princeton U., 1941; MD, Johns Hopkins U., 1944. Diplomate Am. Bd. Internal Medicine. Intern, resident Johns Hopkins Hosp., 1944-46; rsch. fellow Nat. Heart Inst., 1949-51; physician-in-charge heart sta. Johns Hopkins Hosp., 1951-60, physician, 1952—; mem. faculty Johns Hopkins Med. Sch., 1951—, prof. physiology, 1969—. Vis. fellow St. Catherine's Coll. Oxford U., England, 1968; mem. med. adv. panel Am. Inst. Biol. Scis., 1971—; assessor Nat. Med. Rsch. Coun. Australia, 1976—. Author: Hemodynamics, 1989, Cardio-vascular Physiology, 1990; contbr. articles to med. textbooks and med. jours. Capt. med. corps USAAF, 1946—48. Fellow: ACP; mem.: Heart Assn. Md., Am. Heart Assn. (chmn. rsch. com. 1966), Biomed. Engring. Soc., Am. Fedn. Clin. Rsch., Am. Physiol. Soc.

MILONAS, MINOS, artist, designer, poet; b. Heraklion, Crete, Greece, Apr. 28, 1936; came to U.S., 1964, naturalized, 1968; s. Stavros and Maria (Kaplantzis) M.; m. Arlene Watson, Dec. 23, 1963 (div. 1970); m. Sarah Brown, Dec. 1973 (div. 1974); m. Elaine Mauceli, May 26, 1988. BA, Calif. State U., Northridge, 1970; MFA with hons., U. Wash., Seattle, 1972. Freelance writer and poet, Athens, 1960-64; freelance artist L.A., 1964-66; instr. U. Wash., 1971-72, Studio Milonas, Seattle, 1972-76, artist N.Y.C., 1977—, textile designer, 1984-94. One man shows include Second Story Gallery, Seattle, 1971, Henry Art Gallery, Seattle, 1972, Polly Friedlander Gallery, Seattle, 1973, Stavrakakis Gallery, Crete, Greece, 1977, West Broadway Gallery, N.Y.C., 1979, 81, 82, Heraklion Art Gallery, Crete, 1983, Kreonides Gallery, Athens, 1983, 84, Doma Gallery, N.Y.C., 1988, Hellenic Cultural Ctr., N.Y., 1990, 93, Cypriot Consulate, N.Y.C., 1990; exhibitions in group shows at Calif. State U., Northridge, 1968-69, Mcpl. Art Gallery, L.A., 1969, U. Wash. Libr., Seattle, 1971, 72, Panaca Gallery, Bellevue, Wash., 1973, Mercer Island Art Gallery, Seattle, 1973, Henry Art Gallery, Seattle, 1973, Tacoma Art Mus., 1973, 75, N.W. Watercolor Soc., 1974, Gordon Woodside Gallery, Seattle, 1974, Coll. of the Cisciyous, Calif., 1975, Laguna Gloria Art Mus., Austin, Tex., 1975, Redmonds (Wash.) Arts Festival, 1975, Univ. Dist. Arts Festival, Seattle, 1976, Bellevue Art Mus., 1976, Sunne Savage Gallery, Boston, 1976, Cretan Artists, Stavrakakis Gallery, Heraklion, Crete, 1978, Internat. Drawing Biennale, Cleveland, Eng., 1981-82, Bowes Mus., Barnard Castle, Eng., 1982, Shipley Art Gallery, Gateshed, Eng., 1982, House of Commons, London, 1982, Haggin Mus., Stockton, Calif., 1985-86, U. N.D., Grand Forks, 1987, Greek Cultural Ctr., Springfield, Mass., 1987, 89, Del Bello Gallery, Toronto, Ont., Can., 1987, Ball State U., Muncie, Ind., 1989, Morin-Miller Galleries, N.Y.C., 1989-90, Columbia (Md.) Coll., 1989, Grand Prospect Hall, Bklyn., 1990, Kenneth Raymond Gallery, Boca Raton, Fla., 1993-96, Pan Cretan ARt Exhbn. Reythmnon Mcpl. Art GAllery, Crete, Greece, 2003—, Melina Mevkouri Cultural Ctr., Athens, 2003; author: The Small Caravan, 1962, short stories; author 9 books of poetry in Greek, From A to Z, Poems in English, 2003, Look Out Manhattan, Poems in English, 2004; videos include Multimedia Artist, 1988, 500 Definitions--Art Is, 1991; donated paintings to various orgns. Recipient 4 Sculpture awards Summer Art Festivals, 1970-76, 2 Merit awards Greek Cultural Ctr., 1987; U. Wash. grantee, 1970; U. Wash. scholar, 1971. Mem. Nat. Artists Equity Assn., Inc., N.Y. Artists Equity Assn., Inc., Poetry Soc. Am., Greek-Am. Writers Assn., Acad. Am. Poets, Poets House. Democrat. Home and Office: 790 11th Ave Apt 39A New York NY 10019-3521

MILONE, FRANCIS MICHAEL, lawyer; b. Phila., June 18, 1947; s. Michael Nicholas and Frances Theresa (Fair) Milone; m. Maida R. Crane, Nov. 25, 1991; children: Michael, Matthew. BA, LaSalle Coll., 1969; MS, Pa. State U., 1971; JD, U. Pa., 1974. Bar: Pa. 1974, U.S. Dist. Ct. (ea. dist.) Pa. 1974, U.S. Dist. Ct. (mid. dist.) Pa. 1979, U.S. Dist. Ct. (ea. dist.) Mich. 1983, U.S. Ct. Appeals (3d cir.) 1978, U.S. Ct. Appeals (4th and 5th cirs.) 1979, U.S. Supreme Ct. 1979. Assoc. Montgomery, McCracken, Walker & Rhoads, Phila., 1974—77; ptnr. Morgan, Lewis & Bockius, Phila., 1981—. Mem.: ABA (labor and litig. sects.), Phila. Bar Assn., Pa. Bar Assn. Home: 912 Field Ln Villanova PA 19085-2003 Office: Morgan Lewis & Bockius 1701 Market St Philadelphia PA 19103-2903 E-mail: fmilone@morganlewis.com.

MILORO, PROTOPRESBTER FRANK, church official, religious studies educator; b. Wilmington, Del., Jan. 26, 1947; m. Constance Ann Evanisko, Apr. 20, 1969; children: Alexandra, Stephanie, Christopher. Grad. summa cum laude, Saviour Sem., 1969; grad. with high honors, St. Vincent Coll., 1972; attended, U. Pitts. Ordained to Diaconate and Priesthood, 1969. Assigned St. John's Ch., Ligonier, Pa., 1969-72, St. Stephen's Ch., Latrobe, Pa., 1969-72, St. John's Ch., Rahway, N.J., 1972-76; dir. Camp Nazareth, diocesan dir. youth, 1976-86; dean Christ the Saviour Sem.; elevated to dignity of Very Rev., 1985; sec. to bishop; instr. homiletics and parish administrn.; diocesan chancellor Am. Carpatho-Russian Orthodox Diocese, 1990—; dean Christ the Savior Cathedral, 1997—. Chaplain Ea. Orthodox residents Polk Ctr., Commonwealth Pa., established chapel. Assoc. editor The Ch. Messenger. Russian Orthodox. Office: 312 Garfield St Johnstown PA 15906-2122

MILSOM, ROBERT CORTLANDT, banker, director; b. Butler, Pa., Dec. 15, 1924; s. Robert C. and M. Ethel (Leyland) M. BS, John Carroll U., 1948. With PNC Bank (formerly Pitts. Nat. Bank), 1948-90; asst. sec., asst. cashier customer relations div. PNC Bank, 1953-56, asst. v.p. loan div., 1956-60, v.p. charge comml. loan group, 1960-65, sr. v.p. charge comml. banking div., 1965-68, exec. v.p., 1968-72, pres., 1972-85, chmn., CEO, 1985-90, also bd. dirs., 1972—; vice chmn., dir. PNC Bank Corp, 1972-90. Bd. dirs. PNC Bank N.A., PNC Equity Mgmt. Corp., Exec. Svc. Corps., Foxwall Med. Svc.; chmn. bd. trustees Mercy Hosp. Pitts., 1994—. Bd. dirs. Pitts. Mercy Health System, Inc., Pitts. Ballet Theatre, Regional Indsl. Devel. Corp.; hon. trustee John Carroll U., Cleve.; mem. adv. bd. Mon Valley Renaissance program California U. Pa. Mem. Duquesne Club of Pitts., Fox Chapel Golf Club of Pitts., Laurel Valley Golf Club, Rolling Rock Club. Office: PNC Bank 5th Ave & Wood St Pittsburgh PA 15222 also: PNC Bank NA P1-POPP-23-3 1 Pnc Plz Pittsburgh PA 15222-2709

MILSTED, AMY, biomedical educator; BSEd, Ohio State U., 1967; PhD, CUNY, 1977. Lectr. Hunter Coll./CUNY, 1970-76; instr. Carnegie-Mellon U., Pitts., 1976-77; postdoctoral fellow Muscular Dystrophy Assn./Carnegie-Mellon U., Pitts., 1978-79; rsch. assoc. Case Western Res. U., Cleve., 1979-82; rsch. chemist VA Med. Ctr., Cleve., 1982-87; project staff The Cleve. Clin. Found., 1987-89; asst. staff dept. brain and vascular rsch. Cleve. Clinic Found., 1989-93; grad. faculty Sch. Biomed. Scis. Kent (Ohio) State U., 1995—; assoc. prof. dept. biology U. Akron, Ohio, 1993-2000, prof. biology, 2000—. Contbr. articles to profl. jours. Fellow Am. Heart Assn.; mem. AAAS, Inter-Am. Soc. Hypertension, Am. Chem. Soc., Endocrine Soc., Assn. Women in Sci. Office: Univ Akron Dept Biology Asec 279 Akron OH 44325-3908 E-mail: milsted@uakron.edu.

MILSTEIN, ELLIOTT STEVEN, law educator, academic administrator; b. Oct. 19, 1944; s. Samuel M. and Mildred K. Milstein; m. Bonnie Myrun, Oct. 1, 1967 (div. Oct. 1992); 1 child, Jacob. BA, U. Hartford, 1966, LLD (hon.), 1997; JD, U. Conn., 1969; LLM, Yale U., 1971; LLD (hon.), Nova Southeastern U., 2001. Bar: conn. 1969, D.C. 1972, U.S. Dist. Ct. Conn. 1969, U.S. Ct. Appeals (D.C.) 1972. Lectr. law U. Conn. Clin. Program, 1969-70; staff counsel New Haven Legal Assistance Assn., 1971-72; asst. prof. law, dir. clin. programs Washington Coll. Law Am. U., 1972-74, assoc. prof., dir. clin. programs, 1974-77, prof., dir. clin. programs, 1977-88, interim dean, 1988-90, dean, 1990—. Prof. law, Washington Coll. Law Am. U., 1995—; co-dir. Nat. Vets. law Ctr., 1978-84; cons. Calif. Bar Bd. of Bar Admissions, Nat. Conf. Bar Examiners, law tng. Practising Law Inst., N.Y.C.; chmn. D.C. Law Students in Ct. Program, 1982-83; mem. Law Tchrs. for Legal Svcs. Bd. dirs. Alliance for Justice, 1996-97. Ford Urban Law fellow, 1971-72. Mem. ABA (skills tng. com. 1983-85, govt. rels. com. 1992—), ACLU, Soc. Am. Law Tchrs., Assn. Am. Law Schs. (chmn. sect clin. edn. 1982, accreditation com. 1984-86, chmn. standing com. clin. edn. 1993—, exec. com. 1996-2001, pres.-elect 1999, pres. 2000, William Pincus award for outstanding contbns. to clin. legal edn. 1992). Democrat. Home: 3216 Brooklawn Ct Bethesda MD 20815-3941 Office: Am U Washington Coll Law 4801 Massachusetts Ave NW Washington DC 20016-8196

MILSTEIN, LAURENCE BENNETT, electrical engineering educator, researcher; b. Bklyn., Oct. 28, 1942; s. Harry and Sadie (Kaplan) M.; m. Suzanne Barbara Hirschman, Oct. 3, 1969; children: Coreen Roxanne, Renair Marissa. BEE, CUNY, 1964; MSEE, Poly. Inst. Bklyn., 1966, PhD in Elec. Engring., 1968. Mem. tech. staff Hughes Aircraft Co., El Segundo, Calif., 1968-69, staff engr., 1969-72, sr. staff engr., 1972-74; asst. prof. Rensselaer Poly. Inst., Troy, NY, 1974-76, U. Calif.-San Diego, La Jolla, 1976-79, assoc. prof., 1979-82, prof. elec. engring., 1982—, chmn. dept., 1984-88. Cons. Hughes Aircraft Co., Culver City, Calif., 1976—78, Lockheed Missiles and Space Co., Sunnyvale, Calif., 1978—93, Motorola Satellite Comm., 1992—96, InterDigital Comm. Corp., 1992—96, Golden Bridge Tech., 1995—99; cons. various govt. agys., pvt. cos., 1975—. Co-editor: Tutorials in Modern Communications, 1983; Spread Spectrum Communications, 1983; contbr. articles to profl. jours. Recipient Outstanding Tchr. award Warren Coll., U. Calif.-San Diego, La Jolla, 1982, Disting. Tchg. award, 1999; grantee Army Rsch. Office, 1977-84, 86-89, 91-2001, Office of Naval Rsch., Arlington, Va., 1982—, TRW, San Diego, 1983-89, 92-97, NSF, 1993—. Fellow IEEE (Millennium medal 2000, Edwin Armstrong Achievement award 2000, MILCOM long term tech. achievement award 1998, F.W. Ellersick MILCOM prize paper award 2002), IEEE Coms. Soc. (bd. govs. 1983, 85-87, 93-95, v.p. for tech. activities 1990-91), IEEE Info. Theory Soc. (bd. govs. 1989-94). Jewish. Office: U Calif San Diego Dept Elec Computer Engring La Jolla CA 92093 Office Phone: 858-534-3096. Business E-mail: milstein@ece.ucsd.edu.

MILSTEIN, MONROE GARY, retail executive; b. N.Y.C., Jan. 14, 1927; s. Abe Herman and Ann Ethel (Isaacs) M.; m. Henrietta Haas, Dec. 22, 1949; children— Lazer, Andrew, Stephen BS, NYU, 1946. Pres. Monroe G. Milstein Inc., N.Y.C., 1947—; chmn. bd., pres., chief exec. officer Burlington Coat Factory Warehouse Corp., N.J., 1972—; dir. Fidelity Bank & Trust Co. of N.J., 1972—. Trustee, pres. bd. Long Beach Pub. Library, N.Y., 1967-76; pres. bd. trustees Nassau Library System, Roosevelt Field, N.Y., 1971-73 Recipient Man of Yr. awards Coat and Suit Buyers Assn., 1984, Long Beach C. of C., Youth Service award B'nai B'rith Mem. Am. Gen. Mdse. Assn., U.S. C. of C. Clubs: Dads (Long Beach) (pres. 1969). Lodges: B'nai B'rith (v.p. 1960-62). Jewish. Avocations: fishing; reading; music.

MILSTEIN, RICHARD CRAIG, lawyer; b. NYC, July 16, 1946; s. Max and Hattie (Jacobson) Milstein; children: Brian Matthew, Rachel Helanie. AA-(hon.), Miami-Dade Jr. Coll., 1966; BA cum laude, U. Miami, Fla., 1968; JD, 1973. Bar: Fla. 1974, US Dist. Ct./Fla. 1974, US Ct. Appeals (5th cir.) 1974, US Ct. Appeals (11th cir.) 1982. Assoc. August, Nimkoff & Pohlig., Miami, Fla., 1974—76; mng. ptnr. Jepeway, August, Gassen & Pohling, Miami, 1976—78, August, Pohlig & Milstein, P.A., Coral Gables, Fla., 1980—83; sr. ptnr. Milstein & Wayne, Coral Gables, 1983—85; ptnr. Tescher & Milstein, PA, Coral Gables, 1986—90, Akerman, Senterfitt & Eidson, P.A., 1990—. Named to U. Miami Iron Arrow Hon. Soc., U. Miami, 1998—; recipient Extraordinary Voices Award, Mothers' Voices S. Fla., 2000, Establishment of the Richard C. Milstein Excellence Award, Dade County Bar Assoc., 1999, Outstanding Alumnus Award, U. Miami Sch. of Law, 1999, Tobias Simon Pro Bono Service Award, FL Supreme Ct., 1996, John Minor Wisdom Professional and Public Service Award, American Bar Association Section of Litigation, 1996, Pro Bono Service Award for the Eleventh Judicial Circuit, FL Bar Pres., 1996, Pro Bono awards, 1986, Pro Bono Service Award for the Eleventh Judicial Circuit, FL Bar Pres., 1986. Mem.: U. Miami Law Alumni, Fla. Bar Assn., Coral Gables Bar Assn., Dade County Bar Assn., Am. trial Lawyers Assn., ABA, Nat. Coun. Aging, Nat. Acad. Elder Law, Am. Coll. Trust and Estate Counsel, Dade County Cultural Alliance, U. Miami, South Fla. Inter-Profl. Council Inc., South Fla. Mediation Ctr., Ops. SafeDrive, Met. Dade County Ind. Rev. Panel, Acad. Fla. Trial Lawyers, Miami Coalition Inc., Ptnr. for Youth, Metro Dade County Cultural Affairs Coun., Dade County Vol. Lawyers for Arts, Bet Shira Congregation, Dance Umbrella Inc., Zeta Epsilon Nu, Alpha Kappa, Phi Kappa Phi, Delta Pi, Phi Alpha Theta, Omicron Delta Kappa, Delta Theta Mu, Phi Theta Kappa. Democrat. Office: Akerman Senterfitt & Eidson One SE 3rd Ave Fl 28 Miami FL 33131

MILSTEIN, RICHARD SHERMAN, lawyer; b. Westfield, Mass., May 9, 1926; s. Abraham and Sarah (Yudman) M. BA, Harvard U., 1948; JD, Boston U., 1952. Bar: Mass. 1952, U.S. Supreme Ct. 1959. Ptnr. Ely & King, Springfield, Mass., 1954-95, Chaplin & Milstein, Boston, 1984-91; sr. counsel Robinson, Donovan, Madden & Barry P.C., Springfield, 1995-98. Dir. Mass. Continuing Legal Edn., 1969-80; cons. dir., 1980—. Commr. Springfield Parking Authority, 1984—90; trustee Cmty. Music Sch., Springfield, 1994—96, Springfield Symphony Orch., 1995—99, Springfield Libr. Mus. Assn., 1990—2000, Baystate Hosp. Found., 2001—03; overseer Mass. Supreme Jud. Ct. Hist. Soc., 1995—, Boston Lyric Opera, 1999—; trustee Baystate Hosp., v.p., 1995—97; vice chmn. Westfield Acad., 1980—99; chmn. Horace Smith Fund, 1977—93; bd. dirs. Boston Ctr. for Adult Edn., 1998—, v.p., 1998—2003; bd. overseers Huntington Theater, Boston, 1999—; mem. vis. com. Mus. Fine Arts, Boston, 2002—. Lt. comdr. USCGR, 1952—64. Recipient Am. Law Inst.-ABA Harrison Tweed Spl. Merit award for contbn. to CLE, 1997, Mass. Bar Cmty. Svc. award, 1998, William Pynchon award for Cmty. Svc. City of Springfield, 1999. Fellow Am. Coll. Trust and Estate Counsel, Mass. Bar Found. (life); mem. Am. Law Inst. (life), Am. Bar Found. (life). Home: 300 Boylston St Boston MA 02116-3923 also: Mass Continuing Legal Edn 10 Winter Pl Boston MA 02108-4751 Home (Winter): 330 S Ocean Blvd Apt 2E Palm Beach FL 33480 Office Phone: 617-350-7006 x 1241. E-mail: rsmilstein@aol.com., rsmilstein_ab@post.harvard.edu.

MILSTEN, ROBERT B. lawyer; b. Tulsa, Nov. 6, 1932; s. Travis I. and Regina (Jankowsky) M.; m. Jane Herskowitz, June 24, 1956; children: Stuart Paul, Leslie Jane. BS, Ind. U., 1954; LL.B., U. Okla., 1956; postgrad., So. Meth. U., 1959. Bar: Okla. 1956, U.S. Ct. of Appeals 1956, U.S. Tax Ct 1956. Practiced in, Oklahoma City, 1962—; govt. atty. Office Chief Counsel, IRS, 1958-62; atty. Fuller, Smith, Mosburg & Davis, 1962-63; sr. counsel Andrews, Davis, Legg, Bixler, Milsten & Price, Inc., 1964—, mem. firm, 1966—, dir., 1977-82, 96-98. Mem. S.W. region IRS/Bar Liaison Com., 1994-97. Past pres., trustee Temple B'nai Israel. Served as lt., JAGC USAF, 1956-58. Mem. ABA (com. civil and criminal tax penalties sect. taxation 1962—98), Okla. Bar Assn., Fed. Bar Assn. (2d v.p. local chpt. 1976), Econ. Club Okla., Quail Creek Golf and Country Club, Men's Dinner Club, Phi Delta Phi (treas. 1955-56) Office Phone: 405-272-9241.

MILSTONE, LEONARD MATTHEW, physician, educator, researcher; b. Newark, N.J., Oct. 19, 1944; s. Jacob Haskell and Vivian Kaufman M.; m. Ellen Block, Aug. 21, 1967; children: Jenya, Aaron Michael. BS in Chemistry, Yale Coll., 1966; MD, Yale U., 1970. Diplomate Am. Bd. Dermatology. Resident U. Oreg. Med. Sch., Portland, Oreg., 1970-71, 71-72; rsch. assoc. NIH, Bethesda, Md., 1972-75; resident Yale-New Haven Hosp., New Haven, 1975-77, attending physician, 1978—; faculty, prof. Yale U. Sch. of Medicine, New Haven, 1977-93, 93—; staff physician VAMC, West Haven, Conn., 1981—, chief, dermatology svc., 1988—. Cons. Alcide Corp., Farmingdale, N.Y., 1982-86, Novartis Pharm., East Hanover, N.J., 1997—; vis. prof. Ben Gurion U., Beersheva, Israel, 1990. Editor: Endocrine, Metabolic and Immunologic Functions of Keratinocytes, 1988; assoc. editor Jour. Investigative Dermatology, 1992—; contbr. over 75 articles to profl. jours. Bd. dirs. Congregation Mishken Israel, Hamden, Conn., 1980-83; chmn. med. adv. bd. Found. for Ichthyosis and Related Skin Types, Ardmore, Pa., 1989—, bd. dirs. Lt. comdr. USPHS, 1972-75. Recipient Anna Fuller Faculty award Yale U.

Sch. Medicine, 1977-80; rsch. grantee NIH, Bethesda, 1986—, Vet.'s Adminstrn., Washington, 1980-90. Fellow Am. Acad. Dermatology; mem. AAAS, Soc. Investigative Dermatology, Soc. for Molecular Medicine, Am. Soc. Gene Therapy, Am. Dermatol. Assn. Jewish. Avocations: sports, gardening, music, breadmaking.

MILTON, CATHERINE HIGGS, social service entrepreneur; b. N.Y.C., Jan. 6, 1943; d. Edgar Homer and Josephine (Doughty) Higgs; m. A. Fenner Milton (div.); m. Thomas F. McBride, Aug. 25, 1974 (dec. Oct. 31, 2003); children: Raphael McBride, Luke McBride. BA, Mt. Holyoke Coll., 1964, PhD (hon.), 1992. Reporter, travel writer Boston Globe, 1964-68; with Internat. Assn. Chiefs Police, Washington, 1968-70; asst. dir. Police Found., Washington, 1970-75; spl. asst. U.S. Treasury Dept., Washington, 1977-80; project staff Spl. Com. Aging/Senate, Washington, 1980-81; spl. asst. to pres., founder/exec. dir. Stanford (Calif.) U. Haas Ctr. for Public, 1981-91; exec. dir. Commn. for Nat. and Cmty. Svc., Washington, 1991-93; v.p. Corp. for Nat. Svc., Washington, 1993-95; exec. dir. Presidio Leadership Ctr., 1995-96; exec. dir. U.S. Programs Save the Children, Westport, Conn., 1996—2002; pres. Friends of the Children, Portland, Oreg., 2002—. Mem. U.S. Atty. General's Task Force on Family Violence, 1981-82; chair nat. forum Kellogg Found., 1990. Author: Women in Policing, 1972, Police Use of Deadly Force, 1976; co-author: History of Black Americans, 1965, Team Policing, Little Sisters and the Law, 1970. Bd. mem. Youth Svc. Calif., L.A., 1986-91, Trauma Found., San Francisco, 1982-90; spl. advisor Campus Compact, 1986-91 Nat. Kellogg Found. fellow, Battle Creek, Mich., 1985-88; recipient Dedication and Outstanding Efforts award Bd. Suprs., Santa Clara, Calif., 1989, Outstanding Vol. Contbn. award Strive for Five, San Francisco, 1991, Dinkelspiel award Stanford U., 1991; named Outstanding Campus Adminstr. COOL, 1987. Avocations: backpacking, skiing, hiking, travel. Home: 3652 SE Oak St Portland OR 97214 Office: Friends of the Children 44 NE Morris St Portland OR 97214

MILTON, CHAD EARL, lawyer; b. Brevard County, Fla., Jan. 29, 1947; s. Rex Dale and Mary Margaret (Peacock) M.; m. Ann Mitchell Bunting, Mar. 30, 1972; children: Samuel, Kathleen, Kelsey. BA, Colo. Coll., 1969; JD, U. Colo., 1974; postgrad., U. Mo., 1976-77. Bar: Colo. 1974, Mo. 1977, U.S. Dist. Ct. Colo. 1974, U.S. Dist. Ct. (we. dist.) Mo. 1977. Counsel Office of Colo. State Pub. Defender, Colo. Springs, 1974-76; pub. info. officer, counsel Mid-Am. Arts Alliance, Kansas City, Mo., 1977-78; claims counsel Employers Reinsurance Corp., Kansas City, Mo., 1978-80; sr. v.p. Media/Profl. Ins., Kansas City, Mo., 1981-2000; sr. v.p. nat. practice leader, intellectual property & media Marsh, Kansas City, Mo., 2000—. Reporter, photographer, editor Golden (Colo.) Daily Transcript, 1970; investigator, law clk. Office of Colo. State Pub. Defender, Denver, Golden, 1970-74; participant Annenberg Project on the Reform of Libel Laws, Washington, 1987-88; adj. prof., comm. and advt. law Webster U., 1989-93; lectr. in field. Pres. bd. dirs. Folly Theater, 1992-94. Mem. ABA (chair intellectual property law com. of the torts and ins. practice sect., forum com. on comm. law, ctrl. and Ea. European law initiative), Mo. Bar Assn., Kansas City Met. Bar Assn., Libel Def. Resource Ctr. (editorial bd., exec. com.). Avocations: tennis, golf, skiing, sailing, antique maps. Home: 8821 Alhambra St Shawnee Mission KS 66207-2357 Office: Marsh 2405 Grand Blvd Kansas City MO 64108-2510 Office Phone: 816-556-4365. E-mail: chad.e.milton@marsh.com.

MILTON, CHRISTIAN MICHEL, insurance executive; b. London, Nov. 13, 1947; came to U.S., 1978; s. Frank Harry and Gismonde Marie Susini; m. Rana Nikpour, Mar. 31, 1985. Claims clk. Stewart Smith Co., London, 1966-67; mgr. reins. claims Henry Head & Co., London, 1967-73; asst. v.p. reins. div. Airco, Hamilton, Bermuda, 1974-78, Nat. Union Fire Ins. Co., Pitts., 1980-81, Am. Internat. Group Inc., N.Y.C., 1978-80, 81-85, v.p. reins. div., 1985—. Bd. dirs. Nat. Union Fire Ins. Co., N.Y.C., Am. Home Ins. Co., N.Y.C.; lectr. reins. Ins. Soc. N.Y., 1988—. Avocation: reading. Office: Am Internat Group Inc 110 William St New York NY 10038-3901

MILTON, JAMES W. metal products executive; Exec. v.p., pres. Milton Can. Co. Bway Corp., Atlanta, Ga. Office: Bway Corp 8607 Robets Dr Ste 250 Atlanta GA 30350

MILTON, JOHN CHARLES DOUGLAS, nuclear physicist, researcher; b. Regina, Sask., Can., 1924; s. William and Frances Craigie; m. Gwendolyn Margaret Shaw, Oct. 10, 1953; children: Bruce F., Leslie J.F., Neil W.D., Theresa M. A.M. in Music, U. Man., 1943, B.Sc. with honors, 1947; MA, Princeton U., 1949, PhD in Physics, 1951. Asst. rsch. officer Atomic Energy Can., Ltd., Chalk River, Ont., 1951-57, assoc. rsch. officer, 1957-62, sr. rsch. officer, 1962-70, prin. rsch. officer, 1970-91, head nuclear physics br., 1967-83, dir. physics div., 1983-85, v.p. physics and health scis., 1986-90, researcher emeritus, 1990-97. Vis. scientist Lawrence Berkeley Lab., 1960-62, Centre de Recherches, Strasbourg & Bruyeres-le-Chatel, 1975-76; chmn. nuclear physics grants Natural Sci. and Engring. Research Council, 1977-82; adv. bd. TRIUMF 1984-92; bd. dirs. Can. Fusion Fuels Tech., 1986-90, Tokamak de Varennes, 1986-90. Pres. Deep River Hort. Assn., 1997-98. Fellow Royal Soc. Can., Am. Phys. Soc.; mem. Can. Assn. Physicists (pres. 1992). Home: 3 Alexander Pl Deep River ON Canada K0J 1P0

MILTON, JOHN P. ecologist, educator, author, photographer; b. Jersey City, N.J., Nov. 30, 1938; s. John Jr. and Barbara (Potter) M. BS, U. Mich., 1962, MS, 1963. Dir. internat. programs divsn. Conservation Found., Washington, 1963-72; pres., chmn. Threshold Found., Washington, 1973—. Vis. scholar Woodrow Wilson Internat. Sch. for Scholars, Washington, 1972-73; vis. prof. U. Ill., Springfield, 1978-80; pres. Sacred Passage and the Way of Nature, Bisbee, Ariz., 1985—. Author: Future Environments of North America, 1966, Nameless Valleys, Shining Mountains, 1970, The Careless Technology: Ecology and International Development, 1972, Ecological Principles for Economic Development, 1973, Alaska, The Last Great Wilderness, 1973, The Future of America, 1977, The Galapagos, 1980, Ecological Planning in the Nepalese Terai, 1981, Sky Above, Earth Below, 1999. Mem. NAS (com. mem.), Am. Assn. Scis. (com. mem.), Ecol. Soc. Am. Avocations: camping, hiking, canoeing, meditation, vision quest. Office: Sacred Passage & The Way of Nature PO Box CZ Main St Bisbee AZ 85603 E-mail: info@sacredpassage.com.

MILTON, JOSEPH PAYNE, lawyer; b. Richmond, Va., Oct. 24, 1943; s. Hubert E. and Grace C. Milton; children: Michael Payne, Amy Barrett, David King; m. Cela Cabler Milton, Apr. 8, 1989. BS in Bus. Adminstrn., U. Fla., 1967, JD, 1969. Bar: Fla. 1969, U.S. Ct. Appeals (5th cir.) 1971, U.S. Supreme Ct. 1972, U.S. Ct. Appeals (11th cir.) 1981. Assoc. Toole, Taylor, Moseley & Gabel, Jacksonville, 1969-70; ptnr. Toole, Taylor, Moseley, Gabel & Milton, Jacksonville, 1971-78, Howell, Liles, Braddock & Milton, Jacksonville, 1978-89, Milton & Leach, Jacksonville, 1990-95, Milton, Leach & D'Andrea, Jacksonville, 1996—. Mem. Mayor's Blue Ribbon Task Force; mem. Law Ctr. Coun., U. Fla. Coll. Law, 1972-78, mem. alumni coun., 1995—; campaign chmn. N.E. Fla. chpt. March of Dimes, 1973-74, v.p., 1974-75; pres. Willing Hands, 1974-75; chmn. attys.' divsn. United Way, 1977; pres. Civic Round Table of Jacksonville, 1980-81; mem. exec. com. Jacksonville Area Legal Aid, Inc., 1982-83; chmn. pvt. bar involvement com. Legal Aid Bd. Dirs., 1982-83. Recipient Outstanding Svc. award for individual contbns. in support of legal svcs. for the poor, 1981. Fellow: Soc. Lawyers for Pub. Svc., Southeastern Admiralty Law (com., dir. Port, Jacksonville 1996—99), Am. Bar Found., Internat. Soc. Barristers; mem.: ATLA, Am. Judicature Soc., Acad. Fla. Trial Lawyers, Maritime Law Assn. U.S. (mem. com. professionalism 1996—), Nat. Assn. R.R. Trial Counsel (exec. com. 1979—, v.p. southeastern region 1984—86, pres.-elect 1989—90, pres. 1990—91), Jacksonville Assn. Def. Counsel (pres. 1981—82, lectr. CLE programs, guest lectr. U. Fla. Nat. Assn. R.R. Trial Counsel), Fla. Coun. Bar Assn. Pres. (exec. com. 1982—88, v.p. 1984, pres. 1985—86), Fla. Bar (grievance com. 1975—77, chmn. grievance com. 1976, 4th jud. cir. nominating commn. 1980—82, voluntary bar liaison com. 1982—83, mem. exec. coun. for trial sect. 1982—89, chmn.-elect 1986—87, chmn. 1987, 1988, bd. govs. 1988, charter mem. admiralty and maritime law bd. cert. 1996—2000, chmn. 1998, chmn. 4th jud. cir. professionalism com. 1998—, bd. cert civil trial lawyer, bd. cert. admiralty and maritime law, recipient Outstanding Professionalism Program 1999, 2001), Jacksonville Bar Assn. (young lawyers sect. 1974—75, pres. 1980—81, Lawyer of Yr. award 1999), Am. Bd. Trial Advs. (pres. Jacksonville chpt. 1997, FLABOTA bd. mem. 1997—, treas. 1999, nat. bd. mem. 1999—, pres.-elect 2000, charter, treas. 2004, chpt. selected as Best in Nation 1997, Jacksonville chpt. Trial Lawyer of Yr. 2000, selected as Fla. Trial Lawyer of Yr. 2000, named Master In Trial Master of Yr. 2003), Country Club Sapphire Valley (N.C.), Gulf Life Tower Club, Univ. Club, San Jose Country Club. Republican. Home: 4655 Corrientes Cir N Jacksonville FL 32217-4329 Office: Milton Leach Whitman D'Andrea Charek & Milton PA 815 S Main St Ste 200 Jacksonville FL 32207-8181

MILTON, RICHARD HENRY, retired diplomat, children's advocate; b. Bowling Green, Ky., Sept. 30, 1938; s. Lester Thomas and Rose Ann (Jesse) M.; m. Evy M. Miller, Aug. 28, 1964; children: Christopher, Ann. Student, W.Va. U., 1956-57; BA, Marshall U., 1960, MA, 1964. Tchr., Columbus, Ohio, 1960-61; tchr. Sidney, Ohio, 1964-65; fgn. svc. officer U.S. Dept. State, Washington, 1965-94; dep. asst. dir. ACDA, Washington, 1982-83; consul gen. U.S. consulate gen., Guayaquil, Ecuador, 1984-87; polit. advisor U.S. Space Command, Peterson AFB, Colo., 1987-90, 92-94; v.p. Am. Fgn. Svc. Assn., U.S. Dept. State, Washington, 1990-91. Vis. prof. USCG Acad., New London, Conn., 1977-79. Ct. apptd. spl advocate Colo. 4th Jud. Dist., 1993—, Cmty. Partnership for Child Devel., 1995—2002, Protect our Children Coalition, 1996. Served to 1st lt. U.S. Army, 1961-63 Congl. fellow Am. Polit. Sci. Assn., 1974-75; recipient Dist. Vol. of Yr. award Ct. Apptd. Spl. Advocate, 1998, State Vol. of Yr. award, 1999, Nat. C.A.S.A. Vol. of Yr. award, 2000. Home: 2022 Devon St Colorado Springs CO 80909-1618

MILTON-JONES, DELISHA, professional basketball player; b. Riceboro, Ga., Sept. 11, 1974; d. Beverly Milton; m. Roland Jones, June 30, 2003. BA in Sports Mgmt., U. Fla. Forward Portland Power, 1997—99, L.A. Sparks, 1999—. Forward Ekaterinburg team/EuroLeague, Russia, 2002—; mem. USA Basketball Women's Sr. Nat. Team, 2004. Recipient gold medal, Olympic Games, 2000, World Championships, 1998, 2002, U.S. Olympic Cub, 1999, World Univ. Games, 1997, U.S. Olympic Festival, 1994. Office: Los Angeles Sparks 555 N Nash St El Segundo CA 90245*

MILUNAS, J. ROBERT, health care organization executive; b. Aug. 7, 1947; s. Joseph John M.; m. Glenetta Graham; children: Amy, Joseph, Anna Kate. BS, Tulane U., 1969; postgrad., Samford U., 1973; MBA, Ga. State U., 1977. Mgr. internal and govt. reporting, corp. contr.'s staff Arvin Industries Inc., Columbus, Ind., 1977-80; mgr. consol. acctg., corp. contr.'s staff Mattel Inc., Hawthorne, Calif., 1980-82; asst. contr. Times Mirror Cable TV Inc., Irvine, Calif., 1982-83; Western Divsn. contr. SCA, Santa Ana, Calif., 1983-84; v.p., corp. contr. Tchrs. Mgmt. Investment Corp., Newport Beach, Calif., 1984-86; v.p., CFO Beech St. Inc., Irvine, 1987-89; v.p. fin. and adminstrn. ConsumerHealth Inc., Newport Beach, Calif., 1989-93; pres. Aegis Consulting Svcs., Dana Point, Calif., 1993—. 1st lt. U.S. Army Transp. Corps., 1969-71. Decorated Bronze Star. Office Phone: 404-321-4232. *Life is a precious gift to be nurtured daily through interaction with friends and family and helping others achieve their potential.*

MILUNSKY, AUBREY, geneticist, pediatrician, medical educator; b. Johannesburg, Nov. 3, 1936; came to U.S., 1969; 1 child, Jeffrey M. MB, BCh, U. Witwatersand, Johannesburg, 1960, DSc, 1982; postgrad., Gt. Ormond St. Hosp., London, 1965. Diplomate Am. Bd. Pediatrics, Am. Bd. Med. Genetics. Intern Johannesburg Gen. Hosp./Baragwanath Hosp., Johannesburg, 1961; resident in internal medicine and pediat. Baragwanath Hosp., 1961-64; pediat. registrar Queen Mary's Hosp. for Children, Surrey, Eng., 1965-66; asst. pediatrician New England Med. Ctr. Tufts U., Boston, 1966-70, from instr. to asst. prof. pediat. Sch. Medicine, 1966-70; rsch. fellow and assoc. in neurology Mass. Gen. Hosp./Harvard Med. Sch., Boston, 1969-70; dir. Birth Defects and Genetics Clinic Mass. Gen. Hosp., Boston, 1971-73, asst. pediatrician, 1971-82, assoc. dir. Cystic Fibrosis Clinic, 1975-79; asst. prof. pediatrics Harvard Med. Sch., Boston, 1971-81; prof. pediatrics and ob-gyn. Sch. Medicine, dir. Ctr. for Human Genetics, assoc. physician Univ. Hosp. Boston U., 1981—, prof. pathology, 1985—, Endowed chair human genetics, 1991—; pediatrician Boston City Hosp., 1981—. Mem. Mass. State Genetics Adv. Bd., 1983-84; profl. adv. bd. Nat. Tuberous Sclerosis Assn., 1990-93; quality assurance com. New England Regional Genetics Group, 1990-96. Author: The Prenatal Diagnosis of Hereditary Disorders, 1973, Know Your Genes, 1977, How to Have the Healthiest Baby You Can., 1987, Choices, Not Chances: An Essential Guide to your Heredity and Health, 1989, Heredity and Your Family's Health, 1992, Your Genetic Destiny: Know Your Genes, Secure Your Health, Save Your Life, 2001; editor: Clinics in Perinatology, Vol. II, 1974, The Prevention of Genetic Disease and Mental Retardation, 1975, Genetic Disorders and the Fetus: Diagnosis, Prevention and Treatment, 1979, 5th edit., 2004, Coping with Crisis and Handicap, 1981, (with G.J. Annas) Genetics and the Law I, 1976, Genetics and the Law II, 1980, Genetics and the Law III, 1986, (with E.A. Friedman and L. Gluck) Advances in Perinatal Medicine, 1981, Vol. II, 1982, Vol. III, 1983, Vol. IV, 1985, Vol. V, 1986; mem. editl. bd. Am. Jour. Law and Medicine, 1974-93, Am. Jour. Med. Genetics, 1977-94, Bioethics Digest, 1977-78, Prenatal Diagnosis, 1980-90, 92—, Intelligence Reports in Ob-Gyn., 1982-88, Fetal Therapy, 1986—; peer reviewer New England Jour. Medicine, Pediatrics, Am. Jour. Med. Genetics, Am. Jour. Ob-Gyn., Am. Jour. Law and Medicine, Am. Jour. Pub. Health, Prenatal Diagnosis, Fetal Therapy, Ob-Gyn., Epidemiology, Jour. Pediatrics; contbr. over 300 articles to profl. jours. Recipient First Place Film award Nat. Coun. Family Rels. Media Awards Co., 1990, Tinsley Harrison award So. Soc. for Clin. Investigation, 1991; Aubrey Milunsky Endowed Chair in Human Genetics named in his honor Boston U., 1991. Fellow Am. Coll. Med. Genetics (founding), Royal Coll. Physicians (diploma in child health 1965); mem. Am. Pediat. Soc., Am. Soc. Human Genetics (social issues com. 1983-87), Am. Soc. Law and Medicine (v.p. 1982-83, pres.-elect 1983-85, pres. 1985-86, bd. dirs. 1986-88, 90-93), Soc. for Pediat. Rsch., Mass. Med. Soc. Office: Boston U Sch Medicine Ctr for Human Genetics 715 Albany St Boston MA 02118-2307

MIMS, JOYCE ELAINE, lawyer; b. Chgo., Mar. 6, 1942; d. Thomas Samuel Mims and Hortense Bernice (Wade) Miller; m. John Young. B.A., U. Wis., 1964; M.A., Northwestern U., 1965; J.D., NYU, 1975. Bar: Ill. 1976. Tchr. lang. Lane Tech. High Sch., Chgo. Bd. Edn., 1965-67; edn. specialist IBM World Trade Corp., N.Y.C., 1968-69; adminstr. lectr. CUNY-Brooklyn, 1969-75; assoc. firm Bell, Boyd & Lloyd, Chgo., 1975-78; atty. Am. Hosp. Supply Corp., Evanston, Ill., 1978-82, div. counsel, 1982-83, asst. gen. counsel, 1983— . Mem. Evanston Zoning Bd. Appeals, 1977-82; bd. dirs. Evanston Community Devel. Corp., Evanston Hosp. Corp.; Anderson del. Rep. Nat. Conv., 1980. NAACP Scholar, 1960; Chessmen Men's Club scholar, 1960. Mem. ABA, Chgo. Bar Assn., Nat. Slavic Honor Soc. Office: 30 W Monroe St Chicago IL 60603-2495

MIMS, LLOYD LEE, dean, conductor, vocalist; b. Bradenton, Fla., July 29, 1950; m. Marilyn L. Williamson, Aug. 17, 1973; 1 child, Virginia Louise. MusB in Edn., U. So. Miss., 1973, MusM in Voice Performance, 1976; D in Musical Arts, So. Bapt. Theol. Sem., 1983. Prof. music So. Bapt. Theol. Sem., Louisville, 1983—2000, dean Sch. Ch. Music, 1993—2000; dean Sch. Music and Fine Arts Palm Beach Atlantic U., West Palm Beach, Fla., 2000—. Adj. prof. Ind. U.-S.E., Jeffersonville, 1979—83; music dir., prin. condr. Sem. Cmty. Orch., Louisville, 1980—2000. Ordained min. of music First Bapt. Ch., Collins, Miss., 1972—79. Named Regional Finalist, Met. Opera Nat. Coun., 1973. Mem.: Nat. Assn. Tchrs. Singing (dist. gov. Ky. 1992—94, regional gov.-S.W. 2004—). Office: Palm Beach Atlantic Univ 901 South Flagler Dr PO Box 24708 West Palm Beach FL 33416 E-mail: lloyd_mims@pba.edu.

MIMS, WILLIAM CLEVELAND, state legislator, lawyer; b. Harrisonburg, Va., June 20, 1957; s. David Lathan and Lurleen Shirley (Stovall) M.; m. Jane Ellen Rehme, Dec. 20, 1980; children: Katherine Grace, Emily Anne, Sarah Joy. AB, Coll. of William & Mary, 1979; JD, George Washington U., 1984; LLM, Georgetown U., 1986. Bar: Va. Legis. asst. Congressman Paul Trible, Washington, 1981-82; dep. legis. dir. Senator Paul Trible, Washington, 1983-85; chief of staff Congressman Frank Wolf, Washington, 1986-87; atty. Hazel & Thomas, P.C., Leesburg, Va., 1987-91, Worcester, Mims & Atwill, P.C., 1993—2002, Mims, Atwill & Leigh, P.C., Leesburg, 2002—; mem. Va. Gen. Assembly, Richmond, 1991—, del., 1992-98, senator, 1998—. Adj. prof. law George Mason U., 2002—; mem. Va. Housing Commn., 1994—, chmn. 2000—2003; mem. Va. Code Commn., 2000, chmn., 2003—. Bd. dirs. Dulles Area Transp. Assn., Herndon, Va., 1994—, Marshall Home Preservation Fund, Leesburg, 1992—, Youth for Tomorrow, 1995-97; treas., bd. dirs. Loudoun Bar Assn., Leesburg, 1988-89; active Nat. Eagle Scout Assn., 1992–. Flemming fellow, 1995-96. Mem. Va. Bar Assn. (Boyd-Graves Conf. 1996—, bd. govs. 2002—), Va. Trial Lawyers Assn., Christian Legal Soc., No. Va. Transp. Assn. Republican. Episcopalian. Office: Mims Atwill & Leigh PC PO Box 741 Leesburg VA 20178-0741

MIN, BALSHIK, pathologist; b. Seoul, Jan. 15, 1942; s. Young-Ock and Yang-Hee (Kim) M.; m. Jungsoon Ahn, Apr. 25, 1970; children: James, Susan. MD, Seoul Nat. U., 1966. Pathologist Faxton-St. Luke's Healthcare, Utica, NY, 1978—, dir. of labs., 1984—; pathologist Centrex Clin. Labs., New Hartford, NY, 1978—. Dir. of labs. Centrex Clin. Labs., New Hartford, 1990-96. Capt. Korean Army, 1966-70. Fellow Coll. Am. Pathologists; mem. AMA, Am. Soc. Clin. Pathology, Nat. Soc. Histotechnology, Ctrl. N.Y. Acad. Medicine. Avocations: reading, classical music, gardening, golf. Office: Faxton-St Lukes Healthcare 1676 Sunset Ave Utica NY 13502-5416 Office Phone: 315-624-5264.

MIN, DAVID B. chemist, educator, research scientist; b. Seoul, Korea, Sept. 12, 1942; arrived in U.S.A, 1965; s. Yun S. Min and Sun D. Yoon; m. Hyung Ok Lee, Aug. 1, 1953; children: Peter K., Stephen K. BS, Seoul Nat. U., Republic of Korea, 1965; MS, U. Minn., Mpls., 1968; PhD, Rutgers U., New Brunswick, N.J., 1973. Mgr. CP, Best Foods Rsch. Ctr., Union, NJ, 1976—79; prof. Ohio State, Columbus, 1979—. Hon. prof. Rutgers U., 1976—79; cons. Ministry of Agr., Seoul, 2001—; sci. editor Jour. of Food Sci., Chgo., 2001—. Author: Flavor Chemistry of Foods, 1998, Chemistry of Food Lipids, 2002. Pres. Korean Cath. Ch., Columbus, Ohio, 2000—02. Recipient Rsch. Achievement award, Inst. of Food Technologists, 1995, Disting. Sr. Faculty Rsch. award, Ohio State, 1999, Rsch. award, Korean Soc. of Food Sci. and Tech., 2002; fellow, Am. Oil Chemicals Co., 2001, Inst. of Food Technologists, 2002. Roman Catholic. Achievements include development of singlet oxygen oxidation of foods; research in oxygen quenching to improve flavor stability of foods; mechanism of light sensitivity of riboflavin. Avocations: golf, travel. Home: 1306 Lakeside Pl Worthington OH 43085 Office: Ohio State Univ 2015 Fyffe Rd Columbus OH 43210 Office Phone: 614-292-7801. E-mail: min.2@osu.edu.

MINA, JOHN LOUIS (IVAN MINEA), religious studies educator, archivist; b. Nancy, France, Jan. 31, 1950; came to U.S. 1951; s. Albert and Mila (Koenig) M. BA with highest honors, U. Calif., Santa Barbara, 1972; MA, U. Calif., Berkeley, 1974, PhD, 1979. Lectr. Centre D'Etudes Russes, Meudon, France, 1984-85; vis. asst. prof. U. Ky., Lexington, 1987-88; prof. Sts. Cyril and Methodius Sem., Pitts., 1990-95; archivist Met. Archdiocese of Pitts., Byzantine Rite, 1997—. Contbr. articles to profl. jours. Mem. Cath. Hist. Soc. West Pa., Pitts. Recipient Dobro Slovo, U. Calif., Berkeley, 1980; U. Calif. Regents scholar, 1968; Fulbright fellow, 1972. Mem. Assn. Cath. Diocesan Archivists, KC (4th degree), Phi Beta Kappa. Byzantine Catholic. Avocations: travel, foreign affairs. Home: 318 Park Ave Clairton PA 15025-1758 Office: 66 Riverview Ave Pittsburgh PA 15214-2253 E-mail: ascension1@trueyellow.net.

MINA, MICHAEL, chef, restaurant owner; b. Cairo; m. Diane Mina; 1 child, Samuel Jordan. Grad., Culinary Inst. Am., 1989. Formerly mem. staff Aureole Restaurant, N.Y.C.; formerly in charge pastry divsn. Hotel Bel Air, L.A.; chef de cuisine Aqua, San Francisco, 1991—93, exec. chef, 1993—; ptnr. Aqua at the Bellagio Resort, Las Vegas, 1998—, Pisces, Burlingame, Calif., 1999—. Nominee Best Chef, Calif., James Beard Found., 2001; named Grey Poupon Rising Star Chef of Yr., 1997. Office: Aqua Restaurant 252 California St San Francisco CA 94111

MINAHAN, DANIEL FRANCIS, lawyer, retired manufacturing executive; b. Orange, N.J., Dec. 3, 1929; s. Alfred A. and Katherine (Kelly) M.; m. Mary Jean Gaffney, May 2, 1953; children: Daniel F. Jr., John A. AB magna cum laude, U. Notre Dame, 1951; JD magna cum laude, U. Conn., 1964; grad., Advanced Mgmt. Program, Harvard, 1975. Bar: Conn. 1964, U.S. Supreme Ct 1969, U.S. Ct. of Appeals (2d cir.), U.S. Dist. Ct. Conn. 1971. Mgr. indsl. engring. Uniroyal, Inc., Naugatuck, Conn., 1952-59, mgr. indsl. relations, 1959-64, dir. labor relations N.Y.C., 1964-66; v.p. indsl. relations and labor counsel Phillips Van Heusen Corp., N.Y.C., 1966-69; v.p. personnel-adminstrn. Broadway-Hale Stores, Inc., L.A., 1969-70; v.p. employee relations, sec. Magnavox-N.Am., Philips Corp., 1970-73, v.p. ops., group exec., 1973-83, sr. v.p. adminstrn., 1984-89, exec. v.p., 1989-93, vice-chmn., 1991-93; vice-chmn. nat. found. bd. Robert Anderson Sch. Mgmt., U. N.Mex., 1993-98; pvt. practice, 1998—. Trustees adv. coun., Fairfield U., mem. dean's coun. Grad. Sch. Bus. Co-author: The Developing Labor Law, 1971. Chmn. bd. Internat. Fedn. Keystone Youth Orgns., London and Chgo., 1984-88; vice-chmn. nat. found. bd. Anderson Sch. Mgmt., U. N.Mex., 1993-98. With USMC. Mem. The Forum for World Affairs, Conn. Bar Assn., Harvard Club, Club Internat. (Chgo.).

MINAI, OMAR AHMAD, physician; b. Lahore, Pakistan; s. Idris Ahmad and Riaz Fatima Minai; m. Beena Ahmad, Dec. 7, 1998. MB BS, Aga Khan U., Karachi, Pakistan, 1990. Diplomate Am. Bd. Internal Medicine, Am. Bd. Pulmonary Medicine, Am. Bd. Critical Care Medicine, Am. Bd. Sleep Medicine. Intern in internal medicine U. Conn., Farmington, 1992-93, resident in internal medicine, 1992-96; fellow in pulmonary and critical care medicine Cleve. Clin. Found., 1996-99, staff physician in pulmonary and critical care medicine, 1999—. Contbr. Mem.: ACP, Am. Thoracic Soc., Am. Coll. Chest Physicians. Office: Cleve Clinic Found 9500 Euclid Ave Ste A-90 Cleveland OH 44195-0001

MINANEL, SHELLEY, writer, artist; b. New Rochelle, N.Y. parents Benjamin and Mary (Regelson) Lipman. Student, Cooper Union Art, 1939-42. Pres. S. Minanel & Assocs., Marina Del Rey, Calif., 1980—; author Papier-Mache Press, Watsonville, Calif., 1987—. Mem. adv. bd. Internat. Biog. Ctr., Cambridge, Eng., 1997—. Artist: (book) Artist's Market, 1985; contbr. poetry to anthologies, including When I Am an Old Woman I Will Wear Purple, 1987, I Am Becoming the Woman I Want, 1994, There Is No Place Like Home for the Holidays, 1997; contbr. poetry and artwork to publs., including Sailing, Light, Aerobics Mag., Personal Computer Age, Redbook, Ensign, Dawn, others. Mem. Pub. Citizen, Washington, 1996—. Recipient 2d pl. award for poetry N.Mex. Poetry Soc., 1989, Hon. Mention for poetry Writer's Market Digest, 1997. Mem. Sierra Club. Avocations: reading, bicycling, songwriting. Home: # 370C 14021 Marquesas Way # 370C Marina Dl Rey CA 90292-6061 Office: S Minanel Assocs 1402 Marquesas Way Marina Del Rey CA 90292

MINAR, PAUL G. design consultant; b. Phoenix, July 12, 1932; s. Aaron Crowther and Ione Anna (Schmid) Mortensen. Student, Ariz. State U., 1950-54, John F. Kennedy U., 1978-80, Antioch West U., 1980. Sound effects technician, TV stage mgr. Sta. KHJ-AM-TV, L.A., 1955-63; displayer W.&J. Sloane Furniture Co., Beverly Hills, Calif., 1963-66, Bullock's Dept. Store, L.A., 1966-68, Macy's Dept. Store, San Francisco, 1968-70; interior designer Lloyd's Furniture Co., San Diego, 1970-71, Bonynge's Furniture Co., Oakland, Calif., 1971-72, Breuner's Furniture Co., Oakland, 1972-74; design cons. The Other Artist, San Francisco, 1974—. Archival rschr. and conservation Petaluma Hist. Mus., 1994—; profl. numerologist; lectr. in onomatology. Author: Numbers: The Energy Force in Your Name, 2003; writer, producer (documentary) The Modern Nursing Home, 1959. Vol. talent agt. San Francisco Symphony Black and White Ball, 1983; mem. Fine Arts Mus. of San Francisco. Mem. Inst. Noetic Scis., Petaluma Mus. Assn., Interant. Assn. Numerologists, Calif. Soc. Psychical Study. Democrat. Roman Catholic. Avocations: wilderness exploration, tennis, classical music, parapsychology, world history. Office: The Other Artist 3200 Buchanan St San Francisco CA 94123-3517

MINARD, JOSEPH M. state legislator; b. Charleston, W.Va., Jan. 5, 1932; m. Mary Contento; children: Michelle, Marion, Marcia, Michael, Maria, Samuel. BS, W.Va. U. Mem. W.Va. U., Charleston, 1999—. Mem. banking and ins. com., confirmations com., govt. orgn. com., interstate cooperation com., judiciary com., mil. com., natural resources com. Past pres. Harrison County Cath. Sch. Bd. With U.S. Army. Mem. W.Va. Hospitality Assn., VFW, Am. Legion, Columbian Club, Serra, KC, Moose, Lions, Elks. Democrat. Roman Catholic. Office: WVa Senate 1900 Kanawha Blvd E Rm 219W Charleston WV 25305-0009 also: 510 Haymond Hwy Clarksburg WV 26301-3876

MINARDI, RICHARD A., JR., lawyer; b. Mobile, Ala., Aug. 15, 1943; s. Richard A. and Martha F. (Beck) Minardi; m. Frances Archer Guy, Oct. 21, 1989. BA, Yale U., 1965, LLB, 1968. Bar: Va. 1969. Assoc. McGuire Woods & Battle, Richmond, Va., 1968-71; ptnr. Staples, Greenberg Minardi & Kessler, Richmond, 1971-86, Mays & Valentine, Richmond, 1986-2000, Troutman Sanders LLP, Richmond, 2001—. Mem.: ABA, Richmond Bar Assn., Va. Bar Assn. Home: 211 Santa Clara Dr Richmond VA 23229-7152 Office: Troutman Sanders LLP PO Box 1122 Richmond VA 23218-1122 E-mail: rick.minardi@troutmansanders.com.

MINARIK, ELSE HOLMELUND (BIGART MINARIK), author; b. Aarhus, Denmark, Sept. 13, 1920; d. Kaj Marius and Helga Holmelund; m. Walter Minarik, July 14, 1940 (dec.); 1 child, Brooke Ellen; m. Homer Bigart, Oct. 3, 1970 (dec.). BA, Queens Coll., 1942. Tchr. 1st grade, art Commack (N.Y.) Pub. Schs., 1950-54. Author children's books: Little Bear, 1957, Father Bear Comes Home, 1959, Little Bear's Friend, 1960, Little Bear's Visit, 1961, No Fighting, No Biting, 1958, Cat and Dog, 1960, The Winds That Come From Far Away, 1960, The Little Giant Girl and the Elf Boy, 1963, A Kiss for Little Bear, 1968, What If, 1987, Percy and the Five Houses, 1988, It's Spring, 1989, The Little Girl and the Dragon, 1991, Am I Beautiful, 1992. Mem. PEN Club. Home: 30 Gebig Rd Nottingham NH 03290 Office: care Greenwillow Books 1350 Ave Americas New York NY 10019

MINARIK, JOSEPH JOHN, economist, researcher; b. Lancaster, Pa., July 27, 1949; s. Joseph John and Helen Elizabeth M.; m. Eileen Marie Dowds; children: Mara Christina, Sara Elizabeth. BA, Georgetown U., 1971; MA, Yale U., 1972, M.Phil., 1973, PhD, 1974. Rsch. assoc. Brookings Instn., Washington, 1974-81; dept. asst. dir. Congl. Budget Office, Washington, 1981-84; sr. rsch. assoc. Urban Inst., Washington, 1984-88; exec. dir. Joint Econ. Com. U.S. Congress, Washington, 1988-90; exec. dir. for policy, chief economist House Budget Com., 1991-93; assoc. dir. econ. policy Office Mgmt. and Budget, 1993-2001. Author: Making Tax Choices, 1985, Making America's Budget Policy, 1989; contbr. articles to profl. jours. Fellow NSF, 1971-74, Yale U., 1971 Mem. Am. Econ. Assn., Nat. Tax Assn. Democrat. Home: 11656 Mediterranean Ct Reston VA 20190-3401 Office: House Budget Com 216 O'Neill Ho Office Bldg Washington DC 20515 E-mail: joseph.minarik@mail.house.gov.

MINAYA, OMAR, professional sports team executive; b. Valverde Mao, Dominican Republic; Scout Tex. Rangers, 1985—97; dir. pers. and internat. scouting, 1995—97; sr. asst. gen. mgr. N.Y. Mets, 1997—2002; v.p. Montreal (Can.) Expos, 2002—, gen. mgr., 2002—. Office: Olympic Stadium 4549 Pierre de Coubertin Ave Montreal QC Canada H1V 3N7*

MINC, HENRYK, mathematics professor; b. Lodz, Poland, Nov. 12, 1919; s. Izrael and Haja (Zyngler) M.; m. Catherine Taylor Duncan, Apr. 16, 1943; children: Robert Henry, Ralph Edward, Raymond. MA with honors, Edinburgh (Scotland) U., 1955, PhD, 1959. Tchr. Morgan Acad., Dundee, Scotland, 1956-58; lectr. Dundee Tech. Coll., 1957-58, U. B.C., Vancouver, Canada, 1958-59, asst. prof., 1959-60; assoc. prof. U. Fla., Gainesville, 1960-63; prof. U. Calif., Santa Barbara, 1963-90, prof. emeritus, 1990—. Vis. prof. Technion Israel Inst. Tech., Haifa, 1969-80. Author: A Survey of Matrix Theory and Matrix Inequalities, 1964, Russian translation, 1972, Chinese translation, 1990, Introduction to Linear Algebra, 1968, Spanish translation, 1968, Modern University Algebra, 1966, Elementary Linear Algebra, Spanish translation, 1971, New College Algebra, 1968, Elementary Functions and Coordinate Geometry, 1969, Algebra and Trigonometry, 1970, College Algebra, 1970, College Trigonometry, 1971, Integrated Analytic Geometry and Algebra with Circular Functions, 1973, Permanents, 1978, Russian translation, 1980, Chinese translation, 1991, Nonnegative Matrices, 1988, Chinese translation, 1991; contbr. over 80 rsch. articles to math. jours., 9 rsch. papers to archaeol. and ancient numismatic jours., articles to Burns Chronicle; referee and reviewer math. jours. 2nd lt. Polish Army, 1940-48, France, U.K. Recipient Lester Ford award Math. Assn. Am., 1966, rsch. contract Office Naval Rsch., 1985-88, Air Force Office Sci. Rsch. grantee, 1960-83, Lady Davis fellow, 1975-78. Fellow: Soc. Antiquaries of Scotland; mem.: Saltire Soc., Scots. Lang. Soc., Scottish Soc. Santa Barbara (past chieftain), Robert Burns World Fedn. (hon. pres.), Am. Math. Soc., James Hogg Soc., L.A. Burns Club. Democrat. Home: 4076 Naranjo Dr Santa Barbara CA 93110-1213 Office: U Calif Dept Math Santa Barbara CA 93106 E-mail: hmincburns@cox.net.

MINCER, JACOB, economics educator; b. Tomaszow, Poland, July 15, 1922; came to U.S., 1948; s. Isaac and Dora (Eisen) M.; m. Flora Kaplan, 1951; children: Deborah, Carolyn. BA, Emory U., 1950; PhD, Columbia U., 1957; LLD honoris causa, U. Chgo., 1991. Asst. prof. CUNY, 1954-59; assoc. prof. Columbia U., N.Y.C., 1960-62, prof. econs., 1962—. Mem. research staff Nat. Bur. Econ. Research, N.Y.C., 1960—. Author: Schooling, Experience and Earnings, 1974, Studies in Human Capital, 1993, Studies in Labor Supply, 1993; author, editor: Economic Forecasts and Expectations, 1969. Contbr. numerous articles to profl. publs. Recipient IZA prize in Labor Econs., 2002; postdoctoral fellow U. Chgo., 1957-58; Guggenheim fellow, N.Y.C., 1971. Fellow Am. Statis. Assn., Econometric Soc., Am. Econ. Assn. (Disting.); mem. NAS, Am. Acad. Arts and Scis., Nat. Acad. Edn. Home: 448 Riverside Dr New York NY 10027-6801 Office: Columbia U Dept Econs 118th St at Amsterdam Ave New York NY 10027

MINDELL, EARL LAWRENCE, nutritionist, writer; b. St. Boniface, Man., Can., Jan. 20, 1940; came to U.S., 1965, naturalized, 1972. s. William and Minerva Sybil (Galsky) M.; m. Gail Andrea Jaffe, May 16, 1971; children: Evan Louis-Ashley, Alanna Dayan. BS in Pharmacy, N.D. State U., 1963; PhD in Nutrition, Pacific We. U., 1985; master herbalist, Dominion Herbal Coll., 1995. Pres. Adanac Mgmt. Inc., 1979—; instr. Dale Carnegie course; lectr. on nutrition, radio and TV. Author: Earl Mindell's Vitamin Bible, Parents Nutrition Bible, Earl Mindell's Quick and Easy Guide to Better Health, Earl Mindell's Pill Bible, Earl Mindell's Shaping Up With Vitamins, Earl Mindell's Safe Eating, Earl Mindell's Herb Bible, Mindell's Food as Medicine, Earl Mindell's Soy Miracle, 1995, Anti-Aging Bible, 1996, Secret Remedies, 1997, Supplement Bible, 1998, Nutrition and Health for Your Dog, 1998, Prescription Alternatives, 2003, Vitamin Bible for the 21st Century, 1999, Dr. Earl Mindell's Secrets of Natural Health, 2000, Arthritis Miracle, 2000, Peak Performance Bible, 2000, Diet Bible, 2002, Allergy Bible, 2003; columnist: Let's Live mag., The Vitamin Supplement, The Vitamin Connection, Health 'N Fit, Unsafe at Any Meal, 2002; contbr. articles on nutrition to profl. jours., to profl. jours. Fellow Brit. Homeopathic Inst., Scottish Inst. Homeopathy; mem. Beverly Hills, Rancho Park, Western Los Angeles Regional C. of C., Am. Pharm. Assn., Am. Acad. Gen. Pharm. Practice, Am. Inst. for History of Pharmacy, Am. Nutrition Soc., Internat. Coll. Applied Nutrition, Nutrition Found., Nat. Health Fedn., Orthomolecular Med. Assn., Internat. Acad. Preventive Medicine, City of Hope Club, Beverly Hills Rotary, Masons, Shriners. Home and Office: 621 N Palm Dr Beverly Hills CA 90210-3414 Office Phone: 310-550-0161.

MINDELL, EUGENE ROBERT, surgeon, educator; b. Chgo., Feb. 24, 1922; s. Leon and Tillie (Rosenthal) M.; m. June A. Abrams, Sept. 19, 1945; children: Barbara, Ruth, David, Douglas. BS, U. Chgo., 1943, MD, 1945. Diplomate Am. Bd. Orthopaedic Surgery (bd. dirs. 1977-84, pres. 1983-84). Resident in orthopaedic surgery U. Chgo. Clinics, 1948-52; instr. U. Chgo., 1952; mem. faculty dept. orthopaedic surgery Sch. Medicine SUNY, Buffalo, 1953—, prof. Sch. Medicine, 1964—; chmn. dept. SUNY Sch. Medicine, Buffalo, 1964-88, dir. orthopaedic oncology Sch. Medicine, 1988—. Mem. bd. mgrs. Erie County Med. Ctr., 1990-96. Assoc. editor Jour. Bone and Joint Surgery, 1984-88, trustee, 1991—; dep. editor Clin. Orthopaedics and Related Rsch. representing Musculoskeletal Tumor Soc., 1997—; contbr. articles to profl. jours. Lt. (j.g.) M.C. USNR, 1946-48. Eugene R. Mindell Endowed Chair of Orthopaedic Surgery established in his honor SUNY, Buffalo, 1996; recipient Disting. Svc. award Alumni U. Chgo. Sch. Medicine, 1990, award for achievement in health care D'Youville Coll., 2002; NRC fellow, 1949-50. Fellow ACS; mem. Am. Acad. Orthopaedic Surgeons (bd. dirs. 1991-92), Am. Orthopaedic Assn. (v.p. 1990-91), Assn. Orthopaedic Chmn., Am. Assn. Surgery of Trauma, Am. Orthopaedic Rsch. Soc. (pres. 1972-73, residency rev. com. 1985-91), Musculoskeletal Tumor Soc. (pres. 1989-90), Coun. Musculoskeletal Specialty Socs. (chmn. elect 1991, chmn. 1992). Jewish. Home: 85 Depew Ave Buffalo NY 14214-1509 Office: 100 High St Buffalo NY 14203-1126

MINDES, GAYLE DEAN, education educator; b. Kansas City, Mo., Feb. 11, 1942; d. Elton Burnett and Juanita Maxine (Mangold) Taylor; m. Marvin William Mindes, June 20, 1969 (dec.); 1 child, Jonathan Seth; m. Matilde Delich-Funes Mindes Jun. 27, 2002. BS, U. Kans., 1964; MS, U. Wis., 1965; EdD, Loyola U., Chgo., 1979. Tchr. pub. schs., Newburgh, N.Y., 1965-67; spl. educator Ill. Dept. Mental Health, Chgo., 1967-69; spl. edn. supr. Evanston (Ill.) Dist. 65 Schs., 1969-74; lectr. Loyola U., Chgo., 1974-76, Coll. St. Francis, Joliet, Ill., 1976-79; asst. prof. edn. Oklahoma City U., 1979-80; prof. sch. edn. DePaul U., 1993-99, acting dean, 1998-99, prof. edn., 1999—, dir. EdD program, 2000—02, chair tchr. edn., 2003. Lectr. Northeastern Ill., U. Chgo, 1974, North Park Coll., Chgo., 1978; vis. asst. prof., rsch. assoc. Roosevelt U. Coll. Edn., Chgo, 1983-87, Albert A. Robin campus prof., dir. R&D dir. tchr. edn., dir. early childhood, dir. grad. edn. ctr., 1993; search com. multicultural student affairs, v.p. advancement, DePaul U., co-chair tcng., learning, tech. com, 2000—, mem. strategic planning univ. com., 2004; chair Roosevelt U. Senate, 1986-89; trustee Roosevelt U., 1987-93; co-chair ILAEYC Bldg. Bridges; faculty adv. com. to univ. plan. and info. tech. DePaul U. Sch. Edn., panel on grievances, 1995-99, comprehensive pers. devel. com., 1995-99; tng. sub-com. adv. Ill. Dept. Children & Family Svcs., 1993-95; panel of advisers comprehensive pers. devel. sys. Ill. State Bd. Edn., 1995-99; mentor, cons. to partnerships project tng. early intervention svcs. U. Ill. Champaign; panelist Ill. Initiative for Articulation between Ill. Bd. Higher Edn. and Ill. Cmty. Coll. Bd., Early Childhood Assessment Sys.; co-chair, panelist Bansenville Pub. Schs.; cons. in field; project evaluator Chgo. Tchr. Collaborative, Dept. Edn., 1999-2004; chair U. Tchg. Learning Tech. com., 2001-; mem. ISBE/NCATE Partnership Com., 2002, Ill. State Bd. Ednl. Content Expert panel, 2003. Author: Assessing Young Children, 1996, 2d edit., 2003; (with Marie Donovan) Building Character: Five Enduring Themes for a Stronger Early Childhood Curriculum PK-3, 2000; editor: DePaul U. Sch. Edn. Newsletter; co-author: Planning a Theme Based Curriculum for 4's or 5's, 1993, Assessing Young Children: 1996, Encyclopedia of Children's Play, 1997; mem. editl. bd. Ill. Sch. R&D, Ill. Divsn. Early Childhood Edn. Adv. Com. to Ill. Bd. Edn.; cons. editor: NAEYC, 2003; contbr. articles to profl. jours. Bd. dirs. North Side Family Day Care, 1981; northside affiliate Mus. Contemporary Art, 1991-96; active Gov's Task Force on Alternative Rts. to Cert., 1999; edn. adv. com. Okla. Dept. Edn., 1979-80; adv. bd. bilingual early childhood program Oakton C.C.; adv. bd. early childood tech. assistance project Chgo. Pub. Schs., Lake View Mental Health, 1986-90; planning com. Lake View Citizens Coun. Day Care Ctr., 1978-79; local planning coun. Ill. Dept. Child and Family Svcs.; childcare block grant tng. sub. com.; chair teen com. Florence G. Heller JCC, membership com.; adv. bd. Harold Washington Coll. Child Devel., regional tech. assistance grant LICA; mem. parents. com. Francis W. Parker Sch.; mem. assessment task force Dept. Human Svcs., City of Chgo., 2001-02; trustee Congregation Kol Ami., 2000-03. U. Kans. scholar, 1960, Cerebral Palsy Assn. scholar, 1965; U. Wis. fellow in mental retardation, 1964-65. Fellow: Am. Orthopsychiat. Assn.; mem.: ASCD, Found. for Excellence in Tchg. (selection com. Golden Apple 1989—94), Ill. Assn. for Edn. Young Children (co-chair bldg. bridges project), Ill. Coun. for Exceptional Children, Coun. for Exceptional Children, Am. Ednl. Rsch. Assn., Nat. Assn. for Edn. Young Children (tchr. edn. bd. 1990—94, editl. rev. bd., editl. panel 2003—), Pi Lambda Theta, Phi Delta Kappa, Alpha Sigma Nu. Office: DePaul Univ Sch Of Edn Chicago IL 60614 Office Phone: 773-325-7769. Business E-Mail: gmindes@depaul.edu.

MINDLIN, PAULA ROSALIE, retired reading educator; b. N.Y.C., Nov. 27, 1944; d. Simon S. and Sylvia (Naroff) Bernstein; m. Alfred Carl Mindlin, Aug. 14, 1965; 1 child, Spencer Douglas. BA in Edn., Bklyn. Coll., 1965; MS in Edn., Queens Coll., 1970, Specialist Sch. Adminstrn, 1973. Tchr. Dist. 16 Pub. Sch., Bklyn., 1965-68; reading tchr. Dist. 29 Pub. Sch. and Dist. 16, Bklyn., 1968-85; instr. insvc. courses Cmty. Sch. Dist. 29, Queens Village, NY, 1984-93, reading coord. Reading/Comm. Arts Program, 1985-90, dir. reading, 1990-94. Adj. lectr. York Coll., 1989; dir. Chpt. 1 Program (Nat. Recognition 1994, U.S. Sec. of Edn.); curriculum cons., 1997—98. Recipient svc. award N.Y. State Reading Assn. Coun., 1996. Mem. Internat. Reading Assn., Queensboro Reading Coun. (pres. 1994-96, Educator of Yr. award 1994), Nassau Reading Coun. Avocations: reading, gardening.

MINEAR, SARAH M. state legislator; b. Parsons, W.Va., Aug. 11, 1949; m. Robert W. Minear (dec.). Student, Fairmont State Coll., WVa. U., W.Va. Bus. Coll. Mem. W.Va. Senate, Charleston, 1995—. Mem. agr. com., edn. com., fin. com., govt. orgn. com., interstate cooperation com., natural resources com., rules com. Bd. dirs. Tucker County Arts Coun., Ohio-W.Va. YMCA Leadership Ctr.; charter mem. Tucker County Devel. Authority, Allegheny Front Regional Devel. Authority; founder Tucker Cmty. Endowment Found., W.Va. Grantmakers Assn. Mem. W.Va. Forestry Assn., Tucker County C. of C., W.Va. Farm Bur., Tucker County Farm Bur.; mem. W.Va. Rep. Com., Tucker County Rep. Exec. Com. Presbyterian. Office: WVa Senate 1900 Kanawha Blvd E Rm 441M Charleston WV 25305-0009 also: HC 70 Box 450 Davis WV 26260-9721 Fax: (304) 866-4880. E-mail: smminear@aol.com.

MINEHART, JEAN BESSE, tax accountant; b. Cleve., Nov. 8, 1937; d. Ralph and Augusta Besse; m. Ralph Conrad Minehart, Aug. 28, 1959; children: Patricia Minehart Miron, Deborah Minehart Rust, Elizabeth, Stephen. BA, Mass. Wellesley Coll., 1959; MEd, U. Va., 1971. Rsch. assoc. Age Ctr. of New Eng., Boston, 1959-61; substitute tchr. Charlottesville (Va.) Sch. System, 1976-81; tax acct. H&R Block, Charlottesville, 1982-94, Huey & Bjorn, Charlottesville, 1994—. Past pres. Ephphatha Village Housing for the Deaf, Charlottesville, 1984-87; bd. dirs. Tues. Evening Concert Series, Charlottesville, 1990-94; sec., bd. dirs. Family Svc., Inc., Charlottesville, 1987-91; bd. dirs. Westminster Organ Concert Series; elder Westminster Presbyn. Ch., 1979-81, 94-96. Scholar, Wellesley Coll. scholar. Mem. LWV (v.p., treas. 1991-95) Blue Ridge Wellesley Club (pres. Charlottesvillechpt. 1989-91, dorm rep. 1996—). Avocations: reading, music. Home: 1714 Yorktown Dr Charlottesville VA 22901-3034 Office: Huey & Bjorn 408 E Market St Ste 207 Charlottesville VA 22902-5261 Office Phone: 434-971-7642.

MINEKA, SUSAN, psychology educator; b. Ithaca, N.Y., June 2, 1948; d. Francis Edward and Muriel Leota (McGregor) M. BA in Psychology magna cum laude, Cornell U., 1970; PhD, U. Pa., 1974. Lic. psychologist, Ill. Prof. psychology U. Wis., Madison, 1974-85, U. Tex., Austin, 1986-87; prof. Northwestern U., Evanston, Ill., 1987—. Co-dir. Panic Treatment Ctr., EvanstonHosp., 1988-99; mem. NIH Panic Consensus Panel, 1991. Editor Jour. Abnormal Psychology, 1990-94; contbr. articles to profl. jours. Grantee NSF and NIMH, 1988-97; fellow Ctr. for Advanced Study in the Behavioral Scis., Stanford, Calif., 1997-98. Fellow APA (bd. sci. affairs 1992-94, chair 1994, pres. divsn. 12, sect. 3 1995), Am. Psychol. Soc., Psychonomic Soc. (bd. dirs. 2001, 04); mem. Assn. for Advancement Behavior Therapy, Midwestern Psychol. Assn. (pres.-elect 1995-96, pres. 1996-97), Internat. Primatol. Soc., Internat. Soc. for Rsch. on Emotion, Soc. for Rsch. in Psychopathology (mem. exec. bd. 1992-94, 2000-03), Phi Beta Kappa, Sigma Xi. Democrat. Office: Northwestern U Psychology Dept Evanston IL 60208-0001

MINER, JACQUELINE, political consultant; b. Dec. 10, 1936; d. Ralph E. and Agnes (McGee) Mariani; m. Roger J. Miner, Aug. 11, 1975; children: Laurence, Ronald Carmichael, Ralph Carmichael, Mark. Ind. polit. cons., Hudson, NY; instr. history and polit. sci. SUNY, Hudson, 1974—79. Mem. nat. steering com. Fund for Am.'s Future, 2d cir. Hist. Com.; mem. White House Outreach Working Group on Central Am.; candidate for Rep. nomination U.S. Senate, 1982; co-chair N.Y. state steering com. George Bush for Pres. campaign, 1986—88; del. Rep. Conv., 1992, GOP Conv., 1992; Rep. county committeewoman, 1958—76; vice chmn. N.Y. State Ronald Reagan campaign, 1980, N.Y. State Rep. Com., 1991—93; co-chmn. N.Y. State Reagan Roundup Campaign, 1984—86; chmn. Coll. Consortium for Internat. Studies. Mem.: PEO, U.S. Supreme Ct. Hist. Soc. Address: 1 Merlins Way Hudson NY 12534-4157

MINER, JOHN BURNHAM, industrial relations educator, writer; b. N.Y.C., July 20, 1926; s. John Lynn and Bess (Burnham) M.; children by previous marriage: Barbara, John, Cynthia, Frances; m. Barbara Allen Williams, June 1, 1979; children: Jennifer, Heather. AB, Princeton U., 1950, PhD, 1955; MA, Clark U., 1952. Lic. psychologist, N.Y. Rsch. assoc. Columbia U., 1956-57; mgr. psychol. svcs. Atlantic Refining Co., Phila., 1957-60; mem. faculty U. Oreg., Eugene, 1960-68; prof., chmn. dept. orgnl. sci. U. Md., College Park, 1968-73; rsch. prof. Ga. State U., Atlanta, 1973-87, Disting. prof., 1974; pres. Orgnl. Measurement Systems Press, Eugene, Oreg., 1976—; prof. human resources SUNY, Buffalo, 1987-94, chmn. dept. orgn. and human resources, 1989-92; profl. practice Eugene, Oreg., 1995—. Cons. McKinsey & Co., N.Y.C., 1966-69; vis. lectr. U. Pa., Phila., 1959-60; vis. prof. U. Calif., Berkeley, 1966-67, U. South Fla., Tampa, 1972; researcher on orgnl. motivation, theories of orgn., human resource utilization, bus. policy and strategy, entrepreneurship. Author many books and monographs including Personnel Psychology, 1969, Personnel and Industrial Relations, 1969, 73, 77, 85, The Challenge of Managing, 1975, (with Mary Green Miner) Policy Issues Personnel and Industrial Relations, 1977, (with George A. Steiner) Management Policy and Strategy, 1977, James A. Hamilton-Hosp. Adminstrs. Book award 1982, 86), (with M.G. Miner) Employee Selection Within the Law, 1978, Theories of Organizational Behavior, 1980, Theories of Organizational Structure and Process, 1982, People Problems: The Executive Answer Book, 1985, The Practice of Management, 1985, Organizational Behavior: Performance and Productivity, 1988, Industrial Organizational Psychology, 1992, Role Motivation Theories, 1993, (with Donald P. Crane) Human Resource Management: The Strategic Perspective, 1995, The 4 Routes to Entrepreneurial Success, 1996, (with Michael H. Capps) How Honesty Testing Works, 1997, A Psychological Typology of Successful Entrepreneurs, 1997, Organizational Behavior: Foundations, Theories and Analyses, 2002; contbr. numerous articles, papers to profl. jours. With U.S. Army, 1944—46, ETO. Decorated Bronze Star, Combat Infantryman's badge. Fellow APA, Acad. of Mgmt. (editor Jour. 1973-75, pres. 1977-78), Soc. for Personality Assessment, Am. Psychol. Soc.; mem. Soc. for Human Resource Mgmt., Indsl. Rels. Rsch. Assn., Internat. Coun. for Small Bus., Strategic Mgmt. Soc., Internat. Pers. Mgmt. Assn., Human Resource Planning Soc. Republican. Home and Office: 34199 Country View Dr Eugene OR 97408-9440 Office Phone: 541-484-2715.

MINER, JOHN H.F. computer company executive; BSEE, Tulane U.; MBA, U. Oreg. With Intel Corp., 1983—, gen. mgr. desktop motherboard and PC bldg.-blocks bus., v.p. and gen. mgr. Comm. Products Group, gen. mgr. Enterprise Server Group, v.p., 1996—, v.p. and gen. mgr. Intel Capital, 2002—03, pres. Intel Capital, 2003—. Office: 2200 Mission College Blvd Santa Clara CA 95052

MINER, MICHAEL E. neurosurgery educator; b. Louisville, July 25, 1943; s. Gerald Lamont and Alice Mae (Murphy) M.; m. Mildred Elizabeth Kennedy, 1972 (dec. July, 1978); children: Caroline, Matthew, Amanda, Nicholas; m. Mary Ann Bruton, 1980 (dec. Dec., 1992). BS, U. Kans., Lawrence, 1965; MD, U. Kans., Kansas City, 1969, PhD, 1975. Diplomate in neurological surgery Am. Bd. Psychiatry and Neurology. Prof. Ohio State U., 1975—, dir. divsn. neurosurgery, 1984—. Neurosurg. dir. Por Cristo, Boston, 1983—. Author: Neurotrauma, 1986; contbr. articles on neurosurg. disorders to profl. jours. Chmn. Houston Child-Safe Com., 1986—. Served to capt. U.S. Army, 1965-75. Grantee NIH, 1983-87; named Outstanding Tchr., U. Tex., 1984. Mem. Peruvian Surg. Soc., Am. Assn. Neurol. Surgeons (cert.), Soc. Neurol. Surgeons, Ohio State Neurosurg. Soc. (pres. 1995-96). Avocations: running, civil war history. Office: Univ of Tex Med Sch at Houston Dept of Immunology & Organ Transplant 6431 Fannin St # 148 Houston TX 77030-1501 also: Ohio State Univ Hosps Divsn Neurosurgery N1021 Doan Hall 410 W 10th Columbus OH 43210

MINER, ROGER JEFFREY, judge; b. Apr. 14, 1934; s. Abram and Anne M. Miner; m. Jacqueline Mariani; 4 children. BS, SUNY; LLB cum laude, N.Y. Law Sch., 1956; postgrad., Bklyn. Law Sch., Judge Advocate Gen.'s Sch., U. Va.; LLD (hon.), N.Y. Law Sch., 1989, Syracuse U., 1990, Albany Law Sch./Union U., 1996; attended, Emory U. Bar: N.Y. 1956, U.S. Ct. Mil. Appeals 1956, Republic of Korea 1958, U.S. Dist. Ct. (so. and ea. dists.) N.Y. 1959. Ptnr. Miner & Miner, Hudson, NY, 1959—75; corp. counsel City of Hudson, 1961—64; asst. dist. atty. Columbia County, 1964, dist. atty., 1968—75; justice N.Y. State Supreme Ct., 1976—81; judge U.S. Dist. Ct. (no. dist.) N.Y., 1981—85; sr. judge U.S. Ct. Appeals (2d cir.), Albany, NY, 1997—2002. Adj. assoc. prof. criminal law State U. Sys., NY, 1974—79; adj. prof. law N.Y. Law Sch., 1986—96, Albany Law Sch. Union U., 1997—; lectr. state and local bar assns.; lectr. SUNY, Albany, 1985; with N.Y. Law Sch. Bd. Trustees, 1991—96; hon. trustee N.Y. Law Sch. bd. trustees, 1996—; mem. jud. coun. 2d Cir., 1992—96; chmn. 2d Cir. Com. on Hist. and Commemorative Events, 1989—94; with Cameras in the Courtoom Com., 1993—96, No. Dist. Hist. Com., 1981—85, State, Fed. Jud. Coun. of N.Y., 1986—91, chmn., 1990—91, Jud. Conf. on U.S. com. on fed.-state jurisdiction, 1987—92; trustee Practicing Law Inst., 1995—2002. Mng. editor: N.Y. Law Sch. Law Rev.; contbr. articles to law jours. 1st lt. JAGC U.S. Army, 1956—59, capt. USAR, ret. Named Columbia County Man of Yr., 1984; recipient Dean's medal for disting. profl. svc., N.Y. Law Sch., Disting. Alumnus award, Charles W. Froessel award for Valuable Contbn. to Law, Albany Jewish Fedn. award, Abraham Lincoln award, Cmty. Svc. award, Kiwanis, others, Ellis Island medal of honor. Mem.: ATLA, ABA, Columbia County Magistrates Assn., Am. Soc. Writers on Legal Subjects, Fed. Bar Coun., Fed. Judges Assn., Am. Judicature Soc., Am. Law Inst., Columbia County Bar Assn., Assn. of Bar of City of N.Y., N.Y. State Bar Assn., B'nai Brith, N.Y. Law Sch. Alumni Assn. (hon.; bd. dirs.), Supreme Ct. Hist. Soc., Columbia County Hist. Soc., Elks (past exalted ruler). Jewish. Office: US Ct Appeals 445 Broadway Ste 414 Albany NY 12207-2926

MINER, THOMAS HAWLEY, international entrepreneur; b. Shelbyville, Ill., June 19, 1927; s. Lester Ward and Thirza (Hawley) M.; m. Lucyna T. Minciel, July 22, 1983; children: Robert Thomas, William John. Student, U.S. Mil. Acad., 1946-47; BA, Knox Coll., 1950; JD, U. Ill., 1953. Bar: Ill. 1954. Atty. Continental Ill. Nat. Bank & Trust Co., Chgo., 1953-55; pres. Harper-Wyman Internat. (S.A.), Venezuela and Mex., 1955-58, Hudson Internat. (S.A.), Can. and Switzerland, 1958-60, Thomas H. Miner & Assoc., Inc., Chgo., 1960—; chmn. Miner, Fraser & Gabriel Pub. Affairs, Inc., Washington, 1982-88, Miner Systems, Inc., 1981—. Bd. dirs. Lakeside Bank, Worldschool, Bright Oceans Internat. Corp.; chmn. Ill. dist. export coun. U.S. Dept. Commerce, 1971—; sec. Consular Corps. Chgo., 1986—88; chmn. Mid-Am. China Mgmt. Tng. Ctr., Global Software Source, Geo Vision, Inc., U.S.-Iraq Bus. Alliance. Chmn. bd. dirs. Sch. Art Inst. Chgo., 1977-81; bd. govs., life mem., sustaining fellow Art Inst. Chgo.; former chmn. UN Assn., Chgo.; founder, chmn. Mid-Am. Com., 1968—; former mem. bd. dirs. UNICEF, NAM, Internat. Trade Policy Com. and Working Group on Commonwealth of Ind. States and Ea. Europe; trustee 4th Presbyn. Ch., Chgo., Roosevelt U., Chgo., 1996; bd. advisors Mercy Hosp.; vice chmn. Chgo. Sister Cities; mem. adv. bd. Internat. Inst. Edn.; bd. dirs. Internat. Sister Cities. With USNR, 1945-46; mem. Pres. Coun. U. Ill. Found. Capt. U.S. Army, 1946-47. Decorated comdr. Crown of the Kingdom of Belgium, 2003, commendatore Ordine al Merito della Repubblica Italiana; recipient Alumni Achievement award Knox Coll., 1974, Gold Medallion award Internat. Visitors Ctr. Chgo., 1989; named One of Chgo.'s 10 Outstanding Young Men, 1962, Chicagoan of

Year Chgo. Assn. Commerce and Industry, 1968, Alumni of Month Coll. Law U. Ill., Nov. 1970, Aug. 1984; hon. consul Republic of Senegal, 1970-88. Mem. Am. Mgmt. Assn., Chgoland C. of C., Mid-Am. Arab C. of C. (founder, former pres.), Chgo. Bar Assn., Chgo. Com., Chgo. Coun. Fgn. Rels. (past dir.), Coun. of the Ams., Internat. Trade Club (past dir., pres.), Japan-Am. Soc., Nat. Coun. U.S.-China Trade, Nat. Acad. Scis. (pres. coun.), English Speaking Union (dir., past chmn.) Trade and Econs. Coun. USA-CIS (dir.), U.S.-Russia Bus. Coun., Mus. Contemporary Art, Newcomen Soc. N.Am., U.S.-China Bus. Coun., U.S.-Arab C. of C. (bd. dirs.), U.S.-Mex. C. of C. (bd. dirs.), Thomas Minor Soc., Chgo. Club, Econ. Club, Grant Park Concerts Soc., Chgo. Farmers Club, Mid-Am. Club, Univ. Club (Washington), Univ. Club (Milw.), Hillsboro Club (Fla.), Tryall Golf and Beach Club (Jamaica), Rotary, Phi Delta Phi, Phi Gamma Delta Capitis China. Office: 150 N Michigan Ave Chicago IL 60601-7553 also: 2400 Virginia Ave NW Washington DC 20037-2612 also: Miner Farms Shelbyville IL 62565 Office Phone: 312-236-8745. Personal E-mail: ltminer@aol.com. Business E-Mail: tminer@mid-americacenter.com.

MINES, MICHAEL, lawyer; b. Seattle, May 4, 1929; s. Henry Walker and Dorothy Elizabeth (Bressler) M.; m. Phyllis Eastham, Aug. 24, 1957; children: Linda Mines Elliott, Sandra, Diane Paull, Michael Lister. BA, U. Wash., 1951, JD, 1954. Bar: Wash. 1954, U.S. Dist. Ct. (we. dist.) Wash. 1957, U.S. Dist. Ct. Mont. 1970, U.S. Ct. Appeals (9th cir.) 1961, U.S. Supreme Ct. Assoc. Skeel, McKelvy, Henke, Evenson & Uhlman, Seattle, 1956-66, ptnr., 1966-68, Hullin, Roberts, Mines, Fite & Riveland, Seattle, 1968-75, Skeel, McKelvy, Henke, Evenson & Betts, Seattle, 1975-79, Betts, Patterson & Mines, 1978—. Moderator Wash.-No. Idaho conf. United Ch. of Christ, 1975-76; trustee Plymouth Housing Group, 1991-97; chair adult edn. bd. Plymouth Congl. Ch., Seattle, 1998-2001. With U.S. Army, 1954-56. Mem. ABA, Wash. State Bar Assn., Seattle-King Bar Assn., Am. Coll. Trial Lawyers (state chair 1984-85), Internat. Acad. Trial Lawyers (bd. dirs. 1991-96), U. Wash. Law Sch. Alumni Assn. (trustee, pres. bd. dirs. 1995-97). Home: 2474 Crestmont Pl W Seattle WA 98199-3714 Office: Betts Patterson Mines PS One Convention Ctr Ste 1400 701 Pike St Seattle WA 98101-3927 E-mail: mpmines@aol.com., mmines@bpmlaw.com.

MINETA, NORMAN YOSHIO, secretary of transportation; b. San Jose, Calif., Nov. 12, 1931; s. Kay Kunisaku and Kane (Watanabe) M.; m. Danealia; children: David, K., Stuart S.; stepchildren: Robert M. Brantner, Mark Brantner. BS, U. Calif.-Berkeley, 1953; D of Pub. Svc., Santa Clara U., 1989; HHD (hon.), Rust Coll., 1993. Agt./broker Mineta Ins. Agy., San Jose, 1956-89; mem. adv. bd. Bank of Tokyo in Calif., 1961-75; mem. San Jose City Coun., 1967-71; vice mayor City of San Jose, 1969-71, mayor, 1971-75; mem. 94th-104th Congresses from 13th (now 15th) Calif. dist., 1975-95; subcom. surface transp., 1989-92; former dep. Dem. whip; ranking minority mem. transp. and infrastructure com.; sr. v.p., mng. dir. transp. sys. & srvs. Lockheed Martin, Washington, 1995-2000; sec. U.S. Dept. Commerce, 2000-2001, U.S. Dept. Transp., Washington, 2001—. Chmn. fin. com. Santa Clara County (Calif.) Council Chs., 1960-62; commr. San Jose Human Relations Commn., 1962-64, San Jose Housing Authority, 1966— Precinct chmn. Community Theater Bond Issue, 1964; mem. spl. gifts com. Santa Clara County council Boy Scouts Am., 1967; sec. Santa Clara County Grand Jury, 1964; bd. dirs. Wesley Found., San Jose State Coll., 1956-58, Pacific Neighbors, Community Council Cen. Santa Clara County, Japan Soc., San Francisco, Santa Clara County chpt. NCCJ, Mexican-Am. Community Services Agy.; mem. exec. bd. No. Calif.-Western Nev. dist. council Japanese Am. Citizens League, 1960-62, pres. San Jose chpt., 1957-59; bd. regents Smithsonian Instn., 1979-95; chmn. Smithsonian vis. com. for Freer Gallery, 1981-95; mem. bd. regents Santa Clara U.; chmn. Nat. Civil Aviation Rev. Commn., 1997; mem. Smithsonian Nat. Bd., 1996—. Served to lt. AUS, 1954-56. Mem. Greater San Jose C. of C., Nat. Assn. Indsl. Ins. Agts., Calif. Assn. Indsl. Ins. Agts., San Jose Assn. Ind. Ins. Agts. (dir. 1960-62), North San Jose Optimists Club (pres. 1956-58), Jackson-Taylor Bus. and Profl. Assn. (dir. 1963). Democrat. Methodist. Office: US Dept Transp 400 Seventh St SW Washington DC 20590 *Personal philosophy: My two greatest responsibilities are accountability and accessibility to everyone I represent, and to anyone who comes to me for help.*

MINETREE, JAMES LAWRENCE, III, retired military officer, educator; b. Balt., Feb. 21, 1937; s. James Lawrence and Rhoda (Blossom) M.; m. Martha Milling, Apr. 9, 1983; children: James Lawrence IV, Peter Milling, Jennifer Grace, Margaret Warner; stepchildren: Rachael, Aubrilyn. B, U. Nebr., Omaha, 1971; MA, U. So. Calif., L.A., 1973. Commd. 2d lt. U.S. Army, 1964, advanced through grades to lt. col., 1979; mem. Nat. Intelligence Coun. CIA, Langley, Va., 1979-82; ret. U.S. Army, 1982; with GE Aerospace Sys., Reston, Va., 1982-85; sr. cons. Fed. Emergency Mgmt. Agency, 1985; dir. Crisis Mgmt. Info. Sys. BDM, Tysons Corner, Va., 1985-86; pres. Analytical Scis. Inc., Vienna, Va., 1986-90; founder Nat. Inst. for Urban Search and Rescue, Santa Barbara, Calif., 1982—; adj. prof. U. Md. U. Coll., College Park, 1992—; founder, pres. Wilson Inst. for Humanitarian Assistance, Springfield, Va., 1998—. Trustee Nat. Assn. Search and Rescue, Fairfax, Va., 1984—88; mem. nat. adv. bd. Congl. Fire Svcs. Inst., Washington, 1990—96; designated army strategist. Author. U.S. Govt. rep. European Coun., Athens, Greece, 1990; conceived U.S. Nat. and Internat. Urban Search and Rescue Teams, 1987; disaster mgmt. officer Fed. Emergency Mgmt. Agy., Washington, 1993—2000. With USCG Res., 1954—58. Decorated Legion of Merit (2), Bronze Star (2), Air medal, Meritorious Svc. medal, Army Commendation medal (3), Vietnam Cross of Gallantry, Civic Action medal, others, Dominican Republic and Republic of Vietnam; recipient Presdl. citation Pub. Svc. The White House, Washington, 1995. Mem. VFW, Nat. Def. Exec. Res., Assn. U.S. Army, Am. Legion. Republican. Episcopalian. Avocations: humanitarian assistance, education, sailing, skiing, pastoral ministry. Home: Grace Hill Farm RR1 Box 52-1 Millboro VA 24460 E-mail: peteminetree@mqwnet.com.

MING, JENNY J. retail apparel company executive; married; 3 children. B.A. clothing merchandising, San Jose State U. Mdse. mgr. brand activewear Gap Inc., 1986, v.p., divsn. mdse. mgr., co-creator Old Navy subs., 1994—, sr. v.p. merchandising, Old Navy, 1994—96, exec. v.p. merchandising, Old Navy, 1996—99, pres., Old Navy, 1999—, mem., sr. oper. com., 1999—. Bd. dirs. E.piphany, Inc. Bd. dirs. Big Brothers Big Sisters, San Francisco; mem. Com. of 100. Office: Gap Inc 1 Harrison St San Francisco CA 94105-1602

MING, SI-CHUN, pathologist, educator; b. Shanghai, Nov. 10, 1922; arrived in US, 1949, naturalized, 1964; s. Sian-Fan and Jan-Teh (Kuo) M.; m. Pen-Ming Lee, Aug. 17, 1957; children: Carol, Ruby, Stephanie, Michael, Jeffrey, Eileen. *Ancestor Ming Tzeche was a top disciple of Confucius, known for filial piety. Father-in-law Lee Jie, a geologist, supervised the initial archaeological search of the Peking Men fossil in China in 1927.* MD, Nat. Central U. Coll. Medicine, China, 1947. Resident in pathology Mass. Gen. Hosp., Boston, 1952-56; assoc. pathologist Beth Israel Hosp., Boston, 1956-67; asst. prof. pathology Harvard U. Med. Sch., 1965-67; assoc. prof. U. Md., 1967-71; prof. Temple U., Phila., 1971-93, prof. emeritus, 1993—, acting chmn. dept. pathology, 1978-80, dep. chmn. dept. path., 1980-86. Mem. Internat. Study Group on Gastric Cancer; mem. Internat. Gastric Cancer Assn.; U.S. rep. WHO Collaborating Ctr. for Primary Prevention, Diagnosis and Treatment of Gastric Cancer, 1984-98; hon. prof. Tianjin Med. Coll., Shanghai Second Med. U., Fourth Mil. Med. U., China, 1988—. *Initiated research on the immunological suppression of DNA synthesis in human and experimental animal tumors using tritiated thymidine as a marker in 1964.* Author: Tumors of the Esophagus and Stomach, 1973, supplement, 1985, Precursors of Gastric Cancer, 1984, Pathology of the Gastrointestinal Tract, 1992, 2d edit., 1998; mem. editl. bd. World Jour. Gastroenterology, 1998—, Gastric Cancer, 1998—. Nat. Cancer Inst. sr. fellow Karolinska Inst. Stockholm, 1964-65. Mem. AAAS, U.S. Canadian Acad. Pathology, Am. Soc. Investigative Pathology, Am. Gastroenterol. Assn., N.Y. Acad. Scis. Achievements include development of classification method for stomach carcinoma based on the growth pattern of the cancer; establishment of pathological criteria for the premalignant lesions of the digestive tract. Office: 3400 N Broad St Philadelphia PA 19140-5104 E-mail: ming@temple.edu.

MING, YAO, professional basketball player; s. Yao Zhi Yuan and Fang Feng Di. Studied, Shanghai Physical & Sport Technic Edn. Inst., Shanghai Foreign Lang. Inst. Player Shanghai Sharks, Chinese Basketball Assn., 1997—2002, Houston Rockets, Nat. Basketball Assn., 2002—. Ctr. Western Conf. NBA All-Star Game, 2003, 04; mem. Chinese Olympic Basketball Team, Athens, 2004. Named NBA All-Rookie First Team, 2002; named to People Mag. 100 most influential people, 2004; recipient Laureus World Newcomer of Yr. award, 2003. Achievements include 1st player to be #1 overall pick to come from an internat. basketball league; appeared on covers of Sports Illustrated, The Sporting News, ESPN the Mag. SLAM, Inside Stuff and Basketball Digest; featured in Visa, Apple Computer and Gatorade TV commercials. Avocation: computer games. Office: Houston Rockets 2 Greenway Plz Ste 400 Houston TX 77046-1099

MINGE, DAVID, former congressman, lawyer, law educator; b. Clarkfield, Minn., 1942; m. Karen Aaker; children: Erik, Olaf. BA in History, St. Olaf Coll., 1964; JD, U. Chgo., 1967. Atty. Faegre & Benson, Mpls., 1967-70; prof. law U. Wyo., 1970-77; atty. Nelson, Oyen, Torvik, Minge & Gilbertson, 1977-93; mem. 103d-106th Congresses from 2nd Minn. Dist., 1993-2001; judge Minn. Ct. Appeals, Minn., 2002—. Cons. Ho. Jud. Com., Subcom. Adminstrv. Law U.S. Congress, 1975; chair Agrl. Law Sect., Minn. State Bar Assn. 1990-92, adv. bd. Western Minn. Legal Svcs., 1978-84; bd. dirs. Legal Advice Clinics, Ltd., Hennepin County, Western Minn. Vol. Atty. Program; lectr. U. Minn., Morris, 2001-02 Coord. Montevideo area CROP Walk for the Hungry; clk. Montevideo Sch. Bd., 1989—92; dir. Montevideo Cmty. Devel. Corp.; steering com. Clean Up the River Environ., 1992. Fellow Kellogg Found. Food and Soc. fellow, 2002; scholar, Woodrow Wilson Ctr. for Internat. Studies, 2002. Mem.: Minn. Bar Assn. Office: 25 Dr Martin Luther King Jr Blvd Saint Paul MN 55155

MINGER, TERRELL JOHN, public administration and natural resource institute executive; b. Canton, Ohio, Oct. 7, 1942; s. John Wilson and Margaret Rose M.; m. Judith R. Arnold, Aug. 7, 1965; 1 child, Gabriella Sophia. BA, Baker U., 1966; MPA, Kans. U., 1969; postgrad., MIT, 1975; Loeb fellow, Harvard U., 1976-77; postgrad, Stanford U., 1979; MBA, U. Colo., 1983. Asst. dir. admissions Baker U., 1966-67; asst. city mgr. City of Boulder, Colo., 1968-69; city mgr. City of Vail, Colo., 1969-79; pres., CEO Whistler Village Land Co., Vancouver, B.C., Can., 1979-81; v.p., gen. mgr. Cumberland S.W. Inc., Denver, 1981-83; exec. asst. dep. chief of staff to Gov. Colo., 1983-87; pres., CEO Sundance (Utah) Inst. for Resource Mgmt., 1986—, Sundance Enterprises Ltd., 1988-91. Adj. prof. grad. sch. pub. affairs U. Colo., 1983—, Sch. Bus. U. Denver, 1992—; bd. dirs. Colo. Open Lands, Inc.; participant UN Conf. on Environment and Devel., Rio de Janeiro, 1992; chmn. environ. adv. bd. Wal-Mart, Inc., 1990—; co-chmn. task force sustainable consumption World Bus. Coun. Sustainable Devel.; co-chmn. N.Am. Telecom./Environ. Taskforce; dir. Stapleton Found. Sustainable Cities, 2000-; chmn. Environ. Excellence Task Force Telecomm. Industry; environ. advisor Salt Lake City Olympic Com. Editor: Greenhouse/Glasnost-The Global Warming Crisis, 1990, Val Symposium Papers, 1970-79; author, editor: Growth Alternatives for Rocky Mountain West, 1976, Future of Human Settlements in the West, 1977. Spl. del. UN Habitat Conf. Human Settlements, spl. rep. to UN Environ. Program, 1992, coord. UN Global Youth Forum, 1993-94, co-chmn. conf. on environ. and mktg., N.Y.C., 1993; founder Vail Symposium, advisor UN Environ. Program Telecom. Charter, Nairobi, Kenya, 1999; co-founder, bd. dirs. Colo. Park Found., 1985—; chair World Alpine Championship Conf., Vail, Colo., 1999; founding mem. Greenhouse/Glasnost U.S./USSR Teleconf. with Soviet Acad. Scis., 1989—; mem. pres. task force Commn. on Sustainable Devel., 1994—; co-chmn. Golf and Environ. Conf., Pebble Beach, Calif., 1995; founder, pres. Western Rendezvous, 1995—; bd. dirs. Piton Found., 1996; co-chair UN Sustainability Roundtable for Europe and No. Am., 2002. Nat. finalist White House Fellowship, 1978; recipient Colo. Soc. Landscape Arch. award, 1999; named one of B.C.'s Top Bus. Leaders for the '80s, 1980. Mem. Urban Land Inst., Colo. Acad. Pub. Adminstrn. (charter, founding mem. 1988), Colo. City Mgmt. Innovation award 1974-76), Western Gov.'s Assn. (staff coun., chmn. adv. com. 1985-86), Flatirons Athletic Club, Lewis and Clark Nat. Bicentenial Commn. (commr. 2000-2005). Home: 785 6th St Boulder CO 80302-7416 Office: Ctr for Resource Mgmt Malo Mansion 100 E 8th Ave Denver CO 80203-1846

MINGHELLA, ANTHONY, film director, screenwriter; b. Ryde Isle of Wight, Eng., Jan. 6, 1954; Dir. (films) Mr. Wonderful, 1993, Play, 2000; dir., screenwriter (films) Truly, Madly, Deeply, 1991 (BAFTA award for Best Original Screenplay, 1992), The English Patient, 1996 (Acad. award for Best Dir. 1997, Dir.'s Guild Am. award for feature directing 1997), The Talented Mr. Ripley, 1999 (National Board of Review award for Best Dir., 1999) Cold Mountain, 2003 (National Board of Review award for Best Adapted Screenplay, 2003), exec. prodr. (films) Iris, 2001, Heaven, 2002, The Quiet American, 2002, screenwriter (TV series) Grange Hill, 1978, Boon, 1986, Inspector Morse, 1987, The Storyteller, 1987. Office: MacCortendale & Holton 1640 5th St Ste 205 Santa Monica CA 90401-3325*

MINGLE, JAMES JOHN, lawyer; AB in English, St. Joseph's Coll., Phila., 1968; JD, U. Va., 1973. Bar: Md. 1974, Va. 1990, N.Y. 1996. Asst. to pres. Frostburg State Coll., 1973-77, adj. prof. bus. law, 1975-77; asst. atty. gen. State of Md., 1977-89; chief counsel state Md. univ. and coll. sys. U. Md., Md. Pub. TV, 1981-89; gen. counsel U. Va., Charlottesville, 1989-95, lectr. law, 1994-95; gen. counsel, sec. corp., adj. prof. law Cornell U., Ithaca, NY, 1995—. Adj. prof. law U. Md., 1984-88; asst. to bus. mgr. Phila. 76ers NBA Club, 1968-69; city atty. City of Frostburg, Md., 1974-76; joint adv. bd., Cornell Med. Coll., Qatar, 2001—. Mem.: Nat. Assn. Coll. and Univ. Attys. Office Phone: 607-255-3903. Business E-Mail: jjm19@cornell.edu.

MINGLE, JOHN ORVILLE, engineer, educator, lawyer, consultant; b. Oakley, Kans., May 6, 1931; s. John Russell and Beulah Amelia (Johnson) M.; m. Patricia Ruth Schmitt, Aug. 17, 1957; children: Elizabeth Lorene, Stephen Roy. BS, Kans. State U., Manhattan, 1953, MS, 1958; PhD, Northwestern U., 1960; JD, Washburn U., 1980. Bar: Kans., Wyo., U.S. Patent Office; registered profl. engr., Kans. Tng. engr. Gen. Electric Co., Schenectady, 1953-54; mem. faculty Kans. State U., 1956-90, prof. nuclear engring., 1965-90, prof. emeritus, 1990—. Black & Veatch Disting. prof., 1973-78; dir. Inst. Computational Research Engring., 1969-88; exec. v.p., patent counsel Kans. State U. Research Found., 1983-88. Instr. Northwestern U., 1958-59; vis. prof. U. So. Calif., 1967-68; cons. govt. and industry; engring. legal cons. 1990—. Author: The Invarient Imbedding Theory of Nuclear Transport, 1973; also articles. Bd. dirs. Laramie Regional Airport, 1994-97. Officer AUS, 1954—56, lt. U.S. Army, 1954—56. Mem. ABA (chairperson sci. and tech. phys. scis. com. 1982-92), NSPE (sect. exec. com. 1985-87, chmn. 1985-86), Am. Nuclear Soc. (sect. pres. 1976-77), Am. Inst. Chem. Engrs. (profl. devel. com. 1982-95), Am. Soc. Engring. Edn. (chmn. Midwest sect. 1985-86, exec. com. 1984-87), Profl. Engrs. in Edn. (vice chmn. 1978-80, workshop chairperson 1983), Kans. Engring. Soc. (past chpt. pres.), Kans. Bar Assn., Licensing Execs. Soc., Sigma Xi (past chpt. pres., lectr.), Soc. Univ. Patent Adminstrs. (exec. com. 1985-87, v.p. cen. region 1985-87). Home: 1409 Downey St Laramie WY 82072-1867 Office Phone: 307-742-0171. *In times past workaholic behavior produced prudent contributions. Now in our world of paradox, the philosophy has been turned on its head, and an iota of "wisdom work" often overshadows everything else.*

MINGO, JAMES WILLIAM EDGAR, lawyer; b. Halifax, N.S., Can., Nov. 25, 1926; s. Edgar Willard and Lila Theresa (McManus) M.; m. Edith Peppard Hawkins, July 6, 1953; children: Sarah M. (Mrs. J.P. Camus), James A., Johanna E., Nancy S. (Mrs. S.J. Overgaard-Thomsen), Charles H. BA, Dalhousie U., Halifax, 1947, LL.B., 1949; LL.M., Columbia U., 1950; LL.D. (hon.), St. Mary's U., 1981; LL.D. (hon), Dalhousie U., 1998. Bar: N.S. 1950, Queen's counsel 1966. Ptnr. Stewart, McKelvey, Stirling & Scales (and predecessors), Halifax, 1958—, assoc., 1950-57, chmn. exec. com., 1979-92. Pres., dir. Canning Investment Corp. Ltd., Halifax; Minas Basin Pulp & Power Co. Ltd., Hantsport, N.S., Minas Basin Holdings Ltd., Hantsport, The Great Ea. Corp. Ltd., Charlottetown, P.E.I. and Halifax, Toronto, Oxford Frozen Foods Ltd., Oxford, N.S.; trustee Forum for Young Canadians. Mem. Halifax-Dartmouth Port Commn., 1955-83, chmn., 1960-83; chmn. Halifax Grammar Sch., 1971-73; mem. Halifax Port Authority, 1972-84; chmn. nat. treasury com. Liberal Party Can., 1976-85; dir. N.S. Legal Aid, 1977-80; mem. Med. Rsch. Coun. Working Group on Human Experimentation, 1977-78. Mem. Can. Bar Assn. (exec. com. 1973-76, spl. com. on legal ethics 1969-75, 84-87), N.S. Barristers Soc. (pres. 1975-76), Order of Canada, Halifax club, Saraguay club, Royal N.S. Yacht Squadron club, Ashburn club. Office: Box 997 Tower I Purdy's Wharf Halifax NS Canada B3J 2X2

MINI, ANNE ALEXANDRA APOSTOLIDES, writer, educator; b. Oakland, Calif., Sept. 30, 1966; d. Norman and Kleo Varvara (Apostolides) M. AB, Harvard U., 1988; MA, U. Chgo., 1991; PhD, U. Wash., 1995. Freelance writer, Seattle, 1995—; pres. Thesisadvisor.com, 2000—03; owner First Reader Editing, Seattle, 2002—. Lectr., tchg. asst. U. Wash., Seattle, 1991-95, Nancy Hartsock Rotating Chair, 1995. Author: The General Strike of 1934, 1988, Alexis de Tocqueville in Historical Context, 1991, An Expressive Revolution, 1995, Security Issues, 1996, Favorite Son, 1999, Background Noise, 2001, The Buddha in the Hot Tub, 2003, Is That You Pumpkin?, 2004. Precinct com. officer Seattle Dem. Com., 1996-2000; del. King County Dem. Ctrl. Com., Seattle, 1996-2000, mem. bylaws com., 1999; polit. campaign cons., 1998—; mem. Wash. State Dem. Platform Com., 1998, 2000; Wash. state del. Dem. Nat. Conv., 2000. Recipient Zola Award, 2004; grantee, U. Wash., 1985, 1990, U. Chgo., 1989—91, Vt. Studio Ctr., 2004; Radcliffe scholar, 1984—88, Norcroft Writing fellow, 2002. Avocations: 18th and 19th century french liberalism, gourmandry, viticulture. Office: PO Box 27242 Seattle WA 98165 E-mail: authoress1@foxinternet.com.

MINICHELLO, DENNIS, lawyer; b. Cleve., June 9, 1952; s. Ernest Anthony and Mary Theresa (Rocci) M.; m. Janine Stevens, Feb. 14, 1987. BA in Econs., MA in Econs., Ohio U., 1974; JD, Northwestern U., 1978. Bar: U.S. Dist. Ct. (no. dist.) Ill., U.S. Ct. Appeals (7th cir.), Supreme Ct. Ill., U.S. Supreme Ct. Assoc. Haskell & Perrin, Chgo., 1978-84; ptnr. Tribler & Marwedel, Chgo., 1984-89, Keck, Mahin & Cate, Chgo., 1989—97; shareholder Marwedel, Minichellot & Reeb, P.C., 1997—. Contbr. articles to profl. jours. Bd. dirs. Great Lakes Naval and Maritime Mus. Fulbright scholar, 1974-75. Mem. ABA, Ill. State Bar Assn., Chgo. Bar Assn. (mem. transp. com.), Maritime Law Assn. (proctor), The Propeller Club U.S. (pres. 1983-84), Port Chgo., Transp. Lawyers Assn., Conf. of Freight Counsel, Midwest High Speed Rail Coalition (pres. 2000—), Def. Rsch. Inst. Roman Catholic. Avocations: reading, exercise. Office: Marwedel Minichello & Reeb PC 10 S Riverside Plz Ste 720 Chicago IL 60606-3709 Office Phone: 312-902-1600 ext 5065. Business E-Mail: dminichello@mmr-law.com.

MINICK, MICHAEL, publishing executive; b. Albany, NY, Mar. 26, 1945; s. Jason and Ruth Isabelle (Solomon) M. Student, U. Va., 1963-66; BA in History, L.I. U., 1968. Editorial dir. Mag. Mgmt., N.Y.C., 1969-73; mng. editor Gentlemen's Quarterly, N.Y.C., 1975-76; pub., ptnr. Beauty Digest, N.Y.C., 1978-90; pub. Pa. Ofcl. Wine and Liquor Quar., N.Y.C., 1985—, Ohio Liquor Quar., 1990—. Author: The Kung Fu Exercise Book-Health Secrets of Ancient China, 1974, The Wisdom of Kung Fu, 1974; contbr. numerous articles to popular mags. Mem.: Pa. Wine and Spirit Assn., 25 Yr. Club of Ind. Distbrs. Democrat. Home: 440 W 22nd St New York NY 10011-2526

MINICUCCI, RICHARD FRANCIS, lawyer, former hospital administrator; b. N.Y.C., Jan. 16, 1947; s. Daniel Michael and Marie Felice (Trotta) M.; m. Nancy Jean Moran, Aug. 16, 1969; children: Jonathan, Elizabeth, Richard. BA, Rutgers Coll., 1969; MHA, Duke U., 1971; JD, Memphis State U., 1976. Bar: Tenn. 1977, N.Y. 1978. Adminstrv. asst. Duke Hosp., Durham, N.C., 1971; health planner Mid-South Med. Ctr. Coun., Memphis, 1971-73; dir. adminstrn. Memphis & Shelby County Hosp. Authority, 1973-77; assoc. Hayt Hayt & Landau, Great Neck, N.Y., 1977-81, ptnr., 1981-89, Nixon Peabody LLP (Nixon Hargrave Devans & Doyle, LLP), Garden City, N.Y., 1989—. Lectr. various health law assns. Editor: New York Environmental Law Handbook, 2d edit.; author: Residency Training Program Accreditation, 1st-5th edits., Mastering the Accreditation Process, 1999; editor-in-chief Accreditation Alert, Trouble in Academia: Ten Years of LItigation in Medical Education, 2003. Co-chmn. fund raising Luth. High Sch., Brookville, N.Y., 1991. Capt. U.S. Army, 1971-79. Mem. Am., Nassau Bar Assn., Am. Health Lawyers Assn. Republican. Roman Catholic. Avocations: tennis, skiing, hockey, travel. Office: Nixon Peabody LLP 990 Stewart Ave Ste 350 Garden City NY 11530-4838

MINICUCCI, ROBERT A. business executive; b. Waterbury, Conn., May 7, 1952; s. Arnold A. and Mary (Garafola) M.; m. Jill Hanau, June 18, 1988; children: Robert A. Jr., Alexandra H. BA, Amherst (Mass.) Coll., 1975; MBA, Harvard U., 1979. CPA. Staff acct. Price Waterhouse, Boston, 1975-77; assoc. Lehman Bros., N.Y.C., 1979-82, v.p., 1982-85, sr. v.p., 1985-88, mng. dir., 1988-91; sr. v.p., treas. Am. Express Co., 1991-92; CFO First Data Corp., N.Y.C., 1992-93; gen. ptnr. Welsh, Carson, Anderson & Stowe, N.Y.C., 1993—. Bd. dirs. Amdocs Ltd. Inc., Attachmate Corp., Global Knowledge Network Inc., BancTec, Inc., Alliance Data Systems, Inc. Home: 10 Thomas Pl Rowayton CT 06853 Office: Welsh Carson Anderson Stowe 320 Park Ave Ste 2500 New York NY 10022-6815

MINIEAR, J. DEDERICK, software company executive, consultant; b. Columbia City, Ind., Oct. 10, 1959; s. Gary Allen and Mallory Virgean (Dederick) M.; m. Lisa Anne Lattimer, July 30, 1983 (div. May 1991); 1 child, Andrew Ross. BA in Econs. and Computer Studies, Northwestern U., 1982. Head data processing Holcomb & Hoke, Mfg., Indpls., 1982-85; systems engr. Elec. Data Systems, Kokomo, Ind., 1985-87; cons. Healthcare Adminstrv. Systems, Indpls., 1987-89, Software Synergy Inc., Indpls., 1989-90, Indecon, Inc., Indpls., 1990-94, Source Cons., Indpls., 1994-97; founder, owner, CEO Aerosoft, Inc., Indpls., 1989—. Computer cons. Ind. Basketball Hall of Fame, New Castle, 1989-90. Author, found. mem.: Northwestern Rev., 1982; author PC graphics, advt. diskettes, fitness log, screen saver software and video. Pvt. promoter Pres.'s Coun. on Phys. Fitness and Sport, Indpls., 1991—, Nat. Assn. Gov.'s Couns. on Phys. Fitness and Sports. Mem. Christian Coalition (press liaison 1995-96), Full Gospel Businessmen Fellowship Internat. (local sec. 1991—), Gideons Intenat. (local v.p. 2000—). Methodist. Avocations: jogging, weightlifting, basketball. Office: Aerosoft 6827 Kentland Dr Indianapolis IN 46237-9410

MINIERE, MICHAEL ANTHONY, mathematician, educator; b. Plainfield, N.J., Apr. 3, 1945; s. Matthew Salvatore Miniere and Josephine Mineire; m. Lynn Marie Gauker, Aug. 18, 1996; children: Nicole, Samantha, Michael Jr. AA, Hagerstown (Md.) C.C., 1969; BSc, Montclair (N.J.) State U., 1985; MSc, Stevens Inst. Tech., 1987, PhD, 1997. Freelance musician, 1969—87; tchg. asst. Stevens Inst. Tech., Hoboken, NJ, 1987—92; prof. Dept. Math. Middlesex County Coll, Edison, NJ, 1992—. Adj. prof. math. Rutgers U., New Brunswick, NJ, 1999—; bus. dir. Coll. Gifted Programs, Parsippany, NJ, 1992—. Mem.: Am. Math. Soc., The Math. Assn. Am., Phi Kappa Phi. Republican. Roman Catholic. Avocations: fishing, swimming, boating, kayaking. Home: 5 Campbell Rd Kendall Park NJ 08824-1302 Office: Middlesex County College 2600 Woodbridge Ave Edison NJ 08818

MINIKES, STEPHAN MICHAEL, ambassador, lawyer, banker; b. Berlin, Aug. 29, 1938; came to U.S., 1949; naturalized, 1957; married; 1 child. BS, Cornell U., 1961; JD, Yale U., 1964. Bar: N.Y. State 1965, U.S. Ct. Appeals 2nd Circuit, 1967, U.S. Supreme Ct. 1972, U.S. Ct. Mil. Appeals, 1973, D.C. 1977. Assoc. firm Milbank, Tweed, Hadley & McCloy, N.Y.C., 1964-68, Borden & Ball, N.Y.C., 1968-72; counsel to spl. cons. for energy Pres. U.S., 1973; counsel to chief Naval Ops., Washington, 1972-74; sr. v.p. Export-Import Bank of U.S., Washington, 1974-77; resident mng. partner firm Butler & Binion, Houston and Washington, 1977-84, Thelen Reid & Priest, N.Y., L.A., San Francisco, and Wash., 1984—2001; amb. Org. Security and Coop. in Europe, Vienna, 2001—. Contbr. articles to profl. jours. Mem. exec. com. Yale U. Law Sch., 1979-82, 86-89, 93-97; trustee, chmn. fin. com. Washington Opera, 1979-84. Mem. ABA, Fed. Bar Assn., D.C. Bar Assn., Assn. of Bar of

City of N.Y., Am. Soc. Internat. Law, Am. Coun. Germany (bd. dirs.), Cornell U. Alumni Assn., Yale U. Alumni Assn. (law sch. rep. 1981-83, 86-90). Clubs: Yale (Washington), Metropolitan (Washington). Mailing: 9850 OSCE Pl Dulles VA 20189 9850

MINISI, ANTHONY S. lawyer; b. Sept. 18, 1926; s. Anthony F. and Leonora (Petoia) M.; m. Rita Marie Hentz, Jan. 8, 1949; children: Claire, Anthony J., Joseph J., Brian A. BS, U. Pa., 1948, JD, 1952. Player N.Y. Giants NFL, 1948; law clk. to presiding judge Ct. of Common Pleas #6, Phila., 1952-54; counsel Wolf, Block, Schorr and Solis-Cohen, Phila., 1954—. Past pres., vice chmn. Robert E. Maxwell Meml. Football Club, Eastern Assn. Intercoll. Football Ofcls. Past chmn. Com. of Seventy, Phila.; former mem., past pres. Bd. of Edn., Tredyffrin/Easttown Joint Sch. Dist.; mem., chmn. bd. supr. Easttown Twp.; past v.p. Cmty. Svcs. Planning Coun., Phila.; trustee U. Pa.; trustee, mem. exec. com. U. Pa. Health Sys.; chmn. Clin. Care Assocs. U. Pa. Health Sys.; former mem., vice-chmn. Pa. State Bd. Law Examiners. Served to maj. USAR. Mem. ABA (ho. of dels.), Pa. Bar Assn., Phila. Jr. Bar Assn. (past pres.), Def. Lawyers Am., Assn. Trial Attys. Am., Phila. Bar Assn. (bd. of govs., past chmn.), Phila. Trial Lawyers Assn., Fed. Bar Assn., Lawyers Club (past pres.), Justinian soc., Union League (Phila.). Republican. Roman Catholic. Office: Wolf Block Schorr & Solis-Cohen SE Corner 15th & Chestnut Sts Philadelphia PA 19102

MINISSALE, ANTHONY A. hospital administrator; m. Adele Minissale; children: Anthony, Angela. DO, Phila. Coll. Osteo. Medicine. Diplomate Am. Bd. Osteopathic Medicine. Intern Green Cross Gen. Hosp., Cuyahoga Falls, Ohio; resident gen. surgery Parkview Hosp., Phila.; v.p. med. affairs, dir. med. edn. Meml. Hosp., York, Pa. Fellow: Am. Coll. Osteo. Surgeons; mem.: York County Osteo. Med. Soc., Pa. Osteo. Surg. Soc. (founder, chmn.), Pa. Osteo. Med. Assn., Am. Osteo. Assn. (pres.-elect 2001—02, pres. 2002—03). Office: Memorial Hosp PO Box 15118 325 S Belmont St York PA 17403-2608 Address: Am Osteo Assn 142 E Ontario St Chicago IL 60611

MINK, MAXINE MOCK, real estate company executive; b. Lakeland, Fla., Jan. 17, 1938; d. Idus Frank and Elizabeth (Warren) Mock; student Fla. So. Coll.; children: Lance Granger, Justin Chandler. With Union Fin. Co., Lakeland, Fla., 1956-62; ptnr./owner S & S Ent. & Arrow Lake Mobile Home Pk., Lakeland, 1957-66; head bookkeeper Seaboard Fin., Lakeland, 1964-68; ptnr. Custom Chem., Inc., Lakeland, 1968-75, Don Emilio Perfumers, Newport Beach, Calif., 1978-79; owner Maxine Mink Public Relations, Newport Beach, 1978-83; fine homes and relocation specialist Merrill Lynch Realty, Newport Beach, 1985-90, Tarbell Realtors, Newport Beach, 1990-93, Prudential Calif. Realty, Newport Beach, 1993-95, Grubb & Ellis Real Estate, 1996-97, Prudential Calif. Realty, Newport Beach, 1997-2001, Mink Realty, Newport Beach, 2002—. Bd. dirs. Guild of Lakeland Symphony Orch., 1972-75; mem. Lakeland Gen. Hosp. Aux., 1974-76, Mus. Modern Art. Mem. NAFE, Newport Beach C. of C., Hoag Hosp. Aux., Orange County Music Center Guild. Republican. Clubs: Balboa Bay, Sherman Library and Gardens, The 552. Office: PO Box 1262 Newport Beach CA 92659-0262

MINKEL, HERBERT PHILIP, JR., lawyer; b. Boston, Feb. 11, 1947; s. Herbert Philip and Helen (Sullivan) M. BA, Holy Cross Coll., 1969; JD, NYU, 1972. Bar: Mass. 1973, N.Y. 1976, U.S. Dist. Ct. Mass. 1973, U.S. Dist. Ct. (so. dist.) N.Y. 1976. Law clk. U.S. Dist. Ct. Mass., Boston, 1972-73; assoc. Milbank, Tweed, Hadley & McCloy, N.Y.C., 1973-79; ptnr. Fried, Frank, Harris, Shriver & Jacobson, N.Y.C., 1979-94; mem. adv. com. on bankruptcy rules Jud. Conf. U.S., 1987-93; sr. ptnr. Minkel and Assoc., N.Y.C. and Boston, 1994—. Adj. assoc. prof. NYU Law Sch., 1987-94. Contbg. author: American Bankers Assn. Bankruptcy Manual, 1979; contbg. editor: 5 Collier on Bankruptcy, 15th edit., 1979-96; contbr. articles to profl. jours. Bd. advisors Internat. Yacht Restoration Sch., Newport, R.I., Spl. Olympics, Spl. Smiles. Root-Tilden scholar NYU, 1969-72. Mem. ABA, Nat. Bankruptcy Conf., Assn. Bar City of N.Y. Home: 68 Bumps River Rd Osterville MA 02655-1525 Office: Minkel and Assocs 131 E 62d St New York NY 10021 also: 112 Revere St Boston MA 02114 Business E-Mail: hminkel@nyc.rr.com.

MINKER, JACK, computer scientist, educator; b. Bklyn., July 4, 1927; s. Harry and Rose (Lapuck) M.; m. Rita Goldberg, June 24, 1951 (dec. Oct. 11, 1988); children: Michael Saul, Sally Anne; m. Johanna Cartee Weinstein, Jan. 19, 1997. BA cum laude with honors in Math., Bklyn. Coll., 1949; MS in Math., U. Wis., 1950; PhD in Math., U. Pa., 1959. Grad. teaching asst. U. Wis., 1949-50; tchr. math. Erasmus Hall High Sch., Bklyn., 1950-51; engr. Bell Aircraft Corp., Buffalo, 1951-52; mgr. info. tech. sect. RCA, Bethesda, Md., 1952-63; dir. tech. staff Auerbach Corp., Washington, 1963-67, tech. cons., 1967-72; mem. Faculty NIH Grad. Sch., 1965-66; vis. mem. faculty U. Md., 1967-68, assoc. prof. computer sci., 1968-71, prof., 1971-98, prof. emeritus, 1998—, 1st chmn. dept. computer sci., 1974-79; cons., speaker, lectr. in field; cons. NSF, 1979-82, chmn. adv. bd. on computer sci., 1980-82. Prof. Inst. Advanced Computer Studies, 1986—; vice-chmn. Com. Concerned Scientists, 1973—; past mem. U.S. Nat. Com. for Fedn. Info. Documentalists. Author: (with H. Gallaire and J.M. Nicolas) Logic and Data Bases a Deductive Approach, 1984; editor: (with H. Gallaire and J.M. Nicholas) Advances in Data Base Theory, vol. 1, 1980, vol. 2, 1984, (with H. Gallaire) Logic and Data Bases, 1978, Foundations of Deductive Databases and Logic Programming, 1988, (with J. Lobo and A. Rajasekar) Foundations of Disjunctive Logic Programming, 1992; editor: Logic-Based Artificial Intelligence, 2000; founding editor-in-chief Theory and Practice of Logic Programming, 2000-2001; contbr. articles to profl. jours.; publs. reviewer; mem. editl. bd. numerous jours. Vice chmn. Com. Concerned Scientists, 1972—. With U.S. Army, 1945-46. Recipient U. Md. Presdl. medal, 1996; named Disting. Scholar-Tchr. U. Md., 1997-98, fellow Acad. Excellence in Tchg. and Learning, 2002—. Fellow: IEEE (editl. bd. Expert Info.Sys. jour.), ACM, AAAS, Am. Assn. Artificial Intelligence; mem.: Assn. Computing Machinery (chmn. nat. program com. 1968—69, vice chmn. com. on sic. freedom and human rights 1979—89, founding, Outstanding Contbn. award 1985). Jewish. Office: U Md Dept Computer Sci Dept and Inst Advanced Computer College Park MD 20742-0001 Business E-Mail: minker@cs.umd.edu.

MINKOFF, ALICE SYDNEY, interior designer stylist; b. Washington, Jan. 29, 1948; d. Lawrence and Ellen (Altman) Glassman; children: Adam Pollin, Shane Pollin, Jacob, Sam. Student, U. Md. Owner Fredrick, Miley & Assocs., Inc., 1983—2003, Showroom at Washington Design Ctr., 1983—2003. Interior designer for homebuilders, 1975-82; interior designer high end residential homes and hotel interiors, 1980—. Vol. Food and Friends, Washington, 1991—; chair Heartstrings, Washington, 1990; active AIDS Awareness. Mem. NOW, ACLU, Nat. Trust Hist. Preservation, Nature Conservancy, Human Rights Campaign, Dem. Nat. Com., HillPac. Avocations: gourmet cooking, travel, antiques. Home and Office: 3018 New Mexico Ave NW Washington DC 20016-3519

MINKOFF, JACK, retired economics educator; b. N.Y.C., Jan. 29, 1925; s. Isidore and Yetta (Fine) M.; m. Anne B. Johnson, June 19, 1948; children—Ellen, Paul. AB, Cornell U., 1948; A.M., Columbia U., 1950, PhD (Ford Found. fellow), 1960. Instr. econs. Western Res. U., 1952-53; instr. econs. Sarah Lawrence Coll., 1959-60; prof. econs., chmn. dept. social sci. Pratt Inst., Bklyn., 1960—, acting dean Sch. Liberal Arts and Scis., 1985-86, dean, 1986-93, acting provost, 1993-95, prof. econs., 1996—2002, ret., 2002. Served with USAAF, 1943-45. Social Sci. Rsch. Coun. fellow, 1950-51. Mem. Phi Beta Kappa. Home: 57 Ruxton Rd Great Neck NY 11023-1528

MINKOFF, JOHN, applied mathematics, signal processing, and engineering educator; b. Bklyn. s. Alvin Minkoff and Mollie Schwartz; m. Susan Alder, Nov. 19, 1966; 1 child, John. BSEE, Columbia U., 1962, MSEE, 1963, PhD, 1967. Rsch. engr. Columbia U., NYC, 1964-67, rsch. assoc., 1967-73; mgr. analysis activities Riverside Rsch. Inst., NYC, 1973-77; mem. tech. staff Bell Tel. Labs., Whippany, NJ, 1977-86; disting mem. tech. staff ATT/Lucent Techs. Bell Labs., Whippany, 1986—2001; staff scientist ITT Aerospace Comm. Divsn., 2001—. Adj. prof. elec. engring. Polytech. U. NY, 1989-90; adj. prof. applied math. NYU, NYC, 1990-95. Author: Signals Noise and Active Sensors, 1992, Signal Processing Fundamentals and Applications for Communications and Sensing Systems, 2002; contbr. articles to profl. jours. Music dir. Hawthorne (NJ) Symphony Orch. NSF grantee, 1975. Mem. Am. Phys. Soc. Jewish. Avocation: music. Home: 578 Jones Rd Englewood NJ 07631 Office: ITT Aerospace Comm Divsn 100 Kingsland Rd Clifton NJ 07014 Fax: 973-284-2849. Office Phone: 973-284-2011. Business E-Mail: john.minkoff@itt.com.

MINKOWITZ, MARTIN, lawyer, former state government official; b. Bklyn., 1939; s. Jacob and Marion (Kornblau) M.; m. Carol L. Ziegler; 1 son from previous marriage, Stuart Allan. AA, Bklyn. Coll., 1959, BA, 1961; JD, Bklyn. Law Sch., 1963, LLM, 1965. Bar: N.Y. 1963, U.S. Supreme Ct. 1967, U.S. Tax Ct. 1974, all four U.S. Dist. Cts. N.Y. Ptnr. Minkowitz, Hagen & Rosenbluth, N.Y.C., 1964-76; gen. counsel State of N.Y. Workers' Compensation Bd., N.Y.C., 1976-81; dep. supt. and gen. counsel State of N.Y. Ins. Dept., N.Y.C., 1981-88; instr. CUNY, 1975; ptnr. Stroock & Stroock & Lavan, N.Y.C., 1988—. Adv. bd. Coll. Ins., 1987-90; adj. prof. law N.Y. Law Sch., N.Y.C., 1982—; lectr. ABA, N.Y. C. of C., Practicing Law Inst., N.Y. State Bar Assn., Nat. Assn. Ins. Commrs., Nat. Conf. Ins. Legis.; hearing officer N.Y.C. Transp. Dept., 1970-75; cons. City Coun. N.Y.C. 1969. Author: West's New York Workers' Compensation, 2003; (with others) Rent Stabilization and Control, 1973, Handling the Basic Workers' Compensation Law Case, 1996, West's New York General Practice, 2003; co-author: Workers Compensation, Insurance and Law Practice-The Next Generation, 1989; commentaries to McKinney's Consol. Laws, 1982—; mem. editl. bd. Jour. Occupl. Rehab. U. Rochester, 1991—; contbr. articles to profl. jours. Bd. dirs., sec. Kingsbay YM-YWHA, Bklyn., 1978-99, elected dir. emeritus, 1999—; pres. bd. dirs. Shore Terrace Co-op., Bklyn., 1982-83; co-chmn. exec. bd., met. coun., nat. v.p. Am. Jewish Congress, N.Y.C., 1983-91; bd. dirs. Met. Coord. Coun. on Jewish poverty, 1993—, Nat. Conf. for Cmty. and Justice (bd. dir. N.Y. divsn. 1994-2001, nat. bd. trustees 1995-2001, chair N.Y. divsn. 1998-2001). Recipient cert. meritorious svc. Bklyn. Law Sch., Outstanding Pub. Svc. award Ind. Ins. Agt. Assn., citation outstanding performance State of N.Y. Workers' Compensation Bd., Disting. Leadership award N.Y. Claims Assn., City of Peace award State of Israel Bonds, Brotherhood award NCCJ, Man of Yr. award Congregation B'Nai Avraham, Bklyn., 2003. Fellow N.Y. State Bar Found.; mem. N.Y. County Lawyers Assn. (chmn. unlawful practice of law com. 1982-86, mem. profl. ethics com. 1985-91, chair worker's compensation com. 1988-91, bd. dirs. 1997-2002, chair profl. ethics com. 2001—, bd. dirs. exec. bd. 2003—), N.Y. State Bar Assn. (mem. ho. of dels. 1999-2003, chmn. unlawful practice of law com. 1981-83, mem. com. on profl. ethics 1981-84, chmn. com. profl. discipline 1988-92, Sustaining Mem. of Yr. award 1995), Soc. Ins. Receivers, Bklyn. Law Sch. Alumni Assn. (v.p. bd. dirs. 1984-92, pres. elect 1993-94, pres. 1995-96). Office: Stroock Stroock & Lavan 180 Maiden Ln Fl 17 New York NY 10038-4937 Office Phone: 212-806-6256. Business E-Mail: mminkowitz@stroock.com.

MINKOWYCZ, W.J. mechanical engineering educator; b. Libokhora, Ukraine, Oct. 21, 1937; came to U.S., 1949; s. Alexander and Anna (Tokan) M.; m. Diana Eva Szandra, May 12, 1973; 1 child, Liliana Christine Anne BS in Mech. Engring., U. Minn., 1958, MS in Mech. Engring., 1961, PhD in Mech. Engring, 1965. Asst. prof. U. Ill., Chgo., 1966-68, assoc. prof., 1968-78, prof., 1978—. Cons. Argonne Nat. Lab, Ill., 1970-82, U. Hawaii, Honolulu, 1974-94. Founding editor-in-chief (jour.) Jour. Numerical Heat Transfer, 1978—; editor: Internat. Jour. Heat and Mass Transfer, 1968-, Rheologically Complex Fluids, 1972, Internat. Comms. in Heat and Mass Transfer Jour., 1974-, Handbook of Numerical Heat Transfer, 1988, (book series) Computational and Physical Processes in Mechanics and Thermal Sciences, 1979-, Advances in Numerical Heat Transfer, 1996-, Vol. 1, 1997, Vol. 2, 1999—; contbr. articles to profl. jours. Recipient Silver Circle for Excellence in Teaching, U. Ill.-Chgo., 1975, 76, 81, 86, 90, 94, Harold A. Simon award Excellence in Teaching, 1986, Ralph Coats Roe Outstanding Tchr. award Am. Soc. Engring. Edn., 1988, U. Ill. Disting. Tchr. award, 1989. Fellow ASME (Heat Transfer Meml. award 1993); mem. Sigma Xi, Pi Tau Sigma. Republican. Ukrainian Catholic. Office: U Ill Dept Mech Engring Mail Code 251 842 W Taylor St Chicago IL 60607-7021 Office Phone: 312-996-3467. E-mail: wjm@uic.edu.

MINKUS, JEROME BERNARD, mathematician, educator; b. Bklyn., June 1, 1936; s. Max and Anna Minkus. BS, Cornell U., 1958; MS, U. Chgo., 1959, PhD in Math., 1963. Tchr. U. Calif., Berkeley, 1962—63, Cooper Union, NYC, 1968—69, San Francisco State U., 1983—85, 1988—89, 1995—97; ind. scholar San Francisco, 1997—. Contbr. articles to profl. jours. Mem.: Am. Math. Soc. Achievements include research in topology, group theory, number theory. Office: PO Box 4295 Berkeley CA 94704-0295

MINNA, MARIA, member of Canadian Parliament; b. Pofi, Frosinone, Italy, Mar. 14, 1948; arrived in Can., 1957. Grad. in Sociology with honors, U. Toronto. Policy advisor to former Ont. Premier David Peterson; pres. COSTI-IIAS Immigrant Svcs.; v.p. pub. affairs cons. co., Toronto; M.P. from Beaches-Woodbine dist. Ho. of Commons, Toronto, 1993-97, MP from Beaches-East York dist. Ottawa, Ont., Can., 1997—; parliamentary sec. Min. Citizenship and Immigration, 1996—98; chmn. to social policy com. Nat. Liberal Caucus, 1998—99, min. for internat. cooperation, 1999—2002. Life-long liberal, mem. Nat. Platform Com., 1988; apptd. vice chair standing com. Human Resources Devel., 1994. Contbr. reports on cmty. devel. and provision of svcs. to immigrants and minority groups. Former mem. campaign cabinet United Way Gtr. Toronto; former dir. Nat. Coun. Welfare Recipient Premio Italia nel Mondo award, 2001, President's Award, Indo-Canada Chamber of Commerce, 2001, Outstanding Leadership Award, RESULTS Canada, 2002. Mem. Nat. Congress Italian-Canadians (former exec. dir. Toronto dist., former pres.). Liberal. Office: House of Commons 406 West Block Ottawa ON Canada K1A 0A6 also: 1912 Danforth Ave M4C1J4 Toronto ON Canada E-mail: Minna.M@parl.gc.ca.*

MINNAUGH, MARK J, food products/retail grocery executive; CFO, sr. v.p. Giant Eagle, Inc., Pitts. Office: Giant Eagle Inc 101 Kappa Dr Pittsburgh PA 15238-2833

MINNELLI, LIZA, singer, actress; b. Los Angeles, Mar. 12, 1946; d. Vincente and Judy (Garland) M.; m. Peter Allen, 1967 (div. 1972); m. Jack Haley, Sept. 15, 1974 (div.); m. Mark Gero, Dec. 4, 1979 (div. 1992); m. David Gest, March 16, 2002 (div.). Appeared in Off-Broadway revival of Best Foot Forward, 1963; appeared with mother at London Palladium, 1964; nightclub debut at Shoreham Hotel, Washington, 1965; appeared in Flora, the Red Menace, 1965 (Tony award), The Act, 1977 (Tony award), The Rink, 1984, Victor Victoria; films include Charlie Bubbles, 1967, The Sterile Cuckoo, 1969, Tell Me That You Love Me, Junie Moon, 1970, Cabaret, 1972 (Oscar award), That's Entertainment, 1974, Lucky Lady, 1975, A Matter of Time, 1976, Silent Movie, 1976, New York, New York, 1977, Arthur, 1981, Rent A Cop, Arthur on the Rocks, 1988, Stepping Out, 1991; recorded You Are For Loving, 1963, Tropical Nights, 1977, Liza Minnelli at Carnegie Hall, 1987, Results, 1989, Maybe This Time, 1996, Gently, 1996, Minnelli on Minnelli, 2000, (with Herbie Hancock, Johnny Mathis, Donna Summer); (TV films) Parallel Lives, 1994, The West Side Waltz, 1995, Jackie's Back!, 1999; appeared on TV in own spl. Liza With a Z, 1972 (Recipient Emmy award); other TV appearances include Goldie and Liza Together, 1980, Baryshnikov on Broadway, 1980, The Princess and the Pea, Showtime, 1983, A Time to Live, 1985, Sam Found Out, 1988, Liza Minnelli Live from Radio City Music Hall, PBS (Emmy nomination, Music Program Performance, 1993), The West Side Waltz, 1990, The Wonderful World of Oz: 50 Years of Magic, 1990, A Century of Cinema, 1994, My Favorite Broadway: The Leading Ladies, 1999; internat. tour with Frank Sinatra, Sammy Davis Jr., 1988. Awarded the Brit. equivalent of the Oscar for Best Actress, 1972, Italy's David di Donatello award (twice), the Valentino award. Address: Capitol Records Inc 1750 Vine St Hollywood CA 90028-5209 also: Angel EMI Guardian Records 304 Park Ave S New York NY 10010-5339

MINNEMAN, KENNETH PAUL, pharmacology educator; b. Sacramento, Calif., Sept. 1, 1952; s. John Jesse and Esther Annette Minneman; children: Jennifer, Rebecca, Jeffrey. BS, MIT, 1974; PhD, U. Cambridge, England, 1977. Asst. prof. pharm. Emory U., Atlanta, 1980-85, assoc. prof. pharm., 1985-90, prof. pharm, 1990-2000, Charles Howard Candler prof. pharm., 2000—. Author: Human Pharmacology: Molecular to Clinical, 1998 (Excellence award PhRMA Found. 2000). Biomed. rsch. grantee NIH, 1981—; postdoctoral fellow U. Colo. Med. Ctr., Denver, 1977-80. Mem. AAAS, Am. Soc. Pharm. & Exptl. Therapeutics (exec. coun. 1999-2002), Soc. Neurosci., Internat. Soc. Neurochem. Home: 206 Eleventh St Atlanta GA 30309 Office: Emory U 1510 Clifton Rd Atlanta GA 30322 Fax: 404-727-0365. Office Phone: 404-727-5985. Business E-Mail: kminneman@pharm.emory.edu.

MINNER, RUTH ANN, governor; b. Milford, Del., Jan. 17, 1935; m. Roger Minner (dec.), 3 children. Student Del. Tech. and Community Coll. Office receptionist Gov. of Del., 1972-74; mem. Del. Ho. of Reps., 1974-82; mem. Del. Senate, 1982-92; lt. gov. State of Del., Dover, 1993-2001, gov., 2001—. Mem. Dem. Nat. Com., 1988. Office: Office Gov William Penn St Tatnall Bldg 3d Fl Dover DE 19901

MINNER, THOMAS O. marketing executive; b. Chgo., Jan. 3, 1956; s. Robert Schermerhorn and Arleen Minner; m. Mary Anderson; children: Allison, Brent, Courtney, Drew, Summer, Annie. BS in Bus. Adminstrn., U. Ill., 1978; MBA, Northwestern U., 1980. Mktg. mgmt. trainee PPG Industries, Inc., Pitts., 1978—79; market devel. mgr. Gould Inc., Mpls., 1980—89; v.p., gen. mgr. Automotive Battery divsn. GNB Techs., Atlanta, 1990—96; pres., CEO GNB Technologies, Inc., Atlanta, 1997—2000; pres. Transp. Bus. Group, Exide Tech., 2000—02, Champion Performance Products, LLC, 2002—. Bd. dirs. Students in Free Enterprise. Mem. Battery Coun. Internat. (bd. dirs.), City of Atlanta Chamber (bd. advisors 1995-2002). Home: 3485 Newport Bay Dr Alpharetta GA 30005-7820 Office: Champion Performance Products LLC 5490 McGinnis Village Pl Alpharetta GA 30005

MINNERLY, ROBERT WARD, retired headmaster; b. Yonkers, N.Y., Mar. 21, 1935; s. Richard Warren and Margaret Marion (DeBrocky) M.; m. Sandra Overmire, June 12, 1957; children: Scott Ward, John Robert, Sydney Sue. AB, Brown U., 1957; MAT, U. Tex., Arlington, 1980. Tchr., coach Rumsey Hall Sch., Washington, Conn., 1962-64, Berkshire Sch., Sheffield, Mass., 1964-70, asst. head, 1969-70, headmaster, 1970-76; dir. Salisbury (Conn.) Summer Sch. Reading and English, 1970; prin. upper sch. Ft. Worth Country Day Sch., 1976-86; headmaster Charles Wright Acad., Tacoma, 1986-96; admin. cons. The Edn. Group, 1996-2000; interim dir. Harold E. LeMay Mus., 2001—02; exec. dir. R. Merle Plamer Minority Students Scholarship Found., 2004—. Cons. Tarrant County Coalition on Substance Abuse, 1982-84; mem. mayor's task force Tacoma Edn. Summit, 1991-92; bd. dirs. World Cultural Interaction, Gig Harbor, Wash. Contbr. articles to profl. jours. Bd. dirs. Tacoma/Pierce County Good Will Games Art Coun., 1989, Multicare Found., Tacoma, 2002, Tacoma Baseball Found., 2003—; mem. exec. com. Am. Leadership Forum, 1991-95; bd. dirs. Broadway Ctr. for Performing Arts, Tacoma, 1988-94, 96-98, mem. exec. com., 1990-93; elected Wash. State Bd. Edn., 1996-2001; bd. dirs. Tacoma Youth Choir, 2000-03. Named Adminstr. of Yr. Wash. Journalism Edn. Assn., 1991; recipient Columbia award, Wash. Fedn. Ind. Schs., 2000. Mem. Pacific N.W. Assn. Ind. Schs. (chmn. long-range planning com. 1989-92, exec. com. 1990-92, 91, v.p. 1994). Republican. Presbyterian. Home and Office: 4214 39th Avenue Ct NW Gig Harbor WA 98335-8029

MINNERS, HOWARD ALYN, federal agency administrator, preventive medicine physician, researcher; b. Rockville Center, N.Y., Sept. 1, 1931; s. Howard A. and Marie Henriette (Soberski) M.; m. Gretchen Paffenbarger, Oct. 25, 1958; children: Todd, Bradford. AB, Princeton U., 1953; MD, Yale U., 1957; MPH, Harvard U., 1960. Diplomate Am. Bd. of Preventive Medicine; cert. Nat. Bd. of Med. Examiners. 2d. lt. USAF, 1956; intern Wilford Hall USAF Hosp., San Antonio, 1957-58; resident Sch. of Aerospace Medicine, USAF, Brooks AFB, Tex., 1960-62; advanced through grades to maj. USAF, 1966; advanced through grades to rear adm. USPHS, ret., 1987; dir. office rsch. promotion and devel. WHO, Geneva, Switzerland, 1977-80; dir. Office of Sci. Advisor Agy. Internat. Devel., Washington, 1981-91; dep. dir. Office Internat. Health USPHS and Asst. Surgeon Gen., 1980-81. Assoc. dir. NIH NIAID, 1966-77; astronaut flight surgeon NASA, Houston, 1962-66. Pres. Model A Ford Found., 1994-2000. Fellow World Acad. Art and Sci., Am. Coll. Preventive Medicine; mem. AAAS, Internat. Found. Sci. Stockholm (pres., chmn. bd. trustees 1991-97), Yale Med. Alumni Fund (chmn. bd. trustees, 2003-). Avocations: antique automobile restoration, advertising history.

MINNESTE, VIKTOR, JR., retired engineering executive; b. Haapsalu, Estonia, Jan. 15, 1932; s. Viktor and Alice (Lembra) M. BSEE, U. Ill., 1960. Elec. engr. Bell & Howell Co., 1960-69; microstatics divsn. A-M Co., 1969-71, multigraphics divsn., 1972-73; elec. engr. bus. products group Victor Comptometer Co. (merged with Walter Kidde Corp.), Chgo., 1973-74, svc. mgr. internat. group, 1974-75, supr. elecs. desing group, 1975-82; project engr. Warner Electric, 1982-84; systems engr. Barrett Elecs., 1984-85; phone engr. Williams Elecs., 1986-88; cons. engr., 1988-92; ind. contractor, 1993-95; ret., 1995. Pub. Motteid/Thoughts, 1962-68. Chmn. Estonian-Ams. Polit Action Com., 1968-72. With AUS, 1952-54. Home and Office: 3134 N Kimball Ave Chicago IL 60618-6856

MINNEY, MICHAEL JAY, lawyer; b. Lancaster, Pa., Aug. 15, 1948; s. Jay W. and Mary Jane (Erisman) M.; m. Barbara Ann Dunlap, June 28, 1975; 1 child, Michael Jayson. Student, U.S. Mil. Acad., 1967; BA, Ohio Wesleyan U., 1970; JD, Villanova U., 1973. Bar: Pa. 1973, U.S. Dist. Ct. (ea. dist.) Pa. 1974, U.S. Supreme Ct. 1977, U.S. Ct. Appeals (3d cir.) 1979. Ptnr. Minney, Mecum & Kohr, Lancaster, 1975-78, 1978-84; sole practice Lancaster, 1973-75, 84—. Regional council Govs. Justice Commn., Harrisburg, Pa., 1975-78; commr. Pa. Commn. on Sentencing, Harrisburg, 1979-81. Candidate U.S. House of Reps., 16th Dist., Pa., 1974, 76; bd. dirs. United Cerebral Palsy, Lancaster, 1976-84, pres. 1983-84; mem., prin. Bring Back Baseball to Lancaster. Named one of Outstanding Young Men of Am., 1976. Mem. Lancaster County Bar Assn., Pa. Bar Assn., James Buchannan Found. for the Preservation of Wheatland (treas, 1998-99, v.p. 2001, pres. 2002—), Elks, Conestoga Country Club (Lancaster). Republican. Lutheran. Avocations: running, golf, photography. Office: 145 E Chestnut St Lancaster PA 17602-2740 Office Phone: 717-299-5647.

MINNICH, DIANE KAY, legal association administrator; b. Iowa City, Feb. 17, 1956; d. Ralph Maynard Minnich and Kathryn Jane (Obye) Tompkins. BA in Behavioral Sci., San Jose State U., 1978. Tutorial program coord./instr. Operation SHARE/La Valley Coll., Van Nuys, Calif., 1979-81; field exec. Silver Sage Girl Scout Coun., Boise, Idaho, 1981-85; continuing legal edn. dir. Idaho State Bar/Idaho Law Found. Inc., Boise, 1985-88, dep. dir., 1988-90, exec. dir., 1990—. Sec.-treas. Western States Bar Conf., 2001—; bd. dirs. Atty. Liability Protection Soc.--A Fmily of Profl. Svc. Cos.; mem. adv. bd. legal asst. program Boise State U. Mem. Assn. CLE Adminstrs., Chgo., 1985-90; bd. dirs. Silver Sage coun. Girl Scouts, Boise, 1990-93, 99-2001, mem. nominating com., 1990-94, 97-2001, chair nominating com., 1991-92; mem. legal asst. program adv. bd. Boise State U. Named one of Outstanding Young Women in Am., 1991. Mem. Nat. Orgn. Bar Execs. (membership com. 1992-97, chair 1996-97), Zonta Club Boise (pres. 1991-92, bd. dirs. 1989-93), Rotary Club Boise (chair mem. com. 1994-97, bd. dirs. 1996-97, 99—, pres. 2003-04). Avocations: jogging, golf. Office: Idaho State Bar Idaho Law Found PO Box 895 525 W Jefferson St Boise ID 83702-5931 Home: 1118 Harrison Blvd Boise ID 83702-3448

MINNICK, BRUCE ALEXANDER, lawyer; b. New London, Conn., Apr. 16, 1943; s. Robert Wood Minnick and Nedra Louise (Alexander) Wiesman; m. Judith Anita Saxon, Sept. 23, 1967 (div. 1981); children: Audra Anne, Lisa Michelle; m. Charlotte Ann Springfield, Apr. 10, 1983 (div. 1991); 1 child, Matthew Alexander; m. Debra C. Williams, July 3, 1997; 1 stepchild, Brandy Michelle Williams. AA, Broward Community Coll., 1970; BS with honors, Fla. State U., 1971, JD, 1977. Bar: Fla. 1978, U.S. Dist. Ct. (no. dist.) Fla. 1979, U.S. Dist. Ct. (mid. and so. dists.) Fla. 1982, U.S. Supreme Ct. 1981, U.S. Ct. Appeals (11th cir.) 1982, U.S. Tax Ct. 1983, U.S. Ct. Claims 1983, U.S. Dist. Ct. (ea. dist.) Mich. 1990; cert. Expert in Labor and Employment Law, The Fla. Bar, 2003. Asst. v.p., asst. comptroller PAN Am. Bank Miami, 1971—74; staff dir., counsel rules com. Fla. Ho. Reps., Tallahassee, 1976-78; v.p., gen. counsel Fla. Credit Union League, Tallahassee, 1978-80; asst. atty.

gen. dept. legal affairs State of Fla., Tallahassee, 1981-86; ptnr. Mang, Rett & Collette, P.A., Tallahassee, 1986-93, Mang, Rett & Minnick PA, Tallahassee, 1994-95; pvt. practice Bruce A. Minnick PA, Tallahassee, 1996—. Chief adv. Fla. Commn. on Ethics, 1995-96; lectr. state agys., 1982—, Fla. Bar, 1986—; pres. Civil Rights Dispute Resolution Ctr.; v.p. Fed. Dispute Resolution Ctr. Mem. Leon County Dist. Adv. Com., 1980-82, 92-94; mem. exec. com. Leon County Dems., 1984-2000.—. Mem. ABA (labor sect., local govt. and law sect.), Fla. Bar Assn. (chmn. com. labor sect. 1987-91, mem. exec. coun. labor sect. 1989-93, founding chmn. Fed. Ct. practice com. 1990-92, del. to 11th Cir. Jud. Conf. 1990-92, com. chmn. govt. lawyer sect. 1991-2000—, rep. mem. pub. rels. com. 1991-93, cert. expert labor and employment law 2003), Tallahassee Bar Assn., Fa. Govt. Bar Assn., Fla. Women Lawyers Assn., Fed. Bar Assn. (pres.-elect Tallahassee chpt. 1995, pres. 1996), Govs. Club, Univ. Ctr. Club, Golden Eagle Country Club, Phi Alpha Delta. Christian Scientist. Avocations: golf, astronomy, writing. Home: 9017 Eagles Ridge Dr Tallahassee FL 32312-4046 Office: 3116 Capital Cir NE Ste 10 PO Box 15588 Tallahassee FL 32317-5588 Fax: 850-385-8414. Office Phone: 850-386-9444. E-mail: minnicklaw@prodigy.net.

MINNICK, DAVID MICHAEL, lawyer; b. Las Vegas, Nev., Apr. 24, 1956; s. Carl Wallace and Myrtle Ada (Perry) M.; m. Nancy Sue Grosse. BS in Agrl. Journalism, U. Mo., 1978, JD, 1981. Agt. real estate and ins. Phillips Petroleum Co., Odessa, Tex., 1981; asst. cir. atty. Cirt. Atty.'s Office, St. Louis, 1982-85; pvt. practice Troy, Mo., 1985-86; asst. pros. atty., 1985-86; litigation counsel, assoc. v.p. A.G. Edwards & Sons, St. Louis, 1986-90; mng. dir., gen. counsel Morgan Keegan & Co., Memphis, 1990-98; pvt. practice Kansas City, Mo., 1998-2000; sr. regional atty. NASD Regulation, Inc., Kansas City, 2000—. Arbitrator NASDR, N.Y. Stock Exch., Am. Stock Exch., 1995—; litigation adv. com. The Bond Mkt. Assn., 1997—. Contbr. articles to profl. jours. Bd. dirs. YMCA, Memphis, 1993-96; vol. Teach for a Day Programs, Memphis Ptnrs., 1994-96. Mem. Securities Industry assn. (legal and compliance div.), Econ. Club of Memphis, Masons, Shriner. Avocations: ranching, farming, running, hunting, college football. Office: NASD Regulation Inc 120 W 12th St Ste 900 Kansas City MO 64105

MINNICK, MALCOLM DAVID, lawyer; b. Indpls., July 5, 1946; s. Malcolm Dick and Frances Louise (Porter) M.; m. Heidi Rosemarie Klein, May 24, 1972. BA, U. Mich., 1968, JD, 1972. Bar: Calif. 1972, U.S. Dist. Ct. (ctrl. dist.) Calif. 1972, U.S. Ct. Appeals (9th cir.) 1984, U.S. Dist. Ct. (no. dist.) Calif. 1986, U.S. Supreme Ct. 1986. Assoc. Lillick McHose & Charles, LA, 1972-78; ptnr. Lillick & McHose, LA, 1978-91, Pillsbury Winthrop LLP, San Francisco, 1991—. Group mgr. Creditors Rights and Bankruptcy Group, 1993-98; panelist Calif. Continuing Edn. of Bar, LA, 1982-86, 88, Practicing Law Inst., 1992, 93, 94, Banking Law Inst., 1999, 2000; bd. govs. Fin. Lawyers Conf., LA, 1981-84; mem. exec. com. Lillick & McHose, 1982-85. Co-author: Checklist for Secured Commercial Loans, 1983. Pres. Ross Sch. Found., 1997-98. Mem. ABA (corp., banking and bus. law sect.), Calif. Bar Assn. (Uniform Comml. Code com. 1983-86), LA County Bar Assn. (exec. com. comml. law and bankruptcy sect. 1987-90), Bar Assn. San Francisco (comml. law and bankruptcy sect.), LA Country Club, Univ. Club (bd. dirs. 1983-86, pres. 1985-86). Avocation: golf. Office: Pillsbury Winthrop LLP 50 Fremont St San Francisco CA 94105-2230 Office Phone: 415-983-1351. Business E-Mail: dminnick@pillsburywinthrop.com.

MINNICK, MARY E. food products executive; MBA, Duke U. With sales dept. Coca-Cola USA; previous pres. S. Pacific divsn. The Coca-Cola Co., Australia; previous pres. Coca-Cola Japan; exec. v.p., pres., CEO Asia The Coca-Cola Co., Atlanta, 2001—. Mem. Dean's Coun. John F. Kennedy Sch. Bus., Harvard U.; bd. visitors Fuqua Sch. Bus. Named one of most powerful women in the bus. world, Fortune mag. Office: The Coca-Cola Co PO Box 1734 Atlanta GA 30301

MINNIGH, JOEL DOUGLAS, library director; b. Greenville, Pa., Apr. 9, 1949; s. Wendell Ellsworth and Frances Alene (Hyde) M.; m. Margaret Beth Crowther, Dec. 26, 1972; children: Bradley Dean, Douglas Knox. BA, Allegheny Coll., 1971; MLS, U. Pitts., 1975. Cert. libr., Pa. Asst. libr. Wilkinsburg (Pa.) Pub. Libr., 1976-77, head libr., 1977—. Bd. dirs. Goodwill Industries Pitts., 1980-90, Mulberry Sr. Citizens Ctr., Wilkinsburg, Pa., 2001--; vice chmn. bd. dirs. Bach Choir Pitts., 1984-87; sec., bd. dirs. United Meth. Ch. Union, Pitts., 1987-88; elder, deacon Fox Chapel Presbyn. Ch., 1987—, soloist, 1998—. Recipient honor Goodwill Industries Pitts., 1990, citation Pa. Senate, 1991. Mem. Pa. Libr. Assn. (treas. S.W. chpt. 1988-89, 2004—), Allegheny County Libr. Assn. (pres. librs. adv. coun. 2001-02, bd. dirs. 2002—), Wilkinsburg C. of C. (dir. 1998—2003, sec. 1999—2003). Republican. Avocations: travel, cooking, gardening, music, reading. Home: 1009 Blackridge Rd Pittsburgh PA 15235-2719 Office: Wilkinsburg Pub Libr 605 Ross Ave Pittsburgh PA 15221-2145

MINNIS, KAREN, state representative; b. Portland, Oreg., July 20, 1954; m. John Minnis, 1972; 3 children. Student, Clark C.C., 1978. Small bus. owner, 1995—97; legis. aide State Rep. John Minnis, 1987—98; mem. Oreg. Ho. of Reps., 1998—; majority leader, 2001—03. Spkr. of the Ho., 2003—. Republican. Office: 900 Court St NE Rm 269 Salem OR 97301 Office Phone: 503-986-1200.

MINNITI, MARTHA JEAN, home healthcare company executive; b. Shamokin, Pa., Dec. 13, 1951; d. Charles and Betty Minniti; m. James Hill, Apr. 19, 1986; 1 child, Katharine. Diploma, Bryn Mawr (Pa.) Hosp. Sch. Nursing, 1973; BS in Psychology magna cum laude, Rosemont Coll., 1979; postgrad., U. Pa., 1992—. RN, Pa. Staff nurse Chestnut Hill (Pa.) Hosp., 1973-76; staff-charge nurse Phila. Coll. Osteo. Medicine, 1976-78, Med. Staff, Phila., 1978-80; CEO The SNI Cos., Flourtown, Pa., 1980—. Contbr. articles to profl. jours. Mem. ANA, AACN, Am. Orgn. Nurse Execs., Am. Holistic Nurses Assn., Am. Hosp. Assn., Pa. Nurses Assn., Sigma Theta Tau (Kappa Chi chpt.).

MINNIX, BRUCE MILTON, television and theatre director; b. Hendersonville, N.C., Apr. 26, 1923; s. Bruce Milton and Jane Irene (Leverett) M.; m. Corinne McClure, Aug. 5, 1950; 1 child, Tracy Logue. BA, U. N.C., 1948. Mem. faculty New Sch., N.Y.C., 1977-80; adj. prof., Bklyn., 1985; AT&T sales tng. program, 1987. Dir. numerous TV shows including: U.S. Steel Hour, 1961-62, Merchant of Venice, 1962, Essay on Doors, 1963, Never Too Young, 1965-66, On Being Black, 1969, The Haggadah Oratorio, 1981, Search for Tomorrow, 1968-74, All My Children, 1978-79, Another World, 1981, Texas, 1981-82, Body Talk, 1983, As the World Turns, 1985-86; The Cradle Will Rock, 1986 (Emmy nomination), Minolta Tng. series Minolta Info. Network, 1980-81; dir. Citibank, 1984, N.J. Bell (AT&T), 1985; dir. Victorian Cape May A Video Visit to a Town out of Time, 1988 (medal Houston Film Festival), dir. Pitney Bowes Copier Intro 1992, Time Warner Cable 1991; producer, writer: Mt. Washington Valley, A Video Visit in Four Seasons, 1990; Actor: Music Video by Little Texas What Might Have Been, 1993. Mayor, City of Cape May, N.J., 1972-76; founding mem., 3-term pres. Mid-Atlantic Center for Arts. Served with USN, 1943-45. Mem. Dirs. Guild Am.

MINOGUE, JOHN P. academic administrator, educator, priest; b. Chgo., Jan. 1946; B in Philosophy, St. Mary of the Barrens; MDiv, Deandreis Inst. Theology, 1972; M in Theology, DePaul U., 1975; PhD in Ministry, St. Mary of the Lake Sem., 1987. Ordained Vincentian priest, 1972. Vincentian priest Congregation of the Mission; instr. theology, dir. clin. pastoral placement programs St. Thomas Sem., Denver, 1972-76; instr. grad. theology, asst. then acad. dean DeAndreis Inst., 1976-83; pres. DePaul U., Chgo., 1993—. Trustee DePaul U., 1991—; bd. dirs. DePaul U. Corp., 1981-91; adj. prof. Sch. New Learning DePaul U., 1984—, instr. law and med. ethics Coll. Law DePaul U., 1989—; asst. prof. clin. ob.-gyn. Northwestern U.; instr. health care ethics St. Joseph Coll. Nursing, Joliet, Ill., Northwestern Sch. Nursing, Chgo.; cons. nat. health care ethics, patient decision-making, mem. Congregation of the Missions Bd. mem. Children's Meml. Hosp. Mem.: NASA (bd. mem.). Office: De Paul U Office of the Pres 55 E Jackson Blvd 22nd Fl Chicago IL 60604-2287*

MINOGUE, ROBERT BROPHY, retired nuclear engineer; b. Covington, Ky., Jan. 31, 1928; s. Joseph and Catherine Ann (Brophy) M.; m. Marie Joan Clarke, June 12, 1954; children: Patrick, Margaret, Marie, Francis. BS, Thomas More Coll., 1949; MS, U. Cin., 1951; grad., Oak Ridge Sch. Reactor Tech., 1952. Nuclear engr., then head nuclear tech. sect. naval reactors br. AEC, Washington, 1952-56; head research reactor design and enngring., then head nuclear power plant engring. sect. Gen. Atomic div. Gen. Dynamics Corp., 1957-67; chief spl. projects br. div. reactor standards AEC, Washington, 1967-72, asst. dir., then dep. dir. regulatory standards, 1972-74; dir. office standards devel. Nuclear Regulatory Commn., Washington, 1975-80, dir. office research, 1980-86; pvt. practice Temecula, Calif., 1986—. U.S. mem. sr. adv. group Safety Standards IAEA, 1974-86; mem. Com. on Interagy. Radiation Research and Policy Coordination, 1982-86. Author: Reactor Shielding Design Manual, 1956; patentee: Triga Research Reactor. Served with AUS, 1946-48. Recipient Bernard F. Langer award, ASME, 1982. Roman Catholic. Home and Office: 29743 Marhill Cir Temecula CA 92591-1809

MINOR, CLARA MAE, election judge; b. Altapass, N.C., Dec. 3, 1931; d. David Wilkerson Sullins, and Carrie Mae Schism; m. Lawrence Alfred Minor, Oct. 27, 1950; children: Lawrence, Charles, Beverly, John. Grad. h.s., Canton, Ohio, 1949. Sales clk. JC Penney Co., Canton, 1973-80; presiding judge Stark County Election Bd., Canton, 1983—. Pres., mem. PTA, Hubbard, Ohio, 197-72. Mem. DAR, Daus. Am. Colonists, Daus. War of 1812. Republican. Methodist. Avocations: reading, collector ladies antique watches and compacts.

MINOR, GEORGE GILMER, III, drug and hospital supply company executive; b. 1940; married. BA, Va. Mil. Inst., 1963; MBA, U. Va., 1966. With Owens & Minor, Inc., Richmond, Va., 1963—, mgr. sales Acme Candy Co. div., 1966-68, mgr. retail mktg., 1968-73, div. mgr. wholesale drug br., 1973-77, v.p., 1977-80, exec. v.p., 1980-81, pres. 1981-1999, chmn. 1994-, CEO, 1981—, also bd. dirs. Office: Owens & Minor Inc 4800 Cox Rd Glen Allen VA 23060-6292

MINOR, HALSEY, multimedia company executive; married; 3 children. BA in Anthropology, U. Va., 1987. Investment banker Merrill Lynch Capital Markets, San Francisco, 1987—89; founder, CEO Global Publishing Corp., 1989—90; cons. Russell Reynolds Associates, 1991—92; chmn., CEO CNET: The Computer Network, San Francisco, 1992—2000; chmn. emeritus CNET Networks, Inc., 2000—; founder, chmn., CEO Grand Central Communications, 2000—. Bd. dirs. salesforce.com, inc. Office: Grand Central Communications 50 Fremont St 16th Fl San Francisco CA 94105 Office Phone: 415-344-3200. Office Fax: 415-344-3250.

MINOR, JOSEPH EDWARD, civil engineer, educator; b. Corpus Christi, Tex., June 2, 1938; s. William Smoot Jr. and Irene (Schiller) M.; m. Treva Ann Edmiston, Sept. 3, 1960; children: Joseph Edward Jr., Sharon Diane. BSCE, Tex. A&M U., 1959, M of Engring., 1960; PhD, Tex. Tech U., 1974. Registered profl. engr., Tex., Mo., Fla. Sr. rsch. engr. Southwest Research Inst., San Antonio, 1962-69; P. Whitfield Horn prof. Tex. Tech U., Lubbock, 1969-88; Thomas Reese prof., chmn. dept. civil engring. U. Mo., Rolla, 1988-93, rsch. prof., 1993—. Pres. Insulating Glass Cert. Council, N.Y., 1986-89; vis. prof. Tex. A&M U., Kingsville, 2003-. Contbr. articles to profl. jours. Served with USAR. Recipient Disting. Engr. award Tex. Tech U., 1989, Disting. Svc. award Nat. Hurricane Conf., 1999; Nat. Def. fellow, 1959-60; Fulbright scholar, 1978. Fellow ASCE (pres. Tex. sect. 1984-85, award of honor 2003); mem. Nat. Soc. Profl. Engrs. Presbyterian. Avocation: fishing. Office: Joseph E Minor PE Consulting Engineer PO Box 603 Rockport TX 78381-0603 E-mail: josephminor@sbcglobal.net.

MINOR, MARIAN THOMAS, elementary and secondary school educational consultant; b. Richmond, Va., Apr. 16, 1933; d. James Madison and Florence Elwood (Edwards) M. BS, U. Va., 1955; MEd, William and Mary Coll., 1968; postgrad., Va. Commonwealth U., 1987-88. Cert. guidance, health and phys. edn. Educator Richmond (Va.) Pub. Schs., 1955-90, ednl. cons., 1990—. Educator Sch. Nursing Med. Coll. Va., Richmond, 1958-68; camp dir. Manakin, Va., 1956-68; nat. basketball ofcl. Richmond (Va.) Bd. Ofcls., 1952-77; mem. faculty adv. com. Albert Hill Middle Sch., Richmond, 1965-90, dept. chmn., 1960-90, Tchr. of Yr., 1980; textbook adoption Richmond (Va.) Pub. Sch., 1975, 85, curriculum planner, 1978-79, 82-83, 84-85; PTA coord. Albert Hill Middle Sch., Richmond, 1985-89, chmn. self-study and accreditation team, 1987-88. Mem. Sherwood Park Civic Assn., Richmond, 1960-98; v.p. alumni weekend Mary Washington Alumni Assn., Fredericksburg, Va., 1965, 66, v.p. annual giving, 1967; chmn. basketball ofcl. examiners Richmond Bd. Women Ofcls., 1966-76; bd. dirs., homeowner adv., constrn. crewman, family svcs. com. Habitat for Humanity, 1994-2002, Blitz Build 2000 adv. chmn.; mem. exec. com. Northminster Bapt. Ch., 1991-94, 99-2002, deacon, clk., 97-99, worship team, 1999—, premises chair, 1991-94, mem. by-laws revision com., 1986, 98, 99, srs. task force chmn., v.p., sr. fellowship, regional Befriender Ministry adv. coun. Recipient J.C. Penney Golden Rule award, 1996, Outstanding Vol. award Habitat for Humanity, 1998, Outstanding Svc. award Albert Hill PTA, 1988. Mem. AAUW, AAHPERD, Va. Health Phys. Edn. Assn., Va. Ret. Tchrs. Assn., Train Collectors Assn., King and Queen Hist. Soc., Mortar Bd., Alpha Phi Sigma, Kappa Delta Pi. Republican. Avocations: genealogy, local history. Home and Office: 1507 Brookland Pky Richmond VA 23227-4707

MINOR, MARK WILLIAM, allergist; b. Steubenville, Ohio, May 19, 1956; s. Garland Edgar Minor and Norma Jean McKenzie Shidock; m. Rachael Anne Hatfield, Aug. 15, 1987; children: Megan, Emily. BS in Biology magna cum laude, U. Miami, 1978; MD, W.Va. U., 1982. Resident in internal medicine W.Va. U., Charleston; fellow in allergy/immunology U. So. Fla., Tampa; staff physician Holmes Regional Hosp., Melbourne, Fla.; clin. asst., prof. medicine U. South Fla. Contbr. articles, referee Jour. Allergy and Clin. Immunology, So. Med. Jour. Fellow Am. Coll. Allergy, Asthma, and Immunology, Am. Coll. Physicians; mem. Am. Acad. Allergy and Immunology, Alpha Omega Alpha. Office: 2290 W Eau Gallie Blvd #205 Melbourne FL 32935

MINOR, ROBERT ALLEN, lawyer; b. Washington, Oct. 20, 1948; s. Robert Walter and Joan (Allen) M.; m. Sue Ellyn Blose, June 13, 1981; children: Robert Barratt, Sarah Allen. AB in English, Duke U., 1970; JD, Ohio State U., 1975. Bar: Ohio 1975, U.S. Dist. Ct. (so. dist.) Ohio 1976, D.C. 1979. Assoc. Vorys, Sater, Seymour & Pease, LLP, Columbus, Ohio, 1975-82, ptnr., 1982—. Author seminar articles. With U.S. Army, 1970-72. Mem. Ohio Bar Assn., Columbus Bar Assn., Athletic Club Columbus, Scioto Country Club. Republican. Presbyterian. Office: Vorys Sater Seymour & Pease LLP PO Box 1008 52 E Gay St Columbus OH 43215-3161

MINOR, RONALD RAY, minister; b. Aliceville, Ala., Nov. 3, 1944; s. Hershel Ray and Minnie Ozell (Goodson) M.; m. Gwendolyn Otella Newsome, July 25, 1970; 1 child, Rhonda Rene. BA in Ministerial, Southeastern Bible Coll., 1971, BA in Secondary Edn., 1973; DDiv, Southern Bible Coll., 1984. Ordained to ministry Pentecostal Ch. of God, 1968. Gen. sec. Pentecostal Ch. of God, Joplin, Mo., 1979—, dist. supt. Philadelphia, Miss., 1975-79, pastor Bartow, LaBelle, Fla., Orient Park Tabernacle, Tampa, Fla. Pres. Pentecostal Young People's Assn., Fla. and Miss.; sec. Gen. Bd. Pentecostal Ch. of God, Joplin, 1979; bd. dirs. Nat. Assn. Evangs., Wheaton, Ill., 1981-96; adv. coun. Am. Bible Soc., N.Y.C., 1979-2003; sec. Commn. Chaplains, Washington, 1991-95. Home: 2625 Markwardt Joplin MO 64801-5353 Office: Pentecostal Ch of God 4901 Pennsylvania Ave Joplin MO 64804-4947 Office Phone: 417-624-7050. Business E-Mail: ronaldm@pcg.org.

MINOTTI, MARK ANTHONY, assistant principal; b. S.I., N.Y., July 23, 1974; s. Frank Thomas and Christine Marie (Palma) M. BS in Chemistry, Wagner Coll., 1996, MS in Edn., 1998; diploma in ednl. adminstrn./supervision, St. John's U., 1999, EdD in Instructional Leadership, 2001. Assoc. dir. music St. Charles Ch., S.I., 1992—; tchg. asst. Wagner Coll., S.I., 1993-96; instr. chemistry St. Joseph-by-the-Sea H.S., S.I., 1996-99; asst. prin. St. Francis de Sales and St. Lucy Acad., N.Y.C., 1999—. Author website Chemtacular.com, 1997. Asst. coord. St. Charles Sports Program, S.I., 1992—; mem. young people's forum Archdiocese N.Y., 1994. Megerle Sc. scholar Wagner Coll., 1993-96, Alumni scholar, 1996-98. Fellow Internat. Union Pure and Applied Chemistry; mem. ACS, ASCD, Nat. Sci. Tchrs. Assn., Nat. Assn. Secondary Sch. Prins. Republican. Roman Catholic. Avocations: music, piano, travel, reading, education. Office: St Francis de Sales and St Lucy Acad 116 E 97th St New York NY 10029-7201

MINOW, JOSEPHINE BASKIN, civic volunteer; b. Chgo., Nov. 3, 1926; d. Salem N. and Bessie (Sampson) Baskin; m. Newton N. Minow, May 29, 1949; children: Nell, Martha, Mary. BS, Northwestern U., 1948. Asst. to advt. dir. Mandel Brothers Dept. Store, Chgo., 1948-49; tchr. Francis W. Parker Sch., Chgo., 1949-50; vol. in civil and charitable activities, 1950—; bd. dirs. Juvenile Protective Assn., Chgo., 1958—, pres., 1973-75. Bd. dirs. Parnham Trust, Beaminster, Dorset, England. Author: Marty the Broken Hearted Artichoke, 1997. Founder, coord. Children's divsn. Hospitality and Info. Svc., Washington, 1961-63; mem. Caucus Com., Glencoe, Ill., 1965-69; co-chmn. spl. study on juvenile justice Chgo. Cmty. Trust, 1978-80; chmn. Know Your Chgo., 1980-83; bd. dirs. Chgo. Coun. Fgn. Rels., 1977-2003, hon. life mem., 2003; trustee Chgo. Hist. Soc., Ravinia Festival Assn.; mem. women's bd. Field Mus., U. Chgo.; founding mem., v.p. women's bd. Northwestern U., 1978; bd. govs. Chgo. Symphony, 1966-73, 76-; mem. Citizens Com. Juvenile Ct. of Cook County, 1985-96; exec. com. Northwestern U. Libr. Coun., 1974-96; co-chair grandparents' adv. com. Chgo. Children's Mus., 1999; bd. dirs. Jane Addams Juvenile Ct. Found. Recipient spl. award Chgo. Sch. and Workshop for Retarded, 1975, Children's Guardian award Juvenile Protective Assn., 1993. Mem. Hebrew Immigrant Aid Soc. (bd. dirs. 1977-98, award 1988), Friday Club, Northmoor Country Club, The Arts Club. Democrat. Jewish. Office: Chgo Hist Soc Clark St at North Ave Chicago IL 60614

MINOW, NEWTON NORMAN, lawyer, educator; b. Milw., Wis., Jan. 17, 1926; s. Jay A. and Doris (Stein) Minow; m. Josephine Baskin, May 29, 1949; children: Nell, Martha, Mary. BS, Northwestern U., 1949, JD, 1950, LLD (hon.), 1965, U. Wis., Brandeis U., 1963, Columbia Coll., 1972, Govs. State U., 1984, De Paul U., 1989, RAND Grad. Sch., 1993, U. Notre Dame, 1994, Roosevelt U., 1996, Barat Coll., 1996, Santa Clara U. Sch. Law, 1998. With firm Mayer, Brown & Platt, Chgo., 1950-51, 53-55; law clk. to Hon. Fred. M. Vinson, 1951-52; adminstrv. asst. to Ill. Gov. Stevenson, 1952-53; spl. asst. to Adlai E. Stevenson in presdl. campaign, 1952, 56; ptnr. firm Stevenson, Rifkind & Wirtz, Chgo., N.Y.C. and Washington, 1955-61; chmn. FCC, Washington, 1961-63; exec. v.p., gen. counsel, dir. Ency. Brit., Chgo., 1963-65; ptnr. Sidley Austin Brown & Wood, LLP, Chgo., 1965-91, sr. counsel, 1991—. Former trustee, past chmn. bd. dirs., adv. trustee Rand Corp.; past chmn. Chgo. Ednl. TV; chmn. pub. rev. bd. Arthur Andersen & Co., 1974—83; trustee Carnegie Corp. N.Y., 1987—97, chmn. bd. trustees, 1993—97; prof. com. policy and law Northwestern U., 1987—2003; dir. Annenberg Washington Program, 1987—96. Author: (book) Equal Time: The Private Broadcasters and the Public Interest, 1964; co-author: Presidential Television, 1973, Electronics and the Future, 1977, For Great Debates, 1987, Abandoned in the Wasteland: Children, Television, and the First Amendment, 1995, As We Knew Adlai. Bd. govs. Pub. Broadcasting Svc., 1973—80, chmn. bd. dirs., 1978—80; co-chmn. presdl. debates LWV, 1976, 1980, co-chmn. presdl. debates commn., 1993—; chmn. bd. overseers Jewish Theol. Sem., 1974—77; trustee Notre Dame U., 1964—77, 1983—96, life trustee, 1996; trustee Mayo Found., 1973—81, Northwestern U., 1975—87, life trustee, 1987—; trustee Chgo. Orchestral Assn., 1975—87, life trustee, 1987—. With U.S. Army, 1944—46. Named one of Am.'s 10 Outstanding Young Men, 1961; recipient George Foster Peabody Broadcasting award, 1961, Ralph Lowell award, 1982, Lifetime Achievement award, Am. Lawyer, 2004. Fellow: Am. Acad. Arts and Scis., Am. Bar Found.; mem.: Northwestern U. Alumni Assn. (medal 1978), Century Club (N.Y.C.), Chgo. Club, Comml. Club (pres. 1987—88). Democrat. Office: Sidley Austin Brown & Wood LLP Ste 4800 10 S Dearborn St Chicago IL 60603 E-mail: nminow@sidley.com.

MINSHALL, GREG, computer programmer; b. Carmel, Calif., Apr. 21, 1952; s. Glenn Almon and Martha Jane (Hardesty) M.; m. Maria Concepción Gonzalez, Dec. 30, 1976 (div. Jan. 1984); children: Matthew, Cecilia; m. Carol Ann Mendel, Oct. 4, 1987 (div. Feb. 1992); children: Oriana, Jacob. BA in Math., U. Calif., Berkeley, 1985. Computer programmer Stanford Linear Accelerator Ctr., Menlo Park, Calif., 1969-70, 72-73; computer programmer/engr. Inst. for Advanced Computation, Sunnyvale, Calif., 1978-80; computer programmer U. Calif., Berkeley, 1980-88; cons., 1984-88; computer programmer Novell, Inc., Walnut Creek, Calif., 1988-95, Ipsilon Networks, Inc., Mountain View, Calif., 1995—97; founder Siara Sys., 1998—2002. Mem. IEEE, Internet Engring. Task Force, Assn. for Computing Machinery, Usenix.

MINSKY, BRUCE WILLIAM, lawyer; b. Queens, N.Y., Sept. 28, 1963; m. Jill R. Heinter, May 1992; children: Aryeh Hanan, Elisheva Yael, Calev Betzalel, Refael Akiva. BA in Polit. Sci., Boston U., 1985; JD, Southwestern U., 1988; LLM in Am. Banking, Boston U., 1989. Bar: Calif. 1988, Conn. 1989, N.Y. 1990, U.S. Dist. Ct. (ea. and so. dist.), U.S. Ct. Appeals. Assoc. Quirk & Bakalor, N.Y.C., 1989-91; house counsel, v.p. Banco Popular N.Am., N.Y.C., 1991—, Banco Poplur N. Am., 1999. Atty. Monday Night Law Pro Bono Svcs., N.Y.C. Mem. Assn. of Bar of City of N.Y. (mem. young lawyers com. 1993-95). Avocations: music, sports, literature. Office: 7 W 51st St New York NY 10019-6910

MINSON, DIXIE L. legislative staff member; Student, Weber State U. Dir. dept. bus. regulation Utah's Divsn. Consumer Protection; dep. chief of staff Office of Gov. Norman H. Bangerter, Utah; commr. safety, health and indsl. accidents divsn. Indsl. Commn. Utah; state dir. Office of Senator Robert F. Bennett, Salt Lake City, 1993—. Active Utah Hearing Panel for Safety Auto and Inspection Stas., League Utah Consumers; Utah liaison U.S. Product Safety Commn.; v.p. Wester Assn. Worker's Compensation Bd. and Commn.; rep. Funeral Svc. Consumer Action Panel for Western States and Hawaii. Mem. Nat. Assn. Govtl. Labor Ofcls., Nat. Assn. Consumer Agy. Adminstrs., Nat. Assn. Unemployment Ins. Appellate Bds. Office: 1779 W 550 N Clearfield UT 84015

MINTER, DAVID LEE, English literature educator; b. Midland, Tex., Mar. 20, 1935; s. Kenneth Cruse and Frances (Hennessy) M.; m. Cynthia Caroline Sewell, Dec. 22, 1957; children: Christopher Sewell, Frances Elizabeth. BA, N. Tex. State U., 1957, MA, 1959; BD, Yale U., 1961, PhD, 1965. Univ. lectr. Hamburg (W. Ger.) U., 1965-66; lectr. Yale U., 1966-67; asst. prof. Rice U., Houston, 1967-69, assoc. prof., 1969-74, prof., 1974-80; prof. English Emory U., Atlanta, 1981-89, Asa G. Candler prof. Am. lit., 1989-90, dean Coll. Arts and Scis., 1981-90, v.p. arts and scis., 1984-90; Libbie Shearn Moody prof. English Rice U., Houston, 1990-99, interim vice provost, univ. libr., 1995-96, interim provost, 1999-2000, Bruce and Elizabeth Dunlevie prof. English, 1999—2002. Author: The Interpreted Design as a Structural Principle in American Prose, 1969, William Faulkner: His Life and Work, 1980, 82, 91, 97, French edit., 1984, Korean edito., 1999, A Cultural History of the American Novel: Henry James to William Faulkner, 1994, 96, Faulkner's Questioning Narratives: Fiction of the Major Phase, 2001, 04; editor: Twentieth-Century Interpretations of Light in August, 1969, The Norton Critical Edit. of The Sound and the Fury, 1987, 93; co-editor: The Harper American Literature, 1986, 93, 96, 97, The Columbia Literary History of the United States, 1987 (Italian edit. 1990, Chinese edit. 1994, Japanese edit. 1997); also articles and revs. Fulbright Travel fellow, 1966; Nat. Endowment for Humanities fellow, 1969-70; Am. Council Learned Socs. grantee, 1975; Fred Harris Daniels fellow, 1980 Mem. MLA, Am. Lit. Group, Am. Studies Assn., Phi Beta Kappa. Methodist. Home: 2145 Swift Houston TX 77030-1215 Office: Rice U Dept English PO Box 1892 Houston TX 77251-1892

MINTER, JERRY BURNETT, electronic component company executive, engineer; b. Ft. Worth, Oct. 31, 1913; s. Claude Joe and Roxie (Ayers) M.; m. Monica Rose Hanlon, Mar. 2, 1940; children: Claude, Mark (dec.), Byron, Claire, Maureen. BSEE, MIT, 1934. Engr. Boonton (N.J.) Radio Corp., 1935-36, Ferris Instruments Co., Boonton, 1936-39; v.p., chief engr. Measurements Corp., Boonton, 1939-53; pres. Components Corp., Denville, N.J.,

1946—. Contbr. articles to tech. jours. Pilot CAP, Morristown, N.J., 1947-50. Fellow IEEE (life, past chmn. No. N.J. sect.), Audio Engring. Soc. (past pres.), Radio Club Am. (life, pres. emeritus, past pres., Armstrong medal 1968); mem. AIAA, Am. Soc. for Metals (life), N.Y. Acad. Scis., Soc. Motion Picture and TV Engrs. (life), Internat. Soc. Photo-Optical Instrumentation Engrs., Quiet Birdmen. Achievements include 26 patents in field. Home: 48 Normandy Heights Rd Morristown NJ 07960-4613 Office: Components Corp 6 Kinsley Pl Denville NJ 07834 Office Phone: 973-627-0290. Business E-Mail: jminter@componentscorp.com.

MINTER, PHILIP CLAYTON, retired communications company executive; b. Sydney, Australia, Aug. 9, 1928; came to U.S., 1957; s. Roy Dixon and Adeline Claire (Bradly) M.; m. Mary Bashford Schettler, Jan. 24., 1959 (dec. July 1999); children: Elizabeth C., Margaret S. BSc with honours, U. Sydney, 1951; MS, U. Wyo., 1958; PhD, U. Wis., 1960. Tchr. King's Sch., Parramatta, Australia, 1951-57; mng. dir. Motivational Rsch. Assocs., Sydney, 1960-62; dir. rsch. Nat. Fund Raising Coun., Sydney, 1962-65; project dir. USDA, Ft. Collins, Colo., 1965-67; chief info. pesticides program USPHS, Atlanta, 1967-68; mgr. data bases div. Pa. Rsch. Assocs., Phila., 1968-70; pres. Ednl. Communications Inc., King of Prussia, Pa., 1970-94. Pres. Svc. Tng. Ltd., Kenilworth, Eng., 1976-88; cons. Westinghouse Learning Corp., 1972. Author: Handbook for Pesticide-Chemicals Program Coordinators, 1967. Recipient Terry Magill award Australia Soc., N.Y., 1994. Mem. Soc. Automotive Engrs., Sci. Rsch. Soc. Am., Royal Heritage Soc. (bd. dirs.), U. Wis. Alumni Assn. (bd. dirs. Delaware Valley br.), Australian/Am. C. of C. Phila. (pres.), Union League, Brit. Officers Club Phila. (pres. 1992-93), Sloane Club (London), Sigma Xi. Republican. Episcopalian. Home: 1576 Stapler Dr Yardley PA 19067-4214 E-mail: aacc@comcast.net.

MINTO, DAVID W. aeronautical engineer; b. Corpus Christi, Tex., Mar. 23, 1951; s. William and Mary Lois Minto; m. Cathy Jo Albaugh, Jun 14, 1975 (div. Aug. 1991); children: Megan, David, Jennifer; m. Barbara Lee Ebel, Nov. 9, 1991. BS in Astron. Engring., USAF Acad., Colo., 1973; MS in Aero. and Astronautics, Purdue U., West Lafayette, Ind., 1974. Commd. USAF, 1973, advanced through grades to lt. col.; flight test engr. 6585th Test Group, Holloman AFB, N.Mex., 1974—78; chief flight test engring. San Antonio Air Logistics Ctr., Tex., 1979—82; staff officer HQ Air Force Sys. Command, Andrews AFB, Md., 1982—84; exec. officer program integration divsn. Air Force Secretariat, Washington, 1984—88; program mgr. AGM-130 Air-to-Ground Weapons Program Office, Eglin AFB, Fla., 1988—90; comdr. 846th Test Squadron, Holloman AFB, 1990—96; tech. dir. Holloman High Speed Test Track, Holloman AFB, 1996—. Co-author: (book) Advanced Hypersonic Ground Test Facilities, 2002. Decorated Air Force Commendation medal with 2 oak leaf clusters, Meritorious Svc. medal with 3 oak leaf clusters; recipient Air Force Outstanding Logistics Mgr. award, Air Force Assn., 1978, Outstanding Chief Engr. award, AFMC, 2002. Mem.: AIAA (sr.; chmn. propulsion subcom., ground test tech. com. 2002—03, chmn. pub. subcom., ground test tech. com. 2000—02), Internat. Test and Evaluation Assn. Achievements include transition of AGM-130 air-to-ground missile from development into production; development of world record rocket sled test capability which achieved velocity of 6800 mph; of world's fastest maglev vehicle. Avocations: golf, hunting, fishing, poker. Office: 846th TS/CA 1521 Test Track Rd Holloman Afb NM 88330

MINTON, DWIGHT CHURCH, manufacturing executive; b. North Hills, N.Y., Dec. 17, 1934; s. Henry Miller and Helen Dwight (Church) M.; m. Marian Haven Haines, Aug. 4, 1956; children: Valerie Haven, Daphne Forsyth, Henry Brewster. BA, Yale U., 1959; MBA, Stanford U., 1961. With Church & Dwight Co., Inc., Princeton, N.J., 1961—, asst. v.p., 1964-66, v.p., 1966-67, pres., 1967-81, chief exec. officer, 1969-95, chmn., 1981—, chmn. bd., 1966—2001, chmn. emeritus, 2001—. Bd. dirs. Crane Corp. Trustee Atlanta U., 1971-88, Morehouse Coll., 1971—, Spelman Coll., 1971-80; v.p., bd. dirs. Greater Yellowstone Coalition, 1991-99. With U.S. Army, 1956-57. Mem. Chem. Mfrs. Assn. (bd. dirs. 1980-83), Grocery Mfrs. Am. (dir. 1983-87). Clubs: Racquet and Tennis, Yale, Lotos. Office: Church & Dwight Co Inc 469 N Harrison St Princeton NJ 08540-3510

MINTON, HENRY LEE, psychology educator; b. N.Y.C., Nov. 20, 1934; s. Irving and Sophie (Shapiro) M.; m. Sheila Gay Cohen, Jan. 27, 1963 (div. Dec. 1983); 1 child, Gregory. BA, NYU, 1956; MA, So. Ill. U., 1958; PhD, Pa. State U., 1962. Asst. prof. Calif. State U., L.A., 1963-65, SUNY, Albany, 1965-67; assoc. prof. Miami U., Oxford, Ohio, 1967-70; prof. psychology U. Windsor, Ont., Can., 1970-2000, prof. emeritus, 2000—. Author: Differential Psychology, 1980, Lewis M. Terman, 1988, Currents of Thought in American Social Psychology, 1991, Departing from Deviance, 2002. Grantee Social Sci. and Humanities Rsch. Coun., Ottawa, Ont., 1995-98. Fellow APA; mem. Cheiron Soc. Avocations: painting, travel. Home: 670 Camden Ct Rochester Hills MI 48307-4590 E-mail: hlminton@aol.com.

MINTON, JERRY DAVIS, lawyer, consultant, retired banker; b. Ft. Worth, Aug. 13, 1928; s. Robert Bruch and Anna Elizabeth (Davis) M.; m. Martha Drew Fields, Nov. 28, 1975; children: Marianne, Martha, John Morgan. BBA, U. Tex., Austin, 1949, JD, 1960; grad. cert., Nat. Trust Sch., Northwestern U., 1960. Of counsel Michener, Larimore, Swindle, Whitaker, Flowers et al., 1991—96; adv. dir. Kanaly Trust Co., Houston, 1992-2000. Vice chmn. 1st Nat. Bank Ft. Worth, 1982-84; chmn., CEO 1st City Nat. Bank Ft. Worth, 1986-91. Pilot USAF, 1951-55, pilot Tex. Air N.G., 1955-57; capt. USAFR Ret. Decorated D.F.C., Air medal with 3 oak leaf clusters. Mem. State Bar Tex., Tarrant County Bar Assn., Soc. Descs. of Washington's Army at Valley Forge, SAR, SCV, Mil. Order Stars and Bars, Mil. Order World Wars, D.F.C. Soc., Order Quiet Birdmen, Order of Daedalians, River Crest Country Club, Breakfast Club, Wildcatters Club, Sigma Iota Epsilon, Phi Delta Phi. Episcopalian. Home: 5404 El Dorado Dr Fort Worth TX 76107-3236

MINTON, JOHN DEAN, historian, educator; b. Cadiz, Ky., July 29, 1921; s. John Ernest and Daisy Dean (Wilson) M.; m. Betty Jo Redick, June 8, 1947; children— John Dean, James Ernest. AB in Edn, U. Ky., 1943, MA in History, 1947; PhD, Vanderbilt U., 1959. Instr. history U. Miami, Fla., 1951; tchr. Broward County Pub. Sch. Sys., U. Miami evening divsn., 1951-53; prin. Trigg County (Ky.) H.S., 1953-58; prof. history We. Ky. U., Bowling Green, 1958-86, ret., dean Grad. Coll., 1964-71, v.p. for adminstrv. affairs, 1970-79, interim pres., 1979, v.p. for student affairs, 1981-86, part-time prof., 1986-96. Author: The New Deal in Tennessee, 1932-1938, 1979; contbr. articles to profl. jours. Former mem. Gen. Bd. Discipleship, United Meth. Ch.; with Louisville Bd. Discipleship; lay spkr. Louisville Conf. Meth. Ch.; bd. dirs. Higher Edn. Found., Meth. Ch., Jesse Stuart Found. Served with USNR, 1943-46. Mem. NEA, Ky. Edn. Assn., So. Hist. Assn., Ky. Hist. Soc., Bowling Green C. of C. (bd. dirs.), Civitan Club (pres. Cadiz 1956), Phi Alpha Theta, Phi Eta Sigma, Kappa Delta Pi Home: 645 Ridgecrest Way Bowling Green KY 42104-3818

MINTON, JOSEPH PAUL, retired safety organization executive; b. Houston, Oct. 20, 1924; s. Joseph Marion and Stella (Fite) M.; m. Nancy Fettig, June 19, 1948; children: Joan M., Michael J., Jean A., Mary B., John E., Diane C. BS in Air Transp., Purdue U., 1949; Grad., U.S. Air Force Air Command and Staff Coll., 1958. Commd. 2d lt. USAF, 1944, advanced through grades to col., 1966, combat, World War II, assigments in crew, staff and command, ret., 1967; v.p. Purdue Airlines Inc., Lafayette, Ind., 1967-68, pres., CEO, 1969-71; mng. dir., chief exec. officer Saber Air Ltd., Singapore, 1971-73; sr. v.p. Brit. Caledonian Airways, N.Y.C., 1974-76; mng. dir. Nat. Transp. Safety Bd., Washington, 1977-78; exec. dir. Nat. Safety Coun., Washington, 1978-88. Decorated D.F.C. with oak leaf cluster, Air medal with 3 oak leaf clusters, 3 battle stars, Air Force Commendation medal with oak leaf cluster. Roman Catholic. Address: 1720 Lake Shore Crest Dr Apt 15 Reston VA 20190-3243

MINTON, KENT W. lawyer; b. Independence, Mo., May 16, 1955; s. Roy V. and Donabelle M. Minton; m. Karen S. MacDonald, Oct. 21, 1989; children: Kathy, Megan, Abby. BS, Ctrl. Mo. State U., 1976; postgrad., U. Tulsa, 1979-80; JD, U. Mo., Kansas City, 1982. Bar: Mo. 1982, U.S. Dist. Ct. (we. dist.) Mo. 1982, U.S. Ct. Claims 1986. Assoc. Paxton, Block et al, Independence, 1982-83, Holliday & Holliday, Kansas City, 1983-85; ptnr. Raymond, Raymond & Minton, Kansas City, 1985-96, Stewart, Cook, Constance, Stewart, Minton & Wight LLC, Independence, 1996—. Bd. dirs. Comprehensive Mental Health Svcs. Found., Independence. Contbr. chpt. to book. Mem. Mo. Bar (trust law revision subcom.), Kansas City Metro Bar Assn. (probate com.). Office: Stewart Cook Constance Stewart Minton & Wight LLC 501 W Lexington Ave Independence MO 64050-3648

MINTON, O.R. (RICK MINTON), state legislator, real estate broker; b. Orlando, Fla., Jan. 1, 1950; BS in Fruit Crops, 1972, MS in Agrl. Mgmt. and Resource Devel., 1973. Mem. Fla. Ho. of Reps., Tallahassee, 1992—. Vice-chmn. water and resource mgmt. com.; mem. transp. and econ. devel. appropriations com., health care stds. and regulatory conform com.; real estate broker. Supr. St. Lucie County Soil and Water Conservation Dist.; past pres. Fla. Assn. Conservation Dists.; mem. adv. com. St. Lucie County Infrastructure, High-Speed Rail Com. Democrat. Methodist. Avocations: fishing, hunting, golf, aviation, history. Office: State Capitol Rm 207 Tallahassee FL 32399 Also: 5353 W Atlantic Ave Ste 402A Delray Beach FL 33484-8102

MINTON, TORRI, journalist; b. San Rafael, Calif., Oct. 7, 1956; d. John and Mary. BA in Ethnic Studies, U. Calif., Berkeley, 1983; M of Journalism, Columbia U., 1984. Reporter Associated Press, San Francisco, 1984, San Francisco Chronicle, 1986—, assigning editor, 2000—. Vice chmn. San Francisco Chronicle No. Calif. Newspaper Guild, 1992, 97, 2000; rep. assembly del., 1992, 93, 94, 95, 96; instr. newswriting U. Calif., Berkeley, 1995—; instr. journalism, lead advisor Golden Gater Newspaper, San Francisco State U., 2000; instr. journalism U. San Francisco, 2000—. Community devel. vol. Oper. Crossroads Africa, Tiriki, Kenya, 1979. Mem. Phi Beta Kappa. Office: San Francisco Chronicle 901 Mission St San Francisco CA 94103-2905 E-mail: tminton@sfchronicle.com.

MINTON, YVONNE FAY, mezzo-soprano; b. Sydney, Australia; d. Robert Thomas and Alice Violet M.; m. William Barclay, Aug. 24, 1965; children— Malcolm Alexander, Alison Elizabeth. Ed., Sydney Conservatorium of Music, 1960-61. Mezzo-soprano with all maj. orchs. in, Australia, 1958-61; moved to, London, 1961, joined, Royal Opera House, Covent Garden, 1965-70, guest artist, Cologne (Germany) Opera, 1969—, U.S. debut as Octavian in Der Rosenkavalier, 1970; appeared, with Lyric Opera, Chgo., 1970, Met. Opera, N.Y.C., 1973, San Francisco Opera, 1974, Paris Opera, 1974, Bayreuth, 1974, Salzburg, 1978; sings regularly with maj. symphony orchs. throughout world, 1968—; recs. include The Knot Garden, 1970, Cosi Fan Tutte, 1971, Lulu, 1979; maj. vocal works include Mahler songs with, Chgo. Symphony. Comdr. Order Brit. Empire, 1980 Hon. mem. Royal Acad. Music. Office: care Ingpen & Williams 7 St Georges Ct 131 Putney Bridge Rd London SW15 2PA England

MINTZ, ALBERT, lawyer; b. New Orleans, Oct. 19, 1929; s. Morris and Goldie (Goldblum) M.; m. Linda Barnett, Dec. 19, 1954; children— John Morris, Margaret Anne. BBA, Tulane U., 1948, JD, 1951. Bar: La. 1951; cert. tax specialist, estate and adminstrn. specialist. Since practiced in, New Orleans; ptnr. Montgomery, Barnett, Brown, Read, Hammond & Mintz, Hurwitz-Mintz Realty Cos., New Orleans. Bd. dirs. Strauss Distbrs., Avrico, Inc. Mem. editl. bd. Tulane Law Rev. Adv. bd. Law Sch. Tulane U.; chmn., dir. adv. bd. Tulane Summer Lyric Theater; bd. dirs. Tulane Ctr. Stage Talent and Shakespearean Theatre; bd. dirs. Jewish Cmty. Ctr., New Orleans, 1965-72, Jewish Fedn., 1968-, Home for Jewish Aged, 1968-71, Jewish Family Svc., New Orleans, 1968-72; trustee, bd. mgrs. Touro Infirmary Hosp. and Found. chosen as the 1999 recipient of the Judah Touro Society Awd. for his outstanding contribution to the hosp. and its foundation; trustee Jewish Endowment Found.; charter mem. La. Hist. Assn.; bd. trustees, mem. Temple Sinai. Recipient Tulane Outstanding Alumnus award, Class of 1951, 2001, Outstanding Vol. award Tulane U., 2003, Role Model award Young Leadership Coun., 2004. Mem. ABA, La. Bar Assn. (lectr., publ. on corp., tax, real estate law), New Orleans Bar Assn. (exec. com. 1971-74), Am. Law Inst., U.S. Hist. Assn., New Orleans C. of C. (chmn. com. civic affairs and state legis. 1968-69), City Energy Club, Tulane Bus. Sch. Emeritus Club (chmn. exec. com., pres. 2004), Phi Delta Phi, Omicron Delta Kappa, Zeta Beta Tau. Jewish. Home: 1915 State St New Orleans LA 70118-6251 Office: 3200 Energy Ctr 1100 Poydras St New Orleans LA 70163-1101 Office Phone: 504-585-7635. E-mail: amintz@monbar.com.

MINTZ, BETH ANN, sociology educator; b. Norwich, Conn., Dec. 7, 1948; d. Isador B. and Ruth C. (Ringel) M.; 1 child, Rebecca Ilene. BA, CCNY, 1970; MA in Sociology, SUNY, Stony Brook, 1974, PhD in Sociology, 1978. Instr. sociology SUNY, 1975—77; asst. prof. sociology U. Vt., Burlington, 1977—82, assoc. prof., 1982—89, chair women's studies, 1987—89, prof. sociology, 1989—, chair, dept. sociology, 1996—2004. Author: (with Michael Schwartz) The Power Structure of American Business, 1985; contbr. articles and reports to profl. jours. Mem. task force gender bias in legal sys. Supreme Ct. of Vt. Vt. Bar Assn., 1989—91; mem. human rights task force City of Burlington, 1992; bd. dirs. Green Mountain Fund for Popular Struggle, 1993—2003, Vt. Consumer Campaign for Health, Domestic Abuse Intervention Project, No. New England Tradeswomen Assn., 2000—04. Faculty scholar Harvard U., 1984-85; MIT fellow, 1984-85. Mem.: Ea. Sociol. Soc., Sociologists for Women in Soc., Am. Sociol. Assn. (coun. 1991—93, com. on coms. 1992—93, chmn. polit. sociol. sect. 1995—96, editl. bd., Social Problems 1997—). Office: U Vt Sociology Dept 31 S Prospect St Burlington VT 05405-1704 Office Phone: 802-656-2163.

MINTZ, DANIEL HARVEY, endocrinologist, educator, academic administrator; b. N.Y.C., Sept. 16, 1930; s. Jacob A. and Fanny Mintz; m. Dawn E. Hynes, Jan. 15, 1961 (dec.); children: David, Denise, Debra; m. Marge Kleiman, Nov. 30, 1996. BS cum laude, St. Bonaventure Coll., 1951; MD, N.Y. Med. Coll., 1956. Diplomate Am. Bd. Internal Medicine. Intern Henry Ford Hosp., Detroit, 1956-57; resident Georgetown med. div. D.C. Gen. Hosp., Washington, 1957-59, Georgetown U. Hosp., Washington, 1958-59; fellow medicine Nat. Inst. Arthritis and Metabolic Diseases, 1959-60, Am. Diabetes Assn., 1960-61; practice medicine, specializing in diabetes and endocrinology U. Miami. (Fla.) Sch. Medicine, prof. medicine, 1969—, Mary Lou Held prof. medicine, 1981-96, chief div. endocrinology and metabolism, dept. medicine, 1969-80, Sci. dir. Diabetes Research Inst., 1980-96, sci. dir. emeritus, 1996—; asst. prof. medicine Georgetown U. Sch. Medicine, 1963-64; assoc. prof. medicine U. Pitts. Sch. Medicine, 1964-69; chief svc. Georgetown U. Med. div. D.C. Gen. Hosp., Washington, 1963-64; chief medicine Magee-Women's Hosp., Pitts., 1964-69. Guest prof. U. Geneva, 1976—77. Contbr. articles to profl. jours. Fellow: ACP; mem.: Am. Assn. Physicians, So. Soc. Clin. Investigation, Ctrl. Soc. Clin. Investigation, Am. Soc. Clin. Investigation, Am. Fedn. Clin. Rsch., Am. Diabetes Assn., Endocrine Soc. Office: U Miami Diabetes Rsch Inst PO Box 016960 R-77 Miami FL 33101-6960

MINTZ, JACK MAURICE, think tank executive, economics educator; b. Edmonton, Alta., Can., Mar. 6, 1951; s. David Benjamin and Clara (Abramovich) M.; m. Eleanor Janice Schwartz, Aug. 31, 1975; children: Avi Ilan, Gaela Lana. B.A. with honors, U. Alta., Edmonton, 1973; M.A., Queen's U., Kingston, Ont., Can., 1974; Ph.D., U. Essex, Colchester, Eng., 1980. Cons. Econ. Council Can., Ottawa, Ont., 1974-75; assoc. prof. econs. Queen's U., Kingston, 1978-89; prof. J.L. Rotman Sch. Mgmt., U. Toronto, 1989-; pres., CEO, C.D. Howe Inst.; bd. dirs. Brascan, Ont. Financing Authority, CHC Ltd. Author: Most Favored Nation, 2001 (Donner prize, Davis prize); contbr. articles to profl. jours. Mem. Can. Jewish Congress, 1982-; trustee Hillel Acad. Sch., Ottawa, 1985-; pres. Kingston Jewish Cmty. Coun., 1982-84; bd. dirs. Royal Ont. Mus. Found. Commonwealth fellow Eng., 1975-78; postdoctoral fellow Social Sci. and Humanities Rsch. Coun. Can., 1981-82, Inst. Mgmt., 1984. Mem. Can. Econs. Assn., Am. Econs. Assn., Am. Fin. Assn. Lodge: B'nai B'rith Youth Orgn. (internat. pres. 1969-70, exec. mem. 1983-84). Avocations: running, squash. Office: CD Howe Inst 125 Adelaide St E M5C 1L7 Toronto ON Canada

MINTZ, JOEL ALAN, law educator; b. N.Y.C., July 24, 1949; s. Samuel Isaiah and Eleanor (Streichler) M.; m. Meri-Jane Rochelson, Aug. 25, 1975; children: Daniel Rochelson, Robert Eli. BA, Columbia U., 1970, LLM, 1982, JSD, 1989; JD, NYU, 1974. Bar: N.Y. 1975, U.S. Dist. Ct. (so. and ea. dists.) N.Y. 1982, U.S. Ct. Appeals (2d cir.) 1982. Atty. enforcement div. EPA, Chgo., 1975-76, chief atty. case devel. unit, 1977-78, policy advisor to regional adminstr., 1979; sr. litigation atty. Office Enforcement, EPA, Washington, 1980-81; asst. prof. environ. law Nova U. Law Ctr., Ft. Lauderdale, Fla., 1982-85, assoc. prof., 1985-87, prof., 1987—. Author: State and Local Government Environmental Liability, 1994, Enforcement At the EPA: High Stakes, 1995; author: (with others) Environmental Law, 4th edit., 2000, State and Local Taxation and Finance In A Nutshell, 2nd edit., 2000; contbr. articles to legal jours. and treatises. Mem. ABA, Environ. Law Inst. Assocs., Fla. Bar (assoc.), Internat. Coun. Environ. Law, Internat. Union for Conservation of Nature (commn. on environ. law), Assn. Am. Law Schs. (exec. com., state and local govt. law sect.), Ctr. for Progressive Regulation (scholar), Phi Alpha Delta. Avocations: reading, fitness walking, canoeing. Home: 2060 NE 209th St Miami FL 33179-1628 Office: Nova Southeastern U Law Ctr 3305 College Ave Fort Lauderdale FL 33314-7721 Office Phone: 954-262-6160. Business E-Mail: mintzj@nsu.law.nova.edu.

MINTZ, M. J. lawyer; b. Phila., Oct. 29, 1940; s. Arthur and Lillian (Altenberg) Mintz; m. Judith E. Held; children: Robert A., Christine L. BS, Temple U., 1961, JD, 1968. CPA Pa., D.C.; bar: D.C. Atty. adv. to judge U.S. Tax Ct., Washington, 1968-70; asst. gen. counsel Cost of Living Coun. Exec. Office of Pres., Washington, 1971-73; ptnr. Dickstein, Shapiro & Morin, Washington, 1973—. Adj. prof. George Mason U. Law Sch., Va., 1974—78; advisor U.S. Sec. Labor, Employee Ret. Income Security Act, 1974, Adv. Coun., Washington, 1982—85. Contbr. articles to profl. jours. Apptd. by Pres. Ronald Reagan to adv. com. Pension Benefit Guaranty Corp., 1987, reapptd. and designated chmn. by Pres. George Bush; apptd. by Gov. George Allen of Va. Bd. Va. Pub. Bldg. Authority, 1996—2001, reapptd. by Gov. James Gilmore, 2001—; Rep. candidate Fairfax County Bd. Suprs., 1971. Fellow: Nat. Assn. Watch & Cook Collectors (star), Freeman of the Worshipful Co. of Clockmakers (London); mem.: AICPA, ABA, Antiquarian Horological Soc. (London), Naval Club (London), Chappaquiddick Beach Club, Met. Club (Washington), Belle Haven Country Club, Cosmos Club. Avocation: antiquarian horologist.

MINTZ, MARSHALL GARY, lawyer; b. Detroit, May 28, 1947; BA, UCLA, 1968, JD, 1971. Bar: Calif. 1972. Law clk. appellate dept L.A. County Superior Ct., 1971-72; ptnr. Kelly Lytton Mintz & Vann, LLP, L.A., Calif., 1995-2001; of counsel Sidley & Bell LLP, L.A., 2001—03; mem. Mintz & Werner, L.A., 2003—. Moderator, panelist Calif. Continuing Edn. of Bar, 1980—; mem. arbitration adminstrv. com. L.A. County Superior Ct., 1979, mem. 1984 Olympics spl. settlement panel; mem. arbitration panel L.A. Superior Ct., 1999—. Mem. ABA, State Bar Calif., L.A. County Bar Assn. (arbitrator arbitration and client rels. com. 1978-99), Assn. Bus. Trial Lawyers (bd. govs. 1976-77, program chmn. 1976). Office: 1801 Century Park E Ste 2400 Los Angeles CA 90067-2326 Office Phone: 310-556-9692. E-mail: mgmintz@earthlink.net.

MINTZ, MAX M. historian; b. London, Aug. 21, 1919; came to U.S., 1920; s. Samuel and Janie (Stein) M.; widowed. BSS, CCNY, N.Y.C., 1941; MA, NYU, N.Y.C., 1947, PhD, 1957. Tchg. asst. NYU, N.Y.C., 1946-48; prof. history State U. N.Y., Plattsburgh, 1948-51; tool engr. Internat. Bus. Machines, Poughkeepsie, N.Y., 1951-63; from asst. prof. to prof. history So. Conn. State U., New Haven, 1963-85, prof. emeritus history, 1985—. Author: Gouverneur Morris, 1970, Generals of Saratoga, 1990, Seeds of Empire, 1999. With U.S. Army, 1944—46, ETO. Grantee NEH, 1983, Am. Philosophical Soc., 1983; John Adams fellow U. London, 1996; Eccles Ctr. fellow Brit. Libr., 1996. Mem. Orgn. Am. Historians. Democrat. Unitarian Universalist. Avocations: woodworking, walking. Home: 104 Norman Rd Hamden CT 06514 Office: So Conn State U 501 Crescent St Hamden CT 06515

MINTZ, MORTON ABNER, author, former newspaper reporter; b. Ann Arbor, Mich., Jan. 26, 1922; s. William and Sarah (Solomon) M.; m. Anita Inez Franz, Aug. 30, 1946; children— Margaret Ruth, Elizabeth Diane (dec.), Roberta Joan, Daniel Robert. AB in Econs, U. Mich., 1943. Reporter St. Louis Star-Times, 1946-50; reporter, asst. city editor St. Louis Globe-Democrat, 1951-58; reporter Washington Post, 1958-88. Former chair Fund for Investigative Journalism. Author: The Therapeutic Nightmare, 1965, By Prescription Only, 1967, The Pill: An Alarming Report, 1969, At Any Cost: Corporate Greed, Women, and the Dalkon Shield, 1985, (with Jerry S. Cohen) America, Inc.: Who Owns and Operates the United States, 1971, Power, Inc.; Public and Private Rulers and How to Make Them Accountable, 1976, (with others) In the Name of Profit: Profiles in Corporate Irresponsiblity, 1972, More Bucks, Less Bang: How the Pentagon Buys Ineffective Weapons, 1983. Recipient Heywood Broun, Raymond Clapper, George Polk awards for journalism, 1962, A.J. Liebling award, 1974, Worth Bingham Meml. award, 1976, Columbia Journalism award, 1983, Hugh M. Hefner First Amendment award for lifetime achievement, 1996. Mem.: Com. Concerned Journalists. E-mail: mintzm@earthlink.net.

MINTZ, NORMAN NELSON, investment banker, educator; b. N.Y.C., Sept. 18, 1934; s. Alexander and Rebecca (Nelson) M.; m. Marcia Lynn Belford, Aug. 27, 1960; children: Geoffrey Belford, Douglas Nelson. AB, Bucknell U., 1955; PhD, NYU, 1966. Asst. gen. mgr. Ross Products Inc., N.Y.C., 1957-59; media analyst Benton & Bowles Inc., N.Y.C., 1960; asst. prof. fin. Syracuse (N.Y.) U., 1965-69; asst. prof. econs. Columbia U., N.Y.C., 1968-72, assoc. dean Grad. Sch. Arts and Scis., 1972-77, dep. provost, 1977-80, acting provost, 1978-79, sr. v.p., 1980-82, exec. v.p. for acad. affairs, 1982-89, exec. v.p., ret., 1990—; mng. dir. Loeb Ptnrs. Corp., 1990—. Economist U.S.-P.R. Commn. on Status of P.R., 1965-66; bd. dirs. Loeb Holding Corp., Loeb Ptnrs. Corp., Sr. Network, Inc., Comm. Mgmt. Sys., Inc., Exxel/Atmos, Inc., Evare, L.L.C., Intersections, Inc., Loeb Arbitrage Fund. Author: Monetary Union and Economic Integration, 1970; contbr. articles to profl. jours. Dir. Citizens Budget Commn., Conf. on Jewish Social Studies, 1975—94, N.Y.C. Coun. on Econ. Edn., 1993—. 1st lt. Signal Corps. U.S. Army, 1955—57. Earhart Found. fellow, 1963-65. Mem. Am. Econ. Assn., Am. Fin. Assn., Royal Econ. Soc., India House Club, Phi Beta Kappa, Omicron Delta Epsilon. Office: care Loeb Ptnrs 61 Broadway New York NY 10006-2701 Office Phone: 212-483-7041. E-mail: nmintz@loebpartners.com.

MINTZ, SAMUEL ISAIAH, English language educator, writer; b. N.Y.C., Nov. 20, 1923; Nathan and Anna (Sheinkman) M.; m. Eleanor Streichler, Mar. 2, 1947; children: Joel Alan, Jonathan. BA, Bklyn. Coll., 1948; MA, Columbia U., 1949, PhD, 1958. Prof. City Coll. N.Y., N.Y.C., 1948-86, prof. doctoral faculty, 1965-86, prof. emeritus, 1986—, CUNY Grad. Ctr., N.Y.C., 1986—. English faculty Cambridge U., Eng., 1964-65; vis. prof. Columbia U., N.Y.C., 1969-70, Barnard Coll., N.Y.C., 1987-89; vis. fellow Wolfson Coll. Oxford U., 1973. Author: The Hunting of Leviathan, 1962, 2d edit., 1996; editor: From Smollett to Henry James, 1980; founder, editor History Ideas Newsletter, N.Y.C., 1954-60; contbr. articles to profl. jours. With Army Air Force, 1943-46. Fulbright fellow Cambridge U., 1956-57, rsch. scholar, 1964-65, Guggenheim fellow, 1964. Office: City U NY Grad Sch 365 5th Ave New York NY 10016-4309

MINTZ, SHLOMO, conductor, violist; b. Moscow, Oct. 30, 1957; came to U.S., 1974; s. Abraham and Eve (Labko) M.; m. Corina Ciacci; children: Eliav David, Alexander. Studied with Ilona Feher; Diploma, Juilliard Sch. Music, 1979. Judge internat. Tchaikovsky Competition, Moscow, 1990; juror queen Elisabeth Internat. Music Competition, Brussels, 1993. Concerto debut with Israel Philharm.; violin solo recordings include Violin Concertos by Mendelssohn and Bruch (Grand prix du Disque Diapason d'or), 1981, Complete Sonatas and Partitas for Solo Violin by J.S. Bach, The Miraculous Mandarin-Two Portraits (with Abbado/Chicago Symphony Orchestra) by Bartok, Compositions and Arrangements (with Clifford Benson, piano) by Kreisler, Violin Concerto; also Bruch: Violin Concerto Number 1 (with Abbado/Chgo. Symphony Orchestra) by Mendelssohn, Twenty-Four Caprices by Paganini, Two Violin Concertos (with Abbado/London Symphony Orchestra) by

Prokofiev, The Four Seasons (with Stern, Perlman, Mehta) by Vivaldi, Vivaldi violin concertos, Vols. I & II (with Israel Chamber Orch.), 1992, Collection String Symphonies, Vol. III to X, (with Israel Chamber Orch., 1992, Violin and Viola Sonatas by Chostakovich (with V. Postnikova); apptd. music advisor, chief condr., soloist Israel Chamber Orch., 1989-93; artistic advisor, prin. guest condr. Limburg Symphony Orch., Maastricht, The Netherlands, 1994; condr. London Symphony Orch., Berlin Radio Symphony, Balt. Symphony, Detroit Symphony, Rotterdam Philharm.; soloist with Montreal Symphony, Nat. Symphony, Washington, Carnegie Hall, Tonhalle Orch. of Zurich, Spanish Nat. Orch., Israel Philharm., others. Recipient Premio Accademia Musicale, Chigiana Siena, Italy, 1984. Uses Zahn violin made by Stradivarius, and a Carlo-Guiseppe Testrove viola. Office: ICM Artists Inc 40 W 57th St Fl 16 New York NY 10019-4098

MINTZ, SUSAN ASHINOFF, apparel manufacturing company executive; b. N.Y.C., Dec. 7, 1949; d. Lawrence Lloyd and Thelma B. Ashinoff; m. Robert Mintz; children: Geoffrey, Tyler. BA, Finch Coll., 1971; MPA, NYU, 1977. Menswear advt. asst. New Yorker Mag., N.Y.C., 1971-72; assoc. Staub Warmbold & Assocs., Inc., exec. search co., N.Y.C., 1972-80; exec. v.p. Muhammad Ali Sportswear, Ltd., N.Y.C., 1980-81; pres. Forum Sportswear, Ltd., N.Y.C. and Portsmouth, Va., 1981—; group v.p., bd. dirs. Coronet Group, Portsmouth, 1985—. Trustee Dean Jr. Coll. Named to Outstanding Young Women in Am., U.S. Jaycees, 1980. Mem.: Beacon Hill Club. Office: 2615 Elmhurst Ln Portsmouth VA 23701-2736

MINTZ, SUZANNE, association executive; b. Feb. 1946; m. Steven Mintz. BA, Queens Coll., City U. NY; MS, U. Md. Architect; pres., co-founder Nat. Family Caregivers Assn., Wash., DC, 1993—. Bd. dirs. Nat. Patient Safety Found.; adv. bd. Easter Seals, Nat. Assn. Hosp. Hospitality Houses. Author: Love, Honor and Value: A Family Caregiver Speaks Out About the Choices and Challenges of Caregiving, 2002; writer about caregiver issues. Recipient Lilly Welcome Back award for lifetime achievement, 2004. Achievements include has testified before Congress about caregiver issues. Office: Nat Family Caregivers Assn 10400 Conn Ave #500 Kensington MD 20895-3944 Office Phone: 800-896-3650. Office Fax: 301-942-2302.

MINTZ, WALTER, investment company executive; b. Vienna, Feb. 23, 1929; came to U.S., 1938, naturalized, 1945; s. Maximilian and Ilse (Schueller) M.; m. Sandra Jane Earl, Aug. 27, 1971. BA, Reed Coll., 1950; postgrad. in econs, Columbia, 1950—51, postgrad. in econs, 1953—54. Asso. editor Barrons mag., 1951-53, 54-56; with Shearson Hammill Co., 1956-70, dir. research, 1962-69, exec. v.p. charge investment div., 1965-70; partner Cumberland Assocs., investment mgmt., 1970-85; spl. ltd. ptnr. Cumberland Ptnrs., investment ptnrship., 1982—. Bd. dirs. Merrill Lynch Phoenix Fund, Merrill Lynch Fed. Securities Trust, 1982—2001. Trustee Reed Coll., 1971—2001, vice chmn. bd. trustees, 1991—98, chmn. bd. trustees, 1998—2002; trustee Manhattan Inst., 1990—2002, vice chmn., 1994—; bd. dirs. Citizens Union Found. of N.Y.C., 1985—. Mem. N.Y. Soc. Security Analysts (bd. dirs. 1969-75) Home: 2 E 88th St New York NY 10128-0555 Office: Cumberland Assocs Rm 3803 1114 Avenue Of The Americas New York NY 10036-7775

MINTZER, DAVID, physics educator; b. N.Y.C., May 4, 1926; s. Herman and Anna (Katz) M.; m. Justine Nancy Klein, June 26, 1949; children: Elizabeth Amy, Robert Andrew. BS in Physics, Mass. Inst. Tech., 1945, PhD, 1949. Asst. prof. physics Brown U., 1949-55; research asso. Yale U., 1955-56, assoc. prof., dir. lab. marine physics, 1956-62; prof. mech. engring. Northwestern U., Evanston, 1962-91, prof. physics and astronomy, 1968-91, prof. emeritus mech. engring., prof emeritus physics and astronomy, 1991—; assoc. dean McCormick Sch. Engring. and Applied Sci., 1970-73, acting dean, 1971-72, v.p. for rsch., dean sci., 1973-86, spl. asst. to pres., 1986-87, prof. emeritus mech. engring., physics and astronomy, 1991—. Mem. mine adv. com. Nat. Acad. Sci.-NRC, 1963-73; mem. Ill. Gov.'s Commn. on Sci. and Tech., 1987-88; mem. adv. bd. Applied Rsch. Lab. Pa. State U., 1976-82, chmn., 1980-81. Contbr. numerous chpts. to books, papers to profl. publs. Trustee EDUCOM interuniv. communications coun., 1975-83, vice chmn., 1977-78, chmn., 1978-81; trustee Adler Planetarium, 1976-92, life trustee, 1992—; bd. dirs. Rsch. Park, Inc., Evanston, 1986-92, treas., 1986-91; trustee Ill. Math. and Sci. Acad., 1986-97, mem. exec. com., 1989-95, chmn. alliance coun., 1991-93; chmn. bd. dirs. Heartland Venture Capital Network, Inc., 1987-90; bd. dirs. Tech. Innovation Ctr., Inc., 1990-92, treas., 1990-92. Fellow Am. Phys. Soc., Acoustical Soc. Am.; mem. ASME, Am. Astron. Soc., Sigma Xi, Tau Beta Pi, Pi Tau Sigma. Achievements include research on underwater acoustics and rarefied gas dynamics. Office: 990 N Lake Shore Dr #16A Chicago IL 60611-1343 E-mail: dmin@northwestern.edu.

MINTZER, JACOBO E. physician, researcher; b. Argentina; m. Olga Brawman; children: Jonathan, Adam. BA, Latin Am. Rabbinical Sem., Buenos Aires, 1978; MD, Buenos Aires U., 1978. Diplomate Am. Bd. Psychiatry & Neurology, Am. Bd. Gen. Psychiatry, Israel Bd. Psychiatry & Neurology. Intern, resident Hadassah-Hebrew U., Jerusalem, 1979-85; fellow in geriatric psychiatry UCLA, 1985-87; asst. prof. U. Miami (Fla.) Sch. Medicine, 1987-91; assoc. prof. Med. U. S.C., Charleston, 1991-98, prof., 1998—; staff physician Ralph H. Johnson VA Med. Ctr.; prof. physiology and neuroscience Med. U. S.C., 2003. Dir. geriatric psychiatry and fellowship programs Med. U. S.C., Charleston, 1991—, Inst. Rsch. Minority Tng. on Mental Health and Aging; co-dir. Alzheimer's Rsch. & Clin. Program, 1997—; mem. clin. ctrs. and spl. projects rev. com. NIMH, 1997-99. Contbr. articles to profl. jours. Scholar geriatric psychiatry edn. scholar, Med. U. S.C. Found. Mem.: Am. Assn. Geriatric Psychiatrists, Am. Assn. Geriatric Psychiatry, Am. Psychiatric Assn. (chairperson com. ethnic minority elderly 1996—99, coun. on aging 2001). Jewish. Office: Med U SC Alzheimer's Rsch and Clin Programs 5900 Core Rd Ste 203 North Charleston SC 29406-6076 E-mail: mintzerj@musc.edu.

MINTZ-HITTNER, HELEN ANN, physician, researcher; b. Houston, Aug. 12, 1944; d. Bert and Jeanette (Haydis) Mintz; m. David Hittner, Sept. 8, 1968 (div. May 11, 1989); children: Susan Michelle Hittner children: Miriam Annette Hittner Tondera, George Jacob Hittner. BA, Rice U., Houston, 1965; MD, Baylor Coll. of Medicine, Houston, 1969. Lic. Tex. Bd. of Med. Examiners, 1969. Pediat. intern Baylor Affiliated Hosps., Houston, 1969—70, ophthalmology resident, 1970—73; pediatric ophthalmology fellow Tex. Children's Hosp., Houston, 1973—74; pediatric ophthalmologist pvt. practice, Houston, 1974—95; Alfred W. Lasher III prof. pediat. ophthalmology U. of Tex. Houston Med. Sch., 1995—. Author: several rsch. reports and jour. articles. Fellow: Am. Acad. of Ophthalmology (Honor award 1975—86); mem.: N.Y. Acad. of Medicine, N.Y. Acad. of Sci., Ciba Found., Soc. of Heed Fellows (life), Assn. for Rsch. in Vision and Ophthalmology, Am. Assn. for Pediat. Ophthalmology and Strabismus, Phi Beta Kappa (life), Alpha Omega Alpha (life). Liberal. Jewish. Achievements include discovery of Primary etiology of retinopathy of prematurity; research in Genetic linkage of aniridia to chromosome 11p13 (PAX6); Genetic identification of anterior segment dysgenesis on chromosome 10q25 (PITX3); Genetic identification of anterior segment dysgenesis on chromosome 1p32 (FOXE3); Genetic identification of anterior segment dysgenesis on chromosome 20p11.2 (VSX1). Home: 2400 N Braeswood Blvd #125 Houston TX 77030-4357 Office: U of Tex-Houston Med Sch 6410 Fannin St #920 Houston TX 77030-5204 Office Phone: 713-704-2345. Personal E-mail: mintzhittner@aol.com. Business E-Mail: helen.a.mintz-hittner@uth.tmc.edu.

MINUDRI, REGINA URSULA, librarian, consultant; b. San Francisco, May 9, 1937; d. John C. and Molly (Halter) M. BA, San Francisco Coll. for Women, 1958; MLS, U. Calif., Berkeley, 1959. Reference libr. Menlo Park (Calif.) Pub. Libr., 1959-62; regional libr. Santa Clara County (Calif.) Libr., 1962-68; project coord. Fed. Young Adult Libr. Svcs. Project, Mountain View, Calif., 1968-71; dir. profl. svcs. Alameda County (Calif.) Libr., 1971, asst. county libr., 1972-77; libr. dir. Berkeley Pub. Libr., 1977-94; city libr. San Francisco Pub. Libr., 1997-2000. Lectr. U. San Francisco, 1970-72, U. Calif., Berkeley, 1977-81, 91-93, San Jose State U., 1994-97; cons., 1975-90; mem. adv. bd. Miles Cutter Ednl., 1992-98. Author: Getting It Together, A Young Adult Bibliography, 1970; contbr. articles to publs. including Sch. Libr. Jour., Wilson Libr. Bull. Bd. dirs. No. Calif. ACLU, 1994-96, Cmty. Memory, 1989-91, Berkeley Pub. Libr. Found., 1996-99; bd. dirs. Berkeley Cmty. Fund, 1995-99, chair youth com., 1994-96; mem. bd. mgrs. ctrl. br. Berkeley YMCA, 1988-93. Recipient proclamation Mayor of Berkeley, 1985, 86, 94, Citation of Merit, Calif. State Assembly, 1994; named Woman of Yr., Alameda County North chpt. Nat. Women's Polit. Caucus, 1985, Outstanding Alumna, U. Calif. Sch. Libr. and Info. Scis., Berkeley, 1987, Lifetime Achievement award Berkeley Cmty. Fund, 2001. Mem. ALA (pres. 1986-87, exec. bd. 1980-89, coun. 1979-88, 90-94, Grolier award 1974), Calif. Libr. Assn. (pres. 1981, coun. 1965-69, 79-82), LWV (dir. Berkeley chpt. 1980-81, v.p. comm. svcs. 1995-97). Office: Reality Mgmt 836 The Alameda Berkeley CA 94707-1916

MINUTA, JOSEPH J. architect; s. Vincent and Jean (McHenry-Early) Minuta; m. Laurie Jean Solfaro; 1 child, Isabella Carmelina. A in Applied Sci., Orange County C.C., Middletown, N.Y., 1989—92; BArch with Honors, Pratt Inst., 1992—96. Ncarb, Wash. DC, 2002, Canadian Architectural Certification Board, Can., 2002. Draftsman Cuomo Engring. PC, Stewart Internat. Airport, NY, 1990—92; engring. technician Tectonic Engring. Consultants, PC, Highland Mills, NY, 1993—94; design and drafting mgr. CONTINENTAL CABLEVISION (now Media One), Peekskill, NY, 1994—96; cadd mgr./arch. intern DeGraw & DeHaan Architects, Middletown, NY, 1996—98; comml. constrn. adminstr. Denker Cackovic Architects PC, Nyack, NY, 1998—99; archtl. project mgr. Carter & Burgess, Inc., Hartford, Conn., 1991—2001; archtl. services mgr. BPplc/Castrol N.Am., Inc., Wayne, NJ, 2001—03; pres. & dir. Bldg. Archtl. Services Entity, Inc. a subs. of BP PLC, Wayne, NJ, 2001—03; prin. Joseph J. Minuta Architecture, New Windsor, NY, 2001—. Bd. mem. Town of New Windsor Zoning Bd. of Appeals, New Windsor, NY, 2003—; adj. instr. Orange County C.C., Middletown, NY, 2004—. Pub., Architecture - Industry Specific Services Means the Nuances are Understood, 2002, Designing a Lube/Wash Facility, 2002, The Installed Marketer, 2002, abstract illustration, Mapping the Mist, 1995, computer aided design, Reinforced Concrete Design Program, 1994, propsal, JFK Airport, 1994, Fulton Landing, 1993, exhibitions include Mus. of Nat. History, 1992, prin. works include display and archives, Pratt Inst., 1992—96. Bd. mem. NY State Coun. on the Arts, Monroe, NY, 2001—02, McQuade Childerens Svcs., New Windsor, NY, 2004—; committeeman New Windsor Rep. Com., New Windsor, NY, 2002—04. Mem.: AIA, Orange County C. of C., Builders Assn. Hudson Valley, Internat. Conf. Bldg. Officials, Nat. Fire Protection Agy., PADI Diving Soc. Roman Catholic. Avocation: scuba diving. Office: Joseph J Minuta Architect 345 Windsor Hwy New Windsor NY 12553 Office Phone: 845-565-0055. Personal E-mail: jjmarchitect@hvc.rr.com. E-mail: jjmarchitect@hvc.rr.com.

MINZNER, DEAN FREDERICK, aviation company executive; b. July 20, 1945; s. Frederick Louis and Winifred (Hughes) M. BA, Franklin and Marshall Coll., 1967; MBA, Columbia U., 1972. Dist. exec. Greater N.Y. couns. Boy Scouts Am., N.Y.C., 1972-76; sales exec. Coast Avia, Long Beach, Calif., 1976-78, Performance Aircraft, Inc., Hayward, Calif., 1978; owner, pres. Western Aviation Consultants, Inc., Hayward, 1978-82, Cal-Pacific Assocs., Inc., Hayward, 1979—, Cal-Pacific Enterprises, Hayward, 1982—. Mem. Assn. MBA Execs., Columbia U. Grad. Sch. Bus. Alumni Assn., Aircraft Owners and Pilots Assn. Office: PO Box 6206 Hayward CA 94540-6206 E-mail: dminz@hotmail.com.

MINZNER, PAMELA BURGY, state supreme court justice; b. Meridian, Miss., Nov. 19, 1943; BA cum laude, Miami U., 1965; LLB, Harvard U., 1968. Bar: Mass. 1968, N.Mex. 1972. Pvt. practice, Mass., 1968—71, Albuquerque, 1971—73; adj. prof. law U. N.Mex., Albuquerque, 1972—73, asst. prof., 1973—77, assoc. prof., 1977—80, prof. law, 1980—84; judge N.Mex. Ct. Appeals, Albuquerque, 1984—94, chief judge, 1993—94; justice N.Mex. Supreme Ct., Santa Fe, 1994—, chief justice, 1999—2001. Mem. faculty Inst. Preparativo Legal U., N.Mex. Sch. Law, 1975, 79; participant NEH Summer Seminars for Law Tchrs. Stanford Law Sch., 1982, U. Chgo. Law Sch., 1978. Author (with Robert T. Laurence): A Student's Guide to Estates in Land and Future Interests: Text, Examples, Problems & Answers, 1981, 2d edit., 1993. Mem.: ABA, State Bar N.Mex. (co-editor newsletter 1979—83, bd. dirs. 1978—79, 1983—84, sect. on women's legal rights and obligations), Gamma Phi Beta. Democrat. Avocations: reading, bridge, movies. Office: Supreme Ct Bldg 237 Don Gaspar Ave Santa Fe NM 87501-2178

MIOTKE, DAVID ROY, music educator; b. Appleton, Wis., Nov. 30, 1956; s. George Charles and Mary Mae Miotke; m. Sherril Grace Miotke, Oct. 23, 1982. BS, Carroll Coll., 1979. Band dir., music tchr. Reedsburg (Wis.) Sch. Dist., 1979—. Instrumental dir. Choraliers Show Choir, Reedsburg, 1981—2004; tech. coord. Cal Ctr., Reedsburg, 1999—. Composer: (full band commn.) Shiva Dance, 1989, March for Bosiphus, 1989. Hand bell choir dir. St. John Luth. Ch., Reedsburg, 1992—. Recipient Woodson Outstanding Tchr. award, Reedsburg Edn. Found., 2002. Mem.: Wis. Youth Band Dirs. Assn. (pres.), Music Educators Nat. Conf. Avocation: working puzzles, writing music, painting. Office: Webb Mid Sch 707 N Webb Ave Reedsburg WI 53959 Office Phone: 608-524-2328. E-mail: david.miotke@verizon.net.

MIOTTO, MARY ELIZABETH G. pediatrician; b. NYC, Apr. 9, 1964; MD, George Wash. U. Sch. Medicine, 1992. Intern Children's Nat. Med. Ctr., Washington, 1992—93, resident, 1993—95; attending physician INOVA Fairfax Children's Hosp., Falls Church, Va.; staff Marlborough Hosp., Mass. Mem. working group Pediat. Leadership Alliance. Recipient Excellence in Medicine Leadership award, AMA Found., 2004. Mem.: AMA, Am. Acad. Pediat. Office: Marlborough Hosp 157 Union St Marlborough MA 01752

MIQUELON, MIRIAM F. former prosecutor, lawyer; b. Elmhurst, Ill. children: Aaron, Rachel. Grad., U. Ariz., 1975, DePaul U., 1978; LLM in Taxation, Chgo.-Kent Coll. Law; postgrad. in Taxation, DePaul U.; postgrad. in History, Northwestern U. Lawyer, Houston, Stone, McGuire, Benjamin & Kocoras, Miquelon and Assocs., 1981—88, Keck, Mahin & Cate, Chgo., 1988—91; asst. U.S. atty. Ea. Dist. N.Y., Bklyn., 1991—93, So. Dist. Ill., 1993—99; asst. spl. counsel to Spl. Counsel John C. Danforth, 1999—2000; asst. U.S. atty. So. Dist. Ill., 2000—02, U.S. atty., 2002—03. Adj. prof. law Washington U. Sch. Law, St. Louis; adj. faculty Northwestern U. Coll. Law, Chgo. Recipient Chief Postal Inspector's award, U.S. Postal Inspection Svc., 2001, Spl. commendations, FBI, Drug Enforcement Adminstrn., U.S. Customs Svc., IRS. Avocations: volunteering, sports activities.

MIR, RONEN, museum director; b. Rehovot, Israel, July 28, 1957; arrived in US, 1986; s. Gur Arieh and Sara Mir; m. Debby F. Ross, July 15, 1986; children: Shlomo G., Adva R. BS in math, physics, Hebrew U., Israel, 1979; MS in physics, Weizmann Inst. of Sci., Israel, 1982; PhD in physics, Weizmann Inst. of Sci., 1987; postdoctorate in physics, U. Wash., 1988. Cert. musicology Tel Aviv U., 1999. Asst. prof. U. Wash., Seattle, 1988—90; assoc. scientist Ind. U., Bloomington, 1990—93; scientific dir. Clore Garden of Sci., Rehovot, Israel, 1993—98; guest scientist Fermi Nat. Accelerator Lab, Batavia, Ill., 1999—; exec. dir. Scitech Hands on Mus., Aurora, Ill., 1999—. Contbr. articles various profl. jours. Recipient Mayor's award, City of Aurora, 2001. Office: Scitech Hands on Mus 18 W Benton Aurora IL 60506 Home: 1698 Beverly Pl Highland Park IL 60035 Office Fax: 630-859-8692. E-mail: ronen@scitech.mus.il.us.

MIRABELLO, FRANCIS JOSEPH, lawyer; b. Ft. Lauderdale, Fla., Mar. 2, 1954; s. Frank Guy and Mary (Sorce) M.; m. Marianna Hay O'Neal, Aug. 5, 1978; childen: Diana H., A. Paul. BS in Civil Engring., Princeton U., 1975; JD, Harvard U., 1978. Bar: Calif. 1978, Pa. 1981, Fla. 1983. Assoc. Irell & Manella, Los Angeles, 1978-81; ptnr. Morgan, Lewis & Bockius, Phila., 1981—. Lectr. law Villanova (Pa.) U. Law Sch., adj. prof. law U. Pa., Phila. Mem. ABA, ACTEC. Clubs: Merion Cricket, Phila. Skating, Commonwealth Nat. Golf. Avocations: tennis, golf. Office: Morgan Lewis & Bockius 1701 Market St Philadelphia PA 19103-2903

MIRABELLO, MARK LINDEN, history professor; b. Toledo, May 6, 1955; s. Paul Joseph and Regina Joan (Baranski) M. BA, U. Toledo, 1977; MA, U. Va., 1979; PhD, U. Glasgow (Scotland), 1988. Instr. honors program U. Toledo, 1984-87; sr. instr. European history Shawnee State U., Portsmouth, Ohio, 1987-88, asst. prof. European history, 1988-93, chair honors program, 1990—, assoc. prof. European History, 1993—; vis. assoc. prof. European history Nizhni Novgorod State U., Russia, 1994. Dir. Ian B. Cowan Award for Outstanding Work in Hist. Studies, Shawnee State U., Portsmouth, 1990—; cons. The Open Air, Shawnee State U. newspaper, Portsmouth, 1992—, The Univ. Chronicle Shawnee State Univ. Newspaper, Portsmouth, 1992—; co-founder, advisor Ar Tyr Ar Fraternity Shawnee State U., Portsmouth, 1992—. Author: The Odin Brotherhood: A True Narrative of a Dialogue with a Mysterious Secret Society, 1992, The Crimes of Jehovah: A Brief Selection from the Bible, 1996, The Cannibal Within, 2002. Co-founder, adviser Delta Tau Omega fraternity, Shawnee State U., Portsmouth, 1992—. Honored by Asatru Sogulega Bokasafn, 1996; named Hon. Ky. Col. by Gov's. Office, 1998. Mem. Am. Hist. Assn., Ohio Acad. History, Fortean Soc. (London), Internat. Fortean Orgn., Planetary Soc. Avocation: fortean research. Home: 940 2nd St Portsmouth OH 45662-4303 Office: Dept History Shawnee State U Portsmouth OH 45662 Office Phone: 714-351-3351. E-mail: mmirabello@shawnee.edu.

MIRACLE, DORIS JEAN, retired medical/surgical nurse; b. Louisville, July 23, 1931; d. Bernard Louis and Catherine Federle; m. Earl Miracle, Aug. 31, 1951; 1 child, David. Surg. nurse Norton Hosp., Louisville, Norton-Children's Hosp., Louisville. Contbr. poems to poetry anthologies, Theatre of the Mind, 2003, Internat. Libr. Poetry, 2003; poetry (albums) Sounds of Poetry, 2003; contbr. articles to profl. jours., poems to mags. Recipient Editors Choice award, 2003. Mem.: Gaslight Writers, Ky. Writer's Coalition, Internat. Soc. of Poets, Soc. Children's Book Writers and Illustrators. Avocations: reading, poetry, astronomy, art, music.

MIRACLE, GORDON ELDON, advertising educator; b. Olympia, Wash., May 28, 1930; s. Gordon Tipler and Corine Adriana (Orlebeke) M.; m. Christa Stoeter, June 29, 1957; children: Gary, Gregory, Glenn. BBA, U. Wis., 1952, MBA, 1958, PhD, 1962. Case officer, civilian intelligence analyst U.S. Army, Fed. Republic Germany, 1955-57; instr. commerce U. Wis. Grad. Sch. Bus., Madison, 1958-60; instr., then asst. prof. mktg. U. Mich., Ann Arbor, 1960-66; assoc. prof. advt. Mich. State U., East Lansing, 1966-70, chmn. PhD program in mass media, 1973-74, chmn. dept., 1974-80, prof. advt., 1970-99, prof. emeritus, 1999—. Vis. prof. mktg. mgmt. N. European Mgmt. Inst., Oslo, 1972-73; cons., lectr. in field. Author: Management of International Advertising, 1966; co-author: International Marketing Management, 1970, Advertising and Government Regulation, 1979, Instructor's Manual for International Marketing Management, 1971, European Regulation of Advertising: Supranational Regulation of Advertising in the European Economic Community, 1986, Voluntary Regulation of Advertising: A Comparative Analysis of the United Kingdom and the United States, 1987, (in Korean) Cultures in Advertising: Advertising in Cultures, 1990; contbr. articles to scholarly and profl. jours.; editor: Marketing Decision Making: Strategy and Payoff, 1965, Sharing for Understanding, Proc. Ann. Conf. Am. Acad. Advt., 1977. Served with AUS, 1952-55. Recipient first Biennial Excellence in Advt. award, U. Ill., 1995; Ford Found. fellow, 1961-62, 64, Am. Assn. Advt. Agys. fellow Marsteller, Inc., 1967, Advt. Ednl. Found. fellow McCann-Erickson Hakuhodo, 1985, Fulbright rsch. fellow Waseda U., Tokyo, 1985; recipient numerous grants; recipient Viktor-Mataja medal Austrian Advt. Rsch. Assn., Vienna, 1999. Fellow: Am. Acad. Advt. (treas., exec. com. 1978—79); mem.: Internat. Advt. Assn., Internat. Advt. Assn. ((ednl. accreditation com. 1993—95, internat. advt. edn. group 1996—2001), Am. Mktg. Assn., Acad. Internat. Bus. (sec., exec. com. 1973—75), Adcraft Club Detroit. Home: 10025 Oak Island Dr Laingsburg MI 48848-8718 Office: Mich State U Dept Advt East Lansing MI 48824 E-mail: miracle@msu.edu.

MIRANDA, CARLOS SA, food products company executive; b. Fall River, Mass., Nov. 16, 1929; s. Carlos Sa and Annette (Pratt) M.; m. Natalie Cardoso, Jan. 5, 1949; children: Carla, Lucy, John. BS in Mech. Engring., Marquette U., 1956. With internat. divsn. Kellogg Co., Battle Creek, Mich., 1964—65; gen. mgr. Kellogg Co. Brazil, 1965—80; v.p. Kellogg Internat., Battle Creek, 1980—89; gen. mgr. Kellogg's Spain, 1983—84; country dir. internat. exec. svc. corps. Costa Rica, 1990—91; mediator Fla. County Cts., 1994—. Recipient Pero Vaz Caminha award, Brazil, 1976; conferred title Comdr. of Legion of Honor of Marshal Rondon, Brazil, 1971. Mem. ASME. Independent. Roman Catholic. Home: 8949 Wildlife Loop Sarasota FL 34238

MIRANDA, DANIEL FRANK, lawyer, real estate executive; b. Corona, Calif., June 16, 1953; s. Frank R. and Mary A. (Cintas) M.; m. Jacqueline Fry, Dec. 28, 1975; children— David Frank, Kate Elise. A.B., U. Calif.-Berkeley, 1975; J.D., (Stone scholar), Columbia U., 1979. Bar: Ill. 1979. Assoc., Sonnenschein, Carlin, Nath & Rosenthal, Chgo., 1979-81; v.p., legal and corp. sec. The Westport Co. (Conn.), 1981-84; project exec. dir. 666 Assocs., Chgo., 1981-84; pres. First Columbia Corp., Chgo., 1984-88; pres. The M Corp., 1988—; dir. Dade Savs. & Loan Assn., Miami, 1984, Greater N. Michigan Ave. Assn., Chgo.; trustee 4th Presby. Ch., Chgo.; mem. Lincoln Park Zoo Aux. Bd., Chgo. Mem. ABA, Ill. State Bar Assn., Chgo. Bar Assn. *

MIRANDA, ROBERT NICHOLAS, publishing company executive; b. Bklyn., July 9, 1934; m. Marilyn H. Pils, May 25, 1958; children: Marilyn, Robert, Susan, Lori, Jennifer. AA in Acctg. and Bus. Adminstrn., SUNY, Farmingdale, 1967. Pres. Pergamon Press, Inc., Elmsford, NY, 1965—92; chmn., CEO Cognizant Communication Corp., Elmsford, 1992—; owner Miranda Press, 2002. Bd. dirs., exec. v.p., vice chmn. Soc. and Assoc. Svc. Corp., McLean, Va., 1979-82; bd. dirs., chmn. electronics com. Copyright Clearance Ctr., 1984-93. Pub. Acupuncture and Electro Therapeutics Rsch., Analgesia, Bird Behavior, Cancer Prevention Internat., Cell Transplantation, Festival Mgmt. and Event Tourism, Gene Expression, Info. Tech. and Tourism, Life Support and Biosphere Sci., Oncology Rsch., Tourism Analysis, Technology: Jour. of Regulatory Sci., Failure and Lessons Learned in Info. Tech., Pacific Tourism Rev., Tourism, Culture and Comm., Tourism Dynamic Book Series, Tourism in Marine Environments, Habitation: An Internat. Jour. Served with USNR, 1954-59. Mem. Coun. Sci. Editors, Internat. Soc. Intelligent Systems (founder, bd. dirs., fin. dir. 1992—). Avocations: hunting, fishing, horseback riding. Office: Cognizant Comm Corp 3 Hartsdale Rd Elmsford NY 10523-3701 Office Phone: 914-592-7720. E-mail: cogcomm@aol.com.

MIRANDA-LEVI, JASON, film producer, writer; s. Jose Antonio Miranda and Mercedes Bertolin-Levi; m. Maria L Maria Luisa Echaurren, Nov. 24, 1962; 1 child, Mychele Lita Ohre. BS, Fordham U., 1954—58; JD, St. Johns U., 1958—61. Lic.: NY (Attorney) 1963. Pvt. law practice, NY, 1964—74. Prodr.: (film and telvision) Han Matado a Un Cadaver; (TV series) Cara a Cara; author: (novels) The Spanish Enigma; exhibitions include Photographic Surrealism. Lance cpl. USMC, 1951—53, Korea. Recipient Dama del Paraguas, City of Barcelona, Spain, 1973, La Font de Canaletas, City Coun. of the City of Barcelona, Spain, 1973, Medal of San Jordi, Province of Barcelona, Barcelona, Spain, 1976, Font de Canaletas, City Coun. of Barcelona, Spain, 1975. Mem.: SAG, NY Bar. R-Consevative. Jewish. Avocations: antique watch collector, travel, reading, haute cuisine. Personal E-mail: jmlevi@sbcglobal.net.

MIRANTE, ARTHUR J., II, real estate company executive; b. Hackensack, N.J., Aug. 25, 1943; s. Arthur J. and Mildred (Spaluzzi) M.; m. Elizabeth McMillan, Oct. 2, 1993; children: Arthur, Claudia, Matthew. BS, Coll. of the Holy Cross, 1965; JD, St. John's U., 1968. Bar: 1968. Sole practice, N.Y.C., 1966-71; asst. to gen. counsel Cushman & Wakefield, N.Y.C., 1971-77, gen. counsel, 1977-81, nat. dir. asset mgmt., 1981-82, exec. v.p., dir. N.Y. area, 1982-84, pres., chief exec. officer, 1984—. Home: 211 E 70th St New York NY 10021-5205 Office: Cushman & Wakefield Inc 51 W 52nd St Rm 700 New York NY 10019-6119*

MIRE, WELDON J. oil industry executive, human resources specialist; B of Fgn. Lang., U. La., 1971; postgrad., U. Costa Rica. Joined Halliburton, Houston, 1978, ESG country v.p. for Indonesia, bus. develop. mgr. for Asia, dir. strategic bus. develop. & mgr. of tools. testing and tubing conveyed perforating prod. service line, v.p. human resources, 2002—. Office: Halliburton 10200 Bellaire Blvd Houston TX 77020-5299

MIRELS, HAROLD, aerospace engineer; b. N.Y.C., July 29, 1924; s. Hyman and Lily (Efron) M.; m. Nell Segal, Oct. 4, 1953; children: Lily, Laurence Franklin, Jeremy Mark. BSME, Cooper U., 1944; MSME, Case Inst. Tech., 1949; PhD in Aero. Engring., Cornell U., 1953. Sect. head NACA, Cleve., 1944-57; br. chief NASA, Cleve., 1957-61; dept. head Aerospace Corp., El Segundo, Calif., 1961-78, assoc. dir., 1978-84, prin. scientist, 1984-93; cons., 1993—. Co-inventor continuous wave chem. laser. Recipient Tech. Achievement award Cleve. Tech. Socs., 1960. Fellow AIAA (Fluid and Plasmadynamics award 1988), Am. Phys. Soc.; mem. Nat. Acad. Engring. Home: 3 Seahurst Rd Palos Verdes Peninsula CA 90274-3700

MIRENDA, ROSALIE M. nursing educator, administrator; b. Phila., Sept. 22, 1937; d. Achille and Anna Pierotti; m. Anthony D. Mirenda, Sept. 9, 1961; children: Anthony D. Jr., John A., Rosalie A. BSN, Villanova U., 1959; MS in Nursing, U. Pa., 1978; DNSc, Widener U., 1992. Staff nurse, tchr. St. Agnes Med. Ctr., Phila., Mercy Cath. Med. Ctr., Darby, Pa.; prof., v.p. for acad. affairs Neumann Coll., Aston, Pa. Pres. Neuman Systems Model Trustee Group Inc. Contbr. articles to profl. jours. Chmn. Bd. trustees Sch. Holy Child, Drexel. Recipient Bronze medal; named Prof. of Yr. Coun. Adv. Support Edn., 1987, Outstanding Educator of Am., 1975, Outstanding Nurse award, 1990. Mem. ANA, NLN, AAUW, Sigma Theta Tau, Delta Tau. Office: Neumann Coll Libr 1 Neumann Dr Aston PA 19014-1277

MIRIN, STEVEN MARTIN, psychiatrist; b. Bklyn., Jan. 24, 1942; s. Harry and Gertrude Mirin; m. Margaret S. McKenna; children: Jonathan, Daniel, Benjamin, Nicholas. BA, SUNY, Binghamton, 1963; MD, SUNY, Syracuse, 1967. Intern San Francisco Gen. Hosp., 1967-68; dir. narcotic antagonist rsch. unit McLean Hosp., Belmont, Mass., 1973-77, dir. outpatient psychopharmacology svc., 1977-82, chief clin. evaluation svc., 1982-83, acting gen. dir., 1988-91, gen. dir., psychiatrist in chief, 1991-94, CEO, psychiatrist in chief, 1994-97; med. dir. Westwood (Mass.) Lodge Hosp., 1983-88; prof. psychiatry Harvard Med. Sch., 1991—. Pres. McLean Health Svcs., Belmont, 1989-97; trustee MGH Inst. Health Professions, Boston, 1991-97; invited testimony appropriations subcom. on labor HHS U.S. Ho. of Reps., 1994, U.S. Senate, 1994, appropriations sucbom. on def. U.S. Ho. of Reps., 1994, appropriations subcom. on VA, HUD and ind. agys., 1995. Author: The Heroin Stimulus, 1979, Cocaine, 1986; author, editor: Psychiatric Treatment: Advances in Outcome Research, 1991. Fellow Am. Coll. Psychiatrists, Am. Psychiat. Assn. (trustee 1993-96, med. dir. 1997—); mem. Am. Acad. Psychiatrists in Alcoholism and Addictions (founding), Group for the Advancement of Psychiatry, Mass. Assn. Psychiat. Health Sys. (pres. 1994-96). Avocation: fishing.

MIRISOLA, LISA HEINEMANN, air quality engineer; b. Glendale, Calif., Mar. 25, 1963; d. J. Herbert and Betty Jane (Howson) Heinemann; m. Daniel Carl Mirisola, June 27, 1987; 1 child, Ian Cataldo. BSME, UCLA, 1986. Cert. engr.-in-tng., Calif. Air quality engr. South Coast Air Quality Mgmt. Dist., Diamond Bar, Calif., 1988—. Chancellor's scholar UCLA, 1981. Mem. ASME, NSPE, Soc. Women Engrs. Office: South Coast Air Quality Mgmt Dist 21865 Copley Dr Diamond Bar CA 91765-4178 E-mail: lmirisola@aqmd.gov.

MIRK, JUDY ANN, retired elementary school educator; b. Victorville, Calif., June 10, 1944; d. Richard Nesbit and Corrine (Berghoefer). BA in Social Sci., San Jose (Calif.) State U., 1966, cert. in teaching, 1967; MA in Edn., Calif. State U., Chico, 1980. Cert. elem. edn. tchr., Calif. Profl. psychology trainee John F. Kennedy U., Orinda, Calif., 1997—99; tchr. Cupertino (Calif.) Union Sch. Dist., 1967-95; lead tchr. lang. arts Dilworth Sch., San Jose, 1988-90, mem. supt.'s adv. team, 1986-90, mem. student study team, 1987-95; ret. Mem. student study team, 1987-95; mem. Dilworth Sch. Site Coun., 1981-95. Mem. The Commonwealth Club of Calif, Phi Mu. Green Party. Avocations: photography, natural history, watercolors. Home: 2075 Redwood Dr Santa Cruz CA 95060-1238

MIRKARIMI, PAUL B. materials scientist, researcher; s. Sal and Kay Mirkarimi; m. Laura W. Mirkarimi; 1 child, Claire A. BS, U. Ill., 1987; PhD, Northwestern U., 1992. Scientist Sandia Nat. Labs., Livermore, Calif., 1995—97, Lawrence Livermore (Calif.) Nat. Lab., 1997—2000, group leader, 2000—. Contbr. articles to profl. jours. Recipient R&D 100 award, R&D Mag., 2003, Excellence in Tech. Transfer award, Fed. Lab. Consortium for Tech Transfer, 2003. Mem.: Am. Vacuum Soc., Internat. Soc. for Optical Engring., Materials Rsch. Soc. Achievements include patents in field; patents pending in field. Office: Lawrence Livermore Nat Lab MS L-395 7000 East Ave Livermore CA 94550

MIRKIN, BERNARD LEO, clinical pharmacologist, pediatrician; b. Bronx, N.Y., Mar. 31, 1928; s. Max and Esther M.; m. Phyllis Korduner, Aug. 1954 (dec. 1982); children: Lisa Mia, Mara Rebecca; m. Sarah Solotaroff, 1986; stepchildren: Jennifer, Rachel, Jacob. AB, NYU, 1949; PhD, Yale U., 1953; MD, U. Minn., 1964. Asst. prof. pharmacology SUNY, Downstate Med. Center, 1954-60; Ford Found. postdoctoral fellow Karolinska Inst., Stockholm, 1960-61; USPHS post-doctoral fellow Yale U., 1961-62; resident in pediatrics U. Minn. Hosp., Mpls., 1964-66; asst. prof. U. Minn. Med. Sch., Mpls., 1966-67, asso. prof., 1967-72; prof. pediatrics, pharmacology and biol. chemistry, dir. div. clin. pharmacology U. Minn. Health Sci. Ctr., 1972-89; prof. pediatrics and molecular pharmacology Northwestern U. Med. Sch., Chgo., 1989—; head, dir. rsch. Inst. for Edn. and Rsch. Children's Meml. Hosp., Chgo., 1989—99; assoc. dean rsch. Northwestern U. Med. Sch., 1994—96; dir. rsch. emeritus Inst. for Edn. and Rsch. Children's Meml. Hosp., Chgo., 2000—. Cons. Office of Technology Assessment, U.S. Congress, WHO, U.S. Pharmacopeia, PhARMA Found., Nat. Inst. Health; fellow Jesus Coll., Oxford U., 1974. Author: Perinatal Pharmacology and Therapeutics, 1976, Clinical Pharmacology: A Pediatric Perspective, 1978. postdoctoral fellow Karolinska Inst. Stockholm 1960-61 Served with M.C. U.S. Army, 1954-56. Mem. AAAS, Soc. Pediat. Rsch., Am. Assn. Cancer Rsch., Am. Pediat. Soc., Am. Soc. Pharm. Exptl. Therapeutics, Am. Soc. Clin. Pharm. and Therapeutics. Home: 427 Greenleaf St Evanston IL 60202-1328 Office: Childrens Meml Inst Edn and Rsch Mailcode # 117 2300 N Childrens Plz Chicago IL 60614-3363 E-mail: b-mirkin@northwestern.edu.

MIRKIN, CHAD A. chemistry professor; BS in Chemistry, Dickinson Coll., 1986; PhD, Pa. State U., 1989. Asst. prof. chemistry Northwestern U., Evanston, Ill., 1991-95, assoc. prof. chemistry, 1995-97, prof. chemistry, 1997-2000, George B. Rathmann prof. chemistry, 2000—. Contbr. articles to profl. jours. NSF postdoctoral fellow MIT, 1989-91; recipient Beckman Young Investigators award, 1992-94, Disting. New Faculty award Camille and Henry Dreyfus Found., 1991-96, Young Investigator Rsch. award NSF, Young Prof. award DuPont, Young Investigator award ONR, Inventors award B.F. Goodrich, Wilson prize, award in pure chemistry Am. Chem. Soc.; grantee USN. Mem. Am. Chem. Soc. Achievements include research nanotechnology biosensors and new ligand design in synthetic organometallic chemistry. Office: Northwestern U Dept Chemistry 2145 Sheridan Rd Evanston IL 60208-3113 E-mail: camirkin@chem.nwv.edu.

MIRKIN, GABE BARON, allergist, pediatrician, medical educator, writer, radio personality; b. Brookline, Mass., June 18, 1935; s. Mitchell and Vera (Baron) M.; children: Gene, Jan, Jill, Geoffrey, Kenny; m. Diana Purdie Rich, 1998. BA, Harvard U., 1957; MD, Baylor U., 1961. Diplomate Am. Bd. Pediatrics, Sub Bd. Allergy, Am. Bd. Allergy and Immunology, Am. Bd. Sports Medicine. Resident in pediatrics Mass. Gen. Hosp., Boston, 1961-63; fellow allergy, immunology, dermatology Johns Hopkins Hosp., Balt., 1963-65; allergy, immunology, dermatology, sports medicine pvt. practice, Silver Spring, Md., 1966—. Tchg. fellow pediat. Harvard Med. Sch., 1962-63; tchg. fellow allergy and immunology Johns Hopkins Med. Sch., 1963-65; asst. prof. dept. phys. edn. U. Md., College Park, 1976-83; assoc. clin. prof. dept. pediat. Georgetown U. Sch. of Medicine, 1984—. Author: The Sportsmedicine Book, 1978, Getting Thin, 1983, Dr. Gabe Mirkin's Fitness Clinic, 1986, The Complete Sportsmedicine Book for Women, 1985, 2d rev. edit. 1991; (with Shangold) Women and Exercise, 1988, Dr. Gabe Mirkin's Fatfree, Flavorfull Book, 1995; (with Diana Mirkin) The 20 Gram Diet, 1995, The 20/30 Fat and Fiber Diet Plan, Dr. Gabe Mirkins Pocket Guide to Fitness & Sports; (with Rich) The Whole Grains Cookbook, 1997, The Good Food Book, 2001, Healthy Heart Miracle, 2004; author (newsletter) The Mirkin Report, 1990—; columnist: N.Y. Times, 1978-89, United Features, 1989-94, Washington Post, 1976, Singer Media Corp., 1994-99; appearances on P.M. Mag. WDVM-TV, Washington, 1979, House Party, NBC TV, 1990, The Learning Channel; host internationally syndicated radio talk show, 1996-2003; daily radio spots on fitness and nutrition, CBS Radio Stations News Svc., 1979—; host talk show on health fitness and nutrition, KMOX Radio, St. Louis, 1982-98; nightly talk show host NBC Washington, WRC, 1982-84, 87—, WNTR, 1984-86; weekly spots for Physicians Radio Network, 1984-85; daily talk show syndicated by Sun Radio Network, 1992; weekly talk show WEEI, Boston, 1993-94, others; columnist and contbg. editor to health and fitness mags.; contbr. articles to profl. jours., chpts. to books. Major USAF, 1968-70. Fellow Am. Coll. Allergists, Am. Assn. Cert. Allergists, Am. Assn. for Clin. Immunology and Allergy, Am. Acad. Pediatrics, Am. Acad. Allergy and Immunology. Avocation: bicycle tandem riding. Office: 10901 Connecticut Ave Kensington MD 20895-1645 Office Phone: 301-942-9837. E-mail: gabe@drmirkin.com.

MIRMAN, JOEL HARVEY, lawyer; b. Toledo, Dec. 3, 1941; s. Benjamin and Minnie (Krapifko) M.; children: Lisa, Julie, Benjamin. BBA, Ohio U., 1963; JD, Ohio State U., 1966. Bar: Ohio 1966, U.S. Dist. Ct. (so. dist.) Ohio 1966, U.S. Supreme Ct. 1972. Ptnr. Topper, Alloway, Goodman, DeLeone & Duffey, Columbus, Ohio, 1966-85, Benesch, Friedlander, Coplan & Aronoff, 1986-93; shareholder Buckingham, Doolittle & Burroughs, Columbus, 1994—2003; ptnr. Gamble Hartshorn & Johnson, LLC, Columbus, 2004—. Lectr. Ohio CLE Inst., Columbus, 1972—; mem. Supreme Ct. of Ohio Commn. on Certification of Specialists. Author direct examination CLE materials; contbr. articles to profl. jours. Mem. Ohio Elections Commn., 1976-80, vice-chmn. 1980. Named one of Ohio's Top 100 Super Lawyers, 2004, Best Lawyers in Am., 2003—04. Mem. Worthington Hills Country Club, Worthington Hills Civic Assn. (pres. 1992-93). Office: Gamble Hartshorn & Johnson LLC 1 E Livingston Ave Columbus OH 43215 Office Phone: 614-324-5985. E-mail: mirman@ghjlaw.com.

MIRONOVICH, ALEX, publisher; b. Brooklyn, N.Y., Nov. 30, 1952; s. Peter Mironovich and Olga Sachrina; m. Cynthia Ann Wuss, July 23, 1983; children: Brittany, Nicholas. BA in psychology, City U., N.Y.C., 1970-74. Sales rep. House Beautiful mag., N.Y.C., 1976-79, Sawyer Ferguson Walker, N.Y.C., 1979-82, Creative Ideas for Living, N.Y.C., 1982-83, Parents mag. G and J, N.Y.C.; assoc. pub. Y.M. Gruner and Jahr, N.Y., 1986-88, pub., 1988; assoc. pub. Better Homes and Gardens, N.Y.C., 1993—95; pres. pub. group, exec. v.p. Playboy Enterprises Inc., Chgo., 1998—2001; CEO Vibe/Spin Ventures, 2001—, pub., 2003. Group pub. N.W. Traveler and Mature Outlook, 1998—99. Office: 205 Lexington Ave New York NY 10016

MIROSHNICHENKO, ANATOLY S. astronomer, researcher; b. Saint-Petersburg, Russia, Oct. 9, 1961; s. Sergei N and Elena A Miroshnichenko; m. Tatyana A Sheikina, Aug. 18, 2001; m. Tatiana R. Popova, Aug. 13, 1988 (div. July 2, 2001); m. Julia O Mumina, Oct. 16, 1982 (div. Jan. 7, 1987); 1 child, Alexander A.; children: Olga A Sheikina, Vladimir A., Anna A., Nadezhda A. BS, Saint-Petersburg State U., Russia, 1978—83; PhD, Pulkovo Obs., Saint-Petersburg, Russia, 1983—91. Engr. Pulkovo Obs., Saint-Petersburg, Russia, 1983—87, jr. rsch. assoc., 1987—93, rsch. assoc., 1993—94, sr. rsch. assoc., 1994—97; post-doctoral rsch. assoc. U. of Toledo, 1997—98; sr. rsch. assoc. Pulkovo Obs., 1998—99; post-doctoral rsch. assoc. U. of Toledo, 1999—2002, rsch. asst. prof., 2002—. Grantee Rsch. grant, NASA, 1997-1998, Long-Term Stellar Astrophysics grant, 1999-2003, Rsch. grant, US Civilian Rsch. & Devel. Found., 2000-2001, Small rsch. grant, Am. Astron. Soc., 2001. Mem.: Am. Astron. Soc. Home: 4942 Burkewood Ct Apt 201 Sylvania OH 43560 Office: U Toledo 2801 WBancroft St Toledo OH 43606

MIROWSKI, PHILIP EDWARD, economics professor; b. Jackson, Mich., Aug. 21, 1951; s. Edward and Elizabeth Mirowski. BA, Mich. State U., 1973; MA in Econs., U. Mich., 1976, PhD in Econs., 1979. Asst. prof. U. Santa Clara, Calif., 1978-81, Tufts U., Medford, Mass., 1981-84, assoc. prof. econs., 1984-90; Carl Koch prof. econs. and history and philosophy of sci. U. Notre Dame, Ind., 1990—. Vis. assoc. prof. Yale U., New Haven, 1987-88; vis. prof. Tinbergen Inst., Erasmus U., Rotterdam, Holland, 1991, U. Paris, 1997, U. Modena, Italy, 1998, Santa Fe Inst., 2001; Fulbright sr. fellow, 2003, Internat. Ctr. for Advanced Studies, NYU, 2004. Author: Reconstruction of Economic Theory, 1986, Against Mechanism, 1988, More Heat Than Light, 1989, Machine Dreams, 2002, Science Bought and Sold, 2002, Effortless Economy of Science, 2004; editor: Natural Images in Economics, 1994, Edgeworth on Chance, 1994, College Works of William Thomas Thornton, 1999; mem. editorial bd. History Polit. Econ., Duke U., 1986—, Social Concept, 1988-94, Jour. Instnl. Econs., 2004—, Jour. History of Econ., 2001—; contbr. articles to profl. jours. Mem. AAAS, Am. Econs. Assn., History Sci. Soc., History Econs. Soc., Soc. for Social Studies of Sci., Philosophy of Sci. Assn. Office: U Notre Dame 400 Decio Hall Notre Dame IN 46556

MIRRA, SUZANNE SAMUELS, neuropathologist, researcher; BA, Hunter Coll., 1962; MD, SUNY, Bklyn., 1967. Instr. pathology Yale U. Sch. Medicine, New Haven, 1971-73; staff pathologist Atlanta VA Med. Ctr., Decatur, Ga., 1973-97; asst. prof. pathology Emory U. Sch. Medicine, Atlanta, 1973-80, assoc. prof. pathology, 1981-93, prof. pathology, 1993-97; prof., chair dept. pathology SUNY Health Sci. Ctr., Bklyn., 1997—. Dir., prin. investor Emory Alzheimer's Disease Ctr., Atlanta, 1991—97. Mem. editl. bd. Arch Pathol. Lab. Med., 1988-2000, Jour. Neuropathology Exptl. Neurology, 1991-95, Brain Pathology, 1995-99, Alzheimer's Disease Reviews, 1995-2000. Recipient Albert E. Levy Sci. Faculty Rsch. award Emory U., 1987, Disting. Alumnus Achievement award SUNY, 1992; named to Hunter Coll. Hall of Fame, 1996. Fellow Coll. Am. Pathologists (Presdl. award 1987,89, Herbert Lansky award 1990, chair neuropathology commn. 1992-95); mem. Am. Assn. Neuropathologists (v.p. profl. affairs 1992-97, pres. 1999-2000), Alzheimer's Assn. (bd. dir. Atlanta chpt. 1987-97, nat. bd. dir. 1997—), Alpha Omega Alpha, mem., 2002. Office: SUNY Health Sci Ctr 450 Clarkson Ave Brooklyn NY 11203-2056 Office Phone: 718-270-1291. Business E-Mail: suzanne.mirra@downstate.edu.

MIRRER, LOUISE, language educator, consultant; b. N.Y.C., Apr. 27, 1953; d. Gerald Paul and Mildred (Friedelbaum) M.; m. Philip Singer, Sept. 1, 1974 (div. Nov., 1984); 1 child, Philip Mirrer-Singer; m. David Halle, Mar. 6, 1947; children: Carla, Malcolm. BA, U. Pa., 1973; Diploma in Linguistics, Cambridge U., Eng., 1975; MA, Stanford U., 1977, PhD, 1980. Asst. prof. Spanish and Portuguese Fordham U., NYC, 1979-86, assoc. prof., 1986-91, prof. and dept. chair, 1991-94; prof. and chair Spanish & Portuguese dept. U. Minn., Mpls., 1994—95, prof. Spanish & Portuguese, 1994—99, vice provost arts, sci. & engring., 1995—97; vice chancellor for academic affairs CUNY, NY, 1997—2000, prof. Hispanic & Luso-Brazilian studies & medieval studies, 1997—. Bd. advisors Medieval Feminist Newsletter, 1991—; project dir. Japan Found. Grant, 1992-94; editorial bd. mem. Hispanic Issues U. Minnesota Press, 1995-; pres. NY Historical Soc., 2004- Author The Language of Evaluation: A Sociolinguistic Approach to the Story of Pedro el Cruel in Ballad and Chronicle, 1986, Women, Jews, and Muslims in the Texts of Reconquest Castile, 1996; co-author (with David Halle) Prints of Power, 1991; editor Upon My Husband's Death: Widows in the Literature and Histories of Medieval Europe, 1992; contributor Medieval Crime and Social Control, 1999, Women in Medieval Western European Culture, 1999, Charting Memory: Recalling Medieval Spain, 1999. Recipient McKnight fellowship, U. Minn., 1995, YWCA Women Achievers award, 2000, Leadership award Asian-Am. Rsch. Institution, 2003; grantee Littauer Found., 1993, NY Coun. for Humanities, 1994, fellow council on Institutional Cooperation, 1995-96; named one of 50 Most Influential Women in NY, NY Post, 2003. Mem. Governor's Interagency Council on Women, NY State Commissioner's Policy Advisory Com. Governing Bd. (vice chair), Alliance for Minority Participation, NY Acad. of Sci. Working Group for NY Tech. Council, Exec. Com. Modern Language Assn. Div. on Medieval Spanish Literature (chair 1999-2000, mem. delegate assembly 1988-91), Nominating Com. Internat. Assocn. of Hispanists, 1999-, bd. dirs. NY Structural Biology Ctr., bd. advisors Gateway Inst. for Pre-Coll. Edn., Asian-Am. Rsch. Inst., Soc. Medieval Feminist Scholarship, 1991-. Achievements include application of sociolinguistic methodology to orally composed texts; feminist approaches to medieval Spanish literature. Office: CUNY 535 E 80th St New York NY 10021*

MIRRLEES, SIR JAMES ALEXANDER, economics professor; b. Minnigaff, Scotland, July 5, 1936; s. George Barlas MacNab and Nan Lindsay (Purdie) M.; m. Gillian Marjorie Hughes, July 29, 1961 (dec. 1993); children: Catriona, Fiona; m. Patricia Wilson, May 12, 2001. MA, Edinburgh U., Scotland, 1957; BA, Cambridge U., Eng., 1959, PhD, 1963; DLitt (hon.), Warwick U., Eng., 1982, Portsmouth U., 1997, Brunel U., 1997, Edinburgh U., Scotland, 1997, Oxford U., 1998. Lectr. in econ. U. Cambridge, England, 1963-68; Edgeworth prof. econs. U. Oxford, England, 1968-95; prof. polit. economy U. Cambridge, England, 1995—2003; prof. Chinese U. Hong Kong, 2003—. Author: Project Appraisal and Planning for Developing Countries (with Little), 1974; contbr. articles to profl. publ. Recipient Nobel Prize in Economics, 1996. Fellow Brit. Acad., Fellow Roy. Soc. of Edinburgh, Econometric Soc. (pres. 1983-84); mem. Royal Econ. Soc. (pres. 1989-92), Foreign Assoc. of Natl. Acad. Sci., Am. Econ. Assn. (hon.), Am. Acad. Arts and Sci., Assn. Univ. Tchr. Econ. (chmn. 1983-87). Office: Trinity Coll CB2 ITQ Cambridge England Office Phone: +44 1223 339 516., +852 2609 7831.

MIRRO, JOHN, engineering company executive; Student, MIT, Cambridge, Mass. Pres. Conmec, Inc., Bethlehem, Pa. Office: Conmec Inc 1480 Valley Center Pky Bethlehem PA 18017-2264

MIRSKY, ALLAN FRANKLIN, psychologist, researcher; b. N.Y.C., Feb. 2, 1929; s. Harry Leroy and Charlotte (Copans) M.; m. Carol Patricia Vogel, June 24, 1951 (dec. 1983); children: Laura Ann, Richard Daniel; m. Constance Catharine Duncan, July 4, 1986. BS, City Coll. N.Y., 1950; MS, Yale U., 1952, PhD, 1954. Diplomate Am. Bd. Profl. Psychology; cert. clin. Neuropsychology. Rsch. psychologist Nat. Inst. Health, Bethesda, Md., 1954-61; asst. prof. to prof. Boston U., Mass., 1961-80; chief lab. of psychology and psychopathology NIH, Bethesda, Md., 1980-95, chief sect. on clin. and exptl. neuropsychology, 1995—. Cons. NIH, NSF, NRC, Washington, 1965-93, WHO, 1992—; adj. prof. Johns Hopkins U., Balt., 1987—. Editor, author: Education and The Brain, 1978, Elements of Petit Mal Epilepsy, 1988. Comdr. USPHS, 1954-61. Rsch. grant NSF, NIH, 1961-80; recipient Career award NIMH, 1961-80, Outstanding Achievement in Psychology City Coll. N.Y., 1989. Fellow AAAS, APA (pres. divsn. comp. and physiol. psychology 1982-83, pres. divsn. clin. neuropsychology 2001—), Am. EEG Soc., Am. Coll. Neuropsychopharmacology; mem. Internat. Neuropsychological Soc. (pres. 1972), Cosmos Club. Achievements include contributiions to the neuropsychology of attention, schizophrenia and petit mal epilepsy. Home: 5502 Spruce Tree Ave Bethesda MD 20814 Office: NIMH 5415 W Cedar Ln Ste 203B MSC 2615 Bethesda MD 20892-2615

MIRSKY, ARTHUR, geologist, department chairman; b. Phila., Feb. 8, 1927; s. Victor and Dorothy M.; m. Patricia Shorey, Dec. 22, 1961; 1 dau., Alexis Catherine. Student, Bklyn. Coll., 1944-45, 46-48; BA, U. Calif., 1950; MS, U. Ariz., 1955; PhD, Ohio State U., 1960. Cert. geologist, Ind. Field uranium geologist AEC, S.W. U.S., 1951-53; cons. uranium geologist Albuquerque, 1955-56; asst. dir. Inst. Polar Studies, Ohio State U., 1960-67; adj. asst. prof. geology Ohio State U., 1964-67; from asst. prof. geology to prof. Ind. U.-Purdue U., Indpls., 1967-94, prof. emeritus, 1994—, coord. geology, 1967-69, chmn. dept. geology, 1969-93. Contbr. articles to profl. jours. Served with USN, 1944-46. Mem. AAAS, AAUP, Am. Inst. Profl. Geologists, Geol. Soc. Am., Nat. Assn. Geosci. Tchrs., Am. Geol. Inst., Soc. Sedimentary Geology, Ind. Acad. Sci., Sigma Xi. Office: Indiana U-Purdue U Dept Geology 723 W Michigan St Indianapolis IN 46202-5132 Office Phone: 317-278-0229. E-mail: amirsky@iupui.edu.

MIRSKY, PHYLLIS SIMON, librarian; b. Petach Tikva, Israel, Dec. 18, 1940; d. Allan and Lea (Prizant) Simon; m. Edward Mirsky, Oct. 21, 1967; 1 child, Seth (dec.). BS in Social Welfare, Ohio State U., 1962; postgrad., Columbia U., 1962-63; AMLS, U. Mich., 1965. Caseworker field placement Children's Aid Soc., N.Y.C., 1962-63; hosp. libr. hosp. and instns. divsn. Cleve. Pub. Libr., 1963-64; reference libr. UCLA Biomed. Libr., 1965-68, reference/acquisitions libr., 1968-69, head cons./continuing edn. Pacific S.W. Regl. Med. Libr. Sv., 1969-71, asst. dir. Pacific S.W. Regl. Med. Libr. Sv., 1971-73, faculty coord. Biomed. Libr. program Cen. San Joaquin Valley Area Health Edn. Ctr., 1973-77, assoc. dir. Pacific S.W. Regl. Med. Libr. Sv., 1973-79; head reference sect., coord. libr. assoc. program Nat. Libr. of Medicine, Bethesda, Md., 1979-81; asst. univ. libr., scis. U. Calif.-San Diego, La Jolla, 1981-86, acting univ. libr., 1985, 92-93, 98-99, asst. univ. libr. adminstrv. and pub. svcs., 1986-87, assoc. univ. libr. adminstrv. and pub. svcs., 1987-92, assoc. univ. libr., 1993-95; dep. univ. libr., 1995—. Guest lectr. Libr. Schs. UCLA and U. So. Calif., 1967-78, Grad. Sch. Libr. Sci. Cath. U., Washington, 1980, Grad. Sch. Libr. and Info. Sci. UCLA, 1984; mem. task force on role of spl. libr. nationwide network and coop. programs Nat. Commn. on Libr. and Info. Svcs./Spl. Libr. Assn., 1981-83; facilitator AASLD/MLA Guidelines Scenario Writing Session, L.A., 1984; mem. users coun. OCLC Online Computer Libr. Ctr., Inc., 1991-94; U. Calif.-San Diego rep. Coalition for Networked Info., 1992—; instr. Assn. Rsch. Librs., Office Mgmt. Studies, Mgmt. Inst., 1987; peer reviewer Coll. Libr. Tech. and Cooperation Grant Program U.S. Dept. Edn., 1988-94; cons. Nat. Libr. Medicine, Bethesda, Md., 1988, San Diego Mus. Contemporary Art Libr., La Jolla, Calif., 1993, Salk Inst., 1995; mem. Libr. of Congress Network Adv. Com., 1994-96, chair steering com., 1995-96. Contbr. articles to profl. jours. and bulls. Mem. fin. com. City of Del Mar, 1995-98, chair, 1997-98, facility adv. com., 2000—. NIH fellow Columbia U., 1962-63; sr. fellow UCLA/Coun. on Libr. Resources, 1987. Fellow Med. Libr. Assn. (bd. dirs. 1977-80); mem. ALA (site visitors panel com. on accreditation 1990-92, libr. adminstrn. and mgmt. assn. 1990-92), Med. Libr. Group Soc. Calif. and Ariz. (sec. 1970-71, v.p. 1971-72, pres. 1972-73), Documentation Abstracts, Inc. (bd. dirs. 1985-90, vice chair bd. dirs. 1988-90), Med. Libr. Assn. (pres. 1984-85), U. Mich. Sch. Libr. Sci. Alumni Assn. Office: U Calif San Diego U Libr 0175G 9500 Gilman Dr La Jolla CA 92093-0175

MIRZA, HUMAIR, cardiologist, educator; b. Karachi, Pakistan, Feb. 18, 1966; arrived in U.S., 1993; s. Hasan and Qamar Jehan Mirza; m. Mahwash Khan, Dec. 20, 2001. MBBS, Dow Med. Coll., Karachi, 1991. Diplomate Am. Bd. Internal Medicine, Am. Bd. Cardiology, Am. Bd. of Interventional Cardiology. Rsch. fellow nephrology and hypertension SUNY, Stony Brook, 1993—96, resident interanl medicine, 1994—97, chief med. resident, 1997—98, asst. clin. instr., 1994—2001, cardiology fellow, 1998—2001, interventional cardiology fellow, 2001—02, asst. prof. medicine and cardiology, 2002—, asst. program dir., cardiology fellowship program; mem. med. bd. Univ. Hosp., SUNY, Stony Brook, 1999—2002, mem. grad. sch. med. edn. com., 1997—2002. Contbr. articles to profl. jours. (Pfizer Abstract award, 2001). Grantee Nat. Kidney Found., 1994—96. Mem.: ACP, Am. Soc. Internal Medicine. Avocations: classical music, tennis, jogging, theater. Office: SUNY Health Sci Ctr Bldg T 17 Stony Brook NY 11794 E-mail: humirza@excite.com.

MIRZA, LEONA LOUSIN, elementary school educator, director; b. Chgo., July 1, 1944; d. Max B. and Opal Lousin; m. David B. Mirza; children: Sara Anush, Elizabeth Ann. BA in Math., North Park Coll., Chgo., 1965; MA in Edn., Western Mich. U., Kalamazoo, 1967, EdD in Edn., 1972; cert. in computer studies, North Park Coll., 1983. Specialist in elem. curriculum and adminstrn. Tchr. Kalamazoo Pub. Schs., 1965-69; prof. math. edn. North Park U., Chgo., 1969-2001, asst. acad. dean, 1999—2001; dir. Inst. for Internat. and Cultural Studies, 2001—. Editor The Ill. Math. Tchr., 1992-95; contbr. articles to profl. jours. Chmn. adv. com. on edn. in Ill., 1975-77. Mem. Nat. Coun. Tchrs. Math., Ill. Coun. Tchrs. Math., Ill. Assn. Colls. of Tchr. Edn., Ill. Assn. Tchrs. Edn. in Pvt. Colls. (officer 1974-86). Home: 5241 N Sawyer Ave Chicago IL 60625-4715 Office: 3225 W Foster Ave Chicago IL 60625-4823 Office Phone: 773-244-5731. E-mail: lmirza@northpark.edu.

MIRZA, MUHAMMAD ZUBAIR, medical products executive, engineering consultant, inventor, product development company executive, researcher; b. Jhelum, Punjab, Pakistan, Nov. 13, 1949; came to U.S., 1971; s. Muhammad Siddique and Shehr (Bano) M.; m. Tahira Beena, Aug. 12, 1977; children: Sarah, Nadia, Sana. Grad., Cadet Coll., Hasan Abdal, Pakistan, 1967; AS in Respiratory Therapy, St. Joseph/VA Hines Hosps., Chgo., 1974; BS in Biology, U. Ill., Springfield, 1976; MS in Product Design for Health Care, U. Ill., Chgo., 1978. Respiratory therapist St. Joseph Hosp., Chgo., 1974-79; assoc. engr. J.G.G. & Assocs., Woodbridge, N.J., 1979; product devel. engr. Becton-Dickinson Respiratory Sys., Lincoln Park, N.J., 1979-82; biomed. product devel. cons. M. Zubair Mirza Cons., Saddle Brook, N.J., 1982-86; co-founder, v.p. R & D, bd. dirs. Critichem, Inc. (acquired by Becton-Dickinson Corp. 1986), Little Falls, N.J., 1982-86; mgr. advanced devel. engring. Becton-Dickinson, Critichem Group, Fairlawn, N.J., 1986-88; dir. biomed. engring./tech. and equipment planning Shifa Internat. Hosp., Islamabad, Pakistan, 1989-90; pres. M. Zubair Mirza Cons., Wyckoff, Elmwood Park, Teaneck, NJ, 1988—; pres., ameer Natural Solutions, Inc., Wyckoff, Elmwood Park and Teaneck, 1991—. Rsch. asst. in sigh reflex in man, Sch. Medicine, So. Ill. U., Springfield, 1976; rsch. assoc. Office of Spl. Edn., Springfield, 1975-76, designer spl. edn. facility; rsch. assoc. to sr. cons. WHO, Geneva, 1977-78, designer self-health care kit. Author: Islamization of Business, 1994; patentee on respiratory monitor, 1992, respiratory monitoring device, 1993, trocar system, 1994, mechanical trocar insertion aparatus, 1995, pocket electronic spirometer, 1998, transportable sign or message holder, 2001, others. Trustee, v.p. Islamic Edn. Found. N.J., 1995—99, active Muslim, Jewish & Christian Dialogues, 1994—; ameer The Spirit of Medina (a comprehensive Islamic Cmty. Devel. Soc./Inst.), 1997—; mem. Am. Islamic Arbitration Assn., 1998—, mem. cmty.project coms., constn. review com., conflict review bd., election com. and others. Avocations: inventing, writing, reading, camping. Office: 526 John St Teaneck NJ 07666 E-mail: nsi@juno.com.

MISA, ELENA MAY, physical therapist; b. Cebu City, The Philippines, May 3, 1958; came to U.S., 1984; d. Tereso Justo and Lolita (Locaylocay) M.; 1 child, Nina Mae. AB in English, Velez Coll., Cebu City, 1979; BS in Phys. Therapy, Cebu Dr.'s Coll., Cebu City, 1982. Lic. phys. therapist, Tex. Staff phys. therapist S.K. Ajmani, MD, Houston, 1984-88; asst. supr. Twelve Oaks Hosp., Houston, 1988-90; staff phys. therapist L.I.F.E. Phys. Therapy, Houston, 1990-93; contract phys. therapist Stambush Phy. Therapy, Houston, 1990-94; clin. coord. Therapy and Rehab. Svcs., Plainview, Tex., 1994—99; rehab. mgr. Prairie House Living Ctr., Plainview, Tex., 1999—. Life teen core mem. Sacred Heart Ch., Plainview, 2000—, catechist, 1999—. Mem. Internat. Assn. Healthcare Practitioners, Palm Beach Gardens, Fla., 1996—. Roman Catholic. Home: 1509 Floydada St Plainview TX 79072-3655 Office: Prairie House Living Ctr Rehab Dept 1301 Mesa Dr Plainview TX 79072

MISA, KENNETH FRANKLIN, management consultant; b. Jamaica, N.Y., Sept. 24, 1939; s. Frank J. and Mary M. (Soszka) M. BS in Psychology cum laude, Purdue U., 1963; PhD in Psychology, St. John's U., 1966. Cert. mgmt. cons.; lic. psychologist, Calif. Staff psychologist Rohrer, Hibler & Replogle, L.A., 1966-67; assoc. A.T. Kearney, Inc., L.A., 1968-71, sr. assoc., 1972-74, prin., 1975-78, v.p., ptnr., 1979-86; pres. HR Cons. Group, 1987—. Mem. APA, Am. Psychol. Soc., Calif. State Psychol. Assn., Soc. for Human Resources Mgmt., Human Resources Planning Soc., Indsl. Rels. Rsch. Assn., Soc. for Indsl. and Orgnl. Psychology, World Affairs Coun. L.A., Town Hall So. Calif., Glendale C. of C., Jonathan Club. Republican. Roman Catholic. Home: 804 S Orange Grove Blvd Pasadena CA 91105-1715 Office: HR Cons Group 100 N Brand Blvd Ste 200 Glendale CA 91203-2642 Office Phone: 818-241-0060. Home Fax: 626-441-9584. Personal E-mail: kfmhrcg@aol.com.

MISA, THOMAS J. history educator, writer; b. May 31, 1959; BS, M.I.T., 1981; PhD, U. Penn., 1987. Prof. History Ill. Inst. Tech., Chgo., 1987—. Office Phone: 312-567-7967. Business E-Mail: misa@iit.edu.

MISCELLA, MARIA DIANA, humanities educator; b. NYC, July 11, 1929; d. Nicola and Giovanna (Tangorra) Torelli; m. Emilio Miscella, Feb. 27, 1954 (dec. Sept. 30, 1996); children: Delia, Marisa, Giuliana. Tchr. Degree, Istituto Magistrale, Lecce, Italy, 1946; postgrad., U. Naples, 1946-48; BA, Hunter Coll., 1954, MA, 1972. Cert. secondary educator NY. English corr. GE Co., Rome, 1950-51; corr. Spanish & French Pettinos Import & Export Co., N.Y.C., 1952-53; tchr. Italian Harrison (N.Y.) H.S., 1967-87, St. John's U., Queens, N.Y., 1987-89; lectr. Italian various orgsn., N.Y. State, 1987—; lectr. Italian lit. and history various colls. and univs., N.Y., 1987—. Moderator of club Harrison (N.Y.) H.S., 1967-87. Mem. Little Neck (N.Y.) Civic Assn., 1970-95, Am. Assn. Ret. People, Douglaston, N.Y., 1994—; founder, treas. Italian Am. Women's Ctr., 1997—. Recipient scholarship Columbia U., 1954, Letter of Commendation, Bd. Regents, Albany, N.Y., 1980, Cert. Recognition and Gratitude for Contbn. to the Arts and Dedication to Cmty., N.Y.C. Coun., 2004; named Woman of Yr., Consortium of L.I. Italian Am. Orgns., 1992. Mem. AAUW (hostess, v.p. 1990-93, cert. of commendation 1996), Am. Assn. Tchrs. of Italian (sec. Societa Onoraria Italica 1979-91), Ams. Italian Heritage (bd. mem. 1982—, Women of the Yr. 2004), Sons of Italy (John Marino Lodge cultural com. mem 1994—, Merit award 1995), Assn. Italian Am. Educators (dir./historian by-laws com. 2000), N.Y. State United Tchrs., Am. Fedn. Tchrs., Nat. Italian Am. Found., Douglaston Women Club, Retirees Club. Roman Catholic. Avocations: reading, writing, travel, going to theatre, playing bridge.

MISCHKE, CARL HERBERT, retired religious association executive; b. Hazel, S.D., Oct. 27, 1922; s. Emil Gustav and Pauline Alvina (Polzin) M.; m. Gladys Lindloff, July 6, 1947; children: Joel, Susan Mischke Blahnik, Philip, Steven. BA, Northwestern Coll., Watertown, Wis., 1944; M.Div., Wis. Luth. Sem., Mequon, 1947. Ordained to ministry Evang. Lutheran Ch. Parish pastor Wis. Synod, 1947-79; pres. Western Wis. Dist. Evang. Luth. Ch., Juneau, 1964-79; v.p. Wis. Luth. Synod, Milw., 1966-79, pres., 1979-93; retired, 1993. Lutheran.

MISCHKE, FREDERICK CHARLES, retired manufacturing executive; b. Benton Harbor, Mich., Sept. 21, 1930; s. Fred William and Clara Adeline (Ruhno) M.; m. Kathleen Ann Schultz, Nov. 19, 1955 (dec. Aug. 1980); children: Stephanie Ann, Michael Frederick (dec. Oct. 12, 1996), Eric William; m. Lori Ann Leonard, Dec. 23, 1983. AA, Lake Mich. Coll., 1956; BBA, Western Mich. U., 1958. CPA, Ind., Mich. Staff acct. Lybrand, Ross Bros. & Montgomery, Chgo., 1958-63, supr. acctg. Niles, Mich., 1963-65; v.p., treas. Skyline Corp., Elkhart, Ind., 1965-91, ret., 1991. Vol. Svc. Corps. Ret. Execs., 1992—, local v.p., 1993-99, treas. 2000—; chmn. Meml. Endowment Fund Luth. Ch., 1995—. Mem. AICPA, Ind. Assn. CPAs (Civic Achievement award, 1976), Mich. Assn. CPAs, Fin. Execs. Inst. (Michiana chpt. pres. 1974-75), Elcona Country Club (pres. 1975), Rotary (local pres. 1976-77). Republican. Lutheran. Avocations: photography, boating, golf. Home: 23322 Greenleaf Blvd Elkhart IN 46514-4508

MISE, JESSE SHERDEN, structural engineer, consultant; b. Jonesville, Va., July 13, 1933; s. Clabe Moss and Gladys Elizabeth (Orr) M.; m. Betty Joy Curtiss, July 8, 1984; children: Nancy Miller, Linda Andrews, Doug Hinshaw. BS in Math., Tenn. Tech., 1957. Registered profl. engr., Tenn., Mo. Road designer Va. Dept. Hwys., Petersburg, 1958-64; structural designer various archtl., engring. firms, 1964-67; structural engr. Combustion Engring., Windsor, Conn., 1967-72, Tenn. Eastman, Kingsport, 1973-76, TVA, Knoxville, 1976-87, ABB Environ., Knoxville, 1988-91; cons. Jesse S. Mise, P.E., Knoxville, 1992—; chief engr. James Thomas Engring., Knoxville, 1992—. Author: Engineers Guide to Unusual Opportunities, 1972. Mem. Patriots of East Tenn., Knoxville, 1996—. Mem. ASCE, Nat. Coun. of Examiners for Engring. and Surveying, 1993—. Home and Office: 5704 Melstone Dr Knoxville TN 37912-4629 Office Phone: 865-689-3702. Personal E-mail: jessemise@aol.com.

MISHAL, DEVADATT M. obstetrician/gynecologist; b. Ratnagiri, India, Mar. 15, 1948; came to U.S., 1973; MD, Bombay U., 1973. Diplomate Am. Bd. Obstetrics and Gynecology. Intern Lower Bucks Hosp., Bristol, Calif., 1973-74; resident in obstetrics, gynecology Cooper Hosp. U. Med. Ctr., Camden, Calif., 1977-80; pres. of staff Downey (Calif.) Regional Med. Ctr., Calif.; staff Presby Inter Cmty. Hosp., Whittier, Calif., St. Francis Med. Ctr., Lynwood, Calif.; pvt. practice, group partnership Downey, Calif., 1982—; pres. med. staff Downey Regional Med. Ctr., Downey, Calif., 1999—2001. Chmn. obstetrics, gynecology Downey (Calif.) Regional Med. Ctr., 1992—96, 2002—; mem. staff L.A. County Med. Assn. Mem. ACOG, Am. Assn. of Gynecological Laparoscopists, Calif. Med. Assn. (L.A. chpt.), L.A. County Med. Assn. Office: 8500 Florence Ave Downey CA 90240-4015 also: 12446 Washington Blvd Whittier CA 90602-1005

MISHEL, LAWRENCE, economics research director; BA, Pa. State U., 1974; MA, Am. U., 1977; PhD in Econs., U. Wis., 1982. Prof. of Econs. Cornell U., Ithaca, N.Y., 1982-83; economist UAW, Detroit, 1983-85, IUD, AFL-CIO, Washington, 1986-87; rsch. dir. Econ. Policy Inst., Washington, 1987—. Co-author: (book) The State of Working America, 1991.

MISHELEVICH, DAVID JACOB, medical company executive, consultant; b. Pitts., Jan. 26, 1942; s. Benjamin and Sarah (Bachrach) M.; m. Bonnie Gray McKim, Dec. 6, 1981; 1 child, Cory Jane. BS in Physics, U. Pitts., 1962; MD, Johns Hopkins U., 1966, PhD in Biomed. Engring., 1970. Lic., Md., Tex. Intern in medicine Balt. City Hosps. (now The John Hopkins Bayview Med. Ctr.), 1966-67; active duty U.S. Pub. Health Svc., 1967—69, inactive reserve, 1969—; staff assoc. Nat. Inst. Neurol. Diseases and Stroke, NIH, Bethesda, Md., 1967-69; exec. v.p. Nat. Ednl. Consultants, Balt., 1971-72; prof., dept. chairperson, dir. med. computing resources ctr. U. Tex. Health Sci. Ctr., Dallas, 1972-82; attending physician/sr. attending physician internal med. Dallas County Hosp., Dist. Parkland Meml. Hosp., 1973-82; v.p. computer and software tech. EAN-TECH, Mountain View, Calif., 1983-84; CEO Garden Gate Software, Cupertino, Calif., 1984-86; dir., then v.p. and gen. mgr. applications and rsch. divsn. IntelliCorp, Inc., Mountain View, 1986-89; v.p. mktg. and sales Viewpoint Engring., Mountain View, 1989-90; v.p. engring. AirWays Med. Techs., Inc., Palo Alto, Calif., 1991-93; dir., then v.p. R&D, chief tech. officer Circadian, Inc., San Jose, Calif., 1993-95, v.p., gen. mgr. AirWays Asthma Ctrs. divsn., 1995-96; CEO Sterling Healthcare Outcomes, Inc., Cupertino, 1996—2002, Playa del Rey, Calif., 2002—; founder, exec. v.p., chief tech. officer QENM.com, 1999-2001; chief tech. officer HealthShore, Inc., 2001—; lead technologist Outbreak! Music Sys., 2002—; chief tech. officer TeleCath, 2003—. Pres. Mishelevich Assocs., Dallas, 1982-83, Cupertino, 1990-91, cons. prof. of neurosurgery, Stanford U. Sch. Medicine, 2003-; mem. biomed. libr. rev. com. NIH-Nat. Libr. Medicine, 1978-82; cons. in field. Former tech. reviewer IBM Sys. Jour., Jour. of AMA; rev. IEEE computer Soc. Internet, 2001—; contbr. numerous articles to profl. jours.; patentee in field. V.p. Dallas chpt. Am. Jewish Congress, 1980-84, Am. Jewish Fund, 1980-81; pres. Westport Bch. Club Villas, Homeowners Assn., 2003-. Fellow Am. Coll. Med. Informatics; mem. AAAS, IEEE and IEEE Computer Soc. (exec. bd. tech. com. on computational medicine 1981-83), Am. Assn. for Artificial Intelligence, Assn. for Computing Machinery (chair Dallas chpt. 1974-75), Am. Med. Informatics Assn., Internat. Tandem Users Group (past pres.), Model T Ford Club of Am., Phi Beta Kappa, Omicron Kappa. Democrat. Jewish. Home and Office: 7301 Vista del Mar #B111 Playa Del Rey CA 90293 E-mail: david@mishelevich.com. *Working with computers for some forty years has made me particularly sensitive to human needs and productivity. Two principles in which I believe are the human resources principle (maximize people's strengths and minimize or neutralize their weaknesses so they perform personally and professionally better than they would otherwise expect of themselves), and the optimality principle (I would rather do a 92% job in two weeks than a 97% job in 2 years).*

MISHELL, DANIEL R., JR., obstetrician, gynecologist, educator; b. Newark, May 7, 1931; s. Daniel R. and Helen Mishell; m. Carol Goodrich; children: Sandra, Daniel III, Tanya. BA, Stanford U., 1952, MD, 1955. Diplomate Am. Bd. Ob-Gyn. (examiner 1975-95, bd. dirs., dir. subspecialty divsn. reproductive endocrinology 1985-89, pres. 1986-90, chmn. 1990-94). Intern L.A. County Harbor Gen. Hosp., Torrance, 1955-56; resident in internal medicine Bellevue Hosp., N.Y.C., 1956-57; resident in ob-gyn. UCLA-Harbor Gen. Hosp., Torrance, 1959-63; rsch. fellow Univ. Hosp., Uppsala, Sweden, 1961-62; from asst. prof. to assoc. prof. dept. ob-gyn. UCLA Sch. Medicine, 1963-69; prof. U. So. Calif., L.A., 1969—, assoc. chmn. dept., 1972-78, chmn. dept. ob/gyn., 1978—. Editor-in-chief Contraception, 1969—; editor Jour. Reproductive Medicine, 1982—, Year Book of Obstetrics and Gynecology, 1987—, Year Book of Infertility, 1989-96; adv. com. Core Jours. in Ob-gyn., 1982—; mem. editl. bd. New Trends in Gynecology and Obstetrics, 1998—. Capt. USAF, 1957-59. Recipient Lester T. Hibbard award U. So. Calif., L.A., 1983, Joseph Bolivar DeLee Humanitarian award Chgo. Lying-In Hosp., 1985, Arthur and Edith Wippman Sci. Rsch. award Planned Parenthood Fedn. Am., 1992, Disting. Scientist award Soc. Gynecologic Investigation, 1994. Mem. Am. Gyn-Ob Soc., Am. Soc. Reproductive Medicine, Am. Coll. Obstetricians and Gynecologists, Am. Fedn. Clin. Rsch., Endocrine Soc., Soc. for Gynecologic Investigation (pres. 1985-86), L.A. Ob-Gyn. Soc. (v.p. 1984-85, pres. 1985-86), Assn. Profs. Gynecology and Obstetrics (exec. coun. 1982-85), Pacific Coast Fertility Soc. (pres. 1973-74), Salerni Collegium, L.A. Athletic Club, Phi Beta Kappa, Alpha Omega Alpha. Avocations: tennis, fishing. Office: U So Calif 1240 N Mission Rd Los Angeles CA 90033-1019 E-mail: mishell@hsc.usc.edu.

MISHKIN, BARBARA FRIEDMAN, lawyer; b. Phila., Feb. 19, 1936; d. Maurice Harold and Gertrude (Sanders) F.; m. Martin S. Thaler, Mar. 22, 1958 (div. 1970); children: Diane Sanders, Paul Sanders, David Emile, Amy Suzanne; m. Mortimer Mishkin, May 27, 1971. AB, Mount Holyoke Coll., 1957; MA, Yale U., 1958; JD, Am. U., 1981. Bar: D.C. 1982, U.S. Supreme Ct. 1989, U.S. Ct. Appeals (4th cir.) 1995. Research psychologist NIMH, Bethesda, Md., 1968-69; spl. asst. to chief judge U.S. Ct. Appeals (D.C. cir.), Washington, 1970-71; spl. asst. to scientific dir. Nat. Inst. Child Health, Bethesda, 1971-74; asst. staff dir. Nat. Commn. for the Protection of Human Subjects, Washington, 1974-78; staff dir. Ethics Adv. Bd. HEW, Washington, 1978-80; dep. dir. Pres.' Commn. on Ethics in Medicine and Research, Washington, 1980-83; assoc. Hogan and Hartson, Washington, 1983-89, counsel, 1990-93; ptnr. Hogan & Hartson, 1994—. Cons. Ctr. for Law and Health Scis., Boston, 1970-73; cons., lectr. Johns Hopkins U. Sch. of Medicine, Balt., 1971-73; bd. dirs. Bon Secours Health Systems, Inc., Columbia, Md., 1984-90. Contbr. numerous articles on health law, med. ethics and biomed. research to jours. in field. Mem. policy bd. Legal Counsel for the Elderly, Washington, 1984-88, vice chair, 1988-90; trustee Mt. Holyoke Coll., 1985-90; mem. Mayor's Adv. Task Force on Hospice Licensure, Washington, 1985-87; bd. dirs. Hebrew Home Greater Washington, 1987-91. Mem. ABA (chair sect. on health and environment 1988-92, chair com. on regulating rsch. 1996-98), D.C. Bar Assn. (subcom. rights of the elderly and the handicapped 1985-92, Pro Bono Atty. Yr. 1988), AAAS (com. on sci. freedom and responsibility 1986-92, AAAS/ABA Nat. Conf. Lawyers and Scientists 1992, ABA co-chair 1993-97), Am. Soc. Law, Medicine and Ethics (bd. dirs. 1995-98). Home: 5610 Wisconsin Ave Apt 402 Chevy Chase MD 20815-4429 Office: Hogan & Hartson Columbia Sq 555 13th St Washington DC 20004 Office Phone: 202-637-5680. Business E-Mail: bfmishkin@hhlaw.com.

MISHKIN, MORTIMER, neuropsychologist; b. Fitchburg, Mass., Dec. 13, 1926; AB, Dartmouth Coll., 1946; MA, McGill U., Montreal, Can., 1949, PhD, 1951; DSc (hon.), McGill U., 2004. Asst. in research and physiology and psychiatry Yale U. Med. Sch., New Haven, Conn., 1949-51; research assoc. Inst. of Living, Hartford-Conn. and NYU Bellevue Med. Ctr., N.Y.C., 1951-55; research psychologist, sect. on neuropsychology NIMH, Bethesda, Md., 1955-75, research physiologist, Lab. of Neuropsychology, 1976-78, chief sect. cerebral mechanisms Lab. of Neuropsychology, 1979-80, chief Lab. of Neuropsychology, 1980-97, assoc. dir. basic rsch. DIRP, 1994-97, chief sect. cognitive neuroscience, 1997—. Part-time instr. psychology Howard U., 1956-58; vis. scientist Nencki Inst. Exptl. Biology, Warsaw, Poland, winter 1958, 68, Tokyo Met. Inst. Neuroscis., summer 1978, Oxford U. Dept. Exptl. Psychology, summer 1979, Inst. Child Health U. Coll. London, 1993; mem. psychol. scis. panel NIH, 1959-61, exptl. psychology study sect., 1965-69; mem. NIMH Assembly of Scientists Council, 1962-64, 72-74; mem. NIMH Scientist Promotion Rev. Com., 1984-86; mem. adv. com. Cognitive Neurosci. Inst., 1982-86; mem. NIH Fogart Internat. Scholars-in-Residence Adv. Panel, 1985-89, McDonnell Found. Study panel, 1987-89; adv. bd. McDonnell-Pew Program Cognitive Neurosci., 1989-94; cons. Developmental Cognitive Neurosci. Unit, Inst. Child Health, U. Coll. London, 1990—, vis. prof., 2000—; active Human Frontier Sci. Program, 1992-94, chmn. 1993; adv. bd. Ctr. for the Neural Basis of Cognition, U. Pitts. and Carnegie Mellon U., 1994-96, chair, 1999; adv. bd. La. State U. Neurosci. Ctr., 1994-96, Frontier Rsch. Program, RIKEN, Japan, 1994-96, Zanryl Krieger Mind-Brain Inst., Johns Hopkins U., 1994-2000, Cognitive and Behavioral Neurosci. Panel, SUNY, Stony Brook, 1996, Mental Health and Neurosci. Clin. Rsch. Ctr., U. N.C., Chapel Hill, 1996-98, Krasnow Inst., George Mason U., Fellow Mentor Program, 1997-2002. Cons. editor Jour. Comparative and Physiol. Psychology, 1963-73, Exptl. Brain Rsch., 1965—, Brain Rsch., 1974-78, Neuropsychologia, 1963-92, Human Neurobiology, 1981-87, Jour. Cognitive Neurosci., 1989—, Jour. NIH Rsch., 1989-97, Cerebral Cortex, 1990-95, Advances in Neurobiology, 1990—, Handbook Behavioral Neurology, 1991—, Current Opinion in Neurobiology, 1991—, Neurobiology of Learning and Memory, 1992—, Learning and Memory, 1993—, Jour. Internat. Neuropsychol. Soc., 1995-99, Internat. Encyclopedia of the Social and Behavioral Scis., 1998-2002; reviewing editors Sci., 1985-93; assoc. editor Neuroreport, 1990-2000; contbr. numerous articles to profl. jours., also abstracts and book revs. Served to lt. (j.g.) USNR. Recipient U.S. Presdl. Disting. Rank award, 1992, Karl Spencer Lashley prize Am. Philos. Soc., 1996, Found. Ipsen Neuronal Plasticity prize, 1995, Med. Rsch. award Met. Life Found., 2000. Fellow AAAS (chair-elect 1990-91, chair 1991-92, past chair 1992-93), APA Assn. (officer, divsn. 6 mem. at large 1964-66, coun. rep. 1967-69, pres. 1968-69); mem. NAS (officer, sect. 52 chmn. 1989-92), Ea. Psychol. Assn., Internat. Brain Research Orgn. (officer, rep.-at-large governing coun. 1993-98), Internat. Neuropsychol. Soc., Internat. Neuropsychol. Symposium, Internat. Primatological Soc., Internat. Soc. Neuroethology, Soc. Exptl. Psychologists (Howard Crosby Warren medal 1998), Soc. Neurosci. (officer, pres.-elect 1985-86, pres. 1986-87, past pres. 1987-88), Inst. Medicine, Sigma Xi, Phi Beta Kappa. Achievements includes research in behavioral and cognitive neuroscience in primates. Office: NIMH Lab Neuropsychology 49 Convent Dr Msc 4415 Bldg 49 Bethesda MD 20892-0001 Business E-Mail: mishkinm@mail.nih.gov.

MISHKIN, PAUL J. lawyer, educator; b. Trenton, N.J., Jan. 1, 1927; s. Mark Mordecai and Bella (Dworetsky) M.; m. Mildred Brofman Westover; 1 child, Jonathan Mills Westover. AB, Columbia U., 1947, JD, 1950; MA (hon.), U. Pa., 1971. Bar: N.Y. State bar 1950, U.S. Supreme Ct. bar 1958. Mem. faculty Law Sch. U. Pa., Phila., 1950-72; prof. law U. Calif., Berkeley, 1972-75, Emanuel S. Heller prof., 1975—2000, Emanuel S. Heller prof. emeritus, 2000—. Cons. City of Phila., 1953; reporter study div. jurisdiction between state and fed. cts. Am. Law Inst., 1960-65; mem. faculty Salzburg Seminar in Am. Studies, 1974; Charles Inglis Thompson guest prof. U. Colo., 1975; John Randolph Tucker lectr., 1978, Owen J. Roberts Meml. lectr., 1982; vis. fellow Wolfson Coll., Cambridge U., 1984; vis. prof. Duke U. Law Sch., 1989. Author: (with Morris) On Law in Courts, 1965, (with others) Federal Courts and the Federal System, 2d edit, 1973, 3d edit, 1988; contbr. articles to profl. jours. Trustee Jewish Publ. Soc. Am., 1966-75, Ctr. for Law in the Pub. Interest, 2001-04; mem. permanent com. Oliver Wendell Holmes Devise, 1979-87. With USNR 1945-46. Rockefeller Found. rsch. grantee, 1956; Center for Advanced Study in Behavioral Scis. fellow, 1964-65; recipient Russell Prize for Excellence in Teaching, 1996. Fellow Am. Acad. Arts Scis., Am. Bar Found.; mem. Am. Law Inst., Order of Coif, Phi Beta Kappa. Home: 91 Stonewall Rd Berkeley CA 94705-1414 Office: U Calif Sch Law Boalt Hall Berkeley CA 94720

MISHLER, CLIFFORD LESLIE, publisher; b. Vandalia, Mich., Aug. 11, 1939; s. Nelson Howard and Lily Mae (Young) M.; m. Sandra Rae Knutson, Dec. 21, 1963 (dec. July 8, 1972); m. Sylvia M. Leer, Feb. 27, 1976; children: Sheila, Sharon, Susan. Student, Northwestern U., 1957-58. Author, pub. ann. edits. Ann. Studies U.S. and Can. Commemorative Medals and Tokens, 1958-63; assoc. editor Numismatic News, Krause Publs., Iola, Wis., 1963-64, editor, 1964-66, numismatic editor all publs., 1966-75, exec. v.p., pub. all numismatic publs., 1975-78, exec. v.p., pub. all products, 1978-88, sr. v.p., pub. all Numismatic products, 1988-89, sr. v.p. ops., 1989-90; pres. Krause Publs., Iola, Wis., 1991-99. Chmn. bd. dirs. Krause Publs., 2000-02; bd. dirs. First State Bank Iola, 1972-83, Scandinavia Telephone Co., 1981-97, TDS Telecom cmty. bd., 1997-2000; ex-officio dir. Iola Old Car Show, Inc., 1985-2003; mem. coins and medals adv. panel Am. Revolution Bicentennial Commn., 1970-75; mem. ann. assay commn. U.S. Mint, 1973. Co-author: Standard Catalog of World Coins, ann. 1972—; contbr. articles New Book Knowledge, ann. 1969-81. Mem. Wis. Commemorative Quarter Coun., 2001—03; bd. dirs. William R. Higgins, Jr. Found., 1991—. Recipient The Internat. Vreneli Preistrager: The "Friendly Prize" for lifetime numismatic achievements, Munzen-Revue, Basel, Switzerland, 2001, Numis. Amb. award, Numis. News/Balt., Md., 2003. Fellow Am. Numismatic Soc. (life, coun. mem. 1997-2003, trustee 2003—); mem. Am. Numismatic Assn. (life, medal of merit 1983, Farran Zerbe Meml. Disting Svc. award 1984, Glen Smedley meml. dedicated svcs. award 1991, Lifetime Achievement award 1997, Numismatist of Yr. 2002, hall of fame 2004), Token and Medal Soc. (life, pres. 1976-78, editor jour. 1964-68, Disting. Svc. award 1966, 80), Numismatists of Wis. (life, pres. 1974-76, Meritorious Svc. award 1972), Soc. Internat. Numismatics (award of excellence 1981), Blue Ridge Numismatic Assn. (life, hall of fame 1994), Tex. Numismatic Assn. (life, hall of fame 1993), Ind. State Numismatic Assn. (life, founders award 1993), Ctrl. States Numismatic Soc. (life, medal of merit 1984), Iola Lions (Melvin Jones fellow 1996). Home: 100 Island Dr Iola WI 54945-9485 Office: 105 N Main St Iola WI 54945-0001

MISHLER, JOHN JOSEPH, sculptor, art educator; b. Nazareth, Ethiopia, May 28, 1948; came to U.S., 1949; s. Dorsa J. and Mary K. (Diller) M.; m. Phyllis M. Emerson, June 27, 1970; 1 child, Nathan M. BA, Goshen (Ind.) Coll., 1972; MFA, U. Tenn., 1977. Assoc. prof. art Goshen Coll., 1985—. Executed sculptors for Recreation Ctr., Goshen Coll., 1995, Chandler Grade Sch., Goshen, 1995, U. Notre Dame, 1996, also pvt. comms; exhbns. include Midwest Mus., Elkhart, Ind., 1992, Western Mich. U., Kalamazoo, 1992, U. Notre Dame, Ind., 1995-96, Midwest Mus. Am. Art, Elkhart, 1995 (Purchase award), Michiana Regional Airport, South Bend, Ind., 2002, Krasl Art Ctr., St. Joseph, Mich., 2002, Art & Cultural Ctr., Fall Brook, Calif., 2002, Field Mus., Chgo., 2002, Sculpture in the Park 2002, Loveland, Chgo., 2002, Pier Walk 2002, Navy Pier, Chgo., 2002. Genesis grantee, 1995; recipient 2 purchase awards Elkhart (Ind.) Regional Midwest Mus. Art, 1997.*

MISHLER, JOHN MILTON (YOCHANAN MENASHSHEH BEN SHAUL), natural sciences educator, administrator, artist; b. Cairo, Ill., Sept. 25, 1946; s. John Milton and Mary Jane (Woodbury) M.; m. Mary Therese Stember, Apr. 15, 1972 (div. Nov. 1981); m. Sigrid Ruth Elizabeth Fischer, Dec. 15, 1981; 1 child, Joshua Evan. AA with honors, Orange Coast Coll., Costa Mesa, Calif., 1966; AB in Molecular Biology, U. Calif., San Diego, 1969, ScM in Engring. Scis., 1971; DPhil in Immunohematology, St. John's Coll., Oxford U., 1978. Cert. community coll. instr., Calif. Clin. coord. McGaw Labs., Costa Mesa, 1972-78; rsch. fellow Royal Postgrad. Med. Sch., Eng., 1977-78, Med. U., Cologne, Fed. Republic Germany, 1978-80; br. chief Nat. Heart, Lung and Blood Inst. NIH, Bethesda, Md., 1980-82; prof. med., basic life scis. and pharmacol. U. Mo., Kansas City, 1983-89, asst. vice chancellor, 1983-85, dir. div. basic med. scis., 1985-86, assoc. vice chancellor, 1985-89; prof. nat. scis. U. Md. Ea. Shore, Princess Anne, 1989-94, dean grad. studies and rsch., 1989-91; prof. biology Delaware Valley Coll. Sci. and Agrl., Doylestown, Pa., 1994—, dean of Coll., 1994-95. Frequent nat. and internat. lectr.; chmn. 13 nat. and internat. meeting sects. Author: Pharmacology of Hydroxyethyl Starch. Use in Therapy and Blood Banking, 1982; mem. editl. bd. Jour. Soc. Rsch. Adminstrs., 1987-91; book rev. editor Grants Mag., 1987-89; contbr. over 100 articles to profl. jours. Bd. dirs. Ctr. for Bus. Innovation, Inc., 1987, Bucks Assn. for Retarded Citizens, 1995-96; v.p. Artsbridge, 1999-2000. Sr. rsch. fellow Alexander von Humboldt Foun. (Germany), 1978-80; recipient Outstanding Adminstrn. Svc. award U. Mo., Kansas City, 1987, Excellence award Soc. Rsch. Adminstrn., 1989, Cert. Appreciation, 1991, Silver and Bronze awards Artist Guild of Delaware Valley, 1998, Second prize Chester County Art Assn., 1998, Bd. Dirs. award

Gtr. Norristown Art League, 1998, Award of Merit Westmoreland Art Nats., 1998, Perkins Ctr. for Arts, 2000, Robert Ransley Outstanding Talent award, 1999, 2d prize drawing Ctr. for the Creative Arts, 1999, 1st prize graphics Perkiomen Valley Art Ctr., 1999, 2d prize, 2002, Wayne Art Supply award Wayne Art Ctr., 2002, Pres.'s award Salmagundi Club, 2002, Best of Show/1st Pl. award Louisville Art Assn., 2003, Jerry's Artarama award Montana Watercolor Soc., 2003, honorable mention Associated Artists Southport, 2004, Franklin Square Gallery, 2004. Fellow Internat. Soc. Haematology, Royal Coll. Pathologists; mem. Am. Soc. Hematology, German Soc. Hematology, Nat. Coun. Univ. Rsch. Adminstrn., Nat. Assn. State Univs. and Land-Grant Colls. (mem. exec. com. coun. on rsch. policy and grad. edn. 1990-91), Coun. Grad. Schs., N.Y. Acad. Scis., Sigma Xi. Jewish. Avocations: reading, abstract art painting, writing, music. Home: 475 North St Apt 6F Doylestown PA 18901-3863 Office: Delaware Valley Coll 700 E Butler Ave Doylestown PA 18901-2607 Office Phone: 215-489-2351. Business E-Mail: mishlerj@devalcol.edu.

MISHOE, THOMAS M. dairy products executive; b. Loris, S.C., Apr. 5, 1952; s. Thomas Milton Sr. and Coreina (Cartrette) M.; m. Dana Belinda Jones, May 25, 1974; 1 child, Kathryn Morgan. BA, Hampden-Sydney Coll., 1974; MBA, Va. Polytechnic Inst. & State, U., 1976. CPA, CMA. Various positions to sr. mgr. Ernst & Whinney, Birmingham, 1982—; various to sr. mgr. Capital Markets Group, Birmingham, Ala.; chief fin and adminstrv. officer Goldome Credit Corp., 1993-95; cons. Am South Bank, Birmingham; chief fin. officer, v.p., treas. and sec. Eskimo Pie Corp., Richmond, Va., 1996—. Co-author: Profitability Measurement in Financial Institutions: A Management Approach, 1987. Mem. AICPA, Ala. Soc. CPAs, Va. Soc. CPAs, Sigma Nu. Republican. Baptist. Office: Eskimo Pie Corp 1175 Veterans Memorial Hwy Ronkonkoma NY 11779-7639

MISHRA, SANJAY, music educator; arrived in U.S., 1977; s. Shankar and Sudha Mishra. MusB, Peabody Inst., 1985. Adj. faculty No. Va. C.C., Alexandria, 2000—. Composer: (CD) Blue Incantation, 1995, Rescue, 2000, (films) Port Djema, 1996. Recipient Best Score award, Hampton Film Festival, 1996. Home: 6992 N Fairfax Arlington VA 22213 Office: No Va CC 3001 N Beauregard Alexandria VA 22311 Office Phone: 202-331-4435. E-mail: info@mishra.net.

MISHRA, SANJAY R, physicist; b. Surat, Gujarat, India, Dec. 1, 1966; s. Ramnaresh A and Sita Devi Mishra; m. Shefali Pandey, June 6, 1967; 1 child, Chaitanya. BSc, South Gujarat U., Surat, Gujarat, India, 1987; MSc, South Gujarat U., Surat, 1989; PG Diploma, Gujarat U., Ahmedabad, Gujarat, India, 1990; MS, Pitts. St. U., Pittsburg, Kans., 1992; PhD, U. Mo.-Rolla, Rolla, Mo., 1996. Rsch. assoc. U. Wis., Advance Light Source, LBNL, Berkeley, Calif., 1998—99, Va. Commonwealth U., Advance Light Source, LBNL, Berkeley, Calif., 1996—98; asst. prof. U. Memphis, 1999—. Contbr. scientific papers over 20 presented more than 40 seminars. Treas. India Assn. of Memphis, 2000—01; pres. India Student Orgn., Rolla, Mo., 1994—95; vol. Indian culture and cmty. temple, Memphis, 2000. Recipient Y. G Nayak Award, South Gujarat Univ., 1987, Tau beta Tau, U. Mo.-Rolla, 1995, Best Rsch. Award, Pitts. St. U., 1991, U. Mo.-Rolla, 1995, Merit Honour, South Guarat U., 1989, South Gujarat U., 1987; grantee NSF-MRI, NSF, 2000, Faculty Rsch. Grant, U. Memphis, 2003; scholar Nat. Merite Scholarship, Govt. India, 1985. Mem.: Soc. of Microscopy, Materials Rsch. Soc., Am. Phys. Socieity, Phi Beta Phi, Sigma Phi Sigma. Achievements include first to understanding the effect of substitutional non-magnetic atoms in rare earth iron permanent magnetic materials; research in devel. novel ion-implantation technique to prepare magnetic nanocomposites; understanding nanomechanical properties of bio-implantable polymers; synthesis of magnetic nanocomposite and dilute magnetic semicondutors synthesis of exchanges bias material using ball milling. Home: 4829 Kaye Rd Memphis TN 38117 Office: Univ Memphis Dept Physics Manning Hall 226 Memphis TN 38152 Office Phone: 901-678-3115. Business E-Mail: srmishra@memphis.edu.

MISKIS, CONSTANTINOS I. federal agency administrator; BA, Fla. Internat. U.; JD, U. Fla., 1995. Bar: U.S. Dist. Ct. (so. dist.) Fla., U.S. Dist. Ct. (no. dist.) Fla., U.S. Dist. Ct. (mid. dist.) Fla. From law clk. to assoc. former U.S. Dist. Ct. Judge and former U.S. Atty. Thomas E. Scott; mem. AHCA adv. team Gov. Jeb Bush on Medicaid and HHS Issues; chief Medicaid counsel, dep. gen. counsel Fla. Agy. for Health Care Adminstrn., 1998—2001; gen. counsel, dir. legis. affairs, chief of staff Fla. Dept. Elder Affairs, 2001—02; regional rep. Region IV U.S. Dept. Health and Human Svcs., Atlanta, 2002—. Mem. editl. bd.: Fla. Healthcare Jour.; author: Florida Master Medicaid Guide, 2001; contbr. articles to profl. jours. Mem.: ABA, Tallahassee Bar Assn., Dade County Bar Assn., Fla. State Bar (health laws sect.), Am. Health Lawyers Assn. Office: US Dept HHS Sam Nunn Atlanta Fed Ctr 61 Forsyth St SW Atlanta GA 30303-8909 Office Phone: 404-562-7888.

MISKUS, MICHAEL ANTHONY, electrical engineer; b. East Chicago, Ind., Dec. 10, 1950; s. Paul and Josephine Miskus; m. Daphne Christine Headley, Nov. 19, 1998. BS, AAS in Elec. Engring. Tech., Purdue U., 1972; cert. mgmt., Ind. U., 1972, Ind. Ctrl. Coll., 1974; MA in Orgnl. Mgmt., U. Phoenix, 1996, postgrad., 1997; PhD in Orgnl. Behavior, Columbia U., 1998. Cert. plant engr. IIPFE; registered environ. assessor REA, Calif. Svc. engr. Reliance Electric & Engring. Co., Hammond, Ind., 1972-73; maintenance supr., maintenance mgr. Diamond Chain Co./AMSTED Industries, Indpls., 1973-76; primary and facilities elec. engr. Johnson & Johnson Baby Products Co., Park Forest South, Ill., 1976-81; prin. Miskus Cons., indsl./comml. elec. cons., 1979—; plant and facilities engring. mgr. Sherwin Williams Co., Chgo. Emulsion Plant, 1981-85; with Miscon Assocs., Riverside, Calif., 1985—; acting dir. plant and facilities engring. Bourns Inc., 1982-90; facility mgr. Cardiovascular Devices Inc., 3M Healthcare, 1990—; mgr. Metrology and Corp. Metrology Lab. & ISO 9000, 3M, St. Paul; facilities ops. mgr. Press Enterprise, Riverside, 1997-2001; dir. facilities and plant engring. Shell Solar Industries LP, Camarillo, Calif., 2001—. Instr., lectr. EET program Moraine Valley C.C., Palos Hills, Ill., 1979; instr. cert. program plant engring. U. Calif.; lectr. energy engring., bldg. automation sys. Prairie State Coll., Chicago Heights, Ill., 1980—; mem. adj. faculty, faculty adv. bd. Orange Coast Coll., Costa Mesa, Calif.; bd. dirs., v.p. adminstrn. Internat. Inst. Plant & Facilities Engring.; commr., chmn. Riverside Energy Commn., 1988—; mem. Elec. Industry Evaluation Panel. Mem. faculty adv. bd. Moraine Valley C.C., 1980—. Mem. IEEE, Am. Inst. Plant Engrs. (pres. Pomona chpt. 1989—, chmn. western region VI membership, chm. nat. coun. stds. labs. region II Twin Cities sect. 1995—), Assn. Facility Engrs. (pres. Inland Empire chpt. III 1997—), Assn. Energy Engrs. (sr., So. Calif. chpt.), Assn. Profl. Energy Mgrs. (bd. dirs. Orange County chpt. 1992), Internat. Inst. Plant and Facilities Engring. (dir. tech. 1999—), Illuminating Engring. Soc. N.Am., Internat. Platform Assn., Riverside C. of C., Purdue Alumni Orgn. L.A. (v.p. Inland chpt.), Purdue Club L.A. (v.p. Inland Empire sect.). E-mail: info@iipfe.org.

MISLOW, KURT MARTIN, chemist, educator; b. Berlin, June 5, 1923; came to U.S., 1940, naturalized, 1946; s. Max and Ida (Bingen) M.; m. Jacqueline Ford, 1966; children: Christopher, John. BS, Tulane U., 1944, DSc (hon.), 1975; PhD, Calif. Inst. Tech., 1947; Doctorate (hon.), Free U., Brussels, 1974, Uppsala U., 1977, Düsseldorf U., 1994, Zurich U., 2004. Instr. NYU, 1947-51, asst. prof., 1951-56, asso. prof., 1956-60, prof., 1960-64; Hugh Stott Taylor prof. chemistry Princeton, 1964-88, chmn. dept. chemistry, 1968-74, prof. emeritus, 1988—. Vis. prof. Stanford U., 1960, Calif. Inst. Tech., 1994; M.S. Kharasch vis. prof. U. Chgo., 1989; Univ. lectr. U. London, 1965; J.A. McRae Meml. lectr. Queen's U., 1967; H.A. Iddles lectr. U. N.H., 1972; Solvay lectr. and medalist Free U. Brussels, 1972; E.C. Lee lectr. U. Chgo.; A.A. Vernon lectr. Northeastern U., 1976; PPG lectr. Ohio U., 1977; J. Musher Meml. lectr. Hebrew U. Jerusalem, 1978; North Country lectr., 1978; Honor lectr. Ariz. State U., 1981; E. Ritchie meml. lectr. Sydney U., 1983; Fuson lectr. U. Nev., 1983; Research Scholar lectr. Drew U., 1983; McGregory lectr. Colgate U., 1984; Sandia lectr. U. Alta., 1984; Purves lectr. McGill U., 1985; Arnold lectr. So. Ill. U., 1985; Bergmann lectr. Yale U., 1986; H.C. Brown lectr. Purdue U., 1988; Irvine lectr. U. St. Andrews, 1988; Eyring lectr. Ariz. State U., 1989; Disting. Scientist lectr. Bard Coll., 1991; Syntex Disting. lectr. Colo. State U., 1991; Disting. scientist lectr. Bard Coll., 1991; J.W.T. Spinks lectr. U. Saskatchewan, 1992; Bristol-Myers-Squibb disting. lectr. Syracuse U., 1992; Churchill fellow Cambridge U., 1974-75; mem. adv. panel chemistry NSF, 1963-66; mem. panel medical and organic chemistry NIH, 1963-66. Author: Introduction to Stereochemistry, 1965; also numerous articles; bd. editors: Jour. Organic Chemistry, 1965-70; mem. editl. adv. bd. Monatshefte für Chemie, Topics in Stereochemistry, Accounts of Chem. Rsch., Chem. and Engring. News, Bull des Sociétés Chimiques Belges, Symmetry, Jour. Math. Chemistry. Recipient Solvay medal Free U. Brussels, 1972, Prelog medal, ETH Zurich, 1986, W.H. Nichols medal, 1987, Sci. Achievement award medal CCNY, 1988, Disting. Alumni award Calif. Inst. Tech., 1990, Chirality medal, 1993, Sesquicentennial medal Tulane U., 1997, Arthur C. Cope Scholar award Am. Chem. Soc. 1995; Guggenheim fellow, 1957-58, 74-75, Alfred P. Sloan fellow, 1959-63, Sherman Fairchild disting. scholar Calif. Inst. Tech., 1990, 91, 94. Fellow AAAS, Am. Acad. Arts and Scis.; mem. NAS, AAUP, Am. Chem. Soc. (James Flack Norris award 1975), Academia Nazionale dei Lincei (fgn. mem.), Phi Beta Kappa, Sigma Xi. Office Phone: 609-258-3941. E-mail: kmislow@princeton.edu.

MISNER, CHARLES WILLIAM, physics educator; b. Jackson, Mich., June 13, 1932; s. Francis deSales and Madge B. (Mee) M.; m. Susanne Elisabeth Kemp, June 13, 1959; children: Benedicte Elisabeth, Francis Frithjof, Timothy Charles, Christopher Kemp. BS, U. Notre Dame, 1952; MA, Princeton U., 1954, PhD, 1957. Instr. Princeton U., (N.J.), 1956-59, asst. prof., 1959-63; assoc. prof. physics U. Md., College Park, 1963-66, prof., 1966-2000, assoc. chair physics dept., 1995-99, prof. emeritus, sr. rsch. scientist, 2000—. Vis. fellow Inst. for Theoretical Physics, U. Calif., Santa Barbara, 1980-81, All Souls Coll., Oxford, Eng., 1973, Max Planck-Albert Einstein Inst., Potsdam, Germany, 2000, 2002; vis. faculty Calif. Inst. Tech., 1972, Princeton U., 1969 Author: (with Wheeler and Thorne) Gravitation, 1973, (with Patrick J.Cooney) Spreadsheet Physics, 1991; contbr. articles to profl. jours. Recipient Sci. Centennial award U. Notre Dame, 1965, Dannie Heineman prize (with R. Arnowitt and S. Deser) for math. physics Am. Phys. Soc., 1994; NSF sr. postdoctoral fellow, 1966-67; Guggenheim fellow, 1972-73; Einstein Centennial lectr., 1979. Fellow Am. Phys. Soc., Royal Astron. Soc., Am. Acad. Arts and Scis.; mem. Philosophy of Sci. Assn., Am. Math. Soc. Fedn. Am. Scientists Democrat. Roman Catholic. Office: U Md Dept Physics College Park MD 20742-4111

MISNER, CHARLOTTE BLANCHE RUCKMAN, retired community organization administrator; b. Gifford, Idaho, Aug. 30, 1937; d. Richard Steele and Arizona (Hill) Ruckman; m. G. Arthur Misner, Jr., Aug. 29, 1959; children: Michelle, Mary, Jennifer. BS in Psychology, U. Idaho, 1959. Vol. numerous orgns., India, Mexico, The Philippines, 1962-70; sec., v.p., pres., trustee St. Luke's Hosp., Manila, 1970-84; founding mem., 3d v.p., pres. Am. Women's Club of Philippines, 1980-84; exec. dir. Friends of Oakland (Calif.) Parks and Recreation, 1986-2000, ret., 2000. Active Lincoln Child Ctr., Oakland, 1984—. Recipient Vol. Svc. award Women's Bd. St. Luke's Hosp., 1977, Mid. Sch. Vol. award Internat. Sch.-Manila, 1980. Me. Alpha Gamma Delta (alumnae treas., pres. East Bay 1985-89, province dir. alumnae 1989-98, bd. dirs. alumni devel. 1998—, mem. steering com. centennial capital campaign 1999—), Cum Laude Soc. (hon.). Home: 5304 Woodgrove Ct Concord CA 94521-5422

MISNER, JEFFREY J. air transportation executive; b. 1954; married; 3 children. BA, San Deigo State Univ. With Kenneth Leventhal and Co., Newport, Calif., 1979—81; tax & bus. cons. Ernst & Young, Orange County, Calif., 1981—91; v.p. treas. ops. Continental Airlines Inc., 1995—2000, sr. v.p., CFO, 2001—. Served with USMC, 1971—75. Office: Continental Airlines Inc PO Box 4607 Houston TX 77210-4607

MISNER, LORRAINE, laboratory technologist; b. Fitchburg, Mass., June 24, 1948; d. Cedric Winfield and Pearl Erma (Hallisey) M. BA in Biology, Fitchburg State Coll., 1971; MS in Med. Tech., Anna Maria Coll., 1983. Cert. Novell engr. Lab. technologist Leominster (Mass.) Hosp., 1971-87; rsch. asst. U. Lowell Rsch. Found. (now U. Mass. Lowell Rsch. Found.), 1987-99; sys. engr. TeleSpectrum Worldwide Inc., 1999—. Piccolo Townsend (Mass.) Mil. Band, 1964-93; mem. choir United Ch. of Christ, 1961—. Mem. Am. Soc. Clin. Pathologists (assoc., registrant). Avocations: bowling, music, travel, dance. E-mail: lorraine.misner@hp.com.

MISNER, ROBERT DAVID, electronic warfare and magnetic recording consultant, electro-mechanical company executive; b. Waynesville, Ill., May 1, 1920; s. Oscar and Elizabeth (Nyren) M.; student Ill. Wesleyan U., 1939-42; B.S. in Physics, George Washington U., 1946; postgr. U. Md., 1948; m. Virginia Fuehrer, June 4, 1949; children: Robin Beth, Christie Marie. Mem. staff U.S. Naval Rsch. Lab., Washington, 1942-44, 46—, br. head signal exploitation br., 1965-87; pres. MEMRE Co., 1987—; cons. Served in USNR, 1944-46. Recipient Disting. Civilian Service award USN, 1970; others. Mem. IEEE (sr.), Assn. Old Crows, Sigma Xi. Contbr. articles to profl. jours. Home: 6521 Princeton Dr Alexandria VA 22307-2006 Office: 4555 Overlook Ave SW Washington DC 20375-0001

MISRA, DWIJEN CRISTOBAL, surgeon; b. Boston, Sept. 4, 1958; s. Dwijendra Kumar and Candida Rosario (Cristobal) M.; m. Nancy Ann Snider, Nov. 26, 1988; children: Benjamin, Mary Allison, Nathanial. BS, U. Mich., 1981; MD, Wayne State U., 1986. Diplomate Am. Bd. Surgery. Intern William Beaumont Hosp., Royal Oak, Mich., 1986-87, resident in gen. surgery, 1987-91; pvt. practice Troy, Mich. Mem. staff William Beaumont Hosp., Troy. Fellow ACS; mem. AMA, Am. Soc. Gen. Surgeons, Detroit Surgery Soc., Am. Hernia Soc. Office: 44199 Dequindre Rd Ste 412 Troy MI 48085-1128

MISRA, RAGHUNATH PRASAD, physician, educator; b. Calcutta, W. Bengal, India, Feb. 1, 1928; came to U.S., 1964; s. Guru Prasad and Anandi M.; m. Therese Rettenmund, Sept. 13, 1963; children: Sima, Joya, Maya, Tara. BSc with honors, Calcutta U., 1948; MBBS, Med. Coll., Calcutta, 1953; PhD, McGill U., Montreal, Que., 1965. Diplomate Am. Bd. Anatomical and Clin. Pathology. Asst. prof., dir. kidney lab. U. Louisville Sch. Medicine, 1964-68; asso. investigator and dir. kidney lab Mt. Sinai Hosp., Cleve., 1968-73; asst. prof. Case Western Reserve Med. Sch., Cleve., 1973-76; asst. prof., dir. kidney lab. La. State U., Sch. Medicine, Shreveport, 1976-80, assoc. prof., 1980-86; prof. La. State U., Sch. of Medicine, Shreveport, 1986—98, emeritus prof., 1998—, dir. Ocular Pathology Lab., 1988—. Cons. VA Med. Ctr., Shreveport, 1977-98, EA Conway Meml. Hosp., Monroe, La., 1980-98. Author: Atlas of Skin Biopsy, 1983. Pres. India Assn. of Shreveport, 1979, 81. Recipient Tallisman Fellowship, Mt. Sinai Hosp., 1970-73. Fellow Am. Coll. Pathologists, Am. Soc. Clin. Pathologists, Am. Coll. of Internat. Physicians, U. Calcutta Med. Alumni Assn. Am. (pres. 1992-93), Sigma Xi (pres. 1987-89). Democrat. Hindu. Avocations: photography, travel. Office: La State U Sch Medicine 1501 Kings Hwy Shreveport LA 71103-4228 Office Phone: 318-675-5012. E-mail: rmisra@lsuhsc.edu.

MISRACH, RICHARD LAURENCE, photographer; b. L.A., July 11, 1949; s. Robert Laskin and Lucille (Gardner) M.; m. Debra Bloomfield, Jan. 18, 1981 (div. 1987); 1 son, Jacob Luke; m. Myriam Weisang, Apr. 17, 1989. AB in Psychology, U. Calif., Berkeley, 1971. Instr. Assoc. Students Studio, U. Calif., Berkeley, 1971-77; vis. lectr. U. Calif.-Berkeley, 1982; lectr. U. Calif.-Santa Barbara, 1984. Juror Nat. Endowment Arts, 1986; lectr. Calif. Inst. for Arts, 1990. Exhbns. include Whitney Biennial, 1981, 91, Musée d'Art Moderne, Paris, 1979, Mus. Modern Art, N.Y.C., 1978, Grapestake Gallery, San Francisco, 1979, 81, Young-Hoffman Gallery, Chgo., 1980, Oakland Mus., 1982, 87, San Francisco Mus. Modern Art, 1983, Centre Georges Pompidou, Paris, 1983, L.A. County Mus. Art, 1984, Fraenkel Gallery, San Francsico, 1985, 89, 91, 95, 97, 99, Min Gallery, Tokyo, 1975-87, Univ. Art Mus., Berkeley, Curt Marcus Gallery, 1995, 96, 97, 2000, James Danziger Gallery, 1995, Robert Mann Gallery, N.Y., 1999, Melbourne Internat. Festival, Australia, 1995, G. Gibson Gallery, 2000, High Mus. Art, Atlanta, 2000, others; one person exhbns. at Art Inst. Chgo., 1988, Milw. Art Mus., 1988, Carpenter Ctr., Harvard U., 1988, Fotomann, Inc., N.Y., 1989, 91, Photographers Gallery, 1990, Parco Gallery, Tokyo, 1990, Arles Festival, France, 1990, Jan Kesner Gallery, 1990, 91, 94, 2000, Houston Mus. Fine Arts, 1996, Ctr. Creative Photography, Tucson, 1996, Mus. Contemporary Art, Chgo., 1997, Contemporary Mus. of Art Art, Hawaii, 1997, San Jose Mus. of Art, 1998, Diputacion de Granada, Spain, 1999; art commn. cover Time mag., July 4, 1988; books include Telegraph 3 A.M., 1974, Grapestake Gallery, 1979, (A Photographic Book), 1979, Hawaii portfolio, 1980, Graecism dye-transfer portfolio, 1982, Desert Cantos, 1987, (Internat. Ctr. of Photography award 1988), Bravo 20: The Bombing of the American West, 1990 (Pen Ctr. U.S.A. West award for nonfiction 1991), Richard Misrach, Minn. Gallery, 1988, Violent Legacies, Aperture, 1992, Crimes and Splendors, 1996, Cantos del Desierto, Di putacion de Granada, 1999, The Sky Book, 2000, Richard Misrach: Golden Gate, 2001, Pictures of Paintings, 2002. Guggenheim fellow, 1978; Ferguson grantee, 1976; NEA grantee, 1973, 77, 84, 92; AT&T commn., 1979; Eureka fellow, 1991; recipient Koret Israel prize, 1992. *Photographs are the shadows of reality much like dreams. On the one hand, they appear to literally transcribe the real world, while on the other, they defy our linear concept of time and meaning. Because the primary illusion of photography is fact, it is the most powerful art medium of our time.*

MISS, ROBERT EDWARD, fundraiser; b. Frederick, Md., Oct. 14, 1937; s. Robert Edward Sr. and Anna Theresa (Pazdersky) M.; m. Lee Ann Menendez Devine, Nov. 23, 1964 (div. Feb. 1985); children: Stephen Patrick, David Edward, Sarah Ann; m. Judith F. Schwartz Millman, May 22, 1993. AB, Fordham U., 1963; MA, U. N.C., 1973. Asst. dir. pub. affairs Fordham U., Bronx, N.Y., 1963-65; editor Coun. for Advancement and Support of Edn., Washington, 1965-69; network dir. U. N.C.-TV, Chapel Hill, 1969-79; v.p. City Suburban Workshop, N.Y.C., 1979-81; dir. mktg. comm. Lighthouse, Inc., N.Y.C., 1981-86; ptnr. Mktg. Comm. Policy Group, N.Y.C.-various, 1986-89; v.p. Heartshare Human Svcs., Bklyn., 1989-95; sr. acct. exec. Semple & Bixel, Inc., Nutley, N.J., 1996-97; ptnr. Resource Devel. Coun., Dobbs Ferry, N.Y., 1998—. Author, editor: Teacher's Resources for ETV, 1973, Corp. Strategy for Issues of Aging, 1988; author of poems. Mentor team in tng. Leukemia Soc. of Am. Recipient Gilbert Poetry prize Women in the Moon Pubs., 1995. Mem. Nat. Soc. Fundraising Execs., Acad. Am. Poets, Westchester Assn. Devel. Officers. Democrat. Roman Catholic. Avocations: poetry writing, film/video producing, road racing. Home and Office: 37 Round Hill Rd Dobbs Ferry NY 10522-3310

MISSAN, RICHARD SHERMAN, lawyer, educator; b. Oct. 5, 1933; s. Albert and Hannah (Hochberg) Missan; m. Aileen Louise Missan; children: Hilary, Andrew, Wendy. BA, Yale U., 1955, JD, 1958. Bar: NY 59, US Dist. Ct. (so. and ea. dists.) NY 79, US Ct. Appeals (2d cir.) 93. Assoc. Kaye, Scholer, Fierman, Hays & Handler, NYC, 1962—67; ptnr. Schoenfeld & Jacobs, NYC, 1968—78, Walsh & Frisch, NYC, 1979—80, Gersten, Savage & Kaplowitz, NYC, 1980—87; v.p., gen. counsel Avis, Inc., 1987—88; pvt. practice NYC, 1988—. Spl. prof. law Hofstra U., 1988—; mem. panel mediators U.S. Dist. Ct. (ea. dist.) NY, U.S. Bankruptcy Ct. (so. dist. NY). Revision author: Corporations, New York Practice Guide (Business and Commercial). Mem.: ABA, Assn. Bar City NY (mem. com. corrections, chmn. subcom. legis., chmn. subcom. juvenile facilities, mem. com. atomic energy, mem. com. mcpl. affairs, mem. com. housing urban devel.), Fed. Bar Coun., NY State Bar Assn., Yale Club.

MISSAR, CHARLES DONALD, retired librarian; b. Cleve., July 16, 1925; s. Charles Frank and Genevieve Catherine (Buechele) M.; m. Margaret Mary du Fief, Feb. 17, 1962 (dec.); children: Charles David, Stephen du Fief. Student, Sacred Heart Sem., Detroit, 1943-45, St. Mary's Sem., Cleve., 1945-49; BA, John Carroll U., 1951; MLS, Cath. U. Am., 1960. Referral specialist Libr. of Congress, Washington, 1963-66; ERIC info. specialist U.S. Office Edn., Washington, 1966-72; head Ednl. Reference Ctr. Nat. Inst. Edn., Washington, 1973-78, supervisory libr., 1978-85; sr. libr. U.S. Dept. Edn., 1985-86; sr. editor Computer Scis. Corp. Profl. Svcs. Group, 1986-94, Missar Assocs., Washington, 1994—2001. Agy. rep. Fed. Libr. Com., Washington, 1978-86; ann. lectr. Fed. Libr. Resources Workshop, Catholic U. Am., Washington, 1981-96. Editor: Management of Federally Sponsored Libraries: Case Studies and Analysis, 1995; compiler, author: A Checklist of Ohio Imprints From 1821 to 1825, 1960; editor monthly jour. Tech. Abstract Bull., 1958-60; mem. editl. bd. Online Mag., 1977-80 Bd. dirs. Shrine of the Most Blessed Sacrament St. Pius X Libr., 1995—. Recipient Superior Svc. Group award U.S. Office Edn., 1968, Superior Performance award Nat. Inst. Edn., 1974, 84; inductee Spl. Libraries Assn. Hall of Fame, 1991. Mem. ALA, D.C. Libr. Assn. (treas. 1972-74), Spl. Librs. Assn. (chmn. edn. divsn. 1980-81, chmn. 1989-90), Am. Soc. Info. Sci. (chmn. info. svcs. for edn. group 1984-86), John Carroll Soc., Cleve. Club, Serra Club (pres. 1992-93, 94-96), Arimathean Club, Ohio Soc., Cosmos Club. Roman Catholic. Home: 5617 32nd St NW Washington DC 20015-1622 E-mail: cdmissar@aol.com.

MISSETT, JUDI SHEPPARD, dancer, jazzercise company executive; b. Iowa; BA in Theater, Radio/TV, Northwestern U., Chgo., 1966. Profl. dancer, Chgo., 1966-77; jazzercise instr., choreographer, tchr., 1977—; pres. worldwide dance-fitness franchise orgn. Jazzercise, Inc., Carlsbad, Calif.; prin. JM TV Prodns.; prin. mail-order catalog bus. Jazzertogs. Instr. convs., children's fitness progs. Author: (comprehensive nutrition prog.) The Jazzercise Know More Diet; author weekly fitness column for Los Angeles Times Syndicate; performer, prodr. home exercise videos. Mem. Calif. Gov.'s Coun. on Phys. Fitness & Sports; bd. dirs. San Diego Inner-City Games; contbr. millions of dollars for charities by leading spl., large-scale workout classes. Recognized for contbns. to growth and advancement of fitness industry by Pres. Reagan in his White House Conf. on Women in Bus., 1986, Aerobics and Fitness Assn. Am., Am. Coun. on Exercise, Pres.' Coun. on Phys. Fitness & Sports; named Entrepreneur of Year, Working Woman Mag., 1988; recipient Lifetime Achievement award Internat. Assn. Fitness Profls., 1991, Women Who Mean Bus. award San Diego Bus. Jour., 1995, A Woman of Accomplishment award Soroptimist Internat. of San Diego, 1996; inducted into Internat. Assn. Fitness Profls. Hall of Fame, 1992. Mem. Nat. Fitness Leaders Assn. (exec. dir., Charles Bucher Meml. award 1996). Office: Jazzercise Inc 2460 Impala Dr Carlsbad CA 92008-7226

MISSIMER, THOMAS MICHAEL, geologist; b. Lancaster, Pa., Mar. 10, 1950; s. Jacob M. and Lorraine L. (Bilodeau) M. AB in Geology, Franklin and Marshall Coll., 1972; MS in Geology, Fla. State U., 1973; PhD in Marine Geology and Geophysics, U. Miami, Fla., 1995. Registered profl. geologist, Fla., Ga., Ind., Va., Tex. Hydrologist U.S. Geol. Survey, Ft. Myers, Fla., 1973-75; rsch. assoc. sedimentology U. Miami, Coral Gables, 1975-76; pres. Missimer & Assocs., Inc., Cape Coral, Fla., 1976-92; vice chmn. ViroGroup, Inc., Cape Coral, 1991-93; pres. CDM Missimer, Ft. Myers, 1993-99; v.p. Camp, Dresser & McKee, Inc., Ft. Myers, 1994—2004, CDM Missimer, Ft. Myers, 1999—2004; pres. Missimer Groundwater Sci., Inc., Ft. Myers, 2004—. Mem. Bd. Profl. Geologists, 1991-97, avice chmn., 1993, chmn., 1994; apptd. by Gov. J. Bush to the Fla. Forever Adv. Coun., 1999—2003; mem. tech. adv. com. Gov.'s Com. for a Substantial South Fla., 1995-98, chmn., 1996-98. Author Water supply development for membrane water treatment facilities, 1994, Lender's Guide to environmental liability management, 1996; contbr. hydrogeol. and geol. studies of Southeastern U.S. to sci. jours.; contbr. more than 190 articles to profl. jours. Mem. citizens planning adv. com. Bd. Lee County (Fla.), 1981-82, chmn., 1982-83. Recipient Best Paper award, Internat. Desalination Assn., D.C. World Conf. on Desalination, 1991, Acad. Merit award U. Miami, 1997. Mem. Geol. Soc. Am., Am. Inst. Profl. Geologists (cert. profl. geol. scienitst), Am. Water Resources Assn., Am. Water Works Assn., AAAS, Am. Inst. Hydrology (cert. profl. hydrogeologist), Am. Groundwater Assn. (cert. Hydrogeologist), Fla. Acad. Scis. (chmn. earth and planetary sci. sect. 1973-74, 95), Internat. Desalination Assn., Southeastern Geol. Soc., S.E. Desalting Assn. (bd. dirs. 1996-98). Republican. Home: 3214 Mcgregor Blvd Fort Myers FL 33901-6723 Office: Missimer Groundwater Sci Inc 3214 McGregor Blvd Fort Myers FL 33901 Office Phone: 239-810-3009. E-mail: Missimertom@aol.com.

MISTACCO, VICKI E. foreign language educator; b. Bklyn., Nov. 18, 1942; d. Anthony Sebastian and Lucia (Lalli) M. BA, NYU, 1963; MA, Middlebury Coll., 1964; M of Philosophy, Yale U., 1968, PhD, 1972. Instr. French Wellesley Coll., Mass., 1968-72, asst. prof. French, 1972-78, assoc. prof. French, 1978-84, prof. French, 1984—, chmn., 1978-81. Nat. adv. bd. Sweet Briar Jr. Yr. in France, Va., 1978—. Contbr. articles to profl. jours. Fulbright

fellow, 1963-64, Woodrow Wilson fellow, 1964-67; NEH fellow, 1983-84, 94-95. Mem.: N.E. MLA, MLA, Soc. Internat. pour l'Etude des Femmes de l'Ancien Regime, Women in French, Am. Assn. Tchrs. French, Phi Beta Kappa. Democrat. Roman Catholic. Avocations: photography, travel. Office: Wellesley Coll Dept French 106 Central St Wellesley MA 02481-8268 Office Phone: 781-283-2406. E-mail: vmistacco@wellesley.edu.

MISTRAL, JACQUES, economist; b. Toulouse, France, Sept. 22, 1947; s. Léon and Lucienne (Bataillard) M.; m. Bernadette Tricou, July 1, 1970; 3 children. D Econ. Sci., U Paris, 1976; diploma, Ecole Polytechnique, Paris, 1969. Economist French Ministry of Fin., Paris, 1970—76; prof. econs. U. Paris, 1977—81; rsch. officer Centre D'Etudes Prospectives et D'Economie Mathematique, 1980—84; dep. dir. Nat. Sch. Stats. and Econ. Adminstrn., Paris, 1984—88; econ. adviser Prime Minister of France, Paris, 1988—91; exec. v.p. Axa Group, Paris, London, Beijing, Melbourne, 1992—2000; spl. advisor to Minister of Economy, Fin. and Industry Paris, 2000—01; minister, counselor for econ. and fin. affairs Embassy of France, Washington, 2001—. Mem. adv. bd. Grad. Sch. Econs. and Statistics; bd. dirs. Ctr. d'Etudes Prospectives et d'Economie Internationale. Author: Accumulation, Inflation, Crises (with R. Boyer), 2d edit., 1983, Notre Etat, 2000, Etat t'urgence, 2004, La raison du plies tort, 2004. Lt. arty., French armed forces, 1969. Mem.: Le Cercle des Economistes, Le Siècle, French Def. Econ. Coun., French Coun. Econ. Analysis. Office: Embassy of France 4101 Reservoir Rd Washington DC 20007 Office Phone: 202-944-6380. E-mail: jacques.mistral@tresor.finances.gouv.fr.

MISULIS, KARL EDWARD, physician; b. Saranac Lake, NY, Aug. 6, 1953; s. Edward Victor and Ruth Aileen (Miller) M.; m. Christa Margaret Stoscheck, June 14, 1980; children: Edward Nicholas, Karl Christian. BS with honors, Queens U., 1975; PhD, SUNY, Syracuse, 1980; MD, Vanderbilt U., 1982. Diplomate Am. Bd. Psychiatry and Neurology. Chief resident, neurology Vanderbilt U., Nashville, 1984-85, resident, neurology, 1982-86, asst. prof. neurology, 1986-90, assoc. prof. neurology, 1990-98, prof. neurology, 1998—; neurologist Semmes-Murphey Clinic, Jackson, 1991—. Author: (books) Essentials of Clinical Neurophysiology, 1993, 1997, 2003, Spehlmann's Evoked Potential Primer, 1994, Neurologic Localization and Diagnosis, 1996; editor: Scientific Foundations of Neurology, 1996, Disorders of Mental Status, 1998, Confusion, 1999, Review Manual for Neurology in Clinical Practice, 2000, 2004, Shared Care in Neurology, 2002; contbr. articles to profl. publ. Recipient CIDA award NIH. Fellow Am. Acad. Neurology (Saul Korey award); mem. So. Clin. Neurol. Soc. (v.p. 1994—), AAN (mem. com. on crit. care), Am. Acad. Clin. Neurophysiology, Alpha Omega Alpha. Office: Semmes-Murphey Clin 614 Skyline Dr Jackson TN 38301-3923 E-mail: karl@misulis.net.

MISUREC, RUDOLF, physician, surgeon; b. Dobre Pole, Czechoslovakia, June 27, 1924; came to U.S., 1967; s. Gustav and Hilda (Safar) M.; m. Miluse Kisil, 1951 (div. 1978); children: Peter Clyde, Rudolph Carl; m. Stanislava Cuchal, 1978. MD, Masaryk's U., Brno-Czechoslovakia, 1950. Diplomate Am. Bd. Urology, gen. surgery (Czechoslovakia), thoracic surgery (Czechoslovakia). Intern U. Ill., Chgo., 1967-68, resident in urology, 1968-71, clin. asst. prof. urology, 1975—. Mem. Rep. Presdl. Task Force, 1984, Rep. Presdl. Legion of Merit, 1992. Capt. Czechoslovakia Army, 1950-55. Recipient Cert. of Achievement U.S. Army, 1967, Letter of Appreciation, 1967. Fellow ACS, Internat. Coll. Surgeons, Am. Urol. Assn.; mem. AMA, Chgo. Med. Soc., N.Y. Acad. Scis., Czechoslovak Soc. Arts and Scis. (U.S.). Roman Catholic. Office: 3340 Oak Park Ave Berwyn IL 60402-3420

MITAL, ANIL, engineering educator; b. Barabanki, India, Nov. 13, 1951; came to U.S., 1975; s. Virendra Nath and Malti (Gupta) M.; m. Chetna Gupta, June 12, 1981; children: Anubhav, Aashi. B.E., Allahabad U., 1974; MS, Kans. State U., 1976; PhD, Tex. Tech. U., 1980. Asst. prof. indsl. engring. U. Wis., Platteville, 1979-80; assoc. prof., 1984-92; prof. indsl. engring. and phys. med. and rehab., 1993—; human factors engring. grad. coord. U. Cin., 1981—. Dir. Ergonomics Rsch. Lab., 1981—. Editor-in-chief Internat. Jour. Indsl. Ergonomics, 1986—, Internat. Jour. Indls. Engring.-Theory Applications and Practice, 1994—, Elsevier Book Series in Ergonomics; exec. editor: Internat. Jour. Human Resource Devel. and Mgmt., 1999—; gen. editor: Trends in Ergonomics/Human Factors I, 1984, Applications of Fuzzy Set Theory in Human Factors, 1986, Manual Materials Handling, 1989, A Guide to Manual Materials Handling, 1993, 2nd edit., 1997, Handbook of Expert Systems in Manufacturing and Production Engring., 1994, numerous other ergonomics jours.; contbr. numerous articles to profl. jours. Mem. Big Bros.-Big Sisters, Lubbock, Tex., 1977—. Grantee Nat. Inst. Occupl. Safety and Health, 1982-85, NSF, 1993-96; rsch. grantee Nat. Inst. Disability and Rehab., 1993-97; recipient Gold Medal for performacnce Allahabad U., 1974; named Young Engr. Yr. Engrs. and Scientists Cin., 1984; Jr. Morrow Rsch. Chair, 1982-83. Fellow Human Factors and Ergonomics Soc. (Paul M. Fitts award 1996), Inst. Indsl. Egnrs.; mem. Am. Indsl. Hygiene Assn. (chmn. nat. ergonomics com. 1984-85), Human Factors Soc. Am. (editl. bd., chmn. indsl. ergonomics tech. group 1985-86, Outstanding Contbns. award Tri-State chpt. 1984), Human Factors Soc. Greater Cin. (pres. 1983-84), Inst. Indsl. Engrs. (treas. Cin. chpt. 1983-84, ergonomics divsn. 1987-88, ergonomics divsn. award 1989, Eugene L. Grante award 1988), Soc. Automotive Engrs. (faculty advisor 1987-88, Ralph R. Teetor award 1985), Internat. Soc. Occupl. Ergonomics and Safety (Disting. Accomplishment award 1993), Pi Tau Sigma, Alpha Pi Mu, Tau Beta Pi (faculty advisor 1981-85), Phi Kappa Phi, Omicron Delta Kappa, delta Phi Epsilon, Sigma Xi (Disting. Rsch. award 1984), 100 Mile Joggers. Home: 7242 Cascade Dr West Chester OH 45069-2291 Office Phone: 513-556-2652.

MITAU, LEE R. bank executive; b. St. Paul, 1948; AB cum laude, Dartmouth Coll., 1969; JD magna cum laude, U. Minn., 1972. Bar: Minn. 1972, N.Y. 1973. Law clk. to Hon. George E. MacKinnon U.S. Ct. Appeals (D.C. cir.), 1972-73; ptnr. Dorsey & Whitney, Mpls.; exec. v.p. gen. counsel U.S. Bancorp, Mpls. Adj. prof. law William Mitchell Coll. Law, 1982-83. Office: US Bancorp 601 2nd Ave S Ste 3000 Minneapolis MN 55402-4324

MITBY, JOHN CHESTER, lawyer; b. Antigo, Wis., Jan. 7, 1944; s. Norman Peter and Luvern T. (Jensen) M.; m. Julie Kampen, June 10, 1972; children: Tana, Jenna. BS, U. Wis., 1966, LLB, 1971. Bar: Wis. 1971, Colo. 1992. Ptnr. Axley, Brynelson, LLP, Madison, Wis., 1973—. Mem. adv. bd. U. Wis. Golf Course, 1991-96. Served to capt. C.E., U.S. Army, 1966-68. Mem.: ABA, ATLA, Wis. Acad Trial Lawyers (counsel to bd. attys. for disciplinary actions), Colo. Bar Assn., Dane County Bar Assn., Wis. Bar Assn. (past chmn. litigation sect.), Nat. Acad. Elder Law Attys. Inc. (adv. bd.), Am. Soc. Hosp. Attys., Am. Bd. Trial Advs. (past pres. Wis. chpt.), Acad. Trial Lawyers, Nakoma Country Club (Madison). Home: 726 Oneida Pl Madison WI 53711-2958 Office: Axley Brynelson LLP PO Box 1767 2 E Mifflin St Madison WI 53703-2889 Office Phone: 608-283-6710. E-mail: jmitby@axley.com.

MITCH, WILLIAM EVANS, nephrologist; b. Birmingham, Ala., July 22, 1941; s. William Evans and Mary Elizabeth (Ackerman) M.; m. Frances Alexandra Fisher, Aug. 21, 1965; children: Eleanor Baylor, William Armistead. BA, Harvard Coll., 1963; MD, Harvard Med. Sch., 1967. Intern Brigham & Women's Hosp., Boston, 1967-68, resident, 1968-69; clin. assoc. NIH, Bethesda, Md., 1969-72; resident Johns Hopkins Hosp., Balt., 1972-73, Brigham & Women's Hosp., 1973-74; asst. prof., assoc. prof. dept. pharmacy Johns Hopkins U., Balt., 1974-78; assoc. prof. medicine Harvard Med. Sch., Boston, 1978-87; prof. medicine Emory U. Sch. Medicine, Atlanta, 1987—2002, U. Tex., Galveston, 2002—. Mem. study sect. NIH, 1988-92. Editor: The Progressive Nature of Renal Disease, 1986, 2d edit., 1992, Nutrition and the Kidney, 1988, 4th edit., 2002. Pres. region II Nat. Kidney Found., 1990-92, chmn. sci. adv. bd., 1996-98; chmn. exec. coun. on kidney Am. Heart Assn. Grantee NIH, 1979—. Mem. Am. Soc. Clin. Investigation, Assn. Am. Physicians, Am. Clin. and Climatol. Assn., Am. Soc. Nephrology (pres.), Internat. Soc. Nephrology (treas. 1997—2003). Office: U Tex Galveston 9.138 Med Rsch Bldg 301 University Blvd Galveston TX 77555-1064

MITCHAM, BOB ANDERSON, lawyer, judge; b. Atlanta, July 16, 1933; s. George Anderson and Pearl (Bing) M.; m. Lupe M. Vazquez, Dec. 6, 1969; children: Robert Anderson, Tamara Lynn, Matthew Vazquez, Micah Marissa Vasquez. BS, Fla. So. Coll., 1959; JD, Stetson U., 1962. Bar: Fla. 1963, U.S. Dist. Ct. (mid. dist.) Fla. 1963, U.S. Ct. Appeals (5th cir.) 1965, U.S. Ct. Appeals (11th cir.) 1983, U.S. Supreme Ct. 1988. Ptnr. Mitcham & Honig, Tampa, Fla., 1963-66, Mitcham, Leon & Guito, Tampa, Fla., 1966-68; pvt. practice Tampa, Fla., 1968-82; ptnr. Mitcham, Weed & Barbas, Tampa, Fla., 1982—90. Cir. judge, Tampa, 1990-2001, ret.; lectr. Oxford U., Eng., 1981, U. London, 1987. Contbr. articles to profl. jours. Pres. Young Dem. of Fla., Tampa, 1968; active Davis Island Baptist Church. With USAF, 1952-59. Perry Nichols Trial scholar, 1961. Mem. Criminal Def. Lawyers Hillsborough County (pres. 1981-82), Hillsborough County Bar Assn. (dir. 1981-85), Ybor City C. of C. (dir. 1981-82, chmn. Super Bows XVIII). Republican.

MITCHAM, CARLA J. utilities executive; BS in Indsl. Distbn., MS in Indsl. Tech., Tex. A&M U.; JD, U. Houston. Pres. Reliant Energy ERCOT Supply Reliant Resources, Inc., Houston. Office: Reliant Energy Exec Office PO Box 2286 Houston TX 77252-2286

MITCHARD, JACQUELYN, writer; b. 1953; H.S. English tchr., 1974—76; mng. editor, reporter Pioneer Press, Chgo., 1976—79; reporter The Capital Times, Madison, Wis., 1979—84; metro reporter, columnist Milw. Jour., 1984—88; speechwriter for Donna Shalala, 1989—93. Author: Mother Less Child, 1985, Jane Addams: Pioneer in Social Reform and Activist for World Peace, 1991, Jane Addams: Peace Activist, 1992, The Deep End of the Ocean, 1996, The Rest of Us: Dispatches from the Mothership, 1997, The Most Wanted, 1998, A Theory of Relativity, 2001, Twelve Times Blessed, 2003, Christmas Present, 2003, Starring Prima!, 2004. Office: c/o Jane Gelfman Gelfman Schneider Lit Agts Inc 250 W 57th St New York NY 10107

MITCHELHILL, JAMES MOFFAT, retired civil engineer; b. St. Joseph, Mo., Aug. 11, 1912; s. William and Jeannette (Ambrose) Mitchelhill; m. Maurine Hutchason, Jan. 9, 1937 (div. 1962); children: Janis Maurine Mitchelhill Leas, Jeri Ann Mitchelhill Riney; m. Alicia Beuchat, 1982. BS, Northwestern U., 1934, MSCE, 1935. Registered profl. engr., Mont., P.R., Tex. Engring. dept. C., M., St. P. & P.R.R. Co., Chgo., Miles City, Mont., 1935-45; asst. mgr. Ponce & Guayama R.R. Co., Aguirre, PR, 1945-51, v.p., gen. mgr., 1969-70; mgr. Ctr. Cortada, Santa Isabel, PR, 1951-54; r.r. supt. Braden Copper Co., Rancagua, Chile, 1954-63; staff engr. Coverdale - Colpitts, N.Y.C., 1963-64; asst. to exec. v.p. Ctrl. Aguirre Sugar Co., 1964-67; v.p., gen. mgr. Coddea, Inc., Dominican Republic, 1967-68; asst. to gen. mgr. Land Adminstrn. P.R., La Nueva, 1970-71; with Centrals Aguirre Lafayette and Mercedita, 1971-72; asst. to gen. mgr. Corporacion Azucarera de P.R., 1973-76, asst. to exec. dir., 1977-79, asst. exec. dir. for environ., 1979-82, engring. cons., 1982-92; Kendall County engr., 1985-97; ret., 1997. Fellow: ASCE; mem.: Colegio de Ingenieros y Agrimensores de P.R., Am. Ry. Engring. Assn., Travellers Century Club, Circumnavigators Club, Explorers Club, Sigma Xi, Tau Beta Pi. Home: PO Box 506 Boerne TX 78006-0506

MITCHELL, A. JOE, JR., telecommunications industry executive; m. Connie Mitchell. Founder VarTec Telecom, Dallas, 1989, pres., 1989—2001, pres., CEO, 2001—. Office: VarTec Telecom Inc 1600 Viceroy Dr Dallas TX 75235

MITCHELL, ALLAN EDWIN, lawyer; b. Okemah, Okla., May 13, 1944; m. Neva G. Ream; children: Brian E. Mitchell, Amy E. Harrison. BA in Mass. Comm., Northwestern Okla. State U., Alva, 1991; JD, U. Okla., 1994. Bar: Okla. 1994, U.S. dist. ct. (we. and no. dists.) 1994. Asst. state mgr. Oklahomans for Right to Work, Oklahoma City, 1967-68; exec. dir. London Sq. Village, Oklahoma City, 1968-73; dist. mgr. Farmland Ins. Svc., Oklahoma City, 1974-80, Nat. Farmers Union, Oklahoma City, 1980-85; dist. agt. Prudential Ins., Cherokee, Okla., 1985-89; atty. Hughes & Grant, Oklahoma City, 1994-96, Collins & Mitchell, Cherokee, Okla., 1996—2000; asst. dist. atty Woods County, Okla., 1996—. Mem. Cherokee Bd. Edn., 1985-90; mem. fin. com. Rep. Party of Okla., 1995, state com., 1997X; scoutmaster, 1981-86, bd. mem. Great Salt Plains Coun. Boy Scouts Am.; adult advisor Girl Scouts Am.; pres. United Way Cherokee, 1984; mem. Okla. Sch. Bd. Mems. Legis. Network, 1985-90, state com. Okla. Rep. Party, 1997; vol. Okla. Spl. Olympics, 1996, 97; lay min. Ch. of the Nazarene. Avocations: public speaking, politics, civic activities. Office: Office of Dist Atty Woods County Courthouse Alva OK 73717 Office Phone: 580-327-2171.

MITCHELL, ANDREA, journalist; b. N.Y.C., Oct. 30, 1946; d. Sydney and Cecile Mitchell; m. Alan Greenspan, Apr. 6, 1997. BA, U. Pa., 1967. Polit. reporter KYW Newsradio, Phila., 1967-76; polit. corr. Sta. KYW-TV, Phila., 1972-76; corr. Sta. WTOP-TV, Washington, 1977-78; gen. assignment and energy corr. NBC News, Washington, 1978-81, White House corr., 1981-88, chief congl. corr., 1989-92, chief White House corr., 1993-94, chief fgn. affairs corr., 1995—. Substitute host Meet the Press, 1988--; host MSNBC The Mitchell Report, Decision 2000. Trustee U. Pa., 1995—. Recipient award for pub. affairs reporting Am. Polit. Sci. Assn., 1969, Pub. Affairs Reporting award AP, 1976, AP Broadcast award, 1977; named Communicator of the Yr., Phila. chpt. Women in Comms., 1976, Woman of the Yr., Phila. chpt. Am. Women in Radio and TV, 1989, Lucretia Mott award Woman's Way, 1991, Lifetime Achievement award RTNDA, 2004. Office: NBC News 4001 Nebraska Ave NW Washington DC 20016-2733

MITCHELL, ANDREW (ANDY MITCHELL), Canadian government official; b. Montreal; married, Christine Hodson; 3 children. Grad., Carleton U. Mem. House of Commons, Ottawa, Ont., Can., 1993—, sec. of state (parks), 1997—99, sec. of state (rural development), 1999—2003; mem. bd. of Internat. Economy, 2001; min. Indian affairs and northern devel. Govt. of Canada, Hull, Canada, 2003—. Chair standing com. on natural resources, House of Commons, vice chair ind. com., chair of fed. Ont. govt. caucus task force on Access to Capital by Small Bus., ministerial task force on disability and Canadians, chair No. Ont. Liberal caucus. Active vol., foster parent Children's Aid Soc.; vol. summer theater Muskoka, Elliott Lake Arts Task Force; mem. Elliott Lake and Gravenhurst Econ. Devel. Com. Mem. Ont. C. of C. (dir.), Northeastern Ont. C. of C. (past pres.), Elliott Lake C. of C. (past pres.), Gravenhurst C. of C. (past pres.). Office: House of Commons Ottawa ON Canada K1A 0A6 also: Indian and Northern Affairs Canada Terrasses de la Chaudiere 10 Wellington St North Tower K1A 0H4 ON Canada

MITCHELL, ARTHUR, dancer, choreographer, educator; b. N.Y.C., Mar. 27, 1934; s. Arthur and Willie Mae Mitchell. Student, Sch. Am. Ballet.; D. Arts (hon.), Columbia Coll., Chgo., 1975; cert. of competence, Peter U., 1978; DFA (hon.), City Coll., CUNY, 1979, N.C. Sch. Arts, 1981, L.I. U. Sch. Bus. Pub. Adminstrn., 1982, Fordham U., 1983, Princeton U., 1986, Williams Coll., 1986, Juilliard Sch., 1990; DHS (hon.), Urbana Coll., 1979; DA (hon.), Harvard U., 1987. With William Dollar's Ballet Theatre Workshop, 1954, John Butler Co., 1955; prin. dancer N.Y.C. Ballet, 1955-72; artistic dir., founder Am. Negro Dance Co., N.Y.C., 1966—; founder, dir., choreographer Dance Theatre of Harlem, N.Y.C., 1969—; former resident choreographer, artistic dir. Nat. Ballet Co., Brazil. Tchr. dance Karel Shook Studio, Melissa Hayden Sch., Cedarhurst, L.I., Jones-Haywood Sch. Ballet, Washington. Dancer Kiss Me Kate, Orpheus, Carmen Jones, Allegro, Creation of the World, Episodes, House of Flowers, choreographer with Rod Alexander Newport Jazz Festival, Rhythmetron, 1971, Ode to Otis, 1969, Lil' Gal, 1969, Tones, 1970, Biosfera, 1970, Fun and Games, 1970, Holberg Suite, 1970, Manifestations, 1975, Concerto for Jazz Band and Orch., 1971, Fête Noire, 1971, Spiritual Suite: Dance In Praise of His Name, 1976, Breezin', 1977, The Greatest, 1977, El Mar, 1977, Doin' It, 1978, Porgy and Bess, 1985, Phoenix Rising, 1987, John Henry, 1988, Ribbon in the Sky, 1990, Bach Passacaglia, 1993, dancer tv prodns. A Streetcar Named Desire, PBS dance prodn. Songs of Mahler, Dance in America: Dance Theatre of Harlem, Stravinsky's Firebird, NBC prodn. Creole Giselle, A&E prodn. Fall River Legend. Active Nat. Conf. on Social Welfare, 1973, U.S. Dept. State Dance Adv. Panel; pres. Task Force on Arts and Humanities, 1981; mem. Commn. for Cultural Affairs, N.Y.C., 1982; mem. adv. bd. Arts and Entertainment, N.Y.C.; mem. Partnership, Inc., 1983, Nat. Coun. Arts, 1987, Pres. Commn. on White House Fellowships, 1991. Named to Hall of Fame, NAACP Image Awards, 1986; recipient Changers award, Mademoiselle Mag., 1970, award, North Shore Commn. Arts Ctr., 1980, Capezio Dance award, 1971, Ann. Excellence award, John F. Kennedy Ctr. for Performing Arts, 1980, award, Am. Dance Guild, 1982, Am. Black Achievement award, Ebony Mag., 1983, Pres.'s Cabinet award, U. Detroit, 1982, Paul Robeson award, Actors Equity Assn., 1986, Lion of the Performing Arts award, N.Y. Pub. Libr., 1986, Arnold Gingrich Meml. award, 1987, Banquet of Golden Plate, 1989, Harkness Disting. Artist award, Adelphi U., 1990, Disting. Svc. to Arts award, Am. Acad. Arts and Letters, 1994, Zenith award for Fine Arts, 1994, Handel Medallion, N.Y.C., 1993, Barnard Medal of Distinction, Barnard Coll., 1994, Lifetime Achievement award, Sch. Am. Ballet, 1995, Nat. Medal of Arts, Nat. Endowment Arts, 1995, Living Landmarks award, N.Y. Landmarks of Conservancy, 1995; Conroy fellow, St. Paul's Sch., Concord, N.H., 1982, MacArthur fellow, 1994. Office: Dance Theatre Harlem 466 W 152nd St New York NY 10031-1896

MITCHELL, BART ALLEN, secondary school educator; s. Darrell Ray and Sheila Ann Mitchell; m. Helen Diana Crenshaw, June 30, 1984; children: David Allen, Amanda Ruth. AA with honors, Mineral Area Coll., 1981; BS in Edn., Southeast Mo. State U., 1983; MA in Tchg., Webster U., 1990. Dir., chmn. St. Francis County Ambulance Bd., Farmington, 1994—. Named Sports Photographer of Yr., Mo. Press Assn., 1981. Mem.: Math. Assn. Am., Mo. Coun. Tchrs. Math., Nat. Coun. Tchrs. Math. Democrat. Methodist. Avocations: photography, computers, auto restoration, music. Home: 3652 Hwy O Farmington MO 63640 Office: North County High Sch 7151 Raider Rd Bonne Terre MO 63628 E-mail: bart@mineralarea.edu.

MITCHELL, BETTY JO, writer, publisher; b. May 2, 1931; d. Edith Darrah McWilliams. BA, S.W. Mo. State U.; MSLS, U. So. Calif.; MBA, PhD, Calif. Coast U., 2002. Asst. acquisitions libr. Calif. State U., Northridge, 1967—69, libr. for pers. and fin., 1969-71, acting assoc. libr. dir., 1971-72, assoc. dir. univ. librs., 1972-81; mgr. info. sys. City Santa Monica (Calif.) Rent Control, 1984-93; owner Viewpoint Press, Tehachapi, Calif. Cons. We. Interstate Commn. for Higher Edn. USOE Inst. for Tng. in Staff Devel. Problem Solving; participant workshops in field; spkr. at profl. confs. in field; bd. dirs. Tehachapi Cmty. Orch. Author: ALMS: A Budget Based Library Management System, 1982, The Secret of Hilhouse: An Adult Book for Teens, 1993, The Huckenpuck Papers: The Tale of a Family's Secret and a Young Girl's Search for Self-Esteem, 2001; co-author: Cost Analysis of Library Functions: A Total System Approach, 1978, How to See the U.S. on $12 a Day; contbr. writings to profl. publs.; editor Staff Development column in Spl. Librs., 1975-76. Bd. dirs. San Fernando Valley coun. Girl Scouts U.S., 1974-77, employed pers. com., 1979-81; bd. dirs. Bear Valley Springs Condominium Owners Assn., 1978, Empyrean Found., 1978-81, Tehachapi Cmty. Orch. Found., 1998—, Tehachapi Performing Arts Ctr. Found., 2003—. Mem. AAUP, AAUW, ALA (chmn. various coms.), Assn. Women in Computing (bd. dirs. 1987-89), Nat. Libr. Assn., Author's Guild, Calif. Libr. Assn., Assn. Calif. State U. Profs. (sec., exec. com. 1971-72), Phi Beta Chi, Alpha Mu Gamma. Office: PMB 400 785 Tucker Rd Ste G Tehachapi CA 93561-2523 Fax: 661-821-7515. Office Phone: 661-821-5110.

MITCHELL, BETTY LOU, state legislator, retired operations director; b. Hartford, Conn., Aug. 14, 1937; m. Don David Mitchell; 3 children. Grad., Ellsworth H.S. Various mgmt. positions NYNEX Bell Atlantic; ops. dir. State of Maine, Bell Atlantic, 1989-92; mem. Dist. 10 Maine Senate, Augusta, 1996—. Corporator Bangor Savs. Bank, Ea. Maine Health Care. Mem. bd. dirs., chair long range planning Bangor Brewer YWCA; bd. dirs., chair campaign, chair leadership United Way Ea. Maine; bd. dirs., chair leadership devel. Pine Tree chpt. ARC; mem. Better Bus. Womens Investment Club, Telephone Pioneers Am.; mem. SAD 38 and 48, sch. bd., 1975-85; mem. Bd. Environ. Protection, 1984—; mem. Low Level Radioactive Waste Authority, 1993-94; mem. planning bd. ETNA, 1994-95. Republican. Home: PO Box 6 Etna ME 04434-0006 Office: Maine State Senate 3 State House Sta Augusta ME 04333-0003

MITCHELL, BEVERLY SHRIVER, hematologist, oncologist, educator; b. Balt., May 14, 1944; m. John Robert Pringle; children: Robert Mitchell, Elizabeth Greene. AB summa cum laude in Biochemistry, Smith Coll., 1965; MD, Harvard U., 1969. Hematology fellow U. Mich., Ann Arbor, 1975-77, from instr. to asst. prof. internal medicine, 1977-81, assoc. prof., 1981-87, prof. internal medicine and pharmacology, 1987-91, U. N.C., Chapel Hill, 1991—, divsn. chief hematology/oncology, 1994—2003; assoc. dir. Lineberger Cancer Ctr., Chapel Hill, 1994—. Vis. scientist Fred Hutchinson Cancer Ctr., Seattle, 1984; mem. bd. sci. counselors Cancer Treatment divsn. Nat. Cancer Inst. Recipient Stohlman award Leukemia Soc. Am., 1988. Mem. Am. Soc. Hematology (treas. 1991-96, v.p. 1998, pres. 2000), Phi Beta, Inst. Medicine. Achievements include research in nucleotide metabolism and the development of novel therapies for hematologic malignancies. Office: U NC at Chapel Hill CB # 7295 Lineberger Comprehensive Cancer Ctr Chapel Hill NC 27599-7295

MITCHELL, BRIAN CHRISTOPHER, academic administrator; b. Lowell, Mass., Feb. 23, 1953; s. Christopher Joseph and Doris Katherine (McEvoy) M.; m. Maryjane Murphy, June 28, 1975; children: Jeffrey Ryan, Patrick Joseph. BA, Merrimack Coll., 1974; MA, U. Rochester, 1976, PhD, 1981. Chair history dept. Anna Maria Coll., Paxton, Mass., 1982-85; program officer Nat. Endowment Humanities, Washington, 1985-91; pres. Commn. Ind. Colls. and Univs. Pa., Harrisburg, 1991-98, Washington and Jefferson Coll., Washington, Pa., 1998—. Instr. U. Mass., Lowell, 1977-85; adj. prof. George Mason U., Fairfax, Va., 1988-91; cons. Lowell Nat. Hist. Park, 1977-81, Lowell Heritage State Park, 1977-78. Author: The Paddy Camps: The Irish of Lowell, 1821-1861, 1988, On The North Bank, 1984; editor: Building the American Catholic City, 1986; contbg. author: From Paddy to Stud, 1986. Mem. Pa. Humanities Coun.; mem. Pa. Hist. and Mus. Commn.; chair Pa. selection com. Rhodes Scholarship Trust. Grantee Am. Coun. Learned Socs., 1985, NEH. Mem. Am. Hist. Assn. (Albert J. Beveridge award), Orgn. Am. Historians, Nat. Assn. Ind. Colls. and Univs. Roman Catholic. Office: Washington and Jefferson Coll Pres Office Washington PA 15301

MITCHELL, BRIAN STOKES, actor; b. Seattle, Oct. 31, 1958; s. George Thomas and Lillian (Stokes) M. Prin. actor 12th Night Repertory Co., San Diego, 1977-80; co-star Roots: The Next Generations, L.A., 1980, Trapper John, M.D., L.A., 1980-86, The Good War, L.A., 1987, The Fresh Prince of Bel Air, 1993, In the House, 1996, Crossing Jordan, 2002, Frasier, 2002—03; co-star Mail Kennedy Ctr., Washington, The Music Box Theatre, Broadway, N.Y.C., and Pasadena, Calif., 1987-88; star David Merrick's Broadway play Oh Kay Richard Rodgers Theatre, 1990. Guest tchr., speaker San Diego Jr. Theater, 1984; guest star The White Shadow, 227, Houston Knights, Alf, Night Court, L.A., 1987; voice-over actor, series reg. California Raisins, New Kids on the Block, Kid 'n Play, 1988—; trustee Actor's Fund, 1999—. Appeared in Broadway prodn. Jelly's last Jam, 1992, Kiss of the Spider Woman, 1994-95, Ragtime, Ford Theater for Performing Arts, 1996 (Drama League Disting. Performance award, Can.'s Dora award, Drama League award), Shubert Theatre, L.A., 1997 (L.A. Critics award), Kiss Me Kate, 1999-2001 (Tony Award, 2000, Drama Desk award, Outer Critics Circle award), Do Re Mi, 2000, Carnival, 2001, King Hedley II, 2001, Sweeney Todd, 2002; appeared in National Theater prodn. Man of La Mancha, 2002 (Helen Hayes award); composer: (symphonic suite) 3 Scenes for Clipper Ships, 1983; (Trapper John, M.D. TV scores) The Wunderkind, Friends and Lovers, I Only Have Ice For You, 1984; film work includes Ghost Dad, 1990, (voice) The Prince of Egypt, 1998, Ruby's Bucket f Blood, 2000, Call me Claude, 2001. Ambassador March of Dimes, U.S. Tour, 1984-85; performer USO, European Tour, 1984, Far East/Middle East Tour, 1985, Calif. Orgn. of Police and Sheriffs, L.A., 1986. Recipient Best Pop Song and Composer of Yr. awards Los Angeles Songwriters Showcase, 1986, Drama League Distinguished Performance Award, 1998. Mem. Acad. of TV Arts and Scis. (blue ribbon panelist 1987), ASCAP, Screen Actors' Guild, AFTRA, Actors Equity Assn. Avocations: flying, skiing, composing.

MITCHELL, BRIANE NELSON, lawyer; b. Seattle, July 4, 1953; s. Robert Max and Frances Marie (Nelson) M.; m. Suzanne Harmatz; children: Brianne Nelson, Brittany Suzanne. AB, Columbia U., 1975; JD, U. Idaho, 1978. Law clk. U.S. Ct. Appeals (9th cir.), 1978-80; assoc. Debevoise & Plimpton, N.Y.C., 1980-84, Paul, Hastings, Janofsky & Walker, L.A., 1984-86, ptnr., 1986-93, McCambridge, Deixler & Marmaro, L.A., 1994-95, Shapiro, Mitchell & Dupont LLP, Santa Monica, 1996-2000, Manatt, Phelps & Phillips LLP, L.A., 2000—03. Mem. adv. bd. U. Idaho Law Sch. Mem.: ABA, Calif. Bar Assn., N.Y. State Bar Assn., Idaho Bar Assn. E-mail: NelsMitchell@aol.com.

MITCHELL, BRUCE TYSON, lawyer; b. San Francisco, Nov. 6, 1928; s. John Robert and Lorraine C. (Tyson) M.; m. Adrienne Means Hiscox, Oct. 14, 1951; 1 son, Mark Means. AB with great distinction, Stanford U., 1949, JD, 1951. Bar: Calif. 1952, U.S. Dist. Ct. (no. dist.) Calif 1952, U.S. Ct. Appeals (9th cir.) 1952, U.S. Supreme Ct. 1971. Estate adminstr. Crocker Nat. Bank, San Francisco, 1955-57; atty. Utah Internat. Inc., San Francisco, 1957-87, sec., 1974-87, sr. counsel, 1961—87, ret., 1981; pvt. practice securities arbitrator San Francisco. Mem. non-securities panel arbitrators N.Y. Stock Exch., Pacific Stock Exch., NASD Bd. Arbitrators. Chmn. San Mateo County Rep. Ctrl. Com., 1964-70; mem. Calif. Rep. Ctrl. Com., 1964-74, 77-83; alt. del. Rep. Nat. Conv., 1968; co-chmn. San Mateo (Calif.) County Pres. Ford Com., 1976; mem. bd. visitors sch. law Stanford U., 1980-83; exec. v.p., bd. dirs. San Francisco Jr. C. of C., 1961; bd. dirs. No. Calif. chpt. Arthritis Found., 1972-85, 1987-92, St. Francis Hosp. Found., San Francisco, 1992-98, 99—, hon. dir., 1998-99—. Lt. (j.g.) USNR, 1952-55, Japan. Mem. ABA, Calif. Bar Assn., San Francisco Bar Assn., Am. Judicature Soc., Am. Soc. Corp. Secs. (v.p. 1976-77, dir. 1976-79), Assn. Former Intelligence Officers, Commonwealth Club of Calif. (pres. San Francisco 1973), Stanford Assocs., Pacific Union Club, Olympic Club, Capitol Hill Club, Travelers Century Club, Masons. Congregationalist. Home: 165 Redwood Dr Hillsborough CA 94010-6971 Office: 225 Bush St Fl 16 San Francisco CA 94104-4213

MITCHELL, BURLEY BAYARD, JR., lawyer; b. Oxford, N.C., Dec. 15, 1940; s. Burley Bayard and Dorothy Ford (Champion) M.; m. Mary Lou Willett, Aug. 3, 1962; children: David Bayard, Catherine Morris. BA with honors, N.C. State U., 1966, DHL (hon.), 1995; JD, U. N.C., 1969; LLD (hon.), Campbell U., 1998. Bar: N.C. 1969, U.S. Ct. Appeals (4th cir.) 1970, U.S. Ct. Appeals (3d cir.) 2002, U.S. Supreme Ct. 1972. Asst. atty. gen. State of N.C., Raleigh, 1969-72, dist. atty., 1973-77, judge Ct. Appeals, 1977-79, sec. crime control, 1979-82; justice Supreme Ct. N.C., Raleigh, 1982-94; chief justice Supreme Ct. of N.C., Raleigh, 1995-99; ptnr. Womble Carlyle Sandridge and Rice, Raleigh, 1999—. Served with USN, 1958-62, Asia. Recipient N.C. Nat. Guard Citizen Commendation award, 1982 Mem. ABA, VFW, N.C. Bar Assn., Mensa, Am. Legion, Phi Beta Kappa. Democrat. Methodist. Home: 4301 City of Oaks Wynd Raleigh NC 27612-5316 Office: First Union Cptl Ctr Ste 2100 PO Box 831 Raleigh NC 27602-0831

MITCHELL, CAROL ANN, nursing educator; b. Portsmouth, Va., Aug. 31, 1942; d. William Howell and Eleanor Bertha (Wesarg) M.; m. David Alan Friedman, June 17, 1971 (div. 1988). Diploma, NYU, 1963; BS, Columbia U., 1968, MA, 1971, EdM, 1974, EdD, 1980; MS, SUNY, Stony Brook, 1990. Charge nurse Nassau County Med. Ctr., East Meadow, N.Y., 1963-65; staff nurse Meml. Hosp., N.Y.C., 1965-68; head nurse, supr. Cmty. at Glen Cove (N.Y.), 1969-71; assoc. prof. dept. nursing Queensborough C.C. CUNY, Bayside, 1971-80; assoc. prof. Marion A. Buckley Sch. Nursing Adelphi U., Garden City, N.Y., 1981-88; ednl. cons. Nat. League for Nursing, N.Y.C., 1980-81; prof. sch. nursing SUNY, Stony Brook, 1988-92, chmn. adult nursing, 1988-92; prof. chair Coll. Nursing East Tenn. State U., 1992-95, mem faculty, 1995-96; geriat. nurse practitioner, dir. geriat. evaluation unit Vet. Affairs Med. Ctr., Mountain Home, Tenn., 1997—. Mem. faculty Regents Coll. degrees in nursing program USNY, Albany, 1978-91, cons., 1978—; faculty cons. geriats. Montefiore Med. Ctr., 1991-93. Editor emeritus: Scholarly Inquiry in Nursing Practice, 1983—; contbr. articles to profl. jours. Robert Wood Johnson clin. nurse scholar postdoctoral fellow U. Rochester (N.Y.), 1983-85. Mem.: Am. Geriatrics Soc., Am. Nurses Assn. Avocations: reading, gardening, bicycling, travel, cooking.

MITCHELL, CAROL DENISE, small business owner, writer; b. Los Angeles, Calif., May 12, 1955; d. Zebbie Thomas and Tasceaie Carise Charles; m. Willie Mitchell, Apr. 1, 1994; m. Daryl Dean Thompson, Sr. (div.); children: Shaun Evans Caldwell, Daryl Dean Thompson Jr. Profl. contractor Adminstrv. Services, Concord, Calif., 1995—2002; profl. contractor/owner CDM Security, Concord, Calif., 2002—. On-air news anchor Soul Beat TV, 2000—03. Author: (novels) What Happened to Suzy, 1995; editor A Love Worth Fighting For, 2002; prodr.: (song) I Wanna Go Home, 2000. Vol. NAACP, Oakland, Calif., 2000. Recipient Miss Congeniality 1973, Miss Pomona Valley Paegant, sponsored by JC Penney's, Bank of America Music Award, 1970—73. Democrat. Achievements include being a self-educated African Am. mentor for writers; advocate for abused children and adults. Home and Office: CDM Professional Services PO Box 484 Concord CA 94522 Office Phone: 925-609-9308.

MITCHELL, CAROLYN COCHRAN, foundation administrator's executive assistant; b. Atlanta, Dec. 27, 1943; d. Clemern Covell and Agnes Emily (Veal) Cochran; m. W. Alan Mitchell, Aug. 30, 1964; 1 child, Teri Marie. AB magna cum laude, Mercer U., 1965, M in Svc. Mgmt., 1989. Caseworker Ga. Dept. Family & Children Svc., Macon, 1965-67, Covington, 1967-69; presch. dir. Southwestern Theol. Sem., Ft. Worth, 1969-70; presch. tchr., dir. Noah's Ark Day Care, Bowden, Ga., 1970-72, First Bapt. Ch., Bremen, Ga., 1972-75; preschool tchr., dir. Roebuck Pk. Bapt. Ch., Birmingham, Ala., 1975-79; freelance office mgr. and bookkeeper Macon, 1979-84; asst. to pres. Ga. Wesleyan Coll., Macon, 1984-98; asst. to pres., CEO Medcen Cmty. Health Found., Macon, 1998—. Exec. dir. Ga. Women of Achievement, 1991-95; dir. Macon Arts Alliance, 1987-91; mem. Cultural Plan Oversight Com., 1989-90. Active Get Out the Vote Task Force, Macon, 1981-95, Macon Symphony Guild, 1986-91; dep. registrar Bibb County Bd. Elections, Macon, 1981-95; asst. sec. Ronald McDonald House Ctrl. Ga., 1999-2000. Mem. AAUW (bd. dirs. Ga. chpt., v.p. 1991-93, chair coll.-univ. rels. com. 1993-94, bylaws com. 1991-92, v.p., sec., treas., historian, newsletter editor, Macon chpt., Named Gift Honoree 1988, 2000), NAFE, NOW, Women's Network for Change, Am. Mgmt. Assn., Presdl. Assts. in Higher Edn., Religious Coalition for Reproductive Choice, The Interfaith Alliance, Women's Polit. Orgn. Macon, Sigma Mu. Democrat. Baptist. Office Phone: 478-633-7395. E-mail: mitchell.carolyn@mccg.org.

MITCHELL, CHARLES EDWARD, lawyer, arbitrator; b. Seymour, Ind., July 7, 1925; s. Edward Charles and Lula Belle Thompson M.; m. Julia Viola Sarjeant, Sept. 15, 1951 (dec. Feb. 26, 1994); children: Charles Leonard, Albert Bascom; m. Lloyed Overton, Dec. 24, 2002; stepchildren: Victoria martin, Alexis Martin. Student, Morehouse Coll., Atlanta, 1943-44, 46-47, NYU, 1949; JD, Temple U., Phila., 1954. Bar: D.C. 1970, U.S. Ct. Appeals (3d cir.) 1971, Pa. 1972, U.S. Supreme Ct. 1973, U.S. Ct. Appeals (6th cir.) 1984; cert. labor arbitrator, Am. Arbitration Assn., Fed. Mediation and Conciliation Svc. Tchr. City of Phila., 1954-55; mgmt. trainee Office of Dir. of Fin., Budget Bur., Phila., 1955-56; legal asst. Office of Phila. Dist. Atty., 1956-60; claims rep., claims authorizer U.S. HEW, Social Security Adminstrn., Phila., 1960-64; atty., examiner NLRB, Phila., 1964-72; mgmt. labor counsel E.I. duPont de Nemours & Co., Wilmington, Del., 1972-92; pvt. practice Phila., 1993-99. Labor panel Am. Arbitration Assn.; mem. roster of arbitrators Fed. Mediation and Conciliation Svc. Mem. vestry The Ch. Good Shepherd. 1st class seaman USN, 1944-46. Mem. ABA (mgmt. mem. sect. labor and employment law, practice and procs. com. 1973-92), Fed. Bar Assn. (pres. Del. chpt. 1974-76, nat. chpt. del. 1973-78), Indsl. Rels. Rsch. Assn. (v.p. 1970-72), Phila. Bar Assn. Democrat. Episcopalian. Avocations: golf, tennis, chess, bridge, travel. Office Phone: 215-844-3936. Personal E-mail: cemitchell34mv@aol.com.

MITCHELL, CONNIE, director; m. George Mitchell, Sr.; children: Carlata, George Jr. Tchr. adv. Office Adminstrv./Instrnl. Pers. Detroit Pub. Schs. Dir. Ednll. Enrichment Acad. Active Meth. Children's Home Soc. Named Middle Sch. Tchr. of Yr., Newsweek Mag./WDIV-TV, 1994, Tchr. of Yr., Detroit Pub. Schs., 1994; recipient Golden Apple Tchr. award, Wayne County Regional Edn. Svc. Agy. Mem.: Nat. Bd. for Profl. Tchg. Stds. (bd. mem.), Alpha Kappa Alpha. Office: Detroit Pub Schs Schs Ctr Bldg 3031 W Grand Blvd Detroit MI 48202

MITCHELL, DAVID WALKER, lawyer; b. Oakland, Calif., Nov. 11, 1935; s. Theodore Boyd and Helen Louise (Walker) M.; m. Carolyn Hilliard Graves, July 29, 1961; children: Sarah, Betsy. AB in History, Stanford U., 1957; JD, Harvard U., 1960. Bar: Calif. 1961. Assoc. Kindel & Anderson, L.A., 1961-65, Weir, Hopkins, Donovan, San Jose, Calif., 1965-68; ptnr. Hopkins, Mitchell & Carley, San Jose, 1968-87, McCutchen, Doyle, Brown & Enersen, San Jose, 1987-93, Hoge, Fenton, Jones & Appel, San Jose, 1993-2000, of counsel, 2001—. Bd. dirs. Peninsula Open Space Trust, Menlo Park, Calif., 1982—, pres., 1984-92; bd. dirs. Cmty. Found. Silicon Valley., San Jose, 1977-94, 99-2003; chair bd. trustees United Way Santa Clara County, 1983-85. Fellow Am. Bar Found., Am. Leadership Forum (sr.); mem. Santa Clara County Bar Assn. (trustee 1972-75), San Jose C. of C. (bd. dirs. 1975-80). Mem. United Ch. of Christ. Avocations: music, hiking. Office: Hoge Fenton Jones Appel 60 S Market St Ste 1400 San Jose CA 95113-2396 Business E-Mail: dwm@hogefenton.com.

MITCHELL, DONALD WAYNE, management consultant, investment manager, lawyer, writer; b. San Bernardino, Calif., Nov. 1, 1946; s. Donald Wardell (dec.) and Edith Felice (Wood) M.; m. Carol Bruckner, Nov. 11, 1984; children: Donald Weyland, Mark De Saussure, Mandy Sara, Janis Felicia. AB magna cum laude, Harvard U., 1968, JD, 1971. Bar: Mass. 1971. Project mgr. Boston Cons. Group, 1971-74; dir. strategic planning Heublein, Inc., Farmington, Conn., 1974-77; chmn. Mitchell and Co., Wellesley, Mass., 1977—; pres. Mitchell Investment Mgmt. Co., Inc., Wellesley, 1981—. Chmn. Share Price Growth 100, 1989—, Leading CFOs, 1993—, Outstanding CEOs, 1994—; pres. Leading Exec. Orgns. 100, Inc., 1991—. Co-author: The 2,000 Percent Solution, 1999, The Irresistible Growth Enterprise, 2000, The Ultimate Competitive Advantage, 2003. Chmn. Twenty Times Progress Project, 1995—, vice chmn. law sch. fund gift campaign Harvard U., Cambridge, 1981-82, chmn. law sch fund 10th ann. gift campaign, 1980-81, chmn. law sch. class of 1971 15th reunion, 1985-86, co-chmn. class of 1968 20th reunion Harvard U., 1986-88; bd. dirs. Literacy Vols. Mass., 1993-2001, v.p. strategic planning, 1999-2001. Mem. Harvard Alumni Assn. (bd. dirs. 1986-88), Harvard Law Sch. Assn. (centennial com. 1984-86, treas. 1987-90, bus. com. 1999—). Office: Mitchell and Co 888 Worcester St Wellesley MA 02482 E-mail: ultimatecompetitiveadvantage@yahoo.com.

MITCHELL, EARL NELSON, physicist, researcher; b. Centerville, Iowa, Aug. 30, 1926; s. Earl Nelson and Nina (Swank) M.; m. Marlys Marie Panning, July 23, 1955. AB magna cum laude, U. Iowa, 1949, MS, 1951; PhD, U. Minn., 1955. Research scientist Sperry Rand Corp., St. Paul, 1955-58; asst. prof., then assoc. prof. physics U. N.D., Grand Forks, 1958-62; vis. assoc. prof., then assoc. prof. and prof. physics U. N.C., Chapel Hill, 1962-91, prof. emeritus, 1991—, asst. chmn. dept., 1968-76. Lectr. Hamline U., 1956, 57; cons. Sperry Rand Corp., 1958-62 Contbr. articles to profl. jours.; author textbooks. Mem. Chapel Hill Planning Bd., 1970-71; pres. Chapel Hill Concert Series, 1967-70; mem. bd. for missions to deaf Luth. Ch. Mo. Synod, 1958-64. Served in USNR, 1945-46. Mem.: Am. Soc. Enologists (bd. dirs. ea. sect. 1984—91, pres.-elect 1988, pres. 1989, past pres. 1990), Am. Phys. Soc., N.C. Wine Growers Assn. (pres. 1994—98, past pres. 1998—2003), Phi Eta Sigma, Sigma Xi, Phi Beta Kappa. Democrat. Office: U NC Dept Physics Chapel Hill NC 27599-0001

MITCHELL, EARL WESLEY, clergyman; b. Excelsior Springs, Mo., Mar. 16, 1931; s. Earl Van and Ora Leah (Butterfield) M.; m. Mary Lou Bell, June 8, 1956; children: Susan Yvonne, Randall Bruce. Ordained to ministry Christian Union Ch., 1971. Min. Vibbard (Mo.) Christian Union Ch., 1962-69, Liberty (Mo.) Christian Ch., 1969-77, Barwick Christian Union Ch., Cameron, Mo., 1977-80, Independence (Mo.) Christian Union Ch., 1980-95; assoc. pastor Flack Meml. Christian Union Ch., Excelsior Springs, Mo., 1995—. Former mem. state exec. bd. Christian Union Mo., 1995-98; area rep. Mo. Christian Union USA; former mem. gen. exec. bd., former editor C.U. Witness. Sgt. USAF, 1951-55. Avocations: music, woodworking, painting, photography. Home and Office: 618 Henrie St Excelsior Springs MO 64024-2022

MITCHELL, EDWARD JOHN, economist, retired educator; b. Newark, Aug. 15, 1937; s. Edward Charles and Gladys (Werner) M.; m. Mary Josephine Osborne, June 14, 1958; children: Susan, Edward. BA summa cum laude, Bowling Green State U., 1960; postgrad. (Social Sci. Research Council fellow), Nuffield Coll., Oxford U., Eng., 1963-64, PhD in Econs. (NDEA fellow 1960-63, NSF fellow 1964-65), 1966. Lectr. in econs. Wharton Sch., U. Pa., 1964-65; economist Rand Corp., 1965-68; mem. Inst. Advanced Study, Princeton, N.J., 1968-69; sr. economist Pres.'s Council Econ. Advs., Washington, 1969-72; vis. assoc. prof. econs. Cornell U., 1972-73; assoc. prof. bus. econs. U. Mich., 1973-75, prof., 1975-88, prof. emeritus bus. econs. and pub. policy, 1988—; pres. Edward J. Mitchell Inc., Ann Arbor, 1977—94. Dir. nat. energy project Am. Enterprise Inst., 1974-76; pres. Fountainhead Investment Co., 1984—94. Author: U.S. Energy Policy: A Primer, 1974, Dialogue on World Oil, 1974, Financing the Energy Industry, 1975, Vertical Integration of the Oil Industry, 1976, The Deregulation of Natural Gas, 1983; contbr. articles to profl. jours. Home: 310 Penny Ln Santa Barbara CA 93108-2601 Office: Grad Sch Bus U Mich Ann Arbor MI 48109 E-mail: mitchell296@cox.net.

MITCHELL, EHRMAN BURKMAN, JR., architect; b. Harrisburg, Pa., Jan. 25, 1924; s. Ehrman Burkman and Alice (DeCevee) M.; m. Hermine Strickler, Sept. 25, 1948; children: Eric Ehrman, Marianne. AB, U. Pa., 1947, BArch, 1948; LHD (hon.), Spring Garden Coll., 1989. Asso. architect Bellante & Clauss, 1951-58; partner Mitchell/Giurgola, Assocs., Phila., 1958-85. Dir. Wyck Assn.; lectr. Ohio State U., U. Ariz., U. Utah, Cath. U. Am., Washington U., St. Louis, U. Notre Dame, Dartmouth Coll., U. Ky., U. Md., Temple U.; Phila. lectr. U. Nebr.; lectr. Calif. Poly. State U., U. Brasilia, Boston Archtl. Ctr., Pa. State U., Clemson U., Cornell U.; bd. overseers Temple U. Arch. Sch., U. Pa. Grad. Sch. Fine Arts; arch. design rev. panels U. Pa. Prin. works Nat. hdqrs. Am. Coll. Life Underwriters, Bryn Mawr, Pa. also, Adult Learning Research Center; office bldg. Penn Mut. Life Ins. Co., Phila., Ins. Co. N.Am., Phila.; U. Wash. Law Sch. and Library, Seattle, USIS Cultural Center, Brasilia, Brazil, A.B. Volvo Co. mfg. plant, Chesapeake, Va., New Parliament House, Canberra, Australia. Pres. Citizens Coun. Whitemarch Twp., Montgomery County, Pa., 1963-65, dir., 1963-67; mem. Del. Valley Citizens Transp. Com., 1964—, Citizens Coun. Montgomery County, 1964—; mem. archtl. rev. panel U.S. Fed. Res. System; bd. regents Am. Archtl. Found. With USNR, 1943-46. Recipient Gold medal Artists Guild Phila., Hazlett award Pa. Coun. Arts, 1985, plaque honor Mexican Fedn. Architects; fellow U. Pa. Mus. Fellow Royal Archtl. Inst. Can. (hon.), Royal Australian Inst. Architects; mem. AIA (chpt. dir. Phila. 1965-68, coll. fellows 1969—, nat. dir. 1973-75, v.p. 1977, 1st v.p. 1978, pres. 1979, gold medal Phila. chpt. 1964, 72, 74, silver medal 1973, Nat. Honor award 1974, 75, archtl. firm award 1976), Pa. Soc. Architects (dir. 1966—, sec. 1966, v.p. 1967, pres. 1968, silver medal 1974, 75, 77), Am. Inst. Mgmt. (pres.'s coun. 1967), Pa. Acad. Fine Arts, Pan Am. Fedn. Architects, Nat. Acad. Design, Societe Arquitecto Mexicanos, Beta Theta Pi. Clubs: Carpenter's Co., St. Andrew's Soc. (Phila.). Home: 600 E Cathedral Rd Apt E101 Philadelphia PA 19128-1929

MITCHELL, ELIZABETH MARELLE, family nurse practitioner, nursing educator, medical, surgical nurse; b. Bemis, Tenn., Dec. 2, 1937; d. William Columbus and Ruth Marelle (Wadley) Latham; m. Thomas Alton McNatt, June 20, 1953 (dec. Mar. 1984); children: Glenn McNatt, Craig McNatt, Chris McNatt; m. Charles Leon Mitchell, Sept. 7, 1985; stepchildren: Melanie Campbell, Mike, Allyson Webb. AA in Nursing, Union U., 1965; BSN, U. Tenn., Martin, 1994; MSN, FNP, U. Tenn., Memphis, 1996. RN Tenn., cert. CNOR, BCLS, BCLS instr., BCLS instr. trainer, ACLS, ACLS instr., family nurse practitioner, ANCC. Staff nurse med.-surg. units Jackson (Tenn.)-Madison County Gen. Hosp., 1965-66; physician 1st asst. Jackson Clinic Surgeons, 1966-74; nursing instr. Jackson Area Vo-Tech Sch., 1974-78, nursing instr. supr., 1978-81; supr. oper. rm. Jackson Splty. Hosp. (acquired by Jackson-Madison County Gen. Hosp. 1983), 1981-85; instr. nurse edn. Jackson-Madison County Gen. Hosp., 1985-96; family nurse practitioner Perry County Med. Ctr., 1996—. Nursing adv. bd. mem. Jackson Area Vo-Tech Sch., 1987—96; task force nursing asst. curriculum devel. mem. State of Tenn., Nashville, 1992; clin. skills judge Health Occupations Student Assn. Tenn. State Competition, Nashville, 1992. Tchr. Sun. sch. Malesus Bapt. Ch., Malesus, Tenn., 1975—86. Mem.: ANA, West Tenn. Healthcare Edn. and Tng. Conf. Group (pres. 1987, regional rep. 1988, sec. 1994), Tenn. Nursing Assn., Am. Soc. Healthcare Edn. and Tng. (svc. rep. West Tenn. 1988, Outstanding Regional Rep. Tenn. chpt. 1988), Assn. Oper. Rm. Nurses (program com. 1993, 1994), Am. Acad. Nurse Practitioners, U. Tenn. Martin Nursing Honor Soc., Sigma Theta Tau, Phi Theta Kappa. Avocations: reading, swimming, crafts. Home: RR 3 Box 378 Linden TN 37096-9544 Office: Perry County Med Ctr 115 E Brooklyn St Linden TN 37096

MITCHELL, ELLEN CLABAUGH, investment executive; b. Omaha, Mar. 2, 1942; d. Joseph Franklin and Dorothy (Newton) Carpenter; m. Dixon L. Mitchell, Aug. 25, 1962; 1 child, Lara Ellen. BS in Fin. & Econs., U. Nebr., Omaha, 1965; MBA, Va. Poly. Inst., 1983. Chartered Fin. Analyst. Asst. v.p. Firstier Fin., Omaha, 1965-69, 1971-75, Bridges Investments, Omaha, 1970-71; analyst U.S. Securities and Exchange Commn., Washington, 1983-85; v.p. Nat. Bank of Washington, 1985-87, Foxhall Investment Mgmt., Washington, 1987-93; pres. Mitchell Advisors Inc., Reston, Va., 1993—. Mem. Washington Soc. Investment Analysts, Inst. Chartered Fin. Analysts, Garden Club (v.p., treas. 1980). Episcopalian. Home: 2017 Turtle Pond Dr Reston VA 20191-4045 Office: Mitchell Advisors Inc 2017 Turtle Pond Dr Reston VA 20191-4045

MITCHELL, ERIC EHRMAN, photographer, stock broker; b. Phila., Nov. 24, 1954; s. Ehrman Burkman and Hermine (Strickler) M.; m. Leslie Ann Marsh, Aug. 18, 1984; children: Meredith Hermine, Lauren Calder. BS in Photography and Bus., Skidmore Coll., 1977. Accredited asset mgmt. specialist. Head photographer Phila. Mus. Art, 1978-86; freelance photographer St. Peters, Pa., 1986-94; stockbroker Montanto Securities, Bluebell, Pa., 1994-95, Boenning & Scattergood, Inc., Pottstown, Pa., 1996—, v.p., 1996—. Photographs have appeared in various books, catalogues and mags. worldwide. Planning commr. South Coventry Twp., Chester County, Pa., 1990-96, 2001—, supr., 1992-98; mem. Fedn. No. Chester County Cmtys., Pa., 1992-2003; bd. dirs. Pottstown Meml. Med. Ctr., 2003—. Fellow Paul Harris, 2002. Mem.: Am. Soc. Media Photographers, St. Andrews Soc., Rotary. Avocations: skiing, hiking, woodland management, technical analysis of the stock market. Office: Boenning & Scattergood 601 High St Pottstown PA 19464 Office Phone: 610-327-0600.

MITCHELL, GARRY, management consultant, writer; b. Medicine Hat, Alberta, Can., Mar. 22, 1938; s. Archibald Hugh Mitchell and Isobel Lucielle Barber; m. Valerie Nield, Dec. 16, 1968; 1 child, Heather McCall. B in Edn., U. Alta., Edmonton, 1961; MA, CUNY, N.Y.C., 1976; PhD, NYU, 1989. Broadcaster, Medicine Hat, Edmonton, N.Y.C., 1956-80; chmn. theater dept. Victoria Composite H.S., Edmonton, 1961-64; actor in broadway, TV, movies and regional N.Y.C., 1964-72; sales rep., mgr. Eplo Chems., Holiday Magic, AB Dick, N.Y.C., 1972-76; assoc. prof. Nassau C.C., N.Y., 1976-81; cons., spkr. GM Tng. Specialists, N.Y.C., Yarmouth Port, Mass., 1979—. Author: Total Time Management, 1985, How to Motivate Successfully, 1986, The Trainer's Handbook 1st edition, 1987, 98, The Heart of the Sale, 1996. Mem. Internat. Soc. Gen. Semantics, N.Y. Acad. Scis. Avocations: theater, reading. Address: 16 Mattis Dr Yarmouth Port MA 02675-1327

MITCHELL, GARY EARL, physicist, researcher; b. July 5, 1935; s. Earl Raymond and Delma Kathlene (Lockard) Mitchell; m. Carolyn Fey Stutz, Aug. 4, 1957; children: Scott Frederick, Karen Lee(dec.). BS, U. Louisville, 1956; MA, Duke U., 1958; PhD, Fla. State U., 1962. Rsch. assoc. Columbia U., N.Y.C., 1962—64, asst. prof., 1964—68; assoc. prof. NC State U., Raleigh, 1968—74, prof. physics, 1974—, assoc. head physics dept., 1982—97; assoc. dir. Triangle Univs. Nuclear Lab., 1992—. Sr. scientist Alexander von Humboldt Found., Bonn, Germany, 1975, Bonn, 97. Contbr. numerous articles to sci. publs. Recipient Alumni Disting. Prof. award, NC State U. Fellow: Am. Phys. Soc. (Jesse Beams award 1997); mem.: numerous sci. assns. Avocation: history. Home: 2913 Harriman Rd Durham NC 27705-5423 Office: NC State U Dept Physics PO Box 8202 Raleigh NC 27695-0001 Office Phone: 919-660-2638. Business E-Mail: mitchell@tuml.duke.edu.

MITCHELL, GENEVA BROOKE, hypnotherapist; b. Ringgold, Tex., Feb. 15, 1929; d. Roy Banks and Willie Jewel (Lemons) Shaw; m. Roy David Mitchell, Nov. 30, 1947; children: Ronald, Donald, Joel, Pamela, Annette. D of Clin. Hypnosis, Am. Inst. Hypnotherapy, Calif., 1989. Cert. master hypnotist Hypnosis Tng. Inst., hypnotherapist, advanced investigative and forensic hypnosis. Chiropractic asst., Alamogordo, N.Mex., 1962-79; hypnotherapist Alamogordo Hypnosis and Counseling Ctr., 1980-92, M&M Horses Corp., Tularosa, N.Mex., 1985-92; mgr. Shaw Mobile Home Park, 1986-99; mng. ptnr. Shaw, Mitchell & Mallory, Albuquerque, 1986, mgr., 1987-88; owner A New Image Hyupnosis Ctr., Albuquerque, 1992; ret., 1992. Pres. N.Mex. Chiropractic Aux., 1984-85; mem. Am. Coun. Hypnotist Examiners, 1980-85; hypnotist for tape series; instr. New Forever Trim Life Loss Program; spkr. Am. Bd. Hypnotherapy Conv., 1991. Author: Take the Power, 1991. Charter pres. La Sertoma, Alamogordo, 1957; pres. Oreg. Sch. PTA, Alamogordo, 1958, La Luz Sch. Parents Club, N.Mex., 1962; sec. N.Mex. Jr. Rodeo Assn., 1964; co-founder Pre-Sch. La Luz, 1969; active N.Mex. Govs. Coun. on Youth, 1969; bd. dirs. Otero county Jr. Rodeo Assn., N.Mex., 1968; dir. self-hypnosis sch. Recipient Spkrs. award Life Found., 1984. Mem. Am. Assn. Profl. Hypnotherapists, Ladies for Life (Appreciation award 1984, 90), N.Mex. Ladies Life Fellowship (pres. 1983, bd. dirs. 1985), S.W. Hypnotherapy Examining Bd., Internat. Chiropractic Assn. Aux. (pres. 1994—, conv. chmn. 1993), Ladies for Life Chiropractic Orgn. (pres. elect 1993). Avocations: golf, painting, swimming, martial arts, writing. E-mail: gbmitchell@aol.com.

MITCHELL, GEORGE CHARLES, diplomat, international consultant, mediator, educator, writer; b. Aug. 6, 1920; s. Charles Peter and Athena N. (Kapotas) Mitchell; m. Nina Catherine Chaconas, Oct. 22, 1955; children: Martina, Melinda, Marlena. BS, U. Nebr., Kearney, 1941; postgrad., U. Nebr., Lincoln, 1941-42; cert., Oxford U., 1947; MA, Georgetown U., 1947; cert., Acad. Internat. Law, The Hague, The Netherlands, 1948; PhD summa cum laude, Sorbonne U., Paris, 1949; postgrad., Inst. d'Etudes Politiques, Paris, 1947-49, George Washington U. Law Sch., 1959-61, Fgn. Svc. Inst., 1962, 69, U. Pitts., 1974, U.S. Army War Coll., 1980, U.S. Naval War Coll., 1981. News corr., Washington and Western Europe, 1946-49; polit. analyst U.S. Dept. State, Washington, 1951-54, specialist, 1954-55; dep. prin. officer, econ. officer, consul Am. Consulate Gen., Belfast, No. Ireland, 1955-58; fgn. rels. officer, UNESCO rels. staff U.S. Dept. State, Washington, 1958-62; prin. officer, polit. officer, consul Am. Consulate, Arequipa, Peru, 1962-67; dean Consular Corps, 1965-66; polit.-mil. officer, 1st sec. Am. Embassy, Santo Domingo, Dominican Republic, 1967-68; prin. officer, polit.-econ. officer, consul Am. Consulate, San Luis Potosi, Mex., 1968-71; chief Speakers Bur. U.S. Dept. State, Washington, 1971-72, plans officer Bur. Pub. Affairs, 1971-72; exec. dir. World Affairs Coun. Pitts., 1973-91; internat. con., mediator Pitts., 1989—; exec. dir. internat. mgmt. tng. Lang. Ctr., Pitts., 1990-91. Adj. prof. grad. internat. bus. mgmt. Point Pk. U., 1991—2003; internat. mgr. U.S. Arbitration and Mediation, Pa., 1992—93; bd. dirs. Stas. KGFW and KQKY, Kearney, Stas. KKAR and KQKQ, Omaha, Stas. KXNP-KODY, North Platte, 1954—96; leader del. to China World Affairs Coun., 1978; leader del. to Taiwan and Philippines Nat. Coun. World Affairs, 1988. Author: (book) Matthew B. Ridgway: Soldier, Statesman, Scholar, Citizen, 1999; editor: World Affairs Coun. newsletter, Nat. Coun. World Affairs Orgns. newsletter; co-editor: Asian/Pacific Dynamics-Economic, Political, Security, 1984; radio interviewer on internat. affairs, judge (TV series) Battle of Wits; contbr. articles to U.S. govt. publs., profl. jours., newspapers. Founder Prescott Sch., Arequipa; mem. Western Pa. Dist. Export Coun., Pitts., 1979—92; founder, pres. Atheneum Soc., Washington, 1952; founder Am. Soc. Arequipa, 1963. Lt. (j.g.) USNR, 1942—45, ETO. Recipient Meritorious

Honor award, U.S. Dept. State, 1966, Disting. Svc. award, U. Nebr., 1972; scholar AHEPA, 1939. Mem.: Am. Arbitration Assn., Midwest Conf. World Affairs (adv. coun. 1988—90), Assn. Conflict Resolution, Internat. Exec. Svc. Corps, Fgn. Affairs Rels. Corps, Nat. Coun. World Affairs Orgns. (v.p. 1985—87, pres. 1987—89, bd. dirs., exec. com. 1974—91), Com. Present Danger (founding, bd. dirs.), Am. Fgn. Svc. Assn., Rotary, Mortar Bd. Avocations: reading, writing, public speaking, antiques, travel. Home and Office: 3416 Brookdale Dr Upper Saint Clair Pittsburgh PA 15241-1558

MITCHELL, GEORGE ERNEST, JR., animal scientist, educator; b. Duoro, N.Mex., June 7, 1930; s. George Ernest and Alma Thyrza (Hatley) M.; m. Billie Carolyn McMahan, Mar. 14, 1952; children: Leslie Dianne, Karen Leigh, Cynthia Faye. BS, U. Mo., 1951, MS, 1954; PhD, U. Ill., 1956. Asst. prof. animal sci. U. Ill., 1956-60; assoc. prof. U. Ky., Lexington, 1960-67, prof., 1967-98, prof. emeritus, 1998—, dir. grad. studies in animal scis., 1964-96, coord. beef cattle and sheep, 1974-90. Contbr. articles to profl. jours. Served with USAF, 1951-53. Fulbright research scholar New Zealand, 1973-74; Rsch. scholar Japan Soc. for Promotion of Sci., Japan, 1989 Mem. Am. Soc. Animal Sci. (sec. 1969-70, v.p. 1970-71, pres. So. sect. 1971-72, rsch. fellow 1989, Disting. Svc. award 1994), Am. Dairy Sci. Assn., Am. Inst. Nutrition, AAAS, Council for Agrl. Sci. and Tech., Sigma Xi, Alpha Zeta, Gamma Sigma Delta, Omicron Delta Kappa. Democrat. Methodist. Home: 690 Hill N Dale Rd Lexington KY 40503-2164 Office: U Ky 809 W P Garrigus Bldg Lexington KY 40546-0001 Personal E-mail: gmitchel@earthlink.net.

MITCHELL, GEORGE JOHN, former senator, lawyer; b. Waterville, Maine, Aug. 20, 1933; s. George J. and Mary (Saad) M.; m. Heather MacLachlan; children: Andrea, Andrew, Claire. BA, Bowdoin Coll., 1954; LL.B., Georgetown U., 1960. Bar: Maine 1960, D.C. 1960. Trial atty. anti-trust div. U.S. Dept. Justice, Washington, 1960-62; exec. asst. Senator Edmund Muskie, 1962-65; ptnr. Jensen, Baird, Gardner & Henry, Portland, Maine, 1965-77; U.S. atty. Maine, 1977-79; U.S. dist. judge, 1979-80; U.S. senator from Maine, 1980-95; mem. environ. and pub. works com., 1980-95; mem. vet. affairs com., fin. com., 1981-95; mem. nat. ocean policy study group, arms control observer group; ex officio mem. intelligence com.; elected majority leader U.S. Senate, Washington, 1988-95; chmn. Dem. Senatorial Campaign Com., 1984-86; special counsel Verner, Liipfert, Bernhard, McPherson and Hand, Washington, 1996—2002, Preti, Flaherty, Beliveau, Pachios & Haley, Portland, Maine, 1997—; ptnr. Piper Rudnick, Washington, 2002—; chmn. Walt Disney Co., Burbank, Calif., 2004—. Chmn. Maine Democratic Com., 1966-68; nat. committeeman, Maine, 1968-77; asst. county atty. Cumberland County, 1971; chair Internat. Com. on violence in the Middle East, 2001; bd. dirs. FedEx Corp., Staples, Inc., Walt Disney Co., Starwood Hotels & Resorts . Served with U.S. Army, 1954-56; overseer 9-11 Disaster Fund. Chaired Northern Ireland peace talks which led to the Good Friday Agreement, 1998. Office: Piper Rudnick 1200 19th St NW Washington DC 20036-2412*

MITCHELL, GEORGE TRICE, physician; b. Marshall, Ill., Jan. 20, 1914; s. Roscoe Addison and Alma (Trice) M.; m. Mildred Aletha Miller, June 21, 1941; children: Linda Sue, Mary Kathryn. BS, Purdue U., 1935; MD, George Washington U., 1940. Intern Meth. Hosp., Indpls., 1940-41; gen. practice medicine, Marshall, 1946—. Mem. courtesy staff Union and Regional Hosps., Terre Haute, Ind.; clin. assoc. Sch. Basic Medicine, U. Ill.; mem. recruitment and retention com. U. Ill. Coll. Medicine, Rockford; chmn. bd. dirs. 1st Nat. Bank, Marshall. Author: Dr. George-An Account of the Life of a Country Doctor, 1993. Mem. adv. coun. premedicine Eastern Ill. U., 1965-69; alt. del. Rep. Conv., 1968, del., 1972; trustee Lakeland Jr. Coll., 1978-92. Lt. col. USAAF, 1941-45. Named Health Practitioner of Yr. Ill. Rural Health Assn., 1993; recipient Disting. Svc. award, Lake Land Coll., 1992, Purdue Alumni Assn. Citizenship award, 1996. Fellow Am. Acad. Family Physicians (Family Physician of Yr. 1993); mem. AMA, Ill. Med. Soc. (2d v.p. 1980-81), Clark County Med. Soc. (pres.), Aesculapian Soc. of Wabash Valley (pres. 1965), Nat. Rural Health Assn. (Practitioner of Yr. 19951999 Disting. Svc. award), Ill. Rural Health Assn. (bd. dirs.), Clark County Hist. Soc. (pres. 1968-70), Masons (32 degree), Shriners. Methodist. Home: 15923 N Oak Crest Rd Marshall IL 62441-4332 Office: 410 N 2d St Marshall IL 62441-1010 Office Phone: 217-826-5167. Business E-Mail: tblevins@uhhg.org.

MITCHELL, GEORGE WASHINGTON, JR., physician, educator; b. Balt., Apr. 30, 1917; s. George Washington and Katharyne Eugenia (Diggs) M.; m. Anne Jenkins Shriver, Dec. 19, 1942 (div. 1954); children: Beverly Shriver, George Washington III, Anne Jenkins, Edward Diggs; m. Mary Elizabeth McKay, Sept. 14, 1957; children— Bruce McKay, Katharyne Wilcox. AB, Johns Hopkins, 1938, MD, 1942. Diplomate: Am. Bd. Ob-Gyn (dir.). Intern Johns Hopkins Hosp., 1942, resident, 1946-49; gynecologist in chief New Eng. Med. Center Hosp., Boston, 1950-81; prof. ob-gyn Tufts U. Sch. Med., 1954-81, prof. emeritus, 1981—, chmn. dept., 1956-81; prof. ob-gyn U. Tex., San Antonio, 1981—; chief of gynecology U. Tex. Health Scis. Center, San Antonio, 1981-92. Cons. Surgeon Gen. Navy. Served with USNR, 1943-46. Recipient Pub. Svc. award USN, 1977; named to Soc. Scholars Johns Hopkins U., 1991. Fellow ACS, ACOG, Am. Gynecol. and Obstet. Soc.; mem. AMA, Am. Fertility Soc., Soc. Pelvic Surgeons, Mass. Med. Soc., Obstet. Soc. Boston, New Eng. Ob-Gyn. Soc., Soc. Gynecol. Oncologists, So. Atlantic, Tex. Ob-Gyn. Soc., N.Am. Ob-Gyn. Soc., S.W. Ob-Gyn. soc., Johns Hopkins Med. and Surg. Assn., Soc. of Scholars Johns Hopkins U. Office: Dept Obstetrics and Gynecology U Texas Health Sci Ctr San Antonio TX 78284

MITCHELL, GLORIA JEAN, principal, educator; b. Plant City, Fla., Oct. 14, 1945; d. Jessie Mae (Anderson) Smith; m. Thero Mitchell, Sept. 19, 1969; children: Tarra Shariss Patrick, Thero Jr. BS, Bethune-Cookman Coll., 1967; MA, U. Detroit, 1974; postgrad., U. Wash., 1990. Cert. tchr., adminstr. Wash. Tchr. Dade County Schs., Miami, Fla., 1967-71, Agana (Guam) Presch., 1971-72, Detroit Pub. Schs., 1973-76, Prince Williams Schs., Dale City, Va., 1976-81; counselor/tchr. State of Alaska, Ketchikan, 1981-85; tchr. Bellevue (Wash.) Schs., 1985—2000, prin., 1992—96, Seattle Sch. Dist., 1996—. Bd. dirs. YMCA Bothell, Wash., chair sustaining drive, 1994-95; bd. dirs. Cascadia C.C., Bothell, 1996—; mem. Profl. Educators Stds. Bd. Recipient Golden Acorn award PTA-Lake Hills Schs., 1986, Golden Apple award KCTS TV, Seattle, 1994-95; named West Field Vol. of Yr., YMCA, Bothell, Wash., 1987, Woman of Yr., Woodinville (Wash.) Region II Prin. of Yr., Bellevue, 1994 Mem. ASCD, Nat. Alliance Black Sch. Educators, Wash. Alliance Black Sch. Educators (pres.). Avocations: golf, community volunteerism. Office: 1700 E Union Seattle WA 98122

MITCHELL, HENRY ALLEN, JR., lawyer, insurance company executive; b. High Point, NC, Oct. 18, 1935; s. Henry Allen and Connie Estelle (Idol) M.; m. Helen Heck, June 6, 1958; children: Henry Allen III, Michael William, Martha Helen. AB in Econs., Guilford Coll., 1957; JD, Wake Forest U., 1961. Bar: N.C. 1961. Law clk. U.S. Dist. Ct., Greensboro, N.C., 1961-63; assoc. Smith, Leach, Anderson & Dorsett, Raleigh, N.C., 1963-70; dep. gen. counsel Export-Import Bank U.S., Washington, 1970-71; ptnr. Smith, Anderson, Blount & Mitchell, Raleigh, 1971-78, Smith, Anderson, Blount, Dorsett, Mitchell & Jernigan, LLP, Raleigh, 1978—; bd. dirs. Lawyers Mut. Liability Ins. N.C., Raleigh, 1978—, chmn. bd. dirs., 1985—. Bd. dirs., exec. com. Ga. Lawyers Ins. Co., 2002—. Bd. trustees N.C. Symphony Soc., Raleigh, 1991—, vice chmn., 2003—. Mem.: Fellows of Am. Bar Found. (state chair 2003—), N.C. Bar Assn. (v.p. 2003—). Republican. Presbyterian. Avocations: travel, classical music, tennis, hiking. Home: 3424 Williamsborough Ct Raleigh NC 27609-6367 Office: Smith Anderson Blount Et Al 2500 1st Union Capital Ctr 150 Fayetteville Street Mall Raleigh NC 27601-1395 Office Phone: 919-821-6625. E-mail: hmitchell@smithlaw.com.

MITCHELL, JACQUELINE KEATON, English language educator; b. Jackson, Miss., Feb. 15, 1935; d. Randall Calvin and Leanna (Hayes) Anderson; m. William D. Keaton, July 27, 1958 (div. 1966); children: Leslie D., Linda D. AB, Fisk U., 1958; MEd, Washington U., St. Louis, 1972; PhD, Iowa State U., 1984. Tchr. St. Louis Pub. Sch. System, 1963-73, head English Dept., 1972-73, asst. prin., 1972-82; research asst. Iowa State U., Ames, 1982-84; asst. prof. ednl. leadership Tex. Woman's U., Denton, 1984-89, mem. faculty senate, 1988-90; asst. prof. ednl. adminstrn. Iowa State U., Ames, 1989—. Cons. pvt. edn., Metroplex Area, Tex., 1984—, Effective Teaching, Tchr. Evalutation and Instrnl. Leasership; dir. Computer Assisted Tchr. Evaluation, Ames, 1983-84; instr. St. Louis U., 1983; guest lectr. various sch. dists., 1984—. Co-author: Computer Assisted Teacher Evaluation/Suprevision, 1986, Professinal Growth Plans for Texas Teachers: The Appraiser's Guide, 1986, A Compendium of Validated Professional Improvement Commitments, 1986, Writing Professional Growth Plans, 1987; contbr. articles to profl. jours. Washington U. fellow, 1971-72; scholar Iowa State U., 1982-84; recipient Outstanding Acad. Achievement award Minority Student Affairs, 1983, 84. Mem. Assn. for Supervision and Curriculum Devel., Tex. Profs. Ednl. Adminstrn., Assn. Black Journalists (faculty advisor), Tex. Woman's U. (faculty advisor), Phi Delta Kappa, Pi Lambda Theta (faculty advisor), Alpha Sigma. Methodist. Office: Iowa State U Coll Edn & Profl Studies 229N Lagomarcino Hall Ames IA 50010

MITCHELL, JAMES ALBEE, lawyer; b. Grand Rapids, Mich., Aug. 27, 1943; s. Charles Abram and Helen Eloise (Albee) M.; m. Helen Joan Segard, Dec. 29, 1967; children: Christopher Albee, Andrew Charles. B.S. in Chemistry, Mich. Technol. U., 1965; J.D., U. Mich., 1968. Bar: Mich. 1968, U.S. Ct. Customs and Patent Appeals 1974, U.S. Ct. Appeals (Fed. cir.) 1982, U.S. Ct. Appeals (6th cir.) 1974, U.S. Ct. Appeals (5th cir.) 1975, U.S. Ct. Appeals (8th cir.) 1981, U.S. Dist. Ct. (we. dist.) Mich. 1968, U.S. Supreme Ct. 1981. Assoc., Price, Heneveld, Cooper, Dewitt & Litton, Grand Rapids, Mich., 1968-73, ptnr., 1973-; speaker patent, trademark, copyright law; instr. seminar in field. Contbr. articles to legal jours. Exec. com. Kent County Reps., 1974-78, 80-82, 86-88; chmn. Fifth Congl. Dist. Conservative Caucus; state co-chmn. Jack Kemp for Pres.; elder Reformed Ch.; chmn. emeritus Mich. Tech. U.; trustee Mich. Tech. Fund; mem. jud. selection com. We. Dist. Mich.; chmn. bd. control Mich. Tech. U. Mem. ABA, Mich. Bar Assn. (exec. council for patent and trademark sect.), Grand Rapids Bar Assn., L'Association International pour la Protection de la Propriete Industrial, U.S. Patent Law Assn., Mich. Patent Law Assn., Patent and Trademark Inst. Can., Theta Tau (outstanding achievement award). Office: Price Heneveld Cooper DeWitt & Litton 695 Kenmoor Ave SE Grand Rapids MI 49546-2375 Office Phone: 616-949-9610. E-mail: jmitchell@priceheneveld.com.

MITCHELL, JAMES ANDREW, education educator; b. Fort Campbell, Ky., Feb. 16, 1953; s. James Andrew and Joyce Anne (Smith) M.; m. Oana Geodoiu, Aug. 13, 1999; 1 child, Magdalena Amelie. AB, Vassar Coll., 1975; MA, Princeton U., 1979, PhD, 1985. Instr. Princeton (N.J.) U., 1981-82; asst. prof. Haverford (Pa.) Coll., 1981-82, U. Redlands, Calif., 1982-85; escort/interpreter U.S. Dept. State, Washington, 1983-86; project mgr. Delphi Internat. Group, Washington, 1986-89; asst. prof. Mt. Vernon Coll., Washington, 1990—94; assoc. prof. Calif. State U., Northridge, 1994—2003, prof., 2003—. Vis. faculty fellow Am. U. in Kygyzstan, 2001, U. Bucharest, 2001; bd. dirs. South East European Inst. of Internat. Affairs. Contbr. articles to profl. jours. Mem. African policy issues group George Bush for Pres. Campaign, Washington, 1988. Recipient J. William Fulbright fellowship CIES and USIA, U. Bucharest, 1977, fellowship NEH, Washington, 1989, John Parker Compton pre-doctoral fellow Ctr. for Internat. Studies, Princeton U., 1981, rsch. program for devel. studies grantee Woodrow Wilson Sch., Princeton U., 1989. Avocations: fitness profl., aerobic exercise. Office: Dept Polit Sci/Calif State 18111 Nordhoff St Northridge CA 91330-0001 E-mail: james.mitchell@csun.edu.

MITCHELL, JAMES EDWARD, physician, educator; b. Chgo., June 19, 1947; s. James Edward and Elizabeth Latimer M.; m. Karen Antrim, June 14, 1969; children: James, Katherine. BA, Ind. U., 1968; MD, Northwestern U., 1972. Diplomate Am. Bd. Psychiatry Neurology. Intern Ind. U., Mpls., 1979-90; resident Northwestern U., Mpls., 1990-96; from asst. prof. to prof. U. Minn., Mpls., 1979-90, prof., 1990-96; prof., chmn. dept. neuroscience sch. medicine & health sci. U. N.D., Fargo, 1996—. Pres., scientific dir. Neuropsychiat. Rsch. Inst., Fargo, 1996—. Named Tchr. of Yr., N.D. Psychiat. Residents Assn., 1997-98, 98-99. Fellow Am. Psychiat. Assn., Am. Assn. Social Psychiatry; mem. Acad. Eating Disorders (pres.-elect 1999—), Eating Disorders Rsch. Soc. (sec.-treas. 1995—). Avocations: canoeing, art, travel. Office: Neuropsychiat Rsch Inst PO Box 1415 700 1st Ave S Fargo ND 58107 Fax: 701-293-3226. E-mail: mitchell@medicine.nodak.edu.

MITCHELL, JAMES KENNETH, civil engineer, educator; b. Manchester, N.H., Apr. 19, 1930; s. Richard N. and Henrietta (Moench) M.; m. Virginia D. Williams, Nov. 24, 1951; children: Richard A., Laura K., James W., Donald M., David L. BBCE, Rensselaer Poly. Inst., 1951; MS, MIT, 1953, DSc, 1956. Mem. faculty U. Calif., Berkeley, 1958-93, prof. civil engring., 1968-89, chmn. dept., 1979-84, Edward G. and John R. Cahill prof. civil engring., 1989-92, Edward G. and John R. Cahill prof. civil engring. emeritus, 1993—; Via prof. civil engring. Va. Poly. Inst. and State U., Blacksburg, 1994-99, Univ. Disting. prof., 1996-99, Univ. Disting. prof. emeritus, 1999—. Geotech. cons., 1960—. Author: Fundamentals of Soil Behavior, 1976, 2d edit., 1993; contbr. articles to profl. jours. Asst. scoutmaster Boy Scouts Am., 1975-82; mem. Moraga (Calif.) Environ. Rev. Com., 1978-80. Served to 1st lt. AUS, 1956-58. Recipient Exceptional Sci. Achievement medal NASA, 1973, Berkeley citation, 1993, Chief of Engrs. Outstanding Svc. award U.S. Army Corps Engrs., 1999. Mem. ASCE (hon., Huber prize 1965, Middlebrooks award 1962, 70, 73, 2001, Norman medal 1972, 95, Terzaghi lectr. 1984, Terzaghi award 1985, H. Bolton Seed medal 2004, pres. San Francisco sect. 1986-87), NAS, Nat. Acad. Engring. (vice chair civil engring. sect. 2001-03, chair 2003-05), Am. Soc. Engring. Edn. (We. Electric Fund award 1979), NRC (geotech. bd. chmn. 1990-94, bd. on infrastructure and constrn. environ. 1994-96, transp. rsch. bd. exec. com. 1983-87), Internat. Soc. Soil Mechanics and Geotech. Engring. (v.p. N.Am. 1989-94, Kevin Nash Gold medal 2001), Earthquake Engring. Rsch. Inst., Japanese Geotech. Soc. (internat. hon. mem.), Brit. Geotech. Soc. (Rankine lectr. 1991), Sigma Xi, Tau Beta Pi. Office: Va Tech Dept Civil Engring Blacksburg VA 24061-0105 Business E-Mail: jkm@vt.edu.

MITCHELL, JANET ALDRICH, fund raising executive, reference materials publisher; b. Providence, Jan. 12, 1928; d. Norman Ackley and Janet Aldrich; m. Raymond Warren Mitchell, Jan. 9, 1954 (div. 1967); children: Lydia Aldrich, Polly Mitchell Ranson. AB, Smith Coll., 1949; MEd, Rutgers U., 1975. Engaged in devel. various non-profit orgns., 1954-72; dir. devel. Wilson Fellowship Found., Princeton, N.J., 1972-74; dir. spl. projects N.J. Dept. Higher Edn., Trenton, 1974-76; prin., owner Mitchell Guide, 1976—. Cons. numerous non-profit orgns., 1976-86; lectr. Adult Sch., Princeton, 1983-84. Editor: Directory of Woodrow Wilson Fellows, 1968, A Community of Scholars, 1980. Exec. officer Princeton Cmty. Dem. Orgn., 1984—86; elected Princeton Twp. Com., 1987—89; mem. NAACP Legal Def. Fund, 1980—86; trustee N.J. Hist. Soc., 1984—86, Smith Coll. Class of 1949, 1999—. Mem. Princeton Smith Coll. Club (fund agent 1964-69, pres. 1968-70), Princeton Dog Club (bd. dirs. 1962-68). Episcopalian. Avocation: breeding and showing standard poodles. Office: PO Box 626 Pennington NJ 08534 Home: 27 Woosamonsa RD Pennington NJ 08534-3804 E-mail: grantsnj@aol.com.

MITCHELL, JANET BREW, health services researcher; b. N.Y.C., Oct. 20, 1949; d. Robert Moscrip Mitchell and Dorothy Brennan; m. Jerry Lee Cromwell, June 15, 1980; children: Alexander, Genevieve. BA with highest honors, U. Calif., San Diego, 1971; MSW, UCLA, 1973; PhD, Brandeis U., 1976. Rsch. asst. Brandeis U./Worcester Tng. Program in Social Rsch. & Psych., Waltham, Mass., 1973-75; sr. analyst Abt Assocs., Cambridge, Mass., 1975-77; asst. prof. Boston U. Sch. Medicine, 1977-80; pres. Ctr. for Health Econs. Rsch., Waltham, Mass., 1980—. Mem. com. on monitoring access to health care svcs. Inst. Medicine, 1989-92; mem. nat. adv. com. Robert Wood Johnson Health Care Fin. Fellows, 1988-93; cons. VA, 1982-85, NIH, 1983-85, Health Care Financing Adminstrn., 1979—; advisor Physician Reimbursement Study, Congl. Budget Office, 1984-85; mem. adv. panel on physicians & med. tech. Office of Tech. Assessment, 1984-85; mem. health care tech. study sect. Nat. Ctr. for Health Svcs. Rsch., 1984-88; psychiat. social worker UCLA Med. Ctr., 1971-72; med. social worker U. So. Calif., 1972-73, Univ. Hosp. San Diego, 1973. Author (with F.A. Sloan & J. Cromwell) Private Physicians and Public Programs, 1978; contbr. chpts. to 8 books; contbr. numerous articles to profl. jours. Thesis grantee VA, 1976-77. Office: Ctr for Hlth Econ Rsch 411 Waverly Oaks Rd Ste 330 Waltham MA 02452-8448 E-mail: jmitchell@her-cher.org.

MITCHELL, JOAN LAVERNE, research scientist; b. Palo Alto, Calif., May 24, 1947; d. William Richardson and Doris LaVerne (Roddan) M. BS in Physics, Stanford U., 1969; MS in Physics, U. Ill., 1971, PhD in Physics, 1974. Rsch. staff mem. T.J. Watson Rsch. Ctr. IBM, Yorktown Heights, N.Y., 1974-88, 96-98, mgr. T.J. Watson Rsch. Ctr., 1979-88, image tech. cons. mktg. White Plains, N.Y., 1989-91, rsch. staff mem. T.J. Watson Rsch. Ctr. Hawthorne, N.Y., 1991-94, mgr. T.J. Watson Rsch. Ctr., 1992-94, supplemental employee Burlington, N.Y., 1994-96; vis. prof. U. Ill., Urbana, 1996; with IBM Printing Systems Divsn., Boulder, Colo., 1999—, IBM fellow, 2001—. Del. CCITT Study Group XIV, 1978-79, ISO JPEG Com., 1987-94. Co-author: JPEG Still Image Data Compression Standard, 1993, MPEG Video Compression Standard, 1997; contbr. articles to profl. jours. Xerox Indsl. fellow, 1970-71. Fellow IEEE, NAE (elected 2004); mem. Am. Phys. Soc., Soc. for Imaging Sci. and Tech., Sigma Xi (chpt. sec. 1976, v.p. 1977, pres. 1978). Democrat. Achievements include co-inventor on numerous patents. Home: 1172 Fall River Cir Longmont CO 80501 Office: IBM Printing Systems Divsn 6300 Diagonal Hwy MS004N Boulder CO 80301-9270 Office Phone: 303-924-4271.

MITCHELL, JOHN CHARLES, marketing professional; b. Bedford, Ind., May 25, 1947; s. John Lewis and Mary Ellen (Rowe) M.; m. Marie Elizabeth Bruland, Aug. 21, 1971; 1 child, Allison Anne. BA in Econs., Va. Mil. Inst., 1969; MBA, JD, Ind. U., 1975. Bar: Ind., 1975, Fed. Cts., 1975. Brand mgr. Procter and Gamble Co., Cin., 1975-82; group product mgr. RJR/Del Monte, San Francisco, 1982-84; dir. mktg. RJR/Nabisco, Parsippany, N.J., 1984-87, v.p. mktg., 1987-88, v.p., gen. mgr., 1988-90, pres. sales and logistics co., 1991-94, pres. Planters, Lifesavers co. Winston-Salem, N.C., 1994-96; pres. bus. printer divsn. Lexmark Internat., Inc., Lexington, Ky., 1997-99; founder The Collaborative Inst., Chapel Hill, N.C., 2001—. 1st lt. US Army, 1969-71. Inductee Va. Mil. Inst. Sports Hall of Fame, 1981. Republican. Methodist. Avocations: golf, skiing. E-mail: jandmmitchell@nc.rr.com.

MITCHELL, JOHN DIETRICH, theatre arts institute executive; b. Rockford, Ill., Nov. 3, 1917; s. John Dennis Royce and Dora Marie (Schroeder) M.; m. Miriam Pitcairn, Aug. 25, 1956; children: John Daniel, Lorenzo Theodore, Barbarina Mitchell Heyerdahl. BSS, Northwestern U., 1939, MA, 1941; EdD, Columbia U., 1956; HHD (hon.), Northwood U., 1986. Dir., producer Am. Broadcasting Co., N.Y.C., 1942-46; assoc. editor Samuel French, Publ., N.Y.C., 1946-48; assoc. prof. Manhattan Coll., N.Y.C., 1948-58; pres. Inst. for Advanced Studies in the Theatre Arts, N.Y.C., 1958-97. Founder, pres. Eaton St. Press, Key West, Fla., 1994, Mitchell Performing Arts Ctr., Campus Acad., Pa., 2001; bd. dirs. Beneficia Found., Jenkintown, Pa. Author: Staging Chekhov, 1990, Actors Talk, 1991, Gift of Apollo, 1992, Staging Japanese Theatre: Noh and Kabuki, 1995, Men Stand on Shoulders, 1996; author: (aka Jack Royce) The Train Stopped at Domodossola, 1993, Murder at the Kabuki, 1994, Dressed to Murder, 1997, Way to the Towers of Silence, 1997, Bewitched by the Stage, 1997, Troubled Paradise, 1998, The Wallpaper Murder, 1998, Death in the Suit of Lights, 1999, Too Beautiful to Live, 2002, The Sleepers, 2003. Trustee emeritus Northwood U., Midland, Mich., 1972-91; patron Met. Opera, N.Y.C.; golden donor Am. Ballet Theatre. Named hon. conch Key West (Fla.) Commrs., 1994; dedication of Mitchell Performing Arts Ctr., Bryn Athyn, Pa., 2001. Mem. Met. Mus., Key West Arts and Hist. Soc., Spencer Family Assn. Mayflower Soc., Key West Literary Seminar (emeritus), Nippon Club N.Y.C. Mem. Community Ch. Avocations: tai chi chuan, swimming, collecting musical recordings, books. Home and Office: Apts 105-106 W La Brisa 1901 Roosevelt Blvd Key West FL 33040 Fax: 305-296-5827. E-mail: jdm@keysdigital.com.

MITCHELL, JOHN LAURIN AMOS, biological science educator; b. Lincoln, Nebr., July 18, 1944; s. William A. and Ruth Chilla (Cobbey) M.; m. Gail Ann Kurtz, July 13, 1968; children: Jill, Todd. BA, Oberlin Coll., 1966; PhD, Princeton U., 1970. Postdoctoral fellow McArdle Inst. Cancer Rsch., Madison, Wis., 1970-73; asst. prof. No. Ill. U., DeKalb, 1973-78, assoc. prof., prof., 1983—; dir. Ctr. Biochem. Biophys. Rsch., 1997—. Inventor in field; contbr. articles to profl. jours.

MITCHELL, JOHN NOYES, JR., retired electrical engineer; b. Pownal, Maine, Dec. 16, 1930; s. John Noyes and Frances (Small) M.; m. Marilyn Jean Michaelis, Sept. 1, 1956 (dec.); children: Brian John, Cynthia Lynn Mitchell Tumbleson, Stephanie Lee Mitchell Judson; m. Jacqueline A. Starr, Sept. 10, 1999. BSEE, Milw. Sch. Engring., 1957. Registered profl. engr., Ohio. Elec. rsch. engr. Nat. Cash Register Co., Dayton, Ohio, 1957-65; sr. engr. Xerox Corp., Rochester, N.Y., 1965-70, area mgr., 1970-73, Dallas, 1973-76, El Segundo, Calif., 1976-79, tech. program mgr., 1979-85, competitive benchmarking mgr., 1985-92, quality mgr., 1992-97. With USN, 1949—53. Mem. IEEE, Mason. Republican. Episcopalian. Home: 5545 Downham Meadow Sarasota FL 34235-0971 E-mail: jnmitch3@comcast.net.

MITCHELL, JOHN W. pharmaceutical executive; B of Engring., Yale U. Various positions Pfizer, Inc., Bklyn., 1964—68, dir. prodn. planning and inventory control N.Y.C., 1968—72, project dir. constrn and startup new plants, 1972—75, v.p., gen. mfg. ops., 1975—78, pres. profn. pharms., 1978—97, pres. mfg., 1997—99, sr. v.p. global mfg., 1999—2000, pres., team leader global mfg., 2000—, v.p., 2001—. Office: Pfizer Inc 235 E 42d St New York NY 10017

MITCHELL, JON CEANDER, music educator, conductor; b. Chgo., June 18, 1949; s. James William and Violet Linnea Mitchell; m. Ester Morales, Dec. 22, 1973; children: Monica Mitchell Finn, Lydia, David. MusB, Millikin U., 1971; MS in Music Edn., U. Ill., 1972, EdD in Music Edn., 1980. Asst. prof. music Hanover (Ind.) Coll., 1982—87; condr. wind ensemble Carnegie Mellon U., Pitts., 1987—91; asst. prof. music U. Ga., Athens, 1991—92; prof. music U. Mass., Boston, 1992—96, chair dept., 1996—. Music dir. North Pitts. Civic Symphony, Pitts., 1988—92; guest conducting various bands and orchs. Author: (book) From Kneller Hall to Hammersmith, 1990, A Comprehensive Biography of Gustav Holst, 2001; contbr. articles to profl. jours.; condr.: CD Beethoven: Piano Concerto in D, Op. 61, Concerto in D, 2004. Mem.: Coll. Band Dirs. Nat. Assn., Music Educators Nat. Conf., World Assn. Symphonic Bands and Ensembles (asst. editor newsletter 2000, editor WASBE jour. 1994), Condrs. Guild, Phi Kappa Phi. Avocations: travel, model railroading, coaster collecting. Office: Dept Performing Arts U Mass 100 Morrissey Blvd Boston MA 02125-3393

MITCHELL, JONI (ROBERTA JOAN ANDERSON), singer, songwriter; b. Ft. Macleod, Alta., Can., Nov. 7, 1943; d. William A. and Myrtle M. (McKee) Anderson; m. Chuck Mitchell (div.); m. Larry Klein, Nov. 21, 1982. Student, Alta. Coll. Albums Song to a Seagull, Clouds, Ladies of the Canyon, Blue, For the Roses, Court and Spark, 1974, Miles of Aisles, The Hissing of Summer Lawns, 1975, Hejira, 1976, Don Juan's Reckless Daughter, 1979, Mingus, 1979 (Jazz Album of Year and Rock-Blues Album of Year, Downbeat mag., 1979), Shadows and Light, 1980, Wild Things Run Fast, 1982, Dog Eat Dog, 1985, Chalk Mark in a Rainstorm, 1988, Night Ride Home, 1991, Turbulent Indigo, 1994, Hits, 1996, Taming the Tiger, 1998, Both Sides Now, 2000, Travelogue, 2002, screenwriter/actor (films) Love, 1982; contbr. album dog Eat Dog/Wild Things Run Fast, 1996. Named to Rock and Roll Hall of Fame, 1997; recipient Grammy award for Best Folk Performance, 1969, Grammy award for Best Arrangement Accompanying Vocalists (with Tom Scott), 1974. Address: care Reprise Records 3300 Warner Blvd Burbank CA 91505-4632

MITCHELL, JOSEPH PATRICK, architect; b. Bellingham, Wash., Sept. 29, 1939; s. Joseph Henry and Jessie Delila (Smith) Mitchell; m. Marilyn Ruth Jorgenson, June 23, 1962; children: Amy Evangeline, Kirk Patrick, Scott Henry. Student, Western Wash. State Coll., 1957-59; BA, U. Wash., 1963, BArch, 1965. Assoc. designer, draftsman, project architect Beckwith Spangler

Davis, Bellevue, Wash., 1965-70; prin. J. Patrick Mitchell, AIA & Assocs./Architects/Planners/Cons., Kirkland, Wash., 1970—. Charter mem. Northshore Bapt. Ch., 1969, elder, 1984—90; bd. ext. and ctrl. com. Columbia Bapt. Conf., 1977—83; del. Bapt. World Alliance 16th Congress, Seoul, Republic of Korea, 1990, Bapt. World Alliance 17th Congress, Beunos Aires, 1995, Bapt. World Alliance 18th Congress, Melbourne, Australia, 2000; vice-moderator Columbia Bapt. Conf., 1995—96, moderator, 1996—97, overseer ch. ministries bd., pres., 1997—99; charter mem. Cascade Cmty. Ch., 1997—; trustee Bakke Libr./Cultural Ctr., 1994—96; chmn. long range planning com. Lake Retreat Camp, 1965—93; active Deming Hist. Cemetery Assn., 1997—. Recipient Internat. Archtl. Design award, St. John Vianney Parish, 1989. Mem.: AIA, Wash. Farm Forestry Assn., Christian Camping Internat., Christian Mgmt. Assn., Internat. Conf. Bldg. Ofcls., Nat. Coun. Archtl. Registration Bds., Nat. Fedn. Bus., Interfaith Forum Religion, Art, and Architecture (arch. edn. tour. Finland and St. Petersburg, russia 1998, Japan 2000, Spain and Portugal 2002, Switzerland and France 2004, edn. tour China 2001, Scandinavia, Estonia and Russia 2002), Constrn. Specification Inst., Woodinville C. of C. Office: 12620 120th Ave NE Ste 208 Kirkland WA 98034-7511

MITCHELL, JULIE CAROL, mathematician, educator, biochemist, educator; b. Santa Clara, Calif., Oct. 1, 1969; d. Joseph Frederick and Janice Carol (Duncan) Mitchell. BA in Math., San Jose State U., 1992; PhD in Math., U. Calif., Berkeley, 1998. Tchg. assoc. Summer Insts. for Math. Studies, Berkeley, 1994—97; math. software developer U. Calif., Berkeley, 1995—96; postdoctoral fellow U. Calif. San Diego, La Jolla, 1998—2001; rsch. scientist San Diego Supercomputer Ctr., La Jolla, 2001—. Contbr. articles to profl. jours. Fellow, Achievement Rewards for Coll. Scientists Found., 1997, La Jolla Interfaces in Sci., 1998—2001; grantee, U.S. Dept. Energy, 2001—; Regents fellow, U. Calif. Berkeley, 1997. Mem.: Internat. Soc. for Computational Biology, Soc. for Indsl. and Applied Math., Am. Math. Soc. Green Party. Achievements include invention of Fast Atomic Density Evaluator; Pairwise Atomic Density Reverse Engineering method, Variable Precision Distance Lookup method; Image Angle method; Docking Mesh Evaluator. Avocations: travel, music, art, billiards, reading. Office: U Wis Depts Math and Biochemistry 213 Van Vleck Hall 480 Lincoln Dr Madison WI 53706-1388 E-mail: mitchell@math.wisc.edu.

MITCHELL, KAREN FRANCES, artist, jewelry designer; b. Denver, Aug. 24, 1953; d. Harry Francis and Mary Jane Margrete (Jensen-Borg) Mitchell. BFA, U. Colo., 1975; postgrad., Gemological Inst. Am., 1986, Kulicke Jewelry Arts Inst., 1988, Cecilia Bauer Studio, 1992, Fashion Inst. of Tech., 1993, Nat. Acad. Design, 1994. Cert. tchr., art specialist. Jewelry designer, pres. Karen Mitchell Design, Aspen, Colo., 1978—; cultural rschr., cons. various Italian newspapers and mags., NY., Colo., 1992-94, Italian Consulate Cultural Inst., NY, 1992—94. Instr. workshops design and goldsmithing technique; apprentice Van der Schoot Disegno e Fabricazione, Milan, 1989—91. Co-designer, co-author (book) World Gold Coun. Jewelry Trend Book, 1991—95; exhibitions include World Gold Coun., Aaron Faber Gallery, N.Y.C., Yaw Gallery, Mich., SOFA, Chgo., J. Cotter Gallery, Cindy Griem Fine Jewels, Somerhill Gallery, N.C., Facere Gallery, Wash., Concepts Gallery, Calif., Greene & Greene Gallery, NJ, Concepts Gallery, Calif., Greene & Greene Gallery, NJ. Vol. chmn. benefit com. Aspen Art Mus.; co-chmn. benefit com. Aspen Music Festival; mem. Les Dames d'Aspen; vol. Profl. Women's Orgn., Am. Craft Mus., NY, 1993, Coun. Fashion Designers Am., NY, Internat. Design Conf. of Aspen, Screening Com. Aspen Film Fest, Soprano, Aspen Choral Soc.; vol. benefit Aspen Ski Club/U.S. Olympic Equestrian Team, 1995; trustee Aspen Snowmass Coun. Arts. Named Vol. of the Yr., Aspen Art Mus., 2001. Mem.: Jewelry Design Profl.'s Network, Am. Craft Coun., Soc. N.Am. Goldsmiths. Address: PO Box 4885 Aspen CO 81612-4885 E-mail: kmdaspen@hotmail.com.

MITCHELL, KENNETH D. physiologist, educator; b. Musselburgh, Scotland, Mar. 5, 1959; m. Maria Heavens, Sept. 30, 1995. BSc with upper 2d class honors, U. Edinburgh, Scotland, 1981, PhD in Physiology, 1986. Physiology tutor Univ. Med. Sch., Edinburgh, 1981-84; rsch. assoc. dept. physiology and biophysics Nephrology Rsch. and Tng. Ctr. U. Ala., Birmingham, 1984-86, postdoctoral rsch. fellow, 1986-87, rsch. instr., 1987-88, scientist I, 1987-88; asst. prof. dept. physiology Tulane U. Sch. Medicine, New Orleans, 1988-95, assoc. prof., 1995—. Contbr. articles to profl. jours. Fellow Am. Heart Assn. (fellow Coun. High Blood Pressure Rsch. 1993—, Established Investigator award 1995-2000); mem. Am. Physiol. Soc., Am. Soc. Nephrology, Internat. Soc. Nephrology. Office: Tulane U Sch Medicine Dept Physiology SL39 1430 Tulane Ave New Orleans LA 70112-2699 Office Phone: 504-988-2593. Business E-Mail: kdmitch@tulane.edu.

MITCHELL, LAURA ANN, lawyer; b. Miles City, Mont., Oct. 21, 1952; d. Wilmer Ashford and Avis Jean (Baldwin) M.; m. John Walker Ross, Nov. 21, 1981. BA in Polit. Sci. with high honors, U. Mont., Missoula, 1975; JD with honors, George Washington U., 1978. Bar: Mont. 1978. Law clk. to presiding justice U.S. Dist. Ct. for Mont., Billings, 1978-79; assoc. Crowley, Haughey, Hanson, Toole & Dietrich, Billings, 1979-83; ptnr. Crowley, Haughey, Hanson, Toole & Dietrich, 1983-97; atty. pvt. practice, Billings, 1997—. Mem. adv. panel spl. projects Mont. Arts Council, 1980-82; bd. dirs. Billings Preservation Soc., 1988-93, St. Labre Indian Edn. Assn., 1988-94. Mem. Am. Judicature Soc., ABA, Mont. Bar Assn., Yellowstone County Bar Assn. Presbyterian. Avocations: gardening, reading. Office: 611 O'Malley Billings MT 59101

MITCHELL, LEE MARK, communications executive, investment fund manager, lawyer; b. Albany, N.Y., Apr. 16, 1943; s. Maurice B. and Mildred (Roth) M.; m. Barbara Lee Anderson, Aug. 27, 1966; children: Mark, Matthew. AB, Wesleyan U., 1965; JD, U. Chgo., 1968. Bar: Ill. 1968, D.C. 1969, U.S. Supreme Ct. 1972. Assoc. Leibman, Williams, Bennett, Baird & Minow, Chgo. and Washington, 1968-72, Sidley & Austin, Washington, 1972-74, ptnr., 1974-84, 92-94; exec. v.p. and gen. counsel Field Enterprises, Inc., Chgo., 1981-83, pres., CEO, 1983-84, Field Corp., 1984-92; prin. Golder, Thoma, Cressey, Rauner, Inc., Chgo., 1994-98; ptnr. Thoma Cressey Equity Ptnrs., Inc., Chgo., 1998—. Chmn. Chgo. Stock Exch., Inc. Author: Openly Arrived At, 1974, With the Nation Watching, 1979; co-author: Presidential Television, 1973. Bd. visitors U. Chgo. Law Sch., 1984—86, Medill Sch. Journalism, Northwestern U., 1984—91; pres. bd. govs. Chgo. Met. Planning Coun., 1988—91; mem. midwest regional adv. bd. Inst. Internat. Edn., 1987—99; trustee Ravinia Festival Assn., 1989—97, Northwestern U., Northwestern Meml. Hosp.; U.S. del. Brit. Legis. Conf. on Govt. and Media, Ditchley Park, England, 1974; adv. com. LWV Presdl. Debates, Washington, 1979—80, 1982; vice chair Chgo. Met. Planning Coun., 1999—. Mem.: Econ. Mid-Am. Club, ABA, Comml. Club Chgo. Home: 135 Maple Hill Rd Glencoe IL 60022-1252 Office: Thoma Cressey Equity Ptnrs Sears Tower Ste 9200 233 S Wacker Dr Chicago IL 60606-6306 E-mail: LMitchell@thomacressey.com.

MITCHELL, LINDA MARLENE, education educator; b. Atchison, Kans., June 18, 1952; d. Frank Fayne and Marlene Marie Riley; m. John Lee Mitchell Jr., Oct. 16, 1971; children: John Michael, Joseph Lee, Jessica Nicole. BA, Wichita State U., 1986, MA, 1990; PhD, U. Kans., 1997. Lic. speech lang. pathologist; cert. neonatal assessment scale; cert. legal asst. Legal asst. Woodard, Baylock & HErnandez, Wichita, 1979-87; legal asst. to corp. counsel Pizza Hut, Inc., Wichita, 1987-89; infant-toddler svcs. coord., speech/lang. pathologist Rainbows United, Inc., Wichita, 1990-93; rsch. asst. U. Kans., Lawrence, 1993-96; v.p. Futures Unltd., Inc., Wellington, Kans., 1996-97; assoc. prof. dept. curriculum & instrn. Wichita State U., 1997—. Presenter and rschr. in field early childhood special edn.; spl. edn. due process hearing officer State of Kans. Assoc. editor: Jour. Critical Inquiry Into Curriculum and Instrn., 1998—. Grantee multiple grant recipient. Mem. ASCD, Am. Speech-Lang.-Hearing Assn., Nat. Assn. Edn. Young Children, Am. Assn. People with Disabilities, Coun. Exceptional Children, Assn. Persons With Severe Handicaps. Democrat. Avocations: walking, weightlifting, flower gardening, bird watching, hiking, crochet. Office: Wichita State U 1845 Fairmount St Wichita KS 67260-0028

MITCHELL, MARCIA JEANNE, freelance/self-employed writer, events producer; b. San Jose, Calif., Feb. 20, 1932; d. Eugene Lewis Wilcox and Gladys Delphine Shoemaker; m. John Alexander Donnan (div. June 1, 1975); children: Alan James Donnan, Kristen Elizabeth Donnan; m. Thomas Francis Mitchell, June 29, 1985. Student, Colo. State U., 1965—67; BA, Norwich U., Vt. Coll., 1989. Writer, editor Rapid City (S.D.) Jour., 1968—73; cabinet officer, sec. labor S.D. State Govt., Pierre, SD, 1973—75; sr. exec. Corp. for Pub. Broadcasting, Washington, 1975—80; assoc. dir. Am. Film Inst., Washington & L.A., 1980—87; freelance writer, prodr., 1988—. Lectr., seminar leader mgmt. strategies for women, 1980—82; lectr. Crystal Cruise Lines, 1999, Cunard QE2, 2001; motivational sem. spkr. Prodr.: world premieres of maj. motion pictures, 1980—86, A Daughter's Tribute to Fred Astaire, 2001; author: Cosmetics from the Kitchen, 1972, Raindance to Research, 1977, Management Strategies for Women, 1980, 1981, The Spy Who Seduced America: Lies and Betrayal in the Heat of the Cold War, 2002. Past sec. Nat. Assns. Commns. on Women; vice chair Montserrat Found. for Charitable Giving, West Indies, 1995—2001; chair spl. events Hill City (S.D.) Arts Coun., 2001; mem. Montserrat Nat. Trust, Montserrat, 2001; past chair grants com. State Fine Arts Coun., SD; past mem. State Commn. on Status of Women, SD; mem., organizer S.D. Dem. Women, 2001—02; past bd. dirs. Women's Equity Action League, N.Y.C., NY; past chair TV broadcasting com. PBS Sta. WETA-TV, Washington. Recipient 1st pl. feature writing, S.D. Press Women, 1995, 1st pl., Non-fiction Books, 2003. Mem.: Nat. Fedn. Press Women (Top Press Woman of Yr. 1972—73). Roman Catholic.

MITCHELL, MARILYN JUNE, writer, lyricist; d. Francis Vernon Mitchell and Viola Marie Scott Mitchell; m. James Albert Delbridge, June 15, 1947 (dec.); children: Diane Lynn Delbridge, Holly Delbridge, James Michael Delbridge. Student, Duke U., 1944, Miami U., Oxford, Ohio, 1944—47, Santa Barbara (Calif.) City Coll., 1987—88. Securities lic. N.Y. Stock Exch. Model, advt. and TV, N.Y.C., 1954—70; stockbroker Thomson, McKinnon Securities, Denver, 1970—84; v.p. Thomson McKinnon, Denver, 1984—2000; lyricist Nashville, 1988—. Author: Patterns on the Wall; editor: (anthology) Patchwork, An Uncommon Quilt of Words; author many songs; contbr. Recipient 1st pl., 3d pl., Channel City Camera Club, 1988, cert. of recognition poetry excellence, Office of the Mayor, Nashville, 2003. Mem.: DAR, ASCAP, Wordsmith's Ink, Delta Gamma Frat. Avocations: travel, photography, music, theater, writing. Home: 1626 Moores Ct Brentwood TN 37027-2974

MITCHELL, MICHAEL KIEHL, elementary school educator, secondary school educator, security officer, minister; b. Phila., Oct. 27, 1932; B in Edn., U. Miami, 1955; MEd, Tex. A&M U., 1975, PhD, 1978; grad., Internat. Sch. Christian Comm., Front Sight Handgun Tng. Acad., 2000. Ordained to priest Contemporary Cath. Ch., 2002; cert. elem. and secondary edn. Fla., Tex., Alaska, lic. comml. pilot. Tchr. math. Dade County Pub. Schs., Miami Springs, Fla., 1955-60; tchr. elem. Greenwood Sch. Dist., Midland, Tex., 1961-63; from tchr. social studies, English to tng. coord. Midland (Tex.) Sch. Dist., 1963-75; prin. rsch. investigator Tex. A&M U., College Station, 1977-78; project dir. Edn. Profl. Devel. Consortium, Richardson, Tex., 1978-79; sr. rsch. scientist Am. Airlines, Dallas, 1979-83; pres. North Rsch. Inc., Anchorage, Alaska, 1983-84; vocat. edn. curriculum specialist Anchorage Sch. Dist., 1984-87; sci. tchr., dept. head McLaughlin Youth Ctr. Anchorage (Alaska) Sch. Dist., 1987-2001; ret., 2001. Adj. prof. U. Alaska, Anchorage, 1987—89; mem. evaluation team N.W. Accreditation Assn., Anchorage, 1985; instr. Flight and Ground Sch.; security officer Guardian Security, 2003—04, Guardsmark Security, 2004—; security officer, armored car driver, delivery officer Secure-Trans, Inc., 2004—. Dir., v.p. Anchorage Cmty. Theater, 1984—89; vol. United Way, Anchorage, 1984—90; marriage commr. 3d Jud. Dist. Alaska, Anchorage, 1989—93; drum maj. Alaska Highlanders Scottish Bagpipers; vol. Tony Knowles for Gov. Campaign, Anchorage, 1990, 1994, Mark Begich for Mcpl. Assembly Campaign, 1991, Cheryl Clementson for Mcpl. Assembly Campaign, 1993; asst. min. United Meth. Ch., 1990—94; min. Christian Cmty. Fellowship, 1994—; deacon 1st Congl. Ch., Anchorage; online counselor New Hope Online Svcs. Crystal Cathedral Ch. Rev. Robert H. Schuller; min. Sunday ch. svcs. McLaughlin Youth Ctr. Alaska State Reform Sch., 1999—2001. With U.S. Army, 1946—47. Tex. Edn. Agy. fellow, Austin, 1975, Ednl. Profl. Devel. fellow, 1975—78. Mem.: SAG, NTSA, NEA, NRA (life), Am. Correctional Edn. Assn., Anchorage Edn. Assn., Tex. Assn. Aerospace Tchrs. (life), Alaska Sci. Tchrs. Assn. (life), Former Students Assn. Tex. A&M U., Alaska Airmans Assn. (life; bd. dirs. 1983—89), Mensa (life), Vets. Underaged Mil. Svc. (life), Alaskan Aviation Safety Found., Guns Am. (life), Alliance Separation Sch. and State, Clowns of Am., Am. Legion (life), Phi Kappa Phi, Phi Delta Kappa. Libertarian. Avocations: commercial pilot, acting, FAA accident prevention counselor. Home: 6626 Foothill Dr Anchorage AK 99504-2620 Office: Christian Cmty Fellowship 6626 Foothill Dr Anchorage AK 99504 Office Phone: 907-338-6613. Personal E-mail: michaelmitchell@gci.net. *Life has taught me: 1) Regret not the past. 2) Fear not the future. 3) Enjoy the moment.*

MITCHELL, MIKE L. academic administrator; b. Hartville, Mo., Oct. 16, 1949; s. Leroy and Mary Lou Mitchell; m. Joanne Carol Riedel; children: Sharon Dawn Trillo, Michelle Lynn. BS honors in Chemistry, U. Mo., Columbia, Mo., 1971; MS in Chemistry, U. Colo., Boulder, Colo., 1973; PhD Chemistry, Kans. State U., Manhattan, Kand., 1981. Chemistry prof. Bethany Coll., Lindsborg, Kans., 1973—97, v.p. & academic dean, 1997—99, interim pres. & academic dean, 2000—00, provost & academic dean, 2000—03; v.p. academic affairs Medaille Coll., Buffalo, 2003—. Grantee multiple, NSF, Dreyfus Found., U.S. Dept. of Edn., 1973-1997. Avocations: cooking, fishing, hunting. Home: 2035 N Delaware #1B Buffalo NY 14216 Office: Medaille Coll Agassiz Cir Buffalo NY 14214 Business E-Mail: mmitchell@medaille.edu.

MITCHELL, NORMA TAYLOR, history professor; b. Norfolk, Va., Nov. 14, 1936; d. Orville Carson Sr. and Emma (Heal) Taylor; m. Frank Joseph Mitchell, Sept. 5, 1959; 1 child, Anne Mitchell Whisnant. BA in History, Coll. William and Mary, 1958; MA, Duke U., 1962, PhD, 1967. Instr. history and polit. sci. Union Coll., Barbourville, Ky., 1962-64; dean of women Ctrl. Meth. Coll., Fayette, Mo., 1968-70; assoc. prof. history Troy (Ala.) State U., 1970-84, prof. history, 1984-99, prof. emerita, 1999—. Mem. gen. commn. on archives and history United Meth. Ch., 1972-80, chair women's history project, 1977-80; vice chair nat. planning com. Bicentennial of Methodism in Am., 1979-80; hist. lectr. groups within United Meth. Ch., 1972—; lectr., presenter in field. Contbr. chpts. in books; author articles and revs. Lay leader United Meth. Ch., local, state and nat. levels, 1960—, including bd. dirs. United Meth. Bd. Pastoral Care and Counseling, 1984-92, bd. dirs. United Meth. Children's Homes, Ala.-West Fla., 1989-99; del. Southeastern Jurisdictional Confs., 1980; United Meth. Women conf. officer, 1976-80; conf. chair Commn. on Status and Role of Women, 1976-80; bd. dirs. Scarritt-Bennett Ctr., 2003—. Recipient awards and honors; So. Fellowships Fund grantee, 1958-61; Cokesbury Tchg. fellow, 1964-65. Mem. AAUP, NEA, NOW, AAUW (v.p. for membership Troy br. 1995-99, honoree Ednl. Found. 1998-99), Ala. Edn. Assn., Am. Hist. Assn., So. Hist. Assn. (membership com. 1992), So. Assn. Women Historians, Ala. Assn. Historians, Ala. Hist. Assn., North Ala. United Meth. Hist. Soc., Bread for the World, Amnesty Internat., Humane Soc. U.S., Phi Beta Kappa, Phi Kappa Phi, Phi Alpha Theta, Omicron Delta Kappa. Democrat. Avocation: children's and animal rights advocacy. Home: 7 Vandora Pl Durham NC 27705 Office: Troy State U Dept History Bibb Graves Hall 305 Troy AL 36082-0001 E-mail: ntmitchell@earthlink.net.

MITCHELL, ORLAN E. clergyman, former college president; b. Eldora, Iowa, Mar. 13, 1933; s. Frank E. and Alice G. (Brown) M.; m. Verlene J. Huehn, June 10, 1952; children: Jolene R., Stephen M., Nadene A., Timothy M., Mark E. BA, Grinnell Coll., 1955; B.D., Yale U., 1959, M.Div., 1965; D.Min., San Francisco Theol. Sem., 1976. Ordained to ministry United Ch. of Christ, 1959; pastor chs. Sheridan Twp., Iowa, 1954-55, New Preston, Conn., 1956-59, Clarion, Iowa, 1959-69, Yankton, S.D., 1969-77; pres. Yankton (S.D.) Coll., 1977-96; conf. minister Iowa Conf. United Ch. Christ; ret., 1996. Cons. in field. Mem. Sch. Bd., Clarion, Iowa, 1965-69, mem., Yankton, S.D., 1973-77, pres., 1976; bd. dirs. Lewis and Clark Mental Health Center. Mem. S.D. Found. Pvt. Colls., S.D. Assn. Pvt. Colls., Colls. of Mid-Am. Lodges: Kiwanis; Masons. Democrat. Mem. United Ch. Of Christ. Office: 725 Park St Grinnell IA 50112-2235 E-mail: orlanm@pcpartner.net.

MITCHELL, PAMELA ANN, airline pilot; b. Otis AFB, Mass., May 6, 1955; d. Gene Thomas and Rose Margaret (Jones) Mitchell. BFA, Colo. State U., 1975; postgrad., Webster Coll., 1981. Lic. pilot Ill., comml. instr., airline transport pilot, jet rating, Boeing 747 and 727, Boeing 747-400, McDonnell Douglas DC-10. Flight attendant United Airlines, Chgo., 1976-80; owner, operator Deliverance, Unltd. Ferry Co., Aurora, Ill., 1978-81; flight test pilot Cessna Aircraft Co., Wichita, Kans., 1981-82, nat. spokeswoman, 1982-83; airline pilot Rep. Airlines, Mpls., 1983-84; airline pilot, captain Northwest Airlines, Mpls., 1985—; owner, pres. The Global Nomad LLC, 1997—. Mem. Safety Coun. Airline Pilots Assn., 99's Internat. Women Pilots Assn., Internat. Soc. Women Airline Pilots (bd. dirs. 1994-96), Nat. Aviation Club, N.W. Airline Ski Team (capt. 1989-94), Kappa Kappa Gamma. Republican. Presbyterian. Avocations: piano, skiing, tennis, travel, golf.

MITCHELL, PATRICIA EDENFIELD, television executive; b. Swainsboro, Ga., Jan. 20, 1943; d. James Otis and Bernice Tucker Edenfield; m. Jay Addison Mitchell, Aug. 20, 1964 (div. June 1970); 1 child, Mark Addison. BA magna cum laude, U. Ga., 1964, MA, 1965. English instr. U. Ga., Athens, 1965—69; English, drama instr. Va. Commonwealth U., Richmond, 1969—70; researcher, writer LOOK Mag., N.Y.C., 1970; cons., speech writer Garth Assocs., N.Y.C., 1970—71; TV prodr., reporter WB2-TV, Boston, 1971—77; anchor, talk show host WTTG-TV, Washington, 1977—79; corr. NBC-TV Today, N.Y.C., 1984—89, CBS-TV Sunday Morning, N.Y.C., 1989—90; exec. prodr., writer documentaries VU Prodns., L.A., 1990 ; pres. CNN Prodns. and Time Inc. TV TBS, 1992—2000; pres. and CEO PBS, 2000—. Creator, prodr., host, owner Woman to Woman (nationally syndicated program), L.A., 1983—; spkr., conf. leader on women's issues, 1973—; bd. trustees Sundance Inst.; former mem. exec. com. TBS, Inc., CNN Exec. Com.; bd. mem. Internews, 2002—. Mem. adv. com. Nat. Coun. on Rsch. on Women, N.Y.C., 1990—92; mem. adv. bd. Schlesinger Libr. on History of Women, Radcliffe Coll., Cambridge, Mass., 1985—92; media com. Hollywood Women's Polit. Com., L.A., 1989—92; former trustee Metro Atlanta YMCA, High Mus. Art, Atlanta; mem. adv. bd. Santa Barbara Sch. Comm. U. Calif.; pres. Global Green USA (Am. affiliate Mikhail Gorbachev's worldwide conservation orgn.); nat. bd. mem. Girls Inc. Recipient Emmy for Best Daytime Program, TV Acad., 1984, Emmy for Best Host-Daytime, 1971, numerous film festival awards, 1989—92. Avocations: hiking, bicycling, horseback riding, reading. E-mail: pmitchell@pbs.org.

MITCHELL, PATRICK JOHN, financial executive; b. Honolulu, May 24, 1958; s. Bradford William and Frances (Cantwell) Mitchell; m. Catherine Elliott, June 15, 1985; children: Bradford Elliott, Margaret Whiting. BS in Acctg., Pa. State U., 1980. CPA, Pa. Mgr. Arthur Young & Co., Phila., 1980-89; dir. investor rels. Delphi Fin. Group, Inc., Phila., 1989—; asst. v.p. Reliance Standard Life, Phila., 1989-95; v.p., CFO & treas. Westbridge Captial Corp., Fort Worth, 1995—, pres & COO; CEO & chmn. Ascent Assurance Inc. (formerly Westbridge Captial Corp.), Fort Worth, 1998—. Pres. Upper Merion chpt. Am. Cancer Soc., Phila., 1992; chmn. fundraising Utility Emergency Svcs. Fund, Phila., 1992. Mem. AICPA, Pa. Inst. CPAs. Republican. Roman Catholic. Home: 2713 Heritage Hills Dr Fort Worth TX 76109-5516 Office: Ascent Assurance Inc Ste 300 110 W Seventh St Fort Worth TX 76102

MITCHELL, PATSY MALIER, religious school founder and administrator; b. Greenwood, Miss., Aug. 28, 1948; d. William Lonal and Lillian (Walker) Malier; m. Charles E. Mitchell, Apr. 20, 1970; children: Christopher, Kara, Angela. BS in Edn., Delta State U., 1970, MEd, 1974, Edn. Specialist, 1979; MA in Ch. Ministries, Ch. of God Sch. Theology, 1990; PhD in Psychology and Counseling, La. Bapt. U., 1994; D in Edn. Christian Sch. Adminstrn., Baptist Christian U., 1992. Cert. sch. adminstr. Youth, Christian edn. dir. Ch. of God, Minter City, Miss., 1975—, teen talent dir., 1983—, missions rep., 1975—, dist. Christian edn. dir. Cleveland, Miss., 1983-85, sch. adminstr., 1985—. Del. Ch. of God Edn. Leadership, Cleveland, Tenn., 1990; del., spkr. Christian Sch. Internat., Chattanooga, 1991. Contbr. Dir. St. Jude Children's Hosp., Memphis, 1991; vol. 4-H Club, Greenwood, Miss., 1985—91. Named Outstanding Young Women of Am., 1983, Top 10 of 50 Leading Bus. Women in Miss., 2001, Internat. Educator of the Yr., Internat. Biographical Ctr., London, 2003; recipient Cmty. Pride award, Chevron, 1988, Internat. Woman of Yr. award, 1993, One of One Thousand Greatest Ams. Mem.: NAFE, Ch. of God Edn. Assn., Christian Schs. Internat., Christian Sch. Adminstrs., Gospel Music Assn., Ch. of God Sch. of Theology Alumni assn., Delta State Alumni Assn. Republican. Home: 5642 County Rd 544 Minter City MS 38944 Office Phone: 662-299-4592. *The greatest gift that God has given mankind is the capacity to love and encourage others. It is God's gift to us and our gift to others.*

MITCHELL, PAULA LEVIN, biology professor, editor; b. N.Y.C., Nov. 2, 1951; d. Louis X. and Jane (Schanfeld) Levin; m. Forrest Lee Mitchell, July 28, 1979 (div. 1993); children: Robert, Evelyn; m. Edward S. Haynes, June 6, 1994. BA in Biology, U. Pa., 1973; PhD in Zoology, U. Tex., 1980. Rsch. assoc. dept. entomology La. State U., Baton Rouge, 1981-84; vis. prof. dept. biol. scis Tarleton State U., Stephenville, Tex., 1984-93; asst. prof. dept biology Winthrop U., Rock Hill, SC, 1993—99, assoc. prof., 1999—; adj. asst. prof. dept. entomology Clemson Univ., Clemson, SC, 1996—. Adj. asst. prof. dept. biology Tex. Christian U., Fort Worth, 1985-88; editor Entomol. Soc. Am., Lanham, Md., 1986-93. Subject editor Jour. Agrl. Entomology, 1994-98; contbr. articles to profl. jours. Branch sec. AAUW, Stephenville, 1986-87. U. fellow U. Tex., Austin, 1973—76, Fulbright Sr. Rsch. Scholar, New Delhi, India, 2001—02. Mem.: Southwestern Entomol. Soc., S.C. Entomol. Soc. (pres. 2001), Ga. Entomol. Soc., Entomol. Soc. Am. Office: Winthrop U 202 Life Sci Bldg Rock Hill SC 29733-0001 Office Phone: 803-323-2111.

MITCHELL, PAULA RAE, nursing educator, college dean; b. Independence, Mo., Jan. 10, 1951; d. Millard Henry and E. Lorene (Denton) Gates; m. Ralph William Mitchell, May 24, 1975. BS in Nursing, Graceland Coll., 1973; MS in Nursing, U. Tex., 1976; EdD in ednl. Adminstrn., N.Mex. State U., 1996. RN, Tex., Mo.; cert. childbirth educator. Instr. nursing El Paso (Tex.) C.C., 1979-85, dir. nursing, 1985—2003, acting divsn. chmn. health occupations, 1985-86, divsn. dean, 1998-99, dean health occupations, 1999-2000, curriculum facilitator, 1984-86, dean health occupations, math and sci., campus dean, 2000—. Ob-gyn. nurse practitioner Planned Parenthood, El Paso, 1981-86, med. com., 1986-98; cons. in field. Author: (with Grippando) Nursing Perspectives and Issues, 1989, 93; contbr. articles to profl. jours. Founder, bd. dirs. Health-CREST, El Paso, 1981—85; mem. pub. edn. com. Am. Cancer Soc., El Paso, 1983—84, mem. profl. activities com., 1992—93; mem. El-Paso City-County Bd. Health, 1989—91; mem. Govt. Applications Rev. Com. Rio Grande Coun. Govts., 1989—91; mem. collaborative coun. El Paso Magnet H.S. for Health Care Professions, 1992—94; co-chair health and human svcs. task force Unite El Paso Health, 1996—98, mem. steering com., 1999—2000; co-chair health taskforce El Paso Cmty. Legis. Agenda, 1997—99; mem. adv. com. Ctr. for Border Health Rsch., Paso del Norte Health Found., 1998—; mem. Leadership El Paso, 1999; mem. health profl. shortage task force Greater El Paso C. of C., 2001—, mem. health care coun., 2002—; bd. dirs. Border Health Inst., El Paso, 2001—, sec.-treas., 2003—. Capt. U.S. Army, 1972—78. Decorated Army Commendation medal, Meritorious Svc. medal. Named to Women's Hall of Fame, El Paso Commn., 1999, named Outstanding Alumni, N.Mex. State U., 2002-03. Mem. Nat. League Nursing (resolutions com. Assocs. Degree coun. 1987-89, accreditation site visitor, AD coun. 1990—, Tex. edn. com. 1991-92, Tex. 3d v.p. 1992-93, Tex. 1st v.p. 1997-99, nominating com. 1999-2000), Am. Soc. Psychoprophylaxis Obstetrics, Nurses Assn. Am. Coll. Ob-Gyn. (cert. in ambulatory women's healthcare, chpt. coord. 1979-83, nat. program rev. com. 1984-86, corr. 1987-89), Advanced Nurse Practitioner Group El Paso (coord. 1980-83, legis. com. 1984), Am. Phys. Therapist Assn. (commn. on accreditation, site visitor for phys. therapist asst. programs 1991—), Orgn. Assoc. Degree Nursing (Tex. membership chmn. 1985-89, chmn. goals com. 1989—, nat. bylaws com. 1990-95), Am. Vocat. Assn., Am. Assn. Women Cmty. and Jr. Colls., Tex. Orgn. Nurse Execs., Nat. Coun. Workforce Edn. (articulation task force

1986-89, program standards task force 1991-93), Nat. Coun. Instrnl. Adminstrs., Tex. Soc. Allied Health Profls., Tex. Nurses Assn. (pres.-elect dist. one 2002-2003, pres. 2003—2004), Nat. Soc. Allied Health Profls. (edn. com. 1993-96), El Paso C. of C. (healthcare coun. 2001—), Sigma Theta Tau, Phi Kappa Phi. Mem. Christian Ch. (Disciples Of Christ). Home: 4616 Cupid Dr El Paso TX 79924-1726 Office: El Paso C C PO Box 20500 El Paso TX 79998-0500 Office Phone: 915-831-4030. Business E-Mail: paulam@epcc.edu.

MITCHELL, PETER KENNETH, educational consultant; b. Bklyn., June 12, 1949; s. Peter Kenneth and Joan Marie (Hayes) Mitchell; 1 child, Elyse Alexandra. Cert. in French lang. proficiency, U. de Neuchatel, Switzerland, 1969; BA, SUNY, Geneseo, 1970; MS in French, L.I. U., 1975. Tchr. French, Spanish and English Mid. Country Sch. Dist., Selden, NY. 1972-81; tech. asst. to dir. internat. affairs dept. Am. Fedn. Tchrs., Washington, 1981—90; asst. to gen. sec. Internat. Fedn. Free Tchrs. Unions, Amsterdam, Netherlands, 1986—91; exec. dir. Internat. Reading Assn., Newark, Del., 1990-91; owner Insights Out Assocs., Newark, Del., 1992—97. Dir. mktg. Jr. Achievement Del., 1994—99. Contbr. articles to profl. jours. Recipient Father of the Yr. award, Nat. Multiple Sclerosis Soc., 1998. Mem.: Amnesty Internat., Washington U. Club, Blue and Gold Club. Avocations: reading, music.

MITCHELL, RALPH, wholesale distribution executive; B in Commerce, U. N.S.W., Sydney, 1981. Chartered acct. With KPMG Peat Marwick, N.Y. and Sydney, Australia, McKessonHBOC Corp., Dallas; exec. v.p., CFO Daisytek Internat., Allen, Tex., 2000—. Office: Daisytek Internat Corp 1025 Central Expy S Ste 200 Allen TX 75013

MITCHELL, REGINALD EUGENE, mechanical engineering educator; b. Houston, May 16, 1947; s. Clifford Eugene and Juanita Beatrice (Thomas) M.; 1 child, Erika Gene; m. Shirley Ann Myers, Nov. 9, 1990. BS in Chem. Engring., U. Denver, 1968; MS in Chem. Engring., N.J. Inst. Tech., Newark, 1970; ScD in Chem. Engring., MIT, 1975. Mem. tech. staff Sandia Nat. Labs., Livermore, Calif., 1975-89, disting. mem. tech. staff, 1989-91; assoc. prof. mech. engring. dept. Stanford (Calif.) U., 1991—. Recipient Outstanding Tchr. award Tau Beta Pi, 1994. Mem. Nat. Orgn. Black Chemists and Chem. Engrs. (exec. bd., chair western region, Percy Julian award 1987), Combustion Inst., Sigma Xi. Avocations: board games, card games, tennis. Home: 6143 Viewcrest Dr Oakland CA 94619-3728 Office: Stanford U Mech Engring Dept Bldg 520 Rm 520C Stanford CA 94305-3032 Business E-Mail: remitche@stanford.edu.

MITCHELL, RICHARD BOYLE, security consultant; b. St. Louis, June 20, 1947; s. Samuel West and Blair (Boyle) M.; m. Sallie Jean Gear, Dec. 4, 1999; children: Rebecca, Jessica. BS in Mktg., NYU, 1969. Account exec. D.L. Blair Corp., N.Y.C., 1967—70, NW Ayer Advt. Agy., N.Y.C., 1970-74; sr. account exec. Ted Bates Agy., N.Y.C., 1974-75; sr. v.p. DKG Advt., N.Y.C., 1975-81, McCaffrey/McCall, N.Y.C., 1981-86; pres., CEO Marshall Jaccoma Mitchell Advt., N.Y.C., 1986-96; sr. ptnr. Modem Media, N.Y.C., 1996-97; mng. dir., mgmt. cons. MJM Cons., N.Y.C., 1997—2001; pres. 911 Consulting, Wilton, Conn., 2001—. Commr. Wilton (Conn.) Police Dept., 1984-01. Served with USAR, 1969-74. Mem.: Wilton Riding. Democrat. Roman Catholic. Avocations: military history, running, weightlifting. Home: 20 Indian Hill Rd Wilton CT 06897-1319 E-mail: bomitchell@911consulting.net.

MITCHELL, RIE ROGERS, psychologist, counselor, educator; b. Tucson, Feb. 1, 1940; d. Martin Smith and Lavaun (Peterson) Rogers; m. Rex C. Mitchell, Mar. 16, 1961; 1 child, Scott Rogers. Student, Mills Coll., 1958-59; BS, U. Utah, 1962, MS, 1963; postgrad., San Diego State U., 1965-66; MA, PhD, UCLA, 1969. Diplomate Am. Bd. Psychology; registered play therapist, supr.; cert. sandplay therapist. Tchr. Coronado (Calif.) Unified Sch. Dist., 1964-65; sch. psychologist Glendale (Calif.) Unified Sch. Dist., 1968-70; psychologist Glendale Guidance Clinic, 1970-77; asst. prof. ednl. psychology Calif. State U., Northridge, 1970-74, assoc. prof., 1974-78, prof., 1978—. Chmn. dept. ednl. psychology, 1976-80, 2000—, acting exec. asst. to pres. Calif. State U., Dominguez Hills, 1978-79; cons. to various Calif. sch. dists.; pvt. practice psychology, Calabasas, Calif. Author: Sandplay: Past Present & Future, 1994; contbr. numerous articles to profl. jours. Recipient Outstanding Educator award Maharishi Soc., 1978, Woman of Yr. award U. Utah, 1962, Profl. Leadership award Western Assn. Counselor Edn., 1990, Disting. Tchg. award Calif. U. Northridge, 1994. Mem. APA, Calif. Assn. Counselor Edn., Supervision and Adminstrn. (dir. 1976-77), Western Assn. Counselor Edn. and Supervision (officer 1978-82, pres. 1980-81), Assn. Counselor Edn. and Supervision (dir. 1980-81, program chmn. 1981-82, treas. 1983-86, Presdl. award 1986, Leadership award 1987), UCLA Doctoral Alumni Assn. (pres. 1974-76), Am. Ednl. Rsch. Assn., Calif. Women in Higher Edn. (pres. chpt. 1977-78), Calif. Concerns (treas. 1984-86), Sandplay Therpists of Am. (fin. officer 1996-2000, bd. mem. 1993—, media chair, 1995, bylaws chair, 1994-96, exceptions com. chair, 1995-96), Pi Lambda Theta (pres. chpt. 1970-71, chairwoman nat. resolutions 1971-73). Home: 4503 Alta Tupelo Dr Calabasas CA 91302-2516 Office: Calif State U Counselor Edn Dept Northridge CA 91330-0001 Office Phone: 818-677-4976. E-mail: rie.mitchell@csun.edu.

MITCHELL, ROBERT DALE, consulting engineer; b. Worthington, Minn., Aug. 2, 1910; s. Karl V. and Margaret Dumont (Steigleder) M.; m. Carol Sherman Northrop, June 17, 1939; children: Constance Remington, Robert Brown. BS, S.D. State U., 1932; S.M. (grad. fellow), Harvard U., 1939. Engr. J. Emberg, Madison, S.D., 1932-35; instr. S.D. State U., 1935-37; engr. Malcolm Pirnie Engrs., N.Y.C., 1939-42, project engr., ptnr., 1945-70; sr. v.p., sec., chief engr. Malcolm Pirnie, Inc., 1970-75; cons. Malcolm Pirnie Engrs., 1975—. Served to maj. San. Corps AUS, 1942-45. Recipient Distinguished Engr. award S.D. State U., 1977 Fellow Am. Coun. Engring. Cons.; mem. ASCE (life), Am. Water Works Assn., New Eng. Water Works Assn. (Commemorative award 1963) Home: 487 Brackett Rd Rye NH 03870-2204 Office: 104 Corporate Park Dr White Plains NY 10604-3804

MITCHELL, ROBERT JAMES, petroleum company executive; b. Montour Falls, N.Y., Mar. 16, 1925; s. Robert Bowlby and Helen (Bates) M.; m. Pearl Kohnken, Aug. 30, 1947; children: Susan E., LuAnne, Robert James II. Student, Ga. Inst. Tech., 1944, U. Richmond, 1945, Sampson Coll., 1947-48; JD, Valparaiso U., 1953. Adjuster State Farm Mut. Auto Ins., Valparaiso, 1953-54; dist. rep. life ins. Aid Assn. for Luths., Hoffman, Ill., 1954-57; with dept. devel. Valparaiso (Ind.) U., 1957-58; oil prodr. Hoffman, 1958-64; founder, pres., dir. Ego Oil Co., Inc., 1964—; founder, pres., CEO Altec Energy, Inc., 1988—. Author: Spencarian Sonnet, Of Sunshine and Dreams, 1996; The Aleutians, 1998. With USNR, 1941-46, 50-52. Mem. Ind. Petroleum Assn. Am. (dir. 1976—), Delta Theta Phi. Home: Apt 33 502 River Pointe DR Conroe TX 77304-2840

MITCHELL, ROBERT JOSEPH, insurance executive; b. Chgo., Mar. 2, 1947; s. Charles Robert and Rita (Cagney) M.; m. Nancy Telfer, Dec. 24, 1970; children: Laura Magee, Claire Clagett. BS, Loyola U., Chgo., 1970. CLU, ChFC. Asst. cashier Mich. Ave. Nat. Bank, Chgo., 1970-74; asst. v.p. First Nat. Bank of Lake Forest, Ill., 1974-78, United Bank of Skyline, Denver, 1978-79, v.p. comml. loan adminstr., 1979-82; pres., chief exec. officer United Bank of Cherry Creek, Denver, 1982-83; exec. v.p. Capital Nat. Bank, Ft. Worth, 1983-87; ins. agt./broker, CEO Mitchell & Moroneso Ins. Svcs. & Investment Inc., A Highland Capital Co., Ft. Worth, 1987—; pres. The More Fin. Group, Ft. Worth. Bd. dirs., pres. Easter Seals, Ft. Worth, 1988-95, Internat. Sister Cities of Ft. Worth, 1989—; chmn. bd. dirs. Big Bros./Big Sisters of Tarrant County, 1987; priorities com. United Way, 1985—; exec. com. bd. mem. Mus. Sci. and History, Ft. Worth, 1990, Boys and Girls Club Ft. Worth, 1997-2000; bd. dirs. Ptnrs. in Health Found. Recipient Pres. Hon. award Conn. Mut. Life Ins. Co., 1990-91. Mem. Nat. Assn. Life Underwriters (Nat. Quality award 1990-93), Am. Soc. CLUs, Ft. Worth Bus. and Estate Coun., Ft. Worth Million Dollar Roundtable (life, Ct. of Table 1999-2000, 02-03), Ft. Worth Rotary (exec. bd., Paul Harris fellow). Roman Catholic. Avocations: racquetball, squash. Office: Mitchell & Moroneso Ins & Investments 306 W 7th St Ste 888 Fort Worth TX 76102-4912 Office Phone: 817-338-0888.

MITCHELL, ROBERT W. diversified company executive; CFO Ingram Industries Inc., Nashville. Office: Ingram Industries Inc 4400 Harding Road Nashville TN 37205

MITCHELL, ROGER LOWRY, retired agronomy educator; b. Grinnell, Iowa, Sept. 13, 1932; s. Robert T. and and Cecile (Lowry) M.; m. Joyce Elaine Lindgren, June 26, 1955; children: Laura, Susan, Sarah, Martha. BS in Agronomy, Iowa State Coll., 1954; MS, Cornell U., 1958; PhD in Crop Physiology, Iowa State U., 1961. Mem. faculty Iowa State U., 1959-69, prof. agronomy, 1966-69, prof. charge farm operation curriculum, 1962-66; prof. agronomy, chmn. dept. U. Mo., Columbia, 1969-72, 81-83, emeritus prof., 1998—, dean agr., dir. expt. sta., 1983-98, dean extension, 1972-75, emeritus dean, 1998—; v.p. agr. Kans. State U., Manhattan, 1975-80; exec. dir. Mid-Am. Internat. Agrl. Consortium, 1981; ret., 1998. Exec. bd. divsn. agr. Nat. Assn. State Univs. and Land Grant Colls., 1978-80, 85-90, chmn., 1988-89; mem. bd. agr. NRC/NAS, 1983-86. Author: Crop Growth and Culture, 1970; co-author: Physiology of Crop Plants, 1985 Served to 2d lt. USAAF, 1954-56. Danforth fellow, 1956-61; Acad. Adminstrn. fellow Am. Council Edn., 1966-67; recipient Henry A. Wallace award Iowa State U., 1993, Sec.'s Honor award USDA, 1998. Fellow AAAS (chmn. sect. O 1980-81), Am. Soc. Agronomy (pres. 1979-80), Crop Sci. Soc. (pres. 1975-76); mem. Soil Sci. Soc. Am., Coun. Agrl. Sci. and Tech., Sigma Xi, Gamma Sigma Delta, Alpha Zeta, Phi Kappa Phi. Home: 502 W Lathrop Rd Columbia MO 65203-2804 E-mail: mitchellrj@missouri.edu.

MITCHELL, RONNIE MONROE, lawyer, educator; b. Clinton, N.C., Nov. 10, 1952; s. Ondus Corneilius and Margaret Ronie (Johnson) M.; m. Martha Cheryl Coble, May 25, 1975; children: Grant Stephen, Mitchell, Meredith Elizabeth Mitchell. BA, Wake Forest U., 1975, JD, 1978. Bar: N.C. 1978, U.S. Dist. Ct. (ea. dist.) N.C. 1978, U.S. Ct. Appeals (4th cir.) 1983, U.S. Supreme Ct. 1984. Assoc. atty. Brown, Fox & Deaver, Fayetteville, N.C., 1978-81; ptnr. Harris, Sweeny & Mitchell, Fayetteville, 1981-91, Harris, Mitchell & Hancox, 1991-96, Harris & Mitchell, 1997-98, Harris, Mitchell, Burns & Brewer, 1998-2000, Mithchell, Brewer, Richardson, Adams, Burns and Boughman, 2000—. Adj. prof. law Norman Adrian Wiggins Sch. of Law, Campbell U; bd. dirs. Mace, Inc. Contbr. chpts. to books. Chmn. Cumberland County Bd. Adjustment, 1985-92, Cumberland County Rescue Squad, 1986-93; bd. dirs. Cumberland County Rescue Squad, Fayetteville, 1983-91. Recipient U.S. Law Week award Bur. Nat. Affairs, 1978. Mem. ABA, ATLA, Twelfth Judicial Dist. Bar Assn. (pres. 1988-89), N.C. Bar Assn. (councillor Young Lawyers divsn. 1982-85), N.C. Legis. Rsch. Commn. (family law com. 1994), Cumberland County Bar Assn. (mem. family law com., N.C. State Bar Bd. legal specialization), N.C. Acad. Trial Lawyers, Fayetteville Ind. Light Infantry Club, Dem. Men's Club (pres. 1993-94), Moose, Masons. Home: RR 1901 Water Oaks Dr Fayetteville NC 28301-9125 Office: Mitchell Brewer Richardson Adams Burns and Boughman 308 Person St Fayetteville NC 28301-5736

MITCHELL, ROY SHAW, lawyer; b. Sherwood, N.Y., Jan. 16, 1934; s. Malcolm Douglas and Ruth Landon (Holland) M.; m. Nancy Elizabeth Bishop, Aug. 27, 1955; children: Mark E., Jeffrey B., Jennifer R. BS, Cornell U., 1957; JD with honors, George Washington U., Washington, D.C., 1959. Bar: D.C. 1959, Ohio 1960, Va. 1967, U.S. Ct. Fed. Claims 1963, U.S. Supreme Ct. 1965. Atty. Squire, Sanders & Dempsey, Cleve., 1960-61, Hudson & Creyke, Washington, 1961-67, Lewis, Mitchell & Moore, Vienna, Va., 1967-87, Morgan, Lewis & Bockius LLP, Washington, 1987-99; pres., CEO constrn. claims group Hill Internat., Inc., Washington, 1999—2004. Vice-chmn. Ameribanc Savs. Bank, Annandale, Va., 1980-95; trustee Ameribanc Investors Group, Annandale, 1980-95. Co-author: (with others) Handbook of Construction Law and Claims, 1982, 89; contbr. numerous articles to profl. jours. Fellow ABA (pub. contract law sect.), Am. Coll. Construction Lawyers, Va. Bar Assn., D.C. Bar Assn. Presbyterian. Avocation: boating. Home: 5 Jefferson Run Rd Great Falls VA 22066-3200 Office Phone: 571-435-7191. E-mail: roysmitchell@aol.com.

MITCHELL, RUSSELL HARRY, dermatologist; b. Erie, N.D., Oct. 19, 1925; s. William John and Anna Lillian (Sögge) M.; m. Judith Lawes Douvarjo, May 24, 1968 (dec. Mar. 2000); children: Kathy Ellen, Gregory Alan, Jill Elaine, Crystal Anne. BS, BA, U. Minn., Mpls., 1947, BM, 1949, MD, 1951; postgrad., U. Pa., 1968-69. Diplomate Am. Bd. Dermatology. Intern Gorgas Hosp., C.Z., 1951-52; commd. lt. (j.g.) M.C. USN, 1953, advanced through grades to capt., 1968, commdg. officer 1st Med. Bn., 1st Marine divsn., ret., 1981; resident in dermatology U.S. Naval Hosp., Phila., 1967-70; asst. chief out-patient dept. Gorgas Hosp., 1955-64; chief med. and surg. wards Ariz. State Hosp., Phoenix, 1965; pvt. practice Leesburg, Va., 1978—. Staff Loudoun Health Ctr., 1975—; dermatologist Nat. Naval Med. Ctr., Bethesda, Md., 1973-81; asst. prof. Georgetown U. Med. Sch., 1975-85. Contbr. articles to profl. jours. Pres. Archaeol. Soc. Panama, 1962-64. Decorated bronze star with combat V; Vietnam Gallantry Cross with Palm and clasp; Condecoration Vasco Nuñez de Balboa in orden de Caballero (Panamá). Fellow: Am. Acad. Physicians (life), Am. Acad. Dermatology (life), Explorers' Club; mem.: Loudoun County Med. Soc., Am. Soc. Contemporary Medicine and Surgery, Assn. Mil. Surgeons, Assn.Mil. Dermatologists (life), Ctr. for Study of First Americans, Am. Archeology Soc., Marines' Meml. Club (assoc.), Phi Chi. Home: 18685 Woodburn Rd Leesburg VA 20175-9029 Office: 823 S King St Ste J Leesburg VA 20175-3916

MITCHELL, SHAWNE MAUREEN, author; b. Tacoma, Wash., Jan. 09; d. F. King and Nona Margaret Burnside (Hayes) M.; m. J.D. Cook, Spt. 4, 1982; children: Travis, Austin. BA, U. Wash.; postgrad., U. Santa Monica, 1997—. CEO Adventures of the Spirit, Santa Barbara, Calif., 1994—; author, spkr. Soul Style, 1995—; columnist Feng Shui-Soul Style, Calif., 1996—. Cons. real estate, Wash., Calif., 1980—; dir. Small Luxury Hotels, L.A., 1986-87; internat. spkr., author on subject of higher consciousness; internat. spkr. on Feng Shui. Author: Soul Style, 1997, Exploring Feng Shui, Ancient Secrets and Modern Insights, 2001, Creating Home Sanctuaries with Feng Shui, 2002, Simple Feng Shui, 2004; editor: Home Sanctuaries mag.; contbr. articles to profl. jours. Bd. dirs. Montecito (Calif.) Ednl. Found., 1997-99, Los Positas Park Found., Santa Barbara, 1995. Mem. Womens Exec. Network, Seattle Tennis Club. Avocations: boating, hiking, travel, music, art. Office: Adventures of the Spirit Inc PO Box 5765 Santa Barbara CA 93150-5765 Office Phone: 805-565-8885. E-mail: shawne@shawnemitchell.com.

MITCHELL, STEPHEN MILTON, investment company executive; b. Atlanta, Oct. 23, 1943; s. Judge Stephenson and Elizabeth Ruth (Morgan) M.; m. Carolyn Docia Goss, June 29, 1968; children: William Stephenson, Scott Milton, Gregory Stephen. B of Indsl. Engring. with honors, Ga. Inst. Tech., 1965, MS in Indsl. Engring., 1966. Registered profl. engr., Ga. Sr. engr. Lochkeed-Ga. Corp., Marietta, 1966-70; mgr. material control Snapper Power Equipment, McDonough, Ga., 1970-73; pres. Atlanta Processing Co., Conley, Ga., 1973-86; sr. v.p., gen. mgr. Norcom, Inc., Norcross, Ga., 1986-93; chmn., CEO Atlanta Processing B, Inc., Tucker, Ga., 1993-94; CEO Internat. Processing Corp., Atlanta, 1994, Sertec Corp., Atlanta, 1995—, also bd. dirs. Bd. dirs. Atlanta Processing Co., Conley, Ga., Norcom, Inc., Norcross, APB Inc., Tucker, Ga., IPC, Atlanta; mem. exec. com., chmn., bd. dirs. Clairmont Oaks, Inc., 1988—. Bd. dirs., treas. Common Cause, Ga., 1989—; active First Bapt. Ch. of Decatur, Ga., 1968—, chmn. bd. deacons, 1993, 95. Mem. Young Presidents Orgn., World Presidents Orgn., Ga. Tech. Alumni Assn. (trustee 1981-87). Republican. Home: 5268 Browning Way SW Lilburn GA 30047-7029 Office: Sertec Corp 2100 Powers Ferry Rd NW Ste 200 Atlanta GA 30339-5014

MITCHELL, TAWNIA JUANITA, elementary school educator, music educator; b. St. Croix Falls, Wis., July 29, 1969; d. DeWayne Gerhard and Wanda Juanita Gunderson; m. Jeffery Paul Mitchell, Mar. 22, 1997; 1 child, Madelyn Maudene. MusB in Edn., Lawrence U., 1991. Music, vocal tchr. K-12th grade Cambria (Wis.)-Friesland Sch., 1991—93; music, choral tchr. 4th-12th grade Montello (Wis.) Sch. Dist., 1994—96; music, choral tchr. 3rd-12th grade, drama dir. Green Lake (Wis.) Sch. Dist., 1997—. Musician (cellist): Beaver Dam Area Orch., 1992—2003. Mem.: Wis. Choral Dirs. Assn., Music Educators Nat. Conf. Avocations: cello, organ, singing, dance, scrapbooks. Office: Green Lake Sch Dist 612 Mill St Green Lake WI 54941 Business E-Mail: tmitche2@glsd.k12.wi.us.

MITCHELL, TEDDY LEE, physician; b. Columbia, La., Feb. 24, 1962; s. Oliver Clayton nad Mary Elizabeth (Johnston) M.; m. Janet Luisa Tornelli, Apr. 9, 1988; children: Mary Katherine, Oliver Charles, Christopher Tornelli. BS in Biology, Stephen F. Austin State U., 1983; MD, U. Tex. Med. Br., 1987. Diplomate Am. Bd. Internal Medicine, Cert. of Added Qualification-Sports Medicine. Intern U. Tex. Med. Br., Galveston, 1987-88, resident, 1988-90, 90-91; staff physician Cooper Aerobics Ctr., Dallas, 1991—, med. dir. wellness program, 1991—. Mem. Rep. Sen. Inner Cir., Washington, 1993, Heritage Found., Washington, 1993. Capt. U.S. Army Res. Med. Corps, 1988-96. Fellow Am. Coll. Sports Medicine; mem. AMA, Am. Coll. Physicians (cert Merit 1990), Tex. Med. Assn., Dallas County Med. Soc. Methodist. Avocations: exercise, travel, music. Home: 3224 Lovers Ln Dallas TX 75225-7626

MITCHELL, TERENCE EDWARD, materials scientist; b. Haywards Heath, Sussex, Eng., May 18, 1937; came to U.S., 1963, naturalized, 1978; s. Thomas Frank and Dorothy Elizabeth (Perrin) M.; m. Marion Wyatt, Dec. 5, 1959; children: Robin Norman, Jeremy Neil. BA, St. Catharine's Coll., Cambridge (Eng.) U., 1958, MA, PhD in Physics, St. Catharine's Coll., Cambridge (Eng.) U., 1962; ScD, U. Cambridge, 1994. Research fellow Cavendish Lab., Cambridge, 1962-63; asst. prof. metallurgy Case Inst. Tech., 1963-66; assoc. prof. Case Western Res. U., 1966-75, prof., 1975-87, adj. prof., 1987—, chmn. dept., 1983-86, dir. high voltage electron microscopy facility, 1970-82, co-dir. materials research lab., 1982-83; vis. scientist NASA at Ames Lab., Stanford U. and Electric Power Research Inst., Palo Alto, Calif., 1975-76; scientist Ctr. Materials Sci. Los Alamos (N.Mex.) Nat. Lab., 1987—, lab fellow, 1991—; lab fellows chair Los Alamos (N.Mex.) Nat. Lab., 1993-95. Chmn. steering com. Electron Microscopy Ctr. Argonne (Ill.) Nat. Lab., 1979-83; cons. in field; mem. vis. com. metals and ceramics div. Oak Ridge Lab., 1987-91; vis. com. solid state scis. div. Ames Lab., 1987-89; sci. adv. com. Sci. and Tech. Ctr. for Superconductivity, 1989-93. Materials sci. editor Microscopy Rsch. and Technique, 1986—; sr. editor North Am., 1994—; contbr. 400 articles to profl. jours. Pres. Cleve. Ethical Soc., 1970-72; bd. dirs Am. Ethical Union, 1972-74; steward Los Alamos Unitarian Ch., 1992-94; mem. policy com. Univ. Materials Coun., 1986-89; mem. policy com. Argonne Electron Microscopy Steering Com., chmn. 1978-82. Electric Power Research Inst. fellow, 1975-76; NSF grantee, 1966-88; Dept. Energy grantee, 1970-86, 87—; NIH grantee, 1969-72; NASA grantee, 1974-77, 81-87; USAF Office Sci. Research grantee, 1974-85; U.S. Army Research Office grantee, 1970-75, 79-83, EPRI grantee, 1986-89; spl. issue in his honor Philos. Mag. A, Sept. 1998; spl. symposium in his honor TMS Ann. Meeting, San Diego, 2003. Fellow Am. Soc. Metals, Am. Phys. Soc., Am. Ceramics Soc. (assoc. editor jour. 1989-, v.p. 1999-2000), Minerals, Metals & Materials Soc., Los Alamos Nat. Lab., Japan Inst. Metals; mem. Japan Soc. Promotion of Sci., Electron Microscopy Soc. Am. (program chmn. 1981-82, dir. 1984-86, pres.-elect 1994, pres. 1995, past pres. 1996), Materials Rsch. Soc., Soc. Francaise de Microscopie Electronique (sci. com. 1982-90). Office: Los Alamos Nat Lab Ctr Materials Sci Ms # G755 Los Alamos NM 87545-0001 E-mail: temitchell@lanl.gov.

MITCHELL, THEODORE REED, academic administrator; b. San Rafael, Calif., Jan. 29, 1956; s. Theodore Robert and Genevieve Dolores (Doose) Mitchell; m. Christine M. Beckman, July 8, 1995; children: Caroline Mitchell Beckman, Theo Beckman. BA, Stanford U., 1978, MA, 1980, PhD, 1983. Asst. prof. Dartmouth Coll., Hanover, NH, 1981—86, assoc. prof., 1986—87, chair dept. edn., 1987—91; dep. to pres. and provost Stanford U., Calif., 1991—92; dean Sch. Edn. and Info. Studies UCLA, 1992—96, vice chancellor, 1996—98; v.p. for edn. and strategic initiatives The J. Paul Getty Trust, 1998—99; pres. Occidental Coll., 1999—. Trustee Stanford U., 1985—90, Thetford Acad., Vt., 1989—91; bd. dirs. L.A. Edn. Partnership, L.E.A.R.N. Author: Political Education, 1985, Sociology of Education, 1998. Bd. dirs. Children Now, Oakland, Calif., 1994—, Gateway Learning Corp., 1996—. Office: Occidental Coll Office of Pres 1600 Campus Rd Los Angeles CA 90041

MITCHELL, THOMAS EDWARD, JR., communications cabling executive; b. Sacramento, Apr. 12, 1946; s. Thomas Edward and Violet Mae (Southall) M.; m. Terri Kathleen Vance, Apr. 20, 1969; children: Anthony E., Brian C. BA, Nat. U., 1987, MBA, 1988. Enlisted USMC, 1966, advanced through grades to maj., 1980, retired, 1989; sr. exec. Nat. Decision Sys., Encinitas, Calif., 1989-90, Equifax Mktg. Decision Sys., San Diego, 1990-93; exec. v.p., bd. dirs. Holocomm Sys. Inc., San Diego, 1993—. Bd. dirs. Cal-Pacific Steel Structure Inc., Hawaii, Calif. Contbr. articles to profl. jours.; patentee in field. Dir. Toys for Tots, L.A./ORange Counties, Calif., 1974-77. Recipient Silver Star medal U.S. Pres., 1968, Meritorious Svc. medal, Joint Chiefs of Staff Commendation medal, others. Mem. World Trade Assn. (assoc. 1989—), Am. Legion, Internat. Platform Assn. Avocations: restoring old cars, racquetball, golf, history. Home: 3264 Chase Ct Oceanside CA 92056-3809 Office: Holcomm Sys Inc 2131 Palomar Airport Rd Ste 150 Carlsbad CA 92009-1452

MITCHELL, TIMMY J. principal; b. Hammond, Ind., Nov. 2, 1954; s. Thomas E. and Diane E. Mitchell; m. Rhonda J. Matthews, Apr. 18, 1984; 1 child, Terry E.; 1 child from previous marriage, Crystal Marie. BA, Purdue Calumet U., 1995, MS, 2000. Police officer Schererville (Ind.) Police Dept., 1977—97; tchr. Grimmer Mid. Sch., Schererville, 1997—2002; prin. Lincoln Elem. Sch., Roselawn, Ind., 2002—. Mem. Lincoln PTA; D.A.R.E., Officer Friendly Schererville Police Dept., 1990—92. Sgt. USAF, 1972—76. Mem.: Fraternal Order Police. Avocations: motorcycling, motorcross. Office: Lincoln Elem Sch 10280 N 450 E Demotte IN 46310 Fax: 219-345-3488. Business E-Mail: tmitchell@nn.k12.in.us.

MITCHELL, WALTER LOUIS, III, lawyer; b. Orange, N.J., Feb. 20, 1945; s. Walter Louis and Anne (DeBeaux) M.; m. Carol Nash, Apr. 28, 1984; children from previous marriage— Jason Kenyon, Jennifer DeBeaux, David Grant. B.A., Yale U., 1967; J.D., Boston U., 1970. Bar: N.H. 1970, U.S. Dist. Ct. N.H. 1970. Ptnr., Nighswander, Martin & Mitchell, P.A., Laconia, N.H.; mem. N.H. Jud. Council, 1983— . Mem. N.H. Bar Assn. (chmn. mcpl. law sect. 1981-83, v.p. 1982-83, pres.-elect 1983-84, pres. 1984-85), New Eng. Bar Assn. (bd. dirs. 1983-85). Office: Nighswander Martin & Mitchell PA One Mill Plaza Laconia NH 03246

MITCHELL, WAYNE LEE, health care administrator; b. Mar. 25, 1937; s. Albert C. and Elizabeth Isabelle (Nagel) M.; m. Marie Galletti. BA, U. Redlands, Calif., 1959; MSW, Ariz. State U., 1970, EdD, 1979. Social worker various county, state, and fed. agys., 1962-70; social worker Bur. Indian Affairs, Phoenix, Ariz., 1970-77, USPHS, 1977-79; asst. prof. Ariz. State U., 1979-84; with USPHS, Phoenix, 1984—. Lectr. in field. Contbr. articles to profl. jours. Bd. dirs. Phoenix Indian Comty. Sch., 1973-75, ATLATL, 1994-98, Partnership for Comty. Devel. Ariz. State U.-West, 1996-99, Cen. Ariz. Health Sys. Agy., 1982-85; mem. Phoenix Area Health Adv. Bd., 1975, Comty. Behavioral Mental Health Bd., 1976-80, Fgn. Rels. Com., Phoenix; trustee Heard Mus. Anthropology, Phoenix, 1996; apptd. Ariz. State Bd. Behavioral Health Examiners, 2000-2002. With USCG, 1960-62. Recipient Comty. Svc. award Ariz. Temple of Islam, 1980, Ariz. State U., 1996, Dir. Excellence award Phoenix Area IHS Dir., 1992, 93, Nat. IHS Dir.'s award for outstanding svc., 20001; named in Voices and Faces, 2003. Mem. NASW (Lifetime Achievement award 2003), Fgn. Rels. Coun., Am. Hosp. Assn., U.S.-China Assn., Kappa Delta Pi, Phi Delta Kappa, Chi Sigma Chi. Democrat. Congregationalist. Home: PO Box 9592 Phoenix AZ 85068-9592 Personal E-mail: drwlmitch@aol.com.

MITCHELL, WILLIAM CLARK, printmaker, graphic artist; b. Holyoke, Mass., Dec. 15, 1958; s. Ronald Herbert and Ann Theresa (Clark) M.; m. Mary Margaret Malone, Jan. 7, 1984; children: Matthew and Michael (twins). BA in Studio Art, State U. Coll. at Oneonta, N.Y., 1980; student, Boston Mus. Sch., 1980-81. Graphic artist/designer SUNY Coll. at Oneonta, 1978-79; graphic artist Boston Blueprint Co., 1981-83; graphic artist/designer Right on Target, Somersworth, N.H., 1983-84; graphic artist, pre-press specialist U. N.H., Durham, 1984—; educator League of N.H. Craftsmen, Exeter, 1993—. Tchr. screenprinting and children's printmaking League of N.H. Craftsmen. Executed various commns. Mem. N.H. Art Assn., League N.H. Craftsmen, Rochester Print Club. Avocations: hiking, skiing, travel. Home: 102 Watson Rd Dover NH 03820-5801 E-mail: wcmprints@comcast.net.

MITCHELL, WILLIAM D. lawyer; b. Great Falls, Mont., June 15, 1947; s. William Howard and Dorothy Elizabeth (Lane) M.; m. Mary Claire McDonough, Aug. 15, 1973; children: James Edward, Andrew Elliott, Thomas Michael. BA cum laude, U. Wash., Seattle, 1969; MA in Econs., JD, U. Calif., Berkeley, 1976; MLT, Georgetown U., 1982. Bar: Calif. 1977, DC 1978, Del. 1982, Mont. 1981, Fla. 1983, U.S. Ct. Appeals (11th cir.) 1994, U.S. Dist. Ct. (no. dist.) Fla. 1992, U.S. Dist. Ct. (so. dist.) Fla. 1986, U.S. Dist. Ct. (mid. dist.) Fla. 1984, U.S. Dist. Ct. Mont. 1981, U.S. Tax Ct. 1992. Atty. Fed. Trade Commn., Washington, 1976-79; assoc. Koteen & Burt, Washington, 1979-80, Tipp, Hoven & Skjelset, Missoula, Mont., 1980-81, Murdoch & Walsh, Wilmington, Del., 1982-83, Carlton, Fields, Ward, Smith & Cutler, Tampa, 1983-88; of counsel Foley & Lardner, Tampa, 1988-90; ptnr. Langford, Hill, Mitchell, Trybus & Whalen, Tampa, Fla., 1991-92; pres. Mitchell Law Group, Tampa, 1992—. Devel. bd. Sun Coast Gerentology Ctr. Co-author: (book) Employee Fringe and Welfare Benefit Plans, 1988; author: Estate and Retirement Answer Book, 1994, contbr. articles to numerous jours. Lt. U.S. Navy, 1969-72. Mem. ABA (sect. taxation, com. on employee benefits, labor and employment law sect., com. on employee benefits, MEWA subcom., mgmt. co-chair), Greater Tampa Sertoma Club (dir. 1993-96, pres. 1996-97), Tampa Bay Writers Alliance, Mensa. Lutheran. Avocations: creative writing, acting, golf, weightlifting, auto sports.

MITCHELL, WILLIAM EDMUND, electronics executive; b. L.A., Mar. 13, 1944; s. John Stewart and Helen (Fine) M.; m. Jan Marie Scheyer, Feb. 16, 1969; children: Alden, Amanda, Alyssa. BS in Engring., Princeton U., 1966; MS in Engring., U. Mich., 1967. Analyst Exxon Corp., N.Y.C., 1969-72, dept. mgr. Baton Rouge, 1972-73; ops. mgr. Raychem. Corp., Menlo Park, Calif., 1973-76; regional mgr. Raychem Internat., Menlo Park, Calif., 1977-85, v.p., 1985-88; sr. v.p. Raychem Corp., Menlo Park, 1988-93; pres., CEO Nashua (N.H.) Corp., 1993—95; chmn., pres., CEO Sequel Inc., 1995—99; pres. Solectron Global Svcs., 1999—2002; v.p. Solectron Corp., 1999—2002; pres., CEO Arrow Electronics Inc., Melville, NY, 2003—. Bd. dirs. Rogers Corp., Conn. Mem. Orgn. for Corp. Growth, Am. Electronics Assn. (bd. dirs. 1993—), Ladera Oaks Club. Republican. Avocations: swimmming, tennis, books. Office: Arrow Electronics Inc 50 Marcus Dr Melville NY 11747

MITCHELL, WILLIAM F. environmental company executive; b. 1942; Chmn. bd., pres., CEO Environ. Tectonics Corp., Southampton, Pa., 1969—. Office: County Line Indsl Park 125 James Way Southampton PA 18966

MITCHELL, WILLIAM GRAHAM CHAMPION, lawyer, business executive; b. Raleigh, Dec. 24, 1946; s. Burley Bayard and Dorothy Ford (Champion) Mitchell; children: William Graham, Margaret Scripture. AB, U. N.C., 1969, JD with highest hons., 1975. Bar: N.C. 1975, U.S. Dist. Ct. (ea., mid., and we. dists.) N.C. 1976, U.S. Ct. Appeals (4th cir.) 1978. Ptnr. Womble, Carlyle, Sandridge & Rice, Winston-Salem, 1975-87; sr. v.p. for external affairs RJR Nabisco, Atlanta, 1987-89; exec. v.p. R.J. Reynolds Tobacco Co., Winston-Salem, 1988-89; ptnr. Howrey & Simon, Washington, 1990-94; spl. counselor to chmn. bd. True North Comm., Inc., Chgo., 1996; chmn. bd., CEO Global Exch. Carrier Co., Leesburg, Va., 1997-00; pres., CEO Global Comms. Techs. Inc., Reston, Va., 1999-2000; chmn. bd., CEO Convergence Equipment Co., Manassas, Va., 1999-2000; chmn. bd. Qfactor Inc., Bethesda, Md., 2000-01; exec. v.p., gen. mgr. Verisign Inc., Mountainview, Calif., 2001—03; chmn. bd., CEO Network Solutions, Inc., Dulles, Va., 2003—. Bd. dirs. Fed. Agrl. Mortgage Corp., Washington. Mem. Pres.'s Adv. Com. Trade Policy and Negotiations, Indsl. Policy Adv. Com., Washington, 1991—; bd. dirs. Washington Performing Arts Soc., 1988—92; founding trustee Prog. Policy Inst., 1988—; bd. advisors Dem. Leadership Coun., 1988—; vice chmn. fin. Bush Campaign; mem. exec. com. Nat. Assn. Mfrs., Washington, 1988—89, Nat. Fgn. Trade Coun., 1988—89; chmn. Tobacco Inst., Washington, 1988—89. Mem.: ABA (vice chmn. antitrust sect., pvt. litigation com. 1987—89, chmn. FTC com. 1986), Forsyth Country Club, City Club Washington, Georgetown Club, Order of Coif. E-mail: cmitchell@verisign.com., Wgchamp@aol.com.

MITCHELL, WILLIAM J. academic administrator, architecture educator; BArch, U. Melbourne, Victoria, Australia, 1967; M of Environ. Design, Yale U., 1969; MA, U. Cambridge, Eng., 1977. Arch. Yuncken-Freeman Architects, Melbourne, Australia, 1967—68; asst. prof. architecture, urban design UCLA, 1970—74, head architecture, urban design program, 1973—77, assoc. prof. architecture, urban design, 1974—80, prof. architecture, urban design, program head', 1980—86; pres. The Urban Innovations Group, LA, 1973—74; founding ptnr. The Computer-Aided Design Group, Marina Del Rey, Calif., 1978—91; prof. architecture Harvard U., Cambridge, Mass., 1986—89, dir. Master in Design Studies Program, 1986—92, G. Ware and Edythe M. Travelstead prof. architecture, 1989—92; prof. architecture and media arts & sci. MIT, Cambridge, 1992—, dean Sch. of Architecture and Planning, 1992—2003, head media arts and scis. program, 2003—. Vis. critic Yale U., New Haven, 1970—75, Tulane U., New Orleans, 1981; lectr. dept. architecture U. Cambridge, England, 1978—80; vis. prof. U. Calif., Berkeley, 1982, Carnegie-Mellon U., Pitts., 1979—83, U. Sydney, NSW, Australia, 1985; disting. vis. scholar U. Adelaide, SA, Australia. Author: Computer-Aided Architecture Design, 1983, The Logic of Architecture: Design, Computation and Cognition, 1990, The Reconfigured Eye: Visual Truth in the Post-Photographic Era, 1992, City of Bits: Space, Pl., and the Infobahn, 1995, Me++: The Cyborg Self and the Networked City, 2003, e-topia: Urban Life Jim But Not as We Know It, 1999, Info. Tech. and Low-Income Communities, 1999; author: (with others) The Art of Computer Graphics Programming, 1987, The Poetics of Gardens, 1988, The Electronic Design Studio: Architectural Knowledge and Media in the Computer Era, 1990, Digital Design Media, 2d edit., 1991; contbr. numerous articles to profl. jour. Fellow: Royal Australian Inst. Architecture. Office: MIT Media Lab E15-401 77 Massachusetts Ave Cambridge MA 02139-4307

MITCHELL, WILLIAM MARVIN, pathology educator; b. Atlanta, Mar. 3, 1935; s. William Joseph and Marvin Eugenia (Peavy) M.; m. Shirley Ann Crowell, Dec. 22, 1959; children: Alexander James, Keith Townsend, Derek Loren. AS, Vanderbilt U., 1957, MD, 1960; PhD, Johns Hopkins U., 1966. Diplomate Am. Bd. Pathology. Asst. prof. microbiology and medicine Vanderbilt U., Nashville, 1966-70, assoc. prof. pathology, 1970-78, prof., 1978—. Med. dir. Specialized Assays, Nashville, 1981-91; med. dir. Vanderbilt Pathology Lab. Svcs., 1994—; med. dir. Home Health Care Am., 1998—; founder ActivBiotics, Inc., Boston, Genocyte, Inc., Nashville; cons. NIH, DuPont Co., Smith Kline, others. Patentee in field; contbr. articles to profl. jours. Bd. dirs. St. Augustine's Chapel, Nashville, 1981-86, Hemispherx Biopharma, Inc., Phila., 1998—; judge Regional Sci. and Engring. Fair, Nashville, 1985, 88; judge Internat. Sci. Engring. Fair, Nashville, 1992, Birmingham, 1994. Eleanor Roosevelt Internat. Cancer fellow Internat. Union Against Cancer, 1976-77; grantee NIH. Mem. AAAS, Am. Assn. Pathology, Am. Chem. Soc., Am. Soc. Biol. Chemists, Am. Soc. Microbiology, Internat. Acad. Pathology, Am. Soc. Interferon Rsch., Am. AIDS Soc., Sigma Xi. Episcopalian. Avocations: skiing, crafts, music. Office Phone: 615-322-3238. E-mail: bill.mitchell@vanderbilt.edu.

MITCHELSON, MARY SUE, lawyer; b. Joplin, Mo., Mar. 17, 1951; d. L. R. and Mildred (Mathes) M. BA, U. Kans., 1973; JD, Georgetown U., 1976. Asst. dean Georgetown U. Law Ctr., Washington, 1976-78; law clk. to Hon. Harold Greene U.S. Dist. Ct. D.C., Washington, 1978-79; trial atty. civil div. comml. litigation br. U.S. Dept. Justice, Washington, 1979-86, asst. dir. civil div. comml. litigation br., 1986-89; asst. general counsel Clarke Cons. Group, 1989-90; asst. dir., dep. dir. comml. litigation br. Civil Div., Dept. of Justice, 1990-91, 1991-95; dep. general counsel Office of the General Counsel, Office of Pers. Mgt., Washington, 1995-2000; asst. inspector gen. U.S. Dept. Edn., Washington, 2000—. Office: US Dept Edn DIG 330 C St NW Washington DC 20415-0001

MITCHEM, ALLEN P. lawyer; b. Burley, Idaho, Oct. 30, 1918; s. James Edgar and Adah Elizabeth (Allen) Mitchem; m. Katherine I. Webber, Aug. 21, 1993; children: Allen P., James E., Lowell E. AB, Ft. Hays State U., 1940; JD magna cum laude, Washburn U., 1947; LLM, Columbia U., 1948. Bar: Kans. 1947, Colo. 1949. Assoc. prof. Coll. Law, U. Denver, 1948—53; pvt. practice law Denver, 1953—60, 1963—; minority counsel interior and insular affairs com. U.S. Senate, Washington, 1961—62. Vis. lectr. Sch. Law, U. Colo., 1954, 57, 59; lectr. Sch. Law, U. Denver, 1953—63; arbitrator, Denver, 1965—. Contbr. articles to legal rev. Dist. gov. Civitan Internat., 1957—58, judge adv., 1958—59; pres. Denver Execs. Club, 1986—88; chmn. gen. bd. Ctrl. Christian Ch., 1963—65, 1975—76; trustee Endowment Assn. Ft. Hays State U., 1968—78; dir. Colo. Christian Home, Denver, 1974—80; pres. Denver Civitan Club, 1955—56; dir. Denver Area Coun. Chs., 1955, 1957. Capt. USMC, 1942—45. Recipient Alumni Achievement award, Ft. Hays State U., 1970. Mem.: ABA, Denver Bar Assn., Colo. Bar Assn. Home: 420 S Marion Pkwy Apt 2002 Denver CO 80209-5526 Personal E-mail: apmitchem@msn.com.

MITCHEM, CHERYL E. accounting educator; b. South Bend, Ind., June 24, 1947; d. Roy Francis and Marcella Evelyn (Chryst) Drake; m. Allen Pershing Mitchem, Jr., Nov. 28, 1969; children: Michael, Marlo, Megan, Melissa. BA, Tex. Christian U., 1969; MBA, San Diego State U., 1980; PhD, Va. Commonwealth U., 1990. CPA, Va.; cert. mgmt. acct. Vis. prof. acctg. Coll. William and Mary, Williamsburg, Va., 1986-88; adj. prof. acctg. Va. Commonwealth U., Richmond, 1988-89; asst. prof. acctg. Christopher Newport U., Newport News, 1989-91; asst. prof. Va. State U., Petersburg, 1991-93, chair acctg., 1993—2003, assoc. prof., 1998—, acting asst. dean Sch. Bus., 2004—. Contbr. articles to profl. jours. Treas., Greenfield Dragons Athletic Assn., Richmond, 1988-95. Mem. AICPA, Am. Acctg. Assn., Inst. Mgmt. Accts. Mem. Christian Ch. (Disciples Of Christ). Avocations: travel, reading, family activities. Office Phone: 804-524-5831.

MITCHENER, JOHN EDWARD, music educator, musician; b. Laurinburg, N.C., June 30, 1964; s. James Samuel and Sara (Carton) M. BM, N.C. Sch. Arts, Winston-Salem, 1986; MM organ, Eastman Sch. Music, Rochester, N.Y., 1989, MM harpsichord, 1994, D.Mus. Arts, 1995. Organist The Am. Cathedral in Paris, Paris, 1989; dir. music, organist Zion Episcopal Ch., Palmyra, NY, 1991—95; grad. asst. harpsichord Eastman Sch. Music, 1991—92, assoc. instr. organ cmty. edn. divsn., 1992—95; instr. organ Colgate Rochester Divinity Sch., Rochester, 1992—95; grad. tchg. asst. in organ Eastman Sch. Music, 1992—95, grad. tchg. asst. in baroque ensembles, 1994—95; assoc. prof. organ and coll. organist Salem College, Winston-Salem, NC, 1995—; Kenan prof. organ N.C. Sch. of the Arts, Winston-Salem, NC, 1995—. Organist St. Paul's Episc. Ch., Winston-Salem, NC, 2001—, Wesley Meml. United Meth. Ch., High Point, NC, 1996—2001. Musician: (classical organ recitals and concerts) Complete organ works of Johann Sebastian Bach, 2000—03 (Faculty Development Grant from North Carolina School of the Arts, 2001), concerts of Am. music performed througout Europe (Austria, France, Germany, Poland, and Switzerland), 2001, (organ concerts) organ music of Bach performed throughout Europe, 2000, concerts and master classes in USA and Europe, performances heard on Nat. Pub. Radio and Austrian Nat. Radio, —, collaborative artist for 5 CD recordings, —. Mem. exec. com. bd. trustees and chmn. music com. Moravian Music Found., Winston-Salem. Recipient organ competition winner, Music Tchrs. Assn., 1986, Nat. Winner nat. organ competition, Music Tchrs. Nat. Assn., 1986, Winner music competition, N.C. Music Tchrs. Assn. (so. divsn.), 1986, Winner 3rd prize, Dublin Internat. Organ Competition, 1990, Winner Gold Medal in harpsichord, Nat. Conservatory Rueil-Malmaison, France, 1990, Winner Prix d'Excellence in Organ, 1990, Winner Prix de Virtuosité, 1991. Mem.: Moravian Music Found. (pres., bd. trustees), Am. Guild of Organists (Winner AGO competition, Phila. 1987, dean Winston-Salem chpt. 1997—99, Winner organ competition Winston-Salem chpt. 1983). Avocations: golf, reading, running, walking, hiking. Office: NC Sch Arts 1533 S Main St Winston Salem NC 27117-2189 Office Phone: 336-631-1543, etx. 143. Business E-Mail: mitchenerj@ncarts.edu.

MITCHUM, CASSANDRA, poet, writer; b. Greensboro, N.C., June 11, 1950; m. Preston Mitchum Sr., Dec. 17, 1973; children: Preston Jr., Cynthia, Vanessa. Bus. cert., Monroe Bus. Inst., 1970. Receptionist, typist Royal Nat. Bank, N.Y.C., 1970-72, Metcalf & Eddie Engrs., N.Y.C., 1972-74; sec. Bendix Internat., N.Y.C., 1975-80; receptionist Chrysler Corp., N.Y.C., 1980-81; sec. Nat. Assn. Securities, Washington, 1981-83; word processor, sec. Lewis, Kominers & James, Counselors-at-Law, 1983-84, 86. Author numerous poems. Recipient Merit certificate World of Poetry, Sacramento, 1990, Editor's Choice award Nat. Libr. Poetry, 1996-97; named Golden Poet, World of Poetry, Sacramento, 1991; named to Internat. Poetry Hall of Fame, 1997; named one of Best Poets of 1997, 98, Outstanding Poet of 1998. Mem. Internat. Soc. Poets. Democrat. Penecostal. Home: Apt 25 11936 Beltsville Dr Beltsville MD 20705-3151

MITELMAN, BONNIE COSSMAN, editor, writer; b. Flint, Mich., Feb. 15, 1941; d. Maurice B. (dec.) and Frieda H. (Ragir) Cossman; m. Stanley D. Lelewer, Mar. 12, 1961 (div. 1969); children: Joanne, Stephen(dec.); m. Alan N. Mitelman, July 23, 1972; 1 child, Geoffrey. BA, Northwestern U., 1969; MA, Manhattanville Coll., 1977. Copywriter trainee Dancer-Fitzgerald-Sample, Inc., Chgo., 1956—60; advt. copywriter Spiegel, Inc., Chgo., 1961—63; freelance advt. and pub. rels. writer Chgo., N.Y.C., 1963—72; co-founder Mitelman & Assocs., Briarcliff Manor, NY, 1972—92, pub. rels. assoc., 1992—94, asst. dir. publ. rels., 1994—97; dir. internal comm. Anti-Defamation League, N.Y.C., 1997—. Adj. lectr., dept. history Mercy Coll., Dobbs Ferry, NY, 1979—85; contbr. articles N.Y. Times, Am. Experiences, Vol. II, Am. History Illustrated, Working Mother, Reform Judaism, 1977—. Author: Mothers Who Work: Stragtegies for Coping; mem. editl. bd.: Reform Judaism, 1977—. Mem.: Authors Guild, Women in Comm.

MITGANG, LEE DAVID, journalist, writer, educator, foundation administrator; b. N.Y.C., Nov. 12, 1949; s. Herbert and Shirley (Kravchick) Mitgang; m. Gina Saporito, June 17, 1979; 1 child, Caroline. BA in Polit. Sci., U. Mich., Ann Arbor, 1971; MS in History of Polit. Thought, London Sch. Econ., 1972. Corr. bus. and Wall Street, UPI, N.Y.C., 1972-74; bus. writer AP, N.Y.C., 1974-76, urban affairs writer, 1976-80, nat. edn. writer, 1980-91; sr. fellow Carnegie Found. for Advancement of Tchg., Princeton, NJ, 1992-97; pvt. practice cons., journalist Ridgewood, NJ, 1997-2000; dir. comm. Wallace Found., N.Y.C., 2000—, dir. editl. svcs., 2002—. Asst. dir. Hechinger Inst. Edn. and Media Tchrs. Coll., Columbia U., 1999—2000. Co-author: Building Community: A New Future for Architecture Education and Practice, 1996; prin. author: School Choice, 1992; author: Big Bird and Beyond: The New Media and The Markle Foundation, 2000; contbg. editor: Archtl. Record Mag., 1997—2001; mem. editl. bd. Reaching Today's Youth Jour., 1996—. Recipient John Hancock award for Excellence in Bus. Journalism, 1976, Gerald Loeb award for Disting. Bus. and Fin. Journalism, 1977, Sci.-in-Soc. award, Nat. Assn. Sci. Writers, 1989, Disting. Achievement award, Ednl. Press Assn., 1991. Mem.: Edn. Writers Assn. Home and Office: 216 Doremus Ave Ridgewood NJ 07450-4240 Office Phone: 212-251-9780. Business E-Mail: lmitgang@wallacefoundation.org.

MITRA, ATUL, management consultant, educator; s. Ratan Chand and Raj Mitra; m. Ranjana Mitra, July 13, 1987; children: Siddharth, Ariana Simran. BS in Elec. Engring., MREC, Jaipur, India, 1975—81; MTech in Sys. and Mgmt., Indian Inst. Tech., Delhi, 1983—86; PhD, U. Ark., Fayetteville, 1987—93. Engr., sr. engr. NTPC, Delhi, 1982—87; asst., assoc. prof., mgmt. Lyon Coll., Batesville, Ark., 1991—2000; assoc. prof., mgmt. U. N. Iowa, Cedar Falls, 2000—. Vis. scholar Sch. of Indsl. & Labor Rels., Cornell U., Ithaca, NY, 1998; dir., internat. bus. cert. U. N. Iowa, Cedar Falls, 2004—. Chairperson & mem. India Assn. N.E. Iowa, Cedar Falls, 2002. Recipient Citation of Excellence, ANBAR Mgmt. Intelligence, EMRELD, 1997, 1998. Mem.: Sigma Iota Epsilon, Cedar Valley SHRM, Acad. Mgmt. Office: Univ No Iowa Coll Bus Admin BUS 249 Cedar Falls IA 50614 E-mail: atul.mitra@uni.edu.

MITRA, SANJIT KUMAR, electrical and computer engineering educator; b. Calcutta, West Bengal, India, Nov. 26, 1935; came to U.S., 1958; MS in Tech., U. Calcutta, 1956; MS, U. Calif., Berkeley, 1960, PhD, 1962; D of Tech. (hon.), Tampere (Finland) U., 1987; Academician, Acad. Finland, 2000. Asst. engr. Indian Statis. Inst., Calcutta, 1956-58; from teaching asst. to assoc. Univ. Calif., Berkeley, 1958-62; asst. prof. Cornell U., Ithaca, N.Y., 1962-65; mem. tech. staff Bell Telephone Labs., Holmdel, N.J., 1965-67; prof. U. Calif., Davis, 1967-77, prof. elec. and computer engring. Santa Barbara, 1977—, chmn. dept. elec. and computer engring., 1979-82; dir. Ctr. for Info. Processing Rsch., 1993-96. Cons. Lawrence Livermore (Calif.) Nat. Lab., 1974-95; cons. editor Van Nostrand Reinhold Co., N.Y.C., 1977-88; mem. adv. bd. Coll. Engring. Rice U., Houston, 1986-89; mem. adv. coun. Rsch. Inst. for Math. and Computing Sci., U. Groningen, The Netherlands, 1995—; mem. adv. bd. Internat. Signal Processing Ctr., Tampere U. of Tech., Finland, 1997—; external assessor Faculty of Engring., U. Putra Malaysia, Serdang, 1997—2000. Author: Analysis and Synthesis of Linear Active Networks, 1969, Digital and Analog Integrated Circuits, 1980; co-editor: Modern Filter Theory and Design, 1973, Two-Dimensional Digital Signal Processing, 1978, Miniaturized and Integrated Filters, 1989, Multidimensional Processing of Video Signals, 1992, Handbook for Digital Signal Processing, 1993, Digital Signal Processing: A Computer-Based Approach, 1997, 2d edit., 2000, Nonuniform Discrete Fourier Transform and Its Signal Processing Applications, 1998, Digital Signal Processing Laboratory Using MATLAB, 1999, Nonlinear Image Processing, 2000. Named Disting. Fulbright Prof., Coun. for Internat. Exch. of Scholars, 1984, 1986, 1988, Disting. Sr. Scientist, Humboldt Found., 1989; recipient F.E. Terman award, 1973, award, AT&T Found., 1985, Edn. award, IEEE Circuits and Sys. Soc., 1988, Mac Van Valkenburg award, 1999, Golden Jubilee medal, 1999, Blumlein-Browne-Willans premium, IEE, 2000, F.E. Terman award, 1973, AT&T Found. award, 1985, McGraw-Hill/Jacob Millman award, Edn. Soc., 2001, Tech. Achievement award, IEEE Signal Processing Soc., 1996, Soc. award, Tech. Achievement award, European Assn. Signal Processing, 2001, Best Paper award, IEEE Transactions on Circuits and Sys. for Video Tech., 2002. Fellow: IEEE (Golden Jubilee medal 1999, Millennium medal 2000), AAAS, Internat. Soc. Optical Engring.; mem.: Acad. Engring. Mex., U.S. Nat. Acad. Engring., Norwegian Acad. Technol. Scis., Croatian Acad. Arts and Scis., Acad. of Finland, European Assn. for Signal Processing. Achievements include patents for two-port networks for realizing transfer functions; non-reciprocal wave translating device; discrete cosine transform-based image coding and decoding method; method and apparatus for multipath channel shaping; method for embedding and extracting digital data in images and videos. Office: Univ Calif Dept Elec Computer Eng Santa Barbara CA 93106

MITRANY, DEVORA, writer, editor; b. Oak Park, Ill., Mar. 20, 1947; d. John Joseph and Frances Elizabeth (Kirke) Lang. BA cum laude, Beloit Coll., 1969; postgrad., Boston U., 1971-72. Elem. and presch. tchr., Boston, Oak Park, Ill., 1969-72; regional adminstr. TRW Fin. Sys., Wellesley, Mass., 1972-76; mgr. mktg. comm. Computer Sharing Svcs., Denver, 1976-82; dir. corp. comm. Corp. Mgmt. Sys., Denver, 1982-85; sr. copywriter On-Line Software Internat., Ft. Lee, NJ, 1985-86; mgr. corp. comm. Health Mgmt. Sys., N.Y.C., 1986-89; dir. pub. rels. Am. Sephardi Fedn., 1989-92; pres. Mitrell Group, 1992-94; U.S. mktg. dir. Best of Israel, 1994-95; publs. specialist PCS Health Sys., Inc., 1995—98; sci. publs. mgr. AdvancePCS, 1998—2002, consulting med. editor, 2002—. Press release chmn. Nassau Region Hadassah, 1992—94; bd. dirs. Chabad Women, 1995—98, Companion Animal Assn. Ariz., 1999—2000. Dir. pub. rels. Bus. Roundtable Nat. Security, Colo., 1983—84; bd. dirs. Talia Hadassah, 1986—94, co-pres., 1990—92; v.p. edn. Long Beach Hadassah, 1992—94. Named Woman of the Yr., Talia Hadassah, 1993; recipient Nat. Leadership award, Long Beach Hadassah, 1991—92, Talia Hadassah, 1993—94, Vol. of Yr. award, Assisted Living Fedn. Am., 2004. Mem.: Am. Sephardi Fedn. (mem. edn. com. 1987—89), Colo. Conf. Communicators (Denver Advt. Fedn. liaison 1981—84), Denver Advt. Fedn. (bd. dirs. 1981—83, Alfie award 1984), Coun. Sci. Editors (mem. sponsorship com. 2000—, mem. program com. 2001—, chair 2002—), Am. Med. Writers Assn. (mem. biomedical communicators task force 2001—, chair 2003—). Jewish.

MITRE, BLIMA KIRMAYER, pathologist, educator; b. Romania, Aug. 15, 1942; came to U.S., 1968, naturalized, 1978; d. Moses and Regina Kirmayer; m. Ricardo J. Mitre, Oct. 7, 1967; children: Edward, Sandra, Marcie, Richard James. Grad., U. Mayor de San Simon, 1967. Intern Viedma Hosp., Cochabamba, Bolivia, 1967-68; resident in pathology Bapt. Meml. Hosp., Jacksonville, Fla., 1968-70; with Presbyn. Hosp., Pitts., 1970-72, Children's Hosp., Pitts., 1972-73; staff pathologist Passavant Hosp., 1990—; clin. asst. prof. pathology U. Pitts. Med. Sch., 1970—. Mem. ACMS, PMS, Internat. Acad. Pathology, Am. Soc. Clin. Pathologists, Coll. Am. Pathologists, Pa. Assn. Clin. Pathologists. Office: UPMC Passavant Hosp 9100 Babcock Blvd Pittsburgh PA 15237-5815 Office Phone: 412-367-6847. Personal E-mail: bmitre@comcast.net.

MITROVGENIS, JAMES WILLIAM, JR., journalist; b. McAlester, Okla., Feb. 15, 1950; s. James William Sr. and Kula Mitrovgenis; m. Brigitte Dunnebier. Student, U. Okla., 1968-72. Reporter McAlester Daily Dem., 1973—76; news editor Muskogee Phoenix, Okla., 1976—81; night copy editor Daily Oklahoman, Oklahoma City, 1981—86, night news editor, 1986—91, copy editor, 1991—. Mem. NRA, AP Okla. News Execs. (bd. dirs. 1987-89, 1st pl. page one layout award 1987, 2d pl. gen. excellence award 1987, 3d pl. page one layout award 1987, 2d pl. gen. excellence award 1986). Greek Orthodox. Avocations: travel, photography, stock market. Office: Daily Okla 9000 Broadway Ext Oklahoma City OK 73114-3799 Business E-Mail: jmitrovgenis@oklahoman.com.

MITRY, DARRYL JOSEPH, writer, educator; b. Pitts., Feb. 25, 1943; s. Joseph David and Lorraine Marion (Vialc) de Mitry; 1 child, Eden Michelle de Mitry. BA, Calif. State U., L.A., 1967; MA, U. So. Calif., 1968, DPhil, 1971. Pres. S.M.I. Corp., L.A., 1968-70; prof. Calif. State U., San Francisco, 1970-71, U. Redlands, Calif., 1971-73, West Coast U., San Diego, 1996-97; rsch. dir. U. Ky. Med. Ctr., Lexington, 1973-76; lectr. med. econs., dir. bur. bus., econs. San Diego State U., 1976-78, 88-90; pres. Crossover Corp., L.A., 1979-85; cons. dir. Mirch Assocs., Beverly Hills, Calif., 1986-94; pres. Writers Web Global Internet, 1997-99; prof. Nat. U., LaJolla, Calif., 1997—2002, chmn. dept. bus. Sch. Bus. and Tech., 1999-00; pres., CEO Space Market Devel., 1999—2002. Exec. cons. StereoMedia Inc., Burbank, Calif., 1992-94; advisor Internat. Distance Edn., teleconf.-computer Internet, Extended Studies Inst. and Coop. Global Alliance, Europe, Asia, Mid.-East, N.Am., Cen. Am., S.Am., 1997-2002; univ. lead MBA program, 1998-2001, lead internat. bus.-econs. studies, 1997-2002; coun. mem., rsch. cons., fellow Reforming Economies Rsch. Inst., St. Petersburg, Russia, 1998—2002; internat. advisor NEXUS, Paris, 1998-99; vis. prof. Inst. Econs. and Fin., Feodosia, Crimea, Ukraine, 2003-04; internat. diplomacy instr. Norwich Univ., Vt., 2004. Author: Profiles in Price Theory, 1972, Synoptic Guide in Political Economics, 1985, Strategic Initiatives, 1996; editor Bus. Inquiry jour., 1976-78; editor, co-author: Global Leadership in the 21st Century, 1998. Exec. dir. Nat. Living History Inst., San Diego, 1996; co-chair soc. club Am. Cancer Soc., San Diego, 1996; bd. dirs. Animal Rights Legal Fund, Mission Viejo, Calif., 1996. Recipient Golden Baton award San Diego Orch. Assn., 1985, Gallery Honor award Art Assn., San Diego, 1984; Fulbright scholar U.S. Dept. State, 2003-04. Mem. Omicron Delta Epsilon (Disting. Merit award 1971), Sigma Beta Delta (pres. 2000). Avocations: art exhibiting, sculpting, narrating tv and films. Home: 10840 Queen Ave La Mesa CA 91941-7124 Personal E-mail: economics_2000@yahoo.com.

MITSAKOS, CHARLES LEONIDAS, education educator, consultant; b. Lowell, Mass., Oct. 17, 1939; s. Leonidas A. and Vasiliki (Sampatakakis) M.; m. Stella Martakos, June 23, 1963; children: Charles L. Jr., Andria Estelle. BS in Edn., Lowell State Coll., 1961; EdM, Boston U., 1963, EdD, 1977. Tchr., team leader, social studies curriculum specialist Lexington (Mass.) Pub. Schs., 1961-67; social studies coord., cons. Chelmsford (Mass.) Pub. Schs., 1967-78; asst. supt. of schs. Andover (Mass.) Pub. Schs., 1978-83; supt. of schs. Winchester (Mass.) Pub. Schs., 1984-92; clin. faculty supr. Sch. Edn., Boston Coll., Chestnut Hill, Mass., 1992-93; prof. edn., chair dept. edn. Rivier Coll., Nashua, NH, 1993—. Ednl. cons. to schs. and sch. dists. in 15 states, U.S. V.I., U.S. Dept. Def. Dep. Schs. and Ministries of Edn., 1970—; facilitator Sch. Adminstrs. Leading with Tech. (SALT), Bill and Melinda Gates Found. funded project, 2002—; dir. Mid. Sch. Staff Devel. Inst. for Social Desegregation Program, Fairfield County, S.C., 1972; mem. staff, lectr. in team tchg. and social studies edn. NSF Insts., Stanford U., Ind. U., SUNY, Geneseo, Xavier U., U. NC, Boston U., 1968-75; sr. lectr. sch. adminstrn. and curriculum devel. Sch. Grad. Studies, Rivier Coll., 1977-93, numerous others. Author, gen. editor: (multimedia program for elem. sch.) The Family of Man Social Studies Program, 1971-77; co-author: (textbooks) America! America!, 1977, revised 2d edit., 1987, Ginn Social Studies, 1987; author: (workbook) America! America! Workbook, 1982, (textbook) Earth's Geography and Environment, 1991, others. Mem. Coun. Tchr. Edn. NH Dept. Edn., Fin. Com. and Steering Com. So. NH Sch. to Careers Partnership; mem., bd. dirs., past pres. Social Sci. Edn. Consortium; past chmn. task force on teenagers and religious edn. Greek Orthodox Archdiocese of North and South Am.; former trustee U. Lowell; chairperson affirmative action com., chairperson com. to oversee U. Lowell Rsch. Found.; former mem. ad hoc budget com. Town of Winchester; former mem. bd. dirs., chairperson nominating com. and search com. for resident dirs. Andover Com. for A Better Chance; fund-raising chairperson, mem. edn. com., former trustee, newsletter editor local ch. Recipient Disting. Alumni award U. Lowell, Coll. of Edn., 1987. Democrat. Greek Orthodox. Avocations: writing travel articles, mosaic iconography, travel, reading. Office: Rivier Coll 420 Main St Nashua NH 03060-5086 Office Phone: 603-897-8582. E-mail: cmitsakos@rivier.edu.

MITSCHER, LESTER ALLEN, chemist, educator; b. Detroit, Aug. 20, 1931; s. Lester and Mary Athelda (Pounder) M.; m. Betty Jane McRoberts, May 29, 1953; children: Katrina, Kurt, Mark. BS, Wayne U., 1953, PhD, 1958. Rsch. scientist, group leader Lederle Labs., Pearl River, NY, 1958-67; prof. Ohio State U., Columbus, 1967-75, U. Kans., Lawrence, 1975—, chmn. dept. medicinal chemistry, 1975-92; intersearch prof. Victorian Coll. of Pharmacy, Monash U., Melbourne, Australia, 1975—. Cons. NIH, Am. Cancer Soc., Abbott Labs., Pfizer Labs. Author: (with D. Lednicer) The Organic Chemistry of Drug Synthesis, Vol. 1, 1976, Vol. 2, 1980, Vol. 3, 1984, Vol. 4, 1990, The Chemistry of the Tetracycline Antibiotics, 1978; co-author: The Green Tea Book, 1997; editor-in-chief Medicinal Research Reviews, 1995-99; contbr. over 250 articles to profl. jours. Recipient Disting. Alumnus award Sch. Pharmacy, Wayne State U., 1980, 97, Rsch. Achievement award Acad. Pharm. Scis., 1980, 97, Volweiler Rsch. award Am. Assn. Colls. Pharmacy, 1985, Higuchi-Simmons award U. Kans., 1986. Fellow AAAS; mem. Am. Soc. Pharmacognosy (pres. 1992-93), Am. Chem. Soc. (former chmn. councilor medicinal chemistry divsn., Bristol-Myers Smissman rsch. award 1989, Med. Chemistry award 2000), Japanese Antibiotics Assn., Soc. Heterocyclic Chemistry, Internat. Union of Pure and Applied Chemistry (commr. medicinal chemistry divsn.), Internat. Orgn. for Chemistry in Developing Countries (steering com.). Presbyterian. Office: Dept Medicinal Chemistry U Kans Lawrence KS 66045 Business E-Mail: lmitscher@ku.edu.

MITSCHERLICH REYNOLDS, A. CHRISTINE, conservator; d. Eilhard Mitscherlich and Anna Heiman. BFA. Owner, restorer/conservator works of art Restoration Studio, Glens Falls, NY, 1976—. Lectr. in field. Contbr. articles to profl. jours. Mem.: Internat. Conservation Coun. Achievements include research in new methods and materials for invisable repair of antique porclain, pottery, china and related wares. Office: Restoration Studio PO Box 3440 Glens Falls NY 12801 E-mail: anna98@nycap.rr.com.

MITSEFF, CARL, lawyer; b. Detroit, Nov. 16, 1928; s. Frank H. and Katherine (Schaffer) M.; m. Phyllis Schlitters, June 28, 1952; children: C. Randall, Bradley Scott, Julie, Emily, Faye. BS, Wayne State U., 1952, LL.B., 1955. Bar: Mich. 1956. Practiced in Detroit, 1956—; staff atty. Burroughs Corp., 1955-60; mem. firm LeVasseur, Mitseff, Egan & Capp, 1960-80, Mitseff & Baril, 1980-85, Fitzgerald, Hodgman, Cox, Cawthoren & McMahon, 1986-90, Cox & Hodgman, 1990—. Spl. asst. atty. gen. State of Mich.; lectr. in field. Named to Mich. Workers Compensation Hall of Fame, 2000. Mem. ABA, State Bar Mich., Internat. Assn. Ins. Counsel, Internat. Assn. Indsl. Accident Bds. and Commns., Detroit Athletic Club (bd. dirs.), Beavers (pres.), Lochmoor Club, Grosse Pointe Yacht Club, Pi Kappa Alpha, Delta Theta Phi. Home: 612 N Brys Dr Grosse Pointe Woods MI 48236-1247 Office: 1001 Woodward Ave Ste 1000 Detroit MI 48226-1904 Office Phone: 313-963-3210. Personal E-mail: c.mitseff@aol.com.

MITSELMAKHER, GUENAKH, physics educator, researcher; b. Vilnius, Lithuania, Dec. 5, 1945; arrived in U.S., 1991; s. Viktoras and Anna (Bannikova) M.; m. Antonina Lavrova, Aug. 22, 1970; children: Irina, Victor. M Physics, Moscow State U., 1968; PhD in Physics, Joint Inst. Nuclear Rsch., Dubna, Russia, 1974; DS, USSR State Com. Higher Edn., Moscow, 1987. Staff scientist Joint Inst. for Nuc. Rsch., Dubna, Russia, 1968-91, dept. head, 1983-91, dep. dir. lab., 1987-89; staff scientist Superconducting Supercollider Lab., Dallas, 1991-94, Fermi Nat. Accelerator Lab., Batavia, Ill., 1994-98; prof. physics U. Fla., Gainesville, 1995—, dir. Inst. for High Energy Physics and Astrophysics, 2000—, disting. prof. physics, 2004—. Mem. adv. com. Program Fundamental Nuc. Physics, Ministry of Sci. of Russian Fedn., Moscow, 1993-2000; mem. steering com. compact muon solenoid CMS, experiment European Ctr. for Nuc. Rsch., CERN, Geneva, 1997—; cons. to dir. Joint Inst. Nuc. Rsch., Dubna, 2000—. Contbr. over 200 articles to profl. publs. Recipient Commemorative medal, Faculty of Math. and Physics, Charles U., Prague, 2003. Fellow: Am. Phys. Soc.; mem.: AAAS. Achievements include contributions to physics of pions and muons, study of electroweak interactions, particle detectors development. Home: 4929 SW 95th Ter Gainesville FL 32608-4189 Office: U Fla Dept Physics Gainesville FL 32611 E-mail: mitselmakher@phys.ufl.edu.

MITSTIFER, DOROTHY IRWIN, honor society administrator; b. Gaines, Pa., Aug. 17, 1932; d. Leonard Robert and Laura Dorothy (Crane) Irwin; m. Robert Mitchell Mitsifer, June 17, 1956 (dec. Aug. 1984); children: Kurt Michael, Brett Robert. BS, Mansfield U., 1954; MEd, Pa. State U., 1972, PhD, 1976. Cert. home economist. Tchr. Tri-County High Sch., Canton, Pa., 1954-56, Loyalsock Twp. Sch. Dist., Williamsport, Pa., 1956-63; exec. dir. Kappa Omicron Phi, Williamsport, Pa., 1964-86, Kappa Omicron Phi, Omicron Nu, Haslett, Mich., 1986-90, Kappa Omicron Nu, East Lansing, Mich., 1990—. Prof. continuing edn. Pa. State U., University Park, 1976-80; prof. Mansfield (Pa.) U., 1980-86, pres.'s intern, 1984-86. Editor Kappa Omicron Nu Forum, 1986—; contbr. articles to profl. jours. Pres., bd. dirs. Profl. Devel. Ctr. Adv. Bd., Vocat. Edn., Pa. State U., 1980-86. Mem. ASCD, Am. Home Econs. Assn., Mich. Home Econs. Assn. (exec. dir. 1986-96), Am. Vocat. Assn., Am. Soc. Assn. Execs., Assn. Coll. Honor Socs. (sec.-treas. 1976—), Coll. Edn. Alumni Soc. Pa. State U. (pres. 1986-88, bd. dirs. 1980-90), Kappa Delta Pi. Avocations: sewing, camping, fishing. Home: 1425 Somerset Close St East Lansing MI 48823-2435 Office: Kappa Omicron Nu 4990 Northwind Dr Ste 140 East Lansing MI 48823-5031 E-mail: dmitstifer@kon.org.

MITTAL, SUSHIL, religious studies educator; b. Guelph, Ont., Can., Mar. 4, 1967; s. Khyali Ram and Maya Devi Mittal; m. Ritu Agrawal, Jan. 14, 1975; children: Ankur, Aditi. BA, McGill U., Montreal, Can., 1990; MA, Carleton U., Ottawa, Can., 1993; PhD, U. Montreal, Can., 1998. Vis. asst. prof. religion U. Fla., Gainesville, 1998—99; asst. prof. religion Millikin U., Decatur, Ill., 1999—2002, Griswold disting. prof. religion, asst. prof. religion, 2002—. Dir. Internat. Inst. Indian Studies, St. Hyacinthe, Que., Canada, 1994—2004, World Heritage Press Inc, St. Hyacinthe, Que., Canada, 1995—2001; rsch. assoc. Ctr. for the Advanced Study Am. Instns. and Social Movements, Stendhal U., Grenoble, France, 2000—; coord. Gandhi studies program Millikin U., Decatur, 2001—; advisor Encyclopedia of Asia, 2000—02, Dialogue Films, Va., 2002—; mem. Soc. Hindu-Christian Book Award Com., 1997—99. Editor: (book) Development and Change in India, The Hindu World, Religions of South Asia, Surprising Bedfellows: Hindus and Muslims in Medieval and Early Modern India, Handbook for the Study of Hinduism, (journal) Internat. Jour. Hindu Studies, (monograph series) Studies in Religion and Theory, (paper series) Hindu Studies; mem. editl. bd.: Comparative Philosophy and Religion book series, 2002—. Grantee, Infinity Found., 2002, ASIANetwork-Freeman Fellowship, 2000, Am. Acad. Religion, 1999—2000; fellow, Social Scis. and Humanities Rsch. Coun. Can., 1993—97, summer fellow, Shastri Indo-Can. Inst., 1990. Mem.: Soc. for Asian and Comparative Philosophy (sec.-treas.), Am. Acad. Religion. Office: Millikin Univ 1184 West Main St Decatur IL 62522-2084 E-mail: smittal@mail.millikin.edu.

MITTE, ROY F. finance company executive; BS, S.W. Tex. State U., 1953, MEd, 1956. Founder Fin. Industries Corp., Austin, 1972, chmn., CEO, 1985. Establisher Roy F. and Joann Cole Mitte Found. Scholarship program S.W. Tex. State U., 1997. Recipient Disting. Alumnus award S.W. Tex. State U., 1982. Office: Financial Industries Corp 6500 River Pl Blvd Bldg 1 Austin TX 78730-1123

MITTEL, JOHN J. economist, corporate executive; b. L.I., N.Y. s. John and Mary (Leidolf) M.; 1 child, James C. BBA, CUNY. Rschr. econs. dept. McGraw Hill & Co., N.Y.C.; mgr., asst. to pres., Indsl. Commodity Corp., J. Carvel Lange Inc., and J. Carvel Lange Internat., Inc., N.Y.C., 1956-64, corp. sec., 1958-86, v.p., 1964-80, exec. v.p., 1980-86; pres. I.C. Investors Corp., N.Y.C., 1972—, I.C. Pension Adv., Inc., N.Y.C., 1977—. Bd. dir. several corps.; plan adminstr., trustee Combined Indsl. Commodity Corp. and J. Carvel Lange Inc. Pension Plan, 1962-86, J. Carvel Lange Internat. Inc. Profit Sharing Trust, 1969-86, Combined Indsl. Commodity Corp. and J. Carvel Lange Inc. Employees Profit Sharing Plan, 1977-86. Co-author: How Good a Sales Profit Are You, 1961, The Role of the Economic Consulting Firm. Mem. grad. adv. bd. Bernard M. Baruch Coll., CUNY, 1971-72. Mem. Conf. Bd., Am. Statis. Assn., Newcomen Soc. N.Am., Union League (N.Y.C.). Office: 10633 Saint Andrews Rd Boynton Beach FL 33436-4714

MITTELSTADT, MARK, news service executive; Bur. chief AP, Trenton, N.J., 1998—. Office: Assoc Press 50 W State St Ste 114 Trenton NJ 08608-1220

MITTELSTAEDT, ARTHUR HOWARD, JR., educational educator; b. N.Y.C., Sept. 25, 1936; m. Sue Carol Olsen, 1962; children: Kurt Arthur, Karen Maria. BS, Syracuse U., 1958; MPA, NYU, 1963, EdD, 1977. Self-employed landscape designer N.Y. State, 1954-58; asst. landscape architect N.Y.C. Housing Authority, 1959; landscape architect Nassau County Dept. Public Works, 1959-62, Office Joseph Gangemi, N.Y.C., 1959; landscape architect, planning cons. Urban Planning Assocs., Port Washington, N.Y., 1960—, Planning Assocs., Mineola, N.Y., 1961—. Chmn. bd. P.A. Edn. and Recreations Cons., Inc., leisure systems planner, Hempstead, Bohemia and Ronkonkoma, N.Y., 1966—; adj. asst. prof. NYU, 1965-70, Hunter Coll., 1971, So. Conn. State Coll., 1975-77; prof. Merrimack Valley C.C., 1973; assoc. prof. C.W. Post Ctr., L.I. U., 1978-85; participant confs. in field. Contbr. numerous articles, reports to profl. publs. Exec. bd. Nassau County coun. Boy Scouts Am., 1978-84; usher, vestryman St. Stephen's Epis. Ch., Port Washington, 1975-80; corp. bd. dirs. Nassau-Suffolk YMCA, 1975-78; trustee Dikaia Found., 1977-80; trustee Sci. Mus. of L.I. Health and Safety Comm. Nat. Boy Scouts of Am.; chair cmty. safety divsn. Nat. Safety Coun. Capt. USAR, 1958-65. Disting. fellow N.Y. State Recreation and Park Soc. (chmn. various coms. 1973—, pres. 1983-84); mem. Am. Soc. Landscape Architects, Am. Inst. Cert. Planners, Coun. Park and Recreation Cons. (pres.), Nat. Park and Recreation Assn., Comml. Recreation and Tourism Soc. (pres. 1992 and 1998), AAHPER (trustee nat. found. 1974-76), Nassau Recreation, Park and Conservation Soc. (chmn. civic affairs com. 1970-84; profl., presdl. and hon. mention awards 1963-83), recipient numerous nat. awards. Office: Planning Assocs 39 Shadyside Ave Port Washington NY 11050-2416

MITTELSTAEDT, JANET RUGEN, music educator, composer; b. Port Washington, N.Y., Mar. 30, 1941; d. Chester Davis and Harriet Helen (Goodman) Rugen; m. Ronald Edward Mittelstaedt, Aug. 24, 1963; children: Edward D., Amy C. Leimbach, Thomas A. BS in Edn., Bucknell U., 1963; BA in Music, Marylhurst U., 1984; MM in Composition, U. Portland, 1993. Nat. cert. in piano and composition Music Tchrs. Nat. Assn. Tchr. 6th grade Spring Branch Sch. Dist., Houston, 1964-66; piano tchr. Houston, 1964-66, Pitts., 1967-74, Portland, Oreg., 1978—; composition tchr., 1988—. Composer: Solo Snips, 1991, Splashes of Color, 1992, Sonatina for Youth, 1993, Fabric and Frills, 1994, Beehive, 2002, Animal Antics, 2004. Pianist, music coord. Evergreen Presbyn. Ch., Portland, 1994—2000, dir. children's mus., 1996, 1997; youth choir accompanist First Presbyn. Ch., Portland, 2003—. Recipient award, Ernest Bloch Composers Symposium, 1993, spl. awards, ASCAP, 1994, 1995, 1997, 1998, 1999, 2000, 2001, 2002. Mem.: Oreg. Music Tchrs. Assn. (chair Portland program 1999—2001, Portland composition 1998—99, state composition 1992—95, chair Portland ensemble 1992—94, chair Pt. syllabus 1980s, music theory clinician 1980s, music composition clinician 1990—, composition adjudicator 1990—, syllabus adjudicator 2002—, Composer of Yr. 1994), Oreg. Fedn. Music Clubs (chair composition 1980s). Republican. Presbyterian. Avocations: reading, travel, poetry. Home: 4485 NW 187th Ave Portland OR 97229-2911 E-mail: JanRM@worldnet.att.net.

MITTELSTET, STEPHEN, academic administrator; Student, Frank Phillips C.C.; BA summa cum laude, McMurry Coll., 1967; PhD in Higher Edn. Adminstrn./English, U. Tex., 1972. Tchr. adult basic edn. and GED prep. U. Tex., Austin; instr. McMurry Coll., Abilene, Tex., others. Grad. Leadership Dallas, 1978; founder Leadership Richardson, 1985; chair, pres., fund-raising chair Rotary, YMCA, YWCA; bd. dirs. Nat. Inst. Leadership Devel. Mem.: Tex. Higher Edn. Coord. Bd., Continuous Quality Improvement Network, Cmty. Coll. Humanities Assn., Am. Assn. Cmty. Colls. Office: 12800 Abrams Rd Dallas TX 75243-2173

MITTEMEYER, BERNHARD THEODORE, urology and surgery educator; arrived in U.S., 1944, naturalized; BS in Biology, Moravian Coll., 1952, LLD (hon.), 1982; MD, Temple U., 1956; DSc, William Jewell Coll., 1985. Diplomate Am. Bd. Urology, Am. Bd. Quality Assurance and Utilization Rev. Physicians. Rotation intern Santa Barbara (Calif.) Cottage and County Hosps., 1956—57; advanced through grades from capt. to lt. gen. U.S. Army, 1957—81; resident in gen. surgery Fitzsimons Army Med. Ctr., Denver, 1959—61; resident in urol. surgery Tripler Army Med. Ctr., Honolulu, 1962—65; asst. chief urol. surgery svc. urol. residency tng. program Walter Reed Army Med. Ctr., Washington, 1965—68, 1971—74, chief urol. surgery svc. and urol. residency tng. program, 1974—77, chief dept. surgery, 1976—77, comdg. gen., 1980—81; surgeon gen. Dept Army, Washington, 1981—85; ret., 1985—86; sr. v.p., corp. med. dir. Whittaker Health Svcs., L.A., 1985—2002; prof. urology and surgery Tex. Tech U., Lubbock, 1986—, exec. v.p. Health Scis. Ctr., 1986—96; interim dean Tex. Tech U. Sch. Medicine, Lubbock, 1988—90, interim dean, 1995—96; provost Tex. Tech U., Lubbock, 1988—96. Clin. assoc. prof. urology George Washington U. Sch. Medicine, Washington, 1974—85; clin. prof. surgery Uniformed Svcs. U. Health Scis., Bethesda, Md., 1976—; vis. prof., guest lectr. urology U. Mo., U. Pitts., Korea U., Pa. State U., U. Mass., U. Va., Wake Forest U., Armed Forces Inst. Pathology, Walter Reed Army Inst. Rsch., 1975—; ctrl. com. of pub.-acad. liaison Tex. Dept. Mental Health and Mental Retardation, 1990—; managed health care adv. com. ex. Dept. Criminal Justice, 1993—96; presenter in field. Contbr. articles to profl. jours. Trustee Moravian Coll., 1982—86; bd. dirs. Sci. Spectrum, Lubbock, 1988—, Lubbock Symphony Orch., 1989—92, Lubbock Conv. and Visitors Bur., 1991—93. Decorated D.S.M., Legion of Merit with oak leaf cluster, DFC, Bronze Star with V device, Air medal with oak leaf cluster; recipient Comenius award, Moravian Coll., 1978, Founders medal, Assn. Mil. Surgeons, 1978, Alumni Achievement award in health policy, Temple U. Sch. Medicine, 1988. Fellow: ACS, Am. Coll. Quality Assurance and Utilization Rev. Physicians, Am. Coll. Physician Execs.; mem.: AMA (ho. of dels. 1981—85), South Ctrl. Sect. Am. Urol. Assn., Lubbock-Crosby-Garza County Med. Soc. (armed svcs. com. 1988—96), Tex. Med. Assn. (cons. coun. on med. edn. 1987—96), Assn. U.S. Army, Soc. Med. Cons. to Armed Forces, Am. Acad. Med. Dirs., Uniformed Svcs. U. Surg. Assocs., Soc. U. Urologists, Soc. Govt. Svc. Urologists, Am. Urol. Assn., Lubbock C. of C. Home: PO Box 65285 Lubbock TX 79464-5285 Office: Tex Tech U Health Sci Ctr Med Office Plz 3502 9th St Ste 260 Lubbock TX 79415-5305 E-mail: bmittemeyer@cox.net.

MITTEN, DAVID GORDON, classical archaeologist; b. Youngstown, Ohio, Oct. 26, 1935; s. Joe Atlee and Helen Louise (Boyd) M.; children: Claudia Antonia Sabina, Eleanor Elizabeth. BA, Oberlin Coll., 1957; MA in Classical Archaeology, Harvard U., 1958, PhD in Classical Archaeology, 1962. From instr. dept. fine arts to assoc. prof. Harvard U., Cambridge, Mass., 1962-69, James Loeb prof. classical art and archaeology, 1969—; curator ancient art Harvard U. Art Mus., Cambridge, 1976-96, George M.A. Hanfmann curator ancient art, 1996—. Assoc. dir. Harvard-Cornell Sardis Expdn., 1976—; Whitehead vis. prof. archaeology Am. Study of Classical Studies, Athens, Greece, 1990-91. Author: (with S.F. Doeringer) Master Bronzes from the Classical World, 1967; Classical Bronzes: Mus. Art, RISD, 1975, (with Arielle P. Kozloff) The Gods Delight: The Human Figure in Classical Bronze, Cleve. Mus. Art, 1988. Woodrow Wilson fellow Harvard U., 1958; Fulbright fellow Am. Sch. Classical Studies at Athens, 1959-60; Archaeol. Inst. Am. Olivia James fellow, 1969-70; John Simon Guggenheim Found. fellow, 1976-77. Mem. Archaeol. Inst. Am., Assn. Field Archaeology (co-founder), Am. Schs. Oriental Rsch., Brit. Sch. Archaeology (Athens, Greece), Am. Numismatic Soc. Office: Sackler Mus 316 Harvard Univ 485 Broadway Cambridge MA 02138-3845 E-mail: mitten@fas.harvard.edu.

MITTENDORF, ROBERT, physician, epidemiologist; b. Ironton, Ohio, Aug. 6, 1943; s. Robert William and Martha Jane (Whitley) M.; m. Marguerite Jean Herschel, Nov. 10, 1979; children: Jeffrey David, Robert William II, Inga. BS, Ohio State U., 1966; MD, U. Ky., 1974; MPH, Harvard U., 1987, D Pub. Health, 1991. Diplomate Am. Bd. Ob-Gyn. Attending physician St. Margaret's Hosp., Boston, 1977-87; chief of surgery Winthrop (Mass.) Hosp., 1986-88; project dir., collaborative breast cancer study Harvard U., Boston, 1989-91; dir. Office Clin. Rsch. Tufts Sch. Medicine, Boston, 1991-92; dir. health studies, dept. ob-gyn. U. Chgo., 1992-99; prof. Loyola U. Med. Ctr., Maywood, Ill., dir. divsn. gen. ob-gyn, 2000—. Mem. sci. adv. com. anti-epileptic drugs in pregnancy registry Mass. Gen. Hosp., Boston, 1997—; cons. Nat. Ctrs. for Disease Control and Prevention, Atlanta, 1994; bd. dirs. U. Chgo. Health Plan, Chgo., Quadrangle Faculty Club, U. Chgo.; manuscript reviewer The Lancet, 1998. Author: Control of Transmissible Diseases in Health Care, 1995; contbr. articles to profl. jours. Med. dir. Cambridge Econ. Opportunity Com., 1977-78. Capt. USAF, 1966-70. Mem. AMA, Soc. Maternal Fetal Medicine, Soc. Epidemiol. Rsch. Democrat. Achievements include devel. of a linear regression model that permits the more precise determination of the estimated date of confinement in pregnant women (Mittendorf-Williams Rule); discovery that strenuous phys. activity is associated with a reduced risk of breast cancer, using a multivariable logistic regression model. Prin. investigator of the MAGnet Trial (magnesium and neurologic endpoints randomized control trial) to determine if using antenatal magnesium sulfate is associated with the prevention of severe cerebral palsy. Through statis. meta-analysis, discovered that certain prophylactic antibiotics are highly efficacious in preventing the serious infections associated with total abdominal hysterectomy. Home: 5634 S Woodlawn Ave Chicago IL 60637-1623 Office: Loyola U Med Ctr 2160 S 1st Ave Maywood IL 60153-3304 E-mail: rmitten@lumc.edu.

MITTERAND, HENRI C. education educator, writer; b. Vault-De-Lugny, Yonne, France, Aug. 7, 1928; arrived in U.S., 1989; s. Joseph and Helene (Dangauthier) Mitterand; m. Helene T. D'Afflitto, Dec. 24, 1955; children: Marie-Helene, Jacques-Olivier. Lic., U. Paris, 1969, Maitrise, 1950, Agregation, 1951, PhD, 1969; degree (hon.), U. Athens, 1997. From asst. to assoc. prof. U. Besancon, France, 1957-65; assoc. prof. U. Reims, France, 1965-68; prof. U. Paris 8, 1968-78, U. Paris 3, 1978-90, Columbia U., N.Y.C., 1990—. Vis. prof. Stanford U, 1966, U. Toronto, Canada, 1970—93, U. Pa., 1999; editl. cons., Paris, 1971—; mem. numerous adv. bds. in field. Editor: (book) Zola, 5 Vols., 1959—67 (award, 1968), Zola, 15 Vols., 1970; author: Le Discours du roman, 1980, L'Illusion réaliste, 1994, Zola et le Naturalisme, 1986, Le Regard et le Signe, 1987, Le roman á l'oeuvre, 1998, Zola I, 1999, Zola II, 2001, Zola III, 2002. Decorated Officer Palmes Acads., France, Chevalier de la Legion d'Honneur France, Grand Prix de la Ville de Paris, Commandeur des Arts et des Lettres France; recipient Prix de l'Academie Française. Mem.: Soc. Fellows/Columbia U., Acad. du Morvan, Inst. Pierre Larousse, Soc. des Amis de Zola (pres. 1990—), Royal Soc. Can. Avocations: sailing, music, films, reading. Office: Columbia U Broadway/116th St W New York NY 10027 E-mail: hm12@columbia.edu.

MITTERMILLER, JAMES JOSEPH, lawyer; b. Washington, Apr. 13, 1953; s. Jack and Alice Marie (Froeba) M.; m. Elizabeth Gaillard Simons, June 23, 1979; children: Samuel Stoney, Paul Andrew, Laurie Alice, Claire Mary. Student, U. Heidelberg, 1973-74; BA, Claremont McKenna Coll., 1975; JD, U. Calif. Berkeley, 1978. Bar: Calif., U.S. Dist. Ct. (so., ctrl. and ea. dists.) Calif., U.S. Ct. Appeals (9th cir.), U.S. Supreme Ct. Assoc. Sheppard, Mullin, Richter & Hampton, L.A., 1978-86, ptnr., 1986—. Panelist Calif. Continuing Edn. of Bar, L.A. and San Diego, 1984—. Dir. Legal Aid Soc. of San Diego, 1990—, pres., 1998-2000; bd.dirs., LaJolla YMCA, 2001—. Recipient Wiley Manuel Pro Bono award Calif. State Bar, 1992, 2001. Mem. Assn. Bus. Trial Lawyers (bd. dirs. 1998-2001), Am. Inns of Ct., Claremont McKenna Coll. Alumni Assn. San Diego (bd. dirs.). Avocations: swimming, surfing. Office: Sheppard Mullin Richter & Hampton 501 W Broadway Fl 19 San Diego CA 92101-3536

MITTL, RAINER N. ophthalmologist; b. Munich, West Germany, Mar. 19, 1939; came to U.S., 1965; s. Joseph and Maria (Schwickert) M.; m. Janice J. Janoski, June 28, 1970. MD, U. Munich, 1964. Resident in ophthalmology N.Y. Med. Coll., 1967-70; fellow Johns Hopkins Hosp., 1972-73; practice medicine, specializing in ophthalmology N.Y.C., 1973—. Mem. staff Columbia-Presbyn. Med. Ctr. Mem. AMA, ACS, Am. Acad. Ophthalmology, Internat. Coll. Surgeons, Am. Soc. Retina Specialist, N.Y. Athletic club, Univ. Club. Office: Suite 314 Edward S Harkness Eye Inst Columbia-Presbyn Med Center 635 W 165th St New York NY 10032 Office Phone: 212-305-5030. E-mail: MITTLOPHNY@aol.com.

MITTLEBERG, ERIC MICHAEL, pharmaceutical executive; b. NYC, Nov. 7, 1951; s. Irving Ralph and Rose (Schnieder) M.; m. Jane Susan Baumoehl, Dec. 25, 1977; children: Scott, Alyson, Lauren. BS in Pharmacy, St. Johns U., Jamaica, N.Y., 1974, MS in Ind. Pharmaceutics, 1978, PhD in Pharmaceutics, 1982. Registered pharmacist, N.Y. Assoc. scientist Hoffmann-LaRoche Inc., Nutley, N.J., 1974-78; dept. head process improvement Lederle Labs, Pearl River, N.Y., 1978-83; mgr. mfg. devel. Key Pharm., Miami, Fla., 1983-86; dir. prodn. and tech. svcs. Schering Labs, Miami, 1986-89; sr. dir. pharm. devel./tech. svcs. worldwide R.W. Johnson Pharm. Rsch. Inst., Raritan, N.J., 1989-97; v.p. sci./med. affairs Ivax Corp., 1997—. Mem. Internat. Soc. Pharm. Engrs., Acad. Pharm. Sci., Am. Pharm. Assn. Office: IVAX Pharm Inc 140 Legrand Ave Northvale NJ 07647-2403 Business E-Mail: eric_mittleberg@ivax.com.

MITTLER, DIANA (DIANA MITTLER-BATTIPAGLIA), music educator, administrator, pianist; b. N.Y.C., Oct. 19, 1941; d. Franz and Regina (Schilling) Mittler; m. Victor Battipaglia, Sept. 5, 1965 (div. 1982). BS, Juilliard Sch., 1962, MS, 1963; DMA, Eastman Sch. Music, 1974. Choral dir. William Cowper Jr. H.S. and Springfield Gardens Jr. H.S., Queens, NY, 1963-68; coord. music Flushing H.S., Queens, 1968-79; asst. prin. music Bayside H.S., Queens, 1979-86; assoc. prof. music Lehman Coll., CUNY, 1986-87, prof., 1987—, choral dir., 1986—. Cons. ednl. projects New World Records, 1987—; ednl. cons. Flushing Coun. on Culture and the Arts; cons. Sta. WNET; assoc. condr. Queens Borough-Wide Chorus, 1964-70; pianist, founder Con Brio Chamber Ensemble, 1978; faculty So. Vt. Music Festival, 1979-83; soloist with N.Y. Philharm., 1956; solo and chamber music appearances; examiner N.Y.C. Bd. Edn. Bd. Exams., 1985—. Author: 57 Lessons for

the H.S. Music Class, 1983, Franz Mittler: Austro-American Composer, Musician and Humorous Poet, 1993; contbr. articles to music publs.; performance Internat. Summer acad. Mozarteum, Salzburg, Austria, 1995, Weill Recital Hall, 1996, Merkin Hall, 1997, Herbert von Karajan Centrum, Vienna, Austria, 1998, rec. Franz Mittler. Lieder, 1994. Choral dir., accompanist various charitable, religious, mil., civic holiday functions. N.Y. State Regents scholar, 1958-62; scholarships Juilliard Sch. and Eastman Sch. Music; recipient Excellence in Tchg. award, 1993, Prism award, 1996. Mem. Am. Choral Dirs. Assn., Music Edn. Nat. Conf., Golden Key Soc. Democrat. Home: 10857 66th Ave Forest Hills NY 11375-2247 Office: Lehman Coll Music Dept Bedford Pk Blvd W Bronx NY 10468 Office Phone: 718-960-8457. E-mail: dianamittler@aol.com.

MITZNER, KENNETH MARTIN, electrical engineering consultant; b. Bklyn., May 7, 1938; s. Louis Bernard and Dora (Sandler) M.; m. Ruth Maria Osorio, Dec. 26, 1968; children: Camille Lorena Mitzner Zeiter, Esther Jeannette Mitzner Lin, Sharon Michelle Mitzner Mentkowski. BS, MIT, 1958; MS, Calif. Inst. Tech., 1959, PhD, 1964. Mem. tech. staff Hughes Aircraft, Malibu, Calif., 1959-64; prin. engr. B-2 divsn. Northrop Corp., Pico Rivera, Calif., 1964-94; owner Mitzner Sci. and Tech., Oceanside, Calif., 1995—. Instr. U. Calif., Santa Barbara, 1964-65; lectr. in field. Author: (handbook) Demonstrations Against Abortion & Death Selection, 1970; contbr. chpts. to books; contbr. articles to profl. jours. Pres. Mobilization for the Unnamed, Oceanside, Calif., 1970—; bd. dirs. Ams. United for Life, 1971-94, Nat. Right to Life Com., 1980-81, Jewish Life Issues Com., Solana Beach, 1983—; sec. Calif. Pro Life Coun., Sacramento, 1972; mem. L.A. County Select Citizens Com. on Life Support Policies, L.A., 1983-85 Named Patron of Life Calif. Pro Life Coun., 1976, Pres's award, 1979; Howard Hughes fellow, 1959-64; grantee Fullbright Found., Govt. Italy, 1961-62. Fellow IEEE (life); mem. U.S. Nat. Commn. Internat. Union Radio Sci. (del. to 20th gen. assembly), Electromagnetics Acad. Avocations: historic research, stamp collecting/philately. E-mail: kmitzner@aol.com.

MIURA, AKIO, quality assurance management professional; b. Tokyo, Oct. 7, 1936; s. Takeshi and Sakiko (Andoh) Miura; m. Takako Nakatani, Apr. 14, 1968; 1 child, Masahiro. BS, Waseda U., Tokyo, 1959. Cert. quality auditor, Am. Soc. Quality; reliability engr., Am. Soc. Quality, quality engr., Am. Soc. Quality; quality mgr. Am. Soc. Quality, six sigma black belt Am. Soc. Quality, software quality engr. Am. Soc. Quality, registered sr. auditor Registrar Accreditation Bd., Internat. Auditor, Tng. Course Accreditation. Staff mem. Mitsubishi Corp., Tokyo, 1959-75, mgr. indsl. machinery, 1975-78; exec. dir. Kinka Kikai Co., Gifu, 1978-84; asst. gen. mgr. indsl. machinery Mitsubishi Corp., Tokyo, 1984-90; pres. Internat. Quality Sys., Inc., 1990—; sr. cons. N.C. Kist & Assocs., Inc., Naperville, Ill., 1990—2000. Chair Internat. QA Inst., 1991—. Author: Guide for Preparation of Quality Manual, 1992, Practice of ISO 9000, 1994. Fellow: Am. Soc. Quality (cert. qualtiy mgr., internat. coucilor quality audit divsn.); mem.: Internat. Quality Inst. (chmn.). Avocations: baseball, chinese boxing, Karate, fencing, classical music. Home and Office: 3-24-14-703 Shimo-meguro Meguroku Tokyo 153-0064 Japan Fax: +81-3-3712-3399. Office Phone: +81-3-3712-6776. E-mail: a-miura-qad-iqai@mwa.biglobe.ne.jp.

MIURA, IRENE TAKEI, academic administrator; d. Iowa and Jean Abe Takei; m. Neal Isamu Miura, June 26, 1960; children: David Takei, Gregory Ross, Jennifer Miura Yamagishi. BA, U. Calif., Berkeley, 1960; MA in Tchg., Coll. of Notre Dame, Belmont, Calif., 1981; PhD, Stanford U., 1984. Cert. tchr. Calif. Tchr. St. Matthews Episcopal Day Sch., San Mateo, Calif., 1972—81; prof. child devel. San Jose State U., 1984—2000, exec. asst. to the pres., 2000—. Trustee St. Matthews Episcopal Sch., San Mateo, 1990—95, U. Calif. Found., 1997—2001; mem. U. Calif. Bd. Regents, Oakland, 1997—2001; pres. Calif. Alumni Assn., Calif., 1997—99. Author: (book chpts.) Humans as self-constructing living systems: Putting the framework to work (Ford and Ford); mem. editl. adv. bd.: Jour. Ednl. Psychology; author: (book chpts.) Asian perspectives on mathematics education (Bell), The development of arithmetic concepts and skills (Baroody and Dowker); contbr. articles to profl. jours. Vestry mem. St. Matthews Episcopal Ch., San Mateo, 1995—98. Mem.: AAAS, Berkeley Fellows, Internat. Soc. for the Study of Behavioral Devel., Am. Ednl. Rsch. Assn. (Outstanding Study of Yr. award 1994), Am. Psychol. Soc., Soc. for Rsch. in Child Devel., Delta Phi Epsilon, Phi Kappa Phi. Achievements include research in influence of language on children's understanding of number and mathematics concepts.

MIURA, ROBERT MITSURU, mathematician, researcher, educator; b. Selma, Calif., Sept. 12, 1938; s. Richard Katsuki and Frances Yoneko Miura; m. Kathryn Bannai; children: Derek Katsuki, Brian Robert, Jared Bannai Nagae, Sean Takeo. BS, U. Calif.-Berkeley, 1960, MS, 1962; MA, Princeton U., 1964, PhD, 1966. Rsch. assoc. Princeton U. Plasma Physics Lab., 1965-67; assoc. rsch. scientist Courant Inst. Math. Sci., N.Y.C., 1967-68; asst. prof. math. NYU, 1968-71; assoc. prof. math. Vanderbilt U., 1971-75, U. B.C., Vancouver, B.C., Can., 1975-78, prof., 1978—2001; prof. math. sci. and biomed. engring. N.J. Inst. Tech., 2001—, assoc. chmn. math. sci. Editor: Backlund Transformations, 1976, Nonlinear Phenomena in Physics and Biology, 1981, Some Mathematical Questions in Biology-Neurobiology, 1982, Muscle Physiology, 1986, DNA Sequence Analysis, 1986, Plant Biology, 1986; mem. editl. bd. Can. Applied Math. Quar., 1991—; co-editor-in-chief: Analysis and Applications, 2000—, mem. editl. bd.: Integrative Neurosci., 2001—; contbr. articles to profl. jours. Mem. steering com. Ctr. Math. Rsch., U. Montreal, 1990-94; mem. sci. adv. panel, sci. nominating com. Fields Inst., Toronto, 2002—. John Simon Guggenheim fellow, 1980-81; U. B.C. hon. Killam fellow, 1980-81. Fellow Royal Soc. Can.; mem. AAAS (nominating com., math. sect.), Am. Math. Soc., Soc. Indsl. and Applied Math. (chmn. joint com. on math. in life scis. 1981-84), Can. Applied Indsl. Math. Soc., Can. Math. Soc. (internat. affairs com.), Soc. Math. Biology (bd. dirs. 1995-98, nominating com. 1998), Pacific Inst. Math. Sci. (interim exec. bd. 1996), Sigma Xi. Office: NJ Inst Tech Dept Math Sci University Hgts Newark NJ 07102

MIXON, AARON MALACHI, III, medical products executive; b. May 22, 1940; m. Barbara Weber; 2 children. BA, Harvard U., 1962, MBA, 1968. CEO, chmn. Invacare Corp., Elyria, Ohio. Chmn. bd. trustees Cleve. Clinic Found. Office: Invacare Corp 1 Invacare Way PO Box 4028 Elyria OH 44036-2125 Office Phone: 440-329-6000. Office Fax: 440-366-9008.

MIXON, BILLIE LOUISE, language educator; b. Kansas City, Mo., Dec. 06; d. John Henry Ratterree and Ada Louise Babb; m. Charles Wesley Mixon, Mar. 6, 1951 (dec.); children: Mary Frances Damiani, Carol Ann Krendl. BA, Northeastern Univ., Tahlequah, Okla., 1947; BS in Edn., Ark. State Tchrs. Coll., 1950; MEd, U. N. Mex., 1966; elem. supr. endorsement, U. Ariz., 1975. Cert. tchr. Ariz. Reading specialist Amphitheater Jr. H.S., Tucson, 1961—78; reading prof. Pima C.C., 1984—; 2d grade tchr. Casas Adobes Bapt. Sch., Tuscon, Ariz., 1986—96. Guest lectr. U. Ariz. Extension; pvt. reading instr. Tucson Reading and Study Ctr. Sunday sch. tchr. Casas Adobes Bapt. Ch.; vol. children's ch. Thornydale Family Ch., Tucson, 2004; with Ubon Royal Thai Air Force Base, Thailand, 1972—73; with Eglin Air Base Fla., 1973—74; with Hahn Air Base Fed. Republic of Germany, 1974—75, with Spengdahlem Air Base, 1976—77; with Royal Air Force Base Bentwaters Woodbridge, England, 1977; Andrews Air Force Base, 1983—84. Recipient 2d pl. for most creative ways of using lang. master. Baptist. Avocation: writing children's books. Home: 1552 W Oak Shadows Dr Tucson AZ 85737 E-mail: billiemixon@netzero.com.

MIYAGAWA, CHIORI, theater educator, playwright; life ptnr. Hap Tivey. MFA, CUNY, 1989. Asst. lit. mgr. Actors Theatre of Louisville, 1990—91; lit. mgr. Arena Stage, Washington, 1991—92; assoc. artist The Pub. Theater, N.Y.C., 1992—93; artistic assoc. NY Theatre Workshop, N.Y.C., 1993—2000; assoc. prof. theater Bard Coll., Annandale-on-Hudson, NY, 2001—. Playwrith-in-residence Yale Sch. Drama, New Haven, 1996—2000; bd. dir. Alliance of Resident Theatre, N.Y.C., 2003—. Author: (plays) America Dreaming, 1995 (Rockefeller Mulit-Artist Prodn. award, 1994), Nothing Forever (Rockefeller Mulit-Artist Prodn. award, 1995), Yesterday's Window, FireDance, 1997, Jamaica Avenue, 1998, Broken Morning, 1998 (TCG Extended Collaboration grant, 1998), Awakening, 1999 (Japan Found. award, 2000), Woman Killer, 2001, Antigone's Red, 2002. Recipient, Ensemble Studio Theatre/Alfred P. Sloan Found., 2002; fellow, N.Y. Found. for Arts, 1994, Van Lier Playwriting fellow, N.Y. Theatre Workshop, 1997, Asian Cultural Coun., 1999, MacDowell Colony, 2002—03; McNight Playwriting fellow, The Playwrights Ctr., 1998. Democrat. Buddhist. Office: Bard Coll Theater Dept Annandale On Hudson NY 12504 Office Phone: 845-758-7938. E-mail: miyagawa@bard.edu.

MIYAGAWA, ICHIRO, physicist; b. Hiratsuka, Kanagawa, Japan, Mar. 5, 1922; s. Shigejiro and Tsuma (Itoh) M.; m. Mitsuko Yamada, Feb. 10, 1950; children: Shigeru, Haruyo, Mari. BS, Nagoya (Japan) U., 1945; DSc, U. Tokyo, 1954. Asst. prof. U. Tokyo, 1959-62; vis. asst. prof. Duke U., Durham, N.C., 1963-65; asst. prof. physics U. Ala., Tuscaloosa, 1965-66, assoc. prof., 1966-70, prof., 1970-80, Univ. Research prof. physics, 1980-92, prof. emeritus, 1992—. Contbr. articles to profl. jours. Recipient Samuel Ullman award, 1998; USPHS grantee; EPA grantee; NIH grantee. Fellow Am. Phys. Soc.; mem., AAAS, Sigma Xi. Home: 6434 Misty Ridge Dr Birmingham AL 35235- *Finding truth in any work or in any matter, however simple, is rewarding, although painful in many cases. Successful people in every spectrum of society are master discoverers of truth.*

MIYAHIRA, NEAL, state budget and finance administrator; B, M Econs., U. Hawaii. Budget analyst legis. sessions Senate Ways and Means Com., 1978—80; rschr. Senate Health Com., 1981; dep. dir., dep. dir. budget and fin. Dept. Taxation, 1995—98, budget analyst; dir. Hawaii Budget & Fin. Dept., Honolulu, 1999. Chief rsch., 1985—94; chief staff, 1994. Office: Hawaii Budget & Fin Dept PO Box 150 Honolulu HI 96810-0150

MIYAMOTO, CRAIG TOYOKI, public relations executive; b. Joliet, Ill., Oct. 14, 1944; s. Robert Mitsuo Miyamoto, Dorothy Toyoko (Okumura) Miyamoto; m. Diana Chie Ueda, Mar. 24, 1966; children: James Anthony Kazuyuki, Carleton Alan Yasuo. Reporter Alhambra Post-Advocate, Alhambra, Calif., 1968—70; editor Monterey Park Californian, 1970—71; mng. editor So. Calif. Pub. Co., 1971—72; dep. pub. rels. dir. Honolulu Bd. Water Supply, 1972—76, dir. pub. rels., 1976—77; pres. Miyamoto Advt./Pub. Rels., Honolulu, 1977—87; v.p. Profl. Comm., Inc., Honolulu, 1987—95, exec. v.p., 1995—97; prin. Miyamoto Strategic Counsel, Honolulu, 1997—. Asst. prof. U. Hawaii, 1992—95, instr. pub. rels., 1978—80, 1995—, adj. prof., 1995—98, 2002—; reporter Pineapple Post, Honolulu, 1977—88, Aura Publs., Honolulu, 1980—83. Author: How to Earn $2,000 or More Without Hardly Working at All, 1979, Pineapple Post Catalogue, 1984, Environmental Public Relations: A Primer on the Hottest Growth Area of the 90's, 1991, U.S. Corporate Environmental Policy: Philosophy vs Practice at the Dawn of a New Millenium, 1995, Environmental Public Relations and the PRSA Code of Ethics, 1995, Public Relations Ethics 201: Challenges We Just Can't Ignore, 1996. Pres. Honolulu Jaycees, 1975—76; mem. exec. com. 50th State Fair, 1974—76; dir. pub. rels. Hawaii Jaycees, 1974—75, Monterey Park C. of C., 1970—71; bd. dirs. San Gabriel Valley YMCA, 1971—72, Garfield Cmty. Sch. Bd., 1971—72, Am. Heart Assn. Hawaii affiliate; treas. Alzheimer's Assn. of Hawaii, 1991—92; mem. senate Jaycees Internat., 1976—. Named Man of Yr., Honolulu, 1974, Profl. of Yr., Gregg Perry Pub. Rels., 1992; named to Hawaii Pub. Rels. Hall of Honor, 2003; recipient John Armbruster award, 1974, State Svc. award, Hawaii Jaycees, 1974. Fellow: Pub. Rels. Soc. Am. (accredited, bd. dirs. Hawaii chpt., pres., v.p., sec. Hawaii chpt., chmn. South Pacific dist., sec. environ. sect., nat. bd. dirs. 1997—98); mem.: Hawaii Advt. Fedn. (bd. dirs.), Internat. Acad. Bus. Disciplines, Am. Mktg. Assn. (v.p. comm. group Honolulu chpt. 1996—97), Am. Advt. Fedn., Hawaii Stamp and Coin Dealers Assn (pres., v.p.), Mensa. Democrat. Office: PO Box 61414 Honolulu HI 96839-1414

MIYAMOTO, RICHARD TAKASHI, otolaryngologist; b. Feb. 2, 1944; s. Dave Norio and Haruko (Okano) Miyamoto; m. Cynthia VanderBurgh, June 17, 1967; children: Richard Christopher, Geoffrey Takashi. BS cum laude, Wheaton Coll., 1966; MD, U. Mich., 1970; D Engring. (hon.), Rose Hulman Inst. Tech., 2001. Diplomate Am. Bd. Otolaryngology. Intern Butterworth Hosp., Grand Rapids, Mich., 1970—71, resident in surgery, 1971—72; resident in otolaryngology Ind. U. Sch. Medicine, Indpls., 1972—75; fellow in otology and neurotology St. Vincent Hosp. and Otologic Med. Group, L.A., 1977—78; asst. prof. Ind. U. Sch. Medicine, Indpls., 1978—83, assoc. prof., 1983—88, prof., 1988—, chmn., 1987—, chief otology and neurotology dept. otology, head and neck surgery, 1982—, chmn. dept. otolaryngology, 1987—, Arilla DeVault prof., 1991; chief otolaryngology, head and neck surgery Wishard Meml. Hosp., 1979—2002. Mem. editl. bd.: Laryngoscope, Am. Jour. Otology, Otolaryngology - Head and Neck Surgery, European Archives of Oto-Rhino-Laryngology, Anales de Otorrinolaringologia Mexicana; contbr. articles tto profl. jours. Mem. adv. coun. Nat. Inst. Deafness and other Commication Disorders, 1989—94, 2002—; mem. med. adv. bd. Alexander Graham Bell Assn. for the Deaf, The Ear Found. Maj. USAF, 1975—77. Fellow: ACS, Am. Auditory Soc. (mem. exec. com. 1985—2003), Am. Otological, Rhinological and Laryngological Soc. (v.p. mid. sect. 2002—03), Am. Acad. Otolaryngology (gov. 1982—); mem.: Inst. of Medicine of NAS, 2004, Am. Neurotology Soc. (pres.-elect 1999—2000, pres. 2000—01), Collegium Oto-Laryntologicum Amecitiae Sacrum, Royal Soc. Medicine London, Assn. Rsch. Otol. (pres.-elect 2000—01, pres. 2001—), Am. Otol. Soc. (coun. 1992—), Otosclerosis Study Group (coun. 1993—), NY Acad. Scis., Am. Acad. Pediats., Marines Meml. Assn., Cosmos Club of Washington, Wheaton Coll. Scholastic Honor Soc., Psi Iota Xi, Alpha Omega Alpha (pres. Ind. chpt. 2003—). Office: Ind U Sch Med 702 Barnhill Dr Indianapolis IN 46202-5128

MIYASAKI, GEORGE JOJI, artist; b. Kalopa, Hawaii, Mar. 24, 1935; BFA, Calif. Coll. Arts and Crafts, 1957, MFA, 1958. Asst. prof. art Calif. Coll. Arts and Crafts, Oakland, 1958-64; mem. faculty dept. art U. Calif., Berkeley, 1964-94, prof. emeritus. John Hay Whitney fellow, 1957-58; Tamarind printing fellow, 1961; Guggenheim fellow, 1963-64; Nat. Endowment for Arts fellow, 1980-81, 85-86. Mem. NAD. Home: 2844 Forest Ave Berkeley CA 94705-1309

MIYASAKI, NOLA, state agency administrator; BSI in Human Biology, Stanford U.; JD, U. Calif.; postgrad., Keio U., Tokyo, London Sch. Econs. Spl. asst. in tech. Gov. Benjamin Cayetano, Honolulu; exec. dir., CEO High Tech. Devel. Corp., Honolulu, 2000—. Office: Manoa Innovation Ctr 2800 Woodlawn Dr Honolulu HI 96822

MIYASAKI, SHUICHI, lawyer; b. Paauilo, Hawaii, Aug. 6, 1928; s. Torakichi and Teyo (Kimura) M.; m. Pearl Takeko Saiki, Sept. 11, 1954; children: Joy Michiko, Miles Tadashi, Jan Keiko, Ann Yoshie. BSCE, U. Hawaii-Honolulu, 1951; JD, U. Minn., 1957; grad., Army War Coll., 1973. Bar: Minn. 1957, Hawaii 1959, U.S. Supreme Ct. 1980. Examiner U.S. Patent Office, 1957-59; dep. atty. gen. State of Hawaii, 1960-61; mem., dir., sec./treas. Okumura Takushi Funaki & Wee, Honolulu, 1961-90; pvt. practice Honolulu, 1991—; atty. Hawaii Senate, 1961, chief counsel ways and means com., 1962, chief counsel judiciary com., 1967-70; civil engr. Japan Constrn. Agy., Tokyo, 1953-54; staff judge adv., col. USAR, Ft. DeRussy, Hawaii, 1968-79. Local legal counsel Jaycees, 1962; lectr. Nat. Assn. Pub. Accts. Hawaii Chpt. Ann. Conf., 1990, 94, Mid Pacific Inst. Found., Honolulu, 1990, Econ. Study Club of Hawaii, 1990, Meiji Life Ins. Co. Japan, 1992, Cent. YMCA, 1992, City Bank Honolulu, 1997. Legis. chmn. armed services com. C. of C. of Hawaii, 1973; instnl. rep. Aloha council Boy Scouts Am., 1963-78; exec. com., sec., dir. Legal Aid Soc. Hawaii, 1970-72; state v.p. Hawaii Jaycees, 1964-65; dir., legal counsel St. Louis Heights Community Assn., 1963, 65, 73, 91—; dir., legal counsel Citizens Study Club for Naturalization of Citizens, 1963-68; advisory bd. Project Dana Honolulu, 1991—, vice chair, 1991, 92; bd. dirs. Omote Senke Found., 1999—; life mem. Res. Officers Assn. U.S. Served to 1st lt. AUS, 1951-54. Decorated Meritorious Service medal with oak leaf cluster. Mem. ABA, Hawaii Bar Assn., U.S. Patent Office Soc., Hawaii Estate Planning Council, Rotary, Central YMCA Club, Waikiki Athletic Club, Army Golf Assn., Elks, Phi Delta Phi. Office: 1001 Bishop St Ste 1030 Honolulu HI 96813-3408 *Personal philosophy: Study hard, work hard, play hard, love hard, have time for nonsense, help others and be fair to all concerned.*

MIYATA, KEIJIRO, culinary arts educator; b. Tokyo, Mar. 8, 1951; came to U.S., 1967; s. Yataro Miyata and Hekkiken (Liu) Choy; m. Connie Joyce Nelson, Mar. 8, 1976; children: Michelle, Kelly, Adam. Assoc. in Occupational Study, Culinary Inst. Am., Hyde Park, N.Y., 1972, cert. of nutrition, 1991; cert., Seattle Wine Sch., 1991. Cert. exec. chef; cert. culinary educator. Garde mgr. Mid-Pacific Country Club, Kailua, Hawaii, 1972; working chef Waikiki Yacht Club, Honolulu, 1972-74, Sagano Japanese Restaurant, New Rochelle, N.Y., 1974-76; asst. pastry chef Rye Town (N.Y.) Hilton Hotel, 1976-77; working chef The Explorer, Everett, Wash., 1977-79; exec. chef Holiday Inn, Everett, 1979-81, Mill Creek (Wash.) Country Club, 1981; culinary art instr. Everett Community Coll., 1981-85, North Seattle (Wash.) Community Coll., 1985-90, Seattle Cen. Community Coll., 1990—. Cons. Chalon Corp., Redmond, Wash., Chiang-Mai Restaurant, Mukilteo, Wash., 1988, Holiday Inn Crown Plaza, Seattle, Satsuma Japanese Restaurant, 1996. Participant Nagano Winter Olympic Ice Sculpture Festival, Karuizawa, Japan, 1998. Recipient Gold awards Am. Culinary Fedn., Oreg. State Chef's Assn., Portland, 1983, Gold and Bronze medals World Culinary Olympic, Frankfurt, Germany, 1984, 1988, Grand Champion award U.S. Nat. Ice Carving Contest, N.Y.C., 1986, 2d place award, All Japan Ice Carving Assn., Asahikawa, 1988, Ednl. Excellence award Oreg. and Wash. Community coll. Couns. Wash. Fedn. of Tchrs./Am. Fedn. of Tchrs./AFL-CIO, 1988, 1989, ACF Seafood Challenge State finalist, Charlotte, N.C., 1989, New Orleans, 1990, 1st place, Pacific Rim Invitational World Ice Sculpting Classic, 1989, Seymour Ice Sculpting Competition, 1991, 3d Ann. Internat. Ice Sculpting Competition, Lake Louise, Alta., Can., 1993, award of Excellence, Wash. Fedn. Tchrs./Am. Fedn. Tchrs./AFL-CIO, 1993, 1st place, Wash. State Seafood Festival Recipe Contest, Shelton, Wash., 1993, Grand Champion, 1994, 1st place, ICE ART'94 Ice Sculpting Competition, Fairbanks, Alaska, 1994, Most Artistic award Asahikawa Internat. Ice Sculpting Competition, 1996, 1st place Ice Carver's Choice, People's Choice Awards--8th Internat. Ice Carving Championship, Anchorage, Alaska, 1997, selected as Snow Sculpting Team Mem. of Sister City of Portland, Internat. Snow Sculpting Competition, Sapporo, Japan, 1997, participant, Nagano Winter Olympic Ice Sculpture Festival, Karuizawa, Japan, 1998, NICA, Gold Medal Ice Carver's Choice Awd., People's awd., Crystal Gall. of Ice, Internatl. Carving Comp., Alaska, 1999, 1st place, People's Choice Awards--7th Annual Internat. Sculpting Competition, Lake Louise, Alberta, Canada, 2000, 2d Place Hokkaido Newspaper award, Asahikawa Internat. Ice Sculpting competition, 2000, 3rd place team, Ice Alaska, Ice Art, Fairbank, Alaska, 2001, 1st place, People's Choice Award, 9th Ann. Internat. Ice Sculpting Competition, Lake Louise, Alta., 2002, Trustees Lifelong Learning award, Seattle CC, 2003—04. Mem. Wash. State Chefs Assn. (bd. dirs. 1982, 83, 86, 87, 88, cert. chmn. 1986-92, Chef of Yr. 1986), Am. Acad. Chefs, Nat. Ice Carving Assn. Office: Seattle Ctr Cmty Coll 1701 Broadway Seattle WA 98122-2413 E-mail: kmiyat@sccd.ctc.edu.

MIYAZAKI, ANTHONY D. marketing educator, consultant; b. Calif. BA in Mktg., U. of Utah; PhD in Mktg., U. of S.C. Mktg. dir. Rust Instrumentation & Controls, Salt Lake City, 1990—91; mktg. prof. U. of Miami, 1995—2003, Fla. Internat. U., 2003—. Mem.: Acad. of Mktg. Sci., Assn. for Consumer Rsch., Am. Mktg. Assn. Home: PO Box 560751 Miami FL 33256-0751 Office: Florida International University Miami FL

MIYAZAKI, KOICHI, economics professor; b. Yokohama, Japan, Dec. 7, 1949; s. Yoshikazu and Teruko (Inukai) M.; m. Mizuyo Muto, Jan. 16, 1993. BA, Yokohama Nat. U., 1972; MA, U. Tokyo, 1974. Prof. dept. econs. Hosei U., Tokyo, 1986—. Author: A Reform Proposal Concerning the Japanese Commodity Futures Market Institution; contbr. articles to profl. jours.; author: Elucidating the Hellish Trap of Commodity Futures - A Proposal of a Fundamental Reform to Rescue Victims. Mem. Am. Econ. Assn., Tokyo Ctr. for Econ. Rsch., Japanese Econ. Assn. Avocation: tennis. Home: 350-1-108 Katakura-Machi Hachioji-Shi Tokyo 192-0914 Japan Office: Hosei U Dept Econs 4342 Aihara-Machi Machida-Shi Tokyo 194-0298 Japan E-mail: koichi@m.email.ne.jp.

MIYOSHI, MASAO, literature educator, writer; b. Tokyo, May 14, 1928; came to U.S., 1952; s. Katsunai Miyoshi and Hisae Takahama; m. Elizabeth Ann Lester, July 27, 1953 (div. 1977); m. Martha L. Archibald, Apr. 8, 1977; children: Kathy Michele, Owen Malcolm, Melina Cybele. BA, U. Tokyo, 1951; MA, NYU, 1955, PhD, 1963. Instr., lectr. Gakushin U., Tokyo, 1951-52, 54-55; from asst. prof. to assoc. prof. to prof. English U. Calif., Berkeley, 1963-87; Edwin O. Reischauer prof. Japanese studies Harvard U., Cambridge, Mass., 1984-85; Hajime Mori prof. lit. U. Calif., San Diego, 1986—. Vis. prof. U. Chgo., 1978-81; dir. regional seminar, Japanese studies U. Calif., Berkeley, 1980-86, dir. Japanese studies, San Diego, 1989-95; dir. council on East Asian studies, 1997-2000. Author: The Divided Self, 1969, Accomplices of Silence, 1975, As We Saw Them, 1979, Off Center, 1991; editor: Postmodernism and Japan, 1989, Japan in the World, 1993, The Cultures of Globalization, 1998, Learning Places, 2002, (book series) Asia-Pacific: Culture, Politics, and Society. Guggenheim fellow, 1971-72, 75-76. Mem. MLA, Assn. for Asian Studies, Internat. Comparative Lit. Assn. Office: U Calif 9500 Gilman Dr La Jolla CA 92093-5004

MIZE, JOE HENRY, industrial engineer, educator; b. Colorado City, Tex., June 14, 1934; s. Kelly Marcus and Birtie (Adams) M.; m. Betty Bentley, Mar. 16, 1966; 1 dau., Kelly Jean. BS in Indsl. Engring, Tex. Tech. Coll., 1958; MS (Research Found. grantee) in Indsl. Engring, Purdue U., 1963, PhD, 1964. Registered profl. engr., Ala., Okla. Indsl. engr. White Sands Missile Range, N.Mex., 1958-61; grad. research asst. Purdue U., Lafayette, Ind., 1961-64; asso. prof. engring. Auburn (Ala.) U., 1964-69; dir. Auburn (Ala.) U. (Computer Center), 1965-66; prof. engring. Ariz. State U., Tempe, 1969-72; prof., head Sch. Indsl. Engring. and Mgmt. Okla. State U., Stillwater, 1972-80, dir. Univ. Ctr. for Energy Research, 1980-83, Regents prof., 1982-94; v.p. Hong Kong U. of Sci. and Tech., 1994-98; prof., v.p. Hong Kong U. Sci. & Tech., 1994-98; rsch. affiliate engring. sys. divsn. MIT, 1998—. Cons. to Air War Coll., 1968-69, U.S. Army, Ops. Analysis Standby Unit, U. N.C., 1965-69, various mfg. firms, 1964—; program adv. Office of Mgmt. and Budget, Exec. Office of the President, Washington, 1974-79; adv. to NSF, 1974-94, Nat. Center for Productivity and Quality of Work Life, 1973-78; chmn. tech. adv. council So. Growth Policies Bd., 1975-77; accrediting visitor Engrs. Council for Profl. Devel., 1973-80 Author: (with J.G. Cox) Essentials of Simulation (translated into Japanese 1970), 1968, Prosim V.: Instructor's Manual, 1971, Student's Manual, 1971, (with C.R. White and George H. Brooks) Operations Planning and Control, 1971, (with J.L. Kuester) Optimization Techniques with Fortran, 1973, (with W.C. Turner and K.E. Case) Introduction to Industrial and Systems Engineering, 3d edit., 1993 (named Book of Yr., Am. Inst. Indsl. Engrs. 1979), Guide to Systems Integration, 1991; contrbr. articles to profl. jours., more. Recipient Disting. Engring. Alumnus award Purdue U., 1978 Mem. Am. Inst. Indsl. Engrs. (exec. v.p. 1978-80, pres. 1981-82, H.G. Maynard Innovative Achievement award 1977, Gilbreth Indsl. Engring. award 1990), Am. Soc. for Engring. Edn. (sec. govt. rels. com. 1975-76), Nat. Soc. Profl. Engrs., Okla. Soc. Profl. Engrs. (Outstanding Engring. Achievement award 1977, Outstanding Engr. in Okla. 1981), Inst. Mgmt. Scis., Coun. Indsl. Engring. Acad. Dept. Heads (chmn. 1975-76), NAE, Nat. Rsch. Coun., Sigma Xi, Tau Beta Pi, Alpha Pi Mu. Office: Oklahoma State U Dept Indsl Engring Stillwater OK 74078-0001

MIZEL, LARRY A. housing construction company executive; b. 1942; married BA, U. Okla., 1964; JD, U. Denver, 1967. Chmn. bd., chmn. exec. com., dir. MDC Holdings Inc., Denver, 1972—, chmn. bd., pres., CEO, 1988—, chmn. bd., CEO. Office: MDC Holdings Inc 3600 S Yosemite St Ste 900 Denver CO 80237-1867

MIZEL, MARK STUART, orthopedic surgeon; b. N.Y.C., May 23, 1945; s. Harold Henry and Irene (Adelman) M. BSME, Columbia U., 1966, MSME, 1968; MD, Tufts U., 1977. Diplomate Am. Bd. Orthopedic Surgery. Intern George Washington U. Hosp., 1977-78, resident in surgery, 1978-79; resident

Mass. Gen. Hosp., Boston, 1979-82; fellow in foot and ankle surgery Dr. Roger Mann, San Francisco, 1983; practice medicine specializing in orthopedic surgery Orthopedic Ctr. of Lake Worth, Fla., 1983-91; clin. assoc. prof. orthopedics and rehab. U. Miami, Fla., 1989-91; clin. asst. prof. orthopedic surgery Tufts U., Boston, 1991-95; dir. Boston Foot and Ankle Ctr., 1991-95; asst. prof. orthopedic surgery Johns Hopkins U., Balt., 1995-97; assoc. prof. Boston U., 1997-99; assoc. prof. orthop. surgery U. Miami, 2000—02, prof. orthop. surgery, 2002—. Assoc. editor Foot & Ankle; reviewer Jour. Bone and Joint Surgery, Jour. Am. Acad. Orthop. Surgeons. Served as aviator USN, 1969-72; Vietnam. Fellow ACS, Am. Acad. Orthopedic Surgeons, Am. Orthopedic Foot and Ankle Soc. (membership com. 1988-90, orthotics and prosthetics com. 1990-91, chmn. regional rev. subcom., 1993-96). Office: 900 NW 17th St Miami FL 33136-1119 Office Phone: 305-326-6591. E-mail: msmmdltjg@aol.com.

MIZELL, ANDREW HOOPER, III, concrete company executive; b. Franklin, Tenn., Sept. 26, 1926; s. Andrew Hooper Jr. and Jennie McEwen (Fleming); m. Julia Yolanda Mattei, Dec. 20, 1947; children: Andrew Hooper, Julia Fleming; m. Waltraut Hornbostel, Oct. 3, 2002. BA, Vanderbilt U., 1950. Supt. Wescon Constrn. Co., Nashville, 1950-52; acct. McIntyre & Assoc., Nashville, 1952-55; credit mgr. Ingram Oil Co., Nashville, 1955-56, v.p., dir., 1956-62, Comml. Sign & Advt. Co., Nashville, 1957-59, Gen. Properties Co., New Orleans, 1957-62, Minn. Barge & Terminal Co., St. Paul, 1957-62; mgr. real estate and devel., mgr. retail sales Murphy Corp., El Dorado, Ark., 1962-63; pres., chmn. bd. Transit Ready Mix, Inc., Nashville, 1963-92. Pres., Conco, Inc., Apollo Concrete Products, Inc.; ptnr. Mizell Riggs Enterprises. Active United Givers Fund, 1965-66; chmn. Concrete div. Office Emergency Planning, 1965—; mem. Nat. UN Day Com., 1978. Active United Givers Fund, 1965-66; chmn. Concrete divsn. Office Emergency Planning, 1965-92; mem. Nat. UN Day Com., 1978. With USNR, 1944-46. Named Ark. Traveler, 1966, Order Ky. Cols., 1969. Mem. Nat. Ready Mix Concrete Assn. (chmn. membership com. Tenn. sect. 1971-92, chmn. mktg. com. Tenn. chpt. 1973-92), Assn. Gen. Contractors, Tenn. Bldg. Material Assn., Nat. Fedn. Ind. Businessmen, Portland Cement Assn., Nat. Area Bus. and Edn. Radio, Assn. Builders and Contractors, Spl. Indsl. Radio Svc. Industry, Tenn. Road Builders, Boat Owners Assn. U.S., Nashville C. of C., U.S. C. of C., Am. Concrete Indst., Nashville Yacht Club, Nashville City Club, Belle Meade Country Club, Honors Course Club, Commodore Yacht Club (past commodore), Boca Raton Resort and Club, Delray Beach Club, Boca Country Club, Premier Club. Home: 1317 Chickering Rd Nashville TN 37215

MIZELLE, DARY JOHN, composer, educator; b. Stillwater, Okla., June 14, 1940; s. John Dary and Jeanne Rachel Mizelle; m. Disi Yu Yang Mizelle, Mar. 13, 2002; children: Suzette, Adam, Joseph, Agon, Jack. BA, Sacramento State U., 1965; MA, U. Calif. Davis, 1967; PhD, U. Calif. San Diego, 1977. Composer, 1970—; prof. of composition Purchase Coll. SUNY, 1990—. Composer: (music) Radial Energy I and II, 1965—70, (complex of music compositions) SPANDA, 1989—. Achievements include discovery of and explication of multidemensional music. Avocation: yoga. Office: Purchase College SUNY 735 Anderson Hill Rd Purchase NY 10577 Business E-Mail: mizelle@purchase.edu.

MIZER, JOYCE TAYLOR, music educator; b. Staunton, Va., June 16, 1945; d. Wilson and Evelyn Taylor; m. Darryl E. Mizer; children: David Scott, Carol Lynn. MusB Edn., James Madison U., 1966, MusM Edn., 1972. Cert. tchr. Suzuki Assn. of the Americas. Elem. and H.S. band instr. Augusta County Pub. Schools, Fishersville, Va., 1967—84; founder, dir., instr. Suzuki Inst. Sch. of Music, Inc., Sarasota, Fla., 1984—. Guest organist Pentagon, Washington, 1969; guest condr. USAF Band, Washington, 1976. Sec. Va. Band and Orch. Dirs., Charlottesville, 1972—84. Named to, Va. Honor Band, 1984. Mem.: Suzuki Assn. of the Americas (assoc.). Methodist. Avocations: travel, adjudicating musical events. Home: 8951 Huntington Pointe Dr Sarasota FL 34238-3207 Office: Suzuki Inst Sch Music Inc 3100 S Tamiami Trail Sarasota FL 34239 Personal E-mail: drmizer@comcast.net.

MIZER, RICHARD ANTHONY, technology company executive; b. San Francisco, Jan. 7, 1952; s. Conrad Xavier and Sally Jo (Hagan) M. BA in Bioengring. and Econs., U. Calif., San Diego, 1977. Founding ptnr. Microdoctors, Palo Alto, Calif., 1974-94; mgr., ptnr. K-Family Corp. dba Harlow's Night Club, Fremont, Calif., 1977-79, Restaurants Unique Inc. dba Bourbon St., Mountain View, Calif., 1980-83; engring. mgr. Pacific Bell, San Ramon, Calif., 1983-89, tech. staff advanced tech., 1989-92, developer advanced video svcs., 1992-96; asst. v.p. Nuko Info. Sys., Inc., San Jose, Calif., 1996-98; pres., CEO Digital Ventures Diversified Inc., San Jose, Calif., 1998—2003; founder, chief tech. officer CINEvents, Campbell, Calif., 2003—. Exec. prodr.: Cinema of the Future sm, 1992; assoc. prodr. Soccer Fest: World Cup Soccer Final in HDTV to Europe and U.S. theaters from Pasadena Rose Bowl, 1994; exec. in chg. prodn. 50th Anniversary of Signing of UN Charter, 1995. Mem. security staff Republican Task Force, San Francisco, 1984, tech. staff U.S. Olympic Com., Los Angeles, 1984. Mem. IEEE, Nat. Assn. Broadcasters, Soc. Motion Picture and TV Engrs. (western region gov. 1999-2000). Roman Catholic. Avocations: martial arts, auto racing, skiing, triathlon. Office: CINEvents Inc 3960 Howard Hughes Pky Ste 500 Las Vegas NV 89102 Office Phone: 408-246-4949. E-mail: ramizer@cinemaevents.com.

MIZGALA, HENRY F. physician, consultant, retired medical educator; b. Montreal, Can., Nov. 28, 1932; s. Louis and Mary (Ropeleski) M.; m. Pauline Barbara Delaney, Oct. 26, 1957; children: Paul Stephen, Cynthia Louise, Liane Mary Mizgala Sizemore, Melanie Frances Mizgala Dressler, Nancy Elizabeth Mizgala Lewis. BA magna cum laude, Loyola Coll., Montreal, 1953; MD, CM, McGill U., 1957. Rotating intern, then resident in medicine St. Mary's Hosp., Montreal, 1957-59, asst. physician, 1963-66; resident in medicine Royal Victoria Hosp., Montreal, 1959-60; Dazian fellow cardiology Mt. Sinai Hosp., NYC, 1960-61, USPHS fellow cardiology, 1961-62; resident in cardiology Montreal Gen. Hosp., 1962-63, assoc. physician, 1966-74; asst. physician, cons. cardiology Lachine (Que.) Gen. Hosp., 1964-80; mem. faculty McGill U. Med. Sch., Montreal, 1968-74, assoc. prof. medicine, 1973-74; assoc. prof., then prof. Montreal U. Med. Sch., 1974-81; cardiologist Montreal Heart Inst., also dir. CCU, 1974-80; prof. medicine U. B.C., 1980-97, prof. medicine, head divsn. cardiology, 1980-87, prof. medicine emeritus, 1998—; hon. attending med. staff, cardiologist The Vancouver (B.C.) Hosp. and Health Scis. Ctr. Cons. Centre Hosp. Baie des Chaleurs, Gaspe, Que., 1975—80, B.C. Cancer Agy., Vancouver, 1981—; cons. staff Univ. Hosp., U. B.C. site, 1981—94; hon. cons. Montreal Heart Inst., 1980—. Mem. editl. bd. Can. Jour. Cardiology, 1988-99, Jour. Am. Coll. Cardiology, 1992-95; contbr. numerous articles to med. jours. Fellow Royal Coll. Physicians and Surgeons Can., Am. Coll. Cardiology, Am. Heart Assn. (coun. clin. cardiology); mem. Can. Med. Assn., Can. Cardiovasc. Soc. (treas. 1974-90), Que. Med. Assn., B.C. Med. Assn., B.C. and Yukon Heart and Stroke Found. (bd. dirs., sr. bd. dirs.), Alpha Omega Alpha. Office: U BC Divsn Cardiology Dept Med 865 W 10th Ave Vancouver BC Canada V5Z IL7 Business E-Mail: mhenry@interchange.ubc.ca.

MIZIOLEK, ANDRZEJ WLADYSLAW, research physicist; b. Hannover, Fed. Republic Germany, Feb. 17, 1950; s. Ryszard Roman and Irena (Stasinowska) M.; m. Karen Louise Beemon, Nov. 30, 1974 (div. K.L. Beemon); children: Nicole Alicia Beemon Miziolek, Claire Elizabeth Beemon Miziolek; m. Lucy B. Biggs, Oct. 10, 1998. BS in Chemistry magna cum laude, Wayne State U., 1971; PhD in Phys. Chemistry, U. Calif., Berkeley, 1976. Postgrad. rsch. chemist U. Calif., Irvine, 1976-77, asst. rsch. chemist San Diego, 1977-81; rsch. physicist U.S. Army Ballistic Rsch. Lab., Aberdeen Proving Ground, Md., 1981—; sci. advisor Office Naval Rsch., Arlington, Va., 1989; leader applied photochemistry and laser spectroscopy team U.S. Army Ballistic Rsch. Lab., Aberdeen Proving Ground, Md., 1985-95. Chmn. Jannaf Panel on Propellant Combustion, Laurel, Md., 1988; founder/co-chmn. Topical Mtg. in Laser Applications to Chem. Analysis, 1987, 90; chmn. mtg. Internat. Conf. Laser Induced Breakdown Spectroscopy (LIBS 2002). Contbr. 50 articles to profl. jours.; patentee resonance elemental detector; author 100 govt. reports; author: (book) Halon Replacements: Technology and Science, 1995; topical editor: Jour. Applied optics, 1996—. Recipient 3 outstanding achievement awards and 1st prize Army Sci. Conf., 1986, 88, 92. Fellow Optical Soc. Am. (chair tech. group fundamental and applied spectroscopy 1991-93, U.S. Army rep. on DOD Halon Replacement Program NGP 1996—, 10 outstanding army material pers. award 1999); mem. Am. Chem. Soc., Phi Beta Kappa, Sigma Xi. Avocations: piano, tennis, skiing, photography, video. Home: 117 Margate Rd Lutherville MD 21093-5838 Office: Army Rsch Lab AMSRL-WM-BD Aberdeen Proving Ground MD 21005 E-mail: miziolek@arl.army.mil.

MIZRAHI, ABRAHAM MORDECHAY, retired cosmetics and health care company executive, physician; b. Jerusalem, Apr. 16, 1929; came to U.S., 1952, naturalized, 1960; s. Solomon R. and Rachel (Haliwa) M.; m. Suzanne Eve Glasser, Mar. 15, 1956; children: Debra, Judith, Karen. BS, Manchester Coll., 1955; MD, Albert Einstein Coll. Medicine, 1960. Diplomate: Am. Bd. Pediatrics, Nat. Bd. Med. Examiners. Intern U. N.C., 1960-61; pediatric resident Columbia-Presbyn. Med. Center, N.Y.C., 1961-63, NIH fellow in neonatology, 1963-65; assoc. dir. Newborn Service Mt. Sinai Hosp., N.Y.C.; also dir. Newborn Service Elmhurst Med. Center, 1965-67; staff physician Geigy Pharm. Corp., N.Y.C., 1967-69, head cardio-pulmonary sect., 1969-71; sr. v.p. corp. med. affairs USV Pharm. Corp., Tuckahoe, N.Y., 1971-76; v.p. health and safety Revlon, Inc., N.Y.C., 1976-89, sr. v.p. human resources, 1989-94; ret., 1994. Assoc. in pediatrics Columbia U., 1963-67; cons. in neonatology Misericordia-Fordham Med. Ctr., 1967-89; clin. affiliate N.Y. Hosp.; clin. asst. prof. Cornell U. Med. Coll., 1982—. Contbr. articles to profl. jours. Trustee Westchester (N.Y.) Jewish Center. Mem. AMA, N.Y. State and County Med. Soc., Am., N.Y. acads. medicine, Am. Soc. Clin. Pharmacology and Therapeutics, Am. Pub. Health Assn., Am. Occupational Med. Assn. Home: 7 Jason Ln Mamaroneck NY 10543-2108 *The principles that have guided my life are old Biblical concepts. Firstly, that God had created Adam and Eve and all Men are, therefore, brothers and sisters. Secondly, God created Man and, therefore every human being has a spark of God in him. It, therefore, follows that killing diminshes God's presence on earth and saving of a human being increases His presence.*

MIZRAHI, EDWARD ALAN, allergist; b. Tyler, Tex., Aug. 24, 1945; BS in Econs., U. Pa., 1967; MD, U. Fla., 1972. Diplomate Am. Bd. Internal Medicine, Am. Bd. Allergy and Immunology. Intern Med. Coll. Ga., Augusta, 1972-73, resident, 1973-75; fellow Nat. Jewish Hosp., U. Colo., Denver, 1975-77; pvt. practice Jacksonville, Fla., 1977—. Physician Bapt. Med. Ctr., Jacksonville, Meml. Med. Ctr., Jacksonville, St. Luke's Med. Ctr., Jacksonville, St. Vincent's Med. Ctr., Jacksonville, Meth. Hosp., Jacksonville, Orange Park (Fla.) Med. Ctr. Mem. Am. Coll. Allergy, Asthma and Immunology, Am. Acad. Allergy, Asthma and Immunology, Fla. Med. Assn., Fla. Allergy, Asthma and Immunology Soc., Duval County Med. Soc., Southeastern Allergy Assn. Office: Ste A3 3636 University Blvd S Jacksonville FL 32216-4223

MIZRUCHI, MARK SHELDON, sociology and business administration educator; b. New Haven, Dec. 10, 1953; s. Ephraim Harold and Ruth (Trachtenberg) M.; m. Katherine Teves, June 1981 (div. June 1995); 1 child, Joshua. BA, Washington U., 1975; MA, SUNY, Stony Brook, 1977, PhD, 1980. Statis. analyst Albert Einstein Coll. of Medicine, Bronx, N.Y., 1980-83, asst. prof. psychiatry, 1981-87, supr. statis. svcs., 1983-87; asst. prof. sociology Columbia U., N.Y.C., 1987-89, assoc. prof. sociology, 1989-91; prof. sociology and bus. adminstrn. U. Mich., Ann Arbor, 1991—. Author: The American Corporate Network, 1904-1974, 1982, The Structure of Corporate Political Action, 1992; editor (with M. Schwartz) Intercorporate Relations, 1987. Recipient Presdl. Young Investigator award NSF, 1988-93; grantee NSF, 1987-88, 93-95, 99-2000, 2002-03; invited fellow Ctr. for Advanced Study in the Behavioral Scis., 1989. Mem. Am. Sociol. Assn., Acad. Mgmt., Internat. Network for Social Network Analysis, Sociol. Rsch. Assn. Office: Dept Sociology Univ Mich Ann Arbor MI 48104-2590 Office Phone: 734-764-7444. Business E-Mail: mizruchi@umich.edu.

MIZUGUCHI, NORMAN, former state senator; b. Hilo, Hawaii, May 26, 1939; m. Harriet Mizuguchi; 1 child, Reid. BS, Springfield Coll.; MS, Mich. State U.; PhD, U. Utah. Mem. state house State of Hawaii, 1974-78, state senator, 1978—2000, pres. state senate, 1994—2000; pres. Hawaiian Emporium Inc., Sundance Circle Inc.; tchr., edn. officer Dept. of Edn. Sec. Pearl city Makule Softball League; mem. Barbers Point coun., Navy League, Hawaiian Edn. Coun., Hui Kokua Kinipopo Booster Club, Japanese Am. Citizens League Honolulu, Aiea Hongwanji. Democrat.

MKHITARIAN, MARINE, chemical engineer; b. Moscow, Apr. 14, 1956; d. Artavazd and Elena Mkhitarian; m. Aleksan Martirosian, Sept. 25, 1981 (dec. Mar. 1994); 1 child, Hrachia. BS in Chem. Tech., Polytech. U., Yerevan, Armenia, 1979; MS, Mendeleev Inst. Chem. Tech., Moscow, 1991. Sr. R&D chemist Plastpolymer, Yerevan, Armenia, 1979-92; technologist Docdata Calif., Canoga Park, 1995-99; mastering and quality control supr. Crest Nat., L.A., 1999—. Contbr. articles to profl. jours. Fellow Am. Inst. Chemists; mem. AIChE, Am. Chem. Soc., Soc. Plastics Engrs. Avocations: reading, travel, music. Home: Apt A 1528 N Harvard Blvd Los Angeles CA 90027 Office: Crest Nat 6721 Romaine St Hollywood CA 90038 E-mail: marinem@msn.com.

MKHIZE, SIPHIWE FELIX, agriculturist, diplomat; b. Pietermaritzburg, KwaZulu Natal, South Africa, Aug. 20, 1959; s. Virginia Mkhize; m. Sibongile Anna Africa, June 11, 1964; children: Sine M., Fezeka N., Lindo N., Simphiwe N. Diploma in Irrigation Scis., Bari Agronomic Inst., 1981; BSc in Agronomy, Iowa State U., 1986; MS in Soil Chemistry and Fertility, U. of Reading, 1987; MPhil in Environ. Ethics, U. Stellenbosch, Cape Town, South Africa, 1999; PhD, U. Pretoria, 2001. Sr. rsch. fellow Farmer Support Group U. of Natal, Pietermaritzburg, South Africa, 1989—93; devel. coord. Cath. Archdiocese, Durban, South Africa, 1993; dep. dir. internat. rels. Dept. Agr., Pretoira, South Africa, 1997—99, dir. internat. rels., 1999—2001; min. agr. Embassy South Africa, Washington, 2001—. Mem. ANC, Pietermaritzburg, South Africa, 1992—96; mem. dicesan pastoral coun. Cath. Ch., Durban, 1991—96. Mem.: Am. Soc. Agronomy. Roman Catholic. Avocations: travel, soccer, music. Home: 1201 Marion Avenue McLean VA 22101 Office: Embassy of South Africa 3051 Massachusetts Avenue NW Washington DC 20008 Office Phone: 202-274-7989. Personal E-mail: sfmkhize@msn.com. Business E-Mail: smkhize@saembassy.org.

MLADENICH, RONALD E. publishing executive; BA in Bus. Adminstrn., U. Puget Sound, 1965. Buyer Boeing Co., Renton, Wash., 1965-68; sales/contracts Stellar Hydraulics, Sun Valley, Calif., 1968-74; circulation mgr. News Tribune, Tacoma, 1974—, transp. mgr., 1999—. Carl Burkheimer Meml. scholar N.W. Internat. Circulation Execs., 1993. Mem. Internat. Circulation Mgr. Assn. (promotions award chairperson 1986), N.W. Internat. Circulation Execs. (pres. 1984-92), Western Conf. Circulation Execs. (pres. 1985, 86). Office: News Tribune 1950 S State St Tacoma WA 98405-2817

MLOCEK, SISTER FRANCES ANGELINE, financial executive; b. River Rouge, Mich., Aug. 4, 1934; d. Michael and Suzanna (Bloch) M. BBA, U. Detroit, 1958; MBA, U. Mich., 1971. CPA, Mich. Bookkeeper Allen Park (Mich.) Furniture, 1949-52, Gerson's Jewelry, Detroit, 1952-53; jr. acct. Meyer Dickman, CPA, Algaze, Staub & Bowman, CPAs, Detroit, 1953-58; acct., internal auditor Sisters, Servants of Immaculate Heart of Mary Congregation, Monroe, Mich., 1959-66, asst. gen. treas., 1966-73, gen. treas., 1973-76; internal auditor for parishes Archdiocese of Detroit, 1976-78; asst. to exec. dir. Leadership Conf. of Women, Silver Spring, Md., 1978-83; dir. of fin. Nat. Conf. of Cath. Bishops/U.S. Cath. Conf., Washington, 1989-94; CFO Sisters Servants of the Immaculate Heart of Mary, Monroe, Mich., 1994—. Trustee SSIHM Charitable Trust, Monroe, 1988—. Author: (manual) Leadership Conference of Women Religious/Confernce of Major Superiors of Men, 1981. Treas. Zonta Club of Washington Found., Washington, 1983-88, pres., 1992-93; bd. dirs. Our Lady of Good Counsel High Sch., Wheaton, Md., 1983-89. Mem. AICPA, D.C. Inst. CPAs (mem. not-for-profit com. 1992-94, CFOs com. 1990-94. Democrat. Roman Catholic. Office: Sisters Servants Immaculate Heart Mary 610 W Elm Ave Monroe MI 48162-7909

MLYNIEC, WALLACE JOHN, law educator, lawyer, consultant; b. Berwyn, Ill., July 10, 1945; s. Casimir Adele and Adeline Mary Mlyniec; m. Abby L. Yochelson, 1985. BS, Northwestern U., 1967; JD, Georgetown U., 1970. Bar: D.C. 1971, Alaska 1971, U.S. Dist. Ct. D.C. 1971, U.S. Ct. Appeals (D.C. cir.) 1971, U.S. Supreme Ct. 1974. Exec. dir. ABA stds. U.S. Cir. Jud. Conf. on ABA Stds., Washington, 1971-73; dir. Juvenile Justice Clinic Georgetown U., Washington, 1973—, prof. law, 1973—. Lupo-Rico prof. clin. legal studies, 1998—; coord. clin. edn, 1986-89, assoc. dean, 1989—; cons. Nat. Adv. Com. on Juvenile Justice, Washington, 1979-80; chmn. Juvenile Justice Adv. Group, D.C., 1980-82; mem. Nat. Resource Ctr. on Child Abuse and Neglect; cons. in field. Recipient Stuart Stillar Found. award, 1994; Meyer Found. grantee, 1980-82; Swedish Bicentennial fellow, 1985; disting. vis. scholar in pediat. law, Loyola U. Law Sch., 2001. Mem. ABA (adv. com. on family ct. rules 1984, chair com. on juvenile justice 1998—), Am. Assn. Law Schs. (com. on polit. interference 1983-84, chair 1991, standing com. on clin. edn., William Pincus award 1996), DC Bar Assn. (chmn. juvenile justice sect. 1973).

MO, SUCHOON, psychology educator; b. Nagoya, Japan, Apr. 19, 1932; came to U.S., 1955; s. Chihyun and Oksil (Kim) M.; m. Mary Madeleine Lang; children: Blaise, Bernard; m. Judith Carol Oslick, Dec. 26, 1969; childrn: Sage, Daisy, Clifton. BS, Idaho State Coll., 1959; PhD, U. Pa., 1968. Asst. prof. U. Detroit, 1967-73; prof. U. So. Colo., Pueblo, 1973—. Avocations: poetry, martial arts. Home: 1158 S Yerba Santa Dr Pueblo West CO 81007-1947 Office: Psychology Dept U So Colo Pueblo CO 81001

MOAG, RODNEY FRANK, language educator, country music singer; b. Warsaw, N.Y., Oct. 15, 1936; s. Hugh Alexander and Imogene (Hodges) M.; m. Rachel Ann Foley, Feb. 9, 1964 (div. Aug. 1974); children: Robin Gray, Hugh Daniel, Jeffrey Lee. BS, Syracuse U., 1961; MA, U. Wis., 1966, PhD, 1973. Dir. college preparatory program for visually impaired U. Mo., Columbia, 1974; vis. Fulbright prof. U. South Pacific, Suva, Fiji Islands, 1975-78; vis. assoc. prof. U. Mich., Ann Arbor, 1978-80, adj. prof., 1981, vis. assoc. prof., 1982; sr. lectr. U. Tex., Austin, 1981, 83-90, assoc. prof., 1990—2004, prof. emeritus, 2004—. Author: (texts) Fiji Hindi, 1977, Malayalam, 1986; country music artist: several records, 4 CDs, 1995, 2000, 2002. Mng. dir. Amateur Radio Repeaters of Washtenaw, 1984-86; pres. Mich. Repeater Coun., 1985-88; v.p. Austin Amateur Radio Club, 1993-94; vol. programmer, KO-OP, 1995—. Mem. Ctrl. Tex. Bluegrass Assn., Austin Amateur Radio Club, Austin Repeater Orgn., Tex. VHF FM Soc. Avocations: amateur radio, country and bluegrass music. Home: 6909 Miranda Dr Austin TX 78752-3119 Office: U Tex Dept Asian Studies WCH 4-134 Austin TX 78712 E-mail: rodmoag@texas.net., rmoag@mail.utexas.edu.

MOATES, G. PAUL, lawyer; b. May 26, 1947; s. Guy Hart and Virginia Rose (Mayolett) Moates; m. Constance A. Sadler. BA, Amherst Coll., 1969; JD, U. Chgo., 1975. Bar: Ill. 1975, D.C. 1976, U.S. Ct. Appeals (D.C. cir.) 1976, U.S. Supreme Ct. 1980, U.S. Ct. Appeals (6th cir.) 1984, U.S. Ct. Appeals (3d cir.) 1991, U.S. Ct. Appeals (7th cir.) 1993. Assoc. Sidley & Austin, Washington, 1975—82, ptnr., 1982—. Contbr. articles to profl. jours. Mem.: ABA, D.C. Bar Assn., Ill. Bar Assn. Office: Sidley Austin Brown & Wood 1501 K Street NW Washington DC 20005

MOAWAD, ATEF, obstetrician, gynecologist, educator; b. Beni Suef, Egypt, Dec. 2, 1935; came to U.S., 1959; s. Hanna and Baheya (Hunein) M.; m. Ferial Fouad Abdel Malek, Aug. 22, 1966; children: John, Joseph, James. Student, Cairo U. Sch. Sci., 1951-52; MB, BCh, Cairo U. Sch. Medicine, 1957; MS in Pharmacology, Jefferson Med. Coll., 1963. Diplomate Am. Bd. Ob-Gyn; licentiate Med. Coun Can. Rotating intern Cairo U. Hosp., 1958-59, Elizabeth (N.J.) Gen. Hosp., 1959-60; resident in ob-gyn. Jefferson Med. Coll. Hosp., Phila., 1961-64; lect. dept. pharmacology U. Alta., Can., 1966; asst. prof. dept. ob-gyn. and pharmacology U. Alta., Can., 1967-70, assoc. prof., 1970-72; assoc. prof. dept. ob-gyn. and pharmacology U. Chgo., 1972-75, prof. dept. ob-gyn. and pediatrics, 1975—, co-dir. perinatal ctr., 1974-80; obstetrician-gynecologist, chief obstetrics, co-dir. perinatal ctr. The Chgo. Lying-in Hosp. U. Chgo., 1980—. Blum Riese prof. ob-gyn., chief maternal fetal medicine, 2001—, interim chair dept. ob-gyn., 2002—. Vis. investigator dept. ob-gyn. U. Lund, Sweden, 1969. Co-author book chpts., jour. articles. Mem. perinatal adv. com. Chgo. March of Dimes, 1977—, health profl. adv. com., 1983—; mem. perinatal adv. bd. com. State of Ill., 1978—; mem. Chgo. Maternal Child Health Adv. Com., chmn., 1991—; mem. Mayor's Adv. Com. on Infant Mortality, 1991—. Fellow Jefferson Med. Coll., 1960-61, Case Western Res. U., 1964-65; grantee Brush Found., 1966-67, Maternal Fetal Medicine Units Network NIH, 1994; recipient award Phila. Obstet. Soc., 1964, Disting. Tchg. award Am. Profs. Gynecology and Obstetrics, 1993, DeLee Humanitarian award, 2003. Fellow Am. Coll. Ob-Gyn. (Purdue-Frederick award 1978), Royal Coll. Surgeons (Can.); mem. Soc. for Gynecol Investigation, Pharmacol. Soc. Can., Am. Gynecol. and Obstet. Soc., Soc. Perinatal Obstetricians, N.Y. Acad. Scis., Chgo. Gynecol. Soc., Can. Med. Assn., Christian Med. Soc., Edmonton Obstetrics Soc. Office: U Chgo Dept Ob-Gyn 5841 S Maryland Ave MC 2050 Chicago IL 60637-1463 E-mail: amoawad@babies.bsd.uchicago.edu.

MOAZED, KHOSROW L. retired engineering educator; b. Meshed, Iran, Sept. 14, 1930; arrived in U.S., 1943; s. Mohammed and Forough Moazed; m. Carolyn Turner Green, Nov. 14, 1953; children: David Charles, Steven Darius, Elizabeth Ashraf, Maryam Leela. BSc, Rensselaer Poly., 1953, MSc, 1956, Carnegie Mellon U., 1958, PhD, 1959. Registered profl. engr., N.C. Rsch. assoc. Rensselaer Poly. Inst., Troy, NY, 1953—56; GE fellow Carnegie-Mellon U., Pitts., 1956—59; asst. prof. Ohio State U., Columbus, 1959—65, assoc. prof., 1965—68; prof. N.C. State U., Raleigh, 1968—91, prof. emeritus, 1991—, chmn. faculty senate, 1982—83. Prin. sci. officer Nat. Phys. Lab., Teddington, England, 1966; vis. prof. Naval Ocean Sys. Ctr., San Diego, 1985—90. Contbr. scientific papers to profl. jours. Capt., mission pilot CAP, 1995—2002. Grantee, NSF, USAF Office Sci. Rsch., U.S. Army Rsch. Office, Office Naval Rsch. Avocations: flying, art, writing, skiing.

MOBASHER, MAHER ATTIA, academic administrator; b. Elsharkia, Egypt, Dec. 10, 1940; came to U.S., 1970; m. Salwa Fekry Elnakib, June 19, 1983; children: Ahmed, Samer. B in Commerce, Ain Shams U., Egypt, 1963; D in Econs. & Social Devel., Inst. Nat. Devel., Egypt, 1966; MS in acctg., L.I. U., 1975; D in Bus. Adminstrn., Nova Southeastern U., 1995. Acctg. supr. Gen. Orgn. Commerce, Cairo, 1963-70; internal auditor Emigrant Savings Bank, N.Y.C., 1970-73; bank examiner European Am. Bank, N.Y.C., 1973-77; comptroller Cmty. Action. Com. Danbury, Conn., 1977-79; budget ops. mgr. CUNY, Bklyn., 1979-89, bus. mgr., asst. adminstr. Bronx C.C. Bronx, 1989—. Scholar Inst. Nat. Planning, 1964-66; Rsch. grantee Bronx C.C. Found., 1994. Mem. Am. Mgmt. Assn., Am. Assn. Univ. Adminstrs., Nat. Coun. C.C. Bus. Officials, C.C. Bus. Officers Assn., Assn. Coll. Adminstrn. Profls. Office: Bronx CC 181 and University Bronx NY 10453

MOBASHERY, SHAHRIAR, chemist; b. May 17, 1958; BS in Biol. Scis., U. So. Calif., 1980, BS in Chemistry, 1981; PhD, U. Chgo., 1985. Rschr. Rockefeller U., 1986-88; asst. prof. Wayne State U., Detroit, 1989-94, assoc. prof., 1994-97, chair divsn. biochemistry, dept. chemistry, 1996—2000, prof. chemistry, 1997—2003, prof. dept. pharmacology, biochemistry and molecular biology, 2000—03, dir. Inst. Drug Design, 2000—03; Navari Family prof. life scis., dept. chemistry and biochemistry U. Notre Dame, Ind., 2003—. Cons. Salk Inst., 1989-92, Affymax Corp., 1996-98, Procter & Gamble Pharm., 1997-98, Aurora Bioscis., 1998-2000, Guilford Pharm., 2000—; mem. sci. adv. bd. New Biotics, Inc., 2001--; mem. adv. com. biochemistry and endocrinology Am. Cancer Soc., 1994-96, 99-2000; mem. biorganics and natural products study sect. NIH, 2001--; chmn. numerous symposia; speaker in field. Co-author: Resolving the Antibiotic Paradox: Progress in Understanding Drug Resistance and Development of New Antibiotics, 1998; mem. editl. bd. Pharm. and Medicinal Chemistry, 1995—, Jour. Antibiotics, 1998—, Antimicrobial Agents Chemotherapy, 1999—, Biorganic Chemistry, 2000—, Current Organic Synthesis, 2002—, Litt. Organic Chemistry, 2002—, Litt. Drug Designs and Discovery, 2002—, Mini Revs. in Organic Chemistry, 2002—, ad hoc reviewer numerous jours. and orgns.; contbr. articles to profl.

jours.; patentee in field. Mem. AAAS, Am. Chem. Soc., Am. Soc. Microbiology, Sigma Xi. Office: U Notre Dame Dept of Chemistry and Biochemistry 423 Nieuwland Sci Ctr Notre Dame IN 46556

MOBBERLEY, JAMES, music educator, composer; b. Des Moines, June 10, 1954; s. David and Marjorie Mobberley; m. Laura Moore, June 3, 1989; children: Lucas, Jacob. BA in Music, U. N.C., 1978, MusM, 1980; DMA, Cleve. Inst. of Music, 1982. Curators' prof. music U. Mo. Conservatory of Music, Kans. City, 1983—; composer in residence Kans. City (Mo.) Symphony, 1991—98; vis. prof. Ind. U. Sch. of Music, Bloomington, 1998. Composer (composition): (chamber music) Vox Inhumana (Commns. from Koussevitzky and Barlow Founds., 2001), TNT (Nat. Endowment for Arts Composers Fellowship, 1993), Soggiorno (Rome Prize Fellowship, 1989), (piano solo) Give 'em Hell! (Van Cliburn Composers Invitational, 2001), Concerto #1 for Piano and Orch. (Guggenheim Fellowship, 1992). Bd. mem. Walden Sch., San Francisco, 2003—. Recipient Lee Ettelson Composers award, Composers, Inc., 1991, Kazimierz Serocki Competition, League-ISCM (Polish Sect.), 1993, Disting. Composer of Yr., Music Tchrs. Nat. Assn., 1998. Mem.: ASCAP (Std. award 1988—). Avocation: bicycling. Office: Univ Mo Kans City Conservatory of Music 4949 Cherry Kansas City MO 64110 Office Phone: 816-235-2968. Office Fax: 816-235-5265. E-mail: mobberleyj@umkc.edu.

MOBERLY, THOMAS, uniform company executive; b. 1948; With G & K Svcs., Inc., 1974—, exec. v.p., 1993-97, pres., CEO, 2000—. Office: G & K Svcs Inc 5995 Opus Pky Ste 500 Minnetonka MN 55343 Fax: (612) 912-5500.

MOBLEY, BARBARA JEAN, state legislator; b. Dec. 1, 1947; m. James L. Savage, Jr. BS, Savannah State Coll.; MSW, U. Ill.; JD, So. Meth. U. Atty.; mem. Ga. Ho. of Reps., 1992—, mem. higher edn. com., chair ethics com., mem. pub. safety com., mem. judiciary com., 1999. Democrat. Baptist. Home: 3009 Miriam Ct Decatur GA 30032 Office: Ga Ho of Reps 402 LO B Legis Office Bldg Atlanta GA 30334

MOBLEY, EMILY RUTH, library dean, educator; b. Valdosta, Ga., Oct. 1, 1942; d. Emmett and Ruth (Johnson) M. AB in Edn., U. Mich., 1964, AM in Libr. Sci., 1967, postgrad., 1973-76. Tchr. Ecorse (Mich.) Pub. Schs., 1964-65; adminstrv. trainee Chrysler Corp., Highland Park, Mich., 1965-66, engring. libr., 1966-69; libr. II Wayne State U., Detroit, 1969-72, libr. III, 1972-75; staff asst. GM Rsch. Labs. Libr., Warren, Mich., 1976-78, supr. reader svcs., 1978-81; libr. dir. GMI Engring. & Mgmt. Inst., Flint, Mich., 1982-86; assoc. dir. for pub. svcs. & collection devel., assoc. prof. libr. sci. Purdue U. Librs., West Lafayette, Ind., 1986-89, acting dir. librs., assoc. prof. libr. sci., 1989, dean librs., prof. libr. sci., 1989—2004; Esther Ellis Norton Disting. Prof. Libr. Sci. Purdue U., West Lafayette, Ind., 1997—. Adj. lectr. U. Mich. Sch. Libr. Sci., Ann Arbor, 1974-75, 83-86; grants reader Libr. of Mich., 1980-81; project dir. Mideastern Mich. Region Libr. Cooperation, 1984-86; cons. Libr. Coop. of Macomb, 1985-86, Clark-Atlanta U., 1990-91; search com. for new dir. of libr. Smithsonian Instn., 1988; mem. GM Pub. Affairs Subcom. on Introducing Minorities to Engring.; presenter in field. Author: Special Libraries at Work, 1984, numerous other publs.; mem. editl. bd. Reference Svcs. Rev., 1989—2004, Infomanage, 1993-97. Corp. vis. com. for librs. MIT, 1990—2004, Carnegie-Mellon U., 1998—; mem. Ind. Statewide Libr. Automation Task Force, 1989-90; state tech. strategy subcom. on info. tech. and telecomms. Ind. Corp. for Sci. & Tech., 1989; nat. adv. com. Libr. of Congress, 1988; trustee Libr. of Mich., 1983-86, v.p., 1986, long range plan com., 1979-82, task force on document access and delivery, 1977-79; info. project mem. Rep. Nat. Conv., 1980; bd. dirs. Small Farms Assn., Southfield, Mich., Lafayette Symphony Orch., YWCA. Recipient Bausch & Lomb award, 1960, Cert. for Outstanding Performance in Acad. Achievement State of Mich. Ho. of Reps., 1976, Spl. Tribute for Outstanding Contbns. Libr. of Mich. Bd. Trustees, 1986, Disting. Alumnus award U. Mich. Sch. Info. & Libr. Studies, 1989; U. Mich. Regents Alumni scholar, 1960-64; CIC doctoral fellow in libr. sci., 1973-76. Mem. ALA (com. on accreditation, subcom. to rev. 1972, standards for accreditation 1988-89, OLOS minority internship com. 1988-89, nominating com. 1992-93, mem. coun. resolutions com. 1993-97), Assn. Coll. & Rsch. Librs. (task force on libr. sch. curriculum 1988-89, com. on profl. edn. 1990-92), Libr. Adminstrn. & Mgmt. Assn., Assn. Rsch. Librs. (bd. dirs. 1990-93), Spl. Librs. Assn. (pres. 1987-88, fellow 1991, com. mem.), Alpha Kappa Alpha, Phi Kappa Phi, Sigma Xi, Iron Key. Office: Purdue U Librs Stewart Ctr Lafayette IN 47907 Business E-Mail: emobley@purdue.edu.

MOBLEY, JOHN HOMER, II, lawyer; b. Shreveport, La., Apr. 21, 1930; s. John Hinson and Beulah (Wilson) M.; m. Sue Lawton, Aug. 9, 1958; children: John Lawton, Anne Davant. AB, U. Ga., 1951, JD, 1953. Bar: Ga. 1952, U.S. Dist. Ct. D.C. Ptnr. Kelley & Mobley, Atlanta, 1956-63, Gambrell & Mobley, Atlanta, 1963-83; sr. ptnr. Sutherland, Asbill & Brennan, Atlanta, 1983—. Founding chmn. Cmtys. in Schs. of Ga.; bd. dirs. Nat. Cmtys. in Schs.; mem. bd. visitors Emory U.; trustee Canterbury Ct. Episcopal Retirement Home of Atlanta; trustee Episcopal Diocese of Atlanta Found.; twice sr. warden All Saints Episcopal Ch. Capt. JAGC USAF, 1953—55. Recipient Disting. Svc. Scroll, U. Ga. Law Sch. Mem. ABA, D.C. Bar, State Bar Ga., Atlanta Bar Assn., Am. Judicature Soc., Atlanta Lawyers Club, Atlanta Athletic Club, Atlanta Country Club, Commerce Club, Piedmont Driving Club, Georgian Club, N.Y. Athletic Club, Met. Club of Washington, Phi Delta Phi. Home: 4348 Sentinel Post Rd NW Atlanta GA 30327-3910 Office: Sutherland Asbill & Brennan 999 Peachtree St NE Ste 2300 Atlanta GA 30309-3996 Office Phone: 404-853-8128. E-mail: john.mobley@sablaw.com.

MOBLEY, KAREN RUTH, art gallery director; b. Cheyenne, Wyo., Aug. 26, 1961; d. David G. and Marlene G. (Franz) M. BFA, U. Wyo., 1983; MFA, U. Oka., 1987. Sales assoc. Morgan Gallery, Kansas City, Mo., 1984-85; grad. asst. U. Okla. Mus. Art, Norman, 1985-87; dir. Univ. Art Gallery N.Mex. State U., Las Cruces, 1988-93; exec. dir. Nicolaysen Art Mus., Casper, Wyo., 1993-96; dir. Spokane Arts Com., 1997—. Guest artist Oklahoma City C.C., 1986. Paintings exhibited in numerous exhbns. including Phoenix Triennial, 1990, New Am. Talent, Laguna Gloria Art Mus., Austin, Tex., 1992, Adair Margo Gallery, El Paso, 1992, 93, 94, Wyo. Arts Coun. Gallery and Casper Coll., 1995, Mont. State U., 1996, Whitworth Coll., 2004. Trustee Westminster Congl. Ch.; bd. dirs. Spokane Pub. Radio. Wyo. Arts Coun. Individual Artist grantee 1994, Lit. fellow, 1995, 96; named Outstanding Young Women Am. Mem. Am. Assn. Mus., Coll. Art Assn., Wash. State Arts Alliance, Rotary 21, Phi Beta Kappa, Phi Kappa Phi. Office: Spokane Arts Com 808 W Spokane Falls Blvd Spokane WA 99203 Business E-Mail: kmobley@spokanecity.org.

MOBLEY, STACEY J. consumer products company executive; b. Chester, Pa., Nov. 19, 1945; s. James Otis and Retha B. (Hollis) M.; m. Joan Thompson, Aug. 28, 1970; children: Michele. BS in Pharmacy, Howard Univ. Sch. of Pharm., 1968; JD, Howard Univ. Sch. of Law, 1971. Bar: Pa., D.C., U.S. Supreme Ct. Sr. v.p., chief admin. officer and gen. coun. DuPont Co., Wilmington, Del., 1972—83, dir. of Fed. Affairs Wash., DC, 1983—86, v.p. Fed. Affairs, 1986—92, sr. v.p. comm. in External Affairs Wilmington, Del., 1992—99, chief admin. officer, gen. coun., 1999—, sr. v.p., 2001—. Mem. Wilmington Club, Carlton Club. Gov. Ruth Ann Minner appointed Mr. Mobley to chair the Delaware Strategic Econ. Coun., 2001. Office: DuPont Co 1007 Market St Wilmington DE 19898-0001

MOBLEY, TONY ALLEN, foundation administrator, former dean, recreation educator; b. Harrodsburg, Ky., May 19, 1938; s. Cecil and Beatrice (Bailey) M.; m. Betty Weaver, June 10, 1961; 1 child, Derek Lloyd. BS, Georgetown Coll., 1960; MS, Ind. U., 1962, D Recreation, 1965; MRE, So. Sem., Louisville, 1963. Chmn. dept. recreation and pks. Western Ill. U., Macomb, 1965-72, Pa. State U., University Park, 1972-76; prof., chmn. recreation and pks., dean Sch. Health, Phys. Edn. and Recreation Ind. U., Bloomington, 1976—; exec. dir. Ind. U. Found., Bloomington, 2002—. Chair health adv. coun. White River Park Commn., State of Ind., 1979—; v.p Ind. Sports Corp., Indpls., 1983-89; bd. dirs. Nat. Inst. for Fitness and Sport, Indpls., 1984-93; J.B. Nash scholar, lectr. Am. Assn. Leisure and Recreation, Reston, Va., 1985. Contbr. over 50 articles to profl. jours. Bd. dirs. Monroe County YMCA, Bloomington, 1984-88, United Way, Bloomington, 1994—; mem. Gov.'s Coun. for Phys. Fitness and Sport, 1991—. Am. Coun. Edn. adminstrv. internship fellow, N.C. State U., 1970-71. Fellow Am. Acad. Pk. and Recreation Adminstrn. (pres. 1985-86); mem. Nat. Recreation and Pk. Assn. (pres. 1978-79, Nat. Disting. Profl. award 1981), Assn. Rsch., Adminstrn., Profl. Couns. and Socs. (pres. 1986-87, award 1987), Am. Alliance Health, Phys. Edn., Recreation and Dance (Coll. and Univ. Adminstrs. Coun. Honor award 1986, R. Tait McKenzie award 1996), Soc. Pk. and Recreation Edn. (pres. 1974-75, award 1978), Ind. Pk. and Recreation Assn. (Outstanding Profl. award 1985). Avocations: golf, travel. Office: Ind U Found PO Box 500 Bloomington IN 47402

MOBLEY, WILLIAM HODGES, management educator, researcher, author, executive; b. Akron, Ohio, Nov. 15, 1941; BA, Denison U., 1963; PhD, U. Md., 1971. Registered psychologist, Hong Kong. Mgr. employee rels. rsch. PPG Industries, Pitts., 1971-73; prof. U. S.C., Columbia, 1973-80; head dept. of mgmt. Tex. A&M U., College Station, 1980-83, dean. Coll. of Bus. Adminstrn., 1983-86, exec. dep. chancellor, 1986-88, pres., 1988-93; chancellor Tex. A&M U. Sys., College Station, 1993-94; prof. mgmt. Tex. A&M U., College Station, 1980-96; pres. PDI Global Rsch. Consortium, Ltd., Hong Kong, Dallas, London, 1996—2002; prof. mgmt. China Europe Internat. Bus. Sch., Shanghai, 2002—; pres. Legend Global Pacific Ltd., Hong Kong, 2003—, Mobley Group Pacific, 2001—. Vis. fellow Cornell U., 1994, vis. prof. Hong Kong U. Sci. and Tech., 1995-97, U. Hong Kong, 1998. Author: Employee Turnover, 1982, Advances in Global Leadership, vol. I, 1999, vol. II, 2001, vol. III, 2003. Bd. dirs. Internat. Food and Agrl. Devel. and Econ. Coop., U.S. AID, 1992-94; mem. tri-lateral task force on N.Am. Higher Edn. Coop., USIA, 1993-95; trustee SIOP Found., 1998-2001, AMMA Found., Denison U.; mem. Pres. Bush's Commn. on Minority Bus. Devel., 1990-92, U.S. Com. of the Pacific Econ. Coop. Coun., 1995—; bd. dirs. Medici Med. Corp., 1992—, Concept Tech. Ltd., 1999—. Sr. Fulbright scholar Found. for Scholarly Exchange, Republic China, 1978-79; recipient DAAD, Rep. Germany, 1984; Fellow NDEA U.S. Dept. of Edn., 1968-71. Fellow APA, Am. Psychol. Soc.

MOCH, KENNETH IAN, entrepreneur; b. White Plains, N.Y., Sept. 11, 1954; s. Gerald Marvin and Joan Shirley (Kahn) M.; m. Ellen Gray Stolzman, July 27, 1987; 1 child, Jonathan Manley. AB in Biochemistry, Princeton U., 1976; MBA, Stanford U., 1980. Cons. Channing, Weinberg & Co., Inc., N.Y.C., 1976-78, sr. cons. McKinsey & Co., Inc., Chgo., 1980-82; v.p. Liposome Co., Inc., Princeton, N.J., 1982-88; mng. gen. ptnr. Catalyst Ventures, Ltd., Balt., 1988-90; pres., CEO Biocyte Corp., 1990. Mem. Stanford Bus. Sch. Alumni Assn. (pres. N.Y. chpt. 1990—). Avocations: theater, soccer. Office: Alteon Inc 6 Campus Dr Parsippany NJ 07054-4406

MOCH, ROBERT GASTON, retired lawyer; b. Montesano, Wash., June 20, 1914; s. Gaston and Fleeta Belle (Metcalf) M.; m. Barbara M. Kent, Sept. 2, 1940 (dec.); children: Marilynn A., Michael K., Robert M.; m. LaVerne I. Miller, May 29, 1968. BA magna cum laude, U. Wash., 1936; JD, Harvard Coll., 1941. Bar: Mass. 1941, Wash. 1945. Asst. crew coach U. Wash., 1936-39; head crew coach Mass. Inst. Tech., 1939-44; asso. Herrick, Smith, Donald, Farley & Ketchum, Boston, 1941-44; assoc. Eggerman, Rosling & Williams, Seattle, 1945-50, Weter, Roberts & Shefelman, Seattle, 1950-53; ptnr. Roberts & Shefelman, Seattle, 1953-87; of counsel Foster, Pepper & Shefelman, 1988—2001; ret., 2001. Del. Nat. Conf. on Law and Poverty, 1965, Nat. Defender Conf., 1969; chmn. King County Pub. Defender Adv. Com., 1970. Mem. U. Wash. Crew, 1933-36. Recipient Olympic Gold medal, 1936; named to Nat. Rowing Found. Hall of Fame, U. Wash. Hall of Fame, Montesano HS Hall of Fame, 2003. Mem. Wash. Bar Assn. (hon.), U. Wash. Alumni Assn. (pres. 1978-79, Disting. Svc. award 1986), Wash. Alumni Advs. (pres. 1985-87), Rainier Club, Rotary, Phi Beta Kappa, Beta Gamma Sigma, Alpha Kappa Psi, Phi Delta Phi, Phi Gamma Delta. Home: 22975 SE Black Nugget Rd Apt # 459 Issaquah WA 98029-7308

MOCHEL, MYRON GEORGE, mechanical engineer, educator; b. Fremont, Ohio, Oct. 9, 1905; s. Gustave A. and Rose M. (Minich) M.; m. Eunice Katherine Steinicke, Aug. 30, 1930 (dec. Dec. 1982); children: Kenneth R., David G., Virginia June. BSME, Case Western Res. U., 1929; MSME, Yale U., 1930. Registered profl. engr. N.Y., Mass., Pa. Devel. engr. nitrogen div. Allied Chem. Corp., Hopewell, Va., 1930-31; devel. engr. R&D dept. Mobil Corp., Paulsboro, N.J., 1931-37; design and devel. engr. gearing div. Westinghouse Electric Corp., Pitts., 1937-43; rsch. assoc. underwater sound lab. Harvard U., Cambridge, Mass., 1943-45; supr. of tng. steam turbine div. Worthington Corp., Wellsville, N.Y., 1945-49; prof. mech. engr. Clarkson U., Potsdam, N.Y., 1949-71, prof. emeritus, 1971—. Lect. U. Pitts., 1938-43, N.Y. State U. Adult Edn., Wellsville, 1946-49, Oswego, 1965, N.Y. State High Sch. Enrichment Program, Potsdam, 1962-71; cons. Designers for Industry, Cleve., 1953, rsch. engr. Morris Machine Works, Baldwinsville, N.Y., 1954, design engr. Racquette River Paper Co., Potsdam, 1955. Author: Fundamentals of Engineering Graphics, 1960, Pre-Engineering and Applied Science Fundamentals, 1962, Fortran Programming, Programs and Schematic Storage Maps, 1971; co-author: (with Eunice S. Mochel) Funds For Fun, 1983, (with Donald H. Purcell) Beyond Expectations, 1985; contbr. articles to profl. jours. and on internet. Officer, vol. St. Lawrence Valley Hospice, 1983; pres. Mayfield Tenants Assn., 1989-91. Mem. ASME, Am. Soc. Engring. Edn. (advt. mgr. Jour. Engring. Graphics 1963-66, sec. 1966-67, high schs. laision on engring. graphics 1962-65, awards com. chmn. 1965-66), Am. Assn. Ret. Persons (founder St. Lawrence County chpt., income tax counselor 1988-89, medicare/medicaid assistance program counselor 1988—, pres. 1989-90). Republican. Mem. Unitarian Universalist Ch. Home and Office: 17 Elm St Auburn NY 13021-2829

MOCK, DAVID CLINTON, JR., internist; b. Redlands, Calif., 1922; s. David Clinton and Eithel (Benson) M.; m. Marcella Enriqueta Fellin, 1952. AB, U. So. Calif., 1944; MD, M.H.D., Hahnemann Med. Coll., 1948. Intern Hahnemann Hosp., Phila., 1948-49; resident San Mateo (Calif.) County Hosp., 1949-51, 54, VA Hosp., Oklahoma City, 1954-55; research fellow in exptl. therapeutics U. Okla., Oklahoma City, 1956-57, L.N. Upjohn fellow, 1958, dir. exptl. therapeutics unit, 1959-62; dir., preceptorship program, 1968-76; assoc. prof. medicine U. Okla., Oklahoma City, 1963-72, prof., 1972-84, prof. emeritus medicine, 1984—, assoc. dean med. student affairs, 1970-76, assoc. dean postdoctoral edn., 1976-82, dir. continuing med. edn., 1980-83, dir. Transitional Yr. program, 1980-84, dir. History of Medicine program, 1982-84. Chief med. svc., Navajo Base Hosp., Ft. Defiance, Ariz., 1951-53; assoc. faculty homeopathy Royal London Homeopathic Hosp. Capt. USPHS, 1951-99, res.; now ret. Fellow: ACP; mem.: N.Y. Acad. Scis., Am. Fedn. Medical Rsch. Unitarian Universalist. Home: 570 Alameda Blvd Coronado CA 92118-1617

MOCK, FRANK MACKENZIE, lawyer; b. South Bend, Ind., May 17, 1944; s. Frank Carlton and Julia (Baughmann) M.; m. Virginia Johns, Dec. 31, 1974 (div. Feb. 1991); children: Shannon, John, Bridget; m. Christine Mall, June 1995; 1 child, Mackenzie Ann. BA, Duke U., 1966, JD, 1969. Bar: Fla. 1969. Assoc. Mahoney, Adams, Criser, Jacksonville, Fla., 1969-74, ptnr., 1977-92; gen. counsel Builders Investment Group, Valley Forge, Pa., 1974-77; ptnr. Baker & Hostetler, Orlando, Fla., 1992—. Mem. ABA, Am. Coll. Mortgage Lawyers, Duval County Bar Assn., Orange County Bar Assn., Dade County Bar Assn., Palm Beach County Bar Assn., Turnaround Mgmt. Assn. Republican. Episcopalian. Avocations: hiking, fishing, reading. Home: 2147 Santa Antilles Rd Orlando FL 32806-1533 Office: Baker & Hostetler 200 S Orange Ave Ste 2300 Orlando FL 32801-3432

MOCK, JOAN BODET, music educator; b. Houston, Dec. 3, 1937; d. Edward Bodet and Dorothy Crawford; m. Donald P. Garrett, 1966 (dec. 1985); children: William Clifford Garrett, Christopher Paul Garrett; m. Raymond Cecil Mock, July 7, 2002; 1 child from previous marriage, Charles H. Edwards II. B Music Edn., Ind. U., 1960; postgrad., U. N.Mex. Cert. tchr. N.Mex. Tchr. Espanola (N.Mex.) H.S., 1963—66, Hope H.S., Albuquerque, 1978—79; tchr. group piano lessons Piano Store Orgn., Colorado Springs, 1969—70; pvt. tchr. Garrett's Sch. Piano and Voice, Albuquerque; substitute tchr. Albuquerque Pub. Schs. Soloist for Ed Sullivan, Houston, 1956. Performer: Houston Little Theater, 1954—56, Acola Theater, 1970—79, The Ballad Hunter TV Program, 1954—56; dir.: O.P.E.R.A., 1978; contbr. poems to lit. publs. Soloist Christ Unity Ch., Albuquerque, 1988—92. Inst. Work scholar, Ind. U., 1957—60. Mem.: Albuquerque Music Tchrs. Assn., Nat. Music Tchrs. Assn., Nat. Fedn. Music Clubs. Home and Office: 10401 Crosscut Dr NW Albuquerque NM 87114 Office Phone: 505-350-7612.

MOCK, MELINDA SMITH, orthopedic nurse specialist, consultant; b. Austell, Ga., Nov. 15, 1947; d. Robert Jehu and Emily Dorris (Smith) Smith; m. David Thomas Mock, Oct. 20, 1969. ASN, DeKalb Coll., 1972. RN Ga., orthop. nurse specialist, 1976, cert. orthop. nurse, 1988; life care planner 2002. Nursing technician Ga. Bapt. Hosp., Atlanta, 1967, staff nurse, 1979; asst. corr. Harcourt, Brace & World Pub. Co., Atlanta, 1968-69; receptionist, sec. Goodbody & Co., Atlanta, 1969-70; nursing asst. DeKalb Gen. Hosp., Decatur, Ga., 1970-71; staff nurse Drs.' Meml. Hosp., Atlanta, 1972-73; staff nurse, relief charge nurse Shallowford Cmty. Hosp., Atlanta, 1973, charge nurse, 1973-76, head nurse, 1976-79, orthop. nurse specialist emergency rm., 1979; rehab. specialist, sr. rehab. specialist Internat. Rehab. Assocs., Inc., Norcross, Ga., 1981, rehab. supr., 1981-82; cons., founder, propr. Healthcare Cost Cons., Inc., Alpharetta, Ga., 1982-83, cons., founder, pres., 1983—. Legis. com. adv. coun. Ga. Bd. Nursing, Atlanta, 1984—85; adv. coun. Milton HS Coop. Bus. Edn., 1986—89; task force profl. liability ins. Nat. Fedn. Splty. Nursing Orgns., 1987—89; active Congressman Patrick Swindall Sr. Citizen Adv. Coun., 1988, Congressman Ben Jones Vets. Affairs Adv. Coun., 1989—92, White Ho. Conf. Small Bus., 1995; mem. small bus. adv. com., 1997—99; apptd. Congl. Small Bus. Summit, 1998. Atl. del.-at-large Nat. Rep. Conv., 1996; dep. voter registrar Fulton County, Ga., 1983—87; Rep. treas. 23d House Dist.; active various coms. and positions Fulton County Rep. Party, 1989—2001; Rep. treas. 41st House Dist., 1993—97; mem. state exec. com. Ga. Rep. State Com., 1997—99, mem., 1993—2002; 1st vice chairwoman Rep. 6th Congl. Dist., 1993—97, chmn., 1997—99; vice chair 7th Congl. Dist. Ga. Rep. Party, 2003—; del. various convs., 1993—; mem. Chattahoochee Rep. Women, 1989—2001, chmn. campaign com., 1992—94, rec. sec., 1995—2001; chmn. nominating com. House Dist. 23, 1990; mem. steering com. Re-Elect State Rep. Tom Campbell, 1990; mem. campaign staff Re-Elect State Senator Sallie Newbill, 1990, 1992, 1994; mem. health adv. campaign Elect Matt Towery for Lt. Gov., 1990, Elect Bob Barr U.S. Senate, 1991—92; mem. election com. Mark Burkhalter for State Rep.; vol. campaign staff Re-Elect Congressman Newt Gingrich, 1992, 1994, 1996, 1998, Elect Tom Price to State Senate, 1996; mem. campaign staff Cherokee County Reps., 2001—. Recipient Nat. Disting. Svc. Registry award, 1987; named Outstanding Young Women Am., 1984. Mem. Nat. Assn. Orthop. Nurses (nat. policies com. 1981-82, chmn. govt. rels. com. 1987-90, nat. treas. 1991-95, nat. pres. elect 1998-99, pres. 1999-2000, Nurse in Washington intern 1987, 99, legis. contbr. editor news 1989, chmn. legis workshop 1989, co-chmn. legis. workshop 1990, guest editl. Orthop. Nursing Jour. 1988, Ann. Congress del. 1982, 91-94, 96, 98-2001, 2003, Pres.'s award 1992, Outstanding Contbn. to NAON award 1996, chmn. budget and fin. com. 1991-95, nat. bylaws and policies com. 1995-98, bylaws and policies com. Atlanta chpt. 1994-96, pres-elect Atlanta chpt. 1996-97, 2004-05, pres. 1997-98, program dir. 2002-04), Orthop. Nurses Assn. (nat. bd. dirs. 1977-79, nat. treas. 1979-80), Coun. Splty. Nursing Orgns. Ga. (nominating com. 1976-77), Assn. Rehab. Nurses (bd. dirs. Ga. chpt. 1980-81, del. people-to-people program to China 1981), Nat. Fedn. Ind. Bus. (guardian 1988—, leadership coun. 1990—, healthcare task force chmn. 1992—, vice-chmn./fed. liaison Ga. adv. coun. 1995—), Am. Bd. Nursing Specialities (chmn. nominating com. 1993-95, chmn. com. on specialty bd. rev. 1993-95), Ga. Jaycees (dist. 4C rep. Ga. Jaycee Legis. 1984-85), Ga. Seatbelt Coalition, Orthop. Nurses Cert. Bd. (bd. dirs. 1991-96, pres. 1992-93, task force on advanced practice certification 1991-92), North Fulton C. of C. (vice chmn. health svc. effectiveness alliance 1984-85, chmn. 1985-86, co-chmn./editor periodical 1985, 3rd Quarter Workhorse award 1985), Alpharetta Jaycees (adminstrv. v.p. 1984-85, internal v.p. 1985-86), Alpharetta Jaycee Women (bd. dirs. 1983), Ga. Perimeter Coll. Nursing Alumni Assn. (bd. dirs.). Baptist. Avocations: reading, community service activities, scrapbooking. Office: Healthcare Cost Cons Inc PO Box 466 Alpharetta GA 30009-0466 Office Phone: 770-475-9454.

MOCK, ROBERT CLAUDE, architect; b. Baden, Germany, May 3, 1928; came to U.S., 1938, naturalized, 1943; s. Ernest and Charlotte (Geismar) M.; m. Belle Carol Bach, Dec. 23, 1952 (div.); children: John Bach, Nicole Louise; m. Marjorie Reubenfeld, Dec. 20, 1964. BArch, Pratt Inst., 1950; MArch, Harvard U., 1953. Registered arch., N.Y., Conn., N.J., Nat. Coun. Archtl. Registration Bds. Arch. George C. Marshall Space Ctr., Huntsville, Ala., 1950-51; archtl. critic Columbia Sch. Architecture, N.Y.C., 1953-54; dir. facility design Am. Airlines, N.Y.C., 1955-60; founder Robert C. Mock & Assocs., N.Y.C., 1960—. Mem. Mayor's Panel of Archs., N.Y.C. Prin. works include: Shine Motor Inn, Queens, N.Y., 1961 (recipient 1st prize motel category Queens C. of C. 1961), temporary terminal bldg. Eastern Air Lines, La Guardia Airport, N.Y.C., 1961, cargo bldgs United Airlines and Trans World Airlines, Kennedy Airport, N.Y.C., Bridgeport (Conn.) Airport, 1961, Eastern Air Lines Med. Ctr., Kennedy Airport, 1962, ticket office Trans World Airlines Fifth Ave., N.Y.C., 1962, terminal bldgs. Eastern Air Lines and Trans World Airlines, La Guardia Airport, N.Y.C., 1963, 7 bldgs. Mfrs. Hanover Trust Co., 1964-66, kitchen and commissary bldg. Lufthansa German Airlines, 1964, Ambassador Club, La Guardia Airport, 1964, Happyland Sch., N.Y.C., 1965, cargo bldgs. Alitalia and Lufthansa German Airlines, Kennedy Airport, 1965, FAA-Nat. Prototype Air Traffic Control Tower, 1966; Lufthansa German Airlines; Irish Internat. Airlines, El Al Israel Airlines, Varig Brazilian Airlines; passenger terminals Kennedy Airport, 1970; Swiss Air Cargo Terminal, Lufthansa German Airlines, cargo terminals El Al Israel airline cargo terminal, Kennedy Airport, 1972, passenger terminal Aerolineas Argentina, 1974, N.Am. hdqrs. Aerolineas Argentinas, N.Y.C., 1974, corp. hdqrs. Am. Airlines, 1977, N.Am. hdqrs. Varig Brazilian Airlines, N.Y.C., 1977, Norel-Ronel Indsl. Pk., Hollywood, Fla., 1979, N.Am. hdqrs. Irish Internat. Airlines, N.Y.C., 1979, corp. hdqrs. Bankers Trust Co., N.Y.C., 1980, cargo terminal Air India, cargo terminal Flying Tiger, Kennedy Airport, 1982, 2 flight kitchen bldgs. Ogden Food Corp., Kennedy Airport, 1984, 88 and LaGuardia Airport, 1987, Greenwich Assn. Retarded Citizens Sch., 1983, passenger terminal extension Varig Brazilian Airlines, 1985, 3 restaurants La Guardia Airport, 1987, residences Palm Beach, Fla., 1989-92, Bethesda, Md., 1993, 97, 98, 99, (named best custom residence in U.S., Profl. Builder Mag. 2000), Fenwick Island, Del., 1994, Potomac Falls, Md., 1995. Recipient Vol. of Yr. award United Way, 1984. Mem. Am. Arbitration Assn., Harvard Club, Admirals Cove Club. Office: 374 Spyglass Way Jupiter FL 33477-4051

MOCK, THEODORE JAYE, accounting educator; b. Traverse City, Mich., May 28, 1941; s. Raymond Doris and Georgeann (Lardie) M.; m. Mary Jo Icenhower, Mar. 25, 1962; children: Christopher, Cameron BS in Math., Ohio State U., 1963, MBA in Fin., 1964; PhD in Bus. Adminstrn., U. Calif.-Berkeley, 1969. Dir. AIS Research Ctr. UCLA, 1969-73; dir. Ctr. Acctg. Research, Arthur Andersen Alumni prof. acctg. U. So. Calif., 1982—. Vis. prof. Norwegian Sch. Econs. and Bus., Bergen, 1988, Bond U., Gold Coast, Australia, 1990, 92, So. Cross U., Lismore, Australia, 1994, Australia Nat. U., 2002-; adj. prof. U. Maastricht, The Netherlands, 1991—; hon. prof. Hong Kong City U., 1995-98; bd. dirs. Maastricht (The Netherlands) Acctg. Rsch. Ctr., U. Limburg, 1991—; Shaw prof. Nanyang Tech. U., Singapore, 1997, Tang Peng Yey; vis. prof. Nat. U. Singapore, 2000. Author: (monographs) Risk Assessment, 1985, Internal Accounting Control (Am. Acctg. Assn. Wildman medal), 1983, Measurement and Accounting Information Criteria, 1976, Impact of Future Technology on Auditing, 1988, Auditing and Analytic Review, 1989, Belief Functions in Business Decisions, 2000; mem. editorial bd. Auditing: A Jour. of Practice and Theory, 1983-86, 88-93, 99—, editor, 1993-96; mem. editorial bd. The Acctg. Rev., 1972-78, Internat. Jour. Auditing, 1998—. Recipient CPA Faculty Excellence award Calif. CPA Found. for Edn. and Rsch., 1983; Fulbright scholar U. Otago, Dunedin, New Zealand, 1988, U. Limburg, Maastricht, The Netherlands, 1993. Mem. Acctg., Orgns. and Soc. (editorial bd. 1978-93), Am. Acctg. Assn. (dir. rsch. 1982-84, acad. vice chmn. auditing sect. 1990-91, chair auditing sect. 1991-92, Collaboration award with AICPA, 1998, Outstanding Auditing Educator award 2003). Office: U So Calif Sch Acctg Los Angeles CA 90089-0001

MOCKER, HANS WALTER, physicist; b. Teplice, Czech Republic, Feb. 22, 1929; came to U.S., 1960; s. Emil and Marie (Schubert) M.; m. Carol Virginia Vines, Feb. 13, 1981; children: Peter, Nancy. MS in Physics, Inst. Tech., Darmstadt, Germany, 1954; PhD in Physics, U. Innsbruck, Austria, 1959. Sr. rsch. scientist rsch. dept. Honeywell, Mpls., 1960-65, prin. rsch. scientist sys. and rsch., 1965-69, sect. chief sys. and rsch., 1969-78, prin. rsch. fellow sys. and rsch., 1978-93; Ctr. fellow Tech. Ctr.-Alliant Tech. Sys., Mpls., 1991-93; cons. Electro-Optics Laser Sys., Dothan, Ala., 1994—. Physicist Farbenfabriken Bayer, Krefeld, Germany, 1959-60; mem. advanced group on electronic devices Undersec. of Def., Washington, 1977-78; presenter in field. Co-author: Design of Infrared and Laser Systems, 1981; contbr. articles to profl. jours. including Laser Focus, Applied Optics, Applied Physics Letters, IEEE Jour. Quant. Electr. Coach Minn. Soccer Assn., Mpls., 1981-83. Recipient H.W. Sweatt award, 1968, ir-100 award Indsl. Rsch. Mag., 1969, 77, Excellence in Oral Presentation, Soc. Automotive Engrs., 1993; named one of 7 Wonders of Engring., Minn. Soc. Profl. Engrs., 1970. Achievements include patents for apparatus for supervising proportion of magnetically active component in a fluid, for ring laser biased to permit two equal intensity transition frequencies to be generated in opposite directions, for optical system for laser doppler homodyne detection, for relaxation laser synchronizer for pulsed laser operation, for rapidly tunable laser, for method and means for removing claddings from optical fibers, for rapid wavelength switching of IR lasers with Bragg Cells, for laser doppler velocimeter using stable semiconductor or solid-state lasers, for scanning laser helmet mounted sight, for laser cavity helmet mounted sight, for solid-block homodyne interferometer, for look-ahead windshear detector by filtered Raleigh-scattered light. Home: 204 Westbrook Rd Dothan AL 36303-2952

MOCKLER, ESTHER JAYNE, state senator; b. Jackson, Wyo., Sept. 21, 1957; d. Franklin and Nancy (Fisher) Mockler. BA in Polit. Sci., Wellesley Coll., 1980. Legal asst., 1981-84; legal adminstr., 1984-87; rschr., cons., 1987—; exec. dir. Wyo. Dem. Party, 1993-95; mem. from Dist. 44 Wyo. Ho. of Reps., Cheyenne, 1992—96; mem. from Dist. 8 Wyo. Senate, Cheyenne, 1996—. Mem. Audubon Wyo. Bd. Office: PO Box 1857 Cheyenne WY 82003-1857 Office Phone: 307-632-5883.

MOCKLER, ROBERT JOSEPH, management educator; b. St. Louis, May 23, 1932; s. Colman Michael and Veronica (McKenna) M. BA, Harvard U., 1954, MBA, 1959; PhD, Columbia U., 1961. Instr. Rutgers U., N.J., 1959-61; Joseph F. Adams prof. mgmt. St. John's U., Jamaica, N.Y., 1962—. Lectr. in field; owner Real Estate Bus., N.Y.C., 1973-84. Co-author: Strategic Management: A Methodological Approach, 4th edit., 1994, An Information Systems Plan for the Malaysian Agricultural Research and Development Inst., 1993, Expert Systems: An Introduction to Knowledge-Based Systems, 1992; author: Strategic Management: A Research Guide With Comprehensive Bibliographies, 1993, Strategic Management: An Integrative Context-Specific Process, 1993, Strategic Management Cases, 1999, 2003, 2004, Rethinking Strategic Mgmt., 1995, Multinational Cross-Cultural Management, 1997, Multcultural Strategic Alliances, 2000, Expert Knowledge Based Systems, 2002, Winning in Business, 2004; contbr. more than 100 articles to profl. jours. and chpts. to books. 1st lt. Artillery, 1955-57. Recipient Fulbright award, 1993, Innovative Teaching award Decision Sci. Inst., 1990. Avocations: skiing, theater, golf, opera. Office: 114 E 90th St Ste 1B New York NY 10128-1551

MOCKO, GEORGE PAUL, minister; b. Little Falls, N.Y., Feb. 15, 1934; s. George and Anna (Swancara) M.; m. Elizabeth Carol Davidson, Sept. 2, 1956; children: David, Paul, Kristopher, Elissa BA, Hartwick Coll., 1956; BD, Phila. Sem., 1959, STM, 1972; DD (hon.), Gettysburg Coll., 1978. Ordained to ministry Evang. Luth. Ch. in Am., 1959. Pastor Jacob's and Outwood Chs., Pine Grove, Pa., 1959-62; assoc. pastor St Mark's Ch., Wilmington, Del., 1962-65, sr. pastor, 1965-78, Ascension Evang. Luth. Ch., Towson, Md., 1978-91; bishop Del.-Md. Synod Evang. Luth Ch. in Am., Towson, 1991-2000, ret., 2000. Author books; contbr. articles to profl. jours. Mem. Evang. Luth. Ch. Home: 501 Sussex Rd Baltimore MD 21286-7609 E-mail: GPmocko@aol.com. *Colossians speaks of Christ as the one in whom "all things hold together". I know that Christ is the one who holds me together. Proclaiming and living his life, the church holds our society together.*

MODANO, MIKE (MICHAEL MODANO), professional hockey player; b. Livonia, Mich., June 7, 1970; Right wing/ctr. Minn. North Stars, 1988—93, Dallas Stars, 1993—. Mem. U.S. Olympic Hockey Team, Nagano, Japan, 1998, Salt Lake City, 2002, Team U.S.A., Canada Cup, 1991, Team U.S.A., World Cup of Hockey, 1996, 2004. Named to NHL All-Star Game, 1993, 1998—2000, 2003, 2004. Achievements include mem. World Cup Champion Team U.S.A., 1996; mem. Stanley Cup Champion Dallas Stars, 1999. Office: c/o Dallas Stars 2601 Avenue of the Stars Frisco TX 75034*

MODARRES, MOHAMMAD, education educator; b. Esfahan, Iran, Aug. 11, 1952; s. Mohsen and Zahra M.; m. Susan Partovi, Jan. 25, 1984; 1 child, Cena. BS, Tehran Polytecnic, Iran, 1974; MS, MIT, 1977, PhD, 1980. Reliability analyst Sci. Applications, McLean, Va., 1980-82; prof. U. Md., College Park, 1982—; dir. Ctr. for Technology Risk Studies/U. Md., College Park, 1997—. Cons. ISL, Inc., Rockville, Md., 1987—; expert panel mem. Nuclear Regulatory Commn., Rockville, 1991-99; cons. Energy Rsch., Inc., Rockville, 1995—; adv. bd. PLG, Inc., Irvine, Calif., 1983-84. Author: (book) What Every Engineer Should Know About Reliability and Risk Analysis, 1993; co-author: (books) Reliability Engineers and Risk Analysis: A Practical Guide, 1999, Nuclear Power: Assurance Safety for the Future, 1998; contbg. author: Wiley's Ency. of Elec. and Electronics Engring., 1998. Recipient Disting. Scholar-Tchr. award U. Md., 1994-95, Inventor of Yr. award 1996. Fellow Am. Nuclear Soc. (chair human factors divsn. 1996-97, nuclear installations com. safety divsn. program 1997-98); mem. IEEE, Soc. for Risk Analysis. Office: Univ Md 2100 Marie Mount Hall College Park MD 20742-7531

MODE, CHARLES J. mathematician, educator; b. Bismarck, N.D., Dec. 29, 1927; s. Charles and Fannie E. (Hansen) M.; m. Eleanore L. Perdelwitz; 1 dau., Martha Lisa. BS in Genetics, N.D. State U., 1952; MS in Genetics, Kans. State U., 1953; PhD in Genetics, U. Calif., Davis and Berkeley, 1956; postgrad. in stats. (Univ. fellow), N.C. State U., 1956-57. Asst. prof. math. Mont. State U., 1957-59, asso. prof., 1960-62, prof., 1963-66, mem. genetics group, 1957-66; asso. prof. math. stats. SUNY, Buffalo, 1966-70; prof. math. Drexel U., 1970—. Cons. to industry. Author: (books) Multitype Branching Processes - Theory and Applications, 1971, Stochastic Processes in Demography and Their Computer Implementation, 1985, Stochatic Processes in Epidemiology, HIV/AIDS, Other Infectious Diseases and Computers, 2000; contbr. articles to profl. pulbs.; editor (assoc.): (jour.) Math. Bioscis., 1975—. Mem. Inst. Math. Stats., Biometric Soc., Am. Math. Soc., AAAS, Population Assn. Am., Sigma Xi, Phi Kappa Phi, Pi Mu Epsilon. Lutheran. Home: 502 Balsam Rd Cherry Hill NJ 08003-3202 Office: Drexel Univ Dept Math Philadelphia PA 19104 Business E-Mail: cmode@math.drexel.edu.

MODELL, ARTHUR B. professional football team executive; b. Bklyn., June 23, 1925; m. Patricia Breslin, July 25, 1969; stepchildren: John, David. Owner, pres. Cleve. Browns football team (now Baltimore Ravens), 1961—, owner, CEO. Pres. Nat. Football League, 1967-70 Office: Baltimore Ravens 200 Saint Paul Pl Ste 2400 Baltimore MD 21202-2003 also: Baltimore Ravens Ravens Stadium 1101 Russell Street Baltimore MD 21230

MODELL, JEROME HERBERT, anesthesiologist, educator; b. St. Paul, Sept. 9, 1932; s. William and Frieda (Singer) M.; m. Shirley Graves, Nov. 25, 1977; children— Charles, Jack, Julie. BA, U. Minn., 1954, BS, MD, U. Minn., 1957. Intern U.S. Naval Hosp., St. Albans, N.Y., 1957-58, resident, 1958-60; practice medicine specializing in anesthesiology Gainesville, Fla., 1969—; attending staff U.S. Naval Hosp., St. Albans, 1960-61, chief anesthesiology Pensacola, Fla., 1961-63; asso. prof. dept. anesthesiology U. Miami (Fla.) Sch. Medicine, 1963-69; prof., chmn. dept. anesthesiology U. Fla. Coll. Medicine, Gainesville, 1969-92, sr. assoc. dean clin. affairs, 1990-95, exec. assoc. dean, 1996-97, interim dean, 1997; assoc. v.p. U. Fla. Health Sci. Ctr. Affiliations, 1992-96. Assoc. v.p. U. Fla. Health Sci., 1998-2000, emeritus prof. 2000—, courtesy prof. large animal scis., 1999—. Author: The Pathophysiology and Treatment of Drowning and Near-Drowning, 1971, (with others) Introduction to Life Support, 1973; also numerous scientific articles. Served to lt. comdr. USN, 1957-63. Recipient NIH Research Career Devel. award. Mem. AMA, AAAS, Assn. U. Anesthetists, Am. Soc. Anesthesiologists, N.Y. Acad. Scis., Am. Coll. Chest Physicians. Home: PO Box 14347 Gainesville FL 32604-2347 Office: U Fla Coll Medicine PO Box 100254 Gainesville FL 32610-0254 Office Phone: 352-265-8076.

MODELL, JOHN, social sciences educator; b. N.Y.C., June 3, 1941; s. Walter and Merriam (Levant) Modell; m. Judith Schachter, June 2, 1963 (div.); children: Jennifer, Matthew Thelonious; m. Cynthia Garcia Coll, June 25, 2000. AB, Columbia U., 1962, MA, 1963, PhD, 1969; postgrad. (Social Sci. Research Council research tng. fellow), U. Pa., 1969-70. Research asst. Bur. Applied Social Research, Columbia U., 1962-65; lectr. Kingsborough Community Coll., 1965-66; dir. research Japanese Am. Research Project, UCLA, 1966-69; asst. prof. history U. Minn., 1969-72, assoc. prof., 1972-77, prof., 1977-83, Carnegie Mellon U., 1983-99, acting dean Coll. Humanities and Social Scis., 1985-87; prof. edn. and human devel., prof. sociology Brown U., Providence, R.I., 1999—. Rsch. assoc. Phila. Social History Project U. Pa., 1974—85; Cardozo vis. prof. history Yale U., 1991; mem. adv. planning com. Ctr. for Coordination of Study of Social Indicators Social Sci. Rsch. Coun., 1980—85; mem. com. child devel. rsch. and pub. policy NRC, 1981—86; mem. coun. Inter-Univ. Consortium for Polit. and Social Rsch., 1982—86; adv. com. Henry Murray Ctr. for Rsch. in Human Lives Radcliffe Coll.; mem. MacArthur Found. Rsch. Network on Successful Pathways Through Middle Childhood; mem. Network Program on Aging and Social Change Nat. Inst. Aging. Author: The Economics and Politics of Racial Accommodation: The Japanese of Los Angeles 1900-1942, 1977, Into One's Own: From Youth to Adulthood in the United States, 1920-1975, 1989; author: (with others) The Economic Basis of Ethnic Solidarity, 1981, Recent Social Trends in the United States, 1960-90, 1991; editor (, author (with others): The Kikuchi Diary: Chronicle of an American Concentration Camp, 1973; editor: (with others) Theory, Method, and Practice in Social and Cultural History, 1992, Children in Time and Place: Developmental and Historical Insights, 1993. Fellow John Guggenheim Meml., 1978—79. Home: 125 Morris Ave Providence RI 02906-2426 Office: Brown U Dept Edn Providence RI 02912-0001

MODELL, STEPHEN MARK, medical researcher, educator; b. Detroit, June 22, 1958; s. Richard Martin and Sola Jane (Hamburger) M.; m. Wanpen Prasoptham, Jan. 14, 1988; 1 child, Marrisa Lynne. AB in Philosophy, Stanford U., 1980; MD, Med. Coll. Ohio, 1984; MS in Clin. Rsch. Design/Statis. Analysis, U. Mich., 1991. Asst. coord. The Resource for Pub. Health Policy U. Mich. Sch. Pub. Health, Ann Arbor, 1987-89; rsch. asst., dept. psychiatry U. Mich., Ann Arbor, 1989-90, rsch. assoc. Genome Ethics Com., 1992-94; rsch. assoc. Coun. Genetics and Soc. U. Mich. Dept. Health Mgmt. and Policy, Ann Arbor, 1995-98, rsch. dir. genetics policy, 1999—; dissemination activities dir. Mich. Ctr. for Genomics and Pub. Health, 2000—. Mem. pres.'s coun. Med. Coll. Ohio, 1992—. Genome studies sect. editor Ultimate Reality and Meaning, 1995—; editor Studies in Biophilosophy, 1997. Recipient honorable mention Nellie Westerman prize competition in clin. rsch. ethics, Am. Fedn. Clin. Rsch., 1995. Mem. AMA, Am. Fedn. Med. Rsch., N.Y. Acad. Scis., Maimonides Soc., Internat. Soc. Study of Human Ideas on Ultimate Reality and Meaning (bd. dirs. 1994—, treas. 1999-2000, v.p. 2001-02, pres. 2003—). Avocations: book discussion groups, water sports, jogging, hiking, travel. Home: 3086 Deer Creek Ct Ann Arbor MI 48105-9664 Office: U Mich Sch Pub Health SPH-II OCBPH M4157 109 S Observatory St Ann Arbor MI 48109-2029 E-mail: mod@umich.edu.

MODEN, JOLEEN, communications executive; B in Bus. Adminstr. and Actg. CPA. Ptnr. Coopers & Lybrand; v.p., CFO, treas. Signature Home Care Group; dir. corp. audit PepsiCo Inc.; asst. contr. internal audit GTE, 1998—2000; sr. v.p. internal auditing Verizon Comms. Inc., N.Y.C., 2000—. Office: Verizon Comms Inc 1095 Avenue of the Americas New York NY 10036-6797 Office Phone: 212-395-1233.

MODER, JOHN JOSEPH, non-profit administrator; b. St. Louis, Apr. 9, 1948; s. Helen (Freihaut) Moder. BA in English and Philosophy, St. Mary's U., San Antonio, 1970; MA in Philosophy, Fordham U., 1972, PhD in Philosophy, 1977; M Div, U. St. Michael's, 1979. Mem. faculty Assumption High Sch., East St. Louis, Ill., 1973—74, Vianney High Sch., St. Louis, 1975—76; faculty mem. Irish Christian Bros. Sch., Mono Mills, Canada, 1977—79; asst. prof. philosophy St. Mary's U., San Antonio, 1979—86, assoc. prof. philosophy, trustee, co-chmn. peace commn., 1986—88, pres., 1988—2000, Jr. Achievement South Tex., 2000—01; tchr. Alamo Heights H.S., 2001—02; v.p., COO Hispanic Assn. Colls and Univs., 2002—. Bd. advisors Communities-in-Schs., San Antonio, 1988-2000. Avocations: hiking, reading, travel, running. Office: 8415 Datapoint Drive Ste 400 San Antonio TX 78229

MODERACKI, EDMUND ANTHONY, music educator, conductor; b. Hackensack, N.J., July 18, 1946; s. Edmund Joseph and Helen Theresa (Fisher) Moderacki; m. Brenda Wing Moderacki. BA, Montclair State Coll., 1968, postgrad., 1970-71; MA, Hunter Coll., 1970, postgrad., 1970-72, Newark State Coll., 1969-70, Seton Hall U., 1970, Rutgers U., 1976-78, Ctr. for Understanding Media, 1973. Tchr. music pub. schs., River Vale, N.J., 1968—; asst. condr. Ridgewood (N.J.) Symphony Orch., 1969—, trustee, pres., 1986-87, 94-95; artistic dir. Ridgewood (N.J.) Symphony, 2001—; asst. condr. Adelphi Chamber Orch., 1994-95; condr. Project Symphony, 2003. Tuba soloist Rutherford Cmty. Band, Ridgewood Village Band, Waldwick Band, Ridgewood Concert Band, 1978—, trustee, 1985—, guest condr., 1985, 86, 88, 93; mgr. All Bergen High Sch. Band, 1994; condr. All Bergen County High Sch. Band, 2001. Author: Images of America: River Vale. Town historian River Vale; mem. steering com. Bergen County Teen Arts, 1991—. Recipient County Exec. Vol. award, 1991, Tchr. Recognition award Gov. of State of N.J., 1990; Bergen County PTA fellow, 1976. Mem. NEA, Music Educators Nat. Conf., N.J. Orch. Assn. (trustee 1981-85), N.J. Edn. Assn. (alt. del. assembly 1983-93, mem. state membership com. 1986—), Music Educators Bergen County (bd. mem. at-large 1995-97, treas. 1997-2000, pres.-elect 2000-2002, pres. 2002-04), River Vale Edn. Assn. (pres. 1981-83, 88-91, 2000-03), Brigade Am. Revolution (bd. dirs. at large 1991-95, info. officer 1989-95, adj. 1996-2000, editor Brigade Press 2002-), Phi Mu Alpha Sinfonia, Kappa Delta Pi. Home: 740 White Birch Rd Township Of Washington NJ 07676 Office: Woodside Sch Rivervale NJ 07675 Office Phone: 201-358-4000 2801.

MODERY, RICHARD GILLMAN, marketing and sales executive; b. Chgo., Sept. 20, 1941; s. Richard Gustave Modery and Betty Jane (Gillman) Perok; m. Kay Francis Whitby, July 31, 1966 (div. July 1977); children: Stacey Lynn, Marci Kay; m. Anne-Marie Lucette Arsenault, Feb. 27, 1979. Student, Joliet (Ill.) Jr. Coll., 1959-61, Aurora (Ill.) Coll., 1963-65, Davenport Bus. Coll., Grand Rapids, Mich., 1969-71, Northwestern U., Evanston, Ill., 1987. Mktg. products mgr. Rapistan, Inc., Grand Rapids, 1964-75; mgr. estimating, project mgmt., customer svc. E.W. Buschman Co., Cin., 1975-78; exec. v.p. Metzgar Conveyor Co., Grand Rapids, 1979-84; mng. dir. Metzco Internat (ctrl. and S.Am.), Grand Rapids, 1981-84, Transfer Technologies, Inc., Grand Rapids, 1984-87; gen. ptnr., pres., CEO Nat. Monument Co., Grand Rapids, 1986—99; v.p. Translogic Corp., Denver, 1987-88; corp. officer, v.p. mktg., field ops. and sales S.I. Handling Systems, Inc., Easton, Pa., 1988-91; pres. Handling Concepts, Inc., Chgo., 1993—, Modery Sys., Inc., Chgo., 1997—2004. Agt. Muratic-Murata Automated Sys., Inc., 1997—2000. Patentee in field. Commr. City of East Grand Rapids, Mich. Traffic Commn., 1983—86; bd. dirs. Naperville (Ill.) Humane Soc., 2001—. Mem. Internat. Material Mgmt. Soc., Am. Mgmt. Assn., Material Handling Inst. Am., Material Handling Inst. (spkr. nat. confs.), Am. Mktg. Assn., Conveyor Equipment Mfrs. Assn., Material Handling Equipment Distbrs. Assn., Masons (32 degree). Avocations: golf, photography, power walking, computers. Home: 2255 Palmer Cir Naperville IL 60564-5672 Office: Handling Concepts Inc 2255 Palmer Cir Naperville IL 60564-5672 also: Modery Sys Inc 2255 Palmer Cir Naperville IL 60564-5672 Office Phone: 630-904-4642.

MODESITT, CAROL ANN, music, voice educator, opera director; b. Mar. 6, 1947; BA, Utah State U., 1968; MusM, Ea. Ky. U., 1973. Asst. prof. Utah State U., Logan, 1978-84; vis. asst. prof. U. Colo., Boulder, 1984-90; artist in residence Plymouth (N.H.) State Coll., 1990-93; assoc. prof. voice and opera So. Utah U., Cedar City, Utah, 1993—. Author: (ednl. software) Reindeer Ednl. Network, 1999; book reviewer: Nat. Opera Assn. Jour., 1998—; performer (debut recital): Carnegie Hall, 2002. Pres. Cedar City (Utah) Music Arts, 1999—2002, Cedar City Arts Coun., 2002—05. Recipient Contribution to Arts award, Cedar City C. of C., 2001. Mem.: NOW, AAUW, Nat. Opera Assn. (west ctrl. region gov. 1997), Music Tchrs. Nat. Assn. (pres. Cedar City 1997—), Nat. Assn. Tchrs. of Singing (sec. Las Vegas chpt. 1998—, pres. 2004—06). Home: 255 Sunnyview Rd Cedar City UT 84720-2897 Office Phone: 435-865-8166. Home Fax: 435-865-1812.

MODESTINO, JAMES WILLIAM, electrical engineering educator; b. Boston, Apr. 27, 1940; s. William and Mary Elizabeth (Dooley) M.; m. Leone Marie MacDougall, Aug. 25, 1962; children: Michele Marie, Lee Ann. BS, Northeastern U., 1962; MS, U. Pa., 1966; MA, Princeton U., 1968, PhD, 1969. Mem. tech. staff Gen. Telephone Electronics Labs., Waltham, Mass., 1969-70; asst. prof. Northeastern U., Boston, 1970-72; prof. Rensselaer Poly. Inst., Troy, NY, 1972-93, inst. prof., 1993—2001, dir. Ctr. for Image Processing Rsch., co-dir. Internat. Ctr. for Multimedia Edn.; prof., chmn. dept. elec. and computer engring., U. Miami. Vis. prof. U. Calif., San Diego, 1981-82; vis. faculty fellow GE Corp. R&D Ctr., 1988-89; vis. prof. MIT, Cambridge, Mass., 1995-96; pres. Modcom Inc., Ballston Lake, N.Y., 1981—; v.p. ICUCOM Inc., Troy, N.Y., 1986-2001. Recipient Sperry Faculty award Sperry Corp., 1986. Fellow IEEE (S.O. Rice Prize Paper award 1984, mem. bd. of govs. Info. Theory Soc. 1988-92) Avocations: sailing, jogging, tennis, skiing. Office: 1251 Memorial Dr PO Box 248294 Coral Gables FL 33124 E-mail: modestino@ipl.rpi.edu.

MODIANO, ALBERT LOUIS, gas, oil industry executive; b. N.Y.C., Sept. 10, 1953; s. Sam A. and Eve Modiano; m. Carolyn Elizabeth Barker, Sept. 29, 1979; children: Aaron, Sarah Anne. BA cum laude, Hobart Coll., 1975; MA, U. Chgo., 1977; postgrad., Harvard U., 1992. Mem. U.S. Senate, 1980-81; assoc. Am. Petroleum Inst., Washington, 1981-87; dep. dir. Office of Oil Policy U.S. Dept. Energy, Washington, 1987-89; dep. dir. U.S. Minerals Mgmt. Svc., Washington, 1989-93; v.p. U.S. Oil & Gas Assn., Washington, 1993—. Mem. Phi Beta Kappa. Office: Ste 601 901 F St NW Washington DC 20004-1400

MODIE, CHRISTINE M. insurance company executive; BS, U. Vt., 1974. V.p. mutual fund info. svcs. State St. Bank and Trust Co., Quincy; chief info. officer Batterymarch Fin. Mgmt., Inc., Boston; verious sr. level positions Aetna Life Ins. Co., Hartford, Conn.; sr. v.p., chief info. officer Travelers Life & Annuity, 1997—99; exec. v.p., chief info. officer Mass. Life Ins. Co., Springfield, 1999—. Office: Mass Life Ins Co 1295 State St Springfield MA 01111-6001

MODIN, FREDRIK, professional hockey player; b. Sundsvall, Sweden, Oct. 8, 1974; Hockey player Brynas IF, Maple Leafs, 1996-99; left wing Tampa Bay (Fla.) Lightning, 1999—. Office: Tampa Bay Lightning Ice Palace 401 Channelside Dr Tampa FL 33602

MODISETT, JEFFREY A. lawyer, state attorney general; b. Windfall, Ind., Aug. 10, 1954; s. James Richard and Diana T. Modisett; m. Jennifer Ashworth, June 9, 1990; children: Matthew Hunter Ashworth, Haden Nicholas. BA, UCLA, 1976; MA, Oxford (Eng.) U., 1978; JD, Yale U., 1981. Bar: Ind., Calif., D.C. Clk. to Hon. R. Peckham U.S. Dist. Ct. (no. dist.) Calif., San Francisco, 1981—82; asst. U.S. atty. Office U.S. Atty. (ctrl. dist.) Calif., L.A., 1982—88; issues dir. Evan Bayh for Gov., Indpls., 1988; exec. asst. to gov. State of Ind., Indpls., 1988—90; prosecutor Marion County, Indpls., 1991—94; sr. counsel Ice Miller Donadio & Ryan, Indpls., 1995—96; atty. gen. State of Ind., 1997—2000; dep. CEO, gen. counsel Dem. Nat. Conv., 2000; co-CEO TechNet, Palo Alto, Calif., 2000—01; ptnr. Manatt Phelps & Phillips LLP, 2001—02, Bryan Cave LLP, 2002—. Chmn. Gov. Commn. for Drug Free Ind., Indpls., 1989—, Gov. Coun. on Impaired and Dangerous Driving, Indpls., 1989—; pres. Family Advocacy Ctr., Indpls., 1991—94, Hoosier Alliance Against Drugs, Indpls., 1993—96; dir. Cmty. Couns. of Indpls., 1991—93; chmn. Ind. Criminal Justice Inst., Indpls., 1989—90, dir., 1989—; vice chmn. Juvenile Justice and Youth Gang Study Com., Indpls., 1992—94; legal analyst Sta. WTHR-TV, Indpls., 1995—96. Author: Prosecutor's Perspective, 1991—94; editor-in-chief: Yale Jour. Internat. Law, 1980—81. Co-chair Ind. State Dem. Coordinated Campaign, Indpls., 1996. Named Top Lawyer, Indpls. Monthly mag., 1993; named to Sagamore of Wabash, State of Ind., 1995; recipient Spl. Enforcement award, U.S. Customs, 1988, Child Safety Adv. award, Automotive Safety for Children, 1997, STAR Alliance Impact award, 1998, Spirit of Ind. award, Am. Lung Assn., 1999. Mem.: Indpls. Bar Assn., Ind. Bar Assn. Democrat. Avocation: bicycling.

MODISHER, MELVIN WAYNE, obstetrician/gynecologist, educator; b. Sharpsville, Pa., May 9, 1916; MD, Temple U., 1943. Diplomate Am. Bd. Ob-Gyn. Intern Abington Meml. Hosp., 1944; resident in ob-gyn. Bethesda Hosp., Cin., 1946-49; mem. staff U. Hosp., San Diego. Assoc. clin. prof. reproductive medicine Med. Sch. U. Calif. San Diego. Fellow ACS. E-mail: melcor@cts.com.

MODLIN, HOWARD S. lawyer; b. NYC, Apr. 10, 1931; s. Martin and Rose Modlin; m. Margot S. Modlin, Oct. 18, 1956; children: James, Laura, Peter. AB, Union Coll., Schenectady, 1952; JD, Columbia U., 1955. Bar: N.Y. 1956, D.C. 1973. Assoc. Weisman, Celler, Spett & Modlin, P.C., N.Y.C., 1956-61, ptnr., 1961-76, mng. ptnr., 1976-95, pres., 1996—. Chmn. bd. dirs., sec. Gen. DataComm Industries, Inc., Naugatuck, Conn.; bd. dirs. Am.-Book-Stratford Press, Inc., N.Y.C., Fedders Corp., Liberty Corner, NJ, Trans-Lux Corp., Norwalk, Conn. Chmn. bd. dirs. Daus. of Jacob Geriat. Ctr., Bronx, N.Y. Mem. ABA, Assn. of Bar of City of N.Y., D.C. Bar Assn. Office: Weisman Celler Spett & Modlin PC 445 Park Ave New York NY 10022-2606 Office Phone: 212-371-5400.

MODRICH, PAUL L. biochemistry educator; b. Raton, N.Mex., June 13, 1946; BS in Biology, MIT, 1968; PhD in Biochemistry, Stanford U., 1973; postgrad., Harvard U., 1973-74. Asst. prof. chemistry U. Calif., Berkeley, 1974; asst. prof. biochemistry Duke U., 1976, assoc. prof. biochemistry, 1980, prof. biochemistry, 1984, dir. program in genetics, 1989-92, investigator Howard Hughes Med. Inst., 1994—. Contbr. articles to profl. jours.; assoc. editor: Biochemistry, 1992-94, mem. editl. adv. bd., 1986-91, 95—; mem. editl. bd. Nucleic Acids Rsch., 1980-82, Jour. Biol. Chemistry, 1982-83. Recipient award in enzyme chemistry Pfizer, 1983, NAS, 1993, Mott prize in cancer rsch. GM, 1996. Mem. NIH (mem. biochemistry study sect. 1980-84, NIH NIGMS merit award 1986), Am. Soc. Biochemistry and Molecular Biology (councillor 1989-92, 97—, mem. publs. com. 1995-97), Inst. Medicine, 2004. Office: Department of Biochemistry Nanaline H Duke Box 3711 DUMC Durham NC 27710 Office Phone: 919-684-2775.*

MOE, ANDREW IRVING, veterinarian; b. Tacoma, Jan. 2, 1927; s. Ole Andrew and Ingeborg (Gordham) M.; m. Dorothy Clara Becker, June 25, 1950 (dec. Nov. 30, 2001); children: Sylvia Moe McGowan, Pamela Moe Barker, Joyce. BS in Biology, U. Puget Sound, 1949; BA, Wash. State U., 1953, DVM, 1954. Meat cutter Art Hansen, Tacoma, 1943-48; gen. practice as vet. Baronti Vet. Hosp., Eugene, Oreg., 1956-57; vet. regulatory Calif. Animal Health br., resident vet. II Calif. Dept. Food & Agr., Modesto, 1957-64, acting vet.-in-charge Modesto Dist. office, vet. III, 1976-77, ret., 1990—. Watersafety instr. ARC, 1958-61. Capt. Vet. Corps., 1954-56, 62; lt. col. Biomed Scis. Corps. USAF, ret., 1982. Recipient Chief Vet. badge, 1975. Mem. VFW (life, comdr. post 4144 1998-2001, quartermaster 2000-02), No. San Joaquin Vet. Med. Assn. (pres. 1979), Calif. Acad. Vet. Medicine (charter), Mil. Officers Assn. of Am. (charter), Res. Officers Assn. (life), Ret. Officers Assn. (life), Assn. Mil. Surgeons U.S. (life), Sons of Norway, Am. Legion (life), Shriners (bd. dirs. Modesto Shrine 1995), Masons (Illustrious Master Modesto chpt. 1983, Allied Masonic degrees, pres. Modesto Masonic Luncheon Club 1991, 98, Merito-

rious Svc. medal 1992, Man of Yr. award 1999), Scottish Rite (pres. Ctrl. Valley 1997, bd. dirs. 1998-2004), Presido Yacht Club Sausalito (Calif.), Theta Chi, Alpha Psi. Lutheran. Home: 161 Norwegian Ave Modesto CA 95350-3542

MOE, JAMES BURTON, pharmaceutical company executive; b. Hayfield, Minn., Oct. 4, 1940; s. James Herald and Clara Clema (DeVriendt) M.; m. Janice Naomi Nackerud, Nov. 27, 1959; children: Carolyn, Alyson, Jennifer, Bryce. BS, U. Minn., 1962, DVM, 1964; PhD, U. Calif., Davis, 1978. Pvt. vet. practice Dodge Vet. Clinic, Dodge Center, Minn., 1964-66; commd. 1st lt. U.S. Army, 1966, advanced through grades to lt. col., 1979, retired, 1986; dir. divsn. pathology Walter Reed Army Inst. Rsch., Washington, 1980-86; sr. scientist The Upjohn Co., Kalamazoo, 1986-88, dir. drug devel. toxicology, 1988-89, exec. dir. drug safety rsch., 1989-94, v.p. world wide drug safety rsch., 1994-95; v.p. world wide toxicology Pharmacia & Upjohn, Inc., Kalamzoo, Mich., 1995-2000; v.p. global toxicology and metabolism Pharmacia Corp., Kalamzoo, Mich., 2000—03; ind. cons., 2003—. Contbr. articles to profl. jours., chpts. to books. Decorated Bronze Star, Legion of Merit; Calif. Lung Assn. Pulmonary Rsch. grantee, 1976. Mem. Am. Coll. Vet. Pathologists (pres. 1992-93), Soc. Toxicol. Pathologists, U.S. Can. Assn. of Pathology. Lutheran. Avocations: golf, jogging, woodworking. Home: 525 S Burdick St #3706 Kalamazoo MI 49007 Office: Global Toxicology Pharmacia Corp 301 Henrietta St Kalamazoo MI 49007-4940

MOE, JANET ANNE, elementary school educator, church organist; b. Sacramento, May 24, 1946; d. Joseph Robert and Virginia Lou (Jones) Mangan; m. Edward Earl Moe, Aug. 23, 1969 (dec. Aug. 2002); children: Erik John, Erin Jean Moe Mitchell. BA, Calif. Luth. U., 1968; std. secondary tchg. credential, Calif. State U., Sacramento, 1969, crosscultural, lang. and acad. devel. cert. (CLAD), 1996; cert. in Orff Schulwerk Levels I, II and III, U. Calif. Santa Cruz, 1987; MS, preliminary adminstrv. credential, Nat. U., Sacramento, 2001. Elem. tchr. Gloria Dei Luth. Sch., Sacramento, 1969—73; elem. music specialist Sacramento City Unified Sch. Dist., 1982—. All-city elem. choir coord. Sacramento City Unified Sch. Dist., 1999—2001; chorus dir. Sierra Mountain Music Camp, Sacramento, 2001; facilitator Calif. dept. edn. model arts project Sierra Mountain Unified Sch. Dist. Touring choir Sacramento City Coll., Italy, 1998, 1998, 2002, 2002, touring choir in France, Spain, 2002, touring choir in Ireland, Scotland, 2004; touring choir So. Calif. and Hawaii Calif. Luth. U., 1967—68; task force to restore music and the fine arts Sacramento City Unified Sch. Dist., 1999—2000; organist Gloria Dei Luth. Ch., 1970—2002, Luth. Ch. of Good Shepherd, 2003—. Recipient Hon. Svc. award, PTA Bear Flag Sch., Sacramento, 1992. Mem.: NEA, Calif. Music Educators Assn. (elem. rep., mem. bd. Capitol Sect., Save the Music grant 2002, Outstanding Music Educator award 1996, 2003), Nat. Audubon Soc. Republican. Lutheran. Avocations: birdwatching, travel, yoga, reading, hiking, genealogy. Home: PO Box 109 Elk Grove CA 95759-0109

MOE, MICHAEL, diversified financial services company executive; BA in Polit. Sci. and Econs., U. Minn. Cert. fin. analyst. Sr. mng. dir., dir. growth strategy Montgomery Securities; dir. global growth stock rsch., mng. dir. Merrill Lynch, 1998; founder ThinkEquity Ptnrs., San Francisco, chmn., CEO. Advisor Ctr. for Innovation; adv. bd. Edn. Industry Report. Named Best on St., The Wall St. Jour.; named to All American Rsch. Team, Instl. Investor. Mem.: San Francisco (Calif.) Analyst Soc., N.Y. Soc. Security Analysts. Office: ThinkEquity Partners 475 Sansome St Ste 800 San Francisco CA 94111*

MOE, ORVILLE LEROY, racetrack executive; b. Spokane, Wash., Nov. 26, 1936; s. Clarence Orville and Georgia Maria (Lombard) M.; m. Deonne Wesley Schultz, Jan. 11, 1953; children: Kathleen June, Susan Marie, Terry Ann. Co-owner Moe's Sudden Svc. Fuel Co., Spokane, Wash., 1956-74; sec. Gold Res. Mining Corp., Spokane, 1973-89, Bonanza Gold Corp., Spokane, 1973-85; pres., founder Spokane Raceway Park, Inc., 1971—. Regional v.p. Am. Hot Rod Assn., Kansas, Mo., 1968-84, mktg. dir., 1978-84; co-producer Internat. Car Show Assn., Spokane, 1969-90. Co-producer Spokane Auto Boat Speed Show, 1964—. Mem. Nat. Rep. Senatorial Com., 1984—; mem., trustee Rep. Presdl. Task Force, mem. 1992 Presdl. Trust Rep. Nat. Com. Mem. ISCA, Eagles, Am. Hot Rod Assn. (exec. v.p. Spokane, Wash. 1986—), Internat. Footprint Assn., Am. Auto Racing Assn. (regional v.p.). Republican. Avocations: auto racing, mining, collecting and rebuilding autos, fishing, ice hockey. Office: Spokane Raceway Park Inc 101 N Hayford Rd Spokane WA 99224-9510

MOE, RICHARD PALMER, lawyer; b. Duluth, Minn., Nov. 27, 1936; s. Russell James and Virginia Mary (Palmer) M.; m. Julia Neimeyer, Dec. 26, 1964; children— Eric Palmer, Andrew Neimeyer, Alexandra Julia. BA, Williams Coll., 1959; LL.B., U. Minn., 1966. Bar: Minn. 1967, D.C. 1979, N.Y. 1991. Adminstrv. asst. to mayor, City of Mpls., 1961-62; to lt. gov., 1963-66; fin. dir. Minn. Democratic Farmer-Labor Party, 1967-69, chmn., 1969-72; adminstrv. asst. to Sen. Walter F. Mondale of Minn., Washington, 1972-76; chief of staff Vice Pres. Walter F. Mondale, 1977-81; counsel Davis Polk & Wardwell, Washington, 1981-85, ptnr., 1985-92; pres. Nat. Trust for Hist. Preservation, Washington, 1992—. Trustee Ford Found., 1998—. Office: Nat Trust for Hist Preservation 1785 Massachusetts Ave NW Washington DC 20036-2117

MOE, ROGER DEANE, former state legislator, secondary education educator; b. Crookston, Minn., June 2, 1944; s. Melvin Truman and Matheldia (Njus) M.; m. Paulette Moe; four children. BS, Mayville State Coll., 1966; student, Moorhead State Coll., 1969, N.D. State U., 1970. Tchr. Ada (Minn.) H.S., 1966—; v.p. Coleman, Christison Advt. Agy.; mem. Minn. Senate from 2nd dist., St. Paul, 1970—2002; majority leader Minn. State Senate, 1981. Chmn. rules and adminstrn. com., mem. ethics and campaign reform, edn., and higher edn. coms., Minn. State Senate. Ward del. Ada, Minn., 1970; state del. Minn. Dem.-Farmer-Labor Conv., 1970. Mem. NEA, Ada Edn. Assn., Jaycees. Dfl. Office: Rt 3 Box 86A Erskine MN 56535-9532

MOE, RONALD CHESNEY, public administration researcher, consultant; b. San Diego, May 28, 1937; s. Chesney R. and L. Bernice (Weston) M.; m. Carolyn Carr, May 18, 1962 (div. Feb. 1974); children: Steven, Cynthia; m. Grace Tyler, Apr. 30, 1976. BA, Claremont Coll., 1959; MA, Columbia U., 1962, PhD in Pub. Law and Govt., 1968. Asst. prof. San Diego State U., 1967-70; sr. policy advisor Office of Econ. Opportunity, Exec. Office of the Pres., Washington, 1970-71, Cost of Living Coun., Exec. Office of the Pres., Washington, 1971-73; specialist govt. orgns. and mgmt. Congl. Rsch. Svc. Libr. of Congress, Washington, 1973—2002. Cons. OECD, Paris, 1996—, Brookings Instn., Washington, 2003-, Congl. Rsch. Svc., 2003-. Contbr. chpts. in books, articles to profl. jours. Mem. exec. bd. Congl. Chs. of Am., Milw., 1985-89. Capt. U.S. Army Res., 1961-63. Ctr. Study of Am. Govt. fellow Johns Hopkins U., Washington, 1993—; recipient ASPA Louis Brownlow award, 1988, 91, 95-96. Fellow Nat. Acad. Pub. Adminstrn.; mem. Acad. Polit. Sci., Cosmos Club (Washington), Phi Beta Kappa. Republican. Home: 4700 Connecticut Ave NW Apt 407 Washington DC 20008-5609 Office: Congl Rsch Svc Libr Of Congress Washington DC 20540-0001 E-mail: rmoe@crs.loc.gov.

MOE, STANLEY ALLEN, architect, consultant; b. Fargo, ND, May 28, 1914; s. Ole Arnold and Freda Emily (Pape) Moe; m. Doris Lucille Anderson, July 25, 1937 (dec. 2000); children: Willa Moe Crouse, Myra Moe Galther; m. Reiko Izuno, Nov. 11, 2001. BArch, U. Minn., 1936; DEng (hon.), U. ND, 1993. lic. arch. several states; cert. Nat. Coun. Archtl. Registration Bds. Project arch. several firms in Midwest, 1936-42, U.S. Army Corps Engrs., Africa, 1942-43; ptnr. H.S. Starin, Archs. & Engrs., Duluth, Minn., 1943-47; sr. ptnr. Moe & Larsen, Archs. & Engrs., LA, 1947-54; ptnr., gen. mgr., exec. v.p. Daniel, Mann, Johnson & Mendenall, LA, 1954-71, corp. v.p., 1972-79; prin. Stanley A. Moe, AIA, LA, 1979—. Dir. design of major mil. projects in Eritrea, Sudan, Egypt, Yemen for Allied Forces, 1942-43; chmn. control com. DMJM & Assocs., dir. design prototype, tng. & operational facilities Titan I Intercontinental Ballistic Missiles Program USAF, 1958-63; project dir. Space Shuttle facilities Kennedy Space Ctr., 1973; project dir. for design of aircraft maintenance complex Iranian Aircraft Industries, 1978; project mgr. for design of major med. facility program Min. of Def. and Aviation, Saudi Arabia, 1975-76; project mgr. design of Boufarik Internat. Airport, Algeria, 1983. Pres. San. Fernando Valley Young Reps., 1952, Van Nuys (Calif.) Jaycees, 1950. Recipient Disting. Svc. award for cmty. svc. Van Nuys Jaycees, 1949, Sioux award U. ND Alumni Assn., 1985, Trustees Soc. award U. Minn., 1992; inducted into ND Entrepreneur Hall of Fame, 2000. Mem. AIA (Calif. coun.), Rotary, Delta Tau Delta. Republican. Presbyterian. Avocations: world travel, hunting, fishing, historic restoration, woodworking. Home and Office: 447 S Plymouth Blvd Los Angeles CA 90020-4706

MOECK, PETER, crystallographer, materials scientist; s. Adelinde and Erich Moeck; life ptnr. Svoboda Dimitrova; 1 child, Georg Jurkschat. PhD in Crystallography, Humboldt U. of Berlin, Germany, 1991. Cert. Adult Edn. Tchr. 2000. Rschr. Inst. for Semiconductor Physics, Frankfurt/Oder, Germany, 1983—86; rsch. asst. Humboldt U. of Berlin, 1987—91; rschr. Tech. U. of Berlin, 1991—92; post doctoral rschr. Humboldt U. of Berlin, 1992—93; forensic scientist, pub. analyst Ctrl. Forensic Sci. Labs. of the German State Brandenburg, 1993—94; sr. rsch. asst. U. of Durham, England, 1994—97; rsch. assoc. Imperial Coll. London, 1997—98; rsch. fellow U. of Oxford, England, 1998—2000; asst. rsch. prof. U. of Ill., 2000—02; asst. prof. physics Portland State U., Oreg., 2002—. Author about 35 fully refereed papers and 100 others. Recipient Rsch. Innovation award, Rsch. Corp., 2003. Mem.: Am. Phys. Soc., Materials Rsch. Soc., German Soc. for Crystallography. Achievements include invention of Goniometry of direct and reciprocal lattice vectors in transmission electron micrcopy; patents pending for Process for forming semiconductor quantum dots with superior structural stability; development of Direct crystallographic analyses in transmission electron microscopy.

MOE-FISHBACK, BARBARA ANN, counseling administrator; b. Grand Forks, N.D., June 24, 1955; d. Robert Alan and Ruth Ann (Wang) Moe; m. William Martin Fishback; children: Kristen Ann Fishback, William Robert Fishback. BS in Psychology, U. N.D., 1977, MA in Counseling and Guidance, 1979, BS in Elem. Edn., 1984. Cert. elem. counselor Ill. Tchr. United Day Nursery, Grand Forks, 1977-78; social worker Cavalier County Social Svcs., Langdon, N.D., 1979-83; elem. sch. counselor Douglas Sch. Sys., Ellsworth AFB, S.D., 1984-87, Jacksonville (Ill.) Sch. Sys., 1987—2004; h.s. counselor/early years counselor Jacksonville Sch. Dist., 2004—. Vol. Big Sister program, Grand Forks, 1978—84; leader pine to prairie coun. Girls Scouts U.S., 1980—82; tchr. Head Start Program, Grand Forks, 1979; mem. parent com., sec. Abraham Lincoln coun. Boy Scouts Am., 2001—; Sunday sch. tchr., 2001—; leader confirmation team, 2003—. Mem.: AAUW (local br. newsletter editor 1980—81, br. sec. 1981—83), NEA, AACD, Am. Sch. Counselor Assn., Ill. Edn. Assn., Ill. Sch. Counselor Assn., Ill. Assn. Counseling and Devel., Jaycettes (bd. dirs. 1982—83), Kappa Alpha Theta (newsletter, mag. article editor 1976—77). Avocations: cooking, camping, curling, ceramics, creative writing. Home: 291 Sandusky St Jacksonville IL 62650-1844 Office: Jacksonville High Sch 1211 N Diamond Jacksonville IL 62650 Office Phone: 217-243-4384. E-mail: bmoe-fishback@jax117.morgan.k12.il.us.

MOEHLE, JACK P. civil engineer, engineering executive; BSCE, MSCE, U. Ill., 1977, PhD, 1980. Registered civil engr., Calif. From asst. to assoc. prof. U. Calif., Berkeley, 1980-90, prof., 1990—, Roy W. Carlson Disting. prof. civil engring., vice-chair tech. svcs. civil engring., 1990-91, dir. earthquake engring. rsch. ctr., 1991—. Tech. advisor Double Deck Peer Rev. Panel, Caltrans, 1990—; mem. sci. adv. com. Nat. Ctr. Earthquake Engring. Rsch.; proposal reviewer NSF; cons. in field; bd. dirs. Calif. Univs. Rsch. Earthquake Engring., Cooperating Orgns. No. Calif. Earthquake Rsch. and Tech. Contbr. articles to profl. jours.; reviewer tech. papers. Recipient Chi Epsilon Excellence Teaching award, 1986; Regents Jr. Faculty fellow, 1981. Fellow Am. Concrete Inst. (chmn. detail and proportion earthquake resisting structural elements and systems com. 1988—, mem. various coms.); mem. ASCE (publs. sec. com. seismic effects, Huber Rsch. prize 1990), Structural Engrs. Assn. Calif. (mem. seismology com., reinforced concrete com., bd. dirs.), Earthquake Engring. Rsch. Inst. Office: U Calif Berkeley Earthquake Engring Rsch Ctr 1301 S 46th St Richmond CA 94804-4600

MOEHLMAN, MICHAEL SCOTT, lawyer; b. Columbus, Ohio, Apr. 11, 1938; s. Arthur Henry and Marguerite Caroline M.; m. Carol Jean Shafer, Sept. 28, 1963; 1 son, Matthew. BA, Harvard U., 1960; LLB, U. Tex., 1963. Bar: Tex. 1963. With Strasburger & Price, Houston. Bd. dirs. St. Martin's Episcopal Children's Ctr. Fellow Tex. Bar Found.; mem. ABA (com. bank securities), Internat. Bar Assn., Tex. Bar Assn. (com. revision corp. law), Houston Bar Assn. (judicature com.), Tex.-Mex. Bar Assn., Am. Judicature Soc., Houston Bar Found. (chmn. bd. dirs.), Phi Delta Phi. Clubs: Houston (chmn. fin. com., bd. dirs., pres.), Houston Racquet, Houston Yacht, Harvard (Boston), St. Charles Bay Hunting. Episcopalian. Office: Strasburger & Price 1401 McKinney St Ste 2200 Houston TX 77010-4035 Office Phone: 713-951-5684. Business E-Mail: michael.moehlman@strasburger.com.

MOELHMAN, AMY JO, social worker; b. Lafayette, Ind., Mar. 18, 1954; d. Charles and Marian (Young) Moelhman. BS, Ball State U., 1976; MSW, U. Denver, 1979. Lic. clin. social worker, Ind. Social worker Adolescent Crisis Team, Adams County Social Svc., Denver; counselor adolescent boys prog. Pleasant Run Children's Home, Indpls.; group therapist Mothers of Victims of Sexual Abuse, Mid-Town Mental Health, Indpls.; supr. foster care and counseling prog. Children's Bur., Indpls.; mgr. Family Connection Ctr., 1989-90; dir. family programs Vis. Nurse Svc., Indpls., 1990-96; dir. Holy Family Svcs., Cath. Social Svcs., Indpls., 1996—2001; cons. Brown County Family Access Ctr., 1999—; supr. cmty. programs Indpls. Transition Ctr. Casey Family Programs, 2001—. Chair Ind. Coalition of Family-based Svcs., 1992-94; co-chair family preservation com. Marion County Stepahead; part-time faculty masters in social work program Ind. U.-Purdue U., Indpls. Contbr. articles to profl. jours. Mem. NASW, Acad. Cert. Social Workers. Home: 818 E 53rd St Indianapolis IN 46220-3104 E-mail: amoelhman@casey.org.

MOELING, WALTER GOOS, IV, lawyer; b. Quantico, Va., Feb. 16, 1943; s. Walter Goos III and Dorothy M.; m. Nell Frances Askew, Aug. 27, 1965; children: Charles H., Christine E. BA, Duke U., 1965, JD, 1968. Bar: Ga. 1968. Assoc. Powell, Goldstein, Frazer & Murphy, Atlanta, 1968-75, ptnr., 1975—. Bd. dirs. So. Banking Law and Policy Conf., 1989-96, Southeastern Conf. for Bank Dirs., 1996—, Children's Rehab. Ctr., Atlanta, 1982—, Gatchell Home, Atlanta, 1983—; bd. dirs. Frazer Ctr., 1989—, chmn. bd. dirs., 1993. Mem. ABA (mem. banking com. 1986—), Ga. C. of C. (bd. dirs. 1998-2000), Ga. Bar Assn., Ga. Bankers Assn. (assoc., chairperson bank counsel sect. 1992-95, bd. dirs. 1998-2000), Cmty. Bankers Assn. (assoc.), Capital City Club, Willow Point Country Club. Democrat. Unitarian Universalist. Avocations: golf, fly-fishing. Office: Powell Goldstein Frazer & Murphy 191 Peachtree St NE Ste 16 Atlanta GA 30303-1740 Business E-Mail: wmoeling@pgfm.com.

MOELLEKEN, BRENT RODERICK WILFRED, surgeon; b. Vancouver, B.C., Can., Apr. 19, 1960; *married to Dayna Devon, host of NBC's Extra.* BA, Purdue U., 1979; MD, Yale U., 1985; postgrad., Harvard U., 1980-81. Diplomate Am. Bd. Surgery, Am. Bd. Plastic Surgery. Intern U. Calif., San Francisco, 1985-86, resident in gen. surgery, 1986-92, rsch. fellow in plastic surgery, 1988-90, resident in plastic surgery, 1992-94; fellow in aesthetic surgery UCLA, L.A., 1994-95; pvt. practice Beverly Hills, Calif., 1995—, Santa Barbara, Calif., 1995—. Attending surgeon UCLA Hosp., Cedars-Sinai Hosp., L.A.; asst. clin. prof. UCLA. *Private practice in Beverly Hills, Calif. Second office in Santa Barbara, Calif. Featured on ABC's Extreme Makeover, NBC's Dateline and Extra, CNN, Access Hollywood, and Entertainment Tonight for his plastic surgery innovations LiveFill and the superficial cheeklift.* Inventor superficial checklift. Fellow ACS. Achievements include invention of live fill graft; Extreme Makeover surgeon. Office: 120 Spalding Dr, Ste 340 Beverly Hills CA 90212 Office Phone: 310-273-1001. E-mail: drbrent@drbrent.com.

MOELLER, AUDREY CAROLYN, retired energy company executive, corporate secretary; b. Pitts., May 10, 1935; d. Nicholas William and Edith Tecla (Russman) M. Grad. high sch., Pitts. Legal sec. Equitable Resources Inc., Pitts., 1955-72, asst. corp. sec., 1972-80, corp. sec., 1980-86, v.p., corp. sec., 1986-99; also corp. sec. Equitable Resources Inc. subs.; ret., 1999. Com. mem. United Way Allegheny County, Pa., 1978, United Way Southwestern Pa., 1984. Mem.: Pa. Assn. Notaries, Am. Soc. Corp. Secs. (chmn. membership and asst. sec. Pitts. chpt. 1995, treas. 1996, v.p. and program chmn. 1997, pres. 1998), Loyal Christian Benefit Assn. (nat. coun. 1993, pres. br. 331 2000, nat. auditor 2001). Democrat. Roman Catholic. Avocations: choral singing, golf, travel. Home: 1003 Cherry Hill Dr Presto PA 15142

MOELLER, DADE WILLIAM, environmental engineer, educator; b. Grant, Fla., Feb. 27, 1927; s. Robert A. and Victoria (Bolton) M.; m. Betty Jean Radford, Oct. 7, 1949 (dec. Oct. 1998); children: Garland Radford, Mark Bolton, William Kehne, Matthew Palmer, Elisabeth Anne. BSCE, Ga. Inst. Tech., 1947, MS in Environ. Engring., 1948; PhD in Nuc. Engring., N.C. State U., 1957. Commd. jr. asst. san. engr. USPHS, 1948, advanced through grades to san. engr. dir., 1961; rsch. engr. Los Alamos (N.Mex.) Sci. Lab., 1949-52; staff asst. Radiol. Health Program, Washington, 1952-54; rsch. assoc. Oak Ridge Nat. Lab., 1956-57; chief radiol. health tng. Taft San. Engring. Ctr., Cin., 1957-61; officer charge Northeastern Radiol. Health Lab., Winchester, Mass., 1961-66; assoc. dir. Kresge Ctr. Environ. Health, Harvard Sch. Pub. Health, 1966-83, prof. engring. in environ. health, head dept. environ. health scis., 1968-83, dir. Office of Continuing Edn., 1982-84, assoc. dean continuing edn., 1985-93; environ. cons., 1993—; pres. Dade Moeller & Assocs., Inc., 1993—. Cons. radiol. health. Author (textbook) Environmental Health, 3rd edit., 2004; contbr. articles to profl. jours. Chmn. Am. Bd. Health Physics, 1967-70; mem. com. 4 Internat. Commn. on Radiol. Protection, 1978-85; chmn. nat. air pollution manpower devel. adv. com. U.S. EPA, 1972-75; mem. adv. com. reactor safeguards U.S. NRC, 1973-88, chmn., 1976, chmn. adv. com. nuc. waste, 1988-93; chmn. sci. and tech. rev. panel Office of Civilian Radioactive Waste Mgmt., U.S. Dept. Energy, 2003-. Named to Ga. Inst. Tech. Engring. Hall of Fame, 1999; recipient Disting. Engring. Alumnus award, N.C. State U., 2001, Fellow Am. Pub. Health Assn., Am. Nuc. Soc.; mem. AAAS, Am. Acad. Environ. Engrs., Nat. Coun. Radiation Protection and Measurements (hon.), NAE, Health Physics Soc. (pres. 1971-72, Robley D. Evans Commemorative medal 2003). Home and Office: 257 River Island Rd New Bern NC 28562-3669 Office Phone: 252-633-3352.

MOELLER, FLOYD DOUGLAS, lawyer; b. Safford, Ariz., Aug. 16, 1949; s. Floyd Albert and Helen Lou (Posey) M.; m. Tyra Brown, Dec. 18, 1970; children: Kristin, Sam, John, Susan. BS in Police Sci., Brigham Young U., 1972, JD, 1977; MS in Mgmt., Lesley Coll., 1985, MA in Counseling Psychology, 1987; LLM in Tax, Washington Sch. Law, 1987, D of Juridicial Sci., 2001. Bar: N.Mex. 1978, U.S. Dist. Ct. N.Mex. 1978, U.S. Dist. Ct. Ariz. 1978, U.S. Ct. Appeals (10th cir.) 1979, U.S. Tax Ct. 1981, U.S. Supreme Ct. 1981, Navajo Nation, Hopi Tribe, Jicarilla Apache Tribe, White Mountain Apache Tribe, So. Ute Tribe, Ute Mountain Tribe, So. Paiute Coun., Ft. Belknap Indian Ct., Gila River Indian Ct., Mescalaro Apache Ct., S.W. Inter Tribal Ct. Appeals, Zuni Tribal Ct. Assoc. Wade Beavers & Assocs., Farmington, N.Mex., 1978-79; ptnr. Nunn & Moeller, Farmington, 1979; sole practice Farmington, 1979—80; ptnr. Moeller & Burnham, Farmington, 1980-87; sole practice, 1987—. Mem. exec. com. Better Bus. Bur. of 4 Corners, 1978, bd. dirs., 1978—; bd. dirs. Farmington Pub. Library Bd., 1979-86, San Juan Med. Found., San Juan Pub. Library Found., Halvorson House; chmn. local troop coms. Boy Scouts Am., Farmington, 1985—. Capt. USMC, 1972-75. Named diplomat Nat. Bd. Trial Advocacy, 1986. Mem. ABA, J. Reuben Clark Law Soc., Nat. Panel Consumer Arbitrators, Am. Arbitration Assn., N.Mex. Trial Lawyers Assn., N.Mex. State Bar Assn. (CLE, fee arbitration coms. 1985, pres. trial practice sect. 1988), Navajo Nat. Bar Assn., San Juan County Bar Assn., 4 Corners Inn of Ct. Republican. Mem. Lds Ch. Avocations: reading, poetry, gardening, knot tying. Office: PO Box 15249 Farmington NM 87401-5249 Fax: (505) 362-0818. E-mail: dmoeller@acrnet.com.

MOELLER, GALEN ASHLEY, lawyer; b. Ballinger, Tex., Jan. 17, 1950; s. Norbert Edward and Magdaline O. (Kocich) M.; m. Roseann Dominguez, Aug. 12, 1977; children— Tatum Cheree, Taylor Ashley. B.A. in History, St. Mary U., San Antonio, 1972, J.D., 1974. Bar. Tex. 1975, U.S. Dist. Ct. (no. dist.) Tex. 1976. Sole practice, San Angelo, 1975— . Mem. ABA, Tex. Bar Assn., Tom Green County Bar Assn., Tex. Trial Lawyers Assn., Tex. Criminal Def. Lawyers Assn., Sons of Hermann Rowena, Elks, K.C., Lambda Chi Alpha (hon.). Roman Catholic. Office: 331 W Avenue B San Angelo TX 76903-6811 Office Phone: 325-655-4187. E-mail: Gmoe@justice.com, gmoe48@aol.com.

MOELLER, JAMES, retired state supreme court justice; b. Valley, Nebr., Nov. 14, 1933; s. Hans and Marie Grace (Shumaker) M.; m. Nancy Lee Kiely, Dec. 16, 1961; children: Amy Jo, Linda Anne. BA, Nebr. Wesleyan U., 1954; JD with high distinction, George Washington U., 1959. Bar: Ariz. 1959, U.S. Dist. Ct. Ariz. 1959, U.S. Ct. Appeals (9th cir.) 1961. Assoc. Lewis and Roca, Phoenix, 1959-64, ptnr., 1964-70, Moeller Hover Jensen & Henry, Phoenix, 1970-77; judge Maricopa County Superior Ct., Phoenix, 1977-87; assoc. justice Ariz. Supreme Ct., Phoenix, 1987-92, vice chief justice, 1992-96, assoc. justice, 1996-98; ret., 1998—. Editor-in-chief George Washington U. Law Rev., 1958-59. Bd. dirs. Found. for Blind Children, Scottsdale, Ariz., 1964-70, Ariz. Found. Prevention of Blindness, Phoenix, 1966-70; Rep. committeeman, Phoenix and Scottsdale, 1965-69. Served with U.S. Army, 1954-56. Fellow Am. Bar Found., Ariz. Bar Found.; mem. Ariz. Bar Assn., Maricopa County Bar Assn. Presbyterian. Avocations: travel, puzzles, history.

MOELLER, JAMES CHARLES, writer; b. Alameda, Calif, June 7, 1954; s. Wayne Jack Bowen and Barbara Ann (Herrick) Moeller; m. Diana E. Moeller, Feb. 18, 1984; children: Jennifer M., Emmeline J., Abigail C., Clara G. BA SG, Univ. of NE, Omaha, NE, 1987, MA, 1997. First Date Res. Sup. First Data Res., Omaha, 1984—87; trainer Marriott Res. Ctr., Omaha, 1989—2003; adj. prof. Grace Univ., Omaha, 2000—02, Iowa Western C.C., 2003—. Treas. Wordsowers Writers Group, Omaha, 2000—03. Publications: jour. Answering the Call: Omaha Jewry and the War Effort, 1941-1945, 1995, Memories of the Jewish Midwest, 1995; author: (jour. article) Memories of the Jewish MW, 1997, The Death of Raymond Yellow Thunder, 2002; author: Jour. of the West, 2002;; publications: jour. Nebr. Life, 2003, In Nebr. with Lewis & Clark, 2003; author: (mag. article) Nebr. Life, 2003. Del. Rep. Party of Nebr., Lincoln, Nebr., 1996, Rep. Party of Douglas County, Omaha, 1996. Mil. police U.S. Army, 1977—80, Europe. Recipient deans list, Coll. of Arts & Sci./Univ. Nebr., Omaha, 1987. Mem.: Phi Alpha Theta Honors Soc. Republican. Lutheran. Avocations: deer, golf, auto restoration, Star Trek & Sci-Fi, Indian. Home: 4717 N 131st St Omaha NE 68164 Office: Iowa Western Cmty Coll 2700 College Rd Box 4-C Council Bluffs IA 51503

MOELLER, JOSEPH JOHN, JR., university official; b. Jersey City, Feb. 1, 1946; s. Joseph John and Paula (Huneke) M.; m. Linda Lee Recksiek, Aug. 8, 1971. BEng, Stevens Inst. Tech., 1967, MEng, 1969, PhD, 1975. Instr. Stevens Inst. Tech., Hoboken, N.J., 1970-75, asst. prof., 1975-77, dean ednl. devel., 1977-85, mgr. personal computer program, 1983-85, assoc. provost for computing and info. systems, 1985-88, v.p. for info. systems, 1988-92, v.p. for adminstrv. and info. sys., 1992-94, v.p. grad. sch. and rsch., 1994—. Adminstr. N.J. Bus.-Industry-Sci. Edn. Consortium, Hoboken, 1985-92; adminstr. N.J. Intercampus Network, Inc., Steering Com. Adminstr., Hoboken, 1990-93, pres. 1993-97, bd. trustees, 1990—; chmn. Newark Remote Access Ctr., Hoboken, 1988-93. Contbr. articles to profl. jours., chpt. to book. Dir. Hudson County chpt. United Way, 1992-94. Named Outstanding Tchr. of Yr., Stevens Inst. Tech., 1973; honored by N.J. Gen. Assembly for meritorious svc. to edn., 1997. Mem. Assn. Ind. Colls. and Univs. (dir. 1993—), Am. Soc. for Engring. Edn., N.J. Soc. for Info. Mgmt., Sigma Xi, Tau Beta Pi (mem. adv. bd.). Avocations: travel, music. Office: Castle Point On The Hudson Hoboken NJ 07030-5906

MOELLER, JOSEPH (JOE) W. energy executive; b. Holdenville, Okla., 1943; m. Mary Moeller; 3 children. BS in Bus. Adminstrn., Aarhus (Denmark) U.; Degree in Petroleum Mktg., Tulsa, 1966. Joined Koch Industries, Wichita, Kans., 1966, v.p. refined products group, 1980, pres. petroleum group, 1992—95, pres. Koch Industries Internat., 1995—98, pres. Koch Ventures, 1998—99, pres., COO, 1999—, also bd. dirs. Trustee U. Tulsa; mem. 25 Yr. Club Petroleum Industry. Named Outstanding Alumnus, U. Tulsa Coll. Bus. Adminstrn., 1995—96. Office: Koch Industries 4111 E 37th St North Wichita KS 67220

MOELLER, LAURA LEE, former retail executive, library consultant; b. St. Louis, Feb. 20, 1927; d. Edwin Charles and Henrietta Maude (Schelp) Luedde; m. Gerald Herbert Moeller, June 25, 1949; children: Dereck John, Dori Lee, Merry Cay. AB, Harris Tchrs. Coll., St. Louis, 1948; sch. libr. cert., Washington U., St. Louis, 1965. Elem. tchr. Howard Sch., St. Louis, 1948-50, Bay View Sch., Norfolk, Va., 1951; libr. East Ladue Jr. High Sch., St. Louis, 1965-77; mgr., buyer Wornall House Mus. Shop, Kansas City, Mo., 1978-79; co-owner Crabtree & Evelyn London on Plaza, Kansas City, 1979—94. V.p. Women's Coun. U. Mo., Kansas City, 1984—85; active Ch. Libr. Guild, 1990—. Mem.: DAR (treas. Westport chpt. 1992—94, vice regent 1994—96, regent 1996—98), AAUW, Plaza Mchts. Assn. (nominating com. 1981, bd. dirs. 1991—94), Mo. Assn. Sch. Librs. (pres. 1976—77), Rotary Aux., Conservative Capitalists Investment Club (sec. 2002—), Carriage Club. Presbyterian. Avocations: reading, tai chi, line dancing. Home: 6247 Rosewood Shawnee Mission KS 66205

MOELLER, MARY ELLA, retired home economist, educator, radio commentator; b. Southampton, N.Y., Mar. 11, 1938; d. Harry Eugene and Edith Leone (Reester) Parsons; m. James Myron Moeller, Aug. 5, 1961; 1 child, Mary Beth. BS in Home Econs., U. Nebr., 1960; MLS, SUNY, Stony Brook, 1977. Tchr. home econs. Port Jefferson Schs., N.Y., 1960-70; home econs. program asst. Suffolk County Coop. Extension of Cornell U., Riverhead, N.Y., 1972-82; tchr. home econs. Eastport (N.Y.) H.S., 1982-85, South County Schs., Bellport Middle Sch., N.Y., 1985-93; sch. coord. N.Y. state mentoring program Bellport Middle Sch., 1992-95. Host Ask Your Neighbor, Sta. WRIV, Riverhead, 1982-87; trainer Home Econs. Entrepreneurship N.Y. State Edn. Dept., 1986-95; mem. home and career skills regional team N.Y. State Edn. Dept., 1984-86; mem. consumer homemaking adv. bd. Bd. Coop. Edn.; friendly svc. chmn. N.Y. State Ret. Tchrs. L.I. Zone, 1995-2003. Contbr. monthly articles to consumer publs. Chairperson policy bd. South Country Tchrs. Ctr.; mem. East Hampton Town Citizens Adv. com., East Hampton Citizens Adv. Commn., East Hampton Sr. Citizen Adv. Com.; v.p. Friendly Svc., 2000-03. Mem.: DAR (historian 1985, parliamentarian East Hampton chpt.), East End Ret. Tchrs. Assn. (chmn. by laws com. 2003—), N.Y. State Ret. Tchrs. Assn. (v.p. Friendly Svc., L.I. Zone 2000—03, chmn. nominations Long Island zone 2003—, health care coord. 2003—), Suffolk County Home Econs. Assn., Am. Home Econs. Assn. (cert. home economist), N.Y. State Home Econs. Assn., East Hampton Ladies Village Improvement Soc. (bd. dirs.), Daus. of the Founders and Patriots of Am., Eastern Gate Garden Club, Eastern Star (matron 1970). Home: 161 Newtown Ln East Hampton NY 11937-2429 Office: Bellport Mid Sch Kreamer St Bellport NY 11713 E-mail: jasmoel@aol.com.

MOELLER, ROBERT CHARLES (BUD MOELLER), management consultant; b. Washington, Sept. 5, 1954; s. Charles Edward and Ann Joan (Federico) M.; m. Carol Elizabeth Buchanan, June 19, 1976; children: Melaine Elizabeth, Robert Kehne. BChemE, Ga. Inst. Tech., 1976; MBA, Harvard U., 1978. Cons. ERT, Concord, Mass., 1977—78; assoc. Booz, Allen & Hamilton, Bethesda, Md., 1978—81, sr. assoc., 1981—83, prin. San Francisco, 1983—88, v.p., 1988—92; mng. officer Asia/Pacfic Energy Practice, Singapore, 1992—97; ptnr. Accenture, San Francisco, 1998—2002. Chmn. bd. dirs. Nat. Capital YFC, Olney, Md., 1981—83. Contbr. articles to energy and bus. pubs. Chmn. bd. dirs. East Bay Youth for Christ, Concord, Calif., 1983-91; mem. Rep. Presdl. Task Force, Washington, 1984-91; advisor Montgomery County (Md.) Health Dept., 1981; mem. World Affairs Coun., San Francisco Mayor's Fiscal Adv. Com.; adv. YFC Internat., 1992-97; bd. dirs. Emerging Young Leaders, 1998-2001. Mem. Am. Inst. Chem. Engrs., Mensa, Ferrari Owners Club, Sports Car Club of Am., Harvard Bus. Sch. Club (Singapore and San Francisco). Republican. Avocation: profl. auto racing. Address: 1030 Gelston Cir Mc Lean VA 22102 *Personal philosophy: Nothing is ever given; it must be earned.*

MOELLER, SUSAN ELAINE, artist; b. Akron, Ohio, Jan. 27, 1949; d. Guy Raymond and June Elaine (Inherst) Walker; m. Robert Allen Moeller, Aug. 13, 1988. BFA, BA in Edn., Akron U., 1972. Art tchr., dept. head Manchester Sch. Sys., Akron, 1972-79; ad exec. The Repository, Canton, Ohio, 1979-81; art dir. Vic & Walt's, Akron, 1981-85; illustrator Collector's Marketplace Mag., Atwater, Ohio, 1983-85; freelance artist, graphic designer Akron, 1985-94; fine artist, co-owner Creative Images Studio, Cuyahoga Falls, Ohio, 1994-98, Nogal, N.Mex., 1998—; owner Paz de Nogal Gallery and Studio, Nogal, 1998—. Co-owner Creative Images Assocs., Cuyahoga Falls, 1986-98; Nogal, N. Mex., 1998—; graphic cons. Advanced Analytical and Computational Solutions, Inc., Cleve., 1996-97, Akron Chess Club, 1989-97; art juror Cuyahoga Falls H.S., 1997; owner, organizer Paz de Nogal Fine Art Shows, 1998—. Artist, designer: (bd. game) Barnes Publishing, 1984; contbr. poetry and drawing to Cat Fancy Mag., 1994; illustrator: (mag.) Collector's Marketplace, 1983-85, (newspaper) Canton Repository, 1979-81; exhibited N.E. Ohio Fine Art Guild shows, 1996-97. Donor of fine art to various charities, Akron, 1996-98. Recipient Hon. Mention award Kent (Ohio) Art-in-the-Park Com., 1996. Mem. ASPCA, Humane Soc. U.S., Humane Soc. Summit County, Pet Ptnrs. Rescue City (Pet Angel 1997), Lincoln County Humane Soc., Creative Connection, Ohio Arts and Crafts Guild, Cuyahoga Valley Soc. Fine Arts, Lincoln County Soc. Artists. Avocations: antiques, lapidary arts, gardening, writing. Studio: Paz de Nogal PO Box 190 Nogal NM 88341-0190

MOELLERING, JOHN HENRY, aviation maintenance company executive; b. Ft. Wayne, Ind., Feb. 4, 1938; s. Robert Charles and Irene Pauline (Nolde) M.; m. Karla Louise Fritzsche, Dec. 21, 1963; children: John Henry, Matthew C., Ann Elizabeth. BS, U.S. Mil. Acad., 1959; MS, U. Calif., Berkeley, 1962; postgrad., Army Command and Gen. Staff Coll., 1971-72, Army War Coll., 1976-77. Registered profl. engr., La. Commd. 2d lt. U.S. Army, 1959, advanced through grades to lt. gen., 1985; aide de camp Combat Devel. Command, 1961-63; command and staff 24th Inf. Div., Fed. Republic Germany, 1964-67; ops. officer Engr. Group, Vietnam, 1967-68; instr. civil engring., asst. prof. history U.S. Mil. Acad., 1968-71; with Office Army Chief of Staff, Pentagon, 1972-73; White House staff, 1973-74; bn. comdr. 101st Airborne Div., 1974-76; dist. engr. Vicksburg, Miss., 1977-79; exec. to Army Chief of Staff, Pentagon, 1979-81; asst. div. comdr. 9th Inf. Div., Ft. Lewis, Wash., 1981-82; commandant West Point, N.Y., 1982-84; comdg. gen. Ft. Leonard Wood, Mo., 1984-85; asst. to chmn. Joint Chiefs of Staff, Pentagon, Washington, 1985-87; corp. v.p. Automatic Data Processing, Inc., San Ramon, Calif., 1987-90; pres., chief exec. officer Lear Siegler Mgmt. Svcs. Corp., Oklahoma City, 1990-93; pres. UNC Aviation Svcs., Annapolis, Md., 1993-97; pres., CEO Lear Siegler Svcs., Inc., Annapolis, Md., 1997—2002, JM Assocs., Chapel Hill, NC, 2002—. Bd. dirs. USAA Ins. Co., Lear Sigeler Svcs., Inc., Indsl. Coll. of the Armed Forces; frequent lectr. Nat. Def. U.; mem. adv. bd. Sch. Bus. Adminstrn. The Citadel. Editor, contbr.: Evolution of Modern Warfare, 1969, Battalion Commanders Speak Out, 1977. Mem. Sci. Def. Bd., The Pentagon; chmn. Class of '59 fund com. U.S. Mil. Acad., 1984—89. Decorated Def. DSM, Army DSM, Legion of Merit, Bronze Star; White House fellow, 1973-74. Mem.: Nat. Def. Indsl. Assn. (bd. dirs.), Phi Kappa Phi. Office: 50130 Manly Chapel Hill NC 27517-8565 E-mail: johnmoellering@hotmail.com.

MOELLERING, ROBERT CHARLES, JR., internist, educator; b. Lafayette, Ind., June 9, 1936; s. Robert Charles and Irene Pauline (Nolde) M.; children: Anne Elizabeth, Robert Charles, Catherine Irene; m. Mary Jane Ferraro, July 11, 1987. BA, Valparaiso U., 1958, DSc, 1980; MD cum laude, Harvard U., 1962. Diplomate: Am. Bd. Internal Medicine. Intern Mass. Gen. Hosp., Boston, 1962-63, resident, 1963-64, postdoctoral fellow in infectious diseases, 1967-70, resident, 1966-67, mem. infectious disease unit and asst. physician, 1970-76, assoc. physician, 1976-83, hon. physician, 1983—, cons. bacteriology, 1972-87; instr. medicine Harvard U. Med. Sch., Boston, 1970-72, asst. prof., 1972-76, assoc. prof., 1976-80, prof., 1980—; chmn. dept. medicine, physician-in-chief New Eng. Deaconess Hosp., 1981-96; pres., CEO Deaconess Profl. Practice Group, 1995-98; Shields Warren-Mallinckrodt prof. rsch. Harvard U. Med. Sch., Boston, 1981-89, Shields Warren-Mallinckrodt prof. med. rsch., 1989-99, Herrman Blumgart prof. medicine, 1999—; assoc. physician-in-chief Beth Israel Deconess Med. Ctr., 1996—98, physician-in-chief, 1998—; pres. CEO Harvard Medical Fac. Phys. BIDMC, 1998—2003; chmn. bd. dirs., pres., trustee Harvard Med. Faculty Physicians at BIDMC, 2003—. Mem. subcom. on susceptibility testing Nat. Com. for CLin. Lab. Standards, 1976-88; mem. subcom. on antimicrobial agts. and chemotherapy, 1978-80; subcom. on antimicrobiol disc. diffusion suceptibility testing, 1980-88; chmn. data safety monitoring bd. Nat. Inst. Allergy and Infections Disease, NIH, 1997—2002. Mem. editl. bd. Antimicrobial Agts. and Chemotherapy, 1977-81, editor, 1981-85, editor-in-chief, 1985-95; editor European Jour. Clin. Microbial Infectious Diseases, 1990—; consulting. editor Infectious Disease Clinics N.Am., 1986—; editor Les Infections, 1983; editl. bd. New Eng. Jour. Medicine, 1977-81, European Jour.Clin. Microbiology, 1981—, Jour. Infectious Diseases, 1981-85, 89-93, Infectious Disease Alert, 1981-92, Pharmacotherapy, 1982—, Antimicrobial Agts. Ann., 1984-87, Zentralblatt Fur Bacteriologie, Microbiologie and Hygience, 1984—, Jour. of Infection, 1986—, Innovations, 1986-90, Residents Forum in Internal Medicine, 1988-90, Diagnostic Microbiology and Infectious Disease, 1989-90, Internat. Jour. Antimicrobial Agts., 1990—, Infectious Diseases in Clin. Practice, 1991-92, Jour. Infection and Chemotherapy, 1995—, Clin. Infectious Disease, 1999-2004. Served with USPHS, 1964-66. Grantee USPHS, NIH. Master ACP, Am. Acad. Microbiology, Infectious Diseases Soc. Am. (v.p. 1988-89, pres. elect 1989-90, pres. 1990-91, past pres. 1991-92); fellow Royal Coll. Physicians (hon.); mem. Am. Soc. Microbiology, Am. Clin. and Climatol. Assn., Internat. Soc. Chemotherapy, Am. Soc. Clin. Investigation, Assn. Am. Physicians, European Soc. Clin. Microbiology, Am. Fedn. Clin. Rsch., Assn. Profs. Medicine, Roxbury Clin. Records Club, Mass. Med. Soc. (councilor), Brit. Soc. Antimicrobial Chemotherapy, Coun. Biology Editors, Alpha Omega Alpha, Phi Kappa Psi. Home: 49 Longfellow Rd Wellesley MA 02481-5220 Office: Beth Israel Deaconess Med Ctr Dept Medicine 110 Francis St Boston MA 02215-5501 E-mail: rmoeller@bidmc.harvard.edu.

MOELY, BARBARA E. psychology researcher, educator; b. Prairie du Sac, Wis., July 17, 1940; d. John Arthur and Loretta Ruth (Giese) M.; children: John Jacob Moely Wiener, David Andrew Moely Wiener. Student, Carroll Coll., 1958-60; BA, U. Wis., 1962, MA, 1964; PhD, U. Minn., 1968. Asst. prof. U. Hawaii, Honolulu, 1967-71; rsch. psychologist UCLA, 1971-72; asst. prof. Tulane U., New Orleans, 1972-75, assoc. prof. psychology, 1975-85, prof., 1985—, dept. chmn., 1992-96, dir. Office of Svc. Learning, 1999—. Contbr. articles to profl. jours. Grantee U.S. Office Edn., Handicapped Pers. Preparation, 1977-80, Tulane U., 1973, 75, 77-78, 83-84, Inst. for Mental Hygiene, City of New Orleans, 1983-84, 2000, Nat. Inst. Edn., 1983-84, La. Edn. Quality Support Fund, 1988-89, 91-92, 96, HUD, 1997-2003, Annenberg, 1997, HHS, 1997-2002, US Dept. Edn., 1999-2002, Fund for Improvement for Post-Secondary Edn., 2000-03, Corp. Nat. and Cmty. Svc., 2003-. Mem. AAUP (v.p. La. conf. 1992-93, sec. 1993-97, v.p. 1998-2000, pres. Tulane 1992-94), APA, Soc. Rsch. in Child Devel., Am. Ednl. Rsch. Assn., Southwestern Soc. for Rsch. in Human Devel. (pres. 1986-88), Phi Beta Kappa (pres. Alpha chpt. La. 1981-82, sec. 1995-99) Office: Tulane Univ Dept Psychology New Orleans LA 70118 Business E-Mail: moely@tulane.edu.

MOEN, RONALD S. medical association administrator; BS, Concordia Coll.; MS, Purdue U. Pvt. practice psychologist, ND; staff psychologist Blue Island (Ill.) Cmty. H.S. Dist.; exec. dir. Mental Health and Mental Retardation Ctrs., Bell County, Tex.; dir. accreditation program for ambulatory health care Joint Commn. on Accreditation of Healthcare Orgns., Chicago; exec. dirs. Accreditation Assn. for Ambulatory Health Care, Skokie, Ill.; CEO Am. Dietetic Assn., Chicago, 2001—. Mem.: Am. Soc. Assn. Execs. (bd. dirs. 1989—90, 1993—96, v.p. 1997—98), Am. Assn. Orthodontists (Samuel B. Shapiro award 2001, James E. Brophy Disting. Svc. award 2000). Office: Am Dietetic Assn 216 W Jackson Blvd Chicago IL 60606-6995

MOENS, PETER B. biology researcher and educator; b. Sukabumi, Indonesia, May 15, 1931; s. Hendrick P. and Anneke D. (Ritsema van Eck) M.; m. Marja Schröder, May 8, 1953; children: Richard, Theodore, Vivian, Cecilia, Francis. PhD, U. Toronto, 1963. Lectr. biology York U., Toronto, Ont., Can., 1963-64, asst. prof., 1964-67, asso. prof., 1967-71, prof., 1971—2001, chmn. dept. biology, 1981-84, disting. rsch. prof., prof. emeritus, 2001—. Editor: Genome, 1983—, Chromosoma, 1988—2001. Fellow Royal Soc. Can.; mem. Genetics Soc. Am., Can. Soc. Cell Biology, Genetics Soc. Can. (pres. 1979), Am. Soc. Cell Biology Office: York U Dept Biology 4700 Keele St Toronto ON Canada M3J 1P3

MOERBEEK, STANLEY LEONARD, lawyer; b. Toronto, Ont., Can., 1951; arrived in U.S., 1953; s. John Jacob and Mary Emily Moerbeek; m. Carol Annette Mordaunt, Apr. 17, 1982; children: Sarah, Noah. BA magna cum laude, Calif. State U., Fullerton, 1974; student, U. San Diego-Sorbonne, Paris, 1977; JD, Loyola U., 1979. Bar: Calif. 1980; cert. in internat. bus. transactions, bankruptcy and bus. rehab., and civil trial practice. From law clk. to assoc. McAlpin Doonan & Seese, Covina, Calif., 1977-81; assoc. Robert L. Baker, Pasadena, Calif., 1981-82, Miller Bush & Minnott, Fullerton, 1982-83; prin. Law Office of Stanley L. Moerbeek, Fullerton, 1984—. Notary pub. lt. gov. 9th cir. law student divsn. ABA, 1979; judge pro tem Orange County Superior Ct., 1984—. Mem. Heritage Found., Washington, 1989—. Recipient plaque of Appreciation, Fullterton Kiwanis, 1983; Calif. Gov.'s Office scholar, 1970. Mem.: Orange County Bar Assn. (Coll. Trial Advocacy 1985), Calif. Assn. Realtors (referral panel atty. 1985—), Calif. C. of C., Phi Kappa Phi. Roman Catholic. Avocations: history, politics, sports. Office: 1370 N Brea Blvd Ste 210 Fullerton CA 92835-4128 Office Phone: 714-773-5396. Personal E-mail: slmlaw@sbcglobal.net.

MOERDLER, CHARLES GERARD, lawyer; b. Paris, Nov. 15, 1934; came to the U.S., 1946, naturalized, 1952; s. Herman and Erna Anna (Brandwein) M.; m. Pearl G. Hecht, Dec. 26, 1955; children: Jeffrey Alan, Mark Laurence, Sharon Michele. BA, L.I.U., 1953; JD, Fordham U., 1956. Bar: NY 1956, U.S. Supreme Ct. 1962. Assoc. Cravath, Swaine & Moore, N.Y.C., 1956-65; spl. counsel coms. City of N.Y. and judiciary N.Y. State Assembly, 1960-61; commr. bldgs. City of N.Y., 1966-67; sr. ptnr., chmn. litigation dept. Stroock & Stroock & Lavan, N.Y.C., 1967—. Bd. dirs., gen. counsel, dir. N.Y. Post Co., Inc., 1987-92; cons. housing, urban devel. and real estate to Mayor of N.Y.C., 1967-73; mem. com. on character and fitness of applicants for admission to Bar, Appellate divsn. 1st Dept., N.Y., 1977—, vice chmn. 1998—; mem. disciplinary com. appellate divsn. 1st Dept., N.Y., 1998—, commr. N.Y. State Ins. Fund, 1978-97, vice chmn., 1986-94, chmn., 1995-97; mem. Mayor's Com. on Judiciary, 1994-2001; mem. N.Y.C. Housing Devel. Corp., 1997—; bd. dirs. N.Y.C. Residential Mortgage Ins. Corp., 1997—; chmn. bd. dirs. Bank Austria Creditanstalt LLC, 1999-2001; mem. N.Y.C. Bd. Collective Bargaining, 2000—. Mem. editorial bd. N.Y. Law Jour., 1985—; assoc. editor Fordham Law Rev., 1956. Asst. dir. Rockefeller nat. presdl. campaign com., 1964; adv. bd. Sch. Internat. Affairs Columbia U., 1977-80; bd. govs. L.I.U., 1966, trustee, 1985-91; chmn. Cmty. Planning Bds. 8 and 14, Bronx County, 1977-78; nat. bd. govs. Am. Jewish Congress, 1966; bd. overseers Jewish Theol. Sem. Am., 1993-95; trustee St. Barnabas Hosp., Bronx, N.Y., 1985—. Recipient Walker Metcalf award L.I. U., 1966. Mem. Am. Bar Assn., N.Y. State Bar Assn., N.Y. County Lawyers Assn., Internat. Bar Assn., Assn. of Bar of City of N.Y., Free Sons of Israel, Metro. Club. Home: 7 Rivercrest Rd Bronx NY 10471-1236 Office: Stroock Stroock & Lavan 180 Maiden Ln New York NY 10038 E-mail: cmoerdler@stroock.com.

MOESCHL, STANLEY FRANCIS, electrical engineer, management consultant; b. Cin., Mar. 14, 1931; s. Stanley F. and Matilda F. (Trenkamp) M.; m. Kathleen K. Koebel, Aug. 21, 1954; children: Stanley, Melissa, Deborah, Karen. BSEE, Purdue U., 1957. Engr. Honeywell Space Div., St. Petersberg, Fla., 1957-60, engring. mgr., 1960-69, program mgr., 1969-77; dir. engring. Honeywell Avionics Div., Mpls., 1977-80; v.p. gen. mgr. Honeywell Space Div., St. Petersberg, 1980-82, Honeywell Avionics Div., Mpls., 1982-88; pres. Sundstrand Data Control, Redmond, Wash., 1988-92. Bd. mem. Com. of 100, St. Petersberg, 1980-82, Wash. Round Table, Seattle, 1989-92. Bd. dirs. Jr. Achievement, Mpls., 1983-86, Seattle, 1989-92. With USCG, 1951-54, Korea. Mem. IEEE, AIEE, Eta Kappa Nu, Tau Beta Pi. Home: 12826 Yacht Club Cir Fort Myers FL 33919-4635 E-mail: sfmoerchl@aol.com.

MOESCHLER, JOHN BOYER, physician, educator; b. Omaha, Mar. 14, 1950; s. William Joseph and Norma Rose (Boyer) M.; children: Kate, Emily. BS, Creighton U., 1972; MD, U. Nebr., 1975. Bd. cert. Am. Bd. Pediatrics, Am. Bd. Med. Genetics. Intern Univ. Nebr. Med. Ctr., Omaha, 1975-76, resident, 1976-78; fellow Univ. Wash., Seattle, 1978-80; asst. prof., dept. pediatrics Univ. Nebr. Med. Ctr., Meyer Children's Rehab. Inst., Omaha, 1980-83; asst. prof., dept. pediatrics, sect. med. genetics W.Va. Univ. Med. Sch., Morgantown, 1983-85; asst. prof., dept. maternal and child health Dartmouth Med. Sch., Dartmouth-Hitchcock Med. Ctr., Hanover, N.H., 1985-88, assoc. prof., dept. pediatrics, 1988—; dir. Clin. Genetics Program Dartmouth-Hitchcock Med. Ctr., Hanover, 1988—; med. dir., Clinic for Children with Neuromotor Disabilities Dept. Health & Human Svcs., Bur. Spl. Med. Svcs., N.H., 1985-2000; med. dir., Genetic Svcs. Program Dept. Health & Human Svcs., Bus. of Spl. Med. Svcs., N.H., 1988-2000. Bd. dirs. Planned Parenthood of No. New England; attending physician Children's Orthopedic Hosp., Seattle, 1978-80; assoc. dir. Birth Defects Clinic, Children's Meml. Hosp., Omaha, 1982-83; cons. Nebr. State Svcs. for Crippled Children, 1980-83; dir. pediatric rehab. MCRI and Univ. Nebr. Hosp., Omaha, 1982-83; steering com. New England Regional Genetics Group, 1988—; presenter in field. Contbr. articles to Jour. Pediatrics, Am. Jour. Med. Genetics, Am. Jour. Disabled Child, Jour. Ment. Def. Rsch., Jour. Ultrasound Med., Dysmorphology and Clin. Genetics, Jour. Clin. Dysmorphology, Prenatal Diagnosis, Am. Jour. Diseases Children, Devel. Medicine and Child Neurology, Clin. Genetics, and others. Fellow Am. Acad. Pediatrics, Am. Acad. Cerebral Palsy & Devel. Medicine; mem. Soc. for Devel. Pediatrics, Am. Soc. Human Genetics (info. and edn. com. 1990—), Am. Assn. on Mental Retardation, N.H. State Med. Soc., Grafton County Med. Soc. Home: 9 Woodside Rd Durham NH 03824-2120 Office: Ctr for Genetics and Child Devel Dartmouth-Hitchcock Med Ctr Lebanon NH 03756

MOESER, JAMES CHARLES, university chancellor, musician; b. Colorado City, Tex., Apr. 3, 1939; s. Charles Victor and Virginia (James) M.; m. Jesse Kaye Edwards, Jan. 26, 1963 (div. July 1984); children: James Christopher, Kathryn Carter; m. Susan Kay Smith Dickerson, June 21, 1987. B.Mus., U. Tex., 1961, M.M., 1964; postgrad. (Fulbright grantee), Hochschule fur Musik, Berlin, 1961-62; D.MA (Univ. fellow), U. Mich., 1966. Chmn. dept. organ, asst. prof. organ U. Kans., 1966-69, assoc. prof., 1969-74, prof., 1974-86, dean Sch. Fine Arts, 1975-86, Carl and Ruth Althaus disting. prof. organ, 1985-86; organist, choirmaster Plymouth Congl. Ch., Lawrence, Kans., 1967-86; organist nat. conf. Music Tchrs. Nat. Assn., Portland, Oreg., 1972, L.A., 1974; dean Coll. Arts and Architecture, Pa. State U., State College, 1986—91; v.p., academic affairs & provost Univ. S.C., 1991—96; chancellor U. Nebr., Lincoln, Nebr., 1996—2000, U.N.C. - Chapel Hill, Chapel Hill, NC, 2000—. Concert organist, on tour, W. Ger., 1977, Lisbon (Portugal) Festival, 1978, 81, recitals for, Musica Festiva da Costa Verde, Portugal, 1981; organist concerts, W. Ger., 1982, 86, 87; world premier Paul Creston's 3d Symphony for Organ and Orchestra, Kennedy Ctr., Washington, 1982. Bd. govs. Josephson Inst. Ethics, 1998-2002; trustee N.C. Symphony Soc., Inc., 2001—; mem. vis. com. Meml. Ch., Harvard U. Recipient Palmer Christian award U. Mich., 1981, Disting. Alumnus awrd Grad. Sch. U. Tex., 2001; Kent fellow Danforth Found.; Danforth Assoc. Mem. Am. Guild Organists (past dean chpt., nat. dir. student groups 1973-75, nat. chmn. com. on profl. edn. 1983—, chmn. 2d nat. conf. on organ pedagogy 1984, 3d nat. conf. 1986, v.p. 1986—). Episcopalian. Home: 1000 Raleigh Rd Chapel Hill NC 27517-4415 Office: UNC Office of the Chancellor PO Box 9100 Chapel Hill NC 27599-0001 E-mail: james_moeser@unc.edu.

MOESSNER, HAROLD FREDERIC, allergist; b. Lincoln, Nebr., Mar. 29, 1945; s. Samuel Frederick and Helen Lucy (Larson) M.; m. Linda McLeod, Apr. 30, 1972; children: Annie Larson, John Christopher, Sarah Elizabeth. BS with distinction, U. Nebr., 1967; MD, U. Minn., 1971. Diplomate Am. Bd. Pediatrics, Am. Bd. Allergy and Immunology. Intern VA Hosp., Dallas, 1971-72; resident in pediatrics Children's Med. Ctr., Dallas, 1972-74; commd. 2d lt. U.S. Army, 1974-78, advanced through the grades to col., 1980-87; pediatrician Fort Ritchie, Md., 1974-75, U.S. Army Hosp, Augsburg, Germany, 1975-78; fellow in adolescent medicine U. Tex. Health and Sci. Ctr., Dallas, 1978-79; asst. prof. pediatrics Uniformed Svcs., U. Health Scis., Bethesda, Md., 1980-83; fellow allergy and immunology Walter Reed Army Med. Ctr., Washington, 1983-85; chief allergy immunology svc., chief dept. medicine Blanchfield Army Hosp., Fort Campbell, Ky., 1985-87; pvt. practice Nashville, 1987—. Assoc. staff Williamson Med. Ctr., Franklin, Tenn. Contbr. to profl. jours. Fellow Am. Bd. Pediats., Am. Bd. Allergy and Immunology; mem. Am. Acad. Allergy and Immunology, Williamson County Med. Soc., Tenn. Soc. Allergy, Tenn. State Med. Assn., Phi Beta Kappa. Home: 5304 Otter Creek Ct Brentwood TN 37027-4126 Office: 1909 Mallory Ln Ste 308 Franklin TN 37067-8230 also: 251 Hillcrest Dr Ste 101 Clarksville TN 37043-

MOEVS, MARIA TERESA MARABINI, archaeologist; b. Rome, Jan. 31, 1926; came to U.S., 1955, naturalized, 1959; d. Giuseppe and Tosca (Toschi) Marabini; Laurea Lettere, U. Bologna, 1947; Ph.D. summa cum laude, U. Rome, 1951; postgrad. Italian Archaeol. Sch., Athens, 1950-51; m. Robert W. Moevs, Oct. 1, 1953; children— Marina F., Christian R. Insp. antiquities Ministry Edn., Italy, Syracuse, Padua, 1952-53; insp. Central Restoration Inst., Rome, 1953-55; instr. Italian, Harvard U., 1956-57, Douglass Coll., 1965-68, asst. prof. Italian, 1968-72, asso. prof., 1972-77, prof., 1977-81, prof. classics and archaeology, 1981—; mem. Inst. Advanced Study, Princeton, N.J., 1977-78; mem. nat. screening com. Fulbright Am. Grad. Study Program, study in Italy, 1978-79, study in Italy-Greece, 1982-83. Recipient Goffredo Bellonci Spl. Prize, Rome Biennium, 1975-77; Italian Govt. fellow Italian Archaeol. Sch., Rome, 1947-50, Italian Archaeol. Sch. fellow, Athens, 1950-51, Fulbright fellow Am. Acad. Rome, 1952-53; Radcliffe Inst. Ind. Study asso. scholar, 1962-64, Am. Acad. Rome. fellow, 1963-64; NEH fellow, 1986-87. Mem. Archaeol. Inst. Am., Princeton Soc. of Archaeol. Inst. Am. (pres. 1986—), Rei Cretariae Romanae Favtores, Soc. Fellows, Am. Acad. Rome. Author: The Roman Thin Walled Pottery from Cosa, 1973; Gabriele D'Annunzio e le estetiche della fine del secolo, 1976; The Italo-Megarian ware from Cosa, 1980; Aco in Northern Etruria, 1980; Le Muse di Ambracia, 1981; Il Kalathos alessandrino di Bologna, 1983; Penteteris e le tre Horainella Pompe di Tolomeo Filadelfo, 1987. Contbr. articles on Roman pottery from excavations at Cosa, Italy to profl. jours, publs. Home: Blackwell's Mills Belle Mead NJ 08502

MOFENSON, LYNNE MERYL, pediatrician; b. Phila., Oct. 24, 1950; d. Howard Charles and Lois (Stugart) M.; m. Bruce Leslie Katz, Aug. 27, 1972; 1 child, Jessica Ann Mofenson Katz. BA magna cum laude, SUNY at Stony Brook, 1971; MD, Albert Einstein Coll. Medicine, 1977. Diplomate Nat. Bd. Med. Examiners. Intern, residency Pediatric Childrens Hosp., Boston, 1977-79; instr. pediatrics Harvard Med. Sch., Children's Hosp., Boston, 1977-79; chief resident pediatrics U. Mass. Med. Sch., Worcester, 1979-80, fellow infectious disease, 1981-83, assoc. internal medicine & pediatrics, 1982-89; hosp. epidemiologist Marlboro (Mass.) Hosp., 1983-85; pvt. med. practice Northboro, Mass., 1983-85; asst. commr. Communicable Disease Control, Mass. Dept. Pub. Health, Boston, 1985-89; assoc. br. chief for clin. rsch. NICHD, NIH Pediatric Adolescent & Maternal AIDS Br., Bethesda, Md., 1989—2001, br. chief, 2002—. Mem. Cen. AIDS Rev. Bd., Mass. Dept. Social Svcs., 1988-89, subcom. on clin. trials and rsch. Gov.'s Task Force on AIDS, Mass. Dept. Pub. Health, 1988-89, pediatric core com. AIDS Clin. Trials Group, NIH, 1989—; reviewer Year 2000 Nat. Health Objs.; co-chair workshop HIV Infection in Women of Childbearing Age, 1989; mem. working group on PCP prophylaxis in pediatric HIV infection, 1990-91; co-chair workshop perinatal intervention 4th AIDS Vaccine Meeting, 1991, exec. sec. perinatal HIV guidelines working group, 1999—; mem. pediat. antiretroviral guidelines working group and panel in clin. practices for treatment of HIV infections, 1997—; chair. pediat. working group for USPHS guidelines for

treatment, 2001—; mem. working group in antiretroviral treatment guidelines in resource poor settings, 2001-2004; chair pediat. opportunistic infection treatment guidelines, 2002-04; cons. WHO pediat. HIV issues and prevention prenatal HI?V transmission. Mem. editl. bd. Jour. AIDS; sci. adv. bd. AIDScience; contbr. numerous articles to profl. jours. Recipient Pub. Health Svc. Spl. Recognition award, 1992, Commr. Family Resource Program award Dept. Social Svcs., 1989, Teaching award City Boston Sch. System, 1989, Gov.'s Proclamation award, 1989, Citation for Scholastic Achievement Am. Med. Women's Assn., 1977, Neurobiology award Albert Einstein Coll. Medicine, 1974, Regents Scholarship N.Y. State, 1968, Nat. Merit Scholarship Finalist, 1968. Fellow Alpha Omega Alpha, Am. Acad. Pediats. (com. on pediat. AIDS), Infectious Disease Soc. Am.; mem. Mass. Med. Soc., Am. Pub. Health Assn., Am. Soc. Microbiology, Am. Pediatric Soc., Internat. Aids Soc., HIV Medicine Soc., Pediatric Infectious Dis. Soc. Democrat. Jewish. Avocations: nature/hiking, photography, biking. Office: Nat Inst Child Health 6100 Executive Blvd Rm 4B11 Rockville MD 02852 Office Phone: 301-435-6870.

MOFFAT, MARYBETH, consulting company executive; b. Pitts., July 25, 1951; d. Herbert Franklin and Florence Grafe (Knerem) M.; m. Brian Francis Soulier, Nov. 30, 1974 (div.). BA, Carroll Coll., 1973. Indsl. engring. technician Wis. Centrifugal Co., Waukesha, Wisc., 1976-77; indsl. engr. Utility Products, Inc., Milw., 1977-79; mgr. indsl. engring. Bear Automotive (divsn. SPX Corp.), Bangor, Pa., 1980-90; program mgr. Toyota Johnson Controls, Inc. Automotive Systems Group, 1990-2001; pres., CEO Moffat Enterprises, Inc., 2001—. Group home house parent Headwaters Regional Achievement Ctr., Lake Tomahawk, Wis., 1974. Mem. Am. Inst. Indsl. Engrs., MTM Assn. for Standards Rsch., Indsl. Mgmt. Soc., Alpha Gamma Delta (standards chmn. 1971-72). Republican. Methodist. Avocations: skiing, horseback riding, swimming, reading. Personal E-mail: mbmoffat123@cs.com.

MOFFAT, ROBERT W., JR., information technology executive; BS in Econs., Union Coll.; MBA in Mgmt. Info. Sys., Iona Coll. Various mgmt. positions including gen. mgr. personal sys. group, gen. mgr. fin., planning, and bus. sup. IBM Europe IBM, 1978—, sr. v.p., integrated supply chain, 2002—. IBM ptnr. exec. Bell South, Aetna, Carolina Power & Light, Ingram Micro, Progress Energy, CDW, Insight Direct. Office: IBM 1133 Westchester Ave White Plains NY 10604

MOFFATT, HUGH MCCULLOCH, JR., hospital administrator, physical therapist; b. Steubenville, Ohio, Oct. 11, 1933; s. Hugh McCulloch and Agnes Elizabeth (Bickerstaff) M.; m. Ruth Anne Colvin, Aug. 16, 1958; children: David, Susan. AB, Asbury Coll., 1958; cert. in phys. therapy, Duke U., 1963. Lic. in phys. therapy and health care adminstrn. Commd. officer USPHS, 1964, advanced through grades to capt., therapist, 1964-66, Sitka, Alaska, 1970-72, therapist cons. Atlanta, 1968-70, clinic adminstr. Kayenta, Ariz., 1972-73, hosp. dir. Sitka, 1973-78; therapist cons. Idaho Dept. Health, Boise, 1966-68; contract health officer USPHS, Anchorage, 1978-89, ret., 1989; phys. therapy cons. Ocean Beach Hosp., Ilwaco, Wash., 1989—, Harbors Home Health Svcs., Aberdeen, Wash., 1990—. Therapist cons. Our Lady of Compassion Care Ctr., Anchorage, 1979—, Alaska Native Med. Ctr., Anchorage, 1988—. With U.S. Army, 1955-57. Mem. Am. Phys. Therapy Assn., Commd. Officers Assn. USPHS, Res. Officers Assn., Ret. Officers Assn., Am. Assn. Individual Investors, Am. Assn. Ret. Persons, Eagles. Avocations: automobile repairs, woodworking, camping, fishing, church choir.

MOFFATT, JOYCE ANNE, performing company executive; b. Grand Rapids, Mich., Jan. 3, 1936; d. John Barnard and Ruth Lillian (Pellow) M. BA in Lit., U. Mich., 1957, MA in Theatre, 1960; HHD (hon.), Profl. Sch. Psychology, San Francisco, 1991. Stage mgr., lighting designer Off-Broadway plays; costume, lighting and set designer, stage mgr. stock cos., 1954-62; nat. subscription mgr. Theatre Guild/Am. Theatre Soc., N.Y.C., 1965-67; subscription mgr. Theatre, Inc.-Phoenix Theatre, N.Y.C., 1963-67; cons. N.Y.C. Ballet and N.Y.C. Opera, 1967-70; asst. house mgr. N.Y. State Theater, 1970-72; dir. ticket sales City Ctr. of Music and Drama, Inc., N.Y.C., 1970-72; prodn. mgr. San Antonio's Symphony/Opera, 1973-75; gen. mgr. San Antonio Symphony/Opera, 1975-76, 55th St. Dance Theater Found., Inc., N.Y.C., 1976-77, Ballet Theatre Found., Inc./Am. Ballet Theatre, N.Y.C., 1977-81; v.p. prodn. Radio City Music Hall Prodns., Inc., N.Y.C., 1981-83; artist-in-residence CCNY, 1981—; propr. mgmt. cons. firm for performing arts N.Y.C., 1983—; exec. dir. San Francisco Ballet Assn., 1987-93; mng. dir. Houston Ballet Assoc., 1993-95; gen. mgr. Chgo. Music and Dance Theater, Inc., 1995—. Cons. Ford Found., N.Y. State Coun. on Arts, Kennedy Ctr. for Performing Arts., Lensic Performing Arts Ctr, Bloomington, Ill., Sheboygan (Wis.) Theater Found.; mem. dance panels N.Y. State Coun. on Arts, 1979-81; mem. panels for Support to Prominent Orgns. and Dance, Calif. Arts Coun., 1988-92. Appointee San Francisco Cultural Affairs Task Force, 1991; chmn. bd. dirs. Tex. Inst. for Arts in Edn., 1994—; trustee Internat. Alliance of Theatrical Stage Employees Local 16 Pension and Welfare Fund, 1991-94; bd. dirs. Rudolf Nureyev Dance Found., Chgo., 1998—. Mem. Assn. Theatrical Press Agts. and Mgrs., Actors Equity Assn., United Scenic Artists Local 829, San Francisco Visitors and Conv. Bur. (bd. dirs.), Argyle Club (San Antonio). Office: Chicago Music & Dance Theater 205 E Randolph Dr Chicago IL 60601-1210

MOFFATT, KATY (KATHERINE LOUELLA MOFFATT), musician, vocalist, songwriter; b. Ft. Worth, Nov. 19, 1950; d. Lester Huger and Sue-Jo (Jarrott) M. Student, Sophie Newcomb Coll., 1968, St. John's Coll., 1969-70. Rec. artist Columbia Records, 1975-79, Permian/MCA Records, 1982-84, Enigma Records, L.A., 1985, Wrestler Records, L.A., 1987-88, Red Moon Records, Switzerland, 1988-93, Philo/Rounder Records, 1989-96, Round Tower Music, U.K., Ireland, Europe, 1993-96, Watermelon Records, U.S., 1994-96, Panther City Records, New Zealand, 1998, Hightone/HMG Records, 1998-2001, Western Jubilee/Shanachie Records, 2001—, Demon/Westside Records, 2002. Folksinger, Ft. Worth, 1967-68; musician, vocalist, songwriter, rec. artist: (films) Billy Jack, 1970, Hard Country, 1981, The Thing Called Love, 1993; prodn. asst. film, Sta. KIII-TV, Corpus Christi, 1970, audio engr., Sta. KRIS-TV, Corpus Christi, 1970; musician, vocalist in blues band, Corpus Christi, 1970; receptionist, bookkeeping asst., copywriter, announcer, Sta. KFWT, Ft. Worth, 1971, musician, vocalist, songwriter, Denver, 1971-72, on tour, 1973, 75—, Denver, 1974, on tour, 1976-79, European tour, 1977, Can. tour, 1984-85, on tour in Europe, U.S., Can., Asia and Australia, 1985—; albums include Katy, 1976, Kissin' In The California Sun, Am. release, 1977, internat. release, 1978, A Town South of Bakersfield, 1985, Walkin' on the Moon, European release, 1988, U.S. release, 1989, Child Bride, 1990, (duet album with brother Hugh) Dance Me Outside, 1992, (Switzerland only) Indoor Fireworks, 1992, The Greatest Show On Earth A.K.A. The Evangeline Hotel, 1994, Hearts Gone Wild, 1994, Tulare Dust, 1995, (duet album with Kate Brislin) Sleepless Nights, 1996, Midnight Radio, 1996, Angel Town, 1998, Loose Diamond, 1999, Cowboy Girl, 2001, (reissue on CD) Katy/Kissin' in the California Sun, 2002; songs include The Magic Ring, 1971; Gerry's Song, 1973, Kansas City Morning, 1974, Take Me Back To Texas, 1975, (Waitin' For) The Real Thing, 1975, Didn't We Have Love, 1976, Kissin' in the California Sun, 1977, Walkin' on the Moon, 1989. Recipient Record World Album award, 1976; named one of 4 Top New Female Vocalists, Cashbox Singles Awards, 1976; nominee for Top New Female Vocalist, Acad. Country Music, 1985; winner best singer-songwriter category Ft. Worth Weekly Mag. Music awards, 1997. Mem. AFTRA, SAG, NARAS, Am. Fedn. Musicians.

MOFFATT, ROBERT HENRY, accountant, publisher, writer, consultant; b. June 30, 1930; s. James Bigelow and Edwige Edith Moffatt; m. Hannelore Mann, Jan. 7, 1989. Student, Loyola Coll., Montreal, 1948-52, Arcadia U., 1962, UCLA, 1970, 72. Lic. in air navigation, Can.; enrolled agt. Dept. Treasury. Mng. editor, pub. Kings-Annapolis Wings, 1961-66; pres. Valley Pubs. Ltd., Kingston, N.S., Can., 1961-67; exec. dir. Maritime Motor Transport Assn., Moncton, N.B., Can., 1967-68; editor Maritime Truck Transport Rev., Moncton, N.B., Can., 1967-68; dir. custom products divsn. Wolf-Brown Inc., L.A., 1968-77; newsletter pub., writer, 1980—; pvt. practice tax acctg. L.A., 1970—. Columnist, author editls. in mags. Clk., author constn. Village of Greenwood, N.S., 1961-63; chmn. bd. commrs., 1963-66; publicity chmn. Voluntary Econ. Planning Program, province N.S., 1965-66. Lt. Can. Air Force, 1954-60. Mem. Nat. Assn. Enrolled Agts. (newsletter editor, bd. dirs.), Nat. Soc. Pub. Accts. (accredited in taxation, corp. dir.), Calif. Soc. Enrolled Agts. Home and Office: 7509 W 88th St Los Angeles CA 90045-3408

MOFFETT, DAVID MCKENZIE, bank executive; b. Daytona Beach, Fla., Feb. 22, 1952; s. James Denny Jr. and Dorothy McCall (McKenzie) M.; m. Cynthia Ann Daugherty, Aug. 25, 1973 (div. Oct. 1977); m. Katherine Ann Martin, May 26, 1979; children: Jeffrey Martin, Layne McCall, Hilary Marie. BA, Okla. U., 1974; MBA, So. Meth. U., 1975; grad. Stonier Sch. Banking, Rutgers U., 1981. Planning analyst First Nat. Bank & Trust Co., Tulsa, 1975-76, fin. analyst, 1978, v.p., 1978-80, sr. v.p., 1981-86, exec. v.p., 1987—; CFO Firstar Corp., Milw.; CFO, chmn. U.S. Bancorp (formerly Firstar Corp.), Minneapolis, 2001—. Faculty grad. sch. banking U. Wis., 1986; adj. prof. U. Tulsa. Bd. dirs. Leadership Tulsa, Inc., 1985-87, Arts & Humanities Council, Tulsa, 1986, Salvation Army, 1986, St. John's Episc. Ch., Tulsa, 1987. Recipient Chmn.'s award bd. dirs. First Nat. Bank, 1980. Mem. Nat. Asset/Liability Mgmt. Assn. (charter), Bank Adminstrn. Inst. (treasury mgmt. com. 1984, investment banking com. 1987). Republican. Epsicopalian. Clubs: Tulsa, Cedar Ridge Country (Tulsa). Avocations: running, golf, skiing, scuba diving, bicycling. Office: US Bancorp US Bank Pl 601 2nd Ave S Minneapolis MN 55402

MOFFETT, FRANK CARDWELL, architect, civil engineer, real estate developer; b. Houston, Dec. 9, 1931; s. Ferrell Orlando and Jewell Bernice (Williams) M.; m. Annie Doris Thorn, Aug. 1, 1952 (div.); children: David Cardwell (dec.), Douglas Howard; m. Darlene Adele Alm Sayan, June 7, 1985 (div.); m. Vicki Lynn Schultz Harris, May 1, 1999. BArch, U. Tex., 1958. Registered arch.; profl. engr., cert. Nat. Council Archtl. Registration Bds., U.S. Dept. Def., Fallout Shelter Analysis, environ. engring. Arch. Seattle, Harmon, Pray & Detrich, Arnold G. Gangnes, Ralf E. Decker, Roland Terry & Assocs., 1958-64; ptnr. Heideman & Moffett, AIA, Seattle, 1964-71; chief arch. Wash. State Dept. Hwys., Olympia, 1971-77, Wash. State Dept. Transp., Olympia, 1977-87; owner The Moffett Co., Olympia, WA, 1987—. Adv. Wash. State Bldg. Code Counc., 1975-95, instr. civil engrng. tech., Olympia Tech. Commty. Coll., 1975-77; adv. mem. archtl. barriers subcom. Internat. Conf. Building Ofcls.; founder, treas. T.A.A., Inc., P.S., 1988, pres., 1991—; presenter in field. Archtl. works include hdqrs. Gen. Telephone Directory Co., Everett, Wash., 1964; Edmonds Unitarian Ch., 1966; tenant devel. Seattle Hdqrs. Office, Seattle First Nat. Bank, 1968-70; Wash. State Dept. Transp. Area Hdqrs. Offices, Mt. Vernon, Selah, Raymond, Colfax and Port Orchard 1973-87; Materials Lab., Spokane, Wash., 1974; Olympic Meml. Gardens, Tumwater, Wash., 1988, City Anacortes emergency power stas., 1989, L. Albert Residence, 1990, F. Gasperetti Residence, 1991, G. Holbrook Residence, 2000; archtl. barriers cons. State of Alaska, 1978, State of Wash., 1972-94. Co-author: An Illustrated Handbook for Barrier-Free Design, 2nd edit., 1985, 3rd edit., 1987, 4th Edit., 1989, Accessibility Design for All, 1992, 2nd edit., 1995, 3d edit., 1998; Housing and Building Accessibility: The Law in Washington, 1992. Chmn. Planning Commn. of Mountlake Terr., Wash., 1963, 64, mem., 1961-67; mem. State of Wash. Govs. Task Force on Wilderness, 1972-75, Heritage Park Task Force, Olympia, Wash., 1986—; trustee Cascade Symphony Orch., 1971; incorporating pres. United Singles, Olympia, 1978-79; capt. CAP, fin. ofcr. Olympia Squadron; mem. nat. panel profl. advisors to Nat. Multiple Sclerosis Soc., 1993—; bd. dirs. Wash. Coalition Citizens with Disabilities; expert witness Ams. with Disabilities Act of 1990. With USN, 1951-54. Fellow ASCE; mem. AIA (dir. S.W. Wash. chpt. 1980-82, pres.-elect 1985, pres. 1986, dir. Wash. council 1986, archs. in govt. nat. com. 1978-87, chmn. N.W. and Pacific region conf. 1991), Am. Public Works Assn., Inst. Bldgs. and Grounds, Constrn. Specifications Inst., Am. Arbitration Assn. (invited panelist), Washington Soc./Nat. Huguenot Soc. (pres. 1978-80, 85-87, 95-99), Gen. Soc. Mayflower Descs. (gov. Wash. Soc. 1982-83, dep. gov. gen. Gen. Soc., 1998—), SAR (state treas. 1984-85), SCV Sons and Daus. of Pilgrims (gov. Wash. Soc. 1984), Baronial Order of Magna Charta, Aircraft Owners' and Pilots' Assn., Rotary (pres. Edmonds, 1969-70), Olympia, Coll. Club of Seattle. Republican. Baptist. Home and Office: PO Box 7 Hanford CA 93232-0007 E-mail: fmoffett@aol.com., taaae@aol.com.

MOFFETT, JAMES ROBERT, oil and gas company executive; b. Houma, La., Aug. 16, 1938; s. Robert E. and Mary G. (Pollack) M.; m. Louise C. Hohmann, June 5, 1960; children: Crystal Louise, James R. BS, U. Tex., 1961; MS, Tulane U., 1963. Cons. geologist oil and gas industry, New Orleans, 1964-69; v.p. founding ptnr. McMoRan Exploration Co., New Orleans, 1969-74; pres., chief exec. officer McMoRan Oil & Gas Co., New Orleans, 1974-81, 81-85, chmn., chief exec. officer, from 1985, dir., from 1974; vice-chmn. Freeport McMoRan Inc., New Orleans, 1981-85, chmn., chief exec. officer, 1985—, dir., 1981—. Mem. Nat. Petroleum Council, Washington, 1979, Commn. on the Future of South, 1986; bd. dirs. La. Energy Nat. PAC, Metairie, La., 1979, World Trade Ctr., New Orleans, Am. Cancer Soc. Greater New Orleans, Bus. Task Force Edn., Inc.; chmn. bd. La. Coun. Fiscal Reform; chmn. bus. coun. New Orleans and River Region, 1985-87. 2nd lt. U.S. Army, 1961-68, capt. Res. ret. Recipient T award Ex Students Assn. U. Tex., 1960, Hornblower Yr. award Pub. Relations Soc. Am., 1986, Vol. Yr. award Urban League Greater New Orleans, 1987; Minnie Stevens Piper Found. scholar U. Tex., 1960, Jacques E. Yenni, S.J. award Loyola U. of New Orleans for Outstanding Community Svc., Jr. Achievement Bus. Hall of Fame award, 1987, Loyola U. of New Orleans' Integritas Vitae award, 1988; named One of Ten Outstanding Persons of 1985 Inst. for Human Understanding, New Orleans Mem. All Am. Wildcatters, New Orleans Geol. Soc., Petroleum Club New Orleans, Greater New Orleans Mktg. Com. (exec. com. 1987), Geology Found U. Tex. (adv. council 1972-85), Devel. bd. U. Tex., La. Ind. producers Royalty Owners Assn. South La. Mid-Continent Oil Gas Assn. (v.p.), Dinner Steering Com. (Disting, Citizen award 1983, 85 Boy Scouts Am. New Orleans div.), Green Wave Club. Republican. Office: Freeport-McMoRan Copper & Gold 1615 Poydras St New Orleans LA 70112-1254

MOFFETT, SULINDA, nursing association administrator; Exec. dir. Okla. Bd. Nursing, Okla. City. Office: Okla Bd of Nursing 2915 N Classen Blvd Ste 524 Oklahoma City OK 73106-5437

MOFFETT, T(ERRILL) K(AY), lawyer; b. Becker, Miss., July 11, 1949; s. Elmer C. and Mary Ethel (Meek) M.; m. Rita C. Millsaps, Mar. 11, 1972; 1 child, Tara Leigh. BS, U.S. Mil. Acad., 1971; MA in Polit. Sci., U. Hawaii, 1974; JD, U. Miss., 1979. Bar: Miss. 1979, Ala. 1998. Grad. tchr. Am. govt. U. Miss., Oxford, 1977-80; ptnr. Moffett and Thorne, Tupelo, Miss., 1980-88; owner Moffett Law Firm, Tupelo, Miss., 1988—; pros. atty. City of Tupelo, 1989-99. Rep. candidate for U.S. Congress 1st Miss. Dist., 1978, 80; 1st dist. coord. Reagan for Pres., 1980; co-chmn. Lee County George Bush for Pres. Com., 1988, 92; mem. Lee County Rep. Exec. Com., 1980—; chmn. Tupelo Rep. Exec. Com., 1988—; active 1st Bapt. Ch., Tupelo; bd. dirs. Sav-A-Life Tupelo, Inc. Capt. U.S. Army, 1971-76; brig. gen. USAR, 2000—, Miss. Army NG, 1999—. Harvard fellow, 1995-96. Mem. ABA, Miss. State Bar Assn., Lee County Bar Assn., Ala. State Bar Assn., Civitan, Masons, Habitat for Humanity, Phi Sigma Alpha. Avocations: music, hunting, tennis, travel. Home: 1761 N Parc Cir Tupelo MS 38804-9753 Office: Moffett Law Firm PO Drawer 1707 330 N Broadway St Tupelo MS 38802-3926

MOFFIE, H. STEVEN, psychiatrist; b. Chgo., May 5, 1946; s. Samuel Edward and Miriam (Misha) M.; m. Lynn Hansher, June 30, 1968; children: Stacia, Evan. MD, Yale U., 1971. Diplomate Am. Bd. Psychiatry and Neurology. Intern L.A. County-U. So. Calif. Med. Ctr., L.A., 1971-72; resident U. Chgo. Hosps. and Clins., 1972-75; clin. dir. Calhoun-Cleburne Mental Health Ctr., Anniston, Ala., 1975-77, N.W. Med. Health Ctr., Houston, 1978-89; dir. Med. and Psychol. Svcs., Houston, 1983-85; assoc. prof. Baylor Coll. Medicine, Houston, 1985-89; prof. Med. Coll. Wis., Milw., 1989—; supr. Sports Psychiat. Inst., Milw., 1990-94; chief of staff St. Mary's Hill Hosp., Milw., 1990-92. Mem. grant rev. com. NIMH, Washington, 1986; cons. Acad. Managed Care, Milw., 1990—; editor Social Psychiatry Spotlight, Milw., 1998—; chair Socio-Cultural Cmty. Coalition, 1998—. Editor: A Clinician's Manual, 1982, Psychiatry: A Problem-Oriented Approach, 1986, The Ethical Way, 1997, I Have A Vision, 1999. Bd. dirs. Tex. Com. for Humanities, 1988-89, Milw. Ethnic Coun., 1991-94, Alliance for Mentally Ill, Milw., 1993-99. Maj. U.S. Army, 1975-77. Named Exemplary Psychiatrist, Nat. Alliance for Mentally Ill, 1993. Fellow Am. Psychiat. Assn., Am. Orthopsychiat. Assn.; mem. Am. Assn. for Social Psychiatry (pres. 1998—), Am. Assn. Cmty. Psychiatrists (emeritus bd. 1997—, sponsor award for ethical practice 1998), Am. Assn. Psychiat. Adminstrs. (chair ethics com. 1999), Grand Ave. Club (bd. dirs. 1999). Jewish. Avocations: family, music, art, travel, sports. Home: 1200 E Bywater Ln Milwaukee WI 53217-2840 E-mail: rustevie@earthlink.net.

MOFFITT, CAROLYN MULLINS, university official; b. Victoria, Ark. d. Jefferson Forrest and Mabel Mullins: children: James S. Crone, Jr., Jefferson Edward Crone, Laurie Kittrell. BBA, U. Memphis, 1994. Supr. Medicare billing City of Memphis Hosp., 1968-71; dir. budget and reimbursement Regional Med. Ctr., Memphis, 1971-90, bus. mgr. ambulatory svcs., 1990-91; patient accounts mgr. radiology dept. U. Tenn. Med. Group, Memphis, 1992-99; mgmt. analyst, compliance officer U. Tenn. Health Sci. Ctr., Memphis, 1999—. Cons. Meth. Healthcare, Memphis, 1982-84, Brannon McCullough, Primary Health Care Ctr., Memphis, 1990-92; mem. adv. bd. Porter Leath Children's Home, Memphis, 1989-92. Mem. Healthcare Fin. Mgmt. Assn. (cert., fellow, bd. dirs. 1995-96, v.p. 1996-98, pres. 1999-2000, bd. chmn. 2000-2001, compliance officers forum adv. coun. 2001-2004). Avocations: stained glass creations, collectibles, reading, family. Office: U Tenn Health Sci Ctr Ste 807 920 Madison Ave Memphis TN 38163 E-mail: cmoffitt@utmem.edu.

MOFFITT, CHARLES WILLIAM, art gallery director; b. Altoona, Pa., Mar. 24, 1932; s. Charles William and Beatrice Jeanette (Shellenberger) Moffitt; m. Marianne Foley Potter, May 23, 1980 (dec.); children: Michelle Ann Hunt, Charles William III, Deborah K. Moffitt Russell; m. Mary Lou Herold, Nov. 24, 2001; stepchildren: Sherry Marshall, Heather Clayton, Kristin Pfauser. BA, Pa. State U., 1957. Examiner Pa. R.R., Buffalo, 1957-62; asst. to pres. White Cross Stores, Inc., Monroeville, Pa., 1962-65, sec., 1965-70, v.p. adminstrn., sec., 1970-72; dir. labor relations and legal affairs Revco D.S., Inc., Cleve., 1972-75, asst. v.p. personnel, 1974-75; pres. Fashion Wearhouse, Inc., Altoona, Pa., 1975-87; dir., ptnr. Servello Gallery Art, 2002—. Owner Omega Advt. Co.; pres. Olympus I, Inc., 1980-87; agt. Prin. Fin. Group, 1988-90, Variable Annuity Life Ins. Co., 1990-2001. Co-author: Mincemeat Cartoons, Altoona Mirror Newspaper. Bd. dirs. Bedford Springs Music Festival, 1984-87, Blair County Arts Found., 1987-91. Republican. Roman Catholic. Home: RR 5 Box 2324 Altoona PA 16601 Office Phone: 814-946-8922. E-mail: monkmoffitt@aol.com.

MOFFITT, DONALD EUGENE, transportation company executive; b. Terre Haute, Ind., May 22, 1932; s. James Robert and Margaret Mary (Long) M.; m. Billie Duffy, Feb. 21, 1989; 1 child, Jaime. BA, Ind. State U., 1954; postgrad., Ind. U., 1956; grad., Advanced Mgmt. Program, Harvard U., 1972. Acct. Foster Freight Lines, Indpls., 1955-56; with Consol. Freightways Inc., San Francisco, 1956-88, v.p. planning, 1961-69; v.p. fin., motor carrier subs. Consol. Freightways Corp. Del., 1969-75; v.p. fin., treas. parent co. Consol. Freightways Inc., San Francisco, 1975-81, exec. v.p. Palo Alto, Calif., 1981-86; vice chmn. parent co. bd. Consol. Freightways, Inc., Palo Alto, Calif., 1986-88; chmn., CEO Circle Express, Indpls., 1988-90; pres., CEO Consol. Freightways, Inc., Palo Alto, Calif., 1990-96; chmn., CEO Consol. Freightways, Inc. (name now CNF Transp. Inc.), Palo Alto, Calif., 1995—, also bd. dirs. Chmn. bd. dirs. all subsidiaries CNF Transport, 1990—; chmn., pres., CEO CNF Transp. Inc., 1996—. Bd. dirs. Bay Area Coun., Calif. Bus. Roundtable, Conf. Bd., Boy Scouts Am., ARC, Hoover Instn.; bd. dirs., exec. com. Hwy. Users Fedn.; bd. trustees Automotive Safety Found.; bus. adv. coun. Northwestern U. Transp. Ctr. Mem. Nat. C. of C. (vice-chmn., bd. dirs.). Office: CNF Transp Inc 3240 Hillview Ave Palo Alto CA 94304-1201

MOFFITT, RAY, social worker, consultant; b. Moline, Ill., Sept. 1, 1937; s. Ernest R. and Ida L. (Wiggins) M. BS, U. Ill., 1959, MSW, 1966; postgrad. child welfare tng. program, 1995. Cert. social worker, Ill. Social work trainee, grad. sch. field worker various Ill. agencies, 1963-66; social worker, program adminstr. Ill. Soldiers' and Sailors' Children's Sch., Normal, Ill., 1966-73; co-founder, dir. Kaleidoscope, Inc., Bloomington, Ill., 1973-74; pres., dir. Browndale/Kaleidoscope, Inc., various, 1974; field instr. Jane Addams Coll. Social Work U. Ill. at Chgo., 1975-77; social worker Village of Maywood (Ill.), 1977-82, cmty. rep., dir. cmty. rels., 1982-87; founder, dir. Explosonic Rockers Street Jazz Theatrical Troupe, 1987-92; founder, exec. prodr. MWAH! Performing Arts Troupe, 1993—; social worker DuPage County Sheriff's Dept., Wheaton, Ill., 1995—. Collaborator Chgo. Area Project and DuPage County Area Project. Mem. NASW, Acad. Cert. Social Workers, U. Ill. Alumni Assn., Child Care Assn. of Ill., Ill. Alcoholism and Drug Dependence Assn., Boy Scouts Am. (former Explorer advisor), Mental Health Assn. in Ill., Ill. Drug Edn. Alliance, Ill. Assn. Student Assistance Profls., Du Page Intergenerational Village, Alpha Zeta Alumni Assn. Home: 159 Cottage Hill Ave Apt 215 Elmhurst IL 60126-3347

MOFFLY, JOHN WESLEY, IV, magazine publishing executive; b. Phila., Aug. 5, 1926; s. John W. III Moffly and Audrey (Kane) Chancellor; m. Donna Jeanette Clegg, July 11, 1959; children: Jonathan Wesley, Audrey Kane Lkotz. BA, Woodrow Wilson Sch., Princeton U., 1949. NY advt. mgr. House & Home Mag. Time Inc., NYC, 1962-66, NY advt. exec. LIFE Mag., 1967-73, v.p. selling areas mktg. divsn., 1973-87; pres., owner Moffly Publs., Inc., 1987—; pubs. Greenwich, Westport, New Caanan and Darien mags. Bd. dirs. Boys and Girls Club Greenwich, United Way, Greenwich Emergency Med. Svc., Greenwich Adult Day Care; mem. Amb.'s Round Table-Forum, World Affairs. With USAAF, 1944-45. Mem. Greenwich C. of C. (chmn. bd. dirs. 1999-2000, Small Businessman of Yr. 1991), Riverside Yacht Club, Cruising Club Am., Indian Harbor Yacht Club. Republican. Episcopalian. Avocations: sailing, tennis, clay bird shooting, skiing, international studies. Home: 100 Meadow Rd Riverside CT 06878-2520 Office: Greenwich Mag 39 Lewis St Greenwich CT 06830-5558

MOFIDI, MAHYAR, dentist, researcher; s. Manoocher and Rouhi Mofidi. BS, U. Louisville, 1990, DMD, 1993; MPH, U. NC, Chapel Hill, 2000. Dentist Dixie Denta Ctr., Louisville, 1993—98, Cmty. Correctional Ctr., Louisville, 1997—98; intern Quality Mgmt Unit, NC Divsn. Med. Assistance, 1999; post-doctoral fellow, to adj. assoc. prof., to rschr. U. NC, Chapel Hill, 2000—. Cons. Dental Health for Humanity, Anhui Province, China, 1997—98; coord. East Chapel Hill Rotary Club, Haiti, 2000—02. Contbr. articles various profl. jours. Sec. Regional Bahai Council of So. States, Durham, NC, 2001—. Recipient Everett Grad. Student Merit award for outstanding achievement in dental pub. health, Am. Assn. Pub. Health Dentistry, 2001—02, Rsch. award, Am. Acad. Pediat. Dentistry Health Svcs., 2003, Jackson Health Edn. Practice award, 2003. Mem.: Spiritual Assembly Bahai of Durham, Rotary, Alpha Epsilon Lambda. Mem. Bahai Faith. Avocations: tennis, travel, reading, internet, ethnic food. Home: 22 Preakness Dr Durham NC 27713 Personal E-mail: mahyarm@aol.com.

MOGEL, LEONARD HENRY, writer; b. Bklyn., Oct. 23, 1922; s. Isaac and Shirley (Goldman) M.; m. Ann Vera Levy, Oct. 23, 1949; children: Wendy Lynn, Jane Ellen. BBA, CCNY, 1947. Salesman N.Y. Printing Co., N.Y.C., 1946-48; sales mgr. Pollak Printing Co., N.Y.C., 1948-52; advt. dir. Diners Club, Inc., N.Y.C., 1952-56; pub. Diners Club for Signature and Bravo mags., 1956-67; pres. Leonard Mogel Assos., Inc. (nat. advt. reps.), N.Y.C., 1952-67; prin. owner San Francisco Warriors Profl. Basketball Team, 1963-64; pres. Twenty First Century Comm. Inc., N.Y.C., 1967-72; pub. Cheetah and Weight Watchers mags., 1967-75; dir. Regents Pub. Co. divsn. Simon & Schuster, 1960-67; advt. cons. Harvard Lampoon, 1968; pub. Nat. Lampoon, 1970-86, Liberty mag., 1971-73, Ingenue mag., 1973-75, Heavy Metal mag., 1977-86. Adj. prof. NYU Sch. Continuing Edn., 1973—78; panelist Folio Mag. Pub. Conf., 1975—76. Exec. prodr.: (feature films) Heavy Metal, 1981; author: Everything You Need to Know to Make It in the Magazine Business, 1979, Making It in the Media Professions, 1988, Making It in Advertising, 1993, Making It in Public Relations, 1993, Making It in Broadcasting, 1994, Making It in Book Publishing, 1996, Creating Your Career in Communications, the Media and Entertainment, 1998, The Newspaper: Everything You Need to

Know to Make It in the Newspaper Business, 2000, This Business of Broadcasting, 2004. Sponsor Albert Einstein Med. Coll., Birch Wathen Sch., N.Y.C. Served with AUS, 1942-46, CBI. E-mail: mogelpub@aol.com.

MOGENSEN, CHARLES RAY, JR., food service administrator; b. Elizabeth, N.J., May 7, 1946; s. Charles Ray Sr. and Hellen Oakley (Holland) M.; m. Linda Diane Friezer, Apr. 25, 1970; children: Charles Ray III, Jason C., Eric S., Lindsey H. Student, Middlesex County Vocat. Coll., 1972. Cert. food executive, 1979, 1987; lic. real estate agt. NJ. Chef St. Elizabeth Hosp., Elizabeth, N.J., 1969-70; dir. food svcs. Cornell Hall Conv. Ctr., Union, N.J., 1970-96; dir. food svc. Corrections Corp. Am., Elizabeth (N.J.) Detention Ctr., 1996—. Pres. C.R.M. Food Enterprises, Ltd., Kenilworth, N.J., 1971-89; lic. real estate agt. Real Estate Cons., Short Hills, N.J.; owner C.R. Mogensen Antiques, Ltd., Red Bank, N.J. Author: (recipes) Escargots Without Shells, 1979 (citation merit 1979). Mem. Rep. Nat. Com., Washington, 1988; mem. adv. bd. Episcopalian Program for Homeless, Elizabeth, 1990, Union County (N.J.) Coalition for Homeless, 1991. Cpl. USMC, 1964-68, Vietnam. Named N.Y. Dist. winner Gen. Foods Corp., 1981; recipient Cert. of Appreciation Roselle Park (N.J.) First Aid Squad, 1986, award of merit USNR, 1990. Mem. VFW, Vets. of Vietnam War (life), Am. Legion (cert. of appreciation 1999), Royal Arch Masons, Internat. Food Svc. Exec. Assn. (pres. 1977, 79, 85, 86, bd. dirs., treas. 1989-91, Royal Order of Skillet 1987, Humanitarianism award 1987), Am. Correctional Food Svc. Assn., Asia Soc. Avocations: antiques, coins, oriental art. Home: The Harbour Club 708 Sunshine Ct Parlin NJ 08859 Office: Corrections Corp Am Elizabeth Detention Ctr 625 Evans St Elizabeth NJ 07201-2008

MOGENSEN, DENNIS, agricultural products company executive; CFO J.R. Simplot Co., Boise, Idaho. Office: JR Simplot Co PO Box 27 Boise ID 83707-0027

MOGERMAN, SUSAN, state agency administrator; Dir. State of Ill. Historic Preservation Agy., Springfield. Office: State Ill Hist Preservation Agy 500 E Madison Springfield IL 62701-1028

MOGG, JIMMY W. gas industry executive; B in Math., Southwestern Okla. State U., 1971; grad. advanced mgmt. program, Harvard U. With gas supply dept. Panhandle Ea. Pipe Line Co., Liberal, Kans., 1973—80; mgr. forcasting and ops. Panhandle Ea., Kansas City, 1980—86; gen. mgr. gas supply Trunkline Gas Co., Houston, 1986—88; gen. mgr. contracts and ops., gas supply Panhandle Ea., Trunkline, 1988; v.p. gas supply Panhandle Ea., Trunkline, Tex. Ea. Transmission Corp., 1989—91; sr. v.p. Panhandle Ea., 1991; pres. Centana Energy Corp., 1992—94; pres., CEO Duke Energy Field Svcs. LP, Denver, NC, 1994—99, chmn., pres., CEO, 1999—2004, group v.p. Charlotte, NC, 2004—, chief devel. officer, 2004—. Chmn. bd. dirs. TEPPCO Ptnrs. LP. Bd. dirs. Rocky Mountain chpt. Jr. Achievement. Mem.: Gas Processors Assn. (past pres.), Soc. Petroleum Engrs. Office: Duke Energy Corp 526 S Church St Charlotte NC 28202-1803

MOGGE, HARRIET MORGAN, educational association executive; b. Cleve. d. Russell VanDyke and Grace (Wells) Morgan; m. Robert Arthur Mogge (div. 1977); 1 child, Linda Jean. BME, Northwestern U.; postgrad., Ill. State U. Instr. piano, Evanston, Ill., 1954-58; instr. elem. music pub. schs., Evanston, 1959; editl. asst. archivist Summy-Birchard Co., Evanston, 1964-66, asst. to editor-in-chief, 1966-67, cons., 1968-69, ednl. dir., 1969-74, also historian, 1973-74; supr. vocal music jr. high sch., Watseka, Ill., 1967-68; asst. dir. profl. programs Music Educators Nat. Conf., Reston, Va., 1974-84, dir. meetings and convs., 1984-94, mgr. direct mktg. svc., 1981-89; sr. cons. Conv. Cons. Svc., 1993—2003, ret., 2003—. Mng. editor Am. Suzuki Jour., 1972-74, Gen. Music Today, 1987-91; mgr. display advt. Model T Times, 1971—; vice chair editl. bd. Exposition Mgmt., 1991-93. Active various cmty. drives. Mem. Music Educators Nat. Conf., Am. Choral Dirs. Assn., In and About Chgo., Music Educators Assn. (bd. dirs.1973-74), Suzuki Assn. Ams. (exec. sec. 1972-74, Disting. Svc. award 1996), Internat. Assn. Exposition Mgmt. (cert., mem. edn. com. 1979-88, chmn. edn. com. 1985-87, bd. liaison edn. com. 1987-88, bd. dirs. Washington chpt. 1983-85, nat. bd. dirs. 1986-91, nat. v.p. 1989, nat. pres. 1990, Disting. Svc. award 1996), Bus. and Profl. Women's Club Watseka (bd. dirs. 1968-70), Antique Automobile club (registrar ann. meeting 1961-86), Model T Ford Club Internat. (v.p. 1971-72, 76-77, pres. 1981, treas. 1983-87, bd. dirs. 1971-87), Mu Phi Epsilon, Kappa Delta (province pres. 1960-66, 72-76, regional chpts. dir. 1976-78, nat. dir. scholarship 1981-84). Republican. Presbyterian. Home and Office: 1919A Villaridge Dr Reston VA 20191-4824

MOGILNY, ALEXANDER, professional hockey player; b. Khabarovsk, Russia, Feb. 18, 1969; With Buffalo Sabres, 1988—99, capt., 1993—95; with Vancouver Canucks, 1995—99; right wing N.J. Devils, 1999—2001; player Toronto Maple Leafs, 2001—. Mem. USSR Olympic Team, 1988; player NHL All-Star Game, 1992—94. Named to Sproting News All-Star 2d Team, 1992—93, NHL All-Star 2d Team, 1992—93; recipient Gold medal, USSR Olympic Hockey Team, 1988. Office: Toronto Maple Leafs Air Canada Ctr 40 Bay St Ste 300 Toronto ON M5J 2X2 Canada

MOGK, JOHN EDWARD, law educator, association executive, consultant; b. Detroit, Feb. 10, 1939; s. Clifford Anthony and Evelyn Lenore (Paselk) M.; m. Lylas Heidi Goud, Aug. 23, 1964; children: Marja, Tenley, Matthew. BBA, U. Mich., 1961, JD with distinction, 1964; diploma in comparative law, U. Stockholm, 1965. Bar: N.Y. 1966, Mich. 1970. Assoc. atty. Shearman & Sterling, N.Y.C., 1964-68; mem. faculty Wayne State U. Sch. Law, 1968—, dir. grad. studies, 1990-95. Pres. MERRA Rsch. Corp., 1974-94; cons. econ. and urban devel., arbitrator; vis. prof. U. Utrecht, The Netherlands, 2000. Editor Michigan International Lawyer and Utilities Law Rev.; contbr. articles to profl. jours. Chmn. Mich. TOP Task Force, 1972; vice chmn. Mich. Constrn. Code Commn., 1973; mem. exec. com. Southeastern Mich. Coun. Govts., 1970; chmn. Detroit Sch. Boundary Commn., 1970, Downtown Detroit Vacant Bldg. Com., 1991-93; mem. Detroit Bd. Edn., 1970; mgr. Detroit Empowerment Zone Proposal, 1994; project exec. New Detroit Stadium, 1995; pres. Habitat for Humanity Detroit, 1999—. Named Outstanding Contbr. Internat. Law Sect., State Bar of Mich., 2001, Outstanding Wayne State U. Assoc. Prof., 1971, Outstanding Wayne Law Sch. Prof., 1977, 83, 93, 97, 2003, Outstanding Young Man in Detroit, 1972, One of Ten Outstanding Young Men in U.S., 1973, One of Four Outstanding Vols. in U.S., 1974; recipient Presdl. citation Wayne State U., 1977, State of Mich., 1988, 94; Am.-Scandinavian fellow, 1965; vis. fellow U. Warwick, Eng., 1985-86. Mem. ABA, Mich. Bar Assn. (Outstanding Achievement award Internat. Law Sect. 2001), Assn. of Bar of City of N.Y. Home: 1000 Yorkshire Rd Grosse Pointe Park MI 48230-1432

MOGLIA, GREG, education educator; b. Bklyn., Sept. 23, 1942; s. Greg Moglia and Mary Filibert; children: Elizabeth, Jennifer. BS in Chemistry, SUNY, 1964, MS in Chem. Edn., 1965; PhD in Philos. Edn., NYU, 1974. Tchr. chemistry, philos., psychology East Rockaway (N.Y.) HS, 1968—2002; prof. philosophy edn. NYU, N.Y., 1976—. Author: Earth Shattering Poems, 1998; co-author: Roots and Flowers, 2000. Recipient Allan Ginsberg Poetry prize, Passaic County C.C., 2002. Mem.: Live Poet Soc. (writer 1993—). Home: 67 Prime Ave Huntington NY 11743

MOGOL, ALAN JAY, lawyer; b. Balt., July 29, 1946; s. Jesse and Kitty (Stutman) m.; m. Ellen Epstein, June 19, 1969; children: Andrew Stephen, Jonathan David. BA with distinction, U. Va., 1968, JD, 1971. Bar: Md. 1972, U.S. Dist. Ct. Md. 1972, U.S. Ct. Appeals (4th cir.) 1972, U.S. Supreme Ct. 1978. Assoc. Ober, Kaler, Grimes & Shriver, Balt., 1971-77, ptnr., 1978—. Chmn. comml. finance Ober, Kaler, Grimes & Shriver, Balt., 1980-81, 84-85, 91-97, 2002—, chmn. equipment leasing practice group, 1998—; lectr. on continuing edn. Md. Inst. Continuing Profl. Edn. for Lawyers, 1988-92, trustee, 1990-93; spkr. seminars Nat. Health Lawyers Assn., Washington, 1986-87, Rocky Mountain Mgmt., Denver, 1987, Med. Imaging Expo., 1995, Washington, 1995. Co-author: In Structuring the Secured Loan Agreement, 1991, Commercial Finance Guide, 1997, Equipment Leasing, 1999; contbr. articles to profl. jours. and local newspapers. Bd. dirs. Transitional Living Coun., Balt., 1972-92; bd. trustees Md. Inst. of Continuing Profl. Edn. for Lawyers, 1990-93. Fellow Md. Bar Found., Inc., Am. Bar Found., Inc.; mem. ABA, Equipment Leasing Assn. Am. (lawyers com. 1986-89, program com. 1986-91, speaker seminars), Md. Bar Assn. (uniform comml. code com. 1988—, chmn. 1991-93, vice chmn. bus. sect. 1995-96, chmn. bus. sect. 1996-97). Avocation: tennis. Office: Ober Kaler Grimes & Shriver 120 E Baltimore St Ste 800 Baltimore MD 21202-1643 E-mail: ajmogol@ober.com.

MOGRABI, ROBERT, bank executive; b. Cairo, May 5, 1955; s. Joseph I and Simone Mograbi; m. Linda Mograbi, Sept. 9, 1978; children: Joseph, Matthew, Samuel. Positionist EAB, NYC, 1977—78, jr. trader, 1978—80; trader Societe Gen., NYC, 1980—83; chief forward trader Credit Suisse, NYC, 1983—88; mng. dir. Royal Bank of Scotland, 1993—. Avocations: painting, cooking, swimming.

MOGUL, LESLIE ANNE, business development and marketing consultant; b. Balt., Mar. 9, 1948; d. Harry and Elaine Mogul; m. William Kasper. AS, Miami Dade Jr. Coll., 1969; BA, Temple U., 1976; MBA, U. Phoenix, 1996. Accredited pub. rels. Account exec. Gray & Rogers, Inc., Phila., 1976-80; pres. Leslie Mogul, Inc., Phila., 1980-84; v.p. McKinney, Inc., Phila., 1984-87; assoc. dir. comm. Scripps Meml. Hosps., San Diego, 1987-93; dir. pub. rels. Scripps Health, San Diego, 1993, dir. customer rels. and mktg., 1994-95; dir. bus. devel. Harborview Med. Ctr. Hosp., San Diego, 1995-96; cons. Projectworks, San Diego, 1996—, pres., 1996—. Recipient over 25 awards local and nat. pub. rels. and comm. orgns. Mem. Pub. Rels. Soc. Am. (dir.-at-large 1993-94), Alumni Leadership Calif. Office: Project Works PO Box 301395 Escondido CA 92030-1395 E-mail: leslie@projectworksmarketing.com.

MOHAIDEEN, A. HASSAN, surgeon, healthcare executive; b. Ramanathapuram, India, Aug. 14, 1940; s. Abdul and Mariam (Pitchai) Kader; m. Zarina M. Meera, May 30, 1965 (dec. July 1986); children: Ahamed, Mariam, Najeeba, Azeema; m. Laurie J. Kucich, June 23, 1989; children: Yasmin Sara, Leila Jahan. MD, U. Madras, India, 1965; MBA, Wagner Coll., 1996. Diplomate Am. Bd. Surgery, Am. Bd. Quality Assurance and Utilization; cert. physician exec. Am. Coll. Physician Execs. Intern Govt. Stanley Hosp., Madras, 1965-66, Good Samaritan Hosp., West Islip, N.Y., 1967-68; resident in gen. and vascular surgery L.I. Coll. Hosp., Bklyn., 1968-73, asst. attending surgeon, 1973-76, assoc. attending surgeon, 1976-78, attending surgeon, 1978—, chief divsn. vascular surgery, 1980-93, dir. vascular lab., 1981-93; v.p. Bklyn.-Caledonian Hosp. Ctr. (affiliate of NYU), 1994-95; sr. v.p., managed care and exec. vice-chmn. dept. surgery The Bklyn.-Caledonian Hosp. Ctr. (affiliate of NYU), 1995-96; pres., CEO, Health Plan Systems, Inc., Rochelle Park, NJ, 2001—. Asst. surgeon G.H.Q. Hosp., Ramnad, India, 1966-67; assoc. attending surgeon Meth. Hosp., Bklyn., 1982-90, attending surgeon, 1991-97; asst. attending surgeon Bklyn. Caledonian Med. Ctr., 1973-85, mem. courtesy staff, 1985-94, 97—, attending surgeon, 1994-96; attending surgeon Victory Meml. Hosp., Bklyn., 1982—; vis. physician Kings County Hosp. Ctr., Bklyn., 1973-94; clin. instr. in surgery Downstate Med. Ctr., SUNY, Bklyn., 1973-78, clin. asst. prof. surgery, 1978—; mem. exec. com. of med. staff L.I. Coll. Hosp., Bklyn., 1979-93, treas. med. staff, 1982-85, pres., 1985-87, med. chmn. Guild Ball com., 1981, mem. quality assurance com. dept. surgery, 1988-94, chmn. credentials com., 1990-93, quality assurance and risk mgmt. com., 1990-93; bd. dirs. Aetna Health Plans of N.Y., AIDS adv. com., 1987-93, stds. com., 1986-94, quality assurance com.; bd. dirs. Aetna-U.S. Healthcare, 1997; mem. credentials com. Prucare, 1988-92; sr. v.p. managed care Bklyn. Hosp., 1995-96; mem. quality mgmt. com. Oxford Health Plans, 1995-2002; mem. quality improvement com. Chubb Health, N.Y., 1994-96, Cigna (HealthSource), 1997;; mem. credentials com. United Healthcare, 1997—; exec. dir. Mayan Health, PPO, Atlantic Med. Assocs. IPA; pres. Health Plan Sys., Inc. Contbr. articles to med. jours. Fellow ACS (com. on Long Island dist. applicants, 1988-99, bd. dirs. Bklyn.-L.I. chpt.), Royal Coll. Physicians and Surgeons Can. (cert.), Internat. Coll. Surgeons; mem. AMA (Physician's Recognition award), AAAS, Am. Coll. Physician Execs., Med. Soc. of State of N.Y., N.Y. State Soc. of Surgeons, N.Y. Acad. of Scis., Med. Soc. of County of Kings (mediation com., 1979-85), Bklyn. Surg. Soc., Soc. for Non-Invasive Vascular Technicians, Kings Physicians I.P.A. (pres./med. dir., 1985-95), Bklyn. Physicians I.P.A. (v.p., 1985-96, pres.). Avocations: photography, computers, walking. E-mail: hassan@mohaideen.com.

MOHAJER, DINEH, cosmetics company executive; b. Bloomfield Hills, Mich., Sept. 2, 1972; d. Reza and Shahnaz Mohajer. Student, U. So. Calif. Founder, CEO Hard Candy, Inc., Beverly Hills, Calif., 1996—. Office: Hard Candy 729 Farad St Costa Mesa CA 92627-4304

MOHAMED, AHMED A. chemist, researcher; b. Egypt, Aug. 11, 1966; s. Ali A. Mohamed; m. Hanan E. Abdou, Aug. 13, 1992; children: Rowana A., Yara A. Degree in Chemistry, Zagazig U., Egypt, 1988; PhD, U. Maine, 2000. Asst. lectr. dept. chemistry Zagazig (Egypt) U., 1988—92; tchg. asst. U. Maine, Orono, 1996—2000; rsch. assoc. dept. chemistry Tex. A&M U., College Station, 2001—. Co-author: Organic Derivatives of Gold and Silver. Fellow, Robert Welch Found., 2001; scholar, Can. Internat. Devel. Agy., 1993. Mem.: New Eng. Chpt. for Rheumatoid Arthritis, Inter-Am. Photochem. Soc., Am. Chem. Soc., Sigma Xi. Office: Tex A&M U Dept Chemistry College Station TX 77842 Business E-Mail: amohamed@mail.chem.tamu.edu.

MOHAMED, JOSEPH, SR., real estate broker, farmer; b. Omar, W.Va., Mar. 19, 1928; s. Mose and Minnie Elizabeth (Martin) M.; m. Shirley Ida Medeiros; children: Joseph Jr., John W., James R., Leslie Louise. BBA Personnel, Sacramento State U., 1952; postgrad., U. Pacific, U. Calif., Davis, Am. River Coll. Farmer, 1949—; founder comml. trucking operation, 1949-52, 1953; founder Mexican Co. of Agr. and Livestock Ltd., Ensenada, Baja, Calif., Mex., 1953-57; owner Quintair, Inc., Calif., 1954—; contractor, real estate developer, 1949—; owner Joseph's Landscape Svc., Sacramento, 1952-72, Joseph Mohamed Enterprises, 1982—. Pest control adviser, Calif., 1970—. Mem. Rep. Nat. Com., Rep. Presdl. Task Force, Sacramento Regional Arts Coun., 1965—, Govs.' Emergency Drought Task Force, 1977, Civil Affairs Assn., Calif. Rental Assn., 1975—, Sacramento Apartment Assn., Calif. Apartment Assn., Nat. Apartment Assn.; dir. McClellan Aviation Museum Found., Sacramento County Sheriff's Mounted Posse, 1961—. Served with U.S. Army, 1946-48, USAR, 1949-78. Decorated Legion of Merit; recipient Master Aviator Badge. Mem. Sacramento U. Alumni Assn., Sacramento State Horseman's Assn., Calif. State Horseman's Assn., Sacramento Metro. C. of C., Navy League of U.S., Reserve Officer's Assn., Assn. of U.S. Army, Elk Grove C. of C., Sacramento Bd. of Realtors, Calif. Assn. Realtors, Nat. Assn. Realtors, Masons, Shriners.

MOHAMED, MUSTAFA A. management educator; b. Arusha, Tanzania, Dec. 26, 1950; arrived in U.S., 1979; s. Mohamed Fiay and Aziza Kassim; m. Ruth Kiefson, Oct. 5, 1996; children: Karim, Aziza. BA, Inst. Devel. Mgmt., Morogoro, Tanzania, 1976; MS in Mgmt., Mgmt. Edn. Inst., Cambridge, Mass., 1980. Asst. lectr.I Inst. Devel. Mgmt., Morogoro, 1976—79; prof. mgmt. Roxbury C.C., Boston, 1983—. Avocations: travel, crisis hotline. Home: 194 Sherman St Cambridge MA 02140 Office: Roxbury C C 1234 Columbus Ave Cambridge MA 02140

MOHAMMADIAN, ABOLFAZL, civil engineer, educator; s. Ahmad Mohammadian and Saryeh Zandi; m. Maryam Majbouri; 1 child, Kiana. PhD, U. of Toronto, 2001; MSc, Sharif U. of Tech., Iran, 1993; BSc, Iran Univ. of Sci. and Tech., 1992. Professional Engineer, Profl. Engineers Ont., 2000. Rsch. asst. U. of Toronto, Toronto, Canada, 1998—2001; post-doctoral rsch. assoc. McMaster U., Hamilton, Canada, 2001—02; asst. prof. Dept. of Civil Engring., Calif. State U., Sacramento, 2002—03, Dept. Civil and Materials Engring., U. Ill., Chgo., 2003—. Mem. com. on statistical methodology Transportation Rsch. Bd., Nat. Academies. Fellow Post Doctoral Rsch. Fellowship, Natural Sci. and Engring. Rsch. Coun. of Can., 2001; scholar PGSB- Doctoral Rsch. Scholarship, Natural Sci. and Engring. Rsch. Coun. of Can. (NSERC), 2000, OGS - Ont. Grad. Scholarship, Govt. of Ont., 2000. Mem.: Inst. of Transp. Engrs. (student chpt. adv.). Achievements include research in Transportation Planning, Traffic Engineering, Transportation Design, Econometrics, Dynamic Modeling of Household Automobile Transactions. Office: U Ill Dept Civil and Materials Engring 842 W Taylor St Chicago IL 60607-7023

MOHAN, ANNETTE IMELDA, producer, educator; b. Bombay, Sept. 17, 1950; arrived in U.S., 1983; d. Joseph Alexander and Amy (Vaz) Gonsalves. BA, U. Bombay, 1971; MA, Andrews U., 1980, Norfolk State U., 1990. Prodr. Bombay TV, 1972-83; v.p. L.I.F.E., Inc., Virginia Beach, Va., 1983-98, Lathika Internat., Huntsville, Ala., 1998—. Asst. prof. Oakwood Coll., Huntsville, 1998—. Prodr.(shows): Young World, 1975—79, Magic Lamp, 1979—82; exec. prodr.(documentary): Hanged on a Twisted Cross, 1996 (Chris award Columbus (Ohio) Film Festival, 1996),: (films) Nazaraana-The Gift, 1997 (Bronze award Columbus Film Festival, 1997), Father of Preachers, 2001; exec. prodr., exec. prodr.: (films) Here I Stand, 2001, Revolution of Conscience, 2002, In the Footsteps of Martin Luther, 2003, For One English Officer, 2003, In The Footsteps of Martin Luther, 2003. Avocation: Avocations: travel, stamps, coins, cooking. Office: PO Box 5072 Huntsville AL 35814-5072 E-mail: LIFEINCVA@aol.com.

MOHAN, BRIJ, social work educator; b. Mursan, India, Aug. 9, 1939; came to U.S., 1975; s. Ram Pershad and Ram Shree (Devi) Sharma; m. Prem Sharma, Feb. 24, 1967; children: Anupama Sharma, Sanjay M. Sharma. BA, Agra (India) U., 1958, MSW, 1960; PhD, Lucknow (India) U., 1964; DLitt (hon.), M.K. Gandhi Kastic Univ., India, 2004. Rsch. scholar Lucknow U., 1960-63; rsch. supr. U. Lucknow, 1963-64, lectr., 1964-75; acad. specialist U. Wis., Oshkosh, 1975-76; assoc. prof. La. State U., Baton Rouge, 1976-81, dean Sch. Social Work, 1981-86, prof. social work, 1981—, dir. doctoral program, 1997—. Author: New Horizons of Social Welfare and Policy, 1985, Toward Comparative Social Welfare, 1986, Glimpses of International and Comparative Social Welfare, 1989, Denial of Existence, 1987, The Logic of Social Welfare, 1988, Global Development: Post-material values and Social Praxic, 1992, Eclipse of Freedom, 1993, Democracies of Unfreedom, 1996, Unification of Social Work, 1999, Social Work Revisited, 2002, The Practice of Hope, 2003; editor-in-chief New Global Devel.: Jour. Internat. and Comparative Social Welfare; contbr. over 200 articles to profl. jours. Fellow, UNESCO, 1968. Office: La State U Sch Social Work 325 Hp Long Field House Baton Rouge LA 70803-5752 Office Phone: 225-578-1345. Business E-Mail: swmoha@lsu.edu.

MOHAN, JOHN J. lawyer; b. St. Louis, May 22, 1945; s. John Joseph and Virginia Loretta (Durkin) M.; m. Elaine Bronwyn Lipe, May 29, 1982; children: Bryn Elizabeth, John Burke. BS Indsl. Engring., St. Louis U., Sch. Engring. and Earth Scis., 1967; JD, St. Louis U., 1971. Bar: Mo. 1971, Ill. 1971, U.S. Dist. Ct. (we. dist.) Mo. 1971, U.S. Dist. Ct. (ea. dist.) Mo. 1980, U.S. Dist. Ct. (so. dist.) Ill. 1981, U.S. Ct. Appeals (8th cir.) 1987. Asst. prosecuting atty. St. Louis County, 1971-72; asst. cir. atty. St. Louis Cir. Atty's. Office, 1972-74; spl. asst. state's atty. St. Clair County Atty's. Office, Belleville, Ill., 1974—; assoc. Lashley, Caruthers, Theis, Rava & Hamel, St. Louis, 1979-80; ptnr. Schreiber, Tueth & Mohan, Clayton, Mo., 1981-83, Danis, Reid, Murphy, Tobben, Schreiber & Mohan, Ladue, Mo., 1983-87, Hinshaw & Culbertson, St. Louis, 1987-97, Blackwell, Sanders, Peper, Martin, St. Louis, 1998-2000, Tueth, Keeney, Cooper, Mohan & Jackstadt, P.C., 2000—; mcpl. judge City Wildwood, Mo., 2004—. Mem. U. Mo. Law Sch. Found. Scholarship. Mem. ABA, Am. Arbitration Assn. (cert. mediator, arbitrator 1988—), Ill. State Bar Assn., Mo. Bar, Bar Assn. Met. St. Louis, St. Clair County Bar, St. Louis County Bar, Def. Rsch. Inst., Mo. Orgn. Def. Lawyers, Pinnacle Arbitration and Mediation Svcs. (cert. mediator, arbitrator 1997—), Phi Delta Phi. Home: 529 Big Horn Basin Ct Wildwood MO 63011-4818 Office: Tueth Keeney Cooper Mohan Jackstadt PC 425 S Woods Mill Rd Ste 300 Saint Louis MO 63017

MOHAN, KSHITIJ, healthcare company executive; b. India, Jan. 26, 1945; came to U.S., 1965; B in Physics, Patna U., India; M in Physics, U. Colo.; D in Physics, Georgetown U. Various positions U.S. FDA; with White House Office of Mgmt. and Budget; v.p., corp. regulatory affairs Baxter Healthcare, Deerfield, Ill., 1988-90, v.p., scientific affairs for I.V. systems, 1990-95, corp. v.p. rsch. and tech. svcs., 1995—. Bd. dirs. KeraVision, Inc., others; chair Baxter Worldwide Tech. Coun. Mem. Health Industry Mfrs. Assn. (bd. dirs.). Office: King & Spalding 1 Peachtree St Atlanta GA 30303-1763

MOHAN, SANKAR KRISHNAN, mechanical engineer; b. Cochin, Kerala, India, Nov. 25, 1948; life ptnr. Valerie Melburg; 1 child, Gopi. BTech, Indian Inst. Tech., Madras, 1971; MS, Syracuse U., 1983, PhD in Mech. Engring., 2002. Exec. engr. New Venture Gear, East Syracuse, NY, 1988—. Contbr. articles to profl. jours. Mem.: Soc. Automotive Engrs., ASME. Achievements include patents for automotive drivetrain. Office: New Venture Gear Inc 6600 NVG Dr East Syracuse NY 13057 E-mail: mohan@nvg.com.

MOHAN, TUNGESH NATH, television and film producer, film educator; b. Lucknow, India, Oct. 30, 1949; arrived in U.S., 1979; s. Bhola Shambu and Saraswati P. (Devi) Nath; m. Annette Gonsalves Mohan; 1 child, Lathika. BS, Kampur (India) U., 1969; diploma in Cinema, Film and TV Inst. India, Poona, 1972; MA, Andrews U., 1980. Prodr. Bombay TV, 1972-75, 77-79; asst. prof. Film and TV Inst. India, Poona, 1975-77; TV prodr. 700 Club, Virginia Beach, Va., 1980-82; prodr. spl. projects Christian Broadcasting Network, Virginia Beach, 1982-86, Christian Broadcasting Network Cable Prodns., Inc., Virginia Beach, 1986-87; dir. Internat. CBN Prodrs. Group, 1987-89, Internat. North-Star Entertainment Group, LA, 1989-92; mgr. Adventist Comm. Network, Silver Spring, Md., 1992-93; pres. TriAngel Media Corp., Thousand Oaks, Calif., 1992-94. Adj. prof. Film and TV Inst. India, Poona, 1975—79, Spicer Coll., Poona, 1975—79, Hampton (Va.) U., 1980—92; pres. Prodrs. Unit One, Virginia Beach, 1982—, L.I.F.E. Inc., 1993—; cons. Global Comm. Assocs., Virginia Beach, 1987—88, Global TV Syndication, 1998—; dir. Telecom. Ctr., Huntsville, Ala., 1998—. Exec. prodr.: Stand at Ease, 1989—90, A Father of Preachers, 2001; prodr.: Touching the Supernatural, 1992, Midnight Cry, 1994, Master Control, 1994, The Way We Were, 1995, Bought at a Price, 1996, Hanged on a Twisted Cross, 1996 (Chris award for best film, Bronze medal for screenplay Columbus Film Festival, 1996), Inn Keeper, 1996, The Invitation, 1997, The Gift, 1997 (Bronze Plaque for 2d pl. Columbus Internat. Film Fest, 1997), (dir.): Reaalizing the Vision, 2001; exec. prodr.: Father of Preachers, 2001; prodr.(dir.): Here I Stand, 2002, Revolution of Conscience, 2002, The Hymnmaker, 2002, In the Footsteps of Martin Luther, 2002, For One English Officer, 2002, The Dawning, 2002, Thank You, Mr. Hodges, 2003, The Invitation, 2003, Truth to Tell, 2003. Mem.: NATAS, Dirs. Guild Am., Writers Guild Am., Lions. Mem. Seventh-Day Adventist. Avocation: collecting stamps, music, camping, travel, tennis. Office: PO Box 5072 Huntsville AL 35814-5072 Office Phone: 256-881-4266. E-mail: lifeincva@aol.com.

MOHAN IYENGAR, RAJ, automotive executive, researcher; b. Tiruchirapalli, India; s. Krishnaswamy and Rajalakshmi Rengarajan; m. Gayatri Mohan Iyengar; children: Nikitha, Anitha. BE, Madras U., India, 1980; ME, Indian Inst. Sci., Bangalorre, 1982; MS, Rutgers U., New Brunswick, N.J., 1985; ScM, Brown U., Providence, 1986; PhD, Brown U., 1990. Rsch. assoc. Brown U., Providence, 1990, U. Pa., Phila., 1990—91; rsch. scientist Battelle Meml. Inst., Columbus, 1991—99; sr. engr. Rouge Steel Co., Dearborn, Mich., 1999—2001, mgr. auto. platforms, 2001—. Editor: (ASME Jour.of EMT - Special Issue) Integration of Scientific and Engineering Aspects of Structural Materials in High Temperature Applications, 2000, (ASME Journal of PVP - Special Issue) Challenges and Resolution in Structural Life Prediction, 2001, (Fatigue and Fracture of EM&S -Jour.) Materials and Mechanics Issues in Structural Life Prediction, 1998, (ASME - Bound Volume PVP 413) Understanding and Predicting Material Degradation, 2000, (ASME Bound Volume - PVP 391) Advances in Life Prediction Methodology, 1999; assoc. editor Jour. of Pressure Vessel Tech., 2001—; contbr. over 40 articles to profl. jours.; editor (assoc. tech.): Jour. of Pressure Vessel Tech., 2002—. Mem.: ASME, SAE (com. mem. ferrous 2001—), Am. Soc. Metals (Com. mem.- Materials Divsn. nd PVP Divsn. 1997—, Achievement Certificates 1998, 1999, 2000, 2001). Office: Rouge Steel Company PO Box 1631 3001 Miller Rd Dearborn MI 48121 Business E-Mail: rmohan@rougesteel.com.

MOHANTY, CHRISTINE ANN, retired language educator, actress; b. Coaldale, Pa., Jan. 4, 1945; d. Warren Russell and Helen Hargraves; m. Leonard Yehudi Seltzer; 1 child, Kasmira. BA, Queens Coll., Flushing, N.Y., MS Edn., 1972; PhD in English Lit., SUNY, Stony Brook, 1986. Tchr. fgn. langs. Three Village Ctrl. Sch. Dist., Setauket, NY, 1969—2000; asst. prof. Suffolk County C.C., Selden, NY, 1994—. Dir.: (plays) Deathtrap, 1992, Snow Queen, 1995; actor: Stepping Out, 1992, Prelude to a Kiss, 1998, Three Blind Mice, 1999, Social Security, 1999, Arsenic and Old Lace, 2000, Phantom of the Opera, 2000, Wuthering Heights, 2001, The Corn is Green, 2002, The Uninvited, 2002, Little Women, 2002, I Hate Hamlet, 2003, Noel Coward One Acts, 2003, Jekyll & Hyde, 2003, Dancing at Lughnasa, 2004; contbr. articles to profl. jours.; Exhibited in group shows at Bayport (NY) Pub. Libr., 2001—02. Recipient Educator of the Week award, NY55 WLNY-TV, 2000; U. Salamanca scholarship, N.Y. State Edn. Dept., 1990. Mem.: AAUW, Am. Assn. Tchrs. of French (pres. Suffolk county 1990—93, scholarship to France 1982), Long Island Lang. Tchrs., Phi Beta Kappa. Avocations: travel, tennis, creative writing, painting. Home: 109 Edgewater Ave Bayport NY 11705 Personal E-mail: christinemohanty@excite.com.

MOHANTY, MANOJ K. mineral engineer, educator; b. Bhubaneswar, Orissa, India, Mar. 9, 1965; arrived in U.S., 1991; s. Surendra Nath Mohanty, Pramila Mohanty, Kiranbala Mohanty; m. Pragyan "Sheela" P. Mohanty; children: Aadansh children: Anjalika. BS in Mining Engring., REC, Rounkela, India, 1985; PhD, So. Ill. U., 1997. Under mgr. Coal India Ltd., Brajraj Nagar, India, 1985—91; asst. Scientist So. Ill. U., Carbondale, 1994—97, asst. prof., 2000—; sr. process engr. Richwood Industries, Huntington, W.Va., 1998—99. Contbr. articles to profl. jours. Grantee Coal Cleaning Tech. Rsch. grants, Ill. Dept. Commerce and Cmty. Affairs, Clean Coal Rev. Bd., 2000, 2001, Dept. of Energy, 2002—03. Mem.: Soc. Mining, Metallurgy and Petroleum Engrs. (chmn. coal preparation com 2003—, editl. bd. Coal Preparation jour.). Office: So Ill Univ Mining and Mineral Resources Engring Carbondale IL Business E-Mail: mmohanty@siu.edu.

MOHANTY, SUNIL K. finance educator, researcher; b. Cuttack, Orissa, India, Oct. 28, 1958; arrived in came to U.S., 1985; s. Biswanath and Khyana Prava Mohanty; m. Tamera Lyn Bach; children: Rani, Raj. B of Tech., Indian Inst. Tech., Kharagpur, India, 1981; MBA, Minn. State U., 1989; D of Bus. Adminstrn., Cleve. State U., 1993. Jr. engr. Engrs. India Ltd., New Delhi, 1981—83, asst. engr., 1983—85; bus. cons. Small Bus. Devel. Ctr., Mankato, Minn., 1986—87; instr. dept. of mktg. Minn. State U., Mankato, 1988—89; vis. asst. prof. of fin. Hofstra U., Hempstead, NY, 1994—95, assitant prof. of fin., 1995—2001; asst. prof. of fin. U. St. Thomas, Mpls., 2001—, assoc. prof. fin., 2004—. Mem. editl. bd.: Acad. Fin. Studies, 2000—, Acad. Comml. Banking and Fin., 2001—; contbr. articles to profl. jours. (ANBAR Citation of Highest Quality Rating, 1997). Recipient Outstanding Rsch. award, Acad. of Acctg. and Fin. Studies, 2002. Mem.: Allied Acads. Inc. (Outstanding Rsch. award 2002), Fin. Mgmt. Assn. Internat. (assoc.), Ea. Fin. Assn. (assoc.), Am. Fin. Assn. (assoc.), Beta Gamma Sigma, Phi Kappa Phi. Avocations: tennis, swimming, travel. Office: U St Thomas 1000 Lasalle Ave Minneapolis MN 55403 Office Phone: 651-962-4416.

MOHAPATRA, SURYA N. laboratory executive; PhD in Med. Physics, U. London. Sr. v.p. Picker Internat., 1981—99; sr. v.p., COO Quest Diagnostics, Teterboro, NJ, 1999, pres., COO, 1999—2004, pres., CEO, 2004—. Bd. dirs. Vasogen Inc., 1999—. Contbr. articles to profl. jours. Mem.: Royal Coll. Surgeons Eng. (hon.). Achievements include patents in field. Office: Quest Diagnostics One Malcolm Ave Teterboro NJ 07608*

MOHDZAIN, A. ZAIDY, counselor, educator; came to U.S., 1979; s. Mohd Zain Abd Rahman and Siti Katijah Kechik; m. Tracey A. West; children: Andrew, Jasmine. BBA, We. Mich. U., 1980; MPA, U. Ill. Springfield, 1983, MA in Human Devel. Counseling, 1988; PhD of Counselor Edn. & Supervision, Kent State U., 1993. Cert. Nat. Bd. of Cert. Counselors, 1993, lic. Profl. Counselor, Miss., 1994, cert. Sch. Counselor K-12 State of Mo., 2001. Counselor mental health Cmty. Resource Ctr., Centralia, Ill., 1989—90; therapist Kemmerer Village Children's Home, Assumption, Ill., 1990—93; assoc. prof. Delta State U., Cleve., 1993—97, SE Mo. State U., Cape Girardeau, 1997—. Part time lectr. Mara Inst. Tech., Kuala Lumpur, 1984-85. Mem. editol. bd. (the Family Jour.: Counseling & Therapy). Mem. ACA, Internat. Assn for Marriage and Family Counselors, Assn. for Counselor Edn. and Supervision, Chi Sigma Iota. Avocations: camping, travel, hiking, boating, canoeing. Home: 2019 Brink Avenue Cape Girardeau MO 63703-6401 Office: Southeast Missouri State University One University Plaza/MS 5550 Cape Girardeau MO 63701-4799 Office Phone: 573-651-2417. Personal E-mail: zaidymohdzain@yahoo.com. Business E-Mail: zmohdzain@semo.edu. E-mail: zmohdzain@semo.edu.

MOHEBBI, AFSHIN, former telecommunications industry executive; Telecom. engring. cert., UCLA; BSEE, U. Calif., Irvine; MBA, U. Calif. With Pacific Bell, 1983—97; v.p.-bus. mktg. SBC Communications, Inc., 1997; pres., mng. dir. Brit. Telecom., 1997—99; pres., COO Qwest Comm. (merged with US West), 1999—2000, pres., worldwide ops., 2000—01; pres., COO Qwest Communications Internat., Inc., 2001—02. Private investor and advisor in the field.; bd. dir. BearingPoint, Inc., McLean, Va., 2001.

MOHEBBI, ESMAIL, industrial engineer; b. Tehran, Tehran, Iran, Oct. 21, 1964; m. Nooshin Abedini. BS, Tehran Poly. U., 1987; M of Engring., U. Toronto, Ont., Can., 1993, PhD, 1996. Postdoctoral rsch. assoc. U. of Toronto, 1996—97; logistic sys. specialist 3M Can. Co., London, 1997—99; vis. asst. prof. U. of Nebr., Lincoln, 1999—2000, asst. prof., 2000—. Mem.: Inst. of Indsl. Engrs., Inst. for Ops. Rsch. and the Mgmt. Scis. Office: U Nebr 175 Nebraska Hall Lincoln NE 68588-0518 Office Phone: 402-472-8634.

MOHIUDDIN, SYED MAQDOOM, cardiologist, educator; b. Hyderabad, India, Nov. 14, 1934; came to U.S., 1961, naturalized, 1976; s. Syed Nizamuddin and Amat-Ul-Butool Mahmoodi; m. Ayesha Sultana Mahmoodi, July 16, 1961; children: Sameena J., Syed R., Kulsoom S. MB, BS, Osmania U., 1960; MS, Creighton U., Omaha, 1967; DSc, Laval U., Que., Can., 1970. Diplomate Am. Bd. Internal Medcine (cardiovascular disease). Intern Altoona (Pa.) Gen. Hosp., 1961-62; resident in cardiology Creighton Meml. Hosp., also St. Joseph Hosp., Omaha, 1963-65, mem. staff, 1965—; prof. adjoint Laval U. Med. Sch., 1970; practice medicine specializing in cardiology Omaha, 1970—; prof. Creighton U. Med. Sch., 1977—, assoc. dir. div. cardiology, 1983-96; prof. pharmacy practice Creighton U. Sch. Pharmacy, 1986—; dir divsn. cardiology, 1996—; assoc. chair for acad. affairs dept. medicine, 1998—. Vice chmn. dept. medicine Creighton U., Omaha, 2003-; cons. Omaha VA Hosp. Rsch. fellow Med. Rsch. Coun. Can., 1968; grantee Med. Rsch. Coun. Can., 1970; grantee NIH, 1973. Fellow ACP, Am. Coll. Cardiology (gov. for Nebr. 1987-90), Am. Coll. Clin. Pharmacology, Am. Coll. Chest Physicians; mem. AAAS, Am. Heart Assn. (fellow coun. clin. cardiology, bd. dirs. 1973-75), Am. Fedn. Clin. Rsch., Nebr. Heart Assn. (chmn. rsch. com. 1974-76, dir. 1973—), Gt. Plains Heart Com. (Nebr. rep. 1976-84, pres. 1977-78), N.Y. Acad. Scis., Nebr. Cardiovascular Soc. (pres. 1980-81). Democrat. Moslem. Home: 12531 Shamrock Rd Omaha NE 68154-3529 Office: Cardiac Ctr Creighton U 3006 Webster St Omaha NE 68131-2027

MOHL, ALLAN S. social worker; b. Passaic, N.J., Feb. 10, 1933; s. Milton and Ruth (Meisler) M.; m. Judith Klein, Dec. 21, 1958; children: Barbara, Eric, Adam. BA, NYU, 1954, MA, 1956, MSS, 1960; PhD, Columbia Pacific U., 1991. Diplomate Clin. Social Work. Dir. residential social svcs., adminstr. Queens (N.Y.) Soc. for Prevention of Cruelty of Children, N.Y., 1977-80; psychotherapist in pvt. practice Ardsley, N.Y., 1966—; cons., dir. family svcs. Tip Neighborhood House, Bronx, N.Y., 1980-84; sch. social worker Com. on Spl. Edn., Dist. 28, N.Y.C., 1984—2002, Project Liberty, 2003—. Condr. workshop on incestuous families and child sexual abuse; unit dir. Children's Village, Dobbs Ferry, N.Y., 1971-77; cons. Parents Anonymous, South Bronx, N.Y., 1983-84; com. mem. Crisis Intervention Dist. 28, 1995-2002; mem. Queens regional staff devel. com., 1995-98; mem. Queens regional social work awards com., 1996-98. Contbr. articles to profl. jours. Former chmn. Gen. Social Svcs. Adv. Coun. # 6, 1982-83; active participant Bronx Task Force on Child Abuse and Neglect; group leader Project Enable, South Bronx, N.Y., 1965-67; sponsor Parents' Anonymous group, Bronx, 1982-84; vol. White Plains Med. Hosp. Ctr., 1991—. With U.S. Army, 1956-58. NIMH grantee; recipient Editor's Choice award Internat. Libr. Poetry, 1999, 2000, 2002. Mem. NASW (awards com. Queens, N.Y. chpt.), Am. Assn. Marriage and Family Therapy, Am. Orthopsychiat. Assn., N.Y. State Soc. Clin. Social Wk. Psychotherapists, Internat. Assn. Counselors and Therapists, Am. Group Psychotherapy Assn. (assoc. clin. mem.), Internat. Soc. Poets (disting. mem.), N.Y. Acad. Scis. Home: 8 Shorthill Rd Ardsley NY 10502-2020 Office Phone: 914-693-1604.

MOHLER, BRIAN JEFFERY, diplomat; b. Niskayuna, N.Y., May 28, 1948; s. Donald and Rosemary (Brown) M. BA, Johns Hopkins U., 1970, MA, 1972. Economist Congl. Rsch. Svc. Libr. of Congress, Washington, 1973-74; commd. Fgn. Svc. Office, U.S. Dept. State, 1974; staff asst. Bur. Econ. Affairs, Dept. State, Washington, 1974-76, economist, 1979-82; consul Am. Consulate Gen., Strasbourg, France, 1976-78; desk officer European cmty. affairs Bur. European Affairs, Dept. State, Washington, 1982-84; petroleum attache Am. Embassy, Riyadh, Saudi Arabia, 1986-88, counselor for econ. affairs, 1988-90, dep. chief of mission Abu Dhabi, United Arab Emirates, 1990-93; desk officer Japanese affairs Bur. East Asian and Pacific Affairs, Washington, 1984-86; dep. dir. of econs. for Japanese affairs Bur. East Asian and Pacific Affairs, Dept. State, Washington, 1993-95; counselor for econ. affairs Am. Embassy, Tokyo, 1995-99; dir. econ. sanctions policy Bur. Econ. Affairs Dept. State, Washington, 1999-2001, dir. Japanese affairs Bur. East Asian and Pacific Affairs, 2001—03, sr. adviser for Iraq Econ. Reconstrn. Bur. Econ. Affairs, 2003—04, sr. insp. Office of the Insp. Gen., 2004—. 2d lt. U.S. Army, 1972, capt. USAR, 1972-85. Recipient Superior Honor award Dept. of State, 1993, 98, 2003, 04, Meritorious Honor award, 1987, award Sec. of Transp., 1998. Mem.: Japan-Am. Soc. of Washington DC, Am. Fgn. Svc. Assn., Sigma Nu. Roman Catholic. E-mail: mohlerbj@state.gov., bjmohler@hotmail.com.

MOHLER, MARY GAIL, magazine editor; b. Milaca, Minn., Dec. 15, 1948; d. Albert and Deane (Vedders) M.; m. Paul Rodes Trautman, June 5, 1976 (div. 1994); children: Elizabeth Deane, David Albert Rodes, Theodore DeForest Lloyd. BA, U. Calif.-Davis, 1974; MA in Lit., SUNY-Stony Brook, 1976. Asst., then editor-reporter Family Circle Mag., N.Y.C., 1979-81; editorial coordinator Ladies' Home Jour., N.Y.C., 1981, assoc. articles editor, 1982, mng. editor, 1982-93, sr. editor, 1994-98; editor in chief Ladies' Home Jour. Parent's Digest; mng. editor Parents Mag., 1999—2001, editor at large, freelance writer, 2001—. Co-author: Those Who Can...Teach, 1999. Medieval philosophy fellow SUNY-Binghamton, 1978 Mem. MLA, Am. Soc. Mag. Editors, Phi Beta Kappa Clubs: Medieval; Overseas Press. Office: Parents Mag 375 Lexington Ave New York NY 10017-5514

MOHLER, RICHARD ALBERT, JR., academic administrator, theologian; b. Lakeland, Fla., Oct. 9, 1959; s. Richard Albert Sr. and Janet Rae (Johnson) M.; m. Mary Ann Kahler, July 16, 1983; children: Mary Katherine, Christopher Albert. BA magna cum laude, Samford U., 1980; MDiv, So. Bapt. Theol. Sem., Louisville, 1983, PhD, 1989; postgrad., St. Meinrad Sch. Theology, 1985, Oxford (Eng.) U., 1986. Ordained min. So. Bapt. Ch. Pastor Union Grove Bapt. Ch., Bedford, Ky., 1982-87; asst. to pres., coord. found. support, dir. capital funding So. Bapt. Theol. Sem., Louisville, 1983-89, pres., 1993—; editor The Christian Index, Atlanta, 1989-93, prof. christian theology, 1996—. Assoc. dir. The So. Sem. Found., 1983-89; rsch. fellow Ethics and Religious Liberty Commn., 1998—; lectr. in field. Assoc. editor Preaching, 1985-93, contbg. editor, 1993—; gen. editor: The Gods of the Age of the God of the Ages?, 1993; editor-in-chief The So. Bapt. Jour. Theology, 1997—; columnist Religion News Svc., 1998—; sr. corr. World Mag., 1997—; mem. editl. bd. Salem Broadcasting, 1999—; host (radio programs) Truth On the Line, 2001—, The Albert Mohler Program; author daily Crosswalk Commentaries; contbr. articles to profl. jours. Pres., chmn. Coun. of Sem. Pres. of So. Bapt. Conv., 1996—, chmn., Greater Louisville Billy Graham Crusade, 2001. Named one of 40 Rising Evang. Leaders, Christianity Today, 1996, one of 96 Southerners to Watch, Atlanta Jour. and Constitution, 1996, one of 50 Young Leaders Under 40 years of age TIME Mag., one of Emerging Leaders in Edn. CHANGE Mag., 1998. Mem. Am. Acad. Religion, Soc. Biblical Lit., Evang. Theol. Soc., Evang. Philos. Soc., So. Bapt. Hist. Soc., Bapt. Pub. Rels. Assn., So. Bapt. Press Assn., Evang. Press Assn., Nat. Assn. Evangs., Ga. Bapt. Hist. Soc., Rotary Internat., Phi Kappa Phi, Omicron Delta Kappa. Achievements include being named one of 50 young leaders under 40 years of age TIME Mag. Office: So Bapt Theol Sem 2825 Lexington Rd Louisville KY 40280-0001 Office Phone: 502-897-4121. Business E-Mail: presoffic@sbts.edu.

MOHLER, RONALD RUTT, electrical engineering educator; b. Ephrata, Pa., Apr. 11, 1931; s. David Wealand and Elizabeth (Rutt) M.; m. Nancy Alice Strickler, May 6, 1950; children: Curtis Gene, Pamela Louise, Susan Lynn, Anita Marie, John Scott, Andrew Thomas, Jennifer Lee, Lisa Nancy. BS (scholarship), Pa. State U., 1956; MS, U. So. Calif., 1958; PhD, U. Mich., 1965. Designer, trainee Textile Machine Works, Rockwell Internat. Corp., Reading, Pa., 1949-56; staff mem. Hughes Aircraft Co., Culver City, Calif., 1956-58, Los Alamos Sci. Lab., 1958-65; assoc. prof. elec. engring. U. N.Mex., Albuquerque, 1965-69; prof. elec. engring./aerospace, mech. and nuclear engring. U. Okla., 1969-72, prof., chmn. info. and computing scis., 1970-72; dir. Systems Research Center, 1969-72; adj. prof. elec. engring. and nuclear engring. U. N.Mex., Los Alamos Grad. Center, 1959-65; cons. Sandia Corp., Albuquerque, 1966-69, Aerojet-Gen. Corp., Sacramento, 1966; vis. assoc. prof. system sci. UCLA, 1968-69; cons. community health project OEO, Oklahoma City, 1970-71; prof. elec. and computer engring. Oreg. State U., Corvallis, 1972-98, prof. emeritus, 1998—, head dept., 1972-79, 90; pres. Pace Tech., Inc., 1982-97. Vis. prof. U. Rome, 1973, 75, Imperial Coll., London, 1978-79, U.S. Naval Postgrad. Sch., 1983-85, Australian Nat. U., 1988, Sydney U., 1995, 98; cons. Optimization Software, L.A., 1973—, Bonneville Power Adminstrn., 1975—, Internat. Inst. Applied Systems Analysis, 1988—. Author: Optimal Control of Nuclear Reactors, 1970, Bilinear Control Processes, 1973, Nonlinear Systems: Dynamics and Control, vol. 1, 1991, Applications to Bilinear Control, vol. II, 1991, Disease Dynamics, 1993; editor: Theory and Application of Variable Structure Systems, 1972, Variable Structure Systems with Application to Biology and Economics, 1975, Recent Developments in Variable Structure Systems, Economics and Biology, 1979, Nonlinear Time Series and Signal Processing, 1988, assoc. editor Annals of Nuclear Energy, 1973-97; contbr. jours. Chmn. St. Stephens Sch. Bd., Norman, 1970-72. Recipient NATO award, 1979; rsch. grantee NSF, 1966-99, Sandia Labs., 1966-68, 96-97, ONR, 1981-92, NASA, EPRI, BPA, 1990-97; AEC fellow, 1961-65, Hughes fellow, 1956-58; Acad. Sci. exch. scientist to USSR and China, 1980, US-CIS (USSR) Commn. on Engring. Edn., 1991—. Fellow IEEE (life, local chmn. 1975); mem. Control System Soc., Sigma Xi, Tau Beta Pi, Pi Tau Sigma. Democrat. E-mail: ronamoh@aol.com.

MOHLER, STANLEY ROSS, physician, educator; b. Amarillo, Tex., Sept. 30, 1927; s. Norton Harrison and Minnie Alice (Ross) M.; m. Ursula Luise Burkhardt, Jan. 24, 1953; children: Susan Luise, Stanley Ross, Mark Hallock. BA, MA, U. Tex., 1953, MD, 1956. Diplomate Am. Bd. Preventive Medicine. Intern USPHS Hosp., San Francisco, 1956-57; med. officer Center Aging Research, NIH, Bethesda, Md., 1957-61; dir. Civil Aeromed. Rsch. Inst., FAA, Oklahoma City, 1961-66, chief aeromed. applications divsn. Washington, 1966-78; prof., vice chmn. dept. community medicine, dir. aerospace medicine Wright State U. Sch. Medicine, Dayton, Ohio, 1978—. Rsch. assoc. prof. preventive medicine and pub. health U. Okla. Med. Sch., 1961—; vice-chmn. Am. Bd. Preventive Medicine, 1978—, sec.-treas., 1980—. Co-editor: Space Biology and Medicine (5 vols.), 1995 (Life Scis. Book award Internat. Acad. Astronautics); contbr. articles to profl. jours. Bd. dirs. Sr. Citizens Assn. Oklahoma City, 1962—, Flying Physicians Assn., 1961—. Served with AUS, 1946-48. Recipient Gail Borden Rsch. award, Boothby award Aerospace Med. Assn., 1966, FAA Meritorious Svc. award, 1974, Cecil A. Brownlow Publ. award Flight Safety Found., 1998; co-recipient Life Scis. Book award in space, biology and medicine Internat. Acad. Astronautics, 1995. Fellow Geriatrics Soc., Aerospace Med. Assn. (pres. 1983, Harry G. Moseley award 1974, Lyster award 1984, Louis H. Bauer Founders award 1998), Am. Coll. Preventive Medicine, Gerontol. Soc.; mem. AMA, Aircraft Owners and Pilots Assn. (Sharples award 1984, Hubertus Strughold award 1991), Alpha Omega Alpha. Home: 6539 Reigate Rd Dayton OH 45459-3214 Office: Wright State U Sch Medicine PO Box 927 Dayton OH 45401-0927

MOHLER, TERENCE JOHN, psychologist; s. Edward F. and Gertrude A. (Aylward) M.; m. Carol B. Kulczak; children: Renee, John, Timothy. BE, ME, EdS, Toledo U.; PhD, Union Inst., 1979, Walden U. Lic. psychologist, Ohio. Psychologist, sr. ptnr. Psychol. Assocs., Maumee, Ohio, 1970—. Assoc. fellow Inst. for Advanced Study in Rational Psychotherapy, N.Y.C. Served in U.S. Army, 1951-53, Korea. Mem. APA, Ohio Psychol. Assn., Northwestern Ohio Psychol. Assn., Maumee Vly. Psychol. Assn., Soc. Behaviorists, Toledo Acad. Profl. Psychology, Nat. Registry Mental Health Providers, Am. Personnel and Guidance Assn., Ohio Personnel and Guidance Assn., Coun. Exceptional Children, Rotary (Paul Harris fellow), Kappa Delta Phi. Home: 1904 Glen Ellyn Dr Toledo OH 43614-3256 Office Phone: 419-893-0300.

MOHN, MELVIN PAUL, anatomist, educator; b. Cleve., June 19, 1926; s. Paul Melvin and Julia (Jacobik) M.; m. Audrey Faye Lonergan, June 28, 1952; children— Shorey Faye, Andrew Paul AB, Marietta Coll., 1950; Sc.M., Brown U., 1952, PhD in Biology, 1955. Instr. SUNY Downstate Med. Ctr., Bklyn., 1955-59, asst. prof., 1959-63; asst. prof. anatomy U. Kans. Sch. Medicine, Kansas City, 1963-65, assoc. prof., 1965-72, prof., 1972-89, prof. emeritus, 1989—. Cons. Nat. Med. Audiovisual Ctr., Atlanta, 1972; vis. lectr. U. Miami Sch. Medicine, Fla., 1966. Bd. dirs. U. Kans. Med. Ctr. Credit Union, 1968-77, Kansas City Youth Symphony, 1972-77; mem. U.S. Pony Club, 1964-71, Med. Arts Symphony, 1965 71, 90—, Spring Hill Chorale, 1990—. Served with USN, 1944-46, PTO. McCoy fellow, 1950, Arnold biology fellow, 1954 Fellow AAAS; mem. Am. Soc. Zoologists, Am. Assn. Anatomists, Am. Inst. Biol. Sci., Phi Beta Kappa, Sigma Xi, Beta Beta Beta. Clubs: Lions, Rotary,. Lodges: Masons. Republican. Methodist. Home: Yankee Bit Farm 23595 W 223rd St Spring Hill KS 66083-4029 Office: U Kans Med Ctr Dept Anatomy 39th and Rainbow St Kansas City KS 66103

MOHN, RICHARD E. bank executive; Grad., Valley Forge Mil. Acad., Duke U.; MBA, Temple U. Bd. Penn Savs. Bank, 1981—; chmn. bd. Sovereign Bank, FSB, 1989—, Sovereign Bancorp, Wyomissing, Pa. Chmn. Cloister Spring Water Co., Lancaster, Pa. Office: Sovereign Bancorp 1130 Berkshire Blvd Wyomissing PA 19610

MOHNEY, NELL WEBB, religion educator, speaker, author; b. Shelby, N.C., Oct. 31, 1921; d. John Wonnie and Maude (Ferree) Webb; m. Ralph Wilson Mohney, Dec. 31, 1948; children: Richard Bentley, Ralph Wilson Jr. BA, Greensboro Coll., 1943; LHD (hon.), Tenn. Wesleyan Coll., 1982. Dir. youth work Western N.C. Conf., Salisbury, 1945-48; dir. Christian edn. 1st United Meth. Ch., Lenoir, N.C., 1943-45, Washington Pike United Meth. Ch., Knoxville, Tenn., 1952-56; dir. adult ministries 1st Centenary United Meth. Ch., Chattanooga, 1967-73, dir. membership devel., 1973-81, 1st Broad St. United Meth. Ch., Kingsport, Tenn., 1981-87; speaker, seminar leader for bus., profl., religious orgns. S.E. U.S., 1960—. Spkr. Internat. Women's Conf., Crystal Cathedral, 1991, 2001; adj. staff Bd. Discipleship Sect. on Evangelism, Nashville, 1987-96. Author: Inside Story, 1979, Single Out Singles for Ministry, 1989, Don't Put a Period Where God Put a Comma, 1993, How to be Up on Down Days, 1995, Keep on Kicking as Long as You Are Ticking, 1999, Get A Faith Lift, 2000, Develop Your Bounce Back Ability, 2000, From Eve to Esther: What Old Testament Women Say to Women Today, 2001, From Mary to Lydia, 2002, You Can Soar Like An Eagle, 2004; co-author: Parable Churches, 1989, Churches of Vision, 1990, 365 Meditations for Grandmothers, 1996, 365 Meditations for Women, 1997, 2004; contbr. weekly article Chattanooga Free Press, 1977. Recipient Freedom Founds. award for writing, Valley Forge, Pa., 1973, for speaking, 1974, Key to City of Chattanooga, 1979; named Disting. Alumnae Greensboro Coll., 1988, Woman of Distinction in Chattanooga, 1992, Woman of Distinction Hall of Fame, 1993, Tenn. Woman of Yr., 1999. Republican. Home: 1004 Northbridge Ln Chattanooga TN 37405-4214 E-mail: rwmsr@aol.com.

MOHNS, JUDITH, artist, art educator; b. Schenectady, N.Y., Sept. 11, 1963; d. Henry Edward and Malene Dougherty; m. Francois Alain Deschamps; children: Adrien Luc George, Simon Julien Cyril. BFA in photography, SUNY Coll. at New Paltz, 1986, MFA, 1996. Graphic designer Beckwith Barrow Design, Cold Springs, NY, 1988—90; art tchr. Middletown City Sch. Dist., Middletown, NY, 1990—92; vis. fellow U. of Auckland, New Zealand, 1995; adj. instr. Ulster County Cmty. Coll., Stone Ridge, NY, 1998—2001, SUNY Coll. at New Paltz, 2003—. Panel juror N.Y. Found. for the Arts, 2001; juror,women's studio workshop Geraldine R. Dodge Fellowship, 2002. Prin. works include Quartet, 1995, Cartesian Dreams, 1995, prin. works include book Remembrance, 2003. Artist's fellowship, N.Y. Found. for the Arts, 1990, 1997, Book Residency, Nexus Contemporary Art Ctr., 1992. Mem.: Women's Studio Workshop, Coll. Arts Assn.

MOHOLY-NAGY, HATTULA, archaeologist; b. Berlin, Oct. 11, 1933; arrived in U.S., 1937; d. László and Sibyl Pietzsch Moholy-Nagy; m. Roger G. Schneggenburger, June 21, 1987; m. Hans-Rudolf Hug, June 1965 (div. Mar. 1979); children: Andreas Laszlo Hug, Daniel Claude Hug. AB in History, U. Mich., 1955, PhD in Anthropology, 1994; AM in Anthropology, U. Chgo., 1958. Field lab. head Joint Casas Grandes Project of Amerind Found., Dragoon, Ariz., 1958—59; Tikal project rschr. U. Pa. Mus., Phila., 1960—, Tikal project field lab., 1960, field lab. dir., 1961—64; lectr. U. Zurich, 1971—78; rsch. assoc. U. Pa. Mus., 1994—. Reviewer anthropol. books and jours., 1960—; participant profl. meetings, 1974—; lectr. and cons. in field, 1995—. Contbr. articles and monographs to profl. jours. and conf. procs. Mem.: Catalogue Raisonné Scholars Assn., Archaeol. Inst. Am., Soc. for Am. Archaeology, Am. Anthropol. Assn. Home and Office: 1204 Gardner Ann Arbor MI 48104-4321 E-mail: hattula@sprynet.com.

MOHR, CHRISTINA, retired economist; b. San Diego, Calif., June 1, 1949; d. Lloyd Crowell and Joan Watkins, Oliver Watkins (Stepfather); m. Peter Joseph Mohr, July 13, 1989; stepchildren: Robert, Tracie 1 child, Oliver Wise. BS in Polit. Sci, U. Pa., Phila., 1971; MA in Internat. Affairs, George Washington U., Washington, DC, 1979; PhD in Econs., U. Md., College Park, 1993. Cons. World Bank, Washington, 1982; analyst sci. resource Nat. Sci. Found., Washington, 1983—86, speech writer for dir., 1987—93; sci. diplomacy fellow US Agency for Internat. Devel., Washington, 1994—95; sr. analyst Nat. Sci. Found., Washington, 1996—2001; retired, 2001. Commr. People with Disabilities Commn., Montgomery County, Md., 1994—96. Home: 2932 Woodstock Ave Silver Spring MD 20910

MOHR, GARY ALAN, physician; b. Erie, Pa., Aug. 17, 1952; s. Arthur John and Sue (Richardson) m. Christina Wiser; children: Benjamin, Nathan, Elizabeth, Katelyn, Eric. BS, Pa. State U., 1975; MD, Jefferson Med. Coll., 1979. Cert. Am. Bd. Family Practice. Intern, resident in family medicine St. Vincent Health Ctr., Erie, Pa., 1979-82; pvt. practice Canon City, Colo., 1982—. Asst. clin. prof. family medicine U. Colo. Health Scis. Ctr. Founder, treas. Jefferson Soc., Fremont County, Colo., 1991. Fellow Am. Acad. Family Physicians; mem. Fremont County Med. Soc. (past pres.), Mensa. Lutheran. Achievements include climbing Mt. Kilimanjaro, Oct. 2000. Office: 730 Macon Ave Canon City CO 81212-3314 Office Phone: 719-275-1618.

MOHR, JANET ANN, psychiatrist; b. Defiance, Ohio, Feb. 13, 1958; d. Leo Arnold and Keiko Takahashi Mohr; m. Timothy Lyn Hunsucker, Aug. 4, 1984; 1 child, James Hunter Hunsucker. BS, U. Toledo, 1979; MD, Ohio State U., 1982. Diplomat Am. Bd. Psychiatry and Neurology. Intern Baylor and Affiliates, Houston, 1982-83, resident, 1983-86, fellow in child and adolescent psychiatry, 1986-88; pres., psychiatrist Assocs. of Psychiatry P.A., Sugar Land, Tex., 1988-96, Golden Isles Psychiatric Assocs., P.C., Brunswick, Ga., 1996—. Nat. Psychiat. Endowment Fund fellow, 1986. Mem. AMA, Am. Psychiat. Assn., Am. Acad. Child and Adolescent Psychiatry, N.Y. Acad. Scis., Glynn County Med. Soc., Phi Kappa Phi. Office: Golden Isles Psychiat Assocs PC 1421 Lee St Brunswick GA 31520-7132

MOHR, JOHN LUTHER, biologist, environmental consultant; b. Reading, Pa., Dec. 1, 1911; s. Luther Seth and Anna Elizabeth (Davis) M.; m. Frances Edith Christensen, Nov. 23, 1939; children: Jeremy John, Christopher Charles. AB in Biology, Bucknell U., 1933; student, Oberlin Coll., 1933-34, Marine Biol. Lab., Woods Hole, Mass., 1934; PhD in Zoology, U. Calif., Berkeley, 1939; postgrad., Am. U., 1963. Research asso. Pacific Islands Research, Stanford, 1942-44; rsch. assoc. Allan Hancock Found., U. So. Calif., 1944-46, asst. prof., 1946-47, asst. prof. dept. biology, 1947-54, asso. prof., 1954-57, prof., 1957-77; chmn. dept., 1960-62; prof. emeritus, 1977—; vis. prof. summers U. Wash. Friday Harbor Labs., 1956, '57. Rsch. assoc. history and philosophy of sci., NSF, Am. U., 1963, vertebrate zoology Natural History Mus., Los Angeles County, 1996-2003; marine borer and pollution surveys harbors So. Calif. Dept. of Fish and Game, 1948-51, arctic marine biol. rsch., 1952-71; chief marine zool. group U.S. Antarctic rsch. ship Eltanin in Drake Passage, 1962, in South Pacific sector, 1965. Mem. Biol. Stain Commn., 1948-80, trustee, 1971-80, emeritus trustee, 1981—, v.p., 1976-80; bd. dirs. Calif. Natural Areas Coord. Coun., 1981-90. Recipient Guggenheim fellowship, 1957-58 Fellow AAAS (coun. 1964-73, Sr. Scientists and Engrs. Nat. Network), So. Calif. Acad. Scis., Sigma Xi (exec. com. 1964-67, 68, 69, chpt.-at-large bd. 1968-69); mem. Am. Micros. Soc., Marine Biol. Assn. U.K. (life), Am. Soc. Parasitologists, Western Soc. Naturalists (pres. 1960-61), Soc. Protozoologists, Soc. Integrative and Comparative Biology, Ecol. Soc. Am., Calif. Native Plant Soc., Common Cause, Huxleyan, Sierra Club, Phi Sigma, Theta Upsilon Omega. Home: 3819 Chanson Dr Los Angeles CA 90043-1601 Personal E-mail: jmohr10000@aol.com.

MOHR, LAWRENCE CHARLES, physician; b. S.I., N.Y., July 8, 1947; s. Lawrence Charles Sr. and Mary Estelle (Dawsey) M.; m. Linda Johnson, June 14, 1970; 1 child, Andrea Marie. AB with highest honors, U. N.C., 1975, MD, 1979. Diplomate Am. Bd. Internal Medicine. Commd. 2d lt. U.S. Army, 1967, advanced through grades to col., 1989; med. intern Walter Reed Army Med. Ctr., Washington, 1979-80, resident in medicine, 1980-82, chief resident, 1982-83, attending physician, 1984-86, pulmonary fellow, 1986-87; command surgeon 9th Inf. Div., Ft. Lewis, Wash., 1983-84; med. cons. Madigan Army Med. Ctr., Tacoma, 1983-84; White House physician Washington, 1987-93; asst. prof. medicine Uniformed Svcs. U. of the Health Scis., Bethesda, Md., 1984-91; assoc. prof. medicine Uniformed Svcs. U. Health Scis., Bethesda, Md., 1991-94; assoc. clin. prof. medicine George Washington U., Washington, 1990-94; prof. medicine Med. U. S.C., Charleston, 1994—, dir. environ. bioscis. program, 1995—. Attending physician Med. U. Hosp., Charleston, 1994—, Charleston Meml. Hosp., 1994—; mem. Working Group on Disability in U.S. Presidents, 1995—. Editor: International Case Studies in Risk Assessment and Magagement, 1997, Biomarkers, Medical and Workplace Applications, 1998; contbr. articles to profl. jours. and books. Bd. dirs. Internat. Lung Found., Washington; mem. adv. bd. Nat. Mus. Health and Medicine, Washington; mem. sci. adv. bd. Consortium in Environ. Risk Evaluation; prin. investigator Consortium in Molecular Epidemiology and Biomarker Rsch. Decorated Silver Star, Bronze Star with 2 V devices and 3 oak leaf clusters, Purple Heart, Meritorious Svc. medal with oak leaf cluster, Air medal, Army Commendation medal with oak leaf cluster, D.S.M.; recipient Erskine award Walter Reed Army Med. Ctr., 1982; named Outstanding Med. Resident, 1982. Fellow ACP, Am. Coll. Chest Physicians; mem. AMA, Army and Navy Club, Order Mil. Med. Merit, Harbour Club, Phi Beta Kappa. Episcopalian. Avocations: mountain climbing, skiing. Home: 673 Lake Francis Dr Charleston SC 29412-4345 Office: Med U S C Environ Bioscis Program 171 Ashley Ave Charleston SC 29425-0001

MOHR, ROGER JOHN, advertising agency executive; b. Milw., Sept. 8, 1931; s. Reinhold and Clara (Meissner) M.; m. Pauline Spicuzza, Oct. 18, 1958; children: Gregory, Mary Margaret, Kristin, Thomas, Kathleen. BS in Speech, Marquette U., 1953; postgrad. radio and TV, Northwestern U., 1955-56. Staff announcer radio sta. WBKB, West Bend, Wis., 1952, WCAN, Milw., 1952-54; with Arthur Meyerhoff Assos., Inc., Chgo., 1956-80, pres., 1965-80, BBDO, Chgo., 1980-82, chmn., 1982-90, vice chmn. internat., 1991-93; retired, 1993. Chmn. Lake Bluff (Ill.) Plan Commn., 1972-75; mem. Lake Forest (Ill.) Plan Commn., 1994-2000, chmn., 1999-2000; bd. dirs. Chgo. City Ballet, 1982-84, Off the Street Club, 1976-78; mem. adv. coun. Marquette U. Sch. Comm., 1993-99; alderman Lake Forest City Coun., 2000—. Served with AUS, 1954-55. Mem. Am. Assn. Advt. Agys. (chmn. Chgo. coun. 1966-67, sec., treas., nat. bd. dirs. 1976-77), Evans Scholars Alumni Assn. (pres. 1964-65), Western Golf Assn. (bd. dirs. 1980-2000, v.p. 1994-2000, trustee 2000—), Knollwood Club (bd. govs. 1980-85, 89-92), Tavern Club (bd. govs., v.p. 1988-94). Home: 2000 Knollwood Rd Lake Forest IL 60045-1137

MOHRAZ, JUDY JOLLEY, foundation administrator; b. Houston, Oct. 1, 1943; d. John Chesler and Mae (Jackson) Jolley; m. Bijan Mohraz; children: Andrew, Jonathan. BA, Baylor U., 1966, MA, 1968; PhD, U. Ill., 1974. Lectr. history Ill. Wesleyan U., 1972-74; asst. prof. history So. Meth. U., Dallas, 1974-80, coord. women's studies, 1977-81, assoc. prof. history, 1980-94, asst. provost, 1983-88, assoc. provost for student academics, 1988-94; pres. Goucher Coll., Towson, Md., 1994-2000, Virginia G. Piper Charitable Trust, Scottsdale, Ariz., 2000—. Cons. Ednl. Testing Svc., Princeton, N.J., 1984-93, Nat. Park Svcs., Seneca Falls, N.Y., 1992-93; bd. dirs. Balt. Equitable Soc., 1996-2000, The Assocs. First Capital, 1999-2000; bd. visitors U.S. Naval Acad., 1996-2001. Trustee The Lamplighter Sch., 1991-94, St. Mark's Sch. Tex., 1993-94; adv. bd. U. Tex. Southwestern Med. Sch., 1992-94; active Leadership Dallas, 1994; bd. dirs. Nat. Assn. Ind., The Balt. Cmty. Found.; pres. Ariz. Grantmakers Forum, 2003—; mem. Ariz. State Sch. Readiness Bd., 2003-. Recipient Disting. Alumni award Baylor U., 1993; named Woman of Merit, Omicron Delta Kappa, 1993. Office: Virgina G Piper Charitable Trust 6720 N Scottsdale Rd Ste 350 Scottsdale AZ 85253 Business E-Mail: jmohraz@pipertrust.org.

MOHRFELD, RICHARD GENTEL, marketing professional; b. Camden, N.J., Dec. 30, 1945; s. Herbert Henry and Elizabeth Weldon (Gentel) M.; m. Ann Bacon, June 20, 1971 (div. 1975); m. Janice Lee Strickland, July 1, 1978; children: Kathryn Elizabeth, Christopher Hall. BSc in Geology, Dickinson Coll., 1971. Staff geologist Temple U., Phila., 1971-74; pres. Mohrfeld Inc., Collingswood, NJ, 1974—2002; sr. mktg. exec. Quest Environ. & Engring. Svcs., Inc., Clinton, 2002—. Bd. dirs. South Jersey Savs. & Loan Assn., Turnersville, N.J., 1984-2000. Bd. dirs. Boy Scouts Am., Camden County, N.J., 1985—; trustee Knight Park Trustees, Collingswood, 1986—, Health Care Support Found., Inc., 1994—. Sgt. USAF, 1969-71. Mem. ASHRAE, Air Conditioning Contractors Am. (pres. 1986-88), Fuel Mchts. Assn. N.J. (pres. 1992-94), Rotary (pres. Collingswood 1980-81). Episcopalian. Avocations: travel, photography. Home and Office: 314 Auburn Rd Pilesgrove NJ 08098-2602 Office Phone: 609-519-4367. Personal E-mail: m-fuel@comcast.net.

MOHRLANG, ROGER LLOYD, philosopher, educator; b. Hastings, Nebr., Dec. 5, 1941; s. Harold E. and Helen L. Mohrlang; m. Dottie; children: Mark, Becky. BS with hons. in Physics, Carnegie Mellon U., 1963; student in Edn., Columbia U., 1963; student in Ling., U. Okla., 1964—65; MA with hons. in Bib. Studies, Fuller Theol. Sem., 1976; PhD in New Testament, U. Oxford, 1980. Tchr. and interim headmaster Kabarnet (Kenya) Secondary Sch., 1963—64; tchr. geometry Galesburg (Ill.) Sr. HS, 1964—65; phonology dir. Summer Inst. Ling. U. Okla., 1966; rsch. fellow in ling. Ahmadu Bellow U., Nigeria, 1968—74; tchr. Bible translation Fuller Theol. Sem., 1974—75; tutor Keble Coll. U. Oxford, England, 1977—78; from asst. prof. to prof. religion Whitworth Coll., Spokane, Wash., 1978—88, prof. religion, 1988—. Cons. in ling. Wycliffe Bible Translators, Nigeria, 1968—74; vis. assoc. prof. New Testament Fuller Theol. Sem., 1982—84, 1989—90; vis. scholar Wycliffe Hall U. Oxford, 1986, 93; dir. and tchr. seminar Wycliffe Bible Translators, Kenya, 1993; vis. prof. Daystar U., Kenya, 2000—01. Author: Matthew and Paul: A Comparison of Ethical Perspectives, 1984; translator: Holy Bible: New Living Translation, 1992—95, 1998—2002; editor: Vece Yesu Kristi, 1968—75, Melifyi Alekawale Yesu Kristi, 1992—97; commentator New Living Translation Commentary, 1997—2002; contbr. articles to profl. jours. Lay preacher Oxford (Eng.) cir. of Meth. Ch., 1976—78; interim preacher Northview Bible Ch., Spokane, 1989, 1998, mem. preaching team, 2002—. Woodrow Wilson scholar, 1959—63, Gen. Motors scholar, 1959—63, Yale U. fellow, 1976, Duke U. fellow, 1976. Office: Dept Religion and Philosophy Whitworth College Spokane WA 99251

MOHRMAN, HENRY J(OE), JR., lawyer, investment manager; b. St. Louis, Jan. 28, 1948; s. Henry Joseph and Mavis Claire (Lynch) M.; m. Mary Beth Mohrman, Aug. 26, 1969; children: Aaron Henry, Anna Rose. BA, Yale U., 1969; JD, U. Chicago, 1973. Bar: Mo. 1973, Ill. 1974, U.S. Supreme Ct. 1997. Assoc. Greenfield & Davidson, St. Louis, 1973-76; asst. gen. counsel LaBarge, Inc., St. Louis, 1976-77; tax mgr. Ernst & Young, St. Louis, 1977-81; pvt. practice St. Louis, 1982—. Gen. counsel Miss. Valley Equipment Co., St. Louis, 1982—, MKT Mfg., Inc., St. Louis, 1986—, Ronald Coase Inst., 2000—, Whisler Farms LLC, 2002—; prin. Mohrmanlaw LC, 2004—. Mem. ABA, U. Chicago Law Sch. Alumni Assn. (pres. St. Louis chpt. 1986—). Republican. Jewish. Avocations: horsemanship, literature, theater, mathematics. Office: 7751 Carondelet Ave Ste 805 Clayton MO 63105-3369 Office Phone: 314-721-3626.

MOHRMAN, KATHRYN J, academic administrator; BA, Grinnell Coll., 1967; MA, U. Wis., 1969; PhD, George Washington U., 1982. Dean undergrad. studies U. Md., College Park, 1988—93; pres. The Colo. Coll., Colorado Springs, 1993—2002; exec. dir. Hopkins-Nanjing Ctr. for Chinese and Am. Studies, Johns Hopkins U., 2003—. Office: 1619 Massachusetts Ave NW Washington DC 20036 Office Phone: 202-663-5801.

MOHTAR, RABI H. hydrologist; b. Beirut, Nov. 7, 1960; s. Hassan F. and Wadad G. Mohtar. BS, Am. U., Beirut, 1983, MS irrigation sci., 1985; MS engring., Mich. State U., 1992, PhD agricultural engring., 1994. Professional Enginer, Lebanon, 2001. Rsch. assoc. Penn. State U., 1994—96; assoc. prof. Purdue U., West Lafayette, Ind., 1996—. Chmn. Nat. Environ. Regional Rsch. Project, West Lafayette, 1999—2003. Mem.: ASAE (assoc.; com. chair, founder 1994—2003), Gamma Sigma Delta. Home: PO Box 124 Lafayette IN 47902 Office: Purdue Univ ABE West Lafayette IN 47907 Office Phone: 765-494-1791. E-mail: mohtar@purdue.edu.

MOIZE, JERRY DEE, lawyer, government official; b. Greensboro, NC, Dec. 19, 1934; s. Dwight Moody and Thelma (Ozment) M.; m. Margaret Ann Wooten, Aug. 13, 1976; 1 child, Jerry Dee Jr. AB cum laude, Elon (N.C.) Coll., 1957; JD, Tulane U., New Orleans, 1960; diploma, Army Command & Gen. Staff Sch., USAR, 1981. Bar: Colo. 1961, U.S. Dist. Ct. Colo. 1961, U.S. Ct. Mil. Appeals 1962, U.S. Supreme Ct. 1965, N.C. 1965. Legal clk. Air Def. Commd., Colo. Springs, Colo., 1960-61, assistance officer, 1962-63; chief legal assistance divsn. 2nd Army, Ft. Meade, Md., 1964-65; staff JAG, Indiantown Gap Mil. Reservation, 1965; law clk. to hon. Eugen Gordon U.S. Dist. Ct. (mid. dist.) NC, Winston-Salem, 1965-66; dir. Legal Aid Soc. Forsyth County, Winston-Salem, 1966-69; exec. dir. Forsyth Bail Project, Winston-Salem, 1968-69, Lawyer Referral Svc. of Bar of 21st Jud. Dist., Winston-Salem, 1968-69; staff atty. office of gen. counsel FAA, Washington, 1969-70, acting chief admin. & legal resources, 1970-71; staff atty. office of gen. counsel Dept. Housing & Urban Devel., Washington, 1971, counsel Jackson area office, 1971-83, chief counsel Jackson field office, 1983-94; chief counsel Office Gen. Counsel Miss., Jackson, Fla., 1994—; HUD del. Miss. Fed. Exec. Assn., 1997—2000. Lectr. U. W.Va. Conf. on Poverty Law, 1968; HUD program svc. adviser, 2000—. Editor N.C. Legal Aid Reporter, 1968-69, N.C. Legal Aid Directory, 1968, Avlex Legal Index (2nd supplement), 1971, developed Miss. low income housing financing mechanism 1975-76; contbr articles to profl. jours., articles to splty. mags. Dem. candidate NC Ho. of Reps., Guilford County, 1964; mem. mil. com. Forsyth County NC Red Cross, 1967-68; pack leader Andrew Jackson coun. Boy Scouts Am., 1986-92; active Project Adv. Group US Office Econ. Opportunity Legal Svc. Program, 1968-69, Adv. Com. on Housing & Urban Devel., Miss., Law Rsch. Inst., 1980-81, Pilot Mountain Preservation & Park Com., Winston-Salem, 1968-70; mem. Race Com. Whitworth Hunt Races, 1973-76; Am. Master of Foxhounds Assn., 1976-79; adv. Order DeMolay, 1997—; sec. Miss Scottish Games, 1999, v.p. 2000, pres. 2001. Capt. AUS, 1960-65; ret. lt. col. USAR, 1966-87. Decorated Meritorous Svc. medal, Army Commendation medal with oak leaf cluster, Army Res. Forces Achievement medal with three oak leaf clusters, Nat. Def. Svc. medal, Armed Forces Res. medal; named Hon. Knight Mason, 1999; recipient Legion of Honor, Order of De Molay, 2000. Mem.: KT, NRA, N.C. State Bar, Fed. Bar Assn., Sons of Confederate Vets., Caledonian Soc. Miss., The Austin Hunt (joint master of foxhounds 1976—79), Whitworth Hunt (founder, master of foxhounds 1975—76), Miss. Track Club, Miss. Hist. Assn., Iron Bridge Hunt (v.p. 1964—65), Capital Club (Jackson, Miss.), Rosicrucian, Masons (32 degree), Order Ea. Star, Shriners, Pi Gamma Mu. Republican. Episcopal. Avocations: riding to hounds, running, book collecting. Home: 499 S Pear Orchard Rd # 6-C Ridgeland MS 39157 Office: Miss State Dept Housing & Urban Devel Fed Bldg 100 W Capitol 9th Flr Jackson MS 39269

MOJICA, AGNES, academic administrator; Chancellor Inter Am. U. of PR, San German, P.R. Chair governing bd. Hispanic Assn. Colls. and Univs., 1995-96, co-chair leadership group; chair governing bd. Intercollegiate Athletic League, 2001-02. Pres., Consortium of Presidents and Chancellors for the Prevention of the Use and Abuse of Drugs and Alcohol, 1998-2002. Mem., Assn. Industrialists of P.R., Western C. of C., Am. Assn. Higher Edn., Assn. Profl. Women, Altrusa, Rotary (hon.), Alpha Delta Kappa, Phi Delta Kappa. Office: Inter Am U PO Box 5100 San German PR 00683-9801 E-mail: amojica@sg.inter.edu.

MOJTABAI, ANN GRACE, author, educator; b. N.Y.C., June 8, 1937; d. Robert and Naomi (Friedman) Alpher; m. Fathollah Mojtabai, Apr. 27, 1960 (div. 1966); children: Chitra, Ramin. BA in Philosophy, Antioch Coll., 1958; MA in Philosophy, Columbia U., 1968, MS in Libr. Sci., 1970. Lectr. philosophy Hunter Coll., CUNY, 1966-68; libr. CCNY, 1970-76; fellow Radcliffe Inst. Ind. Study, Cambridge, Mass., 1976-78; Briggs-Copeland lectr. on English Harvard U., 1978-83; writer-in-residence U. Tulsa, 1983—, Yaddo Found., Saratoga, NY, 1975, 76. Author: Mundome, 1974, The 400 Eels of Sigmund Freud, 1976, A Stopping Place, 1979, Autumn, 1982, Blessed Assurance, 1986, Ordinary Time, 1989, Called Out, 1994, Soon: Tales From Hospice, 1998. Recipient Richard and Hinda Rosenthal award Am. Acad. and Inst. Arts and Letters, 1983, Lillian Smith award So. Regional Coun., 1986, Lit. Acad. award AAAL, 1993; Guggenheim fellow, 1981-82 Mem. PEN, Mark Twain Soc., Tex. Inst. Letters, Phi Beta Kappa. Home: 2329 Woodside Drive Amarillo TX 79124-1036 Office: U Tulsa Dept English 600 S College Ave Tulsa OK 74104-3126 Office Phone: 918-631-2237. E-mail: ann-mojtabai@utulsa.edu., Agmojtabai@aol.com.

MOK, CARSON KWOK-CHI, structural engineer; b. Canton, China, Jan. 17, 1932; came to U.S., 1956, naturalized, 1962; s. King and Chi-Big (Lum) M.; m. Virginia Wai-Ching Cheng, Sept. 19, 1959. BSCE, Chu Hai U., Hong Kong, 1953; M.C.E., Cath. U. Am., 1968. Registered profl. engr., Md., D.C. Structural designer Wong Cho Tong, Hong Kong, 1954-56; bridge designer Michael Baker Jr., Inc., College Park, Md., 1957-60; structural engr., chief design engr., assoc. Milton A. Gurewitz Assocs., Washington, 1961-65; ptnr. Wright & Mok, Silver Spring, Md., 1966-75; owner Carson K.C. Mok, Cons. Engr., Silver Spring, 1976-81, pres., 1982—. Facility engring. cons. Washington Met. Area Transit Authority, 1985-86; pres. Transp. Engring. and Mgmt. Assocs., P.C., Washington, 1986-2002; adj. asst. prof. Howard U., Washington, 1976-79, adj. assoc. prof., 1980-81. Contbr. articles to profl. jours. Bd. dirs. U.S. Pan Asian Am. C. of C. Sec.; N.Am. trustee China Grad. Sch. Theology, Wayne, Pa., 1972-74, pres., 1975-83, v.p., 1984-91; elder Chinese Bible Ch. Md., Rockville, 1978-80; chmn. Chinese Christian Ch. Greater Washington, 1958-61, 71, elder, 1972-76; dir. Evergreen Family Friendship Svc., Inc., A Pub. Benefit Corp., Colorado Springs, 1993—. Recipient Outstanding Std. of Tchg. award Howard U., 1980, Nat. Merit award U.S. Dept. Transp., 2000. Mem. ASCE, ASTM, Constrn. Specification Inst., Nat. Assn. Corrosion Engrs., Concrete Reinforcing Steel Inst., Am. Inst. Steel Constrn., Am. Concrete Inst., Am. Welding Soc., Prestressed Concrete Inst., Post-Tensioning Inst., Soc. Exptl. Mechanics, Internat. Assn. Bridge and Structural Engring., Pui Ching Mid. Sch. Alumni Assn. (pres. nation's capital chpt. 1991-97). Home: 4405 Bestor Dr Rockville MD 20853-2137 Office: 9001 Ottawa Pl Silver Spring MD 20910-2257 E-mail: ckm9001@aol.com.

MOK, SAMUEL T. federal agency administrator; Grad., Fordham U.; M Acctg., Cath. U., Washington. Chief fin. officer, comptroller U.S. Treasury Dept.; CEO GL Assocs.; mng. mem. Condor Cons., LLC; chief fin. officer U.S. Dept. Labor, Washington, 2002—. With U.S. Army. Decorated Meritorious Unit Citation, Meritorious Svc. medal; recipient James Saylor award Outstanding Svc., Assn. Govt. Accts., Washington. Office: US Dept Labor 200 Constitution Ave NW Washington DC 20210

MOK, WAI YIN, library and information scientist, educator; b. Hong Kong, July 24, 1965; arrived in US, 1985; s. Wai Kwong Mok; m. Kit Yee Cheung, Aug. 19, 1988; children: Rachel Verla, Jonathan Rex, David Eldon. BS in Computer Sci., Brigham Yound U., 1990; MS in Computer Sci., Brigham Young U., 1992, PhD in Computer Sci., 1996. Prof. info. systems Utah State U., Logan, 1999—2001, U. Ala., Huntsville, 2001—. Author: A Comparative Study of Various Nested Normal Forms, A Normal Form for Precisely Characterizing Redundancy in Nested Relations. Richard A. Witmondt faculty fellow, Coll. Adminstrv. Sci., U. Ala., 2002—03. Mem.: IEEE. Mem. Lds Ch. Achievements include research in new normal form for hierarchical databases; A comparative study of various nestd normal forms; A normal form for precisely characterizing redundancy in rested relations. Office: U Ala Dept Acctg and Info Sci Huntsville AL 35899 Personal E-mail: mokw@uah.edu. E-mail: mokw@uah.edu.

MOKODEAN, MICHAEL JOHN, lawyer, accountant; b. Canton, Ohio, Dec. 24, 1923; s. Michael and Elizabeth (Stroia) M.; m. Jean Cristea, Apr. 17, 1950 (dec.); children: Michael Dan, Christine Ann; m. Josephine Woodward, Jan. 28, 1995. BS in Edn, Kent (Ohio) State U., 1948; JD, William McKinley Sch. Law, Canton, 1955. Bar: Ohio 1955; C.P.A., Ohio. Agt. IRS, Canton, 1950-56; self-employed atty. C.P.A., Canton, 1957-69; tax accountant Elmer Fox & Co., Las Vegas, Nev., 1969; mgr. tax and ins. Diebold, Inc., Canton, 1969-74, sec., house counsel, 1974-78, v.p. legal, 1978-87, cons., 1987-89. Part-time instr. tax accounting Walsh Coll., N. Canton, 1963-64, bd. advisers, 1976—; bd. advisers Stark Tech. Coll., Canton, 1972-76 Bd. advisers Doctors' Hosp., Massillon, Ohio, 1986-93. With AUS, 1943-46. Mem. Brookside Country Club. Roman Catholic. Home: 2607 Charing Cross Rd NW Canton OH 44708-1588 E-mail: mokojo75@aol.com.

MOKOTOFF, MICHAEL, pharmaceutical sciences educator; b. Bklyn., Jan. 23, 1939; s. Jack Israel and Pauline (Hochberg) M.; m. Bonnie Faith Arieff, Apr. 22, 1967; children: Jeffrey David, Naomi Joy, Jay Daniel. BS in Pharmacy, Columbia U., 1960; MS, U. Wis., 1963, PhD, 1966. Cert. pharmacist, N.Y. Fellow NIH, Bethesda, Md., 1966-68; asst. prof. U. Pitts., 1968-72; vis. scientist Weizmann Inst. Sci., Rehovot, Israel, 1978; assoc. prof. medicinal chemistry U. Pitts., 1972-85, assoc. prof. pharm. scis., 1985-95, prof. pharm. scis., 1995—. Mem. Pa. Drug, Device and Cosmetic Bd., Harrisburg, 1990-98. Editor, author: (with others) Pharmacokinetics and Pharmacodynamics Vol. 3: Peptides, Peptoids and Proteins, 1991; mem. editl. bd. Jour. Peptide Rsch.; contbr. articles to Jour. Protein Rsch., Jour. Medicinal Chemistry, Jour. Peptide Rsch.; contbr. chpt. to Principles of Medicinal Chemistry, 5th edit., 2002. Fellow Agy. Indsl. Sci. Tech., Tokyo, 1997. Mem. Am. Assn. Colls. Pharmacy, Am. Chem. Soc., Am. Peptide Soc., European Peptide Soc. Achievements include patent for novel peptidyl amino steroids. Office: U Pitts 736 Salk Hl Pittsburgh PA 15261-0001 E-mail: moagie@pitt.edu.

MOKRASCH, LEWIS CARL, neurochemist, educator; b. St. Paul, May 9, 1930; s. Lewis and Anna (Dvorak) M.; m. Jane Carolyn Church, Apr. 20, 1974. BS magna cum laude, Coll. St. Thomas, 1952; PhD, U. Wis., 1955. Rsch. assoc. dept. psychiatry and neurology La. State U. Med. Center, New Orleans, 1956-57, assoc. prof. dept. biochemistry, 1971-76, prof., 1976-92, prof. emeritus, 1992—, acting head dept., 1978-79. Instr. medicine U. Kans. Med. Center, Kansas City, 1957-59, assoc. in medicine, dir. neurochemistry lab., 1959-62; asst. biochemist McLean Hosp., Belmont, Mass., 1960-64, assoc. biochemist, 1964-71; assoc. dept. biol. chemistry Harvard Med. Sch., Boston, 1964-67; asst. prof., 1967-71; adj. assoc. prof. biology Hellenic Coll., Brookline, Mass., 1969-71; staff scientist Neurosciences Research Programs, Brookline, 1970-71; vis. prof. neurology Duke U. Med. Center, 1981-82; lectr. in field Author book written on myelin; contbr. articles to profl. jours.; reviewer: jours. Sci., FASEB. Pres. Belmont Preservation Soc., 1969; candidate Bd. Selectman, Belmont, 1969; active Forsyth County Adult Care Home Cmty. Adv. Com., Hospice, Sr. Fin. Care, Winston-Salem, Reynolda Ho. Mus. Am. Art, Reynolda Gardens, Sr. Svcs. Program, Winston Salem, Citizens Quality Nursing Home Care, 1991-92; sr. leader Duke Long Term Care Program Edn. Com.; mem. edn. com. Shepherd Ctr. Grantee NIMH, 1973-74, Nat. Inst. Neurol. Disability and Blindness, 1957-90, Schlieder Found., 1971-72, 83-84, La. Bd. Regents, 1986-88. Fellow Am. Assn. Clin. Chemists; mem. AAUP, Am. Soc. Neurochemistry (local chmn. 1974), Am. Soc. Biol. Chemists, Soc. Neurosci. (founder, pres. local chpt. 1974-75), Soc. Rsch. Adminstrs. (membership chmn. New Eng. sect.), Nat. Citizens Coalition Nursing Home Reform, Am. Assn. Individual Investors (founder, past pres., sec. Piedmont chpt.). Libertarian. Achievements include first demonstration of adaptive enzyme regulation in animals and allosteric control of fructose bisphosphatase, of incorporation of hydrouracil into transfer RNA, of thermogenic mechanism for arousing hibernators, of metabolic control in hibernation, of altered hydrophobic proteins in neurological disorders, of biosynthesis of hydrophobic proteins and mitochondrial proteins in brain in vitro, of altered transport processes in cells of neurological disease victims, of defective transport of acetylcholine precursors into cells of Alzheimer's victims and that such transport is modulatable; development of coestimation method for ketoses, aldoses, and pentoses; first isolation in pure form of receptor hydrophobic proteins from mammalian brain. Home: 2711 Pilgrim Ct Winston Salem NC 27106 E-mail: DrLewMokasch@aol.com. *Before I entered Science, I regarded it as a Priesthood of individuals dedicated to the service of humanity, whose common goal was the enhancement of human life and the remedying of its ills. After 30 years in Science, I hold this thesis more strongly and have found many colleagues who agree with it. I am certain now that the failures and abuses of Science derive from the use of it for the goals of wealth, fame and power.*

MOKRZECKI, LECH MARIAN, history of education educator; b. Warsaw, Apr. 5, 1935; s. Justyn and Irena (Druhowino) M.; m. Aleksandra Maria Horbowska, Aug. 20, 1983. MA, U. Toruń, Poland, 1956; dipl. cellist, Acad. Music, Gdańsk, Poland, 1962, MA, 1964; PhD, Higher Sch. Pedagogy, Gdańsk, Poland, 1967; DrHabil, U. Gdańsk, Poland, 1975; PhD (hon.), Linköping U., 1998. From asst. to prof. extraordinary Gdańsk U., Poland, 1966-92, prof. ordinary, 1993—. Author: Three Centuries of Gdansk Learning, 1969, 2d edit., 1976, The Study of the Teaching of History, 1973, In the Sphere of the Work of Gdansk Historians in XVII Century, 1974 (Min. of Edn. award 1976), The Beginning of the Knowledge of the Sea in the Former Kingdom of Poland, 1983, The Fortress Vistulamouth, 1978, Traditions of Teaching History to the Close of XVI Century-Selected Countries and Problems, 1992 (Min. of Edn. award 1993), From the Tradition of Teaching History to the End of 16th Century, 1992, Science and Education in Polish Lithuanian COmmenwealth, 2001; co-author, editor: In the Sphere of Culture, Music, Ballet, 1971 (Min. of Culture award 1972), Scientific Copy Books of Gdansk University, Pedagogy History of Education, 1993, 97; co-author: A Significant Social Revolution, 1994. Head, History of Social Sci. Commn., Policy Acad. Sci. Mem. Assn. Internat. pour History of Edn. Belgium, Com. Internat. Scis. History, Commn. History of Historiography Italy, Polish Acad. Scis. (History of Sci. and Tech. com.). Roman Catholic. Avocations: travel, reading poetry. Home: Biała 6-28 80-435 Gdańsk Poland Office: Gdansk U Inst Pedagogy B Krzywoustego 19 80-952 Gdańsk Poland

MOLBEGOTT, LESTER PHILIP, anesthesiologist; b. N.Y.C., N.Y., Sept. 28, 1949; MD, NYU, 1978. Diplomate Am. Bd. Anesthesiology, Am. Bd. Internal Medicine. Intern Albany Med. Ctr., NY, 1978-79, resident internal medicine, 1979-81; resident anesthesiology U. Va. Med. Ctr., Charlottesville,

1983-85; anesthesiologist Monmouth Med. Ctr., Long Branch, NJ; clin. asst. prof. anesthesiology Drexel U., 1985—; pvt. practice Long Branch, 1985—. Mem.: N.J. State Soc. Anesthesiologists, Internat. Anesthesia Rsch. Soc., Am. Soc. Critical Care Anesthesiologists, Am. Soc. Anesthesiologists. Office Phone: 732-923-6980.

MOLDENHAUER, JUDITH A. graphic design educator; b. Oak Park, Ill., Feb. 28, 1951; d. Raymond L. and Jean Marie (Carqueville) M. BFA, U. Ill., 1973; MA, Stanford U., 1974; MFA, U. Wis., 1977. Design supr. N.E. Mo. State U., Kirksville, Mo., 1977-79; asst. prof. design Kansas City Art Inst., Mo., 1979-83; asst. prof. art, graphic design Sch. Art U. Mich., Ann Arbor, 1983-92; vis. lectr. Wayne State U., 1990-92, asst. prof. graphic design, 1992-98, assoc. prof. graphic design, 1998—, area coord. graphic design, 1992—. Free-lance designer The Detroit Inst. Arts, Toledo (Ohio) Mus. Art, Burroughs Corp. (Unisys) Detroit, Detroit Focus Gallery; vis. designer N.S. Coll. Art and Design, 1986; juror Ohio Mus. Assn., 1986, Collaborator Presdl. Initiative "Healthy Start": prenatal and pre-conceptional booklets and ednl. modules designs, 1992—; mem. organizing group health info. design Design Forum; presenter Congress Women's Health Issues, 1997, 98, Internat. Inst. Info. Design, Schwarzenberg, Austria, 1998, Read Me exhbn., Bern, Switzerland, 1999, Expert Forum Manual Design, Malardalen U., Eskilstuna, Sweden, 2000, others; participant design confs. Contbr. articles to profl. jours. Recipient award of distinction, merit award Am. Assn. Museums, 1985, 86, Excellence Design award Beckett Paper Co., 1991, gold award for softcover books Printing & Pub. Competition, 1994, Am. Graphic Design award, 1996, 98; Rackham grantee U. Mich., 1987, grantee Nat. Endowment for Arts, 1988; US-EU FIPSE grantee U.S. Dept. Edn. student and faculty exch. info. design, 2003. Mem. Wood Engraving Network, Univ. and Coll. Designers Assn. (merit award 1979, gold award 1979), Coll. Art Assn. (chmn. panel 1991), Women's Caucus for Art (panel chmn. 1987), Amnesty Internat., Women in Design (excellence award Chgo. 1985, Sierra Club, Audubon Soc. Lutheran. Office: Wayne State U Dept Art and Art History 150 Art Bldg Detroit MI 48202 Office Phone: 313-993-8165., 313-577-2980. E-mail: FrogBoggd@aol.com

MOLDENHAUER, NANCY A. social worker, educator; BSEd, Valparaiso U., 1976; MSW, cert. specialist in aging, U. Mich., 1984. Instr. Meiji Gakuin and Tokyo Med. and Dental U., 1977-81; corp. communication trainer Saito Internat., Inc., Tokyo, 1981-82; conf. coord. Ctr. for Japanese Studies U. Mich., Ann Arbor, 1982-84; gerontol. social worker Turner Geriatric Clinic U. Mich. Hosps., Ann Arbor, 1983-84; med. social worker Mo. Bapt. Med. Ctr., St Louis, 1985-88; geriatric social work specialist Program on Aging Jewish Hosp. Wash. U. Med. Ctr., St. Louis, 1988-92; dir. case mgmt. and corp. svcs. Aging Consult, St. Louis, 1993-95; libr. media specialist, ESL and elem. tchr. Michigan City Area Schs., Ind., 1999—. Adj. prof. Washington U., St. Louis, 1991-95; trainee in aging NIH, 1983-84; dir. Nat. Adult Day Svc. Assn., Nat. Coun. Aging, Washington, 1995-96; registration mgr. Landmark Edn. Corp., Alexandria, Va., 1997-98. Co-author: Positive Attitudes, Positive Aging: A Guide for Positive Actions in Later Life, NASDA Curriculum for Directors and Administrators, Adult Day Services - The Next Frontier, Handbook of Home Health Care Administration. Del. White House Conf. Aging, 1995. Named OWL Woman of Worth, 1993. Mem. NEA, ASCD, NASW, Acad. Cert. Social Workers, Gerontol. Soc. Am., Am. Soc. Aging, Nat. Coun. on Aging, Alzheimer's Assn., Older Women's League (local bd. dirs., pres. 1991-95, nat. bd. dirs., v.p. 1993-96), Challenge Metro (bd. dirs., pres. 1986-90). Avocations: gourmet cooking, restaurants, wine, foreign movies, travel. Office: 107 Kaye Ln Michigan City IN 46360-1730

MOLDENHAUER, WILLIAM CALVIN, soil scientist; b. New Underwood, S.D., Oct. 27, 1923; s. Calvin Fred and Ida (Killam) M.; m. Catherine Ann Maher, Nov. 26, 1947; children— Jean Ann, Patricia, Barbara, James, Thomas BS, S.D. State U., 1949; MS, U. Wis., 1951, PhD, 1956. Soil surveyor S.D. State U., Brookings, 1948-54; soil scientist U.S. Dept. Agr., Big Spring, Tex., 1954-57, soi. scientist Ames, Iowa, 1957-72, Morris, Minn., 1972-75; rsch. leader Nat. Soil Erosion Rsch. Lab., Agrl. Rsch. Svc. U.S. Dept. Agr., West Lafayette, Ind., 1975-85; prof. dept. agronomy Purdue U., West Lafayette, 1975-85, prof. emeritus, 1985—. Contbr. articles to profl. jours. Served with U.S. Army, 1943-46 Fellow Am. Soc. Agronomy, Soil Sci. Soc., Soil Conservation Soc. Am. (pres. 1979), World Assn. Soil and Water Conservation (pres. 1983-85, exec. sec. 1985-2003). Home and Office: 317 Marvin Ave Volga SD 57071-2011

MOLDER, SYBIL AILENE, retired occupational health nurse; b. Djakarta, Indonesia, Nov. 27, 1945; arrived in U.S., 1960; d. Douglas Gordon and Frederika (Dykstra) Ebert; m. Enno Molder, June 24, 1967; children: Sonja, Ingrid. Student, Northeastern U., 1964—66; AS with honors, Tunxis C.C., 1980. RN Conn.; cert. occupl. hearing conservationist. Staff nurse Meriden-Wallingford (Conn.) Hosp., 1980-85; occupl. health nurse Napier Co., Meriden, 1985-88; clin. coord. Miller Meml. Cmty. Ctr., Meriden, 1988-90; clin. dir. Conn. Occupl. Healthcenters, Northern Haven, Milford, 1990-95; team leader State of Conn. Unit 2 Berkley Care, Farmington, 1996—2001; occupl. health nurse Cytec Industries, Inc., Wallingford, 2001—03, ret., 2003. Recipient cert. of recognition, YWCA, 1987. Mem.: Conn. Safety Soc. (v.p. 1987—88), Occupl. Health Nurses Orgn. Home: 136 Knob Hill Rd Meriden CT 06451-4930

MOLDOFF, WILLIAM MORRIS, retired lawyer; b. Phila., Jan. 1, 1921; s. David and Pauline (Arcusin) Moldoff; m. Doris Elaine Johnson (dec.); children: Phillip Douglas, Laura Ellen, Janet Susan Sayers, Allan William. BA, U. Iowa, 1943; JD cum laude, U. Miami, 1950; LLM, U. Mich., 1955. Law editor Lawyers Coop. Pub. Co., Rochester, N.Y., 1952-54, 57-60; instr. Ohio No. U. Coll. of Law, 1955-57; proofreader N.Y. Codes, Rules and Regulations State of N.Y., 1960, adminstrv. asst. to exec. dep. Sec. of State, 1961-63; pvt. practice Nassau, N.Y., 1963-66; vets. claims examiner, rating bd. VA Regional, N.Y.C., 1966-85; ret., 1985. Lt (jg) USNR, 1943—46. Republican. Jewish. Home: 2 Phillips St #151 Nassau NY 12123-0151

MOLDOW, SUSAN, publishing executive; m. Bill Shinker. Various positions to exec. editor Avon Books, 1976—82; editor in chief Dell Books, 1982; editorial dir. Penguin Books, 1988—90; v.p. Viking Penguin Inc., 1988—90; editor in chief Doubleday Publishers, 1990—91; v.p. assoc. pub. and editor in chief, adult trade book div. HarperCollins, 1991—94; pub., v.p. Scribner (Simon & Shuster), N.Y.C., 1994—. Office: Scribner Simon & Shuster 1230 Ave Of The Americas New York NY 10020-1513*

MOLDSTAD, JOSLYN M. pre-school educator, writer; b. Jenera, Ohio, Oct. 8, 1954; d. Wayne F. and Esther Poebler Wiechmann; m. John Arthur Moldstad, July 30, 1977; children: Rachel, John, Matthew, Michael, Andrea, Joshua, Brittany. BSc, Dr. Martin Luther Coll., 1976. Tchr. Elem. Luth. Sch., Wrightstown, Wis., 1976—77; daycare provider Self-Employed, 1978—79; tchr. Luth. Sentinel, 1982—95; daycare provider Self-Employed, 1983—84, 1984—2002; teachers aide Mt. Olive Luth. Sch., Mankato, Minn., 2002—04; preschool tchr. Peace Luth. Ch., Mankato, Minn., 2004—. Contbg. editor: Lutheran Sentinel; author: At Home With Jesus, 1992, (christian novel) Megan's Mountain, 2001. Vol. Rep. Party, Mankato, Minn., 2000, March of Dimes, 1994—2003, Am. Cancer Soc., Mankato, Minn., 1996, 1999, 2000. Republican. Avocations: reading, writing, swimming, walking. Home: 1117 Lori Lane Mankato MN 56001

MOLE, RICHARD JAY, accounting company executive; b. Berea, Ohio, Aug. 10, 1951; s. Wells Warren Jr. and Helen Irene (Buse) M.; m. Kathleen Ann Brennan, Oct. 28, 1978; children: Kevin Michael, Eileen Anne. BBA, U. Notre Dame, 1973; MBA, U. Pitts., 1974. CPA, Ohio, Pa.; CMA, CFM. Staff acct. James P. Ross, CPA, Elyria, Ohio, 1974-75; mgr. acctg. Dean J. Benshoff, PA, Mogadore, Ohio, 1975-77, John P. Hyland, CPA, Cleve., 1980; fin. adminstr. St. Joseph Ch. and Sts. Joseph and John Interparochial Sch., Strongsville, Ohio, 1977-80; v.p., contr. Citadel Alarm, Inc. div. Revco Drug Stores, Inc., Cleve., 1980-82; pres. Richard J. Mole, CPA, Inc., Andover, Ohio, 1982—. Instr. Lorain County C.C., 1975; bd. dirs. Andover Bancorp, Inc., Andover Bank. Chmn. bldg. com., v.p. Andover Pub. Libr., 1983—; mem. Ashtabula County Bd. Mental Retardation, Ashtabula, Ohio, 1987-89; chmn. fin. com. parish coun. Our Lady of Victory Cath. Ch., Andover, 1985-90; bd. dirs. Ashtabula County 503 Corp., 1986-92, pres., 1990-92; bd. dirs. Ashtabula County Revolving Loan Fund, 1986-92, pres., 1990-92; treas., bd. dirs. Civic Devel. Corp. Ashtabula County, 1994—; mem. Leadership Ashtabula County, 1989, grad. charter class; bd. dirs. Pymatuning Area Indsl. Devel. Corp., Andover, pres., 1986-88, 93-94; chmn. Andover Twp. Zoning Commn., 1989-94, mem., 1995, sec., 1996; treas. Andover Civic Improvement Corp., 1992-96, 97—, pres., 1996-97; treas. Andover Found., Inc., 1993—; coach, mgr. Pymatuning Area Youth Orgn., 1987-91, 95, 97-98, pres., 1991-92. Recipient leadership award Civic Devel. Corp., Ashtabula, 1985, Quality of Living award Pymatuning Area Indsl. Devel. Corp., 1986, Best of County award Ashtabula County Growth Partnership, 1992, Leadership award State of Ohio, 1993. Fellow AICPA, Ohio Soc. CPAs, Pa. Inst. CPAs; mem. Inst. Mgmt. Accts., Rotary Internat. (bd. dirs. Andover 1984—, pres. 1985-86, 96-97, treas. 1988-96, 98-99, 2000--, sec. 1987-88, 99-2000, Paul Harris fellow 1993, benefactor Rotary Found. 1999), Andover C. of C. (v.p. 1983-85, treas. 1985-87). Republican. Office: Richard J Mole CPA Inc PO Box 1270 124 S Main St Andover OH 44003-9601 E-mail: rmole@molecpa.com., numbersrus@molecpa.com.

MOLEN, JOHN KLAUMINZER, lawyer; b. Gary, Ind., June 13, 1952; s. Franklin B. and Jane Anne (Klauminzer) M.; m. Susan Wilson Blair, Aug. 10, 1985; children: Mary Wilson, Elisabeth Blair. AB with honors, U. N.C., 1974, MBA, JD with honors, U. N.C., 1978. Bar: Ala. 1978. Assoc. Bradley Arant Rose & White LLP, Birmingham, Ala., 1978-84, ptnr., 1984—. Mem. Rotary Club Birmingham-Sunrise. Presbyterian. Avocations: sailing, swimming. Office: Bradley Arant Rose & White LLP One Federal Pl 1819 5th Ave N Birmingham AL 35203-2104 Office Phone: 205-521-8238. E-mail: jmolen@bradleyarant.com.

MOLER, DONALD LEWIS, educational psychology educator; b. Wilsey, Kans., Jan. 12, 1918; s. Ralph Lee and Bessie Myrtle (Berry) M.; B.S., Kans. State Tchrs. Coll., Emporia, 1939; M.S., U. Kans., Lawrence, 1949, Ph.D., 1951; m. Alta Margaret Ansdell, Nov. 6, 1942; 1 son, Donald Lewis Jr. Tchr., Centralia (Kans.) High Sch., 1939-42, Carthage (Mo.) High Sch., 1946-48; asst. dir. Reading Clinic, U. Kans., 1948-51; dir. reading program Ea. Ill. U., 1951-70, prof. dept. ednl. psychology and guidance, 1963—, chmn. dept., 1963-84, dean Sch. Edn., 1980; vis. scholar U. Fla., 1965. Served with Signal Corps, U.S. Army, 1942-46. Recipient C.A. Michelman award, 1974; Disting Svc. award Ill. Assn. Counselor Educators, 1985. Mem. Ill. Guidance and Pers. Assn. (pres. 1968-69), Ill. Counselor Educators and Suprs., Ill. Coll. Pers. Assn., Am. Pers. and Guidance Assn. (senator 1970-71), Assn. Counselor Edn. and Supervision, Assn. Humanistic Edn. and Devel., Phi Delta Kappa, Xi Phi, Pi Omega Pi, Pi Kappa Delta, Sigma Tau Gamma. Methodist. Assoc. editor Ill. Guidance and Pers. Assn. Quar., 1970-84, mng. editor, 1984— . Home: 407 W Hayes Ave Charleston IL 61920-3303 Office: Ea Ill U Dept Ednl Psychology and Guidance Charleston IL 61920

MOLER, DONALD LEWIS, JR., lawyer; b. Charleston, Ill., Sept. 9, 1955; s. Donald Lewis Sr. and A. Margaret (Ansdell) M.; m. Judith Lynn Enos, Aug. 9, 1986; 1 child, Seth Ansdell; stepchildren, Eric Philip Anderson, Marc Paul Anderson. BA, Ea. Ill. U., 1976, MA, 1977; MA in Pub. Adminstrn., U. Ill., 1983; JD, U. Kans., 1985. Bar: Kans. 1985, U. S. Dist. Ct. Kans. 1985, U.S. Supreme Ct., 1988. Lobbyist League Kans. Mcpls., Topeka, 1985—, exec. dir., 1999—. Adj. prof. law, Washburn U. Sch. of Law, Topeka.; bd. dirs. Natl. League of Cities. Editor: Standard Traffic Ordinance for Kansas Cities, 1986—, Uniform Public Offense Code for Kansas Cities, 1986—. Mem. ABA, Kans. Bar Assn., Topeka Bar Assn. Methodist. Avocation: restoration jaguar automobiles. Home: 401 SW Danbury Ln Topeka KS 66606-2227 Office: League Kans Mcpls 300 SW 8th Ave Topeka KS 66603-3912 Office Phone: 785-354-9565.

MOLER, EDWARD HAROLD, lawyer; b. Oklahoma City, May 26, 1923; s. Harold Stanley and Rosemary (Callahan) M.; m. Donna Blocksom Cram, Sept. 12, 1964; children: John Frederick, Shelley Elizabeth, Christopher Bryan. BA, U. Okla., 1947, LLB, 1948. Bar: Okla. 1948, U.S. Supreme Ct. 1951. Pvt. practice law, Oklahoma City, 1948-52, 61—; asst. mcpl. counselor, 1952-59; mcpl. counselor, 1959-61; spl. justice Okla. Supreme Ct., 1977. Trustee Oklahoma City Mcpl. Improvement Authority, 1960-61; bd. dirs. Mummers Theatre, Inc., 1969—; bd. dirs. Greater Oklahoma City YMCA, 1981-91. 2d lt. USAAF, 1943-45. Mem. ABA, Okla. Bar Assn., Oklahoma County Bar Assn. (bd. dirs. 1963-67, pres. 1968), Rotary, Phi Delta Phi, Phi Gamma Delta (pres. local chpt. 1946, pres. Nu Omega Housing Assn. 1963-65). Home: 2540 NW Grand Blvd Oklahoma City OK 73116-4110 Office: 204 N Robinson Ste 2800 Oklahoma City OK 73102 Office Phone: 405-232-3566.

MOLER, ELIZABETH ANNE, lawyer; b. Salt Lake City, Jan. 24, 1949; d. Murray McClure and Eleanor Lorraine (Barry) M.; m. Thomas Blake Williams, Oct. 19, 1979; children: Blake Martin Williams, Eleanor Bliss Williams. BA, Am. U., 1971; postgrad., Johns Hopkins U., 1972; JD, George Wash. U., 1977. Bar: DC 1978. Chief legis. asst. Senator Floyd Haskell, Washington, 1973-75; law clk. Sharon, Pierson, Semmes, Crolius & Finley, Washington, 1975-76; profl. staff mem. com. on energy and natural resources U.S. Senate, Washington, 1976-77, counsel, 1977-86, sr. counsel, 1987-88; commr. FERC, Washington, 1988-93, chair, 1993-97; dep. sec. Dept. of Energy, Washington, 1997-98, acting sec., 1998; ptnr. Vinson & Elkins, Washington, 1998-99; sr. v.p. Exelon Corp., 2000—02, exec. v.p., 2002—. Mem. ABA, D.C. Bar Assn. Democrat. Office: Exelon Corp Suite 400 East 101 Constitution Ave NW Washington DC 20001 Home: 1537 Forest Ln Mc Lean VA 22101-3317

MOLER, MARY, secondary school educator; d. John and Mary Ann M. AS Math., Casper (Wyo.) Coll., 1977; BS in Math., U. Wyo., Laramie, 1979, MS in Tchg., 1983. Cert. high sch. math. tchr. Wyo. Math. tchr. 7-12 Midwest Sch., Midwest, Wyo., 1979—84; math computer programming tchr. Kelly Walsh H.S., Casper, 1984—91, math. tchr. 10-12 grades, 1991—. Tchg. asst. Western Scholars Program, Spearfish, SD, 1992; ext. class instr. U. Wyo., Casper, Wyo., 1984—87. Mem. Casper Coll. Alumni Assn., Casper, Wyo., 1991—2001. Recipient Presdl. Award for Excellence in Secondary Math. Tchg., NSF, 1986. Mem.: Natrona County Edn. Assn., Wyo. Edn. Assn., NEA (various coms.), Coun. of Presdl. Awardees, Wyo. Coun. Tchrs. Math. (pres. all offices 1984—90). Roman Catholic. Avocations: travel, collecting eggs, exercise. Office: Kelly Walsh High Sch 3500 East 12th St Casper WY 82609-3199 E-mail: Mary_Moler@ncsd.k12.wy.us.

MOLEVER, KEITH, chemist, consumer products company executive; BS in Chemistry, Ariz. State U., 1974. Chemist Dial Corp., Scottsdale, Ariz., 1975—. Contbr. articles to profl. jours. Mem.: Phi Beta Kappa. Office: Dial Corp 15101 N Scottsdale Rd Scottsdale AZ 85254-2101

MOLEY, KEVIN EDWARD, ambassador; Asst. sec. mgmt. and budget U.S. Dept. Health & Human Services, Washington, 1989—92, dep. sec., 1992—93; sr. advisor to Dick Cheney Bush/Cheney Presdl. Campaign, 2000; U.S. permanent rep. to the UN & other internal orgn. in Geneva U.S. Dept. State, Geneva, 2001—. Dir. Pres. Edn. Summit with U.S. Govs., Charlottesville, Va., 1989; vice chmn. Pres.'s Coun. on Mgmt. Improvement, 1989—92; exec. dir. U.S./Pacific Islands Nations Summit, Honolulu, 1990. USMC, 1965—71. Office: UN Palais des Nations CH-1211 Geneva Switzerland*

MOLHO, EMANUEL, publisher; b. N.Y.C., Jan. 27, 1936; s. Isaac Emanuel and Alvira (Altchek) M.; m. Brenda Nadel, Sept. 25, 1965; children— Deborah Rochelle, Brian Emanuel. BA, NYU, 1957; MBA, Wharton Sch., U. Pa., 1960. Pres. French & European Publs., Inc., N.Y.C., 1961—, French & Spanish Book Corp., 1967—. Pres. Librairie de France, Inc., 1961—. Recipient Orden de Merito Civil Spain, 1975 Mem. Am. Booksellers Assn., French-Am. C. of C. in U.S. (exec. com.), Paris Am. Club. Office: Librairie de France Rockefeller Center Promenade 610 5th Ave New York NY 10020-2497

MOLHOLM, KURT NELSON, federal agency administrator; b. Denver, June 24, 1937; s. Ervin Maurice and Helen Pauline (Nelson) M.; m. Sonja Dell Williams, Aug. 17, 1967; children: Kevin William, Paul Nelson. BS, U. Oreg., 1959; MS, George Washington U., 1974; grad., Indsl. Coll. Armed Forces, 1974. Computer specialist D.L.A. Adminstrv. Support Ctr., Alexandria, Va., 1963-65; with Hdqrs. Def. Logistics Agy., Alexandria, 1965-85, chief planning and policy office, 1975-76, chief ADP/T tech. div., 1984-85; adminstr. Def. Tech. Info. Ctr., Alexandria, 1985—. Pres. Nat. Fedn. Abstracting and Info. Svcs., Phila., 1993-94, treas., 1990-93; del. Va. Govs. Conf. Librs. Info. Svcs., 1990, Fed. Libr. Pre-White House Conf. On Librs. Info. Sci., 1990; vice chmn. Fed. Libr. and Info. Ctr. Com., 1992-93, 2002-03; chmn. CENDI Group, 1991-94, 99-2001; mem. NATO Agard Tech. Info. Panel, 1985-91, Internat. Coun. Sci. and Tech. Info., 1993—, treas., 1998-2001, chair editl. bd., 1999-2001, pres. 2001—04; mem. Info. Infrastructure Task Force, 1993-97; chair panel 2 U.S. Nat. Commn. on Librs. and Info. Sci. Comprehensive Assessment of Pub. Info. Dissemination, 2000; NFAIS Conrad Meml. lectr., 2003. 1st lt. U.S. Army, 1960-63. Recipient Meritorious award William A. Jump Meml. Found., 1973. Methodist. Office: Ctr 8725 John J Kingman Rd Fort Belvoir VA 22060-6218 E-mail: kmolholm@dtic.mil., kmolholm@aol.com.

MOLINA, ALFRED, actor; b. London, 1953; m. Jill Gascione. Grad., Guildhall Sch. Music and Drama. Film appearances include Raiders of the Lost Ark, 1981, Meantime, 1983, Number One, 1984, Eleni, 1985, Ladyhawke, 1985, Water, 1985, Letter to Brezhnev, 1986, Prick Up Your Ears, 1987, Manifesto, 1988, Not Without My Daughter, 1991, Enchanted April, 1992, American Friends, 1993, The Trial, 1993, Meverick, 1994, White Fang 2: Myth of the White Wolf, 1994, The Steal, 1994, Species, 1995, Scorpoin Spring, 1995, Hideaway, 1995, Dead Man, 1995, Drowning in the Shallow End, 1989, When Pigs Fly, 1993, White Fang II: Myth of the White Wolf, 1994, Maverick, 1994, The Steal, 1994, Hideaway, 1995, The Perez Family, 1995, Dead Man, 1995, Species, 1995, Nervous Energy, 1995, Before and After, 1996, Mojave Moon, 1996, Anna Karenina, 1997, Scorpion Spring, 1997, Further Gesture, 1997, Boogie Nights, 1997, The Man Who Knew Too Little, 1997, Impostors, 1998, The Treat, 1998, Pete's Meteor, 1998, Dudley Do-Right, 1999, Magnolia, 1999, Chocolat, 2000, Texas Rangers, 2001, Frida, 2002, Plots with a View, 2002, Ape, 2002, My Life Without Me, 2003, Identity, 2003, Coffee and Cigarettes, 2003, Luther, 2003; (TV movies) The Accountant, 1990, Virtuoso, 1991, Angels, 1992, Ashenden, 1992, A Year in Provence, 1993, The Marshal, 1993, Requiem Apache, 1994, The Place of Lions, 1997, Rescuers: Stories of Courage: Two Couples, 1998, Miracle Maker (voice), 2000, Murder on the Orient Express, 2001; (Broadway shows) Art, 1998, Fiddler on the Roof, 2004- (Tony nom. best actor in a musical, 2004); other stage appearances include Destiny, 1977, Troilus and Cressida, 1977, Bandits, 1977, The Bundle, 1977, Frozen Assets, 1977, That Good Between Us, 1977, King Lear, 1977, Dingo, 1978, Irish Eyes and English Tears, 1978, Willie, 1978, Accidental Death of an Anarchist, 1979 (Plays and Players award for most promising new actor), Destry Rides Again, 1982, Dreyfus, 1982, Viva, 1985, The Night of the Iguana, 1992, Molly Sweeney, 1995 (Theatre World award, 1996, Drama Desk award, 1996), True West, 2001, The Cherry Orchard, 2002. Office: William Morris Agy 151 S El Camino Dr Beverly Hills CA 90212-2775*

MOLINA, JOSEPH MARIO, medical administrator; b. Long Beach, Calif., May 16, 1958; s. C. David and Mary R. (Salandini) M.; m. Therese Ann Flynn; children: Carley, Colleen, David, Mary Clare. BA, Calif. State U., Long Beach, 1980; MD, U. So. Calif., 1984. Diplomate Am. Bd. Internal Medicine. Assoc. investigator VA, San Diego, 1988-90; asst. clin. prof. U. So. Calif., L.A., 1990-91; med. dir. Molina Med. Ctrs., Long Beach, 1991-94, v.p. HMO, 1994—96, chmn., pres., CEO, 1996—. Mem. Am. Coll. Physician Execs., Am. Coll. Physicians, Am. Diabetes Assn., Endocrine Soc. Avocation: collecting antique medical books. Office: Molina Med Ctrs Inc 1 Golden Shore St Long Beach CA 90802-4202

MOLINA, MARIO JOSE, physical chemist, educator; b. Mexico City, Mar. 19, 1943; arrived in U.S., 1968; s. Roberto Molina-Pasquel and Leonor Henríquez; m. Luisa Y. Tan, July 12, 1973; 1 child, Felipe. Bachillerato, Acad. Hispano Mexicana, Mexico City, 1959; Ingeniero Químico, U. Nacional Autónoma de México, 1965; postgrad., U. Freiburg, Fed. Republic Germany, 1966—67; PhD, U. Calif., Berkeley, 1972. Asst. prof. U. Nacional Autónoma de México, 1967—68; research assoc. U. Calif.-Berkeley, 1972—73, U. Calif.-Irvine, 1973—75, asst. prof. phys. chemistry, 1975—79, assoc. prof., 1979—82; sr. rsch. scientist Jet Propulsion Lab., 1983—89; prof. dept. earth, atom and planet sci., dept. chemistry MIT, Cambridge, 1989—96, Martin prof. atmospheric chemistry, 1997—, Inst. prof., 1997—. Recipient Tyler Ecology award, 1983, Esselen award for chemistry in pub. interest, 1987, Max-Planck-Forschungs-Preis, Alexander von Humboldt-Stiftung, 1994, Nobel Prize in Chemistry, 1995, Sasakawa prize, UNEP, 1999. Mem.: NAS, Inst. of Medicine, Am. Geophys. Union (Pres.'s Com. on Advisors on Sci. and Tech. 1994—2000), Am. Phys. Soc., Am. Chem. Soc. Achievements include discovery of the theory that fluorocarbons deplete ozone layer of stratosphere. Home: 8 Clematis Rd Lexington MA 02421-7117 Office: MIT Dept of EAPS 77 Mass Ave # 54-1814 Cambridge MA 02139-4307 E-mail: mmolina@mit.edu. *We have to understand our environment to find out if we are tampering with it. One of our accomplishments has been to call attention to society's potential altering of the atmosphere.*

MOLINA, RAFAEL EVENCIO, urologist; b. Havana, Cuba, July 6, 1923; came to U.S., 1961; s. Joseph M. and Maria H. Molina; m. Maria T. Rodriguez (div.); children: Louis R., Maria T., Manuel E., Rafael E. BA, BS, Colegio de Belen, Havana, 1941; MD, U. Havana, 1949. Bd. cert. Am. Bd. Urology. Resident U. Miami, Fla., 1963-66; physician Hoffman Urol., Huntington, W.Va., 1966—2002. Contbr. articles to med. jours. Mem. AMA, ACS, Am. Urodynamic Soc., Am. Urol. Assn., Am. Soc. Nephrology, Cuban Med. Soc. in Exile, Rotary Club, Elks Club, Huntington Area C. of C. Republican. Roman Catholic. Avocation: tennis. Home: 1695 Holderby Rd Huntington WV 25701-4127 Office: 1654 Thirteenth Ave Huntington WV 25701

MOLINA, RON JOSEPH, music educator; b. Antioch, Calif., Sept. 17, 1947; s. Joe Guerrero and Dorothy Mildred Molina; m. Darcy Lauck, Feb. 14, 2003; 1 child, Joseph Michael. A, Diablo Valley Coll., 1966; BA, San Jose State U., 1971. Tchr. vocal music Hollister (Calif.) H.S., 1974—79; regional v.p. Am. Internat., Marina Del Rey, Calif., 1979—82; drama tchr. Bella Vista H.S., Sacramento, 1983—; vocal music tchr. Folsom (Calif.) H.S., 1983—87; dir. choral acitvities Antioch (Calif.) H.S., 1987—. Dir. Internat. Antioch High Sch. Music Masters, 1988—2003. Named Man of Yr., Antioch Civic Arts Commn., 1988, Antioch C. of C., 1991, Hon. Mayor, Rosas, Spain, 2000; recipient Outstanding Cmty. Arts Person, 1991. Mem.: Music Educators Nat. Conf., Am. Choral Dir. Assn., Calif. Music Educators Assn. Avocations: golf, fishing. Office: Antioch High Sch 700 @ 18th St Antioch CA 94509 Office Phone: 925-756-5607. Office Fax: 925-753-1835. Business E-Mail: ronmolina@antioch.k12.ca.us.

MOLINARI, JOSEPH FRANCIS, oculist; b. Worcester, Mass. s. Wallace F. and Antoinette M. (Tortora) Molinari. AA, Ctrl. New Eng. Coll., 1972; BS, New Eng. Coll., 1973, OD, 1974; MEd, Mercer U., 1979; postgrad., Air U., 1998. Staff optometrist Lahey Clin. Med. Ctr., 1977-79; asst. prof. U. Ala., 1979-82; gen. practice optometry Panama City Beach, Fla., 1982—. Consult USAF, Tyndall AFB, 1980—83; chief DS & M vet. affairs, Tallahassee, 1994—. Item writer Nat. Bd. Optometry, Washington, 1980—83, 2003, mem. editl. bd. Mil. Medicine, 2000—; contbr. articles to profl. jours. Pres. Harbour Villas Assn., Inc., 1985—86, Gulf of Mex. Optics Inc., Panama City Beach, 1984—96; chmn. Bay Point Anterior Segment Symposium, Inc., 1984—95. Col. USAFR, 1974—. Named Optometrist of Yr., Armed Forces Optometric Soc., 1999, Biomed. Sci. Corps Individual Mobilization Augmentee of Yr., USAFR, 1996; recipient Spurgeon Eure award, Am. Optometric Found., 1978, 1981—82, Dallas Contact Lens Rsch. award, Brit. Contact Lens Assn., 1984, Outstanding Svc. and Recognition award, Assn. Mil. Surgeons U.S., 1996, 2003, 30 Yr. Recognition, Armed Forces Optometric Soc., 1996. Fellow: Nat. Acads. of Practice (medal), Am. Acad. Optometry (chair disease sect. 2003);

mem.: Am. Coll. Optometry Physicians (diplomate), Neuro-Optometry Soc. (chmn. 1985—88), Fla. Optometric Assn. (del. 1984—85), Am. Legion. Office: 1607 St James Ct Tallahassee FL 32308 E-mail: Joseph.Molinari@med.va.gov.

MOLINARI, MARCO, marketing executive; b. Stockholm, Sept. 15, 1969; m. Lisa Molinari; 2 children. Degree in mktg., St. Louis U.; M in Internat. Bus., Thunderbird U. Formerly with mktg. and sales, various mgmt. positions Goodyear Tire & Rubber Co., Stockholm, past mng. dir., past regional mktg. dir., v.p. sales and mktg. N.Am. Tires, 1996—. Office: Goodyear Tire & Rubber Co 1144 E Market St Akron OH 44316-0002

MOLINARI, SUSAN, congresswoman; b. S.I., N.Y., Mar. 27, 1958; d. Guy V. and Marguerite (Wing) M. BA, SUNY, Albany, 1980, MA, 1982. Former intern for State Senator Christopher Mega; former rsch. analyst N.Y. State Senate Fin. Com.; former fin. asst. Nat. Rep. Gov.'s Assn.; ethnic community liaison Rep. Nat. Com., 1983-84; minority leader N.Y.C. Council, 1986-90; mem. 101st-104th Congresses from 14th (now 13th) N.Y. dist., 1990-97, vice-chair House Rep. Conf.; anchor CBS News Sat. Morning, N.Y.C., 1997-98; Chairman, CEO The Washington Group, 2001—. Author: (book) Representative Mom: Balancing Budgets, Bill and Baby in the U.S. Congress, 1998. Roman Catholic. Office: c/o The Washington Group 1401 K Street NW Washington DC 20005*

MOLINARO, JOSEPH DANIEL, dentist; b. Phila., May 4, 1969; s. Daniel Joseph and Antoinette Marie (Napolio) Molinaro; m. Ellen Catherine Frank, June 14, 2003. BS in biology, Villanova U., 1987—91; DMD, Temple U. Sch. of Dentistry, 1991—95; MS in oral biology, The George Wash. U., 1999—2001. Cert. of residency Nat. Naval Dental Ctr., Bethesda, MD, 2001, diplomate The Fed. Services Bd. of Gen. Dentistry, 2002, Am. Bd. of Gen. Dentistry 2002. Gen. dentist U.S. Naval Dental Ctr. USN, Agana, 1995—97, denatl clinic divsn. officer, 1996—97, gen. dentist USS George Washington CVN 73 Norfolk, Va., 1997—99, dental clinic divsn. officer, 1998—99, resident, comprehensive dentistry Nat. Naval Dental Ctr. Bethesda, Md., 1999—2001, comprehensive dentist, detnal clinic dept. head dental annex br. Indian Head, Md., 2001—. Contbr. articles to profl. jours. Lt. comdr. Dental Corps USN, 1995—, Dental Corps. Decorated Navy and Marine Corps Commendation medal Sec. of USN, Navy and Marine Corps Achievement medal, Humanitarian Svc. medal USN; recipient Martin I. Munin award, Temple U. Sch. of Dentistry, 1995, Commdg. Officer's award for excellence, Commdg. Officer, Nat. Naval Dental Ctr., 2000, Chief of the Dental Corps award, Chief U.S. Naval Dental Corps, 2001; Health Professionals scholarship, USN, 1994—95. Fellow: Acad. of Gen. Dentistry; mem.: ADA, Seminar of Restorative Dentistry (sec. 2000—01, Excellence in Operative Dentistry 2001), Acad. of Operative Dentistry, Edward C. Penick Endodontic Study Club. Roman Catholic. Achievements include completed a study comparing the influence of various dental restorative materials on tooth cusp stiffness. Avocations: travel, reading, sports.

MOLINARO, THOMAS J. lawyer; b. Cleve., June 4, 1952; s. Albert J. and Marilyn Molinaro; children: Daniel, Paul, Marisa, Anna. BS, U. Wis., 1976; JD, U. Wis. Law Sch., 1979. Bar: Wis., U.S. Dist. Ct. (we. and ea. dists.) Wis. Law clk. Wis. Ct. Appeals, Waukesha, 1979-80; assoc. Crooks, Law & Connell, Wausau, 1980-83; ptnr. Brady, Hoover & Molinaro, Wausau, 1983-85, Brady & Molinaro, Wausau, 1986-92; sole practice law Wausau, 1993—2002; ptnr. Grischke, Molinaro & Laughlin, LLSC, Wausau, 2003—. Bd. dirs. Marathon Civic Corp., Wausau, 1988-94, Wausau Area Youth Soccer Assn., 1990-94; membership com. YMCA, Wausau, 1988-90. Mem. ATLA, Wis. Bar Assn., Marathon County Bar Assn. Avocations: antique collecting and restoration, skiing, soccer. Office: 1400 Merrill Ave Wausau WI 54401

MOLINA VILLACORTA, RAFAEL ANTONIO, technology management investment company executive; b. Sept. 5, 1963; s. Rafael Antonio and Rosa Isabel (Villacorta) M.; m. Maria Asuncion Cornejo, Sept. 28, 1985; children: Elisa Maria, Rafael Augusto, Cristian Adolfo, Leonardo Paolo. AA, Sacramento City Coll., 1983; BS, Golden Gate U., 1994. CFO MVM Investments, Sacramento, 1983-85; adminstr. State of Calif., Sacramento, 1985-93; CEO, mng. dir. C & T Investments, Dixon, Calif., 1988—; mng. dir. Data Systems, Los Altos, Calif., 1996—, DASA, S.A. de C.V., 1996—. Dir. MAM Co., Sacramento, 1985-96; CEO, dir. Del Sol Investments, Dixon, 1989-98. Mem. Calif. State Employees Assn., Sacramento, 1985, Am. Mgmt. Assn., Sacramento, 1991; pres. St. Peter's Ch., Dixon, 1992-94. Recipient Outstanding Achievement award Calif. Dept. Health Svcs., 1988, Primary Clinics, 1990. Mem. Am. Mgmt. Assn., Network Profl. Assn., Tele-Comms. Assn., Calif. Microcomputers Users. Roman Catholic. Avocations: travel, computers, reading. Office: C & T Investments Co Ste 013-76 1605-B Siempre Viva Rd San Diego CA 92154 E-mail: rafaelmolina@dasa.net.

MOLINDER, JOHN IRVING, engineering educator, consultant; b. Erie, Pa., June 14, 1941; s. Karl Oskar and Carin (Ecklund) M.; m. Janet Marie Ahlquist, June 16, 1962; children: Tim, Karen. BSEE, U. Nebr., 1963; MSEE, Air Force Inst. Tech., 1964; PhD EE, Calif. Inst. Tech., 1969. Registered profl. engr., Calif. Project officer Ballistic Systems Div., Norton AFB, Calif., 1964-67; sr. engr. Jet Propulsion Lab., Pasadena, Calif., 1969-70; prof. engring. Harvey Mudd Coll., Claremont, Calif., 1970—; prin. engr. Qualcomm Inc., 1996-97, part-time, 1997—; contractor Boeing Satellite Systems, 2000—02. Part-time lectr. Calif. State U., L.A., 1970-74; mem. tech. adv. panel Kinemetrics, Pasadena, 1985-86; part-time mem. tech. staff Jet Propulsion Lab., Pasadena, 1974-97, rep. NASA Hdqrs., Washington, 1979-80; vis. prof. elec. engring. Calif. Inst. Tech., 1982-83. Contbr. articles to profl. jours. Served to capt. USAF, 1963-67. Mem.: IEEE (sr.). Avocations: bicycling, reading, computers. Office: Harvey Mudd Coll Dept Engring 301 E 12th St Claremont CA 91711-5901 Business E-Mail: John_Molinder@hmc.edu.

MOLINE, JACQUELINE, occupational physician; b. Buffalo, Nov. 10, 0662; d. Sheldon Walter and Gloria Bettina Moline; m. Antoine Drye, Nov. 17, 2001. BA, U. Chgo., 1984, MD, 1988; MsC, Mt. Sinai Sch. Medicine, 1993. Diplomate Nat. Bd. Med. Examiners, Am. Bd. Internal Medicine, Am. Bd. Preventive Medicine. Resident in internal medicine Yale U./New Haven Hosp., 1988—91; resident in occupl. medicine Mt. Sinai Sch. Medicine, 1991—93, residency dir. occupl. medicine, 1998—, vice chmn. dept. cmty. and preventive medicine, 2002—. Cons. United Fedn. Tchrs., N.Y.C., 1992—; med. core dir. WTC Worker and Vol. Screening Program, N.Y.C., 2002—. Bd. dirs. JazzReach, N.Y.C., NY, 2002—. Recipient fellowship award, Found. for Occupl. Medicine, 1993, Laborer's award, NY-NJ Laborers, 1999. Mem.: ACP, Am. Coll. Occupl. and Environ. Medicine (bd. dirs. NY 2001—). Office: Mt Sinai Sch Medicine 1 Gustave Levy Pl New York NY 10029 E-mail: jacqueline.moline@mssm.edu.

MOLINEAUX, CHARLES BORROMEO, lawyer, arbitrator, columnist, poet; b. N.Y.C., Sept. 27, 1930; s. Charles Borromeo and Marion Frances (Belter) M.; m. Patricia Leo Devereux, July 2, 1960; children: Charles, Stephen, Christopher, Patricia, Peter, Elizabeth. BS cum laude, Georgetown U., 1950; JD, St. Johns U., 1959. Bar: N.Y. 1959, Mass. 1981, D.C. 1988. From assoc. to ptnr. Nevius, Jarvis & Pilz and successor firms, N.Y.C., 1959-77; ptnr. Gadsby & Hannah, N.Y.C., 1978-80; v.p., gen. counsel Perini Corp., Framingham, Mass., 1980-87; pvt. practice Washington, 1987—. Adj. faculty Internat. Law Inst., Washington, 1989—. Author numerous poems. Mem. adv. bd. Inst. for Transnat. Arbitration; committeeman Rep. Party, Nassau County, NY, 1965—71, mem. exec. com., committeeman Fairfax County, Va., 1969. 1st lt. U.S. Army, 1954—56. Fellow Am. Bar Found.; mem. ASCE, Am. Arbitration Assn. (constrn. ADR task force 1994—), Chartered Inst. Arbitrators, Fedn. Internat. Engrs.-Conseils (Assoc. Gen. Contractors del. constrn. contract com., Louis Prangey award for svc. to profession cons. engring. 1996), Del. Hist. Soc., London Ct. Internat. Arbitration, Fellowship Cath. Scholars. Roman Catholic. Home: 8321 Weller Ave Mc Lean VA 22102-1717 Office: 1660 International Dr Ste 400 Mc Lean VA 22102 Office Phone: 703-287-4232. E-mail: cmlnx@aol.com.

MOLINO, MICHAEL ANTHONY, trade association executive; b. Bklyn., June 25, 1940; s. Angelo T. and Jean (Tepedino) M.; m. Barbara Ann Melzarek, Mar. 20, 1971; children: Michael Richard, Timothy A. BS in History, St. Peter's Coll., Jersey City, 1961; MA in History, U. Mo., Kansas City, 1973. Commd. 2d lt. U.S. Army, 1961, advanced through grades to col., 1983, ops. planner, 1967-68; instr. U.S. Army Command Gen. Staff Coll., Ft. Leavenworth, Kans., 1969-73; tng. coord. U.S. Army in Europe, Erlangen, Fed. Republic Germany, 1973-77, dep. community comdr. Nurenberg, Fed. Republic Germany, 1983-86; dean students Def. Fgn. Lang. Ctr., Monterey, Calif., 1977-79; dean students and adminstrn. Indsl. Coll. Armed Forces, Washington, 1986-88; ret., 1988; asst. exec. v.p. Recreation Vehicle Dealers Assn., Fairfax, Va., 1988-91, v.p., 1991-96, pres., 1996—. Contbr. articles to various publs. Chmn. schs. adv. coun. Dept. Def. Dependent Schs., Nurenberg, 1983-86; v.p. Mid. Franconian Men's Club, Fuerth, Fed. Republic Germany, 1985-86; dir. Springfield (Va.) Babe Ruth Baseball League, 1986-90, pres., 1987-89. Decorated Bronze Star, Legion of Merit; named Knight Order of St. George, U.S. Armor Assn., 1988. Mem. Am. Soc. Assn. Execs. (mem. com. 1991-92), Greater Wash. Soc. Assn. Execs. (career cons 1989, edn. com. 1990-91, vice chmn. edn. com. 1991-92), Ret. Officers Assn., VFW. Roman Catholic. Avocations: writing, jogging, golf. Office: Recreation Vehicle Dealers Assn 3930 University Dr # 100 Fairfax VA 22030-2515

MOLINO, THOMAS MICHAEL, retired military officer; b. Bklyn., Feb. 16, 1947; s. Angelo Thomas and Jean (Tepedino) M.; m. Mary Ellen Thomas, June 3, 1973; children: T. Andrew, Sara Catherine. BA, St. Peter's Coll., 1968; MA, Loyola U., Chgo., 1979. Commd. 2d lt. US Army, 1968, advanced through ranks to col., troop comdr. 2d Squadron, 11th Cav. Rgt., 1970-71, comdr. 2d Squadron 2d Cav. Rgt., 1983-85; spl. asst. to vice chmn. Joint Chiefs of Staff, Pentagon, 1987-89; exec. asst. to comdr. in chief US Army Europe, Heidelberg, Germany, 1990-92; comdr. 2d Cav. Rgt. US Army, Ft. Lewis, Wash. and Ft. Polk, La., 1992-94; chief strategic planning US Army, Pentagon, Washington, 1995-96, ret., 1997; sr. def. analyst Sci. Applications Internat. Corp., 1997-98, v.p., regional security divsn. mgr., 1998-2001, corp. v.p., mgr. strategic analysis and leadership operation, 2001—. Asst. prof. Loyola U. of Chgo., 1976-79. Decorated DSM, Def. Superior Svc. medal, Legion of Merit (3), Republic of Vietnam Honor medal, Air medal, others; fellow-in-residence Harvard U. Ctr. for Internat. Affairs, 1994-95; MIT Seminar XII fellow, 1996-97. Mem. Assn. US Army, VFW, Army-Navy Country Club, 2d Cavalry Assn. (pres.), Woodlands of Fair Lakes Homeowners Assn. (pres.). Roman Catholic. Avocation: golf. Office: 1710 SAIC Dr Mc Lean VA 22102-3701 E-mail: molinot@saic.com.

MOLINO, VIRGINIA LOUISE, lawyer; b. Jersey City, June 12, 1950; d. Nicholas and Jennie (Rocco) M.; m. Gregory S. Smith, June 1, 1985 BA cum laude, NYU, 1972, JD, 1976; MA, U. Wis., 1973. Bar: N.J. 1976, N.Y. 1984. Staff atty. Suburban Propane Gas Corp., Morristown, N.J., 1976-79, assoc. counsel, 1979-81, gen. counsel, 1982-85, McKinsey & Co., Inc., N.Y.C., 1985—. Mem. ABA, N.J. State Bar Assn., N.Y. State Bar Assn., Bar Assn. City of N.Y., Am. Corp. Counsel Assn., Phi Beta Kappa Office: McKinsey & Co Inc 55 E 52nd St Fl 27 New York NY 10055-0183

MOLINS, MARCEL J. lawyer; b. Barcelona, Nov. 1, 1936; s. Pedro and Rosa (Viaplana) M.; m. Martina Molins, Aug. 5, 1963; children: Thomas, Nicole. JD, Barcelona U., 1958; LM, Northwestern U., 1964; JD, Loyola U., Chgo., 1966. Assoc. Baker & McKenzie, Chgo., 1964-70, ptnr., 1970—. Chmn. adv. bd. Instituto Cervantes, Chgo., 1996—. Recipient medalla merito civil Spanish Govt., Madrid, 1997. Office: Baker & McKenzie 130 E Randolph Dr 1 Prudential Plaza Chicago IL 60601 E-mail: marcel.j.molins@bakernet.com.

MOLITOR, GRAHAM THOMAS TATE, lawyer; b. Seattle, Apr. 6, 1934; s. Robert Franklin and Louise Margaret (Graham) M.; m. Carlotta Jean Crate, July 30, 1960; children: Graham Thomas Tate, Anne Therese, Christopher Robert. BS, U. Wash., 1955; LLB, Am. U., 1963. Bar: D.C. 1963. Rsch. asst. U. Wash., Seattle, 1957; bailiff U.S. Criminal Ct. D.C., 1958-59; legis. counsel U.S. Ho. of Reps., Washington, 1961-63; dir. candidate rsch. Rockefeller for Pres. Com., 1963-64, 68; D.C. counsel, asst. dir. govt. rels. Nabisco, Inc., Washington, 1964-70; dir. govtl. rels. Gen. Mills, Inc., Washington, 1970-77; pres., CEO Pub. Policy Forecasting, Inc., Potomac, Md., 1977—; prin. ptnr. Pub. Policy Communicators, 1989-91. Prin., ptnr. Pub. Policy Action Inst., Potomac; adv. bd. Creative Bus. Strategies, Inc.; adj. prof. Grad. Sch. Bus. Am. U., Washington, 1969—75, Washington, 1979—85, Montgomery Coll., Rockville, Md., 1987—88; dir. rsch. White House Conf. on Indsl. World Ahead, 1971—72; mem. White House Adv. Com. on Social Indicators, 1975—76; chmn. Commn. on the Future of Montgomery County, 1986—88; guest lectr. numerous univs.; mem. White House Confs. on Food, Nutrition and Health, 1969—71, White House Conf. on Youth, 1970; bd. dirs. First Global Conf. on the Future, Inc., Can., 1980—; organizing com. Found. for the Future, 1997—, bd. advisors, 1999—, mem. scholar adv. bd., 2001—. Contbg. editor Food Tomorrow Newsletter, 1976-77; co-editor, chmn. editl. bd. Ency. of the Future, 1991-96; cons. editor Hist. Guide to Am. Govt., 1995-97, McMillan Compendium of the Twenty-First Century, 1998-99; editor Technol. Forecasting and Social Change, 1999—; chmn. editl. bd. Future Survey, 1995-97, World Ency. of Police Forces and Correctional Systems, 2003—; mem. bd. editors Hudson Inst. Study of World Food Problems, 1975-77; mem. editl. bd. Bus. Tomorrow Newsletter, 1977-79, Jour. of Futures Studies, 2001—; mem. bd. advisors New Mktg. Techs. Monitor, 1983-85; polit. editor On the Horizon, 1993-95; contbr. articles to profl. jours. Mem. Food Adv. Bd., N.Y.C., 1980-86. Served to 1st lt. U.S. Army, 1958-61. Recipient Disting. Service award Grocery Mfrs. Am., 1973-74, Disting. Service award Nat. Consumer Info. Center, 1974, Disting. Service award Am. Mgmt. Assn., 1975. Fellow: World Acad. Art and Sci. (mem. bd. trustees); mem.: World Future Soc. (gen. chmn. 2d Gen. Assembly 1975, v.p., dir. 1981—94, v.p., legal counsel 1994—, Disting. Svc. award 1975, 2004), E.D. Export Coun., Washington Indsl. Roundtable, Washington Bus.-Govt. Rels. Coun. (mem. exec. com. 2000—, chmn. commn. on Yr. 3000 2001—), Univ. Club, Phi Alpha Delta, Phi Kappa Sigma. Republican. Presbyterian. Home and Office: 2361 Aronimink CIR Fayetteville PA 17222-9242 E-mail: gttmolitor@aol.com.

MOLITOR, MICHAEL A. entrepreneur, consultant; b. Bklyn., Nov. 7, 1965; s. Henry J. and Janet A. (Monti) M.; m. Michele A. Emery, July 8, 1995; 1 child, Michael. BS, Siena Coll., 1987; MBA, Columbia U., 2000. CFP. Fin. aid counselor Janet's Coll. Tuition Aid, Massapequa Park, N.Y., 1987-92; income tax acct. Michael A. Molitor, Massapequa, N.Y., 1988—; owner, fin. aid counseling svc. Molitor Coll. Aid Counseling, Massapequa, 1992—; money mgr. Molitor Money Mgmt., Massapequa, 1992—. Cons. Alive-To-Thrive, Inc., Westchester, N.Y., 1992—, cons., adv. bd. Orphan's Aid Soc., Douglaston, N.Y., 1994—; cons. in field. Author: You Can Afford A College Education, 1992; contbr. articles to profl. jours., various TV talk shows. Con. to Guidance Dept. Massapequa Sch. Dist., Massapequa, 1995-98, mem. Long Island Assn., Hauppauge, N.Y., 1990-92. Recipient Top Producer-Pres. Club Transamerica Funds, Houston, 1993-94, mem. signature Club Oppenheimer Funds, Denver, 1995. Mem. Internat. Assn. Fin. Planning, N.Y. Fin. Air Adminstr. Assn., NAt. Assn. Fin. Aid Adminstr., BMW Car Club Am., Porsche Club Am. Mem. Christian Ch. Avocations: golf, drumming, track driving.

MOLITORIS, BRUCE ALBERT, nephrologist, educator; b. Springfield, Ill., June 26, 1951; s. Edward and Joyce (Tomasko) M.; m. Karen Lynn Wichterman, June 16, 1973; children: Jason, Jared, Julie. BS, U. Ill., 1973, MS in Nutrition, 1975; MD, Wash. U., 1979. Resident Sch. Medicine U. Colo., Denver, 1979-81, nephrology fellow, 1981-84, asst. prof. medicine, 1984-88, assoc. prof. medicine, 1988-93, prof., 1993; dir. nephrology Ind. U. Med. Sch., Indpls., 1993—; vis. scientist U. Colo., MCDB, Boulder, 1989-90, Max Planck Inst., Federal Republic of Germany, 1984-85; dir. Ind. Ctr. Biol. Microscopy, 2002—. NIH reviewer, 1991-94; dir. home dialysis Denver VA Ctr., 1984-93; vis. scientist dept. molecular biology Colo. State U., Ft. Collins, 1998. Mem. editl. bd. Am. Jour. Physiology, 1989-2000, Am. Jour. Kidney Diseases, 1991--; assoc. editor Jour. Investigative Medicine, 1994-99; contbr. articles to profl. jours. Pres. Cherry Creek Village South Homeowners Assn., 1989-90, Pickwick Commons Home Owners Assn., 1999; v.p. Our Father Luth. Ch., Denver, 1989-90; coun. mem. King of Glory Luth. Ch., Indpls., 1999-2002; coach Cherry Creek Soccer Assn., Greenwood Village, 1988-91, Centennial Little League Titans Basketball; bd. dirs. CSSA, 1993. Recipient Upjohn Achievement award, 1979, Liberty Hyde Bailey award, 1973. Mem. Am. Assn. Physicians, Am. Soc. Nephrology (program chmn. 2002-03), Internat. Soc. Nephrology, N.Y. Acad. Sci., Am. Soc. Clin. Investigation, Am. Fedn. for Clin. Rsch. (nat. counselor 1991-94), Western Assn. Physicians. Avocations: bridge, fishing, antiques, hiking. Office: Indiana U Med Ctr R-2 202C 950 W Walnut St Indianapolis IN 46202-5135

MOLL, CURTIS E. manufacturing executive; b. 1933; Diploma, Wesleyan Coll., 1961, So. Meth. U., 1963. Chmn., CEO MTD Products Inc. Office: MTD Products Inc PO Box 368022 Cleveland OH 44136-9722

MOLL, DAVID CARTER, civil engineer; b. Ames, Iowa, Aug. 5, 1948; s. Dale Curtis and Virginia (Carter) M.; m. Margaret E. Newman (div. 1989); 1 child, Megahn Elizabeth; m. Melanie G. Harding, 2004. BSCE, Iowa State U., 1971; cert. advanced study, Am. Grad. Sch. Internat. Mgmt., 1983; MBA with distinction, U. Mich., 1984. Cert. project mgmt. profl. Engr. in tng., Iowa; field engr. Chgo. Bridge & Iron Co., 1971; subcontract supr., field engr. Morrison-Knudsen Internat. Co., Inc., Surinam and Panama, 1976; site supt. engring., asst. supt. constrn. Fluor Corp., Saudi Arabia, 1977-82; group mgr. Cummins Engine Co., Columbus, Ind., 1984-85; mgr. spl. projects Kerr-McGee Coal Corp., Oklahoma City, 1985-88; project mgr. Kerr-McGee Corp., Oklahoma City, 1989, 1993—98, London, 1989-90, Saudi Arabia, 1990—92, Kerr-McGee Environ. Mgmt. Corp., Oklahoma City, 1998—. Lt. USN, 1971—75. Mem. ASCE, AGSIM (leadership circle), Civil Engr. Corps (Meritorious Svc. medal), Am. Soc. Quality Control (constrn. tech. com.), N.Y. Acad. Scis., Am. Legion, Order of the Knoll (Campanile Guild), Marston Club, Project Mgmt. Inst. (Red Earth chpt. dir. fin.), Chi Epsilon. Avocations: cross country skiing, jogging, golf, sailing.

MOLL, DEBORAH ADELAIDE, lawyer; b. Wilmington, Del., Jan. 19, 1946; BA, St. John's Coll., Annapolis, Md., 1969; MA, U. Tex., 1972, JD, 1975. Bar: N.Mex 1977. Law clk. Tex. Ct. Criminal Appeals, Austin, 1975-76, U.S. Ct. Appeals (10th cir.), Santa Fe, 1977-78; asst. atty. gen. N.Mex Atty. Gen., Santa Fe, 1978-84; asst. appellate defender N.Mex Pub. Defender Dept., Santa Fe, 1984-87; staff atty. N.Mex Taxation and Revenue Dept., Santa Fe, 1987-92; shareholder Kemrer-Hayes & Moll, P.A., Albuquerque, 1992; gen. counsel N.Mex Gen. Svcs. Dept., Santa Fe, 1993—. Mem.: N.Mex. State Bar (bd. dirs. bankruptcy sect. 1992, adv. opinion com. 1993—96, bd. dirs. pub. law sect. 1996—, chair pub. law sect. 1997—98, bd. dirs. employment law sect. 1999—2003, chair ad hoc com. 2001, com. establish legal specialization constrn. and pub. contracts 2002—). Avocation: photography. Office: NMex Gen Svcs Dept 715 Alta Vista St Santa Fe NM 87505-4108 Office Phone: 505-827-2000. E-mail: Deborah.Moll@state.nm.us.

MOLL, GEORGE WILLIAM, pediatrician, educator; b. Milw., Nov. 23, 1947; s. George William, Sr. and Laverne Delores (Klein) M.; m. Susana Valdez Ramos, June 24, 1978; children: Christina, Teresa. BA in Chemistry cum laude, Carleton Coll., 1969; PhD in Biochemistry, U. Chgo., 1975, MD, 1977. Diplomate Nat. Bd. Med. Examiners; diplomate in pediatrics and pediat. endocrinology Am. Bd. Pediatrics; cert. PALS, CPR. Pediatric resident Mott Children's Hosp., U. Mich., Ann Arbor, 1977-79; pediatric endocrinology fellowship Wyler Children's Hosp., U. Chgo., 1979-81; asst. prof. pediatrics U. Chgo., 1981-85, Emory U. Sch. Medicine, Atlanta, 1985-87; assoc. prof. pediatrics U. Miss. Med. Ctr., Jackson, 1987-93, prof. pediatrics, 1993—; assoc. staff pediatric endocrinology Little Co. of Mary Hosp., Evergreen Park, Ill., 1981-85, The Meth. Hosps., Gary and Merrillville, Ind., 1981-85; staff pediatric endocrinologist The Emory Clinic, Atlanta, 1985-87, Henrietta Egleston Hosp. for Children, Atlanta, 1985-87, Grady Meml. Hosp., Atlanta, 1985-87; staff Emory Univ. Hosp., 1987, dir. pediatric endocrinology; staff U. Miss. Med. Ctr., Jackson, 1987—. Contbr. articles to profl. jours. Active Diabetes Found. of Miss., Inc., 1998, Juv. Diabetes Found. Internat., 1998, Filipino-Am. Assn. of Miss., 1990—, Chronic Disease Coalition of Miss., 1996—. Recipient med. scientist NIH scholarship/grant U. Chgo., 1970-77, Andrew Mellon Found. fellowship, 1981-82, Med. Excellence award So. Med. Assn., 1995; grantee Am. Lung Assn., 1987-89, Eli Lilly Co., Mobil Oil Co., 1991, Diabetes Rsch. and Edn. Found., Inct., 1992, Pharmacia & Upjohn, 1998, others. Fellow Am. Acad. Pediatrics, Am. Coll. Endocrinology; mem. AAAS, Nat. Bd. Med. Examiners (comprehensive task force for reprodn./endocrinology 1989-90), Chgo. Endocrine Club (sec. 1984-85), N.Y. Acad. of Sci., Am. Fedn. for Med. Rsch., Lawson Wilkins Soc. for Pediat. Endocrinology, Midwest and So. Soc. for Pediatric Rsch., Miss. State Med. Assn., Cen. Miss. Med. and Pediatric Soc., The Endocrine Soc. (regional rep. U.S. Pharmacopeia Quinquennial), Am. Diabetes Assn., Juv. Diabetes Found., Sigma Xi, others. Achievements include isolation of a bovine brain protein kinase and establishment of a protein kinase assay employing a novel PEI-cellulose thin-layer system as part of a PhD Biochemistry; established a novel modified flow-dialysis system for steady state hormone action studies; assisted the delineation of a LH-receptor defect related to precocious puberty and a novel genetic mutation in thyroid binding globulin in males. Avocations: carpentry, general handicrafts, electronics, computer repair work. Office: Univ Miss Med Ctr 2500 N State St Jackson MS 39216-4500 E-mail: gmoll@ped.umsmed.edu.

MOLL, JOHN LEWIS, retired electronics engineer; b. Wauseon, Ohio, Dec. 21, 1921; s. Samuel Andrew and Esther (Studer) M.; m. Isabel Mary Sieber, Oct. 28, 1944; children: Nicolas Josef, Benjamin Alex, Diana Carolyn. B.Sc., Ohio State U., 1943, PhD, 1952; Dr. h.c., Faculty Engring., Katholieke U. Leuven, (Belgium), 1983. Elec. engr. RCA Labs., Lancaster, Pa., 1943-45; mem. tech. staff Bell Telephone Labs., Murray Hill, N.J., 1952-58; mem. faculty Stanford U., 1958-69, prof. elec. engring., 1959-69; tech. dir. opto-electronics Fairchild Camera and Instrument Corp., 1969-74; dir. integrated circuits labs. Hewlett-Packard Labs., Palo Alto, Calif., 1974-80, dir. IC structures research, sr. scientist, 1980-87, dir. Superconductivity Lab., 1987-90, mem. tech. staff, 1990-96; ret., 1996. Author: Physics of Semi Conductors, 1964; co-author Computer Aided Design and VLSI Device Development, 1985, rev. edit., 1988; inventor (with Ebers) first analytical transistor model, 1953, still valid and useful for circuit design. Recipient Howard N. Potts medal Franklin Inst., 1967, Disting. Alumnus award Coll. Engring., Ohio State U., 1970, Benjamin C. Lamme medal Coll. Engring., Ohio State U., 1988, Vladimir Karapetoff award Eta Kappa Nu, 1995; Guggenheim fellow, 1964, C&C Award, NEC Fund Integration Comm. and Computers, 1997. Fellow IEEE (Ebers award 1971, Thomas A. Edison medal 1991), Am. Acad. Arts and Scis.; mem. Am. Phys. Soc., Nat. Acad. Engring., Nat. Acad. Scis. Home: 1 W Edith Ave # A105 Los Altos CA 94022-2770 E-mail: John1Moll@aol.com.

MOLL, JOSEPH EUGENE, chemical engineer, chemical company executive; b. Evansville, Ind., Sept. 3, 1950; s. Jacob Eugene and Mary Ann (Zenthoefer) M., m. Karen Jean Pennington, Aug. 20. 1977; children: Laura, Angela, Jared. BS in Chem. Engring., Purdue U., 1972. Cert. ofcl. USS Swimming. Mem. mfg. mgmt. staff GE, Selkirk, NY, 1972-74, Danville, Ill., 1972—74, product devel. engr. Pittsfield, Mass., 1974-75; tech. specialist Betz Labs., Kokomo, Ind., 1975-78, account mgr. Evansville, 1978-88; account exec. GE Betz, 1988-90, area mgr., 1990—92, sr. acct. rep., 1992—. Mem. Mayor's Tech. Adv. Com., Mt. Vernon, Ind., 1983— Instr. ARC, Evansville, 1971-73; ofcl. Ill. High Sch. Assn., Danville, 1972-73; min. of the word St. Matthew's Ch., Mt. Vernon, Ind., 1980—; amb. Promise Keepers Men's Ministry, 1994—, Sunday sch. tchr., 1996—; asst. cubmaster Boy Scouts Am., 1993-96, asst. scoutmaster, 1997—. Mem. AICE (v.p. 1971-72), Tech. Assn. of Pulp and Paper Industry, Am. Water Works Assn., Purdue Alumni Assn. (life), John Purdue Coaches Club, Elks, Omega Chi Epsilon, Triangle Fraternity. Roman Catholic. Avocations: golf, weight training, swimming, bible study. Home and Office: 28 Parkridge Dr Mount Vernon IN 47620-9405 E-mail: joseph.moll@gesm.ge.com.

MOLL, LLOYD HENRY, banker; b. Reading, Pa., June 26, 1925; s. Lewis J. and Katie (Rothermel) M.; m. Luise G. Keiper, Oct. 25, 1947; children: Lloyd E., Darryl M. BA, Albright Coll., Reading, 1952. Aircraft engine installer War Dept., 1942-47; tire inspector Firestone Tire & Rubber Co.,

Pottstown, Pa., 1947-48; asst. mgr. Household Fin. Corp., Reading, 1952-57; v.p. Meridian Asset Mgmt. Inc. and Meridian Trust Co. (formerly Am. Bank & Trust Co. of Pa.), Reading, 1957-94; v.p. sales and mktg. Investors Trust Co., Wyomissing, Pa., 1995—. Co-founder, past dir. Estate Planning Council of Berks County. Served with AUS, 1945-47. Mem. Am. Inst. Banking. (dir., chmn. bank relations Berks County chpt., pres. 1972-73), Toastmasters (pres. Reading club 1992), Optimists (pres. Reading club 1978-79). Democrat. Home: 213 W 39th St Crestwood Reading PA 19606 Office: Investors Trust Co 2201 Ridgewood Rd #180 Wyomissing PA 19610-1190 *Although it has been known to fail me on occasion I try to live by my understanding of the "Golden Rule". When it does fail me I'm usually able to discount such failure by recounting in my mind the many times it has been a two-way street or by convincing myself that I didn't try hard enough in this particular instance. All too often it comes to me much later that the other fellow's interpretation of the "Golden Rule" was far superior to mine. When this happens I have added to my learning. When it does not happen, it forces me to try that much harder to avoid "PERFECTION".*

MOLLARD, JOHN DOUGLAS, engineering and geology executive; b. Regina, Sask., Can., Jan. 3, 1924; s. Robert Ashton and Nellie Louisa (McIntosh) M.; m. Mary Jean Lynn, Sept. 18, 1952; children: Catherine Lynn, Jacqueline Lee, Robert Clyde Patrick. BCE, U. Sask., 1945; MSCE, Purdue U., 1947; PhD, Cornell U., 1952; LLD (hon.), U. Regina, 1995. Registered profl. engr., profl. geologist Sask., Alta. and B.C., Can. Resident constrn. engr. Sask. Dept. Hwys. and Transp., 1945; grad. asst. Purdue U., West Lafayette, Ind., 1946-47; rsch. engr. sch. civil engring. Cornell U., Ithaca, NY, 1950-52; air surveys engr., soil and water conservation and devel. Prairie Farm Rehab. Adminstrn., Govt. of Can., 1947-50, chief, airphoto analysis and engring. geology divsn., 1953-56; pres. J.D. Mollard and Assocs. Ltd., Regina, 1956—. Aerial resource mapping surveys tech. adv. Colombo plan, Govts. Ceylon and Pakistan, 1954-56; adv. Shaw Royal Commn. on Nfld. Agr.; lectr. in field. Author: Landforms and Surface Materials of Canada, 8 edits.; co-author: Airphoto Interpretation and the Canadian Landscape, 1986; contbr. over 100 articles to profl. publs. Organizer, canvasser United Appeal campaigns; former bd. dirs. Regina Symphony Orch.; gov. gen. Can. Adrian Clarkson Rideau Hall. Decorated officer Order of Can.; named to Engring. Alumni Wall of Distinction, U. Sask., 2000; recipient First Meritorious Achievement award, Lt. Gov. Sask., 2002, Engring. Achievement award, Assn. Profl. Engrs. Sask., 1984, Massey medal, Royal Can. Geog. Soc., 1989, Allied Arts medal, Royal Archtl. Inst. Can., 1998, Sask. Geotech. Achievement award, Sask. Geotech. Group, 2002. Fellow: ASCE, Engring. Inst. Can. (Keefer medal 1948, Julian C. Smith medal 1999), Internat. Explorers Club, Can. Acad. Engring., Geol. Soc. Can., Geol. Soc. Am., Am. Soc. Photogrammetry and Remote Sensing (award for contbns. airphoto interpretation and remote sensing 1979); mem.: Can. Soc. Petroleum Engrs., Geol. Soc. Sask., Regina Geotech. Soc., Can. Geotech. Soc. (1st R.M. Hardy Meml. Keynote lectr. 1987, Thomas Roy award with engring. geology divsn. 1989, R.F. Legget award 1992), Assn. Cons. Engrs. Can., Regina YMCA (former dir.), Rotary (former dir. Regina club). Mem. United Ch. of Can. Avocations: jogging, reading, golf, tennis, nature study. Home: 2900 McCallum Ave Regina SK Canada S4S 0R2 Office: 810 Avord Tower 2002 Victoria Ave Regina SK Canada S4P 0R7 Fax: 306-352-8820. Office Phone: 306-352-8811. E-mail: mollard@jdmollard.com.

MOLLEN, EDWARD LEIGH, pediatrician, allergist, clinical immunologist; b. Richmond, Va., May 13, 1946; s. Irving Roth and Ruth (Damsky) M.; m. Mary Viola Jeffrey, Dec. 14, 1975; children: Shawn, Michael, Eric, Christopher. BS in Chemistry, Coll. William and Mary, 1968; MD, Med. Coll. Va., 1972. Diplomate Am. Bd. Pediatrics, Am. Bd. Allergy and Immunology. Resident in pediatrics Med. Coll. Va., Richmond, 1972-75, fellow in allergy and immunology, 1975-77; practice allergy and pediatric allergy and clin. immunology Allergy Assocs. of Richmond, 1977-85; pvt. practice allergy/pediatric allergy and clin. immunology Richmond, 1985—. Fellow Am. Acad. Allergy, Asthma and Immunology, Am. Acad. Pediatrics; mem. Med. Soc. Va., Richmond Acad. Medicine, Asthma and Allergy Soc. Va. Avocations: bicycling, running, gardening. Office: 5855 Bremo Rd Ste 702 Richmond VA 23226-1926 Office Phone: 804-288-5216. E-mail: elmollenmd@aol.com.

MOLLENAUER, LINN FREDERICK, retired physicist; b. Washington, Pa., Jan. 6, 1937; BS of Engring. Physics, Cornell U., 1959; PhD in Physics, Stanford U., 1965. Asst. prof. physics U. Calif., Berkeley, 1965—72; rsch. staff Bell Labs./Lucent Techs., Holmdel, NJ, 1972—2003; ret., 2003. Co-editor (with J.C. White): Tunable Lasers, 1987. Recipient Ballantine medal, Franklin Inst., 1986, Rank prize in Photonics, 1991; fellow, Bell Labs., 2000. Fellow: IEEE (LEOS Disting. Lectr. award 1991, LEOS Quantum Electronics award 2001), AAAS, Optical Soc. Am. (R.W. Wood prize 1982, Charles Hard Townes award 1997); mem.: NAE. Achievements include first to demonstrate optical soliton propagation, leading to the realization of soliton-based, ultra-high-capacity lightwave communication. Office: Bell Labs Lucent Technologies Rm 4C-306 Crawfords Corner Rd Holmdel NJ 07733 E-mail: linn@lucent.com.

MOLLENHAUER, JUDE, musician, music educator; b. Quincy, Ill., Dec. 16, 1939; d. George Lewis Mollenhauer and Jessie Margret Siepker; children: Jude Christine Webster, Jennifer Lisa Webster. MusB, Curtis Inst. Music, Phila., 1962; MA, U. Pa., 1969. Prin. harpist Opera Co. Phila., 1964—83; solo harpist Pa. Ballet Co. Orch., Phila., 1974—83; prin. harpist Cin. Symphony Orch., 1984—85, Columbus Symphony Orch., Ohio, 1985—; faculty Otterbein Coll., Westerville, Ohio, 2001—. Faculty Capital U., Columbus, 2004—. Musician: (CDs) An English Fantasy for Viola and Harp, 2002, About Foreign Lands and People for Flute and Harp, 2003, Holiday Harps, 2003. Office: Columbus Symphony Orch 55 E State St Columbus OH 43215

MOLLENKOTT, VIRGINIA RAMEY, English literature and language educator, author, guest lecturer; b. Phila., Jan. 28, 1932; d. Robert Franklin and May (Lotz) Ramey; m. Frederick H. Mollenkott, June 17, 1954 (div. July 1973); 1 child, Paul F. BA, Bob Jones U., 1953; MA, Temple U., 1955; PhD, NYU, 1964; D in Ministries (hon.), Samaritan Coll., 1989. Chair English dept. Shelton Coll., Ringwood, N.J., 1955-63, Nyack (N.Y.) Coll., 1963-67; English dept. chair William Paterson U. of N.J., Wayne, 1972-76, prof. emeritus, 1997—, prof. English, 1967—97. Asst. editor Seventeenth Century News, N.Y.C., 1965-75; stylistic cons. New International Version of the Bible, Am. Bible Soc., 1970-78; translation com. An Inclusive Language Lectionary, Nat. Coun. Chs., 1980-88; bd. dirs. Pacem in Terris, Warwick, N.Y., 1980—, Kirkridge Conf. Ctr., Bangor, Pa., 1980-91, Upper Room AIDS Ministry, Harlem, N.Y.C., 1989-94; adv. bd. Program on gender and soc. Rochester (N.Y.) Divinity Sch., 1993—; manuscript evaluator Jour. of Feminist Studies in Religion, Cambridge, Mass., 1994—; contbg. editor The Witness, 1994-2000, 02—, The Other Side, 2003—; lectr. in field. Author: Adamant and Stone Chips, 1967, In Search of Balance, 1969, Women, Men and the Bible, 1977 1st rev. edit. 1988, Korean translation, 1981, Speech, Silence, Action, 1980, (with others) Is the Homosexual My Neighbor? A Positive Christian Response, 1978, rev. edit. 1994 (Integrity award 1979), The Divine Feminine: Biblical Imagery of God as Female, 1983, in German 1985, French, 1990, Italian, 1993; (with others) Views from the Intersection, 1984, Godding: Human Responsibility and the Bible, 1987, Sensuous Spirituality: Out from Fundamentalism, 1992 (N.J. Lesbian and Gay Achievement award 1992), Omnigender: A Trans-Religious Approach, 2001 (Lambda Literary award 2002, Ben Franklin award 2002), (with others) Transgender Journeys, 2003; editor: Women of Faith in Dialogue, 1987, Adam Among the Television Trees, 1971; editl. bd. Studies in Theology & Sexuality, 1997—. Recipient Lifetime Achievement award, Sr. Action in a Gay Environment, 1999. Mem. MLA (exec. com. religion and lit. 1976-80), Women's Inst. for Freedom of the Press (assoc.), Milton Soc. Am. (exec. com. 1974-76). Democrat. Episcopalian. Avocations: travel, gardening, grandmothering. Home and Office: 11 Yearling Trl Hewitt NJ 07421-2510 Office Phone: 973-853-4287. E-mail: jstvrm@warwick.net.

MOLLER, ANDREW K. finance company executive; CPA. Acctg. positions with Ladbroke Racing Canterbury, Inc., B Dalton Bookstores, Arthur Andersen LLP; asst. contr. Christopher & Banks, 1992—94, contr., 1995—98, v.p. finance, CFO, 1998—99, sr. v.p., CFO, 1999—. Office: 2400 Xenium Ln N Minneapolis MN 55441

MOLLER, JAMES HERMAN, pediatrician, educator; b. Fresno, Calif., Aug. 12, 1933; s. Leonard Hansen and Eloise Jean (Hunter) M.; m. Carol Suzanne Eymann, Sept. 8, 1957; children: James, Elizabeth. AB, Stanford U., 1954, MD, 1958. Instr. pediat. U. Minn., Mpls., 1965-66, asst. prof., 1966-70, assoc. prof., 1970-73, prof., 1973—, Dwan prof., 1975—, interim head pediat., 1976-78, 97-99, chief pediat., 1976-78, head pediat., 1999—2003; chief of staff U. Minn. Hosp., Mpls., 1984-89. Vis. prof. Nat. Heart & Lung Inst., London, 1989-90, Inst. Child Health, London, 1989-90. Bd. dirs. U. Minn. Hosp., 1984-89, Mpls. Children's Health Ctr., 1975-78, Children's Hosp., St. Paul, 1975-78, Minn. Assn. Pub. tchg. Hosps., Mpls., 1984-89, Variety Club Heart Assn., Mpls., 1980-83. Capt. U.S. Army, 1961-63. Fellow Am. Acad. Pediat. (exec. bd. 1991-92, dist. chmn. 1991-92, alternate dist. chmn. 1985-91, Ross Edn. award 1989), Am. Coll. Cardiology; mem. Am. Heart Assn. (pres. 1993-94, v.p. 1986-91, bd. dirs. 1986-95, award of Merit 1989), Am. Fedn. Clin. Rsch., Am. Pediatric Soc., Am. Bd. Pediat. Nat. Bd. Med. Examiners, Midwest Soc. Pediatric Cardiology Soc., Minn. Med. Assn. (interspltly. coun. 1979-82, resource group child health 1980-82), Minn. Acad. Medicine, Mpls. Met. Pediatric Soc, No. Pediatric Cardiology Soc. (pres. 1978-79), Midwest Soc. Pediatric Rsch. Soc. Pediatric Rsch., Hennepin County Med. Soc. (bd. dirs. 1986-89), Irish Am. Paediatric Soc., British Paediatric Cardiac Assn., Coun. Med. Splty. Socs. (bd. dirs., 1991—), Sub-bd. Pediatric Cardiology (chmn. 1992—), Internat. Heart Found. (pres. 1997-98), World Heart Fedn. (bd. dirs. 1999). Independent. Congregationalist. Avocations: gardening, travel, oriental carpets, reading. Home: 4816 Sheridan Ave S Minneapolis MN 55410-1917 Office: U Minn 420 Delaware St SE Minneapolis MN 55455-0374 Business E-Mail: molle002@umn.edu.

MOLLEUR, JOSEPH, religious studies educator; b. North Adams, Mass., Aug. 7, 1962; s. Michael Joseph and Theresa Ann Molleur; m. Linda Marie May, Dec. 5, 1992. BA, Grinnell Coll., 1984; MA, Episcopal Divinity Sch., Cambridge, Mass., 1995; PhD, Boston Coll., 1999. Postdoctoral fellow Boston Coll., Chestnut Hill, Mass., 1999—2001; asst. prof. religion Cornell Coll., Mount Vernon, Iowa, 2001—, chair, religion dept., 2004—. Author: Divergent Traditions, Converging Faiths, 2000. Mem.: AAUP, Soc. Hindu-Christian Studies, Am. Acad. Religion, Phi Beta Kappa. Episcopalian. Office: Cornell Coll Dept Religion 600 First St W Mount Vernon IA 52314 Office Phone: 319-895-4237.

MOLLEUR, RICHARD RAYMOND, lawyer; b. Adams, Mass., May 14, 1932; s. Raymond Emory and Germaine (Ouellette) M.; m. Rita M. Desaulniers, Sept. 5, 1955; children: Denis Richard, Michelle Annette, Suzanne Nicole, Celeste Marie. AB, Assumption Coll., Worcester, Mass., 1954; JD, Georgetown U., 1957. Bar: D.C. 1958. Counsel Office of Architect of the Capital, Washington, 1957-60; trial atty. U.S. Dept. Justice, Washington, 1960-65; dir. D.C. bail project Georgetown Law Center, Washington, 1965-66, D.C. bail agy., 1966, asst. dean, asso. prof. law, 1967-69; v.p., gen. counsel Fairchild Industries, Inc., Germantown, Md., 1979-85; ptnr. Herron & Burchett, 1986-90, Winston & Strawn, 1990; corp. v.p., gen. counsel Northrop Corp., L.A., 1991—. Author: Bail Reform in Nation's Capital, 1966. Recipient Alumni Achievement award Georgetown Law Center, 1966 Office: Northrop Corp 1840 Century Park E Los Angeles CA 90067-2199

MOLLICA, JOSEPH A. pharmaceutical executive; b. 1940; Various positions, sr. v.p. drug devel. Ciba-Geigy, Ardsley, NY, 1966—86; v.p. med. products E.I. Du Pont De Nemours & Co., Inc., Wilmington, Del., 1987—90; CEO Du Pont Mercke Pharm. Co., Wilmington, Del., 1991—93; CEO, chmn. Pharmacopeia, 1994—. Office: Pharmacopeia Inc Po Box 5350 Princeton NJ 08543-5350 Business E-Mail: mollica@pharmacop.com.

MOLLICA, SANTO, percussionist, songwriter, performer; b. Bronx, N.Y., Dec. 8, 1958; s. Salvatore and Vincenza Mollica. Student, Fordham, 1974, Hunter, N.Y., 1975-80. Pres., founder Source Unltd. Records, N.Y.C., 1981—. Prodr., writer, dir. (music LP records) American Way, 1985, Music from the Street, 1986, A Night in the Life, 1988, Self-Respect, 1989; dir. Desperate Times by Ed Peterson, 1994, Teaser by Dave Sasser and Mojo Conga Jam, 1996, Summer Heart by Jereme Lodeon, 1997, Home Grown by Tycoon Dog, 1998, Outskirts by Swivelchair, 1998. Office: Source Unltd Records 331 E 9th St New York NY 10003-7721

MOLLISH, JACK JAMES, retired insurance executive; b. Dudley, Pa., June 10, 1918; s. Martin and Helen M.; m. Helen Kocik, Aug. 23, 1947; 1 child: Mary Anne Mollish Seckman. Pres. CEO Nat. Ins. Mgmt. Corp., Clarksburg, W.Va., 1957-2000, Home Crafts Corp., Clarksburg, W.Va., 1981-95. Sec., pres. Clarksburg Life Underwriters, 1968, 69. Mem. Serra Club (pres. 1977—), Lions. Republican. Roman Catholic. Avocations: golf, baseball, reading, hunting. Home: 108 Edgewood Ave Clarksburg WV 26301-9502

MOLLMAN, JOHN PETER, book publisher, consultant electronic publishing; b. Belleville, Ill., Feb. 8, 1931; s. Kenneth John and Maurine (Farrow) M.; m. Carol J. Piper, Apr. 4, 1998; children: Sarah Chase Underhill, Eric Cleburne. BA, Washington U., St. Louis, 1952. Advt. specialist Gen. Electric Co., Schenectady and Boston, 1952-54; mgr. Enterprise Printing Co., Millstadt, Ill., 1956-66; gen. mgr. Monarch Pub. Co., N.Y.C., 1966-67; dir. prodn. Harper & Row Pubs., N.Y.C., 1967-74; pub. Harper's Mag. Press, N.Y.C., 1971-74; v.p. prodn. Random House Inc., N.Y.C., 1974-81; sr. v.p. World Book-Childcraft Inc., Chgo., 1981-88; pres. World Book Pub., 1988-91; pub. cons., 1991-92; dir. intellectual property devel. Multimedia Publishing Microsoft, 1992-96; cons. in electronic pub. Carmel, Calif., 1996—. Mem. vis. com. Washington U.; mem. pub. com. Art Inst. Chgo.; bd. dirs. Yerba Buena Ctr. for the Arts, San Francisco; pres. Internat. ebook Award Found., N.Y. Mem. Golf Club at Quail Lodge, Phi Delta Theta, Sigma Delta Chi, Omicron Delta Kappa. Unitarian Universalist. Home: 25340 Vista Del Pinos Carmel CA 93923-8804 E-mail: pmollman@msn.com.

MOLLOFF, FLORENCE JEANINE, speech and language therapist; b. St. Louis, Aug. 28, 1959; d. Lawrence Allan and Rietta Gertrude (Fiegenbaum) M. BS, Fontbonne Coll., St. Louis, 1983; MEd summa cum laude, Nat. Louis U., St. Louis, 1989; student, Project ACCESS Inst., 1992, Judevine Ctr. Autistic Children Tng., 1992. Cert. speech correctionist, Mo. Intern St. Louis State Sch. for Profoundly Retarded, 1983-84; speech therapist St. Louis Pub. Schs., 1984—; Judvine Ctr. for Autistic Children Tng., 1992; speech/lang. therapist St. Louis Pub. Schs./Autism Program, 1992-93, 97—; speech/lang. therapist Michael Sch. Medically Fragile and Multiply Handicapped Michael Sch. Medically Fragile and Multiply Handicapped, 1993-96; speech and lang. pathologist autism program Buder, 1996—, Buder and Fanning, 1997—2000. Speech, lang. therapist St. Louis Pub. Schs./Michael Sch. for Medically Fragile and Multiply Handicapped, 1993—; ednl. cons. program devel. Mo. Coalition for Environ., St. Louis, Columbia, Kansas City, 1990—; cons., trainer in puppetry Kids on the Block, St. Louis Pub. Schs., 1988—; vol. grant writer West End Restoration Corp.; speech/lang. therapist Mid. Sch. for Medically Fragile and Multiply Handicapped, 1993-96. Author: (pseudonym F.J. Molotschnikov) 91 Seconds to Armageddon, 1999; author, creator transition curriculum: Consultative Resource Program, 1989; creator puppet program: Save Our Astonishing Planet, 1990; ednl. cons. program devel. young St. Louis audiences (adapted program for severe to profoundly handicapped children "Arabian Nights", 1994; editor: Strides Newsletter, St. Louis, 1996-98; contbr. artist St. Louis Internat. Jazz Mus.; vol. grant writer West End Restoration Corp. Educator, lobbyist Coalition for the Environ., St. Louis, 1990, newsletter editor, 2000-01; activist, lobbyist Housing Now, St. Louis, 1989; foster parent Christian Children's Fund, 1986—; activist Habitat for Humanity Internat., 1994—; mem., fundraiser Gateway I Have a Dream Found., 1995—; mem. nat. steering com. (hon.) Pres. Clinton's Re-election 1995; contbg. mem. Dem. Nat. Com., 1995—; vol. grant writer West End Restoration Corp.; mem. Emily's List; participant Cross-Cultural Solutions Project, New Delhi, India, 1998; mem. World Affairs Coun., St. Louis, Mo., 2002. Mem. AAUW, ASCD, Coun. Exceptional Children (state rep. Mo. divsn. for children with communicative disorders 1988-89, presenter nat. conv. 1989), Internat. Platform Assn., Am. Fedn. Tchrs. (bldg. rep. 1992), Nat. Arbor Day Found., Nat. Parks and Conservation Assn., Nat. Women's Polit. Caucus, Mo. Assn. for Augmentative Comm. Systems, Met. St. Louis Women's Polit. Caucus, Emily's List, Am. Med. Writers Assn., Soc. for Tech. Com., NEA (editor Strides newsletter 1996-97, grantee Internet project, sec. St. Louis 1997-99), Mo. NEA, Amnesty Internat., World Affairs Coun. St. Louis. Democrat. Avocations: puppetry, international affairs, running track, film, debate. Home: 9823 Lullaby Ln Saint Louis MO 63114-2510 Office Phone: 314-352-4343. Business E-Mail: fjmolloff@sbcglobal.net.

MOLLOHAN, ALAN B. congressman; b. Fairmont, W.Va., May 14, 1943; s. Robert H. and Helen (Holt) Mollohan; m. Barbara Whiting, Aug. 7, 1976; children: Alan, Robert, Andrew, Karl, Mary Kathryn. AB in Polit. Sci., Coll. William and Mary, 1966; JD, W.Va. U., 1970. Assoc. law firm, 1970-82; mem. U.S. Congresses from 1st W.Va. dist., 1983—; mem. appropriations com., homeland sec. com. With USAR, 1970—83. Mem.: ABA, W.Va. Bar, Elks, Moose. Democrat. Baptist. Office: US Ho Reps 2302 Rayburn HOB Washington DC 20515-0001

MOLLOHAN, BETH M. humanities educator; d. Elmer A. and Winnie M. Mollohan. BA in English, Berea Coll., Ky.; MEd, W.Va. Wesleyan U., Buckhannon. Tchr. Webster County Bd. Edn., Webster Springs, W.Va., 1985—.

MOLLOY, ANGELA MARGARET, advertising, marketing, and public relations executive; b. July 16, 1948; d. John Robert and Angela Margaret (Culotta) Fanto; m. William Francis Molloy, June 24, 1970 (div. Oct. 1978); 1 child, Angela Margaret. BA, Duquesne U., 1970. cert. qualitative rsch. provider Burke Ins., 1995-96. Edtl. asst. Nat. Coun. Internat. Visitors, Washington, 1970-73; dir. devel. DeMatha H.S., Hyattsville, Md., 1973-75; mktg. officer Wash. Fed. Savs. & Loan, Washington, 1978-80; asst. v.p., dir. mktg. Md. Fed. Savs. & Loan, Hyattsville, 1980-83; asst. v.p., dir. mktg. and advt. B.F. Saul Co., Chevy Chase, Md., 1983-86; sr. v.p. Power House Comms. affiliate Gray & Co., pub. rels., Washington, 1986-87; exec. v.p. Susan Davis Advt., 1987-91; ptnr. Gardner, Keaton Molloy Advt., 1991-94; owner Molloy Mktg. Svcs., 1994—. Bd. dirs. YMCA Metro Washington, 1991-95. Mem. soc. Profl. Journalists, Women in Advt. and Mktg., Advt. Club Met. Washington, Mkt. Rsch. Assn., Women of Washington, Amer. Mktg. Assn. Democrat. Roman Catholic. Home: 8601 Castlebar Way Montgomery Village MD 20886-5676 Office Phone: 301-926-4103. E-mail: peggymolloy@comcast.net.

MOLLOY, DAVID SCOTT, JR., labor relations educator; b. Providence, Aug. 17, 1946; s. David Scott and Miriam Virginia (Handy) Molloy; m. Theresa Vinacco; children: Kelsey Allende Molloy, Cady Larkin Molloy. BA, R.I. Coll., Providence, 1970; MA, U. N.H., Durham, 1972; PhD, Providence Coll., 1991. Bus driver R.I. Pub. Transit Authority, Providence, 1973-81; bus. agt. Amalgamated Transit Union, Providence, 1981-84; chief-of-staff U.S. Congresswoman Schneider, Cranston, RI, 1984-86; prof. U. R.I., Kingston, 1986—. Lectr. various labor unions, 1980—; intern dir. Labor Rsch. Ctr., U. R.I., Kingston, 1986—; radio commentator Voice of America, Washington, 1992—. Author: (book) Trolley Wars, 1996; contbr. articles to profl. jours. Mem. exec. bd. Providence Heritage Commn., 1982—92, Leadership R.I., Providence, 1987—90, R.I. Heritage Hall of Fame, 1998—; bd. dirs. R.I. State Humanities Coun., Providence, 1985—95; chmn. Libr. R.I. Hist. Soc., Providence, 1987—93. Recipient Achievement medal, City of Providence, 1986, Scott Molloy Labor Collection award, Smithsonian Instn., 1990, Tchg. Excellence award, Indsl. Rels. Rsch. Assn., 2000, Inst. Labor Studies, 2001. Mem.: AAUP (U. R.I. chmn. PAC 1994—96), AFL-CIO (R.I. adv. exec. bd. 1981—84, Achievement award 1995), Inst. Labor Studies (bd. dirs. 1987—), R.I. Indsl. Rels. Assn. (pres. 1995—96), Blackstone Valley Heritage Corridor (commr. 1988—98), R.I. Labor History Soc. (founder, 1st pres. 1987—2000). Avocations: collecting labor and industrial artifacts, weightlifting. Home: 550 Usquepaugh Rd West Kingston RI 02892-1924 Office: Labor Rsch Ctr 36 Upper College Rd Kingston RI 02881-2005 Office Phone: 401-874-2569. Business E-Mail: molloy@uri.edu.

MOLLOY, DONALD WILLIAM, lawyer; BA, U. Mont., 1968, JD with honors, 1976. Bar: Mont. 1976, U.S. Dist. Ct. Mont. 1976, U.S. Ct. Appeals (9th cir.) 1977, U.S. Supreme Ct. 1984. Aviation lt. USNR, 1968-72; law clk. to James F. Battin U.S. Dist. Ct., Billings, Mont., 1976-78; ptnr. Berger, Anderson, Sinclair & Murphy, Billings, Mont., 1978-81, Anderson, Edwards & Molloy, Billings, Mont., 1981-90, Anderson & Molloy, Billings, Mont., 1990-91; ptnr., sr., owner The Molloy Law Offices, Billings, Mont., 1991-96; judge U.S. Dist. Ct. Mont., Missoula divsn., 1996—. Lawyer rep. 9th Cir. Jud. Conf., San Francisco, 1989-92. Mem. ABA, Yellowstone County Bar Assn. (pres. 1984-95), Mont. Trial Lawyers Assn. (Trial Lawyer of Yr. 1993), Am. Trial Lawyers, Am. Bd. Trial Advocates, Am. Judicature Soc., Mont. Bar Assn., Pa. Trial Lawyer's Assn., Tex. Trial Lawyers Assn. Roman Catholic. Avocations: aviation, pilot. Office: US Dist Ct Dist Mont PO Box 7309 Missoula MT 59807-7309

MOLLOY, GEORGE A. finance company executive; Pres., CEO Liberty Mortgage First Liberty Fin. Corp., Macon, Ga. Office: First Liberty Fin Corp Exec Office 201 2nd St Macon GA 31201-8293

MOLLOY, SYLVIA, Latin American literature educator, writer; b. Buenos Aires, Aug. 29, 1938; came to U.S. 1967; d. Herbert Edward and Margarita Berta (Chasseing) M. Licence es Lettres, U. Paris, 1960, Diplome D'Etudes Superieures, 1961, Doctorat de U. Paris, 1967. Asst. prof. Spanish SUNY, Buffalo, 1967-69; asst. prof. Spanish Vassar Coll., Poughkeepsie, N.Y., 1969-70, Princeton U., Princeton, N.J., 1970-73, assoc. prof., 1973-81, Emory L. Ford prof., 1981-86; prof. Spanish Yale U., New Haven, 1986-90; Albert Schweitzer prof. of Humanities NYU, 1990—. Author: La Diffusion de la Litterature Hispanoamericaine en France, 1972, Las Letras de Borges, 1979, En Breve Carcel, 1981, At Face Value: Autobiographical Writing in Spanish America, 1991; co-author Women's Writing in Latin America, 1991, Hispanisms and Homosexualities, 1998, El Comun Olvido, 2002; author short stories and contbr. articles to profl. jours.; cons., editorial bd. Revista Iberoamericana, 1979-81, 1985-89, Latin Am. Literary Rev., 1985—, Revista de Filología, Buenos Aires, 1985— Fellow Am. Philos. Soc., 1970, NEH, 1976; Social Sci. Research Council grantee, 1983; Guggenheim Found. fellow, 1986-87 Mem. MLA (pres.), Asociacion Internacional de Hispanistas, Instituto Internacional de Literatura Iberoamericana

MOLMENTI, ERNESTO P. surgeon; b. Feb. 5, 1964; BA summa cum laude, Boston U., 1985, MD, 1989. Intern Barnes Hosp.-Washington U. Sch. Medicine, St. Louis, 1989-90, chief resident, 1995—96; instr. dept. anatomy and neurobiology Washington U. Sch. Medicine, St. Louis, 1992-96; fellow, instr., transplant surgeon U. Pitts., 1996-98; asst. prof. surgery S.W. Med. Ctr., U. Tex., Dallas, 1999—2001; transplant surgeon Children's Med. Ctr., Baylor U. Med. Ctr., Dallas, 1999-2001; assoc. prof. surgery Johns Hopkins U., 2001—, surg. dir. kidney-pancreas transplantation, 2001—. Author: Atlas of Liver Transplantation, 2002; contbg. author Washington University Manual of Surgery, 1997, Laporascopic Surgery: Principles and Procedures, Computed Body Tomography with MRI Correlation, 1997, Surgical Clnics of North America, 2000, Clnics in Liver Disease, 2000, Textbook of Critical Care, 2000; contbr. articles to profl. jours. Named Harold C. Case scholar, Boston U., 1984, Internat. scholar, 1984; recipient Avelino Gutierrez Biannual award, Nat. Acad. Medicine Argentina, 1987, Hist. Sci. award, Nat. Acad. Scis. Argentina, 1989, 1990, Excellence in Tchg. award, Washington U. Sch. Medicine, 1991, 1992, Hounsfield award, Soc. Computed Body Tomography Magnetic Resonance, 1995, Young Investigator award, Transplant Soc., 1998, Travel award, Internat. Assn. for the Study of Liver Disease, 1998, Young Investigator award, AST/Am. Soc. Transplant Surgeons, 2000; fellow Abbott Labs. and Crohns and Colitis Found., 1993—94, Faculty Rsch. fellow, ACS,

2002. Mem.: Mem. Argentine Med. Assn. (fgn. corr.), Phi Beta Kappa. Office: The Johns Hopkins Hosp 600 N Wolfe St # 402 Harvey 611 Baltimore MD 21287-8611 E-mail: emolmen1@jhmi.edu.

MOLNAR, BELA, school administrator; b. Elyria, Ohio, May 12, 1951; s. Bela and Olga Margaret (Strong) Molnar; m. Nancy Lynn Campbell, Aug. 9, 1975; children: Eric Bela, Melinda Renee. BA, Heidelberg Coll., 1973; MEd, Cleve. State U., 1977; postgrad., Kent State U., Akron U. Cert. secondary tchr. Ohio, registered baseball and softball ofcl. Ohio H.S. Athletic Assn. Health, phys. edn. tchr. Ford Jr. H.S., Brook Park, Ohio, 1973—79, athletic coach, 1973—79, health, phys. edn. dept. chair, 1977—79; unit prin. Berea H.S., Ohio, 1979—82; asst. prin. Copley H.S., Ohio, 1982—83, prin., 1984—90, Elyria H.S., Ohio, 1990—98, Midpark H.S., Middleburg Heights, Ohio, 1998—. Mem.: Berea Assn. Sch. Adminstrs., Ohio Assn. Secondary Sch. Adminstrs., Nat. Assn. Secondary Sch. Prins., Heidelberg Alumni H Assn. Avocations: jogging, golf, reading. Home: 108 Ashland Ave Elyria OH 44035-8284 Office: Midpark High Sch 7000 Paula Dr Middleburg Heights OH 44130 Office Phone: 216-676-8400.

MOLNAR, DONALD JOSEPH, landscape architecture educator; b. Springfield, Ill., Dec. 24, 1938; s. Joseph and Mabel Irene (Woods) M.; m. Carol Jeanette Smith, Aug. 22, 1958; children: Elaina Deanne, Amy Lynn, Holly Suzanne. BFA in Landscape Architecture, U. Ill., 1960, MFA in Landscape Architecture, 1964. Landscape architect Simonds and Simonds, Pitts., 1961-63; landscape architect campus planning U. Ill., Urbana, 1963-72, asst. dir., planner capital programs Urbana and Chgo., 1971-81; assoc. prof. landscape architecture Purdue U., West Lafayette, Ind., 1981-85, dir. landscape architecture coop. program, 1983—, prof. landscape architecture, 1985—, chair landscape architecture program, 1987—, dir. internat. exch. landscape architecture, 1988—. Cons. to architect, engrs., park agys., 1964—, Mobile Homes Mfrs. Assn., Chgo., 966-76; prin. Profl. Searches for Landscape Archs., employment cons., 2000—; prin. Drumlin Group. Author: Anatomy of a Park, 2d edit., 1986, 3rd edit., 2003; illustrator: Anatomy of a Park, 1971, Visual Approach to Park Design, 1980; developer software CompuPave, 1992, PaveCAD, 1996. Mem., program coord. Champaign (Ill.) Devel. Coun., 1966-78. Named Hon. Parks Commr., Champaign Park Dist., 1981. Fellow Am. Soc. Landscape Architects (licensing com. Ill. chpt. 1968-70, registration com. Ind. chpt. 1982-85, pres. 1991-92, award 1982). Avocations: travel, computers.

MOLNAR, LAWRENCE, lawyer; b. Czygand, Hungary, Apr. 14, 1927; came to U.S., 1954; s. Alexander and Marie (Vavra) M.; m. Virginia Hampton Broome, July 16, 1999. Juris Utriusque Candidatus, Charles U., Prague, Czechoslovakia, 1951; JD, NYU, 1962; LLM, LLD (hon.), Charles U., 1991. Bar: N.Y. 1962, U.S. Dist. Ct. (so. and ea. dists.) N.Y. 1970, Czech Republic, 1991. With U.S. Intelligence, Berlin, 1951-54, Lansen, Naeve Corp., N.Y., 1955-56; asst. mgr. export traffic Intra-Mar Shipping Corp., N.Y., 1957-58; mgr. export traffic Melchior, Armstrong, Ridgefield, N.J., 1958-59; assoc. Hamburger, Weinschenk, N.Y.C., 1963-69; ptnr. Hamburger, Weinschenk, Molnar & Fisher, N.Y.C., 1969—2001; counsel Hamburger, Weinschenk & Fisher, N.Y.C., 2001—. Mem. ABA, Assn. of Bar of City of N.Y., Consular Law Soc. (v.p. 1980—), Fgn. Law Assn., Queens Bar Assn. Office: Hamburger Weinschenk Molnar & Fisher 36 W 44th St New York NY 10036-8102

MOLNAR, VIOLET, mental health nurse; b. Budapest, Hungary; arrived in U.S., 1960; d. Janos Molnar and Erzsebeth Krekacs. ADN, Atlantic Union Coll., 1967; BSN, Walla Walla Coll., 1973. RN Mass., Calif. Staff nurse New Eng. Meml. Hosp., Stoneham, Mass., 1968—70; IV therapist Loma Linda (Calif.) U. Med. Hosp., 1970—72; psychiat. nurse St. Bernardines Med. Ctr., San Bernardino, Calif., 1974—89, Corona Regional Med. Ctr., San Bernardino, 1990—. Pub. spkr. Pres. Lady's Club Friendly Cir., Loma Linda, 1997—99; elder, deaconess, greeter Loma Linda U. SDA Ch., 1975—. Mem.: Rotary Club San Bernardino/Highland (Paul Harris fellow 2001). Avocations: travel, reading, church activities.

MOLNAU, CAROL, lieutenant governor; b. Sept. 17, 1949; m. Steven F. Molnau; 3 children. Attended, U. Minn. Mem. Minn. Ho. of Reps., 1992—2003; commr. Minn. Dept. Transportation; lt. gov. Minn., 2003—. Active Our Saviors Luth. Ch., 4-H, Chaska City Coun. Mem. Agrl. Com., Econ. Devel., Infrastructure & Regulation Fin.-Transportation Fin. Divsn., Fin. Inst. & Ins.: Internat. Trade & Economic Devel. Republican. Office: Office of the Governor 130 State Capitol Saint Paul MN 55155

MOLOFF, ALAN LAWRENCE, military officer, physician; b. Bklyn., Sept. 29, 1954; s. Louis and Muriel Moloff. BS, U. Vt., 1976; DO, U. N.J., 1983; MPH, Harvard U., 1988; student, U.S. Army Command/Gen. Staff Course, 1994-95. Diplomate Am. Bd. Preventive Medicine, bd. cert. aerospace medicine, bd. cert. undersea medicine. Commd. platoon leader U.S. Army, 1976, advanced through grades to col., 1999; intern Fitzsimons Army Med. Ctr., Aurora, Colo., 1983-84; med. officer lst Battalion 10th Spl. Forces Group, Bad Tolz, Germany, 1984-87; resident in aerospace medicine Harvard U., Boston, 1987-89; chief spl. ops. forces divsn. Acad. Health Scis., San Antonio, 1989-92; command surgeon Spl. Forces Command, Ft. Bragg, NC, 1992-93; dep. surgeon U.S. Army Spl. Ops. Command, Ft. Bragg, NC, 1993-94; with command and gen. staff coll. U.S. Army, 1994-95; dep. surgeon 30th Med. Brigade, Heidelberg, Germany, 1995-96; SETAF surgeon, 1995-97; dep. U.S. Army Europe Fwd Surgeon, Hungary, 1995-96; surgeon V Corps, Heidelberg, Germany, 1996-97; comdr. 212th M.A.S.H., Wiesbaden, Germany, 1997-99; fellow environ. policy inst. Army War Coll., 1999-2000; comdr. U.S. Army Aeromed. Ctr., 2000—02, Def. Med. Readiness Tng. Inst., 2002—. Lectr. advanced trauma life support Aerospace Med., Environ. Security, Homeland Security, Undersea Medicine, Med. Support Contingency Ops. Contbr. articles to profl. jours. Active in civic activities. Decorated Legion of Merit, Meritorious Svc. medal with 4 oak leaf clusters, Joint Svc. Commendation medal, S.W. Asian Svc. medal, Army Commendation medal with oak leaf cluster, Joint Army Achievement medal, Armed Forces Svc. medal, Armed Forces Expeditionary medal, NATO medal, Kuwait Liberation medal, Kosovo Campaign medal, German Paratrooper badge, Pathfinder badge, Expert Field Med. badge, Order of Mil. Med. Merit, Master Parachutist award, Ranger, Spl. Forces Qualified Master Flight Surgeon badge, Navy Dive Med. Officer badge, Order of Aeromed. Merit. Fellow: Aerospace med. Assn., Am. Coll. Preventive Medicine; mem.: Spl. Ops. Med. Assn., Assn. Mil. Osteo. Physicians and Surgeons, Soc. U.S. Army Flight Surgeons (life), Assn. Mil. Surgeons U.S., Aerospace Med. Assn. Avocations: skiing, scuba diving, weightlifting, military history, rock climbing. Office: 1706 Stanley Rd Fort Sam Houston TX 78234 Office Phone: 210-221-2109. Business E-Mail: almoloff@dmrti.army.mil.

MOLONEY, DANIEL M. electronics executive; BSEE, U. Mich.; MBA in Mgmt., U. Chgo. Joined Gen. Instrument Corp., 1983; sr. v.p., gen. mgr. broadband IP sys. group Motorola, Inc., exec. v.p., pres., CEO broadband comm. sector, 2002—. Contbr. articles to profl. jours. Office: Motorola Inc 1303 E Algonquin Rd Schaumburg IL 60196

MOLONEY, HERBERT W., III, advertising executive; Retail advt. mgr. The Miami Herald; sales mgr. WPRI-TV; sr. v.p. advt. Phila. Inquirer/Daily News; with Knight-Ridder, Inc., 1973—94; exec. v.p., mktg. and sales TC Advt. (now Vertis), 1994—2000; chief oper. officer Vertis, 2000—. Bd. dirs. Lee Enterprises, Inc. Office: Vertis 250 W Pratt St Baltimore MD 21201

MOLONEY, STEPHEN MICHAEL, lawyer; b. L.A., July 1, 1949; s. Donald Joseph and Madeline Marie (Sartoris) M.; m. Nancy Paula Barile, Jan. 15, 1972; children: Michael, John, Kathleen. Student, St. John's Sem., Camarillo, Calif., 1967-69; BS, U. Santa Clara, 1971, JD, 1975. Bar: Calif. 1975, U.S. Dist. Ct. (cen. dist.) Calif. 1976, U.S. Supreme Ct. 1990. Assoc. Gilbert, Kelly, Crowley & Jennett, L.A., 1975-80, from ptnr. to sr. ptnr., 1980—. Arbitrator, settlement officer Los Angeles Superior Ct., 1985—. Contbr. articles to profl. jours. Dir. Calif. Def. Polit. Action Com., Sacramento, 1991—. With USAR. Recipient Svc. award to Pres. of So. Calif. Def. Counsel, Def. Rsch. Inst., Chgo., 1992. Mem. Assn. So. Calif. Def. Counsel (pres. 1992-93), Calif. Def. Counsel (dir. 1991—), L.A. County Bar Assn. (vols. in parole, 1976-77, exec. com. alternative dispute resolution com. 1992-96), Oakmont Country Club, La Quinta Resort and Club. Democrat. Roman Catholic. Avocations: politics, golf, reading, travel. Office: Gilbert Kelly Crowley & Jennett 1200 Wilshire Blvd Ste 6 Los Angeles CA 90017-1908 E-mail: smm@gilbertkelly.com.

MOLONEY, THOMAS E. lawyer; b. Rockville Ctr., N.Y., Jan. 9, 1949; BS, U. Dayton, 1971; JD, U. Notre Dame, 1974. Bar: Ohio 1974. Prin. Am. Energy Svcs., Inc., Columbus, Ohio. Office: Am Energy Svcs Inc 1105 Schrock Rd Ste 602 Columbus OH 43229-1174

MOLONEY, THOMAS E. insurance company executive; b. 1943; Joined John Hancock Mut. Life, 1965, various mgmt. positions, 1965-89; CFO John Hancock Fin. Svcs., Inc., 1989—. Office: John Hancock Fin Svcs Inc John Hancock Pl Boston MA 02117

MOLONEY, THOMAS JOSEPH, lawyer; b. Bklyn., Oct. 14, 1952; s. Thomas J. and Grace (Nelson) M.; m. Molly K. Heines, Dec. 26, 1976. AB, Columbia U., 1973; JD cum laude, NYU, 1976. Bar: N.Y. 1977, U.S. Dist. Ct. (so. dist.) N.Y. 1977, U.S. Dist. Ct. (ea. dist.) N.Y. 1978, U.S. Ct. Appeals (2d cir.) 1981, U.S. Dist. Ct. (no. dist.) N.Y. 1988, U.S. Ct. Appeals (4th cir.) 1989, U.S. Supreme Ct. 1991. Assoc. Cleary, Gottlieb, Steen & Hamilton, N.Y.C., 1976—84, ptnr., 1984—. Bd. dirs. N.Y. Lawyers for Pub. Interest, N.Y.C., 1986-91; mediator U.S. Bankruptcy Ct. for So. Dist. N.Y., 1995. Asst. counsel Gov.'s Jud. Nominating Com., N.Y.C., 1981-85; chmn. bus. adv. coun. Washington Irving H.S., 1994—. Mem. ABA, Am. Bankruptcy Inst., Assn. of Bar of City of N.Y. (bankruptcy, corp. reorganization coms. 1983-86, chair com. legal assistance 1995-97), Order of Coif. Avocations: chess, golf, dance, travel, wine. Office: Cleary Gottlieb Steen & Hamilton 1 Liberty Plz Fl 38 New York NY 10006-1470

MOLONEY, THOMAS WALTER, consulting firm executive; b. N.Y.C., Feb. 8, 1946; s. Thomas Walter and Anne (Heney) M. BA, Colgate U., 1967; MA, Columbia U., 1970, MPH, 1973, MBA, 1975. Program dir. Nat. Ctr. for Deaf-Blind, New Hyde Park, N.Y., 1971-72; spl. asst. to dir. and dean N.Y. Hosp., N.Y.C., 1973-74; asst. v.p. Robert Wood Johnson Found., 1975-80; sr. v.p. The Commonwealth Fund, N.Y.C., 1980-92; dir. pub. policy and health programs The Inst. for Future, 1992-99; ptnr., owner S/B Futures Inc., Palm Beach, Fla., 1997—. Vis. lectr. Princeton (N.J.) U., 1975-80; bd. dirs. Grantmakers in Health, N.Y.C., 1984—, chmn. bd., 1984-88; mem. health adv. com. GAO, 1987—; mem. health adv. coun. Johns Hopkins U. Sch., Hygiene and Pub. Health, Balt., 1989-91; bd. dirs. Found. Health Svcs. Rsch., Washington, 1985-92; mem. bd. visitors Med. Sch., U. Calif. at Davis, 1988—; mem. vis. com. Grad. Sch. Mgmt. and Urban Policy New Sch. for Social Rsch., N.Y.C., 1988-92; mem. Nat. Bd. Examiners, 1986-90; mem. sr. adv. bd. global leadership program U. Mich. Grad. Sch. Bus., Ann Arbor, 1988—; mem. pres. com. The N.Y. Acad. Scis., 1987-90; policy scholar The Eisenhower Ctr. Columbia U., N.Y.C., 1992—, Inst. Health Policy Studies U. Calif., San Francisco, 1992—. Author books; editor: New Approaches to the Medicaid Crisis, 1983; contbr. articles to profl. jours. Bd. dirs. New Eng. Med. Ctr., Boston, 1982-89. Policy scholar Inst. Health Policy Studies U. Calif., San Francisco, 1992—. Eisenhower Ctr. Columbia U., 1992—. Fellow AAAS; mem. Inst. Medicine, Nat. Acad. Scis., Nat. Acad. Social Ins., N.Y. Acad. Medicine, N.Y. Acad. Scis. (pres' com. 1987-90). Office: S/B Futures Inc Fl 8 1170 N Ocean Blvd Palm Beach FL 33480-3244

MOLONY, MICHAEL JANSSENS, JR., lawyer, arbitrator, mediator; b. New Orleans, Sept. 2, 1922; s. Michael Janssens and Marie (Perret)M.; m. Jane Leslie Waguespack, Oct. 21, 1951; children: Michael Janssens III (dec.), Leslie, Megan, Kevin, Sara, Brian, Ian, Duncan. JD, Tulane U., 1950. Bar: La. 1950, D.C. 1979, U.S. Dist. Ct. (ea. and mid. dists.) La. 1951, U.S. Ct. Appeals (5th cir.) 1953, U.S. Supreme Ct. 1972, U.S. Dist. Ct. (we. dist.) La. 1978, U.S. Ct. Appeals (11th and D.C. cirs.) 1981. Ptnr. Molony & Baldwin, New Orleans, 1950; assoc. Jones, Flanders, Waechter & Walker, New Orleans, 1951-56; ptnr. Jones, Walker, Waechter, Poitevent, Carrere & Denegre, New Orleans, 1956-75, Milling, Benson, Woodward, Hillyer, Pierson & Miller, New Orleans, 1975-91, Chaffe, McCall, Phillips, Toler & Sarpy, New Orleans, 1991-92, Sessions & Fishman, New Orleans, 1993-2000, Molony Law Firm, New Orleans, 2000—. Instr., lectr. Med. Sch. and Univ. Coll. Tulane U., 1953-59; mem. Eisenhower Legal Com., 1952. Mem. bd. commrs. Port of New Orleans, 1976-81, pres., 1978; mem. bd. rev. Assoc. Br. Pilots, 1990—; bd. dirs. La. World Expn. Inc., 1974-84; bd. dirs., exec. com. New Orleans Tourist and Conv. Commn., 1971-74, 78, chmn.; family attractions com. 1973-75; chmn. La. Gov.'s Task Force on Space Industry, 1971-73; chmn. La. Gov.'s Citizens' Adv. Com. Met. New Orleans Transp. and Planning Location of new Miss. River Bridge, 1971-77; mem. La. Gov.'s Task Force Natural Gas Requirements, 1971-72; mem. La. Gov.'s Proaction Commn. for Higher Edn., 1995; mem. Goals Found. Coun. and ex-officio mem. Goals Found., Met. New Orleans, 1969-73; vice chmn. Port of New Orleans Operation Impact, 1969-70, mem. Met. Area Com., New Orleans, 1970-84; trustee Pub. Affairs Rsch. Coun. La., 1970-73, mem. exec. com. Bus./Higher Edn. Coun., U. New Orleans, 1980-94, bd. dirs., 1980-2000, dir. emeritus, 2000—, v.p., 1986-88, pres., 1988-90, chmn. Task Force on Pub. Higher Edn. Funding, 1990-95, chmn. govtl. affairs, 1995-2000, Task Force on Edn./Econ. Devel. Alliances, 1993-95; mem. Mayor's Coun. on Internat. Trade and Econ. Devel., 1978; mem. Mayor's Transition Task Force Econ. Devel., 1994; bd. dirs. La. Partnership for Tech. and Innovation, 1989—, Acad. Sacred Heart, 1975-77, Internat. House, 1985-86, adv. coun., 1985—; bd. dirs. U. New Orleans Found., 1991-2003; mem. vis. com. Sch. Bus. Adminstrn., Loyola U., New Orleans, 1981-2001, trustee Loyola U., 1985-91, vice chmn. bd. trustees, 1990-91; mem. Dean's Coun. Tulane U. Law Sch., 1988-96, vice chmn. bldg. com., 1991-95; bd. dirs., mem. exec. com. Internat. Trade Mart, chmn. internat. bus. com., 1983-85; bd. dirs. World Trade Ctr.-New Orleans, 1983—, mem. port activity com. 1985-91, transp. com. 1991-95, 2000—, govt. affairs com. 1996-99; chmn. Task Force on Internat. Banking, 1982; mem. Mayor's Task Force on Drug Abuse, 1989-90. With USAAC, 1942-46, PTO; capt. JAGDR, USAF, 1950-. Recipient Leadership award AIAA, 1971, Yenni award Loyola U., New Orleans, 1979, New Orleans Times Picayune Loving Cup, 1986, First Citizen of the Learning Soc. Dean's award UNO Met. Coll., 1992; also various civic contbn. awards; co-recipient Silver Anvil award New Orleans chpt. Pub. Rels. Soc. Am., 1991. Fellow Coll. Labor and Employment Lawyers (mem. 5th cir. credentials com.); mem. ABA (labor and employment law and litig. sects., com. equal opportunity law, chmn. regional EEO com. liaison with equal opportunity commn., office of fed. contract compliance programs), D.C. Bar Assn., Fed. Bar Assn., La. Bar Assn. (past sec.-treas., bd. govs. 1957-60, editor jour. 1957-59, sec. spl. supreme ct. com. on drafting code jud. ethics), New Orleans Bar Assn. (dir. legal aid bur. 1954, chmn. standing com. legis. 1968, vice chmn. standing com. pub. rels. 1970-71), Am. Judicature Soc., La. Law Inst. (asst. sec.-treas. 1958-70), Am. Arbitration Assn. (bd. dirs., 1995-98, chmn. reg. adv. coun., chmn. reg. adv. coun. employment law cases, mem. panels-employment, employee benefits, large complex employment and comml. arbitration/mediation cases, Whitney North Seymour Sr. award 1991), So. Inst. Mgmt. (founder), AIM, U.S. C. of C. (urban and regional affairs com. 1970-73), La. C. of C. (bd. dirs. 1963-66), New Orleans and River Region C. of C. (v.p. met. devel. and urban affairs 1969, past chmn. labor rels. coun., bd. dirs. 1970-78, pres. 1971, dir., exec. com. 1972, ex officio mem., bd. dirs. 1979—), Mil. Order Fgn. Wars (vice comdr. La. Commandery 2000-02, comdr. 2003-2004), Nat. Arbitration Forum, Panel Arbitrators, Bienville Club, Pickwick Club, Plimsoll Club, Serra Club, So. Yacht Club, Sigma Chi (pres. alumni chpt. 1956). Roman Catholic. Home: 3039 Hudson Pl New Orleans LA 70131-5337 Office: Molony Law Firm 201 Saint Charles Ave Ste 3500 New Orleans LA 70170-3500 Office Phone: 504-582-1552. Business E-Mail: mjm@mmolony-law.com.

MOLPUS, DAVID LEE, reporter, journalist; b. July 1948; BA in Sociology, U. Miss.; MA in Comm., American U. With NPR, 1979—, staff corr., southeast, 1990—95, investigative reporter, 1995—; regular reporter Morning Edition, All Things Considered. Mem. bd. visitors Trinity Sch., Durham, NC; mem. parents com. Bryn Mawr Coll. Co-recipient Alfred I du-Pont Columbia U. award; recipient Outstanding Journalist award, Am. Legion, Nat. Headliners award, Silver Cindy award, Two Angel awards, Overseas Press Club award, George Foster Peabody award; Jefferson Fellow, U. Hawaii, Neiman Fellow, Harvard U., 1999—2000.

MOLPUS, DICK H. management company executive; b. Philadelphia, Miss., Sept. 7, 1949; s. Richard and Frances (Blount) M.; m. Sally Nash, May 27, 1971; children— Helen Nash, Richard Gregory BBA, U. Miss., 1971. V.p. mfg. Molpus Co., Phila., 1971-80; exec. dir. Gov's Office Fed.-State Programs, Jackson, Miss., 1980-83; sec. of state State of Miss., Jackson, 1984-96; pres., chmn. Molpus Co., Phila., 1996—; pres., dir. Molpus Woodlands Group, Jackson, Miss., 1996—; pres. Timberland Mgmt. Investment Orgn., Jackson, Miss. Dir. Citizens Bank and Trust Co. Vice pres. Miss. Agr. and Forestry Mus., 1979; campaign dir., chmn. bd. United Givers Fund, Nehshoba County, Miss., 1979-80; bd. dirs. Miss. PTA, 1980—; founder Parents for Pub. Schs. orgn., 1989. Recipient Friends of Children award Miss. Assn. Elem. Sch. Adminstrs., 1984, Pub. Ofcl. of Yr. award Miss. chpt. Am. Soc. for Pub. Adminstrn., 1985 Mem. Miss. Forestry Assn. (bd. dirs. 1980-87), Nat. Assn. Secs. of State (pres. 1992), Nature Conservancy (bd. dirs. Miss. chpt.), Sigma Chi, Omicron Delta Kappa, Pi Sigma Alpha (Theta Beta chpt.). Avocations: hiking, tennis, running, reading. Office: 654 N State St Jackson MS 39202

MOLSON, ERIC H. brewery company executive; b. Montreal, Can., Sept. 16, 1937; s. Thomas Henry Pentland and Celia Frances (Cantlie) Molson; m. Jane Mitchell, Apr. 16, 1966; 3 children. AB in chemistry, Princeton U., 1959. With Molson Inc., Montreal, Canada, 1960—, chmn. bd., 1988—; chancellor Concordia University, Montreal, Canada, 1993—. Office: Molson Inc 1555 Notre Dame St E Montreal QC Canada H2L 2R5

MOLTENI, AGOSTINO, pathology educator; b. Como, Lombardy, Italy, Nov. 12, 1933; came to U.S., 1963; s. Enrico and Antonia (Signorini) M.; m. Loredana Brizio, Sept. 5, 1963; children: Claudio Enrico, Ronald Stephen. MD, U. Milan, Italy, 1957; PhD in Pathology, SUNY, Buffalo, 1970. Lic. Italian Bd. Internal Medicine, 1963. Intern and resident in internal medicine U. Milan (Italy), 1957-62; asst. prof. U. Milan, 1957-63; chief rsch. sect. Farmitalia Drug Co., Milan, 1963-65; rsch. assoc. SUNY, Buffalo, 1965-69, asst. prof., 1969-71; assoc. prof. U. Kans., Kansas City, 1971-76; prof. pathology Northwestern U., Chgo., 1976-96, prof. emeritus, 1996—; prof. pathology and pharmacology U. Mo., Kansas City, 1996—, adj. prof. basic med. scis. Vis. prof. Harvard U., 1983-84. Editor, author: Endocrinology and Thermal Trauma, 1990, Menopause Update, 1992; exec. editor Current Pharmaceutical Design, 2000—, Nutrition Rsch., 2003; contbr. articles to profl. jours., chpts. to books. Recipient Sharer in Lasker award Lasker Found., N.Y.C., 1983, Rsch. Career Devel. award NIH, Washington, 1970, award Am. Heart Assn., Chgo., 1982. Fellow Am. Acad. Clin. Biochemistry; mem. Am. Acad. Pathology, Am. Soc. Investigative Pathology, Clin. Chemistry Soc., Endocrine Soc., Am. Assn. Clin. Chemistry. Achievements include patent for captopril as a cancer chemo-preventive agent; research on hypertension and hormonal regulation of cancer. Office: U Mo Truman Med Ctr 2301 Holmes St Kansas City MO 64108-2640

MOLTZ, JAMES EDWARD, investment brokerage company executive; b. Williamsport, Pa., July 25, 1932; s. George N. and Margaret L. (Abell) M.; m. Barbara Vance, Sept. 8, 1956; children: George Wilson, James Clay, John Thomas. BS, Williams Coll., 1954; MBA, Wharton Sch., U. Pa., 1956. Chartered fin. analyst. Fin. analyst Cyrus J. Lawrence Inc., N.Y.C., 1957-62, rsch. dir., 1962-64, gen. ptnr., 1964-71, mng. ptnr., 1971-73; chmn., pres. C.J. Lawrence/Deutsche Bank Securities Corp., N.Y.C., 1973-95; chief investment officer Deutsche Bank Securities, 1996-99; vice chmn. ISI Inc., N.Y.C., 1999—. Mem. fin. com. Williams Coll.; trustee Sterling and Francine Clark Art Inst.; hon. trustee Williamsport-Lycoming Found.; chmn. Woods Hole Oceanographic Inst.; trustee Rockefeller Bros. Fund, Edna McConnell Clark Found. Mem. Fin. Analysts Fedn., N.Y. Soc. Security Analysts (former dir.), Union League Club (N.Y.C.), Wee Burn Country Club (Darien), Windsor Club (Vero Beach), The Links (N.Y.C.). Home: 29 Indian Spring Trl Darien CT 06820-2109 Also: ISI Inc 535 Madison Ave New York NY 10022-4212 E-mail: jmoltz@isimgt.com.

MOLTZON, RICHARD FRANCIS, operations executive; b. Bklyn., Nov. 20, 1941; s. Arthur G. and Joan (Paladino) M.; m. Susan A. Anderson, Feb. 15, 1981; children: Paige, Kimberly, Michael, Keir. BS in Info. Systems Mgmt., U. Md., 1970. Various positions IBM Corp., various locations, 1965—70; plant mgr. Telex Terminal Communications, Inc., Raleigh, NC, 1970—75, Carnes Co. div. Wehr Steel, Sanford, NC, 1975—76; dir., gen. mgr. Modular Computer Systems, Inc., Ft. Lauderdale, Fla., 1980—87; v.p. ops. Profile Corp., Pompano Beach, Fla., 1987—88; dir. mfg. AMF, Inc., Herndon, Va., 1976—79, Documation, Inc., Melbourne, Fla., 1979—90, Concurrent Computer Corp., Oceanport, NJ, 1988—89; v.p. mfg. Internat. Tech. Corp., Clearwater, Fla., 1989—90; pres. The Realty Authority, Inc., 1990—92; v.p. ops. Combustion TEC, Divsn. of Eclipse Combustion, Inc., Orlando, Fla., 1992—99; sr. v.p. ops. Control Ctr. LLC, Orlando, 1999—2001; v.p. product sourcing and mgmt. Environ. Lighting Concepts, Inc., Tampa, Fla., 2002—. With U.S. Army, 1961-64. Mem. KC, Omicron Delta Kappa. Roman Catholic. Avocations: golf, jogging, writing. Office: Environ Lighting Concepts Inc 1214 W Cass St Tampa FL 33606 Office Phone: 813-621-0058. Business E-Mail: rickm@ott-lite.com. E-mail: rsmfl@tampabay.rr.com.

MOLYNEAUX, DAVID GLENN, newspaper travel editor; b. Marion, Ind., Oct. 16, 1945; s. Glenn Ingersol and Barbara Wingate (Draudt) M.; children: Miles David, Rebecca Susan; m. Judi Dash, May 15, 1994. BS in Econs., Miami U., Oxford, Ohio, 1967. Reporter The Plain Dealer, Cleve., 1967-75, city editor, 1976-78, assoc. editor, 1979-80, editorial page editor, 1980-82, travel editor, 1982—. V.p. bd. trustees Soc. Am. Travel Writers Found., 2002—. Editor: 75 Years-An Informal History of Shaker Heights, 1987. Trustee Shaker Heights Pub. Libr., 1987—95. With U.S. Army, 1968-70. Mem. Cleve. Press Club. Office: Plain Dealer 1801 Superior Ave E Cleveland OH 44114-2198

MOLZ, PHILIP JACK, management consultant; b. N.Y.C., Jan. 28, 1929; s. Philip and Mary H. Molz; m. Margaret J. Ralph, July 29, 1978; 1 child, Philene M. BS in Math., CCNY, 1953; PhD in Internat. Bus. Adminstrn., Ky.-Western. Cert. quality auditor; cert. ISO/QS 9000 lead assessor; cert. MBTI instr.; cert. SYMLOG instr.; cert. team facilitator; cert. graphologist IGAS. Accountant, auditor GE, Schenectady, N.Y., 1953-61, treas. Rio, Brazil, 1961-65, CFO Wolfenbüttel, Germany, 1965-68; corp. fin. analyst ITT, N.Y.C., 1968-70; CFO, v.p. fin. adminstrn. Xerox Latin Am., Stamford, Conn., 1970-74; CFO Abbott Labs. Internat., N. Chicago, Ill., 1974-78; sr. CFO Macmillan Pub., N.Y.C., 1978-80; pres., owner TSI Co., Bridgeport, Conn., 1980-85; pres. IJ Cos., Knoxville, Tenn., 1985-89; pres., owner PMP Internat. Group, Kansas City, Kans., 1989—; sr. mgmt. cons. Co-author: Controller's Handbook, 1974, Treasurer's Handbook, 1976, Quality Manual Reference, 1988. With CIC U.S. Army, 1951-53, Korea. Roman Catholic. Avocations: skiing, racquetball, ranching, painting, foreign languages. Home and Office: 11930 Stearns St Overland Park KS 66213-1962 Office Phone: 913-897-0428. E-mail: molzpmpint@aol.com.

MOLZ, REDMOND KATHLEEN, public administration educator; b. Balt., Mar. 5, 1928; d. Joseph T. and Regina (Barry) M. BS, Johns Hopkins U., 1949, MA, 1950; MALS, U. Mich., 1953; DLS, Columbia U., 1976. Librarian I and II Enoch Pratt Free Library, Balt., 1953-56; pub. relations officer Free Library of Phila., 1958-62; editor Wilson Library Bull. H.W. Wilson Co., Bronx, N.Y., 1962-68; chief planning staff Bur. Libraries and Learning Resources U.S. Office Edn., Washington, 1968-73; prof. library sci. Sch. Library Service Columbia U., N.Y.C., 1976-80, Melvil Dewey prof., 1980-93; prof. pub. affairs Sch. Internat. and Pub. Affairs, Columbia U., N.Y.C., 1993-99, prof. emeritus, 2000—. Cons. U.S. Nat. Commn. Librs. and Info. Sci., Washington, 1974-75, U.S. Adv. Commn. Intergovtl. Relations, Washington, 1979-80; mem. nat. adv. coun. The Sheridan Librs., Johns Hopkins U., 1997—. Author: Federal Policy and Library Support, 1976 (Ralph R. Shaw award 1977), National Planning for Library Service, 1935-75, 1984, Library Planning and

Policy Making: The Legacy of the Public and Private Sector, 1990, The Federal Roles in Support of Public Library Services, 1990, The Federal Roles in Support of Academic and Research Libraries, 1991; co-author (with Phyllis Dain) Civic Space/Cyberspace: The American Public Library in the Information Age, 1999; co-editor: The Metropolitan Library (anthology), 1972; author TV script Portraits in Print, 1959. Recipient Leadership Tng. award Fund for Adult Edn., 1956-57; recipient Disting. Alumnus award Sch. Library Sci. U. Mich., 1969, George Virgil Fuller award Columbia U., 1975, Johns Hopkins U. scholar, 1949-50, Horace H. Rackham fellow U. Mich., 1952-53, Columbia U. scholar, 1974-76, Tangley Oaks fellow, 1975-76; Council Library Resources Inc. Officers' grantee, 1974 Mem. ALA (councilor 1972-74, 76-80, exec. bd. 1976-80, chmn. legis. com. 1985-86), Freedom to Read Found. (dir. 1972-79, pres. 1977-79) Office: Columbia U Sch Internat & Pub Affairs New York NY 10027 Business E-Mail: rkm2@columbia.edu.

MOLZ, ROBERT JOSEPH, manufacturing executive; b. Yonkers, N.Y., Mar. 15, 1937; s. Philip and Maria Hilda (Geist) M.; m. Diane Ruth Horowitz, July 31, 1960 (dec. Feb. 2000); children— Jennifer Ann, Erica Beth BS, CCNY, 1960, MA, 1966; PhD, N.Y. Med. Coll., 1969. Tech. svcs. supr. E.I. DuPont de Neumours Co. Inc., Wilmington, Del., 1971-73, product mgr., 1973-75, quality assurance mgr. clin. sys. divsn., 1976, R&D mgr. clin. sys. divsn., 1976-84, asst. dir. R&D divsn. agrl. chem. dept., 1984-86, dir. departmental plans divsn., med. products dept., 1986-88, dir. med. scis. programs, cen. R&D, 1988-91, dir. new bus. devel., Cen. R&D, 1991-92, exec. dir. rsch. support, 1992-96, ret., 1996. Roman Catholic. Home: 306 Dove Dr Newark DE 19713-1212 E-mail: rmolz306@aol.com.

MOMAH, ETHEL CHUKWUEKWE, women's health nurse; b. Iyi-Enu, Ogidi, Nigeria, May 28, 1934; d. Zaccheus C. and Victoria U. (Orizu) Obi; m. Christian C. Momah, Nov. 21, 1959; children: Chukwudi, Adaora, Azuka. SRN, Harrow Hosp., Middlesex, U.K., 1956; SCM, Mothers Hosp., London, 1957; MTD, Midwife Tchrs. Coll., Surrey, U.K., 1964; BS, Upsala Coll., 1988. Cert. inpatient obstetric nurse Nat. Cert. Corp. Nurse-midwife Guy's Hosp., London, 1959; nursing sister, head nurse labor/delivery Univ. Coll. Hosp., Ibadan, Nigeria, 1960-62; midwife tutor Lagos (Nigeria) Island Maternity Hosp., 1963-66; nurse-midwife Brit. Hosp., Paris, 1966, Hosp. Cantonal, Geneva, 1967-78; staff nurse Univ. Hosp., St. Peter's Med. Ctr., New Brunswick, NJ, 1980—85, patient care coord., 1985-90, antenatal testing nurse, 1990—. Named Nurse of Yr. Women's Ambulatory Care Svc. St. Peters Univ. Hosp., 1997. Mem.: Nnewi USA, Inc. (v.p. 2003—), Assn. Women's Health, Obstetric and Neonatal Nurses, Anambra-Enugu States Assn. N.J., Nne-Egwu (dance mother). Office: St Peters Med Ctr New Brunswick NJ 08901 Personal E-mail: chikem@aol.com.

MOMBAERTS, PETER, biology professor; b. Leuven, Belgium, Sept. 27, 1962; s. Leon Mombaerts and Daisy Kortleven. MD, Cath. U. of Leuven Belgium, 1987; PhD in Biology, MIT, 1992. Postdoctoral fellow Columbia U., NY, 1993—95; asst. prof. biology Rockefeller U., N.Y.C., 1995—2001, assoc. prof., 2001—. Recipient Presdl. early career award for scientists and engrs. Pres. of U.S., 1997, career scientist award Irma T. Hirschl Trust, 1997-2000, Takasago award for rsch. in olfaction Assn. for Chemoreception Scis., 2001, Firmenich Fragrance award, 2001; Searle scholar, 1996-99, Basil O'Connor starter scholar March of Dimes Birth Defects Found., 1997-99, scholar Rita Allen Found., 1998-2001; Alfred P. Sloan rsch. fellow, 1997-99, Klingenstein fellow in neuroscis., 1997-2000, McKnight scholar in neurosci., 1997-2000, Guggenheim fellow, 1998-99. Office: Rockefeller U 1230 York Ave New York NY 10021 Fax: 212-327-7310. E-mail: peter@rockefeller.edu.

MOMMSEN, KATHARINA, retired German language and literature educator; b. Berlin, Sept. 18, 1925; came to U.S., 1974, naturalized, 1980; d. Hermann and Anna (Johannsen) Zimmer; m. Momme Mommsen, Dec. 23, 1948. Dr.phil., U. Tübingen, 1956; Dr. habil., Berlin Free U., 1962. Collaborator Acad. Scis., Berlin, 1949-61; assoc. prof. Free U., Berlin, 1962-70; prof. German Carleton U., Ottawa, Can., 1970-74; Albert Guerard prof. lit. Stanford U., 1974-94, ret., 1995. Vis. prof. U. Giessen, Tech. U. Berlin, 1965, State U. N.Y., Buffalo, 1966, U. Calif., San Diego, 1973 Author over 150 publs. on 18th-20th century German and comparative lit.; editor: Germanic Studies in America. Mem. Goethe Soc., Schiller Soc. Home: 980 Palo Alto Ave Palo Alto CA 94301-2223 E-mail: k.mommsen@comcast.net.

MONACELLI, GIANFRANCO, publishing executive; b. Milan; came to U.S., 1965; s. Rodolfo and Isabella (Paolillo) M.; m. Eugenia Hyman; children: Nurit, Fausto, Alexander. Dr., U. Turin, Italy, 1963, Acad. Santa Cecilia, 1964; BS, Mannes Coll., 1967; postgrad., Columbia U., 1969. Gen. mgr. Rizzoli Internat. Bookstore, N.Y.C., 1969-72, v.p., 1972-75; exec. v.p. Rizzoli Internat., Milan, 1975-78; pres., chief exec. officer Rizzoli Internat. Publs., Inc., N.Y.C., 1975-93, Rizzoli Internat. Bookstores, Inc., N.Y.C., 1975-92, Rizzoli Editore Corp., N.Y.C., 1975-89; sr. v.p. RCS Rizzoli Corp., N.Y.C., 1989-93; pres. USITAL Ltd., N.Y.C., 1993—. The Monacelli Press, Inc., N.Y.C., 1994—; v.p. Epikos Security Printing S.A., N.Y.C., 1997—. Trustee Mannes Coll., N.Y.C., 1979-81; pres. Weathersfield Music Festival, Vert., 1993—; mem. vis. com. U. Miami, Coral Gables, Fla., 1988-89. Recipient Met. Home Design 100 award, 1997, collaborative achievement award AIA, 1999; named Pub. of Yr., AIA, 1996. Mem. Century Assn., Am.-Italy Soc. (pres. 1993-94).

MONACO, ANTHONY JOHN, retired health facility administrator, writer; b. Steubenville, Ohio, Oct. 26, 1926; s. Antonio Monaco and Maria Concetta Di Crescentis; m. Wilna Mae Dellinger, Apr. 11, 1953; children: Gregg Anthony, Carol Ann Dawley, Susan Lorraine. BS, Duquesne U., 1949; MPH, U. Pitts., 1958. Exec. dir. So. Ill. Med. Ctr., Mt. Vernon, 1972—79; pres., CEO Healthcare Coun. Nca, Washington, 1980—96. Adminstr. Berwick Hosp., Pa., 1956—72. Author: (albums) The Songs And Wisdom Of David And Solomon, Scriptures From The Orient, The Spirit Is in the Form, The Challenge of Moses, The Mission of Jesus and John, The Recitations of Mohammed. With U.S. Army, 1944—45. Home: 13062 Gorham Way Woodbridge VA 22192-2948

MONACO, ANTHONY PETER, surgery educator, medical institute administrator; b. Phila., Mar. 12, 1932; s. Donoto Charles and Rose (Consalvi) M.; m. Mary Louise Oudens, June 4, 1960; children: Anthony Peter, Marck Churchill, Christopher Donoto, Lisa Oudens. BA in Chemistry, U. Pa., 1952; MD magna cum laude, Harvard U., 1956. Diplomate Am. Bd. Surgery, Am. Bd. Thoracic Surgery. Prof. surgery Harvard Med. Sch., Boston, 1977-95, Peter Medawar prof. transplantation surgery, 1995—, mem. bd. acad. advisors, 1974-83; chief transplantation div. Sears Surg. Research Lab. Boston City Hosp., 1967-73; sci. dir. Cancer Research Inst., New Eng. Deaconess Hosp., Boston, 1980—, chief div. organ transplantation, 1975—; Peter Medacor prof. transplantation surgery Harvard Med. Sch., 1995. Mem. surgery study sect. NIH, 1973-77, mem. clin. sci. study sect., 1983—; mem. adv. com. endstage renal disease Bur. Quality Assurance, HEW, 1975-76; mem. merit rev. bd. immunology VA, Washington, 1977-80; dir. Transplant Ctr. Beth Israel Deaconess Med. Ctr., Boston, 1998. Author: Biology of Tissue Transplantation, 1964; editor: Transplantation Procedures, 1970, 81; jour. Transplantation, 1969—. Trustee New Eng. Organ Bank, Boston, 1970—, chmn., 1981—; bd. dirs. Kidney Found. Mass., 1978-81; mem. Harvard Med. Sch. Alumni Council, 1979-81. Recipient nat. scholar Harvard Med. Sch., 1952-56; recipient Henry Asbury Christian award Harvard Med. Sch., 1956, Lederle Med. Faculty award Harvard Med. Sch., 1968 Fellow Royal Coll. Surgeons, Eng. (hon., The Medowar prize 1998); mem. Transplantation Soc. (charter, v.p. 1971-74, pres. 1985, internat. pres. 1986), Am. Soc. Transplant Surgeons (charter, treas. 1982-85, pres. 1985—), Am. Surg. Assn., Soc. Univ. Surgeons, ACS (pres. Mass. chpt. 1985). Clubs: Harvard (Boston). Home: 25 Farlow Rd Newton MA 02458-2407 E-mail: amonaco@caregroup.harvard.edu.

MONACO, CHRIS, historian, writer, documentary filmmaker; b. Ann Arbor, Mich., June 7, 1950; s. John Monaco and Marilyn Hermine Meeks; life ptnr. Rose Widman. BA, U. of Fla., 1973; MFA, U. of South Fla., 1977. Adv. bd. mem. Conservation Trust for Fla., 2001—. Editor: (book) A Plan for the Abolition of Slavery; dir./writer/prodr. (films) The Far Frontier (Outstanding Achievement, Fla. Trust for Hist. Preservation, 1999), (TV series) Education Showcase (Beacon Award, Nat. Cable TV Pub. Affairs Assn., 1994); author: Moses Levy of Florida: Jewish Utopian, 1782-1854. Bd. mem. Plan Bd., Micanopy, Fla., 1997—99. Recipient Hampton Dunn award, Fla. Hist. Soc., 1998, Flori award, Fla. Ind. Filmmakers Festival, 1979, Award of Excellence, Nat. Cable TV Advt. and Mktg., 1986—87; Faculty-Staff scholarship, U. of South Fla., 1976—77, Individual Artist fellowship, Fla. Fine Arts Coun., 1978. Mem.: So. Jewish Hist. Soc., Fla. Hist. Soc., Orgn. of Am. Historians. Achievements include discovery of the earliest and most important antislavery publication by an American Jew; identified the earliest Jewish communal settlement in the United States, M. E. Levy's Pilgrimage Plantation (1822-1835); established Moses Elias Levy as one of the most significant figures in early American Jewish history. Avocations: graphic arts, photography. Personal E-mail: csmonaco@cs.com.

MONACO, DANIEL JOSEPH, lawyer; b. Easton, Pa., May 12, 1922; s. Federico and Maria (Romano) M.; m. Marian P. Monaco, June 26, 1953 (div.); children: Denise E., Mimi D. AB with honors, Lafayette Coll., 1943; postgrad., U. Mich., 1944—45; MA, U. Chgo., 1946; JD, Stanford U., 1950. Bar: Calif. 1951, U.S. Dist. Ct. (no. dist.) Calif. 1951, U.S. Supreme Ct. 1961. Mem. faculty U. Miami, Fla., 1946-47; founder, of counsel Monaco, Anderlini & Finkelstein, San Mateo, Calif., 1953—; probate judge State of Calif., 1963-67. Real estate broker, Calif., 1957-67; judge pro tem Calif. Mcpl. and Superior Cts. Chmn. San Mateo County Dem. Ctrl. Com., 1960-61, Citizen World Ct.; mem. Calif. State Dem. Exec. Bd.; founder, pres. Circlon Internat., 1978-81; chmn. World Peace Through Law Ctr. com. to establish a Citizens' World Ct.; pres. peninsula com. UN Edni. Sci. & Cultural Orgn., 1955-59; mem. No. Calif. Coun. Fgn. Affairs, San Mateo County Hosp. Found. Bd. With U.S. Army, 1943-46, lt. USAR, 1946-50. Recipient Gentry Mag. Cmty. Stars award, 1997. Mem. ABA, ATLA, UN Assocs.-U.S.A. (pres. San Mateo County chpt. 1958-65), Calif. State Bar Assn., Calif. Trial Lawyers Assn. (bd. govs.), San Mateo County Trial Lawyers Assn. (pres.), World Jurist Assn. (pres. Ams., 1991-93, 2d v.p. 1995-97, 1st v.p. 1997-99, pres. 1999-2001, fin. chmn. 1995-2003, hon. pres. 2003—), Am. Bd. Trial Advs., Internat. Law Assn. World Citizens, Gorbachev Found., The Commonwealth Club, Peninsula Golf and Country Club. Democrat. Avocations: travel, international law. Home: 295 Darrell Rd Hillsborough CA 94010-7109 Office: 400 S El Camino Real Ste 700 San Mateo CA 94402-1744 Fax: 650-348-0962. Office Phone: 650-348-0102. E-mail: dukemonaco@aol.com.

MONACO, GRACE POWERS, lawyer; b. Union City, N.J., Sept. 3, 1938; s. Rea John and Grace Elizabeth (FitzGibbons) Powers; m. Lawrence Anthony Monaco, Aug. 10, 1963; children: Kathleen Rae(dec.), David Gordon, Stephen Michael, Peter Joseph. BA, Coll. Misericordia-Pa., 1960, LittD (hon.), 1979; JD, Georgetown U., 1963. Bar: D.C. 1964. Honor law grad. program Dept. Justice, Washington, 1963—64; pvt. practice Washington, 1965—66; assoc. Wheatley & Wollesen, Washington, 1967—78; ptnr. Fairman, Frisk & Monaco, Washington, 1978—82, White, Fine & Verville, Washington, 1983—88, of counsel, 1988—90; v.p. Emprise, Inc., 1988—91, Med. Care Mgmt. Corp., 1992—; dir. Med. Care Ombudsman Program, 1990—. Contbr. chpts. to books, articles to profl. jours. Chmn. bd. dirs. Candlelighters Childhood Cancer Found., 1978—90; chmn. bd. Capitol Hill Hosp., 1982—85; vice-chmn. Medlantic Healthcare Group, 1982—88, Medlantic Rsch. Found., 1989—95; adv. com. on oncogic drugs FDA, 1988—92; adv. com. on hematologic and neoplastic drugs U.S. Pharmacopeia, 1987—, pub. bd., 1990—2000; pub. mem. data and safety monitoring com. St. Jude's and Children's Oncology Group, 2000—. Named Day of June 28 in her honor, 1987; recipient Nat. award, Am. Cancer Soc., 1978, Achievement award, Capital Hill Cmty., 1985, Lloyd Bentsen Nat. award, 1995, 1997, Lifetime Achievement award, Nat. Coalition for Cancer Survivorship. Mem.: Fed. Energy Regulatory Bar Assn., Am. Health Lawyers Assn., Fed. Bar Assn., D.C. Bar Assn., Women's Bar Assn., Capitol Hill Restoration Soc. Democrat. Roman Catholic. Home: 874 Monument Dr Montross VA 22520 Office Phone: 804-493-7125.

MONACO, JOHN J. molecular genetics research educator; Prof. U. Cin. Sch. of Medicine, Howard Hughes Med. Inst., 1994-2001. Recipient Eli Lilly and Co. Rsch. award in Microbiology and Immunology, Am. Soc. Microbiology, 1995, Investigator award Pharmingen/Am. Assn. Immunologists, 1997. Office: U Cin Sch Medicine Dept Molecular Genetics 231 Albert Sabin Way Cincinnati OH 45267-0524 E-mail: john.monaco@uc.edu.

MONACO, LETITIA ADRIENNE, writer, photographer; d. Joseph Bernard Monaco and June Mary Roberta Hayles Jobic Monaco. BA in Comm. cum laude, Fla. Atlantic U., 1993. Prodr., writer Aug. Sand Productions, Inc., Delray Beach, Fla., 1996—2001; freelance writer, photographer, prodr. Jupiter, Fla., 2001—. Prodr.: (TV series) Travel with Heritage; author: (TV series) Pets N Vets, Discover America, Betsy and the Flag. Scholar, State of Mich., 1984—86. Avocations: swimming, gardening, sailing, painting, travel.

MONACO, ROBERT ANTHONY, radiologist; b. N.Y.C., July 5, 1945; s. Edmond V. and Jean M.; m. Susan Margaret Thompson; children: Kevin, Robert, Christopher, Sarah. BS, Siena Coll., 1967; MD, N.J. Coll. Medicine, 1971. Diplomate Am. Bd. Radiology, Am. Bd. Nuclear Medicine. Radiology resident N.J. Coll. Medicine, Newark, 1971-75; fellow in nuclear medicine med. ctr. NYU, N.Y.C., 1975-76; attending radiologist Med. Ctr. Ocean County, Point Pleasant, N.J., 1976-87, dir. dept. radiology, 1987—, sec. med. staff, 1998-2000. Gen. ptnr Point Pleasant Radiology Group, 1987—; sec. bd. dirs. Found. Med. Ctr. Ocean County, Mid-Coastal IPA, 1997; mng. ptnr. Open MRI of Wall, 1999—. Capt. USAR, 1972-76. Mem. Am. Coll. Radiology, Am. Coll. Nuclear Medicine, Radiol. Soc. N.J. Roman Catholic. Avocations: tennis, fishing, swimming. Home: 13 Bretwood Dr Colts Neck NJ 07722 Office: Open MRI of Wall Rt 34 Wall NJ 07719 Office Phone: 732-974-8060. E-mail: rammdo1@aol.com.

MONAGHAN, CHARLES, writer, editor; b. Bklyn., Sept. 25, 1932; e. Andrew and Pauline (Dunlevy) M.; m. E. Jennifer Walker, Jan. 19, 1933; children: Leila, Anthony, Claire. BA, Manhattan Coll., 1954; MA, NYU, 1958. Copy editor Reuters News Agy., London, 1960-62, N.Y. Times, Paris and N.Y.C., 1962-67; editor Book World supplement to Washington Post and Chgo. Tribune, N.Y.C., 1972-75, Facts on File, N.Y.C., 1975-76; mng. editor Travel & Leisure Mag., N.Y.C., 1977-83; food editor Bergen Record, Hackensack, N.J., 1990-92; Gilder Lehrman fellow Columbia U. Libr., 2002. Author: The Murrays of Murray Hill, 1998; editor: Zagat Survey of N.J. Restaurants, 1996-98; contbr. chpt. to 2 books, more than 500 articles to various publs. Committeeman N.Y. State Dem. Com., 1972-74; dist. leader Kings County Dem. Com., Bklyn., 1972-74; Dem. candidate for state senate, Bklyn., 1976; vice chmn. N.Y. State Dem. Coalition, 1972-75; pres. Ctrl. Bklyn. Ind. Dems., 1970-72, 82-84; co-donor Charles and E. Jennifer Monaghan Collection of Literacy Textbooks, Kenneth Spencer Rsch. Libr., U. Kans., 2001. Mem. Century Club. Home: 2164 Loring Circle Charlottesville VA 22901

MONAGHAN, CRAIG THOMAS, automotive executive; b. Phila. m. Mary Lou Murphy, Jul. 25, 1981; children: Shannon, Connor, Rand. BS industrial engr., Lehigh U., 1980; MBA in fin., Wharton U. Pa., 1985. Cert. mgmt. acct. Financial analyst General Motors, N.Y.C., 1985-87, mgr. overseas fin., 1987-88; dir. corp. fin. Squibb, Princeton, N.J., 1988-90; dir. internat. fin. Bristol-Myers Squibb, N.Y.C., 1990-91; asst. treas. Reader's Digest, Pleasantville, N.Y., 1991-92, controller europe, 1992—98; CFO iVillage.com, 1998-2000, AutoNation, Inc., Fort Lauderdale, FL, 2000—. Capt. U.S. Army, 1980-83. Mem. Inst. Mgmt. Accts. Avocations: fishing, golf, reading. Office: AutoNation Inc 110 SE 6th St Fort Lauderdale FL 33301

MONAGHAN, EILEEN See WHITAKER, EILEEN

MONAGHAN, JOHN J. managing editor; Mng. editor Providence Jour.-Bulletin. Office: Providence Jour-Bulletin 75 Fountain St Providence RI 02902-0050

MONAGHAN, KATHLEEN M. art museum director; b. Waterville, Maine, Sept. 6, 1936; d. Russell Vernon and Gloria Beatrice (LeClair) M. BA in Art History, U. Calif.-Santa Barbara, 1979, MA in Art History, 1981. Curatorial fellow Whitney Mus., N.Y.C., 1979, dir. Equitable Br., 1985-93; asst. curator Santa Barbara Mus., Calif., 1980-81, curator of art, 1983-84; curator, dir. Akron Art Mus., Ohio, 1984-85; dir. The Hyde Collection, Glens Falls, N.Y., 1994; exec. dir. Fresno Metropolitan Museum, Fresno, Calif. Mem. Internat. Com. on Mus., Coll. Art Assn. Address: Fresno Met Museum 1515 Van Ness Ave Fresno CA 93721

MONAGHAN, THOMAS JUSTIN, former prosecutor; JD, U. Nebr. Adj. faculty Coll. St. Mary, Nebr., 1985—91; ptnr. Monaghan, Tiedman & Lynch, Omaha, 1978—93; U.S. atty. Dept. Justice, Omaha, 1993—2001. Office: Monaghan Group 1321 Jones St Omaha NE 68102 E-mail: Tom@TheMonaghanGroup.com.

MONAGHAN, THOMAS STEPHEN, retired restaurant chain executive; b. Ann Arbor, Mich., Mar. 25, 1937; m. Marjorie Zybach, Aug. 25, 1962; children— Mary, Susan, Margaret, Barbara Student, Ferris State Coll., U. Mich.; PhD (hon.), Cleary Coll., 1982, Madonna Coll., 1983, Eastern Mich. U., 1984, So. Fla. U., 1985. Ptnr. Dominick's Pizza, Ypsilanti, Mich., 1960-65; pres., chmn. bd., founder, CEO Domino's Pizza, Inc., Ann Arbor, Mich., 1960-98; ret., 1998. Owner Detroit Tigers, 1983-92. Author: (autobiography) Pizza Tiger. Bd. dirs. Cleary Coll., Ypsilanti, Henry Ford Hosp., Detroit, Detroit Renaissance, U. Steubinville, Ohio, St. Joseph's Hosp. Devel. Bd., Ann Arbor. Served with USMC, 1956-59 Named Entrepreneur of Yr. Harvard U. Bus. Sch., 1984, Pizzaman of Yr. Nat. Assn. Pizza Owners, 1984; recipient Golden Plate award Am. Acad. Achievement, 1984, Golden Chain award Multi Unit Franchise Svc. Orgn., 1986, Horatio Alger award, 1986, Restaurant Bus. Leadership award, 1986, Pope John Paul II Family Fidelity award 1988, Pine Mission's Knights of Charity award, 1990, Semper Fidelis award USMC, 1990. Mem. Internat. Franchise Assn. (Entrepreneur of Yr. 1986), Nat. Restaurant Assn. (Silver Plate award 1985), Mich. Restaurant Assn., Ypsilanti C. of C., U. Mich. Pres.'s Club, Ann Arbor Pres.'s Assn., Missionary Vehicle Assn. (bd. dirs.), AIA (hon.), Mich. Soc. Architects (hon.). Clubs: Barton Hills Country (Ann Arbor). Lodges: K.C. Avocations: collecting frank lloyd wright furniture and memorabilia, classic cars.

MONAHAN, JOHN, medical products executive; BS, Univ. Coll., Dublin, Ireland; PhD in Biochemistry, McMaster U. Group rsch. chief Hoffmann LaRoche, Nutley, NJ, 1981—83; dir. molecular and cell biology Berlex Labs. Schering AG, 1983—88; v.p. R&D Somatix Therapy Corp. (now divsn. Cell Genesys, Inc.), 1989—92; pres., CEO, bd. dirs. Avigen, Inc., Alameda, Calif., 1992—. Office: Avigen Inc Ste 1000 1201 Harbor Bay Pky Alameda CA 94502

MONAHAN, JOHN T. law educator, psychologist; b. N.Y.C., Nov. 1, 1946; s. John Joseph and Dorothy (King) M.; m. Linda Costa, Aug. 24, 1969; children: Katherine, John. BA, SUNY, 1968; PhD, Ind. U., 1972. Asst. prof. U. Calif., Irvine, 1972-80; prof. U. Va., Charlottesville, 1980-84, Doherty prof., 1985—. Dir. mental health law MacArthur Found., Chgo., 1988-98. Author: Predicting Violent Behavior, 1981 (Guttmacher award 1981), Social Science in Law, 1998. Recipient Disting. Contbn. Pub. Policy award APA, Washington, 1990, Isaac Ray award, APA, N.Y., 1996. Mem. APA, Inst. of Medicine Office: U Va Sch Law 580 Massie Rd Charlottesville VA 22903-1738 E-mail: jmonahan@virginia.edu.

MONAHAN, PATRICK, singer; 2 children. Lead singer Train, 1994—. Singer: (albums) Train, 1998, Drops of Jupiter, 2001 (Song "Drops of Jupiter" won Grammy award for Best Rock Song, 2001), My Private Nation, 2003 (Song "Calling All Angels" nom. for Grammy award for Best Rock Vocal Performance by a Duo or Group, 2004), (songs) Meet Virginia, 1999, I Am, 1999, (from Spider-Man 2 soundtrack) Ordinary, 2004. Office: Columbia Records-SONY 1020 E Lafayette St Tallahassee FL 32301*

MONAHAN, THOMAS ANDREW, JR., accountant; b. Erie, Pa., Jan. 23, 1920; s. Thomas Andrew and Margaret (McEnery) M.; m. Patricia Tompkins, Sept. 4, 1948 (div. June 1983); children: Kathleen, Thomas P., Kevin, Margaret, Daniel; m. Rita Fargo, Sept. 3, 1985. BS, U. Pitts., 1942. CPA, Pa. Jr. acct. Price Waterhouse & Co., Pitts., 1942-43; sr. acct. Coopers & Lybrand, Phila., 1944-48; lectr. acctg. U. Pitts., 1948-49; pvt. practice acctg. Erie, 1949—. Lectr. Gannon U., Erie, 1965-78. Contbr. articles to profl. jours. Mem. AICPA (coun. mem. 1981-83), Pa. Inst. CPAs (v.p. 1971-72, coun. mem. 1968-71), Kahkwa Country Club (treas. Erie chpt. 1978-90). Home: 628 Delaware Ave Erie PA 16505-4602 Office: 100 State St Ste 500 Erie PA 16507-1457 Office Phone: 814-459-4345. Personal E-mail: monahan@erie.net.

MONAHAN, THOMAS PAUL, accountant; b. Pitts., Feb. 27, 1951; s. Thomas Andrew and Patricia (Tompkins) M.; m. Ellen McKeithan Easterby, Aug. 2, 1975; children: Kelley Kathleen, Thomas Patrick, Kyle Easterby, Tessa Elizabeth. BS in Acctg., U. S.C., 1973. CPA SC. Staff acct. Rogers, Brigman, Peterson & Co., Columbia, S.C., 1972-75, ptnr., 1975-82; chmn., treas., prin. GMK Assocs., Columbia, 1982—. Chmn., bd. dirs., treas. Devel. Properties, Inc.; trustee, pres. Town Theater Trust, 2000—. Mem. bus. coun. S. Dems., 1986—; bd. dirs. Cultural Coun. of Richland and Lexington Counties; pres. Town Theatre Trust; active Com. of 100. Mem. AICPA, S.C. Assn. CPAs, Columbia Stage Soc. (trustee, bd. dirs.), Spring Valley Country Club, Capital City Club, Palmetto Club, Zeta Beta Tau (trustee emeritus). Home: 1117 Adger Rd Columbia SC 29205-1942 Office: GMK Assoc Ste 2100 1201 Main St Columbia SC 29201-3263 Business E-Mail: tmonahan@gmka.com.

MONAHAN, WILLIAM T. computer company executive; BS in econ., St. Peter's Coll.; MBA, Rutgers U. V.p. electro and communication sys. group 3M, Austin; pres., CEO Nat. Info. Infrastructure Testbed, Inc., 1995—; CEO Imation Corp., Oakdale, Minn., 1996—2004, chmn., 1996—. Mem. bd. dirs. Hutchinson Technology, Inc., Pentair Inc. Office: Imation Corp 1 Imation Pl Oakdale MN 55128-3414

MONAN, JAMES DONALD, university chancellor; b. Blasdell, N.Y., Dec. 31, 1924; s. Edward Roland and Mary Gertrude (Ward) M. AB, Woodstock Coll., 1948, PhL, 1949, STL, 1956; PhD, U. Louvain, 1959; post-doctoral research, Munich, Oxford, Paris; LHD (hon.), Le Moyne Coll., 1973, St. Joseph's Coll., 1973, New Eng. Sch. Law, 1975, Northeastern U., 1975, U. Mass., 1984; LLD (hon.), Harvard U., 1982, Loyola U., Chgo., 1987, Nat. U. Ireland, 1991, Boston Coll., 1996, U. Mass., 1997, Western New Eng. Coll., 2000, Xavier U., 2001. Prof. philosophy Le Moyne Coll., Syracuse, N.Y., 1960-68, v.p., acad. dean, 1968-72; pres. Boston Coll., Chestnut Hill, Mass., 1972-96, chancellor, 1996—. Cons. to N.Y. Jesuit Provincial for Higher Edn., 1966-72; dir. First Nat. Bank Boston, Bank of Boston Corp., 1976-96; interim pres. Assn. Jesuit Colls. and Univs., 1996-97. Author: The Philosophy of Human Knowing, 1952, A Prelude to Metaphysics, 1967, Moral Knowledge and Its Methodology in Aristotle, 1968. Chmn. edn. div. Boston United Way, 1974; chmn. steering com. of coll. pres. under phase II of ct.-ordered desegregation Boston Pub. Sch. System, 1974-76, Coun. for Aid to Edn., 1985-96, The Partnership, 1984-94, Sr. Thea Bowman Black Cath. Ednl. Found., 1989-96, Gov.'s Internat. Trade Adv. Bd., 1992; bd. dirs. Nat. Mentoring Partnership, 1991—, Naval Acad. Endowment Trust, 1998—; co-chair Mass. Mentoring Partnership, 1992-2001, bd. dirs., 1992—; co-chmn. Mass. Summit for Promise of Our Youth, 1997; trustee Le Moyne Coll., 1961-69, 1995—, Fordham U., 1969-75, Boston Coll., 1972-96, Canisius Coll., 1976-82, Georgetown U., 1979-84, Sta WGBH, 1972-96; exec. com. Boston Higher Edn. Ptnrship, 1988-96; mem. com. to Review and Implement Apostolic Constitution Ex Corde Ecclesiae, 1991-96. Mem. Assn. Jesuit Colls. and Univs. (dir., chmn. exec. com. 1983-86), Assn. Ind. Colls. and Univs. Mass. (exec. com. 1988-91, chmn. 1977-78), Nat. Assn. Ind. Colls. and Univs., Harvard Bd. Overseers (com. to visit grad. sch. bus. adminstrn., 1987-93), Nat. Collegiate Athletic Assn. (pres.'s commn. 1984-88), Metaphys. Soc. Am., Jesuit Philos. Assn., Soc. Phenomenology and Existential Philosophy, Soc. Ancient Greek Philosophy. Home: Boston Coll Chestnut Hill MA 02467

MONARCHI, DAVID EDWARD, management scientist, information scientist, educator; b. Miami Beach, Fla., July 31, 1944; s. Joseph Louis and Elizabeth Rose (Muller) M.; 1 child by previous marriage, David Edward. BS in Engring. Physics, Colo. Sch. Mines, 1966; PhD (NDEA fellow), U. Ariz., 1972. Asst. dir. bus. rsch. divsn. U. Colo., Boulder, 1972-75, asst. prof. mgmt. sci./info. sys., 1972-75, assoc. prof. mgmt. sci. and info. sys., 1975-97, prof. info. sys., 1997—, assoc. dir. divsn. info. sci. rsch., 1982-84, chair info. sys. divsn., 1999—. Chair, Information System Divn., 1999—, prin. investigator of socio-econ. environ. systems for govtl. agys., and local govt. orgns., State of Colo., also info. systems for pvt. firms, 1972-77, use of virtual reality in distance learning Colo. Commn. Higher Edn., 1996—. Contbr. numerous articles on socio-econ. modeling, object-oriented sys., info. sys. and artificial intelligence to profl. jours. Mem. Gov.'s Energy Task Force Com., 1974. Mem. IEEE, Inst. for Mgmt. Sci., Assn. Computing Machinery, Am. Assn. Artificial Intelligence. Home: 32 Benthaven Pl Boulder CO 80305-6210 Office: U Colo Grad Sch Bus Boulder CO 80309-0001

MONAS, SIDNEY, retired history educator; b. N.Y.C., Sept. 15, 1924; s. David Joseph and Eva (Kiener) M.; m. Carolyn Babcock Munro, Sept. 5, 1948 (dec. Dec. 1985); children: Erica Beecher Monas, Deborah Gardner Monas Werdmuller, Stephen Sidney; m. Claire Anderson, Nov. 1, 1987. AB, Princeton U., 1948; A.M., Harvard U., 1951, PhD, 1955. Instr. history Amherst (Mass.) Coll., 1955-57; asst. prof. history Smith Coll., 1957-62; prof. history and lit., dir. Russian Studies Ctr., U. Rochester, N.Y., 1962-69; prof. Slavic lang. and history U. Tex., Austin, 1969-93, chmn. dept. Slavic langs., 1969-75; prof. emeritus, 1993—. Fulbright prof. Russian history Hebrew U., Jerusalem, 1966-67; sr. assoc. St. Antony's Coll., Oxford, 1984-85 Author: The Third Section, 1961; editor: Selected Works of N. Gumilev, 1972, Complete Poems of Osip Mandelstam, 1973; editorial bd. Jour. Modern History, 1967-70, Soviet Studies in Literature, from 1968, Am. Hist. Rev, 1980-83, PMLA, 1980-83; editor Slavic Rev., 1985-91; translator: Scenes from the Bathhouse, 1961, Crime and Punishment, 1968, Images of Space, 1997; editor, translator: Selected Essays of Osip Mandelstam, 1977. With AUS, 1943-45. Ford fellow, 1954-55, NEH fellow, 1973-74, fellow Humanities Rsch. Centre Australian Nat. U., 1977, Nat. Inst. Humanities U. Chgo., 1977-78, Rockefeller Humanities fellow, 1984-85 Mem. MLA, Am. Hist. Assn., Am. Assn. Advancement Slavic Studies. Office Phone: 512-471-5001.

MONASTRA, RICHARD J. secondary school educator; b. Phila., June 30, 1946; s. John J. and Carmella C. Monastra; 1 child, Rachel. BA, LaSalle Univ., Phila., 1968; MA, Temple Univ., Phila., 1972; MS, Drexel Univ., Phila., 1974. Lic. tchg. N.J., Pa. Classroom tchr. secondary sch. of Pa., 1968—88, Buena Regional H.S., Buena, NJ, 1989—. Adj. prof. Del. C.C., Media, Pa., 1977—; supr. student tchrs. Interboro H.S.; mentor new faculty Buena Regional H.S. Editor: (in house newspaper) Chalk Talk; author. Named Tchr. of the Yr., Interboro H.S. Mem.: BREA, NJEA, NEA, Assn. of Hist. Edn., Am. Psychology Assn. Achievements include 35 yrs. pub. sch. tchg. Avocation: baseball. Office: Buena Regional H S Weymouth Rd Buena NJ 08310

MONAT, WILLIAM ROBERT, university official; b. Biwabik, Minn., Oct. 9, 1924; s. William Stephen and Milda Aleta (Sundby) M.; m. Josephine Ann Sclafani, Sept. 9, 1951; children: Lise Ann, Kathryn, Margaret, William Michael, Eric. AA, Virginia (Minn.) Jr. Coll., 1947; BA magna cum laude, U. Minn., 1949, PhD, 1956; postgrad., Wayne U., 1949-50. Asst. prof. Wayne U., 1954-57; exec. asst. to Gov. Mich., 1957-60; asso. prof. Pa. State U., 1960-65, prof. polit. sci., 1965-69; asso. dir. Inst. Pub. Adminstrn., 1962-69; majority budget dir. Pa. Ho. of Reps., 1968-69; prof., chmn. dept. polit. sci. No. Ill. U., De Kalb, 1969-71, provost, 1976-78, Regency prof., 1986-92; Regency prof. emeritus, 1992—; pres. No. Ill. U., De Kalb, 1978-84; chancellor Ill. Bd. Regents, 1984-86; prof., dean faculties Baruch Coll., City U. N.Y., 1971-74, v.p. acad. affairs, 1974-76. Cons. USPHS, 1958, Office of Sec. Dept. Labor, 1963-64, Bur. Labor Stads., 1966, Office of Gov. Pa., 1968; bd. dirs. 1st Nat. Bank DeKalb, Castle Bancgroup, Inc. Author: Labor Goes to War, 1965, The Public Library and its Community, 1967, Politics, Poverty and Education, 1968; Editor: Public Adminstration in Era of Change, 1962, The Achieving Institution, 2000; contbr. articles to profl. jours. Mem. Gov.'s Commn. on Sci. and Tech., 1983-87; trustee Grad. Sch. Polit. Mgmt., N.Y., 1986-95; chmn. City of Dekalb Plan Commn.; trustee DeKalb Sanitary Dist., 2002— With AUS, 1943-46. Recipient Outstanding Achievement award U. Minn., 1981; decorated Bronze Star medal. Mem. Am. Polit. Sci. Assn., Am. Soc. Pub. Adminstrn., Phi Beta Kappa. Home: 1605 Mayflower Dr Dekalb IL 60115-1723 E-mail: wmonat@niu.edu.

MONATH, NORMAN, publishing company executive; b. Toronto, Ont., Can. came to U.S., naturalized, 1944; m. Pauline K. Farber, Aug. 30, 1952 (dec. Feb. 1972); children— Richard, Robert, Bruce. Dir. subsidiary rights Simon & Schuster, Inc., 1957-59; now cons.; founding pres. Cornerstone Library, Inc., N.Y.C., 1960—. Composer (with Walt Kelly) Songs of the Pogo, 2003; author: Know What You Want And Get It!, rev. edit., 2002; How To Play Popular Piano, 1984, How To Play Popular Guitar, 1994, (with William Cole) Folk Songs of England, Ireland, Scotland and Wales; editor (with Bobby Short) unpublished songs of Cole Porter; writer songs with Hal David, Sammy Cahn; recs. by Dionne Warwick, Supremes, Mitch Miller, Jerry Vale, Burns and Allen, Burl Ives. Served with Signal Corps AUS, 1942-45. Mem. ASCAP. Inventor Bali word game, 1954. Home: 3545 S Ocean Blvd Apt 101 Palm Beach FL 33480-5716 E-mail: nmonath@cs.com.

MONATH, THOMAS PATRICK, physician; b. Hewlett Harbor, N.Y., Aug. 13, 1940; s. Paul E. and Elizabeth (Burger) M.; m. Jennifer Sanderson Mills, Sept., 25, 1964 (div. 1981); 1 child, Andrea; m. Margaret Blake Garvan, June 25, 1988; 1 child, Nicholas. AB, Harvard U., 1962, MD, 1966. Diplomate Am. Bd. Internal Medicine. Intern, resident Peter Bent Brigham Hosp., Boston, 1966-68, 73-74; med. officer Ctr. Disease Control, Atlanta, 1968-72, dir. div. Vector-Borne Diseases Ft. Collins, Colo., 1974-88; chief virology div. U.S. Army Med. Rsch. Inst. Infectious Diseases, Frederick, Md., 1988-92; chief sci. officer Acambis Inc., Cambridge, Mass., 1992—. Cons. WHO, Geneva, 1974—; chmn. panel on virus diseases Am. Inst. Biol. Scis., Washington, 1978-88; mem. U.S.-Japan Coop. Med. Sci. Program, 1974-78; vis. rsch. fellow U. Ibadan, Nigeria, 1970-72; sr. sci. and tech. adv. to dir. CIA, 1998—. Author, editor: St. Louis Encephalitis, 1980, The Arboviruses, 1988, Field's Virology, 1990, 95; contbr. more than 350 articles to sci. jours. Capt. USPHS, 1968-88, col. U.S. Army, 1988-92. Recipient Presidential Citation, Med. Amateur Radio Coun., 1974, Nat. Young Meml. award Am. Com. on Anthropod-Borne Viruses, 1986, Meritorious Svc. medal UPSHS, 1978. Fellow ACP, Royal Soc. Tropical Med. Hygiene; mem. Am. Soc. Tropical Med. Hygiene (councillor 1976-80, Richard M. Taylor award, 2002, Walter Reed medal 2002), Am. Com. on Arthopod-Borne Viruses (chmn. 1980-82), Am. Soc. Virology, Internat. Soc. Infectious Diseases, Soc. Mucosal Immunology. Democrat. Home: 21 Finn Rd Harvard MA 01451-1925 Office: Acambis 38 Sidney St Cambridge MA 02139-4169 Office Phone: 617-761-4310. E-mail: tom.monath@acambis.com.

MONCK, MAUREEN F. psychoanalyst; b. N.Y.C., Dec. 12, 1938; d. Lawrence Finnerty and Mary Henrietta Crean-Lynch; m. Robert A. Monck, June 16, 1962 (dec. Jan. 1983); children: Merritt Monck-Rowley, Erinna Monck Bernstein, Caitlin Monck-Marcellino. BS, Georgetown U., 1960; PhD, NYU, 1968; MA in Art History, Cooper Hewitt-New Sch., 1999; postdoctoral cert. in adult psychoanalysis, Derner Inst.; postdoctoral cert. in child and adolescent psychotherapy, Adelphi U. Pvt. practice psychoanalyst, Muttontown, NY, 1968—; guest curator Oyster Bay (N.Y.) Hist. Soc., 1997—; supr. of psychotherapy Metro. Ctr. for Mental Health, N.Y.C., 1997—; dir. psychotherapy tng. program L.I. Inst. for Psychoanalysis, East Meadow, NY, 1985—93; dir. nursing program C.W. Post - L.I. Univ., Brookville, NY, 1972—75.

MONCREIFF, ROBERT P. lawyer; b. Evanston, Ill., Mar. 26, 1930; s. W. Philip and Maxine E. M.; m. Elisabeth M.; children: Anne, Philip, Jane. BA, Yale U., 1952; MA, Oxford U., Eng., 1954; LLB, Harvard U., 1957. Bar: Mass. 1957. Assoc. Palmer & Dodge, Boston, 1957-62, ptnr., 1963-95, of counsel, 1995—. City councillor, Cambridge, Mass., 1970-74. Office: Palmer & Dodge LLP 111 Huntington at Prudential Ctr Boston MA 02199-7613 Office Phone: 617-239-0290. E-mail: rmoncreiff@palmerdodge.com.

MONCRIEF, MICHAEL JOSEPH, mayor, former state legislator; b. Houston, Sept. 5, 1943; s. Richard Barto Sr. and Mary Daisy (Wiley) M.; m. Rosemary Brewer, Dec. 31, 1980; children: Troy L., Mitchell K. BS, Tarleton State U., 1968. Ind. oil prodr., Ft. Worth, 1969—; mem. Tex. Ho. of Reps., 1971—72, mem. appropriations com., 1970-72; judge Tarrant County, Tex., 1974—86; mem. Tex. State Senate, 1991—2003; pres. pro tempore Tex. Senate, 2001; mayor City of Ft. Worth, 2003—. Past mem. Tarrant County Drug Abuse Bd., Lone Star Transp. Authority, N. Central Tex. Council of Govts.; mem. Gov.'s Blue Ribbon Commn. on Criminal Justice, many other groups. Bd. dirs. Assn. Retarded Citizens (hon. chmn.), chmn. Neighborhood Resources Devel. Coun., Tarrant County Med., Edn. and Rsch. Found., Tarrant County Mental Health Assn., Drug Treatment Ctr., Tarrant County Juvenile Bd., Ft. Worth State Sch., Inst. Pub. Svc. Tarleton State U., Tex. Affiliate Adv. Com., AHA, Alliance for Children (hon.), Paul Quinn Coll., Tex. Preservation Bd., US Olympic Com., and several others; pres. Neighborhood Health Horizons; past bd. dirs. Gill Children Svcs., Inc., Ft. Worth Libr. Bd., Longhorn Coun. Boy Scouts Am., Tex. Soc. for Prevention of Blindness, North Tex., many others; dir. North Tex. Commn., 2003-; affiliated with Ft. Worth C. of C., Tex. Arts Alliance, Muscular Dystrophy Assn., Inc. and several others. Named Outstanding Cmty. Leader Am., 1970, Outstanding Young Man Am., 1971, Newsmaker of Yr., 1974, 78, Freshman Legislator of Yr., Tex. Legislature, 1971, AARP award, 1997, Common Cause Star of Tex. Pub. Svc. award, 2000, Kiwanis Club ' Community Builder" award, 2002, many other honors. Mem. Tarleton Alumni Assn. (Disting. Alumni 1977), Ind. Petroleum Assn. Am., Am. Judicature Soc., Nat. Coll. Probate Judges, Ft. Worth Res. Police Officers, other profl. orgns. Avocations: skiing, tennis, golf, hunting rattlesnakes and alligators. Office: Office of Mayor 1000 Throckmorton St Fort Worth TX 76102 Business E-Mail: Mayor@fortworthgov.org.

MONCRIEF, WILLIAM ALVIN, JR., oil and gas producer; b. Little Rock, Mar. 27, 1920; d. William Alvin and Elizabeth (Bright) M.; m. Deborah Beggs, Jan. 30, 1947; children: William A. III, R.W., C.B., T.O. BS in Petroleum Engring., U. Tex., Austin, 1942. Registered profl. engr., Tex. Ptnr. Moncrief Oil, Ft. Worth, 1945—; dir. First Republic Bank, Dallas. Regent, U. Tex. system. Served to ensign USNR, 1944-45, PTO. Named Disting. Engring. Grad. U. Tex.-Austin, 1983 Mem.: Shady Oaks of Ft. Worth (pres.); Eldorado (Indian Wells, Calif.); Brookhollow (Dallas). Republican. Episcopalian. Office: Moncrief Oil Moncrief Bldg 9th And Commerce St Fort Worth TX 76102

MONCURE, JOHN LEWIS, lawyer; b. Houston, Nov. 4, 1930; s. Walter Raleigh Daniel and Margaret (Atkins) M.; m. Norma Steed, Dec. 29, 1954 (dec. June 1982); children: John Carter, Michael Lewis, Douglas Lee, Stuart Richard, Mary Margaret; m. Margaret Edmonston, Nov. 12, 1983. BBA, U. Houston, 1953; JD, U. Tex., 1956. Bar: Tex. 1956. Assoc. Butler, Binion, Rice, Cook & Knapp, Houston, 1956-68; ptnr. Prappas, Moncure & Eidman, Houston, 1969-86, John L. Moncure and Assocs., Houston, 1987—. Lectr. bus. law U. Houston, 1958-59, 68-69 Mem. sch. bd. St. Thomas Episcopal Sch., Houston, 1965-78; mem. vestry St. Thomas Episc. Ch., 1975-78. Named Distinguished Alumni Coll. Bus., U. Houston, 1968 Fellow Am. Coll. Probate Counsel; mem. Am., Tex.; Houston bar assns., Assn. Christian Schs. (trustee), Coll. Bus. Alumni Assn. U. Houston (pres., dir.), U. Houston Alumni Fedn. (treas., dir.), Sigma Alpha Epsilon. Republican. Home: 1220 W Clay Houston TX 77019 Office: 1200 River Oaks Tower 3730 Kirby Dr Houston TX 77098-3905 Office Phone: 713-831-6821.

MONDALE, JOAN ADAMS, wife of former Vice President of United States; b. Eugene, Oreg., Aug. 8, 1930; d. John Maxwell and Eleanor Jane (Hall) Adams; m. Walter F. Mondale, Dec. 27, 1955; children— Theodore, Eleanor Jane, William Hall. BA, Macalester Coll., 1952. Asst. slide librarian Boston Mus. Fine Arts, 1952-53; asst. in edn. Mpls. Inst. of Arts, 1953-57; weekly tour guide Nat. Gallery of Art, Washington, 1965-74; hostess Washington Whirl-A-Round, 1975-76; ambassador to Japan, 1993-96. Author: Politics in Art, 1972, Letters from Japan, 1998. Mem. bd. govs. Women's Nat. Dem. Club; hon. chmn. Fed. Coun. on Arts and Humanities, 1978-80; bd. dirs. Associated Coun. of Arts, 1973-75, Reading Is Fundamental, Am. Craft Coun., N.Y.C., 1981-88, J.F.K. Ctr. Performing Arts, 1981-90, Walker Art Ctr., Mpls., 1987-93, Minn. Orch., Mpls., 1988-93, 97-2003, St. Paul Chamber Orch., 1988-90, Northern Clay Ctr., 1988-93, St. Paul, 1988-93, Nancy Hauser Dance Co., Mpls., 1989-93, Minn. Landmarks, 1991-93, Walker Art Ctr., Mpls., 1997-2003; trustee Macalester Coll., 1986—; mem. commn. Nat. Portrait Gallery, 1997—; chair Hiawatha Light Rail Transit Pub. Art and Design com., 2000—. Walker Art Ctr., 2003-. Mem. Phi Beta Kappa Epsilon. Democrat. Presbyterian. Home: 2116 Irving Ave S Minneapolis MN 55405-2541 E-mail: joan.mondale@mac.com.

MONDALE, WALTER FREDERICK, former Vice President of United States, diplomat, lawyer; b. Ceylon, Minn., Jan. 5, 1928; s. Theodore Sigvaard and Claribel Hope (Cowan) M.; m. Joan Adams, Dec. 27, 1955;children: Theodore, Eleanor, William. BA cum laude, U. Minn., 1951, LLB, 1956. Bar: Minn. 1956. Law clk. Minn. Supreme Ct.; pvt. practice law, 1956-60; atty. gen. State of Minn., 1960-64; U.S. senator from Minn., 1964-77; v.p. served under Pres. James Carter U.S., 1977-81; mem. Nat. Security Council, 1977-81; mem. firm Winston & Strawn, 1981-87; U.S. amb. to Japan Tokyo, 1993-96; presidential rep. Indonesia, 1998; ptnr. Dorsey & Whitney, Mpls., 1987—93, 1997—. Author: The Accountability of Power*Toward a Responsible Presidency, 1975; mem. Minn. Law Rev. Dem. nominee for Pres. U.S., 1984. With U.S. Army, 1951-53. Presbyterian. Democrat.*

MONDELLO, MARK T. manufacturing executive; BSME, U. South Fla. Former project mgr. on comml. and def.-related aerospace programs Moog, Inc.; prodn. line supr. Jabil Cir., St. Petersburg, Fla., 1992—93, project mgr., 1993—97, v.p. bus. devel., 1997—99, sr. v.p. bus. devel., 1999—2002, COO, 2002—. Bd. dirs. All Children's Hosp. Office: Jabil Cir 10560 9th St N Saint Petersburg FL 33716

MONDER, STEVEN I. orchestra executive; b. Newark, Mar. 12, 1945; B in Mus. Edn., Coll. Conservatory of Music, 1968, M in Mus. Edn., 1970. Tchr. orch., chorus, humanities McAuley H.S., Cin., 1970-71; prodn. mgr. Cin. Symphony Orch., 1971, asst. mgr., 1971-74, mgr., 1974-76, gen. mgr., 1976-89, exec. dir., 1989-98, pres., 1998—. Prodn. stage mgr. Cin. Opera Co., 1970, 71, adminstr., 1973. Office: Cin Symphony Orch Music Hall 1241 Elm St Cincinnati OH 45210-2231

MONDESI, RAUL, professional baseball player; b. San Cristobal, Dominican Republic, Mar. 12, 1971; Grad. H.S., Dominican Republic. Outfield L.A. Dodgers, 1993-99, Toronto Blue Jays, 2000—. Named N.L Rookie of The Yr., Baseball Writers' Assn. Am., 1994, N.L Rookie of Yr., The Sporting News, 1994; selected to N.L. All-Star Team, 1995. Office: Toronto Blue Jays One Blue Jays Way Ste 3200 Toronto ON Canada M5V 1J1

MONDICH, EDWARD H. protective services official; m. Ruth A. Johnson, Nov. 21, 1990; children: Madison May, Harrison Ross. BA, Ind. U., 1983. Commd. 2d lt. USAF, 1977, advanced through grades, 1990; tchr. algebra Pasadena (Tex.) Ind. Sch. Dist., 1995—98; patrol officer Pasadena Police Dept., 1998—2002, crime scene investigator, 2002—. Author: The Crystalline Rain, 2003. Bd. dirs. Pasadena Police Patrolmen's Union, 2002, polit. action com., 2003—. Mem.: Internat. Assn. Identification. Avocations: writing, guitar, swimming, flying. Office: Pasadena Police Dept 1114 Davis Pasadena TX 77502

MONDINO, BARTLY J. ophthalmologist; b. Sacramento, Calif., May 24, 1945; married; children: Kara, Kristen. BA in Med. Scis., Stanford U., 1967, MD, 1971. Diplomate Am. Bd. Ophthalmology. Intern Stanford (Calif.) U. Hosp., 1971-72; ophthalmology resident N.Y. Hosp., Cornell U., N.Y.C., 1972-75; fellow in cornea, external disease U. Pitts. Sch. Medicine - Eye and Ear Hosp., Pitts., 1975-76, asst. prof. ophthalmology, 1976-79, assoc. prof. ophthalmology, 1979-82; dir. Charles T. Campbell Microbiology Lab. Eye and Ear Hosp., Pitts., 1978-82; assoc. prof. ophthalmology UCLA - Jules Stein Eye Inst., L.A., 1982-83, prof. ophthalmology, 1983—, Wasserman Endowed chair dept. ophthalmology, 1988—; chief cornea-external disease divsn. UCLA, 1991-99, chmn. dept. ophthalmology, 1994—; dir. UCLA - Jules Stein Eye Inst., 1994—; with exec. program for acad. healthcare mgmt. The John E. Anderson Grad. Sch. Mgmt./UCLA, 1992. Bd. dirs. Charles R. Drew U. of Medicine and Sci., L.A., Braille Inst., L.A.; mem. adv. com. Rsch. Study Club, Murrieta, Calif., 1994—, scientific adv. panel on ophthalmology Calif. Med. Assn., San Francisco, 1994—. Editl. bd.: Am. Jour. Ophthalmology, Chgo., 1992—, ophthalmic Surgery and Lasers, 1995—, Ophthalmology Times, 1996—, Ophthalmic Practice (Can.), 1996—; editor-in-chief: EYE Newsletter, 1994—; co-chair corneal diseases program planning panel of Nat. Eye Inst.'s Vision Rsch. Program Planning Subcom., Bethesda, md., 1997—, others. Recipient scholarship Stanford U. Sch. Medicine, Rsch. to Prevent Blindness Manpower award 1983-84, Rsch. to Prevent Blindness Sr. Scientific Investigator's award 1994, various lectureships, others. Mem. AMA, Assn. for Rsch. in Vision and Ophthalmology, Assn. Univ. Profs. of Ophthalmology, Am. Acad. Ophthalmology, Calif. Assn. Ophthalmology, Calif. Cornea Club, Calif. Med. Assn., Contact Lens Assn. of Ophthalmologists, Eye Bank Assn. of Am., L.A. County Med. Assn., L.A. Soc. Ophthalmology, Ophthalmology Rsch. Found., Ophthalmic Surgery and Laser Therapy, Rsch. Study Club. Office: 100 Stein Plz # 2-142 Los Angeles CA 90095-7000 E-mail: mondino@jsei.ucla.edu.

MONDLIN, MARVIN, retail executive, antiquarian book dealer; b. Bklyn., July 1, 1927; s. Samuel and Thelma (Schultz) M.; m. Phyllis Grossman, Oct. 23, 1962 (div. 1968); 1 child, Gerri; m. Irene Szmulewicz, Sept. 4, 1970. Student, Cornell U., 1945; student of Aesthetic Realism, with Eli Siegel, 1945—68; student, CCNY, 1948, Bklyn. Coll., 1969—71. Ptnr. Amory Books, N.Y.C., 1953-59; clk. Strand Book Store, N.Y.C., 1951, estate book buyer, 1959-71, 74-76, sr. exec. v.p., 1976—2004; proprietor Am. Sunbeam Pub., NYC, 1996—. Bus. mgr. Definition Press., N.Y.C., 1957; cataloger U. Cath. de Louvain, Belgium, 1972. Author: Appraisals: A Guide for Bookmen, 1997; co-author: Book Row, An Anecdotal and Pictorial History of the Antiquarian Book Trade, 2003; proofreader, copy editor Dover Publs., N.Y.C., 1958; editor Yearbook of Internat. Assocs., 1974. Mem.: Typophiles, Ephemera Soc. Am., European Soc. History of Phtography, Am. Photog. Hist. Soc., Bibliog. Soc. London, Bibliog. Soc. Am., Appraisers Assn. Am., Camera Club. Avocations: photography, non-silver processes lab. work, natural history, horticulture, music. Home and Office: 889 Broadway Apt 3C New York NY 10003-1219 Office Phone: 212-982-8189. E-mail: marvinmondlin@verizon.net.

MONDRAGON, MARC RENE, dentist, pharmacist, consultant; b. Nogales, Ariz., Jan. 3, 1959; s. Adalbert and Olga (de Leon) Mondragon; m. Kim Ziegler; children: Nicole, Alexis. Student, Washington U., 1977—79; BS in Pharmacy, U. Ariz., 1983; DDS, Marquette U., 1987. Cert. pharmacist Ariz., 1987, dentist. Pharmacist Walgreens, Tucson, 1983—90; pvt. dental practice Tucson, 1987—; dentist St. Elizabeth of Hungry, Tucson, 1987—. Pharmacy cons. Price Smart, San Diego, 2000—. Mem.: ADA, AM. Pharm. Assn., Saguara Bus. Club (pres. 1989—99). Republican. Roman Catholic. Avocations: astronomy, automobiles, family. Office: 3320 N Campbell Ave 100 Tucson AZ 85719 Office Phone: 520-322-0600.

MONDRY, LAWRENCE N. retail sales professional; V.p., nat. mdse. mgr. Highland Superstones, Inc., 1983-88, 88-90; sr. v.p., gen. mdse. mgr. CompUSA, Inc., Dallas, 1990-93, exec. v.p. merchandising, 1993—2000, pres., COO, 2000—03, CEO, 2003—. Office: Comp USA Inc 14951 Dallas Pkwy Dallas TX 75254-7892*

MONDUL, DONALD DAVID, patent lawyer; b. Miami, Fla., Aug. 24, 1945; s. David Donald and Marian Wright (Heck) M.; children: Alison Marian, Ashley Megan; m. Anna Marie Towle, Oct. 12, 1996. BS in Physics, U.S. Naval Acad., 1967; MBA, Roosevelt U., 1976; JD, John Marshall Law Sch., 1979. Bar: Ill. 1979, Fla. 1980, Tex. 1998; U.S. Patent Office 1980; U.S. Ct. Appeals (fed. cir.) 1982; U.S. Supreme Ct. 1990. Commd. ensign USN, 1967, advanced through grades to comdr., 1977; mktg. rep. Control Data Corp., Chgo., 1977-79; patent atty. Square D Co., Palatine, Ill., 1979-81; group patent counsel Ill. Tool Works Inc., Chgo., 1981-87; assoc. Cook, Wetzel & Egan, Chgo., 1987-89; ptnr. Foley & Lardner, Chgo. and Milw., 1989-95; sr. patent atty. IBM, East Fishkill, NY, 1995-96; gen. patent counsel Ericsson, Inc., Richardson, Tex., 1996-99; pvt. practice Dallas, 1999—. Comdr., USNR, 1967-87. Achievements include patents for Electrical Encoding Device; Method and Apparatus for Determining the Product of Two Numbers; Apparatus for Providing Power to Selected Portions of a Multiplying Device; Method and Apparatus for Multiplying a Plurality of N Numbers; Method and for Establishing an Operating Parameter for a Power Supply Device; Apparatus and Method for Locating Objects in a Three-Dimensional Space; Air Baffle Apparatus. Office: 6631 Lovington Dr Dallas TX 75252-2519 Office Phone: 972-758-1955. E-mail: dmondul@aol.com.

MONE, MICHAEL A. social welfare administrator; BS in Pharmacy, U. Fla., 1981, JD, 1985. From atty. to sr. atty. Fla. Dept. Profl. Regulation, 1986-91; staff atty. USP, 1991-93; asst. atty. gen. Office Atty. Gen., State Fla., 1993-96. Contbr. articles to profl. jours. Mem. Nat. Assn. of Bds. of Pharamcy (exec. com. 2002-), The Fla. Bar Assn., Govt. Bar Assn. (bd. dirs. 1994-96), Am. Soc. for Pharmacy Law, Am. Pharm. Assn. (spkr. elect/spkr. ho. dels. 2000-2002), Fla. Pharmacy Assn. (parliamentarian, ho. of dels. 1993-96, 99, vice spkr. 1996-97, spkr. 1997-98), Leon County Pharmacy Assn. (pres. 1995-96), Ky. Pharmacists Assn., Ky. Soc. of Health-System Pharmacists, Am. Soc. of Health-System Pharmacists. Office: Ky Bd Pharmacy 23 Millcreek Pk Frankfort KY 40601-9230

MONE, ROBERT PAUL, lawyer; b. Columbus, Ohio, July 23, 1934; s. Henry P. and Ann E. (Freedlund) M.; m. Lucille L. Willman, May 3, 1960; children: Robert, Maria, Andrew, Richard. BA, U. Dayton, 1956; JD, U. Notre Dame, 1959. Bar: Ohio 1959. Law clk.to presiding judge U.S. Dist. Ct. (no. dist.) Ohio, Cleve., 1960-62; assoc. George, Greek, King, et al, Columbus, 1962-66, ptnr., 1966-79, McConnaughey, Stradley, et al, Columbus, 1979-81, Thompson Hine LLP, Columbus, 1981—. Cpl. U.S. Army, 1959-60. Mem. ABA, Ohio State Bar Assn., Energy Bar Assn., Columbus Bar Assn., Nat. Generation and Transmission Coop. Lawyers Assn. (1st pres.), Rotary. Home: 2300 Tremont Rd Columbus OH 43221-3706 Office: Thompson Hine LLP 10 W Broad St Ste 700 Columbus OH 43215-3435

MONEAR, EDWIN EVERETT, writer; b. Colgate, N.D., July 3, 1917; s. Edwin Ernest and Eleanor Loretta Monear; m. Aileen Glenna Riley, Aug. 31, 1948; children: Robert Gordon, Gail Edwina, Daryl Alan. Student, Newspaper Inst. Am., 1946—47; LLB, LaSalle U., 1955; postgrad., Writer's Digest Sch., 1997—99. Cert. real estate broker Wis., Fla., appraiser Wis. Railroad agt.m telegrapher SooLine Railroad, 1937—49, dispatcher, 1949—52, Duluth South Shore & Atlantic, Marquette, 1952—61, SooLine Railroad, Stevens Point, Wis., 1961—74; realtor Ed Monear Realty, 1963—81, various real estate developers, Ft. Myers, Fla., 1982—95; freelance writer, 1995—. With U.S. Army, 1944—46. Mem.: Shriners, Masons. Avocation: writing. Home: 2828 Jackson St A-3 Fort Myers FL 33901-6203

MONEGRO, FRANCISCO, psychology educator, alternative medicine consultant; b. La Vega, Dominican Republic, Apr. 20, 1949; s. Francisco Monegro-Fdez and Ana A. (Pena) Monegro. Grad. cum laude, Pontifical U., Santiago, Dominican Republic, 1973; grad. psychology, Autonomous U. Santo Domingo, 1978, MD, 1986; MA in Ednl. Psychology, Tech. Inst. Santo Domingo, 1981; PhD in Nutrition, LaSalle U., Mandeville, La., 1993. Cert. natural health profl., hypnotherapist, profl. biofeedback profl.; diplomate in behavioral medicine, diplomate in pain mgmt.; lic. in psychology Autonomous U. Santo Domingo, 1978. Tchr. Peace H.S., Santo Domingo, Dominican Republic, 1975-76; dir. dept. psychology Holy Trinity Ednl. Ctr., Santo Domingo, 1978-80; prof. Sch. Medicine Tech. Inst. Santo Domingo, 1986-87; dir. dept. psychology Interam. U., Santo Domingo, 1988-89; prof. psychology and medicine Autonomous U. Santo Domingo, 1978-89, psychologist, coun-

seling dept., 1979-84; staff mem. spl. edn. Bd. Edn. Dist. X, Bronx, N.Y., 1991-93; founder, chmn. N.Y. Inst. for Holistic Life, N.Y.C., 1991—; prof. psychology CUNY at HCC, Bronx, 1990—. Founder, pioneer in behavioral medicine Behavioral Medicine Clinic, Santo Domingo, 1987-94. Author: Biofeedback-Bio-retroalimentacion, 1988, Holistic Behavioral Medicine, 1993, Biomagnetic Medicine: Secrets and Power of Magnetic Energy, 1996, Psychology and Life Mind, Body and Society, 1997, Commonly Prescribed Psychiatric Drugs. A Guide for Clinicians and Care Takers, 2003, A Guidebook for Behavioral Evaluators, 2003, (interactive CD-ROMs) Psychology and Life, 2000, Developmental Aphasia, 2002, Commonly Prescribed Psychiatric Drugs. A Guide for Clinicians and Care Takers, 2003, A Guide for Behavioral Evaluators, 2003; editor, pub.: BOEST, 1978, Dominican Bull. Behavioral Medicine, 1987, Holistic Life/Vida Holistica, 1991, others. Mem. Dominican Psychol. Assn. (treas. 1978-79), Soc. Behavioral Medicine, Assn. for Advancement of Behavior Therapy, Am. Acad. Pain Mgmt., Assn. for Applied Psychophysiology and Biofeedback. Democrat. Roman Catholic. Avocations: computers, golf, basketball, swimming, travel. Home: PO Box 302 Bronx NY 10458-0302 Office: NY Inst for Holistic Life 976 Mclean Ave Ste 370 Yonkers NY 10704-4105 Office Phone: 718-364-2202. Personal E-mail: holisticlife@msn.com.

MONELLO, JOSEPH D. financial asset management company executive; b. 1945; V.p., contr. Kansas City (Mo.) Southern Industries, Inc., CFO, head fin. svcs. divsn., 1997—. Office: 114 W 11th St Kansas City MO 64105-1804 Fax: 816-983-1459.

MONEO, JOSÉ RAFAEL, architecture educator; b. Tudela, Navarra, Spain, May 9, 1937; s. Rafael and Maria Teresa (Vallés); m. Belén Feduchi; children: Belén, Teresa, Clara Matilde. Degree in architecture, Madrid, 1961, DArch, 1963. Fellow Spanish Acad., Rome, 1963-65; prof. arch. Barcelona, Spain, 1970-80, Madrid, 1981-85, Sch. Design, Harvard U., Cambridge, Mass., 1985—, chmn. dept. arch., 1985-90, Josep Lluís Sert prof. arch., 1991—. Prin. works include Bankinter, Madrid, Logroñó Hall, Mérida Roman Art Mus., Atocha Sta., Madrid, Seville (Spain) Airport, Auditorium of Barcelona, Kursaal Auditorium and Congress Ctr., Thyssen-Bornemesza Mus., Madrid, Davis Mus. Wellesley Coll., Miro Found. Mus., Mallorca, Diagonal Bldg., Barcelona, Museums of Modern Art and Architecture, Stockholm, 1994-98, City Hall Extension, Urcia, 1998, Barcelona Concert Hall & Cultural Ctr., 1999, Kursaal Concert Hall & Cultural Ctr., San Sebastian, 1999, Audrey Jone Beck Bldg., Mus. Fine Arts, Houston, 2000. Recipient Arnold W. Brunner Mem. prize in Architecture, Am. Acad. Arts and Letters, 1993, Pritzker Arch. prize, 1996, Gold medal Internat. Union of Archs., 1996, Antonio Feltrinelli prize, 1998. Office: Harvard U Dept Arch Cambridge MA 02138-3000 E-mail: rmoneo@gsd.harvard.edu.

MONEY, ARTHUR LEWIS, electronics executive; b. Stockton, Calif. m. Sharon Money; children: Jennifer, David. BSME, San Jose State U., 1965; MSME, U. Santa Clara, 1970. Data analysis of space and missile sys. Lockheed Missiles and Space Co., 1962-72; engr., then mgr. and dir. various units ESL Inc., Sunnyvale, Calif., 1972-84, v.p., gen. mgr. signals, analysis and sys. divsn., 1984-89, v.p. advanced programs and devel., 1989-90, pres., 1990-95; v.p., dep. gen. mgr. TRW Avionics and Surveillance Group, Sunnyvale, Calif., 1995; asst. sec. Air Force for Acquisition, Washington, 1996-99; sr. civilian ofcl. officer to Asst. Sec. Def. C3I Air Force Pentagon, Washington, 1998-99; asst. sec. def., chief info. officer Dept. Def., Washington, 1999—. Chmn. United Way campaign Santa Clara County, 1993; bd. dirs. Valley Med. Ctr. Found., Am. Leadership Forum, Santa Clara County Mfg. Group, Silicon Valley Art Fund, San Jose U. Sch. Engring. Mem. AIAA, Am. Electronics Assn., Navy League Am., Assn. Old Crows (exec. mgmt. medal), Air Force Assn., Planetary Soc., Am. Def. Preparedness Assn., Security Affairs Support Assn., Def. and Space Consortium (former chmn.). Office: 6000 Defense Pentagon Washington DC 20301-6000

MONEY, JOHN WILLIAM, retired psychologist, educator; b. Morrinsville, New Zealand, July 8, 1921; came to U.S., 1947, naturalized, 1962; s. Frank and Ruth (Read) M. MA with honors, Victoria U. Coll., New Zealand, 1943; postgrad., U. Pitts., 1947; PhD, Harvard U., 1952; DHL (hon.), Hofstra U., 1992. Jr. lectr. philosophy and psychology U. Otago, New Zealand, 1945-47; part-time vis. lectr. Bryn Mawr Coll., Pa., 1952-53; mem. faculty Johns Hopkins U., Balt., 1951—, prof. med. psychology, 1972-86, assoc. prof. pediatrics, 1959-86, prof. emeritus med. psychology and pediatrics, 1986—; psychologist Johns Hopkins Hosp., 1955—, founder psychohormonal research unit, 1951, founding mem. gender identity com., 1966. Vis. prof. pediats. Albert Einstein Coll. Medicine, 1969, U. Nebr. Coll. Medicine, 1972; vis. prof. endocrinology Harvard U., 1970; vis. prof. ob-gyn. U. Conn., 1975; Rachford lectr. Children's Hosp., Cin., 1969; bd. dirs. Sex Info. and Edn. Coun. U.S., 1965-68, Neighborhood Family Planning Ctr., 1970-82; mem. task force homosexuality NIMH, 1967-69; mem. study sect. devel. and behavioral scis. NIH, 1970-74; mem. task force on nomenclature Am. Psychiat. Assn., 1977-79, 85-87; pres. Am. Found. Gender and Genital Medicine and Sci., 1978—; bd. advisors Elysium Inst., 1980-2000; mem. external com. for rev. of Inst. for Sex Rsch., Ind. U., 1980; mem. sci. adv. bd. Kinsey Inst. for Rsch. in Sex, Gender and Reprodn., 1982-97; hon. chmn. internat. adv. bd. Nat. Inst. Rsch. in Sex Edn., Counseling and Therapy, 1991; Kan Tongpo vis. prof. dept. psychiatry U. Hong Kong, 1994. Mem. editl. bd. numerous jours.; field editor Medicine and Law: an Internat. Jour., 1982-95; subject (book) John Money: A Tribute, 1991, (TV documentary) Coming Home, 1999. Recipient Hofheimer prize Am. Psychiat. Assn., 1956, Gold medal Children's Hosp., Phila., 1966, citation Am. Urol. Assn., 1975, Harry Benjamin medal of honor Erickson Ednl. Found., 1976, Outstanding Contbn. award Md. Psychol. Assn., 1976, Lindemann lectr. pediatrics Cornell U., 1983, Bernadine Disting. lectr. U. Mo., 1985, Maurice W. Laufer Meml. lectr. Bradley Hosp. and Brown U., 1986, Disting. Scholar award Harry Benjamin Internat. Gender Dysphoria Assn., 1987, Outstanding Rsch. Accomplishments award Nat. Inst. Child Health and Human Devel., 1987, Gloria Scientae Polish award, 1991, Lifetime Outstanding award for Treatment of Sex Offenders, 1991, Richard J. Cross award Robert Wood Johnson Med. Sch., 1992, Career Achievement award N.Y. Soc. Forensic Scis., 1994, Coun. of Sex Edn. and Parenthood Internat. award, 1994, gold medal for lifetime achievement World Assn. Sexology, 1995, sexology medal Am. Acad. Clin. Sexology, 1996, Magnus Hirschfeld medal for sexual scis., 2002; named Sexologist of Yr. Polish Acad. Sex. Sci., 1988; James McKeen Cattell fellow Am. Psychol. Soc., 1993; Rm. in his name Kinsey Inst., Ind. U., 2003, wing at Ea. Southland Gallery Inc., Gore, New Zealand, 2003. Fellow: AAAS (life), Soc. Sci. Study Sex (charter, pres. 1974—76, award 1976, Past Pres. award 1987, Kinsey award western regional chpt. 1996, John Money award named in his honor 2003), Nat. Inst. Rsch. Sex Edn., Counseling and Therapy (hon.), Harriet Lane Alumni Soc.; mem.: APA (master lectr. 1975, Disting. Sci. award 1985), Nat. Assn. Sexology (chief patron), Internat. Coll. Pediats., Md. Soc. Med. Rsch., N.Y. Acad. Scis., Internat. Soc. Psychoneuroendocrinology, European Soc. Pediat. Endocrinology (corr.), Asian Fedn. for Sexology (hon.), Soc. Andaluza de Sexologia (hon.), Assn. Sexologists (life), Am. Assn. Sex Educators, Counselors and Therapists (hon. awards 1976, 1985), Columbian Sexol. Soc. (hon.), Czechoslovak Sexology Soc. (hon.; internat. adv. bd. 1995), New Zealand Soc. on Sexology (hon.; life), Soc. Brasileira de Sexologia (hon.), Can. Sex Rsch. Forum (hon.), Assn. Especialistas en Sexologia (hon.), Internat. Acad. Sex Rsch. (charter, award 1991), Lawson Wilkins Pediat. Endocrine Soc. (founder), Soc. Pediat. Psychology, Internat. Orgn. Study Human Devel., Deutsche Gesellschaft fur Sexualforschung. Home: 2104 E Madison St Baltimore MD 21205-2337 Office: Johns Hopkins Hosp Baltimore MD 21205 Business E-Mail: jmoney@mail.jhmi.edu. *It has always been my policy to combine research with clinical care, academic teaching and public education. I have combined a lifelong interest in world travel and in research by lecturing on all continents except Antarctica.*

MONEYPENNY, EDWARD WILLIAM, retail executive; b. Long Branch, N.J., Jan. 28, 1942; s. Edward Henry and Eleanor Kathleen (O'Hagan) M.; m. Connie Wills, Feb. 19, 1966; children: Matthew, Jonathan, Christopher. BS in Acctg., St. Joseph's U., 1964; MS in Acctg. Sci., U. Ill., 1967. CPA, Pa. Audit mgr. Coopers & Lybrand, Phila., 1970-76; mgr. corp. acctg. Sun Co., Inc., Radnor, Pa., 1976-78; v.p. fin. adminstrn. Sun Prodn. Co., Dallas, 1978-81; v.p. fin., CFO Oryx Energy Co. (formerly Sun Exploration and Prodn. Co.), Dallas, 1981-91; sr. v.p. fin., CFO Oryx Energy Co., Dallas, 1992-94, exec. v.p. fin., CFO, bd. dirs., 1994-99; sr. v.p. fin., CFO Fla. Progress Corp., St. Petersburg, Fla., 1999-2000; exec. v.p. fin., CFO Covanta Energy Corp., Fairfield, NJ, 2001; sr. v.p. fin., CFO 7-Eleven, Inc., Dallas, 2002—. Chmn. dean's bus. coun. U. Ill. Sch. Bus., 2000-01, mem. exec. com., dean's bus. coun., 2002-. 1st lt. U.S. Army, 1967-70. Home: 4712 Stonehollow Way Dallas TX 75287-7524 Office: 7-Eleven Inc City Place Ctr East N Haskill and N Central Dallas TX 75204

MONFORTE-MUÑOZ, HECTOR L. pathologist; b. San Diego, Feb. 17, 1959; s. Hector Monforte and Maria De La Luz Muñoz; m. Lana Jill Webster, Nov. 17, 1990; children: Laura, Mariana, Hector. MD, U. Autonoma de Guadalajara, 1984. Diplomate Am. Bd. Pathology, Am. Bd. Pediat. Pathology. Resident in pathology U. Miami - Jackson Meml. Hosp., Miami, Fla., 1985-89; fellow in pathology M.D. Anderson Cancer Ctr., Houston, 1989-90, U. So. Calif. Children's Hosp., L.A., 1990-91; pathologist All Children's Hosp., St. Petersburg, Fla., 1991-93, Children's Hosp. of L.A., 1993—, dir. autopsy program, 1998—, dir. insitu hybridization, 1996—. Contbr. articles to sci. and profl. jours. Recipient Clin. Fellow award Am. Cancer Soc., 1987-88. Fellow Coll. of Am. Pathologists; mem. Soc. for Pediat. Pathology. Roman Catholic. Avocation: model trains and ships. Office: Childrens Hosp LA 4650 Sunset Blvd Box 43 Los Angeles CA 90027-6062

MONG, ROBERT WILLIAM, JR., media executive; b. Fremont, Ohio, Jan. 22, 1949; s. Robert William and Betty (Dwyer) M.; m. Carla Beth Sweet, July 25, 1975 (div. 1979); m. Diane Elizabeth Reischel, Jan. 23, 1988; children: Eric Robert, Elizabeth Diana. BA, Haverford (Pa.) Coll., 1971; graduate exec. bus. program, Stanford U., 1997. Reporter Cin. Post, 1973-75, Capital Times, Madison, Wis., 1975-77; city editor Madison Press Connection, 1977-79; asst. city editor Dallas Morning News, 1979-80, bus. editor, 1980-81, projects editor, 1981-83, asst. mng. editor, 1983-88, dep. mng. editor, 1988-90, mng. editor, 1990 96; pub. Owensboro Messenger-Inquirer, 1996-97; exec. v.p. A.H. Belo Corp., Dallas, 1997-98; pres., gen. mgr. The Dallas Morning News, Dallas, 1998-2001, pres., editor, 2001—. Mem. Am. Soc. Newspaper Editors, Newspaper Assn. Am., Southern Newspaper Pubs. Assn., Am. Press Inst. (bd. dirs.). Office: The Dallas Morning News PO Box 655237 508 Young St Dallas TX 75202-4828 Office Phone: 214-977-8222. Business E-Mail: bmong@dallasnews.com.

MONGAN, JAMES JOHN, healthcare system administrator; b. San Francisco, Apr. 10, 1942; s. Martin and Audrey Vera (Cunningham) M.; m. Jean Trotter Holmes, Apr. 22, 1972; children: John Holmes, Sarah Holmes. Student, U. Calif., Berkeley, 1959-62; BA, Stanford U., 1963, MD, 1967. Intern Kaiser Found. Hosp., San Francisco, 1967-68; med. officer USPHS, Denver, 1968-70; profl. staff mem. U.S. Senate Fin. Com., Washington, 1970-77; dep. asst. sec. for health HEW, Washington, 1977-79; assoc. dir. human resources Domestic Policy Staff, White House, 1979-81; asst. surgeon gen. USPHS, 1979-81; exec. dir. Truman Med. Center, U. Mo., Kansas City, 1981-96; dean sch. medicine U. Mo., Kansas City, 1987-96; pres. Mass. Gen. Hosp., 1996—2002; pres., CEO Partners HealthCare Sys. Inc, Boston, 2003—. Prof. healthcare policy, prof. medicine Harvard Med. Sch.; mem. com. on consequences of uninsured Inst. Medicine; chair adv. com. Commonwealth Fund Task Force; mem. Kaiser Commn. on Medicaid and the Uninsured. Trustee Kaiser Family Found., 1993—2001; chmn. Greater Boston C. of C., 2004—. Mem. NAS, Inst. Medicine, Am. Hosp. Assn. (trustee 1988-91), Am. Assn. Teaching Hospitals. (bd. dirs. coun. tchg hospitals. 1984-90). Office: Partners HealthCare Sys Inc Prudential Tower 800 Boylston St Ste 1150 Boston MA 02199-8001*

MONGE, JAY PARRY, lawyer; b. N.Y.C., Mar. 15, 1943; s. Joseph Paul and Dorothy Emma (Oschmann) M.; m. Julia T. Burdick, 1966 (div. 1994); children: Justin Parry, Lindsay Newton; m. Elizabeth Ann Tracy, 1994. AB, Harvard U., 1966; LLB, U. Va., 1969. Bar: Ill. 1969, N.Y. 1981, N.C. 2003. Assoc. Mayer, Brown, Rowe & Maw, LLP, Chgo., 1969-75, ptnr., 1976-79, N.Y.C., 1980-99, mng. ptnr., 1981-94, ptnr. Charlotte, NC, 2000—. Contbr. legal commentaries Ill. Inst. Continuing Legal Edn., 1974, 78, 81, 84, 87, 93, 96, 2002. Trustee Wagner Coll., 1996-2002. Mem. ABA, Assn. Bar City N.Y., Chgo. Club, Onwentsia Club, Sky Club, Westchester Country Club, Charlotte City Club, Carmel Country Club, Quail Hollow Club. Office: Mayer Brown Rowe & Maw LLP 214 N Tryon St Ste 3800 Charlotte NC 28202 E-mail: jmonge@mayerbrownrowe.com.

MONGUIO, LUIS, Spanish language educator; b. Tarragona, Catalonia, Spain, June 25, 1908; came to U.S., 1939; s. Francisco and Matilde (Primatesta) M.; m. Helen Arnett, Mar. 7, 1933 (dec. Mar. 1976); m. Alicia de Colombi, Aug. 8, 1979. Licenciado en Derecho, U. Madrid, 1928; LLD (hon.), Mills Coll., 1963. Vice consul to 1st clas consul Spanish Fgn. Svc., 1930-39; from instr. to prof. Mills Coll., Oakland, Calif., 1942-43, 46-57; prof. Spanish U. Calif., Berkeley, 1954-75, prof. emeritus, 1975—. Vis. prof. dept. Hispanic and Italian SUNY, Albany, 1981-88, 93-94, hon. prof. Nat. U. of San Marcos, Lima, Peru, 1970—, U. Lima, 1992—. Author: Cesar Vallejo, 1952, es edit., 1960, Poesia postmodernista peruana, 1954, Don Jose Joaquin de Mora y el Peru del Ochocientos, 1967, Notas y estudios de literatura peruana, 1972; editor: Poesias de Don Felipe Pardo Y Aliaga, 1973, others. With AUS, 1944-46. Decorated Knight's Cross Civillian Merit, Spanish Govt., 1931; Teaching fellow Spanish U. Calif., Berkeley, 1940-42, Guggenheim Found. fellow, 1951. Mem. Internat. Inst. Ibero-Am. Literature (pres. 1951-53, mem. editl. bd. 1953-59), MLA (chmn. Spanish Am. lit. group 1951, 61, 66), Am. Soc. Aesthetics, Asociacion Internat. de Hispanistas, Peruvian Acad. Lang. (corr. mem.), others. Home and Office: 24 Berkshire Dr Clifton Park NY 12065-1711

MONHEIT, MOLLY JANE, artist; b. Yakima, Wash., Aug. 5, 1922; d. Laurel LaVergne and Edna (Bracewell) Lugar; m. John Palmer Ruckel (dec. 1952); children: Gail Ruckel, Andrew Ruckel; m. George Monheit, Dec. 7, 1952; 1 child, William. Student, Art Ctr. Sch., Calif., 1942; BA magna cum laude, Wash. State U., 1944; MA, Mills Coll., 1947. Clk., artist, cons. Papyrus, Lafayette, Calif., 1976-97; ret., 1997. Exhibited paintings in Wash., Tex., and Calif.; prin. works represented in permanent collections in pvt. homes and museums in 38 countries; contbr. articles to Bird Watchers Digest. Precinct chmn. Reps., Lafayette, 1954-70; social chmn. Valley View Estates, Lafayette, 1954-80. Recipient fellowship Aurelia Reinhart, 1945-47. Mem. Soc. Western Artists, Am. Women Artists, East Bay Watercolor Soc., Audubon Soc., Am. Field Svc. (pres. 1970), Diablo Art Assn. (pres.), Alpha Gamma Delta. Presbyterian. Avocations: travel on birding trips, track and field (Calif. sr. champion 100m for age group 1980-92). Home: 1107 Magnolia Ln Lafayette CA 94549-3118

MONICA, MARTIN J. law enforcement officer, educator; b. San Francisco; BA in Social Work, San Jose State U., 1980; postgrad., Golden Gate U., 1997—. Officer San Jose (Calif.) Police Dept., 1983—. Editor Am. Assn. for Pub. Adminstrs., San Jose; contbr. articles to Law and Order, Cmty. Policing Consortium. Bd. dirs. Housing Human Svcs., Sunnyvale, Calif. Mem. Latino Police Officers Assn., Hydrocephalaus Assn., Calif. Narcotics Officers Assn., No. Calif. Gang Investigators Assn. Democrat. Roman Catholic. Avocations: running, bicycling, camping, photography. Office: San Jose Police Dept 201 W Mission St San Jose CA 95110-1701 Address: 3061 Harding Ave Santa Clara CA 95051 E-mail: 4acinom@home.com.

MONICAL, ROBERT DUANE, engineering company executive; b. Morgan County, Ind., Apr. 30, 1925; s. William Blaine and Mary Elizabeth (Lang) M.; m. Carol Arnetha Dean, Aug. 10, 1947 (dec. 1979); children: Mary Christine, Stuart Dean, Dwight Lee; m. Sharon Kelly Eastwood, July 13, 1980; 1 stepson, Jeffrey David Eastwood. BSC.E., Purdue U., 1948, MSC.E., 1949. Engr. N.Y.C. R.R., Cin., 1949-51, So. Rwy., Cin., 1951; design engr. Pierce & Gruber (Cons. Engrs.), Indpls., 1952-54; founder, partner Monical & Wolverton (Cons. Engrs.), Indpls., 1954-63, Monical Assocs., Indpls., 1963—, pres., 1975—; v.p. Zurwelle-Whittaker, Inc. (Engrs. and Land Surveyors), Miami Beach, Fla., 1975-90; pres. Monical Engring., Inc., 2004—. Mem. Ind. Adminstrv. Bldg. Council, 1969-75; chmn., 1973-75; mem. Meridian St. Preservation Commn., 1971-75, Ind. State Bd. of Registration for Profl. Engrs. and Land Surveyors, 1976-84, chmn., 1979, 83 Served with USNR, 1943-46, USAR, 1948-53. Mem. ASCE (Outstanding Civil Engr. award Ind. sect. 1987), Cons. Engrs. Ind. (pres. 1969, Cons. Recognition award 1986), Am. Cons. Engrs. Council (pres. 1978-79), Ind. Soc. Profl. Engrs. (Engr. of Yr. 1980), Nat. Soc. Profl. Engrs., Am. Concrete Inst., Am. Inst. Steel Constrn., Indpls. Sci. and Engring. Found. (pres. 1992-93), Am. Legion, Lions, Masons, Shriners. Mem. Christian Ch. Home and Office: 18831 Whitcomb Pl Noblesville IN 46060-8130 Office Phone: 317-770-1266. Personal E-mail: rduane1@aol.com.

MONIRUZZAMAN, MOHAMMED, chemical engineer; b. Rajshahi, Bangladesh, Feb. 15, 1960; came to U.S., 1994; s. Mohammed Abdul Majid and Khukon Bibi. BS, U. Dhaka, Bangladesh, 1982, MS, 1983; D of Engring., Kanazawa U., Japan, 1993. Microbiologist Pfizer Labs. (Bangladesh) Ltd., Dhaka, 1987-88, Rhone-Poulenc (Bangladesh) Ltd., Dhaka, 1988-89; rsch. assoc. dept. chem. engring. Tex. A&M U., College Station, 1994-96; rsch. assoc. dept. microbiology U. Fla., Gainesville, 1996-98; cons. BC Internat., Jennings, La., 1998—. Vis. scientist fermentation biochemistry rsch. unit USDA, Peoria, Ill., 1995-96. Author: (book chpts.) Fuels and Chemicals from Biomass, 1997, Recent Research Developments in Biotechnology and Bioengineering, 1998; patentee in field; reviewer: Applied Biochemistry and Biotechnology, 1995—; contbr. numerous articles and papers to profl. jours. Monbusho scholar Japanese Ministry of Edn., 1989. Mem. Am. Soc. for Microbiology. Achievements include development of cellobiose fermenting bacterial strain by genetic engineering; design and publication of new model for bacterial saccharide metabolism; optimization of steam explosion and ammonia fiber explosion processes for lignocellulose pretreatment; development of unique process for lignocellulose hydrozates fermentation to ethanol by genetically engineered bacteria. Office: BC Internat PO Box 389 11107 Campbell Wells Rd Jennings LA 70546

MONISMITH, CARL LEROY, civil engineering educator; b. Harrisburg, Pa., Oct. 23, 1926; s. Carl Samuel and Camilla Frances (Geidt) M. BSCE, U. Calif., Berkeley, 1950, MSCE, 1954. Registered civil engr., Calif. From instr. to prof. civil engring. U. Calif., Berkeley, 1951—, chmn. dept. civil engring., 1974-79, Robert Horonjeff prof. civil engring., 1986—, prof. emeritus, 1996. Cons. Chevron Rsch. Co., Richmond, Calif., 1957-93, U.S. Army CE Waterways Expt. Sta., Vicksburg, Miss., 1968—, B.A. Vallerga, Inc., Oakland, Calif., 1980-98, ARE, Austin, Tex. and Scotts Valley, Calif., 1978-92; cons. Bechtel Corp., San Francisco, 1982-86. Contbr. numerous articles to profl. jours. Served to 2d lt. C.E., U.S. Army, 1945-47. Recipient Rupert Myers medal U. NSW, 1976; named Henry M. Shaw Lectr. in Civil Engring., N.C. State U., 1993; sr. scholar Fulbright Found., U. NSW, 1971, Nat. Asphalt Pavelent Assn. R.D. Kenyon Rsch. and Edn. award for Outstanding Contbns. for Hot Mix Asphalt Tech., 2002; named Disting. Engring. Alumnus, Coll. Engring., U. Calif., Berkeley, 1996. Fellow: AAAS; mem.: ASTM, NAE, NRC (assoc.), NAS (assoc.), ASCE (hon.; pres. San Francisco sect. 1979—80, ednl. activities com. 1989—91, State of Art award 1977, James Laurie prize 1988), Nat. Assn. of the Nat. Acads., Asphalt Inst. (Roll of Honor 1990), Calif. Asphalt Pavement Alliance, Am. Soc. Engring. Edn., Internat. Soc. Asphalt Pavements (hon.; chmn. bd. dirs. 1988—90), Assn. Asphalt Paving Technologists (hon. W.J. Emmons award 1961, 1965, 1985), Transp. Rsch. Bd. (assoc.; chmn. pavement design sect. 1973—79, K.B. Woods award 1972, 1st disting. lectureship 1992, Roy W. Crum award 1995). Avocations: swimming, stamp collecting/philately. Office: U Calif Dept Civil Engring 215 Mclaughlin Hall Berkeley CA 94720-1712 Office Phone: 510-231-9587. E-mail: clm@maxwell.berkeley.edu.

MONJAN, ANDREW ARTHUR, health science association administrator, educator; b. N.Y.C., Feb. 9, 1938; s. Victor Momjian and Sonia (Sherinian) Dardarian; m. Susan Vollenweider, July 1961 (div. Nov. 1965); m. Usha Bose, Aug. 14, 1969; children: Matthew, Vanessa. BSc, Rensselaer Poly. Inst., 1960; PhD, U. Rochester, 1965; MPH, Johns Hopkins U., 1970. Rsch. asst. Sterling-Winthrop Rsch. Inst., Rensselaer, N.Y., 1960; USPHS rsch. fellow Ctr. for Brain Rsch. U. Rochester, N.Y., 1964-66; asst. prof. depts. psychology and physiology U. Western Ont., London, Can., 1966-69; from asst. prof. to assoc. prof. dept. epidemiology Sch. Hygiene and Pub. Health Johns Hopkins U., Balt., 1971-83; expert epidemiology extramural programs br. NIH, Bethesda, Md., 1983-85, chief neurobiology/immunology programs physiology aging br., 1985-87, acting assoc. dir., 1987, chief neurobiology, acting chief neuropsychology brs., 1987—; exec. sec. Nat. Commn. on Sleep Disorders Rsch., 1990-92. Presenter in field. Contbr. articles to profl. jours. N.Y. State Regents scholar, 1955-59; N.Y. State Regents Grad. Tchg. fellow, 1960-62, USPHS rsch. fellow, 1962-64, 69-70. Mem. Soc. for Neurosci., Sigma Xi. Office: Nat Inst Aging 7201 Wisconsin Ave Msc9205 Ste 350 Bethesda MD 20892-9205 E-mail: am39m@nih.gov.

MONK, ALLAN JAMES, baritone; b. Mission City, B.C., Can., Aug. 19, 1942; m. Marlene Folk; 3 children. Student, Elgar Higgin and Boris Goldovsky. Operatic debut in Old Maid and the Thief, San Francisco, 1967; joined touring co., later main co. San Francisco Opera; appeared with Tulsa Opera, Pitts. Opera, Edmonton Opera, Vancouver Opera, So. Alta. Opera, Chgo. Opera, Balt. Opera, Miami Opera, Colo. Opera, Mont real Opera, Hawaii Opera Theatre, Portland Opera.; 1976. Met. Opera debut as Schaunard in La Boheme, 1976, sang title role in Wozzeck, Wolfram in Tannheuser, Dr. Malatesta in Don Pasquale, Rodrigo in Don Carlo, Sharpless in Madame Butterfly, Herald in Lohengrin; sang with Can. Opera Co. as Abelard in Heloise and Abelard, Macbeth, Rigoletto, Belcore in L'Elisir D'Amoure, Jago in Otello, as Ford in Falstaff, four villains in Les Contes d'Hoffman; with Nat. Arts Ctr. Opera Festival, Ottawa, Ont., Can., title role in Don Giovanni, Almaviva in Le Nozze Di Figaro, gulielmo in Cossi Fan Tutti, Tomsky in Pique Dame, Marcello in La Boheme; Carnegie Hall debut as Vladislav in Dalibor, 1977; European debut as Wozzeck, 1980; solo recitalist; toured with Nat. Arts Ctr. Orch. in USSR, Poland, Italy, 1973; movie debut as Baron Douphol in La Traviata, 1983. Named Artist of Yr. Can. Music Council, 1983, laureat Order of Can., 1985. Office: 14415 Parkland Blvd SE Calgary AB Canada T2J 4L5

MONK, CARL COLBURN, lawyer, academic administrator; b. Sept. 11, 1942; BA in Polit. Sci., Okla. State U., 1965; JD, Howard U., 1971. Bar: D.C. 1971, N.Y. 1973. Assoc. Simpson, Thacher & Bartlett, N.Y.C., 1971-74; from asst. prof. to assoc. prof. Washburn U., Topeka, Kans., 1974-78, from assoc. dean to dean, prof., 1976-88, disting. prof. law, 1988—. Dep. dir. Assn. Am. Law Schs., Washington, 1988-90, exec. dir., 1992—; vis. scholar Bklyn. Law Sch., 1985-86; vis. prof. law W.S. Richardson Sch. Law U. Hawaii Manao, 1990-91; lit. cons. Contbr. articles to profl. jours. Bd. dirs. Kans. Civil Liberties Union. Office: Assn Am Law Schs Ste 800 1201 Connecticut Ave NW Washington DC 20036-2605 E-mail: cmonk@aals.org.

MONK, DIANA CHARLA, artist, stable owner; b. Visalia, Calif., Feb. 25, 1927; d. Charles Edward and Viola Genevieve (Shea) Williams; m. James Alfred Monk, Aug. 11, 1951; children: Kiloran, Sydney, Geoffrey, Anne, Eric. Student, U. Pacific, 1946-47, Sacramento Coll., 1947-48, Calif. Coll. Fine Arts, San Francisco, 1948-51, Calif. Coll. Arts & Crafts, Oakland, 1972. Art tchr. Mt. Diablo Sch. Dist., Concord, Calif., 1958-63; pvt. art tchr. Lafayette, Calif., 1963-70; gallery dir. Jason Aver Gallery, San Francisco, 1970-72; owner, mgr. Monk & Lee Assocs., Lafayette, 1973-80; stable owner, mgr. Longacre Tng. Stables, Santa Rosa, Calif., 1989—. One-person shows include John F. Kennedy U., Orinda, Calif., Civic Arts Gallery, Walnut Creek, Calif., Vallery Art Gallery, Walnut Creek, Sea Ranch Gallery, Gualala, Calif., Jason Aver Gallery, San Francisco; exhibited in group shows at Oakland (Calif.) Art Mus., Crocker Nat. Art Gallery, Sacramento, Le Salon des Nations, Paris. Chair bd. dirs. Walnut Creek (Calif.) Civic Arts, 1972-74, advisor to dir., 1968-72; exhibit chmn. Valley Art Gallery, Walnut Creek, 1977-78; juror Women's Art Show, Walnut Creek, 1970, Oakland Calif. Art. Home and Office: Longacre Tng Stables 1702 Willowside Rd Santa Rosa CA 95401-3922 E-mail: longacrestables@msn.com.

MONK, MEREDITH JANE, artistic director, composer, choreographer, filmmaker, director; b. N.Y.C., Nov. 20, 1942; d. Theodore G. and Audrey Lois (Zellman) Monk. BA, Sarah Lawrence Coll., 1964; ArtsD (hon.), Bard Coll., 1988, U. of the Arts, 1989, Juilliard Sch. Music, 1997, San Francisco Art Inst., 1998, Boston Conservatory, 2001, Bennington Coll., 2002, Cornish Coll. Arts, 2002. Artistic dir., founder Ho. Found. Arts, N.Y.C., 1968—. Bd. dirs. Am. Music Ctr., The Kitchen. Prin. works include 16 Millimeter Earrings, 1966, Vessel, 1971, Quarry, 1976, Recent Ruins, 1979, Turtle Dreams, 1983, The Games, 1983, Book of Days, 1988, Facing North, 1990, Atlas, 1991, Three Heavens and Hells, 1992, Volcano Songs, 1994, American Archeology, 1994, The Politics of Quiet, 1996, Magic Frequencies, 1998, The Impermanence Project, 2004, Mercy, 2001, Possible Sky, 2003, exhibitions include Libr. of Performing Arts, Lincoln Ctr., 1996, Walker Art Ctr., Mpls., 1998, Whitney Mus. Art, 2002, Exit Art, 2002. Recipient Obie award, Village Voice, 1972, 1976, 1985, Creative Arts award, Brandeis U., 1974, Villager award, 1980, 1983, Deutches Kritiker preis, 1981, 1986, Bessie award, 1985, Nat. Music Theatre award, 1986, Dance Mag. award, 1993, John D. and Catherine T. MacArthur award, 1995, Sarah Lawrence Disting. Alumna award, 1996, Samuel Scripps award, 1996, Sigma Phi Omega award, 1987; fellow Guggenheim, 1972, 1982, Norton Stevens, 1993—94, MacDowell Colony. Mem.: ASCAP (award 1980—2000). Office: House Found for Arts 131 Varick St New York NY 10013-1410

MONK, SUSAN MARIE, pediatrician, educator; b. York, Pa., May 7, 1945; d. John Spotz and Mary Elizabeth (Shelly) M.; m. Jaime Pacheco, June 5, 1971; children: Benjamin Joaquin, Maria Cristina. AB, Colby Coll., 1967; MD, Jefferson Med. Coll., 1971. Diplomate Am. Bd. Pediatrics. Pediatrician Children's Med. Ctr., Dayton, Ohio, 1975—; asst. clin. prof. pediat. Wright State U., Dayton, 1976—83, assoc. clin. prof. pediat., 1983—2000, asst. prof. pediatrics, 2000—. Mem. bd. dirs. Children's Med. Ctr., Dayton, 1991-96, chief-of-staff, 1992-94. Mem. Am. Acad. Pediatrics, We. Ohio Pediatric Soc., Pediatric Ambulatory Care Soc. Avocations: reading, gardening, travel, movies, theater. Office: Childrens Health Clinic 730 C Valley St Dayton OH 45404-1845 Office Phone: 937-641-5355.

MONK KIDD, SUE, writer; m. Sandy Monk Kidd; 2 children. BS in Nursing, Tex. Christian U., 1970. Nurse St. Joseph's Hosp., Fort Worth, Tex., Med.Coll. Ga. Contbg. editor: Guideposts; author: God's Joyful Surprise, 1988, When the Heart Waits: Spiritual Direction for Life's Sacred Questions, 1990, The Dance of the Dissident Daughter: A Woman's Journey from Christian Tradition to the Sacred Feminine, 1996, The Secret Life of Bees, 2002 (SEBA Book of Yr. award, 2003); contbr. essays to mags. Recipient Katherine Anne Porter Second prize in fiction, Nimrod/Hardman Awards, 1993, S.C. Fiction Projectaward, S.C. Arts Commn., 1993, 1995, 1997, Isak Dineson Creative Non-Fiction award, 1994, Literal Latte Creative Non-Fiction Third prize, 1999, Bread Loaf scholar, Bread Loaf Writers Conf., 1995; fellow, S.C. Arts Commn., 1993—94, S.C. Acad. Authors, 1994, 1996. Office: c/o Carolyn Coleburn Viking Penguin 375 Hudson St New York NY 10014*

MONKMAN, BETTY CLAIRE, curator; BA, U. N.D.; MA, George Washington U. Registrar Office of the Curator White House, Washington, 1967-80, assoc. curator, 1980-97, curator, 1997—2002. Lectr. on history, arch., changing interiors, decorative and fine arts collections, holiday traditions, archives and documentation of hist. properties in the White House. Author: (with others) Art in the White House: A Nation's Pride, 1992, Our Changing White House, 1995, The White House: Its Historic Furnishings and First Families, 2000, Treasures of the White House, 2001; contbr. articles to profl. jours. Bd. dirs. Mus. City of Washington, 1980-92, Heurich House Fedn., 2002—, N.D. Mus. Art Fedn., 2003—; bd. mgrs. Hist. Soc. Washington, 1980-92, D.C. Bicentennial Commn., 1987-92. Mem. Com. for Preservation White House, Am. Assn. Mus., Soc. for History in Fed. Govt., Cosmos Club.

MONKS, JOHN GARVIE See LOUIS, WILLIAM JOSEPH

MONMONIER, MARK, geographer, graphics educator, essayist; b. Balt., Feb. 2, 1943; s. John Carroll and Martha Elizabeth (Mason) M.; m. Margaret Janet Kollner, Sept. 4, 1965; 1 child, Jo Kerry. BA, Johns Hopkins U., 1964; MS, Pa. State U., 1967, PhD, 1969. Asst. prof. U. Rhode Island, Kingston, 1969-70, SUNY, Albany, 1970-73; assoc. prof Syracuse U., N.Y., 1973-79, prof., 1979-98, Disting. prof. geography, 1998—. Cons. N.Y. State, Albany, 1974-93, Nat. Geog. Soc., 1987, Microsoft Corp., 1993-99, Belmont Rsch., 1995, AT&T Rsch., 1996-97, George Philip Ltd., England, 1996-97; rsch. geographer U.S. Geol. Survey, Reston, Va., 1979-84; dep. dir. N.Y. Ctr. for Geographic Info. and Analysis, 1989-90; Robinson vis. fellow George Mason U., 1985; Ida Beam Disting. vis. prof. U. Iowa, 1985; mem. adv. bd. GIS Law and Policy Inst., 1994-98; adv. bd. Philip Lee Philips Soc.; cons. and expert witness various law firms, 1995—; co-dir. History of Cartography in the Twentieth Century project, 1999--; mem. mapping sci. com. NRC, 2000—. Author: Maps. Distortion and Meaning, 1977, Computer-assisted Cartography, 1982, Technological Transition in Cartography, 1985, Maps with the News, 1989, How to Lie with Maps, 1991, French edit., 1993, 2nd edit., 1996, Japanese edit., 1995, German edit., 1996, Korean edit., 1998, Czech edit., 2000, Spying with Maps, 2002, Mapping it Out, 1993; author Drawing the Line, 1995, Rhumb Lines and Map Wars, 2004, Cartographies of Danger, 1997, Air Apparent, 1999, Bushmanders and Bullwinkles, 2001, Spying with Maps, 2002; co-author: The Study of Population: Elements, Patterns, Processes, 1982, Map Appreciation, 1988; co-editor: History of Cartography Project, 1997—; assoc. editor The American Cartographer, Falls Church, Va., 1977—82; editor: The American Cartographer, 1982—84; assoc. editor Mapping Scis. and Remote Sensing, 1987—97, contbg. editor Cartographica, 1984—, mem. editl. adv. bd. Mercator's World, 1997—2003. Statistician, Police Dept. Syracuse, 1978-80. Fellow John Simon Guggenheim Meml. Found., 1984, centennial fellow Pa. State U. Coll. Earth & Mineral Scis., 1996; recipient Chancellor's citation for Disting. Acad. Achievement, 1993, Disting. Geographer award Pa. Geog. Soc., 2000, O.M. Miller Cartographic medal, Am. Geog. Soc., 2001. Fellow: Am. Congress on Surveying and Mapping; mem.: Soc. History Tech., Philip Lee Phillips Soc., Pa. Acad. Sci. (editl. bd. 1989—2000), N.Am. Cartographic Info. Soc. (editl. bd. 1998—2001), Can. Cartographic Assn. (Award of Distinction 2002), Authors Guild, Am. Cartographic Assn. (pres. 1983—84), Assn. Am. Geographers (Media Achievement award 2000, Globe Book award 2004), Tau Beta Pi, Pi Tau Sigma, Sigma Xi (pres. Syracuse chpt. 2001—02). Roman Catholic. Home: 302 Waldorf Pky Syracuse NY 13224-2240 Office: Syracuse U Dept Of Geography Syracuse NY 13244-1020 E-mail: mon2ier@syr.edu.

MONNICH, JOHN ROBERT, lawyer; b. Detroit, Dec. 9, 1947; s. William Joseph and Sally Jean Monnich; m. Jane Cetrone, June 20, 1970; children: John Robert Jr., Brian William. BBA, U. Notre Dame, 1970; JD, U. Detroit, 1973. Bar: Mich. 1974, U.S. Dist. Ct. (ea. dist.) Mich. 1974, U.S. Ct. Appeals 1976, U.S. Dist. Ct. (we. dist.) Mich. 1987; CLU, CPCU. Assoc. Dinan & Schenden, Troy, Mich., 1974-75, Brian M. Smith, Troy, 1975-76; ptnr. Maybaugh, Wellman & Monnich, Troy, 1976-81, Monnich, Malloy & Delie, Troy, 1981—2001; pvt. practice Royal Oak, 2001—. Roman Catholic. Avocation: sports. Office: # Secondf 225 S Main St Royal Oak MI 48067-2611

MONOHAN, EDWARD SHEEHAN, IV, lawyer; b. Frankfort, Ky., Feb. 12, 1940; s. Edward Sheehan III and Mary (Lally) M.; m. Marilyn Louise Diebold, Aug. 31, 1963; children: Meredith, Edward, Patrick, Megan. BSChemE, Purdue U., 1962; JD, Georgetown U., 1965. Bar: D.C. 1966, Ky. 1966, Ohio 1990, U.S. Supreme Ct. 1975. Assoc. Vest & Ware, Covington, Ky., 1967-74; ptnr. Ware & Monohan, Florence, Ky., 1974-80, Monohan, Hertz & Blankenship, Florence, 1993-2000, Monohan & Blankenship, Florence, 2000—. Pres. Boone County Bar Assn., Florence, 1980-81. City councilman City of Crestview Hills, Ky., 1972-78. Mem. Ky. Bar Assn., Ky. Trial Lawyers Assn., No. Ky. Bar Assn., Louisville Bar Assn., Am. Inns of Ct. (master), Rotary (pres. 1981, 2001). Republican. Roman Catholic. Avocations: sailing, jogging, reading, french. Home: 21 Winding Way Crestview Hills KY 41017-2227 Office: Monohan & Blankenship 7711 Ewing Blvd Ste 100 Florence KY 41042-1814 Fax: 859-283-5155. E-mail: ed@kyattys.com.

MONOS, DIMITRIOS, medical educator, researcher; BS in Biology, U. Patras, Greece, 1975; PhD in Biochemistry and Immunology, Georgetown U., 1981. Vis. fellow lab. tumor immunology & biology Nat. Cancer Inst. NIH, Bethesda, Md., 1982—84; immunopathology fellow dept. pathology & lab. medicine U. Pa., Phila., 1984—86, rsch. assoc. immunology, 1986—88, asst. prof., 1990—96, assoc. prof. dept. pediat., 1996—. Vis. scholar dept. biochemistry & molecular biology Harvard U., 1988—90; prof. human biology and genetics Democritus U. of Thrace Med. Sch., Alexandroupolis, Greece, 1991—; dir. immonogenetics lab. dept. pathology Children's Hosp. Phila., 1996; lectr. in field. Mem. editl. bd.: Clin. and Diagnostic Lab. Clin. Immunology and Immunopathology, ad hoc reviewer: Cancer Rsch., Diabetes, Human Immunology, Jour. Immunology, New Eng. Jour. Medicine; contbr. articles to profl. jours. Recipient New Investigator Rsch. award, NIH, 1986, rsch. award, Am. Diabetes Assn., 1995, Fogarty Internat. fellowship, NIH, 1992; grantee, 1986—, U. Pa., 1987—88, 1995, iabetes Rsch. & Edn. Found, 1990, Juvenile Diabetes Found., 1990—92, Nat. Marrow Donor Program, 1992—94, ADA, 1995—96, 1997—. Mem.: Acad. Clin. Lab. Physicians and Scientists, Am. Soc. Histocompatibility and Immunogenetics, Am. Assn. Immunologists, Sigma Xi. Office: U Pa Sch Medicine Abramson Rsch Ctr 34th St and Civic Center Bd Philadelphia PA 19146-3310

MONOSSON, IRA HOWARD, physician; b. N.Y.C., Mar. 23, 1937; adopted s. Henry M.; s. I. Easer Rosenfield and Yetta Malvin; m. Aviva May Sokol, Sept. 20, 1970; children: Elana, Danielle, Ari. BA, Stanford U., 1959, MD, 1962. Diplomate Am. Bd. Preventive Medicine; cert. in occupational medicine. Intern Montefiore Hosp., Bronx, NY, 1962—63; resident L.A. County Gen. Hosp., 1963-64, Cedars of Lebanon Hosp., L.A., 1964-65; fellow Scripps Clinic and Rsch. Found., La Jolla, Calif., 1965-66; resident U. Calif., Irvine, 1976-77; pvt. practice San Diego, 1966-68, Southington, Conn., 1968-69, Ctrl. Med. Group, L.A., 1969-71; prin., owner Mid-City Med. Group, L.A., 1971-73; ptnr., physician Foley Med. Group, L.A., 1973-74; pub. health physician City of L.A., 1975; chief pub. health med. officer Calif. State Divsn. Occupational Safety & Health, L.A., 1976-82; pvt. practice various, Calif., 1982—. Asst. clin. prof. medicine UCLA Sch. Medicine; asst. clin. prof. preventive medicine U. So. Calif. Sch. Medicine; com. mem. UCLA Inst. Biosafety Com., 1982—; adv. bd. Hazardous Substances Task Force, City of L.A., Calif. State Divsn. Indsl. Accidents, 1984-86, Occupl. Medicine Calif. Med. Assn., 1985-88; cons. in field; spkr. house of delegates Am. Coll. Occupl. & Environ Medicine, 1995; mem. state regulatory bd. Calif. Indsl. Med. Coun., 1990—2003, chmn. 1990-93. Mem. Environ. Occupl. Health com. Am. Lung. Assn. Calif., 1986-89; steering com. of L.A. 2000 project, 1980-81; adv. com. Del Amo/Montrose Superfund Site, 1995—, Permanent Disability Study, Calif. State Commn. Health and Safety and Workers Compensation; mem. L.A. Unified Sch. Dist. Bd. Edn. Ind. Commn. regarding The Belmont Learning Ctr., 1999—. Author: (with others) A Practical Approach to Occupational and Environmental Medicine, 1994; contbr. articles to profl. jours. Fellow Am. Coll. Preventive Medicine, Am. Coll. Occupl. Environ. Medicine (bd. dirs. 1993-95), Royal Soc. Medicine, Am. Acad. Occupl. Medicine; mem. AMA, Calif. Soc. Indsl. Medicine and Surgery (pres. 1995, bd. dirs.). Office: Ste 268W 2001 Santa Monica Blvd Santa Monica CA 90404-2102

MONRAD, ELIZABETH A. corporate financial executive; Grad., Wellesley Coll., 1976; MBA in Fin., MIT. Ptnr. Coopers & Lybrand, Boston; with Gen. RE, 1992—2003; chief fin. officer Gen. Re Corp., 2000—03; exec. v.p., chief fin. officer TIAA CREF, N.Y.C., 2003—. Bd. dirs. Cogate-Palmolivola; mem. standing adv. group Pub. Co. Acctg. Oversight Bd. Mem.: AICPA (past mem. fin. instns. expert panel), Reins. Assn. Am. (past chmn. acctg. com.). Office: TIAA CREF 730 3d Ave New York NY 10017

MONRO, ELIZABETH (BETTY MONRO), federal agency administrator; m. Charles Monro. BA, U. Miss. Dir. fed. legis. Air Transport Assn. of Am.; spl. asst. aviation policy to Sec. Sam Skinner U.S. Dept. of Transp., Washington, 1989—91; chief of staff to adminstr. Gilbert Carmichael Fed. R.R. Adminstrn., 1991—93; chief of staff U.S. Congressman Mac Collins; dep. adminstr. Fed. R.R. Adminstrn., 2001—. Office: Fed RR Adminstrn 1120 Vermont Ave NW Washington DC 20590

MONROE, ERIN, psychiatric nurse practitioner; b. Topeka, Kans., Oct. 10, 1958; d. James Arthur and Virginia Marie Monroe. BA Psychology/Sociology magna cum laude, Bethany Coll., 1981; BSN magna cum laude, Washburn U., 1988; MSN summa cum laude, U. Kans., 1997. RN, Kans.; cert. addictions nurse, psychiatry/mental health nurse; cert. advanced nurse practitioner; cert. group psychotherapist. Lic. mental health technician Topeka State Hosp., 1982-87; staff psychiat. nurse Mennniger's, Topeka, 1988-98, advanced RN practitioner case mgr., 1998-99, primary clinician, 1999-2001, mem. quality assurance investigative com., 1999, Stormont-Vail Regional Health Ctr., Topeka, 2001—02; advanced practice nurse Cin. Children's Hosp. Med. Ctr., 2002—. Contbr. articles to profl. jours. Town rep. McPherson (Kans.) County Family Life Edn. Com., 1979. Mem. ANA, Am. Psychiat. Nurses Assn., Ohio Assn. Advanced Practice Nurses, Kans. State Nurses Assn., Psi Chi (pres., sec. 1979-81), Phi Kappa Phi, Sigma Theta Tau (Eta and Delta chpts.), Beta Tau Sigma. Democrat. Avocations: reading, films, psychoanalysis, art, walking. Office: Cincinnati Children's Hosp Med Ctr 3333 Burnet Cincinnati OH 45229 Home: 3781 Vineyard Woods Dr Cincinnati OH 45255-4699 Office Phone: 513-636-1007. Personal E-mail: emonroe02@yahoo.com.

MONROE, FREDERICK FALES, geologist, oceanographer; b. Washington, May 3, 1936; s. Sheldon McKinley and Fredericka Fales Monroe; m. Lori Rose Farquharson, June 11, 1988; m. Patricia Ann Lynch, July 11, 1971 (div. June 1, 1984); m. Sue Ellen Reeves, Oct. 7, 1963 (div. Oct. 7, 1970); children: Elizabeth Carmela, Patricia Alexis, Calli Grace, Victoria Michelle, John Scott, Lisa Diane Buyan, Christina Lee. BA, Amherst Coll., 1958; MS, The Am. U., 1970; MA, U. Miami, 1977; PhD, The Am. U., 1989. Profl. geologist Va., 1998. Geologist King & Gavaris, Consulting Engineers, N.Y.C., 1960—62; phys. sci. aide U.S. Geol. Survey, Denver, 1962; oceanographer U.S. Army Corps Engrs., Washington, 1962—67; ass't. prof ocean engring. Fla. Atlantic U., Boca Raton, 1967—71; oceanog. cons. Arthur Strock, Inc., 1971—75; fgn. affairs officer U.S. Dept. State, Washington, 1975—. Adj. asst. prof. No. Va. C.C., Alexandria, 2002—; adj. lectr. The Am. U., Washington, 1989—93. Recipient Meritorious Honor award, U.S. Dept. State, 1983, Career Achievement medal, 2001. Fellow: The Explorers Club. Achievements include research in marine resource potential of U.S. Exclusive Economic Zone. Personal E-mail: ffmonroe@hotmail.com.

MONROE, HASKELL MOORMAN, JR., retired university educator; b. Dallas, Mar. 18, 1931; s. Haskell M. and Myrtle Marie (Jackson) M.; m. Margaret Joan (Jo) Phillips, June 15, 1957; children: Stephen, Melanie, Mark, John. BA, Austin (Tex.) Coll., 1952, MA, 1954; PhD, Rice U., Houston, 1961; doctorate (hon.), Austin Coll., 1984. From instr. to prof. Tex. A&M U., 1959-80; asst. dean Tex. A&M U. (Grad. Sch.), 1965-68, asst. v.p. acad. affairs, 1972-74, dean faculties, 1974-80, assoc. v.p. acad. affairs, 1977-80; pres. U. Tex., El Paso, 1980-87; chancellor U. Mo., Columbia, 1987-91, prof. history, 1987-97, chancellor emeritus, prof. history, 1997—; dean faculties emeritus Tex. A&M U., College Station, 1997—. Instr. Schreiner Inst., Kerrville, Tex., summer 1959; vis. lectr. Emory U., summers 1967, 72; faculty lectr. Tex. A&M U., 1972; alumni lectr. Austin Coll., 1980; bd. dirs. City Nat. Bank, Southwestern Bell Corp., Boone County Nat. Bank, SBC Comms., Inc.; history adv. com. Sec. Air Force, 1987-87; orientation com. Dept. Def.-Joint Chiefs, 1986; adv. bd. Army Command and Gen. Staff Sch., 1986-88; trustee Schreiner U., 2000—. Contbr. articles, revs.; editor: Papers of Jefferson Davis, 1964-69; adv. editor: Texana, 1964-71; bd. editorial advisers: Booker T. Washington Papers, 1965-85 . Bd. dirs. Brazos Valley Rehab. Ctr., 1975-77, Salvation Army, El Paso, 1984-87, Columbia, Mo., 1988-97, Crime Stoppers of El Paso, United Way Columbia, 1988-94, Keep Brazos Beautiful, 1999-2003, Washington-on-the-Brazos State Park Assn., 2002-; trustee Bryan Hosp., 1976-79, chmn., 1979; bd. ch. visitors Austin Coll., 1977-78; deacon First Presbyn. Ch., Bryan, 1961-63, elder, 1965-67, 69-71, 73-74, clk. of session, 1973-74, chmn. pulpit nominating com., 1971-72; mem. presbytery's coun. Presbytery of Brazos, 1969-71, mem. resources for the 80s steering com., 1978-80; elder 1st Presbyn. Ch., El Paso, 1984-87, 1st Presbyn. Ch., Columbia, 1994-96; mem. exec. bd. Great Rivers coun. Boy Scouts Am., 1990-97; mem. Pres. Coun. NCAA, 1986-87; chmn. Jefferson Davis award com. Confederate Mus., 1996-97; bd. dirs. Salvation Army, 1989-97, Schreiner U., 1999--. Recipient Citation of Appreciation, LULAC, 1982, Honor award Salvation Army, 1997, also numerous achievement awards; grantee Social Sci. Rsch. Coun., Tex. A&M U., Huntington Libr., Intrafraternity and Sorority Outstanding Tchr. award, 1997; named Ky. Col., 1967; named to Legends of Aggieland, 1998. Mem. Am. Hist. Assn., Orgn. Am. Historians, So. Hist. Assn. Hist. Found. Presbyn. and Reformed Chs. (pres. 1970-72), Coll. Football Assn. (chmn. bd. 1989-90, bd. dirs.), Truman Scholarship Panel, Soc. Conf. Deans Faculties and Acad. V.P.s (pres. 1978), Rotary (El Paso, hon. Columbia, Mo., Bryan, Tex., Paul Harris fellow 1986, 2000). Home: 1005 Sonoma Cir College Station TX 77845-7907 Office: Tex A&M U 6B15 Evans Libr College Station TX 77843 Office Phone: 979-324-4546. Business E-Mail: hmonroe@tamu.edu.

MONROE, JAMES WALTER, retired organization executive; b. Fairfax, SD, Feb. 13, 1936; s. Sherman William and Frances (Burnett) M.; m. Dorothy Lou Gillette, Apr. 1, 1961; children— Steven James, David Walter, Melody Anne, Andrew Scott. Student, Huron (S.D.) Coll., 1954-56, U. Nebr., 1956-57; BA, Nebr. Wesleyan U., 1960. Mgr. Belleville (Kans.) C. of C., 1960-61, Concordia (Kans.) C. of C., 1961-62; asst. chief Div. Nebr. Resources, 1962-65; dir. S.D. Indsl. Devel. Expansion Agy., 1965-67, Nebr. Dept. Econ. Devel., 1967-71; sec. Nebr. Resources Found., 1967-71; exec. dir. Omaha Econ. Devel. Council, 1971-76; pres. Kansas City (Mo.-Kans.) Area Devel. Council, 1976-90; pres., chief exec. officer New Orleans and the River Region C. of C., 1990-96, Metrovision Found., Econ. Devel. Coun. Metro, New Orleans; ret., 1996. Mem. Am. Indsl. Devel. Council, 1965—, chmn. certification bd., 1981-82; sec. labor mgmt. council Greater Kansas City, 1979-90; mem. exec. com. Gov.'s Econ. Devel. Adv. Council, 1979-81. Bd. dirs. Am. Econ. Devel. Coun., 1992—. Served with AUS, 1957-59. Republican. Congregationalist. Home: 413 12th Pl N Edmonds WA 98020-2970

MONROE, JANE D. federal agency administrator; Probation officer; police officer; spl. agt. FBI, Abuquerque, 1985, Tampa, Fla., Washington; spl. agt. criminal divsn. FBI Hdqs., Washington; spl. agt. behavioral sci. unit FBI Acad., Quantico, Va.; supr. white collar crime and pub. corruption squad FBI, San Diego, 1995, coord. hostage negotiation and evidence response teams, 1995—99, asst. spl. agt. in charge Denver, 1999, spl. agt. in charge L.A., 2002, asst. dir. cyber divsn. Washington, 2002—. Office: Fed Bur Investigation J Edgar Hoover Bldg 935 Penn Ave NW Washington DC 20535-0001

MONROE, KENDYL KURTH, retired lawyer; b. Clayton, N.Mex., Sept. 6, 1936; s. Dottis Donald and Helen (Kurth) M.; m. Barbara Sayre, Sept. 12, 1956; children: Sidney, Dean, Loren. AB, Stanford U., 1958, LLB, 1960. Bar: NY 1961, Calif. 1961. Assoc. Sullivan & Cromwell, N.Y.C., 1960-67, ptnr., 1968-94. Chmn. TEB Charter Svcs., Inc., Teterboro, NJ, El Valle Escondido Ranch Ltd. Co., Seneca, N.Mex., Eklund Assn. Clayton, N.Mex., N.Y. Chamber Soloists, N.Y.C.; bd. dirs. Clan Munro Assn., Great Falls, Va., Union County Med. Found., Clayton, N.Mex. Chmn. adv. coun. The Mandala Ctr., Des Moines, N.Mex.; adv. com. Cornerstones Cmty Partnerships, Santa Fe; bd. dirs. N.Mex. Water Dialogue, Corrales, N.Mex., N.Mex. Heritage Preservation Alliance, Santa Fe; dir. emeritus Pub. Health Rsch. Inst., Newark. Mem. State Bar Calif., Assn. of Bar of City of N.Y., N.Mex. Amigos, Met. Club (N.Y.C.). Home: 189 Sayre Rd Seneca NM 88415 Office Phone: 505-451-7454. E-mail: kkmonroe@ptsi.net.

MONROE, KRISTEN RENWICK, political scientist, educator; b. Princeton, Ill., May 17, 1946; d. James Oliver and Gertrude (Renwick) Monroe; m. R.G. Wilmot Lampros, Sept. 26, 1981; children: Alexander Hart Lampros, Nicholas Monroe Lampros, Chloe Lampros-Monroe. AB cum laude, Smith Coll., Northampton, Mass., 1968; MA, U. Chgo., 1970, PhD, 1974. Asst. prof. SUNY, Stony Brook, 1974-77; Killam fellow U. B.C., Vancouver, 1975-76; asst. prof. NYU, N.Y.C., 1977-83; vis. asst. prof. Princeton (N.J.) U., 1983-84; prof. dept. polit. sci. U. Calif., Irvine, 1984—, dir. Ctr. Sci. Study Ethics and Morality, assoc. dir. program polit. psychology. Vis. fellow, assoc. prof. Princeton U., 1990—93. Author: The Heart of Altruism, 1996 (Best Book award in polit. psychology Am. Polit. Sci. Assn.), Presidential Popularity and the Economy, 1984; editor: Economic Approach to Politics, 1991, Contemporary Empirical Political Theory, 1997, Political Psychology, 2001, The Hand of Compassion, 2004. Recipient Mentor of Distinction award Women's Caucus for Polit. Sci.; NEH grantee, NSF grantee; Earhart fellow, Lawrence Rockefeller fellow. Mem.: Midwest Polit. Sci. Assn. (v.p. 1999—2001), Internat. Soc. Polit. Psychology (program chair 1999—2001, mem. coun., v.p. 2003—), Am. Polit. Sci. Assn. (pres. organized sect. in polit. psychology 2001—02, v.p. 2002). Democrat. Office: Univ of Calif-Irvine Dept Political Sci SSPA4103 Irvine CA 92697

MONROE, MELROSE, retired bank executive; b. Flowery Branch, Ga., Apr. 13, 1919; d. Willis Jeptha and Leila Adell Cash; m. Lynn Austin, June 14, 1942. AB in Edn., Ga. State U., 1968. Negotiator Trust Co. Bank, Atlanta, 1962-89, ret., 1989. Mem. Nat. Women's C. of C. (pres. 1987-88), Atlanta Women's C. of C. (dir. 1965-66, pres. Fidelis SS class 1962-63), Nat. Am. Legion Aux. (so. divsn. chmn. aux. Americanism 1995-96, so. divsn. chmn. aux. emergency fund 1996-97, cmty. svc. com.), Am. Legion Aux. (pres. 5th dist. 1986-87, Ga. state chaplain 1989-90, state historian 1991-92, state 2d v.p. 1992-93, 1st v.p. 1993-94, pres. 1994-95, Americanism chmn. so. divsn. 1995-95, chmn. emergency fund 1996-97, mem. cmty. svc. com. 1997-98, nat. historian 1999-00, v. chmn. nat. poppy com. 2000-01), Order Ea. Star (worthy matron 1951-52). Democrat. Home and Office: 6243 Spout Springs Rd Flowery Branch GA 30542-5032

MONROE, ROBERT RAWSON, engineering construction executive; b. Oakland, Calif., Sept. 25, 1927; s. Robert Ansley and Muriel Estelle (Burnham) M.; m. Charlotte Boies Anderson, Oct. 16, 1951; children: Robert Anderson, Nancy Lynn Monroe Sims, Susan Leslie Monroe Gordon. BS in Naval Sci., U.S. Naval Acad., 1950; MA in Internat. Rels., Stanford U., 1962. Commd. ensign USN, 1950, advanced through grades to vice-admiral, 1977; dir. Navy Systems Analysis, 1972-73; comdr. South Atlantic Force, 1973-74; comdr. Operational Test and Evaluation Force USN, 1974-77; dir. Def. Nuclear Agy., 1977-80; dir. Navy Rsch., Devel., Test and Evaluation, 1980-83; ret., 1983; joined Bechtel Nat., Inc., San Francisco, 1984, mgr. def. and space, 1984-89, v.p., 1985, sr. v.p., ptnr., 1987, mgr. mktg. and govt. ops., 1989-91, mgr. spl. projects, 1992-93, mgr. govt. ops. Washington, 1993—2002, sr. counselor, 2002—. Mem. nat. security adv. bd. Los Alamos (N.Mex.) Nat. Lab., 1983—88; mem. tech. evaluation panel U.S. Dept. Energy, 1983—88; mem. engring. adv. com. Oak Ridge (Tenn.) Nat. Lab., 1986—89, Rensselaer Poly. Inst., 1990—91; mem. bd. advisors Office Tech. Assessment, Washington, 1987—89, Nat. Contract Mgmt. Assn., 1986—91; mem. task forces Def. Sci. Bd., Washington, 1983—89; corp. mem. Charles Stark Draper Lab., Cambridge, Mass., 1983—; affiliate mem. Ctr. for Internat. Security and Cooperation, Stanford U., 1989—93; chmn. space transp. subcom. NASA's Adv. Coun., 1995—2001; mem. strategic adv. bd. Nev. Test Site, 1995—99; mem. Nat. Security adv. panel Sandia Nat. Labs., 1996—; mem. threat reduction adv. coun. (nuc. & sci. tech. panels) Dept. Def., 1998—; mem. Enhanced Test Readiness External Rev. Group, 2002—03; mem. threat reduction adv. coun. sci. & tech. panel Dept. Def., 2004—, mem. U.S. nuc. strategy program, 2004—. Decorated Def. D.S.M., USN D.S.M., Legion of Merit, Bronze Star medal with combat device, Joint Svcs. Commendation medal, USN Commendation medal with combat device; Legion of Honor (France). Mem. Nat. Def. Indsl. Assn., Soc. Am. Mil. Engrs. Avocations: tennis, golf, hiking, reading. Home: 2313 Sawdust Rd Vienna VA 22181-3044 Office: Bechtel Nat Inc 1015 15th St NW Ste 700 Washington DC 20005-2636 Office Phone: 202-828-7362.

MONROE, THOMAS EDWARD, industrial corporation executive; b. Ironton, Mo., Nov. 19, 1947; s. Donald Mansfield and Edwina Frances (Carr) M.; children: Thomas Edward II, Katherine Jenna. BA, Drury Coll., 1969; postgrad., Washington U. Sch. Bus. Adminstrn., St. Louis, 1970. Acctg. mgr., asst. contr. Am. Transit Corp., St. Louis, 1970-74; mgr. corp. devel., asst. treas. Chromalloy Am. Corp., St. Louis, 1974-77, v.p. fin., 1977-78, exec. v.p., 1978-82; dir. Chromalloy Fin. Corp., 1976-82, Am. Universal Ins. Co.,

1978-82; chmn. Capital Assocs. Corp., 1982—, Fed. Air Ambulance, The Safe Deposit Co., CompuVault, Inc., James Flying Svc., Inc., Lindbergh Leasing, Inc., Vault II, LLC. Trustee Kingsbury Place Assn., Second Presbyn. Ch. Mem. Algonquin Club (trustee). Presbyterian. Office: Capital Assocs Corp 515 S Lindbergh Blvd Saint Louis MO 63131-2731 E-mail: monroes@swbell.com.

MONROE, WILLIAM LEWIS, human resources executive; b. Detroit, May 11, 1941; s. Lewis Stewart and Ada Jeanette (Williams) Monroe; m. Sharon Lynne Kahal, June 30, 1967; children: Andrea M. Dunk, William J. BA, Western Mich. U., 1963, MA, 1964. Rsch. analyst Chrysler Corp., Detroit, 1965-72, labor economist, 1972-77, mgr. retirement, savs. and unemployment benefit plans, 1977-81; dir. employee benefits W. R. Grace & Co., N.Y.C., 1981-87, v.p. human resources, 1987-2001, bd. trustee, v.p. coun. on employee benefits, 1989-2001, pres. coun. on employee benefits, 1995-96; cons. AON Cons./ASA, Boca Raton, 2001—02. Adj. prof. mgmt. FAU Univ., Boca Raton, 2001; corp. bd. dirs. Internat. Found. Employee Benefits, 1986—88; mem. bus. rsch. adv. coun. U.S. Dept. Labor/Bur. Labor Stats., 1987—96; mem. Human Resources Policy Inst. Boston U., 1993—96. Co-chmn. closing com. PTSA Sch., Birmingham, Mich., 1977; chmn. pers. com. Wilton Presbyn. ch., Wilton, Conn., 1982—86; officer, bd. dirs. Forest Hills Property Owners Assn., Birmingham, 1974—80; mem. exec. bd. Gulf Stream coun. Boy Scouts Am., 1993—99. Served USAR, 1965—71. Mem.: Soc. for Human Resources & Mgmt., Boca Raton Resort and Club. Republican. Presbyterian. Avocation: Avocations: tennis, golf. Office: PO Box 810851 Boca Raton FL 33481-0851 E-mail: bmonroe10@aol.com.

MONSEES, JAMES EUGENE, engineering executive, consultant; b. Sedalia, Mo., Mar. 27, 1937; s. Olen Owen and Ruth Caroline (Weiffenbach) M., m. Leda L. Hoehns, Oct. 8, 1961; children: Brenda G., Mark E. BSCE, U. Mo., 1960, MSCE, 1961; PhDCE, U. Ill., 1970. Registered profl. engr., Ill., Md., Washington, Ohio, Calif., Wash., Colo. Grad. asst. U. Mo., Columbia, 1958-61; project mgr. USAF Spl. Weapons Ctr., Albuquerque, 1961-64; engr. Exxon, Baton Rouge, 1964-66; rsch. assoc. U. Ill., Champaign, 1967-69; sr. v.p. A.A. Mathews, CRS Engrs., Arcadia, Calif. and Rockville, Md., 1969-80; dept. mgr. Battelle Meml. Inst., Columbus, Ohio, 1980-82; v.p.-engr. Lachel L. Hanson & Assocs., Golden, Colo., 1982-83; chief tunnel engr. Metro Rail Transit Couns., L.A., 1983-1990; project mgr. Collider/SSC The PB/MK Team, Dallas, 1990-91; sr. v.p., tech. dir., prin. profl. assoc. Parsons Brinckerhoff, N.Y.C. Mem. Seismic Lifeline Com., San Francisco, 1987—; mem. exec. com. Rapid Excavation/Tunnel Conf., Denver, 1989—. Author: (with others) Guidelines for Tunnel Lining Design, 1984, Mining Handbook, 1992, Tunnel Engineering, 1994, Tunnel Engineering Handbook, 1996. Mem. U.S. Nat. Com. for Rock Mechanics, Wash., D.C., 1983-86, 88-94, Internat. Soc. for Rock Mechanics, 1983—. 1st Lt. USAF, 1961-64. Recipient Mo. Honor award U. Mo., 1992. Fellow ASCE; mem. NAE, Am. Underground Space Assn. (bd. dirs. 1995—), The Moles, Underground Tech. Rsch. Coun. Republican. Avocations: shooting, biking, tennis, reading, dog training. Home: 10141 Hummingbird Cir Orange CA 92861-4155 Office: Parsons Brinckerhoff 505 S Main St Ste 900 Orange CA 92868-4529

MONSELL, THOMAS OLIVER, secondary English educator, writer; b. Greenport, N.Y., Aug. 26, 1933; s. Harry Monroe and Amy Adelle Monsell. BA, Ithaca Coll., 1952—56; MS, SUNY, Albany, 1959—60. Prodn. asst. Robbins Music Corp., N.Y.C., 1957—58; English tchr., drama coach, libr. Lindenhurst Pub. Sch., NY, 1960—88. Founder, dir. Stirling Players Cmty. Theater, Greenport, NY, 1972—; textbook contbr. Henry Holt & Co., Harcourt, Brace, N.Y.C., 1989—94; film & theater critic New York Guardian, 1993—96. Author: (explication) Shakespeare in Perf: Hamlet, 1990, (media criticism) Nixon on Stage and Screen, 1998; co-author (with Antonia Booth): (regional history) Greenport, 2003. Village historian (with James Monsell) City of Greenport, NY, 2000—. Mem.: Shaw Soc., Ibsen Soc. Am., James Jones Lit. Soc., Soc. Mayflower Descendants. Avocations: reading, writing, travel, theater, directing plays for charity benefits. Home: 525 First St Greenport NY 11944

MONSEN, ELAINE RANKER, nutritionist, educator, editor; b. Oakland, Calif., June 6, 1935; d. Emery R. and Irene Stewart (Thorley) Ranker; m. Raymond Joseph Monsen, Jr., Jan. 21, 1959; 1 dau., Maren Ranker. BA, U. Utah, 1956; MS (Mead Johnson grad. scholar), U. Calif., Berkeley, 1959, PhD (NSF fellow), 1961; postgrad. NSF sci. faculty fellow, Harvard U., 1968-69. Dietetic intern Mass. Gen. Hosp., Boston, 1956-57; asst. prof. nutrition, lectr. biochemistry Brigham Young U., Provo, Utah, 1960-63; mem. faculty U. Wash., 1963—, prof. nutrition and medicine, 1984—, prof. nutrition, adj. prof. medicine, 1976-84, chmn. div. human nutrition, dietetics and foods, 1977-82, dir. grad. nutritional scis. program, 1994-99, mem. Council of Coll. Arts and Scis., 1974-78, mem. U. Wash. Press com., 1981—; chmn. Nutrition Studies Commn., 1969-83. Vis. scholar Stanford U., 1971-72; mem. sci. adv. com. food fortification Pan-Am. Health Orgn., São Paulo, Brazil, 1972; tng. grant coordinator NIH, 1976-97. Editor-in-chief Jour. Am. Dietetic Assn., 1983-2003; Editor Emeritus, Jour. Am. Dietetic Assn., 2003—; mem. editorial bd. Coun. Biology Editors, 1992-96; author rsch. papers on lipid metabolism, iron absorption. Bd. dirs. A Contemporary Theatre, Seattle, 1969-72; trustee, bd. dirs. Seattle Found., 1978-95, vice chmn., 1987-91, chmn., 1991-93; pres. Seattle bd. Santa Fe Chamber Music Festival, 1984-85; mem. Puget Sound Blood Ctr. Bd., 1996-99. Grantee Nutrition Found., 1965-68, Agrl. Rsch. Svc., 1969-84; recipient Disting. Alumnus award U. Utah, F. Fischer Meml. Nutrition Lectr. award, 1988, L.F. Cooper Meml. Lectr. award, 1991, L. Hatch Meml. Lectr. award, 1992, Goble Lectr. award Purdue U., 1997. Fellow: Am. Soc. Clin. Nutrition (sec. 1987—90), Am. Inst. Nutrition; mem.: Wash. Heart Assn. (nutrition coun. 1973—76), Am. Soc. Parenteral and Enteral Nutrition, Soc. Nutriton Edn., Am. Dietetic Assn. Office: U Wash PO Box 353410 Seattle WA 98195-3410 E-mail: ermonsen@u.washington.edu.

MONSEN, RONALD PETER, musician, music educator, artist; b. Milw., Sept. 20, 1940; s. Ray Thelmert and Eunice Irene (Friebl) M.; m. Joan Grace Williams, Dec. 21, 1963; children: Dirk Andrew (dec.), Peter Colin, Kirsten Jo. BSc, U. Wis., Milw., 1964; MMus, Northwestern U., Evanston, Ill., 1968; performer's diploma, Royal Acad. Music, London, 1971; D of Mus. Arts, U. Wis., Madison, 1978. Music tchr. Milw. pub. schs., 1964-67; prof. woodwinds Concordia Coll., Moorhead, Minn., 1968-73; prof. clarinet U. Ky., Lexington, 1980—. Clarinet clinican Selmer Co., Elkhart, Ind., 1986—. Clarinet recitalist appearances include Denver, 1983, London, 1984, Seattle, 1986, Cin., 1992; mem. Okla. Clarinet Symphony, 1985. Mem. Internat. Clarinet Assn. (mem. state chair, pres. 1992). Avocations: model railroading, photography, france. Office: Univ Ky Sch Music Coll Fine Arts Lexington KY 40506-0001

MONSER, EDWARD L. electric power industry executive; BA, Ea. Mich. U., 1972; BS in Elec. Engring., Ill. Inst. Tech., 1980. Sr. engr. Rosemount divsn. Emerson, 1981, dir. tech., 1987—89, dir. new products and tech., 1989, v.p. pressure ops., v.p. pressure and temperature, 1994—95, v.p. and gen. mgr. pressure and temperature, 1995—96, pres., 1996—2001; COO Emerson Electric Co., St. Louis, 2001—. Office: Emerson Electric Co 8000 W Florissant Ave Saint Louis MO 63136

MONSKY, JOHN BERTRAND, investment banking executive; b. Montgomery, Ala., May 17, 1930; s. Harry and Belle (Golding) M.; m. Joan Gilbert, June 8, 1952; children: Leslie Joy, John Richard, Harry Robert. BA, Yale, 1952; MBA, Harvard, 1954. Sec. Devoe & Raynolds Co., Inc., Louisville, Ky., 1956-65; v.p., dir. Universal Marion Corp., Jacksonville, Fla., 1965-69, pres., chmn. bd., chief exec. officer, 1969-71, cons., 1971—; vice chmn. ServAmerica, Inc., Jacksonville, 1972-74, co-chmn. bd. dirs., 1974-80, chmn. bd. dirs., 1980—; pres., chmn. bd. dirs. First Fla. Capital Corp., 1985—. Dir. Fla. Wire & Cable Co., Jacksonville, 1975-82 Past pres. bd. trustees Jacksonville Country Day Sch.; bd. dirs. Jacksonville Art Mus.; trustee Bolles Sch., Jacksonville, Jacksonville Symphony Assn. Served with USAF, 1954-56. Mem. Jacksonville Area C. of C. (com. of 100), Jackson County Citizen Involvement Clubs, Harvard Bus. Sch. Club of Ky. (exec. com. 1964-65), Phillips Acad. Andover Alumni Club of Ky. (pres. 1963-64), Epping Forest Cmty. Master Assn. (bd. dirs. 1994—), Yale Club N.E. Fla. (bd. dirs. 1987—), Yale Club of N.Y.C., Harvard Club (Jacksonville), Assn. Yale Alumni (del. 1996—), River Club, Ponte Vedra Club, Epping Forest Yacht Club. Home: Epping Forest 7015 Gaines Ct Jacksonville FL 32217-2672 Office: 300 Wharfside Way # B Jacksonville FL 32207-8153 E-mail: jbmonsky@aol.com.

MONSMA, STEPHEN VOS, political scientist, educator; b. Pella, Iowa, Sept. 22, 1936; s. Martin and Marie Monsma; m. Mary Carlisle, Dec. 19, 1964; children: Martin S., Kristin J. AB, Calvin Coll., Grand Rapids, Mich., 1958; MA, Georgetown U., 1961; PhD, Mich. State U., 1965. Asst. prof. SUNY, Plattsburgh, 1964-67; prof. Calvin Coll., Grand Rapids, Mich., 1967-74; rep. State Legis., Lansing, Mich., 1974-78; senator State of Mich., Lansing, Mich., 1978-82; dir. office quality rev. Dept. Social Svcs., Lansing, Mich., 1985-87; prof. Pepperdine U., Malibu, Calif., 1987—2004, prof. and chair social sci. divsn., 1996-2000, Blanche E. Seaver chair in social sci., 1999—2004, prof. emeritus, 2004; rsch. fellow Henry Inst. for Study of Christianity and Politics, Calvin Coll., Grand Rapids. Author: (books) Pursuing Justice in a Sinful World, 1984, Positive Neutrality, 1993, When Sacred and Secular Mix, 1996, Putting Faith in Partnerships: Welfare-to-Work in Four Cities, 2004; co-author: (book) The Challenge of Pluralism: Ch. and State in Five Democracies, 1997; editor: Ch.-State Rels. in Crisis: Debating Neutrality, 2002; co-editor: Equal Treatment of Religion in a Pluralistic Soc., 1998; corr. editor: Christianity Today. Mem. Natural Resources Commn., Lansing, 1983-85; bd. dir. Ctr. for Pub. Justice, Annapolis, Md., 1996-2002, Bread for the World, Washington, 1991-93. Fellow Ctr. for Pub. Justice, Annapolis, Md.; grantee Earhart Found., 1985, Am. Polit. Sci. Assn., 1995, Smith Richardson Found., 2000, Haynes Found., 2000; vis. scholar, Calvin Ctr. for Christian Scholarship, 1993—94. Mem. Am. Polit. Sci. Assn., Christians in Polit. Sci. (pres. 1994-96). Office: 2605 Golfridge SE Grand Rapids MI 49546 E-mail: smonsma@pepperdine.edu

MONSON, ANGELA ZOE, state legislator; b. Oklahoma City, July 31, 1955; d. Epron Provo Monson. BS, Oklahoma City U., 1976; MPA, U. Okla., 1987. Probation and parole officer Okla. Dept. Corrections, 1976-77; cir. riding city mgr. East Ctrl. Rural Munic Area Coun., 1980-81; fiscal analyst Okla. State Legislature, 1981-84; sales rep. The Equitable, Oklahoma City, 1985-86; exec. dir. Okla. Health Care Project, 1986-90; mem. Okla. Ho. of Reps., 1990—. Mem. Okla. adv. com. U.S. Commn. on Civil Rights, 1984-89. Mem. editl. bd. Primary Care News. Past pres. Okla. chpt. NAACP; past bd. pres. Mary Mahoney Meml. Health Ctr., Neighborhood Svcs. Orgn., Tolliver Alt. Care Co., nat. bd. dirs. State Alliance for Universal Health Care; mem. policy adv. bd. Ctr. for Health Care Access & Reform. Recipient Svc. to Achievement award Black Liberated Arts Ctr., 1981, Outstanding Achievement award Cmty. Health Ctrs. Inc., 1988. Mem. AAUW. Democrat. Baptist. Home: 720 NE 42nd St Oklahoma City OK 73105-7004 Office: Okla Senate State Capitol Oklahoma City OK 73105

MONSON, CAROL LYNN, osteopath, psychotherapist; b. Blue Island, Ill., Nov. 3, 1946; d. Marcus Edward and Margaret Bertha (Andres) Monson; m. Frank E. Warden, Feb. 28, 1981. BS, No. Ill. U., 1968, MS, 1969; D.O., Mich State Coll. Osteo. Medicine, 1979. Lic. physician Mich., diplomate Am. Bd. Osteo., Am. Bd. Family Physicians, Am. Bd. Osteo. Gen. Practice, MSUCOM. Expeditor-psychotherapist H. Douglas Singer Zone Ctr., Rockford, Ill., 1969—71; psychotherapist Tri-County Mental Health, St. Johns, Mich., 1971—76; pvt. practice psychotherapy East Lansing, Mich., 1976—80; intern Lansing Gen. Hosp., Mich., 1979—80, residency dir. family practice, 1988—; pvt. practice osteo. medicine Lansing, 1980—; mem. staff Ingham Regional Med. Ctr., chmn. family practice, 1987—89. Field instr. Sch. Social Work U. Mich., 1973—76; clin. instr. Ctrl. Mich. Dept. Psychology, 1974—75; clin. prof. Mich. State U., 1980—88, asst. prof., 1988—, tng. supr. family medicine residency, 1988—97, faculty devel. fellow, 1994—95, residency dir. family medicine, 1994—97; mem. adv. bd. Substance Abuse Clearinghouse, Lansing, 1983—85, Kelly Health Care, Lansing, 1983—85, Americor Health Svcs., Lansing, 1984—88, Lansing Home Care, Lansing, 1988—94. Fellow: Am. Coll. Family Practice (osteo.); mem.: Am. Coll. Family Physicians (residency insp. 1991—), Mich. Assn. Osteo. Family Physicians (pres.-elect 1994, pres. 1995—96), Nat. Assn. Career Women (conv. com. 1984—), Ingham County Osteo. Assn. (pres. 1993—95, 1996—97), Mich. Osteo. Assn. (program com. 1992—, governance coun. 1996—97, bd. trustees 1997—, pres.-elect 2001—02, pres. 2002—), Internat. Transactional Analysis Assn., Am. Acad. Family Practice, Am. Osteo. Assn. (del. 1994—, health policy fellow 1997—98), Mich. Coun. Grad. Med. Edn. (appointee 1998—, pres. 1999—2002), Lansing Assn. Career Women, Soc. Tchrs. of Family Medicine, Zonta (chmn. service com. Mid Mich. Capital Area chpt.). Avocations: gardening, orchid growing, antique collecting. Office: 2445 Jolly Rd Ste 200 Okemos MI 48864-4572

MONSON, DAN, college basketball coach; b. Spokane, Wash., Oct. 6, 1961; BS in Math., U. Idaho, 1985; MS in Athletic Adminstrn., U. Ala., 1988. Asst. coach Oregon City H.S., 1985-86; grad. asst. U. Ala., Birmingham, 1986-88; asst. coach Gonzaga U., Spokane, 1988-94, assoc. head coach, 1994-97, head coach, 1997-99, U. Minn., 1999—. Dir. Gopherball Basketball Camp, Mpls.; asst. coach World Univ. Games, 1999, USA Basketball's 20-and-under team, 2004. Named Coach of Yr., 1998, Nat. Rookie Coach of Yr., Basketball Times, 1998. Achievements include West. Coast Conf. Champions, 1998; reached NCAA Sweet 16, 1998-99. Office: Univ of Minn Student Devel & Athletics 141 BFAB Minneapolis MN 55455-0100

MONSON, DAVID CARL, school superintendent, farmer, state legislator; b. Langdon, N.D., July 30, 1950; s. Carl Arthur and Shirley Jean (Klai) M.; m. Mary Kathryn Greutman, July 8, 1972; children: Cordell Carl, Cale David, Jared Arthur. Cert. tchr., adminstr., N.D. Sci. tchr. Hankinson (N.D.) Pub. Sch., 1972-75; tchr. Nekoma (N.D.) Pub. Sch., 1975-76; tchr., prin. NeKoma (N.D.) Pub. Sch., 1976-79; tchr., supt. Nekoma (N.D.) Pub. Sch., 1979-80; tchr., prin. Milton (N.D.)-Osnabrock H.S., 1981-84; supt. Adams (N.D.) Pub. Schs., 1984-88; ins. agt. N.Y. Life, Fargo, ND, 1988-95; self-employed ins. agt., Osnabrock, 1988—2003; farmer, 1975—; mem. N.D. Ho. of Reps., Bismarck, 1993—, asst. majority leader, 1998—; supt. Edinburg (N.D.) Pub. Schs., 1995—. Dir. Cavalier County Mut. Ins. Co., Osnabrock, N.D., 1990-98, Northeast Mut. Ins. Co., Cando, N.D., 1998--, N.Am. Indsl. Hemp Coun., 1999—. Leader Bobcats 4-H Club, 1988—2001; pres. Bovre Luth. Ch., Osnabrock, 2002—; mem. sch. bd. dirs. Osnobrock Sch. Bd., 1989—2001. Mem. N.D. Farm Bur., N.D. Coun. Sch. Adminstrs., Eagles, KP (grand sec. N.D. and Sask. 1985-93, award 1990). Republican. Lutheran. Avocations: skiing, gardening, hunting, coin collecting/numismatics. E-mail: dmonson@state.nd.us.

MONSON, DIANNE LYNN, literacy educator; b. Minot, ND, Nov. 24, 1934; d. Albert Rachie and Iona Cordelia (Kirk) M. BS, U. Minn., 1956, MA, 1962, PhD, 1966. Tchr. Rochester (Minn.) Pub. Schs., 1956-59, U.S. Dept. Def., Schweinfurt, West Germany, 1959-61, St. Louis Park (Minn.) Schs., 1961-62; instr. U. Minn., Mpls., 1962-66; prof. U. Wash., Seattle, 1966-82; prof. literacy edn. U. Minn., Mpls., 1982-97, prof. emeritus, 1997—. Chmn. curriculum and instrn. U. Minn., 1986—89. Co-author: Scott Foresman Reading, 2000, New Horizons in the Language Arts, 1972, Children and Books, 6th edit., 1981, Experiencing Children's Literature, 1984, (monograph) Research in Children's Literature, 1976, Language Arts: Teaching and Learning Effective Use of Language, 1988, Reading Together: Helping Children Get A Good Start With Reading, 1991; assoc. editor: Dictionary of Literacy, 1995. Recipient Outstanding Educator award U. Minn. Alumni Assn., 1983, Alumni Faculty award U. Minn. Alumni Assn., 1991. Fellow Nat. Conf. Rsch. in English (pres. 1990-91); mem. ALA, Nat. Coun. Tchrs. English (exec. com. 1979-81), Internat. Reading Assn. (dir. 1980-83, Arbuthnot award 1993, Reading Hall of Fame 1997), U.S. Bd. Books for Young People (pres. 1988-90). Lutheran. Home: 515 S Lexington Pkwy # 604 Saint Paul MN 55116 Business E-Mail: monso001@tc.umn.edu.

MONSON, JAMES EDWARD, electrical engineer, educator; b. Oakland, Calif., June 20, 1932; s. George Edward and Frances Eleanor (Fouche) M.; m. Julie Elizabeth Conzelman, June 25, 1954; children: John, Jamie, Jennifer. BSEE, Stanford U., 1954, MSEE, 1955, PhD in Elec. Engring., 1961. Mem. tech. staff Bell Telephone Labs., Murray Hill, N.J., 1955-56; devel. engr. Hewlett-Packard Co., Palo Alto, Calif., 1956-61; Robert C. Sabini prof. engring. emeritus Harvey Mudd Coll., 1961—. Mem. governing bd. Claremont Unified Sch. Dist., 1966-71, pres., 1969-70; pres. Claremont Civic Assn., 1974-75; bd. dirs. Claremont YMCA, 1978-82, Coastal Health Alliance, 1999-. Fellow NSF, 1954-55, Japan Soc. Promotion Sci., 1984; Fulbright Rsch. grantee, 1975-76; Fulbright sr. lectr., 1980. Fellow IEEE (life); mem. Phi Beta Kappa, Sigma Xi. Home: PO Box 1029 Point Reyes Station CA 94956-1029 Office: Harvey Mudd Coll 301 E 12th St Claremont CA 91711-5901 Personal E-mail: j.monson@ieee.org.

MONSON, JOHN RUDOLPH, lawyer; b. Chgo., Feb. 4, 1941; s. Rudolph Agaton and Ellen Louise (Loeffler) M.; m. Susan Lee Brown, May 22, 1965; children: Elizabeth Louisa, Christina Lee, Donald Rudolph. BA with honors, Northwestern U., 1963; JD with distinction, U. Mich., 1966. Bar: Ill. 1966, N.H. 1970, Mass. 1985. Atty. assoc. Chapman & Cutler, Chgo., 1966-68, Levenfeld, Kanter, Baskes & Lippitz, Chgo., 1968-70, Nighswander, Martin & Mitchell, Laconia, N.H., 1970-71; mem., ptnr. Wiggin & Nourie, P.A., Manchester, N.H., 1972—, pres., 1991-94. Sec., gen. counsel Rock of Ages Corp., 1996-2000. Mem. N.H. Fish and Game Commn., Concord, 1980-94, chmn., 1983-93; sr. bd. dirs. Brown-Monson Found., 1991—; incorporator Cath. Med. Ctr., 1988-95, Optima Health, 1994-99; commr. N.H. Land and Cmty. Heritage Commn., 1998-2000. Fellow Am. Coll. Trust and Estate Counsel, Safari Club Internat. (v.p. 1999-2001, dir.-at-large 1997-99, treas. 2001-02, pres. elect 2002-04, pres. 2004—). Republican. Avocations: skiing, hunting, running. Home: 24 Wellesley Dr Bedford NH 03110-4531 Office: Wiggin & Nourie PA 20 Market St Manchester NH 03101-1931 Office Phone: 603-669-2211.

MONSON, LARRY LEE, music educator; b. Grand Island, Nebr., Oct. 17, 1942; s. Owen H. and Glenna Imojene Monson; m. LaVonne Elise Havekost, Mar. 21, 1964; children: Martin Laurence, Ann Elise, Eric Lee. BA, Midland Luth. Coll., 1965; MA, U. Iowa, 1966. Cert. tchr. Iowa. Dir. music 1st Luth. Ch., Cedar Rapids, Iowa, 1964—67; dir. music and youth Kountze Meml. Ch., Omaha, 1967—69; dir. music 1st Luth. Ch., Sioux Falls, SD, 1969—72, St. Paul Luth. Ch., Davenport, Iowa, 1972—79; choral dir. City HS, Iowa City, 1979—89; dir. choral activities Doane Coll., Crete, Nebr., 1989—, ret. prof. choral music, 2004. Chair music cert. Nebr. State Edn., Lincoln, 1990—93. Bd. dirs. Polley Music Libr., Lincoln, 1989—95. Recipient Outstanding Alumni Achievement award, Midland Luth. Coll., 2001. Mem.: Soc. Preservation and Encouragement of Barbershop Quartet Singing, Internat. Fedn. Choral Music, Am. Choral Dirs. Assn. Avocations: biking, travel, coaching quartets, gardening. Home: 204 Wedgewood Dr Lincoln NE 68510 Office: Doane Coll 1014 Boswell Ave Crete NE 68333 E-mail: larry.monson@doane.edu.

MONSON, ROBERT JOSEPH, education educator; b. St. Paul, July 2, 1947; s. Robert Joseph and Lorraine (Pieruccioni) M.; m. Tracey Monson, Dec. 18, 1970 (dec. 1986); 1 child, Ashley Taylor. BA, St. Thomas Coll., St. Paul, 1969, MA, 1971; PhD, St. Louis U., 1975. Tchr. St. Bernards Schs., St. Paul, 1969-71; asst. prin. Mamaroneck (N.Y.) High Sch., 1975-78; prin. Chapel Hill (N.C.) High Sch., 1978-81; asst. sch. supt. Sch. Dist. South Orange-Maplewood (N.J.), 1981-85; supt. schs. Beachwood (Ohio) pub. schs., 1985-87, Westwood (Mass.) pub. schs., 1987-94, Mendota Heights, Minn., 1994-99; sr. lectr. Lesley Coll., 1990-2000; assoc. prof. Tchrs. Coll. Columbia U., N.Y.C., 1999—. Rsch. cons. NSF, 1975. Contbr. articles to profl. jours. Named Educator of Yr., AGPA, 1981; postdoctoral fellow Harvard U., 1977. Mem. Prins Ctr. Harvard U. (bd. dirs. 1989-91). Roman Catholic. Home: 957 Lake Ave Greenwich CT 06831 Office: 525 W 120th St Box 67 New York NY 10027 Office Phone: 212-678-8118.

MONSON, THOMAS SPENCER, religious organization administrator, former publishing company executive; b. Salt Lake City, Aug. 21, 1927; s. George Spencer and Gladys (Condie) M.; m. Frances Beverly Johnson, Oct. 7, 1948; children— Thomas L., Ann Frances, Clark Spencer. BS with honors in mktg, U. Utah, 1948; MBA, Brigham Young U., 1974, LLD (hon.), 1981. With Deseret News Press, Salt Lake City, 1948-64, mgr., 1962-64; mem. Coun. Twelve Apostles, Ch. of Jesus Christ of Latter-day Saints, 1963-85, bishop, 1950-55; pres. Canadian Mission, 1959-62; mem. first presidency Ch. of Jesus Christ of Latter-day Sts., 1985—; chmn. bd. Deseret News Pub. Co., 1977-96. Vice chmn. Deseret Mgmt. Corp.; pres. Printing Industry Utah, 1958; bd. dirs. Printing Industry Am., 1958-64; mem. Utah exec. bd. U.S. West Communications. Mem. Utah Bd. Regents; mem. nat. exec. bd. Boy Scouts Am.; trustee Brigham Young U. With USNR, 1945-46. Recipient Recognition award, 1964, Disting. Alumnus award U. Utah, 1966; Silver Beaver award Boy Scouts Am., 1971; Silver Buffalo award, 1978; Bronze Wolf award World Orgn. of the Scout Movement, 1993. Mem. Utah Assn. Sales Execs., U. Utah Alumni Assn. (dir.), Salt Lake Advt. Club, Alpha Kappa Psi. Clubs: Exchange (Salt Lake City). Mem. LDS Ch. Office: LDS Ch 47 E South Temple Salt Lake City UT 84150-9701

MONTAG, DAVID MOSES, telecommunications industry executive; b. LA, Apr. 30, 1939; s. Gustave and Esther (Kessler) M; children: Daniel Gershon, Esther Yael, Michael Menachem. Student, UCLA, 1957-61. Tech. writer L.H. Butcher Co., L.A., 1961; phys. sci. lab. technician East L.A. Coll., Monterey Park, 1961—. Pres., dir. Or Chadash, Inc., Monterey Park, 1968—; owner EDUCOMP, Monterey Park, Calif., 1980—; cons. David M. Montag & Assocs., Monterey Park, 1993—; pres. Aquinas Computer Corp.; v.p. Wireless Optical Networks, San Diego, 1996—, R & D Learnfast Corp., Downey, 2001—; ednl. cons. for computer-assisted instrn. V.p., bd. dirs. Coll. Religious Conf., 1968-92; rabbi Congregation Sha'arei Tshuvah, Santa Monica, Calif. Mem. AIAA, Assn. Orthodox Jewish Scientists, Laser Inst. Am., Internat. Sco. Tech. in Edn., Physics Instructional Resource Assn. Home and Office: PO Box 384 Monterey Park CA 91754-0384 Office Phone: 626-398-8501. Business E-Mail: montagdm@elac.edu.

MONTAG, THOMAS W. gynecologist, oncologist; b. Denver, June 29, 1950; MD, U. Minn., 1978. Diplomate Am. Bd. Obstetricians and Gynecologists, Am. Bd. Gynecol. Oncology. Intern flex Hennepin County Med. Ctr., Mpls., 1978-79; resident ob-gyn. Med. Ctr. Hosp. Vt., Burlington, 1979-83; fellow gynecol. oncology U. So. Calif., Los Angeles, 1983-85; mem. staff Maryview Med Ctr, Portsmouth, Va., Chesapeake (Va.) Gen. Hosp., 1980—85; dir. gynecologic oncology U. Colo. H.S.C., 1985—87; pvt. prac. Denver, 1987—90, Burlingame, Calif., 1990—95, Asheville, NC, 1995—99, Cancer Treatment Ctr. of Am., Portsmouth, Va., 1999—; pvt. practice Cheasapeake, Va., 1999—2003; clin. asst. prof. Ea. Va. Med. Sch., Norfolk, 2000—. Fellow ACS, Am. Coll. Ob-Gyn.; mem. Am. Soc. Clin. Oncology, Soc. Gynecol. Oncologists, Western Assn. Gynecologic Oncologists, Internat. Gynecologic Cancer Soc., Mid Atlantic Gynecologic Oncology Soc. Office: 106 Wimbledon Sq Chesapeake VA 23320 Office Phone: 757-436-9898.

MONTAGNIER, LUC ANTOINE, virologist; b. Chabris, Indre, France, Aug. 18, 1932; 3 children. Cert. of Studies on Natural Scis., U. Poitiers, France, 1953, BS, 1955; MD, U. Paris, 1960. Asst. Faculté des Scis, Paris, 1955-60; attaché de recherche Nat. Ctr. Sci. Rsch., Paris, 1960-63, chargé de recherche, 1963-67, maitre de recherche, 1967-72, dir. research, 1974—, head lab. Orsay, France, 1965-72; head viral oncology unit Institut Pasteur, Paris, 1972—, head virology dept., 1982-85, prof., 1974—, head dept. AIDS and Retroviruses, 1990-96; disting. prof., dir. Ctr. for Molecular and Cellular Biology Queens Coll. of the CUNY, 1997-2001. Dir. virology course Institut Pasteur, 1980-85, head dept. AIDS and Retrovirus, 1991-97; mem. responsible research team CNRS; discovered HIV-1 virus, 1983 and HIV-2 virus, 1985; pres. adminstrv. coun. European Fed. for AIDS Rsch., 1988. Author: Vaincre le Sida, 1987, Des virus et des hommes, 1994, AIDS, Oxidative Stress and Cancer, 1997, Virus, in English, 2000. Pres. World Found. for AIDS Rsch. and Prevention, Paris, 1993—. Decorated comdr. Legion of Honor, comdr. Ordre Nat. du Mérite; recipient Lasker prize, 1986, Gairdner prize, 1987, Japan prize, 1988, Warrent Alpert Found. prize, 1998, Prince of Asturias prize, 2000, others. Mem. Acad. Nat. de Médecine, French Acad. Scis. Co-discoverer (with Robert Gallo) of the AIDS virus. Office: World Found AIDS Rsch and Prevention 1 rue Miollis F-75015 Paris France

MONTAGUE, DROGO K. urologist; b. Alpena, Mich., Dec. 11, 1942; s. Frank Wright and Susan Alice (Kidder) M.; children: Mark Andrew, Lisa Joy. Student, U. Mich., 1963, MD cum laude, 1968. Diplomate Am. Bd. Urology. Intern Cleve. Clinic Hosp., 1968-69, resident in gen. surgery, 1969-70, resident in urology, 1970-73; assoc. staff urologist Cleve. Clinic Found., 1973-75, staff urologist, 1975—, head sect. prosthetic surgery, 1981—, urology residence program dir., 1985—, dir. Ctr. for Sexual Function, 1987—; prof. surgery Ohio State U. Coll. Medicine, 1992—. Trainee cardiovascular rsch. tng. program NIH, 1962-68; trustee Am. Bd. Urology, 1989-95, mem. examination com., 1975-80, examiner cert. exam., 1980-88, rep. to Am. Bd. Med. Specialties, 1989-95. Reviewer various publs. in field; contbr. numerous articles to profl. publs., chpts. to books; editor: Disorders of Male Sexual Function, 1988, Surgical Treatment of Erectile Dysfunction, 1993; author audiovisual tapes in field; mem. editl. bd. Jour. Urology. James B. Angell scholar, 1961, 62, Nat. Found. scholar, 1963-68; recipient Russell and Mary Hugh Scott Edn. award, 1989, Iowa Rsch. award, 1967. Fellow ACS; mem. Am. Urolog. Assn. (chmn. sci. exhibits com. North Cen. sect. 1977, mem. residency edn. com. 1979-83, vice chmn. audio visual com. 1989-95, mem. various coms., editor Am. Urolog. Assn. Video Libr. 1995-2000, chmn. audio visual com. 1996-2002), Am. Assn. Genitourinary Surgeons, Cleve. Urolog. Soc. (sec.-treas. 1978-80, v.p. 1980-81, pres. 1981-82, 94-95), Soc. for Study of Impotence (pres. 1995). Office: Cleve Clinic Found Urol Inst 9500 Euclid Ave Cleveland OH 44195-0001

MONTAGUE, EDGAR BURWELL, III, (MONTY MONTAGUE), industrial designer; b. Charlotte, N.C., Aug. 6, 1958; s. Edgar B. Jr. and Mary Sue (Calhoun) M.; m. Nancy Oliver Stallworth, Feb. 25, 1984; children: Nancy Lea, Edgar Eubank. B Environ. Design cum laude, N.C. State U., 1980. Indsl. design Design/Joe Sonderman, Inc., Charlotte, 1980-85; design prin. Bolt (formerly Machen Montague, Inc.), Charlotte, N.Y.C., 1985—, BOLT, Charlotte, 1994—. Holder over 15 design and/or utility patents; work published in Product Design 1-6, Design for Humanity. Designer corp. identity program Habitat for Humanity, Charlotte, 1987 (logo design now used throughout world). Recipient ann. design award Internat. Design mag., 1988-93, ID-40 ID Mag., 1994, Disting. Alumni award N.C. State U., 1999. Mem. Indsl. Designer Soc. Am. (co-founder Carolina chpt., program chmn. 1981-83, vice chmn. 1984, 93, Kudo award for chpt. svc. 1982, Indsl. Design Excellence awards 1989-94). Avocations: travel, art, time with family, coaching soccer. Office: BOLT 1415 S Church St Ste S Charlotte NC 28203-4124 E-mail: monty@boltgroup.com.

MONTAGUE, JOEL GEDNEY, public health officer; b. N.Y.C., July 6, 1932; s. William Pepperrell and Jean Lois (Gedney) M.; m. Shahnaz Emami-Nikou, Dec. 16, 1963; children: Jahan, Maryam. BA, Oberlin Coll., 1956; MA, Johns Hopkins U., 1960; MS in Pub. Health, U. N.C., 1970; postgrad., U. Tehran, 1961. Field rep., mission chief CARE, Iran, Egypt, Tunisia, 1961-68, regional dir., 1968-69, The Population Coun., N.Y.C., 1971-76; dep. dir. Project for Strengthening Health Delivery Systems in Ctrl. and West Africa, Boston, also Ivory Coast, 1976-79; regional dir. Mgmt. Scis. for Health, Boston, 1979-80; head health and hosps. Secretariat of His Highness The Aga Khan, Aiglemont, France, 1980-85; v.p. John Snow Pub. Health, Boston, 1985-89; dir. Am. Friends of AICF, Washington, 1990-92; country rep. John Snow, Cambodia, Cambodia, 1994-97; pvt. pub. health cons., Wellesley, Mass., 1997—. Contbr. articles to profl. jours. Bd. dirs. Nat. Coun. for Internat. Health, 1993-96, Am. Coun. for Nationalities Svcs., 1992-95, U.S. Com. for Refugees, 1991-94; chmn. bd. Ptnrs. for Devel., 1996—. With signal corps U.S. Army, 1956-58. Decorated Medal of Honor, Iranian Red Cross, officer Order of the Republic (Tunisia) Fund; Fulbright grantee, 1961; Ford Found. fellow, 1970-71; Aspen Fund grantee, 1993; hon. fellow Inst. Advanced Study Humanities, U. Edinburgh, Scotland, 1997. Fellow Royal Soc. Tropical Medicine and Hygiene. Home: 24 Maugus Ave Wellesley MA 02481-7617

MONTANA, ENRICO SAKAI, research scientist; b. Youngstown, Ohio, Aug. 2, 1977; s. Enrique C. and Corazon Montana. BS in Molecular Genetics magna cum laude, U. Rochester, 1999; postgrad., MIT, 1999—. DeKiewet Rsch. fellow U. Rochester, N.Y., 1998, ind. rschr., 1998-99. Bausch and Lomb scholar, 1995-99, Xerox scholar, 1995-99, Excellence scholar U. Rochester, 1995-99, Mary Agnes Brandewie scholar, 1995-96; recipient Donald R. Charles Meml. prize, 1999. Mem. Phi Beta Kappa. Office: Ctr Learning And Memory 50 Ames St Bldg E18605 Cambridge MA 02142-1308 E-mail: emontana@mit.edu.

MONTANA, JOSEPH C., JR., former professional football player; b. New Eagle, Pa., June 11, 1956; s. Joseph C. Montana, Sr. and Theresa M. Montana; m. Kim Monses, 1975 (div.); m. Cass Castillo (div. 1983); m. Jennifer Wallace; children: Alexander, Elizabeth. BBA in Mktg., U. Notre Dame, 1978. Quarterback San Francisco 49ers, 1979—93, Kansas City Chiefs, 1993—95; formerly with new bus. devel. dept. Viking Components Inc., Rancho Santa Margarita, Calif., 1999—2000. Mem. Super Bowl Championship Team, 1982, 85, 90. Author (with Alan Steinberg): Cool Under Fire, 1989. Nominee Pro Football Hall of Fame, 2000; named MVP, Super Bowl, 1982, 1985, NFL, 1989, Player of Yr., The Sporting News, 1989, Man of Yr., 1989; named to Pro Bowl, 1981, 1983—85, 1987, 1989, 1990, 1993. Achievements include holding NFL career records for highest completion percentage (63.67), highest passer rating (93.5); NFL single-season record for highest passer rating (112.4), 1989; NFL record for most consecutive games with 300 or more yards passing (5), 1982; most consecutive passes completed (22), 1987. Office: Super Joe Official J Montana Fan Club PO Box 2409 Menlo Park CA 94026-2409

MONTANARI, FRANCO, classicist, educator; b. Sannazzaro de' Burgondi, Italy, May 24, 1950; s. Renzo and Maria (Rastaldi) M.; m. Daniela Manetti, Sept. 21, 1978. Diploma liceale, Liceo Classico U. Foscolo, Pavia, Italy, 1969; laurea in lettere, U. Pisa, Italy, 1973; diploma, Scuola Normale Superiore, Pisa, 1973, perfezionamento, 1974. Contrattista quadriennale U. Pisa, Italy, 1975-77, prof. incaricato, 1977-82, prof. associato, 1982-86; prof. ordinario U. Genova, Italy, 1987—. Pres. XL and XLVIII Entretiens Fondation Hardt, Geneva, 1993, 2001; treas. Bur. of the Fedn. Internat. des Assn. des Etudes Classiques (FIEC), 1994—; mem. Conseil de Fondation and Conseil Scientifique of the Fondation Hardt (Geneva); dir. Centro Italiano dell'Année Philologique. Author: Studi di filologia omerica antica I, 1979, I frammenti dei grammatici Agathokles, Hallanikos, Ptolemaios Epithetes, 1988, Introduzione a Omero, 1990, 1992, Studi di filologia omerica antica II, 1995, GI. Vocabolario della lingua greca, 1995, 2004, Storia della Letteratura Greca, 1998, Prima lezione di Letteratura Greca, Roma-Bari, 2003; editor: Da Omero agli Alessandrini, 1988, La philologie grecque à lépoque hellénistique et romaine, 1994, Omero. Gli aedi, i poemi, gli interpreti, Firenze, 1998, Omero tremila anni dopo, Rome, 2002; mem. editl. bd. Corpus Papiri Filosofici, Florence, Commentaria et Lexica Graeca in Papyris, Florence. Mem. Soc. Internat. de Bibliographie Classique. Home: via San Luca 8 I-56011 Calci Italy Office: Facoltà di Lettere U Genova Via Balbi 4 16126 Genova Italy Office Phone: +39 010 2099724. E-mail: franco.montanari@unige.it.

MONTANEZ, CINDY, state representative; Student, UCLA. Legis. aide Former Councilmember Richare Alarcon; mem. Calif. Assembly, 2002—. Mem. City Coun., San Fernando, 1999—2001; mayor San Fernando, Calif., 2001—02. Democrat. Office: PO Box 942849 Rm 5144 Sacramento CA 94249 Address: 11541 Laurel Canyon Blvd Ste C Mission Hills CA 91345

MONTANEZ, MARY ANN CHAVEZ, counselor, consultant, writer; b. Pasadena, Calif., July 16, 1936; d. Vincent Chavez-Trujillo-Mendibles and Trinidad (Huerta-Molina) Chavez; m. R.E. Montanez, Nov. 17, 1956 (div. June 1976); children: Robert, Eric, (twins) Michael and Manuel. AA, Pasadena City Coll., 1980; BA, Pacific Oaks Coll., 1985, MA in Human Devel., 1988; cert. counseling, Calif. State U., L.A., 1994. Life cert. C.C. counseling and instrn. Placement officer Pasadena (Calif.) C.C. Dist., 1981-90, coll. instr., 1986-90; vocat. rehab. counselor Calif. Dept. Rehab., L.A., 1990—99; exec. dir. Latins Writers & Film Makers, 1998—. Mem. outreach bd. Pasadena Mental Health Assn., 1976-79; field rep. El Centro De Accion Social, Inc., 1976-77; dir. program Pasadena Unified Sch. Dist., 1977-78; coord. outreach, crisis counselor Pasadena Mental Health, 1978-81; cons., field reader Women's Ednl. Equity Act, Washington, 1981; out-placement coord. PCC, 1984; staff recruitment program Pasadena C.C., 1987-88; acad. counselor Multi Cultural Ctr.-Cerritos Coll. Dist., 1990-91. Commr. Commn. on Disabilities, 1990—; adv. bd. mem. Fiesta Educativa, 1991-99; bd. mem. West Side Ctr. on Ind. Living, L.A., 1993-99; mem. credit com. Pasadena Employees Credit Union, 1996; active Huntington Libr., Norton Simon Mus.; mem. Christian Calvery Chapel. Recipient Golden Angel award, 1995. Mem. Soc. Hispanic Hist. Ancestral Rsch., S.W. Oral History Assn. (founding mem., life). Democrat. Roman Catholic. Avocations: writing, history, art. Home: 2533 Glenrose Ave Altadena CA 91001-5049 E-mail: documentary@earthlink.com.

MONTANO, ARTHUR, lawyer; b. Audubon, N.J., 1923; s. Domenick and Theresa (Grasso) M.; m. Ann B. Durkin; children: Sharon Adams, Sandra Bumgardner, Cheryl Ann Hughes, Arthur Jr., Bernadette, Michael. BME, Villanova U., 1950; LLB, Rutgers U., 1954. Bar: N.J. 1955, U.S. Dist. Ct. N.J. 1955, U.S. Ct. Appeals 1967, U.S. Supreme Ct. 1969. Assoc. Orlando, Devine & Tomlin, Camden, N.J., 1955-56, Orlando, Kisselman & Devine, Camden, 1956-58, Kisselman, Devine & Deighan, Camden, 1958-60; ptnr. Kisselman, Devine, Deighan & Montano, Camden, 1960-65, Kisselman, Devine, Deighan, Montano, King & Summers, Camden, 1965-71, Kisselman, Deighan, Montano & Summers, Cherry Hill, N.J., 1971-77; sr. ptnr. Montano, Summers, Mullen & Manuel, Cherry Hill, 1977-88; of counsel Montano, Summers, Mullen, Manuel & Owens, P.A., 1988-99; pvt. practice Audubon, N.J., 1998—. Adj. prof. law Rutgers Law Sch., Camden, N.J., 1984-93; arbitrator Am. Arbitration Assn., state and fed. cts. Navigator AC, U.S. Army, 1943-45. Recipient award for professionalism in law, 1997. Fellow Am. Coll. Trial Lawyers, Am. Bar Found.; mem. N.J. State Bar Assn. (trustee 1977-84), Trial Attys. N.J. (trial bar 1978), Camden County Bar Assn., Tavistock Country Club (Haddonfield, N.J.). Roman Catholic. Office: 1323 Mineo Dr Punta Gorda FL 33950-6637

MONTAÑO, EDGAR J. language educator; b. Tumaco, Colombia, July 23, 1947; arrived in U.S., 1990; s. Manuel A. Montaño and Justa (Torres) de Montaño. BA in Modern Langs., U. De Tunja, Boyaca, Colombia, 1975; MEd in TESOL, Boston U., 1983; MA in Spanish and Lit., So. Ill. U., 1993. Asst. prof. modern langs. U. de Nariño, Pasto, Colombia, 1985—90; bilingual tchr. Migrant Bilingual Program, Cobden (Ill.) Unit Sch., 1991—93; assoc. prof. Spanish John A. Logan Coll., Carterville, Ill., 1993—. Mem.: NEA, TESOL, Ill. Coun. Tchrs. Fgn. Langs., Ill. Edn. Assn., Ill. Migrant Edn. Assn., Internat. Club John A. Logan Coll. Home: 1130 Walkup St Carbondale IL 62901 Office: John A Logan Coll 700 Logan College Dr Carterville IL 62918 Office Phone: 618-985-3741. E-mail: emont22052@aol.com.

MONTE, BONNIE J. performing arts company executive, director, educator; b. Stamford, Conn., Nov. 27, 1954; d. Eugene N. and Ruth M. (Thompson) M. BA, Bethany Coll., 1976; diploma, Hartman Conservatory, Stamford, 1978. Assoc. artistic dir. Williamstown (Mass.) Theatre Festival, 1981-89; casting dir. Manhattan Theatre Club, N.Y.C., 1989-90; artistic dir. The Shakespeare Theatre of NJ, Madison, 1990—. Mem. faculty Drew U., 1991-96; guest artist-in-residence U. Notre Dame, The New Sch.-Eugene Lang. Coll., U. S.C. Recipient Nat. Soc. of Arts and Letters award, N.J., 1997, Alumni Achievement award for arts mgmt. Bethany Coll., 1999; grantee Lotte Crabtree Found., Boston, 1977. Democrat. Avocations: bicycling, archery, writing, travel. Office: Shakespeare Theatre NJ 36 Madison Ave Madison NJ 07940-1434

MONTEAU, NORMAN KEITH, gemologist; b. Balt., Dec. 20, 1957; s. Milton Keith and Vieva Regina (Williams) M.; m. Sandra Lynn Staub, Dec. 7, 1987. Cert. diamond grading, Gemol. Inst., 1981, cert. colored stone grading, cert. gem identification, Gemol. Inst., 1982. Numerous certs. fro Gemol. Inst. Am. Owner, founder Monteau Gemol. Svcs., Woodland Hills, Calif., 1987-91, pres., 1992—; owner, pres. Am. Internat. Gemologists, Beverly Hills, Calif., 1993—; mng. ptnr. The William Staub Co., L.A., 1994—. V.p. bd. dirs. Lynn Meadows, 1999-2000, pres., 2000-2001; appraiser to Archdiocese of L.A., Cath. Ch., 1993—; arbitrator State Farm Ins. Co., 1993—, lectr. nat. retail jewelry stores, insurance cos. others on gemology and values, 1992—; advisor to ins. cos. in Calif. for earthquake property damage assessment, 1994, expert witness L.A. Mcpl. Ct., 1995; jewelry appraiser County of Los Angeles, 1996—; mem. Ptnrs. for Internat. Edn. and Tng./U.S. AID, 1996. Contbr. articles to profl. jours. Recipient Excellence award Aetna Ins. Co., 1992; honored guest of bd. govs. Gemol. Inst. Am., Carlsbad, Calif., 1996. Mem. Nat. Assn. Jewelry Appraisers, Am. Soc. Appraisers, Gemol. Inst. Am. (mem. Pres.'s Cir. 1992—), Calif. Jewelers Assn., Alumni Assn. Gemol. Inst. Am. (charter), Jewelers Bd. of Trade, Woodland Hills C. of C. Avocations: racquetball, mountain climbing, water-skiing, jet car racing, white water rafting. Office: Monteau Gemol Svcs 21250 Califa St Ste 203 Woodland Hills CA 91367-5042

MONTECEL, MARIA ROBLEDO (CUCA ROBLEDO MONTECEL), educational association administrator; b. Laredo, Tex., Jan. 14, 1953; d. Ismael and Paula (Benavides) Robledo; m. Lucas Montecel, Aug. 18, 1979; children: Ismael Gavino, Xavier Mario. BSSW magna cum laude, Our Lady of Lake U., 1972; MEd, Antioch U., 1975; PhD in Urban Edn., U. Wis., 1985. Rsch. asst. D.C. Devel. Assocs., Inc., San Antonio, 1973-75; test designer Dissemination and Assessment Ctr. for Bilingual Edn. U. Tex., San Antonio, 1975-76; grad. rsch. asst. office rsch. Sch. Edn. U. Wis., Milw., 1980-81, program dir. Midwest NODAC dept. cultural founds. Sch. Edn., 1985; evaluator Ctr. for Mgmt. Innovation in Multicultural Edn. Intercultural Devel. Rsch. Assn., San Antonio, 1976-77, dir. bilingual edn. cost analysis project, 1977-78, dir. divsn. rsch., devel. and evalutation, 1978-80, rsch. specialist, 1982-85, dir. Ctr. for Prevention and Recovery Dropouts, 1985-88, 90-92, dir. tng. and tech. assistance, 1988-89, dir. valued youth program, 1988-90, dep. dir., 1992, exec. dir., 1992—. Trustee Our Lady of Lake U. Mem. editorial bd. Tex. Rschr.; contbr. articles to profl. jours. Vol. advocate Alamo Area Rape Crisis Ctr.; mem. rsch. com. Hispanas Unidas; participant Leadership Tex. '85; invited mem. Tex. State Task Force Dropout Prevention; chmn. lifelong learning coun. San Antonio 2000; cons. edn. and immigrant students Mellon Found.; bd. dirs. Mex.-Am. Solidarity Found.; founding bd. dirs. CIVICUS World Alliance Citizen Participation; bd. dirs. community edn. leadership program Mott Found.; mem. nat. adv. coun. Race and Ethnic Studies Inst., Tex. A & M; mem. ednl. review bd. Tex. Ctr. Ednl. Rsch.; mem. nat. adv. bd. ERIC/CRESS, 1994. Recipient High Achievement Commendation, Antioch Coll., 1975, Peter F. Drucker award Coca-Cola Valued Youth Program; Women and Minority Rsch. fellow Nat. Inst. Edn., 1979, Title VII Doctoral fellow U. Wis., 1980-82; named to Top 100 Hispanic Influential, Hispanic Bus., 1997. Mem. Am. Edn. Rsch. Assn., Nat. Assn. Bilingual Edn., Nat. Dropout Prevention Network (charter), Alphi Chi. Roman Catholic. Avocations: reading, writing, fishing, golf. Office: Intercultural Devel Rsch Assn 5835 Callaghan Rd Ste 350 San Antonio TX 78228-1125

MONTEIRO, LOIS ANN, medical science educator; b. Central Falls, R.I., Mar. 22, 1934; d. William Henry and Martha Mae (Leach) Hodgins; m. George Monteiro, Aug. 14, 1958 (div. Feb. 1992); children: Katherine, Stephen, Emily. RN, Roger Williams Hosp., Providence, 1954; BA, Brown U., k1958, PhD, 1970; MS, Boston U., 1960. Asst. prof. Boston U., 1960-65, Brown U., Providence, R.I., 1971-77, assoc. prof., 1978-82, prof., 1983—, chmn. dept., 1985—, assoc. dean medicine, 1991—. Vis. prof. U. Va., 1990, U. Miss., 2002; bd. dirs. Harvard Cmty. Health Plan, 1990-95, Harvard Pilgrim Health Care Plan, New Eng., 1995—. Author: Monitoring Health Status, 1976, Cardiac Rehabilitation, 1980; contbr. articles to profl. jours. Mem. Commn. State of R.I., Providence, 1989—. NSF grantee, 1969, Robert W. Johnson Found. grantee, Princeton, N.J., 1983, NIH grantee, 1987; Bunting Inst. fellow, Cambridge, Mass., 1981, Congrl. fellow House Vets. Affairs Commn., 1998; recipient Am. Sociol. Assn. Spivack award, 1998. Mem. Am. Sociol. Assn., R.I. State Nurses Assn. (pres. 1974-76), Women in Medicine/Assn. Am. Med. Colls. Democrat. Presbyterian. Avocation: collecting books on nursing history. Office: Brown U Dept Med Sci PO Box G-a413 Providence RI 02912-0001 E-mail: lois_monteiro@brown.edu.

MONTEIRO, MARISTELA GOLDNADEL, physician, researcher; b. Niteroi, Brazil, May 15, 1960; s. Christiano Jorge and Myriam (Goldnadel) Monteiro. MD, Escola Paulista de Medicina, Sao Paulo, Brazil, 1983, PhD, 1986. Asst. prof. Escola Paulista de Medicina, 1986-87, adj. prof., 1987—; med. officer WHO, Geneva, 1994-95, scientist, 1996-99, coord. intervention R & D substance abuse dept., 1999-2000, coord. mgmt. substance dependence, 2000—03; regional advisor alcohol, substance abuse Pan Am. Health Orgn., 2004—. Postdoctoral fellow U. Calif. San Diego, 1987-89; advisor Am. Psychiat. Assn. Task Force on Substance Use Disorders, 1989-93; advisor WHO/PSA, Geneva, 1993-94. Editor: Brazil-United States Binational Drug Abuse Research, 1993; contbr. over 90 articles to profl. jours. Mem. Internat. Soc. for Biomed. Rsch. on Alcoholism. Jewish. Avocation: scuba diving. Office: Pan Am Health Orgn 525 23rd St NW Washington DC 20037

MONTEITH, LARRY KING, chancellor emeritus; b. Bryson City, N.C., Aug. 17, 1933; s. Earl and Essie (King) M.; m. Nancy Alexander, Apr. 19, 1952; children: Larry, Carol, Steve. BSEE, N.C. State U., 1960; MSEE, Duke U., 1962, PhD in Elec. Engring., 1965. Registered profl. engr., N.C. Mem. tech. staff Bell Tel. Labs., Burlington, NC, 1960-62, Rsch. Triangle Inst., Raleigh, NC, 1962-66, group leader rsch. sect., 1966-68; adj. asst. prof. elec. engring. N.C. State U., Raleigh, 1965-68, assoc. prof., 1968-72, prof., 1972—, head dept. elec. engring., 1974-78, dean of engring., 1978-89, interim chancellor, 1989-90, chancellor, 1990-98, chancellor emeritus, 1998—. Contbr. articles to profl. jours. With USN, 1952-56. Recipient Disting. Engring. Alumnus award Duke U., 1984, Outstanding Engring. Achievement award N.C. Soc. Engrs., 1990, Disting. Engring. Alumnus award N.C. State U., 1999. Fellow IEEE, Am. Soc. for Engring. Edn.; mem. NSPE (edn. adv. group), Raleigh C. of C. (bd. dirs.), Rotary Internat. (Paul Harris fellow Rotary Found. 1991), Phi Beta Kappa, Sigma Xi, Sigma Iota Rho, Phi Kappa Phi, Eta Kappa Nu, Tau Beta Pi, Sigma Beta Delta.

MONTELEONE, PATRICIA, dean; MD, St. Louis U., 1961. Dean St. Louis U. Sch. Medicine, 1994—. Office: St Louis U Sch Medicine 1402 S Grand Blvd Saint Louis MO 63104-1004

MONTELONGO, MICHAEL, business executive, army officer; b. N.Y.C. m. Debra Tenison; 1 child, Amanda. BS in Gen. Engring., U.S. Mil. Acad.; MBA in Corp. Strategy and Fin., Harvard U., 1988; grad., Command and Gen. Staff Coll., 1992. Commd. 2d lt. U.S. Army, 1977, advanced through grades to lt. col.; with U.S. Mil. Acad., West Point, NY, 1991, asst. prof. social scis. dept., 1988; adviser, spl. asst. to comdr.-in chief U.S. So. Command, 1989; bn. exec. officer, bn. and brigade ops. officer U.S. Army, 1993, spl. asst. to U.S. Army chief of staff, 1994; legis. asst. U.S. Senate, 1995; dir. BellSouth Small Bus. Svcs., 1996; sales exec. and cons. Cap Gemini Ernst & Young, 1998; asst. sec. Air Force fin. mgmt. and comptr. U.S. Dept. Def., Washington, 2001—. Trustee Unite El Paso, 1993; mem. Leadership El Paso Program, 1999. U.S. Army Advanced Civil Schooling fellow, 1986, Inter-Univ. Seminar on Armed Forces and Soc. fellow, 1990, Congl. Hispanic Caucus Inst. fellow, 1992, Army Congl. fellow, 1995. Mem.: Am. Soc. Mil. Comptrollers (pres. 2004), Nat. Soc. Hispanic MBAs (sec.), Assn. West Point Grads. (minority outreach com. 1999—, bd. dirs. Ga. Hispanic voter registration campaign 2000). Office: US Air Force Asst Sec Air Force Fin Mgt & Comptroller 1130 Air Force Pentagon Washington DC 20330-1130

MONTEMARA, WILLIAM J. accountant; BS in Acctg., CUNY; MBA, Boston U. CPA NY. Acct. Coopers & Lybrand (now PricewaterhouseCoopers), NY; audit mgr. Bristol-Myers Squibb Co., NY; with Comcast, Phila., 1993—, v.p. internal audit. Office: Comcast 1500 Market St Philadelphia PA 19102

MONTEMAYOR, CARLOS RENE, advertising agency executive; b. San Antonio, Nov. 21, 1945; s. Raul Martin and Mary (Lyall) M.; m. Marina Cara Cook, Sep. 21, 1967 (div. Dec. 1978); m. Barbara Kay Volmer, Dec. 23, 1979; 1 child, Justin Norman. BBA in Mktg., U. Tex., 1967; MS in Journalism, Northwestern U., 1968. Account exec. Campbell-Ewald Co., Detroit and Cin., 1968-72, Ross Roy Inc., Detroit, 1972-74, Pitluk Group, San Antonio, 1974-76; v.p. GSD&M Advt., San Antonio, 1976-78; mktg. mgr. Church's Fried Chicken, San Antonio, 1978-81; v.p. Ed Yardang & Assocs., San Antonio, 1981-83; pres. Montemayor y Asociados, San Antonio, 1983—2002, vice chmn., 2002—, Global Hue, 2002—. Bd. dirs. USAA Fed. Savs. Bank; past pres. Fiesta San Antonio, Ray Feo XLVII Fiesta, 1995; mem. bd. govs. Cancer Therapy and Rsch. Ctr.; mem. bd. govs., exec. com. S.W. Found.; mem. bd. dirs. ACCION Tex. 2d Lt. USAR, 1968-74. Mem. Club Giraud, Argyle Club, Friends of McNay Club, Govs. Club. Republican. Roman Catholic. Avocations: collecting classic cars, travel, racquet ball. Home: 5 Bitterblue Ln San Antonio TX 78218-1790 Office: 8242 Vicar San Antonio TX 78218-1566 Office Phone: 210-619-2001.

MONTEMURRO, ELIZABETH A, education educator; b. Flemington, NJ, Apr. 13, 1972; d. Anthony and Susan Montemurro; m. Fernando J Charvet, June 2000. BA, Manhattan Coll., 1994; MA, U. of Ga., 1998, PhD, 2001. Contbr. articles to jours. Pre-doctoral tng. grant, Nat. Inst. of Alcohol Abuse and Alcoholism, 1997—2002. Mem.: Ea. Sociol. Soc., Sociologists for Women in Soc., Am. Sociol. Assn., Alpha Kappa Delta, Phi Beta Kappa. D-Liberal. Avocations: writing, walking, travel. Office: Penn State Abington 1600 Woodland Rd Abington PA 19001 E-mail: bmontemurro@hotmail.com.

MONTERO, DARREL MARTIN, social worker, sociologist, educator; b. Sacramento, Mar. 4, 1946; s. Frank and Ann Naake; divorced; children: David Paul, Lynn Elizabeth, Laura Ann, Emily Kathryn. AB, Calif. State U., 1970; MA, UCLA, 1972, PhD, 1974. Postgrad. researcher Japanese-Am. Research Project UCLA, 1971-73, dir. research, 1973-75; assoc. head Program on Comparative Ethnic Studies, Survey Research Ctr. UCLA, 1973-75; asst. prof. sociology Case Western Res. U., Cleve., 1975-76; asst. prof. urban studies, research sociologist Pub. Opinion Survey, dir. urban ethnic research program U. Md., College Park, 1976-79; assoc. prof. Ariz. State U., Tempe, 1979—. Cons. rsch. sect. Viewer Sponsored TV Found., Los Angeles, Berrien E. Moore Law Office, Inc., Gardena, Calif., 1973, Bur. for Social Sci. Research, Inc., Washington, Friends of the Family, Ltd., Nat. Sci. Found. Author: Japanese Americans: Changing Patterns of Ethnic Affiliation Over Three Generations, 1980, Urban Studies, 1978, Vietnamese Americans: Patterns of Resettlement and Socioeconomic Adaptation in the United States, 1979, Social Problems, 1988; mem. editorial bd. Humanity and Society, 1978-80; contbr. articles to profl. jours. Served with U.S. Army, 1966-72. Mem. Am. Sociol. Assn., Am. Assn. Pub. Opinion Research (exec. council, standards com.), Am. Ednl. Research Assn., Council on Social Work Edn., Soc. Study of Social Problems, D.C. Sociol. Soc., Am. Soc. Pub. Adminstrn., Nat. Assn. Social Workers, Pacific Sociol. Assn. Office: Ariz State Univ Sch Social Work Tempe AZ 85281

MONTERO, FERNAN GONZALO, retired advertising executive; b. Buenos Aires, May 22, 1948; came to U.S., 1952; s. Adolfo and Donne (Strang) M. BBA, U. Wis., 1971; M. Journalism in Advt., Northwestern U., 1972. With Young & Rubicam Inc., 1972-82; pres. Young & Rubicam Argentina, Buenos Aires, 1982-85; dep. area mgr. Young & Rubicam Latin Am., Sao Paulo, Brazil, 1985-87; sr. v.p., dir. bus. devel. Young & Rubicam Inc., N.Y.C., 1987-91, chmn., CEO Latin Am., 1991-92, chmn., CEO Europe, Middle East London, 1993-98.

MONTES, LEOPOLDO FELICIANO, dermatologist, educator; b. Buenos Aires, Nov. 22, 1929; came to U.S., 1955, naturalized, 1974; s. Leopoldo A. and Celia (Gaztambide) M.; m. Maria Mercedes Pfeiffer, Nov. 25, 1961; children: Carolina, Mercedes, Ana, Leopoldo, Teresa, William. MD, U. Buenos Aires, 1954; MS, U. Mich., 1959. Intern City of Buenos Aires Hosps., 1954-55; resident in dermatology Pa. Hosp., Phila., 1955-56; resident in dermatology, then instr. U. Mich. Med. Center, Ann Arbor, 1956-60; practice medicine specializing in dermatology Buenos Aires, 1960-63, 82—, Houston, 1963-66, Birmingham, Ala., 1966-81; dermatologist U. Ala., Eye Found.; asst. prof. Baylor U. Coll. Medicine, Houston, 1963—66; mem. faculty U. Ala. Med. Ctr. and Med. Coll. Ala., Birmingham, 1966—, prof. dermatology, 1969—81, assoc. prof. microbiology, 1968—91, prof. emeritus, 1982—; clin.

prof. dermatology U. South Ala., 2002—03. Adj. prof. anatomy Coll. Medicine, U. South Ala., Mobile, 1981-89; adj. prof. large animal surgery and medicine Auburn U. Sch. Veterinary Medicine, 1977—; dir. Dermatology Rsch. Structural Rsch. Ctr., Mobile, 1990—, Vitiligo Unit, 1990. Author: Atlas of Skin Diseases of the Horse, 1983, Vitiligo-Nutritional Therapy, 1999, Scanning Electron Microscopy of Normal and Abnormal Skin, 1985; founding editor Jour. Cutaneous Pathology, 1973-83. Mem. internat. adv. bd. Nat. Vitiligo Found., 2002—. Recipient Rsch. Career Devel. award USPHS, 1965-70; grantee USPHS, NSF, Kresge Found., John A. Hartford Found. Fellow Am. Acad. Dermatology, Am. Acad. Microbiology, Royal Coll. Physicians and Surgeons Can.; mem. AAAS, Am. Soc. Microbiology, Soc. Investigative Dermatology, Histochem. Soc., Am. Soc. Cell Biology, Am. Fedn. Clin. Rsch., Electron Microscope Soc. Am., Internat. Soc. Tropical Dermatology (Asst. sec. gen. 1969-74), Am. Dermatol. Assn., Am. Soc. Dermatopathology, Sigma Xi. Home: Suipacha 1308 1011 Buenos Aires Argentina Office: Paraguay 2302 1121 Buenos Aires Argentina also: Structural Rsch Ctr 120 Novatan Rd Mobile AL 36608 Fax: 5411.4314.4328. Office Phone: 011-5411-4962-4684. E-mail: leopoldo_montes@hotmail.com. *While taking care of a patient I always considered it indispensable to study and research as much as I could about the disease I was treating, to feel I was perhaps the only one in a position to help, to put myself-as Lord Lister said-in the patient's place.*

MONTFORD, JOHN THOMAS, state legislator, academic administrator, lawyer; b. Ft. Worth, June 28, 1943; s. Thomas L. and Jewell F. (Coursey) M.; m. Pamela Jacobs, June 3, 1966 (div.); 1 child, Melinda; m. Debra Kay Mears, Dec. 24, 1975; children: Melonie, John Ross. BA, U. Tex., Austin, 1965, JD, 1968; LLD (hon.), Lubbock (Tex.) Christian U., 1989. Bar: Tex. 1968. Pvt. practice, Lubbock, 1971-78; criminal dist. atty. Lubbock County, 1979-82; state sen. Dist. 28, Lubbock, 1983-96; chancellor Health Scis. Ctr. Tex. Tech. U., 1996—. Adj. faculty Tex. TEch. Coll. of Edn., High Edn. Adminstrn. Program, 1999; founding pres. South Plains Pub. Sch. Found. Trustee S. Park Hosp., Lubbock, 1981-82; bd. dirs., trustee Tex. Boys Ranch, Lubbock, 1982—; chmn. profl. divsn. United Way, Lubbock, 1980; energy com. So. Legis. Conf., 1983; senate appointee So. Growth Policies Bd., 1983; chmn. adv. coun. Lubbock Substance Abuse Prevention Partnership; mem. bd. govs. West Tex. chpt. Multiple Sclerosis; mem. Dean's Roundtable U. Tex. Sch. Law, 1988; mem. Lubbock Symphony Orch. Bd., 1997—; v.p. Jaycees, 1974; adv. group Am. Heart Assn. Tex. affiliate, 1999; co-chmn., adv. coun. Tex. LWV Edn. Fund, 1999; bd. trustees The Nature Conservancy of Tex., 1999. Maj. USMC, 1968-71. Recipient Outstanding Young Man of Lubbock award Jaycees, 1973, Headliner of Yr. award Greater Lubbock Press Club, 1979, Man of Yr./Law Enforcement award Lubbock Optimist Club, 1979, Boss of Yr. award Legal Secs. Assn., 1980, Exec. of Yr., Lubbock Sales Exec. Assn., 1981; named Finest Freshman Tex. Bus. Mag., 1983, Outstanding State Sen. Tex. Youth Commn., 1988, Legislator of Yr. Tex. Pub. Health Assn., 1988, Legislator of Yr. Tex. Pub. Employees Assn. and State Employees, 1989, Outstanding Tex. Leader award John Ben Shepperd Pub. Leadership Forum, 1989, Best New Legislator award Tex. Monthly mag., 1983, Disting. Alumni, L.D. Bell H.S., 1984, Lubbock's Man of the Yr. LWV and Am. Diabetes Assn,. 1987, Disting. Svc. award Tex. C. of C., 1989, Outstanding Legislator in State of Tex., Epsilon Sigma Phi, 1989, Legislator of Yr. award Tex. Soc. Profl. Surveyors, 1989, Legislator of Yr. award 71st Legis., Tex. Mcpl. League, 1989, Tree of Life award Jewish Nat. Fund, 1989; named one of the Ten Best Legislators 71st Legis., Dallas Morning News, Tex. Monthly, 1989, 72d Legis., 1991, Tex. Monthly, 1989, 91, Outstanding Legislator Epsilon Sigma Phi, 1989, Tex. Mcpl. League, 1989; recipient Outstanding Svc. award Tex. Electric Coops., 1989, Pub. Ofcl. award Tex. Pub. Power Assn., 1990, George Woods award in politics NAACP, 1990, Legis. Leadership award 72d Legislator Tex. C. of C., 1992, One of the Seven Best Legislators 73d Legis. Dallas Morning News, 1993, 74th Legis. Dallas Morning News, 1995, One of the Ten Best Legislators 73d Legis. Tex. Monthly, 1993, 74th Legis. Tex. Monthly, 1995, Legislator of Yr. Tex. Pub. Employees Assn., 1993, award Lubbock arts Festival, 1994, award Tex. Mental Health Assn., 1994, honor award Tex. Commn. on the Arts, 1994, Cmty. Statesman award Heritage of Odessa Found., 1995, Legislator of Yr. award Tex. Game Warden's Assn., 1995, Judy coyle Tex. Liberty award Assn. Tex. Profl. Educators, 1995, Man of Yr. in Tex. Colls. & Univs., 1995, Outstanding Legislator award Tex. Police chiefs Assn., 1995, One of Top Ten, Harte-Hanks CComm., Inc., 1995, Newsmaker of 1995, Lubbock Avalanche Jour., One of Friends of Bus. 74th Legis., Tex. Bus. Mag., 1995, Outstanding Legislator, Tex. Jr. Coll. Tchrs Assn., 1995, Integrated Pest Mgmt. award in Excellence, Nat. Found. Integrated Pest Mgmt. Edn., 1996, Paul Harris fellow Rotary Internat., 1997, Founders award Ind. Coll. and Univ. Tex., 1997, Tex. most powerful citizen Lubbock Avalanche-Jour., 1999, Road Hand award Tex. Good Roads Assn., 1999, Declaration of Gratitude Tex. Tech. Sch. Pharmacy, 2000 and numerous others. Mem. State Bar Tex. (com. admissions), Tex. Criminal Def. Lawyers Assn., Tex. Dist. and County Attys. Assn. (life, legis. com.), Western State Water Coun., Tex. Assn. Cmty. Schs. (hon. life), Tex. Heart Inst. (nat. adv. coun. 1991), Lubbock C. of C. (Disting. Svcs. award 1996), Tex. Bar Found., Order of Coif (hon.), Rotary, Lions (Lubbock club), Omicron Delta Kappa, Delta Theta Phi, Phi Kappa Phi, Kappa Sigma (Pres. Commn. 2000), Phi Beta Delta. Office: 1 Buckingham Ct San Antonio TX 78257-1708

MONTGOMERY, ALICE ELIZABETH, vocalist, speech pathologist; b. St. Louis, Oct. 19, 1950; d. Henry Cronbach and Cecile Koven Lowenhaupt; m. Stephen Allen Montgomery; children: Alexander, Benjamin; m. Jonathan Feldman, Dec. 28, 1975 (div. Oct. 1979). BA, U. Mich., 1972; MS, Fontbonne U., St. Louis, 1997. Profl. classical singer, N.Y.C., 1972—86; grant accessor NY State Coun. for the Arts, 1984—86; voice tchr. Webster U., St Louis, 2001—; voice specialist Ctr. for Voice, 2001—. Recipient Finalist, Chgo. Lyric Opera Competition, 1979. Mem.: Nat. Assn. of Tchr. of Singing, Missouri Speech and Hearing Assn., Am. Speech and Hearing Assn. Home: 6933 Kingsbury Blvd Saint Louis MO 63130

MONTGOMERY, AMANDA E. music educator; d. John E. and Elizabeth B. Owens; m. Stefan L. Montgomery, June 20, 1998. MusB, Furman U., 1996; MusM, James Madison U., 1998. Tchg. assoc. James Madison U., Harrisonburg, Va., 1996—98; staff tchr. Farr Music Sch., Greenville, SC, 1998—2000, Furman U., Greenville, SC, 1998—2000, Master's Touch Sch. Music, Grapevine, Tex., 2003—04; tchg. asst. La. State U., Baton Rouge, 2000—03. Presenter in field. Mem.: Coll. Music Soc., Music Tchrs. Nat. Assn., Phi Kappa Lambda. Home: 129 Hobcaw Ln Orangeburg SC 29118

MONTGOMERY, ANN D. federal judge, educator; b. Litchfield, Minn., May 9, 1949; m. Theodore Smetak; 2 children; 1 stepchild. BS, U. Kans., 1971; JD, U. Minn., 1974. Bar: Minn. 1974, U.S. Dist. Ct. Minn., U.S. Ct. Appeals (8th cir.), U.S. Supreme Ct. Law clk. D.C. Ct. Appeals, Washington, 1974-75; asst. U.S. atty. Dist. Minn., Mpls., 1976-83; mcpl. judge Hennepin County, 1983-85; judge Hennepin County Dist. Ct., 1985-94, U.S. Magistrate Ct., 1994-96; federal judge U.S. Dist. Ct., Mpls., 1996—. Adj. prof. U. Minn. Law Sch., Mpls., 1988—; steering com. mem., dir. criminal divsn. Minn. Jud. Coll., 1990-94. Recipient Trial Judge of Yr. award Am. Bd. Trial Advocates, 1996. Mem. FBA, Minn. Dist. Judges Assn., Minn. Bar Assn., Minn. Women Lawyers (Myra Bradwell award 2000), Hennepin County Bar Assn. (Professionalism award 1993), Eighth Cir. Dist. Judges Assn. (pres. 2003—). Office: US Dist Ct 300 S 4th St Minneapolis MN 55415-1320 Fax: 612-664-5097. E-mail: admontgomery@mnd.uscourts.gov.

MONTGOMERY, ANNA FRANCES, elementary school educator; b. Spokane, Wash., Nov. 5, 1945; d. Carl Jacob and Edna Frances (Evans) Kuipers; m. William Lee Montgomery Jr., Oct. 7, 1989. AA, Mid. Ga. Coll., 1965; BS in Elem. Edn., Woman's Coll. of Ga., 1966; MEd, Ga. Coll., 1969, specialist in edn., 1973; studied Brit. edl. sys., London, 1978. Cert. elem. tchr., Ga. Classroom tchr. Muscogee County Sch. Dist., Columbus, Ga., 1966—2002, reading tchr. Title 1 tutorial program, summer 1975, instr. staff devel. program, 1977-80; social sci. lead tchr. Wesley Heights Elem. Sch., Columbus, 1992—2002, chmn. mgmt. team, 1997-98. Tennis and athletic instr. Camp Tegawitha, Tobyhanna, Pa., 1970; social studies textbook adoption com. Muscogee County Sch. Dist., 1977-78, 82-83, 98-99, sick leave com., 1993-95; judge Columbus Regional Social Sci. Fair, 1977, 93-96; basic skills program comprehensive planning task force Muscogee County Sch. Dist., 1995-96, com. to revise the basic skills program in social studies, 1980; presenter in field. Editor: Muscogee County School District's Handbook for Beginning Teachers, 1979. Treas. Wesley Heights PTA, 1983-86; vol. Med. Ctr. Aux., Columbus, 1975-79; pres. pastor's Bible study class St. Luke United Meth. Ch., 1993, 94, 96, 97, 98, mem. Sarah Cir. 11, sec., 1969-71, 78-80, co-chmn., 1974-76, chmn., 1976-78; mem. Bessie Howard Ward Handbells Choir; devel. chmn. Ga. state divsn. Centennial/fellowships com. AAUW, 1974-76. Recipient Valley Forge Tchrs. medal Freedoms Found. at Valley Forge, 1975, Outstanding Tchr. of Yr. award Wesley Hts. Elem. Sch., 1975, Muscogee County Sch. Dist., 1979; named Very Important Lady award Girl Scouts Am., Columbus, 1976, Outstanding Young Woman Am., 1982. Mem. AAUW (chmn. centennial fellowship com. Columbus br. 1973-75), Ga. PTA (hon. life), Profl. Assn. Ga. Educators (life, bldg. rep. Muscogee County chpt. 1983-2002, sec. 1992-94, treas. 1994-98, pres.-elect 1998-2000, Muscogee County's sys. rep. to the state 2000-02, social chmn. 2002-03), Nat. Coun. Social Studies (hostess and registration coms. ann. meeting 1975), Ga. Coun. for Social Studies, Ga. Sci. Tchrs. Assn., Atlanta Alumni Club, Valley Area Sci. Tchrs. (corr. sec. 1996-98), Ga. Coll. Alumni Assn., Mid. Ga. Coll. Alumni Assn., Order of Amaranth (charity 1991-93, 95, truth 1994, assoc. conductress 1996, conductress 1997, assoc. matron 1998, royal matron 1999), Scottish Rite Ladies Aux., Ga. Ret. Educators Assn., Muscogee Ret. Educators Assn., Alpha Delta Kappa (Rho chpt., sec. 1975-76, pres.-elect 1976-78, pres. 1978-80, chaplain, 1996-98), Delta Kappa Gamma (Beta Xi chpt., pres. 1980-82, chmn. pubs. and publicity 1976-78, chmn. profl. affairs 1978-80, nominations com. chair 1980-82, chmn. world fellowship and fund raising 1984-86, 96-2004, chmn. fin. 1990-92, chmn. membership 1994-96, 2000-04), Order Internat. Fellowship in Edn., Wesley Heights Elem. Sch. PTA, Phi Delta Kappa, Phi Theta Kappa. Avocations: reading, organic gardening, travel, fishing, playing clarinet and handbells. Home: 5134 Stone Gate Dr Columbus GA 31909-5573

MONTGOMERY, BETTY DEE, state auditor, former state attorney general, former state legislator; b. Apr. 3, 1948; BA, Bowling Green State U.; JD, Coll. Law U. Toledo, 1976. Former criminal clk. Lucas County Common Pleas Ct.; former asst. pros. atty. Wood County, Ohio, 1977—78, former pros. atty., 1980—88, City of Perrysburg, Ohio, 1978—81; former mem. Ohio Senate Dist. w, 1988—95; former atty. gen. State of Ohio, Columbus, 1994—2002, auditor, 2002—. Former mem. Econ. Devel. Tech. & Aerospace, Agr. & Ways & Means Com.; former vice-chmn. Judiciary Com. Mem. bd. dirs. Ohio Sch. Bd. Atty. Assn. Recipient Women of Achievement award, Toledo Women in Comms., 1984, Govt. Leaders Against Drunk Drivers, MADD, 1990, Senator of the Year, Ohio Hospice Assn., 1991, Disting. Svc. award, Ohio State Bar Assn., 1992, Ohio Women Hall of Fame award, 1996, Public Svc. award, Ohio Assn. of Big Brothers/Big Sisters, 1999, Advocacy award, Ohio Soc. Healthcare Consumer Advocacy, 1999, Child Adv. of the Year, Ohio Ct. Appointed Spl. Advs./Guardian Ad Litem Assn., 1999, Toledo YWCA Milestones award, Women in Govt., 2001, Presdl. award for Pro Bono Svc., The Ohio Legal Assistance Found., 2002, ABA Pro Bono award, to the Office of the Atty. Gen., 2002, Disting. Alumnus award, Bowling Green State Univ., 2003. Mem.: Ohio Prosecuting Atty. Assn. (mem. 1984), Legis. Com., Internat. Prosecutors Assn., Wood County Bar Assn., Alternative Edn. Adv. Com. (former chmn.), Wood County Child Abuse & Neglect Adv. Bd. (former vice-chmn., chmn.), Sexual Abuse Prevention Project, Wood County Sch. (mem. 1981—), Bowling Green C. of C. Republican. Office: Auditor of State 88 E Broad St 5th Fl Columbus OH 43215

MONTGOMERY, CHARLES HARVEY, lawyer; b. Spartanburg, S.C., Jan. 28, 1949; s. Dan Hugh and Ann Louise (Gasque) M.; m. Renée Jean Gubernot, Mar. 27, 1971; children: Charles Scott, Marie Renée. BA, Duke U., 1971; JD, Vanderbilt U., 1974. Bar: N.C. 1974, U.S. Dist. Ct. (ea. dist.) N.C. 1974, U.S. Supreme Ct. 1979, U.S. Dist. Ct. (mid. dist.) N.C. 1991; cert. family law specialist, N.C., 1995. Assoc. Jordan Morris & Hoke, Raleigh, N.C., 1974-75; atty. Wake County Legal Svcs., Raleigh, 1975-76; pvt. practice, Raleigh, 1977; ptnr. Montgomery & Montgomery, Cary, N.C., 1978-79, Sanford Adams McCullough & Beard, Raleigh, 1979-86, Adams McCullough & Beard, Raleigh, 1986-88, Toms Reagan & Montgomery, Cary, 1989-92, Toms & Montgomery, Cary, 1992-93; pvt. practice, Cary, 1993—. Bd. dirs. Br. Bank and Trust, Cary; pres. Family Law Mediation, Inc. Councilman Town of Cary, 1977-81, 83-87; vice-chmn. Wake County Dem. party, Raleigh, 1991-92; commr. Wake County, Raleigh, 1992; bd. dirs. East Cen. Cmty. Legal Svcs., Inc., 1997-2003, State Capitol Found., 1994—. Mem.: ABA, Cary Bar Assn. (organizer 1993—), N.C. Acad. Trial Lawyers (chair family law sect. 1996—98), Wake County Bar Assn. (bd. dirs. 1999—2001), N.C. Bar Assn. (chmn. pub. info. com. 1994—96, dir. family law coun. 1994—97). Methodist. Avocation: sailing. Office: PO Box 1325 590 New Waverly Pl Ste 110 Cary NC 27512-1325 Office Phone: 919-816-9002. Business E-Mail: charles@montylaw.com.

MONTGOMERY, CHARLES HOWARD, retired bank executive; b. Bloomington, Ill., Mar. 23, 1930; s. Dewey H. and Madeline (Wonderlin) M.; m. Diane Dickerson Cohen, Aug. 30, 1978 (dec. Oct. 1996); children: Alison, Douglas; m. Katharine Yang, Oct. 4, 1997. AB, Ill. Wesleyan U., 1951; MS, U. Ill., 1960. CPA, Ill. Auditor Lybrand Ross Bros. & Montgomery, Rockford, Ill., 1955-59; with Abbott Labs., North Chicago, Ill., 1959-67, controller, 1965-67; v.p. finance Anchor Coupling Co., Libertyville, 1967-69; v.p., comptroller First Nat. Bank Chgo., 1969-73, sr. v.p., 1973-75, exec. v.p., 1976-88, comptroller, 1973-88, First Chgo. Corp.; ret. Past chmn. Inter-Assn. Com. Bank Acctg. Served with AUS, 1952-53. Mem. Fin. Execs. Inst., AICPA, Ill. Soc. CPAs, Tau Kappa Epsilon, Phi Kappa Phi, Univ. Club (Chgo.) also: 6321 N Avers Ave Chicago IL 60659-1001 Home: 824 Georgia St Key West FL 33040-7263 E-mail: chmonty@att.net.

MONTGOMERY, CLEOTHUS, minister; b. Henderson, Tex., Dec. 6, 1926; s. Lewis and Amanda (Waters) M.; m. Emma Agusta Tinch (dec. Aug. 23, 1987); children: Michael Dennis, Debra Marie, Pamela Key, Diane Renea, Anthony Cleothus (dec.). BS in Drafting, Calif. Coll., 1951; B in Theology, Union Bapt. Theol. Sem., 1962; M in Theology, Inter Bapt. Theol. Sem., 1965, DD, 1973; D in Sacred Theol. (hon.), Mt. Hope Bible Coll., 1973; M in Ministry, Trinity Theol. Sem., 1990, D in Ministry, 1993. Cert. christian counselor, Tex. Minister Northside Missionary Bapt. Ch., Houston, 1962—. Counselor Chemical Dependency, Houston, 1989-97, Internat. Christian Inst., 1990-97; invited pastor by Campus for Christ to Israel, 1987, Africa, 1990, Russia, 1995-97. Pres. World Christian Tng. Ctr., Houston, 1985-90, Houston Minister Christian Fellowship, 1992-97; chmn. Minister Network Life Gift, Houston, 1988-90, Ministers Against Crime, Houston, 1989-97; treas. Life Investment for Tng., Houston, 1990-97; v.p. Ministerial Adv. to Mayor, Houston, 1995-97; trustee bd. of regency, adv. bd. Coll. of Biblical Studies. With U.S. Army, 1945-46. Mem. NAACP, Am. Assn. Christian Counselors (chemical dependency counselor 1993-97). Democrat. Baptist. Avocations: reading, devotional writings, bowling, travel, jogging. Home: 1407 Laurentide St Houston TX 77029-3411 Office: Northside Missionary Bapt Ch 3202 Bennington St Houston TX 77093-9222

MONTGOMERY, CLIFF WILSON, journalist, writer, researcher; b. Cumberland, Md., Aug. 13, 1965; s. Clifford Ray and Elizabeth Ann Montgomery. European Lit.(hon.), Ed. by pvt. tutor, Charlotte, NC, 1983—91, Am. Lit. (hon.), 1994—98. EastCoast polit. corr. 3 A.M. Mag., Kirkland, Wash., 2000—. Media cons. Sierra Club, Charlotte, NC, 1998. *Among other disclosures, in 2003 he was among the first American journalists to show decisively that Iraq no longer possesses huge stores of chemical and biological weapons or such weapons agents, and was not an immediate nuclear threat, negating a set of concerns which had been the principle rationale behind the second Iraq War. He believes it is the job of any serious journalist to "tell truth to power," however unpopular the truth.* Freelance journalist Washington Spectator, In These Times, Working for Change, Alternet and Political Affairs. Mem. Nat. Trust for Hist. Preservation, 1996—99; activist Amnesty Internat., 1992—96; mem. Pub. Concern Found., 1994—, Archaeol. Inst. of Am., 1999—2000. Independent. Avocations: history, travel, motorcycling. E-mail: clifmn@aol.com.

MONTGOMERY, CONNIE ROGER, writer; b. Radford, Va., Apr. 11, 1945; s. Hobart Leamon and Gladiese Buckner Montgomery; m. Susie Fisher Montgomery, Dec. 31, 1968; children: Darrell, Rhonda, Mark, Beth. AAS in Instrumentation, New River Cmty. Coll., 1978, AAS in Indsl. Elec., 1979. Procedure writer, instrumentation Duke Power, Charlotte, NC, 1996—2000, writer Seneca, SC, 1998—2001, Bridgman, Mich., 2002, maintenance procedure writer Seneca, SC, 2003—. E-5 U.S. Army, 1965—68, Vietnam. Avocations: writing, photography, fishing. Home: PO Box 852 Clover SC 29710 E-mail: info@rogermontgomerypoems.com.

MONTGOMERY, DAN T. construction company executive; Pres. Omni Constrn. Inc., Bethesda, Md. Office: Omni Constrn Inc 7500 Old Georgetown Rd Bethesda MD 20814-6133

MONTGOMERY, DAVID BRUCE, marketing educator; b. Fargo, N.D., Apr. 30, 1938; s. David William and Iva Bernice (Trask) Montgomery; m. Toby Marie Franks, June 11, 1960; children: David Richard, Scott Bradford, Pamela Marie. BSEE, Stanford U., 1960, MBA, 1962, MS in Stats., 1964, PhD in Mgmt. Sci., 1966; D honoris causa, Limburgs U. Centrum, Belgium, 1998. Asst. prof. mgmt. MIT, 1966-69, assoc. prof., 1969-70; assoc. prof. mktg. and mgmt. sci. Stanford U., 1970-73, prof., 1973-78, Robert A. Magowan prof. mktg., 1978-92, Sebastian S. Kregge prof. mktg. strategy, 1992-99, prof. emeritus, 1999—; dean Sch. Bus. Singapore Mgmt. U., 2003—. Prin. The MAC Group Inc., 1969-91; mem. adv. bd. LEK Partnership, London; mem. sci. adv. bd. Univ. Connection, Bonn, Germany; acad. trustee Mktg. Sci. Inst., 1994-2000, exec. dir., 1995-97. Author: (with Glen L. Urban) Management Science in Marketing, 1969, (with Massy and Morrison) Stochastic Models of Buying Behavior, 1970, (with Day et al) Planning: Cases in Computer and Model Assisted Marketing, 1973, (with others) Consumer Behavior: Theoretical Sources, 1973, (with G. J. Eskin) Data Analysis, 1975; editor 5 books; cons. editor Jour. Internat. Mktg., 2000-03; mem. editl. bd. Mgmt. Sci., Jour. Mktg., Jour. Mktg. Rsch., Mktg. Sci., Jour. acad. of Mktg. Sci., Jour. Internat. Mktg.; contbr. more than 100 articles and tech. reports to sci. and profl. jours. Trustee Family Service Assn. of Mid Peninsula, 1972-73. Recipient citation for outstanding contbns. to use of computers in mgmt. edn. Hewlett Packard, 1977, Best Paper award Strategic Mgmt. Soc., 1996. Mem.: Am. Mktg. Assn. (Mahajan award 2002), Inst. Mgmt. Scis., Tau Beta Pi. Republican. Congregationalist. Home: 960 Wing Pl Stanford CA 94305-1020 Office: Stanford U Grad Sch Bus Stanford CA 94305 E-mail: montgomery_david@gsb.stanford.edu.

MONTGOMERY, DAVID CAMPBELL, physicist, researcher; b. Milan, Mo., Mar. 5, 1936; s. Merrill Edward and Ruth E. (Campbell) M.; m. Shirley Arlene Imig, July 20, 1957; children: Kathleen Montgomery Sutton, Elizabeth. Student, U. Mo., 1953-55; BS, U. Wis., 1956; MA, Princeton, 1958, PhD, 1959; D honoris causa, Eindhoven U. of Tech., The Netherlands, 1996. Research assoc. Princeton U., 1959-60; instr. U. Wis., 1961-62; asst. prof. U. Md., 1962-65; assoc. prof. U. Iowa, Iowa City, 1965-70, prof., 1970-77; prof. physics Coll. William and Mary, Williamsburg, Va., 1977-84; prof. Dartmouth Coll., Hanover, N.H., 1984-88, Eleanor and A. Kelvin Smith prof. physics, 1988—2004, Eleanor and A. Kelvin Smith prof. physics emeritus, rsch. prof., 2004—. Vis. prof., rschr. U. Colo., 1966, U. Alaska, 1968, U. Calif.-Berkeley, 1969-70, Bell Labs., 1971, U. Wis., 1989; lectr. Internat. Summer Sch. Theoretical Physics, Les Houches, France, 1972, U. Wis., Madison, 1973; vis. prof. Hunter campus CUNY, 1973-74, U. Nagoya, Japan, 1983, Columbia U., N.Y.C., 1985, Tech. U., Eindhoven, The Netherlands, spring 1992; vis. scientist Nat. Ctr. Atmospheric Rsch., Boulder, Colo., summers 1975, 76, 79, 87, 2002, 2004, Riso Nat. Lab., Roskilde, Denmark, 2001; cons. NASA Hdqs., Washington, 1977-82, JET Joint Undertaking, Culham, U.K., fall 1991; vis. rsch. prof. U. Md., 1977-84; mem. vis. staff Los Alamos Sci. Lab., summers 1977, 78, 79, 80, 81, 86, 91, 92, 94; cons., collaborator, vis. staff mem. Los Alamos Sci. Lab.; former cons. Oak Ridge Nat. Lab., NASA; vis. rschr. Los Alamos Nat. Lab., 1987-88, cons., 1998-2000; J.M. Burgers prof. Eindhoven Tech. U., The Netherlands, 1995-96, 97, 98, 99, 2000, 01, U. Md., 1997; vis. rschr. Courant Inst. NYU, 1997. Former assoc. editor: Physics of Fluids, Internat. Jour. Engring. Sci.; contbr. more than 175 rsch. articles to profl. publs.; also monographs. Fellow Am. Phys. Soc.; mem. N.Y. Acad. Scis., Phi Beta Kappa, Sigma Xi, Pi Mu Epsilon, Phi Mu Alpha. Achievements include introduction of modern fluid turbulence methods into space and controlled fusion theory; developed maximum entropy, or "most probable" states, method of describing coherent structures achieved as a product of turbulent relaxation. Office: Dartmouth College Physics Dept Hanover NH 03755 E-mail: david.c.montgomery@darmouth.edu.

MONTGOMERY, DAVID PAUL, professional baseball team executive; b. Phila. m. Lyn Sagendorph. BA in History, U. Pa., 1968, MBA, 1970. With Phila. Phillies, 1971—, successively mem. sales dept., dir. mktg., dir. sales, formerly exec. v.p., COO, pres., CEO, now mng. ptnr, pres., CEO.

MONTGOMERY, DENISE KAREN, nurse; b. N.Y.C., Dec. 23, 1951; d. Thomas Cornell and Dorothy Marie (Castine) Simons; m. Timothy Bruce Montgomery, July 19, 1974 (div. Feb. 1981); m. Joseph Samuel Montgomery, Aug. 20, 1983. A in Nursing, San Jacinto Coll., 1971. RN, Tex. Charge nurse Aarons Womens Clinic, Houston, 1977; rsch. asst. dept. ob-gyn. Baylor Coll. Medicine, Houston, 1977-81, nursing supr., 1979-81, program coord. population control program, 1979-81; nurse Dr. Eric J. Haufrect, Houston, 1982-83; office mgr., supr. Dr. Samuel Law, Houston, 1983-84, Dr. J.S. Montgomery III, 1987—. Contbr. articles to profl. jours. Recipient Disting. Pub. Svc. award Am. Heart Assn., 1976; numerous rsch. grants. Mem. Nat. Assn. Coll. Ob-Gyn. Republican. Roman Catholic. Home: 8202 N Tahoe Dr Houston TX 77040-1256 Office Phone: 281-955-5300. E-mail: DenMnt@aol.com.

MONTGOMERY, GARY B. manufacturing executive; CFO Amsted Industries Inc., Chgo. Office: Amsted Industries Inc 205 N Michigan Ave Chicago IL 60601

MONTGOMERY, GEORGE CRANWELL, lawyer, former ambassador; b. Chattanooga, Aug. 24, 1944; s. George Donaldson and Mary Elizabeth (Cranwell) M.; m. Carol Lanfear, 1 child, Erynn Elizabeth BA, U. Va., 1966; JD, Vanderbilt U., 1975. Bar: U.S. Ct. Appeals (D.C. cir.) 1976. Mem. legis. staff Senator Howard Baker, Washington, 1975-80; spl. counsel Senate Majority Leader, Washington, 1980-85; U.S. amb. to Oman, 1985-89; atty. Baker, Donelson, Bearman and Caldwell, Washington, 1989—95, partner, 1995—2001, shareholder, 2001—. Bd. visitors Georgetown U. Sch. of Bus. Mem. Coun. on Fgn. Rels. With USN, 1966-72, capt. Res. Mem. ABA, D.C. Bar Assn., Sigma Chi Office: Baker Donelson Bearman & Caldwell 801 Pennsylvania Ave NW Ste 800 Washington DC 20004-2616

MONTGOMERY, GILLESPIE V. (SONNY MONTGOMERY), former congressman; b. Meridian, Miss., Aug. 5, 1920; s. Gillespie M. and Emily (Jones) M. BS, Miss. State U. Mem. Miss. Senate, 1956-66, 90th-104th Congresses from 3rd Miss. Dist., 1967-96; chmn. vets. affairs com., 1981-94; mem. vets. affairs com., chmn. spl. com. on S.E. Asia 90th-102d Congresses, 1978-96; ranking minority mem., 1994-96; mem. armed services. com. 90th-103d Congresses, chmn. select com. on missing persons in southeast Asia, 1975-96; mem. vets. affairs com.; mem. Woodcock Commn., 1977; CEO, pres. The Montgomery Group, Alexandria, Va., 1997—. Pres. Miss. N.G. Assn., 1959; pres. Miss. Heart Assn., 1967-68. Served with AUS, World War II, Korea, ret. maj. gen. Miss N.G. Decorated Bronze Star medal, Combat Inf. Badge; recipient Miss. Magnolia award, 1966, Lifetime Achievement award Mil. Educators & Counselors Assn., 1992. Mem. VFW, Am. Legion 40 and 8, Congl. Prayer Breakfast Group (pres. 1970) Lodges: Masons; Shriners; Scottish Rite. Democrat. Episcopalian. Office: The Montgomery Group 11 Canal Center Plz Ste 104 Alexandria VA 22314-1595

MONTGOMERY, HENRY IRVING, financial planner; b. Dec. 18, 1924; s. Harry Biggs and Martha Grace (Wilkinson) M.; m. Barbara Louise Hook, Aug. 14, 1948; children: Barbara Ruth, Michael Henry, Kelly Ann, Andrew Stuart. Student, U. Iowa, 1942-43, 47-48; BBA, Tulane U., 1952; postgrad., U. Minn., 1976. CFP, Colo. Field agt. OSS, SSU, CIG, CIA, Cen. Europe, 1945-47; pres.

Nehi Bottling Co., Decorah, Iowa, 1952-64; prin. Montgomery Assocs., Mktg. Cons., Trieste, Italy and Iowa, 1965-72; pres. Planners Fin. Svcs., Inc., Mpls., 1972-95, chmn., 1992—. Prin. Montgomery Investment Mgmt., 1992—. Author: Race Toward Berlin, 1945. With U.S. Army, 1943-46, ETO. Decorated Bronze Star; recipient P. Kemp Fain Profl. Svc. award, 1998. Mem. DAV, VFW, Inst. CFPs (bd. dirs. 1977-82, pres. 1980-81, chmn. 1981-82, CFP of Yr. 1984, chmn. fin. products stds. bd. 1984-88), Nat. Assn. Securities Dealers (dist. 8 com. 1988-91, vice-chmn. 1990), Internat. Assn. Fin. Planning (internat. dir. 1976-81, govt. rels. com. 1991—, Minn. chpt. Henry and Andrew Montgomery scholarship co-named in his honor), Investment Co. Inst. (investment adviser com. 1982—), Mpls. Estate Planning Coun., Met. Tax Planning Group (pres. 1984-87), Twin City Fin. Planners (pres. 1976-78), Twin Cities Soc. CFPs, Am. Legion, Elks, Beta Gamma Sigma. Avocation: italian and german languages. Office: Planners Fin Svcs Inc 7710 Computer Ave Ste 100 Minneapolis MN 55435-5417 Office Phone: 952-835-9000.

MONTGOMERY, HUGH EVERETT, JR., civilian military executive; b. Jackson, Miss., July 9, 1944; s. Hugh Everett and Clara (Neelly) M.; m. Liller Markel, May 19, 1966; children: Melinda Dawn, Michelle Elise. BS in Physics and Math., Miss. Coll., 1966; MS in Physics, U. Tenn., 1969, postgrad., 1969-70; diploma, Kennedy Sch. Govt. Harvard U., 1989. Rsch. physicist Naval Surface Warfare Ctr., Dahlgren, Va., 1966-72, dir. tech. br., 1972-79; dir. rsch. Naval Sea Systems Command, Washington, 1979-80; dir. planning and programming Office Naval Tech., Washington, 1980-81; industry ind. R&D mgr. Office Chief Naval Material, Washington, 1981-84; tech. dir. tech. assessment div. Office Chief Naval Ops., Washington, 1985-86, dep. dir. sci. and tech. div., 1986-90, dir. sci. and tech. divsn., 1990-98, dep. dir. test and evaluation and tech. requirements, 1999-2000; tech. dir. Marine Corps Warfighting Lab., 2001—03; exec. dir. Inst. Def. and Homeland Security, 2003—. Exec. dir. Navy sci. and tech. requirements com. Office Chief Naval Ops., 1989-2000, chmn. Navy sci. and tech. working group, 1985-2000; chmn. Navy industry R & D bd. Office Chief Naval Material, 1982-84. Patentee in field; contbr. articles to profl. jours. Organizer, leader Sea Walker's Quartet, Fredericksburg, Va., 1979-99; spokesman Friends of the Rappahannock, Fredericksburg, 1986—, North Ferry Farm Civic Assn., Fredericksburg, 1972-80, Fredericksburg Environ. Group, 1974-78; deacon Ferry Farm Bapt. Ch., 1986—, deacon vice-chmn., 2001, deacon chmn., 2002; tchr., 1974—; mem. devel. commn. Rappahannock Area, 1995—, transp. adv. group, 1994—; transp. adv. com. Spotsylvania County, 1994—; v.p. River Bluffs Owner's Assn., 1995-2000; chmn. Spotsylvania County Planning Commn., 1997, 2000, 04, vice-chmn., 1996. Recipient Navy Disting. Civilian Svc. award, 1992, 2001, Navy Superior Civilian Svc. award, 1987; named Presdl. Meritorious Exec., 1990. Mem. Fed. Exec. Inst. Alumni Assn., River Bluffs Civic Assn., Audubon Soc., Fredericksburg Sister City Assn., Miss. Soc. Washington, Harvard Kennedy Sch. Alumni Assn., Naval Acad. Alumni Assn., Sigma Pi Sigma, Omicron Delta Kappa. Avocations: boating, music, home construction, photography, church activities. Home: 3 River Oak Pl Fredericksburg VA 22407-2321 Office: CIT Tower Ste 600 2214 Rock Hill Rd Herndon VA 20170-4200 Office Phone: 703-689-3034.

MONTGOMERY, JACK SHERWOOD, performing company executive, director; b. Chgo., Apr. 29, 1944; s. Jack Sherwood Montgomery Sr. and Coral Jeanne Montgomey; life ptnr. Leon Irwin Natker, June 16, 1973. BA, San Diego State U., San Diego, Calif., 1967; MFA, Goddard Coll., Plainfield, Vt., 1976. Set designer San Diego Opera Co., 1966—68; artistic dir. Shawnee Summer Theater, Bloomfield, Ind., 1973—80; set designer Drama Divsn. Julliard Sch., N.Y., 1969—70; costume/set designer Alliance Theater, Atlanta, 1970—71; artistic dir. Resident Theater, Kans. City, Mo., 1970—72; concept designer Crown Ctr. Hallmark, Kans. City, 1971—72; set designer Profl. Performing Co., Chgo., 1972—73, co-artistic dir., 1973—79; set designer Chgo. Opera Theater, Chgo., 1974—76; guest lectr. Northwestern U., Evanston, Ill., 1978—83; performer Hull Ho., Chgo., 1980—83; set designer Mo., Kans., Mo., 1968—76; dir. Starlight Opera, San Diego, 1986—88, La Jolla Stage Co., La Jolla, Calif., 1986—87; performer Lawrence Welk Theater, Escondido, Calif., 1987—97; artistic dir. Coronado Playhouse, Coronado, Calif., 1996—98; set designer San Diego Comic Opera, San Diego, 1986—93, assoc. artistic dir., 1993—98; artistic dir. Lyric Opera San Diego, San Diego, 1999—; set designer Drama Divsn. Julliard Sch., N.Y., 1970—71; costume/set deginer Alliance Theater, Atlanta, 1970—71, art and costume designer, 1971—72; artistic dir. Resident Theater, Kans. City, Mo., 1970—72, Resident Theatre, Kans. City, 1971—72; concept designer Crown Ctr. Hallmark, Kans. City, Mo., 1972—72; set designer Profl. Performing Co., Chgo., 1972—72, 1972—73, co-artistic dir., 1973—79; set designer Chgo. Opera Theater, Chgo., 1974—75. Author: (Operas) Rip Van Winkle, 1989. Outreach dir. San Diego Opera, San Diego, Calif., 1986—2004. Mem.: Opera Am. (assoc. Ten Yr. Cert. 2003). Democrat. Avocations: travel, art, opera. Office Phone: 619-231-5714. Personal E-mail: jmontgomery@lyricoperasandiego.com.

MONTGOMERY, JAMES FISCHER, savings and loan association executive; b. Topeka, Nov. 30, 1934; s. James Maurice and Frieda Ellen (Fischer) M.; m. Diane Dealey; children: Michael James, Jeffrey Allen, Andrew Steven, John Gregory. BA in Acctg., UCLA, 1957. With Price, Waterhouse & Co., C.P.A.'s, LA, 1957-60; controller Conejo Valley Devel. Co., Thousand Oaks, Calif., 1960; asst. to pres. Gt. Western Fin. Corp., Beverly Hills, Calif., 1960-64; fin. v.p., treas United Fin. Corp., LA, 1964—69, exec. v.p., 1967—74, pres., 1974—75; chmn., CEO Great Western Financial Corp., Chatsworth, Calif., 1975-96, chmn. bd. dirs., 1996—97; founder, CEO Frontier Bank, Park City, Utah, 1998—2002, chmn., 1998—. Pres. Citizens Savs. & Loan Assn., Los Angeles, 1970-75. Served with AUS, 1958-60. Office: Frontier Bank 1245 Deer Valley Dr PO Box 981180 Park City UT 84098-1180

MONTGOMERY, JERRY LYNN, retired education educator; b. Owensville, Ind., Apr. 21, 1935; s. Philip Matthew and Lois Caroline (Anderson) M.; m. Murelyn Ann Rogers, Sept. 21, 1957 (div. Apr. 1976); stepchildren: Rebecca Williams Slominski, Matthew Williams; m. Gretchen Wendelroth Golzè, May 14, 1977; children: Robin Schneider, Lori Abbott, Vicki Randolph. BS, Purdue U., 1957; MA, Ball State U., 1964, EdD, 1969. Vocat. agrl. Milton (Ind.) Pub. Schs., 1957-58, Carthage (Ind.) Pub. Schs., 1958-61; sci. tchr. Angola (Ind.) City Schs., 1961-66; grad. asst. Ball State U., 1966-69, asst. prof. biology, 1969; edn. prof. Marietta (Ohio) Coll., 1969—2001; sci. educator Project Discovery, Athens, Ohio, 1994-99; Discovery dir. Dist. #11, 1997-98. Goal #4 com. Marietta (Ohio) City Schs., 1993-96, grade 4 profiency test content rev. and rangefinder coms. Ohio Dept. of Edn., Columbus, Ohio, 1994-2002; mem. young engrs. and scientists Marietta Telesis Group, Marietta, 1992-96; vis. prof. physics Ohio State U., 1994; grant evaluator Wash. State Cmty. Coll. and Regional Profl. Devel. Ctr., 1999—; Praxis III evaluator State of Ohio, 1997—; mem. exec. bd. Ohio Math. and Sci. Coalition, 2001—. Recipient Outstanding Educator Martha Holden Jennings Found., 1989. Mem. Assn. of Tchr. Educators (credentials com. 1991-2000), Nat. Sci. Tchrs. Assn., Sci. Edn. Coun. Ohio, Ohio Acad. of Sci., Phi Delta Kappa. Avocations: reading, canoeing, travel, fishing, golf. Home: 105 Rathbone Ter Marietta OH 45750-1443 Office: Marietta Coll 215 5th St Marietta OH 45750-4033 Business E-Mail: montgomj@marietta.edu.

MONTGOMERY, JOEL ROBERT, communications executive, consultant; b. Lexington, Sept. 9, 1946; s. Joseph Gwinn and Lucille O'Hair Montgomery. AA, U. Fla., 1966; BA, Fla. State U., 1968; MEd, EdD, Fla. Internat. U., 1992. Cert. group leader educator MATC, 1978, orgnl. develop. MATC, 1979. Mgmt. cons. Coopers & Lybrand (now PriceWaterhouseCoopers), L.A., 1979—80; regional cons. interaction mgmt. Develop. Dimensions Internat., L.A., 1981—82; pres., cons. coach Resources Inst., Hollywood, Fla., 1982—93; mgr. learning arch. Andersen Cons. (now Accenture), St. Charles, Ill., 1993—98; sr. lead bus. cons. orgnl. change Origin Tech. in Bus. (now Atos-Origin), Dallas, 1999—2000; CEO, performance coach MetaLearning-.com, LLC, Geneva, Ill., 2000—02. With Internat. Inst. Develop. of Human Resources, Bogota, Colombia, 1982; adj. instr. Fla. Internat. U., Miami, 1989—91; performance coach, spkr., cons. Practical Bus. Assessments, Geneva, 2001—02; adj. instr. Lake Forest (Ill.) Grad. Sch. Mgmt., 2002—03; rep. Primerica Fin. Svcs., Carol Stream, Ill., 2002—; bilingual educator Larkin HS, Elgin, Ill., 2003, Meadowdale Elem. Sch., Carpentersville, Ill., 2003—04. *"Joel is truly a genuine, sincere, open person who knows the skills of facilitating groups and working with individuals effectively in his bones. He is what he says he is. This basic integrity has been a hallmark of my experiences with him. He has an active mind and a keen intellect. He is able to take ideas and translate them into workable models."--JHB Joel's style is relaxed and informal, emphasizing coaching and knowledge transfer. A multilingual communicator, he has served clients on five continents. A retirement specialist, Joel helps families improve their lives.* Author: (book) Catalog of Workshop-Seminar Materials for The Resources Institute and INDER-HU, 1983, Human Relations Workbook--The Human Side of Teaching, 1990, (Book) The Development, Application and Implications of a Strategy for Reflective Learning from Experience, 1992; contbr. articles to profl. jours. Mem. ARC, Washington, 1964—, chmn. bd. dirs. Fox River chpt. St. Charles, 1993—96, bd. dirs. Broward County chpt. Ft. Lauderdale, 1990—92. Capt. U.S. Army, 1969—79. Recipient Joint Svc. Commendation medal, U.S. Army, 1975. Mem.: Ednl. Soc. Resource Mgmt., Am. Soc. Tng. & Develop., Orgnl. Develop Network, Internat. Found. Action Learning (leadership team U.S. chpt. 1995—2002), Acad. Human Resources Develop. (bd. dirs. 1997—99). Avocations: swimming, travel. Office: 717 Anderson Blvd Geneva IL 60134-1246 Office Phone: 630-208-0988. Personal E-mail: joelmonty@usa.net.

MONTGOMERY, JOHN RICHARD, pediatrician, educator; b. Burnsville, Miss., Oct. 24, 1934; s. Guy Austin and Harriet Pauline (Owens) M.; m. Dottye Ann Newell, June 26, 1965; children: John Newell, Michelle Elizabeth. BS, U. Ala., 1955, MD, 1958. Intern U. Miss., Jackson, 1958-59, resident in pediat., 1959-60, Baylor Coll. Medicine, Houston, 1960-61, fellow in pediat. infectious diseases and immunoloty, 1964-66, asst. prof. pediat., 1966-70, assoc. prof., 1970-75; chief pediat. programs U. Ala. Sch. Medicine, Huntsville, 1975-95, prof., 1975-97, prof. emeritus, 1997—. Bd. dirs. State Bd. Health, Ala. Bd. Med. Examiners; adv. com. Ala. EMS for Children. Contbr. articles to books and profl. jours. Served with AUS, 1961—62, Korea, ret. col. USAR, 1999. Mem. Soc. Pediat. Rsch., Am. Assn. Immunologists, Infectious Diseases Soc., N.Y. Acad. Scis., Am. Acad. Pediats. (pres. Ala. chpt. 1991-93), Sigma Xi, Phi Beta Kappa. Achievements include assisting in development of germ-free invironmental bubble to protect patient with no natural immunity (patient later subject of movie The Boy in the Plastic Bubble, 1976). Personal E-mail: dnjrmont@bellsouth.net.

MONTGOMERY, JOHN WARWICK (BARON OF KILTARTAN AND LORD OF MORRIS, COMTE DE ST. GERMAIN DE MONTGOMERY), law educator, theologian; b. Warsaw, N.Y., Oct. 18, 1931; s. Maurice Warwick and Harriet (Smith) M.; m. Joyce Ann Bailer, Aug. 14, 1954; 1 child: Catherine Ann; m. Lanalee de Kant, Aug. 26, 1988; 1 adopted child, Jean-Marie. AB in Philosophy with distinction, Cornell U., 1952; BLS, U. Calif., Berkeley, 1954, MA, 1958; BD, Wittenberg U., 1958, MST, 1960; PhD, U. Chgo., 1962; Docteur de l'Université, mention Théologie Protestante, U. Strasbourg, France, 1964; LLB, LaSalle Extension U., 1977; diplôme cum laude, Internat. Inst. Human Rights, Strasbourg, 1978; MPhil in Law, U. Essex, Eng., 1983; D in Civil and Canon Law (hon.), Inst. Religion and Law, Moscow, 1999; LLM, Cardiff U., Wales, 2000; LLD, Cardiff U., 2003. Bar: Va. 1978, Calif. 1979, D.C. 1985, Wash. 1990, U.S. Supreme Ct. 1981, Eng. 1984; lic. real estate broker Calif.; cert. law librarian; diplomate Med. Library Assn.; ordained to ministry Luth. Ch., 1958. Librarian, gen. reference service U. Calif. Library, Berkeley, 1954-55; instr. Bibl. Hebrew, Hellenistic Greek, Medieval Latin Wittenberg U., Springfield, Ohio, 1956-59; head librarian Swift Libr. div. and Philosophy, mem. federated theol. faculty U. Chgo., 1959-60; assoc. prof., chmn. dept. history Wilfred Laurier U. (formerly Waterloo Luth. U.), Ont., Can., 1960-64; prof., chmn. div. ch. history, history of Christian thought, dir. European Seminar program Trinity Evang. Div. Sch., Deerfield, Ill., 1964-74; prof. law and theology George Mason U. Sch. Law (formerly Internat. Sch. of Law), Arlington, Va., 1974-75; theol. cons. Christian Legal Soc., 1975-76; dir. studies Internat. Inst. Human Rights, Strasbourg, France, 1979-81; founding dean, prof. jurisprudence, dir. European program Simon Greenleaf U. Sch. Law, Anaheim, Calif., 1980-88; lic. disting. prof. theology and law, dir. European program Faith Evang. Luth. Sem., Tacoma, 1989-91; from prin. lectr. to reader in law Luton U., Eng., 1991-93, prof. law and humanities, dir. Ctr. Human Rights, 1993-97, emeritus prof., 1997—; disting. prof. apologetics, law, and history of Christian thought, v.p. acad. affairs U.K. and Europe Trinity Coll. and Theol. Sem., Newburgh, Ind., 1997—; disting. prof. law Regent U., Va., 1997-99; sr. counsel European Ctr. Law and Justice, 1997-2001; founding dir. Internat. Acad. of Apologetics, Evangelism and Human Rights, Strasbourg, France, 1997—. Vis. prof. Concordia Theol. Sem., Springfield, Ill., 1964-67, DePaul U., Chgo., 1967-70; hon. fellow Revelle Coll., U. Calif., San Diego, 1970; rector Freie Fakultaten Hamburg, Fed. Republic Germany, 1981-82; lectr. Rsch. Scientists Christian Fellowship Conf. St. Catherines Coll., Oxford U., 1985, Internat. Anti-Corruption Conf., Beijing, China, 1995; Pascal lectr. on Christianity and the Univ., U. Waterloo, Ont., Can., 1987; A. Kurt Weiss lectr. biomed. ethics U. Okla., 1997; adj. prof. Puget Sound U. Sch. Law, Tacoma, 1990-91; founding dir. Internat. Acad. Apologetics, Evangelism and Human Rights, Strasbourg, France, 1997—; Worldwide Adv. Conf. lectr. Inns of Ct. Sch. Law, London, 1998; law and religion colloquium lectr. U. Coll. London, 2000; numerous other invitational functions. Author: The Writing of Research Papers in Theology, 1959, A Union List of Serial Publications in Chicago Area Protestant Theological Libraries, 1960, A Seventeenth-Century View of European Libraries, 1962, Chytraeus on Sacrifice: A Reformation Treatise in Biblical Theology, 1962, The Shape of the Past: An Introduction to Philosophical Historiography, 1962; author: (rev. edit.), 1975; author: The Is God Dead Controversy, 1966; author: (with Thomas J.J. Altizer) The Altizer-Montgomery Dialogue, 1967; author: Crisis in Lutheran Theology, 2 vols., 1967; author: (rev. edit.), 1973; author: Es confiable el Christianismo?, 1968, Ecumenicity, Evangelicals, and Rome, 1969, Where is History Going?, 1969, History and Christianity, 1970, Damned Through the Church, 1970, The Suicide of Christian Theology, 1970, Computers, Cultural Change and the Christ, 1970, In Defense of Martin Luther, 1970, La Mort de Dieu, 1971; author: (with Joseph Fletcher) Situation Ethics: True or False?, 1972; author: The Quest for Noah's Ark, 1972; author: (rev. edit.), 1974; author: Verdammt durch die Kirche, 1973, Christianity for the Toughminded, 1973, Cross and Crucible, 2 vols., 1973, Principalities and Powers: The World of the Occult, 1973; author: (rev. edit.), 1975; author: How Do We Know There is a God?, 1973, Myth, Allegory and Gospel, 1974, God's Inerrant Word, 1974, Jurisprudence: A Book of Readings, 1974; author: (4th edit.), 1992; author: The Law Above the Law, 1975, Cómo Sabemos Que Hay un Dios?, 1975, Demon Possession, 1975, The Shaping of America, 1976, Faith Founded on Fact, 1978, Law and Gospel: A Study for Integrating Faith and Practice, 1978; author: (3rd edit.), 1994; author: Slaughter of the Innocents, 1981, The Marxist Approach to Human Rights: Analysis & Critique, 1984, Human Rights and Human Dignity, 1987, Wohin marschiert China?, 1991, Evidence for Faith: Deciding the God Question, 1991, Giant in Chains: China Today and Tomorrow, 1994, Law and Morality: Friends or Foes?, 1994, Jésus: La Raison Rejoint L'Histoire, 1995; author: (with C.E.B. Cranfield and David Kilgour) Christians in the Public Square, 1996; author: Conflicts of Law, 1997, The Transcendent Holmes, 2000, The Repression of Evangelism in Greece, 2001, Tractatus Logico-Theologicus, 2002, Christ Our Advocate, 2002, History, Law and Christianity, 2002, Heraldic Aspects of the German Reformation, 2003; editor: Lippincott's Evangelical Perspectives, 7 vols., 1970-72, 1970—72, International Scholars Directory, 1973, Simon Greenleaf Law Rev., 7 vols., 1981—88, Global Jour. Classical Theology, 1998—; contbg. editor: Christianity Today, 1965—84, New Oxford Review, 1993—95; author: (films) Is Christianity Credible, 1968, In Search of Noah's Ark, 1977, Defending the Biblical Gospel (11 videocassette series), 1985, (TV series) Christianity on Trial, 1987—93; contbr. articles to acad., theol., legal encys. and jours., chapters to books . Nat. Luth. Ednl. Conf. fellow, 1959-60; Can. Council postdoctoral sr. research fellow, 1963-64; Am. Assn. Theol. Schs. faculty fellow, 1967-68; recipient Angel award Nat. Religious Broadcasters, 1989, 90, 92, Patriarch's Medal, Romanian Orthodox Church, 2003. Fellow Trinity Coll. (Newburgh, Ind.), Royal Soc. Arts (Eng.), Victoria Inst. (London), Soc. for Advanced Legal Studies (U.K.), Acad. Internat. des Gourmets et des Traditions Gastronomiques (Paris), Am. Sci. Affiliation (nat. philosophy sci. and history sci. commn. 1966-70); mem. ALA, European Acad. Arts, Scis. and Humanities (corr. mem., Paris), Acad. Lit. France (titulary mem.), Lawyers' Christian Fellowship (hon. v.p. 1995—), Nat. Conf. U. Profs., Calif. bar Assn. (human rights commn. 1980-83), Internat. Bar Assn., World Assn. Law Profs., Mid. Temple and Lincoln's Inn (barrister mem.), Am. Soc. Internat. Law, Union Internat. des Avocats, Nat. Assn. Realtors, Tolkien Soc. Am., N.Y. C.S. Lewis Soc., Am. Hist. Assn., Soc. Reformation Rsch., Creation Rsch. Soc., Tyndale Fellowship (Eng.), Stair Soc. (Scotland), Presbyn. Hist. Soc. (North Ireland), Heraldry Soc., Soc. of Genealogists, Irish Geneaol. Soc., Am. Theol. Libr. Assn., Bibliog. Soc. U. Va., Evang. Theol. Soc., Internat. Wine and Food Soc., Soc. des Amis des Arts (Strasbourg), Chaîne des Rôtisseurs (commandeur), Athenaeum (London), Players' Theatre Club (London), Sherlock Holmes Soc. London, Soc. Sherlock Holmes de France (hon.), Club des Casseroles Lasserre (Paris), Ordre des chevaliers du Saint-Sepulcre Byzantin (commandeur), Heraldry Soc., Soc. Genealogists, Irish Geneal. Soc., Freeman of City of London, Freeman and Liveryman of Scriveners' Co., Phi Beta Kappa, Phi Kappa Phi, Beta Phi Mu. also: 2 rue de Rome 67000 Strasbourg France Office: No 9 4 Crane Ct Fleet St London EC4A 2EJ England E-mail: 106612.1066@compuserve.com.

MONTGOMERY, JOSEPH WILLIAM, finance company executive; BBA, Coll. William and Mary, 1974. Cert. fin. planner; cert. portfolio mgr. Account exec. Wheat, First Securities, Inc., Lynchburg, Va., 1975-79, Williamsburg, Va., 1979-81, v.p., investment officer, 1981-82, sr. v.p., investment officer, 1982-90; mng. dir. Wachovia Securities, Williamsburg, Va., 1990—. Mem. nat. nominating com. Outstanding Young Am. Program, 1998; bd. dirs. Future Hampton Roads, Inc., 1995—; mem. nat. campaign steering com. Campaign of 4th Century, William & Mary, 1992, bd. vis., 1995-99; mem. commn. tercentenary observanced Coll. William & Mary, 1992; mem. adv. coun. Peninsula White Sox, 1986; bd. dirs. Nat. Conf. Christians & Jews, peninsula chpt., 1986-91; mem. Williamsburg Cmty. Health Found., 1998; dir., treas. Franklin & Gladys Clark Found. Named Top 300 Fin. Advisors in Country, Worth Mag., 1998, The Chancellor's Circle, Coll. William and Mary, 1998, Broker Hall Fame, Rsch. mag., 1996, Top 250 Fin. Advisors, Worth Mag., 1999, 2001, Top 10 Ace Advisers, Ticker Mag., 2000, Best Brokers in Am. award Reg. Rep. Mag., 2002, Am. top 50 Brokers award Reg. Rep. Mag., 2003, Nation's 100 Most Exclusive Wealth Adv. Worth Mag., 2004. Mem. Internat. Assn. Fin. Planning, Inst. Cert. Fin. Planners, Investment Mgmt. Cons. Found., 1998, Soc. of Alumni William & Mary (pres. 1992, treas. 1991, sec. 1990, bd. dirs. 1989, Alumni Medallion 1996). Office: Wachovia Securities 275 McLaws Cir Williamsburg VA 23185

MONTGOMERY, JULIE-APRIL, lawyer; b. Chgo., June 17, 1957; d. Constance Louise Montgomery. BS, U. San Francisco, 1978; MBA, Roosevelt U., 1979; JD, NYU, 1983, LLM in Taxation, 1985. Bar: Ill. 1983, U.S. Dist. Ct. (no. dist.) Ill. 1983, N.Y. 1990, U.S. Supreme Ct. 1995. Legis. advisor Ill. State Senator Charles Chew, Chgo., 1983-84; staff atty. Ill. Indsl. Comm., Chgo., 1984; sole practice Chgo., 1985-86; asst. corp. counsel City of Chgo. Office of Corp. Counsel, 1986—. Co-author Ill. Inst. Cont. Legal Edn. States and Local handbook, 1990; contbr. articles to profl. jours. Instr. Minority Legal Edn. Resources Inc., Chgo., 1983—; vol. March of Dimes Chgo., 1995—; shelter vol. children's program Chgo. Christian Indsl League, 1996—. Mem. ABA, Ill. State Bar Assn. (state local tax sect. 1996—), Ill. Cert. Pub. Accts. Soc. (state and local tax sect. 1995—), Chgo. Bar Assn. (state and local tax sect. 1986—, chmn. com. 1994-95), Phi Alpha Delta, Phi Chi Theta, Alpha Sigma Nu. Lutheran. Avocations: cross-stitching, collecting betty boop, puzzles, movies, history. Office: City of Chgo Corp Counsel 30 N La Salle St Ste 1040 Chicago IL 60602-2503

MONTGOMERY, JUNE C. musician, composer; b. Columbia, S.C., Dec. 12, 1931; d. Joseph Watts Conyers and Justina Wylding; m. Edwin Fleming Montgomery, Dec. 28, 1954; children: Edwin Fleming III, Joseph Watts, James Leighton. BA in Piano with honors, Fla. State U., 1954; BS, U. Fla., 1968. Pvt. piano tchr., Jasper, Fla., 1954—63, Lake City, Fla., 1975—93; music tchr. Orange Park (Fla.) Elem., 1968—74; composer, author Music Encounters, Lake City, 1984—89, David C. Glover Method CPP/Belwin, Miami, Fla., 1988—90, Alfred Pub. Co., Van Nuys, Calif., 1990—. Carilloneur Stephen Foster Meml., White Springs, Fla., 1954—. Author, composer: FUNdamental Musicianship Skills, 1994, Theory Through the Year, 1995, author, composer with M. Mier: Musical Concepts, 1997, author, composer with M. Hinson: Meet the Great Composers, 1995, author, composer: Meet the Great Composers Repertoire Books, 1997, Stories of the Great Composers, 2000, Piano Camp, 1999, Musical Fantasies, 2001, Stories of the Great Hymns, 2002. Named Outstanding Elem. Tchr. Am., Orange Park, 1973. Mem.: Music Tchrs. Nat. Assn., Am. Coll. Musicians, Delta Kappa Gamma. Democrat. Presbyterian. Avocations: crafts, gardening. Home: Rt 8 Box 824 Lake City FL 32055

MONTGOMERY, KAREN E. library and information scientist; b. Madison, Wis., May 25, 1939; d. Guerdon Morris and Mildred Nelson Matthews; m. William Darrell Montgomery, June 17, 1961; children: Anne Elizabeth, Jon Nelson. BA in English Edn., St. Olaf Coll., 1961; postgrad., U. Wis., River Falls, 1977—79. Cataloging asst. U. Calif. Libr., Berkeley, 1962; circulation supr. U. Minn. Libr., Mpls., 1963—64; libr. So. St. Paul (Minn.) Pub. Schs., 1964—65; libr. asst. Am. Bankers Assn., N.Y.C., 1965—66; choir dir. Ezekiel Luth. Ch., River Falls; owner, technician Piano Works, River Falls, 1980—95; asst. cataloger U. Wis. Libr., River Falls, 1989—. Mem. River Falls Pub. Libr. Found. Bd., 2002—. Treas. St. Croix Valley Summer Theatre Friends, River Falls; mem. Cmty. Arts Base, River Falls, 1999—. Mem.: AAUW (pres. River Falls Br. 1995—97, treas. River Falls Br. 1997—2002), Wis. Assn. Acad. Librs., Wis. Libr. Assn. Democrat. Evangelical Lutheran. Avocations: gardening, reading, volunteering, antiques, interior decorating. Home: 75 Woodridge Dr East River Falls WI 54022 Office: U Wis River Falls Chalmer Davee Libr 410 S Third St River Falls WI 54022

MONTGOMERY, KEITH NORRIS, SR., insurance executive, state legislator; b. Natchez, Miss., Sept. 22, 1951; s. Charles Norris Jr. and Miriam (Marron) M.; m. Joan Marie Bishop; children: Keith Jr., Mason, Brenton. BBA, U. Miss., 1974. Sales rep. Boyle-Midway, Monroe, La., 1975-77, Am. Nat. Ins., Jackson, Miss., 1977-79; owner Exec. Benefits, Clinton, Miss., 1979—; state rep. Miss. Ho. of Reps., Jackson, 1993—. Vice chmn. ins. com., mem. conservation, mil. affairs, municipalities, and enrolled bills coms. Miss. Ho. of Reps. City councilman City of Clinton, 1985-93. Master sgt. USAR, 1972—. Mem. Am. Legis. Exch. Coun., Jackson Assn. Health Underwriters (bd. dirs. 1992-94), Clinton C. of C. Republican. Methodist. Home: 104 Countrywood Cir Clinton MS 39056-5717 Office: PO Box 2204 Clinton MS 39060-2204 E-mail: kmontgomery@mail.house.state.ms.us.

MONTGOMERY, LINDA BOUDREAUX, artist; b. Crowley, La., July 27, 1947; d. Edward John Boudreaux and Ellender Earle Murrell; m. Lawrence M. Montgomery, Sept. 16, 1967 (div. Dec. 23, 1980); children: Scott Allen, Brian Michael. BFA, U. La., 1985. Interpreter Montpelier Found., Montpelier Station, Va., 2003; artist Orange, Va., 2003—; exec. dir. The Literacy Coun. of Madison County, Va., 2004. Original painting, Decorations in the Front Hall, Tex. State Capitol, Austin, Tex., 2002 (Ofcl. Tex. Christmas Card for Gov. and Mrs. George Bush), Cities, Suburbs, Countryside, Nat. Bldg., Wash., D.C., 2003 (Hon. Mention for Nat. Trust for Hist. Preservation, 2003); author (illustrator): (children's book) A Colorful Guide to the World Famous Tabasco Pepper Sauce Factory, 1995, A Coloring Guide to the World Famous Jungle Gardens - Wildlife, 1995, A Coloring Guide to the Historic Conrad Rice Mill, 1995, A Colorful Tour of Louisiana's Cajun Country, 1995, A Visit to the Dr. Pepper Museum, 1996, A Visit to the University of Texas at Austin McDonald Observatory, 1996, A Visit to Louisiana's Jean Lafitte National Historic Park & Preserve, 1996, Abbeville - Some Place Special On The Bayou, 1996, A Visit to the Texas Capitol, Austin, Texas, 1997, Una Visita Al Capitolio De Tejas, Austin, Texas, 1997, How Texas Laws Are Made - A Children's Guide, 1997, A Visit to the Alabama Capitol, Montgomery, Alabama, 1997, A Visit to the International UFO Museum & Research Center, Roswell, NM, 1997, A Visit to the Arizona Capitol, Phoenix, Arizona, 1997, A Visit to the California Capitol, Sacramento, California, 1999, A Visit to the Oklahoma Capitol, Oklahoma City, Oklahoma, 2000. Personal E-mail: paintings@customart.com.

MONTGOMERY, MIKE, professional baseball coach; b. Long Beach, Calif., Feb. 27, 1947; m. Sarah Montgomery; children: John, Anne. BA in Phys. Edn., Calif. State U., Long Beach, 1968; MS in Phys. Edn., Colo. State U., 1976. Coach U. Fla., The Citadel, Colo. State U., USCG Acad.; asst. coach Boise State U.; head basketball coach U. Mont., Missoula, 1978-86, Stanford (Calif.) U., 1986—2004; head coach Golden State Warriors, 2004—. Named Head Coach of Yr. USA Men's 22 and Under Select Team, U.S. Basketball Men's Collegiate Com., 1996, U.S. Basketball Devel. Coach of Yr., 1996, U.S. Olympic Com. Basketball Devel. Coach of Yr., 1996. Office: c/o Golden State Warriors 1011 Broadway Oakland CA 94607*

MONTGOMERY, PHILIP O'BRYAN, JR., pathologist; b. Dallas, Aug. 16, 1921; BS, So. Meth. U., 1942; MD, Columbia U., 1945. Diplomate Am. Bd. Pathology, Am. Bd. Clin. Pathology and Forensic Pathology. Intern Mary Imogene Bassett Hosp., Cooperstown, N.Y., 1945-46; fellow in pathology Southwestern Med. Sch., Dallas, 1950-51, asst. prof. pathology, 1953-55, assoc. prof., 1955-61, prof., 1961—, assoc. dean, 1968-70, Ashbel Smith prof. pathology, 1991—; rsch. asst. pathology and cancer rsch. Cancer Rsch. Inst. New Eng. Deaconess Hosp., Boston, 1951-52; spl. asst. to chancellor U. Tex. System, 1971-75. Exec. dir. Cancer Ctr. U. Tex. Health Sci. Ctr. Dallas, 1975-89; pathologist Parkland Meml. Hosp., Dallas, 1952—, Dallas City Zoo, 1955-68; med. examiner DallasCounty, 1955-58; cons. Navarro County Meml. Hosp., Corsicana, Tex., 1952-53, McKinney (Tex.) Vets. Hosp., 1952-65, Lisbons Vets. Hosp., Dallas, 1953—, St. Paul Hosp., Dallas, 1958—, Flow Meml. Hosp., Denton, Tex., 1958-65; pathologist Tex. Children's Hosp., Dallas, 1954-55. Contbr. numerous articles to profl. jours., sci. abstracts, jours. Bd. dirs. Planned Parenthood of Dallas, 1958-63, pres., 1958-60, trustee St. Mark's Sch. Tex., 1958 , v.p., chmn. exec. com. bd. trustee, 1966-68, v.p., 1968-69, pres. 1974-76; trustee Lamplighter Sch., 1967-70; chmn. Dallas Area Libr. Planning Coun., 1970-72, Goals for Dallas Health Task Force com., 1975-76, Fleet Adm. Nimitz Mus. commn., 1979-81; mem. adv. bd. Dallas Citizens coun., chmn. health com. 1988-89; bd. dirs. Met. YMCA, 1960-63, Dallas Coun. on World Affairs, 1962-65; pres., bd. dirs. Damon Runyon, Walter Winchell Cancer Fund, 1974-79; cord. Dallas Arts Dist., 1982-95. Fellow Am. Soc. Clin. Pathologists; mem. Am. Assn. Pathologists and Bacteriologists, Am. Assn. Cancer Rsch., Internat. Acad. Pathology, Am. Acad. Forensic Scis., Soc. Exptl. Biology and Medicine, Internat. Soc. Cell Biology, Biophys. Soc., Am. Soc. Cell Biology, Am. soc. Exptl. Pathology, Tissue Culture Assn., Internat. Fedn. Med. Electronics, Profl. Group Med. Electronics of Inst. Radio Engrs., AAAS, Optical Soc. Tex. (founding), Pan-Am. Med. Assn., AMA, So. Med. Assn., Tex. Med. Assn., AAUP. Home: 6343 Kalani Dallas TX 75368-0001 Office: 5323 Harry Hines Blvd Dallas TX 75390-7208

MONTGOMERY, R. LAWRENCE, department store chain executive; b. 1949; Pres., CEO Black's divsn. Allied Store Corp., 1985-87; sr. v.p., dir. stores, gen. mdse. mgr. Softlines L.S. Ayres divsn. May Dept. Stores, 1987-88; sr. v.p., dir. stores Kohl's Corp., Menomonee Falls, Wis., 1988-93, exec. v.p., 1993-96, vice chmn., 1996—, CEO, 1999—, also bd. dirs. Office: Kohn's Corp N56w17000 Ridgewood Dr Menomonee Falls WI 53051-5660

MONTGOMERY, REX, biochemist, educator; b. Halesowen, Eng., Sept. 4, 1923; came to U.S., 1948, naturalized, 1963; s. Fred and Jane (Holloway) M.; m. Barbara Winifred Price, Aug. 9, 1948 (dec.); children: Ian, David, Jennifer, Christopher. BSc, U. Birmingham, Eng., 1943, PhD, 1946, DSc, 1963. Rsch. assoc. U. Minn., 1951-55; mem. faculty U. Iowa, Iowa City, 1955—, prof. biochemistry, 1963—, assoc. dean U. Iowa Coll. Medicine, 1974-95, v.p. rsch., 1989-90. Vis. prof. Nat. Australian U., 1969-70; mem. physiol. chemistry study sect. NIH, 1968-72; mem. drug devel. contract rev. com., 1975-87; chmn. com. biol. chemistry NAS, 1961-64; pesticide and fertilizer adv. bd. Iowa Dept. Agr., 1990-91; bd. dirs. Wallace Tech. Transfer Found., 1989-93; chmn. bd. dirs. Neurotron Inc., 1990-95; mem. rsch. com. Iowa Corn Promotion Bd., 1995-2001; rsch. dir. Biotech. Byproducts Consortium, 1989—; cons. in field. Author: Chemical Production of Lactic Acid, 1949, Chemistry of Plant Gums and Mucilages, 1959, Quantitative Problems in Biochemical Sciences, 2d edit., 1976, Biochemistry: A Case-Orientated Approach, 6th edit., 1996; mem. editl. adv. bd. Carbohydrate Rsch., 1968-80; mem. editl. bd. Molecular Biotherapy, 1988-92; contbr. articles to profl. jours. Postdoctoral fellow Ohio State U., 1948-49; fellow Sugar Research Found., Dept. Agr., 1949-51 Fellow: Royal Soc. Chemistry. Home: 701 Oaknoll Dr Iowa City IA 52246-5168 Office: U Iowa Coll Medicine Dept Biochemistry Iowa City IA 52242 Office Phone: 319-335-7897. Business E-Mail: rex-montgomery@uiowa.edu.

MONTGOMERY, ROBERT MOREL, JR., lawyer; b. Birmingham, Ala., June 9, 1930; s. Robert Morel and Ella Bernice (Smith) M.; m. Mary Lemerle McKenzie, Mar. 6, 1953; 1 child, Courtnay Elizabeth. BS, U. Ala., 1952; LL.B., U. Fla., 1957. Bar: Fla. 1957; diplomate Acad. Fla. Trial Lawyers. With Howell & Kirby Attys at Law, Jacksonville, Fla., 1957-59; ptnr. Howell, Kirby, Montgomery, Sands & D'Aiuto, Jacksonville, Fla., 1959-66, Howell, Kirby, Montgomery, D'Aiuto, Dean & Hallowes, West Palm Beach, Fla., 1966-75, Montgomery, Lytal, Reiter, Denny & Searcy, West Palm Beach, Fla., 1976-85, Montgomery Searcy & Denny, West Palm Beach, Fla., 1986-89; sr. ptnr. Montgomery & Larson, LLP, West Palm Beach, Fla., 1989—. Civil trial adv. Nat. Bd. Trial Advocacy; lectr. Princeton U., U. Oxford Law Sch. Chmn. Palm Beach Opera; chmn. emeritus Palm Beach Cultural Coun.; co-chmn. The Children's Place at Home Safe, Inc.; founder Armory Art Ctr., Palm Beach Inst. Contemporary Art; trustee Nat. Pub. Radio. 1st lt. AUS, 1952-54. Named Alumnus of Yr. U. Fla. Law Rev., 1983, Philanthropist of Yr. Nat. Assn. Fund Raising Execs., 1990, Honoree for Yr. City of Hope, 1991, Victim Adv. of Yr., Palm Beach County Sheriff's Office, 1997, Child Advocate of the Yr., 1996; recipient Learned Hand award Am. Jewish Com., 1985, Humanitarian award Albert Einstein Coll., 1990, Pub.'s award honor for contbg. most to improving quality of life in Broward and Palm Beach counties, 1992, Great Am. Traditions award B'nai B'rith, 1996, Humanitarian award Albert Einstein Coll. Medicine, 1999, Haym Solomon award Anti-Defamation League, 2000, Palm Beach C.C. Leadership award, 2002, Man of Yr. award Lake Worth Cultural Spotlight Com., 2002, Heartland award Lawton Chiles Found., 2003, Fla.'s Children First!, Inc. award, 2003, Dr. Martin Luther King Jr. Disting. award NAACP, 2004. Mem. ABA, Fla. Bar Assn. (lectr. continuing edn.), Palm Beach County Bar Assn., Trial Lawyers Assn. Am., Inner Circle Advs. Home: 1800 S Ocean Blvd Palm Beach FL 33480-5104 Office: PO Box 3086 West Palm Beach FL 33402-3086 Office Phone: 561-832-2880. E-mail: rmm@rmmjr.com.

MONTGOMERY, ROBERT RENWICK, medical association administrator, educator; b. New Castle, Pa., June 3, 1943; BS in Chemistry, Grove City Coll., 1965; MD, U. Pitts., 1969. Diplomate Am. Bd. Pediatrics. Intern Childrens Hosp. Phila. U. Pa., 1969-70; resident Harriet Lane Svc. Johns Hopkins Hosp., 1972-73, fellow, 1972-73, U. Colo., 1973-76, Scripps Clinic and Rsch. Found., 1976-77; gen. med. officer USPHS, Chinle, Ariz., 1970-71, dep. chief pediatrics Tuba City, Ariz., 1971-72; rsch. clin fellow in pediatric hematology U. Colo., 1973-76; rsch. fellow in molecular immunology Scripps Clinic and Rsch. Found., 1976-77; acting dir. Mountain States Regional Hemphilia Program U. Colo., 1977-78, asst. prof. dept. pediatrics, 1977-80, co-dir. coagulation rsch. labs., asst. dir. mountain sates regional hemophilia program, 1978-80; asst. prof. dept. pediatrics Med. Coll. Wis., 1980-81; dir. hemostasis program Milwaukee Children's Hosp., 1980-84; med. dir. Great Lakes Hemophilia Found., 1980-84; dir. regional homeostasis reference lab. The Blood Ctr. Southeastern Wis., 1981—; cons. hemostasis lab., dept. pathology The Children's Hosp. Wis., 1981—; assoc. prof. dept. pediatrics Med. Coll. Wis., 1981-84; sr. investigator The Blood Ctr. Southeastern Wis., 1982—, section head hemostasis rsch.; scientific dir. Great Lakes Hemophilia Found., 1984-96; assoc. dir. rsch. The Blood Ctr. Southeastern Wis., 1984-86; assoc. clin. prof. dept. pediatrics Med. Coll. Wis., clin. prof. dept. pediatrics, 1986-96, prof. pediatrics, 1996—, vice chmn. rsch. dept. pediatrics, 1998—; dir. rsch. The Blood Ctr. Southeastern Wis., 1986-98; acting sect. head coagulation lab., dept. pathology Med. Coll. Wis., 1986-87; faculty med. tech. Marquette U., Milw., 1986-92; clin. prof. dept. pathology Med. Coll. Wis., 1987—; v.p., dir. rsch. & exec. v.p. and dir. rsch. The Blood Ctr. Southeastern Wis., 1988-96, 96-98. Mem. med. adv. com. Great Lakes Hemophilia Found., 1980-96, exec. com. 1995—; mem. libr. com., human rsch. rev. com. The Blood Ctr. Southeastern Wis., 1981—, mem. rsch. mgmt. group, rsch. strategic planning com., 1983—; mem. subcom. FVIII and von Willebrand factor Internat. Congress Thrombosis and Haemostasis, 1984—; mem. radiation safety com. The Blood Ctr. Southeastern Wis., 1984—; ad hoc reviewer Heart Lung and Blood Inst., NIH, 1984—; mem. Inst. Biosafety com. The Blood Ctr. Southeastern Wis., 1985—; chmn. rsch. review com. Nat. Hemophilia Found., 1987-96, mem. rsch. rev. com., 1996—; ad hoc reviewer com. B Nat. Heart, Lung and Blood Inst., 1991—; chmn. von Willebrand subcom. Hemophilia Rsch. Soc., 1990-97; pres. Hemophilia Rsch. Soc., 1990-93; exec. sec. Hemphilia Rsch. Soc. of N.A., 1993—; mem. med. scientific adv. com. Nat. Hemophilia Found., 1992-95; mem. bd. dirs. Wis. Sickle Cell Disease Comprehensive Ctr., 1992-93; chair med. adv. coun. Great Lakes Hemophilia Found., Milw., 1992-96; mem. blood diseases and resources adv. com. Nat. Heart, Lung, and Blood Inst., 1992-95; prof. pediat. Med. Coll. Wis., 1996—. Sr. asst. surgeon USPHS, Indian Health Svc., 1971-72. Recipient Nat. Rsch. Svc. award Heart Lung and Blood Inst., NIH, 1975-77, Young Investigator award, 1978-81, Established Investigator award Am. Heart Assn., 1982-87, Jack Kennedy Alumni Achievement award Groce City Coll., 1985, Dr. Murray Thelin award Nat. Hemophilia Found., 1991. Mem. AAAS, Am. Soc. Clin. Investigators, Am. Soc. Pediatric Hematology/Oncology, Am. Soc. Hematology, Am. Fedn. Clin. Rsch., Am. Heart Assn., Internat. Soc. Thrombosis and Hemostasis, Soc. Pediatric Rsch., Hemophilia Rsch. Soc. Office: Blood Center of SouthEastern Wis Blood Research Institute 1701 W Wisconsin Ave Milwaukee WI 53233-2113

MONTGOMERY, ROY DELBERT, retired gas utility company executive; b. Indpls., Apr. 24, 1926; s. Lloyd Sipes and Nona Mae (Brummett) M.; m. Barbara Ann Reno, Apr. 21, 1946; children: Stephanie, Rebecca, Jeffrey, Laura. Student, Purdue U., 1950-51; M.E., Internat. Corr. Schs., 1953; A.S. in Mgmt. and Adminstrn., Ind. U., 1973. Registered profl. engr. Ind. Engr. Citizens Gas & Coke Utility, Indpls., 1952-59, supt., 1959-60, dir., 1960-73, exec. dir., 1973-78, v.p., 1978-82, sr. v.p., 1982-86, cons., 1986-88. Contbr. articles to profl. jours. Vice pres. exploring Crossroads of Am. Coun. Boy Scouts Am., Ind., 1978; corp. rep. Jr. Achievement Ind., 1970-82; pres. Fairway Trace at Pendia I, 1994—, Fairway Trace Home Owners Assn., 1995—. Recipient Bronze Big Horn award Boy Scouts Am. Explorer Div., Ind., 1978 Mem. Am. Gas Assn. (merit award 1966), Ind. Gas Assn., Scientec Club Ind., Kiwanis. Republican. Avocations: painting, golf, genealogy.

MONTGOMERY, STEVEN CHARLES, psychologist, minister; b. Sullivan, Ind., Feb. 16, 1958; s. Charles Dean and Ester Lou (Brewer) Montgomery; m. Karen Sue Bennett, Nov. 25, 1978; children: Kendra Michelle, Corey Steven. BA in Theology & Missions, U. Oakland City, 1990; MDiv in Theology & Religious Studies, So. Bapt. Sem., 1992; MA in Counseling Psychology, S.W. Coll. & Sem., 1999, PhD in Counseling Psychology, 2000. Diplomate Am. Coll. Mental Healthcare Practitioners, cert. addictions prevention specialist Nat. Bd. Med. Examiners, alcohol, tobacco & drug counselor Nat. Bd. Med. Examiners, domestic violence counselor Nat. Bd. Med. Examiners, tobacco cessation specialist Nat. Bd. Med. Examiners. Sr. pastor 2nd. Mt. Olive Bapt. Ch., Odon, Ind., 1983—88, Deer Creek Bapt. Ch., Tell City, Ind., 1988—91, Orleans (Ind.) 1st Bapt. Ch., 1991—93; pastor, psychologist Cornerstone Ch. Inc., Franklin, Ind., 1993—. Author: Out of Africa, 2001; contbr. articles to profl. jours. Mem. Gov.'s Commn. for Drug Free Ind.; bd. dirs. Care-Net Pregnancy Ctr. Ind.; mem. Nat. Bd. Addiction Examiners. Mem.: Ind. Addictions Coalition, Nat. Prevention Rsch. Soc., Am. Assn. Pastoral Chaplains & Counselors, Am. Psychol. Assn., Am. Soc. Criminologists, Ind. Assn. Prevention Profls., Nat. Assn. Forensic Counselors, Am. Soc. Aging, Assn. Pastoral Marriage and Family Counselors. Avocations: motorcycling, hill climbing, reading. Home: 1245 Fielding Ln Franklin IN 46131 Office: Christian Therapeutic Intervention 1000 W 375 S Trafalgar IN 46181 E-mail: drstevncm@aol.com.

MONTGOMERY, SUSAN W, interior designer; b. NYC, Feb. 11, 1945; d. Jesse Lee and Travis Katherine Williams; m. Stephen William Montgomery; children: William Lee, Michael James; m. James Sherman Booth, Aug. 12, 1967 (dec. Dec. 1968). BA, Dennison U. French tchr. Saybrook Arrowsmith H.S., Saybrook, Ill.; fine jewelry buyer Bloomingdales, NYC; interior designer Cocobolo, Armonk, NY. Democrat. Avocations: art, antiques, reading. Home: 53 Sunnyside Ave Pleasantville NY 10570 Office Phone: 914-273-4485.

MONTGOMERY, THEODORE ASHTON, physician; b. L.A., Oct. 27, 1923; s. Wayne A. and Hazel (Osmer) M. MD, U. So. Calif., 1947; MPH cum laude, Harvard U., 1955. Diplomate: Am. Bd. Preventive Medicine, Am. Bd. Pediatrics. Intern Los Angeles County Gen. Hosp., 1946-48; intern L.A. Children's Hosp., 1948, resident, 1950-51, St. Louis Children's Hosp., 1951-52; asst. in pediatrics Washington U., St. Louis, 1951-52; instr. pediatrics U. So. Calif., 1952-55; practice medicine specializing in pediatrics, L.A., 1952-54; lectr. pub. health U. Calif., Berkeley, 1960-83. Cons. child health Calif. Dept. Pub. Health, 1954-60, chief maternal and perinatal health, 1960-61, acting chief bur. maternal and child health, 1961-63, asst. chief div. preventive med. services, 1963-66, chief, 1966-68, chief preventive medicine program, 1968-69, dep. dir. of Dept., 1969-73; mem. mental retardation projects rev. com. USPHS, 1965-66, charter mem. surgeon gen.'s adv. com. on immunization practices, 1964-66; mem. task force on alcoholism, drug and narcotic abuse Calif. Commn. on Criminal Justice, 1968-70; chief div. disease control Alameda County Health Care Svcs. Agy., 1973-74; cons. maternal and child health Calif. Dept. Health, Berkeley, 1974-78; chief maternal and child health br. No. Calif. Regional Office, Calif. Dept. Health Svcs., 1978-83; WHO fellow med. care adminstrn., Europe, 1966; co-chmn. Calif. Inter-agy. Council on Tb, 1966-72; vice chmn. Calif. Drug Rsch. Adv. Panel, 1969-70; participant White House Conf. Mental Retardation, 1963, White House Conf. on Mental Retardation Cmty. Ctrs., 1965; Gov's. comm. Calif. Regional Hemodialysis Rev. Com., 1968-73; exec. sec. Gov.'s Population Study Commn., 1966; mem. com. on Tb, Calif. Lung Assn., 1973-74 Author: (with others) Standards and Recommendations for Public Prenatal Care, 1960, Guide to Hearing Testing of School Children, 1961; contbr. articles to med. jours. Bd. dirs. Calif. Interagy. Coun. on Family Planning, 1970-73; chmn. Calif. State Interdepartmental Com. on Food and Nutrition, 1977-79, pres. Clan Montgomery Soc. Internat., 1981-84, regional commr., 1985-91. With M.C. AUS, 1948-50. Fellow Am. Acad. Pediatrics (chmn. Calif. com. Indian health 1973-76, mem. nat. com. on Indian health 1963-79, vice chmn. 1977-79), Am. Pub. Health Assn. (chmn. task force on population policy 1971-72); mem. Alpha Epsilon Delta, Delta Omega. Home: 85 Wildwood Gdns Piedmont CA 94611-3831 E-mail: tmontgo458@aol.com.

MONTGOMERY, THOM MATHEW, health program administrator, counselor; b. Delaware, Okla., Dec. 30, 1942; s. Francis Thomas and Ellen Grace (Whelan) M.; m. Dinah Lee Hicks, Feb. 4, 1961 (div. 1964); children, Laura Diane, Raymond Hunter; m. A.N.D. de Vermandois. Degree, Highlands U., 1966; student, Tulsa U., 1961-64, U. Calif., Irvine, 1980-81, Glencullen U., Dublin, Ireland, 1993—2002. Lic. counselor, Calif. Brokerage mgr. John Hancock Life Ins. Co., Boston, 1964-70; mng. editor Renown Publs., Reseda, Calif., 1970-77; publs. dir. Am. Pub. Health Found., Corona Del Mar, Calif., 1977-79; program adminstr. Life Plus Martin Luther Hosp., Anaheim, Calif., 1979-92; clin. dir. Brookside Inst., Irvine, Calif. Lead counselor Peninsula Recovery Ctr., San Pedro, Calif.; pres. Montgomery Counseling Assocs., Fullerton, 1986—. Author: Ennobled Blood: The Heiresses of Monkstown Castle, A Party for Laura Lee; contbr. articles to profl. jours. Founding mem. Task Force on Alcohol & Drug Abuse for Disabled, Orange County, 1981, Sobriety Faire, Orange County, 1982; bd. dirs. Mid Valley Cmty. Police Coun., San Fernando Valley Employee Assistance Programs. Fellow Am. Pub. Health Found.; mem. Nat. Assn. Alcohol and Drug Abuse Counselors, Internat. Assn. Alcohol and Drug Abuse Counselors, Calif. Assn. Alcohol and Drug Abuse Counselors. Republican. Presbyn. Avocations: chess, hiking, swimming, poetry, drama. Home: 35167 El Diamante Dr Wildomar CA 92595 Office: 213 N Pomona Fullerton CA 92832

MONTGOMERY, VELMANETTE, state senator; b. Tex. Student, U. Ghana; LLD (hon.), St. Joseph's Coll., 1991. Mem. N.Y.C. Dist. 13 Sch. Bd., 1977-80, pres., from 1977; former co-dir. advocacy group Child Care Inc.; mem. N.Y. Senate, Albany, 1984—, ranking Dem. children and families com., ranking Dem. mental health and developmental disabilities com., mem. alcoholism and drug abuse com., mem. crime victims, crime and correction com., mem. edn. com., mem. fin. com., mem. health com., mem. rules com., co-chair Dem. Task Force on Criminal Justice Reform. Fellow Inst. Ednl. Leadership, 1981, Revson Found., 1984. Democrat. also: NY State Senate 306 Legislative Office Bldg Albany NY 12247 Office: Rm 615 30 Third Ave Brooklyn NY 11217-1822 Office Phone: 518-455-3451. Business E-Mail: montgome@senate.state.ny.us.

MONTGOMERY, WILLIAM ADAM, lawyer; b. Chgo., May 22, 1933; s. John Rogerson and Helen (Fyke) Montgomery; m. Jane Fauver, July 28, 1956 (div. Dec. 1967); children: Elizabeth, William, Virginia; m. Deborah Stephens, July 29, 1972; children: Alex, Katherine. AB, Williams Coll., 1955; LLB, Harvard U., 1958. Bar: D.C. 1958, Ill. 1959, U.S. Ct. Appeals (7th cir.) 1959, U.S. Supreme Ct. 1977. Atty. civil divsn., appellate sect. Dept. Justice, Washington, 1958—60; assoc. Schiff Hardin & Waite, Chgo., 1960—68, ptnr., 1968—93; v.p., gen. counsel State Farm Ins. Cos., Bloomington, Ill., 1994—97, sr. v.p., gen. counsel, 1997—99; ptnr. Schiff Hardin & Waite, Chgo., 1999—. Author: (39 corp. practice series) Tying Arrangements, 1984; co-author: Insurance Antitrust and Unfair Trade Practices Law, 2002; contbr. articles to profl. jours. Fellow: Am. Coll. Trial Lawyers; mem.: ABA (coun. antitrust sect. 1989—92), Seventh Cir. Bar Assn. (pres. 1988—89), Chgo. Bar Assn., Econ. Club Chgo., Lawyers Club Chgo. Avocations: skiing, woodturning. Office: Schiff Hardin & Waite 6600 Sears Tower Chicago IL 60606 E-mail: wmontgomery@schiffhardin.com.

MONTGOMERY, WILLIAM D. ambassador; b. Carthage, Mo., Nov. 8, 1945; m. Lynne Germain Montgomery; children: Alexander, Amelia, Katarina. BA, Bucknell U.; MA, George Washington U.; student, Nat. War Coll., 1986-87. With Fgn. Svc., 1974, econ. officer, 1975-78, comml. then polit. officer Moscow, 1979-81; line officer, secretariat staff then exec. asst. to under sec. polit. affairs Dept. State, 1981-84, exec. asst. to dep. sec., 1991-93; dep. chief mission Dar es Salaam, Tanzania, 1984-85, Sofia, Bulgaria, 1988-91; U.S. ambassador, 1993-96; spl. advisor to Pres. and sec. state for Bosnia peace implementation of the Bosnia peace plan, 1996-97; U.S. amb. to Republic of Croatia, 1998-2000; chief of mission U.S. Embassy, Belgrade, Yugoslavia, 2000—01; U.S. amb. to Yugoslavia, 2001—. With U.S. Army, 1967-1970. Decorated Bronze Star, Commendation medal with V device, Combat Infantry Men's badge; Parachute badge; decorated Order of the Horseman of the Madara, Order of the Stara Planina (Bulgaria), Order of Price Trpimir (Croatia); recipient ABA-Ctrl. and East European Law Initiative award for promotions rule of law in Cen. and Ea. Europe. Mem. Am. Fgn. Svc. Assn. Office: 5070 Belgrade Pl Dulles VA 20189-5070

MONTGOMERY-DAVIS, JOSEPH, osteopathic physician; b. Annapolis, Md., Aug. 27, 1940; s. John and Flonila Alice (Sutphin) Swontek. Student, U. Wis., Milw., 1967-70; DO, Chgo. Coll. Osteo. Medicine, 1974. Diplomate Nat. Bd. Examiners for Osteo. Physicians and Surgeons; cert. family practice & osteo. manipulative treatment. Chief technologist nuclear medicine dept. Columbia Hosp., Milw., 1964-70; intern Richmond Heights (Ohio) Gen. Hosp., 1974-75; pvt. practice Raymondville, Tex., 1975—. Mem. med. care adv. com. Tex. Dept. Human Svcs., Austin, 1983—86, Austin, 1990—93, Austin, 2002—, mem. physician payment adv. com., 1991—95, Austin, 2001—; cons. health care issues Tex. Osteo. Med. Assn., 1991—; health officer Willacy County Health Authority, Raymondville, 1984—; mem. med. care adv. com. Tex. Workers Compensation Commn., 1997—2001; clin. assoc. prof. dept. family medicine North Tex. Health Sci. Ctr., Ft. Worth, 2000—. Contbr. articles to profl. jours. With USAF, 1959-63. Mem. Am. Osteo. Assn., Am. Coll. Osteo. Family Physiaicns (spl. Recognition award 1995), Tex. Soc. Am. Coll. Osteo. Family Physicians (pres. 1985-86, Physician of Yr. award 1989, T.R. Sharp Meritorious Svc. award 1999), Tex. Med. Found., Tex. Osteo. Med. Assn. (pres. 1989-90), Tex. Coll. Osteo. Medicine Alumni Assn., Phi Eta Sigma, Sigma Phi. Office: Neighborhood Dr 525 S 10th St Raymondville TX 78580-2593 Office Phone: 956-689-2493.

MONTGOMERY TOBIAS, KAREN TWERDAHL, music educator; b. Chgo., Oct. 9, 1937; d. Edward Ainar Twerdahl and Louise Covington Haynes Twerdahl; m. Clinton Stephens Tobias Jr., May 20, 1995; m. William Thomas Montgomery, Nov. 23, 1966 (div. Jan. 1981); children: William Thomas Jr., Kristen Louise. A, Kendall Coll., 1965; B, New Coll. U. South Fla., 1982; M, Lindenwood U., 1996. Instr. piano pvt. practice, Wilmette, Ill., 1972—, St. Louis, 1972—, Sarasota, Fla., 1972—; tchr. music Des Peies Montessori Sch., St. Louis, 1990—92; ch. organist Christian Sci. Ch., Overland, 1996—99, Northbrook (Ill.) Christian Sci. Ch., 2000—04. Commr. Fine Arts Commn., Wilmette, 2000—. Mem.: North Shore Music Tchrs. Assn. (1st v.p. 2003), Ill. State Music Tchrs. Assn. (chmn. dist. auditions 2001), Sigma Alpha Iota (chair ways & means com. 2001—). Republican. Avocations: swimming, hiking, tennis. Home: 314 Linden Ave Wilmette IL 60091

MONTO, ARNOLD SIMON, epidemiology educator; b. Bklyn., Mar. 22, 1933; s. Jacob and Mildred (Kaplan) M.; m. Ellyne Gay Polsky, June 15, 1958; children: Sarah D. Monto Maniaci, Jane E., Richard L., Stephen A. BA in Zoology, Cornell U., Ithaca, N.Y., 1954; MD, Cornell U., N.Y.C., 1958. Diplomate Am. Coll. Epidemiology. Intern, asst. resident in medicine Vanderbilt U. Hosp., Nashville, 1958—60; USPHS postdoctoral fellow in infectious disease Stanford U. Med. Ctr., Palo Alto, Calif., 1960—62; mem. staff virus diseases sect. mid. Am. rsch. unit Nat. Inst. Allergy and Infectious Disease, Panama, 1962—65; assoc. prof. U. Mich. Sch. Pub. Health, Ann Arbor, 1965—76, prof., 1976—, chmn. dept. population planning and internat. health, 1993—97, dir. Ctr. for Population Planning, 1993—97, dir. U. Mich. Bioterrorism Preparedness Initiative, 2002—. Vis. scientist Clin. Rsch. Ctr., Northwick Park Hosp., Harrow, Eng., 1976; scholar-in-residence bd. on sci. and tech. for internat. devel. NAS and Inst. Medicine, Washington, 1983-84; vis. scientist div. communicable diseases WHO, Geneva, 1986-87; mem. pulmonary diseases adv. com. Nat. Heart, Lung and Blood Inst., Bethesda, Md., 1979-83; mem. nat. adv. coun. Nat. Inst. Allergy and Infectious Diseases, Bethesda, 1989-93, Contbr. articles to med. jours. Recipient career devel. award NIH. Fellow Am. Coll. Epidemiology, Infectious Diseases Soc. Am.; mem. APHA (governing coun. 1978-80), Am. Epidemiol. Soc. (pres.-elect). Achievements include research on respiratory viral infections in the community; demonstration of effectiveness of influenza vaccine in severe disease in the elderly; prevention of spread of influenza virus and treatment of illness, occurrence, causes and treatment of common cold. Office: U Mich Sch Pub Health I 109 Observatory St Ann Arbor MI 48109-2029 Office Phone: 734-764-5453. Business E-Mail: asmonto@umich.edu.

MONTORIO, JOHN ANGELO, magazine editor; b. Montclair, N.J., June 26, 1948; s. John Daniel and Lorraine (DiVita) M.; m. Lois Ann Marco, May 15, 1977; children— John Nicholas, Nicholas Ross BA cum laude in English, Seton Hall U., 1970; MA in English, U. Va., 1972. Sr. editor Gralla Pubs., N.Y.C., 1973-74; assoc. editor Lebhar-Friedman Pubs., N.Y.C., 1974-76; asst. editor Fairchild Pubs., N.Y.C., 1976-77; Sunday mag. editor Washington Star, 1977-81; asst. bus.-fin. editor, dep. home editor N.Y. Times, N.Y.C., 1981-83; Sunday mag. editor Newsday, L.I., N.Y., 1983-92; editor style dept. New York Times, N.Y.C., 1992—. Recipient pubs. award Newsday Inc., 1984 Democrat. Roman Catholic. Office: The NY Times Co 229 W 43d St New York NY 10036-3959

MONTOYA, MICHAEL A. state official, accountant; b. Albuquerque, May 4, 1952; s. Orlando (Reno) and Nancy (Maestas) M. BS, U. Colo., 1982. CPA, N.Mex. Tax mgr. Ernst and Young, Albuquerque, 1985-90; dep. state auditor State of N.Mex., Santa Fe, 1993-94, treas., 1995—. V.p., bd. dirs. Albuquerque Hispano C. of C., 1986-90; bd. dirs. Belen (N.Mex.) C. of C., 1986-90; bd. dirs. Healthnet of N.Mex., Albuquerque, 1987-90, Recreational Health Occupl. Ctr., Inc., Albuquerque, 1986-90. Mem. AICPAs, Assn. Hispanic CPAs. Democrat. Avocations: racquetball, hunting, fishing. Home: PO Box 414 Los Lunas NM 87031-0414 Office: NMex State Treasurer PO Box 608 Santa Fe NM 87504-0608

MONTOYA, PATRICIA T. federal agency administrator; b. Albuquerque; BSN, U. N.Mex., 1975, MA in Pub. Health Adminstrn., 1983. Asst. dir. ANA, Washington, 1987-89; exec. dir. N.Mex. Health Resources, 1989-93; practice mgr. Presbyn. Family Healthcare, Albuquerque, 1993-94; regional dir. HHS, Dallas, 1994-98, commr. adminstrn. children, youth and families Washington, 1998—2001; mem., board of dir. New Mexico Voices for Children, Albuquerque. Office: New Mexico Voices for Children 801 Encino NE Ste F21 Albuquerque NM 87102

MONTOYA, VELMA, economist, policy consultant; b. L.A., Apr. 9, 1938; d. Jose Gutierrez and Consuelo (Cavazos) Montoya; m. Earl A. Thompson; 1 child, Bret L. Thompson. BA in Diplomacy and World Affairs, Occidental Coll., 1959, MA in Internat. Rels., 1960; MS in Econs., Stanford U., 1965; PhD in Econs., UCLA, 1977. Asst. prof. econs. Calif. State U., L.A., 1965-68; vis. assoc. prof. U. So. Calif., 1979; instr. UCLA, 1981-82; staff economist The Rand Corp., Santa Monica, Calif., 1973-82; asst. dir. for strategy, White House Office of Policy Devel. Exec. Office of the Pres., 1982-83; expert economist Office Regulatory Analysis, OSHA, U.S. Dept. of Labor, 1983-85; dir. of Studies in Pub. Policy and Assoc. Prof. of Political Economy, Sch. of Bus. Mgmt. Chapman U., 1985-87; adj. prof. Sch. Bus. Mgmt. Pepperdine U., 1987-88; pres. Hispanic-Am. Pub. Policy Inst., 1984-90; assoc. prof. fin. Sch. Bus. Adminstrn., Calif. State Poly. U., Pomona, 1988-90; mem. Occupl. Safety and Health Rev. Commn., 1990-97; cons. on regulatory and econ. policy, 1997—. Cons. Urban Inst., 1974, Mexican-Am. Study Project UCLA, 1966, Grad. and Profl. Fellowships to the Office of Post Secondary Edn., U.S. Dept. Edn.; editl. referee Contemporary Policy Issues, Economic Inquiry, Policy Analysis, Jour. Econ. Lit.; discussion leader Am. Assembly on Rels. Between the U.S. and Mex.; pres. del. White House Conf. on Aging, 1981; reader of 1988 proposals for the U.S. Dept Edn. for the Improvement and Reform of Schs. and Tchg.; rsch. participant U.S. Dept. Edn. Delphi Assessment of Drug Policies for Use in Minority Neighborhoods, 1989; mem. Hispanic adv. panel Nat. Commn. for Employment Policy, 1981-82; lectr. Brookings Inst. Seminars for U.S. Bus. Leaders; bd. adv. Close-Up Found., 1982-83; discussant Western Econ. Assn. Meetings, 1985, 93; bd. adv. Nat. Rehab. Hosp., 1991-94; mem. nat. exec. adv. bd. Harvard Jour. Hispanic Policy, 1993-95; reader proposals for Hispanic Serving Instns., U.S. Dept. Edn., 2001; mem. regional panel to select White House Fellows, 2002-03. Mem. census adv. com. on hispanic population for 1990 census, 1988—93; mem. adv. com. Senate Rep. Conf. Task Force on Hispanic Affairs, Washington, 1991—; bd. regents U. Calif., 1994—; program rev. com. Los Alamos (N.Mex.) Nat. Lab.; mem. steering com. GetSmarter.org, 1998—99; mem. outreach adv. bd. U. Calif., 1998—; commr. Calif. Postsecondary Edn. Commn., 2000—01, 2004—. Named One of the 100 U.S. Hispanic Influentials Hispanic Bus. Mag., 1982, 90, 97, Woman of the Yr. Mex.-Am. Oportunity Found., 1983, The East L.A. Com. Union, 1979, one of 80 Elite Hispanic Women, Hispanic Bus. Mag., 2002, 03; recipient Freedom Found. at Valley Forge Honor Ecor. Edn. Excellence Cert., 1986, Profl. Achievement award S.E. L.A. Lincoln Club, 2002, Hispanic Leadership award Minorities in Bus. Mag., 2001; Univ. fellow Stanford U., Internat. Rels. fellow Calif. PTA, John Hay Whitney Opportunity fellow; Calif. State Univ. Found. Faculty Rsch. grantee; Marshall scholar, Fulbright scholar. Mem. ASTM (com. on rsch. and tech. planning 1985-87), Am. Econ. Assn. (session chair ann. meetings 1995), Nat. Coun. Hispanic Women (pres. 1997—), State Bar of Calif., Calif. State Bar Ct. (exec. com. 1987-89, disciplinary bd. 1986-89), Western Econ. Assn., Indsl. Rsch. Inst. for Pacific Nations (adv. bd. 1988-89), Salesian Boys and Girls Club (bd. dirs. 1989—), Vets. in Com. Svc. (adv. com. 1989-94), Phi Beta Kappa, Omicron Delta Epsilon, Phi Alpha Theta. Home: 6970 Los Tilos Rd Los Angeles CA 90068-3107 Office Phone: 213-427-8048. E-mail: velmamontoya@earthlink.net.

MONTOYA-AGUILAR, CARLOS, congressman; Pres. World Fedn. of Pub. Health Assns., 2002—. Office: c/o APHA 800 I St NW Washington DC 20001-3710

MONTROLL, ANDREW H. lawyer, councilman; b. Wash., DC, Apr. 11, 1957; s. Elliott W. and Shirley A. Montroll; m. Barbara Anne Komons, July 7, 1996; children: Sarah D., Elliott G. BS in Optics, U. Rochester, 1975—80, MS in Optics, 1980—81; JD summa cum laude, Vt. Law Sch., 1986—89. Bar: Vt. Supreme Ct. 1990. Engr. MRJ, Inc, Oakton, Va., 1981—86; jud. law clk. Vt. Supreme Ct., Montpelier, 1989—90; atty. Burak & Anderson, Burlington, 1990—96; counsel Riser Mgmt. Systems, Burlington, Vt., 1997—. Editor and chief The Vermont Law Review, 1988—89. Author: (book) Critical Connections, Wired for Profit; editor in chief: jour. Vt. Law Rev. Pres. Burlington City Coun., 1994—, city councilor, 1994—; mem. Bd. Civil Authority, Burlington, 2001—; examiner Vt. Bd. Bar Examiners, Montpelier. Recipient Vt. Legal Scholar, Vt. Law Sch., 1989. Achievements include patents for Monolithic semiconductor laser and optical amplifier; Semiconductor laser and optical amplifier. Avocation: photography. Office: Riser Mgmt Sys 200 Church St Burlington VT 05401

MONTRONE, PAUL MICHAEL, scientific instruments company executive; b. Scranton, Pa., May 8, 1941; s. Angelo H. and Beatrice M. (Giancini) M.; m. Sandra G. Gaudenzi, May 30, 1963; children: Michele Marie Cogan, Angelo Henry, Jerome Lawrence. BS in Accounting magna cum laude, U. Scranton, 1962; PhD in Fin., Econs. and Ops. Research, Columbia U., 1965. Ops. analyst Office Sec. Def., Washington, 1965-67; exec. v.p., chief fin. officer Wheelabrator-Frye Inc., Hampton, N.H., 1970-83; exec. v.p. Signal Cos., Inc., La Jolla, Calif., 1983-85, pres. Engineered Products Group Hampton, N.H., 1983-85; exec. v.p. fin. and adminstrn. AlliedSignal Inc., Morristown, N.J., 1985-86; pres. The Henley Group Inc., Hampton, N.H., 1986-92, bd. dirs.; chmn., CEO Wheelabrator Techs. Inc., Hampton, NH, 1987-90; pres., co-owner The Gen. Chem. Group Inc., 1989-94, chmn. bd., 1994-96; vice chmn. Abex Inc., Hampton, 1992-95; pres. Fisher Sci. Internat., Inc., 1997—98, chmn. bd., CEO, 1991—; chmn. bd. GenTex Inc., 1999—. Bd. dirs. Waste Mgmt.; mem. adv. bd. Sintokogio, Ltd. Pres. Met. Opera Assn.; mem. bd. overseers The Bus. Roundtable, Bus. Sch. Columbia U., N.Y.C.; adv. com. Consumer Protection and Quality in the Health Care Industry, Washington. Capt. U.S. Army, 1965-67. Mem.: Brook, University (N.Y.C.); Bald Peak Colony (Melvin Village, N.H.); Lyford Cay (Nassau, Bahamas). Roman Catholic. Office: Gentek 1 Liberty Ln Hampton NH 03842-1808

MONTY, GLORIA, former television producer, film executive; b. Union City, N.J. d. Joseph and Concetta M. (Mango) Montemuro; m. Robert Thomas O'Byrne, Jan. 8, 1952 BA, NYU; MA, Columbia U. Dir. New Sch. Social Rsch., N.Y.C., 1952-53; dir. Old Towne Theatres, Smithtown, N.Y., 1952-56, Abbey Theatre Workshop, N.Y.C., 1952-56; chmn. N.J. Motion Picture & TV Commn., Newark. Cons. ABC Dir. numerous TV programs, including Secret Storm, 1956-72, Bright Promise, numerous episodes ABC Wide World Entertainment; exec. prodr. General Hospital, 1977-86, 90-92, The Hamptons, 1983-85; made-for-TV movies, including Confessions of a Married Man, 1982, The Imposter, 1984; exec. prodr. in devel. for primetime TV 20th Century Fox, 1987-90; head cons. daytime TV ABC, 1987-90; prin. Gloria Monty Prodns. for new ABC daytime drama devel.; co-exec. prodr. While My Pretty One Sleeps, 1994-95, CBS Remember Me, FAMILY CHANNEL, 1995-97, Let Me Call You Sweetheart, 1997—, Moonlight Becomes You, 1997—; made-for-TV movies in assn. with Grosso-Jacobson. Chair Film Commn., State of N.J. Recipient Emmy awards, 1982, 84, Am. Soc. Lighting Dirs. award, 1979, Most Successful TV Show in History of TV award ABC, 1982, Spl. Editors award Soap Opera Digest, 1984, numerous others; named Woman of Yr., Paulist Choristers So. Calif., 1986. Mem. Women in Film, Dirs. Guild Am. (mem. exec. com.), Stuntman's Assn. (hon.), Thunderbird Country Club (Rancho Mirage, Calif.), Bel Air Country Club (Calif.), Deal Country Club, Navesink Country Club. Office: N.J. Motion Picture & TV Commn PO Box 47023 153 Halsey St 5th Fl Newark NJ 07101

MONTY, MITCHELL, landscape company executive; Pres. Suburban Landscape Assocs., Inc., 1981—. Office: Suburban Landscape Associates Inc 20875 N Brady St Davenport IA 52804-9305

MONYPENY, DAVID MURRAY, lawyer; b. Jackson, Tenn., Apr. 29, 1957; s. Kent Brooks Monypeny and Kathryn (Warner) Sadowski. BBA, U. Okla., 1980; JD, U. Memphis, 1983. Bar: Tenn. 1983; CPA, Tenn. Assoc. Glankler, Brown et al, Memphis, 1983-85; acct. Frazee, Thomas & Tate, Memphis, 1985-87; ptnr. Diamond, Finklestein, Monypeny, Memphis, 1987-88, Lowrance & Monypeny, Memphis, 1988-94, Monypeny, Simpson Walker & Schatz, Memphis, 1994-97; sole practice Law Offices of David Monypeny, PLC, 1997—. Tax atty., cons. to nat. entertainers and celebrities. Author: (video) Wiping Out Tax Debt You Can't Afford To Pay, 1993. Mem. Bellevue Ch., Memphis, 1983—; campaign fin. chair Neil Small Chancellor, Memphis, 1990. Featured on TV, in mags. and newspapers for his client's tax settlements; named Bankruptcy Atty. of Yr., 1999, Tax Atty. of Yr., Memphis Bus. Rev., 2000. Republican. Baptist. Avocations: music, video. Office: Law Offices of David Monypeny M PLC 5100 Poplar Ave Ste 2700 Memphis TN 38137-2701

MOODIE, JANICE, professional golfer; b. Glasgow, Scotland, May 31, 1973; Degree in psychology, San Jose State U., 1997. Winner Scottish Ladies title, 1992; mem. team Great Britain, 1994, Ireland Curtis Cup, 1996; turned profl., 1996. Avocations: exercise, movies. Office: PGA 100 International Golf Dr Daytona Beach FL 32124-1092

MOODY, DIXON MCGUIRE, radiologist; b. Tyler, Tex., Jan. 12, 1937; s. Dwight Lyman Moody and Helen Blaine McGuire; m. Lucinda B Blitz, Aug. 15, 1964; children: Abigail Ann (Moody) Sinwell, Susan Eloise (Moody) Prieto, Sarah Katherine. MD, U. of Tex. Southwestern, Dallas, 1963. Diplomate Diagnostic Radiology Am. Bd. of Radiology with subspecialty in diagnostic radiology, 1971, Am. Bd. of Radiology with added qualifications in neuroradiology, 1995. Resident physician Stanford U. Sch of Medicine, Palo Alto, Calif., 1963—70; asst. physician Cornell U. Sch of Medicine, N.Y.C., 1970—71; asst. prof. U. of N.Mex Sch Medicine, Albuquerque, 1971—73; prof. and chief of neuroradiology Wake Forest U. Sch. Medicine, Winston-Salem, NC. Mem. Nat. Adv. Coun. NINDS, NIH, Bethesda, Md., 1994—97, Ctr. for Sci. Rev., NIH, Bethesda, Md., 1998—2004; mem., sci. program com. Radiol. Soc. of N.Am., Oak Brook, Ill. Capt. U.S. Army, 1966—67. Decorated Bronze Star Medal US Army; recipient Alpha Omega Alpha Med. Hon. Soc., U. of Tex. Southwestern Med. Sch., 1963, Established Investigator, Clin. Sci. Award, Wake Forest U. Sch. of Medicine, 2002; grantee Jacob K Javits Neuroscience Investigator, NIH, 1984-2004, Clin. Hypotheses in Neuroscience Imaging Rsch., Charles A Dana Found., 1996-1999. Fellow: Am. Coll. of Radiology; mem.: Am. Soc. of Neuroradiology, Soc. for Neurosci., Radiol. Soc. of N.Am., Forsyth Country Club, Alpha Omega Alpha. Achievements include research in Brain injury during heart surgery due to fat emboli; brain hemorrhage in neonates due to rupture of veins; dementia due to obstruction of veins and loss of capillaries; significant vascular disease in Alzheimer's brains; cause and prevention of brain injury during cardiopulmonary bypass. Avocation: tennis. Office: Wake Forest University School Medicine Medical Center Blvd Winston Salem NC 27157-1088 Office Phone: 336-716-2485. E-mail: dmmoody@wfubmc.edu.

MOODY, FLORENCE ELIZABETH, education educator, retired college dean; b. Penn Yan, N.Y., Sept. 29, 1932; d. James William Southby and Rebecca (Worrall) M. BS, SUNY, Geneseo, 1954; MS, Syracuse (N.Y.) U., 1961; EdD, U. Rochester, N.Y., 1969. Elem. sch. tchr. N.Y. State, 1954-64, 66-68; coord. profl. devel. Eastern Regional Inst. Edn., Syracuse, 1969-71; mem. faculty SUNY, Oswego, 1971-92, prof. elem. edn., 1978-92, assoc. dean profl. studies, 1980-84, dean, 1985-92. Mem. N.Y. State Tchr. Edn. Cert. and Practice Bd., 1983-89; mem. Tchr. Edn. Conf. Bd., 1982-84. Nat. sec. Nat. Women's Party, 1974-76; bd. dirs. Oswego County Extension Svc., 1974-76. NDEA fellow, 1965-66; Danforth assoc., 1978—. Mem. ASCD, Am. Assn. Colls. Tchr. Edn. (pres. N.Y. State chpt. 1983-84), Assn. Tchr. Educators, Am. Ednl. Rsch. Assn., N.Y. State Assn. Tchr. Educators (sec., exec. bd. 1976-78), Order Eastern Star, Kappa Delta Pi, Pi Lambda Theta, Phi Delta Kappa, Delta Kappa Gamma. Home: 44 Franklin Ave Oswego NY 13126 also: 2008 New Bedford Dr Sun City Center FL 33573-6146

MOODY, FRANK G. surgeon; Surgeon dept. surgery Med. Sch. U. Tex., Houston, prof. Recipient Sci. Achievement award AMA, 1995. Office: U Tex Med Sch Dept Surgery 6431 Fannin St Houston TX 77030-1501 Office Phone: 713-500-7241. Business E-Mail: frank.g.moody@uth.tmc.edu.

MOODY, GENE BYRON, engineering executive, small business owner, minister; b. Calhoun, Ga., Aug. 29, 1933; s. Denzel Elwood and Mary Edna (Hughes) M.; m. Willie Earline Chauncey, Sept. 1, 1955; children: Byron Eugene, Iva Marie Levy. BSCE, U. Tenn., 1956. Registered profl. engr., Ala., Ark., Ga., La., Miss., Tex. V.p. S.I.P. Engring. Corp., Baton Rouge, 1968-70; project engr. S.I.P., Inc., Houston, 1970-73; dir. of engring. Jacus Assoc., Mpls., 1972-73; dir. of civil engring. Barnard & Burk, Baton Rouge, 1973-79; project mgr. Process Svcs., Baton Rouge, 1979-80, Salmon & Assoc., Baton Rouge, 1980-81; chief engr. Minton & Assoc., Lafayette, La., 1982; mgr. Assoc. Engr. Cons., Baton Rouge, 1982-86; owner Gene B. Moody, P.E., Baton Rouge, 1986—. Author: Deliverance Manual, 1989; contbr. articles to profl. jours. Tchr. Lake Hamilton Bible Camp, Hot Springs, Ark., 1981—. With U.S. Army, 1957. U. Chattanooga scholar, 1951, U. Tenn. scholar, 1953. Fellow ASCE; mem. Am. Soc. Safety Engrs., La. Soc. Profl. Surveyors, Soc. Automotive Engrs., Inst. Transp. Engrs., La. Engring. Soc., Transp. Res. Rsch. Bd., others. Home and Office: 14930 Jefferson Hwy Baton Rouge LA 70817-5217 Office Phone: 225-755-8870. E-mail: gbmoody@bellsouth.net.

MOODY, GEORGE WALTER, aviation executive; b. London, Mar. 15, 1943; s. George Walter and Margaret (Foster) M.; m. Carol Ann Pettiford, July 11, 1964 (div. 1972); m. Eva Leopoldine Kotek, Jan. 9, 1973; children: Robert Spencer George, Michael David, Stuart Armstrong. Degrees in Elec. and Mech. Engring., Luton (Eng.) Coll., 1964. Chartered engr. Sr. design engr. Brit. Aircraft Corp., Herts, Eng., 1963-68; program mgr., chief engr., gen. mgr. mktg. Redifon Simulation, Sussex, Eng., 1968-75; founder, chmn., pres. George W. Moody Ltd, Sussex, 1975-85, George Moody Inc., Tulsa, 1979-85, Aviation Resources, Inc., Tulsa, 1985—, Aviation Resources Ltd., Sussex, 1985—, George W. Moody Investments, Inc., 1985—, Simulator Mgmt. Corp., 1991—, Aviation Investments, Inc., 1992—. Fellow Inst. Elec. Engrs. (chartered engr.). Home: 2465 E 73rd Pl Tulsa OK 74136-5520

MOODY, JENNIFER JOY, language educator, history professor; d. Charles S. Moody, Jr. and Joyce H. Moody. BA in Internat. Bus., Auburn (Ala.) U., 1978, MA in French Studies, 1982, PhD in History, 2003. Instr. French Messiah Coll., Grantham, Pa., 1983—84; instr. German Auburn (Ala.) U., 1984—86, instr. French, 1996—; grad. tchg. asst. Pa. State U., State Coll., Pa., 1987—89; instr. French and German Meth. Coll., Fayetteville, NC, 1989—91; instr. history and French So. Union State C.C., Opelika, Ala., 2001—; instr. history Tuskegee (Ala) U., 2003—. Translator: French Gastronomy Faced with Globalization, 2002. Republican. Personal E-mail: jmoody@suscc.edu.

MOODY, KATHRYN CURRIER, communications executive, educator; b. Chgo. d. George Edson and Dorothy (Cleveland) C.; children: William Scott, John Currier. BA, U. Mich., 1961, MA, 1970; MEd, Columbia U., 1990, EdD, 1993. Dir. corp. devel. Nickelodeon, N.Y.C., 1981-82; dir. nat. program Sta. WQED, N.Y.C., 1983-84; exec. v.p. Framework II, N.Y.C., 1987-88; pres. Currier Moody Communications, Larchmont, NY, 1988—93; spl. asst. to pres. U. Tex. Med. Sch., Galveston, 1995—2001, dir. Open Gates programs, 1995—2001, asst. prof. neurology, 1995—2001; dir. Ctr. for Understanding Media, 1994—. Editor: Television Awareness Training, 1979, Growing Up on Television, 1980; author: The Children of Telstar, 2000; contbg. author: N.Y. Times Encyclopedia of Television; contbr. articles to profl. jours.; spkr. in field Trustee Larchmont Hist. Soc., 1977-78. Woodrow Wilson fellow Smithsonian Instn., 1978. Mem. Nat. Acad. TV Arts and Scis., N.Y. Women in Communications. Avocations: competitive tennis, poetry, jogging, raising dogs. Office: 38 Oak Ave Larchmont NY 10538-3517

MOODY, LIZABETH ANN, lawyer, educator; b. Johnson City, Tenn., July 11, 1934; d. Robert Alexander and Clara Pauline (Fine) M.; m. Alan Paul Buchmann, Sept. 5, 1959. AB, Columbia U., 1956; LLB, Yale U., 1959. Bar: Conn. 1959, Ohio 1960, U.S. Dist. Ct. Conn. 1960, U.S. Supreme Ct. 1977, U.S. Dist. Ct. (no. dist.) Ohio 1961. Assoc. Goldstein & Peck, Bridgeport, Conn., 1959-60, Slough & Slough, Cleve., 1960-61, 63-66, Ginsberg, Guren & Meritt, Cleve., 1962; ptnr. Metzenbaum, Gaines, Finley & Stern, Cleve., 1967-71; assoc. prof. Cleve. State U., 1970-73, prof., 1973-94, interim dean and prof., 1987-88; vis. prof. U. Toledo, 1976-77; v.p., dean Coll. Law, prof. Stetson U., 1994-99, Disting. univ. prof., 1998—. Rev. authority on civil rights HEW, Washington, 1973—79; vis. prof. Nat. Law Ctr. George Washington U., 1981—82, U. Hawaii, Honolulu, 1988, So. Meth. U., 2004; CEO Law Sch. Admission Svcs., Newtown, Pa., 1991—93; v.p. Stetson U., 1994—99; dir., sec., mem. exec. com. Fla. Health Scis. Ctr., Tampa Gen. Hosp., Fla., 1998—2002; Wallace S. Fugiama Disting. prof. U. Hawaii, Honolulu, 2002; prof. So. Meth. U., 2004. Author: (books) Smith's Review of Corps, 1987, Smith's Review of Estates, 1987; contbr. articles to profl. jours. Pres. Cuyahoga County Econ. and Community Devel., Cleve., 1984-88, Task Force on Violent Crime, Cleve., 1987-88; chmn. audit com. Law Sch. Admission Coun., New Town, Pa., 1988-89, bd. trustees Law Sch. Admission Coun., 1989-94, exec. dir., 1991-93, pres., CEO, dir. Law Sch. Admission Svc., 1991-93; commr. Ohio Ethics Commn., Columbus, Ohio, 1988-91, Ohio Pub. Defender Commn.; v.p., trustee Gt. Lakes Theatre Festival, Cleve., 1972-90; dir., sec. exec. com. Fla. Health Scis. Ctr., 1997—; dir. Cleve. Growth Assn., 1987-88; trustee Acad. Prep., St. Petersburg, Fla., 1999—. Recipient New Frontier award Ams. for Dem. Action, 1977, YWCA Women of Distinction award, 1988, Josephine Irwin award, 1990, award for Excellence in Governance Fl. Health Sci. Ctr., 2002; Day named in her honor, May 8, 1990, Cleve. Mem.: AAUP, ABA (chair non-profit corp. com. 1987—91, bus. law sect. coun. mem. 1993—94, house of dels. 1994—99, accreditation com. 1994—2000, chair internat. programs com. 1995—99, sr. lawyers divsn. coun. 1997—2001, chair accreditation com. 1999—2000, sect. legal edn. coun. 2000—, chair sr. lawyers divsn. coun. 2003—04, chair 2003—04, Glass Cutter award 1997), English Speaking Union (trustee 1986—89), Cleve. Bar Assn. (pres. 1987—88, meritorious svc. award 1987), Ohio State Bar Assn. (coun. of dels. 1981—91, Ohio Bar medal 1992), Am. Law Inst. (ALI-ABA com. 1998—2001, elected mem., adv. com. 2001—), Assn. Am. Law Schs. (exec. com. 1977—81), Tampa Club, St. Petersburg Yacht Club. Office: 1401 61st St S Saint Petersburg FL 33707-3246 Office Phone: 727-562-7848. Business E-Mail: moody@law.stetson.edu.

MOODY, MICHAEL DORN, playwright, entertainer; b. Bangor, Maine, Dec. 29, 1944; s. Elmer Leland and Geraldine Hope (Smith) Moody; m. Anne Littleford Wadsworth, Nov. 27, 1975; children: Nancy Eleanor, Mack Earle. Humanities tchr. Shead HS, Eastport, Maine, 2000—02; mate US Mcht. Marine, internat., ret., 1988—2000; playwright/screenwriter/actor, 1956—. Co-founder The Magnificent Liars (theatrical troupe), Maine, 2000—; entertainment industry instr./tchr. Sunrise Sr. Coll., U. of Maine, 2003; nav. instr. Washington County Tech. Sch., Eastport, Maine, 1999—2000. Author: (plays) The Shortchanged Review, 1975—76 (Orie nom., 1976), The Fool, 1985 (Pulitzer nom., 1985), Spill, 2002. RM3 USN, 1962—66, Gulf of Tonkin, Vietnam. Fellow NEA for Playwriting, US Govt., Nat. Endowment for the Arts, 1976. Mem.: Ensemble Studio Theater, Masons. Avocation: fine furniture design. Home: 810 Leighton Point Road Pembroke ME 04666 Personal E-mail: amoody@midmaine.com.

MOODY, ROBERT ADAMS, neurosurgeon; b. Swampscott, Mass., Oct. 1, 1934; s. George F. and Florence P. M.; m. Claudia; children: Robert Adams, II, Cathy, Paul, Lisa, Sherri. BA, U. Chgo., 1955, BS, 1956, MD, 1960. Intern Royal Victoria Hosp., Montreal, Que., Can., 1960-61; resident in neurosurgery U. Vt. Affiliated Hosps., 1961-66; fellow Lahey Clinic, Boston, 1963-64; asst. prof. neurol. surgery U. Chgo. Med. Sch., 1966-71; sr. clin. instr., then asst. clin. prof. Tufts U. Med. Sch., 1972-74; prof. neurosurgery Abraham Lincoln Med. Sch., U. Ill., Chgo., 1975-81; chmn. div. neurosurgery Cook County Hosp., Chgo., 1974-81, assoc. chmn. dept. surgery, 1976-81; clin. prof. neurosurgery SUNY-Binghamton, 1983—; chmn. neurosurgery Guthrie Clinic, Sayre, Pa., 1981-95; ret., 1995. Contbr. articles med. jours. USPHS fellow, 1957-58 Mem. ACS, Am. Assn. Neurol. Surgeons, Pa. Neurosurg. Soc. (councillor 1986-87, pres.-elect 1988, pres. 1989), Mid-Atlantic Neurosurg. Soc., Ctrl. Neurosurg. Soc. (pres. 1978-79), Alumni Assn. Lahey Clinic Found., Sigma Xi. Office: Guthrie Clinic Guthrie Sq Sayre PA 18840

MOODY, ROBERT LEE, insurance company executive; b. 1936; Chmn., chief exec. officer Nat. Western Life Ins. Co., Austin, Tex., also bd. dirs.; chmn. Am. Nat. Ins. Co., Galveston, Tex., also bd. dirs.; also pres. Moody Bankshares, Inc., Galveston. Pres. Moody Investments, Galveston. Office: National Western Life Insurance Company 850 E Anderson Ln Austin TX 78752-1602

MOODY, RON, actor, writer; b. London, Jan. 8, 1924; s. Bernard and Kate (Ogus) Moodnick. BSc in Econs., U. London, 1953. Appeared in plays: 6 Years Revue, 1959, Candide, 1960, Oliver, as Shylock in Merchant of Venice, 1967, as Polonius in Hamlet, 1972, as Richard in Richard III, 1978, Iago in Othello, 1981, as Harpagon in Moliere's The Miser, Peter Pan, 2000, The Sunshine Boys, 2001, Comedians, 2001; (films) Oliver, 1967, Twelve Chairs, 1970, Dogpound Shuffle, 1973, Wrong is Right, 1981, Where is Parsifal?, 1983, Ghost in Monte Carlo, 1989, Kid at King Arthur's Court, 1995, The Three Kings, 1999, Paradise Grove, 1999, Chopsticks, 2000, Steps, 2000, Revelation, 2001; stage musicals: USA tour HMS Pinafore, 1987, Sherlock Holmes, 1989, Streets of Dublin, 1992, Bertie, 1993, Peter Pan, 1995, The Canterville Ghost, 1998; on TV as Inspector Hart in Nobody's Perfect, ABC-TV, 1980, Dial M for Murder, 1981, Keen Eddie, 2003, The Bill, 2003; dir. (play) Kafka In Love, 1991; author-composer musical comedies Joey, 1966, Saturnalia, 1970, Move Along Sideways, 1971, The Showman, 1976, Nine Lives, 1991; touring Move Along Sideways, 1991, Monologues, 2003; author: (books) The Devil You Don't, 1980, Very Very Slightly Imperfect, Off the Cuff, 1987, The Amazon Box, 1998. Served with RAF, 1943-48. Recipient Golden Globe award, 1968, Moscow Golden Bear award as best actor, 1970, Coco Trophy award, Clowns Internat., 1999; nominated Oscar, 1968. Mem. Am. Acad. Motion Picture Arts and Scis., Variety Club of Great Brit., Actors Equity, Screen Actors Guild, Clowns Internat. (pres. 1984—), Performing Rights Soc. Writers, Soc. Authors. Home: Ingleside 41 The Green Southgate London N14 6EN England Office: Eric Glass Ltd 25 Ladbroke Crescent Notting Hill London WII IP5 England also: The Barry Freed Co 468 N Camden Dr Ste 201 Beverly Hills CA 90210

MOODY, ROSS R. life insurance company executive; Pres. Nat. Western Life Ins. Co., Austin, 1992—. Office: Nat Western Life Ins Co 850 E Anderson Ln Austin TX 78752-1602

MOODY, STANLEY ALTON, entrepreneur, financial consultant; b. Portland, Maine, Oct. 16, 1939; s. Alton Elwood and Mary Gwendolyn (Young) M.; m. Jo-Ann Newton Vercoe, Dec. 15, 1975 (dec. Apr. 1992); children: Karen Elizabeth, Kirt Edward, Leslie Ann; m. Barbara Marie Katkus, June 28, 1992; 1 child, Jonathan Edwards; foster child, Barbara Anne Lane. BSEE, U. Maine, 1962; postgrad., George Washington U., 1963-66; MA in Theol. Studies, Gordon-Conwell Theol. Sem., 1994; PhD in Theology, Trinity Theological Sem., 1999. Ordained to ministry Am. Bapt. Chs. U.S.A., 1996; registered Maine guide. Various positions Eastman Kodak Co., Kelsey-Hayes Co., Components, Inc., 1962-73; prin. Stan Moody Assoc., Augusta, Maine, 1973—; pres. Newton and Moody, Inc., Portland, Maine, 1980-84, Family Bookstores of New Eng., Portland, 1973—. Dir. bus. cons. Maine Devel. Found., 1984-86. Author: Entrepreneurship in Maine, 1985, Telecommunications Design Strategy for Maine, 1986, No Turning Back, 1989, I Will Walk Again, 1993, Crisis in Evangelical Scholarship, 2001. Selectman, Town of Manchester, 2001-2003; candidate for Gov. Maine, 1978; state rep. Maine Ho. of Reps., 2002—; pastor North Manchester Meeting House, 1994—; state rep. State of Maine, 2003; chmn. Greater Portland C. of C. Energy Awareness Task Force, 1977; budget com. Town of Manchester, 1995—; chmn. Manchester Comm. awards Spirit of Am. Found., 1996. Mem. Safari Club Internat. Maine

(v.p. 1993, pres. elect 1994), N. Am. Hunt Club (life). Republican. Avocations: hunting, fly fishing, writing. Home: PO Box 240 Manchester ME 04351-0240 Office: Stan Moody Assoc 98 Readfield Rd Manchester ME 04351-3213

MOODY, WESLEY C. utilities executive; BS, UCLA; postgrad., MIT, So. Meth. U. Registered profl. engr., Calif. Mgr. revenue requirement dept. So. Calif. Edison, 1988, gen. mgr. power prodn., 1992—2000; pres., CEO Edison O&M Svcs. Edison Internat., Rosemead, Calif., 2000—. Office: Edison Internat 2244 Walnut Grove Ave Rosemead CA 91770

MOODY-LAWRENCE, BESSIE, state representative, education educator; b. Chester, S.C., Feb. 14, 1941; d. Robert Douglas Sr. Ayers and Bessie Lewis Akers; m. Lindberg Moody Sr., 1964 (dec.); children: Lindberg Jr., Katrina Joanne, Leah Bess; m. James Earl Lawrence, Feb. 9, 1991; 1 stepchild, Erick C. BS, S.C. State U., 1962; MEd, Winthrop U., 1971; EdD, U. S.C., 1981. Coll. marshal Winthrop U., 1983—97, program coord. elem. edn., 1985—88, assoc. prof. edn.; state rep. dist. 49 S.C. Legis., SC, 1993—, past mem. med., mil., pub. and mcpl. affairs com., mem. edn. and pub. works com. Pacesetter Stennis So. Women in Govt., 1997—98; mem. Joint com. Study Drug and Alcohol Abuse1993, Joint Legis. Com. Children and Families; clk. session Hermon United Presbyn. Ch., 1980—86. Fleming fellow. Mem.: S.C. Assn. Tchr. Educators (pres. 1982—83), NAACP (Laney award 2000), Ctrl. City Optimist (v.p. Rock Hill chpt. 1990—91). Democrat. Office: State Capitol 414C Blatt Bldg Columbia SC 29211 Home: 219 Bowser St Rock Hill SC 29730 E-mail: bam@scstatehouse.net.

MOOERS, CHRISTOPHER NORTHRUP KENNARD, physical oceanographer, educator; b. Hagerstown, Md., Nov. 11, 1935; s. Frank Burt and Helen (Miner) M.; m. Elizabeth Eva Fauntleroy, June 11, 1960; children: Blaine Hanson MacFee, Randall Walden Lincoln. BS, U.S. Naval Acad., 1957; MS, U. Conn., 1964; PhD, Oreg. State U., 1969. Postdoctoral fellow U. Liverpool, Eng., 1969-70; asst. prof. U. Miami, Fla., 1970-72, assoc. prof., 1972-76, U. Del., Newark, 1976-78, prof., 1978-79; prof., chmn. dept. oceanography Naval Postgrad. Sch., Monterey, Calif., 1979-86; dir. Inst. for Naval Oceanography, Stennis Space Ctr., Miss., 1986-89; sci. advisor to dir. Inst. for Naval Oceanography, 1989; rsch. prof. U. N.H., Durham, 1989-91; prof., chmn. divsn. applied marine physics U. Miami, 1991-93, dir. Ocean Pollution Rsch. Ctr., 1992—2002, dir. Ocean Prediction Exptl. Lab., 1993—. Coord. Coastal Ocean Sci. Program, 1991—. Editor Jour. Phys. Oceanography, 1991-96; mng. editor Coastal and Estuarine Studies, 1978-99. With USN, 1957-64. NSF fellow, 1964-67; NATO fellow, 1969-70; Sr. Queen Elizabeth fellow, 1980 Mem.: AAAS, Estuarine Res. Fedn., Marine Tech. Soc., Am. Meteorol. Soc. (chmn. sci.& tech. com. on meterology & oceanography of Coastal Zone 1996—2002), U. Nat. Oceanog. Lab. Sys./Fleet Improvement Com. (chair 1994—97), U.S. Nat. Com. Internat. Union Geodesy and Geophysics (chmn. 1995—99), Ea. Pacific Oceanic Conf. (chmn. 1979—86), Am. Geophys. Union (pres. ocean sci. sect. 1982—84), The Oceanography Soc. (interim councilor 1987—88), Sigma Xi. Achievements include pioneering direct observation of transient coastal ocean currents and fronts plus mesoscale and coastal ocean prediction rsch. Home: 2521 Inagua Ave Coconut Grove FL 33133-3811 Office: U Miami Divsn Applied Marine Physics OPEL/RSMAS 4600 Rickenbacker Causeway Miami FL 33149-1031 Office Phone: 305-361-4088. Business E-Mail: cmooers@rsmas.miami.edu. *My central goal is to understand the ocean as a physical system by combining the interpretation of observations with dynamical theory and numerical models. Special emphasis has been on the dynamics of coastal oceans (continental shelf regions), now the scientific basis for practical mesoscale ocean prediction applied to marginal and semi-enclosed seas and pioneering the development of operational oceanography.*

MOOK, SARAH, retired chemist; b. Bklyn., Oct. 29, 1929; d. Wong and Lie Won (Woo) M. BA, Hunter Coll., 1952; postgrad., Columbia U., 1954—57, postgrad., 1962—65, U. Hartford, 1958—59. Cartographic aide U.S. Geol. Survey Dept. of Interior, Washington, 1952-54; rsch. asst. Mineral Beneficiation Lab. Columbia U., NYC, 1954-57; analytical chemist nuc. divsn. Combustion Engring., Inc., Windsor, Conn., 1957-59; rsch. scientist Radiations Applications Inc., Long Island City, NY, 1959-62; chemist Marks Polarized Corp., Whitestone, NY, 1962-64; sr. chemist NRA Inc. subs. Nuc. Rsch. Assoc., Inc., New Hyde Park, NY, 1964-75; clin. chemist Coney Island Hosp., Bklyn., 1974-84, cmty. bd., 1978-80; assoc. chemist Bellevue Hosp. Ctr., 1984-89, prin. chemist, 1989-95; ret., 1995; instr. ESL, 1999—. Contbr. articles to profl. jours. Mem. adv. com. to state assemblyman State of NY, 1970-72; trustee Park Ave. Christian Ch., 1973-82, sec., 1973-80, vice-chair, 1980-81, chair bd. trustees, 1981-82, pres. Christian Women's Fellowship, 1962-65, elder, 1982—; mem. Neighborhood Adv. Bd. for Cmty. Devel., 1996—, sec., 1996-99, chair 2000-02; mem. Cmty. Bd., 2002—. Named Woman of Yr., N.Y.C. Coun., 2004; recipient Margaret M. McCord Woman of Yr. Meml. award, Sheepshead Bay Hist. Soc., 2004, Woman of Yr. Humanitarian award, NY State Senate, 2004, Disting. Leadership in Cmty. award, NYC Office of Comptr. Mem. Am. Assn. Clin. Chemistry (sec. NY Met. sect. 1999—), AAAS, Am. Chem. Soc., NY Acad. Sci., Van Slyke Soc. Republican. Home: 2042 E 14th St Brooklyn NY 11229-3314

MOOMAW, RONALD LEE, economics professor; b. Orkney Springs, Va., Aug. 1, 1943; s. Leo V. and Vivian (Fansler) M.; m. Juliana Pendleton, Dec. 27, 1971; children: Sara Christina, Kate Winston. BS with highest distinction, U. Va., 1964; PhD, Princeton (N.J.) U., 1976. Vis. asst. prof. U. Va., Charlottesville, 1968-72; asst. prof., assoc. prof. econs. Okla. State U., Stillwater, 1972-83, prof., 1983—, head dept., 1987-93; sr. rsch. assoc. Urban Inst., Washington, 1980-81; vis. assoc. prof. U. B.C., Vancouver, Can., 1983-84. Prof. bus. adminstrn. CBA Assocs., 1994—, Regents prof. 1998-2002; sr. fellow ZEI U. Bonn, 2002-2003. Co-author: Profile of Oklahoma, 1977, Economics and Contemporary Issues, 2004; editor Rev. of Regions L Studies, 2003—; asst. editor Jour. of Econs., 1991—, Jour. of Regional Sci., 1994—; editl. bd. Internat. Regional Sci. Rev., 1995-2001; co-editor: Rev. Regional Studies, 2003—; contbr. articles to profl. jours. Vestryman St. Andrew's Episcopal Ch., Stillwater, 1979-80, treas., 1990-98; mem. budget com. Diocese of Okla., 1994-2000, mem. higher edn. com., 2000--. Woodrow Wilson fellow, 1964, NSF fellow, 1964-66. Mem. Am. Econ. Assn., So. Econ. Assn. (bd. trustees 1989-91, v.p. 1997-1998), Regional Sci. Assn., So. Regional Sci. Assn. (exec. com. 1985-87), Missouri Valley Econ. Assn. (pres.-elect 1995-96, pres. 1996-97), St. Augustine Canterbury Soc. (treas. 2004—), Phi Beta Kappa. Office: Coll Bus Okla State U Stillwater OK 74078-0001 Office Phone: 405-744-7359. Business E-Mail: rmoomaw@okstato.edu.

MOON, CRAIG, publishing executive; Pres. Ark. Gazette, Little Rock, pub.; pres. The News-Press, Ft. Myers, Fla., pub.; v.p. advt. The Cin. (Ohio) Post, 1985—91, The Cin. (Ohio) Enquirer, 1985—91; publisher The Tennessean, Nashville, 1991—2002; exec. v.p. Newspaper Divsn. Gannett Co., Inc., McLean, Va., 2002—03; pres. USA Today, McLean, Va., 2003—, pub., 2003—. Office: USA Today 7950 Jones Branch Drive Mc Lean VA 22107

MOON, DAVID A. manufacturing executive; b. Washington, Aug. 2, 1956; d. Arthur Ray and Lillian (Baker) Moon. PhD in Comm., U.Ill., 1978. Cert.: Police/Nev. (three superiors); industrial employer Ind. Certifications Releases Corp./E Rochell, Nev. Owner,mgr. Indsl. Arts Svc. Firm, Henderson, Nev., 1977; with N.L.R.B., 1977; industrialist I.C.R. Corp., Henderson, Nev., 1980; indusl. authority I.C.R. Corp. TM, Henserson, Nev., 1991—; pres., CEO Teledyne Inc., Ctr. City, 1996; judge US Superior Ct., 1956; owner Ind. Arts Systems Firm, 1972; ind. employer US Gov. Owner (magazines) 25,000 law publ. Recipient 9 First Pl. Blue Ribbon (no. 1) patent and trademark, 1969—72. Mem.: office of Bd. of Gov. Election. Baptist. Office: Indsl Arts Systems Firm 140 E Rochell Rd Henderson NV 89015

MOON, FLETCHER FROE, college librarian, multi-media artist, minister; s. James Lawrence and Lakie Clarice Moon, Dorothy Sawyer Moon (Stepmother); m. Marilyn Nadine Braden, Aug. 14, 1976; 1 child, Mailakia Althea. BA (cum laude), Fisk U., 1972—76; MLS, Vanderbilt U. (Peabody Coll.), 1978—79. Lic. Born Again Ch., 2000, Ordination as Ch. Elder Born Again Ch., 2002; Librarianship N.J. Dept. of Edn., 1980. Libr. asst., spl. collections Fisk U. Libr., Nashville, 1973—76; cameraman/fl. dir./prodn. asst./courier WSM-TV, Nashville, 1975—77; creative/music dir. Larry Sonn Advt. Agy., Nashville, 1977—78; sr. libr. asst., ext. services Nashville Pub. Libr., Nashville, 1977—80; sr. reference libr./adult programming coord. Montclair Pub. Libr., NJ, 1980—83; instr./reference libr. Tenn. State U., Nashville, 1983—88, asst. prof./reference libr., 1988—98, asst. prof./head reference libr., 1998—. Musician (freelance), Nashville, 1972—; prodr., radio/tv commercials Larry Sonn Advt. Agy., Nashville, 1977—78; facilitator, project aero-scan Nashville Pub. Libr., 1978—79; project participant Atlanta U. SLIS Grant, Atlanta, 1985—87; presenter Coun. on Libr. Resources, Fisk U., Nashville, 1989; grant writer Tenn. State U., Nashville, 1990—, grant adminstr./project dir., 1991—94; presenter FIPSE/USDE Project Directors Conf., Wash., 1992—93, Black Caucus of the ALA Conf., Milw., 1994. Musician: (jazz performance) Fisk U. concerts featuring Duke Ellington, Billy Taylor, Eubie Blake, Milt Jackson, Julian Cannonball Adderley, et al, (syndicated TV prodn.) I Owe It All to the Songs That I Sing, (concert tours) The Orchestrated Crowd, Modern Black Mass Choir, other musical groups (Alumni Guest Artist award, 1979); prodr.(facilitator): (heritage tourism drama production) Freedom Trek III; recording artist: documentary film soundtrack The Gift of Black Folk; actor: (plays) Beatrice du Congo; composer (performer): (music/dance collaboration) Ring Dance; singer: (musical revue) The Cotton Club Remembered, editor libr. newsletters and pubs. Performer/supporter Black Expo, Nashville, 1974—76; charter mem. N.J. Black Librs. Network, Montclair, 1980—83; contbr. United Way of Mid. Tenn., Nashville, 1985—2000; campaign vol. Montclair Town Coun., NJ, 1980—82; vol. Howard Gentry vice-mayoral campaign, Nashville, 2002—03; elder Born Again Ch., Nashville, 1972—, trustee, 1996—; facilitator When Men Pray, Nashville, 1998. Recipient Harvard Book Award, Harvard Club of Nashville, 1970, Music award, Fisk U. Jazz Ensemble, 1979, Artist's Portrait, Kay Kato, Newark (NJ) Star-Ledger, 1982, Judge's award, Pride of Tenn. Elks Lodge, 2002—03; grantee Fund for the Improvement of Post Secondary Edn., U.S. Dept. Edn., 1991—94; Presdl. Scholarship, Fisk U., 1973—76, Title II-B Fellowship, Peabody Coll. (Vanderbilt U.), 1978—79. Mem.: ALA (mem. Black Caucus), Tenn. Libr. Assn., Assn. Vanderbilt Black Alumni, Nashville Fisk Club. Mem. Christian Ch. Avocations: reading, creative writing, prayer, walking/light exercise, travel. Office: Tenn State U 3500 John A Merritt Blvd Nashville TN 37220-2336 Office Phone: 615-963-5205. E-mail: fmoon@tnstate.edu.

MOON, HARLEY WILLIAM, veterinarian; b. Tracy, Minn., Mar. 1, 1936; s. Harley Andrew Moon and Catherine Mary (Engesser) Lien; m. Irene Jeannette Casper, June 9, 1996; children: Michael J., Joseph E., Anne E., Teresa J. BS, U. Minn., 1958, DVM, 1960, PhD, 1965. Diplomate Am. Bd. Veterinary Pathologists. Instr. Coll. Vet. Medicine U. Minn., St. Paul, 1960—62, NIH postdoctoral fellow, 1963—65; vis. scientist Brookhaven Nat. Lab., Upton, NY, 1965—66; assoc. prof. Coll. Vet. Medicine U. Sask., Saskatoon, Canada, 1966—68; rsch. vet. Nat. Animal Disease Ctr. Agrl. Rsch. Svc., USDA, Ames, Iowa, 1968—88, ctr. dir., 1988—95; Franklyn Ramnsey chair in veterinary medicine & prof. Ames, Iowa, 1996—; dir. Plum Island Animal Disease Ctr. USDA, 1995—96; prof. in charge Vet. Med. Rsch. Inst., 1996—. Assoc. prof. Iowa State U., Ames, 1970—73, prof., 1972—74; cons. U. N.C., Chapel Hill, 1985—92, Pioneer Hy-Bred Internat., Johnson, Iowa, 1986—92. Contbr. articles reporting rsch. on animal diseases. Recipient Superior Svc. award, USDA. Mem.: NAS, AAAS, NAS, AVMA, Am. Soc. Microbiologists, Am. Coll. Vet. Pathologists, Phi Zeta, Sigma Xi. Avocation: farming. Office: Iowa State University Veterinary Medicine Research Institute 1802 Elmwood Dr Ames IA 50011-0001

MOON, JAMES RUSSELL, technology education educator; b. St. Cloud, Minn., Apr. 12, 1950; s. Glenn Howard and Audrey Katherine (Berg) M.; m. Corrine Mae St. Aubin, July 14, 1978; children: Sheri Ann, Brian Michael. BS, St. Cloud State U., 1972; MS, Bemidji State U., 1975. Tech. edn. tchr. Minnetonka (Minn.) Pub. Schs., 1972—2003, dist. dept. chmn. tech. edn., 1993-95. Voc. standards com. Minn. Dept. Edn., 1995; mem. State Planning Com., 1989-2003. Designer/engr.: Row Crop Tractor, 1975; contbr. articles to profl. jours. Recipient Anchor award Minn. Pub. Schs., 1991, Tchr. Excellence award Internat. Tech. Edn. Assn., 1994, Disting. Tech. Educator Citation, 2002, Minnetonka Co-curricular Advisor of Yr., 2001; named Disting. Tech. Educator, Internat. Tech. Edn. Assn. Mem. Minn. Valley Tech. Edn. Assn. (sec. 1974), Minn. Tech. Edn. Assn. (mem. supermileage state competition com. 1989-2003), Tech. Edn. Tchr. of Yr. 1993, Disting. Svc. award 1991, 92, 94. Joyce Gustafson Meml. award, 2003). Presbyterian. Avocations: antique car restoration, reading technology related, outdoorsman. Home: 2037 20th St SE Buffalo MN 55313-4813 Office: Minn H S 18301 Highway 7 Minnetonka MN 55345-4114

MOON, JOHN C. healthcare company executive; B in Computer Sci., M in Mgmt. Info. Sys., No. Ill. U. With Baxter Internat., Deerfield, Ill., 1983—, v.p. info. tech. renal bus., 1996—2000, chief info. officer, 2000—, v.p., 2002—. Bd. dirs. Global Healthcare Exch. Mem.: Assn. of Info. Tech. Profls., Soc. Info. Mgmt., Pharm. Info. Sys. Assn. Office: 1 Baxter Pkwy Deerfield IL 60015

MOON, JOHN ELLIS VAN COURTLAND, retired historian; b. Geneva, Oct. 25, 1929; arrived in U.S., 1940; s. Carlyle van Courtland and Marie Edmée (Choisy) Moon; m. Palma Roberge (div.); children: John Albert van Courtland, Margaret Hames, Laurelle Conte; m. Joan Mary Farrell, July 24, 1971. AB in History and Lit., Harvard U., 1952, PhD in Am. Civilization, 1968; MA in English and Comparative Lit., Columbia U., 1953. Instr. English Merrimack Coll., North Andover, Mass., 1953—55, Boston U., 1957—58; from instr. to prof. history Boston State Coll., 1958—82; prof. Fitchburg (Mass.) State Coll., 1982—93, prof. emeritus, 1993—. Chmn. com. Coun. Pres., Mass. State Coll. Sys., 1990; vis. prof. Kings Coll., U. London, 1994—95; presenter in field. Author: Confines of Concept: American Strategy in World War II, 1988; co-editor: Biological and Toxin Weapons: Research, Development and Use from the Middle Ages to 1945, 1999; contbr. articles to profl. jours. Grantee, John Kittredge Fund, 1994, John D. and Catherine MacArthur Found., 1994. Mem.: Mass. State Coll. Assn. (pres., Boston State Coll. chpt. 1980—82), Am. Assn. Univ. Profs. (pres., Boston State Coll. chpt. 1970—72, pres. Mass. state conf. 1982—84, William S. Tacey award 1998). Avocations: mountain climbing, book collecting, trekking, travel. Home and Office: 11 Monmouth Ct Brookline MA 02446 Personal E-mail: jevcm@aol.com.

MOON, JOHN HENRY, SR., banker; b. Van Buren, Ark., Aug. 19, 1937; s. B.R. and Alma (Witte) M.; m. Agnes Rose Dickens, Aug. 16, 1958; children: John Henry, Randall Allen. AA, Delmar Coll., Corpus Christi, Tex., 1956; BBA cum laude, Tex. A&M U., Kingsville, 1958. Sr. acct. Tex. Eastern Transp. Co. and subs., 1958-63; exec. v.p., dir. Houston Rsch. Inst., 1963-68; sr. v.p., asst. to chmn. bd., dir. Main Bank, 1968—69; vice chmn. bd., dir. N.E. Bank, 1969; CEO, chmn. bd., dir. Pasadena (Tex.) Nat. Bank, 1970-81; gen. ptnr. Moon and Assocs., Ltd., 1977—. Chmn. bd., pres. Interservice Life Ins. Corp., Phoenix, Cmty. Bank, Houston, 1975-81, Interstate Bank, Houston, 1977-81; chmn. bd., pres. Moon Credit Corp., Pasadena, 1975—, Peoples Bank, Houston, 1983-93; chmn. bd. Cmty. Nat. Bank, Friendswood, Tex., 1981-93; chmn. bd. Peoples Nat. Bank, Pasadena, Tex., 1984-93; dir. San Jacinto River Authority, 1991-93; chmn., pres. Sam Houston Pky. Transp. Corp., 1991-93; bd. dirs. Harris County Indsl. Devel. Corp., 1996-2003, Pro Technologies, Inc., 1987-96, Quality Wire Rope Corp., chmn., 1999—; pres. Sure Found. Inc., 1987—. Past bd. dirs. Pasadena Heart Assn., Salvation Army, Tex. Assn. Prevention of Blindness; past chmn. City of Pasadena Bd. Devel.; past chmn. adv. bd. Pasadena Civic Ctr.; past dir. S.E. Econ. Devel., Inc.; bd. dirs. San Jacinto Coll. Found., 2000-03, chmn., 2002-03. Named Outstanding Young Man of Yr., Pasadena Jr. C. of C., 1973; named to Pasadena Hall of Fame, 1988. Mem. AICPA, Pasadena C. of C. (bd. dirs. S.E. Econ. Devel., Citizen of Yr. 1994), Tex. Soc. CPAs, Tex. Bankers Assn., Rotary (pres. Pasadena Rotary found. 2001—). Home: 310 Del Monte Dr Friendswood TX 77546 Office: PO Box 3487 Pasadena TX 77501 Office Phone: 713-943-7777. Business E-Mail: johnhmoonsr@aol.com.

MOON, MARILYN LEE, economist; b. El Dorado, Kans., July 7, 1947; d. Jesse Morris and Shirley Lois M.; m. J. Douglas Gomery, Jan. 13, 1973. BA in Econs., Colo. Coll., 1969; MS in Econs., U. Wis., 1972, PhD in Econs., 1974. Rsch. assoc. Inst. for Rsch. on Poverty U. Wis., Madison, 1973-74, asst. prof. econs. Milw., 1974-80, assoc. prof. econs., 1980-81; sr. analyst human resources and cmty. devel. divsn. The Congl. Budget Office, Washington, 1981-83; sr. rsch. assoc. Health Policy Ctr. The Urban Inst., Washington, 1983-86; dir. pub. policy inst. AARP, 1986-89; sr. rsch. assoc. The Urban Inst., 1989-94, sr. fellow, 1994—2003; v.p. Am. Insts. for Rsch., 2003—. Cons. The Pepper Commn., 1989. Author: Medicare Now and in the Future, 1993, 2d edit., 1996, The Meaurement of Economic Welfare: Its Application to the Aged, 1977; co-author: Balancing Access, Cost and Politics: The American Context for Health System Reform, 1991, Entitlements and the Elderly: Protecting Promises, Recognizing Realities, 1995; editor: Economic Transfers in the United States, vol. 49, 1984; co-editor: Improving Measures of Economic Well-Being, 1977; columnist The Washington Post, 1993-2000; contbr. articles to profl. jours. Pub. trustee social security and Medicare trust funds, 1995-2000. Ford Found. fellow, 1971-73. Mem. Nat. Acad. Social Ins. (bd. dirs. 1993-2000), Medicare Rights Ctr. (bd. dirs. 1998—), Phi Beta Kappa. Avocations: photography, hiking, reading. Office: Am Insts for Health 10720 Columbia Pike Silver Spring MD 20901 Office Phone: 301-592-2101. E-mail: mmoon@air.org.

MOON, NORMAN K. judge; BA, U. Va., 1959, JD, 1962, LLM, 1988. Bar: (Va.) 1962. With firm Edmunds & Williams (formerly Williams, Robertson & Sackett), Lynchburg, Va., 1962—74; judge 24th Jud. Cir., 1974—84, chief judge, 1982—85; judge Ct. of Appeals of Va., 1985—93, chief judge, 1993—97; judge U.S. Dist. Ct. (we. dist.) Va., 1997—. Vis. lectr. U. Va. Law Sch., Charlottesville, 1975—88. Office: PO Box 657 Lynchburg VA 24505-0657

MOON, RONALD T. Y. state supreme court chief justice; b. Sept. 4, 1940; m. Stella H. Moon. B in Psychology and Sociology, Coe Coll., 1962, LLD, 2001, LLD (hon.), 2001; LLB, U. Iowa, 1965; LLD (hon.), Inha U., Incheon, Korea, 2003. Bailiff, law clk. to Chief Judge Martin Pence U.S. Dist. Ct., 1965-66; dep. prosecutor City and County of Honolulu, 1966-68; assoc. Libkuman, Ventura, Ayabe, Chong & Nishimoto (predecessor firm Libkuman, Ventura, Moon & Ayabe), Honolulu, 1968-72, ptnr., 1972-82; judge 9th div. 1st cir., Cir. Ct., State of Hawaii, Honolulu, 1982-90; assoc. justice Supreme Ct., State of Hawaii, Honolulu, 1990-93, chief justice, 1993—. Adj. prof. law U. Hawaii, 1986, 87, 88; lectr., guest spkr. numerous events. Recipient Disting. Svc. award, Nat. Ctr. for State Cts., 2003, Am. Ctr. for State Cts., 2003, Grand Prize award, Kyungmin Mission Schs., Korea, 2003. Mem. ATLA, ABA, Hawaii Bar Assn. (Golden Gavel award 2001_, Am. Bd. Trial Advocates (pres. 1986-93, nat. sec. 1989-91), Am. Inns of Cts. IV (bencher 1983—), Am. Judicature Soc., Hawaii Trial Judges' Assn., Conf. Chief Justices (bd. dirs.). Office: Supreme Ct Hawaii 417 S King St Honolulu HI 96813-2902 E-mail: Ronald.T.Moon@courts.state.hi.us.

MOON, SEUNGSOOK, sociologist, educator; b. Seoul, Republic of Korea, Oct. 27, 1963; arrived in U.S., 1986; d. Yong-goo Moon and Doh-son Yi; m. Farzin Philip Vahdat, Aug. 3, 1988. BA, Yonsei U., Seoul, 1985; PhD, Brandeis U., 1994. Lectr. social studies Harvard U., Cambridge, Mass., 1993—95; vis. asst. prof. sociology Vassar Coll., 1995—97, asst. prof. sociology, 1997—. Founding mem. SocGlobe; vis. scholar Korea Inst., 2002—03, Harvard U., 2002—03. Contbr. articles to profl. jours.; author: Miliarized Modernity and Gendered Citizenship in South Korea, 1963—2002. Supporter Korean Am. Family Svc., N.Y.C., 1999—2002; editl. bd. Gender & Soc. Jour. Recipient Fulbright Rsch. award, 2004—05; fellow, Brandeis U., 1989—92; Women's Studies Dissertation grantee, 1992, NE Asia Coun. Rsch. grantee, Assn. for Asian Studies, 1995, Gen. Rsch. grantee, Am. Philos. Soc., 1996, Internat. Migration Rsch. Planning grantee, Social Sci. Rsch. Coun., 1997. Mem.: Assn. for Asian Studies, Am. Sociol. Assn., Phi Kappa Phi. Avocations: travel, latin dancing, opera, cooking, gardening. Office: Vassar Coll Maildrop 507 124 Raymond Ave Poughkeepsie NY 12604 E-mail: semoon@vassar.edu.

MOONE, ROBERT H. finance company executive; BA in Psychology, Ohio State U., 1966. With State Auto Fin. Corp., Columbus, Ohio, 1970, br. underwriting mgr., 1980, mgr. sales devel., dir. mktg., dir. sales and mktg., pres., 1996—, CEO, 1999—. Office: State Auto Fin Corp 518 E Broad St Columbus OH 43215-3901

MOONEY, ANDREW P. consumer products company executive; b. Whitburn, Scotland; Cert. Acctg., U.K. Fin. contr. Nike U.K., 1980—82, dir. mktg., 1982—84; various positions to chief mktg. office Nike, Inc., U.S., 1992—99; pres. Disney Consumer Products, Walt Disney Co., Burbank, Calif., 1999—2003, chmn., 2003—. Collaborator various advt. campaigns:. Office: Walt Disney Co 500 S Buena Vista St Burbank CA 91521-9722

MOONEY, BURTON LEE, retired secondary school educator, editor; b. Greenfield, Mass., Dec. 30, 1945; s. James Joseph Mooney and Dorthea Wilberta Atkins; m. Barbara Louise Vosburgh, Apr. 4, 1977 (div. Aug. 4, 1991); m. Lois Ann Hallet, May 30, 1997. BA in English, U. Calif., Chico, 1973; MA in Edn., Rollins Coll., 1981. Tchr. Polk County Sch. Bd., Lakeland, Fla., 1974—2004. Head tchr. Elem. Polk Opportunity Ctr., Lakeland, 1987—94; adj. tchr. Polk C., Winter Haven, Fla., 1983—96; owner, pub. Writer's Helper, Lakeland, 1985—; past editor-in-chief The Pride of Polk City newspaper; editor-in-chief Auburndale Sun newspaper. Author: People, Places, Pets and Animals, 1989, Creative Writing Workbook, 2003; freelance writer. With USAF, 1963-68. Decorated Bronze Star. Mem. VFW (life post 8002-Lakeland), Disabled Am. Vets. (life), Kung Fu Karate Assn. (black belt). Republican. Mem. Lds Ch. Avocations: coaching, music, swimming. Home: 1422 Creekwood Run Lakeland FL 33802 Office: PO Box 8172 Lakeland FL 33809 E-mail: bmoonwrite@aol.com.

MOONEY, HAROLD ALFRED, plant ecologist; b. Santa Rosa, Calif., June 1, 1932; s. Harold Walter and Sylvia Anita Stefany; m. Sherry Lynn Gulmon, Aug. 15, 1974; children— Adria, Alyssa, Arica. AB, U. Calif., Santa Barbara, 1957; MA, Duke U., 1958, PhD, 1960. Assoc. prof. UCLA, 1960—68, Stanford U., Calif., 1968—75, prof. biology, 1975—, Paul S. Achilles prof. environ. biology, 1976—, sr. fellow, Inst. Internat. Studies, 2000—03. Author: Mediterranean-type Ecosystems, 1973, Convergent Evolution in Chile and California, 1977, Components of Productivity of Mediterranean Climate Regions, 1981, Disturbance in Ecosystems, 1983, Physiological of Plants in the Wet Tropics, 1984, Physiological Ecology of North American Plant Communities, 1985, Ecology of Biological Invasions of North America and Hawaii, 1986, Biological Invasions, A Global Perspective, 1989, Biodiversity and Ecosystem Function, 1993, Seasonally Dry Tropical Forests, 1995, CO2 and Terrestrial Ecosystems, 1995, Functional Roles of Biodiversity, 1996, Principles of Terrestrial Ecology, 2002. Served with AUS, 1953-55. Recipient Humboldt award, 1989, Max Planck Forscgungs Preis award Alexander von Humboldt Soc., 1992, Inst. Ecology prize, 1990, Nev. Medal of Sci. award, 2000, Blue Planet prize, 2002; Guggenheim fellow, 1974, Nat. Acad. Scis. fellow, 1982. Fellow AAAS, Am. Acad. Arts and Scis., Am. Philos. Soc.; mem. Ecol. Soc. Am. (pres. 1988-89, Mercer award 1961, Eminent Ecologist 1996), Brit. Ecol. Soc. (hon. mem.), Am. Inst. Biol. Scis. (pres. 1994), Internat. Coun. Sci. Unions (sec. gen. 1996-2002), Botanical Soc. Am. (Merit award, 1983). Office: Dept Biol Scis Stanford Univ Stanford CA 94305-1926 Office Phone: 650-723-1179.

MOONEY, JAMES DAVID, JR., aerial photographer; b. Anderson, Ind., May 20, 1921; s. James David and Jane (Watson) M.; m. Christine Mott, Dec. 29, 1944 (div. 1957); children: Barbara, James II, Richard; m. Gloria van Bomel Schoninger, Dec. 8, 1972. Student, U.S. Naval Acad., 1940-43; naval aviator, USN Flight Sch., 1943; BS in Engring., Princeton U., 1947. Cert. protection profl. Am. Soc. for Indsl. Security; lic. comml. pilot FAA. Supply mgr. Willys-Overland Motors, Inc., Maywood, Calif., 1947-50; contr. F.L. Jacobs Co. Inc., Detroit, 1953-55; spl. rep. U.S. Steel Export Co., Washington, 1956-61; mgr. internat. ops. Armour Rsch. Found., Chgo., 1962-65; v.p. CDC

Sys., Elizabeth, N.J., 1972-74; pres. Cash Control Corp., Mineola, N.Y., 1974-77; cons. J.D. Mooney Assoc., Oyster Bay, N.Y., 1978-98; pres. Aerial Photos by JDM, Inc., 1998—. Author: Long Range Planning, 1967. Police commr. Village of Centre Island, Oyster Bay, 1979-83, mayor, 1983-89. Lt. USN, 1940-45, 51-53. Mem.: N.Y. State Conf. Mayors, Internat. Assn. Chiefs of Police, Aircraft Owners and Pilots Assn., Seawanhaka Corinthian Yacht Club, Piping Rock Club, Cove Neck Tennis Club. Roman Catholic. Avocations: tennis, sailing. Home: 527 Centre Island Rd Oyster Bay NY 11771-5015

MOONEY, JAMES F. telecommunications industry executive; With IBM Corp., 1980—99; COO Baan Co.; CEO, COO Tradeout Inc.; exec. v.p., COO Nextel Comms.; non-exec. chmn. NTL Europe NTL Inc., N.Y., 2003—. Bd. dir. NTL Europe. Office: NTL Inc 110 East 59th St New York NY 10022 also: NTL Europe Inc 22 Suffolk St London SW1Y 4HG England

MOONEY, JAMES HUGH, newspaper editor; b. Pitts., Aug. 18, 1929; s. James H. and Kathryn A. (Hall) M.; m. Eileen Jane Casey, July 30, 1960; children: Mark Hall, Sean Francis, Annina Marie, James Matthew, Lorelei Jane, Paul Adam, Kathryn Celeste. BA in Journalism, Duquesne U., Pitts., 1957. With advt. dept., then editorial dept. Pitts. Post-Gazette, 1953—61; writer-editor Nat. Observer, 1961—77, Nat. Geographic, 1977—79; editor Found. News mag., Washington, 1979—81; press sec. Congressman Mickey Edwards of Okla., Washington, 1982; asst. nat. editor Washington Times, 1982—83; editor Status Report, 1983—92; dir. info. resources Ins. Inst. for Hwy. Safety, 1992—93; editor Western Pa. Medicine, Johnstown, 1993—95, Embassy Flash, Aspen Hill, Md., 1995—96; pres. Mooney Comms., 1997—. Former mem. editl. adv. bd. Nat. Study Ctr. Trauma and Emergency Med. Systems. Served with AUS, 1951-53.

MOONEY, JAMES P. chemicals executive; BA in History, Quincy U. Pres., CEO Mooney Chems., Inc., 1979-91; CEO OM Group Inc., Cleve., 1991—, also chmn. bd. dirs. Mem. Nat. Paint & Coatings Assn., Nat. Fed. Paint, Tech.'s Chems. Mgmt. Coun., Chem. Mfrs. Assn., Cobolt Devel. Inst. (bd. dirs.). Office: OM Group Inc 50 Public Sq,ste 3500 Cleveland OH 44113-2201

MOONEY, JEROME HENRI, lawyer; b. Salt Lake City, Aug. 7, 1944; s. Jerome Henri and Bonnie (Shepherd) M.; m. Carolyn Lasrich, Aug. 10, 1965 (div. Dec. 1978); 1 child, Dierdre Nicole; m. Kaitlyn Cardon, Sept. 23, 1995. BS, U. Utah, 1966, JD, 1972. Bar: Utah 1972, Calif. 1998, U.S. Ct. Appeals (10th cir.) 1974, U.S. Supreme 1984, U.S. Ct. Appeals (7th cir.) 1999, U.S. Ct. Appeals (9th cir.) 2001, U.S. Ct. Appeals (4th cir.) 2002. Sole practice, Salt Lake City, 1972-75, 79-83; sr. ptnr. Mooney, Jorgenson & Nakamura, Salt Lake City, 1975-78, Mooney & Smith, Salt Lake City, 1983-87, Mooney & Assoc., Salt Lake City, 1987-94, Mooney Law Firm, Salt Lake City, 1995-98, Larsen & Mooney Law, Salt Lake City, 1999—. Bd. dirs. Mooney Real Estate, Salt Lake City; mem. Active Music, Calif. Copyright Conf. Mem. Gov.'s Coun. on Vet. Affiars, Salt Lake City, 1982-89; trustee Project Reality, Salt Lake City, 1976—, P.E.A.C.E.; SAMHSA sponsor Project Reality, 1994—; vice chair State Mil. Acad. Assoc. Served with U.S. Army N.G., 1992-93. Mem. ABA (criminal justice sect. U.S. Sentencing Commn. com.), Utah Bar Assn. (chmn. criminal bar sect. 1987-88), Beverly Hills Bar Assn., Nat. Assn. Rec. Industry Profls., Utah NG Assn. (trustee 1976), 1st Amendment Lawyers Assn. (v.p. 1986-88, pres. 1988-89), Nat. Assn. Criminal Def. Lawyers, Families Against Mandatory Minimums (adv. coun.), VFW. Democrat. Jewish. Avocations: sailng, computers. Office: 50 W Broadway Ste 100 Salt Lake City UT 84101-2066 Home: 1950 S 200 W Apt 33 Bountiful UT 84010-7536 E-mail: JerryM@MooneyLaw.com.

MOONEY, JOHN BRADFORD, JR., oceanographer, engineer, consultant; b. Portsmouth, N.H., Mar. 26, 1931; s. John Bradford and Margaret Theodora (Akers) M.; m. Martha Ann Huntley, Dec. 25, 1953 (dec. May 1990); children: Melinda Jean, Pamela Ann, Jennifer Joan; m. Jennie Marie Duca, Nov. 24, 1990. BS, U.S. Naval Acad., 1953; postgrad., George Washington U., 1970, 71, 76; grad. sr. execs. nat./internat. security, Harvard U., 1980. Commd. ens. USN, 1953, advanced through grades to rear adm., 1979; chief staff officer Submarine Devel. Group 1, 1971-73; commdr. Bathyscaphe Trieste II, 1964-66, Submarine Menhaden, 1966-68; comdg. officer Naval Sta., Charleston, S.C., 1973-75; dep. dir. Deep Submergence Systems Div., Office Chief Naval Ops., Washington, 1975-77; comdr. Naval Tng. Ctr., Orlando, Fla., 1977-78; dir. Total Force Planning Div., Office Chief Naval Ops., Washington, 1978-81; oceanographer USN, 1981-83, chief naval rsch., 1983-87, ret., 1987; pres. Harbor Br. Oceanographic Instn., Inc., Ft. Pierce, Fla., 1989-92, marine bd., 1991-94. Mem. marine programs adv. coun. Grad. Sch. Oceanography, U. R.I., Narragansett, 1989—; chmn. study panel on undersea vehicles and nat. needs NRC, 1993—96, mem. adv. com. for postdoctoral and sr. rsch. associateship programs, 1995—2001; mem. panel to visit the former Soviet Union to evaluate undersea tech. for U.S. govt., 1993; chair, 95. At controls of Trieste II when hull of Thresher was found on floor of Atlantic, 1964; coordinated deep search and recovery of hydrogen bomb lost off coast of Spain, 1966; condr. recovery operation from depth of 16,400 feet in Mid-Pacific, 1972. Decorated Legion of Merit with 1 gold star; recipient spl. citation Armed Forces Recreation Assn., 1975, Dist. Eagle Scout award, 1986. Fellow Marine Tech. Soc. (pres. 1991-93), Explorers Club; mem. NAE, Am. Soc. Naval Engrs., Soc. Naval Architects and Marine Engrs., U.S. Naval Inst., Nat. Geog. Soc., Smithsonian Assocs., Masons, Shriners, Order of DeMolay (Legion of Honor), Tau Beta Pi. Avocations: swimming, grandchildren. Home and Office: 2313 Windswept Dr Austin TX 78738 Office Phone: 512-263-2799.

MOONEY, LORI, county official; b. Atlantic City, Aug. 22, 1929; d. Joseph Aloysius and Alice Marie Inemer; m. Charles H. Calvi (div.); children: Joseph P., Stephen C., Christina L.; m. Thomas Christopher Mooney; children: Thomas C., Timothy C. Svc. rep. Bell Telephone Co., Atlantic City, 1950-58; sr. evaluator U.S. Census Bur., N.J., 1960-63; coord. Nat. Sml. Bus. Com. for Johnson and Humphrey, Washington, 1964; owner, mgr. Lori Mooney & Co., Realtors, Atlantic County, N.J., 1965-77; commr. Atlantic County Bd. Elections, 1970—, also chmn., 5 yrs; county clk. County of Atlantic, Mays Landing, 1978-96. Mem. Active Corps Execs., Nat. SBA; chmn. county clk. liaison com. N.J. Supreme Ct., 1984-86. Del. Dem. Nat. Conv., 1972, 76, 84, 88, 96; mem. congl. liaison com. Acad. for State and Local Govts., 1989—; mem. U.S. Senator Bill Bradley's Citizen Adv. Com. Del. Dem. Nat. Conv., 1976, 84, 88, 92, 96, 2000. Recipient Woman of Achievement award N.J. Fedn. Bus. and Profl. Women, 1985, Role Model award The Sun Newspaper, 1989; inducted into Atlantic County Women's Hall of Fame, 2000, Holy Spirit H.S. Inaugural Hall of Fame, 2000. Mem. Internat. Assn. Clks., Recorders, Election Ofcls. and Treas. (N.J. dir. 1988—), Atlantic County Realtors Assn., Bus. and Profl. Women Atlantic County (scholarship chmn. 1982-85), County Officers Assn. N.J. (bd. dirs. 1978-96, pres. 1991-92, 92-93), N.J. Assn. County Clks. (chmn. 1984-86), N.J. Assn. Realtors, Nat. Assn. Realtors, Nat. Assn. Counties, N.J. League Municipalities, Assn. Records Mgrs. and Administrs., Atlantic City Women's C. of C. Home: 100 Carol Rd Linwood NJ 08221-2502 Office: Atlantic County Clks Office Main St Mays Landing NJ 08330-1702

MOONEY, MARILYN, lawyer; b. Pitts., July 29, 1952; d. James Russell and Mary Elizabeth (Cartwright) M. BA summa cum laude, U. Pa., 1973, JD, 1976. Bar: Mass. 1977, D.C. 1985, Pa. 1990, U.S. Dist. Ct. D.C. 1985, U.S. Ct. Appeals (D.C. cir.) 1985, U.S. Supreme Ct. 1986. Atty. E. I. du Pont de Nemours & Co., Wilmington, Del., 1976-84, Washington, 1985; assoc. Fulbright & Jaworski L.L.P., Washington, 1985-90, ptnr., 1990—. Contbr. articles to profl. jours. Mem.: ABA (fed. regulation securities com.), D.C. Bar (corp. fin. and securties law and internat. sections), Internat. Bar Assn. (issues and trading in securities com.), Am. Soc. Corp. Secs. (securities law com.). Office: Fulbright & Jaworski LLP 801 Pennsylvania Ave NW Washington DC 20004-2615 Office Phone: 202-662-4678. E-mail: mmooney@fulbright.com.

MOONEY, MICHAEL EDWARD, lawyer; b. Beloit, Wis., Jan. 21, 1945; s. William C. and Edith (Slothower) M. BA in Econs., St. Norbert Coll., 1966; JD, Boston Coll., 1969. Bar: Mass. 1969, Maine 1969, U.S. Tax Ct. 1975, U.S. Ct. Internat. Trade 1986. Assoc. Nutter, McClennen & Fish, LLP, Boston, 1969-77, sr. ptnr., 1978—, now mng. ptnr. V.p., exec. dir. Fed. Tax Inst. New Eng.; spkr., lectr. numerous seminars. Co-editor: Considerations in Buying or Selling a Business, 1985; mem. bd. editors Accounting and Financial Planning for Law Firms, 1988—. Co-chmn. Metro One Divsn. United Way; bd. dirs. Filene Found. Fellow Am. Coll. Tax Counsel; mem. Boston Bar Assn. (chmn. tax highlights com. 1986-95, mem. fin. com. 1990-92, founder, chmn. summer jobs program, vice chmn. artery bus. com.), Boston Tax Forum. Office: Nutter McClennen & Fish World Trade Ctr West 155 Seaport Blvd Boston MA 02210-2604 Office Phone: 617-439-2000. Personal E-mail: mmooney@nutter.com.

MOONEY, MICHAEL JOSEPH, college president; b. Evansville, Ind., Dec. 15, 1942; s. Joseph Thomas and Marie Louise (DeJean) Mooney; children: Susanne, Julia. AB summa cum laude, St. Meinrad Coll., 1964; STL magna cum laude, Univ. Innsbruck, Austria, 1968; M in Philosophy, Columbia U., 1973, PhD, 1982. Lectr. dept. religious studies, St. Mary's U., Halifax, N.S., Can., 1968-70, Union Theol. Sem., N.Y.C., 1972-74; project coord. Columbia U., N.Y.C., 1973-74, preceptor dept. religion, 1975-76, spl. asst. to exec. v.p. for acad. affairs, 1976-77, asst. provost, 1977-79, assoc. provost, 1979-82, dep. provost, 1982-89; pres. Lewis and Clark Coll., Portland, Oreg., 1989—. Bd. dirs. Reid Hall, Inc., N.Y.C. and Paris, 1977—89; trustee Jour. Philosophy, 1982—; bd. dirs. Roothbert Fund, 1980—92; v.p. Reid Hall, Inc., N.Y.C. and Paris, 1983—89; visitor Inst. for Advanced Study, Princeton, NJ, 1984; trustee Oreg. Ballet Theater, 1992—; mem. Portland Opera Assn., 1992—93; bd. dirs. Nat. Assn. Ind. Colls. and Univs., 1995—99, mem. exec. com., 1997, sec., 1998—99; mem. commn. on internat. edn. Am. Coun. Edn., 1993—95, mem. com. women in higher edn., 1997; mem. Truman Scholarship Finalists Selection Com., 2001—, Lewis and Clark Bicentennial Oreg., 2001—; bd. adv. Music Performance Trust Fund, 2002—. Author: Vico in the Tradition of Rhetoric, 1985 (Gottschalk prize Am. Soc. 18th Century Studies 1985); editor: Renaissance Thought and Its Sources, 1979; co-editor: Toward a Theology of Christian Faith: Readings in Theology, 1968, Vico and Contemporary Thought, 1976, Small Comforts for Hard Times: Humanists on Public Policy, 1977. Trustee Scuola d'Italia, N.Y.C., 1986—89, World Affairs Coun., 1992—2001, pres., 1999—2000. Recipient Rome prize Am. Acad. in Rome, 1989; Roothbert Fund fellow, 1972, Kent fellow Danforth Found., 1972, Woodrow Wilson fellow, 1972, Presdl. fellow Columbia U., 1972, F.J.E. Woodbridge Disting. fellow Columbia U., 1973; NEH grantee, 1984; Cavaliere Ufficiale, Order Merit, Republic of Italy, 1991. Fellow Italian Acad. for Advanced Studies in Am. (sr.); Am. Soc. for Eighteenth-Century Studies, Internat. Soc. for History of Rhetoric, Renaissance Soc. Am., Am. Acad. Religion, Am. Philos. Assn., Phi Beta Kappa (hon.). Office: Lewis & Clark Coll Office Pres 0615 SW Palatine Hill Rd Portland OR 97219-7879

MOONEY, RICHARD EMERSON, writer; b. Plainfield, N.J., Mar. 31, 1927; s. Wandell M. and Alice (Joy) M.; m. Elizabeth B. Coleman, Oct. 30, 1954; children: James C., Stephen E., John B. BA, Yale U., 1947; postgrad. (Nieman fellow), Harvard U., 1955-56. Writer United Press, N.Y.C., 1948-51, econ. reporter Washington, 1951-56, N.Y. Times, Washington, 1957-63, European econ. correspondent Paris, 1963-67, econ. reporter N.Y.C., 1967, asst. to exec. editor, 1968, asst. to mng. editor, 1969, dep. fgn. editor, 1970-72, asst. fin. editor, 1972-76, mem. editl. bd., 1982-95; contbg. editor, 1995-96; v.p. Hartford Courant, 1976-81, exec. editor, 1976-81, dir., 1977-81. Author: (with Edwin L. Dale, Jr.) Inflation and Recession, 1959. Trustee Hartford Courant Found., 1977-81. Served with USNR, 1944-48. Mem. Soc. Silurians (bd. govs. 1998—), Yale Club, The Coffee House. Home and Office: 130 E 67th St New York NY 10021-6136 Office Phone: 212-249-3516. Personal E-mail: remooney@aol.com.

MOONEY, THOMAS ROBERT, lawyer; b. Montclair, N.J., June 16, 1933; s. Thomas Edward and Ruth Evelyn (Meurling) M.; m. Mary Frances Davis, Aug. 23, 1958; children: Terrance Kevin, Rebecca Lee Poyner, Thomas Edward. BA in Econs., Fla. So. Coll., Lakeland, 1956; LLB, JD, Stetson U., St. Petersburg, Fla., 1961. BAr: Fla. 1961, Ga. 1962, U.S. Dist. Ct. (mid. dist.) 1964, U.S. Supreme Ct. 1965. Claims adjuster State Farm Mut. Ins. Co., Atlanta, 1961-63; atty. Maguire, Voorhis & Wells, P.A., Orlando, Fla., 1963-64, Meyers & Mooney, P.A., Orlando, 1964-94, Meyers, Mooney Stanley & Hollingsworth, Orlando, 1994—. Chair Workers Compensation Ednl. Conf., Fla., 1980-81. Chmn. bd. dirs. Epilepsy Assn. Ctrl. Fla., Orlando, 1964-67; bd. dirs. Children's Home Soc., Orlando, 1970-75, chmn., 1970-72. 1st lt. U.S. Army, 1956-58, Korea. Mem. ATLA, ABA, Fla. Bar Assn., Ga. Bar Assn., Acad. Fla. Trial Lawyers (chair workers compensation sect. 1985), Fla. Workers Advocates (bd. dirs. 1992—). Democrat. Methodist. Avocations: skiing, golf, travel, hiking, rafting. Office: Meyers Mooney Stanley & Hollingsworth P A 17 Lake Ave Orlando FL 32801-2730

MOONEY, WILLIAM PIATT, actor; b. Bernie, Mo., May 2, 1936; s. Lowell E. and Louise S. M.; m. Valorie Shaw Goodall, Jan. 13, 1962; children: Sean Goodall, William Norvell. Student Am. theater wing, U. Colo. Pres. William Mooney Assocs., cons. to industry for exec. presentations Appeared in continuing role of Paul Martin on TV series All My Children, 1972-85 (2 Emmy nominations); one-man show Half Horse, Half Alligator & Damn Everything But the Circus, They All Wanted in the Act (The Lindbergh Kidnapping and Trial); stage appearances: Brownsville Raid, We, A Man for All Seasons, Lolita; films: The Next Man, Network, A Flash of Green, Beer, Second Sight, C.A.T. Squad; author/star mus. play Banjo Reb and the Blue Ghost; co-author: ASAP-The Fastest Way to Create a Memorable Speech, 1992, Ready-to-Tell Tales, 1994, A Storyteller's Guide, 1995, Spiders in the Hairdo, 1999, (Grammy nominee 1998), (PBS) With a Dog's Eyes, 1997; recording artist: Why the Dog Chases the Cat, 1997 (ALA Notable Parent's Choice Gold and Naird awards), Spiders In The Hairdo, 1997, More Ready-To-Tell Tales From Around The World, 2000, The Exploding Toilet, 2004. Dir. jazz mus. Jam, 8 yrs. Colo. Univ. Opera Theater, others. Grammy nominee, 1995, 98. Address: 2879 Shadow Creek Dr #105 Boulder CO 80303

MOONVES, LESLIE, broadcast executive; b. N.Y.C., Oct. 6, 1949; s. Herman and Josephine (Schleifer) Moonves; m. Nancy Wiesenfeld, Dec. 17, 1978 (div.); children: Adam, Sara, Michael. BA, Bucknell U., 1971. Devel. exec. Catalina Prodns., Burbank, Calif., 1980—81; v.p. devel. Saul Ilson Prodns. Columbia Pictures TV, Burbank, 1981—82; v.p. movies and mini-series 20th Century Fox, L.A., 1982—85, Lorimar, Inc., Culver City, Calif., 1985—87; exec. v.p. creative affairs Lorimar-Telepictures, Culver City, 1987—90; pres. Lorimar TV, Burbank, 1990—93, Warner Bros. TV, Burbank, 1993—95, CBS Entertainment, L.A., 1995—97; exec. v.p. CBS/Broadcast Group, 1995—97; pres., CEO CBS TV, 1998—2003, chmn., CEO, 2003—04; co-pres., co-COO Viacom Inc., N.Y.C., 2004—. Bd. dirs. KB Home, 2004—. Developer, prodr. (TV series) Dallas, Dark Justice, Guns of Paradise, Knots Landing, Midnight Caller, Sisters, Family Matters, Full House, Perfect Strangers, Family Man, I'll Fly Away, Reasonable Doubts, Step by Step, Hangin' with Mr. Cooper, The Jackie Thomas Show, Crossroads, Homefront, Going to Extremes, Shaky Ground, It Had To Be You, Time Trax, Against the Grain, Lois & Clark: The Adventures of Superman, Cafe Americain, How'd They Do That, Living Single, Family Album, Getting By. Bd. dirs. L.A. Free Clinic; co-chair LA bd. govs. Mus. TV and Radio; bd. trustees Entertainment Industries Coun.; trustee Nat. Coun. for Families and TV, Am. Film Inst. Recipient Gold Medal Award, Internat. Radio and TV Soc., 2003. Mem.: NATAS (exec. com.), Hollywood Radio & TV Soc. (bd. dirs. 1988—91, pres. 1991). Democrat. Jewish. Office: Viacom Inc 1515 Broadway New York NY 10036

MOONWALKER, TU, minister, counselor, artist; b. Feb. 9, 1948; BA, Calif. State U., Sacramento, 1972; BS, U. Calif., Davis, 1973; MA, Tex. Tech. U., 1978, MS, 1979; postgrad., So. Meth. U., 1979. Chef Fairmont Hotel, San Francisco, 1971—72; rsch. and biopsy technician Tex. Tech. U. and Med. Ctr., Lubbock, 1974—78; Native Am. artist Santa Fe, 1979—87; cons. Am. Indian art Wheelwright Mus., Santa Fe, 1984—87; spiritual counselor, tchr. Ctr. for Universal Beingness, Moriarty, N.Mex., 1988—; min., canon Brigade of Light Ch., Cedar Mountain, NC, 1991—. Tech. advisor Am. Playhouse PBS Spl., Crestone, Colo., 1987; chmn. bd. dirs. Crystal Found., Denver, 1988—92, Profit from the Sun, Moriarity, 1999—2001; co-founder Ctr. for Universal Beingness; spkr. in field. *Over 20 years of consulting work to beginning businesses for their start-up structure and management procedure which has added to their success rate. Presently runs a successful portion of the Center for "The Philosophy of Universal Beingness Within the Whole," which offers to the public ongoing classes in such self-help areas as Ministrial Wisdom, Alternative Healing, Leadership, Art of Beingness, Universal Laws and Principles, Spirituality as an Everyday Application. To enhance these presentations, weekend intensives are also being developed and offered to help with awareness and daily application. Tu is now teaching voice lessons to individuals who wish to carry their talents beyond authority, with development of more teaching in the peforming and visual arts for others to explore, expand, and develop their talents.* Dir.(writer): (performances) Karen Lee Dance Theater, 2000—02. Chairperson bd. dirs. Ednl. Opportunity Program Calif. State U., Sacramento, 1971; mem. art com. chair, bd. dirs. YWCA, Lubbock, 1976—77; coun. mem. Sacramento Indian Ctr., 1971; vol. Talking Talons Youth Group, Tijeras, N.Mex., 2000. Named Outstanding Young Woman Am., 1982; recipient Humanitarian award, Friends for Life, Albuquerque, 1996; Wetlands Devel. Fed. grant, U.S. Wildlife, N.Mex., 1999. Mem.: Inst. Noetic Scis., Astron. Soc. Pacific, N.Y. Acad. Scis., Nat. Geog. Birdwatchers Soc., Acad. Am. Poets. Avocations: art, crafts, woodworking, stained glass, poetry and song writing. Office: 30-A Steeldust Ave Moriarty NM 87035

MOOR, KRISTIAN P. insurance company executive; b. N.Y.C. B of Fin., Bryant Coll.; MBA, Pace U. Joined Am. Internat. Group, N.Y.C., 1981, pres. Nat. Union's Mgmt. Liability Divsn., 1995—97; sr. v.p. domestic gen. ins. Am. Internat Group, N.Y.C., NY, 1997—98; exec. v.p. domestic gen. ins. Am. Internat. Group, 1998—. Office: Am Internat Group Inc 70 Pine St New York NY 10270

MOOR, ROY EDWARD, finance educator; b. Riverside, Calif., Oct. 11, 1924; s. Hugh Erin and Clara Viola Moor; m. Beverly A. Colbroth, Aug. 29, 1959; children— Cynthia Ann, Sheryl Lynn BA, UCLA, 1949; PhD, Harvard U., 1958. Vice pres., chief economist Fidelity Bank, Phila., 1965-68; vice pres., chief economist Drexel Firestone, Phila., 1968-71, Warburg Paribas Becker, N.Y.C., 1971-81; sr. v.p., chief economist First Chgo. Corp., 1981-86; prof. fin. Ill. Inst. Tech., Chgo., 1986—. Dir. Nat. Bur. Econ. Research, Cambridge, Mass. Author: Federal Budget as an Economic Document, 1962 Fellow Nat. Assn. Bus. Economists (pres. 1973) Home: 1013 Woodrush Ct Westmont IL 60561-8823 E-mail: rbmoor@kwom.com.

MOORADIAN, ARSHAG DERTAD, internist, educator; b. Aleppo, Syria, Aug. 20, 1953; arrived in U.S., 1981; s. Dertad and Araxi (Halajian) Mooradian; m. Deborah Lynn Miles, June 25, 1985; children: Arshag Dertad, Jr., Ariana Araxie. BS, Am. U., Beirut, 1976, MD, 1980. Diplomate Am. Bd. Internal Medicine. Asst. prof. medicine UCLA, 1985-88; assoc. prof. U. Ariz., Tucson, 1988-91; prof. St. Louis U., 1991. Contbr. articles to profl. jours. Grantee VA, 1985—97. Mem.: Am. Diabetes Assn. (chmn. task force micronutrients 1990—91, chmn. coun. nutrition and metabolism 2000—02), Endocrine Soc., Gerontol. Soc. Am., Am. Fedn. Clin. Rsch. Mem. Armenian Orthodox Ch. Achievements include identification of a potential biomarker of aging; research in on age-related changes in the blood-brain barrier; on age-related changes in thyroid hormone action; on diabetes related changes in the central nervous system. Office: Saint Louis U Med Sch 1402 S Grand Blvd Saint Louis MO 63104-1004 Business E-Mail: mooradad@slu.edu.

MOORCROFT, WILLIAM HERBERT, retired bio-psychologist, educator, researcher; b. Detroit, Mich., Feb. 1, 1944; s. Leonard and Elsie Moorcroft; m. Christina Louise Perrin, Nov. 27, 1971; children: Marcile Louise Cappel, Partick Richard, Andrew William. PhD, Princeton U., 1970. Prof. of psychobiology Luther Coll., Decorah, Iowa, 1971—2002; adj. prof. of psychology Colo. State U., Ft. Collins, Colo., 2001—. Cons. No. Colo. Sleep Consultants, Fort Collins, Colo., 2003—. Author: (textbook) Understanding Sleep and Dreaming, Kluwer Academic / Plenum Press. Mem.: APA, Am. Acad. of Sleep Medicine, Sleep Rsch. Soc., Phi Beta Kappa. Democrat-Npl. Episcopal. Avocations: sailing, internationaltravel. Home: 4443 Vista Dr Fort Collins CO 80526 Office: Psychology Colo State Univ Clark Bldg Fort Collins CO 80523 E-mail: moorbill@comcast.net.

MOORE, ALBERT CUNNINGHAM, lawyer, insurance company executive; b. Miami, Fla., May 31, 1931; s. Elias Richard and Virginia Adelaide (Thompson) Moore; m. Anne Cambreleng Bonynge, Aug. 24, 1957; children: Emily Robinson French, Barbara Raffield, Catherine Anne Bonygne Wells. AB, U. N.C., 1953; JD, U. Va., 1959. Bar: N.Y. 1960. Atty. White & Case, N.Y.C., 1959-69; corporate sec. Studebaker-Worthington, Inc., N.Y.C., 1969-72; sr. v.p., gen. counsel Crum & Forster, 1973-87. Former trustee N.J. Shakespeare Festival; former bd. dirs. DeBordieu Property Owners Assn., DeBordieu Arch. Rev. Bd. With USNR, 1953—56. Mem.: ABA, DeBordieu Club (S.C.), Wilton Ctr. Tennis Club (N.H.), Chi Phi, Phi Alpha Delta. Home: 1318 Debordieu Blvd Georgetown SC 29440-7163

MOORE, ALECIA See PINK

MOORE, ALFRED P. health facility administrator, benefits compensation analyst; BA, St. Vincent Coll.; MS, DSc, U. Pitts. Pres., CEO Am. Mut. Life, Wausau Benefits, Inc., Wausau, Wis., 2000—; v.p. Wausau Ins. Cos., Wausau, Wis., 1996—2000; pres., CEO Wausau Benefits, Inc., Wausau, 2000—. Office: Wausau Benefits Inc 115 W Wausau Ave Wausau WI 54401-2875

MOORE, ALMA DONST, writer, lyricist; b. Albert Alfred and Mary M.; m. Robert Arthur Moore, Apr. 20, 1958 (dec. Feb. 12, 1995). Clk. domestic and juvenile ct., spl. dep. county clk. Warren County Bd. Freeholders Ct. Ho., Belvidere, NJ, 1948—58. Lectr. Sen. Garrett W. Hagedorn NJ State Hosp. Contbg. writer: Soul Food, 1999—; founder The Spotlight, 1948; editor: The Spotlight, 1948, Warren Jour., 1948; author: (lyrics) Lifetime. Coun. mem. Rambai Mukti Mission, Clinton, NJ, 1998—. Recipient Sliver Poet, World Poetry, 1989, Gold Poet, 1999, Homer Diamond, Famous Poets Soc., 1999, Outstanding Achievement in Poetry, Silver Cup, Internat. Soc. Poets, 2003. Mem.: Inter. Soc. of Poets. Home: 71 Grayrock Rd Clinton NJ 08809-1075

MOORE, AMANDA LEIGH See MOORE, MANDY

MOORE, AMY NORWOOD, lawyer; b. Durham, N.C., Sept. 24, 1953; AB summa cum laude, Mt. Holyoke Coll., 1976; MA, U. Va., 1978, JD, 1983. Bar: D.C. 1984, U.S. Ct. Appeals (D.C. and 6th cirs.) 1985, U.S. Tax Ct., 1998. Law clk. to Frank M. Coffin, U.S. Ct. Appeals (1st cir.), 1983-84; ptnr. Covington & Burling, Washington. Articles editor Va. Law Rev., 1982-83. Mem. Phi Beta Kappa. Office: Covington & Burling 1201 Pennsylvania Ave NW Washington DC 20004-2401

MOORE, ANDREA S. state legislator; b. Libertyville, Ill., Sept. 2, 1944; Attended, Drake U. m. William Moore; 3 children. Mem. Ill. Ho. of Reps., 1993—; mem. com. on elections and state govt.; mem. com. on aging; mem. cities and villages com.; mem. environ. and energy com.; mem. labor and commerce com.; mem. com. on healthcare; mem. revenue and commerce com. Republican. Home: 361 S Saint Marys Rd Libertyville IL 60048-9407 Office: Ill Ho of Reps State Capitol Springfield IL 62706-0001 also: 2014-h Stratton Bldg Springfield IL 62706-0001 also: 131 E Park Ave Libertyville IL 60048-2800

MOORE, ANDREW GIVEN TOBIAS, II, investment banker, law educator; b. New Orleans, Nov. 25, 1935; m. Ann Elizabeth Dawson, June 5, 1965; children— Cecily Elizabeth (dec.), Marianne Dawson. BBA, Tulane U., 1958, JD, 1960. Bar: La. 1960, Del. 1963. Law clk. to chief justice Del., Dover, 1963; assoc. firm Killoran & Van Brunt, Wilmington, Del., 1964-70, partner, 1971-76; partner firm Connolly, Bove & Lodge, Wilmington, 1976-82; justice Del. Supreme Ct., Wilmington, 1982-94; sr. mng. dir. Wasserstein Perella & Co., Inc., N.Y.C., 1994-2001, Drsdner Kleinwort Wasserstein, Inc., N.Y.C., 2001—. Mem. Del. Bar Examiners, 1975-82; mem. Del. Gen. Corp. law com., 1969-83; chmn. joint com. Del. Bar Assn.-Del. Bankers Assn., 1978-79; chmn. Del. Jud. Proprieties Com., 1983-94, Del. Bench and Bar Conf., 1988-94; trustee Del. Bar Found., 1984-94; faculty Tulane Inst. European Legal Studies,

Paris Inst., 1990-96, 99; adj. prof. law Georgetown U. Law Ctr., Widener U. Sch. Law, U. Iowa Coll. Law; guest lectr. law Columbia U., Tulane U., U. Toronto, Can., U. Tex., Villanova U., Washington U., St. Louis, U. Iowa, George Mason U., DeVrije U. van Brussel, Cath. U. Louvain La Neuve; mem. pres.'s coun. Tulane U., 1990-96; chmn. Tulane Corp. Law Inst., 1988-95; Lehmann disting. vis. prof. law Washington U., St. Louis, 1994, 96; Mason Ladd disting. vis. prof. U. Iowa, 1995; disting. vis. prof. law St. Louis U., 1995, 96, 99; bd. dirs. Am. Lawyer Media, Inc. Trustee Del. Home and Hosp. for Chronically Ill, Smyrna, 1966-70, chmn., 1966-69; mem. New Castle County Hist. Rev. Bd., Wilmington, 1974-82; mem. Del. Cts. Planning Com., 1982-94; dean's coun. Tulane U. Law Sch., 1988-96; bd. visitors Walter F. George Sch. Law, Mercer U., 1985-91, chmn., 1988-90. With JAGC, USAF, 1960-63. Mem. ABA, La. Bar Assn., Del. Bar Assn. (v.p. 1976-77, exec. com. 1982-83), Am. Judicature Soc. (bd. dirs. 1982-86), Order Barristers, Phi Delta Phi, Delta Theta Phi (hon.), Omicron Delta Kappa Democrat. Presbyterian.

MOORE, ANDREW TAYLOR, JR., banker; b. Tarboro, N.C., June 17, 1940; s. Andrew Taylor and Mary Dare (Allsbrook) M. BA in History, Duke U., 1962; LLB, U.Va., Charlottesville, 1965. Asst. sec. Signet Banking Corp., Richmond, 1965-71, asst. v.p., corporate sec., 1971-75, v.p., corporate sec., 1975-82, sr. v.p., corporate sec., 1982-94. Bd. dirs. Theatre IV, Richmond, Va., 1981-97, Va. State YMCA adv. coun., Lynchburg, 1988—; trustee Hist. Richmond Found., 1993-98; mem. presidents coun. Va. Hist. Soc., 1996—. Presbyterian (elder 1996—). Avocations: jogging; gardening; travel. Home: 2011 Hanover Ave Richmond VA 23220-3539

MOORE, ANN ROY, school system administrator; b. Florence, Ala. BA, Hampton (Va.) U.; MA, EdS, U. No. Ala.; EdD in Curriculum Leadership Pers. and Early Childhood Edn., Vanderbilt U., 1986; cert. in ednl. adminstrn., 1986, cert. in ednl. adminstrn., 1987; cert. supt., Ala. A&M, 1992. Former tchr. pre-sch. and elem. sch. Huntsville (Ala.) City Schs., curriculum specialist, 1978—80, former prin., mgr. elem. edn., dep. supt., 1999—2001, supt., 2001—; former asst. supt. Florence Sch. Sys. Office: Huntsville City Schs 200 White St Huntsville AL 35801

MOORE, ANN S. magazine executive; b. Biloxi, Miss., 1950; d. Monty and Bea Sommovigo; m. Donovan Moore; 1 son, Brendan. BA in Polit. Sci., Vanderbilt U., 1971; MBA, Harvard U., 1978. With Time, Inc., N.Y.C., 1978—; gen. mgr. Sports Illustrated, 1983—89; founding publisher Sports Illustrated for Kids, 1989-91; publisher People mag., 1991—93, pres., 1993—98, People Mag. Group (renamed People/In Style Mag. Group, 2001), 1998—2001; exec. v.p. Time, Inc., 2001—02, chmn., CEO, 2002—. Bd. dirs. Avon Products Inc., 1993; public spkr. bus. and women's issues. Hon. bd. mem. Gilda's Club, N.Y.C.; founder Time to Give Back. Named Pub. Exec. of Yr., Adweek, 1998, 2004 Bus. Statesman, Harvard Bus. Sch.; named one of The 50 Most Powerful Women in Am. Bus., Fortune Mag.; recipient AOL Time Warner Civic Leadership award, 2003. Achievements include guiding People magazine to spin off several popular titles including In Style (domestic and international), Teen People, People en Español, and Real Simple. Office: Time Inc Office of CEO 75 Rockefeller Plaza New York NY 10019*

MOORE, ANNE, physician; b. N.Y.C., Apr. 28, 1944; d. John D.J. and Mary Foote Moore; m. Arnold L. Lisio, Sept. 6, 1969; children: Philip Moore, Mary Foote. BA, Smith Coll., 1965; MD, Columbia U., 1969. Diplomate Am. Bd. Internal Medicine, Am. Bd. Hematology (chmn. 1996), Am. Bd. Oncology. Intern dept. medicine N.Y. Hosp., N.Y.C., 1969-73, assoc. attending physician, 1981-95, attending physician, 1996—; postdoctoral fellow Rockefeller U., 1972-73, hematology-oncology fellow, 1973-75; asst. prof. medicine Cornell U. Med. Coll., N.Y.C., 1975-91, assoc. prof. clin. medicine, 1981-95, prof. clin. medicine, 1996—. Cons. Strang Cancer Prevention Ctr.; lectr., cons., in field. Author: Patient's Guide to Breast Cancer Treatment, 1992, rev. edit., 1997; ad hoc reviewer Am. Jour. Clin. Oncology, 1994, New Eng. Jour. Medicine, 1994, 96, 97; contbr. articles to profl. jours., chpts. to books. Trustee St. David's Sch., 1983-89, HealthCare Chaplaincy, Inc., 1991—; bd. dirs. Camilli Found., 1990—, Cure Myeloma Fund, 1988-98. Recipient award SHARE, 1992, Wholeness of Life award Hosp. Chaplaincy, 1992, Alumnae award Oak Knoll Sch., 1994, Eileen Dreyer Meml. Lectureship award Sass Found. for Med. Rsch., 1996, Commendation award Office of Exec. Nassau County, 1996, award Artists for Breast Cancer Survival, Inc., 2000. Mem. Am. Bd. Internal Medicine (bd. dirs. 1996—), Am. Soc. Hematology, Am. Soc. Clin. Oncology, N.Y. Acad. Scis., Soc. for Study of Blood (membership chmn. 1979-80), N.Y. Met. Breast Cancer Group (membership chmn. 1992-93, sec.-treas. 1993-95, v.p. 1995-96, pres. 1997—), Soc. for Study of Breast Disease, N.Y. Cancer Soc., N.Y. Acad. Medicine (trustee 1998—). Office: Weill-Cornell Med Ctr 428 E 72nd St New York NY 10021-4635

MOORE, ANNETTE B. legislative staff member; b. Salt Lake City, Nov. 8, 1946; Sec., chief adminstrv. officer Utah State Senate, Salt Lake City, 1994—. Mem.: Am. Soc. Legislative Clks. and Secs. (chair mem. and comm. com. 2000—01, chair profl. com. 2001—02, editor Jour of Profl. Com. 2002—03, mem. exec. com. 2003). Office: Utah State Senate State Capitol Rm 319 Salt Lake City UT 84114

MOORE, BEATRICE, religious organization administrator; b. Somerville, Mass., Oct. 6, 1928; d. George and Christina Turner; m. Wendell Moore, May 9, 1953; children: Karl C., Linda Moore Flewelling, Diane Pearl, Larry. BA in Theology and English, Berkshire Christian Coll., Lenox, Mass., 1950. Pres. The Woman's Home and Foreign Mission Soc., Loudon, N.H., past nat. pres. Charlotte, NC, 1987—96; chmn. Nat. Spiritual Life. Sunday sch. tchr., deaconess Loudon Ridge Family Bible Ch.; chair Concord Christian Women's Club, 2002-03; prayer coord. Concord Christian Women's Club, 2003-, Ladies Bible Study leader, 1998-; active Women's Home and Fgn. Mission Soc., Loudon, past pres. N.H. Soc., past pres. ea. region; hostess, contact chmn., prayer adv., Bible club guide Stonecroft Ministries, Friendship Bible Study Guide; past leader 4-H Club. Mem.: Concord Christian Womens Club (chair). Office: Woman's Home & Foreign Mission 845 Loudon Ridge Rd Loudon NH 03307-1712

MOORE, BENJAMIN, theatrical producer; b. Boston, Oct. 25, 1945; s. Charles Frederick and Adeline Reeves (Nichols) Moore; m. Mary Bradford Paine, May 31, 1969 (div. Jan. 1982); m. Barbara Ann Dirickson, June 25, 1983 (div. May 1995); m. Marilyn McGuire, Oct. 9, 1999. BA, Dartmouth U., 1967; MFA, Yale U., 1970. Asst. mng. dir. Yale Repertory Theatre, New Haven, 1969-70; gen. mgr. Westport (Conn.) Country Playhouse, 1970; prodn. dir. Am. Conservatory Theatre, San Francisco, 1970-79, gen. mgr., 1979-81, mng. dir., 1981-85; mng. dir., bd. dirs. Seattle Repertory Theatre, 1985—. Mem. Seattle Arts Commn., 1986—90, chair, 1989; mem. Wash. State Arts Commn. Mem. Wash. State Arts Alliance, League Resident Theatres, Rainier Club. Office: Seattle Repertory Theatre 155 Mercer St Seattle WA 98109-4639

MOORE, BETTY JEAN, retired education educator; b. L.A., Apr. 4, 1927; d. Ralph Gard and Dora Mae (Shinn) Bowman; m. James H. Moore, Nov. 25, 1944 (div. 1968); children: Barbara, Suzanne, Sandra; m. George W. Nichols, Oct. 15, 1983. BA, Pasadena Coll., 1957; MA, U. Nev., 1963; PhD, U. Ill., 1973. Tchr. Calif. Elem. Schs., 1951—63; sec. tchr. Calif. pub. schs., 1963-68; asst. prof. Ea. Ill. U., Charleston, 1968-71; grad. teaching asst. U. Ill., Champaign, 1971-73; asst. prof. to assoc. prof. S.W. Tex. State U., San Marcos, 1973-83, prof. edn., 1983-89, ret., 1989, prof. emeritus, 1995—. Sch. evaluator; cons. in field; reading clinic dir. S.W. Tex. State U., 1974-85; cons. Min. Edn., Rep. of Singapore, 1980, 97; citizen ambassador People to People, China, 1998. Contbr. articles to profl. jours.; author: Teaching Reading, 1984; producer/dir. 5 ednl. videos. Active fund raising various charitable orgns.; vol. reading cons., Ariz. pub. schs., 2000-03. Mem. Internat. Reading Assn. (chpt. pres. 1964-65), Nat. Coun. Tchrs. English, AAUP. Presbyterian. Avocations: reading, writing, swimming, cooking. Office: Tex State U-San Marcos C & I Dept San Marcos TX 78666

MOORE, BETTY JO, legal assistant; b. Medicine Lodge, Kans., July 10, 1921; d. Joseph Christy and Helen Blanche (Hubbell) Sims; m. Harold Frank Moore, June 19, 1941 (dec.); children: Terrance C., Harold Anthony, Trisha Jo. Cert., U. West L.A., 1978; student, Wichita (Kans.) U., 1940-41. Cert. legal asst./escrow officer. Sec. UCLA, 1949-59; escrow officer Security Pacific Nat. Bank, L.A., 1959-62, Empire Savs. & Loan Assn., Van Nuys, Calif., 1962-64; escrow supr. San Fernando Valley Bank, Van Nuys, 1964; escrow officer Heritage Bank, Westwood, Calif., 1964-66; escrow coord. Land Sys. Corp., Woodland Hills, Calif., 1966-67; escrow officer/asst. mgr., real estate lending officer Security Pacific Nat. Bank, L.A., 1967-80; real estate paralegal Pub. Storage, Pasadena, 1980-81; asst. mgr. escrow dept. First Beverly Bank, Century City, Calif., 1982-84; escrow trainer/officer Moore's Tng. Temps Inc., Canoga Park, Calif., 1984—92, legal asst., 1992—. Participant People to People Amb. Program/Women in Mgmt. to USSR, 1989; observer Internat. Fedn. Bus. and Profl. Women's Congress, Washington, 1965, 81, Nassau, Bahamas, 1989, Narobi, Kenya, 1991, Havana, Cuba, 2004. Adv. bd. escrow edn. Pierce Coll., Woodland Hills, Calif., 1968-80. Recipient Cert. of Appreciation, Pierce Coll., 1979, Calif. Fedn. Bus. and Profl. Women, 1989, Nat. Women's History Project, 1995. Mem. Nat. Fedn. Bus. and Profl. Women's Clubs, Calif. Fedn. Bus. and Profl. Women (pres. dist. 1987-88, Calif. Found. chmn. 1988-89, internat. concerns chmn. 1996-97, 2003), Woodland Hills Bus. and Profl. Women ((pres. 1991-92, 94-95), Valley/Sunset Dist. BPW (v.p. legislation/pub. policy 1997-98, 2001-02, 03, Cert. of Appreciation 2002), Tri Valley Dist. Bus. and Profl. Women (legis. chair 1992-93, exec./corr. sec. 1993-94, 94-95), Internat. Fedn. Bus. and Profl. Women, Nat. Women's Polit. Caucus (coord., sec. San Fernando Valley caucus 1986-87, sec. 1990-2003, legis. co-chair 1991-93), Women's Orgn. Coalition San Fernando Valley (sec. 1992, exec. com. L.A. Women's Equality Day 1995, pres. 2002-04), San Fernando Valley Escrow Assn. (bd. dirs. 1962-64), L.A. Women's Family Equity Coalition, U. West L.A. Alumni Assn., Rotary, U.N. Assn., League of Women Voters. Democrat. Methodist. Avocations: reading, musical theater.

MOORE, BILLY DON, video scriptwriter, producer; b. Oklahoma City, Dec. 26, 1956; s. Orval L. and Mary E. (Perry) M.; m. Donna M. Lovelace; stepchildren: Derek, Ryan. BA in Journalism, U. Okla., 1979, MA in Journalism, 1993. Prodn. asst. FAA, Oklahoma City, 1979-81; media technician, supr. Oklahoma City C.C., 1981-85; video prodn. specialist Okla. Dept. Transportation, Oklahoma City, 1985-99; motion picture and broadcast archivist Okla. Hist. Soc., Oklahoma City, 1999—. Owner BVC Video. Editor, photographer (cable series) Connecting, 1983-85, prodr. pub. svc. announcements, (aviation video mag.) Okla. Approach, 1995-99; prodr. documentaries Okla. Pub. TV; prodr., editor, photographer: (TV show) Yesterday. Recipient Crystal award The Communicator, 1998, Telly award excellence, 1998, Aegis award, 1999, Videographer award excellence, 1999, 20th Anniversary Classic Telly award, 1999. Democrat. Baptist. Avocation: writing books on oklahoma history. Office: Okla Hist Soc 2100 N Lincoln Blvd Oklahoma City OK 73105-4907 E-mail: bdmoore@ok-history.mus.ok.us.

MOORE, BOB STAHLY, communications executive; b. Pasadena, Calif., July 3, 1936; s. Norman Hastings and Mary Augusta (Stahly) M. Student, U. Mo., 1954-58, MIT, 1958-62. Dir. news WPEO, Peoria, Ill., 1958—60, KSST, Davenport, Iowa, 1960—62, WIRE, Indpls., 1962—64, WCFL, Chgo., 1964—67; White House corr. Metromedia, Inc., Washington, 1967—71; dir. news Gateway Comm., Altoona, Pa., 1972—74; chief Washington Bur. MBS, 1974—76, v.p. news, 1976—78, White House corr., 1978—81; dir. comm. Fed. Home Loan Bank Bd., Washington, 1981—85; spl. asst. to bd. govs. Fed. Res. Sys., Washington, 1985—. Active ARC. Served with USAF, 1961-63. Recipient profl. awards Ind. News Broadcasters, 1963, Ill. News Broadcasters, 1965, UPI, 1960, 63, 65, AP, 1956, 58, 61, 65, 67, Mo. News Broadcasters, 1956, 61 Mem. Radio and Television News Dirs. Assn. (Profl. award), White House Corrs. Assn., State Dept. Corrs. Assn., Radio-Television Corrs. Gallery (U.S. Capitol), Chgo. Council on Fgn. Relations, Pub. Relations Soc. Am., Nat., Washington, Chgo. press clubs, U.S. Jr., Mo., Ill. chambers commerce, Sigma Delta Chi. Presbyterian. Home: 114 W Arlington Ave Vandalia MO 63382 Office: 20th And Constitution NW Washington DC 20551-0001

MOORE, BRIAN CLIVE, actuary; b. Everett, Wash., Sept. 7, 1945; s. Frederic E. and Kathleen E. (Miller) M.; m. Lorraine Campbell, Feb. 11, 1946; children: Timothy, Jonathan. BA in Math., Yale U., 1970; MA in Math., U. Calif., 1971. Actuarial assoc. INA, Phila., 1971-73; asst. actuary Reliance Ins. Group, Phila., 1973-77, asst. sec., 1977-78, sec., 1978-80, asst. v.p., 1980-84, v.p., 1984-86, sr. v.p., 1986-99; asst. v.p. AIG Mktg., Wilmington, Del., 2000—. With U.S. Army, 1966-68. Fellow Casualty Actuarial Soc.; mem. Am. Acad. Actuaries. Office: AIG Mktg Inc One AIG Ctr Wilmington DE 19803

MOORE, BRUCE, information technology executive; Grad., Stanford U., 1976. With IBM; pres., CEO Diasonics Ultrasound, Inc., Auspex, Santa Clara, 1995—. Office: 2300 Central Expy Santa Clara CA 95050-2516

MOORE, BRUCE E. real estate company executive; CEO Brandywine Real Estate Mgmt. Svcs. Corp., Chedd Ford, Pa., 1989—. Office: Brandywine Real Estate Mgmt Svcs Corp 2 Ponds Edge Dr Chadds Ford PA 19317-9389

MOORE, C. BRADLEY, chemistry professor; b. Boston, Dec. 7, 1939; s. Charles Walden and Dorothy (Lutz) Moore; m. Penelope Williamson Percival, Aug. 27, 1960; children: Megan Bradley, Scott Woodward. BA magna cum laude, Harvard U., 1960; PhD, U. Calif., Berkeley, 1963. Predoctoral fellow NSF, 1960-63; asst. prof. chemistry U. Calif., Berkeley, 1963-68, assoc. prof., 1968-72, prof., 1972-2000, vice chmn. dept., 1971-75, chmn. dept. chemistry, 1982-86, dean Coll. Chemistry, 1988-94, prof. grad. sch., 2000—; v.p. rsch. Ohio State U., Columbus, Disting. prof. math. and phys. sci., prof. chemistry, 2000—03, prof. emeritus, 2003—; prof. chemistry Northwestern U., 2003—, v.p. rsch., 2003—. Assoc. prof. Faculty Scis., Paris, 1970, 75; Miller Rsch. Prof. U. Calif., Berkeley, 1972-73, 87-88; vis. prof. Inst. for Molecular Sci., Okazaki, Japan, 1979, Fudan U., Shanghai, 1979, adv. prof., 1988—; vis. fellow Joint Inst. for Lab. Astrophysics, U. Colo., Boulder, 1981-82; faculty sr. scientist (Chemical Sci. Div.) Lawrence Berkeley Nat. Lab., 1974-2000, divsn. dir., 1998-2000: mem. editl. bd. Jour. Chem. Physics, 1973-75, Chem. Physics Letters, 1980-85, Jour. Phys. Chemistry, 1981-87, Laser Chemistry, 1982—; mem. Basic Energy Scis. adv. com. Office Sci. U.S. Dept. Energy, 2000-03. Editor: Chemical and Biochemical Applications of Lasers; assoc. editor Annual Review of Physical Chemistry, 1985-90; contbr. articles to profl. jours. Trustee Sci. Svc., 1995—, Sci. and Tech. Campus, 2000-03; mem. bd. govs. Ohio Supercomputer Ctr., 2000-03; rsch. officer Coun. of Ohio Bd. of Regents, 2000-03; pres., chmn. bd. Ohio State U. Rsch. Found., 2000-03 Recipient Coblentz award, 1973, E.O. Lawrence Meml. award U.S. Dept. Energy, 1986, Lippincott award, 1987, 1st award Inter-Am. Photochem. Soc., 1988; nat. scholar Harvard U., 1958-60; fellow Alfred P. Sloan Found., 1968, Guggenheim Found., 1969, Humboldt Rsch. award for Sr. U.S. Scientists, 1994. Fellow AAAS, Am. Acad. Arts and Scis., Am. Phys. Soc. (Plyler award 1994); mem. NSF adv. com. for education and human resources directorate, chair subcom. policy and planning 1997-99, NAS (chmn. com. undergrad. sci. edn. 1993-97, class I membership com., 1998-2000, 2002, 2000 nominating com.), Am. Chem. Soc. (past chmn. divsn. phys. chemistry, Calif. sect. award 1977). Avocation: bicycling. Office: Northwestern U Crown 2-223 633 Clark St Evanston IL 60208 E-mail: vp-research@northwestern.edu.

MOORE, CARLETON BRYANT, geochemistry educator; b. N.Y.C., Sept. 1, 1932; s. Eldridge Carleton and Mabel Florence (Drake) M.; m. Jane Elizabeth Strouse, July 25, 1959; children: Barbara Jeanne, Robert Carleton; m. Diane Beets, Apr. 23, 2000. BS, Alfred U., 1954, DSc (hon.), 1977; PhD, Cal. Inst. Tech., 1960. Asst. prof. geology Wesleyan U., Middletown, Conn., 1959-61; mem. faculty Ariz. State U., Tempe, 1961—; nat. rsch. coun. rsch. assoc. NASA Ames Rsch. Ctr., 1974; prof., dir. Ctr. for Meteorite Studies Ariz. State U., Regents' prof., 1988—. Vis. prof. Stanford U., 1974; Prin. investigator Apollo 11-17; preliminary exam. team Lunar Receiving Lab., Apollo, 12-17. Author: Cosmic Debris, 1969, Meteorites, 1971, Principles of Geochemistry, 1982, Grundzügeder Geochemie, 1985; editor: Researches on Meteorites, 1961, Jour. Meteoritical Soc.; contbr. articles to profl. jours. Asteroid 5046 named Carletonmoore in his honor, 2000. Fellow Am. Geophys. Union, Ariz.-Nev. Acad. Sci. (pres. 1979-80), Meteoritical Soc. (life hon., pres. 1966-68), Geol. Soc. Am., Mineral. Soc. Am., AAAS (council 1967-70); mem. Geochem. Soc., Am. Chem. Soc., Am. Ceramic Soc., Sigma Xi. Office: Ariz State U Ctr Meteorite Studies Tempe AZ 85287-2504 Address: PO Box 26137 Tempe AZ 85285 Office Phone: 480-965-3576. Business E-Mail: cmoore@asu.edu.

MOORE, CAROL, state legislator; b. N.Y.C., Jan. 1, 1945; 1 child. BA, Boston U., 1967, MSW, 1971. Psychotherapist, 1968—; mem. dist. Merrimack 19 N.H. Ho. of Reps., 1993—; mem. children, youth and juvenile justice com.; mem. asst. to Dem. leaders. Mem. N.H. Assn. Social Workers, N.H. Women's Lobby (treas. 1983-84, chair 1984-89). Democrat. Avocations: singing, travel, gardening. Home: 38 1/2 S Spring St Concord NH 03301-2427 Office: NH Ho of Reps State House Rm 307 Concord NH 03301

MOORE, CAROL A. academic administrator; b. Newark, N.J., Dec. 8, 1945; d. James Clifford and Helen Mohan Brierley; m. Thomas Eric Moore, Nov. 25, 1967; 1 child, Kimberly Ann. BS in Biology, Montclair St. Coll., N.J., 1967; MA in Biology, Monclair State Coll., N.J., 1972; PhD in Biology, Northeastern Univ., Boston, Mass., 1981. Sci. tchr. H.S. and Jr. H.S., 1967—71; asst. prof. biology Massasoit C.C., Brockton, Mass., 1972—83, divsn. chairperson sci. and tech., asst prof. biology, 1979—83, asst. dean academic affairs, asst. prof. biology, 1983—84; dean academic affairs, chief acadamic officer, prof. biology Lasell Coll., Newton, Mass., 1984—88; dean undergraduate sch., chief acadminc officer, prof. biology Lesley Coll., Cambridge, Mass., 1988—91; provost & v.p. academic affairs, chief academic officer, prof. biology Mercy Coll., Dobbs Ferry, NY, 1992—98; pres. Lyndon State Coll., Lyndonville, Vt., 1998—. Vis. scientist Marine Sci. Inst., Northeastern Univ., Nahant, Mass., 1991—. Contbr. scientific papers to numerous conf., chapters to books, articles to profl. jour. Mem., Vt. higher edn. coun. rep. New Eng. Higher Edn. Bd., 1991—; mem., adv. bd. Vt. Telecom Advancement Ctr. USDA Grant, 2002—, Office of Nursing Workforce Rsch., Planning and Develp., Univ. Vt., 2001—; mem., Vt. bd. dirs. Girl Scout Coun., 2001—; mem. Am. Coun. Edn. Commn. on Women in Higher Edn., 2002—03; mem. Vt. Higher Edn. Coun., 1998—; rep. New Eng. Bd. of Higher Edn., 2002—, pres., 2001—02, v.p., 2000—01, exec. com., 1999—, sec.-treas., 1999—2000, com. on cert. & accreditation, 1998—; bd. dirs. Northeastern Vt. Devel. Assn., 2000—, Northeast Kingdom Learning Svc., 2000—. Grantee Title III Retention Grant, 1995, AAC Cirriculm Devel. Grant, 1990, NSF, 1983. Mem.: Soc. of Devel. and Comparative Immunology, Soc. for Invertebrate Pathology, Nat. Shellfisheries Soc., Am. Soc. of Zoologists (travel award), New Eng. Estuarine Rsch. Soc., Nat/ Assn. for Women Deans, Adminstr., and Counselors, Assn. of Tchr. Educators, Am. Coun. of Edn./ Nat. Identification Program, Nat. Assn. of Academic Affairs Adminstr., Sigma Xi, Phi Sigma. Office: Lyndon State Coll 1001 Coll Rd Lyndonville VT 05851

MOORE, CAROLE IRENE, librarian; b. Berkeley, Calif., Aug. 15, 1944; AB, Stanford U., 1966; MLS, Columbia U., 1967. Reference libr. Columbia U., N.Y.C., 1967-68, U. Toronto, Can., 1968-80, head cataloging, 1980-85, assoc. libr., 1985-86, chief libr., 1986—. Mem. nat. adv. bd. Nat. Libr. Can., Ottawa, 1991-94; bd. dirs. Rsch. Librs. Group. 1994-2000, U. Toronto Press, 1994—. Recipient Disting. Alumni award Columbia U., 1989. Mem. ALA, Can. Libr. Assn., Can. Assn. Rsch. Librs. (pres. 1989-91, bd. dirs. 1996-98). Avocation: gardening. Office: U Toronto Libr 130 Saint George St Toronto ON Canada M5S 1A5

MOORE, CASSANDRA CHRONES, real estate broker and policy analyst; b. Oneonta, N.Y., June 14, 1935; d. Constantine John and Antonia (Laskaris) Chrones; m. Thomas Gale Moore, Dec. 28, 1958; children: Charles Godwin, Antonia Laskaris. BA summa cum laude, Radcliffe Coll., Cambridge, Mass., 1956; MA, Harvard U., 1958; PhD, U. Mich., 1975. Lic. real estate broker, Calif. Lectr. Duquesne U., Pitts., 1962-65, Mich. State U., East Lansing, 1966-68; broker, owner Moore Assocs., Palo Alto, Calif., 1983-85; dir. state and mcpl. legislation Nat. Assn. Realtors, Washington, 1985-87; exec. dir. Fed. Interagy. Coun. on Homeless, Washington, 1987-89; adj. scholar Competitive Enterprise Inst., Washington, 1989—, mem. adv. bd., 1995—; adj. scholar Cato Inst., Washington, 1996—. Author: Haunted Housing, 1997. Co-chmn. Radcliffe Alumnae Lectureship Com., Palo Alto and San Francisco, 1984-2000; mem. nat. com. Radcliffe Alumnae Professorship Fund, 2001-02. Recipient Fulbright fellowship U.S. Govt., Washington, 1956-57. Mem.: Palo Alto Bd. Realtors (dir. 1984, 1985), Tsintzinian Soc. (bd. mem. 1999—, alt. bd. mem. 2001—02), Am. Assn. Small Property Owners (bd. mem. 1997—), Radcliffe Club Peninsula (pres. 1980—82), Phi Beta Kappa. Avocations: hiking, swimming, skiing. Office: 415 Cambridge Ave Palo Alto CA 94306 Business E-Mail: ccmassoc@pacbell.net.

MOORE, CHARLES HEWES, JR., industrial and engineered products executive; b. Coatesville, Pa., Aug. 12, 1929; s. Charles Hewes and Jane Richards (Scott) M.; m. Judith L. McClellan, June 23, 1971; children: Charles Hewes III, James, David, Susan, Kevin, Christopher, Margery, Brian, Amanda. BME, Cornell U., 1952. With Lenape Forge Co. div. Gulf & Western Industries, West Chester, Pa., 1952-73; pres. Lapp div. Interpace Corp., Le Roy, NY, 1973—78; pres., chief exec. officer Allied Thermal Corp. subs. Interpace, 1978-79; sr. v.p., dir. Interpace, 1979-80; exec. v.p., dir. Interpace Corp., Parsippany, N.J., 1980-81; pres., chief exec. officer, dir. Clevepak Corp., 1981-83, 84-86, chief exec. officer, vice chmn. bd., dir., 1983-84; mng. dir. Peers & Co., 1987-88; chief exec. officer Peers Mgmt. Resources, Inc., 1987-88; pres., chief exec. officer Ransburg Corp., Indpls., 1988-92; pres. ITW Finishing Systems and Products, Indpls., 1990-92; exec. v.p. Ill. Tool Works Inc., Glenview, 1991-92; vice-chmn. Advisory Capital Ptnrs., Inc., Greenwich, Conn., 1992—94; chmn. bd. dirs. Xpander Pak Inc., 1994—2000; dir. athletics Cornell U., 1994—99. Dep. to chairs Com. to Encourage Corp. Philanthropy, NY, 1999—2000, exec. dir., NY, 2000—; mem. Pres. Coun. on Physical Fitness & Sports, 2002—. Commr. Smithsonian Am. Art Mus., 2000—; chmn. audit com., pub. sector dir. U.S. Olympic Com., 1992—2000; mem. nat. bd. Smithsonian Instn., 2001—. Recipient Gold medal in 400 meter hurdles, 1952 Olympics, Herbert Adams Meml. award for advancement of Am. sculpture, Nat. Sculpture Soc., 1985. Mem. Pine Valley Golf Club (N.J.), Royal and Ancient Golf Club St. Andrews (Scotland), Cosmos Club (Washington), Blind Brook Golf Club (N.Y.). Republican. Episcopalian. Office: Com to Encourage Corp Philanthropy 110 Wall St Ste 2-2 New York NY 10005

MOORE, CHARLES LOYD, lawyer; b. El Paso, Tex., Aug. 14, 1944; s. Charles McKinney and Alice Adeline (Loyd) M.; m. Peggy Jo ball, Dec. 20, 1969; children: Kirk, Julie. BS in Mil. Engring., U.S. Mil. Acad., West Point, N.Y., 1966; MSME, Calif. Inst. Tech., 1968; JD summa cum laude, So. Meth. U., Dallas, 1975. Bar: N.Mex. 1975, U.S. Dist. Ct. 1975. Commd. 2d. lt. U.S. Army, 1966, advanced through grades to capt., 1968, resigned, 1972; assoc. Keleher & McLeod, P.A., Albuquerque, 1975-79, mem. firm, 1979—. Assisted bd. of bar examiners in writing and grading bar exam questions, Santa Fe, 1990—2000. Contbr. articles to profl. jours. Dist. co-chmn. ann. fund campaign McMurry U., Abilene, Tex., 1988, trustee, 1989—92, Hatton W. Sumners Found., Dallas, 1999—; dir. Robert O. Anderson Schs. Mgmt. Found. Bd., U. N.Mex., 2003—; co-chair N.Mex. Lawyers for Gen. Wesley Clark for Pres. campaign, 2003—04. Decorated Vietnam Svc. medal, Vietnam Campaign medal, Bronze Star, Joint Svc. Commendation medal; named one of Best Lawyers of Am., 1989—90, 1991—92, 1993—94, 1995—96, 1997—98, 1999—2000, 2001—02, 2003—04. Mem. ABA, State Bar of N.Mex. (v.p. young lawyers divsn. 1977-78, chair bus. law sect. 2001), Albuquerque Bar Assn., Phi Delta Phi (Internat. Grad. of Yr. Biennial Conv. 1975), Phi Kappa Phi. Avocations: running, reading. Home: 7929 American Heritage Dr NE Albuquerque NM 87109-3103 Office: Keleher & McLeod PA PO Box Aa Albuquerque NM 87103-1626 Business E-Mail: clm@keleher-law.com.

MOORE, CHRISTOPHER BARRY, industrial engineer; b. Deal, Kent, Eng., Feb. 25, 1938; came to U.S., 1977; s. Ernest Stanley and Millicent Lillian (Harris) M.; m. Jill Irene Porter, July 6, 1963; children: Andrew, Stephen, Jeremy, Jennifer. Diploma mgmt. studies, Barking Regional Coll. Tech., Eng., 1966. Prodn. unit mgr. Plessey Co. Ltd., Ilford, Eng., 1968-70, productivity mgr. Upminster, 1970-72; regional indsl. engr. Ilford, 1972-74; mgr. mfg. devel. No. Telecom Ltd., Montreal, Que., Can., 1974-77, dir. mfg. engring. Nashville, 1977-88; dir. process devel. Nortel Networks, Atlanta,

1988-2000; rsch. advisor Ga. Inst. Tech., 2000—. With RAF, 1956-59. Mem. Inst. Elec. Engrs., Inst. Mgmt. Home: 5167 Killingsworth Trce Norcross GA 30092-1739 E-mail: Chris.Moore@marc.gatech.edu.

MOORE, CHRISTOPHER HUGH, writer; b. Stoke-on-Trent, Eng., June 9, 1950; arrived in Can., 1954; s. M. Vincent and Kathleen A. (Lennox) M.; m. Louise A. Brophy, May 7, 1977; children: Elizabeth, Kate. BA with honors, U. B.C., Vancouver, 1971; MA, U. Ottawa, Ont., Can., 1977. Staff historian Nat. Historic Pks. Svc., Louisbourg, N.S., Can., 1972-75; sec. to bd. Heritage Can. Found., Ottawa, 1977-78; writer, historian Toronto, Ont., 1979—; dir. Access Copyright Licensing Agy., 2001—. Author: Louisbourg Portraits, 1982, 2000, The Loyalists, 1984, 94, Eighteen Sixty-Seven, 1997, The Big Book of Canada, 2002; co-author: Illustrated History of Canada, 1987, The Story of Canada, 1992, Canada: Our Century, 1999. Recipient Gov. Gen.'s Lit. award Can., 1983, Sec. of State Prize Govt. Can., Ottawa, 1985, Mr. Christie's Prize Christie-Brown Ltd., Toronto, 1993. Mem. Writers' Union of Can. (chair contracts com. 1990-94, mem. nat. coun. 1995-97, nat. chair, 1999-00), Can. Hist. Assn. Office: 70 Woodside Ave Toronto ON Canada M6P 1M1 E-mail: cmed@interlog.com.

MOORE, CHRISTOPHER M. lawyer; b. L.A., Oct. 12, 1938; s. Prentiss Elder and Josephine (French) M.; m. Gillian Reed, Sept. 29, 1965; children: Stephanie Kia Conn, Carrie Christine McKay. AB, Stanford U.; JD, Harvard U. Dep. county counsel L.A. County Counsel, 1965-66; ptnr. Burkley & Moore, Torrance, Calif., 1969-74; pvt. practice Law Offices of Christopher Moore, Torrance, 1974-81; ptnr. Burkley, Moore, Greenberg & Lyman, Torrance, 1981-90; prin. Christopher M. Moore & Assoc., Torrance, 1990-2000, Moore, Bryan & Schroff, Torrance, 2000—. Mem. bd. edn. Palos Verdes (Calif.) Peninsula Unified Sch. Dist., 1972-77. Fellow: Am. Acad. Matrimonial Lawyers, Am. Coll. Trust and Estate Counsel; mem.: Palos Verdes Golf Club, L.A. Yacht Club. Avocations: sailing, golf. Office: Moore Bryan & Schroff Ste 490 21515 Hawthorne Blvd Torrance CA 90503-6525 E-mail: chris@mbslawcorp.com.

MOORE, CHRISTOPHER ROBERTSON KINLEY, energy industry consultant; b. Manchester, Eng., Sept. 28, 1954; came to U.S., 1989; s. James Robertson Kinley and Irene (Mason) M.; m. Marian Isabel Pope, Sept. 3, 1977; children: Andrew Christopher, Scott David. BA, U. Cambridge, 1975, MA, 1979. Geologist Brit. Petroleum Co., Scotland, England, Tunisia, 1975-80; sr. geologist Tricentrol Oil Corp., London, 1980-88; planning mgr. ARCO Brit. Ltd., London, 1988-89; from exploration planning advisor to dir. exploration ARCO Internat. Oil & Gas Co., Plano, Tex., 1989-98; Bohai Bay asset mgr. ARCO China Inc., Plano, 1998-99, mgr. China ADT, 1999-2000; mng. dir. Moyes & Co., Inc., Dallas, 2000—. Fellow Geol. Soc. London; mem. Am. Assn. Petroleum Geologists, Soc. Petroleum Engrs., Internat. Assn. Petroleum Negotiators. Home: 15720 Artist Way #3917 Addison TX 75001 Office: Moyes & Co Inc 8235 Douglas Ave Ste 1221 Dallas TX 75225-6012 Office Phone: 214-363-9020. Business E-Mail: cmoore@moyesco.com.

MOORE, CYRUS, language educator; b. Hereford, Tex., Aug. 29, 1951; s. Donald Winfield Moore and Vera Juanita Pickens. Student, U. Chgo., 1970—73; BA in English, Hunter Coll., 1988; MFA in Writing, Bklyn Coll., 1990; PhD in Comparative Lit., CUNY, 2003. Renaissance studies cert. CUNY, 2003. Faculty (spl. programs) Columbia U., N.Y.C., 1998—99; adj. instr. Spanish lang. Lehman Coll., N.Y.C., 2001—01. Translator: First Dream (Primero Sueno, by Sor Juana Ines de la Cruz), 1999, author short stories. Recipient Andrew and Eleanor McGlinchee award for excellence in English Studies, Hunter Coll., 1986, Bernard Cohen Short Story prize, 1988, Randolph and Eliza Guggenheimer prize for disting. work in English Lit., 1988, Prof. Fred J. Nichols Disting. Dissertation award, 2003; fellow, CUNY, 1995; scholar, 1995; Lois Styles scholar, Hunter Coll., 1988. Mem.: MLA, Renaissance Soc. Am. Independent. Personal E-mail: karo8@suryc.com.

MOORE, DANIEL CHARLES, retired anesthesiologist; b. Cin., Sept. 9, 1918; s. Daniel Clark and May (Strebel) M.; m. Betty Maxine Tobias, Aug. 5, 1945 (div. 1988); children: Barbara, Nancy, Daniel, Susan. Grad., Amherst (Mass.) Coll., 1940; MD, Northwestern U., 1944. Diplomate: Am. Bd. Anesthesiologists. Intern Wesley Meml. Hosp., Chgo., 1944, resident, 1945; dir. anesthesia Va. Mason Hosp., Seattle, 1947-72; anesthesiologist (Mason Clinic), 1947-72, sr. cons. in anesthesia, 1972-83. Clin. prof. U. Wash. Sch. Medicine, 1963—89. Author: Regional Block, 1953, Stellate Ganglion Block, 1954, Complications of Regional Anesthesia, 1955, Anesthetic Techniques for Obstetrical Anesthesia and Analgesia, 1964, also papers. Served as capt. M.C. AUS, 1945-47. Recipient Ralph M. Waters award Ill. Soc. Anesthesiologists, Carl Koller Gold medal European Soc. Regional Anaesthesia, 1995. Mem. Am. Soc. Anesthesiologists (1st v.p. 1953-54, 2d v.p. 1954-55, pres. 1958-59, distinguished service award 1976), AMA (sec. anesthesiology sect. 1956-58), Am. Acad. Anesthesiology, Am. Soc. Regional Anesthesia (adv. bd., Gaston Labat award 1977), Wash. Soc. Anesthesiologists (pres. 1949-50), Wash. Med. Soc., King County Med. Soc., Faculty Anaesthetists Royal Coll. Surgeons (hon.), Northwest Forum, Beta Theta Pi, Nu Sigma Nu. Home: Madison Park Pl # 103 2000 43rd Ave E Seattle WA 98112-2704 Office: PO Box 900 Seattle WA 98111-0900 Office Phone: 206-223-6980.

MOORE, DANIEL D. finance company executive; CFO EduTrek Internat. Inc., Atlanta. Office: EduTrek Internat Inc 500 Embassy Row 6600 Peachtree Dunwoody Rd NE Atlanta GA 30328-1649

MOORE, DANIEL EDMUND, psychologist, educator, retired educational administrator; b. Pitts., Dec. 31, 1926; s. John Daniel and Alma Helen (Goehring) M.; m. Rose Marie Blunkosky, Nov. 11, 1949; children: Catherine Chiodo, Claire Marie Moore Caveney, Mary Moore Brilmyer, Suzanne Moore Gray, Elizabeth Moore Sullivan. BSEd, Duquesne U., 1949, MEd, 1952; postgrad., California (Pa.) State Coll., 1954-56, U. Pitts., 1958-59, Mt. Mercy Coll., 1959-60, Cath. U. Am., 1966, W.Va. U., 1970-72. Lic. psychologist; cert. sch. psychologist. Tchr. math. Cecil Twp. Sch. Dist., McDonald, Pa., 1949-52, Pitts. Public Schs., 1952-53; with Mt. Lebanon Twp. (Pa.) Sch. Dist., 1953-88, psychologist, 1954-71, dir. pupil personnel svcs., 1988; psychol cons. Peters Twp. Sch. Dist., McMurray, Pa., 1961-88; psychol. cons. Blackhawk Sch. Dist., Beaver, Pa., 1989—98; psychol cons. Quaker Valley Sch. Dist., Sewickley, Pa., 1989-90; lectr., supr. Grad. and Undergrad. Sch. Edn. Duquesne U.; psychologist DePaul Inst., Pitts., 1992—98. Lectr. ednl. psychology Grad. Sch. Edn., Duquesne U., 1957-92, supr. student tchrs., 1989-92; ednl. cons. St. Francis Schs. Nursing, New Castle and Pitts., 1959-91; mem. test adv. bd. Ednl. Records Bur., 1976-86; hearing officer Right to Edn. Office, Dept. Edn., Harrisburg, Pa., 1975—; in-svc. adv. bd. Pa. Dept. Edn. Hearing Officers. Mem. Chartiers Valley Sch. Dist. Bd., 1963-94, pres., 1971, v.p., 1991; mem. Pkwy. West Tech. Sch. Bd. 1965-67; bd. dirs. secondary sch. rsch. program Ednl. Testing Svc., Princeton, 1971-85; bd. dirs. Robert E. Ward Home for Children, 1975-87, St. Agatha Parish Coun., 1988—, Pathfinder Sch., 1989, v.p., 1990-94, pres. sch. bd., 1991-92; vol. Bridgeville Area Food Bank, 1988—; chairperson Parish 100 Jubilee Ceremony, Goodwill Villa Bd., Goodwill Plaza, Inc., Goodwill Villa Bd. of Incorporators, 1992—; pres. bd. dirs. Goodwill Plaza, 1992—; jubilee chairperson St. Agatha's, Bridgeville, Pa. With USNR, 1945-48. Henry C. Frick grantee, 1970, 73; named Jaycee Educator of Yr. for South Hills Area, Ward Home Outstanding Community Leader, 1984, Outstanding Cmty. Leader, Chartiers Valley Human Rels. Coun., 1998; recipient Human Rels. award Chartiers Valley Inter-relationships Soc., 1998. Mem. Am., Pa. psychol. assns., Coun. Exceptional Children (pres. 1957), Phi Delta Kappa (pres. chpt. 1974-75, chmn. lay awards com. 1979-2001, Svc. Key award 1985). Roman Catholic. Home: 213 Station St Bridgeville PA 15017-1806 Office Phone: 412-221-5217.

MOORE, DARLA D. investment company executive; b. Lake City, S.C. d. Eugene and Lorraine Moore; m. Richard Rainwater, Dec. 13, 1991. BA, U. S.C.; MBA, George Washington U., 1981. Summer intern Sen. Strom Thurmond; rschr. Rep. Nat. Com., 1976; with Chem. Bank, N.Y.C.; pres., CEO Rainwater, Inc., Atlanta, 1994—. Office: Magellan Health Svcs 6666 Powers Ferry Rd NW Ste 110 Atlanta GA 30339-2915

MOORE, DAVID GENE, academic administrator; b. Tonasket, Wash., Oct. 2, 1938; s. Leonard W. and Peggy (Furst) M.; m. Diane Russell, June 15, 1965 (div. 1984); children: John, Kathy, Alan. BA in Polit. Sci., Seattle U., 1960; MBA, U. Puget Sound, 1973; MS in Computer Sci., Kans. State U., 1978; postgrad., U. Mich., 1978—. Commd. 2d lt. U.S. Army, 1960, advanced through grades to col., 1979, ret., 1980; dean mgmt. info. systems Mott Community Coll., Flint, Mich., 1980-82, dean mgmt., 1982-84, pres., 1985-92; pres DeVry Inst. Tech., Los Angeles, CA, 1992-94; pres. Nat. Edn. Centers, Inc., 1994-95; founder, chmn., pres and CEO Corinthian Colleges, Inc., Santa Ana, 1995—. Bd. dirs. Greater Flint Edn. Consortium. Contbr. numerous articles to profl. jours. Bd. dirs. United Way, Flint, 1987—, Human Services Network, Flint, 1988—; chmn. Bus. Resource Ctr., Flint, 1988—; sec. I-75 Corridor, 1987—; active Pvt. Industry Coun., Flint, 1985—. Decorated Silver Stars (2), Legion of Merit (2); recipient numerous civic and profl. awards. Mem. Soc. Automotive Engrs. (chmn. robotics sect. 1986—), Data Processing Mgmt. Assn., COMBASE (bd. dirs.), Coun. North Cen. Community Colls. (bd. dirs.), Mich. Community Coll. Assn. (bd. dirs.), Rotary, Univ. Club. Avocations: skiing, woodworking. Office: Corinthian Colleges Inc 6 Hutton Centre Dr Ste 400 Santa Ana CA 92707-5764

MOORE, DAVID GRAHAM, sociologist, educator; b. Norwich, Conn., May 9, 1918; s. Royal Tolman and Alta Gladys (Jenkin) Moore; m. Margaret Louise Rider, Dec. 2, 1950; children: David G., Kathryn R.; children from previous marriage: Barbara E., Linda C. Turbyville. BA, U. Ill., 1940, MA, 1943; PhD, U. Chgo., 1954. Pers. rsch. We. Electric Co., 1940-41; mem. pers. staff Sears, Roebuck and Co., 1941-43, 46-50; pers. dir. Am. Flange & Mfg. Co., 1943-46; asst. prof. sociology, indsl. rels. U. Chgo., 1950-55, assoc. prof. bus. adminstrn., sociology, dir. exec. program, 1955-56; prof. mgmt. Mich. State U., 1956-58, head dept. pers. and prodn. adminstrn., 1958-61, prof. mgmt., sociology, 1961-63; dean N.Y. State Sch. Indsl. and Labor Rels. Cornell U., 1963-71; sr. v.p. Conf. Bd., N.Y.C., 1971-73, exec. v.p., 1973-79; prof., chmn. dept. bus. adminstrn. U. N. Fla., 1979-86, prof. bus. adminstrn., 1986-89, prof. emeritus, 1991, asst. to pres., 1983-84. Vis. Ford Found. prof. behavioral scis. U. Wis., 1962. Co-author: (book) Human Relations in Industry, 4th edit., 1964, SRA Employee Inventory, 1951, The Enterprising Man, 1964. Mem.: Indsl. Rels. Rsch. Assn., Soc. Applied Anthropology, Am. Sociol. Assn. Home: C205 1000 Vicar's Landing Way Ponte Vedra Beach FL 32082-1331 E-mail: dgmanew@aol.com.

MOORE, DAVID GREGORY, lawyer; b. Winfield, Kans., Nov. 30, 1946; s. Warren Keith and Mary Margaret (Felt) M.; m. Alice Jane Wiley, Feb. 23, 1974; children: Geoffrey Haven Wiley Moore, Caroline Elizabeth Wiley Moore. BA, Albion Coll., 1968; MA, U. Mich., 1971, JD, 1982. Bar: Mich. 1982. Writer, photographer Albion (Mich.) Evening Recorder, 1962-76, editor, 1976-79; assoc. Tuck & Garrison, Albion, 1982-85; mem. Tuck, Garrison & Moore, P.L.L.C., Albion, 1986—. Pres. Albion Vol. Svc. Orgn., 1987-88, 91-92, bd. dirs., 1987-88, 91-92; trustee Albion Civic Found., pres., 1985, 92; chmn. planned giving adv. coun. Albion Coll., 1989-92, mcpl. water study team Greater Albion Alliance 2000, 1991-99; mem. Albion Bd. Edn., 2000—, v.p. 2001—. Named Michigan Minuteman, Greater Mich. Found., Lansing, Mich., 1979. Mem. ABA, Calhoun County Bar Assn. Avocations: cabinetmaking, letterpress printing. Office: Tuck Garrison & Moore PLLC 403 S Superior St PO Box 660 Albion MI 49224-0660

MOORE, DAVID J. media company executive; Grad., Northwestern U. Sales rep. Turner Broadcasting, 1979-82; with Viacom, 1982; founder on-line svc. for physicians, 1993-94; co-founder Petry Interactive, NYC, 1995-98; founder 24/7 Media (formerly Petry Interactive), NYC, 1998—. Bd. dir. Internet Advt. Bur. Mem. Network Advt. Initiative, NE Ill. U. Alumnae Assn.; bd. dir. Nassau and Suffolk Svcs. for Autism. Mem. Internat. Radio and TV Soc., Responsible Electronic Comm. Assn. Achievements include helping launch the Cable Health Network, which eventually became Lifetime; developing and running Medical Television, which was targeted to physicians; developing HealthLink Television, a waiting room service for patients. Office: 24/7 Media Inc 1250 Broadway Fl 28 New York NY 10001-3791 Business E-Mail: David.Moore@247RealMedia.com.*

MOORE, DEBORAH CHANTAY, protective services official, psychotherapist; b. Queens, NY, May 9, 1969; d. Charles Edward and Evelyn Elizabeth Moore. AA, LaGuardia C.C., 1989; BA, York Coll., 1994; MEd, Fordham U., 1997; PhD, Capella U., 2004. Police sgt., counselor N.Y.C. Police Dept., 1991—; founder, owner Personal Enrichment Svcs.; psychotherapist D.C. Moore & Assocs., Queens, 1998—; founder, owner Personal Enrichment Svcs. Cons. mcpl. law enforcement agys., NY, 2000—. Contbr. articles to profl. jours. Recipient Law Enforcement Appreciation award, Kings Dist. Atty. Office, 2001, Congl. Hearing Achievement award, 6th Dist. NY, U.S. Congress Ho. of Reps., 2003, Dem. Achievement award, 2003;, N.Y.C. Police Dept. scholar, 2000. Mem.: Am. Acad. Experts in Traumatic Stress (diplomat), Internat. Assn. Marriage and Family Counselors, Am. Mental Health Counselors Assn., Am. Counseling Assn., Acad. Profl. Law Enforcement, Order Ea. Star. Democrat. Avocations: jogging, travel, reading, soap-making, tennis. Office: Personal Enrichment Svcs DC Moore & Assn Counseling Svcs PO Box 130372 Springfield Gardens NY 11413 Office Phone: 718-288-8548. E-mail: chantay@mindspring.com.

MOORE, DEBRA, lawyer; Grad., U. Utah, 1983. Shareholder Watkiss & Saperstein; employment sect. chief litigation divsn. Utah Atty. Gen.'s Office, 1991—. Instr. legal writing U. Utah Coll. Law, 1993—96; rep. Utah Jud. Coun. Mem.: Utah State Bar (pres.-elect, commn. 1994—2000). Office: Atty Gens Office PO Box 140856 160 E 300 S Fl Salt Lake City UT 84114-0856

MOORE, DEMI (DEMI GUYNES), actress; b. Roswell, N.Mex., Nov. 11, 1962; d. Danny and Virginia Guynes; m. Bruce Willis, Nov. 21, 1987, div. 2000; 3 daughters: Rumer Glenn, Scout LaRue, Tallulah Belle. Studies with Zina Provendie. Actress: (feature films) Choices, 1981, Parasite, 1981, Young Doctors in Love, 1982, Blame it on Rio, 1984, No Small Affair, 1984, St. Elmo's Fire, 1985, About Last Night..., 1986, Wisdom, 1986, One Crazy Summer, 1987, The Seventh Sign, 1988, We're No Angels, 1989, Ghost, 1990, Mortal Thoughts, 1991 (also co-producer), The Butcher's Wife, 1991, Nothing But Trouble, 1991, A Few Good Men, 1992, Indecent Proposal, 1993, Disclosure, 1994, The Scarlet Letter, 1995, Now and Then, 1995 (also prodr.), Undisclosed, 1996, Striptease, 1996, The Juror, 1996, G.I. Jane, 1997, Deconstructing Harry, 1997, Passion of Mind, 2000, Charlie's Angels: Full Throttle, 2003; (TV series) General Hospital, 1982-83; (TV movies) If These Walls Could Talk, 1996 (also exec. prodr.); (voice) The Hunchback of Notre Dame, 1996, The Hunchback of Notre Dame II, 2002; Producer: Austin Powers: International Man of Mystery, 1997, Austin Powers: The Spy Who Shagged Me, 1999, Austin Powers in Goldmember, 2002. Office: Creative Artists Agy Inc 9830 Wilshire Blvd Beverly Hills CA 90212-1825

MOORE, DENNIS, congressman; b. Anthony, Kans., Nov. 8, 1945; m. Stephene; 7 children. BS, U. Kans., 1967; JD, Washburn U., 1970. Bar: Kans. 1970. Asst. atty. gen. State of Kans., 1971-73; pvt. practice, 1973-76; dist. atty. Johnson County, 1977-89; ptnr. Erker & Moore, LLC, 1991-98, Smith, Gill, Fisher & Butts, 1989-91; mem. U.S. Congress from 3d Kans. dist., 1999—. Mem. House Com. on Fin. Svcs. Sci. and the Budget. Elected to Johnson County C.C. bd. trustees, 1993; re-elected, 1997; bd. dirs. Johnson County Safehome, Coalition for Prevention of Child Abuse, Kans. Child Abuse Prevention Coun., CASA (Ct. Appointed Spl. Advocate), United Cmty. Svcs., Cmty. Corrections Adv. Bd.; unsuccessful Dem. candidate for state atty. gen., 1986. With U.S. Army, U.S. Army Res. Democrat. Achievements include personally prosecuting more than 25 felony jury trials; led Consumer Protection Divsn. in the investigation and successful prosecution of a nat. oil co. charged with rigging gas pumps to cheat consumers; established a victim assistance unit; was cited by an ind. cons. hired by the Johnson County Bd. Commrs. as running the most efficient office in Johnson County govt.; served as pres. Kans. County and Dist. Atty.'s Assn. Office: 431 Cannon Hob Washington DC 20515-0001

MOORE, DENNIS DUANE, English educator; b. Greenville, S.C., Oct. 25, 1949; s. Marvin R. Moore and Mildred E. Brown. BA, Clemson U., 1970; MA, U. N.C., 1971, PhD, 1990. Instr. English Greenville (S.C.) Tech. Coll., 1980-82, Clemson (S.C.) U., 1982-84; asst. prof. English U. Tex., El Paso, 1990-91, Fla. State U., Tallahassee, 1991-95, assoc. prof. English, 1995—. Dir. Bryan Hall Learning Cmty., 2000—. Editor: More Letters from the American Farmer: An Edition of Essays in English Left Unpublished by Crevecoeur, 1995; contbr. articles to profl. jours. V.p., program chair Friends of Fla. State U. Librs., 1995—; mem. Friends of Black History Archives, Fla. History Assocs., Mus. Fla. History, Tallahassee. C. Hugh Holman fellow U. N.C. Dept. English, 1989; Rsch. grantee NEH, 1991, 92; fellow in Early Am. History and Culture, Libr. Co. Phila. and Hist. Soc. Pa., jointly, 1988. Mem. Am. Studies Assn. (life mem.), Am. Soc. Eighteenth-Century Studies (life mem.), Soc. Early Americanists (exec. coord. 2001—), Toni Morrison Soc. (charter and life mem.), Internat. Iris Murdoch Soc. (founding mem., life mem., sec.), St. Marks Nat. Wildlife Refuge Assn. (life), Phi Theta Kappa (hon.). Democrat. Unitarian Universalist. Avocations: fly-fishing, birding, canoeing, travel, films. Office: Dept English Fla State U Tallahassee FL 32306-1580 E-mail: dmoore@english.fsu.edu.

MOORE, DONALD FRANCIS, lawyer; b. NYC, Dec. 14, 1937; s. John F. and Helen A. (McLoughlin) M.; m. Alice L. Kalmar; children: Christina M., Marianne, Karen L., Alison A. AB, Fordham U., 1959; JD, St. John's U., Bklyn., 1962. Bar: NY 1962, DC 1970, US Supreme Ct. 1993. Assoc. Paul, Weiss, Rifkind, Wharton & Garrison, NYC, 1962-70, ptnr., 1970-97, of counsel, 1998—. Editor in chief St. John's U. Law Rev., 1962. Served to Capt. U.S. Army, active 1962-64. Mem. NY State Bar Assn., Assn. of Bar of City of NY Roman Catholic. Avocation: fishing. Home: 7 Wedgewood Ct Glen Head NY 11545-2229 Office: Paul Weiss Rifkind Wharton & Garrison Ste 4200 1285 Avenue Of The Americas Fl 21 New York NY 10019-6065

MOORE, DUNCAN THOMAS, optics educator; b. Biddeford, Maine, Dec. 7, 1946; s. Thomas Fogg Moore and Virginia Robinson Wing; m. Gunta Liders, July 1995. BA in Physics, U. Maine, 1969, DSc (hon.), 1995; MS in Optics, U. Rochester (N.Y.), 1970, PhD in Optics, 1974. Asst. prof. U. Rochester, 1974-78, assoc. prof., 1978-86, prof., 1986—, Kingslake prof., 1993—, dean engrng. and applied sci., 1995-97, prof. biomed. engrng., 2001—, exec. dir. Univ., Industry and Govt. Partnership for Advanced Photonics, 2001—02; pres., founder Gradient Lens Corp., Rochester, 1980—97, bd. dirs., 2001—; dir. N.Y. State Ctr. Advanced Optical Tech., Rochester, 1987-94; assoc. dir. technology White House Office Sci. & Technology Policy, Washington, 1997-2000; CEO Infotonics Tech. Ctr. Inc., 2002—04. Vis. scientist Nippon Schlumberger, Tokyo, 1983; Congl. fellow Am. Phys. Soc., Washington, 1993—94; sci. advisor to Sen. John D. Rockefeller IV, W.Va., 1993—94; exec. dir. U. Rochester Industry and Govt. Partnership for Advanced Photonics, 2001—02; mem. environ. and energy svc. rev. com. Idaho Nat. Engrng. and Environ. Lab., 2001—02; mem. vis. com. NASA-Goddard Space Flight Ctr., 2002—; mem. applied engrng. and tech. directorate vis. com. Goddard Space Flight Ctr., 2002—; bd. dirs. Gradient Lens Corp.; lectr. in field. Contbr. numerous articles to profl. jours.; patentee in field. Chmn. Hubble Ind. Rev. Panel, 1990-91; mem. adv. bd. high tech. Rochester C. of C., 1988-93. Recipient Disting. Inventor of Yr. award Rochester Intellectural Property Law Assn., 1993, Grin Optics award Japanese Applied Physics Soc., 1993, Sci. and Tech. award Greater Rochester C. of C., 1992; named Engr. of Yr., Rochester Engrng. Soc., 1999. Mem.: NRC, NAE, Am. Inst. Physics (state dept. fellowship selection com. 2001—), Coalition for Photonics and Optics (chair 1996—97), Forum on Physics and Soc. (exec. com. 1996—97), Coun. Sci. Soc. (co-chair govt. affairs com. 1996—97), Materials Rsch. Soc., Am. Assn. Engrng. Soc. (bd. govs. 1995—97, Nat. Engrng. award 1999), Optical Soc. Am. (bd. dirs. 1987—89, editor Applied Optics 1990—92, bd. dirs. 1992—97, v.p. 1994, pres. 1996, Leadership award 2001), Am. Soc. Precision Engrng., Am. Ceramic Soc. (Edward Orton, Jr. Meml. lectr 2002), Lasers and Electro-Optics Soc. IEEE. Home: 4 Claret Dr Fairport NY 14450-4610 Office: The Inst Optics University of Rochester Rochester NY 14627-0186 Office Phone: 585-275-5248. Business E-Mail: moore@optics.rochester.edu.

MOORE, EDNA GOOGE, primary school educator; b. Aiken, SC, June 16, 1948; d. James and Earthy Lee (Priester) Googe; m. Willie Moore, Dec. 20, 1982; children: Yolanda Catrice Tolbert, Rodney Tremel Bryant, Tarrence stepchildren: Katrina, Julia Tyneka, Jermaine. Diploma, Aiken Tech. Coll., 1998. Kindergarten tchr. Sunshine Ho., Aiken, 1995—99, Second Bapt. Christian Prep. Sch., Aiken, 1999—. Author: (poetry) The Silent Word, 1990 (Appreciation Award, 1992), The Silent Word II, 1991, Because of Christ I, II, and III, 1999, Believing and Receiving God's Blessings, 2004, (song) I Try Not to Slip and Fall, 1992. Bd. mem. Bros. and Sisters of Aiken County, 1994—96; Sunday sch and youth Bible study tchr. Ashley Grove Bapt. Ch., Aiken, 2001—03. Avocations: drawing, writing. Office: Second Baptist Christian Preparatory 343 Laurens St North West Avenue Aiken SC 29809

MOORE, EDWARD WARREN, lawyer; b. Odessa, Tex., July 21, 1959; s. Edward Warren and Gloria (Schroeter) M.; m. JoAnne Bisso; children: Peggy, Barbara. BA in Econs., Princeton U., 1981; JD, So. Meth. U., 1984. Bar: Tex. 1984, U.S. Dist. Ct. (no. dist.) Tex. 1984, U.S. Ct. Appeals (5th cir.) 1984, U.S. Ct. Appeals (10th cir.) 1985. Assoc. Ravkind, Kuehne & Biesel, Dallas, 1984-85; ptnr. Kuehne & Moore, Dallas, 1984-96; pvt. practice, 1996-2000, 2003—; mng. ptnr. Moore & Anderson, 2000—03; COO, Tissue Gen, Inc. Dir. Rsch. Group Tex., Inc.; mentor North Tex. Enterprise Ctr. for Med. Tech. Vol. Ronald McDonald Ho. Children's Med. Ctr. Mem. AAAS, ABA (litigation sect., trial practice sect. and com., product liability, antitrust, intellectual property sect.), ATLA (toxic, environ. and pharm. litigation sect., comml. litigation sect.), State Bar Tex., Dallas Bar Assn., Tex. Trial Lawyers Assn., Dallas Country Club, Safari Club Internat. (life), Dallas Safari Club (life), DSC 100 (vol.). Methodist. Home: 7044 Turtle Creek Blvd Dallas TX 75205-1254 Office Phone: 214-706-9040. E-mail: eddymoor@sprynet.com.

MOORE, ELVI, performing company executive; Mem. faculty U. Chgo.; dir. corp. and found. devel. Nat. Symphony Orch.; with Washington Ballet, 1983—, gen. dir., 1990—, mngng. dir., 1997—. Bd. dirs. Dance/USA; adv. panels Nat. Endowment for Arts, D.C. Commn. Arts and Humanities. Dancer, choreographer, prodr. numerous dance festivals. Office: The Washington Ballet 3515 Wisconsin Ave NW Washington DC 20016-3085

MOORE, EMILY ALLYN, pharmacologist; b. Evansville, Ind., Apr. 3, 1950; m. Robert Alan Yount, Nov. 25, 1972 (div. Feb. 1986); 1 child, Joseph Taylor; m. Robert E. Moore Jr., Aug. 11, 1990; 1 child, Alexander Allyn. AB in Chem. Biology, Ind. U., Bloomington, 1971; MS in Applied Computer Sci., Purdue U., Indpls., 1985; PhD in Pharmacology, Ind. U., Indpls., 1976. Vis. asst. prof. biology Ind. U., Bloomington, 1979, rsch. assoc. in biochemistry Indpls., 1979-81, rsch. assoc., 1982-83, computer programmer for med. genetics, 1983-85, asst. scientist. med. genetics, 1985-87; tech. assessment specialist Boehringer Mannheim Corp., Indpls., 1987, mgr. sci. info., 1987-89; mgr. Tech. Assess, Indpls., 1989-93, quality process analyst, 1993-94. Contbr. articles to profl. jours. Officer or bd. dirs. LWV, Hendricks County, Ind., 1977-84; elder St. Luke's United Ch. of Christ, Speedway, Ind., 1983-85; mem. adv. bd. Operation SMART, Indpls., 1989-90. Achievements include participation in creation of first DNA bank for storage of DNA samples for future use in diagnosis of genetic diseases.

MOORE, EMMETT BURRIS, JR., physical chemist, educator; b. Bozeman, Mont., June 14, 1929; s. Emmett Burris and Iris Marie (Brown) M.; m. Diane Elizabeth Girling, Oct. 1, 1960; children: Karen Elizabeth, Robin Diane. BS in Chemistry with honors, Wash. State U., 1951; PhD in Phys. Chemistry (Shell fellow), U. Minn., 1956. Teaching asst. U. Minn., Mpls., 1951-55, asst. prof. physics Duluth, 1957-59; mem. staff Boeing Sci. Research Labs., Seattle, 1959-73. Lectr. chemistry Seattle U., 1973; dir. power plant siting Minn. Environ. Quality Bd., St. Paul, 1973-76; gen. mgr. Richland (Wash.) Divsn. Olympic Engrng. Corp., 1976-78; staff scientist Pacific N.W. Nat. Lab., 1978-96; mem. environ. engrng. rev. panel EPA, 1989-95; alt. mem. Hanford Adv. Bd., 1995-2000; adj. prof. environ. sci. Wash. State U., 1990—. Author: (book) The Environmental Impact Statement Process and

Environmental Law, 1997, 2d edit., 2000, An Introduction to the Management and Regulation of Hazardous Waste, 2000; contbr. articles to profl. jours. Trustee Mid-Columbia Symphony Soc., 1978-85, v.p., 1980-81, pres., 1981-83; trustee Richland Light Opera Co., 1984-88, bus. mgr., 1984-88. Recipient Land Grant Faculty Excellence award Wash. State U., 1999. Fellow AAAS; mem. Am. Phys. Soc., Am. Chem. Soc. (chmn. Pauling award com. 1971, sec. Puget Sound sect. 1971-73, mem. energy panel of com. on chemistry and pub. affairs 1983-86), Am. Assn. Physics Tchrs. (v.p. Wash. sect. 1965-66, pres. 1966-67), Phi Beta Kappa, Phi Kappa Phi, Phi Eta Sigma, Alpha Chi Sigma, Phi Lambda Upsilon, Sigma Alpha Epsilon (v.p. province 1972-73) Episcopalian (vestryman 1967-69, 76-79, 91, sr. warden 1969, del. diocesan conv. 1969-72). Home: 2323 Greenbrook Blvd Richland WA 99352-8427 Office: Wash State U 2710 University Dr Richland WA 99354-1671 E-mail: ebmoore@wsu.edu.

MOORE, ERNEST CARROLL, III, lawyer; b. Honolulu, Oct. 24, 1944; s. Ernest Carroll Jr. and Frances (Miller) M.; children: Tiffany Meredith, Alyssa Judi. BA, Dartmouth Coll., 1967; JD, So Meth. U., 1974. Bar: Hawaii 1974, U.S. Dist. Ct. Hawaii 1974, U.S. Ct. Appeals (9th cir.) 1974. Ptnr. Torkildson, Katz, Fonseca, Moore & Hetherington, Honolulu, 1974—. Trustee Hawaii Sch. Girls, 1998—. Bd. dirs. Hawaii chpt. ARC, Honolulu, 1979, trustee La Pietra-Hawaii Sch. for Girls, 1998—, Outrigger Duke Kahanamoku Found., 1999-, Bd. of Governors (the Pacific Club). Mem. Am. Acad. Hosp. Attys., Nat. Health Lawyers Assn., Indsl. Relations Research Assn., Soc. for Human Resources Mgmt., Order of Coif, Pacific Club (bd. govs.), Outrigger Canoe Club. Republican. Episcopalian. Avocations: tennis, photography. Office: Torkildson Katz Fonseca Jaffe Moore & Hetherington 700 Bishop St Fl 15 Honolulu HI 96813-4187 Office Phone: 808-523-6000., 808-523-6000. E-mail: ecm@torkildson.com.

MOORE, ERNEST EUGENE, JR., surgeon, educator; b. Pitts., June 18, 1946; s. Ernest Eugene Sr. and Mary Ann (Burroughs) M.; m. Sarah Van Duzer, Sept. 2, 1978; children: Hunter Burroughs, Peter Kitrick. BS in Chemistry, Allegheny Coll., 1968; MD, U. Pitts., 1972. Surg. resident U. Vt., Burlington, 1972-76; chief of trauma Denver Health Med. Ctr., 1976—, chief dept. surgery, 1984—. Prof. surgery, vice chmn. dept., U. Colo., 1985-95; dir. facilities Colo. Trauma Inst., Denver, 1984-95. Editor: Critical Decisions in Trauma, 1987, Trauma, 1988, rev. edits., 1991, 96, 00, Early Care of the Injured, 1989, Surgical Secrets, 1996, rev. edit., 2002, Trauma Manual, 2003; assoc. editor Jour. Trauma, Am. Jour. Surgery, Surgery-Problem Solving Approach, 2d edit., 1994, others; patentee retrohepatic vena cava shunt. Fellow ACS (com. on trauma, vice chair 1990), Soc. Univ. Surgeons (pres. 1989), Am. Assn. Surgery of Trauma (pres. 1993), Internat. Assn. Surgery of Trauma and Surg. Intensive Care (pres. 1998-99), Pan Am. Trauma Assn. (pres. 1991), Southwestern Surg. Congress (pres. 1998), Western Trauma Assn. (pres. 1989). Republican. Avocations: skiing, hockey, hunting, ultra-marathons, fishing. Home: 2909 E 7th Avenue Pky Denver CO 80206-3839 Office: Denver Health Med Ctr Dept Surgery Denver CO 80204 E-mail: ernest.moore@dhha.org.

MOORE, FAY LINDA, systems engineer; b. Houston, Apr. 7, 1942; d. Charlie Louis and Esther Mable (Banks) Moore; m. Noel Patrick Walker, Jan. 5, 1963 (div. 1967); 1 child, Trina Nicole Moore. Student, Prairie View Agrl. and Mech. Coll., 1960-61, Tex. So. U., 1961, Our Lady Lake U., 1993, Software Engring. Inst., 1995, U. Phoenix, 2003—. Cert. ISO 9000 Internal Auditor, 1994-97. Instr. Internat. Bus. Coll., Houston, 1965; keypunch operator IBM Corp., Houston, 1965-67, sr. keypunch operator, 1967-70, programmer technician, 1970-72, asst. programmer, 1972-73, assoc. programmer, 1973-74, sr. assoc. programmer, 1984-87, staff programmer, 1987-92, staff sys. analyst, 1992-96; sr. software quality engr. Loral Space Info. Sys., Houston, 1994—96; owner, pres. AFT Co., Houston, 1993—; sr. software quality engr. Lockheed Martin Corp., Houston, 1996-97; software quality engr. Motorola, Inc., Austin, 1998-2001, quality sys. rev. assessor, 1998-2001, info. tech. quality engr., 2000-2001; prin. sys. engr. Titan Corp., Houston, 2001—. Space shuttle flight support team IBM, 1985—92, mem. space sta. team, 1992—93. Recipient Apollo Achievement award, NASA, 1969, Quality and Productivity award, 1986, 1992, Cert. of Recognition, NASA Office of Space Flight, 2004. Mem. NAFE, Soc. Software Quality, Booker T. Washington Alumni Assn., Ms. Found. for Women, Inc. Democrat. Roman Catholic. Avocation: personal computing.

MOORE, FAYE L. MITCHELL, executive; b. Castalia, N.C., July 3, 1950; d. Frank and Mattie Jane Mitchell; m. Daniel Henry Moore, July 16, 1977; 1 child, Fenita LeSai. BS with honors, N.C. A&T State U., 1976. CPA, Md. Asst. acct. KPMG LLP, Balt., 1976-77, various positions to sr. mgr. Phila., 1977-86; dir. mergers and strategic planning Cigna, Phila., 1986-90; sr. mgr. Mitchell/Titus, N.Y.C., 1990-92; v.p. audit and acquisitions Providian Corp., Frazer, Pa., 1992-95; CFO, treas. Southeastern Pa. Transp. Authority, Phila., 1995—, CEO/gen. mgr., 2002—. Spkr. in field. Trustee Friends Select Sch., Phila., 1997—2002; bd. mem., audit com. United Way Southeastern, Pa., 2003; transp. com. March of Dimes, 2002—; bd. dirs. TCRB/TOPS, 2003—. Recipient Cmty. Svc. award INROADS/Phila., 1993, Nat. Achievement in Govt. award, 2002. Mem. AICPA, NAFE, Md. Assn. CPAs, Nat. Assn. Black Accts., Inc. (life, pres. 1984-86, regional v.p. 1987-88, Profl. Achievement award 1986, chair ea. region student conf. 1997-98, Outstanding Mem. award 1990, Disting. Svc. award 2000), Beta Alpha Psi (Outstanding Alumni 2001, Nat. Achievement award 2002, Women's Transp. Sem. Phila. chpt. 1st Milestone award, conf. of minority tranps. offl., 2000—). Avocations: vacationing with family, crossword puzzles, dance, spectator sports. Home: 5106 Wynnefield Ave Philadelphia PA 19131-2316 Office: Southeastern Pa Transp Authority 1234 Market St Ste 10 Philadelphia PA 19107-3721

MOORE, FLETCHER BROOKS, retired engineering company executive; b. Heiberger, Ala., June 15, 1926; s. Amzi Wallace and Mary Elizabeth (May) M.; m. Margaret Marian Foreman, Sept. 5, 1954; children— Larry Brooks, Ronald Howell. BS in Electronic Engring., Auburn U., 1948; MS in Electronic Engring., Ga. Inst. Tech., 1949. With U.S. Navy Mine Counter-Measures Sta., Panama City, Fla., 1949-52, Army Ballistic Missile Redstone Arsenal, Ala., 1952-60; with Marshall Space Flight Ctr., NASA, Huntsville, Ala., 1960-81; dir. Astrionics Lab. NASA Marshall Space Flight Ctr., 1968-81; chief missile system Teledyne Brown Engring., Huntsville, 1981-83; v.p. Control Dynamics Co., Huntsville, 1983-91; pres. Logicon Control Dynamics, Inc., Huntsville, 1991-94; dep. divsn. dir. Control Dynamics, a Divsn. of bd. Sys., Huntsville, 1996—2002, ret., 2003. Past chmn. alumni engring. coun. Auburn U.; mem. Auburn U. rsch. coun.; vice chairman. Ala. Indsl. Coun. on Engring. Edn.; past mem. adminstrv. sci. adv. coun. U. Ala., Huntsville. Named to State of Ala. Engring. Hall of Fame, Ga. Tech. Engring. Hall of Fame; recipient Algenon Sydney Sullivan award Auburn U., 2002. Mem. AIAA, NASA Alumni League (past pres. Marshall Space Flight Ctr. chpt.). Home: 119 Sherwood Dr SE Huntsville AL 35802-2430 E-mail: bmoore@cdy.bdsys.com.

MOORE, FLORIAN HOWARD, retired electronics engineer; b. Shelby, Ohio, Aug. 23, 1929; s. Carl Leslie and Mona Pearl (Dearth) M.; m. Dorothy Elizabeth Morse, Dec. 19, 1950. AA, Harvard U., 1974. Cert. indsl. maint. electrician; tchg. cert. indsl. electricity, indsl. electronics. With Diebold Inc., Boston, 1955-56; mem. electronics R & D staff Radio Corp. Am., Burlington, Mass., 1956-59; mem. electronics/mech. R & D staff MIT, Cambridge, 1959-74; mem. electricity/electronics/electromech. R & D staff Charles Stark Draper Labs., Cambridge, 1974-76; tchr. indsl. electronics Ashland County Joint Vocat. Sch., Ashland, Ohio, 1976-78; buyer Autocall divsn. Fed. Signal Corp., Shelby, 1978-79; journeyman electrician Excel Wire & Cable divsn. United Tech., Tiffin, Ohio, 1980-86; tchr. indsl. electricity Madison Comprehensive H.S., Mansfield, Ohio, 1986-88; pres., CEO Florian H. Moore & Assocs., Shelby, 1988-2000, ret., 2000. Vol. Ohio Geneal. Libr., Mansfield; foster parent Commonwealth of Mass., 1962-82 (38 children). With USAF, 1948-52. Fellow Internat. Biog. Assn. (dep. dir. gen.); mem. Ohio Geneal. Soc. (v.p. Richland-Shelby gen. chpt. 1993-95, pres. 1995-97), Royal Lincolnshire Regtl. Assn. (life; Am. contingent, 10th foot), DAV (life), Order Internat. Fellowship (charter, U.S. rep. 1995), Masons (32 degree), Kappa Delta Phi (life). Avocations: history, skiing, sky diving, computer programming. Address: Care of Security Natl PO Box 1408 Springfield OH 45501-1408

MOORE, FREDERICK APPEL, administrator; b. Boston, Apr. 25, 1925; s. Robert Webber and Josephine (Appel) M.; m. Cynthia Newton, June 17, 1950 (dec. June 2000); children: Lucinda Moore Hammett, Joanthan Newton, Stephanie Moore Schulz; m. Georgeann Smitt, MAr. 14, 2004. AB, Bowdoin Coll., 1948. CLU. Agt. John Hancock Life Ins. Co., Boston, 1948-56; gen. agy. Mass. Indemnity & Life, Wellesley, 1956-69; 2d v.p. Chubb Life Ins. Co., Concord, NH, 1969-87; owner Moore Ins. & Fin. Svcs., Enfield, 1987-90; dir. gift planning Dartmouth-Hitchcock Med. Ctr., Lebanon, 1990—2004; ret., 2004. Pres. Disability Ins. Tng. Coun., Chgo., 1958-60; treas. Coll. Fin. Planning, Denver, 1973-77; mem. Conn. Valley Estate Planning Coun., Hanover, 1990—. Chmn. planning Bd., Orange, N.H., 1990-2000, Upper Valley Waste Mgmt. Dist., Lebanon, 1990-2000; sr. warden St. Thomas Episcopal. Ch., Hanover, N.H., 1993-95; bd. mem. Upper Valley Planned Giving Coun., 2002--; mem. Phillips Acad. Alumni Coun., Andover, Mass., 2002--. With USMC, 1943-45. Mem. Social Summit Lodge, Scottish Rite, Shriners. Republican. Epsicopalian. Avocations: golf, sailing, tennis, theater, symphony. Home: 1010 Lake Bridge Dr Ormond Beach FL 32174-1480

MOORE, GEORGE C. manufacturing executive; BA in Acctg., Loyola Coll. CPA. Acct. Arthur Andersen, 1977—87; pres., CFO Yield House, 1987—97; group fin. officer Tanaher Tools, Tool Products, Safety and Aviation and Automotive Danaher Corp., 1997—2003, group v.p. fin., 2000—03; exec. v.p. Maytag, Newton, Iowa, 2003—, CFO, 2003—. Office: Maytag 403 West 4th St N Newton IA 50208

MOORE, GEORGE CRAWFORD JACKSON, lawyer; b. Tenn. BA, U. Fla., 1963; PhB in Soviet Law, U. St. Andrews, Scotland, 1966; MA in English Law with honors, Cambridge U., Eng., 1968, LLM in Internat. Law, 1969. Bar: Eng. (Barrister, Inner Temple) 1970, Jamaica 1971, Fla. 1973, Turks & Caicos Islands 1974, U.S. Supreme Ct. 1976, Antigua and Barbuda, Brit. V.I., Grenada, Montserrat, St. Lucia 1977, Anguilla 1999. Legis. asst. to U.S. sen., Washington, 1970-72; asst. pub. defender Palm Beach County, Fla., 1973; pvt. practice West Palm Beach, Fla., 1973—. Founding pres. World Trade Coun. of Palm Beach County, 1981—; chmn. Fla. Coun. Internat. Devel., 1983—84, 2000—03, Fla. Gov.'s Conf. on World Trade and Investment, 1989, Fla. Export Coun. of U.S. Dept. Commerce, 1991—92, Free Trade Agreement of Americas. Editor spl. issues Fla. Bar Jour., 1982, 87, chmn. editorial bd., 1988-89; mem. editorial bd. The Internat. Lawyer jour. of ABA, 1979-84; contbr. articles to profl. jours. Chmn. Fla. Econ. Growth and Internat. Devel. Commn., 1989-90. Fellow: Ctr. Internat. Legal Studies, Soc. Internat. Bus. Fellows (v.p.); mem.: ABA, Fla. Bar (chmn. internat. law sect. 1994—95, bd. cert. specialist in internat. law 1999—, chmn. internat. law cert. bd. 2004—). Office: 105 S Narcissus Ave Ste 812 West Palm Beach FL 33401-5530 Office Phone: 561-833-9000.

MOORE, GEORGE EMERSON, JR., geologist, educator; b. Lebanon, Mo., Jan. 2, 1914; s. George Emerson and Dorothea Louisa (Niewohner) M.; m. Wilma Corrine Leonard, May 20, 1939; children: George E. III, Dana Corinne, Craig G. AB, U. Mo., 1936, MA, 1938; PhD, Harvard U., 1947. Instr. U. Mo., 1938-39; teaching asst. Harvard U., 1940-42, 1946-47; geologist A.P. Green Fire Brick Co., Mexico, Mo., 1942-46; instr. Ohio State U. at Columbus, 1947-48, asst. prof., 1948-57, assoc. prof., 1957-64, prof., 1964-84, prof. emeritus, 1984—. Geologist U.S. Geol. Survey, 1952-83 Fellow Geol. Soc. Am.; mem. Phi Beta Kappa, Sigma Xi. Home: 58 Mulberry Dr Wakefield RI 02879-1416

MOORE, GEORGE EUGENE, surgeon; b. Minn., Feb. 22, 1920; s. Jesse and Elizabeth (MacRae) M.; m. Lorraine Hammell, Feb. 22, 1945; children—Allan, Laurie, Linda, Cathy, Donald. BA, U. Minn., 1942, MA, 1943, BS, 1944, B.M., 1946, MD, 1947, PhD in Surgery, 1950. Intern surgery U. Minn. Hosps., 1946-47; med. fellow gen. surgery, 1947; dir. tumor clinic, 1951-53; sr. research fellow USHPS, 1947-48; faculty U. Minn. Med. Sch., 1948-53, cancer coordinator, 1951-53; chief surgery Roswell Park Meml. Inst., Buffalo, 1953-72, dir., 1953-67; dir. pub. health research N.Y. State Health Dept., Albany, 1967-73; clin. prof. surgery State U. N.Y. at Buffalo, 1962-73, also prof. research biology, 1955-69; dir. surg. oncology Denver Gen. Hosp., 1973-97; prof. surgery U. Colo., 1973-97, prof. emeritus, 1997—. Author: Diagnosis and Localization of Brain Tumors, 1950, Cancerous Diseases, 1970; contbr. 660 articles to profl. jours. Recipient Outstanding Citizen award Buffalo Evening News, 1958, Outstanding Sci. Achievement award, 1959, Disting. Achievement award Modern Medicine mag., 1962, Chancellor's medal U. Buffalo, 1963, Charles Evans Hughes award pub. administrn. Albany, 1963, Bronfman prize Am. Pub. Health Assn., 1964, Tchr. of Yr. award Dept. Surgery, U. Colo., 1977, Disting. Svc. award U. Colo., 1990, Meritorious Svc. Regents award U. Colo., 1990. Mem. Soc. U. Surgs., Halsted Soc., Am. Surg. Assn., Colo. Oncology Found. (pres.). Home: 12048 Black Hawk Dr Conifer CO 80433-7137 Office: Denver Gen Hosp 645 Bannock St PO Box 1806 Denver CO 80201-1806 E-mail: moore@wcox.com. *Individuals are miraculous temporal genetic patterns whose accomplishments will always transcend those of any committee, consensual group, or political assembly; society must provide special early educational opportunities for creative youngsters and those with genius. I hope to see the practical development of cell therapy for the infectious and cancerous diseases and genetic corrections of inherited disorders.*

MOORE, GEORGE W. electronics executive; BSEE, Clemson U.; MBA, Duke U. Jr. engr. IBM, Research Triangle Park, NC, 1978, various engrng. and mgmt. positions, program mgr. strategic planning, 1986—88, mgr. electronic card assembly, 1988—89, mgr. ABS sys. prodn. mgmt. ctr., 1998, gen. mgr. edn. products, 1994—97, v.p. corp. mfg. staff, 1997—2000; corp. officer, exec. v.p. Solectron Corp., Milpitas, Calif., 2000—. Mem.: Nat. Assn. Mfrs. (bd. dirs.). Office: Solectron Corp 777 Gibraltar Dr Milpitas CA 95035

MOORE, GORDON E. electronics company executive; b. San Francisco, Jan. 3, 1929; s. Walter Harold and Florence Almira (Williamson) Moore; m. Betty I. Whittaker, Sept. 9, 1950; children: Kenneth, Steven. BS in Chemistry, U. Calif., 1950; PhD in Chemistry and Physics, Calif. Inst. Tech., 1954. Tech. staff Shockley Semicondr. Lab., 1956—57; mgr. engring. Fairchild Camera & Instrument Corp., 1957—59, dir. R & D, 1959—68; co-founder Intel Corp., Santa Clara, Calif., 1968, exec. v.p., 1968—75, pres., CEO, 1975—79, chmn., CEO, 1979—87, chmn., 1987—95, chmn. emeritus, 1995—. Bd. dirs. Varian Assocs. Inc., Transamerica Corp. Fellow: IEEE (Founders medal 1977); mem.: Am. Phys. Soc., Nat. Acad. Engring. Office: Intel Corp 2200 Mission College Blvd Santa Clara CA 95054-1549

MOORE, GREGORY L. editor; Reporter Dayton Journal Herald, 1976—80, Cleveland Plain Dealer, 1980—83, political editor, 1983—86; asst. metro editor Boston Globe, 1986—94, mng. editor, 1994—2002; editor Denver Post, 2002—. Office: The Denver Post 1560 Broadway Denver CO 80202-1577 E-mail: gmoore@denverpost.com.

MOORE, GUY WILL, retired public information officer, historian, writer; b. Retta, Okla., June 19, 1922; s. Guy Thomas Moore and Pearl Grace Glasgow; m. Hazel Avenell Cartwright, Aug. 31, 1948 (dec. June 18, 1986); children: Anne Elizabeth Tarquinio, March Victoria Dodge. BA in Journalism, U. Okla., 1950, MA in History, 1952. News writer Office of the Army Surgeon Gen., Washington, 1956—57, info, specialist, 1957—59; info. specialist (first) U.S. Army Rsch. and Devel. Command, Washington, 1959—60; dep. info. officer, divsn. gen. med. scis. NIH, Bethesda, Md., 1960—61, staff asst., office of dir. pub. affairs, 1961—64, chief pub. info. sect. office of rsch info., chief supervisory pub. info. specialist, news br., office of comm., 1967—79; ret., 1979. Chmn. pub. info. intern recruitment tng. com. NIH, 1961—79, spkr. grants assoc. seminar, 1971—72; spkr. Am. Coll. Pub. Rels. Assn., Washington, 1970. Author: The Case of Mrs. Surratt, 1954, The NIH: How it Works, 1981; contbg. author: The Surratt Society's In Pursuit of..., 1990; contbr. articles to astronomy jours. Contr. project feeder watch Cornell Lab of Ornithology, 1987—91. Mem.: No. Va. Astronomy Club, Nat. Capitol Astronomers, Surratt Soc. Avocations: astronomy, birdwatching. Home: 224 N Nelson St Arlington VA 22201

MOORE, HAL G. mathematician, educator; b. Vernal, Utah, Aug. 14, 1929; s. Lewis Henry and Nora (Gillman) M.; m. D'On Empey, July 20, 1956; children: David, Nora (Mrs. Bret C. Hess), Alison (Mrs. Samuel M. Smith). BS, U. Utah, 1952, MS, 1957; PhD, U. Calif., Santa Barbara, 1967. Tchr. Salt Lake City Pub. Schs., 1952-53; instr. math. Carbon Jr. Coll., also Carbon H.S., Price, Utah, 1953-55, Purdue U., Lafayette, Ind., 1957-61, adminstrv. asst. dept. math, 1960-61; from asst. prof. math. to assoc. prof. math. Brigham Young U., Provo, Utah, 1961-71, prof., 1971-95, prof. emeritus, 1995—, assoc. chmn. dept. math., 1986-89. Author: Precalculus Mathematics, 2d edit, 1977, (with Adil Yaqub) Elementary Linear Algebra With Applications, 1980, College Algebra and Trigonometry, 1983, A First Course in Linear Algebra, 1992, 3d edit., 1998; contbr. articles to profl. jours. Mem. High Coun., Ch. of Jesus Christ of Latter Day Saints, 1985-91, MTC br. pres., 1991-94, Bishop, 1958-61, 78-82. NSF faculty fellow U. Calif., Santa Barbara, 1964-66. Mem. Am. Math. Soc., Math. Assn. Am. (bd. govs. 1989-92), Utah State Math. Coalition (planning dir. 1990, bd. dirs. 1991-92), Sigma Xi (dir. 1974-80, 82-85, com. chmn. 1982-90), Phi Kappa Phi. Home and Office: 631 W 650 S Orem UT 84058-6027 Office Phone: 801-225-7125. E-mail: mooreh@math.byu.edu. *Revelation and reason can work together to bring human beings closer to the truth of their existence and place in the universe. But charity and love and dedication are as necessary to the success of this union as they are to all others.*

MOORE, HAROLD, food service executive; Student, William Patterson Coll.; degree, Culinary Inst. Am., 1996. Line cook Restaurant Daniel, 1996, sous chef, 1999; with Jean Georges restaurant, 1998; mem. opening team Mercer Kitchen; exec. chef Mantrachet, N.Y.C., 2000—. Walter, NJ. Active ARC, Share Our Strength, Citymeals on Wheels, God's Love We Deliver, Am. Heart Assn., Sloan Kettering. Office: Montrachet 239 West Broadway New York NY 10013-2409

MOORE, HELEN LUCILLE, adult education educator, consultant; b. Watseka, Ill., July 24, 1930; d. John Kenneth and Thelma Mae (Wollschlaeger) Weidert; m. Harold Junior Gossett, June 24, 1948 (div. May 1971); children: Steven, Joyce, Gary, Ricky, Kenny, Jane; m. Herff Leo Moore, Jr., Nov. 24, 1991. AS in Mgmt., Kankakee (Ill.) Jr. Coll., 1969. Sr. sec. Nimz Transp., Watseka, 1948-57; tchg. aide Glenn Raymond H.S., Watseka, 1964-71; asst. pers. and safety mgr. Gt. Plains Bag Co., Jacksonville, Ark., 1971-81; sr. human resources rep. Maybelline Products Co., Inc. divsn. L'Oreal, North Little Rock, Ark., 1981-2000; recruiting dir. StaffMark, Little Rock, 2000—01; adult edn. cons. Dept. Workforce Edn., Little Rock, 2001—. Chmn. Ark. Human Resource Conf., Hot Springs, 1991-92. Contbr. articles to profl. publs. Bd. dirs. Ark. Urban League, Little Rock, 1985-93; co-founder, exec. bd. dirs. Workforce Alliance for Growth in Economy, 1993—; mem. Ark. Gov.'s Workforce Investment Bd. and Exec. Com., 1999—. Recipient Outstanding Ark. Human Resources Profl. award Ark. Human Resources Coun., 1994; named Sr. Inspirational Employee of Yr., ABLE (Ability Based on Long Experience), 1997. Mem.: Ctrl. Ark. Mfg. Pers. Assn. (chmn. 1990—99, co-founder), Ctrl. Ark. Human Resources Assn. (bd. dirs. 1988—90, profl.), Soc. for Human Resource Mgmt. (profl., Outstanding Profl. Mem. award 1989), Nat. Employer Coun. (Ark. chmn. local employer adv. couns. 1989—2000, sch.-to-work com., focus group 1998, Star Performer award 1999), Am. Legion Aux. (life). Office: Dept Workforce Edn Luther S Hardin Bldg Three Capitol Mall Rm 303 Little Rock AR 72034-3315

MOORE, HERFF LEO, JR., management educator; b. San Antonio, Jan. 24, 1937; s. Herff Leo Moore Sr. and Constance (Benesh) Wold; children: Terri Lynne, Christopher Scott, Kimberly Anne. BSBA, The Ohio State U., 1964; MBA, U. Tex., 1968; MS in Community Svcs., U. Rochester, 1976; PhD, U. Tex. at Arlington, 1980. Cert. sr. profl. in human resources (life). Prodn. mgmt., quality assurance officer Sacramento (Calif.) Air Logistics Ctr. USAF, 1964-67; personnel mgmt., adminstrv. cons. Aero. Systems Div. Wright-Patterson AFB, Dayton, Ohio, 1968-73; pers. mgmt. and quality assurance cons. Defense Contract Adminstrv. Svcs. Dist. Hdqrs., Rochester, N.Y., 1973-76; lectr. in mgmt. and doctoral student The Univ. of Tex. at Arlington, 1976-79; asst. prof. bus. adminstrn. Ea. Ky. U., Richmond, 1979-81; assoc. prof. mgmt. East Tex. State U. at Texarkana, 1981-83, Saint John Fisher Coll., Rochester, 1983-85, U. Cen. Ark., Conway, 1985-99, ret., 1999. Pres. H.M.C.C. Mgmt. Group, Conway, 1988—; participant Leadership Texarkana Leadership Tng., 1981-82; mgmt. cons., devel. trainer, Calif., N.Y., Ark., Ohio, N.J., Fla., Ga., Tex., 1964—. Author: (with others) Language, Customs and Protocol: A Guidebook for International Students and Employees, 1992; contbr. numerous articles to profl. jours. Capt. USAF, 1964—76. Recipient Significant Performance Contbr. award Def. Supply Agy., 1975; Nat. scholar Phi Kappa Phi, 1968; named Honor Grad. USAF Officers Tng. Sch., 1964. Mem. Soc. for Human Resource Mgmt. (tng. and devel. com. 1989-94, select panel on edn. 1989-91, coll. rels. com. 1989-92, bd. dirs. area IV 1987-91, sec., treas. Ark. coun. 1986-87), Ark. Human Resources Assn. (pres. 1991-92, bd. dirs. 1991-93), Acad. Mgmt., Soc. Human Resource Mgmt. (superior merit awards student chpt. U. Ctrl. Ark. 1985-90, 93), Alpha Kappa Psi, Phi Kappa Phi, Sigma Iota Epsilon. Mem. Assembly Of God Ch. Avocations: golf, chess, political buttons. Home: 2823 Coll Ave Apt 9 Conway AR 72034

MOORE, HUBERT J. addictions counselor, consultant; b. Oklahoma City, Jan. 2, 1932; s. Hubert and Goldie Edith Moore; m. Mary Alene Jarnet, Dec. 9, 1958 (div. Oct. 1959); 1 child, LeAnne; m. Shirley M. Mumchuck, Apr. 1978 (dec. Nov. 8, 1985); children: Peggy, JoAnn, Lisa, Sharon. AA in Counseling, U. Alaska, 1986, BA in Human Svcs., BA in Psychology, U. Alaska, 1992, BA in Sociology, 1996; MA in Anthropology, U. Mindanao, Philippines, 1998. Cert. addictions counselor II Alaska, Nat. Assn. Alcohol and Drug Abuse Counselors, master forensic counselor and criminal justice specialist Nat. Assn. Forensic Counselors, Nat. Register Addiction Counselors, Calif. Registry Addiction Specialists. Substance abuse counselor II No. Regional Ctr. for Addictions, Fairbanks, Alaska, 1977—85; forensic counselor Fairbanks Correction Facility, 1995—96; addictions cons. Soldotna, Alaska, 1991—. Campaign vol. Rep. Caucus, Soldotna, 1991—. Republican. Moslem. Avocations: philosophic studies, demographic research, motorcycling, moutain climbing, social research. Home and Office: Alternative Counseling PO Box 1057 Soldotna AK 99669

MOORE, HUGH JACOB, JR., lawyer; b. Norfolk, Va., June 29, 1944; s. Hugh Jacob and Ina Ruth (Hall) M.; m. Jean Garnett, June 10, 1972; children: Lela Miller, Sarah Garnett. BA, Vanderbilt U., 1966; LLB, Yale U., 1969. Bar: Tenn. 1970, U.S. Dist. Ct. (mid. dist.) Tenn. 1970, U.S. Dist. Ct. (ea. dist.) Tenn. 1973, U.S. Dist. Ct. (we. dist.) Tenn. 1982, U.S. Ct. Claims, U.S. Ct. Appeals (6th cir.) 1973, U.S. Ct. Appeals (fed. cir.) 1999, U.S. Supreme Ct. 1972. Law clk. U.S. Dist. Ct. (mid. dist.) Tenn., Nashville, 1969-70; trial atty. civil rights divsn. U.S. Dept. Justice, Washington, 1970-73; asst. U.S. atty. Eastern Dist. of Tenn., Chattanooga, 1973-76; assoc. Witt, Gaither & Whitaker, P.C., Chattanooga, 1976-77, shareholder, 1977—2002, also bd. dirs.; shareholder Shumacker, Witt, Gaither & Whitaker, P.C., 2002—. Mem. Commn. Women and Minorities Profession Law, 1995-97; mem. hearing com. Bd. Profl. Responsibility Supreme Ct. Tenn., 1996-2002; mem. mediation and arbitration panel U.S. Dist. Ct. (ea. dist.) Tenn.; cert. arbitrator, cert. mediator Tenn. Rule 31, Nat. Assn. Securities Dealers; cert. arbitrator N.Y. Stock Exch., Nat. Arbitration Forum; mem. adv. commn. on rules of civil and appellate procedure Tenn. Supreme Ct., chmn., 1999—. Contbr. articles to profl. jours. Bd. dirs. Adult Edn. Coun., Chattanooga, 1976-81, pres., 1977-79; bd. dirs. Chattanooga Symphony and Opera Assn., 1981-87, Riverbend Fesitval, 1983-85, 91—, pres., 1995-97, Landmarks Chattanooga, 1983-84, Cornerstones, 1995-98, Orange Grove Sch., 1996-, v.p., 2003-; mem. alumni coun. McCallie Sch., 1980-85; trustee St. Nicholas Sch., 1983-89, chmn., 1986-88. Master Am. Inns of Ct. (Brock-Cooper Inn); fellow Am. Coll. Trial Lawyers, Tenn. State Com., Tenn. Bar Found., Chattanooga Bar Found, Am. Bar Found.; mem. ABA (mem. bd. editors jour. Litigation News 1983-90), Tenn. Bar Assn., Chattanooga Bar Assn. (mem. bd. govs. 1985-87), Mountain City Club, Rotary. Methodist. Home: 101 Ridgeside Rd Chattanooga TN 37411-1830 Office: Schumacker Witt Gaither & Whitaker 1100 Sun Trust Bank Bldg 736 Market St Chattanooga TN 37402 E-mail: hmoore@swgwlaw.com.

MOORE, J STROTHER, science educator, researcher; s. J. Strother and Jessie Louise Moore; m. Jo Anne O'Neil; children: Lisa, Jonathan, Chris. BS, MIT, 1970; PhD, U.Edinburgh, Scotland, 1973. Rsch. mathematician Xerox PARC, Palo Alto, Calif., 1974—76; sr. rsch. scientist SRI, Menlo Park, Calif.; prof. U. Tex., Austin, 1981—87; chief scientist Computational Logic, Inc., Austin, 1987—97; Inman chair U. Tex., Austin, 1997—. Co-author: (software) Boyer-Moore Theorem Prover, 1971. Recipient Current prize in Automatic Theorem Proving, AMS, 1991, Herbrand award, CADE, 1999. Fellow: AAAI. Avocation: rock climbing.

MOORE, J. STUART, information technology executive; married; 5 children. Degree in Computer Scis., U. Calif., Berkeley. With Cambridge Technology Inc.; co-founder, co-chmn., co-CEO Sapient Corp., Cambridge, Mass., 1991—. Office: Sapient Corp 25 First St Cambridge MA 02141*

MOORE, JACQUELYN CORNELIA, labor union official, editor; b. Dec. 25, 1929; d. James C. and Harriette I. Thomas; m. Clarence Carbin Moore, Jan. 19, 1947 (dec. Feb. 1970); children: Clarence Joseph, Janet Elizabeth Moore Marshall. Mail clk. U.S. P.O., Phila., 1966—93; editor Local 509 Newsletter Nat. Alliance of Postal and Fed. Employees, Washington, 1969—74, editl. newsletter chmn., 1969—74, sec. dist. 5, 1972—74, nat. editor Nat. Alliance, 1974—, mem. exec. bd., 1974—, union photographer, 1974—. Dir. 202 Housing for Elderly Corp. bds., Chattanooga, New Orleans, 1981—, Atlanta, 1988—; sec. supervisory com. Nat. Fed. Credit Union, 1977—82, 1984—94, chair, 1994—. Vol. D.C. Voting Rights Corp., Washington, 1979—; sustaining mem. Dem. Nat. Com., 1977—. Mem.: Nat. Press Club, Nat. Bus. and Profl. Women's Club. Roman Catholic. Home: 1102 R St NW Washington DC 20009-4364 Office: 1628 11th St NW Washington DC 20001-5086

MOORE, JAMES ALFRED, ski company executive, lawyer; b. Madisonville, Ky., Oct. 20, 1915; s. Virgil Yandell and Dorothy Ina (Price) M.; m. Lucile Carpenter, June 29, 1970; children by previous marriage: Marjorie M. Eickel, James Kelly, Kathleen M. Marozzi; m. Judith Gallen, June 10, 1995. AB, U. Ky., 1936; LL.B., Harvard U., 1939. Bar: Pa. 1940, D.C. 1969, Va. 1978. Assoc. firm Pepper, Hamilton & Scheetz, Phila., 1940-51, partner, 1951-69, partner firm, 1969-77; pres. Camelback Ski Corp., Tannersville, Pa., 1963-86, chmn., bd. dirs., 1986-93, chmn. emeritus, 1993—. Contbr. articles to various law revs. Bd. dirs. Phila. Soc. for Crippled Children and Adults, 1959-69. Served from ensign to lt. comdr. USNR, 1942-45. Mem. Am. Bar Assn., Am. Law Inst. Republican. Methodist. Office: Camelback Ski Corp PO Box 168 Tannersville PA 18372-0168 Home: PO Box 168 Tannersville PA 18372-0168

MOORE, JAMES CONKLIN, lawyer; b. Albany, N.Y., Dec. 20, 1939; s. James Alexander and Doris Virginia (Conklin) M.; m. Shirley Jean Mitchell, June 17, 1961; children: James, Jennifer, David, Eliza. BS, Cornell U., 1961, LLB, 1964. Bar: N.Y. 1964, U.S. Dist. Ct. (we. dist.) N.Y. 1966, U.S. Dist. Ct. (mid. dist.) Pa. 1981, U.S. Dist. Ct. (no. dist.) N.Y. 1980, U.S. Ct. Mil. Appeals 1965. Assoc. Wiser, Shaw, Freeman, VanGraafeiland, Harter & Secrest, Rochester, N.Y., 1966-74; ptnr. Harter, Secrest & Emery, Rochester, 1974—2003, mediator, arbitrator, 2004—. Author several articles, book chpts. and book revs. Trustee, pres. Friends of Rochester (N.Y.) Pub. Libr., 1993—98; bd. dirs., vice chmn. Geva Theater, Inc.; pres. Legal Connection, Inc., 2002—04; mem. Cornell U. Coun., 1997—2002, Monroe County Bar Found., bd. dirs., 2002—04; chmn. bd. trustees N.Y. Lawyer Assistance Trust, 2001—04. Capt. U.S. Army, 1964—66, Vietnam. Mem. adv. bd. Rochester Area Ednl. TV, 1981-87; elder, trustee Third Presbyn. Ch., Rochester. Fellow: ABA (ho. of dels. 1998—, standing comm. on legal assistance to indigent defendants), N.Y. Bar Found. (bd. dirs. 1997—2000), Am. Coll. Trial Lawyers; mem.: Nat. Conf. Bar Pres. (exec. com. 1999—2002), Monroe County Bar Assn. (chmn. judiciary com. 1982—85, bd. trustees 2004—), N.Y. State Bar Assn. (chmn. ins. sect. 1984—85, ho. del. 1984—87, chmn. task force on liability ins. 1986—87, 1986—87, chmn. com. ins. programs 1988—94, exec. com. 1992—2000, v.p. 1994—97, pres. 1998—99, chmn. nominating com. 2001, ho. del. 1993—), Am. Inst. Law (elected). Republican. Avocations: U.S. history, refinishing old furniture. Home: 251 Windemere Rd Rochester NY 14610-1342 Office: Harter Secrest & Emery 1600 Bausch & Lomb Pl Rochester NY 14604-2711 Office Phone: 585-231-1124. Business E-Mail: jmoore@hselaw.com.

MOORE, JAMES E. state supreme court justice; b. Laurens, S.C., Mar. 13, 1936; s. Roy Ernest and Marie (Hill) M.; m. Mary Alicia Deadwyler, Jan. 27, 1963; children: Erin Alicia, Travis Warren. BA, Duke U., 1958, JD, 1961; Dr. of Humanities (hon.), Lander Univ., 1997. Bar: S.C. 1961, U.S. Dist. Ct. S.C. 1961. Pvt. practice, Greenwood, S.C., 1961-76; cir. judge 8th Jud. Cir. S.C., Greenwood, 1976-91; assoc. justice S.C. Supreme Ct., 1992—. Mem. S.C. Ho. of Reps., Columbia, 1968-76. Mem. S.C. Bar Assn., ABA, Am. Judicature Soc., Baptist. Baptist. Home: 148 Amherst Dr Greenwood SC 29649-8901 Office: PO Box 277 Greenwood SC 29648-0277

MOORE, JAMES L., JR., beverage company executive; b. 1942; BA, Davidson Coll., 1964; MBA, Univ. N.C., 1968. Dist. mgr. Pepsi-Cola Co., 1972-74, mgr. market planning Pepsi-Cola Bottling group, 1974-75, v.p., area mgr. Houston, 1975-76; v.p., gen. mgr. Atlantic Soft Drink, Knoxville, Tenn., 1977-82, v.p. mktg., 1982-83, pres., chief exec. officer, 1983-87, Coca-Cola Bottling Co. Consolidated, 1987—, also dir. 1st lt. U.S. Army, 1972-76. Office: Coca-Cola Bottling Co Consolidated PO Box 31487 Rd Charlotte NC 28231-1487

MOORE, JAMES R. lawyer; b. Longview, Wash., Sept. 14, 1944; s. James Carlton and Virginia (Rice) M.; m. Patricia Riley, Aug. 25, 1967 (div. 1978); 1 child, Katherine M.; m. Christine M. Monkman, July 14, 1979 (div. 1996); stepchildren: Amy McKenna, John McKenna; 1 foster child, Zia Sunseri; m. Kathryn Lindquist, Aug. 26, 1996; stepchildren: Matthew Elggren, Adam Elggren, Erin Elggren, David Heilner. BA, Whitman Coll., 1966; JD, Duke U., 1969. Bar: Wash. 1970, U.S. Ct. Appeals (4th cir.) 1972, U.S. Supreme Ct. 1973, U.S. Ct. Appeals (9th cir.) 1974, D.C., 1995. Law clk. to Hon. J. Barnes U.S. Ct. Appeals (9th cir.), L.A., 1969-70; trial atty. pollution control, land/natural resources div. U.S. Dept. Justice, Washington, 1970-74; asst. U.S. atty. U.S. Atty.'s Office, Seattle, 1974-82; regional counsel U.S. EPA Region 10, 1982-87; counsel Perkins Coie, 1987-88, ptnr., 1989-98; sr. environ. counsel, v.p. Huntsman Corp., Salt Lake City, 1999—; dep. gen. counsel Huntsman Internat., 2002—04, Huntsman LLC, Salt Lake City, 2004—. Spkr. in field. Contbr. articles to profl. jours. Bd. dirs. Environ. Law Inst., 1995-2000; chmn. audit com. Whitman Coll., 1994—, bd. overseers 2003—; mem. Athlete's Hall of Fame Com., 2003—; ethics com. Bd. Environ. Auditors Cert., 1998— Mem. ABA (sect. environment, energy and resources 1987—, vice chmn. in-house counsel com., 2003-04, chmn. 2004—), Wash. State Bar Assn. (environ. and land use sect. 1974—, spl. dist. coun. 1988-95). Democrat. Office: Huntsman Corp 500 Huntsman Way Salt Lake City UT 84108-1235 E-mail: jim_moore@huntsman.com.

MOORE, JANE ROSS, librarian, educator; b. Phila., Apr. 24, 1929; d. John William and Mary M. Ross; m. Cyril Howard Moore, Jr., June 1, 1956 (div. Mar. 1967). AB, Smith Coll., 1951; MLS, Drexel U., 1952; postgrad., Columbia U.; MBA with distinction, NYU, 1965; PhD, Case Western Res. U., 1974. Cataloguer Yale U. Libr., 1952-54; chief tech. processes libr. Lederle Labs., Am. Cyanamid Co., Pearl River, NY, 1954-58; chief serials catalog libr. Bklyn. Coll. Libr., 1958-65, asst. prof., chief catalog divsn., 1965-70, assoc. prof., chief catalog divsn., 1971-73, asso. profc., assoc. libr. adminstrv. svcs., 1973-76; prof., chief libr. Mina Rees Libr., Grad. Ctr., CUNY, 1976-91, prof., chief libr. emerita, 1991—. Lectr. Syracuse U. Grad. Sch. Libr. Sci., 1967, 69, Queens Coll. Grad. Sch. Libr. and Info. Studies, 1967—69, adj. assoc. prof., 1974—76, adj. prof., 1977—86; HEW Title IIB fellow Case Western Res. U. Sch. Libr. Sci., 1970—72; mem. chancellor's task force librs. CUNY, 1979—81; trustee N.Y. Met. Reference and Rsch. Libr. Agy., 1984—93, 2d v.p., 1985—88, v.p., 1988—90, treas., 1991—93. Elder Presbyn. Ch., clk. session, pres. corp.; bd. dirs. Vis. Nurse Assn. Bklyn., 1984—, mem. exec. com., 1987—, vice chmn., 2001—; bd. dirs., mem. exec. com., sec. Vis. Nurse Regional Health Care Sys., Inc., 2001—. Mem.: AAUW, AAUP, ALA (life; membership com. 1967—71, chmn. coun. regional groups, resources and tech. svcs. divsn. 1968—69, dir. divsn. 1968—70, 1975—76, chmn. divsn. cataloging and classification sect. 1975—76), The Typophiles (sec.-treas. 1996—), N.Y. Tech. Svcs. Librs. (pres. 1963—64), Spl. Librs. Assn. Gt. Britain, Chartered Inst. Libr. and Info. Profls. Eng., Am. Printing History Assn., OCLC Users Coun. (SUNY del. 1981—85), Assn. Coll. and Rsch. Librs. (chmn. univ. librs. sect. 1983—84), N.Y. Libr. Assn. (pres. resources and tech. svcs. sect., councilor 1966—67, sec.-treas. acad. and spl. librs. sect. 1973—75, councilor 1975—76, 1978—81, pres. 1979—80), NYU Grad. Sch. Bus. Adminstrn. Alumni Assn. (rec. sec. 1967—69, dir. 1969—70, 1975—79), Princeton Club N.Y., Smith Coll. Club Bklyn. (pres. 1966—68, class treas. 1976—81), N.Y. Libr. Club (sec. 1964—66, coun. 1966—70, 1973—77, 1979—82, pres. 1980—81), Smith Coll. Club N.Y., Archons of Colophon, Phi Kappa Phi. Home: 35 Schermerhorn St Brooklyn NY 11201-4826

MOORE, JANET MARIE, accountant, state official; b. Butler, Pa., Mar. 13, 1947; d. Jesse Robert and Katherine Mae (Pisor) Moore. A in Specialized Bus., New Castle Bus. Coll., 1972. Cost acct. Package Products Inc., Pitts, 1968; audit clk. Liberty Mus. Ins. Co., New Castle, 1968—71; acct. S.R. Snodgrass & Co., CPA, New Castle, 1971—74; clerical supr. Pa. vital records Pa. Dept. Health, New Castle, 1974—2002; ret., 2002; pvt. practice acctg., 1974—. Dog trainer, 1970—. Mem.: NRA (life), New Castle Kennel Club (sec. 1978, dir. 1977—81, v.p. 1979—81), Am. Numismatic Assn., Owner Handler Assn., Studebaker Family Nat. Assn. (life). Democrat. Presbyterian. Home: 371 Ladybug Ln Volant PA 16156

MOORE, JERRY JAY, sales executive, retired archaeologist; b. Ft. Sam Houston, Tex., Jan. 29, 1960; s. Richard Vernal and Irmgard Ludwiga Ottilia (Bennewitz) Moore. Student, Ea. Ill. U., 1980—83. Lab. asst. Archaeol. Investigations Ctr. So. Ill. U., Carbondale, 1979; field/lab. technician Ill. State Mus. Soc., Springfield, 1980, asst. lab. supr. Havana, 1980—81, Am. Resources Group, Ltd., Carbondale, 1983—86; archaeol. technician Midwestern Archaeol. Rsch. Ctr. Ill. State U., Normal, 1986—93; archaeol. asst. U. Ill., Urbana, 1993—94; archaeol. asst. Inst. Archaeology and Anthropology U. S.C., Columbia, 1993—94; merchandising asst. J.C. Penney Co., Champaign, Ill., 1994—2000; sales profl. Bergner's/Saks Inc., Urbana, 2000—02, Dick's Sporting Goods, Inc., Champaign, 2002—. Co-author: monographs; contbr. articles to profl. jours. Scholar, State of Ill., 1978—82. Mem.: SAR, Soc. Collegiate Journalists, Iroquois County Hist. and Geneal. Soc., Soc. of the War of 1812 (U.S. Army Mil. Uniform Ft. Dearborn, Ill. Project 1999—2000, sgt. at arms 2000—), Sons of the Revolution, Sons of Union Vets. of the Civil War (genealogist 1998—), Phi Theta Kappa. Republican. Roman Catholic. Avocations: history, antiques, genealogy. Home: 590 S Park St Paxton IL 60957 Office: 2113 N Prospect Ave Champaign IL 61822 Office Phone: 217-352-4173.

MOORE, JO ELLA, construction executive; b. Morgantown, W.Va., Apr. 13, 1954; d. Steven Kent and Teddie Lynn (Metzger) M. BS in Hort. Sci., N.C. State U., 1976. Grounds maintenance person State of N.C. Gen. Svcs., Raleigh, 1976-77; photography & graphics environ. impact engr. Raleigh-Durham Airport Engring Dept., 1977-80; archtl. woodwork draftsman, project coord., estimator So. Builders & Supplies, Apex, N.C., 1980-84; field office engr. Romeo Guest Assocs., subs. Nello L. Teer Co., Durham, N.C., 1984-85; scheduling/cost engr. Nello L. Teer Co., Durham, 1985-88, project engr., 1988-92; estimator Riverview Millworks, 1994; estimator, project engr. Ranger Constrn., Ft. Pierce, Fla., 1995—98, environl. dir., 1999—. Leader Girl Scouts U.S.A., Durham, 1984. Mem. NAFE, Nat. Assn. Women in Constrn.(pres. Durham chpt. 1987-88, 91) Avocations: photography, camping, sewing, personal defense training, singing. Home: PO Box 12724 Fort Pierce FL 34979-2724

MOORE, JOANNA ELIZABETH, real estate professional; b. Hot Springs, Ark., Dec. 2, 1937; d. Herbert A. and Jewel (Mosier) Casey; m. Merlin Richard Moore, July 13, 1956; children: Melanie Moore Sevcik, Rick Moore, Michelle Moore Folks. Student, Bethany Nazarene Coll., 1956-57, Houston C.C., 1978, U. St. Thomas, 1987-88, 90—. Cert. residential specialist, Residential Sales Coun. of Realtors Nat. Mktg. Inst., accredited buyer rep. Realtor Red Carpet Realtors, Temple, Tex., 1979-80, Century 21, Temple, 1981-85; broker-owner RE/MAX Realtors, Temple, 1986—. Spkr. Homebuilders Assn. seminars, 1985-88, 92. Fund chairwoman Bluebonnet coun. Girl Scouts U.S., 1987, mem. exec. bd., 1989; fund chairwoman March of Dimes, Temple, 1988; pres. Cen. Tex. chpt. Rep. Women's Club, 1983-84. Named Woman of Distinction, Girl Scouts U.S., 1992. Mem. Nat. Assn. Realtors, Tex. Assn. Realtors (mem. Polit. Action com. 1983-92), Temple-Belton Realtors (social chairwoman 1986, legis. chairwoman 1987, edn. chairwoman 1989, bd. dirs. 1998—), Temple Area Homebuilders (builder-realtor com. 1991, Realtor of Yr. 1993, 95, 96), Temple C. of C. (mem. govt. com. 1988, visitation com. 1989, tourist com. 1990, awards com., govt. affairs com. 1992). Home: 7112 Boutwell Dr Temple TX 76502-4204 Office: RE/MAX Realtors 4016 S 31st St Ste 200 Temple TX 76502-3348

MOORE, JOHN DAVID, management consultant; b. Mt. Pleasant, Iowa, Apr. 7, 1937; s. Burris P. and Esther I. (Copenhaver) M.; m. Karen K. Kriegel, June 19, 1957; children: Charles A., Michael J., Susan K., David J. AB, Muscatine (Iowa) C.C., 1961; BBA, Augustana Coll., 1966; postgrad., U. Iowa, 1966-88. Office mgr. Stanley Engring., Muscatine, 1956-64; pers. mgr. Oscar Mayer & Co., Davenport and Perry, Iowa, 1964-68; midwest regional mgr. A.S. Hansen, Lake Bluff, Ill., 1968-73; legal adminstr. Gardner, Carton & Douglas, Chgo., 1973-78, Heller Ehrman White & McAuliffe, San Francisco, 1978-84; v.p., dir. Hildebrandt, Inc., Walnut Creek, Calif., 1984-90; pres. Moore Cons. Inc., Walnut Creek, 1990—. Pres. Libertyville (Ill.) H.S. Bd., 1974, Libertyville Ecumenical Coun., 1975; bd. dirs. Libertyville YMCA, 1969-71. Recipient Muscatine Disting. Svc. award, 1963; named Outstanding State V.P., Iowa Jaycees, 1964, Outstanding Nat. Dir., U.S. Jaycees, 1965. Mem. Assn. Legal Adminstrs. (regional v.p. 1977-78, nat. v.p. 1979-81, nat. pres. 1982-83), Found. Assn. Legal Adminstrs. (pres. 1986-88), Golden Gate Assn. Legal Adminstrs. Republican. Methodist. Home and Office: 3132 Shire Ln Walnut Creek CA 94598-4627 Personal E-mail: jondmor@sbcglobal.net.

MOORE, JOHN EDDY, lieutenant governor; b. Charleston, W.Va., July 13, 1943; s. George Roy and Alvaretta (Hoskins) M.; m. Martha Clay Spangenberg, Aug. 7, 1966; children— Brian Clay, Stacia Hoskins BS in Comemrce, Washington and Lee U., 1965; JD, U. Ky., 1968. Group dir. Rockwell Internat., Cedar Rapids, Iowa, 1974-80, v.p. Dallas, 1980-81; v.p., ptnr. Korn/Ferry Internat., Dallas, 1981-82; sr. v.p. Cessna Aircraft, Wichita, Kans., 1982—2002; lt. gov. State of Kansas, 2003—. Dir. Health Care Plus, Wichita, Kans., Riverside Hosp., Wichita; former mem. Spl. Commn. on Pub. Agenda for Kans.; sec. Kans. Foodbank Warehouse, Wichita; bd. dirs. Booth Meml. Residence, Wichita Mem. Midwest Aerospace Indsl. Relations Council, Machinery and Allied Products Inst. (human resources council), Wichita C. of C. (chmn. state legis. com.), Kans. C. of C. and Industry (bd. dirs.) Republican. Methodist. Avocation: golf. Office: Capitol Ste 212S 300 SW Tenth Ave Topeka KS 66612-1590

MOORE, JOHN EDWARD, marketing professional, freelance writer; b. Watertown, Wisc., Sept. 18, 1920; s. John Martin and Grace Marie (Dent) M.; m. Barbara J. Gates, Sept. 21, 1947 (div. 1957); m. Sally Elizabeth Bond, Oct. 18, 1958; children: Gerald Ian, Helen Louise, Jeffrey Craig, Tracy Patricia. U. Wisc., 1946. Mktg. rsch. mgr. Procter & Gamble (Manila) Phillippines, 1949-57; staff assignment Overseas Div. Procter Gamble, Cin., 1958-62; mkt. rsch. mgr. Procter & Gamble Scandinavia, Newcastle, Tyne, U.K., 1962-64, Export & Spl. Ops., Procter & Gamble A.G., Geneva, Switzerland, 1964-75; assoc. mgr. mkt. rsch. Procter & Gamble, Cin., 1976-79, internat. mktg. rsch. mgr., 1980-84; cons. J.E. Moore, Cin., 1984-95; freelance writer, 1990—. Pres. Philippine (Manila) Radio Broadcasting Corp., 1952-54, mem. European Opinion and Mktg. Congress, 1964-75. Contbr. articles to profl. jours. Chmn. Boy Scouts of Am. Geneva, 1975, pres. Cin. Youth Symphony Orch. 1980-82, Men's com. Cin. Art Mus. 1984-90, Duveneck Assn., 1990-99, fund raiser Art Acad., Cin. 1987; chmn. Duveneck Assn., 1999. With U.S. Army, ETO. Recipient Market Rsch. Pioneer award, Philippines, 1987. Mem. Am. Assn. Individual Investors, Smithsonian Assocs., Am. Assn. Retired Persons, Internat. Visitors Ctr. Episcopalian. Avocations: golf, freelance writing, travel. Home and Office: 6235 Nuevelle Ln Cincinnati OH 45243-2355

MOORE, JOHN EDWIN, JR., academic administrator; b. Aurora, Mo., Nov. 7, 1942; s. John Edwin and Emma Lou (Harback) M.; children: John E. III, Catherine Porter. BA cum laude, Yale U., 1964, MA in Teaching, 1965; EdD, Harvard U., 1971. Tchr. N.C. Advancement Sch., Winston-Salem, 1965-66; rsch. asst. Tech. Edn. Rsch. Ctr., Cambridge, Mass., 1969-70; adminstrv. asst., treas. Kirkwood Sch. Dist. R-VII, St. Louis, 1970-73, asst. supt., treas., 1973-74; adj. prof. U. Mo., St. Louis, 1973-74; v.p. Athens (Greece) Coll., 1974-75; asst. commr. edn. Dept. Elem. and Secondary Edn., Jefferson City, Mo., 1975-83; pres. Drury U., Springfield, Mo., 1983—. Part-time instr. Far-East div. U. Md., 1967-68. Bd. dirs. United Way Ozarks, campaign chmn., 1988; bd. dirs. Mo. Colls. Fund, chmn., 1988-89; bd. dirs. Make-A-Wish Found.; chmn. bd. dirs. Am. Nat. Fish & Wildlife Mus., 1998—. With U.S. Army, 1966-68. Recipient Vincent Conroy Meml. award Harvard Grad. Sch. Edn., 1971; named one of Outstanding Young Men Am., 1973. Mem. Springfield Area C. of C. (v.p. 1988, bd. dirs. Springfieldian of Yr. 1989), Nat. Assn. Intercollegiate Athletics (coun. pres.'s), Rotary (pres. Springfield chpt. 1988-89). Presbyterian (elder). Avocations: hunting, fishing, gardening, conservation. Home: 1234 N Benton Ave Springfield MO 65802-1902 Office: Drury U 900 N Benton Ave Springfield MO 65802-3712

MOORE, JOHN HARTWELL, anthropology educator, consultant; b. Williston, Nd, Feb. 27, 1939; s. William Andrew and Mary Montgomery Moore; m. Shelley Ann Arlen, June 6, 1981; children: Jeremiah, Jessica, Alexandra. BS, U. of Ark., Fayetteville, AR, 1962; Ph. D, NYU, New York, NY, 1974. Anthropology educator U. of Okla., Norman, Okla., 1977—93, U. of Fla., Gainesville, Fla., 1993. Cons. Native Am. Rights Fund, Boulder, Colo., 1979—, Sand Creek Massacre Descendants Trust, Anadarko, Okla., 1991—, Sawridge Indian Band, Slave Lake, Alberta, Canada, 1992—. Author: (book) The Cheyenne; editor: Political Economy of North American Indians. Del. to state conv. Dem. Party, Oklahoma City, 1991—91; chpt. pres. Vietnam Veterans Against the War, West Orange, NJ, 1968—69; state com. Rainbow Coalition, Oklahoma City, 1987—93. Second Lt. U.S. Army, 1962—64, East Asia. Decorated Armed Forces Expeditionary Medal U.S. Army, UN Peacekeeping Medal UN; recipient Governor's Cmty. Svc. Award, State of Okla., 1990. Fellow: Ctr. for Advanced Study in the Behavioral Sciences, Am. Assn. for the Advancement of Science (chair of anthropology sect. 1997—98); mem.: Human Genome Diversity Project (chair north am. cmty. 1998). Democrat. Ethical Culture. Achievements include research in Role of ethnogenesis in human evolution; Rates of gene flow from ethnic inter-marriage. Home: 3328 North West 18 Avenue Gainesville FL 32605 Office: University of Florida 1112 Turlington Gainesville FL 32611 E-mail: moojohn@anthro.ufl.edu.

MOORE, JOHN LEO, JR., journalist, writer, editor; b. Providence, June 24, 1927; s. John Leo and Annabelle Cecilia (Eastwood) Moore; m. Dorothy Dolores Drankwicz, 1952; children: John Leo III, Christopher, Meredith Margaret Moore Poffenberger. AB, Brown U., 1950. Reporter Pawtucket (R.I.) Times, 1950-66, Providence Jour.-Bulletin, 1966; correspondent Carpenter News Svc., Washington, 1966-69; assoc. editor Nat. Jour., Washington, 1969-74; asst. mng. editor Congl. Quarterly, Washington, 1974-78, asst. dir. books, 1978-90; freelance writer, editor Washington, 1990—. Cons. World Bank Internat. Monetary Fund, Washington, 1990—. Editor: Guide to U.S. Elections, 2d edit., 1985, 4th rev. edit., 2001, CQ's Washington Guidebook, 1990, Congressional Ethics, 1992; author: Speaking of Washington, 1993, Elections A to Z, 1999, 2d edit., 2003; co-author: Encyclopedia of American Political History, 2001, Guide to the Presidency, 3d rev. edit., 2002. Committeeman Troop 15 Boy Scouts Am., Pawtucket, 1946—50, committeeman Troop 12, 1964—66; pres. Local 185 Newspaper Guild, Pawtucket, 1964—66; v.p. Cmty. Assn., Severna Forest, Md., 1976—78. Recipient Disting. Reporting Pub. Affairs, Am. Polit. Sci. Assn., 1961, salute, Pawtucket C. of C., 1965, resolution of praise, Pawtucket City Coun., 1966. Mem.: Soc. Profl. Journalists. Roman Catholic. Avocations: photography, home improvement, lawn and garden work, reading, walking. Home and Office: 807 Cottonwood Dr Severna Park MD 21146-2813

MOORE, JOHN NORTON, lawyer, diplomat, educator; b. N.Y.C., June 12, 1937; s. William Thomas and Lorena (Norton) M.; m. Barbara Schneider, Dec. 12, 1981; children: Victoria Norton, Elizabeth Norton. AB in Econs., Drew U., 1959; LLB with honors, Duke U., 1962; LLM, U. Ill., 1965; postgrad., Yale U., 1965-66. Bar: Fla. 1962, Ill. 1963, Va. 1969, D.C. 1972, U.S. Supreme Ct. 1972. Walter L. Brown prof. law, dir. Ctr. Oceans Law and Policy Ctr. for Nat. Security Law, U. Va., 1965-72, 76—. Counselor on internat. law Dept. State, Washington, 1972-73; chmn. Nat. Security Coun. Task Force on Law of Sea and dep. spl. rep. of Pres. and amb. Law of Sea Conf., 1973-76; fellow Woodrow Wilson Internat. Ctr. for Scholars, Washington, 1976; adj. prof. Georgetown Law Ctr., 1978—; mem. Nat. Adv. Com. on Oceans and Atmosphere, 1984-85; mem. U.S. del. Conf. Security and Coop. in Europe, 1984; spl. counsel, dep. agt. for U.S. to World Ct.; former cons. to the Pres.'s Intelligence Oversight Bd., Arms Control and Disarmament Agy., U.S. Info. Agy.; chmn. bd. dirs. U.S. Inst. Peace; co-chmn. with the U.S. assoc. atty. gen. Moscow Seminar on the Rule of Law, 1990; legal advisor during Gulf crisis for Kuwait's Amb. to U.S., including legal adviser to the Kuwait Rep. to UN Boundary Commn., 1991-94. Author: Law and the Indo-China War, 1972 (Phi Beta Kappa award); editor: Law and Civil War in the Modern World, 1976, Readings in International Law, 1979, The Arab-Israeli Conflict, 3 vols., 1976, 4th vol., 1991, Nat. Security Law, 1990, Crisis in the Gulf, 1992, Nat. Security Law Documents, 1995, Treaty Interpretation, The Constitution and the Rule of Law, 2001, The National Law of Treaty Implementation, 2001, Solving the War Puzzle, 2003; editor: The Real Lessons of the Vietnam War, 2002, Civil Litigation Against Terrorism, 2003; bd. editors: Am. Jour. Internat. Law; contbr. articles on oceans policy, nat. security, internat. law, congl.-exec. rels. in fgn. policy, rule of law and democracy-bldg. to profl. jours. Sesquicentennial assoc. Ctr. Advanced Studies, U. Va., 1971-72; adv. bd. law of sea State Dept., 1977-80, adv. bd. internat. law, 1982; chmn. bd. dirs. U.S. Inst. Peace, 1986-89, 89-91; chmn. oceans policy com. Rep. Nat. Com.; com. on exploration of the seas Nat. Acad. Nat. Rsch. Coun., 2002; active Consortium on Intelligence. Recipient Alumni award in arts Drew U., 1976; Compass Disting. Achievement award for significant contbns. to art and sci. of oceanography and marine tech., 1994; NIH fellow Yale U., 1965-66. Mem. ABA (past vice-chmn. sect. internat. law, past 5-term chmn. com. on law and nat. security), Am. Law Inst., Am. Oceanic Orgn. (exec. coun.), Marine Tech. Soc. (exec. coun.), Rhodes Acad. Oceans Law and Policy (founding dir.), Coun. Fgn. Rels., Order of Coif, Cosmos Club, N.Y. Yacht Club, Freedom House (bd. dirs.), Phi Beta Kappa. Republican. Episcopalian. Home: 824 Flordon Dr Charlottesville VA 22901-7810 Office Phone: 434-924-7441. *Life offers opportunity to pursue many worthwhile interests. In selecting among them it has seemed most useful to focus on those issues of sufficiently broad general significance as to justify the efforts of a lifetime. For me that has meant focus on promoting democracy and the rule of law, improving the functioning of government, controlling and reducing war, and the policy choices of the ocean frontier.*

MOORE, JOHN P. microbiologist, immunologist, medical educator; b. Liverpool, Eng., Jan. 20, 1957; BA in Biochemistry, Cambridge U., Eng., 1978, MPhil in Biochemistry, 1979, MA in Biochemistry, 1981, PhD in Biochemistry, 1982. Post-doctoral rsch. asst. dept. biochemistry Cambridge U., 1982—84; vis. scientist labs. Dr. K. Kelly and Dr. M.A. Beaven NIH, Washington, 1985—86; vis. scientist dept. biochemistry Cambridge U., 1985—86; vis. scientist Ludwig Inst. Cancer Rsch., Cambridge, 1986—87; vis. scientist vet. pathology Prof. W.F.H. Jarrett's Lab., Scotland, 1987; sr. rsch. fellow vet. pathology funded by MRC AIDS Directed Programme, Scotland, 1988—89; lectr. U. London, 1989—92; rsch. fellow Chester Beatty Labs. Inst. Cancer Rsch., London, 1989—92; assoc. prof. microbiology Sch. Medicine NYU, N.Y.C., 1992—96; staff investigator Aaron Diamond AIDS Rsch. Ctr., N.Y.C., 1992—2000, dep. sci. adminstr., 1997—2000; assoc. prof. Rockefeller U., N.Y.C., 1996—2000; prof. dept. microbiology and immunology Weill Med. Coll, Cornell U., N.Y.C., 2000—. Chair sub-com. vaccine

R&D com. Office AIDS Rsch.1, 0995; mem. rev. com. Frederick Cancer R&D Ctr. Nat. Cancer Inst., 1995; mem. adult AIDS clin. trials group advanced tech. labs. study sect. Nat. Inst. Allergy and Infectious Diseases, 1995, mem. program project spl. rev. com., 96; mem. steering com. Ctr. AIDS Rsch. Columbia-Rockefeller, 1998—99; mem. faculty com. Fogarty Tng. Program Columbia U., 2000; mem. organizing com. Durban Declaration, 2000; mem. sci. adv. bd. Ctr. AIDS Rsch. U. Mass., 2000; mem. sci. adv. bd. Found. AIDS and Immune Rsch., 2001; mem. standing rev. panel Doris Duke Charitable Found., 2001; lectr. in field; chair AIDS HIV peer rev. panel USAMRDC, 1994; advisor WHO Global Programme on AIDS1, 1994. Editor: Jour. Virology, 1999; mem. editl. bd. Jour. Virology, 1994—, AIDS Rsch. and Human Retroviruses, 1993, AIDS, 1993—99, HIV Molecular Immunology Database, Los Alamos Nat. Lab., 1995, Jour. Exptl. Medicine, 1997, grant reviewer in field, ad hoc reviewer numerous profl. jours. Recipient Stavros Niarchos scholar, Weill Med Coll. Cornell U., 2000, Elizabeth Glaser Scientist award, Pediat. AIDS Found., 1996; grantee, CRC, 1985, U.K. MRC Project, 1985—89, NYU CFAR, 1992, NIH, 1992—2000, Bristol-Myers Squibb, Inc., 1997, Schering-Plough Rsch. Labs., Inc., 1997—2000; Bye-fellow, Downing Coll., 1979. Mem.: Biochemical Soc., Soc. Leukocyte Biology, Cambridge Philos. Soc., Brit. Soc. Cell Biology, N.Y. Acad. Sci., Am. Soc. Microbiology, Am. Soc. Virology, Internat. AIDS Soc. Office: Joan and Sanford I Weill Med Coll Cornell U Dept Microbio and Immunology 1300 York Ave W-805 New York NY 10016*

MOORE, JOHN PLUNKETT DENNIS, publisher; b. Mexico, Mo., Mar. 2, 1931; s. Dennis Talmage and Vona Mae (Vance) M.; m. Lydia Benz Ahern, Aug. 15, 1959, children: Alison Ahern, Lydia Benz, John Talmage, Maude Ahern, Meredith Coleman. Student, Princeton U., 1948-51, U.S. Naval Acad., 1951-53; BA, U. Mo., Columbia, 1953; postgrad., Harvard Law Sch., 1955-56. Coll. traveler The Dryden Press, Inc., N.Y.C., 1957-59; coll. traveler The Macmillan Co., N.Y.C., 1959-60, editor, 1960-67; assoc. exec. editor Columbia U. Press, N.Y.C., 1968-74, editor in chief, 1974-80, pres., 1980-97, also bd. dirs. Bd. dirs., pres. Columbia U. Music Press; bd. dirs. Univ. Presses of Calif., Columbia and Princeton, Chichester, West Sussex, Eng., 1979-97, chmn., 1981-83, 85-87, 96-97; trustee Composer's Recordings, Inc., 1984-97. Author: Columbia University Press: A Historical Sketch, 1893-1993; mem. editl. bd. N.Y. Acad. Scis., 1993-01. Bd. dirs. Greenwich (Conn.) Health Assn., 1970-75; bd. dirs. assoc. Family Centers, Greenwich, Stamford, 1975—; trustee Princeton Libr. in N.Y.C., 1984—; mem. vestry St. Barnabas Ch., Greenwich, 1995-98. With U.S. Army, 1953-55. Mem. Assn. Am. Univ. Presses (chair internat. com. 1994-96, bd. dirs. 1996-97). Clubs: Publishers Lunch (N.Y.C., admissions com. 1996-99), Princeton (N.Y.C.), Faculty House Columbia U. (N.Y.C.), Century Assn. (N.Y.C.); Nassau (Princeton, N.J.), the Book Table (N.Y.C.), The Ch. Club N.Y. (N.Y.C.), Princeton Club So. Calif. (L.A.), The English Speaking Union, The Mystery Club. Episcopalian. Home: 321 Riversville Rd Greenwich CT 06831-3228 also: 1912 Kelton Ave Los Angeles CA 90025 E-mail: jdm123@aol.com.

MOORE, JOHN RONALD, manufacturing executive; b. Pueblo, Colo., July 12, 1935; s. John E. and Anna (Yesberger) M.; m. Judith Russelyn Bauman, Sept. 5, 1959; children: Leland, Roni, Timothy, Elaine. BS, U. Colo., 1959; grad. advanced mgmt. program, Harvard Grad. Sch. Bus., 1981. Mgmt. trainee Montgomery Ward & Co., Denver, 1960-65; distbn. mgr. Midas Internat. Corp., Chgo., 1965-71; v.p., gen. mgr. Midas, Can., Toronto, Ont., 1972-75; pres. Auto Group Midas Internat. Corp., Chgo., 1976-82, pres., chief exec. officer, 1982-98; ret., 1998. Bd. dirs. Lake Forest Grad. Sch. Mgmt., U. Colo. Found., Chgo. Crime Commn.; mem. bus. adv. coun. U. Colo. Sch. Bus.; trustee U. Colo. Found. Mem. Harvard Bus. Sch. Alumni Assn., U. Colo. Alumni Assn., Chgo. Coun. Fgn. Rels., Econ. Club Chgo., Comml. Club Chgo. Republican. *There is very little we accomplish in our lifetime that results from effort we alone expend. All of us should have the wisdom to express our appreciation to our families and associates who have helped us attain our goals and accomplishments— for failure to do so tarnishes our successes and breeds selfishness.*

MOORE, JOHN RUNYAN, agricultural and resource economics educator; b. Columbus, Ohio, Sept. 30, 1929; s. Lawrence Levi and Hazel Marie (Runyan) M.; m. Marjorie Ann Coy, June 14, 1953; children: Lee, Andrew. BSc in Agriculture, Ohio State U., 1951; MSc in Agrl. Econs., Cornell U., 1955; PhD in Agrl. Econs., U. Wis., Madison, 1959. County 4-H Club agt. Ohio Coop. Extension Svc., Steubenville, 1951; grad. rsch. asst. Cornell U., Ithaca, NY, 1953—55, U. Wis., Madison, 1955—58; asst. prof. Mich. State U., East Lansing, 1958—62; mktg. specialist, econ. cons. Ford Found., New Delhi, 1968—70; assoc. prof. U. Md., College Park, 1962—68, prof. in world food situation and food mktg., 1968—95, asst. dean internat. programs, 1979—94, prof. emeritus, 1995—. Econ. cons. FTC, Washington, 1963-64, World Bank, India and Nigeria, 1971-74, Kyrgyz Republic, 1997, U.S. AID, Indonesia, Malawi, Haiti, Liberia and Egypt, various dates, FAO, Beijing, 1990. Co-author: (book) Market Structure of Agriculture Industries, 1964, U.S. Investment In Latin American Food Processing, 1966, Indian Food Grain Market, 1972. Trustee S.E. Consortium for Internat. Devel., 1978-95; chmn. bd. commrs. City College Park Housing Authority, 1996—. Lt. (j.g.) USNR, 1951-53. Recipient Internat. Honor award USDA, Washington, 1985, Cert. of Appreciation, 1986. Mem. Am. Agrl. Econ. Assn. (Thesis award 1960), Am. Econ. Assn., Internat. Agrl. Econ. Assn., Trees for the Future (chmn. bd. trustees 1997—), Rotary (pres. 1998-99). Avocations: photography, travel, gardening, golf. Personal E-mail: JRM36162@cs.com.

MOORE, JOHN STERLING, JR., retired minister; b. Memphis, Aug. 25, 1918; s. John Sterling and Lorena (Bounds) M.; m. Martha Louise Paulette, July 6, 1944; children: Sterling Hale, John Marshall, Carolyn Paulette. Student, Auburn U., 1936-37; AB, Samford U., 1940; ThM, So. Bapt. Theol. Sem., 1944. Ordained to ministry So. Bapt. Conv., 1942. Pastor chs., Pamplin, Va., 1944-48, Amherst, Va., 1949-57; pastor Manly Meml. Bapt. Ch., Lexington, Va., 1957-84, pastor emeritus, 1984—. Mem. Hist. Commn., So. Bapt. Conv., 1968-75; pres. Va. Bapt. Pastor's Conf., 1963. Author: History of Broad Run Baptist Church, 1762-1987, 1987, The History of Second Baptist Church Richmond Virginia, 1998; co-author: Meaningful Moments in Virginia Baptist Life, 1715-1972, 1973; editor Va. Bapt. Register, 1972-2001; contbr. articles to profl. jours. Chmn. Lexington Mayor's Com. on Race Rels., 1962-65; bd. dirs. Stonewall Jackson Hosp., 1967-72, pres., 1969-71; treas. Rockbridge Mental Health Clinic, 1971-84. Recipient Disting. Svc. award Hist. Commn., So. Bapt. Conv., 1988. Mem. Am. Soc. Ch. History, So. Bapt. Hist. Soc. (bd. dirs. 1972-91, pres. 1975-76, sec. 1977-85), Va. Bapt. Hist. Soc. (exec. com. 1963—, pres. 1984-85), Va. Hist. Soc., Masons. Home: 1900 Lauderdale Dr Apt D-115 Richmond VA 23238-3918

MOORE, JOYCE KRISTINA, financial planner, director; b. Phila., June 19, 1955; d. Oscar Herbert Hariu and Virginia Wilson (Guss) Leas; m. William Burns Moore, June 20, 1980 (div. 1990); children: William Patrick, Kristofer Sean. Student, Beloit Coll., 1973-74, U. Pa., 1974-75, Lafayette Coll., 1984-88, Am. Coll., 1991—. ChFC. Photographer Clair Pruett Studios, Drexel Hill, Pa., 1977-80; photographic cons. Dan's Camera City, Allentown, Pa., 1980-81; contr., co-founder BioService, Inc., Bethlehem, Pa., 1985-89; contr. Mega Video Inc., Easton, Pa., 1989-91; spl. rep. John Hancock Fin. Svcs., Allentown, 1990-93; prin. Joyce Moore Fin. Svcs., Macungie, Pa., 1993—. Co-editor: Estate Planning Success for Pennsylvania Residents, 2002. Bd. dirs. Spring Garden Children's Sch., Easton; den leader Cub Scout Pack 31, Williams, Pa., 1991—95, scout leader, 1995—97; mem. Lehigh Valley Estate Planning Coun., 2001—; former mem. Warren County Dem. Com., Phillipsburg, NJ, 1981—83; councilwoman Glendon Borough, 1992—97, coun. v.p., 1996—97; overseer Religous Soc. Friends, 1986—92. Mem.: LWV (bd. dirs. Easton area 1987—91, pres. 1989—90), Pa. Assn. Ins. and Fin. Advisors (bd. dirs. 2002—), First Affirmative Fin. Network, Progressive Asset Mgmt., Social Investment Forum, Lehigh Valley Assn. Ins. Fin. Advisors (bd. dirs. 1995—, pres. 2000—01), Am. Soc. Fin. Svc. Profls. Avocations: needlecrafts, folk music, canoeing. Office: Joyce Moore Fin Svc PO Box 175 Macungie PA 18062-0175 E-mail: joyce@jmfs.com.

MOORE, JULIANNE (JULIE ANNE SMITH), actress; b. Fayetteville, N.C., Dec. 3, 1960; BFA, Boston Univ. With The Guthrie Theater, 1988-89. Actress: (theatre) Serious Money, 1987, Bone-the-Fish, 1988, Ice Cream with Hot Fudge, 1990, Uncle Vanya, (TV soap operas) As the World Turns (Emmy award outstanding ingenue in daytime drama series 1988), The Edge of Night, (TV movies) Money, Power, Murder, 1989, Lovecraft, 1991, (feature films) The Hand That Rocks the Cradle, 1992, The Gun in Betty Lou's Handbag, 1992, Body of Evidence, 1993, Benny & Joon, 1993, The Fugitive, 1993, Short Cuts, 1993, Vanya on 42nd Street, 1994, Roommates, 1995, Nine Months, 1995, Safe, 1995, Assassins, 1995, Surviving Picasso, 1996, The Myth of Fingerprints, 1997, The Lost World: Jurassic Park, 1997, Hellcab, 1997, Boogie Nights, 1997, Chicago Cab, 1998, The Big Lebowski, 1998, Psycho, 1998, Map of the World, 1999, Magnolia, 1999, Cookie's Fortune, 1999, An Ideal Husband, 1999, The End of the Affair, 1999, Hannibal, 2001, Evolution, 2001, The Shipping News, 2001, Far From Heaven, 2002, The Hours, 2002, Marie and Bruce, 2004, Laws of Attraction, 2004. Office: Creative Artists Agy care Kevin Huvane 9830 Wilshire Blvd Beverly Hills CA 90212-1825*

MOORE, JUSTIN EDWARD, information technology executive; b. West Hartford, Conn., June 17, 1952; s. Walter Joseph and Victoria Mary (Calcagni) M. BS in Mgmt. Sci., Fla. Inst. Tech., 1974. Systems assoc. Travelers Ins., Hartford, Conn., 1974-77; data processing programmer R.J. Reynolds Inc., Winston-Salem, N.C., 1977-78; programmer/analyst Sea-Land Svc., Elizabeth, N.J., 1978-79, mgr. market analysis Oakland, Calif., 1979-82; asst. v.p., dir. application systems Fox Capital Mgmt. Corp., Foster City, Calif., 1982-86; mgr. bus. svcs. dept mktg. and pricing Am. Pres. Cos., Ltd., Oakland, 1987-88, dir. mktg. and pricing systems, 1988-89; dir. systems devel. The Office Club, Concord, Calif., 1989-91; dir. MIS Revo, Inc., Mountain View, Calif., 1992-93; account mgr. Imrex Computer Systems, Inc., South San Francisco, 1993-94; project mgr. Exigent Computer Group, Inc., San Ramon, Calif., 1994—. Democrat. Roman Catholic. Avocations: golf, personal computing, investment mgmt. Home: 5214 Jomar Dr Concord CA 94521-2343 Office: Exigent Computer Group Inc 4000 Executive Pky Ste 275 San Ramon CA 94583-4257 Office Phone: 925-866-1692. E-mail: justin_moore@prodigy.net. *Personal philosophy: Strive always to do the right things, at the right time, the right way for the right reasons.*

MOORE, KAREN NELSON, judge; b. Washington, Nov. 19, 1948; d. Roger S. and Myrtle Nelson; m. Kenneth Cameron Moore, June 22, 1974; children: Roger C., Kenneth N., Kristin K. AB magna cum laude, Radcliffe Coll., 1970; JD magna cum laude, Harvard U., 1973. Bar: DC 1973, Ohio 1976, U.S. Ct. Appeals (DC cir.) 1974, U.S. Supreme Ct. 1980, U.S. Ct. Appeals (6th cir.) 1984. Law clk. to Hon. Malcolm R. Wilkey U.S. Ct. Appeals (DC Cir.), Washington, 1973—74; law clk. to Hon. Harry A. Blackmun U.S. Supreme Ct., Washington, 1974—75; assoc. Jones, Day, Reavis & Pogue, Cleve., 1975—77; asst. prof. Case Western Res. Law Sch., Cleve., 1977—80, assoc. prof., 1980—82, prof., 1982—95; judge U.S. Ct. Appeals (6th cir.), Cleve., 1995—. Vis. prof. Harvard Law Sch., 1990—91. Mem. Harvard Law Rev., 1971—73; contbr. articles to profl. jours. Trustee Lakewood Hosp., Ohio, 1978—85, Radcliffe Coll., Cambridge, 1980—84. Fellow: Am. Bar Found.; mem.: Harvard U. Alumni Assn. (bd. dirs. 1984—87), Am. Law Inst., Phi Beta Kappa. Office: US Ct Appeals 6th Cir Carl B Stokes US Courthouse 801 W Superior Ave Cleveland OH 44113-1831

MOORE, KENNETH CAMERON, lawyer; b. Chgo., Oct. 25, 1947; s. Kenneth Edwards and Margaret Elizabeth (Cameron) M.; m. Karen M. Nelson, June 22, 1974; children: Roger Cameron, Kenneth Nelson, Kristin Karen. BA summa cum laude, Hiram Coll., 1969; JD cum laude, Harvard U., 1973. Bar: Ohio 1973, U.S. Dist. Ct. Md. 1974, U.S. Ct. Appeals (4th cir.) 1974, D.C. 1975, U.S. Dist. Ct. (no. dist.) Ohio 1976, U.S. Ct. Appeals (6th cir.) 1977, U.S. Ct. Appeals (D.C. cir.) 1979, U.S. Supreme Ct. 1980. Law clk. to judge Harrison L. Winter U.S. Ct. Appeals (4th cir.), Balt., 1973-74; assoc. Squire, Sanders & Dempsey, Washington, 1974-75, Cleve., 1975-82, ptnr., 1982—, profl. ethics ptnr., 1996—, mem. fin. com., 1990—, chair profl. ethics com., 2003—. Chmn. Ohio Fin. Com. for Jimmy Carter presdl. campaign, 1976; del. Dem. Nat. Conv., 1976; chief legal counsel Ohio Carter-Mondale Campaign, 1976; trustee Hiram Coll., 1997—, mem. exec. com., 1999, chair audit com., 1999, vice chair bd. trustees, 2000—, chair faculty affairs subcom. of faculty and acad. affairs com., 2000—. With AUS, 1970-76. Mem. ABA, Fed. Bar Assn., Ohio Bar Assn., Cleve. Bar Assn., Cleve. City Club. Home: 15602 Edgewater Dr Cleveland OH 44107-1212 Office: Squire Sanders & Dempsey 4900 Key Ctr 127 Public Sq Ste 4900 Cleveland OH 44114-1304

MOORE, KENNETH E. anthropologist, educator, writer; b. Niagara Falls, N.Y., Sept. 19, 1930; s. Gordon Winslow and Marie Frances (Sinclair) M.; 1 child, Christopher T. BA, Mich. State U., 1954; MA, U. Ill., 1967, PhD, 1973. V.p. Wimble, Lane & Assocs., Flint, Mich., 1954-59; dir. pub. rels. Mus. Tent, Clio, Mich., 1956-65; editor McGraw Hill, N.Y.C., 1958-60; prof. anthropology U. Notre Dame (Ind.), 1970-00; prof. emeritus, 2000—; founding chmn. dept. anthropology, 1981-85. Univ. prof. U. Warsaw, 1992-93. Author: Those of the Street, 1976, Dublin Ghetto, 2000; editor, translator (with Anthony Kerrigan and Saul Bellow): Revolt of the Masses, 1985; editor, contbr. Waymarks, 1987; mem. editl. bd. U. Notre Dame Press, 1978-84. Spkr. opening panel Key West (Fla.) Literary Festival, 1986. Rsch. grantee NIH, 1968-71, Wilbur Found., 1990; recipient Faculty award Andrew Mellon Found., 1980. Fellow Am. Anthropol. Assn., Royal Anthropol. Inst.; mem. AAUP, Ctrl. States Anthropol. Soc., Soc. Urban Anthropology, Soc. Study Symbolic Interaction. Roman Catholic. Office: U Notre Dame Dept Anthropology 611 Flanner Hall Notre Dame IN 46556 E-mail: kmoore@nd.edu.

MOORE, KENNETH EDWIN, pharmacology educator; b. Edmonton, Alta., Can., Aug. 8, 1933; came to U.S., 1957, naturalized, 1966; s. Jack and Emily Elizabeth (Tarbox) M.; m. Barbara Anne Stafford, Sept. 19, 1953; children—Grant Kenneth, Sandra Anne, Lynn Susan. BS, U. Alta., 1955, MS, 1957; PhD, U. Mich., 1960. Instr. pharmacology Dartmouth Med. Sch., Hanover, N.H., 1960-61, asst. prof., 1962-66; assoc. prof. pharmacology Mich. State U., East Lansing, 1966-70, prof., 1970—, chmn. dept. pharmacology and toxicology, 1987—2001. Vis. scholar Cambridge (Eng.) U., 1974; instr. Lansing Community Coll., 1975-81; cons. NIH, also pharm. industry. Author 1 book; contbr. articles to profl. jours. Fellow Am. Coll. Neuropsychopharmacology; mem. Am. Soc. Pharmacology and Exptl. Therapeutics (chmn. bd. publs. trustees 1992-96, pres. 1998-2000), Soc. Exptl. Biology and Medicine, Soc. Neuroscis. Home: 4790 Arapaho Trl Okemos MI 48864-1402 Office: Dept Pharmacology Mich State U East Lansing MI 48824 E-mail: moorek@msu.edu.

MOORE, KENNETH JAMES, agronomy educator, scientist; b. Phoenix, June 6, 1957; s. George Taylor and Barbara Joyce (Amy) M.; m. Gina Marie McCarthy Aug. 11, 1979; children: Ellyn Elizabeth, David Taylor, Mark Daniel. BS in Agr., Ariz. State U., 1979; MS in Agronomy, Purdue U., 1981, PhD in Agronomy, 1983. Asst. prof. agronomy U. Ill., Urbana, 1983-87; assoc. prof. N.Mex. State U., Las Cruces, 1988-89; rsch. agronomist Agrl. Rsch. Svc., USDA, Lincoln, Nebr., 1989-93; prof. Iowa State U., Ames, 1993—. Adj. assoc. prof. U. Nebr. Lincoln, 1989-93, prof., 1993-96; sr. rsch. fellow Ag Rsch. Grasslands, New Zealand, 1998; dir. MS in Agronomy Distance Edn. program Iowa State U., 1995—, dir. Crop Advisor Inst., 2000—. Founding editor Crop Mgmt., 2002--; assoc. editor Agronomy Jour., 1989-93, tech. editor, 1994-97; assoc. editor Crop Sci., 1994; editor: Forages: An Introduction to Grassland Ag, 2003, Native-Warm Season Grasses: Research Trends and Issues, 2000, Post-Harvest Physiology and Preservation of Forages, 1995; contbr. chpts. to books. Bd. dirs. Lincoln Children's Mus., 1991-93, Children's Svcs. of Ctrl. Iowa, 1996-97; bd. dirs. Children's Mus. Ctrl. Iowa, 1997-2002, pres., 2000-01; mem. mgmt. com. N.E. YMCA, Lincoln, 1991-93; mem. youth policy forum Lincoln YMCA, 1991-92. Recipient Point of Light award USDA, 1991. Fellow Am. Soc. Agronomy (bd. dirs. 2002—), Crop Sci. Soc. Am. (divsn. chmn. 1990-92, pres. 2003-, exec. com. and bd. dirs. 2002—, Young Crop Scientist award 1993); mem. Am. Forage and Grassland Coun. (Outstanding Young Scientist award 1982, merit award 1991). Republican. Presbyterian. Avocations: swimming, fishing, music. Office: Iowa State U Agronomy Dept 1567 Agronomy Hl Ames IA 50011-0001 Business E-Mail: kjmoore@iastate.edu.

MOORE, KENT, grocery company executive; Audit mgr. Arthur Anderson; v.p., CFO United Supermarkets, 1989-98, sr. v.p., CEO, 1998—.

MOORE, KURT RICHARD, anthropologist, fundraiser, investor; b. Scott AFB, Ill., Oct. 9, 1955; s. Richard Vernal and Irmgard Ludwiga (Bennewitz) M.; m. Josée Lucille Bédard, May 20, 1989 (div. Jan. 1995); m. Gail Ann Smith, Aug. 25, 2001. AB, BFA, U. Ill., 1976; MA, So. Ill. U., 1981, postgrad., 1984-85; cert. fin. planner, Fla. State U., 2001. Grad. tchg. asst. Field Sch. Archaeology So. Ill. U., Carbondale, 1977, grad. tchg. asst. Ctr. Continuing Edn., 1978, archaeol. field/lab. asst. Ctr. Archaeol. Investigations, 1978-79, grad. rsch. asst., 1979-80; archaeologist Ill. State Mus. Soc., Springfield, 1980-82; rsch. archaeologist Am. Resources Group, Ltd., Carbondale, 1982-85; mgr. tech. support TSG, Inc., Carbondale, 1985-86; dir. corp. and found. rels. Le Moyne Coll., Syracuse, N.Y., 1986-87; asst. dir. corp. devel. Cornell U., Ithaca, 1987-89, assoc. dir. major gifts, 1989-91; dir. major gifts and planned giving Crouse Irving Meml. Found., Syracuse, N.Y., 1991-93; dir. planned giving Fla. Inst. Tech., Melbourne, 1993-95; sr. dir. corp. and found. rels. Fla. State U., 1995-2001, dir. corp. R&D, 2001—. Contbr. articles to profl. jours.; author monographs. Bd. dirs. Birdsong Nature Ctr., Thomasville, Ga., 1997—, v.p., 1998-99, pres., 1999-2003; dir. Panhandle Archeol. Soc. Tallahasee, 2003—. Edmund J. James scholar U. Ill., Urbana, 1972-73, John T. Rusher Meml. scholar, 1975-76, So. Ill. U. scholar, 1981-87. Mem. Estate Planning Coun., Soc. Am. Archaeology, Fla. Anthrop. Soc., U.S. Racquetball Assn., Fla. Archaeological Coun., Phi Kappa Phi. Republican. Roman Catholic. Avocations: racquetball, art. Home: 1803 Folkstone Rd Tallahassee FL 32312-4002 Office: Fla State Univ Office Rsch 109 Westcott Bldg Tallahassee FL 32306-1330 E-mail: kmoore@mailer.fsu.edu.

MOORE, LAURENCE JOHN, business educator; b. Greeley, Colo., May 7, 1938; s. John Harold and Ruth Anderson M.; m. Nancy Kay Hibbert, Aug. 31, 1963 (div. Apr. 1996); children: Rebecca Ann, John Andrew, Stefani Ruth. BA in Econs., Monmouth Coll., Ill., 1962; MS in Econs., Ariz. State U., 1965, DBA in Mgmt. Sci., 1970. Dist. mktg. rep. Standard Oil Co. (Ind.), Chgo., 1962-63; sr. analyst long range and capital planning, 1964-66; head quantitative studies Continental Ill. Bank, Chgo., 1966-67; mem. faculty dept. mgmt. sci. Coll. Bus. Va. Poly. Inst. and State U., Blacksburg, 1970—, prof. Coll. Bus., 1977-85, C&P Disting. prof. bus., 1985-96, head dept. Coll. Bus., 1976-83, dir. univ. fin. planning and analysis, 1983-84, dir. univ. planning, 1988-89, Bell Atlantic-Va. prof. of bus., 1996—2002, Verizon prof. bus., 2002—. Cons. in field. Author: (with S.M. Lee, B.W. Taylor) Management Science, 1981, 4th edit., 1993, (with S.M. Lee) Introduction to Decision Sciences, 1975, (with E.R. Clayton) GERT Modeling and Simulation: Fundamentals and Applications, 1976. Served with U.S. Army, 1957-59. Recipient Disting. Service award SE region Am. Inst. Decision Scis., 1977 Fellow Am. Inst. Decision Scis. (pres. 1983-84, Disting. Svc. award 1986); mem. Inst. Mgmt. Sci. (Disting. Svc. award SE region), Inst. for Ops. Rsch. and Mgmt. Sci., Alpha Iota Delta, Beta Gamma Sigma, Omicron Delta Epsilon, Sigma Iota Epsilon. Presbyterian. Home: 1013 Chateau Ct Blacksburg VA 24060-3676 Office: Va Poly Inst and State U Dept Bus Info Tech 1007 Pamplin Hall Blacksburg VA 24061-5102 Office Phone: 540-231-5887. E-mail: ljmoore@vt.edu.

MOORE, LEROI, musician; b. Durham, N.C., Sept. 7, 1961; Student, James Madison U. Mem. (saxophone, flute, whistle, keyboards, clarinet, horn, background vocals) Dave Matthews Band, 1991—. Musician (with Dave Matthews Band): (albums) Remember Two Things, 1993, Crash, 1996, Live at Red Rocks 8.15.95, 1997, Before These Crowded Streets, 1998, Don't Drink the Water, 1998, Everyday, 2001, Busted Stuff, 2002, Central Park Concert, 2003, Gorge, 2004; musician: Best of Columbia Records Radio Hour, Vol. 2, Various Artists, 1996, Code Magneta, Code Magenta, 1996, Live on Letterman: Music from the Late Show, Various Artists, 1997, Scream 2 Original Soundtrack, 1997, Musical Chairs, Hootie & The Blowfish, 1998, In November Sunlight, Soko, 2000, Great Day in C'Ville: Jazz from the Piedmont, Various Artists, 2001, Superfastgo, Peter Griesar, 2003, Toe 2 Toe, Vol. 6, Elephant Man/Vybz Cartel, 2004. Recipient (with Dave Matthews Band) Grammy award for Best Rock Performance by a Duo or Group with Vocal for So Much to Say, 1996, Chmns. award, NAACP Image Awards, 2004. Office: RCA Records 1540 Broadway New York NY 10036*

MOORE, LINDA KATHLEEN, personnel agency executive; b. San Antonio, Tex., Feb. 18, 1944; d. Frank Edward and Louise Marie (Powell) Horton; m. Mack B. Taplin, May 25, 1963 (div. Feb. 1967); 1 child, Mack B.; m. William J. Moore, Mar. 8, 1967 (div. Nov. 1973). Student, Tex. A&I Coll., 1962-63. Co-owner S.R.O. Internat., Dallas, 1967-70; mgr. Exec. Girls Pers. & Modeling Svcs., Dallas, 1970-72, Gen. Employment Enterprises, Atlanta, 1972-88; owner, mgr. More Pers. Svcs., Inc., Atlanta, 1988-94, pres., chmn. bd., 1994—. Contbr. short story to Writer's Digest. Mem. NAFE, Nat. Fedn. Bus. and Profl. Women, Am. Soc. Profl. and Exec. Women, Women Bus. Owners, Nat. Assn. Women Cons., Nat. Assn. Personnel Svcs., Ga. Assn. Personnel Svcs., Women's Clubs, Atlanta C. of C. (speaker's bur.), Better Bus. Bur., Cobb County C. of C. Office: More Pers Svcs Inc Ste 505 2309 W Washington St Stephenville TX 76401-3805

MOORE, LLOYD EVANS, retired lawyer; b. Feb. 10, 1931; s. Bascom Sturgill and Julia M. (Martin) M.; m. Marilyn Moore, June 12, 1955; children: William, Erik, Julia. BA, Ohio State U., 1957, JD, 1958. Bar: Ohio 1959, U.S. Dist. Ct. (so. dist.) Ohio 1962, U.S. Dist. Ct. (ea. dist.) Ky. 1965, U.S. Supreme Ct. 1963. County prosecutor Lawrence County, Ohio, 1973-76; assoc. Moore, Wolfe & Bentley, Ironton, Ohio, 1989-95; ret., 1995. Author: The Jury, 1973, 1988, Face to Face - The Photography of Lloyd E. Moore, 2004. Mem. Ironton Sch. .Bd., 1966-69, pres., 1968-69; bd. dirs. Lawrence County Joint Vocat. Sch., 1966-69. With USMC, 1950-54. Fellow Royal Photog. Soc.

MOORE, LOIS JEAN, health science facility administrator; married; 1 child. Grad., Prairie View (Tex.) Sch. Nursing, 1957; BS in Nursing, Tex. Woman's U., 1970; MS in Edn., Tex. So. U., 1974. Nurse Harris County (Tex.) Hosp. Dist., 1957—; pres., chief exec. officer Harris County Hosp.; adminstr. Jefferson Davis Hosp., Houston, 1977-88, exec. v.p., chief ops. officer, 1988—2001; chief adminstr. U. Tex. Harris County Psychiat. Hosp., Houston, 2001—. Mem. adv. bd. Tex. Pub. Hosp. Assn. Contbr. articles to profl. jours. Mem. Mental Health Needs Council Houston and Harris County, Congressman Mickey Leland's Infant Mortality Task Force, Houston Crack-down Com., Gov.'s task force on health care policy, 1991; chairperson Tex. Assn. Pub. and Nonprofit Hosps., 1991, subcom. of Gov.'s task force to identify essential health care svc., 1992; bd. dirs. ARC, 1991—, Greater Houston Hosp. Coun., March of Dimes, United Way. Recipient Pacesetter award North-East C. of C., 1991; named Nurse of Yr. Houston Area League Nursing, 1976-77, Outstanding Black Achiever YMCA Century Club, 1974, Outstanding Women in Medicine YWCA, 1989. Mem. Am. Coll. Hosp. Adminstrs., Tex. Hosp. Assn. (chmn. pub. hosp. com.), Young Hosp. Adminstrs., Nat. Assn. Pub. Hosps. (bd. dirs., mem. exec. com. Tex. assn.), License Vocat. Nurses Assn., sigma Theta Tau. Home: 3730 S Macgregor Way Houston TX 77021-1506 Office: Univ Texas Harris County Psychiatric Ctr 2800 S Mar Briger Way Houston TX 77266

MOORE, LORI, information technology executive; BS in Polit. Sci., The Am. U. From mgr. to corp. v.p. Microsoft, Redmond, Wash., 1991—2000, corp. v.p. product support svc., 2000—. Office: One Microsoft Way Redmond WA 98052-6399

MOORE, LOUISE HILL, surgical technologist; b. Knoxville, Tenn., July 9, 1950; d. Mary Elizabeth Hill; m. David Oscar Moore; children: Kimberly Hill, Daveisha. Cert. surg. technologist; cosmetologist, aesthetician. Cosmetologist Millers Dept. Store, Knoxville, 1968—70, Austinian Beauty Shop, Knoxville, 1970—74, Hair Fashions E., Knoxville, 1974—78; gen. laborer Alcoa, Alcoa, Tenn., 1978—94; cert. surg. technologist St. Mary's Med. Ctr., Knoxville, 1995, Ft. Sanders Hosp., Knoxville, U. Tenn. Med. Ctr., Knoxville, 1997, safety coord., slip/pack/utility, 1997—. Mem.: Knoxville Writers Guild, Assn. Surg. Technologists. Home: 225 Grata Rd Knoxville TN 37914

MOORE, MALCOLM FREDERICK, manufacturing executive; b. Kankakee, Ill., Sept. 19, 1950; s. Robert Dunham and Josephine Frances (Jones) M.; m. Patricia Claudine Bennert, June 13, 1971; children: Michael Dunham, Emily Suzanne, Marjorie Nicoll. BSBA, Am. U., 1972; M of Mgmt., Northwestern U., 1982. Internat. mktg. mgr., product mgr. FMC Corp., Chgo., 1973-84, mktg. and engring. mgr., 1985-90; cons. Frank Lynn & Assoc., Chgo., 1984-85; v.p., gen. mgr. Lindberg unit of Gen. Signal, Watertown, Wis., 1990-93; pres. Abar Ipsen Industries, Inc., Bensalem, Pa., 1993-96, Centorr Vacuum Industries, Nashua, N.H., 1993-96, Linac Holdings, Inc., Rockford, Ill., 1994-96; pres., CEO Pangborn Corp., Hagerstown, Md., 1996-98; pres., COO Gehl Co., West Bend, Wis., 1999—. Inventor material handling equipment. Episcopalian.

MOORE, MANDY (AMANDA LEIGH MOORE), singer, actress; b. Nashua, NH, Apr. 10, 1984; d. Don and Stacy Moore. Host MTV show, Mandy, 2000. Actor(voice): (films) Dr. Doolittle 2, 2001, The Princess Diaries, 2001, A Walk to Remember, 2002 (MTV Movie award breakthrough performance-female, 2002, Teen Choice awards choice breakout performance-actress, with Shane West Teen Choice awards choice chemistry, 2002), How to Deal, 2003, Chasing Liberty, 2004, Saved!, 2004; singer: (albums) So Real, 1999, I Wanna Be With You, 2000, Mandy Moore, 2001, Coverage, 2003. Office: Epic Records 550 Madison Ave New York NY 10022-3211

MOORE, MARC ANTHONY, university administrator, writer, retired military officer; b. Dallas, July 15, 1928; s. Edward Clark and Mary Cathrine (Spake) M.; m. Mary Joan Donahue, Sept. 5, 1953; children— Daniel, Mary Ellen, Virginia, Andria. BA, So. Meth. U., 1951; MA, George Washington U., 1970; grad., Amphibious Warfare Sch., 1960, Nat. War Coll., 1974; LHD (hon.), Philippine Women's U., 1987. Enlisted man U.S. Marine Corps, 1946-48, commd. 2d lt., 1951, advanced through grades to maj. gen., 1978; regtl. comdr. Camp Pendleton, Calif., 1971; regtl. exec. officer, infantry bn. comdr., 1970; with Joint Chief Staff Ops., Washington, 1977-78; asst. dir. Marine Command and Staff Coll., 1972-73; dir. div. English and history U.S. Naval Acad., 1974-76; comdg. gen. 4th Marine Div., New Orleans, 1978-80; chief of staff U.S. Forces, Japan, from 1980, now ret.; former chancellor San Diego campus, v.p. for devel. Nat. U., 1990-91. Teaching asst. dept. psychology George Washington U., 1974; instr. dept. behavioral sci. U.S. Naval Acad., 1975-76; adj. faculty Nat. U., 1983 Co-founder Leadership 2000; mem. pres. council Calif. State U., San Marcos, 1993-96, 98-2000; mem. bd. advisors Marine Mil. Acad., 1983-95; founder and council advisors mem., Command Mus. and Warfare Leadership Ctr., Marine Recruit Depot, San Diego, 1984—. Decorated Def. Superior Svc. medal, Legion of Merit with combat V, Bronze Star with combat V with oak leaf cluster, Air medal, Def. Meritorious Svc. medal, Order Sacred Treasure (Japan); recipient Disting. Alumni award So. Meth. U., 1981. Mem. Marine Corps Assn., Phi Delta Theta. Roman Catholic. Home: 3611 Lago Sereno Escondido CA 92029-7902

MOORE, MARGARET D. human resources specialist; b. New Haven, Conn., 1948; BA, Smith Coll., 1970; MBA, Columbia U., N.Y.C., 1974. Treasury analyst PepsiCo, 1973—77, asst. treas., 1977—87, v.p. investor rels., 1987—99, sr. v.p. human resources, 1999—; sr. v.p., treas. Pepsi Bottling Group, 1998—99, bd. dirs. Bd. dirs. Michael Foods; mem. corp. adv. coun. Fin. Acctg. Stds. Bd. Office: Pepsico Inc 700 Anderson Hill Rd Purchase NY 10577*

MOORE, MARILYN, federal agency administrator; b. Md. B in Bus. Mgmt., Pers. and Labor Rels. magna cum laude, U. Md., 1990; M in Applied Mgmt., U. Coll. Md., 1997. Pers. staffing specialist U.S. Office Pers. Mgmt., Washington, 1990; mgmt. analyst U.S. Census Bur., chief corr. mgmt./info. mgmt. staff Policy Office, 1998, chief corr. quality assurance; exec. secretariat records mgmt. divsn. FBI, Washington, 2002—. With D.C. Air Nat. Guard, 1986—95. Office: FBI J Edgar Hoover Bldg 935 Pennsylvania Ave NW Washington DC 20535

MOORE, MARK HARRISON, criminal justice and public policy educator; b. Oak Park, Ill., Mar. 19, 1947; s. Charles Eugene and Jean (McFeely) M.; m. Martha Mansfield Church, June 15, 1968; children— Phoebe Sylvina, Tobias McFeely, Gaylen Williams. Student, Phillips Acad., 1962-65; BA, Yale U., 1969; M.Public Policy, Harvard U., 1971, PhD, 1973. Teaching fellow, instr. public policy J.F. Kennedy Sch. Govt., Harvard U., Boston, 1971-73, asst. prof., 1973-74, 75-76, assoc. prof., 1976-79, Guggenheim prof. criminal justice policy and mgmt., 1979—; dir. Hauser Ctr. Non-Profit Orgns. Harvard U., 1998—. Spl. asst. to adminstr., chief planning officer Drug Enforcement Adminstrn., U.S. Dept. Justice, Washington, 1974-75; cons. U.S. Dept. Justice, 1975-76, 81 Author: Buy and Bust: The Effective Regulation of an Illicit Market in Heroin, 1977, Creating Public Value: Strategic Management in Government, 1995, (with others) Dangerous Offenders, 1985, From Children to Citizens: Vol. 1, The Mandate for Juvenile Justice, 1987, (with Malcolm K. Sparrow) Ethics in Government, 1990, (with Malcolm K. Sparrow and David Kennedy) Beyond 911: A New Era for Policing, 1991; editor: (with Joel Fleishman and Lance Leibman) Public Duties, 1980, (with Dean Gerstein) Alcohol and Public Policy, 1981. Dir. Hauser Ctr. for Non Profit Orgns. Mem. Assn. Schs. Public Policy and Mgmt., Phi Beta Kappa Home: 331 Waverley St Belmont MA 02478-2418 Office: JF Kennedy Sch Govt Harvard U 79 Jfk St Cambridge MA 02138-5801 Office Phone: 617-795-1113. Business E-Mail: mark_moore@harvard.edu.

MOORE, MARK TOBIN, art educator, artist, retired museum curator; b. Washington, Jan. 19, 1954; s. Selden George and Dorothy May (Tobin) M.; m. Denise Annette Poole, Oct. 20, 1987 (div. Jan. 1995); 1 child, James Tobin. BA in Art, U. Charleston, 1983; MA in Art, Marshall U., 1985; MFA in Painting, W.Va. U., 2000. Art instr. Ohio U., Ironton, Ohio, 1985-87, Ashland (Ky.) C.C., 1985-87, U. Charleston, W.Va., 1985-87; art specialist U.S. Army Europe/Giessen Arts and Crafts, 1987-91; exhibits coord. W.Va. State Mus., Charleston, 1992-93, exhibits dir., 1993-98; grad. tchg. asst. art dept. W.Va. U., Morgantown, 1999-2000, vis. adj. prof., 2001; asst. prof. art W. Va. State Coll., Institute, 2001—04. Art instr. U. Charleston, 1995-98, W.Va. State Coll. Inst., 1995-98; adj. instr. art dept. Marshall U., Huntington, W.Va., 1998; gallery adv. bd. U. Charleston, 1997; judge various art shows. One-man shows include Sunrise Art Mus., 1996, Sleeth Gallery, W.Va. Wesleyan Coll., 1995, Perspective Galerie, Giessen, 1990, Alderson-Broadus Coll., Phillipi, W.Va., 2001, Cultural Ctr. of Fine Arts, Parkersburg, W.Va., 2002, Hurricane, W.Va., 2002, Robert C. Byrd Fed. Courthouse, Charleston, 2004; group shows include Salon of French and Allied Forces, Palace of Luxemburg, Paris, Ariel Gallery, NYC, 1989, Huntington (W.Va.) Mus. Art, 1992, 94, 97, Gov.'s Mansion W.Va., 1997, Omaha Ctr. for Contemporary Art, 1999, Dairy Barn Cultural Arts Ctr., Athens, Ohio, 2000, 04, Paul Mesaros Gallery, W.Va. U., Morgantown, 2000, OCAF, Athens, Ga., 2002-03 (2d pl. merit award 2002), W.Va. State Mus., 2002-03, Beckley, W.Va., 2002, Avampato Discovery Mus., Clay Ctr., Charleston, W.Va., 2003-04, Fayetteville (NC) State U. Rosenthal Art Gallery, 2003; exhibitions include Cultural Ctr. Fine Arts, Parkersburg, W.Va., 2004, Dairy Barn, 2004, OCAF, Athens, Ga., 2004 With USN, 1972-83. Recipient Arthur Carpenter award for excellence in art, 1985, Merit award Nat. Collage Soc., Cleve., 1998, award of excellence Allied Artists W.Va., Sunrise Mus., Charleston, 1998; WVa./NEA profl. devel. grantee, 2003—. Home: 1210 Dudley Rd Charleston WV 25314 Studio: Blue Door Studios 223 1/2 Hale St Charleston WV 25314 Office Phone: 304-343-6750. Personal E-mail: tobinmrs@aol.com.

MOORE, MARSHA LYNN, retired elementary school educator, counseling administrator; b. Washington, May 19, 1946; d. Marshall Alexander and Doris Virginia (Diggs) Moore. BA, Howard U., 1967; MEd, U. Md., 1973. Sch. counseling K-12, cert. tchr. grades 1-6, sci. resource tchr. grades 1-6. 1st grade demonstration tchr. Anne M. Goding Sch. D.C. Pub. Schs., 1967—72; counselor Balt. County Schs., Towson, Md., 1972—77; fashion coord., mgr. Wallach's Ladies' Store, Nanuet, NY and Livingston, NJ, 1977—80; adult edn. cons., counselor East Orange (N.J.) Adult High Sch., 1980—83; coord. lang. arts Faith Hope Christian Sch., 1983—84; minority counselor Essex County C.C., Newark, 1984—85; equal opportunity fund counselor, instr. Kean Coll., Union, NJ, 1985—87; tchr. 5th grade Randle Highlands Elem. Sch., 1987—90; tchr. 5th and 6th grade Brookland Sch., Washington, 1990—98; 5th grade tchr., math. and sci. resource tchr. Shepherd Elem. Sch., Washington, 1998—2000; tchr. 6th grade math and sci. Bertie Backus Mid. Sch., Washington, 2002—03; ret., 2003. Coord. counselor Summer Youth Program, East Orange, 1982; career fair coord. East Orange Adult H.S., 1981, Essex County C.C., 1985; mem. discipline com. PTA Shepherd Sch., Washington, 1998—2002; liaison, exec. bd., hospitality com., multicultural com. PTA, 2000—02; math.-a-thon coord. St. Jude's, 2000, coord. parent math. workshop, 2000—02, sci. resource tchr., United States, 2000—02; coord. Sci. Careers Expo and 1st Sci. Bee, 2001; co-sponsor Student Coun., 2001—02; facilitator DCACTS, 2001—02; math. tutor, 2000—01; sgt.-at-arms WT Union Sch. Orgn., 2002—03. Editor: Sci. newsletter. Chmn. Teen Lift, NJ, Delteens, Washington; 2d v.p. Washington Pan-Hellenic Coun., 1994—96, fin. sec., 1996—98, co-chair Greek Forum, 1996—98; mentor Best Friends, Inc. Mem.: NAACP, AFT, Nat. Mid. Sch. Assn., Nat. Sci. Tchrs. Assn., Washington Tchrs. Union, U.S. Tennis Assn., Howard U. Alumni Assn. (reunion planning com. 1967, N.J. coord. 1980—87, v.p. Washington 1989—91, pres. 1991—93, parliamentarian Washington chpt. 1999—2001, chairperson membership com. Wash. chpt. 2003—, life mem. Washington chpt.), Schomburg Rsch. Ctr. (N.Y.C.), Kennedy Ctr. for Performing Arts, Friends of Andrew Rankin Chapel (adj. sec. 1994—97, newsletter co-chair, fundraising and archives coms.), Delta Sigma Theta (Diamond Life mem.). Episcopalian. Avocations: tennis, gardening, landscape designing, swimming, travel.

MOORE, SISTER MARY FRANCIS, parochial school educator; b. Bklyn., Aug. 17, 1928; d. Daniel and Mary Frances (Downing) M. B in Social Studies, St. Francis Coll., Bklyn., 1971; M in Elem. Edn., L.I. U., Bklyn., 1976; cert. in adminstrn. and supervision, Manhattan Coll., Riverdale, N.Y., 1988. Joined Sisters of Mercy, Roman Cath. Ch., 1957. Acct. N.Y. Tel. Co., Bklyn., 1945-57; tchr. 2nd grade St. Mary's Sch., Roslyn Heights, N.Y., 1960-62; tchr. 1st grade St. Brigid's Sch., Bklyn., 1962-68; tchr. 2nd and 6th grades St. Jerome's Sch., Bklyn., 1968-74; tchr. 3rd grade St. Bernard's Sch., Bklyn., 1974-81, tchr., prin., 1981-82, prin., 1982-85; tchr. 1st grade Maria Regina Sch., Seaford, 1985—2002. Cooperating tchr. for tchr. tng. program St. Joseph's Coll., Brentwood, L.I., N.Y., 1968-70. Recipient Appreciation award Bergen Beach Civic Assn., Bklyn., 1985, The Thomas Cuite Meml. award Ancient Order of Hibernians, 1993. Mem. Nat. Cath. Edn. Assn. (tchr. assoc.). Roman Catholic. Avocations: reading, walking, baseball, movies, enjoying friends. Office: Maria Regina Sch 4045 Jerusalem Ave Seaford NY 11783-1627

MOORE, MARY FRENCH (MUFFY MOORE), potter, advocate; d. John and Rhoda French; m. Alan Baird Minier, 1982; children: Jonathan Corbet, Jennifer Corbet, Michael Corbet. BA cum laude, Colo. U., 1964. Ceramics mfg., Wilson, Wyo., 1969-82, Cheyenne, Wyo., 1982—. Commr. County Teton (Wyo.), 1976-83, chmn. bd. commrs., 1981, 83, mem. dept. pub. assistance and social svc., 1976-82, mem. recreation bd., 1978-81, water quality adv. bd., 1976-82. Bd. dirs. Teton Sci. Sch., 1968-83, vice chmn., 1979-81, chmn., 1982; bd. dirs. Grand Teton Music Festival, 1963-68, Teton Energy Coun., 1978-83, Whitney Gallery of Western Art, Cody, Wyo., 1995—, Opera Colo., 1998—; mem. water quality adv. bd. Wyo. Dept. Environ. Quality, 1979-83; Dem. precinct committeewoman, 1978-81; mem. Wyo. Dem. Ctrl. Com., 1981-83; vice chmn. Laramie County Dem. Ctrl. Com., 1983-84, Wyo. Dem. nat. committeewoman, 1984-87; chmn. Wyo. Dem. Party, 1987-89; del. Dem. Nat. Conv., 1984, 88, mem. fairness commn. Dem. Nat. Com., 1985, vice-chairwoman western caucus, 1986-89; chmn. platform com. Wyo. Dem. Conv., 1982; mem. Wyo. Dept. Environ. Quality Land Quality Adv. Bd., 1983-86; mem. Gov.'s Steering Com. on Troubled Youth, 1982, dem. nat. com. Compliance Assistance Commn., 1986-87; exec. com. Assn. of State Dem. Chairs, 1989; mem. Wyo. Coun. on the Arts, 1989-95, chmn., 1994-95, Dem. Nat. Com. Jud. Coun., 1989—; legis. aide for Gov. Wyo., 1985, 86; project coord. Gov.'s Com. on Childrens' Svcs., 1985-86; bd. dirs. Wyo. Outdoor Coun., 1984-85; polit. dir., dep. mgr. Schuster for Congress, 1994-95; adminstrv. dir. Freudenthal for Gov., 2002, personnel coord., 2002; mem. pres.' adv. com. on the performing arts John F. Kennedy Ctr. for the Performing Arts, 1999-2001. Recipient Woman of Yr. award Jackson Hole Bus. and Profl. Women, 1981, Dem. of Yr. Nellie Tayloe Ross award Wyo. Dems., 1990. Mem. Alden Kindred of Am., Jackson Hole Art Assn. (bd. dirs., vice chmn. 1981, chmn. 1982), Assn. State Dem. Chairs, Soc. Mayflower Descendents, Pi Sigma Alpha. Home: 8907 Cowpoke Rd Cheyenne WY 82009-1234 E-mail: muffy.moore@bresnan.net.

MOORE, MARY TYLER, actress; b. Bklyn., Dec. 29, 1936; d. George and Marjorie Moore; m. Richard Meeker, 1955 (div. 1961); 1 child, Richard (dec.); m. Grant Tinker, 1963 (div. 1981); m. Robert Levine, 1983. Chmn. bd. MTM Enterprises, Inc., Studio City, Calif. Stage appearances include (Broadway debut) Breakfast at Tiffany's, 1966, Whose Life Is It, Anyway?, 1980, Sweet Sue, 1988, The Players Club Centennial Salute, 1989, Rose's Dilemma, 2003; appeared in TV series Richard Diamond, Private Eye, 1957-59, Dick Van Dyke Show, 1961-66, Mary Tyler Moore Show, 1970-77, Mary, 1978, Mary Tyler Moore Hour, 1979, Mary, 1985, Annie McGuire, 1988, New York News, 1995, Mary and Rhoda, 1998; miniseries Gore Vidal's Lincoln, 1988, New York News, 1995; in TV movies Love American Style, 1969, Run a Crooked Mile, 1969, First You Cry, 1978, Heartsounds, 1984, Finnegan Begin Again, 1984, The Last Best Year, 1990, Thanksgiving Day, 1990, Stolen Babies, 1993 (Emmy award, Outstanding Supporting Actress in a Miniseries or Special, 1993), Payback, 1997, Mary and Rhoda, 2000, Like Mother, Like Son: The Strange Story of Sante and Kenny Kimes, 2001, Miss Lettie & Me, 2002, The Gin Game, 2003, Blessings, 2003; films: X-15, 1961, Thoroughly Modern Millie, 1967, Don't Just Stand There, 1968, What's So Bad About Feeling Good?, 1968, Change of Habit, 1969, Ordinary People, 1980 (Acad. Award nominee for best actress 1981), Six Weeks, 1982, Just Between Friends, 1986, Keys to Tulsa, 1996, Flirting with Disaster, 1996, Reno Finds Her Mom, 1997, Labor Pains, 1999; appeared on Broadway in Whose Life Is It Anyway?, 1980, Sweet Sue, 1987, Labor Pains, 2000, Cheats, 2002; in TV spl. How to Survive the Seventies, 1978, How To Raise a Drug Free Child; author: After All, 1995. Chair Juvenile Diabetes Found., 1985—. Recipient Emmy award Nat. Acad. TV Arts and Scis. 1964-65, 73-74, 76, Golden Globe award 1965, 81, Star on the Hollywood Walk of Fame, 1992; named to TV Hall of Fame, 1985. Office: William Morris Agy care Betsy Berg 151 S El Camino Dr Beverly Hills CA 90212-2775*

MOORE, MATTHEW SCOTT, publisher, deaf advocate, author; b. Indpls., Dec. 31, 1958; s. Scott Moore and JoNelle (Painter) Giegerich. BA in Social Work, Rochester Inst. Tech., 1983. Founder, pres. MSM Prodns., Ltd., Rochester, N.Y., 1984—; pub., co-editor-in-chief Deaf Life, Rochester, 1986—. Flying Words Project, Rochester, 1989—; lectr., spkr. in field; organizer confs. Co-author: For Hearing People Only, 1992, Great Deaf Americans, 2nd edit., 1996; launched several websites; lectr., spkr. in field; conf. organizer. Founder Deaf Rochesterians' Cmty. Ctr. Core Team, 1992; chmn. Third N.Y. State Conf. for Sign-Lang. Instrs., Rochester, 1992; coord. Am. Sign-Lang. Tchrs. Assn. 1st Nat. Profl. Devel. Conf., Rochester, N.Y., 1999. Recipient Recognition cert. World Recreation Assn. of Deaf, 1990, Humanitarian award Delta Sigma Phi, 1991, Pres. award Am. Sign Lang. Tchrs. Assn. Lilac chpt., 1993, Outstanding Alumni award NTID, 1993, Tex. Deaf Caucus award, 1993, Alice Cogswell award Gallaudet U., 1994, Printing Week award, 1995, Disting. Alumni Modern Era award Ind. Sch. Deaf, 1997, Georgianna Elliott award Dallas Deaf Celebration, 1998. Avocations: writing, performing, theater, collecting birdhouses. Office: MSM Prodns Ltd PO Box 23380 Rochester NY 14692-3380

MOORE, MCPHERSON DORSETT, lawyer; b. Pine Bluff, Ark., Mar. 1, 1947; s. Arl Van and Jesse (Dorsett) M. BS, U. Miss., 1970; JD, U. Ark., 1974. Bar: Ark. 1974, Mo. 1975, U.S. Patent and Trademark Office 1977, U.S. Dist. Ct. (ea. dist.) Mo. 1977, U.S. Ct. Appeals (8th, 10th and fed. cirs.). Design engr. Tenneco, Newport News, Va., 1970-71; assoc. Rogers, Eilers & Howell, St. Louis, 1974-80; ptnr. Rogers, Howell, Moore & Haferkamp, St. Louis, 1981-89, Armstrong, Teasdale, Schlafly & Davis, St. Louis, 1989-95, Polster, Lieder, Woodruff & Lucchesi, St. Louis, 1995—. Engr. City of Ladue, Mo., 1998-2000. Bd. dirs. Legal Svcs. Ea. Mo.; mem. Ladue Zoning and Planning Commn., 1998—. With USAR, 1970-76. Mem. ABA, Bar Assn. Met. St. Louis (chmn. young lawyers sect. 1981-82, sec. 1984-85, v.p. 1985-86, chmn. trial sect. 1986-87, pres. 1988-89), Ark. Bar Assn., St. Louis Bar Found. (sec. 1984-85, v.p. 1988-89, pres. 1989-90), The Mo. Bar (chmn. patent, trademark and copyright law com. 1992-94, co-chmn. 1994-95), St. Louis County Bar Assn., Women Lawyers Assn., Am. Intellectual Property Law Assn., Mound City Bar Assn., Phi Delta Theta Alumni (treas. St. Louis chpt. 1987-88, sec. 1988-89, v.p. 1989-90), Racquet Club (St. Louis). Home: 33 Deerfield Rd Saint Louis MO 63124-1412 Office: Polster Lieder Woodruff & Lucchesi 12412 Powers Ct Dr Saint Louis MO 63131-3615 Office Phone: 314-238-2400.

MOORE, MECHLIN DONGAN, communications executive, marketing consultant; b. N.Y.C., May 21, 1930; s. Albere Ethier and Pamela (Robinson) M.; m. Elizabeth Ann Tonkin, Feb. 11, 1956 (dec. 1992); children: Lansing, Pamela; m. Valery Ann Shields, July 14, 1995. AB, Harvard U., 1952. Reporter Washington Post, 1955-59; dir. build Am. better com. Nat. Assn. Real Estate Bds., D.C., 1960-64; dir. info. Urban Land Inst., D.C., 1964-66; exec. v.p. Ctrl. Assn. Seattle, 1966-70; asst. to pres. United Airlines, Inc., Chgo., 1971-72, sr. v.p. external affairs, 1972-74, group v.p. mktg., 1975-76, sr. v.p. pub. affairs, 1976-79; pres. Ins. Info. Inst., N.Y.C., 1979-91; chmn., CEO Informatrix Worldwide SuperSite Devel., 1996-98; pvt. practice Naples, Fla., 1991—; advisor Vertical Net, Inc., 1998-2001; project planning dir. Fla. Gulf Coast Univ. Found., 2004—. Pres. Eagles Mere Water Co., 1993-96; bd. electors Ins. Hall of Fame; bd. govs. Internat. Ins. Seminars. Contbg. author publs. Nat. Assn. Real Estate Bds.; assoc. editor Jour. Property Mgmt. Adv. bd. mem. Traffic Inst. Northwestern U.; past mem. St. George's Vestry, N.Y.C. 1st lt. U.S. Army, 1952-54. Recipient Commendation Ribbon with Metal Pendant U.S. Army, 1954, Disting. Svc. award Central Assn. Seattle, 1972 Mem. Univ. Club, Pelican Marsh Golf Club, Shenorock Shore Club. Republican. Episcopalian. Home: 8711 Spikerush Ln Naples FL 34109 Fax: 941-594-8575. Office Phone: 239-777-1595. E-mail: mmoore7412@aol.com.

MOORE, MELINDA, public health physician; MD, MPH, Harvard U., 1975. Diplomate Am. Bd. Pediat., Am. Bd. Preventive Medicine. With divsn. viral diseases Ctr. Disease Control, Atlanta, 1978-80, with divsn. nutrition, 1980-81, dep. dir. internat. health program office, 1991-96; assoc. dir. Global Health Ctr. Disease Control, Nat. Ctr. Environ. Health, Atlanta, 1998-2000; dep. dir. DHHS Office Global Health Affairs, Rockville, Md., 2000—. Cons. Africa Child Survival Project, Atlanta and Zaire, 1982-87, Zaire SPH, 1987-89, Ctr. for Disease Control HIV Policy Office, 1989-91; acting assoc. dir. Global Health, 1996-97. Office: DHHS Office Global Health Affairs Parklawn Bldg 5600 Fishers Ln Rm 18-105 Rockville MD 20857 E-mail: mmoore@osophs.dhhs.gov., Melinda.Moore@hhs.gov.

MOORE, MICHAEL, film director, writer; b. Flint, Mich., Apr. 23, 1954; m. Kathleen Glynn; 1 child. Actor, dir., prodr. (documentary) Roger & Me, 1989 (Ten Best Films of Yr. list), Bowling for Columbine, 2002 (Academy award Best Documentary Feature, 2003); actor, dir. prodr., writer Canadian Bacon, 1994, Fahrenheit 9/11, 2004 (Palme d'Or, Cannes Film Festival, 2004); dir., creator, host TV Nation, 1994-1995 (Outstanding Informational Series Emmy award, 1995); dir.: (films) Two Mikes Don't Make a Wright, 1992, The Big One, 1997, (TV) The Awful Truth, 1999; former editor Flint Voice newspaper; author: Downsize This! Random Threats from Unarmed America, 1996, Adventures in a TV Nation, 1998, Stupid White Men and Other Sorry Excuses for the State of the Nation!, 2002, Dude, Where's My Country?, 2003. Office: Creative Artists Agy c/o David Tenzer 9830 Wilshire Blvd Beverly Hills CA 90212-1804*

MOORE, MICHAEL WATSON, musician, educator; b. Cin., May 16, 1945; s. Clarence Watson and Jeannette Elizabeth (Gardner) M.; m. Renee Allyn White, Oct. 23, 1993; children: Benjamin Butler, Matthew Satyavan. Attended, Cin. Coll. Conservatory of Music, 1964-65. Bass instr. Summer Stage Bank Clinic, 1969, Eastman Sch. of Music, Rochester, N.Y., 1974-87, U. Bridgeport, Bridgeport, Conn., 1981-83, L.I. U., Bklyn., 1993-96, William Patterson U., Wayne, N.J., 1994-95. String bass player with Cal Collins Trio, Cin., 1965, Woody Evans Trio, Cin., 1965, Woody Herman Band, USO, Africa, Ea. Europe, 1966-67, Marion McPartland Trio, N.Y.C., 1968, Freddie Hubbard Quintet, N.Y.C., 1969-70, Jack Wilkins Trio, N.Y.C., 1971, Chet Baker Quartet, N.Y.C., 1972-73, Phil Woods Quartet, N.Y.C., 1972, Gene Bertoncini Duo, N.Y.C., 1972—, Stan Getz Quartet, N.Y.C., 1973, Tony Bennett, N.Y.C., 1973, Ruby Braff, George Barnes Quartet, N.Y.C., 1973-75, Gerry Mulligan Quartet, N.Y.C., 1974, Benny Goodman Sextet, N.Y.C., 1974-76, Lee Konitz Quartet, N.Y.C., 1975, Teddy Wilson Duo, N.Y.C., 1977, Jim Hall Trio, N.Y.C., 1977, Bill Evans Trio, N.Y.C., 1978, Bob Brookmeyer Quintet, N.Y.C., 1978, Mike Abene, Michael Moore Quintet, N.Y.C., 1978, Zoot Sims Quartet, N.Y.C., 1979, Gary Burton Quartet, N.Y.C., 1981-82, Louis Belson Quartet, N.Y.C., 1982, Roger Kellaway Duo and Trio, N.Y.C., 1980s, Jimmy Rowles Duo, N.Y.C., 1980s, Jon Scoffield Duo and Quartet, N.Y.C., 1980s, Lew Tabackin Trio, N.Y.C., 1980s, Hank Jones Trio, N.Y.C., 1980s, Shelly Mann Trio, N.Y.C., 1980s, Pepper Adams Quartet, N.Y.C., 1980s, Lou Levy Duo, N.Y.C., 1980s, Al Cohen Trio, N.Y.C., 1980s, Jake Hanna Quartet, N.Y.C., 1980s, Rosemary Clooney, N.Y.C., 1987-88, Louis Stewart Trio, Ireland and U.K., 1990, Howard Alden Trio, N.Y.C., 1990s, Warren Vache Trio, N.Y.C., 1990s, Harry Allen Trio, N.Y.C., 1990s, Ken Peplowski Trio, N.Y.C., 1990s, Charlie Byrd Quartet, N.Y.C., 1990s, Dave Brubeck Quartet, 2001—; co-leader duo with Rufus Reid, 1995, with Chris Potter, 1995; leader duo with Bill Charlap, 1995; tour Japan with Harry Allen, 1997; leader trio with Ken Peplowski and Tom Melito, 1998-, Dave Brubeck Quartet, 2001—; composer: Rio Pindare, 1986, Wake Me When It's Over, 1988, The Lilter, 1989, The Old New Waltz, 1992, Zoot's Suite, 1995, Just Me, Just Me, 1995, When I Wage Battle Next, 1999, Moon Dog, 1999; recs. Michael Moore Trio Plays Gershwin, 1993, Michael Moore/Bill Charlap, 1995 (One of the Best Jazz CDs of 95, The New Yorker, 1996), Michael Moore/Rufus Reid Doublebass Delights, 1996 (One of the Best Jazz CDs of 96, The New Yorker, 1997), Michael Moore/Rufus Reid The Intimacy of the Bass, 1999, Michael Moore and His Trio The History of Jazz: Vol. 1, 2000, The Michael Moore Trio The History of Jazz Vol. 2 Dedication, 2002 (One of Best Jazz CDs of 2002, The New Yorker), Video with Rufus Reid, 1998; author: Melodic Improvising in the Thumb Position: Method for Improvisation for the String Bass, 1986, (with Clem Derosa) The Michael Moore Bass Method, 2002; performer: (with Weslia Whitfield) The White House, 1996. Councilman Borough of Bangor, Pa., 1987-88. Mem. ASCAP. Avocation: piano. Home and Office: 5 E 22d St Apt 15M New York NY 10010-5325

MOORE, MIKE, former state attorney general; m. Tisha Moore; 1 child, Kyle. Grad., Jackson County Jr. Coll., 1972; BA, U. Miss., 1974, JD, 1976. Asst. dist. atty. State of Miss., 1977—78, dist. atty., 1979, atty. gen., 1988—2003; atty. Phelps Dunbar, 2004—. Democrat. Office: Phelps Dunbar 111 East Capitol St Ste 600 Jackson MS 39201 Office Phone: 601-352-2300. Office Fax: 601-360-9777.

MOORE, MILES DAVID, journalist; b. Lancaster, Ohio, Mar. 8, 1955; s. Russell Emerson and Dorothy Louise (Camp) Moore. BS in Journalism, Ohio U., 1977. Asst. editor Rubber and Plastics News, Akron, Ohio, 1977-80; Washington reporter Rubber and Plastics News/Tire Bus., Washington, 1980—. Bd. dirs. Word Works, adminstr. Washington prize, 1995—. Co-editor: Winners: A Retrospective of the Washington Prize, 1999—; editor: The Federal Poets, 1992—95; author: The Bears of Paris, 1995, Buddha Isn't Laughing, 1999, Fatslug Unbound, 2000, Rollercoaster, 2004. Recipient Sidney Sulkin prize, Poet Lore, 1998, Poetry prize, Potomac Rev., 1996, Rose Lefcowitz prize, Poet Lore, 1994, Crain award, Crain Comm., Inc., 1991, 2000. Mem.: Fed. Poets, Writer's Ctr., Nat. Press Club. Lutheran. Avocations: reading, walking, theater, movies. Office: Crain Comms Inc 814 National Press Building Washington DC 20045-1801

MOORE, MILO ANDERSON, banker; b. Orange, N.J., Aug. 26, 1942; s. Milo H. and Helen (Wiley) M.; m. Judith J. Colosimo, May 4, 1968; children: Milo Robert, Matthew Wiley, Marykate Bartlett. BS, Ithaca Coll., 1964; MBA, Rutgers U., 1971. Traffic supt. N.Y. Tel. Co., N.Y.C., 1964-71; trust officer Midlantic Nat. Bank, Newark, 1971-76; v.p. Shearson Loeb Rhoades, N.Y.C., 1976-80; sr. v.p. Donaldson Lufkin & Jenrette, N.Y.C., 1980-85; sr. mng. dir. Bear, Stearns & Co., 1985-92; v.p. JP Morgan Pvt. Bank, Morristown, N.J.,

1992—. Advisor Jr. Achievement, Bronx, N.Y., 1967-68; pres. Chatham Jaycees, N.J., 1974; big bros. Morris County Big Bros., Morristown, 1971-81; pres. Stanley Congl. Ch., Chatham, N.J., 1995-97; trustee SAGE Solutions, 1994—, pres., 2002. Mem. Securities Industry Assn. (tax shelter com. 1982-85), Glenburnie Club (pres. 1989—), Canoe Brook Country Club (Summit, N.J.), Beta Gamma Sigma. Office: JP Morgan Chase Pvt Banking 225 South St Morristown NJ 07960-5336 Office Phone: 973-285-2256. E-mail: milo.moore@jpmorgan.com.

MOORE, MINVON, political organization worker; b. Chgo. Attended, U. Ill., Chgo. With Nat. Rainbow Coalition/DNC Voter Project, numerous presdl. campaigns; dep. asst. to Pres. and dep. dir. polit. affairs, 1997—98; asst. to Pres. Bill Clinton and dir. pub. liaison at White House, 1998—2001; COO Dem. Nat. Com. (DNC), 2001—02; co-founder Am. Coming Together, 2003—; prin. Dewey Square Group, 2002—; strategist, sr. advisor to DNC chmn. Terry McAuliffe, 2002—. Named one of 100 Most Powerful Women in Wash., Washingtonian mag., 2001. Office: Dewey Square Group 1001 G St NW Ste 300E Washington DC 20001 Office Phone: 202-638-5616. Office Fax: 202-638-5612. Business E-Mail: mmoore@deweysquare.com.

MOORE, NORMA JEAN, real estate broker; b. Keota, Iowa, Mar. 23, 1935; d. George E. and Eula Margaret (Martin) Dillon; m. Gordon George Moore, Sept. 1, 1956; children: Steven, Ronald, Cynthia Wojcik. BS, Iowa State U., 1957. Tchr. N. Haven H.S., North Haven, Conn., 1957-60, Hicksville (N.Y.) Jr. High, 1960-61; real estate assoc. Brucker Real Estate, Hatboro, Pa., 1978-82; assoc. broker Prudential Felte Real Estate, Willow Grove, Pa., 1982—. Mem. Ea. Montgomory County Bd. of Realtors, Pa. Assoc. of Realtors, Nat. Assoc. of Realtors. Presbyterian. Avocations: sewing, cooking, investing. Home: 163 Greyhorse Rd Willow Grove PA 19090-1646 E-mail: resold@comcast.net.

MOORE, OLIVER SEMON, III, publishing executive, consultant; b. Jersey City, July 26, 1942, s. Oliver S. and Ann Loy (Spics) M.; m. Dina Downing DuBois, Feb. 23, 1961 (div. 1974); 1 child, Deborah; m. Christine Laine Meyers, May 12, 1990; 1 child, Kathryn Laine. BA, U. Va., 1964. Chief bur. Richmond (Va.) Times-Dispatch, 1964-66; corr. Time mag., N.Y.C., 1966-67, contbg. editor, 1967-68; assoc. editor Newsweek, N.Y.C., 1969-71; freelance writer, 1972-75; mng. editor Motor Boating and Sailing, N.Y.C., 1976-78, editor, 1980-82; exec. editor US Mag., N.Y. Times Co., 1978-80; dep. editor Town & Country Mag., N.Y.C., 1982-84; editor Sci. Digest Mag., N.Y.C., 1984-86; pub. dir. Yachting Mag., N.Y.C., 1986-95; editorial dir. Outdoor Life, N.Y.C., 1993-95; v.p. The Outdoor Co., N.Y.C., 1994-95; editor-at-large Motor Boating & Sailing, 1995—2001; pres. Alamo Pub. Svcs., Inc., Detroit, 1995—. Co-founder, chmn. bd. Corp! (Mag.), 1998. Author: (poems) Voices International, 1969; contbg. editor Sports Afield, 1996—; photographer (mags.) Motor Boating and Sailing, Yachting, Working Woman, (books) Lines to a Little Girl, Rancho Paradiso. Recipient Merit award Art Dirs. Club, 1981, award of merit Soc. Publ. Designers, 1981, Excellence in Media award Nat. Arbor Day Found., 1985. Mem. Am. Soc. Mag. Editors, Mag. Pubs. Assn. (nat. mag. award 1995), N.Y. Yacht Club, Grosse Pointe (Mich.) Club, Bayview (Mich.) Yacht Club, The Huntsman (Mich.), Wyndeme Club (Fla.). Republican. Episcopalian. Avocations: sailing, antique cars. Office: Corp! 3645 Crooks Rd Troy MI 48084-1642

MOORE, OMAR KHAYYAM, experimental sociologist; b. Helper, Utah, Feb. 11, 1920; s. John Gustav and Mary Jo (Crowley) M.; m. Ruth Garnand, Nov. 19, 1942; 1 child, Venn. BA, Doane Coll., 1942; MA, Washington U., St. Louis, 1946, PhD, 1949. Instr. Washington U., St. Louis, 1949-52; teaching assoc. Northwestern U., Evanston, Ill., 1950-51; rsch. asst., prof. sociology Tufts Coll., Medford, Mass., 1952-53; researcher Naval Rsch. Lab., Washington, 1953-54; asst. prof. sociology Yale U., New Haven, 1954-57, assoc. prof. sociology, 1957-63; prof. psychology Rutgers U., New Brunswick, N.J., 1963-65; prof. social psychology, sociology U. Pitts., 1965-71, prof. sociology, 1971-89, prof. emeritus, 1989—; scholar-in-residence Nat. Learning Ctr.'s Capital Children's Mus., Washington, 1989-90. Pres. Responsive Environ. Found., Inc., Estes Park, Colo., 1962—; assessor of rsch. projects The Social Scis. and Humanities Rsch. Coun. Can., 1982—; adj. prof. U. Colo., Boulder, 1992—. Contbg. editor Educational Technology; contbr. numerous articles to profl. jours.; patentee in field; motion picture producer and director. Recipient Award The Nat. Soc. for Programmed Instruction, 1965, Award Doane Coll Builder Award, 1967, Ednl. Award Urban Youth Action, Inc., 1969, Award House of Culture, 1975, Cert. of Appreciation, 1986, Cert. of Appreciation D.C. Pub. Schs., 1987, da Vinci Award Inst. for the Achievement of Human Potential, 1988, Cert. of Appreciation Capital Children's Museum, 1988, award Jack & Jill of America Found., 1988, Cert. of Appreciation U.S. Dept. of Edn., 1988, Cert. of Appreciation D.C. Pub. Schs., 1990, Person of Yr. in Ednl. Tech. award Ednl. Tech. mag., 1990. Mem. AAAS, Am. Math. Soc., Am. Psychol. Assn., Internat. Sociol. Assn., Am. Sociol. Assn., Assn. for Symbolic Logic, Assn. for Anthrop. Study of Play, Philosophy Sci. Assn., Psychonomics Soc., Soc. for Applied Sociology, Soc. for Exact Philosophy, Math. Assn. Am. Republican. Avocation: mountain climbing. Home and Office: 1420 Centre Ave Apt 502 Pittsburgh PA 15219-3521 E-mail: vm15219@aol.com.

MOORE, PAMELA RAE, elementary school educator; b. Paulding, Ohio, Feb. 22, 1959; d. Loren J. and Louella I. Thomas; m. Chet Moore, Dec. 10, 1977; children: Amy Renae, Cheryl Kae. BS, Defiance Coll., 1990; MS, St. Francis U., 1995. H.s. learning disabilities tchr., Paulding, 1991—99; mid. sch. reading tchr., 1999—. Home: 819 E Wayne St Paulding OH 45879

MOORE, PAT HOWARD, engineering and construction company executive; b. Laredo, Tex., Sept. 16, 1930; s. Howard Warren and Odette Evelyn (Bunn) M.; m. Elsie Mae Crossman, Mar. 23, 1954; children: Linda Marie Ford, Margaret Ann, Andrew Patrick. BA, Rice U., 1952, BS in Civil Engring., 1953; postgrad., Tulane U., 1956-58. Registered profl. engr., Tex., La. Spl. investigator Army Counter Intelligence Corps., Houston, 1954-56; div. engr. McDermott Inc., Morgan City, La., 1956-58; pres., dir. Navasota Tel. Co., Tex., 1958-63; project mgr. Brown & Root, Inc., Houston, 1963-67, exec. v.p., chief fin. officer, dir., 1990-95; pres., dir. Fluor Ocean Svcs., Houston, 1968-80; sr. v.p. Raymond Internat., Inc., Houston, 1980-86; pres., dir. Martin Moore Inc., Bellaire, Tex., 1986-90; dir. Charter Builders, Inc., Dallas, 1988-90; mgmt. cons. Bellaire, 1996—2003. Adv. dir. Tex. Commerce Bank, Houston, 1979-86; lectr. ethics Rice U., 1996-2003, adj. prof. Rice U., civil and environ. engring. 2003-; bd. dirs. XServ, Inc., Houston. Bd. govs. Rice U., 1984-88. With U.S. Army, 1954-56. Fellow ASCE; mem. Chi Epsilon, Kiwanis (pres. 1960). Home: 124 Chuckwagon Trail Georgetown TX 78628 Office: 124 Chuckwagon Trail Georgetown TX 78628

MOORE, PATRICIA ANN, medical technology investor, consultant; b. Huntington, N.Y., July 16, 1954; d. Joseph Nicholas and Dorothy Patricia (Olszewski) Mamola; m. William Martin Moore, Feb. 15, 1986; children: William Eric, Kyle Martin. BS, U. Santa Clara, 1976. Ops. mgr. Laguna Fed. Savs. & Loan, Orange, Calif., 1977-79; customer svc. rep. Bentley Labs., Irvine, Calif., 1979-80, mgr. custom products, 1980-82, internat. custom product specialist, 1981-82; dist. sales mgr. Am. Bentley Labs., San Francisco, 1982-83, Nellcor, Inc., San Francisco, 1983-84, product mgr. Hayward, Calif., 1984-85, nat. accounts mgr., 1986-88, internat. distbn. mgr., 1985-88; dir. internat. mktg. and sales NATUS Med., Inc., Foster City, Calif., 1989-92; mng. ptnr.seed investment proprietary med. tech. Alpine Ptnrs., Incline Village, 1992—; bd. dirs. Responsive Med. Applications, Incline Village, 1996—. Bd. dirs. Alpine Med. Concepts Incline Village. Designer, patent holder skin-mounted surg. drain holder "Comfort Hold", 1998. Avocations: bicycling, hiking, travel. Office: Alpine Ptnrs 153 Country Club Dr Ste 8 Incline Village NV 89451-9348

MOORE, PATRICK J. paper company executive; b. Sept. 7, 1954; Asst. treas. Jefferson Smurfit Corp., St. Louis, 1987-90, treas., 1990-93, v.p., treas., 1993-94; v.p., gen. mgr. Indsl. Packaging divsn. Indsl. Packaging divsn., St. Louis, 1994-96; v.p., CFO Jefferson Smurfit Corp., St. Louis, 1996—98, Smurfit-Stone Container Corp., Chgo., 1998—2002, pres., CEO, 2002—, chmn., 2003—. Office: Smurfit-Stone Container Corp 150 N Michigan Ave Chicago IL 60601-7568

MOORE, PATRICK S. epidemiologist, researcher, educator; m. Yuan Chang, 1989. MD, U. Utah. With field sta. Ctr. Disease Control and Prevention, Ft. Collins; dep. commr. health City N.Y., 1992; rschr. Columbia U. Sch. Pub. Health, 1993; prof. dept. molecular genetics and biochemistry U. Pitts. Sch. Medicine, 2002—; dir. molecular virology program U. Pitts. Cancer Inst., 2002—. Mem. editl. bd. Virus Rsch., Emerging Infectious Diseases and the Epstein-Barr Virus Report; contbr. articles and revs. in med. lit. Recipient Meyenburg Found. award cancer rsch., Robert Koch prize, N.Y.C. Mayor's award excellence in sci. and tech., Charles S. Mott prize, GM Cancer Rsch. Found., 2003. Achievements include discovery of and characterized the causative agent of Kaposi's Sarcoma-associated Herpes virus (KSHV) or human herpes virus 8 (HHV8), also is linked to other disorders that involve a compromised immune system. Office: U Pa Molecular Genetics and Biochemistry HCCLB 1 8 Pitts Pittsburgh PA 15122

MOORE, PATSY SITES, food service consultant; b. San Marcos, Tex., Mar. 29, 1939; d. Sam W. and Hilda (Wiede) Sites. BS in Home Econs. Edn., S.W. Tex. State U., 1970. Owner, operator Westover Kindergarten and Nursery Sch., San Marcos, 1965-68; food svc. dir. San Marcos Consol. Ind. Sch. Dist., 1975-97; cons. to food svc. industry, San Marcos, 1997—. Cons. in field., 1997—. Mem. steering com. Play Scape/Children's Park, San Marcos, 1992; mem. Hays County Pks. Adv. Bd., City of San Marco Sr. Citizens Adv. Coun.; sr. adv. bd. City of San Marcos, 2000—; adv. bd. Hays County Parks, 1998—; vice chmn. Hays Rep. Club, 2001-2002, sec., 2003. Mem. Am. Sch. Food Svc. Assn., Tex. Sch. Food Svc. Assn., Ctrl. Tex. Sch. Food Svc. Dirs. Assn. (founder, past pres.), Heritage Assn. (mem. bd. dirs. 2003-), Order Eastern Star, San Marcos Fedn. Rep. Women (pres.), Spring Lake Garden Club (sec. 1999, 2000, pres. 2002-03). Lutheran. Avocations: gardening, painting, lapadary. Home and Office: 285 Hilliard Rd San Marcos TX 78666-8905

MOORE, PEARL B. nursing educator; b. Pitts., Aug. 25, 1936; d. Hyman and Ethel (Antis) Friedman; 1 child, Cheryl. BS in Nursing, U. Pitts., 1968, M in Nursing, 1974. Staff nurse Allegheny Gen. Hosp., Pitts., 1957-60; instr. Liliane S. Kaufman Sch. Nursing, Pitts., 1960-70, asst. dir., 1970, dir., 1970-72; cancer nurse specialist Montefiore Hosp., Pitts., 1974-75; coord. Brain Tumor Study Group, Pitts., 1975-83; adj. asst. prof. U. Pitts., 1983—. Contbr. articles in field to profl. publs. Fellow Am. Acad. Nursing; mem. ANA, Oncology Nursing Soc. (exec. dir. 1983—, CEO 1999, Disting. Svc. award 1995), Am. Soc. Clin. Oncology, Am. Soc. Assn. Execs., Nurses Alumnae U. Pitts., Sigma Theta Tau. Home: 5701 Centre Ave Pittsburgh PA 15206 Office: 125 Enterprise Dr Pittsburgh PA 15275

MOORE, POWELL ALLEN, federal government official; b. Milledgeville, Ga., Jan. 5, 1938; s. Jere N. and Sarah (Allen) Moore; m. Pamla Hill Prochnow, Sept. 29, 2001; children: Frances Moore Preston, Powell Allen Jr. BA in Jounalism, U. Ga., 1959. Press sec. to Richard Russell, U.S. Senate, Washington, 1966-71; dep. dir. pub. info. Dept. Justice, Washington, 1971-72; dep. spl. asst. to Pres. for legis. affairs The White House, Washington, 1973-75, cons. pub. affairs, 1975-81, dep. asst. to Pres. for legis. affairs, 1981-82; asst. sec. for congl. rels. Dept. State, Washington, 1982-83; v.p. legis. affairs Lockheed Corp., Washington, 1983-85, Ginn, Edington, Moore and Wade, Washington, 1985-90; pres. ASL Internat., Washington, 1990-93; sr. prin., mng. dir. Capitoline, MS&L, Washington, 1993-98; chief of staff Office of Sen. Fred Thompson, Washington, 1998-2001; asst. secy. for legis. affairs U.S. Dept. Defense, Washington, 2001—. Dir. press Com. to Re-elect the Pres., Washington, 1972; cons. Pres. Ford Com., 1976, Reagan-Bush Com., 1980. Served to capt., inf. U.S. Army, 1959-62. Mem. Belle Haven Country Club, Met. Club. Republican. Episcopalian. Office: US Dept Defense Legislative Affairs 1300 Defense Pentagon Washington DC 20301-1300

MOORE, RACHEL SUZANNE, performing company executive, dancer; b. Davis, Calif., Feb. 19, 1965; d. Charles Vincent and Patricia (Dudley) M. BA, Brown U., 1992; MA, Columbia U., 1994. Dancer Am. Ballet Theatre II, N.Y.C., 1982-84, 1984—88; devel. officer Nat. Cultural Alliance, Wash., 1994—95; dir., coord. Center for Cmty. Devel. & Arts Americans for the Arts, Wash., 1995—97; mng. dir. Ballet Theater of Boston, Boston, 1998; exec. dir. Project STEP, Boston, 1998—2001; dir. Boston Ballet Center for Dance Ed., Boston, 2001—04; exec. dir. Amer. Ballet Theatre, NYC, 2004—. Adjunct dance prof. Emerson Coll., Boston U. Presidential scholar U.S. Dept. of Edn., Washington, 1982. Mem. Am. Guild of Mus. Artists. Democrat. Unitarian Universalist. Office: Am Ballet Theatre 890 Broadway Fl 3D New York NY 10003-1211*

MOORE, RAYBURN SABATZKY, American literature educator; b. Helena, Ark., May 26, 1920; s. Max Sabatzky and Sammie Lou (Rayburn) M.; m. Margaret Elizabeth Bear, Aug. 30, 1947; children: Margaret Elizabeth Moore Kopcinski, Robert Rayburn. AB, Vanderbilt U., 1942, MA, 1947; PhD, Duke U., 1956. Script writer King Biscuit Time, Interstate Grocer Co., KFFA, 1947-50; Vice pres. Interstate Grocer Co., Helena, 1947-50; research and grad. asst. Duke U., 1952-54; asst. prof. English, Hendrix Coll., Conway, Ark., 1954-55, asso. prof., 1955-58, prof., 1958-59; asso. prof. U. Ga., Athens, 1959-65, prof., 1965-90, prof. emeritus, 1990—, chmn. Am. studies program, 1968-90, chmn. div. lang and lit., 1975-90. Vis. scholar Duke U., 1958, 64 Author: Constance Fenimore Woolson, 1963, For the Major and Selected Short Stories of Constance Fenimore Woolson, 1967, Paul Hamilton Hayne, 1972, A Man of Letters in the Nineteenth-Century South: Selected Letters of Paul Hamilton Hayne, 1982; sr. editor: History of Southern Literature, 1985, Selected Letters of Henry James to Edmund Gosse (1882-1915): A Literary Friendship, 1988, The Correspondence of Henry James and the House of Macmillan, 1877-1914: All the Links in the Chain, 1993, The Letters of Alice James to Anne Ashburner, 1873-1878, Resources for American Literary Study, vol. 27 numbers 1 and 2, 2001; mem. editorial bd. U. Ga. Press, 1972-74, Ga. Rev., 1974-82, chmn., 1980-82; contbr. articles, revs. to profl. jours. Adv. bd. Letters of Henry James complete edit., 1995—, editl. bd., 1997—; troop com. Boy Scouts Am., Athens, 1973-75; deacon, elder Presbyterian Ch., 1962—; Lamar Meml. Lectures com. Mercer U., 1984-91. Capt. US Army, 1942-46, PTO. Recipient John Hurt Fisher award South Atlantic Assn. Depts. English, 2000, honoree English Language and Lit., Philoological Assn. of Carolinas, 1990. Mem. MLA (exec. com. Gen. Topics VI 1972-75), Soc. Study So. Lit. (exec. com. 1968-69, 74-79, 85-88, 91-94, v.p. 1981-82, pres. 1983-84), South Atlantic Grad. English Coop. Group (exec. com. 1969-79, chmn. 1971-72), South Atlantic MLA (exec. com. 1975-77, nominating com. 1985-87), Am. Lit. Assn. (chair Simms Soc. Sessions 1993-2003), Va. Hist. Soc., Philological Assn. Carolinas, Edgar Allan Poe Soc., William Gilmore Simms Soc. (exec. com. 1993-94, pres.-elect 1993-95, chmn. Simms sessions Am. Lit. Assn. 1993—), Constance Fenimore Woolson Soc., Blue Key, Phi Beta Kappa, Sigma Chi. Office: U Ga Dept English Park Hall Athens GA 30602-6205

MOORE, RAYMOND A. consultant, retired agriculture educator; b. Britton, S.D., Nov. 16, 1927; s. Arthur L. and Anna (Schuur) M.; m. Marlys Schiefelbein, Jun 17, 1951; children: Craig, Jay, Kent, Jeff. BA in Agrl. Edn. and Econs., S.D. State U., 1951, MS in Agronomy, 1958; PhD in Crop Physiology and Ecology, Purdue U., 1963. Instr. vocat. agriculture Bennett County H.S., Martin, S.D., 1951-56; instr., prof., adminstr. S.D. State U., Brookings, 1956-94, dir. emeritus agrl. expt. sta., 1994—. Cons. Coop. States Rsch. Svcs. USDA, Washington, Producers Renewable Products, St. Paul. Contbr. chpts. to books, articles to profl. jours. With USN, 1945-47. Nat. Sci. Faculty fellow forage & pasture mgmt. CSRS/U.S. Dept. Agriculture, 1965; Citizens Ambassador Program People to People Internat. travel grantee, U.S. Dept. Agriculture travel grantee. Mem. Am. Soc. Agronomy, Kiwanis Internat., Sigma Xi, Gamma Sigma Delta. Avocations: hunting, fishing, gardening, farming. Home: 207 17th Ave Brookings SD 57006-2609 Office: SD State U PO Box 2207 Brookings SD 57007-0001

MOORE, RAYMOND EDWARD, retired physician; b. Groveland, Mass., Sept. 9, 1912; s. Edward Bishop and Louise Maud (Fowler) M.; m. Christine Isobel Vaughan, June 18, 1938; children: Susan, Stephen. BA, Weslyan U., 1933; MD, Tufts U., 1937. Diplomate Am. Bd. Family Practice. Intern R.I. Hosp., Providence, 1937-39; pvt. practice Hampstead, N.H., 1939-97; ret., 1997. Chief of staff Hale Muni Hosp., Haverhill, Mass., 1968-70. Fellow Am. Acad. Family Physicians (pres. N.H. chpt. 1970-72), Phi Beta Kappa. Office: PO Box 865 Hampstead NH 03841-0865 E-mail: raymondmoore@attbi.com.

MOORE, RICHARD, former academic administrator, educator; m. Susan Moore; children: Betsy, Parker. BS in Econs., Claremont Men's Coll., 1955, PhD, 1965; MBA, U. Calif., 1956. Asst. prof. mktg. San Jose (Calif.) State U., 1959-61; instr., divsn. dir. San Bernardino Valley (Calif.) Coll., 1961-66; dean instrn. Moorpark Coll., Calif., 1966-74; pres., supt. Santa Monica (Calif.) Coll., 1974-94; pres. C.C. So. Nev., Las Vegas, 1994-99, Nev. State Coll., Henderson, 2000—02, prof., 2002—. Active C.C. H.S. program Clark County Sch. Dist., Boys & Girls Clubs, Learning and Earning Program, Weekend Coll., Silver Sage Coll., Peace Officers Acad., Video Distance Edn., other acad. programs. Lt. U.S. Army, 1957-59. Office: Nev State Coll 1125 Dawson Ave Henderson NV 89015

MOORE, RICHARD ALAN, landscape architect; b. St. Louis, Jan. 17, 1930; s. Ira Mack and Helen Adoline (Fakes) M.; m. Patricia Ruth Burke, Mar. 15, 1952 (div. 1967); children: Sheryl Louise, Richard Dennis, Sara Lynn, Sandra Lee. BS, U. Mo., 1951; MLA, U. Oreg., 1957. Registered landscape architect, Calif., Hawaii. Asst. prof. landscape architecture Calif. State Poly. Coll., Pomona, 1957-61; assoc. prof., head dept. landscape architecture N.C. State U., Raleigh, 1962-67; pvt. practice landscape architecture Pomona, Calif., 1957-61; dir. land devel. and planning Oceanic Properties Inc., Honolulu, 1967-69; pvt. practice Honolulu, 1969-70, 79—; dir. ops. Eckbo, Dean, Austin & Williams, Honolulu, 1970-71, v.p. ops., 1971-73; pres. EDAW, Inc., San Francisco, 1973-76, chmn. bd., 1976-78; prof. landscape architecture Tex. A&M U., Bryan, 1977-79. Prin. works include Whispering Pines Motor Lodge, N.C., 1964 (award of merit N.C. chpt. AIA 1964), North Shore Devel. Plan, Kauai, Hawaii, 1973, Comprehensive Zoning Ordinance, County of Kauai, 1973 (Am. Soc. Landscape Architects honor award 1973, HUD honor award 1974), Lihue Devel. Plan, Kauai, 1975, Koloa, Poipu, Kalaheo Devel. Plan, Kauai, 1978, Gen. Plan Update, Kauai, 1982, Mililani Town Devel. Plan, 1967-69 (Am. Soc. Landscape Architects merit award 1970), Lanai Land Mgmt. and Devel. Study, 1969 (Am. Soc. Landscape Architects merit award 1970), Wailea Master Devel. Plan, 1971, Kukuiula Devel. Plan, 1983, Lanai Project Dist. Master Plan, 1983-89, Maliu Ridge Devel. Plan, North Kohala, 1985, Mililani Mauka Devel. Plan, 1988, Devel. Plan, Lanai City Comml. Dist., 1990, Dandan Golf Course, Guam, 1991. Fst lt. U.S. Army, 1951-53, Korea. Fellow Am. Soc. Landscape Architects; mem. Masons. Avocations: sports, drawing, painting.

MOORE, RICHARD KERR, electrical engineering educator; b. St. Louis, Nov. 13, 1923; s. Louis D. and Nina (Megown) M.; m. Wilma Lois Schallau, Dec. 10, 1944 (dec. 1999); children: John Richard, Daniel Charles. BS, Washington U. at St. Louis, 1943; PhD, Cornell U., 1951. Test equipment engr. RCA, Camden, N.J., 1943-44; instr. and rsch. engr. Washington U., St. Louis, 1947-49; rsch. assoc. Cornell U., 1949-51; rsch. engr., sect. supr. Sandia Corp., Albuquerque, 1951-55; prof., chmn. elec. engring. U. N.Mex., 1955-62; Black and Veatch prof. U. Kans., Lawrence, 1962-94; prof. emeritus, 1994—; dir. remote sensing lab. U. Kans., 1964-74, 84-93. Pres. Cadre Corp., Lawrence, 1968-87; cons. cos., govt. agys. Author: Traveling Wave Engineering, 1960; co-author: (with Ulaby and Fung) Microwave Remote Sensing, Vol. I, 1981, Vol. II, 1982, Vol. III, 1986; contbr. to profl. jours. and handbooks. Lt. (j.g.) USNR, 1944-46. Recipient Achievement award Washington U. Engring. Alumni Assn., 1978, Outstanding Tech. Achievement award IEEE Geosci. and Remote Sensing Soc., 1982, Louise E. Byrd Grad. Educator award U. Kans., 1984, Irving Youngberg Rsch. award U. Kans., 1989, Australia prize, 1995. Fellow AAAS, IEEE (sect. chmn. 1960-61, Outstanding Tech. Achievement award coun. oceanic engring. 1978); mem., NAE, AAUP, Am. Soc. Engring. Edn., Am. Geophys. Union, Internat. Sci. Radio Union (chmn. U.S. commn. F 1984-87, internat. vice chmn. commn. F 1990-93, chmn. 1993-96), Kiwanis, Sigma Xi, Tau Beta Pi. Presbyterian (past elder). Achievements include research in submarine communications, radar altimetry, radar as a remote sensor, radar oceanography; patent for polypanchromatic radar. Home: 1712 Carmel Dr Lawrence KS 66047-1840 Office: U Kans R S & Remote Sensing Lab 2335 Irving Hill Rd Lawrence KS 66045-7612 E-mail: rmoore@sunflower.com.

MOORE, RICHARD LAWRENCE, structural engineer, consultant; b. Rocky Ford, Colo., Feb. 7, 1934; s. Lawrence and Margaret Kathryn (Bolling) M.; m. Donna St. Clair, Mar. 26, 1972 (div. 1983); 1 child, Andrew Trousdale; m. Margaret Ann Guthrie, May 4, 1984. BSCE, U. Colo., 1957; MS, Princeton U., 1963; PhD, Calif. Western U., Santa Ana, 1975. Registered profl. engr., Mass., Maine, Colo., Pa., Iowa, Nebr., N.Mex., Wyo., Ill., Ark., Mo., ND, Mich., Okla., Mont., N.H. Structural engr. Cameron Engrs., Denver, 1964-66; v.p. Moore Internat., Jeddah, Saudi Arabia, 1967-78; asst. to pres. C.H. Guernsey Co., Oklahoma City, 1979-82; pres. R.L. Moore Co., Boston, 1983—; v.p., dir. Isolink Ing., Basel, Switzerland, 1990—. Nat. chmn. Roof Cons. Inst., Raleigh, N.C., 1988-92; prof. Episcopal Sch. Theology, Denver, 1967-71. Patentee in field. Member Mound City (Mo.) Libr. Bd., 1963-64; pres. Dist. Rep. Party, Boston, 1988—; sr. warden St. John Chrysostom Epis. Ch., Denver, 1966-71. Danforth Found. scholar, 1962. Mem. ASCE, NSPE, Am. Concrete Inst., Nat. Forensic Ctr. Avocations: golf, travel, antique pocket watch collecting. Home and Office: RL Moore Co 534 E Broadway Boston MA 02127-4407

MOORE, ROBERT BYRON, chemical engineer, consultant; b. Bangkok, Nov. 11, 1929; arrived in U.S., 1930; s. William Robert and Ruth Byron Moore; m. Mary Frances Trager, June 18, 1955; children: Robert Byron, Kathryn Lynn. BSChemE, U. Mich., 1952. EIT Tex., La. Process engr. Phillips Chem. Co., Dumas, Tex., 1952—53, Houston, 1955—59; process mgr. Air Products, West Palm Beach, Fla., 1959—61, ops. supt., 1961—63; project engr. Air Products and Chems., Allentown, Pa., 1963—64, New Orleans, 1965—66, project mgr. Allentown, 1967—73; ret., 1999; chem. engring. cons. Hydrogen Tech., 2003—. Mgr. econ. evaluation Air Products and Chems., Allentown, 1974—99; cons. hydrogen gas Ind. Cons., Allentown, 2000—. Contbr. scientific papers to profl. jours. With U.S. Army, 1953—55. Achievements include patents for hydrogen and chemical production. Avocations: tennis, skiing, golf. Home: 2951 Edgemont Ct Allentown PA 18103-5417 E-mail: moorehome@enter.net.

MOORE, ROBERT CRUMLEY, mathematician, educator; BA, So. Adventist U., Collegedale, Tenn., 1975; MS, U. NC, 1979; EdD, U. Ga., 1990. Cert. secondary tchg. N.C. Secondary math. and sci. tchr. Fletcher (N.C.) Acad., 1975—78; prof. of math. So. Adventist U., Collegedale, 1979—. Vis. assoc. prof. math. edn. Mont. State U., Bozeman, 1993—94. Mem.: Nat. Coun. Tchrs. Math., Math. Assn. Am. Office: So Adventist U P O Box 370 Collegedale TN 37315-0370 E-mail: moore@southern.edu.

MOORE, ROBERT HENRY, financial services executive; b. Madisonville, Ky., Sept. 16, 1940; s. William Lee Moore and Robbie (Pritchett) Ruby; m. Diana Churchill, Aug. 17, 1963 (div. 1978); children: Randall Lee, Robin Churchill; m. Patricia Mary George, Oct. 4, 1981; 1 child, Christopher Robert. BA, Davidson (N.C.) Coll., 1962; MA, U. N.C., 1964; PhD, U. Wis., 1972. Asst. dir. admissions Davidson Coll., 1963-64; teaching asst. U. Wis., Madison, 1965-68; staff and faculty U.S. Mil. Acad., West Point, N.Y., 1968-70; lectr., asst. prof. U. Md., College Park, 1970-76, assoc. prof., 1976; cons. U.S. Congress, Washington, 1976-77; emerging issues coordinator The Conf. Bd., N.Y.C., 1977-79; dir. govt. relations Benefacts, Inc., Washington, 1977-78; v.p. Alexander & Alexander, Inc., Washington, 1978-81, Alexander & Alexander Svcs. Inc., N.Y.C., Washington, 1981-85, sr. v.p. corp. rels., 1985-95, sr. v.p. (inactive), 1995-97; chmn., pres. A & A Govt. and Industry Affairs Inc., Washington, 1990-94, Aon Corp., Vienna, Va., 1997—. Del. Nat. Security Affairs Conf., Washington, 1978-82; mem. adv. bd. Career Opportunities Inst., U. Va., Charlottesville, 1982-86, Ctr. for New Am. Work Force,

1992-96; mem. corp. adv. bd. Queens Coll., CUNY, 1985-96; mem. V.P.'s Forum, 1989-94; mem. coun. Conf. Bd. Corp. Comm. Execs., 1990-94; mem. Pub. Rels. Sem., 1993-97; editl. advisor Ctr. for Mind-Body Medicine, Washington, 1998-2000; adv. coun. Mindfulness Practice Ctr. of Fairfax, 1998—; bd. visitors Dictionary of Am. Regional English, 1999—; adv. to chmn. NEH, 1999-2001. Co-author: (with others) School for Soldiers: West Point and the Profession of Arms, 1974 (NYT award 1974), Spreading the Risks: Insuring the American Experience, 2003 (Washington Book Pubs. award 2003); contbr. articles to profl. jours.; contbr. interviews to nat. mags., newspapers, radio and TV. Mem. kitchen cabinet Points of Light Found., 1991-95. With U.S. Army, 1968-70, capt. USAR, 1970-72. Ops. Crossroads Africa fellow, 1960; U. Md. rsch. grantee, 1972, 76. Mem. Nat. Assn. Ins. Brokers (exec. com., bd. dirs., pres. 1985-86, chmn. past presidents adv. coun. 1989-93).

MOORE, ROBERT MADISON, food products executive, lawyer; b. New Orleans, June 21, 1925; s. Clarence Greer and Anna Omega (Odendahl) M.; m. Evelyn Eileen Varva, Apr. 11, 1953; children: Eileen Alexandria Moore Wynne, John Greer. BBA, Tulane U., 1947; JD, U. Va., 1952; LLM (Food Law Inst. fellow), NYU, 1953. Bar: La. 1956, Calif. 1972. Asst. to pres., gen. counsel Underwear Inst., N.Y.C., 1953-55; pvt. practice law New Orleans, 1955-56; asst. gen. atty., dir. Legal services, sec. and gen. atty. Standard Fruit & Steamship Co., New Orleans, 1957-72; v.p., gen. counsel Castle & Cooke Foods, 1972-81, Castle & Cooke, Inc., 1973-81, sr. v.p. law and govt., 1981-82; pres. Internat. Banana Assn., 1983-98; acting exec. dir. Pan Am. Devel. Found., 1999. Dir. Ferson Optics of Del., Inc., 1958-69, Baltime Securities Corp., Pan American Devel. Found. Asst. atty. gen., La., 1960-66. Served with AUS, 1943-46. Mem. ABA, Calif. Bar Assn., La. Bar Assn., SAR (sec. 1960-61), KM, Cosmos Club, Phi Delta Phi, Alpha Tau Omega. Democrat. Roman Catholic. Home: 3323 R St NW Washington DC 20007-2310 E-mail: rmevmoore@aol.com.

MOORE, ROBERT WILLIAM, professional organization executive; b. Claysburg, Pa., June 4, 1924; s. Frank B. and Sarah A. (Edelbute) M.; m. Helen Lingenfelter, July 17, 1948; children: Thomas R., Priscilla Jane. BA, Pa. State U., 1948. With Price Waterhouse & Co., Pitts., 1948-62, mgr., 1955-62; asst. contr. Con-Gas Svc. Corp., Pitts., 1962-65, Consol. Natural Gas Svc. Co., Inc., Pitts., 1966-72, contr., 1972-78, Consol. Natural Gas Co., Pitts., 1972-78; pres. Fin. Execs. Inst., Morristown, N.J., 1978-89, pres. emeritus, 1989—. Mem. Fin. Acctg. Standards Adv. Coun., 1978-89. Bd. dirs. Central Blood Bank, Pitts., 1960-78, treas. corp., 1962-68, chmn. finance com., 1962-68, chmn. bd., 1969-72; mem. exec. bd. Pa. State U. Alumni Council, 1975-83; mem. exec. com. Campaign for Pa. State U., bd. vis.; pres. Pa. State Coll. Bus. Adminstrn. Soc., 1981-83. Served with AUS, 1943-45. Mem. Am., Pa. insts. C.P.A.s, Inst. of Mgmt. Acct., Fin. Execs. Inst., Pa. State U. Alumni Assn., Pa. Soc., Beta Alpha Psi (nat. forum), Delta Tau Delta. Clubs: University (dir., pres. 1975-76), Valley Brook Country (dir. 1968-70, v.p. bd. 1970), Duquesne (Pitts.), University, St. Clair Country. Episcopalian. E-mail: rmoorepgh@msn.com.

MOORE, ROBERT YATES, neuroscience educator; b. Harvey, Ill., Dec. 5, 1931; s. Raymon Irwin and Marie Louise (Fischer) M.; children: Elizabeth Allen, Matthew McCormick, Joshua Gilbert, Thomas Douglas. BA magna cum laude, Lawrence U., 1953; MD with honors, U. Chgo., 1957, PhD, 1962; MD (hon.), Lund (Sweden) U., 1974. Diplomate: Am. Bd. Psychiatry and Neurology. Intern Univ. Hosp., Ann Arbor, Mich., 1958-59; resident U. Chgo., 1959-64, asst. prof. neurology and anatomy, 1964-66, assoc. prof., 1966-70, prof., 1970-74; prof. neurosci. U. Calif., San Diego, 1974-79; prof., chmn. dept. neurology SUNY, Stony Brook, 1979-90; prof. psychiatry, neurology and neurosci. U. Pitts., 1990—, chmn. dept. neurology, 1992-2000. Cons. Contbr. numerous articles to profl. jours. Recipient numerous grants. Fellow Am. Acad. Neurology; mem. Am. Neurol. Assn., Soc. Neurosci., Internat. Brain Research Orgn., Am. Assn. Anatomists. Office: U Pitts Dept Neurology 3471 5th Ave Ste 811 Pittsburgh PA 15213-3232

MOORE, ROGER ADDISON, pediatrician, anesthesiologist; b. Portsmouth, Va., 1948; MD, U. Va., 1973. Diplomate Am. Bd. Pediatrics, Am. Bd. Anesthesiology. Intern Colo. Affil. Hosps., Denver, 1974-75, resident in pediatrics, 1975-77; resident in anesthesiology Hosp. U. Pa., Phila., 1977-79; fellow in pediat. anesthesiology, CCM Children's Hosp., Phila., 1979; chmn. anesthesiology dept. Deborah Heart - Lung Ctr., Browns Mills, NJ, 1993—2004, chair emeritus, 2004—; assoc. prof. anesthesiology U. Pa., 1988-97, clin. assoc. prof. anesthesiology, 1998—. Mem. AMA, Am. Assn. Pediatrics, Am. Soc. Anesthesiologists (treas. 2003—), Soc. Cardiovasc. Anesthesiologists (pres. 2001-03), Alpha Omega Alpha, others. Office: Deborah Heart & Lung Ctr Browns Mills NJ 08015 Address: Soc Cardiovascular Anesthesiologists PO Box 11086 Richmond VA 23230-1086 Office Phone: 609-893-6611. Personal E-mail: rogermoore435@yahoo.com.

MOORE, ROY DEAN, retired judge; b. Chickasha, Okla., Jan. 15, 1940; s. Frank B. and Delia Pauline (Morgan) M.; m. Carolyn Kaye Wood, Aug. 10, 1962; children— Darla Kaye, Jared Dean, Amy Darise. BA, Central State U., 1962, M. Teaching, 1966; JD, Oklahoma City U., 1970; grad., Nat. Coll. State Trial Judges, 1972. Bar: Okla. 1970. Coach debate, instr. dramatics Kingfisher (Okla.) High Sch., 1962-67; instr. English and journalism, head dept. lang. arts. Jarman Jr. High Sch., Midwest City, Okla., 1967-70; pros. atty. City of Lawton, Okla., 1970; spl. dist. judge 5th Jud. Dist. Okla., 1971-72; pvt. practice law Lawton, 1973-90; dist. judge 5th Jud. Dist. Okla., 1990—2002. Pres. Swinney PTA, 1975-76; Editor: Problems in Teaching in the Secondary School, 1966. Pres. Comanche County Mental Health Assn., 1973-74, bd. dirs., 1972-76; co-chmn. Kingfisher County Reps. for Congressman James V. Smith, 1966; mem. state exec. com. Okla. Republican Com., 1973-74, chmn. auditing com., 1977-78; del. Rep. Nat. Conv., 1976; chmn. cts. com. Assn. South Central Okla. Govts. Crime Commn.; chmn. Comanche County Reps. for Reagan for Pres., 1973-83; mem. adv. bd. Jim Taliferro Mental Health Center, 1977-78; del. Nat. Mental Health Assn. Conv., 1975; bd. dirs. Lawton Campfire Girls; elder N.W. Ch. of Christ, 1977—; dir. Back to Bible Campaigns, 1976-2002. Named Outstanding Dist. Judge in State of Okla., Okla. Trial Lawyers Assn., 1999. Mem. Am., Okla., Comanche County bar assns., Okla. Trial Lawyers Assn., Lawton Antique Auto Club, Ford Retractible Club Am., Alpha Psi Omega, Delta Theta Phi. Republican. Mem. Ch. of Christ (elder). Clubs: Fraternal Order of Police, Lion. Home: 2114 NW Atlanta Ave Lawton OK 73505-3923 Personal E-mail: vokal@sbcglobal.net.

MOORE, ROY S. former state supreme court chief justice; m. Kayla Moore; children: Heather, Roy, Caleb, Micah. BS, U.S. Mil. Acad., 1969; JD, U. Ala., 1977. Dep. dist. atty. Etowah County, Ala., 1977—82; pvt. practice Gadsden, Ala., 1982—92; cir. judge 16th Judicial Cir., Gadsden, 1992—2001; chief justice Ala. Supreme Ct., 2001—03. Republican. Baptist.

MOORE, SALLY FALK, anthropology educator; b. N.Y.C., Jan. 18, 1924; d. Henry Charles and Mildred (Hymanson) Falk; m. Cresap Moore, July 14, 1951; children: Penelope, Nicola. BA, Barnard Coll., 1943; LL.B., Columbia U., 1945, PhD, 1957. Asst. prof. U. So. Calif., Los Angeles, 1963-65, assoc. prof., 1965-70, prof., 1970-77, UCLA, 1977-81; prof. anthropology Harvard U., Cambridge, Mass., 1981—, Victor Thomas prof. anthropology, 1991—, dean Grad. Sch. Arts and Scis., 1985-89. Author: Power and Property in Inca Peru, (Ansley Prize 1957), 1958, Law as Process, 1978, Social Facts and Fabrications, 1986, Moralizing States, 1993, Anthropology and Africa, 1994, Law and Anthropology, 2004. Trustee Barnard Coll., Columbia U., 1991-92; master Dunster House, 1984-89. Rsch. grantee Social Sci. Rsch. Coun., 1968-69, NSF, 1972-75, 79-80, Wenner Gren Found., 1983; Guggenheim fellow, 1995-96. Fellow Am. Acad. Arts & Scis., Am. Anthrop. Assn., Royal Anthrop. Inst. (Huxley medallist, lectr. for 1999); mem. Assn. Polit. and Legal Anthropology (pres. 1983), Am. Ethnological Soc. (pres. 1987-88), Assn. Africanist Anthropologists (pres.-elect 1995, pres. 1996-98). Democrat. Office: Harvard U 348 William James Hall Cambridge MA 02138

MOORE, SCOTT, former state official; b. York, Nebr., 1960; m. Danene Tushar, 1989. BA in Polit Sci., U. Nebr. Legis. aide Nebr. Legislature, 1981-86, mem., 1986-94, chair appropriations com., 1991-94; sec. of state State of Nebr., 1995—2000; dir. gov. affairs Union Pacific R.R., 2000—. With Moore & Sons. Office: Union Pacific RR 1416 Dodge St Room 801 Omaha NE 68179 Address: 615 N 62nd St Omaha NE 68132-1958

MOORE, SHIRLEY THROCKMORTON (MRS. ELMER LEE MOORE), accountant; b. Des Moines, July 4, 1918; d. John Carder and Jessie (Wright) Throckmorton; m. Elmer Lee Moore, Dec. 19, 1946; children: Fay, Lynn Dallas. Student, Iowa State Tchrs. Coll., 1937-38, Madison Coll., 1939-41; MCS, Benjamin Franklin U., 1944. CPA. Asst. bookkeeper Sibley Hosp., Washington, 1941-42, Alvord & Alvord, 1942-46, bookkeeper, 1946-49, chief acct., 1950-64, fin. advisor to sr. ptnr., 1957-64; dir. Allen Oil Co., 1958-74; pvt. practice acctg., 1964—. Contbr. articles to profl. jours. Mem. sch. bd. Takoma Acad., Takoma Park, Md., 1970—; mem. hosp. bd. Washington Adventist Hosp., 1974-85; chmn. worthy student fund Takoma Park Seven Day Adventist Ch., 1987-88; trustee Benson Found., 1963-99; vol. Am. Women's Vol. Svc., 1942-45. Recipient Disting. Grad. award Benjamin Franklin U., 1961. Mem. AICPA, D.C. Inst. CPAs (pub. rels. com. 1976—), Am. Women's Soc. CPAs, Am. Soc. Women Accts. (legis. chmn. 1960-62, nat. dir. 1952-53, nat. treas. 1953-54), Bus. and Profl. Women's Club (treas. D.C. 1967-68), Benjamin Franklin U. Alumni Assn. (Disting. Alumni award 1964, charter, past dir.), DAR, Md. Assn. CPAs (charter chmn. membership com. Montgomery Prince George County 1963-64, chmn. student rels. com. 1964-67, pres. 1968-69, mem. fed. tax com. 1971-73). Mem. Seventh Day Adventist Ch. Home and Office: 2401 Pine Lake Dr West Columbia SC 29169-3737

MOORE, SPENCER RONEAL, retired business owner, accounts receivable funder; b. Levelland, Tex., Apr. 3, 1934; s. Joe Bailey and Ida Maye (Williams) M.; m. Valeria a., Dec. 28, 1966. Student, Hartnell Coll., 1952-53. Sales asst. Dick Bruhns, A Man's Store, Salinas, Calif., 1951-52; salesman Pauson's Men's Store, San Francisco, 1953-54; mdse. buyer Hart's Dept. Store, San Jose, Calif., 1954-64; buyer men's, boys Demery's Wurzbergs, Detroit and Grand Rapids, Mich., 1966-70; opers. mgr. Saks Fifth Ave., Woodland Hills, Calif., 1971-74; mdse. mgr. Vornado, Inc., Whittier, Calif., 1974-75; self employed The Mole Hole, La Jolla, Calif., 1976-93; ret., 1994. Mem. Am. Cash Flow Industry, La Jolla Profl. Men's Soc., Kiwanis (Torrey Pines). Democrat. Avocations: golf, travel, reading, family, fitness excercise. Home: 24440 Woodsage Dr Bonita Springs FL 34134-7959 Office: Express Small Bus Funding 17595 S Tamiami Trl Fort Myers FL 33908-4570

MOORE, STEPHEN JAMES, lawyer; b. Kansas City, Mo., Aug. 9, 1947; s. James Andrew and Frances Clare (Kennedy) M. BSBA, Rockhurst U., 1969, BA, 1975; JD, U. Mo., Kansas City, 1977, LLM, 1997. Bar: Mo. 1978, U.S. Dist. Ct. (we. dist.) Mo. 1978, U.S. Ct. Appeals (8th cir.) 1980, U.S. Ct. Appeals (10th cir.) 1981, U.S. Ct. Fed. Claims 1991, U.S. Ct. Appeals (6th cir.) 1997. Law intern Mo. Atty. Gen.'s Office, Kansas City, 1976-77, asst., 1978; assoc. Popham, Conway, Sweeny, Fremont & Bundschu PC, Kansas City, 1978-84, Freilich, Leitner & Carlisle, PC, Kansas City, 1985, Herrick, Feinstein, Kansas City, 1985-86, Freilich, Leitner, Carlisle & Shortlidge, Kansas City, 1986-90; ptnr. Freilich, Leitner & Carlisle, Kansas City, Dallas, L.A., 1987-2000, Aspen, Colo., 1997-2000, Peters, Moore & Jones, LLC, Kansas City, Mo., 2001—02, Peters & Moore, L.L.C., 2002—. Adj. prof. law U. Mo., Kansas City, 1995—. Mem. Friends of Art, Nelson-Atkins Mus. Art, Kansas City, 1988—, Smithsonian Inst., Washington, 1985—, Nat. Trust for Historic Preservation, Washington, 1988—, Libr. of Congress Assocs., The Federalist Soc., Nat. Audubon Soc. Mem. ABA, Assn. Trial Lawyers Am., Kansas City Metro Bar Assn., Sports Car Club Am., Am. Mus. Nat. History, Porsche Club Am., Lake Ozarks Yacht Assn., Boat Owners Assn. U.S., Ancient Order of Hibernians, Delta Theta Phi, Tau Kappa Epsilon. Roman Catholic. Avocations: vintage sportscars, boating. Home: 5840 McGee St Kansas City MO 64113-2132 Office: Peters & Moore LLC 1500 Traders on Grand Bld 1125 Grand Ave Kansas City MO 64106 E-mail: moore@p-mlaw.com.

MOORE, SUSANNA, writer; b. Bryn Mawr, Pa., Dec. 9, 1948; d. Richard Dixon and Anne (Shields) M.; 1 child, Lulu Lenane Sylbert. Author: My Old Sweetheart, 1982 (Am. Book award nomination for best first novel 1983, Sue Kaufman prize for first fiction Am. Acad. Inst. Arts and Letters 1983), The Whiteness of Bones, 1989, Sleeping Beauties, 1993, In the Cut, 1995, One Last Look, 2004. Recipient Literary Lion award N.Y. Pub. Libr., 1993, PEN/Ernest Hemingway citation, Sue Kaugman prize, 1983.

MOORE, TERRY EDWARD, actor, performing company executive; b. Radford, Va., Aug. 11, 1956; s. Stanley Raymond and Elizabeth Anderson Moore; m. Cornelia Duryée, Dec. 29, 1989; children: Tallis Edward, Theophilus Schuyler. BA, Carleton Coll., 1978; MFA, Brandeis U., 1982. Co-founder, co-artistic dir. Seattle Shakespeare Co., 1991—97. Actor: (plays) A Christmas Carol, Howards End (Stellar Performance Yr. Seattle Times, 2002), Billy Bishop Goes to War (Stellar Performance Yr. Seattle Times, 1995). Personal E-mail: terryedwardmoore@earthlink.net. E-mail: terryedwardmoore@earthlink.net.

MOORE, TERRY L. financial executive; CPA, Ohio. CFO, CEO Nationwise Automotive, Inc.; CFO, treas. Shoe Corp. Am.; contr. Drug Emporium, Inc., Powell, Ohio, CFO, 1999—. Office: Drug Emporium Inc 811 14525 Highway 7 Minnetonka MN 55345-3734

MOORE, THOMAS A. lawyer; b. Waterford, Ireland, May 2, 1942; STL, Cath. U., 1968; JD, Fordham U., 1972. Bar: N.Y. 1973, U.S. Dist. Ct. (so. and ea. dists.) N.Y. 1973, U.S. Supreme Ct. 1991. Lawyer Kramer, Dillof, Livingston & Moore, N.Y.C., 1973—. Lectr. in field. Mem.: ATLA (nat. bd. dirs. 1992), Am. Bd. Trial Advs., N.Y. State Trial Lawyers Assn. Office: Kramer Dillof Livingston & Moore 217 Broadway New York NY 10007

MOORE, THOMAS ANDREW, former medical communications company executive; b. Cambridge, Mass., Jan. 28, 1951; s. Leo B. and Christine (Banios) M.; m. Avril Barton, Nov. 8, 1975; children: Thomas, Diana, Juliet. BA in History, Princeton U., 1973. Brand asst. Procter & Gamble Co., Cin., 1973-84, advt. mgr. Beauty Care, 1984-86, gen. mgr. Vidal Sassoon L.A., 1986-88, v.p. Health Care Cin., 1988-91; pres. Procter & Gamble Can., Toronto, Ont., Can., 1991-92; pres. Health Care Procter & Gamble USA, Cin., 1992-96; group v.p. Procter & Gamble Co., Cin., 1992-96; pres., CEO Nelson Communications, 1996—2002, Biopure Corp., Cambridge, Mass., 2002—04. Treas. Alliance Drug Free Can., Toronto, 1991, 92; chmn. Cin. Ballet Co., 1986-91; bd. dirs. Am. Health Found., N.Y.C., 1989—, Mercy Hosp., Anderson, Ohio, 1993—. Mem. Non Prescription Drug Mfrs. Assn. (vice chmn. 1992—), Princeton Club, Union Club, Jasna Polana. Avocations: fly fishing, wine collecting, consumption.

MOORE, THOMAS DAVID, academic administrator; b. Rochester, N.Y., July 26, 1937; s. Robert Franklin and Hilda (Kennedy) M.; m. Virginia Muller, June 13, 1959; children: Kathleen Mary, Michael David, Thomas David. BSS, St. John Fisher Coll., 1959; MS, SUNY, Brockport, 1962; EdD, Rutgers U., 1966. Tchr. Rochester City Schs., 1959-62; grad. asst. Rutgers U., New Brunswick, N.J., 1963-65; from asst. to full prof. Kent (Ohio) State U., 1965-93, asst. v.p. acad. affairs, 1976-83, v.p. faculty affairs and personnel, 1984-86, provost, v.p. acad. and student affairs, 1987-91, prof. emeritus ednl. philosophy, 1991—; provost, v.p. acad. affairs Ctrl. Washington U., 1993-97, prof. edn. and philosophy, 1997—. Roman Catholic. Avocations: sports, film, public affairs, music. Office Phone: 330-524-0688.

MOORE, THOMAS EDWIN, biologist, educator, museum director; b. Champaign, Ill. s. Gerald E. and Velma (Lewis) M.; m. E. Eleanor Sifferd, Feb. 4, 1951; children: Deborah S., Melinda S. BS, U. Ill., 1951, MS, 1952, PhD, 1956. Tech. asst. Ill. Natural History Survey, Urbana, 1950-56; instr. zoology U. Mich., Ann Arbor, 1956-59, asst. prof. zoology, 1959-63, assoc. prof. zoology, 1963-66, prof. biology, 1966—2000, curator insects, 1956—2000, dir. exhibit mus., 1988-93. Vis. prof. Orgn. for Tropical Studies, San Jose, Costa Rica, 1970, 72; bd. dirs. Orgn. Tropical Studies, San Jose, 1968-79; mem. steering com. tropical biome U.S. Internat. Biol. Program, 1969-72; mem. conf. planning com. Nat. Inst. for Environment, 1991-92; mem. steering com. Univ. Colloquium on Environ. Rsch. and Edn., 1991-93, grievance com. U. Mich., 1997-98, faculty handbook com., 1997-98. Co-editor: Lectures on Science Education, 1991, 92, 93; Cricket Behavior and Neurobiology, 1989; author movie 17-Year Cicadas, 1975, TV, 1998; co-author: Singing Insects of N.Am. Website, 2003—. County rep. Huron River Watershed Coun., Ann Arbor, 1988-92; mem. U. Mich. Senate Adv. Com. on Univ. Affairs, 1993-96, vice chair, 1995-96; bd. mem. U. Mich. Acad. Freedom Lecture Fund, 1995—, treas., 1995-98; cons. NSF Visual Tech. in Environ. Curricula, 1994-97; cons. Misery Bay exhibits ParksCanada, 2003-04. Rsch. grantee NSF, 1963-66, 66-69, 96-97, rsch. equipment grantee, 1984-86, rsch. grantee Def. Advanced Rsch. Project Agy./Office of Naval Rsch. 1998-2001 Fellow AAAS, AAUP (pres. U. Mich. chpt. 1996-99, exec. bd. Mich. chpt. 1996-98), Royal Entomol. Soc. London, Linnaen Soc. London; mem. Assn. Tropical Biology (pres. 1973-75), Sigma Xi (pres. U. Mich. chpt. 1994-96, coun. 1993-98). Home: 4243 N Delhi Rd Ann Arbor MI 48103-9485 Office: Mus of Zoology U Mich Ann Arbor MI 48109-1079 Office Phone: 734-763-4766. E-mail: temoore@umich.edu.

MOORE, THOMAS KAIL, magistrate district court judge; b. Idaho Falls, Idaho, Jan. 15, 1938; s. Burton L. and Clara E. (Kail) Moore; m. Judith Diane Gilman, July 30, 1966; children: David T., Jonathan G. AB in Pers. Scis., Harvard U., 1961; JD, Georgetown U., 1967. Bar: D.C., V.I., Va. Law clk. to Hon. John A. Danaher U.S. Ct. Appeals (D.C. Cir.), 1967-68; staff atty. Office Gen. Coun., Office Sec. Dept. Transp., Washington, 1968-69; assoc. Stanford, Reed & Gelenian, Washington, 1969-70; asst. U.S. Atty. U.S. Attys. Office, Washington, 1970-71, U.S. Attys. Office (ea. dist.), Va., 1971-76, prin. asst. Alexandria office, 1974-76; asst. U.S. Atty. U.S. Attys. Office (V.I. dist.), 1976-78; pvt. practive St. Thomas, V.I., 1978-81; shareholder Hoffman & Moore, P.C., St. Thomas, 1981-87; ptnr. Grunert, Stout, Moore & Bruch, St. Thomas, 1987-92; dist. judge U.S. Dist. Ct. (V.I. dist.), 1992—. Editor-in-chief Georgetown Law Journal, 1966-67. Scoutmaster Antilles Sch. Troop; trustee V.I. Montessori Sch. Capt. USAF, 1961-64, USAFR. Mem.: ABA, Va. Bar Assn., V.I. Bar Assn. (judicial), St. Thomas Yacht Club. Avocations: tennis, swimming, sailing. Office: 3013 Estate Golden Rock Ste 216 St Croix VI 00820

MOORE, THOMAS L. state legislator; b. Aiken, S.C., May 8, 1950; s. Lucius L. Jr. and Mae R. (Harrelson) M.; m. Dale J. Moore, Mar. 21, 1971; children: Baylen, Brent. BS, U. S.C., Aiken. Mem. S.C. Ho. of Reps., Columbia, 1979-80, S.C. Senate, Columbia, 1981—. Mem. fish, game and forestry com., gen. com., judiciary com., labor, commerce and industry com., chmn. med. affairs com. Democrat. Office: 305 Gressette Bldg Columbia SC 29202

MOORE, THOMAS LLOYD, librarian; b. Springfield, Ill., Oct. 4, 1942; s. Edward Joseph and Dorothy A. (Menezes) M.; m. Ann Mary Walsh, Aug. 29, 1971; children: Sean Christopher, Martin Thomas, Kathleen Adele. AA, Springfield Coll., 1963; BA, Cardinal Glennon Coll., St. Louis, 1968; MA in Library Sci., Rosary Coll., 1973. Tchr. Little Flower Grade Sch., Springfield, 1963-66; head of adult services Elk Grove Village (Ill.) Pub. Library, 1973-74; dir. Northlake (Ill.) Pub. Library Dist., 1974-75, Danville (Ill.) Pub. Library, 1975-78; adminstrv. librarian Palatine (Ill.) Pub. Library Dist., 1978-81; dir. Wake County Dept. of the Pub. Library, Raleigh, N.C., 1981—; trainer Roger Schwarz & Assocs., Chapel Hill, N.C., 1997—. Bd. dirs. Commit to a Healthier Region, 1991-93, Planned Parenthood of the Capital & Coast, 1993-97, sec., 1994; bd. dirs. Pirates Cove Homeowners Assn., 1992-97, v.p., 1993-94, pres., 1995-96; mem. Libr. Power Adv. Com., 1993-95, Facilitatators Orgnl. Devel. Group, 1995—, ASSIST Wake to Health Coalition, 1992-94. Mem. ALA, N.C. Library Assn. Democrat. Roman Catholic. Office: Wake County Pub Libr 4020 Carya Dr Raleigh NC 27610-2913

MOORE, THOMAS PAUL, retired broadcast executive; b. Danville, Ill., Feb. 29, 1928; s. Lester Rufus and Mabel Ellen (Jackson) M.; m. Jean LaVonne Sather, Aug. 31, 1952; children: Randyl Ellen, Patricia Kay, Gregory Sather. BA, North Cen. Coll., Naperville, Ill., 1952; postgrad., Denver U., 1952-53. Newscaster Sta. KFEL-AM-FM-TV, Denver, 1952-54; sales rep. Sta. KGMC, Englewood, Colo., 1954-56; sales mgr. Sta. KDEN-AM-FM, Denver, 1956-62; pres. Stas. WBCO, WQEL, Bucyrus, Ohio, 1962-98; ret., 1998. Hon. dir. First Fed. Cmty. Bank, 2001—. Lay leader, mem. program council Ohio Sandusky Conf., United Methodist Ch., 1966-69 (pres. gen. laity bd. and laymen's found. 1968-72); mem. Gen Council on Ministries, 1980-84, N.W. Ohio Water Devel. Adv. Com., 1967-69, Sandusky River Basin Water Pollution Study Com., 1968-69; v.p., bd. mgrs. EUB Men, Evang. United Brethren Ch., 1958-68; pres. Rocky Mountain Conf., 1957-61; mem. gen. bd. Nat. Council Christian Chs. Am., 1968-72; charter pres. Bucyrus Bratwurst Festival, Inc., 1968; adv. bd. Bucyrus Salvation Army, 1964-68; mem. planning com. East Ohio Conf., 1972-76 (chmn. commn. on minimum salaries, 1968-72, lay leader, 1972-76); vice chmn. council ministries, mem. episcopal com., 1972-76, head. del. to gen. conf., Portland, Oreg., 1976, Balt., 1984; head del. to Jurisdictional Conf., Sioux Falls, 1976, Duluth, Minn., 1984; pres. United Meth. Communications, 1972-76, mem. gen. council fin. and adminstrn., 1976-80; mem. communications commn. Nat. Council Chs., 1972-76; mem. communications con. Ohio Council Chs.; mem. Episc. com., chmn. New Vision Task Group, both East Ohio Conf., North Cen. Jurisdiction, United Meth. Ch.; mem. exec. com. Council on Ministries, 1980-86; mem. World Meth. Council, 1986-91, World Meth. Conf., 1996; trustee United Theol. Sem., 1972-80; trustee Ohio Northern U., 1986—, mem. exec. com., 1991-2003, chair student affairs com., 1991-95, chair, 1995—; mem. exec. com. East Ohio del. to United Meth. Gen. Conf. and Jurisdictional Conf., 1987-91; sec. Community Improvement Corp., Bucyrus, 1989-91; mem. Overall Econ. Devel. Com. of Crawford County, 1992-96; chmn. Crawford County Traffic Safety Council, 1979-89, 96-98; pres. Crawford County Econ. Devel. Adv. Coun., 1992-96; mem., sec. Crawford County Devel. Bd., Inc., 1997-2000; mem. exec. com. of del. to 1988 Gen. Conf. United Meth. Ch., St. Louis; bd. dirs. Bucyrus Community Hosp., 1992, mem. fin. com., 1993-96, chair nominating com., 1993-96, campaign dir., chair fundraising com., 1993-96, v.p. bd. dirs., 1994-96; chmn. N. Ctrl. Ohio Health Sys., 1996-98; mem. Crawford County Rep. Ctrl. Com., 1998-2001; mem. City of Bucyrus Bd. of Zoning Appeals, 1998-2001; pres. Crawford County Devel. Bd., 2000—; chmn. City of Bodyrus Bd. Zoning Appeals, 2000-01; sec. Bucyrus Pub. Libr Bd., 2004—. Served with USN, 1946-48. Named a Civic Leader of Am., 1968. Mem. Nat. Assn. Broadcasters (legis. liaison 1984-91, mem. small market radio com.), Ohio Assn. Broadcasters (pres. 1982-85), North Ctrl. Ohio Broadcasters Assn. (pres. 1983-84, 96-98, v.p. 1985-96), Bucyrus Area C. of C. (chmn. airport study com. 1967-68, bd. dirs. 1964-67, pres. 1989-91), Rotary (pres. Bucyrus chpt. 1992-93). Office Phone: 419-562-6023. Personal E-mail: tommoore@cybrtown.com., cedbinc@cybrtown.com.

MOORE, THOMAS RONALD (LORD BRIDESTOWE), lawyer; b. Duluth, Minn., Mar. 27, 1932; s. Ralph Henry and Estelle Marguerite (Hero) M.; m. Margaret C. King, Sept. 10, 1955 (dec. May 10, 2003); children: Willard S., Clarissa, Charles R.H. BA magna cum laude, Yale U., 1954; JD, Harvard U., 1957. Bar: N.Y. 1958, U.S. Supreme Ct. 1965. Instr. Harvard Law Sch., 1957-58; with Dewey Ballantine, N.Y.C.; ptnr. Breed, Abbott & Morgan, N.Y.C., Finley Kumble & Wagner, N.Y.C., Law Offices of Thomas R. Moore, N.Y.C. Lectr. Harvard U. Law Sch., Cornell Law Sch., NYU Law Sch., Practising Law Inst., NYC, Las Vegas, New Orleans; lectr. Oxford U. Author: Plantagenet Descent, 31 Generations from William the Conqueror to Today, 1995; co-author: Estate Planning and the Close Corporation; editor-in-chief: Gastronome, bd. editors: The Tax Lawyer; contbr. articles to profl. jours.; cited in popular press and TV commentaries, including 12 media interviews Jan. 24, 2002. Bd. dirs. exec. com. Citymeals on Wheels; bd. dirs. Nat. Soc. to Prevent Blindness, 1973-81, chmn., 1981-83, hon. pres.; sec.-treas., trustee A.D. Henderson Found., Del.; trustee, Fla.; bd. dirs. Phoenix Theatre Inc., Inst. Aegean Prehistory, Found. Future of Man, Am. and Internat. Friends of Victoria and Albert Mus., London; conservator NY Pub. Libr.; trustee Found.

for Renaissance of St. Petersburg (Russia), Malcolm Wiener Found.; pres., bd. dirs. Laurence Levine Charitable Fund., Inc.; bd. dirs. Gov.'s Commn. on Scholastic Achievement; constl. advisor to Pres. George Bush; advisor to King Michael of Romania. Decorated knight Queen Elizabeth II; recipient Coat of Arms, Order of Crown of Charlemagne, Order of Plantagenet, Order of Barons of Magna Charta, Order of Descendants Knights of the Garter, Thomas R. Moore Disting. Pub. Servant award, Nat. Soc. to Prevent Blindness; scholar of House, Class Marshall, Yale; Clare scholar, Cambridge U. Mem.: St. Andrews Soc., St. George Soc., Confrerie de la Chaine des Rotisseurs (nat. pres., dir., exec. com. world coun. Paris), Robert Burns Soc., Nat. Wine Coalition (bd. dirs.), Chevalier du Tastevin, The Pilgrims, Church Club, Univ. Club, Delta Sigma Rho. Republican. Episcopalian. Office: 590 Madison Ave Ste 2100 New York NY 10022 Office Phone: 212-333-8630.

MOORE, THOMAS SCOTT, lawyer; b. Portland, Oreg., Nov. 17, 1937; s. Harry Alburn and Geraldine Elizabeth (Scott) M.; m. Saundra L. Wagner, Sept. 7, 1957 (div. 1974); children: Cindy, Kristin, Thomas, Victoria, Wendy; m. Alice H. Zeisz, Nov. 5, 1976; 1 child, Alice G. BA, Willamette U., 1959, JD cum laude, 1962. Bar: Oreg. 1962, Wash. 2002. Pvt. practice, Portland, 1962—. Contbr. articles to law jours. Republican. Avocation: tennis. Office: Ste 230 5901 SW MacAdam Ave Portland OR 97239-3621

MOORE, THURSTON ROACH, lawyer; b. Memphis, Dec. 10, 1946; s. Richard Charlton Moore and Halcyon Hall (Roach) Lynn; m. Corell Luckhardt Halsey, Sept. 26, 1998. BA with distinction, U. Va., 1968, JD, 1974. Bar: Va. 1974. Rsch. analyst Scudder, Stevens & Clark, N.Y.C., 1968—71; ptnr. Hunton & Williams, Richmond, Va., 1974—. Bd. dirs. Met. Advantage Corp., Richmond. Trustee Va. Aerospace Bus. Roundtable, Hampton, 1989—, Va. Ea. Shore Sustainable Devel. Corp., 1995—2000, bd. dirs. Mary Morton Parsons Found., Charlottesville, Va., The Nature Conservancy, Charlottesville, chmn. Va. chpt. Mem.: ABA (bus. law sect., chmn. ptnrs. com. 1992—96, mem. fed. regulation security com., bus. law coun.), Va. State Bar, Va. Bar Assn. Office: Hunton & Williams Riverfront Plz E Tower 951 E Byrd St Richmond VA 23219-4074

MOORE, TOM WHITE, JR., lawyer; b. July 19, 1943; s. Tom White and Barbara Jeanice (Byrne) Moore; m. Linda Kay Blankinship, Aug. 29, 1967; children: Tom White, Heather Lucille. BS, U. Tenn., 1967; JD, Samford U., Birmingham, Ala., 1970. Bar: Tenn. 1970, U.S. dist. Ct. (mid. dist.) Tenn. 1970, U.S. Ct. Appeals (6th cir.) 1977, cert.: Nat. Elder Law Found. and Tenn. Comn. Legal Edn.and Specialization (elder law specialist) 2001. Assoc. Moore, Henry, Henry, Lewis & Cain, Pulaski, Tenn., 1970—71; ptnr. Henry, Lewis, Cain & Moore, Columbia, Tenn., 1971—74, Cain & Moore, Columbia, 1974—82, Cain, Moore & Peden, Columbia, 1982—87, Moore & Peden, Columbia, 1987—. Served with USANG, 1961—67. Mem.: Maury County Bar Assn. (pres. 1979), Nat. Acad. Elder Law Attys., Tenn. Trial Lawyers Assn. (bd. dir. 1971—), Assn. Trial Lawyers Am., Tenn. Bar Assn., Kiwanis. Home: 1205 Confederate Dr Columbia TN 38401 Office: Moore & Peden PC 700 N Garden St AmSouth Bank 3rd Fl Columbia TN 38401-3355

MOORE, VERNON JOHN, JR., pediatrician, consultant, lawyer; b. Chgo., Mar. 18, 1942; s. Vernon John Moore; m. Rutheva deVera Dizon, Feb. 27, 1979; children: Christopher, Joseph. BS, Loyola U., Chgo., 1964, JD, 1986; MD, U. Ill.-Chgo., 1968. Bar: Ill. 1986, U.S. Dist. Ct. (no. dist.) Ill. 1986. Intern St. Joseph Health Care Ctrs. and Hosp., Chgo., 1968-69, resident in pediat., 1971-74, chief resident, 1972-74, mem. med. staff, 1974-76, 78-86; pvt. practice Chgo., 1974-76, 97—; mem. med. staff Naval Hosp. Great Lakes, 1976-78; med. officer Chgo. Mil. Entrance Processing Sta., 1996—2002, Midwest Ctr. for Youth and Families, Kouts, Ind., 1997—; mem. med. staff Ill. Masonic Med. Ctr., Chgo., 1997—, Swedish Covenant Hosp., Chgo., 1998—, Luth. Gen. Hosp., Park Ridge, Ill., 1998—, Alexian Bros. Med. Ctr., Elk Grove Village, Ill., 2000—02. Asst. dir. pediat. edn. St. Joseph Health Care Ctrs. and Hosp., 1974—76, co-dir., 1978—86, acting chmn. dept. pediat., 1985—86; clin. assoc. prof. pediat. Loyola U., Maywood, Ill., 1981—87; med. cons. CNA Ins. Cos., Chgo., 1987—94; pediat. med. cons. Hartgrove Hosp., Chgo., 1996—, Alexian Bros. Behavioral Health Hosp., Hoffman Estates, Ill., 1999—2001. Part-time staff Senator Everett M. Dirksen, Chgo., 1961—64. With med. corps USNR, 1976—2000, ret. as capt. USNR, 2002. Fellow: Am. Acad. Pediat.; mem.: U. Ill. Pres. Coun., Alumni Assn. Coll. Medicine U. Ill. (alumni councillor 1989—99), U. Ill. Alumni Assn. (bd. dirs. 1983—89). Republican. Roman Catholic. Home: 146 Park Ave River Forest IL 60305-2040 Office: 5758 N California Ave Chicago IL 60659-4726

MOORE, VERNON LEE, retired food products executive, agriculturist, consultant; b. Creston, Iowa, Mar. 29, 1928; s. Newton and Eulalia Pearl (Lewis) Moore; m. Lorene Shirley Burns, Jan. 29, 1949; children: Dianne, Nancy, Jack. BS in Agr., Iowa State U., 1951. Instr. vocat. agrl. Gowrie (Iowa) Sch. Dist., 1951-55; with Land O'Lakes, Inc., Mpls., 1955-88, sr. v.p., 1988; pvt. practice agrl. cons., 1989—. Commr. Civil Svc. Commn., Columbia Heights, Minn., 1974—98; dir. adminstrn. Russian Farm Cmty.; various leadership positions Fridley United Meth. Ch., Minn., 1971—; bd. dirs. exec. com. Agrl. Coop. Devel. Internat., Washington, Am. Inst. Coop., Washington, 1975—88, Minn. 4-H Found., Washington, 1980—91; bd. dirs. Vols. Overseas Coop. Devel., Washington, 1980—88, Coop. Found., St. Paul, 1978—88; mem. adv. com. U. Minn., 1984—91. Recipient Internat. Coop. award, Coop. Coordinating Group, 1987. Mem.: Shriners, Masons, Rotary. Avocations: photography, woodworking, gardening.

MOORE, VINCENT D. humanities educator, writer; b. Strongsville, Ohio, Nov. 11, 1960; s. Thomas J. Moore and Nancy E. Sinclair. BA in psychology, Oberlin Coll., 1980—85; MA in creative writing, Miami U., 1990—92; PhD in english, U. of So. Miss., 1995—98. Asst. prof. of English St. Paul's Coll., Lawrenceville, Va., 2001, Tiffin U., Ohio, 2002—. Faculty sponsor/instr. Tiffin U. Martial Arts Club, Ohio, 2002—. Editor: (book) Religion and Terrorism: An Interfaith Perspective; contbr. articles to profl. jours. Mem.: Popular Am. Culture Assn. Avocations: martial arts, cooking, weightlifting. Office: Tiffin University 155 Miami St Tiffin OH 44883 Office Phone: 419-448-3345. Business E-Mail: moorev@tiffin.edu.

MOORE, VIRGINIA BRADLEY, librarian; b. Laurens, S.C., May 13, 1932; d. Robert Otis Brown and Queen Esther (Smith) Bradley; m. David Lee Moore, Dec. 27, 1957 (div. 1973). BS, Winston-Salem State U., 1954; MLS, U. Md., 1970. Cert. in libr. sci. edn. Tchr. John R. Hawkins H.S., Warrenton, N.C., 1954-55, Happy Plains H.S., Taylorsville, N.C., 1955-58, Young and Carver elem. schs., Washington, 1958-65; libr. Davis and Minor elem. schs., Washington, 1965-72, Ballou Sr. H.S., Kramer Jr. H.S., Washington, 1972-75, 78-80, Anacostia Sr. H.S., Washington, 1975-77, 80-95; libr. I, adult svcs. Greenbelt (Md.) Br. Libr., 1997—. Dir. ch. libr. workshops Asbury United Meth. Ch., Washington, 1972—74, 1976; spkr., presenter Ch. and Synagogue Libr. Assn., 1975, 80, 83, spkr. spring workshop, 99, presenter, 2000; mem. serials com. Prince George's County Meml. Libr. Sys., 2000—; chair-competency based curriculum D.C. pub. schs., 1978—93; chair local arrangements launching Nat. Sch. Libr. Media Month U.S. Capitol, 1985; mem. 1st libr. and info. sci. del. to People's Republic China, 1985; mem. faculty 1st established pub. svc. acad. in nation Anacostia Sr. H.S., 1990—95; coord. Nat. Libr. Week workshop Greenbelt Libr. Prince George's County Meml. Libr. Sys., 2002; presenter in field; host ch. chair Asbury United Meth. Ch., 2004. Author: (bibliography) The Negro in American History, 1619-1968, 1968; (with Helen E. Williams) Books By African-American Authors and Illustrators for Children and Young Adults, 1991; TV script for vacation reading program, 1971, sound/slide presentation D.C. Church Librs.' Bicentennial Celebration, 1976; video script and tchr.'s guide for Nat. Libr. Week Balloon Launch Day, 1983; bibliography Black Literature/Materials, 1987; contbr. articles to profl. jours. Co-chmn. nat. libr. involvement com. Martin Luther King, Jr. Fed. Holiday Commn., 1990—99, chmn., 1996—99; trustee LeRoy C. Merritt Humanitarian Fund, 2002; libr. Mt. Carmel Bapt. Ch., Washington, 1984, chair ch. libr. com., 2000—, ad hoc com. for churchwide programs, 2001—, libr. Sunday Sch. Mother's Day coord., 1990—94, jr. ch. pianist, 1994—97, Sunday Sch. adult dept. pianist, 1984—, co-chmn. African-Am. History Mo. commn., 1996—, chmn. publicity com., 1996—99, com. renovation of Rev. Arthur H. Pace Libr. Multipurpose Rm., vice-chair publicity liaison com., 1999—, soprano sanctuary choir, 1995—, soprano soloist women's day and tribute commemoration, 1998, music com., 1998—; chmn. social responsibilities roundtable Martin Luther King Jr. holiday task force Am. Libr. Assn., 1999—; rec. sec. Washington Pan-Hellenic Coun., 1975. Named outstanding educator, Mt. Carmel Bapt. Ch., 1984; recipient Outstanding Congl. Libr., Ch. and Synagogue Libr. Assn., 2001, certs. of award, D.C. Pub. Libr., 1980, D.C. Pub. Schs., 1983; fellow Grad. fellow, U. Md., 1969; scholar NDEA scholar, Central State Coll., Edmond, Okla., 1969, U. Ky., 1969, Ball State U., 1969. Mem. ALA (councilor-at-large 1983-91, 96—, Freedom to Read Honor Roll, 1999, chmn.), LWV (sec. Prince George's County, Md. 1997-99, v.p. 1999-2000, pres. 2000—), AARP, Internat. Assn. Sch. Librs., NEA (life), Am. Assn. Sch. Librs. (coms. 1973-83, 1987—), D.C. Assn. Sch. Librs. (pres. 1971-73, citation 1973, newsletter editor 1971-75, 83), Intellectual Freedom Com. (chmn. 1983-99), Freedom to Read Found., Soc. Sch. Librs. Internat. (charter), Intellectual Freedom Roundtable (bd. dirs. exec. com. 1989-91), D.C. Libr. Assn., Md. Libr. Assn., Md. Ednl. Media Orgn., Internat. Platform Assn., S.E. Neighbors Club, Am. First Day Cover Soc., Nat. Coun. of Negro Women, Zeta Phi Beta (v.p. chpt. 1972-74), Delta Kappa Gamma (v.p. Alpha chpt. 1990-92, pres. 1992-95, Nu State D.C. membership chmn. 1991-92, 2002-, rec. sec. 1994-95, v.p. 1995-97, liaison U.S. Forum 1995-97, 99—, spkr., state pres. 1997-99, steering com. speaker Soc. Internat. Legislative seminar 1998). Democrat. Achievements include being First Lady Laura Bush's guest at White House to launch Nat. Libr. Week, 2003. Home: 2100 Brooks Dr Apt 721 Forestville MD 20747-1016 Office: Prince Georges County Meml Libr Sys Greenbelt Br Libr 11 Crescent Rd Greenbelt MD 20770-1891

MOORE, VIRGINIA LEE SMITH, elementary school educator; b. Middletown, N.Y., May 13, 1943; d. James William and Anna Van Alst (Suydam) Smith; m. Thomas J. Moore, Oct. 16, 1965 (div. Apr. 1980); 1 child, Christian Thomas. AA in Liberal Arts, Orange County C.C., 1963; BA in Sociology magna cum laude, SUNY, Buffalo, 1965; MS in Edn., SUNY, New Paltz, 1980; MS in Edn. of Gifted, Coll. New Rochelle, 1990, cert. elem. edn., staff devel., 1994; cert. sch. adminstrn., 1994. Cert. elem. tchr., N.Y. Spl. edn. tchr. The Devereux Found., Glen Loch, Pa., 1965-66; elem. tchr. Harris Sch., Coatesville, Pa., 1967, Pine Bush (N.Y.) Cen. Schs., 1967-70, 78-00, substitute tchr., 1970-71; nursery sch. tchr. Olivet Meth. Nursery Sch., Coatesville, Pa., 1976-78, profl. devel. coord. Pine Bush Sch. Dist., 1998. Presenter ednl. workshops Pine Bus Sch. Dist., Haldane Sch. Dist., Cold Spring, NY, Eldred Sch. Dist., Marlboro, NY, Middletown (N.Y.) Tchr. Ctr., N.Y. State Tech. Edn. Assn., Brookhaven Nat. Lab., NY, 1994, Nevele Conference Ctr., Ellenville, NY, 1995, Rochester (N.Y.) Inst. Tech., 1996, SUNY, Oswego, 1996, Rennselaer Poly. Inst., Troy, NY, 1997, Marriot Conf. Ctr., Syracuse, NY, 1999, Sci. Tchrs. Assn. N.Y. State, Nevele Conf. Ctr., Ellenville,, 1995, Internat. Tech. Edn. Assn., Indpls., 1999; participant math., sci. and tech. on elem. level program NSF, 1997—2000. Contbr. articles to profl. jours., sci. and tech. articles to profl. publs. Pres. Redtown Residents' Assn., Middletown, 1988—; sec. Orange County C.C. Alumni Bd. Dirs. Recipient Dean's Acad. Excellence award Coll. of New Rochelle, 1991, Orange County Conservation Tchr. of Yr., 1993, N.Y.S. Conservation Tchr. of Yr., 1993, Presdl. award for excellence in math. and sci. tchg. N.Y. State, 1997; Partnership in Edn. grantee Area Fund Orange County, N.Y., 1991, Energy grantee Orange and Rockland Utilities, 1995, Tech. grantee Mid-Hudson Tchr. Ctr., 1997, 98, Energy grantee N.Y. State Electric and Gas, 1998. Mem. NSTA, Internat. Tech. Edn. Assn. (N.Y. State Elem. Sch. Tchr. Excellence award 1998-99), N.Y. State United Tchrs., Sci. Tchrs. Assn. N.Y. State (Outstanding Sci. Tchr. award 1992, Excellence in Sci. Tchg. award 1995), N.Y. State Tech. Edn. Assn. (Tech. grantee 1999), Phi Beta Kappa. Baptist. Avocations: piano, reading, local environmental issues, development of interactive science museum exhibits. Home: 1672 Route 211 E Middletown NY 10941-3718

MOORE, W. DARIN, minister; b. Mt. Vernon, N.Y., Mar. 25, 1960; s. William David Moore and Constance Louise Farrow; m. Devieta Chevette, June 9, 1984; children: W. Daron, Dana M., Dion B. Student, Livingstone Coll., 1980-84; BS, Purchase Coll., 1995; postgrad., Yale U., 2000—. Ordained elder AME Zion Ch. Pastor Clarksville AME Zion Ch., Monroe, N.C., 1983-84, Morning Star AME Zion Ch., Monroe, 1983-84, Mt. Olivet AME Zion Ch., Greensboro, N.C., 1984-89, Jones Tabernacle, Indpls., 1989-93, Greater Centennial AME Zion Ch., Mt. Vernon, N.Y., 1993—. Presiding elder Indpls. Dist. AME Zion Ch., 1991-93; nat. dir. young adult ministries AME Zion Ch., founding chmn. young adults in Christian ministries. Mem. Guilford County (N.C.) Commn. on Youth, 1988-89; pres. Ch. Fedn., Indpls., 1992-93; founder, chmn. Save Our Seed Ministries, Mt. Vernon, 1994—; trustee Mt. Vernon Bd. Edn., 1998—. Mem. NAACP, Nat. Alliance Black Sch. Educators, Nat. Sch. Bds. Assn., United Black Clergy of Westchester (v.p.), Interdenomination Mins. Assn., Alpha Phi Alpha. African Meth. Episcopal Zion. Avocations: travel, reading, golf. Office: Greater Centennial AME Zion Ch 100 W 4th St Mount Vernon NY 10550-4044

MOORE, WARD WILFRED, medical educator; b. Cowden, Ill., Feb. 12, 1924; s. Cecil Leverett and Velma Leona (Frye) M.; m. Frances Laura Campbell, Jan. 29, 1949; children— Scott Thomas, Ann Gail, Brian Dean, Kevin Lee. AB, U. Ill., 1948, MS, 1951, PhD, 1952; DSc (hon.), Mahidol U., Bangkok, 2001. Instr., rsch. assoc. U. Ill., 1952-54; asst. prof. Okla. State U., Stillwater, 1954-55, Ind. U., Bloomington, 1955-59, assoc. prof., 1959-66, prof. physiology, 1966-89, prof. physiology and biophysics emeritus, 1989—, acting chmn. dept. anatomy, 1971-73, assoc. dean basic med. scis., 1971-89, assoc. dean, dir. med. scis. program, 1976-89. Vis. prof. Postgrad. Med. Center, Karachi, Pakistan, 1963-64; staff mem. Rockefeller Found., 1968-71; vis. prof., chmn. dept. physiology, faculty sci. Mahidol U., Bangkok, Thailand, 1968-71 Served with U.S. Army, 1943-46. Mem. Am. Physiol. Soc., Endocrine Soc., Am. Soc. Nephrology, Soc. Study Reproduction, Am. Assn. Anatomists, Soc. Exptl. Biology and Medicine, Am. Assn. Med. Colls., AAAS, Am. Inst. Biol. Scis., AAUP, Ind. Acad. Sci., Ind. Hist. Soc., Soc. Sons of Am. Revolution, Sigma Xi, Phi Sigma. Home: 3500 E Bradley St Bloomington IN 47401-4201 Office: Indiana U Jordan Hall # 105 Bloomington IN 47405 Personal E-mail: moorew@indiana.edu.

MOORE, WESLEY BOYD, occupational physician; b. Nashville, Nov. 2, 1953; s. Jesse Perry and Anna Lou Moore; m. Regina G. Moore, Sept. 25, 1976; children: Daniel Trent, Amy Leigh, Emily Annette. BS in Chemistry, Middle Tenn. State U., 1975; MD, U. Tenn., 1978. Bd. cert. family medicine and occupl. medicine. Intern, resident family practice U. Pa., Jackson (Tenn.) Madison County Gen. Hosp., 1979-81; emergency physician William Gaw, M.D., Nashville, 1982-85; family physician LaVergne (Tenn.) Med. Clin., 1985-86, Family Med. Ctr., Inc., Antioch, Tenn., 1986-91; staff physician Miller Med. Group, Antioch, 1991-93; co. physician Nissan Motor Mfg., Inc., Smyrna, Tenn., 1989—. Pres. Andrew Jackson chpt. Tenn. Acad. Family Physicians, Nashville, 1983-84; bd. mem. Tenn. Acad. Family Physicians, 1987-93. Founding editor Tenn. Family Physician, 1989, assoc. editor, 1990-99. Fellow Am. Acad. Family Practice; mem. AMA, Am. Coll. Occupl. and Environ. Medicine, Tenn. Coll. Occupl. and Environ. Medicine (bd. mem. 1998-99), LaVergne Men's Club (Man of Yr. award 1989). Office: Nissan Motor Mfg Inc 983 Nissan Dr Smyrna TN 37167-4405

MOORE, WILLIAM BLACK, JR., retired aluminum company executive; b. Jackson, Miss., Sept. 18, 1924; s. William Black and May Isom (Whitten) M.; m. Lillian Wells, Sept. 14, 1946; children: Kathryn Ramsey Moore Dannels, William Black III, Bethany Moore Richmond. BSChemE, U. Louisville, 1945, MSChemE, 1947. Registered profl. engr., Ky. Chem. engr. U. Louisville Rsch. Inst., 1947-49; mktg. mgr. Reynolds Metals, Louisville, 1949-58, dir. mktg. Richmond, Va., 1958-61, regional gen. mgr. St. Louis, 1961-69, v.p. Richmond, 1969-80; ret. Mem. adv. bd. Bay Trust Co. Author: Letters to Rebecca; contbr. articles to profl. jours. Pres. bd. dirs. Rappahannock Found.; pres. Lagniappe Found.; dir. adv. bd. Bay Trust Co., Kilmarnock, Va. Served to Lt. USNR, 1943-47. Mem. AIA (hon.), Indian Creek Club (Kilmarnock, Va.), Country Club of Va. (Richmond). Baptist. Avocations: fishing, farming, genealogy. Home: PO Box 1300 Kilmarnock VA 22482-1300 E-mail: wbmoore@crosslink.net.

MOORE, WILLIAM GROVER, JR., management consultant, retired military officer; b. Waco, Tex. s. William Grover and Annie Elizabeth (Pickens) Moore; m. Marjorie Y. Gardella, Jan. 18, 1943; 1 child, Allyson. Student, Kilgore (Tex.) Coll., 1937—39, Sacramento State Coll., 1951, George Washington U., 1962; grad., Air War Coll., Air U., 1957, Nat. War Coll., 1962. Enlisted U.S. Army Air Force, 1940, commd. 2d lt., 1941, advanced through grades to gen., 1977; comdr. 777th Squadron, 15th AF, Italy, 1944—45, 3535th Maintenance and Supply Group, Mather AFB, Calif., 3d Bomb Group, Korea, 1952; chief bases and units divsn. Hdqrs. USAF, 1952—56; asst. dep. chief of staff ops. Hdqrs. USAF Europe, 1957—61; comdr. 314th Troop Carrier Wing, Stewart AFB, Tenn., 1962—63, 839th Air Divsn., 1963—65; asst. J3 U.S. Strike Command, 1965—66; comdr. 834th Air Divsn., Vietnam, 1966—67; dir. operational requirements Hdqrs. USAF, 1967—70; comdr. 22d AF, 1970—73, 13th AF, 1973; chief of staff Pacific Command, 1973—76; asst. vice chief of staff Hdqrs. USAF, 1976—77; comdr. in chief Mil. Air Lift Command, 1977—79; ret., 1979; pres., COO Emery Air Freight Corp., Wilton, Conn., 1981—83; bus. cons., 1983—. Pres. Met. Nashville Airport Authority, 1984—. Decorated Def. D.S.M., Air Force D.S.M. with 2 oak leaf clusters, Legion of Merit with 4 oak leaf clusters, Silver Star, D.F.C. with oak leaf cluster, Air Medal with 9 oak leaf clusters, Air Force Commendation medal with 10 oak leaf clusters (U.S.), Croix de Guerre with palm France, Armed Forces Honor medal 1st class Vietnam, Republic of China Cloud and Banner, Legion of Honor Republic of the Philippines; named to Minuteman Hall of Fame, 1979; recipient L. Mendel Rivers award of excellence; fellow Jimmy Doolittle fellow in aerospace edn., 1978. Mem.: Am. Ordnance Assn., Nat. Def. Transp. Assn., Air Force Assn. Home: 932 W Main St Franklin TN 37064-2730 Office: Nashville Internat Airport 1 Terminal Dr Ste 501 Nashville TN 37214-4110

MOORE, WILLIAM H., III, investment company executive; Gen. ptnr. Brown Bros. Harriman & Co., N.Y.C. Office: Brown Bros Harriman & Co 59 Wall St New York NY 10005-2808

MOORE, WILLIAM JOHN MYLES, retired electrical engineer, researcher; b. Edinburgh, Scotland, May 3, 1924; arrived in Can., 1928; s. William Harold Moore; m. Ruth Elizabeth Duffy, Aug. 21, 1948; children: Roberta Louise, Marilyn Elizabeth. B in Applied Sci., U. B.C., Can., 1946; postgrad., NRC, Ottawa, Can., summer 1947; M in Engring., McGill U., 1948. Rsch. officer NRC Can., Ottawa, Ont., 1948-51, 55-88, asst. head power engring sect. elec. engring. div., 1988-90, ret., 1990; rsch. officer Can. Armament R&D Establishment, Valcartier, Que., 1951-52, head analysis sect., 1952-54, group leader analysis, control and simulation sects., 1954-55. Cons. prof. Huazhong U. Sci. and Tech., Wuhan, Peoples Republic of China., 1988. Author: The Current Comparator, 1987; holder 10 patents. Fellow IEEE (chmn. Ottawa sect. 1966-67, chmn. Elec. and Electronic Measurement and Test Instrumentation Conf. and Instrumentation and Measurement Symposium 1969, pres. Group on Instrumentation and Measurement 1974, chmn. power systems instrumentation and measurement com. Power Engring. Soc. 1981-82, Morris E. Leeds award, 1987, Centennial medal 1984, A.G.L. McNaughton medal 1991), Assn. Prof. Engrs. Ont. Home: 797 Dunloe Ave Ottawa ON Canada K1K 0K3

MOORE, WILLIAM LEROY, JR., career officer, physician; b. Savannah, Ga., June 1, 1934; s. William Leroy Sr. and Helen Louise (Robbins) M.; m. Anna Elizabeth Ballard, Mar. 15, 1958; children: William L., Christopher A., Mary Beth. Student, Ga. Inst. Tech., 1951-52; AB, Emory U., 1955; MD, Med. Coll. Ga., 1959; postgrad. mil. tng. courses, 1962-94. Diplomate Am. Bd. Internal Medicine, Am. Bd. Infectious Diseases. Commd. capt. U.S. Army, 1962, advanced through grades to maj. gen., 1992; intern Floyd Hosp., Rome, Ga., 1959-60; pvt. practice Rome, 1960-61; resident in internal medicine Brooke Gen. Hosp., Ft. Sam Houston, Tex., 1965-68; rsch. fellow in infectious diseases U. Tex. Southwestern Med. Sch., Dallas, 1968-70; resident in internal medicine Parkland Meml. Hosp., Dallas, 1968-70; gen. med. officer Martin Army Hosp., Ft. Benning, Ga., 1962, 5th Spl. Forces Group, Spl. Warfare Ctr., Ft. Bragg, N.C., 1962-63; gen. internist, group surgeon, commdg. officer 1st Spl. Forces Group, Spl. Action Force, Okinawa, Japan, 1963-65; asst. chief to chief infectious disease svc. Brooke Gen. Hosp., Ft. Sam Houston, Tex., 1970-74; chief internal medicine svc., chief dept. medicine, chief profl. svcs. Eisenhower Army Med. Ctr., Ft. Gordon, Ga., 1978-83; comdr. Frankfurt (Germany) Army Regional Med. Ct., 97th Gen. Hosp., 1983-86; project mgr. Office of Surgeon Gen., Washington, 1986-88; adj. faculty Nat. Def. U., Ft. Lesley J. McNair, Washington, 1986-88; vice comdr. Joint Mil. Med. Command, Randolph AFB, Tex., 1988-91; comdr. Brooke Army Med. Ctr., Ft. Sam Houston, Tex., 1988-91, U.S. Army Med. Dept. Ctr. & Sch., Ft. Sam Houston, Tex., 1991-94; state epidemiologist, dir. communicable & environ. disease Tenn. Dept. Health, 1995-2001; prof. medicine divsn. infectious diseases Vanderbilt U. Sch. Medicine, Nashville, 1994—; chief of staff VA Med. Ctr., Nashville, 2001—02; dir. bur. epidemiology Nashville Davidson Met. Health Dept., 2002—. Clin. assoc. in medicine U. Tex. Southwestern Med. Sch., 1969-70; clin. assoc. prof. medicine U. Tex. Med. Sch., 1970-74; chief. sect. of infectious diseases Med. Coll. Ga., 1974-75, assoc. prof., 1974-78, clin. prof., 1978-83; prin. investigator infectious disease rsch. VA Hosp., Augusta, Ga., 1974-78, asst. chief med. svc., 1974-75, dir. clin . microbiology lab., 1974-78, epidemiologist, 1974-78; head internal medicine infectious disease 97th gen. Hosp., Frankfurt, 1983-86, Walter Reed Army Med. Ctr., 1986-88; clin. prof. medicine U. Tex. Health Sci. Ctr., San Antonio, 1989-94; mem. ref. panel on Am. Hosp. Formulary Svc. of Am. Soc. Hosp. Pharmacists, 1974-78; faculty Advisor Lane-Walker AMSA Free Clinic, Augusta, 1975-78; mem. various coms. and bds., VA Hosp., Augusta, 1974-78. Contbr. articles to profl. jours. Mem. Army Comty. Coun. San Antonio, 1988-94; dir., bd. dirs. Army Med. Dept. Mus. Found. Inc., 1989-94; bd. dirs. San Antonio Area chpt. ARC, 1989. Decorated Army Commendation medal, Meritorious Svc. medal (3), Legion of Merit with three oak leaf clusters, Disting. Svc. medal Army Med. Dept. Regiment, 1994, Order of Mil. Med. Merit; recipient Scholastic Excellence award C.V. Mosby Co., 1959, Laureate award, Am. Coll. Physician, 1996, Dirs. Commendation VA Hosp., Augusta, 1978, Surgeon Gen.'s A Profl. Designer for Internal Med., 1982. Fellow ACP, Infectious Diseases Soc. Am.; mem.: NAS (nat. rsch. coun. 1995-96), Assn. Mil. Surgeons U.S. (mem.-at-large exec. coun. Alamo chpt. 1989), Soc. Med. Cons. to Armed Forces (chmn. com. on cons. activities 1977-79), Am. Heart Assn. (bd. dirs. San Antonio divsn. 1988-89), San Antonio Rsch. Club (sec., pres. 1970-74), Tenn. Med. Assn., Nashville Acad. Medicine, Tenn. Pub. Health Assn., Coun.State and Territorial Epidemiologists. *Strict adherence to moral and ethical principles, willingness to work hard, use all of one's talents to benefit others and take advantage of all of the opportunities one finds to improve one's self while serving others are the elements of success in this life.*

MOORE, WILLIAM THEODORE, JR., judge; b. Bainbridge, Ga., May 7, 1940; s. William T. and Mary (Talbert) M.; m. Jane Hodges, July 18, 1964; children: Sarah S., Mary T. William T III. AA, Ga. Military Coll., 1960; JD, U. Ga., 1964; Law (hon.), Ga. Mil. Coll., 1978; LLM, U. Va., 2001. Bar: Ga. 1964, U.S. Dist. Ct. (so. dist.) Ga. 1964, U.S. Ct. Appeals (5th and 11th cirs.) 1979, U.S. Supreme Ct. 1980. U.S. atty. So. Dist. Ga. U.S. Dept. of Justice, Savannah, 1977-81; ptnr. Corish, Smith, Remler & Moore, Savannah, 1967-77, Sparkman, Harris & Moore, Savannah, 1981-87, Oliver Maner & Gray, Savannah, 1988-94; judge U.S. Dist. Ct. for So. Dist. Ga., Savannah, 1994. Atty. Savannah-Chatham County Bd. Pub. Edn., 1975-77, mem. U.S. Atty. Gen's. Adv. com. D.C. 1978-81. Recipient Spl. Appreciation award Ga. Bur. of Investigation, 1980, U.S. Dept. Treasury Bur. of Alcohol, Tobacco & Firearms, D.C., 1980; Extraordinary Svc. award Savannah Chapt. Fed. Bar Assn., 1980. Fellow Am. Bd. Criminal Lawyers (pres. 1993); mem. NACDL, Nat. Assn. Former U.S. Attys. (bd. dirs. 1984—), Jud. Conf. U.S. (com. on criminal law, sentencing subcomittee), Ga. Assn. Criminal Def. Lawyers (v.p. 1986—), Ga. Bar Assn. Democrat. Episcopalian. Avocations: jogging, weight training, golf, reading. Office: US Dist Courthouse 125 Bull St PO Box 10245 Savannah GA 31412-0445

MOORE, WILLIAM VINCENT, political science educator; b. Columbia, Mo., Apr. 13, 1944; s. Willis and Mabelle (Rogers) M.; m. Suzanne Shelton, July 14, 1967 (div. Feb. 1984); children: Mark, Laura. BA, So. Ill. U., 1966, MA, 1968; PhD, Tulane U., 1975. Instr. Fla. Meml. Coll., Miami, 1968-69,

Xavier U., New Orleans, 1970-72; asst. prof. to assoc. prof. polit. sci. Coll. of Charleston, S.C., 1972-83, prof., 1983-99, disting. prof., 1999—, scholar-in-residence, 1976, dir. summer sessions, 1984-87, chmn. dept., 1987-93, dir., masters in pub. adminstrn. dept., 1993-99. Chmn. S.C. Interagy. Merit Coun., Columbia, 1987-99; instr. jr. statesmen program Northwestern U., Evanston, Ill., 1996; faculty Northampton U. Coll., Northampton, Eng., 2001; mem. adv. com. Charleston Sch. of Law, S.C. Author: Political Extremism in the U.S.A., 1983; co-author: Politics and Government in South Carolina, 1994; contbr. articles to profl. jours. Grantee U. N.C., 1980; rsch. fellow U. S.C., 1983; named Prof. of Yr., S.C. Gov., 1997. Mem. Am. Polit. Sci. Assn., So. Polit. Sci. Assn., S.C. Polit. Sci. Assn. (pres. 1983-84), Phi Kappa Phi (chpt. pres. 1982-84), Pi Sigma Alpha (chpt. pres. 1987-93), Pi Alpha Alpha. Avocations: tennis, racquetball. Home: 378 Cross St Charleston SC 29407-6977 Office: Coll of Charleston Polit Sci Dept Charleston SC 29424 Office Phone: 843-953-5724. Business E-Mail: moorew@cofc.edu.

MOORE, WISTAR, cardiovascular surgeon; b. Feb. 16, 1959; BA, U. N.C., 1981, MD, 1985. Bd. cert. gen. surgery, thoracic surgery. Gen. surgery resident Mass. Gen. Hosp., 1985-90; cardiothoracic resident The Emory Clinic, 1990-93; cardiovasc. surgeon Watson Clinic, Lakeland, Fla., 1993-2000; chief divsn. cardiovasc. thoracic surgery Lakeland Regional Med. Ctr., 1996-2000; cardiovasc. surgeon Cardiovasc. Surgeons, Orlando, Fla., 2000—04, Leesburg-Ocala Heart Inst., 2004—. Fellow ACS, Am. Coll. Chest Physicians; mem. Fla. Soc. Thoracic and Cardiovasc. Surgeons, So. Thoracic Surg. Assn., Soc. Thoracic Surgeons. Office: 700 Doctors Ct Leesburg FL 34748 Office Phone: 352-787-9830.

MOOREFIELD, KENNETH P. ambassador; b. Temple, Tex., July 1943; m. Geraldine Moorefield; 1 child. Grad., U.S. Mil. Acad., 1965; postgrad., Georgetown U., 1972. U.S. amb. to Gabon, Sao Tome and Principe Dept. of State, Washington, 2002—. Decorated Silver Star, Purple Heart. Office: DOS Amb 2270 Libreville Pl Washington DC 20521

MOORE JR, CLETUS B. financial consultant, hotel executive; s. Cletus B Moore Sr and Grace H Moore; m. Phyllis A Land, June 21, 1991; m. Jean Barton, Mar. 21, 1970 (div. Apr. 1, 1987); children: Jennifer L Moore, Christopher B Moore. BS in Bus. Admin., Woodbury U., 1997; MBA, George Fox U., 1995. Asst. gen. mgr. Oxford Inns & Suites, Chico, Calif., 2002—; exec. asst. to pres. Am. Pacific Bus. Ventures, Inc., Portland, Oreg., 1978—85; dir. human resources Emmert Internat., Clackamas, Oreg., 2001—02; v.p. fin., bus. adminstrn. Warner Pacific Coll., Portland, Oreg., 1999—2001; adminstr., ho. rules & pub. affairs commn. Oreg. State Legislature, 70th Session, Salem, Oreg., 1999—99; dir. of campus ops. Western States Chiropractic Coll., Portland, Oreg., 1995—98; v.p., fin. & adminstrn., cfo Urban League of Portland, Portland, Oreg., 1990—95; interim pres. & cfo Urban League Of Portland, Portland, Oreg., 1993—94; v.p., ops. Beutelschies & Associates, Portland, Oreg., 1987—90; devel. officer Brim & Associates, Portland, Oreg., 1985—86. Investment and ins. cons. Primerica Fin. Services Investments, Inc., Portland, Oreg., 1997—. Dir. Downtown Cmty. Housing Inc., Portland, Oreg., Morison Ctr., Child & Family Svcs., Portland, Oreg., 1998—2001, Rosemont Sch. for Girls; dir., pres. Carousel Children's Theater for Children; com. mem. Coun. Youth Drug, Alcohol & Tobacco Use, Oreg.; dir. Governor's Commn. on Sr. Services, Oreg., Adv. Bd., Housing Authority of Portland, Oreg.; commr. Southwood/Woodland Pk. Water Dist., Oreg.; bd. of edn. Mt Hood C.C., Greasham, Oreg., 1999—2003; chmn. Multnomah County Rep. Party, Portland, Oreg., 2000—03. Tech. seargent USAF. Decorated Commendation for Meritorious Svc. - Vietnam USAF, Noteworthy Performance 479th Tactical Hosp. USAF, George AFB; recipient Outstanding Airman of the Month, Comdr., George AFB, 1969. Independent-Republican. Baptist. Avocations: community service, musical theater. Office: Oxford Inns & Suites PO Box 9022 Chico CA 95927-9022 E-mail: b_oxfordsuites@yayoo.com.

MOORE-JUMONVILLE, KIMBERLY, literature educator; b. Lubbock, Tex., Oct. 7, 1958; d. Darrell Paul and Donna (Browning) Moore; m. Robert Stuart Moore-Jumonville, Jan. 1, 1982; 1 child, Annesley. BA in English, Seattle (Wash.) Pacific U., 1981; MPhil in 19th Century Studies, drew U., 1987; PhD in 19th Century Studies, Drew U., 1991. Asst. prof. English Taylor U., Upland, Ind., 1992—98, assoc. prof. English, 1998—2001, Spring Arbor (Mich.) U., 2001—, chmn. English Dept., 2002—. Mem.: Modern Lang. Assn., Christianity and Lit., Dorothy Sayers Soc. Office: Spring Arbor Univ English Dept 106 E Main St Spring Arbor MI 49283 Office Phone: 517-750-6692.

MOORER, MICHAEL, professional boxer; b. Bklyn., Nov. 12, 1967; m. Bobbie Moorer; 1 child, Michael Jr. Champion World Boxing Assn., light heavyweight title, Pittburgh, Pa., 1990, World Boxing Assn. and Internat. Boxing Federation, heavyweight title, Las Vegas, Nev., 1996. Office: Main Event 390 Murray Hill Pkwy East Rutherford NJ 07073-2109

MOORES, JOHN, professional sports team executive; b. July 9, 1944; m. Becky Moores, 1963; children: Jennifer, John Jr. With IBM, Shell Oil; founder, CEO BMC Software, 1980-89, chmn., 1980-92, Peregrine Sys., Inc., Del Mar, Calif., 1990—2000, 2002; founder, chmn. JMI Services, San Diego, 1992—; chmn., co-owner San Diego Padres, 1994—. Mem. adv. bd. San Diego Hall of Champions; bd. dirs. Scripps Rsch., Inc. Trustee Carter Ctr. of Emory U.; founder, chmn. River Blindness Found.; founder Padres Found., 1995—, Padres Scholars Program, 1995—; mem., bd. regents U. Houston, 1991-1994, U. Calif, 1999—, chmn. 2002—. Office: San Diego Padres PO Box 2000 San Diego CA 92112-2000 also: JMI Services 12680 High Bluff Dr Suite 200 San Diego CA 92130*

MOORE-VICULIN, CHARLOTTE ANNE, artist, musician; d. Harry and Virginia Longworth (Dyer) Moore; m. Richard Jerry Viculin, Oct. 15, 1977. BFA, postgrad., Wayne State U. Self-employed portrait artist, mural painter; tchr., performer piano, vocalist Detroit, Livonia and Plymouth, Mich.; music arranger, profl. music judge. Fundraiser Plymouth Symphony League, 1980—95; bd. dirs., former sec. Plymouth Symphony, 1991—96. Named Nat. Career Woman of Yr., Nat. Assn. Career Women, 1991. Mem. Am. Soc. Portrait Artists, Portrait Soc. Am., Nat. Guild Piano Tchrs., Nat. Music Tchrs. Assn., Mich. Music Tchrs. Assn., Nat. Fedn. Music Clubs, Mich. Fedn. Music Clubs (officer), Ann Arbor Area Piano Tchrs. Guild (officer), Livonia Area Piano Tchrs. Forum (officer) Home: 27265 Canfield Dr W Dearborn Heights MI 48127-1044 Office: Charlotte Moore-Viculin Studios of Music and Art 352 N Main St Ste 4 Plymouth MI 48170-1270 Office Phone: 734-459-1112.

MOORHEAD, CARLOS J. former congressman; b. Long Beach, Calif., May 6, 1922; s. Carlos Arthur and Florence (Gravers) M.; m. Valery Joan Tyler, July 19, 1969; children: Theresa, Catharine, Steven, Teri, Paul. BA, UCLA, 1943; JD, U. So. Calif., 1949. Bar: Calif. 1949, U.S. Supreme Ct. 1973. Pvt. practice law, Glendale, Calif., 1949-72; dir. Lawyers Reference Service, Glendale, 1950-66; mem. 93d-104th Congresses from 22d (now 27th) Dist. Calif., 1973-96; mem. judiciary com.; chmn. subcom. on cts. and intellectual property; vice chmn. commerce com.; mem. subcom. on energy & power, subcom. on telecomm. & fin.; dean Calif. Congl. Rep. Delegation. Apptd. to Fed. Cts. Study Com.; sr. fellow Sch. Pub. Policy, UCLA. Pres. Glendale Hi-Twelve Club; mem. Verdugo Hills council Boy Scouts Am.; mem. Calif. Assembly, 1967-72; mem. Calif. Law Revision Commn., 1971-72; pres. 43d Dist. Republican Assembly, Glendale Young Republicans; mem. Los Angeles County Rep. Central Com., Calif. Rep. Central Com.; bd. dirs. Glendale La Crescenta Camp Fire Girls, Inc.; mem. Found. Bd., Glendale Hosp., Glendale C.C.; mem. adv. bd. Salvation Army of Glendale. Served to lt. col. AUS, 1942-46. Recipient Man of Yr. award USO, 1979 Mem. Calif. Bar Assn. L.A. County Bar Assn., Glendale Bar Assn. (past pres.), Glendale C. of C., Masons, Shriners, Lions, Moose, VFW. Presbyterian. Office: 1354 J Lee Cir Glendale CA 91208-1730

MOORHEAD, GERALD LEE, architect; b. Davenport, Iowa, Feb. 18, 1947; s. Wayne Lee and Marilou (George) M. BA, Rice U., 1969, BArch, 1971. Arch. Middleton & Statton, El Paso, Tex., 1967, MA Floyd Assocs., Houston, 1968, CRS Design Inc., Houston, 1969-70, Phillips & Peterson AIA, Houston, 1969-73; arch., v.p. Charles Tapley Assocs., Houston, 1973-83; propr. Lloyd Jones Fillpot Assocs., 1986-87, Gerald Moorhead, Arch., 1983-98; sr. assoc. Bailey Archs., 1998—. Photography exhibited in group shows at Galveston Arts Coun., Tex., 1976, Jewish Cmty. Ctr., Houston, 1977, Cronin Gallery, Houston, 1977; one-man photog. exhbns. include Autry Ho. Gallery, Houston, 1979; editor, photographer: Houston Architectural Guide, 1999, Buildings of Texas; editor: Houston Architectural Ballade, 2000; contbg. editor Tex. Arch., Arthtl. Record; contbr. articles on architecture to profl. publs.; exhbn. curator Houston Mus. Natural Sci., 1990, Mus. Fine Arts, Houston, 1991, FotoFest, Houston, 1996. Treas. Houston Ctr. for Photography, 1985-87. Recipient Spl. award Houston AIA/Houston Home & Garden, 1979, Internat. prize Union Archs. Kazakstan, 1991; named Arch. Laureate of Kazakstan, 1992. Fellow AIA (Honor award Houston chpt. 1979, Young Arch. award Houston chpt. 1985); mem. Soc. Archtl. Historians, Nat. Trust for Hist. Preservation, Tex. Soc. Archs. (1st Honor award 1976, Interiors award 1986, Flowers Journalism award 1995), Rice Design Alliance. Home: 1755 W Main Ave Houston TX 77098-3607

MOORHEAD, GLEN W. (WALLY), III, career officer; b. Smackover, Ark. Student, USAF Acad. Prep. Sch., 1965; BS in Engring. Scis., USAF, 1969; student pilot tng., Columbus AFB, Miss., 1970-71; student combat crew tng., England AFB, La., 1971, 72-73, Myrtle Beach AFB, S.C., 1972-73; student, Squadron Officer Sch., 1975, Fighter Weapons Sch., 1978, Air Command and Staff Coll., 1982, Air War Coll., 1987, U.S. Army War Coll., 1991. Commd. 2d lt. USAF, 1969, advanced through grades to lt. gen., 1998; pilot 8th Spl. Ops., Bien Hoa Air Base, S. Vietnam, 1971-72, various squadrons, Korat Royal Thai AFB, Thailand, 1973; stationed at England AFB, 1973-75, 80-82; operational test pilot, A-10 joint test force 4486th Test Squadron, Edwards AFB, Calif., 1975-76; stationed at Davis-Monthan AFB, Ariz., 1976-77, Nellis AFB, 1977-86; A-10 squadron comdr. 356th Tactical Fighter Squadron, Myrtle Beach AFB, 1986-89; dep. dir. fighter tactics and tng. Hdqs. Tactical Air Command, Langley AFB, Va., 1989-90; various comdr. assignments, 1991-94, 96-97; spl. asst. to Supreme Allied comdr., 1994-96; chief of staff Joint Task Force Provide Promise, Naples, Italy, 1994-96; comdr. Space Warfare Ctr., Falcon AFB, Colo., 1997-98, Air Warfare Ctr., Nellis AFB, 1998-2000; asst. dep. chief of staff USAF Hdqs. Air & Space Ops., Washington, 2000; vice commander US Air Forces in Europe, Ramstein AB, Germany, 2000—02; commander Allied Air Forces Southern Europe, Stabilization Force Air Component and Kosovo Force Air Component, Naples, Italy, and Commander 16th Air Force, USAFE, Aviano AB, Italy, 2002—. Decorated Legion of Merit with oak leaf cluster, D.F.C., Purple Heart, Air medal with 12 oak leaf clusters. Office: APO AE 09604 Aviano AB Italy

MOORHEAD, JOHN COUPER, emergency physician; b. Toronto, Nov. 4, 1949; came to U.S., 1978; s. David Earle and Elizabeth Cook (Couper) M.; married; children: Couper John, Jackson Couper. BA, Queens U., Kingston, Ont., 1971, MD, 1975; MS, NYU, 1989. Emergency physician Oreg. Health Scis. U., Portland, 1978—. Bd. dirs. Am. Bd. Emergency Medicine. Mem. editl. bds. three med. jours.; contbr. articles to profl. jours. Mem. AMA, Oreg. Med. Assn. (pres. 2004—), Am. Coll. Emergency Physicians, Oreg. Coll. Emergency Physicians (bd. dirs.), Assn. Acad. Chairs Emergency Medicine, Soc. Acad. Emergency Medicine. Office: Oregon Health Scis U 3181 SW Sam Jackson Park Rd Portland OR 97239-3079 Business E-Mail: moorhead@ohsu.edu.

MOORHEAD, NILA KATHERINE, music educator; b. Tucson, Ariz., Aug. 18, 1978; d. Peter M. Faber and Nila L. Haworth; m. Cord Christopher Moorhead, Mar. 1, 2003. MusB, Ariz. State U., 1996—2001. Band dir. Gilbert Unified Sch. Dist., Gilbert, Ariz., 2001—. Flute tchr., Ariz., 1996—; piccolo player Tempe Wind Ensemble, Tempe, Ariz., 2001—. Recipient Tchr. of the Month, Desert Ridge Jr. High, 2003, Suddler Silver Scroll award, John Phillip Sousa Found., 2002. Mem.: AMEA, Nat. Flute Assn., Ariz. Flute Soc. (flute choir dir. 1997—98), Music Educators' Nat. Conf. Independent. Episc. Avocations: hiking, reading, flute. Office: Gilbert Unified School District 10211 E Madero Ave Mesa AZ

MOORHEAD, ROLANDE ANNETTE REVERDY, artist, educator; b. Périgueux, France; d. RémyJean and Andrée Marcelle (Lavollée) Reverdy; m. Elliott Swift Moorhead, III, Sept. 30, 1960; children: Edward Marc, Roland Elliott, Rémy Bruce. Degree in liberal arts, Coll. Technique, Nice, France, 1954. Bi-lingual sec., France, 1957-58, French Embassy, Washington, 1959-60, 68-70; chmn. exhibit com. Lauderdale-By-The-Sea Art Guild, Ft. Lauderdale, Fla., 1972-75, v.p., 1972-74, founder group 5 Women Artists; exhibit com. Broward Art Guild, Ft. Lauderdale, Fla., 1976; treas., dir. Alliance Francaise, Miami, Fla., 1973-75. Juror, lectr. in field; invited guest artist Franco-Am. Art Show, Curemonte, France, 1996-97. One-woman shows include numerous galleries, Ft. Lauderdale area, 1971—, Ocean Club Art Gallery, Ft. Lauderdale, 1971-74, Pier 66 Gallery, Ft. Lauderdale, 1973, 75, 76, Ft. Lauderdale City Hall, 1974, 77-78, 81-88, 91-94, 95-2000, St. Basil Orthodox Ch., North Miami Beach, 1977, Galerie Vallombreuse, Biarritz, France, 1977, Gallerie Mooffe, Paris, 1978, Gallerie du Palais des Fêtes, Périgueux, 1978, 88, Le Club Internat., Ft. Lauderdale, 1979, Leonard Gallery, Ft. Lauderdale, 1990-92, Tallahassee (Fla.) Capitol Bldg., 1990, Lighthouse Pt. (Fla.) Gallery, 1990, Hollywood (Fla.) Art and Cultural Ctr., 1987, 89, 90, 91, 93, 95, Ft. Lauderdale Arts Inst., 1991, 93-95, Dover Gallery, Boca Raton, Fla., 1992; Galerie Mouffe, Paris, 1978, Glass Gallery, Pembroke Pines, Fla., 2001; exhibited in group shows Gallery YES, Wilton Manors, Fla., 2001, Wave Gallery, Key west, Fla., Webber Art Center, Ocala, Fla., 2003; Broward Art Guild, 1971, 73, 74, Point of Am. Gallery, Ft. Lauderdale, 1971, 73, Internat. Festival, Miami, 1976, Internat. Salon, Biarritz, 1977, Internat. Summer Salon, Paris, 1977, Fine Art Gallery Show and Competition, Long Galleries, Ft. Lauderdale, 1979, Pembroke Pines (Fla.) City Hall, 1982, Hollywood City Libr., 1982, also area banks, ch. and libr., numerous local art festivals, Schacknow Mus. Plantation, Fla., 2000, Ft. Lauderdale Mus. Art, 2000; represented in permanent collections: Fr. Lauderdale City Hall, DAV Hdqrs., Washington, Associated Aircraft Co., March of Dimes Bldg. (both Ft. Lauderdale), Oakland Pk. Libr., Fla., St. Josephs Convent, St. Augustine, Fla., US Air Force Mus., Ohio, Main Line Fleets, Inc., Palm Beach, Fla., Creditreform, Dusseldorf, Germany, St. Front Cathedral, Périgueux, St. Sacerdoce Cathedral, Sarlat, France, Club Med, Fla. and Caribbean, also numerous pvt. collections US and Europe; author art manual for Broward Arts Coun., Fla., 1986. Recipient Best in Show award Internat. Salon, Biarritz, 1977; named artist in residence Broward County Sch., 1985. Mem. Am. Soc. Portrait Artists, Nat. Assn. Women Artists, Fla. Watercolor Soc., Palm Beach Watercolor Soc., Nat. League Am. Penwomen, Art 24, Périgueux, Internat. Soc. Marine Painters, Am. Watercolor Soc., Cathedral St. Sacerdoce, Nat. Mus. Women in Arts, Nat. Mus. Am. Indian, Gold Coast Water Color Soc. (pres. 1984-87), 2+3 The Artist Orgn., Union des Francais de l'Etranger. Office: PO Box 8692 Fort Lauderdale FL 33310-8692

MOORHEAD, SYLVESTER ANDREW, retired education educator; b. Denver, Feb. 23, 1920; s. Ray Rodney and Cora Margaret (Payne) M.; m. Katherine May Schlessman, July 21, 1945; children: Rodney A., Sylvia Kay, Kent A., Pamela Ann. BA, U. No. Colo., 1942; PhD, Stanford U., 1950. Tchr. secondary sch., Redwood City, Calif., 1947-48, Sunnyvale, Calif., 1948-49; mem. faculty U. Miss., 1949—, prof. edn., 1955—, dean U. Sch. Edn., 1961-85, dean emeritus, 1985—. Contbr. articles profl. jours. Served with USAAF, 1942-45. Mem. NEA (life), Kappa Delta Pi, Phi Delta Kappa. Lodges: Rotary. Baptist. Home: 211 Vivian St Oxford MS 38655-2719

MOORHEAD, THOMAS BURCH, lawyer, corporation and government executive; b. Evanston, Ill., May 3, 1934; s. John William and Jane (Hendrich) M.; m. Christie Barnard, Dec. 31, 1966 (div. June 1992); children: Merrell Hendrich, Hannah Christie, Rachel McGill; m. Elizabeth Howard, May 3, 2002. BA, Yale U, 1956; postgrad., The Hague Acad. Internat. Law, 1958; JD, U. Pa., 1959; LLM, NYU, 1964. Bar: N.Y. 1960, Conn. 1971, U.S. Supreme Ct. 1965. Assoc. Milbank, Tweed, Hadley & McCloy, N.Y.C., 1959-63; assoc. counsel, asst. sec. Hooker Chem. Corp., N.Y.C., 1963-68, dir. indsl. rels., 1968-69, v.p. indsl. rels., 1969-72; v.p. employee rels. Champion Internat. Corp., N.Y.C., 1972-74; v.p. adminstrn. Beker Industries Corp., Greenwich, Conn., 1974-76; v.p. corp. affairs Estée Lauder, Inc., N.Y.C., 1976-84, sr. v.p., 1984-87; v.p. human resources Carter-Wallace, Inc., N.Y.C., 1987—2001; dep. undersec. for internat. affairs U.S. Dept. Labor, Washington, 2001—. Bd. dirs., vice chmn. Transaction Billing Resources, Inc., 1991-97; elected mem. Corp. Culinary Inst. of Am., 1993-2000. Mem. New Canaan (Conn.) Rep. Town Com., 1980-85; elected mem. New Canaan Town Coun., 1985-2001, vice chmn., 1989-98, chmn. 1998-2001; justice of the peace State of Conn., 2001—; bd. dirs. Employment Policy Found., 1993-2001, Les Amis d'Escoffier Soc., 1990-2001, Les Amis d'Escoffier Found., 1990-2001, Yale U. Alumni Fund, 1987-92, Nat. Choral Coun., 1988-93, United Way Tri-State, Inc., 1986-89, United Way New Canaan, 1983-89, pres., 1986-87; mem. Conn. Oversight Commn., Metro-North Commuter R.R., 1985-89; U.S. del. ILO, 1985, 93, 94, 95, 96, 2000, 01, 02, head U.S. employer del., 1994, 95, 96, 2000 and to ILO Asian Regional Meeting, 1997, ILO Ams. regional meeting, 1999, 2002, head U.S. govt. delegation, ILO Assn. Reg. Meeting, 2002, elected v.p. ILO conf., Geneva, 2000, elected mem. governing body ILO, 2001—. Mem. ABA, Assn. of Bar of City of N.Y., Am. Soc. Internat. Law, Met. Club, New Canaan Country Club, Gridiron Club of New Canaan (pres. 1990-2001), Yale Club. Office: 200 Constitution Ave NW Washington DC 20210 Home: 152 E 94TH St Apt 8B New York NY 10128-2578

MOORHOUSE, JOCELYN DENISE, film director; b. Melbourne, Victoria, Australia, Sept. 4, 1960; came to U.S., 1994; d. John Henry Murray and Denise Patricia Moorhouse; m. Paul John Hogan, Feb. 20, 1988. Student, Australian Film and TV Sch., 1981-84. Script editor, writer Channel 7 Drama Unit, Sydney, Australia, 1984-86, Crawford Prodns., Melbourne, 1986-87; series creator, writer ABC TV series c/o the Bartons, Melbourne, 1988-89; screenwriter, dir. various prodns., 1990—. Screenwriter, dir. feature film Proof, 1991; dir. films Pavane, 1983, How to Make An American Quilt, 1995, A Thousand Acres, 1997; prodr., writer Unconditional Love, 2002. Office: Creative Artists Agy 9830 Wilshire Blvd Beverly Hills CA 90212-1804

MOORHOUSE, LINDA VIRGINIA, symphony orchestra administrator; b. June 26, 1945; d. William James and Mary Virginia (Wild) M. BA, Pa. State U., 1967. Sec. San Antonio Symphony, Tex., 1970-71, adminstrv. asst., 1971-75, asst. mgr., 1975-76; exec. dir. Canton (Ohio) Symphony, 1977—. Mem. Ohio Arts Coun. Music Panel, 1980-82, 87-89, Mich. Arts Coun. Music Panel, 1986. Bd. dirs. Stark County unit Arthritis Fedn., 1986-92, treas., 1989-91; bd. dirs. Canton Palace Theatre Assn., treas., 1994-96, pres., 1998-99; active Cen. Stark County United Way Allocations Panel, 1991-96. Mem. Met. Orch. Mgrs. Assn. (pres. 1983-85), Orgn. Ohio Orchs. (pres. 1985-86), Am. Symphony Orch. League (bd. dirs. 1983-85, nat. 1st ladies' site com. 1997—), Stark County Women's Hall of Fame (charter inductee), Soroptimist (Canton, Ohio, Women of Distinction 1992), Nat. First Ladies Libr. Office: Canton Symphony Orch 1001 Market Ave N Canton OH 44702-1024

MOORING, F. PAUL, physics editor; b. Pitt County, N.C., Feb. 6, 1921; s. Benjamin Arthur and Amanda Elizabeth (Congleton) M.; m. Jean Louise Carpenter, Aug. 28, 1948; children: Cecily Hamm, Carol Larson, Margaret Calderon. BA, Duke U., 1944; PhD, U. Wis., 1951. Instr. Duke U., Durham, N.C., 1943-46; teaching asst. U. Wis., Madison, 1946-50, rsch. asst., 1950-51; physicist Argonne (Ill.) Nat. Lab., 1951-83; editor, cons. Am. Inst. Physics, Argonne, 1983—. Adj. prof. St. Louis U., 1966-83. Contbr. articles to profl. jours. Pres. The Ill. Prairie Path, Wheaton, Ill., 1971-93, Ill. Audubon Soc., Wayne, Ill., 1978-81. Fulbright Rsch. fellow U. Helsinki, 1962-63. Mem. AAAS, Am. Phys. Soc. Democrat. Home: 295 Abbotsford Ct Glen Ellyn IL 60137-4803 E-mail: fmooring@aol.com.

MOORMAN, JOHN A. librarian; b. Humboldt, Nebr., Sept. 15, 1947; m. Ileen Mary Geiger, Dec. 20, 1968; children: Johanna Boulden, Jessica Trinoskey, John A. Moorman Jr. AB, Guilford Coll., Greensboro, N.C., 1969; MSLS, U. N.C., 1972; postgrad., U. N.C., Greensboro, 1974-75; PhD, U. Ill., 2002. Pub. svcs. and circulation libr. Guilford Coll., 1972-75; dir. Elbert Ivey Meml. Libr., Hickory, N.C., 1975-80, Brazoria County Libr. System, Angleton, Tex., 1980-86, Oak Lawn (Ill.) Pub. Libr., 1986-88; exec. dir. Cumberland Trail Libr. System, Flora, Ill., 1989-92; city libr. Decatur (Ill.) Pub. Libr., 1992-2000; dir. Williamsburg (Va.) Regional Libr., 2000—. Adj. faculty Cath. U., 2003—. Author: Managing Small Library Collections in Businesses and Community Organizations: Advice for Non-Librarians, 1989. Grad. Decatur Leadership Inst., 1993, Leadership Hist. Triangle, 2003. Mem.: ALA, Va. Libr. Assn. (legis. com.). Mem. Soc. Of Friends. Avocations: travel, reading, woodworking, sports. Home: 8216 Old Mill Ln Williamsburg VA 23188-1135 Office: Williamsburg Regional Libr 7770 Croaker RD Williamsburg VA 23188 Office Phone: 757-259-7777. E-mail: jmoorman@mail.wrl.org.

MOORMAN, RICHARD HAL, IV, lawyer; b. Waco, Tex., Mar. 2, 1950; s. George R. and Billie (Scoggin) M.; m. Lucy Baker, May 24, 1974; children: Theodore Clark, Lydia Anne, Peter Baker. BCE, MIT, 1971; JD, So. Meth. U., 1976. Bar: Tex. 1976, U.S. Dist. Ct. (so. dist., we. dist., ea. dist.) Tex. 1976, U.S. Ct. Appeals (5th cir.) 1976; Bd. Cert. Civil Trial Law and Estate Planning and Probate Law, Tex. Bd. of Legal Specialization. Engr. Turner Collie & Braden, Houston, 1971-72, P.G. Bell Co., Houston, 1972-73; ptnr. Moorman Tate Moorman Urquhart & Haley L.L.P., Brenham, Tex., 1976—. Bd. dirs. Washington County Abstract Co., Brenham; bd. mem. Trinity Med. Ctr. Hosp.; past examiner (2002) Tex. Bd. of Legal Specialization; course dir. State Bar of Tex. Advanced Estate Planning and Probate Seminar. Mem. Tex. Air Control Bd., Austin, 1980-86; past pres. Washington on Brazos State Pk. Assn., Brenham, Brenham Downtown Assn. Named one of Tex. Superlawyers. Fellow Am. Coll. Trust and Estate Counsel, Tex. Bar Found.; mem. ABA (estate gift tax com.), State Bar of Tex. (coun. mem. real estate probate and trust sect.), Washington County C. of C. (pres.); Main Street Bd, Elder: Brenham Bible Ch. Avocations: antiques, hunting, fishing, theology. Office: Moorman Tate Moorman Urquhart Haley LLP 207 E Main St Brenham TX 77833-3754 Office Phone: 979-836-5664.

MOOS, H. WARREN, physicist, astronomer, educator, administrator; b. N.Y.C., Mar. 26, 1936; s. Henry H. and Dorothy E. (Warren) M.; m. Doris Elaine McClure, July 13, 1957; children: Janet, Paul, Daniel, David. BS, Brown U., 1957; MA, U. Mich., 1959, PhD, 1962. Rsch. assoc. Stanford (Calif.) U., 1961-63; acting asst. prof. Johns Hopkins U., Balt., 1963-64, asst. prof., 1964-68, assoc. prof., 1968-71, prof., 1971—, dir. Ctr. for Astrophys. Scis., 1988-93, chmn. Physics & Astronomy, 1993-96. Cons. in field; mem. com. on planetary and lunar exploration NRC/Nat. Acad. Sci., Washington, 1982-86; mem. space and earth sci. adv. com. NASA, Washington, 1984-87; vis. fellow Joint Inst. for Lab. Astrophysics, 1972-73, 80-81. Editor: Optical Properties of Ions in Crystals, 1967; contbr. over 300 articles to profl. jours. Trustee Associated Univs., Inc., 2002—. Sloan Found. fellow, 1965-69. Fellow Am. Phys. Soc.; mem. Am. Astron. Soc., Internat. Astron. Union. Achievements include prin. investigatorof far ultraviolet spectroscopic explorer; co-investigator of Apollo 17 ultraviolet spectrometer, of Hopkins Ultraviolet Telescope, of Voyager ultraviolet spectrometer, of space telescope imaging spectograph; research on ultraviolet astronomy and fusion plasma diagnostics. Office: Johns Hopkins U Dept Physics & Astronomy 34th & Charles Sts Baltimore MD 21218 E-mail: hwm@jhu.edu.

MOOS, RUDOLF H. psychologist, researcher; b. Berlin, Sept. 10, 1934; s. Henry R. and Herta M. (Ehrlich) M.; m. Bernice Schradski, June 9, 1963; children: Karen, Kevin. BA in Psychology, U. Calif. at Berkeley, 1956; PhD, U. Calif.-Berkeley, 1960. Mem. faculty psychiatry Stanford (Calif.) U., 1962—, dir. psychiatry research tng. program, 1967-92, prof. psychiatry, 1972—, dir. social ecology lab., 1967-92; chief research, research career scientist VA Med. Center, Palo Alto, Calif., 1975—, dir. Ctr. for Health Care Evaluation, 1984—2002, dir. Program Evaluation and Resource Ctr., 1990-99. Vis. prof. Inst. Psychiatry, also Maudsley and Royal Bethlem Hosp., London, 1969-70 Author: Issues in Social Ecology, 1974, Evaluating Treatment Environments, 1974, Health and the Social Environment, 1974, Evaluating Correctional and Community Settings, 1975, Human Adaptation Coping with Life Crises, 1976, The Human Context, 1976, Environment and Utopia, 1977, Coping with Physical Illness, 1977, Evaluating Educational Environments, 1979, Coping with Physical Illness: New Perspectives, 1984, Coping with Life Crises: An Integrated Approach, 1986, Alcoholism Treatment: Content,

Process and Outcome, 1990, Group Residential Facilities for Older Adults, 1994, Evaluating Residential Facilities, 1996, The Quality of Psychiatric and Substance Abuse Programs, 1997; mem. editl. bd. Jour. Behavioral Medicine, Internat. Jour. Therapeutic Comtys., Prevention in Human Svcs., Psychosomatic Medicine, Jour. Personality and Social Psychology, 1985-91, Health Psychology: An Internat. Jour., Violence, Agression, and Terrorism, Jour. Substance Abuse, Jour. Applied Gerontology, Jour. Cmty. and Applied Social Psychology, Psychology and Aging, 1986-91, Evaluation and Program Planning, Environment and Behavior, 1987-91, Indian Jour. Clin. Psychology, 1996—, Jour. Studies on Alcohol, 1997, Am. Jour. of Cmty. Psychology, 1998—; assoc. editor: Ency. of Psychological Assessment. Fellow APA, Acad. Behavioral Medicine, Soc. Behavioral Medicine, Am. Orthopsychiat. Assn., Nat. Inst. on Alcohol Abuse and Alcoholism (mem. coun.); mem. Am. Sociol. Assn., Am. Psychosomatic Assn. (mem. coun.). Home: 25661 W Fremont Rd Los Altos CA 94022-1600 Office: Stanford U Dept Psychiatry MC 5550 Palo Alto CA 94305

MOOS, WALTER HAMILTON, pharmaceutical company executive; AB in Chemistry cum laude, Harvard U., 1976; PhD in Chemistry, U. Calif., Berkeley, 1982. Scientist Parke-Davis Rsch. Divsn. Warner Lambert Co., Ann Arbor, Mich., 1982-83, sr. scientist, 1984, rsch. assoc., 1984-86, sr. rsch. assoc., 1986-87, sect. dir. chemistry, 1987-89, dir. chemistry, 1989, sr. dir. chemistry, 1990, v.p. neuroscis. and biol. chemistry, 1990-91; v.p. rsch. devel. Chiron Corp., Emeryville, Calif., 1991-97; chmn., CEO MitoKor, San Diego, 1997—. Adj. asst. prof. dept. medicinal chemistry Coll. Pharmacy, U. Mich., 1990, adj. assoc. prof., 1990-91; adj. prof. dept. pharm. chemistry U. Calif., San Francisco, 1991—; bd. dirs. Rigel Pharm., Biotech. Industry Orgn., Alnis, Anterion, Axiom, Keystone Symposia, Mimotopes, Oncologic, Onyx; presenter to numerous sci. confs. Co-editor: Drug Discovery Technologies, 1990, Cognitive Disorders: Pathophysiology and Treatment, 1991; editor-at-large Medicinal Chemistry, 1988—; cons. editor Bio-Organic and Medicinal Chemistry Letters. Mem. Am. Peptide Soc. (charter mem.), U. Mich. Enzyme Discussion Group (co-founder), ACS Divsn. Medicinal Chemistry (chmn. membership com. 1989, councilor 1990), Am. Chem. Soc. Office: MitoKor Inc 12780 High Bluff Dr San Diego CA 92130

MOOSAZADEH, KIOOMARS, orthopedist, educator, physiatrist, researcher; b. Tehran, Iran, Apr. 27, 1956; arrived in U.S., 1998; s. Yakhazghel Moosazadeh and Mohtaram Banayee; m. Katayoun Ooriel, Apr. 5, 1989; children: Pegah, Kiarash. MD, Shahid Beheshti U., 1989. Cert. med. dr. 2001. Orthopaedic surgeon Emdad Hosp. Health and Med. Scis., Shahrood, Iran, 1989—98; fellow in advanced orthopedic surgery A-O Internat., Switzerland, 1996; asst. prof. Azad U. Shahrood, 1996—98; fellow Hosp. Joint Disease Orthopedic Inst., N.Y.C., 1999—2000; vis. fellow in joint disease orthopedics NYU Hosp., 2000—01; intern Bklyn. Hosp. Ctr., 2001—02; clin. asst. State U. Hosp., Bklyn., 2002—. Permanent mem., cons., med. com. retirement and impairment Social Welfare Orgn., Divsn. of Health Ministry, Shahrood, 1991—98; cons. physician Jewish Charity Hosp., Tehran. With Iranian Mil., 1982—84. Mem.: AMA (assoc.). Achievements include research in Bone Reimplantation Technique. Avocations: carpentry, music. Home: 26 Coolidge Ave Roslyn Heights NY 11577 Office: State Univ Hosp 445 Lenox Rd Brooklyn NY 11203 E-mail: kioomarsmd@hotmail.com.

MOOSE, BRIAN DAVID, illustrator, art director; b. San Mateo, Calif., July 30, 1958; s. Irvin Russel and Gene (Thompson) M.; m. Leca Renee Emerson, 1991. AA in Comml. Art, Coll. of San Mateo, 1981; BFA in Illustration, Calif. State U., Long Beach, 1984. Pvt. practice illustrator, San Mateo, 1977-81, Long Beach, 1981—91, San Francisco, 1991—94, Santa Cruz, Calif., 1994—; creative cons. Walt Disney Prodns., Anaheim, Calif., 1981-84; sr. model builder Walt Disney Co., Anaheim, Calif., 1984—88; dir. art divsn., bd. mem. Am. Space Meml., Washington, 1986—88; designer Creative Network Studios, San Francisco, 1991—94; dir. creative Fractal Design/MetaCreations, Scotts Valley, Calif., 1995—2000; creative dir. Handspring Inc., Mountain View, Calif., 2000—02. Cons., designer Toyota, Design Sci. Internat., L.A., 1986-88, Quadrant Group Inc., L.A., 1986, Toyota Calty Design Rsch., Inc., Newport Beach, Calif., 1986-88, Toyota Hdqrs., Torrance, Calif., 1986-88, Terragrafics, San Francisco, 1990-91, Walt Disney Co., Burbank, Calif., Burnes of Boston, 1993-96. Represented in permanent collection Smithsonian Inst., 1984; exhibited in shows of N.Y. Soc. Illustrators, N.Y.C., 1985, The Soc. of Illustrators (Illustrators 27), Belcher Studios, San Francisco. Mem. Graphic Artist Guild, Soc. Illustrators. Republican. Avocation: sketching. Office: 232 Auburn Ave Santa Cruz CA 95060-6234 Office Phone: 831-469-8951.

MOOSE, CHARLES A. former protective services official; b. Aug. 11, 1953; BA in U.S. History, U. N.C., 1975; MA in Pub. Adminstrn., Portland State U., 1984, PhD in Urban Studies and Criminology, 1993; grad., FBI Nat. Acad. Patrol officer Portland Police Dept., 1975-81, sergeant, 1981-84, lieutenant, 1984-91, capt. of No. Precinct, 1991-92, dep. chief of Ops. Branch, 1992-93, chief of police, 1993—99, Montgomery County, Md., 1999—2003. Co-author (with Charles Fleming): Three Weeks in October, 2003. Bd. dirs. Boys and Girls Club of Portland, Comprehensive Options for Drug Abusers; mem. funding allocation com. Black United Fund Oreg.; mem. Multnomah County Cmty. Action Commn., Police Exec. Rsch. Forum, Bd. Pub. Safety Standards and Tng., Gov.'s Drug and Violent Crime Policy Bd., Gov.'s Juvenile Justice Task Force; bd. dirs. Portland State U. Mem. Am. Soc. Criminology, Nat. Orgn. of Black Law Enforcement Execs., Soc. of Police Futurists Internat., Internat. Assn. Chiefs of Police.

MOOSSA, A. R. surgery educator; b. Port Louis, Mauritius, Oct. 10, 1939; s. Yacoob and Maude (Rochecoute) M.; m. Denise Willoughby, Dec. 28, 1973; children: Pierre, Noel, Claude, Valentine. BS, U. Liverpool, Eng., 1962, MD (hon.), 1965; postgrad., Johns Hopkins U., 1972—73, U. Chgo., 1973—74. Intern Liverpool Royal Infirmary, 1965-66; resident United Liverpool Hosps. and Alder Hey Children's Hosp., 1966-72; from asst. prof. surgery to assoc. prof. U. Chgo., 1975-77, prof., dir. surg. rsch., chief gen. surgery svc., vice chmn. dept., 1977-83; chmn. dept. surgery U. Calif.-San Diego Med. Ctr., 1983—2004, prof., surgery, emeritus chmn., assoc. dean, spl. counsel for clin. affairs, 2004—. Litchfield lectr. U., Oxford, Eng., 1978; praelector in surgery U. Dundee, Scotland, 1979; Hampson Trust vis. prof. U. Liverpool, 1992, G.B. Ong. vis. prof. U. Hong Kong, 1993, Philip Sandblon vis. prof. U. Lund, Sweden. Editor: Tumors of the Pancreas, 1982, Essential Surgical Practice, 1983, 4th edit., 2000, Comprehensive Textbook of Oncology, 1985, 2d edit., 1991, Gastrointestinal Emergencies, 1985, Problems in General Surgery, 1989, Operative Colorectal Surgery, 1993. Fellow Royal Coll. Surgeons (Hunterian prof. 1977); mem. ACS, Am. Surg. Assn., Soc. Univ. Surgeons, Am. Soc. Clin. Oncology, European Surg. Assn. Office: U Calif San Diego Thornton Hosp 9300 Campus Point Dr 7212 La Jolla CA 92037 Office Phone: 858-657-6112. Business E-Mail: amoossa@ucsd.edu.

MOOSSY, JOHN, neuropathologist, neurologist, consultant; b. Shreveport, La., Aug. 24, 1925; s. John Yazbeck and Rose (Ferris) M.; m. Yvonne Reese, Mar. 15, 1951; children: John Jefferson, Joan Marie. MD, Tulane U., 1950. Intern Charity Hosp. of New Orleans, 1950-51, neurology resident, 1951-53; neuropathology fellow Columbia U. Coll. of Physicians and Surgeons, N.Y.C., 1953-54; assoc., lectr. in neuropathology Tulane U. Sch. Medicine, New Orleans, 1954-57; asst. to prof. in pathology, neurology La. State U., New Orleans, 1957-65; prof. pathology, grad. faculty U. Pitts., 1965-67; prof. pathology neuropathology Bowman Gray Sch. of Medicine, Winston-Salem, N.C., 1967-72; prof. pathology and neurology, dir. div. neuropathology U. Pitts., 1972-93, emeritus prof., 1993—. Dir. Cerebrovascular Disease Study, World Fedn. of Neurology, Antwerp, Belgium, 1960-61; cons. Armed Forces Inst. of Pathology, Washington, 1977—, mem. sci. adv. bd., Washington, 1984-86. Editor: Cerebral Vascular Disease Seventh Conference, 1970, Cerebrovascular Diseases 12th Research Conference, 1981; editor-in-chief Jour. Neuropathology and Exptl. Neurology, 1981-91; mem. editorial bd. Archives Neurology, 1982-92. Recipient Excellence in Teaching award U. Pitts. Sch. of Medicine, 1987-88; named Commencement Speaker U. Pitts. Sch. of Medicine, 1989. Mem. Am. Acad. Neurology (sec.-treas. 1963-655), Am. Neurol. Assn. (v.p. 1977-78), Am. Assn. Neuropathologists (pres. 1974-75, Neuropathology award 1992), Internat. Soc. Neuropathology, Coun. Biology Editors.

MOOTE, A. LLOYD, history professor; b. Hamilton, Ont., Can., Mar. 22, 1931; s. Stanley Alanson and Esther Grace (Wood) M.; m. Barbara Brown, Dec. 27, 1956 (div. 1982); children: Karen, Peter, Daphne, Robert; m. Dorothy Carter May, May 30, 1986. BA, U. Toronto, 1954; MA, U. Minn., Mpls., 1956, PhD, 1958. Tchg. asst. U. Minn., Mpls., 1955-58; lectr. U. Toronto, 1958-61; asst. prof. U. Cin., 1961-62; from asst. prof. to prof. history U. So. Calif., L.A., 1962-92, prof emeritus, 1993—. Vis. prof. Queen's U., Kingston, Ont., 1965-66; chmn. gen. edn. program U. So. Calif., 1978-81; mem. Inst. Advanced Study, Princeton, 1988-89; affiliated prof. Rutgers U., 1994—. Author: The Seventeenth Century, 1970, The Revolt of the Judges, 1971, The World of Europe: The Seventeenth Century, 1973, 2d edit., 1979, Louis XIII: The Just, 1989, paperback edit., 1991, (with Dorothy C. Moote) The Great Plague: The Story of London's Most Deadly Year, 2004; co-editor, contbr. issue of French hist. studies on biography, 1996; mem. editl. bd. French Hist. Studies, 1971-74; internat. adv. bd. European History Quar., 1983—. Founder, convener So. Calif. Early Modern French Studies Group, 1980-93, Rutgers, Princeton and Phila. Early Modern History Group, 1994—. Recipient William Koren prize Soc. French Hist. Studies, 1962, creative scholarship award U. So. Calif. Assocs., 1973, faculty book award U. So. Calif. chpt. Phi Kappa Phi, 1990; younger scholar NEH, 1969; grantee Am. Philos. Soc., 1962, Haynes Found., 1973, Wellcome Inst. for History Medicine, 1993-94, Burroughs-Wellcome Fund, 1996; Guggenheim fellow, 1976, fellow U. Essex, Eng., 1993-94, Rutgers Ctr. for Hist. Analysis, 1995-97. Mem. Am. Hist. Assn., Soc. French Hist. Studies (pres. 1984-85), Soc. for Study French History (U.K.), Sixteenth-Century Studies Conf. Home: 149 Meadowbrook Dr Princeton NJ 08540-3664 E-mail: dmoote@erols.com.

MOOTY, JOHN WILLIAM, lawyer; b. Adrian, Minn., Nov. 27, 1922; s. John Wilson and Genevieve (Brown) M.; m. Virginia Nelson, June 6, 1952 (dec. 1964); children: David N., Bruce W., Charles W.; m. Jane Nelson, Jan. 15, 1972. BSL, U. Minn., 1943, LLB, 1944. Bar: Minn. 1944. Ptnr. Gray, Plant, Mooty & Bennett, Mpls., 1945—. Bd. dirs. Internat. Dairy Queen, Inc., Bur. of Engraving, Inc., Riverway Co. and subs., Rio Verde Svcs., Inc., Ariz. Author: (with others) Minnesota Practice Methods, 1956. Chmn. Gov.'s Task Force on Edn., 1981; pres. Citizens League Mpls., 1970; acting chmn. Republican Party of Minn., 1958. Mem. ABA, Minn. Bar Assn., Hennepin County Bar Assn., U. Minn. Alumni Assn. (pres. 1982), Tonto Verde Country Club, Minikahda (Mpls.) Club, Mpls. Club. Home: 8106 Highwood Dr Apt Y232 Bloomington MN 55438-1054 Office Phone: 612-343-3200.

MORA, ALBERTO, lawyer; Grad. with honors, Swarthmore Coll.; JD, U. Miami. Bar: Fla., D.C. Naval gen. counsel Dept. Def., Washington, 2001—; fgn. svc. officer U.S. State Dept., 1975—78; gen. counsel USIA, 1989—93, pres. broadcasting bd. govs., 1995—2001; counsel Greenberg Traurig, Washington. Bd. dirs. Nat. Coun. for Internat. Visitors, Radio Free Asia, Radio Free Europe/Radio Liberty. Editor-in-chief: Law of the Ams.: U. Miami Jour. of Internat. Law. Fellow, Orgn. of Am. States. Mem.: Coun. Fgn. Rels. Office: Dept Def Gen Counsel Navy 1000 Navy Pentagon Washington DC 20350-1000

MORA, FEDERICO, neurosurgeon; b. Guatemala, Guatemala, Jan. 11, 1926; came to the U.S., 1945; s. Carlos Federico and Rosa (Castaneda) M.; m. Natalie Viriginia Ramin, June 30, 1951; children: Federico, Clara Luz, Ana Maria, Claudia Ines, Juan Rafael. Student, Harvard U., 1945—46, MD, 1950. Diplomate Am. Bd. Neurol. Surgery. Pvt. practice neurol. surgery, Guatemala, 1958-59, Albuquerque, 1959-95; asst. prof. surgery and anatomy U. N.Mex. Sch. Medicine, Albuquerque, 1969-70. Capt. USAFR, 1954-56. Mem. Alpha Omega Alpha. Democrat. Avocations: scuba diving, nature studies. Home: 1809 Avenida Alturas NE Albuquerque NM 87110-4956

MORA, JAMES ERNEST, former professional football coach; b. Glendale, Calif., May 24, 1935; s. Mario Joseph and Helen Laverne (Thompson) M.; m. Connie Beatrice Saunders, Dec. 18, 1959; children— James L., Michael J., Stephen P. BS, Occidental Coll., 1957; MA, U. So. Calif., 1967. Asst. coach U. Washington, Seattle, 1975-78, Seattle Seahawks, Seattle, 1978-82, New England Patriots, Foxboro, MA, 1982-83; head coach Philadelphia Stars (name changed to Baltimore Stars), Baltimore, MD, 1983-86, New Orleans Saints, New Orleans, 1986-96, head coach, v.p. L.A., 1994-96; commentator NFC Football, 1997; head coach Indianapolis Colts, Ind., 1998—2002. Served to capt. USMCR, 1957-60 Mem. Am. Football Coaches Assn. Republican. Lutheran. Avocations: working out; golf; skiing; reading; biking.

MORA, KATHLEEN RITA, state judicial administrator; b. Atlantic City, Sept. 24, 1948; d. Francis Bernard and Catena Rose (Borzellino) Gribbin; m. Ben P. Mora, June 28, 1969; children: Michael, Brian. AS, Atlantic C.C., 1977; BS with program distinction, Stockton State Coll., 1984. Sec. The Press of Atlantic City, Pleasantville, N.J., 1966-69, pers. adminstr., 1969-73, adminstrv. asst., 1973-76, fin. asst., 1976-87, acctg. mgr., 1987-89; dir. fin. Atlantic and Cape May counties Superior Ct. N.J., Atlantic City, 1989—. Host Healthline, Sta. WOND, 1989-91. Co-hostess ann. radio broadcast Miss Am. Pageant, 1985—; judge Miss Cape County Pageant, 1979; co-hostess Amb. Program, United Way, bd. dirs. Atlantic County, 1977-78; commentator TV Telethon, March of Dimes, N.J., 1976-85; auditor Miss Atlantic County Pageant, 1990-2000; commentator ARC Ann. Telethon, 1995-97. Recipient Contemporary Woman award McDonalds Corp./Sta. WAYV-AM, 1978, Svc. award 4-H Club Coun., 1985, N.J. Judiciary AQCES award, 1994; named Miss Atlantic City, Women's div. Atlantic City C. of C., 1968-69, Miss United Way, 1975, Outstanding Chairperson, United Way Atlantic County, 1987, Outstanding Young Woman of Atlantic County, Mainland Jaycettes, 1978. Mem. Mid-Atlantic Assn. for Ct. Mgrs. Roman Catholic. Home: 805 N Derby Ave Ventnor City NJ 08406-1121 Office: Superior Ct NJ 1201 Bacharach Blvd Atlantic City NJ 08401-4510

MORA, PHILIPPE, screenwriter, producer, director, painter; b. Paris, Aug. 8, 1949; s. Georges and Mirka Madeleine (Zelik) M.; m. Pamela Mai Krause, Aug. 1, 1980; children: Madeleine Mai, Georges Ritchie Maximillian, Dominic Marceau. Student, La Trobe U., Melbourne, Australia, 1967. Screenwriter, dir., producer, 1969—. Founder Cinema Papers mag., Melbourne, 1967. Dir., writer, prodr. (films) Trouble in Molopolis, 1969, The Howling III: The Marsupials, 1987, Snide and Prejudice, 1997, According to Occam's Razor, 1999, Project 65, 2002; co-writer (film) Double Headed Eagle, 1971; dir., writer: (films) Swastika, 1972 (Blue Ribbon award 1974), Brother Can You Spare a Dime, 1975, Mad Dog, 1976 (John Ford Meml. award 1976), According to Occam's Razor, 2000; dir.: (films) The Beast Within, 1980, The Return of Captain Invincible, 1981, A Breed Apart, 1983, The Howling II, 1984, Death of a Soldier, 1985, Back in Business, 1996; dir. prodr.: Communion, 1990, Art Deco Detective, 1994, Pterodactyl Woman from Beverly Hills, 1994, Precious Find, 1995, Burning Down the House, 1996, Thick and Thin, 1997, Joseph's Gift, 1999; dir., prodr.: (film) Hamlet, 2001; painter exhibited in group shows at Argys Gallery, Melbourne, 1967, Clytie Jessop Gallery, London, 1968-71, Sigi Kraus Gallery, London, 1970-71, Camden Arts Centre, London, 1970, Richard Demarco Gallery, Edinburgh, 1971, Tolarno Gallery, Melbourne, 1971, Watters Gallery, Sydney, Australia, 1972, William Mora Gallery, Melbourne, 1987, Caz Gallery, L.A., 1990, Larrikins in London, 2003, Coll. Fine Arts, Sydney, 2003; represented in permanent collection Nat. Gallery Collection, Canberra, Australia, 1982, Mus. Modern Art Australia; English Lit. exhibition Victorian Edn. Authority, Victoria, Australia, 1966. Mem. Dirs. Guild Am., Acad. Motion Picture Arts and Scis., Australian Film Dirs. Assn. Office: Michael Blaha Esq 2530 Wilshire Blvd Santa Monica CA 90403-4616 E-mail: moracyber@juno.com.

MORABITO, PHILIP A. public relations executive; BS, MBA in Mktg. With Robert Marston & Assocs., N.Y.C.; pres. Pierpont Comms., Houston, 1987—. Adj. prof. Sch. Journalism and Grad. Sch. Bus. U. Houston; spkr., presenter in field. Mem. Am. Mktg. Assn., Internat. Assn. Bus. Communicators, Strategic Interest Group, Publ Rels. Soc. Am. Office: Pierpont Comms Inc 1800 West Loop S Ste 800 Houston TX 77027-3261

MORABITO, ROCCO ANTHONY, urologist; b. Huntington, W.Va., Nov. 23, 1950; s. Nicola F. and Theresa M. (Lobaldo) M.; m. Deborah Gayle Hall, 1973 (div. 1986); m. Brenda Kay Lyons, June 14, 1991; children: Shawn, Chris, Rocco Jr., Justin. BA, W.Va. U., 1972, MD, 1976. Diplomate Am. Bd. Urology, Nat. Bd. Med. Examiners. Surg. residency W.Va. U. Hosp., Morgantown, 1976-78, urol. residency, 1978-81; pres. Huntington (W.Va.) Urol. Assn., 1981—, Midwest Mobile Lithotripsy, Huntington, 1989-96, Tri-State Health Ptnrs., Huntington, 1994-96; pres. med. staff Cabell Huntington Hosp., Huntington, 1991-93, St. Mary's Hosp., 1997-99. Clin. assoc. prof. urology, W.Va. U. Sch. Medicine, 1981—, Marshall U. Sch. Medicine, Huntington, 1981—. Fellow ACS; mem. AMA, Am. Urol. Assn., So. Med. Assn., W.Va. State Med. Assn., Cabell County Med. Soc., W.Va. U. Sch. Medicine Alumni Assn. (chmn. 1989-94). Republican. Roman Catholic. Avocations: tennis, boating, skiing, music, cooking. Home: 20 Kensington Ln Huntington WV 25705-3860 Office: Huntington Urological Assn 2860 3rd Ave Ste 230 Huntington WV 25702-1453

MORADI, AHMAD F. software company executive, consultant; b. Tehran, Persia, Mar. 21, 1955; came to U.S., 1973; s. Akbar and Afsar (Mokaram) M.; m. Lourdes Pernas; l child, Aimee. AS, Broward Community Coll., 1978; BA, Fla. Atlantic U., 1980; PhD, LaSalle U., 1989. Advisor restaurant industries, Miami, Fla., 1974-78; pres. Octa-8, Inc., Ft. Lauderdale, Fla., 1980-82; mgmt. cons. MGI-MCG, Boca Raton, Fla., 1982-83; dir. ops. Datamation, Hollywood, Fla., 1983-85; pres. Software Intelligence Corp., Ft. Lauderdale, 1985—; with ARM Financial Corp., 1987-89; MIS dir., CIO Churchill Tech., Inc., Davie, Fla., 1992—; MIS dir. Westmack Group Holding Co., Delray Beach, 1995—; prin. G4, Inc., Ft. Lauderdale, 1992—; CEO Futuretrak Internat. OTC BB:FTRK, 1998-99, Worldcast Interactive Inc.; with Biomed. Rsch. Techs., 1997—, Interchange Med., Inc., 1999—, Maxwell Rand Inc., 1999—, Netstairs.com, 2000—. Lectr. South Fla. Bus. Jour., 1984-85, Victoria Hosp., Miami, Fla., 1985, Mt. Sinai Hosp., Miami, Fla., 1985, U. Miami, Fla., 1986, Chiropractic Today, 1989; cons., bus., mktg., internat. mktg. and telemarketing mgmt. Software Intelligence Corp., 1985—; systems analyst Softway, Inc., Ft. Lauderdale, 1986; hon. co-chmn. bus. adv. coun. Nat. Leadership Coun.and Nat. Rep. Bus. Commn.; hon. chmn. U.S. Presdl. Bus. Commn., 2002. Named Businessman of Yr., U.S. Presdl. Bus. Commn., 2003; recipient Gold medal, 2002. Mem. Data Processing Mgmt. Assn., Small Bus. Inst. Office Phone: 954-229-0900. E-mail: g4@ix.netcom.com., g41@bellsouth.net., inquiry@g41.com.

MORAHAN-MARTIN, JANET MAY, psychologist, educator; b. N.Y.C., Jan. 13, 1944; d. William Timothy and May Rosalind (Tarangelo) Morahan; m. Curtis Harmon Martin, June 2, 1979; 1 child, Gwendolyn May. AB, Rosemont (Pa.) Coll., 1965; MEd, Tufts U., 1968; PhD, Boston Coll., 1978. Asst. mkt. rsch. analyst Compton Advt. Co., N.Y.C., 1965-67; mkt. rsch. analyst Ogilvy & Mather Advt., N.Y.C., 1967; ednl. rsch. asst. Tufts U., Medford, Mass., 1968-69; counselor Psychol. Inst. Bentley Coll., Waltham, Mass., 1971-72; dir. counseling svcs. Bryant Coll., Smithfield, R.I., 1972-75, psychology instr., 1972-76, asst. prof. psychology, 1976-81, assoc. prof. psychology, 1981-91, prof. psychology, 1991—. Bd. dirs. Multi-Svc. Ctr., Newton, Mass., 1980-82. Contbr. articles to profl. jours., chpts. to books; reviewer APA Conv., 1985—, Teaching of Psychology Jour., 1988—, Collegiate Micro-Computer Jour., 1991, 93, Nat. Soc. Sci. Jour., 1991; mem. editl. bd., spl. edit. editor Cyber Psychology and Behavior. Bd. dirs. Wellesley (Mass.) Community Children's Ctr., 1986-90, Coun. for Children, Newton, Mass., 1984-86. NIMH fellow, 1967-68; NSF grantee, 1974-76, U.S. Office Edn. grantee, 1980. Mem. APA, Mass. Audubon Soc., Internat. Soc. for Online Mental Health (founding mem.), Soc. for Tchg. of Psychology, Soc. Computers in Psychology. Avocations: photography, antiques, gardening, literature. Home: 17 Fuller Brook Rd Wellesley MA 02482-7108 Office: Bryant Coll 1150 Douglas Pike Smithfield RI 02917-1291 E-mail: jmorahan@bryant.edu.

MORALES, DIANE K. former federal agency administrator; b. Houston, July 11, 1946; d. Arthur Clement and Helen Mary (Araiza) M. BA, U. Tex.-Austin, 1968. Account exec. Goodwin, Dannenbaum, Littman & Wingfield, Houston, 1968-70; pub. relations rep. Gittings, Inc., Dallas, 1970-71; asst. buyer, mgr. Neiman-Marcus, Dallas, 1971-80; sr. assoc., mktg. mgr. 3/D Internat., Houston, 1980-81; dep. asst. sec. policy U.S. Dept. Interior, Washington, 1981-83; bd. dirs. CAB, Washington, 1983-86; v.p. Earth Tech. Corp., Washington, 1986-88; pres. Morales Consulting Svc. Co., Washington, 1988-90; dep. asst. sec. def. for logistics U.S. Dept. Def., Washington, 1990—93, dep. under sec. logistics material readiness, 2001—04. Mem. Def. Depot Maintenance Coun.; chmn. Def. Material Mgmt. Bd, Def Transp. Polic Coun., Def. Energy Policy Coun. Pres. Downtown Rep. Women's Club, Dallas, 1979-80, bd. dirs. Dallas County Men's Rep. Club, 1980, Dallas County Women's Rep. Club, 1980; mem. Rep. Women's Fed. Forum, Rep. Nat. Hispanic Assembly. Republican. Presbyterian.

MORALES, EMMITT, mechanical consultant; s. Emilio and Alice Morales; m. Virginia Eilene Lopez, Nov. 27, 1951; children: David, Michael. Grad. h.s., Port Arthur, Tex. Co-owner Tool Tech, Beaumont, Tex., 1999—. With U.S. Army, 1969—71. Church Of Christ. Achievements include patents for stud removal and fastening tool. Avocation: golf. Home: 5260 Stardust Beaumont TX 77706 Office: Tool Tech 5420 Gorman Rd Beaumont TX 77705

MORALES, IRIS C. secondary school educator; d. Vicente and Concepción Morales; 1 child, Loaiza M. Walker-Morales. BA, CCNY, 1975. Tchr. N.Y.C. Bd. Edn., 1975—76, Dept. Edn., Hato Rey, PR, 1976—80, Arlington (Va.) Pub. Schs., 1990—2002, substitute tchr., 2002—. Author: The Metamorphosis, 2003. Avocations: music, tennis, reading, writing. Home: 4939 Americana Dr Annandale VA 22003 Personal E-mail: irroldan@aol.com.

MORALES, JOHN PAUL, television services producer; b. Menard, Tex., May 17, 1963; s. Herb Morales; m. Karen Elain Cox-Morales, Aug. 14, 1993. BAS, Tex. Tech U., 1986. On-air promotion mgr. KTVD-UPN 20, Englewood, Colo., 1996—99; TV svcs. prodr. Denver Police Dept., 2000—. Owner HEDZUP Prodns., Denver, 2000—. Videographer, editor (training video) Intro to Krav Maga (Gold Classic Telly award, 2004). Recipient Telly award, 2002. Mem.: Law Enforcement Video Assn. (Gold Shield and award of honor 2003). Office: Denver Police Acad 8895 Montview Blvd Bldg # 58 Denver CO 80220 Office Phone: 303-370-1522.

MORALES, JOSE, psychotherapist, writer; b. Hatillo, P.R., May 27, 1930; s. Polonio and Marciala (Dorta) M.; m. Ramona Velez, Oct. 24, 1954 (div. Mar. 1976); 1 child, Jose R. Jr.; m. Carmen Iris Lopez, Apr. 12, 1976; 1 child, Delia. BA in Edn., U. P.R., 1960; MSW, NYU, 1968; PhD, U. Calif., Santa Barbara, 1985. Cert. social studies tchr., P.R., N.Y.; cert. social worker, N.Y. Tchr. P.R. Bd. Edn., Arecibo, 1960-63; ednl. counselor Puerto Rican Migration Dept., N.Y.C., 1964; case worker Lincoln Hall, N.Y.C., 1964-66, social worker, 1968-70; social worker, supr. Greenpoint Hosp., Bklyn., 1970-76; social worker VA Hosp., Phila., 1977-80; social work supr. Kings County Hosp., Bklyn., 1981-93; psychotherapist CCM, Bklyn., 1993—. Cons./supr. N.Y. PCC, Bklyn. Author: Puerto Rican Spiritism, 1977 (Meritorious award 1981), Pepito, 1998, El Morro, 1998, Galeria de Heroes de Puerto Rico, 1997 (Meritorious award 1999); freelance journalist Eco Latino, 1993, El Latino Americano, 1997. Co-founder CILI, Bklyn., 1973, ACCEPIA, Bklyn., 1993. Mem. NASW, Am. Psychology Soc., Latin Am. Assn. Poets and Writers (co-founder, sec. 1997—, leadership com. 1998), N.Y. Acad. Scis. Avocations: reading, writing, researching geneology. Home: Bay Ridge Sta PO Box 234 Brooklyn NY 11220-0234 Office: CCM 185 Montague St Fl 9 Brooklyn NY 11201-3608 E-mail: JMora52825@aol.com.

MORALES, JULIO K. lawyer; b. Havana, Cuba, Jan. 17, 1948; arrived in US, 1960; s. Julio E. and Josephine (Holsters) M.; m. Suzette M. Dussault, May 31, 1970 (div. 1978); children: Julio E., Karel A.; m. Barbara A. Miller, July 14, 1979 (div. 1988); 1 child, Nicolas W. BA, Carroll Coll., 1969; JD, U.

Mont., 1972. Bar: Mont. 1972, U.S. Dist. Ct. Mont. 1972, U.S. Ct. Mil. Appeals 1972, U.S. Ct. Appeals (9th cir.) 1980. Law clk. to presiding justice Mont. Supreme Ct., Helena, 1972; sole practice Missoula, Mont., 1973-78, 88—; sr. ptnr. Morales & Volinkaty, Missoula, 1978-88; pvt. practice law Morales Law Office, 1988—. Author: Estate Planning for the Handicapped, 1975. Pres. Rockmont, Inc., Missoula, 1985-2001. Served to 2d lt. U.S. Army, 1972. Named Boss of the Yr., Missoula chpt. Mont. Assn. Legal Secs., 1988. Mem. ABA (dist. rep. 1975-79, exec. com. young lawyer divsn. 1977-79), Mont. Bar Assn. (chmn. law day 1974, 75, 77), Am. Judicature Soc., ATLA, World Assn. Lawyers, Missoula Soccer Assn. (pres. 1983-85), Mont. Sailing Assn. (bd. dirs. 1994—), Nat. Exch. Club (bd. dirs. Yellowstone dist. 1987-88, pres. 1990-91), Missoula Exch. Club, Elks (officer 1999-2001, exalted ruler 2001-02), Phi Delta Phi. Roman Catholic. Avocations: sports, coaching youth, boating, skiing, golf. Office: PO Box 9311 430 Ryman St Missoula MT 59802-4249

MORALES, MARY E. social worker; b. Va., Jan. 14, 1972; d. Juan and Wanda I. Morales. BA in Psychology and BA in Environ. Studies, Yale U., 1994. Social worker Evergreen Children's Svcs., Det., 1994—96; child devel. specialist Klingberg Family Ctr., New Britain, 1998—99; resdl. supr. St. Agnes Family Ctr., West Hartford, Conn., 1997—99; high risk newborn social worker Dept. Children & Families, New Britain, 1999—. Mem. child protection team Bristol (Conn.) Hosp., 1999—. Vol. P.E.P. (Youth at Risk), Plainville, Conn., 1999—; mentor St. Agnes Family Ctr., West Hartford, 1999—. Recipient Conn. Cmty. Svc. award, Yale U., 1991—94, award for outstanding cmty. edn., U. Conn. Med. Sch. Home: 123 Stearns St Bristol CT 06010-5134

MORALES, MICHAEL ANGELO, physician; b. N.Y., May 7, 1959; s. Maurice Johnson Morales and Maria Ceclia Cucaion Aragon; m. Oksana Popoukina Morales, Sept. 29, 1994; m. Emily Jane Essinger (div.); children: Eva Marie, Olive Michelle. Cert. bd. all U.S. Naturopathic Coll., 2001. Owner Lotus Flower Health Foods, Flushing, NY, 1979—81; dir. N.Y. E. W. Macrobiotics Ctr., N.Y., 1981—85; owner/chef Grainary Restaurant, Deer Field Beach, Fla., 1985—94; health cons./dir. N.Y. Macrobiotics Ctr., N.Y., 1994—2000; naturopathic dr. self employed, Queens, NY, 2000—. Lectr., cons. in field; adv. bd. St. Croix Healing Retreat, N.Y., 2002—04. Editor (writer): (newsletter) New York East West Macrobiotics, 1981—85; designer (menu/restaurant), 1985. Mem.: Am. Naturopathic Med. Assn., N.Y. Citiworks. Avocations: history, cooking, yoga, running, bodybuilding. Home: 15007 78th Ave Flushing NY 11367

MORALES, REYNALDO, physicist; BS in Physics, St. Mary's U., San Antonio, 1959; MA in Physics, U. Tex., 1962, PhD in Physics, 1967. Physicist Los Alamos Nat. Lab., N.Mex., 1966—85, 1987—95, 1997—; sci. counselor State Dept., Washington, 1987—95; fgn. affairs specialist ACDA, 1995—96; physicist Dept. of Def./ATSD/NCB, 1996—97. Mem. Army Sci. Bd. Mem.: AAAS, Soc. of Hispanic Profl. Engrs., Soc. for Advancement of Chicanos and Native Ams. in Sci., Am. Phys. Soc. Office: Los Alamos National Lab PO Box 1663 MSM719 Los Alamos NM 87545

MORALES-RAMOS, JUAN ALFREDO, entomologist, researcher; s. Alfredo Morales and Hortencia Ramos De Morales; m. Maria Guadalupe Rojas, Sept. 15, 1985. BS, Autonomous U. Nuevo Leon, Mex., 1977; MS, Higher Coll. of Tropical Agr., Mex., 1982; PhD, Tex. A&M U., 1991. Rschr., lectr. Colegio Superior de Agricultura Tropical, Cardenas, Mexico, 1978—84; rsch. technician Tex. A&M U., Coll. Sta., Tex., 1985—86; rsch. entomologist USDA-ARS Subtropical Agrl. Rsch. Ctr., Weslaco, Tex., 1992—98, USDA-ARS So. Regional Rsch. Ctr., New Orleans, 1998—. Co-author: Natural Enemies and Pest Control: An Integrated Pest Management Concept; contbr. articles to prof. jours. Recipient Scientist of the Yr. award, USDA-ARS, 2002. Mem.: Am. Inst. of Biol. Scis., Soc. Mex. de Control Biologico, Entomol. Soc. of Am., The Mars Soc., The Planetery Soc. Achievements include research in Mass propagation an release technology of the boll weevil parasitoid Catolaccus grandis; development of Artificial Diet for the boll weevil parasitoid Catolaccus grandis; patents for Artificial diet for Ectoparsitoid Insects; first to First Biological Control of a primary insect pest (the boll weevil) in an annual crop (Cotton); First biological control of a primary insect pest by mass propagating a natural enemy using an artificial diet; patents for Bait Matrix for control of Subterranean Termites; first to The use of chemical analysis of food sources for the development of artificial diets and baits for beneficial insects and pests. Office: USDA-ARS Soutern Reginal Research Center 1100 Robert E Lee Blvd New Orleans LA 70124

MORAN, BARBARA BURNS, librarian, educator; b. Columbus, Miss., July 8, 1944; d. Robert Theron and Joan (Brown) Burns; m. Joseph J. Moran, Sept. 4, 1965; children: Joseph Michael, Brian Matthew. AB, Mount Holyoke Coll., S. Hadley, Mass., 1966; M in Librarianship, Emory U., Atlanta, 1973; PhD, SUNY, Buffalo, 1982. Head libr. The Park Sch. of Buffalo, Snyder, NY, 1974-78; prof. Sch. Info. and Libr. Sci. U. N.C., Chapel Hill, 1981—, asst. dean, 1987-90, dean, 1990-98, prof. and dir. internat. programs, 1999—. Participant various seminars; evaluator various edn. progs.; cons. in field; bd. govs. UNC Press, 1998—. Author: Academic Libraries, 1984; co-author: (with Robert D. Stueart) Library and Information Center Management, 6th edit., 2002; contbr. articles to profl. jours., chpts. to books; mem. editl. bd. Jour. Acad. Librarianship, 1992-94, Coll. and Rsch. Libraries, 1996-2002, UNC Press. Coun. Libr. Resources grantee, 1985, Univ. Rsch. Coun. grantee, 1983, 89, others. Mem. ALA, Assn. for Libr. and Info. Sci. Edn., Popular Culture Assn., N.C. Libr. Assn., Beta Phi Mu. Home: 1307 Leclair St Chapel Hill NC 27517-3034 Office: Univ NC Sch Info & Libr Sci Chapel Hill NC 27599-0001 Office Phone: 919-962-8067. Business E-Mail: moran@ils.unc.edu.

MORAN, CHARLES, consumer products company executive; From v.p. fin. CA One Svcs. to pres., COO Del. North Cos., Buffalo, 1992—2003, pres. CA One Svcs., 2004—, COO, 2004—. Office: Delaware North Companies 40 Fountain Plaza Buffalo NY 14202

MORAN, CHARLES A. securities executive; b. Chgo., Feb. 7, 1943; s. Charles W. and Rose B. (Sutcher) M.; m. Donna L. Orbach, Sept. 3, 1967; children: Scott Alan, Erin Lizabeth. AB, Princeton U., 1964; JD, U. Mich., 1967; postgrad. advanced mgmt., Harvard U., 1982. CFP, Certified Employee Benefit Specialist. With Chase Manhattan Bank, N.Y.C., 1967-70; pension trust officer, adminstrv. officer, officer in charge new bus. devel., pension div. Mfrs. Hanover Trust Co., N.Y.C., 1970-87, sr. v.p., officer-in-charge employee benefit trust div., 1979-80; chmn. bd., pres., CEO MH/Edie Investment Counsel (formerly Lionel D. Edie & Co.), N.Y.C., 1980-82, officer-in-charge corp. trust div., 1982-83, officer in charge-global securities group, 1983-87; pres. Govt. Securities Clearing Corp., N.Y.C., 1987-96; asst. prof., faculty fellow, faculty senate Coll. of NJ, Trenton, 1996—99; pres. Strategic Financial Adv., Montclair, N.J., 1996—; prof. Harvard U., Cambridge, summer 1997—; asst. prof., residential coll. adv. bd. Bucknell U., 1999—2003; assoc. prof., dir. fin. planning program SUNY, Cobleskill, 2003—. Dir. Ctr. for Collaborative Sustainability, 2003-; chmn. bd. dirs. Inform, Inc.; past lectr. bus. and econs. Bloomfield Coll.; past lectr. sociology and fin. employee benefits C.W. Post Coll., L.I. U.; cons. Urban Vol. Cons. Group, Inc.; adv. coun. U.S. Dept. Labor; adv. bd. BNA Pension Reporter; mem. Employees Retirement Income Security Act of 1974 Roundtable; industry adv. com. Future Electronic Funds Payments Svcs. Fed. Res.; sec. environ. and bus. sect. Acad. Legal Studies in Bus. Contbr. articles to profl. jours. Mem. Am. Inst. Banking, Am. Employee Benefits Inst. (treas. 1976-79), N.Y. State Bankers Assn. (employees trust com.), Assn. Pvt. Pension and Welfare Plans (dir., mem. exec. com.), ERISA Industry Com. (pres., dir., mem. exec. com., treas.), Am. Bankers Assn. (chmn. employee benefit trust com. 1977-82), Internat. Found. Pension and Welfare Plans, Bank Adminstrn. Inst. (mem. tech. commn.), N.Y. C. of C. (task force on pub. pensions), Fin. Planning Assn. (dir., govt. rels. com., ethics com.), The Inst. of Cert. Fin. Planners (bd. dirs., com. on career devel.), N.J. Soc. Inst. Cert. Fin. Planners (bd. dirs., sec., treas.), World Future Soc., Internat. Soc. Cert. Employee Benefit Specialists, Am. Acad. Mgmt., Am. Soc. Fin. Svcs. Profls., Strategic Mgmt. Soc., Internat. Soc. Cert. Employee Benefit Specialist, Princeton Club, Harvard Bus. Sch. Club of N.Y. E-mail: cmoransfa@yahoo.com.

MORAN, DONALD WILL, consulting company executive; b. Chgo., Nov. 27, 1951; s. William Frederick and Violette Mae (Tillman) M.; m. Catherine Anne Court, Nov. 26, 1977; 1 child, John Savage BS, U. Ill., 1973; postgrad., Southwest Mich. Coll., 1973-74, U. Mich., 1976-77. Adminstrv. asst. Cass County Bd. of Commns., Cassopolis, Mich., 1974-75; planning cons. Mich. Employment Sector Commn., Dowagiac, 1975-76; exec. dir. Barry-Branch St. Joseph Employment & Tng. Consortium, Coldwater, Mich., 1976-77; legis. asst. U.S. Congressman David A. Stockman, Washington, 1977-81; assoc. dir. Exec. Office of Pres. Office of Mgmt. and Budget, Washington, 1981-82, exec. assoc. dir., 1982-85; v.p. ICF, Inc., Washington, 1985—. Contbr. articles to profl. jours. Vice chmn. Republican Campaign Commn., Cassopolis, 1976 Mem. Am. Contract Bridge League Republican. Avocations: golf, bridge, woodworking. Home: 502 Canterbury Ln Alexandria VA 22314-4704

MORAN, ELIZABETH AMES, library director; b. Camden, Maine, June 22, 1940; d. Robie Frank and Dorothy Dyer Ames; m. Andrew Jackson Moran, Dec. 3, 1966; children: Heather Elizabeth, Melissa Ames. BA, U. Maine, 1962; MA in Law & Diplomacy, Fletcher Sch. Law & Diplomacy, 1964; MLS, U. S.C., 1997. Intelligence officer CIA, Washington, 1964-68; sch. libr. Fairfax (Va.) County Schs., 1981-87; libr. Camden (Maine) Pub. Libr., 1988-90, libr. dir., 1990—. Bd. dirs. Camden Tech. Conf., 1997-98; chair Maine Libr. Commn., 2000—. Mem. ALA, Maine Libr. Assn. (pres. 1998-2000), Pub. Libr. Assn. Small Pub. Libr. Assn., Camden Garden Club, Phi Beta Kappa. Republican. Episcopalian. Avocations: sailing, needlecrafts. Home: 32 Atlantic Hwy Northport ME 04849-3010 Office: Camden Pub Libr 55 Main St Camden ME 04843-1794

MORAN, EMILIO FEDERICO, anthropology and ecology educator; b. Habana, Cuba, July 21, 1946; s. Emilio F. Sr. and Caridad B. (Corrales) M.; m. Maria del Carmen Mendez, (div. 1970); m. Millicent Fleming, Dec. 15, 1972 (div. 2003); 1 child, Emily Victoria. BA, Springhill Coll., 1968; MA, U. Fla., 1969, PhD, 1975. Asst. prof. Ind. U., Bloomington, 1975-79, assoc. prof., 1979-84, chmn. dept. anthropology, 1980-87, prof. dept. anthropology, 1984—, Rudy prof. anthropology, 1996—, dir. Anthrop. Ctr. Tng. and Rsch. on Global Environ. Change, 1992—. Co-dir. Ctr. for Study of Instns., Population and Environ. Change, 1996—; leader Focus 1, Land-Use/Cover Change Program, 1999—; vis. prof. soil sci. NC State U., Raleigh, 1984; adv. panelist NSF, Washington, 1987-88, 90. Author: Developing the Amazon, 1981, Human Adaptability, 1982, 2d edit., 2000, The Human Ecology of Amazonian Populations, 1993; editor: The Dilemma of Amazonian Development, 1983, The Ecosystem Concept in Anthropology, 1984, The Ecosystem Approach in Anthropology, 1990, The Comparative Study of Human Societies, 1995, Transforming Societies, Transforming Anthropology, 1996; mem. editl. bd. Jour. Latin Am. Studies (Japan), 1992—, Jour. Forest and Conservation History, 1986-95, Anthrop. Linguistics, 1982-87, World Cultures, 1987-97, Human Ecology, 1993—. Grantee Fulbright Found., 1973, 76, 89, NIMH, 1974, NSF, 1991-93, 93—, Dept. Energy, 1991-95, Wenner-Gren, 1989, NICHD, 1997-2001, 03-, NASA, 1998—, NOAA, 2000—; named A.J. Hanna Disting. Lectr. Rollins Coll., 1985, ERDAS award for best sci. paper, 2000, Robert McNetting award Assn. Am. Geographers, 2002; postdoctoral fellow Tinker Found., 1983-84; Guggenheim Meml. Found. fellow, 1989; named Disting. Ecologist Colo. State U., 1987. Fellow AAAS (nominations com. 1987—, coun. rep. to bd., chmn. section H, 2003—), Am. Anthrop. Assn. (chmn. panel on devel., chmn. task force on environment, pres. anthropology and environ. sect. 1995-98)), Linnean Soc. London. Home: 915 S Baldwin Dr Bloomington IN 47401 Office: Ind U Student Bldg 240 Bloomington IN 47405

MORAN, GREGORY ALLAN, real estate developer, real estate agent; b. Oklahoma City, Okla., Oct. 23, 1962; s. Emet Allan and Joyce (Ladon) M.; m. Bridget Ellen Moran, Aug. 17, 1991; children: Ian Anderson, Conor Alexander, Kathlyn Maeve. BSBA in Fin. and Real Estate, U. Denver, 1985. Rsch. analyst Boettcher & Co., Denver, 1983-85; broker assoc. Del E. Webb Co., Denver, 1985-87, Grubb & Ellis Co., Denver, 1987-90; sr. broker assoc. The Colfax Group, Austin, Tex., 1990-96, Frederick Ross Co., Denver, 1996-98; v.p. leasing Miller Weingarten Realty, LLC, Englewood, Colo., 1998—. Burns fellow U. Denver-Burns Sch. Real Estate, 1999—. Sec., Kappa Sigma-Beta Omicron Housing Corp., Denver, 1996—. Mem. Internat. Coun. Shopping Ctrs. (assoc., state dir. 1997-2000, state govt. rels. dir. 2000-04, state alliance dir. 2004—), Urban Land Inst., Lakewood Country Club. Republican. Roman Catholic. Avocations: alpine skiing, running. Office: Miller Weingarten Realty LLC 850 Englwood Pkwy Ste 200 Englewood CO 80110-2304

MORAN, GREGORY JOHN, emergency medicine physician, educator; b. Kansas City, Mo., July 30, 1961; MD, U. Kans., 1987. Cert. in emergency medicine; cert. in internal medicine; bd. cert. in infectious disease. Intern UCLA, 1987-88, resident in internal medicine, 1988-90, resident in emergency medicine, 1990-92, fellow in infectious diseases, 1993-96; emergency medicine physician Olive View-UCLA Med. Ctr. Assoc. prof. medicine UCLA, 1993—. Mem. Am. Coll. Emergency Physicians, Infectious Diseases Soc. Am., Alpha Omega Alpha. E-mail: gmoran@ucla.edu.

MORAN, JAMES BYRON, federal judge; b. Evanston, Ill., June 20, 1930; s. James Edward and Kathryn (Horton) M.; children: John, Jennifer, Sarah, Polly; stepchildren: Katie, Cynthia, Laura, Michael. AB, U. Mich., 1952; LLB magna cum laude, Harvard U., 1957. Bar: Ill. 1958. Law clk. to judge U.S. Ct. of Appeals (2d cir.), 1957-58; assoc. Bell, Boyd, Lloyd, Haddad & Burns, Chgo, 1958-66, ptnr., 1966-79; judge U.S. Dist. Ct. (no. dist.) Ill., Chgo., 1979—. Dir. Com. on Ill. Govt., 1960-78, chmn., 1968-70; vice chmn., sec. Ill. Dangerous Drug Adv. Coun., 1967-74; dir. Gateway Found., 1969—; mem. Ill. Ho. of Reps., 1965-67; mem. Evanston City Council, 1971-75. Served with AUS, 1952-54. Mem. Chgo. Bar Assn., Chgo. Council Lawyers, Lawyers Club, Phi Beta Kappa. Home: 117 Kedzie St Evanston IL 60202-2509 Office: US Dist Ct 219 S Dearborn St Chambers 1846 Chicago IL 60604-1800 Office Phone: 312-435-5572. E-mail: jbm117@aol.com.

MORAN, JAMES D., III, university administrator; b. Bklyn., Mar. 2, 1951; s. James D. and Monica (Scherzinger) M.; m. Laurette Virginia Miller, Aug. 11, 1973; children: Ryan, Mollie. BA magna cum laude, Duke U., 1973; MS, U. Okla., 1975; PhD, Okla. State U., 1978. Asst. prof. U. Okla., Norman, 1978-80, Va. Poly. Inst. and State U., Blacksburg, 1980-83, assoc. prof., asst. head dept. famly and child devel., 1983-85; prof., head dept. family rels. and child devel. Okla. State U., Stillwater, 1985-89; assoc. dean coll. human ecology U. Tenn., 1989-98, dean, 1998—2002, assoc. vice provost, accreditation and state relations, 2002—03, asst. v.p. acad. affairs, 2004—. V.p. U. Tenn. Rsch. Corp.; mng. dir. Tande Tech. Licensing, 1997-2003. Mem. editl. bd. Home Econs. Rsch. Jour., 1983-85, Family Rels., 1985-91, Creativity Rsch. Jour., 1988-90, Home Econs. Forum, 1990-91, Jour. Family and Consumer Scis., 1993-95. Recipient Outstanding Rsch. award, Va. Home Econs. Assn., 1982, Disting. Alumnus award, Coll. Human Environ. Scis., Okla. State U., 2001. Mem.: Nat. Assn. for Edn. Young Children, Am. Assn. Family and Consumer Scis. (vice chmn. family rels. and child devel. sect. 1985—86, chmn. nominating com. 1987, chair coun. for accreditation 1989, chair strategic planning com. 1989, chair coun. for accreditation 1991, chair collegiate assembly 1995—97, vice chair bd. on human scis. 1999—2001, chmn.-elect 2003, pres. elect 2003—04, pres. 2004—05, named among New Faces to Watch 1984, Leadership award 1986), Phi Kappa Phi, Kappa Omicron Nu. Democrat. Roman Catholic. Avocation: golf. Home: 824 Andover Blvd Knoxville TN 37922-1532 Office: Office of Provost 413 AHT U Tenn Knoxville TN 37996-0184 Office Phone: 865-974-3265. E-mail: jmoran@utk.edu., jdmoran3@aol.com.

MORAN, JAMES JOSEPH, JR., insurance executive; s. James J. and Marilyn A. (Sullivan) M.; m. Mary Therese Stevens, Oct. 6, 1979; children: Sean M., James E., Matthew S. AB cum laude, Boston Coll., 1975, JD, 1978. Bar: Mass. 1978, U.S. Ct. Appeals (1st cir.) 1979, U.S. Dist Ct. Mass. 1979, U.S. Tax Ct. 1979, U.S. Supreme Ct. 1982; CPCU; Assoc. in Reins. Assoc. Haussermann, Davison & Shattuck, Boston, 1978-84, Morrison, Mahoney & Miller, Boston, 1984—87, ptnr., 1988—98; pres. Eastern Casualty Ins. Co., Marlborough, Mass., 1998—2001; sr. v.p, gen. counsel Quincy (Mass.) Mutual Fire Ins. Co., 2001—. V.p., gen. counsel Ind. Property-Casualty Insurers Mass. Inc., 1991-98; bd. dirs. R.I. Insurers Insolvency Fund, 2003—; counsel Mass. Assn. Ins. Agts., 1985-96; ins. broker, Mass.; New Eng. regional regulatory counsel Alliance Am. Insurers, 1994-98; trustee New Eng. Coll. Fin., 1998-2000. Bd. dirs. (gubernatorial appointee) Mass. Pollution Liability Reinsurance Corp., 1988-90. Recipient Econ. Leadership award Orgn. New Equality, 1997. Mem. Internat. Assn. Def. Coun., CPCU Soc. (pres. Boston chpt. 1993-94), Fedn. Ins. Corp. Coun., Ins. Libr. Assn. Boston (trustee 1983—, pres. 1989-90). Roman Catholic. Home: 15 Bramel Cir Walpole MA 02081-2043 Office: Quincy Mutual Fire Ins Co 57 Washington St Quincy MA 02169-9155 Office Phone: 617-770-5199.

MORAN, JAMES M. automotive sales executive; b. 1918; married. Owner Courtesy Motor Sales Inc. (formerly Hudson Motor Franchise Inc.), Chgo., 1947-68; chmn., now hon. chmn. JM Family Enterprises Inc., Deerfield Beach, Fla., 1969—. Office: JM Family Enterprises 100 NW 12th Ave Deerfield Beach FL 33442-1702

MORAN, JAMES MICHAEL, JR., astronomer, educator; b. Plainfield, N.J., Jan. 3, 1943; s. James Michael and Martha (Algermissen) M.; m. Barbara Putney Smith, Nov. 30, 1974; children: Susan Harrison, Michael Putney. BS, U. Notre Dame, 1963; SM, MIT, 1965, PhD, 1968. Mem. staff MIT Lincoln Lab., Lexington, 1968-70; sr. radio astronomer Smithsonian Astrophys. Obs., Cambridge, Mass., 1970—; prof. practice of astronomy Harvard U., Cambridge, 1979-89, Donald H. Menzel prof. astrophysics, 2001—; assoc. dir. Harvard-Smithsonian Ctr. Astrophysics, Cambridge, 1987-92, dir. Submillimeter Array Project, 1996—. Jansky lectr. Nat. Radio Astronomy Obs., 1996; trustee N.E. Radio Obs. Corp., Cambridge, 1983—. Contbr. numerous articles on radio astronomy to profl. publs. Co-recipient Rumford prize Am. Acad. Arts and Scis., 1971; recipient Sr. award Alexander von Humboldt Soc., 1993. Fellow AAAS, IEEE; mem. NAS, Am. Astron. Soc. (Pierce prize 1978), Explorers Club. Achievements include development of technique of very long baseline interferrrometry; research in study of black holes. Home: 93 Anson Rd Concord MA 01742-5704 Office: Harvard-Smithsonian Center for Astrophysics 60 Garden St Cambridge MA 02138-1516 Office Phone: 617-495-7477.

MORAN, JAMES PATRICK, JR., congressman, stockbroker; b. Buffalo, N.Y., May 16, 1945; s. James Patrick and Dorothy (Dwyer) M.; m. Mary Craig, Dec. 27, 1967 (div. 1974); children: Jimmy, Mary; m. Mary Howard; children: Michael, Patrick, Dorothy. BA in Econs., Coll. of Holy Cross, Worcester, Mass., 1967; postgrad., CUNY, 1967-68; MA in Pub. Adminstrn., U. Pitts., 1970. Budget analyst HEW, Washington, 1969-74; budget and fiscal policy specialist, Congl. rsch. Libr. of Congress, Washington, 1974-76; sr. staff appropriations com. U.S. Senate, Washington, 1976-79; city councilman City of Alexandria, Va., 1979—84, vice-mayor, 1982-84, mayor, 1985-91; investment broker A.G. Edwards & Sons, Alexandria, Va., 1979—; mem. U.S. Congress from 8th Va. dist., Washington, 1991—; mem. appropriations com., budget com. Councilman, City of Alexandria, 1979-82, vice-mayor, 1982-84, mayor, 1985—; chmn. No. Va. Transportation Bd., 1988—, United Way, 1977-79; vice chmn. Mental Health Retard and Substance Abuse Bd., 1976-78, vice chmn. D.E.O., 1976-78;dir., Met. Area Council Govts., dir. No. Va. Transp. Commn., 1985—. Recipient Outstanding Citizenship award YMCA, 1983. Mem. C. of C. (dir. 1985-86). Democrat. Roman Catholic. Home: 205 Uhler Ter Alexandria VA 22301-1551 Office: US Ho of Reps 2239 Rayburn Ho Office Bldg Washington DC 20515-4608

MORAN, JERRY, congressman; b. Great Bend, Kans., May 29, 1954; m. Robba A. Moran; 2 children. BS, Kansas U., 1976, JD, 1981. Senator dist. 37 State of Kans., 1989—96, sen. majority leader, 1994—96; mem., asst. majority whip U.S. Ho. of Reps. from 1st Kans. dist., 1997—, mem. agr., transp., infrastructure, vets. affairs coms., chmn. subcom. on gen. commodities; chmn. Rural Health Care Coalition. Republican. Office: US Ho of Reps 1519 Longworth Hob Washington DC 20515-1601

MORAN, JOHN BERNARD, retired government official; b. Saginaw, Mich., Nov. 26, 1936; s. Leo Lewis and Marie Katherine (Langley) M.; m. Diann Marie Markey, May 20, 1963 (div.); m. Barbara Jane Livingston, Aug. 18, 1978; children— Leslie Marie, Leanne Rene, Jeffrey John BS in Metall. Engring., Ill. Inst. Tech., 1959. Sr. automotive specialist Dow Chem. Co., Midland, Mich., 1962-71; program dir. research EPA, Research Triangle Park, N.C., 1971-75, dir. monitoring tech. div. Washington, 1975-76; dir. div. safety research Nat. Inst. for Occupational Safety and Health, Ctrs. for Disease Control, USPHS, HHS, Morgantown, W.Va., 1976-77, 83-88; dir. research and devel. safety products div. Am. Optical Corp., Southbridge, Mass., 1977-80; v.p., dir. ops. Geomet, Inc., Rockville, Md., 1980-83; program dir. Hartford Engring. Tech., Inc., Windsor, Conn., 1988; assoc. dir. health and safety laborers Associated Gen. Contractors, 1988-89; dir. safety and health Laborers Health and Safety Fund, 1989-95; spl. asst. to dep. asst. sec. Worker Health and Safety U.S. Dept. Energy, Washington, 1995; dir. policy OSHA, U.S. Dept. Labor, Washington, 1996; expert cons. to asst. sec. OSHA, Washington, 1996—; expert cons. to CDC Chem./Bioagts., 1996-99, ret.; now cons. in field. Mem. Nat. Mine Health Rsch. Adv. Com., Atlanta, 1980-84; govt. del. ILO, Geneva, 1985; mem. Nat. Adv. Com. on Constrn. Safety and Health, 1985-88, 92-95, Bur. Labor Stats. Rsch., 1991-95, hazardous material transp. info. com. NAS, 1991-93, Hazardous Materials Control Rsch. Inst.; chmn. lead subcom. Bldg. Constrn. Trades Dept., 1991-95; adj. asst. prof. mech. engring. W.Va. U., 1985-88; vis. ext. prof. U. Conn., Storrs, 1988-90; mem. Fed. Facilities Environ. Restoration Com., constrn. com. A 10 Am. Nat. Stds. Inst.; co-chair EPA-Labor Superfund Task Force, 1990-95, 96—; mem. nat. lead task force HUD, 1993-95; cons., expert witness. Patentee; contbr. articles to profl. jours, chpts. to books. Mem. Task Force on Hazardous Materials, Rockville, Md., 1983. chmn. Nat. Tech. Workshops on Safety and Health Issues. Served to capt. USMC, 1959-65 Recipient Bronze medal for commendable service EPA, 1974, Commitment to Life award Nat. Safe Workplace Inst., 1988. Mem. Internat. Soc. Respiratory Protection (pres. 1985-87, bd. dirs. 1987-89), Am. Conf. Govtl. Indsl. Hygienists. Roman Catholic. Home: PO Box 267 Franklinton NC 27525-0267

MORAN, JOHN FRANCIS, cardiologist; b. Chgo., Sept. 5, 1938; MD, Loyola U., Stritch Sch. Medicine, 1964. Cert. cardio. disease 1973. Office: Loyola U Med Ctr 2160 S 1st Ave Maywood IL 60153

MORAN, JOHN GREGORY, musician; b. Arlington, Va., Feb. 1, 1963; s. Charles Carroll and Carol Barbara Moran; m. Risa Browder, July 16, 1988; children: Thomas Edward, Stephen Paul. MusB, Oberlin U., 1985; diploma in Music, Schola Cantorum Basiliensis, Basel, Switzerland, 1989; PhD, U. London, 2001. Cellist Consort of Musicke, London, 1988—93, English Baroque Soloists, London, 1989—92, Les Musiciens du Louvre, Paris, 1990—95, REBEL, N.Y.C., 1997—; tchr. Peabody Conservatory Music, Balt., 2000—. Music dir. Modern Musick, Washington, 2002—. Contbr. articles to profl. jours. Mem.: Viola da gamba Soc. Am., Kindler Cello Soc., Am. Musicological Soc. Democrat. Roman Catholic. Avocations: German literature, French literature. Home: 814 North Daniel St Arlington VA 22201-1944 Office: Peabody Conservatory of Music 1 E Mt Vernon Pl Baltimore MD 21202

MORAN, JULIETTE M. retired chemicals executive; b. NYC, June 12, 1917; d. James Joseph and Louise M. BS, Columbia U., 1938; MS, NYU, 1948. Research asst. Columbia U., 1941; jr. engr. Signal Corps Lab., U.S. Army, 1942-43; with GAF Corp. (formerly Gen. Aniline & Film Corp.), 1943-82; from jr. chemist process devel. dept. to exec. v.p. and dir. GAF Corp., 1953—80, vice chmn., 1982—2002, cons., 1982—95; ret., 1982. Bd. dirs. N.Y. State Sci. and Tech. Found. Recipient Greater N.Y. Advt. award for excellence in communications N.Y. chpt. Assn. Indsl. Advertisers, 1972, Alumni Achievement award N.Y. U. Grad. Sch. Arts and Scis., 1977 Fellow AAAS, Am. Inst. Chemists; mem. Am. Chem. Soc., Comml. Devel. Assn. Home: 10 W 66th St New York NY 10023-6206

MORAN, KATE, sculptor, photographer; b. Langhorne, Pa., Dec. 27, 1958; BA in Visual Arts, Antioch Coll., 1982; cert., Pa. Acad. Fine Arts, Phila., 1988; MFA, U. N.C., 1992. Grad. faculty Pa. Acad. Fine Arts, 2002; instr. Acad. Fine Arts, Phila., 2004, Arcadia U., Glenside, Pa., 2004; bd. artistic advisors Creative Arts Network, Phila., 2002. One-woman shows include Fleisher Art Meml., Phila., 1992, Westby Art Gallery, Rowan Coll. N.J., Glassboro, 1992, More Gallery, Phila., 1995, Lafayette Coll., Williams Ctr. for Arts, Easton, Pa., 1995, John Michael Kohler Arts Ctr., Shebyoyan, Wis., 1996, U. N.C., Chapel Hill, 1997 (also vis. artist, lectr.), Steinbaum Krauss Gallery, N.Y.C., 1997, 98, List Gallery, Swarthmore (Pa.) Coll., 1997, Mangel Gallery, Phila., 1998, Mus. Am. Art, Pa. Acad. Fine Arts, 1998, Bernice Steinbaum Gallery, Miami, Fla., 2000, Olin Gallery, Kenyon Coll., Gambier, Ohio, 2000, Gallery Joe, Phila., 2004; 2 woman shows SPACES, Cleve., 1996, Suzanne H. Arnold Art Gallery, Lebanon Valley Coll. Pa., Annville, 1996; exhibited in group shows, 1991—, including Del. Art Mus., Wilmington, 1991, 93, 96, Print Club, Phila., 1991, New Orleans Mus. Art, 1992, Phila. Art Alliance, 1992, 94, Nexus Gallery, Phila., 1993, Stuart Levy Gallery, N.Y.C., 1993, 94, More Gallery, 1993, 94, Beaver Coll., Glenside, Pa., 1994, Snug Harbor Cultural Ctr., S.I., N.Y., 1995, Woodmere Art Mus., Phila., 1996, Phila. Mus. Art, 1996, 98, Rosenwald-Wolf Gallery, U. Parts, Phila., 1996; represented in permanent collections Mus. Am. Art at Pa. Acad. Fine Arts, Phila. Mus. Art, Woodmore Art Mus., New Orleans Mus. Art, State Mus. Pa., Harrisburg, CIGNA Mus. an Art Collection, Phila., Bryn Mawr (Pa.) Coll. Library; work represented in various publs. Recipient award Friends of Beaver Coll., 1991, purchase award New Orleans Mus. Art, 1992; John Michael Kohler Arts-Industry Residency, 1997, Works on Paper award Pa. Coun. on the Arts, 2000; fellow Pa. Coun. on Arts, 1992-93, 95-96, photography fellow PEW Fellowships in Arts, 1993-94; grantee Leeway Found., 1996-97, 2000; Works on Paper fellow Pa. Coun. Fine Arts, 2002. Home: 357 Leverington Ave Philadelphia PA 19128 Office: The Bernice Steinbaum Gallery 3550 N Miami Ave Miami FL 33127 E-mail: kmor@erols.com.*

MORAN, KEVIN J. book publisher; s. Thomas F. and Loraine Moran; m. Gail Anne Iskra, Dec. 23, 1983; children: Thomas F., Nora K., Conor G., Kevin. BA(hon.), SUNY, 1976. Pub. Hatherleigh Press, Long Island City, NY, 1995—. Mng. editor (non-fiction book) Living with Hepatitis C, Faith of Our Founding Father, The Arab Mind; contbr. reference. Coach Cath. Youth Orgn., New York, NY, 1993—2004. Mem.: Regis Alumni Assn. (assoc.). Democrat-Npl. Roman Catholic. Avocations: fishing, bird watching, hiking. Office: Hatherleigh Press 5-22 46th Ave Long Island City NY 11377 Office Phone: 718-786-5338. Office Fax: 718-706-6087. Personal E-mail: kevin@hatherleighpress.com.

MORAN, MARK, medical products executive; B in Math. and Physics, U. Okla.; MD, Washington U., St. Louis; MBA, Northwestern U. From asst. prof. to clin. assoc. prof. Stanford U. Sch. Medicine; from assoc. dir., to sr. dir. clin. rsch. Searle, Skokie, Ill.; former v.p. med. affairs and v.p. ops. Glycomed Inc. (now Ligand Pharms., Inc.); pres., CEO Ansan Pharms., Inc. (now Discovery Labs., Inc.); founder BioMedicines, Inc., Emeryville, Calif. Inventor in field. Former engring. officer USN. Office: Biomedicines Inc 2000 Powell St Ste 1640 Emeryville CA 94608

MORAN, MARTIN JOSEPH, fundraising company executive; b. Bklyn., Nov. 3, 1930; s. Dominick and Mary (Lydon) Moran; m. Mary Therese Schofield, June 5, 1954; children: Martin Joseph, John P., Maureen M., Thomas S., Robert P., William M., Maria M. BA, St. John's U., 1952. Profl. fundraising cons., 1956—; founder Martin J. Moran Co., Inc., NYC, 1964, pres., 1964—74, chmn. bd., 1974—. Mem. Am. Revolution Bicentennial Commn., Oyster Bay, NY, Massapequa Park Ethics Commn., 1969—72; trustee Notre Dame Coll., S.I, NY, 1969—72, La Salle Acad., NYC, 1971—87; mem. pres.'s coun. Cath. U. P.R., Ponce, 1966—71; mem. Cardinal's Com. for Edn., NYC, 1970—79, Cardinal's Com. for Laity Archdiocese NY, 1979—98, Massapequa Park (NY) Bd. Zoning Appeals, 1972—84, chmn., 1978—84; bd. councilors, sec., treas. Equestrian Order Holy Sepulchre of Jerusalem, 1990—, sec.-treas., 1990—93, pres., 1993—. Served as aviator USNR, 1952—56. Decorated knight Order Holy Sepulchre, Pope Paul VI, Knight of Malta Pope Paul VI, papal Knight of Order of St. Gregory the Gt. Pope John Paul II, knight comdr.; recipient Pietas medal, St. John's U., NY, 1988. Mem.: Am. Assn. Fundraising Counsel (bd. dirs. 1970—75), Navy Hist. Assn., Navy League, Friendly Sons of St. Patrick, Nassau County Hist. Soc., St. John's U. Alumni Assn. (pres. 1987—94), Old Port Yacht Club, Lost Tree Club (N. Palm Beach, Fla.), Madison Sq. Garden Club (NYC), KC. Home: 1300 Lakeshore Dr Massapequa Park NY 11762-1764 also: 677 Village Rd North Palm Beach FL 33408-3329 Office: Martin J Moran Co 1 Penn Plz Ste 1626 New York NY 10119-1626 E-mail: mjmmarty@aol.com.

MORAN, MARY SHANKS, hydrogeologist; b. Biloxi, Miss., Feb. 8, 1950; d. John William and Sara Lillie (Kirklin) Shanks; m. William Madison Moran, June 5, 1971; 1 child, Alice Janette. BS in Geology, Tenn. Tech. U., 1973; MS in Geology, Vanderbilt U., 1977; postgrad., Ohio U., 1979. Cert. and lic. profl. geologist. Hydrologist U.S. Geol. Survey, Nashville, 1974-77; hydrogeologist, rsch. assoc. Oak Ridge (Tenn.) Nat. Lab., 1977-80, hydrogeologist rsch. staff, 1981-85; sr. hydrogeologist Henningson, Durham & Richardson, Knoxville, 1980-81; hydrogeologist Birmingham, Ala., 1985-87; sr. hydrogeologist Sci. Applications Internat., Birmingham, 1987-89; environmental svcs. mgr. Atec Assocs., Birmingham, 1989; chief scientist, prin. Gallet & Assocs., Inc., Birmingham, 1989—. Geotech and environ. cons., 1989—; mem. adv. bd. Geoenviron. Cons., 1995—, Ala. State Drinking Water Act, 1998—; mem. Ala. Bd. Licensure Profl. Geologists, 1996—, Ala. Onsite Sewage Mgmt. Com., 1999—. Co-author: (book) Water Resources Investigations U.S. Geological Survey, 1977, Sourcebook of Hydrologic/Ecological Features Water Resouce Regions of the Conterminous U.S., 1980; contbr. articles to profl. jours. Named Outstanding Young Woman of Am. Mem.: ASCE (mem. geoinst. mem. com. 1999—), ASFE Profl. Firms Practicing Geoscis. (Svc. award 1998), Am. Inst. Profl. Geologists (sect. pres. 1993—95, Svc. award), Geol. Soc. Am., Assn. Groundwater Scientists and Engrs. (dir. 1995—97, Svc. award 1995), Rotary (pres. 1994—95), Sigma Xi. Avocations: horseback riding, needlepoint, field geology, drawing. Home: 913 Masters Ln Birmingham AL 35244-3262 Office: Gallet & Assocs Inc 320 Beacon Pkwy W Birmingham AL 35209-3171 E-mail: mmoran@gallet.com.

MORAN, MELVIN ROBERT, oil industry executive; b. St. Joseph, Mo., Sept. 18, 1930; s. Meyer Moran and Elsie Fine; m. Jasmine Dolores Lindsay, Nov. 22, 1953; children: Marilyn Townsend, Elisa, David. BS in Bus. Adminstrn., U. Mo., 1951. Asst. to supt. Moran Oil Co., Seminole, Okla., 1953-55; mgr., corp. sec. Moran Pipe & Supply Co., Inc., Seminole, 1955-81; mng. ptnr. Moran K Oil, Seminole, 1979—, Moran Oil Enterprises, Seminole, 1979—. Dir. Banc First, Oklahoma City, 1983—. Pres. BNai Brith, 1960—; mayor, councilman City of Seminole, 1965-79; bd. dirs. Seminole Industries Found., 1977—, Communities Found. of Okla., Higher Edn. Alumni Coun., 2004—; chmn. state campaign U.S. Senator David Boren, 1982-94; regent, chmn. Seminole State Coll., 1983-97; trustee Okla. Found. Excellence, 1986—; founder Jasmine Moran Children's Mus., Seminole, 1993; elected bd. dirs. Okla. Heritage Assn., 1999—; active Okla. Tourism and Recreation Commn., 2003. Lt. USAF, 1951-53, Eng. Recipient Philanthropist of Yr. award Okla. Fundraising Execs., 1995, Founders award Seminole State Coll., 2003; named to Hall of Fame, Okla. Heritage Assn., 1997, Oilman of Yr. Seminole Hist. Soc., 2002, Hall of Fame Tulsa Ctrl. H.S., 2003. Mem. Okla. Ind. Petroleum Assn. (dir., pres.), Seminole C. of C. (pres. dir. 1975—, Citizen of Yr. 1975, Hall of Fame 1980), Rotary (pres. 1960, apptd. blue ribbon jud. com. 1998—, apptd. bus. cir. for arts 1998—, apptd. Okla. Arts Coun. 1999, Mem. of Yr. 1997). Democrat. Jewish. Avocation: golf. Office: Moran Oil Enterprises PO Box 1295 Seminole OK 74818-1295 E-mail: melvinmoran@webtv.net., moe@renet.com.

MORAN, PATRICIA, lawyer; b. Wilmington, Del., 1959; BS, U. Scranton, 1981; JD, Villanova U., 1984. Bar: Del. 1984. Atty. Skadden, Arps, Slate, Meagher & Flom LLP, N.Y., ptnr., 1994—. Office: Skadden Arps Slate Meagher & Flom LLP Four Times Square New York NY 10036

MORAN, PATRICIA GENEVIEVE, corporate financial executive; b. Evanston, Ill., July 26, 1945; d. James Moran; children: Christine Coyle, Thomas Beddia, Donald Beddia. Student, Marquette U. Dir. corp. transp. JM Family Enterprises, Inc., 1984, corp. assoc. rels. dir., 1985, v.p., 1985-88; group v.p. sales Southeast Toyota, Deerfield Beach, Fla., 1988-89; pres., CEO JM Family Enterprises, Inc., Deerfield Beach, Fla., 1989—2000, chmn., 2000—. Bd. dirs. Am. Heritage Life Ins. Co. Bd. dirs. Take Stock in Children, Boca Raton Resort and Club. Named One of Top 50 Working Women by Working Woman's Mag. Mem. Nat. Assn. Automobile Dealers, Am. Internat. Automobile Dealers Assn., Fla. Council of 100, Com. of 200. Office: JM Family Enterprises 100 NW 12th Ave Deerfield Beach FL 33442

MORAN, PAUL JAMES, journalist, columnist; b. Buffalo, July 20, 1947; s. Paul James and Frances (Sciortino) M.; m. Kim Maldiner, Mar. 17, 1975 (div. July 1979); m. Colette Stass (div. Jan. 1997); 1 child, Heather. Student, SUNY, Buffalo, 1965-67, Millard Fillmore Coll., 1971-73. Sports editor Tonawanda News, North Tonawanda, N.Y., 1972-75; writer/columnist Fort Lauderdale (Fla.) News/Sun Sentinel, 1975-85, N.Y. Newsday, Melville, 1985—. Cons. Green Country Racing Assn., Tulsa, 1983-85. Author: (with others) Crown Jewels of Thoroughbred Racing; contbr. articles to mags. and newspapers. Sgt. USAF, 1967-71. Recipient Eclipse award Thoroughbred Racing Assn., 1985, 90, Disting. Writing award Am. Soc. Newspaper Editors, 1990, Deadline Writing award Soc. Silurians, 1990, Deadline Reporting award L.I. Press Club, 1991, Disting. Sports Writing award N.Y. Newspaper Pubs. Assn., 1992, (with others) Journalism collection Best Newspaper Writing 1991, Media award L.I. Vet. Med. Assn., 1997, excellence in continuing feature Fla. Mag. Assn., 1999, Best of Manhattan award N.Y. Press, 2002. Mem. N.Y. Turf Writers' Assn. (pres. 1990-92, sec.-treas. 1992-94), Nat. Turf Writers' Assn. (bd. dirs. 1987-90). Republican. Avocations: photography, art collecting. Home: 40 Carnation Ave Floral Park NY 11001-1730 Office: Newsday 235 Pinelawn Rd Melville NY 11747-4250

MORAN, PHILIP DAVID, lawyer; b. Lynn, Mass., June 3, 1937; s. J. Francis and Margaret M. (Shanahan) M.; m. Carole A. Regan, May 12, 1962; children: Maura F., Philip David. AB, Holy Cross Coll., 1958; EdM, Salem State Coll., 1961; JD, Suffolk U., 1968. Bar: Mass., 1968, U.S. Dist. Ct. Mass., 1972, U.S. Supreme Ct., 1988, U.S. Ct. Appeals (1st cir.), 1993. House counsel Viatron Computer Systems Corp., Burlington, Mass., 1968-71; ptnr. Kane & Moran, Lynn, Mass., 1972-78; pvt. practice law Salem, Mass., 1978—; propr. Law Offices of Philip D. Moran P.C., 1993—. Asst. dist. atty. Essex County (Mass.), 1974-78; mem. pres.'s coun. Holy Cross Coll., 1985—, Nat. Inst. Trial Advocacy U. Colo., 1973; gen. chmn. bicentenary com. Maynooth Coll., Boston, 1994-96. Contbg. author: Encyclopedia of Biomedical Policy, 1995. Bd. dirs. Nat. Right to Life Inc., 1977-83, 87—, treas., 1981-83; bd. dirs. Mass. Citizens for Life, 1973—, pres. 1979-80, chmn. 1991-93; mem. Salem Conservation Commn., 1980-89, chmn., 1982-89. With U.S. Army, 1960-66. Recipient Ignatius O'Connor Pro Life award, 1994, Gold medatl St. Patrick Maynooth Coll., Irelnd, 1996, Knight of Malta, 1997, Family, Faith and Freedom award Family Rsch. Coun., 1997, Citizenship award Mass. Family Inst., 1997. Mem. Mass. Bar Assn., Salem Bar Assn., Lynn Bar Assn., Am. Trial Lawyers Assn., Nat. Acad. Elder Law Attys., Murray Inn of Ct., Pro Life Legal Def. Fund (pres. 1997), Hibernian Civil Rights Coalition (bd. dirs. 1997, pres. 1997), Irish Am. Partnership, Nat. Coalition of Pro Life Dems. (bd. dirs., treas. 1999—), Dem State Com., Catholic Alliance (bd. dirs., gen. coun. 1999—). Roman Catholic. Avocations: swimming, reading, gardening, boating, photography. Home: 415 Lafayette St Salem MA 01970-5337 Office: 265 Essex St Salem MA 01970-3419

MORAN, RACHEL, lawyer, educator; b. Kansas City, Mo., June 27, 1956; d. Thomas Albert and Josephine (Portillo) Moran. AB, Stanford U., 1978; JD, Yale U., 1981. Bar: Calif. 1984. Assoc Heller, Ehrman, White & McAuliffe, San Francisco, 1982-83; prof. law U. Calif., Berkeley, 1984—, Robert D. and Leslie-Kay Raven prof. law, 1998—. Vis. prof. UCLA Sch. Law, 1988, 2002Stanford (Calif.) U. Law Sch., 1989, NYU Sch. Law, 1996, U. Miami Sch. Law, 1997, U. Tex. Law Sch., 2000; chair Chicano/Latino Policy Project, 1993-96; dir. Inst. for Study Social Change, 2003—. Contbr. articles to profl. jours. Recipient Disting. Tchg. award, U. Calif. Mem.: ABA, Calif. Bar Assn., Am. Law Inst., Phi Beta Kappa. Democrat. Unitarian Universalist. Avocations: jogging, aerobics, reading, listening to music. Office: U Calif Sch Law Boalt Hall Berkeley CA 94720 Office Phone: 510-643-6351. Business E-Mail: moran@law.berkeley.edu.

MORAN, RONALD WESSON, retired English educator, dean, writer; b. Phila., Sept. 9, 1936; s. Ronald Wesson and Julia Marie (Hagymasi) M.; m. Jane Edith Hetzler, Jan. 31, 1959; (twins) Sally and Ronald Wesson III. BA, Colby Coll., 1958; MA, La. State U., 1962, PhD, 1966. Instr. English La. State U., Baton Rouge, 1963-66; asst. prof. English U. N.C., Chapel Hill, 1966-69, assoc. prof., 1969-75; prof. English Clemson (S.C.) U., 1975-99, head dept. English, 1975-80, asst. dean, 1986-91, assoc. dean, 1991-99, interim dean Coll. Arch., Arts and Humanities, 1999-2000; ret., 2000. Arts and scis. adv. bd. Greenville (S.C.) Tech. Coll., 1986-89; Fulbright lectr., Würzburg, Germany, 1969-70; bd. dirs. Clemson Area Retirement Ctr., Inc. Author: So Simply Means the Rain, 1965, Louis Simpson, 1972, Life on the Rim, 1988, Sudden Fictions, 1994, Getting the Body to Dance Again, 1995, Fish Out of Water, 2000, Ronald Moran: Greatest Hits, 1965-2000, 2001; co-author: Four Poets and the Emotive Imagination, 1976; assoc. editor: South Atlantic Bull., 1975—77, adv. bd.: S.C. Rev., 1980—. Recipient Nat. Looking Glass Poetry Chapbook award, 1994. Mem. Assn. Acad. Affairs Adminstrs.-Southeastern Region (bd. officers 1989-93). Methodist. Home: 114 Princess Ln Clemson SC 29631-2120 E-mail: rmoran@statecom.net.

MORAN, THOMAS HARRY, retired academic administrator; b. Milw., Oct. 21, 1937; s. Harry Edward and Edna Agnes Moran; m. Barbara Ellen Saklad, June 10, 1969; children: David Thomas, Karen Ellen. BS, U. Wis., 1964, MA, 1972, PhD, 1974. Dir. capital budgeting Wis. Dept. Adminstrn., 1962-64; exec. dir. Wis. Higher Ednl. Aids Bd., 1964-69; spl. cons. tax policy Wis. Dept. Revenue, 1973-74; dep. dir. Wis. Manpower Coun., Office of Gov., 1974-76; v.p. bus. and fin., treas. U. Detroit, 1976-78; exec. assoc. v.p. health affairs U. So. Calif., LA, 1979-87, v.p. bus. affairs, 1988—2002, v.p. emeritus, 2002—. USN fellow, 1957-59, U.S. Office Edn. rsch. fellow, 1973. Mem. Am. Assn. Higher Edn., Phi Kappa Phi. E-mail: tmoran@usc.edu.

MORAN, WILLIAM EDWARD, academic administrator; b. White Plains, N.Y., May 28, 1932; s. Frank Joseph and Margaret Mary (Farrell) M.; m. Barbara Carol Baillet, Apr. 20, 1963; children: Kathryn, Kevin, Colin, Christian. AB, Princeton U., 1954; MBA, Harvard U., 1959; PhD, U. Mich., 1967. Mgmt. cons. Booz, Allen & Hamilton, N.Y.C., 1959-61; mem. adminstrv. staff Harvard U., Boston, 1961-63; asst. exec. v.p. SUNY-Stony Brook, 1966-71; chancellor Flint Campus U. Mich., 1971-79, U. N.C., Greensboro, 1979-94; sr. v.p. Connors Investor Svcs., Inc., 1994—. Bd. dirs. Greensboro, N.C. Connors Investor Services, Reading, Pa., Cross Enging. & Sales Co., 2001—, Piedmont Land Conservancy, 2001—, U. N.C. at Greensboro Investment Fund, 2001—. Contbr. articles to profl. jours. Pres. So. Univ. Conf., 1987. Served with USN, 1954-57. Mem. N.C. Assn. Colls. and Univs. (pres. 1992), Princeton Club (N.Y.), Rotary. Home: 5206 Barnfield Rd Greensboro NC 27455-2136

MORAND, PETER, investment company executive; b. Montreal, Que., Can., Feb. 11, 1935; s. Frank and Rose Alice (Fortier) M.; m. Dawn McKell, Oct. 10, 1957; children: Clifford, Tanya. BSc with honors, Bishop's U., Lennoxville, Que., 1956, DCL (hon.), 1991; PhD, McGill U., Montreal, 1959; hon. Doctorate (hon.), U. Ottawa, 2001. NATO postdoctoral fellow Imperial Coll., London, 1959-61; sr. rsch. chemist Ayerst Labs., Montreal, 1961-63; from asst. prof. to prof. chemistry U. Ottawa, 1963—90, acad. asst. vice rector, 1968-71, dean sci.and engring., 1976-81, dir. rsch. svcs., 1981-87, vice rector univ. R&D, 1987—90; pres. Natural Scis. and Engring. Rsch. Coun., Ottawa, 1990-95; pres., CEO Can. Sci. and Tech. Growth Fund, 1996—; chmn. Adherex Techs. Inc., Ottawa, 1998—2002, Inno-centre Ottawa, 2000—02. Bd. dirs. Ottawa Life Scis. Coun., 1996—, Can. Swedish Bus. Assn., Can. Bioscis. Communication Inst., 2001—, Can. Bacterial Diseases Network, 1996—, Inst. on Governance, 2002—. Contbr. articles to profl. jours.; patentee in field. Trustee Royal Ottawa Health Care Group, 1992-2000. Natural Scis. and Engring. Rsch. Coun. grantee, 1964-90. Fellow Chem. Inst. Can. Office: Adherex Techs Inc 600 Peter Morand Cres # 220 Ottawa ON Canada K1G 5Z3

MORANG, DIANE JUDY, writer, television producer, business entrepreneur; b. Chgo., Apr. 28, 1942; d. Anthony Thomas Morang and Laura Ann Andrzejczak. Student, Stevens Finishing Sch., Chgo., 1956, Fox Bus. Coll., 1959-60, UCLA, 1967-69. Mem. staff Chgo. Sun Times, Daily News, 1957, Drury Ln. Theatre, Chgo., 1961-62, AM Show ABC-TV, Hollywood, Calif., 1970-71; creator, owner Internet store. Judge 2 categories regional Emmy Awards, 1985, chair, mem. judging panel, 89; owner www.americanposh.com. Author: How to Get into the Movies, 1978; author, creator: The Rainbow Keyboard, 1991, The Translation of the Code of Music into Numerics; creator: The Best Kids' Show in the World, The Best Dog Treats in the World; contbr. numerous articles to newspapers, mags. Bd. dirs., mem. scholarship com. Ariz. Bruins, UCLA Alumni Assn.; mem. Nat. Mus. Women in the Arts, Washington, D.C.; mem. Nat. Women's Hall of Fame, Seneca Falls, N.Y. Mem. NATAS (mem. Hollywood Emmy Award-winning team Hollywood, Calif. 1971), Ariz. Authors Assn. (bd. dirs.), Amon Carter Mus. Roman Catholic.

MORANO, GERARD JOHN, marketing executive; b. Mount Vernon, N.Y., Oct. 23, 1944; s. Gerard Anthony and Pauline (Ungaro) M.; m. Allison Lenore Folz, June 28, 1975; 1 child, Steven Christopher. BS in Fin., CUNY, 1974; BA in Mktg., Pace U., Pleasantville, N.Y., 1981; MBA, Pace U., White Plains, N.Y., 1982. From fin. planner to mgr. sales promotion ITT Continental, Rye, NY, 1968—84; from dir. mktg. to sr. v.p. mktg. and comm. Quality Bakers Am., Greenwich, Conn., 1984—2000, exec. v.p. QBA, Advt., Inc., Greenwich, Conn., 1992—2000, Solutions Mktg. LLC, Darien, Conn., 2001—. Alumni mentor Pace U., 1988—; fundraiser Vietnam Vets. Meml. Com., Washington, 1980-82; bd. dirs. Vets. Bus. Network, 2001—. With U.S. Army, 1966-68, Vietnam. Decorated Bronze Star; recipient Conspicious Silver Svc. Star and Order of Merit, State of N.Y., 2001. Mem.: Promotional Mktg. Assn., Am. Film Inst., 199th Inf. Assn., Ellis Island Found., Vietnam Vets. Am., Wildlife Conservation Soc. Avocations: photography, videography. Office: Solutions Mktg LLC 30 Old Kings Hwy S Darien CT 06820 Office Phone: 203-655-2614. E-mail: jmorano2000@aol.com.

MORANO, KEVIN R. mining company executive; b. June 28, 1953; m. Ellen Dooley. BS magna cum laude, Drexel U., 1977; MBA, Rider Coll., 1983. Audit supr. Coopers & Lybrand, Newark, N.J.; with contr. dept. ASARCO Inc., N.Y.C., 1978-88, treas., 1989, gen. mgr. Ray Copper Mining and Smelting Complex, 1991, v.p., CFO, 1993-98, exec. v.p., COO, 1999, also bd. dirs.; exec. v.p., CFO Exide Tech., 1999—2001, Lumiens Ltd., 2002—. Bd. dirs. Apex Silver Ltd., Datatwatch Corp., Bear Creek Mining Corp. Mem. AICPA, N.J. Soc. CPA. Office: 375 Park Ave 11th Fl New York NY 10152

MORANT, RICARDO BERNARDINO, psychology educator; b. New Britain, Conn., Feb. 13, 1926; s. J. Ramon and Rosario (Ciscar) M.; m. G. Francisca Giner, Dec. 26, 1955; children— Ramon, Francisca, Dolores, Ricardo. AB, Harvard, 1948; postgrad., Wesleyan Coll., Middletown, Conn., 1948-49; MA, Clark U., 1950, PhD, 1952. From faculty to prof. Brandeis U., Waltham, Mass., 1952—91, Minnie and Harold L. Fierman prof. psychology, 1991—, prof. Volen Nat. Ctr. for Complex Sys., 1994—. Prin. investigator NIMH, Spencer Found., Rothman Found. 1960—; spl. research space perception, body orientation. Bd. dirs. Coun. Pub. Schs., 1970-73; mem. steering com. Sensory Aid Eval. and Devel. Ctr., MIT, 1963-67; chmn. bd. trustees Hiatt Ednl. Programs, 1982-94. Served with USNR, 1946-48. Fellow APA; mem. Psychonomic Soc. Home: 35 Cliff Rd Wellesley MA 02481-3001 E-mail: morant@brandeis.edu.

MORARI, MANFRED, chemical engineer, educator; b. Graz, Austria, May 13, 1951; came to U.S., 1975; s. Manfred and Hilde M.; m. Marina Korchynsky, May 12, 1984. Diploma Chem. Engring., Eidgenoessische Technische Hochschule, Zurich, Switzerland, 1974; PhD in Chem. Engring., U. Minn., 1977; Dr h c, Babes Bolyai U., 2003. Asst. prof. U. Wis., Madison, 1977-81, assoc. prof., 1981-83; prof. chem. engring. Calif. Inst. Tech., Pasadena, 1983-94, McCollum-Corcoran prof., 1991-94, exec. officer, 1990-93, prof. control and dynamical sys., 1993-94; exec. officer, 1993-94; head automatic control lab. ETH. Gulf vis. prof. chem. engring. Carnegie Mellon U., 1987. Contbr. articles to profl. jours. Recipient D.P. Eckman award Am. Automatic Control Coun., 1980. Mem. IEEE (George S. Axelby Outstanding Paper award 1990), NAE, AIChE (A.P. Colburn award 1984, Profl. Progress award 1995, Computing in Chem. Engring. award 2002), Am. Soc. for Engring. Edn. (Curtis W. McGraw rsch. award 1989), Am. Chem. Soc. Home: Laerchentobelstrasse 22 CH-8700 Kuesnacht Switzerland Office: Automatic Control Lab ETH-Z ETL I 29 CH-8092 Zurich Switzerland Office Phone: +41 44 632 7626. E-mail: morari@control.ee.ethz.ch.

MORARIU, CORINA, professional tennis player; b. Detroit, Michigan, Jan. 26, 1978; d. Albin and Rodica Morariu; m. Andrew Turcinovich. Grad., St. Andrews H.S., 1996. Mem. U.S. Nat. Tennis team, 1996. Won Jr. Championship Australian, French and U.S. Opens, 1995, Australia, 1994, Wimbledon, doubles, 1999 (with Lindsay Davenport), Australian Open Mixed Doubles (with E. Ferreira), 2001; winner 1 Career Singles Title, 10 Career Doubles Titles, WTA Tour. Office: USTA 70 W Red Oak Ln White Plains NY 10604-3602 also: ATP Tour 201 Atp Tour Blvd Ponte Vedra Beach FL 32082-3211

MORATH, MAX EDWARD, entertainer, composer, writer; b. Colorado Springs, Colo., Oct. 1, 1926; s. Frederic Palmer and Gladys Hester Nancy (Ramsell) M.; m. Norma Loy Tackitt, Oct. 23, 1953 (div. 1992); children: Kathryn, Christine, Frederic; m. Diane Fay Skomars, May 24, 1993. BA in English, Colo. Coll., 1948; postgrad., Stanford NBC-Radio-TV Inst., Palo Alto, Calif., 1951; MA in Am. Studies, Columbia U., 1996. Touring nationally in concerts and theater Ragtime and Again, 2004—; recs. on Epic, RCA, Vanguard, SoloArt, Omega, Premier; author: The Road to Ragtime, 1999, The NPR Curious Listener's Guide to Popular Standards, 2002; playwright, producer, composer (musical play) Trust Everybody...But Cut the Cards, 2003. Mem. Broadcast Music, Inc. Office: Ste 700 850 7th Ave New York NY 10019-5230 Office Phone: 212-459-0030. Personal E-mail: rathmo@aol.com.

MORAVCSIK, JULIUS MATTHEW, philosophy educator; b. Budapest, Hungary, Apr. 26, 1931; came to U.S., 1949; s. Julius and Edith (Fleissig) M.; m. Marguerite Germain Truninger, Sept. 14, 1954; children: Adrian Clay, Peter Matthew. BA, Harvard U., 1953, PhD, 1959. Asst. prof. U. Mich., Ann Arbor, 1960-66, assoc. prof., 1966-68; prof. Stanford (Calif.) U., 1968—. Lectr. in 25 countries. Author: Understanding Language, 1975, Thought and Language, 1990, Plato and Platonism, 1992, Meaning, Creativity, and the Partial Inscrutability of the Human Mind, 1998., Was Menschen Verbindet, 2003. Recipient Sr. Humanist prize Humboldt Found., 1983; fellow Ctr. Advanced Studies Behavioral Scis., 1986-87, Inst. Advanced Studies, 2001-02. Fellow Inst. Advanced Studies Budapest; mem. Am. Philos. Assn. (pres. Pacific divsn. 1987-88), Am. Soc. Aesthetics (trustee 1988-92), Soc. Ancient Greek Philosophy (pres. 1989-91, bd. dirs. Jour. History Philosophy, James Wilbur Award Value Theory 2000), Hungarian Acad. Arts and Scis. (external mem.). Avocations: golf, tennis. Office: Stanford U Dept Of Philosophy Stanford CA 94305 Office Phone: 650-723-2547. Business E-Mail: julius@csli.stanford.edu.

MORAVEC, CHRISTINE D. SCHOMIS, medical educator; b. L.A., Apr. 26, 1957; BA, John Carroll U., 1978, MS, 1984; PhD, Cleve. State U., 1988. Tchr. Trinity H.S., Garfield Heights, Ohio, 1978-80; grad. teaching asst. dept. biology John Carroll U., Cleve., 1982-84; rsch. assoc. dept. cardiovascular biology Cleve. Clinic Found., 1990-93, project scientist dept. cardiovascular biology, 1990-93, asst. staff dept. cardiovascular biology, 1993-94; asst. prof. dept. physiology & biophys. Case Western Res. U. Sch. Medicine, Cleve., 1993—. Adj. asst. prof. Cleve. State U., 1994—; asst. staff Ctr. Anesthesiology Rsch. Cleve. Clinic Found., 1994—. Contbr. articles to profl. jours. Grad. fellow Cleve. Clinic Found., 1984-88, Postdoctoral fellow, 1988-89, recipient Tarazi fellow, 1989. Mem. Am. Physiol. Soc., Am. Heart Assn. (basic sci.

coun. 1990—; Established Investigatorship award 1995), Ohio Physiol. Soc., Electron Microscopy Soc. Northeastern Ohio, Cardiac Muscle Soc. Office: Cleve Clin Found Ctr Anesthesiology Found 9500 Euclid Ave # FF40 Cleveland OH 44195-0001

MORAVEC, PAUL, composer; b. Buffalo, 1958; Attended, Am. Acad., Rome; BA in music composition magna cum laude, Harvard U., 1990; MusM in music composition, Columbia U., 1982, D Musical Arts in music composition, 1987. Tchg. asst. Columbia U., 1980—84, preceptor, 1985—87; dir. Columbia U. Composers' Colloquium, 1985—87; asst. prof. Dartmouth Coll., 1987—93, assoc. prof., 1993—96; prof., chmn. Adelphi U., 1997—. Vis. assoc. prof. Columbia U., 1996—98; adj. assoc. prof. Hunter Coll., 1998. Composer over seventy orchestral, chamber, choral, and lyric compositions including, (orchestral) Spiritdance, 1989, Adelphony, 1997, Ancient Lights, 1994, Northern Lights Electric, 2000, Tempest Fantasy, 2003, (chamber) The Kingdom Within, 1989, Circular Dreams, 1991, Quintessence, 1999, Octocelli, 2000, (piano solo) Music Remembers, 1983, Piano Triptych, 1991, Characteristics, 1995, (choral) Ave Verum Corpus, 1979, Three Anthems, 1983, A Spirit of Power, 1996, Personals, 1999. Fellow in Music Composition, Nat. Endowment Arts, Rockefeller Found., Goddard Lieberson; Rome Prize Fellowship, Am. Acad. Rome, residency fellowship, Carnargo Found., Charles Ives Fellowship, Am. Acad. Arts Letters. Office: Adelphi U Dept Music Post Hall Second Fl Garden City NY 11530*

MORAWETZ, CATHLEEN SYNGE, mathematician; b. Toronto, Ont., Can., May 5, 1923; arrived in U.S., 1945, naturalized, 1950; d. John Lighton and Elizabeth Eleanor Mabel (Allen) Synge; m. Herbert Morawetz, Oct. 28, 1945; children: Pegeen Morawetz Rubinstein, John Synge, Lida Morawetz Jeck, Nancy. BA, U. Toronto, 1945; SM, MIT, 1946; PhD, NYU, 1951; degree (hon.), Ea. Mich. U., 1980, Smith Coll., 1982, Brown U., 1982, Princeton U., 1986, Duke U., 1988, N.J. Inst. Tech., 1988, U. Waterloo, 1993, U. Dublin, 1996, U. Toronto, 1996. Research assoc. Courant Inst., NYU, 1952—57, asst. prof. math., 1957—60, assoc. prof., 1960—65, prof., 1965—, assoc. dir., 1978—84, dir., 1984—88. Chmn. bd. Sch. Theoretical Physics Dublin Inst. for Advanced Studies, 1995—2000. Former editor various math. jours., author articles in applications of partial differential equations, especially transonic flow and scattering theory. Trustee Princeton U ., 1973—78, Sloan Found., 1980—94. Recipient Nat. medal of Sci., NSF, 1998; fellow Guggenheim, 1967, 1979; grantee Office of Naval Rsch., 1990. Fellow: AAAS, Royal Soc. Can.; mem.: NAS, London Math. Soc., Royal Irish Acad., Soc. Indsl. and Applied Math., Am. Philos. Soc., Am. Acad. Arts and Scis., Am. Math. Soc. (term trustee 1975—85, pres. 1995—97). Office: CIMS 251 Mercer St New York NY 10012-1110

MORAWETZ, THOMAS H. law educator; b. Montreal, July 22, 1942; s. Frederick and Melanie (Landau) Morawetz. AB, Harvard U., 1963; MPhil, Yale U., 1966, JD, 1968, PhD in Philosophy, 1969. Assoc. prof. philosophy Yale U., New Haven, 1969—77; prof. law U. Conn., Hartford, 1977—91, Tapping Reeve prof. law and ethics, 1991—. Vis. prof. various Am. and European univs.; adv. bd. Legal Ethics, London, 1998—, Law and Philosophy, San Diego, 1994—; creator mus. shows on transformational makeup. Author: (book) Criminal Law, 1996, Law's Premises, Law's Promise, 2000, Making Faces, Playing God, 2001; contbr. over 50 articles to profl. jours. Mem. Amnesty Internat. Fellow Wilson Ctr. fellow, Woodrow Wilson Ctr., 1985; Fulbright fellow, 1963. Avocations: collecting books and kaleidoscopes, reviewing modern fiction. Home: 8G Staunton Ct Farmington CT 06032 Office: Univ of Conn Sch of Law 65 Elizabeth St Hartford CT 06105 Office Phone: 860-570-5274. E-mail: tmorawet@law.uconn.edu.

MORBY, JACQUELINE, venture capitalist; b. Sacramento, June 19, 1937; d. Junior Jennings and Bertha (Backer) Collins; m. Jeffrey L. Morby, June 21, 1959; children: Andrew Jennings, Michelle Lorraine. BA in Psychology, Stanford U., 1959; M in Mgmt., Simmons Grad. Mgmt. Sch., Boston, 1978. Assoc. TA Assocs., Boston, 1978-81, gen. ptnr., 1982-89, mng. dir., 1989—2002, prin., 2003—. Bd. dirs. HVL, Inc., Pitts., Softmed Sys. Inc., Bethesda, Md., Ansys, Inc., Canonsburg, Pa., Pacific Life Corp., Newport Beach, Calif., J&B Software, Inc., Bluebell, Pa. Trustee Simmons Coll., Warholl Mus. Mem. Nat. Venture Capital Orgn. Avocations: theater, reading, art, skiing, travel. Office: TA Assocs 125 High St Boston MA 02110-2704 E-mail: jmorby@ta.com.

MORCOS, ANN CONTI, writing and editing company executive; b. Jackson, Miss., Oct. 6, 1947; d. Joseph Salvador Conti and Dorothy Anderson Irwin; m. Kaysar E. Morcors, July 4, 1970 (div. Apr. 1990); children: Laila, Samy. BA in English, U. New Orleans, 1972, MA in English, 1986. Cert. Peace Officers Stds. and Tng., 2002. Instr. English, U. New Orleans, 1983—87; coord. Bogalusa Heart Study, La. State U. Med. Ctr., 1987—92; assoc. editor Ochsner Found. Hosp., 1992—94; pubs. coord. urology dept. Tulane Med. Ctr., 1995—97, exec. asst. chancellor, 1997—99; owner MorcosMedia.com, Metairie, 1999—. Author: The Tale of Nada Nutria, 2002; editor: Archives of Brazilian Card, 1999—, Jour. of Soc. of Laproendoscopic Surgeons, 2000—; bd. editors: Life Scis., 1995; contbr. articles to profl. jours., newspapers. Vol. Ozonana Inn, New Orleans, 2000—; tchr. Sunday sch. Holy Trinity Cathedral, New Orleans, 1997—2000, St. Basil Orthodox Ch., Metairie, 1980—87. Mem.: Soc. for Scholarly Pub., Text and Acad. Authors Assn., European Assn. Sci. Editors, Am. Med. Writers Assn., Coun. Sci. Editors (ann. meeting editor 1999—). Avocations: reading, writing, exercise, travel. Office: MorcosMedia PO Box 1956 Metairie LA 70004-1956 E-mail: acmorcos@cox.net.

MORD, IRVING CONRAD, II, lawyer; b. Mar. 22, 1950; s. Irving Conrad and Lillie Viva (Chapman) M.; m. Julia Ann Russell, Aug. 22, 1970 (div. Apr. 1980); children: Russell Conrad, Emily Ann; m. Kay E. McDaniel, Aug. 31, 1985; children: Kurt August, Clayton Troy. BS, Miss. State U., 1972; JD, U. Miss., 1974. Bar: Miss. 1974, U.S. Dist. Ct. (no. dist.) Miss. 1974, U.S. Dist. Ct. (so. dist.) Miss. 1984. Counsel to bd. suprs. Noxubee County, Miss., 1976-80, Walthall County, Miss., 1980—, Bd. Edn., Walthall County, 1982—, County pros. atty. Noxubee County, Macon, Miss., 1974—80, Walthall County, Tylertown, Miss., 1982—88, Tylertown, 1991—96. Bd. dirs. East Miss. Coun., Meridian, 1978-80, Trustmark Nat. Bank, Tylertown, 1986—, chmn., 2002-; v.p. Macon coun. Boy Scouts Am., 1978, mem. coun., 1979; county crusade chmn. Am. Cancer Soc., Macon, 1976-78, county pres., 1979; chmn. fund dr. fine arts complex Miss. State U., Macon, 1979; Walthall County family master, 1996—, Walthall County Youth referee, 1996—; mem. Local Workforce Investment Bd., 2000—. Recipient Youth Leadership award Miss. Econ. Coun., 1976. Mem. Miss. Assn. Bd. Attys. (v.p. 1985, pres. 1986), Miss. Assn. Sch. Bd. Attys., Miss. State Bar, Am. Judicature Soc. (Torts award 1972), Nat. Fed. Ind. Bus., Miss. State U. Alumni Assn., Walthall County C. of C., Phi Kappa Tau (bd. govs. 1976-80, grad. coun. 1972—, pres. grad. coun. 1977-80, pres. house corp. 1977-80, Alumnus of Yr. Alpha Chi chpt. 1979), Rotary (sec.-treas. 1977, v.p. 1978, pres. Macon 1979, pres. Tylertown club 1986-87), Phi Delta Phi. Office: 729 Beulah Ave Tylertown MS 39667-2709 Office Phone: 601-876-2611. E-mail: icmord@telapex.com.

MORDECAI, BENJAMIN, theatrical producer, drama educator; b. N.Y.C., Dec. 10, 1944; s. Allen Lewis Mordecai and Florence Doris (Goldman) Holl; m. Sherry Lynn Morley, July 20, 1974; 1 child, Rachel Elizabeth. BA, Buena Vista Coll., 1967; MA, Eastern Mich. U., 1968; postgrad., Ind. U., 1968—70. Founder, producing dir. Ind. Repertory Theatre, Indpls., 1971-82; mng. dir. Yale Repertory Theatre, New Haven, 1982-93; assoc. dean Yale Sch. Drama, New Haven, 1992—; mng. ptnr. Benjamin Mordecai Prodns., Inc., N.Y.C., 1992—; ptnr. Prodrs.' Mgmt. Group, 1999—2003, Prodrs. Four, 2003—. Cons. Found. for the Ext. and Devel. of the Am. Profl. Theatre, N.Y.C., 1974; adj. prof. Yale Sch. of Drama, 1982—; ind. cons., New Haven, 1984—. Dir.: (plays) Fables Here and Then, 1972, Dracula, 1973, Bird in the Hand, 1975; assoc. prodr. (plays) Fences, 1987 (Tony award, 1987), Joe Turner's Come & Gone, 1988 (N.Y. Drama Critics Cir. award, 1988), A Walk in the Woods, 1988, gen. mgr. A Walk in the Woods (USSR), 1989; exec. prodr.: (plays) The Piano Lesson, 1990 (N.Y. Drama Critics Cir. award, 1990, Drama Desk award, 1990), Two Trains Running, 1992, Angels in America (N.Y. Drama Critics award, 1993, Tony award, 1993, 1994); prodr.: Redwood Curtain, 1993, Twilight: Los Angeles, 1992, 1994; assoc. prodr. The Kentucky Cycle, 1993; prodr.: Gate of Heaven (U.S. Holocaust Mus.), 1995, August Wilson's Seven Guitars, 1996 (N.Y. Drama Critics award, 1996), Golden Child (Kennedy Ctr.), 1997, (Singapore, N.Y.), 1998, Jitney, 2000 (N.Y. Drama Critics award, 2000), August Wilson's King Hedley II, 2001, August Wilson's Jitney (Nat. Theatre, London), 2001 (Olivier award for best play), Thunder Knocking on The Door, 2002, Endpapers, 2002, Flower Drum Song, 2002, Ma Rainey's Black Bottom, 2003, Sixteen Wounded, 2004; exec. prodr.: Harlem Nutcracker, 1997—99, Moscow Art Theatre's Three Sisters, 1998. Recipient Disting. Svc. award Indpls. Jaycees, 1979, spl. commendation City-County Coun., Inpls., 1982, Robert Whitehead award for outstanding comml. producing, 1993, Spl. Achievement award New Eng. Theatre Conf., 1998, Outstanding Producing award Hollywood NAACP, 1990, 92; named Outstanding Young Alumnus, Buena Vista Coll., 1987. Mem. League of Resident Theatres (exec. com. 1981-91), Assn. Arts Adminstrn. Educators (sec.-treas. 1984-88), Am. Theatre Exch. Initative (bd. dirs. 1987—, pres. 1994—), Writers Theatre (bd. advisors 1983—), Stage Dirs. and Choreographers Found. (bd. dirs. 1990—), League Am. Theatres & Prodrs., Nat. Theatre Conf. Business E-Mail: benjamin.mordecai@yale.edu.

MORDEN, ANNETTE SONJA KNUDSON, education educator; b. Phoenix, Mar. 17, 1940; d. Maynard Wold and Mertie Lucille Knudson; m. Robert Dean Morden, Aug. 5, 1962; children: Kristina, Shauna. BA, U. Northern Iowa, 1962; MA in edn., U. of Northern Iowa, 1966. Math tchr. Rockford Roosevelt, Ill., 1962—65; benthic biologist U. Wis., 1972, 1975, sr. lectr. and dir. math tutoring lab, 1982—. Unit leader and budget, audit and fin. com. League of Women Voters, 1971—73; brownie and girl scout leader Girl Scouts Am., 1963—64, 1977—82; bd. dirs. and exec. bd. YMCA, 1976—81; mem. founding com. and exec. bd. Habitat for Humanity, 1991—94. Mem.: Assn. of U. of Wis. Professionals. Lutheran. Avocations: reading, travel, snorkeling. Home: 1422 N 21st St Superior WI 54880

MORDEN, JOHN REID, security-business intelligence consultant; b. Hamilton, Ont., Canada, June 17, 1941; s. Warren Wilbert and Isabelle Gemmell (Reid) M.; m. Margaret Keens, June 27, 1964; children: Michael, Geoffrey. BA, Dalhousie U., 1962; postgrad., Dalhousie Law Sch., 1962-63; LLD (hon.), Dalhousie U., 2003. With Can. Dept. External Affairs, various worldwide cities, 1963-84; asst. dep. min. native claims Dept. Indian & Northern Devel., Canada, 1984-85; trade and econ. policy Can. Dept. External Affairs, 1985-86; asst. sec. to cabinet Fgn. and Def. Affairs, Can., 1986-87; dir. Can. Security Intelligence Svc., 1987-91; dep. min. fgn. affairs Govt. Can., 1991-94; pres, CEO, Atomic Energy of Can., Ltd., Ottawa, Canada, 1994-98; mng. dir. Kroll Asocs. Can., Toronto, 1999-2000; chmn. KPMG Corp. Intelligence Inc., Toronto, 2000—02; pres. RM & A, Inc., 2002—; exec. dir. CTTEE. Bd. dirs. CAN Inst. Internat. Affairs; mem. adv. bd. Imagis Tech., Inst. for Study Violence and Terrorism; chair bd. govs. Trent U.; chair coun. of chairs Ont. Univs. Mem. internat. adv. coun. York U.; mem. Can. com. Coun. for Security and Cooperation in Asia and Pacific. Decorated Order of Can.; Order of So. Cross (Brazil); recipient Ian L. Macrae award, 1998. Mem. Toronto Hunt Club, Nat. Club. Avocations: photography, music, ballet, reading. E-mail: rmorden@uniic.org.

MORDUKHOVICH, BORIS SHOLIMOVICH, mathematician, educator, researcher; b. Moscow, Apr. 8, 1948; arrived in US, 1988; s. Sholim T. and Rosa Z. (Lyubarsky) M.; m. Margaret A. Gankin, Apr. 29, 1969; children: Yelena, Irina. MS in Applied Math., Byelorussian State U., Minsk, USSR, 1971, PhD in Math., 1973. Rsch. engr. Sci. Rsch. Inst. Automation, Minsk, 1971-73; sr. scientist Byelorussian Sci. Rsch. Inst. Land Reclamation Water Mgmt., Minsk, 1973-88; prof. math. Byelorussian State U., 1973-88, Wayne State U., Detroit, 1989—. Vis. scientist Ctr. Math. Rsch., U. Montreal, 1989, U. Pau, France, 1990, Inst. Nat. Rsch. Info. Autom. (INRIA), Rocquecourt, France, 1990; vis. prof. Inst. for Math. and Its Applications, Mpls., 1993, U. NSW, Sydney, Australia, 1993, Banach Intern. Math. Ctr., Warsaw, 1993; intern Inst. Applications Systems Analysis, Laxenburg, Austria, 1994, 95; U. Uppsala, Sweden, 1995, U. Porto, Portugal, 1995, U. Limoges, France, 1996, Technoin, Haifa, Israel, 1997, Peking U., Beijing, China, 1998, U. Bourgogne, Dijou, France, 1999, U. Chile, Santiago, 2000, U. Paul Sabatier, Toulouse, France, 2000. Author rsch. monographs; contbr. over 200 articles to profl. jours. Mem. Am. Math. Soc., Soc. Indsl. and Applied Math. Avocations: lit., history, tourism. Office: Wayne State U 1150 FAB Dept Math Detroit MI 48202 Office Phone: 313-577-3193. Business E-Mail: boris@math.wayne.edu.

MORDY, JAMES CALVIN, lawyer; b. Ashland, Kans., Jan. 3, 1927; s. Thomas Robson and Ruth (Floyd) M.; m. Marjory Ellen Nelson, Nov. 17, 1951; children: Jean Claire Mordy Jongeling, Rebecca Jane Mordy King, James Nelson. BA in Chemistry, U. Kans., 1947; JD, U. Mich., 1950; postgrad., George Washington U., 1952—53. Bar: Kans. 1950, Mo. 1950; cert. in bus. bankruptcy law, Am. Bankruptcy Bd. Assoc., Morrison, Hecker, Buck, Cozad & Rogers, Kansas City, Mo., 1950-59; ptnr. Morrison & Hecker LLP, Kansas City, 1959-96, sr. counsel, 1996-97, of counsel, 1997-2000. Contbg. author: Missouri Bar Insurance Handbook, 1968, Missouri Bar Bankruptcy Handbook, 1991, also supplements; contbr. articles to profl. jours. Chmn. bd. Broadway United Meth. Ch., Kansas City, 1964-70, chmn. bd. trustees, chmn. fin. com., 1988-90, 94, 2000-2002; bd. dirs. Broadway Child Enrichment Ctr., 1980—; bd. dirs., exec. com. Della C. Lamb Neighborhood House, Kansas City, 1973-80; bd. dirs., treas. Friends of Sacred Structures, Kansas City, 2000—; coun. mem. St. Paul Sch. Theology, Kansas City, 1986-; bd. dirs. Kingswood Sr. Living Cmty., Kansas City, 2004-; del. 17th World Meth. Conf., Rio de Janeiro, 1996. With USN, 1945-46, 51-53, comdr. USNR, ret. Summerfield scholar, 1943-47; recipient Shepherd of the Lamb award Della Lamb Neighborhood House, 1980. Fellow Am. Coll. Bankruptcy, Am. Bar Found. (life); mem. ABA, Am. Judicature Soc., Am. Bankruptcy Inst., Mo. Bar Assn., Kansas City Met. Bar Assn., Lawyers Assn. Kansas City, Workout Profs. Assn. Kansas City, Univ. Club (v.p., bd. dirs. 1983, 86), Barristers Soc., Phi Beta Kappa, Delta Tau Delta (pres. Kansas City alumni chpt. 1965-72, pres. U. Kans. House Corp. 1966-72), Alpha Chi Sigma, Phi Alpha Delta. Avocations: travel, geography (maps), history, music, theology. Home: 8741 Ensley Ln Leawood KS 66206-1615 Office: Stinson Morrison Hecker LLP 2600 Grand Ave Kansas City MO 64108-4606

MORE, DOUGLAS MCLOCHLAN, lawyer; b. N.Y.C., Apr. 21, 1926; s. Morgan Berkeley and Lucinda (Bateson) M.; m. Pamela Bennett Marr, Aug. 6, 1954; children— Robin Maclachlan More Eddy, Alison Marr More Davies. Grad., Phillips Exeter Acad., 1943; BA, Harvard U., 1947; LL.B., Columbia U., 1950. Bar: N.Y. State bar 1950, Conn. bar 1981, Fla. bar 1983. With N.Y. Trust Co., 1950-51; asso. firm Bigham, Englar, Jones & Houston, N.Y.C., 1951-53; fin. analyst Johns-Manville Corp., 1953-54; assoc. firm Kissam & Halpin, N.Y.C., 1954-59; assoc. counsel Hooker Chem. Corp., 1959-63, gen. counsel, 1963-72, v.p., 1967-72; v.p. law Airco, Inc., 1972-75; gen. counsel Beker Industries Corp., 1975-81, v.p., 1975-78, sr. v.p., 1978-81; ptnr. firm More Phillips & Duncan, P.C., Greenwich, Conn., 1981-88, of counsel, 1988—. Served to lt. (j.g.) USNR, 1943-46. Mem. ABA, Conn. Bar Assn., Greenwich Bar Assn., Phi Delta Phi, Phoenix S-K Club, Hasty Pudding Inst. 1770 (Harvard). Home and Office: 27 Skylark Rd Greenwich CT 06830-4624 Office Phone: 203-869-0663.

MORE, JAY, neurosurgeon; b. Newark, May 19, 1960; BSc, McGill U., 1982; MD, N.Y. Med. Coll., 1987. Diplomate Am. Bd. Neurol. Surgeons. Attending surgeon JFK Med. Ctr., Edison, N.J., 1994—; dir. spine surgery N.J. Neuroscience Inst., Edison, 1994—; chief divsn. neurosurgery Muhlenberg Hosp., Plainfield, N.J., 2000—. Asst. prof. Seton Hall U., S. Orange, N.J., 1994—. Mem.: Am. Coll. Physician Execs., N.J. State Neurol. Soc., Joint Sect. Spine and Peripheral Nerve Surgery, Congress Neurol. Surgeons, Am. Assn. Neurol. Surgeons (mem. Think First 1994—).

MORE, PHILIP HARVEY BIRNBAUM, business administration educator; b. San Diego, Jan. 21, 1944; s. Louis and Ruth Laureen (Bay) B.; m. Marlin Sue Van Every, Dec. 26, 1964; 1 child, Brian Philip. BA, U. Calif., Berkeley, 1965; PhD, U. Wash., 1975. Internal cons./analyst Los Angeles County Civil Svc. Commn., 1965-67; tchg. assoc. U. Wash., Seattle, 1972-74; asst. prof. bus. adminstrn. Ind. U., Bloomington, 1975-80, assoc. prof., 1980-85, prof., 1986—. Resident dir. J.F.K. Int., Tiburg U., The Netherlands; vis. scholar Polish Acad. Scis., Hungarian Acad. Scis., Tokyo U., SDA Bocconi, Milan, Italy, Seoul Nat. U., Korea, Dartmouth Coll. Co-author: Organization Theory: Structural and Behavioral Analysis, Modern Management Techniques for Engineers and Scientists, International Research Management: Studies in Interdisciplinary Methods From Business, Government and Academics, 1990; assoc. editor IEEE Transaction on Engring. Mgmt. jour.; contbr. articles to profl. jours., book revs., sects. to books, invited papers Germany, Poland, Eng., Can., Thailand, Hong Kong, Korea. With USAF, 1967-71. NSF fellow, 1974-75, N.Y. Acad. Scis. fellow, 1981; U. Hong Kong Sr. Fulbright scholar, 1981-82. Mem. Acad. Mgmt. (pres. tech. and innovation mgmt. divsn. 1989-90), Engring. Mgmt. Soc., Inst. Ops. Rsch. and Mgmt. Scis., Internat. Assn. for Study of Interdisciplinary Rsch., Beta Gamma Sigma, Beta Alpha Psi, Sigma Iota Epsilon, Sigma Chi. Methodist. Office: Univ So Calif Marshall Sch Bus Los Angeles CA 90089-0808 Business E-Mail: phbmore@marshall.usc.edu.

MOREAN, WILLIAM D. manufacturing executive; s. William E. Morean. Student, Western Mich. U. With Jabil Cir., St. Petersburg, Fla., 1977—, formerly v.p., pres., CEO, bd. dirs., 1978—, chmn. bd. dirs., 1988—. Office: Jabil Cir 10560 9th St N Saint Petersburg FL 33716

MOREHEAD, CHARLES RICHARD, insurance company executive; b. Independence, Mo., Jan. 25, 1947; s. Robert E. and Ruth Elizabeth (Taylor) M.; m. Donna Joyce Shores, Feb. 17, 1968 children: Grant, Blaine. BSBA, U. Mo., 1971. CPA, Fla. (inactive). Mem. staff Peat, Marwick, Mitchell & Co., Kansas City, Mo., 1972-75, audit mgr. Jacksonville, Fla., 1976-83, audit ptnr., 1983-86; treas. Standard Havens, Inc., Kansas City, 1975-76; exec. v.p., treas., CFO Am. Heritage Life Ins. Co., Jacksonville, Fla., 1986-97, pres., COO, 1997-99, pres., CEO, 1999—, also bd. dirs. Mem. AICPA, Fla. Soc. CPA's. Home: 4538 Swilcan Bridge Ln N Jacksonville FL 32224-5617 Office: Am Heritage Life Ins Co 1776 Am Heritage Life Dr Jacksonville FL 32224

MOREHOUSE, DAVID FRANK, geologist; b. Charles City, Iowa, Dec. 8, 1943; s. Neal Francis and Florence E. (Schwendener) M. BS in Gen. Scis., State U. Iowa, 1967; MS in Geology, Iowa State U., 1970; postgrad., Pa. State U., 1970-74. Staff geologist Nat. Gas Survey and Planning and Spl. Projects Div., FPC, Washington, 1974-78; dir. Info. Processing and Interpretation and Analysis Divs. Oil and Gas Info. System, Energy Info. Adminstrn., Washington, 1978-80, sr. supervisory geologist, 1980-95, sr. petroleum geologist, 1996—. Advisor petroleum data sys. U. Okla., Norman, 1975-86; Energy Info. Adminstrn. rep. Am. Gas Assn. Com. on Natural Gas Res., Washington, 1991-95, Potential Gas Com., Boulder, Colo., 1991—; Dept. of Energy rep. Fed. Geog. Data Com. Coordination Group, 1997—; Nat. Critical Infrastructure Task Force Energy Group, 1998—. V.p. Iowa Jr. Acad. Sci., 1961. Recipient awards for outstanding performance Fed. Govt., Washington, 1974—. Fellow Nat. Speleological Soc.; mem. AAAS, AIME, AGI, Am. Geophys. Union, Internat. Assn. Math. Geology, N.Y. Acad. Scis. Congregationalist. Achievements include first evidence that sulfuric acid can be important to speleogenesis; exercising the prin. responsibility for design and establishment of fed. govts. domestic oil and gas reserves estimation and analysis program. Office: Energy Info Adminstrn EI-46 1000 Independence Ave SW Washington DC 20585-0644 E-mail: david.morehouse@eia.doe.gov.

MOREHOUSE, LAWRENCE GLEN, veterinarian, educator, academic administrator; b. Manchester, Kans., July 21, 1925; s. Edwy Owen and Ethel Merle (Glenn) M.; m. Georgia Ann Lewis, Oct. 6, 1956; children: Timothy Lawrence, Glenn Ellen. BS in Biol. Sci., DVM, Kans. State U., 1952; MS in Animal Pathology, Purdue U., 1956, PhD, 1960. Lic. vet. medicine. Veterinarian County Animal Hosp., Des Peres, Mo., 1952-53; supr. Brucellosis labs. Purdue U., West Lafayette, Ind., 1953-60; staff veterinarian lab. svcs. USDA, Washington, 1960-61; discipline leader in pathology and toxicology, animal health divsn. USDA Nat. Animal Disease Lab., Ames, Iowa, 1961-64; prof., chmn. dept. veterinary pathology U. Mo. Coll. Vet. Medicine, Columbia, 1964-69, 84-86, dir. Vet. Med. Diagnostic Labr., 1968-88, prof. emeritus, 1986—. Cons. USDA, to comdg. gen. U.S. Army R&D Command, Am. Inst. Biol. Scis., NAS, to Surg. Gen., Miss. State U., St. Louis Zoo Residency Tng. Program, Miss. Vet. Med. Assn., Okla. State U., Pa. Dept. Agr., Ohio Dept. Agr. Co-editor: Mycotoxic Fungi, Mycotoxins, Mycotoxicoses: An International Encyclopedic Handbook, 3 vols., 1977; contbr. articles on diseases of animals to profl. jours. Active Trinity Presbyn. Ch., Columbia, 1964-2002; bd. dirs. Mo. Symphony Soc., Columbia, 1989-92. Pharmacists mate second class USNR, 1943-46, PTO; 2d. lt. U.S. Army, 1952-56. Recipient Outstanding Svc. award USDA, 1959, merit cert., 1963, 64, Disting. Svc. award U. Mo. Coll. Vet. Medicine, 1987, Dean's Impact award, 1996, Kans. State U. Alumni award, 2004. Fellow Royal Soc. Health London; mem. AAAS, Am. Assn. Vet. Lab. Diagnosticians (E.P. Pope award 1976, chmn. lab. accreditation bd. 1972-79, 87-90, pres. 1979-80, sec.-treas. 1983-87), World Assn. Vet. Lab. Diagnosticians (bd. dirs. 1984-94, dir. emeritus 1994—), N.Y. Acad. Sci., U. S. Animal Health Assn., Am. Assn. Lab. Animal Sci., Mo. Soc. Microbiology, Am. Assn. Avian Pathologists, N.Am. Conf. Rsch. Workers in Animal Diseases, Mo. Univ. Retirees Assn. (pres. 1996-99). Presbyterian. Avocations: classic cars, boating, genealogy. Home: 916 Danforth Dr Columbia MO 65201-6164 Office: U Mo Vet Med Diagnostic Lab PO Box 6023 Columbia MO 65205-6023 E-mail: lmorehou@coin.org.

MOREHOUSE, RICHARD EDWARD, psychology educator; b. LaCrosse, Wis., May 21, 1941; s. Ervin Lenard and Anna Martha (Weiland) Morehouse; m. Rita Spangler, Aug. 20, 1966; 1 child, Lyda Ann. BS, U. Wis., 1971, MST, 1973; PhD, The Union Inst., 1979. Teaching asst. U. Wis., LaCrosse, 1971-72; ednl. cons. Coop. Ednl. Svcs. Agy., LaCrosse, 1972-80; dir. coop. edn. Viterbo U., LaCrosse, 1980-85; from asst. to prof. psychology Viterbo Coll., LaCrosse, 1985—. Dept. chmn. Viterbo U., LaCrosse, 1986—93, chair, 1995—; vis. scholar Tex. Wesleyan U., Ft. Worth, 1993—94. Co-author: Student Study Guide for Human Development Across the Lifespan, 1991, 1994, Beginning Qualitative Research, 1994; co-editor: Analytic Teaching, 1991—96; editor, 1996—; author: Five Year Longitudinal Study of Healthy Families, 2001. Grantee Gifted Edn., Elem. and Secondary Edn. Act, 1976—79, Tchr. Tng., Cmty. Awareness, Wis. Humanities, 1982, Coll., Cmty. Symposium, 1983. Mem.: Am. Psychol. soc. (charter), N.Am. Assn. for Cmty. Inquiry (founder, 1st pres. 1994). Democrat. Unitarian Universalist. Home: 1131 Charles St La Crosse WI 54603-2508 Office: Viterbo Coll 815 9th St S La Crosse WI 54601-4777 Office Phone: 608-796-3710. E-mail: remorehouse@viterbo.edu.

MOREHOUSE, VALERIE JEANNE, librarian; b. Taft, Calif., Jan. 30, 1947; d. Gordon Stanley and Cloe Ozelle (Reed) Hogue; m. Keith Herbert Morehouse, Aug. 22, 1968 (div. 1994); 1 child, Gordon. AA, Taft Coll., 1966; AB in English, U. Calif., Berkeley, 1968; MSLS, Simmons Grad. Sch. Libr. Sci., 1977. Cert. profl. librarian, Mass. Asst. libr. dir. Plymouth (Mass.) Pub. Librs., 1977—82; asst. exec. dir. Southeastern Librs. Coop., Rochester, Minn., 1982—84; libr. automation cons. N.D. State Libr., Bismarck, 1984—89; dist. libr. media dir. Bismarck Pub. Sch. Dist., 1989—97; sys. adminstr. MARINet, San Rafael, Calif., 1997—2000; libr. Temple Isaiah of Contra Costa County, Lafayette, 2001—. Adv. panelist for literature Mass. Coun. on Arts and Humanities, Boston, 1980-82. Editor, writer Libr. A Word to the Wise, 1995-97; author: Anthology: A Collection of Cape Cod Poets, 1974. Legis. chair, membership chair N.D. Libr. Assn., 1987-93; mem. N.D. Gov.'s Libr. Vision 2004 Com., Bismarck, 1995-96; mem. Ctrl. Dakota Libr. Network Bd., Bismarck, 1992—. Recipient Capewide 1st prize for poetry Provincetown Assn. for Living Arts, 1972, Spl. Recognition award COSMEP, 1977, Pres.' award for svc. to librs. N.D. Libr. Assn., 1994. Mem. ALA (chair publs. com. 1985-87, columnist, reviewer The Book List 1977-79), Calif. Libr. Assn., Beta Phi Mu. Avocations: gardening, travel. Office: Temple Isaiah Libr 3800 Mt Diablo Blvd Lafayette CA 94549 E-mail: valmorehouse@earthlink.net.

MOREHOUSE, WARD, III, theater critic, writer, playwright; b. N.Y.C., Aug. 11, 1945; s. Morehouse Ward, II and Joan Marlowe Rahe; m. Elizabeth Haggard, Feb. 10, 1979; 1 child, William. Student, Am. Acad. Dramatic Art, N.Y.C., 1965—66. Make-up editor, reporter N.Y. Post, N.Y.C., 1969—73; staff reporter, staff corr. Christian Sci. Monitor, Boston, 1973—77, N.Y.C.,

1977—82; press rep. NBC News, N.Y.C., 1983—84; freelance drama critic Christian Sci. Monitor, N.Y.C., 1984—2002; Broadway columnist Reuters, N.Y.C., 1993—95, N.Y. Post, N.Y.C., 1994—98; reporter, writer People Mag., People.com, N.Y.C., 1998—2000; drama critic, feature writer Christian Sci. Monitor, N.Y.C., 2000—02; Broadway columnist N.Y. Sun, N.Y.C., 2002—04, AM New York, N.Y.C., 2004—. Author: (book) The Waldorf-Astoria: America's Gilded Dream, 1991, Inside the Plaza: An Intimate Portrait of the Ultimate Hotel, 2001, (plays) The Actors, 1986—87, If It Was Easy, 2001 (Best Play nomination Am. Critics Assn.), The Caedmon School, 2003. Mem.: Drama Desk, Lambs Club. Home: 12 E 86th St Apt 938 New York NY 10028-0514

MOREIRA, MARCIO MARTINS, advertising executive; b. Sao Paulo, Brazil, Nov. 20, 1947; came to U.S. 1980; naturalized, 1990; s. Guido Martins and Maria Rosa (Macrine) M.; children from previous marriage: Joaquim Pedro Rezende Martins Moreira; m. Maria Auxiliadora Godinho, Oct. 18, 1981; children: Eliana Maria Godinho Martins Moreira. Ed., U. Sao Paulo, Brazil, 1970. TV producer-copywriter McCann-Erickson, Sao Paulo, Brazil, 1967-71, creative dir., 1974-77, group creative dir. London, Lisbon and Frankfurt, 1971-74, executive creative dir., 1977-80, internat. creative dir., 1980-88; vice chmn., chief creative officer McCann Erickson Worldwide, N.Y.C., 1988—; vice chmn., regional dir. Asia-Pacific McCann-Erickson Worldwide, N.Y.C., 1995-99, chief creative officer, dir. global brands, 1999—. Lectr. various univs. Author: Terraplenagem, 1968 Liquidacao, 1979; lyricist, 1968—; contbr. articles to profl. jours. U.S. judge, pres. jury Cannes Film Festival, 1989; chmn. bd. judges The New York Festivals. Recipient 5 Clio awards, 1976-89, Gold Lion, Silver Lion, Bronze Lion awards, Cannes, France, H.K. McCann award, Brazil, 1977, Paul Foley award Interpub. Group of Cos., 1983, Terence Cardinal Cooke medal for Disting. Svc. in Health Care, N.Y. Med. Coll., 1994. Mem. Brazilian-Am. C. of C. (bd. dir.). Republican. Roman Catholic. Avocations: cinema, songwriting, cars, speedwalking. Office: McCann-Erickson Worldwide 750 3rd Ave Fl 21 New York NY 10017-2703

MORELAN, PAULA KAY, choreographer; b. Lafayette, Ind., Nov. 24, 1949; d. Dickie Booth and Marian Maxine (Fetterhoff) M.; m. Kerim Sayan, Aug. 10, 1974. Student, U. Utah, 1968-69; BFA, Tex. Christian U., 1972; postgrad., El Centro Coll., 1969-70. Tchr. Rosello Sch. Ballet, Dallas, 1972-74; mgr., tchr. Ballet Arts Co., Dallas, 1974-76, owner, tchr. Ballet Classique, Garland, Tex., 1976-87, Garland Ballet Acad., 1977-87; resident choreographer Garland Civic Theatre, 1988—, lifetime mem., 1998. Asst. to Mythra Rosello, Tex. Civic Ballet, Dallas, 1972-74; assoc. artistic dir. Dance Repertory Theatre Dallas, 1974-75; artistic dir. Dance Repertory Theatre Dallas, 1975-76, Garland (Tex.) Ballet Assn., 1977-90, Classical Ballet Acad., Performing Arts Sch., 1987-90; founder, chairperson Act IV Guild, 2002-. Bd. dirs. Garland Civic Theatre, 2000—. Recipient Leon Rabin award for Best Choreography, 1996, 98, 2000, 2001, Column award, Best Choreographer award 2003, Choreographer of the Yr., 2001, 02, 03. Personal E-mail: pkm@worldnet.att.net.

MORELAND, DIANE CHRISTINA, researcher; b. Manhasset, N.Y., Aug. 8, 1973; d. Diane Jane and Stephen John Nucatola; m. Jeremy Moreland, Sept. 2003. AA, Glendale C.C., Ariz., 1993; BA, Ariz. State U. West, 1995; MS, Tex. Christian U., 1998. Sr. rsch. specialist Ariz. Prevention Resource Ctr., Phoenix, 1999—2000, Casey Family Programs, Phoenix, 2000—. Author: (sci. rsch. article) Jour. of Substance Abuse Treatment, Jour. of Psychoactive Drugs. Mem.: Am. Psychol. Soc. Personal E-mail: moreland@casey.org.

MORELAND, DONALD EDWIN, plant physiologist; b. Enfield, Conn., Oct. 12, 1919; s. Albert Sinclair and Ruth (Cowan) M.; m. Verdie Brown Stallings, Nov. 6, 1954; 1 child, Donna Faye; stepchildren: Frank C., Paul Ziglar. BS in Forestry, N.C. State U., 1949, MS in Plant Physiology, 1950, PhD in Plant Physiology, 1953. Plant physiologist SUNY Coll. Forestry, Syracuse, 1952-53, USDA-Agrl. Rsch. Svc., Raleigh, N.C., 1953-71, rsch. leader, 1972-78, sr. exec., 1979-95, collaborator, 1996—; asst. prof. to prof. N.C. State U., Raleigh, 1953-95, prof. emeritus, 1996—. Mem. toxicology study sect. NIH, USPHS, Bethesda, Md., 1963-67. Editor: Biochemical Responses Induced by Herbicides, 1982; mem. editorial bd. Pesticide Biochemistry and Physiology, 1971-97, Pesticide Sci., 1987-96; contbr. articles to profl. jours. 1st lt. U.S. Army, 1941-46. AEC predoctoral fellow, 1950-52. Fellow AAAS, Weed Sci. Soc. Am. (outstanding rsch. award 1973); mem. Am. Chem. Soc., Plant Growth Regulator Soc. Am., Am. Soc. Plant Physiologists, So. Weed Sci. Soc., Sigma Xi. Avocations: woodworking, surf fishing, square dancing. Home: 1508 Pineview Dr Raleigh NC 27606-2562 Office: NC State U USDA-Agrl Rsch Svc Dept Crop Sci 3127 Ligon St Raleigh NC 27607-5376

MORELLA, CONSTANCE ALBANESE, ambassador, former congresswoman; b. Somerville, Mass., Feb. 12, 1931; d. Salvatore and Mary Christine (Fallette) Albanese; m. Anthony C. Morella, Aug. 21, 1954; children: Paul, Mark, Laura; guardians of: Christine, Catherine, Louise, Rachel, Paul, Ursula. AA, Boston U., 1950, AB, 1954; MA, Am. U., 1967, D of Pub. Svc. (hon.), 1988, Norwich U. and Dickinson Coll., 1989, Mt. Vernon Coll., 1995, U. Md. U. Coll., 1996, USUHS, 1997, U. Md., 1997, Elizabethtown Coll., 1999. Tchr. Montgomery County (Md.) Pub. Schs., 1956-60; instr. Am. U., 1968-70; prof. Montgomery Coll., Rockville, Md., 1970-86; mem. Md. Ho. Dels., Annapolis, 1979-86, U.S. Congress from 8th Md. dist., 1987—2003; mem. sci. com., tech. subcom., basic rsch. subcom., govt. reform com., chair D.C. subcom., mem. civil svc. subcom.; visiting fellow Kennedy School, Harvard, 2003; U.S. permanent rep. to Orgn. for Econ. Co-operation & Devel. U.S. Dept. State, Paris, 2003—. Mem. civil svc., adv. bd. Am. Univ., Washington; U.S. amb. Orgn. Econ. Coop. and Devel., 2003-. Mem. adv. coun. Montgomery County Hospice Soc.; hon. bd. mem. Nat. Kidney Found; active Human Rights Caucus; Congressional Women's Caucus, Older Ams. Caucus, Population and Devel. Caucus; mem. bd. Cafritz Found. Named Glamour Woman of Yr. Glamour mag. 1995, Washingtonian of Yr. 1991; named to Md. Women's Hall of Fame, Md. Women's Hall of Fame, 1994. Republican. Avocations: theater, tennis, reading. Home: USOECD PSC 116 APO AE 09777

MORELLI, CARMEN, lawyer; b. Oct. 30, 1922; s. Joseph and Helen (Carani) Morelli; m. Irene Edna Montminy, June 26, 1943; children: Richard A., Mark D., Carl J. BSBA, Boston U., 1949, JD, 1952. Bar: Conn. 1955, U.S. Dist. Ct. Conn. 1958. Asst. prosecutor Town of Windsor, 1957—58; mem. Conn. Ho. of Reps., 1959—61; atty. Town of Windsor, 1961; rep. Capitol Regional Planning Agy., 1965—72. Mem. Windsor Town Com., 1957—82, chmn., 1964—65, treas., 1960—64, mem. planning and zoning commn., 1965—74, mem. charter revision com., 1963—64; rep. Presdl. Task Force. Served with USN, 1943—45. Mem.: ABA, Am. Arbitration Assn., Windsor Bar Assn. (pres. 1979), Hartford Bar Assn., conn. Bar Assn., Rotary (sgt. arms, sec. 1989—90, pres. 1990—91), Elks, Windsor C. of C. (v.p. 1978). Roman Catholic. Home: 41 Farmstead Ln Windsor CT 06095-1834 Office: 41 Farmstead Lane Windsor CT 06095-2926

MORELLI, MARIO FRANK, philosophy educator; b. Poughkeepsie, NY, Feb. 3, 1945; s. Idalgo and Anna Maria Morelli; m. Roberta Anne McCamy, Jan. 2, 1944; children: Frank Mario, Mark Stephen, Laura Anne. BA, Johns Hopkins U., 1966; PhD, Washington U., 1971. Instr. U. Mo., St. Louis, 1968—70, Kent State U., Ashtabula, Ohio, 1970—72; from asst. prof. to prof. Western Ill. U., Macomb, 1972—99, prof., dept. chair, 1999—. Contbr. articles to profl. jours. Mem.: Am. Philos. Assn., Phi Beta Kappa. Office: Western Illinois Univ 1 University Circle Macomb IL 61455-1367 Business E-Mail: m-morelli@wiu.edu.

MORELLO, CELESTE ANNE, historian, criminologist; b. Norristown, Pa., July 22, 1958; d. Ann M. Morello. Student, Loyola U., Rome, 1978; BA in Classics cum laude, BA in Art History magna cum laude, Chestnut Hill Coll., 1980; MS in Criminology, St. Joseph's U., Phila., 1994; MA in History, Villanova U., 2000; grad., Civilian Police Acad., Phila., 2000. Cert.: Villanova U. (paralegal) 1986. Tchr. history, social studies, sci. Archdiocese of Phila., Phila., 1977-84; lectr. on ancient history of Sicily, 1982—; cons. criminologist in Mafia and LCN history Phila. Police and U.S. Atty.'s Office, 1993—. Pioneer in criminal and Mafia history; petitioner, originator over 20 Phila. hist. sites Pa. Hist. and Mus. Commn. Hist. Marker Program, 1993—; lectr. Villanova U., Phila.; lectr. in field. Author: Beyond History: The Times and Peoples of St. Paul's R.C. Church, 1843-1993, 1992; writer, dir. History of the Mafia and LCN in Philadelphia 1880-1959 for Dept. of Justice, FBI, Phila., 1997, History of South Philadelphia, Introduction, Institute for Service Learning, 1996, Survey of Illicit Narcotics Use in Philadelphia 1900-45 for Dept. of Justice, High Intensity Drug Traffic Area, Philadelphia/Camden, The Phenomenon of the Mafia, 1997, Oral Histories of Three Men: All Mafiosi Before 1930, 1998, The Early Sicilian American Mafia Before 1930, 1998, Case Study of A Western Sicilian Colony in Suburban Philadelphia, 1998, The Philadelphia Italian Market Cookbook, 1999, rev., enlarged edit., 2004, Before Bruno: The History of Philadelphia's Mafia, Book I 1880-1931, 1999, Before Bruno: The History of Philadelphia's Mafia, Book II 1931-46, 2001, The Philadelphia Police's Homicide Records: The First Decades of Investigating and Advancement, 2003, Before Bruno: The History of the Philadelphia Mafia, Book 3, 1946-1959, 2004; contbr. articles to profl. jours, chpts. to books. Founder Sicilian Culture Collection, Hist. Soc. Pa., Phila. Mem. Moyamensing Hist. Soc. (founder), Pa. Hist. Assn., Arba Sicula, Sicilian Lang./Lit. Jour., Internat. Assn. for the Study of Organized Crime. Roman Catholic. Office: 1234 S Sheridan St Philadelphia PA 19147-4820 Office Phone: 215-334-6008.

MORELLO, DANIEL CONWAY, plastic surgeon; b. Vineland, N.J., Nov. 12, 1943; s. John B. and Mina M. (Conway) M.; m. Mona L. Comras; children: Amy, Elise, Kate. BS, U. Notre Dame, 1965; MD, Georgetown U., 1969. Diplomate Am. Bd. Plastic Surgery, Am. Bd. Surgery, Nat. Bd. Med. Examiners. Intern Hahnemann Med. Coll. Hosp., Phila., 1969-70, surgery resident to chief resident, 1970-74; plastic surgery resident to chief resident NYU Med. Ctr. Inst. for Reconstructive Plastic Surgery, N.Y.C., 1974-76; attending surgeon White Plains (N.Y.) Hosp. Med. Ctr., 1976—, chief of plastic surgery, 1992-98; pvt. practice in plastic surgery White Plains, 1976—; emeritus chief, 1998—. Asst. attending surgeon Bellevue Hosp., Manhattan VA Hosp., Manhattan Eye, Ear and Throat Hosp. (all N.Y.C.), 1976-85; attending surgeon Northern Westchester (N.Y.) Hosp. Ctr., 1976—; United Hosp., Port Chester, N.Y., 1976—; cons. Burke Rehab. Ctr., 1977-81; asst. instr. surgery, Hahnemann Med. Coll., 1973-74, clin. instr. plastic surgery, NYU Sch. Medicine, 1974-78, clin. asst. prof. plastic surgery, 1978-86. Contbr. numerous articles to profl. jours., chpts. to books; presenter in field, including co-chair symposia 1993, 95. Bd. dirs., golf chmn. Whippoorwill Club, 1989-95, extensive com. work 1988-95. Fellow ACS; mem. Am. Soc. for Aesthetic Plastic Surgery (ofcl. spokesperson 1988-, bd. dirs. 1991-, treas. 1995-98, v.p. 1998-99, 1999-2000, pres. 2000-01, chair, bd. trustees 2001-02, bd. trustees 2001-04, chair nom. com. 2003-04, chair pub. edn. com. and internat. task force 1994-97, other offices and coms.), Am. Soc. of Plastic and Reconstructive Surgeons (ofcl. spokesperson 1992—, pub. edn. com. and sci. program subcom. 1994-99, also other coms.), Am. Assn. for Accreditation of Ambulatory Surgery Facilities (pres. 1994-98, bd. dirs. 1989—, mem. strategic planning com. 1991—, other offices, coms.), N.Y. Regional Soc. Plastic Surgery (bd. dirs. 1988-91, chair program com. 1987-88, membership com. 1978-80, sec. 1988-90), Med. Soc. State of N.Y., Westchester County Med. Soc. (bd. dirs. 1986-88, extensive com. work, including med.-legal rels. com. 1986—). Avocations: golf, travel, reading. Home: 7 Harbor Dr Port Chester NY 10573 Office: 10 Chester Ave White Plains NY 10601-5112 also: 91 Smith Ave Mount Kisco NY 10549-2810 Office Phone: 914-761-8667.

MORELLO, JOSEPH ALBERT, musician, educator; b. Springfield, Mass., July 17, 1928; s. Joseph Charles and Lilia (LaPalme) M.; m. Jean Ann Mehnert. Grad. high sch., Springfield. Ind. drummer, Springfield, 1945-49; drummer Gil Melé, Stan Kenton, Tal Farlow, Johnny Smith, N.Y.C., 1953-55, Dave Brubeck Quartet, touring worldwide, 1955-68; clinician Selmer Ludwig Drum Co., Elkhart, Ind., 1957-92; leader Joe Morello Quartet, 1979—; clinician DW Drums, Oxnard, Calif., 1993—; rec. artist Digital Music Products Inc., 1993—. Rec. artist Savoy, Capitol, Norgran, Blue Note, Columbia, RCA labels; innovator finger control in jazz drumming; author: Joe Morello Drum Method, The Natural Approach to Technique, 1993, Joe Morello Drum Method 2, 1994, also New Directions in Rhythm, Rudimental Jazz, Off the Record, Master Studies; releases include (with Joe Morello Quartet) Going Places, 1993, Morello's Standard Time, 1994, Marion Mc Partland's Hickory House Trio, 1999, Marion McPartland Trio with Joe Morello, 2002, Rufus Reid Live at Shanghai Jazz, 2002. Named to Hall of Fame, Modern Drummer mag., 1988, Percussive Arts Soc. Hall of Fame, 1993, Am. Jazz Hall of Fame, 2001, Trumpets Jazz Hall of Fame, 2002; recipient New Star award, Downbeat mag., 1955, Melody Maker mag. award, 1963—67, Jazz mag. award, 1964—67, Thomas A. Edison Lifetime Achievement award, 1990, Lifetime Achievement award, Jersey Shore Jazz and Blues Found., 1996, Recognition of Outstanding Leadership award, Kosa Internat. Percussion Workshops, 2002, Lifetime Achievement award, Montreal Drum Festival, 2002, poll winner, Downbeat mag., 1963—65, Playboy mag., 1963—67, Lifetime Achievement award, Sabian Ltd., 2003. Mem.: N.J. Jazz Soc. Avocation: photography.

MORELLO, STEVEN J. federal agency administrator, lawyer; b. Saginaw, Mich., Sept. 17, 1952; m. Francia S. Morello, Apr. 8, 1978; children: Steven Jr., Rebecca. BS in Fgn. Studies, Georgetown U., 1974; JD, U. Detroit, 1977; MBA, Boston U., Heidelberg, Fed. Republic Germany, 1980. Bar: Mich. 1977, Ill. 1984. Atty. contract Northrop Co., Rollings Meadows, Ill., 1982-84; atty., mgr. Digital Equipment Corp., Arlington Heights, Ill., 1984—; army gen. counsel U.S. Dept. Defense, Washington, 2001—. Served to capt. JAGC, U.S. Army, 1978-82. Fellow Nat. Contract Mgmt. Assn. (pres. Chgo. chpt. 1985-86). Office: US Dept Defense Army General Counsel 104 Army Pentagon Washington DC 20310-0104

MOREL-SEYTOUX, HUBERT JEAN, civil engineer, educator; b. Calais, Artois, France, Oct. 6, 1932; came to U.S., 1956; s. Aimé and Suzanne Claire (Rousseau) M.-S.; m. Margery K. Keyes, Apr. 16, 1960; children: Aimée, Claire, Sylvie, Marie-Jeanne. BS, Ecole St. Genevieve, Versailles, France, 1953; MS, Ecole Nationale des Ponts et Chaussées, Paris, 1956; PhD, Stanford U., 1962. Research engr. Chevron Oil Field Research Co., La Habra, Calif., 1962-66; prof. Colo. State U., Ft. Collins, 1966-91, prof. emeritus, 1991—; chargé de recherches U. Grenoble, France, 1972-73; maitre de recherches Ecole des Mines de Paris, Fontainebleau, France, 1982; directeur de recherches ORSTOM, Montpellier, France, 1991—; cons. hydrology Atherton, Calif., 1992—. Cons. AID, Dakar, Senegal, 1985-86, 88, Ministry of Agriculture and Water, Riyadh, Saudi Arabia, 1978-83, City of Thornton, Colo., 1986-88, King Abdulaziz U., Jeddah, Saudi Arabia, 1987, 89, Ford Found., India, 1976, 79, South Fla. Water Mgmt. Dist., West Palm Beach, 1991-93, Battelle Pacific Northwest Labs., Richland, Wash., 1991-94, City of Paris, France, 1992—, Agence de l'Eau Seine-Normandie, 1992-2000, Utah State U., Logan, 1994-95, Reservoir Enging. Rsch. Inst., Palo Alto, 1994-95, Bay Delta Modeling forum, 1997—, U.S. Bur. Reclamation, 1998-2002; vis. prof. Ecole Polytechnique Federale de Lausanne, 1987; vis. scholar Stanford U., 1992-96; adj. prof. U. Colo., Boulder, 1992—; lectr. U. Calif., Berkley, 1993. Editor: Hydrology Days, 1981—2000, 3d Internat. Hydrology Symposium, 1977, Unsaturated Flow in Hydrologic Modeling, 1989. Pres. Internat. Ctr., Ft. Collins, 1984-86. Served to lt. French Army Marine Corps Engrs., 1959-62. Sr. Fulbright scholar, France, 1972-73; recipient Abell Faculty Rsch. award Colo. State U. Coll. Engring., 1985. Mem. Am. Geophys. Union, ASCE (best paper award, Water Resources Planning and Mgmt., 1999), Soc. Petroleum Engrs., Am. Meteorol. Soc., Am. Soc. Agrl. Engrs. Home: 57 Selby Ln Atherton CA 94027-3926 Office: Hydroprose Internat Cons Hydrology Days Publs 57 Selby Ln Atherton CA 94027-3926 Office Phone: 650-365-4080. E-mail: hydroprose@batnet.com.

MORENCY, PAULA J. lawyer; b. Oak Park, Ill., Mar. 13, 1955; AB magna cum laude, Princeton U., 1977; JD, U. Va., 1980. Bar: Ill. 1980, U.S. Dist. Ct. (no. dist.) Ill. 1980, U.S. Ct. Appeals (7th cir.) 1981, U.S. Ct. Appeals (5th cir.) 1990, U.S. Dist. Ct. (ctrl. dist.) Ill. 1999, U.S. Dist. Ct. (ea. dist.) Wis. 2000. Assoc. Mayer, Brown & Platt, Chgo., 1980-86, ptnr., 1987-94, Schiff Hardin & Waite, Chgo., 1994—. Adj. prof. trial advocacy Northwestern U. Sch. Law, Chgo., 1997--; faculty Midwest Regional, Nat. Inst. for Trial Advocacy, 1988—; mem. pres.'s coun. Dominican U., 1998-2002. Author: Cross-Examination of a Franchise Executive, 1995, Insurance Coverage Issues in Franchise and Intellectual Property Litigation, 1996, Re-Emergence of Franchise Class Actions, 1997, Judicial and Legislative Update: ABA Forum on Franchising, 1999, How to Find, Use and Defend Against the Expert Witness, 2000, Dealing With System Change in a High-Tech World, 2001. Mem. ABA (forum franchising, governing com., litig. sect., intellectual property sect.), Chgo. Coun. of Lawyers (bd. govs. 1989-93), Constnl. Rights Found. Chgo. (chair 2001). Office: Schiff Hardin & Waite 7300 Sears Tower Chicago IL 60606

MORENO, ALBERT F. apparel executive, lawyer; B in Econs., San Diego State U., 1966; M in L.Am. Econ. Studies, U. Madrid, 1996; JD, U. Calif., Berkeley, 1970. Regional dir. Legal Svcs. Corp.; asst. gen. counsel Levi Strauss & Co., San Francisco, 1978—81, assoc. gen. counsel, 1981—85, dep. gen. counsel, 1985—94, chief counsel Levi Strauss N.Am., 1994—96, sr. v.p., gen. counsel, 1996—. Mem. worldwide leadership team Levi Strauss & Co.; bd. dirs. Levi Strauss Found. Trustee Tomas Rivera Policy Inst., Nat. Assn. Latino Elected and Apptd. Ofcls. Edn. Fund; former pres., bd. dirs. Nat. Hispanic Corp. Coun. Office: Levi Strauss & Co 1155 Battery St San Francisco CA 94111

MORENO, BARRY, historian, writer; b. LA; s. Rafael S. and Eva Maria Moreno. BA in History, Calif. State U., L.A., 1985. Libr., historian Statue of Liberty and Ellis Island, N.Y.C., 1988—. EEO counselor Nat. Park Svc., NYC, 1988—96. Author: The Statue of Liberty Encyclopedia, 2000, Italian Americans, 2003, Images of America: Ellis Island, 2003, Encyclopedia of Ellis Island, 2004, Images of America: The Statue of Liberty, 2004; (foreword) Ellis Island Interviews, 1997; (bibliography) Statue of Liberty Revisited; cons. for, appeared on numerous film, TV and radio documentaries including Ellis Island: Everyman's Monument, 1991, On the Inside: The Statue of Liberty, 1999, Building a Colossus: The Statue of Liberty, 2001, The Sweetest Sound, 2001, Lady By the Sea: The Statue of Liberty, 2004; contbr. chpts. to books, articles to profl. jours. Recipient EEO Counseling award Statue of Liberty Nat. Monument, 1994. Mem. Mus. Coun. N.Y., Am. Immigration and Ethnic History Soc., Calif. Hist. Soc., Monarchist League, Vaudeville History Soc., English-Speaking Union. Roman Catholic. Avocations: writing, studying languages, reading. Office: Statue of Liberty Nat Monument and Ellis Island Liberty Island New York NY 10004 E-mail: barry_moreno@nps.gov.

MORENO, CARLOS R. state supreme court justice; b. L.A., Nov. 4, 1948; m. Christine Moreno; children: Keiko, Nicholas. BA in Polit. Sci., Yale U., 1970; JD, Stanford U., 1975. Dep. city atty. L.A. City Atty.'s Office; atty. with Mori & Ota (now known as Kelley, Drye & Warren), 1979; apptd. justice Mncpl. Ct., 1986—93; justice L.A. County Superior Ct., 1993—97, US Dist. Ct. (ctrl. dist.) Calif., 1998—2001; assoc. justice Supreme Ct. Calif., 2001—. Bd. visitors Stanford Law Sch.; bd. govs. Assn. Yale Alumni; dir. Arroyo Vista Family Health Ctr. Recipient Criminal Justice Superior Ct. Judge of Yr. award, L.A. County Bar Assn., 1997, For God, For Country and For Yale award, Yale U., 2001. Avocations: theater, opera, crossword puzzles. Office: Calif Supreme Ct 350 McAllister St San Francisco CA 94102-4783

MORENO, DAVID, artist; b. L.A., 1957; BFA, U. Ariz., 1982; postgrad., Calif. Inst. Arts, 1984-85. One-woman shows include Feature, N.Y.C., 1989, 1991, 1993, 1994, 1997, 1999, Ctr. Contemporary Art, Chgo., 1990, 1992, U. Galleries-Ill. State U., Normal, 1991, Neuberger Mus. Purchase Coll. SUNY, 1997, exhibited in group shows at Ctr. Contemporary Art, Chgo., 1989, 1991, Alcolea Gallery, N.Y.C. and Barcelona, 1990, Gallery 400 U Ill. Chgo., 1992, 1994, Galerie Jennifer Flay and Urbi et Orbi, Paris, 1992, Randolph St. Gallery, Chgo., 1993, 808 Penn Modern, Pitts., 1993, Roger Merians Gallery, N.Y.C., 1995, Feature, 1995, 1996, 1998, Carla Stellweg Gallery, 1996, Caren Golden Fine Art, 1997, Mus. Modern Art, 1997, ANP, Antwerp, Belgium, 1998, The Elmhurst (Ill.) Art Mus., 1998, Anna Kustera Gallery, N.Y.C., 1998, others. Recipient awards in painting, sculpture, printmaking, photography and craft media, Louis Comfort Tiffany Found., 1997. Office: 2604 Dellana Ln Ste 100 Austin TX 78746-5746

MORENO, ERNEST H. college president; BA in Polit. Sci., Calif. State U., L.A.; MPA in Ednl. Adminstrn., Calif. State U., Long Beach. Employee rels. specialist, pers. analyst L.A. Cmty. Coll. Dist., 1969-78, asst. dir. of labor rels., 1978-85; v.p. acad. affairs East L.A. Coll., 1991-93, pres., 1993—. Instr. L.A. Trade Tech. Coll., 1976-84, West L.A. Coll., 1984-94. Bd. dirs. Santa Marta Hosp.; pres., bd. trustees Santa Clarita C.C. Dist.; bd. trustees L.A. County Med. Ctr. Sch. of Nursing; chmn. ARC; mem. pers. com. United Way, East L.A. Occpl. Ctr., Bienvenidos Family Ctr., LAPD Hispanic Cmty. Forum. With U.S. Army, 1970-72. Mem. Assn. of Negotiations and Contract Adminstrs., Assn. of Calif. Coll. Adminstrs., Am. Coun. on Edn. (commr.), Hispanic Assn. of Colls. and Univs., East L.A. Rotary, East L.A. C. of C., Am. Diabetes Assn. Office: East Los Angeles Coll 1301 Avenida Cesar Chavez Monterey Park CA 91754-6001

MORENO, FERNANDO, lawyer, educator; b. Santurce, P.R., Oct. 17, 1934; s. Esteban and Maria (Salas) M.; m. Rosario Gonzalez, Dec. 21, 1957; children: Rosario, Esteban, Marie, Fernando. BA, U. P.R., 1955, postgrad. in pub. adminstrn., 1955—56, JD magna cum laude, 1973; LLM in Ocean and Coastal Law, U. Miami, 1982, PhD, 1998. Bar: P.R. 1974, U.S. Dist. Ct. P.R. 1974, U.S. Ct. Appeals (1st cir.) 1974. Treas. Gonzalez R. Investment Corp., P.R., 1958-79, dir., 1958-83; lectr. Sch. Law, U.P.R., 1973—79; sr. law lectr. marine sci. program U. Miami, 1982—. Office mgr., personnel dir., in-house counselor at law, dir. Gonzalez Rodriguez Investment Corp., Catalan Gonzalez & Co., Inc., Indsl. Gonzalez, Inc., Santurce, 1958-79. Mem. U. P.R. Law Rev., 1971-73, chmn. San Juan Mail Users Coun., 1968. Mem. ABA, P.R. Bar Assn., P.R. Philatelic Soc. (founder 1952, pres. 1967-68), Sigma Xi. Home: PO Box 248698 Coral Gables FL 33124 E-mail: fmoreno@rsmas.miami.edu.

MORENO, HELENA, newscaster; b. Xalapa, Veracruz, Mex. Grad. in Journalism, So. Meth. U., Dallas. Intern for Hillary Clinton White House, Washington; gen. assignment reporter, fill-in anchor WTOC-TV, Savannah, Ga.; reporter WDSU News Channel 6, New Orleans, 2000—. Office: WDSU News Channel 6 846 Howard Ave New Orleans LA 70113

MORENO, VERONICA, food products executive; m. Eduardo Moreno. Co-founder Olè Mexican Foods, Norcross, Ga., 1987—. Named Nat. Hispanic Businesswoman of Yr., U.S. Hispanic C. of C., 2001, Latina Entrepreneur of Yr., Hispanic Bus. Mag., 2004. Office: Ole Mexican Foods Inc 6585 Crescent Dr Norcross GA 30071

MORENO-CABRAL, CARLOS EDUARDO, cardiac surgeon; b. Zacatecas, Mex., Nov. 4, 1951; s. Manuel Julio Moreno and Dominga Cabral; m. Elaine Nakamura; children: Rodrigo, Iza, Daniel. MD, Nat. U. Mex., 1976. Diplomate Am. Bd. Thoracic Surgery. Resident in gen. surgery U. Hawaii, 1977-80, Mich. State U., 1980-82; fellow in cardiac surgery Stanford (Calif.) U., 1982-84, 86-88; tng. in thoracic surgery SUNY, Bklyn., 1984-86; dir. cardiac transplant program St. Francis Hosp., Honolulu, 1989—. Author: Postoperative Management in Adult Cardiac Surgery, 1988. Fellow ACS; mem. Soc. Thoracic Surgeons, European Assn. Cardio-Thoracic Surgery. Avocation: photography. Office: 1380 Lusitana St Ste 912 Honolulu HI 96813-2448 E-mail: cemoreno@aol.com.

MORENO DELGADILLO, MARIO E. educational association administrator, educator; b. Nuevo Laredo, Tamaulipas, Mex., June 24, 1961; s. Jose Luis Moreno Garza and Judith Elena Delgadillo Arreola; m. Maria Isabel Zepeda Bustos, Mar. 30, 1985; children: Mario Alberto Moreno Zepeda, Andrea Isabel Moreno Zepeda, Lara Victoria Moreno Zepeda. BA in Acctg., ITESM, Monterrey, NL, Mex., 1984, MS in Mgmt., 1989; MS in Acctg., U. Ill., Urbana Champaign, Urbana, Ill., PhD, 1999—. CPA Mexican, Instituto Mexicano de Contadores Publicos, 1985. Cost analyst Cigarrera La Moderna, Monterrey, Mexico; gen. acct. Lamosa, Monterrey, Mexico; dir. acctg. dept. ITESM, Monterrey, Mexico, 1994—96, assoc. prof. acctg.; assoc. v.p. Morton Coll., Cicero, Ill., 2003—. Newspaper editor, coord. El Informador de Champaign Urbana, Champaign, Ill., 2003—. Treas. El Informador de Champaign Urbana,

Champaign, Ill. Mem.: Assn. for the Study of Higher Edn. (assoc.), Am. Ednl. Rsch. Assn. (assoc.). Office: Morton College 3801 S Central Ave Cicero IL 60804 Office Phone: 708-656-8000 ext. 240. Business E-Mail: mario.moreno@morton.edu.

MORENO-DUCHENY, DENISE, state senator; m. Al Moreno-Ducheny. Student, Univ. Lund (Sweden); BA in History, Pomona Coll.; JD, Southwestern U., 1979. Bar: Calif. Lawyer; trustee San Diego CC Dist. Governing Bd; mem. Calif. State Assembly, 1994—2000, Calif. State Senate, Sacramento, 2000—. Chair Housing and Cmty. Devel. Com.; mem. Agriculture and Water Resources Com., Banking, Commerce and Internat. Trade Com., Budget Com., Judiciary Com., Vets. Affairs, Calif. Border Environ. Cooperation Commn.; commr. San Diego County Regional Governance Efficiency Commn., State Commn. on the Califs.; mem. Latino Legis. Caucus, Women's Caucus; lectr. in field. Trustee Anza-Borrego State Park Found.; bd. dirs. San Diego Natural Hisotry Mus. Mem.: Calif. C.C. Trustees Assn. (bd. dirs.), Assn. Latino C.C. Trustees Calif. (chair, co-founder). Democrat. Mailing: State Capitol Rm 2062 Sacramento CA 95814 Office: 637 3rd Ave Ste C Chula Vista CA 91910

MOREST, DONALD KENT, neuroscientist, educator; b. Kansas City, Mo., Oct. 4, 1934; s. F. Stanley and Clara Josephine (Riley) M.; m. Rosemary Richtmyer, July 13, 1963 (dec. 2002); children: Lydia, Claude. BA, U. Chgo., 1955; MD, Yale U., 1960. Sr. asst. surgeon USPHS, Bethesda, Md., 1960-63; asst. prof. U. Chgo., 1963-65; asst. to assoc. prof. Harvard Med. Sch., Boston, 1965-77; prof., dir. Ctr. for Neurol. Scis. U. Conn. Health Ctr., Farmington, 1977—; prof. commn. scis. U. Conn., Storrs, 2002—. Cons. NIH, Bethesda, 1975—, European Commn. Contbr. articles to profl. jours. and books. Recipient Loeser award U. Conn. Health Ctr., Farmington, 1982; Career Devel. awardee NIH, 1971; named Javits neurosci. investigator NIH, 1984, Claude Pepper awardee, 1990. Mem. Am. Assn. Anatomists (C. Judson Herrick award 1966), Soc. for Neurosci., Assn. for Rsch. in Otolaryngology, Conn. Acad. Sci. and Engring. (elected), Cajal Club (pres. 1980). Avocations: flute, badminton. Home: 18 Shady Ln West Simsbury CT 06092-2232 E-mail: kent@neuron.uchc.edu.

MORETTI, EDWARD CHARLES, environmental engineer, consultant; b. Pitts., Feb. 8, 1962; s. Raymond and Mary Nancy (Corvari) M.; m. Deborah Benson, May 6, 1989; 1 child, Matthew. BSChE, U. Pitts., 1984; M Pub. Mgmt., Carnegie Mellon U., 2001. Engr., prototype ops. GE, Schenectady, N.Y., 1985-86; sr. engr. Radian Corp., Research Triangle Park, N.C., 1986-90, SAIC, Monroeville, Pa., 1990-92; mgr. environ. compliance Michael Baker Corp., Coraopolis, Pa., 1992—2003; prin. Moretti Cons. Group, Carnegie, Pa., 2003—. Course instr. AIChE Continuing Edn. Program, Ctr. for Profl. Advancement, Inst. Gas Tech. Author: Current and Potential Future Industrial Practices for Reducing and Controlling Volatile Organic Compounds, 1993, Practical Solutions for Reducing Volatile Organic Compounds and Hazardous Air Pollutants, 2001; contbr. Ency. Environ. Analysis and Remediation, 1997; contbr. articles to profl. jours., including Chem. Engring. Progress. Mem. AIChE, Air and Waste Mgmt. Assn., Assn. Iron & Steel Engrs. Avocations: tennis, theater. Office: Moretti Consulting Group 314 E Main St Carnegie PA 15106 E-mail: emoretti@moretticonsulting.com.

MORETTI, ROBERT JAMES, psychologist, educator; b. Chgo., Aug. 28, 1949; s. James John and Elva Eve (Bonini) M.; m. Carol L. Curt, Dec. 6, 1986. BS in Psychology, Loyola U., Chgo., 1971, PhD in Clin. Psychology, 1982; MA in Behavioral Sci., U. Chgo., 1976; diploma in analytical psychology, Jung Inst., Chgo., 1997. Lic. clin. psychologist, Ill. Rsch. fellow Ill. State Psychiat. Inst., Chgo., 1974-76; clin. asst. prof. Loyola U. Sch. Dentistry, Chgo., 1976-81; asst. prof. behavioral scis. Northwestern U. Dental Sch., Chgo., 1981-91, assoc. prof., 1991—2000. Asst. dir. clin. tng., dir. health psychology Northwestern U. Med. Sch., 1988-93; asst. prof. Grad. Sch., Northwestern U., 1986-91, assoc. prof., 1991—; faculty mem. C.G. Jung Inst., Chgo., 1993—, mem. tng. com., 1999-2000, faculty mem., Evanston, 2004—; staff Northwestern Meml. Hosp.; sr. faculty AIDS Mental Health Edn. and Evaluation Project, 1986-89, dir. relaxation and epilepsy project, 1991—; pvt. practice clin. psychology, 1983—; Jungian analysis, 1997—. Mem. editl. bd. Jour. of Am. Analgesia Soc., 1987-93; contbr. articles to profl. jours., chpts. to books. Served with Ill. Army Nat. Guard, 1971-77. Kellogg fellow Am. Fund Dental Health, 1981. Mem. APA, Ill. Psychol. Assn., Assn. Applied Psychophysiology and Biofeedback, Soc. Personality Assessment, Internat. Stress Mgmt. Assn., Chgo. Soc. Jungian Analysts (sec. 1999-2001, v.p. 2002—), Internat. Assn. for Analytical Psychology, Inst. Noetic Scis., Assn. for Study of Dreams, Internat. Assn. Near-Death Studies. Home: 3458 N Normandy Ave Chicago IL 60634-3717 Office: 151 N Michigan Ave Apt 801 Chicago IL 60601-7543 Office Phone: 312-540-9014. E-mail: r-moretti@northwestern.edu.

MORETTO, JANE ANN, nurse, public health officer; b. Belgium, Ill., Apr. 9, 1934; d. Bernard James and Mildred Bertha (Sutton) Moretto; BSN, St. Joseph Coll., Emmitsburg, Md., 1969; RN, Ill. Relief head nurse, staff nurse Mercy Hosp., Urbana, Ill., 1955-57; staff nurse in psychiatry VA Hosp., Danville, Ill., 1957-59; staff nurse pulmonary disease VA Hosp., Long Beach, Calif., 1959-60, staff nurse surg. unit, L.A., 1960-61, staff nurse oper. rm., 1961-64; commd. lt. comdr. USPHS, 1969, advanced through grades to capt., 1975—; staff nurse USPHS Hosp., Galveston, Tex., 1964-66, staff nurse tumor ICU, Balt., 1967, asst. oper. rm. supr., New Orleans, 1969-71, oper. rm. supr., Brighton, Mass., 1971-78, dep. dir. nursing, dir. insvc. edn. Carville, La., 1978-80, dir. nurses Gillis W. Long Hansen's Disease Ctr., 1980-91, clin. nurse cons. lower extremity amputation prevention program Carville Diabetic Foot Program, 1991-95; cons., lectr. in field. Inventor teaching foot model. Recipient Superior Performance award, USPHS Hosp., Galveston, 1966, Outstanding Svc. medal Dept. Health Human Svcs.-Pub. Health Svc., 1986 (citation, 1990, Unit Commendation award USPHS, 1981, Isolated Hardship award USPHS, 1981, Hazardous Duty award USPHS, 1992, Commendation medal USPHS, 1993); named Nurse of Yr., Baton Rouge Dist. Nurses Assn., 1991. Mem. Am. Nurses Assn., La. Nurses Assn., La. Hosp. Assn., La. Soc. Nursing Svc. Adminstrs., Nat. Assn. for Uniformed Svcs., Assn. Mil. Surgeons of U.S., Assn. Oper. Rm. Nurses, Alumnae Assn. of Schlarman High Sch., Alumnae Assn. of St. Joseph Coll., Commd. Officers Assn. USPHS. Roman Catholic. Home: 1741 Cobble Ln Mount Dora FL 32757-6251

MOREWITZ, STEPHEN JOHN, behavioral scientist, consultant, educator; b. Newport News, Va., May 14, 1954; s. Burt M. and Ruth (August) M., Lora Friedman (stepmother). BA, Coll. William and Mary, 1975, MA, 1978; PhD, U. Chgo., 1983. Rsch. asst. Michael Reese Hosp., Chgo., 1979-84; asst. social scientist Argonne (Ill.) Nat. Lab., 1984-85; asst. to dean, asst. prof. U. Ill., Chgo., 1988-92, sr. rsch. splst., 1991-92; vol. rsch. staff San Francisco Gen. Hosp., 1993-97; pres. S. Morewitz, PhD & Assocs., Chgo. and Buffalo Grove, Ill., 1988—, San Francisco, 1992—. Part-time sociology faculty DePaul U., Chgo., 1985—; mem. faculty St. Elizabeth's Hosp., 1987—88; assoc. prof. Calif. Coll. Podiatric Medicine, 1997—2000, prof., rsch. dean, 2000—02; adj. prof. Calif. Sch. Podiatric Medicine, 2003—; cons. in field; lectr. Calif. State U., 2004. Co-author: Medical Malpractice, 1996; author: Sexual Harassment and Social Change, 1996, Stalking and Violence, 2003, Domestic Violence and Maternal Child Health, 2004; contbr. articles to profl. jours., chapters to books. Vol. docent Garfield Farm Mus., LaFox, Ill., 1979—; curator Saving of S.S. Quanza, Chgo., 1991—. Mem. Am. Pub. Health Assn. (Top 10 Injury Poster award 2000), Am. Diabetes Assn. (profl. sect.), Assn. for Behavioral Scis. and Med. Edn., Am. Sociol. Assn. (cert., nat. finalist med. sociology), Soc. Behavioral Medicine, Generalist in Med. Edn., Sociol. Practice Assn., Soc. Study Social Problems (divsn. chmn., Outstanding Scholar award 2003). Avocations: theater, museum design, swimming, environmental preservation, farming. Office: S Morewitz PhD & Assocs PMB M858 28 E Jackson Blvd 10 Fl Chicago IL 60604

MOREY, CARL REGINALD, musicologist; b. Toronto, Ont., Can., July 14, 1934; s. Reginald Donald and Julia Beatrice (Mabey) M.; m. Lorna Ann Dalton, June 2, 1960 (dec.); 1 child, Rachel Adriana MusB, U. Toronto, 1957; MusM, Ind. U., 1961, PhD, 1965. Asst. prof. Wayne State U., Detroit, 1962-63; assoc. prof. U. Windsor, Ont., 1964-70; prof. music U. Toronto, 1970-2000, dean faculty of music, 1984-90, Jean A. Chalmers prof., dir. Inst. for Can. Music, 1991-2000. Author: Music in Canada: A Research and Information Guide, 1997; MacMillan On Music, 1997, An Opera Sampler, 1998, Opera Viva, 2000; editor: (musical) Works of Glenn Gould (Schott), 1995, 96, 97, 99, 2004. Avocation: swimming. Home: 540 Palmerston Blvd Toronto ON Canada M6G 2P5 Office: U Toronto Faculty of Music Toronto ON Canada M5S 2C5 E-mail: carl.morey@utoronto.ca.

MOREY, CHARLES LEONARD, III, theatrical director; b. Oakland, Calif., June 23, 1947; s. Charles Leonard Jr. and Mozelle Kathleen (Milliken) M.; m. Mary Carolyn Donnet, June 10, 1973 (div. 1975); m. Joyce Miriam Schilke, May 29, 1982; 1 child, William. AB, Dartmouth Coll., 1969; MFA, Columbia U., 1971. Artistic dir. Peterborough (N.H.) Players, 1977-88, Pioneer Theatre Co., Salt Lake City, 1984—. Actor: N.Y. Shakespeare Festival, Playwrights Horizons, New Dramatists, ARK Theatre Co., Ensemble Studio Theatre, Cubiculo, Folger Theatre, Syracuse Repertory Theatre, Theatre by Sea, others; over 200 plays acted in or directed; guest dir. Ensemble Studio Theatre, ArK Theatre, Am. Stage Festivel, McCarter Theatre, Pioneer Theatre Co., PCPA Theatrefest, The Repertory Theater of St. Louis, Meadow Brook Theatre, Utah Shakespearean Festival; author Laughing Stock and Alexandre Dumas and the Lady of the Camelias, new adaptations Alexandre Dumas' The Three Musketeers, Bram Stoker's Dracula, Charles Dickens' A Tale of Two Cities, Victor Hugo's The Hunchback of Notre Dame, Alexandre Dumas' The Count of Monte Cristo. Trustee Utah Arts Endowment, Inc., Nat. Theatre Conf.; panelist Nat. Endowment for Arts. Mem. Soc. Stage Dirs. and Choreographers, AEA, SAG, AFTRA, Salt Lake City C. of C. (Honors in the Arts award 1991), Utah Assn. Gifted Children (Community Svc. award 1991), Peterborough Players (Edith Bond Stearns award 1990). Democrat. Episcopalian. Office: Pioneer Theatre Co 300 S 1400 E Salt Lake City UT 84112-0660 E-mail: chuck@ptc.utah.edu.

MOREY, PHILIP STOCKTON, JR., mathematics professor; b. Houston, July 11, 1937; s. Philip Stockton and Helen Holmes (Wolcott) M.; m. Jeri Lynn Snyder, Sept. 5, 1964; children: William Philip, Christopher Jerome. BA, U. Tex., 1959, Ma, 1961, PhD, 1967. Asst. prof. math. U. Nebr., Omaha, 1967-68; assoc. prof. Tex. A&I U., Kingsville, 1968-76; prof. Tex. A&M U., Kingsville, 1976—. Lectr. U. Tokyo, 1976, U. Hokkaido, 1977, 88. Contbr. articles to Tensor N.S., Internat. Jour. Engring. Sci, Tex. Jour. Sci. Recipient Researcher of Yr. awrd Tex. A&I Alumni Assn., 1985. Mem. Tex. Acad. Sci. (chmn. math. sect. 1982, 85, 99), Am. Math. Soc., Tensor Soc., (Japan). Achievements include research in extensor analysis, tensor analysis, differential geometry, mathematical physics. Home: 1514 Lackey St Kingsville TX 78363-3199 Office: Tex A&M Univ Dept Math Kingsville TX 78362 E-mail: kfpsm00@tamuk.edu.

MOREY, ROBERT HARDY, communications executive; b. Milw., Sept. 5, 1956; s. Lloyd W. and Ruby C. (McElhaney) M. AA, Ricks Coll., 1978; BA, Brigham Young U., 1983. Program dir. Sta. KABE-FM, Orem, Utah, 1982-83, sales mgr., 1983; nat. mgr. ops. Tiffany Prodns. Internat., Salt Lake City, 1983-84; account exec. Osmond Media Corp., Orem, 1984; corp. sec., bd. dirs. Positive Communications, Inc., Orem, 1984—87, chief exec. officer, 1987—; gen. mgr. Sta. KSRR, Orem, 1985—; pres. K-Star Satellite Network, Orem, 1986—89, Broadcast Media Svcs., Orem, 1987—; gen. mgr. Sta. KMGR, Salt Lake City, 1993; ops. mgr. KQMB-FM, Salt Lake City, 1994-95, gen. mgr., 1995-98; gen. mgr. KCFM, 1998—. With Ams. Freedom Festival at Provo, 2002—; guest lectr. various colls. and univs. Chmn. Rep. voting dist., Orem, 1984. Recipient Community Service award Utah Valley Community Coll., 1983; named one of Outstanding Young Men in Am. U.S. Jaycees, 1983. Avocations: reading, collecting stamps. Home: PO Box 828 Orem UT 84059-0828 Office: Sta KSRR Ventura Media Ctr 1240 E 800 N Orem UT 84097-4318

MOREYRA, ABEL E. physician, medical educator; b. Mar del Plata, Argentina, Dec. 2, 1941; came to U.S., 1972; s. Genaro and Emilia (Basso) M.; m. Maria Elena Moreyra; children: Maria Eugenia, Maria Evelina, Fernando Abel. MD, U. Nacional de La Plata, Argentina, 1967. Fellow Cleve. Clinic Found., 1972-75; asst. prof. medicine UMDNJ-Robert Wood Johnson Med. Sch., New Brunswick, N.J., 1975-83, assoc. prof., 1983-95, prof., 1995—. Fellow ACP, Am. Coll. Cardiology; mem. Am. Coll. Angiology. Office: UMDNJ-RW Johnson Med Sch CN-19 Rm 582A New Brunswick NJ 08903 E-mail: moreyrae@umdnj.edu.

MORFOPOULOS, V. metallurgical engineer, materials engineer; b. Athens, Greece, Oct. 22, 1937; BS, Purdue U., 1958; MS, Columbia U., 1961, ScD in Engring. Sci., 1964. Rsch. assoc. metall. engring. Purdue U., 1957-60; rsch. engr. U.S. Steel Corp., 1961; instr. chem. CUNY, 1961-63; rsch. engr. Argonne Nat. Lab., 1963, Am. Iron & Steel, Columbia U., 1964-65, sr. metall. sci., 1965-66; tech. dir. R&D testing Am. Standards Testing Bur., 1966—. Cons. govt. and industry, 1966—; mem. Int. Commn. Chem. Thermodyn. & Kinetics; mem. Transp. Rsch. Bd., Nat. Rsch. Coun. Mem. AAAS, Am. Inst. Mining, Metall. Petroleum Engrs., Am. Soc. Engr. Edn., Assn. Cons. Chemists and Chem. Engrs., N.Y. Acad. Sci. Achievements include research and consulting in fields of corrosion and oxidation phenomena. low and high temperature thermodynamics, liquid metals and compounds, surface phenomena, electrometallurgy and electrode phenomena, electrical and magnetic properties of matter, failure and stress analysis, metal finishing, joining and working. Office: Am Standards Testing Bur Inc 40 Water St New York NY 10004-2626 E-mail: worldteck@aol.com .

MORFORD, JOANN (JOANN MORFORD-BURG), state senator, investment company executive; b. Miller, SD, Nov. 26, 1956; d. Darrell Keith Morford and Eleanor May (Fawcett) Morford-Steptoe. BS in Agrl.-Bus., Comml. Econs., S.D. State U., 1979; cert. in personal fin. planning, Am. Coll., 1992. Chartered fin. cons., CLU. Agrl. loan officer 1st Bank System, Presho, S.D., 1980-82, Wessington Springs, S.D., 1982-86, Am. State Bank, Wessington Springs, 1986; registered investment rep. ARM Fin. Svcs. Inc., Wessington Springs, 1986-96; Miller, 1997—; mem. S.D. State Senate, Wessington Springs, 1990-96, majority whip, 1993-94, minority whip, 1995-96, mem., 1990-97, Miller, 1997-98; ins. agt. Western Fraternal Life Assn., 2001—03. Mem. senate appropriations com. 1993-98; chair senate ops. and audit com. 1993, 94; mem. ops. and audit com., 1995-98; mem. Nat. Conf. State Legislators' Assembly of Fed. Issues Environ. Com., 1994-98, vice chair, 1996-97. Mem. Midwestern-Can. task force Midwest Conf., 1990-94; transp. com., commerce com., taxation com. SD State Senate, Pierre, 1990-92; treas. twp. bd. Wessington Springs, 1990-92; active Wessington Springs Sch. Improvement Coun., 1992-95.; fin. com. United Meth. Ch., Miller, SD, 2001—. Fleming fellow Ctr. Policy Alternatives, 1996. Mem.: S.D. Farmers Union, Girl Scouts of Nyoda Council (bd. dirs.), Bus. and Profl. Women (2nd v.p. 2002), S.D. State U. 4-H Alumni Assn., Future Farmers Am. (adv. bd. Wessington Springs chpt. 1984—96), Alumni Coun. Young Polit. Leaders (China delegation 1996, host El Salvador delegation 1999), Order Ea. Star (various offices 1980—). Democrat. Home and Office: PO Box 21 Miller SD 57362-0021

MORFORD, JOHN A. investment company executive; CFO V.T. Inc., Shawnee Mission, Kans. Office: VT Inc PO Box 795 Shawnee Mission KS 66201-0795

MORFORD, LYNN ELLEN, state official; b. Peoria, Ill., June 17, 1953; d. Raymond Scott Jr. and Georgiana (Woodhall) M. BA, Millikin U., 1975; MA, U. Ill. was Sangamon State U., Springfield, Ill., 1984. News reporter Stas. WJBC-WBNQ, Bloomington, Ill., 1975-76, Sta. WSOY-AM-FM, Decatur, Ill., 1976-78, Stas. WXCL-WZRO-FM, Peoria, 1978, Sta. KACY-AM-FM, Ventura, Calif., 1978, Sta. WKAN, Kankakee, Ill., 1979-82; freelance news reporter Sta. WMAQ, Chgo., 1982; news dir. Stas. WXCL-WKQA-FM, Peoria, 1983; press sec. Ill. Ho. of Reps. Rep. Press Office, Springfield, 1984-85; chief Press Office, Ill. Dept. Commerce and Community Affairs, Springfield, 1986-95, comms. coord., 1995—. Mem. adv. bd. Ill. AP, 1983; radio news contest judge Okla. AP, 1983; bd. dirs. Ill. News Broadcasters Assn., 1980-84; mem. Gov.'s Conf. on Mgmt. of Illinois River, 1997—. Mem. adv. bd. Leadership Ill., 1992—, spring conf. chair, 1994; Springfield St. Patrick's Day Parade Com., 1991-99; chmn. pub. rels. film fund raiser Vachel Linds ay Assn., Springfield, 1989; mem. Springfield Jr. League, 1990-91; mem. Samaritans St. John's Hosp., Springfield, 1995—, Ill. River Econ. Devel. Action Team, 1996-97, Orlene Moore Scholarship Com., 1996—, Student of Yr. Selection Com., 1996; pres., bd. trustees Sherman Pub. Libr. Dist., 1995—; elder Buffalo Hart Presbyn. ch., 1998—; pres. Buffalo Hart Women's Assn., 1997—; mem. Town and Country Women's Assn., 1998—. Recipient Best Contbr. award Ill. AP, 1983; Robert Howard scholar Sangamon State U., 1983; named to Hon. Order of Ky. Cols., 1992. Mem. Order of Ea. Star. Presbyterian. Avocations: golf, competitive sewing and baking (state fair champion), vocal music, gardening, decorating. Home: 2 Willow Hill Dr Sherman IL 62684-9769 Office: Ill Dept Commerce and Community Affairs 620 E Adams St Springfield IL 62701-1615 E-mail: lmorford@commerce.state.il.us.

MORFORD, THOMAS, administrator; b. May 11, 1946; BA, Canisius Coll., 1968; MA, Syracuse U., 1971. Dir. office survey & cert. health stds. & quality bur. Health Care Fin. Adminstrn., 1979-82, deputy dir. health stds. & quality bur., 1982-86, dir. health stds. & quality bur., 1986-92; deputy dir. office rsch. integrity Office of Asst. Sec. for Health, 1992-95; assoc. adminstr. ops. & mgmt. Health Resources & Svcs. Adminstrn., Rockville, Md., 1995-97, dep. adminstr., 1997—2001; dep. dir. Johns Hopkins U. Urban Health Inst., Balt., 2001—. Contbr. articles to profl. jours. Office: Johns Hopkins U Urban Health Inst 111 Market Pl Ste 850 Baltimore MD 21202 Business E-Mail: tmorford@jhsph.edu.

MORGA BELLIZZI, CELESTE, editor; b. N.Y.C., Mar. 8, 1921; d. Louis and Emma (Macari) Morga; m. John J. Bellizzi, Sept. 1, 1942; children: John J., Robert F. Student, Columbia U., 1940-41, SUNY, Albany, 1970. Cert. med. lab. technician. Medical lab. technician USMC Hosp., N.Y.C., 1942, Woman's Hosp., N.Y.C., 1942-52; spl. investigator N.Y. State Atty. Gen.'s Office, Albany, 1958-65; editor Internat. Drug Report publ., The Narc Officer publ. Internat. Narcotic Enforcement Officers Assn., Albany, 1965—. Dir. Albany Inst. History and Art, 1988-90, N.Y. State Press Women, Albany, 1987; advisor UN Non-govtl. Orgns. Drug Com., N.Y.C., 1980-90, White House Conf. Drug Free Am., Washington, 1987; mem. com. Bethlehem Drug Prevention Program, Delmar, N.Y., 1987-90, Action Commn. Narc Edn., Delmar, 1984-90; v.p. Women's Rep. Party Albany, 1972 Recipient Pres.'s award INEOA, 1982, Disting. Svc. award Houston Police Dept., 1981. Mem. Nat. Fedn. Press Women, Nat. Press Club, Univ. Club, Albany Country Club, Aberdeen Country Club. Avocations: painting, golf, tennis. Office: Internat Narcotic Enforcement Officers Assn 112 State St Albany NY 12207-2005 Office Phone: 518-463-6232.

MORGAN, ALAN VIVIAN, geologist, educator; b. Barry, Glamorgan, Wales, Jan. 29, 1943; emigrated to Can., 1964, naturalized, 1977; s. George Vivian Williams and Sylvia Nesta (Atkinson) M.; m. Marion Anne Medhurst, June 14, 1966; children: Siân Kristina, Alexis John. B.Sc. with honors in Geology and Geography, U. Leicester, Eng., 1964; M.Sc. in Geography, U. Alta., Calgary, Can., 1966; PhD in Geology, U. Birmingham, Eng., 1970. Postdoctoral fellow U. Western Ont. and U. Waterloo, Ont., Can., 1970-71; asst. prof. earth scis. and man-environ. studies U. Waterloo, 1971-78, assoc. prof. earth scis., 1978-85, prof., 1985—, assoc. dir. Quaternary Scis. Inst., 1992-97, dir. Quaternary Scis. Inst., 1997—2004. Mem. Brit. Schs. Exploring Soc. Ctrl. Iceland Expdn., 1960; rep. Can. Geosci. Coun., 1977-83, exec. dir., 1988-94, adminstrv. dir., 1996-2001; mem. com. on global change Royal Soc. Can., 1988-91, mem. com. on pub. awareness of sci., 1989-94; coord. global change Geol. Survey Can., 1990-92; sr. officer Internat. Geosci. Edn. Orgn., 2000—, sec.-treas., 2003—; dir. Can. Prize Awards Found., 2000—, Can. Prize Found., 2001-; chair Can. Geosci. Edn. Network, 2003—. Author 6 field guides; editor newsletter OYEZ, 1990-94; contbr. articles to numerous profl. publs.; dir., prodr. documentary film The Heimaey Eruption, 1974. Recipient award for MS thesis Can. Soc. Petroleum Geologists, 1967, Bancroft award Royal Soc. Can., 1994, John H. Moss award Nat. Assn. Geology Tchrs., 1995, J. Willis Ambrose medal Geol. Assn. Can., 1997. E.R.W. Neale medal Geol. Assn. Canada, 1998; Charles Lapworth scholar, 1970; Nat. Scis. and Engring. Rsch. Coun. Can. grantee, 1971— Fellow Geol. Assn. Can. (hon. life, sec.-treas. 1975-83, disting. fellow), Geol. Soc. Am.; mem. Am. Quaternary Assn. (pres. 1990-92), Can. Quaternary Assn. (pres. 1987-89), Brit. Quaternary Research Assn., Internat. Union Quaternary Research (sec. gen. XII congress 1983-87). Office: U Waterloo Dept Earth Scis Waterloo ON Canada N2L 3G1

MORGAN, ALBERT GEORGE LEONARD, retired airline pilot, writer; b. West Terre Haute, Ind., Mar. 23, 1922; s. Kingsley John and Juliet Freda (Gardner) M.; m. Margaret Clark May, Nov. 27, 1943; children: Terry Len, Juliet Kathryn. Student, U. Louisville, 1948. Lic. airline transport pilot FAA. Photogrammetrist Park Aerial Surveys, Inc., Louisville, 1945-46; capt. Braniff Internat., Dallas, 1949-82; owner Morgan Aviation Books, Dallas, 1955-75; writer, pub. Dallas, 1955-99. Investor, Palm Harbor, Fla., 1993-99; cons. U.S. Dept. Justice, Washington, 1988. Author: Crackup!, 1968, Aviation Hall of Fame, 1970, View From the Cockpit, 1985, Vectors, 1992, others; prodr.: Fasten Seat Belts, 1969, Aircraft of the Vietnam War, 1971, The Lady Be Good, 1982, others; co-author: (with G. Bradford) 50 Famous Tanks, 1967, (with T.L. Morgan) The Boeing Scrapbook, 1978; contbr. articles on aviation to profl. jours. With Royal Can. Air Force, 1941-42, U.S. Army Air Forces, 1942-45, Ky. Air N.G., 1946-49. Recipient writing awards Aviation and Space Writers Assn., 1977, 78. Mem. Am. Aviation Hist. Soc., Air Line Pilots Assn., Braniff Internat. Silver Eagles. Presbyterian. Avocations: aviation history research, accident research, collecting rare books. Office: PO Box 6190 Palm Harbor FL 34684-0790 E-mail: bnf747@aol.com.

MORGAN, ALLEN B., JR., securities executive; b. 1942; BA, U. N.C., 1965. Branch mgr. Courts & Co., Memphis, Tenn., 1965-69; founder Morgan Keegan & Co., Inc., Memphis, 1969, now chmn. bd. dirs. Vice chmn. Regions Fin. Corp.; chmn. Regions Morgan Keegan Select Funds, Securities Industry Assn., 2002. Office: Regions Fin PO Box 10247 Birmingham AL 35202-0247*

MORGAN, ANDREW LANE, urologist, educator; b. May 13, 1920; s. James Albert and Elsie Edna (Johnson) M.; m. Miriam Cleary, June 9, 1951; children: Andrew Lane, Christine, Martha, James. Exch. fellowship, St. John's U., Shanghai, China, 1939—40; BA, Dartmouth Coll., 1942; MD, Cornell U., 1945. Diplomate Am. Bd. Urology. Intern Lenox Hill Hosp., N.Y.C., 1945-46; resident Queen's Med. Ctr., Honolulu, 1948-50, Yale U., 1950-52; practice medicine, specializing in urology Honolulu, 1952-87; ret., 1987. Chmn. dept. surgery Queen's Med. Ctr., 1979; clin. prof. urology John Burns Sch. Medicine, U. Hawaii; mem. renal transplant team St. Francis Med. Ctr. Past pres. Hawaii Med. Libr., 1957-58. Served to capt., AUS, 1946-48. Fellow ACS; mem. AMA, AM. Urol. Assn. (past pres. Western sect.), Hawaii Med. Assn., Societe Internationale d'Urologie, Honolulu County Med. Soc. (bd. govs. 1970-76, treas. 1978-79), Pacific Club (Honolulu). Episcopalian. Home: 44 Puako Beach Dr Kamuela HI 96743-9707

MORGAN, ANNE MARGARET BARCLAY, artist, author, psychologist; b. Washington, June 20, 1952; d. George A. and Margaret R. (Taylor) Morgan; m. Harper Brent Mashburn, Aug. 3, 2001. PhD in Psychology, U. Vienna, Austria, 1977; MA in Art History, U. Fla., 1990. Lectr. on contemporary art; design cons. for serene environments, spiritual healing. Prodr.(dir., writer): (art documentaries including) Video Art to Virtual Reality, 1992; exhibitions include, U.S. and Eruope; contbr. articles and revs. to profl. jours. and books; contbg. editor: Sculpture Mag. Mem. APA, Coll. Art Assn., Internat. Assn. Art Critics (southeastern rep.). Office: 1119 NW 36th Dr Gainesville FL 32605-4944

MORGAN, ANNE MARIE G. broadcast journalist, educator; b. Paducah, Ky., Apr. 23, 1955; d. Ralph Edward and Vera Christine Gill; m. Michael William Morgan, Nov. 19, 1977; children: Deborah, Jon, James. BA in Govt. and Psychology, Coll. William and Mary, 1976; MA in Polit. Sci., U.

Richmond, 1997; postgrad. in Pub. Policy, Va. Commonwealth U., 1998. HS tchr. James-City County Sch., Williamsburg, Va., 1977, Colonial Hts. Sch., Va., 1977-79; TV and radio journalist Capitol News, Richmond, Va., 1984—, Va. Pub. Broadcasting, Richmond, Va., 1987—, WRIC TV and WTVR TV, Richmond, 1984—2000; broadcast news anchor Va. News Network, Richmond, Va., 2000—02; journalist WVTF Radio, Roanoke, 2002—. Asst. prof. polit. sci. U. Richmond, Va., 1998—. Author: (with others) Controversies in American Public Polity, 1999, Opposing Viewpoints Series, 1991. Sec. Parents' Guidance/Pupil Pers. Guidance Com., Powhatan, Va., 1996—98; bd. dirs. Va. Pub. Broadcasting, Richmond, 2000—02, Va. Adv. Coun. Adult Edn. and Literacy, Richmond, 1999—2002, Coun. Child Care and Early Childhood Devel., Richmond, 1995—96; chair bd. dirs. State Bd. for Cmty. Colls., Richmond, 1997—2002; chair Va. Coun. Status of Women, Richmond, 1994—2002. Recipient Gov. proclamation Anne Marie Morgan Day in Commonwealth Va., Gov. Va., 1997; Meritorious award Va. Assoc. Press Broadcasters, 2002. Mem.: Soc. Profl. Journalists, Soc. Profl. Journalists (Va. profl. chpt.), Nat. Fedn. Press Women, Va. Press Women, Capitol Corrs. Assn., Am. Polit. Sci. Assn., Pi Sigma Alpha. Avocations: music, singing, mentoring.

MORGAN, ARDYS NORD, school improvement consultant; b. South Bend, Ind., Nov. 1, 1946; d. Arthur August and Janet Ardis (Eide) Nord; children: Elizabeth Elayne, Matthew Richard. BS in Elem. Edn., Ind. U., Bloomington, 1968; MS in Elem. Edn., Ind. U., Indpls., 1972; reading cert., Ind. U., South Bend, 1982; EDS, Ind. U., Bloomington, 1992; adminstr. lic., Ind. U.-Purdue U., Indpls., 1989; EdD in Curriculum and Sch. Adminstrn., Ind. U., 1994. Tchr., South Bend, 1968-69, 73-87; adminstr. dept. instrn. and curriculum, 1987-90; tchr. Indpls., 1969-70; resident lectr. Ind. U./Purdue U., Indpls., 1970-73, adminstr., 1989; mem. adj. faculty Ind. U., South Bend, 1985-90, acting program dir. elem. and secondary edn., 1990-92; asst. supt. schs. Michigan City (Ind.) Area Schs., 1992-94; supt. Union North United Schs. Corp., 1994-96; ednl. cons., tech. and staff devel. in curriculum Lightspan Partnership, San Diego, 1997-99; pres. Sch. Improvement Partnership, Inc., Granger, Ind., 1999—. Cons. on implementation of tech., mid. grades and effective teaching strategies, elem. curriculum, reading and lang. arts, fed. and state projects, staff devel. Recipient Disting. Alumni award div. edn. Ind. U., South Bend, 1990. Lilly Endowment fellow, 1987. Home: 51550 Stratton Ct Granger IN 46530-8342 Office: Sch Improvement Partnership 51550 Stratton Ct Ste 300 Granger IN 46530-8342

MORGAN, ARLENE NOTORO, university administrator; b. Phila., July 27, 1945; d. James Vincent and Mary Rose (Actis-Grande) Notoro; m. David J. Morgan, Mar. 3, 1948; children: Elizabeth, Lauren. BS in Journalism, Temple U., 1967. Reporter Delaware County Daily Times, Chester, Pa., 1967-69, Phila. Inquirer, 1969—, dep. metro editor, 1990-91, sr. editor, asst. mng. editor, 1991-2000, reader advocate columnist, 1998-2000; asst. dean Columbia U. Grad. Sch. Journalism, N.Y.C., 2000—. Bd. dirs. Friends Hosp., Phila., 1978—; mem. adv. bd. Temple U., La. State U.; mem. Am. Soc. Newspaper Editors Journalism Credibility Project; dir. Columbia Race Project. Recipient Phila. Newspapers Inc. Employee Recognition award, 1987, Excellence in Diversity award Knight Ridder, 1995; Media Studies Ctr. fellow Freedom Forum, 1996-97. Mem. Soc. Profl. Journalists., Newspaper Assn. Am. (diversity com.). Roman Catholic. Avocations: ballet, travel, opera and art appreciation, advocate to the mentally ill. Office: Columbia Univ 2960 Broadway New York NY 10027-6900 E-mail: am494@columbia.edu.

MORGAN, BETSY STELLE, lawyer; b. Terre Haute, Ind., Mar. 15, 1963; BA, DePauw U., 1985; JD, John Marshall Law Sch., 1988. Bar: Ill. 1989. With Baker & McKenzie, Chgo., 1988—, counsel, 1997—2002, ptnr., 2002—. Co-chair N.Am. Pro Bono Initiative Baker & McKenzie, Chgo. Author: United States Business Immigration Manual, 2003. Office: Baker and McKenzie One Prudential Plz 130 E Randolph Dr Chicago IL 60601

MORGAN, BEVERLY CARVER, pediatrician, educator; b. NYC, May 29, 1927; d. Jay and Florence (Newkamp) Carver; children: Nancy, Thomas E. III, John E. MD cum laude, Duke U., 1955. Diplomate Am. Bd. Pediat. (oral examiner 1984-90, mem. written examination com. 1990—), Nat. Bd. Med. Examiners. Intern, asst. resident Stanford U. Hosp., San Francisco, 1955-56; clin. fellow pediat., trainee pediatric cardiology Babies Hosp.-Columbia Presbyn. Med. Ctr., NYC, 1956-59; rsch. fellow cardiovasc. diagnostic lab. Columbia-Presbyn. Med. Ctr., NYC, 1959-60; instr. pediat. Coll. Physicians and Surgeons, Columbia U., NYC, 1960; dir. heart sta. Robert B. Green Meml. Hosp., San Antonio, 1960-62; lectr. pediat. U. Tex., 1960-62; spl. rsch. fellow in pediatric cardiology Sch. Medicine, U. Wash., Seattle, 1962-64, from instr. to prof. pediat., 1962-73, chmn. dept. pediat., 1973-80; mem. staff U. Wash. Hosp., chief of staff, 1975-77; mem. staff Harborview Med. Ctr., Children's Orthop. Hosp. and Med. Ctr., dir. dept. medicine, 1974-80; prof., chmn. dept. pediat. U. Calif., Irvine, 1980-88, prof. pediat. and pediatric cardiology, 1980—; pediatrician in chief Children's Hosp. Orange County, 1988. Mem. pulmonary acad. awards panel Nat. Heart and Lung Inst., 1972-75; mem. grad. med. edn. nat. adv. com. to sec. HEW, 1977-80; mem. Coun. on Pediatric Practice; chmn. Task Force on Opportunities for Women in Pediat., 1982; mem. nursing rev. com. NIH, 1987-88. Contbr. articles to profl. jours.; mem. editl. bd. Clin. Pediat., Am. Jour. Diseases of Children, Jour. of Orange County Pediatric Soc., Jour. Am. Acad. Pediat., LA Pediatric Soc. Recipient Women of Achievement award Matrix Table, Seattle, 1974; Disting. Alumnus award Duke U. Med. Sch., 1974; Ann. award Nat. Bd. Med. Coll. Pa., 1977; Career Devel. award USPHS, 1966-71; Moseby scholar, 1955. Mem. Am. Acad. Pediat. (chmn. com. on pediat. manpower 1984-86), Am. Coll. Cardiology, Soc. for Pediat. Rsch., Am. Fedn. Clin. Rsch., Am. Pediat. Soc., Assn. Med. Sch. Pediat. Dept. Chmn. (sec.-treas. 1981-87), Western Soc. for Pediat. Rsch., Alpha Omega Alpha. Office: U Calif Irvine Med Ctr Dept Pediatrics 101 The City Dr S Orange CA 92868-3201 Office Phone: 714-456-6483. Business E-Mail: bcmorgan@uci.edu.

MORGAN, BEVERLY HAMMERSLEY, middle school educator, artist; b. Wichita Falls, Tex. d. Vernon C. and Melba Marie (Whited) Hammersley; m. Robert Lewis Morgan, Sept. 21, 1957 (div. 1972); children: Janet Claire, Robert David. BA, So. Meth. U.; MA, U. Ala., 1980, AA certification, 1982; postgrad., U. Tex., 1991—. Cert. art tchr., Tex., Ala.; cert. elem. tchr., Ala. Tchr. art Ft. Worth Pub. Schs., 1955-60; tchr. English, Lincoln County Schs., Fayetteville, Tenn., 1961-62; elem. tchr. Huntsville (Ala.) Pub. Schs., 1960-61, 62-68, tchr. art, 1972-92, 93-94. One-woman shows include U. Ala., 1980, Huntsville Art League, 1981, and various other art gallerys, art shows and exhbns. Mem. HAL Gallery, Huntsville, Madison County Sr. Art Gallery. Mem. Huntsville Mus. Art, Am. Contract Bridge League. Republican. Avocations: bridge, travel, collecting Hammersley English bone china. Home: 12027 Chicamauga Trl SE Huntsville AL 35803-1544

MORGAN, BRUCE RAY, international consultant; b. Los Angeles, Oct. 28, 1932; s. Francis Raymond and Rose Hall (Black) M.; m. Bette Jeanne Moore, Oct. 7, 1957; children: Michael John, Brian Leo, Jeanne Anne. AA, Sacramento Jr. Coll., 1952; BS, U. Calif.-Berkeley, 1954, LL.B., 1957. Bar: Calif. 1957. Judge adv. USAF, Saudi Arabia and Morocco, 1958-61; atty. firm Thelen, Marrin, Johnson & Bridges, San Francisco, 1961-67; dep. dir. Peace Corps, Nepal, 1967-68, dir, 1968-70; exec. dir. Center Research and Edn., Denver, 1971-75; dir. U.S. representation to Saudi Arabia-U.S. Joint Commn. on Econ. Coop., Riyadh, 1975-76; pres. Bruce Morgan Assocs., Inc., Washington, 1976—. Editor: Calif. State Bar Jour. Legis. Rev, 1957. Served with USAF, 1958-61. Mem. U.S., Calif. bars. Office: Bruce Morgan Assocs 3014 New Mexico Ave NW Washington DC 20016-3519 E-mail: bmorgan@bmainc.com.

MORGAN, CATHERINE MARIE, psychologist, writer; b. Duluth, Minn., Mar. 27, 1947; m. Ralph Morgan, 1967; 1 child, Andrew. BS, U. Nebr., 1968; MEd, U. Okla., 1973; PhD, Okla. State U., 1987; postgrad. Menninger Found., Psychotherapy Tng. Program, 1987-89. Child devel. specialist Southwest Guidance Ctr., Wheatland, Okla., 1973-74; pvt. practice Family Counseling Assocs., San Antonio, 1974-75; psychol. asst. Edmond Guidance Ctr., Okla., 1975-82; psychol. asst. supr. Southeast Guidance Ctr., Del City, Okla., 1982-86; psychol. intern Cleve. County Health Dept., Moore, Okla., 1986-87; psychologist Cen. State Hosp., Norman, Okla., 1987-89; pvt. practice assocs. in psychology Edmond, Okla.; vice chair bd. mgrs. Integris Mental Health; pres. Assocs. in Psychology, 1988—. Mem. AAUW, APA, Okla. Psychol. Assn., Am. Bus. Women's Assn., P.E.O., Kappa Delta Pi. Avocations: writing, reading, knitting, racquetball. Office: 3545 NW 58th St Ste 220 Oklahoma City OK 73112-4725

MORGAN, CHARLES OXFORD, JR., lawyer; b. Miami, Fla., Jan. 21, 1940; s. Charles O. and Corabel (Klefeker) M.; m. Marabel Hawk, June 25, 1964; children: Laura M. Horton, Michelle R. Knott. BA, Wheaton (Ill.) Coll., 1962; JD, U. Miami, Fla., 1965; LLM in Taxation, NYU, 1966. Bar: Fla. 1965. Assoc. Peters, Maxey & McDonald, Miami, 1966-68; ptnr. Peters, Maxey, Short & Morgan, Miami, 1969-82; pvt. practice Miami, 1983—. Author: Jesus On Line, 1995. Exec. dir. Don Shula Found., Inc., Miami, 1991—; chmn. bd. dirs. Tyndale Theol. Sem., Amsterdam, Holland, 1989-92; dir. Miami Heart Inst., 1982-84, Billy Graham Evangelistic Assn., Mpls., 1983—. Office: 1300 NW 167th Ste 3 Miami FL 33169-5738

MORGAN, CHARLES RUSSELL, lawyer; b. New Orleans, La., Oct. 15, 1946; s. Charles and Marian E. (Wetzel) M.; children: Charles Bradford, William Russell, Elizabeth Anne. BA, U. N.C., 1968; JD, Columbia U., 1971. Bar: N.Y. 1973, Ill. 1981, Ohio 1994. Law clk. to cir. judge US Ct. Appeals, Washington, 1971-72; atty. Davis Polk & Wardwell, NYC, 1972-80; sr. staff counsel Household Internat., Inc., Prospect Heights, Ill., 1980-83; v.p., asst. gen. counsel Kraft, Inc., Glenview, Ill., 1983-85, v.p., sr. corp. counsel, 1985-88; v.p., gen. counsel, sec. Chiquita Brands Internat., Cin., 1988-95; ptnr. Mayer Brown & Platt, Chgo., 1995-98; exec. v.p., gen. counsel BellSouth Corp., Atlanta, 1998— V.p., sec., dir. John Morrell & Co., Inc. Contbg. editor The Corp. Counselor, 1986—, The Environmental Corporate Counsel Report. Recipient Spirit of Excellence Award, Am. Bar Assoc., Corp. Legal Diversity Award, Am. Corp. Counsel Assoc., 2000, Nat. Diversity Leadership Award, Coalition of fBar Assoc. of Color, Diversity 2000 Award, Minority Corp. Coun. Assoc. Mem. ABA (chmn. corp. counsel com. 1983-86, chmn. comm. com. 1986—), Am. Law Inst., Am. Corp. Counsel Assn. (bd. dirs.), Am. Arbitration Assn. (bd. dirs.), Legal Club Chgo., Army-Navy Club of Washington. In Nov., 2000, Morgan was appointed by the Chief Justice of the Supreme Court of Ga. as Chair of the Supreme Court's Blue Ribbon Commission on Indigent Defense. Office: BellSouth Corp 1155 Peachtree St NE Ste A Atlanta GA 30309-3610

MORGAN, CHRISTINA, venture capital firm executive; Student, Am. U., Beirut; BS in Fin., MBA in Fin., Ariz. State U. With Memorex, Qume Corp., 1977-82; securities analyst Hambrecht & Quist LLC Investment Bankers, San Francisco, 1982-84, investment banking prin., 1984-90, mng. dir., 1990-94, mng. dir., co-head investment banking, 1994—, Chase H&Q, San Francisco. Bd. dirs. Visigenic Software. Office: Chase H&Q 1 Bush St San Francisco CA 94104-4425

MORGAN, CLARA MCMAHON, publishing consultant; b. Ironton, Ohio, Nov. 10, 1955; d. Nicholas G. McMahon and Barbara Ann Jarrett; m. Richard D. Brown, June 18, 1977 (div.); m. George Pidcock Morgan, Oct. 8, 1983; children: David Christopher, Sean Jarrett. BS, Miami U., Oxford, Ohio, 1977; postgrad. in MS in Edn. program, U. Phoenix. Health ministries coord. Synod the Covenant Presbyn. Ch., Columbus, Ohio, 1977-82; dir. Nat. Abortion Rights Action League of Ohio, Columbus, 1982-84; orgnl. devel. cons. PC (USA), 1988—92, Cmty. Involvement Coun., Tarpon Springs, Fla., 1992—95; substitute tchr. Tarpon Springs Elem. Sch., 1992—95; ednl. cons. Houghton Mifflin Co., Boston, 1995—. Co-author: Responsibility and Respect, 1992. Sec., treas. Harbor Woods Homeowners Assn., Palm Harbor, Fla., 1992—94; cmty. involvement coord. Tarpon Springs Elem. Sch., 1993—95, chair sch. adv. coun., 1992—95; founder, bd. dirs. Presbyn. Affirming Reproductive Options, Louisville, 1991—; bd. dirs. Presbyn. Health, Edn. and Welfare Assn., Louisville, 1978—86, 1997—2000; elder Presbyn. Ch. USA, 1993—. Mem.: ASCD, AAUW, Nat. Sci. Tchrs. Assn., Nat. Coun. Tchrs. Math., Fla. Reading Assn., Internat. Reading Assn. Democrat. Avocations: photography, travel, gourmet cooking, piano. Office Phone: 727-939-9446.

MORGAN, CLYDE NATHANIEL, dermatologist; b. Bell County, Tex., Nov. 2, 1923; s. Xenophen William and Rhoda Ella (Deck) M.; m. Birdie Joyce Rich, Mar. 3, 1951; children: Clyde Nathaniel Jr., Reinette Jean, Nancy Elaine. *Dr. Morgan is a descendant of Morgan ap Morgan, the first white settler in West Virginia, of Captain David Morgan, Indian fighter and Captain in the American Revolution, and of James Morgan who assisted in establishing American independence while acting in the capacity of private and Indian spy under Captain James Brenton and Colonel John Evans in 1778. Family tradition has it that Captain David Morgan taught George Washington how to survey. Wife, Birdie Morgan, was a delegate to the Republican National Convention in 1984.* BS, Abilene Christian Coll., 1948; MD, U. Tex., Galveston, 1953. Assoc. prof. biology Abilene (Tex.) Christian Coll., 1954-56; pvt. practice Abilene, 1954-67; dermatologist, 1969—. *Presented research papers on the development of special techniques in the cryosurgical treatment of benign and malignant lesions if the skin before the American College of Cryosurgery meetings in New Orleans and New York City; before the Southern Medical Association meeting in San Antonio; before the World Congress of cryosurgery meetings in San Remo, Italy, and Manila, Philippines; and before the Indian Cryogenics Council in Calcutta. Invited guest lecturer at the Jadavpur University Medical School in Calcutta, India.* Contbr. articles to profl. jours. Mem. AMA, SAR (chpt. pres. 1997-99, award 1995), Am. Coll. Cryosurgery, Internat. Soc. Cryosurgery, Tex. Med. Assn., So. Med. Assn., Tex. Dermatologic Soc., Taylor-Jones-Haskell County Med. Soc. Republican. Mem. Ch. Of Christ. Avocations: golf, fishing, hunting, cryogenics research. Home: 1718 Cedar Crest Dr Abilene TX 79601-3228 Office: 1166 Merchant St Abilene TX 79603-5014 Office Phone: 325-673-4242. E-mail: clybird@juno.com.

MORGAN, CONSTANCE LOUISE, real estate executive; b. Denver, July 24, 1941; d. Willis Stephen and Evelyn (Rutar) Claus; m. Robert M. Morgan, Jan. 3, 1963; children: Stephen, Melayne. BS, U. N. Mex., 1963. Lic. real estate broker; Fla. master gardener, 1996. Realtor, assoc. Investors Realty, Tallahassee, 1980-82, br. mgr., 1982-83; pres., broker Connie Morgan Realty, Inc., Tallahassee, 1983-96, Constance L. Morgan, Broker, Tallahassee, 1996—; founder Network for Ind. Brokers, 1989-93. Chmn. docents Fla. Gov.'s Mansion, Tallahassee, 1979-80; pres. Newcomers-Univ. Women, Tallahassee, 1968, Hunters Crossing Homeowners Assn., 1998-99; bd. dirs. Tallahassee Symphony Orch., 1990-96; bd. dirs. Rotary Youth Camp, Inc., 1995—, Tallahassee United Way. Mem. Nat. Assn. Realtors, Fla. Assn. Realtors, Tallahassee Bd. Realtors (chmn. Multiple Listing Svc. 1984, 94), Tallahassee Cmty. Realty Group, Tallahassee C. of C. (bd. dirs. 1984-86, 89-92), Rotary, Chi Omega (treas. 1962), Phi Gamma Nu (pres. 1962). Home and Office: 3322 Remington Run Tallahassee FL 32312-1462

MORGAN, DAHLIA, museum director, art educator; BA, McGill U., Montreal, 1958; postgrad., Sir George Williams U., Montreal, 1968-69, U. Miami, Fla., 1974. Lectr. Mus. of Fine Arts, Montreal, 1965-70; lectr./rschr. Sir George Williams U., Montreal, 1968-70; grad. asst. dept. art and art history U. Miami, Fla., 1971-74; adj. prof. visual arts dept. Fla. Internat. U., Miami, 1975-77, vis. rof. visual arts dept., 1978-79, faculty visual arts dept., 1979—, dir. Art in State Bldgs. Program, 1984—, dir. Art Mus., 1980—. Lectr. in field; curator numerous exhbns.; panelist NEA Mus. Grants, 1993, Cultural Advancement Grants, 1990, 92; cons. Fed. Gen. Svcs. Adminstrn., 1992, Metro-Dade Art in Pub. Places Program, 1992. Prodr. numerous catalogues to exhbns. Juror South Miami Art Fair Photo Group; bd. dirs. Nat. Found. for Advancement in the Arts, 1984—; founder Friends of the Frost Art Mus. Support Group at Fla. Internat. U., 1984—; chmn. State of Fla. Art in Bldgs., 1984—; chmn. Art in Pub. Places, Dade County, Fla., 1980-84. Recipient 3d Ann. MAXIE award Miami Arts Exchange, 1990; grantee Fla. Endowment for Humanities, 1986, Metro Dade County Cultural Affairs Coun., 1986, Fla. Internat. U., 1990, 91; U. Miami-Coral Gables merit scholar, fed. scholar. Mem. Assn. Coll. and Univ. Mus. and Galleries, Am. Assn. Mus., Coll. Art Assn. Am., Fla. Mus. Dirs. Assn., Fla. Higher Edn. Arts Network, Internat. Coun. Mus. (fine arts com.), Miami Cultural execs. Coun., Southeastern Mus. Assn., Fla. Cultural Action Alliance, Phi Kappa Phi. Office: Frost Art Mus Fla Internat U University Park PC # 110 11200 SW 8th St Miami FL 33199-0001

MORGAN, DAVID, communications media executive; Bur. chief Phila. Reuters Am., Inc., 1997—. Office: Reuters Am Inc 1818 Market St Ste 2530 Philadelphia PA 19103-3698

MORGAN, DAVID O. physiologist, educator; BSc in Animal Biology with 1st class honors, U. Calgary, Can., 1980; PhD in Endocrinology, U. Calif., San Francisco, 1986. Postdoctoral fellow dept. biochemistry and biophysics U. Calif., San Francisco, 1986—87, postdoctoral fellow dept. microbiology and immunology, 1987—89, asst. prof. dept. physiology, 1989—95, assoc. prof. depts. physiology and biochemistry and biophysics, 1995—97, prof. depts. physiology and biochemistry and biophysics, 1997—. Program mem. U. Calif. San Francisco Comprehensive Cancer Ctr.; mem. Herbert Boyer Program in Biol. Scis. Contbr. articles to profl. jours. Recipient Amoco Can. Petroleum scholarship, 1976—80, Province of Alta. scholarships, 1976—80, Alta. Heritage Found. for Med. Rsch. studentship, 1981—86, Helen Hay Whitney Found. postdoctoral fellowship, 1987—89, Searle Scholar award, 1990—93, March of Dimes Basil O'Connor Starter Scholar award, 1990—92, Rita Allen Found. Scholar award, 1991—96. Office: U Calif Box 0444 San Francisco CA 94143-0444

MORGAN, DENNIS ALAN, retired federal official, education educator; b. St. Joseph, Mo., Feb. 1, 1947; s. John Frederick and Eunice L. (Seiter) M.; divorced; 1 child, Tracey Melinda. BA, U. Mo., 1969; MS, U. So. Calif., 1973; PhD, Pacific Western U., 1991. With Dept. of Navy, Washington, 1969—2002, dir. joint programs and acquisition reform, 1984—2002; prof. Coll. So. Md., 2004—. Lectr. in field. Author: The Pechora Intercept, 1988, Act of Contrition, 1991. Curators scholar U. Mo., 1965. Mem. SAR, Mensa, Nat. Geog. Soc., Lambda Chi Alpha. Republican. Avocations: reading, writing, travel, geneology. Home: 21625 Weatherby Ln Lexington Park MD 20653-2539 Personal E-mail: den979@yahoo.com.

MORGAN, DENNIS KEITH, lawyer; b. St. Louis, Dec. 12, 1947; s. Charles Gustave and Justine Estelle (Picarelli) M.; children: James, Elizabeth, Rebecca. BJ, U. Mo., 1970, JD, 1972; LLM, Washington U., St. Louis, 1978. Bar: Mo. 1972, U.S. Dist. Ct. (we. dist.) Mo. 1972, Ill. 1978, U.S. Dist. Ct. (ea. dist.) Mo. 1978, U.S. Ct. Appeals (8th cir.) 1978, Tex. 1981, U.S. Tax Ct. 1981, U.S. Ct. Mil. Appeals 1981., Pa. 2003. Spl. counsel U.S. Dept. Energy, 1979—80; exec. v.p. adminstrn., gen. counsel, corp. sec. So. Union Co., Wilkes-Barre, Pa., 1981—. Mem. exec. com. Austin Visual Arts Assn., 1999—2002; bd. dirs. Austin Symphony Orch., 2000—02; trustee Everhart Mus. Maj. JAGC USAR, 1970—86. Mem. ABA, Tex. Bar Assn., Mo. Bar Assn., Pa. Bar Assn., Am. Gas Assn. (legal com.), So. Gas Assn. (legal com.). Lutheran. Avocations: teaching, history, travel. Office: So Union Co One PEI Ctr Wilkes Barre PA 18711 Home: 1104 Tennyson Close Moosic PA 18507 Office Phone: 570-820-2402. E-mail: dmorgan@southernunionco.com.

MORGAN, DENNIS RICHARD, lawyer; b. Jan. 3, 1942; s. Benjamin Richard and Gladys Belle (Brown) Morgan. BA, Washington and Lee U., 1964; JD, U. Va., 1967; LLM in Labor Law, NYU, 1971. Bar: Ohio 1967, Va. 1967, U.S. Ct. Appeals (4th cir.) 1968, U.S. Ct. Appeals (6th cir.) 1971, U.S. Supreme Ct. 1972. Law clk. to chief judge U.S. Dist. Ct. (ea. dist.) Va., 1967—68; mem. Marshman, Snyder & Seeley, Cleve., 1971—72; dir. labor rels. Ohio Dept. Adminstrv. Svcs., 1972—75; asst. city atty. Columbus, Ohio, 1975—77; dir. Ohio Legis. Reference Bur., Columbus, 1979—81; assoc. Clemans, Nelson & Assocs., Columbus, 1981; pvt. practice Columbus, 1978—92. Lectr. in field; guest lectr. Cen. Mich. U., 1975; judge moot ct. Ohio State U. Sch. Law, 1981, 83, grad. divsn., 73, 74, 76; guest lectr. Baldwin-Wallace Coll., 1973; legal counsel Dist. IV Comms. Workers Am., 1982—88; pers. dir. Pub. Utilities Commn., Ohio, 1989—91; asst. atty. gen. State of Ohio, 1991—2003. Negotiator Franklin County United Way, 1977—81; regional chmn. ann. alumni fund-raising program U. Va. Sch. Law; mem. Greater Hilltop Area Commn., 1989—; pres. Woodbrook Village Condominium Assn., 1985—; vice-chmn. Franklin County Dem. Party, 1976—82; dem. com. person Ward 58, Columbus, 1973—; chmn. rules com. Ohio State Dem. Conv., 1974; co-founder, trustee Greater West Side Dem. Club; bd. dirs. Hilltop Civic Coun., Inc., 1997—99. Capt. U.S. Army, 1968—70. Recipient Am. Jurisprudence award, 1967; scholar Robert E. Lee Rsch., 1965. Mem.: Am. Judicature Soc., Fed. Bar Assn., Indsl. Rels. Rsch. Assn., Columbus Metropolitan club (charter), Pi Sigma Alpha. Roman Catholic. Home: 1261 Woodbrook Lane G Columbus OH 43223-3243 E-mail: denmorgan@earthlink.net.

MORGAN, DIRCK, broadcast journalist; b. L.A., Feb. 3, 1954; s. Phillip Barton and Katherine (Ramirez) Segall; m. Ellen Tomoye Matsumoto, Dec. 1, 1993; 1 child, Makena Sunao. AA, Pierce Coll., 1973. Assignment editor KFWB/Group W. Westinghouse, L.A., 1972-74; corp. comm. specialist Northrop Corp., L.A., 1975-78; news dir. Stas. KARM, KFIG, Fresno, Calif., 1978-84; editor, anchor Sta. KGIL, L.A., 1984-85; fin. anchor Sta. KWHY-TV, L.A., 1985-87; cmty. resources specialist Optimist Boys Home, L.A., 1985-87; reporter Sta. KFWB, CBS, L.A., 1988—. Media crisis mgmt. instr. L.A. County Fire Dept., 1990—, L.A. Police Dept., 1991—, LAUSD, 1996, Calif. State Mil. Res., L.A., 1990-95. Helicopter airborne reporter Sta. KFWB, 1988-91, broadcast series on L.A. riots, 1992 (L.A. Press Club award), L.A. Police Dept. Ballistics, 1994 (L.A. Press Club award), Radio TV News Assn. Instr., announcer Kenkojuku World Karate, L.A., 1984-92; host Nissei Week, L.A., 1990-98. Recipient 19 Golden Mike awards Radio and TV News Assn. Mem. L.A. Police Protective League (hon. life). Avocations: Karate, japanese koi fish, firearms, classic cars. Office: KFWB/CBS 6230 Yucca St Los Angeles CA 90028-5295

MORGAN, DONNA EVENSEN, lawyer; b. Bklyn., Feb. 28, 1957; d. Edward Ivar and Judith (Larsen) Evensen; m. Charles S. Morgan, Sept. 3, 1988. BA, Colgate U., 1979; JD, U. Mich., 1984. Bar: Ill. 1985. Assoc. Chapman and Cutler, Chgo., 1985-86, Kirkland and Ellis, Chgo., 1987-89, Mayer Brown Rowe & Maw, Chgo., 1989—. Office: Mayer Brown Rowe & Maw 190 S La Salle St Ste 3100 Chicago IL 60603-3441 Office Phone: 312-701-7138. Business E-Mail: dmorgan@mayerbrownrowe.com.

MORGAN, EDMUND SEARS, retired history professor; b. Mpls., Jan. 17, 1916; s. Edmund Morris and Elsie Sears (Smith) M.; m. Helen Theresa Mayer, June 7, 1939; children: Penelope, Pamela; m. Marie Caskey, June 22, 1983. AB, Harvard U., 1937, PhD, 1942. Instrument maker Radiation Lab., MIT, 1942-45; instr. U. Chgo., 1945-46; asst. prof. Brown U., 1946-49, asso. prof., 1949-51, prof., 1951-55, acting dean grad. sch., 1951-52; prof. Yale U., 1955-65, Sterling prof., 1965-86, prof. emeritus, 1986—. Rsch. fellow Huntington Libr., 1952-53; Johnson rsch. prof. U. Wis., 1968-69 Author: The Puritan Family, 1944, Virginians at Home, 1953; author: (with Helen M. Morgan) The Stamp Act Crisis, 1953; author: The Birth of the Republic, 1956, The Puritan Dilemma, 1958, The Gentle Puritan, 1962, Visible Saints, 1963, Roger Williams, 1967, So What About History, 1969, American Slavery American Freedom, 1975, The Challenge of the American Revolution, 1976, The Meaning of Independence, 1976, The Genius of George Washington, 1980, Inventing the People, 1988, Benjamin Franklin, 2002, The Genuine Article, 2004; mem. editl. bd.: N.E. Quar.; contbr. articles and revs. to hist. jours. Trustee Smith Coll., 1984-89. Recipient Nat. Humanities medal, 2000. Mem.: Am. Acad. Arts and Scis., Orgn. Am. Historians (pres. 1971—72), Royal Hist. Soc., Brit. Acad., Am. Philos. Soc., Am. Antiquarian Soc., Mass. Hist. Soc., Colonial Soc. Mass.

MORGAN, ELIZABETH, plastic surgeon; b. Washington, July 9, 1947; d. William James and Antonia (Bell) Morgan; 1 child, Elena. BA magna cum laude, Harvard U., 1967; postgrad. (fellow), Oxford U., 1967, 70; MD, Yale U., 1971; PhD in Psychology, U. Canterbury, Christchurch, New Zealand, 1995. Diplomate Am. Bd. Surgery, Am. Bd. Plastic Surgery. Intern Yale-New Haven Hosp., 1971-72, resident, 1972-73, 76-77, Tufts-New Eng. Med. Center, Boston, 1973-76, Harvard-Cambridge (Mass.) Hosp., 1977-78; col-

umnist Cosmopolitan mag., 1973-80; pvt. practice specializing in cosmetic plastic surgery Washington, 1978-87, McLean, Va., 1998—, Chevy Chase, Md., 1998—. Assoc. faculty Am. U. Dept. Law, Justice and Soc., 1998. Author: The Making of A Woman Surgeon, 1980, Solo Practice, 1982, Custody, A True Story, 1986, The Complete Book of Cosmetic Surgery for Men, Women and Teens, 1988. Fellow: ACS, Am. Soc. Aesthetic Plastic Surgeons, Am. Soc. Plastic Surgeons; mem.: APSCA, APA, Am. Profl. Soc. Abused Children, Internat. Soc. Study Dissociation. Episcopalian. Office: Chevy Chase Bldg 5530 Wisconsin Ave Ste 1135 Chevy Chase MD 20815-4302 Fax: 301-951-8128. Office Phone: 301-951-8122. E-mail: mail@drelizabethmorgan.com.

MORGAN, ETHEL BRANMAN, accountant, retired electronics engineer; b. N.Y.C., Jan. 16, 1914; d. Morris and Dina Branman; m. Donald Arol Morgan, Mar. 14, 1936; children: Margaret Voelkel, Barbara Weeks, John T., Janet Katich, Ethel Lynn. BS, U. Ala., 1964. Mathematician Army Missile Command, Redstone Arsenal, Ala., 1964-67, computer specialist, 1967-71, lead engr. air def. sys. command control software, 1971-73; pvt. practice tax acctg., fin. cons. Huntsville, Ala., 1974—. Pres. Huntsville-Madison County Coun. on Aging, 1980-82; vice chmn. Citizens Adv. Com. to Small Claims Ct., 1980-83; bd. dirs. Madison County Sr. Ctr., 1979-83, Mdison County Coun. on Aging, 1978-82, Redstone Village, 1997—. Mem. AAUW (legis. chair Huntsville br. 1980-82), Nat. Soc. Pub. Accts., Nat. Assn. Enrolled Agts., Ala. Soc. Pub. Accts., Ala. Soc. Enrolled Agts. (treas. 1983-89), Phi Beta Kappa. Office: PO Box 4312 Huntsville AL 35815-4312 also: 10100 Hillview Dr Apt 342 Pensacola FL 32514-5439

MORGAN, EVAN, retired chemist; b. Spokane, Wash., Feb. 26, 1930; s. Evan and Emma Anne (Klobucher) M.; m. Johnnie Lu Dickson, Feb. 14, 1959; 1 child, James. BS, Gonzaga U., 1952; MS, U. Wash., 1954, PhD, 1956. Staff chemist IBM Corp., Poughkeepsie, N.Y., 1956-60; group supr. Olin Mathieson Co., New Haven, 1960-64; assoc. prof. chemistry High Point (N.C.) Coll., 1964-65; sr. rsch. chemist Reynolds Metals Co., Richmond, Va., 1965-72; chemist Babcock & Wilcox, Lynchburg, Va., 1972-95, Lynchburg Tree Steward, Lynchburg, 1995—2002; ret., 2002—. Mem. Am. Chem. Soc. Home: 5128 Wedgewood Rd Lynchburg VA 24503-4208 E-mail: emorgan@worldnet.att.net.

MORGAN, EVELYN BUCK, retired nursing educator; b. Phila., Nov. 3, 1931; d. Kenneth Edward and Evelyn Louise (Rhineberg) Buck; m. John Allen McGeary, Aug. 15, 1958 (div. 1964); children: John Andrew, Jacquelyn Ann McGeary Keplinger; m. Kenneth Dean Morgan, June 26, 1965 (dec. 1975). Grad., Muhlenberg Hosp. Sch. Nursing, Plainfield, N.J., 1955; BSN summa cum laude, Ohio State U., 1972, MS, 1973; EdD, Nova U., 1978. RN, N.J., Ohio, Fla., Calif.; cert. clin. specialist ANCC; cert. advanced RN practitioner, Fla. Staff nurse Muhlenburg Hosp., 1955-57; indsl. nurse Western Electric Co., Columbus, Ohio, 195-59; supr. Mt. Carmel Hosp., Columbus, 1960-65; instr. Grant Hosp. Sch. Nursing, Columbus, 1965-72; cons. Ohio Dept. Health, Columbus, 1972-74; prof. nursing Miami (Fla.)-Dade C.C., 1974-96, prof. emerita, 1996—; pvt. practice family therapy, Ft. Lauderdale, Fla., 1982—. Family therapist Hollywood Pavilion Hosp., 1977-82; founder Elder Reach, Inc., care mgmt. co., 1998. Sustaining mem. Dem. Nat. Com., 1975— Mem. ANA, Nat. Guild Hypnotists, Am. Nurses Found., Am. Holistic Nurses Assn., Fla. Coun. Psychiat. and Mental Health Clin. Specialists, Sigma Theta Tau. Roman Catholic. Personal E-mail: emorgan288@aol.com.

MORGAN, FRANK EDWARD, II, lawyer; b. Burlington, Vt., May 16, 1952; s. Robert Griggs and Ruth (Jepson) M. First Class Cert. Merit, U. Edinburgh, Scotland, 1973; AB with honors, Brown U., 1974; LLM, Cambridge U., Eng., 1976; JD, U. Va., 1978. Bar: Mass. 1978, N.Y. 1990. Assoc. Gaston & Snow, Boston, 1978—82; v.p., gen. counsel Madison Fund, Inc. and Adobe Resources Corp., N.Y.C., 1982—87; ptnr. Gaston & Snow, N.Y.C., 1987—91, Mayer, Brown & Platt, N.Y.C., 1991—96, Dewey Ballantine, N.Y.C., 1996—2003; pres., COO Coller Capital, Inc., N.Y.C., 2003—. Mem. ABA, N.Y. State Bar Assn., Am. Soc. Internat. Law. Republican. Congregationalist. Home: 14 Sutton Pl S New York NY 10022-3071 Office: Coller Capital Inc 410 Park Ave Ste 530 New York NY 10022 Business E-Mail: morgan@collercapital.com.

MORGAN, FRANK T. business educator, consultant; b. Shamokin, Pa., July 8, 1944; s. Burgess Sherman and Marion Regina (Lewis) M.; m. Nancy Ida Bishop, May 30, 1970; children: Elizabeth Marion, Douglas Bishop. AB, Princeton U., 1966; MS, Pa. State U., 1967; postgrad., Stevens Inst. Tech., Hoboken, N.J., 1976-79; PhD, Calif. Coast U., 1983. Cert. sr. profl. in human resources. Plant pers. mgr. Gen. Foods, Jacksonville, Fla., 1967-69, assoc. placement mgr. White Plains, N.Y., 1969-70, mgr. sales devel., 1970-71; mgr. orgn. devel. Berol Corp., Daubury, Conn., 1971-73, v.p. human resources, 1973-78, sr. grop v.p. internat., 1978-87; prof., dir. exec. edn. U. Va. Darden Grad. Sch. Bus., Charlottesville, 1987-94; global dir. exec. edn. U. N.C., Chapel Hill, 1994-99; dir. exec. devel. The Dow Chem. Co., Midland, Mich., 1999—. Bd. dirs. Danbury Med. Ctr., 1977-85; chmn. Danbury Edn. Adv. Coun., 1978-86; pres. Morgan Assocs., Charlottesville, 1987—. Contbr. articles to publs. Mem. Am. Psychol. Assn., Am. Soc. for Tng. and Devel., Soc. for Pers. and Human Resources (chair), Consortium for Exec. Edn. Republican. Episcopalian. Avocations: sailing, tennis, history. Office: The Dow Chem Co Edc Midland MI 48674-0001

MORGAN, GAYLIN F. public relations consultant; b. Cedar Falls, Iowa, Nov. 3, 1938; BS in Journ., Bus., Iowa State U., 1962. Creative dir. Reiman Assocs., 1965-75; pres. Morgan & Myers, Jefferson, Wis., 1976-97, cons., 1997—. Address: 304 E Linden Dr Jefferson WI 53549-2146 E-mail: gfmorgan@charter.net.

MORGAN, GREGORY PAUL, financial planner; b. Cocoa Beach, Fla., Sept. 9, 1958; s. Paul Leo and Mickey Maxine (Cooper) M. BS in Psychology magna cum laude, Pepperdine U., 1980. Cert. fin. planner. Fin. analyst Williams & McCombs, Inc., Arlington, Tex., 1980-83; fin. advisor Balanced Fin., Dallas, 1983-86; ptnr. Strategic Fin. Group, Arlington, 1986—. Chmn. coun. Lowry Fin. Svcs., West Palm Beach, Fla., 1987—; pres. Strategic Fin.Mgmt., 1989; lectr. numerous orgns. Big Bros. Am. United Way, Dallas, 1986—. Named to Bloomberg Top 200 Wealth Mgrs., 2003. Mem. Inst. Cert. Fin. Planners, Internat. Assn. for Fin. Planners, Inst. Chartered Fin. Analysts, Great S.W. Tax and Estate Planning Coun., Dallas Assn. Investment Analysts. Avocations: tennis, basketball, water- and snow-skiing. Office: 5310 Harvest Hill Rd Ste 146 Dallas TX 75230-5893 Home: 581 Indian Rock Dr Coppell TX 75019

MORGAN, GWYN, oil and gas executive; b. Carstairs, Alta., Can., Nov. 4, 1945; BSc in Mech. Engring., U. Alta., 1967; postgrad., Cornell U. Petroleum engr. Alta. Energy Resources Conservation Bd.; mgr. ops. and engring. Consolidated Natural Gas Ltd., Consolidated Pipelines Ltd., Norlands Petroleums Ltd.; with Alta. Energy Co., Ltd., Calgary, 1975—2002; pres., CEO En Cana Corp., Calgary, 2002—. Bd. dirs. HSBC-Bank N.Am. Trustee Fraser Inst.; dir. Inst. of the Ams.; vice-chair Can. Coun. Chief Execs.; gov. Coun. for Can. Unity; mem. adv. bd. Accenture Energy; mem. Am. Petroleum Inst. Avocations: sailing, hiking, skiing, physical fitness, bicycling. Office: EnCana Corp 1800-855 2d St SW Calgary AB Canada T2P 2S5

MORGAN, HARRY NEW, education educator; b. Blenheim, Va., June 6, 1926; s. John Alexander and Cheyney (Lewis) M.; children: Parris Mitchell, Lawrence Milan. BS, NYU, 1949; MSW, U. Wis., 1969; EdD, U. Mass., 1970. Cert. social worker, N.Y. Dir. N.E. region Head Start, N.Y.C., 1965-67; program coord. Bank St. Coll., N.Y.C., 1967-70; prof. and chmn. African-Am. Studies Ohio U., Athens, 1970-72, Syracuse (N.Y.) U., 1972-84; prof. and chmn. earl chldhood edn. U. West Ga., Carrollton, 1984—. Conducted rsch. studies on cmty. and classroom issues, 1984-95. Author: Affective Education for Cognitive Development, 1967, The Learning Community, 1970, Historical Perspectives on the Education of Black Children, 1995, Cognitive Styles and Classroom Learning, 1997, The Imagination of Early Childhood Education, 1999, Real Learning: A Bridge to Cognitive Neuroscience, 2003. Bd. dirs. Marcy Settlement House, Bklyn., 1962-65; pres., co-founder bd. Met. Sch. for Arts, Syracuse, 1975; founder housing cooperative, Syracuse. Mem. APA, Am. Ednl. Rsch. Assn., Assn. Study of African Am. Life and History. Avocation: antiques. Home: 2284 Lakeview Pky Villa Rica GA 30180-8082 Office: State U West Ga Maple St Carrollton GA 30118-0001 E-mail: hmorgan@westga.edu.

MORGAN, HELEN GAYLE, music educator; b. Jackson, Mo., Jan. 30, 1951; d. Julius Kirk and Ann Carter Morgan. BS, U. So. Miss., 1973, MS in music edn., 1974. Music tchr. Pisgah HS, Sandhill, Miss., 1974—81; choir dir., German tchr. Northwest Rankin HS, Brandon, 1981—. Violinist Jackson Symphony Orchestra, 1974—84. Mem. First Baptist Ch., 1974—. Mem.: Music Educator's Nat. Conf., Am. Choral Dirs. Assn. Baptist. Avocations: violin, cross stitch. Home: 1936 Meadowbrook Rd Jackson MS 39211 Office: NW Rankin HS 5805 Hwy 25 Brandon MS 39047

MORGAN, HENRY COKE, JR., judge; b. Norfolk, Va., Feb. 8, 1935; s. Henry Coke and Dorothy Lea (Pebworth) M.; m. Margaret John McGrail, Aug. 18, 1965; children: A. Robertson Hanckel Jr., Catherine Morgan Stockwell, Coke Morgan Stewart. BS, Washington and Lee U., 1957, JD, 1960; LLM in Jud. Process, U. Va., 1998. Bar: Va. 1960, U.S. Dist. Ct. (ea. dist.) Va. 1961, U.S. Ct. Appeals (4th cir.) 1964. Asst. city atty. City of Norfolk, 1960-63; ptnr. Pender & Coward, Virginia Beach, Va., 1963-92; vice chmn., gen. counsel Princess Anne Bank, 1986-92; judge U.S. Dist. Ct. (ea. dist.) Va., 1992—. Served with U.S. Army, 1958-59. Episcopalian. Office: US Dist Ct Eastern Dist Va Walter E Hoffman US Courthouse 600 Granby St Ste 183 Norfolk VA 23510-1915 E-mail: henry_morgan@vaed.uscourts.gov.

MORGAN, HUGH JACKSON, JR., bank executive; b. Nashville, Aug. 10, 1928; s. Hugh Jackson and Robert Ray (Porter) M.; m. Ann Moulton Ward, Aug. 28, 1954; children— Ann, Grace, Caroline, Hugh AB, Princeton U., N.J., 1950; LL.B., Vanderbilt U., Nashville, 1956; A.M.P., Harvard Bus. Sch., 1976. Bar: Tenn. 1956. Practice law Miller & Martin, Chattanooga, 1956-60; atty. So. Natural Gas Co., Birmingham, Ala., 1961-65, gen. atty., 1966-70, v.p., 1971-78, pres., 1982-84, chmn. bd., 1984-87; v.p. Sonat Inc., Birmingham, Ala., 1973-78, sr. v.p., 1979-84, exec. v.p., 1984, vice chmn. bd., 1984-87; vice chmn. Nat. Bank of Commerce, Birmingham, Ala., 1987-90, chmn., 1990—2003. Bd. dirs. Atrion Corp. Chmn. Birmingham Airport Authority, 1986-2000; trustee Children's Hosp. Ala., Birmingham, 1974— . Served to lt. (j.g.) USN, 1950-53. Recipient Bennett Douglas Bell Meml. prize Vanderbilt Law Sch., 1956 Mem. Order of the Coif. Clubs: Mountain Brook (pres. 1972), Redstone, (Birmingham); Belle Meade (Nashville); Linville Golf (N.C.). Lodges: Rotary. Home: 3121 Brookwood Rd Birmingham AL 35223-2016 Office: Nat Bank of Commerce 1927 1st Ave N Birmingham AL 35203-4058

MORGAN, JACK M. lawyer; b. Portales, N.Mex., Jan. 15, 1924; s. George Albert and Mary Rosana (Baker) M.; m. Peggy Flynn Cummings, 1947; children: Marilyn, Rebecca, Claudia, Jack. BBA, U. Tex., 1948, LLB, 1950. Bar: N.Mex. 1950. Sole practice law, Farmington, N.Mex., 1956—. Mem. cmty. bd. dirs. Wells Fargo, Farmington, N.Mex. Mem. N.Mex. State Senate, 1973-88. Served with USN, 1942-46. Mem. N.Mex. Bar Assn., S.W. Regional Energy Coun. (past chmn.), Kiwanis, Elks. Republican. Office: PO Box 2151 Farmington NM 87499-2151 E-mail: jmorgansr@fisi.net.

MORGAN, JACOB RICHARD, cardiologist; b. East St. Louis, Ill., Oct. 10, 1925; s. Clyde Adolphus and Jennie Ella Henrietta (Van Ramshorst) M.; m. Alta Eloise Ruthruff, Aug. 1, 1953; children: Elaine, Stephen Richard. BA in Physics, BBA, U. Tex., 1953; MD, U. Tex., Galveston, 1957. Diplomate Am. Bd. Internal Medicine, Am. Bd. Cardiology. Ensign USN, 1944, advanced through grades to capt., 1969; intern U.S. Naval Hosp., Oakland, Calif., 1957-58, chief medicine Taipei, Republic of China, 1962-64; internal medicine staff San Diego, 1964-67, chief cardiology, 1969-73; ret., 1973; dir. medicine R.E. Thomas Gen. Hosp., El Paso, Tex., 1973-75; asst. clin. prof. medicine U. Calif., San Diego, 1970-73; prof. medicine, assoc. chmn. dep. Tex. Tech U. Sch. Medicine, Lubbock and El Paso, 1973-75; pvt. practice National City, Calif., 1976—; dir. cardiology Paradise Valley Hosp., National City, 1976-88. Presenter in field. Contbr. articles on cardiology to sci. jours. Recipient Casmir Funk award, 1972. Fellow ACP, Am. Coll. Cardiology, Am. Coll. Chest Physicians, Am. Heart Assn. (coun. on clin. cardiology). Avocation: golf. Home: 9881 Edgar Pl La Mesa CA 91941-6833 Office: 2409 E Plaza Blvd National City CA 91950-5101 Office Phone: 619-475-4200.

MORGAN, JACQUI, illustrator, painter, educator, writer; b. N.Y.C., Feb. 22, 1939; d. Henry and Emily (Cook) Morganstern; m. Onnig Kalfayan, Apr. 23, 1967 (div. 1972); m. Tomás Gonda, Jan. 1983 (dec. 1988). BFA with honors, Pratt Inst., Bklyn., 1960; MA, CCNY, 1978. Textile designer M. Lowenstein & Sons, N.Y.C., 1961-62, Fruit of the Loom, N.Y.C., 1962; stylist-design dir. Au Courant, Inc., N.Y.C., 1966—; assoc. prof. Pratt Inst., Bklyn., 1977—. Guest lectr. U. Que., Syracuse U., Warsaw TV & Radio, Poland, NYU, Parsons Sch. Design, N.Y.C., Sch. Visual Arts, N.Y.C., Va. Commonwealth U., Fashion Inst. of Tech., others; mem. profl. juries; curator Tomás Gonda retrospective exhbn.; condr. workshops. One-person shows include Soc. Illustrators, N.Y.C., 1977, Art Dirs. Club, N.Y.C., 1978, Gallerie Nowe Miasto, Warsaw, 1978, Gallerie Baumeister, Munich, W.Ger., 1978, Hansen-Feuerman Gallery, N.Y.C., 1980, Krannert Mus./U. Ill., 1998, Art Gallery at Marywood U., Scranton, Pa., 1998; group shows include Mus. Contemporary Crafts, N.Y.C., 1975, Smithsonian Instn., Washington, 1976, Mus. Warsaw, 1976, 78, Mus. Tokyo, 1979, Nat. Watercolor Soc., 1989, Salmagundi Club, 1990, New Eng. Watercolor Soc. Open, 1990, Miss. Watercolor Grand Nat., 1990, Illustration West 29, 1990, Adirondack Nat., 1990, Die Verlassenen Schuhe, 1993, N.Y. restaurant Sch., 1994, Lizan-Tops Gallery, 1996, The Art Club, 2000, Museum at Fashion Inst. Am., 2003; represented in permanent collections: Smithsonian Instn., Mus. Warsaw; author, illustrator: Watercolor for Illustration; produced 3 instrnl. watercolor videos; series of prints pub., 1995; series of plates publ., 1995; co-curator Tomas Gonda Retrospective, Va. Commonwealth U., Rutgers U., Carnegie Mellon U., others in U.S., Museo Del Arte Moderno, Buenos Aires, Ulmer Mus., Ulm, Germany; illustrator Lights Along the Path, 1999, The Healing Garden, 1999; contbr. articles to profl. jours. Recipient more than 200 awards from various orgns. including Soc. Illustrators, Fed. Design Coun., Comm. Arts Mag., Am. Inst. Graphic Arts, N.Y. Art Dirs. Club, Print Design Ann. Mem. Graphic Artists Guild (dir. 1975-79), Soc. Illustrators, Women Artists of the West, Pa. Watercolor Soc. Studio: 176 E 77th St Apt 11C New York NY 10021-1910 Office Phone: 212-772-0627. *Finally, I understand that it's the pleasure of the process and the internal knowledge of improvement that gives the greatest satisfaction.*

MORGAN, JAMES C. computer equipment company executive; b. 1938; BSME, MBA, Cornell U.; DEng (hon.), De Anza Coll., 1994. Corp. staff Textron Inc., 1963—72; sr. ptnr. West Ven Mgmt., San Francisco, 1972—76; pres. Applied Materials, Inc., Santa Clara, Calif., 1976—87, CEO, 1977—2003, chmn. bd., 1987—, vice chmn. pres. export coun., 2003—. Apptd. by Pres. Clinton to Commn. U.S.-Pacific Trade and Investment Policy, 1996; mem. Nat. Adv. Com. Semiconductors, 1988—92; bd. dirs. Cisco Sys.; apptd. to U.S.-Japan Sector Govt. Commn., 2002. Co-author: Cracking the Japanese Market: Strategies for Success in the New Global Economy. Named Internat. Citizen of Yr., World Forum of Silicon Valley, 1995; named to Jr. Achievement Hall of Fame, 1991; recipient Cmty. Svc. award, NCCJ, 1995, Nat. Medal of Tech., Pres. Clinton, 1996. Mem.: Semiconductor Equipment and Materials Internat. (dir. emeritus, past pres.), Pacific Basin Econ. Coun. (chmn.'s circle), Coun. Competitiveness, Nat. Ctr. Asia-Pacific Econ. Cooperation (bd. dirs.), Congrl. Econ. Leadership Inst. (bd. dirs.), World Presidents Orgn., Semiconductor Equipment and Materials Internat./SEMATECH (past bd. dirs.), Am. Electronics Assn. (past bd. dirs.). Office: Applied Materials Inc 3050 Bowers Ave Santa Clara CA 95054-3298

MORGAN, JAMES H. investment company executive; Grad., Vanderbilt U., 1969. With Hornblower & Weeks, Bach Halsey Stuart Shields, Interstate/Johnson Lane, Charlotte, N.C., 1986-89; pres. Morgan Investments, Inc., 1989—90; pres., COO Interstate/Johnson Lane, Charlotte, NC, 1990-94, pres., CEO, 1994-99, Wachovia Securities, Inc., 1999, cons., 2000—01; chmn. Morgan Semones & Assoc., 2001—. Bd. dirs. Krispy Kreme, Winston Salem, NC. Lt. USN. Recipient One-Yr. Investing Derby, Smart Money mag. Office: Morgan Semones Assocs 4201 Congress St #155 Charlotte NC 28209*

MORGAN, JAMES JOHN, environmental engineering educator; b. N.Y.C., June 23, 1932; s. James and Anna (Treanor) M.; m. Jean Laurie McIntosh, June 15, 1957; children— Jenny, Johanna, Eve, Michael, Martha, Sarah BCE, Manhattan Coll., 1954; MSCE, U. Mich., 1956; postgrad., U. Ill., 1956-60; PhD, Harvard U., 1964; ScD (hon.), Manhattan Coll., 1989. Instr. civil engring. U. Ill., Urbana, 1956-60; assoc. prof. U. Fla., Gainesville, 1963-65, Calif. Inst. Tech., Pasadena, 1965-69, prof. environ. engring., 1969-87, Marvin L. Goldberger prof. environ. engrng. sci., 1987—, dean of students, 1972-75, dean grad. studies, 1981-84, v.p. student affairs, 1980-89; exec. officer environ. engrng. sci., 1993-96. Mem. environ. studies bd., NRC, 1974-80; chmn. Acid Deposition Sci. Adv. Com., Calif., 1983-98; chmn. Gordon Rsch. Conf. on Environ. Sci.; Water, 1970. Author: (with Werner Stumm) Aquatic Chemistry, 1970, 2d edit., 1981, 3rd edit. 1996; editor Environ. Sci. and Tech., 1966-74; contbr. articles to profl. jours. Recipient Stockholm Water prize, 1999, Clarke Water prize, 1999. Mem. ASCE (award 1997), Am. Chem. Soc. (award 1980), AAAS, Am. Soc. Limnology and Oceanography (editorial bd. 1977-80), Nat. Acad. Engring., Assn. Environ. Engring. Profs. (award 1981, 83, 94), Am. Water Works Assn. (award 1963), Sigma Xi, Chi Epsilon. Democrat. Roman Catholic. Avocations: tennis; folk music. E-mail: morgan. E-mail: morgan_j@caltech.edu.

MORGAN, JAMES PHILIP, pharmacologist, cardiologist, educator; b. Cin., Jan. 13, 1948; s. James Weldon and Dorcas Adele (Meyer) M.; m. Kathleen Greive, Dec. 22, 1973; children: James Patrick, Jonathan Michael. BS, U. Cin., 1970, PhD, 1974, MD, 1976. Diplomate Am. Bd. Internal Medicine, Am. Bd. Cardiovascular Disease. Fellow in internal medicine Mayo Clinic, Rochester, Minn., 1976-79, fellow in cardiovascular disease, 1979-83; asst. in medicine Beth Israel Hosp., Boston, 1983—. Instr. pharmacology U. Cin., 1975—76; asst. prof. pharmacology, instr. medicine Mayo Clinic, 1981—83; asst. prof. medicine Harvard U., Boston, 1983, assoc. prof., 1988—96, Herman Dana prof. medicine, 1996—; affiliate faculty, dept. pharmacology Harvard Med. Sch., 1986—; chief and prgram dir. cardiovascular divsn. Beth Israel Hosp., 1994—2001, vice chmn. medicine, 2000—. Contbr. articles to profl. jours. Recipient Young Investigators award Am. Coll. Cardiology, 1982, Balfour award Mayo Clinic, 1983, Advanced Cardiac Life Support Spl. Recognition award Mayo Clinic, 1983, Rsch. Career Devel. award NIH, 1985-90. Mem. AMA, Am. Heart Assn., Biophys. Soc. Am. Soc. Pharmacology and Exptl. Therapeutics, Masons. Avocation: philatelics. Office: Beth Israel Deaconess Med Ctr 330 Brookline Ave Boston MA 02215-5400 Business E-Mail: jmorgan@caregroup.harvard.edu., jmorgan@biomc.harvard.edu.

MORGAN, JANE HALE, retired library director; b. Dines, Wyo., May 11, 1926; d. Arthur Hale and Billie (Wood) Hale; m. Joseph Charles Morgan, Aug. 12, 1955; children: Joseph Hale, Jane Frances, Ann Michele. BA, Howard U., 1947; MA, U. Denver, 1954. Staff Detroit Pub. Libr., 1954-87, exec. asst. dir., 1973-75, dep. dir., 1975-78, dir., 1978-87; ret., 1987. Mem. Mich. Libr. Consortium Bd.; exec. bd. Southeastern Mich. Regional Film Libr.; vis. prof. Wayne State U., 1989—. Trustee New Detroit, Inc., Delta Dental Plan of Mich., v.p. Delta Dental Fund, Delta Dental Plan of Ohio; v.p. United Southwestern Mich.; pres. Univ.-Cultural Ctr. Assn.; bd. dirs. Rehab. Inst., YWCA, Met. Affairs Corp., Literacy Vols. Am., Detroit, Mich. Ctr. for the Book, Interfaith Coun.; bd. dirs., v.p. United Comty. Svcs. Met. Detroit; chmn. Detroiters for Adult Reading Excellence; chmn. adv. coun. libr. sci. U. Mich.; mem. adv. coun. libr. sci. U. Mich., mem. adv. coun. libr. sci. Wayne State U.; dir. Met. Detroit Youth Found.; chmn. Mich. LSCA adv. coun.; mem. UWA Literacy Com., Attys. Grievance Com., Women's Commn., Mich. Civil Svc. Rev. Com.; vice-chair Mich. Coun. for Humanities; v.p. Commn. for the Greening of Detroit; adv. com. Headstart; mem. Detroit Women's Com., Detroit Women's Forum, Detroit Exec. Svc. Corps.; sec., treas. Delta Dental Fund, pres., 1999. Recipient Anthony Wayne award Wayne State U., 1981, Summit award Greater Detroit C. of C.; named Detroit Howardite of Year, 1983 Mem. ALA, AAUW, Mich. Libr. Assn., Women's Nat. Book Assn., Assn. Mcpl. Profl. Women, NAACP, LWV, Women's Econ. Club (bd. dirs.), Sorosis Club (v.p.), Alpha Kappa Alpha (pres.). Democrat. Episcopalian.

MORGAN, JOE LEONARD, investment company executive, retired professional baseball player, commentator; b. Bonham, Tex., Sept. 19, 1943; Student, Oakland City (Ind.) Coll.; BA in Phys. Edn., Calif. State U.-Hayward, 1990. Infielder Houston Astros, 1962-71, 2nd baseman, 1980, Cin. Reds, 1972-79, San Francisco Giants, 1981-82, Phila. Phillies, 1983, Oakland A's, 1984; pres. Joe Morgan Investments Inc., Oakland, 1984—; baseball analyst Sta. WLWT-TV, Cin., 1985; college baseball analyst ESPN, 1985-88, analyst ESPN Sunday Night Baseball, 1990—; analyst GiantsVision, 1986-90, ABC-TV, 1988, NBC-TV, 1994—; analyst Oakland Athletics Baseball Sports Channel, 1995—; pres. J.L. Morgan Enterprises Inc. Owner, pres. Joe Morgan Beverage Co., 1988—. Named Most Valuable Player Tex. League, 1964; Rookie of Yr. in Nat. League Sporting News, 1965; Most Valuable Player Nat. League, 1975, 76; Maj. League Player of Year. Sporting News, 1975, 76; named to Nat. League All-Star Team, 1970, 72-79, Nat. League Comeback Player of the Year Sporting News, 1982, Nat. League Player of the Year Sporting News, 1975, Nat. League All Star Team Sporting News, 1972, 73-77; recipient Silver Slugger award Sporting News, 1982; elected to Baseball Hall of Fame, 1990; recipient CableACE award, 1990. player World Series, 1972, 75-76, 83. Office: ESPN Espn Plz Bristol CT 06010-1099 also: J L Morgan Enterprises Inc PO Box 815 Alamo CA 94507-0815

MORGAN, JOHN BRUCE, hospital care consultant; b. Youngstown, Ohio, Oct. 25, 1919; s. John Benjamin and Ida May (Lane) M.; m. Marian Frampton, July 11, 1969; children: John B., Carolyn, Leonard, Suzanne (dec.). BS, Miami U., 1941; MBA, Harvard U., 1946. Field rep. Gen. Motors Acceptance Corp., Youngstown, 1941; pres. Asso. Hosp. Service, Inc., Youngstown, 1947-74, Hosp. Care Corp. (Blue Cross), Cin., 1974-83, cons., 1983—; pres. Health Maintenance Plan, Cin., 1974-83, Health Care Mutual, Cin., 1974-83. Chmn. bd. govs., chmn. exec. com. Blue Cross Assn., Chgo., 1981-82; chmn. bd. Community Life Ins. Co., Worthington, Ohio, 1979-83; mem. joint exec. com. Blue Cross-Blue Shield Assns., mem. joint bds., Chgo.; mem. bus. adv. com. Miami U., Oxford, Ohio. Gen. chmn. United Fund campaign, Youngstown, 1965; pres. Cancer Soc., 1965; chmn. bd. trustees Ch. of the Palms, 1996. Served with AUS, 1942-46. Mem. Am. Hosp. Assn. (Justin Ford Kimball award 1983), Ohio Hosp. Assn., Ohio C. of C. (bd. dirs.), Youngstown Area C. of C. (pres. 1966-67), Delray Beach, Fla. C. of C., Delray Dunes Golf and Country Club (bd. dirs., v.p.), Rotary (bd. dirs. Delray Beach club, pres. 1992, Paul Harris fellow), Masons, Elks, Sigma Alpha Epsilon, Delta Sigma Pi. Mem. United Ch. of Christ. Home: 9 Slash Pine Dr Boynton Beach FL 33436-5524 Office: 1351 William Howard Taft Rd Cincinnati OH 45206-1721

MORGAN, JOHN DAVIS, consultant; b. Newark, Feb. 14, 1921; s. John Davis and Caroline Frommel (Schaller) M.; m. Leta Maude Bretzinger, June 27, 1953; children: John Davis III, Bret Zinger. BS, Pa. State U., 1942, MS, 1947, PhD, 1948, E.M., 1950; grad. extension course, Indsl. Coll. of Armed Forces, Washington, 1953. Asst. for materials and stockpile policies Nat. Security Resources Bd., Washington, 1948-51; dir. materials rev. div. DPA, Washington, 1951-53; materials expert ODM, Washington, 1953-56; mem. staff President's Cabinet Com. on Mineral Policy, 1953-54; cons. bus. and def. problems in metals, minerals and fuels Washington, 1956-71; mem. nat. def. exec. res. for ODM, 1956-58, OCDM, 1958-61, Office Emergency Planning, 1961-71, Emergency Minerals Adminstrn., 1972-95; mem. spl. stockpile advisory com. to ODM, 1957-58; com. on scope and conduct of materials research NAS, 1959-60, then, mem. com. on mineral sci. and tech., 1966-70; mem. Interagy. Adv. Com. on Mining and Mineral Research, 1977-95. Head dept. sci. and math. Daytona Beach C.C., Fla., 1961-71; asst. dir. mineral position analysis U.S. Bur. Mines, Dept. Interior, Washington, 1971-74, acting dir. bur., 1973-74, 77-78, assoc. dir. mineral and materials supply/demand analysis, 1974-79, chief staff officer, 1979-95, Interior Dept. liaison to Com. Internat. Econ. Policy Staff, 1973-77, to Econ. Policy Bd. Staff, 1974-77, to Dept. Def. Materials Steering Group, 1975-78, to FPA-FEMA Stockpile Com.,

1975-88, to Winter Energy Emergency Planning Group of Dept. of Energy, 1977-81; alt. Interior rep. Trade Policy Rev. Group, 1975-81; chmn. minerals rev. com. Non-Fuel Minerals Policy Study, 1978; chmn. materials supply task force NSC Stockpile Study, 1983-87; liaison to Dept. Def. Stockpile Com., 1988-95; mem. Def. Logistics Agy. Market Impact Com., 1988-95; mem. Def. Dept. Adv. Com. Operation and Modernization of Stockpile, 1993-95; U.S. rep. UN Sci. Conf. on Resources, 1949; lectr. numerous univs. including Nat. Def. U., War Coll., Indsl. Coll., Def. Intelligence Coll., Army War Coll., 1949—; hon. prof. Indsl. Coll., 1983—; invited spkr. nat. meetings sci. and engring. socs., 1949—. Author: Domestic Mining Industry of the U.S. in World War II, 1949; corr.: Mining Ann. Rev., London, 1958-95; contbr. articles to profl. jours. Served from 2d lt. to maj. Corps Engrs. AUS, 1942-46. Decorated Bronze Star; recipient Distinguished Service gold medal Interior Dept., 1976; named Meritorious Exec. Sr. Exec. Service, 1983 Fellow Soc. Am. Mil. Engrs.; mem. Sci. Research Soc. Am., Soc. Mining Engrs. (Disting. mem.), AIME (nat. Krumb lectr. 1973, Legion of Honor 1989), Sigma Xi, Tau Beta Pi, Sigma Tau, Pi Mu Epsilon, Phi Lambda Upsilon, Phi Kappa Phi, Phi Eta Sigma, Sigma Gamma Epsilon. Clubs: Cosmos (Washington). Home: 5013 Worthington Dr Bethesda MD 20816-2748

MORGAN, JOHN DERALD, electrical engineer; b. Hays, Kans., Mar. 15, 1939; s. John Baber and Avis Ruth (Wolf) M.; m. Elizabeth June McKneely, June 23, 1962; children: Laura Elizabeth, Kimberly Ann, Rebecca Ruth, John Derald. BSEE, La. Tech. U., 1962; MS, U. Mo., Rolla, 1965, Degree in Elec. Engring. (hon.), 1987; PhD, Ariz. State U., 1968. Registered profl. engr., forensic engr., Mo., N.Mex. Elec. engr. Tex. Eastman div. Eastman Kodak Co., 1962-63; instr. U. Mo., Rolla, 1963-65, Ariz. State U., 1965-68; asso. prof. elec. engring. U. Mo., Rolla, 1968-72, Alcoa Found. prof. elec. engring., 1972-75, chmn. elec. engring., 1978-85, assoc. dir. Ctr. Internat. Programs, 1970-78, Emerson Electric prof., 1975-85; dean engring. N.Mex. State U., 1985-99; v.p. univ. advancement U. Ala. in Huntsville, 1999—; exec. sec. U. Ala. Huntsville Found., 1999—. Nat. adv. com. Engring. Exploring; cons. to industry. Author: Power Apparatus Testing Techniques, 1969, Computer Monitoring and Control of Electric Utility Systems, 1972, Control and Distribution of Megawatts Through Man-Machine Interaction, 1973, Electromechanical and Electromagnetic Machines and Devices, 1986, Wolf Brethren, 2003; also articles. Pres. bd. trustees First United Meth. Ch., Rolla, 1971-73, pres. adminstrv. bd., 1978-79; v.p., mem. bd. adminstrn. People to People, 1976, bd. dirs., cubmaster Ozarks dist. Boy Scouts Am., 1960-79, asst. dist. commr., 1971-73, cubmaster Yucca coun., 1986-90, coun. commr., 1989-90, asst. scout master, 1990-99, dist. com. Sunshine Dist., dist. chmn. Meramec dist., 1978-80, engring. exploring nat. com.; chmn. Creek Dist., 2000—, bd. mem., Greater Ala. Coun. No. Svc. Dist., 2000—; bd. dirs. Partners of the Americas. Recipient Scouters Key award and Scouter Tng. award Ozarks coun., Boy Scouts Am., 1971, Dist. award of merit 1977, Silver Beaver award, 1982, Cub Leader award, Webelos Leader award, Dist. Com. Key award, James West Soc. award, Sunshine Dist. Yucca coun.; T.H. Harris scholar, 1959-61; John H. Horton scholar, 1961-62. Fellow: IEEE (chmn. internat. practices subcom. 1972—79, chmn. ednl. resources subcom. 1973—78, chmn. 1979—85, sec. PSE com., vice chmn., award of Merit St. Louis sect., Educators award St. Louis sect., honor award St. Louis sect., Centennial award 1984), Nat. Acad. Forensic Engrs.; mem.: PSI, ASTM, Am. Soc. Engring. Edn. (chair bylaws com. 1999—2001), N.Mex. Soc. Profl. Engrs. (N.Mex. Engr. of Yr. 1993), NSPE (bd. govs., nat. dir., vice chmn., S.W. chmn. Profl. Engrs. in Edn. v.p., mem. Steinman Coun.), SAR (Tenn. Valley chpt. sec.), Rotary Internat. (Paul Harris fellow 1997), Phi Kappa Phi, Omicron Delta Kappa, Eta Kappa Nu, Tau Beta Pi, Sigma Xi, Epsilon Gamma (grand master, grand procurator), Kappa Sigma (faculty and alumni advisor). Home: 113 Lansdowne Dr Madison AL 35758-7613 Office: U Ala in Huntsville Alumni House 102 Huntsville AL 35899-0001

MORGAN, JOHN K. chemicals executive, electronics executive; BS in Engring. Tech., Purdue U.; MBA, Ind. U. From mgmt. to pres., chief devel. officer Acuity Brands Inc., Atlanta, 1979—2004, pres., 2004—, chief devel. officer, 2004—. Office: Acuity Brands Inc 1170 Peachtree St NE Atlanta GA 30309*

MORGAN, JOYCE ELIZABETH, retired elementary school educator; b. Pitts., June 8, 1940; d. Richard Gailbreth and Pauline (Wasil) Cunningham; m. John R. Morgan; children: Janet Lynn, Jennifer Ann, Joy Ellyn, Jamie Elizabeth. BS, Calif. State U., 1962. Elem. tchr. Chartiers Valley Sch. Dist., Pitts., 1971—99; ret., 1999. Mem. Tchrs. & Adminstrs. for Better Schs. Com., 1993-94. Facilitator Our Lady of Grace Bible Sch., Scott Twp., 1975-78, CCD tchr., 1978-82, mem. choir, 1982-85, mem. folk group choir, 1990-93, tchr. children's liturgy, 1993-94; mem. Eucharistic Ministry, 1994-2004. Republican. Roman Catholic. Avocations: reading, landcaping, plants, travel, golf.

MORGAN, KATHRYN LAWSON, retired historian, educator; 1 child, Susan Morgan Crooks MA, Howard U., 1952, U. Pa., 1967, PhD, 1970. Asst. prof. U. Del., Newark, 1970-71; lectr. Swarthmore Coll., Pa., spring 1970, prof. history and folklore, 1972—95, Sara Lawrence Lightfoot Prof. History emerita, 1995. Vis. assoc. prof. Bryn Mawr Coll., 1972-75, Haverford Coll., 1972-74, U. Calif.-Berkeley, winter 1975; cons. Research for Better Schs., Phila., 1968-69, Black History Mus., Phila., 1966-76, Smithsonian Instn., 1974-76, Ednl. Film Service, 1977 Author: Children of Strangers; Stories of a Black Family, 1980, transl. Brazilian-Portuguese, 2002, Books Across the Seas, Selected for Youth, 1981; contbr. articles to profl. jours., mags. Grantee Smithsonian Instn.-Am. Philos. Soc., 1983; Danforth Found. fellow, 1968—70, sr. rsch. scholar, Swarthmore Coll., 2003. Avocations: traveling; storytelling; theatre; music. Office: Swarthmore Coll Dept Hist Swarthmore PA 19081

MORGAN, KERMIT JOHNSON, lawyer; b. Henderson, Iowa, Feb. 13, 1914; s. Samuel Jr. and Jennie Amelia Morgan; m. Georgina R. Morgan, Oct. 12, 1940 (dec. 1958); children: Georgina Morgan Street, Wilson S.; m. Ortrud Impol, Dec. 9, 1960. BA, U. Iowa, 1935; JD, U. So. Calif., 1937. Bar: Calif. 1939. Pvt. practice, LA, 1940—45, 1971—80, 1991—, Santa Monica, Calif., 1991—; ptnr. McBain & Morgan, L.A., 1945-65, Kermit Morgan, 1971—80, McBain, Morgan & Roper, L.A., 1965—71, Morgan & Armbrister, L.A., 1980-91. Mem. ABA, Am. Bd. Trial Advs. (diplomate, nat. pres. 1973, pres. L.A. 1972), Assn. Def. Trial Attys. (bd. dirs. 1982-85), Internat. Assn. Ins. Counsel, Hon. Order of Blue Goose, Calif. State Bar, Assn. So. Calif. Def. Counsel (bd. dirs. 1966-67), L.A. Bar Assn. Republican. Congregationalist. Avocation: golf. Home: 2108 Stradella Rd Los Angeles CA 90077-2325 Office: 3420 Ocean Pk Blvd Santa Monica CA 90405 Office Phone: 310-314-4764.

MORGAN, LARRY RONALD, minister; b. Springhill, La., Mar. 12, 1936; s. Woodrow Wilson Morgan and Alma Elizabeth (Dunn) Burch; m. Elizabeth Dianne Baker, May 24, 1958; children: Elizabeth Denise Morgan Davis, Dennis Kevin. ADiv, Bapt. Missionary Assn. Theol. Sem., Jacksonville, Tex., 1990. Ordained to ministry Bapt. Ch., 1971. Clk., carrier U.S. P.O., Springhill, La., 1956-71; assoc. pastor Webb Chapel Bapt. Ch., Dallas, 1971-72, pastor, 1972-99, First Bapt. Ch., Springhill, La., 1999—. Clk., trustee Bapt. Missionary Assn. Sem., Jacksonville, 1983-86; chmn. bd. trustees Bapt. Progress, Dallas, 1984-87. Pres. PTA Browning Elem. Sch., Springhill, 1969-70. With USAR, 1959-66. Mem. Bapt. Missionary Assn. Am. (v.p. hdqrs. Little Rock 1985-86, pres. 1986-88, v.p. Am. 1996-98, pres. 1998-2000), Dallas County Bapt. Assn. (moderator 1982-84), Bapt. Missionary Assn. of La. (moderator 2000—)., Springhill Baptist Assn. (moderator 2001-). Baptist. Home: 611 Butler St Springhill LA 71075-2519 Office Phone: 318-539-2610. Personal E-mail: ronaldmorgan1@juno.com.

MORGAN, LEON ALFORD, retired utility executive; b. Washington, Dec. 29, 1934; s. Albert Lewis and Alice Viets (Alford) M.; children: David Richard, Sherry Alice; m. Jacqueline Jamieson, Feb. 14, 1993. BSEE, Worcester (Mass.) Poly. Inst., 1957. Registered profl. engr., Conn. With United Illuminating Co., New Haven, 1957-94, gen. ops. mgr., then v.p. ops., 1973-76, exec. v.p., 1976-83, sr. v.p. fin., 1984-94. Republican. Episcopalian. Home: 43 Forest Brook Rd Guilford CT 06437-2245 E-mail: lamwpi57@comcast.net.

MORGAN, LINDA GAIL, producer; b. Tallahassee, May 14, 1952; d. Thomas Mitchell Morgan Sr. and Helen Frances (Rives) Stokes. BS, Fla. State U., 1974. Prodn. mgr. Valley Forge Ballet-5th World Peace Youth Culture Festival, Honolulu, 1985, Salute to Lady Liberty, Madison Square Gardens, 1986, U.S. Constn. 200 Yr. Anniversary Parade, Phila., 1986-89, Columbus Day Parade, N.Y.C., 1988, Gift of the White Bird Parade-Landmark Entertainment, Oita, Japan, 1990-91, 1996 Olympic Opening and Closing Ceremonies-Centenniel Events, Inc., Olympic Stadium, Atlanta, 1996, Super Bowl XXXI Half Time Show, New Orleans, 1997, N.Y. Jets Halftime Show, Meadowlands Stadium, N.J., 1997; prodn. state mgr. Walt Disney Bus. Prodns., 1998; coordinating prodr. (musical) This Is America, The New World, Freedom Music, Santa Monica, Calif., 1989, California Traditional Music Festival, Human Rights Lectr. Series, Soka U. Am., L.A., 1992-95, The Genius and the Great, L.A., 1993, Every Child Deserves a Chance, L.A., 1994, A Tribute to Burt Reynolds, L.A., 1994, Celebrate the Garnet and Gold IV Honoring Charles Nelson Reilly, L.A., 1995, Leisure Quest Internat./Entertainment Devel. Group, Burbank, Calif., 1997; artist agt., co. gen. mgr. Zoli Mgmt., Inc., N.Y.C., 1986-89; orch. prodn. mgr. All Am. Gen. Meeting, Spectrum, Phila., 1987; asst. prodn. mgr. 8th World Peace Culture Festival, Fukuoka, Japan, 1987, This Is America, Madison Square Gardens, 1988, 1991 Olympic Festival Opening Ceremonies Radio City Spl. Events, Dodger Stadium, L.A., 1991; prodn. staff Inauguration Mayor of Atlanta, Civic Ctr., Atlanta, 1998; event mgr. Coke on Ice World of Coca Cola, Atlanta, 1997-98, Disney Events Productions, 1998-2003; prodr. Anheuser-Bush Creative Svcs., 2001-. Mem. Soka Gakkai Internat. (arts divsn. culture dept. 1995-99), Fla. State U. So. Calif. Alumni Assn. (bd. dirs. 1991-95, Garnet/Gold award 1995), Internat. Spl. Event Soc., Alpha Chi Omega. Democrat. Buddhist. Avocations: arts, needlepoint, antiques, piano, gardening.

MORGAN, LINDA JOAN, former federal agency administrator; b. Chester County, Pa., May 19, 1952; m. Michael E. Karam; 1 child, Meredith Lyn. AB in Hispanic Studies, Vassar Coll., 1973; JD, Georgetown U., 1976; postgrad., Harvard U., 1991. Assoc. Welch & Morgan, Washington, 1976-78; staff counsel U.S. Senate Com. on Commerce, Sci. and Transp., 1978-86, gen. counsel, 1987-94; mem. ICC, Washington, 1994-96, chmn., 1995-96, Surface Transp. Bd., Washington, 1996—2003. Mem. D.C. Bar Assn., Bar of Supreme Ct. of U.S., Women's Bar Assn., Women's Transp. Seminar. Democrat.

MORGAN, LUCY WARE, journalist; b. Memphis, Oct. 11, 1940; d. Thomas Allin and Lucile (Sanders) Keen; m. Alton F. Ware, June 26, 1958 (div. Sept. 1967); children: Mary Kathleen, Andrew Allin; m. Richard Alan Morgan, Aug. 9, 1968; children: Lynn Elwell, Kent Morgan AA, Pasco Hernando C.C., New Port Richey, Fla., 1975; student, U. South Fla., 1976-80. Reporter Ocala Star Banner, Fla., 1965-68, St. Petersburg Times, Fla., 1967-86, capitol bur. chief, 1986—. Assoc. editor and bd. dirs. Times Pub. Co. Recipient Paul Hansel award Fla. Soc. Newspaper Editors, 1981, First in Pub. Service award Fla. Soc. Newspaper Editors, 1982, First Place award in pub. service Fla. Press Club, 1982, Pulitzer award for investigative reporting Columbia U., 1985, First Place award in investigative reporting Sigma Delta Chi, 1985; named to Kappa Tau Alpha Hall of Fame, 1992. Home: 7030 Spencer Dr Tallahassee FL 32312-3548 Office: St Petersburg Times 336 E College Ave Tallahassee FL 32301-1551

MORGAN, LYNN, sports association executive; BS in Mktg., U. Ga. Dir. sales devel., Olympic mktg. mgr. Cox Enterprises, Inc., Atlanta, 1991—2001; pres., CEO Women's United Soccer Assn., N.Y.C., 2001—03. Bd. dirs. Atlanta Sports Coun., Atlanta Thunder; gen. mgr. Atlanta Beat Women's United Soccer Assn. Bd. dirs. Salvation Army, Atlanta Ad Club, Atlanta Arts and Bus. Coun.

MORGAN, M. JANE, computer systems consultant; b. Washington, July 21, 1945; d. Edmond John and Roberta (Livingstone) Dolphin (dec.); 1 child, Sheena Anne. Student, U. Md., 1963-66, Montgomery Coll., 1966-70; BA in Applied Behavioral Sci with honors, Nat.-Louis Univ., 1987, MS in Mgmt., 1991; postgrad. diploma in info. resource mgmt, Am. U., 1995; cert., USDA Grad. Sch., 2000; postgrad. diploma, State U. Calif., Northridge, 2002. With HUD, Washington, 1965-84, computer specialist, 1978-84; pres., CEO Systems and Mgmt. Assocs., 1983-91; dir. systems engring. Advanced Tech. Systems, Inc., Vienna, Va., 1984-86, sr. cons., 1989; chief tech. staff Tech. and Mgmt. Svcs., Inc., 1986-89; sr. computer scientist Integrated Systems divsn. Computer Scis. Corp., 1989-90; computer systems specialist gen. svcs. adminstrn. U.S. Govt., 1991—2001; divsn. dir. U.S. Gen. Svcs. Adminstrn., 2001—. Mgmt. cons. Author: Rapid Identification of Critical Staff, 1991. Bd. dirs. PL Active. Mem. Federally Employed Women (life, nat. exec. v.p. 1998-2000), Order Eastern Star. Episcopalian.

MORGAN, MARABEL, writer; b. Crestline, Ohio, June 25, 1937; d. Howard and Delsa (Smith) Hawk; m. Charles O. Morgan, Jr., June 25, 1964; children— Laura Lynn, Michelle Rene. Ed., Ohio State U. Pres. Total Woman, Inc., Miami, Fla., 1970—. Pub. speaker. Author: The Total Woman, 1973, Total Joy, 1976, The Total Woman Cookbook, 1980, The Electric Woman, 1985, The Home on the Range Cookbook, 1995. Office: c/o Total Woman Inc 1300 NW 167th St Ste 3 Miami FL 33169-5738

MORGAN, MARIANNE, corporate professional; b. Muncie, Ind., Oct. 13, 1940; d. Clarence Wilson and Mary Estle (Shafer) M. BA, Calif. State U., Long Beach, 1962; MS, U. So. Calif., 1968. Lic. real estate salesperson, Fla. Lab. technician Ball Meml. Hosp. Pathology Lab, Muncie, 1956-61; sr. libr. asst. Anaheim (Calif.) Pub. Libr., 1963-68; coll. libr. Orange Coast Coll., Costa Mesa, Calif., 1968-73; exec. v.p. Brady Products, Inc., Clearwater, Fla., 1973—. Bd. dirs. Brady Products, Inc., Clearwater, Suncoast Fluid Power, Inc., Clearwater. Fiction book reviewer, Libr. Jour., 1969-73; photography pub. in Irvine mag., 1973. Named Alice Miriam Kitselman Scholar, Kitselman Estate, Muncie, 1958. Mem. Nat. Water Well Assn., Boat Owners of the U.S., U.S. Tennis Assn., Sea Ray Boat Owners Club, RVing Women, Carefree Club, Sapphire Lakes Country Club, The Cliffs Country Club. Republican. Avocations: boating, tennis, photography, travel, raising akc bulldogs.

MORGAN, MARILYN, federal judge; b. 1947; m. James R. Grube; 1 child, Terrence M. Adamson. BA, Emory U., 1969, JD, 1976. Bar: Ga. 1976, Calif. 1977. Ptnr. Morgan & Towery, San Jose, Calif., 1979-88; bankruptcy judge U.S. Bankruptcy Ct. (no. dist.) Calif., 1988—. Mem. bankruptcy adv. com. U.S. Dist. Ct., 1984-88; law rep. 9th Cir. Jud. Conf., 1987-88. Mem. adv. bd. Downtown YMCA, 1984-88; dir. The Women's Fund, 1987-88; bd. dirs. Consumer Credit Counselors of San Francisco, 1999—, Cathedral Found., 2001—. Mem. Santa Clara County Bar Assn. (chmn. debtor and creditor and insolvency com. 1979, 81, treas. 1982, pres. 1985-86), Santa Clara County Bar Assn. Law Found. (trustee 1982, 86-88, pres. 1985, law related edn. trustee 1986-88), Nat. Assn. Bankruptcy Trustees (founding mem., v.p., sec. 1981-88), Rotary Club San Jose (bd. dirs. 1992-95), Nat. Assn. Bankruptcy Trustees (founder). Office: US Bankruptcy Ct 280 S 1st St Rm 3035 San Jose CA 95113-3010

MORGAN, MARY E. publishing executive; married; 1 child. B, SUNY Binghamton. Adv. dir. Fitness Mag., 1992—94; assoc. group pub. Parents and Child Mag., 1994—95; assoc. pub. Ladies Home Journal, 1995—97; v.p., pub. Health Mag., 1997—2003, Redbook, 2003—. Mem. editl. bd. Pharmaceutical Executive Magazine. Mem.: Nat. Assn. of Chain Drug Stores, Cosmetic Exec. Women (philanthropy com.), Advt. Women of N.Y. (mem. bd. dirs.), Advt. Club of N.Y. Office: Redbooks 224 West 57th St New York NY 10019

MORGAN, MARY LOU, retired education educator, volunteer; b. Chgo., Mar. 5, 1938; d. William Nicholas and Esther Lucille (Galbraith) Wanmer; m. James Edward Morgan, May 30, 1963. BA in Bus. Edn. and Econs., Wichita State U., 1971, MEd in Student Pers. and Guidance, 1974; postgrad., Kans. State U., 1986. Cert. bus. tchr., Kans. Reservationist Braniff, Wichita, Kans., 1961-62; stenographer, fin. analyst, clk.-typist Boeing Co., Wichita, 1962-68, tng., pers. and records positions, 1979-93; pers. cons. Rita Pers. Svc., Wichita, 1974-75; adminstrv. aide, manpower specialist, job developer City of Wichita, 1975-76; account exec., employment counselor Mgmt. Recruiters, 1976-77; pers. mgr., patient cons. Women's Clinic, 1977; vocat. rehab. counselor State of Kans., Parsons, 1977-79; pvt. detective Investigation Svcs., Wichita, 1981-84; instr. career devel. Wichita State U., 1988-90. Paralegal asst. Turner & Hensley, Wichita, 1975. Coord. funding Women's Crisis Ctr., Wichita, 1975; docent Carver Mus., Hoover Mus.; vice chmn. Hist. Preservation Commn.; founder, coord. Ann. Women's Chautauqua; Precinct committeewoman Wichita Dem. Com., 1992—94; pres. Jasper County-Newton County Dems., 1998; mem. Grover Beach Dems., 2001—, sub., co-chair, chmn. precinct walkers voter registration, 2004; bd. dirs. City of Wichita, Wichita Commn. on Status of Women, 1988—91. Mem.: ACLU, NOW (founder, 1st pres., v.p. program chmn. Wichita chpt. 1969—93, asst. state coord. polit. action com. Wichita chpt. 1993—95, at-large state bd. Joplin com. 1994—95, 1997—98, 1999—2000, at-large state mem. Grover Beach chpt. 2001—), AARP, AAUW (bd. dirs. edn., equity, women's issues Joplin br. 1999—2000, Grover Beach br. 2001—, pres. Grover Beach br. 2002—04, mem. state pub. policy com. 2003—04, br. pub. policy chair 2004—), LWV (v.p. issues study Joplin area league 1998—2000, Grover Beach league 2001—, off board dir. 2002—03, bd. dirs. 2003—04), So. County Hist. Soc. Avocations: waterskiing, boating, collecting victorian clothing, travel.

MORGAN, MARY LOUISE FITZSIMMONS, fund raising executive, lobbyist; b. N.Y.C., July 22, 1946; d. Robert John and Mary Louise (Gordon) Fitzsimmons; m. David William Morgan, Aug. 7, 1971; children: Mallory Siobhan, David William. BA, Marquette U., 1964; MA, Catholic U., Wash., 1966. Asst. prof. Monmouth U., West Long Branch, N.J., 1966-69; campaign dir. United Way, N.Y.C., 1969-80; pres. Morgan Communications, N.Y.C., 1980-82; capital campaign dir. YMCA of Greater N.Y., 1982-85; dir. devel. N.Y. Med. Coll., Valhalla, 1985-88; counsel Challenger Ctr., Va., 1988-89; v.p. Ctr. Molecular Medicine & Immunology, Newark, 1989-92, Garden State Cancer Ctr., Newark, 1989-92; chief devel. and pub. affairs officer Mental Health Assn., White Plains, N.Y., 1993-95; dir. external affairs St. Vincents Svcs., 1996—. Adj. prof. Iona Coll., New Rochelle, N.Y., 1994-95; dir. Meth Ch. Home for Aged, Riverdale, N.Y., Casita Maria Inc., N.Y.C., 1975-95; pres., founding dir. Achievement Rewards for Coll. Scientists Inc., 1978-80. Sec. Darien (Conn.) Dem. Town Com., 1984—, vice chmn. Darien nominating com. 1986—. Recipient 50th Anniversary award Casita Maria Inc., N.Y.C., 1984, Iris award Bus. Communicators of Am., 1991, Nat. Depression Awareness Campaign award NMHA, 1994, Am. Graphic Design award, 2002. Mem. Nat. Soc. Fund Raising Execs., Nat. Soc. Hosp. Adminstrn., Spring Lake (N.J.) Bath and Tennis Club. Democrat. Roman Catholic. Avocations: golf, gardening, tennis. Office: 66 Boerum Pl Brooklyn NY 11201-5705 E-mail: MaryL.Morgan@svs.org.

MORGAN, MATTHEW R. journalist; b. Willingboro, NJ, Apr. 23, 1975; s. C. Goodwyn and Janice R. Morgan. BA, Ariz. State U., 1997. Assoc. editor West Valley View, Litchfield Pk., Ariz., 1998—2000; mng. editor Virgo Pub. Inc., Phoenix, 2000—; owner Greek Review publication. Recipient Best Sports Beat Coverage award, Ariz. Newspaper Assn., 1999.

MORGAN, MICHAEL B. retired music educator; b. Muncie, Ind., Oct. 24, 1948; s. Betty J. Morgan; children: Stacie Lynn Carpenter, Tricia Michelle. BS in Music Performance, Excelsior Coll., Albany, N.Y., 1999; MEd, Northwestern State U., La., 2002. Cert. tchr. La., 2002. Sr. instr. Armed Forces Sch. of Music, Norfolk, Va., 1980—85; NATO band leader Supreme Hdqs. Allied Powers Europe, Mons, Belgium, 1985—90. SACS facilitator La. State Bd. of Edn., Baton Rouge, 2002—. Composer: (military march) Shape International March, numerous jazz and combo arrangements. 1st sgt. U.S. Army, 1966—2001. Mem.: Dist. V Band Dirs. Assn. (assoc.; pres. 2002—04), La. Band Dirs. Assn. (assoc.), La. Music Educators Assn. (assoc.; asst. state jazz chmn. 2002—03), MENC (assoc.). Achievements include organized first NATO international band for the Supreme Command of Europe; development of rehearsal techniques manual for the Military School of Music.

MORGAN, MICHAEL BREWSTER, publishing company executive; b. L.A., Dec. 30, 1953; s. Brewster Bowen and Eleanor (Boysen) M.; m. Debra Hunter, July 20, 1986. BA, Conn. Coll., 1975. Coll. sales rep. Addison Wesley Pub. Co., Chapel Hill, NC, 1977—81, sponsoring editor Reading, Mass., 1981—84; chief exec. officer Morgan Kaufmann Pubs., San Francisco, 1984—2002; CEO, Morgan and Claypool Pubs., San Rafael, Calif., 2002—. Mem. Am. Assn. for Artificial Intelligence, Assn. for Computing Machinery. Office: Morgan and Claypool Pubs 40 Oak View Dr San Rafael CA 94903

MORGAN, MICHAEL VINCENT, lawyer; b. July 31, 1947; s. Stanley William and Alice (Michalski) M.; m. Susan Wanda Staub, Aug. 21, 1970; children: Jason, Allison. BA, U. Detroit, 1969, JD, 1972. Bar: Mich. 1972, U.S. Dist. Ct. (ea. dist.) Mich. 1972. Chmn. Lic. Appeal Bd. Mich. Dept. State, Detroit, 1972-73; pvt. practice Detroit, 1973-75, Troy, Mich., 1975—. Lectr. in field. Editor: Michigan Drunk Driving Law & Practice, 1986, 3rd edit. 1999; contbr. articles to profl. publs. Bd. dirs. U. Detroit Nat. Alumni Bd., 1974-77. Recipient Athletic Dirs. award U. Detroit, 1983. Mem. Mich. Bar Assn., U. Detroit Law Alumni Assn. (bd. dirs. 1996—), Titan Club (bd. dirs. 1982-86), Advocates Club (Detroit). Roman Catholic. Office: 3155 W Big Beaver Rd Ste 100 Troy MI 48084-3006

MORGAN, NEIL, writer, newspaper editor, lecturer, columnist; b. Smithfield, N.C., Feb. 27, 1924; s. Samuel Lewis and Isabelle (Robeson) M.; m. Caryl Lawrence, 1945 (div. 1954); m. Katharine Starkey, 1955 (div. 1962); m. Judith Blakely, 1964; 1 child, Jill. AB, Wake Forest Coll., 1943. Columnist San Diego Daily Jour., 1946-50; columnist San Diego Evening Tribune, 1950-92, assoc. editor, 1977-81, editor, 1981-92; assoc. editor, sr. columnist San Diego Union-Tribune, 1992—. Syndicated columnist Morgan Jour., Copley News Service, 1958—; lectr.; cons. on Calif. affairs Bank of Am., Sunset mag. Author: My San Diego, 1951, It Began With a Roar, 1953, Know Your Doctor, 1954, Crosstown, 1955, My San Diego 1960, 1959, Westward Tilt, 1963, Neil Morgan's San Diego, 1964, The Pacific States, 1967, The California Syndrome, 1969, (with Robert Witty) Marines of Margarita, 1970, The Unconventional City, 1972, (with Tom Blair) Yesterday's San Diego, 1976, This Great Land, 1983, Above San Diego, 1990, (with Judith Morgan) Dr. Seuss & Mr. Geisel, 1995, (with Judith Morgan) Roger: The Biography of Roger Revelle, 1997; (forewards) Under Cover for Wells Fargo, 1999, San Diego's Navy, 2001; conbr. non-fiction articles to Nat. Geog., Esquire, Redbook, Reader's Digest, Holiday, Harper's, Travel and Leisure, Ency. Brit. Lt. USNR, 1943-46. Recipient Ernie Pyle Meml. award, 1957, Bill Corum Meml. award, 1961, Disting. Svc. citation Wake Forest U., 1966, Grand award for travel writing Pacific Area Travel Assn., 1972, 78, Fourth Estate award San Diego State U., 1988, The Morgan award Leadership Edn. Awareness Devel. San Diego, 1993; co-recipient Ellen and Roger Revelle award, 1986; named Outstanding Young Man of Yr. San Diego, 1959, 1st place news commentary, Calif. News Pub. Assn., 1993, Harold Keen award, 1996, Chancellors medal, U. Calif., San Diego, 2000; named Mr. San Diego, Rotary, 1999. Mem. Authors Guild, Soc. Profl. Journalists (award for best column 1999), Soc. of Am. Travel Writers, Bohemian Club, Phi Beta Kappa. Home: 7930 Prospect Pl La Jolla CA 92037-3721 Office: PO Box 120191 San Diego CA 92112-4106 E-mail: neil.morgan@uniontrib.com.

MORGAN, PATRICIA, financial consultant, former Republican party chairman; Chairwoman Rep. Party, East Providence, RI Rep. State Ctrl. Com., West Warwick, 2001—03; fin. cons. Smith Barney, Providence, 2003. Office: GOP RI 643 East Ave Warwick RI 02886

MORGAN, PAUL WILLIAM, engineer, researcher; b. Highland Park, Mich., June 29, 1952; s. Kenneth Hayden and Margaret Anne (Rourk) M.; children: Paul James, Thomas Edward, Anna Florence. BSEE, Wayne State U., 1975. Design engr. Marposs Gauges, Madison Heights, 1977-79, Lebow Assocs., Troy, Mich., 1979-80, quality mgr., 1980-81; project engr. Eaton-Lebow, Troy, 1981-83, sr. project engr., 1983-92; chief engr. Key Transducers, Sterling Heights, Mich., 1992-98; pres. Engineered Measurement Syss., Redford, Mich., 1998—. Inventor and patentee in field. Achievements include inventions, patents, and the manufacturing of unique, high precision, torque-

meters for NASA, Nat. Lab., aerospace and automotive applications. Home: 5976 Dwight Ave Waterford MI 48327-1329 Fax: 313-255-0487. Office Phone: 313-255-2200. E-mail: EMSTorque@aol.com.

MORGAN, RAYMOND F. plastic surgeon; b. Pitts., Apr. 24, 1948; s. Edwin J. and Alberta (Hirt) M.; m. Sue Ann; children: Ryan Frederic, Alexander Evan, Elizabeth Anne. BS, U. Pitts., 1969, MEd, DMD, U. Pitts., 1972; MD, W.Va. U., 1976. Diplomate Am. Bd. Plastic Surgery, Am. Bd. Hand Surgery. Intern Johns Hopkins U. Hosp., Balt., 1976-77, resident surgery, 1977-80, resident plastic surgery, 1980-82; resident hand surgery Union Meml. Hosp., Balt.; staff U. Va. Health Scis. Ctr., Charlottesville, M.T. Edgerton prof., chmn. dept. plastic surgery, 1988—. Mem. ACS, Soc. Univ. Surgeons, So. Surg. Assn., Am. Soc. for Surgery of the Hand, Am. Assn. Plastic Surgeons. Office: U of Va Dept Of Plastic Surgery Charlottesville VA 22908-0001

MORGAN, RAYMOND FRANKLIN, education educator; b. Crisfield, Md., Dec. 19, 1943; s. Raymond Franklin and Anna Marie (Evans) M.; m. Susan Morgan, July 1, 1978; children: Jonathan, Christopher. BA, Randoph-Macon Coll., 1966; MEd, U. Va., 1970, EdD, 1974. Tchr. English and reading Chesterfield Pub. Schs.; English tchr. York Acad. and Miller Sch. of Albemarle; asst./assoc. prof. grad. program dir. in reading, then prof. edn. Old Dominion U., Norfolk, Va., 1974—. Presenter, spkr., cons. in field. Co-author: Reading for Success, 1996, Reading to Learn in the Content Areas, 5th edit., 2003, others; co-author: The Psychology of Human Development, 2d edit., 1985, 3rd edit., 1993, Critical Reading-Thinking Skills for the College Student, 1985, 2d edit., 1986; mem. editl. bd. Reading in Va., Reading Improvement; contbr. over 60 articles to profl. jours. Recipient Tonelson award Darden Coll. Edn., over 3.7 million dollars in grants for svc. and rsch. Mem.: Nat. Soc. for the Study of Edn., Coll. Reading Assn., Assn. Lit. Scholars Critics, Internat. Reading Assn., Phi Kappa Phi. Avocation: golf. Home: 5298 W Valleyside Ct Virginia Beach VA 23464-2606 Personal E-mail: rmorgvbva@aol.com. Business E-Mail: rmorgan@odu.edu.

MORGAN, RAYMOND VICTOR, JR., university administrator, mathematics educator; b. Brownwood, Tex., May 10, 1942; s. Raymond Victor and Lovey Lucile (Tate) M.; m. Mary Jane Folks, Aug. 13, 1967; children: Jason Wesley (dec.), Jeremy Victor. BA, Howard Payne U., 1965; MA, Vanderbilt U., 1966; PhD, U. Mo., 1969. Asst. prof. So. Meth. U., Dallas, 1969-75; assoc. prof. Sul Ross State U., Alpine, Tex., 1975-82, math. dept. chmn., 1976-85, prof., 1982—, dean of scis., 1979-86, exec. asst. pres., 1985-90, pres., 1990—96. Bd. dirs. Tex. Internat. Edn. Consortium. Author textbook: Agricultural Mathematics, 1978; author articles. Bd. dirs. Texas Rural Cmtys., 1998—, chair bd. dirs., 2003—; founder regional commr. Alpine Soccer League, 1984; v.p. coach Alpine Baseball League, 1983; pres. Alpine PTA, 1982-83; founder, pres. So. Meth. U. Faculty Club, 1973-75; mem. exec. com. Tex. Assn. Coll. and Univ. Student Pers. Adminstrs., 1990-92; mem. commn. on colls. class of 2003 So. Assn. of Colls. and Schs. NSF grantee, 1979. Mem. Am. Assn. Higher Edn., Tex. Assn. Coll. Tchrs. (chpt. v.p. 1978-79), Math. Assn. Am. (chmn. Tex. sect. 1985-86), Chihuahuan Desert Rsch. Inst. (bd. dirs.), Lions Club (pres. 1979-80, Lion of Yr. 1980, 83), Alpine Country Club. Republican. Mem. Ch. Of Christ. Avocations: motocycling, golf, shooting. Home: PO Box 1341 Alpine TX 79831-1341 Office: Sul Ross State U E Highway 90 PO Box C114 Alpine TX 79831-0114 Office Phone: 432-837-8032. Business E-Mail: rvmorgan@sulross.edu.

MORGAN, RICHARD ERNEST, political scientist, educator; b. Centre County, Pa., May 17, 1937; s. James Ernest and Helen Estelle (Hogge) M.; m. Jean Mary Yarbrough, 1996. AB, Bowdoin Coll., Brunswick, Maine, 1959; A.M., Columbia U., 1961, PhD, 1967. Instr. in govt. Columbia U., 1962-63, 65-67, asst. prof. govt., 1967-68; asso. prof. govt. Bowdoin Coll., 1969-75, William Nelson Cromwell prof. constl. law and govt., 1975—. Fellow in law and govt. Harvard U. Law Sch., 1968-69; research dir. Twentieth Century Fund Project on Polit. Surveillance in Am., 1975-79 Author: The Politics of Religious Conflict, 1968, The Supreme Court and Religion, 1972, (with others) American Politics: Directions of Change, Dynamics of Choice, 1979, Domestic Intelligence: Monitoring Dissent in America, 1980, Disabling America: The Rights Industry in Our Time, 1984, People, Power and Politics, 1994; contbg. editor, City Journal, 1998—; contbr. articles to profl. publs.; editor: (with James E. Connor) The American Political System: Introductory Readings, 1971. Chmn. Spl. Commn. on Legis. Compensation, State of Maine, 1973-74; chmn. Maine adv. com. U.S. Commn. on Civil Rights, 1985-87. Served to 1st lt. U.S. Army, 1963-65. Mem. Am. Polit. Sci. Assn., New. Eng. Polit. Sci. Assn. (pres. 1988-89). Republican. Episcopalian. Home: 55 Otter Brook Rd South Harpswell ME 04079-9802 Office: Bowdoin Coll Brunswick ME 04011

MORGAN, RICHARD GREER, lawyer; b. Houston, Dec. 23, 1943; s. John Benjamin (stepfather) and Audrey Valley (Brickwede) Haus; children: Richard Greer, Jonathan Roberts. AB in History, Princeton U., 1966; JD, U. Tex., 1969. Bar: Tex. 1969, D.C. 1970, Minn. 1976, U.S. Ct. Appeals (D.C. cir.) 1970, U.S. Ct. Appeals (5th and 9th cirs., temporary emergency ct. appeals) 1976. Atty., advisor to commr. Lawrence J. O'Connor, Jr. Fed. Power Commn., Washington, 1969-71; assoc. Morgan, Lewis & Bockius, Washington, 1971-75; ptnr. O'Connor & Hannan, Washington, 1975-89, Lane & Mittendorf, Washington, 1989-97, Shook, Hardy & Bacon, L.L.P., Houston, 1997—2003; pres., mng. ptnr. Preis, Kraft & Roy, 2000—. Bd. dirs. Hexagon, Inc.; instr. law seminars; lectr. in field. Author: Gas Lease and Royalty Issues, Natural Gas Yearbook, 1989, 90, 91, 92, 2002; contbr. articles on energy law to profl. jours. Bd. dirs. Mighty Spl. Music Makers, U. Tex. Law Sch. Found. Mem. ABA, Fed. Bar Assn., Energy Bar Assn. (bd. dirs.), D.C. Bar Assn., Princeton Alumni Coun., Princeton Alumni Assn. Houston, Energy Law Found. (pres.). Office: Preis Kraft & Roy Ste 600 2000 Bering Dr Houston TX 77057 Office Phone: 713-355-6062. Business E-Mail: rmorgan@pkrlaw.com.

MORGAN, ROBERT, writer, educator; b. 1943; BA, U. N.C., 1965; MFA, U. N.C., Greensboro, 1968. Tchg. asst. U. N.C., Greensboro, 1967—68; instr. Salem Coll., Winston-Salem, NC, 1968—69; lectr. Cornell U., Ithaca, NY, 1971—73, asst. prof., 1973—78, assoc. prof., 1978—84, prof. English, 1984—, Kappa Alpha prof. English, 1992—. Author: (poetry) Zirconia Poems, 1969, The Voice in the Crosshairs, 1971, Red Owl, 1972, Land Diving, 1976, Trunk and Thicket, 1978, Groundwork, 1979, Bronze Age, 1981, At the Edge of the Orchard Country, 1987, Sigodlin, 1990, Green River: New and Selected Poems, 1991, Topsoil Road, 2000, The Strange Attractor: New and Selected Poems, 2004, (novels) The Blue Valleys, 1989, The Mountains Won't Remember Us, 1992, The Hinterlands, 1994, The Truest Pleasure, 1995, Gap Creek, 1999 (So. Book award), This Rock, 2001, Brave Enemies: A Novel of the American Revolution, 2003, (essays) Good Measure, 1993. Recipient N.C. award for lit., James G. Hanes Poetry award, Jacaranda Rev. Fiction prize; fellow, Nat. Endowment for the Arts, 1968, 1974, 1981, 1987, Guggenheim Found., 1988—89; Bellagio fellow, Rockefeller Found. Office: Goldwin Smith Hall Dept English Cornell U Ithaca NY 14853 also: c/o Algonquin Books PO Box 2225 Chapel Hill NC 27515-2225

MORGAN, ROBERT GEORGE, accounting educator, researcher; b. Sanford, Maine., Feb. 20, 1941; s. George Andrew and Katherine (Gray) M.; children: Robert George, Katherine Neva. BA, Piedmont Coll., Demorest, Ga., 1968; MAcctg., U. Ga., 1971, PhD, 1974. CPA, N.C.; cert. mgmt. acct. Asst. prof. acctg. U. Wyo., Laramie, 1974-76, Drexel U., Phila., 1976-80; assoc. prof. acctg. U. N.C., Greensboro, 1980-83; prof. acctg. Loyola Coll., Balt., 1983-85; chmn. dept. acctg. East Tenn. State U., Johnson City, 1985-92, prof. acctg., 1985—. Editor jour. The Mgmt. Rev., 1983-85; contbr. articles to profl. jours. Treas. Running Brook PTA, Columbia, Md., 1984-85. Mem. AICPA, Inst. Mgmt. Accts. (pres. East Tenn. chpt. 1995-96), Am. Acctg. Assn., Acad. Acctg. Historians, Tenn. Soc. Acctg. Educators (pres. 1986-87), Beta Gamma Sigma, Beta Alpha Psi. Presbyn. Avocation: golf. Office: E Tenn State U Dept Acctg PO Box 70710 Johnson City TN 37614-0710 Home: 401 Belleair Ln Bristol VA 24201-1508 E-mail: morgan@etsu.edu., morganjewellry@msn.com.

MORGAN, ROBERT MARION, educational research educator; b. Ponca City, Okla., Feb. 5, 1930; s. Perry Harrison and Velma Beatrice (Stowe) M.; m. Constance Louise Claus, Jan. 3, 1963; children— Stephen, Melayne. BS, Okla. State U., 1955, MS, 1956; PhD, Ohio State U., 1958; LLD, Dongah U., Pusan, Korea. Asst. prof. U. N.M., 1958-62; pres. Gen. Programmed Tchg. Corp., Palo Alto, Calif., 1961-64; v.p. Ranchers Corp., Albuquerque, 1962-64; dir. ednl. systems Litton Industries, College Park, Md., 1964-66; dep. dir. divsn. vocational rsch. U.S. Office Edn., Washington, 1966-68; prof., head dept. ednl. rsch. Fla. State U., Tallahassee, 1968-74; dir. Center for Ednl. Tech., 1968-75, Learning Systems Inst., 1975—2003, prof. emeritus, 2003. Lectr. Catholic U. Am., 1966-68, Seoul (Korea) Nat. U., 1970-71; cons. AID, Republic of Brazil, Korea, Italian Air Force, Navy Dept., U.S. Naval Acad.; Chmn. Fla. R & D, Council, 1969—; sch. bd. U. Sch., Tallahassee, 1969-74. Author: Programmed Instruction-A Concept of Learning, 1963, An Educational Systems Analysis for the Republic of Korea, 1970; contbr. articles to profl. jours. Bd. dirs. U.S. Coalition for Edn. for All, 1992—; trustee Aerospace Ednl. Found. With AUS, 1949-52. Fellow Royal Soc. Arts; mem. Am. Ednl. Research Assn., Am. Psychol. Assn., Nat. Soc. for Programmed Instrn., Am. Mgmt. Assn., Rotary, Sigma Xi. Republican. Presbyterian. Home: 3322 Remington Run Tallahassee FL 32312-1462 Office: Fla State Univ C4605 University Ctr Tallahassee FL 32306 Office Phone: 904-644-2572. Business E-Mail: rmorgan@lsi.fsu.edu.

MORGAN, ROBERT P. music theorist, educator; b. Nashville, July 28, 1934; s. Hugh J. and Robert (Porter) M.; m. Carole Ann Montgomery, June 12, 1965. BA, Princeton U., 1956, MFA, 1960, PhD, 1969; MA, U. Calif., 1958. Instr. U. Houston, 1963-67; asst. prof. Temple U., Phila., 1967-70, assoc. prof., 1970-75, prof., 1975-79, U. Chgo., 1979-89, Yale U., New Haven, 1989—. Vis. prof. U. Pa., Phila., 1976-78, Yale U., 1987; adv. bd. Fromm Music Found., Chgo., 1984-89. Author: Twentieth Century Music, 1991; mem. editorial bd. Critical Inquiry, 1980—, Studies in the Criticism and Theory of Music, 1981—, Composers of the Twentieth Century; composer orch., chamber ensemble, voice and piano works; articles in field. Grantee German Govt., 1960-62; Woodrow Wilson fellow, 1956-57, NEH sr. fellow, 1983-84. Mem. Am. Musicol. Soc. (council mem. 1982-85), Soc. for Music Theory (bd. dirs. 1985—), Coll. Music Soc., Yale Club (N.Y.C.) Democrat. Office: Yale Univ Dept Music New Haven CT 06520-8310

MORGAN, ROBIN EVONNE, poet, author, journalist, activist, editor; b. Lake Worth, Fla., Jan. 29, 1941; 1 child, Blake Ariel. Grad. with honors, The Wetter Sch., 1956; student, pvt. tutors, 1956-59, Columbia U.; DHL (hon.), U. Conn., 1992. Free-lance book editor, 1961-69; editor Grove Press, 1967-70; editor, columnist World column Ms. Mag., NYC, 1974-87, editor in chief, 1989-93, cons. editor, 1993—, columnist, 2003—. Vis. chair and guest prof. women's studies New Coll., Sarasota, Fla., 1973; disting. vis. scholar, lectr. Ctr. Critical Analysis of Contemporary Culture, Rutgers U., 1987, U. Canterbury, Christchurch, New Zealand, 1989, U. Denver Grad. Sch. Internat. Affairs, 1996-97; invited spl. cons. UN com. UN Conv. to End All Forms Discrimination Against Women, Sao Paulo and Brasilia, Brazil, 1987; mem. adv. bd. ISIS (internat. network women's internat. cross-cultural exch.); spl. advisor gen. assembly conf. on Gender UN Internat. Sch., 1985-86; free-lance journalist, lectr. cons., editor, 1969—; invited speaker numerous confs., orgns., acad. meetings, US and abroad. Author, compiler, editor: Sisterhood Is Powerful: An Anthology of Writings from the Women's Liberation Movement, 1970, Swedish edit., 1972, Sisterhood Is Global: The International Women's Movement Anthology, 1984, U.K. edit., 1985, Spanish edit., 1994, Feminist Press edit., 1996, Sisterhood Is Forever:The Women's Anthology for A New Millennium, 2003; author: (nonfiction) Going Too Far: The Personal Chronicle of a Feminist, 1978, German edit., 1978, The Anatomy of Freedom: Feminism, Physics and Global Politics, 1982, 2d edit., 1994, fgn. edits. UK, 1984, Germany, 1985, Argentina, 1986, Brazil, 1992, The Demon Lover: On the Sexuality of Terrorism, 1989, UK edit., 1989, Japanese edit., 1992, Italian edit., 1998, revised US edit., 2002, The Word of a Woman: Feminist Dispatches 1968-91, 1992, 2d edit., 1994, UK edit., 1992, Chinese edit., 1996, A Woman's Creed, English, Arabic, French, Italian, Sanskrit, Hindi, Russian, Spanish, Portuguese, Chinese and Persian edits., 1995, Saturday's Child: A Memoir, 2000, (fiction) Dry Your Smile: A Novel, 1987, U.K. edit., 1988, The Mer-Child: A New Legend, 1991, German edit., 1995, Korean edit., 2000, (poetry) Monster: Poems, 1972, Lady of the Beasts: Poems, 1976, Death Benefits: Poems, 1981, Depth Perception: New Poems and a Masque, 1982, Upstairs in the Garden: Selected and New Poems, 1968-88, 1990, A Hot January: Poems 1996-1999, 1999, (plays) In Another Country, 1960, The Duel, 1979; poetry editor: The New Woman: Anthology, 1969; contbr. numerous articles, essays, book revs., poems to various publs.; presenter poetry readings, univ., poetry ctr., radio, TV, others, 1970—. Mem. 1st women's liberation caucus CORE, 1965, Student Nonviolent Coordinating Com., 1966; organizer 1st feminist demonstration against Miss Am. Pageant, 1968; founder, pres. The Sisterhood is Powerful Fund, 1970; founder, pres. NY Women's Law Ctr., 1970; founder NY Women's Ctr., 1969; co-founder, bd. dir. Feminist Women's Health Network, Nat. Battered Women's Refuge Network, Nat. Network Rape Crisis Ctr.; bd. dirs. Women's Fgn. Policy Coun.; adv. trustee Nat. Women's Inst. for Freedom of Press; founding mem. Nat. Mus. Women in Arts; founder Sisterhood is Global Inst. (internat. think-tank), 1984, officer, 1989-97, chair adv. bd., 1997-2004, pres., 2004—; co-organizer, U.S. mem. ofcl. visit Coalition of Philippines Women's Movement, 1988; chair NY state com. Hands Across Am. Com. for Justice and Empowerment, 1988; mem. adv. bd. Global Fund for Women, Equality Now. Recipient Front Page award for disting. journalism, Wonder Woman award for internat. peace and understanding, 1982, Feminist of Yr. award Fund for Feminist Majority, 1990; Human Rights Activism Award from Equality NOW, 2002, Feminist Press award, 2003; writer-in-residence grantee Yaddo, 1980; grantee Nat. Endowment for Arts, 1979-80, Ford Found., 1982, 83, 84. Mem. Nat. Mus. Women in Arts, Feminist Writers' Guild, Media Women, N.Am. Feminist Coalition, Pan Arab Feminist Solidarity Assn. (hon.), Israeli Feminists Against Occupation (hon.). Office: c/o Edite Kroll Literary Agency 12 Grayhurst Park Portland ME 04102-3601

MORGAN, RONALD BRIAN, retired aerospace engineer, advocate, writer; b. Jamaica, N.Y., Nov. 12, 1935; s. Raymond Edward and Gladys Irene Morgan; m. Eileen Marie Crowley, Dec. 19, 1959 (dec.); children: Glen, Genevieve, Mary, Mark, Brian. EE, Manhattan Coll., Bronx, N.Y., 1955. Design engr. Douglas Aircraft Co., Santa Monica, Calif., 1955—68; lead engr. and group leader McDonnell Douglas Corp., Kennedy Space Ctr., Fla., 1968—75; supr. Planning Rsch. Corp., Cocoa Beach, 1975—83; sec.-treas. Exec-Invest, Inc., 1979—83; prin. engr. McDonnell Douglas Corp., Merritt Island, 1983—93; author and lectr. self-employed, Cocoa Beach, 1998—2001; owner and pres. Ronald B. Morgan Publ., Merritt Island, 2001—; founder, pres. Am. Millennium Found., Inc., 2004. Co-founder and 2nd pres. PRC Mgmt. Assoc., Cocoa Beach, Fla., 1975—82; co-founder and by-laws chmn. Profl. Businessmen's Assn., 1970—72. Author: The Am. Spirit in the New Millenium, 2001, (play) No Time for Planners, 1970—72. Senate pres. Fla. Silver-Haired Legislature, Merritt Island, Fla., 2001—, CEO, 2004; bd. dirs. Joe Realino Meml. Fund, Cocoa Beach, Fla., 2001—, Sr. Resource Alliance, Viera. Recipient Apollo Program Honoree, NASA, 1969, Space Shuttle Return to Flight Group Achievement award, NASA, Kenedy Space Ctr., 1989, Congressional Record citation, 2001. Mem.: AARP Avocacy Team (Fla. coord. 2002—03), Brevard Tomorrow/Leadership Brevard (mem. govt. working group 2000—04). Roman Catholic. Achievements include invention of electrical "T" connector; design of first aircraft emergency lighting system used on commercial aircraft; first series of hand-held elec./electronic test equipment for commercial aircraft; first integrated logistics system for all NASA Kennedy Space Ctr. facilities, systems and equipment; integrated logistics system for the mirror fusion project at the Lawrence Livermore Labs; first integrated data system used for configuration mgmt. of Spacelab payloads flown on the Space Shuttle at Kennedy Space Ctr. Avocations: historical research, law research, legislative bills, senior issues. Office: Ronald B Morgan PO Box 540998 Merritt Island FL 32954

MORGAN, RONALD E. retired federal air traffic director; m. Kathy Morgan; children: Timothy, Rebecca. Charter pilot, flying instr., Calif.; from air traffic controller to tower mgr. L.A. Air Route Traffic Control Ctr., Palmdale, Calif., 1970-88; staff mem. FAA, Washington, 1988-92, dir. NAS System Engring. Svc., 1992-94, assoc adminstr. system engring. and devel., 1994-95, dir. office System Arch. and Program Evaluation, 1995-96, dir. air traffic, 1996-2001, ret., 2001. Acting assoc. adminstr. for air traffic svcs., 1998. Office: FAA Office Air Traffic 800 Independence Ave SW Washington DC 20591-0001 Fax: (202) 267-5456.

MORGAN, RUTH PROUSE, academic administrator, educator; b. Berkeley, Calif., Mar. 30, 1934; d. Ervin Joseph and Thelma Ruth (Prcesang) Prouse; m. Vernon Edward Morgan, June 3, 1956; children: Glenn Edward, Renée Ruth. BA summa cum laude, U. Tex., 1956; MA, La. State U., 1961, PhD, 1966. Asst. prof. Am. govt., politics and theory So. Meth. U., Dallas, 1966-70, assoc. prof., 1970-74, prof., 1974-95; prof. emeritus, 1995—; asst. provost So. Meth. U., Dallas, 1978-82, assoc. provost, 1982—86, provost ad interim, 1986-87, provost, 1987-93, provost emerita, 1993—; v.p. Chem. Abatement Tech., Inc., 1995—. Tex. state polit. analyst ABC, N.Y.C., 1972-84. Author: The President and Civil Rights, 1970, Governance By Decree: The Impact of the Voting Rights Act in Dallas, 2004; mem. editl. bd. Jour. of Politics, 1975-82, Presdl. Studies Quar., 1980—; contbr. articles to profl. jours. Active Internat. Women's Forum, 1987—, City of Dallas Redistricting Commn., 2001; trustee Hockaday Sch., 1988-94, The Kilby Awards Found., 1993-95; bd. dirs. United Way, Met. Dallas, 1993-99; adv. com. U.S. Army Command and Gen. Staff. Coll., 1994-97; founder Archives of Women of the Southwest, 1992, chmn. adv. com. 1995-99; mem. Dallas Women's Found. Mem. Am. Polit. Sci. Assn., So. Polit. Sci. Assn. (mem. exec. coun. 1979-84), Southwestern Polit. Sci. Assn. (pres. 1982-83, mem. exec. coun. 1981-84), The Dallas Assembly, The Dallas Forum of Internat. Women's Forum (pres. 1996-97), Charter 100 Club (pres. 1991-92), Ctr. for the Study of the Presidency, Dallas Summit Club (pres. 1992-93), Phi Beta Kappa, Pi Sigma Alpha, Phi Kappa Phi, Theta Sigma Phi. Avocations: photography, travel.

MORGAN, SAMUEL P(OPE), physicist, applied mathematician; b. San Diego, July 14, 1923; s. Samuel Pope and Beatrice Marie (Summers) M.; m. Mary Caroline Annin, Jan. 23, 1948; children: Caroline Gail, Lesley Anne, Alison Lee, Diane Elizabeth. BS, Calif. Inst. Tech., 1943, MS, 1944, PhD in Physics, 1947. Mem. tech. staff AT&T Bell Labs., Murray Hill, N.J., 1947-59, head dept. math. physics, 1959-67, dir. computing tech., 1967-70, dir. computing sci. research center, 1967-82, disting. mem. tech. staff, 1982-95, Lucent Tech./Bell Labs., 1996-98, ret., 1998. Research, publs. on electromagnetic theory, applied math., queueing theory; patentee in field. Fellow IEEE (life); mem. AAAS, Am. Phys. Soc., Sigma Xi. Home: 4113 Fellowship Rd Basking Ridge NJ 07920-3906

MORGAN, STANLEY CHARLES, plastic and reconstructive surgeon; b. Phoenix, July 23, 1935; s. Fred Charles and Hazel (King) M.; m. Doris Anne Duke, Sept. 8, 1956; children: Pamela Anne, Cheryl Lynn, Mark Thomas. BS, U. Ariz.; MD, St. Louis Sch. Medicine. Diplomate Am. Bd. Plastic Surgery. Intern UCLA Ctr. Health Svcs., 1961-62, resident plastic surgery, 1966-68; resident gen. surgery Wadsworth Vets. Hosp., L.A., 1962-66; practice medicine specializing in plastic surgery Pasadena, Calif., 1970—. Asst. clin. prof. U. So. Calif. Sch. Medicine, Los Angeles, 1981—, UCLA Ctr. Health Scis., 1970-81. Lt. col. U.S. Army, 1968-70. Fellow ACS, Am. Soc. Plastic and Reconstructive Surgeons, Am. Soc. Aesthetic Plastic Surgery, Calif. Soc. Plastic Surgeons.

MORGAN, STEPHEN CHARLES, academic administrator; b. Upland, Calif., June 2, 1946; s. Thomas Andrew and Ruth Elizabeth (Miller) M.; m. Ann Marie McMurray, Sept. 6, 1969; 1 child, Kesley Suzanne. BA, U. La Verne, 1968; MS, U. So. Calif., 1971; EdD, U. No. Colo., 1979. Devel. officer U. La Verne, Calif., 1968-71, asst. to pres., 1971-73, dir. devel., 1973-75, v.p. devel., 1975-76, pres., 1985—; dir. devel. U. So. Calif., L.A., 1976-79; exec. dir. Ind. Colls. No. Calif., San Francisco, 1979-85. Dir. Ind. Colls. So. Calif., L.A., 1985—. Bd. dirs. Mt. Baldy United Way, Ontario, Calif., 1988-98, McKinley Children's Ctr., San Dimas, Calif., 1989-99, LeRoy Haynes Ctr. for Family and Children's Svcs., 2000—; chair nat. com. on higher edn. Ch. of Brethren, Elgin, Ill., 1988-90; dir. Pomona Valley Hosp. Med. Ctr., 1992-98, 99—, Inter Valley Health Plan, 1992-97, PFF Bank and Trust, 2001—. Mem. Assn. Ind. Calif. Colls. and Univs. (exec. com. 1989—, vice-chmn. 1996-2000, chmn. 2000-2002), L.A. County Fair Assn. (bd. dirs., chmn. 2002—), Western Coll. Assn. (exec. com. 1992-98, pres. 1996-98), Western Assn. Schs. and Colls. (sr. accrediting commn. 1996-2001), Pi Gamma Mu. Avocations: orchid culture, fly fishing, golf. Home: 2518 N Mountain Ave Claremont CA 91711-1579 Office: U LaVerne Office Pres 1950 3rd St La Verne CA 91750-4401 E-mail: morgans@ulv.edu.

MORGAN, SUSAN H. state representative; b. Nanaimo, Sept. 1, 1949; m. Kip Morgan; 3 children. AS, Lane C.C., 1977. Office mgr. Morgan Loggin, M&M Hardwoods, 1978—90; mgr. info. sys. Weyerhauser Pole Facility, 1990—93; sales rep. C&D Lumber Co., 1993—98; mem. Oreg. Ho. of Reps., 1998—. Mem. planning adv. com. South Umpqua County, 1980—98; mem. adv. bd. Myrtle Creek Pub. Libr., 1988—96. Mem.: Oreg. Lands Coalition (founding). Republican. Office: 900 Court St NE H-381 Salem OR 97301

MORGAN, THEODORE, economist; b. Middletown, Ohio, May 31, 1910; s. Ben and Anna Louella (Knecht) M.; m. Catharine Moomaw, June 30, 1943; children: Stephanie H., Marian, Laura S. AB, Ohio State U., 1930, AM, 1931, BSE, 1931; MA, Harvard U., 1940, PhD, 1941. Asst. prof. Randolph-Macon Women's Coll., Lynchburg, Va., 1941-42; teaching fellow, tutor, instr. Harvard U., Cambridge, Mass., 1940-41, 42-47; advisor, dep. gov. Cen. Bank of Ceylon, Colombo, 1951-53; assoc. prof. to prof. U. Wis., Madison, 1947-80, prof. emeritus, 1980—. Vis. prof. U. Singapore, 1967-69, Gadjah Mada U., Yogjakarta, Indonesia, 1959-60, Nankai U., Tianjin, China, 1990, U. Manchester, Eng., 1980-82, Sussex U., Brighton, Eng., 1975-76; sr. staff Coun. Econ. Advisors, Washington, 1964-65; advisor Ministry of Econ. Affairs. Govt. Thailand, Bangkok, 1970; rsch. fellow Resource Systems Inst. East-West Ctr., Honolulu, 1985-86. Author: Hawaii, A Century of Economic Change, 1948, Income and Employment, 1947, Introduction to Economics, 1950, 56, Economic Development, 1975, and others. Mem. Royal Econ. Soc. (life), Am. Econ. Assn. Mem. Unitarian Ch. Avocations: tennis, bicycling, skiing, hiking. Home: 3534 Topping Rd Madison WI 53705-1441 Office: U Wis Social Sci # 7313 Madison WI 53706

MORGAN, THOMAS I. retail executive; Employee Genuine Parts Co.; exec. v.p. S. P. Richards Co.; CEO, pres., COO U.S. Office Products Co., Washington; pres., COO Hughes Supply Inc., Orlando, Fla., 2001—03, pres., CEO, 2003—. Office: Hughes Supply Inc Corp Office One Hughes Way Orlando FL 32805*

MORGAN, THOMAS ROWLAND, retired marine corps officer; b. Allentown, Pa., Jan. 6, 1930; s. Harry Campbell and Olwen (Pierce) M.; m. Barbara A. Croze, June 29, 1957; children— Lynn A., Susan E., Beth E. BA in History, Colgate U., 1952; student, Marine Corps Command and Staff Coll., 1965-66; MA in Edn., U. Va., 1973. Commd. 2d lt. USMC, 1952, advanced through grades to gen., 1986; naval aviator Naval Air Sta., Pensacola, Fla., 1953-54; asst. maintenance officer 3d Marine Aircraft Wing, El Toro, Calif., 1954-55; personnel officer Marine Aircraft Group Western Pacific, 1954-55; aide to comdg. gen. 1st Marine Aircraft Wing, Pacific, 1955; asst. ops. officer Marine Aircraft Group, Kaneohe Bay, Hawaii, 1956-57; squadron pilot, ground tng. officer Marine Attack Squadron, Hawaii, 1957-59; flight instr. Naval Air Sta., Olathe, Kans., 1959; personnel officer, aircraft maintenance officer Marine Fighter Squadron, Beaufort, S.C., 1959-61; exec. officer Hdqrs. and Maintenance Squadron, Atsugi, Japan, 1961-62; fleet liaison officer Marine Corps Air Sta., Yuma, Ariz., 1962-65; comdr. Marine Fighter Attack Squadron, Beaufort, 1966-67; group ops. officer, officer-in-charge DaNang DASC, Vietnam, 1968-69; exec. officer Marine Corps Air Sta., Quantico, Va., 1969-71; exec. officer Naval ROTC unit U. Va., 1971-73; chief war plans br. J-5 U.S. European Command Hdqrs., Stuttgart, Fed. Republic Germany, 1973-76; asst. to dep. chief of staff requirements and programs Hdqrs. U.S. Marine Corps, Washington, 1976-77; asst. div. comdr. 3d Marine Div., Okinawa, Japan, 1977-78; asst. chief of staff C-5 Combined Forces Command, Seoul, 1978-80;

dep. comdr. FMF Pacific, Camp Smith, Hawaii, 1980-81; dep. chief of staff for requirements and programs Hdqrs. Marine Corps, Washington, 1981-85, dep. chief staff for plans, policies and ops., acting Chief of Staff, 1985-86, asst. commandant, 1986-88, ret. Decorated D.S.M., Def. Superior Service medal, Legion of Merit, Bronze Star medal, Meritorious Service medal, Air medal; Order of Nat. Security medal, Cheonsu medal (Korea) Mem. Am. Legion Avocations: golf, skiing, water sports. E-mail: tmorgva@cox.net.

MORGAN, TIMI SUE, lawyer; b. Parsons, Kans., June 16, 1953; d. James Daniel and Iris Mae (Wilson) Baumgardner; m. Rex Michael Morgan, Oct. 28, 1983; children: Tessa Anne, Camma Elizabeth. BS, U. Kans., 1974; JD, So. Meth. U., 1977. Bar: Tex. 1977, U.S. Dist. Ct. (no. dist.) Tex. 1978, U.S. Ct. Appeals (5th cir.) 1979, U.S. Tax Ct. 1980; cert. tax law specialist. Assoc. Gardere & Wynne, Dallas, 1977-79, Akin, Gump, Strauss, Hauer & Feld, Dallas, 1979-83, ptnr., 1984-86; of counsel Stinson, Mag & Fizzell, Dallas, 1986-88; sole practice Dallas, 1988—. Adj. lectr. law So. Meth. U., 1989-90, 92-98. Bd. dirs. Dallas Urban League Inc., 1987-91. Mem. State Bar Tex. (mem. taxation sect.), Dallas Bar Assn., So. Meth. U. Law Alumni Coun. (sec. 1985-86), Order of Coif, Beta Gamma Sigma. Republican. Episcopalian.

MORGAN, VICTORIA, performing company executive, choreographer; BFA, U. Utah, 1973, MFA magna cum laude, 1976. Prin. dancer Ballet West, 1969-78, San Francisco Ballet, 1978-87; resident choreographer San Francisco Opera, 1987—97; artistic dir. Cin. Ballet, 1997—. Dancer with lead roles in numerous classical, neoclassical and modern ballets including works by George Balanchine, Forsythe, and Kudelka, lead roles for TV and films, choreographer creating over 40 works for 20 ballet and opera cos. across U.S. including Utah Ballet, Pacific Northwest Ballet, Glimmerglass Opera, N.Y.C. Opera and Cin. Opera. Office: Cincinnati Ballet 1555 Central Pkwy Cincinnati OH 45214-2863*

MORGAN, VIRGINIA MATTISON, magistrate judge; b. 1946; BS, Univ. of Mich., 1968; JD, Univ. of Toledo, 1975. Bar: Mich. 1975, Federal 1975, U.S. Ct. Appeals (6th cir.) 1979. Tchr. Dept. of Interior, Bur. of Indian Affairs, 1968-70, San Diego Unified Schs., 1970-72, Oregon, Ohio, 1972-74; asst. prosecutor Washtenaw County Prosecutor's Office, 1976-79; asst. U.S. atty. Detroit, 1979-85; magistrate judge U.S. Dist. Ct. (Mich. ea. dist.), 6th circuit, Detroit, 1985—. Mem. bd. Fed. Jud. Ctr., 1997-2001; mem. jud. conf. U.S. Com. on Long Range Planning, 1993-96. Recipient Spl. Achievement award Dept. of Justice, Disting. Alumni award U. Toledo, 1993. Fellow Mich. State Bar Found.; mem. FBA (chpt. pres. 1996-97), Fed. Magistrate Judges Assn. (pres. 1995-96). Office: US Courthouse 231 W Lafayette Blvd Detroit MI 48226-2700

MORGAN, WILLIAM ADAMS, lawyer; b. Detroit, Dec. 5, 1956; s. Thomas Oliver and Katharine (Eagerton) M.; m. M. Gwen Herrin, Aug. 29, 1987. BA in Polit. Sci. cum laude, Ill. Wesleyan U., 1979; JD, U. Ill., 1982. Bar: Ill. 1982, U.S. Dist. Ct. (no. dist.) Ill. 1982, U.S. Ct. Appeals (7th cir.) 1996. Atty. Pope Ballard Shepard & Fowle, Chgo., 1982-91; assoc. gen. counsel, personal injury/workers' compensation Bd. of Edn. of the City of Chgo., 1991—. Recipient Recognition of Outstanding Svc. award Intergovtl. Risk Mgmt. Agy., 1996. Mem. ABA, Ill. State Bar Assn., Appellate Lawyers Assn. (bd. dirs. 2000-01, treas. 2001-02, sec. 2002-03, v.p. 2003-04, pres. 2004-05). Avocations: gourmet cooking, wine collecting, travel, photography. Home: 1925 W Bradley Pl Chicago IL 60613-3513 Office: Bd of Edn of City of Chgo 125 S Clark St Ste 700 Chicago IL 60603-5200 E-mail: wmorgan@csc.cps.k12.il.us.

MORGAN, WILLIAM BRUCE, naval architect; b. Fairfield, Iowa, Dec. 20, 1926; s. Orville Burns and Mary Verle (Balderson) M.; m. Mary Maxine Gillam, June 21, 1950; children: Margaret Ann, Ann Elise. BS in Marine Engring., U.S. Mcht. Marine Acad., 1950; MS in Hydraulic Engring., U. Iowa, 1951; DEng in Naval Architecture, U. Calif., 1961. Hydraulic engr. David Taylor Model Basin, Bethesda, Md., 1951-52, naval architect, 1952-58, naval architect supr., 1958-62, head propeller br., 1962-70; head hydromechanics div. David Taylor Naval Ship R&D Ctr. (formerly David Taylor Model Basin), Bethesda, 1970-79, head hydromechanics directorate, 1979—2001; ret. Chmn. exec. com. Am. Towing Tank Conf., 1983-86; mem. exec. com. Internat. Towing Tank Conf., 1984-90. Co-inventor ventilated propeller, supercavitating propeller with air ventilation; contbr. articles to profl. jours. Recipient Navy Disting. Civilian Svc. award USN, 2000, Navy Superior Civilian Svc. award, 1974, Navy Meritorious Svc. award, 1967, Meritorious Exec. award Office of Pres., 1987, William Froude medal Royal Instn. Naval Architects, 1989, Capt. Robert Dexter Conrad award USN, 1993, Gibbs Bros. medal NAS, 1997; named to U. Iowa Disting. Engring. Alumni Acad., 1999. Fellow Soc. Naval Architects and Marine Engrs. (hon. life; exec. com. 1985—, Davidson medal 1986), ASME (chmn. fluids engring. div. 1981-82); mem. NAE, Schiffbautechnische Gesellschaft, Am. Soc. Naval Engrs. (Gold Medal award 1993), Chinese Soc. Naval Architects and Marine Engrs. (hon.), Sigma Xi. Presbyterian. Home: 110 Upton St Rockville MD 20850-1836 E-mail: wbmorgan@erols.com.

MORGAN, WILLIAM FRANCIS, JR., police chief; b. Hartford, Conn. s. William Francis and Nancy M.; m. Kathleen Buckley, Oct. 12, 1985. B.Criminal Justice, U. New Haven, 1982; JD, Quinnipiac Coll., Hamden, Conn., 1998; Cert., FBI Nat. Acad., Quantico, Va., 1999. Bar: Conn. 1998. Police officer Conn. State Capitol Police, Hartford, 1985-89, sr. police officer, 1989-97, sgt., 1997-99, lt., 1999-2000, chief of police, 2000—. Mem. consumer adv. network Nat. Criminal Justice Ref. Svc., Rockville, Md., 2000. Recipient Samuel J. Lucian award Police Officer Tng. Coun., 1986, Trooper Allen Tuskowski award, 1986, Legis. Staff Achievment award Nat. Conf. State Legislators, 2002, John Everhardt Trooper award Nat. Legis. Svcs. and Security Assn., 2002. Mem. Nat. Legis. Svc. and Security Assn. (regional 3 chair 1997-98, 3d trustee 1998-99, 1st trustee 1999-2002). Office: Conn State Capitol Police 210 Capitol Ave Hartford CT 06106

MORGAN, WILLIAM J. accounting company executive; b. Bklyn., Jan. 12, 1947; s. William J. and Emma T. (Kraft) M.; m. Patricia A. Maltz, Mar. 23, 1968; children: Michele, Jennifer. BS, St. John's U., 1968. CPA, NY Conn., NJ. Ptnr. KPMG LLP, Stamford, Conn., audit staff, 1968-72, audit supr., 1972-74, audit mgr., 1974-77, ptnr.-in-charge pvt. bus. adv. svc. NYC, 1977-79, nat. office, ptnr.-in-charge recruiting, 1979-82, ptnr. comml. health care practice Short Hills, NJ, 1982-91, ptnr.-in-charge NJ audit practice, 1989-91, mng. ptnr. Fairfield/Westchester counties practice, 1991-94, ptnr. in charge met. NY area mfg., retail and distbn. practice, 1993-96, ptnr. in charge global accts., 1996-98, mng. ptnr. Stamford office, 1996—2003. Mem. Bus. Unit Planning Task Force, 1987—90, mem. compensation com., 1990—91, bd. dirs., 1991—2003, chmn. profit distbn. com., 1991—95, mem. future direction com., 1991—93, pension task force, 1991—92, chmn. compensation com., 1997—2003, mem. bd. process com., 1997—2002, mem. nominating com., 2002—03; bd. dirs. KPMG Americas, 1999—2003. Acctg. adv. bd. Grad. Sch. Bus. Fordham U., 1979—82; mem. standardization com. Nat. Retail Mchts. Assn., 1979; trustee Tri County Scholarship Fund, 1984—91; v.p., exec. com., adv. bd. Fairfield coun. Boy Scouts Am., 1993—95; bd. dirs. Stamford Symphony, 1995—99; bd. dirs., chmn. bus. ops. com. heritage affiliate Am. Heart Assn., 1997—2000; chmn. Fairfield County Info. Exch., 1992—94; chmn. bd. SACIA, the Bus. Coun. of Fairfield Co., 2001—03, bd. dirs., 1993—2004, Inroads Fairfield and Westchester County chpt., 1992—95; mem. Bus. Execs. for Nat. Security, 1995—99, Ambs. Roundtable, 1995—99; exec. com. Conn. Policy and Econs. Coun., 1998—2003. Recipient Stamford Good Scout award, 1999, Walter H. Wheeler Disting. Leadership award, 2000. Mem. AICPA (small bus. devel. com. 1979-81, acctg. lit. awards com. 1983-86), NJ Soc. CPAs (chmn. acctg. and auditing stds. com. 1988-90, trustee 1990-92, pub. rels. task force, 1987, subcom. health care acctg. 1983-86), NY State CPAs (retail acctg. com. 1975-78, com. on edn. in coll. and univs. 1978-82), Nat. Assn. Accts. (dir. manuscripts 1975-77, v.p. NY chpt. 1977-81, pres. NY chpt. 1981-82, nat. publs. com. 1982-83, com. acad. rels. 1983-84, nat. dir. 1983-86, Disting. Svc. award 1975), Health Care Fin. Mgmt. Assn. (NJ chpt. chmn. auditing com. 1982-83, legis. task force com. 1985-86, chmn. joint ventures com., 1987-88), Swedish Am. C. of C. (bd. dirs. 1995—, exec. com. 2000-), Fairmount Country Club (bd. govs., treas. 1987-90), Woodway Country Club, Conn. Golf Club (bd. govs. 2003-). Roman Catholic. Office: KPMG LLP 3001 Summer St Stamford CT 06905-4317

MORGAN, WILLIAM JASON, geophysics educator; b. Savannah, Ga., Oct. 10, 1935; married; 2 children. BS, Ga. Inst. Tech., 1957; PhD in Physics, Princeton U., 1964. Rsch. assoc. Princeton U., 1964-66, from asst. prof. to assoc. prof., 1966-77, prof. geophysics, 1977—. Recipient Japan prize, 1990, co-Recipient James b. Macelwane Young Investigator medal Am. Geophysical Union, 1995, Nat. Medal of Science award, 2002. Mem. NAS, 1982-, Am. Geophys. Union, European Union Geol. Sci. Achievements include research in mantle convention, heat flow, plate tectonics, marine geophysics. Office: Princeton U Dept Geosciences 417 Guyot Hall Princeton NJ 08544-0001 E-mail: wjmorgan@princeton.edu.*

MORGAN, WILLIAM LIONEL, JR., physician, educator; b. Honolulu, Nov. 18, 1927; s. William Lionel and Lucy Salisbury (Grimes) M.; m. Joan Brunjes, Apr. 10, 1954; children: Nancy Salisbury, Linda Pittman. BA cum laude, Yale U., 1948; MD magna cum laude, Harvard U., 1952. Diplomate: Am. Bd. Internal Medicine. (mem. bd. 1973-80, mem. residency review com. 1975-80, chmn. residency rev. com. 1979-80). Intern Mass. Gen. Hosp., Boston, 1952-53, resident in medicine, 1953-54, 56-57, fellow in cardiology, 1957-58; asso. physician div. cardiovascular disease Henry Ford Hosp., Detroit, 1958-62; asso. prof. medicine U. Rochester (N.Y.) Sch. Medicine and Dentistry, 1962-65, prof., 1966-89, prof. medicine emeritus, 1989—, asso. chmn. dept. medicine, 1966 89; dir. med. residency program Strong Meml. Hosp., 1962—89. Author: (with G.L. Engel) The Clinical Approach to the Patient, 1969. Served with USPHS, 1954-56. Mem. ACP (Master), Am. Clin. and Climatol. Assn., Phi Beta Kappa, Alpha Omega Alpha Home: 160 Collingsworth Dr Rochester NY 14625-2024

MORGAN, WILLIAM NEWTON, architect, educator; b. Jacksonville, Fla., Dec. 14, 1930; s. Thomas and Kathleen (Fiske) M.; m. Bernice E. Leimback, July 31, 1954; children: William Newton, Dylan Thomas. AB magna cum laude, Harvard Coll., 1952, MArch Grad. Sch. of Design, 1958. Pres. William Morgan Architects, P.A., Jacksonville, Fla., 1961—. Critic various archtl. schs.; lectr. in field; adj. prof. of art history, Jacksonville U., 1995-96, U. North Fla., 1997; Beinecke-Reeves Disting. Prof. Architecture, U. Fla., 1998-99. Prin. works include Fla. State Mus., Jacksonville Police Meml. Bldg., Pyramid Condominium, Ocean City, Md., Fed. Cts. and Offices, Ft. Lauderdale, Fla., Westinghouse World Hdqs., Orlando, Fla., Neiman-Marcus store, Ft. Lauderdale, 1st Dist. Ct. Appeal, Tallahassee, Fla., Conf. Ctr., Tallahassee, U.S. Embassy, Khartoum, Sudan, U.S. Courthouse, Tallahassee; author: Prehistoric Architecture in the Eastern United States, 1980, Prehistoric Architecture in Micronesia, 1988, Ancient Architecture of the Southwest, 1994, Precolumbian Architecture in Eastern North America, 1999. Subject of The Architecture of William Morgan (Paul Spreiregen) 1987, Images Master Architect Series: William Morgan (Robert McCarter), 2002; Fulbright grantee to Italy, 1958-59; grantee Graham Found. Advanced Studies Arts, 1973; Lehman fellow Harvard U., 1957, Wheelwright fellow 1964-65, fellow NEA, 1991; Sam Gibbons Eminent scholar Fla. A&M U. and U. South Fla. Fellow AIA (past chmn. com. design) AIA Inst. honor for rsch. into the beginnings of archtl. creativity 1998, Fla. 2000 Millenium award honor for design 2000). Office: William Morgan Architects 220 E Forsyth St Jacksonville FL 32202-3328 Office Phone: 904-356-4195. Personal E-mail: wnmorgan@aol.com.

MORGAN, WILLIAM RICHARD, mechanical engineer; b. Cambridge, Ohio, Mar. 27, 1922; s. Wilbur Alfred and Treva Beatrice (Minto) M.; m. Marjorie Eleanor Stevens, Feb. 17, 1946; children: Carol M. Morgan Dingledy, William R., Jr. BSME, The Ohio State U., 1944; MSME, Purdue U., 1950, PhD in Mech. Engring., 1951. Registered profl. engr., Ohio. Power plant design engr. Curtiss Wright Corp., Columbus, Ohio, 1946-47; instr., rsch. fellow Purdue U., West Lafayette, Ind., 1947-51; supr. exptl. mech. engring. GE, Cin., 1951-55, mgr. controls analysis, devel. Aircraft Gas Turbine Divsn., 1955-59, mgr. XV5A vertical take-off and landing aircraft program, 1959-65, mgr. acoustic engring. Flight Propulsion Divsn., 1965-69, mgr. quiet engine program Flight Propulsion Divsn., 1969-71; pres. Cin. Rsch. Corp., 1971-73; v.p., COO SDRC Internat., Cin., 1973-79; engring. and mgmt. cons. Cin., 1979—. Author of papers presented at Brookhaven Nat. Lab., AEC Heat Transfer Symposium, 1954, ASME Fall Meeting, Thermal Conductivity of Insulation Material for Use in Nuclear Reactors, 1957, Am. Inst. Aero. Engrs. Ten-Ton V/STOL Lift Fan Transport, 1961, Dynamics Loads Symposium, XV5A Dynamic Load Characteristics, 1963, Joint Meeting of AGARD-Nato on Aircraft Engine Noise and Sonic Boom, 1969, ASME Meeting, Analytical Prediction of Fan/Compressor Noise, 1969. Lt. j.g. USNR, WWII. Westinghouse Rsch. fellow. Mem. ASME, Masons, Sigma Xi, Pi Tau Sigma, Pi Mu Epsilon. Achievements include patents in Humidity Detection and Indicating Instrument, Stall Prevention/Acoustic Tip Treatment, Acoustic Treatment, Inlet Noise Reduction Configuration. Home and Office: 312 Ardon Ln Cincinnati OH 45215-4102

MORGAN, WILLIAM V. oil and gas pipeline and storage executive; Pvt. practice law, Washington; legal and mgmt. positions Fla. Gas Transmission Co., Transwestern Pipeline Co., No. Natural Gas Co.; vice chmn., pres. Kinder Morgan, Inc., Houston, Kinder Morgan Energy Ptnrs., 1997—. Office: Kinder Morgan Inc 1301 McKinney St Ste 3400 Houston TX 77010

MORGAN-PRAGER, KAROLE, lawyer, publishing executive; Assoc. Morrison & Foerster, L.A., 1987—92; assoc. gen. counsel Times Mirror Co., 1992—95; gen. counsel, corp. sec. McClatchy Co., Sacramento, 1995—, v.p., 1998—. Office: McClatchy Co Legal Dept 2100 Q St Sacramento CA 95818-6899

MORGANROTH, FRED, lawyer; b. Detroit, Mar. 26, 1938; s. Ben and Grace (Greenfield) M.; m. Janice Marilyn Cohn, June 23, 1963; children: Greg, Candi, Erik. BA, Wayne State U., 1959, JD with distinction, 1961. Bar: Mich. 1961, U.S. Dist. Ct. (ea. dist.) Mich. 1961, U.S. Ct. Claims 1967, U.S. Supreme Ct. 1966; trained matrimonial arbitrator. Ptnr. Greenbaum, Greenbaum & Morganroth, Detroit, 1963-68, Lebenbom, Handler, Brody & Morganroth, Detroit, 1968-70, Lebenbom, Morganroth & Stern, Southfield, Mich., 1971-78; pvt. practice, Southfield, 1979-83; ptnr. Morganroth & Morganroth P.C., Southfield, 1983-94, Morganroth, Morganroth, Alexander & Nye, P.C., Birmingham, Mich., 1994-98, Morganroth, Morganroth, Jackman & Kasody, PC, Bloomfield Hills, Mich., 1999—. Mem. ABA (family law sect. 1987—), Mich. Bar Assn. (hearing panelist grievance bd. 1975—, Oakland County family law com. 1988—, vice chmn. 1992-93, chair 1993—), State Bar Mich. (mem. family law coun. of family law sect. 1990—, treas. 1993-94, chmn.-elect 1994-95, chmn. 1995-96), Detroit Bar Assn., Oakland Bar Assn. (cir. ct. mediator 1984—), Am. Arbitration Assn. (Oakland County family law com. 1985—, vice chmn. 1992-93, chmn. 1993-94, trained matrimonial arbitrator), Detroit Tennis Club (Farmington, Mich., pres. 1978-82), Charlevoix Country Club, Tam-O-Shanter Country Club. Jewish. Avocations: commercial pilot, golf. Home: 30920 Woodcrest Ct Franklin MI 48025-1435 Office: 40701 Woodward Ave Ste 250 Bloomfield Hills MI 48304 E-mail: fmmman1@aol.com.

MORGANS, BOB D. minister; b. Claremore, Okla., June 29, 1956; s. John Henry Morgans and Rhodana Mae Sutherland; m. Barbara Kay Carter, May 8, 1976; children: Bobby Dean, Deana Marie. BS, Tarkio Coll., Mo., 1986. Pastor United Pentecostal Ch., Trenton, Mo., sr. pastor Athens, Ohio, 1998—. Home missions dir. sect. eight United Pentecostal Ch., Kans. City, Mo., 1991—97. Author: (book) How to Pray with a Child to Receive the Holy Ghost (Best Seller, 2001), How to Pray with an Adult to Receive the Holy Ghost, No Fear, Just Believe, How to Receive Your Miracle, (video) Worldwide Children's Crusades. Coord. for ann. walk Multiple Sclerosis Soc., Trenton, Mo., 1990—94. Mem.: Children's Evangelist Assn. Avocation: travel. Home: 4807 Fisher Rd Athens OH 45701-9334 Personal E-mail: bmorgans@frognet.net.

MORGANTE, JOHN-PAUL, human resources specialist; b. Yonkers, N.Y., June 26, 1962; s. Enzo and Teresa (DellaToffola) M.; m. Ellen Rothberger, May 26, 1984; children: Camden Anne, Bethany Nicole, Hailee Marie. BA, U. So. Calif., L.A., 1984. Ordained to ministry Christian Ch., 1987; cert. profl. in human resources; sr. profl. human resources. Adminstrv. dir. MCM Internat., Lomita, Calif., 1984-87; dir. human resources, 1987-91; exec. dir. Champions for Christ, Austin, Tex., 1991-93; pres. Annimar Assocs., Austin, 1991—95; OD and tng. officer Tex. Dept. Health, Austin, 1995-97; mgr. human resources The TFE Group, Augusta, Ga., 1997-99, sr. mgr., 2000; corp. human resources mgr. Morris Comms. Corp., Augusta, Ga., 2000—01, asst. dir. corp. human resources, 2001—03; dir. human resources and adminstrn. Talla-Com Industries, Tallahassee, 2003—. Contbr. to profl. jours. Mem. ctrl. com. Orange County (Calif.) Reps., 1988-89; intern U.S. Rep. Robert Badham, Washington, 1983, campaign worker, 1984; intern Assemblyman Curt Pringle, Garden Grove, Calif., 1988; campaign worker U.S. Senator Chic Hecht, 1982, U.S. Rep. Robert Dornan, 1984, Reagan-Bush, 1984, Tex. State rep. Terry Keel, Austin, 1996, Leadership Austin program Austin C. of C., 1994; mem. solicitation bd. City of Austin, 1996-97; del. Dist. 14 Rep. Conv., Austin, 1996; bd. dirs. Area II Soc. for Human Resource Mgmt. 2002-03; mem. nat. nominating com. Outstanding Young Ams., 1996-2001; peer moderator Nat. Issues Conv., Phila., 1996; campaign work George W. Bush, 2000; moderator, Mayor's Initiative on Race, Tallahassee, 2003. Recipient Rep. Presdl. Legion of Merit, Presdl. Commemorative Honor Roll, 1991, Staff Mem. of Yr., 1987; commd. Hon. Texan by Gov. George Bush, 1995. Mem. ASTD, Soc. for Human Resource Mgmt. (Area II bd. dirs. 2002-03), Augusta-Aiken Soc. for Human Resource Mgmt. (sec. 2000, pres. elect, 2001, pres. 2002), Big Bend Soc. Human Resource Mgmt. (exec. bd. 2003—). Avocations: golf, travel, jazz. Office: Talla-Com Industries 1721 W Paul Dirac Dr Tallahassee FL 32310 E-mail: jpmorgante@annimar.com.

MORGENROTH, EARL EUGENE, entrepreneur; b. Sidney, Mont., May 7, 1936; s. Frank and Leona (Ellison) M.; children: Dolores Roxanna, David Jonathan, Denise Christine BS, U. Mont., 1961. From salesman to gen. mgr. Sta. KGVO-AM Radio, Missoula, Mont., 1958-65; sales mgr. Stas. KGVO-TV, KTVM-TV and KCFW-TV, Missoula, Butte, Kalispell, Mont., 1965-66, gen. mgr., 1966-68, Sta. KCOY-TV, Santa Maria, Calif., 1968-69; v.p., gen. mgr. Western Broadcasting Co., Missoula, 1966-69, gen. mgr., pres., 1969-81, numerous cos., Mont., Calif., Idaho, P.R., Ga., 1966-84; pres., chmn. Western Broadcasting Co., Missoula, 1981-84, Western Comm., Inc., Reno, 1984-90; prin. Western Investments, Reno, 1984—. Chmn. Western Fin., Inc., Morgenroth Music Ctrs. Inc., Mont. Band Instruments, Inc., E&B Music Inc., Times Square, Inc., Rio Plumas Ranches, LLC; mem. presdl. adv. coun. U. Mont., 1994—, mem. biol. scis. adv. coun., 1999—. Mem. Mont. Bank Bd., Helena; commencement spkr. U. Mont., 1988, mem. pres.' adv. coun., 1992--, mem. biol. scis. adv. coun., 2001--; bd. dirs. U. Mont. Found., 1985-95. With. U.S. Army, 1954-57. Named Boss of Yr. Santa Maria Valley J.C.s, 1968, Alumnus of the Yr., U. Mont. Bus. Sch., 1998. Mem. U. Mont. Century Club (pres.), Missoula C. of C. (pres.), Rocky Mountain Broadcasters Assn. (pres.), Craighead Wildlife-Wildlands Inst. (bd. dirs. 1991-97), Boone and Crockett Club (pres. 2001-02), Grizzly Riders Internat. (bd. dirs., v.p. 1991-), Bldg. A Scholastic Heritage (bd. dirs. 1987-97). Republican. Methodist.

MORGENSEN, JERRY LYNN, construction company executive; b. Lubbock, Tex., July 9, 1942; s. J.J. and Zelline (Butler) M.; m. Linda Dee Austin, Apr. 17, 1965; children: Angela, Nicole BCE, Tex. Tech U., 1965. Area engr. E.I. Dupont Co., Orange, Tex., 1965-67, div. engr. La Place, La., 1967-73; project mgr. Hensel Phelps Constrn. Co., Greeley, Colo., 1973-78, area mgr., 1978-80, v.p., 1980-85, pres., CEO, 1985—. Office: 420 6th Ave Greeley CO 80631-2332

MORGENSON, GRETCHEN C. reporter; b. State College, Pa., Jan. 2, 1956; BA in English and History, Saint Olaf Coll., 1976. Asst. editor Vogue Mag., 1976—81; stock broker Dean Witter Reynolds, N.Y.C., 1981—84; staff writer Money Mag., 1984—86; editor, investigative bus. writer Forbes Mag., 1986—93; exec. editor Worth Mag., 1993—95; mng. editor Forbes Mag., 1996—98; asst. bus. and fin. editor NY Times, 1998—. Author: Forbes Great Minds of Business, 1997; co-author: The Woman's Guide to the Stock Market, 1981; author: (with Campbell R. Harvey) The New York Times Dictionary of Money and Investing: The Essential A-to-Z Guide to the Language of the New Market, 2002; co-author: (with Allen R. Myerson (editor), Floyd Norris) The New Rules of Personal Investing: How to Prosper in a Changing Economy, 2001. Recipient Gerald Loeb award, 1998, 2002, Pulitzer Prize for beat reporting, 2002, TJFR Group/MasterCard Internat. Bus. News Luminaries award, 2003. Office: NY Times 229 W 43d St New York NY 10036*

MORGENSTEIN, WILLIAM, shoe company executive; b. Bklyn., Jan. 11, 1933; s. Samuel and Jeanne Marie (Mittentag) M.; m. Sylvia Dove, June 8, 1952; children: Lee Brian, David Barry. BS in Fin., U. Ala., 1955. Salesman Greenwald Shoe Co., Birmingham, Ala., 1954-56; sr. buyer Melville Shoe Corp., N.Y.C., 1958-67; pres. Kitty Kelly Shoe Co., N.Y.C., 1967-70; exec. v.p. A.S. Beck Shoes, N.Y.C., 1970-71, Sandia Internat., Englewood Cliffs, N.J., 1971-75; pres., chief exec. officer Marquesa Internat. Corp., Englewood, N.J., 1975-95; sr. acct. mgr. Signature Group divsn. Montgomery Ward, 1995-99; v.p. Advanceme.com Inc., 1999—. Internat. cons. footwear exporting, 1965—. Served with U.S. Army, 1956-58. Mem. Footwear Distbrs. and Retailers Am. (vice-chmn., bd. dirs., exec. com.), Internat. Footwear Assn. (vice-chmn., exec. com. 1986—, chmn. 1989—, pres.), 210 Assn. (Pres.' Circle 1987), Toastmasters (past pres. Teaneck, N.J. chpt.). Republican. Jewish. Avocations: history, golf. Office Phone: 888-700-8181 132. E-mail: bmorgens@aol.com., bmorgenstein@advanceme.com.

MORGENSTERN, LEON, surgeon; b. Pitts., July 14, 1919; s. Max Samuel and Sarah (Master) M.; m. Laurie Mattlin, Nov. 27, 1967; 1 son, David Ethan. Student, CCNY, 1936-37; BA magna cum laude, Bklyn. Coll., 1940; MD, N.Y. U., 1943. Diplomate: Am. Bd. Surgery. Intern Queens Gen. Hosp., Jamaica, N.Y., 1943-44, fellow, asst. resident in pathology, 1947-48, resident in surgery, 1948-52; practice medicine, specializing in surgery LA, 1953—, Bronx, N.Y., 1959-60; dir. surgery Cedars of Lebanon Hosp., LA, 1960—73, Cedars-Sinai Med. Ctr., LA, 1973—88, emeritus dir. surgery, 1989—, dir. bioethics program, 1995—; prof. surgery UCLA Sch. Medicine, 1973-90, prof. surgery emeritus, 1990—. Asst. prof. surgery Albert Einstein Coll. Medicine, N.Y.C., 1959-60; adj. prof. bioethics U. Judaism, L.A., 1996—; dir. Ctr. Health Care Ethics Cedars-Sinai Med. Ctr., 1998—. Assoc. editor Mount Sinai Jour. Medicine, 1984-88; contbr. articles to profl. publs. Served to capt. M.C. U.S. Army, 1944-46. Mem. Soc. for Surgery Alimentary Tract, Soc. Am. Gastrointestinal Endoscopic Surgeons (hon.), Am. Gastroent. Assn., L.A. Surg. Soc. (pres. 1977), ACS (sec.-treas. 1976-77, pres. 1978, bd. dirs. So. Calif. chpt. 1976-84, gov.-at-large), Internat. Soc. Surgery, Western Surg. Assn., Pacific Coast Surg. Assn., AMA, Calif. Med. Assn., L.A. County Med. Assn., Am. Surg. Assn., others. Home: 5694 Calpine Dr Malibu CA 90265-3812 Office Phone: 310-423-9636. Business E-Mail: morgenstern@cshs.org.

MORGENSTERN, LEWIS B. medical educator; Grad., U. Mich.; postgrad., U. Tex. Resident in neurology Johns Hopkins Hosp., Balt.; assoc. prof. neurology U. Tex. Med. Sch., Houston, 1994—2002. Recipient Clinician Scientist award, Am. Heart Assn., 1996. Mem.: Alpha Omega Alpha. Office: U Mich Health Sys TC 1920/0316 1500 E Medical Center Dr Ann Arbor MI 48109

MORGENSTERN, MATTHEW, computer scientist; b. N.Y.C. BSEE, Columbia U., 1968, MSEE and Computer Sci., 1970; MS in Computer Sci. and Mgmt., MIT, 1975, PhD in Computer Sci., 1976. Asst. prof. computer sci. Rutgers U., New Brunswick, N.J., 1976-82; research computer scientist Info. Scis. Inst., U. So. Calif., Los Angeles, 1982-84; sr. computer scientist SRI Internat., Menlo Park, Calif., 1984-90; dir. R & D programs advt. info. tech. divsn. Xerox, Cambridge, Mass., 1990-92; prin. scientist Xerox Design Rsch. Inst./Cornell U., Ithaca, N.Y., 1992—. Cons. Hewlett-Packard Corp., Palo Alto, Calif., 1990, Cornell U., 1996—; prin. investigator U.S. Govt. DARPA projects on heterogeneous databases and metadata repositories, 1992—. Co-author: Database Security VIII, 1994; contbr. articles to profl. jours. Mem.

IEEE, Am. Assn. Artificial Intelligence, Assn. Computing Machinery, Sigma Xi, Tau Beta Pi, Eta Kappa Nu. Office: Xerox Design Research Inst Cornell Univ 603 Rhodes Hall Theory Ctr Ithaca NY 14853-3801 E-mail: mmorgen@alum.mit.edu.

MORGENSTERN, NORBERT RUBIN, civil engineering educator; b. Toronto, Ont., Can., May 25, 1935; s. Joel and Bella (Skornik) M.; m. Patricia Elizabeth Gooderham, Dec. 28, 1960; children: Sarah Alexandra, Katherine Victoria, David Michael Gooderham. BASc, U. Toronto, 1956, DEng h.c., 1983; DIC, Imperial Coll. Sci., 1964; PhD, U. London, 1964; DSc h.c., Queen's U., 1989. Rsch. asst., lectr. civil engring. Imperial Coll. Sci. and Tech., London, 1958-68; prof. civil engring. U. Alta., Edmonton, Can., 1968-83, Univ. prof., 1983—, chmn. dept. civil engring., 1994-97. Cons. engr., 1961— Contbr. articles to profl. jours. Bd. dirs. Young Naturalists Found., 1977-82, Edmonton Symphony Soc., 1978-85. Decorated Order of Can.; recipient prize Brit. Geotech. Soc., 1961, 66, Huber prize ASCE, 1971, Legget award Can. Geotech. Soc., 1979, Alta. order of Excellence, 1991; Athlone fellow, 1956. Fellow Royal Soc. Can., Can. Acad. Engring., Indian Nat. Acad. Engring. (fgn.); mem. U.S. Nat. Acad. Engring. (fgn. assoc.), Royal Acad. Engring. (fgn. mem.), Cancian Geosci. Coun. (pres. 1983), Order Can., Can. Geotechnical Soc. (pres. 1989-91), Internat. Soc. for Soil Mechanics and Found. Engring. (pres. 1989-94), Royal Glenora Club, Athenaeum (London), various other profl. assns. Home: 106 Laurier Dr Edmonton AB Canada T5R 5P6 Office: U Alta Dept Civil Engring Edmonton AB Canada T6G 2G7

MORGENSTERN, ROBERT TERENCE, lawyer; b. N.Y.C., Aug. 23, 1944; s. Carl G. and Jean C. (Madden) M.; m. Nancy G. Golden, June 29, 1968; children: Cynthia, John, Kathryn, Brian. BA, Villanova U., 1966, JD, 1969. Bar: N.J. 1969, U.S. Supreme Ct. 1986; cert. civil trial atty. Assoc. Dolan & Dolan, Newton, N.J., 1969-74, officer, dir., 1975—. Mem. ABA, Assn. Trial Lawyers Am., N.J. Fedn. Planning Officials, Sussex County Bar Assn. (v.p.), N.J. State Bar Assn., Rotary. Roman Catholic. Home: 44 Deire Dr Sparta NJ 07871-1134 Office: Dolan & Dolan PA 53 Spring St & 1 Legal Ln PO Box D Newton NJ 07860-0605 Office Phone: 973-383-1600.

MORGENSTERN, SHELDON JON, symphony orchestra conductor; b. Cleve., July 1, 1938; s. Irwin Arthur and Harriet Sue Morgenstern; m. Patricia Lou Bradshaw; 1 child, Sali Sharpe Hagan. MusB, Northwestern U., 1961; MusM, New Eng. Conservatory, 1966; DMA (hon.), Greensboro (N.C.) Coll., 1986. Mem. conducting staff New Eng. Conservatory, 1965-66; music dir. Greensboro Symphony Orch., 1967-74; prin. guest condr. Betica Philharm., Seville, Spain, 1978-82, Polish Radio Orch., Warsaw, 1990—. Music advisor Miss. Symphony Orch., 1985-86; bd. mem. Istanbul (Turkey) Internat. Festival, 1975—, Company for Televised Theatre; mus. cons. U.S. Dept. Interior for Wolf Trap Farm Park, 1972; mem. adv. bd. Avery Fisher Award, 1978—; music dir. Ea. Music Festival, Greensboro, 1962-98, music dir. emeritus, 1998—. Author: No Vivaldi in the Garage, 2001. Recipient O'Henry award City of Greensboro, 1980, Long Leaf Pine award State N.C., 1989, Nat. Alumni award Northwestern U., 1990. Home: Airans/Farges Ch des Charmys 01550 Collonges France E-mail: 105017.2535@compuserve.com.

MORGENTHALER, DAVID TURNER, venture capitalist; b. Chester, S.C., Aug. 5, 1919; s. Henry W. and Elizabeth (Taylor) M.; B.S. in Mech. Engring., M.S., Mass. Inst. Tech., 1941; m. Lindsay Anne Jordan, May 17, 1945; children— David T., Gary J., Todd W., Gaye Elizabeth. Sales mgr. Ervite Corp., 1945-47; mech. engr. Copes Vulcan div. Blaw-Knox Co., 1947-50; v.p., dir. sales Delavan Mfg. Co., Des Moines, 1950-57; pres. Foseco, Inc., Cleve., 1957-68; chmn. bd. Foseco Technik Ltd., Birmingham, Eng., 1964-68; chmn. bd. API Instruments Co., 1968-70, dir., 1963-70; chmn. bd. Mfg. Data Systems, Inc., Ann Arbor, Mich., 1969-81; chmn. exec. com., dir. LFE Corp., Waltham, Mass., 1970-85; founding ptnr. Morgenthaler Assocs.; mng. ptnr. Morgenthaler Ventures, 1981—; dir. Hauserman, Inc., Cleve., Tartan Labs., Inc., Pitts., Three Phoenix Co.; bd. dirs., Ribozyme Pharmaceuticals, 1992-02, chmn., 1995-02; ons. Brentwood Assocs.; trustee Cleve. Clinic Found.; bd. overseers Case Western Res. U. Served to capt., AUS, 1941-45. Mem. Nat. Venture Capital Assn. (past pres.), Chief Execs. Orgn., Inc. (past pres.), Young Pres. Orgn. (sr. v.p., bd. dirs.), Sigma Nu. Clubs: Westwood Country, Union, Pacific Union, Lyford Cay. Home: 13904 Edgewater Dr Cleveland OH 44107-1416 Office: 50 Public Sq Ste 2700 Cleveland OH 44113

MORGENTHALER-LEVER, ALISA, lawyer; b. St. Louis, June 3, 1960; d. Gerald Thomas and Mary Louise (Neece) M. BA, S.W. Mo. State U., 1982; JD, Cornell U., 1985. Bar: N.Y. 1986, D.C. 1988, Calif. 1990. Law clk. City of Springfield, Mo., 1981; atty. bd. govs. Fed. Res. Sys., Washington, 1984, staff atty., 1985-86; assoc. Kirkpatrick & Lockhart, Washington, 1986-88, Stroock & Stroock & Lavan, Washington, 1988-89; ptnr. Christensen, Miller, Fink, Jacobs, Glaser, Weil & Shapiro, L.A., 1989—. V.p., sec., bd. dirs. L.A. Retarded Citizens Found.; v.p., bd. dirs. Malibu Riviera III Homeowners Assn. Mem. ABA, Calif. Bar Assn. (del. to com. on adminstrn. justice), D.C. Bar Assn., N.Y. Bar Assn., L.A. County Bar Assn. (jud. appts. com.), Beverly Hills Bar Assn., Century City Bar Assn., Women Lawyers Assn. of L.A. (bd. dirs.), 3019 Third St. Owners Assn. (v.p. bd. dirs.), Order of Omega, Phi Alpha Delta, Rho Lambda, Phi Kappa Phi, Pi Sigma Alpha, Gamma Phi Beta. Office: Christensen Miller Fink Jacobs Glaser Weil & Shapiro 10250 Constellation Blvd 19th Fl Los Angeles CA 90067-5010 E-mail: amorgenthaler@chrismill.com.

MORGENTHAU, ROBERT MORRIS, prosecutor; b. N.Y.C., July 31, 1919; s. Henry Jr. and Elinor (Fatman) M.; m. Martha Pattridge (dec.); children: Joan, Anne, Elinor, Robert P., Barbara; m. Lucinda Franks, Nov. 19, 1977; children: Joshua, Amy. Grad., Deerfield (Mass.) Acad., 1937; BA, Amherst Coll., 1941, LLD (hon.), 1966; LLB, Yale U., 1948; LLD (hon.), N.Y. Law Sch., 1968, Syracuse Law Sch., 1976, Albany Law Sch., 1982, Colgate U., 1988. Bar: N.Y. 1949. Assoc. firm Patterson Belknap & Webb, N.Y.C., 1948-53, ptnr., 1954-61; U.S. atty. So. Dist. N.Y., 1961-62, 62-70; dist. atty. New York County, 1975—. Former pres. N.Y. State Dist. Attys. Assn.; lectr. London Sch. Econs., 1993. Chmn. Police Athletic League; trustee Baron de Hirsch Fund; chmn. Gov.'s Adv. Com. on Sentencing, 1979; counsel N.Y. State Law Enforcement Coun.; chmn. A Living Meml. to the Holocaust-Mus. of Jewish Heritage; Dem. candidate for Gov. of N.Y., 1962; trustee Temple Emanu-El, N.Y.C.; bd. dirs. P.R. Legal Def. and Edn. Fund. Lt. comdr. USNR, 1940—45. Recipient Emory Buckner award Fed. Bar Coun., 1983, Yale Citation of Merit, 1982, Fordham-Stein prize, 1988, Thomas Jefferson award in law U. Va., 1991, Brandeis medal U. Louisville, 1995, Omanut award Yeshiva U., 1995, Trumpeter award Nat. Consumers League, 1995, Frank S. Hogan award N.Y. State Dist. Atty's. Assn., 2000, Lone Sailor award USN Meml. Found., 2000; named Man of Yr., Fed. Law Enforcement Assn. Found., 2004; Matheson-Morgenthau Disting. Professorship in Law named in his honor, Va. Law Sch. Fellow Am. Bar Found.; mem. ABA, N.Y. State Bar Assn. (award for Excellence in Pub. Svc. 2001), Assn. of the Bar of the City of N.Y., N.Y. County Lawyers Assn. (Disting. Pub. Svc. award 1993), Amherst Alumni Assn. (hon. pres. 2001), Phi Beta Kappa. Office: Office Dist Atty 1 Hogan Pl New York NY 10013-4311

MORGESE, VINCENT JOHN, neurosurgeon; b. Whippany, N.J., Apr. 23, 1961; s. Albert Nicholas and Irma Nittoli Morgese; m. Victoria C. Morgese, Apr. 1, 1990; children: Elizabeth, Albert. BA in Biophysics, Johns Hopkins U., 1983; MD, Brown U., 1987. Diplomate Am. Bd. Neurologic Surgery. Resident neurosurgery Loma Linda (Calif.) U., 1987-93; pvt. practice neurosurgeon Napa, Calif., 1993—. Recipient Good Citizenship award DAR, N.J., 1979. Mem. AMA, Am. Assn. Neurol. Surgeons, Congress Neurol. Surgeons, Calif. Assn. Neurol. Surgeons, Calif. Med. Assn., Napa County Med. Assn. Office: 980 Trancas St Ste 12 Napa CA 94558-2933

MORGISON, F. EDWARD, investment broker; b. Clay Center, Kans., Oct. 4, 1940; s. Fred and Lena Edna (Chaput) M.; m. Karen Lorene Herdman, Nov. 21, 1964; 1 child, Diana Michelle. BA in Math., Emporia State U., 1963; MSBA, U. Mo., Columbia, 1964; postgrad., U. Mo., Kansas City. Cert. purchasing mgr.; registered securities agt., Mo., Kans., Ill., 2001. Computer programmer U. Mo. Med. Ctr., Columbia, 1964-65; adminstrv. and budget analyst Urban Renewal Project, Independence, Mo., 1965-66; acct. exec., bank broker Stifel Nicolaus & Co., Kansas City, Mo., 1966-73; pres., CEO Will-Mor Investment Sys., Kansas City, Mo., 1973-75; br. mgr. Edward Jones & Co., Kansas City, 1975; editl. and exec. asst. to Morgan Maxfield for U.S. Congress, Kansas City, 1976; sr. acct. exec., merger and acquisitions specialist Rowland & Co., Kansas City, 1976-77; chmn. bd., pres., CEO Mo. Securities, Inc., Kansas City, 1977-78; v.p., regional mgr. Charles Schwab & Co., Kansas City, 1978-79; v.p. Profl. Assistance, Kansas City, 1979-81; exec. v.p. J. Penner & Assocs., Kansas City, 1981-82; pres. J. Penner & Co., Kansas City, 1982-83; acct. exec., registered broker Lowell H. Listrom & Co., 1981-84; pres., CEO First Allen Securities, Inc., 1983-89, Venture House, Kansas City, 1989—. Agt. Offerman & Co., Kansas City, 1979-81, CEO Morgison & Assoc., Kansas City, 1979-81; fiscal dir. Housing Authority of Kansas City, 1981; dir., sec. Hubach Group, Inc., 1987-88; treas. Skytrader Corp., 1986-89, Emergency Sys. Svcs., 1986-87, Internat. Tex. Industries, Inc., San Antonio, 1986-88; chmn. bd., treas. Masters Mark, Inc., 1986-89; CFO Am. Utilicraft Corp., 1992-97, v.p. purchasing, 1997--; acct. exec. N.Y. Stock Exch., Am. Exch., 1965-89. Recipient Bausch and Lomb Sci. award, 1959, Sci. award Lambda Delta Lambda, 1962. Mem. NRA (life), U. Mo. Alumni Assn. (life), Emporia State U. Alumni Assn. (life), U.S. Chess Fedn. (life), Mensa (life). Home: 1000 NE 96th Ter Kansas City MO 64155-2145

MORGNER, AURELIUS, economist, educator; b. N.Y.C., May 23, 1917; s. Oscar A. and Anna G. (Hoffmeister) M. BS in Bus. Adminstrn., U. Mo., 1938, MA in Econs., 1940; PhD, U. Minn., 1955. Investigator Dept. Labor, 1941; project dir. Employment Stblzn. Research Inst., 1941-42; instr. bus. adminstrn. U. Minn., 1942-46; lectr. Northwestern U., 1946-47; assoc. prof. Tex. A&M U., 1947-56, prof., 1956-58; vis. prof. U. São Paulo, Brazil, 1958-60, dir. grad. social studies, 1959-60; prof. econs. U. So. Calif., L.A., 1960—, chmn. dept., 1962-69; prof. internat. econs. Sch. Internat. Relations, 1960—. Pub. panel mem. Chgo. Regional War Labor Bd., 1943-45; pub. rep. minimum wage com. Dept. Labor, 1942,43; cons. Govt. Eucador, 1965-68, Govt. Guyana, 1968, state Nev., 1970, Philippines, 1971-72, Yemen Arab Republic, 1974-75; U.S. State Dept. vis. lectr., Brazil, summer 1966 Co-author: Local Labor Markets, 1948, Problems in Economic Analysis, 1948, Problems in the Theory of Price, 1954 (trans. Spanish 1965, Portuguese 1967). Ford faculty fellow Columbia U., 1954-55 Mem. So. Calif. Econ. Assn. (pres. 1965-66), Am. Econs. Assn., Western Econ. Assn., Am. Arbitration Assn., Internat. Studies Assn. Office: U So Calif Dept Econs Los Angeles CA 90089-0001

MORGRIDGE, JOHN P. computer systems network executive; m. Tashia Morgridge; three children. BBA, DSc (hon.), U. Wis.; MBA, Stanford U. Mktg. profl. Honeywell Info. Systems, 1960-80; v.p. mkgt., sales and svc. Stratus Co., Inc., 1980-86; pres., chief ops. officer GRiD Systems (now part of Tandy Corp.), 1986-88; pres., CEO Cisco Systems, 1988-95, pres., CEO, chmn., 1995-98, chmn., 1998—. Recipient Leadership in Tech. award Tech. Corps, 1988. Office: Cisco Systems 170 W Tasman Dr San Jose CA 95134-1700

MORI, ALLEN ANTHONY, academic administrator, consultant; b. Hazleton, Pa., Nov. 1, 1947; s. Primo Philip and Carmella (DeNoia) M.; m. Barbara Epoca, June 26, 1971; 1 child, Kirsten Lynn. BA, Franklin and Marshall Coll., Lancaster, Pa., 1969; MEd, Bloomsburg U. Pa., 1971; PhD, U. Pitts., 1975. Spl. edn. tchr. White Haven (Pa.) State Sch. and Hosp., 1969-70, Hazleton Area Sch. Dist., 1970-71, Pitts. Pub. Schs., 1971-74; supr. student tchrs. U. Pitts., 1974-75; prof. spl. edn. U. Nev., Las Vegas, 1975-84; dean coll edn. Marshall U., Huntington, W.Va., 1984-87; dean coll. edn. Calif. State U., L.A., 1987—2003, provost, v.p. acad. affairs Dominquez Hills, 2003—. Hearing officer pub. law 94-142 Nev. Dept. Edn., Carson City, 1978—; mem. Nev. Gov.'s Com. on Mental Health and Mental Retardation, 1983-84; cons. Ministry Edn., Manitoba, Can., 1980-82; pres. Tchr. Edn. Coun. State Colls. and Univs., 1993-94. Author: Families of Children with Special Needs, 1983; co-author: Teaching the Severely Retarded, 1980, Handbook of Preschool, Special Education, 1980, Adapted Physical Education, 1983, A Vocational Training Continuum for the Mentally and Physically Disabled, 1985, Teaching Secondary Students with Mild Learning and Behavior Problems, 1986, 93, 99; author numerous articles, book revs. and monographs. Bd. dirs. Assn. Retarded Citizens San Gabriel Valley, ElMonte, 1989-94. Recipient grants U.S. Dept. Edn., 1976-91, Nev. Dept. Edn., W.Va. Dept. Edn., Calif. State U. Chancellor's Office. Mem. Assn. Tchr. Educators, Coun. for Exceptional Children (div. on Career Devel. exec. com. 1981-83), Nat. Soc. for Study of Edn., Phi Beta Delta, Phi Delta Kappa, Pi Lambda Theta. Avocations: wine collecting, travel. Office: Calif State U Dominguez Hills 1000 E Victoria Carson CA 90747

MORI, MARIKO, artist; b. Tokyo, 1967; Student, Bunka Fashion Coll., Tokyo, 1986-88, Byam Shaw Sch. Art, London, 1988-89, Chelsea Coll. Art, 1989-92, Whitney Mus. Am. Art, 1992-93. One-woman shows include Geneva Project Room, N.Y.C., 1993, Shiseido Gallery, Tokyo, 1995, Am. Fine Arts Co., N.Y., 1995, Galerie Emmanuel Perrotin, Paris, 1996, Ctr. Nat. D'Art Contemporain Grenoble, Italy-Nordic Pavilion Venice Biennale, 1997, L.A. County Mus. Art, 1998, Mus. Contemporary Art, Cgo., 1998, Serpentine Gallery, London, 1998, Andy Warhol Mus., Paris, 1998, Bklyn. Mus. Art, Kunstmus. Wolfsburg, 1999, Fondazione Prada, Milan, 1999, Ctr. Pompidou, Paris, Ctr. Nat. Photography, 2000, Mus. Contemporary Art, 2002, Tokyo, 2004. Office: c/o Eyestorm 2nd Fl 547 W 27th St New York NY 10001

MORI, TOSHIKO, architecture educator; Student, Cooper Union, 1970—71, BArch, 1976; AM (hon.), Harvard U., 1996. Registered Arch., Fla., Maine, N.Y., NCARB cert. Arch. Edward Larrabee Barnes and Assocs., 1976—81, Toshiko Mori Arch., 1981—; prof. architecture Grad. Sch. Design Harvard U., 1995—2001, Robert P. Hubbard prof. arch. Grad. Sch. Design, 2002—, chair dept. architecture Grad. Sch. Design, 2002—. Arch. Tod Williams and Assocs., 1972—73, ELS Design Group Urban Design, 1973—74; vis. critic Grad. Sch. Design Harvard U., 1989, 94; Eero Saarinen vis. prof. Sch. Architecture Yale U., 1992, vis. critic Sch. Architecture, 93, Columbia U., 1994; lectr. in field. Advisor Greenwich Village Soc. Historic Preservation; mem. adv. bd. Montreal Mus. Decorative Art McDonald Stewart Found. Recipient prize for urban design, Abraham Kazan Fund, 1976, Henry Adams Cert. of Achievement, AIA, 1976, The One Show Merit award, 1981, N.Y.C./AIA Design Award Citation Interior Architecture, 1988, N.Y.C./AIA Design award in interior architecture, Internat. Assn. Lighting Designers, 1989, 11th Ann. Interiors award for best retail design, Shinkenchiku/Ctrl. Glass Internat., 1990, Renovation award, C. of C., Rockport, Rockland, Maine, 1995, Silver medal in exhbn. design at MOMA, Art Dirs. Club, 1999, N.Y.C./AIA Design award, 1998, 2000. Office: Harvard Design Sch 202 Gund Hall 48 Quincy St Cambridge MA 02138

MORIAL, MARC HAYDEL, former mayor, association executive; b. New Orleans, Jan. 3, 1958; s. Ernest and Sybil M.; m. Michelle Miller; 1 child, Mason; 1 child from previous marriage, Kemah. Bar: La. Legis. intern U.S. Sen. Russell Long, Washington, 1979; dir. U. Pa. Office of Supportive Svcs., Phila., 1979-80; summer assoc. U.S. Atty. U.S. Dist. Ct. (so. dist.) N.Y., 1982; legis. asst. U.S. Rep. George T. Leland, Washington, 1983; atty. Barham & Churchill, New Orleans, 1983-85; pvt. practice New Orleans, 1985—; mem. La. Senate, Baton Rouge, 1991-93, mem. revenue and fiscal affairs com., commerce com., labor and indsl. rels. com., select com. crime & drugs, intergovtl. rels. com., Pres. Clinton's action com. on crime & drugs, senate select com. on econ. devel.; mayor City of New Orleans, 1993—2002; ptnr. Adams & Reese, 2002—03; pres. Nat. Urban League, N.Y.C., 2003—. Adj. prof. law, polit. sci. Xavier U. La., New Orleans, 1988-90. Del. Nat. Rainbow Coalition Conv., 1986, La. State Dem. Conv., 1986, Dem. Nat. Conv., Atlanta, 1988; cooperating atty. NAACP Legal Def. Fund, mem. nat., New Orleans br.; gen. counsel La. Assn. Minority and Women Owned Businesses, Inc., La. Voter Registration/Edn. Crusade; cooperating atty. Minority Bus. Enterprise Legal Def. and Edn. Fund; divestment coord., legal advisor New Orleans Anti-Apartheid Coalition, 1983—; bd. dirs. La. ACLU, La. Spl. Olympics, Milne Boys Home; mem. project steering com. Voting Rights Law Reporter; mem. Young Leadership Coun., Friend of New Orleans Ctr. for Creative Arts. Recipient Chmns. award Congl. Black Caucus, 1989, Outstanding Svc. award Lutcher (La.) H.S., 1990, La. NAACP Cmty. Svc. award, 1988; named Legis. Rookie of Yr. Baton Rouge Bus. Report, 1992, All Rookie Team by polit. columnist John Maginnis, 1993, Legis. Newcome of Yr., 1992. Mem. ABA (standing com. on world order under law 1982-83), Nat. Bar Assn., La. State Bar Assn. (Pro Bono Pub. award 1988), La. Assn. Criminal Def. Attys., Nat. Conf. Black Lawyers, Amnesty Internat. USA, Transafrica, Louis A. Martinet Legal Soc. New Orleans, La. Trial Lawyers Assn. (pres. adv. coun.), Nat. Black Law Students Assn. (nat. bd. dirs. 1981-83), Alpha Phi Alpha. Office: Nat Urban League 120 Wall St 8th Fl New York NY 10005

MORIARTY, DONALD WILLIAM, JR., bank executive; b. Amarillo, Tex., Sept. 15, 1939; s. Donald William and Lorraine Julia (Walck) Moriarty; m. Rita Ann Giller, Nov. 28, 1964; children: Mary Kathleen, Jennifer Ann, Anne Marie, Kerry Lee, Erin Teresa. Student, St. Benedict's Coll., 1957-59, 60-61; BSc, Washington U., 1962; MSc, St. Louis U., 1965, PhD, 1970. Cost acct. Emerson Electric, St. Louis, 1959-63; grad. fellow in econs. St. Louis U., 1963-65, instr., 1965-68; asst. prof. U. Mo., St. Louis, 1968-70; with Fed. Res. Bank of St. Louis, 1968-83, v.p., 1971-74, sr. v.p., controller, 1974-77, 1st v.p., 1977-83; sr. v.p. Gen. Bancshares Corp., 1983-86; exec. v.p. Commerce Bancshares, Inc., 1986-87; bank cons., 1987-89; pres., CEO, bd. dirs. Duchesne Bank, St. Peters, Mo., 1989-95; sr. cons. Universal Fin. Group, Inc., 1996—2003; assoc. prof. bus. Fontbonne U., St. Louis, 1998—. Vis. instr. Webster Coll., 1975—82; adviser City of Des Peres, Mo., chmn. fin. com., 1976—78, chmn. mgmt. com., 1978—81, mem. pers. commn., 1978—81, mem. planning and zoning com., 1981—83; bd. dirs. Mid-Am. Payments Exch., Duchesne Bank. Mem. parent's coun. Creighton U., Omaha, 1995—97; mem. adv. bd. St. Joseph Acad., 1982—86; mem. pres.'s coun. St. Louis U., 1983—; dist. chmn. Boy Scouts Am., 1991—93, vice chmn., 1994—2001; trustee, chmn. St. Joseph Hosp., 1982—93; bd. dirs. ea. Mo. region NCCJ, 1987—93. Recipient Alumni Merit award, St. Louis U., 1979. Mem.: Am. Mgmt. Assn., Am. Fin. Assn., Am. Econ. Assn., Alhpa Kappa Psi, Beta Gamma Sigma.

MORIARTY, GEORGE MARSHALL, lawyer; b. Youngstown, Ohio, Sept. 16, 1942; s. George Albert Moriarty and Caroline (Jones) Bass; m. Elizabeth Bradley Moore, Sept. 11, 1965 (div. 1986); children: Bradley Marshall, Caroline Walden, Sarah Cameron; m. Phyllis A.N. Thompson, May 2, 1998. BA magna cum laude, Harvard U., 1964, LLB magna cum laude, 1968. Bar: Mass. 1969, U.S. Dist. Ct. Mass. 1973, U.S. Ct. Appeals (1st cir.) 1976, U.S. Ct. Appeals (D.C. cir.) 1984, U.S. Claims Ct. 1983, U.S. Supreme Ct. 1976, U.S. Ct. Appeals (2d cir.) 1997. Law clk. to Hon. Bailey Aldrich U.S. Ct. Appeals (1st cir.), Boston, 1968-69; law clk. to Hon. Warren Burger, Hon. Hugo Black, Hon. Potter Stewart, Hon. Byron White U.S. Supreme Ct., Washington, 1969-70; spl. asst. to Hon. Elliot L. Richardson, Dept. Health, Edn. & Welfare, Washington, 1970-71, exec. asst., 1971-72; assoc. Ropes & Gray, Boston, 1972-77, ptnr., 1977—. Bd. dirs. Ptnrs. Healthcare Sys. Pres. Boston Athenaeum; chmn. Brigham and Women's Hosp. Mem. ABA, Am. Law Inst., Boston Bar Assn., Somerset Club, Tavern Club, Met. Club. Office: Ropes & Gray 1 Internat Pl Boston MA 02110

MORIARTY, JOHN, opera administrator, artistic director; b. Fall River, Mass., Sept. 30, 1930; s. John J. and Fabiola Marie (Ripeau) M. MusB summa cum laude, New Eng. Conservatory, 1952, DM, 1992. Artistic adminstr. Opera Soc. of Washington, 1960-62, Santa Fe Opera, 1962-65; dir. Wolf Trap Co., Vienna, Va., 1972-77; chmn. opera dept. Boston Conservatory, 1973-89, New Eng. Conservatory, 1989—. Prin. condr. Central City Opera, Denver, 1978—, artistic dir., 1982-98, artistic dir. emeritus, 1998—; panelist Nat. Inst. Music Theater, 1985, 86, 87, Conn. Arts Coun., 1982, 84; adjudicator various contests including Met. Opera auditions, 1965—. Author: Diction, 1975. Bd. dirs. Wm. Matheus Sullivan Found.; trustee Boston Concert Opera; recs. on Cambridge Records, Newport Classics, Parnassus Records; adv. bd. Shoshana Found. Recipient Frank Huntington Beebe award, Boston, 1954, Disting. Alumni award New Eng. Conservatory Alumni Assn., 1982, Gold Chair award Central City Opera House Assn., 1988. Mem. Nat. Opera Assn., Sigma Alpha Iota, Delta Omicron, Pi Kappa Lambda. Office: New Eng Conservatory 290 Huntington Ave Boston MA 02115-5018 also: Cen City Opera House Assn 621 17th St Ste 1601 Denver CO 80293-1601

MORIARTY, JOHN KLINGE, electronics engineer, consultant; b. Washington, Feb. 6, 1956; s. John Klinge and Mary (Cozart) M.; m. Elizabeth Rouse, Dec. 31, 1987; children: Maire Elizabeth, John Lank, Harris James. BS in Physics, Va. Poly. Inst. and State U., 1981; M of Engring. in Elec. Engring., Clemson U., 1996. Project engr. Delco Electronics divsn. G.M.C., Kokomo, Ind., 1981-84; staff engr. Hekimian Labs., Gaithersburg, Md., 1984-85; sr. LSI design engr. Case Comms., Inc., Columbia, Md., 1985-86; ind. electronics cons. Gaithersburg, 1986-88; mem. tech. staff Bell Labs., Reading, Pa., 1988-97; ind. electronics cons. Reading, 1997—. Cons. Squire Comms., Miami, Fla., 1986, Delco Electronics Corp., Kokomo, 1986—88, Mfg. Networks Inc., San Francisco, CPClare Corp., Beverly, Mass., Wireless Sys. Techs., Inc., San Jose, Calif.; mem. tech. adv. bd. SOMA Networks, Inc., San Francisco; tutorial presenter West Med. Design and Mfg. Conf., Anaheim, Calif., 1991, East Med. Design and Mfg. Conf., N.Y.C., 1991; sen. mem Tech. Staff Legerity Luc, 2003—. Contbr. articles to profl. jours. including IEEE Jour. Solid State Cirs., Procs. IEEE Custom Integrated Cirs., Cancer Treatment Reports. Recipient Supplier Recognition award Hughes Aircraft Corp., 1992. Mem. IEEE, IEEE Electron Device Soc., IEEE Solid State Cirs. Soc., IEEE Cirs. and Sys. Soc. Achievements include patents in field. Home: 2557 River Rd Reading PA 19605-2840 E-mail: jmoriarty@ieee.org.

MORIARTY, JOHN TIMOTHY, transportation consultant, writer; b. Cleve., Jan. 23, 1939; s. James Joseph and Margaret (Healy) Moriarty; m. Angela Marie Veneziano, June 29, 1968; children: Patrick J., Sean Gerald. Student, John Carroll U., 1957, Cleve. State U., 1964—67. Traffic analyst, Cleve., 1957—82; transp. cons. Norfolk So. R.R., Cleve., 1982—. Author: One Square Mile of Mayhem, 1998, Honest John, 1998, The Phantom Employee, 1998, Sister Mommy, 1999, Thin Ice, 2001, Streets of Gold, 2001. With U.S. Army, 1961—63. Mem.: Ill. Internat. Freight Coun. Roman Catholic. Avocations: basketball, billiards, reading. Home: Apt 2615 1111 Independence Ave Akron OH 44310-1896

MORIARTY, MICHAEL EUGENE, retired humanities educator; b. Goshen, Ind., Feb. 7, 1941; s. Frank B. and LaVon Edith M. BA, St. Francis Coll., 1965; MA, Western Mich. U., 1968; PhD, Ind. U., 1971. Ouiseau de passage litéraire, Passim, 1971-85; assoc. prof. lang. arts Valley City (Md.) State U., 1986-96; adj. assoc. prof. humanities U. Phoenix, Maitland, Fla., 1998-2000. Interim chair comms. arts and social scis. Valley City State U., 1995-96. Author: Semiotics of World Literature, 1996; contbr. articles to profl. jours. Mem. MLA, Masons, Linguistic Cir. of Manitoba and N.D. (life). Buddhist. Avocations: gardening, hiking, human rights activism. Home: 8255 Deming Dr Orlando FL 32825-8219 E-mail: mmoriar2@bellsouth.net.

MORICE, WILLIAM DANIEL, business and tax counselor; b. May 6, 1946; s. John Lowry and Evelyn Mae (Brown) M.; m. Kay Iris Mason, June 14, 1975; children: Elizabeth Anne, Charlotte Katherine, Michelle Alexandra. BSEE, U. Md., 1973; MBA, Emory U., 1976. CPA, Md. Tech. rep. Xerox Corp., Washington, 1965-66, So. Ry., Atlanta, 1973; cons. Mantech of N.J., Washington, 1975, Peat Marwick Mitchell & Co., Washington, 1976-82; prin. Booz Allen & Hamilton, Inc., Bethesda, Md., 1982-84; owner Gen. Bus. Services, Bethesda, 1985-98; CEO Gen. Tax Svcs., Inc., 1996-98; v.p. Century Small Bus. Solutions, Inc., 1998-2000; ea. region mgr. Fiducial, Inc., 2000—03, dir. field operations, 2003—. Pres. Apple Limousine Inc., 1988—, Morice and Blohm LLC, 1995-98. Bd. dirs., treas. Nat. Pbt. Bus. Polit. Fund. With U.S. Army, 1966-69. Mem. Md. Assn. Accts., Capital Area Franchise Assn. (bd. dirs.), Beta Gamma Sigma, Tau Kappa Epsilon, Terrapin Club, Friends of Kennedy Ctr. (founding mem.), River Hill Music Boosters (founder). Republican. Episcopalian. Office: Fiducial Inc 10480 Little Patuxent Pkwy Ste 300 Columbia MD 21044 E-mail: william.morice@fiducial.com., bill@moriceclan.com.

MORIE, G. GLEN, lawyer, manufacturing executive; BA, Bowdoin Coll., 1964; LLB, U. Pa., 1967. Bar: Wash. 1968. Pvt. practice law, Wash., 1970-73; asst. counsel PACCAR, Inc., Bellevue, Wash., 1973-79, asst. gen. counsel, 1979-82, gen. counsel, 1983-85, v.p., gen. counsel, 1985—. Office: PACCAR Inc PO Box 1518 Bellevue WA 98009-1518

MORIN, JOYANN HAUGE, education educator; d. Harry Adrian and Anna (Barnec) Hauge; m. Dale Arthur Morin, May 21, 1954; children: David Dale, Angelique Marie, Debra Kay(dec.). AA, ElCamino Coll., 1967; BA in History, Calif. State U., Dominguez Hills, 1969, MA, 1977; EdD in Curriculum and Instrn., U. So. Calif., 1986. Elem. tchg. credential Commn. on Tchr. Credentialing, Calif. Elem. tchr. St. Catherine Laboure Sch., Torrance, Calif., 1969—71, L.A. Unified Sch. Dist., 1971—77; curriculum coord. L.A. Sch. Dist., 1977—84; prof. Calif. State U., Northridge, 1984—93, L.A., 1993—, prof. emeritus, 2002. Presenter in field. Author: (textbook) Social Education Instruction, 2003; contbr. articles to profl. jours. Recipient Spl. Merit award, Edn. Jour., 1996; Innovative Tchg. grant, Calif. State U., L.A., 1994. Mem.: AAUP, Calif. Coun.on the Edn. Tchrs., Nat. Coun. for the Social Studies. Avocations: creative writing, researching. Home: 24848 Quigley Canyon Rd Newhall CA 91321 Office: Calif State Univ 5151 State University Dr Los Angeles CA 90032-8140

MORIN, LEE MILLER EMILE, astronaut; b. Manchester, N.H., Sept. 9, 1952; married; 2 children. BS in Math./Elec. Sci., U. N.H., 1974; MS in Biochemistry, NYU, 1978, MD, 1981, PhD in Microbiology, 1982; MPH, U. Ala., Birmingham, 1988. With Media Lab., MIT, 1974; resident in gen. surgery Bronx Mcpl. Hosp. Ctr., Montefiore Hosp. Med. Ctr., N.Y.C.; commd. lt. USN, 1982, advanced through grades to capt., 1998; undersea med. officer Naval Undersea Med. Inst., Groton, Conn., 1983; med. officer, diving med. officer, submarine med. officer USS Henry M. Jackson; naval flight surgeon, diving med. officer Naval Aerospace Med. Inst., Pensacola, Fla.; pvt. practice in occupl. medicine Jacksonville, Fla.; flight surgeon Operation Desert Shield, 1990; spl. project officer Naval Aerospace Med. Inst.; dir. warfare specialty programs Naval Aerospace and Operational Med. Inst., resident in aerospace medicine; astronaut NASA, 1996, mission specialist. Decorated Navy Commendation medal, Navy Achievement medal, Nat. Def. medal; recipient Excellence in Mil. Medicine award, Chmn. Joint Chiefs of Staff, 1994, Sustaining Membership Lecture award, Assn. Mil. Surgeons of U.S., 1996. Mem.: Soc. U.S. Naval Flight Surgeons, Undersea and Hyperbaric Med. Soc., Force Recon Assn., Aerospace Med. Assn. Avocations: amateur machinist, math, jogging. Office: Astronaut Office/CB NASA Johnson Space Ctr Houston TX 77058

MORIN, LOUIS, government agency administrator; b. Que., Can., Sept. 29, 1941; s. Paul-Emile and Jeanne Dechene) M.; m. Marthe Champoux, Sept. 12, 1970; children: Francois, Antoine, Brigitte. BA, Coll. Jesuites, 1962; LLL, U. Laval, 1965. Atty. Grondin LeBel Morin, Que., Canada, 1966—77; judge Que. Labor Ct., 1977—2002, chief judge, 1990—98; pres. Que. Labour Rels. Bd., 2002—. Mem. Que. Jud. Coun., Montreal, 1992-96; tchr. labor law U. Laval, Que., 1989. Mem. Can. Bar Assn., Que. Bar Assn., Que. Young Bar Assn. (pres. 1975-76), Que. Judge's Assn. (pres. 1989-90). Avocations: skiing, bicycling. Office: Que Labor Rels Bd 200 chemin Sainte-Foy 6 etage Quebec City PQ Canada G1R 5S1 E-mail: louis-morin@crt.gouv.qc.ca.

MORIN, PIERRE JEAN, retired management consultant, social services administrator; b. Quebec City, Que., Can., Aug. 5, 1931; s. Augustin Norbert and Yvonne (Gaudry) M.; m. Colette Poulin, Apr. 3, 1954; children: Anne, Gilles, Louis. BS, Concordia U., Montreal, 1964; MS, Laval U., Que., 1970, D.Sc., 1973. Quality control technician Dow Brevery, Montreal, Que., 1952-56; research assoc. Royal Victoria Hosp., Montreal, 1957-67; coordinator of research Que. Heart Inst., 1967-73; dir. research labs. Laval Hosp., Que., 1973-80, lectr. dept. medicine, 1973-77; dir. gen. Community Service Ctr., 1980-88; mgmt. cons., 1988-91; ret., 1991. Cons. Que. Minister of Environ., 1975-84. Contbr. articles to profl. jours. and news media. Schering Travelling fellow, 1971 Mem. AAAS Roman Catholic. Home: 336 Rg Castor Leclercville QC Canada G0S 2K0 *Well assumed failure may be a must towards later success.*

MORIN, YVES-CHARLES, linguistics educator, researcher; b. St. Germain, Yvelines, France, Nov. 7, 1944; arrived in Can. 1972; s. Georges and Denise (Montaudouin) M.; 1 child, Yannig Lic., U. Paris, 1967; Diploma in Engring., Ecole Centrale, 1967; MA in Linguistics, U. Mich., 1970, PhD in Computer Sci., 1971. Engr. Mil. Radar Estab., Pontoise, France, 1971-72; asst. prof. U. Montreal, Montreal, Que., Can., 1972-76, assoc. prof., 1967-82, prof., 1982—, mem. exec. com. Faculty of Arts and Scis., 1984-86. Invited prof. Bourguiba Inst., Tunis, Tunisia, 1977; mem. cons. bd. Humanities and Social Scis. Research Council of Canada, Ottawa, 1980-83; vis. scholar Centre d'Etudes Metriques de Nantes (France), 1994. Contbr. articles to profl. jours. Served to lt. Logistics-Radar, 1971-72; France Harkness fellow Commonwealth Fund, 1967; Camargo Found. fellow, 2002. Mem. Linguistic Soc. Am., Can. Linguistic Soc., Can. Jour. Linguistics, Société Asiatique, Sigma Xi, Phi Kappa Phi Office: U Montreal Dept Linguistics CP 6128 Montreal QC Canada H3C 3J7

MORING, JOHN FREDERICK, lawyer; b. Farmville, Va., Oct. 30, 1935; s. Scott O'Ferrall and Margaret Macon (Mitchell) M.; m. Margaret Ann Clarke, Mar. 30, 1959; children: Martha, Elizabeth, Scott, Lee. BS, Va. Poly. Inst., 1957; JD, George Washington U., 1961. Bar: Va. 1961, D.C. 1962, U.S. Supreme Ct. 1964; cert. mediator civil disputes Supreme Ct. Va. 2004. Assoc. Morgan, Lewis & Bockius, Washington, 1961-68, ptnr., 1969-78, Jones, Day, Reavis & Pogue, Washington, 1978-79; founding ptnr. Crowell & Moring, Washington, Irvine, N.Y.C., London, Brussels, 1979-2000. Sec. Associated Gas Distbrs., Inc., 1977-2000. Local gas utility columnist: Nat. Gas Jour., 1989—2000; mem. editl. bd. Natural Gas Contracts, 1994—2001. Mem. nat. panel neutrals Am. Arbitration Assn., 2003—; chmn. bd. dirs. Washington Legal Counsel for Elderly, 2000—01; Rep. candidate 23d Dist./Va. Gen. Assembly, Alexandria, 1973; mem. bd. govs. St. Stephen's and St. Agnes Sch., Alexandria, 1989—95; pres. St. Stephen's Found., Inc., 1990—93; sr. warden Immanuel Ch. on the Hill, Alexandria, 1988, 1989; trustee Ch. Schs. of Diocese of Va., 1996—; mem. bd. govs. St. Margaret's Sch., Tappahannock, Va., 2002—. 2d lt. U.S. Army, 1958. Mem.: ABA (natural resources law sect. 1982—86, coun.), Am. Arbitration Assn., Fed. Energy Bar Assn. (sec. 1963—66, pres. 1982—83), Indian Creek Yacht and Country Club (Kilmarnock, Va.). Episcopalian. Avocations: golf, fishing, canoeing. Home: PO Box 224 White Stone VA 22578 Office: Crowell & Moring 1001 Pennsylvania Ave NW Fl 10 Washington DC 20004-2595 also: 2010 Main St Irvine CA 92614-7203 also: 180 Fleet St London ECAA2 HD England also: 590 Madison Ave Ste 2100 New York NY 10022 also: 27 Ave Des Arts B-1040 Brussels Belgium Office Phone: 202-624-2570. E-mail: fmoring@rivnet.net.

MORINI, ANGELO SYLVESTER, food company executive; b. New Castle, Pa., Sept. 30, 1942; s. Angelo Salterno and Lisa (Ricutti) M.; m. Dagmar Rose Zindren, Apr. 19, 1975; children: Matthew, Brian, Jamie. BBA, Youngstown State U., 1968. With Morini Markets, Ellwood, Pa., 1955-60, USX, Pitts., 1964-68, Pillsbury Co., Pitts., 1968-69, Gen. Foods Co., Pitts., 1969-70, Feasta Foods, New Castle, 1970-71; pres., founder Galaxy Cheese Co., New Castle, 1971—. Inventor cheese subsititute-Formage. Served with USN, 1960-63. Mem. Inst. Food Tech. Avocations: golf, hiking. Home: Oak Tree Ct West Middlesex PA 16127 Office: Galaxy Foods Co 2441 Viscount Row Orlando FL 32809-6217

MORIOKA, BRENNON T. engineering executive, political organization worker; b. Hawaii; BS in Civil Engring., U. Calif.; PhD in Civil Engring., U. Hawaii, 1999. Sr. geotechnical engr. URS Corp., Honolulu. Chmn. Rep. Party, Hawaii. Mem.: ASCE (chmn. geotechnical com.), Hawaii Soc. Profl. Engrs. (named Young Engr. of Yr.). Office: URS Corp 615 Piikoi St 9th Fl Honolulu HI 96814-3141*

MORIS, LAMBERTO GIULIANO, architect; b. Siena, Tuscany, Italy, Mar. 29, 1944; came to U.S., 1972; s. Gualtiero Luigi and Giovanna (Avanzati) M.; m. Tracy P. Schilling, 1970 (div. 1985); children: Giacomo, Stefano; m. Beverly Chiang, Mar. 28, 1986; 1 child, Christopher. MA in Arch., U. Florence, Italy, 1970. Assoc. Marquis Assocs., San Francisco, 1972-78, prin., 1978-85, Simon Martin-Vegue Winkelstein Moris, San Francisco, 1985—. Tchr. San Francisco City Coll., 1982—84; juror DuPont Antron Design Awards, 1989, AIA Hon. Awards, 1995, AIA Interior Architecture Awards, Chgo. chpt., 1997; mem. interior design adv. coun. Acad. Art Coll., San Francisco, 1992—2001; lectr. AIA Nat. Conf., 1996, Aircraft Interiors Expo, Canne, France, 2000, Aircraft Interiors Conf. and Exhbn., Long Beach, Calif., 2001, AIA- Italy Summit, San Francisco, 2003. Mem. design com. Clairmont Pines Task Force, 1991; charter mem. Forecast 21 Principals Roundtable, 1993; mem. Bldg. Industry Conf. Bd. (BICB), 2001—; mem. bd. dirs. ItaLingua Inst., 1984—. Mem.: FAIA (mem. selection com. 2003), AIA (mem. internat. com. 2003), Interior Architecture, No. Calif. chpt., Am. Inst. Architects, Coll. Fellows, Am. Inst. Architects (corp. mem. 1979—), Am. C. of C. in Italy, Oakland Met. C. of C., Accademia Italiane della Cucina, Cath. Prof. Bus. Club, San Francisco Opera Assn., Il Cenacolo (bd. dirs. 1991), San Francisco Heritage Assn., Engr. Club. Roman Catholic. Avocations: coin collecting/numismatics, skiing, travel. Office: SMWM 989 Market St 3d Fl San Francisco CA 94103 Office Phone: 415-882-3003. Office Fax: 415-882-0709. Business E-Mail: lmoris@smwm.com.

MORISCO, JERID SIMON, music educator, conductor; b. Rockmart, Ga., Nov. 18, 1967; s. Ann Floyd and Gary Dewayne Galloway. MusB, Shorter Coll., Rome, Ga., 1990; MusM, Sam Houston State U., Huntsville, Tex., 1992; degree in Edn. Specialist, Lincoln Meml. U., Harrogate, Tenn., 2001; post grad. in Musical Arts, Shenandoah U., Winchester, Va., 2001. Cert. tchr. Ga., 1998. Tenor Atlanta Symphony Orch. Chorus, 1989—90; asst. prof. music Gulf Coast C.C., Panama City, 1993—97; dir. choral studies Mt. Eden H.S., Hayward, 1997—98; adj. prof. Shorter Coll., Marietta, Ga., 1999—; music specialist Marietta City Schs., Ga., 1999—; artistic dir. / founding condr. The Marietta Master Chorale, Inc., Ga., 2001—. Recipient Going the Extra Mile award, Marietta Kiwanis Club, 1999. Mem.: Internat. Kodaly Soc., Orgn. Am. Kodaly Educators, Internat. Soc. for Music Edn., Music Educators Nat. Conf., Ga. Music Educators Assn., Am. Choral Dirs. Assn., Conductors Guld, Phi Theta Kappa, Pi Kappa Lambda, Phi Mu Alpha. Episcopalian. Home: 3210 Hudson Rd Marietta GA 30060 Office: The Marietta Master Chorale 105 Park St Marietta GA 30060 Personal E-mail: jerid_morisco@hotmail.com.

MORISHITA, AKIHIKO, trading company executive; b. Osaka, Japan, Oct. 14, 1941; came to U.S., 1981; s. Sueyoshi and Toshiko Morishita; m. Fumiko Okamura; children: Shizuko, Kumiko, Okamura. BA in Econs., Wakayama U., Wakayama, Japan, 1965. Mgr. Hanwa & Co. Ltd., Osaka, 1965-80; cons. oil dept. Pacific Southwest Trading Co., San Diego, 1981-82; exec. Pacific Marine Bunkering, Inc., L.A., 1982—. Mem. Woodland Hills Country Club. Home: 4610 Don Pio Dr Woodland Hills CA 91364-4205 E-mail: a.morishita@worldnet.att.net.

MORISKY, DONALD E. director, medical educator; b. Kalamazoo, Mich., Dec. 30, 1945; s. Marvin F. Morisky; m. Susan Mageuflor Morisky, June 26, 1971; children: Philip M., Marty M. ScD, Johns Hopkins U., 1981. Assoc. prof. UCLA Sch. of Pub. Health, 1987—94, prof., vice chair, 1994—2003, prof., 1994—, chair, 2004—. Asst. prof. UCLA Sch. of Pub. Health, Los Angeles, Calif., 1982—87. Recipient Disting. Career Fellow, Soc. of Pub. Health Edn. and Am. Acad. Health Behavior, 2003; grant, NIH, Ctrs. for Disease Control, 1987—. Fellow: Am. Acad. Health Behavior, Coun. Epidemiology Rsch.; mem.: APHA (chairperson 1985—86, Early Career Award 1986), Delta Omega (pres. 2000—02). Achievements include research in longitudinal assessments of behavioral interventions on health status; self-reported medication taking behavior assessment tool; HIV/AIDS prevention interventions in the Philippines; tuberculosis control programs for hispanic adults and adolescents. Home: 2020 Glencoe Ave Venice CA 90291-4007 Office: UCLA 650 Charles E Young Dr S Los Angeles CA 90095-1772 Office Phone: 310-825-8508. E-mail: dmorisky@ucla.edu.

MORISON, JOHN HOPKINS, casting manufacturing company executive; b. Milw., June 29, 1913; s. George Abbot and Amelia (Elmore) M. m. Olga de Souza Dantas, July 29, 1944; children: Maria de Souza Dantas, John Hopkins III. AB, Harvard U., 1935; LLD, New Eng. Coll., 1973. Various positions Bucyrus-Erie Co., South Milwaukee, Wis., U.S. and Latin Am., 1935-49; pres., dir. Hitchiner Mfg. Co., Inc., Milford, N.H., 1949-93, chmn. bd., 1973-93, chmn. emeritus, 1994—. Pres., treas. Upland Farm Inc., Peterborough, N.H., 1986-98, sec., 1967—; chmn. RiverMead Retirement Community, Peterborough, N.H., 1991-96, trustee 1991—. Commr. N.H. Commn. on Arts, 1967-77; mem. regional exec. com. Boy Scouts Am., Framingham, Mass., 1970-76; mem. exec. com., pres., N.H. Coun. on World Affairs, 1955-76; trustee Canterbury Shaker Village, 1982-96; trustee Land Use Found. N.H., 1970-75, World Peace Found., 1962-90, Currier Gallery Art, 1969-2000, trustee emeritus, 2000—; pres. bd. dirs. Matthew Thornton Health Plan, 1972-82; bd. dirs. Forum on N.H.'s Future, 1979-81; pres., distbg. dir. N.H. Charitable Fund, 1968-79; mem. corp. MacDowell Colony; v.p. bd. govs. N.H. Public TV, 1979-89. Lt. (j.g.) USNR, 1943-46. Recipient Lifetime Achievement award N.H. Bus. and Industry Assn., 1993, N.H. High Tech. Coun., 1996, Granite State award U. N.H., 1994. Mem. Somerset Club. Unitarian Universalist. Home: PO Box 2001 Milford NH 03055-2001

MORISON, WARWICK LINDSAY, dermatologist, educator, consultant; b. Sydney, Australia, Mar. 31, 1941; came to U.S., 1975; s. Frank and Jean M.; m. Browyn Jones, Mar. 27, 1971. MB, BS, U. Sydney, 1963, MD, 1975. Diplomate Am. Bd. Dermatology. Asst. prof. dermatology Harvard Med. Sch., Boston, 1980-81, Johns Hopkins U., Balt., 1981-85, assoc. prof., 1984-95, prof., 1995—. Sr. rsch. scientist Nat. Cancer Inst., Frederick, Md., 1981-85. Adv. com. Skin Cancer Found., N.Y.C., 1983—, Nat. Psoriasis Found., Portland, Oreg., 1994—. Assoc. editor Jour. Photodermatology, 1999—. Fellow Royal Coll. Physicians, Am. Acad. Dermatology; mem. Photomedicine Soc. (pres. 1999—), Am. Soc. Photobiology, Soc. Invesigative Dermatology, British Assn. Dermatology, Wine and Food Soc. Md. (bd. govs.). Avocations: travel, gardening, wine and food appreciation. Office: Johns Hopkins Greenspring 10753 Falls Rd S-355 Lutherville MD 21093 E-mail: wmorison@jhmi.edu.

MORISSEAU, NAN KRUGER, television personality; b. Oklahoma City; d. Albert William and Lillie Mae (Kubala) K.; m. Fay Edwin Morisseau Esq., III, June 8, 1974; children: Katherine, Paul. BS, U. Okla., 1972; postgrad., U. Houston, 1986-90. Fashion designer Charm of Hollywood, L.A., 1972-74, Jackson Sq., New Orleans, 1974-75; buyer Federated Dept. Stores Foleys Houston, 1975-80; stockbroker Prudential Securities, Houston, 1980-86; pres. The Newport Beach (Calif.) Recital Series, 1995-99, also bd. dirs.; pres. Cachet' Prodns. Internatl., Newport Beach, 1994—, Golden Girl Jewelry, Newport Beach, 1997—; TV talk show host Rise & Shine with Nancy Morgan Pacific Family Entertainment, Fountain Valley, Calif., 1997—, also bd. dirs., 1996-97. Author (plays) White Russian, 1988, Meyerhold, 1990, (screenplay) Triumph of The Spirit, 1992; actor (situation comedy) Student Union, 1992, (play) Charon Unleashed, 1993. Hostess Chamber Music Salons, 1995-99; pres. Friends of Newport Beach Recital Series, 1995—; bd. dirs. Orange County Philharm. Soc., Big Canyon, Calif., 1996-97. Vol. Ctr. devel. grantee, 1996; recipient Bronze medal Nastar Downhill Skiing, 1996. Mem. AAUW (chair classical music sect. 1997), Womens Diversity Forum, North Orange County Computer Club, Arts Orange County. Avocations: skiing, surfing, computer graphics, music, ballet. Home and Office: Cachet Prodns Internatl 77 Montecito Dr Corona Del Mar CA 92625-1018

MORISSETTE, ALANIS, musician; b. Ottawa, ON, Canada, June 1, 1974; Singer: (albums) Alanis, 1991, Now is the Time, 1992, Jagged Little Pill, 1995, Supposed Former Infatuation Junkie, 1998, Under Rug Swept, 2002, Feast On Scraps, 2002, So-Called Chaos, 2004; actor: (films) Dogma, 1999, Jay and Silent Bob Strike Back, 2001. Recipient Grammy award for Album of Yr., Best Female Rock Vocal Performance, Best Rock Song, Best Rock Album, 1996. Address: Maverick Recording Co 9348 Civic Center Dr Ste 100 Beverly Hills CA 90210-3606*

MORITA, RICHARD YUKIO, microbiology and oceanography educator; b. Pasadena, Calif., Mar. 27, 1923; s. Jiro and Reiko (Yamamoto) M.; m. Toshiko Nishihara, May 29, 1926; children— Sally Jean, Ellen Jane, Peter Wayne BS, U. Nebr., 1947; MS, U. So. Calif., 1949; PhD, U. Calif., 1954. Microbiologist Mid-Pacific Expdn., 1950, Danish Galathea Deep-Sea Expdn., 1952, Trans-Pacific Expdn.; Postdoctoral fellow U. Calif., Scripps Inst. Oceanography, 1954-55; asst. prof. U. Houston, 1955-58; asst. prof., assoc. prof. U. Neb., 1958-62; prof. microbiology and oceanography Oreg. State U., Corvallis, 1962-89, prof. emeritus microbiology and oceanography, 1989—. Prog. dir. biochemistry NSF, 1968-69; Disting. vis. prof. Kyoto Univ.; cons. NIH, 1968-70; researcher in field. Contbr. articles to sci. lit. Patentee in field. Served with U.S. Army, 1944-46 Grantee NSF, 1962—, NIH, 1960-68, NASA, 1967-72, Office Naval Research, 1966-70, Dept. Interior, 1968-72, NOAA, 1975-82, Bur. Land Mgmt., 1982, EPA, 1986—; recipient awards including King Fredericus IX Medal and Ribbon, 1954, Sr. Queen Elizabeth II Fellowship, 1973-74, Hotpack lectr. and award Can. Soc. Fellow Japan Soc. for Promotion Sci.; mem. Am. Soc. Microbiology (Fisher award). Home: 1515 NW 14th St Corvallis OR 97330

MORITSUGU, KENNETH PAUL, physician, government official; b. Honolulu, Mar. 5, 1945; s. Richard Yutaka and Hisayo Joan (Nishikawa) M.; children: Erika Lizabeth, Vikki Lianne (deceased), Emily Renee. Student, Chaminade Coll. Honolulu, 1963-65; BA in Classical Langs. with honors, U. Hawaii, 1967; MD, George Washington U., 1971; MPH, U. Calif., Berkeley, 1975; DSc (hon.), Coll. Osteopathic Medicine, U. New Eng., 1988, Midwestern U., 1993; D Pub. Svc. (hon.), U. North Tex., 1994; DHL (hon.), Western U. Health Scis., 2002, Alliant Internat. U., 2002; DDL (hon.), Phila. Coll. Osteo. Medicine; DHL (hon.), Campbell U., 2003. Diplomate Am. Bd. Preventive Medicine (fellow); cert. correctional health profl. Intern USPHS Hosp., San Francisco, 1971-72, resident, 1972-75; commd. USPHS, 1968, advanced through grades to med. dir., 1979; promoted to rank of rear adm., asst. surgeon gen., 1988; staff med. officer USPHS Hosp., San Francisco, 1972-75, regional cons. med. manpower planning and devel. HEW, San Francisco, 1976-78, chief internat. edn. programs br. Washington, 1978, dep. dir. divsn. medicine, 1978; dir. Bur. Health Professions, div. medicine HHS, Rockville, Md., 1978-83, dir. Nat. Health Service Corps, 1983-87, dep. dir. Bur. Health Professions, 1987; med. dir. Fed. Bur. Prisons Dept. Justice, Washington, 1987-98; dep. surgeon gen. USPHS, Rockville, Md., 1998—, acting surgeon gen., 2002. Decorated D.S.M., knight grand cross Mil. and Hospitaller Order St. Lazarus of Jerusalem; named Disting. Alumnus, George Washington U., 2002; recipient Commendation medal, Meritorious Svc. medal, Outstanding Svc. medal, Surgeon Gen.'s medallion, Surgeon Gen.'s medal, Dirs. award, U.S. Marshal's Svcs., John D. Chase award, AMSUS, Nathan Davis award, AMA, Disting. Svc. award, ACHSA, DSM award, U.S. Dept. Justice, Fed. Bur. Prisons, Health Leader of Yr., Commd. Officers Assn. Fellow Am. Coll. Preventive Medicine, Royal Soc. Health, Royal Soc. Medicine; mem. APHA, Assn. Tchrs. Preventive Medicine, Assn. Mil. Surgeons U.S., Res. Officers Assn., Mensa, Am. Guild Organists, Am. Acad. Physicians Assts. (hon.), Delta Omega, Omicron Delta Kappa. Office: USPHS Office of Surgeon Gen 5600 Fishers Ln Ste 18-67 Rockville MD 20857-0001 Personal E-mail: 1samurai@cox.net.

MORITZ, DONALD BROOKS, mechanical engineer, consultant; b. Mpls., June 17, 1927; s. Donald B. and Frances W. (Whalen) M.; m. Joan Claire Betzenderfer, June 17, 1950; children: Craig, Pamela, Brian. BS in Mech. Engring., U. Minn., 1950; postgrad., Western Res. U., 1956-58. Registered profl. engr., Ill. Minn., Ohio. V.p., gen. mgr. Waco Scaffold Shoring Co., Addison, Ill., 1950-72; group v.p. Bliss and Laughlin Industries, Oak Brook, Ill., 1972-83; sr. v.p. AXIA Inc. (formerly Bliss and Laughlin Industries, Oak Brook, 1983-84, exec. v.p., chief operating officer, 1984-88; cons. Exec. Svc. Corps Chgo., 1988—; pres. Image-A-Nation, Unltd., 1988—. Bd. dirs. Am. Photographic Acad. Patentee in field. Served with USN, 1945-46. Mem. ASME, Scaffold and Shoring Inst. (founder, past pres.), Mensa, Five Seasons Country Club. Office: Moritz and Assocs PO Box 305 Clarendon Hills IL 60514-0305

MORITZ, MILTON EDWARD, security consultant; b. Reading, Pa., Sept. 5, 1931; s. Edward Raymond and Anna May M.; m. Elizabeth Ann Walls, June 6, 1952; children: Betsy Ann Moritz Koppenhaver, Stephen Edward, Sandra E. Student, U. Md., 1950-51, Fla. State U., 1959-60. Enlisted U.S. Army, 1949, chief warrant officer 3, 1968, spl. agt. M.I.; ret., 1970; safety and security dir. Harrisburg (Pa.) Hosp., 1970-72; security mgr. Sprint, Carlisle, Pa., 1972-94; prin. Moritz Assocs., Harrisburg, 1994—. Lectr., instr. Harrisburg Area Community Coll.; mem. Indsl. Security Adv. Coun. Assoc. editor: Protection of Assets Manual. Pres. Greater Harrisburg Crime Clinic, 1974. Decorated Bronze Star with oak leaf cluster. Mem. Am. Soc. Indsl. Security (past pres., chmn. bd. dirs.), Assn. Former Intelligence Officers, Internat. Narcotic Enforcement Officers Assn., Pa. Crime Prevention Assn. (bd. dirs). Republican. Lutheran. Home and Office: 7723 Avondale Ter Harrisburg PA 17112-3805 Office Phone: 717-545-6551. Business E-Mail: mickmoritz@cs.com.

MORITZ, TIMOTHY BOVIE, psychiatrist; b. Portsmouth, Ohio, July 26, 1936; s. Charles Raymond and Elisabeth Bovie (Morgan) M.; m. Joyce Elizabeth Rasmussen, Oct. 13, 1962 (div. Sept. 1969); children: Elizabeth Wynne, Laura Morgan; m. Antoinette Tanasichuk, Oct. 31, 1981; children: David Michael, Stephanie Lysbeth. BA, Ohio State U., 1959; MD, Cornell U., 1963. Diplomate Am. Bd. Psychiatry and Neurology. Intern in medicine N.Y. Hosp., N.Y.C., 1963-64, resident in psychiatry, 1964-67; spl. asst. to dir. NIMH, Bethesda, Md., 1967-69; dir. Community Mental Health Ctr., Rockland County, N.Y., 1970-74, Ohio Dept. Mental Health, Columbus, Ohio, 1975-81; med. dir. psychiatry Miami Valley Hosp., Dayton, Ohio, 1981-82; med. dir. N.E. Ga. Community Mental Health Ctr., Athens, Ga., 1982-83, Charter Vista Hosp., Fayetteville, Ark., 1983-87; clin. dir. adult psychiatry Charter Hosp., Las Vegas, Nev., 1987-94; pvt. practice psychiatry Las Vegas, 1997—; med. dir. Problem Gambling Cons., Las Vegas, 2000—. Prof. Wright State U., Dayton, Ohio, 1981-82; asst. prof. Cornell U., N.Y.C., 1970-73; mem. human subjects biomed. scis. rev. com. U. Nev., Las Vegas, 2000-2001; cons. NIMH, Rockville, Md., 1973-83. Author: (chpt.) Rehabilitation Medicine and Psychiatry, 1976; mem. editorial bd. Directions in Psychiatry, 1981— Dir. dept. mental health and mental retardation Gov.'s Cabinet, State of Ohio, Columbus, 1975-81. Recipient Svc. award Ohio Senate, 1981, Svc. Achievement award Ohio Gov., 1981. Fellow Am. Psychiat. Assn. (disting. life, Disting. Svc. award 1981); mem. AMA, Nev. Assn. Psychiat. Physicians, Nev. State Med. Assn., Am. Assn. Chronic Fatigue Syndrome, Clark County Med. Soc., Cornell U. Med. Coll. Alumni Assn., Ohio State U. Alumni Assn. (life). Office: 2330 Paseo del Prado Ste C-109 Las Vegas NV 89102-4336 Office Phone: 702-363-3633. Personal E-mail: TBMoritz@earthlink.net.

MORIYAMA, IWAO MILTON, statistician, consultant; b. San Francisco, Jan. 26, 1909; s. Saburo and Reki Moriyama; m. Toshiko Kako Moriyama; children: Halley Isao, Ken. BS, U. Calif., Berkeley, 1931; MPH, Yale U., 1934, PhD, 1937. Chief mortality analysis Nat. Office of Vital Stats. USPHS, Washington, 1946—61, dir. Office of Health Stats., Nat. Ctr. for Health Stats. Rockville, Md., 1961—74, assoc. dir. internat. stats. Nat. Ctr. Health Stats., 1974—75; chief epidemiology and stats. dept. Radiation Effects Rsch. Found., Hiroshima, Japan, 1975—78; dep. exec. dir. Internat. Inst. for Vital Registration and Stats., Bethesda, Md., 1978—86, pres. and exec. dir., 1986—; chief epidemiology and stats. dept. Atomic Bomb Casualty Commn., Hiroshima, 1971—73. Vis. prof. faculty of medicine U. Tokyo, Japan, 1988; collaborator program for accelerated improvement of civil registration and vital stats. in developing countries UN/WHO; mem. expert panel on health stats. WHO, Geneva, 1950—75, head US delegation Internat. Conf. for 9th Decennial Revision of Internat. Classification of Diseases, 1975; lectr. Am. U., Washington, 1965; vis. lectr. biostatistics U. Calif., Berkeley, 1967; project officer Longitudinal Study of Survival and Outcome of a Birth Cohort, Safdarjung Hosp., New Delhi, 1969—89, Longitudinal Studies in Human Reprodn.,

Christian Med. Coll., Vellore, India, 1973—89; biostatistician vital stats. divsn. Bur. of Census, US Dept. Commerce, 1940—46; exec. sec. US Nat. Com. on Vital and Health Stats., 1949—75; editl. cons. Demography, 1966—75; cons. in field. Recipient Disting. Svc. award, US Dept. HEW, Halbert L. Dunn award, Nat. Assn. Pub. Health Stats. and Info. Sys. Fellow: APHA, Population Assn. Am., AAAS, Am. Statis. Assn.; mem.: Internat. Epidemiol. Assn., Am. Epidemiol. Soc., Cosmos Club, Sigma Xi, Delta Omega. Home: 7120 Darby Rd Bethesda MD 20817-2914 E-mail: imoriyama@comcast.net.

MORK, GORDON ROBERT, historian, educator; b. St. Cloud, Minn., May 6, 1938; s. Gordon Matthew and Agnes (Gibb) Mork; m. Dianne Jeannette Muetzel, Aug. 11, 1963; children: Robert, Kristiana, Elizabeth. BA, Yale U., 1960; MA, U. Minn., 1963, PhD, 1966. Instr. history U. Minn., Mpls., 1966; lectr., asst. prof. U. Calif., Davis, 1966-70; mem. faculty Purdue U., West Lafayette, Ind., 1970—, assoc. prof., 1973-94, prof. history, 1994—, dir. honors program humanities, 1985-87, dir grad. studies history, Am. studies, 1987-93, mem. Jewish studies com., 1980—, head dept. history, 1998—2003; resident dir. Purdue U.-Ind. U. Program, Hamburg, Germany, 1975-76. Rsch. fellow in humanities U. Wis., Madison, 1969—70; mem. test devel. com. advanced placement European history Ednl. Testing Svc., 1993—99, chair, 1995—99; cons. Coll. Bd. and Ednl. Testing Svc., 1999—. Author: Modern Western Civilization: A Concise History, 3d edit., 1994; editor: The Homes of Ober-Ammergau, 2000; mem. adv. bd. Teaching History, 1983—, History Teacher, 1986—2002. Mem. citizens task force Lafayette Sch. Corp., 1978—79; bd. dirs. Ind. Humanities Coun., 1986—89; elder Ctrl. Presbyn. Ch., Lafayette, 1973—75, deacon, 1996—99, trustee, 2001—04; bd. dirs., sec. Murdock-Sunnyside Bldg. Corp., 1980—. Mem.: Com. History in Classroom (treas. 1990—93), Soc. History Edn., German Studies Assn., Am. Hist. Assn., Internat. Soc. History Didactics (v.p. 1991—95, 1996—2000), Phi Beta Kappa. Home: 1521 Cason St Lafayette IN 47904-2642 Office: Purdue U Dept of History West Lafayette IN 47907-2087 Business E-Mail: gmork@purdue.edu.

MORKOÇ, HADIS, electrical engineer, educator; b. Senkaya, Erzurum, Turkey, Oct. 2, 1947; came to U.S., 1971; s. Mustafa and Saadet (Metin) M.; m. Amy C. Ahlberg, Sept. 5, 1975; 1 child, Erol Taner. MS, Tech. U., Istanbul, 1969; PhD, Cornell U., 1975. Postdoctoral fellow Cornell U., Ithaca, N.Y., 1975-76; mem. tech. staff Varian Assocs., Palo Alto, Calif., 1976-78; prof. elec. engring. U. Ill., Urbana, 1978-97, Va. Commonwealth U., 1997—. Disting. vis. scientist Calif. Inst. Tech., Pasadena, 1987-88; cons., Motorola, IBM, AT&T, others. Author: Principles and Technology of ModFETs, 1991, Nitride Semiconductors and Devices, 1999; contbr. chpts. to 37 books, 1050 articles to profl. jours. Fellow IEEE, AAAS, Am. Phys. Soc.; mem. Math. Rsch. Soc., Optical Soc. Am., Sigma Xi, Eta Kappa Nu, Sigma Phi Sigma. Achievements include invention of fastest transistor in world. Home: 2403 Lake Loreine Ln Richmond VA 23233-2523 Office: Va Commonwealth U PO Box 843072 601 W Main St Richmond VA 23284-9052 E-mail: hmorkoc@vcu.edu.

MORLAND, JOHN KENNETH, sociology and anthropology educator; b. Huntsville, Ala., July 4, 1916; s. Howard Cannon and Ethel Mae (Cowan) M.; m. Margaret Louise Ward, Feb. 26, 1949; children: Carol, Katherine, Evelyn. BS, Birmingham So. Coll., 1938; B.D., Yale U., 1943; PhD, U. N.C., 1950. Instr. Yale in China Middle Sch., Changsha, Hunan, 1943-46; exec. sec. Yale in China Assn., New Haven, 1946-47; asst. prof. Coll. William and Mary, Williamsburg, Va., 1949-53; Charles A. Dana prof., chmn. dept. sociology and anthropology Randolph Macon Woman's Coll., Lynchburg, Va., 1953-87; rsch. analyst City of Lynchburg, 1989-94. Cons. U.S. Dept. Edn., Dept. Commerce, NEH, So. Regional Coun. NSF, Ednl. and Rsch. Found., Lynchburg, Va. Author: Social Problems in the United States, 1975, Millways of Kent, 1958, (with John Williams) Race, Color and the Young Child, 1976, (with Jack Balswick) Social Problems: A Christian Understanding and Response, 1990; contbr., editor: The Not So Solid South, 1971. Pres. bd. nat. ministries Am. Bapt. Chs., USA, 1973-79. Named Eminent Laureate of Va., 1981; recipient Disting. Alumnus award Birmingham-So. Coll., 1985, Nat. Conf. Christians and Jews Humanitarian award, 1994; Fulbright scholar Chinese U., Hong Kong, 1966-67; grantee NSF, Taiwan, 1975, U.S. Dept. Edn., 1972, Liberty Bell award Lynchburg Bar Assn., 1997. Fellow Am. Anthropol. Assn.; mem. Am. Sociol. Assn., So. Sociol. Soc., Va. Social Sci. Assn. (pres. 1963), AAUP (pres. 1962), Phi Beta Kappa. Home: 1619 Dogwood Ln Lynchburg VA 24503-1923 Office: Randolph Macon Woman's Coll Lynchburg VA 24503-1526

MORLAND, RICHARD BOYD, retired educator; b. June 27, 1919; s. Howard Cannon and Ethel May (Cowan) M.; m. Jessie May Parrish, Mar. 17, 1949; 1 child, Laura. AB, Brimingham-So. Coll., 1940; MEd, Springfield Coll., 1947; PhD, N.Y. Univ., 1958. Phys. dir. YMCA, Frankfort, Ky., 1940—41; dir. athletics, head basketball coach Fla. So. Coll., 1947—50; from head basketball coach and chmn. dept. phys. edn. to sr. active prof. Stetson U., Deland, Fla., 1952—89; lectr. in edn. NYU, 1950—51; sr. active prof. Stetson U., Deland, Fla., 1989—90; ret., 1990. Chmn. grad. coun, 1962-69, chmn. dept. edn., 1969-75; head basketball coach Stetson U., Deland, Fla., 1952-57. Contbr. articles to profl. jours. Lt. USNR, 1941-45. Decorated 11 battle stars, USS Lexington; named to Stetson U. Sports Hall of Fame; named Hon. Ky. Col. Gov. Ky., 1945; recipient McEniry award for Excellence in tchg., 1983, Richard B. Morland Disting. Alumni award named in his honor; bronze bust by Harry Messersmith dedicated, 1992; So. Fellowships Fund fellow 1957-58. Mem. Philosophy of Edn. Soc. (pres. region 1963-64), Fla. Coun. Deans and Dirs. Tchr. Edn. (pres. 1974-75), Fla. Founds. Edn. and Policy Studies Soc. (exec. bd. 1987-90), DeLand Country Club, Omicron Delta Kappa, Phi Alpha Theta, Kappa Delta Pi, Phi Delta Kappa (pres. region 1977-78, editl. bd. 1978-83, named Regional Educator of Yr. 1991, panel gallup poll on edn., 1995), Kappa Alpha. Home: 524 N Mcdonald Ave Deland FL 32724-3643

MORLEY, HARRY THOMAS, JR., real estate executive; b. St. Louis, Aug. 13, 1930; s. Harry Thomas and Celeste Elizabeth (Davies) M.; m. Nelda Lee Mulholland, Sept. 3, 1960; children: Lisa, Mark, Marci. BA, U. Mo., 1955; MA, U. Denver, 1959. Dir. men's student activities Iowa State Tchrs. Coll., 1955-57; dir. student housing U. Denver, 1957-60; pvt. practice psychol. consulting St. Louis, 1960-63; dir. adminstrn. County of St. Louis, Mo., 1963-70; regional dir. HUD, Kansas City, Mo., 1970-71, asst. sec. adminstrn., 1971-73; pres. St. Louis Regional Commerce and Growth Assn., 1973-78, Taylor, Morley, Inc., St. Louis, 1978—. Teaching cons.-lectr. Washington U., St. Louis, 1962-70; bd. dirs. Mid-Am. Alliance Corp. and Life Ins. Co. Bd. dirs., mem. exec. com. St. Louis Coll. Pharmacy; past chmn. Better Bus. Bur.; chmn. Mo. Indsl. Devel. Bd., Mo. State Hwy. Commn.; bd. dirs. St. Luke's Hosps., St. Johns Hosp., Downtown St. Louis, Inc., Laclede's Landing Redevel. Corp. Served with USN, 1951-53. Mem. Am. Nat. Assn. Homebuilders, St. Louis Homebuilders Assn. (pres.), St. Louis Advt. Club, Mo. Athletic Club, St. Louis Club, Noonday Club, Castle Oak Country Club, Round Table Club, Sunset Country Club. Republican. Methodist. Home: 14238 Forest Crest Dr Chesterfield MO 63017-2818 Office: 17107 Chesterfield Airport Chesterfield MO 63005 E-mail: harrym@taylormorley.com.

MORLEY, JOHN EDWARD, physician; b. Eshowe, Zululand, South Africa, June 13, 1946; came to U.S., 1977; s. Peter and Vera Rose (Phipson) M.; m. Patricia Morley, Apr. 4, 1970; children: Robert, Susan, Jacqueline. MB, BCh, U. Witwatersrand, Johannesburg, South Africa, 1972. Diplomate Am. Bd. Internal Medicine, subspecialty cert. endocrinology and geriatrics. Asst. prof. Mpls. VA Med. Ctr. and U. Minn., 1979-81; assoc. prof. U. Minn., Mpls., 1981-84; prof. UCLA San Fernando Valley, 1985-89; dir. GRECC Sepulveda (Calif.) VA Med. Ctr., 1985-89; Dammert prof. gerontology, dir. div. geriatric medicine St. Louis U. Med. Ctr., 1989—; dir. geriatric rsch., edn. and clin. ctr. St. Louis VA Med. Ctr., 1989—. Author: (with others) Nutritional Modulation of Neuronal Function, 1988, Neuropeptides and Stress, 1988, Geriatric Nutrition, 1990, 2d edit., 1995, Medical Care in the Nursing Home, 1991, 2d edit., 1997, Endocrinology and Metabolism in the Elderly, 1992, Memory Function and Aging Related Disorders, 1992, Aging and Musculoskeletal Disorders, 1993, Aging, Immunity and Infection, 1994, Sleep Disorders and Insomnia in the Elderly, 1993, Quality Improvement in Geriatric Care, 1995, Focus on Nutrition, 1995, Applying Health Services Research to Long-Term Care, 1996, Cardiovascular Disease in Older People, 1997, Hydration and Aging, 1997, Advances in Care of Older People with Diabetes, 1999, Endocrinology of Aging, 1999, Science of Geriatrics, 2000, Subacute Care, 2000; mem. editl. bd. Peptides, 1983—, Internat. Jour. Obesity, 1986-89, Jour. Nutritional Medicine, 1990—, Clinics in Applied Nutrition, 1990-92; editor geriatrics sect. Yearbook of Endocrinology, 1987-2001, Nursing Home Medicine, 1992-97, Clin. Geriatrics, 1992-97, Sandwich Generation, 1997, others; editor Jour. Gerontology: Med. Scis., 2000—. Mem. adv. bd. Alzheimer's Assn., St. Louis, 1990-92; mem. adv. com. for physicians Mo. Divsn. Aging, Jefferson City, 1990-2001; bd. dirs. Mo. Assn. Long Term Care Physicians, 1991—, Long Term Care Ombudsman Program, St. Louis, 1992, Fund for Psychoneuroimmunology, 1990-2001, Hamilton Hts. Health Resource Ctr., 1992—. Recipient Mead Johnson award, Am. Inst. Nutrition, 1985, Cmty. Svc. award, BREM, 1997, Robert H. Bollinger Disting. Acad. award, U. Kans., 1997, Longevity prize, Ispen Found., 1999, Circle award, Am. Dietetics Assn., 2001, Nasher/Manning award, Am. Geriatric Soc., 2002. Mem. ACP (geriatrics subcom. 1991-92), Am. Soc. Clin. Investigation, Endocrine Soc., Am. Fedn. Clin. Rsch., Am. Acad. Behavioral Sci., Gerontology Soc. Am., Am. Diabetes Assn., Am. Soc. Pharmacy and Therapeutics, Soc. for Neurosci., La Asociacion de Gerontologica y Geriatrica, A.C. (hon.), Assn. Dirs. Geriatric Acad. Programs. Office: Saint Louis U Sch Medicine 1402 S Grand Blvd Rm M238 Saint Louis MO 63104-1004

MORLEY, JUDY MATTIVI, historian, educator, preservation consultant; b. Denver, Colo., Mar. 11, 1965; d. Rudolph August and Alice Marie (Vodicka) Mattivi; m. Troy Morley, Aug. 2, 1986 (div. Jan. 9, 2002); 1 child, Kinsey Nicole. BS in Journalism, U. Colo., 1987, MA in History, 1995; PhD in History, U. N.Mex., 2002. Sr. acct. exec. Graham Advert., Colo. Springs, Colo., 1988—92; dir. of devel. Western Hist. Assoc., Albuquerque, 1999—2001; instr. U. Colo., Denver, 2001—03, Met. State Coll., Denver, 1999—2003; resource devel. mgr. Downtown Denver Partnership, 2003—04; pres., owner Denver History Tours, LLC, 2004—. Conf. coord. Ctr. for the SW, Albuquerque, 2002. Author: (book) Making History: Hist. Preservation & the Creation off W. Civic Identity, 2003, Centenniae Anada, 1904-2004: A Pictorial History; contbr. articles to profl. jours. Vol. Colo. Hist. Soc., Denver, 1993—99. Recipient Frederick G. Boehm prize, U. N.Mex., 1999; L. Dudley Phillips fellow, 2000. Mem.: Am. Planning Assoc., Orgn. of Am. Hist., Western History Assn. Democrat. Avocations: reading, bicycling, skiing, jewelry-making. Home: 7606 S Cove Cir Centennial CO 80122 Office Phone: 720-234-7929.

MORLEY, LAWRENCE WHITAKER, geophysicist, remote sensing consultant; b. Toronto, Feb. 19, 1920; s. George Whitaker and Mary Olive (Boyd) M.; divorced; children; Lawrence, Patricia, Chris, David (dec.); m. Beverly Anne Beckworth; step-children: Sandra Wellman, Stephen Burdett, Richard Burdett. BA, U. Toronto, 1946, MA, 1949, PhD, 1952; DSc (hon.) (hon.), York U., Toronto, 1974; Dr Environ. Studies (hon.), U. Waterloo, 2001. Dir. geophysics div. Geol. Survey Can., Ottawa, 1952-71; founding dir. gen. Can. Centre for Remote Sensing, Ottawa, 1971-80; founding exec. dir. Inst. for Space and Terrestrial Sci., Toronto, 1987-91; pres. Teledetection Internat., 1991—. Sci. counselor Can. High Commn., London. Lt. Can. Navy, 1941-45. Decorated Order of Can. Fellow Royal Soc. Can., Can. Aeronautics and Space Inst., Royal Can. Geog. Soc.; mem. Can. Soc. Remote Sensing (founding pres. 1971-74), Am. Geophys. Union, Am. Soc. Phototogrammetry and Remote Sensing, Soc. Exploration Geophysicists, Can. Geophys. Union, Can. Geomatics Inst. Home and Office: 16 Raglan St Ste 307 Collingwood ON Canada L9Y 4Y2 E-mail: l.morley@rogers.com.

MORLEY, LLOYD ALBERT, electrical engineering educator; b. Provo, Utah, Oct. 28, 1940; s. John Jr. and Dorothea (Nielsen) M.; m. Jo Ann Bryant, Feb. 22, 1975; 1 child, Paul Loring. BS in Mining Engring., U. Utah, 1968, PhD in Mining Engring., 1972. Tchg. asst., rsch. assoc. U. Utah, Salt Lake City, 1968-71; asst. prof. mining engring. Pa. State U., University Park, 1971-75, assoc. prof., 1975-80, prof., 1980-85; prof., head dept. mineral engring. U. Ala., Tuscaloosa, 1985-93, endowed chair mining engring., 1993-99, prof. elec. engring., 1996—, assoc. dept. head elec. and computer engring., 1997-99, interim head, 1999-2000, head, 2000—. Cons. Jim Walter Resources, Inc., Brookwood, Ala., 1987-98, Pitts. and Midway Coal Mining Co., Englewood, Colo., 1990-98, Drummond Co., Inc., Birmingham, Ala., 1991-98. Author: Mine Power Systems, 1990; contbr. articles to profl. jours. Staff sgt. USNG, 1958-66. Recipient Wilson Outstanding Teaching award Pa. State U., 1980; Outstanding Rsch. Report awards U.S. Bur. Mines, 1983-84, grantee, 1971-87. Fellow IEEE (bd. dirs. 1991-92, 94, 97-99, v.p. publs. 1994, 99, v.p. tech. activities 1997, 98); mem. Industry Applications Soc. IEEE (Mining Best Paper awards 1984, 88, 90, pres. 1988, Disting. lectr. 1991, Disting. Svc. award 1995), Power Engr. Soc., Computer Soc. Standards Assn., Phi Kappa Phi, Eta Kappa Nu. Avocations: high-fidelity systems, classic sports cars, rose growing, music. Office: U Ala Dept Electrical and Computer Engring PO Box 870286 Tuscaloosa AL 35487-0286 Office Phone: 205-348-0672. Business E-Mail: lmorley@coe.eng.ua.edu.

MORLEY, MICHAEL B. public relations executive; b. Madras, India, Nov. 18, 1935; s. Gordon and Violet M.; m. Ingrid Hellman, Aug. 20, 1957; children: Andrew, Helen, Ann. Attended, Eastbourne Coll. Dir. Harris & Hunter Pub. Rels., 1960-67; mng. dir. Daniel J. Edelman, 1967; pres. Edelman Internat., 1970, Edelman N.Y., 1994—; dep. chmn., pres. Edelman Worldwide, 2000—. Comms. Advt. and Mktg. Edn. Found. fellow, 1981; decorated Knight of First Class, Order of Lion, Rep. Finland, 1978. Mem. Internat. Pub. Rels. Assn., Internat. Pub. Rels., Brit. C. of C., Japan Soc., Bus. Coun. Internat. Understanding, Inc., Korea Soc. Home: 1 Devon Pl Cresskill NJ 07626-1608 Office: Edelman Pub Rels Worldwide 200 E Randolph St Fl 62 Chicago IL 60601-6436

MORLEY, MICHAEL P. research and development company executive; BS, Rochester (N.Y.) Inst. Tech.; MS in Mgmt., MIT, 1987. From with Divsn. Film Testing to exec. v.p. Eastman Kodak Co., Rochester, NY, 1964—2000, exec. v.p., 2000—, chief adminstrv. officer, 2000—. Chmn. bd. Nat. Action Coun. Minorities in Engring., Inc.; bd. dirs. Charter One Bank F.S.B., Indsl. Mgmt. Coun.; bd. govs. Al Sigl Ctr.; bd. govs. Sloan Sch. MIT, Mass.; bd. trustees Rochester (N.Y.) Inst. Tech.; chmn. Personnel Roundtable. Fellow Sloan fellowship, 1986. Office: Eastman Kodak Company 343 State St Rochester NY 14650

MORLEY, WILLIAM GEORGE, retired military officer, educator; b. Stockton, Calif., June 4, 1924; s. George Irwin and Helen Geers M.; m. Marian Elise Morley, Nov. 24, 1945; children: Susan Elise, John Philip, Kristina, Kevin James. BS in Polit. Sci., Georgetown U., 1956. Commd. 2d lt. USAF, 1943, advanced through grades to lt. col., dir. combat airlift ops. 815th Air Divsn., 1969—70, ret., 1973; exec. administr. Arnold Air Soc., Washington, 1973-90. Mo. valley liaison officer USAF Acad., St. Louis, 1960-63. V.p. Greater Lake Palstine Coun., Chandler, Tex., 1997-2002. Decorated Bronze Star; recipient Disting. Svc. award USAF. Mem. AF Assn. (advisor 1976-90, Citation 1990), Arnold Air Soc. (trustee Silver Wings 1990—). Republican. Roman Catholic. Avocations: golf, real property development, writing. Home: Emerald Bay 134 Marina Dr Bullard TX 75757 Office: Blue Heron Publs Emerald Bay Profl Ctr Bullard TX 75757 E-mail: blueheronpub@yahoo.com.

MORLOCK, CARL GRISMORE, physician, medical educator; b. Crediton, Ont., Can., Sept. 11, 1906; came to U.S., 1934, naturalized, 1939; s. Charles Edward and Emma (Grismore) M.; m. Katherine Ruth Mercer, Sept. 18, 1937; children: Anne Louise, William Edward. BA, U. Western Ont., 1929, MD, 1932; fellow internal medicine, Mayo Found., Grad. Sch. U. Minn., 1934-37; MS in Medicine, U. Minn., 1937. Intern Victoria Hosp., London, Ont., 1932-33, resident, 1933-34; practice medicine specializing in internal medicine and gastroenterology Rochester, Minn., 1934—; assoc.prof. internal medicine Mayo Found., 1949-62, prof. clin. medicine, 1962-72; prof. medicine Mayo Med. Sch., 1972—. Contbr. articles on gastrointestinal subjects to med. jours. Fellow ACP; mem. Am., Minn. med. assns., Osler Med. Soc., Am. Gastroent. Assn., Gideons Internat. Sigma Xi, Alpha Omega Alpha. Baptist. Home: 211 2nd St NW # 401 Rochester MN 55901-2807 Office: Mayo Clinic 200 1st St SW Rochester MN 55905-0002

MORMAN, DEAN SMITH, accountant, consultant; b. Owosso, Mich., Jan. 4, 1936; s. Corneilius Frank and Alliene Delight Morman; m. Christine Marie Paletta, Oct. 26, 1985; m. Betty Ann Branham, Aug. 7, 1954 (div. Oct. 21, 1985); 1 child, Dawn Denise Bogert. BBA, Kettering U. (GMI), Flint, Mich., 1959. Acctg. mgr. Ctrl. Foundry Divsn., GMC, Saginaw, Mich., 1954—63; mgr. of material control Midland-Ross Corp., Cleveland, Ohio, 1963—66; various mgmt. and exec. positions IBM Corp., Armonk, NY, 1966—88; pres. Self Funded Svcs., Ocean City, NJ, 1989—2009; bus. controls mgr. Atlantic City Coin and Slot Svc. Co., Pleasantvile, NJ, 1999—2002. Author: (poem) The Living Sea, 2003, (essay) Pets, 2003. Treas. South Jersey Cancer Fund, Brigantine, NJ, 1991—2000, St. Andrew by-the-Sea Luth. Ch., Atlantic City, 1988—99. R-Consevative. Lutheran. Avocations: travel, reading, creative writing.

MORNEAU, WILLIAM, pension and benefits company executive; Pres., CEO Morneau Sobeco, Toronto. Office: Morneau Sobeco 895 Don Mills Rd Ste 700 Toronto ON Canada M3C 1W3

MORNING, JOHN, graphic designer; b. Cleve., Jan. 8, 1932; s. John Frew and Juanita Kathryn (Brannan) M.; m. Carole Ann Coleman, Jan. 24, 1964 (div. July 1984); children: Ann Juanita, John Floyd. BFA, Pratt Inst., 1955. Art dir. McCann-Erickson, Inc., N.Y.C., 1958-60; pvt. practice design N.Y.C., 1960—. Bd. dirs. Dime Savings Bank N.Y. Trustee Wilberforce U., 1986-, CUNY, 1997-, Rockefeller BRos. Fund, 1999-, Charles Stewart Mott Found., 2000-; trustee com. on edn. Mus. Modern Art; chmn. bd .trustees Pratt Inst., Bklyn., 1988—99; vice chmn. N.Y.C. Cultural Affairs Adv. Commn., 1994—2000; dir. N.Y. Coun. for Humanities, 1999—; Bd. dirs. N.Y. Landmarks Conservancy, Charles E. Culpepper Found., 1990-, Henry St. Settlement, chmn., 1979-86, Bklyn. Acad. Music, 1993, Lincoln Ctr. Inst., 1993, Vivian Beaumont Theater, 1995-; bd. dirs. Mus. African Art, N.Y.C., co-chair, 1991-94. With U.S. Army, 1956—58. Recipient Alumni medal Pratt Inst., 1972, Presdl. Recognition award Pres. of U.S., 1984, Lillian D. Wald Humanitarian award, 1992. Mem.: Assn. Governing Bds. Colls. and Univs. (bd. dirs., chmn. 1998—2000), Am. Acad. Dramatic Arts (trustee 1988—95). Republican. E-mail: 110733.3622@compuserve.com .

MORONEY, JAMES M., III, publishing executive, broadcast executive; m. Barbara Moroney; 5 children. BA in Am. Studies, Stanford U., 1978; MBA, U. Tex., 1983. With Petry TV, NY; acct. exec. Belo stas. WFAA, KFDM-TV, Beaumont, Tex., 1978—84; local sales mgr. WFAA, 1985; controller Belo, Dallas, 1989, asst. to pres. co.'s broadcast divsn., 1990—92; gen. sales mgr. KOTV, pres., gen. mgr., 1992, promoted to pres., gen. mgr., 1993, v.p. broadcast divsn., 1993; exec. v.p. TV Group, 1995, promoted to pres., 1997; exec. v.p. Belo, 1998—2001; founding pres. Belo Interactive (subs. of Belo), 1999; pub., CEO Dallas Morning News, 2001—. Mem. Dallas Citizens Coun.; mem. bd. dirs. TV Bur. Adv., Goodwill Industries, Dallas, Tulsa, United Way Tulsa, Cath. Charities Tulsa, Jr. Achievement Tulsa, Gilcrease Mus. Tulsa, Cistercian Perp. Sch. Dallas, Greater Dallas Chamber, State Fair Tex.; mem. bd. dirs. Coll. Comm. U. Tex. Austin. Named Pub. of Yr., Editor & Pub. mag., 2004. Office: Dallas Morning News PO Box 655237 Dallas TX 75265-5237 Address: 508 Young St Dallas TX 75202-4808*

MORONEY, JOHN RODGERS, economist, educator; b. Dallas, Jan. 29, 1939; s. John Rodgers and Irene (Lewis) M.; m. Margaret Cecil Kearny, May 30, 1959; children: John Rodgers, Stephen Kearny, Helen, Michael Edward; m. Carmen Lambert, May 22, 1993. BA, So. Meth. U., 1960; PhD, Duke, 1964. Asst. prof. econs. Fla. State U., 1964-66; assoc. prof. econs. Mich. State U., 1966-69; mem. exec. com. Inst. Pub. Utilities, 1968-69; prof. econs., chmn. dept. Tulane U., New Orleans, 1969-81; prof., head dept. econs. Tex. A&M U., College Station, 1981—. Vis. prof. econs. M.I.T., 1975-76; Schmidt internat. prof. A.B. Freeman Sch. Bus., Tulane U., New Orleans, 1998—; pres. Moroney Econ. Rsch. Assocs., 1992—. Author: The Structure of Production in American Manufacturing, 1972, Exploration, Development, and Production: Texas Oil and Gas, 1997; editor, contbr.: Income Inequality: Trends and Internat. Comparisons, 1979, Economic Aspects of New Technology, 1980, Formal Energy and Resource Models, 1982; editor: Econometric Models of the Demand for Energy, 1984; editor, contbr.: Energy, Capital, and Technological Change, 1987, Energy, Growth, and the Environment, 1992, Energy Prices and Production, 1994, Sustainable Economic Growth, 1995, Energy Supply and Demand, 1997, Fuels for the Future, 1999; mem. editl. bd. Bus. Topics, 1968-69, So. Econ. Jour, 1975—. Social Sci. Research Council faculty research fellow, 1969; NSF research fellow, 1975-76, 77-79 Mem. Am. Econ. Assn., So. Econ. Assn. (exec. com. 1975—, v.p. 1980), Royal Econ. Assn., Econometric Soc., Phi Beta Kappa. Home: 210 Fireside Cir College Station TX 77840-1877 Office: Dept Econs Tex A&M U College Station TX 77843-4228 Office Phone: 979-845-1363. Business E-Mail: jmoroney@econmail.tamu.edu.

MORONEY, MICHAEL JOHN, lawyer; b. Jamaica, N.Y., Nov. 8, 1940; s. Everard Vincent and Margaret Olga (Olson) M.; children: Sean, Megan, Matthew. BS in Polit. Sci., Villanova U., 1962; JD, Fordham U., 1965; Police Sci. (hon.), U. Guam, 1976. Bar: Hawaii 1974, U.S. Dist. Ct. Hawaii 1974, U.S. Ct. Appeals (9th cir.) 1974, Guam 1976, U.S. Dist. Ct. (Guam dist.) 1976, U.S. Ct. Claims 1976, U.S. Tax Ct. 1976, U.S. Ct. Mil. Appeals 1977, U.S. Supreme Ct. 1977, High Ct. Trust Ters. 1977, U.S. Dist. Ct. (No. Mariana Islands) 1983. Spl. agt. FBI, Memphis and Nashville, 1965-67, Cleve. and Elyria, Ohio, 1967-71; spl. agt., prin. legal advisor FBI, U.S. Dept. Justice, Honolulu, 1971-97; v.p. Merrill Corp., Honolulu, 1997-2000; mgr. Investigative Svcs. Worldwide, 2000—; mng. dir. Paradise Meml. Park, LLC, Honolulu, 2000—; pres., mgr. ISW, LLC, 2000—. Bar examiner and applications rev. com. Supreme Ct. Hawaii, 1980—; pres. Hawaii State Law Enforcement Assn., 1985-86; mem. and del. to congress Gov.'s Task Force on Hawaii's Internat. Role, 1988; mem. Charter Commn., City and County of Honolulu, 1998-2000; mem. Consular Corps of Hawaii, 1997-2000; regent Harris Manchester Coll., Oxford U., 2000—. Gov.'s task force, del. gov.'s congress on Hawaii's Internat. Role, 1988—; apptd. hon. consul gen. Republic of Palau; pres. Tommy E. Remongesau, Jr., 2002—, pres. Kunio Nakamura, 1999, 2002—. Recipient Govs. Award for outstanding contbns. to law enforcement Govt. of Guam, 1974, 76, cert. of appreciation Supreme Ct. Hawaii, 1981, Honolulu Police Commn., 1984, 86; named Fed. Law Enforcement Officer of Yr., State of Hawaii, 1992, Outstanding Career award in law enforcement and commitment to Hawaii State Law Enforcement Ofcls. Assn., 1998. Mem. ABA, Hawaii Bar Assn., Guam Bar Assn., Inst. Jud. Adminstrn., Hawaii State Law Enforcement Ofcls. Assn., Hilo Yacht Club, Oahu Country Club, Plaza Club, Rotary Club Honolulu. Address: 7858 Makaaoa Pl Honolulu HI 96825-2848 Office: Paradise Meml Park LLC 1154 Fort Street Mall Ste 300 Honolulu HI 96813-2712 Fax: 808-599-5004. E-mail: mmoro007@aol.com.

MORONI, MARIO, humanities educator; b. Tarquinia, Viterbo, Italy, Aug. 17, 1955; arrived in U.S., 1989; s. Manfredo Moroni and Paola Capotondi; m. Olivia Wendy Holmes, June 10, 1989; 1 child, Jacopo Holmes. Laurea, U. Rome, 1979; M, Northwestern U., 1991, PhD, 1995. Vis. asst. prof. Northwestern U., Evanston, Ill., 1996—97; vis. faculty Yale U., New Haven, 1997—99; asst. prof. U. Memphis, 1999—2001; Paganucci asst. prof. Colby Coll., Waterville, Maine, 2001—. *Author of six volumes of poetry, one of short stories, two volumes of literary criticism, and co-editor of two volumes of essays. Major fields of scholarly research European and Italian literature from romantic to the present. Created minor in Italian studies at Colby College in 2001.* Mem.: Italian Poetry Soc. Am. (exec. com. 1996—99), Am. Assn. Tchrs. Italian, Am. Assn. Italian Studies, Modern Lang. Assn. Democrat. Avocations: travel, soccer. Office: Colby College Waterville ME 04901 Office Phone: 207-872-3119.

MOROOKA, HIROSHI, neurosurgeon; b. Kurashiki, Okayama, Japan, Aug. 28, 1946; s. Shigeru and Akiko (Kobayashi) M.; m. Michiko Ninomiya, June 6, 1976; children: Takatoshi, Hanako, Teruko. MD, U. Okayama, 1971, D

Med. Sci., 1978. Diplomate Japanese Bd. Neurol. Surgery. Clin. asst. neurosurgery U. Okayama Med. Sch., 1972-77, instr. neurosurgery, 1980-83, asst. prof. neurosurgery, 1984-86; rsch. assoc. neurology U. Miami (Fla.) Med. Sch., 1977-79; chief neurosurgery Okayama Rousai Hosp., 1987-92, Bizen City Hosp., 1993-95, Okayama Saidaiji Hosp., 1996—. Author: Cytoprotection & Cytobiology, 1995-97, Medical Biochemical & Chemical Aspects of Free Radicals, 1989, Intracranial Pressure VII, 1989, Brain Edema IX, 1993. Recipient Nat. Rsch. grant, 1981. Mem. Japan Neurol. Soc., Societas Neurologica Japonica, N.Y. Acad. Scis., Am. Heart Assn. Liberal Dem. Christian. Avocations: golf, go (7th degree). Home: 880-165 Minato 703 8266 Okayama Japan Office: Okayama Saidaiji Hosp 8-41 Saidaiji Nakano Honmachi Okayama 704-8192 Japan Office Phone: 086-943-2211. Business E-Mail: morooka@okym.enjoy.ne.jp.

MOROSO, MICHAEL JOSEPH, aerospace engineer; b. Centerville, Iowa, Jan. 26, 1923; s. John and Antonietta (Sartor) M.; m. Jody Mary Scripter, June 16, 1951; children— Barbara, Michael, Robert, Philip. BSME, U. Wis., 1952. Naval aviator, Pensacola, Fla.; designer Douglas Aircraft Co., Santa Monica, Calif., 1952-65; engr., scientist McDonnell Douglas launch ctr. Vandenberg AFB, Calif., 1965-70; engr., sci. specialist McDonnell Douglas Astronautics Co., Huntington Beach, Calif., 1970-76; sr. propulsion engr. Northrop Corp., Hawthorne, Calif., 1976-79; staff engr. Douglas Aircraft Co., Long Beach, Calif., 1979— . Served to lt. USN, 1943-47. Mem. advancement com. Boy Scouts Am., Santa Maria, Calif., 1966-69; Little League mgr., coach, Santa Maria, 1967-69. Assoc. fellow AIAA; mem. So. Calif. Profl. Engrs. Assn., Am. Legion (adjutant, fin. officer 1950-65), Douglas Mgmt. Club. Democrat. Roman Catholic. Home: 964 Lansing Ln Costa Mesa CA 92626-2821 Office: 3855 N Lakewood Blvd Long Beach CA 90846-0003

MOROWITZ, HAROLD JOSEPH, biophysicist, educator; b. Poughkeepsie, N.Y., Dec. 4, 1927; s. Philip Frank and Anna (Levine) M.; m. Lucille Rita Stein, Jan. 30, 1949; children: Joanna Lynn, Eli David, Joshua Alan, Zachary Adam, Noah Daniel. BS, Yale U., 1947, MS, 1950, PhD, 1951. Physicist Nat. Bur. Stds., 1951-53, Nat. Heart Inst., Bethesda, Md., 1953-55; mem. faculty Yale U., 1955-88, assoc. prof. biophysics, 1960-68, prof. molecular biophysics and biochemistry, 1968-88, master Pierson Coll., 1981-86; mem. faculty George Mason U., Fairfax, Va., 1988—, Robinson prof. biology and natural philosophy, 1988—; dir. Krasnow Inst. for Advanced Study, 1993-98. Chmn. com. on models for biomed. rsch. NRC, 1983-85, mem. bd. on basic biology, 1986-92. Author: Life and the Physical Sciences, 1964, (with Waterman) Theoretical and Mathematical Biology, 1965, Energy Flow in Biology, 1968, Entropy for Biologists, 1970, (with Lucille Morowitz) Life On The Planet Earth, 1974, Ego Niches, 1977, Foundations of Bioenergetics, 1978, The Wine of Life, 1979, Mayonnaise and the Origin of Life, 1985, Cosmic Joy and Local Pain, 1987, The Thermodynamics of Pizza, 1991, Beginnings of Cellular Life, 1992, (with James Trefil) The Facts of Life, 1992, Entropy and the Magic Flute, 1993, The Kindly Dr. Guillotin, 1997, The Emergence of Everything, 2002; editor Complexity, 1994-2002; contbr. articles to profl. jours. Mem. sci. adv. bd. Santa Fe Inst., 1991-97, co-chmn. sci. adv. bd., 2000—. Mem. Biophys. Soc. (exec. com. 1965), Nat. Ctr. for Rsch. Resources (coun. 1987-92). Office: George Mason U Mail Stop 2A1 Krasnow Inst Advanced Study Fairfax VA 22030 Office Phone: 703-993-4334.

MOROZ, PAVEL EMANUEL, research scientist; b. Leningrad, Russia, 1928; came to U.S., 1976. Degree in Medicine, Pavlov Med. Inst., Leningrad, 1952, MD in Cytology and Biophysics, 1960. Rsch. scientist various insts., Leningrad, 1952-75. Author: (in Russian) A Book of Aphorisms, 2002; contbr. articles to profl. jours. Mem. N.Y. Acad. Scis. Achievements include research in the effects of the force of gravity and centrifugal force on the cell and development of centrifuge microscope; analysis of the physical limits of biological evolution, particularly of the vertical posture in man. Home: 15-17 Willet St Apt 3K New York NY 10002

MORPHY, JAMES CALVIN, lawyer; b. Pitts., Jan. 16, 1954; s. Robert Samson and Autumn (Phillips) M.; m. Priscilla Winslow Plimpton, July 11, 1981; children: Calvin, Katherine, Victoria. BA, Harvard U., 1976, JD, 1979. Bar: N.Y. 1980. Assoc. Sullivan & Cromwell, N.Y.C., 1979-86, ptnr., 1986—, mng. ptnr. com., 1992—, mng. ptnr. M&A group, 1995—. Author (contbg.): (treatise) New York and Delaware Business Entities: Choice Formation, Operation, Financing, and Acquisition, 1997, Transactional Lawyer's Deskbook, 2001. Trustee Greenwich Acad. Mem. ABA (com. on fed. securities law 1992—), Assn. Bar of City of N.Y., Wianno Club (bd. govs.), Greenwich Country Club, Harvard Club N.Y., Wianno Yacht Club, Phi Beta Kappa. Office: Sullivan & Cromwell 125 Broad St Fl 28 New York NY 10004-2489

MORPHY, JOHN, manufacturing executive; b. Rochester, N.Y., Aug. 14, 1947; s. John and Mary (Kelleher) M.; m. Marcia Price, June 5, 1971; children: Jaime, Matthew. BS in Acctg., Le Moyne Coll., Syracuse, N.Y., 1969. CPA, N.Y. Mgr. Arthur Andersen & Co., Rochester, 1969-76; v.p., controller Computer Consoles Inc., Rochester, 1976-85; v.p., CFO Goulds Pumps Inc., Seneca Falls, N.Y., 1985; group v.p. Gould's Pumps, Inc., 1992-95; v.p., dir. of fin. Paychex, Inc., Rochester, N.Y., 1996—. Office: Paychex Inc 911 Panorama S Rochester NY 14625-0397

MORREALE, JOSEPH CONSTANTINO, higher education administrator, public administration educator, economic and financial consultant; b. Bronx, N.Y., Oct. 26, 1944; s. Joseph Vincent Morreale and Grace (Soricelli); m. Barbara McAdorey; children: Gwenn F., Margaret I., Adam J.; stepchildren: Neil J., Michael D., John D. BA, Queens Coll. CUNY, 1967; MA, SUNY, Buffalo, 1969, PhD in Econs., 1972; MS in Higher Ednl. Adminstrn., SUNY, Albany, 1989. Asst. prof. econs. Western Mich. U., Kalamazoo, 1970-74; rsch. assoc. U. Wis., Madison, 1974-75; asst. to assoc. prof. health svcs. adminstrn., econs. Grad. Sch. Pub. Health U. Pitts., 1975-79; assoc. to prof. econs., environ. studies Bard Coll., Annandale-On-Hudson, N.Y., 1979-88; vis. rsch. fellow Grad. Sch. Edn., H.E. Adminstrn. SUNY, Albany, 1988-89; prof., chmn. dept. pub. adminstrn. Grad. Sch. Pace U., White Plains, N.Y., 1989-96; vice provost for planning assessment and instnl. rsch. Pace U., N.Y.C., Westchester, 1996-98, v.p. planning, assessment, rsch. and acad. support, 1998—, sr. assoc. provost, v.p., 2001—. Health care and govt. fin. cons. to fed. agencies, state and local govts., pvt. firms, 1979—; adj. prof. law Pace U., 1990-96; adj. prof. pub. adminstrn. Grad. Sch. Pub. Affairs, SUNY-Albany, 1990-96; vis. prof. U. Lancaster, Eng., 1984-85; rsch. assoc., bd. dirs. Hudsonia Environ. Rsch., Annandale, 1985-95; fin. planner Prudential Fin. Svcs., Newburgh, N.Y., 1987-89. Author: Health Care Economics, 1977, Post Tenure Review and Renewal: Experienced Voices, 2002; editor: The U.S. Medical Care Industry, 1974, Post-tenure Review: Policies, Practices, Precautions, 1997; contbr. articles to profl. jours. Appoint pub. rep. Westchester County Deferred Compensation Bd., Mt. Kisco Planning Bd. Recipient NDEA fellowship, 1967-70, Pharm. Mfg. Assn. fellowship, 1969-70, post-doctoral fellowship Health Econ. Rsch. Ctr. U. Wis., 1974-75, rsch. fellowship Grad. Sch. Edn. SUNY-Albany, 1988-89, ACE fellowship UNC, Charlotte, 1995-96, sr. rsch. fellow Harvard IEM Inst., 2000. Mem. Am. Soc. for Pub. Adminstrn., Am. Econ. Assn., Am. Ednl. Fin. Assn., Assn. Instl. Rsch., Am. Assn. Higher Edn., Am. Coun. Edn. (fellow 1995-96), N.Y. State Govt. Fin. Officers Assn. (bd. dirs. 1990-95). Mem. Soc. Of Friends. Avocations: photography, tennis, music, environ. concerns. Office: Pace U VP 1 Pace Plz New York NY 10038-1598

MORREIM, E. HAAVI, medical ethics educator; b. Austin, Minn., July 21, 1950; d. Paul Eugene and Florence Adeline Morreim. BA in Philosophy, St. Olaf Coll., 1972; MA in Philosophy, U. Va., 1976, PhD, 1980. Med. philosopher program in human biology and soc. U. Va. Sch. Medicine, Charlottesville, 1980-82, asst. prof. philosophy in medicine, 1982-84; from asst. to assoc. prof. dept. human values and ethics U. Tenn. Coll. Medicine, Memphis, 1988—93, prof. dept. human values and ethics, 1993—. Adj. prof. philosophy Va. Commonwealth U., Richmond, 1980; vis. prof. philosophy St. Olaf Coll., Northfield, Minn., 1982; Andrew Mellon vis. asst. prof. humanities and medicine Georgetown U. Sch. Medicine, Washington, 1983; sr. vis. rsch. scholar Kennedy Inst. Ethics, Georgetown U., 1983; manuscript reviewer; presenter and lectr. in field. Author: Balancing Act: The New Medical Ethics of Medicine's New Economics, 1991, Holding Health Care Accountable: Law and the New Medical Marketplace, 2001; mem. editl. adv. bd. Jour. Medicine and Philosophy; bd. editors: Jour. Law, Medicine and Ethics, IRB: Ethics and Human Research; contbr. articles to profl. jours. Active Hastings Ctr. Mem. Am. Health Lawyers Assn., Am. Soc. Law, Medicine, and Ethics, Am. Soc. for Bioethics and Humanities, Phi Beta Kappa. Avocations: running, high-performance automobile driving, photography, skiing. Office: Univ Tenn Coll Medicine 956 Court Ave Ste B328 Memphis TN 38163-2814 Office Phone: 901-448-5725. Business E-Mail: hmorreim@utmem.edu.

MORREL, WILLIAM GRIFFIN, JR., banker; b. Lynchburg, Va., Aug 25, 1933; s. William Griffin and Virginia Louise (Baldwin) M.; m. Sandra Virginia Coats, Jan. 31, 1959; children: William Griffin, John Coats, Elisabeth White, Jere Coleman. BS, Yale U., 1955; postgrad. Rutgers U., 1965-67. With Md. Nat. Bank, Balt., 1955-84, asst. v.p., 1959, v.p., 1964, sr. v.p., 1975-84, mgmt. com. 1979-84, chmn. three lending coms., others; pres., bd. dirs. Md. Nat. Overseas Investment Corp.; chmn. bd. London Interstate Bank Ltd.; chmn. bd. dirs. Md. Internat. Bank; sr. v.p., chief operating officer Abu Dhabi Internat. Bank, Inc., 1984-86, pres., chief exec. officer Heritage Internat. Bank, 1986-89; dir., pres., CEO Madison Fin. Group, 1989-97, chmn., 1997—2003; CEO, chmn. The Valley Fin. Group, Balt., 1989—; pres., chief exec. officer Summit Bancorp, Balt., 1990-92; consul of the Netherlands at Balt., 1978-84. Mem. Balt. Consular Corps, 1978-84; chmn. Md. World Trade Efforts Commn., 1983-84; mem. Md. Trade Policy Council, 1985-88; vice chmn. Dist. Export Council, 1983—. Contbr. articles to profl. jours. Sr. fellow Ctr. for Internat. Banking Studies, Darden Grad. Bus. Sch. U. Va., 1978-91. Served with U.S. Army, 1956-58. Mem. Bankers Assn. for Fgn. Trade (bd. dirs. 1975-78), Robert Morris Assocs. (nat. bd. dirs. 1984-88), Internat. Lending Council (bd. dirs., chmn., 1978-80), Md. Hist. Soc. (trustee), Balt. Council Fgn. Relations (trustee), Econ. Devel. Council. Republican. Presbyterian. Clubs: Yale, Farmington Country, Elkridge, Md. Club. Home and Office: 6 Beechdale Rd Baltimore MD 21210-2207 E-mail: grifbank@aol.com.

MORRELL, GENE PAUL, liquid terminal company executive, consultant, b. Ardmore, Okla., Oct. 4, 1932; s. Paul T. and Etta L. (Weaver) M.; m. Jan A. Foster, Aug. 20, 1954; children: Jeffrey T., Kelly Ann, Rob Redman. BS in Geology, U. Okla., 1954, LLB, 1962. Bar: D.C. 1973. Geologist Gilmer Oil Co., Ardmore, Okla., 1957-59, atty.-geologist, 1962-63; pvt. practice Ardmore, 1963-69, ofcl. Dept. Interior, Washington, 1969-72, v.p. Lone Star Gas Co., Washington, 1972-76; sr. v.p. United Energy Resources, Inc., Houston, 1976-86; vice chmn. Petro United Terminals, Inc., Houston, 1986-98; cons. on investments, 1998—. Contbr. articles to profl. jours. Commr. City of Ardmore, 1967-69, vice-mayor, 1968. Mem. D.C. Bar Assn., Am. Assn. Petroleum Geologists, River Oaks Country Club (Houston), Phi Alpha Delta, Sigma Alpha Epsilon. Episcopalian.

MORRILL, BILLIE ALBERTA, librarian; b. Hartford, Conn., Aug. 25, 1942; d. Clifford Kenneth Worland and Alberta Molly Schwartz; m. Richard Melvin Morrill, June 11, 1966; 1 child, Celeste. LTA cert., Three Rivers C.C., Norwich, Conn., 1993, AS in Gen. Studies, 1998. Asst. editor Travelers Bull. Travelers Ins. Co., Hartford, 1970—73, head spkrs. bur., 1973—75; copywriter G. Fox & Co., Hartford, 1979—83; freelance writer, 1983—87; reference libr. East Lyme Pub. Libr., Niantic, Conn., 1987—. Author poetry; contbr. articles to profl. jours. Charter mem., pres. Travelers Toastmistress Club, Hartford, 1970—75. Recipient Trustee's medallion, Three Rivers C.C., 1998. Mem.: Poets of the Sound (facilitator 1998—), Conn. Poetry Soc., LTA Alumni Assn., Phi Theta Kappa. Methodist. Avocations: writing, reading, walking. Office: East Lyme Pub Libr 39 Society Rd Niantic CT 06357-1100

MORRILL, JOYCE MARIE, social worker, educator; b. Rockland, Maine, Dec. 27, 1939; d. Henry Higgins and Julia Ellen (Philbrook) Thompson; m. Edward Morrill, Sept. 7, 1972; 1 son, Gregory Hodgman; 1 stepchild, Shawn Morrill. BA, U. Hartford, 1964; MSW, Hunter Coll., 1972. Co-host Today in Conn. Program Sta. WHNB-TV, Hartford, 1964—65; clin. social worker, field instr. Rehab. Inst., NYC, 1972—78; dir., founder Wellness Svcs., Jamaica Estates, NY, 1979—95; pres. Morrill Support, 1996—. Photographer-artist. Mem.: NASW, Inst. Noetic Scis., Alliance of Queens Artists, Profl. Woman Photographers. Home and Office: 181-38 Midland Pky Jamaica NY 11432 E-mail: Joyce@morrillsupport.com.

MORRILL, PENNY CHITTIM, art historian; b. San Antonio, Feb. 4, 1947; d. Jack Robert and Dorothy Born (Sutherland) Chittim; m. James Agrippa Morrill, July 12, 1969; children: Jackson Forrest, Julia Chiltipin. BA with honors, Tulane U., 1969; MA, U. Pa., 1971; PhD, U. Md., 2001. Program coord. Cancer Rsch. Found. Am., Alexandria, Va., 1990-95; adj. prof. Md. Inst. Coll. Art, Balt., 2000, Corcoran Coll. Art, Washington, 2003, Georgetown U., 2004. Curator and catalogue author for traveling exhbn. Maestros de Plata: William Spratling and the Mex. Silver Renaissance, San Antonio Mus. of Art., 1998-2004. Author: Silver Masters of Mexico, 1996, Mexican Silver, 1994; contbr. articles to profl. jours. Vol. teen pregnancy prevention Nat. ARC, Washington, 1986-98; participant Coro Women in Leadership, Washington, 1988; adv. com. Betty Ford Breast Health Ctr., Washington, 1997-98; adv. com. Nat. Rehab. Hosp., Washington, 1991—, bd. dir.; mem., v.p. Newcomb Coll./Tulane U. Alumnae Bd., 1990-94; mem., pres. Lyceum Mus., Alexandria, 1992-97; mem., editor, pres. Hist. Alexandria Found., 1980-89; curator exhbn. Carlyle House Mus., Alexandria, 1980. Recipient Achievement award Jr. League of Phila., 1985, Award for RAP and AMAZE, Nat. ARC, 1988, Spirit of Volunteerism award Jr. League of Washington, 1992, Recognition award Nat. Rehab. Hosp., 1997. Mem. Coll. Art Assn., Am. Soc. Jewelry Historians. Episcopalian. Avocations: knitting, gardening.

MORRILL, R. LAYNE, real estate broker, executive, professional association administrator; m. Brenda Morrill; 1 child, Rochelle Dawn. Cert. real estate broker. Pres. Shepherhd of the Hills, Realtors, Kimberling City, Branson, Mo., 1960—; mem. exec. com. Nat. Assn. Realtors, 1988—, pres., 1998—99, also bd. dirs. and mem. exec. com., 1988—. Regional v.p. Nat. Assn. Realtors, Ark., Kans., Mo., Okla., 1988; chair realtors polit. action com., 88; dir. Bank Kimberling city, Mo., Rural Mo. Cable TV, Inc. White River Valley Electric Coop., Branson, Mo., KAMO Electric Coop., Vinita, Okla., Nat. Rural utilities Coop. Fin. Corp., Herndon, Va. Mem.: Tri-Lakes Bd. Realtors (pres.), Mo. Assn. Realtors (pres., bd. dirs. 1962—, Realtor of the Yr. award 1979). Office: Nat Assn Realtors 430 N Michigan Ave Chicago IL 60611-4011

MORRILL, RICHARD LESLIE, university administrator; b. Weymouth, Mass., June 4, 1939; s. Duncan Russel and Violet Erma (Gibson) M.; m. Martha Leahy, June 24, 1964; children: Katie, Amy. AB in History magna cum laude, Brown U., 1961; B.D. in Religious Thought, Yale U., 1964; PhD in Religion, Duke U., 1968. Instr. Wells Coll., Aurora, N.Y., 1967-68; asst. prof. Chatham Coll., Pitts., 1968-74, assoc. prof., 1974-77, assoc. provost and asst. to pres., 1973-77; assoc. provost Pa. State U., University Park, 1977-79; pres. Salem Coll. and Acad., Winston-Salem, N.C., 1979-82, Centre Coll., Danville, Ky., 1982-88, U. Richmond, Va., Va., 1988-98, chancellor, 1998—. Bd. dirs. Ctrl. Fidelity Banks, Inc.; v.p. So. Univ. Conf., 1993—; chmn. Assoc. Colls. of the South, 1993-94; v.p. So. Univ. Conf., 1993—; mem. governing coun. Wye Faculty Seminar, 1994—; mem. presdl. adv. com. KPMG Peat Marwick, 1989—; cons. edn. divsn. Lilly Endowment, 1990—. Author: Teaching Values in College, 1980; contbr. articles to profl. jours. Bd. dirs., mem. program com. Teagle Found., 1989—; mem. nat. bd. visitors Ind. U. Ctr. on Philanthropy, 1991—; mem. commn. on leadership devel. Am. Coun. on Edn., 1992-94; trustee Williamsburg Investment Trust, 1993—; mem. Richmond Symphony Coun., 1995—; mem. Va. Coun. for Internat. Edn., 1995-96; bd. dirs. Assn. Am. Colls. and Univs., 1996—. Woodrow Wilson fellow, 1961-62; James B. Duke fellow Duke U., 1964-67 Mem. Soc. for Values in Higher Edn. (dir. 1981-84), Am. Acad. Religion, Am. Soc. for Christian Ethics, Am. Assn. Higher Edn., So. Assn. Colls. and Schs. (commr. 1985—), Coll. Athletic Conf. (chmn. 1985-87), Council Ind. Ky. Colls. and Univs. (sec. 1984-86, v.p. 1986-88, exec. com. 1984-86), Assn. Presbyn. Colls. and Univs. (exec. com. 1984-86), Phi Beta Kappa. Clubs: University. Lodges: Rotary. Home: 7000 River Rd Richmond VA 23229-8532 Office: U Richmond Office of Chancellor Boatwright Library Richmond VA 23173-1903

MORRILL, THOMAS CLYDE, insurance company executive; b. Chgo., July 1, 1909; s. Walter and Lena Elpha (Haney) M.; m. Hazel Janet Thompson, Oct. 18, 1930; children: Dorothy Mae (Mrs. Gerald L. Kelly), Charles T. Student, Cen. Coll. Arts and Scis., Chgo., 1928-29, Northwestern U., 1929-30. With Alfred M. Best Co., Inc., 1929-45, assoc. editor, 1940-45; with N.Y. State Ins. Dept., 1945-50, dep. supt. ins., 1947-50; with State Farm Mut. Automobile Ins. Co., Bloomington, Ill., 1950-77, v.p., 1952-77; chmn. bd. State Farm Fire and Casualty Co., Bloomington, 1970-86, State Farm Gen. Ins. Co., Bloomington, 1970-91; cons. State Farm Ins. Cos., Bloomington, 1991—. Founder, chmn. dir. Ins. Inst. for Hwy. Safety; co-founder, dir. Hwy. Loss Data Ins. Chmn. exec. subcom. Nat. Hwy. Safety Adv. Com., 1971-73; chmn. tech. com. on transp. White House Conf. on Aging, 1971; mem. Pres.'s Task Force on Hwy. Safety. Mem.: Union League Club (Chgo.).

MORRIS, ALBERT JEROME, medical company executive; b. N.Y.C., Jan. 3, 1919; s. Peter and Minnie (Miller) M.; Barbara McLeod, Feb 6, 1943; children: Peter A., Lee Ellen Morris Guenther, Lisa Ann Morris Rasche. BS in Electronics, U. Calif., Berkeley, 1941; MS in Electronics, Stanford U., 1948, Degree of Engr., 1950. Registered profl. engr., Calif. Founder Morris Defibrilator Co., 1949; sr. v.p., co-founder Levinthal Elec. Products, Palo Alto, Calif., 1953-60; pres., dir. Radiation at Stanford, Palo Alto, 1960-63; pres., chief exec. officer Energy Systems Inc., Palo Alto, 1963-66, Genesys Systems Inc., Palo Alto, 1967-84, Biosys, Palo Alto, 1983-88, chmn. bd., 1989; also chmn. bd. TurboEnergy Systems, Phoenix, 1989-90; chmn. bd., chief exec. officer Neural Systems Corp., Palo Alto, 1991—. Cons. to schs. of engring., Stanford U. and 18 other major univs.; chmn. San Francisco coun. Western Electronics Mfrs. Assn., 1965; chmn. bd. Western Electronics Show and Conv., Calif., 1961, Neural Sys. Corp. Author over 50 papers on ship stabilization, high power electronics, med. electronics and continuing edn. Recipient Best Paper award IEEE/ASEE Frontiers in Edn. Conf., 1978. Fellow IEEE, Sigma Chi Iota; mem. AAAS. Avocations: tennis, golf.

MORRIS, ALVIN LEONARD, retired dentist, educational administrator; b. Detroit, July 2, 1927; s. Frank and Lulu (Cornett) M.; m. Arlene Teschler, Feb. 1, 1947 (dec. Apr. 1974); children: Jeffry, Gregg, Beth; m. Beverly Hackman, 1975. Student, U. Ill., 1944-45; D.D.S., U. Mich., 1951; PhD, U. Rochester, 1957; D.Sc. (hon.), U. Md., 1983. Intern Letterman Army Hosp., San Francisco, 1951-52; postdoctoral research fellow NIH, 1954-57; head dept. oral diagnosis U. Pa. Sch. Dentistry, 1957-61; dean U. Ky. Coll. Dentistry, Lexington, 1961-68; asst. v.p. U. Ky. Coll. Dentistry (Med. Center), 1968-69, v.p. adminstrn. univ., 1970-75; exec. dir. Assn. for Acad. Health Centers, Washington, 1975-79; prof. dental care systems Sch. Dental Medicine, asso. v.p. health affairs U. Pa., 1979-87, sr. assoc. Leonard Davis Inst. Health Econs., Wharton Grad. Sch., 1980-87, prof. emeritus, 1987-89; research prof. Health Services Research Ctr./Sch. of Dentistry, U. N.C., Chapel Hill, 1987-89. Cons. Dental Corps, U.S. Army, 1960-70, VA, 1962-75, U.S. Dept. Def., 1969-72; pub. health service cons. dental study sect. USPHS, 1963-67; also chmn.; cons., lectr. USN Dental Sch.; cons. Army Med. Service Adv. Com. Preventive Dentistry, 1967-71; mem. Nat. Adv. Council Edn. Health Professions, 1968-72; bd. dirs. Nat. Center Health Edn., 1977-84; adv. com. Ednl. Testing Service, 1977-82; chmn. adv. com. Nat. Preventive Dental Demonstration Program, 1976-83 Served with inf. AUS, 1944-46; to 1st lt. Dental Corps 1951-54. Recipient Pierre Fauchard medal, 1974, Henry Spenadel medal, 1982, Callahan medal, 1991. Fellow Internat., Am. colls. dentists; mem. ADA (Disting. Svc. award 1985), Inst. Medicine of NAS, AAAS, Internat. Assn. Dental Rsch., So. Conf. Dental Deans and Examiners (pres. 1964-65), Sigma Xi. Presbyterian (deacon, trustee). Home: 302 Briarcliff Ln Danville KY 40422

MORRIS, ANN HASELTINE JONES, social welfare administrator; b. Springfield, Mo., Feb. 3, 1941; d. Mansur King and Adelaide (Haseltine) Jones; m. Ronald D. Morris, Nov. 29, 1963 (div. 1990); children: David, Christopher. BA in Edn. and Art, Drury Coll., 1963. Art instr. Ash Grove (Mo.)/Bois D'Arc Pub. Sch. Dist., 1963-64; instr. Drury Coll., Springfield, 1966-67; tchr. Springfield R-12 Sch. Dist., 1974-86; exec. dir. S.W. Ctr. for Ind. Living, Springfield, 1986—. Adv. com. Springfield R-12 Spl. Edn., 1993—; tech. cons. and alternative dispute resolution mediator Ams. with Disabilities Act EEOC, Dept. of Justice Network, 1993—; peer reviewer Office Spl. Edn. and Rehabilitative Svcs. Bd. dirs. Ozark Greenways, 1991-93, Springfield Deaf Relay, 1988-90; adv. task force Allied Health Program Devel. S.W. Bapt Univ., 1988; mem. Drury Coll. Women's Aux., 1984-96, conservator of the peace, handicap parking enforcement action team, 1991—; bd. treas. Mo. Parent Act, 1989-91, Diversity Network of the Ozarks, 1990—; svc. coord. Youthnet, 1990—; community adv. bd. Rehab. Svcs., St. John's Regional Health Care Ctr., 1988-91; mem. Springfield Homeless Network, 1989—, others; apptd. to Mo. Gov.'s Coun. on Disability; pres. Statewide Ind. Living Coun; mem. Gov.'s Commn. on Home and Cmty. Based Svcs., 2000-2001. Mem. NOW (sec. 1991), P.E.O., Mo. Assn. of Ctrs. for Ind. Living (v.p. 1990-97), Mo. Assn. for Social Welfare (bd. treas. 1989-95), Nat. Assn. of Ind. Living Ctrs. (AIDS task force 1993-96), Assn. of Programs for Rural Ind. Living, Nat. Soc. of Fund Raising Execs., Mo. Rehab. Assn., C. of C. (healthcare divsn.), Zeta Tau Alpha. Home: 1748 E Arlington Rd Springfield MO 65804-7742 Office Phone: 417-886-1188.

MORRIS, ARLENE MYERS, marketing professional; b. Washington, Pa., Dec. 29, 1951; d. Frank Hayes Myers and Lula Irene (Slusser) Kolcun; m. John L. Sullivan, Feb. 17, 1971 (div. July 1982); m. David Wellons Morris, July 27, 1984. BA, Carlow Coll., 1974; postgrad., Western New England Coll., 1981-82. Sales rep. Syntex Labs., Inc., Palo Alto, Calif., 1974-77; profl. sales rep. McNeil Pharm., Spring House, Pa., 1977-78, mental health rep., 1978-80, asst. product dir., 1981-82, dist. mgr., 1982-85, new product dir., 1985-87, exec. dir. new bus. devel., 1987-89, v.p. bus. devel., 1989-93, Scios Inc., Mountain View, Calif., 1993-96, Coulter Pharma., 1996—. Mem. Found. of Ind. Colls., Phila., 1989. Mem. Pharm. Advt. Coun., Am. Diabetes Assn., Am. Acad. Sci., Healthcare Bus. Womens Assn., Lic. Execs. Soc. Office: Coulter Pharm 600 Gateway Blvd South San Francisco CA 94080-7014

MORRIS, ASHLEY, information scientist, educator; b. DeFuniak Springs, Fla., Oct. 20, 1963; s. Kenneth Eugene and Dorothy Morris; m. Hana Zizková, May 15, 1999. BS, U. So. Miss., 1985, MS, 1995; PhD, Tulane U., 1999. Software specialist Digital Equipment Corp., Culver City, Calif., 1987—89; cons. Ashley Morris Cons., LA, 1989—93, AT&T, Seattle, 1993—94; instr. Oracle, Redwood Shores, Calif., 1997—98; prof. U. Idaho, Moscow, 1998—2000, DePaul U., Chgo., 2000—. Cons. H.A. Morris, Inc., New Orleans, 1994—, Oracle, Atlanta, 1997—98; rschr. Naval Rsch. Lab., Stennis Space Ctr., Miss., 1997—98. Contbr. articles to profl. articles. Grantee, Oracle, 1999, U. Idaho, 1999; Nat. Leadership grant, Inst. Mus. & Libr. Svcs., 1998, Rsch. grant, U. Idaho, 1999, Cobase grant, Nat. Acad. Scis., 2003—04. Mem.: IEEE Computer Soc., Assn. Computing Machinery, Internat. Fuzzy Sets Assn., N.Am. Fuzzy Info. Processing Soc., Upsilon Pi Epsilon. Avocations: music, hockey, travel. Office: DePaul Univ 243 S Wabash Ave Chicago IL 60604 Office Phone: 312-362-8252. Office Fax: 312-362-6116. Personal E-mail: ashley@ashleymorris.com. Business E-Mail: amorris@acm.org.

MORRIS, BRIAN, advertising executive; Pres. Dailey & Assoc., L.A., Calif. Office: Dailey & Assoc 8687 Melrose Ave Ste G300 West Hollywood CA 90069-5725

MORRIS, BUCKNER STUART, lawyer; b. Charleston, W.Va., Jan. 7, 1922; s. Donnally H. and Anne Byrne (Buckner) M. A.B., W.Va. U., 1943; J.D., U. Va., 1947. Bar: Va. 1947, Tenn. 1948. With legal dept. Provident Life & Accident Insurance Co., Chattanooga, 1947-84, v.p., gen. counsel, 1974-84; counsel Spears, Moore, Rebman & Williams, Chattanooga, 1984—. Served to sgt. U.S. Army, 1943-45. Decorated Purple Heart (3 clusters). Mem. Assn. Life Insurance Counsel (bd. govs.), Chattanooga Bar Assn., ABA, Tenn. Bar Assn. Republican. Presbyterian. Clubs: Mountain City (Chattanooga); Fairyland (Lookout Mountain). Office: Blue Cross Bldg Chattanooga TN 37402

MORRIS, CARLOSS (WILLIAM MORRIS), lawyer, insurance company executive; b. Galveston, Tex., June 7, 1915; s. William Carloss and Willie (Stewart) M.; m. Doris Poole, Dec. 2, 1939; children: Marietta (Mrs. Morgan Maxfield), William Carloss III, Malcolm Stewart, Melinda Louise (Mrs. Glen Ginter). BA with distinction, Rice Inst., 1936; JD with highest honors, U. Tex., 1939. Bar: Tex. 1938. With Stewart Title Guaranty Co., Houston, 1939—, pres., 1951-75, chmn. bd. dirs., chief exec. officer, 1975-91; chmn. bd. dirs., co-chief exec. officer Stewart Info. Services Inc., 1975-2000; chmn. exec. com. Stewart Title Guaranty Co., 1975—. Stockholder Morris, Lendais, Hollrah and Snowden, Houston. Chmn. Interdisciplinary Commn. on Housing and Urban Growth, 1974-77; chmn. Star Hope Mission, 1951-90, hon., 1991—; pres. Tex. Safety Assn., 1950-51; bd. dirs. Goodwill Industries; bd. dirs., mem. exec. com. Billy Graham Evangelistic Assn., 1956-2000, adv. dir., 2000—; chmn. Baylor Coll. Medicine, 1968, trustee, 1952—; trustee, deacon 1st Bapt. Ch., Houston, chmn. bd. deacons, 1987-89; trustee Baylor U., 1952-72, past vice chmn. bd. dirs.; trustee Oldham Little Ch. Found., B.M. Woltman Found. Recipient Book of Golden Deeds award Exch. Club of Houston, 1974, Disting. Svc. awrad Tex. Soc. Sons Am. Revolution, 1988, Gen. Maurice Hirsch award Soc. for Fund Raising Execs., 1988, George Washington Honor medal Freedoms Found. at Valley Forge, 1990; inducted into Tex. Bus. Hall of Fame, 1995. Fellow Am. Bar Found., State Bar Tex. Found.; mem. ABA (past chmn. younger lawyers sect.), Tex. Bar Assn., Tex. Young Lawyers Assn. (past pres.), Chancellors, Order of Coif, Phi Delta Phi, Alpha Tau Omega. Clubs: River Oaks Country, University. Lodges: Kiwanis. Office: 1980 Post Oak Blvd Ste 800 Houston TX 77056-3826

MORRIS, CHRISTOPHER DAVID, lawyer; b. Rochester, Ind., Mar. 25, 1957; s. William Laurence Morris and Maxine (Bailey) Bearss; m. Jeannine Kreiter, June 20, 1986. BA, Kalamazoo (Mich.) Coll., 1979; JD, Cooley Law Sch., Lansing, Mich., 1983. Bar: Mich. 1984, U.S. Dist. Ct. (we. dist.) Mich. 1984, U.S. Ct. Appeals (6th cir.) 1988. Assoc. Ryan, Jamieson and Hubbell, Kalamazoo, 1984-86; ptnr. Ryan, Jamieson, Hubbell and Morris, Kalamazoo, 1986-89; assoc. Varnum, Riddering, Schmidt and Howlett, Kalamazoo, 1989-90; ptnr. Ryan, Jamieson and Morris, Kalamazoo, 1990—2003; mng. ptnr. Ryan, Jamieson, Morris, Ryan and Smith, Kalamazoo, 2003—. Adj. mem. Mich. Workers' Compensation Appeal Bd., 1991-92; spl. asst. atty. gen., 2003. Mem. ABA, Mich. Bar Assn., Kalamazoo County Bar Assn. Home: 9830 E Shore Dr Kalamazoo MI 49002-7477 Office: 121 W Cedar St Kalamazoo MI 49007-6221

MORRIS, CLAYTON LESLIE, priest; b. Eugene, Oreg., June 23, 1946; s. Joseph William Morris and Betty Fern (Rasmussen) Morris Darby; m. Mary Susan Pacquer, Dec. 30, 1968; children: Andrea Christine, Jonathan William. B Music, Willamette U., 1968; MA in Theology, Grad. Theol. Union, 1971, PhD in Theology, 1986; MDiv, Ch. Div. Sch., 1971. Ordained priest Episcopal Ch., 1971. Assoc. priest St. Andrew's Ch., Saratoga, Calif., 1971-74; rector St. Mark's Ch., King City, Calif., 1974-79; organist, choirmaster St. Paul's Ch., Oakland, Calif., 1979-80; teaching fellow, instr. Ch. Div. Sch., Berkeley, 1979-86; dir. music All Souls Ch., Berkeley, Calif., 1980-86; assoc. rector St. Mark's Ch., Palo Alto, Calif., 1986-91; staff officer liturgy and music Episc. Ch. Ctr., N.Y., 1991—. Mem. N.Am. Acad. Liturgy, Assn. Anglican Musicians, Assn. Diocesan Liturgy and Music Commns., Consultation on Common Texts, Associated Parishes Coun. Office: Episcopal Church Ctr 815 2nd Ave New York NY 10017-4503

MORRIS, DANIEL ROBERT, language educator; b. McCammon, Idaho, Sept. 8, 1953; s. Robert Green and Lula Cammack Morris; m. Cindy Lee Landon, May 6, 1977; children: Jessica Lee Malan, Rebecca Jean, Jacob Daniel, David Robert, Camille Danielle. PhD in Romance Langs., U. Oreg., 1985; BA in French and Math Edn. cum laude, Brigham Young U., 1977; MA in French, U. Utah, 1979. Cert. secondary sch. French tchr. Utah, 1977. Resident dir., sys. study abroad programs U. Oreg., Poitiers and Lyon, France, 1987—89; prof. French So. Oreg. U., Ashland, Oreg., 1982—, chair, fgn. langs. and lits., 1997—. Dir. So. Oreg. Fgn. Lang. Articulation, Ashland, Oreg., 1997—; chair, faculty senate So. Oreg. U., Ashland, Oreg., 1993—94. Author: From Heaven to Hell: Imagery of Earth, Air, Water and Fire in the Novels of Georges Bernanos; contbr. articles to profl. jours. Bishop LDS Ch., Ashland, Oreg., 1991—96. Mem.: Fgn. Langs. and Lits. Assn. Greater Siskiyous, Pacific N.W. Confedn. Lang. Tchrs., Confedn. in Oreg. for Lang. Tchrs. (exec. bd. 2001—03, Outstanding Post-secondary Lang. Tchr. award 2001), Am. Coun. on Tchg. of Fgn. Langs., Phi Delta Phi, Phi Sigma Iota (faculty advisor 1990—97), Phi Kappa Phi (pres. So. Oreg. U. chpt. 1997—98). Office: Southern Oreg U Dept Fgn Langs Ashland OR 97520 E-mail: morris@sou.edu.

MORRIS, DAVID, publishing executive; Grad., St. Anselm Coll. From NY adv. mgr. Entertainment Weekly to assoc. pub. Time Inc., NYC, 1991—2000, pub., Entertainment Weekly, 2000—03, pub., Sports Illustrated, 2003—. Office: Time Inc Sports Illustrated Bldg 135 W 50th St 3rd Fl New York NY 10020

MORRIS, DESMOND (JOHN), zoologist, writer, artist; s. Harry Howe Morris and Dorothy Marjorie (Hunt) Fuller; m. Ramona Joy Baulch, July 30, 1952; 1 son, Jason. BSc, Birmingham (Eng.) U.; DPhil, Oxford (Eng.) U.; DSc (hon.), Reading (Eng.) U., 1998. Rsch. worker zoology U. Oxford, Eng., 1954-56; head Granada T.V. and Film Unit, Zool. Soc. London, 1956-59, curator mammals, 1959-67; dir. Inst. Contemporary Arts, London, 1967-68; rsch. fellow Wolfson Coll., Oxford, 1973-81. Author: Biology of Art, 1962, Apes and Monkeys, 1965, Big Cats, 1965, Mammals: A Guide to the Living Species, 1966, The Naked Ape, 1968, The Human Zoo, 1969, Intimate Behavior, 1971, Manwatching: A Field Guide to Human Behavior, 1977, The Soccer Tribe, 1981, The Book of Ages, 1983, The Art of Ancient Cyprus, 1985, Bodywatching: A Field Guide to the Human Species, 1985, The Illustrated Naked Ape, 1986, Catwatching, 1986, Dogwatching, 1986, The Secret Surrealist, 1987, Catlore, 1987, The Animals Roadshow, 1988, The Human Nestbuilders, 1988, Horsewatching, 1988, The Animal Contract, 1990, Animalwatching, 1990, Babywatching, 1991, Christmas Watching, 1992, The World of Animals, 1993, The Human Animal, 1994, Body Talk, A World Guide to Gestures, 1994, The Naked Ape Trilogy, 1994, Illustrated Cat Watching, 1994, Illustrated Babywatching, 1995, Illustrated Dogwatching, 1996, Catworld: A Feline Encyclopedia, 1996, The Human Sexes, 1997, Illustrated Horsewatching, 1998, Cool Cats: The 100 Cat Breeds of the World, 1999, Body Guards, 1999, Dogs: A Dictionary of Dog Breeds, 2001, Peoplewatching, 2002, The Nature of Happiness, 2004, The Naked Woman, 2004, others; co-author: (with Ramona Morris) Men and Snakes, 1965, Men and Apes, 1966, Men and Pandas, 1966, The Giant Panda, 1981, Gestures: Their Origins and Distribution, 1979; autobiography Animal Days, 1979, The Naked Eye, 2000; editor: Primate Ethology, 1969, (fiction) Inrock, 1983; contbr. numerous articles to zool. jours.; one-man shows include Mayor Gallery, London, 1997, Pub. Art Gallery, Buxton, 1997, Keitelman Gallery, Brussels, 1998, Rossaert Gallery, Antwerp, 1998, Witteveen Gallery, Amsterdam, 1999, Mus. Modern Art, Ostend, 2002, others. Address: care Jonathan Cape RandomCH 20 Vauxhall Bridge Rd London SWIV 2SA England E-mail: dmorris@mail.sci-net.co.uk.

MORRIS, DOLORES ORINSKIA, psychologist, psychoanalyst; PhD, Yeshiva U., N.Y.C., 1974; cert. psychoanalysis and psychotherapy, NYU, 1980. Pvt. practice psychologist, N.Y.C., 1980—. Supr. postdoc. program in psychotherapy and psychoanalysis NYU, 1990—. E-mail: domorris@worldnet.att.net.

MORRIS, DONALD ARTHUR ADAMS, college president; b. Detroit, Aug. 31, 1934; s. Robert Park and Margaret Lymburn (Adams) M.; m. Zella Mae Stormer, June 21, 1958; children: Dwight Joseph, Julie Adams. BA, Wayne State U., 1961; M.P.A., U. Mich., 1966, PhD, 1970; LLD (hon.), Olivet Coll., 1987. Copy boy Detroit Times, 1952-55, reporter, 1955-57, edn. writer, 1957-60; adminstrv. asst. Wayne State U., Detroit, 1960-62; mng. editor news service U. Mich., 1962-64, spl. programs, 1964-68; mgr. Met. Detroit Devel. Program, 1968-71; v.p. for devel. Hobart and William Smith Colls., Geneva & N.Y., 1971-76, exec. v.p., 1976-77; pres., prof. polit. sci. Olivet (Mich.) Coll., 1977-92; pres. emeritus Olivet Coll., Mich., 1992—, cons., 1992-93. Trustee Mich. Intercollegiate Athletic Assn., 1977-92, chair, 1978-79, 85-86, 90-91; trustee Assn. Ind. Colls. and Univs. Mich., 1977-92, chair, 1984-85; cons. evaluator North Ctrl. Assn. Colls. and Schs., 1986-92; mem. Mich. Jud. Tenure Commn., 1991-94; mem. Newspaper Guild of Detroit, 1952-60, exec. bd., 1958-60. Contbr. articles to profl. jours. Trustee Olivet Coll., 1977-92, Mich. Coll. Found., 1977-92, exec. com., 1989-92; trustee Ecumenical Inst. Jewish-Christian Studies, 1988-89; mem. Mich. Higher Edn. Assistance and Student Loan Authorities, 1986—2002, chair, 1989-94; bd. dirs. Planned Parenthood of Finger Lakes, N.Y., 1973-77, pres., 1975-77; bd. dirs., treas. Genesee Regional Family Planning Program N.Y., 1975-77; trustee Coun. Higher Edn., United Ch. of Christ, 1977-92, mem. exec. com., 1982-92, chair, 1986-88; trustee Glen Lake Cmty. Libr. Bd., 1993—, pres., 1994-99; mem. Sleeping Bear Noontiders, 1993—, sec., 1995, v.p. 1996-97, pres., 1997-98, South Manitou Meml. Soc., 1980—, chair nominating com., 1996-97, pres., 1997—; dir. Dorado # 4 Assn., 1998—, pres., 2000—; mem. So. Ariz. Scottish Soc., 1998—, Chris-Craft Antique Boat Club, 1999—, Mayo Smith Soc., 1985—; bd. dirs. Friends of the Tucson-Pim Pub. Libr., 2002—. Mem. Am. Assn. for Higher Edn., Leelanau Athletic Club, U. Mich. Alumni Assn. (life), U. Mich. Alumni Club Grand Traverse, U. Mich. Alumni Club Tucson, Friends of Tucson-Pima Pub. Libr., Sigma Delta Chi, Omicron Delta Kappa, Alpha Lambda Epsilon, Kappa Sigma Alpha, Gamma Iota Sigma, Alpha Mu Gamma, Phi Mu Alpha Sinfonia, Rotary (local pres. 1987-88, Paul Harris fellow). Congregationalist. Home (Summer): 8330 S Dunns Farm Rd Maple City MI 49664-8721 Home (Winter): 6551 E Dorado Blvd Tucson AZ 85715-4705

MORRIS, DONALD G. engineering company executive; b. Santa Barbara, Calif., Nov. 19, 1943; BSBA, North Ga. Coll. and State U., 2000, MS in Pub. Adminstrn., 2001. Various to mgr. engr. Goetze Corp. of Am., LaGrange, Ga., 1986—89; plant mgr. Jakes Mfg., Greenwood, Miss., 1989—92; CEO Morris & Assocs., Gainesville, Ga., 1992—. Contbr. articles to profl. jours. Recipient Leadership award, Wall Street Jour., 2000. Mem.: Fabricators and Mfrs. Assn., Soc. Die Cast Engrs. Office: Morris & Assoc 7412 Barkers Bend Dr Murrayville GA 30564

MORRIS, DOUGLAS PETER, recording company executive; b. Far Rockaway, N.Y., Nov. 23, 1938; s. Walter and Mary (Lerner) Morris; m. Monique Jequel, Mar. 20, 1964; children: Walter, Peter. BA, Columbia Coll., 1960. Gen. mgr. Robert Mellin, Inc., N.Y.C., 1964—65; writer. producer Laurie Records, Inc., NYC, 1965—69, v.p., gen. mgr.; owner Big Tree Records (acquired by Atlantic Records), NYC, 1970—78; pres. ATCO Records, Swan Song and Rolling Stones Records (subs. of Warner Music), 1978, Atlantic Records, NYC, 1980—90; co-chmn., co-CEO Atlantic Recording Group, NYC, 1990—94; chmn., COO, pres. Warner Music-U.S., 1994—95; chmn., CEO Universal Music Group (formerly MCA Music Ent.), NYC, 1995—. Cons. Ampex Records, 1968. Composer: (songs) Sweet Talkin Guys, 1968, Smoking in the Boys' Room, 1970; prodr.: (song) Wave on Wave, 2003. With U.S. Army, 1962—64. Named Man of Yr. in Record Industry, United Jewish Appeal, 1981; scholar, Paragon Oil, 1954, Columbia Coll., 1960. Mem.: ASCAP. Office: Universal Music Group 1755 Broadway Fl 7 New York NY 10019-3743*

MORRIS, EARLE ELIAS, JR., retired state official, business executive; b. Greenville, S.C., July 14, 1928; s. Earle Elias and Bernice (Carey) M.; m. Jane L. Boroughs, Apr. 12, 1958; children: Lynda Lewis, Carey Mauldin, Elizabeth McDaniel, Earle Elias III; m. Carol Telford, Oct. 4, 1972; 1 son, David Earle (dec.). BS, Clemson Coll., 1949, LLD; D.Pub. Svc. (hon.), U. S.C., 1980, S.C. State Coll., 1990; Dr. Med. Sci., U. S.C.; LLD (hon.), The Citadel, Cen. Wesleyan Coll.; HHD (hon.), Lander Coll., Francis Marion Coll., 1984, U. Charleston, 1992; DHL, Winthrop U., 1996. V.p., dir. Pickens Bank, 1956-69, Bankers Trust S.C., Pickens, 1968-75; pres. Gen. Ins. Agy., Pickens, 1970—; ptnr. Morris Realty Co., Pickens; mem. S.C. Ho. of Reps., 1950-54, S.C. Senate, 1954-70; lt. gov. State of S.C., 1971-75, comptr. gen., 1976-99. Bd. dirs. S.C. Bus. Alliance for Transp; dir. Brunswick Worsted Mills, S.C. Devel. Corp., Pickens Savs. & Loan Assn.; hon. consul Republic of Korea. Pres. Clemson U. Found., 1984-85; state dir. Selective Svc. Sys. Served to brig. gen. S.C. N.G., maj. gen. S.C. S.G. Decorated Legion of Merit, Meritorious Svc. medals; recipient Algernon Sydney Sullivan award, 1980, Donald L. Scantlebury award, 1985, Nations Most Valuable Pub. Ofcl. award, 1993, Pub. Svc. award Am. Legion, 1993, Living Legend award S.C. Hist. Found., 1997, Clemson Medallion award 1997, Order of the Palmetto; named Disting. Alumnus, Clemson Coll. Mem. Nat. Assn. State Comptrollers (pres. 1982), Nat. Assn. State Auditors, Comptrollers and Treasurers (pres. 1988-89), S.C. Nat. Guard Assn. (pres. 1980-81), S.C. Jr. C. of C., S.C. Rehab. Assn. (v.p.), Govtl. Acctg. Standards Adv. Coun. (chmn. 1989-96), Fin. Acctg. Found. (trustee 1985-88, 96—, v.p. 2000-01), S.C. Retirees Assn. (pres.), Blue Key, Palmetto Club, Faculty Club (Columbia), Poinsett Club (Greenville), Masons, Shriners, Lions (hon., life), Order of Saint Stanislas (grand chancellor, Knight Grand Cross), Order of white Eagle of Saint Stanislas, Sovereign Mil. Order Swabia, Order of Polonia Restituta (knight comdr., 2d class), Knights of Malta. Presbyterian (elder, former deacon, synod trustee). Home: 159 Lake Murray Ter Lexington SC 29072-9103 *In my personal, public and professional life I have tried to follow the Biblical admonition of "loving mercy, doing justly, and walking humbly.".*

MORRIS, EDWARD J(AMES), JR., retired insurance agent, small business owner; b. Jersey City, Jan. 9, 1936; s. Edward James Sr. and Mary Alice (Carr) M.; m. Joan M. O'Keefe, Sept. 17, 1955; children: Edward James III, Glenn D., Gary J. Student, Drakes Bus. Coll., 1953; cert. ins. broker, Vale Tech. Inst., 1962. CLU, Chartered Fin. Cons. Part-time salesperson Stanley Home Products, Jersey City, 1958-60; selector Am. Stores, South Kearny, N.J., 1957-62; owner Ed Morris State Farm Agy., Jersey City, 1962-72; owner, mgr., restaurateur E&J Morris Enterprises, Inc., New Bern, N.C., 1972-79; owner, mgr. Morris Ins. Agy., Jackson, N.J., 1979-82; spl. agt., reg. rep. Morris Fin. and Ins. Agy., Matawan, N.J., 1982-92; owner, mgr. Sunset Selections, Scottsdale, Ariz., 1992-98, ret., 1998. Agt. emeritus Prudential Ins. Cos., Scottsdale, 1992—. Contbr. articles to profl. jours. Mem. com. Boy Scouts Am., Jersey City, 1966-72; basketball coach Our Lady of Mercy Ch., Jersey City, 1967-69; treas., basketball coach Coll. Little League, Jersey City, 1966-71; mcpl. chmn. Citizens for Goldwater, Jersey City, 1963-64. Sgt. USMC, 1954-57. Avocations: boxing, cooking, wine, investments, writing.

MORRIS, EDWARD WILLIAM, JR., lawyer; b. Medford, Oreg., Apr. 12, 1943; s. Edward William and Julia Loretta (Sullivan) M.; m. Margaret Ellen McKenna, 1976; children: John McKenna, Elizabeth Anne. BS, Fordham Coll., 1965, JD, 1971. Bar: N.Y. 1973. Dir. Drug Products Co., Inc., Union City, N.J., 1968-71; asst. arbitration dir. N.Y. Stock Exch., N.Y.C., 1971-73, arbitration dir., 1973-74, asst. sec., arbitration dir., 1974-89, v.p. arbitration, 1989-91, chief hearing officer, 1991—2003. Mem. Securities Industry Conf. on Arbitration, N.Y.C., 1977—; lectr. in field. Served to sgt. U.S. Army, 1965-68, Vietnam. Mem. ABA, Am. Arbitration Assn. (comml. law com. 1983—), N.Y. County Lawyers Assn. (sec. com. on arbitration 1983—), High Mountain Golf Club. Home: 67 Arlton Ave Allendale NJ 07401-1331 E-mail: emoris1@prodigy.net.

MORRIS, EUGENE JEROME, retired lawyer; b. N.Y.C., Oct. 14, 1910; s. Max and Regina (Cohn) M.; m. Terry Lesser, Mar. 28, 1934 (dec. Sept. 1993); 1 child, Richard S.; m. Blanche Bier Funke, June 22, 1994. BSS., CCNY, 1931; LL.B., St. John's U., 1934. Bar: N.Y. 1935. Practiced, N.Y.C., 1935-99; sr. and founding partner firm Demov, Morris & Hammerling, 1946-87; v.p., sr. counsel Ea. region Am. Title Ins. Co., N.Y.C., 1990-93; of counsel Spector & Feldman, 1991-99; ret., 1999. Adj. prof. land use regulation NYU Grad. Sch. Pub. Adminstrn., 1978-81; adj. prof. legal issues in real estate, Real Estate Inst. NYU, 1988—; spl. master Supreme Ct. State of N.Y., 1979-99; arbitrator Civil Ct. N.Y., 1994-99. Editor weekly column N.Y. Law Jour., 1965-87, It's the Law, Real Estate Forum, 1982-87; editor-in-chief N.Y. Practice Guide: Real Estate, 4 vols., 1986, Real Estate Development, 4 vols., 1987; contbr. articles to profl. jours. Mem. N.Y. State Tax Revision Commn., 1977-80, N.Y.C. Rent Guidelines Bd., 1983-85. Served with AUS, 1943-45. Recipient Justice award N.Y. sect. Am. Jewish Congress, 1996. Mem. ABA (chmn. spl. com. housing and urban devel. 1970-73, coun. sect. real property, probate and trust law 1971-74, assoc. editor Real Property, Probate and Trust Jour. 1979-86, editor Real Property, Probate and Property mag., articles editor 1986-94), Am. Judges Assn., Assn. Bar City N.Y. (chmn. com. housing and urban devel. 1971-74, com. on lectures and continuing edn. 1980-83, coun. on jud. adminstrn. 1989-92)), N.Y. State Bar Assn. (exec. com. 1980-97, chmn. com. meetings and lectrs. 1982-92, CLE com. 1984-90, ho. of dels. 1986-95, co-editor Real Property Jour. 1995-97, Professionalsim award 2002), Citizens Union, Lambda Alpha (bd. dirs. 1990-98, pres. N.Y. chpt. 1990-93, sec. 1993-95, treas. 1996-97). Home: 200 Central Park S New York NY 10019-1415 Home Fax: 212-983-0874. Personal E-mail: specfeld@aol.com. *After 70 years of marriage and 65 years of practicing law, I have retired. However, like the old fire horse when the bell rings I run; thus I am still teaching real estate law as an Adjunct Professor at the New York Universitsy Real Estate Institute, am counsel to my firm and stay active in bar associations, civic groups and fraternities. I am always an optimist at work, with friends, and with my family.*

MORRIS, FRANK CHARLES, JR., lawyer, educator; b. Pitts., May 11, 1948; s. Frank Charles and Mary Louise Morris; m. Kathleen Williams; children: Frank Charles III, Alexander Greg. BS with distinction, Northwestern U., 1970; JD, U. Va., 1973. Bar: Pa. 1973, U.S. Ct. Appeals (4th and 7th cirs.) 1974, D.C. 1975, U.S. Ct. Appeals (1st, 2d and 9th cirs.) 1975, (U.S. Ct. Appeals (10th cir.)) 1976, U.S. Supreme Ct. 1976, U.S. Ct. Appeals (5th and D.C. cirs.) 1977, U.S. Dist. Ct. D.C. 1977, U.S. Dist. Ct. (ea. dist.) Wis. 1980, U.S. Dist. Ct. (ea. dist.) Pa. 1993, U.S. Ct. Appeals (6th, 7th and 8th cirs.) 1987, U.S. Ct. Appeals (11th cir.) 1981, U.S. Dist. Ct. Md. 1985, U.S. Ct. Appeals (3d cir.) 1991. Rsch. asst. Bernard Dunau, Washington, 1972—73; appellate ct. br. atty. NLRB, Washington, 1973—76; assoc. McGuiness & Williams, Washington, 1976—78, Epstein Becker & Green, P.C., Washington, 1978—80, ptnr., 1981—88, sr. ptnr., 1988—. Mem. adj. faculty Law Sch. Cath. U. Am., Washington, 1979—80, adj. prof. law, 1984—; adj. prof. law, Law Sch. George Washington U., Washington; mem. faculty Sch. Indsl. and Labor Rels. EEO study program, Cornell U., N.Y.C., 1979—, ALI-ABA course Employment Discrimination and Civil Rights Actions, 1988, Trial Evidence, Civil Practice, and Effective Litigation Techniques in Fed. and State Cts.; co-chair ALI-ABA Fed. Jud. Ctr., Video Law Rev., Ams. with Disabilities Act, 1992; co-chair video law rev. ALI-ABA How to Present and Challenge Experts in Employment Cases, 1994; co-chair Current Devels. in Employment Law, 1994—; faculty Litigating Employment Cases: Views from the Bench Georgetown U., 1998—; spkr., lectr. in field. Author: Current Trends in the Use (and Misuse) of Statistics in Employment Discrimination Litigation, 1977, 2d edit., 1978; editor-in-chief The Equal Employer Newsletter, 1981—86, editl. adv. bd. ADA Policy & Law, 1992—, Corp. Counsel's Guide to ADA, 1993—. Dir. Northwestern U. Alumni Admissions Coun., Washington Area Coun., 1978—81. Named to Outstanding Young Men of Am., U.S. Jaycees, 1982; recipient Sustained Superior Performance award, NLRB Gen. Counsel, 1974, cert. commendation for outstanding performance, 1975, commendation for collective bargaining, Social Security Adminstrn. Commr., 1988. Mem.: ABA (labor and employment law, adminstrv. and litigation sects.), Fed. Bar Assn., D.C. Bar Assn. (adminstrv. law, labor rels. and litigation divsns.), Pa. Bar Assn., Northwestern U. Alumni Club (bd. govs. 1975—), John Evans Club of Northwestern U., D.C. Rd. Runners Club.

MORRIS, G. RONALD, industrial executive; b. East St. Louis, Ill., Aug. 30, 1936; s. George H. and Mildred C. M.; m. Margaret Heino, June 20, 1959; children: David, Michele, James. BS in Metall. Engring, U. Ill., 1959. Metall. engr. Delco-Remy divsn. Gen. Motors Corp., 1959-60; factory metallurgist Dubuque Tractor Works, John Deere Co., Iowa, 1960-66; with Fed.-Mogul Corp., 1966-79, v.p., group mgr. ball and roller bearing group, 1979; pres. Tenneco Automotive divsn. Tenneco, Inc., Deerfield, Ill., 1979-82; pres., CEO PT Components, Inc., Indpls., 1982-88; vice-chmn. Rexnord Corp., Indpls., 1988-89; chmn., pres., CEO CTP Holdings Inc., 1986-88; chmn. Integrated Technologies, Inc., Indpls., 1990-92, also bd. dirs.; pres., CEO Western Industries, Inc., Milw., 1991-99. Chmn. bd. dirs. Milnot Holding Corp., St. Louis; bd. dirs. NN, Inc., Erwin, Tenn., Hines Hort, Inc., Irvine, Calif. Mem. Pres.'s Coun., U. Ill., mem. sr. adv. bd. Sch. Materials Sci. and Engring; mem. U. Ill. Found. Mem. ASM, SAE, U. Ill. Alumni Assn. (bd. dirs.), The Landings Club (Savannah, Ga.), Masons, Scottish Rite, Kiwanis Internat. Republican. Presbyterian. E-mail: savannahronm@aol.com.

MORRIS, GARY, oil industry executive; BBA, St. Edwards U. V.p. fin. Brown & Root; contr. Halliburton Co.; v.p. fin. Halliburton Energy Svcs.; sr. v.p. Halliburton Co., exec. v.p., CFO. Office: 01-7th Fl 4100 Clinton Dr Houston TX 77020-6237

MORRIS, GERALD DOUGLAS, newspaper editor; b. Boston, May 7, 1937; s. George Christopher and Lucy Bell (MacPhee) M.; m. Elaine Louise Owen, Nov. 13, 1964 (div. 1976); children: Laura Louise, Douglas Owen; m. Mary Elizabeth Simpson Stevens, Apr. 15, 1977; children: Jeffrey David Stevens Morris, Wendy Elizabeth Stevens Morris. Student, Boston U., 1959. Reporter Patriot Ledger, Quincy, Mass., 1961-66; copy editor Boston Globe, 1966—, travel editor, 1989—. Syndicated columnist Globe-Trotting, 1970—. Author: Boston Globe Guide to Boston, 1989, New England under Sail, 1993, Guide to Cape Cod, 1999. Chmn. Canton (Mass.) Cable Adv. Bd., 1990-92; bd. dirs. Lowell Thomas Found., 1997. With U.S. Army, 1959-61. Mem. Soc. Am. Travel Writers (chmn. N.E. chpt. 2000—), Skal Club Boston, Lions (pres. Canton 1969-70, 80-81). Avocations: photography, travel. Home: 873 Harris Ave Woonsocket RI 02895-1824 Office: Globe Newspaper Co 135 Morrissey Blvd Boston MA 02125-3310

MORRIS, GORDON JAMES, financial company executive, consultant; b. Mt. Vernon, Ohio, Oct. 6, 1942; s. R. Hugh and Betty Jane (Roberts) M.; m. Janet Ann Swanson, Aug. 28, 1965 (div. 1971); m. Nancy Joan Meyfarth, July 26, 1975 (div. Oct. 1998); 1 child, Lawrence Hugh; m. Phyllis J. Hersha, Jan. 1, 2000. Student, Ohio State U., 1960-61; BA, Otterbein Coll., 1966; postgrad. in law, Capital U., Bexley, Ohio, 1967-68; postgrad., Coll. Fin. Planning, Denver, 1983-90, Inst. Cert. Fund Specialists, 1991. Registered investment advisor; cert. fin. planner; cert. fund specialist; lic. living trust advisor; cert. divorce planner. Asst. to pres. Jaeger Machine Co., Columbus, Ohio, 1968-73; rep. Equitable Fin. Svcs., Sarasota, Fla., 1974-81; pres. Beacon Wealth Mgmt. (formerly Morris & Assocs., P.A.), Sarasota, 1981—; co-gen. ptnr. Beacon Bridge Loan Pool, Ltd., 1994-97. Chmn. bd. dirs. MAP Fin. Group, Inc., Sarasota, 1985-89; co-owner U.S.I.S.L. West Fla. Fury Soccer Team, 1996-98; bd. dirs., v.p. Soccer Resource Group, Sarasota, 1997-99, Radyx Capital Ptnr., Tampa, 1999-2003, seminar lectr. High Mark Ins. Svcs., Inc. Past columnist The Creative News. Past chmn. West Coast chpt. March of Dimes, Bradenton, Fla., bd. dirs., 1986-88; v.p. All Sch. Kids, Inc., 1998-99; pres. Epilepsy Found. S.W. Fla., Inc., 1986-87. Mem. Inst. Cert. Fin. Planners, Million Dollar Roundtable, Sertoma (pres. local club 1979-80). Republican. Methodist. Home and Office: 3822 Countryside Ln Sarasota FL 34233-2122 Office Phone: 941-929-0070. E-mail: striker.five@comcast.net.

MORRIS, GRANT HAROLD, law educator; b. Syracuse, N.Y., Dec. 10, 1940; s. Benjamin and Caroline Grace (Judelson) Morris; m. Phyllis Silberstein, July 4, 1967; children: Joshua, Sara. AB, Syracuse U., 1962, JD, 1964; LLM, Harvard U., 1971. Bar: N.Y. 1964. Atty. N.Y. Mental Hygiene Law Recodification Project, Inst. Public Adminstrn., N.Y.C., 1964-66; from asst. prof. to assoc. prof. Wayne State U. Law Sch., 1967—70, prof., 1970-73, dean acad. affairs, 1971-73; prof. U. San Diego Law Sch., 1973—, Univ. prof., 1996-97, acting dean, 1977-78, 88-89, assoc. dean grad. legal edn., 1978-81, interim dean, 1997-98; prof. law in psychiatry Wayne State U. Med. Sch., 1970-73; adj. prof. U. Calif. Med. Sch., San Diego, 1974-84, clin. prof. dept. psychiatry, 1984—. Legal counsel Mich. Legis. Com. to Revise Mental Health Statutes, 1970-73; organizer law and psychiatry sect. Assn. Am. Law Schs., 1973, chmn., 1973-74; patients advocate, San Diego County, 1977-78; cons. Criminal Code Commn., Ariz. Legis., 1974; reporter task force on guidelines governing roles of mental health profls. in criminal process Am. Bar Assn. standing com. on assn. standards for criminal justice, 1981-84; cert. rev. hearing officer San Diego Superior Ct., 1984-90, ct. commr./judge pro tem, 1990-92, mental health hearing officer, 1992-97; hearing officer San Diego Housing Commn., 1988-92; mem. exec. com. sect. law and mental disability Assn. Am. Law Schs., 1990-97. Author: The Insanity Defense: A Blueprint for

Legislative Reform, 1975; co-author: Mental Disorder in the Criminal Process: Stan Stress and the Vietnam/Sports Conspiracy, 1993; editor, contbr.: The Mentally Ill and the Right to Treatment, 1970. Mem. Atascadero State Hosp. adv. bd., 2000—, chair, 2003—. Mem. Phi Alpha Delta (faculty adv. 1970-73, 75-92). Home: 8515 Nottingham Pl La Jolla CA 92037-2125 Office: U San Diego Law Sch 5998 Alcala Park San Diego CA 92110-2492 Office Phone: 619-260-2321. E-mail: gmorris@sandiego.edu.

MORRIS, HENRY MADISON, JR., education educator; b. Dallas, Oct. 6, 1918; s. Henry Madison and Ida (Hunter) M.; m. Mary Louise Beach, Jan. 24, 1940; children: Henry Madison III, Kathleen Louise, John David, Andrew Hunter, Mary Ruth, Rebecca Jean. BS with distinction, Rice Inst., 1939; MS, U. Minn., 1948, PhD, 1950; LLD, Bob Jones U., 1966; LittD, Liberty U., 1989. Registered profl. engr., Tex. Jr. engr. Tex. Hwy. Dept., 1938-39; from jr. engr. to asst. engr. Internat. Boundary Commn., El Paso, 1939-42; instr. civil engring. Rice Inst., 1942-46; from instr. to asst. prof. U. Minn., Mpls., also research project leader St. Anthony Falls Hydraulics Lab., 1946-51; prof., head dept. civil engring. Southwestern La. Inst., Lafayette, 1951-57, Va. Poly. Inst., Blacksburg, 1957-70; v.p. acad. affairs Christian Heritage Coll., San Diego, 1970-78, pres., 1978-80; dir. Inst. for Creation Rsch., 1970-80, pres., 1980-96, pres. emeritus, 1996—. Author (with Richard Stephens): (report) Report on Rio Grande Cosnervation Investigation, 1942; author: 2d edit That You Might Believe, 1946; author: (with Curtis Larson) (book) Hydraulics of Flow in Culverts, 1948; author: The Bible and Modern Science, 1951, rev. edit, 1968; author: (with John C. Whitcomb) The Genesis Flood, 1961; author: Applied Hydraulics in Engineering, 1963, The Twilight of Evolution, 1964, Science, Scripture and Salvation, 1965, Studies in The Bible and Science, 1966, Evolution and the Modern Christian, 1967, Biblical Cosmology and Modern Science, 1970, The Bible has the Answer, 1971, Science and Creation: A Handbook for Teachers, 1971; author: (with J.M. Wiggert) Applied Hydraulics, 1972; author: A Biblical Manual on Science and Creation, 1972, The Remarkable Birth of Planet Earth, 1973, Many Infallible Proofs, 1974, Scientific Creationism, 1974;: 2d edit, 1985, Troubled Waters of Evolution, 1975, The Genesis Record, 1976, Education for the Real World, 1977, 1991, (book) The Scientific Case for Creation, 1977, The Beginning of the World, 1977, 2d edit, 1991, Sampling the Psalms, 1978, King of Creation, 1980, Men of Science, Men of God, 1982, 2d edit, 1988, Evolution in Turmoil, 1982, The Revelation Record, 1983, History of Modern Creationism, 1984, 2d edit, 1993, The Biblical Basis for Modern Science, 1984, 2002, Creation and the Modern Christian, 1985, Science and the Bible, 1986, Days of Praise, 1986, The God Who is Real, 1988, 2d edit., 2000, The Remarkable Record of Job, 1987; author: (with Martin Clark) The Bible Has the Answer; author: (with Gary E. Parker) What is Creation Science?, 1982; author: 2d edit., 1988, The Long War Against God, 1989; author: (with John D. Morris) Science, Scripture and the Young Earth, 1989; author: The Bible Science and Creation, 1991, Creation and the Second Coming, 1991, Biblical Creationism, 1993, The Defender's Bible, 1995, The Modern Creation Trilogy, 1996, The Heavens Declare the Glory of God, 1997, That Their Words May be Used Against Them, 1998, The Origin of Earth and its People, 1999, Defending the Faith, 1999, Treasures in the Psalms, 2000, Solomon and His Remarkable Wisdom, 2001, God and the Nations, 2002, The Incredible Journey of Jonah, 2003, Miracles, 2004. Fellow AAAS, ASCE, Am. Sci. Affiliation; mem. Am. Soc. Engring. Edn. (sec.-editor civil engring. divsn. 1967-70), Trans-Nat. Assn. Christian Schs. (pres. 1983-95), Creation Rsch. Soc. (pres. 1967-73), Am. Geophys. Union, Geol. Soc. Am., Am. Assn. Petroleum Geologists, Geochem. Soc., Gideons (pres. La. 1954-56), Phi Beta Kappa, Sigma Xi, Chi Epsilon, Tau Beta Pi. Baptist. Home: 6733 El Banquero Pl San Diego CA 92119-1129 Office: Inst for Creation Rsch 10946 Woodside Ave N Santee CA 92071 *The Bible is the inerrant word of God and thus should be believed and obeyed in all things.*

MORRIS, HENRY MADISON, III, minister, speaker, writer, consultant; b. El Paso, Tex., May 15, 1942; s. Henry Madison and Mry Louis (Beach) M.; m. Janet Deckman, July 25, 1965; children: Henry M., Scotta Marie. BA summa cum laude, Christian Heritage Coll., 1976; MDiv, Luther Rice Sem., 1977; DMin, 1978; MBA, Pepperdine U., 1989. Ordained to ministry Bapt. Ch., 1968. Regional mgr. Integon Ins. Co., Greenville, S.C., 1969-75; pastor Hallmark Bapt. Ch., Greenville, S.C., 1969-75; assoc. prof. Bible Christian Heritage Coll., El Cajon, Calif., 1977-78; adminstrv. v.p., 1978-80; pastor First Bapt. Ch., Canoga Park, Calif., 1980-86; chief adminstrv. officer, CFO SunGard Fin. Sys. Inc., Canoga Park, 1986-94; v.p. sales and mktg., 1994-96; adminstrv. pastor Ch. at Rocky Peak, Chatsworth, Calif., 1996-99; regional sales mgr. SunGard Ins. Sys., 2000—01; exec. v.p. Inst. for Creation Rsch., Santee, Calif., 2002—. Lectr. in field; cons. World Pubs., 1995; commr. Transitional Assn. Christian Colls. and Schs., 2003—. Author: Baptism: What is It?, 1977, Explore the Word, 1978, Churches: History and Doctrine, 1980, After Eden, 2003; co-author: Many Infallible Proofs, 1996, Sampling the Psalms, 1999; contbg. editor: The Defenders Bible, 1995. Served with U.S. Army, 1959-66. Republican. Office: Inst for Creation Rsch 10996 Woodside Ave N Santee CA 92091 Office Phone: 972-506-3035.

MORRIS, IAIN, information technology executive; b. Scotland; B in Tech. and Bus. Studies, U. Strathclyde, Glasgow, Scotland. With Motorola, 1978—2001; pres. embedded and personal sys. orgn. Hewlett Packard Co., 2001—02, sr. v.p. mobility and emerging techs., 2002—03; sr. v.p. personal connectivity solutions group Advanced Micro Devices, Sunnyvale, Calif., 2004—. Office: Advanced Micro Devices ONe AMD Pl PO Box 3453 Sunnyvale CA 94088-3453*

MORRIS, JACK G. architecture educator, writer; b. Clark County, Wash., June 1, 1920; s. Thomas Frank and Hazel Ann (Ditmer) Morris; m. Rosalind Vallens, Mar. 16, 1945 (dec. Nov. 1990); children: Jane, Wendy, Virginia, Thomas. Jr. cert., U. Oreg., 1942; BA, Stanford U., 1948; Calif. tchg. credential, UCLA, 1950; cert. in environ. design, U. Calif., Irvine, 1981. Tchr. Union H.S., Perris, Calif., 1950—53, LaPuente, Calif., 1953—76; archtl. designer, draftsman, carftsman various cos. and contractors, Calif., 1976—86; tchr. archtl. drafting and rendering various cmty. colls., Orange County, Calif., 1986—91; freelance writer Calif., 1994—2002. Bd. mem. ext. program in environ. design U. Calif. Irvine Ext., 1978—83. Author: (memoir) One Angel Left, 2000. Chmn. Orange County Stanford Annual Fund, Stanford U., 1980—85, Stanford Alumni Assn., Stanford Club, 1985—86; art therapy vol. Spring Lake Village, Santa Rosa, Calif., 2002—03. Capt. USMC, 1942—46, PTO. Mem.: Stanford Assocs., Stanford Faculty Club (assoc.). Democrat. Avocation: watercolor painting. Home: 5555 Montgomery Dr C-205 Santa Rosa CA 95409

MORRIS, JAMES BRUCE, internist; b. Rochester, NY, May 13, 1943; s. Max G. and Beatrice Ruth (Becker) M.; m. Susan Carol Shencup, July 31, 1966; children: Carrie, Douglas, Deborah, Rebecca. BA, U. Rochester, 1964; MD, Yale U., 1968. Diplomate Am. Bd. Internal Medicine, Am. Bd. Infectious Diseases. Intern SUNY, Buffalo, 1968-69, resident, 1969-70, 72-73, chief resident, 1973; pvt. practice medicine & infectious diseases Plantation, Fla., 1974—. Chmn. infection control com. Lauderdale Lakes Gen. Hosp., 1974-76; chmn. infection control com. Plantation Gen. Hosp., 1976-80, 83-85, chmn. pharmacy com., 1980-81, chmn. tissue com., 1982; sec., program chmn. dept. medicine Bennett Community Hosp., 1978-80, chmn. dept. medicine, 1980-81, vice chief staff, 1981-83; chmn. infection control com. Fla. Med. Center, 1980-82; chief staff Humana Hosp. Bennett, 1983-85, trustee, 1983-88, chmn. infection control com., 1985-87; clin. assoc. prof. U. Miami Med. Sch., 1975—. With USAR, 1970-72. Named one of Top Docs in South Fla., Miami Metro; recipient Recognition, Town & Country Guide to Primary Care Physicians; fellow, U. Miami, 1974. Fellow ACP; mem. AMA, Am. Soc. Microbiology, Infectious Diseases Soc. Am., Am. Soc. Internal Medicine, Fla. Med. Assn., Broward County Med. Assn. Office: Morris Sklaver Mestre & Denney MD PA 7353 NW 4th St Plantation FL 33317-2202 Office Phone: 954-584-6320.

MORRIS, JAMES CARL, architect; b. Richmond, Va., Sept. 2, 1930; s. James Carl and Florence Virginia (Hey) M.; m. Frances Parrott Wooten, June 9, 1952; children: James Carl Jr., David Palmer. Student, N.C. State U., 1948-50; BS in Bldg. Constrn., Va. Polytechnic Inst., 1952. Cert. Nat. Coun. Archtl. Registration Bds. Archtl. draftsman Va. Electric & Power Co., Richmond, Va., 1955-56, Marcellus, Wright & Son, Richmond, 1956-57; architect C.W. Huff, Jr., Richmond, 1957; ptnr. to prin./owner Huff-Morris Architects, Richmond, 1966—. Pres. Point of Rocks Devel. Corp., Chesterfield, Va., 1986—; ptnr. Rivermont Assocs., Chesterfield, 1987—, JCM Partnership, Chesterfield, 1988—. Contbr. articles to profl. jours. Bd. dirs. Chesterfield Preservation Commn.; deacon Branch's Ch., Richmond, 1986-90; chmn. Va. Bapt. Extension Bd., Richmond, 1991-2001, 2004-; mem. 250th anniversary com. Chesterfield County, 1999. With U.S. Army, 1953-54. Recipient award of Merit S.S. Bd. of So. Bapt., Nashville, Excellence in Masonry Design award Va. Masonry Coun., Richmond. Mem. AIA (past pres. Richmond chpt.), Constrn. Specifications Inst., Interfaith Forum on Religion, Art & Architecture, Commonwealth Club of Va. Avocations: woodworking, fishing, hunting. Office: Huff-Morris Arch PC 8 N 1st St Richmond VA 23219-2102 Home: 5907 Village Lake Ct Richmond VA 23234-6945 E-mail: architecture@huffmorris.com.

MORRIS, JAMES E. lawyer, judge, educator; b. Rochester, N.Y., Nov. 20, 1942; s. Ira H. and Hortense Morris; m. Ruth J. Myers, June 15, 1965 (div. Oct. 1977); children: Kim I., Deborah M. Field; m. Virginia B. Morris, Aug. 22, 1983; children: Katelyn E., Eric W. BS, Syracuse U., 1964, LLB, 1967. Bar: N.Y. 1967. Ptnr. Morris and Morris, Rochester, N.Y., 1967—; asst. dist. atty. County of Monroe, Rochester, N.Y., 1968-72; Brighton Town justice Town of Brighton, N.Y., 1972—. Adj. prof. Monroe C.C., Rochester, 1975—; mem. criminal procedure law adv. bd. N.Y. State Office Ct. Adminstrn., 1980-86. Author: You Can Win Big in Small Claims Court, 1981, 2002, Victim Aftershock, 1983; co-author: New York Village, Town and District Courts Guide, 1995. Mem., past pres. Med. Motor Svc. at Al Sigl Ctr., Rochester, N.Y., 1971—. Brighton Fire Dept., 1985—; mem. Convalescent Hosp. for Children, Rochester, 1980s. Mem. N.Y. State Bar Assn., N.Y. State Trial Lawyers Ass., N.Y. State Magistrates Assn. (past pres.), Am. Soc. Writers on Legal Subjects, Monroe County Bar Assn.; fellow Am. Coll. Civil Trial Mediators. Republican. Office: Morris and Morris Attorneys 120 Corporate Woods #240 Rochester NY 14623-1455

MORRIS, JAMES MALACHY, lawyer; b. Champaign, Ill., June 5, 1952; s. Walter Michael and Ellen Frances (Solon) M.; m. Mary Delilah Baker, Oct. 17, 1987; children: James Malachy Jr., Elliot Rice Baker, Walter Michael, Nicholas Aidan. Student, Oxford U. (Eng.), 1972; BA, Brown U., 1974; JD, U. Pa., 1977. Bar: N.Y. 1978, U.S. Dist. Ct. (so. and ea. dists.) N.Y. 1978, Ill. 1980, U.S. Tax Ct. 1982, U.S. Supreme Ct. 1983; admitted to Barristers Chambers, Manchester, Eng., 1987. Assoc. Reid & Priest, N.Y.C., 1977-80; sr. law clk. Supreme Ct. Ill., Springfield, 1980-81; assoc. Carter, Ledyard & Milburn, N.Y.C., 1981-83; sole practice N.Y.C., 1983-87; counsel FCA, Washington, 1987—; acting sec., gen. counsel FCS Ins. Corp., McLean, Va., 1990-98. Cons. Internat. Awards Found., Zurich, 1981-2002, Pritzker Architecture Prize Found., N.Y.C., 1981-2002, Herbert Oppenheimer, Nathan & VanDyck, London, 1985—. Contbr. articles to profl. jours. Mem. ABA, Ill. Bar Assn., N.Y. State Bar Assn., N.Y. County Lawyers Assn., Assn. Bar City N.Y., Brit. Inst. Internat. and Comparative Law, Am. Inst. Parliamentarians, Lansdowne Club (London), Casanova (Va.) Hunt Club. Office: PO Box 1407 Mc Lean VA 22101-1407

MORRIS, JAMES PEPPLER, bass; b. Balt., Jan. 10, 1947; s. James Deal and Geraldine (Peppler) M.; m. Joanne Frances Vitali, Nov. 15, 1971; 1 child, Heather Frances; m. Susan Louise Quittmeyer, Jan. 3, 1987; children: (twins) Daniel Robert and Jennifer Louise. Student, U. Md., 1965-66, Peabody Conservatory, 1966-68; studied with Nicola Moscona, Phila. Acad. Vocal Arts, 1968-70; studied with Rosa Ponselle. Recorded with Angel Records div. EMI and Deutche Grammophone, Sony, Phillips. Debut at Met. Opera, N.Y.C., 1971, singer, 1970—, opera and concert singer throughout U.S., Can., S.Am., Europe, Australia, Japan, 1970—; featured roles include Philip II in Don Carlos, Horace Tabor in The Ballad of Baby Doe, Scarpia in Tosca, title roles in The Flying Dutchman, Don Giovanni, Le Nozze di Figaro, Macbeth, Boris Godunov, Der Fliegende Holländer, the 4 villains in Tales of Hoffmann, Mephistopheles in Faust, Claggart in Billy Budd, Wotan/Wanderer in Wagner's Ring, Iago in Otello; recs. include Wotan in two separate Ring Cycles, The Flying Dutchman, operas by Wagner, Offenbach, Mozart, Massenet, Verdi, R. Strauss, Gounod, (with Dame Joan Sutherland) Donizetti, Puccini, Bellini, Thomas, orchestral works including Haydn's Creation, Beethoven's 9th Symphony, Mozart and Fauré Requiems, arias by Verdi and Wagner. Recipient Grammy award for rec. of Wagner's Ring Cycle. Mem. Actors Equity (Can.), Am. Guild Mus. Artists. Office: care Colbert Artists Mgmt Inc 111 W 57th St New York NY 10019-2211

MORRIS, JANE ELIZABETH, home economics educator; b. Marietta, Ohio, Nov. 28, 1940; d. Harold Watson and LaRue (Graham) M. Student, U. Ky., 1960; BS, Marietta Coll., 1962, postgrad., 1963; MA, Kent State U., 1970, postgrad., 1985-87, Coll. Mt. St. Joseph, 1984-86, John Carroll U., 1986, Ashland Coll., 1987. Cert. high sch. tchr., Ohio. Tchr. home econs. Chagrin Falls (Ohio) Mid. and High Sch., 1963-95; pres. JEM Creations, Inc., 1995—. Head cheerleading advisor Chagrin Falls H.S., 1970-80, freshman class advisor, 1981-82, head fine and practical arts dept., 1982-84, sophomore class advisor, 1982-85, 87-89, mem. prin.'s cabinet, 1987-88, tchr., adminstr. adv. coun., 1990-93. Vice chmn. The Elec. Women's Round Table, Inc., Cleve., 1968, chmn., 1969-71; treas. Trees Condominium Assn., 1981-83, pres., 1991-94; active Chagrin Falls chpt. Am. Heart Assn., Am. Cancer Soc., Geauga County Humane Soc., Valley Save a Pet; pres. Eagles Nest Condo Assn., 1999-2002. Mem. AAUW, NEA, PEO, Career Edn. Assn., Ohio Edn. Assn., Ohio Retired Tchrs. Assn., Chagrin Falls Edn. Assn. (bldg. rep. 1986-95, negotiating team 1990, negotiating com. 1993, commendation State of Ohio rep. assembly 1995), Nat. Soc. Arts and Letters (treas.), Marietta Coll. Alumni Assn. (mem. Mid Ohio Valley chpt.), Washington County Hist. Soc., Marietta Photographic Soc., Friends of the Mus. Campus Martius Mus., Order Ea. Star (mem. Marietta chpt. no. 59), Alpha Xi Delta (treas. alumni bd.). Methodist. Avocations: swimming, interior design, sewing, gourmet cooking.

MORRIS, JEFFREY BRANDON, law educator; b. N.Y.C., Jan. 8, 1941; s. Richard B. and Berenice (Robinson) M.; m. Dona Gene Baron, July 9, 1972; children: David Brandon, Deborah Helaine. AB, Princeton U., 1962; JD, Columbia U., 1965, PhD in Polit. Sci., 1972. Bar: N.Y. 1967, U.S. Supreme Ct. 1970, D.C. 1978, U.S. Dist. Ct. D.C. 1978. Lectr., instr., asst. prof. CUNY, N.Y.C., 1968-74; spl. asst. to provost Columbia U., N.Y.C., 1974-76; jud. fellow U.S. Supreme Ct., Washington, 1976-77, rsch. assoc. adminstrv. asst. chief justice, 1977-81; asst. prof. polit. sci. U. Pa., Phila., 1981-88; vis. assoc. prof. Bklyn. Law Sch., N.Y.C., 1988-90; from assoc. prof. to prof. law Touro Law Sch., Huntington, N.Y., 1990—. Rapporteur Nat. Conf. on Causes Population Dissatisfaction, with Popular Dissatisfaction Adminstrn. of Justice, St. Paul, 1976; cons. bicentennial exhibitions Independence Nat. Hist. Park, 1986. Author: Federal Justice in the Second Circuit, 1988, U.S. District Court Eastern District N.Y., 1965-90, 1992, Making Sure We are True to Our Founders, 1997, Brooklyn Law School: The First Hundred Years, 2001, Calmly to Poise the Scales of Justice, 2001; co-author: A Pocket History of the United States, 9th rev. edit., 1992; editor: Encyclopedia of American History, 1982, 7th edit., 1996; assoc. editor Yearbook, Supreme Ct. Hist. Soc., 1979-83. Mem. Brookings Conf. on Interbr. Rels., Williamsburg, Va., 1980, 81. Jewish. Avocations: opera, dance, theater. Home: 234 Forest Rd Flushing NY 11363-1303 Office: Touro Law Sch 300 Nassau Rd Huntington NY 11743-4346 E-mail: jeffreym@tourolaw.edu.

MORRIS, JEFFREY SELMAN, orthopedic surgeon; b. Johannesburg, June 26, 1948; arrived in Can., 1979; came to U.S., 1990; s. Israel and Anna Riva (Belikoff) M.; m. Carol Parker, Jan. 21, 1973 (div. 1986); children: Amit, Leora; m. Cheryl Tyler, Aug. 16, 1997; 1 stepchild, Jennifer Tyler. BSc, U. Witwatersrand, Johannesburg, 1970, B of Medicine, B of Surgery, 1973. Cert. pvt. pilot, FAA. Rotating intern Natalspruit Hosp., South Africa, 1974, surg. resident, 1975-76; resident in orthopedic surgery Cen. Emek Hosp., Afula, Israel, 1977-79, Queen's U., Kingston, Ont., Can., 1979-82; orthopedic surgeon Port Arthur Clinic, Thunder Bay, Ont., 1983-86, Joseph Brant Meml. Hosp., Burlington, Ont., 1986-90, Beachwood (Ohio) Orthopedic Assocs., 1990-98; sole practitioner Twinsburg, Cuyahoga Falls, Ohio, 1998—. Mem. active staff South Pointe Hosp., Cleve.; assoc. staff Hillcrest Hosp., Cleve., Cuyahoga Falls Gen. Hosp.; provisional staff Summa Health Sys., Akron, Ohio. Contbr. articles to profl. jours., chpt. to book. Med. advisor Arthritis Soc., Thunder Bay, 1983-86. Mem. ACS, Am. Bd. Independent Med. Examiners, Am. Bd. Forensic Medicine, Can. Med. Assn., Ont. Med. Assn., Can. Orthopedic Assn., Ont. Orthopedic Assn., Ohio Orthopedic Soc., Cleve. Orthopedic Soc., Royal Coll. Physicians and Surgeons (Can.), Can. Soc. Surgery of the Hand, Ohio Med. Assn. Jewish. Avocations: music, tennis, theater, aviation. Office: PO Box 1027 Hudson OH 44236-6227 also: Falls Group Bldg Ste 104 3033 State Rd Cuyahoga Falls OH 44223-2545

MORRIS, JOHN, composer, conductor, arranger; b. Elizabeth, N.J. s. Thomas Arthur and Helen (Sherratt) M.; m. Francesca Bosetti; children: Evan Bosetti, Bronwen Helen. Student, Julliard Sch. Music, 1946-48, U. Wash., 1947, New Sch. Social Research, 1946-49. Composer (film) The Producers, The Twelve Chairs, The Gamblers, Blazing Saddles (nominated Acad. award 1976), The Bank Shot, Young Frankenstein, Sherlock Holmes Smarter Brother, Silent Movie, The Last Remake of Beau Geste, The In-Laws, The World's Greatest Lover, In God We Trust, High Anxiety, The Elephant Man (nominated Acad. award 1981), Table for Five, History of the World Part I, Yellowbeard, The Doctor and the Devils, Clue, To Be or Not To Be, Woman in Red, Johnny Dangerously, Haunted Honeymoon, Dirty Dancing, Spaceballs, Ironweed, The Wash, Stella, Life Stinks; (Broadway stage plays) My Mother, My Father and Me, Doll's House, Camino Real; (mus.) A Time for Singing; (off-Broadway) Take One Step, Young Andy Jackson, N.Y. Shakespeare Festival Much Ado About Nothing, Peer Gynt, Richard III, Love's Labor's Lost, Electra, As You Like It, Comedy of Errors, Titus Andronicus, Henry IV Parts 1 and 2, Romeo and Juliet, Hamlet, The Cherry Orchard, Stratford Connecticut Shakespeare Festival The Tempest, Julius Caesar, Antony and Cleopatra, Measure for Measure, Twelfth Night, Lincoln Ctr. King Lear; (TV) Fresno, Katherine Anne Porter, Ghost Dancing, The Firm, The Mating Season, Splendor in the Grass, The Electric Grandmother, The Scarlet Letter, The Adams Chronicles, Georgia O'Keeffe, The Franken Project, The Tap Dance Kid (Emmy award 1986), Make Believe Marriage, ABC After Sch. Spl. Theme, Making Things Grow Theme, The French Chef Theme, The Desperate Hours, The Skirts of Happy Chance, Infancy and Childhood, The Fig Tree, The Little Match Girl, Our Sons, The Last to Go, The Last Best Year, The Sunset Gang, Coach Theme, Favorite Son, Journey Into Genius, When Lions Roared, Scarlett Mini Series, With God On Our Side, Ellen Foster, Murder in a Small Town, The Lady in Question, Tribute to Julie Harris, Only Love, Blackwater Lightship, documentary films; mus. supr., condr., arranger numerous TV spls., Broadway and off-Broadway shows and recs. including Anne Bancroft Spl. #1 (Emmy award), 'S Lemmon 'S Gershwin 'S Wonderful (Emmy award), Hallmark Christmas Spls.; (Broadway) Peter Pan, Bells Are Ringing, Bye-Bye Birdie, All-American, Wild Cat, Kwanmina, Baker Street, Mack and Mabel, Much Ado About Nothing; (off-Broadway) Hair; (records) Wildcat, All-American, Bells Are Ringing, First Impressions, Bye-Bye Birdie, Kwamina, Baker Street, Rodgers and Hart, George Gershwin vols. I and II, Jerome Kern, Lyrics of Ira Gershwin, Cole Porter, others. Mem. ASCAP, Acad. Motion Picture Arts and Scis., Soc. Composers and Lyricists, Am. Fedn. Musicians. Avocations: computers, humorous poetry, cooking. Office: Alan Stein 345 E 56th St # 10J New York NY 10022 E-mail: jmorris319@hotmail.com.

MORRIS, JOHN SELWYN, philosophy educator, college president emeritus; b. Tonypandy, Wales, July 2, 1925; came to U.S., 1954, naturalized, 1993; s. Jenkin and Hannah M. (Williams) M.; m. Enid Elry Walters, Apr. 10, 1954; 1 child, Paul John. BA, Univ. Coll. South Wales and Monmouthshire, 1951; MA, Cambridge (Eng.) U., 1953; student, Union Theol. Sem., 1957-60; MA, Colgate U., 1961; PhD, Columbia U., 1961; LL.D. (hon.), Hartwick Coll., 1979; LHD (hon.), Elmyra Coll., 1990; DLitt, Skidmore Coll., 1991. Ordained to ministry Presbyterian Ch., 1954; minister Vernon (N.Y.) and Vernon Center Presbyn. chs., 1954-57; instr. Colgate U., Hamilton, N.Y., 1960-63, asst. prof., 1963-66, asso. prof., 1966-70, prof. philosophy and religion, 1970-79, dir. div. humanities, 1970-72, dir. div. univ. studies, 1972-73, provost, dean of faculty, 1973-79, acting pres., 1977; prof. philosophy Union Coll., Schenectady, 1979-90, pres., 1979-90; chancellor Union U., 1979—90; pres. emeritus, rsch. prof. philosophy Union Coll., Schenectady, 1990—. Leverhulme vis. fellow U. Exeter, Eng., 1968-69; chmn. Commn. Ind. Colls. and Univs., 1984-86; trustee Cazenovia Coll., N.Y. Trustee Skidmore Coll.; chancellor New England Coll., N.H. With RAF, 1943-47. Recipient Disting. Svc. award Colgate U. Alumni Corp., 1978, Schenectady Patroon award, 1989, Union Coll. Founders Medal, 1990; fellow Cardiff U. Mem. AAUP, Am. Philos. Assn., Am. Acad. Religion, Royal Inst. Philosophy, Soc. for Study Theology, Nat. Welsh Am. Found. (bd. advisors). Office: Union Coll Humanities Ctr Schenectady NY 12308

MORRIS, JOHN WOODLAND, II, businessman, former army officer; b. Princess Anne, Md., Sept. 10, 1921; s. John Earl and Allice (Cropper) M.; m. Geraldine Moore King, May 12, 1947; children: Susan K., John Woodland III. BS, U.S. Mil. Acad., 1943; MS, U. Iowa, 1947; postgrad., Army War Coll., 1961-62, U. Pitts., 1966. Commd. 2d lt. U.S. Army, 1943, advanced through grades to lt. gen., 1976; dep. dist. engr. Savannah, Ga., 1952-54; resident engr. Goose Bay, Labrador, 1955-57; staff officer Office Chief Engrs., 1957-60; comdg. officer 8th Engr. Bn., Korea, 1960-61; dist. engr. Tulsa, 1962-65; dep. comdt. U.S. Mil. Acad., 1965-67; dep. chief legis. liaison Office Sec. Army, Washington, 1967-69; comdg. gen. 18th Engr. Brigade, Vietnam, 1969-70; div. engr. Missouri River Div., Omaha, 1970-72; dir. civil works Office C.E., Washington, 1972-75; dep. chief engr. U.S. Army, 1975-76, chief engr., 1976-80; ret., 1980; exec. dir. Royal Volker Stevin, 1980-84; pres. J.W. Morris Ltd., 1981—; prof. U. Md., 1983-86; chmn. bd., CEO, PRC Engring., 1986-88. Engr. advisor, cons. Zorc, Rissetto, Weaver & Rosen, 1988-92; engr. advisor Seltzer & Rosen, 1992-98; bd. dirs. Air Water Tech., Morganti Constrn. Co., Search Techs. Inc., Thaco Rsch. Inc., Dutra Corp.; mem. adv. bd. AMEC Ltd. Mem. Indian Nations coun. Boy Scouts Am., 1962-65; chmn. Water Resources Congress, 1988-90; trustee U.S. Mil. Acad. Assn. Grads, 1986—; advisor dean engring. and math. U. Vt., 1990-96. Decorated Legion of Merit with three oak leaf clusters, Army D.S.M., Def. D.S.M.; recipient Merit award Am. Cons. Engrs. Council; Palladium medal Audubon Soc.; award of excellence Constrn. Industry Inst., 1997. Fellow ASCE (Disting. Constructor award 2000); mem. AIA (hon.), Internat. Navigation Congress (v.p.), U.S. Soc. Mil. Engrs. (pres.), Nat. Acad. Engrs. (Founders award 1996), U.S. Com. on Large Dams (past chmn. environ. effect com., named Constrn. Man of Yr. 1977, Navigation Hall of Fame 1990, Golden Beaver award for engring. 1995, Golden Eagle award, 1998, Acad. of Dist. Eng. U. Iowa, 1998, Dist. Grad. of U.S. Mil. Acad., 1998). Episcopalian. E-mail: morrisJ@aol.com.

MORRIS, JOSEPH ANTHONY, retired health science association administrator; b. Marboro, Md., Mar. 6, 1918; s. Charles Lafayette and Essie (Stokes) M.; m. Ruth Savoy, Nov. 1, 1942; children: Carol Ann, Marilyn T., Joseph A., Larry A. BS, Cath. U. Am., 1940, MS, 1942, PhD, 1947. Asst. scientist Josiah Macy, Jr. Found., N.Y.C., 1943-44; virologist Depts. Agr., Interior, Laurel, Md., 1944-47; virologist, chief hepatitis virus rsch. Walter Reed Army Inst. Rsch., Washington, 1947-56; virologist, asst. chief, dept. virus and rickettsial dis. U.S. Army Med. Command, Japan, 1956-59; virologist chief sect. respiratory diseases divsn. biologics stds. NIH, Bethesda, Md., 1959—2003. Dir. slow, latent and temperate virus br. FDA, Bethesda, 1972-76; lectr. dept. microbiology U. Md., College Park, 1977-79; vice-chmn. Bell of Atri, Inc., College Park, 1979-82, chmn., 1983; cons. Commn. on Influenza, Armed Forces Epidemiologic Bd., 1960—, Nat. Inst. Neurol. Diseases and Blindness, 1962—. Mem. Soc. Tropical Medicine and Hygiene, Soc. Am. Microbiologists, Soc. Exptl. Biology and Medicine, Am. Assn. Immunologists, N.Y. Acad. Scis. Achievements include discovery of respiratory sycytial virus; research on infectious hepatitis, respiratory diseases of virus etiology and zoonosis. Home: 23E Ridge Rd Greenbelt MD 20770-0714 Office: PO Box 40 College Park MD 20741-0040

MORRIS, JOSEPH RAYMOND, business and economics educator; b. Stuckey, Ga., May 29, 1939; s. Joseph Alton and Ora Lou (Hinson) M.; m. Joyce Marilyn Speiller, Mar. 17, 1984; children from previous marriage: Theresa, Marianne, Jennifer. BA, Nova U., 1986, M of Internat. Bus.

Adminstrn., 1988. Sales profl. Dixie Pllywood Corp. Inc., Miami, Fla., 1964-68; sales mgr. Bradley Plywood Corp. Inc., Savannah, Ga., 1968-73; mgr. City Motel Inc., Franklin, N.C., 1973-78; pres., owner Coweee Gem Shop, Franklin, 1973-78; with Eastern Airlines Inc., Miami, 1978-90; adj. prof., then full-time/part-time prof. Broward C.C., Ft. Lauderdale, Fla., 1989—. Adj. prof. Palm Beach C.C., Boca Raton, Fla., 1995, Fla. Internat. U., Miami,1990—, Lynn U., Boca Raton, 1998—; instr. part-time Nova Southeastern U., Ft. Lauderdale, 1996—, Johnson & Wales U., 2000—. With USN, 1956-64. Recipient Enterpreneurship Inst. Svc. award, 1998, Fla. Inernat. U. Cmty. Svc. award, 1997. Mem. Am. Inst. Econ. Rsch., Acad. Internat. Bus., Franklin Gem and Mineral Soc.,, Lions (pres. Franklin chpt. 1976-77, v.p. 1973-75, chmn. western counties 1977-78), Civitans (treas. 1982-83), Toastmasters, Masons, Shriners. Republican. Baptist. Avocations: golf, swimming, community service, time with students. Home and Office: PO Box 292104 Davie FL 33329-2104

MORRIS, JUSTIN ROY, food scientist, consultant, enologist, research director, science administrator; b. Nashville, Ark., Feb. 20, 1937; s. Roy Morris; m. Ruby Lee Blackwood, Sept. 5, 1956; children: Linda Lee, Michael Justin. BS, U. Ark., 1957, MS, 1961; PhD, Rutgers U., 1964. Instr. Rutgers U., New Brunswick, NJ, 1964-67; ext. horticulturist U. Ark., Fayetteville, 1964-67, from asst. to assoc. prof., 1967-75, prof., 1975-85, univ. prof., 1985-97, disting. prof., 1997—, dir. Inst. Food Sci. and Engring., Ctr. Food Processing and Engring., 1995—. Cons. viticulture sci. program Fla. A&M U., Tallahassee, 1979—81; cons. viticulture and enology program Grayson City Coll., Denison, Tex., 1987—97; cons. J. M. Smucker Co., 1982—91. Assoc. editor: Am. Jour. Enology and Viticulture, 1985; co-author: (book) Small Fruit Crop Management, 1990, Quality and Preservation of Fruits, 1991, Modern Fruit Science Text Book, 1995; contbr. chapters to books; publ. (to sci. jour. articles) over 345 rsch. articles. Apptd. by gov. Ark. Wine Prodrs. Coun., 2002—. Recipient Rsch. award, Nat. Food Processors Assn., 1982, Food Processors 49er Leadership award, 1998, Food Sci. Rsch. award, 1998, award of merit, Am. Wine Soc., 1999, John White Outstanding Team award, 2002, So. Region Grape Rsch. award, 2003, Outstanding Alumnus award, U. Ark. Horticulture Dept., 2003; Spitze Land grantee, 1997. Fellow: Inst. Food Technologists (co-organizer fruit and vegetable divsn. 1987—), Am. Soc. Hort. Sci. (assoc. editor 1985, Gourley award 1979, Outstanding Rsch. award 1983); mem.: Am. Soc. Enology and Viticultures (chairperson 1996—97, Disting. Achievement award ea. sect. 1995, Nat. Merit award 1996), Food Processors Guard Soc. (life Grape Team Rsch. award 2002, Outstanding Grape and Wine Rsch. award So. Region 2003), Coun. Agrl. Sci. and Tech. (chmn. nat. concerns 1987—91, bd. dirs. 1987—93, pres.-elect 1993, pres. 1994, 1995), Ozark Food Processers Assn. (exec. v.p. 1988—), Gamma Sigma Delta. Achievements include development of mechanical cane fruit harvester; mechanical strawberry harvester; modified grape harvester for wine grapes; mechanical shoot positioner for grapes; mechanized systems for the production, harvesting, handling and utilization of grape juice and wine. Office: U Ark Inst Food Sci and Engring 2650 N Young Ave Fayetteville AR 72704-5690 Office Phone: 501-575-4040. Business E-Mail: jumorris@uark.edu.

MORRIS, LEIGH EDWARD, mayor, retired hospital executive officer; b. Hartford City, Ind., Dec. 26, 1934; s. Fredus Orlando and Martha (Malott) M.; m. Marcia Renee Meredith, Oct. 7, 1967; children: Meredith Anne, Curtis Paul. BS in Commerce, Internat. Coll., 1954; BSBA, Ball State U., 1958; M in Health Adminstrn., U. Minn., 1972. Mem. labor relations staff Borg-Warner Corp., Muncie, Ind., 1961-64; various positions then personnel mgr. Internat. Harvester Co., Ft. Wayne, Ind., 1964-70; pres. Huntington (Ind.) Meml. Hosp., 1972-78, La Porte (Ind.) Hosp., 1978-2000; ret.; mayor City of LaPorte. Bd. dirs. First of Am. Bank of Ind., Am. Hosp. Svcs., Inc., Health Forum, Inc.; chmn., bd. dirs. Am. Hosp. Pub. Co.; chmn. La Porte Devel. Corp., 1980-81. Chmn. La Porte chpt. ARC, 1984-86; bd. dirs. John G. Blank Ctr. for the Arts. With U.S. Army, 1958-60. Recipient Disting. Alumni award Ball State U., Muncie, Ind., 1968, James A. Hamilton award U. Minn., Mpls., 1972, Trustees award Am. Hosp. Assn., 1996. Fellow Am. Coll. Healthcare Adminstrn. (life), Health Care Fin. Mgmt. Assn.; mem. APHA, Am. Hosp. Assn. (trustee, regional chmn. 1985-89), Soc. for Healthcare Planning and Mktg. (bd. dirs.), Soc. Ind. Pioneers (bd. dirs.), Ind. Hosp. Assn. (chmn. 1980-81), La Porte C. of C. (chmn. 1981-82). Republican. Presbyterian. Avocations: classic cars, civic affairs. Home: 424 Lake Shore Dr La Porte IN 46350-2917 Office Phone: 219-362-8220.

MORRIS, LOIS LAWSON, retired education educator; b. Antoine, Ark., Nov. 27, 1914; d. Oscar Moran and Dona Alice (Ward) Lawson; m. William D. Morris, July 2, 1932 (dec.); 1 child, Lavonne Morris Howell (dec.). BA, Henderson U., 1948; MS, U. Ark., 1951, MA, 1966; postgrad., U. Colo., 1954, Am. U., 1958, U. N.C., 1968. History tchr. Delight H.S., Ark., 1942-47; counselor Huntsville Vocat. Sch., 1947-48; guidance dir. Russellville Pub. Sch. Sys., Ark., 1948-55; asst. prof. edn. U. Ark., Fayetteville, 1955-82, prof. emeritus, 1982—. Edn. cons. Ark. Pub. Schs., 1965-78. Author: Biographical Essays, 2000; contbr. 2 articles to profl. jours. including Ark. Biography, 2000. Mem. Hist. Preservation Alliance Ark.; pres. Washington County Hist. Soc., 1983-85, Pope County Hist. Assn.; mem. Ark. Symphony Guild; charter mem. Nat. Mus. in Arts; bd. dirs. Potts Inn Mus. Found. Named Ark. Coll. Tchr. of Yr., 1972; recipient Plaque for Outstanding Svcs. to Washington County Hist. Soc., 1984. Mem. LWV, AAUW, NEA, Washington County Hist., Soc. (exec. bd. 1977-80), Ark. Edn. Assn., Ark. Hist. Assn., Pope County Hist. Assn. (pres. 1991-92), The Ga. Hist. Soc., U. Ark. Alumni Assn., Sierra Club, Nature Conservancy, Ark. River Valley Arts Assn., Phi Delta Kappa, Kappa Delta Pi, Phi Alpha Theta. Democrat. Episcopalian. Address: 1601 W 3d St Russellville AR 72801-4725

MORRIS, MAC GLENN, advertising bureau executive; b. Bessemer City, N.C., Jan. 24, 1922; s. Manly T. and Erin C. (Cline) M.; m. Janelle Connevey, July 27, 1946; children— Robert S., Janelle C., Patricia A., John Logan. AB, Davidson Coll., 1942. Space salesman Progressive Farmer mag., N.Y.C., 1946-52; exec. v.p., advt. dir. This Week mag., 1952-68; pres. Newspaper One, N.Y.C., 1968-71; sr. v.p. nat. sales Newspaper Advt. Bur., N.Y.C., 1972-87; proprietor MGM Assocs., Princeton, N.J., 1987—. Bd. dirs. Princeton Bank & Trust Co. divsn. Chem. Bank N.J., N.A., now owned by P.N.C. Bank, N.Y.C. Served to 1st lt., pilot USMCR, World War II. Decorated D.F.C. (2), Air medal (7). Mem. Newcomen Soc. in N. Am., Pi Kappa Phi. Presbyn. (deacon). Club: Springdale Golf (Princeton, N.J.) (bd. govs.). Home and Office: 383 Herrontown Rd Princeton NJ 08540 *I am always an optimist at my work, with friends, and with my family.*

MORRIS, MARCIA A. language educator; d. William H and Kathleen E Morris; m. Martin J O'Mara, Sept. 7, 1974; children: David M O'Mara, Daniel M O'Mara. PhD, Columbia U., 1987. Prof. Georgetown U., Washington, 1987—. Author: Saints and Revolutionaries: The Ascetic Hero in Russian Literature, The Literature of Roguery in Seventeenth- and Eighteenth-Century Russia. Office: Slavic Languages Georgetown University 37th & O Sts NW Washington DC 20057-1050

MORRIS, MARGARET ELIZABETH, marketing professional; b. N.Y.C., Nov. 1, 1962; d. John Daniel and Jean Bingham (MacCollom) M. BA in English, Georgetown U., 1984. Cert. Rubenfeld Synergy Method, 1997; cert. scuba diver: openwater, rescue diver, divemaster, emergency first responder instr., PADI. Mem. staff mktg. programs AT&T Nat. Fed. Mktg., Arlington, Va., 1985; mktg. tech. cons. AT&T Nat. Fed. Systems, Washington, 1985-87; tech. cons. computer mktg. Cin. Bell Tel. Co., 1987-89, mktg. tech. cons., 1989-95; sr. acct. exec.-strategic accts., 1995—. Tutor (vol.) Ptnrs. in Edn. Editor: (newsletter) District Action Project RAP, 1981-82; contbr. chpt. to book. Intern Citizen's Complaint Ctr., Washington, 1981-82; asst. coach River City Volleyball Club; coach CYO Girls Volleyball; vol. tech. amb. Corryville Cath. Sch.; vol. coord. SPCA Cin.; participant Leukemia and Lymphoma Soc. Am. Team in Tng., Suzuki Rock n Roll Marathon, San Diego, 2000, Walt Disney World Marathon, Orlando, 2001, Flying Pig Marathon, Cin., 2001, Mayor's Midnight Sun Marathon, Anchorage, 2002, Las Vegas Internat. Marathon, 2003, Marine Corps Marathon, 2003. Named Salesperson of Yr., 1997, Corp. Vol. of Yr., SPCA Cin., 2001. Mem.: Telephone Pioneers Am. (Pioneer Vol. of Yr. 2000). Office: Cin Bell Tel Co 201 E 4th St Rm 102-1136 Cincinnati OH 45202-4122

MORRIS, MARIE SCHUESSLER, dean; d. Robert Keith Schuessler and Marie Esther Sosnowski; m. Keith Alan Morris, Mar. 1, 1958; children: Jesse Schuessler, Alexander Robert. Doctorate, George Mason U., 1993. Nursing faculty Ea. Mennonite U., Harrisonburg, Va., 1984—94, nursing dept. chair, 1994—98, assoc. dean, 1998—2000, academic dean, 2000—. Sunday sch. shepherd Zion Mennonite Ch., Va., 2002—04. Office Phone: 540-432-4106. Office Fax: 540-432-4444.

MORRIS, MARK WILLIAM, choreographer; b. Seattle, Wash., Aug. 29, 1956; s. William and Maxine (Crittenden) Morris. Studied with, Verla Flowers and Perry Brunson; D (hon.), Boston Conservatory of Music, Juilliard Sch., L.I. U., Pratt Inst., Bowdoin Coll. Artistic dir. Mark Morris Dance Group, N.Y.C., 1980—, Théâtre Royal de la Monnaie, Brussels, 1988—91; co-founder White Oak Dance Project, 1990; owner Mark Morris Dance Ctr., Bklyn., 2001—. Performed with Lar Lubovitch Dance Co., Hannah Kahn Dance Co., Laura Dean Dancers and Musicians, Eliot Feld Ballet, Koleda Balkan Dance Ensemble. Choreographer Mort Subite, Boston Ballet, 1986, Esteemed Guests, Joffrey Ballet, 1986, Nixon in China, Houston Grand Opera, 1987, L'Allegro, il Penseroso ed il Moderato, 1988, Drink to Me Only With Thine Eyes, Am. Ballet Theatre, 1988, Orfée et Euridice, Seattle Opera, 1988, Dido and Aeneas, 1989, Ein Herz, Paris Opera Ballet, 1990, The Death of Klinghoffer, Théâtre de la Monnaie, 1991, The Hard Nut, 1991, Great Performances/Dance in Am. The Hard Nut, 1992, Maelstrom, San Francisco Ballet, 1994, The Office, 1994, Lucky Charms, 1994, Pacific, San Francisco Ballet, 1995, Platée, Royal Opera Covent Garden, 1997, Sandpaper Ballet, San Francisco Ballet, 1999, Four Saints in Three Acts, 2000, Sang-Froid, 2000, A Garden, San Francisco Ballet, 2001, Gong, Am. Ballet Theatre, 2001; dir.: Die Fledermaus, 1988, Dido and Aeneas, 1995, Falling Down Stairs, 1997 (Emmy award, 1997), The Capeman, Kolam, 2002. Recipient Dance and Performance award, 1984, 1990; fellow, Guggenheim Found., 1986, MacArthur Found., 1991. Office: Mark Morris Dance Group 3 Lafayette Ave Brooklyn NY 11217

MORRIS, MAX KING, foundation executive, former naval officer; b. Springfield, Mo., Oct. 23, 1924; s. Lee Howard and Aldyth (King) M.; m. Mary Jane Bull, June 19, 1952; children: Jane, William, Mary. BS, U.S. Naval Acad., 1947; MA in Internat. Law, Tufts U., 1960, MA in Internat. Econs., 1961, PhD, 1967. Commd. ensign U.S. Navy, 1947, advanced through grades to rear adm., 1972; carrier pilot with combat duty in Korea and Vietnam, 1947-71; comdr. jet squadron U.S.S. America, 1965-67; maj. command at sea, 1969-70; comdt. U.S. Naval Acad., 1971-73; Joint Chiefs of Staff rep. UN Law of Sea Conf., 1973-77; ret., 1977. Pres. Thalassa Rsch. Co., Jacksonville, Fla., 1977—; trustee Arthur Vining Davis Founds., Fla. Author: Politico-Military Coordination in the Armed Forces, 1968; Contbr. numerous articles to naval and legal jours. Served with arty. U.S. Army, 1942-44. Decorated D.S.M., Legion of Merit (2), Air medal (5) Mem. Internat. Inst. Strategic Studies (London), Council on Fgn. Relations, Middle East Inst., U.S. Naval Inst. Clubs: N.Y. Yacht, Fla. Yacht; Belfry (London); Ponte Vedra (Fla.). Home: 4123 Duval Dr Jacksonville Beach FL 32250-5813

MORRIS, MICHAEL DAVID, chemistry professor; b. N.Y.C., Mar. 27, 1939; s. Melvin M. and Rose (Pollock) M.; m. Leslie Tuttle, June 5, 1961; children: Susannah, David, Rebecca, Ari. BA in Chemistry, Reed Coll., 1960; PhD in Chemistry, Harvard U., 1964. Asst. prof. Pa. State U., University Park, Pa., 1969; assoc. prof. U. Mich., Ann Arbor, 1969-82, prof., 1982—. Assoc. chmn. U. Mich., Ann Arbor, 1992-97. Editor: Spectroscopic and Microscopic Imaging of the Chemical State, 1993; mem. editorial bd. Applied Spectroscopy, 1994— (Gold medal N.Y. sect. 1993), Spectrochim Acta Rev., 1987-92, editor, 1993. Recipient Anachem award Assn. Analytical Chemists, 1997. Mem. Am. Chem. Soc. (award in Spectrochemical Analysis Divsn. Analytical Chemistry 1995), Soc. Applied Spectroscopy (Strock award 1995), Microbeam Analysis Soc. Office: Univ Mich Dept Chemistry Ann Arbor MI 48109 E-mail: mdmorris@umich.edu.

MORRIS, MICHAEL G. utilities executive; b. Fremont, Ohio, Nov. 11, 1946; married, Linda Lindstrom, 1970; two children. BS, Ea. Mich. U., MS, 1973; JD cum laude, Detroit Coll. Law, 1981. With environ. dept. Commonwealth Assocs., Jackson, Mich., 1973—76; pres. ANR Gathering Co.; exec. v.p. mktg., transp. and gas supply ANR Pipeline Co., 1982—87; pres. Colo. Interstate Gas Co., 1987—88; exec. v.p., natural gas & mktg. Consumers Energy subsidiary of CMS Energy Corp., 1988—92, COO, 1992—94, pres., CEO, 1994—97; chmn., pres., CEO Northeast Utilities, Berlin, Conn., 1997—2003; pres., CEO Am. Electric Power Co., Springfield, Mass., 2004—, chmn., 2004—. Exec. com., trustee Inst. Gas Tech.; trustee Ea. Mich. U. Found.; trustee Detroit Coll. Law, Delta Sigma Phi Found.; mem. Olivet Coll. Leadership Adv. Coun.; bd. dirs. Libr. Mich. Found.; bd. regents Ea. Mich. U., 1997—. Recipient Disting. Alumnus award Ea. Mich. U., 1995. Mem. Mich. Bar Assn., Delta Sigma Phi (pres.). Office: Am Electric Power Co 1 Riverside Plz Columbus OH 43215-2372*

MORRIS, NANCY B. lawyer; b. Bklyn. m. Craig Morris; children: David, Michael. JD cum laude, Pace U., White Plains, N.Y., 1991. Bar: N.Y., N.J., U.S. Dist. Ct. (so. dist.) N.Y., U.S. Dist. Ct. N.J. Assoc. Law Office of Anne Glickman, New City, N.Y., 1992-96; pvt. practice New City, 1996—. Mem. Rockland County Bar Assn., Rockland County Women's Bar Assn. (officer, dir. 1995—). Office: 2 New Hempstead Rd New City NY 10956-3635 Office Phone: 845-638-8000. E-mail: nmorris@attorney.com.

MORRIS, NAOMI CAROLYN MINNER, clinical pediatrician, medical researcher, educator, health facility administrator; b. Chgo., June 8, 1931; d. Morris George and Carrie Ruth (Auslender) Minner; m. Charles Elliot Morris, June 28, 1951; children: Jonathan Edward, David Carlton. BA magna cum laude, U. Colo., 1952, MD, 1955; MPH magna cum laude, Harvard U., 1959. Diplomate Am. Bd. Preventive Medicine. Rotating intern LA County Gen. Hosp., 1955-56; clin. fellow in pediat. Mass. Gen. Hosp., Boston, 1957; pub. health physician Mass. Dept. Health, Boston, 1957-58; clin. pediatrician Norfolk King's Daus. Hosp., Va., 1959-61; from rsch. assoc. to prof. dept. maternal/child health Sch. Pub. Health, U. NC, Chapel Hill, NC, 1962-70, 71-74, chair dept., 1975-77; prof., dir. cmty. pediat. U. Health Sci., Chgo. Med. Sch., Ill., 1977-80; prof. Sch. Pub. Health, U. Ill., Chgo., 1980—, dir. cmty. health sci. divsn., 1980-95. Advisor to chief pub.health officer, Guam, 1970-71; mem. liaison com. with Lake County Med. Soc. 1978-80; nursing divsn. adv. com. Lake County Health Dept., 1978-98; resource person Ill. 1980 White Ho. Conf. on Children, 1979-80; participant Enrich-A-Life series Chgo. Dept. Health, 1984-85, Ill. Health and Hazardous Substance Registry Pregnancy Outcome Task Force, 1984-86; mem. profl. adv. bd. Beethoven Project Ctr. Child Devel., 1986-96; mem. planning com. for action to reduce infant mortality Chgo. Inst. Medicine, 1986-89; founding mem. Westside Futures Infant Mortality Network, 1986; mem. Ill. vital stats. supplement Ill. Dept. Pub. Health, 1987; investigator and team leader Rev. Mo. Families Maternal and Child Health State Svcs., 1989; mem. children and youth 2000 task force MacArthur Found., 1992—; active Ill. Caucus on Teenage Pregnancies, 1978—, Chgo. Dept. Health Child Health Task Force, 1982-83, HSC Interprofessional Edn. Com., 1983-84, Med. Task Force Project Life, 1983-88, Women's Studies Curriculum Com., 1985-90, Com. Rsch. on Women, 1985-90, Mayor's Adv. Com. on Infant Mortality, 1986-2002, Coun. for Integrated Svc. Sys., 2001-02, Cmty. Access Program, 2002—, Gov. Adv. Com. on Infant Mortality, 1988-96, Ctr. for Rsch. on Women Fellowship Com., 1993-98; cons. pediat. nursing resources group Ill. Dept. Pub. Health, 1983-84; cons. Cook County Hosp. Study of Preventive Childhood Obesity, 1983-84, Chgo. Dept. Pub. Health Coun. for an Integrated Svc. Sys., 2001-02. founder and dir. MCH training program, 1983-03 Contbr. chapters to books, articles to profl. jours. Mem. Ill. MCH Coalition, 1994—, Voices for Ill. Children, 1993—, Children and Youth 2000, 1992—. Recipient Jonas Salk Lifetime Achievement award, March of Dimes, 2003. Fellow APHA (task force on adolescence maternal and child health sect. 1977-85, sec. 1979-80, cons. manpower project 1982-83, publ. bd. 1985-87, coun. pediat. rsch. to Am. Acad. Pediats. 1985-92, APHA, Martha May Eliot award outstanding contbns. to field of maternal and child health 1999-, Am. Coll. Preventive Medicine, Am. Acad. Pediats. (Ill. chpt. com. on sch. health, 1992-94, and com. adolescent health 1993—); mem. Ambulatory Pediat. Assn., Assn. Tchrs. Maternal and Child Health (exec. com. 1981-87, com. on tng. and continuing edn. needs of MCH/CCS dirs. 1982-83, liaison com. to fed. DCMH office 1983-87, pres. 1983-85), Chgo. Pediat. Soc. (Disting. Svc. award 2002), Phi Beta Kappa, Alpha Omega Alpha, Delta Omega, Sigma Xi. Avocations: photography, swimming, reading, classical music, travel. Office: U Ill Chgo Sch Pub Health 1603 W Taylor St Chicago IL 60612-4246

MORRIS, NIGEL W. financial executive; BA, Univ. London, 1983; MBA, London Bus. Sch., 1985. Cons. Strategic Planning Assoc., 1985-88; exec. v.p., Bank Card Divsn. Signet Banking Corp., 1988-94; pres., CEO Capital One Fin. Corp., Falls Church, Va., 1994—. Office: 2980 Fairview Park Dr Ste 1300 Falls Church VA 22042-4525

MORRIS, OWEN GLENN, engineering corporation executive; b. Shawnee, Okla., Feb. 3, 1927; s. Vestus and Myrtle (Lindsey) M.; m. Joyce Gast; children: Deborah Moree, Janine Inez. BS in Mech. Engring, U. Okla., 1947, M.Aero. Engring., 1948; postgrad., U. Va., 1952-53, Va. Poly. Inst., 1955-56, Coll. William and Mary, 1957-58. Aero., research scientist NASA, Langley Field, Va., 1948-61, mgr. mission engring. Apollo to mgr. sys. integration space shuttle Houston, 1961—74, mgr. sys. integration space shuttle, 1974—80; pres. Eagle Engring., 1980-86; pres., chief exec. officer Eagle Aerospace, Houston, 1987-90, chmn., chief exec. officer, 1990-93, chmn. bd., 1992—. Served with USNR, 1943-46. Recipient U.S. Medal of Freedom, 1972, NASA Distinguished Service medal, 1973, NASA Exceptional Service medal, 1969, Outstanding Leadership medal NASA, 1979. Asso. fellow Am. Inst. Aeros. and Astronautics; mem. Am. Astronautical Soc., Acad. Model Aeros., Tau Beta Pi, Tau Omega. Presbyterian (elder 1964—). Club: Rotary. Home: 14914 Timberland Ct Houston TX 77062-2922

MORRIS, RALPH WILLIAM, chronopharmacologist; b. Cleveland Heights, Ohio, July 30, 1928; s. Earl Douglas and Viola Minnie (Mau) M.; m. Carmen R. Mueller; children: Christopher Lynn, Kirk Stephen, Timothy Allen and Todd Andrew (twins), Melissa Mary. BA, Ohio U., Athens, 1950, MS, 1953; PhD, U. Iowa, 1955; postgrad., Seabury-Western Theol. Sem., 1979-81, McHenry County Coll., 1986-88. Research fellow in pharmacology, then teaching fellow U. Iowa, 1952-55; instr. dept. pharmacology Coll. Medicine, 1955-56; asst. prof. dept. pharmacognosy and pharmacology Coll. Pharmacy, 1956-62, assoc. prof., 1962-69; prof. Med. Center, U. Ill., Chgo., 1969-98, prof. emeritus, 1998, adj. prof. dept. pharmacodynamics, 1998-2000. Mem. adv. com. 1st aid and safety Midwest chpt. ARC, 1972-83; cons. in drug edn. to Dangerous Drug Commn., Ill. Dept. Pub. Aid, Chgo., Ill. Dept. Profl. Regulataions, Ill. Dept. Corrections and suburban sch. dists.; adj. prof. edn. Coll. Edn., U. Ill., Chgo., 1976-85; vis. scientist San Jose State U., Calif., 1982-83, St. George Med. Sch., Grenada, 1994. Referee and contbr. articles to profl. and sci. jours., lay mags., radio and TV appearances. Trustee Palatine (Ill.) Pub. Libr., 1967-72, pres., 1969-70; trustee North Suburban Libr. System, 1968-72, pres. 1970-72, mem. long-range planning com., 1975-81; chmn. Ill. Libr. Trustees, 1970-72, intellectual freedom com.; mem. Title XX Ill. Citizens Adv. Coun., 1981-83; trustee McHenry (Ill.) Pub. Libr. Dist., 1987-89, pres., 1987-89; trustee St. Gregory's Abbey, Three Rivers, Mich., 1989-96; bd. dirs. North Suburban Libr. Found., Wheeling, Ill., 1998-99; bd. dirs. United Campus Ministry U. Ill. at Chgo., 1983-87; pres. R.W. Morris & Assocs., 1988—; v.p. Lake Barrington Shores Condo X Assn., bd. dirs., 1999—; mem. archtl. commn. Lake Barrington Shores Master Bd., 1999—. Recipient Golden Apple Teaching award U. Ill. Coll. Pharmacy, 1966; cert. of merit Town of Palatine, 1972 Mem. AAAS, Am. Assn. Coll. Pharmacists, Internat. Soc. Chronobiology, European Soc. Chronbiology, Am. Soc. Pharmacology and Exptl. Therapeutics, Am. Library Trustee Assn., Ill. Library Trustee Assn. (v.p. 1970-72, dir. 1969-72), Sigma Xi, Rho Chi, Gamma Alpha. Episcopalian. Home and Office: 584 Shoreline Dr Lake Barrington IL 60010-3883 Personal E-mail: raphaelmor@aol.com.

MORRIS, ROBERT, education educator; b. Akron, Ohio, Nov. 21, 1910; s. Joseph and Katherine (Spielberger) Schmaltz; m. Sara Goldman, Dec. 20, 1940. AB, U. Akron, 1931; MSc, Western Res. U., 1935; DSW, Columbia U. Sch. Social Work, 1959; D of Humane Letters (hon.), Brandeis U., 1984. Prin. welfare officer UNRRA, 1945; regional dir. social services VA, Chgo., 1946-48; social planning cons. Council Jewish Fedns. and Welfare Funds, N.Y.C., 1948-58; prof. social planning Brandeis U., Waltham, Mass., 1959-68, Kirstein prof. social planning, 1968-83, Kirstein prof. social planning emeritus, 1983—. Cardinal Medeiros lectr. U. Mass., Boston, 1983—, lectr. Harvard U. Sch. Pub Health, 1974-88; prof. Inst. Health Professions, Mass. Gen. Hosp., 1980-83, U. Md. cons. adj. prof., 1999—; mem. adv. com. Aging Rsch., U.S. Dept. Health, Edn. and Welfare, 1971, Helen Keller Internat. Found. on the Overseas Blind, 1971-74; mem. spl. med. adv. group VA, Washington, 1969-71; cons. on Geriatric Rsch., Nat. VA, 1974-78, U.S. Office of Human Devel. Svcs., 1978-79; v.p. Vis. Nurses Assn., Boston, 1979-92; mem. Fed. Adv. Coun. on Aging Rsch., Mass. State Health Coord. Coun., 1984-85; vice chmn. Mass. Health Data Consortium, 1979-89; chmn. Internat. Rev. Com. Brookdale Inst. for Gerontology and Adult Human Devel., Israel, 1982-83, cons., 1984-85; chmn. Am. Found. for the Blind Com. on Geriatric Blindness, 1969-74; adv. com. Md. Dept. Health and Mental Health, 1993-95; pub. policy com. Nat. Coun. on the Aging, 1993-95, Ctr. for Health Planning, Program and Devel., U. Md. Baltimore County, 2000-03. Author: Feasible Planning for Social Change, 1966, Urban Planning and Social Policy, 1968, Centrally Planned Change, 1964, Trends and Issues in Jewish Social Welfare in the U.S., 1966, Encyclopedia Social Work and Social Welfare, 1971, Toward a Caring Society, 1974, Centrally Planned Change: A Re-Examination of Theories and Concepts, 1974, Social Policy of the American Welfare State, 1979, 2d edit., 1985, Allocating Resources for the Aged and Disabled, 1981, Rethinking Social Welfare: Why Care for the Stranger, 1986, Retirement Reconsidered, 1988, Economic Roles for the Elderly, 1987, 88, Testing the Limits of Social Welfare; International Perspectives on Policy Changes in Nine Countries, 1988, International Perspectives on State and Family Support for the Elderly, 1993, The National Government and Social Welfare, 1997, Personal Assistance: The Future of Home Care, 1998, Welfare Reform 1996-2000: Is There a Safety Net, 1999, Social Work at the Millenum, 2000; editor Jour. of Social Work, 1960-72, Jour. Aging and Social Policy, 1983—. Cons. NIMH, 1964-70; chmn. adv. bd. Mass. Dept. Welfare, 1968-69; profl. adv. com. Easter Seal Soc., 1971-80; mem. Mass. Gov.'s Commn. on Nursing Homes, 1962-67, on Aging, 1962-67, on Hosp. Costs, 1967, Mass. Soc. Prevention Blindness, 1971-75; organizer Odyssey Forum on Federal Social Policy, 1995—. With AUS, 1943-44. Fulbright award, Italy, 1965-66, 68, Ford Found. fellow U.K., 1969-70; recipient rsch. awards Ford Found., 1960-65, Treuhaft Found., 1964, 72, Max and Anna Levinson Fund, 1970, 72, U.S. Pub. Health Svcs., 1957, 59, 65, NSF, 1975-78, W.K. Kellog Found., 1997, Retirement Rsch. Found., 1998, Louis Lowy award Mass. Gerontology Soc., 1994. Fellow AAAS, APHA, Gerontol. Soc. Am. (Kent award 1988, Maxwell Pollack award 1992, pres. 1966-67), Mass. Pub. Health Assn. (Lemuel Shattuck medal 1976), Ctr. for Applied Gerontology (Heritage award 1987), Commonwealth of Mass. and Assn. for Gerontology in Higher Edn. (Spl. Recognition award 1987), Columbia U. Sch. Social Wor (centennial award for leadership in edn.). Home: 830 W 40th St Apt 353 Baltimore MD 21211-2164 Office: Univ Mass Boston MA 02125

MORRIS, ROBERT CRANE, management training executive; b. El Centro, Calif., July 22, 1937; s. George Howser Morris and Lillian Cauthen Barnhouse; m. Susanne Rockne, Feb. 17, 1968. BS, U. Calif., Davis, 1961, MS, 1972; PhD, Mich. State U., 1984. Vol. U.S. Peace Corps, Lyallpur, Pakistan, 1961-63, asst. dir. Lahore, Pakistan, 1963-64; cons. Swedish Internat. Devel. Agy., Stockholm, 1965; dir. overseas ops. sch. partnership program U.S. Peace Corps, Washington, 1966-68; dir. info. ctr. Internat. Secretariate Vol. Svc., Washington, 1968-69; fellow Social Sci. Rsch. Coun., Colombia, 1972-74; faculty dept. comm. Mich. State U., 1974-78; exec. dir. Mgmt. Tng. and Devel. Inst., Washington, 1978—. Chmn. Mgmt. Tng. & Devel. Inst., Singapore, 1995-97. Author: Overseas Volunteer Programs; guest editor Rural Africana, 1977; editor, mgmt. comm. series SUNY Press, Albany, 1994—.

Adv. com. Indus Found., 1997—. Mem. ASTD, Soc. Internat. Devel., Assn. Internat. Educators. Avocation: guitar. Home: 1230 4th St SW Washington DC 20024-2302 E-mail: rands.morris@verizon.net.

MORRIS, ROBERT DARRELL, reading education educator; b. Durham, NC, Nov. 25, 1947; s. Robert James and Lily B. (O'Kelly) M.; m. Verda Wilson Ingle, July 20, 1978; children: Joseph, Katherine. BA in Psychology, Randolph-Macon Coll., 1972; MA in Psychology, U. Richmond, 1976; EdD in Reading Edn., U. Va., 1980. Spl. edn. tchr. Culpeper (Va.) County Schs., 1974-76; assoc. prof. edn. Nat. Coll. Edn., Evanston, Ill., 1979-89; prof. edn. Appalachian State U., Boone, N.C., 1989—. Dir. reading clinic Nat. Coll. Edn., 1981-87, Appalachian State U., 1989—; dir. Howard St. Tutoring Program, Chgo., 1979-85; creator, cons. Early Steps Reading Intervention Program, various cities, 1987—. Author: Howard Street Tutoring Manual, 1999; contbr. articles to profl. jours. Mem. Nat. Reading Conf., Internat. Reading Assn. (Exemplary Reading Program award 1987), Internat. Dyslexia Assn. Avocations: basketball, football, baseball, fishing, blues music. Office: Appalachian State U Reading Clinic Boone NC 28608-0001

MORRIS, ROBERT GEMMILL, retired foreign service officer; b. Des Moines, July 20, 1929; s. Robert William and Iva May (Gemmill) M.; m. Beverly Schupfer, July 3, 1955; children: Robert William II, John Schupfer, Richard Edward. BS, Iowa State U., 1951; postgrad., Charles Francis U., Graz, 1951-52; MS, Calif. Inst. Tech., 1954; PhD, Iowa State U., 1957. Asst. prof. S.D. Sch. Mines and Tech., Rapid City, 1958-59, assoc. prof., 1959-62, prof., head dept. physics, 1962-68; phys. sci. officer Office of Naval Research, Washington, 1968-73, dir. electronics program, 1973 74; U.S. fgn. service officer U.S. Dept. State, Washington, 1974-78; counselor for sci. and technol. affairs U.S. Mission to OECD, Paris, 1978-82, U.S. Embassy, Bonn, Fed. Republic Germany, 1982-85; dep. asst. sec. of state for sci. and tech. affairs Washington, 1985-87; fgn. svc. officer U.S. Embassy, Buenos Aires, 1987-90, Madrid, 1990-92. Contbr. articles to profl. jours. Fulbright scholar, Austria, 1951; Swiss govt. fellow, Zurich, 1957. Fellow APS; mem. Am. Fgn. Service Assn.

MORRIS, ROBERT LOUIS, management consultant; b. Phila., Aug. 24, 1932; s. Joseph Aloysius and Philomena Mary Ellen (Clauser) M.; m. Elizabeth Marie Smyth, Sept. 10, 1955; children: Robert L., Thomas J., Lawrence F., Elizabeth M., Mary Ellen, Richard B. BS, Drexel U., 1955; MS, U. Pa., 1957; postgrad., U. Cin., 1965-66, U. Chgo., 1969-71. Group leader Proctor & Gamble Co., Miami Valley Labs., 1958-68; dir. computing svcs. rsch. & devel. divsn. Kraft, Inc., Glenview, Ill., 1968-71; dir. rsch. and process devel. Continental Baking Co., St. Louis and Rye, N.Y., 1971-77, v.p. tech. affairs, 1978-92; tech. dir. food and chem. products ITT, Inc., N.Y.C., 1977-78; pres. Mng. Tech., Inc., Williamsburg, Va., 1992—, Regu-Tech. Assocs., Inc., Lightfoot, Va., 1997—. Patentee in field. Bd. dirs. Fundacion Chile, Santiago, 1978-79, 83-85; mem. Greenwich Rep. Town Meeting, 1977. With AUS, 1957. NSF fellow, 1955-56, Wilson S. Yerger fellow, 1956-57. Fellow Am. Inst. Chem. Engrs.; mem. Assn. Rsch. Dirs., Indsl. Rsch. Inst. (bd. dirs. 1988-91), Am. Assn. Cereal Chemists, bd. dirs. Olde Towne Med. Ctr., Williamsburg, 2000—, vice chr. 2003-04, Ford's Colony Golf Club. Roman Catholic. Office: The MTI Group PO Box 679 Lightfoot VA 23090-0679 Office Phone: 757-258-9105. E-mail: rlmatmti@tni.net.

MORRIS, RONALD ANTHONY, county official; b. Wilmington, Del., Nov. 8, 1946; s. Elwood and Sophia (Ptak) M.; m. Barbara Marie Szostkowski, July 16, 1976. BS, U. Balt., 1970; MBA, Widener U., 1975. Cert. govt. fin. mgr. Cost acct. Atlas Chem. Industries, New Castle, Del., 1966-67; sr. cost acct. Bethlehem Steel Corp., Balt., 1967-70; sr. acct. J.K. Lasser & Co., CPAs, Wilmington, 1970-71; dep. dir. fin. City of Wilmington, 1971-74; acctg. supr. New Castle County, 1974-75, controller, 1975-80, budget and acctg. mgr., 1980-97, CFO, 1997—. Recipient Achievement award Nat. Assn. Counties, 1990, 92, 94, EXSL award Nat. Ctr. for Pub. Productivity, 1990, Award of Excellence, Nat. Assns. County Info. Officers, 1989. Mem. Del. Assn. Govtl. Fin. Officers (v.p. 1990-94), Am. Soc. Pub. Adminstrn., Del. Assn. for Pub. Adminstrn. (coun. mem. 1980-82), Govt. Fin. Officers Assn., U.S. and Can. (com. mem. 1989—, Fin. Reporting Achievement award 1981-2002, Disting. Budget Presentation award 1991-2002, award for Excellence 2004, Achievement award 2004), Am. Acctg. Assn., Nat. Assn. Accts., ICMA, New Castle County Econ. Devel. Coun., Rotary Club of Wilmington (Del.). Avocations: beach, classic cars, coins, currency. Business E-Mail: rmorris@co.new-castle.de.us.

MORRIS, RONALD LEW, oil and gas company executive; b. Jacksonville, Fla., Feb. 17, 1946; s. Joel and Lillian Morris; m. Lynda Lea Johnson, Jan. 1967 (div. Oct. 2000); children: Adria Jenny, Adam Poff; m. Yan Wang, Feb. 2001; children: Oliver Wang, Mattie Wang. BSc in Aero. Engring., U. Okla., 1970; MSc in Mech. Engring., Colo. State U., 1972. Project coord. Danish Undergrounds Consortium, Copenhagen, 1979-83; mgr. planning and econs. Texaco Ltd., London, 1983-84; drilling mgr., dist. engr. Texaco North Sea UK, Aberdeen, Scotland, 1984-89; portfolio evaluations mgr. Texaco USA, Midland, Tex., 1989-91; asst. gen. mgr. Texaco-Angola, Luanda, 1991-96; v.p., mng. dir. Texaco Exploration Myanmar Inc., Yangon, 1996-98; mng. dir. CACT-Ops. Group, Shekou, China, 1998—2001; gen. mgr. Ori Ox Energy Assocs. Ltd., Hong Kong, Beijing, 2001—. Chmn. bus. mgmt. seminar 7th Oil & Gas Conf., Beijing, 2000. Contbr. articles to profl. jours. Instr. Jr. Achievement and Young Astronauts, Midland, 1990-93; cub scout leader Boy Scouts Am., Aberdeen, 1986-88. Recipient Friendship award, Guangdong, China, 2001, Regional Svc. award, Soc. Petroleum Engrs. Asia Pacific, 2003. Mem. Am. C. of C., Soc. Petroleum Engrs. Avocations: golf, travel, pilot. Home: Dong Run Feng Jing Yuan 2-901 Beijing 100016 China Mailing: PMB 258 4096 Piedmont Ave Oakland CA 94611-5221

MORRIS, RUSTY LEE, architectural consulting firm executive; b. Glenwood Springs, Colo., Nov. 28, 1940; d. Raymond M. and Raylene Pearl Marie (Hendrick) Morris; m. Robert W. Sosa, Nov. 20, 1995; children: Thomas John, Michael Joseph (dec.), Michelle Renee Bentley. Student, York Christian Coll., 1974-75, U. Nebr., 1975-76, Mesa State Coll., 1992-95; BS in Orgnl. Mgmt. summa cum laude, Colo. Christian U., 1996; postgrad., Union Inst., 1996—; MS in Mgmt., Colo. Christian U., Cin., 1997; postgrad. in forensic criminology, Union Inst., Cin. Specialist comm. security Martin-Marietta Corp., Larson AFB, 1962-63; communications security specialist classified def. project Boeing Aerospace Div., Larson AFB, Wash., 1963-64; with F.W. Sickles div. Gen. Instrument Corp., Chicopee, Mass., 1965-68; adminstr. judicial affairs J. Arthur Hickerson, Judge, Springfield, Mass., 1969-71; researcher Mont. United Indian Assn., Helena, 1970-72; adminstrv. asst. Vanderbilt U. Hosp., Nashville, 1980-82; paid bus. supr. Sears Svc. Ctr., Grand Junction, Colo., 1987-89; founder, chief exec. officer Vast Spl. Svcs., Grand Junction, 1988—; courier U.S. Census Bur., Grand Junction, 1990; spl. program coord. Colo. Dept. Parks and Recreation, Ridgway, 1990-91. Acad. athletic program founder, coord. Mesa State Coll., 1992-93, math. and sci. rep., student govt., 1992—, athletic coun., 1993—, student health ctr. com., 1993—, faculty search com., 1993; founder, CEO Rolling Spokes Assn.; world cons. on archtl. contracts for structural and/or outdoor recreational facilities. Author: Abuse of Women with Disabilities, 1996. Vol. Easter Seals Soc., 1964-67, vol. instr. Adult Literacy Program, 1984-87; vol. T.V. host Muscular Dystrophy Assn. Am., 1975-94; bd. dirs. Independent Living Ctr., 1985-87, Handicap Awareness Week, 1989; trails com. Colo. State Parks and Outdoor Recreation, 1988—; condr. seminars Ams. With Disabilites Act, 1989—; cons. Bur. Reclamation, 1988—, Bur. Land Mgmt., 1989—; staff trainer Breckenridge Outdoor Recreation Ctr., 1989-90; emergency svcs. officer Colo. Civil Air Patrol, Thunder Mountain Squadron, 1989—; bd. dirs. Handicap Awareness, 1989; dir. com. Colo. State Trails Commn., 1989-90; mem. Dem. Nat. Com., 1991—; dist. com. Grand Junction Sch. Dist., 1992—; mem. Restore the Com., Avalon, 1993—; bd. dirs., presenter No. Colo. chpt. Colo. Orgn. of Victim Assistance; with victim assistance Mesa County Sheriff's Dept., 1993—. Recipient Hometown Hero award, 1993. Mem. AAUW, Internat. Platform Assn., Handicap Scholarship Assn. (bd. dirs. 1994, award 1993), Nat. Orgn. Victim Assistance (presenter 1988—), Nat. Coun. Alcoholism and Drug Abuse (vol. 1987—), Mother's Against Drunk Driver's (bd. dirs. Mesa County chpt., v.p. 1985—), Concerns of Policy Survivors, Club 20 of Western Colo. (mem. com. status), Great Outdoor Colo., Grand Junction C. of C., Grand Junction Symphony, Mus. Western Colo., Mesa State Coll. Geology Club, Toastmasters (Able Toastmaster, winner speech contests 1985-87). Home and Office: 1617 S Jean St Kennewick WA 99337-4173

MORRIS, SANDRA K. computer company executive; b. Paxtang, Pa., 1954; BS with honors and distinction, U. Del., 1976, MS, 1981; postgrad., U. Pa. Faculty mem. U. Del.; with RCA Corp. David Sarnoff Rsch. Ctr.; product mgr. Intel Corp., 1985, v.p. e-bus. group, 1999—2002; CIO, and V.P. Intel Corp, 2002—. Co-author: Multimedia Application Development Using Indeo video and DVI Technology, 1982. Office: Intel Corp PO Box 58119 2200 Mission College Blvd Santa Clara CA 95052-8119

MORRIS, SHARON HUTSON, city manager; BA in Home Econs., Calif. State U., 1976; MA in Urban Planning, UCLA, 1979. Legislative analyst So. Calif. Gas Co., L.A., 1983-86, dist. mgr., 1986-90, cmty. outreach coord., 1990; dir. intergovt. affairs South Coast Air Quality Mgmt. Dist., Diamond Bar, Calif., 1990-94; commr. Bd. Pub. Works City of L.A., 1994-96, dep. mayor Office of Mayor Richard J. Riordan, 1996-97, gen. mgr. Dept. Animal Regulation, 1997-98, exec. dir. Dept. on Disability, 1998—; alt. pub. mem. South Coast Air Quality Hearing Bd., 1998—. Mem. KCET cmty. adv. bd. Hollywood Cmty. Housing Corp. Recipient Outstanding Alumna award Calif. State U., L.A., 1997. Mem. Am. Assn. Blacks in Energy, Nat. Forum for Black Pub. Adminstrn., The Ethnic Coalition (bd. dirs.), Women of Color, Inc. (past co-presiding officer), Calif. League Conservative Voters (bd. dirs.), Alpha Kappa Alpha, Phi Kappa Phi. Office: City Los Angeles Dept Disability 700 E Temple St Rm 380 Los Angeles CA 90012-4046

MORRIS, STANLEY E. international financial consultant; b. Hayward, Calif., Feb. 17, 1942; s. Richard Ellsworth and Lavila (Gibson) M.; 1 child, Courtney. BA, San Jose State Coll., 1963; MA, Columbia U., 1967. Intern mgmt. HEW, Washington, 1968-71, dir. operational planning, 1971-73; dep. assoc. dir. Office Mgmt. and Budget, Washington, 1973-79; sr. fellow, lectr. U. Md., College Park, 1980-81; assoc. dep. atty. gen. U.S. Dept. Justice, Washington, 1981-83; dir. U.S. Marshals Svc., Washington, 1983-89; dep. dir. Office of Nat. Drug Control Policy, Exec. Office of the Pres., Washington, 1989-91; chief of staff Under Sec. of the U.S. Treasury, Washington, 1992-94; dir. Fin. Crimes Enforcement Network, Vienna, Va., 1994-98. Bd. mem. Transparency Internat., 1998—; cons., expert Coun. of Europe, 1998—. Recipient Sec.'s Spl. Citation HEW, 1973, Presdl. Meritorious Exec. award, 1983, Pres.'s award Nat. Sheriffs Assn., 1988, Presdl. Disting. Exec. award, 1996. Mem. Assn. Fed. Investigators (pres. 1991—).

MORRIS, STEPHEN BURRITT, marketing information executive; b. Morristown, N.J., Aug. 13, 1943; s. Grinnell and Cornelia Rogers (Kellogg) M.; m. Victoria Ann French, Feb. 18, 1967; children: Christopher Jackson, Robin Taylor BA, Yale U., 1965; MBA, Harvard U., 1969. With product mgmt. Gen. Foods Corp., White Plains, NY, 1969—83, gen. mgr. Maxwell House Coffee div., 1983-85, v.p., 1983-87, pres. Maxwell House div., 1986-87; founder, dir. Spectra Mktg. Systems Inc., Chgo., 1987-90; pres., CEO Vid Code Inc., Waltham, Mass., 1990-92; pres., CEO, Arbitron Inc., N.Y.C., 1992—. Bd. dirs. John B. Stetson Co. Trustee N.Y. Theatre Workshop, 1995; bd. dirs. Advt. Rsch. Found.; trustee David Parsons Dance Co., 2003. Served to 2d lt. USMCR, 1965-66. Avocations: tennis, gardening. Home: 300 Mt Holly Rd Katonah NY 10536-3546 Office: Arbitron Inc 142 W 57th St Fl 11 New York NY 10019-3397

MORRIS, STEPHEN OWENS, psychiatrist; b. Muncie, Ind., Jan. 17, 1948; s. Edmond Deny and Martha Jean (Owens) Morris. BA, Ind. U., 1970, MD, 1973. Diplomate Am. Bd. Psychiatry and Neurology, 1986. Intern Edward W. Sparrow Hosp., Lansing, Mich., 1973—74; staff psychiatrist Inst. of Living, Hartford, Conn., 1977—78, Maricopa Med. Ctr., Phoenix, 1978—94, Comcare/ABS/Value Options, 1994—2004; psychiatrist pvt. practice, Paradise Valley, 1985—. Mem.: Phoenix Psychiat. Coun., Am. Psychiat. Assn. Avocations: scuba diving, exercise, weightlifting, jet skiing. Office: 7125 E Lincoln Dr #214B Paradise Valley AZ 85253 Office Phone: 480-991-5015.

MORRIS, STEVEN LYNN, engineering consultant, retired career officer; b. Dallas, Dec. 7, 1952; s. William Ira and Alta Faye (McCarley) M.; m. Jacqueline Ann Fenter, July 30, 1977; children: Steven Sean, Michael Wayne. BS in Engring. Scis., USAF Acad., 1975; MS in Aero. Engring, Air Force Inst. Tech., 1980; PhD in Aerospace Engring., Tex. A&M U., 1989. Registered profl. engr., Tex. Commd. 2d lt. USAF, 1975, advanced through grades to lt. col., 1991, ret., 1999; assoc. prof., dep. head dept. aeronautics USAF Acad., Colo., 1989-99; engring. specialist SRS Techs., Colorado Springs, Colo., 1999-2000; sr. cons. Engring. Systems, Inc., 2000—. Named Outstanding Young Man Am., Jaycees, 1981. Fellow AIAA (assoc., flight mechanics tech. com. 1991-94, 98-2001, mem. applied aerodynamics tech. com. 2003—, dep. dir. for edn. region V 1992-94, dep. dir. for precoll. outreach region V 1998-2002); mem. USAF Acad. Assn. Grads., Soc. Automotive Engrs., Air Force Assn., Tex. A&M U. Assn. Former Students, Tau Beta Pi, Sigma Gamma Tau. Baptist. Avocations: running, photography, hiking. Home: 5331 Wells Fargo Dr Colorado Springs CO 80918 Office: Engring Systems Inc Ste 106 4775 Centennial Blvd Colorado Springs CO 80919 Office Phone: 719-535-0400. E-mail: slmorris@esi-co.com.

MORRIS, STEVLAND See **WONDER, STEVIE**

MORRIS, THERESA JANETTE (TJ MORRIS), vocalist, writer, composer, publishing executive; d. Nathaniel Burton Thurmond and Theresa Mae Bolton, Charlie E. Thomas (Stepfather), Louise Hotard (Stepmother); m. Thomas Ray Morris; children: Angela Dawn Parrish, Lauren Michelle Parrish, Stephanie Esther Parrish, Ginger Theresa-Fay Parrish. Student, Ill. Acad. of Bus. and Pub. Security, 1985—86. Cert. Naval health sci. and edn. U.S. Naval Acad. Hosp. Corps, Ill., 1985; Ill. Sec. of State, 1986, lic. comml. driver Okla., 1985. Investigator U.S. Adv. Commn. on Intergovernmental Resources, Birmingham, Ala., 1977—80; govt. gen. svc. investigator U.S. Navy, Honolulu, 1980—93; singer, songwriter self-employed, 1993—; founder Bluegrass Events, Inc., Beaver Dam, Ky., 2003—. Pub. rels. cons. American Culture Internat. Rels., Beaver Dam, Ky., 2002, ABC, TJ Morris Agy., Morris Prodns.; event prodr. Bluegrass Events, Inc.; event coord. Bill Monroe Found., 2002; author/biographer, investigative reporter, columnist Ohio County Messenger Newspaper, 2000—03; firearm tng. security officer Ill. Acad. of Bus./Pub. Security. Composer Bluegrass Train songs, (CDs) American Bluegrass Country Style, Bluegrass Mama, Blues Jukes, Uplifting America. Vol. various cmty. events. Named a Lucky 7 Founder, Entrepreneurial Life, 2003; recipient Artist of Hawaii award, State of Hawaii, 1989—93. Mem.: BMI, IBMA, The Rosine Assn. (assoc.; singer/musician 1995—2004, Vol. award 2003), Ohio County Ky. C. of C. (assoc.), Bill Monroe Found. (assoc. Vol. Svc. award 2002), SETI (corr.; vol. sci. 2002). Republican. Achievements include patents in field. Avocations: songwriting, arts. Home: 656 Carolyn Ln Beaver Dam KY 42320-9769 Office: ACIR/ABC mag Morris Agy 656 Carolyn Ln Beaver Dam KY 42320-9769 Office Phone: 270-691-3031. Personal E-mail: mstjmorris@aol.com. E-mail: acirl@aol.com.

MORRIS, THOMAS WILLIAM, symphony orchestra administrator; b. Rochester, N.Y., Feb. 7, 1944; s. William H. and Eleanor E. M.; m. Jane Allison, Aug. 7, 1965; children: Elisa L., Charles A., William H. AB, Princeton U., 1965; MBA, Wharton Sch. U. Pa., 1969. Adminstrv. asst., Ford Found. fellow for adminstrv. interns in arts Cin. Symphony, 1965-67; payroll clk. bus. office Boston Symphony Orch., 1969-71, asst. mgr. bus. affairs, 1971-73, mgr., 1973-78, gen. mgr., 1978-86, v.p. spl. projects and planning, 1986; pres. Thomas W. Morris and Co., Inc., Boston, 1986-87; exec. dir. Cleve. Orch., 1987—2004; artistic dir. Ojai Music Festival, 2004—. Chmn. policy com. Maj. Orch. Mgrs., 1977-79; chmn. orch. panel Nat. Endowment for Arts, 1979-80. Chmn. Cleve. Cultural Coalition, 1992-95; mem. Cleve. Bicentennial Commn., 1993-97; mem. bd. overseers Curtis Inst. Music, 1998—. Mem. Am. Symphony Orch. League (dir. 1977-79) Office: 2533 Fairmount Blvd Cleveland OH 44106

MORRIS, VALERIE, news correspondent; b. Phila. BA in journalism, San Jose State U.; M in broadcast journalism, Columbia U. Grad. Sch. Journalism. Morning drive anchor KCBS Radio, LA; anchor KCBS-TV, LA; researcher, gen. assignment reporter, anchor KRON-TV and KGO-TV, San Francisco; gen. assignment reporter, weekend anchor WPIX-TV, NY; joinged CNN, 1996; co-anchors CNNfn's The Flipside; anchor CNNfn's Smart Assets, 1996—. Recipient Three Calif. Emmy awards for breaking news events and special reports, Black Woman Yr. award, Outstanding Contbn. to Broadcasting award, Am. Women in Radio and TV, Award Courage, Nat. Orgn. Women. Mem.: Delta Sigma Theta. Office: CNN 5 Penn Plz Fl 20 New York NY 10001-1810 Office Phone: 212-714-7800.

MORRIS, VALERIE BONITA, performing arts administrator; b. Beverly, Mass., May 22, 1947; d. Glen Franklin and Helen (Benjamin) M.; m. Boris Bohun-Chudyniv, Jan. 7, 1975; children: Alexander, Anya. BA, Am. U., 1968; MA, U. Mich., 1972. Promotions dir. McCarter Theatre, Princeton, N.J., 1972-73; assoc. mgr. Jorgensen Auditorium, Storrs, Conn., 1973-74; dir. art mgmt., chair performing arts Am. U., Washington, 1974-98, chair faculty senate, 1989-91; dean Sch. Arts Coll. of Charleston, S.C., 1998—. Exec. editor Jour. Arts Mgmt., Law and Soc., 1982-88, 90—; co-editor: Future of the Arts, 1990, The Arts in an New Millennium, 2003. Bd. dirs. Everyday Theatre, Washington, 1990-93, The Support Ctr., 1980-98, The Theatre Lab, 1994—, Charleston Symphony, 1998—, ABC Project, 1999—, Scaae, 2000-, ICFAD, 2004—. Named one of Outstanding Women of Am., 1983. Mem. Assn. Arts. Adminstrv. Edn. (sec. treas. 1989-91, pres. 1997-98), Am. Coun. for Arts (rsch. adv. coun.), Assn. Performing Arts Presenters, Internat. Coun. Fine Arts Deans, Omicron Delta Kappa. Home: 710 Willow Lake Rd Charleston SC 29412-9164 Office: Coll of Charleston 66 George St Charleston SC 29424-1407 Office Phone: 843-953-8222. E-mail: morrisv@cofc.edu.

MORRIS, WILLIAM CHARLES, investor; b. St. Louis, Apr. 15, 1938; s. Barney Lockhart and Kathryn (Evers) M.; m. Susan VanAvery Follett, Aug. 26, 1961; children: Edward F., David L., Kenneth V. SB in Chem. Engring., MIT, 1960; MBA, Harvard U., 1963. Assoc. Mobil Chem. Co., N.Y.C., 1963-66; with Lehman Bros., NYC, 1967—84; chmn. Carbo Ceramics Inc., Dallas, 1987—, J&W Seligman & Co., Inc., N.Y.C., 1988—. Chmn. Tri-Continental Corp., NYC, 1988—, Seligman Group of Investment Cos., NYC, 1988—. Mng. dir. Met. Opera Assn., NY, 1995—, pres., CEO, 2003—; trustee Woods Hole (Mass.) Oceanog. Instn., 2001—. Ensign USCGR, 1961. Office: J & W Seligman & Co Inc 100 Park Ave New York NY 10017-5598

MORRIS, WILLIAM OTIS, JR., lawyer, educator, writer; b. Fairmont, W.Va., Dec. 2, 1922; s. William Otis and Flora Helois (Preston) M.; m. Hazel Irene Kolbus, May 28, 1948; children: Barbara Ann, Melinda Lou. Student, Fairmont State Coll., 1940-41; AB, Coll. William and Mary, 1944; LLB, U. Ill., 1946, JD, 1968; HDC, Nicholas Copernicus U., Torun, Poland, 1992; LLD, Fairmont State U., 2003. Bar: Va. 1945, Ill. 1946, U.S. Supreme Ct. 1949. Prof. bus. law U. Ill., 1947-55; assoc. prof. law Stetson U., 1955-58; prof. law W.Va. U., Morgantown, 1958-94, prof. emeritus law, 1994—. Vis. U. Vienna, Austria, Nat. U., Singapore, Nat. U., Seoul, Korea, U. Sydney, Australia, East China Inst. of Law and Politics, U. Thessaloniki, Greece. Author: Dental Litigation, 1972, 2d edit., 1977, The Law of Domestic Relations in West Virginia, 1975, Veterinarian in Litigation, 1976, Revocation of Professional License, 1985, Handbook of Dental Law, 1994, The Dentist's Legal Advisor, 1994; mem. bd. editors Jour. Law and Ethics in Dentistry, Med. Malpractice Prevention, Clin. Jour.; contbr. articles to profl. jours. Decorated Merit medal (Poland); recipient Spl. award Nat. U. Seoul, Old Guard Medallion Coll. William and Mary, 1994, Lifetime Achievement Award Dentistry, 1994. Fellow Cleve. Clinic Med. Inst.; mem. ATLA, Va. Bar, Ill. Bar, W.Va. Trial Lawyers Assn., Order of Coif, Order of White Jackets, Sir Robert Boyle Soc. Republican. Lutheran. Home: 644 Bellaire Dr Morgantown WV 26505-2421 Office Phone: 304-599-2664. E-mail: bajrmig@webtv.net.

MORRIS, WILLIAM SHIVERS, III, newspaper executive; b. Augusta, Ga., Oct. 3, 1934; s. William Shivers Jr. and Florence (Hill) M.; m. Mary Sue Ellis, Jan. 18, 1958; children: William Shivers IV, John Tyler, Susie Blackmar. AB in Journalism, U. Ga., 1956. Asst. to pres., pub. Southeastern Newspapers and Augusta Newspapers, 1956-60; v.p., dir. Savannah Newspapers, Inc. and Savannah News-Press, Inc., Ga., 1960-63, Southeastern Newspapers Corp., 1963-65, chmn. bd., CEO, Banner-Herald Pub. Co., Athens, Ga., 1965, Morris Comm. Corp., Augusta, Southwestern Newspapers Corp., N. Am. Publs., Inc., Fla. Pub. Co., Jacksonville; chmn. bd., CEO, pub. Augusta Chronicle, Athens Star, and Augusta Herald, Ga., 1966-94, Augusta Chronicle and Athens Star, Ga., 1966—; pub. Juneau Empire; CEO Morris Comm. Corp., Augusta, 1999—. Bd. dirs. Ga. Power Co., Atlanta, So. Co., Atlanta, AP. Trustee Augusta Coll. Found.; bd. regents Univ. System Ga., 1967-73. Capt. USAF, 1956-58. Hon. mem. Golden Quill Soc., 1960. Mem. Am. Newspaper Pubs. Assn., Southeastern Newspaper Pubs. Assn. (dir. 1966—), So. Newspaper Pubs. Assn., Internat. Press Inst. Presbyterian (elder). Clubs: Pinnacle (Augusta) (pres.); University (N.Y.C.); Oglethorpe (Savannah); Commerce (Atlanta). Office: Morris Communications Corp PO Box 936 Augusta GA 30903-0936 also: Amarillo Globe-News Div PO Box 2091 Amarillo TX 79166-0001

MORRISEY, MARENA GRANT, art museum administrator; b. Newport News, Va., May 28, 1945; BFA in Interior Design, Va. Commonwealth U., 1967, MA in Art History, 1970. With Orlando (Fla.) Mus. Art, 1970—, exec. dir., 1976—. Former v.p., chmn. mus. svcs. com., mem. ad hoc com. on collections sharing and long range planning com., past chmn. exhbns. and edn. com. Am. Fedn. Arts; former mem. nat. adv. coun. George Washington U. Clearinghouse on Mus. Edn.; former mem. accreditation com. Nat. Found. for Interior Design Edn. Rsch. Former mem. strategic planning adv. coun. Orange County Sch. Dist.; former mem. advt. rev. bd. BBB; former mem. Orlando Pub. Art Adv. Bd., Orlando Leadership Coun., Orlando Hist. Bldg. Commn.; mem. art selection com. Orlando Internat. Airport, former chmn.; former mem. bd. dirs. Sta. WMFE-TV; bd. dirs. New World Sch. of Arts; vol. Sister Cities of Orlando; mem. internat. arts and culture com. Metro Orlando Internat. Affairs Commn. Named Orlando's Outstanding Woman of Yr. in Field of Art; recipient Fla. State of Arts award. Mem. Am. Assn. Mus. (former mem. governing bd., accreditation commn., profl. stds. and practices com., internat. coun. of mus.), Assn. Art Mus. Dirs. (comm. and publs. com.), Southeastern Mus. Conf. (past pres.), Fla. Art Mus. Dirs. Assn. (past pres.), Fla. Assn. Mus. (former bd. dirs.), Greater Orlando C. of C. (past mem. steering com. Leadership Orlando), Jr. League Orlando-Winter Park, Rotary Club Orlando (program com. Orlando, membership com., chmn. fund. com., Paul Harris fellow). Office: Orlando Museum of Art 2416 N Mills Ave Orlando FL 32803-1483 Office Phone: 407-896-4231. E-mail: mgmorrisey@omart.org.

MORRISEY, MICHAEL A. health economics educator; b. Crookston, Minn., Mar. 20, 1952; s. Charles Arthur and Eleanor E. (LaFleur) M.; m. Elaine M. Mardian, Aug. 26, 1972; children: Michelle Ann, David Michael. BA, No. State U., Aberdeen, S.D., 1974; MA in Econs., U. Wash., 1975, PhD in Econs., 1979. Rsch. asst., specialist Battelle HARC, Seattle, 1976—79; sr. economist Am. Hosp. Assn., Chgo., 1979-85; sr. economist, asst. dir. Hosp. Rsch. & Ednl. Trust, Chgo., 1983-85; vis. scholar Northwestern U., Evanston, Ill., 1984-85; assoc. prof. U. Ala., Birmingham, 1985-88, prof., 1988—, disting. faculty investigator, 1999-2000; dir. Lister Hill Ctr. for Health Policy, Birmingham, 1990—. Dep. editor Med. Care, Cleve., 1987—96; mem. Pa. Mandates Benefits Rev. Panel, Harrisburg, 1987—, Ala. Task Force on Rural Health Care Crisis, 1989; mem. health svcs. devel. grants rev. com. Agy. for Health Care Rsch. and Quality, Rockville, Md., 1992—96; cons. in field. Author: Price Sensitivity in Health Care, 1992, Cost Shifting in Health Care, 1994, Managed Care and Changing Health Care Markets, 1998; mem. editl. bd. Health Svcs. Rsch., 1985-94, Health Affairs, 1998—, Jour. Gerontology, 1998-2001, Health Svcs. and Outcomes Rsch. Methodology, 1999—, Health Adminstrn. Press, 1999-2002, Med. Care Rsch. and Rev., 2000—; contbr. more than 120 articles to profl. jours. Recipient John D. Thompson prize in health svc. rsch., Assn. Univ. Programs in Health Adminstrn., 1991, UAB Pres. award for excellence in tchg., 2000—01; fellow, Employee Benefits Rsch. Inst.; grantee, Nat. Ctr. Health Svcs. Rsch., NIH, Agy. for Health Care Rsch. and Quality, Robert Wood Johnson Found.; Adj. scholar, Am. Enterprise

Inst., 2002—. Mem.: Internat. Health Econs. Assn. (treas. 1994—2000, sec.-treas. 2000—), Acad. Health (chmn. com. 2000), Am. Econ. Assn. Republican. Roman Catholic. Office: UAB Sch Pub Health Birmingham AL 35294-0022 Office Phone: 205-975-8966.

MORRISH, THOMAS JAY, golf course architect; b. Grand Junction, Colo., July 6, 1936; s. Wilbur Merle and Margaret Beula (Cronk) M.; m. Louise Ann Dunn, Apr. 2, 1965; children: Carter J., Kimberly L. Coder. AA, Mesa Coll., Grand Junction, 1956; BS in Landscape and Nursery Mgmt., Colo. State U., 1964. Golf course arch. Robert Trent Jones, Montclaire, N.J., 1964-67, George Fazio, Jupiter, Fla., 1967-69, Desmond Muirhead, Newport Beach, Calif., 1969-72, Jack Nicklaus, North Palm Beach, Fla., 1972-83; prin. Jay Morrish & Assocs. Ltd., Flower Mound, Tex., 1983—. Prin. golf course designs include: Troon Golf & Country Club, Scottsdale, Ariz., Las Colinas Sports Club, Irving, Tex., Mira Vista, Ft. Worth, Foothills Golf Course, Phoenix, Forest Highlands, Flagstaff, Ariz. (One of 100 Top Golf Courses in World, Golf mag., Golf Digest), Bentwater on Lake Conroe, Houston, Shadow Glen Golf Club, Olathe, Kans. (Best New Private Course, Golf Digest 1989), Troon North Golf & Country Club, Scottsdale (One of 100 Top Courses in U.S., Golf mag.), Harbor Club on Lake Oconee, Greensboro, Ga., Loch Lomond, Scotland, The Country Club of St. Albans, Mo., Broken Top, Bend, Oreg., Dauble Eagle Club, Galena, Ohio (one of Top 100 Courses in World, Golf Mag.), Buffalo Creek Golf Course, Rockwall, Tex., La Cantera, San Antonio (Best New Pub. Course of 1995, Golf Digest Mag.), numerous others. Edn. grantee State of Colo., 1961-64; Trans-Miss. golf scholar, 1962-64; named Architect of Yr. Golf World Mag., 1996. Mem. Am. Soc. Golf Course Archs. (pres. 2002), Dallas Safari Club. Republican. Avocation: hunting. Office: PO Box 271559 Flower Mound TX 75027-1559

MORRISON, ANNE DEINLEIN, law librarian; b. Balt., Md., July 3, 1962; d. John Frederick and Mary Katherine Kress Deinlein; m. Jeffrey Morrison, Nov. 7, 1992; children: Ian, Katherine. BA in English, Towson State U., 1980—84; MA in Legal & Ethical Studies, U. of Balt., 1990—94. Asst. libr. Piper & Marbury Law Firm, Balt., 1984—93; law libr. Semmes, Bowen & Semmes, Balt., 1994—95, Prince George's County Law Libr., Upper Marlboro, Md., 1997—. Pres. Law Libr. Assn. of Md., 1994—95. Editor: (newsletter) Law Libr. Assn. of Md. Newsletter. Coord. Girl Scouts of Ctrl. Md., Shipley's Choice, 2002—03. Mem.: State Ct. and County Law Libraries SIS (exec. bd. mem. 2003—), Law Libr. Assn. of Md., Spl. Libraries Assn., Am. Assn. of Law Libraries. Office: Prince George's County Law Libr 14735 Main St Rm 172 Upper Marlboro MD 20772 Business E-Mail: admorrison@co.pg.md.us.

MORRISON, ASHTON BYROM, pathologist, medical school official; b. Northern Ireland, Oct. 13, 1922; came to U.S., 1955; s. Samuel and Henrietta (Good) M.; m. Claire Morris, M.D.; 1 dau., Mary Claire. MB, Queen's U, Belfast, No. Ireland, 1946; PhD, Queens U., Belfast, No. Ireland, 1950, MD (hon.), 1988; MD, Duke U., 1946. Intern Royal Victoria Hosp., Belfast, 1947; asst. lectr. Queens U., 1947-52; registrar dept. exptl. medicine Cambridge U., 1952-55, dir. med. studies Corpus Christi Coll., 1954-55; assoc. Duke U., N.C., 1955-58; asst. prof. pathology U. Pa. Sch. Medicine, 1958-61; assoc. prof. U. Rochester Sch. Medicine, 1961-65; prof. pathology, chmn. dept. Rutgers U. Med. Sch., 1965-80; v.p. acad. affairs Eastern Va. Med. Authority, 1980-83; dean Eastern Va. Med. Sch., 1980-83; prof. pathology Robert Wood Johnson Med. Sch.-U. Medicine and Dentistry N.J., Camden, 1983-93; assoc. dean in charge Robert Wood Johnson Med Sch.-U. Medicine and Dentistry N.J., Camden, 1983-89, prof. pathology emeritus, 1993-96, prof. pathology and lab. medicine emeritus, 1997—; prof. pathology Ea. Va. Med. Sch., 1994—. 22nd Scott Heron lectr. Royal Victoria Hosp., Belfast, No. Ireland, 1978. Recipient Disting. Alumnus award Duke U. Med. Sch., 1987. Mem. Am. Assn. Investigative Pathologists (emeritus), Am. Physiol. Soc. (emeritus), Soc. Exptl. Biology and Medicine (emeritus), Am. Soc. Nephrology (emeritus). Home: 3518 Rue De Fleur Columbus OH 43221

MORRISON, BARBARA SHEFFIELD, Japanese translator and interpreter, consultant, educator; b. Morristown, N.J., Dec. 22, 1958; d. Barclay Morrison and Pauline Morison O'Gorman; m. Michael Missiras, Nov. 2, 1991. BA, Wesleyan U., 1980; postgrad., Middlebury Coll., 1983; MA in Japanese Lit., Columbia U., 1998; postgrad., U. N.D., 2001—. Mem. Bklyn. Waterfront Coalition, N.Y. Group Shows, 1985-91; real estate salesperson Huberth & Peters, Inc., N.Y.C., 1986-88, Joseph Hilton & Assoc., N.Y.C., 1989; real estate systems rsch. cons. N.Y.C., 1989-92; pres. Redgate, Minn., 1990—. Tchr. The Bus. English Ctr., Tokyo, 1980-83; bilingual adminstrv. asst. The Chiba Bank, Ltd., N.Y.C., 1985-86; adj. instr. langs. dept. Minn. State U., 1999; instr. English Composition U. N.D., 2001–. One woman show, Soho, N.Y., 1992, The Pyramid Gallery, Rochester, N.Y., 1993, Spirit Rm. Gallery, Fargo, N.D., 1999; translator: Coltrane: A Player's Guide to His Harmony, 1994, American House Styles: A Concise Guide, 1997, Abstracts for the Proposed Shinto Dictionary, 1999. Mem. Fargo Moorhead Heritage Soc. (sec. 2001–). Avocations: painting, gardening. Home and Office: 703 5th St S Moorhead MN 56560-3403 Business E-Mail: morrison@mnstate.edu.

MORRISON, BRUCE ANDREW, government executive, public affairs consultant; b. N.Y.C., Oct. 8, 1944; s. George and Dorothea A. (Meyer) M.; m. Nancy A. Wanat, Sept. 22, 1991; 1 child, Drew. S.B., MIT, 1965; MS, U. Ill., 1970; JD, Yale U., 1973; Litt.D. (hon.), Quinnipac Coll. Staff atty. New Haven Legal Assistance Assn., 1973-74, mng. atty., 1974-76, exec. dir., 1976-82; mem. 98th-101st Congresses from 3d Conn. dist., 1983-91; chmn. L.I. Sound Caucus, chmn. Third World Debt Caucus. Chmn. judiciary subcom. on immigration, refugees, and internat. law U.S. Ho. of Reps.; chmn. Fed. Housing Fin. Bd., 1995-2000; co-chmn. ad hoc com. on Irish affairs; mem. U.S. commn. on immigration reform, 1991-97; chair Irish Ams. for Clinton-Gore, 1992, 96; chair Ams. for a New Irish Agenda, 1993-95; vice chmn. GPC Internat., 2000-2001; chmn. Morrison Pub. Affairs Group, 2001-. Mem. Nat. Dem. Ethnic Coordinating Com.; bd. dirs. Rock Mountain Mut. Housing Assn., Alliance for Responsible Cuba Policy. Mem. ABA, Conn. Bar Assn., New Haven County Bar Assn., Am. Immigration Lawyers Assn. Democrat. Lutheran. Office: 6004 Onondaga Rd Bethesda MD 20816 Office Phone: 301-263-1142. Personal E-mail: b.a.m@att.net.

MORRISON, CHARLES E. think-tank executive; b. Billings, Mont., 1944; m. Chieko Hayashi; children: Karen, Erica, Kenneth, Douglas. BA in Internat. Studies, MA, PhD, Johns Hopkins U. Legis. asst. U.S. Senate, 1972-80; part-time sr. rsch. assoc. Japan Ctr. for Internat. Exch., 1980-92; asst. to pres. East-West Ctr., 1986-92, dir. program on internat. econs. and politics, 1992-95, pres., 1998—; chair U.S. Consortium of APEC Study Ctrs., 1996-98. Editor: Asia-Pacific Security Outlook books, 1997—; author: wide range of books, papers and analyses; widely quoted by major news media on issues of regional cooperation, internat. rels., U.S. Asia policy and trade policies, U.S.-Japan rels. Mem.: U.S. Asia Pacific Coun. (founding mem. 2003). Office: East West Ctr 1601 E West Rd Honolulu HI 96848-1601

MORRISON, CHERYL LYNN, petroleum engineer, project manager; b. Galveston, Tex., Mar. 12, 1953; d. John Lipuscek and Dorothy Eloise (Weed) Morrison. BS in Biology, U. Ala., Tuscaloosa, 1975, BS in Petroleum Engring., 1979. Assoc. ops. engr. Getty Oil Co., Mobile, Ala., 1979—82, prodn. engr. Kilgore, Tex., 1982—85; drilling engr. Mobil Oil Co., Lafayette, La., 1985—87, Houston, drilling supr., 1987—89; drilling rep. Chevron USA, Lafayette, 1989—90, Bakersfield, Calif., 1990—96, petroleum engr., 1996—99, project mgr., 1999—2000, Chevron Texaco, San Ramon, Calif., 2000—. Mem. Soc. Petroleum Engrs. (sec., treas., bd. dirs. 1979-), Tex. State Profl. Engrs. Methodist. Home: PO Box 2568 San Ramon CA 94583-7568 Office: Chevron Texaco Co 60901 Bollinger Canyon Rd San Ramon CA

MORRISON, CRAIG O. chemicals executive; Sr. operational and bus. mgmt. pos. GE Co., 1990—93; pres., gen. mgr. Van Leer, Inc., 1993—98, Alcan Pharm. and Cosmetic Packaging, divsn. Alcan, Inc., Millville, NJ, 1998—2002; pres., CEO Borden Chem., Columbus, Ohio, 2002—. Office: Borden Chemical 180 E Broad St Columbus OH 43215

MORRISON, DALE F. food company executive; b. N.D. BS in BA, U. N.D., 1971. With Gen. Foods, 1972-81, Pepsico, 1981-95, mng. dir. Walkers Smiths Snack Foods, pres. frito-Lay North, pres. Hostess Frito-Lay Can.; pres. Pepperidge Farm Campbell Soup Co., 1995-96, pres. internat. and specialty foods and sr. v.p., pres., CEO, 1997-2000. Bd. dirs. U. N.D. Found. Mem.: U. N.D. Alumni Assn. (bd. dirs.). Office: Campbell Soup Co Campbell Pl Camden NJ 08103-1799

MORRISON, DARREL GENE, landscape architecture educator; b. Orient, Iowa, June 20, 1937; s. Raymond Delbert and Rosy Christina (Mensing) M.; m. Dawna Lee Hauptman, June 29, 1963 (div. Sept. 1987); children: Jon David, Scott Darrel. BS in Landscape Architecture, Iowa State U., 1959; MS in Landscape Architecture, U. Wis., 1969. Landscape arch. Md. Nat. Capital Park and Plan Commn., Silver Spring, 1962-64, T.D. Donovan & Assocs., 1964-66, City Washington, 1966-67; rsch. asst. U. Wis., Madison, 1967-69, mem. faculty, 1969-83, John Bascom prof., 1978; dean environ. design U. Ga., Athens, 1983-92, prof. environ. design, 1992—2002, prof. emeritus, 2002—. Co-editor: Landscape Jour., 1981-88. With U.S. Army, 1960-62. Recipient Disting. Tchg. award U. Wis., 1976, Bracken medal Pa. State U., 1996, Tchg. award Am. Hort. Soc., 1998, Hutchinson medal Chgo. Hort. Soc., 1998; named Outstanding Educator, Coun. Educators in Landscape Architecture, 1977, 94. Fellow Am. Soc. Landscape Architects (v.p. 1987-89). Address: 3501 S Barnett Shoals Rd Watkinsville GA 30677-2240 E-mail: darrelmo@uga.edu.

MORRISON, DAVID, science administrator, researcher; b. Danville, Ill., June 26, 1940; s. Donald Harlan Morrison and Alice Lee (Douglass) Guin; m. Nancy Dunlap, June 19, 1966 (div. 1977); m. Janet L. Irick, Aug. 23, 1981. BA, U. Ill., 1962; PhD, Harvard U., 1969. Prof. astronomy U. Hawaii, Honolulu, 1969-88, vice chancellor rsch., 1983-85, dir. IRTF telescope, 1985-88; dep. assoc. adminstr. NASA Office Space Sci., Washington, 1981; chief space sci. divsn. NASA Ames Rsch. Ctr., Moffett Field, Calif., 1988-96, dir. astrobiology and space rsch., 1996—2001, chief scientist NASA Astrobiology Inst., 2001—. Pres. Astron. Soc. of the Pacific, San Francisco, 1982-84; chmn. Divsn. for Planetary Scis., Washington, 1980-81; councillor Am. Astron. Soc., Washington, 1982-85; pres. Internat. Astron. Union Commn. on Planets, 1991-94. Author: Exploration of the Universe, 1987, 91, 95, The Planetary System, 1988, 96, Cosmic Catastrophes, 1989, Exploring Planetary Worlds, 1993, Voyages Through the Universe, 1996; editor: Satellites of Jupiter, 1982; contbr. articles to profl. jours. Fellow AAAS, 1982, Com. for Sci. Investigation of Claims of Paranormal, 1983, Calif. Acad. Sci. Achievements include advanced research for Voyager and Galileo planetary exploration missions. Home: 14660 Fieldstone Saratoga CA 95070 Office: NASA Ames Rsch Ctr MS 240-1 Moffett Field CA 94035 Office Phone: 650-604-5094. Business E-Mail: dmorrison@arc.nasa.gov.

MORRISON, DAVID FRED, communications executive; b. Columbus, Ohio, Aug. 15, 1953; s. Fred Liew and Sophie Ann (Snider) M.; 1 child, Ian. BA, Stanford U., 1975; MBA, U. So. Calif., 1978. Sr. corp. planning analyst Tiger Internat., L.A., 1978-80, mgr. new bus. devel., 1980-81; dir. planning and controls Hall's Motor Transit Co., Mechanicsburg, Pa., 1981-82; mng. dir., gen. mgr. Consol. Freightways Export-Import Svc., San Francisco, 1984-86; asst. treas. McKesson Corp., San Francisco, 1987-90, treas., 1990-91; dir. strategic planning Consol. Freightways, Inc., Palo Alto, Calif., 1982-84, 86-87, v.p., treas., 1991-96; exec. v.p., CFO Consol. Freightways Corp., 1996-99; CEO The Ladder Group, 1999—. Bd. dirs. Am. Sports Inst., Mill Valley, Calif., 1992-99; trustee Ctrl. States Pension Fund, 1997-99. Fellow State of Calif., 1977, Commerce Assocs., 1977. Mem. Fin. Execs. Inst. (silver medal 1978), Turnaround Mgmt. Assn, San Francisco Treas. Club (pres.). Avocations: bicycling, scuba, skiing.

MORRISON, DONALD FRANKLIN, statistician, educator; b. Stoneham, Mass., Feb. 10, 1931; s. Daniel Norman and Agnes Beatrice (Packard) M.; m. Phyllis Ann Hazen, Aug. 19, 1967; children: Norman Hazen, Stephen Donald. BS in Bus. Adminstrn, Boston U., 1953, AM, 1954; MS, U. N.C., 1957; PhD, Va. Poly. Inst. and State U., 1960; MA (hon.), U. Pa., 1971. Mem. staff Lincoln Lab., M.I.T., 1956; cons. math. statistician NIMH, Bethesda, Md., 1956-63; mem. tech. staff Bell Labs., Holmdel, N.J., 1967; mem. faculty, dept. stats. Wharton Sch., U. Pa., 1963-99, prof. stats., 1973-99, chmn. dept., 1978-85, prof. emeritus, 2000—. Author: Multivariate Statistical Methods, 3d edit., 1990, Applied Linear Statistical Methods, 1983; editor: The American Statistician, 1972-75; assoc. editor: Biometrics, 1972-74; contbr. articles to profl. jours. Served with USPHS, 1956-58. NSF grantee, 1966 Fellow Am. Statis. Assn., Inst. Math. Stats.; mem. Internat. Statis. Inst., Royal Statis. Soc., B&M R.R. Hist. Soc., Nat. R.R. Hist. Soc., R.R. and Locomotive Hist. Soc., N&W Hist. Soc., Bridge Line Hist. Soc., N.E. Elec. Rwy. Hist. Soc. Democrat. Lutheran. Home: 118 E Brookhaven Rd Wallingford PA 19086-6327 E-mail: donaldm@wharton.upenn.edu.

MORRISON, DONALD GRAHAM, business educator, consultant; b. Detroit, Feb. 26, 1939; s. Roderick and Ethelyne (Murray) M.; m. Sherie Leaver, Sept. 12, 1964; children: Heather Margaret Felix, Tracey Michelle Oliva. BSM.E., MIT, 1961; PhD in Ops. Research, Stanford U., 1965. Instr. Stanford U., Calif., 1965-66, vis. prof., 1982-97; mem. faculty Columbia U., N.Y.C., 1966-87, prof., 1973-87, Armand G. Erpf prof. bus., 1985-87; William E. Leonard prof. Anderson Grad. Sch. Mgmt., UCLA, 1987—. Vis. prof. U. Calif., Berkeley, 1970-71; cons. in field, UCLA faculty athletic rep. to NCAA. Editor in chief Mgmt. Sci., 1983-90; founding editor Mktg. Sci., 1980-82. Elder Hitchcock Presbyn. Ch., Scarsdale, N.Y., 1978-84, Westwood Presbyn. Ch., L.A., 1991-94, 95-98; treas. Scarsdale Jr. H.S. PTA, 1977-78; acad. trustee Mktg. Sci. Inst., 1986-92; mem. Decision, Risk and Mgmt. Sci. rev. bd. NSF, 1989-91. Recipient Lifetime Achievement in Mktg. Rsch. Award, AMA, 2001, Disting. Educator of Yr. Award, McGraw-Hill/Irwin, 2002. Mem. Inst. Mgmt. Sci. (pres. 1990-92), Ops. Rsch. Soc. Am., Am. Statis. Assn. Presbyterian. Avocations: golf, jogging, bridge. Office: UCLA Anderson Grad Sch Mgmt 110 Westwood Plz Los Angeles CA 90095-0001

MORRISON, DONALD WILLIAM, lawyer; b. Portland, Oreg., Mar. 31, 1926; s. Robert Angus and Laura Calista (Hodgson) M.; m. Elizabeth Margaret Perry, July 25, 1953; children: Elizabeth Laura, Carol Margaret. BSE.E., U. Wash., 1946; LL.B., Stanford U., 1950. Bar: Oreg. 1950, Calif. 1950, N.Y. 1967, Ill. 1968, Ohio 1974. Assoc. Pendergrass, Spackman, Bullivant & Wright, Portland, 1950-57, ptnr., 1957-60; gen. atty. Pacific N.W. Bell, Portland, 1960-66; atty. AT&T, N.Y.C., 1966-68; counsel Ill. Bell Telephone Co., Chgo., 1968-74; v.p., gen. counsel Ohio Bell Telephone Co., Cleve., 1974-91; of counsel Arter & Hadden, Cleve., 1992—2003. Trustee Citizens League Rsch. Inst.; trustee, pres. Cleve. Chamber Music Soc.; trustee Cleve. Coun. on World Affairs; mem. adv. com. Cleve. Play House, Cleve. Bot. Garden; trustee Cleve. Archaeol. Soc., Archael. Inst. Am. With USN, 1943—50. Recipient various bar and civic appreciation awards. Mem. ABA, Ohio State Bar Assn., Bar Assn. Greater Cleve., Oreg. State Bar Assn., Calif. Bar Assn., Rowfant Club.

MORRISON, FRED BEVERLY, real estate consultant; b. Gt. Neck, N.Y., May 21, 1927; s. Fred B. and Beverly (Fitzgerald) M.; m. Janet Thornton Johnson, May 22, 1948; children— Jane, Susan, Martha, James, Ann, David. BA, Columbia U., 1948, LLB, 1951. Bar: D.C. 1952. Asst. gen. counsel ARC, Washington, 1951-54; nat. exec. sec., voluntary home mortgage program Housing and Home Fin. Agy., Washington, 1954-57; investment v.p. mortgages Met. Life Ins. Co., N.Y.C., 1957-67; pres. Lomas & Nettleton Co., Dallas, 1967-76; pres., CEO Western Mortgage Corp., L.A., 1976-78; exec. v.p. real estate industries div. Crocker Nat. Bank, L.A., 1978-84; pres. Pearce, Urstadt, Mayer & Greer, N.Y.C., 1984-89; real estate cons., 1989—. Bd. dirs. Guardian Life Ins. Co., MetLife Internat. Real Estate Equity Shares, Guardian Trust Co.; chmn. Fed. Nat. Mortgage Assn. Adv. Com., 1981. Mem. Mortgage Bankers Assn. Am. (gov. 1979-84). Clubs: Union League (N.Y.C.). Home: 947 Post Rd Wakefield RI 02879-7521

MORRISON, GAIL, internist, nephrologist, educator; BA in Biology, Chemistry magna cum laude, Boston U., 1967; MD, U. Pa., 1971. Diplomate Am. Bd. Med. Examiners, Am. Bd. Internal Medicine, Am. Bd. Nephrology. Instr. dept. continuing edn. Boston U., 1966-67; clin. fellow Harvard U., Boston, 1971-72; intern Beth Israel Hosp., Boston, 1971-72; jr. asst. resident Georgetown U. Hosp., Washington, 1972-73; staff physician clin. ctr. NIH, Bethesda, Md., 1973-74, staff assoc. Nat. Heart & Lung Inst., 1973-74; fellow in nephrology renal electrolyte sect. U. Pa. Hosp., Phila., 1974-76, rsch. fellow in nephrology renal electrolyte sect. NIH, 1975-76, asst. prof. medicine, 1982-83; from asst. prof. to assoc. prof. medicine U. Pa. Sch. Medicine, Phila., 1976-94, prof. medicine, 1994—; attending Phila. Vets. Adminstrn. Med. Ctr., 1976-77, U. Pa. Health Sys., 1996—. Asst. dir. dialysis unit U. Pa. Hosp., Phila., 1976-77, assoc. dir., 1977-82, dir. renal outpatient prog., 1976-82, dir. outpatient dialysis unit, 1979-84, acting dir. dialysis prog. for inpatient and outpatient dialysis units, 1981-82, dir., 1982-86; acad. coord. dept. medicine U. Pa. Hosp., Phila., 1985-96; assoc. chmn. dept. medicine for student edn. U. Pa. Sch. Medicine, Phila., 1986-96, acting assoc. dean for clin. curriculum, 1991, assoc. dean for clin. curriculum, 1991-95, vice dean for edn., dir. acad. progs., 1995—, mem. numerous acad., search, planning, steering, alumni, budget, nutrition coms., others; cons., advisor in field; presenter, co-dir., tchr., leader workshops, symposiums, confs. Author: (with A. Goroll) Core Medicine Clerkship: A Curriculum Guide, Manual for Curriculum 2000, 1996; editor: (with others) Introduction to Clinical Medicine, 2d rev. edit., 1995, Concepts in Basic Science, 1995, Essentials of Nutrition: A Case-Based Approach, 1995; mem. editorial bd. Am. Jour. Medicine, 1996-99; author papers, reviews, abstracts, chpts. to books; contbr. articles to profl. jours. Grantee Pa. Sch. Nursing, 1989-90, Heinz Endowment Fund, 1990-95, U. Pa. Sch. Medicine, 1993-95, 93-96, 97-98. Fellow ACP, Coll. Physicians of Pa. (mem. sect. on pub. health and preventive medicine 1995—); mem. AAAS, Internat. Soc. Nephrology, Am. Soc. Nephrology, Am. Fedn. for Clin. Rsch., Am. Assn. Med. Colls. Women's Liaison Officer, Pa. Soc. Nephrology (coun. mem. network #24 federally funded end-stage renal disease orgn. 1978-83, mem. facility planning bd. 1979-80, chmn. 1980-82, mem. exec. com. 1980-82, ad-hoc mem. med. review bd. 1980-82, mem. nomination and credential com. 1982-83), Southeastern Nat. Kidney Found. (bd. dirs. 1984-88), Phi Beta Kappa, Sigma Xi, Alpha Omega Alpha. Home: 1040 Stony Ln Gladwyne PA 19035-1136 Fax: 215-573-4289. Office Phone: 215-898-8034.

MORRISON, GARY RAY, instructional technology educator, researcher; b. Bedford, Ind., Nov. 17, 1948; s. Glenn Molar and Betty Ann Morrison. BS in Edn., Ind. U., 1971, EdD, 1977. Instrnl. designer U. Mid-Am., Lincoln, Nebr., 1976-78, Solar Turbines Internat., San Diego, 1978-80, GE Corp. Consulting Group, Bridgeport, Conn., 1980, Tenneco Oil Co. E&P, Houston, 1980-84; prof. U. Memphis, 1984-98, Wayne State U., Detroit, 1998—. Author: Designing Effective Instruction, 4th edit., 2000 (L.C. Larson award 1995), Integrating Computer Technology in the Classroom. Mem. Assn. Ednl. Comm. and Tech. (pres. rsch. and theory div. and div. instrnl. design), Am. Ednl. Rsch. Orgn. Office: Wayne State Univ 399 Edn Detroit MI 48202 E-mail: Gary_Morrison@wayne.edu.

MORRISON, GLENN, neurosurgeon; b. Phila., June 16, 1940; married, 3 children. AB, Colgate U., 1962; MD, Case Western Reserve U., 1967; postgrad., Nat. Comm. Disease Ctr., 1968. Diplomate Am. Bd. Neurological Surgery, Am. Bd. Pediatric Neurological Surgery. Intern Cleve. Met. Hosp., 1968; resident in neurosurgery Univ. Hosps. Cleve., 1970-74; with Neurosurg. Assocs., Coral Gables, Fla., 1974-85, Baptist Hosp., Miami, 1974—; pvt. prac. Coral Gables, 1985—2000; chief pediatric neurological surgery Miami Children's Hosp., 1986—. Prof. dept. neurological surgery, U. Miami Sch. Med., dir. pediat. neurosurg. alliance; cons. divsn. children's med. svcs. state of Fla. Lt. Cmdr. USPHS, 1968-70. Recipient Nat. Found. Rsch. award, 1967. Fellow ACS (sec., treas. greater Miami chpt. 1979-83, pres. 1983-85, interview com. 1980—); mem. AMA, Am. Assn. Neurol. Surgeons, Congress Neurol. Surgeons, Am. Acad. Pediats., Am. Heart Assn., Neurol. Soc. Am., Internat. Soc. Pediat. Neurosurgery, So. Neurosurg. Soc. (v.p. 1989-90, treas. 1992-95, pres. 1996-97), Fla. Neurosurg. Soc. (pres. 1982), Greater Miami Neurosurg. Soc. (pres. 1978), numerous others. Office: Miami Children's Hosp 3200 SW 60th Ct Ste 301 Miami FL 33155-4071 Office Phone: 305-662-8386.

MORRISON, GLENN LESLIE, minister; b. Cortez, Colo., Feb. 26, 1929; s. Ward Carl Morrison and Alma Irene (Butler) Anderson; m. Beverly Joanne Buck, Aug. 26, 1949; children: David Mark, Betty Jo Morrison Mullen, Gary Alan, Judith Lynn Morrison Oltmann, Stephen Scott. Student, San Diego State U., 1948-49, Chabot Coll., 1968-69. Ordained ministry Evang. Ch. Alliance, 1961. Dir. counseling follow-up Oakland (Calif.) Youth Christ, 1954-56; pres. Follow Up Ministries, Inc., Castro Valley, Calif., 1956—. Assoc. pastor 1st Covenant Ch., Oakland, 1956-58; exec. dir. East Bay Youth Christ, Oakland, 1960-66; supervising chaplain Alameda County (Calif.) Probation Dept., 1971-90; vol. chaplain Alameda County Sheriff's Dept., 1971—; founder, dir. God Squad Vol. Program Prison Workers, 1972—; seminar leader Calif. Dept. Corrections, Sacramento, 1978—, mem. chaplains coordinating com., 1988—. Author: Scripture Investigation Course, 1956. Mem. Am. Correctional Assn., Am. Protestant Correctional Chaplains Assn. (regional pres., sec. 1980-86, nat. sec. 1986-88, nat. 2nd v.p. 1996-98). Office: Follow Up Ministries Inc PO Box 2514 Castro Valley CA 94546-2514 Personal E-mail: fumi2000@msn.com.

MORRISON, GORDON MACKAY, JR., investment company executive; b. Boston, Jan. 18, 1930; s. Gordon Mackay and Alice (Blodgett) M.; m. Barbara J. Lee, June 15, 1954; children: Lee (dec.), Leighton, Faith. AB, Harvard U., 1952, MBA, 1954. Regional mgr. Bankers Leasing Corp., Boston, 1965-68; portfolio mgr. Loomis, Sayles and Co., Boston, 1969-71; sr. v.p. Ft. Hill Investors Mgmt., Boston, 1972-75; chmn. bd. Bradford Gordon Inc., Boston, 1977—2001; gen. ptnr. Bradford Gordon Ptnrs., Boston, 1977—. Trustee East Boston Savs. Bank, 1962-91; trustee Meridian Fin. Svcs., Inc., 1991-2002, hon. trustee, 2002–. Bd. dirs. The New Eng. Hosp., 1961-96, emeritus, 1996—. Republican. Congl. Club: Harvard. Lodge: Masons. Home: 5 Neptune Ln Biddeford ME 04005-9594 Office: Bradford Gordon Ptnrs 50 Congress St Boston MA 02109-4027

MORRISON, GREGORY BERNARD, information systems specialist; b. Washington, Dec. 19, 1959; s. Carl Edward and Evelyn Patricia (Goodwin) M.; m. Patrice Hinton, May 20, 1981 (div. June 1989); children: Krystina, Michael, Matthew; m. Debra Dobson, 1993. BS in Math. and Physics magna cum laude, S.C. State U., 1982; MS in Indsl. Engring., Northwestern U., 1987. Mgr. info. svcs. Prudential Ins. Co. Am., Newark, 1989-90, dir. and group systems exec., 1990-93, dir. info. svcs. Roseland, NJ, 1993—2000, v.p. info. svcs., 2000—02; COO RealEstate.com, 2000; v.p., chief info. officer Cox Enterprises, Inc., Atlanta, 2002—. Bd. dirs. Met. YMCA, West Orange, N.J., 1990—, Minority Interchange, Inc., Newark, 1989-93. Capt. U.S. Army, 1982-89. Fellow U.S. Army, 1986. Mem. Ops. Rsch. Soc. Am., 100 Black Men N.J., Masons, Phi Beta Sigma. Avocations: golf, gardening. Home: 2718 Bonar Hall Path Duluth GA 30097-7462 Office: Cox Enterprises Inc 6205 Peachtree Dunwoody Rd Atlanta GA 30328*

MORRISON, GUS (ANGUS HUGH MORRISON), mayor, engineer; b. Buffalo, Sept. 13, 1935; s. John Weir and Mary (Norton) Morrison; m. Joy Rita Hallenbarter, Feb. 7, 1959; children: Frank, Gloria, Heather. Technician Bell Aircraft Corp., Niagara Falls, N.Y., 1956-58, Lockheed Missiles and Space Corp., Sunnyvale, Calif., 1958-63, test engr., 1963-78, group engr., 1978-86, dept. mgr., 1985—89; ret., 1994. Mayor Fremont, Calif., 1985-99, 94—, council mem., 1978-85, 91-94, planning commr., 1977-78; bd. dirs. Tri City Ecology Ctr., 1976—. Served with USN, 1953-56. Democrat. Roman Catholic. Avocations: computers, photography, seriography. Office: Office Mayor PO Box 5006 Fremont CA 94537-5006

MORRISON, H. ROBERT, municipal official; b. Pitts., Apr. 7, 1938; s. Hugh and Gertrude Mary (Gehenio) Morrison; m. Meredith Wollenberg, Dec. 8, 1979; children: Hugh Robert Jr, Justin William, Elizabeth Jeanne. BA in English, Howard U., 1969. Master govt. treas. Writer Nat. Geog. Soc., Washington, 1969-73, editor ednl. filmstrips, 1973-77, sr. writer, 1977-88, mng. editor nat. geography bee, 1988-89; elected treas. City of Falls Church,

Va., 1993—. Bd. dirs. Falls Church Cable Access Corp., pres., 1990—93; bd. dirs. Tinner Hill Heritage Found.; exec. bd. dirs. Tapestry Theatre, Alexandria, Va. Contbg. author: book As We Live and Breathe, 1971, The Ocean Realm, 1978, America's Majestic Canyons, 1979, Mysteries of the Ancient World, 1979, America's Magnificent Mountains, 1980, America's Hidden Corners, 1983, Exploring America's Valleys, 1984, America's Seashore Wonderlands, 1985; co-author: America's Atlantic Isles, 1981. Vice chmn. Falls Church Dem. Com., 1988—89, 1998—99. With U.S. Army, 1961—64. Mem.: NAACP, Treas. Assn. Va. (bd. dirs. 1996—97), Clan Morrison N.Am. (life), St. Andrew's Soc. Washington. Avocations: reading, personal computing, photography, TV production, historic preservation. Home: Bonnie Briar 502 Walden Ct Falls Church VA 22046-2628 Office: City Hall 300 Park Ave Falls Church VA 22046-3332 Personal E-mail: hbobm@aol.com. Business E-Mail: fctreas@aol.com.

MORRISON, HARRIET BARBARA, retired education educator; b. Boston, Feb. 23, 1934; d. Harry and Harriet (Hanrahan) M. BS, Mass. State Coll., 1956, MEd, 1958; EdD, Boston U., 1967. Elem. tchr. Arlington (Mass.) Pub. Schs., 1956-67; instr. U. Mass., 1967; asst. prof. edn. No. Ill. U., Dekalb, 1967-71, assoc. prof., 1971-85, prof., 1985-97; ret., 1997. Author: The Seven Gifts, 1988; editor Vitae Scholasticae. Mem. ASCD, Am. Ednl. Studies Assn., Philosophy of Edn. Soc., Midwest Philosophy Edn. Soc., Ill. ASCD, Pi Lambda Theta. Home: 834 S 8th St Dekalb IL 60115-4551

MORRISON, HARRY, chemistry professor; b. Bklyn., Apr. 25, 1937; s. Edward and Pauline (Sommers) M.; m. Harriet Thurman, Aug. 23, 1958; children: Howard, David, Daniel. BA, Brandeis U., 1957; PhD, Harvard U., 1961. NATO NSF postdoctoral fellow Swiss Fed. Inst., Zurich, 1961-62; rsch. assoc. U. Wis., Madison, 1962-63; asst. prof. chemistry Purdue U., West Lafayette, Ind., 1963-69, assoc. prof., 1969-76, prof., 1976—, dept. head, 1987-92, dean Sch. Sci., 1992—2002. Mem. acad. adv. com. Indsl. Rsch. Inst., 1993-96. Contbr. numerous articles to profl. jours. Bd. fellows Brandeis U. Mem. Am. Chem. Soc., Am. Soc. Photobiology, Inter-Am. Photochem. Soc., Coun. for Chem. Rsch. (chmn. 1995), Phi Beta Kappa, Sigma Xi. Office: Purdue Univ Dept Chemistry Brown Bldg West Lafayette IN 47907-2084 Office Phone: 765-494-5246. Business E-Mail: hmorrison@purdue.edu.

MORRISON, JAMES FRANK, optometrist, state legislator; b. Colby, Kans., Apr. 11, 1942; s. Lloyd Wayne and Catherine Louise (Beckner) M.; m. Karen Jean Carr, Aug. 25, 1963; children: Mike, Jeff, Scott. Student, U. Kans., 1960-64; BS, OD, So. Coll. Optometry, 1967. Pvt. practice, 1969-75; founder, chief staff N.W. Kans. Ednl. Diagnostic and Referral Ctr. Children, Inc., Colby; asst. chief engr. Sta. KXXX-FM, 1977-80, chief engr., 1980-82; prof. vision dept. Colby Community Coll., 1979-84; mem. Kans. Ho. Reps., Topeka, 1992—. Cubmaster pack 140 Cub Scouts Am., 1970-80, dist. chmn., 1977-79. Fellow Am. Acad. Optometry, Coll. Optometrists in Vision Devel.; mem. Am. Optometric Assn., Am. Soc. Broadcast Engrs., Kans. Soc. Broadcast Engrs. (founder, pres. 1970-71), Kans. Optometric Assn., Kans. Assn. Children with Learning Disabilities, Mo. Optometric Assn., Thomas County Assn. Retarded Children, Rotary, Lions, Kiwanies (pres. 1971-72), Masons, Shriners. Rotary. Mem. Assemblies of God. Ch. Avocations: amateur radio, photography, astronomy. Home: 3 Cottonwood Dr Colby KS 67701-3902 Office: Morrison Optometric Assocs 180 W 6th St Colby KS 67701-2315

MORRISON, JAMES FREDERICK, management consultant; b. Evanston, Ill., Aug. 12, 1933; s. Paul Leslie and Carolyn Lola (Rosemeier) M.; m. Myra Val Wokoun, June 22, 1957; children: Myra Hollie Morrison Nielsen, Cynthia Leslie Morrison. BA, Northwestern U., 1955, MBA, 1958. CPA Wis. Accounting mgr. Froedtert Malt Corp., Milw., 1958-61; asst. controller, asst. v.p. Northwestern Nat. Ins. Co., Milw., 1961-65; controller Eutectic Welding Alloys Corp., Flushing, NY, 1965-68; internal auditor Sterling Drug, NYC, 1968-69; controller Internat. Flavors and Fragrances, NYC, 1970-76, mng. dir., v.p. Europe London, 1977-80, v.p. new bus. group U.S. NYC, 1981-84, v.p. export and communications U.S. Hazlet, NJ, 1984-96, cons., 1996—99. Instr. fin. Marquette U., 1960—65. Co-chmn. Milw. Festival of Arts, 1965; treas. Manhasset Student Aid Assn., 1970—71; mem. Manhasset Bd. Edn., NY, 1970—75, v.p., 1975, United Fund Manhasset, 1971—72; elder First Presbyn. Ch., Red Bank, NJ, 1996—2000, 2003—; pres. bd. trustees First Presbyn. Ch., Red Bank, 1997—2000; chmn. priorities com. United Way Monmouth County, 1992—93, strategic planning com., 1995—97, bd. dir., 1991—99, Monmouth Ocean Found. for Ednl. Enhancement, 1996—2002. Lt. USAF, 1955—57, lt. USAFR, 1958—68. Mem. AICPA, Fin. Exec. Inst. (pres. L.I. chpt. 1975-76), Internat. Trade Facilitation Coun. (vice-chmn. 1991-92), Wis. Soc. CPA's, Internat. Commerce Club NJ, Systems and Procedures Assn. (pres. Milw. chpt. 1965), Culver Acad. Alumni Club Milw. (pres. 1965), Internat. Sr. Amateur Golf Soc. (treas. 1998—), Eastern Sr. Golf Assn. (treas. 1994-98, 2d v.p. 1999-2000, 1st v.p. 2000-02, pres. 2002—, internat. team capt. 1994-2001), Rumson Country Club (bd. dir. 1996—), Beta Gamma Sigma. Presbyterian. Avocations: golf, travel. Home and Office: 124 Silvermist Ct Little Silver NJ 07739-1813

MORRISON, JAMES R. retired banker; b. Duluth, Minn., May 1, 1924; s. Earl Angus and Jessie (McLean) M.; m. Clarice Mae Wolf, June 5, 1949; children— Kenneth, Alan, Jane, Richard MBA, U. Chgo., 1976. Br. mgr. Parkersburg State Bank, Iowa, 1947-49; asst. cashier Bank of Sparta, Wis., 1949-50; cashier Tobacco Exchange Bank, Edgerton, Wis., 1950-53; sr. v.p. Fed. Res. Bank Chgo., 1953-89, ret. Bd. dirs. Bank of Tokyo-Mitsubishi Chgo., 1994-98; chmn. subcom. on credits and discounts Fed. Res. Sys., Chgo., 1984-86; mem. Mt. Prospect Fin. Commn., 1989-2001. Served with U.S. Army, 1943-46, ETO Home: 13590 Crosscliffe Pl Rosemount MN 55068-3557

MORRISON, JAMES WILLIAM, JR., lobbyist, government relations consultant; b. Bluefield, W.Va., Jan. 14, 1936; s. James William and Winnie Ella (Hendricks) M.; m. Marva Elizabeth Tillman, Aug. 8, 1957 (div.); children: Traquita Renee, James William III; m. Jean Murray Barber, May 15, 2001; 1 stepchild, Susannah Claire. BA, W.Va. State Coll., 1957; MPA, U. Dayton, 1970. Inventory mgr. Dayton Air Force Depot/Def. Electronics Supply Ctr., 1959-63; mgmt. specialist Air Force Logistics Command, Dayton, 1963-72; exec. asst. to dir. mgmt. sys. NASA, Washington, 1972-74; sr. mgmt. assoc. Exec. Office of Pres. Office Mgmt. and Budget, 1974-79; asst. dir. econ. and govt. U.S. Office of Pers. Mgmt., 1979, dir. congl. rels., 1979-81, assoc. dir. compensation, 1981-87; sr. mgt. CNA Ins. Co., 1987-88; pres. Morrison Assocs., 1988—. Vis. lectr. pub. exec. project SUNY Albany, 1974-76. Contbr. articles to profl. jours. Mem. adv. com. Dayton Bd. Edn., 1971. With U.S. Army, 1957-59. Recipient Presdl. Rank award of Disting. Exec., 1985. Mem. Alpha Phi Alpha, Pi Delta Phi, Pi Alpha Alpha. Republican. Presbyterian. Home: 35056 N 80th Way Scottsdale AZ 85262 Office Phone: 480-515-2859. Personal E-mail: jwmorrison@cox.net.

MORRISON, JELENA, technologist, educator; d. Johanna Gertrude and Vid Spacoje Savic. BS(hon.), N.E. Ill. U., 1973, M in Math. Edn., 1989. Edn. K-9 Ill., 1973, edn. 9-12 Ill., 1979, bilingual edn. Ill., 1993, ESL edn. Ill., 1993. H.s. math tchr. Ctrl. Jr. H.S., Evergreen Park, Ill., 1973—79, Proviso East H.S., Maywood, Ill., 1979—99; instrnl. technologist Proviso West H.S., Hillside, Ill., 1999—. Workshop presenter - tchr. topics Proviso Twp. 209, Maywood, Ill., 1999—; writer ednl. curriculum Proviso Twp. H.S., Hillside, Ill., 1999—; sch. photographer Proviso West H.S., Hillside, Ill., 2000—; home schooling instr. U. Nebr.-Lincoln, 2002—. Filmmaker (animated short film) The Insect Reaction (Best Film, 1992). Walk animals mem. Humane Farming Assn., Chicago, 2003. Named 1 of Top 10 Tchrs. in US nat. TV documentary, Arnold Shapiro Prodns., 1984, featured spkr. Channel 5 More You Know Edn., Channel 5 Nat. TV, 1984; recipient Larry Schlessbauer Tech. award, West 40 Ednl. Ctr., 1988, 2001. Mem.: Ill. Fedn. Tchrs. Avocations: photography, filmmaking, dance, designing costumes. Home: 3228 N Newland Chicago IL 60634 Office: Proviso W HS 4701 W Harrison St Hillside IL 60162 Office Phone: 708-202-6220. Home Fax: 708-449-3636. Personal E-mail: jxm73@hotmail.com.

MORRISON, JOHN HADDOW, JR., engineering company executive; b. Bozeman, Mont., Aug. 24, 1933; s. John Haddow Sr. and Rosalie (Lehrkind) M.; m. Shirley Easbey, Sept. 11, 1954; children: Robert, Richard; m. Minh Le, Apr. 25, 2001. BS, Mont. State U., 1955. Registered profl. engr., Mont., Ariz., Calif.; registered land surveyor, Mont. Project engr. Morrison-Maierle, Inc., Helena, Mont., 1957—64, chief airport design, 1964—73, chief exec. officer, 1973—88, chmn., 1998—2000, dir. emeritus, 2000—; pres. Morrison-Maierle Ariz. Inc., Helena, 2000—02. Bd. dirs. Mont. State U. Found., Inc., 1983—, chmn. 1992-94; sec.-treas. Helena YMCA, 1977-80. With U.S. Army 1955-57. Mem. ASCE (pres. Mont. sect. 1971-72), NSPE (pres. Helena chpt. 1968-69, Outstanding Young Engr., Helena chpt. 1965), Cons. Engrs. Council Mont. (past sec., past v.p., pres. 1986-87). Lodges: Kiwanis, Masons. Methodist. Avocations: golf, photography. Home: 2415 E Windsong Dr Phoenix AZ 85048 Office: Morrison-Maierle Inc Ste 201 80 E Rio Salado Pkwy Tempe AZ 85281-9108 E-mail: jmorrison@m-m.net.

MORRISON, JOHN HORTON, lawyer; b. Sept. 15, 1933; BBA, U. N.Mex., 1955; BA, U. Oxford, 1957; JD, Harvard U., 1962. Bar: Ill. 1962, U.S. Supreme Ct. 1966. Assoc. Kirkland & Ellis, Chgo., 1962-67, ptnr., 1968-99. Named Hon. Officer Most Excellent Order Brit. Empire, 1994; Rhodes scholar. Mem. ABA, Internat. Arbitration (arbitrator, mediator London Ct.), Internat. Bar Assn., Assn. Am. Rhodes Scholars (pres. 1998—), Chgo. Internat. Dispute Resolution Assn. (dir.). Home: 2717 Lincoln St Evanston IL 60201-2042 Personal E-mail: johnhmorrison@post.harvard.com. Business E-Mail: jmorrison@kirkland.com.

MORRISON, JOHN M. bank executive; Owner, CEO Ctrl. Bank Group, Golden Valley, Minn.; interim chmn., CEO Allina Health Sys., 2001—02, bd. chmn., 2004—. Mem. Fairview U. Med. Ctr. Bd., Fairview Health Sys. Corp. Bd.; chmn. exec. com. bd. trustees U. St. Thomas; former mem. bd. govs., chmn. bd.'s fin. com. U. Minn. Acad. Health Ctr.; former mem. Johns Hopkins Medicine bd. visitors Johns Hopkins U. Mem.: U. St. Thomas Sch. Law (mem. bd. govs., founder John. M. Morrison Ctr. Entrepreneurship). Office: Allina Hosps and Clinics 710 E 24th St Minneapolis MN 55404

MORRISON, K. JAYDENE, education counseling firm executive; b. Cherokee, Okla., Aug. 22, 1933; d. Jay Frank and Kathryn D. (Johnson) Walker; m. Michael H. Morrison, July 11, 1955 (dec. 1991); children: Jay, Mac. BS, Okla. State U., 1955, MS, 1957; postgrad., U. Colo., 1965, Ctrl. State U., Okla., 1967—70, postgrad., 1984, U. Denver, 1981—82. Lic. coun. Okla., marriage and family therapist, cert. sch. psychologist, counselor. Psychologist Cushing Pub. Schs., Okla., 1955—57, Indpls. Pub. Schs., 1958—59; counselor, tchr. spl. edn. Helena-Goltry Pub. Schs., Okla., 1965—73; psychometrist Okla. State Title III Program, Alva; sch. psychologist Okla. State Dept. Edn., Enid, 1977—85; pres., dir. Ventures in Learning, Inc., Helena, 1984—. Career counselor, Oklahoma City, 1985—86; rural specialist Okla. Conf. Chs. AG LINK, 1986—88; v.p., sec./treas. Okla. Made, Inc., Oklahoma City, 1988—89; sch. psychologist Okla. City Pub. Schs., 1988—93; therapist and pub. sch. liason Chisholm Trail Counseling Svc., 1993—95; coord. Statewide Farm Stress Program, 1994—95; therapist Greenleaf Drug/Alcohol Rehab., 1988—89; sec., treas. Okla. Pure; part-time counselor Clayton Clinic, 1987—89; cons. Okla. Family Inst., 1990—93; with Dept. Edn. Behavior Mgmt. Ctrl. Dist., Hawaii, 1995—. Author: Coping with ADD/ADHD, 1995; co-author: Coping With a Learning Disability, 1992. Chmn. Alfalfa County Excise and Equalization Bd., Cherokee, 1979—83; asst. state coord. Okla. Am. Agr. Movement, Oklahoma City, 1982—83; co-chmn. Alfalfa County Dem. Party, Cherokee, 1976—83; sec.-treas. 6th Dist. Okla. Dem. State Exec. Bd., 1983—87; counselor United Meth. Counseling Ctr., 1987—88; mem. Elder Christian Ch. Named Citizen of Yr., Okla. chpt. Nat. Assn. Social Workers, 1988; recipient Tchr. of Yr. award, Helena Masonic Lodge, 1967, Spl. award, Okla. Women for Agr., 1979. Mem.: Okla. Assn. Learning Disabilities, Garfield County Interagy. Task Force, Okla. Sch. Psychologists Assn., Nat. Assn. Sch. Psychologists, Okla. Soc. Advancement Biofeedback, Biofeedback Soc. Am., Chi Omega Alumni, Delta Kappa Gamma. Office: PO Box 917 Nederland CO 80466-0917 Office Phone: 303-258-3976. Business E-Mail: JaydeneMor@aol.com.

MORRISON, KENNETH DOUGLAS, author, columnist; b. Mpls., Apr. 1, 1918; s. Kenneth Mortimore and Florence Myrtle (Sutton) M.; m. Helen Curtis, Feb. 25, 1943; children: Kenneth D., Sally, Steven C., Mary. AB, Carleton Coll., 1940; grad. study, U. Miami, 1940-41, U. Minn., 1941. Free lance writer, Mpls., 1941; editor publs. Minn. Dept. Conservation, 1942-47; Minn. rep. to Nat. Audubon Soc., 1947-49, dir. pub relations, editor Audubon mag., 1949-56, v.p., 1955-56; dir. Mountain Lake Sanctuary and Singing Tower Am. Found., 1956-80, dir. environ. concerns, 1980-82, fellow, 1982-83; syndicated nature-conservation newspaper columnist 4 papers, 1985—. Audubon tour lectr., 1958-63; interviewer naturalists Wildlife Unltd., TV sta. WOR-TV, N.Y.C., 1951- 52; Mem. Minn. Bird Commn., 1951-54; trustee emeritus Fla. Nature Conservancy; trustee Fla. Conservation Found.; v.p., trustee Conservation 70's; mem. Gov. Fla. Natural Resources Com., State Parks Adv. Council, 1971-79 Author: Favorite Birds of America, 1951, Favorite Animals of America, 1951, Mountain Lake Almanac, 1984; Compiler: (with Mrs. M. E. Herz) Where to Find Birds In Minnesota, 1950. Bd. dirs. Defenders Wildlife; adv. bd. Webber Coll., 1969— . Recipient Gov. Fla. Wildlife Conservation award, 1960, Gulf Oil Conservation award, 1982, Feinstone Environ. award SUNY, 1987, Carleton Coll. Disting. Achievement award, 1990, Grassroots Leadership award Fla. Nature Conservancy, 1996. Mem. Wilson Ornithol. Soc., Wilderness Soc., Greenpeace, Native Plant Soc., Fla. Audubon Soc. (pres., Award of Merit 1964, Cruickshank Conservation award 1993), Hawk Mountain Sanctuary Assn. (bd. sponsors), Nature Conservancy, Sierra Club, Friends of Earth, Green Horizon Land Trust (bd. dirs. 1999—), Pi Delta Epsilon. Methodist. Home: 1351 Hollister Rd Babson Park FL 33827-9684 *We ought to keep in mind that we are mammals and that we need to renew regularly our contact with the basic, simple life of soil, sun, water, animals and trees.*

MORRISON, L. WARREN, computer engineer; BSEE, CCNY, 1951; MS in Med. and Indsl. Electronics, Bklyn. Poly. Inst., 1951—52; PhD in Elec. Engring., U. So. Calif., 1969. Pres. Direct Data Corp., 1971—83; asst. v.p. BDM Internat., Inc., 1984—89; chief scientist Info. Technologies Group, 1990—; vis. scientist Software Engring. Inst., Carnegie Mellon U., Pitts., 1994—. Mem. Army Sci. Bd., 1978—87, 1996—. Contbr. articles to profl. jours. Recipient Cert. of Appreciation for Patriotic Civilian Svc., 1987, Recognition for Outstanding Performance, Office of Dep. Chief of Staff for Ops. and Plans, Dept. of Army, 1987. Mem.: IEEE, N.Y. Acad. Scis., Eta Kappa Nu. Office: Software Engineering Inst Carnegie Mellon Univ 4500 Fifth Ave Pittsburgh PA 15213-3890

MORRISON, MARTIN, computer systems analyst; b. Oakland, Calif., Mar. 28, 1947; s. Raymond Earl and June (Cabral) M. AB with distinction, U. Calif., Berkeley, 1967, MA, 1969, postgrad., 1969-73. Certified (life) nat. tournament dir.; cert. jr./community coll. tchr. (life), Calif. Instr. classics and English composition U. Calif. at Berkeley, 1967-73; instr. legal argument Boalt Hall Law Sch., 1972; with exec. office CF Air Freight, Inc., 1979-83, asst. to traffic mgr. for spl. projects, 1982-83, computer systems mgr., 1982-83; computer systems analyst Qantel Bus. Computers, 1983-86, sr. computer systems analyst, 1986-92; sr. tech. writer Shared Med. Systems, 1992-96, supr. tech. writing, 1996-98, mgr. tech. writing, 1998—2000; lead tech. writer Kaiser Permanente, 2001—. Mem. Amateur Chamber Music Players, 1978—. Author: Writing Argument, 1972, USCF Yearbooks, 1974-76, Official Rules of Chess, 1975, 77, Chess Competitor's Handbook, 1980, Latin Works for Transparent Language Computer Program, 1992-93; editor: Chess Voice, 1968-73, Keeping Ancient Rome Alive, 1987-89; contbg. author: Fundamentals of Management, 3d edit., 2000; chess editor: Oakland Tribune, 1965-66; columnist Via Lorenzo, 1987-88, Metric Today, 1985—; pub., bus. mgr. Chess Life & Rev., 1977-78, Bancroft Music Sch., 1958-60. Asst. concertmaster Berkeley Chamber Chorus and Orch., 1980-83; concertmaster Oakland Philharm., 1987-90, bd. dirs., corp. sec., 1988-90; 1st violin Albany Trio, 1987-91, Mostly Baroque Ensemble, 1999-2000; vol. staff Chabot Sci. Ctr., 1981-84, chmn. computer system mgmt. staff; sec., treas. AstroSoft, 1983-87. Schola Gregoriana San Francisco, 1989-92, Schola Cantemus, 1992-95; dir. St. John Schola, 1995—. Fellow U.S. Metric Assn. (life, chmn. consumer edn. com. 1984—, Spl. Citation 1986, cert. advanced metrication specialist 1987); mem. Am. Philol. Assn., Am. Classical League, Eastbay Astron. Soc. (bd. dirs. 1981-84, v.p. 1983-84), Internat. Assn. Chess Press (v.p. 1973-77), Soc. for Tech. Comm. (sr.), Chess Journalists Assn. (pres. 1972-75), World Chess Fedn. (internat. life arbiter, mem. rules com. 1973-78, chmn. 1976-78), U.S. Chess Fedn. (bd. dels. 1968-78, 1st v.p. Pacific Region 1972-73, nat. sec. 1972-75, tech. dir. 1973-76, exec. dir. 1976-78, Disting. Vol. award, 1982, Spl. citation, 1984, Disting. Svc. award 1995), Calif. Alumni Assn. (life, scholarship com., chmn. 1987-93, Disting. Chmn. award 1990), San Lorenzo Garden Homes Assn. (v.p./sec. 1985-86, pres. 1986-92), Mensa, Phi Beta Kappa.

MORRISON, MICHAEL CHRISTOPHER, advertising executive; b. Phila., Mar. 29, 1976; s. Steven D. Morrison and Anne Fenstamaker Mosteller. BS in Bus. Adminstrn., Pa. Coll. of Tech., 2000. Gen. laborer Tory Belt & Leather, Co., Williamsport, Pa., 1992—99; advt. mgr./sales mgr. Gregory Welteroth Advt., Inc., Montoursville, Pa., 2000—. Poetry/songs, Voodoo. Fund raiser Alzheimer's Rsch. Fund, Williamsport, Pa., 2003; mem. Young Men's Rep. Club, Williamsport, Pa., 1997—2003. Conservative. Avocations: golf, landscaping, writing, musician. Home: 2426 Waldman Dr Williamsport PA 17701 Office: Gregory Welteroth Advertising Inc 356 Laurens Rd Montoursville PA 17754 Office Phone: 570-433-3366. Office Fax: 570-433-4764. E-mail: mike.morrison@gwa-inc.com.

MORRISON, MICHAEL DEAN, lawyer, law educator; BA with high honors, Okla. U., 1971, JD, 1974. Bar: Okla. 1975, Kans. 1975, Tex. 1981, U.S. Ct. Appeals (5th cir.) 1980, U.S. Dist. Ct. (ea., no. and so. dists.) Tex. 1983, U.S. Dist. Ct. (wc. dist.) Tex. 1980, U.S. Dist. Ct. (we. dist.) Okla. 1975, U.S. Supreme Ct. 1979. Pvt. practice, Wichita, Kans., 1974-75; asst. dir. Law Ctr. Okla. U., 1975-77, asst. prof., 1977-80, assoc. prof., 1980-82, prof. law, 1982-90, William J. Boswell chair of law, 1990—. Mayor City of Waco, 1996—2000; ordained elder 1st Presbyn. Ch. Waco, stated clk. of session, 1996—98. Mem. Order of Coif, Phi Beta Kappa. Office: PO Box 97288 Waco TX 76798-7288

MORRISON, PATRICE B. lawyer; b. St. Louis, July 8, 1948; d. Frank J. and Loretta (S.) Burgert; m. William Brian Morrison, Aug. 12, 1969; 1 child, W. Brett. AB, U. Miami, 1971, MA, 1972, JD, Am. U., 1973, LLM in Taxation, Georgetown U., 1978. Bar: Fla. 1975, D.C. 1977, N.Y. 1983. Atty. U.S. Dept. Treas., Washington, 1975-79; atty., ptnr. Nixon Hargrave Devans & Doyle, LLP, Palm Beach County, Fla., 1980-89, Nixon Peabody LLP (formerly Nixon, Hargrave, Devans & Doyle), Rochester, N.Y., 1989—. Bd. dirs. Rochester Friendly Sr. Svcs., Inc., 1996—. Bd. dirs. Alzheimer's Assn., Rochester, 1990-95, Nat. Women's Hall of Fame, 1990-92; mem. Rochester Women's Network; mem. exec. com. Estate Planning Coun. Rochester, 1992-95; dir. Cloverwood Sr. Living, Inc., 2000—. Mem. Am. Immigration Lawyers Assn. Republican. Office: Nixon Peabody LLP PO Box 31051 Rochester NY 14603-1051

MORRISON, PATRICIA B. retail executive; CIO GE Indsl. Sys. Gen. Electric; CIO Quaker Oats Co., Office Depot, Inc., Delray Beach, Fla., 2002—. Office: Office Depot Inc 2200 Old Germantown Rd Delray Beach FL 33445

MORRISON, PATRICIA KENNEALY, author; b. N.Y.C., Mar. 4, 1946; d. Joseph Gerard and Genevieve Mary (McDonald) Kennealy; m. James Douglas Morrison, June 24, 1970 (dec. July 3, 1971). Student, St. Bonaventure U., 1963-65; BA, Harpur Coll., 1967. Editor Jazz & Pop Mag., N.Y.C., 1968-71; sr. copywriter RCA Records, N.Y.C., 1971-73; copy dir. CBS Records, N.Y.C., 1973-79, New Sch., N.Y.C., 1979-81; author, pres., CEO Lizard Queen Prodns., Inc., N.Y.C., 1984—. Author: The Copper Crown, 1984, The Throne of Scone, 1986, The Silver Branch, 1988, The Hawk's Gray Feather, 1990, The Oak Above the Kings, 1994, The Hedge of Mist, 1996, Blackmantle, 1997, The Deer's Cry, 1998, Strange Days: My Life With and Without Jim Morrison, 1992; contbr.: Rock She Wrote, 1995; tech. advisor, actress The Doors, 1990-91. Mem.: Sovereign Mil. Order of Temple of Jerusalem (dame), Mensa. Office: Lizard Queen Prodns Inc 151 1st Ave Ste 120 New York NY 10003-2965 also: Ralph Vicinanza Literary Agy 303 W 18th Street New York NY 10011 E-mail: patriciamorrison@lycos.com.

MORRISON, PAUL A. lawyer; b. Mo., June 11, 1958; s. John Coulter and Rita (Dickey) Morrison; m. Delmara Faye Bayliss, May 11, 1988 (div. 1995); children: Hunter, Gracie; m. Mary Beth Bradley, Oct. 5, 1996. BA with honors, U. So. Miss., 1984; JD, Washington and Lee U., 1987. Bar: Va. 1987, U.S. Dist. Ct. (ea. dist.) Va. 1989, U.S. Ct. Appeals (4th cir.) 1990, U.S. Supreme Ct. 1998. Mng. ptnr. Morrison & Bayliss, Leesburg, Va., 1987—89, 1992—95, Morrison, Bayliss & Briel, Leesburg, 1989—92, Howard, Morrison & Howard, Warrenton, Va., 1998—; atty. Clark, Scott & Sullivan, Mobile, Ala., 1995—96; pvt. practice Warrenton, 1996—98. Neutral case evaluator Fauquier County Bar, 2000—02. Mem.: ABA, ATLA, Loudoun County Bar Assn. (bd. dirs. 1993), Va. Trial Lawyers Assn. Home: 5568 Valley Green Dr Broad Run VA 20137 Office: Howard Morrison and Howard 1 Wall St Warrenton VA 20186 Office Phone: 540-349-1155. Business E-Mail: paul.morrison@starband.net.

MORRISON, PORTIA OWEN, lawyer; b. Charlotte, N.C., Apr. 1, 1944; d. Robert Hall Jr. and Josephine Currier (Hutchison) M.; m. Alan Peter Richmond, June 19, 1976; 1 child, Anne Morrison. BA in English, Agnes Scott Coll., 1966; MA, U. Wis., 1967; JD, U. Chgo., 1978. Bar: Ill. 1978. Ptnr. Piper Rudnick LLP, Chgo., 1978—. Lectr. in field. Pres. Girl Scouts of Chgo. Mem.: ABA, CREW Chgo., Chgo. Fin. Exch., Pension Real Estate Assn., Chgo. Bar Assn. (real property com., subcom. real property fin., alliance for women), Am. Coll. Real Estate Lawyers (pres.-elect, bd. govs.). Office: Piper Rudnick LLP 203 N La Salle St Ste 1800 Chicago IL 60601-1210 E-mail: portia.morrison@piperrudnick.com.

MORRISON, RICHARD DRURY, health policy consultant, medical educator; b. Logan, W.Va., Nov. 14, 1935; s. William Cline Morrison and Gladys Leone Rogers-Morrison-Taylor; m. Carolee Benefico, Oct. 15, 1971 (div.). PhD, Va. Commonwealth U., Richmond, 1988; MA, Coll. of William and Mary in Va., Williamsburg, 1985; BA, Christopher Newport Coll., Newport News, Va., 1976. Adj. asst. prof. Old Dominion U., Norfolk, Va., 1999—2003. Cons. in evidence based medicine Ea. Va. Med. Sch., Norfolk, 1999—2003. Cons. and fellow Am. Internat. Health Alliance, Washington, 1996—98, UCSF Ctr. for the Health Professions, Pew Charitable Trusts, San Francisco, 1994—96; dep. dir. Va. Dept. of Health Professions, Richmond, 1984—94; dicrector of membership services AVMA, Chgo., 1963—65; asst. dir. Am. Assn. of Dental Schools, Chgo., 1965—69. Author (more than 50): (published health policy reviews) On Request. Specialist 5 US Army, 1956—59, Fort Lee, Virginia. Achievements include serving on bd. of dir. Coun. on Licensure, Enforcement and Regulation; The Center for Public Affairs, Virginia Commonwealth University; consulting, Bur. of Health Professions, US Department of Health & Human Services; bd. of dr., v.p., Citizen Advocacy Ctr; cons., Inst. of Medicine, Nat. Acad. of Sciences; cons., The Pew Charitable Trusts; cons., Robert Wood Johnson Found; intern, Va. Joint Legis. Audit and Review Cmmn; intern, The Va. Crime Cmmn; cons. and sr. rsch. fellow, The Williamson Institue, Medical Coll. of Va; mem., Task Force of Pres. Carter's Cmmn.on Mental Health. Avocations: international travel, creative writing.

MORRISON, ROBERT LEE, physical scientist; b. Omaha, Nov. 22, 1932; s. Robert Alton and Lulu Irene (Ross) M.; m. Sharon Faith Galliher, Feb. 19, 1966; children: Dennis, Karyn, Cheryl, Tamara, Traci. BA, U. Pacific, Stockton, Calif., 1957, MS, 1960. Chief chemist Gallo Winery, Modesto, Calif., 1957-66; rsch. scientist Lawrence Livermore Nat. Lab., Livermore, Calif., 1966-69, sr. rsch. scientist, 1973-93; pres. Poolinator, Inc., Gardena, Calif., 1970-72; owner R.L. Morrison Techs., Modesto, 1993—. Cons., speaker, presenter in field. Contbr. numerous articles to profl. jours.; patentee in field. Recipinet Excellence in Nuclear Weapons award U.S. Dept. Energy, 1990, others. Mem. Am. Chem. Soc. Avocations: fishing, skiing, scuba diving, photography. Home: 1117 Springcreek Dr Modesto CA 95355-4820

MORRISON, ROGER BARRON, geologist; b. Madison, Wis., Mar. 26, 1914; s. Frank Barron and Elsie Rhea (Bullard) M.; m. Harriet Louise Williams, Apr. 7, 1941 (dec. Feb. 1991); children: John Christopher, Peter Hallock and Craig Brewster (twins). BA, Cornell U., 1933, MS, 1934; postgrad., U. Calif., Berkeley, 1934—35, Stanford U., 1935—38; PhD, U. Nev., 1964. Registered profl. geologist, Wyo. Geologist U.S. Geol. Survey, 1939-76; vis. adj. prof. dept. geoscis. U. Ariz., 1976-81, Mackay Sch. Mines, U. Nev., Reno, 1984-86; cons. geologist; pres. Morrison and Assocs., Morrison Cons. Corp., 1978—. Prin. investigator 2 Landsat-1 and 2 Skylab earth resources investigation projects NASA, 1972-75. Author 3 books; co-author 1 book; co-editor 2 books; editor Quaternary Nonglacial Geology, Conterminous U.S., Geol. Soc. Am. Centennial Series, vol. K-2, 1991; mem. editl. bd. Catena, 1973-88; contbr. over 250 articles to profl. jours. Fellow Geol. Soc. Am.; mem. AAAS, Internat. Union Quaternary Rsch. (mem. Holocene and paleopedology commns., chmn. work group on pedostratigraphy), Am. Soc. Photogrammetry and Remote Sensing, Internat. Soil Sci. Soc., Am. Quaternary Assn., Colo. Sci. Soc., Geol. Soc. Nev. Achievements include research in on Quaternary geology and geomorphology, hydrogeology, environmental geology, neotectonics, remote sensing of Earth resources, paleoclimatology, pedostratigraphy; technology for converting waste wood, garbage, municipal solid waste, natural gas, landfill gas, etc. to mixed-alcohol motor fuel; development of of forest and range land and a new town in western Paraguay; research in nuclear waste issues at Yucca Mtn., Nev. Home and Office: 7500 N Calle Sin Envidia Apt 8104 Tucson AZ 85718-7361 E-mail: rbmorrison@earthlink.net.

MORRISON, SARAH LYDDON, author; b. Rochester, N.Y., May 19, 1939; d. Paul William and Winifred (Cowles) Lyddon. BA, U. Vt., 1961. Sec. asst. Glamour mag., N.Y.C., 1961-63, Vogue mag., N.Y.C., 1963-65; asst. editor Venture mag., N.Y.C., 1966-71; dir. pub. rels. for tourism Commonwealth of P.R., N.Y.C., 1971-75; asst. Am. Legion, Washington, 1988-98; owner Sarah Lyddon Morrison Pub. Rels., Washington, 1999—. Author: The Modern Witch's Spellbook, 1971, Book II, 1983, The Modern Witch's Dream Book, 1985, The Modern Witch's Book of Home Remedies, 1988, The Modern Witch's Book of Healing, 1991, The Modern Witch's Book of Symbols, 1997, Modern Witch's Guide to Magic and Spells, 1998. Mem. Washington Club, DAR (dir. pub. rels. Emily Nelson chpt. 1999, 2000), Colonial Dames XVII. Avocations: travel, reading, swimming, rock music, cooking. E-mail: sarahlyd@aol.com.

MORRISON, SCOTT DAVID, management consultant, small business owner; b. Duluth, Minn., May 8, 1952; s. Robert Henry and Shirley Elaine (Tester) M. (dec. 1990); m. Jana Louise Bergeron, May 29, 1976; chilren: Robert Scott (dec. 1999), Matthew John. Cert. in welding, Duluth Area Inst. Tech., 1971; student, U. Wis.-Superior, 1976-77; A in Mfg. Mgmt., N. Hennepin C.C., 1985; BA, Concordia Coll., St. Paul, 1988; MBA, St. Thomas U., St. Paul, 1991. Cert. in quality tech., Am. Soc. Quality, 1985; lic. vocat. instr., Minn. Cert. welder Litton Ship Systems, Pascagoula, Miss., 1971-72, Barko Hydraulics, Superior, Wis., 1972-76, Am. Hoist and Derrick Co., Mpls., 1977-79, cert. level II non-destructive exam. insp., 1979-80; quality supr. Colight Inc., Mpls., 1980, Tol-O-Matic, Inc., Mpls., 1980-82; quality assurance engr. ADC Telecommunications, Mpls., 1982-84, design assurance engr., 1985-86, product assurance engr., 1986-87, sr. product assurance engr., quality improvement facilitator, 1987-88, product engr. supr., 1988-90, mgr. design assurance, quality assurance, component engring., 1990-92; dir. quality and reg. affairs Waters Instruments, Inc., 1992-96, sr. quality engr., 1996, corp. quality sys. mgr., 1996-98; corp. mfg. and quality Compaq Computer Corp., Houston, 1996-98; sys. engr., sr. cons. Dimension Product Group, 1998-99, Dell Computer Corp., Austin, Tex., 1998—, quality engr., sr. cons. Transactional Line of Bus., 1999—, mgr. quality syss. application team project, 2000, supplier quality engr., sr. cons., 2000—01; sr. cons. ABS Cons. Mgmt. Sys. divsns., Houston, 2001—; mgr. Mgmt. Systems Cons., 2002—03; owner Dimensions in Quality, LLC, 2003—, Quality Environ. Safety and Health Consulting. Judge U.S. Amateur Boxing Fedn., Mpls., 1978-87, 95-97; examiner Minn. Quality Award Minn. Coun. for Quality, 1993, 95, Tex. Quality Award, 1997; mem. quality coun. Am. Electronics Assn., 1994-95; mem. bd. dirs. Rochester Quality Coun., 1994-95; examiner Malcolm Baldridge Nat. Quality award Nat. Inst. Standards and Technology, 1994-95, sr. examiner, 1996-97, alumni examiner, 1999-2000; site visit rschr. broad prize edn., 2002-04; reviewer fellowship grant applications ASQ, 1996; adj. instr. Riverland Technical Coll., Rochester, Minn., 1995; lic. profl. boxing judge Tex. Dept. Licensing and Regulation, 1996—; cert. lead quality auditor British Standards Internat., 1996, cert. lead environ. system auditor, 2001; facilitator Malcolm Bridge Nat. Quality Award Regional Conf., 1997; cons. in field. Recipient Technical Excellence award ADC Telecoms., 1987, 88. Mem. ASTM, Am. Soc. Quality (cert. quality engr. cert. quality auditor, cert. quality mgr., cert. six sigma black belt, chmn. host and attendance subcom. 1986-87), Am. Welding Soc., Soc. Mfg. Engrs., Internat. Platform Assn. Roman Catholic. Home and Office: 18 Seneca Pl The Woodlands TX 77382-5353

MORRISON, SHELLEY, actress; b. N.Y.C., Oct. 26, 1936; d. Maurice Nissim and Hortense Mitrani; m. Walter R. Dominguez, Aug. 11, 1973. Student, L.A. City Coll., 1954—56. Presenter Alma awards, 2001—02, Imagan Awards, 2001, Nosotros Golden Eagle awards, 2002. Actress: (films) Interns, 1962, The Greatest Story Ever Told, 1964, Castle of Evil, 1965, Divorce, American Style, 1965, How to Save a Marriage, 1966, Funny Girl, 1967, Three Guns for Texas, 1969, Man and Boy, 1971, Blume in Love, 1972, McKenna's Gold, 1967, Breezy, 1973, People Toys, 1973, Rabbit Test, 1975, Max Dugan Returns, 1982, Troop Beverly Hills, 1988, Fools Rush In, 1996, others, (TV movies) The Girl Who Came Giftwrapped, Three's a Crowd, 1969, Once an Eagle, 1974, The Night That Panicked America, 1975, Kids Don't Tell, 1984, Cries From the Heart, 1994, Columbo: It's All In the Game, Lassie: A New Beginning, others, (TV series) Laredo, 1965-67, The Flying Nun, 1966-70, First and Ten, 1987, I'm Home, 1990, The Fanelli Boys, 1990, Love, Lies and Murder, 1990, Playhouse 90, Dr. Kildare, The Fugitive, Gunsmoke, Marcus Welby, General Hospital, and many others, 1960-70, Man of the People, Sisters, 1991, 92, Murder She Wrote, 1992, Johnny Bago, 1993, Columbo, 1993, L.A. Law, 1994, Live Shot, 1995, Courthouse, Home Improvement, 1997, Nothing Sacred, 1997, Prey, 1997, Nearly Yours, 1998; recurring role in Will & Grace, 1998—, series regular 1999—; TV guest appearances include Prey, Nothing Sacred, L.A. Law, Busting Loose, Marcus Welby, M.D., Occasional Wife, Between the Lines, Home Improvement, Murder, She Wrote, The Bold Ones, Divorce Court, Soap, The Streets of San Francisco, Dr. Kildare, Man of the People, The Partridge Family, My Favorite Martian, The Outer Limits, The Robert Taylor Show, numerous others; (voice over animated cartoon comml.) Handy Nanny, 2003, (A&E) Letters, 2003, numerous others, (stage prodns.) Pal Joey, 1956, Bus Stop, 1956, Only in America, 1960, Orpheus Descending, 1960, Spring's Awakening, 1962, over 65 other prodns., 1956-1970, also appeared in The Mikado, Pal Joey, Anastasia, Orpheus Descending, A Streetcar Named Desire, Sweet Bird of Youth, The Crucible, Zoo Story, Rashomon, Desk Set, Pygmalian, The Would-Be Gentleman, Comedy of Errors, Tiger at the Gates, The Rose Tattoo, Orpheus Descending, Come Back Little Sheba, The Odd Couple, Only in America, El Camino Real, Hamlet, Country Girl, Romeo and Juliet, Cotton Candy, Point of View, Coney Island of the Mind, Last of the Aztecs, numerous others; prodr., writer live shots, 1975—; prodr. (with husband Walter Dominguez) documentary Mexican culture, 2003. Condr. seminars (with husband Walter Dominquez) about Native Americans to keep traditions and ceremonies flourishing. Honored (with husband Walter Dominguez) for work with homeless City of L.A., 1985, for work during L.A. riots, 1992; nominated for Alma awards SAG, 2000, 2001, 2002; recipient SAG award for Will and Grace. Mem. SAG, AFTRA, Actors Equity Assn. Democrat.

MORRISON, STACY LYNNE, magazine editor; b. Jenkintown, Pa., Jan. 17, 1969; d. Robert Isaac and Sharon Lee (Wiley) Morrison; m. Christopher Cole Shannon, Oct. 1, 1994. BA, Washington & Lee U., 1990. Editl. asst. Mirabella mag., NYC, 1991-92, asst. editor, 1992-93, assoc. features editor, 1993-95; mng. editor J. Crew Group Inc., NYC, 1995, Time Out New York, NYC, Conde Nast Sports for Women; editor-in-chief Modern Bride, 1998—2000, ONE, 2000—01; exec. editor Marie Claire, NYC, 2001—04; editor-in-chief Redbook, NYC, 2004—. Office: Redbook 224 W 57th St New York NY 10019*

MORRISON, STEPHEN GEORGE, lawyer; b. Pasadena, Calif., Aug. 10, 1949; s. Ira George and Virginia Lee (Zimmer) M.; m. Gail Louise Moore, June 10, 1972; 1 child, Gregory Stephen. BBA, U. Mich., 1971; JD, U. S.C., 1975. Ptnr. Nelson, Mullins, Riley & Scarborough, Columbia, S.C., 1975—. Adj. prof. U. S.C., Columbia, 1973-75, 82—; pres. Defense Rsch. Inst., 1995-96; exec. v.p., gen. counsel, sec., chief adminstrv. officer Policy Mgmt. Sys. Corp.; presenter in field. Author/editor: Products Liability Pretrial Notebook, 1989, South Carolina Appellate Practice Handbook, 1986. Bd. dirs. S.C. Com. Humanities, Columbia, 1986—, S.C. Gov. Sch. Arts, Columbia, 1988-95; pres., bd. dirs. Richland County Pub. Defender Assn., Columbia, 1991-95. Fellow S.C. Bar Found.; mem. Internat. Assn. Defense Coun., Lawyers for Civil. Justice (bd. dirs. 1995—, pres. elect 1997—). Democrat. Episcopalian. Avocations: fishing, country music, chamber music, physics, history. Home: 2626 Stratford Rd Columbia SC 29204-2342 Office: Nelson Mullins Riley & Morrison 1330 Lady St Fl 3 Columbia SC 29201-3300

MORRISON, TONI (CHLOE ANTHONY MORRISON), novelist; b. Lorain, Ohio, Feb. 18, 1931; d. George and Ella Ramah (Willis) Wofford; m. Harold Morrison, 1958 (div. 1964); children: Harold Ford, Slade Kevin. BA in English, Howard U., 1953; MA, Cornell U., 1955. Tchr. English and humanities Tex. So. U., 1955-57, Howard U., 1957-64; editor Random House, N.Y.C., 1965—; assoc. prof. English SUNY, Purchase, NY, 1971-72, Schweitzer Prof. of the Humanities Albany, NY, 1984-89; Robert F. Goheen Prof. of the Humanities Princeton Univ., Princeton, NJ, 1989—; chair, creative writing pgm. Princeton U. Visiting prof., Yale Univ., 1976-77, Bard Coll., 1986-88. Author: The Bluest Eye, 1969, Sula, 1973 (National Book award nomination 1975, Ohioana Book award 1975), Song of Solomon, 1977 (National Book Critics Circle award 1977, American Acad. and Inst. of Arts and Letters award 1977), Tar Baby, 1981, (play) Dreaming Emmett, 1986, Beloved, 1988 (Pulitzer Prize for fiction 1988, Robert F. Kennedy Book award 1988, Melcher Book award Unitarian Universalist Assn. 1988, National Book award nomination 1987, National Book Critics Circle award nomination 1987), Jazz, 1992, Playing in the Dark: Whiteness and the Literary Imagination, 1992, Nobel Prize Speech, 1994, Birth of a Nation'hood: Gaze, Script & Spectacle in the O.J. Simpson Trial, 1997, Paradise, 1998, The Big Box, 2002, The Book of Mean People, 2002, Love, 2003; editor: The Black Book, 1974, Race-ing Justice, En-Gendering Power: Essays on Anita Hill, Clarence Thomas, and the Construction of Social Reality, 1992; lyricist: Honey and Rue, 1992. Recipient New York State Governor's Art award, 1986; Washington College Literary award, 1987; Elizabeth Cady Stanton award National Organization for Women; Nobel prize in Literature Nobel Foundation, 1993. Mem. Author's Guild (council) Office: Princeton U Writing Program 305 Nassau St Princeton NJ 08544-2003

MORRISON, VAN, musician, songwriter; b. Belfast, Ireland, Aug. 31, 1945; s. George and Violet Morrison; 1 child, Shana. Founder, lead singer rock group Them, 1964-67, albums include Them, 1965, Them Again, 1966, Them featuring Van Morrison, 1972; solo career, 1967—; albums include Blowin' Your Mind, 1967, Astral Weeks, 1968, Moondance, 1968, Best of Van Morrison, 1970, His Band and Street Choir, 1970, Tupelo Honey, 1971, St. Dominic's Preview, 1972, Hard Nose the Highway, 1973, It's Too Late To Stop Now, 1974, TB Sheets, 1974, Veedon Fleece, 1974, This Is Where I Came In, 1977, A Period of Transition, 1977, Wavelength, 1978, Into the Music, 1979, Common One, 1980, Beautiful Vision, 1982, Inarticulate Speech of the Heart, 1983, Live at the Grand Opera House Belfast, 1984, A Sense of Wonder, 1985, No Guru, No Method, No Teacher, 1986, Poetic Champions Compose, 1987, (with The Chieftains) Irish Heartbeat, 1988, Live for Ireland, 1988, Avalon Sunset, 1989, Enlightenment, 1990, The Best of Van Morrison, 1990, Hymns to the Silence, 1991, Bang Masters, 1991, The Best of Van Morrison, 1993, Too Long in Exile, 1993, A Night in San Francisco, 1994, Days Like This, 1995, The Healing Game, 1997, Tell Me Something, 1997, The Philosopher's Stone, 1998, Brown Eyed Girl, 1998, Brown Eyed Beginnings, 1998, The Masters, 1999, Super Hits, 1999, New York Sessions '67: Bang Demos, 1999, Back On Top, 1999, The Skiffle Sessions: Live in Belfast 1998, 2000; composer numerous hit singles including Gloria, 1965, Brown Eyed Girl, 1967, Moondance, 1968, Domino, 1970, Wild Night, 1971; composer TV film Drei Amerikanische LP's, 1969, films Dusty and Sweets McGee, 1971, Slipstream, 1974, Lamb, 1986, Moondance, 1995, Beyond the Clouds, 1995; actor films The Day the Music Died, 1977, The Last Waltz, 1978, Van Morrison in Ireland, 1980, Ready Steady Go, 1983, TV series (voice) Irish in America: The Long Journey Home, 1998. Inducted into Rock and Roll Hall of Fame, 1993; recipient Grammy award for Best Pop Collaboration With Vocals, 1995, 97.

MORRISON, WILLIAM DAVID, lawyer; b. Aug. 19, 1940; s. Maxey Neal and Mary Fuller (Chase) M.; m. Barbara Heath, Aug. 25, 1962 (div.); children: David Conrow, Stephen Munro, John Pomeroy; m. Sandra Elizabeth Butter, Mar. 16, 1983; children: Charles Nicholas, Sophie Natasha. BA, Princeton U., 1962; LLB, Yale U., 1965. Bar: N.Y. 1966, Calif. 1975. Assoc. Winthrop, Stimson, Putnam & Robert, N.Y.C., 1965-74; ptnr. Erickson & Morrison, and predecessor firms, L.A., 1974—79, LeBoeuf, Lamb, Leiby & Macrae, N.Y.C., 1979-88, Bryan Cave, St. Louis, 1988-97, Sidley, Austin, Brown & Wood, N.Y.C., 1997—2002; sr. cons. MEC Internat. Ltd., London, 2002—; sr. legal advisor The Trinity Group, London, 2003—. Lectr. on Saudi Arabian law; active Royal Inst. Internat. Affairs (Chatham House). Mem. ABA, Calif. Bar Assn., Internat. Bar Assn., Royal Geog. Soc., Internat. Inst. for Strategic Studies, The Pilgrims, Brooks, City of London Club, Marks Club, Annabel's, RAC Club, Princeton Club (N.Y.C.). Home: 34 Norland Sq London WII4PU England Office: The Trinity Group 22 Upper Grosvenor St London W1K 7PE England Office Phone: (+44) (0) 20 7229 5187. Business E-Mail: wd.morrison@btinternet.com.

MORRISON, WILLIAM FOSDICK, business educator, retired electrical company executive; b. Bridgeport, Conn., Mar. 14, 1935; s. Robert Louis and Helen Fosdick (Mulroney) M.; m. E. Drake Miller, Dec. 14, 1957 (div. Sept. 1972); children: Donna Drake, Deanne Fosdick, William Fosdick; m. Carol Ann Stover, Nov. 20, 1972. BA in Econs., Trinity Coll., 1957. Mgr. purchasing dept. Westinghouse Electric Co., Lima, Ohio, 1960—68, mgr. mfg. Upper Sandusky, Ohio, 1969, gen. mgr. Gurabo, 1970—71, mgr. tng. Pitts., 1972—84, program mgr. Sunnyvale, Calif., 1984—89, procurement project dir., 1990—94; prof. San Jose State U., Calif., 1993—, Golden Gate U., San Francisco, 1995—; lead negotiator Advanced Micro Devices, Santa Clara, Calif., 1995—97; prof. U. Calif., Berkeley, 1996—2002, Menlo Coll., 1998—2001; faculty adv. Beta Gamma Sigma, 2002—. Negotiation cons. and trainer, 1969—; lead negotiator ReSound Corp., 1998-99; mgr. renovation project San Jose State U., 1999-2000. Author: The Pre-Negotiation Planning Book, 1985, The Human Side of Negotiations, 1994; contbr. articles to profl. jours. Bd. dirs. Valley Inst. of the Theatre Arts, Saratoga, Calif., 1986-90, Manhattan Playhouse, 1989-94; chmn. Sensory Access Found. Golf Tournament, 1995-96. Served to capt. USAFR, 1958-64; mem. protocol office World Cup USA, 1994. Named Man of the Yr. Midwest Lacrosse Coaches Assn., 1983, recipient Service award U.S. Lacrosse Assn., 1982. Mem.: Nat. Assn. Purchasing Mgmt. (pres. Lima chpt. 1966—67, dir. nat. affairs 1967—68, dist. treas. 1968—70), The Propeller Club (sec., San Francisco port 2002—), Circumnaviagators Club (founder, pres. San Francisco chpt. 2001—), Sunnyvale Golf Assn. (vice-chmn. 1985, chmn. 1986, handicap scorer 1992—93, chmn. 1993), Elks. Avocation: golf. Home: 3902 Duncan Pl Palo Alto CA 94306-4550 Office: San Jose State U Coll of Bus 1 Washington Sq San Jose CA 95112-3613 E-mail: wfmorrison@earthlink.net.

MORRIS-ROGERS, CHERYL-ANN, daycare provider, director, educator; b. Chgo., Feb. 26, 1958; d. Richard Lee and Ruth Hortence (Davis) M. AA, Cen. YMCA Coll., 1979; BA, DePaul U., 1982. Cert. in child devel. Supr. C.E.T.A. Program, Chgo., 1979; asst. dir. WLS AM/FM Radio Pub. Affairs, Chgo., 1981-82; educator Auburn Pk. Day Care, Kindergarten, Chgo., 1982-83, pres., dir., 1983—; educator, pres., dir. Lakefront Children's Acad., Chgo., 1999—. Cons. in field. Mem. NAACP, Chgo., 1988—, United Negro Coll. Fund, Chgo., 1988—; com. mem. Election Judge Loretta Hall Morgan, Chgo., 1989; vol. Election Mayor Harold Washington, Chgo., 1987. Recipient Child Devel. award Love Drops Mag., 1987; named to Dean's List, 1980. Mem. Nat. Assn. Women-Bus. Owners, League Black Women, Preschool Owners Assn., Nat. Assn. for Edn. Young Children, Chgo. Assn. for Edn. Young Children. Avocations: reading, writing, swimming, camping, travel. Office: Auburn Pk Day Care 741 W 79th St Chicago IL 60620-2423 also: Lakefront Childrens Acad 400 E Randolph St Chicago IL 60601-7329

MORRISS, FRANK, writer, educator; b. Pasadena, Calif., Mar. 28, 1923; s. B. Gerard Morriss and Regina Spann; m. Mary Rita Moynihan, Feb. 11, 1950 (dec. Oct. 23, 1996); children: Patricia, Mary Ellen Hill, Regina, Gerard. BS in Philosophy magna cum laude, Regis Coll., Denver, 1943; JD, Georgetown U., 1948. Editor Register Newspapers, Denver, 1949—61, 1963—67; assoc. editor Vt. Cath. Tribune, Burlington, 1961—63; contbg. editor The Wanderer, St. Paul, 1967—; educator Colorado Cath. Acad., Wheat Ridge, Colo., 1973—. Bd. dirs. Wanderer Forum Found., St. Paul, 1969—; policy expert Heritage Found., 1995—. Author: Saints In Verse, Two Chapels, (lectrs. on CD) Saints Speak to Modern World. Founder Colo. Cath. Acad., Wheat Ridge, 1970—2002. Sgt. U.S. Army, 1943—45, PTO. Recipient Frederic Ozanam award, Soc. Cath. Social Scientists, 2003. Mem.: Fellowship of Cath. Scholars, VFW. Republican. Roman Catholic. Home: 3505 Owens Street Wheat Ridge CO 80033

MORRISS, FRANK HOWARD, JR., pediatrics educator; b. Birmingham, Ala., Apr. 20, 1940; s. Frank Howard Sr. and Rochelle (Snow) M.; m. Mary J. Hagan, June 29, 1968; children: John Hagan, Matthew Snow. BA, U. Va., 1962; MD, Duke U., 1966. Diplomate Am. Bd. Pediatrics, Am. Bd. Perinatal and Neonatal Medicine. Intern Duke U. Med. Ctr., Durham, N.C., 1966-67, resident in pediatrics, 1967-68, fellow in neonatology, 1970-71, U. Colo., Denver, 1971-73; asst. prof. to prof. U. Tex. Med. Sch., Houston, 1973-86; prof. U. Iowa Coll. Medicine, Iowa City, 1987—, chmn. dept., 1987—2004. Editor: Role of Human Milk in Infant Nutrition and Health, 1986; contbr. numerous articles to profl. jours, chpts. to books. Lt. comdr. USN, 1968-70. NIH grantee, 77-87, 90—. Mem. Am. Pediatric Soc., Soc. Pediatric Rsch., Am. Acad. Pediatrics, Soc. Gynecol. Investigation, Midwest Soc. Pediatric Rsch. Office: U Iowa Hosps & Clinics Dept Pediatrics Iowa City IA 52242 Office Phone: 319-384-6530.

MORRISSEY, CHARLES THOMAS, historian, educator; b. Newton, Mass., Nov. 11, 1933; s. Leonard Eugene and Margaret (McCarthy) M. AB, Dartmouth Coll., 1956; MA, U. Calif., Berkeley, 1957. Instr. Dartmouth Coll., Hanover, N.H., 1961-62; oral historian Harry S. Truman Library, Independence, Mo., 1962-64; chief oral history project John F. Kennedy Libr., Washington, 1965-66; dir. Vt. Hist. Soc., Montpelier, 1966-71, 73-75; dir. oral history project Ford Found., 1971-73; adj. prof. history U. Vt., Burlington, 1969-73, 75-85; dir. Oral History and Archives Office, cons. Baylor Coll. Medicine, Houston, 1985—2003. Vis. instr. oral and pub. history Portland State U., 1979—82, 1984—2001, 2003—, Vt. Coll., Montpelier, 1985—2000, 2002—; lectr. in field. Author: Vermont: A Bicentennial History, 1981, (with others) Vermont, 1985; editor: Oral History Assn. Newsletter, 1968-71, Vermont History, 1967-71, 73-76, Internat. Jour. Oral History, 1985-89; contbg. editor: Vermont Life mag., 1969-81, editor, 1982-83; also articles; radio commentator Sta. WDEV, Waterbury, Vt., 1982—; columnist Hardwick (Vt.) Gazette, 1997—. Recipient Harvey Kantor award New England Assn. Oral Historians, 1980. Fellow Ctr. for Rsch. on Vt.; mem. Oral History Assn. (pres. 1971-72), Nat. Coun. on Pub. History (coun. 1980-82), Assn. Oral History Educators, Sharpshooters Club (North Fayston, Vt.), Cosmos Club (Washington).

MORRISSEY, EDMOND JOSEPH, classical philologist; b. N.Y.C., June 5, 1943; s. William J. and Anne K. (Gaffney) M.; m. Patricia M. Hanlon, Oct. 11, 1987; children: William, Edmond, Kathleen, Patrick, Jennifer, Lisa, Paula. AB summa cum laude, Boston Coll., 1965; BA, U. Oxford, 1967, MA, 1971, Harvard U., 1969, PhD, 1974. Seminarian Pope John XXIII Nat. Sem., Weston, Mass., 1974-77; collaborator prof. Sterling Dow Harvard U., Cambridge, Mass., 1977-95. Cons. in pub. and photoreprodn. Author: Studies in Inscriptions Listing the Agonistic Festivals, 1974, A Quinquagesimal History of the Church of St. Bernadette, 1987; contbr. articles to profl. jours. Pres., chmn. adminstrn. fin., St. Bernadette's Ch., Archdiocese of Boston, 1980—; founding dir. Theol. Lectures Series, Randolph, Mass., 1978—, Randolph Hist. Commn., 1988—; staff vol. Cardinal Medeiros Program for Handicapped, 1980-82; treas., bd. dirs. Randolph Community Food Pantry, 1994—. Marshall scholar, 1965-67; Wilson scholar, 1965—; Gen. Motors scholar, 1962-65; Ford Found. fellow, 1967-69; Harvard U. fellow, 1969-71 Mem. Am. Inst. Archaeology, Am. Philol. Assn., Alumni Assn. Harvard, Oxford U. Alumni Assn., Boston Coll. Alumni Assn. Democrat. Roman Catholic. Home: 4 Bennington St Randolph MA 02368-2106 E-mail: EdmondusM@msn.com.

MORRISSEY, JOHN CARROLL, SR., lawyer; b. N.Y.C., Sept. 2, 1914; s. Edward Joseph and Estelle (Caine) M.; m. Eileen Colligan, Oct. 14, 1950; children: Jonathan Edward, Ellen (Mrs. James A. Jenkins), Katherine, John, Patricia, Richard, Brian, Peter. BA magna cum laude, Yale U., 1937, LLB, 1940; JSD, N.Y. U., 1951; grad., Command and Gen. Staff Sch., 1944. Bar: N.Y. State 1940, D.C. 1953, Calif. 1954, U.S. Supreme Ct. 1944. Asso. firm Dorsey and Adams, 1940-41, Dorsey, Adams and Walker, 1946-50; counsel Office of Sec. of Def., Dept. Def., Washington, 1950-52; acting gen. counsel def. Electric Power Adminstrn., 1952-53; atty. Pacific Gas and Electric Co., San Francisco, 1953-70, assoc. gen. counsel, 1970-74, v.p., gen. counsel, 1975-80; individual practice law San Francisco, 1980-2000. Dir. Gas Lines, Inc. Bd. dirs. Legal Aid Soc., San Francisco; chmn. Golden Gate dist. Boy Scouts Am., 1973-75; commr. Human Rights Commn. of San Francisco, 1976-89, chmn., 1980-82; chmn. Cath. Social Svc. of San Francisco, 1966-68; adv. com. Archdiocesean Legal Affairs, 1981—; regent Archdiocesan Sch. of Theology, St. Patrick's Sem., 1994-99; dir. Presidio Preservation Assn., 1995-99. Served to col. F.A. U.S. Army, ETO, 1941-46. Decorated Bronze star, Army Commendation medal. Mem. NAS, AAAS, ABA, Calif. State Bar Assn., Fed. Power Bar Assn., N.Y. Acad. Scis., Calif. Conf. Pub. Utility Counsel, Pacific Coast Electric Assn., Pacific Coast Gas Assn., Econ. Round Table of San Francisco, World Affairs Council, San Francisco C. of C., Calif. State C. of C., Harold Brunn Soc. Med. Rsch., Electric Club, Serra Club, Commonwealth Club, Yale Club of San Francisco (pres. 1989-90), Pacific-Union Club, Sometimes Tuesday Club, Sovereign Mil. Order Malta, Phi Beta Kappa. Roman Catholic. Home: 2030 Jackson St San Francisco CA 94109-2840 Office: 1661 Pine St # 1135 San Francisco CA 94105 E-mail: dadjcm@aol.com.

MORRISSEY, MARY, state representative; b. Vennington, Vt., Mar. 26, 1957; State rep. Vt. Ho. Reps., 1996—. Bd. dirs. Southwestern Vt. Med. Ctr. Mem. Bennington Rep. Com., 1991—, Bennington County Rep. Com., 1992—; recording sec. Bennington Bd. Civil Authority; bd. dirs. Old Castle Theatre, 1986-89, exec. bd. 1989, guild 1985—); bd. dirs. Bennington County Choral Soc., 1985-88. Mem. Bennington Bus. and Profl. Women (pres. 1991-93), Bennington Crimestoppers (bd. dirs. 1992—, vice-chmn. 1996), Rotary, Cath. Daus. Am. Office: 228 Dewey St Bennington VT 05201-2222

MORRISSEY, MARY F. (FRAN), human resource consulting company executive; Cert. profl. employer specialist. Acctg., tax profl., small bus. cons., 10 yrs.; formre owner, mgr. profl. employer orgn.; co-founder, pres., CEO, Staff Mgmt., Inc., Rockford, Ill., 1983—. Part-owner John Morrissey, Accts., Rockford; presenter to state and fed. legislators, regulatory agys. and profl. orgns.; sec., mem. bd. Merc. Bank; bd. dirs. Inst. for Accreditation Profl. Employer Orgns. Bd. dirs. Swedish Am. Health Sys., Rockford; active numerous civic orgsn. Named One of Top 25 Women Bus. Owners, Crain's Chgo. Bus., 1993, 95, Connie Tremulis award for bus. owners YWCA, Rockford, 1998. Mem. Soc. for Human Resource Mgmt. (accredited sr. profl. in human resources), Nat. Assn. Profl. Employer Orgns. (past bd. dirs. and past pres.), former mem. profl. stds. com., also former chmn., past mem. comm. network, mgmt. performance, membership, govt. affairs, and edn. coms.), Midwest Assn. Profl. Employer Orgns. (past pres.), Nat. Assn. Women Bus.

Owners (One of Top 25 Women Bus. Owners 1993, 95), Rockford Area C. of C. (coun. of 100, Woman Bus. Owner of Yr. 1998)), Rockford Women's Club, also others. Office: Staff Mgmt Inc 5919 Spring Creek Rd Rockford IL 61114-6447 Fax: 815-282-0515.

MORRISSEY, MICHAEL JOSEPH, investment banker; b. Mount Holly, N.J., June 26, 1947; s. Edward Francis and Winifred (Monahan) M.; m. Joanne Stone, June 5, 1982; children: Scott Christopher, Nathanial Joseph Cake. AB, Boston Coll., 1969; MBA, Dartmouth Coll., 1971; grad. Corp. Fin. Mgmt. Program, Harvard U., 1979. Security analyst Philo Smith & Co., Inc., Stamford, Conn., 1971-73, Kidder Peabody & Co., Inc., N.Y.C., 1973-74, asst. v.p., 1974-76, v.p., 1976-77, Dean Witter Reynolds, Inc., N.Y.C., 1977-78, Crum and Forster, Morristown, N.J., 1978-80, sr. v.p., 1980-83; pres. Firemark Investments, Morristown, NJ, 1983-85, chmn. bd., 1985—; exec. v.p. Manhattan Nat. Corp., N.Y.C., 1985, pres., chief operating officer, 1985-86. Bd. dir. Fin. Pacific Ins. Group, Calif., Post Acute Care Inc., Pa., Online Benefits Inc., NYC. Recipient CFA award, 1977. Fellow Assn. Investment Mgmt. and Rsch.; mem. Internat. Ins. Soc., Young Pres.' Orgn., Pk. Ave. Club, Dartmouth Club (N.Y.C.), Spring Brook Country Club. Republican. Presbyterian. Office: FireMark Investments 200 W De Vargas St Santa Fe NM 87501 Office Phone: 505-989-8384. E-mail: mjm@firemarkinv.com.

MORRISSEY, PATRICIA A. commissioner; AA Liberal Arts, Hartford C.C., 1964; BA Psychology, Stetson U., 1966; M.Ed. Spl. Edn., Pa. State U., 1971; PhD Spl. Edn., Pa. State U., 1974. Sr. assoc. Booz Allen Hamilton, McLean, Va.; commr. adminstrn. and devel. disabilities U.S. Health and Human Svcs. (HHS), 2001—. With Senate, Ho. of Reps., Pres. Ronald Regan; with Senate Ticket to Work and Work Incentives Improvement Act Wis. Gov. Thomson's Office; with Pres. George W. Bush's New Freedom Initiative. Republican. Office: 200 Independence Ave SW Washington DC 20201 Business E-Mail: pmorrissey@acf.dhhs.gov.*

MORRIS-TYNDALL, LUCY, construction executive; married; 2 children. From sec. to cost engr. Swinerton & Walberg, San Francisco, 1977—92, asst. project mgr., 1992—94, with mgmt. and consulting br., 1994—97, v.p., ops. mgr., 1997—99; chief info. officer Swinerton Inc. (formerly Swinerton & Walberg), San Francisco, 1999—. Recipient Julia Morgan award, YWCA of Oakland, 1996, Medal of Excellence, Women at Work, 2002. Mem.: AGC of Calif. (info. tech. task force), Constrn. Info. Execs. Office: Swinerton Inc 260 Townsend St San Francisco CA 94107

MORRONE, FRANK, electronic manufacturing executive; b. Marano Marchesato, Cosenza, Italy, May 13, 1949; s. Luigi and Emma (Molinaro) M.; m. Katherine Ann Kuehn, Feb. 1, 1975; children: Louis H., Cecilia E., Joseph V. BSEE, U. Wis., 1972; MBA, Northwestern U., 1993. Project engr. 3M Co., St. Paul, 1972—73; product engr., mgr. Eaton Corp., Kenosha, Wis., 1973—79; chief elec. engr. Tree Machine Tool, Racine, Wis., 1979—80; v.p. engring. MacPower divsn. Manu-Tronics, Inc., Kenosha, 1980—84, exec. v.p., 1984—99, bd. dirs., sec., 1988—99; v.p. ops. Sanmina Corp., 1999—2001, sr. v.p., 2001—. Mem. exec. bd. southeast coun. Boy Scouts Am., Racine, 1987—; bd. dirs. Kenosha Libr., 1987-98, U. Wis.-Parkside Benevolent Found., 2000—; mem. mgmt. coun. Lakeview Tech. Acad., 1997-99. Mem. IEEE, Kenosha County Club (bd. dirs.). Office: Sanmina Corp 8701 100th St Pleasant Prairie WI 53158-2202

MORRONI, JOHN, state legislator, banker; b. Chgo., Feb. 16, 1955; BA in History, Loyola U., 1977. Mem. Fla. Ho. of Reps., Tallahassee, 1992—. Chmn. regulated svcs. com.; mem. edn. K/12 com., election reform com., ednl. facilities select com. Mem. adv. bd. U. South Fla., 1994—; bd. dirs. Pinellas County Industry Coun.; mem. Clearwater (Fla.) Hist. Preservation Bd., 1988-91. Mem. Largo C. of C., Gateway C. of C. Republican. Roman Catholic. Avocations: beach volleyball, reading, collecting presidential memorabilia coins. Office: State Capitol Rm 408 HOB 402 Monrose St Tallahassee FL 32399-1300

MORROS, STEPHEN VINCENT, marketing professional, educator; b. Birmingham, Ala., July 24, 1968; s. Joe (Stepfather) and Diana Johnson; life ptnr. Lee Morrison, June 21, 1997. MusM in Edn., BA in Music, Jacksonville State U., 1993. Assoc. dir. band, choir Mortimer Jordan H.S., Morris, 1995—2000; mktg. and sales coord. Emageon, Birmingham, 2000—01, mgr. mktg., 2001—. Composer: (percussion ensemble composition) Quartet For 1 Stick (Superior Medal, 1997), Dreamscape (Superior Medal, 1999), (percussioin ensemble composition) Ostinato (Superior Medal, 1998). Mem. PFLAG, 1998—2002; mem. steering com. Equality Ala., Birmingham, 2002; mem. Human Rights Campaign, Birmingham, 1997—2002; mem. choir Dawson Meml. Bapt. Ch., Birmingham, 1994—97. Recipient Cert. of Achievement, Collegiate Music Educators Nat. Conf., 1995. Mem.: Percussive Arts Soc. (assoc.; chpt. web master 1999—2002), Omicron Delta Kappa (life), Kappa Delta Pi (life), Phi Mu Alpha (life; sec. 1987—90, Alumnus of Yr. 1991). Democrat. Avocations: travel, cooking, reading, music, computers. Home: 2516 Arlington Crescent Birmingham AL 35205 Office: Emageon 1200 Corporate Drive Suite 400 Birmingham AL 35242 Personal E-mail: svmdrum@bellsouth.net. E-mail: smorros@emageon.com.

MORROW, ARDYTHE LUXION, adult education educator, researcher; b. Elgin, Ill., Aug. 30, 1955; children: Winona, Justin. PhD, U. Tex., Houston, 1991. Prof. Eastern Va. Med. Sch., Norfolk, 1992—2001; assoc. dir. Ctr. for Pediatric Rsch., Norfolk, 1998—2001; prof. U. Cin. Coll. Medicine, 2001—; dir. Ctr. for Epidemiology and Biostats., Cin. Children's Hosp. Med. Ctr., 2001—. Tech. advisor WHO, 2001—. Mem. editl. bd.: Jour. Human Lactation; contbr. articles to profl. jours. Recipient Young Investigator award Internat. Soc. for Rsch. in Human Milk and Lactation, 1997, Faculty Rsch. award Eastern Va. Med. Sch., 1999, Human Milk Program Project grant NIH, 2003—; fellow Exec. Leadership in Acad. Medicine program MCP Hahnemann U., 2000-01; Jackie Schnell Meml. scholar Rice U., Brown Coll., 1974. Mem.: Milk Club/Pediat. Acad. Soc. (chair 2002—), Am. Pediat. Soc., Am. Coll. Epidemiology. Bahai Faith. Avocations: travel, music. Home: 6234 Orchard Ln Cincinnati OH 45213 Office: Ctr Epidemiology and Biostats Cin Children's Hosp 3333 Burnet Ave Cincinnati OH 45229 Office Phone: 513-636-7626.

MORROW, BARRY NELSON, screenwriter, producer; b. Austin, Minn., June 12, 1948; s. Robert Clayton and Rose Nell (Nelson) M.; m. Beverly Lee McKenzie, Mar. 3, 1969; children: Clayton McKenzie, ZoeAnna Rachel. BA, St. Olaf Coll., 1970; DHL (hon.), U. La Verne, Calif., 1990. Media specialist U. Iowa, Iowa City, 1974-81; freelance screenwriter Los Angeles, 1981-90; pres. Morrow-Heus Prodns., 1990-00. Storywriter (TV film) Bill, 1981 (Emmy award 1982); screenwriter: (TV films) Bill: On His Own, 1983, Conspiracy of Love, 1987, Silent Victory, 1988, The Karen Carpenter Story, 1989, (feature film) Rain Man, 1988 (co-recipient Acad. award Best Original Screenplay 1989); screenwriter, exec. prodr.: Christmas on Division Street, 1991; exec. prodr.: Switched at Birth, 1991 (Emmy nomination), Gospa, 1995, The Fifties, 1997, Behind the Mask, 1999; screenwriter, prodr. Race the Sun, 1996; monologist: Bill for Short, 1992. Recipient Pres.'s award Am. Acad. for Devel. Medicine, 1978, Outstanding Contbn. award Mid-Am. Congress on Aging, 1983, SI award NASW, 1991, Pope John XXIII award Viterbo Coll., 1992. Mem. Writers Guild Am. West, Acad. TV Arts and Scis., Acad. Motion Picture Arts and Scis., Motion Picture Screen Cartoonists Guild.

MORROW, BILL, state legislator; b. Monterey Park, Calif., Apr. 19, 1954; married; 1 child. BA, U. Calif., L.A., 1976; JD, Pepperdine U., 1979. Commd. officer, mil. judge adv. USMC, 1979-87; civil litig. atty., 1987—; mem. Calif. State Assembly, 1993-98, Calif. State Senate, 1998—, vice chmn. judiciary com., mem. coms. on transp., ins., govtl. orgn., energy. Active Spl. Olympics, Boys and Girls Club, Salvation Army. Named Legislator of Yr. Orange County League of Cities., Legislator of Yr. Pro-Life PAC Orange County, 1995, Civil Justice Reform Legislator of Yr. Orange County Citizens Against Lawsuit Abuse, 1996, Legislator of Yr., Calif. Rep. Assembly, 1996, Legislator of Yr. Golden State Mobilehome Owners League Calif., 1997, Small Bus. Legislator of Yr. Calif. Rep. Assembly, 2002, Legislator of Yr. Calif. Rifle and Pistol Assn., 2002. Mem. NRA, Am. Legion, Marine Corps League, Gun Owners Calif., Ducks Unlimited, Calif. Waterfowl Assn., Oceanside C. of C., San Juan C. of C., North County Armed Forces, Amvets, Kiwanis, YMCA. Republican. Protestant. Office: State Capitol Rm 4048 Sacramento CA 95814 also: 27126A Paseo Espada # 1621 San Juan Capistrano CA 92675-2725 also: 2755 Jefferson St Ste 101 Carlsbad CA 92008-1714 E-mail: bill.morrow@assembly.ca.gov.

MORROW, BRUCE WILLIAM, educational administrator, business executive, consultant, author; b. Rochester, Minn., May 20, 1946; s. J. Robert and Frances P. Morrow; m. Jenny Lea Morrow. BA, U. Notre Dame, 1968, MBA in Mgmt. with honors, 1974, MA in Comparative Lit., 1975; grad., U.S. Army Command and Gen. Staff Coll., 1979. Cert. project mgmt. profl. Project Mgmt. Inst., 2003. Chmn. elem. German U. Notre Dame, 1973-75; co-mgr. Wendy's Old Fashioned Hamburgers, South Bend, Ind., 1976-77; adminstrn. mgr. Eastern States Devel. Corp., Richmond, Va., 1977; v.p. JDB Assocs., Inc., Alexandria, Va., 1976-78; sr. cons. Data Base Mgmt., Inc., Springfield, Va., 1979-80; owner Aardvark Prodns., Alexandria, 1980-82; sys. analyst/staff officer Hdqrs., Dept. Army, Washington, 1980-84; chmn. bd. Commonwealth Dominion Corp., Sierra Vista, Ariz., 1982—. Strategic planner, dep. comdr. Fort Pickett, Blackstone, Va., 1986—89; dir. continuing edn. Southside Va. C.C., Alberta, 1989—91; co-founder S.W. Bus. Group, Tucson, 1995—99; pres. Sierra Vista Golf, Inc., Ariz., 1994—95; Cochise County team leader Ariz. Coun. Econ. Conversion, 1994—95; mem. com. Ariz. Small Bus. Initiative, 1994—99; internet webmaster, 1996—; exec. dir. Southea. Ariz. Contrs. Assn., 1997—98; corp. adminstr. Garcia Cos., Sierra Vista, Tucson, Phoenix, 1997—99; property adminstr. Brown & Root Svcs., Ft. Huachuca, Ariz., Land Between the Lakes, Ky., 1999—2000, logistics coord., 2001—02; dir. assessment ctr. Transport. Security Agy. NCS Pearson, Nashville, 2002—, dir. assessment ctr. TSA project, Fresno, Calif., 2002—; project specialist Dyncorp Internat., Irving, Tex., 2004—. Author (radio series) Survival in the Computer Jungle, 1986, (classroom text) Introduction to Computers, 1988, 2d edit., 1993, Defense Conversion Handbook, 1995, business Assessment Manual, 1996, Employee Manual Guide, 1996, Business Plan Guide, 1996, Marketing Plan Guide, 1996, (screenplay) Gray Rock, 2000; contbg. columnist Notre Dame mag., 1974-86; exec. prodr. (motion picture) Beneath the Law, 1995-96; composer songs. Active Boy Scouts Am., 1960-69, firefighter Roanoke Wildwood Vol. Fire Dept., 1991-93. Lt. col. USAR, ret. Decorated Bronze Star, Army commendation medals, Army Achievement medal, Meritorious Svc. medals, Parachutist's badge, Army Gen. Staff badge. Mem. VFW (life), Nat. Eagle Scout Assn., Lake Gaston C. of C. (bd. dirs.), Am. Legion, Sierra Vista Area C. of C., Lions (v.p. local club), Friends Internat. (Am. v.p. 1969-71, Boeblingen, Germany), Order of DeMolay, Beta Gamma Sigma, Delta Phi Alpha. Office: Commonwealth Dominion Corp 334 Landing Strip Rd Hardin KY 42048-9413 E-mail: cdc@theriver.com.

MORROW, DAVID ANDREW, secondary school educator; b. Van Buren, Maine, Dec. 5, 1950; s. Laurence and Anne Marie (Lavoie) M; m. Robertine Thibodeau, June 20, 1975. BS magna cum laude, U. So. Maine, 1981; student, U. Maine. Indsl. arts/tech. and vocat. tchr. Van Buren (Maine) Community High/Mid. Sch., 1971-87; tech. edn. tchr. Ashland (Maine) Community High/Mid. Sch., 1987—. With USN, 1969-71. Recipient Tchr. Excellence award Internat. Tech. Edn. Assn., Maine, 1992. Mem. NEA, Internat. Tech. Edn. Assn. (Tchr. Excellence award 1993), Tech. Edn. Assn. Maine (Tech. Tchr. of Yr. 1993), Maine Tchrs. Assn., Ashland Tchrs. Edn. Assn., Assn. Supervision and Curriculum Devel., Aroostook Tech. Edn. Assn. Maine. Roman Catholic. Avocations: photography, computers, canoeing, skiing, playing guitar. Home: 9 Skyview Dr Presque Isle ME 04769-2460 Office: Ashland Comty High Sch Hayward St Ashland ME 04732

MORROW, ELIZABETH HOSTETTER, sculptress, museum administrator, farmer, educator; b. Sibley, Mo., Feb. 28, 1947; d. Elman A. and Lorine H. Morrow; married, 1970 (div. 1979); children: Jan Pawel, Lorentz Arthur. Student, William Jewell Coll., 1958-59, Colo. Coll., 1959-60, U. Okla., 1960-62; BFA, U. Kans., 1964, MFA, 1967; postgrad., U. Minn., 1965, U. Kans., 1968. Pres. E. Morrow Co., Kansas City, Mo., 1966-67; head dept. art U. Hawaii, Honolulu, 1968-69, Tarkio (Mo.) Coll., 1970-74; exec. dir. Pensacola (Fla.) Mus. Art, 1974-76; pres., owner Blair-Murrah Exhbns., Sibley, Mo., 1980—. Pres. bd. trustees, CEO Blair-Murrah, Inc., 1991—; sec.-treas. Coun. for Cultural Resources, 1995—. Del. White House Conf. on Small Bus., 1986. Lew Wentz scholar U. Okla., 1960-62. Mem. Internat. Coun. of Mus., Internat. Coun. Exhbn. Exch., Internat. Soc. Appraisers, Am. Assn. Mus., Canadian Assn. Mus., Internat. Trade Club of Greater Kansas City, Nat. Assn. Mus. Exhibitions, Ft. Osage Hist. Soc., Hist. Six MileCemetery Bd., Friends Art, Internat. Com. Fine Arts, Internat. Com. Conservation, Internat. Sculpture Ctr., DAR, Delta Phi Delta. Independent. Avocations: historical and cultural activities, antique cars, midwest farm auctions, genealogy. Home: RR # 1 Sibley MO 64088 Office: Blair-Murrah Vintage Hill Orch Sibley MO 64088 also: 7 rue Muzy PO Box Nr 554 1211 Geneva Switzerland Office Phone: 816-249-9400. E-mail: elizabethmorrow@blair-murrah.org., exhibits@blair-murrah.org.

MORROW, GEORGE J. pharmaceutical company executive; m. Katherine Morrow; 3 children. BA, Southampton Coll.; MA in Biochemistry, Bryn Mawr Coll.; MBA, Duke U. V.p., gen. mgr. sales and mktg. divsn. Glaxo, Inc., 1992, v.p. comml. ops., 1993; mng. dir. Glaxo Wellcome UK; pres., CEO Glaxo Wellcome Inc., Research Park Triangle, NC, 1999—2001; exec. v.p., worldwide sales and mktg. Amgen, Inc., Thousand Oaks, Calif., 2001—. Office: Amgen Inc 1 Amgen Ctr Dr Thousand Oaks CA 91320-1799

MORROW, GEORGE LESTER, retired oil and gas executive; b. New Haven, Apr. 27, 1922; s. Lester W.W. and Esther (Morrow) M.; m. Mary L. Evenburg, Dec. 28, 1946; children: Susan Morrow Donaldson, William, John, Thomas. BS, Rutgers U., 1943; MBA, U. Chgo., 1954. With Peoples Gas Light and Coke Co., Chgo., 1947-77, v.p. ops., 1966-71, pres., 1971-77; also dir.; pres. Natural Gas Pipeline Co. Am., 1977-83; vice chmn., dir. Midcon Corp., 1983-87. Capt. AUS, 1943-46. Mem. Sarasota Yacht Club, Lake Zurich Golf Club. Presbyterian. Home: 801 N Beverly Ln Arlington Heights IL 60004-5724

MORROW, GRANT, III, medical research director, pediatrician; b. Pitts., Mar. 18, 1933; married, 1960; 2 children. BA, Haverford Coll., 1955; MD, U. Pa., 1959. Intern U. Colo., 1959-60; resident in pediat. U. Pa., 1960-62, fellow neonatology, asst. instr., 1962-63, instr., 1963-66, assoc., 1966-68, asst. prof., 1968-70, assoc. prof., 1970-72, U. Ariz., 1972—78, prof., 1974-78, assoc. chmn. dept., 1976-78; med. dir. Columbus (Ohio) Children's Hosp., 1978-94; prof. neonatology and metabolism, chmn. dept. Ohio State U., 1978-94; med. dir. divsn. molecular and human genetics Children's Hosp. Rsch. Found., Columbus, 1994-98. Med. dir. Children's Rsch. Inst., Columbus, Ohio, 1978—. Mem. Am. Pediat. Soc., Am. Soc. Clin. Nutrition, Soc. Pediat. Rsch. Achievements include research on children suffering inborn errors of metabolism, mainly amino and organic acids. Office: Children's Rsch Inst 700 Childrens Dr Columbus OH 43205-2696 Fax: (614) 722-2716. Office Phone: 614-722-2708. E-mail: morrowg@pediatrics.ohio-state.edu.

MORROW, JAMES FRANKLIN, lawyer; b. Shenandoah, Iowa, Oct. 23, 1944; s. Warren Ralph and Margaret Glee (Palm) M. BS, Kans. State U., 1967; JD, U. Ariz., 1973. Bar: Ariz. 1973, U.S. Dist. Ct. Ariz. 1973. Ptnr. Bilby, Shoenhair, Warnock & Dolph, Tucson, 1973-83, Quarles & Brady Streich Lang LLP, Tucson, 1984—. Mng. editor U. Ariz. Law Rev., 1972-73. Past chmn. bd. trustees Palo Verde Mental Health Svcs.; past pres. U. Ariz. Alumni Assn.; past chmn. bd. Palo Verde Hosp., Ariz. Tech. Devel. Corp.; past pres. bd. Cath. Cmty. Svcs.; past chmn. bd. dirs. U. Ariz. Found. Capt. U.S. Army, 1967-70. Mem. Am. Coll. Real Estate Lawyers, Am. Coll. Mortgage Attys., State Bar Ariz. (cert. real estate specialist, adv. com. real estate specialists, past chmn. real estate property sect.), Pima County Bar Assn., Calif. Bar Assn. Democrat. Roman Catholic. Avocation: golf. Office: Quarles & Brady Streich Lang LLP Ste 1700 One South Church Ave Tucson AZ 85701

MORROW, JAMES THOMAS, energy executive; b. Seattle, Apr. 24, 1941; s. James Elroy and Helen Margaret (Helzer) M.; 1 child, Shannon F. BSEE, BS in Gen. Sci., Oreg. State U., 1964; MBA, U. Santa Clara, 1966, PhD, 1973. Registered profl. engr.; registered investment advisor. Engr. Gen. Electric Co., San Jose, Calif., 1964—66; engring. mgr. Beckman Instruments, Inc., Palo Alto, Calif., 1966—69; pres. MSA Cons., Inc., Portland, Oreg., 1969—75; asst. prof. U. Portland, 1969—75; mgr. A.T. Kearney, Inc., San Francisco, 1975—78; v.p. mktg. Pierce Pacific Mfg., Portland, 1978—79; chmn., CEO Lanco Internat., Inc., Clackamas, Oreg., 1979—81; regional mgr., v.p. Case & Co., Portland, 1981—82; chmn. bd., exec. v.p. Morley Fin. Svcs. Inc., 1982—94; exec. v.p., chmn. bd. Biojet, Med. Systems Ltd., 1985—94; ptnr. WAM Partnership, 1987—96; sec.-treas. Environ. Waste of Am., Inc., Seattle, 1992—94; chmn., pres., CEO Capital Devel. Group, Inc., Portland, 1994—96; chmn., CEO USA/China Design and Mfg. Inc., Tianjing, China, 1994—95, The Apollo Fin. Group, N.Y.C., 1996—98; pres., chmn., CEO G.I.C. Acceptance Corp., Portland, 1992—; chmn., CEO Turtle Cove Resort, Anacortes, Wash., 2000—, Olympic Healthcare Tech., Inc., Portland, N.Y.C., 1998—2002; pres., CEO, dir. Naanovo Energy, Inc., Calgary, Alta., Canada, 2003—; sr. v.p. El Rincon Resort, Cabo San Lucas, Mexico, 2002—03. Chmn. bd. dirs. Ship Harbor Resort and Marina, Inc., 1998-2004, Turtle Cove Resort, Inc., 1998, Olympic Capital, Inc., 1998-2003; bd. dirs. Naanove Energy, Accucom Data Network, Inc., Pierce Pacific Mfg., Lanco Internat., Energy Guard, Inc., G&R Devel. Co., Inc., MSA Cons., Inc.; sec.-treas. Everybody's Record Co., Inc. Contbr. articles to profl. jours., chpts. to textbooks; patentee biojector needleless syringe. Bd. dirs. Found. for Oreg. Rsch. and Edn., Jr. Achievement, First August Fin., Inc., Met. Youth Symphony; chmn. steering com. R.S. Dow Neurol. Scis. Inst.; mem. Russian ANT-25 Aviation Com. Mem. Oreg. Pilots Assn. (pres. Beaverton chpt.). Republican. Congregationalist. Home: 3721 NW Port Ave Lincoln City OR 97367

MORROW, JASON DREW, medical and pharmacology educator; b. St. Louis, Mar. 30, 1957; s. Ralph Ernest and Vera Rowena (Cummings) M.; m. Lisa Lee Hyman, Mar. 26, 1983; children: Jeremy Nash, Stephanie Rose. BA magna cum laude, Vanderbilt U., 1979; MD, Washington U., St. Louis, 1983. Diplomate Am. Bd. Internal Medicine, Am. Bd. Infectious Diseases. Med. intern, resident Vanderbilt U. Hosp., Nashville, 1983-86, Hugh J. Morgan chief med. resident, 1987-88, rsch. fellow in clin. pharmacology, 1988-91; sr. rsch. fellow dept. pharmacology Vanderbilt U., Sch. Medicine, Nashville, 1991-94, asst. prof. pharmacology and medicine, 1994-95; assoc. prof. Vanderbilt U., Nashville, 1995-99, F. Tremaine Billings prof. medicine, 1999—, dir. Eicosanoid Core Lab. dept. pharmacology, 1992—; clin. fellow in infectious diseases Barnes Hosp./Washington U., 1986-87; staff physician in medicine and infectious diseases VA Med. Ctr., Nashville, 1991—; dir. med. scholars program Vanderbilt Med. Sch., 1997—, assoc. dean, 2003—. Mem. internat. adv. com. 9th Internat. Conf. on Prostglandins and Related Compounds, Florence, Italy, 1994, 10th Conf., Vienna, Austria, 1996; dir. Rsch. Ctr. Pharm. and Drug Toxicology, Vanderbilt Med. Sch., 1999—. Contbr. over 300 articles, revs. and papers to sci. jours., chpts. to books. Physician Nashville Union Rescue Mission, 1988-00. Recipient Physician-Scientist award NIH, 1990-91, grantee; recipient Rsch. Found. Devel. award Internat. Life Scis. Inst., 1992-96, Burroughs Wellcome Fund award in Transitional Rsch., 1999—; Centennial Clin. Pharmacology fellow Boehringer-Ingelheim, 1990-91, Howard Hughes Med. Inst. Physician rsch. fellow, 1991-94; grantee Liddle Med. Rsch., 1996. Mem. AMA, ACP, AAAS, Am. Fedn. Clin. Rsch., Am. Soc. Clin. Investigation, So. Soc. Clin. Investigation, Infectious Diseases Soc. Am., Am. Soc. Pharmacology Exptl. Therapeutics, Am. Soc. Biochemistry and Molecular Biology, Phi Beta Kappa. Avocations: running, fishing, outdoors. Home: 6408 Eastbourne Dr Brentwood TN 37027-4802 Office: Vanderbilt U Dept Pharmacology 23rd And Pierce Ave Nashville TN 37232-0001

MORROW, JENNIFER LEIGH See LEIGH, JENNIFER JASON

MORROW, LESLEY MANDEL, literacy and elementary education educator; BS, Syracuse U.; MA, N.J. City U.; PhD, Fordham U. Cert. early childhood tchr., elem. tchr., reading specialist K-12, supr., prin. Tchr. Bradford Elem. Sch., Montclair, NJ, 1964—68; demonstration tchr. Lab. Elem. Sch. William Paterson U., NJ, 1968—70; instr. edn. dept. Chapman Coll., Orange, Calif., 1970—71; instr. learning and tchg. dept. St. John's U., NY, 1971—74; instr. comm. scis. dept. and early childhood dept. Kean U., NJ, 1974—79; asst. prof. edn. dept. Douglas Coll. Rutgers U., New Brunswick, NJ, 1979—85, assoc. prof. Grad. Sch. Edn., 1986—91, chair dept. learning and tchg., 1991—93, 2000—02, prof. literacy and early childhood/elem. edn. Grad. Sch. Edn., 1991—. Coadjutant faculty N.J. City U., 1974—76, Fordham U., 1974—76, William Paterson U., 1974—76; cons. in field; author Scott Foresman Basal Reading Series, 1991—97; mem. adv. bd. Sesame Street PBS Children's TV Workshop, 1993—98; sr. author William H. Sadlier Reading Programs, 1998—; mem. adv. bd. Reading Rainbow PBS Program, 2002—. Recipient Disting. Achievement for Excellence in Ednl. Journalism award, Ednl. Press Assn. Am., 1989, Literacy award, N.J. Reading Assn., 1996, Spl. Svc. award, 2000, grants and scholarships in field. Fellow: Nat. Conf. on Rsch. in English; mem.: Nat. Assessment Ednl. Progress (adv. bd. 1992, 1994), Internat. Reading Assn. (pres. 2003—, Outstanding Tchr. Educator of Reading award 1995). Office: Rutgers The State U NJ Grad Sch Edn Rm 206A 10 Seminary Pl New Brunswick NJ 08901-1183

MORROW, MONICA, medical educator; b. Abington, Pa., Sept. 16, 1953; d. James Robert and Maxine Cooper Morrow; m. Virgil Craig Jordan, OBE, PhD, DSc. BS magna cum laude, Pa. State U., 1974; MD, Jefferson Med. Coll., 1976. Diplomate Am. Bd. of Surgery. Fellow in surg. oncology Meml. Sloan Kettering Cancer Ctr., New York, NY, 1981—83; asst. prof. of surgery SUNY Health Sci. Ctr. at Bklyn, Brooklyn, NY, 1983—88; assoc. prof. of surgery U. of Chgo., Chicago, Ill., 1988—93, Northwestern U., Chicago, Ill., 1993—97, prof. of surgery, 1997—2004; chmn. dept. surgical oncology and G. Willing Pepper chair cancer rsch. Fox Chase Cancer Ctr., Phila., 2004—. Dir., cancer dept. ACS, Chgo., 1999—2001; exec. dir. Am. Joint Com. on Cancer, Chgo., 1999—2001; mem. Nat. Cancer Policy Bd., Inst. of Medicine, Washington, 1999—2002; co-chair Joint Com. of the ACS, Am. Coll. of Radiology, and Coll. of Am. Pathologists on Standards for Breast Conservation, 2000—02. Editor: (book) Managing Breast Cancer Risk, American Joint Committee on Cancer Staging Manual, sixth edition, Diseases of the Breast, Breast Diseases: A Problem Based Approach. Recipient Distinguished Alumni, Pa. State U., 2002; grantee Prin. Investigator, Avon Found. Ctr. of Excellence Grant, 2000 - Present, Co-Principal Investigator, Specialized Program of Rsch. Excellence in Breast Cancer Grant, Nat. Cancer Inst., 2000-2005. Mem.: Am. Surg. Assn., Am. Soc. of Clin. Oncology (bd. of directors 1998—2001), Soc. of Surg. Oncology (exec. com. 2003—), Soc. of Surg. Oncology (exec. com. 1993—96). Avocations: travel, history, wine. Office: Fox Chase Cancer Ctr 333 Cottman Ave Philadelphia PA 19111-2497

MORROW, NANA KWASI SCOTT DOUGLAS, choreographer, director, writer, filmmaker, educator; b. NYC, Jan. 29, 1954; s. Alfredo and Lorraine (Lopez) Morro. Honor grad., N.Y.C. H.S. of Performing Arts; BFA in Dance, SUNY, Purchase, 1976; MA in Choreography, UCLA, 1986. Ordained interfaith min. 2004. Prin. instr. Phil Black Dance Studio, N.Y.C., 1969-77; dir. dance divsn. No. Ill. U., DeKalb, 1976-78; artistic dir., resident choreographer No. Ill. Repertory Dance Co., 1976-78; artistic dir. Scott Morrow Dance Theatre Co. and Sch., L.A., 1978-85; prin. instr. Mary Tyler Moore Los Angeles Dance Ctr., 1979-80; resident dance master South Coast Repertory Acting Conservatory, Calif., 1979-82; vis. prof. Wright State U., Ohio, 1981; ballet master, resident choreographer Empire State Ballet, Buffalo, 1984-85; asst. prof. U. Kans., Lawrence, 1985-88. Choreographer Morrow Dance Theatre-in-Residence, U. Kans., 1985-88, 92d St. Dancer Ctr., YMHA and YWHA, NYC, 1989; founder, dir. Jazz Dance Ministry for Racial Reconciliation, Peace and Healing, N.Y.C., 1988—; assoc. dir., dir. edn. pub. sch. dance programs K-12, Bronx Dance Theatre Performing Arts Ctr., NYC, 1990-93; faculty Internat. Summer Sch. Royal Acad. Dancing, NYC, 1991-92, Calif. State U. Sys. Summer Inst. for Tchg. and Learning, 1994; sr. faculty Lilly Conf. on Coll. Tchg., Miami U., Ohio, 1991-2001; dance specialist State Edn. Dept. Summer Inst. on Assessment in Arts, NY, 1992; founder, dir. in chief Inst. Advancement Edn. Dance, NYC, 1992-02; adv. bd. Internat. Found. for

Performing Arts Medicine, 1992—; adv. Performing Arts Medicine Ctr., Kessler Inst. Rehab., NJ, 1995—; Walter H. Annenberg disting. vis. artist-scholar The Renaissance Sch., NYC, 1995-96; cons. presenting and commissioning program Nat. Endowment for Arts, 1993-95; peer rev. panel Fund for Innovation in Edn. US. Edn. Dept., 1993-94; co-chmn. dance edn. com. World Dance Allliance: Americas Ctr., 1993-97; internat. artistic advisor Noyam Exptl. Dance Co. and Rsch. Project, Ghana, 1998—; founder, min. in chief Embassy of Sekyere Kwamang Traditional Area, Asante Nation, Ghana to the U.S.A., 1998—; internat. adv. bd. Ctr. for Nat. Culture, Kumasi, Astante Nation, Ghana, 2001—; co-founder and co-pastor Of One Blood Ministries, N.Y.C., 2004—. Choreographer: (mus. theater) Broadway Musical Classics on International Tour, (musical stage rev) Bebop Hot! Celebrating the Music of Dizzy Gillespie & Charlie Parker, (film musicals) Chestnuts, Rainbows Edn., (documentary film) Broadway Babies: Long Forgotten Performers of the Vaudeville Era, (teleseries) Adventures of Hans Christian Andersen, (telespecial) Rapsodia Afrikiko: A Celebration in Dance, (indsl. show) Le Parfum Salvador Dali, (nightclub) The African Room, N.Y.C.; choreographer, asst. Broadway musical Safari 300: A Musical Experience of 300 Years of Black Culture, Song & Dance, N.Y.C.; film dir., editor Of One Blood: Returning Home to Africa, 1999 (Best Documentary Film award Black Internat. Cinema Festival); co-author, dir., choreographer, co-star (nat. stage prodn.) Realizing the Dream: Celebrating the Enduring Spirit of Rev. Dr. Martin Luther King Jr.; world premieres presented at festivals including Morningside Dance Festival, NYC, Mid Am. Dance Festival, L.A. Dance Kaleidoscope Festival, Middfest Internat., Ohio, Smithsonian Instn's Duke Ellington Festival, Washington, Marche Internat. de Disque et de l'Edition Musicale, Cannes, France, Anokyekrome Festival, Kumasi, Asante Nation, Ghana, Royal Performance King Nana Barimah Abeyie Ntori Nimpah II, Sekyere Kwamang, Asante Nation, Ghana, Black Internat. Cinema Festival, Berlin; creator over 40 ballets; contbr. to profl. publs. including African Profiles USA Mag., African Personality Mag., African Press. Nat. Festival for the Performing Arts Choreographers fellow, 1989; Josephine & Randolph Stewart African Heritage Fund Edn. and Rsch. grantee, 1997; named Master Educator and Disting. Fellow, Am. Bd. Master Educators, 1987; Alvin Ailey scholar, Sch. Am. Ballet scholar, Harkness House for Ballet Arts scholar; recipient Grand Prize for Choreography, Ann. Internat. Artistic Impression Competition, 1991, citation U.S. Edn. Dept., 1993, contbns. to growth and advancement of performing arts award, U.S. Arts Coun. Co-op, 1993, instrnl. approach recognized as an ednl. innovation Internat. Bur. Edn., UNESCO, 1996; named Traditional Chief and Spl. Advisor in Edn. and Human Devel. to King, Sekyere Kwamang, Asante Nation, Ghana, 1997, Pan-African and Humanitarian Vision award African Profiles USA mag., 2001. Office: Embassy Sekyere Kwamang Trad Area US Asante Nation Rep Ghana The Belvedere 84-12 35th Ave Jackson Heights NY 11372 E-mail: nanasmorrow@hotmail.com.

MORROW, PATRICK DAVID, English educator; b. L.A., Oct. 1, 1940; s. Patrick Francis and Mary Lillian (Keefe) M.; m. Joyce Mae Rothschild, June 14, 1984; children: Milan Elizabeth, Christopher Patrick, Paul Issac Hotchkiss, Judith Spenceley, Mary Vehrs. Student, Sacramento State Coll., 1958-61; BA, U. So. Calif., 1963; MA, U. Wash., 1965, PhD, 1969. Asst. prof. English U. So. Calif., 1969-75; assoc. prof. English, prof. Auburn (Ala.) U., 1975—. Vis. assoc. prof. Am. studies U. N.Mex. and Idaho State U., summers, 1972, 73; cns. Ctr. Western Studies, Augustana Coll. Author: The Popular and the Serious in Select Twentieth Century American Novels, 1991, Katherine Mansfield's Fiction, 1993, Post-Colonial Essays on South Pacific Literature, 1998, others. Mem. Local Multiple Sclerosis Support Group. Fulbright grantee U. Canterbury, Christchurch, New Zealand, 1981, U. South Pacific, Suva, Fiji, 1989, rsch. grantee Auburn U., 1993, 95. Mem. MLA, Assn. Am. Australian Lit. Studies. Democrat. Jewish. Avocations: music, sports. Office: Auburn U Dept English Auburn AL 36849-0002 E-mail: merropd@mail.auburn.edu.

MORROW, RICHARD MARTIN, retired oil company executive; b. Wheeling, W.Va., Feb. 27, 1926; B.M.E., Ohio State U., 1948. With Amoco Corp., 1948-91; v.p. Amoco Prodn. Co., 1964-66; exec. v.p. Amoco Internat. Oil Co., 1966-70, Amoco Chem. Corp., 1970-74, pres., 1974-78, Amoco Corp., 1978-83, chmn. chief exec. officer, 1983-91; ret., 1991. Trustee U. Chgo. and Rush-Presbyn. St. Luke's Med. Ctr. Office: 200 E Randolph Dr Ste 6952 Chicago IL 60601-7704

MORROW, SANDRA KAY, librarian; b. Levelland, Tex., Jan. 6, 1944; d. Oran Eiland and Martha Jane Johnson; m. Troy Leon Morrow; children: Paul, Kile. AA, Lubbock Christian U., 1964; BS in Edn., Abilene Christian U., 1966. Cert. libr. sci. U. Tex., 1973. Tchr. Andrews Sch. Dist., Andrews, Tex., 1966—68, New Deal Sch. Dist., New Deal, Tex., 1970—71, Ector County Sch., Odessa, Tex., 1971—72; libr. Austin Sch. Dist., Austin, Tex., 1974—77; tchr. Brentwood Christian Sch., Austin, 1984—. Originator Christian Librarians' Conf., Searcy, Ark., 1996—2003; presenter in field; dir. Yearly Booklist for primary, intermediate and Jr. H.S., 1992—. Creator Children's Crown award, 1992, Lamplighter award, 1996, Children's Crown Gallery award, 2000; ministry leader Westover Hills Ch. of Christ, Austin, 1977—2002, nursery dir., 1975—85. Recipient Disting. Alumni Award, Lubbock Christian U., 2002. Mem.: Nat. Christian Sch. Assn. (awards dir. 1996—, Christian Educator of Yr. award 2001), Tex. Christian Schools Assn. (Tchr. of Yr. award 2001), Tex. Libr. Assn. Republican. Mem.Church Of Christ. Avocations: reading, gardening, jogging, music. Home: 8308 Grayledge Drive Austin TX 78753 Office: National Christian School Association 11908 North Lamar Boulevard Austin TX 78753 Business E-Mail: smorrow@brentwoodchristian.org.

MORROW, SUSAN DAGMAR, psychic, medium educator, writer, consultant; b. Harrisburg, Pa., July 10, 1932; d. William Lime and Margaret Louise (Deckard) Brubaker; m. Henry Taylor Morrow, June 9, 1952 (div. Mar. 1984); children: Quenby Anne, Christopher Brian. Student, Carnegie Inst. Tech., 1950-52, U. Ariz., 1952-54, U. Calif., Berkeley Ext., 1960-72, Foothill Coll., 1980-81. Self-employed psychic, psychic tchr., Palo Alto, Calif., 1976-80, Mountain View, Calif., 1980—; medium, psychic, tchr Seekers Quest Profl. Ctr., San Jose, Calif., 1983—. Tchr. Sunnyvale Community Ctr., 1977-87; tchr. San Andreas Health Coun., Palo Alto, 1981-83; lectr. U. Calif., Berkeley, 1978, Foothill Coll., Los Altos, Calif., 1980; lectr. in field; medium, cons. in cases of mental disorientation to psychologists, Palo Alto and Mountain View, 1978—, to detectives and police in cases of missing persons, animals or property, 1983—, pvt. tutor, medium, cons. past lives, archeological information, 1990—. Contbr. articles on psychic awareness to various publs. Mem. Assn. Psychic Practitioners (co-founder, v.p. 1982-83, editor and writer newsletter 1982-83), Mountain View C. of C., Mind Being Found., Assn. Rsch. and Enlightenment, Inst. Noetic Sci., Friends of the Animals. Democrat. Episcopalian. Avocations: physical mediumship, painting, swimming, sailing. Office Phone: 650-814-4909.

MORROW, WALTER EDWIN, JR., electrical engineer, university laboratory administrator; b. Springfield, Mass., July 24, 1928; s. Walter Edwin and Mary Elizabeth (Ganley) M.; m. Janice Lila Lombard, Feb. 25, 1951; children: Clifford E., Gregory A., Carolyn F. S.B., M.I.T., 1949, S.M., 1951. Mem. staff Lincoln Lab., MIT, Lexington, Mass., 1951-55, group leader, 1956-65; head div. communications MIT Lincoln Lab., 1966-68, asst. dir., 1968-71, asso. dir., 1972-77, dir., 1977-98, dir. emeritus, 1998—. Contbr. articles to profl. publs. Recipient award for outstanding achievement Pres. M.I.T., 1963, Edwin Howard Armstrong Achievement award IEEE Communications Soc., 1976 Fellow IEEE, Nat. Acad. Engring. Achievements include patent for synchronous satellite, electric power plant using electrolytic cell-fuel cell combination. Office: MIT Lincoln Lab PO Box 73 Lexington MA 02420-9108

MORROW, WILLIAM CLARENCE, judge, lawyer, mediator; b. Austin, Tex., Aug. 9, 1935; s. Theodore Faulkner and Gladys Lee (Ames) M.; m. Sheila Beth Pfost, June 29, 1973; children: Scott Fitzgerald Morrow, Elizabeth Ann Rettig, Shana Lynn Proctor. BA, Baylor U., 1957; JD, So. Meth. U., 1962. Bar: Tex. 1962. Trial atty. SEC, Ft. Worth, 1963-65; former ptnr. Cotton, Bledsoe, Tighe, Morrow & Dawson, Lynch, Chappell and Alsup; v.p. Magnatex Corp., Midland, 1980-86; v.p., gen. counsel, sec. Elcor Corp., Midland, 1986-88; county judge Midland County, Tex., 1999—. Mem. Tex. Jail Standards Commn., Austin, Tex., 2002—. Mem. Midland City Coun., 1992-95, Tex. Jail Commn., 2002-, mayor pro tem, 1994-95; former vice chmn. Tex. Rehab. Commn.; pres. Found. Mental Health and Mental Retardation Permian Basin; pres. United Way of Midland, 1985, Indsl. Found. Midland, 1987; trustee Midland Cmty. Theatre, 1980—, chmn., 1995-96; elder First Presbyn. Ch., Midland. Mem. Coll. of State Bar Tex., Tex. Bar Assn., Midland County Bar Assn., Tex. Coll. of Probate Judges, Phi Delta Phi. Home: 3110 Gulf Ave Midland TX 79705-8205 Office: 200 W Wall Ste 006 Midland TX 79701-4512

MORROW, WILLIAM EARL, retired government official; b. Perryopolis, Pa., Oct. 22, 1923; s. Robert Ferguson and Daisy (Johnson) M.; m. Danna Katunaric, Apr. 26, 1958; children: Jamie Johnson, Tammara Marie, Kim Ina, William Joseph, Geoffrey Sean. BS in Psychology, Waynesburg Coll., 1948; MA, U. Pitts., 1953; LLD (hon.), U. Zagreb, 1958; postgrad., U. Md., 1969, Indsl. Coll. Armed Forces, 1969-70. With Survey Rsch. Ct. U. Mich., 1947; auditor, employment interviewer, then asst. dir. pers. Jones & Laughlin Steel Corp., 1948—54; exec. coord. Peoples Cab Co., 1954; labor-mgmt. adviser, policy coord. Arabian Am. Oil Co., Saudi Arabia, 1954—57; pers. expert UN/ILO, 1957—58; cons., 1958—59; tng./program officer AID U.S. Dept. State, 1959—65; adminstrv. officer Bur. Internat. Labor Affairs Labor Dept., 1965—68, dep. divsn. chief, 1968—72, projects dir., 1973—80; asst. dir. Office Fgn. Rels., 1980—86; exec. sec. Employee Retirement Income Security Act Office of Sec. Labor U.S. Dept. Labor, 1986—95; ret., 1995. Guest prof. U. Coll. W.I., 1960-64; lectr. Prince George's Community Coll., 1965-97; lectr. U. Md., 1967-97; adj. prof. U. Md., 1997-2003. Mem. Tantallon (Md.) Citizens Assn. With USAF, 1942-44. Mem. Indsl. Rels. Rsch. Assn., Prince George's County Bd. Realtors, Am. Fedn. Govt. Employees, Am. Soc. Tng. Dirs., Am. Legion, D.A.V., Masons, Scottish Rite, Shriners, Tantallon on the Potomac Golf and Country Club (control com.), U. Md. Faculty Club, Dominion Valley Golf and Country Club, Psi Chi Iota, Phi Alpha Theta, Delta Sigma Phi. Methodist. Home (Winter): Village Walk on Palmer Ranch 8308 Jesolo Ln Sarasota FL 34238 Home (Summer): Dominion Valley Golf and Country Club 5726 Wheelwright Way Haymarket VA 20169 E-mail: willmorrow@aol.com.

MORROW, WINSTON VAUGHAN, financial executive; b. Grand Rapids, Mich., Mar. 22, 1924; s. Winston V. and Selma (von Egloffstein) M.; m. Margaret Ellen Staples, June 25, 1948 (div.); children: Thomas Christopher, Mark Staples; m. Edith Burrows Ulrich, Mar. 2, 1990. AB cum laude, Williams Coll., 1947; JD, Harvard U., 1950. Bar: R.I. 1950, U.S. Dist. Ct., U.S. Supreme Ct. Assoc. atty. Edwards & Angell, Providence, 1950-57; exec. v.p., asst. treas., gen. counsel, bd. dirs. Avis, Inc. and subs., 1957-61; v.p., gen. mgr. Rent A Car div. Avis, Inc., 1962-64, pres., bd. dirs., 1964-75; chmn., chief exec. officer, bd. dirs. Avis, Inc. and Avis Rent A Car System, Inc., 1965-77; chmn., pres., bd. dirs. Teleflorists Inc. and subs., 1978-80; pres. Westwood Equities Corp., L.A., 1981-95, CEO, 1984-95, also bd. dirs.; chmn., pres., chief exec. officer Ticor Title Ins. Co., 1982-91, also bd. dirs.; chmn. TRTS Data Svcs. Inc., 1985-91; bd. dirs. AECOM Tech. Corp., L.A., 1990-99. Mem. Pres.'s Industry and Govt. Spl. Travel Task Force, 1968, travel adv. bd. U.S. Travel Svcs., 1968-76, L.A. City-wide Airport Adv. Com., 1983-85; co-chmn. L.A. Transp. Coalition, 1985-91. Mem. juvenile delinquency task force Nat. Coun. Crime and Delinquency, 1985-86, L.A. Mayor's Bus. Coun., 1983-86, Housing Roundtable, Washington, 1983-85, Calif. Bus. Roundtable, 1985-90; chmn., pres. Spring St. Found., 1991—; bd. dirs. Police Found., Washington, 1983-91; trustee Com. for Econ. Devel., Washington, 1987-91; trustee Adelphi U., 1970-75. Decorated Stella Della Solidarieta Italy, Gold Tourism medal Austria. Fellow The Huntington; mem. R.I. Bar Assn., Car and Truck Rental Leasing Assn. (nat. pres. 1961-63), Am. Land Title Assn. (bd. govs. 1989-90), L.A. Area C. of C. (bd. dirs. 1983-90), Williams Club, L.A. Tennis Club, Phi Beta Kappa, Kappa Alpha. Home: 4056 Farmouth Dr Los Angeles CA 90027-1314 also: Meadowview Farm 286 Cushing Corner Rd Freedom NH 03836-0221

MORSCH, THOMAS HARVEY, lawyer; b. Oak Park, Ill., Sept. 5, 1931; s. Harvey William and Gwendoyne (Maun) M.; m. Jacquelyn Casey, Dec. 27, 1954; children: Thomas H. Jr., Margaret, Mary Susan, James, Kathryn, Julia. BA, Notre Dame U., 1953; BSL., Northwestern U., 1953, JD, 1955. Bar: Ill. 1955, D.C. 1955. Assoc. Crowell & Leibman, Chgo., 1955-62; ptnr. Leibman, Williams, Bennett, Baird & Minow, Chgo., 1962-72, Sidley & Austin, Chgo., 1972-97, counsel, 1998-2000. Bd. dirs. Chgo. Lawyers Com. for Civil Rights Under Law, chmn., 1982-83; bd. dirs. Pub. Interest Law Initiative, pres., 1993-95; No. Dist. Ill. Civil Justice Reform Com., 1991-95, Ill. Equal Justice Commn., 1999—2003; mem. vis. com. Law Sch. Northwestern U., 1989-90, dir. Small Bus. Opportunity Ctr., 1998—, assoc. clin. prof., 1998-2003, clin. prof., 2003—. Pres. Republican Workshops of Ill., 1970; gen. counsel Ill. Com. to Re-elect the Pres., 1972; mem. LaGrange Plan Commn., Ill., 1972-80, LaGrange Fire and Police Commn., 1968-72; trustee LaGrange Meml. Hosp., 1983-89; mem. adv. bd. Cath. Charities of Chgo., 1985—, Kellogg Ctr. for Nonprofit Mgmt., 2001—. Fellow Am. Coll. Trial Lawyers; mem. ABA, Ill. State Bar Assn., Chgo. Bar Assn. (bd. mgrs. 1979-81), DC Bar, 7th Cir. Bar Assn., Northwestern Law Sch. Alumni Assn. (pres. 1988-89), Chgo. Bar Found. (bd. dirs., pres. 1995-97), Univ. Club (Chgo.), LaGrange Country Club, Palisades Park Country Club (Mich.), Point O'Woods Country Club (Mich.). Roman Catholic. Home: 301 S Edgewood Ave La Grange IL 60525-2153 Office: Northwestern U Sch Law 357 E Chicago Ave Chicago IL 60611 E-mail: tmorsch@law.northwestern.edu.

MORSE, ANN LAWRANCE, photographer; b. Wilmington, Dela., Mar. 22, 1937; d. Clarence Wanton Balis and Eleanor Silliman Hawkes; m. Kingsley Morse, Dec. 1984 (dec. July 1993); 1 child, Emilio C Orecchia. BA in art hist., Vassar Coll., 1955—59. Mem. adv. bd. Stieglitz Soc., Met. Mus. of Art; mem. adv. bd., fellow of photography Mus. of Modern Art; mem. adv. bd. Bard Coll., Ctr. for Photography at Woodstock. One-woman shows include Dutchess County Arts Coun., Milbrook, NY, 1998, Ctr. St. Gallery, Jackson Hole, Wyo., 1996, Tiglieto Gallery, Kent, Conn., 1993, MAG, Alvin Ailey, Milbrook, NY, 1991, Mid-Hudson Arts and Sci. Ctr. Gallery, Poughkeepsie, NY, 1991, 1990, Art Ctr., Port Jervis, NY, 1990, Bardavon Opera House Gallery, 1990, Vassar Bros. Inst., Poughkeepsie, NY, 1989, Mid-Hudson Arts and Sci. Ctr. Gallery, 1988, Bardavon Opera House Gallery, 1988, Cultural Ctr. of No. Am., Madrid, Spain, 1980, exhibited in group shows at Gallery at Mill St. Loft, Poughkeepsie, NY, 2002, Time and Space Ltd. Gallery, Hudson, NY, 2002, Samuel Dorsky Mus., New Paltz, NY, 2001, Gallery at Merritt Bookstore, Millbrook, NY, 2000, Candice Perish Gallery, Katonah, NY, 2000, White Plains Libr. Gallery, 2000, Rye Arts Ctr., 1999, Howland Ctr., 1999, Soho 20 Gallery, 1998, Coll. Ctr. Gallery at Vassar College, 1992, Coll. Ctr. Gallery at Vassar Coll., 1997, Coffey Gallery, 1997, Schoolhouse Gallery, Croton Falls, NY, 1997, Barett House Galleries, 1997, Carrie Haddad Gallery, 1996, Cunneen-Hackett Galleries, 1996, Marist Coll., 1995, Gallery at Hastings on Hudson, 1995, Pelham Art Ctr., 1995, Brownson Gallery, 1994, Dutchess County Arts Assn., 1994, Evolving Images Gallery, 1994, Gallery on the Circle, 1993, Mt. Guilian Gallery, 1992, Sarah Lawrence Gallery, 1992, Allan Brown Gallery, 1991, University Place Galleries, 1991, The Armory, 1991, The Interlude Gallery, 1991, The Hudson River Mus., 1990, The Butler Gallery at Marymount Coll., 1990, Pike St. Art Ctr., 1990, Thorne Gallery, 1990, Albany Ctr. Gallery, 1989, Mt. Top Gallery, 1988, Allan Brown Galleries, 1986, Ctr. for Photography at Woodstock, 1985, Galleria Redor, 1982, Galleria Durero, Madrid, 1981, Galleria Nacional Palma de Mallorca, Spain, 1965, Galleria Nacional, Madrid, 1965. Recipient First prize, Hudson River Photography Exhbn., THe Gallery, Hastings on Hudson, 1991, Best of Photography, Photographers Forum, 1989, First prize, B/W Photography, Dutchess County Art Assn., 1986, First prize, Color Photography, T.V. Espanola, 1977.

MORSE, DANIEL E. biochemistry educator, science administrator; b. N.Y.C., May 20, 1941; BA, Harvard U., 1963; PhD in Molecular Biology, Albert Einstein Coll. Medicine, 1967. Fellow in molecular genetics Stanford U., 1967-69; from Silas Arnold Houston asst. prof. to Silas Arnold Houston assoc. prof. med. sch. Harvard U., 1969-73; prof. molecular genetics and biochemistry U. Calif., Santa Barbara, 1973—, chmn. sect. molecular biology and biochemistry dept. biol. sci., 1981-85, chmn. Marine Biotechnology Ctr., 1986—. Mem. NRC, U.S. Nat. Com. Internat. Union Biol. Sci., 1986—; chmn. task force biotechnology in ocean sci. NSF, 1987—. Fellow AAAS; mem. Am. Soc. Molecular Biology and Biochemistry, Am. Soc. Limnology and Oceanography, Am. Soc. Microbiology, Am. Soc. Zoology, N.Y. Acad. Sci., Internat. Soc. Chem. Ecology. Achievements include research on molecular mechanisms controlling reproduction, larval metamorphosis, development and gene expression; signal molecules, receptors, and transducers; molecular marine biology; molecular neurobiology; molecular chemosensory mechanisms. Office: U Calif Marine Biotech Ctr Dept Biology Santa Barbara CA 93106

MORSE, DUANE D(ALE), lawyer; b. Stevens Point, Wis., Sept. 19, 1950; s. Douglas D. and Rosemary (Adamson) M.; m. Diane C. Crampton, June 23, 1973; children: Jason V., Julia C. BA, Northwestern U., 1972; JD magna cum laude, U. Mich., 1979. Bar: D.C. 1980, U.S. Dist. Ct. D.C. 1981, U.S. Ct. Appeals (D.C. cir.) 1987, U.S. Dist. Ct. Md. 1989, U.S. Ct. Appeals (4th cir.) 1990, Va. 2002. Law clk. to judge U.S. Ct. Appeals (6th cir.), Nashville, 1979-80; assoc. Wilmer, Cutler & Pickering, Washington, 1980-86, ptnr., 1987—. Editor Mich. Law Rev., 1977-79; contbr. articles to profl. publs., chpt. to book. Mem. ABA, Am. Bankruptcy Inst., Order of Coif. Office: Wilmer Cutler Pickering Hale and Dorr LLP 1600 Tysons Blvd Fl 10 Mc Lean VA 22102 Office Phone: 703-251-9740. E-mail: duane.morse@wilmerhale.com.

MORSE, EDWARD J. automotive executive; b. 1949; Former pres. Morse Ops., Ft. Lauderdale, 1970; pres., CEO Ed Morse Chevrolet, Inc., Ft. Lauderdale, Fla., 1979—, chmn., CEO. Office: Morse Operations Inc 6363 NW 6th Way Ste 400 Fort Lauderdale FL 33309-6188

MORSE, EDWARD LEWIS, petroleum industry executive; b. N.Y.C., Jan. 5, 1942; s. Jonah Benjamin and Rebecca (Freiberg) M.; m. Linda Kasle Jones, Aug. 15, 1965; children: Michael Ari, Molly Rachel. BA, Johns Hopkins U., Balt., 1963; MA, Johns Hopkins U., Washington, 1966; PhD, Princeton U., 1969. Asst. prof. internat. politics Woodrow Wilson Sch. Princeton (N.J.) U., 1969-75; sr. rsch. fellow Coun. on Fgn. Rels., N.Y.C., 1975-78; exec. asst. to undersec. econ. affairs U.S. Dept. State, Washington, 1978-79, dep. asst. sec. for internat. energy policy, 1979-81; dir. internat. affairs Phillips Petroleum Co., Bartlesville, Okla., 1981-84; mng. dir. Petroleum Fin. Co., Ltd., Washington, 1984-96; pres., publisher Petroleum Intelligence Weekly, N.Y.C., 1988-99, The Oil Daily Co., N.Y.C., 1996-99; exec. Hess Energy Trading Co., N.Y.C., 1999—. Author: Foreign Policy and Interdependence in Gaullist France, 1973, Modernization and the Transformation of International Relations, 1976; contbr. articles to various publs. Office: HETCO 1185 Avenue Of The Americas New York NY 10036-2601 E-mail: elmorse@hess.com., edmorse@aol.com.

MORSE, F. D., JR., dentist; b. Glen Lyn, Va., Apr. 5, 1928; s. Frank D. and Ida Estell (Davis) M.; m. Patsy Lee Apple, Feb. 4, 1967; 1 child, Fortis Davis; m. Nancy Zink; 1 child, Pamela Marie. Student, U. Va., 1945; BS, Concord Coll., 1951; DDS, Med. Coll. Va., 1955. Freelance photographer, 1950-56; practice dentistry, 1958—; mem. staff Giles Hosp., Pearisburg, 1958-86. Served from asst. dental surgeon to sr. asst. dental surgeon USPHS, 1955-57; assigned to USCG, 1957-58. Honors scholar U. Va. Mem. AAAS, ADA, S.W. Va. Dental Assn., Assn. Mil. Surgeons, Nat. Assn. Advancement Sci., Fedn. Dentaire Internat., Internat. Platform Assn., W.Va. Collegiate Acad. Sci., Kiwanis, Beta Phi. Achievements include research in dental ceramics and roof coatings. Home: 116 Tazewell St Pearisburg VA 24134 Office: Giles Profl Bldg Pearisburg VA 24134 Office Phone: 540-921-3523.

MORSE, GARY H. construction executive; Pres., CEO The Villages, Fla., 1972—. Office: The Villages 1100 Main St Lady Lake FL 32159-7732

MORSE, JEROME SAMUEL, government administrator, trade specialist; b. Worcester, Mass., Feb. 25, 1947; s. Manuel and Bernice Morse; m. Burnham Marie Spottswood, Oct. 25, 1970; children: Jordana Eve, Alexander Lewis. BA in Internat. Rels., Clark U., 1969; MA in Internat. Affairs, George Washington U., 1971. Internat. trade specialist U.S. Dept. Commerce, Washington, 1970-78, dep. dir. export awareness divsn., 1978-82, dep. dir. World's Fair staff, 1982-84, project mgr. trade devel., 1984-92, dir. planning and mgmt. divsn., 1992—2002, dir. office of machinery, 2002—. Author: The Complete Guide to Operating An Import/Export Business, 1989. Mem. fundraising com. McLean (Va.) H.S. Choral Parents Assn., 1997-2001; mem. McLean Theater Alliance, 1998—, treas., 2000—. Recipient Congl. fellowship Am. Polit. Sci. Assn., 1979. Mem. Multinational Mktg. Assocs. (v.p. 1986-90), Phi Beta Kappa. Democrat. Jewish. E-mail: Jerry_Morse@ita.doc.gov. Avocation: collecting boston red sox memorabilia. Home: 1935 Rockingham St Mc Lean VA 22101-4923 Office: US Dept Commerce ITA TD/TM/OM Rm 4310 Washington DC 20230-0001 Office Phone: 202-482-1180. E-mail: Jerry_Morse@ita.doc.gov.

MORSE, JOHN B., JR., corporate financial executive; From product dir. to chmn., CEO Johnson & Johnson, 1953—89; ptnr. Price Waterhouse, 1972; v.p., CFO Washington Post Co., Washington, 1989—, v.p., contr., 1989—. Mem.: AICPA, Inst. Newspaper Fin. Execs. Office: Washington Post Co 1150 15th St NW Washington DC 20071

MORSE, JOHN M. book publishing executive; Sr. v.p., publisher Merriam-Webster Inc., Springfield, Mass., pres., publisher, 1997—. Office: Merriam Webster Inc 47 Federal St PO Box 281 Springfield MA 01102

MORSE, KAREN WILLIAMS, academic administrator; b. Monroe, Mich., May 8, 1940; m. Joseph G. Morse; children: Robert G., Geoffrey E. BS, Denison U., 1962; MS, U. Mich., 1964, PhD, 1967; DSc (hon.), Denison U., 1990. Rsch. chemist Ballistic Rsch. Lab., Aberdeen Proving Ground, Md., 1966-68; lectr. chemistry dept. Utah State U., Logan, 1968-69, from asst. to assoc. prof. chemistry, 1969-83, prof. chemistry dept., 1983-93, dept. head Coll. Sci., 1981-88, dean Coll. Sci., 1988-89, univ. provost, 1989-93; pres. Western Wash. U., Bellingham, 1993—. Mem., chair Grad. Record Exam in chemistry com., Princeton, N.J., 1980-89, Gov.'s Sci. Coun., Salt Lake City, 1986-93, Gov.'s Coun. on Fusion, 1989-91, ACS Com. on Profl. Tng., 1984-92; cons. 1993; nat. ChemLinks adv. com. NSF, 1995; bd. advisor's orgn. com. 2008 summer Olympic Games, Seattle, 1995; faculty Am. Assn. State Colls. and Univs. Pres.'s Acad., 1995, 96; chair Wash. Coun. of Pres., 1995-96; bd. dirs. Whatcom State Bank; NCAA Divsn. II Pres.'s Coun., 1999—, CHEA bd., 2000—; Nat. Rsch. Coun. Chem. Svcs. Roundtable, 1999—. Contbr. articles to profl. jours. Mem. Cache County Sch. Dist. Found., Cache Valley, Logan, 1988-93; swim coach, soccer coach; trustee First United Presbyn. Ch., Logan, 1979-81, 82-85; adv. bd. Sci. Discovery Ctr., Logan, 1993, KCTS-TV, Bellingham, 1996—, Seattle Opera Bd., 1999—; mem. bd. dirs. United Way, Whatcom County, 1993—; exec. com. Bellingham-Whatcom Econ. Devel. Com., 1993—. Recipient Disting. Alumni in Residence award U. Mich., 1989, Francis P. Garvan and John M. Olin medal, 1997. Fellow AAAS; mem. Am. Chem. Soc. (Utah award Salt Lake City and Cen. dists. 1988, Garvan-Olin medal 1997), Am. Assn. State Colls. and Univs. (mem. policy and purposes com. 1995, chair 1996), Bus. and Profl. Women Club (pres. 1984-85), Philanthropic Edn. Orgn., Phi Beta Kappa, Sigma Xi, Phi Beta Kappa Assocs., Phi Kappa Phi, Beta Gamma Sigma. Avocations: skiing, biking, photography. Office: Western Washington U Office Pres 516 High St Bellingham WA 98225-5946

MORSE, LARRY EUGENE, botanist, conservationist; b. Dayton, Ohio, Nov. 15, 1947; s. Carson Clark and Dorothy Virginia (Clum) Morse. BS, Mich. State U., E. Lansing, 1966—70; AM, Harvard U., Cambridge, Mass., 1970—71, PhD, 1972—79. Staff botanist Dayton Mus. of Natural History, Ohio, 1969; rsch. asst. Smithsonian Instn., Washington, 1971—72, N.Y. Bot. Garden, Bronx, 1976—78; chief botanist The Nature Conservancy, Arlington, Va., 1979—2000; North Am. botanist NatureServe, Arlington, Va., 2001—. Founder, convener Plant Conservation Roundtable, Washington, 1981—88. Author: (book) Computer Programs for Specimen Identification; co-editor: Rare Plant Conservation: Geographical Data Organization; contbr. chapters to books, articles to profl. jours. Fellow, NSF, 1970, Woodrow Wilson Fellowship Found., 1970. Mem.: New Eng. Bot. Club, Mich. Bot. Club, Bot. Soc. of Wash. (pres. 1985—86, mem., centennial symposium com. 2001), Ottawa

Field-Naturalists' Club (life), So. Appalachian Bot. Soc. (life), Internat. Assn. for Plant Taxonomy (life). Achievements include development of a methodology for plant specimen identification with computers; guidelines for conservation status reports (co-developer); a methodology for conservation status ranking, The Nature Conservancy (co-developer); a methodology for invasiveness assessment of non-native plants, NatureServe (co-developer); design of central scientific databases, The Nature Conservancy (co-designer). Avocations: nature photography, contra dancing, stamp collecting/philately. Home: 1306 Corbin Pl NE Washington DC 20002 Office: NatureServe 1101 Wilson Blvd #1500 Arlington VA 22209

MORSE, LEONARD J. epidemiologist, public health service officer; MD, U. Md., 1955. Intern infectious diseases U. Md. Med. Sys., resident infectious diseases; fellow internal medicine New Eng. Med. Care Hosps.; pvt. practice Worchester, Mass.; ret., 1996; med. dir. New Bedford Cmty. Health Ctr., 1996—2001; prof. clin. medicine, family medicine, cmty. health U. Mass. Med. Sch., Worcester; pub. health commr. Worcester, 2001—. Mem.: AMA Found. (immediate past chair Coun. Ethical and Jud. Affairs, Pride in Profession award 2004), Am. Soc. History Medicine, Am. Med. Writers Assn., Am. Soc. Microbiology, Infectious Diseases Soc. Am., Am. Soc. Internal Medicine, Mass. Med. Soc. (pres. 1993—94, past chmn. Com. Ethics and Discipline, Lifetime Achievement award 1997, Grant V. Rodkey award 1997), Am. Coll. Physicians (Named Internist of Yr. Mass. chpt. 1998). Office: Worcester Pub Health 25 Meade St Worcester MA 01610

MORSE, M. HOWARD, lawyer; b. Louisville, May 30, 1959; s. Marvin Henry and Betty Anne (Hess) M.; m. Laura E. Loeb, Apr. 17, 1988; children: Elizabeth L., Marni L. AB summa cum laude, Dartmouth Coll., 1981; JD cum laude, Harvard U., 1984. Bar: D.C. 1984, U.S. Ct. of Internat. Trade 1985, U.S. Ct. Appeals (fed. cir.) 1985, U.S. Dist. Ct. D.C. 1986, U.S. Ct. Appeals (D.C. cir.) 1986, U.S. Ct. Appeals (4th cir.) 1987. Assoc. Arnold & Porter, Washington, 1984-88; atty. FTC Bur. Competition, Washington, 1988-91, dep. asst. dir. for policy, 1991-93, asst. dir., 1993-97; ptnr. Drinker, Biddle & Reath, Washington, 1998—. Adj. prof. law Georgetown Law Ctr., Washington, 1995—2000. Mem.: ABA (chair computer industry com. 1996—99, chair intellectual property com. 1999—2002, coun. 2002—, mem. antitrust sect.), D.C. Bar Assn., Intellectual Property Owners Assn., Phi Beta Kappa. Office: Drinker Biddle & Reath 1500 K St NW Ste 1100 Washington DC 20005-1209 Office Phone: 202-842-8883. E-mail: howard.morse@dbr.com.

MORSE, MARVIN HENRY, retired judge; b. Mt. Vernon, NY, July 19, 1929; s. Frank Irving and Lillian (Seeger) M.; m. Betty Anne Hess, Dec. 27, 1953; children: Martin Albert, Michael Howard, Lee Anne. AB, Colgate U., 1949; LLB, Yale U., 1952. Bar: N.Y. 1952, Ky. 1956, Md. 1964, U.S. Supreme Ct. 1960, U.S. Ct. Appeals (6th cir.), U.S. Dist. Ct. (we. dist.) Ky., U.S. Ct. Mil. Appeals, U.S. Ct. Claims, U.S. Ct. Appeals (D.C. cir.), U.S. Ct. Appeals (fed. cir.), U.S. Dist. Ct. (no. dist.) Tex., U.S. Dist. Ct. Hawaii. Pvt. practice, Louisville, 1956-62; asst. counsel Office of Gen. Counsel Dept. Navy, Washington, 1962-65, Office of Gen. Counsel Office Sec. Def., Washington, 1965-68; asst. gen. counsel GSA, Washington, 1968-70, U.S. Postal Svc., Washington, 1970-73; adminstrv. law judge Fed. Energy Regulatory Commn., Washington, 1973-75, Postal Rate Commn., Washington, 1975-77, CAB, Washington, 1977-80; dir. adminstrv. law judges Office Pers. Mgmt., Washington, 1980-82; chief adminstrv. law judge SBA, Washington, 1982-87, asst. adminstr. hearings and appeals, 1985-87; adminstrv. law judge Exec. Office of Immigration Rev. Dept. Justice, Washington, 1987—2002; temp. mem. Bd. of Immigration Appeals, 1998—2002; ret., 2002. Mem. Adminstrv. Conf. of U.S., 1980-84, govt. mem., 1985-86, 87-95, liaison mem.; faculty and faculty coord. The Nat. Jud. Coll., 1977, 79-80. Author: (with S. Groner) ABA Handbook chpt. on adminstrv. law, 1981, (with Lucy Moran) Troubling the Waters: Human Cargos, 2002. Trustee Washington area chpt. Am. Digestive Disease Soc., 1976-87. With JAGC, USAF, 1952-56, to col. USAFR, ret. 1979. Decorated USAF Legion of Merit; recipient Disting. Svc. award Am. Digestive Disease Soc., 1980. Mem. ABA (exec. com. 1977-82, 84-87, chmn. 1980-81, conf. adminstrv. law judges, del. ho. of dels. 1984-87, lawyers in govt. com. 1985-86, jud. selection, tenure and compensation com. 1987-93, govt. pub. sect. lawyers divsn., coun. 1996-02), Fed. Bar Assn. (nat. coun. 1976—, chmn. career svc. sect. 1983-86, chmn. judiciary sect. 1986-88, sect. coord. 1988-90, sec. 1991-92, del. to ABA ho. of dels. 1992-93, 97-99, v.p. 1993-94, pres.-elect 1994-95, pres. 1995-96), Am. Law Inst., Fed. Adminstrv. Law Judges Conf. (exec. com. 1975-77, 82-96, 2000-01), Nat. Assn. Adminstrv. Law Judges (hon.), Fed. Am. Inn of Ct. (coun. 1990-92, pres. 1992-94). Home: 2425 Gulf of Mexico Dr Longboat Key FL 34228: 2425 Gulf of Mexico Dr Longboat Key FL 34228-3287 E-mail: bhmmhm@aol.com.

MORSE, PETER HODGES, ophthalmologist, educator; b. Chgo., Mar. 1, 1935; s. Emerson Glover and Carol Elizabeth (Rolph) M. AB, Harvard U., 1957; MD, U. Chgo., 1963. Diplomate: Am. Bd. Ophthalmology. Intern U. Chgo. Hosp., 1963-64; resident Wilmer Inst. Johns Hopkins Hosp., Balt., 1966-69; fellow, retina service Mass. Eye and Ear Infirmary, Boston, 1969-70; asst. prof. ophthalmology, chief retina service U. Pa., 1971-75, assoc. prof., 1975, U. Chgo., 1975-77; prof. ophthalmology, 1979-93; sec. dept. ophthalmology, 1976-77; chief retina service, prof., 1979-93; clin. prof. ophthalmology U. S.D. Sch. Medicine, Sioux Falls, 1993—. Prof. La. State U., 1978; chmn. dept. ophthalmology, chief retina service Ochsner Clinic and Found. Hosp., New Orleans, 1977-78; clin. prof. Tulane U., 1978 Author: Vitreoretinal Disease: A Manual for Diagnosis and Treatment, 1979, 2d edit., 1989, Practical Management of Diabetic Retinopathy, 1985; co-editor: Disorders of the Vitreous, Retina, and Choroid; bd. editors Perspectives in Ophthalmology, 1976—, Retina, 1980—; contbr. articles to profl. jours. Served with USNR, 1964-66. Fellow ACS, Coll. Ophthalmologists Eng., Am. Acad. Ophthalmology, Royal Soc. Health (Eng.), Royal Coll. Ophthalmologists (Eng.); mem. AMA, La. Med. Soc., Orleans Parrish Med. Soc., New Orleans Acad. Ophthalmology, La. Ophthalmol. and Otolaryngol. Soc., Miss. Ophthalmol. and Otolaryngol. Soc., Assn. Rsch. Vision and Ophthalmology, Retina Soc., Soc. Heed Fellows, Ophthalmol. Soc. U.K., Pan Am. Assn. Ophthalmology, Oxford Ophthalmol. Congress, All-India Ophthalmol. Soc., Soc. Eye Surgeons, Vitreoretinal Soc. (India), Sigma Xi. Republican. Episcopalian. Home: 1307 S Holly Dr Sioux Falls SD 57105-0221 Office: Sioux Valley Clin Dept Ophthalmology 1100 E 21st St Sioux Falls SD 57105-1002

MORSE, RICHARD JAY, human resources specialist, consultant; b. Detroit, Aug. 2, 1933; s. Maurice and Belle Rosalyn (Jacobson) M. BA, U. Va., 1955; MA in Clin. Psychology, Calif. State U., L.A., 1967. Area pers. adminstr. Gen. Tel. Co. of Calif., Santa Monica, 1957-67; sr. v.p. human resources The Bekins Co., Glendale, Calif., 1967-83; pvt. cons. human resources and orgn. devel. Cambria, 1983—. Contbr. articles to profl. jours. Fund raiser various orgns., So. Calif., 1970—. Mem. Internat. Soc. Performance Improvement (founding mem. 1958—). Republican. Jewish. Avocations: travel, tennis, walking, swimming. Home and Office: 6410 Cambria Pines Rd Cambria CA 93428-2009 Office Phone: 805-927-3457. Personal E-mail: dickmorse@earthlink.net.

MORSE, ROBERT HARRY, lawyer; b. Bklyn., May 25, 1941; s. Soll and Rachel Morse; m. Sandra Goldstein, July 22, 1967; children: Lisa Jennifer, Eric Jeffrey. BSEE with honors, MIT, 1963, MSEE with honors, 1964; JD, Harvard U., 1967. Bar: N.Y. 1968, D.C. 1978, Md. 1985. Assoc. Kenyon & Kenyon, Reilly, Carr & Chapin, N.Y.C., 1967-71; trial atty. antitrust divsn. Dept. Justice, Washington, 1971-74, sr. trial atty., 1974-78; ptnr. Peabody, Lambert & Meyers, Washington, 1978-82, Galland, Kharasch, Morse & Garfinkle, Washington, 1982-96, Ropes and Gray, Washington, 1997-2000; pres., CEO Esrom Consulting LLC, Rockville, Md., 2000—; ptnr. Farkas & Morse LLC, Washington, 2003—. Dir. Earle Palmer Brown Cos., 1984-98. Mem. nat. capital area coun. Boy Scouts Am., gen. counsel, 1991-94, exec. bd. dirs., 1990—, pres. 2001-02, chmn., 2002-2003. Recipient Spl. Achievement award Dept. Justice, 1973, Meritorious award Dept. Justice, 1976, Silver Beaver award Boy Scouts Am., 1999. Mem.: ABA, Patent Bar, D.C. Bar Assn., Nat. Alumni Assn. MIT (bd. dirs. 1986—88), MIT Club Washington (sec. 1981—82, pres. 1983—84), Eta Kappa Nu, Tau Beta Pi, Sigma Xi. Office Phone: 202-337-7802. E-mail: esrom4consulting@aol.com., rmorse@farkasmorse.com., rhmorse@comcast.net.

MORSE, ROBERT PARKER, investment company executive; b. Nyack, N.Y., May 8, 1945; s. Robert Willard Parker and Julia (Larson) M.; m. Sarah Morgan Cumings, Sept. 23, 1978; children: Robert Bradley St. Clair, Parker Morgan, Sarah Spencer. BS in Econs., U. Pa., 1967; student in advanced currency theory, Adelphi Suffolk U., 1970-71. V.p. Am. Express/W.H. Morton Divsn., N.Y.C., 1970-74; sr. v.p., ptnr. William G. Campbell & Co., Inc., N.Y.C., 1975-80; chmn., CEO Morse, Williams & Co., Inc., N.Y.C., 1981—. Bd. dirs. Optix Networks, Inc., eLottery, Inc. Gov. Soc. Mayflower Descs., N.Y., 1993-98; trustee Plimoth Plantation, Mass., 1994-2000, Bermuda Biol. Sta. Rsch., 1983-2000, Gen. Svc. Bd., N.Y., 1981-93, trustee, chmn. fin. English Spkg. Union, 1998—, U.S. del. internat. coun., English Spkg. Union, London, 2002; bd. assocs. The Whitehead Inst., MIT, 1996—; bd. dirs. Arlington Inst., 1995-2001; chmn. bd. The Wall Street Fund, 1984—. Lt. USNR, 1967-78. Mem. Am. Def. Preparedness Assn., Pilgrims of U.S., River Club, Bond Club N.Y., U.S. Naval Inst., Union Club, N.Y. Yacht Club, Links Club, River Club. Episcopalian. Avocations: sailing, skiing, reading, golf, tennis, squash. Office: Morse Williams & Co Inc 230 Park Ave Rm 1635 New York NY 10169-1602 Office Phone: 212-856-8200. Business E-Mail: rpm@morsewilliams.com.

MORSE, SAUL JULIAN, lawyer; b. Jan. 17, 1948; s. Leon William and Goldie (Kohn) M.; m. Anne Bruce Morgan, Aug. 21, 1982; children: John Samuel, Elizabeth Miriam. BA, U. Ill., 1969, JD, 1972. Bar: Ill. 1973, U.S. Dist. Ct. (so. dist.) Ill. 1976, U.S. Ct. Appeals (7th cir.) 1983, U.S. Supreme Ct. 1979, U.S. Tax Ct. 1982. Law clk. State of Ill. EPA, 1971-72, Ill. Commerce Commn., 1972, hearing examiner, 1972-73, trial atty., 1973-75; asst. minority legal counsel Ill. Senate, 1975, minority legal counsel, 1975-77; mem. Ill. Human Rights Commn., 1985-91; dir., treas., chair grievance com. Ill. Comprehensive Health Ins. Plan, 1987—2002; gen. counsel Ill. Legis. Space Needs Commn., 1978-92; pvt. practice Springfield, Ill., 1977-79; prnr. Gramlich & Morse, Springfield, 1980-85; prin. Saul J. Morse and Assocs., 1985-87; ptnr. Morse, Giganti and Appleton, 1987-92; v.p., gen. counsel Ill. State Med. Soc., 1992—2004; of counsel Brown, hay & Stephens, LLP, Springfield, Ill., 2004—. Lectr. in continuing med. edn., 1986-90; counsel symposia; adj. asst. prof. med. humanities So. Ill. Sch. Medicine; pres. Springfield Profl. Baseball, LLC. Bd. dirs. Springfield Ctr. for Ind. Living, 1984-89, Ill. Comprehensive Health Ins. Plan Bd., 1987-2002, United Way Ctrl. Ill., Inc., 1991-97, G.I.N.I. Inst., 2002, Hope Sch., Springfield, 1996-2003, Springfield Jewish Fedn., 1992-95; bd. dirs. United Cerebral Palsy Land of Lincoln, v.p., 2002; mem. task force on transp. Rep. Nat. Com., 1979-80; mem. Springfield Jewish Cmty. Rels. Coun., 1976-79, 97-2002; bd. dirs. internat. Post Polio Health Internat., 2002-, Springfield Jewish Fedn. Endowment; mem. spl. com. on zoning and land use planning Sangamon County Bd., 1978; treas. City of Leland Grove, 1999—; exec. com. AMA and State Med. Socs. Litig. Ctr., 1999-2004, chmn. 2004; commr. Ill. Guardianship and Advocacy Commn., 2002; mem. chancellor's cmty. adv. coun. U. Ill., Springfield, 2002-; bd. dirs. Vis. Nurse Assn. Ctrl. Ill., 2004-. Named Disabled Adv. of Yr., Ill. Dept. Rehab. Svcs., 1985; recipient Chmn.'s Spl. award Ill. State Med. Soc., 1987, Susan S. Suter award as outstanding disabled citizen of Ill., 1990. Mem. ABA (vice-chmn. medicine and law com. 1988-90, tort and ins. practice sect., forum com. on health law), Am. Assn. Health Lawyers, Am. Soc. Law and Medicine, Ill. State Bar Assn. (spl. com. on reform of legis. process 1976-82, spl. com. on the disabled lawyer 1978-82, young lawyers sect. com. on role of govt. atty. 1977-80, chmn. 1982, sect. coun. adminstrv. law, vice-chmn. 1981-82), Sangamon County Bar Assn., Am. Soc. Med. Assn. Counsel, Phi Delta Phi. Home: 1701 S Illini Rd Springfield IL 62704-3301 Office: Brown Hay Stephens LLC PO Box 2459 205 S Fifth St Ste 750 Springfield IL 62705 Office Phone: 217-544-8491. E-mail: saulmorse@sbcglobal.net., smorse@bhslaw.com.

MORSE, STACEY ANN, art studio owner; b. Arcadia, Calif., Jan. 18, 1964; d. Lewis Richard and Phyllis Juanita (Verdugo) Corbet; m. Stuart Hopkins Morse, June 6, 1987; children: Merill Leann, True Corbet. BFA, Maryville U., St. Louis, 1989. With William Tao & Assocs., St. Louis, 1984-87; comml. photographer Voyles Photography, St. Louis, 1988-94; fine art photographer Stacey A. Morse Photography, St. Louis, 1987—; cons. Chesterfield Arts Inc., Chesterfield, Mo., 1996—; co-owner, v.p. Morse Fine art Studios, Inc., Chesterfield, 1994—. Exec. dir. Chesterfield Arts, Inc., Chesterfield, Mo., 2002—. Mem. Reg. Commerce and Growth Assn., St. Louis, 1997. Recipient Young Alumni award Maryville U., 1992, Byron lee Fine Arts award, 1988. Mem. Nat. Soc. Arts & Letters, Art St. Louis, St. Louis Chamber Orch. 2002-(bd.mem). Avocations: tennis, skiing, backpacking. Office: Morse Fine Art Studios Inc PO Box 74 Chesterfield MO 63006-0074 Office Phone: 636-458-0886.

MORSE, STEPHEN SCOTT, virologist, epidemiologist, immunologist, educator; b. NYC, Nov. 22, 1951; s. Murray H. and Phyllis Morse; m. Marilyn Gewirtz, Feb. 1991. BS, CCNY, 1971; MS, U. Wis., 1974, PhD, 1977. NSF trainee dept. bacteriology U. Wis., Madison, 1971-72, rsch. asst., 1972-77; Nat. Cancer Inst. rsch. fellow Med. Coll. Va./Va. Commonwealth U., Richmond, 1977-80, instr. microbiology, 1980-81; asst. prof. microbiology Rutgers U., New Brunswick, N.J., 1981-85; rsch. assoc. Rockefeller U., N.Y.C., 1985-88, asst. prof., 1988-96, adj. faculty, 1996—; program mgr. Def. Advanced Rsch. Projects Agy., 1996-2000; asst. prof. to assoc. prof. epidemiology, Mailman Sch. Pub. Health, Columbia U., 1996—, dir. Ctr. Pub. Health Preparedness, Mailman Sch. Pub. Health, 2000—. Cons. U.S. Congress Office Tech. Assessment, Washington, 1989; chair conf. on emerging viruses NIH, 1989; mem. com. microbial threats to health, chair subcom. on viruses Inst. Medicine-NAS, 1990—92; steering com. Forum on Emerging Infections, 1996—; chair program for monitoring emerging diseases (ProMED) Fedn. Am. Scientists, 1993—, mem. com. future biothreats, 2003—. Author: Emerging Viruses, 1993, Evolutionary Biology of Viruses, 1994; sect. editor: Ctr. for Disease Control and Prevention Jour., Emerging Infectious Diseases, 1995—2002, mem. editl. bd.: Emerging Infectious Diseases, 2003—, Biosecurity and Bioterrorism, 2003—. Fellow: N.Y. Acad. Scis. (vice chair microbiology sect. 1994—96, chair 1996—98); mem.: Marine Biology Lab., Am. Assn. Immunologists, Am. Soc. Microbiology, Sigma Xi. Office: Columbia U Mailman Sch Pub Health Ctr Pub Health Preparedness 722 W 168th St New York NY 10032-3722 Business E-Mail: ssm20@columbia.edu.

MORSE, SUZANNE ROWENA, education educator; b. Berkeley, Calif., June 17, 1957; d. Anthony Perry and Barbara Vernon Morse. BA, U. Calif., Berkeley, 1980, PhD, 1988. Postdoctoral rschr. Harvard U., Cambridge, Mass., 1988—91; prof. Coll. of Atlantic, Bar Harbor, Maine, 1991—. Newlin chair botany Coll. Atlantic, Bar Harbor, Maine, 2004—. Mem.: Bioneers, Maine Orgn. Farmers and Gardeners, Ecological Soc. Am. Office Phone: 707-288-5015 308.

MORSE, THEODORE FREEMAN, dean, writer; b. Marlboro, Mass., Dec. 29, 1943; s. Harry Freeman and Kathryn (Nunn) Morse; m. Nancy Adams, Nov. 23, 1993; children: Alexander, Sarah, Timothy, Sussanah. BA in History, Middlebury Coll., 1965; MA, Tufts U., 1967. Head, history dept. Kent Sch., Kent, Conn., 1970—86, Scarsdale (N.Y.) H.S., 1986—89, Forman Sch., Litchfield, Conn., 1991—94; head, history dept., and dean Antilles Sch., St. Thomas, 1995—. Cons. Coll. Bd. (apptd. chief reader, advanced placement in U.S. History), Princeton, NJ, 1980—. Author: Excellence in U.S. History, 1984, Colonizers and Colonists, 1997, Investigating China, 2000. Grantee Fulbright scholar, 1980, 1982. Fellow: Asian Studies Soc., Orgn. Am. Historians. Democrat. Buddhist. Avocations: hockey, mountain climbing, canoeing, golf. Home: Box 7968 St Thomas VI 00801 Office: Antilles Sch Frenchman's Bay St Thomas VI 00802

MORSELL, FREDERICK ALBERT, performing company executive, educator, consultant; b. NYC, Aug. 3, 1940; s. John Albert and Marjorie Ellen Morsell. B in liberal arts, Dickinson Coll., 1962; M in theatre arts, Wayne State U., 1974. Pres. Fremarto Enterprises, Inc., Emigrant, Mont., 1991—. Author: (novels) Presenting Mr. Frederick Douglass, 1990, (plays), 2003. Bd. mem. Frederick Douglass Mus., Washington, 2004—, Hall Fame for Caring Am., Washington, 2004—. 1st lt. U.S. Army, 1962—65, Japan. Office: Fremarto Enterprises Inc PO Box 382 Emigrant MT 59027 Office Phone: 406-333-4970. Office Fax: 406-333-4145. E-mail: fremarjo@att.net.

MORSHED, MOQBUL MONTY, civil and environmental engineer; b. Rajshahi, Bangladesh, July 17, 1962; came to U.S., 1986; s. M. Rahman and Khojesta Fasiha (Akhter) Sarkar; m. Tahmina Rahman, Jan. 3, 1991. BSCE, Bangladesh U., 1984; MSCE, Wayne State U., 1987. Registered profl. engr., Fla., Pa., Oreg. Asst. engr. Bur. Cons. Engrs. Ltd., Dhaka, Bangladesh, 1984-86; civil/environ. engr. CH2M Hill, Phila., 1987-92; sr. environ. engr. Oreg. Dept. of Environ. Quality, Portland, 1992—2001; sr. project engr., project mgr. SCS Engrs., Tampa, Fla., 2001—03; sr. project mgr. Santa Ana Watershed Project Authority, Riverside, Calif., 2003—. Recipient 1st grade Merit scholarship Rajshahi, Bangladesh Bd. Edn., 1977-84. Mem. ASCE, Nat. Soc. Profl. Engrs., Fla. Engring. Soc., Chi Epsilon. Home: 31202 Garnedside Ln Menifee CA 92584 Office Phone: 951-354-4245. Business E-Mail: mmorshed@sawpa.org.

MORSI, ABD EL WAHAB, artist; b. Fakos, Egypt, Feb. 23, 1931; s. Abdulwahab Mursi; married; 2 children. BA in Fine Arts, Cairo U., 1957; diploma, High Inst. Art Edn., 1958; spl. studies in graphic field, San Vernando, Spain, 1971. Staff Documentary Ctr. Egyptian Monuments, 1958-74; gen. dir. exhbns. Ministry of Egyptian Culture, 1974-80, gen. dir. art museums, 1980-90. Min. of Edn., 1977. Exhbns. include Biennial of Alexandria, Egypt, 1957, 59, 61, 68, 70, 96, Internat. Exhbn. Belgrade, 1961, Internat. Biennial Young Artists, Paris, 1965, Palette Bleue Gallery, Paris, 1965, Internat. Exhbn. African Art, Dakar, 1966, Biennial of Venice, 1968, Sport Biennial, Madrid, 1969, Toison Gallery, Spain, 1972, Nika Exhbn., Japan, 1973, Biennial of Rabat, Morocco, 1975, Kany Carmer Exhbn., Nice, France, 1975, Gallery Contemporain, Geneva, Holland Biennial of Venice, 1975, Internat. Exhbn. African Art, Lagos, Nigeria, 1976, Exhbn. Egyptian Graphic Art, West Germany, 1979, numerous galleries in Cairo, exhbns. in Paris, 1999, Mus. Modern Art Cairo, 1969, Ekhnaton Gallery, Cairo, 1964, Goethe Inst., Cairo, 1970, 1979, exhbns. Frankfurt, Prais, Austria, Finland, Paris, 1981-82, Khan El Magraby, Cairo, 1996-98, others; represented in collections Roil Mus., Madrid, White House, U.S., Mus. Barcelona, Nat. Mus. Jordan, Mus. Modern Art, Cairo, Mus. Alexandria, Mus. Port Said, Egypt, Mus. Teito Grade, Yugoslavia. Recipient 2d prize Biennale Exhbn. at Alexandria, 1970, prize Biennale Exhbn. at Barcelona, Spain, 1971, prize Biennale Exhbns., Paris, Madrid. Mem. Fine Arts Grads. Assn. Avocation: creative art. Address: 7 Sharia Dr Mustafa al-Nagdi al-Sirkh Quarter Shubra Cairo Egypt E-mail: khaled2003@yahoo.com.

MORTENSEN, ARVID LEGRANDE, lawyer; b. July 11, 1941; s. George Andrew and Mary Louise (Myers) M.; m. Elaine Marie Mains, Aug. 2, 1968; children: Marie Louise, Anne Catherine, Joseph Duncan, Susan Kumari. BS in English and Psychology, Brigham Young U., 1965, MBA in Mktg. and Fin., 1967; JD cum laude, Ind. U., 1980. Bar: Ind. 1980, U.S. Supreme Ct. 1983, Mo. 1985, D.C. 1985; CLU; accredited estate planner; cert. dive master Profl. Assn. Diving Instrs.; lic. amateur radio operator FCC, amateur extra class. Agt. Conn. Mut. Life Ins. Co., Salt Lake City, 1967-68, agt., br. mgr. Idaho Falls, Idaho, 1968-74; with Rsch. and Rev. Svc. Am., Inc./Newkirk Assocs., Inc., Indpls, 1974-83, sr. editor, 1975-79, mgr. advanced products and seminars, 1979-80, sr. mktg. exec., 1980-83; tax and fin. planner Indpls., 1980-85, St. Louis and Chesterfied, Mo., 1985-90, Tampa Bay, Fla., 1990-91, Orange County, Calif., 1991—. Mem. sr. mgmt. com., v.p. Allied Fidelity Corp., 1983-85, Allied Fidelity Ins. Co., 1983-85, Tex. Fire and Casualty Ins. Co., 1983-85; v.p., bd. dirs. Gen. Am. Ins. Co., St. Louis, 1985-86, v.p., 1985-90; pvt. practice law, Indpls., 1980-85, St. Louis, Chesterfield and Bridgeton, Mo., 1985-90, Tampa Bay, 1990-91, Orange County, 1991—. Author: Employee Stock Ownership Plans, 1975, Fundamentals of Corporate Qualified Retirement Plans, 1975, 78, 80, Buy-Sell Agreements, 1988, The Key Executive Sale, 1989, (with Norman H. Tarver) The IRA Manual, 1975-87 edits., The Keogh Manual, 1975, 77, 78, 80 edits., The Section 403 (b) Manual, 1975, 77, 78, 80, 84, 85, 87 edits., sole author, 1991, 93, 94, edits., (with Leo C. Hodges) The Life Insurance Trust Handbook, 1980; contbr. articles to profl. jours.; editor-in-chief various tax and fin. planning courses; bd. editors Ind. Law Rev., 1977-78. Active Ch. Jesus Christ of Latter-day Saints, Denver, Idaho Falls, Indpls., St. Louis, Chesterfield, Tampa Bay Area and Orange County, Calif. Mem. Assn. Advanced Life Underwriting, Mo. Bar Assn., D.C. Bar Assn., Ind. Bar Assn., Am. Soc. CLUs. Office: 620 Newport Center Dr Ste 1100 Newport Beach CA 92660-8011 also: PO Box 6362 Laguna Niguel CA 92607-6362 Office Phone: 949-363-7132. E-mail: alm@webworldinc.com.

MORTENSEN, GORDON LOUIS, artist, printmaker; b. Arnegard, N.D., Apr. 27, 1938; s. Gunner and Otillia Ernestine (Reiner) M.; m. Phoebe Hollis Hansen, Apr. 10, 1965 (div. 1968); m. Linda Johanna Sisson, Dec. 7, 1969. BFA, Mpls. Coll. Art and Design, 1964; postgrad., U. Minn., 1969-72. One-man shows include Minn. Mus., St. Paul, 1967, Concept Art Gallery, Pitts., 1981, 1983, 1985, 1987, 1989, 1991, 1993, C.G. Rein Galleries, Mpls., 1978, 1980, 1985, 1989, 1991, 1993, others, exhibited in group shows at Miami U., Oxford, Ohio (1st pl. award, 1977), Phila. Print Club (George Bunker award, 1977), 12th Nat. Silvermine Guild Print Exhbn., New Canaan, Conn., 1976, 1978, 1980, 1983, 1986, 1994, 1996 (Hearsch Mag. award, 1978, Purchase award, 1983, 1986), 4th Miami Internat. Print Biennial (4th pl. award, 1980), Rockford Internat., 1981, 1985 (Juror's award, 1981), Boston Printmakers Nat. Exhbn., 1977, 1979, 1980, 1981, 1983, 1997, 2003 (Purchase award, 1977, 1979, 1983, Juror's Accomodation), others, Represented in permanent collections Achenbach Found. Graphic Arts at Palace Legion of Honor, San Francisco, Bklyn. Mus., Phila. Mus. Art, Libr. of Congress, Minn. Mus. Art, Met. Mus. and Art Ctr., Miami, Fla., Mus. Am. Art, Washington, Art Inst. Chgo., Mus. Art at Carnegie-Mellon Inst., Pitts., Walker Art Ctr., Mpls., Dulin Gallery Art, Knoxville, Tenn., Phila. Mus. Art, Tokyo Fuji Art Mus., numerous corp. collections; profiled in numerous art jours. Served with USMC, 1957-60. Mem. Boston Printmakers, Phila. Print Club, L.A. Printmaking Soc., Albany Print Club, Am. Print Alliance. Home and Office: 4153 Crest Rd Pebble Beach CA 93953-3052 Office Phone: 831-625-0960.

MORTENSEN, ROBERT HENRY, landscape architect, golf course architect; b. Jackson, Mich., June 9, 1939; s. Henry and Charlotte Marie (Brown) M.; divorced; children: Phillip, Paul, Susan, Julia. B in Landscape Architecture, Ohio State U., 1961; M in Landscape Architecture, U. Mich., 1965. Registered landscape arch., Va., Md. Landscape arch. various firms, Louisville, 1960, 61-63; with Ohio Divsn. Pks., Columbus, 1960-61; landscape arch. various firms, Toledo, 1963, 65-67; pvt. practice Ann Arbor, Mich., 1963-65; ptnr. firms Toledo, 1967-78; pres. Harvey Jones and Assocs., Clearwater, Fla., 1979-81; owner Mortensen Assocs., Toledo and Falls Church, Va., 1979-85; prin. Mortensen, Lewis & Scully, Inc., Vienna, Va., 1985-93; owner Mortensen Assocs., McLean, Va., 1993. Assoc. prof. U. Mich. Grad. Sch., 1973; vis. lectr. Ohio State U., 1965—, Bowling Green (Ohio) State U., 1969—, U. Mich., 1971, Purdue U., 1971, Mich. State U., 1973—, U. Mass., 1986—; mem. archtl. environ. rev. com. Ohio Arts Coun., 1974-78; adj. prof. Dept. Landscape Architecture, U. Md., 1992—; chmn. Merrifield Master Plan Task Force, 1998-2001. Editor: Handbook of Professional Practice, 1972, Marketing Landscape Architectural Services to the Federal Government, 1974. Mem. Ohio Bd. Unreclaimed Strip Mined Lands, 1973-76; mem. Lucas County facilities rev. com. Health Planning Assn. N.W. Ohio, 1972-76, chmn. maternal and child health subcom., 1972-74; bd. dirs. No. Va. Cmty. Appearance Alliance, 1988—2002, chair, 1991, pres., 1994. Recipient Disting. Svc. award Health Planning Assn. N.W. Ohio, 1973, Disting. Alumni award U. Mich. Sch. Natural Resources, 1985, Disting. Alumnus award Ohio State U. Coll. Engring., 1985. Fellow Am. Soc. Landscape Architects (trustee 1977-82, v.p. 1982-83, pres.-elect 1983-84, nat. pres. 1984-85, del. to Internat. Fedn. Landscape Architects 1987-92, del. Internat. Landscape Alliance 1994-2000); mem. Ohio Soc. Landscape Architects (pres. 1969-74), Landscape Inst. U.K. (hon. corr.), Toledo C. of C. (chmn. sts. and hwys. transit com. 1972-73), Greater Merrifield Bus. and Profl. Assn. (bd. dirs. 1993-2002, chmn. bd. dirs. 1998, pres. 1997), Washington Golf and Country Club (officer, bd. mem. 1999—, pres. 2002-03), Sigma Phi Epsilon. Home: 6843 Churchill Rd Mc Lean VA 22101-2822 Office: Mortensen Assocs 6843 Churchill Rd Mc Lean VA 22101 Office Phone: 703-917-1515. E-mail: rhmort@aol.com. *One of the best continuing educational experiences for a practising professional is to teach students what you have learned. They respond in a critical and ever-so-fresh "so what" atmosphere, and demand more of you sometimes than you demand of yourself. Thus, there is learning on both sides of the lectern.*

MORTENSEN, VIGGO, actor; b. N.Y.C., N.Y., Oct. 20, 1958; Degree in Govt. and Spanish, St. Lawrence U., 1980. Actor: (TV miniseries) George Washington, 1984; (TV films) Once In a Blue Moon, 1990; (films) Witness, 1985, Salvation!, 1987, Fresh Horses, 1988, Prison, 1988, Leatherface: Texas Chainsaw Massacre III, 1990, Young Guns II, 1990, Reflecting Skin, The, 1990, Tripwire, 1990, Indian Runner, The, 1991, Boiling Point, 1993, Ruby Cairo, 1993, Carlito's Way, 1993, Young Americans, The, 1993, Ewangelia wedlug Harry'ego, 1993, Desert Lunch, 1994, Floundering, 1994, Crew, The, American Yakuza, 1994, Crimson Tide, 1995, Black Velvet Pantsuit, 1995, Prophecy, The, 1995, Gimlet, 1995, Albino Alligator, 1996, Portrait of a Lady, The, 1996, Daylight, 1996, G.I. Jane, 1997, Pistola de mi hermano, La, 1997, Perfect Murder, A, 1998, Psycho, 1998, Walk on the Moon, A, 1999, 28 Days, 2000, Lord of the Rings: The Fellowship of the Ring, 2001, Lord of the Rings: The Two Towers, 2002, Lord of the Rings: The Return of the King, 2003, Hidalgo, 2004. Office: Creative Artists Agy 9830 Wilshire Blvd Beverly Hills CA 90212-1825

MORTENSEN-SAY, MARLYS, school system administrator; b. Yankton, SD, Mar. 11, 1924; d. Melvin A. and Edith L. (Fargo) Mortensen; m. John Theodore Say, June 21, 1951; children: Mary Louise, James Kenneth, John Melvin, Margaret Ann. BA, U. Colo., 1949, MEd, 1953; Adminstrv. Specialist, U. Nebr., 1973. Tchr. Huron (S.D.) Jr. H.S., 1944-48, Lamar (Colo.) Jr. H.S., 1950-52, Norfolk Pub. Sch., 1962-63; sch. supr. Madison County, Madison, Nebr., 1963-79. Mem. ASCD, NEA (life) AAUW, Am. Assn. Sch. Adminstrs., Dept. Rural Edn., Nebr. Assn. County Supts., N.E. Nebr. County Supts. Assn. Assn. Sch. Bus. Ofcls., Nat. Orgn. Legal Problems in Edn., Nebr. Edn. Assn., Nebr. Sch. Adminstrs. Assn. Republican. Methodist. Home: 1222 W S Airport Rd Norfolk NE 68701-1349

MORTENSON, KRISTIN OPPENHEIM, violinist; b. San Antonio, Tex., July 14, 1964; d. Russell E. and Martha Kunkel Oppenheim; m. Gary Curtiss Mortenson; children: Leah Marie, Sarah Grace. Attended, U. Tex., 1984; MusB, La. State U., 1987, MusM, 1988. Violinist Austin Symphony Orch., Austin, Tex., 1981—84, Baton Rouge Symphony, Baton Rouge, 1985—89; violin/viola tchr. Pvt. Music Studio, Manhattan, Kans., 1989—; violinist Wichita Symphony Orch., Wichita, Kans., 1991—93, Des Moines Symphony, Des Moines, 1993—2001; assoc. concertmaster Topeka Symphony Orch., Topeka, 2001—. Violinist/violist Heartland String Ensemble, Manhattan, Kans., 2001—. Assistant editor The International Trumpet Guild Jour., 2001, violinist (live performances with) Ray Charles, Dionne Warwick, Bob Hope, Shirley Jones, Marvin Hamlisch, Rich Little, La., Kans., Nebr. Mem. Lee Sch. Site Coun., Manhattan, Kans., 2000—02; pres. Lee Sch. PTO, Manhattan, Kans., 2000—01; sec. Grandview Hills Neighborhood Assn., Manhattan, Kans., 2000—02. Mem.: Am. String Tchrs. Assn. (state pres. La. 1988—89), Pilot Club of Manhattan (editor Pilot Times 2001—), Sigma Alpha Iota (life; pres. U. Tex. 1983—84, Coll. Honor award, Sword of Honor 1984). Home: 522 Westview Dr Manhattan KS 66502

MORTENSON, M. A., JR., construction executive; Chmn., pres., ceo M. A. Mortenson Co., Mpls., 1960-98, chmn., CEO, 1998—. Office: M A Mortenson Co 700 Meadow Ln N Ste 710 Minneapolis MN 55422-4817

MORTENSON, THOMAS THEODORE, medical products executive, management consultant; b. Hallock, Minn., Dec. 18, 1934; s. Theodore William and Esther (Hanson) M.; m. Alice L. Girdvain, June 27, 1958; children: Kim M., Laura Dee Mortenson Pavlides. BSBA, U. ND, 1956, postgrad., 1957—58. Sales rep. Johnson & Johnson, Detroit, 1960-66, tng. and product dir. New Brunswick, NJ, 1967-72; dir. market devel. C.R. Bard, Murray Hill, NJ, 1973-75; gen. mgr. MacBick, Murray Hill, 1976-78; dir. mktg. Bard Med. Systems, Murray Hill, 1979-81, dir. sales, 1982; dir. sales/mktg., bd. dirs. Bac-Data Med. Info. Systems, Totowa, NJ, 1983-84; v.p. mktg. and sales United Med. Corp., Haddonfield, NJ, 1985—86; exec. v.p. Daltex Med. Scis., West Orange, NJ, 1987-92; dir. ConMed Corp., Utica, NY, 1993—. Guest lectr. Am. Mgmt. Assn., 1971, Mktg. Scis. Inc., NYC, 1978, Internat. Novel Drug Delivery Techs., Tustin, Calif., 1987. With U.S. Army, USMC reserves, 1953—58. Mem. Am. Mgmt. Assn. (instr. 1971), Berkeley Swim Club (Berkeley Heights, NJ, pres. 1979-82, bd. dirs. 1974-84). Avocations: auto model collecting, woodworking, gardening, WWII history. Home: 44 Ironwood Rd New Hartford NY 13413-3906 Office: 525 French Rd Utica NY 13502 Office Phone: 800-765-8375 ext. 3134.

MORTHAM, SANDRA BARRINGER, former state official; b. Erie, Pa., Jan. 4, 1951; d. Norman Lyell and Ruth (Harer) Barringer; m. Allen Mortham, Aug. 21, 1950; children: Allen Jr., Jeffrey. AS, St. Petersburg Jr. Coll., 1971; BA, Eckerd Coll. Cons. Capital Formation Counselors, Inc., Bellair Bluffs, Fla., 1972-74; commr. City of Largo, Fla., 1982-86, vice mayor, 1985-86; mem. Fla. Ho. of Reps., 1986-94, Rep. leader pro tempore, 1990-92, Rep. leader, 1992-94; Sec. of State State of Fla., 1995-98; pub. affairs dir., CEO, exec. v.p. Fla. Med. Assn., 1999—. Bd. dirs. Performing Arts Ctr. & Theatre, Clearwater, Fla.; exec. com. Pinellas County Rep. Com., Rep. Nat. Com. Named Citizen of Yr., 1990; recipient Tax Watch Competitive Govt. award, 1994, Bus. and Profl. Women "Break the Glass Ceiling" award, 1995, Fla. League of Cities Quality Floridian award, 1995, also numerous outstanding legislator awards, achievement among women awards from civic and profl. orgns. Mem. Am. Legis. Exch. Coun., Nat. Rep. Legislators Assn., Largo C. of C. (bd. dirs. 1987—, pres.), Largo Jr. Woman's Club (pres., Woman of Yr. award 1979), Suncoast Community Woman's Club (pres., Outstanding Svc. award 1981, Woman of Yr. award 1986), Suncoast Tiger Bay, Greater Largo Rep., Belleair Rep. Woman's, Clearwater Rep. Woman's, Tallahassee Rep. Woman's Club (pres. 1999-2000), Fla. Fedn. Rep. Women (2d v.p.). Republican. Presbyterian. Home: 6675 Weeping Willow Way Tallahassee FL 32311-8795 E-mail: smortham@aol.com.

MORTILLARO, LOUIS FRANCIS, psychologist; b. Ft. Dodge, Iowa, Dec. 8, 1944; s. Louis and Catherine (Perri) M.; m. Linda Vivian Tapp Johnson, Sept. 18, 1982 (div. July 1994); children: Ross, Darren. BS, Loyola U. L.A., 1966; MS, MPA, U. So. Calif., 1974; PhD, U.S. Internat. U., San Diego, 1978; cert. in neuropsychology, Fielding Inst., Santa Barbara, Calif., 1998. Lic. psychologist, Nev.; lic. MFT, Nev. Chief psychologist Clark County Juvenile Ct., Las Vegas, Nev., 1971-78, JHC Rehab. Ctr., Las Vegas, Nev., 1978-89; pvt. practice Las Vegas, Nev., 1989—; psychology dir. Nev. Pain and Rehab. Ctr., Las Vegas, 1990-95; chief psychologist Novacare Pain and Rehab. Ctr., Las Vegas, 1995—; evaluator Las Vegas Metro Police Dept., 1995-98. Mem. Bd. Psychol. Examiners, Nev., 1992-2000, pres., 1998-2000. Co-author: (chpt.) Field Events and Theory for Counselors, 1975; assoc. prodr., Ask Rita TV show, 2003—; contbr. articles to profl. jours. Pres., bd. dirs. Big Bros./Big Sisters, Las Vegas, 1984-86; bd. dirs. Boys and Girls Club, Las Vegas, 1986—, Youth Charities of So. Nev. Recipient Outstanding Svc. award Big Bros./Big Sisters, 1978, 83, Outstanding Svc. award Boys and Girls Club, 1992, 97, Outstanding Svc. award Nev. State Bd. Psychol. Examiners, 2000. Mem. APA, AAMFT, Nat. Acad. Neuropsychology, Nev. State Psychol. Assn. (past treas. 1975-76, 91-92, pres. elect 2001, pres. 2002-2003, Psychologist of Yr. 2002-03), Phi Kappa Phi. Avocations: golf, structured exercise, travel. Office: 501 S Rancho Dr Ste F-37 Las Vegas NV 89106-4834 E-mail: lfmort@aol.com.

MORTIMER, DAVID WILLIAM, electronics engineer; b. Redding, Calif., June 8, 1962; s. Walter L. and Phyllis B. (Winters) M.; m. Jenene McGhie, Sept. 20, 1997. BSEE, Brigham Young U., 1988; MBA, Syracuse U., 1997. Devel. engr. Scala Electronics, Medford, Oreg., 1988-89; asst. sta. mgr. Holzkirchen Radio Free Europe/Radio Liberty, Munich, 1989-90, asst. sta. mgr. Spain Playa de Pals, 1990-93, ops. dir. Portugal Lisbon, 1993-95, tech. asst. Prague, Czech Republic, 1995; project mgr. Siemens Transp. Sys., Sacramento, 1999—; acting mng. dir. Portugal Radio Free Europe/Radio Liberty, Lisbon, 1995. Mem. IEEE, Aircraft Owners and Pilots Assn., Nat. Eagle Scout Assn. (life.), Project Mgmt. Inst. (cert. project mgmt. profl.).

MORTIMER, JOHN H. home heating equipment manufacturing executive; b. Australia; BSEE, Monash U. (formerly Caufield, Inst. of Tech.), Melbourne; MS with distinction, U. Pa. Registered profl. engr., N.J. Joined Inductotherm, Melbourne, Australia, 1969, design engr., 1969-71, mng. dir., 1971-79, chief engr., 1979, v.p. engring., 1980-84; pres. Inductotherm Corp., N.J., U.S., 1984-97, chmn., 1998, chmn., CEO, 1998—; pres., CEO Inductotherm Furnace and Tech. Group, Rancocas, N.J., 1998—. Mem. IEEE 9sr.), Nat. Fire Protection Inst. (nat. code panel).

MORTIMER, KENNETH P. retired academic administrator; Pres. Western Wash. U., Bellingham, 1988-93, U. Hawaii Sys., Honolulu, 1993—2001. Office: U Hawaii Sys Bachmann Hall 202 2444 Dole St Honolulu HI 96822-2302

MORTIMER, MARY R. counselor; b. Muskegon, Mich., Oct. 22, 1945; d. Frederick A. Moldenauer and Margaret Olive Murray; m. Colin J. Casey, 1979 (dec. 1990); m. Eugene C. Mortimer, Dec. 30, 1994; stepchildren: stepchildren: Peter C. Casey, Harold E. Mortimer, Margaret H. Cinnella. BS in Criminology, Coll. of Santa Fe, 1986; MA in Counseling, Webster U., 1991. Nat. cert. counselor; lic. counselor, N.Mex. Mktg. rep. U.S. West, Albuquerque, 1963-72, disbursing agt., 1972-78, benefit adminstr., 1978-86, purchasing agt., 1986-90; mental health counselor Cottonwood Treatment Ctr., Los Lunas, N.Mex., 1990-94; vol. mental health counselor Taos Ski Valley (N.Mex.) EMS, 2000—. Vol. breast helpline Am. Cancer Soc., Albuquerque, 1991-98, Reach to Recovery, Albuquerque, 1994-2001, Taos, 1999—, Early Support, Albuquerque, 1998-2000, Taos, 1999—, Breast Self Exams in Sch. Edn., Albuquerque, 1991-98, N.Mex. Breast Cancer Core Team, Albuquerque, 1994-2000, People Living Through Cancer, Albuquerque, 1996-2000, Nat. Breast Cancer Coalition, Albuquerque, 1998—, LEAD, Albuquerque, 1998—, Rio Grande Coalition, Albuquerque, 1995-99; cert. vol. firefighter Taos Ski Valley Vol. Fire Dept., 1991—; vol. wilderness 1st responder Taos Ski Valley Emergency Med. Sys., 2000—; vol. critical incident stress counselor N.Mex. Critical Incident Stress Mgmt. Team, Taos Ski Valley, 2000—; vol. peer reviewer Dept. Def. Rev. Panel for Breast Cancer Rsch., Washington, 2000; vol. spkr., fundraiser United Way of Ctrl. N.Mex., Albuquerque, 1991-2000. Recipient Nat. Jefferson award Am. Inst. Pub. Svc., 1991, vol. recognition award Albuquerque chpt. ARC, 2000, recognition in Celebrating Life, S.W. divsn. ARC, 2000, named Vol. of Yr., 1997, featured vol. annual report cover, 1997, Am. Cancer Soc. Avocations: backpacking, hiking, whitewater canoeing, skiing.

MORTIMER, RICHARD WALTER, mechanical engineer, educator; b. Phila., Dec. 7, 1936; s. Horace and Almira Duffield (Matthews) M.; m. Doris Claire Ridler, June 29, 1957; children: Patrick Lee, David Walter, James Matthew, Daniel Scott. BSME, Drexel U., 1962, MSME, 1964, PhD, 1967. Prof. Drexel U., Phila., 1967—, assoc. dean grad. sch., 1974-76, head dept. mech. engring., 1976-85, assoc. v.p. acad. affairs, 1985-89. Mem. exec. com. Engring. Accreditation Com., N.Y.C., 1986-91. Contbr. over 40 articles to profl. jours. Pres. Haverford (Pa.) Twp. Sch. Dist., 1980-83. With U.S. Army, 1958-60. With U.S. Army, 1958—60. Recipient Achievement award Am. Soc. Nondestructive Testing, 1973, Best Tech. Paper award, 1973; fellow NASA, 1967, 68; grantee numerous orgns. including NASA, USAF, NSF, 1967-87; Fellow Members awd., Am. Soc. for Engineering Education, 1992. Fellow Am. Soc. Engring. Educators; mem. ASME (mem. numerous coms., bds. and chairs 1976-92). Republican. Episcopalian. Achievements include research in fields of structural dynamics and composite materials.

MORTIMER, WENDELL REED, JR., judge; b. Alhambra, Calif., Apr. 7, 1937; s. Wendell Reed and Blanche (Wilson) M.; m. Cecilia Vick, Aug. 11, 1962; children: Michelle Dawn, Kimberly Grace. AB, Occidental Coll., 1958; JD, U. So. Calif., L.A., 1965. Bar: Calif. 1966. Trial atty. Legal div. State of Calif., L.A., 1965-73; assoc. Thelen, Marrin, Johnson & Bridges, L.A., 1973-76, ptnr., 1976-93; pvt. practice San Marino, Calif., 1994-95; judge L.A. Superior Ct., 1995—, mem. complex litigation panel, 2000—. With U.S. Army, 1960-62. Mem. ABA, Internat. Acad. Trial Judges, Los Angeles County Bar Assn., Calif. Judges Assn., Am. Judicature Soc., Am. Judges Assn., Legion Lex., Am. Bd. Trial Advocacy (nat. bd. dirs., exec. com. L.A. chpt.), San Marino City Club (bd. dirs., v.p.), Pasadena Bar Assn., Balboa Yacht Club. Home: 1420 San Marino Ave San Marino CA 91108-2042

MORTLOCK, ROBERT PAUL, microbiologist, educator; b. Bronxville, N.Y., May 12, 1931; s. Donald Robert and Florance Mary (Bellaby) M.; m. Florita Mary Welling, Sept., 1954; children: Florita M., Jeffrey R., Douglas P. BS, Rensselaer Poly. Inst., N.Y., 1953; PhD, U. Ill., Urbana, 1958. Asst. prof. microbiology U. Mass., Amherst, 1963-68, assoc. prof. microbiology, 1968-73, prof. microbiology, 1973-78, Cornell U., Ithaca, N.Y., 1978-99, prof. emeritus, 2000. Editor: Microorganisms as Model Systems for Studying Evolution, 1984, The Evolution of Metabolic Function, 1992. Served to 1st lt. U.S. Army, 1959-61 Fellow Am. Acad. Microbiology; mem. AAAS, Am. Soc. Microbiology, Northeastern Microbiologists, Physiology, Ecology and Taxonomy (pres. 1984-91). Office: Cornell U Dept Microbiology Wing Hall Ithaca NY 14852 Business E-Mail: rpm2@cornell.edu.

MORTON, BRIAN, writer, editor; b. N.Y.C., July 8, 1955; s. Richard Paul and Tasha (Brisman) Morton. BA, Sarah Lawrence Coll., 1978. Instr. grad. dept. English, NYU, N.Y.C., 1992-94, 98—, acting dir. Grad. Creative Writing Program, 2003—; tchr. 92d St. YMCA, N.Y.C., 1993-98; instr. New Sch. Social Rsch., N.Y.C., 1995-97; exec. editor Dissent Mag., N.Y.C., 1994-99; instr. Sarah Lawrence Coll., Bronxville, NY, 1998—. Author: (novels) The Dylanist, 1991, Starting Out in the Evening, 1998, A Window Across the River, 2003; book rev. editor: Dissent Mag., 1988—2000. Finalist PEN/Faulkner award, 1999; recipient Koret Jewish Book award for fiction, 1998, Acad. Lit. award, Am. Acad. Arts and Letters, 2000; fellow Guggenheim, 2001. Office: Sarah Lawrence Coll One Mead Way Bronxville NY 10708

MORTON, CRAIG RICHARD, real estate investor; b. Mpls., Dec. 8, 1942; s. William Charles and Patricia Louise (Hare) M.; m. Barbara Jean Larsen, 1998; children: Kelly McCall, Bradley Winslow; step-son Thomas Paul Caspers. Student, U. Philippines, Quezon City, 1961-62; BA in Geography of Southeast Asia, U. Minn., 1966; postgrad., St. John's Coll., Annapolis, 1966. Vol. U.S. Peace Corps, Philippines, 1966-68; v.p. Rent Mgmt., Inc., Mpls., 1970-80; pres. Diversified Hawaiian Investments, Inc., Mpls., 1981-99, Craig R. Morton & Assoc., Inc., Mpls., 1980-2000, No. Am. Land Corp., 1992—. Founder 49 real estate ltd. partnerships, Minn., N.Mex., Hawaii, Tex.; real estate developer Enchanted Lakes, Minn., 1990; pres. Am. Forex Corp., 1995-98, Sweet Magnolia HOA, 2001—, Royal Palms HOA, 2002—, Ashby Cove HOA, 2003—, Space Coast Barter, 2003—. Am. Field Svc. scholar to Pakistan, 1960. Mem. Soc. Mayflower Descs., Jaguar Club Minn., Country Classics Car Club, Rotary (Paul Harris fellow), Order of DeMolay, Boy Scouts Order of Arrow, Loyal Order of Moose, Internat. Arabian Horse Assn. Republican. Avocations: Jaguar automobiles, reading, stamp collecting/philately, woodsmanship, raising arabian horses. Home: 3569 Muirfield Dr Titusville FL 32780

MORTON, CYNTHIA C. geneticist; Geneticist Brigham & Women's Hosp., Boston. Recipient Warner-Lambert/Parke-Davis award Am. Soc. Investigative Pathology, 1997. Office: Brigham & Women's Hosp 75 Francis St Boston MA 02115-6106 E-mail: cmorton@partners.org.

MORTON, DAVID K. language educator; b. York, Pa., Mar. 24, 1962; s. Harold Pete E. Morton and Charlotte Herman Huber, F. Bud G. Huber (Stepfather); m. Maranda T. Boyd, June 19, 1999; children: P. Chase, Mark D. BA, Fla. State U., Tallahassee, 1985. Instrnl. cert. level II Pa. Dept. of Edn. Tchr. English Dallastown (Pa.) Area H.S., 1985—, asst. girls' volleyball coach, 1986—93, head boys' volleyball coach, 1986—97, 2001—02, head girls' volleyball coach, 2001—02. Mem. Pa. Interscholastic Athletic Oversight Coun., Harrisburg, 2001—. Mem.: Pa. Coaches Assn. (sec., founder), Keystone Regional Volleyball Assn. (dir. jr. boys' devel. 1990—96, newsletter editor 1996—2000), Dallastown Area Edn. Assn., Pa. Volleyball Coaches' Assn. (life; pres. 1998—2004, 1998—, dist. III boys' rep. 1989—95), North Town Volleyball Club (dir., coach 1988—97). United Ch. Of Christ. Avocations: volleyball, reading, writing. Office: Dallastown Area HS 700 New School Ln Dallastown PA 17313

MORTON, DONALD CHARLES, astronomer; b. Kapuskasing, Ont., Can., June 12, 1933; s. Charles Orr and Irene Mary (Wightman) M.; m. Winifred May Austin, Dec. 12, 1970; children: Keith James, Christine Elizabeth. BA, U. Toronto, 1956; PhD, Princeton U., 1959. Astronomer U.S. Naval Rsch. Lab., Washington, 1959-61; from rsch. assoc. to sr. rsch. astronomer with rank of prof. Princeton (N.J.) U., 1961-76; dir. Anglo-Australian Obs., Epping and Coonabarabran, Australia, 1976-86; dir. gen. Herzberg Inst. Astrophysics, NRC of Can., Ottawa and Victoria, 1986—2000; rschr. emeritus NRC of Can., 2001—. Contbr. numerous articles to profl. jours. Fellow Australian Acad. Sci.; mem. Internat. Astron. Union, Royal Astron. Soc. (assoc. 1980), Astron. Soc. Australia (pres. 1981-83, hon. mem. 1986), Royal Astron. Soc. Can., Am. Astron. Soc. (councilor 1970-73), Can. Astron. Soc. Australian Inst. Physics (Pawsey Meml. lectr. 1985), Can. Assn. Physicists, U.K. Alpine Club, Am. Alpine Club, Alpine Club Can. Avocations: mountain climbing, rock climbing, ice climbing, marathon running. Office: Herzberg Inst Astrophysics NRC Can 5071 W Saanich Rd Victoria BC Canada V9E 2E7 Office Phone: 250-363-8313.

MORTON, DONALD JOHN, librarian; b. Bklyn., Jan. 11, 1931; s. Ellwood Stokes and Gladys (Hassler) M.; m. Ann Mayo Tilden, Aug. 16, 1958; children— Saundra Kay, Donald John, Mary Ann. BS, U. Del., 1952; MS, La. State U., 1954, PhD, U. Calif. at Berkeley, 1958; MS in Libr. Sci., Simmons Coll., 1969, Dr. Arts in Library Sci, 1976. Asst. prof. botany N.M. State U., Las Cruces, 1957-58; asst. prof. plant pathology N.D. State U., Fargo, 1959-61; plant pathologist Agr. Dept., Tifton, Ga., 1961-65; asso. prof. plant pathology U. Del., Newark, 1965-68; librarian Northeastern U., Boston, 1968-70; head librarian, asst. prof. history of medicine U. Mass. Med. Sch., Worcester, 1970-74, dir. libr., assoc. prof. libr. sci., 1974-94, libr. cons., 1994—; tchr. med. librarianship Worcester State Coll., 1974-94; libr. cons., 1994—; computer cons. Hampton Hist. Soc., 1995—; libr. advisor Exeter (N.H.) Hosp., 1996—. Cons. in field; mem. adv. com. med. librarianship Simmons Coll., 1972-94; mem. task force com. New Eng. Regional Libr. Svc., 1971-94; mem. cooperating staff Worcester Found. Exptl. Biology, 1972-94; chmn. Coun. Developing Med. Librs., 1974; pres. North Atlantic Health Scis. Librs., 1974-75, Worcester Area Coop. Librs., 1974-75. Contbr. articles to profl. jours. Mem. Oliver Wendell Holmes endowment com. Boston Med. Libr., 1973-74, U. Mass. Bicentennial Com., 1973-75. Mem. Am. Assn. Univ. Adminstrs., Simmons Coll. Libr. Sch. Alumni Assn. (pres. 1975-76), Worcester Art Mus., Worcester Hist. Soc., Northboro Hist. Soc., Hampton Hist. Soc., N.H. Hist. Soc., Am. Soc. Info. Sci., ALA, Mass. Libr. Assn., Med. Libr. Assn. (chmn. New Eng. group 1974-75), Mycol. Soc. Am., Spl. Librs. Assn., New Eng. Coll. Librarians, Piscataqua Pioneers Hereditary Soc., Sigma Xi, Phi Kappa Phi, Phi Sigma, Delta Tau Delta, Alpha Zeta. Home: 314 High St Hampton NH 03842-4004

MORTON, EDWARD JAMES, insurance company executive; b. Ft. Wayne, Ind., Nov. 8, 1926; s. Clifford Leroy and Clara Marie (Merklein) M.; m. Jean Ann McClernon, Apr. 30, 1949; children: Marcia Lynn, Anne; m. Matthild Schneider, Sept. 19, 1986; 1 child, Katherine. BA, Yale U., 1949. With John Hancock Mut. Life Ins. Co., Boston, 1949—, v.p., then sr. v.p., 1967-74, exec. v.p., 1974-82, pres., chief operating officer, 1982-86, chmn., chief exec. officer, 1987-92, also bd. dirs. Trustee Gettysburg Coll. 1990-2002, trustee emeritus, 2002—; hon. life overseer Children's Hosp. Fellow Soc. Actuaries; mem. Actuaries Club Boston, Comml. Club Boston, Phi Beta Kappa. Office: John Hancock Life Ins Co PO Box 111 C-01-03 Boston MA 02117-0111

MORTON, FRED J. lawyer; b. El Paso, Tex., Nov. 13, 1935; s. R.A.D. and Julianne (More) M.; m. Anne Adele Reynolds, July 19, 1960; children: Chris, Anne, John, Robert, Peter, Mary Virginia, Thomas, Mary Katherine. BA, U. Tex., El Paso, 1957; LLB, U. Tex., Austin, 1958. Bar: Tex. 1958. Asst. U.S. atty., El Paso, 1961-65; U.S. commr. cts., 1966-71. Trustee, Southwestern Children's Home Trust, El Paso, 1983—; pres. El Paso County Hist. Soc., 1967. Fellow U. Tex. Law Sch. Ctr. for Pub. Policy Dispute Resolution, 1996. Mem. Tex. Bar Assn., El Paso Trial Lawyers Assn. (pres. 1972), El Paso Bar Assn. (pres. 1985), Sigma Alpha Epsilon, Phi Delta Phi. Democrat. Roman Catholic. Home: 1101 Montana Ave El Paso TX 79902-5509 E-mail: fredmorton713@msn.com.

MORTON, FREDERIC, author; b. Vienna, Oct. 5, 1924; s. Frank and Rose (Ungvary) M.; m. Marcia Colman, Mar. 28, 1957; 1 dau., Rebecca. BS, Coll. City N.Y., 1947; MA, New Sch. Social Research, 1949. Author: The Hound, 1947, The Darkness Below, 1949, Asphalt and Desire, 1952, The Witching Ship, 1960, The Schatten Affair, 1965, Snow Gods, 1969, An Unknown Woman, 1976, The Forever Street, 1984, Crosstown Sabbath, 1987, (biography) The Rothschilds, 1962 (Nat. Book award finalist), A Nervous Splendor-Vienna 1888/9, 1979 (Nat. Book award finalist), Thunder at Twilight-Vienna 1913/14, 1989; books translated into 14 langs.; actor (documentary made in English and German) Crosstown Sabbath, 1995 (broadcast in Austria, Germany, Switzerland, P.B.S. Stas., U.S.); contbg. editor: Vanity Fair; contbr. to publs. including Best Am. Short Stories, Best Am. Essays of 2003, and other anthologies, N.Y. Times, Harper's mag., Atlantic mag., Nation, Playboy, Esquire, N.Y. Mag., Hudson Rev., Wall Street Jour., Vanity Fair, L.A. Times, others; columnist Village Voice, Conde-Nast Traveler, Wall Street Jour. Recipient Author of Year award Nat. Anti-Defamation League, B'nai B'rith; Hon. Professorship award Republic of Austria, 1980, Tom Osborne Disting. lectureship U. Nebr., 1989; Dodd, Mead Intercollegiate Lit. fellow, 1947; Yaddo residence fellow, 1948, 50; Breadloaf Writers' Conf. fellow, 1947; Columbia U. fellow, 1953; recipient Golden Merit award City of Vienna, 1986, City of Vienna medal of honor in gold, 2001, Cross of Honor for Achievements in Arts, Republic of Austria, 2003. Mem. Author's Guild (exec. coun.), P.E.N. Home: 110 Riverside Dr New York NY 10024-3715 Office: Sandra Diskstra Agy OMB 515 1155 Camino Del Mar Del Mar CA 92014 *As a writer I'm trying to tell the truth interestingly.*

MORTON, HUGH WESLEY, producer, director; b. Pasadena, Calif., Dec. 8, 1931; s. Hugh Wesley Morton and Timey Delacey Hopper; m. Paula Dozois, Nov. 30, 1951 (dec. May 1954); m. Norma Antonia Daloisio, Apr. 22, 1965 (div.); 1 adopted child, Wil Guido. BA, Northwestern U., 1954; BS, U. Mont., 1959; MA, U. Oreg., 1961. Mailboy, prodn. office clk. Paramount Prodns., Hollywood, Calif., 1962-64; dir., tchr. Profl. Theatre Workshop, Desilu Studios, Hollywood, 1964-66; asst. to contr. Columbia Pictures TV, Hollywood, 1966-68, asst. to exec. v.p. TV prodn., 1968-75; asst. to studio pres. The Burbank (Calif.) Studios, 1975-78; dir. Hollywood Central, Glendale, Calif., 1978-82; spl. events prodr., dir. studio facilities Fox Studios/News Corp., L.A., 1982-97; vol. oncology, sr. peer counseling Providence St. Joseph Hosp., Burbank, Calif., 1997—; cons. on call IV Prodns., L.A., 1997—. Prodr. 400 TV episodes, 50 films; author: Assistant Director's Handbook, 1973. Mem. Mus. of Arts, City of Hope, L.A.; libr. assoc. Coll. Canyons; prodr. Ciba Geigy, L.A.; prodr. various spl. events. Named Vol. of Yr. Providence St. Joseph Hosp., 1998; recipient Outstanding Support award White House Comms. Agy., 1994, Outstanding Svc. award C. of C., 1983, Award of Merit Media Workshop Found. Mass Comm. and Educating Am. Youth; Fulbright scholarship Alternate Royal Acad. Mem. Acad. of TV Arts and Scis., Screen Actors Guild, Am. Fedn. of TV and Radio Artists, Internat. Alliance of Theatrical State Employees Artists and Allied Crafts of the U.S., Calif. State Sheriff's Assn., Canyon Theatre Guild, Met. Mus. of Art (assoc.), Wildlife Sta., Calif. State Parks Assn., L.A. County Mus. of Arts, L.A. Natural History Mus., The Colony Playhouse. Avocations: hiking, gardening, singing, reading. Office: IV Prodns PO Box 2517 Toluca Lake CA 91610

MORTON, JAMES CARNES, JR., automotive executive; b. Duncan, Okla., May 8, 1945; s. James Carnes and Syble Lyda (Looney) Morton; m. Susan Phillips, May 25, 1968; children: James III, Terrissa Anne, Scott Thomas. BA, Westminster Coll., 1967; JD, U. Mo., 1972. Bar: Mo. 1972. Tax acct. Arthur Andersen Co., St. Louis, 1972-74; tax atty. Gen. Dynamics Corp., St. Louis, 1974-76; asst. gen. counsel Michelin Tire Corp., Greenville, SC, 1976-86; gen.

counsel Michelin Tire Corp. and Michelin Tires (Can.) Ltd., Greenville, 1990-92; dir. pub. rels. and govt. affairs Michelin Tire Corp., Greenville, 1986-92; exec. dir. external rels. Michelin N.Am., Inc., Greenville, 1992-96, v.p. pub. rels. and govt. rels., 1996-2000; sr. v.p. fin. & adminstrn., bd. dirs. Nissan North Am., Inc., Gardena, Calif., 2000—. Bd. dirs. Nissan Can., Inc. Bd. dirs. Greenville Symphony Orch., 1986—89, United Way Greenville, 1987—88, Greenville YMCA, 1988—89; mem. S.C. Reorganization Commn., 1985—98; trustee S.C. Gov.'s Sch. Sci. and Math., 1996—99; mem. sch. bd. Christ Ch. Episcopal Sch., Greenville, 1997—2000; vice chmn. S.C. Ports Authority, 1999—2000; pres. Nissan Found., 2003—. Lt. U.S. Army, 1967—70, capt. Mo. N.G., 1970—72. Recipient Alumni Achievement award, Westminster Coll., 2003. Mem.: ABA, Mo. Bar Assn. (non-resident), Alliance Automobile Mfrs. (bd. dirs. 2000—03), Rubber Mfrs. Assn. (bd. dirs. 1995—2000, mem. govt. affairs com., mem. tire mgmt. com.), Assn. Internat. Automobile Mfrs. (bd. dirs., mem. exec. com. 2000—), LA Urban League (bd. dirs. 2001—, chmn. audit com. 2004—), S.C. C. of C. (mem. exec. com. 1981—84, 1986—95, bd. dirs., pres. 1993—94, chmn. 1994—95, Recognition award 1982), Calif. C. of C. (bd. dirs. 2001—), Greater Greenville C. of C. (chmn. govt. affairs com. 1990, bd. dirs. 1990—93, chmn. legis. affairs com. 1996—98), Rolling Hills Country Club, Greenville Country Club. Presbyterian. Avocation: golf. Office: Nissan NAm Inc PO Box 191 Gardena CA 90248-0191 Business E-Mail: jim.morton@nissan-usa.com.

MORTON, JOËLLE, musician, editor; d. Raymond and Lynn Fancher; m. Brian Morton, Dec. 19, 1991. DMA, U. of So. Calif., 1993—97. Musician/clinician/lectr. Freelance performer on violas da gamba, violoni and period double basses, 1997—; gen. editor Internat. Soc. of Bassists, Dallas, 1999—. Author: (scholarly articles) The Early History of the G Violone Jour. of the Viola da Gamba Soc. of Am., editor Bass World mag., Jour. of Bass Rsch.; contbr. gen. interest articles Chamber Music: An Art of Speaking and Listening Simultaneously, Evolution Theory: A Bass By Any Other Name? Back to the Future: The Renaissance of the Violone, Haydn's Missing Double Bass Concerto, Performance Practice. Mem.: Viola da Gamba Soc. of Greater N.Y. (bd. mem. 1998—2002), Internat. Soc. of Bassists (life; bd. mem. 1999—2003), Pi Kappa Lambda. Home: 560 Riverside Dr #5D New York NY 10027 Personal E-mail: bm120@columbia.edu.

MORTON, LOUIS GEORGE, retired social sciences educator; b. St. Louis, May 21, 1928; s. Louis George and Helen (Kesl) Morton; m. Mary Ann Moore, Dec. 5, 1954; children: Robert, David, James. BS in Edn., Mo. U., 1953; MA, Western State Coll., Gunnison, Colo., 1966, cert. in edn. specialist, 1971. Tchr. history Ctrl. HS, Grand Junction, Colo., 1961—66; prof. polit. sci. Mesa State Coll., Grand Junction, 1966—95, prof. emeritus, 1995—, pres. faculty senate, 1988—90, dept. chmn. social scis., 1991—92. Pres. Ctrl. CEA, Grand Junction, 1965—66. Author: A Student's Guide to the U.S. Constitution, 1987, A Citizen's Guide to the U.S. Constitution, 1993, The First 75 Years History Mesa State College, 2003. 1st lt. USAF, 1946—53. NSF grantee, U. Mo., 1966, U. Tex., 1975. Mem.: Mesa State Coll. Emeriti Assn. (pres. 1997—98), Colo. Ret. Sch. Employees Assn. (pres. 2004—), Mesa County Ret. Sch. Employees Assn. (pres. 2000—01), Am. Legion. Democrat. Methodist. Avocations: numismatist, philately, writing. Home: 1111 Horizon Dr # 403 Grand Junction CO 81506 Business E-Mail: lmorton@iopener.net.

MORTON, MARILYN MILLER, retired genealogy and history educator, lecturer, researcher, travel executive, director; b. Water Valley, Miss, Dec. 2, 1929; d. Julius Brunner and Irma Faye (Magee) Miller; m. Perry Wilkes Morton Jr., July 2, 1958; children: Dent Miller Morton, Nancy Marilyn Morton Driggers, E. Perian Morton Dyar. BA in English, Miss. U. for Women, 1952; MS in History, Miss. State U., 1955. Cert. secondary tchr. Tchr. English, speech and history Starkville (Miss.) H.S., 1952-58; part-time instr. Miss. State U., 1953-55; spl. collection staff Samford U. Libr., Birmingham, Ala., 1984-92; lectr. genealogy and history, instr. Inst. Genealogy & Hist. Rsch., Samford U., Birmingham, 1985-93, assoc. dir., 1985-88, exec. dir., 1988-93; founding dir. SU Brit. and Irish Inst. Genealogy & Hist. Rsch. Samford U., Birmingham, 1986-93; owner, dir. Marilyn Miller Morton Brit-Ire-U.S. Genealogy, Birmingham, 1994—95, 1994—95. Instr. genealogy classes Samford U. Metro Coll., 1986-94; former lectr. nat. conf. Fedn. of Geneal. Soc. Contbr. articles to profl. jours. Miss. state pres. Future Homemakers Am., 1947-48; active Birmingham chpt. Salvation Army Aux., 1982-87. Named to Miss. U. for Women Hall of Fame, 1952. Fellow Irish Geneal. Rsch. Soc. London; mem. Nat. Geneal. Soc. (mem. nat. program com. 1988-92, lectr. nat. meetings), Antiquarian Soc. Birmingham (sec., 2d v.p. 1982-84), DAR (regent Cheaha chpt. 1977-78), Daus. Am. Colonists (regent Edward Waters chpt. 1978-79), Nat. League of Am. Penwomen, Phi Kappa Phi (charter mem. Samford U. chpt. 1972). Avocations: reading, research, travel, bridge, chess. Home: PO Box 660562 Birmingham AL 35266-0562

MORTON, MARY MADELINE, family nurse practitioner; b. Bronx, N.Y., Aug. 7, 1952; d. David E. and Frances P. (Perrone) Bennett; children: Anthony, Kathryn; m. Robert B. Morton, May 25, 1991. AAS in Nursing-RN with distinction, Pace U., 1989, BSN summa cum laude, 1994, MSN, 1996. Cert. LPN; RN, N.Y.; cert. family nurse practitioner. Med. asst. C.A. Vera, MD, Bronx, 1970-79; staff nurse med.-surg., pediatric, orthopedic and cardiac units Hudson Valley Hosp. Ctr., Peekskill, N.Y., 1986-96; office nurse William Higgins, MD, Mohegan Lake, N.Y., 1993-95; pvt. practice, 1998—; dir. Med. Clinic St. Vincent's Hosp, Westchester, N.Y., 1997-98; nurse practitioner Skyview Health Care Ctr., Croton, N.Y., 1996-97. Camp nurse Summer Trails Day Camp, Somers, N.Y., summer, 1992; clin. instr./lectr. LPN program Bd. Cooperative Ednl. Svcs. Tech. Ctr., Yorktown Height, N.Y., 1994-95; adj. prof. Pace U. Leinhard Sch. Nursing, Pleasantville, N.Y., 1995. Tchr. religious edn. St. Mary's Ch., Katonah, N.Y., 1988, 89. Mem. ANA, N.Y. State Coalition of Nurse Practitioners, Sigma Theta Tau, Alpha Chi. Democrat. Roman Catholic. Home: PO Box 455 Lincolndale NY 10540-0455

MORTON, MICHAEL JAMES, software engineer; b. Long Beach, Calif., Apr. 15, 1969; s. Thomas James and Carol Ann Morton. B in Computer Sci., U. Calif., Irvine, 1994. Photo finisher One Hour Moto Photo, Lake Forest, Calif., 1988-94; software engr. Quarterdeck Corp., Marina Del Rey, Calif., 1994-96, Connect-3, Los Alamitos, Calif., 1996-97, Beckman Instruments, Fullerton, Calif., 1997—. Co-founder Tru Justice LLC, Claremont, Calif., 1996—. Mem. Phi Beta Kappa (sponsor, contbr.). Libertarian. Avocations: automobiles, electronics/circuit design, photography, aviation, horology. Home: 6260 E Via Ribazo Anaheim CA 92807-2334 Office: 4300 N Harbor Blvd Fullerton CA 92835-1091 E-mail: morton555@worldnet.att.net.

MORTON, MICHAEL RAY, retail company consultant; b. Memphis, Nov. 10, 1952; s. James Ray and Margaret Regina (Stevens) M.; m. Mary Elizabeth Harkness; children: Mary Harkness, Margaret Jeanne, Molly Ray. BBA, U. Miss., 1973; MBA, U. Denver, 1975. Cost acct. Dover Corp., Memphis, 1975-76; internal auditor W.R. Grace and Co., Memphis, 1976-78, sr. fin. analyst N.Y.C., 1979-80, v.p. Handy Dan div. San Antonio, 1981-82; chief fin. officer, sec., treas. Home Ctrs. Am., San Antonio, 1983; sr. v.p. Builders Square K-Mart Corp., San Antonio, 1984-89; pres. Orion Strategic Solutions, Inc., 1989-95; mng. ptnr. Critical Path Strategies, Boerne, Tex., 1996—. Bd. dirs. Builders Design Inc., Dania, Fla., 1989-91, treas., 1985-87, Materials Evolution Devel. USA. CEO, bd. dirs., 2001—; bd. dirs., v.p. Tex. Ind. Newspapers, Inc., San Antonio; mem. exec. com. Home Ctr. Industry Conf.; bd. dirs., Critical Path Strategies, 1995—. Bd. dirs. Friends of Cibolo Wilderness, pres., 2001—, Cibolo Land Trust Conservancy. Mem. Boerne C. of C. (amb. 1981), Home Ctr. Leadership Coun. Republican. Roman Catholic. Avocations: running, golf, reading. Home: 8060 Pimlico Ln Boerne TX 78015-4705 Office: 33 FM 474 Boerne TX 78006

MORTON, MIKE, consumer products executive; CFO H.T. Hackney Co., Knoxville, Tenn. Office: 502 S Gay St Knoxville TN 37902-1503

MORTON, RICHARD, lawyer, financial consultant; b. Jamaica, N.Y., Sept. 25, 1925; s. Lawrence and Irma (Gross) M.; m. Helen Malone, May 9, 1965; children: Bruce, Greg, Terri L. Sloan. BSBA, U. Denver, 1949; postgrad., Stetson Coll. Law, 1961; JD, U. Miss., 1963; LLM, Yale U., 1964. Bar: Miss. 1963, Fla. 1971. Builder, developer, N.Y., Fla., 1962-60; prof. law U. Ga., Athens, 1965-68; pvt. practice law Miami, 1971—; mng. ptnr. Morton Towers, 1988-97. Pres. S. Fla. Savs. & Loan, Miami, 1980-84; bd. dirs. Bank of Fla., Founders Nat. Mortgage Corp.; of counsel Katz, Barron, Squitero & Faust, 1998—; adv. com. Apt. Investment & Mgmt. Co., Denver. Contbr. articles to profl. jours. Served to 1st. lt. U.S. Army. Decorated Bronze Star. Office: 2699 S Bayshore Dr Fl 7 Miami FL 33133-5408 Home: 17215 Courtland Ln Boca Raton FL 33496 E-mail: richardmorton@msn.com.

MORTON, SAMANTHA, actress; b. Nottingham, Eng., May 13, 1977; d. Peter and Pamela; 1 child, Esme. Actor: (TV miniseries) Band of Gold, 1995, The History of Tom Jones, a Foundling, 1997; (TV series) Soldier Soldier, 1991, Max and Ruby, 2002; (TV films) The Token King, 1993, Emma, 1997, Jane Eyre, 1997; (films) The Future Lasts a Long Time, 1996, Under the Skin, 1997, This is the Sea, 1998, Sweet and Lowdown, 1999 (Acad. award nomination for best supporting actress, 2000), Jesus' Son, 1999, The Last Yellow, 1999, Eden, 2001, Morvern Callar, 2002, Minority Report, 2002, In America, 2002 (Acad. award nomination for best actress, 2004), Code 46, 2003. Mailing: c/o CAA 9830 Wilshire Blvd Beverly Hills CA 90212*

MORTON, SCOTT VINCENT, finance company executive; b. Natick, Mass., May 10, 1958; s. Earl Douglas Morton and Emma Jane Harman. V.p. Seed Money Assocs., Largo, Fla., 1993—2002; pres. UncleScott.com, Largo, 1997—; v.p. Morton-Bros.com, Largo, 2000—02; pres. Flabeep.com, Largo, 2004—. Author: (novel) Clouds Jumping. Fin. contbr. Salesian Missions, New Rochelle, NY, 1987—98; mem., fin. contbr. Harley Owners Group, Milw., 1983—94, AFL/CIO, Internat. Brotherhood Elec. Workers, Attleboro, Mass., 1978—79. Specialist 4th class U. S. Army, 2/35 F.A., 1980—82, Fort Stewart, Ga. Mem.: Smithsonian Instn. Independent. Avocations: motorcycling, fishing, boating.

MORTON, STEPHEN DANA, chemist, consultant; b. Madison, Wis., Sept. 7, 1932; s. Walter Albert and Rosalie (Amlie) M. BS, U. Wis., 1954, PhD, 1962. Asst. prof. chemistry Otterbein Coll., Westerville, Ohio, 1962-66; postdoctoral fellow water chemistry, pollution control U. Wis., Madison, 1966-67; water pollution rsch. chemist WARF Inst., Madison, 1967-73, head environ. quality dept., 1973-76; mgr. quality assurance Raltech Sci. Svcs., 1977-82; pres. SDM Cons., 1982—. Author: Water Pollution-Causes and Cures, 1976. 1st lt. Chem. Corps, AUS, 1954-56. Mem. AAAS, Am. Chem. Soc. Home and Office: 1126 Sherman Ave Madison WI 53703-1620

MORTON, WILLIAM GILBERT, JR., stock exchange executive; b. Syracuse, N.Y., Mar. 13, 1937; s. William Gilbert and Barbara (Link) M.; m. Margaret Halleron, Nov. 26, 1982; children: Andrew Baker, William Gilbert III, Sarah Ellsworth, Kate Spencer. BA, Dartmouth Coll., 1959; MBA, NYU, 1965. Asst. v.p. Discount Corp. N.Y., 1960-67; co-mgr. trading, sr. v.p., dir. Mitchell Hutchins Inc., 1967-79; mng. stock exch. floors, sr. v.p., dir. Dean Witter Reynolds Inc., 1979-85; chmn., CEO Boston Stock Exch. Inc., 1985-2001, chmn. emeritus, 2001—02. Chmn. allocation com. NY Stock Exch., floor ofcl., 1976—81, com. mem., 1970—85; bd. dirs. Radio Shack Corp., Ft. Worth, The Griswold Co., NY, J.P. Morgan Funds. Bd. dirs. Vt. Acad., Saxton's River, 1984-90, Boston 2000 Commn., 1998-2001, Nat. Football Found. and Coll. Hall of Fame, N.Y.; trustee search com. Dartmouth Alumni Coun., 1988-91; trustee Berklee Coll. Music, Stratton Mountain Sch., Stratton, Vt. With USMC, 1959-65. Mem. NASD (nominating com. 2003—), Boston Econ. Club, Mass. Bus. Roundtable, Nat. Orgn. Investment Profls., Racquet and Tennis Club N.Y.C., Stratton Mt. Country Club (Vt.), Colo. Arlberg Club (Winter Park), Brae Burn Country Club (Newton), Ekwanok Country Club (Vt.), Royal Poinciana Club (Fla.), Stock Exch. Luncheon Club N.Y.C., Theta Delta Chi. Republican. Presbyterian. Office: 304 Newbury St #560 Boston MA 02115

MORTVEDT, JOHN JACOB, soil scientist, researcher; b. Dell Rapids, SD, Jan. 25, 1932; s. Ernest R. and Clara (Halvorson) M.; m. Marlene L. Fodness, Jan. 23, 1955; children: Sheryl Mortvedt Jarratt, Lori Mortvedt Klopf, Julie Mortvedt Stride. BS, SD State U., 1953, MS, 1959; PhD, U. Wis., 1962. Soil chemist TVA, Muscle Shoals, Ala., 1962-87, sr. scientist, 1987-92, regional mgr. field programs dept., 1992-93; ext. soils specialist Colo. State U., Ft. Collins, 1994-95, ext. environ. and pesticide edn. specialist, 1996—. Agr. cons. U.S. Borax, 1997—. Co-author: Fertilizer Technology and Application, 1999; editor: Micronutrients in Agriculture, 1972, 2d edit., 1991; contbr. articles to profl. jours. 1st lt. U.S. Army, 1953-57. Fellow AAAS, Soil Sci. Soc. Am. (pres. 1988-89, editor-in-chief 1982-87, Profl. Svc. award 1991, Disting. Svc. award 1996), Am. Soc. Agronomy (exec. com. 1987-90, Agronomic Svc. award 2003); mem. Internat. Union Soil Sci., Colombian Soil Sci. Soc. (hon.), Exch. Club (pres. Florence, Ala. chpt. 1987-88), Toastmasters (pres. Florence chpt. 1964-65), Phi Kappa Phi. Avocations: photography, golf. Office: Colo State U Dept Soil And Crop Scis Fort Collins CO 80523-1170

MORVANT, BARBARA L. nursing administrator; Exec. dir. La. State Bd. Nursing, Metairie. Office: La State Bd Nursing 3510 N Causeway Blvd Ste 601 Metairie LA 70002-3531

MORVILLO, ROBERT GUY, lawyer; b. N.Y.C., Jan. 22, 1938; s. M. Victor and Marie (Santeramo) M.; m. Catherine A. Shields, Apr. 20, 1963; children: Christopher, Gregory, Edward, Robert. AB, Colgate U., 1960; JD, Columbia U., 1963. Bar: N.Y. 1964, U.S. Dist. Ct. (so. dist.) 1964, U.S. Ct. Appeals (2nd cir.) 1964, U.S. Ct. Appeals (3rd cir.) 1979, U.S. Suprmem Ct. 1982, U.S. Ct. Appeals (10th cirs.) 1983. Law clk. to Hon. William B. Herlands U.S. Dist. Ct. (so. dist.), N.Y.C., 1963-64, asst. U.S. atty., 1964-68, chief trial counsel fraud unit, 1970-71, chief criminal div., 1971-73; assoc. Reavis & McGrath, N.Y.C., 1968-70; prin. Morvillo, Abramowitz & Grand, P.C. and predecessors, N.Y.C., 1973—. Lectr. Columbia Law Sch., N.Y.C., 1974-85. Columnist, N.Y. Law Jour., N.Y.C., 1982—; editor, White Collar Crime: Business and Regulatory Offenses, 1990. Fellow Am. Coll. Trial Lawyers; mem. ABA, Assn. of Bar of City of N.Y., N.Y. State Bar Assn., N.Y. Coun. of Def. Lawyers (bd. dirs. 1987—). Office: Morvillo Abramowitz Grand Iason & Silberberg PC 565 Fifth Ave New York NY 10017 Office Phone: 212-880-9400. E-mail: rmorvillo@magislaw.com.

MOSATCHE, HARRIET SANDRA, writer, psychologist, researcher; b. Bklyn., Apr. 10, 1949; d. Charles Morris and Ruth (Green) Rosenberg; m. Ivan Lawner, Feb. 19, 1983; children: Robert Alexander Lawner, Elizabeth Kim Lawner. BA cum laude, Bklyn. Coll., Bklyn., 1970; MA, Hunter Coll., N.Y.C., 1972; PhD, CUNY, N.Y.C., 1977. Lectr. in psychology Hunter Coll., N.Y.C., 1973-76, instr. in psychology, 1976-77; asst. prof. Coll. of Mt. St. Vincent, Riverdale, N.Y., 1977-83, chairperson psychology dept., 1978-84, assoc. prof., 1983-84; writer, cons. pvt. practice New Rochelle, N.Y., 1985—. Adj. asst. prof. Manhattan Coll., Riverdale, 1978—83, adj. assoc. prof., 1983—85; adj. prof. Coll. of New Rochelle, 1990—92; dir. program devel. Girl Scouts U.S.A., 1986—88, 1992—2002, sr. dir., rsch. program, 2002—; spkr. in field. Author: Searching: Practices & Beliefs of Religious Cults & Human Potential Groups, 1984, Preventing Youth Suicide, 1987, Facing Family Crises, 1988, Preventing Teenage Pregnancy, 1989, Too Old for This, Too Young for That! Your Survival Guide for the Middle School Years, 2000, Girls: What's So Bad About Being Good?, Getting to Know the Real You: 50 Fun Quizzes Just for Girls, 2002; online advice columnist: "Ask Dr. M", 1997—, columnist: mag. Adam, 2002; contbr. articles to profl. jours. Active Spring Creek Assn. for Retarded Children, 1975—80; leader Girl Scouts U.S.A., 1993—; bd. dirs. Assn. Grad. Ctr. CUNY Alumni, 1979—80, All Day Kindergarten Task Force, New Rochelle, 1989—90. Recipient Gold award, Nat. Assn. Parenting Publs., 2000, Woman of Excellence award, New Rochelle C. of C., 2002; rsch. grantee, NSF, 1996—2000, Nat. Inst. on Aging NIH, 1982—84, summer rsch. grantee, Coll. of Mt. St. Vincent, 1981. Mem. APA, Ea. Psychol. Assn., Soc. Children's Book Writers and Illustrators. Avocations: piano, dance, reading. E-mail: hmosatche@girlscouts.org.

MOSBAUGH, PHILLIP GEORGE, urologist, educator; b. Noblesville, Ind., Jan. 15, 1938; s.Ward C. and Frances J. Mosbaugh; m. Vera A. Deganutti Green, Jan. 21, 1963 (dec. May 2000); children: Anne R. Mosbaugh Knapp, Virginia G. AB, Ind. U., Bloomington, 1959; MD, Ind. U., Indpls., 1963. Diplomate Am. Bd. Urology. Intern Orange County Hosp., Orange, Calif., 1963-64; resident in gen. surgery and urology Ind. U. Med. Ctr., Indpls., 1964-68; pvt. practice, Indpls., 1970—. Asst. clin. prof. urology Ind. U. Sch. Medicine, 1975—; mem. med. adv. bd. on interstitial cystitis ALZA Pharms., 1988—, mem. spkr.'s bur., 1998—. Contbr. articles to med. jours., including Jour. Urology. Capt. M.C., USNR, 1968-70. Fellow ACS; mem. Interstitial Cystitis Assn. (med. advisor Ind. chpt. 1987—). Republican. Roman Catholic. Avocations: golf, travel, reading, crosswords. Home: 623 Round Hill Rd Indianapolis IN 46260-2915 Office: Urology of Ind LLC 1801 Senate Blvd Ste 655 Indianapolis IN 46202-1259

MOSBERG, HENRY I. pharmacist, educator, medicinal chemist; b. Jan. 29, 1949; BS, U. Ill., 1971, PhD, 1976. Postdoctoral rsch. assoc. U. Ill., Urbana, 1976—78, U. Ariz., Tucson, 1978—81, rsch. asst. prof. dept. chemistry, 1981—83; from asst. prof. to assoc. prof. U. Mich. Coll. Pharmacy, Ann Arbor, 1983—95, prof., 1995—. Ad hoc reviewer Human Frontier Sci. Program, Rsch. Corp., Med. Rsch. Coun. Can., NSF, NIH; mem. biochemistry rev. subcom. NIH, Nat. Inst. on Drug Abuse, 1989—93; mem. program com. Internat. Narcotic Rsch. Conf., 1996. Mem. editl. bd.: Jour. Medicinal Chemistry, Jour. Peptide Rsch., Letters in Peptide Sci.,:. Recipient Nat. Merit scholarship, 1967—71, James scholar, U. Ill., 1967—71, grad. fellowship, 1971—72, predoctoral fellowship, NIH, 1973—76, postdoctoral fellowship, Nat. Rsch. Svc. award, 1977—78, Rsch. Scientist Devel. award, NIH, Nat. Inst. Drug Abuse, 1989—99. Mem.: AAAS, Am. Chem. Soc., Protein Soc., Am. Chem. Soc. (ad hoc reviewer petroleum rsch. fund), Am. Peptide Soc. (awards com., publs. com., nominating com.), Phi Lambda Upsilon, Phi Kappa Phi. Achievements include research in modeling of opioid receptors and other GPCRs and of other membrane-bound proteins; synthesis and studies of nitric oxide synthase-derived calmodulin-binding peptides; design and synthesis of opioid peptide ligands and of peptidomimetics; developments of the theory of protein structure. Office: U Mich Coll Pharmacy 428 Church St Ann Arbor MI 48109

MOSBO, JOHN ALVIN, dean; b. Davenport, Iowa, June 11, 1947; s. Alvin Oswald and Marie Lindeen Mosbo; m. Anna Marie Mosbo, Dec. 14, 1968; children: Kristina, Julie. BA, U. No. Colo., 1969; PhD, Iowa State U., 1973. Faculty mem. Ball State U., Muncie, Ind., 1973-86; dept. head James Madison U., Harrisburg, Va., 1986-94; coll. dean U. Ctrl. Ark., Conway, 1994-98, provost, 1998—2001; dean faculty, v.p. for acad. affairs Gustavus Adolphus Coll., St. Peter, Minn., 2001—. Cons. Merck Co., 1991-94, AMP, Inc., 1988, Anchor-Hocking, 1985-86. Author: (with others) Inorganic Reactions and Methods, 1991; contbr. articles to profl. publs. Bd. dirs. Staunton (Va.) Civic Dance Co., 1991-94, Faulkner County (Ark.) United Way, 2000-01. Student Rsch. grant NSF, 1993-95, Equipment grant Hewlett-Packard, 1992, Merck Co., 1991-92, NSF, 1991. Mem. AAAS, Am. Assn. of Higher Edn., Am. Chem. Soc., Am. Conf. of Acad. Deans, Coun. of Undergrad. Rsch., Sigma Xi. Avocations: softball, jogging, bicycling, in-line skating. Office: Gustavus Adolphus Coll 800 W College Ave Saint Peter MN 56082

MOSCHELLA, SAMUEL L. dermatology educator; b. East Boston, Mass., Apr. 22, 1921; BS, Tufts U., 1943, MD cum laude, 1946. Diplomate Am. Bd. Dermatology. Intern in medicine Boston City Hosp., 1946-47; resident in dermatology U.S. Naval Hosp., Phila., 1948, St. Albans, 1951; postgrad. in skin and cancer Bellevue Hosp., N.Y.C., 1952-53; chief dermatology U.S. Naval Hosp., Phila., 1953-54, chief dermatology, asst. chief medicine, Guantanamo Bay, Cuba, 1948-51, chief dermatology, Chelsea, Mass., 1956-62, chmn. dept. dermatology, Phila., 1962-67; chmn. dept. dermatology Lahey Clinic Med. Ctr., Burlington, Mass., 1969-82; clin. prof. dermatology Harvard U. Med. Sch., Boston, 1980-91, prof. emeritus, 1991—. Cons. U.S. Naval Hosp., Phila., 1967-72, U. Pa. Grad. Sch., 1962-67, Harvard Sch. Tropical Medicine, 1975—, Nat. Hansen's Disease Ctr., Baton Rouge, 2002—. Author/editor: (with otherw) Dermatology, 3d edit., 1992; contbr. articles to profl. jours.; also papers, book chpts. Fellow ACP; mem. AMA, Am. Acad. Dermatology, Am. Dermatol. Assn., Am. Soc. Dermapathology, Internat. Leprosy Assn., Internat. Soc. Dermatology, New Eng. Dermatologic Soc., Mass. Acad. Dermatology, Mass. Med. Soc., soc. Investigative Dermatology Home: 887 Commonwealth Ave Newton MA 02459-1036 Office: Lahey Clinic Med Ctr 41 Mall Rd Burlington MA 01805-0002 E-mail: samuel.l.moschella@lahey.org.

MOSCHELLA, WILLIAM EMIL, state attorney general; b. 1968; BA, U. Va.; JD, George Mason Univ. Sch. of Law. Gen. coun. House Commn. on Rules, 1999, chief investment coun.; chief Legis. Coun. and Parliamentarian House Commn. on the Judiciary, 1999—2003; asst. Atty. Gen. Legis. Affairs U.S. Dept. of Justice, Washington, 2003—. Office: Robert F Kennedy Bldg Ten St and Constitution Ave NW, Rm 1145 Washington DC 20530

MOSCHOS, MICHAEL CHRISTOS, lawyer; b. Worcester, Mass., Jan. 8, 1941; s. Constantine Mina and Vassiliky (Strates) M.; m. Mary Patricia Dermody, Feb. 20, 1977 (div. Dec. 1991); children: Charles, Michael Patrick; m. Susan Smith Harrington, June 6, 1998; 1 stepchild, Katherine L. BBA cum laude, U. Mass., 1962; JD, Boston U., 1965. Bar: Mass. 1965, N.Y. 1970, U.S. Dist. Ct. Mass. 1982, U.S. Supreme Ct. 1982. Lawyer Investors Group, N.Y.C., 1968-72; assoc., spl. counsel Cabot, Cabot, Forbes, Boston, 1972; pvt. practice Boston, 1973, Worcester, 1979—. Spl. counsel Esso-Pappas, S.A., Athens, Greece, 1969-70; investment banker, counsel Worcester Bancorp., 1974-79; cons. atty. Baskins-Sears Esq., N.Y.C., 1979; counsel Downtown Worcester Bus. Devel. Corp., 1974-76. Legal officer Worcester Heritage Soc., 1975-82; mems. coun. Worcester Art Mus., 1975-83; incorporator Worcester Natural History Soc., 1977-98; spl. counsel, acting mng. dir. Hellenic Bottling Co., S.A., Hellenic Canning Industries, S.A., Internat. Canning Industry, S.A., Athens, Greece, 1973. Capt. U.S. Army, 1965-67. Mem. Worcester County Bar Assn. Greek Orthodox. Home: 4004 Brompton Cir Worcester MA 01609-1160 Office: 250 Commercial St Ste 210 Worcester MA 01608 Office Phone: 508-753-8993.

MOSCICKA, DOROTA, engineer; arrived in U.S., 1992; d. Bernard Moscicki and Krystyna Moscicka. BS in Applied Math., N.J. Inst. Tech., 1999, MS in Computer Sci., 2001. Engr. Optical Networking Group Lucent Technologies, Holmdel, NJ, 1999—. Avocations: reading, travel, classical music, other cultures.

MOSCICKI, RICHARD A. health products executive; b. 1952; BS, Northwestern U., MD, 1976. Immunologist Mass. Gen. Hosp./Harvard Med. Sch., 1979-92; dir. med. affairs Genzyme Corp., Cambridge, Mass., 1992, v.p. med., clin. and regulatory affairs, 1993, sr. v.p., 1996, chief med. officer, 1994—. Office: 500 Kendall St Cambridge MA 02142-1108 Office Fax: 617-252-7600. E-mail: kathy.alpert@genzyme.com.

MOSCINSKI, DAVID JOSEPH, educational administrator, school psychologist; b. Stevens Point, Wis., Mar. 23, 1948; s. Edward Marcel and Helen Mary (Prondzinski) M.; m. Sharon Lynn Krueger, Aug. 14, 1971; children: Andrew, Jonathan, Matthew. BS, U. Wis., Stevens Point, 1970; MEd, U. Wis.-Stout, Menomonie, 1972; EdS, U. Wis., Milw., 1998. Cert. sch. psychologist, dir. spl. edn. and pupil svcs., K-12 prin., dist. adminstr. Sch. psychologist Coop. Ednl. Svcs. Agy. #8, Appleton, Wis., 1972-78, Freedom (Wis.) Area Sch. Dist., 1978-86, dir. pupil svcs., 1986-92, asst. supt., 1992-2000, dist. adminstr., 2000—; community prevention coord. Project Pre-Action, Outagamie County, Wis., 1979—. Cons. Wis. Dept. Pub. Instrn., Madison, 1981-90; mem. pupil performance testing com. Wis. Supt.'s Adv. Com., 1989-92. Contbg. author Wis. Sch. Psychologist Jour., 1985-87, Sch. Psychology Programs and Practices, 1989. Pres. Huntley PTA, Appleton, 1984-86, Appleton North Booster Club, 1993-96; big brother Fox Valley Big Bros. Assn., coach Appleton Recreation Dept., 1982-86, Appleton Little League, 1987-93; tchr. Sunday sch. Faith Luth. Ch., 1989-2001, chair stewardship com., 1996-98. Recipient Outstanding Program award Outagamie County Cmty. Bd., 1980, Achievement award Nat. Assn. Counties, 1986, Prevention Coords. Recognition award, 1987, Red Smith Svc. award, 1997. Mem. NASP (del. adv. bd. 1985-89), Wis. Sch. Psychologists Assn. (pres.

1985, President's award 1986), Sch. Prevention-Intervention Network (bd. dirs. 1984-88, svc. award 1985), Wis. Assn. Alcohol and Other Drug Abuse (best program award 1983), Wis. Coun. Adminstrs. Pupil Svcs. (bd. dirs. 1987-93, pres. 1989-90, President's award 1991), Fedn. Pupil Svcs. Assn. (bd. dirs. 1985-91), Phi Delta Kappa (nominations com. 1984). Avocations: fishing, hunting, golf, computers. Home: 2613 N Viola St Appleton WI 54911-2263 Office: Freedom Area Sch Dist PO Box 1008 Freedom WI 54131-1008 E-mail: dmoscinski@new.rr.com.

MOSELEY, CARLOS DUPRE, music executive, musician; b. Laurens, S.C., Sept. 21, 1914; s. Carlos Roland and Helen Allston (DuPre) M. BA magna cum laude, Duke, 1935; postgrad., Phila. Conservatory Music, 1941-44; student piano with Harold Morris, Olga Samaroff, Sophia Rosoff; LHD (hon.), Wofford Coll., 1966, Duke U., 1985; MusD (hon.), Converse Coll., 1971; DFA (hon.), U. S.C., 1989; LHD (hon.), The Juilliard Sch., 1995. Head fgn. information research div. OWI, N.Y.C., 1944-45; chief music sect. State Dept., Washington, 1946-48; music officer Office Mil. Govt. for Bavaria, Munich, Germany, 1948-49; chief fine arts and exhibits sect. reorientation br. Army Dept., N.Y.C., 1949-50; dir. Sch. Music, prof. music U. Okla., 1950-55; dir. press and pub. relations N.Y. Philharmonic Symphony Soc., N.Y.C., 1955-59, assoc. mng. dir., 1959-61, mng. dir., 1961-70, pres., 1970-78, vice chmn., 1978-83, chmn., 1983-85, chmn. emeritus, 1985—. U.S. del. to UNESCO Music Conf., Paris, 1948; U.S. del Internat. Music Coun., Paris, 1953; mem. music panel Nat. Endowment for Arts, 1967-69, N.Y. State Coun. on Arts, 1973-77, Nat. Coun. on Arts, 1985-91; life trustee Converse Coll., 1998—. Soloist, N.Y. Philharmonic Orch., N.Y.C. Symphony, Berkshire Music Center Orch., San Diego Symphony, Portuguese Nat. Symphony, Lisbon, Vt. Symphony, others. Dir. Fan Fox and Leslie R. Samuels Found., Eleanor Naylor Dana Charitable Trust; hon. dir. Charles A. Dana Found.; mem. Lincoln Ctr. coun. Lincoln Ctr. for Performing Arts, 1961-78; chmn. performing arts adv. com. Asia Soc., 1970-91; mem. Met. Opera Assn.; dir. N.Y. Philharm. Winner MacDowell Nat. Young Artists Competition, 1939; recipient N.Y.C. Mayor's medal of honor for arts and culture, 1978, Disting. Svc. citation U. Okla., 1989, Order of the Palmetto, State of S.C., Nat. citation Nat. Fedn. Music Clubs, 1991, Lifetime Achievement award S.C. Gov.'s Sch. of the Arts, 1995, Lotus award Young Coun. Artists, N.Y.C., 1999. Mem. Met. Opera Assn., Century Assn. (N.Y.C.), Piedmont Club (S.C.), Phi Beta Kappa, Mu Phi Epsilon, Pi Kappa Lambda, Phi Eta Sigma.

MOSELEY, CHRIS ROSSER, marketing executive; b. Balt., Apr. 13, 1950; d. Thomas Earl and Fern Elaine (Coleman) Rosser; m. Thomas Kenneth Moseley. BA with honors, The Coll. of Wooster, 1972. Asst. dir. advt. and promotion Sta. WBAL-TV, Balt., 1972-74; dir. pub. rels. Mintz & Hoke Advt. Inc., Hartford, Conn., 1974-75; promotion mgr. Sta. WFSB-TV, Hartford, 1975-77; audience promotion mgr. Sta. WTVJ-TV, Miami, Fla., 1977-78; pres. CMA Mktg. Cons., Hyde Park, N.Y., 1979-82; promotion mgr. Ind. Network News-Sta. WPIX-TV, N.Y.C., 1982-84; sr. v.p., mgmt. supr. Christopher Thomas Muller Jordan Weiss, N.Y.C., 1984-89, Earle Palmer Brown/N.Y., N.Y.C., 1989-90; sr. v.p. advt., promotion Discovery Networks, U.S., Bethesda, Md., 1990-99; exec. v.p. mktg. ABC, Inc., N.Y.C., 1999—2000; exec. v.p. worldwide mktg. and brand strategy Hallmark Channel, Studio City, Calif., 2000—. Recipient Best Bus.-to-Bus. award Art Direction mag., 1984, award of achievement in media rels. and edn. Nat. Resources Coun. Am., 1991, Best Editorial Excellence award Mag. Age, 1992, Best Overall Mktg. Campaign award MIP/MIPCOM, 1994, 1st Place Print award: Media Promotion, London Internat. Advt. awards, 1993, Gold award Broadcast Designers, 1993, Mktg. 100 award Ad Age, 1995, Cable Marketer of Yr. award Ad Age, 1995. Mem. CTAM (chair, Mark award 1995, 96, co-chair 1997, bd. dirs. 1997), NCTA (conv. com. 1995, 96, Vanguard award for mktg. 1996, named One of 2002 Multichannel News' Wonderwomen of Yr.), WIC, AWNY, PROMAX Internat. (chair 1996-97), CTPAA. Democrat. Avocations: horticulture, travel. Home: 5224 Los Encantos Way Los Angeles CA 90027 Office: Hallmark Channel 12700 Ventura Blvd Ste 100 Studio City CA 91604-6201

MOSELEY, CLIFFORD WAYNE, writer, poet; b. Odessa, Tex., Aug. 10, 1947; s. Leylon Ivan and Josephine Opal Moseley; m. Cathryn Lualice Brotherton, Oct. 11, 1968; children: Clifford Wayne Jr., Patrick Lee. AAS, Odessa Coll., 1989; B in Bus. Mgmt., U. Tex. Permian Basin, Odessa, 1994. Enlisted U.S. Army, 1968, advanced through grades to SFC, 1982; ret., 1985; with Ready Reserves, 1985—89. Writer tech. manuals, Dover, NJ, 1971—75. Contbr. poems to Tomorrow's Dreams, 1995. Decorated Bronze Star, 1971; nominee Tex. Scout of Yr., Boy Scouts Am., 1966. Republican. Avocation: collecting military paraphernalia. Home and Office: 4280 Bonham Ave Odessa TX 79762 E-mail: Cliff_Moseley@yahoo.com.

MOSELEY, JAMES FRANCIS, lawyer; b. Charleston, SC, Dec. 6, 1936; s. John Olin and Kathryn (Moran) M.; m. Anne McGehee, June 10, 1961; children: James Francis Jr., John McGehee. AB, The Citadel, 1958; JD, U. Fla., 1961. Bar: Fla. 1961, U.S. Supreme Ct. 1970. Pres. Moseley, Warren, Prichard & Parrish, Jacksonville, Fla., 1963—. Chmn. jud. nominating com. 4th Jud. Cir., 1978-80 Assoc. editor: American Maritime Cases; contbr. articles on admiralty, transp. and ins. law to legal jours. Pres. Jacksonville United Way, 1979; chmn. bd. dirs. United Way Fla., 1992-93, S.E. regional coun. United Way, 1992-96; trustee Jacksonville Cmty. Found.; chmn. bd. trustees Jacksonville Pub. Libr.; trustee Libr. Found., sec., 1987-91; trustee CMI Am. Found.; chmn. Jacksonville Human Svcs. Coun., 1989-91; chmn. bd. trustees United Way N.E. Fla., 1995-97; bd. govs. United Way Am., 1996-2002. Recipient Meritorious Pub. Svc. award/medal U.S. Dept. Transp./USCG, 1998. Fellow Am. Coll. Trial Lawyers, Am. Bar Found.; mem. ABA (ho. of del. 2002—), Jacksonville Bar Assn. (pres. 1975), Fla. Coun. Bar Pres. (chmn. 1979), Maritime Law Assn. U.S. (exec. com. 1978-81, chmn. navigation com. 1981-88, v.p. 1992-96, pres. 1996-98), Comm. Maritime Internat. (titulary), Com. on Collision (Lisbon Rules), Fed. Ins. Corp. Counsel (chmn. maritime law sect.), Internat. Assn. Def. Counsel (chmn. maritime com. 1989-91), Am. Inns of Ct. (master of bench), Assn. of Citadel Men (bd. dirs. 1989-93, exec. com. 1994, Man of Yr. award 1992, Palmetto medal 2001), Citadel Inn of Ct. (sr. bencher), Deerwood Club, River Club, India House (NYC), Army Navy Club (Washington), St. John's Dinner Club (pres. 1988). Home: 7780 Hollyridge Rd Jacksonville FL 32256-7134 Office: Moseley Warren Prichard & Parrish 1887 West Rd Bay St Jacksonville FL 32216-4542 Office Phone: 904-356-1306.

MOSELEY, JAMES R. federal agency administrator, farmer; b. Peru, Ind. BS in horticulture, Purdue U. Owner Ag Ridge Farms, Clarks Hill, Ind.; mng. ptnr. Infinity Pork LLC, Clarks Hill; asst. sec. agr. natural resources and environ. USDA, 1990—92; dir. agrl. svcs. and regulations. State of Ind., Purdue U., West Lafayette, 1992—95; dep. sec. agr. USDA, Washington, 2001—. Agrl. advisor to adminstr. U.S. Environ. Protection Agy., 1989—90; chmn. industry negotiating team Am. Clean Water Found. Nat. Environ. Dialogue on Pork Prodn., 1997; cons. Nat. Assn. State Depts. Agr., 1995. Past. mem. editl. bd. Farm Jour. Pub., past polit. analyst. Office: USDA Office of the Sec 1400 Independence Ave SW Washington DC 20250

MOSELEY, JOHN TRAVIS, university administrator, research physicist; b. New Orleans, Feb. 26, 1942; s. Fred Baker and Lily Gay (Lord) M.; m. Belva McCall Hudson, Aug. 11 1964 (div. June 1979); m. Susan Diane Callow, Aug. 6, 1979; children: Melanie Lord, John Mark, Stephanie Marie, Shannon Eleanor. BS in Physics, Ga. Inst. Tech., 1964, MS in Physics, 1966, PhD in Physics, 1969. Asst. prof. physics U. West Fla., Pensacola, 1968-69; sr. physicist SRI Internat., Menlo Park, Calif., 1969-75, program mgr., 1976-79; vis. prof. U. Paris, 1975-76; assoc. prof. U. Oreg., Eugene, 1979-81, dir. chem. physics inst., 1980-84, prof. physics, 1984—, head physics dept., 1984-85, v.p. rsch., 1985-94, v.p. acad. affairs, provost, 1994-2001, sr. v.p., provost, 2001—. Mem. exec. com., coun. on acad. affairs NASULGC, 1994-2000, chair, 1996-97; bd. dirs. Oreg. Resource and Tech., Portland; mem. com. on Atomic and Molecular Sci., 1983-85. Contbr. numerous articles to profl. jours. Mem. So. Willamette Rsch. Corridor, Eugene, 1985—, Lane Econ. Devel. Com., Eugene, 1988-94; bd. dirs. Eugene/Springfield Metro Partnership, 1985—, Oreg. Bach Festival, Eugene, 1987-94, Eugene Arts Found., 1995-97. Recipient Doctoral Thesis award Sigma Xi, 1969; Fulbright fellow, 1975; numerous rsch. grants, 1969—. Fellow AAAS, Am. Physical Soc.; mem. AAUP, Am. Chem. Soc. Avocations: skiing, backpacking. Home: 2140 Essex Ln Eugene OR 97403-1851 Office: U Oreg Office of Sr VP and Provost Eugene OR 97403-1258 E-mail: jtm@uoregon.edu.

MOSELEY, JULIA W. music teacher, historic preservationist; b. Tampa, Fla., Mar. 21, 1919; d. Hallock Preston and Ruby Winifred Moseley. BA, Agnes Scott Coll., Decatur, Ga., 1940. Nat. cert. music tchr. Asst. food and fashion editor Atlanta Constn., 1940-41; credit report typist, publicist, fund raiser Mchts. Assn. Tampa, 1942-43; teletype operator, writer/editor, commodities marketer USDA, Atlanta, 1943-47; self-employed music tchr. Atlanta, 1945-47; hist. rschr. New Orleans, 1947—48; self-employed music tchr., 1948—; also cattle raiser, citrus grower; preservationist Moseley Homestead, Brandon, Fla., 1948—. Author, editor: Come to My Sunland, 1997; co-author: Internet Lake Atlas, 1999, Recipes and Remembrances, 1999; composer song Brandon, Brandon. Mem. Brandon Citizens Adv. Com.; established Timberly Trust, Inc., 1994; worked with Historic Tampa/Hillsborough Cunty Preservation Bd., 1983-92; spokesperson to Hillsborough County Bd. Commrs. on land use and preservation, 1966-99; mem. Brandon Task Force involved with county devel. issues; mem. hist. com. Brandon Centennial Celebration, 1990. Elizabeth Ordaway Dunn Found. grantee, 1998. Mem.: Fla. State Music Tchrs. Assn. (past officer), Limona Acad. Arts, Letters and Scis. (past officer and dir.), Art Publ. Soc. (Guild tchr.), Nat. Fedn. Music Clubs, Nat. Guild Piano Tchrs., Music Tchrs. Nat. Assn., Tampa Music Tchrs. Assn. (officer), Fla. Breeding Bird Atlas, Tampa Preservation, Inc., Nature Conservancy, Fla. Trust for Historic Preservation, Nat. Trust for Historic Preservation, Friday Morning Musicale Club. Avocations: bird watching, reading, walking, photography, star gazing. E-mail: ttland@hotmail.com.

MOSELEY, MARC ROBARDS, sales executive; b. L.A., July 14, 1954; s. Thomas Robards and Doris Cecile (Tye) M.; m. Laura Hoon Hamilton, 1999. Student, U. Ky., 1972-74, U. Ga., 1977-78; BA, La. Tech. U., 1985; postgrad., Western Mich. U., 1986. Svc. rep. Ky. Mortgage Co., Lexington, 1973; loan rep. Termplan Fin. Co., Atlanta, 1975-77; sr. cons. Co-Ordinated Planning Assocs., Atlanta, 1979-80; sales rep. Nat. Starch & Chem. Corp., Monroe, La., 1980-84; v.p. sales Ednl. Funding Svc., Monroe, 1984-85; tech. sales rep. polymer divsn. Ralston Purina, St. Louis, 1985-87; account mgr. Protein Techs. Internat. Polymer Group subs. Ralston Purina, St. Louis, 1988-90, sr. account mgr., 1990-92, area dir. market ops., 1992-96; dir. industry mgmt. and bus. devel. Polymer Group subs. Dupont Ag Enterprise, 1996-98; dir. strategic accounts Polymer Group Dupont Soy Polymers, 1999—2002; reional sales rep. Phila. Mixing Solutions, Palmyra, Pa., 2004—. V.p. sales and mktg. RANA Enterprises, Inc., Atlanta, 1991-98; dir. Radiant Chem., Atlanta, 1992-2001; v.p., dir. Bishop Pharm. Co., Inc., West Monroe, La., 1994-96. Mem. TAPPI Greater Atlanta, U. Ky. Alumni Assn. (bd. dirs. 1991-97, exec. v.p. Ga. sect. 1992-94). Avocations: water and snow skiing, basketball, music, golf. Home: 12220 Brookfield Club Dr Roswell GA 30075-1265 Office: Philadelphia Mixing Solution 1221 E Main St Palmyra PA 17078 E-mail: mrmosley@mindspring.com.

MOSELEY-BRAUN, CAROL, former senator, former ambassador; b. Chgo., Aug. 16, 1947; d. Joseph J. and Edna A. (Davie) Moseley; m. Michael Braun; 1973 (div. 1986); 1 child, Matthew. BA, U. Ill., Chgo., 1969; JD, U. Chgo., 1972. Asst. U.S. atty. U.S. Dist. Ct. (no. dist.) Ill., 1973-77; mem. Ill. Ho. of Reps., 1979-88; recorder of deeds Cook County, Ill., 1988-92; U.S. senator from Ill. Washington, 1993-99; Am. ambassador to New Zealand and Samoa U.S. Dept. State, 1999—2001; adj. prof., mgmt. DePaul U., 2002.

MOSELLIE, ANTHONY, architect; BSc in Arch., U. Mich., 1984. Arch. Welton Becket Assocs., 1984—85, Murphy Jahn Archs., PC, N.Y.C., 1986—88; from arch. to prin. Kohn Pedersen Fox Assocs., N.Y., 1986—99, prin., 1999—. Mem. Airports Cons. Coun.; design jury U. Pa. Contbr. articles to profl. jours. Mem.: AIA, Am. Assn. Airport Execs. Office: KPF Assocs 111 W 57th St New York NY 10019*

MOSELY, JACK MEREDITH, thoracic surgeon; b. Hodge, La., July 20, 1917; s. Charles Hodge and Lucille (Hays) M.; m. Kathryn L. Stephenson, Apr. 30, 1954 (div. May 1972); children: Kathryn S. Mosely-Bennett, Jack Meredith Jr.; m. Elberta Pate, Sept. 23, 1995. BS, La. State U., Baton Rouge, 1939; MD, La. State U., New Orleans, 1943. Diplomate Am. Bd. Surgery, Am. Bd. Thoracic Surgery. Intern Univ. Hosp., Mpls., 1943-48, resident in surgery, head resident, instr. Syracuse, N.Y., 1946-48, 49-50; fellow in surgery Lahey Clinic, Boston, 1948-49; resident in thoracic surgery Herman Kiefer Hosp., Detroit, 1952-53; instr. thoracic surgery Tulane U. Med. Sch., New Orleans, 1953; pvt. practice thoracic surgery, New Orleans, 1953, Santa Barbara, Calif., 1953—. Chmn. health sect. Welfare Planing Coun., Santa Barbara, 1955-57; mem. Atty. Gen.'s Vol. Adv. Coun., State of Calif., 1974-75; chmn. dept. thoracic and cardiovascular surgery Cottage Hosp., Santa Barbara, 1995—. Pres. bd. dirs. Wood Glen Hall, Santa Barbara, 1971-73. Capt. M.C., U.S. Army, 1944-46. Fellow ACS, Am. Thoracic Soc., Pan Am. Med. Assn., Southeastern surg. Congress; mem. Valley Club of Montecito. Avocations: golf, travel, reading, gardening. Home: 134 Coronada Cir Santa Barbara CA 93108-1825 E-mail: drmose@aol.com.

MOSELY, TEED M. career officer; BA in Polit. Sci., Tex. A&M, 1971, MA in Polit. Sci., 1972. Commd. 2d lt. USAF, 1971, advanced through grades to brig. gen., 1996; various assignments 338th Flying Tng. Squadron, 78th Flying Tng. Wing, Webb AFB, Tex.; mission comdr., instr. pilot, flight lead 7th Tactical Fighter Squadron, 49th Tactical Fighter Wing, Holloman AFB, N.Mex., 1977-79; weapons and tactics officer, F-15 mission comdr. 18th Tactical Fighter Wing, Kadena AB, Japan, 1979-83, flight examiner, instr. pilot, 1979-83; course officer Air Command and Staff Coll., Maxwell AFB, Ala., 1983-84; chief tactical fighter br. Hdqrs. USAF, the Pentagon, Washington, 1984-87; comdr. F-15 divsn., instr. pilot USAF Fighter Weapons Sch., Nellis AFB, Nev., 1987-89; course officer Nat. War Coll., Washington, 1989-90, chief of staff of the AF chair, 1990-92; comdr. 33rd Ops. Group, 33rd Fighter Wing, Eglin AFB, Fla., 1992-94; chief AF Gen. Officer Matters Office Hdqrs. USAF, The Pentagon, Washington, 1994-96; comdr. 57th Wing, Nellis AFB, Nev., 1996-97; dep. dir. for politico-mil. affairs Asia/Pacific and Middle East, the Joint Staff, Washington, 1997—. Decorated Air medal, Legion of Merit with oak leaf cluster, Air Force Achievement medal. Office: Office Sec of Air Force 1160 Air Force Pentagon Washington DC 20330-1160

MOSEMANN, LLOYD KENNETH, II, business executive; b. Lancaster, Pa., May 16, 1936; s. Lloyd Kreider and Beatrice Elizabeth (Frey) M.; m. Arlene K. White, Sept. 6, 1957; children— Gigi Renee Mosemann Falke, Lloyd Kenneth III, Douglas Lamar, Holly Joy AB in Social Sci., U. Chgo., 1957, AM in Internat. Rels., 1959. Gen. supply officer Navy Electronics Supply Office, Great Lakes, Ill., 1958-62; inventory mgmt. specialist Def. Electronics Supply Ctr., Dayton, Ohio, 1962-63; head integrated-retail supply and support br. Naval Supply Systems Command, Washington, 1963-69; dep. chief logistics support analysis office Def. Logistics Agy., Alexandria, Va., 1969-71; dep. for supply and maintenance Office Sec. of Air Force, Washington, 1971-74; dep. asst. sec. for logistics and communications Dept. Air Force, Washington, 1974-91, dep. asst. sec. for comm., computers and logistics, 1991-93, dep. asst. sec. for comm., computers and support systems, 1993-96; software and acquisition cons., 1996-97; sr. v.p. corp. devel. Sci. Applications Internat. Corp., McLean, Va., 1997—. Mem. Air Force Exec. Resources Bd., 1981—95. Decorated DSM; recipient Meritorious Svc. medal Sec. Air Force, 1977, Exceptional Civilian Svc. medal sec. Air Force, 1979, 81, 82, 87, 96, Meritorious Sr. Exec. award Pres. of U.S., 1982, 87, Def. Meritorious Civilian Svc. medal, 1985. Mem. Soc. Logistics Engrs. (bd. advisers 1983—, Founders medal 1983, H. Mark Grove award for excellence in software mgmt. 1996, Govt. Computer News Hall of Fame 1996, Fed. Computer Week "100" award 1996), Am. Def. Preparedness Assn. (bd. dirs. 1974-83), Nat. Inst. for Urban Search and Rescue (exec. bd. dirs. 1990—). Home: 10013 Blake Ln Oakton VA 22124

MOSENA, DAVID R. museum administrator; M in City Planning, U. Tenn. Dir. rsch. Am. Planning Assn., Chgo.; mem. staff City of Chgo., 1984-89, planning commr., 1989-91, chief of staff, 1991-92, aviation commr., 1992-96; pres. CTA, 1996—97; pres., CEO Museum of Science and Industry, Chicago, 1997—. Chmn. bd. dirs. U. Chgo. Lab. Schs. Office: Museum of Science and Industry 5700 S Lake Shore Dr Chicago IL 60637*

MOSER, C. THOMAS, lawyer; b. Seattle, Aug. 10, 1947; s. Carl Thomas and Helen Louise (Felton) M.; m. Deborah J. St. Clair, Sept. 25, 1976; children: Nicole, Lauren. BA, Cen. Wash. U., 1972; M in Pub. Adminstrn., George Washington U., 1974; JD, Gonzaga U., 1976. Bar: Wash. 1977; U.S. Dist. Ct. (we. dist.) Wash. 1977, U.S. Dist. Ct. (ea. dist.) Wash. 1980, U.S. Ct. Appeals (9th cir.) 1980, U. S. Supreme Ct. 1981. Dep. pros. atty. Skagit County Pros. Atty., Mount Vernon, Wash., 1976-77, chief civil dep., 1979-80, pros. atty., 1980-86, San Juan County Pros. Atty., Friday Harbor, Wash., 1977-79; pvt. practice Mount Vernon, 1987—. Hearing examiner pro tem Skagit County, 1992—. Author: Gonzaga Law Review, 1975. Bd. dirs. Wash. Environ. Coun., Seattle, 1971-72, Padilla Bay Found., Skagit County, Wash., 1988; bd. trustees Wash. Assn. County Ofcls., Olympia, 1983; exec. bd. North Pacific Conf. Evang. Covenant Ch., vice sec. 1991-96; bd. trustees Skagit Valley Coll., 2000—. Sgt. U.S. Army, 1967-69, Korea. Recipient Silver Key award ABA Student Law Div., 1976, Legion of Honor award Internat. Order DeMolay, Kansas City, Mo., 1982, Chevalier award 1982. Mem. ATLA, Nat. Coll. Advocacy (advocate), Wash. State Trial Lawyers Assn. (bd. govs. 1990-92, 96-97), Wash. Assn. Pros. Attys. (bd. dirs. 1983-85), Skagit County Bar Assn. (pres. 1995-96), Kiwanis Club Mt. Vernon, Affiliated Health Svc. (ethics com.), Christian Legal Soc. Democrat. Evangelical. Avocations: skiing, golf, woodworking. Office: 411 Main St Mount Vernon WA 98273-3837

MOSER, DEBRA KAY, medical educator; BSN magna cum laude, Humboldt State U., Arcata, Calif., 1977; M in Nursing, UCLA, 1988, D in Nursing Sci., 1992. RN, Calif., Ohio; cert. pub. health nurse, Calif. Staff nurse, relief supr. med.-surg. fl. Mad River Cmty. Hosp., Arcata, 1977-78, staff/charge nurse intensive care/cardiac care unit, 1978-86; clin. nursing instr. Humboldt State U., Arcata, 1985-86; staff/charge nurse surg. ICU Santa Monica (Calif.) Hosp., 1987-88; spl. reader UCLA Sch. Nursing, 1990-91, rsch. assoc., 1986-91, clin. rsch. nurse, 1988-92, project dir., 1991-92, asst. prof., 1992-94; asst. prof. dept. adult health and illness Ohio State U. Coll. Nursing, Columbus, 1994-98, assoc. prof. dept. adult health and illness, 1998—. Mem. working group on ednl. strategies to Prevent Prehosp. Delay in Patients at High Risk for Acute Myocardial Infraction, Nat. Heart Attack Alert Program, NIH, Nat. Heart, Lung and Blood Inst., 1993-95; abstract grader sci. sessions program Am. Heart Assn., 66th Sci. Sessions, 1993, 96; grad. advisor Sigma Theta Tau-Gamma Tau chpt., 1993-94; mem. med. adv. com. Westside YMCA Cardiac Rehab. Program, 1993-94; mem. Task Force on Women, Behavior and Cardiovasc. Disease NIH, Nat. Heart, Lung and Blood Inst., 1991; coord. cont. care CHF cmty. case mgmt. Mt. Carmel Health Sys., Columbus, Ohio, 1997—; presenter in field. Reviewer Am. Jour. Critical Care, 1992—, Heart and Lung, 1991—, Progress in Cardiovasc. Nursing, 1993—, Heart Failure: Evaluation and Care of Patients With Left-Ventricular Systolic Function, 1993, Intensive Coronary Care, 5th edit., 1994, Rsch. in Nursing & Health, 1995—, Jour. Am. Coll. Cardiology, 1995; co-editor Jour. Cardiovasc. Nursing, 1997—; mem. editl. bd. Am. Jour. Critical Care, 1994—, Jour. Cardiovasc. Nursing, 1995—; contbr. articles to profl. jours., chpts. to books. Recipient scholarship UCLA, 1988-90, scholarship Kaiser Permanente Affiliate Schs., 1990, Ednl. Achievement award LA-AACN, 1990, Alumni rsch. award UCLA, 1990, rsch. abstract award AACN-IVAC, 1993, Heart Failure Rsch. prize AHA Coun. Cardiovascular Nursing/Otsuka Am. Pharm., Inc., 1995; grantee Sigma Theta Tau-Gamma Tau chpt., 1989-90, AACN, 1989-90, 92-93, NIH, Nat. Ctr. Nursing Rsch., 1990-92, UCLA Program in Psycheuroimmunology, 1992-93, UCLA Sch. Nursing, 1993, UCLA Acad. Senate, 1993-94, AACN/Sigma Theta Tau Internat., 1994-95, NIH, Nat. Inst. Nursing Rsch., 1991-96, Sigma Theta Tau Epsilon chpt., 1995, Ohio State U., 1995, Nat. Am. Heart Assn., 1995—. Mem. AACN (Critical Care Rsch. Abstract award 1995, 98), Am. Heart Assn. Coun. Cardiovasc. Nursing (New Investigator award 1995, Heart Failure Rsch. prize 1995), Am. Psychol. Soc., Heart Failure Soc. Am., AHA (fellow Coun. Cardiovascular Nursing), Sigma Theta Tau (mem. rsch. com. 1990-94, Excellence in Rsch. award Gamma Tau chpt. 1993). Office: Ohio State U Coll Nursing Dept Adult Health & Illness 1585 Neil Ave Columbus OH 43210-1216 Home: Apt 1010 4390 Clearwater Way Lexington KY 40515-6375

MOSER, DIANE, state agency administrator; AAS in Data Processing and BSBA in Acctg., U. So. Colo., 1978. CPA Colo. Auditor various acctg. firms, Denver, 1978—85; with Denver Technol. Ctr., 1985—95, acctg. mgr.; prin. acctg. Wyo. Dept. Agr., 1995—99; comptroller Wyo. Bus. Coun., Cheyenne, 1999—. Office: Wyoming Business Council 214 W 15th St Cheyenne WY 28002

MOSER, DONALD BRUCE, magazine editor; b. Cleve., Oct. 19, 1932; s. Donald Lyman and Kathryn (McHugh) Moser; m. Penny Lee Ward, Dec. 20, 1975. BA, Ohio U., 1957; postgrad., Stanford U., 1957—58, U. Sydney, 1959—60. With Life mag., 1961—72, West Coast bur. chief, 1964—65, Far East bur. chief, 1966—69, asst. mng. editor, 1970—72; free-lance writer, 1972—77; exec. editor Smithsonian mag., Washington, 1977—80, editor, 1980—, editor-in-chief. Author: The Peninsula, 1962, The Snake River Country, 1974, A Heart to the Hawks, 1975, Central American Jungles, 1976, China-Burma-India, 1978. With U.S. Army, 1953—55. Stegner fellow, 1957—58, Fulbright scholar, 1959—60. Mem.: Phi Beta Kappa. Office: Smithsonian Mag Arts & Indsl Bldg MRC 951 Washington DC 20560-0951

MOSER, EUGENE PAUL, JR., retired secondary school educator; b. Alexandria, La., Oct. 8, 1943; s. Eugene Paul and Sally Dawkins Moser; m. Dianna Lynn Michael; children: Eugene Paul III, Sarah Elizabeth. AB, Coll. of William and Mary, 1961—65. H.s. tchr. Hampton City Schools, Hampton, Va., 1968—99, substitute tchr., 1999—. Author: Skinny Dipping and Other Stories, Into Joy From Sadness. First lt. Army - F.A., Ft. Gordon, GA, 2nd Inf. Div, Korea. Decorated Va. N.G. Bronze Star. Episc. Achievements include co-founder, Operation Footlocker, the Mobile Military Brat Monument. Avocations: photography, cooking, water gardening, model railroading. Home: 9 Ward Dr Hampton VA 23669-3646 Personal E-mail: steamgene@aol.com.

MOSER, FRANKLIN GEORGE, neuroradiologist, researcher; b. N.Y.C., Jan. 17, 1956; s. Alexander Sander and Belle (Herz) M.; m. Caroline Labiner, Aug. 25, 1984; children: Claire Irene, Julia Hannah. BS, Yale U., 1977; MD, McGill U., Montreal, Can., 1981. Diplomate Am. Bd. Radiology, Am. Bd. Neuroradiology. Intern in surgery and medicine Sir Mortimer Davis Hosp., Montreal, 1981-82; resident in radiology Mt. Sinai Med. Ctr., N.Y.C., 1982-85; fellow in radiology Neurologic Inst. N.Y. Columbia U., N.Y.C., 1985-86, asst. prof. radiology, 1986-87; asst. prof. radiology, dir. neuroradiology Montefiore Med. Ctr., N.Y.C., 1987-90; chief neuroradiology Lenox Hill Hosp., N.Y.C., 1990-92; dir. clin. & intervtnl. neuroradiology, dir. outpatient radiology Cedars-Sinai Med. Ctr., L.A., 1992—. Contbr. articles to profl. jours. Mem. Am. Soc. Neuroradiology (sr.), Am. Soc. Theraputic and Interventional Neuroradiology, Radiol. Soc. N.Am., Am. Coll. Radiology, Soc. Rsch. Nervous and Mental Disease, Am. Roentgen Ray Soc., Am. Soc. Spine Radiology, Calif. Radiol. Soc., N.Y. Radiol. Soc., N.Y. Neurosurgical Soc. (hon.), L.A. Radiol. Soc., Yale Club. Avocations: arts & crafts, furniture, pottery. Office: Cedars Sinai Med Ctr 8700 Gracie Allen Dr Los Angeles CA 90048-3811 E-mail: moser@cshs.org.

MOSER, HUGO WOLFGANG, physician; b. Switzerland, Oct. 4, 1924; came to U.S., 1940, naturalized, 1943; s. Hugo L. and Maria (Werner) M.; m. Ann Boody, Dec. 28, 1963; children— Tracey, Peter, Karen, Lauren. MD, Columbia U., 1948; A.M. in Med. Sci, Harvard U., 1956. Intern Columbia-Presbyn. Med. Center, N.Y.C., 1948-50; asst. in medicine Peter Bent Brigham Hosp., Boston, 1950-52; research fellow dept. biol. chemistry Harvard U., 1955-57; asst. resident, resident in neurology Mass. Gen. Hosp., 1957-59, asst. neurologist, 1960-67, assoc. neurologist, 1967-69, neurologist, 1969-76. Teaching fellow neuropathology Harvard Med. Sch., 1959-60, instr. neurology, 1960-64, assoc. in neurology, 1964-67, asst. prof., 1967-69, assoc. prof., 1969-72, prof., 1972-76; dir. research and tng. Walter E. Fernald State Sch., 1963-68, asst. supt., 1968-73, acting supt., 1973-74, supt., 1974-76; dir. Center for Research on Mental Retardation and Related Aspects of Human Devel.,

dir. univ. affiliated facilities for mentally retarded, 1965-74; co-dir. Eunice Kennedy Shriver Center for Mental Retardation, Inc., 1969-74; pres. John F. Kennedy Inst., Balt., 1976-88; prof. neurology and pediatrics Johns Hopkins U., 1976—. Author: (with others) Mental Retardation: An Atlas of Diseases with Associated Physical Abnormalities, 1972; Contbr. (with others) articles to med. jours. Served with AUS, 1943-44; to capt. U.S. Army, 1952-54. Recipient Hower award Child Neurology Soc., 1994, Becker award German Soc. for Neuropediats., 1999, Frank Ford award Internat. Child Neurology Assn., 2002. Mem. Am. Acad. Neurology, Am. Assn. Mental Deficiency, Am. Assn. Neuropathologists, Am. Neurol. Assn., Internat. Soc. Neurochemistry, Am. Pediatrics Soc., Sigma Xi, Alpha Omega Alpha. Home: 100 Beechdale Rd Baltimore MD 21210-2209 Office: Kennedy Inst Inc 707 N Broadway Baltimore MD 21205-1832 Office Phone: 443-923-2750. Business E-Mail: moser@KennedyKrieger.org.

MOSER, JEFFERY RICHARD, state agency administrator, public affairs and public management executive, artist, writer, former state official; b. Miller, S.D., Feb. 8, 1961; s. Richard and Ardessa Joan (Yost) M. Student, U. Minn., 1979-84, Duke U., 1995, Northwestern U., 1997. Cert. lay minister; cert. in pub. policy and pub. fin.; cert. CPR, Am. Red Cross. Lab asst., intern U. Minn. Dept. Limnology, Mpls., 1980-81; exec. intern pub. affairs dept. Target Corp., Mpls., 1982; Nat. Farmers Union, Nat. Youth Adv. Coun., Denver, 1980-81; intern/asst. for legis. and policy Minn. Agri-Growth Coun., Bloomington, 1984-85; field office asst. U.S. Congressman Thomas A. Daschle, Aberdeen, S.D., 1986; pvt. cons. to non-profit orgns., 1986-89; notary pub. State of S.D., 1986-99; acting camp dir. S.D. Farmers Union Edn. Program, 1987-88; small bus. owner, 1986—; exec. dir. S.D. Assn. Towns and Twps., 1990-95; dep. state treas. to treas. Richard D. Butler State of S.D., Pierre, 1995-99; dir. econ. & co-op devel. Nat. Farmer's Union, Aurora, Colo., 1999—. Participant 4-H/UN/USAID Presdl. young adult exch. program to Kenya and Botswana, Africa, summer 1985. Vol. U. Minn. Hosps., 1979-83, U. Minn. Dept. Minn. Unions, Mpls., 1983-84; gen. election poll watcher Hand County Rural precincts, 1988; past mem. Beadle County Dems., Hand County Dems., Brown County Dems., Hughes County Dems., v.p., 1997-98, Arapahoe County Dems., 1999—; del. State Dem. Conv., 1990, 92, 94; alt. del. Nat. Dem. Conv., Chgo., 1996, Clinton for Pres., 1992; nom. Dem. candidate State Auditor, 1994, U.S. House, 1998; donor S.D. Dems., Dem. Nat. Com.; Dem. Nat. Senate Task Force; Dem. Congl. Campaign Com.; chair, del. Selection/Affirmative Action Com., 1996; Clinton-Gore, mem. State Adv. Com., 1996; at. del. Dem. Nat. Conv., 1996; mem. Hughes County Steering Com. to Re-Elect Senator Tom Daschle, 1997-98; dem. candidate S.D. at-large dist. U.S. Ho. of Rep., 1998; vol. leader, advisor, and state fair judge S.D. 4-H Program, 1981-94; bd. dirs. S.D. Rural Devel. Coun., 1993-95, S.D. State Adv. Com. for Green Thumb, Inc., 1993-95; mem. task force Nat. Urban Comparative Risk Environ., 1994, Common Cause S.D., 1991-94; dist. edn. dir. S.D. Farmers Union, 1988-93; dir. Minn. Union Coordinating Bd., U. Minn., 1982-84; bd. dirs. Golden Razor Hair Salon, Inc., Mpls., 1983-84, bd. dirs. Internat. Study & Travel Assn., Mpls., 1982-83; mem. Rose Hill Presbyn. Ch., Clan Campbell Soc. (N.Am.), E. River Sierra Club, Rocky Mountains/Hi Plains Group Sierra Club, S.D. AG Heritage Mus., S.D. Com. for World Food Day, S.D. Bread for the World, Dakota Rural Action, S.D. Project Prosperity Coalition, S.D. Farmers Union, S.D. Horticulture Soc., Dakota Rural Action, South Dakotans For the Arts, Wilson Ctr., Am. Mus. Nat. Hist., Smithsonian Assocs., Lib. Congress, Oscar Howe Art Ctr., Siouxland chpt. Alzheimer's Assn., S.D. Health Care Reform Coalition, S.D. Artists Network, S.D. Hist. Soc., Colo. Pub. Radio (donor), 9th Jud. Circuit Ct. Soc., Nat. Resource Defense Coun., Nat. Audubon Soc., Internat. 4-H Programs; host family Botswana Agr. Exch. Program, 1992; Presbytery of S.D., sec. Congl. Devel. Ministry, 1988-91, Advocacy Devel. Ministry unit, 1992-93, ch. camp dean, moderator Soc. Witness and Action Com., 1995-99, mem. com. representation, 1995-99, mem. com. Self-Devel. People, 1995-99; exec. Presbytery Search com., 1995-96, active Am. Heart Assn. Pierre Area Heart Walk, 1995, 97; vol. coord. Bread for the World Hunger Awareness event, Huron, 1993; mem. planning com. 1993 Regional 4-H Leaders Forum, Sioux Falls; past del. rep. S.D. Nat. 4-H Congress, 1981; past del. rep. Nat. Farmers Union Nat. conf., Presbyn. Ch. USA Gen. Assembly, Presbyn. Ch. USA Consultation on Sustainable Devel., 1995, Nat. 4-H Coun. Master Communicators Conf., Albuquerque, Presbyn. Ch. USA Synod Lakes and Prairies Workshop on Representation and Nominations, Rochester, Minn., 1997, Common Cause Nat. Leadership conf., Washington, 1993, Sharing Global Harvests Nat. Tng., Nat. Assn. Towns and Twps. Am.'s Town Meeting, Washington, 1992, strategic leadership for state execs. course Duke U., 1995, Inst. Pub. Fin. Northwestern U., 1997; bd. co-chair Huron Postal Customer Adv. Bd., 1993-95; bd. dirs. S.D. Peace and Justice Ctr., sec.-treas., 1994, v.p., 1995, dir. 1994-97; copywriter Minn. Ag. Manual, 1985; active Fed. Credit Union. Mem. Nat. Audubon Soc., S.D. Hort. Soc., Phi Beta Kappa, Omicron Delta Kappa, Mortar Bd., Golden Key. Democrat. Address: PO Box 1682 Aurora CO 80040-1682

MOSER, M(ARTIN) PETER, lawyer; b. Balt., Jan. 16, 1928; s. Herman and Henrietta (Lehmayer) M.; m. Elizabeth Kohn, June 14, 1949; children— Mike, Moriah, Jeremy AB, The Citadel, Charleston, S.C., 1947; LLB, Harvard U., 1950. Bar: Md. 1950, U.S. Supreme Ct., U.S. Ct. Appeals (4th cir.). Asst. states atty. City of Balt., 1951, 53-54; assoc. Blades Rosenfeld, Balt., 1950, 53-54; ptnr. Frank, Bernstein, Conaway & Goldman and predecessor firms, Balt., 1955-90, co-chmn. firm, 1983-86; counsel, 1991-92; of counsel Piper Rudnick LLP, 1992—. Instr. U. Balt. Law Sch., 1954-56, 86, U. Md. Law Sch., 1986-87. Contbr. articles to profl. jours. Del., chmn. local govt. com. Md. Constl. Conv., 1967-68; mem. Balt. City Planning Commn., 1961-66, Balt. Regional Planning Council, 1963-66, Md. Commn. to Study Narcotics Laws, 1965-67, Mayor's Task Force on EEO, 1966-67, Met. Transit Authority Adv. Council, 1962, Com. to Revise Balt. City Planning Laws, 1962, Com. to Revise Balt. City Charter Provision on Conflicts of Interest, 1969-70; mem. Citizens Adv. Com. on Dist. Ct., chmn., 1971, Dist. Adv. Bd. for Pub. Defender System for Dist. 1, 1973-85; mem. Atty. Grievance Commn. of Md., 1975-78, chmn. 82-86; chmn. Md. State Ethics Commn., 1987-89; bd. dirs. Sinai Hosp., 1983—, Lifebridge Health Sys., 1998—, Ct. of Appeals Comm. to Study the Model Rules, 1983-86, 2002-. Served with JAGC, U.S. Army, 1951-53 Fellow: Balt. Bar Found. (pres. 1970—71), Md. Bar Found., Am. Bar Found. (pres. 2002—04); mem.: ABA (ho. of dels. 1978—2002, bd. govs. 1984—87, 1992—96, treas. 1993—96), Lawyers' Round Table Club, Wednesday Law Club, Balt. Bar Assn., Md. State Bar Assn. (pres. 1979—80). Democrat. Jewish. Office: Piper Rudnick LLP 6225 Smith Ave Baltimore MD 21209-3600 Office Phone: 410-580-4218.

MOSER, MARVIN, physician, educator, writer; b. Newark, Jan. 24, 1924; s. Sol and Sophia (Markowitz) M.; m. Joy Diane Lipez, July 1, 1954; children: Jill, Stephen, John. AB, Cornell U., 1943; MD, Downstate Coll. Medicine, N.Y.C., 1947. Diplomate: Am. Bd. Internal Medicine, subbd. cardiovascular disease; cert. specialist in hypertension Am. Soc. Hypertension. Intern univ. div. Kings County Hosp., N.Y.C., 1947-48, resident in medicine, 1948-49, Montefiore Hosp., N.Y.C., 1949-50; Nat. Heart Assn. fellow Mt. Sinai Hosp., N.Y.C., 1950-51; charge vascular service Walter Reed Army Hosp. Med. Centre, Washington, 1951-53; practice medicine specializing in cardiology White Plains, N.Y., 1953-95; assoc. physician cardiology Montefiore Hosp., 1953-75, in charge hypertension sect., 1960—74. Attending physician cardiology White Plains Hosp., 1968-95, chief cardiology, 1969-78; adj. physician in cardiology Grasslands Hosp., Valhalla, N.Y., 1953-60; attending physician in medicine in charge Hypertension Clinic, Westchester County Med. Center, Valhalla, 1974-84; asst. clin. prof. medicine Albert Einstein Coll. Medicine, 1965-75; clin. prof. medicine N.Y. Med. Coll., 1974-84, Yale U. Sch. Medicine, 1984—; sr. med. cons. nat. high blood pressure program NIH, 1975-2002, mem. nat. high blood pressure coordinating com., 1976—; chmn. Joint Nat. Com. Hypertension, 1975-76, vice-chmn., 1979, mem., 1984-88, 92, 96; mem. exec. com. Nat. Citizens for Treatment High Blood Pressure, 1976-78, vice chmn., 1978-88; mem. N.Y. State Adv. Com. on Hypertension, 1977-84; chmn. Nat. Conf. on High Blood Pressure Control, 1979; mem. select panel on hypertension in Am. Congl. Subcom. on Aging, 1978-79; cons. cardiology N.Y. State Dept. Health, Gen. Hosp., Saranac Lake, N.Y., 1980-90; med. dir. Westchester County Hypertension Program, N.Y., 1979-88. Author: (with A.M. Master, M. Moser, H. Jaffee) Cardiac Emergencies and Heart Failure, 2d edit., 1955, (with A. Goldman) Hypertensive Vascular Disease, 1967, Hypertension, A Practical Approach, 1975, Lower Your Blood Pressure and Live Longer, 1988; co-editor, contbr. Yale University School of Medicine Heart Book, 1992, Week by Week to a Strong Heart, 1992, Heart Healthy Cooking for all Seasons, 1996, Clinical Management of Hypertension, 1996, 7th edit., 2003, Myths, Misconceptions and Heroics, the Story of the Treatment of Hypertension, 1997, 2002, (with J. Sowers) Management of Cardiovascular Risk Factors in Diabetes, 2001; editl. bd. Preventive Cardiology, 1998—, Jour. Medicine and Sports, 1999-2004;; assoc. editor Angiology, 1976-85; bd. editors Primary Cardiology, 1975-78, assoc. editor-in-chief, 1978-96; editor-in-chief Jour. of Clin. Hypertension, 1999—. Chmn. Narcotics Guidance Coun., Scarsdale, 1968-72; trustee Scarsdale Bd. Edn., 1970-73, Trudeau Inst., Nat. Hypertension Found., 1992-2001, Nutrition 21, 1997—, Comprehensive Neuroscience; bd. dirs. Third Ave. Value and Small Cap Funds, 1994—; pres. Hypertension Edn. Found., 1977—. Served U.S. Army, 1941-46; capt. M.C. USAF, 1951-53. Recipient Achievement awards Nat. High Blood Pressure Edn. Program, 1985, 97, award Internat. Soc. Hypertension, 2004; grantee Nat. Heart Inst., 1958-62. Fellow: ACP, Am. Heart Assn. ((various offices: pres. coun. geriatric cardiology 1996-97, others)), Am. Coll. Cardiology, Royal Coll. Physicians and Surgeons (hon.); mem.: Century Country Club. Home and Office: 13 Murray Hill Rd Scarsdale NY 10583 Personal E-mail: moserbp@aol.com.

MOSER, MICHAEL R. newspaper editor; b. Shelby, Ohio, May 27, 1952; s. Roger and Patricia (Welch) M.; m. Gayle Overby, Aug. 20, 1985 (div. Nov. 1997); children: Maggie, Amber, Skye, Tess. Assoc. of Fire Sci., Shelton State Coll. Editor Ctrl. Ala. Advertiser, Clanton, 1972-75, Englewood (Ohio) Independent, 1975-78, St. Clair News-Aegis, Pell City, Ala., 1978-83, Crossville (Tenn.) Chronicle, 1984—. City planner Crossville Regional Planning Commn., 1989—. Actor Cumberland County Playhouse, 1989—; author: The Beauty of Riverside, 1992. Bd. dirs. Cumberland Teen Ranch, Crossville, 1988-90, Cumberland County Playhouse, 1992—. Recipient Helen Byrd award Cumberland County Playhouse, 1992. Mem. Nat. Newspaper Assn. (numerous awards 1985—), Tenn. Press Assn., Kiwanis, soc. Profl. Journalists. Office: Crossville Chronicle PO Box 449 Crossville TN 38557-0449 Home: 81 Rhodendrum Cir Crossville TN 38555-5355

MOSER, R. KEVIN, clinical psychologist, educator; b. Reading, Pa., Aug. 29, 1963; s. Richard H. and Evelyn M. Moser; m. Shannon Elizabeth Timpane, Aug. 4, 1990; children: Lily Mae, Grace Elizabeth. BS in Biochemistry Summa Cum Laude, Albright Coll., 1985; MA in Counseling Psychology, Calif. Inst. Integral Studies, 1989; PhD in Clin. Psychology, New Sch. U., 1996. Lic. Psychology CA, 2000, NY, 1998. Psychiat. childcare worker Burt Children's Ctr., San Francisco, 1986—87; therapist Boyer Marin Lodge, Woodacre, Calif., 1988—90, Mt. Sinai Hosp. Dept. Psychiat. Rehab., N.Y.C., 1990—94; predoctoral psychology intern Albert Einstein Coll. Medicine North Ctrl. Bronx Hosp., Bronx, NY, 1994—95; psychology fellow Albert Einstein Coll. of Medicine Bronx Psychiat. Ctr., 1995—96; sr. psychologist Coney Island Hosp. Dept. Psychiatry, Bklyn., 1997—98; chief psychologist Coney Island Hospital-Child Devel. Ctr., Bklyn., 1998—2000; program dir. TALK Line Family Support Ctr., San Francisco, 2000—03, clin. and tng. dir., 2003—. Clin. psychologist Pvt. Practice, San Francisco, 2002—; asst. prof. adj. faculty Calif. Inst. Integral Studies, San Francisco, 2002. Contbr. articles to profl. jours. Buddhist scholar and practioner. Recipient Original Biochemical Rsch., MSD Lab, 1985. Buddhist. Achievements include research in Biology of Plasmid DNA. Avocations: travel, poetry & literature, painting, classical music. Office: 2142 Sutter St #2 San Francisco CA 94115

MOSER, RICHARD PETER, neurosurgeon; b. Fort Wayne, Ind., Dec. 4, 1948; s. Virgil and M. (Lynch) M.; m. Plaree Madoo; children: Sunil, Risha, Erik. BS, Loyola U., Chgo., 1971, MD, 1974. Resident neurosurgery U. Minn., Mpls., 1975-81; fellow neurosurgery Karolinska Inst., Stockholm, 1981-82; assoc. prof. U. Tex., Houston, 1982-92; neurosurgeon Surg. Neurology Assocs., Elk Grove Village, Ill., 1992—; chmn. dept. surgery NCH, Arlington Heights, Ill., 2000—; asst. prof. neurosurgery U. Ill., Chgo. Bd. dirs. Am. Cancer Soc., Arlington Heights, Ill.; council Chgo. Med. Soc., 1994-95. Author: Pineal Region Tumors, 1984, Prognosis in Neurological Diseases, 1993; contbr. articles to profl. jours. Grantee Dunn Found., 1988; recipient Saul Korcy award Am. Acad. Neurology, 1974. Fellow ACS; mem. AMA, Am. Assn. Neurol. Surgeons, Am. Soc. Clin. Oncology, Ill. State Med. Soc. (del.), Chgo. Med. Soc. (councilor), Congress Neurol. Surgeons. Roman Catholic. Home: 1530 Rfd Long Grove IL 60047-9507 Office: Busse Ctr for Specialty Medicine 880 Central Rd Arlington Heights IL 60005 Office Phone: 847-398-6464.

MOSER, ROBERT HARLAN, internist, educator, writer; b. Trenton, N.J., June 16, 1923; s. Simon and Helena (Silvers) Moser; m. Linda Mae Salsinger, Mar. 18, 1989; children from previous marriage: Steven Michael, Jonathan Evan. BS, Loyola U., Balt., 1944; MD, Georgetown U., 1948. Diplomate Am. Bd. Internal Medicine. Commd. 1st lt. U.S. Army, 1948, advanced through grades to col., 1966, intern D.C. Gen. Hosp., 1948—49, fellow pulmonary disease D.C. Gen. Hosp., 1949—50, bn. surgeon, 1950—51; asst. resident Georgetown U. Hosp., 1951—52; chief resident Georgetown U. Hosp. U.S. Army, 1952—53, chief med. service U.S. Army Hosp., 1953—55, Wurzburg, Germany, 1955—56, resident in cardiology Brooke Gen. Hosp., 1956—57, asst. chief dept. medicine Brooke Gen. Hosp., 1957—59, chief Brooke Gen. Hosp., 1967—68, fellow hematology U. Utah Coll. Medicine, 1959—60, asst. chief U.S. Army Tripler Gen. Hosp., 1960—64, chief William Beaumont Gen. Hosp., 1965—67, chief Walter Reed Gen. Hosp., 1968—69, ret., 1969; chief of staff Maui (Hawaii) Meml. Hosp., 1969—73, chief dept. medicine, 1975—77; exec. v.p. Am. Coll. Physicians, Phila., 1976—86; v.p. med. affairs The NutraSweet Co., Deerfield, Ill., 1986—91. Assoc. prof. medicine Baylor U., 1958—59; clin. prof. medicine Hawaii U., 1969—77, Washington U., 1970—77, Abraham Lincoln Sch. Medicine, 1974—75; adj. prof. medicine U. Pa., 1977—86, Northwestern U., 1987—91; adj. prof. Uniformed Svcs. U. Health Scis., 1979—97; clin. prof. medicine U. N.Mex. Coll. Medicine, 1992—96, emeritus, 1996—; flight contr. Project Mercury, 1959—62; cons. mem. med. evaluation team Project Gemini, 1962—66; cons. Project Apollo, 1967—73, Tripler Gen. Hosp., 1970—77, Walter Reed Army Med. Ctr., 1974—86; sr. med. cons. Canyon Cons. Corp., 1991—; mem. cardiovascular and renal adv. com. FDA, 1978—82; chmn. life scis. adv. com. NASA, 1984—87, mem. adv. coun., 1983—88; chmn. gen. med. panel Hosp. Satellite Network, 1984—86; mem. adv. com. NASA Space Sta., 1988—93; mem. Dept. Def. Com. on Grad. Med. Edn., 1986—87, Life Scis. Strategic Planning Study Group, 1986—88; mem. space studies bd. NRC, 1988—93, space exploration initiation study, 1990; mem. NASA Space Sta. Commn., 1992—93, mem. com. adv. tech. human supp. space, 1996—97; mem. med. adv. bd. the patient coun. GE Healthcare, 2001—. Editor, chief divsn. sci. publs. Jour. AMA, Chgo., 1973—75, contbg. editor Med. Opinion and Rev., 1966—75, chmn. editorial bd. Diagnosis mag., 1986—89, mem. editorial bd. Hawaii Med. Jour., Family Physicians, Archives of Internal Medicine, 1967—73, Western Jour. Medicine, 1975—87, Chest, 1975—80, Med. Times, 1977—84, Quality Rev. Bull., 1979—91, The Pharos, 1991—, book rev. editor, 2000—, mem. editorial bd. Travel Medicine, 1994—96; contbr. over 200 articles to med. sci. jours. and med. books; author: Diseases of Medical Progress, 1955, 1969, House Office Training, 1970, Decade of Decision, 1992, Past Imperfect A Personal History of Life In and Around Medicine, 2003; co-author Adventures in Medical Writing, 1970, editor chief divsn. sci. publs. Jour. AMA, Chgo., 1973—75, contbg. editor Med. Opinion and Rev., 1966—75, chmn. editl. bd. Diagnosis mag., 1986—89; contbr. articles to med. sci. jours. and med. books. Master: ACP (exec. v.p. 1977—86); fellow: Am. Clin. and Climatol. Assn., Am. Coll. Cardiology, Royal Coll. Physicians and Surgeons Can. (hon.); mem.: AMA (adv. panel registry of adverse drug reactions 1960—67, coun. on drugs 1967—73), Soc. Med. Cons. to Armed Forces, Coll. Physicians Phila., Chgo. Soc. Internal Medicine, Nat. Assn. Physician Broadcasters, Inst. Medicine-NAS, Am. Osler Soc., Am. Therapeutic Soc., Am. Med. Writers Assn., Alpha Omega Alpha, Alpha Sigma Nu. Democrat. Jewish. Avocations: hiking, international travel, white water rafting, distance bicycling. Home and Office: 943 E Sawmill Canyon Pl Green Valley AZ 85614 Office Phone: 520-399-2526.

MOSER, ROBERT LAWRENCE, pathologist, health facility administrator; b. Passaic, N.J., Mar. 22, 1952; s. Robert George and Marjorie Ann (Frankenberger) M.; m. Rosemarie Scolaro, June 16, 1978; children: Rachel Ann, Alexander Robert. BA in Biology magna cum laude, Lafayette Coll., 1974; MD Microbiology/Internal Med. with honors, Hahnemann Med. Coll., 1978. Diplomate Am. Bd. Pathology, Am. Bd. Anatomic Pathology, Am. Bd. Clin. Pathology, Am. Bd. Forensic Medicine. Intern, fellow dept. pathology The Johns Hopkins Hosp., Balt., 1978-79, resident, fellow dept. pathology, 1979-81, chief resident, fellow dept. pathology, 1981-82, resident, fellow dept. lab. medicine, 1982-84; cons. pathologist Perry Point (Md.) VA Med. Ctr., 1983-84; pathologist Helene Fuld Med. Ctr., Trenton, N.J., 1984-88; med. dir. St. Francis Med. Ctr., Trenton, 1988—, dir. clin. info. sys., 1995—, Franciscan Health Sys., 1995-96, Cath. Health Initiatives, 1996—2000. Pres. Pathology Assocs., Lawrenceville, N.J., 1981—. Contbr. articles to profl. jours. Fellow Coll. Am. Pathologists, Coll. Physicians of Phila.; mem. Am. Med. Informatics Assn., Med. Soc. N.J., Mercer County Med. Soc., Ctrl. Jersey Ind. Physician Assn. (v.p. 1994-95, sec.-treas. 1995-96, exec. v.p. 1997—), Ea. Pathology Assn. (v.p. 1996-2003), Phi Beta Kappa. Avocations: golf, gardening, skiing.

MOSER, ROYCE, JR., preventive medicine physician, educator; b. Versailles, Mo., Aug. 21, 1935; s. Royce and Russie Frances (Stringer) M.; m. Lois Anne Hunter, June 14, 1958; children: Beth Anne Moser McLean, Donald Royce. BA, Harvard U., 1957, MD, 1961; MPH, Harvard Sch. Pub. Health, Boston, 1965. Diplomate Am. Bd. Preventive Medicine (trustee 1989-98). Commd. officer USAF, 1962, advanced through grades to col., 1974; resident in aerospace medicine USAF Sch. Aerospace Medicine, Brooks AFB, Tex., 1965-67; chief aerospace medicine Aerospace Def. Command, Colorado Springs, Colo., 1967-70; comdr. 35th USAF Dispensary Phan Rang, Vietnam, 1970-71; chief aerospace medicine br. USAF Sch. Aerospace Medicine, Brooks AFB, 1971-77; comdr. USAF Hosp., Tyndall AFB, Fla., 1977-79; chief clin. scis. divsn. USAF Sch. Aerospace Medicine, Brooks AFB, 1979-81, chief edn. divsn., 1981-83, sch. comdr., 1983-85, ret., 1985; prof. dept. family and preventive medicine U. Utah Sch. Medicine, Salt Lake City, 1985—, vice chmn. dept., 1985-95; dir. Rocky Mountain Ctr. for Occupl. and Environ. Health, Salt Lake City, 1987—2003. Cons. in occupl., environ. and aerospace medicine, Salt Lake City, 1985—; presenter in field. Author: Effective Management of Occupational and Environmental Health and Safety Programs, 1992, 2d edit. 1999; contbr. book chpts. and articles to profl. jours. Past pres. 1st Bapt. Ch. Found., Salt Lake City, 1987-89; chmn. numerous univ. coms., Salt Lake City, 1985—; bd. dirs. Hanford Environ. Health Found., 1990-92; preventive medicine residency rev. com. Accreditation Coun. Grad. Med. Edn., 1991-97; ednl. adv. bd. USAF Human Sys. Ctr., 1991-96; chmn. long-range planning com. Am. Bd. Preventive Medicine, 1992-95; mem. alumni coun. Harvard Sch. Pub. Health, 2003-. Decorated Legion of Merit (2); recipient Harriet Hardy award New Eng. Coll. Occupl. and Environ. Medicine, 1998, Rutherford T. Johnstone award Western Occupl. and Environ. Med. Assn., 2002. Fellow Aerospace Med. Assn. (pres. 1989-90, chair fellows group 1994-97, Harry G. Mosely award 1981, Theodore C. Lyster award 1988, Eric Liljencrantz award 2001), Am. Coll. Preventive Medicine (regent 1981-82), Am. Coll. Occupl. and Environ. Medicine (v.p. med. affairs 1995-97, Robert A. Kehoe award 1996); mem. Internat. Acad. Aviation and Space Medicine (selector 1989-94, chancellor 1994-98), Soc. of USAF Flight Surgeons (pres. 1978-79, George E. Schafer award 1982), Phi Beta Kappa. Avocations: photography, fishing. Home: 664 Aloha Rd Salt Lake City UT 84103-3329 Office: Rocky Mountain Ctr Occupl & Environ Health 391 Chipeta Way Ste C Salt Lake City UT 84108 Office Phone: 801-581-8719. Business E-Mail: Royce.Moser@hsc.utah.edu.

MOSER, WILLIAM OSCAR JULES, mathematics professor; b. Winnipeg, Can., Sept. 5, 1927; s. Robert and Laura (Fenson) M.; m. Beryl Rita Pearlman, Sept. 2, 1953; children— Marla, Lionel, Paula. B.Sc., U. Man., 1949; MA, U. Minn., 1951; PhD, U. Toronto, 1957. Lectr. U. Sask., 1955-57, asst. prof., 1957-59; asso. prof. U. Man., 1959-64, McGill U., 1964-66, prof., 1966-97, prof. emeritus, 1997—. Author: (with H.S.M. Coxeter) Generators and Relations for Discrete Groups, 1957, 4th edit., 1980, (with E. Barbeau, M. Klamkin) 500 Mathematical Challenges, 1995, also research papers; editor: Can. Math. Bull, 1962-70, Can. Jour. Math., 1982-85. NRC fellow, 1951-53; Can. Coun. leave fellow, 1971. Mem. Am. Math. Soc., Can. Math. Soc. (pres. 1975-77), Math. Assn. Am. Office: McGill U Dept Math 805 Sherbrooke St W Montreal QC Canada H3A 2K6 E-mail: moser@math.mcgill.ca.

MOSES, ABE JOSEPH, international financial consultant; b. Springfield, Mass., July 15, 1931; s. Mohammed Mustapha and Fatima (Merriam) M.; m. Donna C. Moses (dec. 1987); children: James Douglas, John C., Peter J.; m. Mary Jo Morris, Aug. 25, 2001. BA, Amherst Coll., 1955; MA in Internat. Affairs, Johns Hopkins U., 1957. Legis. aide Sen. J.F. Kennedy, 1955-57; fgn. service officer Dept. State, 1960-65; v.p., gen. mgr. Libyan Desert Oil Co., Texfel Petroleum Corp., Tripoli, Libya, 1965-67; v.p. adminstrn., fin. Occidental Petroleum Corp., Libya, 1967-70; v.p. fin., dir. Northrop Corp., 1970-74; chmn. Transworld Trade Ltd., Washington, 1971—; v.p., mng. dir. world adv. group Chase Manhattan Bank, 1974-80; pres. Berkshire Properties, 1976-95; pres., COO, Grolier Internat., Inc., Danbury, Conn., 1980-82; CEO, dir. Galadari Bros., Dubai, United Arab Emirates, 1982-86; internat. bus. and fin. cons. Traxol, Dubai, 1986—; fin. cons. Govt. Costa Rica, 1986-89. Chmn. Aviation Sys. Corp., Northampton, Mass., 1974, Dillon Internat., Akron, Ohio, 1986—; mng. dir. Sheraton Suites Akron, Cuyahoga Falls, Ohio, 1990—; owner's rep. Monarch Sheraton Hotel, Springfield, Mass., 1993-95; bd. dirs., v.p. Morgan Freeport Co., Hudson, Ohio; bd. dirs. Seeds of Peace, Washington; gen. ptnr. BPM Ltd. Partnership, 1995—. Pres., bd. dirs. Riverside Comty. Urban Redevel. Corp.; mem. exec. com., bd. dirs. Near East Found., N.Y.C., 1978—; pres. Riverfront Ctr. Assn., Cuyahoga Falls, 1992-95; bd. dirs. Gulfcoast Radio Ptnrs., 1997-99, Capitol City Radio Ptnrs., 1998-2000, Ind. Radio Ptnrs., Monroe (La.) Radio mems., LLC, Commonwealth Opera Co., Northampton, Mass., 2002—. Capt. USAF, 1957-60. Ford Found. fellow Johns Hopkins U., 1955, Barr Found. fellow, 1955-57. Mem.: Assn. Sheraton Franchise Owners N.Am. (bd. dirs. 2004—). Democrat. Home: 16 Highmeadow Rd Northampton MA 01062-2625 Office: Riverside CURC 1989 Front St Cuyahoga Falls OH 44221-3811 Office Phone: 330-920-7502. E-mail: abejmoses@comcast.net.

MOSES, ALFRED HENRY, lawyer, writer, diplomat; b. Balt., July 24, 1929; s. Leslie William and Helene Amelia (Lobe) Moses; m. Carol Whitehill, Nov. 24, 1955; children: Barbara, Jennifer, David, Amalie. BA, Dartmouth, 1951; postgrad., Woodrow Wilson Sch., Princeton U., 1951-52; JD, Georgetown U., 1956. Bar: D.C. 1956. Assoc. Covington & Burling, Washington, 1956-65, ptnr., 1965-94, 97—; spl. advisor, spl. counsel Pres. Jimmy Carter, Washington, 1980-81; amb. to Romania, 1994-97; Pres. spl. emissary for Cyprus, 1999-2001; founder, gen. counsel Promontory Interfin. Network, LLC, 2003—. Legal advisor minority rights Dem. Nat. Com., Washington, D.C. Commn. Urban Renewal; commr. Pub. Housing, Fairfax County, Va., 1971—72; chmn. UN Watch, Geneva, 2001—; chmn. nat. bd. Hebrew Coll., Newton Ctr., Mass., 2002—; lectr. in field. Contbr. articles to profl. jours. Pres. Am. Jewish Com., 1991—94; bd. dirs. Paralysis Cure Rsch. Found., 1978—81; trustee Phelps Stokes Fund, N.Y.C., 1978—84, Jewish Publ. Soc., 1989—94, Haifa U., 1988—90; co-chmn. legal divsn. United Givers Fund, Washington, 1975—76; mem. Coun. Fgn. Rels., N.Y.C., 1977—; pres. Nat. Children's Island, Washington, 1975—76, Golda Meir Assn., 1986—88, nat. chmn., 1988—93; mem. bd. regents Georgetown U., 1986—92. Mem.: ABA, D.C. Bar Assn., Met. Club. Democrat. Jewish. Home: 7710 Georgetown Pike Mc Lean VA 22102-1431 Office: 1201 Pennsylvania Ave NW Washington DC 20004-2401

MOSES, BONNIE SMITH, lawyer, educator; b. Phila., Jan. 20, 1955; d. D. Ralph (dec.) and Mercedes McKinley (Harrison) S.; m. Richard Moses, July 8, 1978; children: Michelle Irene, Jacquelyn Elyse. BS in Psychology summa cum laude, Pa. State U., 1975; JD, Temple U., 1978, LLM in Taxation, 1981. Bar: Pa. 1978, U.S. Dist. Ct. (ea. dist.) Pa. 1978, U.S. Ct. Appeals (3d cir.) 1980, U.S. Tax Ct. 1981, U.S. Supreme Ct. 1986. Law clk. Ct. Common Pleas, Phila., 1978-79; assoc. Leonard M. Sagot Assocs., Phila., 1979-80, mng. assoc. Jenkintown, Pa., 1980-84; ptnr. Dessen, Moses & Sheinoff, Phila., 1984—. Adj. prof. bus. law Arcadia U., Glenside, Pa., 1982—. Co-author The

Physician's Guide to Medical Practice, 2003; Contbr. articles to law jours. Bd. dirs. Phila. Jewish Archives, v.p., chair nom. com., Jewish Heritage Program; v.p., chmn. personnel Girls Inc. of Greater Phila.; mem. Leadership Coun. Phila.; vol. Lawyers for the Arts; mentor, Women's Law Caucus, Temple U. Law Sch. Fellow Pa. Bar Assn.; mem. ABA, AAUW, NAFE, Pa. Bar Assn., Phila. Bar Assn., Montgomery County Bar Assn., Am. Prepaid Legal Svcs. Inst. (chmn. conf. com. 2001—), Temple Law Alumni Assn. (exec. com.), Ogontz Campus Alumni Assn., Phi Beta Kappa, Phi Kappa Phi (Woman of Vision award). Office: Dessen Moses & Sheinoff 600 Easton Rd Philadelphia PA 19090 Office Phone: 215-658-1400. Business E-Mail: bmoses@dms-lawyer.com.

MOSES, EDWIN, former track and field athlete; b. Dayton, Ohio, Aug. 31, 1955; m. Myrella Moses. Student, Morehouse Coll. Fin. cons. Robinson-Humphrey Co., Atlanta; founder Platinum Group. Olympian hurdler; Worlds Top Ranked Intermediate Hurdler, 1987. Chmn. U.S. Olympic Com. Substance Abuse Com., 1989—. Holder world record 400 meter hurdle; Olympic gold medalist, 1976, 84; 1st U.S. athlete to be voted delegate to Internat. Amateur Athletic Fedn.; named Sportsman of the Yr. U.S. Olympic Com.; named to U.S. Track & Field Hall of Fame, 1994. Mem. Internat. Amateur Athletics Assn. (pres.), U.S. Olympic Com. (exec. com.).

MOSES, GREGORY H., JR., health services administrator; m. Johnella Moses. Lead engagement ptnr. Sister Mercy Health Corp.; ptnr.-in-charge Healthcare Consulting Group, N.Y., N.J.; ptnr. Coopers & Lybrand; pres., COO United Am. Healthcare Corp., Detroit, 1998—. Office: United American Health Care 300 River Place Dr Ste 4700 Detroit MI 48207-5069 Fax: 313-393-7944.

MOSES, HAMILTON, III, academic neurologist, management consultant, hospital executive; s. Hamilton Jr. and Betty Anne (Theurer) M.; m. Elizabeth Lawrence Hormel, 1977 (dec. 1988); m. Alexandra McCullough Gibson, 1992. BA in Psychology, U. Pa., 1972; MD, Rush Med. Coll., Chgo., 1975. Clk. Nat. Hosp. for Nervous Diseases, London, 1974; intern in medicine Johns Hopkins Hosp., Balt., 1976-77, resident in neurology, 1977-79, chief resident, 1979-80, assoc. prof. neurology, 1986-94, vice chmn. neurology and neurosurgery, 1980-88, v.p., 1988-94, dir. Parkinson's Ctr., 1984-94; dir. neurol. inst., prof. neurology and neurosurgery and mgmt. U. Va., Charlottesville, 1994-97; sr. advisor Boston Cons. Group, 1995—; prof. Darden Sch. Bus. U. Va., Charlottesville, 1994-98; cons. neurologist Mass. Gen. Hosp., Boston, 1997—; vis. prof. neurology and psychiatry Harvard U. Sch. Medicine, Boston, 1997-99; chmn. The Alerion Inst., 2003—. Sr. advisor Ptnrs. Healthcare, Boston; spl. advisor Nat. Health Svc., Eng., 1988-91. Editor, major author: Principles of Medicine, 1985-96; editor newsletter Johns Hopkins Health, 1988-94; contbr. numerous articles to med. jours. Mem. com. on med. ministries Episcopal Diocese Md., Balt., 1987; bd. dirs. Valleys Planning Ct.; trustee McLean Hosp., Belmont, Mass., 1997—. Fellow Am. Acad. Neurology (sec. 1989-91), Royal Soc. Medicine (U.K.) (overseas fellow 2000—); mem. Am. Neurol. Assn., Md. Neurol. Soc. (pres. 1984-86), Movement Disorders Soc. Republican. Avocations: landscape photography, sailing. Office: PO Box 150 North Garden VA 22959-0150 also: 4800 Hampden Ln Bethesda MD 20814-2930

MOSES, HAROLD L. oncologist; MD, Vanderbilt U., 1962. Rschr. NIH, 1965—68; faculty Vanderbilt U., Nashville, 1985—, prof. cancer biology, the Benjamin F. Byrd Jr. prof. of clin. oncology, prof. pathology and prof. medicine, 1993—, dir. Vanderbilt-Ingram Cancer Ctr., 1999—, chair dept. cell biology, 1985—98. Dir. Frances Williams Preston Rsch. Labs. T.J. Martell Found., 1993—; clin. oncologist Mayo Clinic, Rochester, Minn., 1973—85; mem. nat. dialogue on cancer, vice chair cancer rsch. team, char parent com. Nat. Cancer Inst., mem. bd. sci. counselors. Mem.: Am. Assn. for Cancer Rsch. (past pres.), Assn. of Am. Cancer Insts. (pres.), Inst. Medicine, 2004. Office: Vanderbilt-Ingram Cancer Ctr 691 Preston Bldg Nashville TN 37232

MOSES, JEFFREY WARREN, cardiologist, educator; b. Bklyn., May 12, 1948; s. Julian and Mildred Moses; m. Laurie Levinberg, Nov. 4, 1983; children: Ariel, Jarret, Chandler, Harrison. BA, Yale U., 1970; MD, U. Pa., 1974. Intern Presbyn.-U. Pa., Phila., 1974—75, resident in medicine, 1975—77, fellow in cardiology, 1978—80; asst. instr. U. Pa., Phila., 1975—77; med. adv. staff Blue Cross/Blue Shield Greater N.Y., 1977—78; asst. med. dir. Equitable Life Soc., N.Y.C., 1977—78; asst. attending physician N.Y. Hosp., N.Y.C., 1980—87, asst. dir. adult cardiac catheterization lab., 1980—83, dir. clin. electrophysiology, 1981—87, assoc. dir. adult cardiac catheterization lab., 1983—87, assoc. attending physician, 1987; instr. medicine Cornell U. Med. Coll., N.Y.C., 1980—81, asst. prof., 1981—87, assoc. prof. clin. medicine, 1987; chief interventional cardiology Lenox Hill Hosp., N.Y.C., 1987—, assoc. attending physician, 1987—88, sr. attending physician, 1988—; clin. assoc. prof. medicine NYU Sch. Medicine, N.Y.C., 1993—96, clin. prof. medicine, 1996—. Fellow: ACP, Soc. Cardiac Angiography and Intervention, Am. Coll. Cardiology. Office: Lenox Hill Hosp 130 E 77th St New York NY 10021 E-mail: jmoses@leroxhill.net.

MOSES, JOEL, computer scientist, educator; b. Petach Tikvah, Israel, Nov. 25, 1941; came to U.S., 1954, naturalized, 1960; s. Bernhard and Golda (Losner) M.; m. Margaret A. Garvey, Dec. 27, 1970; children: Jesse, David. BA, Columbia U., 1962, MA, 1963; PhD, MIT, 1967. Asst. prof. dept. elec. engring. and computer sci. MIT, Cambridge, 1967-71, assoc. prof., 1971-77, prof., 1977—, assoc. dir. Lab for Computer Sci., 1974-78, assoc. head computer sci. and engring., dept. elec. engring. and computer sci., 1978-81, head dept., 1981-89, D.C. Jackson prof., 1989-99, dean Sch. Engring., 1991-95, provost, 1995-98, prof. engring. sys. divsn., 1999—, Inst. prof., 1999—. Vis. prof. Harvard Grad. Sch. Bus. Adminstrn., 1989-90; vis. adj. sr. rsch. scientist Columbia U. FU Found. Sch. Engring. and Applied Sci., 1998. Editor: The Computer Age: A Twenty Year View, 1979; co-originator Knowledge Based System Concept; developer MACSYMA system for formula manipulation. Recipient Achievement award MIT Lab. for Computer Sci., 1985. Fellow IEEE, AAAS, Am. Acad. Arts and Scis.; mem. NAE, Assn. for Computing Machinery, Am. Soc. Engring. Edn. (Centennial cert.). Office: MIT Computer Sci Artificial Intelligence Lab 32-249 Cambridge MA 02139 E-mail: moses@mit.edu.

MOSES, KAREN, editor; B Journalism, U. N.Mex. Gen. assignment reporter Pioneer Press, Chgo., 1977; reporter, then regional editor Gallup Ind.; asst. city editor Albuquerque Jour., city editor, asst. mng. editor, 1994—2001, mng. editor, 2001—. Office: Albuquerque Jour 7777 Jefferson NE PO Drawer J Albuquerque NM 87103*

MOSES, LINCOLN E. statistician, educator; b. Kansas City, Mo., Dec. 21, 1921; s. Edward Walter and Virginia (Holmes) Moses; m. Jean Runnels, Dec. 26, 1942; children: Katherine, James O'D., William C., Margaret, Elizabeth; m. Mary Louise Coale, 1968. AB, Stanford, 1941, PhD, 1950. Asst. prof. edn. Columbia Tchrs. Coll., 1950—52; faculty Stanford U., 1952—, prof. stats., 1959—, exec. head dept., 1964—68; assoc. dean Stanford U. (Sch. Humanities and Scis.), 1965—68, 1985—86, dean grad. studies, 1969—75; faculty Stanford U. (Med. Sch.), 1952—; adminstr. Energy Info. Adminstrn., Dept. of Energy, 1978—80. L.L. Thurstone disting. fellow U. N.C., 1968—69; com. mem., intermittently Am. Friends Svc. Com., 1954—, chmn. No. Calif. chpt., 1972—76, 1984—88. Bd. dirs. Am. Found. for AIDS Rsch., 1992—97. Fellow Guggenheim, 1960—61, Ctr. for Advanced Study in Behavioral Scis., 1975. Fellow: Inst. Math. Stats. (coun. 1969—72), Am. Acad. Arts and Scis.; mem.: Internat. Statis. Inst., Biometric Soc. (pres. Western N.Am. region 1969), Am. Statis .Assn. (coun. 1966—67), Inst. Medicine of NAS. Office: Stanford U Med Ctr Divsn Biostats Stanford CA 94305

MOSES, MARK S. state representative; b. Medford, Mass., May 25, 1948; m. Kyong Soon; children: Michelle, John(dec.), James, Michael, Matthew, Madalyn, Mitchell. BS in Physics, U. Tex., 1973. Vice chair Makakilo/Kapole/Honokai Hale Neighborhood Bd. #34, 1995—97; mem., minority whip Hawaii Ho. of Reps. Mem. Ctrl. Oahu Regional Pk. Adv. Com.; cmty. rep. City and County of Honolulu Planning Adv. Group; pres. Hawaii Commn. of Performance Stds. Maj. USMC, 1966—91. Mem.: DAV, ALA, Am. Legion. Republican. Office: State Capitol Rm 310 415 S Beretania St Honolulu HI 96813 E-mail: repmoses@capitol.hawaii.gov.

MOSES, ORAL, music educator; s. Otis Moses and Elveta Lewis-Moses. D, U. Mich., 1984. Opera singer Mich. Opera Theater, Detroit, 1983—84; prof. voice Kennesaw State U., Ga., 1984—. Vis. prof. U. Cape Coast, Ghana, 2003; part-time recitalist, 1984—. Performer: (albums) Deep River: Art Songs and Spirituals, 1995, Amen-African American Composers of 20th Century, 2001, Spirituals in Old Zion, 2001, Third Day-A Worship Album, 2001. Artistic dir. Cobb County Choir, Marietta, Ga., 1988—. With U.S. Army, 1966—69. Recipient Achievement award, NAACP, 1990; grantee, Harvard U., 1986, Boston Coll., 1992; Salzburg fellow, Salzburg Sem., Austria, 1976, Thomas J. Watson fellow, Fisk U., Munich, Germany, 1975—76. Mem.: Soc. Am. Music, Nat. Assn. Tchrs. Singing. Avocations: gardening, music. Office: Kennesaw State U Dept Music 100 Chastain Rd Kennesaw GA 30144

MOSES, RAPHAEL JACOB, lawyer; b. Girard, Ala., Nov. 6, 1913; s. William Moultrie and Anna (Green) M.; m. Marian Eva Beck, Aug. 22, 1938 (dec. Feb. 1976); 1 child, Marcia (Mrs. William S. Johnson); m. Fletcher Lee Westgaard, Jan. 20, 1979. AB, U. Colo., 1935, JD, 1937. Bar: Colo. 1938. Practiced in, Alamosa, 1938-62, Boulder, 1962—; pres. Moses, Wittemyer, Harrison & Woodruff (P.C.), from 1970, now of counsel. Spl. asst. atty. gen. Rio Grande Compact, 1957-58; mem. Colo. Water Conservation Bd., 1952-58, chmn., counsel, 1958-76, cons., 1976-77; research asso., faculty law U. Colo., 1962-66, vis. lectr., 1966-76, resident counsel, 1964-66, regent, 1973-74; grad. faculty Colo. State U., 1963-67; mem. Western States Water Council, 1965-77, chmn., 1966-70. Trustee Rocky Mountain Mineral Law Inst., 1964-66; bd. dirs. U. Colo. Found., 1977-97, chmn., 1977-79, mem. chancellor's adv. coun., 1981-97; bd. dirs. Colo. Open Lands, 1983-91, U. Colo. Improvement Corp., 1980-90, Colo. Endowment for Humanities, 1986-89; mem. adv. bd. Natural Resources Ctr., U. Colo. Sch. Law, 1983-92, chmn., 1986-88; mem. Sr. Citizens Adv. Bd., Boulder, Colo., 2003—. Served to lt. (s.g.) USNR, 1942-45. Decorated Purple Heart; recipient William E. Knous award U. Colo. Sch. Law, 1971, Norlin award U. Colo., 1972; Raphael J. Moses Disting. Natural Resources professorship established U. Colo., 1994. Fellow Am. Bar Found. (life), Colo. Bar Found. (trustee 1977-90), Am. Coll. Trial Lawyers; mem. ABA (chmn. water rights com. sect. natural resources 1959-60), Colo. Bar Assn. (pres. 1959-60, Award of Merit 1972), San Luis Valley Bar Assn. (pres. 1942), Am. Counsel Assn., Order of Coif (hon.) Presbyterian (elder). Clubs: Boulder Country; Garden of the Gods (Colorado Springs). Home: 4913 Clubhouse Cir Boulder CO 80301-3715 E-mail: RayMoise@aol.com.

MOSES, WINFIELD CARROLL, JR., state legislator, construction company executive; b. Ft. Wayne, Ind., Feb. 20, 1943; s. Winfield C. and Helen A. (O'Neil) M.; children: Elizabeth, Christopher. AB in Econs, Ind. U., 1964, MBA in Fin, 1966. Apt. builder, Ft. Wayne, 1966—; mem. Ft. Wayne City Coun., 1972-79; mayor City of Ft. Wayne, 1980-87; mem. Ind. Ho. of Reps., Indpls., 1992—. Founding pres. Washington House, 1973-76, Citizen Energy Coalition, 1974-75; active Art Mus.; mem. Ind. Urban Enterprise Zone Bd., Ind. Bus. Modernization Bd. Mem. C. of C., Rotary. Democrat. Unitarian Universalist. Office: 6000 N Oak Blvd Fort Wayne IN 46818-2438

MOSETTIG, MICHAEL DAVID, television producer, writer; b. Washington, July 21, 1942; s. Erich and Ann (Nelson) M.; m. Anne L. Groer. Student, Ind. U., 1960-61; BA in Polit. Sci., George Washington U., 1964; MA in European History, Georgetown U., 1968. Reporter Leslie E. Carpenter News Bur., Washington, 1961-65, Newhouse Nat. News Svc., Washington, 1965-69, UPI, London and Brussels, 1969-70; editor, reporter Nat. Jour., Washington, 1970-71; producer NBC News, Washington and N.Y.C., 1971-79; assoc. Grad. Sch. Journalism Columbia U., N.Y.C., 1979-83; prodr. MacNeil/Lehrer News Hour, 1983-85, sr. prodr. fgn. affairs and def., 1985-95, News Hour with Jim Lehrer, 1995—. Mem. Internat. Inst. for Strategic Studies, London, Coun. Fgn. Rels., N.Y. Author: DeGaulle and His Anglo-Saxon Allies, 1968, (with Ronald Müller) Revitalizing America, 1980. With USCGR, 1966-68, USNR, 1968-78. Herman Lowe Meml. scholar Washington chpt. Sigma Delta Chi; Joan Barone award Radio-TV Corrs. Assn., Nat. Emmy award, 1997. Mem. Cosmos Club. Home: 2500 Q St NW # 640 Washington DC 20007

MOSHER, CHARLES D. mayor, real estate manager; b. Portland, Oreg., Dec. 14, 1941; s. Harold Clarke and Leona (Hostetler) M.; m. Betty C. Mosher, June 12, 1965; ch ildren: Jeffrey, Jason, Janelle. BS, Oreg. State U., 1965; MBA, Portland State U., 1972. Audit mgr. U.S. Gen. Acctg. Office, Seattle, 1965-93; prin. EXECURENT, Bellevue, Wash., 1976—; mem. City Coun., City of Bellevue, 1996—, dep. mayor, 1998-99, mayor, 2000—02. Exec. sec. Pacific N.W. Intergovtl. Audit Forum, Seattle, 1977—79; bd dirs Sound Transit, Wash. State Mcpl. Rsch. Coun. Chmn. Cascade Water Alliance, Bellevue, 1999-2000; mem. energy, environment and natural resources steering com. Nat. League of Cities, Washington, 1999—; chair Bellevue Planning Commn., 1994-95, Wash. State citizen's adv. com. on pipeline safety, Olympia, 2000—; pres. Whispering Heights and Collingwood Cmty. Assn., 1991-92; chmn. Newport Covenant Ch., 1986-87; exec. com. Rep. Mayors and Local Govt. Ofcls., 2000-01, sec.-treas., 2001—. U.S. Nat. Bank scholar, Portland, 1959-65. Fellow Am. Water Resources Assn. (nat. pres. 1993); mem. Assn. Wash. Cities (dist. 7 dir. 1997-2001, sec. 2000-01, v.p. 2001-2002, pres. 2002—), Advance Bellevue (bd. dirs. 1998-2001, Best of Bellevue award 1998). Republican. Avocations: dahlias, gardening, skiing, running, geneology. Home: 4730 154th Pl SE Bellevue WA 98006 Office: City of Bellevue PO Box 90012 11511 Main St Bellevue WA 98009-9012 E-mail: chuck@mosher.net.

MOSHER, DONALD ALLEN, artist; b. Malden, Mass., Oct. 11, 1945; s. Allen M. and Florence C. (Post) M.; m. Christine Ann Crivello, Feb. 15, 1969; 1 child, Heather Ann. Cert., Vesper George Sch. Art, Boston. Comml. artist Stop & Shop Corp., Boston, 1971-75, Rich's Dept. Store, Salem, Mass., 1975-81; profl. artist Rockport, Mass., 1972—. Exhibited Am. Watercolor Soc. and NAD, Butler Inst., Chgo., Cleve. Meml. Gallery, SUNY, Mystic Seaport Mus., New Bedford Whaling Mus., Mint Mus. Fine Arts, Tuskegee Inst., numerous others. Recipient more than 150 awards from various art assns. Mem. Rockport Art Assn. (v.p. 1988-92, curator 1988-94), New Eng. Watercolor Soc., Guild of Boston Artists, Copley Soc., Salmagundi Club, Am. Artists Profl. League, North Shore Art Assn., Whiskey Painters Am., Am. Soc. Marine Artists, Acad. Artists Assn., Hudson Valley Arts Assn. Home: 13 Main St Rockport MA 01966-1512

MOSHER, ROGER L. lawyer; Ptnr. Mosher, Pooley, Sullivan & Hendren, Palo Alto, Calif. Office: Mosher Pooley Sullivan & Hendren 525 University Ave Ste 1410 Palo Alto CA 94301-1910

MOSHER, SALLY EKENBERG, lawyer, musician; b. N.Y.C., July 26, 1934; d. Leslie Joseph and Frances Josephine (McArdle) Ekenberg; m. James Kimberly Mosher, Aug. 13, 1960 (dec. Aug. 1982). MusB, Manhattanville Coll., 1956; postgrad., Hofstra U., 1958-60, U. So. Calif., 1971-73, JD, 1981. Bar: Calif., 1982. Musician, pianist, tchr., 1957-74; music critic Pasadena Star-News, 1967-72; mgr. Contrasts Concerts, Pasadena Art Mus., 1971-72; rep. Occidental Life Ins. Co., Pasadena, 1975-78; v.p. James K. Mosher Co., Pasadena, 1961-82, pres., 1982—, Oakhill Enterprises, Pasadena, 1984—; assoc. White-Howell, Inc., Pasadena, 1984-94; real estate broker, 1984-96. Harpsichordist, lectr., composer, 1994—; pub. Silver Wheels Pub., ASCAP. Musician (CD recs.) William Byrd: Songs, Dances, Battles, Games, 1995, From Now On: New Directions For Harpsichord, 1998; author: People and Their Contexts: A Chronology of the 16th Century World; contbr. articles to various publs. Bd. dirs. Jr. League Pasadena, 1966-67, Encounters Concerts, Pasadena, 1966-72, U. So. Calif. Friends of Music, L.A., 1973-76, Calif. Music Theatre, 1988-90, Pasadena Hist. Soc., 1989-91, I Cantori, 1989-91; bd. dirs. Pasadena Arts Coun., 1986-92, pres., 1989-92, chair adv. bd., 1992-93; v.p., bd. dirs. Pasadena Chamber Orch., 1986-88, pres., 1987-88; mem. Calif. 200 Coun. for Bicentennial of U.S. Constn., 1987-90; mem. Endowment Adv. Commn., Pasadena, 1988-90; bd. dirs. Foothill Area Cmty. Svcs., 1990-95, treas., 1991, vice chair, 1992-94, chair, 1994-95; sec., bd. dirs. Piano Spheres, 2001-02, pres., 2002—. Manhattanville Coll. hon. scholar, 1952-56. Mem. ABA, Calif. Bar Assn., Assocs. of Calif. Inst. Tech., Athenaeum, Kappa Gamma Pi, Mu Phi Epsilon, Phi Alpha Delta. Home: 1260 Rancheros Rd Pasadena CA 91103-2759 Fax: 626-795-3146. E-mail: sally@cyberverse.com.

MOSHER, SUE A. computer consultant; b. Havre, Mont., Aug. 21, 1953; d. Richard B. and Malinda Grace (Simpson) Billingsley; m. Robert Allen Mosher, June 21, 1986; 1 child, Ann Maura. BA in Sociology, Coll. of William & Mary, Williamsburg, Va., 1974. Asst. music dir. Sta. WOWI-FM, Norfolk, Va., 1974-75; news dir. Sta. WNOR-AM/FM, Norfolk, Va., 1976-77; reporter, editor, writer Sta. WSOC-AM/FM, Charlotte, N.C., 1977-79; editor, writer AP Broadcast Svcs., N.Y.C., 1979-82, asst. broadcast editor, 1982-83, gen. broadcast editor N.Y.C. and Washington, 1983-85, asst. dir. adminstrn. Washington, 1985-87, asst. dir. tech. devel., 1989-94; prin. Slipstick Sys., Arlington, Va., 1994—2001; pres. Turtleflock, LLC, 2001—. Author: AP NewsDesk User's Manual, 1991, Microsoft Exchange User's Handbook, 1997, Microsoft Outlook E-mail and Fax Guide, 1998, Teach Yourself Microsoft Outlook 2000 Programming in 24 Hours, 1999, Microsoft Outlook 2000 E-mail and Fax Guide, 2000, Microsoft Outlook Programming, 2002; outlook editor Windows NT Mag. Exch. Adminstr., 1998-; contbg. editor: Inside Windows: Networking Edition, 1994; contbr.: Spl. Edition Using Windows NT Workstation 3.51, 1996, Spl. Edition Using Windows NT Workstation 4.0, 1996, Microsoft Office Expert Solutions, 1996. Trustee, Universalist Nat. Meml. Ch., Washington, 1990-91, 2001-. Mem. Soc. Tech. Comm.

MOSHFEGH, MOUSSA, surgeon; b. Tehran, Iran, Jan. 17, 1947; MD, U. Tehran, 1972. Diplomate Am. Bd. Surgery. Resident in gen. surgery Sinai Med. Ctr., Tehran, Iran, 1974-78; intern Kern Med. Ctr., Bakersfield, Calif., 1980-81, resident in gen. surgery, 1981-85; pvt. practice LA. Mem. staff Cedars-Sinai Med. Ctr., L.A., Midway Hosp., L.A., Greater El Monte Hosp., Whittier Med. Ctr., Brotman Med. Ctr., L.A., Suburban Hosp., L.A.; chmn. dept. surgery Greater El Monte Cmty. Hosp., 1993—94, 1997—98, chmn. emergency svcs., 1995—96, chmn. credential com., 1998—2002, chief of staff, 2003—. Fellow ACS; mem. AMA, Am. Soc. Gen. Surgeons, Internat. Coll. Surgeons. Office: 6221 Wilshire Blvd Ste 616 Los Angeles CA 90048-5201 Office Phone: 323-933-3810. Personal E-mail: drmmoshfegh@sbcglobal.net.

MOSHKIN, NICKOLAY V. financial consultant, litigation consultant; s. Venedict F. Moshkin and Olga H. Moshkina; m. Marianna A. Moshkina, Jan. 21, 1994; 1 child, Artem N. MS in applied math. and physics(hon.), Moscow Inst. of Physics and Tech., Russia, 1992; PhD in econ., Yale U., 2000. Assoc. Cornerstone Rsch., New York, NY, 2001—. Office: Cornerstone Rsch 599 Lexington Ave New York NY 10022 E-mail: nmoshkin@cornerstone.com.

MOSHMAN, JACK, statistical consultant; b. Richmond Hill, N.Y., Aug. 12, 1924; s. Morris and Sadye (Posner) M.; m. Annette Gordon, Aug. 10, 1947; children: Gordon, Marc, Sherri, Ira. BA, NYU, 1946; MA, Columbia U., 1947; PhD, U. Tenn., 1953. Instr. Queens Coll., Flushing, N.Y., 1946-47, U. Tenn., Knoxville, 1947-53; statistician AEC, Oak Ridge, Tenn., 1948-50; sr. statistician Oak Ridge (Tenn.) Nat. Labs., 1950-54; mem. tech. staff Bell Tel. Labs., Murray Hill, N.J., 1954-57; v.p. C-E-I-R Inc., Washington, 1957-66; mng. dir. EBS Mgmt. Cons., Washington, 1966-68; sr. v.p. Leasco Systems & Rsch., Bethesda, Md., 1968-69; pres. Moshman Assocs. Inc., Bethesda, Md., 1970—. Adj. prof. Rutgers U., 1963-66; professorial lectr. George Washington U., 1959-62; chmn. Inst. for Safety Analysis, Rockville, Md., 1975-89, mem. office of mgmt. and budget adv. com. on statistical policy. Editor: Faith, Hope & Parity, 1967; author Ency. sect. Computers & Politics, 1985, 90, 93; contbr. articles to profl. jours. Trustee Babbage Found., St. Paul, 1983-87; pres. Moshman Charitable Found., Bethesda, 1996—; v.p. Eleanor & George Kokiko Sr. Found., Bethesda, 1997—. With U.S. Army, 1943-46, ETO. Fellow Am. Statis. Assn. (coun. 1956, 58); mem. Am. Fedn. Info. Processing Soc. Am. (bd. dirs., pres. 1986-87), Assn. for Computing Machinery (sec. 1956-64, v.p 1965), Inst. for Math. Stats., Inst. for Mgmt. Scis., Ops. Rsch. Soc. Am., Biometrics Soc. Avocation: psephology. Office: Moshman Assocs Inc 4340 East West Hwy Bethesda MD 20814-4411 Office Phone: 301-229-3000. Personal E-mail: jmoshman@aol.com.

MOSICH, ANELIS NICK, accountant, writer, educator, consultant; b. Croatia, Aug. 30, 1928; came to U.S., 1939, naturalized, 1951; s. Dinko and Josephine (Ursich) M.; m. Dorothy V. Rasich, June 15, 1958; children: Lori, Lisa, Jeffrey. BS, UCLA, 1951, MBA, 1953, PhD, 1963. CPA, Calif. Mem. faculty UCLA, 1955-63, Calif. State U., Northridge, 1963-64; examiner for Calif. State Bd. Accountancy, 1964-70; prof. acctg. U. So. Calif., LA, 1964-74, William C. Hallett prof. acctg., 1974-81, Ernst & Young prof., 1981-90, chmn. acctg. dept., 1970-74, 77-78, prof. emeritus, 1993. Cons. various bus. orgns., 1953—; expert witness; guest spkr. various profl. and bus. groups in Calif., Oreg., NY, Tex., Fla. and Hawaii, 1963—93; bd. dirs. Metro-Goldwyn-Mayer, Inc. Author: Intermediate Accounting, rev. 6th edit., 1989, Financial Accounting, 1970, 75, Accounting: A Basis for Business Decision, 1972, Modern Advanced Accounting, 4th edit., 1988, The CPA Examination: Text, Problems and Solutions, 1978; editor: Education column Calif. CPA Quar., 1965-66; contbg. editor: Education and Professional Training column Jour. Accountancy, 1971-77; contbr. numerous articles to jours. and acctg. Mem. productivity commn. City of L.A., 1993—94; bd. dirs. Bill Hannon Found. With U.S. Army, 1953—55. Fellow UCLA, 1963; recipient Dean's award Sch. Bus. Adminstrn., U. So. Calif., 1973, 78, Fred B. Olds Support Group award U. So. Calif., 1994, Disting. Svc. award for Leventhal Sch. Acctg., 1999. Office: U So Calif Leventhal Sch Acctg University Park Los Angeles CA 90089-1425

MOSICH, NICHOLAS JOSEPH, lawyer; b. San Pedro, Calif., July 2, 1951; s. Nicholas Andrew and Barbara Yvonne (Chutuk) M.; m. Susanne Melinda Wolf, Dec. 18, 1976 (dec. Jan. 1998); m. Jessica V. Schutte, Dec. 22, 2002; children: Nicholas Daniel, Andrea Michelle. BA, Santa Clara U., 1974; JD, Pepperdine U., 1977. Bar: Calif. 1977, U.S. Dist. Ct. (so. dist.) Calif. 1979, U.S. Dist. Ct. (ctrl. dist.) Calif. 1980. Assoc. Forgy & Inadomi, Santa Ana, Calif., 1978-83, ptnr., 1983-92, Mosich & Fotone, 2002. Bd. dirs. Young Men's Christian Assn., Santa Ana, 1980-87. Mem. ABA, Orange County Bar Assn., Assn. Trial Lawyers Am. Republican. Roman Catholic. Office: 2204 E 4th St Ste 100 Santa Ana CA 92705-4071

MOSIER, HARRY DAVID, JR., physician, educator; b. Topeka, May 22, 1925; s. Harry David and Josephine Morrow (Johnson) M.; m. Nadine Oclea Merilatt, Aug. 24, 1949; children: Carolyn Josephine Mosier Pohlmeyer, William David, Daniel Thomas, Christine Elizabeth Mosier Mahoney; m. Marjorie Knight Armstrong, Sept. 26, 1963. BS magna cum laude, U. Notre Dame, 1948; MD, Johns Hopkins U., 1952. Diplomate Am. Bd. Pediatrics, Am. Bd. Pediatric Endocrinology. Intern Johns Hopkins Hosp., Balt., 1952-53; resident in pediat. Los Angeles Children's Hosp., 1953-54, resident pediatric pathology, 1954-55; fellow pediatric endocrinology Johns Hopkins U., 1955-57; asst. prof. pediat. UCLA, 1957-61, assoc. prof., 1961-63; dir. rsch. Ill. State Pediatric Inst., Chgo., 1963-67; assoc. prof. U. Ill., 1963-67; prof. pediat. U. Calif.-Irvine, 1967—2002, emeritus, 2002—, head divsn. pediat. endocrinology, 1967-2000; staff Children's Hosp. Med. Ctr., Long Beach, Calif., 1970—, U. Calif. Irvine Med. Ctr., Orange, 1979—; dist. cons. Med. Bd. Calif., 1995—. Contbr. articles to med. jours. With AUS, 1943-46, col. U.S. Army Med. Corps, 1990-91, Persian Gulf War. USAR Med. Corps, 1952-62, 83-93 (ret.). Office: U Calif Dept Pediat 101 City Dr S Orange CA 92868-3201

MOSIER, JOHN, education educator, writer; b. Bentonville, Ark., July 9, 1944; s. Frank Byerley (Stepfather) and Helen Friedel; m. Sarah Elizabeth Spain, Dec. 7, 1985; m. Janice Elaine Meer, May 23, 1963 (div. Feb. 2, 1982); children: Therese Groves, Katherine Johnston, Elise Howard. BA, Tulane U., 1964, MA, 1966, PhD, 1968. Assoc. dean Loyola U., New Orleans, 1968—71, dep. provost, 1971—75, editor, New Orleans rev., 1984—91, prof. of English, 1986—, chair, dept. of English, 1988—92. Camera d'or jury Cannes Film Festival, 1978—82. Contbg. editor: Iste e Cinema, 1976—80, OAS, Am. Mag., 1980—90, New Orleans Art Review, 1990—, Film e Historia,

1991—93; author: The Myth of the Great War (nominated Pulitzer Prize in History, 2001), Institutional Research to 1970, The Blitzkrieg Myth, 2003; editor: Women and Men Together, 1976; contbr. chapters to books. Cash award, La. State Bd. of Regents Quality Support Fund, 1992. Office: Loyola University 6363 Saint Charles Ave New Orleans LA 70118 Office Phone: 504-865-2296. E-mail: jmosier@loyno.edu.

MOSK, RICHARD MITCHELL, judge; b. L.A., May 18, 1939; s. Stanley and Edna M.; m. Sandra Lee Budnitz, Mar. 21, 1964; children: Julie, Matthew. AB with great distinction, Stanford U., 1960; JD cum laude, Harvard U., 1963. Bar: Calif. 1964, U.S. Supreme Ct. 1970, U.S. Ct. Mil. Appeals 1970, U.S. Dist. Ct. (no., so., ea., and cen. dists.) Calif 1964, U.S. Ct. Appeals (9th dist.) 1964. Staff Pres.'s Commn. on Assassination Pres. Kennedy, 1964; rsch. clk. Calif. Supreme Ct., 1964-65; ptnr. Mitchell, Silberberg & Knupp, L.A., 1965-87; prin. Sanders, Barnet, Goldman, Simons & Mosk, PC, L.A., 1987-2000; justice Calif. Ct. Appeal, 2nd Dist., 2001—. Spl. dep. Fed. Pub. Defender, L.A., 1975—76; instr. U. So. Calif. Law Sch., 1978; judge Iran-U.S. Claims Tribunal, 1981—84, 1997—2001, substitute arbitrator, 1984—97; mem. L.A. County Jud. Procedures Commn., 1973—82, chmn., 1978; co-chmn. Motion Picture Assn. Classification and Rating Adminstrn., 1994—2000; mem. panel Ct. Arbitration for Sport-Geneva, 1998—2001. Contbr. articles to profl. jours. Mem. L.A. City-County Inquiry on Brush Fires, 1970; bd. dirs. Calif. Mus. Sci. and Industry, 1979-82, Vista Del Mar Child Ctr., 1979-82; trustee L.A. County Law Libr., 1985-86; bd. govs. Town Hall Calif., 1986-91; mem. Christopher Commn. on L.A. Police Dept., 1991; mem. Stanford U. Athletic Bd., 1991-95. With USNR, 1964-75. Hon. Woodrow Wilson fellow, 1960; recipient Roscoe Pound prize, 1961. Mem.: ABA (coun. internat. law sect. 1986—90), Am. Law Inst., L.A. County Bar Assn., Beverly Hills Bar Assn., Internat. Bar Assn., Am. Bar Found., Phi Beta Kappa. Office: Ct Appeal 300 S Spring St Los Angeles CA 90013

MOSKAL, ANTHONY JOHN, former dean, professor, management and education consultant; b. South Amboy, N.J., May 31, 1946; s. Anthony Joseph and Jennie (Salamon) M.; m. Kathryn Jean Coakley, July 8, 1978; 1 child, Nicole Elizabeth. AB, Villanova (Pa.) U., 1968, MA, 1972; MEd, Ga. State U., 1974; PhD, Columbia Pacific U., San Rafael, Calif., 1987. Prin. instr. U.S. Army, Ft. Benning, Ga., 1969-71; research mgr. Blue Cross and Blue Shield, Columbus, Ga., 1972-74; sales rep. J.C. Penney Co., Parlin, N.J., 1974-76; dean of students Alliance Coll., Cambridge Springs, Pa., 1976-77; tchr. Sayreville (N.J.) pub. schs., 1977-79; county 4-H agt. Rutgers U., New Brunswick, 1979-86; pres. Eagle Assocs., South Amboy, N.J., 1985—. Adj. faculty Georgian Ct. Coll., Lakewood, NJ, 1987—, U.S. Army Command and Gen. Staff Coll., Ft. Leavenworth, Kans., 1989—2000, Nat. Def. U., Washington, 1991—2000; cons. dir. Union County Ednl. Svcs. Commn., 2000—; cons. in mgmt., leadership, edn., volunteerism, youth programs, career planning; spl. liaison to Mcpl. Bd. Edn., Sayreville, 1991—95, Sayreville, 2000—; area admissions rep. U.S. Mil. Acad., 1984—91. Contbr. articles to profl. jours. Mem. Boy Scouts Am.; counselor, mem. dist. com. Ctrl. N.J. Coun. Boy Scouts Am., 1982—; pres., bd. dirs. Vol. Action Ctr., Middlesex County, NJ, 1979—87; pres. Sayreville War Meml. H.S. Band Parents Assn., 1994—96; county committeeman Middlesex County, 1990—94, 2000—; dir. religious edn. Sacred Heart Parish, South Amboy, NJ, 1988—91. With U.S. Army, 1969—71, with U.S. Army, 1990—92, lt. col. USAR. Decorated Meritorious Svc. medal, Army Commendation medal (2), Mil. Outstanding Vol. Svc. medal; recipient Order of the Arrow award Boy Scouts Am., 1960, 20th Century award of Achievement, Nat. Assn. Chiefs of Police, Desert Shield/Desert Storm medal State of N.J., Disting. Svc. medal State of N.J.; United Way of Ctrl. Jersey grantee, 1984, others. Mem.: ASCD, Holy Name Soc., U.S. Army Officer Candidate Alumni Assn., Am. Fedn. Police (award of merit 1989, legion of honor 1990, J. Edgar Hoover Meml. medal 1991, St. Michael the Archangel award 1992, patriotism award 1993), Nat. Assn. Ext. 4-H Agts. (regional contact 1981—83, cert. appreciation 1983), Res. Officers Assn., Mil. Police Regtl. Assn., N.J. Assn. 4-H Agts. (pres. 1985—86, outstanding svc. citation 1981, 1987), Vietnam Vets. of Am. (life; rec. sec., honor guard), Nat. Infantry Assn. (life), Nat. Eagle Scout Assn., Am. Legion, K. of C. (3d degree officer, dir. coun. activities, vol. coord. fife and drums corps, degree team co-capt., 4th degree officer, color corps comdr., dist. degree team, diocesan degree team, Family of Mo., 4th degree Family of Yr., Dist. Color Corps Man of Yr., Assembly Color Corps Man of Yr., Knight of Mo. (3), 3d degree Family of Yr.), Kiwanis, Pi Gamma Mu, Epsilon Sigma Phi, Alpha Phi Omega. Republican. Roman Catholic. Avocations: reading, music, recreational camping, travel, woodworking. Office: Eagle Assocs 166 Luke St South Amboy NJ 08879-2231 Office Phone: 908-317-8634. Personal E-mail: ajmoskal@verizon.net.

MOSKIN, JOHN ROBERT, historian, editor, writer; b. N.Y.C., May 9, 1923; s. Morris and Irma (Rosenfeld) M.; m. Doris Marianne Bloch, Oct. 7, 1948 (div. 1978); children: Mark Douglas, David Scott, Nancy Irma; m. Lynn Carole Goldberg, Apr. 10, 1986. Grad., Horace Mann Sch., 1940; BS, Harvard U., 1944; MA, Columbia U., 1947. Reporter Boston Post, 1941-42, Newark News, 1947-48; asst. to gen. mgr. N.Y. Star, 1948-49; editor Westport (Conn.) Town Crier, 1949; med. editor Look mag., N.Y.C., 1950-51, articles editor, 1951-53, sr. editor, 1956-66, fgn. editor, 1966-71; mng. editor Woman's Home Companion, 1953-56; sr. editor Collier's, 1956; editor at large Saturday Rev., 1972-75; sr. editor World Press Rev., 1976-87, contbg. editor, 1987-93; editl. dir. Aspen Inst., 1977-83. Editl. dir. Commonwealth Fund, 1984-87, sr. editl. advisor, 1987-93. Author: (with others) The Decline of the American Male, 1958, Morality in America, 1966, Turncoat, 1968, The U.S. Marine Corps Story, 1977, 82, 87, 92, Among Lions, 1982, (with Julia Vitullo-Martin) The Executive's Book of Quotations, 1994, Mr. Truman's War, 1996, 2002; editor: The Marines, 1998; mem. editl. adv. com. Dimensions mag, 1970-71, Present Tense, 1973-90. Trustee Scarsdale Adult Sch., 1965—72, chmn., 1969—70; mem. comm. screening com. Coun. Internat. Exch. Scholars, 1974—77, Pres.'s Coun. Heritage Coll., 1995—; bd. dirs. SIECUS, 1972—80, Jerusalem Found., 1977—2003, Marine Corps Hist. Found., 1979—82, 1989—95, Faculty for Continuing Med. Edn., 1983—86, Authors Guild Found., 2000—, Lotos Club Found., 2000—; mem. Dana Reed Prize com. Harvard U., 1947—2000, mem. com. Class of 1944, 1943—. Served with AUS, 1943—46. Recipient Benjamin Franklin Gold medal for pub. svc. Woman's Home Companion, 1955, Page One award Newspaper Guild N.Y., 1965, Sidney Hillman Found. award, 1965, National Headliners award, 1967, Overseas Press Club award, 1969, citation for excellence, 1971, Disting. Svc. award Marine Corps Combat Corrs. Assn., 1978, 99, Nat. Jewish Book award, 1983, Disting. Svc. award Marine Corps Hist. Found., 1996, Gen. O.P. Smith award Marine Corps Heritage Found., 1999. Mem.: PEN, Nat. Press Club (Washington), Fgn. Editors Group (chmn. 1970—71), Am. Hist. Assn., Soc. Mil. History, Authors Guild, Lotos Club (bd. dirs. 1988—90, 1994—2002, pres. 1991—94), Harvard Club (N.Y.C.), The Century Assn., Overseas Press Club (gov. 1975—79), Sigma Delta Chi (nat. freedom of info. com. 1964, 1971). Home: 945 5th Ave New York NY 10021-2655 also: 157 Jerusalem Rd Tyringham MA 01264 E-mail: jrmedit@att.net.

MOSKIN, MORTON, lawyer, director; b. N.Y.C., Mar. 28, 1927; s. Barnett and Sonia (Burr) M.; m. Rita Lee Goldberg, June 15, 1952; children: Tina, Ilene, Jonathan. BA, Pa. State Coll., 1947; LLB, Cornell U., 1950. Assoc. White & Case, N.Y.C., 1950—61, ptnr., 1962—94, cons., 1995—. Chmn. exec. com. Mallinckrodt, Inc. (formerly IMCERA, previously Internat. Minerals & Chem. Corp.), St. Louis, 1988-91, chmn. corp. governance com., 1993-97; dir. Crum & Forster, 1973-82, sec. BT Mortgage Investors, Garden City, N.Y., 1975-82. Editor (with Field): New York and Delaware Business Entities: Choice, Formation, Operation, Financing, Acquisitions, 1997, Transactional Lawyer's Deskbook: Advising Business Entities, 2001; editor: Commercial Contracts: Strategies for Drafting and Negotiating, 2002. Bd. dirs. Fedn. Employment and Guidance Svcs.; bd. dirs., pres. Henry M. Blackmer Found., N.Y.C.; bd. dirs. Achievement Found., Stamford, Conn., pres., 1988-94; bd. dirs. Jewish Cmty. Svcs. L.I., 1974-93, pres., 1984-87. Fellow Am. Bar Found.; mem. ABA, N.Y. State Bar Assn., N.Y. County Lawyers Assn. (dir. 1981-86, 99-2002), Norfolk (Conn.) Country Club, Cornell Club N.Y. Home: 1160 Park Ave Apt 15B New York NY 10128-1212 Office: White & Case 1155 Ave of Americas New York NY 10036-2711 E-mail: mmoskin@whitecase.com.

MOSKOS, CHARLES C. sociology educator; b. Chgo., May 20, 1934; s. Charles and Rita (Shukas) M.; m. Ilca Hohn, July 3, 1966; children— Andrew, Peter. BA cum laude, Princeton, 1956; MA, UCLA, 1961, PhD, 1963; LHD (hon.), Norwich U., 1992, Towson U., 2002. Asst. prof. U. Mich., Ann Arbor, 1964-66; assoc. prof. sociology Northwestern U., Evanston, Ill., 1966-70, prof., 1970—. Fellow Progressive Policy Inst., 1992—; mem. Presdl. Commn. on Women in the Mil., 1992. Author: The Sociology of Political Independence, 1967, The American Enlisted Man, 1970, Public Opinion and the Military Establishment, 1971, Peace Soldiers, 1976, Fuerzas Armadas y Societdad, 1984, The Military--More Than Just A Job?, 1988, A Call to Civic Service, 1988, Greek Americans, 1989, Soldiers and Sociology, 1989, New Directions in Greek American Studies, 1991, The New Conscientious Objection, 1993, All That We Can Be, 1996, Reporting War When There Is No War, 1996, The Media and the Military, 2000, The Postmodern Military, 2000. Chmn. Theodore Saloutos Meml. Fund; mem. Archdiocesean Commn. Third Millenium, 1982-88; mem adv. bd. Vets. for Am., 1997—; mem. Congl. Commn. on Mil. Tng. and Gender-Related Issues, 1998-99, Nat. Security Study Group, 1998-2001. Served with AUS, 1956-58. Decorated D.S.M., Fondation pour les Etudes de Def. Nat. (France), S.M.K. (The Netherlands); named to Marshall rsch. chair ARI, 1987-88, 95-96; Ford. Found. faculty fellow, 1969-70; fellow Wilson Ctr., 1980-81, guest scholar, 1991; fellow Rockefeller Found. Humanities, 1983-84, Guggenheim fellow, 1992-93, fellow Annenberg Washington Program, 1995; grantee 20th Century Fund, 1983-87, 92-94, Ford Found., 1989-90; recipient Nat. Educator Leadership award Todd Found., 1997, Book award Washington Monthly, 1997, Honored Patriot award Selective Svc. Sys., 1998; Pub. Policy fellow Wilson Ctr., 2002; Eisenhower chair Royal Mil. Acad. Netherlands, 2002. Mem. Am. Sociol. Assn., Internat. Sociol. Assn. (pres. rsch. com. on armed forces and conflict resolution 1982-86), Am. Polit. Sci. Assn., Inter-Univ. Seminar on Armed Forces and Soc. (chmn. 1987-99), Am. Acad. Arts and Scis. Greek Orthodox. Home: 2440 Asbury Ave Evanston IL 60201-2307

MOSKOS, HARRY, writer, former newspaper editor; b. Chgo., Oct. 8, 1936; m. Victoria Marie Poulos; 3 children. BA, U. N.Mex., Albuquerque, 1958. With Albuquerque Tribune, 1953-59; editor Grants (N.Mex.) Daily Beacon, 1959-60; newsman AP, Albuquerque, 1960, state editor, 1961-63, chief of bur. Honolulu, 1963-69; city editor Albuquerque Tribune, 1969-73, mng. editor, 1973—80; editor El Paso Herald-Post, 1980—84, Knoxville News-Sentinel, 1984—2001; columnist, letters editor Albuquerque Jour., 2001—. Office: 7777 Jefferson St NE Albuquerque NM 87109 E-mail: hmoskos@abqjournal.com.

MOSKOVITS, MARTIN, chemist, educator, dean; BSc, U. Toronto, Can., 1965, PhD, 1971. Founder OHM Distbrs. and Mfrs., Ltd., 1966—70; rschr. Alcan R&D/Alcan Internat., 1970—75; prof. U. Toronto, 1982—99, chmn. chemistry, 1993—99; prof. phys. chemistry U. Calif., Santa Barbara, 2000, dean sci., 2000—. Mem. adv. bd. NRC Steacie Inst. Molecular Scis.; bd. dirs. Can. Overseas Internat. Coll., Hong Kong, Sansum Med. Rsch. Inst., 2003. Editor, co-author: Science and Society: The John C. Polanyi Nobel Laureates Lectures; editor: Nanostructured Materials: Clusters, Composites, and Thin Films, Cryochemistry, Metal Clusters, Chemistry and Physics of Matrix Isolated Species; mem. Jour. Chem. Physics. Recipient Gerhard Hertzberg award, Spectroscopy Soc. of Can., 1993, 400th Anniversary Johannes Marcus Marci medal, Czech Spectroscopy Soc., 1995, CSC EWR Steacie award, 1999; Killam fellow, 1989—91, Guggenheim fellow, 1986—87. Fellow: Royal Soc. Can. (Surface and Colloid Sci. award 1993). Achievements include patents for heterogeneous catalyst and process for its manufacture 590kb; process for manufacture of quantum dot and quantum wire semiconductors; nanoelectric devices with Martin Moskovits. Office: U Calif Santa Barbara Divsn Sci Cheadle Hall Santa Barbara CA 93106-2080 Business E-Mail: mlpsdean@ltsc.ucsb.edu.

MOSKOVITZ, JIM, radio, television and film producer, writer; b. L.A., Aug. 14, 1958; s. Mayer and Charlotte (Creamer) M.; m. Joyce Ferro, Nov. 25, 1989. BA in Pol. Sci., Stanford U., 1980. Pres. JMJ Films, Inc., N.Y.C., 1991—, Marathon Sports Group, Inc., 1998—. Writer/prodr. Pat Summerall's Sports in Am., N.Y.C., 1990-97, Instant Replay with R. MacLean, Toronto, 1992-97, Talking Sports with Tim McCarver, 1998-2000, The Tim McCarver Show, 2000—. Author: Pat Summerall's Sports in America, 1997, The 12 Greatest Rounds of Boxing: The Untold Stories, Sports Illustrated, 2000; developer (motion picture) The Boys of Summer, 1999; writer, dir., prodr. (television special) Grand Slam!, 1989; writer, prodr. (TV show) Tim McCarver Show, 1998—, (Showtime) The 12 Greatest Rounds of Boxing: The Untold Stories, 2000 Recipient Sports Video of Yr. award Video Magazine, N.Y.C., 1989, Video Review, N.Y.C., 1990, silver medal Internat. Radio Awards, N.Y.C., 1996; named finalist Internat. Radio Awards, N.Y.C., 1994. Mem. Assn. Composers, Authors, Producers, Israel Policy Forum, Peace Now, Stanford Alumni Assn. Avocations: baseball, history, politics. Office: JMJ Films Inc 11 W 84th St Apt 4 New York NY 10024-4761 Fax: 212-724-7712.

MOSKOW, MICHAEL H. federal official; b. Paterson, N.J., Jan. 7, 1938; s. Jacob and Sylvia (Edelstein) M.; m. Constance Bain, Dec. 18, 1966; children: Robert Bain, Eliot Marc, Lisa Danielle. AB, Lafayette Coll., Easton, Pa., 1959; MA in Econs., U. Pa., 1962, PhD, 1965. Instr. econs. Lafayette Coll., 1964-65; asst. prof. mgmt. Drexel Inst. Tech., Phila., 1963-64, 65-67; assoc. prof. econs., dir. Bus. Econ. and Bus. Research, Temple U., Phila., 1967-69; sr. staff economist Council Econ. Advisers, Washington, 1969-70; exec. dir. Constrn. Industry Collective Bargaining Commn., 1970-71; dep. under sec. U.S. Dept. Labor, 1971-72, asst. sec. for policy, evaluation and research, 1972-73; asst. sec. for policy devel. and research HUD, 1973-75; dir. Council on Wage and Price Stability, 1975-76; under-sec. labor U.S. Dept. Labor, 1976-77; cons. Com. for Econ. Devel., 1977; dir. corp. devel. and planning Esmark, Inc., 1977-78, v.p. corp. devel. and planning, 1978-80; exec. v.p. Estronics, Inc. div. Esmark, Inc., 1980-82; pres. Velsicol Chem. Corp. div. N.W. Industries, Inc., Chgo., 1982-84; v.p. corp. devel. Dart & Kraft, Inc., Northbrook, Ill., 1985-86; v.p. strategy and bus. devel. Premark Internat. Inc. (spinoff from Dart & Kraft), Deerfield, 1986-90; amb. Washington, 1991-93; prof. strategy and internat mgmt. Northwestern U. Kellogg Grad. Sch. Mgmt., Evanston, Ill., 1993-94; pres. Fed. Reserve Bank Chgo., 1994—. Bd. dirs. Conrail, Inc., 1994. Author: Teachers and Unions, 1966, Labor Relations in the Performing Arts: An Introductory Survey, 1970; co-author: Collective Negotiations for Teachers, 1966, Collective Bargaining in Public Employment, 1970, Strategic Planning in Business and Government, 1978; co-editor: Readings on Collective Negotiations in Public Education, 1967, Employment Relations in Higher Education, 1969, Women and Work, 1987; contbr. articles to profl. jours. Bd. trustees U. Chgo. Hosp., 1980-90. 1st lt. AUS, 1959-60. Mem. Indsl. Rels. Rsch. Assn. (pres. 1987), Nat. Bur. Econ. Rsch. (bd. dirs., exec. com.), Comml. Club Chgo. (civic com.), Econ. Club Chgo. Home: 400 Sheridan Rd Winnetka IL 60093-2628 Office: Fed Reserve Bank Chgo 230 S La Salle St Chicago IL 60604-1496*

MOSKOWITZ, ARNOLD X. economist, strategist, educator; b. N.Y.C., Jan. 27, 1944; s. Morris and Millie (Kozichovsky) M.; m. Sandra Moskowitz; children: Nicole, Alex Michael Archangel. BS in Elec. Engring., CCNY, 1966; MS in Indsl. Mgmt., Poly. Inst. N.Y., 1970; MPhil, NYU, 1979, PhD in Econs. and Fin., 1985. Analyst Grumman Corp., N.Y.C., 1968-70; assoc. economist Dean Witter Reynolds, Inc., N.Y.C., 1970-74, first v.p., economist, 1975-82, sr. v.p., economist, 1983-89; sr. v.p., dir. investment strategy County NatWest U.S.A., N.Y.C., 1989-90; chmn. Moskowitz Capital Cons. Inc., N.Y.C., 1990—. Lectr. New Sch. Social Research, 1978—; adj. assoc. prof. fin. Pace U., N.Y.C., 1980-82; pres. Money Marketers NYU, 1988-89. Contbr. articles to profl. jours.; chpts. to books, including Security Selection and Active Portfolio Management; contbr. to Ency. of Economics, How to Beat Wall Street Mem. Am. Econ. Assn., Nat. Econ. Club, Nat. Assn. Bus. Economists, Atlantic Soc., Beta Gamma Sigma Jewish. Office: Moskowitz Capital Cons 200 E 94th St Apt 719 New York NY 10128-6027 *Our guidelines for success starts with our principles to provide the highest level of service to our customers and treat our employees as partners in the business. Our goal is to maintain the highest level of integrity in dealing with clients and workers in order to maximize our performances.*

MOSKOWITZ, HERBERT, management educator; b. Paterson, NJ, May 26, 1935; s. David and Ruth (Abrams) Moskowitz; m. Heather Mary Lesgnier, Feb. 25, 1968; children: Tobias, Rebecca, Jonas. BS in Mech. Engring., Newark Coll. Engring., 1956; MBA, U.S. Internat. U., 1964; PhD, UCLA, 1970. Rsch. engr. GE, 1956-60; systems design engr. Gen. Dynamics Convair, San Diego, 1960-65; asst. prof. Purdue U., West Lafayette, Ind., 1970-75, assoc. prof., 1975-79, prof., 1979-85, Disting. prof., 1985-87, James B. Henderson Disting. prof., 1987-91, Lewis B. Cullman Disting. prof. mfg. mgmt., 1991—, dir. Dauch Ctr. Mgmt. Mfg. Enterprises. Cons. AT&T, Inland Steel Co.; adv. panelist NSF, 1990—. Author: Management Science and Statistics Texts, 1975—90; contbr. articles to jours. in field. Bd. dirs. Sons of Abraham Synagogue, Lafayette; mem. Lafayette Klezmorem, 1973—. Capt. USAF, 1956—60. Recipient Disting. Doctoral Student award, UCLA Alumni Assn., 1969—70; Fulbright Rsch. scholar, 1985—86. Fellow: Decision Scis. Inst. (sec. 1985—87, v.p. 1978—80); mem.: Ops. Rsch. Soc. Am./Inst. Mgmt. Sci. (liaison officer 1977—, panelist, advisor NSF and Fulbright Scholar program 1993—), Pi Tau Sigma, Tau Beta Pi. Jewish. Avocations: jewish music, tennis. Home: 1430 N Salisbury St West Lafayette IN 47906-2420 Office: Purdue U Krannert Grad Sch Mgmt Dauch Ctr Mgmt Mfg Enterprises West Lafayette IN 47907-2056

MOSKOWITZ, JAY, health sciences administrator; b. N.Y.C., Jan. 9, 1943; s. Murray and Helene Moskowitz; m. Joanne Cathy Schindelheim, Dec. 27, 1970; children: Michael Bradley, Andrew Cory. BS, Queens Coll., 1964; postgrad., CUNY, 1965; PhD, Brown U., 1969. From research assoc. in pharmacology to dep. dir. NIH, 1969—93, dep. dir. for sci. policy & tech. transfer, prin. dep. dir., 1993; various positions Nat. Heart, Lung and Blood Inst., 1976-86, acting dir. Nat. Inst. on Deafness and Other Communication Disorders, 1988-90, dep. dir., 1993-95; sr. assoc. dean for rsch. devel., prof. pub. health scis. Wake Forest U. Sch. Medicine, Winston-Salem, NC, 1995—2001, sr. assoc. dean, 1997—2001; assoc. v.p. health sci. rsch. Pa. State U., 2002—, vice dean rsch. coll. medicine, 2002—, prof. medicine, 2002—. Contbr. articles to profl. jours. Served to lt. comdr. USPHS. Recipient Meritorious award William A. Jump Meml. Found., 1977, Dir.'s award NIH, 1978, Superior Svc. award USPHS, 1980, performance awards Sr. Exec. Svc., Presdl. Meritorious Exch. Rank award 1989, Disting. Svc. award HHS, 1991, Disting. Svc. award Nat. Inst. on Deafness and Other Comm. Disorders, 1994. Mem. AAAS, Soc. Exptl. Biology and Medicine, N.C. Inst. Medicine. Jewish. Home: 1760 Adeline Dr Mechanicsburg PA 17050 Office: Penn State College Medicine 500 University Hershey PA 00033 Office Phone: 717-531-7199. Business E-Mail: jmoskowitz@psu.edu.

MOSKOWITZ, JOEL STEVEN, lawyer; b. N.Y.C., Jan. 14, 1947; s. Jack I. and Myra (Shor) M.; m. Anna Boucher; children: David, Michael, Ellen. BA, UCLA, 1967, JD, 1970. Bar: Calif. 1971, U.S. Ct. Appeals (9th cir.) 1971, U.S. Ct. Appeals (D.C. cir.) 1975, U.S. Supreme Ct. 1975, U.S. Ct. Appeals (2d cir.) 1979. Dep. atty. gen. Calif. Dept. Justice, Sacramento, 1970-83; dep. dir. Calif. Dept. Health Svcs., Sacramento, 1983-85; of counsel Gibson, Dunn & Crutcher, L.A., 1985-88, ptnr., 1988-96, Moskowitz, Brestoff, Winston & Blinderman LLP, 1996—. Author: Environmental Liability in Real Property Transactions, 1995; contbr. articles to legal publs. Mem. Phi Beta Kappa. Office: 1880 Century Park E Ste 300 Los Angeles CA 90067-1631 Office Phone: 310-373-9790. Business E-Mail: jsm6@ix.netcom.com.

MOSKOWITZ, MICHAEL ARTHUR, neuroscientist, neurologist; b. N.Y.C., May 26, 1942; s. Irving Lawrence and Clara (Dranoff) M.; m. Mary Henderson, May 18, 1991; 1 child, Jenna Rachel. AB, Johns Hopkins U., 1964; MD, Tufts U., 1968; MSc (hon.), Harvard U., 1992. Diplomate Am. Bd. Psychiaty and Neurology, Am. Bd. Internal Medicine. Intern Yale U. Dept. Medicine, 1968-69, resident, 1969-71; resident in neurology Peter Bent Brigham Children Hosp., 1971-74; asst. prof. Med. Sch., Harvard U., Boston, 1975-79, assoc. prof., 1979-92; prof. divsn. health sci. and tech. Harvard-MIT, Boston, 1992—. Established investigator Am. Heart Assn., 1980-85; neurophysiologist and assoc. neurologist Mass. Gen. Hosp., Boston, 1981—; H.J. Barnett lectr. Canadian Heart Assn., Queens U., Kingston, Ont., 1993—, Witter lectr. U. Calif., San Francisco, 1994—, Barraquer-LaFora lectr. Spanish Neurol. Soc., Barcelona, Spain, 1994—, Decade of the Brain lectr. Am. Acad. Neurology, 1995, Briggs lecture dept. pharmacology U. Tex., San Antonio, 1995, Richardson lectr. Canadian Neurol. Assn., 1998, John Graham lectr. Am. Assn. Study Headache, Merck Sharpe Dohme Neurosci. lectr. Birmingham, Eng., 2000, Soriano lectr. Am. Neurol. Assn., 2003, Dr. Chaimn Mayman lectr. Beth Israel HOsp., Boston, 2003, others; chmn. sci. adv. bd. Max Plank Inst., Kön; program project dir. stroke and migraine NIH program projects, NIH rev. study sect. mem. 1982-85, 88-91, 97—; 2nd internat. hon. lectr. European Stroke Conf., 1997; cons. pharm. industry; chmn. sci. adv. bd. Max Planck Inst., U. of Ottawa, Can., Queen's Neurosc. Inst.; mem. sic. adv. bd. Queen's Med. Ctr., Honolulu, U. Ottawa. Editl. bd. Stroke, Acta Neurol. Scandinavica Cephalalgia, Jour. Cerebral Blood Flow & Metabolism, Cerebrovascular Disease; editor: Animal Models of Headache, 1996; basic sci. editor Stroke (AHA jour.); contbr. numerous articles to profl. jours; patentee in field. MIT postdoctoral fellow, 1974-76, Alfred Sloan Found. fellow, 1978-80; recipient Enrico Greppi award Italian Neurology Soc., 1986, 88, Tchr.-Investigator award Nat. Inst. Disease and Stroke, 1975-80, Zülch prize Max-Planck Soc./Inst., 1996, John Graham award AASH, 1998, Arnold Friedman award Am. Headache Soc., Top 200 Most Highly Cited in Neurosci., ISI; rsch. grantee Bristol-Myers Squibb, 1993—, MGH Interdepartmental Stroke Ctr. Mem. Am. Heart Assn. (nat. rsch. com. 1991-96, exec. com. stroke coun. 1991-96), Am. Neurol. Assn. (Soriano lectr., 2003, 04), Am. Heart and Stroke Assn. (co-chair program com. 2001—), Am. Acad. Neurology, Am. Pain Soc., Soc. Neurosci., Internat. Soc. for Cerebral Blood Flow and Metabolism (bd. dirs., pres. 2001—), Internat. Symposium Pharm. of Cerebral Ischemia, Can. Neurol. Soc. (hon.). Achievements include research in neuroscientific, neurology literature including stroke and migraine. Office: Mass Gen Hosp Charleston Navy Yard 149 13th St Charlestown MA 02129-2020

MOSKOWITZ, ROLAND WALLACE, internist; b. Shamokin, Pa., Nov. 3, 1929; MD, Temple U., 1953. Intern Temple U. Hosp., Phila., 1953-54; fellow in internal medicine Mayo Clinic, Rochester, Minn., 1954-55, 57-60; mem. staff U. Hosps. Cleve.; prof. medicine Case Western Res. U. Sch. Medicine, Cleve. Mem.: ACR, Alpha Omega Alpha. Office: Parkway Med Ctr 3609 Park East Dr STe 307N Beachwood OH 44122 E-mail: rolliemoskowitz@aol.com.

MOSKOWITZ, STANLEY ALAN, financial executive; b. N.Y.C., June 8, 1956; s. Sol and Kate (Mermelstein) M.; m. Eve Kronenberger, Sept. 20, 1981; children: Alana, Kate. BA, Queens Coll., 1978; MBA in Fin., St. John's U., 1980. Sr. credit analyst Mfrs. Hanover Leasing Corp., N.Y.C., 1979-81; gen. ptnr. Exec. Leasing Co., N.Y.C., 1981-83; pres. Execulease Corp., Elmont, N.Y., 1983-97; pres., CEO QuesTech Fin. LLC, Danbury, Conn., 1997—2003. Bd. dirs. UFA/Fedn. of Greenwich, Conn., 1995—, treas., 1997—2003. Named finalist, Ernst & Young Entrepreneur of Yr., 2001. Mem. Ea. Assn. Equipment Lessors (chmn. pub. rels. 1985-90, bd. dirs. 1988-92, Meretorious Svc. award 1986-87, chmn. ethics com. 1991-92), Omicron Delta Epsilon. Republican. Jewish. Avocations: reading, bicycling. Office: QuesTech Fin LLC 98 Mill Plain Rd Danbury CT 06811-6101 Office Phone: 203-778-1000 13. E-mail: sammy@qtfc.com.

MOSLER, BRUCE E. real estate company executive; Grad., Duke U., 1980. Exec. v.p. Cushman & Wakefield, Inc., N.Y.C., pres. U.S. ops., 2000—, also bd. dirs. Bd. mem. Modell Found., Urban Tech.; mem. bd. govs., exec. com. Real Estate Bd. N.Y.; mem. profl. svcs. adv. coun. Lower Manhattan Devel. Corp. Bd. mem. Intrepid Mus. Found. Named Property Svcs. Exec. of Yr., Comml. Property News, 2002; named one of 40 Under 40, Crain's N.Y. Bus., 1994; recipient Deal of the Yr. award, Real Estate Bd. N.Y., 1999, 2000. Office: Cushman & Wakefield Inc 51 W 52nd St New York NY 10019-6178*

MOSLEY, EVERETT L. federal agency administrator; m. Alice Mosley; 1 child, Damian. B Acctg., Crambling State U. From entry level to asst. inspector gen. audit USDA, Washington, 1969—80, regional inspector gen. audit, 1980—88; deputy asst. inspector gen. audit USDA/OIG, 1988—94; deputy inspector gen. USAID, 1994—2000, inspector gen., 2000—. Office: USAID RRB 1300 Pennsylvania Ave NW Washington DC 20523-2901

MOSLEY, GLENN RICHARD, religious organization administrator, minister; b. Akron, Ohio, May 23, 1935; s. James Garfield and Viola Mildred (Wiseman) M.; m. Martha Lorella Mitchell, July 17, 1952; children: Glenn R. Jr., Tracey, Susan, Kristin, Robert. BA, MA, Wayne State U., 1974; PhD, Walden U., 1976; MS in Adminstrn., Cen. Mich. U., 1991; DD (hon.), Unity Sch. Christianity, Kansas City, Mo., 1976. Ordained to ministry Unity Ch., 1961. Letter writer, student min. Silent Unity Prayer Soc., Kansas City, Mo., 1957-59; min. Unity Ch., Flushing, N.Y., 1959-64, Des Moines, 1964-65, co-min. N.Y.C., 1965-68; min. Unity Temple, Detroit, 1968-75, Unity Ch., Akron, 1975-85; pres., CEO Assn. Unity Chs., Lee's Summit, Mo., 1985—. Author, co-author of nine books; mem. editl. staff Jour. Thanatology, 1966-76; contbr. numerous articles and monographs to profl. jours. Mem. AAAS, John Templeton Found. (Sewanee, Tenn., judge for Templeton prize for progress in religion), Rep. Presdl. Coun. Office: Assn Unity Chs 401 SW Oldham Pkwy Lees Summit MO 64081-2747 *The Religious Truth message we teach is eternal, and the techniques for teaching it work best for me when I develope new ways to teach which meet a great diversity of learning styles. There are almost zero days left in the current millennium; what an exciting period in which to live and teach.*

MOSLEY, JESSIE BRYANT, retired science educator; b. Houston, Nov. 30, 1903; d. William and Emma Bryant; m. Charles Clint Mosley (dec.); children: Charles Mosley, Jr., Gene Lavell, Wilma Emma Clopton. LHD, BS, Jarvis Christian Coll.; LHD (hon.), Tougaloo Coll.; lifetime tchr.'s cert. Cert. libr. sci. Teen cons. YWCA, Jackson, Miss., 1950—60; bank teller State Mut. Fed. Savs. and Loan, Jackson, Miss., 1960—65; tchr. Jackson Pub. Schs., Jackson, Miss., 1965—70; founder Smith Robertson Mus. and Cultural Ctr., Jackson, Miss., 1970, dir., 1970—90, mus. dir., 1970—90. Author: The Negro In Mississippi History, 1950, The History of the Women's Movement in Mississippi, 1978. State convener Nat. Coun. Negro Women, Jackson, 1977—2001; mem. LeFleur's Bluff Links, Jackson, 1970, 100 Black Women, Jackson, 1990, Miss. Humanities Coun., Jackson, 1990; founder Farish St. Dist. Neighborhood Found., Jackson, 1980; mem. Jackson Urban League, 1967, Nat. Bus. League, Jackson, 1968, Integrated Ch. Women United, Jackson, 1960, Fedn. of Colored Women's Clubs, Jackson, 1950; chmn. Iwy, Jackson, 1977; chaperone Y-Teens, Jackson, 1950. Named Dr. Jessie B. Mosley Health and Human Services Bldg., Hinds County, 1990, Dr.Jessie B. Mosley St., City of Jackson, 1990, Disting. Black Citizen, U. Miss., 1990, Mary McCleod Bethune Living Legend, NCNW, 1998; recipient Carter G. Woodson award, NEA, Outstanding and Dedicated Svc. award, NCNW, 1978, Disting. Svc. to Religious and Civic Orgn. award, United Christian Ch., 1984, Oustanding Leadership award, NCNW, 1996, Outstanding Achievement-Civics, Arts and Culture award, NOBW, 1998-1999, Years of Endearing and Committed Svc. award, Nat. Coun. of Negro Women, 2000, Resolution for Life-Long Svc. award, NCNW, 2000, Cmty. Partners award, State Instns. Higher Learning bd. trustees, 2000. Mem.: AAUW, Alpha Kappa Alpha (hon. Dedicated Svc. to Cmty. 1986). Home: 1968 Wingfield Cir Jackson MS 39209-7101

MOSLEY, RAYMOND A. federal agency administrator; b. Greenville, Miss., July 27, 1947; s. Raymond Clay and Grace Elizabeth (Correro) M.; m. Julia A. Fisk. BA, Miss. State U., 1969; postgrad., Georgetown U. Dir. Records Appraisal Disposition Divsn., Nat. Archives, 1981-84; dep. asst. archivist Fed. Records Ctrs., 1984-89, chief of staff, 1989-94; asst. archivist Spl. and Regional Archives, 1994-96; dir. Fed. Register, 1996—. Office: Nat Archives and Records Adminstrn 800 N Capitol St NW Washington DC 20408-0001 E-mail: raymondamosley@hotmail.com., ray.mosley@fedreg.nara.gov.

MOSLEY, WALTER, writer; b. L.A., 1952; m. Joy Kellman. Student, Goddard Coll., City Coll., CUNY; grad., Johnson State Coll. Author: Devil in a Blue Dress, 1990 (Shamus award Private Eye Writers Am. 1990, Edgar award nomination Mystery Writers Am. 1990), A Red Death, 1991, White Butterfly, 1992, Black Betty, 1994, RL's Dream, 1995, A Little Yellow Dog, 1996, Gone Fishin', 1997, Always Outnumbered, Always Outgunned: The Socrates Fortlow Stories, 1998, Blue Light, 1998, Walkin' the Dog, 1999, Workin' on the Chain Gang: Contemplating Our Chains at the End of the Millennium, 1999, Fearless Jones: A Novel, 2001, Futureland, 2001, Bad Boy Brawley Brown, 2002, What Next: An African American Initiative Toward World Peace, 2003, Six Easy Pieces, 2003, Fear Itself, 2003, The Man in My Basement, 2004, Little Scarlet, 2004; writer, prodr. movie Devil in a Blue Dress, 1995. Recipient Anisfield Wolf award, Risktaker award Sundance Inst., 2004. Office: care W W Norton 500 5th Ave Fl 6 New York NY 10110-0699*

MOSLEY, WILEY HENRY, medical educator; MD, U. Okla.; MPH, Johns Hopkins U. Resident Johns Hopkins Hosp., Balt.; head epidemiology divsn. Cholera Rsch. Lab. CDC, Dhaka, Bangladesh, 1965-71; prof., chmn. dept. population dynamics, dir. Population Ctr. Johns Hopkins U., Balt., 1971-77, prof. population dynamics, internat. health, infectious dis., 1985—, chmn. dept. population dynamics, 1985-98. Cons. WHO, NAS, UN Population divsn., World Bank, many others; dir. Cholera Rsch. Lab., Bangladesh, 1977-79; sr. assoc. Population Coun. and vis. prof. population studies U. Nairobi, Kenya, 1979-81; child survival program officer Ford Found., Jakarta, Indonesia, 1982-84. Contbr. over 120 articles to profl. jours. With USPHS, 1961-63, 64-71. Mem. APHA, Internat. Epidemiol. Soc., Am. Epidemiol. Soc., Population Assn. Am. Office: Johns Hopkins University Sch Hygiene/Pub Health 615 N Wolfe St Baltimore MD 21205-2103

MOSMAN, MICHAEL W. prosecutor; BA, Utah State U.; JD, Brigham Young U. Assoc. Miller, Nash, Portland, Oreg., 1986—88; asst. U.S. atty. Dist. Oreg. U.S. Dept. Justice, 1988—2001, U.S. atty. Dist. Oreg., 2001—. Office: 1000 SW 3rd Ave Ste 600 Portland OR 97204-2902

MOSMANN, TIM, microbiologist, educator, immunologist; PhD, 1973. Rsch. scientist DNAX Rsch. Inst., 1982—90; chmn. immunology U. Alberta, 1990—99; prof. U. Rochester, NY, 1999—. Contbr. articles to profl. jours. Office: Univ Rochester School Medicine and Dentistry 601 Elmwood Ave Box 609 Rochester NY 14642

MOSORA-STAN, FLORENTINA IOANA, physics educator; b. Cluj, Romania, Jan. 7, 1940; arrived in Belgium, 1968; d. Oprea and Cornelia (Stanescu) M.; m. Stephan Stan, Jan. 22, 1977; 1 child, Guy Bart. B in Biol. Sci. with highest distinction, U. Bucharest, Romania, 1961, B in Phys. Sci. with highest distinction, 1967, PhD in Biophysics cum laude, 1971. Cert. biologist and physicist. Rsch. fellow U. Bucharest, 1967-71, U. Liege, Belgium, 1971-74, maitre de conferences, 1974-75; head rsch. fellow Inst. Physics, U. Liege, Belgium, 1975-79, lectr., 1979-88, prof., 1988—. Author: Elements of General Physics and Biophysics, vol. 1, 1974, vol. 2, 1975, Introduction to the Mechanics of Physiologic Fluids, 1984-85, Mechanics of Microcirculation, 1990: Editor: Biomechanical Transport Processes, 1991. Mem. European Med. Rsch. Coun. Devel. of Resch. in Nutrition and Stable Isotopes, 1991—. Decorated officer Ordre of Leopold II, (Belgium), 1981, comdr. Ordre de la Couronne (Belgium, 1992; recipient Agathon de Potter prize Royal Acad. Belgium, 1982. Mem. Stareso Oceanographic Rsch. Calvi (sci. coun. 1987—), Isotopes Stables (v.p. 1987—), Inst. Recherches Marines et Interactions Air-Mer (pres. 1989—), Hemo Liege (founder), Belgian Soc. Biophysics, Internat. Soc. Rsch. Circulation and Environ. Diseases, N.Y. Acad. Scis. Roman Catholic. Avocations: swimming, gymnastics. Home: Residence Verdi Av Blonden 7 4000 Liège Belgium Office: U Liege Inst Physics B5 4000 Liège Belgium

MOSQUEIRA, CHARLOTTE MARIANNE, dietitian; b. L.A., July 26, 1937; d. Leo and Magdalene Tollefson; children: Mark, Michael. BA, St. Olaf Coll., 1959; postgrad., U. Oreg. Med. Sch., 1959-60; MA, Ctrl. Mich. U., 1980. Registered dietitian. Dir. dietetics Riverside Meth. Hosp., Columbus, Ohio, 1977-79; dir. nutrition and food svcs. Fresno (Calif.) Cmty. Hosp. and Med. Ctr., 1980-91; mem. faculty Dept. Enology and Food Sci. Calif. State U., Fresno, 1984-93; dir. nutritional svcs. Emanuel Med. Ctr., Turlock, Calif., 1991-97, Bapt. Health Med. Ctr., Little Rock, CMM Food Svc. Solutions, 2004. Mem. Am. Dietetic Assn., Calif. Dietetic Assn. Lutheran. E-mail: charlotte500@msn.com.

MOSS, ADAM WENDER, editor; b. Bklyn., May 6, 1957; s. Paul and Abigail (Wender) M. BA, Oberlin Coll., 1979. Assoc. editor Rolling Stone Collected Papers, N.Y.C., 1979-81; asst. editor, assoc. editor, sr. editor, mng. editor, dep. editor Esquire mag., N.Y.C., 1981-87; editor in chief 7 Days, N.Y.C., 1987-90; cons. editor N.Y. Times, N.Y.C., 1991—93; editorial dir. The N.Y. Times Mag., N.Y.C., 1993—98, editor, 1998—2003; assoc. mng. editor N.Y. Times, 2002—03; asst. mng. editor N.Y. Times, features, N.Y.C., 2003—04; editor N.Y. Mag., N.Y.C., 2004—. Named Editor of the Yr., Advt. Age, 2001. Office: NY Mag 444 Madison Ave New York NY 10022*

MOSS, AMBLER HOLMES, JR., lawyer, former ambassador; b. Balt., Sept. 1, 1937; s. Ambler Holmes and Dorothea Dandridge (Williams) M.; m. Serena Welles, May 6, 1972; children: Ambler H., Benjamin Sumner, Serena Montserrat, Nicholas George Oliver. BA, Yale U., 1960; JD, George Washington U., 1970. Bar: D.C., Fla. Joined Fgn. Svc., Dept. State, 1964; vice consul Barcelona, 1964-66; adviser U.S. del. to OAS, 1966-69; Spanish desk officer Dept. State, Washington, 1968-70; assoc. Coudert Bros., Washington, 1971-73, resident atty. Brussels, 1973-76; mem. U.S. Negotiating Team for Panama Canal treaties, 1977; dep. asst. Sec. of State, Washington, 1977-78; amb. to Panama, Am. Embassy, Panama City, 1978-82; of counsel Greenberg, Traurig, LLP, Miami, 1982-87, 95—; prof. U. Miami, Fla., 1984—, dean Grad. Sch. Internat. Studies, 1984-94. Bd. dirs. Espirito Santo Bank of Fla. Mem. Panama Canal Consultative Com., 1995-2000. With USN, 1960-64. Mem. ABA, Am. Soc. Internat. Law, Inter-Am. Bar Assn., Am. Fgn. Svc. Assn., Coun. Fgn. Rels., Am. Legion, Inter-Am. Dialogue (Washington), Navy League, Greater Miami C. of C. (gov. 1983-86), Royal Inst. Internat. Affairs (London), Internat. Inst. Strategic Studies (London), Army and Navy Club, Order of the Coif. Address: 5711 San Vicente St Coral Gables FL 33146-2724

MOSS, ARTHUR HENSHEY, lawyer; b. Reading, Pa., July 26, 1930; s. John Arthur and Christine Bracken (Henshey) M.; m. E. Leslie Fritz, Feb. 1982; 1 child by previous marriage, John Arthur. AB, Williams Coll., 1952; JD, U. Pa., 1955. Bar: Pa. 1956. Assoc. Montgomery, McCracken, Walker & Rhoads, Phila., 1960-69, ptnr., 1969-2000, of counsel, 2000—. Editor U. Pa. Law Rev., 1953-55; contbr. articles to profl. jours. Pres. Wayne Civic Assn., 1964—65; commr. gen. assembly Presbyn. Ch. (U.S.A.), 1983; steward, deacon Wayne Presbyn. Ch., 1966—72, 1979—84, 1989—95, ruling elder, 1966—72, 1979—84, 1989—95, clk. of session, 1973—74, 1978—89, trustee, 1987—93, Presbytery of Phila., 1984, 1994—2001, treas., 1996—2001; chmn. Radnor-Haverford-Marple Sewer Authority, 1968—83; bd. dir. John Bartram Assn., 1987—2002, treas., 1989—2002, emeritus dir., 2002—; trustee Radnor Twp. Meml. Libr., 2001—. Mem. Radnor Hist. Soc. (dir., sec. 1978-90), Broadacres Trouting Assn., Athenaeum of Phila., Merion Golf Club, Edgemere Club. Home: 200 Walnut Ave Wayne PA 19087-3423 Office: Montgomery McCracken Walker & Rhoads 123 S Broad St Philadelphia PA 19109-1030 Office Phone: 215-772-1500. E-mail: wwww.esq@verizon.net.

MOSS, ARTHUR JAY, physician; b. White Plains, N.Y., June 21, 1931; s. Abraham Loeb and Ida (Bank) M.; m. Joy Folkman, June 23, 1957; children: Katherine, Deborah, David. BA, Yale U., 1953; MD, Harvard U., 1957. Resident Mass. Gen. Hosp., 1957-58, 60-61; fellow in cardiology med. ctr. U. Rochester, N.Y., 1961-65, from asst. to assoc. prof. sch. medicine and dentistry, 1966-71, clin. assoc. prof., 1971-82, clin. prof., 1982-91, prof. medicine, 1991—, dir. heart rsch. follow-up program med. ctr., 1971—. Mem. cardiology adv. com. Nat. Heart, Lung, and Blood Inst., NIH, 1980-82, chmn., 1982-84, mem. epidemiology and disease control study sect., 1998—. Author: Antiarrhythmic Agents, 1973; editor: Clinical Aspects of Life-threatening Arrhythmias, 1984, QT Prolongation and Ventricular Arrhythmias, 1992, Noninvasive Electrocardiology, 1995; editor-in-chief Ann. Noninvasive Electrocardiology, 1996—; mem. editl. bd. Am. Jour. Cardiology, 1988—, Jour. Am. Coll. Cardiology, 1997-2001. Lt. USNR, 1958-60. Mem. Assn. Am. Physicians, Alpha Omega Alpha. Home: 581 Claybourne Rd Rochester NY 14618-1224 Office: Univ Rochester Med Ctr PO Box 653 Rochester NY 14642-8653 Office Phone: 585-275-5391. Business E-mail: heartajm@heart.rochester.edu.

MOSS, BEN FRANK, III, art educator, painter; b. Phila., Feb. 28, 1936; s. B. Frank Jr. and Helen Charlotte (Figge) M.; m. Jean Marilyn Russel, Aug. 26, 1960; children: Jennifer Kathleen, Benjamin Franklin IV. BA, Whitworth Coll., 1959; postgrad., Princeton Theol. Seminary, 1959-60; MFA, Boston U., 1963; MA (hon.), Dartmouth Coll., 1993; studied with Walter Murch, Karl Fortess and Herman Keys. Instr. Gonzaga U., Spokane, Wash., 1964-65; assoc. prof., dir. MFA and vis. artist program Fort Wright Coll., Spokane, 1965-72; acting dean, co-founder Spokane Studio Sch., 1972-74; prof. painting and drawing Sch. Art and Art History U. Iowa, Iowa City, 1975-88; George Frederick Jewett prof. art Dartmouth Coll., Hanover, N.H., 1993—. Chmn. studio art dept. Dartmouth Coll., Hanover, 1988-94, Vt. Studio Ctr., Johnson, 1990; area head painting U. Iowa, 1985; artist-in-residence Queens Coll., U. Melbourne, Australia, 1993-94; vis. artist, lectr. Northwest Mo. State U., Maryville, 1996, Houghton (N.Y.) Coll., 1996, Gordon Coll., Wenham, Mass., 1996, Northwestern U., Evanston, Ill., 1997, Colo. State U., Ft. Collins, 1997, Ravenscroft Sch., Raleigh, N.C., 1997, Coe Coll., Cedar Rapids, Iowa, 1998, Seattle Pacific U., 2002, Bowling Green U., Ohio, 2003, Williams Coll., Willamstown, Mass., 2003, numerous others. Represented by Pepper Gallery, Boston, Francine Seders Gallery, Ltd., Seattle, Susan Conway Galleries, Washington; one-man shows include Susan Conway Galleries, 1990, Dartmouth Coll., 1989, 94, Kraushaar Galleries, 1981, 83, 87, Swarthmore Coll., Pa., 1984, Stony Brook (N.Y.) Sch., 1982, Saint-Gaudens, Picture Gallery, Cornish, N.H., 1981, Kans. State U., 1980, Francine Seders Gallery, Seattle, 1979, 82, 99, Hudson D. Walker Gallery, Fine Arts Work Ctr., Provincetown, Mass., 1978, Arnot Art Mus., Elmira, N.Y., 1977, Kirkland Coll., Clinton, N.Y., 1977, Juniper Tree Gallery, Spokane, 1975, Middlebury (Vt.) Coll., 1971, Seligman Gallery, Seattle, 1967, 69, Cheney Cowels Meml. Mus., Spokane, 1967, Loomis Chaffee Sch., 1995, Tasis England Am. Sch., 1994, Queens Coll., U. Melbourne, 1994, Houghton Coll., 1996, Gordon Coll., 1996, N. W. Mo. State U., 1996, Princeton Theol. Sem., 2001, Taylor U., Upland, Ind., 2002, Bedford Art Mus., Mass., 2003, Brattleboro Mus. and Art Ctr., 1995, Nat. Acad. and Design, 1995, Messiah Coll., 1995, 97, 99, 2001, 2003, Phillips Exeter Acad., 1995, Susan Conway Galleries, 1993, 96, Chase Gallery City Hall, Spokane, 1993, Colby-Sawyer Coll., New London, N.H., 1992, Pepper Gallery, Boston, Mass., 1998, 2000, Idaho State U., Pocatello, 1972, Kouros Gallery, N.Y.C., 2001, Augustana Coll., Rock Island, Ill., 2002, New England Coll., Henniker, N.H., 2003, others; exhibited in group shows at Blair Acad., Blairstown, N.J., 1996, Albright Knox Gallery, Buffalo, N.Y., 1995-96, Smith Coll., North Hampton, Mass., 1996, Nat. Acad. Design, N.Y.C., 1995, Boston U., 1995, Brattleboro (Vt.) Mus. and Art Ctr., 1995, Susan Conway Galleries, 1989—, Middlebury Coll. Mus. Art, Babcock Galleries, N.Y.C., Albany Inst. History and Art, Owensboro (Ky.) Mus. Fine Art, Westmoreland Mus. Art, Greenburg, Pa., Md. Inst. & Coll. Art, 1993-94, Gallery 68, 1992, Vt. Studio Ctr. Visiting Critics, Vergennes, 1992, 79th Ann. Maier Mus. Art, Randolph, Macon Women's Coll., Lynchburg, Va., 1990, Del. Ctr. Contemporary Arts, Wilmington, 1988, U. Iowa, 1976, 78, 80, 82, 84, 86, 88, Bladen Meml. Mus., Fort Dodge, Iowa, 1987, Phila. Mus. Art, 1986, Union League Club, N.Y.C., 1986, Blackfish Gallery, Portland, 1986, Columbia (S.C.) Mus. Art, 1985, Columbus Mus. Art, 1982-86, Paine Art Ctr., Oshkosh, Wis., 1985, Burpee Art Ctr., Rockford, Ill., 1985, Ill. State U., Normal, 1985, Wilkes Coll., Wilkes-Barre, Pa., 1985, Albright-Knox Mus., Buffalo, N.Y., 1984, Ark. Art Ctr., Little Rock, 1984, Millersville (Pa.) U., 1983, Fairfield (Conn.) U., 1983, Marion Koogler McKay Inst., San Antonio, 1983, Boston City Hall Gallery, 1983, Cedar Rapids (Iowa) Mus. Art, 1982, Montclair (N.J.) Jr. League, 1981, Iowa Arts Coun., Des Moines, 1980-81, Pepper Gallery, Boston, 1997-98, Spheris Gallery Fine Art, 1997, The Art Spirit Gallery of Fine Art, Walpole, N.H., 1997, Coeur d' Alene, Ind., 1998, numerous others. Sr. Faculty fellow Va. Ctr. for Creative Arts, 1996, Dartmouth Coll., 1993, MacDowell Colony, 1992, Devel. grant U. Iowa, 1980, 86; Summer fellowship U. Iowa, 1979, Rsch. and Travel grantee Ford Found., 1979-80, Yaddo Found., 1965, 72, Travel grantee U. Iowa Found., 1986,; recipient Disting. Alumni award Boston U., 1988 Mem. NAD (academician mem.), Coll. Art Assn. Independent. Presbyterian. Avocations: music, poetry, travel, tennis. Office: Dartmouth Coll Hb 6081 Studio Art Hanover NH 03755

MOSS, BERNARD, virologist, researcher; b. N.Y.C., July 26, 1937; s. Jack and Goldie (Altman) M.; m. Toby Frima Lieberman, Dec. 25, 1960; children: Robert, Jennifer, David. BA, NYU, 1957, MD, 1961; PhD, MIT, 1967. Diplomate Am. Bd. Med. Examiners. Intern Children's Hosp., Boston, 1961-62; investigator, sect. head NIH, Bethesda, Md., 1966—, lab. chief, 1984—. Mem. adv. bd. Virus Res., 1984—, Current Opinion Biotech., 1989—. Assoc. editor Virology Jour., 1976-92, editor., 1992—; mem. editorial bd. Jour. of Virology, 1972—, Antimicrobial Agts. and Chemotherapy, 1973-79, Jour. Biol. Chemistry, 1982-87; AIDS rsch. Human Retroviruses, 1989—; contbr. more than 600 articles to profl. jours. Mem. adv. com. Am. Cancer Soc., N.Y.C., 1983-86; bd. dirs. Found. Advanced Edn. in Scis., Bethesda, 1985-91; mem. NIH AIDS vaccine selection com., 1989—. Served as med. dir. USPHS, 1966-98. Named one of 100 Most Innovative Scientists of 1986, Sci. Digest; recipient Solomon A. Berson Alumni Achievement award Sch. Medicine, NYU, Meritorious Svc. medal USPHS, Disting. Svc. medal USPHS, Dickson prize in medicine, Invitrogen award for eukaryotic gene expression, ICN Internat. prize in Virology, Taylor Internat. prize in medicine., Bristol-Myers Squibb Award, Distinguished Achievement in Infectious Disease Research, 2000. Fellow AAAS; mem. Am. Soc. for Biochemistry and Molecular Biology, Am. Acad. Microbiology, Am. Soc. Microbiology, Am. Soc. Virology (pres. 1995), Nat. Acad. Sci., Phi Beta Kappa, Sigma Xi, Alpha Omega Alpha. Office: NIH 4 Center Dr Bethesda MD 20892-0445 E-mail: bmoss@nih.gov.

MOSS, BILL RALPH, lawyer; b. Amarillo, Tex., Sept. 27, 1950; s. Ralph Voniver and Virginia May (Atkins) M.; 1 child, Brandon Price. BS with honors, West Tex. A&M U., 1972, MA, 1974; JD, Baylor U., 1976; cert. regulatory studies program, Mich. State U., 1981. Bar: Tex. 1976, U.S. Dist. Ct. (no. dist.) 1976, U.S. Tax Ct. 1979, U.S. Ct. Appeals (5th cir.) 1983. Briefing atty. Ct. Appeals 7th Supreme Jud. Dist. Tex., Amarillo, 1976-77; assoc. Culton, Morgan, Britain & White, Amarillo, 1977-80; hearings examiner Pub. Utility Commn. Tex., Austin, 1981-83; asst. gen. counsel State Bar Tex., Austin, 1983-87; founder, owner Price & Co. Publs., Austin, 1987-97; asst. gen. counsel Tex. Ethics Commn., Austin, 1997—2004; asst. atty. gen. antitrust and civil medicaid fraud div. Office Atty. Gen., Tex., 2004—. Instr., lectr. West Tex. State U., Canyon, Ea. N.Mex. U., Portales, 1977-80; spkr. in field. Active St. Matthew's Episcopal Ch.; election inspector State of Tex., 1998—. Mem. ABA, Tex. Bar Assn., Nat. Orgn. Bar Counsel, Internat. Platform Assn., Capitol of Tex. Rotary Club, Alpha Chi, Lambda Chi Alpha, Omicron Delta Epsilon, Phi Alpha Delta, Sigma Tau Delta, Pi Gamma Mu. Home: 506 Explorer St Lakeway TX 78734-3447 Office: Office of Atty Gen William P Clements Bldg 300 W 15th St 9th Fl Austin TX 78701 E-mail: bill.moss@oag.state.tx.us.

MOSS, CARL ARTHUR, psychologist; b. Port Huron, Mich., Aug. 12, 1940; s. August Carl and Frances Elizabeth Moss; m. Patricia Elizabeth Howe, Feb. 13, 1965; children: Miriam, Anne Elizabeth. AA, Port Huron Jr. Coll., Mich., 1960; BS, Ea. Mich. U., 1966, MS, 1973. Cert. sch. psychologist Mich. Psychologist Port Huron Area Schs., 1967—. Trustee Port Huron Mus., 1970—76, bd. pres., 1974—76; founding mem. Riverside Heritage Assn., Port Huron, 1972—78; active Olde Town Dist. Com., Port Huron, 2000—; mem. Port Huron Hist. Dist. Commn.; sec. bd. dirs. Wills Sainte Claire Automobile Mus., Marysville, Mich. With U.S. Army, 1963—69. Recipient Spirit of Port Huron award for civic involvement, 2002. Episcopalian. Avocations: civil war history, antiques. Home: 1617 Military St Port Huron MI 48060

MOSS, CARL MICHAEL, minister, religious studies educator; b. Danville, Ill., Feb. 10, 1950; s. Carl Wesley and Mabel Jenkins Moss; m. Virginia Porter, Feb. 10, 1950; children: Rebecca Sekeres, Abigail Rosser, Carrie McLean. B.A., Lipscomb U., Nashville, TN, 1968—72; M.A., Harding U. Grad. Sch. of Religion, Memphis, TN, 1972—73; MDiv, So. Bapt. Theol. Sem., Louisville, KY, 1976—79, PhD, 1979—82. Assoc. dean, coll. of bible and ministry, prof. of bible and Greek Lipscomb U., Nashville, 1983—; min. Middletown Ch. of Christ, Louisville, 1975—83; meadowbrook ch. of christ; pulpit min. Ctrl. Ch. of Christ, Nashville, 1991—. Author: (book) Lord, Sometimes I Don't Feel Saved (Sabbatical, 2001), When God Reigns: Studies in the Parables of Jesus; actor: (book) Coll. Press NIV Commentary: 1, 2 Timothy & Titus; translator: (book) NKJV Greek Interlinear, The NKJV Greek English Interlinear New Testament; contbr. book Man of God. Grantee Grant for Greek Rsch., Lipscomb U., 1983, Summer Grant for Travel to the Holy Lands, 1984, Sabbatical, 2001-2002. Mem.: Am. Acad. of Religion, Evang. Theol. Soc., Soc. of Bibl. Lit. Church Of Christ. Avocations: travel, computer assisted learning. Home: 508 Adamwood Drive Nashville TN 37211 Office: Lipscomb University 3901 Granny White Pike Nashville TN 37204-3951 Office Phone: 1-615-279-6051. Office Fax: 1-615-279-6052. Personal E-mail: michael.moss@lipscomb.edu. E-mail: michael.moss@lipscomb.edu.

MOSS, CARRIE-ANNE, actress; b. Vancouver, British Columbia, Can., Aug. 21, 1967; Actress in films: Flashfire, 1993, The Soft Kill, 1994, Terrified, 1995, Sabotage, 1996, Secret Life of Algernon, 1997, Lethal Tender, 1997, New Blood, 1999, The Matrix, 1999, Memento, 2000, The Crew, 2000, Red Planet, 2000, Chocolat, 2000, The Matrix Reloaded, 2003; tv movies: Doorways, 1993; television appearances: L.A. Law, 1986, Baywatch, 1989, Dark Justice, 1991, Silk Stalkings, 1991, Street Justice, 1992, Nightmare Cafe, 1992, Forever Knight, 1992, Matrix, 1993, Models Inc., 1994, Nowhere Man, 1995, Nowhere Man, 1996, F/X: The Series, 1996, Viper, 1997.

MOSS, CHARLES, advertising agency executive; b. Bklyn., Sept. 7, 1938; s. Samuel and Celia (Liebes) Moskowitz; m. Margo Jean Schekman, July 3, 1963 (div.); 1 child, Robert Evan; m. Susan Dukes Calhoun, Mar. 18, 1977; children: Mary Calhoun, Samuel Calhoun. BA cum laude, Ithaca Coll., 1961. Copywriter Doyle, Dane, Bernbach, N.Y.C., 1962-65; group copy supr. J. Tinker & Partners, N.Y.C., 1965-66; creative dir. Wells, Rich, Greene, Inc., N.Y.C., 1968-74, pres., chief operating officer, 1971-76, vice chmn., corp. creative dir., 1976—, also bd. dirs.; now chmn. Moss/Dragoti (ptnr. co. DDB Worldwide), N.Y.C. Author (with Stan Dragoti) film Dirty Little Billy, 1971. Mem. adv. bd. NYU Sch. Continuing Edn.; mem. creative rev. bd. Com. for Drug Free Am. Served with AUS, 1962-68. Recipient Gold Key Copy Club, 1968, 1st prize Clio award, 1968, 1st prize Art Dirs. Club, 1968; Andy award N.Y. Advt. Club, 1968, spl. Tony award, Golden Apple award for I Love New York advt. campaign 1978, Clio Classic Hall of Fame award 1983, 86, Gold medal for Hertz Corp., Internat. Film Festival, 1995. Mem. Writers Guild Am., Screen Authors Guild. Avocations: golf, tennis. Office: Moss Dragoti 437 Madison Ave New York NY 10022-7001

MOSS, CHARLES JOSEPH, III, (CHUCK MOSS), writer, broadcaster; b. Norfolk, Va., Aug. 31, 1953; s. Charles Joseph Jr. and Sally Jane (Brown) M.; m. Alice Northrop Heaton, June 30, 1979; children: Elizabeth Northrop, Carolyn Woods. BA, Mich. State U., 1975; JD, U. Detroit, 1979. Bar: Mich. 1979. Asst. prosecuting atty. Genesee County, Flint, Mich., 1979-81; pvt. practice law Ferndale, Mich., 1981-85; polit. writer/columnist Birmingham, Mich., 1985—; co-host WTVS TV56, 1996—. Host talk show WWNT Internet, 1997—. Mem. Birmingham Traffic Safety Bd., Oakland County Pub. Transit Auth. Bd., 1996—; commr. City of Birmingham, 1997-2000, mayor, 2000; commr. Oakland County, 2001—. Recipient award for radio commentary UPI, 1989. Mem. Optimists. Address: 1184 Dorchester Dr Birmingham MI 48009-5900 Office Phone: 248-642-1820.

MOSS, DAVID, music company executive; Cert., Musician's Inst. in Hollywood, 1985; B of commerce in mktg and fin., Concordia U., 1989. Dir., sch. of fine arts Saidye Bronfman Ctr. for the Arts, 1994—96, exec. dir., 1996—2003; gen. dir. Montreal Opera, 2003—. Founding mem., mem. exec. com. Culture Montreal; apptd. to Groupe Conseil pour la Politique Culturelle

de Montreal, 2002; appt. to bd. La Vitrine Culturelle de Montreal, 2003. Office: L'Opera de Montreal 260 Maisonneuve Blvd W Montreal PQ H2X 1Y9 Canada Office Phone: 514-985-2222.

MOSS, DOUGLAS, architectural firm executive; BArch, Tex. Tech. U. Assoc. Hardy, Holzman, Pfeiffer Assocs. LLP, N.Y.C., prin., 2002—03, ptnr., 2003—, mng. dir. Co-founder internet co.; lectr. in field. Mem.: AIA (mem. profl. practice com., com. on edn. N.Y. chpt.). Office: HHPA 19th Fl 902 Broadway New York NY 10010*

MOSS, EDWARD R. publishing executive; m. Christine Moss; children: Matthew, Lindsey stepchildren: Vanessa, Graham, Shannon; 1 child, Megan. Degree, Va. Commonwealth U. Various mgmt. positions Freedom Comms., Thomson Newspapers, Tribune Co.; v.p. sales Freedom Media Enterprises; pres. Gorilla Newspaper Networks 21st Century Newspapers Inc., Pontiac, Mich., 2003—04; pres. The Oakland Press, Pontiac, 2004—, pub., 2004—. Office: The Oakland Press 48 W HuronSt Pontiac MI 48342*

MOSS, ELIZABETH LUCILLE (BETTY MOSS), retired transportation executive; b. Ironton, Mo., Feb. 13, 1939; d. James Leon and Dorothy Lucille (Russell) Rollen; m. Elliott Theodore Moss, Nov. 10, 1963 (div. Jan. 1984); children: Robert Belmont, Wendy Rollen. BA in Econs. and Bus. Adminstrn., Drury Coll., 1960. Registrar, transp. mgr. Cheley Colo. Camps, Inc., Denver and Estes Park, 1960-61; office mgr. Washington Nat. Ins. Co., Denver, 1960-61; sec. White House Decorating, Denver, 1961-62; with Ringsby Truck Lines, Denver, Oakland, Calif., and L.A., 1962-67, System 99 Freight Lines, L.A., 1967-69, terminal mgr. Stockton, Calif., 1981-84; with Yellow Freight System, L.A., 1969-74, Hayward, Calif., 1974-77, ops. mgr. Urbana, Ill., 1977-80; sales rep. Calif. Motor Express, San Jose, 1981; regional sales mgr. Schneider Nat. Carriers, Inc., No. Calif., 1984-86; account exec. TNT-Can., Nev. and Cen. Calif., 1986-88; mgr. Interstate-Intermodal Divs. HVH Transp., Denver, 1988-89; regional sales mgr. MNX, Inc., Northern Calif., 1989-91; sales dir., nat. accts. mgr., terminal mgr. Mountain Valley Express, Manteca, Calif., 1992—2003; ret., 2003. Chmn. op. coun. for San Joaquin and Stanislaus Counties Calif. Trucking Assn., 1983-84, Truck Accident Reduction Projects, San Joaquin County, 1987-88. Mem. Econ. Devel. Coun. Stockton C. of C., 1985-86; active Edison High Sch. Boosters, 1982-88. Mem.: Calif. Trucking Assn. (tri county unit steering com. 2001—03), So. Calif. Round Table (bd. dirs. 1993—2001), Coun. Logistics Mgmt., Oakland Traffic Club, Ctrl. Valley Traffic Club, Stockton Traffic Club (bd. dirs. 1982—84, Trucker of Yr.), Nat. Def. Transp. Assn. (bd. dirs. 1986—87), Delta Nu Alpha (bd. dirs. Region 1 1982—84, v.p. chpt. 1984—85, pres. chpt. 1985—86, chmn. bd. 1985—87, regional sec. 1987—88, Outstanding Achievement award 1986, 1988). Methodist. Avocation: reading. Home: One Parkway Pl 2A 350 S John Q Hammons Pkwy Springfield MO 65806 E-mail: MossBetty@sbcglobal.net.

MOSS, ERIC OWEN, architect; b. L.A., July 25, 1943; BA, UCLA, 1965; MArch with honors, U. Calif., Berkeley, 1968, Harvard U., 1972. Prof. design So. Calif. Inst. Architecture, 1974—; prin. Eric Owen Moss Archs., Culver City, Calif., 1975—; Eliot Noyes chair Harvard U., Cambridge, Mass., 1990; Eero Saarinen chair Yale U., New Haven, 1991. Lectr. Hirshhorn Mus. Symposium, Washington, 1990, Nat. AIA Conv., 1990, Mus. Contemporary Art, L.A., 1991, N.Y. Archtl. League, 1991, Archtl. Assn. Ireland, Dublin, Archtl. Assn., London, 1991, Royal Coll. Art, London, 1991, Smithsonian Inst., Washington, 1992, U. Calif., Berkeley, 1992, Osterreichiaches Mus. fur Angewandte Kunst, Vienna, Austria, 1992, UCLA, 1992, Royal Danish Acad. Fine Arts, Copenhagen, 1993, U. Lund, Sweden, 1993, Mus. Finnish Architecture, Helsinki, 1993, Royal Acad. Arts, London, 1993, U. Pa., Phila., 1994, others; tchr. U. Tex., Austin, 1983, Wash. U., St. Louis, 1984, U. Ill., Chgo., 1985, Tulane U., New Orleans, 1985, U. Minn., Mpls., 1985, Columbia U., N.Y.C., 1986, Rice U., Houston, 1988; participant various confs. Exhbns. of work include World Biennial of Architecture, Sofia, Bulgaria, 1989, Salle des Tirages du Credit Foncier de France, Paris, 1990, Bartlett Sch. Architecture and Urban Design, London, 1991, Gallery of Functional Art, Santa Monica, Calif., 1992, GA Gallery, Tokyo, 1992, Mus. fur Gestaltung Zurich, Switzerland, 1993, Santa Monica (Calif.) Mus. Art, 1993, Fonds Regional D'Art Contemporain du Centre, 1993, Aspen (Colo.) Art Mus., 1993, Centro de Arte y Comunicacion, Buenos Aires, 1993, Contemporary Arts Ctr., Cin., 1993, Philippe Uzzan Galerie, Paris, 1993, Contemporary Arts Ctr., Tours, France, 1993, Internat. Exhbn. Contemporary Architecture, Havana, Cuba, 1994, others. Recipient Progressive Architecture Design award, 1978, 92, Winning Interior Archtl. Record award, 1984, Interiors Design award, 1991. Fellow AIA (L.A. awards 1977, 79, 83, 88, 90, Calif. Coun. awards 1981, 86, 88, L.A. Honor awards 1991, Nat. Honor awards 88, 89, Calif. Coun. Urban Design/Adaptive Re-Use awards 1991, Nat. Interior Design awards 1992, 94, L.A. Design awards 1992, 93). Achievements include being subject of monographs and numerous articles in mags. and jours. Office: 8557 Higuera St Culver City CA 90232-2535

MOSS, GERALD S. dean, medical educator; b. Cleve., Mar. 4, 1935; s. Harry and Lillian (Alter) M.; m. Wilma Jabak, Sept. 1, 1957; children: William Alan, Robert Daniel, Sharon Lynn. BA, Ohio State U., 1956, MD cum laude, 1960. Diplomate Am. Bd. Surgery (apptd. assoc. examiner com. 1989); lic. Ill. Intern Mass. Gen. Hosp., Boston, 1960-61, resident, 161-65; from asst. prof. to assoc. prof. dept. surgery Coll. Medicine U. Ill., Chgo., 1968-72, prof., 1973-77, 89—, head dept. surgery, 1989, dean, 1989—; prof. dept. surgery Pritzker Sch. Medicine U. Chgo., 1977-89. Tutor in surgery Manchester (Eng.) Royal Infirmary, 1964; asst. chief surgical svcs. VA West Side Hosp., Chgo., 1968-70; attending surgeon dept. surgery Cook County Hosp., Chgo. 1970-72, chmn. 1972-77; dir. surgical rsch. Hektoen Inst. for Med. Rsch., Cook County Hosp., 1972-77, Michael Reese Hosp. and Med. Ctr., Chgo., 1977-89, chmn. dept. surgery, 1977-89, chief svc. 1989, trustee, 1981, and numerou coms.; appointed to Nat. Rsch. Coun., NAS, 1966-68, Ad Hoc Subcom., NAE, 1970, Ad Hoc Study Sect., 1970, del. to Third Joint U.S-USSR Symposium, 1983, Blood Diseases and Resources Adv. Com., 1984-88, Planning Com. for discussing key blood problems, Nat. Heart and Lung Inst., 1987, chmn. Plasma and Plasma Products Com., 1979, bd. dirs., 1983, v.p., 1985, Ad Hoc Transition Com., Am. Blood Commn., 1989, Panel on Rsch. Opportunities, Office Naval Rsch. Program, 1987, exec. com., coord. com., Nat. Blood Edn. Program, 1988, Tech. Adv. Task Force Am. Hosp. Assn., 1988, chmn. review panel contract proposals, NIH, 1975, program project site visit, 1976, chmn. site-visit review group, 1977, adv. com. Blood Resources Work group, 1978, Planning Com. for Consensus, 1987, Small Bus. Innovation Rsch., 1988, Med. Rsch. Scv. Merit Review Bd. VA, 1978-81, Liaison Com. Graduate Med. Edn. AMA, 1979, and numerous other coms. for various med. organizations; cons. Nat. Heart and Lung Inst., Transfusion Medicine Acad. Awardees Program; vis. prof. Montefiore Med. Ctr. Bronx, N.Y., 1986, Ohio State U., 1988, U. N.Mex., Albuquerque, 1989, Seton Med. Ctr., Austin, Tex., 1990, U. Ill. Coll. Medicine, Peoria, 1991; guest lectr., participant numerous meetings, symposiums; cons. in field. Contbr. numerous articles to profl. jours., chpts. to books. With USN, 1965—68, Vietnam. Teaching fellow Harvard Med. Sch., 1962; recipient Stitt Lectr. award Assn. Mil. Surgeons U.S.A., 1981; grantee U.S. Navy, 1969-84, U.S. Army, 1971-74, 75-78, NIH, 1969, 83-84, Dept. Pub. Health, 1973, HEW, 1974-77, UpJohn, 1974, Northfield Labs. 1985-89. Fellow ACS (pre and postoperative care com. 1975-83, rep. Am. blood commn. 1977—, mem. various coms., speaker various symposiums), Am. Soc. Surgery Trauma; mem. Am. Surgical Assn. (rep. Nat. Soc. Med. Rsch. 1984-88), Am. Trauma Soc., Am. Physicians Fellowship (rep. Israel Med. Assn.), Assn. Acad. Surgery (chmn. membership selection com. 1973-75, pres. elect 1974-75, pres. 1975-76, exec. coun. 1977-79), Soc. Univ. Surgeons (rep. Nat. Soc. Med. Rsch. 1973-77, com. Surgical Edn. 1979-81), Ctrl. Surgical Soc. (rep. Nat. Soc. Med. Rsch. 1973-77), Shock Soc. (chmn. planning com. 1986, chmn. program com. 1986, pres. elect 1986-87, pres. 1987-88), Soc. for Surgery Alimentary Tract (mem. com. west north ctrl. region 1978-82), Internat. Soc. Blood Transfusion, Surgical Biology Club II, Nat. Soc. for Med. Rsch., Collegium Internationale Chirugiae Digestivae, Societe Internationale de Chirugie, Sigma XI, Alpha Omega Alpha (faculty advisor 1972-73). Office: U Ill Coll Medicine Chgo 1853 W Polk St # M/C 784 Chicago IL 60612-4316 Office Phone: 312-996-3500. E-mail: gmoss@uic.edu.

MOSS, KATE, model; b. Croydon, England, Jan. 16, 1974; With Storm Agy., England, Women Model Mgmt., N.Y.; model Calvin Klein Jeans. Appeared in films Unzipped, 1995, Catwalk, 1995, Beautopia, 1998, Blackadder Back and Forth, 1999, Original Copies, 1999, (TV films) Inferno, 1992, Naomi Conquers Africa, 1998, (TV series) French and Saunders, 1987. Office: Storm Model Mgmt 5 Jubilee Pl 1st Fl London SW3 3TD England

MOSS, LESLIE OTHA, protective services official; b. Detroit, Mar. 8, 1952; s. Lonnie and Emma (Robinson) M. BA, U. Mich., 1982, postgrad., 1990—. Cert. protection officer, security supr. Dept. Homeland Security, protection profl. Technician oper. rm. Sinai Hosp., Detroit, 1972-75; nurses' technician Detroit Osteo. Hosp., 1976-83; supr. Southfield (Mich.) Placement Ctr., 1983-85; rsch. asst. Wayne County Commr.'s Office, Detroit, 1985-86; fin. aid counselor Wayne State U., 1986-87; probation officer Dept. Corrections State of Mich., 1988—; exec. asst. Human Rights Dept., City of Detroit; rsch. asst. Law Dept. City of Detroit, 1990; asst. pers. mgr. Detroit Osteo. Hosp., 1991-93, Highland Pk. C.C., 1991-93; mental health worker Mich. Health Ctr.-Adult Mental Health and New Ctr. Hosp., Detroit, 1992-94; legal technician Ptnrs. Against Crime, Detroit, 1994; social work technician, 1994. Sgt. of arms Detroit Police Res., 1987—; intern, assoc. prodr. local TV sta., Detroit, 1993; mem. bd. advisors, mem. bd. govs. Am. Biog. Rsch. Inst., dep. gov., 1994; exec. cons. in field., 1993—; asst. pers. mgr., 1993—. Bd. advisors Am. Biog. Inst., 1994; active re-election com. Mayor Coleman A. Young, Detroit, 1989-93; patient care counselor; adv. various causes, including industrialized Am., higher edn., automotive quality. Recipient Twentieth Century Achievement award Biog. Centre, 1994, Spl. Recognition award Detroit Pub. Sch. Sys., 1992, Internat. Man of Yr. award, 1992-93; award for mass media svc. participation Barden Cable Vision, Detorit, 1991, Man of the Yr. award, 1996, Disting. Alumni Award Mumford H.S. Detroit, 1996, Most Outstanding Men of the Twentieth Century award, 1999; named Most Admired Man of Decade, 1994, Disting. Alumnus, Detroit Pub. Schs. Mich., 1995, Most Admired Man of the Yr., State of Mich., 1995; named to Internat. Honors Hall of Fame, 1998, Millenium Hall of Fame, 1998; inducted 500 Leaders of Influence Pub., 2000. Mem. NAFE, NAACP (advisor 1989), Internat. Order of Merit, Assn. Pre-Med Students (cons. 1988—), Assn. Psychologists, Am. Biog. Rsch. Inst. Assn. (mem. bd. govs. 1993, dep. gov.), Internat. Platform Assn., U. Mich. Alumni Assn., Golden Key Internat. Honor Soc. (life), Kappa Alpha Psi, Phi Theta Kappa. Home and Office: 1190 Seward St Apt 306 Detroit MI 48202-2336

MOSS, LOGAN VANSEN, lawyer; b. Atlanta, Apr. 17, 1957; s. Joseph Henry Moss and Elsie Louise (McCown) Daniels. BA, Bates Coll., 1979; JD, U. Tulsa, 1982; MTS, Ave Maria U., 2003. Bar: Okla. 1982, U.S. Dist. Ct. Okla. 1982, Maine 1984, U.S. Dist. Ct. Maine 1984, U.S. Supreme Ct. 1986, Tex. 1991. Law clk. to presiding justice Okla. Ct. Appeals, Tulsa, 1982-84; assoc. Strout, Payson et al, Rockland, Maine, 1984-87, Joseph M. Cloutier & Assocs., Camden, Maine, 1987-88, Armstrong & Assoc., Tulsa, Okla., 1988-91; asst. gen. counsel Temple-Inland Forest Products Corp., Diboll, Tex., 1991—2002; gen. counsel litig. Temple-Inland Inc., Austin, Tex., 2003—. Republican. Roman Catholic. Avocation: catholic studies. Office: Temple Inland Corp 1300 S Mopac Expy Austin TX 78746 Office Phone: 512-434-8050. E-mail: loganmoss@templeinland.com.

MOSS, MADISON SCOTT, editor; b. Charlotte, N.C., May 23, 1948; s. James Madison and Nellie Lee (Jenkins) M. BA in English, U. N.C., 1970. Editl. aide NASW, Inc., Washington, 1974, promotions specialist, 1974-79, assoc. editor, 1979-80, editor, 1980-90, mng. editor, 1990—. Creator numerous videos. Campaign coord. Eugene McCarthy for Pres., Rutherford County, N.C., 1968. Recipient award for Pub. Excellence Comms. Concepts, 1993, 94, 95, 96, 97, 98, Bronze award newspaper gen. excellence Soc. Nat. Assn. Publs., 1996, Silver award, 1997. Mem. Am. Assn. Ret. Persons, U. N.C. Gen. Alumni Assn., Am. Found. AIDS Rsch. Democrat. Avocations: video producing, creating digital art and animations, reading. Office: NASW Inc 750 1st St NE Ste 700 Washington DC 20002-4241 Business E-Mail: Smoss@naswdc.org.

MOSS, MELVIN LIONEL, anatomist, educator; b. N.Y.C., Jan. 3, 1923; s. Maurice and Ethel (Lander) M.; m. Letty Salentijn, Apr. 1970; children (by previous marriage)— Noel Morrow, James Andrew. AB, N.Y. U., 1942; D.D.S., Columbia, 1946, PhD, 1954. Mem. faculty Columbia, 1954—, prof., 1967-93; prof. emeritus, 1993; also dean Columbia (Sch. Dental and Oral Surgery.). Recipient Lederle Med. Faculty award, 1954-56 Fellow AAAS, Royal Anthrop. Soc. Gt. Britain; mem. Am. Assn. Anatomists, Am. Assn. Phys. Anthropologists, Internat. Assn. Dental Research (craniofacial biology award), Am. Soc. Zoologists, Sigma Xi, Omicron Kappa Upsilon. Achievements include research, numerous publs. on skeletal growth and application of computer-assisted methods of numerical and graphic analysis of growth. edu. Home: 560 Riverside Dr New York NY 10027-3202 Office Phone: 212-305-5647. E-mail: MLM7@columbia.

MOSS, MYRA ELLEN (MYRA MOSS ROLLE), philosophy educator; b. L.A., Mar. 22, 1937; m. Andrew Rolle, Nov. 5, 1983. BA, Pomona Coll., 1958; PhD, The Johns Hopkins U., 1965. Asst. prof. Santa Clara (Calif.) U., 1968-74; prof. Claremont McKenna Coll., 1975—, chmn. dept. philosophy, 1992-95. Assoc. dir. Gould Ctr. for Humanities, Claremont, Calif., 1993-94; adv. coun. Milton S. Eisenhower Libr./Johns Hopkins U., 1994-96, 2001–. Author: Benedetto Croce Reconsidered, 1987, Mussolini's Fascist Philosopher: Giovanni Gentile Reconsidered, 2004; translator: Benedetto Croce's Essays on Literature & Literary Criticism, 1990; co-author: Values and Education, 1998; assoc. editor Special Issues; Journal of Value Inquiry, 1990-95 (Honorable Mention, Phoenix award); cons. editor Jour. Social Philosophy, 1988—; assoc. editor: Value Enquiry Book Series, 1990-95; editor: The Philosophy of José Gaos, by Pio Colonnello, Value Inquiry Book Series, 1997. Bogliasco fellow, Liguria, Italy, 2000. Mem. Am. Philos. Assn., Am. and Internat. Soc. for Value Inquiry, Soc. for Aesthetics, Collingwood Soc. (life), Phi Beta Kappa (hon.). Avocations: gardening, horseback riding. Office: Claremont McKenna Coll 850 Columbia Ave Claremont CA 91711-3901

MOSS, NANCY EVANS, nurse midwife, women's health nurse; b. Louisville, Sept. 20, 1944; d. Howard Heath and Emily Trimble (Muir) Evans; m. Edward Jewell Moss Jr., Dec. 21, 1984; children: Catherine Howard Rehm, Keith Hayes Rehm. Diploma, Norton Meml. Infirmary, Louisville, 1967; BSN, U. Pitts., 1973; MS in Nursing, U. Ky., 1975; PhD in Health Edn., U. Utah, 1991. Cert. Am. Coll. Nurse Midwives. Mem. clin. faculty dept. ob-gyn. U. Utah Coll. Medicine, Salt Lake City; asst. prof. U. Ky. Coll. Nursing, Lexington; asst. prof., dir. nurse midwifery ednl. program East Carolina U., Greenville, N.C.; prof., dir. nurse-midwifery ednl. program U. Cin. Mem. Am. Coll. Nurse-Midwives (bd. dirs.), Sigma Theta Tau. Home: 518 Fawn Run Dr Highland Heights KY 41076-3790

MOSS, PATRICIA L. bank executive; m. Greg Moss; children: Jennifer, Jeffrey. BS in bus. adminstrn., Linfield Coll., Oreg.; masters studies Portland State U.; certification ABA Comml. Banking Sch., U. Okla. From mem. staff to pres., CEO Cascade Bancorp, Bend, Oreg., 1977—99, pres., CEO, 1998—; CEO Bank of the Cascades, Bend, Oreg., 1998—. Bd. dirs. Cascade Bancorp, Bank of the Cascades, Aquilla Tax-Free Trust of Oreg., Ctrl. Oreg. Ind. Health Svcs., MDU Resources Group Inc., 2003—. Adv. bd. Oreg. State U. Cascade Campus. Named Disting. Citizen of Yr., Bend C. of C., Ctrl. Oreg. Bus. Woman of Yr. Mem.: Ind. Cmty. Bankers Assn. Am., Oreg. Bankers Assn. (bd. dir.), Oreg. Women's Forum. Office: Cascade Bancorp 1100 NW Wall St Bend OR 97701

MOSS, RANDY, professional football player; b. Feb. 13, 1977; 2 children. Student, Marshall U. Wide receiver Minn. Vikings, 1998—. Named Rookie of Yr., NFL, 1998, Most Outstanding Player, NFL Pro-Bowl, 2000; named to NFL Pro-Bowl, 1998—2000, 2002—03; recipient Espy Award for Breakthrough Athlete of the Yr., 1999. Achievements include first round draft pick NFL, 1998; led NFL in recieving touchdowns, 1998, 2000, 2003; holds NFL record for receptions in first five seasons (414), 2002; holds NFL record for fewest games to reach 5,000 career receiving yards (59 games); holds every receiving record at Marshall Univ. Office: MN Vikings 9520 Viking Dr Eden Prairie MN 55344 3898

MOSS, RICHARD L. physiology educator; b. Fond du Lac, Wis., Nov. 2, 1947; s. Robert C. and Lenore H. Moss; m. Susan L. Rusch, Aug. 17, 1968; 1 child, James P. BS in Biology, U. Wis., Oshkosh, 1969; PhD in Physiology and Biophysics, U. Vt., 1975. Rsch. assoc. Boston Biomed. Rsch. Inst., 1975-79; asst. prof. physiology U. Wis., Madison, 1979-83, assoc. prof., 1983-87, prof., 1987—, chair dept. physiology, 1988—. Dir. U. Wis. Cardiovascular Rsch. Ctr., 1995—; mem. cellular pharmacology and physiology rsch. study com. Am. Heart Assn., Dallas, 1990-93, Established Investigator, 1981-86; mem. physiology study sect. NIH, 1994—. Mem. editl. bd. Biophys. Jour., 1985-92, Jour. Gen. Physiology, 1987-91, Am. Jour. Physiology: Cellular, 1990-96, Physiol. Revs., 1985-91, Jour. Physiology (London), 1995—; contbr. articles to Biophys. Jour., Circulation Rsch., Nature, Jour. Physiology. NRSA fellow NIH, 1976-78. Achievements include research on regulation of heart and skeletal muscle contraction by selective extraction and/or exchange of regulatory protein from permeabilized muscle preparations, implicating role of thick filament proteins (i.e. light chain-2 and C-protein) in regulation of tension and kinetics of contraction. Office: U Wis Med Sch 1300 University Ave Madison WI 53706-1510

MOSS, RICHARD SPENCER, communications executive; b. Portland, Oreg., May 26, 1949; s. Harry and Mary Louise (Ruckdeschel) M., divorced, children: Emily Anne, Paul Spencer, Kathryn Elizabeth, Brian Richard. AA, Mount Hood C.C., 1975; BA in Comm., U. Portland, 1977. Publs. mgr. First Nat. Bank Oreg., Portland, 1977; mgr. employee comm. Ga.-Pacific Corp., Portland, 1977-80; dir. alumni and cmty. rels. U. Portland, 1980-84; dir. employee comm. NERCO Inc., Portland, 1984-87; pres. R.S. Moss & Assocs., Corp. Comms, Portland, 1987—. Bd. dirs. Vietnam Vets. of Oreg. Meml. Fund, Inc. With USN, 1969-73; Vietnam. Recipient Arnold's Admirables award The Ragan Report, 1982, Award of Excellence Annual Reports, Comm. Arts mag., Design Annual, 1989-90, Excellence award Soc. for Tech. Comms., 1989. Mem. Pub. Rels. Soc. Am., Internat. Assn. Bus. Communicators (chpt. dir., chpt. pres. 1985-86, Gold Quill award 1979, 83), Portland Advt. Fedn., Vietnam Vets. Am. (chpt. dir., state coun. dir.), bd. dirs., Vietnam Vets. of Oregon Meml. Fund. Republican. Roman Cath. Home and Office: 716 Smith Ave Lebanon PA 17042-7138

MOSS, ROGER WILLIAM, historian, writer, administrator; b. Zanesville, Ohio, Jan. 31, 1940; s. Roger William and Dorothy Elizabeth (Martin) M.; m. Gail Caskey Winkler, 1981; children by previous marriage: Elizabeth Moss McQuiston, Victoria Stiles Moss. BS in Edn., Ohio U., 1963, MA, 1964; postgrad., Attingham, Eng., 1966; PhD, U. Del., 1972. Staff Peace Corps, Cameroon, 1962-63; curator of rare books Ohio U., 1962-64; lectr., dept. history U. Del., 1966-68, U. Md., 1967-68; exec. dir. Athenaeum of Phila., 1968—. Lectr. to adj. prof. architecture U. Pa., Phila., 1981—2004. Publs. include Morgan Collection, 1965, Master Builders, 1972, Century of Color, 1981, Biographical Dictionary of Philadelphia Architects, 1985, Philadelphia, 1986, Victorian Interior Decoration, 1986, Victorian Exterior Decoration, 1987, Lighting for Historic Buildings, 1988 (Joel Polsky prize 1989), The American Country House, 1990, Philadelphia Victorian, 1998, Historic Houses of Philadelphia, 1998, Historic Sacred Places of Philadelphia, 2004; gen. editor Athenaeum Libr. of Nineteenth-Century Am. series, 1975—; editor: Paint in America, 1994; contbr. articles to profl. jours. Bd. dirs. Conservation Ctr. for Art and Hist. Artifacts, 1984-96, chmn., 1993-95, Woodlands Cemetery Co., 1990-99, Rsch. Librs. Group, 1993-96; exec. com., Phila. Area Consortium Spl. Coll., Librs., 1988-93; bd. dirs., sec. Christopher Ludwick Found., 1969—; bd. dirs. Brit. Cathedrals and Hist. Chs. Found., sec.-treas., 1996-2001, pres., 2002-04, bd. dirs. Abraham Lincoln Found., 1996—; bd. dirs., sec., treas. Victorian Soc. in Am., 1969-88; assoc. Nat. Preservation Inst., 1982-93; bd. dirs. Hist. House Assn. Am., 1978-83, Com. for Preservation of Archtl. Records, 1978-80, Phila. Area Cultural Consortium, 1977-82, also treas., Mus. Coun. Phila., 1976-78; sec. Hopkinson House Coun., 1982-93, Clivden Coun., Nat. Trust for Hist. Preservation, 1974-81, 84-86, Harriton House, 1969-81, Friends of Laurel Hill, 1978-83. NEH grantee, 1983-85; recipient Biddle award Preservation Alliance, 2004. Fellow Royal Soc. Arts; mem. Carpenters' Co. (hon.), Soc. Archtl. Historians, Soc. Preservation New Eng. Antiquities, Castine Yacht Club, Phila. Club. Office: Athenaeum of Phila 219 S 6th St Philadelphia PA 19106-3794 Office Phone: 215-925-2688. E-mail: rwmoss@philaathenaeum.org.

MOSS, THOMAS E. prosecutor; Grad., U. Idaho; JD, U. Idaho Coll. Law. Prosecuting atty. Bingham County Dist. Ct., 1967—71, 1979—99; ptnr. Moss, Cannon and Romrell, Blackfoot, Idaho; U.S. atty. U.S. Dept. of Justice, Idaho, 2001—. Mem.: Idaho Ho. of Reps. Office: PO Box 32 Boise ID 83707-0032

MOSS, THOMAS HENRY, science association administrator; b. Cleve., June 27, 1939; s. Joseph Harold and Elsa Margaret (Lemkau) M.; m. Kathleen Goddard, May 31, 1966; children: Ellen, Joseph, Cheryl, David. AB, Harvard U., 1961; PhD, Cornell U., 1965. Cons. analyst govtl. sci. policy U.S. Govt. Office Mgmt. and Budget, Washington, 1963-67; research physicist IBM Corp., Yorktown, N.Y., 1967-74, 75-76; staff dir., sci. advisor Office of Congressman George E. Brown, Washington, 1976-79; staff dir. subcom. sci., research and tech. Ho. of Reps., Washington, 1979-82; prof. physics, dean grad. studies and research Case Western Res. U., Cleve., 1982-96; exec. dir. Govt.-Univ.-Industry Roundtable, 1996—2001; with Nat. Acad. Scis, Washington; dir. Univ. relations Ohio Aerospace Inst., 2001—03. Adj. prof. physics Columbia U., N.Y.C., 1966-76; mem. nat rev. com. Office of Nuclear Waste Isolation, Columbus, 1983-87; bd. dirs. Univ. Tech. Inc., Cleve.; bd. dirs. Ctr. Great Lakes, Chgo., 1985-89; v.p. Edison Poymer Innovation Corp., Independence, Ohio, 1986-90. Editor: The Three Mile Island Nuclear Accident-Lessons, 1981; asst. editor Environ. Profl. mag.; cons. editor Sci, Tech. and Human Values Environ. mag.; contbr. articles to profl. jours. Treas. Lake Bancroft Cmty. Assn., Falls Church, Va., 1980; mem. adv. bd. Small Bus. SBIR Program, Cleve., 1983-85; mem., v.p. Shaker Heights (Ohio) Bd. Edn., 1989-96; chmn. N.E. Region Ohio Systemic Statewide Initiative in Sci. and Math. Edn., 1992-95. ASME fellow, 1995-96, NSF fellow Nobel Instn., 1966-67. Fellow Am. Phys. Soc. (chmn. forum on physics and soc. 1990-91), Nat. Coun. Univ. Rsch. Adminstrs. (Nat. Innovation Program award 1987), Scientists Inst. Pub. Info. (Disting. Svc. award Harlem Prep. Sch. 1971), AAAS (chmn. com. on sci., engring. and pub. policy 1989-91, chmn. sect. X 1998-99, exec. com. sect. P 2004—). Avocations: gardening, camping. Office Phone: 703-914-2854.

MOSSAVAR-RAHMANI, BIJAN, oil and gas company executive; b. Tehran, Iran, June 14, 1952; arrived in U.S., 1978; s. Morteza and Fatemeh (Mohtashem-Nouri) Mossavar-R.; m. Sharmin Batmanghelidj, Oct., 1980. BA, Princeton U., 1974; MS, U. Pa., 1975; MPA, Harvard U., 1982. Oil and energy columnist Kayhan Group of Newspapers, Iran, 1975-78; energy policy analyst Govt. of Iran, 1976-78; vis. rsch. fellow The Rockefeller Found., N.Y., 1978-80; rsch. coord. internat. natural gas study Harvard U., Mass., 1982-85, asst. dir. Energy and Environ. Policy Ctr., 1985-87; pres. Apache Internat., Inc., Houston, 1988-96; chmn. bd. Mondoil Corp., N.Y.C., 1996—, Foxtrot Internat. LDC, Abidjan, Cote d'Ivoire, 1999—. Author: Energy Policy in Iran, 1981; co-author: OPEC and the World Oil Outlook, 1983, World Natural Gas Outlook, 1984, The OPEC Natural Gas Dilemma, 1986, Energy Security Revisited, 1987, Natural Gas in Western Europe, 1987, Lower Oil Prices: Mapping the Impact, 1988, Competition and Realignment in Global Energy Markets, 1997, Energy Policies and Markets: New Trends or Old Cycles, 2001, Energy Liberalization and Regulation Revisited, 2002, Thinking the Unthinkable, 2003; mem. editl. adv. bd. Offshore mag., 1992-94. Bd. dirs. U.S.-Angola C. of C., 1990-92, Persepolis Found.; mem. coun. Internat. Exec. Svc. Corps, 1991-96; mem. vis. com. Dept. Islamic Art Met. Mus. Art, 2003-; mem. internat. coun. Belfer Ctr. for Sci. and Internat. Affairs, Harvard U., 2004-. Decorated Comdr. de l'Ordre Nat. de Cote d'Ivoire. Mem. Denver U. Club, Nassau Club, Harvard Club of N.Y. Address: 953 Fifth Ave New York NY 10021 Office Phone: 212-535-9930.

MOSSAWIR, HARVE H., JR., retired lawyer; b. Morton, Miss., Aug. 9, 1942; s. Harve H. and Madeline (Price) M.; children: Anna Christine, Karen Elyse; m. Judy S. Bardugo, Aug. 5, 1985; 1 child, Leigh Sarah. BA with honors, U. Ala., 1964; MA in Econs., U. Manchester, 1965; JD with honors, U. Chgo., 1968. Bar: Calif. 1970. Asst. prof. U. Ala. Law Sch., Tuscaloosa, 1968-69; assoc. Irell & Manella, L.A., 1969-74, ptnr., 1974-94, of counsel, 1994-96. Mem. bd. editors U. Chgo. Law Rev., 1966-68; contbr. articles to profl. jours. Fulbright scholar, 1964-65, Floyd Russell Mecham scholar, 1965-68. Republican. E-mail: labard1@yahoo.com.

MÖSSBAUER, RUDOLF LUDWIG, physicist, researcher; b. Munich, Jan. 31, 1929; s. Ludwig and Erna M.; m. E. Pritz, 1957 (div. 1983); 3 children; m. Christel Braun, 1985. Ed., Technische Hochschule, Munich; DSc (hon.), Gustaphus Adolphus Coll., 1963, U. Lille, France, 1963, Oxford U., 1973, U. Leicester, Eng., 1975; Dr. honoris causa, U. Grenoble, France, 1974, U. Madrid, 1975, U. Leuven, 1976, U. Saarbrücken, 1985, Eötvös Loránd U., Budapest, Hungary, 1989, U. Montreal, 1989, U. Birmingham, U.K., 1998. Research asst. Max-Planck Inst., Heidelberg, Fed. Republic Germany, 1955-57; research fellow Technische Hochschule, Munich, 1958-60, Calif. Inst. Tech., 1960, sr. research fellow, 1961, prof. physics, 1961; prof. exptl. physics Tech. U. Munich, 1964-72, 77-97, prof. emeritus, 1997—. Dir. Inst. Max von Laue, Grenoble, France and German-French-Brit. High Flux Reactor, 1972-77. Author publs. on recoilless nuclear resonance absorption and neutrino physics. Decorated Order for Merit for Scis. and Arts (Germany); recipient Research Corp. award, 1961, Röntgen prize U. Giessen, 1961, Elliott Cresson medal Franklin Inst., Phila., 1961, Nobel prize for physics, 1961, Guthrie medal Inst. Physics (London), 1974, Lomonossov medal Acad. Sci. USSR, 1984, Einstein medal Albert Einstein Soc., Bern, 1986,mem. of Order of Merit for Arts and Scis., Bonn, Germany, 1996. Fellow Franklin Inst. (life); mem. Deutsche Physikalische Gesellschaft, Deutsche Gesellschaft der Naturforscher und Aerzte, Deutsche Akademie der Naturforscher Leopoldina, Am. Phys. Soc., European Phys. Soc., Indian Acad. Scis., Am. Acad. Sci. (fgn.), Am. Acad. Arts Scis. (fgn), Nat. Acad. Scis. (fgn. assoc.), Bavarian Acad. Scis., Academia Nazionale dei XL Roma, Pontifical Acad. Scis., Acad. Sci. USSR (fgn.), Acad. European Scis. Arts des Letters France, Hungarian Acad. of Scis., Internat. Acad. Scis., Internat. Acad. of Science, Munich, Acad. Europe U.K., French Phys. Soc. (hon.), Brit. Inst. Physics (hon.)., Academia Scientiarum et Artium Europaea. Office: Tech U Munich Dept Physics E15 85748 Garching Germany

MOSSBERG, WALTER, columnist; b. Warwick, RI; m. Edith Mossberg; children: Steven, Jonathan. B in Politics, Brandeis U.; MA, Columbia U.; LLD (hon.), U. RI, 2001. Reporter, editor Wall St. Jour., NYC, 1970—, dep. Washington bur. chief, 1983-87, sr. corr., asst. news editor, 1987-91, creator, author personal tech. column, 1991—. Author: The Wall Street Journal Book of Personal Technology, (weekly column) Jour., Mossberg's Mailbox, The Mossberg Solution, The Mossberg Report; contbg. editor SmartMoney, The Wall Street Journal Mag. Personal Bus.; co-editor Labor Letter. Named Most Influential Computer Journalist in Nation, Mktg. Computers Mag., Most Influential Journalist Writing About Computers, Tech. Mktg. mag., 1995—2001; recipient Loeb award for Commentary, 1999, Nat. Headliner award, 2001. Office: Dow Jones & Co World Fin Ctr 200 Liberty St New York NY 10281

MOSSE, PETER JOHN CHARLES, financial services executive; b. Mtarfa, Malta, Sept. 8, 1947; came to U.S., 1977; s. John Herbert Charles and Barbara Haworth (Holden) M.; m. Christine Marielle St. Preux, Oct. 17, 1994. BA, Oxford U., 1969; MBA, U. Pa., 1971; MA, Oxford U., 1989. Bank officer N.M. Rothschild & Sons Ltd., London, 1971-76; spl. projects officer banking Bumiputra Mcht. Bankers Berhad, Kuala Lumpur, Malaysia, 1976-77; v.p., treas., sec. NMR Metals Incorp., N.Y.C., 1977-79, exec. v.p., 1979-83; sr. v.p. Rothschild, Inc., N.Y.C., 1983-90; v.p., CFO, The Arista Group Inc., N.Y.C., 1991-93; U.S. rep. Travelex Fin. Svcs. Ltd., London, 1994-95; ptnr. Creelman Fine Arts, N.Y.C., 1995—2003; fellow Royal Soc. Arts, London, 2003—. Treas. Circumnavigators Found., 2004—. Mem. Pilgrims of the U.S., St. George's Soc. N.Y. (life), Oxford U. Alumni Soc. (exec. com. 1994-96), Gold Inst. (co. rep., bd. dirs. 1985-90), Silver Inst. (co. rep., bd. dirs. 1989-90), Copper Club, Commodity Exch., Inc. (co. rep. 1979-90), Circumnavigators Club, Travelers Century Club. Episcopalian. Avocations: travel, trains. Home and Office: 353 E 72nd St Apt 33D New York NY 10021-4622

MOSSINGHOFF, GERALD JOSEPH, patent law expert, educator; b. St. Louis, Sept. 30, 1935; m. Jeanne Carole Jack, Dec. 29, 1958; children: Pamela Ann Jennings, Gregory Joseph, Melissa M. Ronayne. BSEE, St. Louis U., 1957; JD with honors, George Washington U., 1961. Bar: Mo. 1961, D.C. 1965, Va. 1981. Project engr. Sachs Electric Corp., 1954-57; dir. congl. liaison NASA, Washington, 1967-73, dep. gen. counsel, 1976-81; asst. Sec. Commerce, commr. patents and trademarks U.S. Patent Office, 1981-85; pres. Pharm. Rsch. and Mfrs. Am., Washington, 1985-96; Cifelli prof. intellectual property law George Washington U., Washington, 1996—; sr. counsel Oblon, Spivak, McClelland, Maier & Neustadt, Arlington, Va., 1997—. Amb. Paris Conv. Diplomatic Conf.; adj. prof. George Mason U. Law Sch. Recipient Exceptional Svc. medal NASA, 1971, Disting. Svc. medal, 1980, Outstanding Leadership medal, 1981, Jefferson medal, 2000; Disting. Alumnus George Washington U., 1996; granted presdl. rank of meritorious exec., 1980; Disting. Pub. Svc. award Sec. of Commerce, 1983 Fellow Am. Acad. Pub. Adminstrn.; mem. Reagan Alumni Assn. (bd. dirs.), Cosmos Club, Knights of Malta, Order of Coif, Eta Kappa Nu, Pi Mu Epsilon. Home: 1530 Key Blvd Penthouse 28 Arlington VA 22209-1532 Office: Oblon Spivak McClelland Maier & Neustadt 1940 Duke St Alexandria VA 22314 Office Phone: 703-412-7073.

MOSSO, LYLE DAVID, financial executive; b. Pasadena, Calif., Aug. 13, 1926; s. Joseph Ernest and Marian (Ure) M.; m. Lee McVoy Pierce, June 11, 1955; children: Janet, Andrew, Jocelyn. BBA magna cum laude, Washburn U., 1950, D in Commerce (hon.), 1982; MA in Econs, U. Minn., 1951. CPA, Va. With Santa Fe Ry., 1942-44; instr. econs. and acctg. Washburn U., 1954-55; with U.S. Treasury Dept., 1955-77, commr. accounts, 1971-73, dep. asst. sec. treasury, 1973-75, asst. sec., 1975-77; with Fin. Acctg. Stds. Bd., 1978-96; vice chmn. Fin. Acctg. Standards Bd., 1986-87; adj. prof. acctg. Fordham U., 1996—; chmn. Fed. Acctg. Stds. Adv. Bd., 1997—. Arbitrator Am. Arbitration Assn., 1997—. Contbr. articles to profl. jours. Mem. Comptr. Gen.'s Acctg. Stds. Adv. Coun., 1987-90; mem. charter revision commn. City of Stamford, 1986-87, Can.-U.S. Adv. Group on Fed. Reporting, 1984-86; alt. trustee Nat. Gallery Art, 1975-77; dir. Stamford Emergency Med. Svc., 1993-94. 1st lt. AUS, 1944-46, 51-53. Recipient Alexander Hamilton award Treasury Dept., 1977, Braden award Case Western Res. U., 2002. Mem. AICPA (Elijah Watt Sells award 1962), Va. Soc. CPAs (Gold medal 1962), Am. Acctg. Assn., Assn. Govt Accts. (dir. Washington chpt. 1972-73, Disting. Leadership award 1977, Elmer Staats award 1990), Treasury Hist. Assn. (pres. 1978), Tau Delta Pi, Pi Gamma Mu, Phi Kappa Phi. Home: 111 Saddle Hill Rd Stamford CT 06903-2307 Office: 441 G St NW Ste 6814 Washington DC 20548-0001

MOSSOP, GRANT DILWORTH, geologist, researcher; b. Calgary, Alta., Can., Apr. 15, 1948; s. Cyril S. and Freida E. (Dilworth) Mossop; m. Ruth Shaver, May 24, 1969; children: Jenny, Jonathan, David. BSc in Geology, U. Calgary, 1970, MSc in Geology, 1971; PhD, DIC in Geology, Imperial Coll., U. London, 1973. Postdoctoral fellow U. Calgary, Canada, 1974; asst. rsch. officer Alta. Rsch. Coun., Edmonton, 1975—77, assoc. rsch. officer, 1977—80, head geol. survey dept., 1980—84, sr. rsch. officer, 1985—91; dir. Geol. Survey of Can., Calgary, 1991—2001, rsch. scientist, 2001—. Acad. visitor dept. earth sci. Oxford U., England, 1984—85. Project mgr., editor: Geological Atlas of Western Canada Sedimentary Basin. Fellow: Geol. Assn. Can. (pres. 1986—87); mem.: Can. Soc. Petroleum Geologists. Home: 68 Colleen Cres SW Calgary AB Canada T2V 2R3 Office: Geol Survey Can 3303 33d St NW Calgary AB Canada T2L 2A7 E-mail: gmossop@nrcan.gc.ca.

MOSS-SALENTIJN, LETTY (ALEIDA MOSS-SALENTIJN), anatomist, educator; b. Amsterdam, The Netherlands, Apr. 14, 1943; came to U.S., 1968; d. Ewoud and Johanna Maria (Schoonhoven) Salentijn; m. Melvin Lionel Moss, Apr. 17, 1970. DDS, State U. Utrecht, Netherlands, 1967, PhD, 1976. Asst. prof. histology State U. Utrecht, 1967-68; asst. prof. Columbia U., N.Y.C., 1968-74, assoc. prof., 1974-86, prof., 1986—, Edwin S. Robinson prof., 1999—, dir. dental radiology, 1980-86, dir. grad. program dental sci., 1986—, dir. postdoctoral affairs, 1987-90, asst. dean postdoctoral programs, 1990-94, assoc. dean acad. affairs, 1994—. Author: Orofacial Histology & Embryology, 1972; Dental and Oral Tissues, 1980, 2d edit., 1984, 3d edit., 1990; contbr. chpts. to books, articles to profl. jours. Fellow Royal Microscopical Soc., Am. Coll. Dentists; mem. Am. Assn. Anatomists, Internat. Assn. Dental Rsch., Am. Soc. Biomechs., Sigma Xi (chpt. sec. 1980-87, pres. 1987-89, 98-99), Omicron Kappa Upsilon (pres. local chpt. 1987). Avocation: stained glass art. Home: 560 Riverside Dr Apt 20K New York NY 10027-3239 Office: Columbia U/SDOS Assoc Dean Academic Affairs 630 W 168th St New York NY 10032-3702 Office Phone: 212-305-8334. Business E-Mail: lm23@columbia.edu.

MOST, JACK LAWRENCE, lawyer, consultant; b. N.Y.C., Sept. 24, 1935; s. Meyer Milton and Henrietta (Meyer) M.; children: Jeffrey, Peter; m. Irma Freedman Robbins, Aug. 8, 1968; children: Ann, Jane. BA cum laude, Syracuse U., 1956; JD, Columbia U., 1960. Bar: N.Y. 1960, U.S. Dist. Ct. (so. and ea. dists.) N.Y. 1963. Assoc. Hale, Grant, Meyerson and O'Brien, N.Y.C., 1960-66; dep. assoc. dir. OEO, Exec. Office of The Pres., Washington, 1965-67; asst. to gen. counsel C.I.T. Fin. Corp., N.Y.C., 1968-70; corp. counsel PepsiCo, Inc., Purchase, N.Y., 1970-71; v.p. legal affairs Revlon, Inc., N.Y.C., 1971-76; asst. gen. counsel Norton Simon, Inc., N.Y.C., 1976-79; ptnr. Rogers Hoge and Hills, N.Y.C., 1979-86, Finkelstein Bruckman Wohl Most & Rothman LLP, N.Y.C., 1986-97, mng. ptnr., 1990-93, Ferster Bruckman Wohl Most & Rothman LLP, 1997-98; ptnr. Goetz, Fitzpatrick, Most & Bruckman LLP, 1999—2002, Goetz Fitzpatrick, LLP, 2003—. Corp. sec. Requa, Inc., Flowery Beauty Products, Inc., 1987—. Contbr. articles to profl. jour. and mags. Bd. dirs. Haym Salomon Home for the Aged, 1978-91, pres., 1981-91; bd. dirs. The Jaffa Inst. for Advancement Edn., 1994-95; bd. dirs. Jewish Fellowship of Hemlock Farms, 1995-2001, treas., 1996-98, sec. 1998-99; bd. dirs., 1992—, pres. Haym Salomon Found., 1992-99; mem. bd. advisors Touro Coll. Health Scis., 1989-90. Mem. ABA (food, drug and cosmetic law com., trademark and unfair competition com.), N.Y. State Bar Assn. (food, drug and cosmetics sect.), YRH Owners Corp. (bd. dirs., pres. 1989-92), Lords Valley Country Club (bd. govs. 1984-90, 1st v.p. 1987-88, 2d v.p. 1989-90), Zeta Beta Tau, Omicron (trustee Syracuse chpt. 1988-91). Jewish. Home: 429 E 52nd St New York NY 10022-6430 Office: Goetz Fitzpatrick LLP One Penn Plz New York NY 10119 E-mail: jmost@goetzfitz.com.

MOST, NATHAN, mutual fund executive; b. L.A., Mar. 22, 1914; s. Bernard and Bertha (Saltzman) M.; m. Evelyn Rosenthal, July 10, 1964; children—Stephen, John, Robert, Barbara. BA, UCLA, 1935. Exec. v.p. Getz Bros. & Co., San Francisco, 1945-60; pres. Carad Corp., Palo Alto, Calif., 1961-64; exec. v.p. James S. Baker Co., San Francisco, 1964-65, Pacific Vegetable Oil Corp., San Francisco, 1965-70, Am. Import Co., San Francisco, 1970-74; pres. Pacific Commodities Exchange, San Francisco, 1974-76; spl. asst. to chmn. Commodity Futures Trading Commn., Washington, May-Dec. 1976; pres. Amex Commodities Exch., N.Y.C., 1977-80; v.p. new products devel. Am. Stock Exch., 1980—96, sr. v.p., 1996—2002; pres., chmn., CEO iShares Inc., Wilmington, Del., 1990—92; pres., chmn. bd., CEO iShares Trust, 2000—; chmn. emeritus, bd. dirs. iShares Inc. and iShares Trust, Wilmington, 1992—. Pres. Amex Commodities Corp., Inc., N.Y.C., 1982-96; v.p. Calif. Council Internat. Trade, 1966-67; pres. Commodity Club San Francisco, 1970—; bd. dirs. San Francisco-Pacific Commodity Exch., 1970—, San Francisco World Trade Assn., 1970—, World Affairs Council No. Calif., 1953-65; pres. San Francisco World Trade Assn., 1956-58; pres., chmn. bd. IShares Trust, San Francisco, 2000—. *Designer and creator of the first Exchange Traded Fund, the Standard and Poor's Depository Receipt — the SPDR- launched in 1993-while at the American Stock Exchange in charge of new product development 1977-1996. As a member of the AMEX staff during 1994-1996, acted as consultant for Morgan Stanley in developing their MSCI WEBS now iShares, the first ETF's based on foreign shares. 1998-2002 served as an independent consultant for Barclays Global Investors in the development of their iShares program.* Councilman Atherton, Calif., 1959-64. Named one of 30 most influential people in the world of investing, Smart Money. Mem. Export Mgmt. Assn. No. Calif. (pres. 1972—), San Francisco Commodity Club (dir.). Home: 602 Laurel Ave Apt 704 San Mateo CA 94401 Office Phone: 650-348-7650. Personal E-mail: natemost@aol.com.

MOSTAFA, JAVED, information scientist, educator; b. Chittagong, Bangladesh, July 31, 1966; came to U.S., 1984; s. Ghulam Mustafa and Jobeda Khatun; m. Sigma Salahuddin, June 7, 1991. BSc magna cum laude, N.W. Okla. State U., 1987; MA, Ohio State U., 1990; PhD, U. Tex., 1994. Dir. info. processing lab U. Tex., Austin, 1991-92; asst. prof. Ind. U., Bloomington, 1994—, Victor Yngve asst. prof., 1998-2000, Victor Yngve assoc. prof. info. sci., 2000—, assoc. prof. Sch. Informatics, 2000—. Adj. asst. prof. computer sci. dept. Ind. U., Inpls., 1996—02, adj. assoc. prof. 2001-, rschr. web lab. 1996-97,Core Facility Cognitive Sci. Ind. U. Bloomington,1999-; vis. scholar sys. engrng. dept. Chinese U. Hong Kong, 1998. Author: Easy Internet Handbook, 1994; contbr. articles to profl. jours. Grantee NSF, 1999, 2000, North Ctrl. Regonal Ednl. Lab., 2002, Eli Lilly & Co., 1999, Inst. Mus. and Libr. Svcs., 2001. Fellow Ctr. Social Informatics; mem. AAAS, Am. Assoc. Adv. Sci. Am. Soc. Info. Sci., Assn. Computing Machinery, IEEE computer Soc. mem. editrl. bd. ACM Transactions Info. Sys. Am. Assn. for the Advancement of Sci., IEEE Computer Soc., bd. dir. ACM Trans. on Info. Sys., Phi Kappa Phi. Avocations: reading, travel, jogging, racquetball. Home: 6456 Deerwood Ct Greenwood IN 46143 Office: Ind U SLIS # 025 10th & Jordan Ave Bloomington IN 47405-1801

MOSTELLER, FREDERICK, mathematical statistician, educator; b. Clarksburg, W.Va., Dec. 24, 1916; s. William Roy and Helen (Kelley) M.; m. Virginia Gilroy, May 17, 1941; children: William, Gale. ScB, Carnegie Inst. Tech. (now Carnegie-Mellon U.), 1938, MSc, 1939, DSc (hon.), 1974; AM, Princeton U., 1942, PhD, 1946; DSc (hon.), U. Chgo., 1973, Wesleyan U., 1983; D. of Social Scis. (hon.), Yale U., 1981; LLD (hon.), Harvard U., 1991. Research assoc. Office Pub. Opinion Research, 1942-44; spl. cons. research br. War Dept., 1942-43; research mathematician Statis. Research Group, Princeton, applied math. panel Nat. Devel. and Research Council, 1944-46; mem. faculty Harvard U., 1946—, prof. math. stats., 1951-87, Roger I. Lee prof., 1978-87, prof. emeritus, 1987—, chmn. dept. stats., 1957-69, 75-77, chmn. dept. biostats., 1977-81, chmn. dept. health policy and mgmt., 1981-87; dir. Tech. Assessment Group, 1987—; dir. Ctr. for Evaluation Am. Acad. Arts and Scis., 1994—. Vice chmn. Pres.'s Commn. on Fed. Stats., 1970-71; mem. Nat. Adv. Council Equality of Ednl. Opportunity, 1973-78, Nat. Sci. Bd. Commn. on Pre-coll. Edn. in Math., Sci. and Tech., 1982-83; Fund for Advancement of Edn. fellow, 1954-55; nat. tchr. NBC's Continental Class-room TV course in probability and stats., 1960-61; fellow Center Advanced Study Behavioral Sciences, 1962-63, bd. dirs., 1980-86; Guggenheim fellow, 1969-70; Miller research prof. U. Calif. at Berkeley, 1974-75; Hitchcock Found. lectr. U. Calif., 1985. Co-author: Gauging Public Opinion (editor Hadley Cantril), 1944, Sampling Inspection, 1948, The Pre-election Polls, 1948, 49, Stochastic Models for Learning, 1955, Probability with Statisticial Applications, 1961, Inference and Disputed Authorship, The Federalist, 1964, The National Halothane Study, 1969, Statistics: A Guide to the Unknown, 3d edit., 1988, On Equality of Educational Opportunity, 1972, Sturdy Statistics, 1973, Statistics By Example, 1973, Cost, Risks and Benefits of Surgery, 1977, Data Analysis and Regression, 1977, Statistics and Public Policy, 1977, Data for Decisions, 1982, Understanding Robust and Exploratory Data Analysis, 1983, Biostatistics in Clinical Medicine, 1983, 3d edit., 1994, Beginning Statistics with Data Analysis, 1983, Exploring Data Tables, Trends and Shapes, 1985, Medical Uses of Statistics, 1986, 2d edit., 1992, Quality of Life and Technology Assessment, 1989, Fundamentals of Exploratory Analysis of Variance, 1992, Meta-analysis for Explanation, 1992, Doing More Good Than Harm, 1993, Medicine Worth Paying For, 1995; author articles in field. Trustee Russell Sage Found.; mem. bd. Nat. Opinion Research Center, 1962-66. Recipient Outstanding Statistician award Chgo. chpt. Am. Statis. Assn., 1971, Boston chpt., 1989, named Sports Statistician of 1996; recipient Myrdal prize Evaluation Research Soc., 1978, Paul F. Lazarsfeld prize Council Applied Social Research, 1979, R.A. Fisher award Com. of Pres.'s of Statis. Socs., 1987, Medallion of Ctrs. for Disease Control, 1988. Fellow AAAS (chmn. sect. U 1973, dir. 1974-78, pres. 1980, chmn. bd. 1981), Inst. Math. Statistics (pres. 1974-75), Am. Statis. Assn. (v.p. 1962-64, pres. 1967, Samuel S. Wilks medal 1986), Social Sci. Research Council (chmn. bd. dirs. 1966-68), Math. Social Sci. Bd. (acad. governing bd. 1962-67), Am. Acad. Arts and Scis. (council 1986-88), Royal Statis. Soc. (hon.); mem. Am. Philos. Soc. (council 1986-88), Internat. Statis. Inst. (v.p. 1986-88, pres.-elect 1989, pres. 1991-93), Math. Assn. Am., Psychometric Soc. (pres. 1957-58), Inst. Medicine of Nat. Acad. Scis. (council 1978), Nat. Acad. Scis., Biometric Soc. Office: 1 Oxford St Cambridge MA 02138-2901

MOSTELLER, JAMES WILBUR, III, data processing executive; b. Ft. Riley, Kans., June 21, 1940; s. James Wilbur Jr. and Ruth Renfro (Thompson) M.; m. Sandra Josephine Stevenson, Oct. 13, 1962; children: Margaret, Steven, Michael. BS in Econs., Rensselaer Poly. Inst., 1962; MBA, Temple U., 1971. Cert. in data processing. Data processing sys. analyst Philco-Ford, Ft. Washington, Pa., 1966-69; data processing analyst and supr. Merck Sharp & Dohme, West Point, Pa., 1969-75; dir. mgmt. info. sys. KELCO divsn. Merck and Co., San Diego, 1975-87; dir. info. mgmt. Advanced Sys. divsn. United Technologies, San Diego, 1987-88; computer scientist Navy Personnel Research and Devel. Ctr., San Diego, 1988-97; head prodn. sys. Navy SPAWAR Sys. Ctr., 1997—. Bd. dirs. New Horizons Montessori Sch., Ft. Washington, 1974-75; leader youth programs North County YMCA, 1977-81; mem. San Diego Rsch. Park Com., 1978-86; 1st v.p., mem. exec. com. San Diego Space and Sci. Found., 1985-92; trustee emeritus Reuben H. Fleet Sci. Ctr., 2003—. With USN, 1962-66, capt. res., 1966-93. Mem. Data Processing Mgmt. Assn., Assn. Sys. Mgmt., Naval Res. Assn. (life), U.S. Naval Inst. (life), Royal Scottish County Dance Soc. (chmn. San Diego br. 2001-03), La Playa Yacht Club, Beta Gamma Sigma, Sigma Alpha Epsilon (chpt. pres. 1961-62). Office: Navy SPAWAR Sys Ctr D0294 San Diego CA 92152-5001

MOSTELLER, ROBERT P. law educator; b. 1948; BA, U. N.C., 1970; MA, Harvard U., 1975; JD, Yale U., 1975. Bar: N.C. 1975, D.C. 1976. Law clk. to Hon. Braxton Craven U.S. Ct. Appeals (4th cir.), Asheville, NC, 1975-76; atty., chmn. trial div., tng. dir. D.C. Pub. Defender Svc., 1976-83; assoc. prof. Duke U., Durham, NC, 1983-87, prof., 1987-2001, Harry R. Chadwick, Sr. prof., 2001—, sr. assoc. dean, 1989-91, chair acad. counsel, 1998-2000. Mem. Phi Beta Kappa (pres. 1969-70). Office: Sch Law Duke U Durham NC 27708

MOSTER, MARY CLARE, public relations executive; b. Morristown, N.J., Apr. 7, 1950; d. Clarence R. and Ruth M. Moster; m. Louis C. Williams, Jr., Oct. 4, 1987. BA in English with honors, Douglass Coll., 1972; MA in English Lit., Univ. Chgo., 1973. Accredited pub. rels. counselor. Editor No. Trust Bank, Chgo., 1973-75, advt. supr., 1975-77, communications officer, 1977-78; account exec. Hill & Knowlton, Inc., Chgo., 1978-80, v.p., 1980-83, sr. v.p., 1983-87, sr. v.p., mng. dir., 1987-88; staff v.p. comms. Navistar Internat. Corp., Chgo., 1988-93; v.p. corp. comms. Comdisco, Inc., Rosemont, Ill., 1993—2002; sr. v.p. L.C. Williams and Assocs., Chgo., 2002—. Bd. dirs. The Pegasus Players, 1993-2000. Author poetry, poetry translation. Bd. govs. Met. Planning Coun., Chgo., 1988-94; fellow Leadership Greater Chgo., 1989-90; bd. dirs. New City YMCA, Chgo., 1986-92; corp. devel. bd. Steppenwolf Theatre Co., Chgo., 1988-90; mem. The Chgo. Network, 1994—, bd. dirs., 1996-99. Mem. Nat. Investor Rels. Inst. (bd. dirs. 1988-89, 90-99, pres. Chgo. chpt. 1998-99), Arthur W. Page Soc., Pub. Rels. Soc. Am., Internat. Women's Forum. Avocations: sailing, cross country skiing, book groups. Office: L C Williams & Assocs 150 N Michigan Ave Ste 3800 Chicago IL 60601 Office Phone: 312-565-3900.

MOSTILLO, RALPH, medical association administrator; s. Joseph and Antoinette Mostillo. BA in Chemistry magna cum laude, Rutgers U., Newark, 1972; MA in Biochemistry, Princeton (NJ) U., 1974, PhD in Biochemistry, 1978. Rsch. fellow Princeton U., 1972-78; sr. scientist drug regulatory affairs Hoffmann-La Roche, Inc., Nutley, NJ, 1979-85; founder, chmn., CEO Am. Cancer Assn., Nutley, 1986—. With USN, 1962—66, Vietnam. Fellow, NIH, 1972—78. Mem.: NY Acad. Scis., Am. Mktg. Assn., Am. Mgmt. Assn., Am. Chem. Soc., Vietnam Vets. Am., Am. Legion, Phi Beta Kappa, Sigma Xi. Achievements include research in on molecular transport systems in E. coli as general models for drug delivery into cells. Home: PO Box 505 Nutley NJ 07110-0505 Office: Am Cancer Assn PO Box 87 Nutley NJ 07110-0087

MOST-LEVIN, CAROL LYNN, physician, geriatrician; b. Long Island, N.Y., Sept. 1, 1959; d. Herbert Jules and Jean (Friedman) Most; m. Ronald Mitchell Levin, June 17, 1979; children: Jay Samuel, Marc Andrew, Eric Brian. BA magna cum laude, La Salle Coll., Phila., 1981; MD, Med. Coll. Pa., 1985. Diplomate Nat. Bd. Med. Examiners; diplomate in internal medicine and geriatric medicine Am. Bd. Internal Medicine. Intern and resident Abington (Pa.) Meml. Hosp., 1985-88; pvt. practice, 1988-95, 2001—; internist Abington Meml. Hosp., 1995-2001, mem.-at-large med. exec. com., 1999—2002. Med. dir. U.S. Homecare, Phila., 1991-94; clin. instr. Temple U., Phila., 1995-96; instr. Jefferson U., 1996—; med. sch. interviewer Alleghany U., 1995-97; spkr. in field. Contbr. articles to mag., jours. Recipient First prize Eleanor Dixon Writing/Rsch. Competition, 1988. Fellow ACP; mem. AMA (Physician's Recognition award 1991, 94, 97, 2000, 03), Am. Geriatrics Soc., Pa. Med. Soc., Montgomery County Med. Soc., Delaware Valley Geriatrics Soc. Avocations: travel, cooking, decorating. Office: Levin and Most-Levin Med Assocs LLC 6921 B Frankford Ave Philadelphia PA 19135 Home: 4838 Noras Path Rd Charlotte NC 28226-3463 E-mail: cmlmdfacp@aol.com.

MOSTO, PATRICIA, environmental scientist, educator; b. Buenos Aires, Dec. 6, 1950; arrived in U.S., 1977; d. Alberto Pdro Mosto and Lia Ester Cagnoni; 1 child from previous marriage, Lara Cascallar. Lic., U. Buenos Aires, 1973, PhD, 1995; MA, U. Tex., 1980; MS, Drexel U., 1993. Asst. curator U. Tex., Austin, 1978—82; water lab rschr. Dept. Pub. Work, L.A., 1985—88; water lab dir. Dept. Water & Power, L.A., 1988—89; rsch. asst. Drexel U., Phila., 1989—92, Acad. Nat. Sci., Phila., 1992—93; from asst. prof. to assoc. prof. Rowan U., Pitman, NJ, 1993—2004, prof., chair, 2004—. Rsch. cons. U. So. Calif., L.A., 1983—85, Rohm & Haas, Phila., 1997—99, Naval Svc. Investigation, Buenos Aires, 1995—. Author: Practical Limnology, 1986, Fresh Water Ecosystems, 1995; contbr. articles to jours. Bd. dirs. Pitman Environ. Commn., 1996—; judge Coriell Sci. Fair, NJ, 1999—; cons. LandiSewage Authority, NJ, 2000—. Recipient 26 grants. Mem.: Am. Assn. Higher Edn., Am. Chem. Engrng. Soc., Phycological Soc. Am., Phi Kappa Phi. Avocations: camping, movies, cards. Home: 523 Grandview Ave Pitman NJ 08071 Office: Rowan U 201 Mullica Hill Rd Glassboro NJ 08028 Office Phone: 856-256-4834. Business E-Mail: mosto@rowan.edu.

MOSTOFF, ALLAN SAMUEL, lawyer, consultant; b. N.Y.C., Oct. 19, 1932; s. Morris and Ida (Goldman) M.; m. Alice Tamara Popelowskuy, July 31, 1955; children: Peter Alexander, Nina Valerie. BS, Cornell U., 1953; MBA, NYU, 1954; LLB, N.Y. Law Sch., 1957. Bar: N.Y. 1958, D.C. 1964. Assoc. Olwine Connelly Chase O'Donnell & Weyher, N.Y.C., 1958-61; atty. SEC, Washington, 1962-66, asst. dir., 1966-69, assoc. dir., 1969-72, dir. divsn. investment mgmt. regulation, 1972-76; ptnr. Dechert Price & Rhoads, Washington, 1976—2002, Dechert, Washington, 2000—03; ptnr. emeritus, sr. counsel Dechert LLP, Washington, 2002—03, of counsel, 2004—; pres. Mut. Fund Dirs. Forum, 2002—. Adj. prof. Georgetown U. Law Ctr., 1972-82; mem. Fin. Acctg. Standards Adv. Bd., 1982-86; mem. adv. bd. Investment Lawyer, 2000—, BNA Securities Regulation and Law Report, 1977-87. Mem. ABA, Assn. of Bar of City of N.Y., Fed. Bar Assn. (past chmn. exec. coun. securities regulation com. 1990-92), Am. Law Inst. Home: 6417 Waterway Dr Falls Church VA 22044-1325 Office: Mutual Funds Dirs Forum Two Lafayette Ctr 1133 21st St NW Ste 780 Washington DC 20036 Office Phone: 202-775-2100. E-mail: allan.mostoff@mfdf.com.

MOSTOVOY, MARC SANDERS, conductor, music director; b. Phila., July 1, 1942; s. Ira and Floretta (Schiff) M. MusB, Temple U., 1963; postgrad., U. Pa., 1964-66; pvt. study in U.S.A., France, 1950-66; MusD (hon.), Combs Coll. Music, 1980; diploma, Acad. Music, Nice, France. Conductr, music dir. Concerto Soloists of Phila., 1964—; also bd. dirs., 1964—. Cultural advisor to gov. Commonwealth of Pa., Harrisburg, 1971—77; music dir. Mozart on the Sq., Phila., 1980—91; music advisor Walnut St. Theater, Phila., 1970—75;

mem. music adv. panel Pa. Coun. on the Arts, 1991—92. Condr.: numerous nat. and internat. concert tours with Concerto Soloists Chamber Orch. of Phila., artistic dir.: Laurel Festival of the Arts, 1990—95; editor: various music compositions. Program adv. com. Nat. Mus. Am. Jewish History, 1985-86; bd. dirs. Citizens for the Arts in Pa., 1984-86. Recipient Orpheus Club award, 1958, Govs. citation Commonwealth of Pa., 1976, Mayors citation City of Phila., 1984; Temple U. scholar, 1960-63. Mem. Mus. Fund Soc. Phila., Greater Phila. C. of C. (adv. com. arts and cultural coun. 1984-88). Jewish. Office: The Chamber Orch Phila 5th Fl 1520 Locust St Philadelphia PA 19102 E-mail: mmostovoy@chamberorchestra.org, Info@chamberorchestraofphiladelphia.org.

MOSTOW, GEORGE DANIEL, mathematics professor; b. Boston, July 4, 1923; s. Isaac J. and Ida (Rotman) M.; m. Evelyn Davidoff, Sept. 1, 1947; children: Mark Alan, David Jechiel, Carol Held, Jonathan Carl. BA, Harvard U., 1943, MA, 1946, PhD, 1948; DSc (hon.), U. Ill., Chgo., 1989. Instr. math. Princeton U., 1947-48; mem. Inst. Advanced Study, 1947-49, 56-57, 75, mem. bd. of trustees, 1982-92; asst. prof. Syracuse U., 1949-52; asst. prof. math. Johns Hopkins U., 1952-53, assoc. prof., 1954-56, prof., 1957-61; prof. math. Yale U., 1961-66, James E. English prof. math., 1966-81, Henry Ford II prof. math., 1981-98, chmn., 1971-74, prof. emeritus, 1998—. Vis. prof. Conselho Nat. des Pesquisas, Inst. de Matematica, Rio de Janiero, Brazil, 1953-54, 91, U. Paris, 1966-67, Hebrew U., Jerusalem, 1967, Tata Inst. Fundamental Rsch., Bombay, 1970, Inst. des Hautes Etudes Scientifiques, Bures-Sur-Yvette, 1966, 71, 75, Japan Soc. for Promotion of Scis., 1985, Eidgenossische Technische Hochschule, Switzerland, 1986; chmn. U.S. Nat. Com. for Math, 1971-73, 83-85, Office Math. Scis., NRC, 1975-78; mem. sci. adv. coun. Math. Scis. Rsch. Inst., Berkeley, Calif., 1988-91; mem. sci. adv. com., bd. govs. Weizmann Inst., Israel, 1987—2003; bd. govs. Tel Aviv U., 1990-2000; mem. Harvard Grad. Coun., 1988-91; mem. vis. com. dept. math. Harvard U., 1975-81, MIT, 1981-94; Ritt lectr. Columbia U., 1982, Bergman lectr. Stanford U., 1983, Sachar lectr. Tel Aviv U., 1985, Karcher lectr. U. Okla., 1986, Markert lectr. Pa. State U., 1993. Assoc. editor Annals of Math., 1957—64, Trans. Am. Math. Soc., 1958—65, Am. Scientist, 1970—82, Geometriae Dedicata, 1985—90, bd. cons. Jour. D'Analyse Mathématique, 1994—; editor: Am. Jour. Math., 1965—69; assoc. editor Am. Jour. Math., 1969—79; author rsch. articles:. Fulbright rsch. scholar, Utrecht U., The Netherlands; Guggenheim fellow 1957-58 Mem. AAAS, NAS (chmn. sect. math. 1982-84), Am. Math. Soc. (pres. 1987-88, Steele prize for Paper of Lasting Importance 1993), Internat. Math. Union (chmn. U.S. del. to Gen. Assembly Warsaw 1982, exec. com. 1983-86), Phi Beta Kappa, Sigma Xi. Home: 25 Beechwood Rd Woodbridge CT 06525-1309 Office: Yale Univ Dept Mathematics New Haven CT 06520 E-mail: george.mostow@yale.edu.

MOSTOWYCZ, LEONIDAS, radiologist; b. Ukraine, Oct. 4, 1919; came to U.S., 1957; MD, U. Innsbruck, 1951. Intern Sts. Mary & Elizabeth Hosp., Louisville, 1957-58; resident U. Clinics, Innsbruck, 1952-55, U. Hosps., Innsbruck, 1955-57, U. Louisville Hosp., 1961-64; prof. emeritus U. Ky. Coll. Medicine, 1994—. Cons. in radiology for new ind. East European states. Mem. AMA, Am. Coll. Radiology, Radiol. Soc. N.Am., Urkanian Med. Assn. N.Am., Ky. Med. Assn.

MOTAMED, THOMAS FIROUZ, insurance company executive; BA, Adelphi U., 1971; JD, Delaware Law Sch., 1975. Sci. faculty Malvern Prep. Sch., Pa., 1975-76; field underwriter New York Life, Carle Place, NY, 1976-77; exec. v.p. Chubb & Son Inc. (subs. of Chubb Corp.), Warren, N.J., 1977—. Office: Chubb Corp 15 Mountain View Rd Warren NJ 07059 E-mail: tmotamed@chubb.com.

MOTE, CLAYTON DANIEL, JR., university president, mechanical engineer, educator; b. San Francisco, Feb. 5, 1937; s. Clayton Daniel and Eugenia (Isnardi) M.; m. Patricia Jane Lewis, Aug. 18, 1962; children: Melissa Michelle, Adam Jonathan. BSc, U. Calif., Berkeley, 1959, MS, 1960, PhD, 1963; Doctorate (hon.), Tashkent State Tech. U., 2001; DSc, Ohio State U., 2001; Dr Sci. and Tech. (hon.), Carnegie Mellon U., 2004. Registered profl. engr., Calif. Asst. specialist U. Calif. Forest Products Labs., 1961-62, asst. mech. engr., 1962-63; lectr. mech. engring. U. Calif., Berkeley, 1962-63, asst. prof., 1967-69, asst. research engr., 1968-69, assoc. prof., assoc. research engr., 1969-73, prof., 1973-98, vice chmn. mech. engring. dept., 1976-80, 83-86, chmn. mech. engring. dept., 1987-91, vice chancellor univ. rels., FANUC chair mech. systems, 1991-98; research fellow U. Birmingham, Eng., 1963-64; asst. prof. Carnegie Inst. Tech., 1964-67; Glen L. Martin Inst. prof. engring. U. Md., College Park, 1998—, pres., 1998—. Vis. prof. Norwegian Inst. Wood Tech., 1972—73, vis. sr. scientist, 1976, 78, 80, 84, 85; cons. in engring., design and analysis; cons. in engring. NAE, 1988, Nat. Acad. Arts and Sci., 2004; sr. scientist Alexander Von Humboldt Found., Germany, 1988, Japan Soc. for Promotion of Sci., Japan, 1991. Mem. editl. bd. Soma Jour. Sound and Vibration, Machine Vibration; contbr. articles to profl. jours.; patentee in field. NSF fellow, 1963-64, Sr. Scientist fellowship Japan Soc. Promotion Sci., 1991, Berkeley fellow, 2001; recipient Disting. Teaching award, U. Calif., 1971, Pi Tau Sigma Excellence in Teaching award, U. Calif., 1975, Humboldt Prize, Fed. Republic Germany, 1988, Disting. Engring. Alumnus award U. Calif., 2001, Frederick W. Taylor Rsch. medal. Soc. Mfg. Engrs., 1991, Hetenyi award Soc. Exptl. Mechanics, 1992, Eagle award Met. Washington chpt. ARCS, 2000. Fellow: AAAS (coun. del. Sect M 2003—), NAE (coun. 2002—, former program com., peer com.), ASME (hon.; chmn. San Francisco sect. 1978—79, nat. chmn. noise control and acoustics 1980—84, v.p. environ. and transp. 1986—90, Blackall award 1975, Disting. Svc. award 1991, Charles Russ Richards award 1994, Rayleigh lectr. 1994), Acoustical Soc. Am., Internat. Acad. Wood Sci.; mem.: ASTM (com. on snow skiing F-27 1984—87), Orthopaedic Rsch. Soc., Am. Soc. Biomechanics, Am. Acad. Mechanics, Am. Soc. Engring. Edn. (Ralph Coast Roe award 1997), Internat. Soc. Skiing Safety (hon.; sec. 1977—85, bd.dirs. 1977—, chmn. sci. com. 1985—, v.p.), Nat. Soc. Collegiate Scholars, Golden Key Nat. Honor Soc., Phi Kappa Phi, Omicron Delta Kappa, Tau Beta Pi, Pi Tau Sigma, Sigma Xi. Home: Pres' Residence One Presidential Dr College Park MD 20740 Office: Office of Pres U Md Main Adminstrn Bldg College Park MD 20742-5025 Office Phone: 301-405-5803. Business E-Mail: dmote@umd.edu.

MOTES, CARL DALTON, lawyer; b. May 31, 1949; s. Carl Thomas and Orpha Jeanette (McGauley) M.; m. Maria Eugenia Aguirre, Apr. 19, 1975. AA with honors, St. Johns River Jr. Coll., 1969; BA, Fla. State U., 1971, JD with honors, 1974. Bar: Fla. 1974, U.S. Dist. Ct. (cen., no. and so. dists.) Fla. 1975, U.S. Ct. Appeals (11th cir.) 1980. Assoc. Maguire, Voorhis & Wells P.A., Orlando, Fla., 1975-79, ptnr., 1979-97, Motes & Sears P.A., Winter Park, Fla., 1998-99, Motes & Carr, P.A., Orlando, 1999—; asst. to pres. Fla. Bar, Tallahassee, 1974-75. Dir. Legal Aid Soc., Orlando, 1979-83, pres., 1983-84; lectr. at various Bar Assns. and edni. insts. Mem. editl. bd. Jour. Trial Advocate Quar., 1981-91, chmn., 1989-91; contbr. articles to profl. jours. Active in Planning & Zoning Bd., Altamonte Springs, Fla., 1977-79, Capital Funds Project Rev. Com., Cen. Fla., 1983; bd. dirs. Cen. Fla. coun. Boy Scouts Am., mem. exec. bd., v.p. adminstrn. 1993-94. Mem. Internat. Assn. Def. Counsel, Fla. Def. Lawyers Assn. (bd. dirs. 1989-94, sec., treas. 1991-92, pres.-elect 1992-93, pres. 1993-94), Fla. Bar, Fedn. of Def. and Corp. Counsel, Orange County Bar Assn. (sec. 1979-80, exec. coun. 1980-83, named Outstanding Mem. 1981-82, Outstanding Com. Chmn. 1977), Fla. State U. Coll. Law Alumni Assn. (bd. dirs. 1975-78, pres. 1979), Def. Rsch. Inst. (state chair 1994), Phi Delta Phi. Republican. Office: Motes & Carr PO Box 149205 Orlando FL 32802-9205 Fax: 407-897-6949. E-mail: carl@moteslaw.com.

MOTHKUR, SRIDHAR RAO, radiologist; b. Mothkur, India, Oct. 5, 1950; came to U.S., 1975; naturalized. s. Venkat Rao and Laxmi Bai (Gundepally) M.; m. Sheila Rama Rao Paga, Nov. 30, 1973; children: Swathi, Preethi, Venkat Krishna. Student, Coll. Arts and Sci. Osmania U., Hyderabad, India, 1966; MB, BS, Osmania U., Hyderabad, India, 1972, DPH, 1974; MPA, Ind. U. N.W., 2000. Diplomate Am. Bd. Radiology. Rotating intern Osmania Gen. Hosp., Hyderabad, 1972-73, internal medicine intern, 1973, resident in surgery, 1974-75; resident Resurrection Hosp., Chgo., 1975-76; resident in radiology Luth. Gen. Hosp., Park Ridge, Ill., 1976-79, chief resident radiology, 1978-79; with rotations in nuclear medicine, angiography and neuroradiology Rush-Presbyn. St. Luke's Med. Ctr., Chgo., 1978; chmn. and med. dir. dept. radiology Louise Burg Hosp., Chgo., 1979-85, Shriner's Hosp., Chgo., 1986-88; fellow in ultrasound and computered tomography U. Ill., Chgo., 1988-89, fellow in magnetic resonance imaging, 1988-89; staff radiologist St. Anthony Hosp., Michigan City, Ind., 1989—, med. dir. MRI Ctr., 1989—; pvt. practice, Michigan City, 1989—; staff radiologist Kingwood Hosp., Michigan City, 1989-94, Charter Hosp., Behavioral Health Sys. Ind., Michigan City, 1994-96; pres. Michigan City Radiologists, Inc., Michigan City, 1998—2003; med. dir. dept. diagnostic imaging St. Anthony Meml. Med. Ctr., Michigan City, 2004—. Cons., radiologist Med. Group Michigan City, 1989—98, Franklin Clin. and Med. Watch, Michigan City, 1989—; spl. staff radiologist Christ hosp. Med. Ctr., Oak Lawn, Ill., 1988—89, Jasper County Meml. Hosp., Rensselaer, Ind., 1994—, United Diagnostic Svcs., Westchester, Ill., 1979—2000; dir. MRI Ctr. Meml. Hosp., 1989—97; med. dir. interventional radiology St. Anthony and Meml. Hosp., Michigan City, 1989—93; clin. asst. prof. radiology U. Ill., Chgo., 1990—2004; cons. radiologist Health Partners Medical Group, St. Francis, 2004—; others in field. Mem. Chinmaya Mission, Vishva Hindu Parishad. Fellow: Internat. Coll. Angiology, Am. Coll. Angiology, Am. Coll. Internat. Physicians; mem.: AMA, AmAm. Assn. Therapeutic and Interventional Neuroradiology, La Porte County Med. Soc., Telugu Assn. Greater Chgo., Chgo. Med. Soc., Ind. Med. Soc., Ill. Med. Soc., Ind. Assn. Physicians Indian Origin, India Med. Assn. N.W. Ind. (bd. dirs. 1999—2001), Am. Assn. Radiologists Indian Origins, Ind. Interventional Radiol. Assn., Tristate Telugu Assn., Indian Radiol. and Imaging Assn., Ind. Assn. Physicians from India, Soc. Magnetic Resonance in Medicine, Soc. Cardiovascular and Interventional Radiology, Soc. Magnetic Resonance Imaging, Am. Coll. Healthcare Execs., Am. Telugu Assn., Am. Soc. Head and Neck Radiology, Am. Coll. Emergency Physicians, Am. Diabetes Assn., Am. Assn. Physicians of Indian Origin, Am. Roentgen Ray Soc., Telugu Assn., Radiol. Soc. N.Am., Am. Assn. Andhra Brahmins, Internat. Soc. Krishna Consciousness, Pi Alpha Alpha. Republican. Home: 1457 Sand Creek Dr Chesterton IN 46304-3393 Office: Michigan City Radiologists Inc 8865 W 400 N Ste 115 Michigan City IN 46360-9223

MOTLEY, CONSTANCE BAKER (MRS. JOEL WILSON MOTLEY), federal judge, former city official; b. New Haven, Sept. 14, 1921; d. Willoughby Alva and Rachel (Huggins) Baker; m. Joel Wilson Motley, Aug. 18, 1946; 1 son, Joel Wilson, III. AB, NYU, 1943; LLB, Columbia U., 1946. Bar: N.Y. 1948. Mem. Legal Def. and Ednl. Fund, NAACP, 1945-65; mem. N.Y. State Senate, 1964-65; pres. Manhattan Borough, 1965-66; U.S. dist. judge So. Dist. N.Y., 1966-82, chief judge, 1982-86, sr. judge, 1986—. Author: Equal Justice Under Law, 1998. Mem. N.Y. State Adv. Council Employment and Unemployment Ins., 1958-64. Mem. Assn. Bar City N.Y. Office: US Dist Ct US Courthouse 500 Pearl St New York NY 10007-1316 E-mail: constance_motley@nysd.uscourts.gov.

MOTOYAMA, KEIICHI, mechanical engineer, consultant; b. Yokohama, Kanagawa, Japan, May 25, 1953; s. Kakuju and Yoshiko Motoyama; m. Kazue Motoyama, Mar. 20, 1983. BS in Aerospace Engring., Nat. Def. Acad., Yokosuka, Japan, 1977; MS in Structural Engring., U. Tsukuba, Japan, 1983, PhD in Structural Engring., 1986. Tech. officer Def. Agy., Tokyo, 1977—89; engr. Honda R & D, Wako, Japan, 1989—92; rsch. engr. Miss. State U., Starkville, 1992—95; prin. engr. Honda R & D Am., Starkville, 1992—95; engr. Honda R & D, Wako, 1995—99; sr. cons. Mech. Dynamics Japan, Tokyo, 1999—2001, consulting dir., 2001—. Contbr. articles to profl. jours. Lt. comdr. Japanese Mil., 1977—80. Mem.: AIAA, Japan Soc. Computational Engring. and Sci., Japan Soc. Mech. Engrs. (rsch. com. design engring.), Japan Soc. Civil Engring. (rsch. com. impact engring.), Soc. Naval Archs. Japan, U.S. Naval Inst. (life). Achievements include patents for measuring of multi-point loads; method and apparatus for estimating loads imposed on structural body; aerodynamic noise reduction via optimization technique; aerodynamic noise test equipment; aerodynamic noise reduction via optimization technique. Office: MSC Software Corp 2300 Traverwood Dr Ann Arbor MI 48105-2195 also: MSC Software Ltd Shinjuku First West 8F 23-7 Nishishinjuku 1-chome Shinjuku-ku Tokyo 160-0023 Japan

MOTRONI, HECTOR JOHN, manufacturing executive; b. Havana, Cuba, Dec. 2, 1943; came to U.S., 1956; s. Marco Antonio and Lilia Ines (Suarez) M.; m. Myra Helene Egan, Aug. 9, 1969; children: Marcus Alan, Melissa Aimee. BA, Dartmouth Coll., 1966, BE, 1967, ME, 1968. Engr. USPHS, Bethesda, Md., 1969-71; various positions Xerox Corp., Stamford, Conn., 1971-99, corp. sr. v.p., chief staff officer, 1999—2002, corp. sr. v.p., chief staff and ethics officer, 2003—. Bd. dirs. Prep for Prep. Trustee Temple Israel, Westport, Conn., 1981-84; bd. adv. Outward Bound USA, 1998; bd. dirs. Nat. Action Coun. for Minorities in Engring. Named Hispanic Achiever of Yr., Hispanic Corp. Achievers, 1997; named on of 50 Most Important Hispanics in Bus. and Tech. Hispanic Engrs. and Info. Tech. Mag., 2003, 04; recipient Eagle award Nat. Eagle Inst., 1997. Mem. Nat. Policy Assn. (bd. dirs., chmn. com. new Am. realities 1996-2002), Dartmouth Soc. Engrs. (pres. 1977-85), Dartmouth Coll. Alumni Coun. (chmn. communications 1983-88), Coun. of the Ams. (adv. bd. 1983-89), Forum for World Affairs (bd. dirs. 1996-2001). Avocation: running. Office: Xerox Corp PO Box 1600 Stamford CT 06904-1600

MOTSENBOCKER, REX ALAN, construction company executive; b. Norman, Okla., Dec. 14, 1962; s. Rex Albert and Nondace Nadine (Bonner) M.; m. Karla Doreen Miller, Nov. 14, 1992. BS in BA, Calif. State U., Sacramento, 1984; BS in Constrn. Engring., Ariz. State U., 1986; MBA in Fin. magna cum laude, Western Internat. U., Phoenix, 1994; postgrad., So. Calif. U., Newport, 1994—. Cert. fin. cons. Project coord. Tibshraeny Bros., Mesa, Ariz., 1986; project mgr. Joe E. Woods, Tempe, Ariz., 1986-87; project engr. Sundt Corp., Phoenix, 1987—; pres. Master Investments, Phoenix, 1994—; CFO Master Builders Devel., LLC, Las Vegas, Nev., 1994—; mgr., CFO Remington Estates Devel., L.L.C., Phoenix, 1995—. Bd. dirs. bullion Recovery Sys., Inc., Phoenix. Author: Financial Aspects of Investing in Mexico, 1994. Team leader Senator McCain Re-election Campaign, Phoenix, 1992-94; project dir. Christmas in April, Phoenix, 1989-93. Mem. Project Mgrs. Inst. (v.p. membership 1990—), Am. Mgrs. Assn., Constrn. Mgmt. Assn., Phoenix C. of C., Nat. Asbestos Council, Ariz. State U. Alumni Assn. (v.p. bd. 1994—), Delta Mu Delta (v.p. 1993—). Republican. Avocations: triathlons, singing. Home: 15833 N 7th Dr Phoenix AZ 85023-4435

MOTT, EARL, artist, poet, writer; b. San Augustine, Texas, May 9, 1949; s. J.B. and Lillie Mae M.; m. Frances Katherene Mott, Oct. 30, 1975 (dec. Apr. 1993); children: Amber Katherene Fanning; stepchildren: Ricky Lynn Plunk, Gary Lee Plunk, Jamey Leon Plunk. Student, Art Instrn. Schs., 1968—71, Virginia Blackmon, 1973—74, Foster Caddell's Art Sch., 1977. Author, artist: Secrets From an Oil Painting Diary, 1988; artist: The Best of Portrait Painting, 1998; artist, poet: The Unseen Hand, 2003; contbr. articles to profl. publ.; one man shows at Angelina Coll., 1975, 82, 83, 87, Kurth Meml. Libr., 2001; group shows at Mus. East Tex., 1995, others. With USN, 1968—70. Recipient numerous awards for paintings. Mem.: Oil Painters of Am. Baptist. Avocations: poetry, reading, hiking, writing, photography. Home and Office: 304 Paul Ave Lufkin TX 75901 E-mail: art_tailored@yahoo.com.

MOTT, FREDERICK B., JR., publishing executive; Pub. Post-Tribune, Gary, Ind., 1991—95; pres., publ. The State, Columbia, SC, 1995—. Office: The State 1401 Shop Rd Columbia SC 29201-4814

MOTT, JOHN C. judge; b. LeRoy Twp., Pa., May 23, 1955; s. Charles S. and H. Grace (Spencer) M.; m. Brenda K. Bailey, Aug. 19, 1972; children: Reeve A., Nicholas H., Adam R. BA with high honors, Mansfield U., Pa., 1977; JD, Dickinson Sch. of Law, Carlisle, Pa., 1980. Bar: Pa. 1980, U.S. Dist. Ct. (mid. dist.) Pa. 1983. Assoc. firm Vineski, Brann, Williams and Caldwell, Troy and Canton, Pa., 1980-83; ptnr. firm Vineski, Brann, Williams, Caldwell and Mott, Troy and Canton, Pa., 1984-87; judge Ct. of Common Pleas Bradford County, Towanda, Pa., 1988—. Committeeman Bradford County Republican Com., Pa., 1982-87, chmn., 1984-85; deacon Canton Ch. of Christ (Disciples), 1982-88, chmn. steward-ship com. 1983-84, elder 1989—; Bradford County crusade chmn. Am. Cancer Soc., Sayre, Pa., 1983-84; dir. N.Y.-Pa. Health System Agy., Binghamton, N.Y., 1984-85, Troy Community Hosp., Pa., 1983-85. Mem. Bradford County Bar Assn. (sec.-treas. 1980-82), Pa. Bar Assn., Pa. Conf. State Trial Judges (jud. ethics com., exec. com.), Masons, Lions (pres. 1983-84), Elks. Office: Bradford County Courthouse Main St Towanda PA 18848 Office Phone: 570-265-1709.

MOTT, MARY ELIZABETH, retired educational administrator; b. West Hartford, Conn., July 10, 1931; d. Marshall Amos and Mary Herman Mott. BA, Conn. Coll. for Women, 1953; MA, Western Res. U., 1963. Cert. tchr., Ohio; cert. computer tchr., Ohio. Mgr. sales promotion Cleve. Electric Illuminating Co., 1953-60; tchr. Newbury Bd. Edn., Ohio, 1960-67, West Geauga Bd. Edn., Chesterland, Ohio, 1967—97, ret., 1997. Chmn. state certification com. in computers ECCO, Mayfield, Ohio, 1983—, exec. bd., 1980—. Asst. dir. West Geauga Day Camp, Chesterland, 1968. Mem. Ednl. Computer Consortium Ohio, West Geauga Edn. Assn. (exec. bd. 1975-97), Delta Kappa Gamma. E-mail: pci238@aol.com.

MOTT, RANDALL D. computer company executive; B of Math., U. Ark. Various positions Wal-Mart, 1978—94, sr. v.p., chief info. officer, 1994—97, mem. exec. com., 1997; sr. v.p., chief info. officer Dell, Inc., Round Rock, Tex., 2000—. Named Chief Info. Officer of Yr., Info. Week Mag., 1997. Office: Dell Inc 1 Dell Way Round Rock TX 78682-2222

MOTT, ROBERT LEWIS, writer, sound effects artist; b. Nyack, N.Y. s. Morgan Edward and Grace (Groben) M.; m. Catherine O'Keefe, June 28, 1947 (div. 1974); children: Susan Patricia, Gail Ann, Cathee Caron, Nancy Jean; m. Cinda M. Yank, Dec. 28, 1985. Grad., NYU, 1947-50. Freelance writer, 1951—; sound effects artist CBS, N.Y.C., 1951-69, NBC, Burbank, Calif., 1970-89. Writer (children's record) Rocket to Mars, 1954, (cartoon series) Cool McCool, 1956, (Broadway mus.) Girls Against the Boys, 1958; comedy writer The Ed Sullivan Show, Garry Moore Show, Andy Williams Show, Dick Van Dyke Show, Red Skelton Show; author: Sound Effects: Radio, TV and Film, 1988, Sound Effects: Who Did It and How, in the Era of Live Broadcasting, 1993 (Best Lit. List, Choice Mag. 1993), Radio Live! Television Live! When Horses Were Coconuts!, 2000. Served with USMC, 1943-45, ETO. Decorated 4 campaign battle stars; recipient 3 Emmy award nominations Acad. TV Arts and Scis., 1986, 87, Byron Kane award, Lifetime achievement award Soc. to Preserve and Encourage Radio Drama, Variety and Comedy, Diamond Cir. award, Pacific Pioneer Broadcasters; named to Acad. of T.V. Arts and Sci. Mem. Writers Guild Am., Pacific Pioneer Broadcasters. Home: 396 Miller Way Arroyo Grande CA 93420-2004

MOTT, RODNEY, metal products executive; V.p., gen. mgr. Nucor Steel; pres., CEO Internat. Steel Group, Richfield, Ohio, 2002—. Named Mgr. of Yr., New Steel Mag., 1995. Mem.: Am. Iron and Steel Engrs. (pres. 1998). Office: Internat Steel Group 3250 Interstate Dr Richfield OH 44286

MOTT, STEWART RAWLINGS, business executive, political activist; b. Flint, Mich., Dec. 4, 1937; s. Charles Stewart and Ruth (Rawlings) M.; m. Kappy Wells, Oct. 13, 1979 (div. Mar. 1999); 1 child, Samuel Apple Axle. Grad., Deerfield (Mass.) Acad., 1955; BS in Bus. Adminstrn, BA in Comparative Lit, Columbia, 1961, postgrad. English lit., 1961-62. Exec. trainee various cos., 1956-63; English instr. Eastern Mich. U., 1963-64; corp. dir. U.S. Sugar Corp., Clewiston, Fla., 1965—98. Investor various diversified cos., 1968—. Founder Flint Cmty. Planned Parenthood, 1963; pres. S.R. Mott Charitable Trust, 1968—; pres., founder Spectemur Agendo, N.Y.C. and Flint, 1965—; bd. dirs. Fund For Peace, N.Y.C., 1967-90, Nat. Com. for Effective Congress, N.Y.C., 1968-, Planned Parenthood Fedn. Am., 1964-81, Am. Commn. on U.S.-Soviet Rels., 1977-92, Citizens Research Found., 1977-97, Ams. for Dem. Action, 1978-90, Friends of Family Planning, 1979-84, Voters for Choice, 1979-89; bd. dirs., founder Fund Constl. Govt., 1974-; bd. dirs. Population Action Council, 1978-82; maj. donor McCarthy, McGovern, Anderson campaigns. Mem. Phi Beta Kappa. *At age 18 I realized that two problems confront planet earth that dwarf and aggravate all conventional problems: namely the threat of nuclear war and the continuing worldwide population explosion. Coming to grips with these realities, I decided to dedicate my life to help find solutions to these two problems through public service in philanthropy and politics.*

MOTTELSON, BEN R. physicist; b. Chicago, July 9, 1926; naturalized Danish citizen, 1971. s. Goodman and Georgia (Blum) M.; m. Nancy Jane (Reno), 1948 (dec. 1975); 3 children;m. Britta Marger (Siegumfeldt), 1983. B.Sc., Purdue U., 1947; PhD, Harvard U., 1950; hon. degrees, Purdue U., U. Heidelberg, Fed. Republic Germany, Lund U., Sweden, Liverpool U., Eng. Sheldon traveling fellow Inst. Theoretical Physics, Copenhagen, 1950—51, U.S. AEC fellow, 1951—53; with theoretical study group CERN, Copenhagen, 1953—57; prof. Nordic Inst. for Theoretical Atomic Physics, Copenhagen, 1957—; dir. European ctr. Theoretical Studies in Nuc. Physics and Related Areas, Trento, Italy, 1980—97. Physicist Neils Bohr Inst., Copenhagen; bd. dir. Nordita; vis. prof. U. Calif., Berkeley, 1959, Berkeley, 84; adj. prof. Niels Bohr Inst., Copenhagen, 1994; Feshbach lectureship, 96. Author: Nuclear Structure, vol. 1, 1969, vol. 2 (with A. Bohr), 1975; numerous other publications in field. Recipient Nobel prize for physics, 1975. Mem.: Norwegian Acad. of Sci. and Letters, Polish Acad. of Sci., Kroatian Acad. Sci. (fgn. assoc.), Finnish Soc. Sci. and Letters, European Acad. of Arts, Sci., and Letters, Kgl. Fys. Graf, Lund, Sweden, Am. Acad. Arts and Letters, Royal Dan. Acad. Sci. and Letters, Nat. Acad. Sci. (fgn. assoc.). Address: NORDITA and The Niels Bohr Inst Blegdamsvej 17 DK-2100 Copenhagen Denmark Business E-Mail: mottelson@nordita.dk.

MOTTER, THOMAS FRANKLIN, medical products executive; b. Modesto, Calif., June 27, 1948; s. Thomas Dean and Beverley June (Mosier) M.; m. Wanda Lenice Parker, Feb. 9, 1968 (div. Jan. 1972); children: Eric Franklin (dec.), Katrina Lenice; m. Jerry Ann Averill, Oct. 24, 1976; children: Heidi Marika, Courtney Averill. AA, Cabrillo Jr. Coll., Santa Cruz, Calif., 1968; BA, Stephens Coll., 1970; MBA, Pepperdine U., 1975. Social worker County of Santa Cruz and Amador, 1970-77; nat. dir. mktg. Humphrey Instruments/SmithKline, San Leandro, Calif., 1978-88; internat. gen. mgr. HGM Med. Lasers, Salt Lake City, 1988-89; pres., CEO Paradigm Med. Industries Inc., Salt Lake City, 1989—. Mem. Nat. Ski Patrol, Stockton, 1973-79; v.p. Sandy (Utah) Pony Baseball, 1994-95; coach Kearns (Utah) Am. Legion Baseball, 1995-96. Capt. U.S. Army, 1970-76. Named Mem. Nat. Adult Baseball Assn. (mem. Nat. Championship team), Am. Legion, Sons of the Am. Revolution Utah State Chpt., Knight Orthodox Order of the Knights of the Hosp. of St. John of Jerusalem. Episcopalian. Avocations: skiing, hardball baseball, coaching, fly fishing, hunting. Office: Paradigm Med Industries Inc 2355 S 1070 W Salt Lake City UT 84119-1552

MOTTO, JEROME ARTHUR, psychiatry educator; b. Kansas City, Mo., Oct. 16, 1921; MD, U. Calif., San Francisco, 1951. Diplomate Am. Bd. Neurology and Psychiatry. Intern San Francisco Gen. Hosp., 1951-52; resident Johns Hopkins Hosp., Balt., 1952-55; sr. resident U. Calif., San Francisco, 1955-56, from instr. to prof., 1956—91, prof. emeritus, 1991—. Contbr. articles to profl. jours. With AUS, 1942-46, ETO. Fellow: Am. Psychiatric Assn. (life; disting. fellow).

MOTTOLA, THOMAS, former entertainment company executive; b. Bronx, NY; m. Mariah Carey, 1993 (div.); m. Thalia Sodi, 2000. Pres., CEO Sony Music Entertainment Inc, N.Y.C., chmn., CEO, 1998—2003.

MOTULSKY, ARNO GUNTHER, internist, geneticist, educator; b. Fischhausen, Germany, July 5, 1923; arrived in U.S., 1941; s. Herman and Rena (Sass) Molton; m. Gretel C. Stern, Mar. 22, 1945; children: Judy, Harvey, Arlene. Student, Cen. YMCA Coll., Chgo., 1941—43, Yale U., 1943—44; BS, U. Ill., 1945, MD, 1947, DSc (hon.), 1982, MD (hon.), 1991. Diplomate Am. Bd. Internal Medicine, Am. Bd. Med. Genetics. Intern, fellow, resident Michael Reese Hosp., Chgo., 1947-51; staff mem. charge clin. investigation dept. hematology Army Med. Service Grad. Sch., Walter Reed Army Med. Ctr., Washington, 1952-53; research assoc. internal medicine George Washington U. Sch. Medicine, 1952-53; from instr. to assoc. prof. dept. medicine U. Wash. Sch. Medicine, Seattle, 1953-61, prof. medicine, prof. genetics, 1961—; head div. med. genetics, dir. genetics clinic Univ. Hosp., Seattle, 1959-89; dir.

Ctr. for Inherited Diseases, Seattle, 1972-90. Attending physician Univ. Hosp., Seattle; cons. Pres.'s Commn. for Study of Ethical Problems in Medicine and Biomed. and Behavioral Rsch., 1979—83; cons. various coms. NRC, NIH, WHO, and others. Editor: Am. Jour. Human Genetics, 1969—75, Human Genetics, 1969—97. Fellow Commonwealth Fund in human genetics, Univ. Coll., London, 1957—58, Ctr. Advanced Study in Behavioral Scis., Stanford U., 1976—77, Inst. Advanced Study, Berlin, 1984; scholar John and Mary Markle in med. sci., 1957—62. Fellow: AAAS, ACP; mem.: Am. Philos. Soc., Am. Acad. Arts and Scis., Inst. of Medicine, Am. Assn. Physicians, Am. Soc. Clin. Investigation, Am. Soc. Human Genetics, Western Soc. Clin. Rsch., Genetics Soc. Am., Am. Fedn. Clin. Rsch., Internat. Soc. Hematology, NAS. Home: 4347 53rd Ave NE Seattle WA 98105-4938 Office: U Wash Medicine and Genome Scis PO Box 357730 Seattle WA 98195-7730 Office Phone: 206-543-3593. E-mail: agmot@u.washington.edu.

MOTZ, DIANA GRIBBON, judge; b. Washington, July 15, 1943; d. Daniel McNamara and Jane (Retzler) Gribbon; m. John Frederick Motz, Sept. 20, 1968; children: Catherine Jane, Daniel Gribbon. BA, Vassar Coll., 1965; LLB, U. Va., 1968. Bar: U.S. Dist. Ct. Md. 1969, U.S. Ct. Appeals (4th cir.) 1969, U.S. Supreme Ct. 1980. Assoc. Piper & Marbury, Balt., 1968—71; asst. atty. gen. State of Md., Balt., 1972—81, chief of litigation, 1981—86; ptnr. Frank, Bernstein, Conaway & Goldman, Balt., 1986—91; judge Md. Ct. of Special Appeals, 1991—94, U.S. Ct. Appeals (4th Cir.), 1994—. Mem.: ABA, Fed. Cts. Study Com., Lawyers Round Table, Md. Bar Found., Am. Bar Found., Am. Law Inst., Balt. City Bar Assn. (exec. com. 1988), Md. Bar Assn., Wranglers Law Club. Roman Catholic. Office: 920 US Courthouse 101 W Lombard St Ste 920 Baltimore MD 21201-2611

MOTZ, JOHN FREDERICK, federal judge; b. Balt., Dec. 30, 1942; s. John Eldered and Catherine (Grauel) M.; m. Diana Jane Gribbon, Sept. 20, 1968; children: Catherine Jane, Daniel Gribbon AB, Wesleyan U., Conn., 1964; LLB, U. Va., 1967. Bar: Md. 1967, U.S. Ct. Appeals (4th cir.) 1968, U.S. Dist. Ct. Md. 1968. Law clk. to Hon. Harrison L. Winter U.S. Ct. Appeals (4th cir.), 1967-68; Assoc. Venable, Baetjer & Howard, Balt., 1968-69; asst. U.S. atty. U.S. Atty.'s Office, Balt., 1969-71; assoc. Venable, Baetjer & Howard, Balt., 1971-75, ptnr., 1976-81; U.S. atty. U.S. Atty.'s Office, Balt., 1981-85; judge U.S. Dist. Ct. Md., Balt., 1985—, chief judge, 1994—2001. Trustees Friends Sch., Balt., 1970-77, 1981-88, Sheppard Pratt Hosp., 1987-97, 99—. Mem.: ABA, Am. Coll. Trial Lawyers (mem. bd. editors. Manual of Complex Litigation (4th), mem. Judicial Panel on Multidist. Litigation), Am. Law Inst., Am. Bar Found., Md. State Bar Assn. Republican. Mem. Soc. Of Friends. Office: US Dist Ct 101 W Lombard St Rm 510 Baltimore MD 21201-2605

MOTZ, KENNETH LEE, former farm organization official; b. Grand Junction, Colo., Mar. 6, 1922; s. Harold I. and Acquila (Ulmer) M.; m. Margaret Florence Mitchell, Oct. 9, 1948; children: Gwendolyn Ann, Stephen Mitchell. AA, Mesa Jr. Coll., 1942; BSBA, Denver U., 1947. Bookkeeper Farmers Union Mktg. Assn., Denver, 1942-43; asst. sec. Nat. Farmers Union, Denver, 1947-50, 59-66, sec.-treas., 1966-72, 85-86, treas., asst. sec., 1972-85, retired, 1987; treas. Green Thumb, Inc., 1980-85, sec.-treas., 1985-86, retired, 1987. Ins. acct. Nat. Farmers Union Ins. Cos., Denver, 1952-59. Sec. uniform pension com. Nat. Farmers Union, 1959-93; Dem. precinct committeeman, 1960-68; elder Calvary Presbyn. Ch. Maj. USMCR, ret. 1982. Recipient Svc. award Farmers Union, 1991. Mem. Nat. Presby. Mariners, Masons, Delta Sigma Pi. Presbyterian. Home: 2018 Fairway Hills Dr Huntsville AL 35802-4329

MOTZER, ROBERT JOHN, oncologist, educator; b. Paterson, N.J., Nov. 20, 1954; s. John William and Muriel M.; m. Sara Evelyn Gaylord, June 30, 1979; children: Katherine, Rachel, Andrew. BA, Hope Coll., Holland, Mich., 1977; MD, U. Mich. Med. Sch., 1981. Assoc. chmn. Meml. Sloan Kettering Cancer Ctr., New York, 1996—, attending physician, 2000—; prof. Cornell U. Med. Coll., 1998—. Contbr. over 150 articles to profl. jours.; lectr. in field. Recipient Career devel. award, Am. Cancer Soc., Mid-career Devel. award, NIH, 1999—. Mem. Am. Soc. Clin. Oncology, Am. Assn. Cancer Rsch., Kidney Cancer Assn. (exec. bd.). Office: Meml Sloan Kettering Cancer Ctr 1275 York Ave New York NY 10021-6094 E-mail: motzerr@mskcc.org.

MOUGHAN, PETER RICHARD, JR., lawyer; b. Phila., July 29, 1951; s. Peter Richard and Catherine L. (Gavin) M.; m. Janice Billick, Aug. 3, 1974 (div. Aug. 2000); children: Peter Richard III, Gavin Patrick, Jacob Daniel. BA, Wheeling Coll., 1973; MS, Gonzaga U., 1975, MBA, JD, Gonzaga U., 1977. Bar: Pa. 1977, N.Mex. 1980. Legal rschr. Am. Law Inst.-ABA, Phila., 1977-78; claim rep. Allstate Ins., Phila., 1978-79; assoc. Larry D. Beall, P.A., Albuquerque, 1979-81; pvt. practice law Moughan Law Firm, Albuquerque, 1981—. Mem.: K.C., Albuquerque Aardvarks Rugby Football Club (chmn. 1980—84), Ancient Order of Hibernians (Albuquerque) (pres. 1984—85, 1992—), Phi Alpha Delta. Office: PO Box 715 Albuquerque NM 87103-0715 Home: 623 San Pedro Dr SE Albuquerque NM 87108 E-mail: moughan2@lawyer.com., moughan2@yahoo.com.

MOUL, MAXINE BURNETT, state official; b. Oakland, Nebr., Jan. 26, 1947; d. Einer and Eva (Jacobson) Burnett; m. Francis Moul, Apr. 20, 1972; 1 child, Jeff. BS in Journalism, U. Nebr., 1969; DHL (hon.), Peru State Coll., 1993. Sunday feature writer, photographer Sioux City Iowa Jour., 1969-71; reporter, photographer, editor Maverick Media, Inc., Syracuse, Nebr., 1971-73, editor, pub., 1974-83, pres., 1983-90; grant writer, asst. coord. Nebr. Regional Med. Program, Lincoln, 1973-74; lt. gov. State of Nebr., Lincoln, 1991-93; dir. Dept. Econ. Devel., Lincoln, 1993-99; pres. Nebr. Cmty. Found., 1999—. Mem. Dem. Nat. Com., Washington, 1988-92, Nebr. Dem. State Ctrl. Com., Lincoln, 1974-88; del. Dem. Nat. Conf., 1972, 88, 92; mem. exec. com. Nebr. Dem. Party, Lincoln, 1988-93. Recipient Margaret Sanger award Planned Parenthood, Lincoln, 1991, Champion of Small Bus. award Nebr. Bus. Devel. Ctr., Omaha, 1991, Toll fellowship Coun. State Govts., Lexington, Ky., 1992. Mem. Bus. and Profl. Women, Nebr. Mgmt. Assn. (Silver Knight award 1992), Nat. Conf. Lt. Govs. (bd. dirs. 1991-93), Nebr. Press Women, Women Execs. in State Govt., Cmty. Devel. Soc., U. Nebr.-Lincoln Journalism Alumni. Democrat. Avocations: reading, gardening. Office: Nebr Cmty Found 317 S 12th St Lincoln NE 68508-2108

MOUL, WILLIAM CHARLES, lawyer; b. Columbus, Ohio, Jan. 12, 1940; s. Charles Emerson and Lillian Ann (Mackenbach) M.; m. Margine Ann Tessendorf, June 10, 1962; children: Gregory, Geoffrey. BA, Miami U., Oxford, Ohio, 1961; JD, Ohio State U., 1964. Bar: Ohio 1964, U.S. Dist. Ct. (so. dist.) Ohio 1965, U.S. Ct. Appeals (2d cir.) 1982, U.S. Ct. Appeals (6th cir.) 1984, U.S. Ct. Appeals (3d cir.) 1985. Assoc., ptnr. George, Greek, King, McMahon & McConnaughey, Columbus, 1964-79; ptnr. McConnaughey, Stradley, Mone & Moul, Columbus, 1979-81; ptnr.-in-charge Thompson, Hine & Flory, Columbus, 1981-89, exec. com., 1989-98. Chmn. Upper Arlington Civil Svc. Commn., Ohio, 1981-86. Mem. ABA, Ohio State Bar Assn. (labor sect. bd. dirs. 1983—), Columbus Bar Assn. (chmn. ethics com. 1980-82), Lawyers Club Columbus (pres. 1976-77), Athletic Club, Scioto Country Club, Wedgewood Country Club, Masons. Lutheran. Home: 2512 Danvers Ct Columbus OH 43220-2822 Office: Thompson Hine LLP 10 W Broad St Ste 700 Columbus OH 43215-3435 Office Phone: 614-469-3220. E-mail: william.moul@thompsonhine.com.

MOULD, JEREMY RICHARD, astronomer; b. Bristol, Eng., July 31, 1949; s. Michael Thomas and Sheila Patricia (Pickering Clarke) Mould; m. Joan Mary Milesi, Dec. 11, 1971; children: Helen, Kate. BSc with honors, U. Melbourne, Australia, 1971; PhD, Australian Nat. U., 1975. Rsch. fellow Royal Greenwich (Eng.) Obs., 1976; postdoctoral fellow Kitt Peak Nat. Obs., Tucson, 1976—78, asst. astronomer, 1980—82; Carnegie fellow Hale Obs., 1978—79; prof. Calif. Inst. Tech., Pasadena, 1982—93, exec. officer for astronomy, 1987—90; prof. Australian Nat. U., Canberra, 1993—2001; dir. Mt. Stromlo & Siding Obs., Weston, Australia, 1993—2001, Nat. Optical Astronomy Obs., Tucson, 2001—. Mem. Anglo Australian Telescope Bd., 1993—2001, chair, 1999; mem. Australia Telescope Steering Com., 1995—2000; mem. space sci. adv. com. NASA. Mem.: Australian Acad. Sci., Assn. Univ. Rsch. Astronomy (bd. dirs. 1997—2001), Astron. Soc. Pacific, Astron. Soc. Australia, Am. Astron. Soc. Office: NOAO 950 N Cherry Ave Tucson AZ 85726-6732

MOULDER, T. EARLINE, musician; b. Buffalo, Mo., Oct. 11; d. Earl Young and Ruby M. (Phillipot) M.; m. R. David Plank, Dec. 21, 1980; children: Jeannine Stanton, Jon Stanton, Timothy Stanton. AB in Biology and French, Drury Univ., 1973; studied piano with Soulima Stravinsky, 1961; M in Music, Ind. U., 1963; D in Musical Arts, U. Kansas, 1991; pvt. organ study, Andre Marchal, Paris, France, 1971. Concert organist, 1964—; exec. editor Drury Coll. Mirror, Springfield, Mo., 1971-73; rschr. Am. U., Beirut, 1973; journalist U.S. Naval Res., Springfield and Treasure Island, Calif., 1975-77; organist King's Way Meth. Ch., Springfield, Mo., 1983-93; chair organ dept. Drury U., Springfield, Mo., 1968—, univ. organist, 1991—. Lectr. recitals on Jewish music, 1991—; translator, Profl. documents, 1990—. Author: Organ Works of Elsa Barraine, 1995, Music of Alice Jordan, 1998; composer organ composition The Crucifixion, 1995; contbr. articles to profl. jours. Charter mem. Nat. Mus. Am. Indian, 1994—. Recipient Teaching fellow U. Kans., Drury Mirror award Rank I Mo. Coll. Newspaper Assn. Mem. Mortar Bd., Sigma Alpha Iota, Alpha Lambda Delta, Pi Delta Phi, Beta Beta Beta, Pi Kappa Lambda, Organ Hist. Soc., Am. Guild Organist. Home: 3563 E Linwood Dr Springfield MO 65809-2131 Office: Drury Univ 900 N Benton Ave Springfield MO 65802-3712 Address: 95 rue de Seine 75006 Paris France Office Phone: 417-873-7376. Personal E-mail: dplank@msn.com. Business E-Mail: emoulder@drury.edu.

MOULDS, ERIC SHANNON, professional football player; b. Lucedale, Miss., July 17, 1973; Student, Miss. State U. Wide receiver, kickoff return Buffalo Bills, 1996—. Achievements include first round draft pick NFL, 1996. Office: Buffalo Bills 1 Bills Dr Orchard Park NY 14127-2296

MOULDS, WILLIAM J. retired aeronautical engineer; b. Newton, Kans., Mar. 7, 1933; s. William J. and Edith M. (Cox) Moulds; m. Myra Teresa Cummins, Dec. 28, 1955; children: Michael J., Robert W., Barbara L., Anne T. Moulds-Laughlin, Patrick L., Margaret L. Moulds-Vittitow. BSME, U. N.Mex., 1957; MSME, N.Mex. State U., 1970. Registered profl. engr., N.Mex. Rsch. engr. rsch. lab. Allis-Chalmers, Cin., 1956—57; supr. aero. engr. Air Force Spl. Weapons Ctr., Albuquerque, 1958—63; sr. aero. rsch. engr. Air Force Weapons Lab., Albuquerque, 1963—72, theoretical rsch. engr., 1972—79, chief tech. svcs. divsn., staff rsch. engr. to comdr., 1979—89; ret., 1989. Contbr. articles to profl. jours.; patentee in field. Vol. Barrett House; founder, 1st pres. U. N.Mex. Sch. Engring Alumni Assn.; bd. dirs. N.Mex. State Bd. Registration for Profl. Engrs. and Land Surveyors, 1990—95, chmn. com. on rules, regulations and statues, 1992; com. mem. Barrett Found. Named to Sociedad de Ingenieros as Ingeniero Eminente, New Mex. State U., 1993; recipient Honor award, U. N.Mex. Sch. Engring., 2000. Republican. Roman Catholic. Home: 1401 Cardenas NE Albuquerque NM 87110-6623

MOULE, WILLIAM NELSON, electrical engineer, consultant; b. Highland Park, Mich., Sept. 13, 1924; s. Hollis Creager and Kate DeEtte (Hill) Moule; m. Barbara Ann Bagley, June 27, 1953; children: Janice Louise, Robert Hollis(dec.), Linda Anne, Nancy Lynn Moule Moles. BSEE, Mich. State U., 1949; MSEE, U. Pa., 1957. Reg. profl. engr., N.J. Design engr. Radio Corp. of Am., Camden, NJ, 1949—59, sr. design engr. Moorestown, NJ, 1959—67; sr. engr. Emerson Elec. Co., St. Louis, 1967—70, Emerson Elec. Rantec Divsn., Calabasas, Calif., 1970; sr. staff engr. Raytheon Co., Santa Barbara, Calif., 1970—73, ITT Gilfillan, Van Nuys, Calif., 1973, Jet Propulsion Lab., Pasadena, Calif., 1973—79; sr. rsch devel. engr. Lockheed Advanced Devel. Co., Burbank, Calif., 1979—2000, cons. engr., 2000—. Patentee numerous inventions, 1956—. Dir. nat. alumni bd. Mich. State U., East Lansing, 1984-87; pres. Big Ten Club of So. Calif., L.A., 1992. Staff sgt. USAAF, 1943-46. Mem. IEEE (sr., L.A. chpt. sec., treas. Antennas and Propagation soc. 1987-89, vice chmn. 1989-90, chmn. 1990-91), 305th Bombardment Group Meml. Assn. (life; pres. 2000-2001). Democrat. Presbyterian. Avocations: travel, photography, genealogy. Home: 5831 Fitzpatrick Rd Calabasas CA 91302-1104 Office: 5831 Fitzpatrick Rd Calabasas CA 91302-1104 Office Phone: 818-888-9567. Personal E-mail: wmoule@qnet.com.

MOULIN, JANE ANN FREEMAN, ethnomusicology educator, researcher; b. Oak Park, Ill., Mar. 4, 1946; d. James Frederic and Georgia Charlotte (Rahn) Freeman; m. Jacques Edouard Moulin, Apr. 26, 1975; children: Jean-Philippe Keala, Marie-Chantal Mahala. BA in Music cum laude, U. Hawaii, 1969; MA in Music, UCLA, 1971; PhD in Music, U. Calif., Santa Barbara, 1991. Libr. Music Libr UCLA, 1970-71; tchr. English Companions, Osaka, Japan, 1972; dancer Te Maeva and Tahiti Nui, Papeete, Tahiti, 1973-76; rsch. fellow U. Auckland, New Zealand, 1989; fellow East-West Ctr., Honolulu, 1984-85, 91; assoc. prof. Hawaii Loa Coll., Kaneohe, 1980-92; prof. U. Hawaii, Honolulu, 1992—, chmn. ethnomusicology program, 1993—98, 1999—2003, chmn. undergrad. studies in music, 2001—04. Dir. Europa Early Music Consort, Honolulu, 1981-2000; primary rschr. field work in French Polynesia, 1973-77, 85, 89, 95, 98, 2000, Territorial Survey Oceanic Music, Marquesas Islands, 1989; cons. Video series Dancing, WNET Channel 13, N.Y.C., 1989-92. Author: The Dance of Tahiti, 1979, Music of the Southern Marquesas Islands, 1994, (audio catalog) Music of the Southern Marquesas Islands, 1991, ency. and jour. articles on Tahitian and Marquesan performing arts, field recordings of Tahitian and Marquesan music; editl. bd. Jour. Perfect Beat, 1993—, Pacific Islands Monograph Series, 1997—; video documentarian Fesitval of Pacific Arts, 1992, 96, 2000, 04. Bd. dirs. Tahiti-USA Assn., Honolulu, 1997-2000; mem. adv. bd. folk arts State Found. Culture and Arts, Honolulu, 1985-87; bd. dirs. Hawaii Assn. Music Socs., Honolulu, 1983-88. Recipient Regents' fellowship U. Calif., 1970-71, 88-89, rsch. grant UNESCO/Archives of Maori and Pacific Music, Auckland, 1989, Regents' award for excellence in tchg. U. Hawaii, Honolulu, 1997, First Prize Thèse-Pac Assn. Competition, New Caledonia, 1994. Mem. Soc. Ethnomusicology (mem. coun. 1995-97), Internat. Coun. Traditional Music, Polynesia Soc., Pacific Arts Assn., Viola da Gamba Soc. Am. Avocations: Tahitian dance, hula, consort playing. Office: U Hawaii Music Dept 2411 Dole St Honolulu HI 96822-2329

MOULLETTE, JOHN BRINKLEY, retired corporate trainer, consultant; b. Camden, N.J., Jan. 23, 1927; s. Clarence Earle Moullette and Margaret Dorothea Philipsen; m. Lillian Marie Laye, Jan. 30, 1954 (div. 1979); children: John, Bruce, Jeanne, Edward, Jennifer. BEd, Trenton (N.J.) State Coll., 1957; MEd, Rutgers U., 1966, EdD, 1970. Cert. vocat.-tech. inst adminstr. N.J. Instr. tech. writing Salem County Tech. Inst., Penns Grove, N.J., 1961-65; supr. vocat. edn. N.J. State Dept. Edn., Trenton, 1965-66; lectr. in edn. Rutgers U., New Brunswick, N.J., 1966-70; assoc. prof. Wash. State U., Pullman, 1970-71; rsch. prof. Ohio State U., Columbus, 1971-75; mgr. proposal devel. Telemedia, Inc., Chgo., 1975-77; mgr. edn. and tng. Royal Saudi Naval Forces, Dammam, 1977-79; mgmt. and profl. trainer Saudi Aramco, Dhahran, Saudi Arabia, 1980-89, ret., 1989. Cons. Royal Saudi Naval Forces naval tech. tng. facilities, Dammam, Saudi Arabia, 1990-91, tng. ship Tarpon Springs, Fla., 1991-93, UN Devel. Program, Internat. Labor Orgn. Nat. Tng. Secretariat, Phnom Penh, Kingdom of Cambodia, 1993-94, Mil. Sea Lift Command USNS Comfort, 1996. Author: Technical Writing, 1969, Training Start-Up and Planning Guide, 1989, International Relations, 1993. Sgt. USMC, 1944-46, PTO, 1950-52, Korea; quartermaster/boatswain U.S. Mcht. Marine, 1946-49. Recipient Disting. Svc. award Grad. Sch. Edn., Rutgers U., New Brunswick, 1992. Mem.: Am. Legion (comdr. China Post #1, Dhahran 1986, 1988), Phi Delta Kappa, Epsilon Pi Tau. Avocations: scuba diving, offshore sailing, pioneer trekking, camping. Office: Internat Tng Consultants 3937 Winding Rd Fort Garland CO 81133

MOULTHROP, EDWARD ALLEN, architect, artist; b. Rochester, N.Y., May 22, 1916; s. Ray Josiah and Jetta (McDonald) M.; m. Mae Elizabeth Crotser, Jan 31, 1942; children: Mark, Philip, Samuel, Timothy. B.Arch., Western Res. U., 1939; M.F.A., Princeton, 1941. Asst. prof. architecture Ga. Inst. Tech., 1943-46, asst. prof. physics, 1944-46; chief designer Robert and Co. Asso. Architects and Engrs., Atlanta, 1948-72; prin. Edward Allen Moulthrop (architect and cons.), Atlanta, 1972—. 1st chmn. Ga. Art Commn., 1954-65 Exhibited in Watercolor U.S.A., 1962, USIA crafts traveling show to Russia, 1970., 1970, to Europe, 1990-93, Wichita Nat. Decorative Arts and Ceramics Exhbn., 1972, Ga. artists exhibit, High Mus. Art, Atlanta, 1971, 72, 74, Vatican Mus., Italy, 1978, Art of Woodturning show, Smithsonian Renwick Gallery, Washington, 1993—; represented in permanent collections Mus. Modern Art, N.Y., Met. Mus. Art, N.Y., Phila. Mus. Art, Chgo. Art Inst., The White House, Mint Mus. Art, Charlotte, N.C., High Mus. of Art, Atlanta, Boston Mus. Fine Arts, Ariz. State U. and Mus., Chgo. Art Inst., Copenhagen Mus. Art, Detroit Inst. Arts, Arkansas Arts Ctr. Decorative Arts Mus., Am. Craft Mus., N.Y., Renwick Gallery Mus. Am. Art, Smithsonian Inst., Mobile Mus. Art, Columbus Mus., Ga.; pvt. collections include Met. Mus. Art; instnl. collections include a. Gov.'s Office, Ga. Inst. Tech., Ga. State U., Atlanta Hist. Soc., Shepard Spinal Clinic, (permanent trophy and ann. trophies) Vintage Invitational Golf Tournament, White Ho. Collection Am. Crafts; corp. collections include So. Bell Hdqs., Atlanta, First Am. Bank, Nashville, Charlotte, Coca-Cola Co. World Hdqrs., St. Louis, Columbia Pictures, M.C.I., Hallmark, Phillip Morris, Cox Communication Co., IBM, Fuqua Inds., Atlanta, Rockefeller Ctr. Rainbow Room; spl. invited exhbts. Artists in Ga. High Mus. Art, Atlanta, 1971, 72, 74, The Vatican Mus., Rome, Internat. Exhbn.,Smithsonian Instn., 1978, Renwick Gallery Smithsonian Instn., 1978, XII Olympics Art Exhbn., Lake Placid, N.Y., 1980, Art for Use Nat. Crafts Exhbn. Am. Craft Mus., N.Y., 1980, Twenty-Fifth Anniversary Exhbn. Am. Craft Exhbn., 1981, Am. Craft Mus., N.Y., 1986, U.S. Info Agy. Ea. Europe, 1986-89; one man exhbn. High Mus. Art, 1987, U.S Info. Agy. European exhbn., overseas exhbn., 1992-95, 95-98; pubs. include Wall St. Jour., N.Y. Times, Village Voice, Atlanta Jour., Ariz. Republic, So. Accents, Creative Ideas, Home Mechanics, Fine Woodworking, American Craft, The Woodworker (with cover Great Britain), Holz und Elfenbein (with cover German), World of Wood, Popular Woodworking, Woodturning, Great Britain, Forbes Mag. Recipient Nat. Design award Am. Inst. Steel Constrn. 1959, 67, 1st purchase award for crafts Atlanta Arts Festival 1963, 64, 67, 72, 74, 77, 78, Atlanta Arts Festival First awards in crafts, 1963, 65, 67, 69, 73, 74, 77, 78, Craftsman U.S. award of merit 1966, Judges Choice award Western Colo. Center for Arts 1973, Purchase award 1975, Prize award, 1975, prize Marietta Coll. Crafts Nat. 1974, 76, prize awards Marietta Crafts Nat. Exhbn., Ohio, 1974, 75, 76, selected for exhibited 1973, 77, 78, N.C. prize awards Piedmont Regional Biennial Crafts Exhbns. Mint Mus. Art, Charlotte, 1974, 76, 78, Craftwork prize Am. Crafts Council 1976, 78, Prize awards, Am. Crafts Coun. S.E. Regional Biennial Crafts Exhbns., 1976, 78, Craftsmanship medal Atlanta chpt. Am. Instn. Archs., 1978, Ga. Assn. Am. Instn. Archs., 1980, Ga. State Gov's. award in Arts, 1981, Ga. Gov.'s Award in Arts 1981, Disting. Achievement award Ariz. State U., 1999. Fellow AIA (pres. Ga. chpt. 1953), Am. Craft Coun., Am. Craft Coun., 1987; mem. Ga. Engring. Soc. (pres. 1958, spl. hon. mem. 1969), Am. Craftsmens Coun. (Ga. rep. 1973-75), Ga. Designer Craftsmen (pres. 1975-76). Achievements include providing gifts for President Clinton, Queen Margrethe of Denmark and President Earnesto of Mexico. Home and Office: 180 Dickerson Road NE Marietta GA 30067

MOULTON, EDWARD QUENTIN, civil engineer, educator; b. Kalamazoo, Nov. 16, 1926; s. Burt Frederick and Esther (Fairchild) M.; m. Joy Wade, Jan. 2, 1954; children: Jennifer Fairchild, Charles Wade, David Frederick II, Alison Joy. BS, Mich. State U., 1947; MS, La. State U., 1948; PhD, U. Calif., Berkeley, 1956; DSc (hon.), Wittenberg U., 1980; LLD (hon.), Xavier U., 1983, Wilmington Coll., 1983. Registered profl. engr., Ohio. Instr. civil engring Mich. State U., 1947; hydraulic engring. fellow La. State U., 1947-48; engr. U.S. Waterways Expt. Sta., Vicksburg, Miss., 1948; rsch. fellow U. Wis., 1948-49; asst. prof. civil engring. Auburn U., 1949-50; lectr. civil engring. U. Calif., Berkeley, 1950-54; asst. prof. civil engring. Ohio State U., 1954-58, assoc. prof., 1958-64; asst. dean Ohio State U. (Grad. Sch.), 1958-62, assoc. dean Grad. Sch., Coll. Arts and Scis., chmn. geodetic sci., 1962-64; dean off-campus edn., asso. dean faculties for personnel budget, prof. engring. mechanics Ohio State U. Grad. Sch., Columbus, 1964-66; dir. Coll. Sci. and Engring. Dayton campus Miami U.-Ohio State U., 1963-66; pres. U. S.D., 1966-68; exec. asst. to pres. Ohio State U., 1968-69, sec. bd. trustees Ohio Agr. Devel. Ctr., 1968-79, prof. civil engring., 1968-79, v.p. adminstrv. ops., 1969-70, exec. v.p. adminstrv. ops., 1970-71, exec. v.p., 1971-73, v.p. bus. and adminstrn., 1973-79, v.p., sec. emeritus, 1984—; chancellor Ohio Bd. Regents, 1979-84, chancellor emeritus, 1984—; exec. v.p. Cranston Securities Co., 1984; pres. Lake Erie Coll., 1985-86; pres., gen. mgr. Columbus Symphony Orchestra, 1986-88, mem. trustees cir., 2000—. Cons. civil engring. 1954—. Author articles, reports, bulls. on environ. engring. and edn. Trustee Blue Cross Ctrl. Ohio, 1971-77, 80-82, Columbus Symphony Orch., 1980-85, Riverside Meth. Hosp., 1979-95, chmn. fin. and assets com., 1983-94, treas., 1988-94, vice-chmn., 1994-95; nat. adv. coun. for small bus. to U.S. Sec. Treasury, 1975-76; steering com. Devel. Com. Greater Columbus, 1970-1980, chmn., 1978-79; nat. adv. coun. SBA, 1973-76; bd. dirs. Columbus Safety Coun., 1970-79; bd. mem. Greater Columbus Arts Coun., 1970-78, Mid-Ohio Health Planning Commn., 1973-74, Am. Univs. for Rsch. in Astronomy, 1972-79, Ohio Transp. Rsch. Ctr., 1979-83, U.S. Health Corp. (now Ohio Health), 1995-97; chmn. Grant/Riverside Meth. Hosps., 1995-97, mem. trustees' coun., 1998—, trustee emeritus, 1999—; vice-chmn. Ohio Higher Edn. facilities Commn., 1979-83; bd. mem. Ohio Sch. and Coll. Bd. Registration, 1979-83, Ohio Ednl. TV Commn., 1979-83, Midwest Edn. Commn., 1979-85; chmn. Columbus Symphony Grand Ball, 1983; chmn. judging Internat. Sci. and Engring. Fair, 1984. With USN, 1945-46, PTO. Fellow ASCE; mem. Ohio Hist. Soc. (bd. dirs. 1979-83), State Higher Edn. Exec. Officers (exec. com. 1981-83), Meml. Soc. Columbus Area (pres. 1999-2000, bd. mem.), Ohio Commodore, Scioto Country Club, Faculty Club (Columbus), Athletic Club Columbus, Sigma Xi, Tau Beta Pi, Pi Mu Epsilon, Chi Epsilon, Delta Omega, Romophos, Sigma Alpha Epsilon. Congregationalist. Home: 1303 London Dr Columbus OH 43221-1541

MOULTON, HUGH GEOFFREY, lawyer, retired business executive; b. Boston, Sept. 18, 1933; s. Robert Selden and Florence (Bracq) M.; m. Catherine Anne Clark, Mar. 24, 1956; children: H. Geoffrey, Cynthia C. Moulton Bassett. BA, Amherst Coll., 1955; LL.B., Yale U., 1958; postgrad. Advanced Mgmt. Program, Harvard U., 1984. Bar: Pa. 1959. Assoc. Montgomery, McCracken, Walker-Rhoads, Phila., 1958-66, ptnr., 1967-69; v.p., counsel Dolly Madison Industries, Inc., Phila., 1969-70; sec. Alco Std. Corp., Valley Forge, Pa., 1970-72, v.p. law, 1973-79, v.p., sec., gen. counsel, 1979-83, sr. v.p., gen. counsel, 1983-92, exec. v.p., chief adminstrv. officer, gen. counsel, 1992-94; exec. v.p. Alco Std. Corp. now IKON Office Solutions Inc., Valley Forge, Pa., 1994-96, Unisource Worldwide, Inc., 1997-99; ret., 1999. Pres. Wissahickon Valley Watershed Assn., Ambler, Pa., 1975-78, treas., 1978—; mem. Pa. Coun. for Econ. Edn., bd. dirs., 1985-95; trustee Arcadia U., 1991—, chair, 1998-02; Montgomery Co. Lands Trust (trustee 2000—), Whitemarsh Found. (trustee, pres. 2002—). Mem. Am. Corp. Counsel Assn. (bd. dirs. Delaware Valley chpt. 1984-88, pres. 1986-87), Nature Conservancy (trustee Pa. chpt. 1991—, chmn. 1993-97), Sunnybrook Golf Club (Plymouth Meeting, Pa.), Cape Cod Nat. Golf Club (Harwich, Mass.), Lemon Bay Golf Club (Englewood, Fla.). Home: 300 Williams Rd Fort Washington PA 19034-2015 E-mail: hgmoulton@att.net.

MOULTON, JENNIFER T. city official, architect; BA cum laude, Colo. Coll., 1971; MArch with honors, U. Colo., Denver, 1978. Registered arch., Colo. Corp. legal asst. Davis, Graham & Stubbs, Denver, 1972-75; mem. staff Ctr. for Cmty. Devel. and Design, Denver, 1976-77; assoc. Barker Rinker Seacat & Ptnrs., Archs., Denver, 1978-84; v.p., owner Anthony Pellecchia Archs., P.C., Denver, 1984-89; pres. Hist. Denver, Inc., 1989-91; dir. Denver Planning and Devel. Office, 1992—. Mem. master plan com. Colo. Coll., Colorado Springs, 1994-95, juror Ctrl. States Regional Awards of Excellence, 1995; team mem. Mayor's Inst. for City Design, Harvard U., 1996, Design Workshop for Oklahoma City, Nat. Endowment for Arts, 1995; mem. dean's search com. Sch. Architecture and Planning, U. Colo., Denver, 1986, mem. dean's adv. com., 1986-89, vis. lectr., 1979-81; instr. corp. paralegal courses U. Denver Coll. Law, Arapahoe C.C., C.C. Denver, 1973-75; lectr. Jr. League Denver, 1987-88, Colo. Coll. Alumni Assn., 1985. Prin. works include Grant Humphries Mansion restoration, Denver, also offices for Colo. Coun. on Arts and Humanities in carriage house therein, Washington Park Pavilion restoration, Denver, Goss Residence, Boulder, Colo., Georgetown (Colo.) Downtown Redevel. Project, Georgetown Loop R.R. Master Plan, Malo Mansion project, Denver. Founder, pres. Women for Downtown Housing, 1980-81; co-chmn. urban design and land use task force comprehensive plan adv. com. City of

Denver, 1986-87, mem. parks and recreation adv. com., 1983-89; atrustee, chmn. preservation com. Hist. Denver, Inc., 1986-89; mem. Citizens for Denver's Future, 1989; vice chmn. Colo. Passenger Tramway Safety Bd., 1981-89; mem. design competition jury Denver Pub. Libr., 1990-91; chmn. design rev. com. Cul. Denver Pub. Libr., 1992-94; trustee Colo. Hist. Found., 1990—; mem. South Platte River Commn., 1995— Recipient Disting. Svc. award U. Colo. Sch. Architecture and Planning, 1987, Louis T. Benezet award for outstanding profl. achievements Colo. Coll., 1991. Mem. AIA (chmn. design awards program Denver chpt. 1983, bd. dirs. 1977-87, treas. 1982, sec. 1983, 2d v.p. 1984, pres.-elect 1985, pres. 1986), Colo. Soc. Archs. (chmn. design awards program 1980-82). Office: Denver Planning & Devel Office 200 W 14th Ave Ofc Ste 203 Denver CO 80204-2732

MOULTON, PAUL DOUGLAS (PETE MOULTON), information technology consultant; b. Binghamton, N.Y., Sept. 1, 1944; s. Fredrick Douglas and Helene Marjorie (Cole) M.; children: Susan Jennifer, Jeremy Matthew. BS in Math., Clarkson Coll. Tech., 1966, MS in Indsl. Mgmt., 1968. Instr. indsl. mgmt. Clarkson Coll., Potsdam, N.Y., 1967-68; tech. staff Sanders Data Systems, Inc., Nashua, N.H., 1968-71; grad. asst. Pa. State U., University Park, 1971-72; computer specialist Nat. Weather Svc., Silver Spring, Md., 1972; mgr. Info. & Communication Applications, Inc., Rockville, Md., 1972-75, Rehab. Group, Inc., Arlington, Va., 1975-77; supr. spl. projects U.S. Senate, Washington, 1977-80; sr. cons. specialist telecommunications policies and programs Gen. Electric Info. Svcs. Co., Rockville, 1980; dir. The Moulton Co., Columbia, Md., 1981—. Internat. lectr., cons. in PCs and telecomms. Author: Hard Disk Quick Reference, Que Corporation, 1989, A+ Certification and Repair Guide, 2000, 02, The Telecommunications Survival Guide, 2001, Small Office/Home Office LANS, 2002; host DialANerd radio show WITK and WCBM, Balt., 1998-2001; exec. prodr., host Technically Correct TV show WMAR ABC-TV2, Balt. N.Y. Regent scholar. Mem. IEEE, Am. Inst. Indsl. Engrs. (sr.). Home and Office: 7146 Rivers Edge Rd Columbia MD 21044-4235

MOULTON, SARA, chef, magazine editor; married; 2 children. Grad., U. Mich., 1974, Culinary Inst. Am., 1977; postgrad. stagaire with a master chef, Chartres, France, 1979. With Julia Child and More Co., 1979; mem. test kitchen Gourmet mag., 1984—88, exec. chef, 1988—; host Sara's Secrets, Food Network, Cooking Live, Food Network; exec. chef Good Morning Am., food corr., 1997, food editor; sous chef La Tulipe, NY; co-founder NY Women's Culinary Alliance; instr. Peter Kump's NY Cooking Sch. Author: Sara Moulton Cooks at Home, 2002; co-author (with Jean Anderson): Good Morning America Cut the Calories Cookbook, 2000. Office: Sara Moulton Enterprises Inc 130 W 24th St 3B New York NY 10011 Business E-Mail: sara@saramoulton.com.

MOULTON, WILBUR WRIGHT, JR., lawyer; b. Pensacola, Fla., Dec. 3, 1935; s. Wilbur Wright and Evelyn (Nobles) M.; m. Ann Arnow, Nov. 10, 1978; 1 child, Kelly Arnow. BA, Duke U., 1957; LLB, U. Va., 1959; LLM in Taxation, NYU, 1964. Bar: Fla. 1959; cert. tax lawyer, Fla. Assoc. Beggs & Lane, Pensacola, 1964-69; gen. counsel The Moulton Trust, Pensacola, 1970-74; pvt. practice, Pensacola, 1974-83; ptnr. Carlton, Fields, Ward, Emmanuel, Smith & Cutler, P.A., Pensacola, 1983-2000, Moulton, McEachern & Walker (formerly Carlton, Fields et al), Pensacola, 2000—. Pres. Pensacola Heritage Found., 1971-72, Lakeview Ctr., Inc., Pensacola, 1975-77, dir. emeritus, 1984; chmn. bd. Lakeview Found., Inc., Pensacola; bd. trustees Pensacola Mus. Art; trustee Roberts Cemetery, 1962—, Roberts Cemetery Trust, 1987—; mem. adv. com. Switzer Bros. Charitable Found., 2000—. Lt. USNR, 1960-64. Mem. ABA, Fla. Bar Assn., Estate Planning Coun. N.W. Fla. (pres. 1978), Escambia-Santa Rosa Bar Assn. (pres. 1988-89), Rotary, Pensacola Country Club, Pensacola Yacht Club. Republican. Episcopalian. Avocations: reading, travel. Office: Bank of Am Bldg 5041 Bayou Blvd Ste 300 Pensacola FL 32503 Fax: 850-969-0566. Business E-Mail: wmoulton@pensacolalegal.com.

MOULTRIE, FRED, geneticist, researcher; b. Albertville, Ala., Apr. 18, 1923; s. Walter Louis and Minnie Alma (Bodine) M.; m. Frances Grace Aldridge, May 28, 1947; children: Marilyn R. Moultrie Phillips, Elizabeth Anne Moultrie Becker, Janet Carol Moultrie Gauger. BS, Auburn U., 1948, MS, 1949; PhD in Genetics, Kan State U., 1953. Asso. prof. Auburn U., 1951-55, prof., 1955-56; geneticist Arbor Acres Farm, Inc., Glastonbury, Conn., 1956-59, research coordinator, 1959-62, v.p., dir. research, 1962-64, exec. v.p., 1964-72, pres. domestic div., 1972-73; pres. Corbett Breeders, Westover, Md., 1973-81; v.p., dir. research Corbett Enterprises, Inc., 1973-81, Kennebec Internat., 1981-84; geneticist Perdue Farms, Salisbury, Md., 1984-88; genetics cons., 1988—. Served with USCGR, 1942-46. Mem. World's Poultry Sci. Assn., Am. Poultry Sci. Assn., Poultry Breeders Am. (pres. 1967-68), Sigma Xi, Phi Kappa Phi, Alpha Zeta, Gamma Sigma Delta. Clubs: Masons. Home and Office: 30390 Southampton Bridge Rd Salisbury MD 21804-2497

MOULY, EILEEN LOUISE, financial planner; b. Milw., Apr. 18, 1955; d. George Joseph and Gertrude Mary (DuBois) M. BBA in Acctg. summa cum laude, U. Miami, Coral Gables, Fla., 1977, MBA, 1978. CPA, Fla.; cert. fin. planner, personal fin. specialist. Acct. Main Hurdman, CPA's, Miami, Fla., 1979-82, Coopers & Lybrand, CPA's, West Palm Beach, Fla., 1982-83, Pannell Kerr Forster CPA's, Miami, 1983-84; cert. fin. planner Consortium Group, Miami, 1984-86; ptnr., fin. planner Evensky & Brown, Miami, 1986-91; pres. Mouly Fin. Mgmt. Inc., Miami, 1991—. Instr. U. Miami, 1987-90, Fla. Internat. U., 1987-90; speaker in field. Mem. AICPA, Fla. Inst. CPAs (bd. dirs. 1991-93, bd. govs. 2000-01, sec. South Dade chpt. 1993-94, treas. 1994-95, v.p. 1995-96, pres. 1997-98, 99-2000), Fin. Planning Assn., Registry Fin. Planning Practitioners, Inst. CFPs (cert., v.p. greater Miami chpt. 1987-91), Leadership South Dade. Office: Mouly Fin Mgmt Inc 290 NW 165th St Plz 300 Miami FL 33169-6457

MOUNT, WILLIE LANDRY, state legislator; b. Lake Charles, La., Aug. 25, 1949; d. Lee Robert and Willie Veatrice (McCullor) Landry; m. Benjamin Wakefield Mount, Aug. 19, 1976. BS, McNeese State U., 1971. Geophys. asst. La. Land and Exploration, Lake Charles, La., 1971-76; pharm. rep. Lederle, Lake Charles, 1976-80; realtor Mary Kay Hopkins, Lake Charles, 1976-87; co-owner Paper Place, Lake Charles, 1991-95; mayor City of Lake Charles, 1993—2000; mem. La. State Senate, 2000—, mem. select com. on consumer protection, mem. jud. C, health and welfare, legis. audit adv. commn., mem. state tech. adv. commn., joint juvenile justice commn., millennium port com., sch. fin. rev. commn., mem. edn. com., vice chair joint legis. com. on capital outlay, chmn. revenue and fiscal affairs com. Gov. Violent Crime & Homicide Task Force, Baton Rouge, 1993—95; mem. steering com. La. conf. Mayors bd. pres. La. Asset Mgmt. Pool Bd., 1997. Guest condr. Lake Charles Symphony, 1992; active La. Mcpl. Assn., Baton Rouge, 1995-98; pres. Jr. League of Lake Charles; mem. state interagy. coordinating coun. Dyslexia Study Com.; mem. adv. bd. S.W. La. Literacy Coalition; mem. adv. coun. Pet Overpopulation; active First United Meth. Ch., La. Meth. Conf., McNeese State U. Found., Prevent Child Abuse bd. Micro-Enterprise Devel. Alliance of La. Bd., McNeese State U. Found. Bd., St. Patrick Hosp. Bd. Councillors, Coastal Plain Conservancy Bd., United Way, Children's Miracle Network; exec. com. Coun. for a Better La. Recipient Spiritual Aims award Kiwanis Club, 1991, Cmty. Svc. award, 1995, Citizen of Yr. 1996-97, Dorthea Combre award NAACP, 1994, La. Mcpl. Assn. Cmty. Achievement award, 1995-97, Disting. Citizen award Boy Scouts Am., 1999, Patron Architecture, 2000, Disting. Alumni award McNeese State U., 2000, Golden Apple award Delta Kappa Gamma, 2002, Disting. Svc. award La. Restaurant Assn., 2002, Spl. Friend of La. Mcpl. Assn. award, 2003, Wilton Bellard Jr. award S.W. La. Ctr. for Health Svcs., Ron Schroeder award MEDAL; named Woman of Yr., Quota Club, 1991, Citizen of Yr., Women's com. S.W. La., 1992, Woman of Yr., Pub. Ofcl. of Yr. Msgr. Cramers KC, Pub. Ofcl. of Yr., NASW, 1997, Legislator of Yr., La. Orthopaedic Assn., Champion for Children, Prevent Child Abuse. Mem. LWV, S.W. La. Mayor's Assn. (chmn. 1993-94). Home: 205 Shell Beach Dr Lake Charles LA 70601-5933 Office: PO Box 3004 Lake Charles LA 70602-3004 E-mail: lasen27@legis.state.la.us.

MOUNTAIN, CLIFTON FLETCHER, surgeon, educator; b. Toledo, Apr. 15, 1924; s. Ira Fletcher and Mary (Stone) M.; m. Merel Ann Grey; children: Karen Lockerby, Clifton Fletcher, Jeffrey Richardson. AB, Harvard U., 1946; MD, Boston U., 1954. Diplomate Am. Bd. Surgery. Dir. dept. statis. rsch. Boston U., 1947-50; cons. rsch. analyst Mass. Dept. Pub. Health, 1951-53; intern U. Chgo. Clinics, 1954, resident, 1955-58, instr. surgery, 1958-59; sr. fellow thoracic surgery Houston, 1959. Mem. staff U. Tex. Anderson Cancer Ctr.; asst. prof. thoracic surgery U. Tex., 1960-73, assoc. prof surgery, 1973-76, prof., 1976-94, prof. emeritus, 1995—, prof. surgery Sch. Medicine, 1987—, chief sect. thoracic surgery, 1970-79, chmn. thoracic oncology, 1979-84, chmn. dept. thoracic surgery, 1980-85, cons. dept. thoracic and cardiovascular surgery, 1996—, chmn. program in biomath. and computer sci., 1962-64, Mike Hogg vis. lectr. in S. Am., 1967; prof. surgery U. Calif., San Diego, 1996—; pres., chmn. Mountain Found. for Lung Cancer Rsch. and Edn., 1997—; mem. sci. mission on cancer USSR, 1970-78, and Japan, 1976-84; mem. com. health, rsch. and edn. facilities Houston Cmty. Coun., 1964-78; cons. Am. Joint Com. on Cancer Staging and End Result Reporting, 1964-74, Tex. Heart Inst., 1994-96; mem. Am. Joint Com. on Cancer, 1974-86, chmn. lung and esophagus task force; mem. working party on lung cancer and chmn. com. on surgery Nat. Clin. Trials Lung Cancer Study Group, NIH, 1971-76; mem. plans and scope com. cancer therapy Nat. Cancer Inst., 1972-75, mem. lung cancer study group, 1977-89, chmn. steering com., 1973-75, mem. bd. sci. counselors divsn. cancer treatment, 1972-75; hon. cons. Shanghai Chest Hosp. and Lung Cancer Ctr., Nat. Cancer Inst. of Brazil; sr. cons. Houston Thorax Inst., 1994-96. Editor The New Physician, 1955-59; mem. editl. bd. Yearbook of Cancer, 1960-88, Internat. Trends in Gen. Thoracic Surgery, 1984-91; contbr. articles to profl. jours., chpts. to textbooks. Chmn. profl. adv. com. Harris County Mental Health Assn.; bd. dirs. Harris County Chpt. Am. Cancer Soc. Lt. USNR, 1942-46. Recipient award Soviet Acad. Sci., 1977, Garcia Meml. medal Philippine Coll. Surgeons, 1982, Disting. Alumni award Boston U., 1988, Disting. Achievement U. Tex. M.D. Anderson Cancer Ctr., 1990, Disting. Svc. award Internat. Assn. for the Study of Lung Cancer, 1991, Disting. Alumnus award Boston U. Sch. of Medicine, 1992, ALCASE Internat. award for excellence, 1997, Rudolf Nissen medal German Soc. Cardiovascular and Thoracic Surgery, 1998, named hon. pres. First Internat. Congress on Thoracic Surgery, 1997; Fellow ACS Am. Coll. Chest Physicians (chmn. com. cancer 1967-75), Am. Assn. Thoracic Surgery, Inst. Environ. Scis., N.Y. Acad. Sci., Assn. Thoracic and Cardiovascular Surgeons of Asia (hon.), Hellenic Cancer Soc. (hon.), Chilean Soc. Respiratory Diseases (hon., hon. pres. 1982). Mem. AAAS, Am. Assn. Cancer Rsch., AMA, So. Med. Assn., Am. Thoracic Soc., Soc. Thoracic Surgeons, Soc. Biomed. Computing, Am. Fedn. Clin. Rsch., Internat. Assn. Study Lung Cancer (pres. 1976-78), Am. Radium Soc., European Soc. Thoracic Surgeons, Pan-Am Med. Assn., Houston Surg. Soc., Soc. Surg. Oncology, James Ewing Soc., Sigma Xi. Achievements include conception and development of program for application of mathematics and computers to the life sciences, of resource for experimental designs, applied statistics and computational support; concept and implementation of multidisciplinary, site specific cancer mgmt. clinics; first clinical use of physiological adhesives in thoracic surgery; demonstration of clinical behavior of undifferentiated small cell lung cancer; first laser resection of lung tissue at thoracotomy; development of international system for staging of lung cancer. Office Phone: 858-454-6028. Business E-Mail: cmountain@ucsd.edu.

MOUNTAIN, JEFFREY RICHARDSON, engineering educator; s. Clifton Fletcher and Marilyn I. Mountain; m. Gaye Lynne Hostutler; children: Jennifer Rene, Rachel Elizabeth. BSME, U. Tex., Arlington, 1989, MSME, 1990, PhD, 1994. Registered profl. engr., Tex.; cert. master plumber Tex. State Bd. Plumbing Examiners. Lectr. dept. gen. engring. U. Ill., Urbana, 1997—98; assoc. prof. of mech. engring. U. of Tex., Tyler, 1998—. Contbr. articles to tech. jours. Recipient Best Prof. of Yr. award, Engring. Students Assn., 2000—01; Engring. Edn. and Ctrs. grantee, NSF, 2003, Course Curriculum and Laboratory Improvement grantee, 2000. Mem.: ASME (chmn. 2001—03, Disting. Svc. award 2002), Am. Soc. of Engring. Educators, Alpha Xi, Pi Tau Sigma, Tau Beta Pi. Avocation: sailing. Office: U Tex Tyler 3900 University Blvd Tyler TX 75799

MOUNTCASTLE, KENNETH FRANKLIN, JR., retired stockbroker; b. Winston-Salem, NC, Oct. 8, 1928; s. Kenneth Franklin and May M.; m. Mary Katharine Babcock, Sept. 1, 1951; children: Mary Babcock, Laura Lewis, Kenneth Franklin, Katharine Reynolds. BS in Commerce, U. N.C., 1950. With Mountcastle Knitting Co., Lexington, N.C., 1952-55, Reynolds & Co., N.Y.C., 1955-71, Reynolds Securities Inc. (formerly Reynolds and Co.), N.Y.C., 1971-95; sr. v.p. Reynolds Securities Inc., N.Y.C., 1974-78, Dean Witter Reynolds (formerly Reynolds Securities Inc.), N.Y.C., 1978-95; ret., 1995. Trustee New Canaan (Conn.) Country Sch., 1962-68, Ethel Walker Sch., Simsbury, Conn., 1973-85, Coro Found., 1980—, nat. chmn., 1986-89; past bd. dirs., past pres. Mary Reynolds Babcock Found., Winston-Salem; past bd. visitors U. N.C., Chapel Hill,; bd. dirs. Inform, NYC, Fresh Air Fund, NYC, Giraffe Project, Bus. Execs. Nat. Security. With U.S. Army, 1950-52. Mem. Country Club of New Canaan, Wee Burn Country Club (Darien, Conn.), Old Town Club (Winston-Salem), Racquet and Tennis Club, Ocean Forest Golf Club (Sea Island, Ga.), Sea Island Club, Pine Valley Golf Club, Stock Exch. Luncheon Club, Down Town Assn. (NYC). Office: 49 Locust Ave Ste 104 New Canaan CT 06840-4764

MOUNTCASTLE, VERNON BENJAMIN, neurophysiologist; b. Shelbyville, Ky., July 15, 1918; s. Vernon and Anne-Francis Marguerite (Waugh) Mountcastle; m. Nancy Clayton Pierpont, Sept. 6, 1945; children: Vernon Benjamin III, Anne Clayton, George Earle Pierpont. BS in Chemistry, Roanoke Coll., Salem, Va., 1938, DSc (hon.), 1968; MD, Johns Hopkins U., 1942; DSc (hon.), U. Pa., 1976, Northwestern U., 1985, U. Minn., 1995; MD (hon.), U. Zurich, 1983, U. Siena, 1984, U. Santiago, Spain, 1990. House officer surgery Johns Hopkins Hosp., 1942—43; mem. faculty Johns Hopkins Sch. Medicine, 1946—, prof. physiology, 1959, dir. dept., 1964—80, Univ. prof. neurosci., 1980—92, prof. emeritus, 1992—; dir. Bard Labs. Neurophysiology Johns Hopkins U., Balt., 1981—91. Spl. rsch. physiology brain; chmn. physiology study sect., mem. physiology tng. com. NIH, 1958—61; adv. coun. Nat. Eye Inst., 1971—74; vis. prof. Coll. de France, Paris, 1980. Editor-in-chief: Jour. Neurophysiology, 1961—64, editor, contbr.: Med. Physiology, 12th edit., 1968, Med. Physiology, 13th edit., 1974, Med. Physiology, 14th edit., 1980, with G.M. Edelman: The Mindful Brain, 1978,: Perceptual Neuroscience: The Cerebral Cortex, 1998, author articles in field. Lt. (s.g.) M.C. USNR, 1943—46. Recipient Lashley prize, Am. Philos. Soc., 1974, F.O. Schmitt prize and medal, MIT, 1975, Sherrington prize and Gold medal, Royal Acad. Medicine, London, 1977, Horowitz prize, Columbia U., 1978, Helmholtz prize, 1982, Fyssen Internat. prize, Paris, 1983, Lasker award, 1983, Nat. Medal Sci., 1986, Zotterman prize and medal, Swedish Physiol. Soc., 1989, award in neurosci., Fidia Fedn., 1990, Australia prize, 1993. Mem.: AAAS (McGovern prize and medal 1990), NAS (chmn. sect. on physiology 1971—74, award in neurosci. 1998), Acad. Sci. (Finland, fgn.), Royal Soc. London (fgn.), Acad. Scis. (France, fgn.), Nat. Inst. Medicine, Am. Philos. Soc. (councillor 1979—82), Soc. Neurosci. (pres. 1970—72, Gerard prize 1980), Harvey Cushing Soc., Am. Acad. Arts and Scis., Am. Physiol. Soc., Physiol. Soc. London (hon.), Am. Neurol. Assn. (hon. Bennett lectr. 1978), Sigma Xi, Phi Chi, Alpha Omega Alpha, Phi Beta Kappa. Home: 15601 Carroll Rd Monkton MD 21111-2009 Office Phone: 410-566-4271. E-mail: mountcastle@mbi.mb.jhu.edu.

MOUNTCASTLE, WILLIAM WALLACE, JR., philosophy and religion educator; b. Hanover, N.H., July 10, 1925; s. William Wallace and Grace Elizabeth (Zottarelli) M.; m. Ila M. Warner (div.); children: Christine, Susan, Gregory, Eric; m. Barbara Kaye Griffin, Oct. 19, 1979; 1 child, Cathleena; stepdaughter, Dasha. BA, Whittier Coll., 1951; STB, Boston U., 1954, PhD, 1958. Ordained to ministry United Meth. Ch. Asst. prof. philosophy and religion High Point (N.C.) Coll., 1958-60; mem. So. Calif. Ann. Conf. United Meth. Ch., 1954-60; assoc. prof., head dept. philosophy Nebr. Wesleyan U., Lincoln, 1960-63, prof., head dept. philosophy, 1963-67; mem. Neb. Ann. Conf. United Meth. Ch., 1960-95; prof. philosophy Fla. So. Coll., Lakeland, 1967-69; assoc. prof. philosophy and religion U. W. Fla., Pensacola, 1969-79, prof. philosophy and religion, 1979—, M.L. Tipton prof. philosophy and religion, 1980—2003, emeritus M.L. Tipton prof., 2003. Author: Religion in Planetary Perspective, 1979, Science Fantasy Voices and Visions of Cosmic Religion, 1996; contbr. articles to profl. jours. Fighter pilot USAAF, 1942-48, PTO. Mem. NEA/United Faculty Fla., Am. Assn. Religion, Am. Philos. Assn., Democrat. Home: 4549 Sabine Dr Gulf Breeze FL 32563-9253 Office: U West Fla Dept Phil-Religious Studies Pensacola FL 32514

MOUNTJOY, DENNIS LEE, state official; b. Pasadena, Calif., Feb. 12, 1957; children: Tammy, Nicholas. Grad. h.s., Monrovia. V.p., gen. mgr. Mountjoy Constrn., 1978—88; owner constrn. co., 1988—; state assembly mem. Dist. 59 Calif. State Assembly, 2000—. Vice-chair housing and comty. devel. com.; mem. ins. com.; mem. transp. com.; mem. VA com.; mem. Calif. Rep. Assembly. Mem. San Gabriel Valley Caucus. Mem.: Lincoln Club. Republican. Mailing: Rm 3141 PO Box 942849 Sacramento CA 94249 Office: Ste A 135 W Lemon Ave Monrovia CA 91016

MOUNTJOY, HELEN W. educational association administrator; married; 3 children. Grad., Vanderbilt U. Mem. Ky. State Bd. Edn., 1991—, chairperson, 1998—. Mem. Ky. Literacy Partnership; mem. edn. adv. com. Coun. State Govts.; mem. Owensboro adv. bd. BB&T Bank. Chairwoman Daviess County Sch. Bd.; chair Owensboro Mercy Health Sys. Bd. Trustees, Leadership Owensboro Bd. Recipient Disting. Svc. award, Nat. Assn. State Bds. Edn., 2002. Mem.: Owensboro C. of C. (mem. edn. com., mem. citizens com. on edn.). Address: 449 Browns Valley Rd Utica KY 42376

MOUNTZ, LOUISE CARSON SMITH, retired librarian; b. Fond Du Lac, Wis., Oct. 20, 1911; d. Roy Carson and Charlotte Louise (Scheurs) Smith; m. George Edward Mountz, May 4, 1935 (dec. Oct. 3 1951); children: Peter Carson, Pamela Teeters Mountz McDonald. Student, Western Coll. for Women, 1929-31; AB, The Ohio State U., 1933; MA, Ball State U., 1962; postgrad., Manchester Coll., 1954, Ind. U., 1960-61. Cert. tchr., Ind. Tchr. Monroeville (Ind.) H.S., 1953-54, Riverdale H.S., St. Joe, Ind., 1954-55; libr. High Sch., Avilla, Ind., 1955-58; head libr. Penn H.S., Mishawaka, Ind., 1958-67, Northwood Jr. H.S., Ft. Wayne, Ind., 1967-69, McIntosh Jr. H.S., Auburn, Ind., 1969-74; dir. Media Ctr. DeKalb Jr. H.S., Auburn, Ind., 1974-78; ret., 1978; cons. media ctr. planning Penn-Harris-Madison Sch. Corp., Mishawaka, 1966-67. Author: Biographies for Junior High Schools and Correlated Audio-Visual Materials, 1970; contbr. articles to profl. jours. Bd. dirs. DeKalb County chpt. ARC, 1938-42, 51-53, DeKalb County Heart Assn., 1946-52, DeKalb County Cmty. Concert Assn., 1946-58, Am. Field Svc. Mishawaka chpt., 1960-67; mem. Ft. Wayne Philharmonic Orch. Assn., Ft. Wayne Art Mus., DeKalb County Hist. Soc., Garrett Hist. Soc., DeKalb County Genealogy Soc., Acres Landtrust, Preservation of DeKalb County Heritage Assn., DeKalb Meml. Hosp. Women's Guild, also life mem. Mem. Ind. Sch. Librarians Assn. (dir. 1963-67), Internat. Assn. Sch. Librarianship, Ind. Assn. Ednl. Communication and Tech., Assn. Ind. Media Educators, Nat. Ret. Tchrs. Assns., Nat. Trust Hist. Preservation, Hist. Landmarks Found. Ind., Delta Kappa Gamma (charter mem., Beta Beta chpt.), Kappa Kappa Kappa (pr. officer 1941-45, pres. Alpha Chi chpt. 1938-40, organizer Garrett Assoc. chpt. pres. Garrett Assoc. chpt. 1971-73), Greenhurst Country Club, Ft. Wayne's Women's Club, Athena Lit. Club (hon.), Ladies Lit. Club of Auburn (hon.), Delta Delta Delta (house pres.). Methodist.

MOUNTZ, WADE, retired health service management executive; b. Winona, Ohio, Nov. 19, 1924; s. Lowell J. and Ethel M. (Coppock) M.; m. Betty G. Wilson, June 3, 1946; children: David John, Timothy Wilson. BA, Baldwin-Wallace Coll., 1948; MHA, U. Minn., 1951; LHD (hon.), Ky. Wesleyan Coll., 1991. With Norton Meml. Infirmary, Louisville, 1951-69, adminstr., 1958-69; pres. Norton-Children's Hosps., Inc., Louisville, 1969-81, NKC, Inc., Louisville, 1981-85, vice chmn., 1985-87; pres. emeritus Norton Healthcare, 1987—. Vice chmn. Comprehensive Health Planning Council Ky., 1968-73, chmn., 1973-79; bd. dirs. Louisville chpt. ARC, 1961-74; trustee Blue Cross Hosp. Plan, 1959-72; trustee Am. Hosp. Assn., 1971-76, chmn. bd., 1975. Served with A.C., USNR, 1943-45. Recipient Disting. Service award Ky. Hosp. Assn.; Disting. Layman award Ky. Med. Assn. Fellow Am. Coll. Hosp. Healthcare Execs. (life, gold medal), Masons. Home and Office: 9 Muirfield Pl Louisville KY 40222-5074

MOURA, JOSE, wine consultant; b. Ponce, P.R., Dec. 6, 1961; s. Santiago Moura and Juana Castellar; children: Sharon, José E., José F. BBA in Mktg., U. P.R., 1985; M Direct Mktg., NYU, 1992. Wine cons. Banfi Vintner's, N.Y., 1988-97, Czaznove Opici Wine Corp., N.Y., 1999—; wine columnist, restaurant critic El Diario, La Prensa, N.Y., 1994-99; food and wine editor El Puente Latino.com, N.Y., 2000—; sales mgr. Codorniu Internat. U.S.A., 2000—. Mem. tasting panel Wine & Spirits Mag., N.Y., 1997-99; cons. N.Y. City TV Sta., 1993, Indian TV Network, N.Y., 1993; lectr. in field. Author: Al Pan Pan y al Vino Vino, 1997; editor Food and Wine, 2000; columnist Hablando de Vinos, 1994-99. Mem. adv. bd. Pub. Sch. 1987, 1997; vol. Hispanic Commn. on AIDS, 1996; baseball coach West Side League, N.Y.C.; basketball coach Save Heaven League, N.Y.C. Home: Urbanizacion San Antonio Cll 2 U5 Ponce PR 00731

MOURA, JOSÉ MANUEL FONSECA, electrical engineer, educator; b. Beira, Mozambique, Portugal, Jan. 9, 1946; s. José Saraiva and Maria José (Fonseca) M.; m. Maria Tereza Fernandes, 1969 (div. 1981); 1 child, Barbara Fernandes; m. Maria Manuela Veloso, 1981; children: André Veloso, Pedro Veloso. Engenheiro Electrotecnico, Instituto Superior Tecnico, Lisbon, 1969; MS in Elec. Engring., MIT, 1973, ScD in Elec. Engring. and Computer Sci., 1975. Prof. auxiliar Instituto Superior Técnico, Lisbon, 1975-78, prof. aggregado, 1978, prof. catedrático, 1979-86; prof. Carnegie Mellon U., Pitts., 1986—. Vis. assoc. prof. elec. engring. and computer sci. MIT, Cambridge, 1984-86, vis. prof. elec. engring., 1999-2000; vis. scholar U. So. Calif., Los Angeles, summers 1978, 79, 80, 81. Editor: (with others) Nonlinear Stochastic Problems, 1983, Acoustic Signal Processing for Ocean Exploration, 1993; contbr. articles to profl. jours.; holder 6 patents. Fellow IEEE (editor-in-chief trans. on Signal Processing 1995-99, v.p. publs. Signal Processing Soc. 2000-02, govs. 1999-2002, v.p. publs. Sensors Coun. 2000-02, editl. bd. Proc. 1999-2003, TAB periodicals com., chair TAB Trans. editors com. 2002-03, Millenium medal 2000, Signal Processing Soc. Meritorious Svc. award 2003); mem. NAS Portugal (corr. mem.), Am. Math. Soc., Soc. Indsl. and Applied Math., Ordem dos Engenheiros. Office: Carnegie-Mellon U Dept Elec & Computer Enging 5000 Forbes Ave Pittsburgh PA 15213-3890 E-mail: moura@ece.cmu.edu.

MOURASHKIN, BORIS V. composer, sound therapist, poet, performer, producer; b. Kemerovo, Siberia, Feb. 27, 1949; BA in Musical Theory and Composition, Novosibirsk Mus. Coll., 1976; MA in Music Theory and Composition, M.I. Glinka Conservatory, 1980. Head rsch. lab. (Bio-Energetic Music) for Bio-Energetic and Ecology of Consciousness Russian Fedn., Inst. Human Ecology, Acad. Tech. Scis., Moscow, 1993—. Prof., composer various styles of music including choir music, piano composition, compositions for string orchs., incidental music, musical scores for films and plays;compositions include Jungle Passion, Odd & Even, Two-Step for Lovers, The Stirrings of Love, Blizzard Dance, Without End..., Dedicated to Alfred Schnittke (a musical poetry and dialogue), 1987, others; music editor Novosibirsk-Telefilm, 1980-83; rec. engr., composer, film actor TV, 1980-90; composer: This Is Us, O Lord!, 1991, Kama Sutra, 1991, Points of Light, 1994, Healing Music, 1994, Bio-Energetic Psychotropic Music, Touching the Mystical of Outer Space (dedicated to Steven Spielberg, Jeffrey Katzenberg and David Geffen), Night of Open Doors, 1995, author: (poetry and prose) The Existence of Man Begins with Protest (a tribute to V.M. Schukschin), The Broom's Solo, God Loves the Righteous; Cds include Howl of the Siberian Wolf, 2000, Tribute to the East, 2000; inventor, founder Bio-Enegetic Psychotropic Music, Healing Power of Music, 1983; founder, dir., prodr. Golden Fund of Documentary Films (extraordinary Russian-Americans); contbr. various articles to newspapers and mags. Vol. Siberian Orphanage, 1972-89, Siberian Prison, 1976-89, St. Christopher-Ottilie Home, Bio-Energetic Psychotropic Music Therapy Workshops for mentally and retarded children, Sea Cliff, N.Y., 1992-94, Gift of Life, Inc., 1993, Manhattan Psychiat. Ctr. workshops with Bio-Energetic, Psychotropic Music with mentally disordered people, Wards Island, N.Y., 1997; bd. dirs., mem. adv. bd. Tchertkoff Meml. & Cultural

Found.; hon. mem. operation kids program Nat. Police Def. Found., 1999. Named Famous Poet, Famous Poets Soc., 1998, One of Best Poets of 2000 Internat. Libr. Poetry, 2000; recipient award of recognition Famous Poets Soc., 1998, Poet of the Yr. medallion Famous Poets Soc., 1999, Diamond Homer trophy Famous Poets Soc., 1999, Internat. Poet of Merit award medallion Internat. Soc. Poets, 1999, Pres. Recognition Lit. Excellence The Drifting Sands, Nat. Libr. Poetry, 1999. Fellow Internat. Informatization Acad. UN (academician, prof., SciD Art of Music Alternative Music Therapy, PhD Art of Science Practical Elaboration and Expertise BioSound Therapy Tech. and Soundpsycho-neuro-reflective immunotherapy); mem. Internat. Union Info., World Assn. Edn. Worlddidac, Nat. Acad. Rec. Art & Scis. Inc., Internat. Soc. Poets (disting.; Internat. Poet of Merit award medallion 1999, Poet of Yr. 1999, Prometheus Muse of Fire trophy 2000), Broadcast Music, Inc., Cinematographer's Union of Russian Fedn., Nat. Authors Registry. Home: 165 Brown St Sea Cliff NY 11579-1601 E-mail: bmourashkin@yahoo.com.

MOURNING, ALONZO, retired professional basketball player; b. Chesapeake, Va., Feb. 8, 1970; m. Tracy Mourning; children: Alonzo III, Myka. Student, Georgetown U. Player Charlotte Hornets, SC, 1992—95, Miami Heat, 1995—2003, NJ Nets, 2003. Mem. Dream Team II, 1994; player All-Star Game, 1994. Named to NBA All-Rookie 1st team, 1993.

MOUROU, GERARD A. research administrator; BS in Physics, U. Grenoble, France, 1967; MS in Physics, U. Orsay, France, 1970; PhD in Physics, U. Paris, 1973. Sci. cooperant Université Laval, Quebec, Canada, 1970-73; postdoctoral fellow San Diego State U., 1973-74; scientist Lab. for Laser Energetics U. Rochester, N.Y., 1979-88, group leader Picosecond Rsch. Group, Lab. for Laser Energetics, 1979-88, sr. scientist Lab. for Laser Energetics, 1981-88, assoc. prof. Inst. Optics, 1983-87, divsn. dir. Ultrafast Science Divsn., Lab. for Laser Energetics, 1986-88, prof. Inst. Optics, 1987-89; prof. Dept. Elec. Engring. and Computer Scis., Coll. Engring. U. Mich., 1988—, dir. Ctr. for Ultrafast Optical Science NSF and Tech. Ctr., 1991—. Vis. prof. U. Tokyo, Japan, 1994; prof. physics, mcpl. chair Université Joseph Fourier, Grenoble, France, 1994; mem. editl. bd. Laser Focus. Contbr. numerous articles to scientific jours. Recipient R.W. Wood prize Optical Soc. of Am., 1995. Fellow Optical Soc. Am. Achievements include numerous patents in field including apparatus for switching high voltage pulses, light activated solid state switch, avalanche effect light activated solid state switching, microwave pulse generation with light activated semiconductor switch and control of transmission of microwaves using light activated semiconductors, laser system using organic dye laser and laser amplifier for generation of picosecond laser pulses, sweep drive circuit for streak camera image converter, photoelectron switching in semiconductors in the picosecond domain, measurement of electrical signal with Ps resolution, electro-optical wide band signal measurement system, CW pumped variable repetition rate regenerative laser amplifier, amplification of ultrashort pulses with Nd: glass amplifiers pumped by alexandrite free running laser. Office: Univeristy of Michigan Ctr for Ultrafast Optical Science 2200 Bonisteel Blvd Rm 6117 Ist Ann Arbor MI 48109-2099

MOUSEL, CRAIG LAWRENCE, lawyer; b. St. Louis, July 22, 1947; s. George William and Charlotte (Howard) M.; m. Polly Deane Burkett, Dec. 21, 1974; children: Donna, Dennis, D'Arcy. AB, U. So. Calif., 1969; JD, Ariz. State U., 1972. Bar: Ariz. 1973, U.S. Dist. Ct. Ariz. 1973, U.S. Ct. Appeals (9th cir.) 1973, U.S. Dist. Ct. (cen. dist.) Calif. 1984, Colo. 1993; registered lobbyist, Ariz. Adminstrv. asst. to Hon. Sandra O'Connor Ariz. State Senate, Phoenix, 1971-72; asst. atty. gen. Ariz. Atty. Gen.'s Office, Phoenix, 1973-75; ptnr. Sundberg & Mousel, Phoenix, 1975—. Spl. counsel City of Chandler, 1991 Hearing officer Ariz. State Personnel Bd., 1976-80, spl. appeals counsel, 1978—; hearing officer Ariz. Outdoor Recreation Coordinating Commn., 1975; dep. state land commr. Ariz. State Land Dept., 1978; precinct capt. Rep. Com.; mem. Ariz. Kidney Found., Orpheum Theatre Found., Phoenix Zoo Curators Club; sponsor Phoenix Art Mus.; varsity baseball coach Valley Luth. H.S., 1995-97, St. Mary's H.S., 2000; asst. baseball coach St. Mary's H.S., 1997-99. Fellow Ariz. Bar Found.; mem. ABA, ATLA, Ariz. Bar Assn., Maricopa County Bar Assn., Sports Lawyers Assn., Internat. Platform Assn., Ariz. Club, Am. Baseball Coaches Assn., Nat. High Sch. Baseball Coaches Assn., Ariz. Baseball Coaches Assn., USC Ptnrs. Alumni Group, U. So. Calif. Alumni Assn., Ariz. State U. Alumni Assn., Ariz. State Coll. Law Alumni Assn. Office: Sundberg & Mousel 934 W Mcdowell Rd Phoenix AZ 85007-1730 Office Phone: 602-252-7223. Personal E-mail: mousel@mindspring.com.

MOUSER, LES, advertising executive; Pres., COO Campbell Mithun Esty, Mpls., 1999—, CEO, 2001—. Office: care Campbell Mithun Esty 222 S 9th St Minneapolis MN 55402-3389

MOUSSAVI, RAMYAR, podiatrist; b. Tehran, Iran, Apr. 24, 1972; d. Abdol Moussavi and Mandana Saberi. DPM, Temple U., 2002. Diplomate Am. Bd. Podiatry. With Angeles Foot & Ankle Inst., L.A. Mem.: Am. Bd. Podiatric Surgery. Home: 100 S Doheny Dr # 221 Los Angeles CA 90048 Office: Angeles Foot and Ankle Inst 1551 W Olympic Blvd Los Angeles CA 90015 Office Phone: 213-383-3942. Office Fax: 213-383-4413.

MOUSSOUTTAS, MICHAEL M. medical educator; b. NYC, Sept. 7, 1968; s. Constantine and Christina Moussouttas; m. Maria Iuanow, Nov. 5, 2000. BA, NYU, 1990; MD, SUNY Syracuse, 1994. Lic. N.Y., 1995, diplomate Am. Bd. Neurology 1999. Intern North Shore U. Hosp., Manhasset, NY, 1994—95; resident Mt. Sinai Hosp., NYC, 1995—98; neurovascular fellow Yale-New Haven Hosp., 1998—2000; asst. prof. N.Y. Med. Coll., Valhalla, 2000—03, Seton Hall U. Neuroscience Inst., Edison, NJ, 2003—. Neurovascular program dir. N.Y. Med. Ctr., 2000—03. Contbr. articles to profl. jours. Mem.: AMA, Neurocritical Care Soc., Am. Heart Assn., Am. Acad. Neurology. Greek Orthodox. Avocations: sports, chess, travel. Office: Neuroscience Inst 65 James St Edison NJ 08818

MOW, ROBERT HENRY, JR., lawyer; b. Cape Girardeau, Mo., Dec. 10, 1938; s. Robert H. Sr. and Ann Elise (Beck) M.; m. Jody K. Boggs, Aug. 29, 1987; children: Robert M., Brynn A., W. Brett, Rebecca M., W. Kirk, Allison M. Student, Westminster Coll., 1956-57; AB with distinction, U. Mo., 1960; LLB magna cum laude, So. Meth. U., 1963. Bar: Tex. 1963, U.S. Dist. Ct. (no. dist.) Tex. 1965, U.S. Dist. Ct. (so. dist.) Tex. 1969, U.S. Dist. Ct. (ea. and we. dists.) Tex. 1976, U.S. Ct. Claims 1973, U.S. Ct. Appeals (5th cir.) 1972, U.S. Ct. Appeals (11th cir.) 1981, U.S. Ct. Appeals (fed. cir.) 1994, U.S. Supreme Ct. 1978. Assoc. Carrington, Johnson & Stephens, Dallas, 1963-69; ptnr. Carrington, Coleman, Sloman & Blumenthal, Dallas, 1970-85, Hughes & Luce, LLP, Dallas, 1985, mng. ptnr., 2003—. Editor-in-chief Southwestern Law Jour., 1962-63. Trustee First Bapt. Acad., chair, 1999-2002. Served to 1st lt. U.S. Army, 1963-65. Fellow Am. Coll. Trial Lawyers; mem. Dallas Assn. Def. Counsel (chmn. 1976-77), Tex. Assn. Def. Counsel (v.p. 1981-82), Am. Bd. Trial Advocates (pres. Dallas chpt. 1983-84), Dallas Bar Fellows (chmn. 2003-04). Republican. Baptist. Office: Hughes & Luce LLP 1717 Main St Ste 2800 Dallas TX 75201-4685 Office Phone: 214-939-5448. E-mail: mowb@hughesluce.com.

MOW, VAN C. engineering educator, researcher; b. Chengdu, China, Jan. 10, 1939; B. Aero. Engring., Rensselaer Poly. Inst., 1962, PhD, 1966. Mem. tech. staff Bell Telephone Labs., Whippany, N.J., 1968-69; assoc. prof. mechanics Rensselaer Poly. Inst., Troy, N.Y., 1969-76, prof. mechanics and biomed. engring., 1976-82, John A. Clark and Edward T. Crossan prof. engring., 1982-86; prof. mech. engring. and orthopedic bioengring. Columbia U., N.Y.C., 1986—98, chmn. dept. biomed. engring. Fu Found. Sch. Engring. and Applied Sci., 1998—; dir. Orthopedic Rsch. Lab., Columbia-Presbyn. Med. Ctr., N.Y.C., 1986—, Stanley Dicker prof. biomed. engring., 1998—. Vis. mem. Courant Inst. Math. Sci., NYU, 1967-68; vis. prof. Harvard U., Boston, 1976-77; chmn. orthopaedics and musculoskeletal study sect. NIH, Bethesda, Md., 1982-84; hon. prof. Sichuan U., 1981, Shanghai Jiao Tong U., 1987, Shanghai U., 1983, Hong Kong Poly. U., 2003, Zhejiang U., 2004, Beighong U., 2004; chmn. grants rev. bd. Orthopaedic Rsch. Edn. Found., 1992-96; bd. dirs. Hoar Rsch. Found., 1993—; chmn. adv. com. divsn. Med. Engring. Rsch. Nat. Health Rsch. Inst., Taiwan, 1999—; cons. in field. Assoc. editor Jour. Biomechanics, 1981—, Jour. Biomech. Engring., 1979-86; chmn. editorial adv. bd. Jour. Orthopedic Rsch., 1983-90; adv. editor Clin. Orthopedic Rel. Rsch., 1993—; contbr. numerous articles to profl. jours. Founder Gordon Research Conf. on Bioengring. and Orthopedic Sci., 1980. NATO sr. fellow, 1978; recipient William H. Wiley Disting. Faculty award Rensselaer Poly. Inst., 1981; Japan Soc. for Promotion Sci. Fellow, 1986, Fogarty Sr. Internat. fellow, 1987; Alza disting. lectr. Biomed. Engring. Soc., 1987; H.R. Lissner award ASME, 1987, Kappa Delta award AAOS, 1980, Giovani Borelli award, 1991. Fellow ASME (chmn. biomechanics divsn. 1984-85, Melville medal 1982, R.H. Thurston lectr., Van C. Mour medal), Am. Inst. Med. Biol. Engring.; mem. NAE, Orthopaedic Rsch. Soc. (pres. 1982-83), Am. Soc. Biomechanics (founding), Internat. Soc. Biorheology, U.S. Nat. Com. on Biomechanics (sec.-treas. 1985-90, chmn. 1991-94), Nat. Acad. Engring., Inst. of Medicine, Nat. Acad. Scis., Academia Sinica. Office: Dept Biomed Engring Columbia U 351 Engring Terr MC 8904 1210 Amsterdam Ave New York NY 10027 Business E-Mail: vcm1@columbia.edu.

MOW, WILLIAM, apparel executive; b. Apr. 19, 1936; BEE, Rensselear; PhD, Purdue U., 1967. With Honeywell Inc., Boston, 1963-65; program mgr. Litton Industries, L.A., 1967-69; founder, pres., chmn. bd. MacroData Corp., L.A., 1969-76; sci. advisor Cutler Hammer, L.A., 1976-77; with Bugle Boy Industries, Inc., Simi Valley, Calif., 1977—, now chmn., CEO. Office: Bugle Boy 2900 N Madera Rd Simi Valley CA 93065-6230

MOWATT, E. ANN, women's voluntary leader, lawyer; BA in History, Dalhousie U., Halifax, Nova Scotia, 1982, LLB, 1985. Barrister, solicitor Patterson Palmer, 1986—2001; small claims adjudicator Patterson Palmer Hunt Murphy, 1999-2001; dir. gen. survivors and high performance Income Security br. Human Resources Devel. Can., 2001—. Bd. dirs. YMCA-YWCA of Saint John N.B., Can., 1987-93; also mem. exec., fin., social action, and camp coms., pres., 1991; bd. dirs. YWCA of Can., 1989-98, chair constn. task force, mem.-at-large, treas., v.p., pres., 1995-97, past pres., 1997-98; bd. dirs. Coalition of Nat. Vol. Orgns., 1994-2001, chair; pres. Saint John chpt. Multiple Sclerosis Soc. Con., 1987-88, bd. dirs. Atlantic divsn., 1988-97, mem. nat. bd. dirs., 1992-95, 97-2001, pres. Atlantic divsn., 1993-95. Mem. Can. Bar Assn. (mem. N.B. coun. 1986-89), Law Soc. N.B. (mem. legal aid com. 1989-92), Eclectic Reading Club Avocations: reading, films, camping, canoeing, theater. Home: 114 Orange St Saint John NB Canada E2L 1M4 also: Apt 1416 160 Chapel St Ottawa ON Canada K1N 8P5 E-mail: ann.mowatt@hrdc-drhc.gc.ca.

MOWBRAY, ROBERT NORMAN, natural resource management consultant, forest ecologist; b. Warren, Pa., Feb. 26, 1935; s. Leonard Kelly and Jean Elizabeth (Lowes) M.; m. Sonia de los Angeles Baquerizo, June 7, 1969; children: Norma Mercedes, Elizabeth Laning. BA, Dartmouth Coll., 1957; M of Forestry, Yale U., 1963; postgrad., Duke U., 1966-70. Rsch. asst. forest ecology Duke U., Panama, 1967, Ecuador, 1968—70, U. Tenn., Knoxville, 1970-71; rsch. asst. ecology Oak Ridge (Tenn.) Nat. Labs., 1971-72; reclamation crew chief Tenn. Mountain Mgmt., Knoxville, 1972; assoc. dir. agr. and environment Peace Corps, Asunción, Paraguay, 1972-78; agrl. devel. officer U.S. Agy. for Internat. Devel., San Jose, Costa Rica, 1978-80, U.S. AID, Kingston, Jamaica, 1980-83, Washington, 1983-88, 90-91, forestry devel. officer Quito, Ecuador, 1988-90, sr. forest ecologist, natural resource mgmt. specialist Washington, 1991-94; internat. natural resource mgmt. cons., Reston, Va., 1994—. Forestry vol. Peace Corps, Ecuador, 1963-66, editor tech. newsletter, 1964-66; botany vol. The Nature Conservancy, 1997-98. Author: (with others) Natural Resource Management and Conservation of Biodiversity and Tropical Forests in Ecuador-A Strategy for USAID, 1989, Lebanon Environmental Policy Assessment, 1999, Forestry and the Environment: Costa Rica Case Study, 1994, Assessment of USAID Biological Diversity Protection Programs: Costa Rica Case Study, 1994, Conservation of Forests and Biodiversity in Lebanon, 2002; editor (spl. issues) NicAvance, 1995-96; contbr. articles to profl. jours. Vol. Reston Assn. Environ. Adv. Com., chmn. Natural Areas Subcom., mem. Watershed subcom., 2000—. Recipient U.S. Forest Svc. Chief's Internat. Forestry award, 1994. Mem. World Wildlife Fund, Nature Conservancy, Assn. for Tropical Biology, Internat. Soc. Tropical Foresters, Friends of the Nat. Zoo, Nat. Coun. Returned Peace Corps Vols., Soc. Conservation Biology. Avocations: gardening, photography. Home and Office: 2218 Wheelwright Ct Reston VA 20191-2313 Office Phone: 703-758-1959. Personal E-mail: rnmowbray@worldnet.att.net.

MOWE, GREGORY ROBERT, lawyer; b. Aberdeen, Wash., Feb. 23, 1946; s. Robert Eden and Jeannette Effie (Deyoung) M.; m. Rebecca Louise Nobles, June 14, 1969; children: Emily, Tom. BA, U. Oreg., 1968, MA, 1969; JD magna cum laude, Harvard Law Sch., 1974. Bar: Oreg. 1974, U.S. Dist. Ct. Oreg. 1974, U.S. Ct. Appeals (9th cir.) 1974. Assoc. atty. Stoel Rives Boley Jones & Grey, Portland, Oreg., 1974-79, ptnr., 1979—. Pres. bd. dirs. Planned Parenthood of Columbia/Willamette, Portland, 1989-90. 1st lt. U.S. Army, 1969-71, Vietnam. Mem. ABA, Phi Beta Kappa. Office: Stoel Rives Boley Jones & Grey 900 SW 5th Ave Ste 2300 Portland OR 97204-1229 Office Phone: 503-294-9458. Business E-Mail: grmowe@stoel.com.

MOWEN, JOHN C. business educator; b. Charlottesville, Va., Nov. 13, 1943; s. John Calvin and Hope Hopkins Mowen; m. Maryanne Myers, June 12, 1971; children: Katherine, Cara. BA, William & Mary U., 1969; PhD, Ariz. State U., 1977. Prof. in bus. Okla. State U., Stillwater, 1978—. Cons. in field; bd. dirs. Consumer Credit Counseling Svc., Oklahoma City. Pres. Payne County United Way, Stillwater, 1996; co-chair House Campaign for Dem. Legislator, Stillwater, 1976; founder, bd. dirs. Mission of Hope Shelter for Homeless, Stillwater, 1987-98. Capt. U.S. Army, 1969-73, Vietnam. Decorated Bronze Star; recipient Best Article award Jour. Personal Selling, 1992. Mem. APA, Am. Mktg. Assn. (Best Article award 1998), Soc. for Consumer Psychology, Assn. for Consumer Rsch., Stillwater C. of C. (bd. dirs. 1997—), CCCS Ctrl. Okla. (bd. dirs. 1998-99). Avocations: golf, water gardening. Office: Okla State U Coll Bus Stillwater OK 74078-0001 E-mail: jcmmkt@okstate.okway.edu.

MOWER, MORTON MAIMON, cardiologist; b. Balt., Jan. 31, 1933; MD, U. Md. Sch. Medicine, 1959. Diplomate Am. Bd. Internal Medicine, Am. Bd. Cardiovac. Disease. Intern U. Md. Hosp., Balt., 1959-60; resident Sinai Hosp., Balt., 1960-63, fellow in cardiology, 1965-66; v.p. med. scis. Guidant Corp., St. Paul, 1989—96; assoc. prof. medicine Johns Hopkins U. Sch. Medicine, Balt.; prof. physiology and biophysics Howard U. Sch. Medicine. Named to Nat. Inventors Hall of Fame, 2002. Fellow: ACP, Am. Coll. Chest Physicians, Am. Coll. Cardiology; mem.: Am. Soc. Internal Medicine, Am. Fedn. Clin. Rsch. Home: 3908 N Charles St Apt 1001 Baltimore MD 21218-1753 Office Phone: 410-243-1127. E-mail: mmower@aol.com.

MOWERS, KATHY A. mathematics professor; d. Alfred Lee and Evaline R. Reed; m. Patrick W. Mowers; children: Jeremy W., Jonathan M. MA in Tchg., Ind. U., 1975. Cert. med. technologist Am. Soc. of Clin. Pathologists, 1985. Prof. math. Owensboro Cmty. and Tech. Coll., Ky., 1989—. Author: (textbook) Intermediate Algebra: An Introduction to Functions Through Applications, 1999, Elementary Algebra: A Prerequisite for Functions, 1999 (1999). Sec. Pilot Internat. Club of Owensboro, Ky., 2003—04; chair Green River Home Health, Owensboro, Ky., 2002—. Recipient Math. Achievement and Svc. award, Ky. Coun. of Tchrs. of Math., 1991. Mem.: Am. Math. Assn. of Two-Yr. Colls. (assoc.; midwest v.p. 1997—2003, pres.-elect 2003—, INPUT Award 2003). Office: Owensboro Cmty and Tech Coll 4800 New Hartford Rd Owensboro KY 42303

MOWERY, ANNA RENSHAW, state legislator; b. Decatur, Tex., Jan. 4, 1931; d. Lafayette William and Early Virginia (Bobo) Renshaw; m. Wesley Harold Mowery, June 2, 1951; children: Jeanette Mowery Hefferman, Mark William, Timothy Dean, Marianne Mowery Fichera. BA, Baylor U., 1951; MA, Ctrl. State U, 1967. Tchr. Ft. Hood (Tex.) Pub. Schs., 1951-52; petroleum landman Ft. Worth, 1979-82; dist. dir. U.S. Congl. Dist. 6 Joe Barton, Ft. Worth, 1985-86; polit. cons., pres. Trinity Assocs., Ft. Worth, 1987-88; state rep. Tex. House Reps., Ft. Worth, 1988—. Chmn. Tarrant County (Tex.) Rep. Party, 1975-77; mem. Tex. Rep. Exec. Com., Ft. Worth, 1980-84, Greater Ft. Worth Literacy Coun., 1990—; mem. adv. bd. Sr. Citizen Svcs./Tarrant County, Ft. Worth, 1988—. Recipient 4-H Clubs Am. Alumni award, 1990; nominee Newsmaker of Yr., Ft. Worth Press Club, 1974, 76. Mem. Tex. Women's Alliance, Mowery's Policy Forum. Republican. Baptist. Home: 4108 Hildring Dr W Fort Worth TX 76109-4722 Office: 6421 Camp Bowie Blvd Fort Worth TX 76116-5401 also: Tex House of Reps State Capitol Austin TX 78768-2910

MOWERY, GERALD EUGENE, publishing executive, writer; b. Buena, Wash., Mar. 7, 1927; s. Jennings Bryan and Opal Mae Mowery; children: Colleen, Theresa, Rhonda, Laura, Victoria, Charles, Peggy. Degree in bus., Kinmen's U. Lic. pub. acct., Wash. Supr. Boeing Airplane Co., Seattle, 1968-78; owner Jerry's Coin, Book and Frame Shops, Puyallup, Wash., 1978-85, Rudolph Maurer Pub., Puyallup, Wash., Tampa, Fla., 1985—. Author and pub. more than 152 books including All Matter Originates from Electrons, Positrons and Neutrinos, 1981, E=GM Squared, 1994, The Revised Periodic Table of Elements, The Four Unacknowledged Elements, 1999; co-author with Gene Buck: The Entrepreneurs Favorite Short Stories, Favorite Poems, Favorite Facts and Stuff; author, publ. Adjusted Periodic Table of Elements, 1982, 93, 97, 98, 2001; author children's books The Adventures of Alexander Smiriotes series including Alexander Simiriotes Rides his Alligator Through Tampa, Alexander Visits Athens, Greece, Chelsea Thompson Visits Seattle. Achievements include defining the atomic mass make up of sub atomic particles and their relationship to carbon 12; prepared (atomic mass) sub atomic particle table from the equation atomic mass squared x 938.27231 equals measured MeV Values; illustrated that elements are periodic functions of neutrons and are not periodic functions of atomic number; established that isotopes have a periodic progression and are not randomly added; established the theory and concept of compact neutrons as the basis for the periodic table; illustrated that the configuration and measurements of elements are paired with themselves, that all atoms are paired in a solid state, singular in a gas state, and both paired and unpaired in a liquid state; confirmed and illustrated how matter has a periodic atomic mass progression from the subatomic particles through the elements; put on a firm basis the theory that subatomic particles are the result of Proton Fractures at certain points in the 27 electron/proton chain and releasing energy (MeV) in the process; illustrated that elements and periodic functions of electrons. Address: 203 South G St #217 Tacoma WA 98405 E-mail: GEMowery@msn.com.

MOWERY, WARD FRANKLIN, retired music educator; s. Walter James and Mary Elizabeth Mowery; m. Anita Mae Hitchcock, June 12, 1960; children: Dale Richard, Angela Denise Mowery-Bemus. BS, Ohio State U., 1962, PhD, 1993; MS, MMusic, U. Ill., 1968. Nationally registered music educator, 1991, cert. tchr. Ohio, Assn. Christian Schs. Internat. Tchr. River View Local Schs., Warsaw, Ohio, 1962—63, Lima Shawnee Local Schs., Lima, Ohio, 1963—65; instr. Wilkes Coll., Wilkes-Barre, Pa., 1968—69; tchr. Lincolnview Local Schs., Van Wert, Ohio, 1969—74; music ministry The Mowerys, Lima, 1974—85; assoc. prof. Bluffton Coll., Ohio, 1976—90, adj. prof., 1990—99; tchr. Lima City Schs., 1989—99, Christian Acad. Louisville, 1999—2002. Prin. bassist Lima Symphony Orch., Lima, 1977—99; ch. musician Lyndon Christian Ch., Louisville, 1999—, SE Christian Ch., Louisville, 1997—. Composer musical compositions. Served with USN, 1955—58, Hawaii. Mem.: MENC (adjudicator 1978—95). Republican. Achievements include Mowery's music ministry performed over 1600 concerts 1974-1985; Numerous former students now major teachers. Avocations: music performance, church music, physical conditioning. Home: 7215 Quail Ridge Road Louisville KY 40291-1878 Personal E-mail: wamowery@aol.com.

MOWLANA, HAMID, international relations and communication educator; b. Tabriz, Iran, Feb. 25, 1937; came to U.S., 1958; s. Karim Seyyed Agha Mowlana and Robab Ibrahimi; m. Bonnie J. Byrnes. BA equivalent, U. Tehran and Northwestern U., 1959; MS, Northwestern U., 1960, PhD, 1963. Asst. prof. U. Tenn., Knoxville, 1965-68; assoc. prof. Am. U., Washington, 1968-71, prof., 1971—, dir. internat. comm. studies, 1968—. Vis. prof. various univs., 1968-2000. Author: Global Information and World Communication, 1986, 96, The Passing of Modernity, 1992, Global Communication in Transition, 1997, others. Mem. Internat. Assn. Media and Comm. Rsch. (pres. 1994-98). Avocations: walking, photography, gardening, tennis. Office: Am U Sch Internat Svc Washington DC 20016 E-mail: mowlana@american.edu.

MOWLAVI, ARIAN S. plastic surgeon; b. Kansas City, Mo., Feb. 22, 1971; s. Dory S. and Zari S. Mowlavi. MD, U. Calif., 1998. Cert. plastic surgeon Calif., 1994. Resident So. Ill. U., Springfield, 1998—. Mem.: Plastic Surgery Residents Affiliate Group (assoc.), Phi Betta Kappa, Alpha Omega Alpha. Achievements include research in Plastic Surgery Education Foundation Junior Clinical Research Award. Arlington, IL June 13, 2003; Resident's Research Day (First Prize).Springfield, IL May 15, 2003; Investigator Category Essay (First Prize). Arlington, IL May 2, 2001; Combined Research Symposium (First Prize). Springfield, IL April 18, 2001; Basic Science Research Award. ASRM. Palm Springs, CA. January 17, 2004. Home: 23451 Dorrielle Court Laguna Niguel CA 92677 Office: Cosmetic Surgery Clinics 31542 South Pacific Coast Hwy South Laguna CA 92677 Personal E-mail: amowlavi@hotmail.com.

MOWRIS, GERALD WILLIAM, lawyer; b. Grand Forks, N.D., Oct. 2, 1948; s. Robert Earl and Lillian Vivian (Zavoral) M.; m. Alice Hulick, Apr. 2, 1970 (div.); m. Susan Leah Sachtjen; children: Danae E., Jeffrey W. Student, Mich. State U., 1966-67; JD, U. Wis., 1973. Bar: Wis. 1973, U.S. Dist. Ct. (we. dist.) Wis. 1973, U.S. Ct. Appeals (7th cir.) 1984, U.S. Ct. Mil. Appeals 1984. Asst. dist. atty. Dane County Dist. Atty.'s Office, Madison, 1973-79; ptnr. Pellino, Rosen, Mowris & Kirkhuff, Madison, 1979—. Bd. dirs. YMCA of Met. Madison, 1991-94; mem. ARC Cmty. Svcs., Madison, 1980—, past pres., appointed by gov. Wis. Sentencing Commn., 2003-. Maj. USAR, 1970-92. Mem. State Bar Wis. (co-chmn. com. for local bar leaders 1995-97, bd. govs. 1999-2000, pres. 2001-02), Dane County Bar Assn. (pres. 1994-95), Wis. Assn. Criminal Def. Lawyers (pres. 1995-96), Nat. Assn. Criminal Def. Lawyers, Wis. Acad. Trial Lawyers, Nat. Ski Patrol (patroller 1967—). Avocations: skiing, fishing, hiking, canoeing, golf. Office: Pellino Rosen Mowris & Kirkhoff SC 131 W Wilson St Ste 1201 Madison WI 53703-3243 Office Phone: 608-255-4501. Fax: 608-255-4345. E-mail: gmowris@prmk.com., gmowris@prmk.com.

MOWRY, FRANK HENRY, journalist, photojournalist; b. Oak Ridge, Tenn., Sept. 11, 1952; s. Ralph Lenord Mowry and Estella Elise Dietz. Student, U. Kans., 1972-77. Journalist, pub. affairs specialist USN Comdr. 6th Fleet, Gaeta, Italy, 1985-89, USN, Yokosuka, Japan, 1990-92, Naval Support Facility, Diego Garcia, Brit. Indian Ocean Terr., 1990-98; journalist, copy editor Pacific Stars & Stripes, Tokyo, 1992-94; journalist, photojournalist, broadcaster radio & TV Am. Forces Network, Sigonella, Italy, 1994-97; journalist, photojournalist, webmaster USN Comdr. in Chief Pacific Fleet, Pearl Harbor, Hawaii, 1999—2002; writer, editor Bur. Land Mgmt., North Palm Springs, Calif., 2003—. Contbr. pub. affairs Y2K, 1999. Instr., ARC, Yokosuka, 1992-94. Journalist 1st class, USN, Hawaii, 1996-2002. Petty officer 1st class USN, 1996. Mem. VFW (life), Nat. Press Photographers Assn., Soc. Profl. Journalists, Nat. Profl. Photoshop Assn. Democrat. Avocation: experiencing world cultures. Home and Office: 3155 E Ramon Rd Apt 603 Palm Springs CA 92264-7974 Office: Bur Land Mgmt Palm Springs-South Coast Field Office 690 W Garnet Ave North Palm Springs CA 92258 Fax: 760-521-4899. Office Phone: 760-251-4822. Personal E-mail: mowryfh@worldnet.att.net.

MOWRY, ROBERT WILBUR, pathologist, educator; b. Griffin, Ga., Jan. 10, 1923; s. Roy Burnell and Mary Frances (Swilling) M.; m. Margaret Neilson Black, June 11, 1949; children: Janet Lee, Robert Gordon, Barbara Ann. BS, Birmingham So. Coll., 1944; MD, Johns Hopkins U., 1946. Rotating intern U. Ala. Med. Coll., 1946-47, resident pathology, 1947-48; sr. asst. surgeon USPHS-NIH, Bethesda, Md., 1948-52; fellow pathology Boston City Hosp., 1949-50; asst. prof. pathology Washington U., St. Louis, 1952-53, U. Ala. Med. Ctr., Birmingham, 1953-54, assoc. prof. pathology, 1954-57; prof.

U. Ala. Med. Center, Birmingham, 1958-89, prof. emeritus, 1989—, prof. health svcs. adminstrn., 1976-84, dir. Anat. Pathology Lab., 1960-64, dir. grad. programs in pathology, 1964-72. Sr. scientist U. Ala. Inst. Dental Research, 1967-72, dir. autopsy services, 1975-79; vis. scholar dept. pathology U. Cambridge, Eng., 1972-73; cons. FDA, 1975-81 Author: (with J.F.A. McManus) Staining Methods: Histologic and Histochemical, 1960; mem. editorial bd. Jour. Histochemistry and Cytochemistry, 1960-75, Stain Tech., 1965-90, AMA Archives of Pathology, 1967-76, Biotechnics and Histochemistry, 1991—. Served with USPHS, 1948-52. Mem. Am. Soc. Investigative Pathology, Internat. Acad. Pathology, Biol. Stain Commn. (v.p. 1974-76, pres. 1976-81, trustee 1966—), Am. Assn. Univ. Profs. Pathology, Phi Beta Kappa, Sigma Xi, Delta Sigma Phi, Alpha Kappa Kappa. Presbyterian. Achievements include perfection of staining methods for complex carbohydrates (Alcian blue and colloidal iron) and insulin (Alcian blue-aldehyde fuchsin); showed the utility of these in diagnostic histopathology. Home: 6605 N Quail Hollow Rd Apt 323 Memphis TN 38120-1337

MOXLEY, JOHN HOWARD, III, internist; b. Elizabeth, N.J., Jan. 10, 1935; s. John Howard Jr. and Cleopatra (Mundy) Moxley; m. Doris Banchik; children: John Howard IV, Brook, Mark. BA, Williams Coll., 1957; MD, U. Colo., 1961; DSc (hon.), Sch. Medicine Hannemann U. Diplomate Am. Bd. Internal Medicine. Intern Peter Bent Brigham Hosp., Boston, 1961—62, resident in internal medicine, 1962—66; with Nat. Cancer Inst., USPHS, 1963—65; asst. to dean, instr. medicine Harvard Med. Sch., Boston, 1966—69; dean Sch. Medicine, U. Md., 1969—73; vice chancellor health scis., dean Med. Sch., U. Calif.-San Diego, 1973—79; asst. sec. for health affairs Dept. Def., Washington, 1979—81; sr. v.p. Am. Med. Internat., Beverly Hills, Calif., 1981—87; pres. MetaMed. Inc., Playa Del Rey, Calif., 1987—89; mgr. dir. Korn/Ferry Internat., L.A., 1989—. Cons. FDA, NIH; dir. Nat. Fund for Med. Edn., 1986—, chmn., 1993—; dir. Henry M. Jackson Found. for Adv. Mil. Medicine. Contbr. articles to profl. jours. Dir. Polyclinic Health Svcs. Games of XXIII Olympiad. Recipient Gold and Silver award, U. Colo. Med. Sch., 1974, commr.'s citation for outstanding svc. to over-the-counter drug study, FDA, 1977, spl. achievement citation, Am. Hosp. Assn., 1983, Sec. of Def. medal for disting. pub. svc., 1981. Fellow: ACP, Am. Coll. Physician Execs. (disting.); mem.: AMA (chmn. coun. sci. affairs 1985), Am. Hosp. Assn. (trustee 1979—81), Soc. Med. Adminstrs., Calif. Med. Assn. (chmn. sci. bd. 1970—83, councilor), Inst. Medicine NAS, San Diego C. of C., Rotary, Alpha Omega Alpha. Office: Korn Ferry Internat 1800 Century Park E Ste 900 Los Angeles CA 90067-1512 E-mail: moxleyj@kornferry.com.

MOY, AUDREY, retired retail buyer; b. Bronx, N.Y., May 6, 1942; d. Ferdinand Walter Melkert and Stella (Factorow) Schroff; m. Edward Moy, Aug. 16, 1974. BA in Biology, Hunter Coll., 1964, MA in Biology, 1966. Asst. buyer Bonwit Teller, N.Y.C., 1961-68; dept. mgr. Franklin Simon, N.Y.C., 1968; asst. buyer Saks Fifth Ave, N.Y.C., 1968-73; buyer Martins, Bklyn., 1973, Boyer Belk Store Svcs, N.Y.C., 1974-97. Mem.: AAUW. Avocations: cooking, antique collecting, gardening.

MOY, MARY ANASTASIA, lawyer; b. Melrose Park, Ill., Aug. 13, 1964; d. Kenneth Kwok and Chuk Ying (Tsang) M. BA cum laude, Wellesley Coll., 1986; JD, U. Pa., 1989. Bar: N.Y. 1991, D.C. 1993, U.S. Dist. Ct. (so. and ea. dists.) N.Y. 1992. Law clk. to Hon. Glenn E. Mencer U.S. Dist. Ct. (we. dist.), Pitts., 1989-90; assoc. Thelen, Reid & Priest, N.Y.C., 1990—93, Ladas & Parry, N.Y.C., 1993—98, 1999—2000, ptnr., 2001—, Bristol-Myers Squibb Co., N.Y.C., 2000—01. Assoc. counsel N.Y. State Gov.'s Jud. Screening Com. for 1st Jud. Dept., 1991-92. Articles editor U. Pa. Jour. of Internat. Bus. Law, 1988-89. Mem. Asian Am. Bar Assn. of N.Y., Internat. Trademark Assn. Republican. Avocations: opera, music, dance, travel. Office: Ladas & Parry 26 W 41st St New York NY 10023

MOY, RICHARD L. virologist; BA in Biochemistry, Columbia U., 1996—2000; PhD in Microbiology, Mt. Sinai Sch. of Medicine-NYU, 2001—. Lab. technician Aaron Diamond AIDS Rsch. Ctr. (ADARC)-Rockefeller U., N.Y.C., 2000—01; ph.d. student Mt. Sinai Sch. of Medicine, N.Y.C., 2001—. Recipient Semifinalist, 55th Ann. Westinghouse Sci. Talent Search, Sci. Svc., 1996; fellow (T32) Tng. Program in Mechanisms of Virus-Host Interactions, NIH (NIH), 2001-2, Student Internship (awarded twice), Elizabeth Glaser Pediatric AIDS Found., 1999, 2001. Mem.: AAAS, Am. Soc. for Biochemistry and Molecular Biology (assoc.). Office: Mt Sinai Sch of Medicine One Gustave L Levy Pl Box 1124 New York NY 10029 E-mail: richard.moy@mssm.edu.

MOY, RONALD LEONARD, dermatologist, surgeon; b. Stuttgart, Germany, June 10, 1957; s. Howard Leonard Stephen and Jenny (Yee) M.; m. Lisa Wing Lan Lin, Aug. 10, 1986; children: Lauren, Erin. Grad., Rensselaer Poly. Inst., 1977, Albany Med. Coll., 1981. Dir. Mohs micrographic surgery div. dermatology UCLA, 1988-93, dir. dermatologic surgery div. dermatology, 1988-93, co-chief div. dermatology, 1992-93; chief dermatologic surgery VA-West Los Angeles Med. Ctr., 1988—. Gov. apptd. Med. Bd. Calif., 2000—. Author: Atlas of Cutaneous Flaps and Grafts, 1990, Facial Rejuvenation, 1999; editor: Principle and Practice of Dermatologic Surgery, 1993, Facial Rejuenation, 2000; editor-in-chief: Dermatologic Surgery, 1997—2001; editl. bd. Archives Facial Plastic Surgery, Jour. Am. Acad. Cosmetic Surgery; contbr. articles to profl. jours. Bd. dirs. L.A. Costal unit Am. Cancer Soc., 1988. Recipient J. Lewis Pipkin award in dermatology Nat. Student Rsch. Forum, 1981, Henry Christian award Am. Fedn. Clin. Rsch., T-cell and Cytokine Patterns in Skin Cancer award NIH, 1992. Fellow: Am. Acad. Cosmetic Surgery, Am. Acad. Dermatology (Gold award 1986); mem.: Am. Acad. Facial Plastic Surgery, L.A. County Med. Assn. (pres. Bay dist. 1997—98), Assn. Acad. Dermatologic Surgeons (bd. dirs. 1992—95), Am. Coll. Mohs Micrographic Surgery and Cutaneous Oncology (bd. dirs. 1992—95), Am. Soc. Dermatologic Surgery (bd. dirs. 1993—96, v.p. 2001—02, pres. 2003—04). Roman Catholic. Office: 100 UCLA Med Plz Ste 590 Los Angeles CA 90024-6992

MOYA, FRANCISCO SAEZ, consumer products company executive; b. 1951; Pres. Play by Play Toys and Novelties Europe, vice chmn., 1998—; also bd. dirs. Office: Play By Play Toys & Novelties Inc 1153 E Commerce St San Antonio TX 78205-3305 Fax: 210-824-6565.

MOYA, PATRICK ROBERT, lawyer; b. Belen, N.Mex., Nov. 7, 1944; s. Adelicio E. and Eva (Sanchez) Moya; m. Sara Dreier, May 30, 1966; children: Jeremy Brill, Joshua Dreier. AB, Princeton U., 1966; JD, Stanford U., 1969. Bar: Calif. 1970, Ariz. 1970, DC 1970, U.S. Dist. Ct. (no. dist.) Calif. 1970, U.S. Ct. Claims 1970, U.S. Tax Ct. 1970, U.S. Ct. Appeals (DC cir.) 1970, U.S. Supreme Ct. 1973. Assoc. Lewis and Roca, Phoenix, 1969—73, ptnr., 1973—83; sr. ptnr. Moya, Bailey, Bowers & Jones, P.C., Phoenix, 1983—84; ptnr., mem. nat. exec. com. Gaston & Snow, Phoenix, 1985—91; ptnr. Quarles & Brady LLP, Phoenix, 1991—2003, mem. nat. exec. com., 2000—02; exec. v.p. Insight Enterprises, Inc., Tempe, Ariz., 2002—, chief adminstrv. officer, 2002—03, sec., 2002—, gen. counsel, 2002—. Instr. sch. of law Ariz. State U., 1972; bd. dirs. BIGE Real Estate, Inc., PlusNet Techs., Ltd., Plusnet, plc. Mem. Paradise Valley Bd. Adjustment, 1976-80, chmn., 1978-80; mem. Paradise Valley Town Coun., 1980-82; bd. dirs. Phoenix Men's Arts Coun., 1973-81, pres., 1979-80; bd. dirs. The Silent Witness, Inc., 1979-84, pres., 1981-83; bd. dirs. Enterprise Network, Inc., 1989-94, pres., 1991-92; bd. dirs. Phoenix Little Theatre, 1973-75, Interfaith Counseling Svc., 1973-75; precinct committeeman Phoenix Rep. Com., 1975-77; dep. voter registrar Maricopa County, 1975-76; mem. exec. bd. dirs. Gov.'s Strategic Partnership for Econ. Devel.; pres. GSPED, Inc.; mem. of Steering Com. for Sonora-Ariz. Joint Econ. Plan; mem. Gov.'s Adv. Com., Ariz. and Mex., Ariz. Corp. Commn. Stock Exch. Adv. Coun., Ariz. Town Hall. Mem. ABA, Nat. Hispanic Bar Assn., Los Abogados Hispanic Lawyers Assn., Nat. Assn. Bond Lawyers, Ariz. Bar Assn., Maricopa County Bar Assn., Paradise Valley Country Club, Univ. Club. Office: Insight Enterprises Inc 1305 W Auto Dr Tempe AZ 85284

MOYA, SARA DREIER, educational association administrator; b. N.Y.C., June 9, 1945; d. Stuart Samuel and Hortense (Brill) Dreier; m. P. Robert Moya, May 30, 1966; children: J. Brill, Joshua D. BA, Wheaton Coll., Norton, Mass., 1967; postgrad., Mills Coll., Oakland, Calif., 1967-68; MPA, Ariz. State U., 1995, PhD, 2002. Mem. Paradise Valley (Ariz.) Town Coun., 1986-98, vice mayor, 1990-92; instr. advanced pub. exec. programs Ariz. State U. Chmn. Gov.'s Homeless Trust Fund Oversight Com., 1991—; pres. Ctr. for Acad. Precosity, Ariz. State U., Tempe, 1987-95; bd. dirs. Ariz. Assn. Gifted and Talented; participant 3d session Leadership Am., 1990; mem. steering com. Maricopa County Homeless Continuum of Care, 1999—, mem. planning subcom., 2000—; mem. planning com. N.E. Valley Family Advocacy Ctr., 2001—; adj. prof. planning and landscape arch. Ariz. State U. Mem. Citizens Adv. Bd. Paradise Valley Police Dept., 1984-86, Valley Citizens League Task Force on Edn., bd. trustees Paradise Valley Sch., 2002—, Socio-Economic Indications Group, 2002—, Pewate Sch. Found., 2002—; bd. dirs. Valley Leadership Inc., 1988-94; chair Maricopa Assn. Govts. Task Force on Homeless, 1989-92, 95-98; mem. Emergency Food and Shelter Program, FEMA bd. Maricopa County and Ariz., 1989—, chmn., 1996—; dir. Valley Youth Theater, 1990-93, Maricopa County Homeless Accomodation Sch., 1991—. Mem. ASPA (bd. dirs. 1996-98, pres. 1999-2000), Ariz. Women in Mcpl. Govt. (sec. 1988-89, bd. dirs. 1986—, pres. 1989-90), Western Social Sci. Assn., Ariz. State U. Students of Pub. Affairs Network (sec./treas. 1996-98), Data Network for Human Svcs. (bd. dirs. 1990-93), Maricopa Assn. Govts. (regional coun. 1988-98, vice-chmn. mag. regional devel. policy com. 1989-91, chair 1992-98, mag. joint econ. devel./human resources subcom. 1990-94, mag. youth policy adv. com. 1994-98, blue ribbon com. 1995-97, vision 2025 com. 1997-2000, chair urban features subcom. 1998-2000, valley vision 2025 steering com. 1999-2000), Maricopa Assn. Govts. (air quality policy com. 1994-96), Ariz. Acad., Ariz. Planning Assn. (bd. dirs., citizen planner, 1996 98), Paradise Valley Country Club, Phi Kappa Phi, Pi Alpha Alpha. Republican. Avocations: travel, golf, reading. Home: 5119 E Desert Park Ln Paradise Valley AZ 85253

MOYA, STEVE, managed health care company executive; BA in Urban Affairs, U. So. Calif.; postgrad., Va. Poly. Inst. and State U. Formerly sr. v.p. Manning, Selvage and Lee, N.Y.C.; founder Moya Villanueva & Assocs.; former v.p. strategic planning and comm. LatinWorks Mktg., Austin, Tex.; former prin. Growth Strategies Consulting; sr. v.p., chief mktg. officer Humana, Inc., Louisville. Office: Humana Inc 500 W Main St Louisville KY 40202

MOYARS-JOHNSON, MARY ANNIS, university official; b. Lafayette, Ind., July 19, 1938; d. Edward Raymond and Veronica Marie (Quigg) Moyars; m. Raymond Leon Molter, Aug. 1, 1959 (div. 1970); children: Marilyn Eileen Molter Davis, William Raymond Molter Johnson, Ann Marie Molter Guentert; m. Thomas Elmer Johnson, May 25, 1973 (div. 1989); children: Thomas Edward, John Alan, Barbara Suzanne. BS, Purdue U., 1960; MA, Purdue U., West Lafayette, Ind., 1991, postgrad., 1985—. Grader great issues Purdue U., West Lafayette, 1960-63, writer edn. films, 1962-65, publicity dir. convocations and lectures, 1969-74, devel. officer Sch. Humanities, 1979-88, asst. to dir. Optoelectronics Rsch. Ctr., 1989-90, mgr. indsl. rels. Sch. Elec. and Computer Engrng., 1990—2002, assoc. v.p. for info. tech., for comm., 2002—04; tchr. English and math. Benton Community Schs., Fowler, Ind., 1966-69; pub. rels. dir. Sycamore Girl Scout Coun., Lafayette, Ind., 1974-78; dir. pub. info. Ind. Senate, Majority Caucus, Indpls., 1977-78; sr. script writer Walters & Steinberg, Lafayette, 1988-89; ret., 2004. Author: Colonial Potpourri, 1975, Ouiatanon--The French Post Among the Ouia, 2000; co-author: Historic Colonial French Dress, 1982, 2nd edit., 1998; contbr. articles to profl. jours. Bd. govs. Tippecanoe County Hist. Assn., Lafayette, 1981-97. Mem. Women in Comms., Inc. (Pres. award 1983, pres. Lafayette Chpt., 2004), Ctr. for French Colonial Rsch. (dir. 1986-89, editor 1988-89), Palatines to Am., Ind. History Assn., Ind. Hist. Soc., French Colonial Hist. Soc. Roman Catholic. Avocations: history, genealogy, embroidery. Home: 924 Elm Dr West Lafayette IN 47906-2246 Office: Purdue Info Tech Young Hall West Lafayette IN 47906-3560 E-mail: mamoyars@indy.net.

MOYER, ALAN DEAN, retired newspaper editor; b. Galva, Iowa, Sept. 4, 1928; s. Clifford Lee and Harriet (Jacques) M.; m. Patricia Helen Krecker, July 15, 1950; children: Virginia, Stanley, Glenn. BS in Journalism, U. Iowa, 1950. Reporter, copy editor Wis. State Jour., Madison, 1950-53; reporter, photographer Bartlesville (Okla.) Examiner-Enterprise, 1953; telegraph editor Abilene (Tex.) Reporter-News, 1954-55; makeup editor Cleve. Plain Dealer, 1955-63; mng. editor Wichita (Kans.) Eagle, 1963-70; exec. editor Wichita Eagle and Beacon, 1970-73; mng. editor Phoenix Gazette, 1973-82, Ariz. Republic, 1982-89; ret., 1989. Pres., dir. Wichita Profl. Baseball, Inc., 1969-75; mem. jury Pulitzer Prizes, 1973-74, 85, 86, 88. Mem. AP Mng. Editors Assn. (dir. 1973-78), Am. Soc. Newspaper Editors, Wichita Area C. of C. (dir. 1970-72), Sigma Delta Chi. Office: Phoenix Newspapers Inc 200 E Van Buren St Phoenix AZ 85004-2238 E-mail: moyeralan@cox.net.

MOYER, ANNA BLACKBURN, retired secondary and elementary school educator; b. Lock Haven, Pa., Nov. 27, 1938; d. Edwin Conley and Charlotte Catherine (Eisenhower) Blackburn; m. John C. Moyer, May 28, 1960; 1 child, Johanna Lee Moyer Michalik. BS in English cum laude, Lock Haven State Coll., 1962; MEd, Pa. State U., 1976; postgrad., Lock Haven U., 1996-97. Cert. tchr. Pa. English, journalism tchr., reading specialist Lock Haven Area Sch. Dist., 1962-64; devel. reading tchr. Bellefonte (Pa.) Area Sch. Dist., Pa., 1970-73; devel., remedial reading tchr., student govt. adv. Williamsport (Pa.) Area Sch. Dist., Pa., 1975-95; title 1 reading tchr. Lose Elem. Sch., 1995—2000; title 1 tchr. Cochran Elem. Sch., Williamsport, 1999—2000, St. Boniface Elem. Sch., 1996—2000; ret., 2000. Speaker in field. Coord. Williamsport Students Engaged in Real Vol. Efforts, 1990-1995 Mem. Delta Kappa Gamma. Republican. Avocations: needlecrafts, reading, cooking. Home: Dunrovin Lane 14707 Coudersport Pike Lock Haven PA 17745

MOYER, BERNADETTE ANN, writer, small business owner; b. Hazelton, Pa., Oct. 7, 1959; d. Bernard M. and Inez S. (Totani) O'Connell; m. Randall H. Moyer, Dec. 2, 1978 (dec. Feb. 1983); 1 child, Ariane M.; m. Brian T. Sahm, Aug. 1, 1998; children: (twins) Briana, Brandon. Student, Bryn Mawr U., 1977-79; BS in Bus., Towson U., 1988. Lic. real estate broker, Md. Realtor O'Conor, Piper & Flynn, Lutherville, Md., 1986-96; pub. Two Bee..., Hunt Valley, Md., 1997—, retail store owner, 1997—; events mgr. The Children's Guide, Balt., 2000—. Author: Two Bee..., 1997, Angel Stacey, 1998, Caesar Salad, 1999, But...We Are Twins, 1998, Bare Breasted Heart, 1999; contbg. author: Surviving Ophelia, 2001. Active Bush Campaign Rep. Orgn., Towson, Md., 2000; pub. spkr. Young Widowed, Balt., 1999; rm. mother Hampton Elem. Sch., Lutherville, Md., 2000-01; vol. Boyu Scouts Am., Hunt Valley, Md., 1998—. Mem. Nat. Pubs. Network, Md. Pubs. Assn., Toastmasters, Internat. Poets (hon.). Republican. Roman Catholic. Avocations: travel, reading, cooking, writing, speaking. Home: 1210 Malbay Dr Lutherville MD 21093

MOYER, DAVID S. executive search consultant; BA in History, SUNY, Purchase, 1975. Spl. asst. for pub. affairs Grumman Corp., Bethpage, N.Y., 1975-76; instr. R.T.Y., Inc., N.Y.C. and Miami, Fla., 1976-77; exec. v.p. Wesley-Brown, Ltd., N.Y.C. and L.A., 1977-83; v.p. Paul Stafford Assocs. Ltd., N.Y.C., 1983-90, Fenwick Ptnrs., Inc., N.Y.C., 1990-91, Moyer, Sherwood Assocs., Inc., Stamford, Conn., 1991-97, N.Y.C., 1997—. Contbr. articles to profl. publs. Bd. dirs. The Helicon Found., N.Y.C., 1999—. Mem. Assn. Exec. Search Cons. (bd. dirs. 2003—), Stamford Yacht Club (chmn. membership com. 1993-97). Office: 1285 Ave Americas 35th Fl New York NY 10019

MOYER, F. STANTON, financial executive, advisor; b. Phila., June 7, 1929; s. Edward T. and Beatrice (Stanton) M.; m. Ann P. Stovell, May 16, 1953; 1 child, Alice E. BS in Econs., U. Pa., 1951. Registered rep. Smith, Barney & Co., Phila., 1951-54, Kidder, Peabody & Co., Phila., 1954-60; mgr. corp. dept. Blyth Eastman Dillon & Co., Inc. (formerly Eastman Dillon, Union Securities & Co.), Phila., 1960-65, instl. sales mgr., 1965-67, gen. partner, 1967-71, 1st v.p., 1971-74, sr. v.p., 1974-80; v.p., resident officer Kidder, Peabody & Co. Inc., Phila., 1980-86; chmn. Pa. Mcht. Group Ltd., Radnor, 1987-88; exec. v.p. Rorer Asset Mgmt., Phila., 1990-92; chmn. Mercer Capital Mgmt., 1992-93, Global Mgmt. Group, Inc., 1993-95; mng. dir. Avonwood Capital Corp., 1995-97; chmn. Main Line Capital Ptnrs. Inc., 1997—. Trustee U. Pa., 1978-83, Hosp. of U. Pa., 1978-87; bd. dirs. Atwater Kent Mus., Phila., 1983—. Mem. Racquet Club (Phila.), St. Anthony Club (Phila.), Merion Cricket Club (Haverford, Pa.), Gulph Mills Golf Club (King of Prussia, Pa.), Gulf Stream Golf Club (Fla.), Gulf Stream Bath and Tennis Club, Delta Psi. Republican. Episcopalian. Home: 445 Caversham Rd Bryn Mawr PA 19010-2901 also: 3 Little Club Rd Gulf Stream FL 33483 Office Phone: 610-527-5015. Personal E-mail: growthguy@aol.com.

MOYER, H. WAYNE, political science educator; b. Phila., Aug. 18, 1939; s. H. Wayne and Ruth Stevens Moyer; m. Helen Johnson, June 29, 1963. BA with honors, U. Va., 1961; MA in Internat. Rels., Yale U., 1969, MPhil in Polit. Sci., 1972, PhD in Polit. Sci., 1976. Instr. polit. sci. Grinnell (Iowa) Coll., 1972-76, asst. prof., 1976-79, assoc. prof., 1979-86, prof. polit. sci., 1986—, Rosenfield prof., 1985—. Author: Agricultural Policy Reform: Politics and Process in the USA and EC, 1990, Agricultural Policy Reform: Politics and Process in the EU and U.S. in the 1990s, 2002. Lt. USN, 1961-67. Mem. Am. Polit. Sci. Assn., Internat. Studies Assn., Iowa Conf. Polit. Sci., European Union Studies Assn. Democrat. Avocations: sailing, gardening. Home: 890 Juniper Ave Kellogg IA 50135 Office: Grinnell Coll 1131 Park St Grinnell IA 50112 E-mail: moyer@grinnell.edu.

MOYER, HOMER EDWARD, JR., lawyer; b. Atlanta, Nov. 20, 1942; s. Homer Edward and Mildred Joye (Wilkerson) M.; m. Beret Butter, July 6, 1974; children: Bronwen, Homer, Eli, Kaia Joye. BA, Emory U., 1964; LLB, Yale Law Sch., 1967. Bar: Ga. 1967, D.C. 1973. Assoc. Covington & Burling, Washington, 1973-76; from dep. gen. counsel to gen. counsel U.S. Dept. of Commerce, Washington, 1976-81; ptnr. Miller & Chevalier, Washington, 1981—. Author: The R.A.T. (Real-World Aptitude Test): Preparing Yourself for Leaving Home, 2001; co-author: Export Controls as Instruments of Foreign Policy, 1988, Justice and the Military, 1972. Bd. visitors Emory U., Atlanta, 1987-91; chmn. Friends of CEELI Inst. Mem. ABA (chmn. internat. law and practice sect. 1990-91, chmn. trade com. 1984-86, chmn. Cen. and East European Law Initiative 1990-2002, chmn. Friends of the CEELI Inst., chmn. Moscow conf. on law and bilateral econ. rels. 1990), Coun. on Fgn. Rels. Episcopalian. Office: Miller & Chevalier 655 15th St NW Ste 900 Washington DC 20005-5799

MOYER, J. KEITH, newspaper editor; Exec. editor The Fresno (Calif.) Bee, pub., 1997—. Office: The Fresno Bee 1626 E St Fresno CA 93786-0002

MOYER, JAMES ARTHUR, music educator, department chairman; b. Shamokin, Pa., Jan. 26, 1959; s. Robert Charles and Bertha Jean Moyer; m. Rosalie Mariel Coveleski, May 30, 1987. MusB, Susquehanna U., 1980; MusM, U. Okla., 1982, Mus D, 1989. Assoc. prof. Millikin U., Decatur, Ill., 1986—98; acct. exec. Holocomb's Edn. Resource, Cleve., 1998—2000, Apple Computer, Cupertino, Calif., 2000—02; chair, music dept. Marywood U., Scranton, Pa., 2002—. Timpanist Allentown (Pa) Band, 2000—; percussionist, extra Allentown (Pa) Symphony, 2000—. Musician: (cd) Something Old, Something New, 1995; arranger: Marimba Solo Grand Overture, 1992; composer: Four-Mallet Method for Marimba, 1990. Mem.: Am. Fed. of Musicians, Phi Beta Phi, Pi Kappa Lambda. Home: 3567 Southwood Dr Easton PA 18045 Office: Marywood U 2300 Adams Ave Scranton PA 18509 E-mail: jamoyer@mac.com.

MOYER, KEITH J. publishing executive; m. Marilyn Moyer; 3 children. Exec. editor Fresno (Calif.) Bee, 1994—97, pres., 1997—2001; pub. Mpls. (Minn.) Star Tribune, 2001—. Office: Star Tribune 425 Portland Avenue Minneapolis MN 55488

MOYER, MICHAEL EDWARD, lawyer; b. Allentown, Pa., Apr. 3, 1952; s. Howard Charles and Elizabeth (Sherer) M.; children: Kyle, Joshua. BA, Temple U., 1974, JD, 1977. Bar: Pa. 1977, U.S. Dist. Ct. (ea. dist.) Pa. 1977, U.S. Dist. Ct. (mid. dist.) Pa. 1998, U.S. Ct. Appeals (3d cir.) 1991, U.S. Supreme Ct. 1986. Asst. dist. atty. Lehigh County Dist. Atty., Allentown, 1977-81, 84-88; asst. pub. defender Lehigh County Pub. Defender, Allentown, 1981-84; pvt. practice Allentown, 1981—. Mem. Bar Assn. of Lehigh County (pres. 1997), Nat. Assn. Criminal Def. Lawyers, Pa. Criminal Def. Attys., Pa. Bar Assn., Am. Inn Ct. Office: 523 W Linden St Allentown PA 18101-1415

MOYER, R. CHARLES, finance educator, consultant; b. Reading, Pa., July 11, 1945; s. Ralph Charles and Jane Anne (Huls) M.; m. Sally Louise Prizer, May 19, 1973; children: Laura Prizer, Craig Prizer. BA in Econs., Howard U., 1967; MBA, U. Pitts., 1968, PhD in Fin., 1971. Asst. prof. fin. U. Houston, 1971-76; fin. economist U.S. Maritime Adminstrn., Washington, 1973-74; assoc. prof. Lehigh U., Bethlehem, Pa., 1976-77; from assoc. prof. to prof. U. N.Mex., Albuquerque, 1977-80; prof., chmn. fin. dept. Tex. Tech U., Lubbock, 1980-87; GMAC ins. chair in fin., Babcock Grad. Sch. Wake Forest U., Winston-Salem, NC, 1988—, dean Babcock Grad. Sch. of Mgmt., 1996—2003; dir. King Pharm., Inc., Bristol, Tenn., 2000—; dean emeritus Wake Forest U., Winston-Salem, NC, 2003—. Pres., founder R.O.E. Cons. Group, Lubbock, 1978; cons. Pub. Svc. Co. N.Mex., 1978—, KN Energy, Denver, 1979—, Gas Co. N.Mex., 1985—, San Diego Gas Electric Co., 1986—; bd. dirs. Inst. Banking Fin. Studies, 1982-86; mem. adv. bd. Amarr Garage Door Co., Winston-Salem. Author: Managerial Economics, 10th edit., 2005, Contemporary Financial Management, 9th edit., 2003, Financial Management with Lotus 1-2-3, 1986, Contemporary Financial Management Fundamentals, 2004; contbr. numerous articles to profl. jours. Vice-chmn. Lubbock Gen. Hosp. Found., 1985-88. Capt. U.S. Army, 1969-71. Fed. Res. Bank Cleve. fellow, 1970-71. Mem.: We. Fin. Assn., Ea. Fin. Assn., So. Fin. Assn. (v.p. 1990—93, pres. 1993), Am. Econs. Assn., Am. Fin. Assn., Fin. Mgmt. Assn. (bd. dir. ombudsman 1985—87, v.p. 1988—, sec.-treas. 1994—2002), Twin City Track Club, Old Town Club, Bermuda Run Country Club, Beta Gamma Sigma, Phi Beta Kappa. Avocations: tennis, golf, bicycling. Office: Wake Forest U Babcock Grad Sch PO Box 7659 Winston Salem NC 27109-7659 Office Phone: 336-758-5413.

MOYER, THOMAS J. state supreme court chief justice; b. Sandusky, Ohio, Apr. 18, 1939; s. Clarence and Idamae (Hessler) M.; m. Mary Francis Moyer, Dec. 15, 1984; 1 child, Drew; stepchildren: Anne, Jack, Alaine, Elizabeth. BA, Ohio State U., 1961, JD, 1964. Asst. atty. gen. State of Ohio, Columbus, 1964-66; pvt. practice law Columbus, 1966-69; dep. asst. Office Gov. State of Ohio, Columbus, 1969-71, exec. asst., 1975-79; assoc. Crabbe, Brown, Jones, Potts & Schmidt, Columbus, 1972-75; judge U.S. Ct. Appeals (10th cir.), Columbus, 1979-86; chief justice Ohio Supreme Ct., Columbus, 1987—. Sec. bd. trustees Franklin U., Columbus, 1986-87; trustee Univ. Club, Columbus, 1986; mem. nat. council adv. com. Ohio State U. Coll. Law, Columbus. Recipient Award of Merit, Ohio Legal Ctr. Inst.; named Outstanding Young Man of Columbus, Columbus Jaycees, 1969. Mem. Ohio State Bar Assn. (exec. com., council dels.), Columbus Bar Assn. (pres. 1980-81), Critchon Club, Columbus Maennerchor Club. Republican. Avocations: sailing, tennis. Office: Ohio Supreme Ct 30 E Broad St Fl 3 Columbus OH 43215

MOYERS, BILL D. journalist; b. Hugo, Okla., June 5, 1934; s. John Henry and Ruby (Johnson) M.; m. Judith Davidson, Dec. 18, 1954; children: William Cope, Suzanne, John. BJ with honors, U. Tex., 1956; grad. student, U. Edinburgh, Scotland, 1956-57; MDiv with honors, Southwestern Baptist Theol. Sem., 1959; DFA (hon.), Am. Film Inst. Personal asst. to Senator Lyndon B. Johnson, 1960; assoc. dir. Peace Corps, 1961-62, dept. dir., 1963; spl. asst. to Pres. Johnson, 1963-67, press sec., 1965-67; pub. Newsday, Garden City, N.Y., 1967-70; editor-in-chief Bill Moyers Jour. (weekly pub. affairs program on pub. TV), 1971-76, 78-81; chief corr. CBS Reports, CBS-TV, 1976-78; sr. news analyst CBS News, CBS-TV, 1981-86; exec. editor Pub. Affairs TV, Inc., 1986—. Author, editor: Listening to America, 1971, Report from Philadelphia, 1987, The Secret Government, 1988; editor: Joseph Campbell and the Power of Myth, 1988, A World of Ideas, 1989, 2d edit., 1990, Healing and the Mind, 1993, Genesis, 1996, Fooling With Words, 1999. Pres. The Florence and John Schumann Found., 1991—. Recipient over 30 Emmy awards, Ralph Lowell medal for contbn. to pub. TV, George Peabody award, 1976, 80, 85-86, 88-90, 99, 2000, 04, DuPont-Columbia U. Silver Baton, 1979, 86, 88, Gold baton award, 1991, 99, George Polk award,

1981, 86, career achievement award Internat. Documentary Assn., Eric Barnouw award Orgn. Am. Historians, medal of excellence N.Y. State Bd. Regents, James Madison award Nat. Broadcasting Editl. Assn., Communicator of Decade award Religious Comm. Congress, Elmer Holmes Bibst award NYU, Religious Liberty award Am. Jewish Com., 1995, Walter Cronkite award for excellence in journalism, 1995, The Fred Friendly First Amendment award, 1995, NEH Charles Frankel prize for outstanding contbns. to cultural life, 1997; elected to TV Hall of Fame, 1995. Fellow AAAS; mem. Am. Philos. Soc. Office: Pub Affairs TV Inc 450 W 33rd St New York NY 10001-2603

MOYERS, JUDITH DAVIDSON, television producer; b. Dallas, May 12, 1935; d. Henry Joseph and Eula E. (Dendy) Davidson; m. Bill D. Moyers; children: William Cope, Suzanne, John. BS, U. Tex., 1956; LittD (hon.), L.I. U., 1989, SUNY, 1990. Pres., exec. prodr. Pub. Affairs TV, N.Y.C., 1987—; exec. editor NOW, 2001—. Exec. prodr. TV documentaries (Emmy 1980, 93, 98, 2001, DuPont 1999, Christopher 1990, Parker 1992, Gold Hugo 1991, Humanitas prize 1995); exec. editor Now with Bill Moyers, 2001-; contbr. articles to profl. jours., newspapers, mags. Trustee SUNY, 1976-90; commr. U.S. Commn. UNESCO, Washington, 1977-80, White House commn. Internat. Yr. of Child, Washington, 1978-80; mem. jud. selection com. State N.Y., 1992-93; dir. Pub. Agenda Found. Recipient Christopher award, 2004. Mem. Acad. TV Arts and Scis., Century Club. Mem. Congregational Ch. Office: Pub Affairs TV Inc 450 W 33rd St Fl 7 New York NY 10001-2603

MOYERS, SYLVIA DEAN, retired medical librarian; b. Independence, W.Va., Oct. 22, 1936; d. Wilkie Russell and Ina Laura (Watkins) Collins; m. Paul Franklin Moyers, June 29, 1957; children: Tammy Jeanne, Thomas Paul, Tara Sue. Student, Am. Med. Record Assn., 1977—79. Sec. Teets Lumber Co., Terra Alta, W.Va., 1954-58, Preston County News, 1958-60; med. record clk. med. record dept. Hopemont (W.Va.) Hosp., W.Va., 1960-75, dir., 1975-88; sec. The Terra Alta Bank, 1990-95; ret., 1995. Charter mem., past mother advisor Order of Rainbow Girls (Terra Alta Assembly No. 26), past grand editor Mountain Echoes; vol. Preston Meml. Hosp., ARC, Salvation Army, Am. Cancer Soc., Boy Scouts Am., Muscular Dystrophy Assn.; active Kingwood Fire Dept. Aux. Mem.: Preston County Hist. Soc., Preston Meml. Hosp. Aux., Kingwood Civic Club. Republican. Methodist. Home: 120 Miller Rd Kingwood WV 26537-1321

MOYER-STAKER, DENISE ELANE, music educator; b. Kans. City, Kans., Aug. 4, 1956; d. Audrie F. and Marvin M. Moyer; m. Robert V. Staker, Oct. 4, 1996. MusB in edn., Conservatory of Music, U. Mo., Kans. City, 1974—78; MusM in edn., Conservatory of Music, U. Mo., 1979—81. Cert. Teaching, Choral, Instrumental Music, K-12 Mo.-Life. Tchr. vocal, instrumental music, Kans., 1978—99, 1978—99, 1978—99; prof. music Ctrl. Fla. CC, Lecanto, 2001—. Musician, spkr., Citrus County, Fla., 2000—. Contbr. articles; dir.: (choir) all-state choir, rainbow girls, 1983—85; performer (spkr.): Music Educators Conf., 1979; prodr.(spkr.): Music Educators Conf., 1981. Pres. Mil. Order Cootie Aux., Hampton, Va., 1998—99. E-4, musician USN, 1991—95, NATO, Naples, Italy. Recipient Fla. All-State q.m., VFW, 2001-2003; scholar Conservatory Women's Com. scholarship, Conservatory Women's Com., 1974-78. Mem.: Mu Phi Epsilon Profl. Music Alumni (assoc.; chaplain 1974—78), Grand Cross Color (life; state recorder 1980—81), VFW (life; adj., q.m. 2001—03), Order Rainbow Girls (life; state dean 1984—85, All-State q.m. 2001-2003). Avocations: reading, music, public speaking, volunteering. Home: 2395 N Annapolis Ave Hernando FL 34442 Office: Central Fla CC 3800 S Lecanto Highway Lecanto FL 34461 Personal E-mail: pribble9@naturecoast.net. Business E-Mail: stakerd@cf.edu.

MOYES, JERRY C. transportation executive; Chmn., pres., CEO Swift Transp. Co., Inc., Phoenix, 1974—. Office: Swift Transp Co 2200 S 75th Ave Phoenix AZ 85043-7410 also: PO Box 29243 Phoenix AZ 85038-9243 Fax: 623-907-7380.

MOYES, NORMAN BARR, journalism educator, writer, photographer; b. Fairmont, W.Va., Aug. 26, 1931; s. Roland Dare and Lillian T. (Barr) M.; div. 1980; children: Christine, Mark, Elizabeth. AB in English/Spanish, West Liberty State Coll., 1963; MA in English, W.Va. U., 1956; PhD in Comm., Syracuse (N.Y.) U., 1968. Instr. West Liberty (W.Va.) State Coll., 1955-58; prof. Syracuse U., 1958-63; prof. journalism Boston U., 1963—. Author: Journalism in the Mass Media, 1970, Mass Media Journalism, 1975, Journalism, 1984, Journalism Resource Book, 1985, Battle Eye, 1995. With U.S. Army, 1953-55. Named Outstanding Alumnus West Liberty State Coll., 1992. Avocation: photography. Office: Boston U 640 Commonwealth Ave Boston MA 02215-2422 Home: 67 Colborne Rd Apt 4 Brighton MA 02135-4130 E-mail: nmoyes@bu.edu.

MOYLAN, DOUGLAS, state attorney general; b. Guam; m. Deborah Moylan. B in Bus. Admin., U. Notre Dame, 1988; JD, Santa Clara U., 1991. Bar: Guam Bar Admissions 92, Calif. Bar Admissions 1992, cert.: D.C. Ct. of Appeals 1993. Law clk. Judge Alberto C. Lamenora Superior Ct. Guam, 1991, staff atty., 1991—93; atty. with Robert Torres P.C. Legis. Counsel, 24th, 25th, 26th Guam Legis., 1993—96; small claims ct. referee Superior Ct. Guam, 1995—97; pvt. practice Moylan & Van de Veld Law Offices, 2002; atty. gen., 2002—. Bd. mem. Guam Election Commission, 1996—2000. Bd. mem. Guam's Election Commn. Bd. Office: Judicial Ctr Bldg Ste 2-200E 120 W OBrien Dr Hagatna GU 96910

MOYLAN, JAMES JOSEPH, lawyer; b. Forest Hills, N.Y., Feb. 3, 1948; s. James Gerard and Jessie Cora (Geary) M.; m. Barbara Chesrow, Aug. 29, 1970; children: James, C., Joseph O., Alicia G. BSBA, U. Denver, 1969, JD, 1971. Bar: Colo. 1972, D.C. 1972, Ill. 1975, U.S. Dist. Ct. Colo. 1972, U.S. Supreme Ct. 1975. Trial atty. SEC, Washington, 1972-75; assoc. gen. counsel Chgo. Bd. Options Exch., Ill., 1975-77; assoc. Abramson & Fox, Chgo., 1977-80; ptnr. Bowen, Knepper & Moylan Ltd., Chgo., 1980-82, Moylan & Early, Ltd., Chgo., 1983-84; prin. James J. Moylan and Assocs., Ltd., Chgo., 1984-95; ptnr. Arnstein & Lehr, Chgo., 1995-2000, Tressler, Soderstrom, Maloney & Priess, Chgo., 2000—03. Adj. prof. law IIT Chgo. Kent Coll. Law, 1976-2002; former pub. dir. MidAm. Commodity Exch. divsn. Chgo. Bd. Trade, Chgo. Contbr. articles to profl. jours. Mem.: ABA (sect. corp., banking and bus. law, sect. litigation), D.C. Bar Assn., Chgo. Bar Assn., Ill. State Bar Assn. (sect. coun. mem.), Theta Chi (grand chpt. 1993—2000, funds bd. 2000—). Republican. Roman Catholic. Office Phone: 970-870-0730.

MOYLAN, KALEO, lieutenant governor; s. Kurt S. and Judith G. Moylan; m. Julie R. Cruz; children: Alyssa Lehua, Jada Pomaikai. BA, U. Colo.; JD, U. Puget Sound. Senator 25th and 26th Guam Legis., chmn. com. on housing, gen. govt. svcs. and fgn. affairs, com. on ways and means, chmn. ways and means com.; lt. gov. Guam, Anigua, 2003—. Office: Ricardo J Bordallo Governors Complex Adelup GU 96910 Mailing: PO Box 2950 Hagatna GU 96932 Office Phone: 671-475-9380. Business E-Mail: ksmoylan@ite.net.

MOYLAN, STEVE, publishing executive; BA, Boston Univ.; MA, Univ. of San Francisco. Pres, CEO Infoworld, San Mateo, 2000—. Office: 28 E 28th St New York NY 10016

MOYLE, PETER BRIGGS, fisheries and biology educator; b. May 29, 1942; s. John Briggs and Evelyn (Wood) M.; m. Marilyn Arneson, June 11, 1966; children: Petrea Ruth, John Noah. BA, U. Minn., 1964, PhD, 1969; MS, Cornell U., 1966. Asst. prof. Calif. State U., Fresno, 1969-72; from asst. prof. to prof. U. Calif., Davis, 1972—, chmn. dept. wildlife and fisheries, 1982-87, Pres.'s chair in undergrad. edn., 2003—. Head, Delta Native Fishes Recovery Team, 1993-95. Author: Inland Fishes of California, 1976, 2d edit., 2002, Fishes: An Introduction to Ichthyology, 5th edit., 2003, Fish: An Enthusiast's Guide, 1993. Fellow Calif. Acad. Sci.; mem. Am. Fisheries Soc. (life, award of excellence West divsn. 1991, Outstanding Educator award 1995), Ecol. Soc. Am., Am. Soc. Ichthyologists and Herpetologists, Soc. Conservation Biology, Natural Heritage Inst. (v.p. 1994—). Home: 612 Eisenhower St Davis CA 95616-3031 Office: U Calif Dept Wildlife Fish & Conservation Biolog 1 Shields Ave Davis CA 95616 E-mail: pbmoyle@ucdavis.edu.

MOYLES, PHILIP VINCENT, JR., financial services company executive; b. N.Y.C., July 14, 1964; s. Philip Vincent and Anne Kane Moyles; m. Beth O'Connor. BA in History, Kenyon Coll., 1986; postgrad., Dartmouth Coll., 2000. Mgmt. trainee Rollins Burdick Hunter Co., Chgo., 1986-87; assoc. Johnson & Higgins, N.Y.C., 1987-90; sr. acct. rep. Marsh & McLennan Inc., N.Y.C., 1990-91, asst. v.p., 1991-93, v.p., 1993-95, sr. v.p., 1995-96; mng. dir., practice leader mergers and acquisitions Marsh Inc., N.Y.C., 1996—. Mem. Union League Club N.Y., Allegheny Country Club (Sewickley, Pa.). Republican. Roman Catholic. Office: Marsh Inc 1166 Ave of Americas New York NY 10036

MOYNA, JOHN LAWRENCE, priest; b. NYC, Aug. 20, 1945; s. John Lawrence and Margaret Mary (Healy) Moyna. BA, St. Joseph's Sem. Coll., 1969; MDiv, Christ the King Sem., 1975. Ordained Roman Catholic Priest Diocese of Albany, 1973. Assoc. pastor St. Clare's Ch., Colonie, NY, 1973—75, St. Mary's Ch., Clinton Heights, NY, 1975—79, St. Pius X Ch., Londonville, NY, 1979—83, St. John the Evangelist Ch., Schenectady, NY, 1983—86; pastor St. Mary's Ch., Coxsackie, NY, 1986—; chaplain N.Y. State Dept. of Corrections, 1996—. Dean Suburban Albany, NY, 1982—83. Co-chmn. Ministerial Assoc., Coxsackie; mem. Presbyterial Coun., Albany, 1975—79, 1988—93, chmn., 1991—93. Mem.: Am. Correctional Assn., Acad. Correctional Health Profls. Roman Catholic. Achievements include development of hospice tng. for prison inmates. Home and Office: St Mary's Ch 80 Mansion St Coxsackie NY 12051 Office Phone: 518-731-8800.

MOYNAHAN, JOHN DANIEL, JR., retired insurance executive; b. Chgo., Dec. 10, 1935; s. John Daniel and Helen (Hurley) M.; m. Virginia Thomas, Oct. 10, 1959; children: Laura, Mark, Tricia, Kate. BA cum laude, U. Notre Dame, 1957. With Met. Life Ins. Co., N.Y.C., 1957—, regional v.p., from 1971, with nat. div. group nat. accounts, 1979-80, sr. v.p. group life and health ops., 1980-86, exec. v.p., 1986-97; ret., 1997.

MOYNAHAN, JULIAN LANE, English language educator, author; b. Cambridge, Mass., May 21, 1925; s. Joseph Leo and Mary (Shea) M.; m. Elizabeth Rose Reilly, Aug. 6, 1945; children: Catherine (dec.), Brigid, Mary Ellen. AB, Harvard U., 1946, A.M., 1951, PhD, 1957. Cataloguer, rare books asst. Boston Pub. Library, 1948-49, 51; teaching fellow Harvard U., 1951-53; instr. English Amherst Coll., 1953-55; instr., asst. prof. English Princeton, 1955-63; Fulbright lectr. Am. and English lit. Univ. Coll., Dublin, 1963-64; assoc. prof. English Rutgers U., 1964-66, prof., 1966-93, disting. prof., 1976-93, prof. emeritus, 1993—. Vis. prof. U. Wyo., summer 1965, Harvard U., summer 1967, Bread Loaf Sch., 1969, NYU, 1997; NEH vis. prof. Manhattanville Coll., 1972; Gauss lectr. Princeton U., 1975; vis. scholar English dept. U. Utah, spring 1980; lectr. N.J. Coun. for Humanities, 1998, 99. Author: Sisters and Brothers, 1960, The Deed of Life, A Critical Study of D.H. Lawrence, 1963, Pairing Off, 1969, Vladimir Nabokov, 1971, Garden State, 1973, Where the Land and Water Meet, 1979, Anglo-Irish: The Literary Imagination in a Hyphenated Culture, 1995; editor: (D.H. Lawrence) Sons and Lovers: Text, Criticism, Backgrounds, 1968, 77, The Viking Portable Thomas Hardy, 1977; contbr. revs. and criticism to N.Y. Times Book Rev., T.L.S., Washington Post Book World, N.Y. Rev. Books; contbr., mem. editl. bd. The Recorder, Jour. Am. Irish Hist. Soc., 1994—. Bicentennial preceptorship Princeton, 1960-63, grants-in-aid Am. Coun. Learned Socs., Am. Philos. Soc.; mem. Pulitzer Prize Fiction Jury, 1981, chmn., 1987; mem. Friends of Princeton U. Libr., 2002—. Served with AUS, 1943-44. 7500 creative writing award Nat. Found. Arts, 1966; Ingram-Merrill award, 1967; NEH fellow, 1975; Guggenheim fellow, 1983-84. Mem. MLA, PEN, Harvard Club of Princeton. Democrat. Home: 136 Bayard Ln Princeton NJ 08540-3041 Address: Apt 9B London Ter 405 W 23d St New York NY 10011 also: Chatham Lodge Oldcastle Kells County Meath Ireland

MOYNE, JOHN ABEL, computer scientist, linguist, educator; b. Yezd, Iran, July 6, 1920; came to U.S., 1956, naturalized, 1965; s. Abul Kasim and Sogra (Afshar) M.; m. Claudia Wienert, July 4, 1963; children: David, Nicholas, Parvin. BA, Georgetown U., 1959, MA, 1960; PhD, Harvard U., 1970. With Brit. Govt., Iran and India, 1943-52, market rsch. officer Tehran, 1952; linguist U.S. Govt., Cyprus, 1953-56; rsch. assoc. Georgetown U., Washington, 1960-63; mgr. applied linguistics dept. IBM Corp., Cambridge, Mass., 1963-71; prof., chmn. computer sci. dept. Queens Coll. CUNY, Flushing, 1971-81, chmn. divsn. math. and natural scis., 1978-81, chmn. univ. faculty for PhD in Computer Sci., 1978-82, exec. officer Grad. Sch. PhD Program in Linguistics, 1983-88, prof. linguistics and computer sci., 1971—91, prof. emeritus linguistics and computer sci., 1991—. Author, co-author: Hafiz of Shiraz, 1946, Life in India, 1949, Open Secret, 1984, Understanding Language: Man or Machine, 1985, Unseen Rain, 1986, Rumi: These Branching Moments, 1988, This Longing Poetry, Teaching Stories, and Letters of Rumi, 1988, LISP: A First Language for Computing, 1991, Say I Am You, 1994, The Essential Rumi, 1995, Rumi and the Sufic Tradition: Essays on the Mowlavi Order and Mysticism, 1998, The Drowned Book, 2004; contbr. articles to profl. jours., chpts. to books. Grantee EURATOM, AEC, NSF, CUNY. Mem. Linguistics Soc. Am., Brit. Inst. Engring. Tech., The Acad. Am. Poets. Democrat. Home: 40 Prospect Ave Sea Cliff NY 11579-1029 Office: CUNY PhD Program Linguistics Grad Ctr 365 5th Ave New York NY 10016-4334 E-mail: jmoyne@post.harvard.edu., jmoyne@gc.cuny.edu.

MOYNE, YVES M. water treatment executive; b. Jallieu, Isere, France, May 23, 1955; came to U.S., 1994; PhD, Hautes Etudes Commerciales, Paris, 1980; M in Econs., U. La Sorbonne, Paris, 1980. Sr. KPMG Peat Marwick, Paris, 1980-83; fin. controller Lyonnaise Des Eaux, Paris, 1983-86, mgr. orgn., 1986-88, group dir. for Hong Kong, China, Macau Hong Kong, 1988-91; exec. dir. The Macau Water Supply Co., 1988-91; v.p., fin. and adminstr. Degremont, Rueil, France, 1991-94; chmn., pres., CEO INFILCO Degremont, Inc., Richmond, Va., 1994—; chmn., CEO Aquasource North Am., Richmond, Va., 1996—; CEO Degremont N.Am. Rsch. & Devel. Ctr., 1997—. V.p. JOUD, Crolles, France, 1994; advisor to French Govt. for Fgn. Trade, 1995—; dir. Greater Richmond Tech. Coun., 1996—; prof. U. Paris IV, Creteil, 1981; lectr. pub. utility mgmt., S.E. Asia, and China. Author survey: For a Better Knowledge of The Consumers' Habits, 1978. With French Air Force, 1976-77, Istres, France. Mem. French Am. C. of C. (bd. dirs. 1997—; exec. v.p. Washington 1997-98). Avocations: architecture, skiing. Office: INFILCO Degremont Inc 2924 Emerywood Pkwy Ste B Richmond VA 23294-3751

MOYNIHAN, BRIAN T. finance company executive; b. 1960; m. Susan Berry; 3 children. Grad., Brown U., U. Notre Dame. Dep. gen. coun. FleetBoston Fin. Corp., Boston, 1993—94, mng. dir., corp. strategy and devel., 1994—2000, Sr. VP, 1998—99, exec. vp., 1999—, exec. vp., wealth mgmt. and brokerage, 2000—. Bd. dirs. YouthBuild Boston. Office: FleetBoston Fin Corp 100 Federal St Boston MA 02110

MOYNIHAN, GARY PETER, industrial engineering educator; b. Little Falls, NY, Mar. 5, 1956; s. Peter H. and Frances S. (Ferjanec) M.; m. Eleanor T. McCusker, Mar. 10, 1984; children: Andrew Ross, Keith Patrick. BS in Chemistry, Rensselaer Polytech. Inst., 1978, MBA in Opsl. Mgmt., 1980; PhD in Indsl. Engring., U. Ctrl. Fla., 1990. Prodn. supr. Am. Cyanamid, Bound Brook, N.J., 1978-79, Nat. Micronetics, Kingston, N.Y., 1980-81; assoc. mfg. engr. Martin Marietta Aerospace, Orlando, Fla., 1981-82, indsl. engr., 1982-85, sr. indsl. engr., 1985-87, group indsl. engr., 1987-90; asst. prof. indsl. engring. U. Ala., Tuscaloosa, 1990-96, assoc. prof., 1996—2001, prof., 2001—. Cons. in field. Contbr. articles to profl. jours. Regents scholar N.Y. State Bd. Regents, 1974-78; rsch. fellow NASA, 1992-93, 98-99; rsch. grant BellSouth Telecomm., 1994-96; recipient Outstanding Tchg. award AMOCO Found., 1993-94, Ralph R. Teetor Engring. Educator award Soc. Automotive Engrs, 2000. Mem.: IEEE (sr.), Aerospace and Def. Soc. (v.p. fin. and adminstrn. 1994—97), Inst. Indsl. Engrs. (sr.; chpt. dir. 1991—95, chpt. pres. 1996—97, regional v.p. 2004, Outstanding Faculty Adv. SE Region award 2004). Achievements include design and development of information systems applications for the aerospace and foundry industries; 4 software copyrights. Office: U Ala Dept Indsl Engring Tuscaloosa AL 35487-0001

MOYNIHAN, JAMES J. architectural firm executive; Pres., CEO Heery Internat., Atlanta. Office: Heery Internat 999 Peachtree St NE Ste 500 Atlanta GA 30309-3953

MOYNIHAN, JAMES M. bishop; b. Rochester, N.Y., July 16, 1932; Student, St. Bernard's Sem., Rochester, N.Am. Coll., Rome, Gregorian U. Ordained priest Roman Cath. Ch. 1957. Bishop Diocese of Syracuse, Syracuse, NY, 1995—. Office: 240 E Onondaga St Syracuse NY 13202-2608

MOYNIHAN, JOHN BIGNELL, retired lawyer; b. N.Y.C., July 25, 1933; s. Jerome J. and Stephanie (Bignell) M.; m. Odilia Marie Jacques, Nov. 13, 1965; children: Blair, Dana. BS, Fordham U., 1955; JD, St. John's U., N.Y.C., 1958. Bar: Tex. 1961, U.S. Supreme Ct. 1965, U.S. Dist. Ct. (we. dist.) Tex. 1968, U.S. Ct. Appeals (5th cir.) 1973. Sole practice, Brownsville, Tex., 1961-62; asst. city atty. City of San Antonio, 1962-63; sole practice San Antonio, 1963-65; estate tax atty. IRS, San Antonio, 1965-73; dist. counsel EEOC, San Antonio, 1974-79; asst. U.S. atty. Office U.S. Atty., San Antonio, 1980-87, sr. litigation counsel, 1987-94; sole practice San Antonio, 1995-98; ret., 1998. Chmn. reform and renewal com., San Antonio Roman Cath. Archdiocese, 1968. Served with U.S. Army, 1958-60; lt. col. USAFR (ret.), 1986. Mem. San Antonio Bar Assn. (chmn. state and nat. legis. com. 1972-73, Meritorious Svc. award 1968), Fed. Bar Assn. (bd. dirs. San Antonio chpt. 1983—, pres. elect 1986, pres. 1987), KC (pres. 1967). Home: 11011 Whispering Wind St San Antonio TX 78230-3746 E-mail: jmoynihan@rr.satx.com.

MOYNIHAN, WILLIAM J. museum executive; b. Little Falls, N.Y., Apr. 8, 1942; s. Bernard J. and Mary A. (Flynn) M.; m. Irene A. Sheilds, July 2, 1966; children: Patricia, Erin, Sean. BA, SUNY, Binghamton, 1964; MA, Colgate U., 1966; PhD, Syracuse U., 1973. From asst. to assoc. prof. Colgate U., Hamilton, NY, 1973—77, from asst. to assoc. dean faculty, 1977—80, dean students, 1980—83, dean coll., 1983—88; v.p.m. dir. Am. Mus. Natural History, NYC, 1988—95; pres., CEO Milw. Pub. Mus., 1995—2002; ret., 2002. Bd. dirs. N.Y. State Mus.; adv. com. arts and culture Congressman J. Nadler, N.Y.C., 1993-95. Adv. editor Curator jour., 1991-95. Mem. Am. Mus. Assn., Am. Assn. Museums (mem. ethics com., bd. dirs.), Wis. Acad. of Scis., Arts and Letters (councillor-at-large 1995-02), Univ. Club. Home: 84 Eaton St Hamilton NY 13346

MOYSE, HERMANN, III, banker; b. Baton Rouge, Dec. 28, 1948; s. Hermann Jr. and Marie Louise (Levy) M.; m. Janet Lee Doise; children: Allison Leze, David Hermann, Aaron Lewis. BA, Coll. of Emporia, 1970; MSW, La. State U., 1973. Asst. dir. Capital Area Health Planning Agy., 1973-74; research assoc. La. State U., Baton Rouge, 1974-78; trainee to v.p. City Nat. Bank, Baton Rouge, 1978—, sr. v.p., 1985-94, also bd. dirs., chmn., 1994-98; owner, pres. HM3 Corp., 1999—. Sec.-treas. Melrose Devel. Corp., Baton Rouge, 1986-87; bd. dirs. La. Cos., Charter Chambers, LLC; CEO Health Net One, 1999; adv. bd. Iberra Bank, 2004—; pres. WRKF Radio, 2003-04; chmn. La. State U. Health Care Svcs. Found., 2002—. Mem. Istrouma Council Boy Scouts Am.; mem. Capital Area United Way Agy. Svcs. Div., Baton Rouge, 1979-86, 88-91, vice chmn. 1981, bd. dirs., 1987—, chmn., 1989-90; v.p. Arts Coun. Greater Baton Rouge, 1990—; 1st v.p. La. Arts & Sci. Ctr., Baton Rouge, 1985—, pres., 1988; mem. Community Funds for Arts, 1989-90; mem. Arts & Humanities Coun., 1990—, v.p., 1991—, treas., 1992; mem. Community Funds for the Arts, 1989—, vice chmn., 1992; pres. Cath. Community Life Office, Baton Rouge, 1981, Baton Rouge Speech and Hearing Found., 1986, pres. 1983, treas., 1981; mem. St. Joseph's Acad. Adv. Bd., v.p., 1986-88, pres., 1987-88; bd. dirs. St. James Place; treas. Baton Rouge Crisis Intervention Ctr., 1984-85, v.p., 1987, pres., 1987; sec. St. Joseph's Children's Home, 1980; bd. dirs. Crime Stoppers, Inc., 1986—, v.p., 1989, pres. 1991—; pres. Mid City Devel. Alliance, 1991-93, 97—; mem. adv. bd. Tau Ctr., 1990-93; trustee Episc. High Sch., 1990-92; treas. La. Delta Svc. Corps. Inc., 1995—; bd. trustees Gen. Health Sys., Inc, 1994-98, La. Nature Conservancy, 2001—, Our Lady of Lake Coll., 2001—, sec., 2003—; mem. Baton Rouge Crimestoppers, chmn. fin. com., 1997—; chmn. First Commerce Cmty. Devel. Corp., 1993-99. Mem. La. Bankers Assn. (fed. affairs com. 1990—), La. Coun. Econ. Edn. (trustee 1987, regional v.p. 1990—, Community Vol. Activist award 1988), NCCJ (chpt. bd. dirs. 1988, treas. 1995), City Club, Baton Rouge Country Club. Democrat. Jewish.

MOZILO, ANGELO R. diversified financial services company executive; BS, Fordhan U., 1960; LLD with hon., Pepperdine U. Ptnr., co-founder Countrywide Credit Industries, Inc., Calabasas, Calif., 1969—, CEO, 2000—, also vice chmn.; chmn., CEO Countrywide Home Loans, Inc. subs., Calabasas, Calif., chmn., CEO, pres. Vice chmn. Office: Countrywide Credit Industries Inc 4500 Park Granada Calabasas CA 91302-1613*

MOZLEY, PAUL DAVID, retired obstetrics and gynecology educator; b. Decatur, Ala., Oct. 27, 1928; s. James Howard and Ruth Dianne (Brindely) M.; m. Mary Dale Goss, Aug. 30, 1983; children from previous marriage: Susan Ruth, Paul David Jr., Sally Robin. BA, U. Ala., 1950; MD, Med. Coll. Ala., 1955. Diplomate Am. Bd. Ob-Gyn, Am. Bd. Psychiatry and Neurology. Commd. lt. USN, 1955, advanced through grades to capt., 1970; resident ob-gyn Corona (Calif.) and San Diego Naval Hosp., 1956-59; resident in psychiatry Bethesda, Md., 1964-66, Phila. Naval Hosp., 1969-70; staff gynecologist U.S. Naval Hosp., Yokosuku, Japan, 1959-62, chief gynecologist Memphis, 1962-64, dir. med. services Naples, Italy, 1966-68, comdg. officer, 1969; chmn. neuropsychiatry Naval Regional Med. Ctr., Portsmouth, Va., 1970-75; ret., 1975; assoc. prof. psychiatry Eastern Va. Med. Sch., Norfolk, 1975-77, prof., interim chmn. dept., 1977-78, vice chmn. psychiatry, 1978-79; prof., dir. undergrad. edn. Dept. Ob-Gyn Sch. Medicine, East Carolina U., Greenville, 1979-84; prof. ob-gyn, chmn. dept., Coll. Community Health Scis. U. Ala., Tuscaloosa, 1984-99, prof. ob-gyn, assoc. chmn. dept. Sch. Medicine, 1984-99, prof., chmn. emeritus Sch. Medicine, prof. emeritus obstetrics, 1999—; ret., 2002. Dir. psychiat. services Norfolk Gen. Hosp., 1975-79; chmn. dept. ob-gyn DCH Regional Med. Ctr., Tuscaloosa, 1986—; obstetrician Baldwin Clinic; cons. med. liability law legal firms., Ala., Tenn., 1980—. Contbr. numerous articles to profl. jours. Mem. Regional Parental Adv. Council, Montgomery, Ala., 1986-87; sponsor Tuscaloosa Symphony Assn. Recipient Meritorious Service medal Pres. U.S., 1975, Surgeon Gen.'s Merit award, 1975, Attending of Yr. award Residents in Psychiatry, 1979, Clin. Sci. Course award Dept. Ob-Gyn grad. class, 1982, Eastern Va. Sch. Medicine; named one of Outstanding Young Men in Am., Jaycees, 1964 Fellow ACS, Am. Coll. Ob-Gyn (chmn. various programs 1974, 76, 77, Chmn.'s award clin. research 1969, life), Am. Psychiat. Assn. (Continuing Med. Edn. Standards award 1977, life); mem. AMA (Physician's Recognition award 1986), Am. Soc. Psychosomatic Ob-Gyn (founding mem., pres. 1979-80, chmn. nominating com. 1981, permanent steering com. 1982), Va. Ob-Gyn Soc., Assn. Acad. Psychiatry, Va. Med. Soc., N.C. Neuropsychiat. Assn., Pitt County Med. Soc., Med. Assn. Ala., Ala. Psychiat. Assn., LWV, Torch Club (Portsmouth), Alpha Epsilon Delta. Democrat. Mem. Ch. of Christ. Avocations: cabinetry, goldsmithing. Home: 563 N Mobile St Fairhope AL 36532-2609

MRACHEK, LORIN LOUIS, lawyer; b. Fairmont, Minn., Jan. 5, 1946; s. Louis L. and Kathleen (Loring) M.; m. Elizabeth Moss, Aug. 31, 1968; children: Kathleen Elizabeth, Louis Moss. BA with honors, Fla. State U., 1968; MBA, JD, Columbia U., 1974. Bar: Fla. 1974, Va. 1977, U.S. Ct. Mil. Appeals 1977, U.S. Supreme Ct. 1978; cert. in civil trial law and bus. litigation Fla. Bar Bd. Certification; cert. in bus. bankruptcy law Am. Bd. Bankruptcy Certification; cert. in civil trial advocacy Nat. Bd. Trial Advocacy. Commd. 2d lt. USMC, 1969, advanced through grades to capt., 1974, chief def. counsel Marine Corps. Recruit Depoit, 1975-77, resigned, 1977; spl. asst. to gen. counsel U.S. Ry. Assn., Washington, 1977-78; shareholder Gunster, Yoakley, Valdes-Fauli & Stewart, P.A., West Palm Beach, Fla., 1978-2000; founding shareholder Page, Mrachek, Fitzgerald & Rose, West Palm Beach, Fla., 2000—. Mem. leadership coun. Fla. State U. Coll. Arts. and Scis. Editor-in-chief Columbia Jour. Law and Social Problems, 1973-74; contbr. articles to profl. jours. Fellow Am. Coll. Trial Attys.; mem. ABA, Am. Bankruptcy Inst., So. Fla. Bankruptcy Bar Assn. Avocations: running, tennis, golf. Office: 505 S Flagler Dr Ste 600 West Palm Beach FL 33401-5941 E-mail: lmrachek@pm-law.com.

MRACKY, RONALD SYDNEY, marketing and media executive, tourism consultant; b. Sydney, Australia, Oct. 22, 1932; came to U.S., 1947, naturalized, 1957; s. Joseph and Anna (Janousek) M.; m. Sylvia Frommer, Jan. 1, 1960; children: Enid Hillevi, Jason Adam. Student, English Inst., Prague, Czechoslovakia, 1943-47; grad., Parsons Sch. Design, N.Y.C., 1950-53; postgrad., NYU, 1953-54. Designer D. Deskey Assocs., N.Y.C., 1952-53; art dir., designer ABC-TV, Hollywood, Calif., 1956-57; creative dir. Neal Advt. Assocs., L.A., 1957-59; pres. Richter & Mracky Design Assocs., L.A., 1959-68; pres., CEO Richter & Mracky-Bates divsn. Ted Bates & Co., L.A., 1968-73, Regency Fin., Internat. Fin. Svcs., Beverly Hills, Calif., 1974-76; sr. ptnr. Sylron Internat., L.A., 1973—, mgmt. dir. for N.Am. Standard Advt.-Tokyo, 1978-91. CEO, Std./Worldwide Cons. Group, L.A., Tokyo, 1981-87; officer, bd. dirs. Theme Resorts, Inc., Denver, 1979—; prin., officer Prodn. Travel & Tours, Universal City, 1981—, Eques Ltd., L.A., 1988-93; mng. ptnr. GO! Pubs., 1993—; cons. in field; exec. dir. Inst. for Internat. Studies and Devel. L.A., 1976-77; mng. ptnr. Africa Consult Group, 1998—. Dir. MedicusTravel.com, 2003—; mem. editl. bd., mktg. dir. The African Times and Africa Quar., 1990—; contbr. articles to profl. jours With U.S. Army, 1954-56. Recipient nat. and internat. awards design and mktg. Mem. Am. Mktg. Assn., Africa Travel Assn. (amb.-at-large, internat. secretariat), L.A. Publicity Club, Pacific Asia Travel Assn., S.Am. Travel Assn., Am. Soc. Travel Agts. Office: Ste 115 6363 Wilshire Blvd Los Angeles CA 90048 Office Phone: 818-760-7740. Personal E-mail: sylron-1@mindspring.com. Business E-Mail: medicustravel@earthlink.com.

MRAK, ROBERT EMIL, neuropathologist, educator, electron microscopist; b. Oakland, Calif., Dec. 18, 1948; s. Emil Marcel and Vera Dudley (Greaves) M.; m. Paula Elizabeth North, Oct. 18, 1980; children: Lara North, Eric North, Ian North. BS in Math., U. Calif., Davis, 1970, MD, 1975, PhD in Zoology, 1976. Diplomate Am. Bd. Pathology, Am. Bd. Neuropathology. Resident in pathology Vanderbilt U. Hosp., Nashville, 1976-78, fellow in molecular biology, 1978-80; asst. prof. pathology Vanderbilt U., 1980-84, U. Ark. for Med. Scis., Little Rock, 1984-87, assoc. prof. pathology and anatomy, 1987-93, prof. pathology and anatomy, 1993—98, chief neuropathology, 1999—, dir. neuropathology core, Alzheimer Disease Core Ctr., 2001—, prof. pathology, anatomy and neurobiology, 1998—. Chief electron microscopy VA Hosp., Little Rock, 1984-98; cons. in neuropathology Ark. Children's Hosp., Little Rock, 1984—. Editl. bd. mem. Jour. Neuropathy & Explt. Neurology, 1996-99, Human Pathology, 1996—, contbr. articles and abstracts to profl. jours. Rsch. grantee VA, 1980-83, 86-89, Muscular Dystrophy Assn., 1981-85, NIH, 1986-90, 95—. Mem. Am. Assn. Neuropathologists, Soc. for Neurosci., U.S. and Can. Acad. Pathology. Avocations: running, skiing. Office: U Ark for Med Scis #517 4301 W Markham St Little Rock AR 72205-7101 E-mail: mrakroberte@uams.edu.

MRAZEK, DAVID ALLEN, pediatric psychiatrist; b. Ft. Riley, Kans., Oct. 1, 1947; s. Rudolph George and Hazel Ruth (Schayes) M.; m. Patricia Jean, Sept. 2, 1978; children: Nicola, Matthew, Michael, Alissa. AB in Genetics, Cornell U., 1969; MD, Wake Forest U., 1973. Lic. psychiatrist, child psychiatrist, N.C., Ohio, Colo., D.C., Va., Md., Minn., Ariz. Lectr. child psychiatry Inst. of Psychiatry, London, 1977-79; dir. pediatric psychiatry Nat. Jewish Ctr. for Immunology and Respiratory Medicine, Denver, 1979-91; chmn. psychiatry Children's Nat. Med. Ctr., Washington, 1991-98; chair psychiatry and behavioral scis. George Washington U. Sch. Medicine, 1996-2000; dir. Children's Rsch. Inst. Neurosci., 1995-98; chair psychiatry and psychology Mayo Clinic, Rochester, Minn., 2000—; prof. psychiatry and pediatrics Mayo Sch. Medicine, Rochester, 2000—; dir. Mayo Clinic S.C. Johnson Genomics of Addictions Program, 2004—. Asst. prof. psychiatry U. Colo. Sch. Medicine, 1979-83, assoc. prof. psychiatry and pediatrics, 1984-89, prof., 1990-91; prof. psychiatry and pediatrics George Washington U. Sch. Medicine, 1991-2000, Leon Yochelson prof. psychiatry and behavioral scis.; dir. Am. Bd. Psychiatry and Neurology, 2003-. Contbr. chapters to books, articles to profl. jours. Recipient Rsch. Scientist Devel. awards NIMH, 1983-88, 88-91, Irving Phillips Meml. award for outstanding rsch. in prevention Acad. Child and Adolescent Psychiatry, 2000. Fellow Am. Acad. Child Psychiatry, Royal Soc. Medicine, Am. Psychiat. Assn. (Blanche F. Ittleson award 1996, Agnes Purcell McGavin award 1999), Royal Coll. Psychiatrists, Am. Coll. Psychiatrists; mem. Group for the Advancement of Psychiatry, Colo. Child and Adolescent Psychiatry Soc. (pres. 1984), Benjamin Rush Soc., Am. Bd. Psychiatry Neurology (bd. dirs. 2003—). Office: Mayo Clinic Dept Psychiatry/Pschology 200 1st St SW Rochester MN 55905 Office Phone: 507-284-8891. Office Fax: 507-266-3319. Business E-Mail: mrazek.david@mayo.edu.

MRKVICKA, EDWARD FRANCIS, JR., financial writer, publisher, consultant; b. Aurora, Ill., Oct. 17, 1944; s. Edward Francis Sr. and Ruth Caroline (Phillips) M.; m. Madelyn Helen Rimnac, July 1, 1972; children: Edward Francis III, Kelly Helen. Cert. comml. pilot, U. Ill., 1965; diploma, Dept. Def., 1967, Bank Mktg. Assn., 1972, grad. cert., 1973. Mktg. officer Downers Grove (Ill.) Nat. Bank, 1964-72; asst. v.p., mktg. officer Bank of Westmont, Ill., 1972-73; v.p., cashier 1st State Bank Hanover Park, Ill., 1973-76; pres. 1st Nat. Bank Marengo, Ill., 1976-81, Reliance Enterprises, Inc., Fin. News Syndicate, Omni, Fin. Group, Eagle Publishing, Marengo, 1981—. Adv. coun. Am. Monetary Found., Fullerton, Calif., 1987; mem. panel of experts Boardroom Reports, 1990—. Pub.: (newletter) Money Insider; author: Battle Your Bank-And Win!, 1984, Moving Up, 1985; (with others) The Complete Book of Personal Finance, 1987, The Bank Book, 1989, 91, 94, 1,037 Ways to Make or Save Up to $100,000 This Year Alone, 1991, The Rational Investor, 1992, Your Bank is Ripping You Off, 1997, 99, J.K. Lasser's Pick Winning Stocks, 2000; contbr. articles to profl. jours. and newspapers; fin. columnist Nat. Enquirer, 1996—. Bd. dirs. DuPage County Lung Assn., Downers Grove, 1970, Western Suburbs Combined Com. Appeal, Downers Grove, 1971, McHenry County Easter Seals Clinic, Woodstock, Ill., 1979; v.p., treas. Marengo/Union Chamber, 1980; Am. rep. Cans. for Constitutional Money, 1990—. Sgt. USAF, 1965-69. Mem. Nat. Writers Union. Republican. Avocations: bowling, fishing. Office: Reliance Enterprises Inc PO Box 413 Marengo IL 60152-0413

MROCHEK, MICHAEL JOHN, physician; b. Ames, Iowa, Mar. 3, 1960; m. Diana Jo Ayoub, June 27, 1987; children: Justin, Jena. BA in Chemistry, U. Tenn., 1982; MD, U. Tenn., Memphis, 1986. Diplomate Am. Bd. Phys. Medicine and Rehab., Am. Bd. Electrodiagnostic Medicine, Am. Bd. Ind. Med. Examiners. Commd. 2d lt. U.S. Army, 1982, advanced through grades to maj., 1992; intern William Beaumont Army Med. Ctr., 1986-87; resident Walter Reed Army Med. Ctr., 1988-91; chief phys. medicine and rehab. William Beaumont Army Med. Ctr., El Paso, Tex., 1992-94; outpatient med. dir. Rio Vista Rehab. Hosp., El Paso, 1994—; pvt. practice El Paso Orthopedic Surgery Group, 1996—. Fellow Am. Acad. Phys. Medicine and Rehab., Am. Assn. Electrodiagnostic Medicine; mem. AMA, Tex. Med. Assn., El Paso County Med. Soc. Avocations: hunting, fishing, hiking, camping, swimming. Office: 1720 Murchison Dr El Paso TX 79902-2908

MROZ, GLENN D. academic administrator; BS in Forest Mgmt., Mich. Technol. U., 1974, MS in Forest Soils, 1976; PhD in Silviculture, N.C. State U., 1983. Instr. dept. forestry Mich. Technol. U., Houghton, 1980—83, asst. prof. dept. forestry, 1983—86, assoc. prof. Sch. Forest Resources and Environ. Sci., 1986—91, prof. Sch. Forest Resources and Environ. Sci., 1991—, program coord. forest ecology and mgmt. Sch. Forest Resources and Environ. Sci., 1997, assoc. dean Sch. Forest Resources and Environ. Sci., 1999—2000, interim dean Sch. Forest Resources and Environ. Sci., 2000—01, dean Sch. Forest Resources and Environ. Sci., 2001—, interim pres., 2004—. Trustee Mich. del. Great Lakes Forestry Alliance. Mem.: AAAS, Soc. Wetland Scientists, Soil Sci. Soc. Am., Soc. Am. Foresters, Nat. Assn. Profl. Forestry Schs. and Colls. (Mich. Technol. univ. rep.), Xi Sigma Pi, Sigma Xi. Office: Mich Technol Univ Sch Forest Resources and Environ Sci 1400 Townsend Dr Houghton MI 49931-1295*

MROZ, JOHN EDWIN, political scientist; b. Lowell, Mass., May 1, 1948; s. Edwin T. and Margaret Mary (Little) M.; m. Karen Linehan, June 17, 1972; children: Jonathan E.R., Jessica, Jeffrey. BA, cert. Soviet and East European studies, U. Notre Dame, 1970; AM, Northeastern U., 1972; MA, MALD, Tufts U., 1974. Exec. sec. UN Assn. Greater Boston, 1971-73; exec. v.p., dir. Middle East Studies, Internat. Peace Acad., Inc., N.Y.C., 1976-81; pres. Inst. East West Studies, N.Y.C., 1981—; cons., U.S. Govt. intermediary in Middle East, U.S. Dept. State, 1981-82; cons. Fgn. Svc. Inst., Dept. State, 1977-81; cons. Coun. of Europe, Strasbourg, Fed. Republic Germany, 1989—, East European govts., 1990—. Author: Beyond Security: Private Perceptions Among Arabs and Israelis, 1980. Contbr. articles to profl. jours. Teaching fellow NSF, 1971-72. Decorated Officer's Cross of Order of Merit Fed. Republic of Germany, 1991. Mem. Coun. on Fgn. Rels., Internat. Inst. Strategic Studies. Republican. Avocations: travel, falconry. Office: Inst East West Studies 700 Broadway New York NY 10003-9536

MRUK, CHARLES KARZIMER, agronomist; b. Providence, Sept. 23, 1926; s. Charles and Anna (Pisarek) M. BS in Agr., U. R.I., 1951, MS in Agronomy, 1957. Soil scientist soil conservation svc. Dept. Agr., Sunbury, Pa., 1951; insp. Charles A. McGuire Co., Providence, 1952; claims insp. R.R. Perishable Inspection Agy., Boston, 1953-55; asst. in agronomy U. R.I., 1955-57; agronomist Hercules Inc., 1957-79, tech. salesman, 1957-79; sr. tech. sales rep. BFC Chems., Inc., 1981-82; are devel. supr. Ea. States, 1982-84, ret., 1984. Cons. turf maintenance Olympic Stadium and Grounds, Mexico City, 1968, Fenway Park, Boston, 1963-70; bd. mem. L. Troll/G.C.S.A.N.E. Turf Rsch. Fund; advisor Mass. TurfGrass Conf. and Trade Show, Chicopee. Author and editor articles on turf culture and fertilizers, 1960-81. Mem. Rep. Ward Com., Providence, 1963-76. With USN, 1944-46. U.S. Golf Assn. Green Sect. grantee, 1955-57. Mem. Am. Soc. Agronomy, New Eng. Sports Turf Mgrs. Assn. (life), R.I. Golf Course Supts. Assn., Mass. Turf and Lawn Grass Coun. (dir., mem. planning com., chmn. fin. com., 1987, pres., 1987-89), VFW, Am. Registry Cert. Profls. in Agronomy (cert. agronomist), Sigma Xi, Alpha Zeta. Mem. Polish National Ch. Home: 75 Burdick Dr Cranston RI 02920-1517

MRUK, EUGENE ROBERT, retired marketing professional, urban planner; b. Buffalo, Sept. 12, 1927; s. Stanley and Lucy Ann (Wolanski) M.; m. Florence Helen Guzy, Apr. 15, 1950; children: Linda, Lawrence, Edith, Ginny. AA in Engring., U. Buffalo, 1966, BA in Sociology, 1970; cert. sys. analysis & application admin., U. Wis., 1971; MA in Econs., U. Buffalo, 1974. Asst. dir. planning City of Buffalo, 1958-70; commr. planning Erie County, N.Y., Buffalo, 1970-74; dir. socioecon. studies Ecology and Environment, Inc., Buffalo, 1974-79, dir. transp. system studies, 1979-81, dir. bus. devel., 1981-86, v.p. sales and mktg., 1986-90, sr. v.p. sales and mktg. nat. and internat., 1990-94, cons., 1994-96; ret., 1996. Pvt. practice planning cons. Buffalo area, 1950-64; v.p. rsch. and planning coun. WNY, 1971-74; mem. indsl. adv. bd. dept. chem. engring. SUNY, Buffalo. Author various mcpl. govt. plans. Coord. Econ. Devel. program, Buffalo, 1966; exam. cons. Civil Svc. Commn. City of Buffalo, 1974; grand marshal Gen. Pulaski Parade com., Buffalo, 1972; trustee Villa Maria Coll. Buffalo, 1992-93. Named Man of Yr. in Govt. Am-Pole Eagle newspaper, 1970; gold medal sr. olympics, N.H., N.Y., 2003. Mem. Am. Assn. Cert. Planners, Am. Planning Assn. (Disting. Leadership award N.Y. upstate chpt. 1992), Profl. Businessmen's Assn., Fr. Kolbe Soc./Polish Union of Am. (pres. 1995-2000). Democrat. Roman Catholic. Avocations: tennis, senior olympic basketball, photography, oil and acrylic painting. Home: 3 Dennis Ln Cheektowaga NY 14227-1301

MSEZANE, ALFRED ZAKELE, physics educator; b. Springs, Transvaal, South Africa, Dec. 31, 1938; came to US, 1978; s. Albert and Esther (Mbuli) M.; m. Gail Patrick, Nov. 30, 1969; children: Temba, Lambda. BSc, U. South Africa, 1962; BSc (hon), 1964; MSc, U. Sask. (Can.), 1968; PhD, We. Ont., 1973; DSc (hon.), U. Fort Hare, South Africa, 1998. Rsch. assoc. U. Witwatersrand, Johannesburg, South Africa, 1968-69, Ga. State U., Atlanta, 1974-76; instr. U. New Brunswick, Fredericton, Can., 1976-78; vis. prof. La. State U., Baton Rouge, 1978-80; from asst. prof. to assoc. prof. physics Morehouse Coll., Atlanta, 1980-83; prof. physics Atlanta U., 1983-89; chmn. physics dept., 1986-89; prof. Clark Atlanta U., 1989—; chmn. physics dept., 1991-92. Dir. NSF Ctr. Theoret. Studies of Phys. sys., 1991—; bd. dirs. Nat. alliance Rsch. Ctrs. Excellence, acting chmn., 1998—; chmn. physics and astronomy group U. Ctr. Ga., 1983-84; rev. NSF Dept. Edn., NASA, Dept. Energy; vis. prof. Inst. Theoret. Atomic and Molecular Physics, Harvard Ctr. Astrophysics, 1994; Martin Luther King, Jr. Meml. vis. prof. Wayne State U., 1998; presenter in field. Contbr. articles to profl. jours.; referee Phys. Rev. A, Jour. Phys. B., others Trustee Marist Sch., Atlanta, 1998—; del. to China People to People, Spokane, Wash., 1990; soccer coach YMCA, Decatur, Ga., 1980-90, Baton Rouge, 1978-80; treas. East Lake Cmty. Assn., 1983-89; mem. J. Erkine Love Fellowship Com. World Univ. Svc. scholar, 1965-67, Witwatersrand U. scholar, 1968-69; rsch. grantee NSF, 1983—, DOE, Acad. Applied Sci., 1981—, USAF Office Sci., 1994-97, edn. grantee NASA, 1998—; recipient Bursary Rotary Club, 1962, Bursary City Coun. Springs, 1960-62, Sir Oppenheimer Meml. Bursary Anglo am. Corp., 1965, 69, Bouchet award Am. Phys. Soc., 1999; recognized as exemplary immigrant Atlanta Jour.-Constitution, 1993. Fellow Am. Phys. Soc.; mem. AAAS, Nat. Phys. Sci. Consortium (bd. dirs. 1989-91, 97—, fellowship com.), Am. Phys. Soc. (mem. subcommittee on internat. sci. affairs), Black Physicists, Sigma Pi Sigma. Office: Clark Atlanta U Dept Physics 223 James P Brawley Dr SW Atlanta GA 30314-4358 E-mail: amsezane@ctsps.cau.edu.

MSHANA, PAMELA MARIVA, secondary school educator; b. Pomona, Calif., Sept. 28, 1969; d. Gadi Mshana and Patricia Ann Mshana-Caraway; 1 child, Mariva Jamilla Mshana-Dawes. BFA, NYU, 1991; MEd, Azusa Pacific U., 2003. Writer, rschr. Kundola Prodns., N.Y.C., 1991—93; drama/playwright instr. House of Praise Pvt. Playhouse, Moreno Valley, Calif., 1994—96; tchr. lang. arts Pomona Unified Sch. Dist., 1999—. Author: (plays) Ebony, 1990, A Toast to Leslie, 1990, Girls in Search of Cover, 2003. Finalist Young Playwrights Festival, The Dramatist Guild, 1987, Internat. Young Playwrights Festival, Sydney Opera House, 1989; recipient 3d Pl. award, NAACP Nat. Young Poets Contest, 1984. Avocations: theater, film arts, reading.

MUBASHIR, BASHAR A. internist, oncologist, hematologist; b. Pakistan, June 12, 1944; MBBS, Nishtar Med. Coll., Multan, Pakistan, 1967. Diplomate Am. Bd. Internal Medicine, Am. Bd. Oncology, Am. Bd. Hematology. Intern Toledo Hosp., 1968-69; resident in internal medicine Univ. Medicine and Dentistry of N.J., Newark, 1969-71; fellow in hematol. oncology U. Tex.-Md Anderson Hosp., Houston, 1971-73; fellow in med. hematology Case Western Res. U. Hosp., Cleve., 1973-74; pvt. practice Akron. Mem. staff St. Thomas Hosp. Med. Ctr., Akron; assoc. prof. medicine Northeastern Ohio U., Akron. Fellow ACP. Office: 444 N Main St Akron OH 44310-3110

MUCCI, GARY LOUIS, lawyer; b. Buffalo, Nov. 12, 1946; s. Guy Charles and Sally Rose (Battaglia) M.; m. Carolyn Belle Taylor, May 4, 1991. BA cum laude, St. John Fisher Coll., 1968; JD, Cath. U., 1972. Bar: N.Y. 1972. Law clk. to Hon. John T. Curtin U.S. Dist. Ct., Buffalo, 1972-74; assoc. atty. Donovan Leisure Newton & Irvine, N.Y.C., 1974-75, Saperston & Day P.C., Buffalo, 1975-80, sr. ptnr., 1980—2001; ptnr. Hiscock Barclay, 2001—. Chmn. bd. Buffalo Philharm. Orch., 1985-86; pres. Hospice Buffalo, 1986-87; mem. N.Y. State Coun. on the Arts, 1987-2000; chmn. Citizens Com. on Cultural Aid, Buffalo, 1992-98; trustee St. John Fisher Coll. Recipient Brotherhood award NCCJ, Buffalo, 1983; named Man of Yr. William Paca Soc., 1984. Mem. Erie County Bar Assn., N.Y. State Bar Assn. Home: 27 Tudor Pl Buffalo NY 14222-1615 Office: Hiscock Barclay 3 Fountain Plz Ste 1100 Buffalo NY 14203-1486 Office Phone: 716-856-5400. Home Fax: 716-885-5175. Business E-Mail: gmucci@hiscockbarclay.com.

MUCCIA, JOSEPH WILLIAM, lawyer; b. N.Y.C., May 31, 1948; s. Joseph Anthony and Charlotte (Mohring) M.; m. Margaret M. Reynolds, June 29, 1985. BA magna cum laude, Fordham U., 1970, JD, 1973. Bar: N.Y. 1974, U.S. Dist. Ct. (so. dist.) N.Y. 1974, U.S. Dist. Ct. (ea. dist.) N.Y. 1980, U.S. Ct. Appeals (2d cir.) 1974, U.S. Ct. Appeals (D.C. cir.) 1980, U.S. Supreme Ct. 1980. Assoc. Cahill Gordon & Reindel, N.Y.C., 1973-82; ptnr. Corbin Silverman & Sanseverino, N.Y.C., 1983—2001, Brown Raysman Millstein Felder & Steiner LLP, N.Y.C., 2002—. Assoc. editor Fordham Law Rev., 1972-73. Mem. ABA (litigation sect.), N.Y. County Lawyers Assn., Fed. Bar Coun., N.Y. State Bar Assn. (com. litigation sect.), Phi Beta Kappa, Pi Sigma Alpha. Office: Brown Raysman et al 900 3d Ave New York NY 10022 Office Phone: 212-895-2930. E-mail: jmuccia@brownraysman.com.

MUCHIN, ALLAN B. lawyer; b. Manitowoc, Wis., Jan. 10, 1936; s. Jacob and Dorothy (Biberfeld) M.; m. Elaine Cort, Jan. 28, 1960; children: Andrea Muchin Leon, Karen, Margery Muchin Goldblatt. BBA, U. Wis., Manitowoc, 1958, JD, 1961. Gen. counsel IRS, Chgo., 1961-65; assoc. Altman, Kurlander & Weiss, Chgo., 1965-68, ptnr., 1968-74; co-mng. ptnr. Katten Muchin Zavis Rosenman, Chgo., 1974-95, chmn. emeritus, 1995—. Bd. dirs. Chgo. Bulls, Chgo. White Sox, Alberto-Culver Co., Acorn Investment Trust; bd. visitors U. Wis. Law Sch.; trustee Noble St. Charter Sch. Pres. Lyric Opera Chgo., 1993—; mem. adv. com. Am. Com. for Weizmann Inst. of Sci., Chgo., 1991—. Mem. Econ. Club Chgo., Comml. Club Chgo. Avocations: travel, tennis, reading. Office: Katten Muchin Zavis Rosenman 525 W Monroe St Ste 1600 Chicago IL 60661-3693

MUCHMORE, DON MONCRIEF, retired museum, foundation, educational, financial fund raising and public opinion consulting firm administrator, banker; b. Wichita, Kans., Dec. 26, 1922; s. Floyd Stephen and Ivy Fay (Campbell) Muchmore; m. Virginia Gunn, June 18, 1949 (div. Dec. 1978); children: Melinda, Marcia. BA, Occidental Coll., Los Angeles, 1945; postgrad., U. So. Calif. Law Sch., 1945, UCLA. Intern Nat. Inst. Pub. Affairs, Washington, 1944; exec. asst. to congressman Washington, 1946-48; teaching asst. UCLA, 1949-50; mem. faculty San Diego State U., 1950-51; asst. prof., adminstr. Calif. State U., Long Beach, 1951-56; pres., CEO The Campbell Found., L.A., 1956—2002; spl. asst. to supt. pub. instrn. Calif. Dept. Edn., Sacramento, 1956-57; exec. mus. dir. Calif. Mus. Sci. and Industry, L.A., 1957-62, 82-89; exec. v.p., chief exec. officer Calif. Mus. Found., L.A., 1957-62, 82-89; dep. dir. (on loan from mus.) Calif. Dept. Fin., Sacramento, 1960; exec. vice chancellor Calif. State Colls. and Univs. System, Long Beach, 1962-64; first exec. asst. to chmn. and chief exec. officer Calif. Fed. Savs. and Loan Assn., L.A., 1964-66; sr. v.p. Calif. Fed. Savs. and Loan Assn, L.A., 1966-82; pres., CEO PE Conservation Svcs., Inc., 1990-94; ret., 2002. Chmn. bd. dirs., CEO Opinion Rsch. of Calif. Opinion Surveyors, The State Poll and Mktg. Surveys, Inc., Long Beach, 1948—71; syndicated by L.A. Times, 1961—70; also M-R Assocs. Campaigns; cons. in pub. opinion mus. mgmt. and fund raising, 1948—71; chmn., CEO, cons. DMM & Assocs., Long Beach, 1961—2002; sec., treas. EVENUP for the Homeless, 1994—97; mem. Inst. Mus. Svcs., 1983—88. Contbr. chapters to books. Participant in pub. opinion work Dem. and Rep. Campaigns, 1954—72; mem., chmn. 4 presdl. commns., 1970—82, Just Say No Internat., 1989—91, Reading is Fundamental, 1989—, The Buckley Sch., 1989—90; cons. overseas traveling sci. exhibit, planning mus., 1984—96; sr. adminstr., advisor, cons. PCS (South Ctrl. L.A.) Sr. Citizens, 1995—96; cons. Long Beach com. Improvement League, 1995—96; lead cons. New Solution to Homeless, 1993—98; prin. officer Peruvians Cultural Exhibit, 1988—96; prin. cons. cultural exhibit Wonders of World, 1992—95, Queensway Bay, Long Beach, 1992—98; bd. dirs. Bus. Tele Network, 1995—97; active Even up for the Homeless, 1996—98; cons. Christian Outreach Agy., 1998—99; pres. Harborplace Tower Home Owners Assn., 1999—; pres. bd. trustees East Village Cmty. Ch., 1998—, pres., 1998—2001. Named Chpt. Advisor of Yr., Sigma Alpha Epsilon, 1999, Pollster of Yr., Newsweek, 1968; recipient Highest Mus. Edn. award, Sigma Alpha Epsilon, 1992, Citizen of Yr. award and numerous other awards from nat., state and local groups; scholar Elks Nat. scholar. Mem.: AAAS, Calif. Mus. Assn. (pres. 1960, bd. dirs. 1982—88), Am. Polit. Sci. Assn., Am. Assn. Pub. Opinion Rsch., Assn. Sci. and Tech. Ctrs. (bd. dirs. 1982—88), Am. Assn. Mus. Mailing: 123 4th Ave Unit 312 NW Puyallup WA 98371

MUCHMORE, ROBERT BOYER, engineering consultant executive; b. Augusta, Kans., July 8, 1917; s. Ray Boyer and Charlotte (McPherron) M.; m. Betty Vaughan, Jan. 29, 1944; children: Andrew Vaughan, Douglas Boyer. BS, U. Calif., Berkeley, 1939; degree in Elec. Engring., Stanford U., 1942. Project engr. Sperry Gyroscope Co., Garden City, N.Y., 1942-46; sr. mem. tech. staff Hughes Aircraft, Culver City, Calif., 1946-54; v.p., chief scientist TRW Systems, Redondo Beach, Calif., 1954-73, cons. Sonoma, Calif., 1973—. Lectr. in engring. UCLA, 1954-58. Author: Essentials of Microwaves, 1952. Fellow IEEE; mem. AAAS, Assn. Computing Machinery, Sierra Club. Home: 4311 Grove St Sonoma CA 95476-6046 E-mail: rbm@sonic.net.

MUCHMORE, ROBERT CHARLES, JR., oil industry executive; BBA with honors, So. Meth. U., 1975. CPA Tex., 1977. Teller, mail rm. clk. Preston State Bank (not Bank One), 1971—75; staff auditor Arthur Andersen LLP, Dallas, 1975—78; internal auditor Otis Engring Corp. (not Halliburton Energy Svcs.), 1978—79, fin. reporting supr., 1979—80, internat. acctg. coord., 1980—82, internat. controller, 1982—83, internat. tax mgr., 1983—84, mgr. L.Am. fin. & adminstrn., 1984—85; mgr. internat. fin. systems Halliburton Energy Svcs., Houston, 1985—87, mgr. internat. fin. svcs., 1987—89, mgr. Europe/Africa regional fin. and adminstrn., 1989—96; v.p., controller Halliburton Co., 1996—2003, v.p. fin. controls, 2003—. Mem.: AICPA, Fin. Exec. Inst., Tex. Soc. CPA's. Office: Halliburton 10200 Bellaire Blvd Houston TX 77020-5299

MUCHNICK, RICHARD STUART, ophthalmologist, educator; b. Bklyn., June 21, 1942; s. Max and Rae (Kozinsky) Muchnick; m. Felice Dee Greenberg, Oct. 29, 1978; 1 child, Amanda Michelle. BA with honors, Cornell U., 1963, MD, 1967. Diplomate Am. Bd. Ophthalmology, Nat. Bd. Med. Examiners. Intern in medicine N.Y. Hosp., N.Y.C., 1967—68, now assoc. attending ophthalmologist Pediatric Ophthalmology Clinic; resident in ophthalmology, 1970—73; practice medicine, specializing in ophthalmology, notably strabismus and ophthalmic plastic surgery, 1974—. Attending surgeon, chief Ocular Motility Clinic Manhattan Eye, Ear and Throat Hosp., N.Y.C.; clin. assoc. prof. ophthalmology Cornell U., N.Y.C., 1984—; clin. rschr. strabismus, ophthalmic plastic surgery, 1973—. Served with USPHS, 1968—70. Recipient Coryell Prize Surgery, Cornell U. Med. Coll., 1967. Fellow: ACS, Am. Acad. Ophthalmology; mem.: AMA, Manhattan Ophthal. Soc., Greater N.Y. Soc. Pediat. Ophthalmology and Strabismus, N.Y. Acad. Medicine, N.Y. Soc. Clin. Ophthalmology, Internat. Strabismological Assn., Am. Assn. Pediatric Ophthalmology and Strabismus, Am. Soc. Ophthalmic Plastic and Reconstructive Surgery, 7th Regt. Tennis, Lotos, Alpha Epsilon Delta, Alpha Omega Alpha. Office: 69 E 71st St New York NY 10021-4213 Office Phone: 212-744-1726.

MUCINO-QUINTERO, VICTOR HUGO, mechanical engineering educator, consultant; b. Mexico City, Jan. 2, 1952; arrived in U.S., 1985; s. Alfonso Mucino-Reyes and Marcelina Quintero-Elizondo; m. Elisabeth Sanchez, Jan. 26, 1990; children: Andrea, Veronique. BSME, Poly. Inst. Mex., Mexico City, 1974; M Engring., U. Wis., Milw., 1977, DEng, 1981. Registered prof. engr., Wis., W.Va. Rsch. assoc. J. I. Case Co., Racine, Wis., 1977-80; prof. Nat. U. Mex., Mexico City, 1981-85; prof. mech. engring. W.Va. U., Morgantown, 1985—. Dir. indsl. outreach program in Mex. W.Va. U.; indsl. cons. Contbr. articles to profl. jours., including ASME Jour. Mech. Design, Indsl. Tribology, SAE Trans., Jour. Sound and Vibrations, others. Mem.: ASME, Am. Soc. Engring. Educators, Acad. Engring. Mex., Soc. Automotive Engrs. (Ralph Teetor award 1995). Avocations: music, poetry. Office: WVa U PO Box 6106 Morgantown WV 26506 E-mail: vmucino@wvu.edu.

MUCKENFUSS, CANTWELL FAULKNER, III, lawyer; b. Montgomery, Ala., Apr. 25, 1945; s. Cantwell F. and Dorothy (Dauphine) M.; m. A. Angela Lancaster, June 25, 1978; children: Alice Paran Lancaster, Cantwell F. IV. BA, Vanderbilt U., 1967; JD, Yale U., 1971. Bar: N.Y. 1973, D.C. 1976. Law clk. to presiding justice U.S. Ct. Appeals (6th cir.), 1971-72; atty., project developer Bedford Stuyvesant D and S Corp., Bklyn., 1972-73; spl. asst. to the dir. FDIC, Washington, 1974-77, counsel to the chmn., 1977-78; sr. dep. comptroller for policy Office of the Comptroller of the Currency, Washington, 1978-81; ptnr. Gibson, Dunn & Crutcher LLP, Washington, 1981—. Mem. editorial adv. bd. Issues in Bank Regulation, Rolling Meadows, Ill., 1977-91, Electronic Banking Law and Commerce Report, 1996—; mem. bd. advisors Rev. Banking and Fin. Svcs., N.Y.C., 1985—; bd. dis. Fair Tax Edn. Fund, Washington, 1987-90. Served with USNG, 1968-70, USAR, 1970-74. Recipient Spl. Achievement award U.S. Dept. Treasury, 1979, Presdl. Rank award

U.S. Govt., 1980. Mem. ABA, Fed. Bar Assn. Clubs: Kenwood Country (Bethesda, Md.); Yale (N.Y.C.). Democrat. Episcopalian. Office: Gibson Dunn & Crutcher LLP 1050 Connecticut Ave NW Ste 900 Washington DC 20036-5306

MUCKENHOUPT, BENJAMIN, retired mathematics educator; b. Newton, Mass., Dec. 22, 1933; s. Carl Frederick and Sarah Joanna (Boell) M.; m. Mary Kathryn Heath, Aug. 29, 1964; children: Margaret, Carl Edward. AB, Harvard U., 1954; MS, U. Chgo., 1955, PhD, 1958. Instr. DePaul U., Chgo., 1958-59, asst. prof. math., 1959-60; faculty Rutgers U., New Brunswick, N.J., 1960-91, prof. math., 1970-91. Vis. assoc. prof. Mt. Holyoke Coll., 1963-65; visitor Inst. Advanced Study, Princeton, N.J., 1968-69, 75-76; vis. prof. SUNY-Albany, 1970-71 Contbr. articles to profl. jours. NSF rsch. grantee, 1965-88; Rutgers Rsch. Coun. fellow, 1968-69. Mem. Am. Math. Soc., Math. Assn. Am., Phi Beta Kappa, Sigma Xi. Home: 196 Woodfern Rd Neshanic Station NJ 08853-4054 E-mail: muckenho@post.harvard.edu.

MUCKERMAN, NORMAN JAMES, priest, writer; b. Webster Groves, Mo., Feb. 1, 1917; s. Oliver Christopher and Edna Gertrude (Hartman) M. BA, Immaculate Conception Coll., 1940, M. in Religious Edn., 1942. Ordained priest Roman Catholic Ch., 1942. Missionary Redemptorist Missions, Amazonas, Para, Brazil, 1943-53, procurator missions St. Louis, 1953-58; pastor, adminstr. St. Alphonsus Ch., Chgo., 1958-67, St. Gerard, Kirkwood, Mo., 1967-71; mktg. mgr. circulation Liguori Pubs., Liguori, Mo., 1971-76; editor Liguorian Mag., Liguori, Mo., 1977-89. Author: How to Face Death Without Fear, 1976, Redemptorists on the Amazon, 1992, Preparation for Death, 1998, Into Your Hands, 2001, From the Heart of St. Alphonsus, 2002; contbg. editor: Liguorian, 1989—95. Recipient Nota Dez award Caixa Fed. Do Para, Brazil, 1958 Mem. Cath. Press Assn. (cons. 1971-95, bd. dirs. 1976-85, pres. 1981-84, St. Francis De Sales award 1985). Avocations: golf, travel, reading. Office Phone: 636-223-1441.

MUDAVANHU, BLESSING, research scientist; b. Harare, Mashonaland, Zimbabwe, May 26, 1971; s. Jackson and Gladys Mudavanhu; m. Mutsa Tongoona, July 22, 1996. BS in Gen. Math. and Stats., U. Zimbabwe, Harare, 1993, BS in Math., 1995; M in Fin. Engring., U. Calif., Berkeley, 2002; MS, U. Wash., 1998, PhD, 2002. Rsch. asst. U. Wash., Seattle, 1996—2001; derivatives quantitative analyst Am. Internat. Group, N.Y.C., 2002—. Fellow U. of Zimbabwe Math. fellow, 1995; scholar Fulbright scholar, U.S. Govt., 1996—98. Mem.: Internat. Assn. for Fin. Engrs., Soc. for Indsl. and Applied Math., Am. Math. Soc., Fulbright Assn. (bd. dirs. Puget Sound chpt. 2000—02).

MUDD, DANIEL H. mortgage company executive; married; 4 children. BA in History, U. Va.; MPA in Econs. and Internat. Affairs, Harvard U. With GE Capital, 1991-99, v.p. bus. devel.; pres., CEO GE Avis Fleet Svcs., Brussels; pres. Asia Pacific GE Capital, 1996-99, pres., CEO, 1999; vice chmn., COO, bd. dirs. Fannie Mae, Washington, 2000—. Officer USMC. Robert Bosch Found. fellow, 1989. Office: Fannie Mae 3900 Wisconsin Ave NW Washington DC 20016-2892

MUDD, JOHN O. lawyer; b. 1943; BA, Cath. U., 1965, MA, 1966; JD, U. Mont., 1973; LLM, Columbia U., 1986; JSD of Law, 1994. Bar: Mont. 1973. Pntr. Mulroney, Delaney, Dalby & Mudd, Missoula, Mont., 1973-79; lectr. U. Mont., Missoula, 1973-74, 75-76, prof. law, dean, 1979-88; ptnr. Garlington, Lohn & Robinson, Missoula, 1988—99; sr. v.p. Providence Svcs., 2000—, also bd. dirs. Pres. Mid-Continent Assn. Law Schs., 1982—83; chmn. bd. dirs. Ascension Health. Editor: Mont. Law Rev., 1972—73. Chmn. Mont. Commn. Future of Higher Edn.; elected Dem. candidate U.S. Senate, 1994; bd. dirs. St. Patrick Hosp., 1985—90. With U.S. Army, 1967—73. Mem.: State Bar Mont., Am. Judicature Soc. (bd. dirs. 1985—89).

MUDD, JOHN PHILIP, lawyer; b. Washington, Aug. 22, 1932; s. Thomas Paul and Frances Mary (Finotti) M.; m. Barbara Eve Sweeney, Aug. 10, 1957; children: Laura, Ellen, Philip, Clare, David. BSS, Georgetown U., 1954; JD, Georgetown Law Center, 1956. Bar: Md. 1956, D.C. 1963, Fla. 1964, Calif. 1973. Pvt. practice, Upper Marlboro, Md., 1956-66; v.p., sec., gen. counsel Deltona Corp., Miami, Fla., 1966-72; sec., gen. counsel Nat. Community Builders, San Diego, 1972-73; gen. counsel Continental Advisers (adviser to Continental Mortgage Investors), 1973-75, sr. v.p., gen. counsel, 1975-80, Am. Hosp. Mgmt. Corp., Miami, 1980-89; legal coord. Amerifirst Bank, Miami, 1989-92; v.p., legal counsel Cartaret Savs. Bank, Morristown, N.J., 1991-93, cons., 1991-92; gen. counsel Golden Glades Hosp., Miami, 1992-93, Bank of N.Am., Miami, 1994—. Gen. counsel Golden Glades Hosp., Miami, 1992-93; cons. FSLIC, 1988-89, J.E. Robert Cos., Alexandria, Va., 1988-89, Real Estate Recovery, Inc., Boca Raton, Fla., 1991-92, Bank N.Am., Ft. Lauderdale, Fla., 1992; dir. Unitower Mortgage Corp., Miami, Fla.; dir. Unitower Mortgage Corp., Miami; pres. Marquette Realty Corp., Miami. Former mem. Land Devel. Adv. Com. N.Y. State; chmn. student interview com. Georgetown U.; bd. dirs. Lasalle High Sch., Miami; corp. counsel Com. of Dade County, Fla.; trustee Golden Glades Gen. Hosp., Miami, Fla., 1992—, gen. counsel, 1991—, Bank of North Am., Miami, 1992—. Mem. Fla. Bar Assn., Calif. Bar Assn., Md. Bar Assn., D.C. Bar Assn., Fla. State Bar (exec. com. on corp. counsel com.). Democrat. Roman Catholic. Home: 607 Velarde Ave Coral Gables FL 33134-7044 Office: Bank of North Am Golden Glades Med Plz 8701 SW 137th Ave Ste 301 Miami FL 33183-4498

MUDD, ROGER HARRISON, news broadcaster, educator; b. Washington, Feb. 9, 1928; s. Kostka and Irma Iris (Harrison) M.; m. Emma Jeanne Spears, Oct. 26, 1957; children: Daniel H., Maria M., Jonathan, Matthew M. AB, Washington and Lee U., 1950; MA, U. N.C., 1953. Tchr. Darlington Sch., Rome, Ga., 1951-52; reporter Richmond News Leader, Va., 1953; news dir. Sta. WRNL, Richmond, 1953-56; reporter radio and TV Sta. WTOP, Washington, 1956-61; corr. CBS, 1961-80; chief Washington corr. NBC, 1980-87; Congl. corr. MacNeil/Lehrer News Hour, 1987-92; prof. journalism Princeton U., 1992-94, Washington & Lee U., 1995-96. Host The History Channel, 1995—. Trustee Randolph-Macon Women's Coll., Lynchburg, Va., 1971-78, Robert F. Kennedy Journalism Awards Com., 1971-78, Blue Ridge Sch., Dyke, Va., 1978-84; bd. dirs. Fund for Investigative Journalism, PEN/Faulkner, 1985-92, Va. Found. for Humanities, Va. Hist. Soc., 1988-94, RIAS Berlin Commn., 1996-99, Va. Found. for Ind. Colls., 1997—, Nat. Portrait Gallery Commn., 1997—, Civil War Trust, 1999-01; mem. adv. com. Mt. Vernon Ladies Assn., Eudora Welty Found., 2002—; bd. dirs. Media Gen., 1998-01. With AUS, 1945-47. Mem. Radio-TV Corr. Assn. (chmn. exec. com. 1969-70), Am. Antiquarian Soc.

MUDD, SIDNEY PETER, former beverage company executive; b. St. Louis, Jan. 21, 1917; s. Urban Sidney and Hallie Newell (Perry) M.; m. Ada Marie Herbermann, Oct. 22, 1942; children: Sidney Peter, Ada Marie, Peter, Michael, Mary, Elizabeth, Catherine. AB magna cum laude, St. Louis U., 1938; L.H.D., Coll. New Rochelle, N.Y., 1974; LHD, Iona Coll., 1985. Distr. Joyce Seven-Up, Chgo., 1938, sales mgr., 1939, coordinator N.Y. ops., 1941, v.p. charge ops., 1949-51; exec. v.p. N.Y. Seven-Up Bottling Co., Inc., New Rochelle, 1951-63, pres., 1963-73, dir., 1952-84, chmn. bd., 1973-84; pres. Joyce Beverages, Inc. (Joyce Advt.), 1973-84; past chmn. bd. Joyce Beverages/N.Y., N.J., Conn., Ill., Wis. Past dir. Joyce Beverages Inc., Joyce Advt., Joyce Beverages/N.Y., N.J., Conn., Chgo., Washington, Wis., Ill., Joyce Assocs.; dir., vice-chmn. Westchester Fed. Savs. Bank; bd. dirs. Marine Midland Bank Regional Bd., chmn. 1987-88. Past pres., bd. trustees St. Joseph's Hosp., N.Y.C., St. Francis Hosp.; chmn. Westchester County Assn.; past bd. lay advisers St. Agnes Hosp., White Plains; past chmn. bd. trustees Coll. of New Rochelle; past bd. dirs. U.S. Cath. Hist. Soc.; former trustee St. Louis U.; bd. dirs., v.p. John M. and Mary A. Joyce Found.; chmn. N.Y. Industry-Labor Com. for Resource Recovery; bd. dirs. Am. Alliance Resource Recovery Interests, Westchester Pub. Issues Inst., 2001-; pres. New Rochelle Devel. Council; bd. dirs. Keep Am. Beautiful, Inc.; chmn. Westchester 2000, 1984-2000. Served with USNR. Decorated Knight of Malta, knight Equestrian Order of Holy Sepulchre; recipient St. Louis U. Alumni award, 1967, Dr. Martin Luther King, Jr. award New Rochelle Community Action Agy., 1978, New Rochelle K.C. Civic award, 1978, Outstanding Citizen award New Rochelle YMCA, 1979, Disting. Service award Westchester region NCCJ, 1980, Medallion award Westchester Community Coll. Found., 1981; honoring resolution N.Y. State Senate, 1982; honoring resolution N.Y. State Assembly, 1982; honoring proclamation County of Westchester, City of Yonkers, City of White Plains, 1982; ARC award of excellence, 1983, Man of Yr. award Beverage Industry, 1974, Disting. Service award Sr. Personnel Employment Council, 1986, Disting. Achievement award Mental Health Assn., 1987, Disting. Citizen award New Rochelle Hosp. Med. Ctr., 1990; named to St. Louis U. Sports Hall of Fame, 1976, Beverage World Hall of Fame, 1984. Mem. Nat. Soft Drink Assn. (dir., pres. 1974-76, Disting. Achievement award 1980), N.Y. State Soft Drink Assn. (pres. 1966-67, Disting. Service award 1985, 86), Theta Kappa Phi, Crown and Anchor Soc. (St. Louis U.), Westchester County Assn. (Chmn.'s award 2002). Clubs: Winged Foot Golf (Westchester) (founder, past v.p., dir.); Sales and Mktg. Execs. *A happy life, a successful life is a life lived in love; love of God; love of self, love of others. To love and be loved is life's greatest reward on earth.*

MUDGE, LEWIS SEYMOUR, theologian, educator, university dean; b. Phila., Oct. 22, 1929; s. Lewis Seymour and Anne Evelyn (Bolton) M.; m. Jean Bruce McClure, June 15, 1957; children: Robert Seymour, William McClure, Anne Evelyn. BA, Princeton U., 1951, M Div, 1955, PhD (Kent fellow), 1961; BA with honors in Theology, Oxford (Eng.) U., 1954, MA (Rhodes scholar), 1958. Ordained to ministry Presbyn. Ch., 1955. Presbyn. univ. pastor Princeton, 1955-56; sec. dept. theology World Alliance Ref. Chs., Geneva, 1957-62; minister to coll. Amherst Coll., 1962-68, asst. prof. philosophy and religion, 1962-64, assoc. prof., 1964-70, prof. philosophy and religion, 1970-76, chmn. dept. philosophy and religion, 1968-69, 75-76; dean faculty, prof. theology McCormick Theol. Sem., Chgo., 1976-87, San Francisco Theol. Sem., 1987—; prof. Grad. Theol. Union, Berkeley, Calif., 1987-95; dir. Ctr. for Hermeneutical Studies, Grad. Theol. Union/U. Calif., Berkeley, 1990-97; Stuart prof. theology Grad. Theol. Union, Berkeley, Calif., 1995—. Mem. commn. on faith and order Nat. Council Chs., 1965-70; sec. spl. com. on confession faith United Presbyn Ch., 1965-67, chmn. spl. com. on theology of the call, 1968-71; chmn. theol. commn. U.S. Consultation on Ch. Union, 1977-89; co-chmn. Internat. Ref.-Roman Cath. Dialogue Commn., 1983-90; observer Extraordinary Synod Bishops, 1985. Author: One Church: Catholic and Reformed, 1963, Is God Alive?, 1963, Why is the Church in the World?, 1967, The Crumbling Walls, 1970, The Sense of a People: Toward a Church for the Human Future, 1992, The Church as Moral Community, 1998, Rethinking the Beloved Community, 2001; also numerous articles and revs.; editor: Essays on Biblical Interpretation (Paul Ricoeur), 1980, (with James Poling) Formation and Reflection: the Promise of Practical Theology, 1987, (with Thomas Wieser) Democratic Contracts for Sustainable and Caring Societies, 2000. Pres. Westminster Found. in New Eng., 1963-67; chmn. bd. Nat. Vocation Agy., 1972-75; mem. com. selection Rhodes Scholars, Vt., 1966, Wis., 1983-85, Iowa, 1986. Mem. Phi Beta Kappa. Democrat. Home: 2444 Hillside Ave Berkeley CA 94704-2529 Office: Grad Theol Union 2905 Dwight Way Berkeley CA 94704-2514 E-mail: lewismudge@comcast.net.

MUDRY, MICHAEL, pension and benefit consultant; b. Lucina, Czechoslovakia, Dec. 5, 1926; (parents Am. citizens); s. John Zaleta and Helen (Molchan) M.; m. Kendall Archer, June 17, 1960; children: F. Goodrich Archer, Benjamin Kendall. BA, U. Conn., 1951. Sr. v.p. Hay/Huggins Co. Inc., Phila., 1956-93; self-employed pension and benefit cons. Wayne, Pa., 1994—. Former actuary Ch. Pensions Conf. Contbr. articles to profl. jours. Bd. mem., actuary Am. Coun. on Gift Annuities, Indpls., 1978—. Served with U.S. Army, 1945-46. Fellow: Conf. Cons. Actuaries, Soc. Actuaries; mem.: Internat. Assn. Cons. Actuaries, Internat. Actuarial Assn., Am. Acad. Actuaries, Tri-State Jazz Soc. (bd. dirs. 2001—, treas. 2001—).

MUECKE, CHARLES ANDREW (CARL MUECKE), former federal judge; b. N.Y.C., Feb. 20, 1918; s. Charles and Wally (Roeder) M.; m. Claire E. Vasse; children by previous marriage: Carl Marshall, Alfred Jackson, Catherine Calvert. BA, Coll. William and Mary, 1941; LL.B., U. Ariz., 1953. Bar: Ariz. 1953. Rep. AFL, 1947-50; reporter Ariz. Times, Phoenix, 1947-48; since practiced in Phoenix; with firm Parker & Muecke, 1953-59, Muecke, Dushoff & Sacks, 1960-61; U.S. atty. Dist. Ariz., 1961-64, U.S. dist. judge, 1964—97, sr. judge, 1984—97. Mem. Phoenix Planning Commn., 1955-61, chmn., 1960; chmn. Maricopa County Dem. Party, 1961-62. Maj. USMC, 1942-45, USMCR, 1945-60. Mem. Fed. Bar Assn., Ariz. Bar Assn., Maricopa Bar Assn., Dist. Judges Assn. Ninth Circuit, Phi Beta Kappa, Phi Alpha Delta, Omicron Delta Kappa.

MUEGGE, LYN, advertising executive; CFO, exec. v.p. Publicis & Hal Riney (formerly Hal Riney & Ptnrs. Inc.), San Francisco. Office: Publicis & Hal Riney 2001 The Embarcadero San Francisco CA 94133-5200*

MUEGGLER, ERIK, anthropologist, educator; BA, Cornell U., 1987; MA, Johns Hopkins U., 1990, PhD, 1996. Faculty mem., dept. anthropology U. of Mich., assoc. prof., 2001—. Author: (book) The Age of Wild Ghosts; contbr. articles in The Jour. of Asian Studies, Cultural Anthropology, Modern China. Grantee Advanced Study in China grant, NAS, 1991, fellowship, NEH, 1996. Office: U of Mich Dept of Anthropology Rm 1020 L S & A Bldg 500 S State St Ann Arbor MI 48109-1382

MUEHLBAUER, JAMES HERMAN, manufacturing executive; b. Evansville, Ind., Nov. 13, 1940; s. Herman Joseph and Anna Louise (Overfield) M.; m. Mary Kay Koch, June 26, 1965; children: Stacey, Brad, Glen, Beth, Katy. BSME, Purdue U., 1963, MS Indsl. Adminstrn., 1964. Registered profl. engr., Ind., 1970. Engr. George Koch Sons, Inc., Evansville, 1966-67, chief estimator, 1968-72, chief engr., 1973-74, v.p., 1975-81, dir., 1978—, exec. v.p., 1982-98, Koch Ent., Inc., 1999—; pres. George Koch Sons LLC, 1999—2003, chmn., 2003—04; pres. Koch Air LLC, 2003—. V.p., bd. dirs. Brake Supply Co., Evansville, Gibbs Die Casting Corp., Henderson, Ky., Uniseal, Inc., Evansville; bd. dirs. Fifth Third Bank Indiana, George Koch Sons (Europe) Ltd., Lichfield, Eng., Red Spot Paint & Varnish Co., Inc., Evansville, George Koch Sons de Mex., Monterrey, George Koch Sons GmbH, Cologne. Co-author: Tool & Manufacturing Engineering Handbook, 1976; patentee in paint finishing equipment. Bd. dirs., past pres. Evansville Indsl. Found., 1980—; bd. dirs., past pres., past campaign chmn. United Way S.W. Ind., Evansville, 1983—; bd. dirs., past vice-chmn. Univ. So. Ind. Found., Evansville, 1988-2001; bd. dirs. Deaconess Hosp., Evansville, 1986—, treas., 1991-96, vice-chmn., 1999-2003, chmn., 2003-; bd. dirs. Cath. Found. Southwestern Ind., 1998-2004 dir. bd. visitors U. So. Ind. Sch. Bus., 1997—, chmn., 2001-02; bd. dirs. Ind. Assn. United Ways, 2000—, Alliance Indpls., 1993-2004, pres. 1999; mem. Brute Soc., Cath. Diocese Evansville, 1997, Equestrian Order of the Holy Sepulchre of Jerusalem, 1996—. Named Engr. of Yr. S.W. chpt. Ind. Soc. Profl. Engrs., 1983; recipient Tech. Achievement award Tri-State Coun. for Sci. and Engring., Evansville, 1984, Purdue U. Alumni Citizenship award, 1991. Mem. Soc. Mfg. Engrs. (past nat. chmn. finishing and coating tech. divsn.), ASME, NSPE, Evansville Country Club, Evansville Petroleum Club, Evansville Kennel Club (bd. dirs. 1997-2001). Republican. Roman Catholic. Home: 2300 E Gum St Evansville IN 47714-2338 Office: Koch Enterprises 14 S 11th Ave Evansville IN 47744-0001 Office Phone: 812-962-5260. E-mail: jhm@kochllc.com., jmuealbauer@kochair.com.

MUEHLEISEN, GENE, retired protective services administrator, state official; b. San Diego, Dec. 28, 1915; s. Adolph and Vesta C. (Gates) M.; m. Elsie Jane Conover, Sept. 14, 1940 (dec. Mar. 17, 1999); 1 son, John Robert. Student, San Diego State Coll., 1935—39, San Diego Jr. Coll., 1957. U.S. pk. ranger Yosemite Nat. Pk., summers 1936-39, 79-84; with San Diego Police Dept., 1940-60, dir. tng., 1957-59, commdg. officer patrol divsn., capt., 1958-60; exec. dir. Commn. on Peace Officer Stds. and Tng., Calif. Dept. Justice, Sacramento, 1960-65, 67-76; assoc. dir. Pres.'s Commn. on Law Enforcement and Adminstrn. of Justice, Nat. Crime Commn., 1965-67; chmn. police sci. adv. com. San Diego Jr. Coll., 1957-60, police sci. faculty, 1957-60; staff instr. San Diego Police Acad., 1954-60; guest instr. police adminstrn. Sacramento State Coll., 1964; grad. FBI Nat. Acad. 51st Session, 1953, pres. of class, guest faculty, 1963-66; cons. Ford Found. Internat. Assn. Chiefs of Police Project, 1964-67. Cons. U.S. Nat. Pk. Svc., 1965-84, spl. asst. to regional dir. Western region, 1977-79; adviser Royal Can. Mounted Police, 1961—; guest lectr., 1960—. U.S. rep. Interpol Symposium on Police Edn. and Tng., Paris, 1965; mem. adv. com. FBI, 1972—; vice-chmn. Calif. Commn. Peace Officer Stds. and Tng., 1959—60; chmn. police svcs. task force Calif. Coun. Criminal Justice, 1968—78; mem. Atty. Gen.'s Commn. Police and Cmty. Rels., 1971—, Gov.'s Pub. Safety Planning Coun., 1974—; bd. dirs. San Diego Hist. Soc.; chmn. Atty. Gen.'s Com. on Law Enforcement Stds., 1957—59; mem. adv. com. on police tng. Ford Found., 1964—. Active duty USN, 1940—45, WWII, capt. USNR, 1940—75. The Gene Muehleisen Nature Area, Valley Oak Pk., Sacramento dedicated, 1992. Mem. Nat. Conf. Police Assns. (com. chmn.), Calif. Peace Officers Assn. (com. chmn.), Peace Officers Rsch. Assn. Calif. (pres. 1959-60, com. chmn.), Am. Soc. Pub. Adminstrn. (dir. San Diego County chpt.), Nat. Assn. State Dirs. Law Enforcement Tng. (pres. 1972-73), Am. Corrections Assn., Calif. Assn. Adminstrn. of Justice Educators, Pk. Rangers Assn. of Calif., Internat. Police Assn. (life, v.p. region 29 USA), Internat. Assn. Chiefs of Police (life), Calif. Pks. and Recreation Soc. (Citizen of Yr. 1992), Sacramento Tree Found. (tech. adv. com. 1983—), Kiwanis, San Diego Ski Club (founder, pres.). Home and Office: 4221 Corona Way Sacramento CA 95864-5301

MUEHLNER, SUANNE WILSON, library director; b. Rochester, Minn., June 29, 1943; d. George T. and Rhoda (Westin) Wilson. Student Smith Coll., 1961-63; A.B., U. Calif.-Berkeley, 1965; M.L.S., Simmons Coll., 1968; M.B.A., Northeastern U., Boston, 1979. Librarian, Technische Univ. Berlin, Germany, 1970-71; earth and planetary scis. librarian MIT Libraries, Cambridge, 1968-70, 1971-73; personnel librarian, 1973-74, asst. dir. personnel services, 1974-76, asst. dir. pub. services, 1976-81; dir. libraries Colby Coll., Waterville, Maine, 1981—. Mem. ALA, New Eng. Assn. Coll. and Research Librarians (sec.-treas. 1983-85, pres. 1986-87), Maine Libr. Assn. (chmn. intellectual freedom com. 1984-88, OCLC Users Coun., 1988-95), Nelinet (bd. dirs. 1985-91, chair 1989-91). Office: Colby Coll Miller Libr Waterville ME 04901

MUELLER, ANNE, legislator; b. Atlanta, Oct. 5, 1929; d. Howard Raymond O'Quin and Bessie Kate (Bell) Brace; m. Hans Kurt Mueller, June 22, 1953; children: Yvonne Marie Key, Heidi Spivey, Mark Jennings. BS in Zoology, U. Ga., 1951. Registered med. technologist. Med. technologist Grady Hosp., Atlanta, 1953—, St. Joseph Hosp., Atlanta, 1957, Meml. Hosp., Waycross, Ga., 1958-59; legislator Ga. Ho. of Reps., 1983—. Mem. Savannah (Ga.) area Rep. Women, sec., 1980-81, v.p., 1981-82, Ga. Fedn. of Rep. Women, Savannah, dist. dir., 1986—. Republican. Baptist. Home: 13013 Hermitage Rd Savannah GA 31419-2840 Office: GA House of Reps State Capitol Atlanta GA 30334-9003

MUELLER, BETTY JEANNE, social work educator; b. Wichita, Kans., July 7, 1925; d. Bert C. and Clara A. (Pelton) Judkins; children— Michael J., Madelynn J. MSSW, U. Wis., Madison, 1964, PhD, 1969. Asst. prof. U. Wis., Madison, 1969-72; vis. asso. prof. Bryn Mawr (Pa.) Coll., 1971-72; asso. prof., dir. social work Cornell U., Ithaca, N.Y., 1972-78, prof. human svcs. studies, 1979-96, prof. policy and mgmt., 1996-98, prof. emeritus, 1998—. Nat. cons. Head Start, Follow Through, Appalachian Regional Commn., N.Y. State Office Planning Svcs., N.Y. State Dept. Social Svcs., N.Y. State Divsn. Mental Hygiene, Nat. Congress PTA, ILO; mem. internat. adv. com. Family Resources Tng. Ctr., Singapore, 1999—. Author: (with H. Morgan) Social Services in Early Education, 1974, (with R. Reinoehl) Computers in Human Service Education, 1989, Determinants of Human Behavior, 1995; contbr. articles to profl. jours. Recipient Fulbright Rsch. award, 1990; grantee, HEW, 1974—76, 1979—80, State of N.Y., 1975—95, Israeli Jewish Agy., 1985—87. Mem. Leadership Am., Chi Omega. Democrat. Unitarian Universalist. Home: 412 Highland Rd Ithaca NY 14850-2216 Office: Cornell U Policy and Mgmt 108 MVR Hall Ithaca NY 14853 Business E-Mail: bjm5@cornell.edu.

MUELLER, CARL RICHARD, theater arts educator, author; b. St. Louis, Oct. 7, 1931; s. Anton John and Bonita Blanche (Lacy) M. BS, Northwestern U., 1954; MA, UCLA, 1960, PhD, 1967; cert., Freie U., Berlin, 1961. Prof. theater dept. Sch. Theater, Film and Television UCLA, 1967—; dramaturg New Theatre, Inc., L.A., 1975-2000. Cons. U. Calif. Press, 1972—. Translator plays published include Buechner: Complete Plays and Prose, 1963, Brecht: The Visions of Simone Machard, 1965, Brecht: The Measures Taken, 1977, Hauptmann: The Weavers, 1965, Hebbel: Maria Magdalena, 1962, Strindberg: A Dream Play and The Ghost Sonata, 1966, Strindberg: Five Major Plays, 2000, Schnitzler: La Ronde and Game of Love, 1964, Hofmannsthal: Electra, 1964, Wedekind: The Marquis of Keith, 1964, Wedekind: The Lulu Plays, 1967, Wedekind: Four Major Plays, 2000, Zuckmayer: The Captain of Koepenick, 1972, Horváth: Tales from the Vienna Woods, 1998, Schnitzler: Four Major Plays, 1999, Sophocles: The Complete Plays, 2000, Pirandello: Three Major Plays, 2000, Kleist: Three Major Plays, 2000, Wedekind: Four Plays, vol. 2, 2002, Strindberg: Five Major Plays, vol. 2, 2002, Aeschylus: The Complete Plays, vol. 1, Oresteia, 2002, Aeschylus: The Complete Plays, vol. 2, Four Plays, 2002, Goethe: Faust, 2004; translator plays produced include Anon: The Puppet Play of Dr. Johannes Faustus, Hauptmann: The Beaver Coat, Schnitzler: Dr. Bernhardi, Schnitzler: Anatol, Sternheim: The Underpants, Brecht: Mother Courage, Brecht: Caucasian Chalk Circle, Brecht: The Trial of Joan of Arc, Brecht: In the Jungle of Cities, Brecht: Man is Man, Brecht: He Who Says Yes, Brecht: He Who Says No, Brecht: The Exception and the Rule, Brecht: Round Heads, Peaked Heads, Brecht: Schweyk in the Second World War, Kleist: The Broken Jug, 1992, Lessing: Nathan the Wise, 1993, Toller, The Blind Goddess, 1993, Sophokles, Elektra, 1994, Zweig, Volpone, 1995, Sternheim, The Snob, 1996; gen. editor Visual Resources, Inc., 1976-2000; theater editor Mankind mag., 1975-82; editor New Theater/Teatro Nuevo, 1985-87; author catalogue and slides A Visual History of European Theater Arts, 1978, A Visual History of European Experimental Theater, 1983, Greek and Roman Classical Theatre Structures and Performance Iconography, 1991, Medieval Theater and Performance Iconography, 1991, The Theater of Meyerhold, 1992, Stanislavsky and the Moscow Art Theater, 1992, The Commedia dell'Arte, 1992, Russian Scene and Costume Design, vols. 1 and 2, 1993, The Baroque Stage, 1993, 18th and 19th Cen. European Theater Structures, Performance Iconography and Costume Designs, 1994, Renaissance Theater Structures, Performance Iconography and Costume Designs, 1994, The Genius of the Russian Theatre 1900-1990, 1995, 20th Century World Theater, From Appia to Dali, 1900-50, vol. 1, 1996, 20th Century World Theater, From Mother Courage to Hair, 1951-68, vol. 2, 1996, 20th Century World Theater, From Svoboda to Hockney, 1968-91, vol. 3, 1996, The Genius of the Russian Theater, From Meyerhold to the Present, 1996, Contemporary European Experimental Theater, vol. 1, Italy and Germany, 1996, The Classical Experience: The Greek Theater and Its World, 1996, The Classical Experience: The Roman Theater and Its World, 1996; dir.: (plays) Spring's Awakening, Endangered Species, Hedda Gabler, My Body, Frankly Yours, Hamlet, Macbeth, Dionysos. Served with U.S. Army, 1954-56. Recipient Samuel Goldwyn Creative Writing award Goldwyn Found., 1959; Fulbright exchange grantee Berlin, 1960-61 Mem. Internat. Arthur Schnitzler Research Assn., UCLA Center for Medieval and Renaissance Studies (mem. adv. com. 1980-83) Democrat. Office: UCLA Dept Theater Sch Theater Film TV 102 E Melnitz Box 951622 Los Angeles CA 90095-1622 E-mail: cmueller@tft.ucla.edu. *Communication has always been the primary goal of my life. The challenge of passing on to generations of new students the life sustaining ideas of human culture is formidable; the joy of searching out new ideas and methods of thought and action is a privilege of which far too few of us take proper advantage.*

MUELLER, CHARLES BARBER, surgeon, educator; b. Carlinville, Ill., Jan. 22, 1917; s. Gustav Henry and Myrtle May (Barber) M.; m. Jean (Mahaffey), Sept. 7, 1940; children: Frances Ann, John Barber, Richard Carl, William Gustav. BA, U. Ill., 1938; MD, Washington U., St. Louis, 1942; LHD (hon.), Blackburn Coll., 1987; DSC (hon.), State Univ. of N.Y., Syracuse, 2002; DSc (hon.), McMaster U., 2003. Intern, then resident in surgery Barnes Hosp., St. Louis, 1942-43, 46-51; asst. prof. Wash. U. Med. Sch., 1951-56; prof. surgery, chmn. dept. State Univ. of N.Y. Med. Sch., Syracuse, 1956-67; prof. surgery Mc Master U. Med. Sch., Hamilton, Canada, 1967—, chmn. dept., 1967-72. Contbr. articles to profl. journals. Served in USNR, 1943—46. Decorated Purple Heart with 2 oak leaf clusters, Bronze Star; recipient

Favorite Son Award So. Ill. Med. Soc., 1996; Jackson Johnson fellow, 1938-42; Rockefeller post war asst., 1946-49; Markle scholar, 1949-54. Mem. ACS (v.p. 1987-88, Disting. Svc. Award 1984), Am. Surg. Assn., Ctrl. Surg. Assn., Soc. Univ. Surgeons, Assn. Acad. Surgery, Royal Coll. Physicians and Surgeons (Duncan Graham Disting. Svc. Award 1992), Phi Beta Kappa, Sigma Xi, Alpha Omega Alpha, Phi Kappa Phi. E-mail: cbarbermueller@cogeco.ca.

MUELLER, CHARLES FREDERICK, radiologist, educator; b. Dayton, Ohio, May 26, 1936; s. Susan Elizabeth (Wine) W.; m. Kathe Louise Lutterbei, May 28, 1966; children: Charles Jeffrey, Theodore Martin, Kathryn Suzanne. BA in English, U. Cin., 1958, MD, 1962. Diplomate Am. Bd. Radiology, Am. Bd. Nuclear Medicine. Asst. prof. radiology U. N.Mex., Albuquerque, 1968-72, assoc. prof. radiology, 1972-74, Ohio State U., Columbus, 1974-79, acting chmn. dept. radiology, 1975, prof. radiology, 1979—2002, prof. radiology, dir. post grad. program radiology, 1980-2000, acting chmn. dept. radiology, 1990—93, prof. emeritus, 2002—. Bd. dirs. Univ. Radiologists, Inc., Columbus, v.p., 1980—86; pres., founder Ambulatory Imaging, Inc., Columbus, 1985—2002. Author: Emergency Radiology, 1982; contbr. articles to profl. jours.; editl. bd. Emergency radiology, 1995-2002; editor Internat. Trauma, Am. Jour. Roentgenology, 1997-2004. Com. chmn. Boy Scouts Am., Columbus, 1980—84; vol. Columbus Free Clinic, 2003, Franklin Park Conservatory, 2003—. Research grantee Ohio State U. 1975, Gen. Electric Co., 1986-88; Gold medalist ASER, 2001. Fellow Am. Coll. Radiologists; mem. AMA, Assn. Univ. Radiologists, Am. Roentgen Ray Soc., Am. Soc. Emergency Radiology (founder 1988, pres. 1993-94, Gold medal 2001), Radiol. Soc. N.Am., N.Mex. Soc. Radiologists (pres. 1973-74), Ohio State Radiol. Soc. (pres. 1986-87). Republican. Presbyterian. Avocations: flying, fly fishing, hiking. Office: Ohio State Univ Hosps Dept Radiology 410 W 10th Ave Columbus OH 43210-1240

MUELLER, CHARLES WILLIAM, electric utility executive; b. Belleville, Ill., Nov. 29, 1938; s. Charles A. and Clara R. (Jorn) M.; m. Janet Therese Vernier, July 9, 1960; children: Charles R., Michael G., Craig J. BSEE, St. Louis U., 1961, MBA, 1966. Registered profl. engr., Mo., Ill. Engr. Union Electric Co., St. Louis, 1961-75, supervisory engr., 1975-77, asst. dir. corp. planning, 1977-78, treas., 1978-83, v.p. fin., 1983-88, sr. v.p. adminstrv. svcs., 1988-93; pres., CEO Ameren Corp., St. Louis, 1994-98, pres., CEO, chmn., 1998—. Dep. chmn. The Fed. Res. Bank of St. Louis; chmn. bd. Webster U.; bd. dirs. Electric Energy Inc., Regional Commerce and Growth Assn., Edison Electric Inst., Angelica Corp., United Way of Greater St. Louis, BJC Health Sys., Kiel Ctr. Corp.; dir. Assn. of Edison Illuminating Cos., St. Louis Children's Hosp., St. Louis Sci. Ctr., Civic Progress, The Mcpl. Theatre Assn. Mem. IEEE, Mo. Athletic Club, St. Clair Country Club, The Bogey Club, Saint Louis Club. Avocations: tennis, boating, travel. Office: Ameren Corp 1901 Chouteau Ave Saint Louis MO 63103-3003

MUELLER, CHERONE, religious organization administrator, writer, minister; b. The Dalles, Oreg. Diploma in Acctg., diploma in Bus. Mgmt., Chemeketa Coll., Oreg., 1984; DD (hon.), World Christianship Ministries, Calif., 2002. Ordained Minister World Christianship Ministries, 2002. Founder Cherone Faith Ministry, Jacksonville, 1999—, pres., CEO, 2000—. Ordained min. A Call to Worship Ch., Jacksonville, 2001—. Author: (book) At San Jose Make a Left, Dancing Around the Throne, (poetry) Dream Away (Editors Choice award Internat. Libr. Poets, 2002, 2004), You Have Done it Before-You Will Do it Again (Best Poet and Poem of 2001), Sands of Time (Best Poet and Poem of 2002), Walking In The Rain, (poem) Side By Side (Best Poem, 1986), Jesus, You Are My Lord, 2003, Keep A Hold of His Hand (Best Poem/Poet, 2003), When Life Is In a Turmoil, 2003 (Best Poem & Poet award, 2003). V.p. singles group Salem UPC, 1983—91, choir, 1982—91, treas. ladies aux., 1984—90, v.p. Singles Group, 1983—91; nursery caregiver First UPC, Jacksonville, 1995—97; Sunday sch. tchr. Christ Ch. Jacksonville, 1997—98, praise singer, fellowship coord., 1997—2001; dir. 'daughters of zion' (praying for our children) UPC Internat., Jacksonville, 1999—2001. Named Pastor of the Month, Radio WAYR, Jacksonville, Fla. June, 2003; recipient Editor's Choice award for outstanding achievement in poetry, Internat. Libr. of Poetry, 2001, 2002, 2003, 2004. Master: World Christianship Ministries (licentiate; rev. 2002). Avocations: sewing, cooking, crocheting, sign language, drawing. Office: Cherone Faith Ministry PO Box 47077 Jacksonville FL 32247-7077 Personal E-mail: cheronefaith@mail.com.

MUELLER, DIANE, hotel executive; m. Tim Mueller; children: Ethan, Erica. V.p., co-owner Okemo Mountain Resort, Ludlow, Vt., 1982—. Mem. Vt. State Bd. Edn., 1998—, chmn., 2003—; past mem. Green Mountain Union H.S. Bd., Chester; founder Okemo Cmty. Challenge. Named Citizen of the Yr., Vt. C. of C., 2001. Office: Okemo Mountain Resort 77 Okemo Ridge Rd Ludlow VT 05149

MUELLER, EDWARD ALBERT, retired transportation engineer executive; b. Madison, Wis., May 12, 1923; s. Edward F. and Lulu (Wittl) M.; m. Margaret Wetzel, Sept. 12, 1953; children: Lynn, Karen. Student, U. Wis., 1941-43; BCE, Notre Dame U., 1947; cert. in traffic, Yale U., 1953, postgrad., 1952—53, Fla. State U., 1955-62; MCE, Catholic U. Am., 1967. Registered profl. engr., Fla. Project engr. Carl C. Crane, Inc., 1947-50; engr. Ammann & Whitney, Inc., Milw., 1950-52; rsch. asst. Yale U., 1953-55; asst. dir., dir. traffic and planning div. Fla. State Rd. Dept., Tallahassee, 1955-63; engr. traffic and ops. Transp. Rsch. Bd., Washington, 1963-70; sec. Fla. Dept. Transp., Tallahassee, 1970-72; exec. dir. Jacksonville (Fla.) Transp. Authority, 1972-80; mgr. transp. div. Reynolds, Smith & Hills, 1980-83; v.p. Morales and Shumer Engrs., Inc., 1983-95. Occasional lectr. U. Fla., 1971-76, U. N.Fla., 1974-76 Author: Steamboating on the St. Johns, 1979, Ocklawaha River Steamboats, 1983, St. Johns River Steamboats, 1986, Perilous Journeys, 1990, Upper Mississippi River Ratting Steamboats, 1995, Steamships of the Two Henrys, 1996, Along the St. Johns and Ocklawaha River, 1999, Queen of Sea Routes, 2000, The Savannah Line, 2001; contbr. engrng. articles to profl. jours. Mem. Fla. Com. of 100, 1970-72; bd. dirs. Luth. Social Svcs., Jacksonville, 1982-94, v.p., 1981-91; regional v.p. Fla.-Ga. dist. Luth. Laymen's League, 1982-92; curator Jacksonville Maritime Mus., 1990-99, mem. exec. com., 1989-95, pres., 1993-95, exec. dir., 1995-99. Recipient Disting. Svc. award Coll. Engring., U. Fla., 1975, Samuel Ward Stanton award for life achievement Steamship Hist. Soc. Am., 2001; named one of top 10 pub. works ofcls. in U.S., 1978. Mem. Southeastern Assn. State Hwy. Ofcls. (pres., v.p. 1971-72), Engrs. in Govt. (chmn., vice-chmn. sec.), Fla. Engring. Soc. (pres. Northeast chpt. 1982-83, Engr. of Yr. Tallahassee chpt. 1972, Jacksonville chpt. 1974, award for outstanding tech. achievement 1976, outstanding svc. to engring. profession 1989, James Shivler award 1993), Inst. Transp. Engrs. (pres. 1977, disting. svc. award Fla. sect. 1976), Fla. Transit Assn. (pres. 1974-75), Fla. Engring. Found. (sec. 1986-95). Lutheran. Home: 4734 Empire Ave Jacksonville FL 32207-2136 E-mail: eamu27@hotmail.com.

MUELLER, GARY ALFRED, software engineer; b. Denver, Oct. 6, 1950; s. Alfred Henry and Verna Mae (Ashmore) M. BS in Mineral Engring. Physics, Colo. Sch. Mines, 1972, BS in Mineral Engring. Math., 1973; BSEE and Computer Sci. with honors, U. Colo., Denver, 1975; MSEE, U. Colo., Boulder, 1995. Registered profl. engr., Colo. Computer programmer, mathematician U.S. Geol. Survey, Denver, 1977-81; mem. tech. staff AT&T Bell Labs., Denver, 1982-84; adv. software engr. Storage Tech. Corp., Louisville, Colo., 1985—2001; cons., 2002—. Mem.: Assn. for Computing Machinery, IEEE (sr.), Tau Beta Pi, Kappa Mu Epsilon, Eta Kappa Nu.

MUELLER, GERHARD G(OTTLOB), retired financial accounting standard setter, retired educator; b. Eineborn, Germany, Dec. 4, 1930; came to U.S., 1952, naturalized, 1957; s. Gottlob Karl and Elisabeth Charlotte (Hossack) M.; m. Coralie George, June 7, 1958; children: Kent, Elisabeth, Jeffrey. AA, Coll. of Sequoias, 1954; BS with honors, U. Calif.-Berkeley, 1956, MBA, 1957, PhD, 1962; D Econs. (hon.), Swedish Sch. Econs. and Bus. Adminstrn., 1994; D Laws (hon.), Kwansei Gakuin U., 2000. CPA (ret.), Wash. Staff acct. FMC Corp., San Jose, Calif., 1957-58; faculty dept. acctg. U. Wash., Seattle, 1960-96, assoc. prof., 1963-67, prof., 1967-96, chmn. dept., 1969-78, dir. grad. profl. acctg. program, 1979-90, sr. assoc. dean, 1990-95, acting dean, 1994, Hughes M. Blake prof. internat. bus. mgmt., 1992-95, Julius A. Roller prof. acctg., 1995-96, mem. fin. acctg. stds. bd., 1996—2001; ret., 2001. Dir. U. Wash. Acctg. Devel. Fund, Overlake Hosp. Med. Ctr., Bellevue, 1984-96, chmn. bd. trustees, 1991-93; cons. internat. tax matters U.S. Treasury Dept., 1963-68; cons. Internat. Acctg. Rsch., 1964-96; vis. prof. Cranfield Sch. Mgmt., Eng., 1973-74, U. Zurich, Switzerland, 1973-74; lectr. in field. Author: International Accounting, 1967; co-author: Introductory Financial Accounting, 3d edit., 1991, A Brief Introduction to Managerial and Social Uses of Accounting, 1975, International Accounting, 1978, 2nd edit., 1992, Accounting: An International Perspective, 1987, 4th edit., 1997; editor: Readings in International Accounting, 1969, Accounting-A Book of Readings, 2d edit., 1976, A New Introduction to Accounting, 1971, A Bibliography of Internat. Accounting, 3d edit., 1973, Essentials of Multinational Accounting—An Anthology, 1979, Frontiers of International Accounting, 1986, AACSB Curriculum Internationalization Resource Guide, 1988; contbr. chpts. to books, numerous articles to profl. jours. Recipient U. Wash. Disting. Tchg. award, 1983, Disting. Svc. award, U. Wash., 1984; Ford Found. fellow, 1958—59, Price Waterhouse Internat. Acctg. Rsch. fellow, 1962—64. Fellow Acad. Internat. Bus.; mem. AICPA (internat. practice exec. com. 1972-75, exec. coun. 1987-89, Disting. Achievement in Acctg. Edn. award 2000), Am. Acctg. Assn. (pres. 1988-89, acad. v.p. 1970-71, chmn. adv. bd. internat. acctg. sect. 1977-79, Wildman medal 1986, Nat. Outstanding Educator 1981, Disting. Internat. Lectr. in Black Africa 1987, Outstanding Internat. Acctg. Educator 1991), Wash. Soc. CPAs (pres. 1988-89, Outstanding Educator award 1985, Pub. Svc. award 1995), Acctg. Edn. Change Commn. (chmn. 1994-96), Beta Alpha Psi (Acad. Acct. of Yr. 1987), Beta Gamma Sigma (Disting. scholar 1978-79), Alpha Gamma Sigma. Home: 15794 Dovewood Ct Poway CA 92064-2282 E-mail: gmueller@u.washington.edu. *It has always been important to me to associate with people and tangible and intangible things of the highest quality. I make it a practice to set clear goals and then pursue them actively. A broad world view on all aspects of life engenders more success and happiness than special interest perspectives. I welcome change in professional matters, but seek constancy in personal and family affairs. Fate has played a role in my successes. I believe in God, Protestant ethics, and the merits of classical academic scholarship.*

MUELLER, GERRY, realtor, investor, former internet executive; b. N.Y.C., Mar. 17, 1944; s. John and Mary (Choisy) M.; m. Debra Pritt, Sept. 17, 2000. BA, St. Johns U., 1965; MBA, Adelphi U., 1970. Mktg. exec. IBM, White Plains, N.Y., 1967-84; pres., gen. mgr. Prodigy Network, White Plains, 1985-97; now realtor and investor. Avocations: wine collecting, golf. Home: 6738 N Ocean Blvd Ocean Ridge FL 33435

MUELLER, I. LYNN, strategic planning and communications consultant; b. Cin., Feb. 2, 1941; s. Irwin Ludwig and Helen Marie (Bloomfield) Mueller; m. Maria Rose Cavallino; children: Shallah Whitney, Geoffrey Koskinen. BBA, U. Cin., 1964, MBA, 1966; postgrad., George Washington U., 1966-68. V.p., founder Robert-Lynn Assoc., Ltd., Washington, 1968-72; spl. asst. N.Y. State Assembly Spkr., Albany, 1971-74; v.p. adminstrn. and fin. Epsilon Data Mgmt., Boston, 1974-75; founder, sr. v.p. First Tuesday Comms., Buffalo, N.Y., 1974-78; v.p. cmty. affairs Gardenway Mgmt., Troy, N.Y., 1976; pres. ILM Enterprises, Old Chatham, N.Y., 1977-91; exec. dir. Minority Leader, N.Y. State Assembly, Albany, 1983-91; founder Decision Strategies Group, Albany, 1991—. Contbr. chpt. to book. Trustee Chatham (N.Y.) Meth. Ch., 1992-94; mem. Chatham Sch. Bd., 1990-93; Cons. to Gov. George Pataki Transition Com., 1994; advisor Morris Meml. Bd., Chatham, 1984-98; alumni rep. George Washington U., Albany, 1993—. Mem. Nat. Space Soc., Planetary Soc., Cin. Soc. (pres. 1961-62), McMicken Soc., Sigma Sigma, Omicron Delta Kappa, Alpha Kappa Psi, Beta Alpha Psi. Republican. Presbyterian. Avocations: basketball, tennis, sailing, bridge, reading non-fiction. Office: Decision Strategies Group Ste 2001 One Commerce Plz Albany NY 12210 Business E-Mail: lynnmueller@decisionstrategiesgroup.com.

MUELLER, JOHN ERNEST, political science educator, dance critic and historian; b. St. Paul, June 21, 1937; s. Ernst A. and Elsie E. (Schleh) M.; m. Judy A. Reader, Sept. 6, 1960; children: Karl, Karen, Susan AB, U. Chgo., 1960; MA, UCLA, 1963, PhD, 1965. Asst. prof. polit. sci. U. Rochester, N.Y., 1965-69, assoc. prof., 1969-72, prof., 1972-2000, prof. film studies, 1983-2000, founder, dir. Dance Film Archive, 1973—; prof. polit. sci., Woody Hayes chair of nat. security studies Ohio State U., 2000—. Lectr. on dance in U.S., Europe, Australia, 1973—; OP-ED columnist Wall St. Jour., 1984—, L.A. Times, 1988—, N.Y. Times, 1990—; mem. dance panel NEA, 1983-85; columnist Dance Mag., 1974-82; dance critic Rochester Dem. and Chronicle, 1974-82; mem. adv. bd. Dance in Am., PBS, 1975; mem. editl. bd. Ohio State U., 2000—04. Author: War, Presidents and Public Opinion, 1973 (book selected as one of Fifty Books That Significantly Shaped Public Opinion Rsch. 1946-95 Am. Assn. Pub. Opinion Rsch. 1995), Dance Film Directory, 1979, Astaire Dancing: The Musical Films, 1985 (de la Torre Bueno prize 1983), Retreat From Doomsday: The Obsolescence of Major War, 1989, Policy and Opinion in the Gulf War, 1994, Quiet Cataclysm: Reflections on the Recent Transformation of World Politics, 1995, Capitalism, Democracy, and Ralph's Pretty Good Grocery, 1999; co-author: Trends in Public Opinion: A Compendium of Survey Data, 1989; editor: Approaches to Measurement, 1969, Peace, Prosperity, and Politics, 2000; co-editor Jour. Policy Analysis and Mgmt., 1985-89; mem. editl. bd. Pub. Opinion Quar., 1988-91, Jour. Cold War Studies, 1999—, Ohio State U. press, 2001—; prodr. 12 dance films/recorded commentator on 2nd soundtrack of laser disc edit. Swing Time, 1986; co-adapter (musical) A Foggy Day, 1998; prodr. Shaw Festival Niagara-on-the-Lake, Ont., 1998, 99. Grantee NSF, 1967-70, 74-75, NEH, 1972-73, 74-75, 77-78, 79-81; Guggenheim fellow, 1988. Mem. Am. Acad. Arts and Scis., Am. Polit. Sci. Assn., Dance Critics Assn. (bd. dirs. 1983-85). Home: 420 W 5th Ave Columbus OH 43201-3159 Office: Ohio State U Polit Sci Dept Columbus OH 43210-1373 Office Phone: 614-247-6007.

MUELLER, KATHRYN LUCILE, occupational and environmental medicine educator; b. Lincoln, Nebr., Feb. 14, 1951; d. Roland Fredrick and Elizabeth (Brown) M.; m. Rex A. Logemann, Apr. 27, 1978; children: Elizabeth C., Alexander F. BA, U. Nebr., 1973, MD, 1977; MPH, Med. Coll. Wis., 1994. Diplomate Am. Bd. Preventive Medicine in Occupl. Medicine. Instr. Rush Med. Sch., Chgo., 1981-87; asst. prof. U. Colo. Health Scis. Ctr., Denver, 1987-98, dir. student and occupational health svcs., 1989-96, assoc. prof. surgery and preventive medicine, 1998—; med. dir. Colo. Divsn. Worker's Compensation, Denver, 1991—. Project med. dir. Christ Hosp. EMS program, Chgo., 1983-87; physician advisor Emergency Med. Svcs. State of Colo., Denver, 1991-92; peer reviewer Tomes Plus, 1991—; oral bd. examiner Am. Bd. Emergency Medicine, Ill., 1992-95; chair first test com. Am. Bd. Ind. Med. Examiners, 1994-95. Mem. editl. bd.: Guides Newsletter AMA, 1996—. Am. Coll. Emergency Medicine fellow, 1983-2002; Robert Wood Johnson grantee, 1998-2000. Fellow Am. Coll. Occupl. and Environ. Medicine (chair com. state legis. affairs 1996-2002, co-chair coun. on govtl. affairs 2002-, bd. dirs. 2000-04, sec.-treas. 2004—); mem. Rocky Mountain Acad. Occupl. and Environ. Medicine (bd. dirs. 1992-94, pres. 1997). Avocations: cross country skiing, travel, reading. Office: U Colo Health Scis Ctr 4200 E 9th Ave B 211 Denver CO 80262-0001

MUELLER, KURT M. hotel executive; Pres. Motels Am., Des Plaines, Ill.; CFO MOA Hospitality Inc., Des Plaines, Ill., 1997—, pres., CFO. Office: Hospitality Inc 701 Lee St Ste 1000 Des Plaines IL 60016-4555

MUELLER, LISEL, writer, poet; b. Hamburg, Germany, Feb. 8, 1924; BA in Sociology, U. Evansville; postgrad., Ind. U. Vis. faculty Goddard Coll., 1977-80, Warren Wilson Coll., 1983, 85-86; vis. lectr. U. Chgo., 1984; disting. writer-in-residence Wichita State U., 1981. Author: Dependencies, 1965, 2d edit. 1998, Life of a Queen, 1970, The Private Life, 1976, Voices from the Forest, 1977, The Need to Hold Still, 1980, Waving from Shore, 1989, Second Language, 1986, Learning to Play by Ear, 1990, Alive Together: New & Selected Poems, 1996 (Pulitzer prize). Recipient Pulitzer prize for poetry, Nat. Book award for poetry, Carl Sandburg award, Ruth Lilly Poetry prize, 2002, Jacob Glatstein Meml. prize, Eunice Tietjens Meml. prize; NEA fellow. Mem.: Poetry Ctr. Chgo. (founding mem.). Office: La State U Press PO Box 25053 Baton Rouge LA 10894-5053

MUELLER, LOIS M. psychologist; b. Milw., Nov. 30, 1943; d. Herman Gregor and Ora Emma (Dettmann) M. BS, U. Wis., Milw., 1965; MA, U. Tex., 1966, PhD, 1969. Cert. family mediator; lic. psychologist, Ill., Fla. Postdoctoral intern VA Hosp., Wood, Wis., 1969-71; counselor, asst. prof. So. Ill. U. Counseling Ctr. and dept. psychology, Carbondale, 1971-72, coord. personal counseling, asst. prof., 1972-74, counselor, asst. prof., 1974-76; individual practice clin. psychology Carbondale, 1972-76, Clearwater, Fla., 1977-90, Port Richey, Fla., 1990—. Family mediator, 1995—; mem. profl. adv. com. Mental Health Assn. Pinellas County, 1978, Alt. Human Services, 1979-80; cons. Face Learning Center, Hotline Crisis Phone Service, 1977-87; advice columnist Clearwater Sun newspaper, 1983-90; pub. speaker local TV and radio stas., 1978, 79; talk show host WPLP Radio Sta., Clearwater, 1980-83, WTKN Radio Sta., Tampa Bay, 1988-89, WPSO Radio Sta., New Port Richey, 1991. Contbr. articles to profl. jours. Campaign worker for Sen. George McGovern presdl. race, 1972; sec. bd. dirs. PACE Ctr. for Girls of Pasco; bd. dirs. Suncoast Girl Scout Coun. Mem. APA, Fla. Psychol. Assn., Pinellas Psychol. Assn. (founder, pres. 1978), Am. Soc. Clin. Hypnosis, Fla. Soc. Clin. Hypnosis, Calusa Bus. & Profl. Women (pres., Woman of Yr. 1999), West Pasco C. of C., Cmty. Svc. Coun. Office: 6709 Ridge Rd Ste 109 Port Richey FL 34668-6851

MUELLER, MARGARET S. musician, educator; b. Creston, Iowa, Dec. 3, 1924; d. Homer Cowan and Pearl Callahan Snodgrass; m. John Storm Mueller, June 10, 1958; 1 child, Laura Marjorie Mueller Woods. Student, Kans. U., 1943-46; MusB, Oberlin Conservatory, 1950, MusM, 1958. Instr. piano N.D. State Tchrs. Coll., Minot, 1950-51; instr. piano and organ Iowa State U., Ames, 1951-55, Randolph-Macon Woman's Coll., Lynchburg, Va., 1957-58; prof. organ and theory Salem Coll., Winston-Salem, N.C., 1958-95, prof. emerita, 1995—. Performing artist organ various concerts throughout the U.S. and Europe, 1953—; organist St. Paul's Episcopal Ch., Winston-Salem, 1963—2001; judge André Marchal Internat. Competition, Biarritz, France, 2001. Grantee Fulbright Assn., Frankfurt, Germany, 1955-56, Aeolian grantee, Paris, 1956-57. Mem.: Nat. Guild Piano Tchrs. (judge piano and organ), Winston-Salem Profl. Piano Tchrs. Assn., Music Tchrs. Nat. Assn. (judge piano and organ), Organ Hist. Soc., Am. Guild Organists (judge state, regional and nat. competitions 1965—, performing artist organ nat. and regional convs. 1973, 1976, 1987, 1993), Pi Kappa Lambda, Mu Phi Epsilon. Democrat. Episcopalian. Home: 1524 Sharon Rd Winston Salem NC 27103-1816 Office: Salem Coll Salem Square Winston Salem NC 27108

MUELLER, MARK CHRISTOPHER, lawyer; b. Dallas, June 19, 1945; s. Herman August and Hazel Deane (Hatzenbuehler) M.; m. Linda Jane Reed. BA in Econs., So. Meth. U., 1967; MBA in Acctg., 1969, JD, 1971. Bar: Tex. 1971, U.S. Dist. Ct. (no. dist.) Tex. 1974, U.S. Tax Ct. 1974; CPA, Tex. Acct. Arthur Young & Co., Dallas, 1967-68, A.E. Krutilek, Dallas, 1968-71; pvt. practice law Dallas, 1971—; assoc. L. Vance Stanton, Dallas, 1971-72. Instr. legal writing and rsch. So. Meth. U., Dallas, 1970-71, instr. legal acctg., 1975; unauthorized practice of law com. Supreme Ct. Tex. Leading articles editor Southwestern Law Jour., 1970-71. Mem. NRA, Tex. Bar Assn., Tex. State Rifle Assn., Tex. Soc. CPA's, Dallas Bar Assn., SAR, Sons Republic Tex., Sons of Union Vets. of Civil War, Sons Confederate Vets., Mil. Order Stars and Bars, Order of Coif, Dallas Hist. Soc., Dallas County Pioneer Assn., Rock Creek Barbeque Club, Masons, Shriners, York Rite, Grotto, Scottish Rite (32 degree Knight Commdr. Ct. of Honor), Beta Alpha Psi, Phi Delta Phi, Sigma Chi. Home: 7310 Brennans Dr Dallas TX 75214-2804 Office: 6510 Abrams Rd Ste 565 Dallas TX 75231-7292 Office Phone: 214-221-6888.

MUELLER, NANCY, food products executive; BS in chemistry, Russel Sage Coll., 1965. Founder, pres. Nancy's Specialty Foods, Newark, Calif., 1977—. Bd. trustees Rensselaer Polytechnic Inst., Palo Alto Med. Found.; bd. dirs. Sr. Coord. Coun. Palo Alto; mem. Com. 200; bus. adv. coun. Stanford Grad. Sch. Office: Nancys Specialty Foods 6500 Overlake Pl Newark CA 94560-1084

MUELLER, NANCY SCHNEIDER, retired biology educator; b. Wooster, Ohio, Mar. 8, 1933; d. Gilbert Daniel and Winifred (Porter) Schneider; m. Helmut Charles Mueller, Jan. 27, 1959; 1 child, Karl Gilbert. AB in Biology, Coll. of Wooster, 1955; MS in Zoology, U. Wis., 1957, PhD in Zoology, 1962. Instr. zoology U. Wis., Madison, 1966; asst. prof. poultry sci. and zoology N.C. State U., Raleigh, 1968-71; vis. prof. biology N.C. Ctrl. U., Durham, 1971-73, assoc. prof., 1973-79, prof., 1979-93; ret., 1993. Vis. scientist U. Vienna, Austria, 1975. Contbr. articles, abstracts to profl. publs. Mem. Am. Soc. Zoologists, Am. Ornithologists Union, Cooper Ornithol. Soc., Wilson Ornithol. Soc., Wis. Acad. Sci., Arts and Letters, N.C. Acad. Sci., LWV (bd. dirs. 1988—, natural resources com. 1988—), Sigma Xi. Avocations: bird migration, conservation and environmental issues. Home: 409 Moonridge Rd Chapel Hill NC 27516-5576

MUELLER, O. THOMAS, molecular geneticist, pediatrics educator; b. Berlin, Aug. 17, 1950; arrived in U.S., 1955; s. Heinz Carl and Gertrud (Jung) M.; m. Mary Gail Craig, April 24, 1976; children: Cara Lynne, Kyle Thomas, Eric Andreas. BA, Lehigh U., 1972; PhD in biol. chemistry, Pa. State U., 1978. Diplomate: Am. Bd. Med. Genetics in Molecular and Biochemical Genetics. Postdoctoral fellow U. Colo. Med. Ctr., Denver, 1978-80; rsch. asst. Roswell Park Meml. Inst., Buffalo, N.Y., 1980-84, rsch. affiliate, 1984-87; assoc. prof. pediats. U. So. Fla., Tampa, 1987—; dir. molecular genetics All Children's Hosp., St. Petersburg, Fla., 1994—. Contbr. numerous articles to scientific jours. including Human Genetics, Am. Jour. Med. Genetics, Am. Jour. Human Genetics, Jour. Biol. Chemistry, and others. Avocations: triathlons, sailing. Home: 2001 Point Overlook Dr NE Saint Petersburg FL 33703-3435 Office: Dept Pathology All Children's Hosp 801 6th St S Saint Petersburg FL 33701-4816 Office Phone: 727-767-8985. Business E-Mail: otmuelle@hsc.usf.edu.

MUELLER, PAUL HENRY, retired bank executive; b. NYC, June 24, 1917; s. Paul Herbert and Helen (Cantwell) M.; m. Jean Bonnel Vreeland, Sept. 10, 1949; 1 child, Donald Vreeland. BS, NYU, 1940; AB, Princeton U., 1941; LittD (hon.), Heriot-Watt U., Edinburgh, Scotland, 1981; LHD (hon.), Bloomfield Coll., 1991. From page to sr. v.p. Citibank N.A., 1934—65, sr. v.p., 1965—74, chmn. credit policy com., 1974—82; chmn. Saab-Scania Am. Inc., 1982—90; ret., 1990. Joined U.S. Fgn. Svc., served in Panama, Cairo, Washington, 1941-43; asst. adminstrv. sec. UN Montary and Fin. Conf., Bretton Woods, N.H., 1944; divisional asst. Dept. State, 1946; sec. West Indian Conf., 2d session, St. Thomas, V.I., 1946; vis. lectr. U. Va., 1980-2001; founding chmn., sr. fellow Ctr. Internat. Banking Studies, 1977-91. Author (contbg.): Offshore Lending by U.S. Commercial Banks, 1975, 2d edit., 1981, Bank Credit, 1981, Classics in Commercial Bank Lending, 1981, Vol. II, 1985, Loan Portfolio Management, 1988, Credit Culture, 1994, Credit Risk Management, 1995; author: (with Leif H. Olsen) Credit and the Business Cycle, 1979; author: Learning from Lending, 1979, Credit Doctrine for Lending Officers, 1976, 1981, 2d edit., 1997, Credit Endpapers, 1982, Perspective on Credit Risk, 1988, In a Nutshell, 2002; contbr. articles to profl. jours. Trustee Bloomfield Coll., N.J., 1983-91, vice chmn., 1987-88, chmn., 1988-91, trustee emeritus; treas. Marcus Wallenberg Found. (U.S.), 1984—. Served from 2d lt. to capt. USMCR, 1944-59. Decorated Royal Order Polar Star (Sweden); recipient Alumni award Grad. Sch. Credit and Fin. Mgmt., Dartmouth Coll., 1958, Disting. Svc. award Robert Morris Assocs., 1981. Mem. Bankers Assn. Fgn. Trade (hon., v.p. 1976), Pilgrims, SAR, Swedish-Am. C. of C. USA (chmn. 1989-90, hon. dir.), Royal Econ. Soc. (U.K.), Univ. Club (N.Y.C.), Beta Gamma Sigma. Republican. Presbyterian. Home: 75 Rotary Dr Summit NJ 07901-3131

MUELLER, PEGGY JEAN, dance educator, choreographer, rancher; b. Austin, Tex., June 14, 1952; d. Rudolph George Jr. and Margaret Jean (Locke) M.; m. John Yerby Tarlton, June 24, 1972 (div. June 1983). BS in Home Econs., Child Devel., U. Tex., Austin, 1974. Dance tchr. Shirley McPhail Sch. Dance, Austin, 1972-75, Jean Tarlton Sch. Dance, Alpine, Tex., 1975-77, College Station, Tex., 1977-80, Sul Ross State U., Alpine, 1975-77, Tex. A&M U., College Station, 1977-80, A&M Consol. Community Edn., Coll. Station, 1977-78, Jean Mueller Sch. Dance, Austin, 1980—, U. Tex., Austin, 1980—. Dancer, contest judge Gt. Tex. Dance-Off, Austin, 1985—86; mem. equestrian com. Austin Travis County Livestock Show and Rodeo, 1980—92, chmn. trail

ride, 1986—, Star Tex. Fair and PRCA Rodeo, 2000—; trial boss, pres. Austin Founders Trail Ride, 1986—; trail boss Bandera Longhorn Cattle Dr. and Trail Ride, 1990, 91; choreographer, head cheerleader Austin Texans Pro Football Team, 1981; dance tchr. Austin Ballroom Dancers, 1988, the Austin Club, 1997, 98; dancer, agt. George Strait/Bud Light Comml. Auditions, 1990; head contest judge Am.'s Ultimate Dance Contest, Austin, 1994; contest judge Two-Stepping Across Am., Austin, 1994; hon. trial boss Dream Catcher Ranch Trail Ride, Franklin, Tex., 1995, 96, Grapevine/Housgon Country Donkey, Mule and Horse Trail Ride, 1997, 2000. Dancer Oklahoma, Austin, 1969, Kiss Me Kate, Austin, 1970; choreographer, lead role Cabaret, Alpine, 1976, (mini-series) True Women, 1997. Active Women's Symphony League Austin, 1972—, Settlement Club, Austin, 1987—; recreation chmn. St. Martin's Evang. Luth. Ch., Austin, 1972—; hon. trail boss St. Jude Children's Rsch. Hosp. Trail Ride, Austin and Kyle, Tex., 1991. Recipient Outstanding Trail Rider of Yr. award Wild Horse Trail Ride, Okla., 1984; named Tex. First Lady Trail Boss, Gov. Mark White, Mayor Frank Cooksey, Austin City Coun., 1986, Judge Bill Aleshire, Travis County Commrs., 1989, Outstanding Intramural Sports Team Mgr.-Player, Tex. A&M U., 1978-79. Mem. Tex Assn. Tchrs. of Dancing, Inc., U.S. Twirling and Gymnastics Assn., Univ. Tex. Ex-Students Assn., Tex. Execs. in Home Econs., Am. Vet. Med. Assn. Aux. (v.p. 1978-79, pres. 1979-80), Am. Horse Shows Assn., Internat. Arabian Horse Assn., Austin Women's Tennis Assn. (v.p. 1985-86, pres. 1986-90, spl. events chmn. 1990-92, advisor 1990—, winner 2d ann. Harriet Crosson Outstanding Player & Community Svc. award), Women's Team Tennis of Austin Assn. (pres.-elect 1992-93, pres. 1993-94), Capital Area Tennis Assn. (membership com. 1991, 92), Houston Salt Grass Trail Ride Assn., San Antonio Alamo Trail Ride Assn., Ft. Worth Chisholm Trail Ride Assn., U. Tex. Longhorn Alumni Band, Austin C. of C., Am. Bus. Women's Assn., Austin Alumnae Panhellenic Assn. (1st v.p. 1989-90, rush forum chmn. 1990, pres. 1990-91, parliamentarian 1991-92), Lone Grove Cmty. Club (treas. 199697, v.p. 1997-99, pres. 1999—, exec. trustee 1997-99, exec. dir. 1999-2000), Omicron Nu (v.p. 1973-74), Jr. Austin Woman's Club (historian 1990-91), Austin Country Club (team tennis captain 1994-95, player 1994—, dance tchr. 1993-96), Zeta Tau Alpha (Austin Alumnae Chpt., alumnae photographer, social advisor 1982-87, treas. 1987-89, publicity chmn. 1989, Easter Seals fundraiser, Honor Cup winner 1990, pres. 1991-92, internat. convention official del. 1988, 92, nominating chmn. 1992-93, mem. yearbook com. 1992-94, 2d v.p. 1993-94). Clubs: Cen. Tex. Arabian Horse, Capitol Area Quarter Horse Assn., Jr. Austin Woman's, Austin Country. Republican. Avocations: theater, piano, drums, sports, travel. Home and Office: PO Box 5868 Austin TX 78763-5868 E-mail: aftr@USATrailRides.com.

MUELLER, ROBERT LOUIS, business executive; b. Denver, Aug. 25, 1927; s. George Winchester and Ruth Mabel (Cole) M.; m. Sue McCoy, July 3, 1949; children: Robert, Richard, Edward, Mark; m. Susan Galbraith, June 23, 1985. BSMechE, Yale U., 1948. Chief computer Western Geophys. Co., Mont., Wyo., Colo., Tex., 1949-50; dist. mgr. Armco Steel Corp., Colo., Ohio, N.Y., 1950-63, L.B. Foster Co., N.Y.C., 1963-66; v.p. Wheeeling Pitts. Steel Co., W.Va. and Pa., 1966-75; chmn., pres., chief exec. officer Connors Steel Co., Ala., 1975-82; pres., chief exec. officer Judson Steel Co., Calif., 1982-87; pres., COO Proler Internat., Houston, 1987-94, also bd. dirs., 1987-94, cons., 1994—; dir. Employee Solutions, Inc., 1995—; pres. Mueller Resources, Inc., Sedona, Ariz., 1993—. Co-author: Handbook of Drainage and Construction Products, 1954. With USN, 1945-46. Mem. ASCE, Assn. Iron and Steel Engrs., Duquesne Club (Pitts.), Houston City Club, Sedona Racquet Club, The Sedona 30.

MUELLER, ROBERT SWAN, III, federal agency administrator, lawyer; b. N.Y.C., Aug. 7, 1944; s. Robert Swan Jr. and Alice (Truesdale) M.; m. Ann Standish, Sept. 3, 1966; children: Cynthia, Melissa. BA, Princeton U., 1966; MA, NYU, 1967; JD, U. Va., 1973. Bar: Mass., U.S. Dist. Ct. Mass., U.S. Ct. Appeals (1st cir.), Calif., U.S. Dist. Ct. (no. dist.) Calif., U.S. Ct Appeals (9th cir.). Assoc. Pillsbury, Madison & Sutro, San Francisco, 1973-76; asst. U.S. atty. U.S. Atty.'s Office, No. Dist. Calif., San Francisco, 1976-80; chief unit spl. prosecutions, Calif. no. dist. U.S. Atty.'s Office, San Francisco, 1980-81, chief criminal div., 1981-82, chief criminal div. Mass. dist. Boston, 1982-85, 1st asst. U.S. atty. in Boston, 1985, U.S. atty. for Mass. dist., 1986-87, dep. U.S. atty. for Mass. dist., 1987-88; ptnr. Hill and Barlow, Boston, 1988-89; asst. to atty. gen. for criminal matters U.S. Dept. Justice, Washington, 1989-90, asst. atty. gen. for criminal div., 1990-93; lawyer Hale & Dorr, Washington, 1993—95; US atty, Calif no. dist U.S. Dept of Justice, 1998—2001, acting dep. U.S. Atty. Gen., 2001; dir. F.B.I. U.S. Dept. Justice, Washington, 2001—. Capt. USMC, 1967-70; Vietnam. Decorated Bronze Star, Purple Heart, Vietnamese Cross of Gallantry. Office: FBI J Edgar Hoover Bldg 935 Pennsylvania Ave NW Washington DC 20535-3404

MUELLER, SHARON LEE (SHERRY MUELLER), educational organization executive; b. Chgo., Aug. 17, 1943; d. LeRoy Elmer Arthur and Lucille Viola (Armborst) M. BA, Am. U., 1965; MA in Law and Diplomacy, Tufts U., 1966, PhD, 1977. Group leader Experiment in Internat. Living, 1969; cross-cultural trainer Nat. 4-H Found., 1970-71; cons. U.S. Dept. State, 1972, contract escort officer, 1970-77; cons. Fletcher Sch. Law and Diplomacy, 1976-81; lectr. dept. polit. sci. U. R.I., Kingston, 1975-77; adj. prof. Sch. Internat. Svc. Am. U., Washington, 1981-87; program officer Inst. Internat. Edn., Washington, 1978-82, dir. prof. exch. programs, 1982-96; exec. dir. Nat. Coun. for Internat. Visitors, Washington, 1996—2001, pres., 2001—. Mem. editl. adv. bd. Internat. Educator, 1991—; bd. dir. Nat. Coun. for Internat. Visitors, 1983-88; bd. dir., trustee World Learning, 1999-. Author: Careers in International Education, Exchange, and Development, 1998; contbr. chpts. to books; guest editor, contbr. Internat. Educator, 1992. Mem. exec. com. Internat. Student House, Washington, 1992-95; usher Foundry Meth. Ch., Washington, 1990—; mem. The Pres.'s Cir. Coun., Am. U., Washington, 1988-98, chair, 1996-98. Recipient Alumni Recognition award Am. U., 1990, award of appreciation Nat. Coun. for Internat. Visitors, 1988, award of appreciation World Ctr. for Tng. and Devel., 1988, Disting. Alumni award Lake Park High Sch., 1995, Outstanding Svc. award U.S.I.A., 1996. Mem. Nat. Press Club (assoc.), Sch. Internat. Svc. Alumni Assn. The Am. U. (founding pres. 1981-83), Sigma Iota Rho (hon.), Cosmos Club. Home: 1317 N Lynnbrook Dr Arlington VA 22201-4918 Office: NCIV 1420 K St NW Ste 800 Washington DC 20005-2500 Office Phone: 202-842-1414.

MUELLER, SHIRLEY ANNE, lawyer, real estate broker; b. Miami, Fla., Aug. 25, 1950; d. Robert Peter and Arvella Gertrude (Feldkamp) M.; divorced; children: Peter, Tybe, Samantha. AA in Journalism, Miami Dade Jr. Coll., 1970; BA in Philosophy, U. Calif., Berkeley, 1972; JD, Benjamin Cardozo Sch. Law, N.Y.C., 1982. Dir. children's advt. div. Coun. Better Bus. Bur., N.Y.C., 1973-79; assoc. Cutner & Rathkopf, N.Y.C., 1983-87; pres. Uncommon Properties, Inc., N.Y.C., 1990-94; pvt. practice N.Y.C., 1994—; assoc. broker Sotheby's Internat. Realty, N.Y.C., 2002—. Mem. fundraising com. Children's Air Ctr. N.Y. Hosp., N.Y.C., 1988—99, Nightingale Bamford Schl, N.Y.C., 1987—98; bd. dirs. Am. Symphony Orch., N.Y.C., 2003—. Roman Catholic. Avocations: reading, music, travel, dance. Home: 3601 S Flagler Dr West Palm Beach FL 33405 Office: 379 W Broadway 2d Fl New York NY 10024 Office Phone: 917-331-6691. Personal E-mail: shirleyamueller@hotmail.com.

MUELLER, THOMAS JAMES, engineering educator, researcher; b. Chgo., May 25, 1934; s. John Anthony and Margaret Mary (Staudenmaier) M.; m. Sarah Ann Holthaus, Nov. 18, 1961; children: Mark, Monica, Annmarie, Matthew, James. BSME, Ill. Inst. Tech., 1956; MSME, U. Ill., 1958, PhD in Gas Dynamics, 1961. Asst. prof. U. Ill., Urbana, 1961-63; sr. rsch. scientist United Tech., East Hartford, Conn., 1963-65; assoc. prof. U. Notre Dame, Ind., 1965-69, prof. aero. engring., 1969-88, assoc. dean engring., 1985-88, dept. chair, 1988-96, Roth-Gibson prof., 1988—. Vis. scientist Von Karman Inst., Brussels, 1973-74; cons. ARO, Inc., Tullahoma, Tenn., 1966-70, Lockheed-Ga. Co., 1980-82, AGARD, NATO, paris, 1983-84, Office Naval Rsch., Arlington, Va., 1999—. Co-author: Fr. T. Hesburg Commitment, Compassion, Consecration, 1989; editor: Low Reynolds Number Aerodynamic, 1989, Fixed and Flapping Wing Aerodynamics for Micro Air Vehicles Applications, 2001, Aeroacoustic Measurements, 2002; contbr. over 180 articles to profl. publs. in aerodynamics, propulsion, flow visualization and acoustics. Mem. Fellow ASME, AIAA (edn. achievement award 1980-81, aerodynamics award 2003), Royal Aero. Soc.; mem. Supersonic Tunnel Assn. (pres. 1994-95). Avocations: music, reading, investing. Home: 1535 Hoover Ave South Bend IN 46615 Office: U Notre Dame 112 Hessert Ctr Notre Dame IN 46556 Office Phone: 574-631-7073.

MUELLER, WAYNE DENNIS, music educator; b. Scottsbluff, Nebr., Apr. 20, 1947; s. Roger Wayne Mueller and Lorraine Rose Marie Eisenach; m. Mitzi Marie Hummel, Aug. 22, 1969; 1 child, Robert. Bachelors in Music Edn., U. of Nebr., Lincoln, NE, 1970. Cert. Teaching Certificate, K-12 Music Nebr. 6-12 vocal / instrumental music Thedford Pub. Schools, Thedford, Nebr., 1970—70; 7-12 vocal / instrumental music Morrill Pub. Schools, Morrill, Nebr., 1970—72; 7-12 vocal music Mitchell Pub. Schools, Mitchell, Nebr., 1972—73; sales and instrumental repair Jay's Music, Scottsbluff, Nebr., 1973; 6-12 instrumental music North Platte Pub. Schools, North Platte, Nebr., 1974—. Musician Mcpl. Band, North Platte, Nebr., 1975—, Sandhills Symphony, North Platte, Nebr., 1975—; condr. Sandhill Symphony, North Platte, Nebr., 1994—2000; musical dir. Cmty. Playhouse, North Platte, Nebr., 1995. Pres., sec., elder, choir dir. Beautiful Savior Luth. Ch., North Platte, Nebr., 1980—2002; soccer referee Am. Youth Soccer Orgn., North Platte, Nebr., 1985—90. Recipient Art Beat Award, North Platte Chamber of Commerce, 1996; Music grantee for accelerated program, North Platte Pub. Sch. Found., 2000—03. Mem.: Nebr. Music Edn. Assn., North Platte Edn. Assn. (pres. 1974—2002), Optimist Club. Lutheran. Avocations: golf, coaching football and baseball, coaching football and baseball, coaching football and baseball, community musical events. Home: 2607 West Philip Avenue North Platte NE 69101 Office: North Platte Public Schools 1000 West Second Street North Platte NE 69101

MUELLER, WILLARD FRITZ, economics professor; b. Ortonville, Minn., Jan. 23, 1925; s. Fritz and Adele C. (Thormaehlen) M.; m. Shirley I. Liesch, June 26, 1948; children: Keith, Scott, Kay. BS, U. Wis., 1950, MS, 1951; PhD, Vanderbilt U., 1955. Asst. prof. U. Calif., Davis, 1954-57; prof. U. Wis., 1957-61, prof. agrl. and applied econs. Dept. Econ. Sch. Law, 1969—; chief economist small bus. com. U.S. Ho. of Reps., 1961; chief economist, dir. bur. econs. FTC, 1961-68; exec. dir. President's Cabinet Com. on Price Stability, 1968-69. Expert House and Senate Com., 1960—86; cons. in field. Past bd. editors Rev. Ind. Orgn., Antitrust Law and Econ. Rev., Antitrust Bull., Jour. Reprints for Antitrust Law and Econs. Served with USN, 1943-46, mem. Economic Policy Inst., 1987-1990. Recipient Distinguished Service award FTC, 1969 Fellow Am. Agrl. Econs. Assn.; mem. Am. Econ. Assn., Am. Agr. Econ. Assn. (profl. excellence awards in policy contbn. 1980, in communications 1985, in rsch. discovery 1988). Assn. Evolutionary Econs. (pres. 1974-75), Indsl. Orgn. Soc. (pres. 1989-90), Argus Econ. Svcs. (pres. 1985—). Unitarian Universalist. Home: 121 Bascom Pl Madison WI 53726-3975 Office: U Wis 427 Lorch St Madison WI 53706-1513 Personal E-mail: wfritzmueller@aol.com.

MUELLER, WILLYS FRANCIS, JR., retired pathologist; b. Detroit, July 15, 1934; s. Willys Francis and Antoinette Frances (Stimac) M.; m. Dolores Mae Vella, Aug. 25, 1956; children: Renee Ann, Willys Francis, Paul E., Mark A., Maria D., Beth M., Matthew P. MD, U. Mich., 1959. Intern Providence Hosp, Detroit, 1959-60, resident, 1960-62, Wayne County Gen. Hosp., Eloise, MIch., 1962-64; asst. pathologist Grace Hosp., Detroit, 1964; assoc. pathologist Hurley Hosp., Flint, Mich., 1964-66, Hurley Med. Ctr., Flint, 1968-97, dir. lab., 1981-97; chief dep. med. examiner Genesee County, Mich., 1971-79, ret., 1979—. Pres. Pathology Assos. Inc.; assoc. clin. prof. Coll. Human Medicine, Mich. State U.; med. dir. blood svcs. Wolverine region/Great Lakes region ARC, 1981-96. Editor Bull. of Genesee County Med. Soc. Served with U.S. Army, 1966-68. Fellow Am. Soc. Clin. Pathologists, Coll. Am. Pathologists, Am. Acad. Forensic Scis.; mem. AMA (Physicians Recognition awards), Mich. State Med. Soc., Mich. Soc. Pathologists (sec.-treas. 1981-83, pres. 1985), Genesee County Med. Soc. (pres. 1987), Mich. Assn. Blood Banks (bd. dirs., pres. 1992), Nat. Assn. Med. Examiners, K.C. Republican. Roman Catholic. Home: 1096 Berkshire Ln Tarpon Springs FL 34688-7624

MUELLER-HEUBACH, EBERHARD, medical educator; b. Berlin, Feb. 24, 1942; came to U.S., 1968; s. Heinrich Gustav and Elisabeth (Heubach) M.; m. Cornelia Rosemarie Uffmann, Sept. 6, 1941; 1 child, Oliver Maximilian. MD, U. Koeln, 1966. Intern U. Koeln (Germany) Women's Hosp., 1967-68, Middlesex Gen. Hosp., New Brunswick, N.J., 1968-69; rsch. fellow Columbia U., 1969-71; resident Columbia-Presbyn. Med. Ctr., N.Y.C., 1971-74, chief resident, 1974-75; asst. prof. Magee-Women's Hosp. U. Pitts., 1975-81, assoc. prof. Magee-Women's Hosp., 1981-89; prof., chmn. ob-gyn. Sch. Medicine Wake Forest U., Winston-Salem, 1989—2002, prof. ob-gyn., 2002—. Mem. editl. bd.: Ob-Gyn, 1999—2002. Mem. Am. Gyn.-Ob Soc. (asst. sec. 1999-2001, sec. 2002-2004), Soc. Gynecol. Investigation, The Perinatal Rsch. Soc., Coun. Univ. Chairs Ob-Gyn. (pres. 1998-2000). Avocations: horses, travel, arts. Office: Wake Forest U Bapt Med Ctr Medical Center Blvd Winston Salem NC 27157-0001 E-mail: emueller@wfubmc.edu.

MUENCH, KARL HUGO, clinical geneticist; b. St. Louis, May 3, 1934; MD, Washington U., St. Louis, 1960. Diplomate Am. Bd. Med. Genetics. Intern Barnes Hosp., St. Louis, 1960-61; fellow in biological chemistry Stanford U. Sch. Medicine, 1961-65; staff mem. Jackson Meml. Hosp., Miami, Fla.; prof. medicine U. Miami Sch. Medicine. Mem. AMA, ACP, Am. Coll. Med. Genetics. Office: U Miami Sch Med Div Genetic Med PO Box 16960 Miami FL 33101-6960 Office Phone: 305-243-6652. E-mail: kmuench@med.miami.edu.

MUETH, JOSEPH EDWARD, lawyer; b. St. Louis, Aug. 8, 1935; s. Joseph and Marie Clare (Reher) M.; m. Ellen Agnes O'Heron, Dec. 24, 1973; children: Erin R., Patricia A. B.Chem. Engring., U. Dayton, 1957; LL.B., Georgetown U., 1960, LL.M., 1961. Bar: Calif. 1964. Practice law, L.A.; ptnr. Wills, Green & Mueth, L.A., 1974-83; pvt. practice law Calif., 1983-94; of counsel Sheldon & Mak, Pasadena, Calif., 1994—. Adj. prof. law U. Calif. Hastings Coll. Law, San Francisco, 1972-75; lectr. Claremont Grad. Sch., 1982—. Author: Copyrights Patents and Trademarks, 1974. Chmn. bd. Rio Hondo council Camp Fire Girls Inc., 1967-72. Mem. AAAS, Am., Los Angeles County bar assns., State Bar Calif., N.Y. Acad. Scis., L.A. Athletic Club. Home: PO Box 3369 1217 Seal Way Seal Beach CA 90740-6419 Office: 225 S Lake Ave Ste 800 Pasadena CA 91101-4858

MUETHER, CHARLES ALEXANDER, writer, educator; b. Port Jefferson, NY, Nov. 14, 1964; s. Herbert Robert and Anne Muether; m. Kristie Jo Muether, Aug. 27, 1988. MA Curriculum and Devel., Dordt Coll., Sioux Center, Iowa, 1997, BA English and Secondary Edn., 1987; postgrad., Mid-Am. Reformed Seminary. English and drama educator Pella Christian, Pella, Iowa, 1989—2001; prin., educator Volga Christian, Volga, SD, 1988—89. Writer Wioarey Press, Des Moines, 2000—02. Author: (book) Theatre in the Middle; editor: Assessing the Whole Child. Deacon, elder, v.p. Covenant Ref. Ch., Pella, Iowa, 2002; mem. Grace Ref. Presbyn. Ch., Covenant Ref. Ch. Recipient Walmart Tchr. of the Yr. Award, Walmart, 2000, Golden Apple Award, Who-TV, 1995. Mem.: Nat. Coun. of Teachers of English. Independent. Avocations: reading, photography, model railroading. Home: 310 Prairie Street Pella IA 50219

MUFSON, MAURICE ALBERT, infectious diseases physician, educator; b. N.Y.C., July 7, 1932; s. Max and Faye M.; m. Diane Cecile Weiss, Apr. 1, 1962; children: Michael Jeffrey, Karen Andrea, Pamela Beth. AB, Bucknell U., 1953; MD, NYU, 1957. Intern Bellevue Hosp., N.Y.C., 1957-58, resident, 1958-59; chief resident Cook County Hosp., Chgo., 1965-66; sr. surgeon USPHS Lab. Infectious Diseases, NIH, 1961-65; from asst. prof. medicine to prof. U. Ill., 1965-76; prof. Marshall U., 1976—2002, prof. emeritus, 2002—, chmn. dept. medicine, 1976—2000, chmn. emeritus, 2000—. Vis. scientist Karolinska Inst., 1984-85. Contbr. articles to profl. jours. Served with U.S. Navy, 1959-61. WHO grantee, 1967; recipient Meet-the-Scholar award Marshall U., 1986, Rschr. of Yr. award Sigma Xi, Marshall U., 1989, Solomon A. Berson Alumni Achievement award in health sci. NYU Sch Medicine, 1997; co-recipient Louis Weinstein award Jour. Clin. Infectious Diseases, 1994; named to Greater Huntington Wall of Fame, 2002. Master ACP (traveling scholar 1987, Laureate award W.Va. chpt.), Infectious Diseases Soc. Am.; mem. AMA, Soc. Exptl. Biology and Medicine, Ctrl. Soc. Clin. Rsch., So. Soc. Clin. Investigation, W.Va. State Med. Assn., Assn. Profs. Medicine (counselor 1992-95, pres.-elect 1995-96, pres. 1996-97, past pres. 1997-98), Alpha Omega Alpha. Office: Marshall U Sch Medicine 1600 Med Ctr Dr Ste G500 Huntington WV 25701 Office Phone: 304-691-1050. E-mail: maurice@ezwv.com., mufson@marshall.edu.

MUFTI, AFTAB A. civil engineering educator; b. Sukkur, Sind, Pakistan, Apr. 24, 1940; arrived in Can., 1963; s. Abdul Wahid D. and Shah Jahan M.; children: Javed, Alex; m. Zehra Mehdi, Sept. 22, 2000. BCE, NED Engring. U., Karachi, Sind, 1962; MCE, McGill U., Montreal, 1965, PhD, 1969. Registered profl. engr., Man., B.C. Asst. prof. McGill U., 1969-72; assoc. prof., head dept. comp. sci. Acadia U., Wolfville, Nova Scotia, 1972-76, prof., dir. Sch. Comp. Sci., 1976-80; prof. civil engring. Dalhousie U., Halifax, 1980-2000; pres. ISIS Can. Network of Ctrs. of Excellence U. Man., Winnipeg, Can., 2000—, prof. structural engring., 2000—. Pres. Advanced Composite Materials in Bridges and Structures Network of Can.; judge Can. Cons. Engring. Awards, 1987; earthquake cons. Lepereau Nuclear Power Plant and Confedn. Bridge. Author: Elementary Computer Graphics, 1982, Bridge Engineering, 1994; editor: Advanced Composite Materials in Bridges and Structures, 1972, Finite Element Method in Civil Engineering, 1993, Developments in Short and Medium Span Bridge Engineering, 1994, Bridge Superstructures New Developments, 1996; contbr. numerous articles to refereed jours., also conf. papers. Vol. fireman Wolfville Fire Dept., 1976-77. Recipient award for Distinction in Engring., Assn. Profl. Engrs. of Nova Scotia, 1996, award of merit Consulting Engrs. Man., 2003, award of excellence Consulting Engrs. Man., 2003, award of recognition Natural Scis. and Engring. Rsch. Coun., 2004, award of appreciation ISIS Can. Rsch. Network, 2004. Fellow Can. Acad. Engring., Engring. Inst. Can. (Phelp Johnson prize 1969), Can. Soc. Civil Engring. (Whitman Wright award 1990, Pratley award 1993), ASCE (Lt. Govs. award Engring. Excellence in Nova Scotia 1996, IRF award 1997, ACI design award 1998, Nova award 2000). Achievements include patents for Bridge Deck and Steel Free Bridge Deck. Office: ISIS Can Admin Ctr U Man A250-96 Dafoe Rd Winnipeg MB Canada R3T 2N2 Office Phone: 204-474-7476. Office Fax: 204-474-7519. Business E-Mail: muftia@cc.umanitoba.can.

MUFTU, SINAN, mechanical engineer, educator; b. St. Louis, Mo., Jan. 15, 1964; s. Yunus and Gulgun Muftu; m. Lynne Hilda Brum, Oct. 7, 1995; children: Serra Ayshe, Emre Yunus. BS, Middle East Tech U., 1987, MS, 1989, U. Rochester, 1990, PhD, 1994. Tchg. asst. METU, Aukara, Turkey, 1988—89; rsch. asst. U. Rochester, 1989—96, post doctoral fellow, 1996, Penn State, 1995—96, MIT Haystack Obs., Chelmsfold, Mass., 1995—97, rsch. staff mem., 1998—2000; assoc. prof. Northeastern U., Boston, 2000—. Mem. exec. com. ISPS Divsn. of the Am. Soc. of Mech. Engring., 2000—, chair exec. com., 2003—. Contbr. articles to profl. jours. Recipient Best Paper award, Info. Storage and Processing Systems Divsn. of the Am. Soc. of Mech. Engineers. Mem.: Soc. of Indsl. and Applied Math., Materials Rsch. Soc., Am. Soc. Mech. Engring. Achievements include patents for. Office: Northeastern U Dept Mech Engring 334 S N 02115

MUGERAUER, ROBERT W., JR., architecture educator; B in Liberal Studies, U. Notre Dame, 1967; PhD in Philosophy, U. Tex., 1973. Faculty mem. Grand Valley State Coll., Mich., 1975—80; various positions including assoc. acad. den, acad. dean, acad. v.p., acting exec. v.p. St. Edward's U., Austin, Tex., 1980—84; with U. Tex., 1985—2000; Sid Richardson Centennial chair arch. and planning U. Tex. Sch. Arch., Austin, 1990—2000, assoc. prof., 1990—2000; prof. urban design and planning U. Wash., Seattle, 2000—, dean Coll. Arch. and Urban Planning, 2000—. Author: Intrepretations on Behalf of Place: Environmental Displacements and Alternative Responses, 1994, Environmental Interpretations: Tradition, Deconstruction, and Hermeneutics, 1997. Named a Most Important Midcareer Rschr.-Tchr., Environ. Design Rsch. Assn., 1996; recipient Excellence Tchg. award, U. Tex. Sch. Arch., 1988—89, Outstanding Tchr. award, 1993, 2000. Mem.: Internat. Assn. for Philosophy and Environment (sec.), Internat. Assn. for Study Traditional Environments (mem. steering com.). Office: U Wash Sch Arch 224 Gould Hall Box 355726 Seattle WA 98195-5726*

MUGGENBURG, BRUCE AL, veterinary physiologist; b. May 2, 1937; s. Elmer Carl and Gladys O. (Bakke) M.; m. Marianne Nordgren, June 18, 1960 (dec. 1976); m. Carolyn Seale, July 16, 1977; children: Katherine Ann, Carl Thor, Virginia Hope. BS, U. Minn., St. Paul, 1959, DVM, 1961; MS, U. Wis., 1964, PhD, 1966. Asst. prof. U. Wis., Madison, 1966-69; sr. scientist Lovelace Inhalation Toxicology Rsch. Inst., Albuquerque, 1969—. Vis. prof. U. do Rio Grande dul Sol, Porto Alegre, Brazil, 1966—68; clin. rsch. prof. dept. medicine U. N.Mex., Albuquerque, 1988—2000, clin. profl. coll. pharmacy, 1993—2000. Contbr. articles to profl. jours. Mem. AVMA, Am. Thoracic Soc., Am. Physiol. Soc., Health Physics Soc., Radiation Rsch. Soc., Scandinavian Club of Albuquerque (pres. 1983, 87, 88). Lutheran. Home: 2805 Calle Del Rio NW Albuquerque NM 87104-3141 Office: Lovelace Respiratory Rsch Inst 2425 Ridgecrest Dr SE Albuquerque NM 87108 E-mail: bmuggenb@lrri.org.

MUGGERIDGE, DEREK BRIAN, dean, engineering consultant; b. Godalming, Surrey, U.K., Oct. 10, 1943; arrived in Can., 1956; s. Donald William and Vera Elvina (Jackson) M.; m. Hanny Meta Buurman, Dec. 4, 1965; children: Karen Julie, Michael Brent. BS in Aero. Engring., Calif. State Polytech. U., 1965; MASc in Aerospace Engring., U. Toronto, 1966, PhD in Aerospace Engring., 1970. Spl. lectr. U. Toronto, Ont., Can., 1971; indsl. post-doctoral fellow Fleet Mfg. Co., Fort Erie, Ont., 1970-72; from asst. prof. to prof. Meml. U. of Nfld., St. John's, 1972-93, univ. rsch. prof., 1990-93; dir. Ocean Engring. Rsch. Ctr., 1982-93; dean Okanagan U. Coll., Kelowna, B.C., Can., 1993—, assoc. v.p. rsch., 1998—. Pres. Offshore Design Assocs. Ltd., St. John's, Nfld., 1980—; sec., ptnr. Nfld. Ocean Cons., St. John's, 1981-93; ptnr. LNF Joint Venture Ltd., St. John's, 1984-90; vis. prof. Norweigan Inst. Tech., Trondheim, Norway, 1976, NRC, Ottawa, Can., 1976, U. Victoria, B.C., 1988-89. Co-author: Ice Interaction with Offshore Structures, 1988; contbr. articles to profl. jours.; contbr. conf. articles, reports. U. Toronto Grad. fellow, 1965, Nat. Rsch. Coun. Can. Grad. fellow U. Toronto, 1966-70. Mem. Assn. Profl. Engrs. & Geoscis. of Province of B.C. Marine and Naval. Avocations: windsurfing, sailing, rock collecting. Home: 16438 Carr's Landing Rd Lake Country BC Canada V4V 1C3 Office: Okanagan Univ Coll 3333 College Way Kelowna BC Canada V1V 1V7

MUGLIA, ROBERT L. information technology executive; BS in Computer Sci., U. Mich., 1981. Devel. mgr. ROLM Co.; with Microsoft, Redmond, Wash., 1988, v.p. enterprise storage svcs. group, 2001—03, sr. v.p., windows server div., 2003—. Mem. Sr. Leadership Team, Bus. Leadship Team, Microsoft. Office: Microsoft One Microsoft Way Redmond WA 98052-6399*

MUGNAINI, ENRICO, neuroscience educator; b. Colle Val d'Elsa, Italy, Dec. 10, 1937; came to U.S., 1969. children: Karin E., Emiliano N.G. MD cum laude, U. Pisa, Italy, 1962. Microscopy lab. rsch. fellow dept. anatomy U. Oslo Med. Sch., 1963, asst. prof., head of electron microscopy lab., 1964-66, assoc. prof., 1967-69; prof. biobehavioral scis. and psychology, head lab. of neuromorphology U. Conn., Storrs, 1969-95; E.C. Stuntz prof. cell biology, dir. Inst. for Neurosci., Northwestern U., Chgo., 1995—. Vis. prof. Dept. Anatomy Harvard U., Boston, 1969-70; traveling lectr. Grass Found., spring 1986, fall 1990. Mng. editor USA Anatomy and Embryology Jour., 1989—; contbr. more than 150 articles to books and jours. Recipient Decennial Camillo Golgi award Acad. Nat. dei Lincei, 1981, Sen. Javits Neurosci. Rsch. Investigator award NIH, 1985-92. Mem. AAAS, Am. Assn. Anatomists, Am. Soc. Cell Biology, Internat. Brain Rsch. Orgn., Internat. Soc. Developmental Neurosci., Norwegian Nat. Acad. Scis. and Letters, Soc. Neurosci., Cajal Club (pres. 1987-88). Office: U Northwestern Inst Neurosci 5-474 Searle Bldg 320 E Superior St Chicago IL 60611-3010

MUHAMMAD, MUHSIN, II, professional football player; b. Lansing, Mich. m. Christa; children: Jordan Taylor, Chase Soen. Student, Mich. State U. Wide receiver Carolina Panthers, 1996—. Founder M2 Found.; spokesperson Men For Change group that generates money and awareness for a battered women's shelter. Named to Pro Bowl, 1999; named Panther's Man of Yr. for his cmty. efforts, 1999. Office: Carolina Panthers 800 S Mint St Ste 2 Charlotte NC 28202-1502

MUHICH, BRIAN WILLIAM, insurance broker; b. Champaign, Ill., Jan. 28, 1978; s. Frank William and Virginia May Muhich; m. Leah Joi Leonard, Apr. 6, 2001. BSBA, U. Ill., 2000. Comml. benefits broker Ins. Plans Agy., Inc., Schaumburg, Ill., 2000—. Author: (christian hymns) Book of Songs (I & II). Office: Ins Plans Agy Inc 1320 Tower Rd Ste 102 Schaumburg IL 60173 Office Phone: 847-885-5611. E-mail: info@ipa-agency.com.

MÜHLANGER, ERICH, ski manufacturing company executive; b. Aug. 26, 1941; arrived in U.S., 1971, naturalized, 1975; s. Alois Mühlnager and Maria (Stückelschweiger) Mühlanger; m. Gilda V. Oliver, July 13, 1973; 1 child, Erich. A in Engring., Murau Berufsschule Spl. Trade, Austria, 1959; student, Inst. Tech. and Engring., Weiler Im Allgau, Germany, 1963—65. Salesman Olin Ski Co. (Olin-Authier), Switzerland, 1965—67, mem. mktg. dept., 1967—67, svc. and mfg., 1969—71, quality control insp., 1971—77, supr., 1977—78, gen. foreman, 1978—83, process control mgr., 1983—88; dir. mfg. Entech Corp., 1988—89; prodn. mgr. metallizing divsn. Risden Corp., Thomaston, Conn., 1989—94, quality process engr., 1994—. Pres. Bus. Consolidating Svcs. Internat., Rocky Hill, Conn., 1989—, quality control technician, 1990—, quality process request divsn., fragrance divsn., 1993—; pres. Cons. Svcs. Internat. Chartered mem. Presdl. Task Force, trustee; preferred mem. U.S. Senatorial Club. Served to cpl. Austrian Air Force, 1959—60. Mem.: Mgmt. Club, Am. Soc. Quality Control, Am. Mgmt. Assn., Screenprinting Assn. Am. Roman Catholic. Home: 13 Clemens Ct Rocky Hill CT 06067-3218 Office: 60 Electric Ave Thomaston CT 06787-1617 also: Bus Consolidating Svcs Internat Rocky Hill CT 06067

MUHLBACH, ROBERT ARTHUR, lawyer; b. Los Angeles, Apr. 13, 1946; s. Richard and Jeanette (Marcus) M.; m. Kerry Eldene Mahoney, July 26, 1986. BSME, U. Calif., Berkeley, 1967; JD, U. Calif., San Francisco, 1976; MME, Calif. State U., 1969; M in Pub. Adminstrn., U. So. Calif., 1978. Bar: Calif. 1976. Pub. defender County of Los Angeles, 1977-79; assoc. Kirtland & Packard LLP, Los Angeles, 1979—85, ptnr., 1986—2001, sr. ptnr., 2001—. Chmn. Santa Monica Airport Commn., Calif., 1984-87, chmn., bd. dirs. Hawthorne Airport Cmty. Assn. Inc. Served to capt. USAF, 1969-73. Mem. ABA, AIAA, Internat. Assn. Def. Counsel, Am. Bd. Trial Advs. Office: Kirtland & Packard LLP 2361 Rosecrans Ave 4th Fl El Segundo CA 90245 Office Phone: 310-536-1000. Business E-Mail: ram@kirtland-packard.com.

MUHLBERGER, RICHARD CHARLES, former museum administrator, writer, educator; b. Engelwood, N.J., Jan. 20, 1938; s. George Albert and Margaret Bertha (Heins) M. AA, Calif. Concordia Coll., 1958; BA, Wayne State U., 1964; MA in Art History, Johns Hopkins U., 1967. Curator mus. edn. Worcester Art Mus., Mass., 1966-72; chmn. edn. Detroit Inst. Arts, 1972-75; dir. Mus. Fine Arts and George Walter Vincent Smith Art Mus., Springfield, Mass., 1976-87; vice dir. for edn. Met. Mus. Art, N.Y.C., 1987-89; dir. Knoxville (Tenn.) Mus. Art, 1990-91; adj. prof. art history Western New England Coll., Springfield, Mass., 1991—. Guest curator Mus. Am. Folk Art, 1997-98; mem. adv. panel NEH, 1976-78, Mass. Coun. on Arts and Humanities, 1979-81; mem. policy panel, mus. program Nat. Endowment Arts, 1981-83. Author: The Bible in Art, The New Testament, 1990, The Bible in Art, The Old Testament, 1990, The Christmas Story, 1990, What Makes a Raphael a Raphael, 1993, What Make a Bruegel a Bruegel, 1993, What Makes a Rembrandt a Rembrandt, 1993, What Makes a Monet a Monet, 1993, What Makes a Degas a Degas, 1993, What Make a Van Gogh a Van Gogh, 1993, What Makes a Leonardo a Leonardo, 1994, What Makes a Goya a Goya, 1994, What Makes a Cassatt a Cassatt, 1994, What Makes a Picasso a Picasso, 1994, The Unseen Van Gogh, 1998, American Folk Marquetry, 1998, Charles Webster Hawthorne: Paintings and Watercolors, 1999. Woodrow Wilson fellow, 1965-66; recipient Outstanding Young Man award Greater Worcester Jaycees, 1970 Mem. Am. Assn. Museums (chmn. com. on edn. 1974-76, councilor 1988-91), New England Mus. Assn. (pres. 1985-87), Phi Beta Kappa. Home: 41 Smithfield Ct Springfield MA 01108-3129

MUHLENBRUCH, CARL W. civil engineer; b. Decatur, Ill., Nov. 21, 1915; s. Carl William and Clara (Theobald) M.; m. Agnes M. Kringel, Nov. 22, 1939; children: Phyllis Elaine Wallace, Joan Carol Wenk. BCE, U. Ill., 1937, CE, 1945; MCE, Carnegie Inst. Tech., 1943; LLD, Concordia U., River Forest, Ill., 1995. Rsch. engr. Aluminum Rsch. Labs., Pitts., 1937-39; cons. engring., 1939-50; mem. faculty Carnegie Inst. Tech., 1939-48; assoc. prof. civil engring. Northwestern U., 1948-54, lectr. in Civil Engring., 1998—; pres. TEC-SEARCH, Inc. (formerly Ednl. and Tech. Consultants Inc.), 1954-67, chmn. bd., 1967—. Pres. Profl. Ctrs. Bldg. Corp., 1961-77; lectr. civil engring., 1997—. Author: Experimental Mechanics and Properties of Materials; contbr. articles to profl. jours. Treas., bd. dirs. Concordia Coll. Found.; dir. Mo. Luth. Synod, 1965-77, vice chmn. 1977-79. Recipient Stanford E. Thompson award, 1945. Mem. Am. Econ. Devel. Coun. (cert. econ. developer), Am. Soc. Engring. Edn. (editor Ednl. Aids in Engring.), NSPE, ASCE, Univ. Club (Evanston), Rotary (dist. gov. 1980-81, dir. svc. projects Ghana and the Bahamas), Sigma Xi, Tau Beta Phi, Omicron Delta Kappa. Home and Office: Tec-Search Inc 4071 Fairway Dr Wilmette IL 60091-1005 Office Phone: 847-256-2750.

MUHLENFELD, ELISABETH S. college president, educator, author; b. Washington, Nov. 12, 1944; d. Merle Roberts and Cornelia Elizabeth (Herring) Showalter; m. Edward F. Muhlenfeld, Sept. 10, 1966 (div. 1975); children: Allison Elisabeth, David Edward; m. Laurin A. Wollan, Jr., June 5, 1982; stepchildren: Ann Louise Wollan, Laurin A. Wollan III. BA in Philosophy, Goucher Coll., 1966; MA in English, U. Tex., Arlington, 1973; PhD, U. S.C., 1978. Rsch. asst., adminstrv. asst. So. Studies program U. S.C., Columbia, 1975-78; asst. prof. English Fla. State U., Tallahassee, 1978-82, assoc. prof., 1982-87, dir. undergrad and grad. studies, assoc. chmn. dept. English, 1987-96, prof. English, 1987-96, dean undergrad. studies, 1984-86; pres. Sweet Briar (Va.) Coll., 1996—. Mem. ABA Commn. on Coll. and Univ. Legal Studies, 1991-94. Author: Mary Boykin Chesnut: A Biography, 1981; editor: William Faulkner's Absolom, Absolom: A Critical Casebook, 1984, The Private Mary Chesnut: The Unpublished Civil War Diaries, 1984. Mem. Capital Women's Network. NEH Dir.'s grantee, 1983-84. Mem. MLA, St. George Tucker Soc. (charter fellow), So. Assn. Women Historians, William Faulkner Soc. (charter mem; sec.-treas. 1991-94), Phi Kappa Phi (exec. bd., pres. 1992-93). Office: Sweet Briar Coll Pres's Office Box C Sweet Briar VA 24595

MUHLERT, JAN KEENE, art museum director; b. Oak Park, Ill., Oct. 4, 1942; d. William Henry and Isabel Janette (Cole) Keene; m. Christopher Layton Muhlert, Jan. 1, 1966; 1 son, Michael Keene. BA in Art and French, Albion (Mich.) Coll., 1964; MA in Art History, Oberlin (Ohio) Coll., 1967; student, Neuchatel (Switzerland) U., Inst. European Studies, Paris, Inst. de Phonetique, Acad. Grande Chaumiere. Asst. curator Allen Meml. Art Mus., Oberlin, 1967-68; asst. curator 20th Century painting and sculpture Nat. Collection Fine Arts, Smithsonian Instn., Washington, 1968-73, assoc. curator, 1974-75; dir. U. Iowa Mus. Art, 1975-79, Amon Carter Mus., Ft. Worth, 1980-95, Palmer Museum of Art, University Park, Pa., 1996—. Author museum brochures, catalogues. Mem. Nat. Mus. Act. Adv. Coun., 1980—83; vis. com. Allen Meml. Art Mus. Oberlin Coll., Ohio, 1992—2003; chair adv. com. North Tex. Inst. Educators on the Visual Arts, U. North Tex., 1992—95. Grantee Nat. Endowment Arts-Donner Found., 1979; recipient Friend of Art Edn. award Tex. Art Edn. Assn., 1994. Mem. Assn. Art Mus. Dirs. (trustee 1981-82, 84-86, 92-93, chmn. govt. and art com. 1982-84, chmn. profl. practices com. 1990-92), Western Assn. Art Mus. (regional rep. 1978-79), Am. Assn. Mus. (commn. for new century 1981-84, gen. co-chair 1993 ann. meeting), Am. Arts Alliance (dir. 1980-86, vice-chmn. 1982-84). Office: Palmer Museum of Art Pa State U Curtin Rd University Park PA 16802-2507

MUHLSCHLEGEL, HARRY J. transportation company executive; m. Karen B. Muhlschlegel. CEO Jevic Transp. Inc., Delanco, N.J., 1981—, pres., 1981-97. Office: Jevic Transp Inc 600-700 Creek Rd Delanco NJ 08075 Fax: 609-764-6724.

MUHN, JUDY ANN, psychologist, trainer, genealogist; b. Detroit, Dec. 29, 1952; d. Wilbur William and Dolores Eleanor (Sutinen) Nimer; m. Dennis James Muhn, June 6, 1975. BS, Mich. State U., 1975; EdM, Boston U., 1992; MA in Counseling, U. San Francisco, 1997. Registered marriage, family and child counselor intern.; lic. psychologist, Mich. Legis. aide press sec. to Calif. state senator, 1982-84; dir. pub. rels. Tierra del Oro coun. Girl Scouts U.S., 1984-86, mgr. mem. devel. San Antonio area coun., 1986-90; counselor Yuba City Indian Health Ctr., 1997; intervention counselor Sutter-Yuba Mental Health, 1997-98; counselor, intern White Ho. Cmty. Counseling Ctr., 1998; pvt. practice Wixom, Mich., 1998—. Adj. faculty Henry Ford C.C., 1998—2001, Oakland C.C., 1998—2001, U. Md.; therapist Brighton (Mich.) Hosp., 2000—01, Advanced Counseling Svcs., Brighton, 2001—03; spkr. in field. Bd. dirs., chmn. pub. affairs com. Planned Parenthood Clinton County, NY, 1980-81; bd. dirs. Family Planning Advs., Albany, 1981, Planned Parenthood San Antonio, 1987-89; co-founder Womanspirit Rising, 1987-89; pres. Planned Parenthood Assn. Sacramento Valley, 1982-84; founder Women's Roundtable, Plattsburgh, 1981; sec. San Antonio Coun. Native Ams., 1986-89; dep. exec. dir. U. Santo Tomas Alumni Assn., 1998-2001; dir. adult devel. and vol. svcs. Girl Scouts of Met. Detroit, 2002—. Mem. Am. Soc. Tng. and Devel., Met. Detroit Vol. Adminstrs., San Antonio Women's C. of C. (bd. dirs. 1989), Nat. Wildlife Fedn., Greenpeace, Amnesty Internat., Sierra Club. Office Phone: 313-972-4475. Business E-Mail: jmuhn@gsfmd.org.

MUI, JIMMY KUN, architect; b. Hong Kong, Sept. 1, 1958; arrived in U.S.A., 1971; s. Yuk-on and Kum-Ngor (Yuen) M.; m. Susan (Yew), Sept. 23, 1989; children: Deborah Yoke-Kit, Peter Wai-Loon. BArch, State Univ. N.Y., Buffalo, 1982, postgrad., 1982—84. Registered architect, N.Y. Architecture aide N.Y.C. Dept. of Health, 1978; intern architect Niagara Frontier Transp. Authority, Buffalo, 1983; architect, drafter Bradley Corp. Pk., Blauvelt, NY, 1984—85; asst. architect City of N.Y. Dept. of Housing Preservation and Devel., 1985—87, N.Y.C. Bd. Edn., NY, 1987—91; prin. arch. J.K. Mui Design, N.Y.C., 1989—; project coord. N.Y.C. Pub. Sch., 1991—98; pres. Mui Enterprises Internat., Bronx, NY, 1994—2000; constrn. mgr. Fedayeen Constrn. Co., LLC, Ctrl. Bklyn., 1998—2000; pres. Mui Enterprises, Inc., N.Y.C., 2001—. Mem. CCM Assoc., LLC, Norwich, Conn., 2001—03. Vice chmn. bd. dir. Hong Kong Students Assn. N.Y., Inc., 1989-91, chmn., 1987-89, pres., 1986; sec. Moy Shee Family Assn., N.Y.C., 1999-2000, pres., 2001-02, advisor, 2003—; bd. dir. Moy's Clan Assn., 2002—, World Moy Clan's Assn., 2002—. Recipient N.Y. State Regent Scholarship Award, 1977-81, Husted Eward Scholarship, State Univ. N.Y., 1980. Roman Catholic. Home: 2237 Haviland Ave Bronx NY 10462-5202 Office: 230 Grand St Ste 402A New York NY 10013 Office Phone: 212-941-9242. Business E-Mail: jimmy@jkmui.com.

MUILENBURG, JOHN POWELL, minister; b. Grand Rapids, Mich., Oct. 26, 1911; s. Teunis William and Sena Muilenburg; m. Virgina Louise Turpin, Apr. 2, 1944; children: Peter, Jonathan, Stephan, Bartholomew. BA, Hope Coll., Holland, Mich., 1933; ThM, Princeton Theology Sem., 1938; MDiv, New Brunswick Theology Sem., New Brunswick, N.J., 1936. Pastor Ref. Ch. in Am., Rocky Hill, NJ, 1938—40, asst. pastor Kingston, NY, 1940—41, missionary to China N.Y., 1942—50, missionary to Philippines, 1952—67, exec. staff nat. coun. of ch., 1967—76. Town coun. Town of Penney Farms, Fla., 1995—98, mayor, 1999—2000. Recipient A.J. Muste award, New Brunswick Theology Sem., 1986. Democrat. Reformed Ch. In Am. Avocations: tennis, golf, music, sailing. Home: 4400 Ott St Penney Farms FL 32079

MUIR, DONALD M. electronics company executive; BBA in Acctg., U. Mass.; MBA in Fin., Boston U. Various positions Prime Computer, Inc., Natick, Mass.; contr. customer svc., mgr. mfg. planning Stratus Computer, Marlboro, Mass., dir. fin. and adminstrn., treas.; CFO Am. Power Conversion Corp., West Kingston, R.I., 1995—. Office: Am Power Conversion Corp 132 Fairgrounds Rd Kingston RI 02892

MUIR, HELEN, journalist; b. Yonkers, N.Y., Feb. 9, 1911; d. Emmet A. and Helen T. (Flaherty) Lennehan; m. William Whalley Muir, Jan. 23, 1936; children: Mary Muir Burrell, William Torbert. With Yonkers Herald Statesman, 1929-30, 31-33, N.Y. Evening Post, 1930-31, N.Y. Evening Jour., 1933-34, Carl Byoir & Assocs., N.Y.C., Miami, 1934-35; syndicated columnist Universal Svc., Miami, 1935-38; columnist Miami Herald, 1941-42; children's book editor, 1949-56; women's editor Miami Daily News, 1943-44; freelance mag. writer numerous nat. mags., 1944—. Drama critic Miami News, 1960-65. Author: Miami, U.S.A., 1953, expanded edit., 2000, Biltmore: Beacon for Miami, 1987, 3d rev. edit., 1998, Frost in Florida: A Memoir, 1995. Trustee Coconut Grove Libr. Assn., Friends U. Miami Libr., Friends Miami-Dade Pub. Libr.; vis. com. U. Miami Librs.; bd. dirs. Miami-Dade County Pub. Libr. Sys., chmn. emeritus, 1999. Recipient award Delta Kappa Gamma, 1960, trustees and friends award Fla. Libr. Assn., 1973, award Coun. Fla. Librs., 1990, trustee citation ALA, 1984, spirit of excellence award, 1988; named to Fla. Women's Hall of Fame, 1984, Miami Centennial '96 Women's Hall of Fame; named chmn. emeritus Metro-Dade Libr. Sys., 1999. Mem.: ALA (named leading libr. adv. 20th Century), Authors' Guild, Soc. Women Geographers (meritorious svc. award 1996, Fla. Groups First Woman of World award 2000), Women in Comms. (Cmty. Headliner award 1973), Biscayne Bay Yacht Club, Cosmopolitan Club (N.Y.C.), Fla.Women's Press Club (award 1963). Home: 3855 Stewart Ave Miami FL 33133-6734

MUIR, J. DAPRAY, lawyer; b. Washington, Nov. 9, 1936; s. Brockett and Helen Cassin (Dapray) M.; m. Louise Rutherfurd Pierrepont, July 16, 1966. AB, Williams Coll., 1958; JD, U. Va., 1964. Bar: Md., Va., D.C. 1964, U.S. Supreme Ct. 1967. Ptnr. Ruddy & Muir, LLP, Washington; asst. legal advisor for econ. and bus. affairs U.S. Dept. State, 1971-73. Mem. U.S. del. to Joint U.S./USSR Comml. Commn., 1972; chmn. D.C. Securities Adv. Com., 1981-84, mem. 1985-88. Bd. editors Va. Law Rev, 1963-64; contbr. articles to profl. jours. Bd. dirs. Trust Mus. Exhbns., 1997—, Internat. Fedn. Insts. Advanced Study, 1992—97. Lt. (j.g.) USNR, 1958—61. Mem. Am. Arbitration Assn. (panel of comml. arbitrators, 1997—), D.C. Bar (chmn. internat. law div. 1977-78, chmn. environ., energy and natural resources div. 1982-83), Met. Club (Washington), Chevy Chase (Md.) Club. Home: 3104 Q St NW Washington DC 20007-3027 Office: 1717 K St NW Ste 600 Washington DC 20036 Business E-Mail: muirlaw@aol.com.

MUIR, MALCOLM, federal judge; b. Englewood, N.J., Oct. 20, 1914; s. John Merton and Sarah Elizabeth Muir; m. Alma M. Brohard, Sept. 6, 1940 (dec. 1985); children: Malcolm, Thomas, Ann Muir, Barbara (dec.), David Clay. BA, Lehigh U., 1935; LL.B., Harvard U., 1938. Sole practice, Williamsport, Pa., 1938-42, 45-49, 68-70; mem. firm, 1949-68; judge U.S. Dist. Ct. (mid. dist.) Pa., 1970—. Active charitable orgns., Williamsport, 1939-70 Mem. ABA, Pa. Bar Assn. (pres.-elect 1970) Avocation: reading. Office: US Dist Ct Ste 401 240 W 3rd St Williamsport PA 17701-6461

MUIR, PATRICIA ALLEN, professional association administrator; b. Dallas, Nov. 4, 1929; d. Jack Charleton Allen and Anna Patricia (Hovis) Allen Atchison; m. Lester Doyle Rader, Jr., Aug. 4, 1950 (dec. Sept. 1950); 1 child, Lester Doyle III; m. Perren James Muir, June 2, 1956 (div.); children: Edward John, Patricia Jane. Grad., Our Lady of Victory Coll., 1948; student, George Washington U., 1948-49, Washington Sch. for Sec., 1949-50. Traffic mgr. Am. Storage Co., Washington, 1960-69; asst. sec. Ind. Tele. Pioneer Assn., Washington, 1969-76; adminstrv. asst. ALA, Washington, 1977-98, staff liaison to Fed. Libr. Round Table, 1991-98, staff liaison to Armed Forces Libr. Round Table, 1991-98, staff liaison to Govt. Documents Round Table, 1991-98; office mgr. Fed. Documents Clearing House, Washington, 1998-2000; cons., 2000—. Columnist, contbr. The Ind. Pioneer, 1969-76. V.p. Friendship House Child Devel. Ctr. Parents, Washington, 1978, pres., 1979—83; mem. parish coun. St. Peter's Cath. Ch., 1987—91, mem. edn. and spiritual devel. com., 1986—, chair, 1988—91, coord. Bible study, 1999—2003; vol. St. Peter's Interparish Sch. Reading Program, 2001—02. Mem. Ladies Ancient Order of Hibernians (state pres. 1991-97, nat. budget com. 1996-98, nat. elections com. 1998—, nat. constn. com. 1998-02, nat. rules of order com. 2000-02). Avocations: travel, genealogy, reading, writing. Home: 343 11th St SE Washington DC 20003-2105

MUIR, RUTH BROOKS, counselor, substance abuse service coordinator; b. Washington, Nov. 27, 1924; d. Charles and Adelaide Chenery (Masters) B.; m. Robert Mathew Muir, Nov. 26, 1947 (dec. Feb. 20, 1996); children: Robert Brooks, Martha Louise, Heather Sue. BA in Art, Rollins Coll., Winter Park, Fla., 1947; MA in Rehab. Counseling, U. Iowa, 1979. Cert. substance abuse counselor, Iowa. Program advisor Iowa Meml. Union, Iowa City, 1959-66; counselor, coord. Mid Eastern Coun. on Chem. Abuse, Iowa City, 1976-81; patient rep. Univ. Hosp., Iowa City, 1982-85; rsch. project interviewer dept. psychiatry U. Iowa Coll. Medicine, 1985-88; pvt. practice family counselor, 1984—. Docent U. Iowa Mus. of Art, 1999—. Art exhibited at Iowa City Sr. Ctr., 1987, 92, Iowa City Art Ctr., 1989, U. Iowa Hosp., 1991, Great Midwestern Ice Cream Co., 1991, Summit St. Gallery, 1995, Iowa City C. of C., 2001, Iowa City's First Art Walk March, 2003; creator, coord. therapeutic series Taking Control, Iowa City Sr. Ctr., 1986-87, Art Walk Lorenz Boot Shop, 2003. Vol. coord. art exhibits Sr. Ctr., Iowa City, 1992-94, Iowa City Arts Exhbn. Com., 1996, Arrowmont Sch. Art, 1996—, Arrowmont Amb., 1996-98; treas. bd. dirs. Crisis Ctr., Iowa City, 1976-77; sec. coun. elders Sr. Citizens Ctr., Iowa City, 1976-78; pres. Unitarian-Universalist Iowa City Women's Fedn., 1985; friend U. Iowa Mus. Art, docent, 1999—; active Opera Supers, Iowa City Unitarian U.N. Envoy; fgn. rels. coun., bd. dirs. annual changing family conf. U. Iowa, 1986 92; non govtl. rep. Earth Summit Global Forum, 1992; care review bd. Mental Health Homes, 1997-99; bd. dirs. Arts Iowa City, 2002—. Mem.: AAUW (state cultural rep. 1990—92, Iowa City chpt. co-chair for programs 1998—99), Health Care: Health Svcs., Nat. League Am. PEN Women (membership chair 2002—04, v.p. 2004—), Iowa City Unitarian Soc. (adult program com. 1993—94, unitarian care com. 1993—, membership com.), Nat. Soc. Colonial Dames, U. Iowa Print and Drawing Study Club (bd. dirs. 2003—04), Pi Beta Phi (pres. alumnae club 1995—97). Home and Office: 6 Glendale Ct Iowa City IA 52245-4430 Office Phone: 319-337-7287. Business E-Mail: ruthmuir@inav.net.

MUIR, WARREN ROGER, chemist, executive; b. N.Y., 1945; s. Ernest Roger and Phyllis (Stirn) M.; m. Jo-Ann McNally; children: Amy, Douglas, Michael, Gregory, Daniel. AB in Chemistry cum laude, Amherst Coll., 1967; MS in Chemistry, Northwestern U., Evanston, Ill., 1968, PhD in Chemistry, 1971; postgrad. in epidemiology, Johns Hopkins U., 1975-77. Sr. staff mem. environ. health council on Environ. Quality, EPA, Washington, 1971-78; dir. Office of Toxic Substances, EPA, 1978-81; pres. Hampshire Rsch. Assocs., Inc., 1981-99, Hampshire Rsch. Inst., 1987-99; exec. dir. divsn. earth and life studies NRC/Nat. Acad. Scis., 1999—. Assoc. environ. health scis. Johns Hopkins U., 1981-99; rsch. prof. biology Am. U., 1985; sr. fellow INFORM, 1982-95; mem. Nat. Conf. Lawyers and Scientists, 1987-89; bd. environ. scis. and toxicology Nat. Rsch. Coun., 1997-99 Contbr. articles on environ. quality to profl. jours. Mem., chair several Nat. Rsch. Coun. coms.; pres. Children's Friendship Project for No. Ireland, 1997-99, bd. dirs. 1995—, chair 1997-2002, bd. dirs. HasNa, Inc., 2003-. Recpient NSF Acad. award, 1966, Howard Waters Doughty prize Amherst Coll., 1967, Forris Jewett Moore fellow, 1967; comdr., 1996, officer brother Most Venerable Order of St. John, 1992; co-recipient Adminstrs. award U.S. EPA, 1992, Cmty. Svc. award Nat. Acads., 2003. Mem.: AAAS, Am. Chem. Soc. Home: 9426 Forest Haven Dr Alexandria VA 22309-3151

MUIR, WILLIAM KER, JR., political science educator; b. Detroit, Oct. 30, 1931; s. William Ker and Florence Taylor (Bodman) M.; m. Paulette Irene Wauters, Jan. 16, 1960; children: Kerry Macaire, Harriet Bodman. BA, Yale U., 1954, PhD, 1965; JD, U. Mich., 1958. Bar: N.Y. 1960, Conn. 1965. Instr. U. Mich. Law Sch., 1958-59; assoc. firm Davis Polk & Wardwell, NYC, 1959-60; lectr. in polit. sci. Yale U., 1960-64, 65-67; from assoc. to ptnr. Tyler Cooper Grant Bowerman & Keefe, New Haven, 1964-68; prof. emeritus polit. sci. U. Calif., Berkeley, 1968-98, dept. chmn., 1980-83; speechwriter v.p. U.S., 1983-85; columnist Oakland (Calif.) Tribune, 1992-93; writer Gov. of Calif., Sacramento, 1994. Sr. cons. Calif. State Assembly, Sacramento, 1975-76; cons. Oakland Police Dept., 1969-74; vis. prof. polit. sci. Harvard U., summers 1976, 79; vis. prof. Hawaii Pacific U., 2000, U. Ariz., 2002. Author: Prayer in the Public School, 1967, later republished as Law and Attitude Change, 1974, Police: Streetcorner Politicians, 1977, Legislature: California's School for Politics, 1982, The Bully Pulpit: The Presidential Leadership of Ronald Reagan, 1993, An Understanding of Democracy, 2003, Power and American Democracy, 2003, memoirs, 2003. Mem. Berkeley Police Rev. Commn., 1981-83; chmn. New Haven Civil Liberties Coun., 1965-68; Rep. candidate Calif. State Assembly, 1996. Recipient Hadley B. Cantril Meml. award, 1979, Disting. Tchg. award U. Calif., Berkeley, 1974, Phi Beta Kappa No. Calif. Assoc. Excellence in Tchg. award, 1994. Mem. Am. Polit. Sci. Assn. (Edward S. Corwin award 1966). Republican. Presbyterian. Home: 59 Parkside Dr Berkeley CA 94705-2409 Office: Dept Polit Sci U Calif Berkeley CA 94720-1950 E-mail: sandymuir@aol.com.

MUIR, WILLIAM LLOYD, III, academic administrator; b. Norton, Kans., Mar. 20, 1948; s. John Thomas and Rosalie June (Benton) M. BBA, Kans. State U., 1977. Asst. sec. of state State of Kans., Topeka, 1971-72, fin. adminstr. atty. gen. office, 1972-79, comptr. Office of Gov., 1979-87, sec. of cabinet, 1979-87, asst. sec. adminstrn., 1986-87; dir. econ. devel. Kans. State U., Manhattan, 1987-91, asst. to v.p. for cmty. rels., 1991—2002, faculty rep., senator Student Governing Assn., 1992—, mem. union governing bd., 1997—, asst. v.p. for cmty. rels., 2002—. Chmn. housing appeals bd. City of Manhattan, 1996—; trustee Kans. State U. Found., 1993—; mem. Leadership Kans., 1989; state officer Native Sons and Daus., 1997—2002, pres., 2001; mem. Kans. Territorial Sesquicentennial Commn., 2003—, Kans. Capitol Area Plaza Authority, 2004—; bd. dirs. United Way Riley County, 1989—99, chmn., 1992; treas. Flint Hills Regional Leadership Program, 2002—. Mem.: Nat. Geog. Soc., Friends of Cedar Crest Assn., Sierra Club, Blue Key, Masons (Scottish Rite), Alpha Kappa Psi, Alpha Tau Omega (nat. officer, bd. govs. Alpha Tau Omega Found.). Episcopalian. Avocations: travel, volunteer work, advising. Home: 2040 Shirley Ln Manhattan KS 66502-2059 Office: Kansas State U 122 Anderson Hall Manhattan KS 66506-0100 Office Phone: 785-532-6269. Business E-Mail: billmuir@ksu.edu.

MUIRHEAD, JAMES RUSSELL, federal judge; b. Phillipsburg, Pa., Apr. 11, 1941; BS, Cornell U., 1963, LLB, 1966. Bar: N.H. 1966. Pvt. practice, Manchester, N.H., 1966-95; magistrate judge for N.H., U.S. Fed. Ct., Concord, N.H., 1995—. Office: WB Rudman US Courthouse 55 Pleasant St Concord NH 03301-3954

MUIRHEAD, VINCENT URIEL, retired aerospace engineer; b. Dresden, Kans., Feb. 6, 1919; s. John Hadsell and Lily Irene (McKinney) M.; m. Bobby Jo Thompson, Nov. 5, 1943; children: Rosalind, Jean, Juleigh. BS, U.S. Naval Acad., 1941; BS in Aero. Engring, U.S. Naval Postgrad. Sch., 1948; Aero. Engr., Calif. Inst. Tech., 1949; postgrad., U. Ariz., 1962, 64, Okla. State U., 1963. Midshipman U.S. Navy, 1937, commd. ensign, 1941, advanced through grades to comdr., 1951; nav. officer U.S.S. White Plains, 1945-46; comdr. Fleet Aircraft Service Squad, 1951-52; with Bur. Aeros., Ft. Worth, 1953-54; comdr. Helicopter Utility Squadron I, Pacific Fleet, 1955-56; chief staff officer Comdr. Fleet Air, Philippines, 1956-58; exec. officer Naval Air Tng. Center, Memphis, 1958-61; ret., 1961; asst. prof. U. Kans., Lawrence, 1961-63, assoc. prof. aerospace engring., 1964-76, prof., 1976-89, prof. emeritus, 1989—, chmn. dept., 1976-88. Cons. Black & Veatch (cons. engrs.), Kansas City, Mo., 1964— Author: Introduction to Aerospace, 1972, 5th edit., 1994, Thunderstorms, Tornadoes and Building Damage, 1975. Decorated Air medal. Fellow AIAA (assoc.); mem. Am. Acad. Mechanics, Am. Soc. Engring. Edn., Tau Beta Pi, Sigma Gamma Tau. Mem. Ch. of Christ (elder 1972-96). Achievements include research on aircraft, tornado vortices, shock tubes and waves Home: 503 Park Hill Ter Lawrence KS 66046-4841 Office: Dept Aero Engring Univ Kans Lawrence KS 66045-0001 E-mail: vmuirhead

MUJICA, BARBARA LOUISE, language educator, writer; d. Louis and Frieda (Kline) Kaminar; m. Mauro E. Mujica, Dec. 26, 1966; children: Lillian Louise, Mariana Ximena, Mauro Eduardo Ignacio. AB, UCLA, 1964; MA, Middlebury Coll., 1965; PhD, NYU, 1974. Instr. French UCLA, 1963-64; assoc. editor modern langs. Harcourt Brace Jovanovich, N.Y.C., 1966-73; instr., asst. prof. Romance langs. CUNY, 1973-74; prof. Spanish Georgetown U., Washington, 1974—. Mem. faculty NEH Summer Inst., 1980. Author: (book) A-LM Spanish, Levels I-IV, 1969—74, Readings in Spanish Literature, 1975, Calderon's Characters: An Existential Point of View, 1980, Pasaporte, 1980, rev. edit., 1984, Aqui y ahora, 1979, Entrevista, 1982, Iberian Pastoral Characters, 1986, Texto y Espectáculo, 1987, Et in Arcadia Ego, 1990, Texto y Vida: Introduccion a la Literature Española, 1990, Antología de la Literatura Española: La Edad Media, 1991, Renacimiento y Siglo de Oro, 1991, Siglos XVII y XIX, 1999, Texto y Vida: Introduccion a la Literature Hispano-Americana, 1992, Looking at the Comedia in the Year of the Quincentennial, 1993, Premio Nobel, 1997, Books of the Americas, 1997, El Texto Puesto en Escena, 2000, (novels) Sanchez Across the Street, 1997, The Deaths of Don Bernardo, 1990, Far From My Mother's Home, 1999, Frida: A Novel, 2001; editor: (book) Milenio, 2002, Teresa de Jesus: Espiritualidad y feminismo, Comedia Performance Jour.; editor, pub. Verbena: Bilingual Rev. of Arts, 1979—85, sr. assoc. editor, bd. dirs. Washington Rev., mem. editl. bd. Bull. of Comediantes Hispana. Named winner, E.L. Doctorow Internat. Fiction Competition, 1992; named one of 50 Best Op Eds of Decade, N.Y. Times, 1990; recipient Pangolin prize best short story, 1998, Hoepner award for fiction; grantee, Spanish Govt., 1987, Poets and Writers of N.Y.; Penfield fellow, 1971. Mem.: MLA (pres. Golden Age sect.), Assn. Hispanic Classical Theater (bd. dirs.). Office: Georgetown U Dept Spanish Washington DC 20057-1039

MUJICA, MAURO E. architect; b. Antofagasta, Chile, Apr. 20, 1941; came to U.S., 1965, naturalized, 1970; s. Mauro Raul and Graciela (Parodi-Blayfus) M.; m. Barbara Louise Kaminar, Dec. 26, 1966; children: Lillian Louise, Mariana Ximena, Mauro Eduardo Ignacio III. BArch, MArch, Columbia U., 1971. Head designer Columbia U. Office Archtl. Planning, N.Y.C., 1966-71; project mgr. Walker, Sander, Ford & Kerr, Architects, Princeton, N.J., 1971-72; prin. Mauro E. Mujica, Architect, N.Y.C., 1972-74; dir. internat. divsn. Greenhorne & O'Mara, Inc., Riverdale, Md., 1974-78; ptnr. Mujica & Reddy Architects, Washington, 1978-80; prin. Mauro E. Mujica, Architect, Washington, 1980-81; ptnr. Mujica & Berlin Investment Bankers, Washington, 1982-85, Mujica Keppie Henderson Internat., Washington and Glasgow, Scotland, 1981-83, Mujica-Seifert Architects, Washington and London, 1983-87; pres.,CDEO, The Pace Group, Washington, 1987-91; ptnr. Pace/Walsh Internat., London and Washington. Chmn. bd., CEO, U.S. English Found., Washington, 1993—; hon. mem. Emmanuel Coll. Cambridge (Eng.) U., 1995; mem. adv. bd. U.S.-U.K. Fulbright Commn., 1995-2000.

MUJUMDAR, VILAS SITARAM, structural engineer, researcher; b. Indore, India, June 26, 1941; arrived in U.S., 1968; s. Sitaram and Kamala (Kulkarni) Mujumdar; m. Ingrid M. Dietrich, Mar. 1, 1969. BSCE, Vikram U., India, 1961; MS, U. Roorkee, India, 1962; MBA, U. Santa Clara, Calif., 1980; D in Pub. Adminstrn., U. So. Calif., 2000. Registered profl. engr., U.S., Can., Eng., structural engr., Calif. Design engr. U.S.D. & Co., India, 1962-65, Donovan H. Lee & Ptnrs., London, 1965-66; asst. chief engr. Francon & Spancrete Ltd., Montreal, Canada, 1966-68; gen. mgr., dir. engring. Modular Constructors, Woburn, Mass., 1968-70; sr. project engr., tech. mgr. LeMessurier Assocs., Cambridge, Mass., 1970-74; v.p. Precast Sys. Cons., Woburn, 1974-77; prin. structural engr. Ecodyne Corp., Santa Rosa, Calif., 1977-79; v.p. Foster Engring., Inc., San Francisco, 1979-81, 3D/Internat. Inc., Houston, 1981-85; pres. VSM Assocs., Santa Rosa, 1985-88; v.p. BSHA, Inc., San Diego, 1988-90; pres. McNamara, Salvia, Mujumdar, Inc., San Diego, 1990-92; chief ops. Divsn. State Arch. Dept. Gen. Svcs., Calif., 1992-2000; exec. dir. Concrete Masonry Assn. Calif., Nev., 2000—02; program dir. NSF, 2003—. Mem. steering con. U.S.-Japan Seismic Rsch.; chmn. several earthquake engring. coms. Author: (book) Concrete Design Manual, Structural Engineer Review Course; contbr. articles to profl. jours. Recipient Gold medal, numerous awards; Merit scholar, Govt. India, 1957—62. Fellow: ASCE, Am. Concrete Inst., Inst. Structural Engrs. U.K.; mem.: Soc. Risk Analysis, Masonry Soc. (mem. code com., mem. tech. activities com.), Structural Engrs. Assn. Calif. (chmn. seismology com. 1992—93), Prestressed Concrete Inst., Beta Gamma Sigma (hon. bus. soc.). Achievements include invention of pre-cast concrete buidling system. Home: 9905 Trosby Ct Vienna VA 22181 E-mail: vilas.mujumdar@earthlink.net.

MUKAMAL, DAVID SAMIER, sign manufacturing company executive; b. Baghdad, Iraq, Oct. 6, 1944; arrived in US, 1950; s. Abraham Sassoon and Mary (Murad) M.; m. Anitamarie Costa, July 31, 1970; children: Adam Scott, Rebecca Kate. BBA in Econs. with honors, Bryant Coll., 1970; MBA in Fin. Mgmt., Iona Coll., 1975. Budget analyst USV Pharm./Revlon, Inc., Tuckahoe, N.Y., 1970-72; sr. budget officer Met. Transp. Authority, N.Y.C., 1972-74; sr. fin. analyst Am. Airlines, Inc., Dallas, 1974-82; chmn. DSM Industries Inc.; pres. All State Signs, Richardson, Tex., 1982—, Framed Enterprises, Inc., Irving, Tex., 1995-99. With USN, 1965-66. Recipient Jerremiah Clarke Barber award Bryant Coll., 1970. Mem. Dallas Apt. Assn., Tex. Sign Mfrs. Assn., Internat. Sign Assn., La Cima Club (bd. dirs.), Omicron Delta Epsilon. Republican. Jewish.

MUKASEY, MICHAEL B. federal judge; b. 1941; AB, Columbia U., 1963; LLB, Yale U., 1967. Assoc. Webster Sheffield Fleishchmann Hitchcock & Brookfield, 1967-72, Patterson, Belknap, Webb & Tyler, 1976-88; asst. U.S. atty. U.S. Dist. Ct. (so. dist.) N.Y., 1972-76, dist. judge, 1988—. Lectr. in law Columbia Law Sch. Contbr. articles to profl. jours. Office: US Dist Ct US Courthouse 500 Pearl St New York NY 10007-1316

MUKERJEE, DEBDAS, environmental health scientist, educator; b. Darjeeling, India; came to U.S., 1959. s. Suresh Chandra and Bidyutlata Mukerjee; m. Bhaisa Freny Dee, July 15, 1959; 1 child, Shaibal. BSc with honors, Calcutta (India) U., 1954, MSc, 1957; PhD, U. Ky., 1962. Rsch. prof. pathology Jefferson Med. Coll., Thomas Jefferson U., Phila., 1974-80; sr. sci. advisor, environ. health scientist U.S. EPA Environ. Criteria Assessment Office, Cin., 1980-91; environ. health scientist U.S. EPA Nat. Ctr. for Environtl. Assessment, Cin., 1991—; adj. prof. toxicology Inst. Toxicology, U. Kiel (Germany) Med. Sch., 1990—. Adj. prof. environ. toxicology Ohio No. U., Ada, 1998-2001; assoc. prof. pathology, dir. divsn. basic rsch. U. Tex. Med. Br., Galveston, 1969-74; asst. prof. biology M.D. Anderson Hosp. & Tumor Inst., U. Tex. Cancer Ctr., Houston, 1966-69; mem. NATO/Com. Challenges of Modern Soc. Study on Internat. Info. Exch. of Dioxins and Related Compounds, 1985-88. Contbr. articles to profl. jours., chpts. to books. Sir J.C. Bose rsch. scholar Bose Inst., Calcutta, 1958; recipient silver medal for commendable svc. to EPA, 1980, Silver medal USEPA, 2002. Mem. AAAS, World Affairs Coun. Greater Cin., N.Y. Acad. Scis. Achievements include pioneering in risk assessment of dioxins, pcbs, children's risk from aggregate exposures to environmental pollutants; methodology of risk assessment, xenoestrogen related feminization of males in human, in vitro transformation of cells from cancer genetic susceptible persons; human secondary trisomy chromosome, transclocation between sex and somatic chromosomes, sex chromosome abnormalities. Avocations: comparative religion, philosophy of life, reading, writing. Office: US EPA Nat Ctr Environ Assessment Cincinnati OH 45268-0001 Office Phone: 513-569-7572. Business E-Mail: mukerjee.debdas@epa.gov.

MUKERJEE, PASUPATI, chemistry professor; b. Calcutta, India, Feb. 13, 1932; s. Nani Gopal and Probhabati (Ghosal) M.; m. Lalita Sarkar, Feb. 29, 1964 (dec.); [illegible] Mina Maitra, Nov. 14, 1998. B.Sc., Calcutta U., 1949, M.Sc., 1951; Ph[illegible] So. Calif., 1957. Lectr., vis. asst. prof. U. So. Calif., 1956-57; rsch [illegible] khaven Nat. Lab., L.I., 1957-59; reader in phys. chemistry [illegible] ation of Sci., Calcutta, 1959-64; guest scientist U. Utrecht, [illegible] ientist chemistry dept. U. So. Calif., 1964-66; vis. assoc. [illegible] on, 1966-67, prof. Sch. Pharmacy, 1967-94, emeritus [illegible] of. Indian Inst. Tech., Kharagpur, 1971-72; mem. [illegible] urface chemistry Internat. Union Pure and Applied [illegible] to profl. jours.; mem. editl. bd. Jour. Colloid and [illegible] ian Jour. Pharm. Scis., 1978-85, Colloids and Surfaces, 1980-86. Grantee USPHS, NSF, Nat. Bur. Stds., Petroleum Rsch. Fund. Fellow AAAS, Acad. Pharm. Scis., Am. Inst. Chemistry; mem. Am. Chem. Soc. (editorial bd. Langmuir 1985-86), Am. Pharm. Assn., Acad. Pharm. Scis., Rho Chi. Home: 5526 Varsity Hl Madison WI 53705-4652 Office: 777 Highland Ave Madison WI 53705-2222 Office Phone: 608-262-7289.

MUKERJEE, SHAIBAL, environmental scientist; b. Lexington, Ky., Sept. 29, 1962; s. Debdas and Freny Dee (Bhaisa) M.; m. Mamta Syal, Oct. 3, 1997. BS, Xavier U., 1986; MS, U. Cin., 1988, PhD, 1991. Rsch. phys. scientist EPA, Research Triangle Park, N.C., 1991—. Guest editor Environ. Internat., 1997, Sci. Total Environment, 2001. Mem. Internat. Soc. Exposure Analysis, Air and Waste Mgmt. Assn. (chair U.S.-Mex. border air quality sessions 1999). Achievements include research in atmospheric characterization and modeling of incinerator emissions, environmental and exposure studies in U.S.-Mexico border region, wind sector analysis for source apportionment air studies, transboundary air pollution assessments, and development of risk apportionment concept.

MUKHERJEE, AMIYA K. metallurgy and materials science educator; PhD, Oxford (Eng.) U., 1962. Prof. U. Calif., Davis. Recipient Alexander von Humboldt award Fed. Republic Germany, 1988, Albert Easton White Disting. Tchr. award Am. Soc. Materials, 1992, Pfeil medal and prize Inst. Materials, 1993, U. Calif. prize and citation, 1993, Anatoly Bochvar medal U. Moscow, 1996, Inst. medal Max Planck Inst. for Metallforschung, 1997. Office: U Calif Davis Dept Chem Engring & Material Sci Davis CA 95616 E-mail: akmukherjee@ucdavis.edu.

MUKHERJEE, ASIT BARAN, geneticist, educator; b. Suri, India; came to U.S., 1963; s. Shyama Pada and Sabasana (Chatterjee) M.; m. Tapani Ghoshal; 1 child, Deepro. BS, U. Utah, 1965, MS, 1966, PhD, 1968. Rsch. assoc. Upstate Med. Ctr., Syracuse, N.Y., 1968-69, Columbia U. Med. Ctr., N.Y.C., 1969-70; instr. Albert Einstein Coll. Medicine, N.Y.C., 1970-72; from asst. prof. to prof. Fordham U., N.Y.C., 1972-83, prof., 1983—. Author, co-author monographs, book chpts.; contbr. over 50 articles to profl. jours. Tchg. fellow U. Utah, 1965-67, Presl. fellow, 1967-68, NIH fellow, 1969-70; grantee W. Alton Jones Found., 1973-83, Whitehall Found., 1977-83, NIH, Minority Access to Rsch. Career, 1984-89. Mem. Gerentol. Soc. Am., Am. Soc. Human Genetics. Office: Fordham U 441 E Fordham Rd Bronx NY 10458-9993 Business E-Mail: mukherjee@fordham.edu.

MUKHERJEE, BHARATI (MRS. CLARK BLAISE), author, English educator; b. Calcutta, India, July 27, 1940; d. Sudhir Lal and Bina (Banerjee) M.; m. Clark L. Blaise, Sept. 19, 1963; children: Bart Anand, Bernard Sudhir. BA, U. Calcutta, 1959; MA, U. Baroda, India, 1961; MFA, U. Iowa, 1963, PhD, 1969. Instr. in English Marquette U., Milw., 1964-65; instr. U. Wis., Milw., 1965; lectr. McGill U., Montreal, Que., Can., 1966-69, asst. prof. English, 1969-73, assoc. prof., 1973-78, prof., 1978-79, Skidmore Coll., Saratoga Springs, N.Y., 1979-84; assoc. prof. Montclair (N.J.) State College, 1984-87; prof. CUNY, 1987-89, U. Calif., Berkeley. Vis. prof. of writing U. Iowa, Iowa City, 1979, 82; vis. prof. Emory U., Atlanta, 1983. Author: The Tiger's Daughter, 1972, Wife, 1975, (with Clark Blaise) Days and Nights in Calcutta, 1977, Darkness, 1985, The Middleman and Other Stories, 1988 (Nat. Book Critics Circle award 1989), (with Clark Blaise) The Sorrow and the Terror, 1988, Jasmine, 1989, The Holder of the World, 1993, Leave It to Me, 1997, Desirable Daughters, 2002, The Tree Bride, 2004; contbr. short stories, essays and book revs. to several jours. Grantee McGill U., 1968, 70, Can. Arts Coun., 1973-74, 77, Shastri Indo-Can. Inst., 1976-77, Guggenheim Found., 1978-79, Can. Govt., 1982; recipient 1st prize Periodical Distbn. Assn., 1980, NEA award, 1986. Mem. PEN. Hindu. Office: U Calif Dept English 322 Wheeler Hall Berkeley CA 94720-1030*

MUKHERJEE, BHRAMAR, statistician, educator; b. Calcutta, India, Oct. 22, 1973; arrived in U.S., 1996; d. Ashok and Ira Mukhopadhyay; m. Yashowanto M. Ghosh, July 31, 1996; 1 child, Mrittika Ghosh. BSc in Statis., Presidency Coll., Calcutta, India, 1991—94; MS in Applied Stats. and Data Analysis, Indian Statis. Inst., Calcutta, India, 1994—96; MS in Math. Sci., Purdue U., West Lafayette, Ind., 1999, PhD in Stats., 2001. Rsch. asst., tchg. asst. Dept. Stats., Purdue U., West Lafayette, Ind., 1996—2001, vis. asst. prof., 2001; intern Eli Lilly and Co., Indpls., 2000; vis. scholar Stanford U., Calif., 2002; asst. prof. Dept. Stats., U. Fla., Gainesville, 2002—. Reviewer Jour. of Statis. Planning and Inference; contbr. articles to profl. jours. Grantee, Purdue Rsch. Found., 1998—2000, NSF, 2002—03; Debesh-Kamal scholar, The Ramakrishna Mission, India, 1996. Mem.: Internat. Indian Statis. Assn. (exec. bd. mem., rep. of young profl. statisticians 2003—), Am. Statis. Assn. (jour. reviewer, mem., com. on minorities in stats. 2004—). Avocations: theater, literature, music, art. Home: The Reserve at Kanapaha Apt 321 4440 SW Archer Rd Gainesville FL 32608 Office: Dept Stats Univ Fla 226 Griffin-Floyd Hall Gainesville FL 32611-8545 Business E-Mail: mukherjee@stat.ufl.edu.

MUKHERJEE, PRACHETA, management educator, researcher, consultant; b. Kanpur, India, Sept. 2, 1951; came to U.S., 1984; s. Shyamapada and Gouri (Banerjee) Mukherjee; m. Krishna Chakravarty, Feb. 28, 1981. BSc with honors, Ranchi (Bihar) U., 1972; MBA, Indian Inst. Mgmt., Calcutta, West Bengal, 1975; MS, U. Kans., 1988, PhD, 1992. Trainee account rep. Hindustan Thompson Assocs., Calcutta, 1975-76; sr. acct. Calcutta Electric Supply Corp., 1976-84; grad. teaching and rsch. asst. U. Kans., Lawrence, 1984-89; asst. prof. mgmt. Slippery Rock U. Pa., 1989—95, vis. faculty Sch. Bus., 2002—04. Researcher, consultant in field. Mem. Acad. Mgmt. (nominee doctoral consortium U. Kans. 1987), Inst. for Ops. Rsch. and Mgmt. Scis., Beta Gamma Sigma. Avocations: photography, stamp collecting/philately, international travel. Home: 227 W Cooper St # 20 Slippery Rock PA 16057-1533

MUKHERJEE, SANDEEP, gastroenterologist, educator; b. Kuala Lumpur, Selangor, Malaysia, Nov. 5, 1968; s. Ajit Kumar and Gaitri Hena Mukherjee. MBBCh, U. Wales, Cardiff, 1991. Diplomate Am. Bd. in Internal Medicine, 1996, gastroenterology Am. Bd. in Internal Medicine, 1999, cert. Ednl. Commn. Fgn. Med. Grad., 1991, lic. Ednl. Commn. Fgn. Med. Grad., 1993. Staff physician Omaha VA Med. Ctr., 2000—. Asst. prof. internal medicine U. Nebr. Med. Ctr., 2000—. Contbr. articles to profl. jours. Recipient, Dulwich Coll., 1982, Travel award, Gastroent. Rsch. Group and Am. Gastroent. Assn., 1998—99, Am. Assn. of Transplantation, 2000, Millenium Award, Vietnam Vets. Am. State Coun. Nebr., 2001; Janssen Pharm. scholar, World Congress of Gastroent., 1998, Wyeth-Averst Ednl. fellow, Am. Gastroent. Assn., 1999. Fellow: Royal Coll. Physicians Can. (cert. internal medicine 1998); mem.: Am. Coll. Gastroenterology, Am. Assn. for Study of Liver Diseases, Nebr. Gut Club. Office: Univ Nebr Med Ctr 983285 Nebraska Med Ctr Omaha NE 68198-3285 Office Phone: 402-559-8859. E-mail: smukherjee@surgery.unmc.edu.

MUKHERJEE, SANDIP KUMAR, cardiologist; b. India, Oct. 28, 1961; came to U.S, 1965; s. Tridib and Debdasi (Chatterjee) M.; m. Sholeh Moghaddam, Dec. 21, 1985; children: Mina, Alexander. BS, Tex. A&M U., 1982; MD, Tex. Tech U., 1988. Diplomate Am. Bd. Internal Medicine, Am. Bd. Cardiovascular Disease. Intern and resident in internal medicine Yale U. Sch. Medicine, New Haven, 1988-91, chief med. resident, 1991-92, fellow in cardiovascular medicine, 1992-95, asst. clin. prof. medicine, 1996—; ptnr. pvt. practice Cardiology Assocs. of New Haven. P.C. Co-dir. NIH/NHLBI study, 1996—; dir. cardiovascular workshop Yale Med. Sch.; presenter in field. Editl. fellow Med. Letter, 1997—; contbr. articles to profl. jours. Fellow Am. Coll. Cardiology; mem. AMA, ACP, Am. Heart Assn. Clin. Cardiology Coun., Beta Beta Beta. Office: Cardiology Assn New Haven 40 Temple St Ste 6A New Haven CT 06510-2715

MUKHOPADHYAY, INDRANATH, communications engineer, researcher; s. Sibkinkar and Chhabi Mukhopadhyay; m. Suvra Roychoudhury, July 8, 1987; 1 child, Anirban. PhD, U. NB, Can., 1986. EECE, Indian Inst. of Tech., 1981. Sr. rsch. assoc. U. Akron, Ohio, 2000—02; prof. Dakota State U., Madison, SD, 2002—. Scientist Ctr. of Advanced Tech., Indore, M.P., India, 1990—2000. Contbr. articles various profl. jours. Recipient U. Gold medal, Burdwan U., 1976. Mem.: Indian Laser Assn. (life). Office: Dakota State U 820 N Washington Ave Madison SD 57042 E-mail: mukhopai@pluto.dsu.edu.

MUKOYAMA, JAMES HIDEFUMI, JR., securities executive; b. Chgo., Aug. 3, 1944; s. Hidefumi James and Miye (Maruyama) M.; m. Kyung Ja Woo, June 20, 1971; children: Sumi Martha, Jae Thomas. BA in English, U. Ill., 1965, MA in Social Studies, 1966; honor grad., U.S. Army Inf. Sch., 1966; grad., U.S. Army Command and Gen. Staff Coll., 1979, U.S. Army War Coll., 1984. Registered prin., sr. registered options prin. Nat. Assn. Securities Dealers. Commd. 2d lt. U.S. Army, 1965-70; with USAR, 1970—, brig. gen., 1987-90, maj. gen., 1990-95; asst. dept. mgr. Mitsui & Co. (USA), Inc., Chgo., 1971-74; mem. Chgo. Bd. Options Exch., 1976-90; allied mem. N.Y. Stock Exch., 1982-84; v.p. Lefta Advt., Chgo., 1976-90, Fltte Brokerage, Chgo., 1990-95; exec. v.p., COO Regal Discount Securities, 1995—. Mem. exec. bd. Hillside Free Meth. Ch., Evanston, Ill., 1982-93; dir. Chgo. coun. Boy Scouts Am., 1993-95; bd. dirs. Nat. Japanese Am. Meml. Found., 1995—. Decorated Silver Star, Legion of Merit, Purple Heart, 3 Bronze Stars; Vietnamese Army Cross of Gallantry; Japanese Army Parachutist badge; recipient cert. of merit Korean Army, others. Mem. VFW (life), U. Ill. Alumni Assn. (life), Assn. U.S. Army, U.S. Army Warr Coll. Alumni Assn. (life), Army Res. Assn. (pres., founder 1992—), Mil. Order Purple Heart (life), Am. Legion (life), Res. Officers Assn. (life), Sr. Army Res. Comdrs. Assn. (life), Nat. Infantryman's Assn. (life). Home: 4109 Tracey Ct Glenview IL 60025-2468 Office: Royal Discount Securities 950 Milwaukee Ave Ste 102 Glenview IL 60025-3766

MUKUNDA, RAM, communications executive; MSEE and Math., U. Md. Fixed income analyst Caine Gressel et al; advisor strategic planning INTELSAT; pres., CEO Startec Global Comm. Corp., Bethesda, Md., 1998—. Named Greater Washington Entrepreneur of Yr., 1998. Office: 10411 Motor City Dr Bethesda MD 20817-1008

MULALLY, ALAN R. aerospace company executive; b. Aug. 4, 1945; m. Nicki Mulally; 5 children. BS, MS, U. Kans.; M in Mgmt., MIT. With Boeing Def. and Space Group, Seattle, 1969—, v.p. 777 engring., v.p., gen. mgr. 777 divsn., sr. v.p. airplane devel., 1994—96, pres., 1997-99; exec. v.p Boeing Co., 1997—; pres. Boeing Comml. Air Group, 1999—. Mem. adv. bd. NASA, U. Wash., U. Kans.; mem. sci. adv. bd. USAF. Alfred P. Sloan fellow, 1982; recipient Leadership Tomorrow Program award, Seattle C. of C., 1984, One of 25 Bus. Leaders award, Puget Sound Bus. Jour., 1985, Disting. Engring. Svc. award, U. Kans. Engring. Sch., 1994, Laurels award, Aviation Week and Space Tech. mag., 1996, Engr. of Yr. award, Design News, 1996, Robert J. Collier Trophy (on behalf of 777 team), Nat. Aero. Assn., 1996. Fellow Royal Aero. Soc. (Eng.), AIAA (Tech. Mgmt. award 1986, Reed Aeronautics award 1996); mem. NSPE (Industry Engr. of Yr. 1978), NAE. Avocations: private pilot, reading, tennis, golf. Office: Boeing Comml Air Group MC 21-89 PO Box 3707 Seattle WA 98124-2207 Office Phone: 253-773-2500.

MULARKEY, MIKE, professional football coach; Degree in Kinesiology and Sociology, U. Minn. Tight end Minn. Vikings, 1983—88, Pitts. (Pa.) Steelers, 1989—91; coach offensive line Concordia Coll., 1993; coach quality control Tampa Bay (Fla.) Buccaneers, 1994; coach tight end Pitts. (Pa.) Steelers, 1996—2000, offensive coord., 2001—03; head coach Buffalo (N.Y.) Bills, Orchard Pk., NY, 2004—. Office: One Bills Drive Orchard Park NY 14127*

MULARZ, THEODORE LEONARD, architect; b. Chgo., Nov. 6, 1933; s. Stanley A. and Frances (Baycar) Mularz; m. Ruth L. Larson, Nov. 9, 1963; children: Anne Catherine, Mark Andrew. BArch, U. Ill., 1959. Registered arch., Colo., Oreg. Prin. Theodore L. Mularz, AIA Architects, Aspen, Colo., 1981-90; v.p. Benedict-Mularz Assocs., Inc., 1978-81; pvt. practice Ashland, Oreg., 1990—. Prin. works include numerous archtl. projects, including comml., indsl., religious, recreational, residential and hist. restoration. Vice-chmn. Pitkin County Bd. Appeals, 1972—90; mem. Colo. Bd. Examiners Archs., 1975—85, pres., 1976—80, v.p., 1978; vice-chmn. City of Aspen Bd. Appeals, 1985—90; mem. adv. com. City of Aspen Planning/Bldg. Dept., 1989; bd. dirs. Rogue Valley Symphony, Ashland, 1990—92, treas., 1991—92, chmn. fin. com., 1991—92; mem. Oreg. Bd. Examiners Archs., 1996—2000. With USCGR, 1953—55. Fellow: AIA; mem.: Colo. Soc. Archs. (Cmty. Svc. award 1975), Nat. Coun. Archtl. Registration Bds. (profl. conduct com. 1977—78, procedures/docs. com. 1978—82, chmn. edn. com. 1982—83, bd. dirs. 1982—87, chmn. 1983—84, mem. interprofessional coun. registration 1984—85, exec. com. 1984—87, internat. rels. com. 1984—89, interant. oral exam. com. 1984—89, v.p. 1985, pres. 1985, 1986, broadly experienced arch. interview com. 1987—2001), Aspen Hist. Soc. (com. chmn. 1963—64), Aspen C. of C. (past dir., pres., v.p.), Rotary (dir. Ashland Found. 2001—03, pres. 2001—02). Roman Catholic. Studio: 793 Elkader St Ashland OR 97520-3307 E-mail: tmularz@aol.com.

MULASE, MOTOHICO, mathematics professor; b. Kanazawa, Japan, Oct. 11, 1954; came to U.S., 1982; s. Ken-Ichi and Mieko (Yamamoto) M.; m. Sayuri Kamiya, Sept. 10, 1982; children: Kimihico Chris, Paul Norihico, Yurika. BS, U. Tokyo, 1978; MS, Kyoto U., 1980, DSc, 1985. Rsch. assoc. Nagoya (Japan) U., 1980-85; JMS fellow Harvard U., Cambridge, Mass., 1982-83; vis. asst. prof. SUNY, Stony Brook, 1984-85; Hedrick asst. prof. UCLA, 1985-88; asst. prof. Temple U., Phila., 1988-89; assoc. prof. U. Calif., Davis, 1989-91, prof., 1991—, vice chair dept. math., 1995-96, chair dept. math., 1998—2001, 2004—. Mem. Math. Scis. Rsch. Inst., Berkeley, Calif., 1982-84, Inst. for Advanced Study, Princeton, N.J., 1988-89; vis. prof. Max-Planck Inst. for Math., Bonn, Germany, 1991-92, Kyoto U., 1993, 94, Humboldt U., Berlin, Germany, 1995, 1996, 2002. Contbr. articles to profl. jours. Treas. Port of Sacramento Japanese Sch., 1990-91. Mem. Am. Math. Soc. (com. on internat. affairs 1993-96). Avocation: music. Office: U Calif Dept Math Davis CA 95616 Business E-Mail: mulase@math.ucdavis.edu.

MULCAHY, ANNE MARIE, printing company executive; b. Rockville Centre, N.Y., Oct. 21, 1952; BA in English and Journalism, Marymount Coll., 1974. Sales rep., various mgmt. positions Xerox Corp., 1976-91, v.p. human resources, 1992-95, v.p., staff officer customer ops., 1996-97, sr. v.p., chief staff officer, 1998, pres. gen. mkts. ops., 1999—2000, pres., COO, 2000—01, pres., CEO, 2001—02, chmn., CEO, 2002—. Bd. dirs. Target Corp., Fannie Mae, Fuji-Xerox Corp., Catalyst. Office: Xerox Corp 800 Long Ridge Rd Stamford CT 06904-1227

MULCAHY, GABRIEL M. pathologist; b. Jersey City, Feb. 16, 1929; s. Joseph Alphonsus and Anna Elizabeth Mulcahy; m. Vesna Maria Mulcahy, May 24, 1958; children: Mary, Michael, Robert, Richard, Thomas, John, Gabriel Jr. AB, St. Peter's Coll., Jersey City, 1950; MD, Georgetown U., 1954. Diplomate Nat. Bd. Med. Examiners, Am. Bd. Pathology. Intern St. Michaels Hosp., Newark, 1954-55; med. officer U.S. Pub. Health Svc., Crownpoint, N.Mex., 1955-57, resident in pathology Seattle, 1957-59, Staten Island, N.Y., 1959-61, chief pathology svc. Detroit, 1961-62; with pathology faculty Creighton U., Omaha, 1962-69; dir. pathology Jersey City Med. Ctr., 1969-78; mem. pathology faculty Univ. Medicine and Dentistry N.J., Newark, 1978-2001; chief lab. med. Univ. Hosp., Newark, 1978-2001. Mem. editl bd.: Annals of Clin. and Lab. Sci., 2000—; contbr. articles to profl. jours. Mem. adv. bd. St. Ann's Home for the Aged, Jersey City, 1973-89, sec., 1973-83; pres. bd. edn. St. Paul's Parish Sch., Jersey City, 1973-78. Mem. AAAS, Am. Soc. Human Genetics, Am. Assn. Blood Banks, Assn. Clin. Scientists (sci. coun. 1999—), Coll. Am. Pathologists, Soc. Med. Decision Making. Roman Catholic. Avocations: history, philosophy, philology, photography. E-mail: mulcahy@comapp.org., mulcahy21@comcast.net.

MULCAHY, JOAN CATHERINE, elementary school educator; b. Bridgeport, Conn., Feb. 16, 1937; d. Timothy John Jr. and Mary Elizabeth (Kluge) Mulcahy; m. Harry Curtiss Williams (div.). BA, So. Meth. U., Dallas, 1958; MA, Columbia U., N.Y.C., 1959. Cert. speech pathologist, tchr. of deaf, supr. spl. edn. Cons., tester Care Options for Kids, Dallas; tchr. spl. edn. Focus Learning Acad., Dallas; coord. speech and spl. edn. Honors Acad., Dallas; lead tchr. juvenile justice Brown Schs., Dallas; vocat. tchr. Carrollton Farmer's Br.,

Dallas; head speech pathologist Shelton Sch., Dallas; tchr. deaf and speech pathologist Dallas Pub. Schs.; coord. spl. edn. Mesquite Pub. Schs., Dallas; chief hearing dept. Dallas Soc. for Crippled Children. Vol. Big Brothers Big Sisters, 1970—76, Channel 13, Genesis for Battered Women. Scholar, So. Meth. Univ., Tchrs. Coll. Columbia U. Achievements include research in Pie baldism testing the deaf. Home: 5023 Stanford Ave Dallas TX 75009 Office Phone: 214-879-0027. E-mail: jcmulcahy@sbcglobal.net.

MULCAHY, ROBERT EDWARD, management consultant; b. Cambridge, Mass., Mar. 2, 1932; s. George Frances and Hazel (Douglas) M.; m. Ethel Walworth, Nov. 14, 1953; children: Linda, Scott, Steven, Susan. BS, Lowell Textile Inst., 1953. With Allied Chem. Corp., Morristown, N.J., 1953—; from engr. to mktg. mgr. Nat. Aniline div. Allied Corp., 1953-63, from dir. indsl. mktg. to v.p.-mktg. Fibers div., 1963-69, asst. to group v.p., corporate office, 1969, v.p. and gen. mgr.-consumer group Fabricated Products div., 1969-71, pres. Fibers div., 1971-74, group v.p., 1974-75, pres., dir., 1975-79, asst. to chmn. and dir., 1979-80; sr. assoc. The Corp. Dir., Inc., N.Y.C., 1981-83; pres. Counselors to Mgmt. Inc., 1984—.

MULCH, ROBERT F., JR., physician; b. Quincy, Ill., June 21, 1951; s. Robert Franklin and Martha Jo (Nisi) M.; m. Barbara Ann Best, Apr. 5, 1975; children: Matthew, Luke. BS, U. Ill., 1973; MD, Rush Med. Coll., Chgo., 1977. Diplomate Am. Bd. Family Practice; cert. in geriatrics. Intern Riverside Meth. Hosp., Columbus, Ohio, 1977-78, resident in family practice, 1978-80; family physician Hillsboro (Ill.) Med. Ctr., 1980—; ptnr., assoc. med. dir. Springfield Clin., 1998—; med. staff, v.p. Hillsboro Area Hosp. Asst. clin. prof. family medicine So. Ill. U., Springfield, 1981—90; reviewer Ctrl. Ill. Peer Rev. Orgn.; v.p. med. staff Hillsboro Area Hosp. Fellow Am. Acad. Family Practice; mem. AAFP, Am. Coll. Physician Execs. Lutheran. Avocations: computers, swimming. Office: Hillsboro Med Ctr SC 1250 E Tremont St Hillsboro IL 62049-1912 Office Phone: 217-532-6911. E-mail: rmulch@consolidated.net., rmulch@springfieldclinic.com.

MULCHAHEY, TERRY S. human resources executive, management consultant; b. Laurium, Mich., May 3, 1948; m. Patricia Brooks Mulchahey. BA with honors, Mich. State U., 1970; MS in Indsl. and Labor Rels. Studies, Cornell U., 1973. Various human resources positions Mobil Corp., Princeton, NJ, 1976—85; mgr. employee rels. Rubbermaid, Inc., Wooster, Ohio, 1984—89; dir. human resources and labor rels. KLM Royal Dutch Airlines, Elmsford, NY, 1989—95; v.p. human resources Alper Holdings USA, N.Y.C., 1995—98, Uniscribe Profl. Services, Inc., Norwalk, Conn., 1998—99; prin. The Hyde Hazen Group, Ridgefield, Conn., 1999—. Mem.: Am. Arbitration Assn. (labor mgmt. edn. com. 1991—94), Internat. Assn. Corp. and Profl. Recruiters (nat. bd. mem., chmn. Fairfield/Westchester chpt. 1994—96), US Squash Racquets Assn. (life), Cornell Club N.Y.C. Episcopalian. Office: The Hyde Hazen Group 406 North Street Ridgefield CT 06877 Office Phone: 203-438-9676.

MULCHANDANI, ASHOK KIMATRAI, chemical engineer, educator; b. Ajmer, India, Oct. 21, 1956; s. Kimatrai C. and Kalawanti M.; m. Priti Vadhva, Nov. 18, 1990; children: Anjali, Divya. B of Tech., Nagpur U., India, 1976; M of Tech., Indian Inst. Tech., Bombay, 1978; PhD, McGill U., Montreal, Can., 1985. Design engr. Vulcan-Laval Ltd., Pune, India, 1978-80; rsch. assoc. Laval U., St. Foy, Can., 1985-87, Biotech. Rsch. Inst., Nat. Rsch. Coun. Can., Montreal, 1987-90; asst. prof. dept. chem. U. Western, London, Ont., Can., 1990-91; asst. prof. dept. chem. & biochem. engring. U. Calif., Riverside, 1991-95, assoc. prof. dept. chem. & environ. engring., 1995-99, prof. dept. chem. & environ. engring., 1999—, chair dept. chem. & environ. engring., 2000—. Faculty rsch. participant U.S. Dept. Energy, Oak Ridge Nat. Lab, 1999-2000; cons. in field; editor-in-chief Applied Biochemistry and Biotechnology. Editor: Biosensors for Process Monitoring and Control, 1995, Protocols and Techniques in Enzyme and Microbial Biosensors, 1998, Protocols and Techniques in Affinity Biosensors, 1998, Chemical and Biological Sensors for Environmental Monitoring, 2000. Recipient Rsch. Intiation award NSF, 1993-96, Rsch. Participation award Dept. Energy Faculty, 1999-2000; grad. fellow U. Grants Commn., New Delhi, India, 1976-78. Mem. AIChE, Am. Chem. Soc. Avocations: music, tennis, squash, badminton. Office: U Calif Dept Chem & Environ Engring Bourns Hall Riverside CA 92521

MULDAUR, DIANA CHARLTON, actress; b. N.Y.C., Aug. 19, 1938; d. Charles Edward Arrowsmith and Alice Patricia (Jones) M.; m. James Mitchell Vickery, July 26, 1969 (dec. 1979); m. Robert J. Dozier, Oct. 11, 1981. BA, Sweet Briar Coll., 1960. Actress appearing in: Off-Broadway theatrical prodns., summer stock, Broadway plays including A Very Rich Woman, 1963-68; guest appearances on TV in maj. dramatic shows; appeared on: TV series Survivors, 1970-71, McCloud, 1971-73, Tony Randall Show, 1976, Black Beauty, 1978; star: TV series Born Free, 1974, Hizzoner, 1979, Fitz & Bones, 1980, Star Trek: The Next Generation, 1988-89; NBC miniseries and TV series A Year in the Life, 1986; TV movie Murder in Three Acts, The Return of Sam McCloud, 1989; TV series L.A. Law, 1989-91; motion picture credits include McQ, The Lawyer, The Other, One More Train to Rob, Mati, etc. Bd. dirs. Los Angeles chpt. Asthma and Allergy Found. Am.; bd. advisors Nat. Ctr. Film and Video Preservation, John F. Kennedy Ctr. Performing Arts, 1986. Recipient 13th Ann. Commendation award Am. Women in Radio and TV, 1988, Disting. Alumnae award Sweet Briar Coll., 1988. Mem. Acad. Motion Picture Arts and Scis., Screen Actors Guild (dir. 1978), Acad. TV Arts and Scis. (exec. bd., dir., pres. 1983-85), Conservation Soc. Martha's Vineyard Island. Office: Bauman Bedanty & Shaul 5757 Wilshire Blvd Ste 473 Los Angeles CA 90036

MULDER, DAVID S. cardiovascular surgeon; b. Eston, Sask., Can., July 28, 1938; s. Peter and Laura (Lovie) M.; m. Norma D. Johnston, Aug. 19, 1961; children— Scott D., Lizabeth J., John C. MD, U. Sask., 1962; M.Sc., McGill U., 1964. Intern, resident in surgery Montreal Gen. Hosp., McGill U., 1963-67; resident in cardiac surgery U. Iowa, 1967-69; surgeon-in-chief Montreal Gen. Hosp., 1977-98; prof. surgery McGill U., 1979—; chmn. dept. surgery, 1993-98. Contbr. articles to med. jours. Fellow: ACS, Royal Coll. Surgeons Can.; mem.: Soc. Thoracic Surgeons (named Order Can. 1997), Am. Assn Thoracic Surgery, Am. Assn. Trauma, Nat. Hockey League Team Physicians Assn., Soc. Univ. Surgeons. Conservative. Home: 76 Sunnyside Ave Westmount QC Canada H34 1C2 Office: Montreal Gen Hosp Room L-512 Montreal QC Canada H3G 1A4 Office Phone: 514-935-4888. E-mail: David.Mulder@muhc.mcgill.ca., dsmulder@sympatico.ca.

MULDER, DONALD WILLIAM, physician, educator; b. Rehobath, N.Mex., June 30, 1917; s. Jacob D. and Gertrude (Hofstra) M.; m. Gertrude Ellens, Feb. 22, 1943. BA, Calvin Coll., 1940; MD, Marquette U., 1943; MS, U. Mich., 1946. Intern Butterworth Hosp., Grand Rapids, Mich., 1943-44; resident U. Hosp., Ann Arbor, Mich., 1944-46, Denver, 1947-49; asst. prof. medicine in neurology U. Colo., 1949-50; prof. neurology Mayo Found. Faculty, 1964—, Mayo Med. Sch., 1973—; cons. neurology Mayo Clinic, Rochester, Minn., 1950—, gov., 1962-69, chmn. dept. neurology, 1966-71, pres. staff, 1971—, Andersen prof. neurology, 1977-83, prof. emeritus, 1983—; sci. advisor ALS. Contbr. articles on neuromuscular disease to sci. jours. Ret. capt. USNR. Recipient Disting. Alumni award Calvin Coll., 1992. Fellow A.C.P., Am. Acad. Neurology; mem. Am. Neurol. Assn. (hon.). Office: 200 1st St SW Rochester MN 55905-0001 Home: Apt 1307 211 2nd St NW Rochester MN 55901-2897

MULDER, EDWIN GEORGE, retired minister, church official; b. Raymond, Minn., Mar. 25, 1929; s. Gerrit and Etta (Dresselhuis) M.; m. Luella Rozeboom, June 14, 1952; children: Timothy, Mary, Mark, Elizabeth. BA, Cen. Coll., Pella, Iowa, 1951, DD (hon.), 1979; BD, Western Theol. Sem., Holland, Mich., 1954. Ordained to ministry Ref. Ch. in Am., 1954. Pastor Reformed Ch. in Am., 1954—, v.p. particular N.J. Synod, 1975-76, pres. particular N.J. Synod, 1976-77, v.p., then pres. Gen. Synod, 1978-80; chmn. bd. dirs. Relgion in Am. Life, 1995—. Chair U.S. Ch. Leaders, 1989-94; mem. exec. com. World Alliance Reformed Chs., 1990-97, Nat. Coun. Chs., 1991; mem. cen. com. World Coun. Chs., 1991-94; gen. sec. Reformed Ch. in Am., 1983-94. Trustee Cen. Coll., 1968-94; assoc. min. Marble Collegiate Ch., N.Y.C., 1995—. E-mail: emulder@marblechurch.org.

MULDER, PATRICIA MARIE, education educator; b. South Bend, Ind., Dec. 28, 1944; d. Ervin James and Carmen Virginia (Sheeley) Anderson; m. James R. Mulder, Dec. 27, 1964; children: Todd Alan, Scott Robert. BA, Western Mich. U., 1967. Freelance writer, photographer, Berrien Springs, Mich., 1980—; tchr. Eau Claire (Mich.) Pub. Schs., 1969-70; staff writer, sales rep. Jour. Era, Berrien Springs, 1979-81; sales rep. Berrien County Record, Buchana, Mich., 1981-82; account exec. WHFB Radio Palladium Pub. Co., St. Joseph, Mich., 1982-86; substitute tchr. Berrien County Intermediate Dist., 1986-89; instr. Southwestern Mich. Coll., Dowagiac, 1989-96, cons. Writing Ctr., 1996—; corp. trainer, 2000—. Editor The Positive Image newsletter, 1980—, The F Stop, 1982-90; author: Poetry Anthologies, 1989—; staff writer Decision Point, 1988-89; newsletter editor Fernwood Nature Photographers, 1980—. Ofcl. photographer Ind. and Internat. Spl. Olympics, Notre Dame, 1986. Named Emerging Artist Ind. Coun. for the Arts, 1989, Honor award Southwestern Coun. of Camera Clubs, 1988, Photographer of the Yr. Berrien County Photographic Artists, 1987, 90. Mem. AAUW, Nat. Authors Registry, Meth. Profl. Women (sec. 1990—), Berrien County Artists (v.p. 1986), Berrien County Photographic Artists (v.p. 1984), Southwestern Mich. Coun. Camera Clubs, Berrien Springs Camrea Club (v.p. 1980—). Methodist. Avocations: writing, photography, painting, watercolor painting. Home: 10252 Castner Dr Berrien Springs MI 49103-9602 Office: Southwestern Mich Coll 58900 Cherry Grove Rd # 316L Dowagiac MI 49047-9726

MULDOON, JAMES PETER, JR., government agency administrator; b. Grand Rapids, Mich., Mar. 7, 1960; s. James Peter Muldoon and Jane Northen; m. Reeta Roy, Aug. 1, 1987. BA, St. Louis U., 1982; MA, Miami U., Oxford, Ohio, 1983. Corr. analyst The White House, Washington, 1984—85; rsch. asst. Am. Enterprise Inst., Washington, 1985—86; dir. edn. program UN Assn. of USA, N.Y.C., 1986—96; vis. scholar Shanghai Acad. Social Scis., 1996—99; sr. rsch. fellow Carnegie Coun. on Ethics and Internat. Affairs, N.Y.C., 1999—2000; sr. fellow Ctr. for Global Change and Governance, Rutgers U., Newark, 2000—. Author: The Architecture of Global Governance, 2003; editor: Multilateral Diplomacy and the UN Today, 2d edit., 2005; contbr. book Guide to International Politics and Diplomacy, 2002. Active Lake Forest (Ill.) Caucus Com., 2003—. Named Man of Yr., Midwest Model UN, 1986, UN50 honoree, UNA of St. Louis, 1995; recipient Pres. award, St. Louis U. Student Govt. Assn., 1981. Mem.: Carnegie Coun. on Ethics and Internat. Affairs, Chgo. Coun. Fgn. Rels., Acad. Polit. Sci., Acad. Coun. for the UN Sys., Internat. Studies Assn., UN Assn. of the USA (pres. N.J. divsn. 2000—02). Home: 182 Washington Cir Lake Forest IL 60045

MULDOON, PAUL, creative writing educator, poet; b. Portadown, No. Ireland, 1951; came to U.S., 1987; BA in English Lang. and Lit., Queen's U., Belfast, No. Ireland, 1973. Prodr. arts programs radio BBC No. Ireland, 1973-78, sr. prodr. arts programs radio, 1978-85, TV prodr., 1985-86; Judith E. Wilson vis. fellow Cambridge U., 1986-87; creative writing fellow U. East Anglia, 1987; writer-in-residence 92d St. Y, N.Y.C., 198; Roberta Holloway lectr. U. Calif., Berkeley, 1989; lectr. Princeton (N.J.) U., 1990—, prof., 1995—, dir. creative writing program, 1993—2002, Howard G.B. Clark '21 prof., 1998—; prof. poetry U. Oxford, Eng., 1999—. Part-time tchr. writing divsn. Sch. of Arts, Columbia U., 1987-88; part-time tchr. creative writing program Princeton U., 1987-88; vis. prof. U. Mass., Amherst, 1989-90. Author: (poetry) Knowing My Place, 1971, New Weather, 1973, Spirit of Dawn, 1975, Mules, 1977, Immram, 1980, Why Brownlee Left, 1980, Out of Siberia, 1982, Quoof, 1983, Selected Poems 1968-83, 1986, Meeting the British, 1987, Madoc: A Mystery, 1990, Incantata, 1994, The Prince of the Quotidian, 1994, The Annals of Chile, 1994, Hay, 1998, Moy Sand and Gravel, 2002, others, (criticism) To Ireland, I, 2000, (opera libretto) Shining Brow, 1993, Bandanna, 1999, (TV play) Monkeys, 1989, (translation from Irish) The Astrakhan Cloak, 1993, (children's book) The O-O's Party, 1981, The Noctuary of Narcissus Batt, 1997; editor: (poetry) The Scrake of Dawn, 1979, The Faber Book of Contemporary Irish Poetry, 1986, The Essential Byron, 1989, The Faber Book of Beasts, 1997; contbr. to anthologies. Recipient Eric Gregory award, 1972, Sir Geoffrey Faber Meml. award, 1980, 91, T.S. Eliot prize, 1994, Acad. award in lit. Am. Acad. Arts and Letters, 1996, Irish Times prize for poetry, 1997, Pulitzer Prize for poetry, 2003, Griffin Internat. prize excellence in poetry, 2003; John Simon Guggenheim Meml. fellow, 1990. Fellow Royal Soc. Lit.; mem. Am. Acad. Arts and Scis., Aosdana. Office: Princeton Univ Creative Writing Program Princeton NJ 08544-0001

MULDOON, ROBERT JOSEPH, JR., lawyer; b. Somerville, Mass., Nov. 16, 1936; s. Robert Joseph and Catherine Eileen (Hurley) M.; m. Barbara Joyce Mooney, Aug. 24, 1968; children: Andrew Robert, Catherine Lane, Timothy John. AB, Boston Coll., 1960, MA, 1961, LLB, 1965. Bar: Mass. 1965, U.S. Tax Ct. 1966, U.S. Supreme Ct. 1970. Law clk. Supreme Jud. Ct. Mass., 1965-66; assoc. Withington, Cross, Park & Groden, Boston, 1966-71, ptnr., 1972-82, Sherin and Lodgen, LLP, Boston, 1982—. Mem. Bd. Bar Examiners Mass.; chmn. Nat. Conf. Bar Examiners, 1985-86; pres. Mass. Continuing Legal Edn., Inc., 1992-94. Trustee Boston Coll. H.S., 1990-96, chmn. bd. trustees, 1995-96. Fellow Am. Coll. Trial Lawyers; mem. Am. Law Inst., Boston Bar Assn., Curtis Club, Nisi Prius Club, Tavern Club. Office: Sherin and Lodgen LLP 101 Federal St Boston MA 02110 E-mail: rjmuldoon@sherin.com.

MULDOWNEY, MICHAEL PATRICK, finance executive; b. Chgo., Oct. 8, 1963; s. James Joseph and Clare (Sexton) M.; m. Daniela Nicoletta Pernis, Apr. 25, 1992; children: Michael James, Patrick Nicholas. BA, St. Ambrose U., 1985. CPA, Ill., Mass. Acctg. mgr. Fletcher Engring., Des Plaines, Ill., 1985; asst. auditor Marsh & McLennan Cos., Chgo., 1986, auditor London, 1987, sr. auditor N.Y.C., 1988; asst. corp. contr. Temple, Barker & Sloane, Lexington, Mass., 1989; regional contr. Temple, Barker & Sloane/Strategic Planning Assocs., Lexington, 1990; dir. fin. and adminstrn. Mercer Mgmt. Consulting, Lexington, 1991, corp. contr. N.Y.C., 1992-97; v.p. fin. Nextera Enterprises, Lexington, 1997-98, CFO, 1998—, COO, 2003—. Mem. Boston mgmt. com. Mercer Mgmt., Lexington, 1994-96; chmn. Fin. Execs. Mgmt. Consulting Firm, Boston, 1995. Chmn. United Way fundraiser Mercer Mgmt. Consulting, Lexington, 1992, chmn. co. fundraiser, 1993; trustee Meadowbrook Water Trust, Dover, Mass., 1993-97. Mem. AICPA, Ill. Soc. CPA's, Mass. Soc. CPA's, Fin. Execs. Inst., Wellesley Country Club (Tennis champion 1995-98), Boston Coll. Club. Avocation: tennis. Office: Nextera Enterprises Inc 4 Cambridge Ctr Cambridge MA 02142

MULDROW, TRESSIE WRIGHT, psychologist; b. Marietta, Ga., Feb. 1, 1941; d. Festus Blanton and Louise Williams Wright Summers; 1 child, DeJuan Denise. BA, Bennett Coll., 1962; MS, Howard U., 1965, PhD, 1976. Rsch. asst. W.C. Allen Corp., Washington, 1966-68; pers. rsch. psychologist Dept. Navy, Washington, 1968-73, Office Pers. Mgmt., CSC, 1973-79; chief adv. coun. on alternative selections procedures Office Pers. Mgmt., Washington, 1979-86, chief consultative svcs., 1986-91, chief multidimensional assessment br., 1992-94; spl. advisor Office of Diversity, 1994-95; leader Bus. Re-engring. Task Force, 1995-96, acting divsn. dir. Assessment Svcs. Divsn., 1996-97; dir. Performance Am., 1998-2000, sr. scientist, 2000—, exec. advisor, 2002—. Lectr. Howard U., 1979, guest lectr., 1999—; chair bd. dirs. U.S. Premier Fed. Credit Union, 2004. Contbr. articles to profl. publs. Mem. Washington Inter-Alumni coun. United Negro Coll. Fund, 1970—, pres., 1988—92; trustee Bennett Coll., vice chmn., 1985—90; v.p. Family Life Ctr. bd. Boys and Girls Club of Washington, 1984—90; loaned exec. Combined Fed. Campaign, 2001—02; nat. fundraising chair Bennett Coll. Alumnae, 2001—, sr. advisor employment svcs., 2001—. Named Alumna of Yr., United Negro Coll. Fund, 1971, Outstanding Alumna, Morehouse Coll., 1978, Bennett Coll., 1993, Outstanding Woman, Am. Bus. Women's Assn., 1994, Outstanding Loaned Exec. to Combined Fed. Campaign, 2001; recipient Individual Achievement award, United Negro Coll. Fund, 1984, Exemplary Performance award, 1995, Outstanding Leadership award, Washington Inter-Alumni Coun., Dirs. award for excellence, 2000, 2001, 2002, Outstanding Alumnus award, United Negro Coll. Fund, 2001. Mem.: Bennett Coll. Alumnae Assn. (nat. pres. 1978—85, 1993—97), Delta Sigma Theta. Presbyterian. Office: 1900 E St NW Washington DC 20415-0001 Office Phone: 202-606-2491. Personal E-mail: muldro@starpower.net.

MULÉ, ANN C. oil industry executive; b. Phila., Pa., Oct. 22, 1956; BA magna cum laude, St. Joseph's U., 1978; JD cum laude, Villanova U., 1981. Bar: Pa. 1981, U.S. Supreme Ct./ 1988. From atty. to chief governance officer Sunoco Inc., Phila., 1980—2002, chief governance officer, 2002—. Bd. dir. Phila. (Pa.) Zoo; adv. bd. Ctr. Corp. Governance, U. Del. Mem.: ABA, Am. Corp. Counsel Assn. (vice chmn. exec. counsel, mem. corp. and securities law com.), Phila. (Pa.) Bar Assn., Pa. Bar Assn. (chmn. bus. law sect., mem. bd. govs., chmn. com. securities regulation, mem. title 15 task force), Am. Soc. Corp. Secs. (bd. dir., mem. exec. steering com., mem. nat. conf. com., mem. corp. practices com.), Alpha Sigma Mu (chmn. moot ct. bd.). Office: Sunoco Inc Ten Penn Center 1801 Market St Philadelphia PA 19103-1699

MULFORD, DAVID CAMPBELL, ambassador, former finance company executive; b. Rockford, Ill., June 27, 1937; s. Robert Lewis Mulford and Theodora Henie Countryman; m. Jeannie Louise Simmons, Oct. 19, 1985; children: Robert Ian, Edward Maitland. BA in Econs. cum laude, Lawrence U., 1959; postgrad., U. Cape Town, South Africa, 1960; MA in Polit. Sci., Boston U., 1962; PhD, Oxford U., 1966; LLD (hon.), Lawrence U., 1984. White House fellow U.S. Dept. Treas., Washington, 1965-66, under asst. sec. internat. affairs, 1984-89; dir. White Weld & Co., N.Y.C. and London, 1966-74; sr. investment advisor Saudi Arabian Monetary Agy., Riyadh, 1974-84; asst. sec. internat. affairs Dept. of Treas., 1984-89; under sec. treasury internat. affairs U.S. Treas. Dept., Washington, 1989-92; vice chmn. CS First Boston, N.Y.C., 1992—93; chmn. Credit Suisse First Boston, London, 1993-98, internat. chmn., 1998—2003; U.S. amb. to India U.S. Dept. State, New Delhi, 2004—. Author: Northern Rhodesia General Election, 1962, Zambia: The Politics of Independence, 1967. Trustee Lawrence U., 1986—. Decorated Legion d'Honneur, 1990, recipient Order of May Merit Pres. Argentina, 1993, Officers Cross of the Medal of Merit Pres. Poland, 1995; Rotary Internat. fellow Oxford U., U. Cape Town, 1961-62, Woodrow Wilson fellow Boston U., Oxford U., 1962, Ford Found. fellow St. Anthony's Coll., Oxford, 1963-65; named Disting. Alumni Boston U., 1992; Disting. scholar Ctr. Strategic and Internat. Studies, Washington, 1993—. Mem. Coun. Fgn. Rels., White House Fellows Assn., Metropolian Club (Washington). Republican. Office: US Dept State 9000 New Delhi Pl Washington DC 20521-9000*

MULFORD, RICHARD ALBERT, mechanical engineer, professional society administrator; b. Phila., Dec. 13, 1930; s. William Abernathy and Jeanne Ann (Roy) Mulford. BSME, U. Pa., 1952, MS in Mech. Engring., 1957; Diploma in Bus., Dartmouth Coll., 1985. Registered profl. engr., Pa. Engr. Phila. Elec. Co., 1952-64, sr. engr., 1964-67, project mgr., 1967-85, staff engr., 1985-91; exec. dir. Engrs. Club of Phila., 1991—. Vol. Paoli Meml. Hosp., Pa., 1991—; donor Phila. Orch. Assn., 1980—; treas., donor Phila. Engring. Found., 1991—. Recipient Disting. Svc. award, Pa. Soc. Profl. Engrs., 1991, 1998, D. Robert Yarnall award (Outstanding Engring. Alumnus), U. Pa., 1981, Alumni award of merit, 1993, Presdl. award, Phila. sect. ASCE, 2002, Outstanding Svc. award, Del. Valley Engrs. Week Coun., 2003. Fellow: Engrs. Club Phila. (sec.-treas. 1953—, George Washington medal 1988); mem.: NSPE, Union League Phila. (scholarship trustee 1963—), Racquet Club Phila. Republican. Achievements include patents in field. Avocations: classical music, antique cars, home and lawn maintenance. Home: 1231 Wisteria Dr Malvern PA 19355-9736 Office: Engrs Club of Phila 215 S 16th St Ste 36 Philadelphia PA 19102-3349 Office Phone: 215-985-5701. Business E-Mail: info@engrclub.org.

MULGAONKAR, PRASANNA G. computer scientist; B.Tech. in Elec. Engring., Indian Inst. Tech., Kanpur, 1979; MS in Computer Sci., Va. Poly. Inst. and State U., 1981, PhD in Computer Sci., 1984. Computer scientist robotics lab. SRI Internat., Menlo Park, Calif., 1984—90, dir. machine vision and robotics program, 1990—93, dir. advanced automation tech. ctr., 1993—. Sci. adv. com. Def. Sci. Bd.; bd. visitors NSF; mem. Army Sci. Bd., 2002—; bd. dirs. AddressFree Corp. Contbr. over 50 articles to profl. hours., chpts. to books. Mem.: ASME (emeritus chair exec. com. for material handling engring. divsn.), IEEE Computer Soc. Office: SRI International 333 Ravenswood Ave Menlo Park CA 94025-3493

MULHAUSER, CRAIG H. energy executive; BS in Aerospace Engring., MS, U. Cin. Formerly with NASA; formerly with aircraft engine and power systems group GE; sr. v.p. sales and svc. Ams., v.p. worldwide aftermarket bus. Pratt & Whitney, Conn., 1995—97; v.p. Ford Motor Co., 1997—2000; pres. Visteon Automotive Systems, 1997—2000; chmn., CEO Exide Techs., Princeton, NJ, 2000—. Mem. U. Cin. Found. Mem.: Motor Equipment Mfrs. Assn. Office: Exide Techs 210 Carnegie Ctr Ste 500 Princeton NJ 08540*

MULHAUSER, FREDERICK VAN NORDEN, lawyer; b. Pomona, Calif., Apr. 16, 1943; s. Frederick Ludwig Jr. and Margaret Marie (Lehman) M.; m. Karen Webber, Aug., 1968; 1 child, Christopher. AB magna cum laude, Harvard Coll., 1964; MA, Yale U., 1966; EdM, Harvard U., 1982; JD, Georgetown U., 2001. Spl. asst. Rep. John Brademas, U.S. Ho. of Reps., Washington, 1973-74; sr. rsch. assoc. U.S. Nat. Inst. Edn., Washington, 1974-83; evaluator, asst. dir. program evaluation divsn. U.S. GAO, Washington, 1983-93; litigation screening coord. Nat. Capital area chpt. ACLU, Washington, 1993—2001, staff atty., 2001—. Adj. lectr. Am. U., Washington, 1981-83; adj. prof. U. DC Law Sch., 2002—. Bd. editors, co-chair Harvard Ednl. Rev., 1967-69; contbr. articles and revs. to profl. jours, chpts. to books; author GAO evaluation reports and testimony to Congress, 1983-93. Mem. neighborhood sch. bd. D.C. Pub. Schs., Washington, 1978; bd. dirs. DC Prisoners Legal Svcs. Project, Washington, 2004—. Woodrow Wilson Found. fellow, 1964, Upham scholar Harvard U., 1966, edn. policy fellow Ford Found./Inst. for Ednl. Leadership, Washington, 1973, ACLU Alan Barth award, 2001. Mem. DC Bar Assn., Country Music Assn., Washington Area Music Assn. Avocation: music. Home: 319 7th St NE Washington DC 20002-6103 Office: ACLU/NCA 1400 20th St NW Ste 119 Washington DC 20036-5920 Office Phone: 202-457-0800.

MULHEARN, CHRISTOPHER MICHAEL, lawyer; b. Providence, June 14, 1969; s. Michael R. and Judith A. Mulhearn; m. Melissa L. Mulhearn. BA in Polit. Sci., Marquette U., 1991; JD, Cleveland-Marshall Coll. Law, 1994. Bar: R.I. 1994, U.S. Dist. Ct. R.I. 1995, Mass. 1995, U.S. Dist. Ct. Mass. 1996. Assoc. Rodio & Brown, Ltd., Providence, 1994-96, Tate & Elias, Providence, 1996-99, Carroll, Kelly & Murphy, Providence, 1999; prin. Christopher M. Mulhearn, Esq., Counselor at Law, P.C., Providence, 1999—2001; sr. litigation assoc. Ferrucci, Russo, PC, Providence, 2001—. Bd. dirs. Children's Shelter of Blackstone Valley, Inc., Pawtucket, R.I., 1996-2002; mem. alumni bd. dirs. Bishop Hendricken H.S., Warwick, R.I., 1996-2004, bd. dirs. Aids Care Ocean State 2002-. Mem. ABA, Mass. Bar Assn., R.I. Bar Assn. Avocations: golf, music. Home: 449 Narragansett Pkwy Warwick RI 02888-4002 Office: Ferrucci Russo PC 55 Pine Street, 4th Floor Providence RI 02903 E-mail: cmulhearn@frlawri.com.

MULHERN, EDWIN JOSEPH, lawyer; b. Bklyn., Mar. 8, 1927; s. Edward Thomas and Jennie (Keenan) M.; m. Maureen P. Purcell, Oct. 2, 1964; children: Edwin T., Deborah J., Kevin T. BBA, St. John's U., 1950, LLB, 1954. Bar: N.Y. 1954, U.S. Dist. Ct. (ea. and so. dists.) N.Y. 1954, U.S. Supreme Ct. 1960. Sr. acct. Susquehanna Mills Inc., N.Y.C., 1947-53; chief acct. Rockwood Chocolate Co., Bklyn., 1953-54; trial atty. Allstate Ins. Co., Freeport, N.Y., 1954-57; claims rep. State Farm Ins. Co., Hempstead, N.Y., 1957-58; sole practice, Bellmore, N.Y., 1958-70, Mineola, N.Y., Carle Place, N.Y., 1970—; mem. joint grievance com. for 10th jud. dist. (N.Y.), 1981-89. Pres. Christian Bros. Boys' Assn., 1975-82; bd. dirs. Legal Aid Soc. of Nassau County, 1980—. Served with USAAF, 1945-46. Mem. ABA, N.Y. State Bar Assn., Nassau Bar Assn. (bd. dirs. 1981-83, chmn. admissions com. 1979, chmn. grievance com. 1980-82), Suffolk County Bar Assn., Nassau Lawyers Assn. (pres. 1975, exec. dir. 1993—, Man of Yr. 1981), Criminal Ct. Assn. of Nassau County (pres. 1976), Criminal Cts. Bar Assn.

County, Am. Assn. Trial Lawyers. Clubs: University of L.I. (Hempstead), K.C. (new Hyde Park, N.Y.). Office: 1 Old Country Rd Ste 145 Carle Place NY 11514-1801 Office Phone: 516-294-8000.

MULHERN, MARTIN ROBERT, engineer; b. New Brunswick, N.J., June 12, 1946; s. Thomas Desmond and Helen Casserly M. BS in Civil Engring., U. Calif., Berkeley, 1968; MS in Civil Engring., U. Wash., 1982. Cert. inshore/offshore hydographer Am. Congress of Surveying and Mapping; unltd. master merchant marine lic. USCG. Structures weights engr. The Boeing Co., Everett, Wash., 1968; capt. NOAA Corps., Silver Spring, Md., 1969-98; cons. Boulder, Colo., 1998-2001. NOAA rep. U. Nat. Oceanographic Lab. System, Silver Spring, 1992-96; comdg. officer NOAA ship Whiting. Recipient H. Arnold Karo award Soc. of Am. Mil. Engrs., 1980, 88. Mem. The Oceanography Soc. (charter, life mem.), Soc. Am. Mil. Engrs. (life), Am. Geophys. Union (life), The Hydrographic Soc. Achievements include conducting geodetic and hydrographic surveys with the Nat. Ocean Survey, extensive duty with labs. and hdqtrs. of the Office of Atmospheric and Oceanographic Rsch. Office: PO Box 19545 Boulder CO 80308-2545 E-mail: mmulhern@attglobal.net.

MULHERN, PATRICK J. lawyer, banker; b. NYC, Mar. 17, 1928; s. John J. and Beatrice (Gilholly) Mulhern; m. Joan F. Cassidy, June 14, 1952; children: John, Eileen, Barbara. BS, Fordham U, 1952, JD, 1955. Bar: NY 1955. Atty. US Dist. Ct. (so. dist.), NY Assoc. counsel Sherman & Sterling, 1955—66; v.p. cashier's adminstrn. Citibank NA, NYC, 1966—79; sr. v.p. Office of Gen. Counsel, 1979—80, sr. v.p., gen. counsel, 1980. USAR, 1946—47. Mem.: Fed. Bar Assn., ABA, Am. Soc. Corp. Sec., Assn. Bar City of NY, Unqua Corinthian Yacht, NYC Univ., KC Kiwanis. Office: Citicorp 399 Park Ave New York NY 10022-4614

MULHOLLAND, KENNETH LEO, JR., health care facility administrator; b. Chgo., July 16, 1943; s. Kenneth Leo Sr. and Virginia May (Groble) M.; m. Betty Lou Bledsoe, Feb. 18, 1978; children: Arthur G. Pope (dec.), Michelle Rae Pope Nobles. BS, Loyola U., 1969; M in Mgmt., Northwestern U., 1974. RN. Nurse VA Med. Ctr., Chgo., 1970-72, health care adminstr. tng., 1972-74, assoc. dir. tng. Lexington, Ky., 1976-77, assoc. dir. Muskogee, Okla., 1977-79, Knoxville, Iowa, 1979-81, acting dir., 1981, assoc. dir. Richmond, Va., 1981-83, dir. Bronx, N.Y., 1983-85, Memphis, 1985—. Pres. Memphis Area Fed. Exec. Assn., 1988—; bd. dirs. Memphis chpt. ARC, 1985—, Health Sys. Agy., Memphis, 1985-87; mem. citizen's adv. bd. St. Joseph's Hosp., 1993—; mem. dean's adv. bd. Grad. Sch. Bus., Christian Brothers U., 1996—. Recipient Presdl. Rank award for meritorious executive, 1989. Mem. Memphis Area Fed. Exec. Assn. Lodges: Rotary. Home: 2024 Thorncroft Dr Germantown TN 38138-4017 Office: VA Med Ctr 1030 Jefferson Ave Memphis TN 38104-2127

MULHOLLAND, PAUL A. gas industry executive; BS, Drexel U., 1975, MBA, 1978. Mgr. fin., mergers and acquisitions Sunoco Inc., Phila., 1993—97, dir. corp. fin., 1997—2000, treas., 2000—, Sunoco Logistics Ptnrs., 2002—. Office: Sunoco Inc Ten Penn Ctr 1801 Market St Philadelphia PA 19103-1699

MULHOLLAND, S. GRANT, urologist; b. Springfield, Ohio, Sept. 1, 1936; s. Stanford Wallace and Florence Kathryn (Grant) M.; m. Ruth Fritz, Aug. 21, 1961; children: David, Michael, Mark, John. BS, Dickinson Coll., Carlisle, Pa., 1958; MD, Temple U., 1962; MS, U. Va., 1966. Intern Reading (Pa.) Hosp., 1962-63; resident in surgery Tampa (Fla.) Gen. Hosp., 1963-64; resident in urology U. Va., Charlottesville, 1964-68; urologist U.S. Naval Hosp., St. Albans, N.Y., 1968-70; epidemiologist Grad. Hosp. of U. Pa., Phila., 1971-74, asst. urologist, 1970-77; chief urologist Phila. Gen. Hosp., 1972-77; asst. surgeon Children's Hosp. Phila., 1974-77; urologist Hosp. U. Pa., Phila., 1974—77; chmn. dept. urology Thomas Jefferson U. Hosp., Phila., 1977—2002. Cons. VA Ctr., Phila., 1974-77, Bryn Mawr Hosp., VA Hosp., Wilmington, Del., 1977—. Author: Antibiotic Treatment, 1996, Urinary Tract Infections, 1999—2001, Prostate Cancer, 1999—2000, Bladder Defense Mechanisms, 2000—02. Lt. comdr. USN, 1968-70. Grantee NIH, Jefferson U., 1989. Fellow ACS; mem. Am. Urol. Assn. (pres. 1988-89), Phila. Urol. Assn. (pres. 1988-89), Internat. Soc. Urology, AMA, Phila. Country Club (Gladwyne, Pa.). Republican. Avocations: golf, fishing, skiing. Home: 1783 Sheedermill Rd Birchrunville PA 19421 Office: Jefferson Med Coll 1025 Walnut St # 1112 Philadelphia PA 19107-5001 E-mail: grant.mulholland@jefferson.edu.

MULHOLLAND, WILLIAM DAVID, JR., retired bank executive; b. Albany, N.Y., June 16, 1926; s. William David and Helen E. (Flack) M.; m. Nancy Louise Booth, June 22, 1957; children: William David III, Charles Douglass, James Andrew, John Alexander, Elizabeth Helen, Madeline Louise, Sarah Alexandra, Caroline Marie, Bruce Henry. AB cum laude, Harvard U., 1950, MBA, 1952; LLD, Meml. U., 1972, Queens U., 1988. Mem. staff Morgan Stanley & Co., N.Y.C., 1952-61, gen. ptnr., 1962-69; pres., chief exec. officer Brinco Ltd., Montreal, Que., Can., 1970-74, Churchill Falls (Labrador) Corp. Ltd., 1970-74; pres. Bank of Montreal, 1975-81, chief exec. officer, 1979-89, chmn. bd., 1981-90. Bd. dirs., mem. exec. com. Bank of Montreal, Can. Pacific Ltd., Upjohn Co.; bd. dirs. Brooks Fashion Stores, Kimberly-Clark Corp., Rio Tinto-Zinc Corp., Standard Life Assurance Corp., Consolidated Bathhurst Corp.; chmn. exec. com. Bank of Montreal, Upjohn, Can. Life gov. Douglas Hosp., Montreal; hon. v.p. Quebec provincial coun. Boy Scouts Can.; mem. adv. coun. Ecole des Hautes Etudes Commerciales, Montreal; mem. adv. coun. Ctr. Can. Studies Sch. Advanced Internat. Studies Johns Hopkins U.; bd. dirs. Atlantic Salmon Fedn., St. Michael's Coll. Found., Mounted Police Found., Conf. Bd. Can., Monreal Symphony Orch.; trustee Hudson Inst., Queen's U., Kingston, Can. Olympic Trust; fin. com. Queen's U.; nat. co-chmn. Can. Coun. Christians and Jews. Served as officer, inf. U.S. Army, 1944-46, PTO. Decorated Knight Comdr.'s Cross (Badge and Star) Order of Merit, Fed. Republic of Germany, 1989, Prime Minister's medal State of Israel, 1987; recipient Human Rels. award, Good Servant's medal Can. Coun. Christians and Jews, 1985. Mem. Mount Royal Club (Montreal), Caledon Riding and Hunt Club, Toronto Club. Roman Catholic. Office: Bank of Montreal 302 Bay St Ste 400 Toronto ON Canada M5X 1A1

MULHOLLEM, PAUL B. finance company executive; m. Valerie Mulhollem; 1 child, Claire Jean. Grad., U. Minn., 1971. From mng. dir. to sr. v.p. Archer Daniels Midland Co., Decatur, Ill., 1993—2001, pres., 2001—. Office: Archer Daniels Midland Co 4666 Faries Pkwy Decatur IL 62526

MULKERN-KOLOSEY, SANDY KATHLEEN, college counselor, educator, realtor; b. Needham, Mass., Apr. 09; d. Thomas Joseph and Elizabeth (Bjornson) Mulkern; m. Michael George Kolosey, July 15, 1972; 1 child, Michael Thomas Kolosey. AA, Coll. of Marin, Kentfield, Calif., 1989, AS/Dental Asst., 1990; BA in Clin. Psychology, San Francisco State U., 1991; MA in Counseling/Psychology, U. San Francisco, 1993, postgrad., doctoral student in organ. and leadership, U. San Francisco. Cert. in pupil pers. svcs., psychol. svcs. Acad. advisor, counselor Santa Rosa (Calif.) Jr. Coll., 1992—. Ednl. cons., San Francisco Bay area, 1994; career coach and workshop facilitator, Sonoma County. Mem. AAUW, APA, Alumni Assn. U. San Francisco and San Francisco State U., Golden Key Nat. Honor Soc., Psi Chi, Alpha Gamma Sigma, Phi Delta Kappa. Avocations: bicycling, reading, computers, travel, real estate investing. Home: PO Box 750401 Petaluma CA 94975-0401 Office: ReMax 775 Baywood Dr Petaluma CA 94954

MULKEY, JACK CLARENDON, library director; b. Shreveport, La., Oct. 31, 1939; s. Jack Youmans and Hilda Lillian (Beatty) M.; m. Mary Lynn Shepher[illegible]0, 1971; 1 child, Mary Clarendon. BA, Centenary Coll., 1961; pos[illegible] scholar), U. Dijon, France, 1961-62, Duke U. Law Sch., [illegible]tate U., 1969. Jr. exec. Lykes Bros. S.S. Co., 1964-66; asst. [illegible]enary Coll. of La., 1966-67; head reference services and [illegible]rt Pub. Library, 1968-71; dir. Green Gold Library [illegible]71-73; mgmt. cons. Miss. Library Commn., 1973-74, [illegible]1976-78, Jackson Met. Library System, 1978-85; [illegible]y, 1986-2000; State Librarian of Ark., 2000—. Adj. [illegible] Libr. Sci., 1979—; treas., bd. dirs. Southeastern Library Network (SOLINET), 1985-86; cons. in field; mem. White House Conf. Taskforce on Libraries and Info. Services, 1980—. Chmn. Miss. Govs. Conf. on Libraries, 1979; chmn. Miss. delegation White House Conf. on Libraries, 1979; hon. del. White House Conf. on Librs., 1991. Served with USAF, 1963-64. Mem. ALA (chmn. state libr. agy. sect. 1995-97), Southeastern Libr. Assn. (bd. dirs. 1994—), Miss. Libr. Assn. (pres. 1981-82), Ark. Libr. Assn. (exec. bd. dirs. 1994—), Chief Officers of State Libr. Agys., Phi Alpha Delta, Beta Phi Mu, Omicron Delta Kappa, Phi Kappa Phi. Episcopalian. Home: 1805 Martha Dr Little Rock AR 72212-3840 Office: 1 Capitol Mall Little Rock AR 72201-1049 Office Phone: 501-682-1526. Personal E-mail: jmulkey@webtv.net.

MULL, GALE W. lawyer; b. Hillsdale, Mich., Sept. 8, 1945; s. Wayne E. and Vivian M. (Bavin) M.; m. Holly Ann Allen, Aug. 2, 1969 (div. Nov. 1983); 1 child, Carter B.; m. Jeanne Anne Haughey, Aug. 18, 1985. BA, Mich. State U., 1967; MA in Sociology, Ind. U., 1969; JD, Emory U., 1972. Bar: Ga. 1972, U.S. Dist. Ct. (no. dist.) Ga. 1972, U.S. Ct. Appeals (5th cir.) 1973, U.S. Ct. Appeals (11th cir.) 1981. Instr. sociology Clemson (S.C.) U., 1968-69, Spelman Coll., Atlanta, 1969-70; pvt. practice, Atlanta, 1972-75; ptnr. Mull & Sweet, Atlanta, 1975-81; pres. Gale W. Mull, P.C., Atlanta, 1981—. Bd. dirs. BOND Community Fed. Credit Union, Atlanta, 1975-81; directing atty. Emory Student Legal Services, Atlanta, 1975-91; Sociology instr. Clemson U., Clemson, S.C., 1968-69, Spelman Coll., Atlanta, Ga., 1969-70. Pres. Inman Park Restoration, Inc., Atlanta, 1972—74, BASS Orgn. for Neighborhood Devel., Inc., 1974—78; mem. Housing Appeals Bd., Atlanta, 1982—88, Mayor's Task Force on Prostitution, 1984—86; bd. dirs. Trinity Towers, Inc., 1999—2000; vestry St. John's Episc. Ch., 1992—99, 2003—, sr. warden, 1998—99; bd. dirs. St. John's Episcopal Day Sch., 1992—97, Bethlehem Ministries, 1997—, ACLU Ga., 1981—92, sec. bd. dirs., 1983—85, cooperating atty., 1972—. Mem. ABA, Ga. Bar Assn., Atlanta Bar Assn., Lawyers Club Atlanta. Clubs: Quail Unltd. (bd. dirs., sec. 1984-86). Office: 2149 Rugby Ave Atlanta GA 30337 Office Phone: 404-761-6600. E-mail: galewmull@mindspring.com.

MULL, ROBERT W. filmmaker, curator; b. Great Bend, Kans., Mar. 8, 1953; s. Charles Laverne and Mary Anne Mull; m. Donna Lee Howell, May 24, 1976 (div. Jan. 1980). B in Gen. Studies, U. Kans., 1976; MA, Ea. Wash. U., 1982. Curator Yakima (Wash.) Valley Mus., 1981—85, Pacific Sci. Ctr., Seattle, 1985—88; ind. documentary filmmaker Wash., 1981—93; ind. writer, 1993—. Cons. Wash. Commn. for Humanities, Olympia, 1982—85; founder, officer Wash. State Folklife Coun., Olympia, 1983—87; mem. planning com. Wash. 1989 Centennial, Seattle, 1988—89. Author: The Lupus Kid and Other Stories, 2002; prodr.: (documentaries) When Court Adjourned, 1982 (PBS award, 1983), Something To Win the War, 1985 (TLC award, 1987). Grants writer Harbor Assn. Vols., Westport, Wash., 1996—2000; publicist Seattle Housing Authority, 1999—2003. Named Alumnus of Yr., Ea. Wash. U., 1996; grantee, Wash. Commn. for Humanities, 1981, Wash. Centennial Commn., 1988. Mem.: Olive Ridge Cmty. Coun., Ea. Wash. U. Alumni Assn., N.W. chpt. Lupus Found. (event chmn. 2002, bd. dirs. 2003—). Congregationalist. Avocations: travel, reading, volunteer work. Home: 1700 17th Ave #608 Seattle WA 98122

MULLA, ZUBER, epidemiologist; b. Gujarat, India; BA, U. Ariz., Tucson, 1991; MSPH, U. South Fla., 1994, PhD, 2001. Epidemiologist Fla. Assn. of Pediatric Tumor Programs, Tampa, Fla., 1994—97; regional epidemiologist Fla. Dept. of Health, Orlando, Fla., 1998—2002; asst. prof. epidemiology U. Tex.-Houston Sch. Pub. Health, El Paso, Tex., 2002—. Dean's alumni adv. bd. U. South Fla. Coll. Pub. Health, Tampa, Fla., 1995—98. Contbr. articles to profl. jours., chpt. to book. Mem.: Am. Coll. Epidemiology, Delta Omega. Achievements include investigation of anthrax outbreak in Florida in 2001; research in treatment of invasive group A streptococcal infections. Office: U Tex Sch Pub Health 1100 N Stanton St Suite 110 El Paso TX 79902 E-mail: zmulla@sph.uth.tmc.edu.

MULLAINATHAN, SENDHIL, education educator, researcher; BA in Computer Sci., Economics and Math., Cornell U., 1990—93; PhD in Economics, Harvard U., 1993—98. Asst. prof. MIT, 1998—2000, Mark Hyman Jr. Career Devel. asst. prof., 2000—02, Mark Hyman Jr. Career Devel. assoc. prof., 2002—. Faculty rsch. fellow/labor and corp. fin. Nat. Bur. of Econ. Rsch., 1998—; cons. Harvard Inst. for Internat. Devel., 1998—2000; mem., Behavioral Economics Roundtable Russell Sage Found., 2001—; referee Am. Econ. Rev., Econometrica, Jour. of Polit. Econ., Jour. of Pub. Econ., Quar. Jour. of Econ., Rev. of Econ. Studies, Rev. of Fin. Studies, Rand Jour. of Econ. Contbr. numerous articles in var. profl. jours.; author: (paper) Do CEOs Set Their Own Pay? The Ones Without Principals Do (Best Paper award, Corp. Governance Libr., 2000). Grantee Harvard U. Merit fellowship, Harvard U., 1993—96, Sumner Slichter fellowship, 1996—97, rsch. grant, Am. Compensation Assn., 1996, Chiles Found. fellowship, Harvard U., 1997—98, Russell Sage Found. small grants program (joint with Marianne Bertrand), 1997, Citicorp rsch. grant (joint with Marianne Bertrand), 1999—, award #9986268 (joint with Marianne Bertrand), NSF, 2000—02, Sloan Found. fellow, 2001—03, Zvi Griliches Nat. fellow, Nat. Bur. of Econ. Rsch., 2001, Olin Found. fellow, 2002—03, MacArthur fellow, 2003—08. Office: E52-252c Dept of Econ MIT 50 Memorial Dr Cambridge MA 02142-1347

MULLALLY, MEGAN, actress; b. LA, Nov. 12, 1958; d. Carter Mullally, Jr. and Martha Mullally; m. Michael Katcher (div.); m. Nick Offerman, Sept. 20, 2003. Student, Northwestern U. Actor: (TV films) Rainbow Drive, 1990, Winchell, 1998; (TV series) Ellen Burstyn Show, 1986; (TV films) Everything Put Together, 2000, Lifetime, The Pact, 2002; (TV series) My Life and Times, 1991, Fish Police, 1992, Rachel Gunn, RN, 1992, Will and Grace, 1998— (Emmy Award Supporting Actress in a Comedy, 2000, Outstanding Comedy Series award, 2000, Am. Comedy Award, 2001, Outstanding Female Actor Award, 2001, Screen Actors Guild award Oustanding Actress in a Comedy Series, 2001, 2002, 2003); (Broadway plays) Grease, 1994, How to Succeed in Business Without Really Trying, 1995—96; (films) Once Bitten, 1985, Last Resort, 1986, About Last Night, 1986, Anywhere But Here, 1999, Best Man in Grass Creek, 1999, Everything Put Together, 2000, Monkey Bone, 2001, Stealing Harvard, 2002; actor, actor: (films) Speaking of Sex, 2001, (voice) Teacher's Pet, 2004. Office: The Gersh Agency PO Box 5617 Beverly Hills CA 90210 also: Will and Grace KoMut Entertainment 4024 Radford Ave Studio City CA 91604

MULLAN, DONALD WILLIAM, archbishop; b. Galt, Ont., Apr. 26, 1937; s. William James and Lillian Maude (Sachs) M.; m. Cathy Templeman. Met. bishop Christ Cath. Ch. Internat.; pastor Cathedral of St. Luke, Niagara Falls. Trustee Bd. Edn., Preston, Ont., 1962-68, Waterloo County, Ont., 1969-70, Wellington County, Ont., 1971-72. Mem. Order of Noble Companions of the Swan (grand prelate), Moose, Scouts of Can. E-mail: dmullan1@cogeco.ca.

MULLAN, FITZHUGH, public health physician; b. Tampa, Fla., July 22, 1942; s. Hugh and Mariquita (MacManus) Mullan; children: Meghan Elizabeth, Jason Michael, Caitlin Patricia. BA, Harvard U., 1964; MD, U. Chgo., 1968; DSc, U. Osteo. Medicine, 1993; LHD, Coll. Osteo. Medicine Pacific, 1993. Intern Jacobi Hosp., Bronx, 1968—70; resident Lincoln Hosp., Bronx, 1970—72; physician Nat. Health Svc. Corps., Santa Fe, 1972—75; dir. Nat. Health Svc. Corps, Rockville, Md., 1977—81; scholar-in-residence Inst. Medicine, Washington, 1981—82; sr. med. officer NIH, Bethesda, Md., 1982—84; sec. for health and environment State of N.Mex., Santa Fe, 1984—85; assoc. prof. Johns Hopkins Sch. Hygiene and Pub. Health, Balt., 1986—88; dir. pub. health history project Office of Surgeon Gen., Rockville, 1988—90; dir. bur. health professions USPHS, Rockville, 1990—96; contbr. editor Health Affairs, Bethesda, 1996—; clin. prof. pediats. and pub. health George Washington U., 1996—; staff physician Upper Cardozo Cmty. Health Ctr., 1996—. Author: White Coat, Clenched Fist: The Political Education of an American Physician, 1976, Vital Signs: A Young Doctor's Struggle With Cancer, 1983, Plagues and Politics: The Story of the United States Public Health Service, 1989; contbr. articles to profl. jours. Fellow: Am. Acad. Pediats.; mem.: Inst. of Medicine of NAS, Am. Assn. for History of Medicine, APHA, AMA. Office: Health Affairs 7500 Old Georgetown Rd Ste 600 Bethesda MD 20814-6133

MULLAN, JOHN H. science administrator; b. Middletown, NY, Apr. 16, 1942; BA cum laude, St. Johns U.; LLB, Columbia U.; LLM in Taxation, NYU. Bar: NY 1968, Calif. 1997. From staff to dep. gen. counsel Grumman Corp., LA, 1975—94; from east coast litigation counsel to sr. corp. counsel Northrop Grumman Corp., LA, 1994—99, corp. v.p., sec., 1999—. Woodrow Wilson fellow, Stanford U., 1964—65. Office: Northrop Grumman Corp 1840 Century Park E Los Angeles CA 90067-2199

MULLANE, DENIS FRANCIS, insurance executive; b. Astoria, N.Y., Aug. 28, 1930; s. Patrick F. and Margaret (O'Neill) M.; m. Kathryn Mullman, June 28, 1952; children: Gerard, Kevin, Denise. BS in Mil. Engring, U.S. Mil. Acad., 1952; LHD (hon.), U. Conn., 1988, St. Joseph's Coll., 1990; LLD (hon.), U. Hartford, 1993, Trinity Coll., Hartford, Conn., 1995; MS in Fin. Svcs., The Am. Coll., Bryn Mawr, Pa., 1995. CLU. With Conn. Mut. Life Ins. Co., Hartford, 1956—, v.p., 1969-72, sr. v.p., 1972-74, exec. v.p., 1974-76, pres., 1977—, chief exec. officer, 1983-85, chmn., chief exec. officer, 1985-90, chief exec. officer, pres., 1990-93; chmn. Mulane Enterprises, Inc., Hartford, Conn., 1994—; with Mullane Enterprises, West Hartford, Conn., 1994—. Bd. dirs. Conn. Natural Gas Co.; chmn. The Am. Coll., Bryn Mawr, Pa., 1993-96; chmn. joint planning com. Am. Coll. and Soc. Fin. Svcs. Profls., 1996-99. Dir. U.S. Chamber, 1991-95. 1st lt. C.E., U.S. Army, 1952-56. Recipient John Newton Russell award, 1987, Knight of St. Gregory award, Disting. Grad. award USMA, 2004. Mem.: Assn. Grads. U.S. Mil. Acad. (pres. 1989—93), Nat. Assn. Ins. and Fin. Advisors, Am. Soc. Corp. Execs. Republican. Roman Catholic. Office: Mullane Enterprises Inc 29 S Main St Hartford CT 06107-2449 Office Phone: 860-561-7650.

MULLANE, JOHN FRANCIS, pharmaceutical company executive; b. N.Y.C., Mar. 10, 1937; s. John Gerard and Rita Ann (Hoben) M.; m. Ruth Ann Cecka, Nov. 17, 1962; children— Rosemarie, Michael, Kathleen, Therese, Thomas MD, SUNY, 1963, PhD, 1968; JD, Fordham U., 1977. Bar: N.Y. 1978, D.C. 1979. Assoc. med. dir. Ayerst Labs. div. Am. Home Products Corp., N.Y.C., 1973-75, dir. clin. research, 1975-76, v.p. clin., 1977, v.p. sci., 1978-82, sr. v.p., 1982, exec. v.p., 1983-88; pres. Mullane Health Care Cons., N.Y.C. and Sarasota, Fla., 1989—; dir. drug devel. DuPont Med. Products, Wilmington, Del., 1990; sr. v.p. DuPont-Merck, Wilmington, 1991-94; exec. v.p. Amylin Pharms., 1994-96. Contbr. articles to profl. jours. Served to lt. col. U.S. Army, 1970-73 Recipient Upjohn Achievement award, 1970; N.Y. Heart Assn. Crawford-Maynard fellow, 1966-68 Fellow Am. Coll. Clin. Pharmacology; mem. ABA, Am. Soc. Clin. Pharmacology and Therapeutics, Am. Assn. Study of Liver Diseases, Misty Creek Country Club. Roman Catholic. Avocation: golf. Home and Office: 9047 Misty Creek Dr Sarasota FL 34241-9542

MULLANEY, JOANN BARNES, nursing educator; b. Newport, R.I., Dec. 7, 1943; d. Elliott Calvert and Betty (Dawson) Barnes; m. Charles Patrick Mullaney, June 3, 1967 (div. 1973); 1 child, Mark Andrew. Diploma in Nursing, Newport Hosp. Sch. Nursing, 1965; BSN, Salve Regina Coll., Newport, 1976; BSN/MS in Psychiat. Mental Health Nursing, Boston Coll., 1977; PhD in Edn., U. Conn., 1983. RN, R.I.; clin. specialist, ANCC. Instr. Salve Regina U., Newport, 1979-83, asst. prof., 1983-85, sr. level coord., 1983-94, assoc. prof. nursing, 1985-95, prof., 1995—. Psychiat. clin. specialist in pvt. practice The Center, Middletown, R.I., 1990—, utilization reviewer, Providence, 1990-92, ednl. cons., 1990—. Contbr. to book: Psychiatric Care Planning, 1989 (ASN Book of Yr. 1988). Mem. Atty.-Gen.'s Task Force on Domestic Violence, Providence, 1994; mem. Health Care Reform Coalition, Providence, 1993—, Nat./R.I. Action Not Gridlock Coun., 1993—; mem. R.I. House and Senate Women's Health Issues Commn., 1995. Recipient Air Force Nurse Educator award, 1988; grantee HEW, 1976, NIMH, 1977, 91-94, Lilly Co., 1994; Mass. Assn. Colls. Nursing scholar, 1995. Mem. ANA, AAUW, AAUP, New Eng. Orgn. Nursing, Ea. Nursing Rsch. Soc., Soc. Edn. and Rsch. in Psychiat. Nursing, R.I. State Nurses' Assn. (pres.-elect 1992-93, pres. 1993-95, pres. ex-officio 1995—), Mass. Assn. Coll. Nursing Rsch., Sigma Theta Tau (Delta Upsilon chpt.), Phi Lambda Theta. Home: 242 Gibbs Ave Newport RI 02840-2829

MULLANEY, THOMAS JOSEPH, lawyer; b. N.Y.C., Feb. 9, 1946; s. James Joseph and Dorothy Mary (Fulling) M.; m. Christine E. Hampton, Aug. 16, 1969; children: Richard, Jennette. BA, Fordham U., 1967; JD, U. Va., 1970; LLM, NYU, 1971. Bar: Va. 1970, N.Y. 1971, U.S. Dist. Ct. (so. and ea. dists.) N.Y. 1972, U.S. Ct. Appeals (2d cir.) 1972, U.S. Supreme Ct. 1975. Assoc. Brown, Wood, Ivey, Mitchell & Petty, N.Y.C., 1970-79, Law Offices of John M. Kenney, Garden City, N.Y., 1979-84; ptnr. Abrams, Thaw & Mullaney, N.Y.C., Farmingdale, N.Y., 1985-91; dir., sr. counsel law dept. Merrill Lynch & Co., Inc., N.Y.C., 1991—. Capt. JAGC, U.S. Army, 1971-74. Mem. Va. State Bar Assn., N.Y. State Bar Assn. Republican. Roman Catholic. Home: 104 Huntington Rd Garden City NY 11530-3122 Office: 222 Broadway Fl 14 New York NY 10038-2510 E-mail: thomas_mullaney@ml.com.

MULLARE, T(HOMAS) KENWOOD, JR., lawyer; b. Milton, Mass., Jan. 19, 1939; s. Thomas Kenwood and Catherine Marie (Leonard) M.; m. Joan Marie O'Donnell, May 27, 1967; children: Jennifer M. Cedrone, Tracy K., Jill M. Hegarty, Joyce M. AB, Holy Cross Coll., 1961; LLB, Boston Coll., 1964. Bar: Mass. 1964. Atty. New Eng. Electric Sys., 1964-69; v.p., gen. counsel, sec. AVX Corp., NYC, 1970-73; v.p., gen. counsel, clk. Tyco Labs., Inc., Exeter, NH, 1974-77; v.p., gen. counsel, sec. SCA Svcs., Inc., Boston, 1978-83; spl. counsel Houghton, Mifflin Co., Boston, 1984-85, v.p., dir. bus. software divsn., 1985-92; pres. North River Capital Co., Inc., Norwell, Mass., 1990—; gen. counsel, sec. Aztec Tech. Ptnrs., Inc., Braintree, Mass., 1999—2002; prin., owner Law Office T. Kenwood Mullare, Norwell, 2002—. Bd. dirs. Friendship Home, Inc. Mem. regional adv. bd. com. Mass. Dept. Mental Retardation, 1994-97; bd. dirs. Barque Hill Assn., Norwell, 1980-84, pres., 1981-83; pres. Ch. Hillers, Norwell, 1983-84; bd. dirs. South Shore Assn. for Retarded Citizens, Weymouth, Mass., 1993-98, chmn., 1995-97. Mem. Boston Bar Assn., Am. Corp. Counsel Assn. Home: 31 Barque Hill Dr Norwell MA 02061-2815

MULLARKEY, MARY J. state supreme court chief justice; b. New London, Wis., Sept. 28, 1943; d. John Clifford and Isabelle A. (Steffes) M.; m. Thomas E. Korson, July 24, 1971; 1 child, Andrew Steffes Korson. BA, St. Norbert Coll., 1965, LLD (hon.), 1989; LLB, Harvard U., 1968. Bar: Wis. 1968, Colo. 1974. Atty.-advisor U.S. Dept. Interior, Washington, 1968-73; asst. regional atty. EEOC, Denver, 1973-75; 1st atty. gen. Colo. Dept. Law, Denver, 1975-79, solicitor gen., 1979-82; legal advisor to Gov. Lamm State of Colo., Denver, 1982-85; ptnr. Mullarkey & Seymour, Denver, 1985-87; justice Colo. Supreme Ct., Denver, 1987—, chief justice, 1998—. Fellow: Colo. Bar Found., ABA Found.; mem.: ABA, Denver Bar Assn. (Jud. Excellence award 2003), Colo. Women's Bar Assn. (Mary Lathrop award 2002), Colo. Bar Assn., Thompson G. Marsh Inn of Ct. (pres. 1993—94). Office: Supreme Ct Colo Jud Bldg 2 E 14th Ave Denver CO 80203-2115

MULLARKEY, MAUREEN T. game company executive; BS, U. Tex., 1980; MBA, U. Nev., 1988. From fin. analyst to CFO Internat. Game Tech., Reno, 1989—2001, CFO, 2001—, exec. v.p., 2003—, treas., 2003—; CFO Zoho Corp., 2000—01. Office: International Game Technology 9295 Prototype Dr Reno NV 89521

MULLEN, DANIEL ROBERT, finance executive; b. Swedesboro, N.J., Apr. 17, 1941; s. Harold Legrand and Gladys (DeVault) M.; m. Elizabeth A. Willers, Dec. 17, 1977; children: William H., Jonathan O. BS in Fin., Ariz. State U., 1966, postgrad., 1966-67. Appraiser Ariz. Dept. Revenue, 1966-68; financial analyst Amerco, Inc., Phoenix, 1968-70, treas., 1970-82; pres., dir. Continental Leasing Co., 1980—; v.p. Southwest Pipe and Supply Co., 1982; treas. Talley Industries, Inc., 1982-93, v.p., 1993-98; COO Friendship Publs., 1998-99. Bd. dirs. C. Myers Corp., Amerco. Del. Ariz. Presdl. Dem. Conv., 1972; bd. dirs. Big Sisters of Ariz., 1975, Found. for Blind Children, 1984-90, Phoenix Little Theatre, 1985-91, Kachina Country Day Sch., 1988-94, New Way Sch., 1994-2000, Interfaith Coop. Ministries, 2003-, With U.S. Army, 1959-62. Ariz. Soc. CPAs grantee, 1964-65 Mem. Fin. Execs. Internat. Home: 3627 E Medlock Dr Phoenix AZ 85018-1505

MULLEN, EDWARD JOHN, JR., Spanish language educator; b. Hackensack, NJ, July 12, 1942; s. Edward J. and Elsie (Powell) M.; m. Helen Cloe Braley, Apr. 2, 1971; children: Kathleen, Julie Ann. BA, W.Va. Wesleyan Coll., 1964; MA, Northwestern U., 1965, PhD, 1968. Asst. prof. modern langs. Purdue U., West Lafayette, Ind., 1967-71; assoc. prof. Spanish U. Mo., Columbia, 1971-78, prof. Spanish, 1978—. Author: La Revista Contemporáneos, 1972, Carlos Pellicer, 1977, Langston Hughes in the Hispanic World and Haiti, 1977, The Life and Poems of a Cuban Slave: Juan Francisco Manzano 1797-1854, 1981, Critical Essays on Langston Hughes, 1986, Sendas Literarias: Hispanomerica, 1988, El cuento hispánico, 1980, 84, 89, 94, 2000, 04, Afro-Cuban Literature: Critical Junctures, 1998; editor: The Harlem Group of Negro Writers (Melvin B. Tolson), 2001; co-editor Afro-Hispanic Rev., 1987—. Recipient Diploma de Honor Inst. de Cultura Hispánica, 1964; Woodrow Wilson fellow, 1964-65; Northwestern U. fellow, 1965-67; Rsch. grant U. Mo., 1972, 76; grantee Am. Council Learned Socs., 1979 Mem. MLA, Am. Assn. Tchrs. Spanish and Portuguese, Assn. of Depts. Fgn. Langs. (pres. 1989-91). Home: 207 Edgewood Ave Columbia MO 65203-3413 Office: U Mo Dept Romance Langs 143 Arts And Sci Bldg Columbia MO 65211-0001 Office Phone: 573-882-5041. E-mail: mullene@missouri.edu.

MULLEN, EDWARD K. paper company executive; CEO Newark Group, Cranford, NJ, to 1997, chmn. bd. dirs., 1997—. Office: Newark Group 20 Jackson Dr Cranford NJ 07016-3609

MULLEN, EILEEN ANNE, human resources executive; b. Phila., Feb. 14, 1943; d. Joseph Gregory and Helen Rita (Kane) M.; m. William John Raschiatore (dec.). BS in English, St. Joseph's U., 1967; MA in English, Villanova U., 1978. Cert. tchr., Pa. Tchr. St. Anastasia Sch., Newtown Square, 1960-67, West Cath. Girls H.S., 1967-74; mgr. staff tng. and devel. ASTM, Phila., 1974-96, dir. human resources, 1996—. Instr. lit., speech and communications Widener U., Chester, Pa. and Wilmington, Del. Contbg. author articles on comms. tng. programs; contbr. articles to profl. jours. Mem. ASTD (pres. Phila./Del. Valley chpt. 1980-81, Outstanding Leadership as Pres. award 1981), Soc. for Human Resource Mgmt. Democrat. Roman Catholic. Office: ASTM 100 Barr Harbor Dr West Conshohocken PA 19428-0700 E-mail: emullen@astm.org.

MULLEN, GEORGE D. artist; BA, U. of Colo., Boulder. Artist Studio Revolution (www.StudioRevolution.com), Del Mar, Calif., 1993—; chmn. The Cyber Nation of Freedom (www.CyberNationofFreedom.com), San Diego, 2000—. Oil painter, 250 Plus Paintings; author: (book) Peace in the Mid. East, (document) Liberation of the Individual, The Return To Common Sense (A Purely Secular Argument Against Abortion), The Return To Common Sense - Part II. Chmn. The CyberNation of Freedom (www.CyberNationofFreedom.com), San Diego, Calif., 2000—03. Mem.: Rotary Internat. (pres. of mission valley rotary club 1995—96). Office: StudioRevolution PO Box 2806 Del Mar CA 92014 E-mail: gmullen@studiorevolution.com.

MULLEN, GRAHAM C. federal judge; b. 1940; BA, Duke U., 1962, JD, 1969. Bar: N.C. 1969. Ptnr. Mullen, Holland, Cooper, Morrow, Wilder & Sumner, 1969-90; judge U.S. Dist. Ct. (we. dist.) N.C., Charlotte, 1990—. Lt. USN, 1962-66. Mem. N.C. Bar Assn. (bd. govs. 1983-88), Mecklenburg County Bar Assn. Office: US Courthouse 401 W Trade St Rm 230 Charlotte NC 28202-1619 E-mail: gmullen@ncwd.net.

MULLEN, J. THOMAS, lawyer; b. Evanston, Ill., Aug. 27, 1940; BSE, Princeton U., 1963; JD cum laude, U. Mich., 1967. Bar: Ill. 1967. Ptnr. Mayer, Brown, Rowe & Maw, Chgo.; ptnr.-in-charge London office, 1974-78. Bd. dirs. Legal Assistance Found. Chgo., 1979-85. Mem. ABA, Chgo. Bar Assn., Chgo. Coun. Lawyers. Office: Mayer Brown Rowe & Maw 190 S La Salle St Ste 3100 Chicago IL 60603-3441 E-mail: tmullen@mayerbrownrowe.com.

MULLEN, MARIE, actress; Founding mem., co-founder Druid Theatre Co., 1975. Appeared in numerous prodns. including the Beauty Queen of Leenane (Tony award, 1998, Obie award), The Loves of Cass McGuire, Silverlands, The Playboy of the Western World, Lovers' Meeting, the Colleen Bawn, The Shaughraun, A Doll's House, Much Ado About Nothing, 'Tis Pity She's a Whore, Famine, Drama at Inish, Conversations on a Homecoming, The Power of Darkness, The Plough and the Stars, the Cavalcaders, The Man of Mode, Love of the Nightingale, Man Who Came to Dinner, King Lear, Big Maggie, 2001 (Irish Theatre award nominee); TV/films appearances include The Butcher Boy, 1997, The Van, 1996, Snakes and Ladders, The Disappearance of Finbarr, 1996, Circle of Friends, Family, 1995, Dancing at Lughnasa, 1998, When Brendan Met Trudy, 2000, Disco Pigs, 2001. Address: Druid Theatre Co Chapel Ln Galway Ireland

MULLEN, MAUREEN ANN, social worker; b. Chgo., Mar. 22, 1949; d. Robert Vincent and Mary Geraldine M. BA, U. Ill., 1971; MEd, Coll. of William and Mary, 1974; MSW, Univ. Ill., 1990; postgrad., U. Chgo., 1985, 86. Programmer Computer Task Group, N.Y.C., 1980-81; analyst, programmer Guy Carpenter, N.Y.C., 1981-82; analyst C.N.A. Ins., Chgo., 1982-84; analyst, programmer Lakeshore Nat. Bank, Chgo., 1984-85; sales support Sterling Software, Chgo., 1986; owner Mullen Designs, Chgo., 1987; dir. of social svcs. Vista Health, Fayetteville, Ark., 2002—03; employee assistance counselor Ark. Employee Assistance Program, Fayetteville, 2003—. Prodr., host (TV show) Ozarks Live!. Vol. Samaritans hotline, Chgo., 1986; mem. adv. bd. Lakeview Mental Health Ctr., Chgo., 1986; mem. Chgo. Coun. on Fgn. Rels., 1986—87; chmn. fundraiser Habitat for Humanity, 1987; vol. Manic Depressive and Depressive Assn. and Nat. Alliance for Rsch. into Scizophrenia and Depression, 1988, Wilmette Sch. Bd. Caucus, 1997, mem. endowment fund com., 1996, 1997; vol. Chgo. Bot. Garden, 1999; spkrs. chmn. Fayetteville Freedom Festival, 2003; vol. Thomas Hynes campaign, Chgo., 1987, New Trier Dem. Orgn., 2000; bd. dirs. N.W. Ark. Mental Health Assn., 2002—, chmn. sch. libr. book project, 2003, 2004; bd. dirs. Cmty. Access TV, Fayetteville, 2003. Recipient Fat Cat award, Cmty. Access TV, Fayetteville, 2004; Ill. State scholar, 1971. Mem.: ACLU, NOW, Sierra Club, Dem. Nat. Com., So. Poverty Law Ctr. Avocations: painting, poetry, backpacking, photography, acting. Home: 3246 Autumn Ct Fayetteville AR 72703

MULLEN, MICHAEL G. career military officer; b. L.A. m. Deborah Morgan; children: John, Michael. Graduate, U.S. Naval Acad., 1968; MSc in Ops. Rsch., Naval Postgraduate Sch., 1985. Enlisted USN, 1968, advanced through grades to adm., 2003; stationed on USS Collett, USS Blandy; comdr. USS Noxubee, 1973-75; company officer, exec. asst. U.S. Naval Acad., 1975-78; chief engr. USS Fox, 1978-80; exec. officer USS Sterett, 1981-83; comdr. USS Goldsborough, 1985-87; dir. divsn. officer course Surface Warfare Officer's Sch., 1987-89; staff asst. for navy programs Office of the Sec. Defense, 1989-91; comdr. USS Yorktown, 1992-94; from dir. surface officer distribution divsn. to dep. dir. Bureau of Naval Personnel, 1994-96; comdr. Cruiser-Destroyer Group 2, 1996-98; dir. surface warfare divsn. Office of Chief of Naval Ops., 1998—2000; comdr. SECOND fleet/ Striking Fleet Atlantic, 2000—01; dep. chief naval ops., resources, requirements & assessments U.S. Navy, 2001—03, vice chief naval ops., 2003—04; comdr. US Naval Forces Europe, 2004—, Regional Command South, Naples, Italy, 2004—. Office: Comdr US Naval Forces Europe PSC 802 Box 2 FPO AE 09499-0002*

MULLEN, MICHAEL M. real estate company executive; B in Fin., Loyola U. Co-founder, v.p. sales FCLS; exec. v.p. mktg. and acquisitions, chief investment and devel. officer Ctr. Point Properties Trust, Oak Brook, Ill., 1993—97, v.p., COO, 1997—2001, pres., COO, 2001—. Bd. mem. Brauvin Capital Trust. Mem.: Nat. Assn. Office Indsl. Properties (bd. mem.). Office: Center Point Properties Trust 1808 Swift Dr Oak Brook IL 60523*

MULLEN, MICHAEL T. lawyer; b. Evanston, Ill., Apr. 15, 1956; s. George Martin and Marguerite (Tully) M.; m. Patricia Reilly, Apr. 24, 1987; children: Claire, Catherine, Michael, Conor. BA, Marquette U., 1978; JD, Loyola U., 1981. Bar: Ill. 1981, U.S. Dist. Ct. (no. dist.) Ill. 1981, U.S. Ct. Appeals (7th cir.) 1981, U.S. Supreme Ct., 2000. Asst. atty. gen. Ill. Atty. Gen., Chgo., 1981-85; asst. U.S. atty. U.S. Atty., Chgo., 1985-90, 90-92, dep. chief, 1990-92; ptnr. Mullen & Minella, Chgo., 1992-98, Paul B. Episcope, Ltd., Chgo., 1998—. Contbr. articles to profl. jours. Trustee Village of Western Springs (Ill.), 1995—. Recipient Spl. Achievement award for sustained superior U.S. Dept. Justice, 1988, performance award 1990; named to Loyola Acad. Athletic Hall of Fame. Mem. Ill. State Bar Assn., Ill. Trial Lawyers Assn., West Suburban Bar Assn. lawyer for multiple cases with multimillion dollar jury verdicts and settlements. Office: Paul B Episcope Ltd 77 W Washington St Ste 300 Chicago IL 60602-2896 Office Phone: 312-782-6636. Business E-Mail: mtm@episcopeltd.com.

MULLEN, PETER P. lawyer; b. N.Y.C., Apr. 8, 1928; m. Cecilia Kirby; 5 children. AB cum laude, Georgetown U., 1948; LLB, Columbia U., 1951. Bar: N.Y. 1951. Ptnr. Skadden, Arps, Slate, Meagher & Flom LLP, N.Y.C., 1961-98, exec. ptnr., 1981-94, of counsel, 1998—. Co-chmn. Cardinal's Com. Laity Archdiocese N.Y., 1989-2003; bd. dirs., sec., treas., Eye Surgery, Inc. Formerly mem., pres. Bd. Edn. Pub. Schs., Bronxville, N.Y., 1979-81; chmn. Skadden Fellowship Found., 1988—; bd. dirs., vice-chmn. Lawrence Hosp., Bronxville, 1984-89; bd. dirs., sec. Project Orbis Internat., 1985-, Georgetown U., Washington, 1982-99, chmn., 1985-92; bd. dirs. Legal Aid Soc., 1987-93, Vols. Legal Svcs., Inc., 1988-99, United Way Bronxville, 1985-93, New Milford Hosp. Found., 1997-, Practicing Attys. Law Students, 1988-99; trustee Lawyer's Commn. Civil Rights Under Law, 1984-99; chmn. Gregorian U. Found., 1989—; bd. dirs., exec. com. Vatican Obs. Found., 1993. Named Man of Yr. Cath. Big Bros., 1987; recipient John Carroll award Georgetown U., 1984, John Carroll Medal Merit, 1988, Thomas More award Lawyers Com. Cardinal's Com. of the Laity, 1996, Elizabeth Ann Seton award Nat. Cath. Edn. Assn., 1998; named Stone scholar Columbia U., 1951. Mem. Am. Bar Assn., N.Y. State Bar Assn. (com. securities regulation 1980-83), Assn. Bar City N.Y. (com. corp. law 1964-67, com. admissions 1965-68, com. securities regulation 1970-73), Soc. Friendly Sons St. Patrick (N.Y., pres. 1989-90), Knight Malta. Office: Skadden Arps Slate et al LLP 4 Times Sq New York NY 10036-6522

MULLEN, ROD, nonprofit organization executive; b. Puyallup, Wash., Aug. 2, 1943; s. Charles Rodney and Grace Violet (Fritsch) M.; m. Lois Fern Tobiska, May 3, 1963 (div. Jan. 1977); children: Cristina, Charles, Moneka; m. Naya Arbiter, Oct. 17, 1977. Student, U. Idaho, 1961-63; AB in Polit. Sci., U. Calif., Berkeley, 1966; postgrad., San Francisco Art Inst., 1968. Dir. Oakland (Calif.) facility Synanon Found., Inc., 1971-72, dir. San Francisco facility, 1972-73, dir. Tomales Bay (Calif.) facility, 1976-78, dir. Synanon edn. programs, 1973-76; treatment dir. nat. programs Vision Quest, Inc., Tucson, 1981-82; dir. resources and devel. Amity, Inc., Tucson, 1982-84, exec. dir., 1984-95; founder, pres., CEO, Amity Found., Porterville, Calif., 1995—. Mem. Nat. Adv. Com. on Substance Abuse Prevention, 1990-96; adv. bd. Ctr. for Therapeutic Cmty. Rsch., Nat. Devel. and Rsch. Insts., NYC, 1991-2002; cons. Calif. Office Criminal Justice Planning, Sacramento, 1993; prin. investigator program Nat. Inst. on Drug Abuse, 1990-93; pres. Calif. Therapeutic Com.; videographer Prodigal Daughters, 2002, TC Pioneers, 2003, Voices From Circle Tree Ranch, 2004. Dir.: (documentaries) Prodigal Daughters, 2002, TC Pioneers, 2003; contbr. chapters to books, articles to profl. jours. Mem. Am. Correctional Assn., Therapeutic Coms. of Am. (pres. Calif. sect. 2004—). Office: Amity Found PO Box 713 Porterville CA 93258-0713 Office Phone: 559-783-2813. Business E-Mail: rmullen@amityfdn.org.

MULLEN, RON, insurance company executive; b. Tex., Aug. 8, 1939; s. Durward Lacy and Blanche V. (Coulson) M.; m. Carole King, Dec. 29, 1959; children: Lacy Lynne Holcomb, Misty Kay. Student, Abilene Christian Coll., 1957-58, San Antonio Coll., 1958-59; BBA, S.W. Tex. State U., 1965. C.L.U., Chartered Fin. Cons. City council mem. City of Austin, 1977-83, mayor, 1983-85; mgr. Prin. Fin. Group, Austin, 1965-98, Ron Mullen & Assocs. Inc., Austin, 1966—, InNet Fin. Group; prin. Prime Fin. Opportunities. Chmn. TML Ins. Trust Fund Com., 1983—; mem. Gov.'s Task Force on State Employees Health Ins. Benefits, Austin, 1984 Chmn. Austin Transp. Study Com., Austin, 1983—, Greater Austin-San Antonio Corridor Coun., 1984—, Social Policy Adv. Com., Austin, 1979-80, March of Dimes campaign, Austin, 1974-75; co-chmn. Consumers United for Rail Equity, Austin, 1983—; v.p. Austin Symphony Orch., 1974-75; mem. exec. com. Capital Area Planning Coun., Austin, 1976—, exec. bd. Tex. Mcpl. League, Austin, 1983—, Gov.'s Task Force on Indigent Health Care, Austin, 1984, Tex. Adv. Commn. on Intergovtl. Rels., Austin, 1981—; chmn. Infant Parent Tng. Ctr., 1985-98; bd. dirs., chmn. South MoPac Transp. Com., 1986-87; life mem. Austin Jaycees, bd. dirs., 1974-75; vice-chmn. Mental Health Mental Retardation Bd.; vice chmn. South Tex. Audio Reader Svc.; bd. dirs. BBB, Inc., Hyde Park Bapt. Sch., 1999—; mem. nat. com. Assn. Ins. and Fin. Advisers, Austin, 1999—. Recipient Road Hand award Tex. Dept. Hwys. and Transp., 1985, award for regional statesmanship Greater Austin-San Antonio Corridor Commn.; named Boss of Yr., Treaty Oaks chpt. Am. Bus. Women's Assn., 1978, Nat. Mgr. of Yr., Bankers Life Ins. Co., 1977, 82, 84-85, Alumnus of Yr. Austin Jaycees, 1988-90. Mem. Am. Coll. Life Underwriters (pres.), Tex. Assn. Life Underwriters (pres. 1997-98), Austin Assn. Life Underwriters (pres. 1974-75), Austin Gen. Agts. and Mgrs. Assn. (pres. 1978-80), Sales and Mktg. Execs. of Austin (pres. 1972-73), Downtown Rotary (pres. 1996-97). Baptist. Home: 6902 Mesa Dr Austin TX 78731-2822 Office Phone: 512-973-9993. E-mail: ron9991@msn.com.

MULLEN, RUSSELL EDWARD, agricultural studies educator; b. Atlantic, Iowa, Sept. 4, 1949; AA, Southwestern C.C., Creton, Iowa, 1969; BS in Agriculture, N.W. Mo. State U., 1971, MS in Edn., 1972; PhD in Crop Physiology and Mgmt., Purdue U., 1975. Grad. asst. N.W. Mo. State U., Maryville, 1971-72; grad. teaching asst. Purdue U., West Lafayette, Ind., 1972-74, grad. instr., 1974-75, temporary asst. prof., 1975-76; asst. prof. U. Fla., Gainesville, 1976-78; from asst. prof. to prof. Iowa State U., Ames, 1978—86, prof., 1986—. Recipient Ensminger Interstate Disting. Tchr. award Nat. Assn. Colls. Tchrs. Agriculture, 1992, Am. Soc. Agronomy Resident Edn. award, 1999; Am. Soc. Agronomy fellow, 1998. Office: Iowa State U Dept Agronomy 1126 Agronomy Hl Ames IA 50011-0001

MULLEN, TERRI ANN, retired special education educator; b. St. Louis, Apr. 01; d. William Earl and Sophia Kinniff; m. Thomas Patrick Mullen; children: David, Mark, Debi. BS in Edn., S.E. Mo. State U.; M in Sch. Adminstrn., Calif. State U., 1978, M in Spl. Edn., 1981; EdD in Institutional Mgmt., Pepperdine U., 1985. Cert. spl. edn., std. sec., std. elem., adminstrv. svc. K-12, cmty. coll. instr. Tchr. Irvine (Calif.) Unified Sch. Dist., 1972-84; lectr., spl. edn. Calif. State U., Fullerton, 1989-90; asst. prin. Moreno Valley (Calif.) Unified Sch. Dist., 1984-85; adminstr. of spl. svcs. Centralia Sch. Dist., Buena Park, Calif., 1984-89; elem. prin. Capistrano Unified Sch. Dist., San Juan Capistrano, 1989-93; spl. edn. tchr., dept. chair Moreno Valley (Calif.) Unified Sch. Dist., 1993—. Chair, cmty. staff edn. planning com. Santiago Elem. Sch., Irvine Unified Sch. Dist., 1981; dir., staff devel. for spl. programs pers. Centralia Sch. Dist., Buena Park, 1984-89; workshop presenter Assn. of Calif. Sch. Adminstrs. Conf., San Francisco, 1983. Author: Resource Book of Classroom Interventions for the Collaborative Teaching Model, 1994, Tips of the Trade for the Classroom Aide, 1984; contbr. articles to profl. jours. Adv. bd. for sp. edn. Calif. State U. Fullerton, 1988-89. Recipient Cmty. Svc. award Disneyland, 1992, 93; named Outstanding Educator of Yr. Rotary Club, 1983. Mem. Coun. for Exceptional Children, Kappa Delta Pi, Phi Kappa Phi. Avocations: roller skating, fashion design, interior design, computer applications, writing. E-mail: tmullen@pacbell.net.

MULLEN, WILLIAM JOSEPH, III, military analyst, retired career officer; b. Plattsburg, N.Y., Dec. 26, 1937; s. William Joseph Jr. and Georgia (Cook) M.; m. Norma Sturgeon, Aug. 6, 1962; 1 child, William Joseph IV. BS, U.S. Mil. Acad., West Point, N.Y., 1959; MS in Internat. Affairs, George Washington U., 1971. Commd. 2d lt. U.S. Army, 1959, advanced through grades to brig. gen., 1987; various assignments in U.S., Vietnam, Korea, Panama, Germany, Saudi Arabia, 1959-92; mem. staff, faculty U.S. Mil. Acad., West Point, 1967-70; comdr. 1st Brigade, 1st Inf. Div., Ft. Riley, Kans., 1983-86; asst. div. comdr. 5th Inf. Div., Ft. Polk, La., 1986-87; comdg. gen. U.S. Army Combined Arms Tng. Activity, Ft. Leavenworth, Kans., 1987-89, 1st Inf. Div. (Forward), Germany, 1989-91; dep. dir. ops. J3 Forces Command, Ft. McPherson, Ga., 1991-92; sr. mgr. mil. tng. and analysis sys. BDM Fed., Inc., Monterey, Calif., 1992-98; sr. program mgr. tng. mgmt. sys. Northrop Grumman Mission Sys., Monterey, 1998—. Co-author: Changing an Army, An Oral History of Gen. W.E. DePuy, 1979; contbr. articles, book revs. to Mil. Rev. Decorated D.S.C., D.S.M. Mem. Assn. U.S. Army, Soc. of 1st Div. (chpt. officer 1968, assoc. 1989-93, trustee found. 1989-93, bd. dirs.), Legion of Valor, Nat. Infantry Assn. (Order of St. Maurice). Avocations: sports, reading. *When in doubt, I have always found direction from the guidance explicit in the 1st Infantry Division's motto, "Duty first!".*

MULLENDORE, JAMES MYERS, lawyer; b. Charlottesville, Va., Mar. 21, 1946; s. James M. and Elaine (Gregg) M.; m. Kristine B. Mullendore; children: Margaret E., Sean T. BS, W.Va. U., 1968; JD, U. Va., 1975. Bar: Mich. 1975, U.S. Dist. Ct. (we. dist.) Mich. Ptnr. Mullendore & Thrall, Greenville, Mich., 1975—. Pres., v.p. Greenville Bd. Edn., 1976-82; ofcl. Mid-Am. Football Conf., 1985-86, Big Ten Football Ofcls., 1987-2001,—; bd. dirs. United Way Greenville, 1978-83; chmn. controlled substances adv.com. State Mich., 1994-2001; bd. dirs. Danish Festival Inc, 1997-2000. Mem. ABA, Assn. Trial Lawyers Am., Mich. Trial Lawyers Assn., U.S. Football League (ofcl. 1983), Greenville Area C. of C. (chmn. bd. dirs.), Rotary (v.p. 1983-84). Congregationalist. Home: 7678 Greenbrier NE Rockford MI 49341 Office: PO Box 40 Greenville MI 48838 Office Phone: 616-754-4611.

MULLENDORE, WALTER EDWARD, retired economist; b. Harrah, Okla., Apr. 22, 1940; s. Newton and Ida Minnie (Lohmann) M.; m. Edra Janell Havenstrite, July 4, 1963; children: Matthew Edward, Karen Kay, Mark Andrew. BS, Okla. State U., 1961, MS, 1963; PhD in Econs., Iowa State U., 1968. Grad. asst. Okla. State U., 1961-63; instr. Iowa State U., 1965-67, mem. faculty dept. econs. U. Tex., Arlington, 1968—2002, prof., 1975—2002, dean Coll. of Bus., 1980—93; ret., 2002. Contbr. articles to profl. jours. Served with U.S. Army, 1963-65. Mem. Mo. Valley Econ. Assn. (v.p. 1980-81, pres. 1982-83), Gt. S.W. Rotary (pres. 1989-90), Omicron Delta Epsilon. Methodist. Home: 8003 John T White Rd Fort Worth TX 76120-3611

MULLENIX, LINDA SUSAN, lawyer, educator; b. N.Y.C., Oct. 16, 1950; d. Andrew Michael and Roslyn Marasco; children: Robert Bartholomew, John Theodore, William Joseph. BA, CCNY, 1971; M Philosophy, Columbia U., 1974; PhD Pres.'s fellow, 1977; JD, Georgetown U., 1980. Bar: D.C. 1981, U.S. Dist. Ct. D.C. 1981, U.S. Ct. Appeals (D.C. cir.) 1981, U.S. Supreme Ct. 1986, Tex. 1991, U.S. Ct. Appeals (5th cir.) 1995. U. Md. European divsn., Ramstein, Germany, 1974; instr. N.Y. Inst. Tech., N.Y.C., 1976; assoc. prof., lectr. George Washington U., Washington, 1977-80; asst. prof. Am. U., Washington, 1979; assoc. Pierson, Ball & Dowd, Washington, 1980-81; clin. prof. Loyola U. Law Sch., L.A., 1981-82; asst. prof. Cath. U. Law Sch., Washington, 1984-86; assoc. prof., 1986-90; prof., 1990; Reuschlein disting. vis. chair Villanova Law Sch., 2000. Vis. asst. prof. CCNY, 1977, Cooper Union Advancement Sci., Art, N.Y.C., 1977, Loyola U. Law Sch., L.A., 1982-83, Cath. U. Law Sch., Washington, 1983-84; jud. fellow U.S. Supreme ct. and fed. Jud. Ctr., 1989-90; Bernard J. Ward Centennial prof. U.S. Tex., 1991-2001, Morris and Rita Atlas chmn. in advocacy, 2001—; vis. prof. Harvard Law Sch., 1994-95, Mich. Law Sch., 1996; adj. instr. Fordham U., N.Y.C., 1975-76, adj. asst. prof., 1977; resident scholar Rockefeller Found. Bellagio (Italy) Study Ctr., 2002. Author: Mass Tort Litigation: Cases and Materials, 1996, Civil Procedure Roadmap, 1997, Casenotes: Federal Courts, 1997, ExamPro: Civil Procedure, 1998, Civil Procedure, 2004; co-author: Understanding Federal Courts, 1998, Federal Courts in the Twenty-First Century, 1996, 2d edit., 2002; Moore's Federal Practice and Procedure, 1991, 97; editor bibliographies Polit. Theory, A. Jour. Polit. Philosophy, 1972-74, The Tax Lawyer Jour., 1978-80; columnist The National Law Jour., 1998—; contbr. editor review of U.S. Supreme Ct. Cases; co-reporter Report and Plan of Civil Justice Reform Act Adv. Group, S.d., Tex., 1991; assoc. reporter ALI, Restatement of the Law Governing Lawyers; contbr. articles to profl. jours. Alt. del. Dem. State Conv., 1980. Fellow NDEA, 1971-74; N.Y. State Regents Scholar, 1967-71. Mem. ABA (reporter task force on class actions 1995-97), Am. Law Inst., D.C. Bar Assn. (com. on ethics, CLE and the Model Rules 1987), Am. Assn. Law Schs. (exec. com. sect. on civil proc. 1987-88, exec. com. sec. on conflicts of law 1991-92,chair prof. devel. com. 1991-93), Jour. Legal Edn. (editl. bd. 1997-1999), Phi Beta Kappa. Home: 722 Crystal Creek Dr Austin TX 78746-4730 Office: U Tex Sch Law 727 E Dean Keeton St Austin TX 78705-3224 Office Phone: 512-232-1375.

MULLENS, DELBERT W. automotive executive; CEO Wesley Ind., Inc., Bloomfield Hills, MI. Office: Wesley Ind Inc 43173 Woodward Ave #329 Bloomfield Hills MI 48302-5005

MULLENS, WILLIAM REESE, retired insurance company executive; b. Franklin, Tenn., Sept. 12, 1921; s. William Pope and Elizabeth (Reese) M.; m. Katherine Ann Jones, Nov. 24, 1945; children: Jo Ann Mullens Sanditz, Carol Ann Mullens Slegers. BA, Vanderbilt U., 1942. With Bus. Men's Assurance Co., Kansas City, Mo., 1947-75, exec. v.p., dir., 1969-75; pres., dir. J.C. Penney Life Ins. Co., 1975-82; pres. Gt. Am. Res. Ins. Co., 1975-84, dir., 1975-89. Dir. Nat. Fidelity Life Ins. Co., 1986-89 Served to lt. comdr. USNR, 1943-46. Fellow Soc. Actuaries; mem. Phi Beta Kappa, Alpha Tau Omega. Presbyterian. Home: One McKnight Pl Apt 118 Saint Louis MO 63124

MULLER, BARBARA ANN, allergist; b. Teaneck, N.J., Jan. 10, 1957; MD, Med. U. Guadalajara, 1982. Diplomate Am. Bd. Allergy and Immunology, Am. Bd. Internal Medicine. Intern U. Medicine Dentistry N.J./Hackensack Med. Ctr., 1983-84; resident in internal medicine Hackensack Med. Ctr., 1984-87, chief resident in internal medicine, 1987-88; fellow in allergy and immunology U. Iowa Hosps., Iowa City, 1988—90, asst. prof. allergy-immunology, 1995—97, assoc. prof. allergy-immunology, 1997—2003, prof. allergy-immunology, 2003—; dir. ambulatory care programs internal medicine U. Iowa Hosps. and Clinics, Iowa City, 1993—2003; dir. U. Iowa Health Plans, 1996—; dir. care mgmt. program U. Iowa, 1997—; dir. Anticoagulation Case Mgmt. Svc., 1999—2003; sr. asst. dir. med. ops. U. Iowa Hosp. and Clinics, 2003—; asst. dean U. Iowa, 2003—. Mem.: ACP/ASIM, Am. Coll. Physician Execs., Am. Coll. Allergy and Immunology, Am. Acad. Allergy and Immunology. Office: U Iowa Hosps and Clinics A&I 1303 JCP Iowa City IA 52242 Office Phone: 319-356-3694. Business E-Mail: barbara-muller@uiowa.edu.

MULLER, CAROLYN BUE, physical therapist, volunteer; b. Crosby, N.D., Feb. 24; d. Sigurd Christian and Eleanor (Rushfeldt) Bue; m. Willard Chester Muller, Jan. 27, 1945; children: Marolyn Jean, Barbara Anne, Nancy Eleanor. BA, St. Olaf Coll., 1940; cert. in phys. therapy, Harvard U., 1944. Assoc. dir. younger girls and phys. edn. sect. YWCA, Syracuse, N.Y., 1940-43; phys. therapist Valley Forge Hosp., Phoenixville, Pa., 1944-45; med. records libr. Trust Territory of Pacific Islands, Truk, Caroline Islands, 1951-52. Founder, prin. organizer Am. Cmty. Sch., Truk, 1952, Lincoln Sch., Katmandu, Nepal, 1956, Am. Cmty. Sch., Mogadiscio, Somali Republic, 1958, Kampala, Uganda, 1966; panelist workshop Wash. Commn. for Humanities, Yakima, 1996. Author: Living in Uganda, 1967; cartographer: Maudie - An Oregon Trail Childhood, 1993. Charter registrar Clallam County Mus. and Hist. Soc., Port Angeles, Wash., 1977-87; vol. reading tutor Port Angeles Sch. Dist., 1980—; cmty. coord. UNICEF, Port Angeles, 1982-85; rep. Target Wash. Seminar, Seattle, 1984; rep. Asia-Can. Women in Mgmt. Conf., Victoria, B.C., Can., 1985; regional judge Wash. State Nat. History Day Contest, Port Angeles, 1985-2002; selection judge Wash. State Inquiring Mind Lecture Series, Seattle, 1989, 90, 96, organizer/coord., Inquiring Mind Lecture Series 1983-2002; Wash. state judge Nat. History Day Contest, Ellensburg, Wash., 1993-2003; bd. dirs. Wash. State Friends of the Humanities, 1991-94; trustee Wash. Commn. for the Humanities, 1995-97; pres. Am. Women's Club, Katmandu, 1957-58, Mogadiscio, 1959-60; v.p. Internat. Women's Club, Saigon, South Vietnam, 1971; mem. selection com. Evergreen State Soc. Awards, 1998, 99. Recipient Women Making a Difference award Soroptimist Internat., 1984, Outstanding Vol. award Citizens' Ednl. Ctr. N.W., 1988, Evergreen award Evergreen State Soc., 1992. Mem. AAUW (br. pres. 1980-84, Edn. Found. scholarship in her name 1996). PEO (rec. sec. 1984-85, v.p. 1985-86, pres. 1987-89, chaplain 1994, Internat. Peace scholarship in name 1990, state chmn. Internat. Peace scholarship 1989-90), W

Athletic Club. Avocations: growing flowers, cross-country walking, painting, reading, travel. Home: 3624 S Mount Angeles Rd Port Angeles WA 98362-8910 E-mail: muller@tenforward.com.

MULLER, CHARLOTTE FELDMAN, economist, educator; b. N.Y.C., Feb. 19, 1921; d. Louis and Lillian (Drogin) Feldman; m. Jonas N. Muller, 1942 (dec.); m. Carl Schoenberg, 1970; children: Jeremy Lewis Muller, Sara Linda Muller. AB, Vassar Coll., 1941; A.M., Columbia U., 1942, PhD in Econs., 1946. Instr. econs. Bklyn. Coll., 1943; lectr. Barnard Coll., 1943-46; asst. prof. Occidental Coll., 1947; asst. study dir. Survey Rsch. Ctr., U. Mich., 1948; rsch. assoc. U. Calif., Berkeley, 1948-50; lectr. Yale U. Sch. Pub. Health, 1952-53; asst. prof. Columbia U. Sch. Pub. Health, 1957-67; assoc. dir. Ctr. for Social Rsch. CUNY, 1967-86, prof. econs., 1978-91, prof. emerita, 1991—, prof. sociology, 1982-91, prof. urban studies Ctr. for Social Rsch., 1967-78; v.p. CUNY Acad. for Humanities and Scis., 1985-88; prof. health econs. Mt. Sinai Sch. Medicine, 1986-91, prof. emerita, 1991—, dir. div. health econs., 1988-91, prof. dept. geriatrics, 1990-91, assoc. dir. Internat. Longevity Ctr.-USA, Ltd., 1991-97, sr. economist Internat. Longevity Ctr.-USA, Ltd., 1998—, co-dir. rsch. program Internat. Longevity Ctr.-USA, Ltd., 1999—. Cons. Health Care Financing Adminstrn., U.S. VA; disting. alumna speaker Vassar Centennial, 1971. Author: Health Care and Gender, 1990; mem. editorial bd. Am. Jour. Pub. Health, 1980-84, Women and Health, Rsch. on Aging; contbr. numerous articles on health econs. to profl. publs. Mem. N.Y.C. Mayor's Com. on Prescription Drug Abuse, 1970-73; bd. dirs. Alan Guttmacher Inst., 1972-81, CUNY Rsch. Found., 1985-91; vice chmn. Med. and Health Rsch. Assn., N.Y.C.; mem. health care tech. study sect. Nat. Ctr. Health Svcs. Rsch., 1976-79; mem. commn. on nat. policy Am. Jewish Congress, 1980-91. Ford/Rockefeller Founds. grantee, 1972-73, 75-76; Russell Sage Found. grantee, 1985-90. Mem.: APHA, Am. Econ. Assn. Jewish. Achievements include presenting report on Economic Status of Older Women to UN 2nd World Assembly on Aging., Madrid, 2002. Office: Internat Longevity Ctr-USA Ltd 60 E 86th St New York NY 10028-1009 E-mail: charlottem@picusa.org.

MULLER, DAVID WEBSTER, architectural designer; b. Norwich, Conn., Aug. 25, 1956; s. Richard Johnson and Barbara Alice (Reading) M.; 1 stepchild, Shannon. BA in Polit. Sci., George Washington U., 1978. Rsch. assoc. Rep. Nat. Com., Washington, 1978-80, dep. dir. spl. projects, 1981-83; western field dir. Nat. Rep. Congl. Com., Washington, 1983-85; v.p. Russo Watts & Rollins, Sacramento, 1985-86; campaign mgr. Chavez for U.S. Senate, Silver Spring, Md., 1986; v.p. Russo Watts & Rollins, Sacramento, 1987-89; cons. Sacramento, 1989; pvt. investor, 1990—2000; project mgr. Kokoro Country Houses, 2002; loan cons. Royalty Fin., Newport Beach, Calif., 2004. Archtl. design and restoration Muller/West, 1990-2001; founding mem. The M.I.N.D. Inst. Med. Investigation of Neurodevelopmental Disorders, U. Calif. Davis Med. Ctr., Sacramento. Mem. Nat. Coun. for Arts and Scis. at George Washington U., centennial com. Corona del Mar, 2004; bd. trustees Nautical Mus., Newport Beach, Calif., 2003—; crew leader Habitat for Humanity, Orange, Calif., 2002—. Mem.: Corona del Mar C. of C. Avocations: boating, photography, fiction writing, international travel, kayaking. Home: 512 Begonia Ave Corona Del Mar CA 92625-1728 Office: 512 Begonia Ave Corona Del Mar CA 92625-2011 Office Phone: 949-675-6153. Personal E-mail: dmuller4385@aol.com.

MULLER, EDWARD ROBERT, lawyer; b. Phila., Mar. 26, 1952; s. Rudolph E. and Elizabeth (Steiner) M.; m. Patricia Eileen Bauer, Sept. 27, 1980; children: Margaret Anne, John Frederick. AB summa cum laude, Dartmouth Coll., 1973; JD, Yale U., 1976. Assoc. Leva, Hawes, Symington, Martin & Oppenheimer, Washington, 1977-83; dir. legal affairs Life Scis. group Whittaker Corp., Arlington, Va., 1983-84; v.p. Whittaker Health Svcs., Arlington, Va., 1984-85; v.p., gen. counsel, sec. Whittaker Corp., L.A., 1985-93, chief adminstrv. officer, 1988-92, CFO, 1992-93, bd. dirs., 1993-99; v.p., gen. counsel, sec. BioWhittaker, Inc., Walkersville, Md., 1991-93; pres., CEO, bd. dirs. Edison Mission Energy, Irvine, Calif., 1993-2000. Bd. dirs. GlobalSantaFe Corp., Houston, 1997—, Interval, Inc., Marina del Rey, Calif., 2000—, Strategic Data Corp., Santa Monica, Calif., 2001—, The Keith Cos., Inc., Irvine, Calif., 2001—, RigNet, Inc., Houston, 2002—, RealEnergy, Inc., Woodland Hills, Calif., 2003—; mem. Brookings Task Force on Civil Justice Reform, 1988—89; chmn. U.S.-Philippines Bus. Com., 1998—2000; adv. bd. Tennenbaum Capital Ptnrs., LLC, L.A., 1997—2003; mem. Coun. on Fgn. Rels., 1998—, Pacific Coun. on Internat. Policy, 1988—, corp. bd. advisors, 2001—; dep. chmn. Contact Energy Ltd., Wellington, New Zealand, 1990—2000; bd. dirs. Oasis Residential, Inc., Las Vegas, 1995—98. Trustee Exceptional Children's Found., L.A., 1988-94, treas., 1988-93; co-chair Internat. Energy Devel. Coun., Washington, 1993-2000; bd. govs. Jr. Achievement of Orange County and the Inland Empire, 1995-96; mem. Pres. Leadership Coun., Dartmouth Coll., 2003-. Home and Office: 502 20th St Santa Monica CA 90402-3028 Office Phone: 310-917-1546.

MULLER, ERNEST H. geology educator; b. Tabriz, Iran, Mar. 4, 1923; (parents U.S. citizens); s. Hugo Arthur and Laura Barnett (McComb) M.; m. Wanda Custis, Apr. 7, 1951; children: Ruth Anne, David Stewart, Katherine Lee. BA, Wooster Coll., 1947; MS, U. Ill., 1949, PhD, 1952. Geologist U.S. Geol. Survey, Washington, 1947-54; asst. prof. geology Cornell U., Ithaca, N.Y., 1954-59; assoc. prof. Syracuse U., N.Y., 1959-63, prof., 1963-89, interim chmn. dept. geology, 1970-71, 79-81, prof. emeritus, 1989—. Seasonal geologist N.Y. Geol. Survey, 1956-76; geologist Am. Geog. Soc., Chile, 1959; rsch. assoc. Natural History Mus., Reykjavik, Iceland, 1968-69; vis. prof. Alaska Pacific U., Anchorage, 1979; Erskine vis. prof. U. Canterbury, Christchurch, New Zealand, 1974; mem. Bering Glacier (Alaska) Rsch. Group, 1988—, N.Y. Pleistocene Stratigraphy. Author: Geology of Chautauqua County, New York, 1964, Seaway Trail Rocks and Landscapes, 1987. 1st lt. USAAF, 1943-46. Fellow Geol. Soc. Am. (geomorphology panel 1962-64, 66-68, 75-77, 97-99), AAAS; mem. Am. Quaternary Assn. (counselor 1982-86), Glaciological Soc., Nat. Assn. Geology Tchrs., Sigma Xi. Home: 874 Livingston Ave Syracuse NY 13210-2936 Office: Syracuse Univ 204 Heroy Geology Lab Syracuse NY 13244-0001

MÜLLER, GENE ALAN, historian, consultant; b. Grand Island, Nebr., Jan. 10, 1943; s. Ludwig Frederick Alex and Erma Gertrude (Gorin) M.; m. Diana June Currey; children: Michelle Nicole Müller-Mehta, Alyssa Katherine, Alexandra Mariel, Nicholas Christian. B.A. cum laude, Midland Lutheran Coll., Fremont, Nebr., 1965; NYU in Spain scholar, U. Madrid, 1963-64; Fulbright-Hays scholar, U. Nacional Tucuman, Argentina, 1965-66; M.A., U. Kans., Lawrence, 1969, Ph.D., 1982. Asst. instr. U. Kans., 1967-73; asst. prof. history Ft. Hays State U., Kans., 1973-74; bilingual historian El Paso Community Coll., Tex., 1974—; project reviewer Nat. Endowment Humanities, 1978—. Author: The Church in Poverty: Bishops, Bourbons, and Tithes in Spanish Honduras, 1700-1821; A Select Bibliography on the Catholic Church in Latin America, The Status of the Clergy and the Condition of the Church Wealth in Mexico: 1800-1850, Dr. Tomas Ruiz: Founder of Univ. of Nicaragua and Precursor of C.Am. Independence, 1777-1819, John Gorin of Fairfax County, Virginia: Defender of Mt. Vernon in 1781; also articles, book revs., chpts. in books. Mem., v.p. El Paso Council Internat. Visitors, 1982-83, pres., 1983-85; pres. So. N.Mex./El Paso br. Lutheran Brotherhood, v.p. Thrivent fraternal chpt., 2003—; bd. dirs. Nat. Council for Internat. Visitors, Leadership El Paso, Class VIII; pres. El Paso chpt. Am. Field Service; mem. El Paso County Coun. for the Social Studies, regional chairperson, Regional Fulbright Tchr. Exchg. Interview Com.; pres., bd. dirs. El Paso Mission Trails Assn.; moderator Nat. Issues Forums, 1985—; coordinator NCIV/USAID Midwinter Seminar, El Paso, 1983-86, NEH Summer Seminar U. Tex., El Paso, 1986[illegible] asst. Luth. Quad Parish of Western, Kans. Am. Field Service scholar [illegible]land, 1960; NDFL Title VI fellow U. Kans., 1969; Ford Fou[illegible]caragua, 1969, Central Am., 1970; OAS fellow to Guate-[illegible]ht summer grantee, Brazil, 1982, Netherlands, 1983; sr. [illegible]osta Rica, 1987, Fulbright-Alfonso Gevcio Robles sr. [illegible]2-93, Fulbright-Hays, Nepal and India, 2003; recipient [illegible] award, 1988, Outstanding Alumni award Midland [illegible] Energy Found. award, 1993-94, EPCC Faculty [illegible] NISOD Master Tchr. Award, 2004. Mem. Am. [illegible]ssn., Latin Am. Studies Assn., Conf. Latin Am. Studies, Tex. Cath. Hist. Assn., Rocky Mountain Council Latin Am. Studies, Midwest Assn. Latin Am. Studies., Fulbright Assn. (pres. del Norte chpt. 1989—). Democrat. Home: 10708 Vista Lomas Dr El Paso TX 79935-3611 Office: El Paso Community Coll PO Box 20500 El Paso TX 79998-0500 E-mail: genem@epcc.edu.

MULLER, HENRY JAMES, journalist, magazine editor; b. Garmisch-Partenkirchen, Germany, Feb. 10, 1947; came to U.S., 1953; s. Henri Jacques and Helga (Mensch) M.; m. Maggie McComas, June 19, 1968. BA, Stanford U., 1968. Tchr. U.S. Peace Corps, Ethiopia, 1968-70; chief Vancouver (B.C., Can.) bur. Time mag., 1971-73, European econ. corr., 1973-77, chief Paris bur., 1977-81, world editor, 1982-85, chief of corrs., 1986-87, mng. editor, 1987-93; editorial dir. Time Inc., 1993-2000, editor-at-large, 2000—. Faculty mem. profl. pub. course Stanford (Calif.) U., 1989—; bd. visitors Columbia Journalism Sch., 1998—. Trustee Stanford U., 1991-2001, Carnegie Corp., 1992-2000, Overseas Press Club, 1993-97; dir. Media Action Internat., 2000—. Recipient David Brower Environ. Journalism award Sierra Club, 1990, Gerald Loeb award for disting. bus. and fin. journalism, 1992. Mem. Am. Soc. Mag. Editors (bd. dirs. 1991-95), Coun. of Fgn. Rels. Avocations: hiking, reading, skiing. Office: Time Inc Time & Life Bldg 1271 Avenue Of The Americas New York NY 10020-1300 E-mail: henry_muller@timeinc.com.

MULLER, H(ENRY) NICHOLAS, III, retired foundation administrator; b. Pitts., Nov. 18, 1938; s. Henry N. Jr. and Harriet (Kerschner) M.; m. Nancy Clagett, June 20, 1959 (div. 1985); children: Charles T., Brook W.; m. Carol A. Cook, Jan. 4, 1986. BA, Dartmouth Coll., 1960; PhD, U. Rochester, 1968. Instr. Dartmouth Coll., Hanover, NH, 1964; lectr. Mt. Allison U., Sackville, Canada, 1964—66; asst. prof., prof. history U. Vt., Burlington, 1966—78, asst. dean Coll. Arts, Scis., 1969—70, assoc. dean Coll. Arts, Scis., 1970—73, dir. Living, Learning Ctr., 1973—78; pres. Colby-Sawyer Coll., New London, NH, 1978—85; dir. State Hist. Soc. Wis., Madison, 1985—96; pres., CEO Frank Lloyd Wright Found., Scotsdale, Ariz., 1996—2002; ret., 2002. Dir. Standex Internat. Corp., Salem, NH, 1984; mem. State Hist. Records Adv. Bd., 1985—96, Gov. Coun. Tourism, 1987—96; chmn. Wis. Burial Sites Bd., 1988—96; trustee Nat. Trust Hist. Preservation, 1989—98; chair Wis. Submerged Cultural Resources, 1993—96. Co-author: An Anxious Democracy, 1982; co-editor: Science, Technology and Culture, 1974, In a State of Nature, 1982; sr. editor Vt. Life mag., 1975-87; editor Vt. History, 1977-85. Fin. chmn. Vt. Bicentennial Commn., 1970—77; trustee Vt. Hist. Soc., 1972—85, 2003—, v.p., 1975—82; chmn. Vt. Coun. Hist. Preservation, 1975—78; chair Bicentennial Com., Burlington, 1976; mem. NH Postsecondary Edn. Commn., 1983—85; trustee, pres. Taliesin Preservation, Inc., 1991—2001; mem. Wis. Sesquicentennial Commn., 1995—99; trustee Frank Lloyd Wright Found., 1996—; v.p. Ind. Coll. Univ. Coun. Ariz., 1998—2000, mem. bd., 1998—2002; interim chmn. Taliesin Archs., 2000—01; counselor Essex Cmty. Fund; bd. dirs. Wis. Preservation Fund Inc., 1989—, USS Wis., 1989—93; trustee Ethan Allen Homestead Trust, 2002—, treas., 2003—; dir., vice chmn. Essex Cmty. Heritage Orgn., NY, 2003—; trustee Smith House Health Care Ctr., Willsboro, NY, 2004—. Fellow: Ctr. Rsch. on Vt.; mem.: Am. Assn. State and Local History (councillor 1988—91), Vt. Archeol. Soc. (pres. 1971—74), Nat. Coun. Pub. History (bd. dirs. 1988—90), Madison Club.

MULLER, JENNIFER, choreographer, dancer; b. Yonkers, N.Y., Oct. 16, 1944; d. Don Medford and Lynette (Heldman) Muller. BS, Juilliard Sch. Music, 1967. Instr. in dance H.S. Performing Arts, 1967-72, Sarah Lawrence Coll., 1968-72, The Juilliard Sch., 1969-70, Nederlands Dans Theater, 1971-76, Utah rep., 1973-74, Centre Nat. de la Dance, Paris, 1998, Acad. Isola Danzo, Venice, 1999-2001, Atelier de Paris, 1999, Institut del Teatre de Barcelona, 2001, Centro Andaluz de Danza-Seville, 2003; commns.: Alvin Ailey Am. Dance Theatre, N.Y.C., 1977, 85, 2003, Festival d'Avignon, France, 1980, Lyon Opera Ballet, France, 1984, Aterballetto, 1988, Ballet Stagium, 1991, Dansgroep Krisztina de Chatel, 1992, Tanz-Forum Staatsoper Koln, Sachsische Staatopera-Dresden, ARTSCAPE-Balt., 1991, 95, Aterballetto, Italy, 1993, Les Ballet Jazz de Montreal, 1994, Ballet du Nord, France, 1995, White Wave Rising, 1996, Bat Dor Dance Co., Israel, Nederlands Dans Theatre 3, Ballet Contemporaneo, Argentina, Ohio Ballet, 2000, Dance Inst. U. Akron, 2003; cons. Met. Mus. Art, 1971-72. Mem. Pearl Lang Dance Co., N.Y.C, 1959-63, prin. dance, Jose Limon Dance Co., N.Y.C., 1963-71, assoc. dir., choreographer, prin. dancer, Louis Falco Dance Co., N.Y.C., 1968-74; founder, dir., choreographer: Jennifer Muller/The Works, N.Y.C., 1974-; choreographic works include: Nostalgia, 1971, Rust, 1971, Cantata, 1972, Tub, 1973, An American Beauty Rose, 1974, Biography, 1974, Speeds, 1974, Winter Pieces, 1974, Clown, 1974, Four Chairs, 1974, Wyeth, 1974, White, 1975, Strangers, 1975, Beach, 1976, Crossword, 1977, Predicaments for Five, 1977, Mondriaan, 1977, Lovers, 1978, Solo, 1979, Conversations, 1979, Chant, 1980, Terrain, 1981, Shed, 1982, Kite, 1983, Souls, 1984, The Enigma, 1986, Fields, 1986, Couches, 1986, Life/Times, 1986, Darkness and Light, 1986, Interrupted River, 1987, Occasional Encounters, 1988, City, 1988, The Flight of a Predatory Bird, 1989, Refracted Light, 1990, RIGHTeous About Passing (on the LEFT), 1990, Woman with Visitors at 3am, 1991, Regards, 1991, arm in arm in arm..., 1991, Thesaurus, 1991, Glass Houses, 1991, 2-1-1/Attic, 1992, Momentary Gathering, 1992, The Waiting Room, 1993, The Politician/Peeling the Onion, 1993, Orbs, Spheres and Other Circular Bodies, 1993, HUMAN/NATURE-A Response to the Longhouse Gardens, 1993, Pierrot, 1993, Desire-That DNA Urge, 1994, Point of View (A Case of Persimmons and Picasso), 1994, The Spotted Owl, 1995, Some Days are Like That, 1995, Promontory, 1996, Fruit, 1996, The Dinner Party, 1996, A Broken Wing, 1996, Ricochet, 1997, Degas Revisited, 1998, Dialectics Part I, 1998, Spores, Solitude & Summer Humming, 1999, Beethoven-Not Four Naught, 2000, aSOlo, 2000, Hymn for Her, 2000, Time Treading, 2000, China Project: Sagone; Suk Road; Dancing Waves, 2001, The Door, 2001, Never in The Same Room, 2002, To Live Alone..., 2002, Moon, 2002, It's a c#!* City, 2002, Prayer, 2003, Bounce, 2003, Footprints, 2003, Flowers, 2004, Ecstatic Poems, 2004, A Candle at Both Ends, 2004; choreographer for theatrical prodns.: Frimbo, 1980, The Death of von Richthofen..., 1982, Fame, The Musical, 1988, Up Against It, 1989, The Seven Deadly Sins, 1990, Signature, 1990, Esther, 1993, Once Around the City, 1998, 2001; dir. Le Jongleur, 2000. Recipient Best Performance award Berlin Festival, 1977, Acad. award Juilliard Sch. Music, 1967, Carbonell award, 1989; grantee Nat. Endowment for Arts, 1971-77, 80-85, 86-87, 87-88, Creative Artists Pub. Svc., 1976-77, N.Y. State Coun. on Arts, 1976-77, 78-79, 85-93, N.Y.C. Dept. Cultural Affairs, 1978-79, 94-2003, N.Y.C. Dept. Youth and Cmty. Devel., 2001-03. Mem. Am. Guild Mus. Artists, Soc. Stage Dirs. and Choreographers, World Arts Coun. (founding mem.). Home and Office: The Muller/Works Found Inc 131 W 24th St New York NY 10011-1942 E-mail: jenniferm@compuserve.com., theworksnyc@compuserve.com.

MULLER, JEROME KENNETH, photographer, art director, editor; b. Amityville, NY, July 18, 1934; s. Alphons and Helen (Haberl) M.; m. Nora Marie (Nestor), Dec. 21, 1974. BS, Marquette U., 1961; post grad., Calif. State U., Fullerton, 1985-86; MA, U. Calif., San Diego, 1988; post grad., Newport Psychoanalytic Inst., 1988-90. Comml. and editorial photographer, NYC, 1952-55; mng. editor Country Beautiful mag., Milw., 1961-62, Reproductions Rev. mag., NYC, 1967-68; editor, art dir. Orange County (Calif.) Illustrated, Newport Beach, Calif., 1962-67, art editor, 1970-79, exec. editor, art dir., 1968-69; owner, CEO Creative Svcs. Advt. Agy., Newport Beach, Calif., 1969-79. Founder, CEO, Mus. Graphics, Costa Mesa, Calif., 1978—; tchr. photography Lindenhurst (NY) HS, 1952-54, comic art U. Calif., Irvine, 1979, publ. design Orange Coast Coll., Costa Mesa, Calif., 1997-2002; guest curator Fiftieth Anniversary Exhbn. Mickey Mouse, 1928-78, The Bower's Mus., Santa Ana, Calif., 1978. *Exhibitions Organized: The Cartoon Show, Laguna Beach Art Mus, 1972. Indianapolis Mus of Art, 1977, Everson Mus of Art, Syracuse, 1978, Memorial Art Gallery, Rochester, 1979; The Moving Image, San Jose Mus, 1980, Mus of Science and Industry, Chicago, William Rockhill Nelson Gallery, Kansas City, 1981, Newport Harbor Art Mus, Calif, Mus of Albuquerque, 1982, Boston Mus of Science, 1983, Pensacola Mus of Art, 1984; The American Comic Strip, U. of Texas, 1981, Duke U, Midwest Mus of Am Art, 1982, U of Chicago, The Parthenon, Nashville, 1983, Albrecht Art Mus, St Joseph, Mo, Wichita Art Mus, 1984, Monterey Peninsula Mus of Art, 1985.* One-man shows include Souk Gallery, Newport Beach, 1970, Gallery Two, Santa Ana, Calif., 1972, Cannery Gallery, Newport Beach, 1974, Mus. Graphics Gallery, 1993, White Gallery Portland State U., 1996, U. Calif., Irvine, 1997, Nat. Telephone and Comm., Irvine, Calif., 1998, Robert Mondavi Wine and Food Center, Costa Mesa, 2000; author: Rex Brandt, 1972, Publication Design and Production, 2000; contbr. photographs and articles to mag. Mem. Cultural Arts Com., City of Costa Mesa, CA., 2000-2002. With USAF, 1956-57. Recipient, two silver medals Twentieth Ann. Exhbn. Advt. and Editorial Art in West, 1965. Mem.: Laguna Beach Art Mus., Art Mus. Assn. Am., Met. Mus. Art, Mus. Modern Art (N.Y.C.), Orange County Mus. Art, Alpha Sigma Nu. Home: 2438 Bowdoin Pl Costa Mesa CA 92626-6304 Office: PO Box 11155 Costa Mesa CA 92627-1155

MULLER, JOHN BARTLETT, university president; b. Port Jefferson, NY, Nov. 8, 1940; s. Frederick Henry and Estelle May (Reeve) M.; m. Barbara Ann Schmidt, May 30, 1964 (dec. 1972); m. Lynn Anne Spongberg, Oct. 10, 1987. AB in Polit. Sci., U. Rochester, 1962; postgrad. in apologetics, Westminster Sem., Phila., 1962-63; MS in Psychology, Purdue U., 1968, PhD in Psychology, 1975. Asst. prof. psychology Roberts Wesleyan Coll., Rochester, N.Y., 1964-66, acting chmn. div. behavioral sci., dir. instl. research, 1967-70; vis. asst. prof. psychology Wabash Coll., Crawfordsville, Ind., 1970-71; research assoc. Ind. U.-Purdue U., Indpls., 1971-72; prof. psychology, v.p. for acad. affairs Hillsdale (Mich.) Coll., 1972-85; pres. BMW Assocs., Osseo, Mich., 1984-85, Bellevue (Nebr.) U., 1985—. Bd. dirs. Nebr. Ind. Coll. Found., Omaha, Assn. Ind. Colls. Nebr., Lincoln; bd. advisors Wells Fargo Bank of Omaha, Applied Info. Mgmt. Inst., Gt. Western Bank. Contbr. articles to profl. jours. and textbooks. Bd. govs. Boys Club of Omaha. Nat. Inst. Mental Health fellowship Purdue U., 1963, Nat. Tchg. fellowship Fed. Govt., 1967, Townsend fellowship U. Rochester, 1962. Mem. APA, Bellevue C. of C. (bd. dirs. 1989-95), Phi Beta Kappa, Phi Kappa Phi. Republican. Home: 13303 Lochmoor Cir Bellevue NE 68123-3770 Office: Bellevue U Office of the Pres 1000 Galvin Rd S Bellevue NE 68005-3098 E-mail: jmuller@bellevue.edu.

MULLER, MERVIN EDGAR, computer scientist, statistician, educator; b. Hollywood, Calif., June 1, 1928; s. Emanuel and Bertha (Zimmerman) Muller; m. Barabara McAdam, July 13, 1963; children: Jeffrey McAdam, Stephen McAdam, Todd McAdam. AB, UCLA, 1949, MA, 1951, PhD, 1954. Instr. in math. Cornell U., 1954-56; rsch. assoc. in math. Princeton (N.J.) U., 1956-59, sr. scientist stats. and elec. engring., 1968-69; sr. statistician, dept. mgr. IBM, N.Y.C., White Plains, 1956-64; prof. computer sci. and stats. U. Wis., 1964-71; prof. computer sci. George Mason U., 1985; dept. dir. World Bank, Washington, 1971-81, sr. advisor, 1981-85; Robert M. Critchfield prof. computer info. sci. Ohio State U., 1985-98, prof. emeritus, 1994-98, dept. chair, 1985-94. Chair sci. and tech. info. bd. NRC, NAS; bd. dirs. Advanced Info. Tech. Ctr., Columbus, Ohio. Mem. editl. bd. Computation and Stats., 1990, Jour. Computational and Graphical Stats., 1990; contbr. articles to profl. jours. Trustee First Unitarian Ch., Bethesda, Md., 1975—79. Rsch. grantee, AT&T, Columbus, 1987. Fellow: World Acad. Productivity Sci., Am. Statis. Assn.; mem.: Internat. Assn. Statis. Computing (sci. sec. 1979—83, pres. 1977—79), Internat. Statis. Inst. (mem. steering com. Internat. Rsch. Ctr. 1987—89). Avocations: reading, jogging, walking, bridge. Home: 4171 Clairmont Rd Upper Arlington OH 43220-4501 Office: Ohio State U Dept Computer Info Sci Rm 395 2015 Neil Ave Columbus OH 43210-1210 E-mail: mmuller@columbus.rr.com.

MULLER, PETER, lawyer, entertainment company executive, retail company executive, consultant; b. Teplitz-Sanov, Czechoslovakia, Mar. 4, 1947; came to U.S., 1949; s. Alexander and Elizabeth Rudolpha (Weingarten) M.; m. Irene Smolarski, Nov. 18, 1971 (div. 1973); children: Chloe, Aurora; m. Esther Unterman Meisler, Jan. 4, 1987 (div. 1995). BA, NYU, 1968, JD cum laude. Entertainment editor Ambience mag., N.Y.C., 1978-79, Women's Life mag., N.Y.C., 1980-81; sole practice N.Y.C., 1984—; entertainment writer Jewish Press; chief exec. officer Producers Releasing Corp., N.Y. and Nev., 1987-88, pres. entertainment div., 1987-88; pres., founder Muller Entertainment Group, N.Y.C. and Calif., 1988—; pres., chief oper. officer ACA Joe, Inc., San Francisco and N.Y.C.; also bd. dirs. ACA Joe Inc., San Francisco and N.Y.C. Expert tech. adv. svc. for attys., Pa., 1987—; lectr. entertainment and comm. bus. to various orgns.; adj. prof. NYU, UCLA. Author: Show Business Law, 1991, The Music Business: A Legal Perspective, 1994. Bd. dirs. NYU Coll. Arts and Sci.; vol. Lawyers for the Arts, N.Y.C., 1987—. Mem. ABA (forum on entertainment and sports industries, forum on copyright, trademark and patent law), N.Y. State Bar Assn., NYU Alumni Assn. (bd. dirs. 1987—, v.p. bd. dirs., coun.), Assn. of Am. Mgmt. Assn. (pres.). Avocations: sports, swimming, history, writing, travel. Office Phone: 212-358-3406.

MULLER, RALPH W. hospital administrator; b. Oct. 26, 1945; married. BA in economics, Syracuse U., NY, 1966; MA in govt., Harvard U., Cambridge, Mass., 1968. Asst. to commr. Nicholas Johnson FCC, Washington, 1967; assoc., health care consulting Orgn. for Social and Tech. Innovation, Cambridge, Mass., 1969-70; rsch. asst. to Prof. Samuel H. Beer Harvard U., 1967—68, teaching fellow, govt., and resident tutor, 1969—72; govt. instr. Suffolk U., Boston, 1972—74; budget dir., dept. of public welfare Commonwealth of Mass., Boston, 1975—78, dep. commr., dept. public welfare, 1978—80; dir. fin. planning and budget U. Chgo., 1980—83, assoc. v.p. budget, computing and info. sys., 1984, v.p., hospitals and clinics and dep. dean, divsn. biological sciences, 1985—86; pres., CEO U. Chgo. Hospitals and Health Sys., 1986—2003; CEO U. Pa. Health Sys., 2003—. Fellow: AAAS; mem.: Coun. of Tchg. Hospitals (chmn. 1997—98), Am. Assoc. of Med. Colleges (AAMC) (chmn. 1999—2000). Office: U Pa Health Sys 3400 Spruce St Philadelphia PA 19104*

MULLER, RICHARD STEPHEN, electrical engineer, educator; b. Weehawken, NJ, May 5, 1933; s. Irving Ernest and Marie Victoria Muller; m. Joyce E. Regal, June 29, 1957; children: Paul Stephen, Thomas Richard. ME, Stevens Inst. Tech., Hoboken, N.J., 1955; MSEE, Calif. Inst. Tech., 1957, PhD in Elect. Engring. and Physics, 1962. Test engr. Wright Aero/Curtiss Wright, Woodridge, N.J., 1953-54; mem. tech. staff Hughes Aircraft Co., Culver City, Calif., 1955-61; instr. U. So. Calif., L.A., 1960-61; asst. prof., then assoc. prof. U. Calif., Berkeley, 1962-72, prof., 1973—. Guest prof. Swiss Fed. Inst. Tech., 1993; founder, dir. Berkeley Sensor and Actuator Ctr., 1985—; chmn. sensors electron devices NRC Army Rsch. Lab., 2003—, chmn.microsystem tech. Helmholtz Assn., Germany, 2003—; chmn. steering com. Internat. Sensor and Actuator Meeting. Co-author: Device Electronics for Integrated Circuits, 1977, 3d, rev. edit., 2002, Microsensors, 1990; editor-in-chief IEEE/ASME Jour. Microelectromech. Sys., 1998—; contbr. over 200 articles to profl. jours. Pres. Kensington (Calif.) Mcpl. Adv. Coun., 1992-98; trustee Stevens Inst. Tech., 1996—. Fellow Hughes Aircraft Co., 1955-57, NSF, 1959-62, NATO postdoctoral fellow, 1968-69, Fulbright fellow, 1982-83, Alexander von Humboldt prize, 1993, Tech. U. Berlin, 1994; Berkeley citation, 1994, Stevens Renaissance award, 1995, Career Achievement award Internat. Conf. on Sensors and Actuators, 1997. Fellow IEEE (life, Cledo Brunetti award 1998, Millennium prize 2000); mem. IEEE Press Bd., NAE, NRC (chmn. sensors adv. bd. U.S. Army Rsch. Lab. 2003—, liaison between NAE and NRC 2003—), Nat. Acad. Engring., Nat. Materials (adv. bd. 1994-98), Electron Devices Soc. (adv. com. 1984-98), Helholtz Assn. Germany (sensors and actuators com. 2003—). Achievements include 18 U.S. and foreign patents; construction of first operating micromotor. Office: U Calif Dept EECS # 1770 401 Cory Hall Berkeley CA 94720-1770 Office Phone: 510-642-0614. Personal E-mail: rsmuller@pacbell.net. Business E-Mail: r.muller@ieee.org.

MULLER, ROBERT JOSEPH, gynecologist; b. New Orleans, Dec. 5, 1946; s. Robert Harry and Camille (Eckert) M.; m. Susan Philipsen, Aug. 22, 1974; children: Ryan, Matt. BS, St. Louis U., 1968; BS, MSc, Emory U., 1976; MD, La. State U., New Orleans, 1981; cert. in emergency mgmt., FEMA, 1998; cert. in Mgmt., Auburn U., 2001, MBA, 2003. Intern Charity Hosp., New Orleans, 1981-82; resident La. State U. Affiliate Hosp., 1982-85; resident staff physician La. State U. Med. Ctr., New Orleans, 1981-85; pvt. practice Camellia Women's Ctr., Slidell, La., 1985—; staff physician Tulane Med. Ctr., New Orleans, 1986—. Med. dir. Northshore Regional Med. Ctr., Slidell, 1987—, chief staff, 1998; mem. adv. bd. Auburn U., 2004, vice chair governing bd., 2004; med. dir. New Orleans Police Dept., 1981-95, S.W. La. Search and Rescue, Covington, La., 1986—, St. Tammany Parish Sheriff

Dept., Covington, 1989—, commdr., 1990—, Camellia City Classic, Slidell, 1989—, Crawfishman Triathalon, Mandeville, La., 1988—, Res-Q-Med Laser Team, 1984—. Contbr. articles to profl. jours. Recipient Commendation Medal New Orleans Police Dept., 1986, 87, 89, Medal Valor St. Tammany Parish Sheriff Office, Covington, 1990, Cert. Valor S.E. La. Search and Rescue, Mandeville, 1990; named one of Outstanding Young Men of Am., 1984. Mem. Am. Coll. Ob-Gyn., La. State Med. Soc., Profl. Assn. Diving Instrs. (divemaster 1991, asst. instr. 1995), So. Offshore Racing Assn. (med. dir. 1982—), Offshore Profl. Racing Tour (med. dir. staff 1990—), Am. Power Boat Assn. (med. staff 1984-89). Roman Catholic. Avocations: scuba diving, boating, shooting. Home: 1181 Yorktown Dr Slidell LA 70461-3023 Office: Camellia Womens Ctr 105 Smart Pl Slidell LA 70458-2039 Office Phone: 985-641-2100. Personal E-mail: rmullermd@aol.com.

MULLER, STEVEN, international studies educator, academic administrator; b. Hamburg, Germany, Nov. 22, 1927; came to U.S., 1940, naturalized, 1949; 0. Werner Adolph and Marianne (Hartstein) M.; m. Margie Hellman, June 19, 1951 (dec. July 1999); children: Julie, Elizabeth; m. Jill E. McGovern, Feb. 5, 2000. BA, UCLA, 1948; BLitt (Rhodes scholar), Oxford (Eng.) U., 1951; PhD, Cornell U., 1958. Asst. prof. Haverford (Pa.) Coll., 1956-58; mem. faculty and adminstrn. Cornell U., 1958-71, dir. Ctr. Internat. Studies, 1961-66, v.p. pub. affairs, 1966-71; provost Johns Hopkins U., 1971-72, pres., 1972-90, pres. emeritus, 1990—, fellow Fgn. Policy Inst., disting. lectr., 1993—. Cons. Dept. Def., 1962-67, ACDA, 1967-77; bd. dirs. Orgn. Resources Counselors, Inc., Atlantic Coun. of the U.S. Author: Documents on European Government, 1963; co-editor: From Occupation to Cooperation, 1992, In Search of Germany, 1996; editor: Universities in the Twenty First Century, 1996. Trustee, chmn. St. Mary's Coll., 1991—2003; trustee German Marshall Fund of the US. Decorated comdr. Order of Merit (Fed. Republic of Germany), commendatore Republic of Italy. Mem. Am. Inst. Contemporary German Studies (co-chmn. emeritus), Coun. Fgn. Rels., Am. Polit. Sci. Assn., Internat. Inst. Strategic Studies, Am. Assn. Rhodes Scholars, Phi Beta Kappa, Cosmos Club (Washington). Office: Johns Hopkins U Sch Advanced Internat Studies 1619 Massachusetts Ave NW Washington DC 20036-2213 Office Phone: 202-663-5821. Business E-Mail: kareese@jhu.edu.

MULLER, WILLARD C(HESTER), writer; b. Havre, Mont., May 7, 1916; s. Chester Rudolph and Clara (Hansen) M.; m. Carolyn Elfrid Bue, Jan. 27, 1945; children: Marolyn Jean, Barbara Anne, Nancy Eleanor. BA, Stanford U., 1941; MPA, Maxwell Grad. Sch. Govt. Adminstrn., 1943; student, Nat. War Coll., 1961-62. Newspaper reporter, short story writer Bremerton (Wash.) Daily Searchlight, 1934-36; White House corr. Bremerton Daily Searchlight and Port Angeles Evening News, 1941; mgmt. analyst USDA, 1942, 46-47; mem. staff for food, agr. and forestry U.S. Dept. Army and U.S. High Commr. for Germany, Munich and Frankfurt, Fed. Republic Germany, 1948-50; dist. adminstr., Am. consul U.S. Trust Territory of Pacific Islands, Truk, Caroline Islands, 1951-55; dep. dir. ICA, U.S. Ops. Mission to Nepal, Kathmandu, 1956-58; dir. U.S. Ops. to Somali Republic, 1958-61, Office East and Southern African Affairs, AID, Dept. State, Washington, 1962-65, AID, Kampala, Uganda, 1965-70, assoc. dir. for land reform Saigon, Republic of Vietnam, 1970-73, ret., 1973, cons., 1974-81; free lance writer, 1973—. Author various short stories; contbr. articles to profl. jours. Chmn. steering com. 4-state program dialogue on peace Pacific NW dist. Am. Luth. Ch., Tacoma, 1983-85; mem. Clallam br. Wash. State Centennial Commn., 1986-89; mem. Food Bank Bd., Port Angeles, Wash., 1986-90. Lt. USNR, 1943-45, PTO. Mem.: Am. Fgn. Svc. Assn., Am. Soc. Pub. Adminstrn., Kiwanis. Avocations: horseback riding, world travel. Home and Office: 3624 S Mount Angeles Rd Port Angeles WA 98362-8910 Office Phone: 360-457-1892. E-mail: muller@tenforward.com.

MULLER, WILLIAM ALBERT, III, retired library director; b. Savannah, Ga., Jan. 1, 1943; s. William Albert Jr. and Julia Catherine (Cleary) M.; m. Claudya Barbara Burkett, Dec. 12, 1965 (div. 1986); 1 child, Martha Genevieve; m. Pamala Qualls, Apr. 9, 1988; 1 child, Tabitha Wade. BA, Ga. So. Coll., 1966; MLS, Emory U., 1969. Dir. War Woman Regional Libr., Elberton, Ga., 1969-73; rsch. libr. City of Savannah, 1973-75; dir. Mason County Pub. Libr., Point Pleasant, W.Va., 1976-78; pub. rels. cons. Eastern Shore Regional Libr., Salisbury, Md., 1978-81; dir. Brooke County Pub. Libr., Wellsburg, W.Va., 1982-84, McDowell Pub. Libr., Welch, W.Va., 1984-88, Bristol (Va.) Pub. Libr., 1988—2000; ret. Dir. Albermarle Regl. Libr., Winton, N.C., 2003-; sec. So W.Va. Libr. Automation Corp., Beckley, 1984-87, pres. 1987-88, S.W. Info. Network Group, Abindgdon, Va., 1990-91, treas. (swing) 1993—; bd. dir. Albermarle Regional Libr., Winton, N.C. Fundraiser Paramount Fund, Bristol, 1989; acct. exec. United Way Fund of Bristol, 1991; bd. dirs. Mid-Atlantic Chamber Orch., Bristol, 1988-92, treas., 1992; bd. dirs. Bristol Preservation Soc., 1988-98, Nat. Ctr. for Quality, 1992-98, Main St. Bristol, 1991-95, treas., 1994; bd. dirs. Jr. Achievement, 1992-99, pres., 1997-99; bd. dirs. Vol. Bristol, 1998; bd. dirs., vol. chair Racefest 98, 99. Democrat. Avocations: gardening, cabinetry, photography, travel, model railroads. Home: 406 Holly Hill Rd Murfreesboro NC 27855 Office Phone: 252-287-9753. E-mail: unclebillm@yahoo.com.

MULLER, WILLIAM HENRY, JR., surgeon, educator; b. Dillon, S.C., Aug. 19, 1919; s. William Henry and Octavia Elizabeth (Bethea) M.; m. Hildwin Clare Headly, Mar. 23, 1946; children: William Henry III, Marietta John Lewis. BS, The Citadel, 1940, DS (hon.), 1972; MD, Duke U., 1943; DHL (hon.), Med. U. S.C., 1977. Diplomate Am. Bd. Thoracic Surgery, Am. Bd. Surgery (rep. conf. com. grad. tng. in surgery). Intern Johns Hopkins Hosp., Balt., 1944, asst. surgery, asst. resident, 1944-46, resident gen. surgery, instr. surgery, 1948-49, resident cardiovascular surgery, 1949; practice gen. surgery Dillon, 1947-48; asst. prof. surgery UCLA, 1949-53, assoc. prof. Sch. Medicine, 1953-54; attending specialist thoracic surgery Wadsworth VA Hosp., Los Angeles; chief sect. cardiovascular surgery Los Angeles County-Harbor Gen. Hosp., Torrance, Calif.; cons. surgery St. John's, Santa Monica Hosps., 1949-54; cons. cardiovascular surgery U.S. Naval Hosp., San Diego, 1953-54; Stephen H. Watts prof. surgery, chmn. dept. U. Va. Sch. Medicine, 1954-82, v.p. health affairs, 1976-88, univ. prof. surgery and health policy, 1988-90, S. Hurt Watts prof. surgery emeritus, 1990—, v.p. for health affairs emeritus; surgeon-in-chief U. Va. Hosp., 1954-82; chmn. S.E. Surg. Congress; mem. Pres.'s Panel on Heart Disease, 1972; past chmn. surgery study sect. NIH; mem. exec. com., div. med. scis. NRC. Mem. editorial bd.: Am. Jour Surgery, Annals of Surgery, Am. Surgeon; contbr. articles to med jours. Trustee, mem. exec. com. Duke U. Served as capt. M.C. AUS, 1946-47. Named One of 10 Outstanding Young Men of Yr. U.S. Jr. C. of C., Calif. Jr. C. of C., 1952; recipient Disting. Alumni award (1st award) Duke U. Med. Ctr., 1969; Thomas Jefferson award U. Va., 1982; McCallie Sch. Alumni Achievement award, 1986; Paul Harris fellow Nat. Rotary Found., 1988. Fellow ACS (past chmn., forum com. fundamental surg. problems, regent 1971—, chmn. bd. regents 1976-78, pres.-elect 1979); mem. Internat. Soc. Surgery, Internat. Cardiovascular Soc. (past v.p.), AMA, Am. Surg. Assn. (pres. 1974-75), So. Surg. Assn. (pres. 1975), Pacific Coast Surg. Assn., Am. Assn. Thoracic Surgery, Soc. Univ. Surgeons (past pres.), Soc. Surgery Alimentary Tract, Assn. Acad. Surgeons, James IV Assn. Surgeons (v.p. U.S.), Med. Soc. Va., Albemarle County Med. Soc., Soc. Vascular Surgery (past pres.), Am. Heart Assn. (chmn. surgery research study com., mem. central research com.), Va. Surg. Soc, Halsted Soc., Johns Hopkins Soc. Scholars, Raven Soc., Sigma Xi, Alpha Omega Alpha, Phi Chi Home: 900 Flordon Dr Charlottesville VA 22901-7844

MULLER, WILLIAM MANNING, corporate lawyer; b. N.Y.C., Mar. 20, 1959; s. Eugene Lee and Patricia Anne (Manning) M. AB, Brown U., 1981; JD, Northwestern U., 1987. Bar: N.Y. 1989, Conn. 1989, Ga. 1996. Assoc. Milbank, Tweed, Hadley & McCloy, N.Y.C., 1987-90; legal counsel Rockefeller & Co., Inc., N.Y.C., 1991-93; assoc. Reid & Priest, N.Y.C., 1993-95; counsel Turner Broadcasting Sys., Inc., Atlanta, 1995—97, sr. counsel, 1997—2001, v.p. and regional counsel, 2001—. Mem. ABA, Conn. Bar Assn., State Bar Ga., Assn. Bar City of New York, TV Assn. Programmers (chmn. govt. and legal affairs com.), Univ. Club New York. Office: Turner Broadcasting Sys Inc One CNN Ctr Atlanta GA 30303

MULLER JR. THOMAS G, music educator; b. Medford, Oreg., Aug. 3, 1969; s. Thomas G and Jeanne C Muller; m. Jennifer J Brooks, Aug. 12, 1997; 1 child, Sarah K Muller. B in music edn., U. of Oreg., 1989—95. Education TSPC/Oreg., 1995. Tchr. Reynolds Mid. Sch., Fairview, Oreg., 1999—; mid. sch. band chair Oreg. Music Educator's Assn., Oreg., 1997—. Instrumental music coord. Reynolds Sch. Dist., Fairview, Oreg., 2003—. Mid. sch. band chair Oreg. Music Educators Assn., 1997. Recipient Sallie Mae First Class Tchr., Sallie Mae, 1995, Hon. Membership, Alpha Delta Kappa, 1996. Democrat-Npl. Avocations: french horn, travel, gourmet cooking. Home: 2434 SE Darling Ave Gresham OR 97080 Office: Reynolds Middle School 1200 NE 201st Ave Fairview OR 97024 Personal E-mail: jjbmtgm@aol.com. E-mail: tom_muller@reynolds.k12.or.us.

MULLETTE, JULIENNE PATRICIA, health facility administrator; b. Sydney, Australia, Nov. 19, 1940; came to U.S., 1953; d. Ronald Stanley Lewis and Sheila Rosalind Blunden (Phillips) M.; m. Fred Gillette Sturm, Nov. 24, 1964 (div. Dec. 1969); m. Kenneth Walter Gillman, Dec. 28, 1971 (div. Dec. 1978); children: Noah Khristoff Mullette-Gillman, D'Dhaniel Alexander Mullette-Gillman. BA, Western Coll. for Women, Oxford, Ohio, 1961; postgrad., Harvard U., 1964, U. Sao Paulo, Brazil, 1965, Inst. Philosophy, Sao Paulo, 1965, Miami U., Oxford, 1967-69. Tchr. English, High Mowing Sch., Wilton, N.H., 1962-64, Stoneleigh-Prospect Hill Sch., Greenfield, Mass., 1964; seminar dir. Western Coll. for Women, 1967-69; pres. Family Tree, Home U., Montclair, NJ, 1978—88; dir. Pleroma Holistic Health Ctr., Montclair, 1980—. Dir. Astrological Rsch. Ctr., Sydney, Australia, 1983; founder Spiritual Devel. Rsch. Group, 1986—; pvt. astrology counselor, 1962—; guest on radio & TV shows, 1962—; lectr. worldwide, 1963—; founder Pleroma Found. for Astrological Rsch. & Studies, 1990; breeder, trainer exotic animals; mem. Woodstock Pub. Access Com., 1993—. Author: The Moon-Understanding the Subconscious, 1973; contbr. articles to profl. jours.; editor (founding): KOSMOS Mag., 1968—78, Jour. Astrological Studies, 1970—; contbg. columnist: mags; hostess (radio talk shows) The Julienne Mullette Show, 1985—, others, —, (TV series) You and the Cosmos, Woodstock, NY, 1992—, The Julienne Mullette Show Connections TV, Newark, NJ, 1985—. Founder local chpt. La Leche League, Montclair, 1974; founding pres. The Internat. Astrology Forum, 2000. Mem. AAUW (chmn. cultural affairs Montclair chpt. 1987—), NAFE, Spiritual Devel. Group (founder), Internat. Soc. Astrological Rsch. (founding pres. 1968-78), Cosmos Hyperspace Astrological Origins and Supergravity Studies (founder), Am. Fedn. Astrologers (cert.), Belgian Soc. Astrology, Am. Assn. Humanistic Psychology, Internat. Llamas Assn., Internat. Soc. Astrological Studies and Rsch. (founder 2002). Avocations: tennis, local theatre, singing. E-mail: julienne@nep.net.

MULLIGAN, BRIAN C. film company executive; Former co-chmn. Universal Pictures, Universal City, Calif.; exec. v.p., CFO Seagram's, 1999—2001; chmn. Fox TV, 2001; venture capitalist, advisor to Marvin Davis, 2001—. Bd. mem. Roxio, 2003—.*

MULLIGAN, DONALD, retail grocery company executive; CFO DeMoulas Super Mkts., Tewksbury, Mass. Office: DeMoulas Super Markets 875 East St Tewksbury MA 01876 Office Fax: (978) 640-8390.

MULLIGAN, ELINOR PATTERSON, lawyer; d. Frank Clark and Agnes (Murphy) Patterson; m. John C. O'Connor; children: Christine Fulena, Valerie Clark, Amy O'Connor, Christopher Criffan O'Connor; m. William G. Mulligan, Dec. 6, 1975. BA, U. Mich.; JD, Seton Hall U., 1970. Bar: N.J. 1970. Assoc., Springfield and Newark, 1970-72; pvt. practice, Hackettstown, N.J., 1972; ptnr. Mulligan & Jacobson, N.Y.C., 1973-91, Mulligan & Mulligan, Hackettstown, 1976—. Atty. Hackettstown Planning Bd., 1973-86, Blairstown Bd. Adjustment, 1973-95; sec. Warren County Ethics Com., 1976-78, sec. Dist. X and XIII Fee Arbitration Com., 1979-87, mem. and chair, 1987-91, mem. dist. ethics com. XIII, 1992—; mem. spl. com. on atty. disciplinary structure N.J. Supreme Ct., 1981—; lectr. Nat. Assn. Women Judges, 1979, N.J. Inst. Continuing Legal Edn., 1988—. Contbr. articles to profl. jours. Named Vol. of Yr., Attys. Vols. in Parole Program, 1978. Fellow Am. Acad. Matrimonial Lawyers (1st woman pres. N.J. chpt. 1995-96); mem. ABA, Warren County Bar Assn. (1st woman pres. 1987-88), N.J. State Bar ASsn., N.J. Women Lawyers Assn. (v.p. 1985—), Am. Mensa Soc., Union League Club (N.Y.C.), Baltusrol Golf Club (Springfield, N.J.), Panther Valley Golf and Country Club (Allamuchy, N.J.), Kappa Alpha Theta. Republican. Home: 12 Goldfinch Way Hackettstown NJ 07840-3007 Office: 933 County Road 517 Hackettstown NJ 07840-4654 Office Phone: 908-852-0202. E-mail: llp-nj@mindspring.com., elinormulligan@mulligansavage.com.

MULLIGAN, JEREMIAH T. lawyer; b. Rochester, N.Y., 1944; BA, St. Bernard's Seminary and Coll., 1966; JD, Fordham U., 1970. Mem. Curtis, Mallet-Prevost, Colt & Mosle, N.Y. Office: Curtis Mallet-Prevost Colt & Mosle 101 Park Ave Fl 34 New York NY 10178-0061 Business E-Mail: jmulligan@cm-p.com.

MULLIGAN, JOSEPH FRANCIS, physicist, science historian, educator; b. N.Y.C., Dec. 12, 1920; s. Joseph Lawrence and Mary (Collins) M.; m. Eleanor Lee Wells 1984. Student, Fordham Coll., 1938-39, 41-43; AB, Boston Coll., 1945, MA, 1946; PhD in Physics, Cath. U. Am., 1951. Instr. physics St. Peter's Coll., Jersey City, 1946-47; faculty Fordham U., 1955-68, assoc. prof. physics, 1963-68, chmn. dept., 1956-64, dean Grad. Sch. Arts and Scis., dean liberal arts faculty, 1964-67; prof. physics U. Md., Baltimore County, 1968-89, prof. emeritus, 1989—, dean for grad. studies and rsch., 1968-82. Mem. adv. com. grad. fellowship program NDEA, 1960-63 Author: Practical Physics: The Production and Conservation of Energy, 1980, Introductory College Physics, 2d edit., 1990, translated into 3-vol. Italian edit., Fisica, 1993; editor: Heinrich Rudolf Hertz (1857-1894): A Collection of Articles and Addresses, 1994; contbr. articles to profl. jours. Bd. dirs. Excel Interactive Sci. Mus., Salisbury, 1998-2000. NSF fellow U. Calif, San Diego, 1961-62 Mem. AASA, Am. Phys. Soc., Am. Assn. Physics Tchrs., History of Sci. Soc., Sigma Xi, Sigma Pi Sigma. Home: 228 Canal Park Dr Apt G103 Salisbury MD 21804-3750 E-mail: jmull68640@aol.com.

MULLIGAN, MICHAEL DENNIS, lawyer; b. St. Louis, Mar. 9, 1947; s. Leo Virgil and Elizabeth (Leyse) M.; m. Theresa Baker, Aug. 7, 1971; children: Brennan, Colin. BA in Biology, Amherst Coll., 1968; JD, Columbia U., 1971. Bar: Mo. 1971, U.S. Dist. Ct. (ea. dist.) Mo. 1972, U.S. Ct. Appeals (8th cir.) 1982, U.S. Tax Ct. 1985. Law clk. to judge U.S. Dist. Ct. (ea. dist.) Mo., 1971-72; assoc. Lewis, Rice & Fingersh, L.C., St. Louis, 1972-80, ptnr., 1980—. Mem. editl. bd. Estate Planning Mag., 1985—. Served as cpl. USMC, 1968-70. Fellow Am. Coll. Trust and Estate Counsel; mem. ABA (mem. real property, probate and trust, and taxation sects.), Mo. Bar Assn. (mem. probate and trust, taxation sects.). Office: Lewis Rice & Fingersh LC 500 N Broadway Ste 2000 Saint Louis MO 63102-2147 Office Phone: 314-444-7757. E-mail: mmulligan@lewisrice.com.

MULLIGAN, ROBERT, film director, producer; b. N.Y.C., Aug. 23, 1925; s. Robert Edward and Elizabeth (Gingell) M. Grad., Fordham U. Dir.: TV prodns. including Philco Playhouse, Suspense, Playhouse 90; film prodr./dir.: films Fear Strikes Out, Come September, The Spiral Road, To Kill a Mockingbird, Love with the Proper Stranger, Inside Daisy Clover, Summer of '42, Bloodbrothers, Same Time Next Year, The Other, Kiss Me Goodbye, Nickel Ride, Stalking Moon, Baby the Rain Must Fall, Pursuit of Happiness, Up the Down Staircase, Clara's Heart, The Man in the Moon. Office: Ste 675 1901 Avenue Of The Stars Los Angeles CA 90067-6098

MULLIKIN, THOMAS WILSON, mathematics professor; b. Flintville, Tenn., Jan. 9, 1928; s. Houston Yost and Daisy (Copeland) M.; m. Mildred Virginia Sugg, June 14, 1952; children: Sarah Virginia, Thomas Wilson, James Copeland. Student, U. South, 1946-47; AB, U. Tenn., 1950; postgrad., Iowa State U., 1952-53; A.M., Harvard, 1954, PhD, 1958. Mathematician Rand Corp., Santa Monica, Calif., 1957-64; prof. math. Purdue U., 1964-93, interim v.p., dean grad. sch., 1991-93, dean grad. sch., prof. math emeritus, 1993—. Served with USNR, 1950-52. Mem.: AAAS, Am. Math. Soc. Home: 104 Club Ct Cape Carteret NC 28584-9736

MULLIN, GENE, state legislator; b. San Francisco, Apr. 21, 1937; m. Terri Mullin; children: Jennifer, Kevin. BA in Polit. Sci., U. San Francisco, 1960. Lifetime secondary tchg. credential U. San Francisco, 1967. Tchr. govt. South San Francisco High Sch., 1967—99; mem. planning commn. City of South San Francisco, 1972—80, mem. city council, 1995—, mayor, 1998, 2001—02; mem., dist. 19 Calif. State Assembly, 2002—. Chair negotiations com. South San Francisco CTA, 1986—90; lectr., cons. Inst. Local Self Govt., 1989—97, Ctr. Youth Citizenship, 1999—; vice chair Labor and Employment Com.; mem. Edn. Com., Housing and Cmty. Devel. Com., Human Svcs. Com., Local Govt. Com., Vets. Affairs Com.; pres. Soutn San Francisco Classroom Tchr.'s Assn., 1992—95. Author: 2 books on local govt. JAG gen. corps U.S. Army, 1959—60. Mem.: Assn. Bay Area Govts. (mem. exec. com. 1999—), San Mateo County Retired Tchrs. Assn., Young Men's Inst. Democrat. Roman Catholic. Mailing: PO Box 942849 Rm 2170 Sacramento CA 94294 Office: 1528 S El Camino Real Ste 302 San Mateo CA 94402

MULLIN, JAMES ALBERT, executive; b. Mpls., Nov. 6, 1934; s. Gerald Thomas and Ruth Krammerer M.; m. Franchelle Collison, Apr. 20, 1968; children: John, Andrew, Charles, Anna. BA, U. Minn., 1956; MBA, U. Pa., 1960. Line & staff mgmt. Gen. Mills, Inc., Mpls., 1960-73; v.p. Ellerbe Architects & Engring., Mpls., 1973-77; treas., dir. Solar Energy Resource Ctr., Mpls., 1977-79; sr. v.p., CAO Opus Corp., Mpls., 1979-91; dir. resource devel. Archdiocese St. Paul/Mpls., St. Paul, 1991—; exec. dir. Cath. Cmty. Found., St. Paul, 1992—. Dir. Opus North Corp., Chgo., 1990-2001; chmn. Archdiocesan Fin. Coun., St. Paul, 1990-91; deputy Minn. Bus. Partnership, Mpls., 1983-89. Trustee James J. Hill Ref. Libr., St. Paul, 1985-93, Mpls. Soc. Fine Arts, 1975-79, St. Thomas Acad., St. Paul, 1980-85, St. Therese Southwest, Hopkins, Minn., 1993-2001. Capt. U.S. Army, 1956-58. Decorated Commendation medal. Mem. Minikahda Club, Skylight Club, Minn. Club, Knights of Holy Sepulcher (knight comdr. 1994-2001). Roman Catholic. Home: 1700 W 26th St Minneapolis MN 55405 Office: Cath Cmty Found 328 W Kellogg Blvd Saint Paul MN 55102 E-mail: mullinj@archspm.org.

MULLIN, LEO FRANCIS, airline executive; b. Concord, Mass., Jan. 26, 1943; s. Leo F. and Alice L. (Fearns) M.; m. Leah J. Malmberg, Sept. 10, 1966; children: Jessica, Matthew. AB, Harvard U., 1964, MS, 1965, MBA, 1967. Assoc. McKinsey & Co., Washington, 1967-73, prin., 1973-76; sr. v.p. strategic planning Consol. Rail Corp., Phila., 1976-78; sr. v.p. 1st Chgo. Corp., 1981-84, exec. v.p., 1984-91; chmn. Am. Nat. Bank and Trust Co. Chgo. subs. 1st Chgo., Chgo., 1991-93; pres., COO 1st Chgo. Corp., Chgo., 1993-95; vice chmn. Unicom/Commonwealth Edison, Chgo., 1995—97; CEO Delta Airlines, Atlanta, 1997—2003, chmn. bd. dirs., 1999—. Bd. dirs. Pittway Corp., Inland Steel Industries, Inc. Vice chmn. Chgo. Urban League, 1993—; chmn. bd. trustees Field Mus. Natural History, 1994—; bd. dirs. Chgo. chpt. Juvenile Diabetes Found., 1985—, Met. Planning Coun., 1983—, Children's Meml. Hosp., Chgo., 1989—, Chgo. Coun. Fgn. Rels., 1994—; mem. Chgo. Econ. Devel. Commn., 1992-95; trustee Northwestern U., 1992—. Mem. Chgo. Club, Harvard Club of Chgo., Econ. Club of Chgo.*

MULLIN, PATRICIA JONES, banker; b. Long Branch, N.J., Oct. 27, 1955; d. George Edwin and JoAn Layden Jones; m. Peter William Mullin, Apr. 5, 1986; children: Ryan Peter, Connor Patrick. BBA, St. Mary's Coll., Notre Dame, Ind., 1977; MBA, Roosevelt U., 1982. Cert. cash mgr. Officer First Chicago, 1977-83; asst. v.p. Fidelity Bank, Phila., 1983-84; v.p. State St. Bank, Boston, 1984—99, Citizens Bank, Boston, 1999-2000; v.p., team leader Sovereign Bank, Boston, 2000—. Mem. Assn. Fin. Profls., Treasury Mgmt. Assn. New Eng. (pres., bd. dirs. 1994—), Boston Club, St. Mary's Club of Boston (bd. dirs. 1994-96). Roman Catholic. Avocations: quilting, needlecrafts, hiking, swimming. Office: Sovereign Bank 75 State St Boston MA 02109-1829

MULLIN, PATRICK ALLEN, lawyer; b. Newark, Jan. 13, 1950; s. Gerard Vincent and Frances Regina (Magnanti) M. BA, William Paterson U., 1972, MEd, 1974; JD, NYU, 1979, LLM in Taxation, 1990; postgrad., Harvard Law Sch., 1979; Gerry Spence's Trial Lawyers Coll., Duboise, Wyo., 1997. Bar: N.J. 1979, D.C. 1980, N.Y. 1990; cert. criminal trial atty. N.J. Supreme Ct. Law clk. to Hon. Dickinson R. DeBevoise, U.S. Dist. Ct. N.J., Trenton, 1979-80; assoc. Charles Morgan Assocs., Washington, 1980-81; pvt. practice, Hackensack, NJ, 1985—; instr., 1985—. Mem. Practitioners Adv. Group U.S. Sentencing Commn.; lectr. Seton Hall Law Sch., 2001, 02, 04, ATLA, 2003; instr. Gerry Spence's Trial Lawyers Coll. Contbr. articles to profl. jours. Mem. ABA. Roman Catholic. Avocations: jogging, martial artist. Address: 25 Main St # 200 Hackensack NJ 07601-7015 also: 305 Madison Ave Ste 449 New York NY 10165-0006 Office Phone: 201-488-5500. Home Fax: 201-487-2848. E-mail: mullin.law@verizon.net.

MULLINAX, A. R. energy executive; b. Cameron, Tex. BBA in Acctg., Tex. A&M; grad. exec. program, Stanford U. CPA Tex. From internal audit staff to sr. analyst corp. planning. Tex. Eastern Corp., Tex., 1977—80, from supr., mgr. natural gas acctg. area to v.p. info. svcs. and controls, 1985—96; sr. v.p. shared svcs. Duke Power Co., 1997—99; pres., CEO DukeNet Comm., 2002; exec. v.p. bus. svcs. Duke Energy Corp., Charlotte, NC, 2003—. Mem.: AICPA, Tex. Soc. CPAs. Office: Duke Energy Corp 526 S Church St Charlotte NC 28202-1803

MULLINAX, PERRY FRANKLIN, rheumatologist, allergist, immunologist; b. Quebec City, Que., Can., June 7, 1931; MD, Med. Coll. Va., 1955. Diplomate Am. Bd. Allergy and Immunology, Am. Bd. Diagnostic Lab. Immunology, Am. Bd. Internal Medicine, Am. Bd. Rheumatology. Intern Yale Med. Ctr., New Haven, 1955-56, resident in medicine, 1958-59; fellow in medicine Mass. Gen. Hosp., Boston, 1959-61; fellow in microbiology immunology Washington U., St. Louis; fellow in biology MIT, Boston, 1962-63; mem. faculty dept. internal medicine Med. Coll. Va./Va. Commonwealth U., 1963—, prof. internal medicine, 1977-2000, emeritus prof. internal medicine, 2000—. Mem. AAAS, Am. Coll. Rheumatology. Office: Med Coll Va PO Box 980263 Richmond VA 23298-0263 E-mail: pfmullin@hsc.vcu.edu.

MULLINEAUX, DONAL RAY, geologist; b. Weed, Calif., Feb. 16, 1925; s. Lester Ray and Mary Lorene (Drew) M.; m. Diana Suzanne Charais, Nov. 21, 1951; children: Peter, Lauren, Keith. Student, U. Wash., 1942, BS in Math., 1947, BS in Geology, 1949, MS in Geology, 1950, PhD in Geology, 1961. Drilling insp. U.S. Army C.E., 1948; geologist U.S. Geol. Survey, 1950-86; contracting geologist, 1987-90; scientist emeritus U.S. Geol. Survey, 1990—. Author articles on volcanic activity and hazards, Mt. St. Helens, other Cascade Range volcanoes, stratigraphy and engring. geology of Puget Sound Lowland, Wash. With USNR, 1943-54, active duty, 1943-46, 51-53. Rsch. fellow Engring. Expt. Sta. U. Wash., 1949-50. Fellow Geol. Soc. Am. (E.B. Burwell Jr. award 1983); mem. Colo. Sci. Soc. Home: 14155 W 54th Ave Arvada CO 80002-1513 Office: PO Box 25046 Denver CO 80225-0046 Personal E-mail: dondiana@mullineaux.us.

MULLINIX, EDWARD WINGATE, lawyer; b. Balt., Feb. 25, 1924; s. Howard Earle and Elsie (Wingate) M.; m. Virginia Lee McGinnes, July 28, 1944; children: Marcia Lee Ladd, Edward Wingate. Student, St. John's Coll., 1941-43; JD summa cum laude, U. Pa., 1949. Bar: Pa. 1950, U.S. Supreme Ct. 1955; cert. BBB Auto Line arbitrator. Assoc. Schnader Harrison Segal & Lewis LLP, Phila., 1950-55, ptnr., 1956-92, now sr. coun. Mem. adv. bds. Antitrust Bull., 1970-81, BNA Antitrust and Trade Regulation Report, 1981-94; mem. Civil Justice adv. group U.S. Dist. Ct. (ea. dist.) Pa., 1998—; mem. Civil Justice Reform Act of 1990 adv. group U.S. Dist. Ct. (ea. dist.) Pa., 1991-98; co-chmn. Joint U.S. Dist. Ct./Phila. Bar Assn. Alternative Dispute Resolution Com., 1990-2002; cons. on revision of local civil rules U.S. Dist. Ct. (ea. dist.) Pa., 1995—; mem. adv. com. U. Pa. Law Sch. Ctr. Professionalism, 1988-92; mediator U.S. Dist. Ct. (ea. dist.) Pa.; judge Day Forward and Commerce case mgmt. programs, chmn. adv.

merce program Ct. Common Pleas of Phila. County; advocate, mem. steering com. in elderly-victim-assistance program Phila. Dist. Atty.'s Office Elder Justice Project; faculty participant Pa. Bar Inst. and other CLE programs. Trustee Sta. KYW-TV Project Homeless Fund, 1985-86. Served with USMCR, 1943-44; to lt. (j.g.) USNR, 1944-46. Fellow Am. Bar Found. (life), Am. Coll. Trial Lawyers (emeritus, mem. complex litig. com. 1980-91, vice-chmn. com. 1981-83); mem. ABA (spl. com. complex and multidist. litig. 1969-73, co-chmn. com. 1971-73, coun. litig. sect. 1976-80), Pa. Bar Assn., Phila. Bar Assn., Hist. Soc. U.S. Dist. Ct. (ea. dist.) Pa. (bd. dirs. 1984—, pres. 1991-94), Juristic Soc., Order of Coif, Union League (Phila.), Socialegal Club (Phila.), Aronimink Golf Club (Newtown Sq., Pa.). Republican. Presbyterian. Home: 251 Chamounix Rd Saint Davids PA 19087-3605 Office: 1600 Market St Ste 3600 Philadelphia PA 19103-7286 Office Phone: 215-751-2442. E-mail: ewm@shsl.com.

MULLINS, CHARLES BROWN, physician, academic administrator; b. Rochester, Ind., July 29, 1934; s. Charles E. and Mary Ruth B. (Bamberger) M.; BA, N. Tex. State U., 1954; MD, U. Tex., 1958; m. Stella Churchill, Dec. 27, 1955; children: Holly, David. Diplomate Am. Bd. Internal Medicine. Intern, U. Colo. Med. Ctr., Denver, 1958-59; resident in internal medicine Parkland Meml. Hosp., Dallas, 1962-64; USPHS rsch. fellow U. Tex. Southwestern Med. Sch., Dallas, 1964-65; chief resident medicine Parkland Meml. Hosp., 1965-66; USPHS spl. rsch. fellow cardiology br. Nat. Heart Inst., Bethesda, Md., 1967-68; practice medicine specializing in cardiology, Dallas, 1966-81; sr. attending staff Parkland Meml. Hosp., dir. med. affairs, 1977-79; asst. prof. medicine U. Tex. Southwestern Med. Sch., Dallas, 1968-71, assoc. prof., 1971-75, dir. clin. cardiology, 1971-77, prof., 1975-79, clin. prof. medicine, 1979-81; prof. medicine U. Tex. Health Sci. Ctr., Dallas, 1981-; exec. vice-chancellor health affairs U. Tex. System, 1981-2001, spl. projects dir., 2001-02; CEO Dallas County Hosp. Dist., 1979-81. Contbr. articles to profl. jours. With M.C., USAF, 1959-62. Fellow ACP, Am. Coll. Cardiology (Tex. gov. 1974-77, chmn. bd. govs. 1976), Am. Heart Assn. Coun. on Clin. Cardiology; mem. AMA, Am. Fedn. Clin. Rsch., Assn. Acad. Health Ctrs., Assn. Univ. Cardiologists, Laennec Soc., Alpha Omega Alpha. Office: 5323 Harry Hines Blvd Dallas TX 75390-9166 Office Phone: 214-648-4370.

MULLINS, DAVID ROY, chemist, researcher; b. Passaic, N.J., Apr. 4, 1956; m. Mary Celia Janes, May 21, 1978. BS, Coll. of William and Mary, Williamsburg, VA, 1978; PhD, U. Tex., Austin, 1984. Postdoctoral rsch. assoc. U. Tex., Austin, 1984—86, Oak Ridge Nat. Lab., Tenn., 1986—88, rsch. scientist, 1988—. Sec.- treas. Jefferson Mid. Sch. PTO, Oak Ridge, 2001—03; pres. Aid to Distressed Families of Anderson County, 1991—93; treas. First Presbyn. Ch., Oak Ridge, 1996—2003, bd. mem., 1996—2003. Mem.: Am. Vacuum Soc. (sec. - treas. (Oak Ridge chpt.) 1998—2003). Achievements include development of raman spectroscopy from single crystal metal surfaces; research in soft X-ray photoelevtron spectroscopy using synchrotron radiation; surface science of metal oxide surfaces; surface science of sulfur containing molecules with metals. Office: Oak Ridge Nat Lab PO Box 2008 MS 6201 Oak Ridge TN 37831-6201 E-mail: mullinsdr@ornl.gov.

MULLINS, JAMES LEE, library administrator; b. Perry, Iowa, Nov. 29, 1949; s. Kenneth Wiley and Lorene (Gift) M.; m. Kathleen Stiso, May 10, 1986; 1 stepchild, Michael Stiso. BA, U. Iowa, 1972, MA, 1973; PhD, Ind. U., 1984. Instr. Ga. So. U., Statesboro, 1973-74; assoc. law librarian Ind. U., Bloomington, 1974-78, dir. library South Bend, 1978-96; dir. Falvey Meml. Libr., Villanova U., 1996-2000; assoc. dir. for adminstrn. MIT, Cambridge, 2000—04; dean libraries Purdue U., West Lafayette, Ind., 2004—. Contbr. articles to profl. publs. Mem. exec. com. South Bend Art Ctr., 1984—89; mem. Mayor's Task Force Redevel., South Bend, 1986; pres. Fischoff Nat. Chamber Music Assn., 1989—91, Gov. Conf. on Libr. Planning Com., 1989—91, Mich. Freenet bd., 1993—96, Ind. Coop. Libr. Svcs. Authority, 1993—94; mem. Hugh Atkinson Award Com., 2001—; mem. planning com. Lama Nat. Inst., 2001—02, IFLA mktg. & mgmgt. sect. standing com., 2003—07. Mem. ALA, LAMA (program com. 1997-2001, exec. com. 1998-2000), Ind. Libr. Assn., Assn. Coll. and Rsch. Librs. (stds. com. 1994-2000, stds. & accreditation com, 2000-02), Ind. Libr. Endowment Bd. (pres. 1988-91), Rotary. Avocations: reading, gardening, cross country skiing, historic preservation. Home: 144 Creighton Rd West Lafayette IN 47906 Office: Purdue Univ 504 W State St West Lafayette IN 47907 Business E-Mail: jmullins@purdue.edu.

MULLINS, JEFFREY ALAN, historian, educator; PhD, Johns Hopkins U., 1998. Prof. St. Cloud State U., Minn., 1999—. Faculty Rsch. fellowship, Emory U., 2003-2004. Mem.: Am. Hist. Assn. Office: St Cloud State U 720 4th Ave S Saint Cloud MN 56301-4498 Office Phone: 320-308-6134.

MULLINS, JEROME JOSEPH, real estate developer, consulting engineer; b. Reedsville, Wis., June 3, 1925; s. James Raymond and Anna (Wilhelm) M.; m. Carol M. Fessler, Sept. 12, 1949; children: Maureen, Brian, Mallory, Bradley, Jerome J. Jr. BSCE, U. Wis., 1950. Registered prof. engr., land surveyor, Wis.; lic. real estate broker and appraiser, Wis. Engr. Gen. Engring. Co., Baraboo, Wis., 1950-51; engring. mgr. George Nelson & Sons, Inc., Madison, Wis., 1951-56, Weiler & Strang Architects/Engrs., Madison, 1956-64; pres. Sample-Mullins Architects/Engrs., Madison, 1964-69; chief exec. officer J.J. Mullins & Assocs., Inc., Madison, 1969—. Pres. Bayview Found., Madison, 1968-72, Greater Madison Conv. and Visitors Bur., 1976-78; bd. dirs. Downtown Madison, Inc., 1976—. Madison Conv. and Visitors Bur., 1986-90; mem. Madison Taxicab Com., 1977-78. Officer USN, 1943-46, PTO. Recipient award Capital Community Citizens, 1974, appreciation award Madison Conv. and Visitors Bur., 1976-79, 87-89, U. Wis. Athletics, 1983, Employer of Yr. award Goodwill Industries South Cen. Wis., 1981, award Downtown Madison, Inc., 1986, award for support Badger State Games, 1989. Mem. NSPE, AIA (assoc.), Nat. Bd. Realtors, Nat. Constrn. Specifications Instr., Wis. Soc. Profl. Engrs., Profl. Engrs. in Pvt. Practice, Wis. Soc. Registered Land Surveyors. Avocations: boating, hunting, reading. Office: 401 N Carroll St Madison WI 53703-1803

MULLINS, OBERA, retired microbiologist; b. Egypt, Miss., Feb. 15, 1927; d. Willie Ree and Maggie Sue (Orr) Gunn; m. Charles Leroy Mullins, Nov. 2, 1952; children: Mary Artavia, Arthur Curtis, Charles Leroy, Charlester Teresa, William Hellman. BS, Chgo. State U., 1974; MS in Health Sci. Edn., Governors State U., 1981. Med. technician, microbiologist Chgo. Health Dept., Chgo., 1976—, now pers. asst. III, to 1999; ret., 1999. Mem. AAUW, Am. Soc. Clin. Pathologists (cert. med. lab. technician), Ill. Soc. Lab. Technicians. Roman Catholic. Home: 9325 S Marquette Ave Chicago IL 60617-4131

MULLINS, RUTH GLADYS, nurse; b. Westville, N.S., Can., Aug. 25, 1943; came to U.S., 1949, naturalized, 1955; d. William G. and Gladys H.; m. Leonard E. Mullins, Aug. 27, 1963 (dec.); children: Deborah R. Jenkins, Catherine M., Leonard III. BS in Nursing, Calif. State U., Long Beach, 1966; MSN, UCLA, 1973; PhD, Columbia Pacific U. Cert. pediatric nurse practitioner. Pub. health nurse Los Angeles County Health Dept., 1967-68; nure Meml. Hosp. Med. Ctr., Long Beach, 1968-72; dir. pediatric nurse practitioner program Calif. State U., Long Beach, 1973-97, asst. prof., 1975-80, assoc. prof., 1980-85, prof., 1985—, coord. accelerated BSN program, 2003—. Health svc. credential coord. Sch. Nursing Calif. State U., Long Beach, chmn., 1979-81, coord. grad. programs, 1985-92; mem. Calif. Maternal, Child and Adolescent Health Bd., 1977-84; vice chair Long Beach/Orange County Health Consortium, 1984-85, chair 1985-86. Author: (with B. Nelms) Growth and Development: A Primary Health Care Approach; contbg. author: Quick Reference to Pediatric Nursing, 1984; assoc. editor Jour. Pediatric Health Care, 1985— [illegible] grantee HHS, Divsn. Nursing Calif. Dept. Health. Fellow Nat. Assn [illegible] Nurse Assocs. and Practitioners (exec. bd., pres. 1990-91), Nat. F[illegible]lty. Orgns. (sec. 1991-93); mem. APHA, Nat. Alliance N[illegible]verning body 1990-92), Assn. Faculties Pediatric Nurse [illegible] L.A. and Orange County Assn. Pediatric Nurse [illegible](treas. 1998—), Am. Assn. Univ. Faculty. Democrat. [illegible]il Ave Huntington Beach CA 92647-4232 Office: [illegible]g 1250 N Bellflower Blvd Long Beach CA [illegible] Phone: 562-985-4476. E-mail: [illegible]llins@csulb.edu.

MULLIS, KARY BANKS, biochemist; b. Lenoir, N.C., Dec. 28, 1944; s. Cecil Banks Mullis and Bernice Alberta (Barker) Fredericks; m. nancy Mullis; children: Christopher, Jeremy, Louise. BS in Chemistry, Ga. Inst. Tech, 1966; PhD in Biochemistry, U. Calif., Berkeley, 1973; DSc (hon.), U. S.C., 1994. Lectr. biochemistry U. Calif., Berkeley, 1972, postdoctoral fellow San Francisco, 1977—79, U. Kans. Med. Sch., Kansas City, 1973—76; scientist Cetus Corp., Emeryville, Calif., 1979—86; dir. molecular biology Xytronyx, Inc., San Diego, 1986—88; cons. Specialty Labs, Inc., Amersham, Inc., Chiron Inc. and various others, Calif., 1988—96; chmn. StarGene, Inc., San Rafael, Calif.; v.p. Histotec, Inc., Cedar Rapids, Iowa; v.p. molecular biology chemistry Vyrex Inc., La Jolla, Calif.; Distinguished Researcher Children's Hospital and Research Institute, Oakland, Calif. Disting. vis. prof. U. S.C. Coll. of Sci. and Math. Contbr. articles to profl. jours.; patentee in field. Named Scientist of Yr., R&D Mag., 1991, Calif. Scientist of Yr., 1992; named to National Inventors Hall of Fame, 1998; recipient Preis Biochemische Analytik award, German Soc. Clin. Chem., 1990, Allan award, 1990, award, Gairdner Found. Internat., 1991, Nat. Biotech. award, 1991, Robert Koch award, 1992, Chiron Corp. Biotechnology Rsch. award, Am. Soc. Microbiology, 1992, Japan prize, Sci. and Tech. Found. Japan, 1993, Nobel Prize in Chemistry, Nobel Foundation, 1993. Mem.: Inst. Further Study (dir. 1993—), Am. Acad. Achievement, Am. Chem. Soc. Achievements include invention of invention of Polymerase Chain Reaction (PCR).*

MULLMAN, MICHAEL S. lawyer; b. N.Y.C., Sept. 17, 1946; s. Herbert and Harriet (Weissman) M.; m. Ellen Mullman, 1975; children: Jeremy, Cassie. BA in Polit. Sci. cum laude, Union Coll., Schenectady, N.Y., 1968; JD, Columbia U., 1971. Bar: N.Y. 1972, U.S. Ct. Appeals (2d cir.), U.S. Dist. Ct., 1975. Ptnr. Schonwald, Schaffzin & Mullman, N.Y.C., 1980-89, Tenzer Greenblatt LLP, N.Y.C., 1989-99; adminstrv. ptnr. in charge N.Y. Blank Rome LLP, N.Y.C., 2000—, mem. exec. com., distbn. com., ptnr. bd. Bd. editors Columbia Jour. Law and Soc. Problems, articles edition, 1970-71. Nott scholar Union Coll., 1967, Harlan Fiske Stone scholar Sch. Law Columbia U., 1971. Mem. Bar Assn. N.Y.C., Phi Beta Kappa. Avocations: tennis, skiing, reading, gardening. Office: Blank Rome LLP The Chrysler Bldg 405 Lexington Ave New York NY 10174-0002

MULLNER, ROSS MICHAEL, healthcare educator; b. Chgo., Jan. 8, 1949; s. John Michael and Jean Mullner; m. Linda Cheryl Fantozzi, Dec. 20, 1974; children: Erik Michael, Jason Matthew. BS in Edn., Chgo. State U., 1971; MS, U. Ill., 1973; MPH, U. Ill., Chgo., 1974; PhD, U. Ill., 1976. Dir. rsch. Am. Hosp. Assn., Chgo., 1978—86; assoc. prof. U. Ill., Sch. Pub. Health, 1986—. Cons. Mt. Sinai Hosp., Chgo., 1999—. Author: Deadly Glow; The Story of the Radium Dial Painter Tragedy, From Yellow Fever to the Aids Epidemic; contbr. articles to profl. jours. Office: University of Illinois at Chicago 1603 W Taylor Street Chicago IL 60612-4394 Office Phone: 312-996-5758. Business E-Mail: mullner@uic.edu. E-mail: rmullner@comcast.net.

MULLOY, PATRICK ALOYSIUS, lawyer; b. Wilkes-Barre, Pa., Sept. 14, 1941; s. Hugh Patrick and Ellen Mary (Meagher) M.; m. Marjorie Baumer; children: Maura Alice, Daniel Patrick, Claire Ellen. BA magna cum laude, King's Coll., 1963; MA, U. Notre Dame, 1965; JD with honors, George Washington U., 1971; LLM, Harvard U., 1978. Bar: D.C. 1972, Pa. 1972, U.S. Ct. Appeals (D.C., 2d, and 9th cirs.) 1975, U.S. Supreme Ct. 1975, U.S. Ct. Appeals (5th and 9th cirs.) 1976. Fgn. service officer U.S. Dept. State, Washington, 1965-72; trial lawyer Dept. Justice, Washington, 1973-77, sr. lawyer antitrust div., 1978-82; Congl. fellow U.S. Congress, 1983; minority gen. counsel U.S. Senate Banking Com., 1984-86, gen. counsel, 1987-89, sr. counsel, internat. affairs advisor, 1989-92, chief internat. counsel, 1993-94, chief internat. coun. (minority), 1995-98; asst. sec. market access and compliance Internat. Trade Adminstrn., U.S. Dept. Commerce, Washington, 1998-2001. Apptd. asst. sec., exec. br. commn. on security and coop. in Europe by Pres. Clinton, 1999-2001; apptd. commr. Joint House Senate U.S.-China Econ. and Security Rev. Commn., Washington, 2001—; adj. prof. internat. trade law Cath. U. Law Sch., Washington, 2002-, George Mason Law Sch., Arlington, Va., 2003-. Home: 304 W Masonic View Ave Alexandria VA 22301-2419 Office: US China Security Rev Commn Hall of States Ste 602 444 N Capitol St NW Washington DC 20001 Office Phone: 202-624-1412. E-mail: pamulloy@aol.com., pmulloy@uscc.gov.

MULRONEY, BRIAN (MARTIN BRIAN MULRONEY), former prime minister of Canada; b. Baie Comeau, Que., Can., Mar. 20, 1939; s. Benedict and Irene (O'Shea) M.; m. Mila Pivnicki, 1973; 4 children. BA, St. Francis Xavier U., LLD, 1979; LLL, U. Laval, Que.; LLD (hon.), Meml. U. Nfld., Nfld., 1980, U. W.I., 1993, Tel Aviv U., 1994, Ctrl. Conn. State U., 1994, Barry U., 1995. Ptnr. Ogilvy Renault, Montreal, Canada, 1965-76; exec. v.p. Iron Ore Co. Can., Montreal, 1977-83, 1976-77, pres., 1977-83; mem. Parliament Can. from Ctrl. N.S., Ottawa, 1983-84; mem. Parliament Can. from Manicouagan, 1984-88; mem. Parliament Can. from Charlevoix, 1988-93; leader of Her Majesty's Loyal Opposition, 1983-84; prime min., 1984-93; royal commr. Cliche Commn. investigating violence in Que. constrn. industry, 1974; sr. ptnr. Ogilvy Renault, Montreal, 1993—. Chmn. internat. adv. bd. Barrick Gold Corp., The J.P. Morgan Chase Corp.; mem. internat. adv. coun. Power Corp. Can.; mem. adv. bd. The China Internat. Trust and Investment Corp.; mem. Hicks Muse Tate & Furst Ind. News and Media, PLC; mem. internat. adv. coun. Inst. Internat. Studies; bd. dirs. Archer Daniels Midland Co., Barrick Gold Corp., The Trizec Properties Inc., Power Corp., Quebecor World Inc.; chmn. Forbes, NYC. Author: Where I Stand, 1983. Trustee Montreal Heart Inst.; mem. internat. adv. coun. Les Hautes Etudes Commerciales l'Université de Montréal. Named Grand Officer, Ordre Nat. du Que.; recipient Companion of the Order of Can. Office: Ogilvy Renault 1981 McGill College Ave Ste 1100 Montreal QC Canada H3A 3C1 E-mail: bmulroney@ogilvyrenault.com.

MULRONEY, DERMOT, actor; b. Alexandria, Va., 1964; m. Catherine Keener, 1990; 1 child, Clyde. Student, Northeastern U.; BS, Northwestern U., 1985. Appeared in films Sunset, 1988, Young Guns, 1988, Staying Together, 1989, Longtime Companion, 1989, Survival Quest, 1990, Bright Angel, 1991, Career Opportunities, 1991, Where the Day Takes You, 1992, Point of No Return, 1993, Samantha, 1993, The Thing Called Love, 1993, Silent Tongue, 1993, Bad Girls, 1994, There Goes My Baby, 1994, Angels in the Outfield, 1994, Box of Moonlight, 1996, Bastard Out of Carolina, 1996, Kansas City, 1996, The Trigger Effect, 1996, My Best Friend's Wedding, 1997, Where the Money Is, 1999, Goodbye Lover, 1999, Trixie, 2000, The Safety of Objects, 2001, Lovely & Amazing, 2001, Investigating Sex, 2001, About Schmidt, 2002, Undertow, 2004, Something Borrowed, 2004; tv appearances include Fame, 1982, Sin of Innocence, 1986, Daddy, 1987, Long Gone, 1987, Unconquered, 1989, The Heart of Justice, 1993, The Last Outlaw, 1993, My Best Friend's Wedding, 1997, Box of Moonlight, 1997, Friends, 2003, (mini-series) Family Pictures, 1993, (spls.) The Drug Knot, 1986; prodr. (film) Living in Oblivion, 1995. Office: Internat Creative Mgmt 8942 Wilshire Blvd Beverly Hills CA 90211 Address: PMK/KBH Ste 700 8500 Wilshire Blvd Beverly Hills CA 90211*

MULROW, PATRICK JOSEPH, medical educator; s. Patrick J. and Delia (O'Keefe) M.; m. Jacquelyn Pinover, Aug. 8, 1953; children: Deborah, Nancy, Robert, Catherine. AB, Colgate U., 1947; MD, Cornell U., 1951; MSc (hon.), Yale U., 1969. Intern N.Y. Hosp., 1951-52, resident, 1952-54; instr. physiology Med. Coll. Cornell U., 1954-55; research fellow Stanford U., 1955-57; instr. medicine Yale U., 1957-60, asst. prof., 1960-66, assoc. prof., 1966-69, prof. medicine, 1969-75; chmn. dept. medicine Med. Coll. Ohio, Toledo, 1975-95, prof. medicine, 1975—. Chmn. ednl. com. Council for high blood pressure rsch. Am. Heart Assn., 1968-70, mem. exec. com., 1986-96, vice-chmn. of coun., 1990-92, chmn. 1992-94, past chmn., 1995-96; mem. study sect. NIH, 1970-74. Editorial bd. Jour. Clin. Endocrinology and Metabolism, 1966-70, 75-79, Endocrine Rsch., 1974—, Jour. Exptl. Biology and Medicine, Hypertension, 1994-98; contbr. articles to profl. jours. With USNR, 1944-46. Mem. ACP, Am. Soc. Clin. Investigation, Assn. Am. Physicians, Am. Physiol. Soc., Endocrine Soc., Am. Fedn. Clin. Rsch., Am. Clin. and Climatol. Assn., Am. Heart Assn. (nat. rsch. com., chmn. cardiovasc. regulation rsch. study com. 1986-91), Assn. Profs. Medicine, Assn. Program Dirs. in Internal Medicine, Cen. Soc. Clin. Rsch. (pres. 1988-89), Internat. Soc. Hypertension, World Hypertension League (sec.-gen. 1995—), Inter-Am. Soc. Hypertension, Sigma Xi (pres. Yale chpt. 1965-66), Alpha Omega Alpha. Home: 9526 Carnoustie Rd Perrysburg OH 43551-3501 Office: Med Coll Ohio Dept Medicine 3120 Glendale Ave Toledo OH 43614-5809 Office Phone: 419-383-3707. Business E-Mail: pmulrow@mco.edu.

MULRYAN, HENRY TRIST, mineral company executive, consultant; b. Palo Alto, Calif., Jan. 6, 1927; s. Henry and Marian Abigail (Trist) M.; m. Lenore Hoag, Aug. 25, 1948; children: James W., Carol. Student, Yale U., 1945-46; AB in Econs., Stanford U., 1948; postgrad., Am. Grad. Sch. Internat. Bus., 1949, Columbia U., 1983. V.p. mktg. Sierra Talc Co., South Pasadena, Calif., 1955-65, United Sierra, Trenton, N.J., 1965-67, v.p., gen. mgr., 1967-70, pres., 1970-77; v.p. Cyprus Mines Corp., Los Angeles, 1978-80; sr. v.p. ops. Cyprus indsl. minerals div. Amoco Minerals Co., Englewood, Colo., 1980-85; pres. Cyprus Indls. Minerals Co., Englewood, 1985-87; v.p. Cyprus Minerals Co., Englewood, 1985-87, sr. v.p. mktg., corp. adminstr., 1987-89; pres. Mineral Econs. Internat., 1989—. Vol. exec., Internat. Exec. Svc. Corps., Zimbabwe, 1998, Romania, 1998, Jordan, 2000, 01, 02, 04, Armenia, 2003; pres. Jonathan Art Found., 2004—. Served with U.S. Army, 1944-46. Mem.: Jonathan (Los Angeles), Rotary (pres. South Pasadena club 1964-65) (bd. dirs. Princeton, N.J. club 1969-75). Office: 539 Muskingum Ave Pacific Palisades CA 90272-4252 E-mail: htmulryan@gte.net.

MULRYAN, LENORE HOAG, art curator, author; b. Lompoc, Calif., Aug. 25, 1927; d. William Thomas and Lois Lorraine (Fratis) Hoag; m. Henry Trist Mulryan; children: Patricia Trist (dec.), James William, Carrie M. Neal. BA, UCLA, 1979, postgrad., 1979—81; Cert., Am. Inst. Fgn. Trade, Glendale, Ariz., 1949. Vis. art curator UCLA Fowler Mus. Cultural History, 1982—2004; art curator, editor, cons. Internat. Exec. Svc. Corps, 1998. Dir. fine art print calendars for Chapin Sch., Princeton, NJ, 1971-73; co-chair Fine Arts Tours, Princeton, 1973; cons. Internat. Exec. Svc. Corp., Zimbabwe, 1998, Romania, 1998; curator UCLA Fowler Mus. Nat. History. Author, curator, editor: (books/exhbns.) Mexican Figural Ceramists and Their Works, 1982, Nagual in the Garden: Fantastic Animals in Mexican Ceramics, 1996, Ceramic Trees of Life: Popular Art from Mexico, 2003, UCLA Fowler Mus. Cultural History, 2003—; curator Wilmot Collection of Mexican Art, 1982-91. Mem. Eisenhauer Disting. Fgn. Leader Program U. So. Calif. Mem. Delphians (pres. 1963-64), Westwood Village Rotary Club (chair Amb. Scholarship Selection com. 1996—). Avocations: music, art, yoga, travel.

MULSANT, BENOIT HENRI, psychiatry educator, medical researcher; b. Paris, Feb. 28, 1960; arrived in U.S., 1985; s. Henri Edmond and Francoise Emilie Mulsant; m. Sharon Jane Laufenberg, Feb. 17, 1995; children: Louise Sharon, Sophie Sharon. MD, U. Laval, Que., Can., 1983—84; MS, Carnegie Mellon U., 1989. Lic. Am. Bd. of Psychiatry and Neurology. Assoc. prof. psychiatry U. Pitts., 1996—2004, prof. psychiatry, 2004—; med. dir. ECT svc. U. Pitts. Med. Ctr., 1994—. Prin. investigator federally-funded and industry-sponsored clin. rsch. trials on psychiat. disorders in geriatric patients. Contbr. articles to profl. jours., chpts. to books. Recipient Jr. Investigator award, Am. Assn. for Geriatric Psychiatry, 1994, Ann. Award for Merit, Nat. Psychiat. Endowment Fund, 1990, Laughlin fellowship, Am. Coll. of Psychiatrists, 1990, NIH Career Development award. Mem.: Internat. Coll. Geriatric Neuropsychopharmacology (founding mem. 2001), Am. Psychiat. Assn. Office: U Pitts - WPIC 3811 O'Hara St Pittsburgh PA 15213

MULTHAUP, MERREL KEYES, artist; b. Cedar Rapids, Iowa, Sept. 27, 1922; d. Stephen Dows and Edna Gertrude (Gard) Keyes; m. Robert Hansen Multhaup, Apr. 7, 1944; children: Eric Stephen, Robert Bruce. Student, State U. Iowa, 1942—43, Rice U., 1971. Tchg. faculty Summit (NJ) Art Assn., 1956-60; art instr. studio classes Springfield, NJ, 1954-55, Bloomfield (NJ) Art Group, 1955-56, Westport, Conn., 1962-63; tchg. faculty Hunterdon Art Ctr., Clinton, NJ, 1985-92. Numerous one-woman shows including Summit Art Assn., 1955, Papermill Playhouse, NJ, 1957, 1959, 1960, 1978, 1979, Benedict Gallery, NJ, 1976, Coriell Gallery, 1995; exhibited in group shows at Nat. Assn. Women Artists, NYC, 1957-2001 (awards in figure painting), Hartford (Conn.) Athanaeum Mus., 1961 (1st prize), Highgate Gallery, NYC, Waverly Gallery, NYC, Leicester Gallery, London, Silvermine Gallery, Conn., Pendut Gallery, Tex., Benedict Gallery, Sidney Rothman Gallery, NJ, Stamford (Conn.) Mus., Bridgeport (Conn.) Mus., Montclair (NJ) Mus., Newark Mus., Coriell Gallery, Albuquerque; (traveling exhibit) Nat. Assn. Women Artists, 1996—, Travel USA, 1999, New World Art Ctr., NYC, 1998-99, Gallery Art 54, NYC, 1997, Atelier 14 Gallery, NYC, 2000-02; more than 30 commd. portraits. 1960–. Bd. dirs., exhbn. chmn. Summit Art Assn., 1950-60, Silvermine Guild of Art, New Canaan, Conn., 1960-64; bd. dirs. Artist's Equity of NJ, 1977-84, chmn. state-wide event, 1983, 86; artist's adv. coun. Hunterdon Art Ctr., Clinton, 1988-92; pres. Four Hills Neighbors, 1998-2000. Recipient awards in juried exhbns. in Iowa, Pa., NJ, Conn., NYC. Mem. Nat. Mus. for Women in Arts (charter mem.), Nat. Assn. Women Artists Inc. (awards for figure painting 1957, 80-89), Silvermine Nat. Portrait Group of Artists. Avocations: entertaining, singing, dance, playing the piano, reading. Home: 1321 Stagecoach Rd SE Albuquerque NM 87123-4320

MULVA, JAMES JOSEPH, oil company executive; b. Oshkosh, Wis., June 19, 1946; m. Miriam Mulva; 2 children. BBA in Fin., U. Tex., 1968, MBA in Fin., 1969. Mgmt. trainee, treas. Phillips Petroleum Co., Bartlesville, Okla., 1973, asst. treas. London, 1974, mgr. fgn. exch. and investment Bartlesville, Okla., 1976, v.p., treas. Europe/Africa div. London, 1980, mgr. corp. and planning Bartlesville, Okla., 1984, asst. treas., 1985, treas., 1986, v.p., treas., 1988—90, chief fin. officer, 1990—99, pres., COO, 1994—99, vice-chmn., pres. & CEO, 1999, chmn., CEO, 1999—. Officer Navy, 1969—73. Roman Catholic. Office: Phillips Petroleum Co 18 Phillips Bldg Bartlesville OK 74003*

MULVA, PATRICK T. oil industry executive; b. Green Bay, Wis. BBA, Notre Dame U.; MBA, U. Tex. Fin. analyst ExxonMobil Corp., Baton Rouge, 1976, exec. asst. to pres. U.S. affiliate, 1987, asst. contr. internat. affiliate, fin. dir. Malaysia, 1991, upstream to asst. contr., 1993; contr. Imperial Oil Ltd., 1996, sr. v.p. fin. and adminstrn., 1998—2002, contr., 2000—02; v.p. investor rels. and sec. ExxonMobil Corp., 2002—. With USAF, 1972—75. Office: ExxonMobil Corp 5959 Las Colinas Blvd Irving TX 75039-2298

MULVANEY, MARY FREDERICA, systems analyst; b. NY, Nov. 27, 1945; d. Michael Joseph and Mary Catherine (Clapper) Mulvaney. BA, Marymount Coll., 1967; MA, U. Va., 1968; MS in Computer Sci., Marymount U., 1999. Cert. data processor Inst. Cert. Computer Profls. Computer systems analyst Dept. of Def., Ft. Meade, Md., 1968-74; sr. programmer analyst Planning Rsch. Corp., McLean, Va., 1974-83; mem. tech. staff Fed. Systems Group TRW, Inc., Fairfax, Va., 1983-90, engr., scientist, 1994—2002; sr. mem. tech. staff GTE Govt. Sys. Corp., Rockville, Md., 1990-94; software engr. Northrop Grumman, Fairfax, 2003—. Mem.: IEEE, Cath. Assn. Scientists and Engrs., Computer Measurement Group, Data Processing Mgmt. Assn. Roman Catholic. Office: Northrop Grumman Mission Sys 12900 Federal Sys Park Dr Fairfax VA 22033

MULVANEY, MARY JEAN, physical education educator, department chairman; b. Omaha, Jan. 6, 1927; d. Marion Fowler and Blanche Gibons (McKee) M. BS, U. Nebr., 1948; MS, Wellesley Coll., 1951; LHD (hon.), U. Nebr., 1986. Instr. Kans. State U., Manhattan, 1948-50, U. Nebr., Lincoln, 1951-57, asst. prof., 1957-62, U. Kans., Lawrence, 1962-66; assoc. prof. U. Chgo., 1966-76, prof., 1976-90, prof. emeritus, 1990—, chmn. women's divsn., 1966-76, chmn. dept. phys. edn. and athletics, 1976-90; mem. vis. com. on athletics MIT, 1978-81, Wellesley Coll., 1978-79. Dir. athletics U. Chgo., 2003—; mem. selection com. U. Chgo. Athletics Hall of Fame, 2004. Recipient Honor award Nebr. Assn. Health, Phys. Edn. and Recreation, 1962, U. Nebr. Alumni Achievement award, 1998; named to U. Chgo. Athletics Hall of Fame, 2003; Office of Dir. Athletics, U. Chgo., named in honor, 2003. Mem. AAHPERD, Nat. Collegiate Athletic Assn. (mem. coun. 1983-87), Collegiate Coun. Women Athletic Adminstrs., Midwest Assn. Intercollegiate Athletics for Women (chmn. 1979-81), Nat. Assn. Collegiate Dirs. of Athletics (mem. exec. com. 1976-80, Hall of Fame 1990), Ill. Assn. Intercollegiate Athletics for Women (chmn. 1978-80), Univ. Athletic Assn. (sec. 1986-90, mem. exec. com.

1986-90, mem. dels. com. 1986-90, chmn. athletic adminstr.'s com. 1986-88), Mortar Bd., Alpha Chi Omega. Home: 5821 Kennelley Ct Lincoln NE 68516-3799 E-mail: maryjeanmulvany@aol.com.

MULVEE, ROBERT EDWARD, bishop; b. Boston, Feb. 15, 1930; s. John F. and Jennie (Bath) T. BA, PhB, U. Sem. Ottawa, 1953; MRE, Am. Coll., Louvain, Belgium, 1957; D Canon Law, Lateran U., Rome, 1964; DD (hon.), Rivier Coll., Nashua, N.H., 1979. Ordained priest Roman Cath. Ch., 1957. Asst. chancellor of diocese, 1964—72; named monsignor, 1966; elevated to domestic prelate, 1970; named chancellor, 1972; aux. bishop Roman Catholic Diocese of Manchester, NH, 1977—85; bishop of Wilmington Del., 1985—95; coadjutor bishop Roman Cath. Diocese of Providence, 1995—97; bishop Providence, 1997—. Trustee Nat. Shrine Imaculate Conception, Washington, 1987. Mem.: Nat. Conf. Cath. Bishops/ U.S. Cath. Conf. (adminstrv. com. and bd. dirs. 1986, com. on pers. and adminstrv. svcs. 1987), Nat. Conf. Cath. Bishops (campaign for human devel. com. 1985, joint com. Orthodox and Roman Cath. Bishops 1986, chmn. bd. bishops Am. Coll. of Louvain, Belgium 1986, Cath. Relief Services bd. 1987). Office: One Cathedral Sq Providence RI 02903-3695

MULVEY, GERALD JOHN, meteorologist; b. Cambria Heights, N.Y., Dec. 20, 1949; s. George Patrick and Estelle Florence M.; m. Katherine Louise Strick, July 7, 1973. BS in Physics, York Coll., Jamaica, N.Y., 1971; MS in Atmospheric Sci., SUNY, Albany, 1973; PhD in Atmospheric Sci., Colo. State U., 1977. Cert. cons. meteorologist, CCM. Rsch. assoc. dept. atmospheric sci. Colo. State U., 1977—78; mgr. dept. atmospheric physics Meteorology Rsch., Inc., Altadena, Calif., 1978—80; sr. rsch. engr. Lockheed Missiles and Space, Sunnyvale, Calif., 1980—97; advanced programs mgr. Lockheed Martin Western Devel. Labs., 1997—98; lectr. dept. geoscis. San Francisco State U., 1995—98; advanced programs mgr. Lockheed Martin Global Telecomm., Sunnyvale, Calif., 1998—99; prin. sys. engr. DIVA Sys. Corp., Redwood City, Calif., 1999—2002; sr. mgr. Northrop Grumman, 2002—. Co-author: Environmental Impacts of Artificial Ice Nucleating Agents, 1978; contbr. articles to profl. jours. including Analytical Chemistry and Jour. Applied Meteorology. Mem. Cupertino (Calif.) Libr. Commn., 1989—93; v.p. bd. dirs. Cupertino Libr. Found., 2000—01. Mem. AAAS, Am. Meteorological Soc., Internat. Soc. Measurement and Control (v.p. Santa Clara valley 1996-97), Sigma Xi. Roman Catholic. Achievements include verifying/documenting of long range transport of active cloud nucleating agents. Office: Nothrop Grumman Mission One Space Rsch Park R10/1791 Redondo Beach CA 90278 Office Phone: 310-812-5196. Business E-Mail: gerry.mulvey@ngc.net.

MULVIHILL, JAMES EDWARD, periodontist, educator; b. Cleve., Sept. 24, 1940; s. John F. and Teresa J. (Carlos) M.; m. May Jane Forino, 1963; children— Karen, Kristen, Jason BA, Coll. of Holy Cross, 1962; DMD, Harvard U., 1966. Asst. dean for student affairs, coordinator Harvard-VA continuing edn. program Harvard Sch. Dental Medicine, Boston, 1970-71; dean clin. campus L.I. Jewish-Hillside Med. Ctr., Queens Hosp. Ctr. Affiliation, Jewish Inst. for Geriatric Care, Health Scis. Ctr. SUNY-Stony Brook, 1971-80; v.p. for edn. and research L.I. Jewish-Hillside Med. Ctr., New Hyde Park, N.Y., 1975-80; v.p., provost for health affairs, exec. dir. Health Ctr., prof. periodontics U. Conn., Farmington, 1980-92; attending periodontist John Dempsey Hosp., U. Conn. Health Ctr., Farmington, 1982-92; pres. John Dempsey Fin. Corp., Farmington, 1988-92; sr. v.p. for health policy The Travelers Corp., Hartford, Conn., 1992-94; chmn. bd. The Travelers Health Co., Hartford, 1992-93; sr. fellow in health policy Assn. of Acad. Health Ctrs., 1994; pres., CEO Managed Health, Inc., 1994, Comty. Health Plan of Queens/Nassau, New Hyde Park, N.Y., 1994-95, Forsyth Dental Ctr., Boston, 1995-96, Juvenile Diabetes Found. Internat., 1996-99; dir. instnl. advancement and corp. rels. Am. Dental Edn. Assn., 2000—; asst. to pres. So. Maine Med. Ctr., 2000—01; chief dept. dentistry Harvard U. Health Svcs., 2003—. Cons. in field Author: (with others) Guide to Foreign Medical Schools, 1975, Editorial Instructions for Dental Authors, 1979-80, 1979, Human Subjects Research: The Operational Handbook for IRB's, 1982, 2d edit., 1984, Japanese edit., 1987; also articles, chpt. in book Bd. dirs. William Gies Found., Nat. Fund for Med. Edn., Found. for Blood Rsch. Recipient Disting. Alumnus award Harvard Sch. Dental Medicine, 1982, Disting. alumnus award Holy Cross Coll., 1991. Fellow AAAS, Am. Coll. Dentistry, Internat. Coll. Dentistry; mem. ADA, Am. Acad. Periodontology, Conn. State Dental Assn. (Fones award 2004), Harvard Dental Alumni Assn., Alpha Sigma Nu, Sigma Psi. Avocations: golf, gardening, photography. Address: 117 Kings Hwy Kennebunkport ME 04046-5606 Personal E-mail: mulvi@adelphia.net.

MULVIHILL, KEITHLEY D. lawyer; b. Pitts., Oct. 16, 1956; s. Bernard H. and Doris L. M.; m. Donna Colella, 1980; children: Michael, Mary Katherine. BA in History, Ind. U. Pa., 1978; JD, U. Pitts., 1981. Bar: Pa. 1981, U.S. Dist. Ct. (we. dist.) Pa. 1981, U.S. Ct. Appeals (3d cir.) 1982; CPCU. Assoc. Rose, Schmidt, Hasley & DiSalle, Pitts., 1981-88, shareholder, 1988-2001; ptnr., head litigation dept. Leech, Tishman, Fuscaldo & Lampl, Pitts., 2001—03; mng. ptnr. Pitts. office Rawle & Henderson LLP, 2003—. Spl. master Ct. of Common Pleas of Allegheny County, Pa.; commr. Municipality of Mt. Lebanon, Pa., 1999—, v.p. 2002, pres., 2003. Mng. editor U. Pitts. Law Rev., 1980—81. Mem. Allegheny County Dem. Com; rep. Mt. Lebanon South Hills Area Coun. of Govts.; mem. St. Bernard Roman Cath. Ch. (past mem. parish coun.). Mem. ABA, Pa. Bar Assn., Pa. Def. Inst. (treas. 1998—), Allegheny County Bar Assn., Assn. Def. Trial Attys. (Pa. state chair), Fed. Rsch. Inst., CPCU Soc. (pub. rels. chmn. Allegheny chpt.). Office: Rawle & Henderson LLP Ste 910 Henry W Oliver Bldg 535 Smithfield St Pittsburgh PA 15222 E-mail: kmulvihill@rawle.com.

MULVIHILL, PETER JAMES, fire protection engineer; b. Honolulu, Jan. 24, 1956; s. James H. and Jane A. (Norton) M. BSCE, Worcester (Mass.) Poly. Inst., 1978. Registered fire protection engr., Nev., Utah. Sr. engr. Indsl. Risk Insurers, San Francisco, 1978-84; fire protection engr. Aerojet Gen. Corp., Sacramento, 1984-87, Reno Fire Dept., 1987-93; fire protection engr., bn. chief Boise (Idaho) Fire Dept., 1993-95; cons. Rolf Jensen & Assocs., Inc., Lehi, Utah, 1995-96, fire protection engr. Las Vegas, Nev., 1996-99, v.p., engring. mgr., 2004—; mgr. western region Fire Protection Mgmt., Inc., Las Vegas, 1999—2002, v.p., western region, 2003. Part-time instr. univ. extension U. Calif., Davis, 1993-95, Truckee Meadows Community Coll., Reno, 1988-93. Mem. Gov.'s Blue Ribbon Commn. to Study Adequacy of State Regulations concerning Highly Combustible Materials, Carson City, Nev., 1988, Nev. State Bd. Fire Svs., 2001—, chmn., 2003—04; mem. Nev. Fire Svc. Standards and Tng. Com., 2003—04. Mem.: ASCE, Fire Marshals Assn. Utah, Internat. Assn. Fire Chiefs, Nat. Fire Protection Assn. (alt. com. air conditioning and profl. qualifications for fire insps.), No. Nev. Fire Marshals Assn. (pres. 1992—93), Soc. Fire Protection Engrs. Office: Ste 650 101 Convention Center Dr Las Vegas NV 89109-2001 Office Phone: 702-699-5391.

MULVIHILL, WILLIAM J. former health science association administrator; BBA, U. Cinn.; MEd, Ohio U. V.p. Ohio River Valley chpt. Arthritis Found., 1984-87, chair, 1987-90, midwest. area vice chair, 1988-90, chair fin. devel. com., 1991-93, vice chair of couns., 1993, treas., 1994-96, sr. vice chair, 1996-98, chair, 1998—2001; mem. board Alliance for Lupus Research. Mem. com. on appointments, salary and personnel com., exec. com.; assoc. dir. athletics for external affairs U. Cinn., exec. dir. athletic team scholarships. Mem. Coun. for Advancement and Support of Edn., Nat. Assn. Collegiate Dirs. of Athletics, Nat., Assn. Athletic Devel. Dirs. Office: Alliance For Lupus Research 28 W 44th St #1217 New York NY 10036-6600

MULVILLE, DANIEL R. federal agency administrator; b. Washington, D.C., Dec. 7, 1939; BSME, George Washington U., 1962, M Engring., 1977; PhD in Structural Mechs., Cath. U., 1974; postgrad., Coll. Armed Forces, 1986. Mech. engr. Naval Rsch. Lab., 1962—79; program mgr. structures rsch. Office Naval Rsch., 1975; structures tech. mgr. Naval Air Sys. Command, 1979—86; dep. dir. materials and structures divsn. Office Aeronautics and Space Tech. NASA, Washington, 1986—90, dir. engring. and quality mgmt. divsn. Office Safety and Mission Assurance, 1990—94, dep. chief engr., 1994—95, chief engr., 1995—99, assoc. dep. adminstr., 1999—, acting adminstr., 2001. Office: NASA Hdqrs Mail Code A 300 E St SW Washington DC 20546

MUMA, LESLIE M. data processing executive; Pres. Fiserv, Brookfield, Wis., 1984—, vice chmn., 1995-99, CEO, 1999—, chmn. bd. dirs., 2000—. Office: Fiserv 255 Fiserv Dr Brookfield WI 53045

MUMFORD, BEVERLY JEAN, paralegal; b. Washington, Mar. 27, 1949; Assoc. Degree in Transp. Mgmt., LaSalle U., 1977; Environ. Sci. Diploma, Calif. State U., 1993, Thomas Edison State Coll., 1993; BS/MBA-Bus. Adminstrn., Chadwick U., 1995. Transp. asst. Interstate Commerce Commn., Indpls., 1977—79, paralegal specialist Washington, 1979—84; legal staff asst. Armed Svcs. Bd. of Contract Appeals, Falls Church, Va., 1987—89; paralegal specialist Mil. Sealift Command, Far East, Yokohama, Japan, 1989—94, Def. Fin. and Acctg. Svc. (former Spouse Divsn.), Cleve., 1994—2001. Author: Prevention of Sexual Harassment in the Workplace, 1992. Decorated Navy Unit Commendation Cert./Mil. Sealift Command, (Desert Shield/Desert Storm), Yokohoma; named to Women's Inner Circle of Achievement. Mem.: Ohio State Bar Assn., Nat. Environ. Health Assn., Nat. Paralegal Assn., Internat. Platform Assn. Republican. Baptist. Avocations: golf, horseback riding, collecting antiques. Home and Office: Mumford And Mumford 1213 Missouri Ave Lorain OH 44052-3139

MUMFORD, CHRISTOPHER GREENE, corporate financial executive; b. Washington, Oct. 21, 1945; s. Milton C. and Dorothea L. (Greene) Mumford. BA, Stanford U., 1968, MBA, 1975. Cons. Internat. Tech. Resources Inc., 1974; asst. v.p. Wells Fargo Bank, San Francisco, 1975-78; asst. treas. Arcata Corp., San Francisco, 1978-82, v.p. fin., 1982-87, exec. v.p. fin., 1987-94. Gen. ptnr. Scarff, Sears & Assocs., San Francisco, 1986—95; mng. dir. Questor Ptnrs. Fund, L.P., San Francisco, 1995—98; v.p. bd. dirs. Triangle Pacific Corp., Dallas, 1986—88, Norton Enterprises Inc., Salt Lake City, 1988—90, Crown Pacific Ptnrs., Portland, Oreg., 1991—, Ryder TRS, Inc., Miami, Fla., 1996—98, Ockham PLC, London, 1996—98, Impco Technologies, Inc., Cerritos, Calif., 1998—2000. Office: PO Box 1340 Mill Valley CA 94942-1340 Office Phone: 415-601-6800. E-mail: cgmumford@aol.com.

MUMFORD, DAVID BRYANT, mathematics professor; b. Worth, Sussex, Eng., June 11, 1937; came to U.S., 1940; s. William Bryant and Grace (Schiott) M.; m. Erika Jentsch, June 27, 1959 (dec. July 30, 1988); children: Stephen, Peter, Jeremy, Suchitra; m. Jenifer Moore, Dec. 29, 1989. BA, Harvard U., 1957, PhD, 1961; D.Sc. (hon.), U. Warwick, 1983, Norwegian U. Sci. Tech., 2000, Rockefeller U., 2001. Jr. fellow Harvard U., 1958-61, assoc. prof., 1962-66, prof. math., 1966-77, Higgins prof., 1977-97, chmn. dept. math, 1981-84; U. prof. Brown U., 1996—. V.p. Internat. Math. Union, 1991-94, pres., 1995-98. Author: Geometric Invariant Theory, 1965, Abelian Varieties, 1970, Introduction to Algebraic Geometry, 1976, 2 and 3 Dimensional Patterns of the Face, 1999, Indra's Pearls, 2002. Recipient Fields medal Internat. Congress Mathematicians, 1974; MacArthur Found. fellow, 1987-92. Fellow Tata Inst. (hon.); mem. Accad. Nazionale dei Lincei, Nat. Acad. Scis., Am. Acad. Arts and Scis., Am. Philosophical Soc. Office: Brown U 182 George St Providence RI 02912-9056 Home: Brown Univ #Box-F Providence RI 02912-0001

MUMFORD, LAWRENCE R. composer, educator; s. Richard W. and Mary Margaret Mumford; m. Donna L. Mumford, Mar. 9, 1996. BA in Music, George Washington U., 1975; MMus, Peabody Conservatory, Balt., 1976; DMus, U. So. Calif., L.A., 1989. Cert. tchr. Ind. U., Bloomington, 1977. Music accompanist Glendale Coll., Calif., 1990—91; music prof. The Master's Coll., Santa Clarita, Calif., 1992—2004; adj. music prof. Calif. State U., Northridge, 1993—94, Concordia U., Irvine, Calif., 2001—04; prof. music Vanguard U., Costa Mesa, 2004—. Compositions and arrangements published by 6different cos. Recipient Composition Prize, Culver Chamber Soc., 1999. Mem.: Soc. for Music Theory, Soc. of Composers, Inc., Music Tchrs. Assn. of Calif. (branch pres. 1989—90, pres. emeritus), Pi Kappa Lambda, Phi Beta Kappa. Home: 15 Cortona Irvine CA 92614 Office: Vanguard U 55 Fair Dr Costa Mesa CA 92626 Business E-Mail: lmumford@masters.edu.

MUMFORD, STEPHEN DOUGLAS, research scientist; b. Louisville, Aug. 28, 1942; s. Adrian Leroy and Mildred Margaret (Cardwell) M.; m. Judy Sheng-Ju Lee, Dec. 26, 1966; children: Christopher Lee, Sonia Lea. BS in Agr., U. Ky., 1966; MPH in Internat. Health/Population Study, U. Tex., Houston, 1971, DrPH in Health Svcs. Adminstrn., 1975. Indsl. hygienist Ky. State Dept. Health, Frankfort, 1966-67; rsch. asst. dept. ob.-gyn. Baylor Coll. Medicine, Houston, 1973-75; rsch. statis. aide population studies U. Tex., Houston, 1971-75, rsch. asst. dept. reproductive biology/endocrinology, 1971-76; dir. rsch., sr. vasectomy counselor Planned Parenthood of Houston, 1972-76; adminstr. Nat. Swine Flu Immunization Program/Houston/Harris County, Tex., 1976-77; from sect. leader design/analysis divsn. to scientist Internat. Fertility Rsch. Program, Research Triangle Park, N.C., 1977-83; pres. Ctr. for Rsch. on Population and Security, Research Triangle Park, N.C., 1984—. Author: The Pope and the New Apocalypse: The Holy War Against Family Planning, 1986, American Democracy and the Vatican: Population Growth and National Security, 1984, Population Growth Control: The Next Move is America's, 1977, The Decision-Making Process that Leads to Vasectomy: A Guide for Promoters, 1977, Vasectomy Counseling, 1977, The Life and Death of NSSM 200: How the Destruction of Political Will Doomed a U.S. Population Policy, 1996; contbr. numerous articles to profl. jours., chpts. to books; contbr. editor The Churchman, 1991-98. Mem. Alan Guttmacher Inst., Assn. for Vol. Sterilization, Environ. Def. Fund, Fund for Feminist Majority, Nat. Abortion Rights Action League, Population Inst., Population Ref. Bur., Ams. United for Separation of Ch. and State, Religious Coalition for Abortion Rights. Capt. U.S. Army, 1966-70. Recipient Cert. of Appreciation for Outstanding Contbns. to Advancing the Cause of Reproductive Rights, Feminist Caucus of Am. Humanist Assn., 1986, Humanist Disting. Svc. award, 1981, Margaret Mead Leadership prize in population and ecology, 1981, Award for Outstanding Single Project in Area of Human Rels., U.S. Jaycees, 1974-75, Award for Outstanding Chmn. of a Single Project in Area of Human Rels., 1974-75. Mem. AAAS, Am. Humanist Assn., Am. Pub. Health Assn. (population sect.), Ams. for Immigration Control, Ams. for Religious Liberty, Fedn. for Am. Immigration Reform, Internat. Epidemiol. Assn., Negative Population Growth, Carrying Capacity Network, Soc. for Epidemiologic Rsch., Zero Population Growth, NOW Avocations: gardening, fruit growing, woodworking, fishing, running. Home: 322 Azalea Dr Chapel Hill NC 27517-8105 Office: Ctr Rsch Population PO Box 13067 Research Triangle Park NC 27709 Office Phone: 919-933-7491. Personal E-mail: smumford@mindspring.com.

MUMFORD, WILLIAM PORTER, II, retired lawyer; b. Kewanee, Ill., July 13, 1920; s. Harold E. and Mary K. (Harry) M.; m. Jean N. Hagemann, Nov. 22, 1951; children— William Porter III, James F., Michael E. BS in Accounting, U. Ill., 1943, JD, 1949. Bar: Ill. 1949, Oreg. 1955; C.P.A., Ill., Oreg. Jr. acct. Price Waterhouse & Co., Chgo., 1949-51; practiced in Chgo., 1951-54, Grants Pass, Ore., 1955-57, Eugene, Oreg., 1957—; mem. firm McAdams & Kirby, 1951-55; sr. acct. B.K. Herndon & Co., 1955-57; ptnr. Thompson, Mumford, Anderson & Fisher, 1957-86, ret., 1986. Eugene campaign mgr. Hatfield for Gov., 1960-62; Chmn. bd. trustees Oreg. State Library. Served to capt., inf. AUS, 1943-46. Mem. Am. Legion, Elks Club, Pi Kappa Alpha, Phi Alpha Delta. Republican. Home: 2064 Musket St Eugene OR 97408-4624

MUMM, CHRISTOPHER ERIC, lawyer, county government official; b. Reno, Dec. 9, 1950; s. Hans Heinrich and Yolanda Victoria (Erickson) M.; m. Stephanie Wasile, Nov. 27, 1984; children: Melody Anishka, Alexander Matthew. AAS in Real Estate, Truckee Meadows C.C., 1976; JD, Nev. Sch. Law, 1985. Bar: Nev. 1987, Calif. 1987; lic. real estate broker, Nev. Dep. appraiser Washoe County, Reno, 1976-80, dep. tax assessor, 1980—2001; ind. real estate broker Reno, 1979—; pvt. practice law, 1987—. Chief tribal ct. judge Pyramid Lake Indian Reservation, 1994-98. Pres. PTA, Sparks Mid. Sch., 1999, Alice Maxwell Elem. Sch., 1998. With U.S. Army, 1970-72. Mem. Calif. Bar Assn., Nev. Bar Assn., Soc. Real Estate Appraisers (v.p. edn. Reno chpt. 1984-86), Internat. Assn. Assessing Ofcls., Nev. Jr. C. of C. (pres. 1986), U.S. Jaycees (exec. bd. dirs. 1986, amb., sen.), Acquarian Toastmasters (pres. 1988), Sertoma. Republican. Roman Catholic. Home: 3815 Moorpark Ct Sun Valley NV 89433-8240 Office Phone: 775-331-1770. E-mail: judgemumm9@sbcglobal.net.

MUMM, STEVEN ROBERT, geneticist, educator; s. Harry John and Louisa Elizabeth Mumm; m. Kimberly Allen Baker, May 27, 1978; children: Eric Anderson, Emily Baker. BS in Biochemistry, U. Mo., 1978, MS in Chemistry, 1983; PhD in Cellular and Molecular Biology, St. Louis U., 1991. Asst. prof. medicine Washington U. Sch. Medicine, St. Louis, 1999—. Mem. sci. staff Shriners Hosps. for Children, St. Louis. Contbr. articles to profl.jours. Predoctoral trainee, NIH, 1984—88, postdoctoral trainee, 1994—95, Markey postdoctoral fellow, Washington U. Sch. Medicine, 1992—94, postdoctoral fellow, Shriners Hosps. for Children, 1995—97. Mem.: Am. Soc. Bone and Mineral Rsch., Am. Soc. Human Genetics, Am. Soc. Microbiology. Office: Washington U Sch Medicine Saint Louis MO Office Phone: 314-454-8779. E-mail: smumm@wustl.edu.

MUMMA, ALBERT GIRARD, JR., architect; b. Long Beach, Calif., July 2, 1928; s. Albert Girard and Carmen (Braley) M.; m. Janeal Thomas Woolf, Dec. 24, 1973; children: Eugenia M. Villagra, Albert Girard III, Peter Brenaman. B.Arch., U. Va., 1951. Designer McLeod & Ferrara, Architects, Washington, 1951-56; assoc. Deigert & Yerkes, Architects, 1956-62; prin. Mumma & Assocs., Washington, 1962—. Archtl. designer hotel div. Marriott Corp., 1980-82 Prin. archtl. works include Nat. Arboretum Hdqrs. Bldg. 1961, Finnmark Sq., Silver Spring, Md., 1964, Inverness townhouses, Potomac, Md., 1971, Post Office and Fed. Bldg., Elkins, W.Va., 1971, U.S. Trade Fairs in Spain, Finland, Japan, El Salvador, Poland 1963-72, Fallswood housing project, Falls Church, Va., 1972, Bristow Village townhouses, Annandale, Va., 1972-73, Marriott Hotel, Dayton, Ohio, 1982, Plaza Venetia, Biscayne Bay, Miami, Fla., 1983, Houston Med. Ctr. Hotel, Newark Airport Hotel, 1984, pvt. residences, No. Neck, Rappahanock River, Lancaster County, Va., 1993-2004, subdivision and townhouse projects, Washington, Md., Va., Pa., 1962—. Served with USMC, 1945-47. Recipient Design award Washington Bd. Trade, 1964; winner Newark Airport Hotel Competition, 1981. Mem. AIA (medal 1951), Rappahannock River Yacht Club, Indian Creek Yacht and Country Club, Moran Creek Yacht Club.

MUMMA, MICHAEL JON, physicist, researcher; b. Lancaster, Pa., Dec. 3, 1941; s. John Henry and Violet Lyndell (Baxter) M.; m. Sage Bailey Tower, Aug. 20, 1966; children: Peter Robb, Amy Elizabeth. AB in Physics with honors, Franklin and Marshall Coll., 1963; PhD in Physics, U. Pitts., 1970. Grad. research asst. U. Pitts., 1963-70; astrophysicist NASA Goddard Space Flight Center, Greenbelt, Md., 1970-76, head br. Infrared and Radio Astronomy, 1976-84, assoc. chief Lab. Extraterrestrial Physics, 1984-85, head Planetary Systems br., 1985-90, chief scientist Lab. Extraterrestrial Physics, 1990—, dir. Ctr. Astrobiology, 2003—; adj. research assoc. in physics Pa. State U., 1978-81, prof. physics, 1981-88. Mem. numerous working groups and adv. coms. NASA, Nat. Bur. Standards, NSF, Nat. Acad. Scis., 1973—; lectr. in field. Contbr. numerous articles to profl. publs., 1970—; editor: The Study of Comets, Vols. 1, 2, 1976, Vibrational-Rotational Spectroscopy for Planetary Atmospheres, vols. 1, 2, 1982, Astrophysics from the Moon, 1990. Recipient NASA medal for Exceptional Sci. Achievement, 1988, 97; Kershner award for physics, 1962; Coll. Trustee's scholar Franklin and Marshall Coll., 1963., Asteroid 8340 named "Michael J. Mumma" by Internat. Astron. Union, 1999. Fellow Am. Phys. Soc., Washington Acad. Sci.; mem. AAAS, Am. Astron. Soc., Am. Geophys. Union, Internat. Astron. Union, Sigma Pi Sigma. Achievements include discovery of natural lasers in atmospheres of Mars, Venus, and Jupiter; first detection of water vapor in comets, discovery of formaldehyde, methanol, methane, and ethane in comets; discovery of x-rays in comets; first definitive measurements of deuterium and hydrogen on Mars and Venus; first absolute wind measurements on Venus and Mars; invention of tunable diode laser heterodyne spectrometer and other advanced instruments; development of Doppler-limited infrared spectroscopy for laboratory and astrophysical applications, of absolute calibration procedures in vacuum ultraviolet, of molecular branching ratio technique for intensity calibration in vacuum ultraviolet; measurement of many absolute cross sections in vacuum ultraviolet; research on atomic and molecular physics and chemistry, on comets, on planetary atmospheres, on infrared astronomy, on high-resolution spectroscopy, and in the field of dissociative excitation of molecules. Office: Code 690 Goddard Space Flight Ctr Greenbelt MD 20771-0001

MUMMANENI, PADMAJA, research scientist, educator; d. Ram Mohan Rao and Lakshmiswaramma Mummaneni. BSc in Life Scis., Delhi U., India, 1980, MSc, 1982, PhD, 1989. Postdoctoral rsch. fellow U. Ky., Lexington, 1989—96; staff fellow NIH, Bethesda, Md., 1996—2000; scientist Neuralstem Inc., Gaithersburg, Md., 2000—03; project scientist lead Neuronascent Inc., Md., 2004—. Guest lectr. Found. for Advanced Edn. in the Scis. NIH, Bethesda, Md., 1998—2000, juror, 1998—2000, sci. adv. bd. Contbr. articles to profl./peer-reviewed jours. Fellow: AAAS, Am. Soc. of Cellular and Molecular Biology, N.Y. Acad. Scis.; mem.: Am. Women In Sci. Hindu. Avocations: painting, art. Home: 10513 Montrose Ave Bethesda MD 20814 Office: FDA 1451 Rockville Pike Rockville MD 20852

MUMPOWER, JERYL L. academic administrator; m. Edwina Dorch; 1 child, Sarah. BA, Coll. William and Mary; PhD in Social and Quantitative Psychology, U. Colo. Dir., policy analyst NSF; assoc. dir. Rockfeller Inst. Govt.; prof. pub. adminstrn., pub. policy and info. sci. U. Albany, SUNY, 1984—, dir. Ctr. for Policy Rsch., assoc. provost, dean grad. studies, interim provost, v.p. for acad. affairs, 2004—. Contbr. chapters to books, articles to profl. jours. Office: Univ Albany SUNY UAB 400 1400 Washington AVe Albany NY 12222*

MUNAS, FALIES A. psychiatric physician; b. Colombo, Sri Lanka, Aug. 30, 1946; came to U.S., 1972; s. M.H.M. and C.P. M. MBBS, MD, Christian Med. Coll., Vellore, India, 1971. Diplomate Am. Bd. Psychiatry and Neurology. Dir. geropsychiatry Trinity Meml. Hosp., Cudahy, Wis., 1991-95; dir. clin. svcs./chief of staff De Paul Hosp., Milw., 1996-97; dir. behavioral medicine VA Med. Ctr., Marion, Ill., 1998-2000; assoc. clinical prof. of psychiatry S.I.U. Sch. Medicine, Springfield, Ill., 1999—. Pres. Extended Family Svcs. Corp., Big Bend, Wis., 1989-97; assoc. clin. prof. psychiatry So. Ill. U. Sch. Medicine, Springfield, 1999—. Home: 23107 Galatia Post Rd Pittsburg IL 62974-1832 Office: VA Med Ctr 2401 W Main St Marion IL 62959-1188 Personal E-mail: filmunas@hotmail.com.

MUNASINGHE, MOHAN, development economist; b. Colombo, Sri Lanka, July 25, 1945; s. Peter Munasinghe and Flower Wickramasinghe; m. Sria Gooneratne, May 8, 1970; children: Anusha, Ranjiva. BA with honors, Cambridge (Eng.) U., 1967, MA, 1968; SM, MIT, 1969, EE, 1970; PhD in EE, McGill U., Montreal, Can., 1973; MA in Econs., Concordia U., 1975. Sr. advisor World Bank, Washington, 1996—2002; chief energy advisor Govt. of Sri Lanka, 2002—. Vis. prof. Am. U., Washington, 1977-81, Inst. Tech. Policy in Devel., SUNY, 1982-88, Energy Ctr. U. Pa., Phila., 1988-94, UN U./Inst. for Advanced Studies, 1997—; disting. vis. prof. environ. mgmt. Colo. U., Sri Lanka, 1995-2001; vice chair intergovernmental panel on climate change, Geneva, 1997—; disting. vis. prof. Yale U., 2004—; sr. advisor Min. of Environment, Sri Lanka, 1995-98; pres. Lanka Internat. Forum Environ. & Sustainable Devel., Sri Lanka, 1996-2002; sr. advisor to pres. Office of Pres. of Sri Lanka, Colombo, 1982-87, chmn. computer and info. tech. coun., 1983-86; divsn. chief World Bank, Washington, 1987-96; sr. rsch. fellow Ctr. Internat. Devel. and Conflict Mgmt. U. Md., College Park, 1987-90; pres.-emeritus Sri Lanka Energy Mgmt. Assn., Colombo, 1985—, pres. 1983-85; advisor U.S. Pres.'s Coun. on Environ. Quality, 1990-92; chancellor Internat. Water Acad., Norway, 1999—; chmn. Munasinghe Inst. Devel., 1999—. Author: 81 books including Economics of Power System Reliability and Planning, 1979, Energy Economics, Demand Management and Pricing, 1983, Rural Electrification for Development, 1987, Integrated National E[illegible] Planning and Management, 1988, Computers and Informatics in D[illegible] Countries, 1989, Energy Analysis and Policy, 1990, Electric P[illegible]

ics, 1990, Water Supply and Environmental Management, 1992, Energy Modelling and Policy, 1992, Environmental Economics & Sustainable Development, 1993, Economywide Policies and the Environment, 1994, Protected Area Economics & Policy, 1994, Defining & Measuring Sustainability, 1995, Natural Disasters & Environment, 1995, Property Rights in Social and Ecological Context, 1995, Environmental Impacts of Macroeconomic Policies, 1997, Climate Change Policy, 1998, Sustainomics, 1999; author over 300 tech. papers; mem. editl. bd. Energy Jour., Environ. and Devel. Econ., Environ. Econ. and Policy Studies, Internat. Jour. Elec. Power and Energy Systems, Open Economics Review, Pacific and Asian Jour. of Energy, Utilities Policy. Recipient Outstanding Scientists Gold medal Lions Internat., 1985, Exceptional Contbns. award Internat. Assn. Energy Econs., 1987, prize for Outstanding Achievement Latin Am. and Caribbean Energy Conf., 1988, award for Outstanding Contbns. World Water Congress, 1995, Global Green award Internat. Fedn. Environ. Journalists, 1998, award for unique and innovative contbns. U.S. Assn. Energy Econs., 2003; Grass fellow MIT, 1968, fellow Beijer Internat. Inst.-Royal Swedish Acad. Scis. Fellow Nat. Acad. Scis. (Sri Lanka), Third World Acad. Scis. (Italy), World Water Acad. (Norway), Royal Soc. Arts, (U.K.) Inst. Elec. Engrs. (U.K., Beauchamp prize 1967), Inst. Engrs. (Sri Lanka); mem. IEEE, Am. Econ. Assn., Am. Phys. Soc., Sri Lanka Assn. Adv. Sci., Sri Lanka Econ. Assn. Mailing: 10 De Fonseka Pl Colombo Sri Lanka

MUNCH, DOUGLAS FRANCIS, pharmaceutical and health industry consultant; b. Bronx, N.Y., Mar. 15, 1947; s. Robert Joseph and Isabel (Fiordelisi) M.; m. Janice Ann Davis, Apr. 3, 1976 (div. Aug. 2003): children: Sarah Christine, Eric Christopher. BSChemE, Villanova U., 1969; MS, U. Calif., Santa Barbara, 1974; PhD, Johns Hopkins U., 1978. Project engr. Grumman Aerospace Corp., Bethpage, N.Y., 1969-73; postdoctoral fellow U. South Ala., 1978-80; program mgr. Travenol Labs., Round Lake, Ill., 1980-82; dir. Kimberly Clark Corp., Atlanta, 1982-86; pres. Biomed. Products Group Inc., Roswell, Ga., 1986-87; cons., pres. D.F. Munch & Assocs., Roswell, 1986-88; pres., CEO, dir. Sphinx Pharmaceuticals, Inc., Durham, N.C., 1988-89; v.p., dir. Orthopharm Corp.-Advanced Care Products, Johnson & Johnson, Raritan, N.J., 1989-93; pres. D.F. Munch, Ltd., Basking Ridge, N.J., 1993—. Bd. dirs. Percura, Inc., Irvine, Calif.; adv. bd. mem. dept. biomed. engring. and Whitaker Biomed. Engring. Inst., chmn., 2001—, Johns Hopkins Sch. Medicine, 1997—; advisor Queensland N.Am. Biotech. Group, Australia, 2001—. Author: Cardiovascular Pharmacology, 1981; contbr. articles to profl. jours. Pres. Hollyberry Civic Assn., Roswell, 1980-87, Roswell Neighborhood Network, 1987, Basking Ridge (N.J.) Little League, 1992-97; elder Basking Ridge Presbyn. Ch., 1992-95; mem. BME bd. dirs. Johns Hopkins Med. Sch., Balt., 1997—; trustee Philharm. Orch. N.J., 2000—, treas., 2000—. Recipient Apollo Achievement award NASA, 1969; Profl. Achievement award Villanova U., 1987; NIH fellow, 1974-78. Fellow Royal Soc. Medicine; mem. Am. Physiol. Soc., Biomed. Engring. Soc., Johns Hopkins Med. and Surg. Assn. Avocations: woodworking, music, camping, bicycling, swimming. Home: 94 Countryside Dr Basking Ridge NJ 07920

MUNCK, ALLAN ULF, physiologist, educator; b. Buenos Aires, July 4, 1925; came to U.S., 1945, naturalized, 1959; s. Carl and Elisabeth (Schmidt) M.; m. Claire Brosi, Oct. 5, 1957; children— Alexander Charles, Ingrid Claire, Kirsten Tanya. BS in Chem. Engring, Mass. Inst. Tech., 1948, MS, 1949, PhD in Biophysics, 1956. Chem. engr., Ducilo, Buenos Aires, 1949-50; mem. staff Huntington Lab. Mass. Gen. Hosp., Boston, 1956-57, Worcester Found. Exptl. Biology, Shrewsbury, Mass., 1957-59; mem. med. sch. faculty Dartmouth Coll., 1959—; prof. physiology Dartmouth Med. Sch., 1967—2001, prof. physiology emeritus, 2001—. Marius Tausk prof. Leiden U., The Netherlands, 1998. Served with Argentine Army, 1949. Mem. Physiol. Soc., Endocrine Soc., Am. Soc. Biochemistry and Molecular Biology. Home: PO Box 114 Norwich VT 05055-0114 Office: Dartmouth Med Sch Dept Physiology Lebanon NH 03756 E-mail: allan.u.munck@dartmouth.edu.

MUNCY, ESTLE PERSHING, physician; b. Tazewell, Tenn., Apr. 9, 1918; s. William Loyd and Flora Media (Monday) M.; m. Dorothy Davis, Dec. 31, 1946 (div. Apr. 1980); children: Robert H., Teresa A., Dorothy J., Estle II,James; m. Jean Marie Hayter, Mar. 19, 1985. AB, Lincoln Meml. U., 1939; MD, U. Tenn., 1943. Resident Dallas Meth. Hosp., 1948; tchg. resident Tufts Med. Sch., Boston, 1949-50; physician Jefferson City, Tenn., 1950-96. Author: The Muncys in the New World, 1988, People and Places in Jefferson County, Tennessee, 1994. Alderman Jefferson City, 1974-77; chmn. Jefferson City Planning Commn., 1976-79. Capt. M.C., U.S. Army, 1944-46. Recipient Commendation for work on Tenn. history Gov. Don Sundquist, Jefferson award Am. Inst. Pub. Svc., 1995, Covenant Health Platinum award, 2000; named to Lincoln Meml. U. Lit. and Profl. Halls of Fame, 1997. Mem. Tenn. Heart Assn. (pres. 1966-67), Hamblen County Med. Soc. (pres. 1960-61), Jefferson County Hist. Soc. (pres. 1993-94, historian 1995—). Republican. Baptist. Avocations: photography, gardening. Home: 1428 Russell Ave Jefferson City TN 37760-2216

MUND, GERALDINE, judge; b. L.A., July 7, 1943; d. Charles J. and Pearl M. BA, Brandeis U., 1965; MS, Smith Coll., 1967; JD, Loyola U., 1977. Bar: Calif. 1977. Bankruptcy judge U.S. Ctrl. Dist. Calif., 1984—, bankruptcy chief judge, 1997—2002. Past pres. Temple Israel, Hollywood, Calif.; past mem. Bd. Jewish Fedn. Coun. of Greater L.A. Mem. ABA, L.A. County Bar Assn. Office: 21041 Burbank Blvd Woodland Hills CA 91367-6606 Office Phone: 818-587-2840.

MUND, LORRAINE G. English studies educator, writer; b. Glemsford, Suffolk, Eng. d. Mario and Joan Muselli; m. Joseph Mund, May 29, 1965; children: Jemine, Lorna, Kristin. BA in English, St. Josephs Coll., 1962; MA in English, Columbia U., 1964; PhD in English, La Salle U., 1997. Asst. prof. Five Towns Coll., Merrick, N.Y., 1976-78; instr. SUNY, Old Westbury, N.Y., 1978-96. Part-time instr. SUNY, Stony Brook, 1997-99; adj. prof. Nassau Coll., Garden City, N.Y., 1974—; workshop dir. East Meadow (N.Y.) Sch., 1995, 96; dir. Old Westbury Poetry Ctr., 1994-96; guest spkr. Rotary, Hicksville, N.Y., 1997, 98, 99. Author numerous short stories; author: Poetry, Like an IV...., 2000; editor Poetry Jour. SUNY, 1994-96. Performer, singer Camcos, N.Y. chpt. Mem. Internat. Found. Freedom Women (spkr.), Women's Faculty Assn. Avocations: teaching, writing, conducting workshops. Home: 40 Alpine Ln Hicksville NY 11801

MUNDAY, ROBERT STEVENSON, priest, academic administrator; b. Benton, Ill., Oct. 19, 1954; s. Robert Meade and Kathryn (McCollum) M.; m. Christina Ellen Karroll, July 31, 1976. BA, So. Ill. U., 1976; MDiv, Mid-Am. Bapt. Theol. Sem., Memphis, 1979, PhD, 1984; MLS, Vanderbilt U., 1986; postgrad., Duquesne U., U. of the South, Sewanee, Tenn. Ordained priest Episcopal Ch., 1990. Chaplain St. Jude Children's Rsch. Hosp., Memphis, 1981-84; instr. Mid-Am. Bapt. Theol Sem., Memphis, 1984-86; libr. dir. Trinity Episcopal Sch. for Ministry, Ambridge, Pa., 1986—2001, prof. systematic theology, 1986—2001, assoc. dean for administrn., 1987-94, assoc. dean planning and policy, 1994-97, assoc. dean for libr. and info. svcs., 1997—2001; pres., dean Nashotah House Theol. Sem., Wis., 2001—. Dep. to the gen. conv. Episcopal Ch., 1994, 97, 2000, 03, prof. Systematic Theology, 2001--. Chmn. bd. dirs. Life Choices, Memphis, 1984-86; bd. dirs. Cen. Pitts. Crisis Pregnancy Ctr., 1989-2001, pres., 1990-95; bd. dirs. Pregnancy Care Ctrs. Pitts., 1995-2001, pres., 1996-2001; bd. dirs. S.Am. Missionary Soc., 2001--. Mem. Nat. Orgn. Episcopalians for Life (bd. dirs., pres. 1991-94), Fairfax Va., Theol. Edn. Commn., Episcopal Synod Am., Am. Acad. Religion, Am. Theol. Libr. Assn., Brotherhood St. Andrew (life), Fellowship of St. Alban and St. Se[illegible]gius, Oblate, Order of St. Benedict. Office: Nashotah House Theol Sem [illegible] Mission Rd Nashotah WI 53058 Home: 2777 Mission Rd Nashota[illegible]-9790 *Life is about possibility and transformation—the possi[illegible]ed above mere human existence to be the creatures we [illegible] of God. The possiblility of that transformation is the [illegible]tion in Jesus Christ.*

[illegible]LE, writer, artist; b. Haskell, Tex., Mar. 10, 1949; [illegible] Laverne Stuteville, June 19, 1981. BA, West [illegible] ranch editor Abilene (Tex.) Reporter-News, [illegible]man Tex. and Southwestern Cattle Raisers Assn., Fort Worth, 1972-74; info. dir. Tex. Cattle Feeders Assn., Amarillo, 1974; freelance writer Arlington, Tex., 1974-76; dir. field svcs. Simmental Shield Mag. Am. Simmental Assn., Arlington, Tex., 1975; editl. dir. The Cattleman Mag. Tex. and Southwestern Cattle Raisers Assn, Fort Worth, 1976-78; news dir. Tex. and Southwestern Cattle Raisers Assn., Fort Worth, 1978-81, adminstrv. asst. media and govt. rels., 1981-95, exec. v.p., 1995-2001. Asst. sec. Tex. and Southwestern Cattle Raisers Found., Fort Worth, 1995-2001; sec.-treas. Tex. and Southwestern Cattle Raisers Assn. Ins. Svcs., Inc., Ft. Worth, 1995-2001, Tex. and Southwestern Cattle Raisers Assn. Legal Def. Fund, 1995-2001. Editor: TSCRA News Update, 1979-1995(1st pl. gen. excellence Livestock Pubs. Coun. 1986, 88, 90-91, 2d pl., 1989). Bd. dirs. Hist. Camp Bowie, Inc., Fort Worth, 2001. Capt. U.S. Army, 1971-99. Mem. AARP, Southwestern Cattle Raisers Assn. (treas. polit. action com. 1995-2001). Avocations: reading, painting, cartooning, travel, collectibles. Home: 3415 Bristol Rd Fort Worth TX 76107 E-mail: cowscribe@msn.com.

MUNDELL, ROBERT ALEXANDER, economist, educator; b. Kingston, Ont., Can., Oct. 24, 1932; s. William C. and Lila (Knifton) Mundell; m. Barbara Sheff, Oct. 14, 1957 (div. 1972); children: Paul Alexander, William Andrew, Robyn Leslie; m. Valerie Sophia Natsios, Nov. 10, 1998; 1 child, Nicholas Robert. BA, U. B.C., Can., 1953; postgrad., U. Wash., 1953—54, London Sch. Econs. and Polit. Sci., 1955—56; PhD, MIT, 1956; postdoc., U. Chgo., 1956—57; PhD (hon.), Renmin U. China, 1985, U. Paris, 1992. Instr. econs. U. B.C., Vancouver, Canada, 1957—58; acting asst. prof. econs. Stanford U., Calif., 1958—59; vis. prof. econs. Sch. Advanced Internat. Studies, Johns Hopkins U. Ctr., Bologna, Italy, 1959—61; sr. economist research dept. IMF, Washington, 1961—63; vis. prof. econs. McGill U., Montreal, Canada, 1963—64; Rockefeller vis. research prof. internat. econs. Brookings Instn., Washington, 1964—65; prof. Grad. Inst. Internat. Studies, Geneva, 1965—75; Ford Found. vis. research prof. econs. U. Chgo., 1965—66, prof., 1966—71; prof. econs., chmn. dept. U. Waterloo, Canada, 1972—74; prof. econs. Columbia U., N.Y.C., 1974—. Marshall lectr. Cambridge U.,, 1974; economist Can. Royal Commn on Price Spreads on Food Products, 1957; mem. joint fiscal mission to Peru OAS and Inter-am. Devel. Bank, 1964; cons. FRS, IBRD, 1966—, U.S. Treasury Dept., 1969—74, EEC, 1970—73, UN, Govt. Panama; organizer, participant internat. confs.; lectr. numerous univs. and profl. orgn. meetings; hon. prof. Renmin U. China, Beijing. Author: The Internat. Monetary System- Conflict and Reform, 1965, Man and Economics, 1968, International Economics, 1968, Monetary Theory- Interest, Inflation and Growth in the World Economy, 1971; contbr. articles to profl. jours.; co-editor: Monetary Problems of the International Economy, 1969, Trade Blaance of Payments and Growth, 1971, The International Monetary System, 1977; editor: Jour. Polit. Economy, 1966—70, Global Disequilibrium in the World Economy, 1989, 1992, Building the New Europe, 1991, Debt, Deficit and Economic Importance, 1990, Inflation and Growth in China, 1996. Named Companion of Order of Can., 2003; recipient James Rueff medal, 1983, Nobel prize in Econs., 1999; fellow, Guggenheim, 1970—71; grantee, NSF, 1967—70. Fellow: AAAS, 1998; mem.: Am. Econ. Assn. (Disting. fellow 1997). Office: Dept Econs Columbia U 1031 Internat Affairs 420 W 118th St # Mc3308 New York NY 10027-7213*

MUNDHEIM, ROBERT HARRY, law educator; b. Hamburg, Germany, Feb. 24, 1933; m. Guna Smitchens; children: Susan, Peter. BA, Harvard U., 1954, LLB, 1957; MA (hon.), U. Pa., 1971. Bar: N.Y. 1958, Pa. 1979. Assoc. Shearman & Sterling, N.Y.C., 1958-61; spl. counsel to SEC Washington, 1962-63; vis. prof. Duke Law Sch., Durham, N.C., 1964; prof. law U. Pa., Phila., 1965—. Univ. prof. law and fin., 1980-93, dean, 1982-89, Bernard G. Segal prof. law, 1987-89; co-chmn. Fried, Frank, Harris, Shriver & Jacobson, NYC, 1990-92; exec. v.p., gen. counsel Salomon Inc., 1992-97; sr. exec. v.p., gen. counsel Salomon Smith Barney Holdings, Inc., 1997-98; of counsel Shearman & Sterling, 1999—; gen. counsel U.S. Dept. Treasury, Washington, 1977-80, trustee, pres. Am. Acad. in Berlin, 2000—; chmn. legal adv. bd. NASDAQ, chmn. legal adv. bd. NASD; pres. Appleseed Found.; trustee New Sch. U.; coun. Am. Law Inst.; bd. dirs. eCollege, Arnhold & S. Bluchroder; gen. counsel Chrysler Loan Guarantee Bd., 1980; mng. dir., mgmt. bd. Salomon Bros. Inc., NYC, 1992-97; overseer Curtis Inst. Fin., 2000—; supervisory bd. Hypo Real Estate. Author: Outside Director of the Publicity Held Corporation, 1976; American Attitudes Toward Foreign Direct Investment in the United States, 1979; Conflict of Interest and the Former Government Employee: Re-thinking the Revolving Door, 1981; chmn. adv. bd. Jour. Internat. Econ. Law, 1996-97. Trustee SEC Hist. Soc. With USAF, 1961-62. Recipient Alexander Hamilton award U.S. Dept. Treasury, 1980, Harold P. Seligson award Practicing Law Inst., 1988, Francis J. Rawle award, ABA-ALI, 1992, Anti-Defamation League Human Rels. award, 1999. Mem. ABA (task force on corp. responsiblity), Am. Law Inst., San Diego Securities Regulation Inst. (exec. com.). Office: Shearman & Sterling 599 Lexington Ave Fl 16 New York NY 10022-6069

MUNDIE, CRAIG R. information technology executive; BEE, M in Info. Theory and Computer Sci., Ga. Inst. Tech. Software developer Data Gen. Corp., 1972; co-founder, CEO Alliant Computer Systems Corp., 1982—92; head consumer platforms divsn. Microsoft, Redmond, Wash., 1992, v.p., advanced consumer tech. group, 1993, sr. v.p. advanced strategies, sr. v.p., chief tech. officer of advanced strategies and policy, 2002—. Mem. Nat. Security Telecom. Adv. Com., Pres. Clinton, 2000. Office: Microsoft One Microsoft Way Redmond WA 98052-6399

MUNDINGER, DONALD CHARLES, retired college president; b. Chgo., Sept. 2, 1929; s. George Edward and Bertha (Trelkenberg) M.; m. June Myrtle Grubbe, June 17, 1951; children: Debra Sue, Donald William, Mary Ruth (dec.). Student, U. Ill., 1947-48; BA, Concordia Coll., River Forest, Ill., 1951, LLD (hon.), 1982; MA, Northwestern U., 1952; PhD, Washington U., St. Louis, 1956; DH (hon.), MacMurray Coll., Jacksonville, Ill., 1984, Ritsumeikan U., Kyoto, Japan, 1992; LLD (hon.), Ill. Coll., Jacksonville, 1993; postdoctoral study, Cambridge U. (Eng.), 1967-68. Asst. prof. polit. sci., chmn. dept. Augustana Coll., Sioux Falls, S.D., 1956-58; asst. prof. govt. Valparaiso (Ind.) U., 1958-61, assoc. prof., 1961-65, prof., 1965-73; dean Valparaiso (Ind.) U. (Coll. Arts and Scis.), 1965-67; dir. Overseas Center, Cambridge, Eng., 1967-68, v.p. acad. affairs, 1968-73; pres. Ill. Coll., Jacksonville, 1973-93; chmn. Fedn. Ind. Ill. Colls. and Univs., 1975-78; chmn. non-public adv. com. Ill. Bd. Higher Edn., 1988-91. Postdoctoral fellow Center Study Higher Edn., U. Mich., 1964-65; chmn. bd. Council Ind. Colls., 1988-90. Contbr. articles to profl. jours. Mem. Ill. State Bar Assn. (com. on fed. judicial and related appointments 1983-89), Nat. Assn. Ind. Colls. and Univs. (commn. on new initiatives, 1988-90), Pi Sigma Alpha, Phi Eta Sigma. Home: 3803 Pheasant Walk Dr Valparaiso IN 46383-2205

MUNDINGER, MARY O'NEIL, nursing educator; b. Fredonia, N.Y., Apr. 27, 1937; d. Thomas Lewis and Dorothy (Hanselman) O'Neil; m. Paul C. Mundinger, Aug. 23, 1958; children: Paul Jr., Ann Mundinger Schimenti, Thomas, Elizabeth. BS, U. Mich., 1959; MA, Columbia U., 1974, PhD, 1981. Adminstr., instr. Tchrs. Coll. Columbia U., N.Y.C., 1975; adj. instr. Pace U., N.Y.C., 1975-77, asst. prof., 1977-82; asst. prof. nursing, dir. grad. program Columbia U. Sch. Nursing, N.Y.C., 1982-83, assoc. prof. nursing, dir. grad. program, 1983-84, assoc. prof., assoc. dean adminstrv. affairs, 1984-85, assoc. prof., asst. dean faculty of medicine, 1986—, dean, Centennial prof. health policy, 1986—. Bd. dirs. Conn. Hospice, Branford; adv. group steering com. N.Y. Acad. Medicine, N.Y.C., 1992—; regional adv. com. Nat. Network Librs. of Medicine, N.Y.C., 1992—; Robert Wood Johnson health policy fellows bd. Inst. Medicine, Washington, 1990—, Health Svcs. Improvement Fund, N.Y.C., 1992—, health policy adv. com. Sen. Edward Kennedy, Washington, 1985—, med. adv. bd. Walt Disney Imagineering (Wonders of Life), Orlando, Fla., 1988-89; charter mem. health care tech., Inst. Medicine, NAS, 1985—. Author: Home Care Controversy: Too Little, Too Late, Too Costly, 1983 (Book of Yr. 1984), Autonomy in Nursing, 1980 (Book of Yr. 1981). Recipient grant W.K. Kellogg Found., 1989, grant Katzenbach Found., 1986. Avocations: skiing, reading. Office: Office of Dean of Nursing 630 W 168th St Box 6 New York NY 10032-3702 Fax: (212) 305-1116.

MUNDT, BARRY MAYNARD, management consultant; b. San Francisco, June 28, 1936; s. Kenneth Francis and Janet (Doughty) M.; m. Sally Hanscom, June 13, 1960; children: Kevin Warren, Trevor Stevens, Stacey Corbin BS in Indsl. Engring., Stanford U., 1959; MBA, U. Santa Clara, 1964. Registered indsl. engr., Calif. Statistician Aerojet-Gen., Sacramento, 1957-58; reliability engr. Lockheed Missiles, Sunnyvale, Calif., 1959-61; mgmt. engr. C-E-I-R, Inc., Los Altos, Calif., 1961-65; sr. cons. Peat, Marwick, Livingston & Co., Los Angeles, 1965-68; mgr., prin. Peat, Marwick, Mitchell & Co., Atlanta, 1968-84; ptnr.-in-charge, ops. mgmt. cons. KPMG Peat Marwick Main & Co., N.Y.C., 1984-88; internat. mgmt. cons. ptnr. KPMG Internat., N.Y.C. and Amsterdam, The Netherlands, 1988-92; mgmt. cons., ptnr. KPMG Peat Marwick U.S., Montvale, N.J., 1992-95; prin. The Strategy Facilitation Group, Rowayton, Conn., 1995—. Pres. Thomas Place Assoc., 1998—. Author-editor: Managing Public Resources, 1982; co-author Il Manager Pubblico (Italy), 1986; mem. editl. bd., contbg. author Handbook of Industrial Engineering, 3rd edit., 2001; contbr. articles to profl. jours. Mem. ann. campaign Atlanta Symphony Orch., 1974-82, Atlanta Arts Alliance, 1976-81; del. to assembly United Way of Met. Atlanta, 1974-84; bd. chmn., mem. Brandon Hall Sch., Atlanta, 1980—2002. Fellow Inst. Indsl. Engrs. (treas. 1976-81, pres. 1982-83, asst. treas. 1985-92); mem. Thomas Pl. Assn. (pres.), Norwalk Yacht Club. Episcopalian. Avocations: golf, boating. Home and Office: 21 Thomas Pl Norwalk CT 06853-1500 Office Phone: 203-831-9107. Personal E-mail: bmundt@optonline.net.

MUNDY, PETER, psychology educator; b. Port of Spain, Trinidad and Tobago, May 13, 1954; s. Philip Mundy and Daphne Hyde; m. Kim Fuller, July 13, 1986; 1 child, Erin Fuller. PhD, U. of Miami, 1981. Lic. psychology Fla. Clin. asst. prof. UCLA Neuropsychiat. Inst., 1986—91; prof. psychology U. of Miami, Coral Gables, Fla., 1991—. Exec. dir. Ctr. for Autism and Related Disabilities, Coral Gables, 1993—. Contbr. papers to sci. jours. Mem.: Soc. of Rsch. on Child Devel. (assoc.). Office: U Miami 5665 Ponce De Leon Blvd Coral Gables FL 33146

MUNERA, GERARD EMMANUEL, manufacturing executive; b. Algiers, Algeria, Dec. 2, 1935; s. Gabriel and Laure (Labrousse) M.; m. Paule A. Ramos, July 28, 1959; children: Catherine, Philippe, Emmanuelle, Jean-Marie. M Math., M Physics, M Chemistry, Ecole Poly., Paris, 1956; CE, Ecole Ponts et Chaussees, Paris, 1959. Chief county engr. Dept. Rds. and Bridges, South Algiers, 1959-62; cons. French Ministry Fgn. Affairs, Argentina, 1962-66; sr. v.p. fin. Camea Group Pechiney Ugine Kuhlmann, Buenos Aires, 1966-70, chmn. bd., chief exec. officer, 1976-77; exec. v.p. Howmet Aluminum Corp., Greenwich, Conn., 1976-77, pres., chief operating officer, 1977-79, pres., chief exec. officer, 1980-83; corporate v.p. nuclear fuels Pechiney, Brussels, 1983-85; vice chmn., chief exec. officer Union Minière, Brussels, 1985-89; head corp. planning and devel. RTZ, London, 1989-90; pres., CEO Minorco USA, Englewood, Colo., 1990-94, also bd. dirs.; chmn. and CEO Latin Am. Gold, Inc., N.Y.C., 1994-96, Synergex Inc., 1996—. Bd. dirs. Nevsun Resources, Inc., Meridian Gold Inc., Dynamic Materials Corp., Inc., Twin Mining Ltd.; chmn., CEO, Arcadia Inc., mng. ptnr. Synergex Group LLC. Patentee low-income housing system. Served with French Air Force, 1956-57. Decorated officer Legion of Honor (France). Roman Catholic. Office: Arcadia 60 Bonner St Stamford CT 06902-6610 Office Phone: 203-869-3919.

MUNERA, PEDRO ANTONIO, child and adolescent psychiatrist; b. Granollers, Spain, May 16, 1970; s. Pedro Munera and Dolores Cordoba; m. Sherry Lynn Rowlett, Mar. 7, 2003. MD, Univ. Autonoma de Barcelona, Barcelona, 1994. Psychiatry Am. Bd. of Psychiatry and Neurology, 2002. Child and adolescent psychiatrist Weems Cmty. Mental Health Ctr., Meridian, Miss., 2003—; clin. asst. prof. Dept of Psychiatry, U. of Miss., Jackson, Miss., 2003—. Chmn. mems. in tng. com. Tex. Soc. of Psychiat. Physicians, Austin, 1998—2000; mem. resident and early career psychiatrist com. Am. Acad. of Child and Adolescent Psychiatry, Washington, 2002—. Author: (book review) Jour. of the Am. Acad. of Child and Adolescent Psychiatry, (case report) Jour. of the Am. Acad.of Child and Adolescent Psychiatry (Resident of the Yr., Pharm. Co. grant, 2001), Jour. of Child and Adolescent Psychopharmacology. Mem.: Miss. Psychiat. Assn. (assoc.), Am. Acad. of Child and Adolescent Psychiatry (assoc.; residents and early career psychiatrists com. 2002—03), Am. Psychiat. Assn. (assoc.). Roman Catholic. Avocations: travel, reading. Office: U of Miss Med Ctr 2500 N State St Jackson MS 39216 Personal E-mail: pmunera@pol.net.

MUNERLYN, LORRAINE, administrative secretary, writer; b. Flint, Mich., Dec. 23, 1958; d. Lurane Allen; m. Raydell Munerlyn, Sr., Nov. 16, 1979; children: Raydell, Jr., Jordan Earl, Stephanie. Deputized Correctional Chaplain Forgotten Man Min., Mich., 2002. Line worker Gen. Motors V-8 Engine, Flint, Mich., 1977—79, Gen. Motors Buick Plant, Flint, Mich., 1980—81, Gen. Motors Buick, Olds, Cadillac, Lake Orion, Mich., 1984—92; deputized chaplain Forgotten Man Ministries, Grand Rapids, Mich., 2002—; adminstrv. sec. Five Fold Outreach Ministries, Flint, Mich., 2002—. Author: (collection of poems) From God's Lips To My Ears Insp. Poems (Life As It Lay); composer: (poetry in songs) Project Song of Praise- songs Guardian Angel's Love with Amerecord, (songs) America At War: Unforgettable Men & Women at War. Recipient Award of Merit in Writing, Amherst Soc., 2001, Hon. Mention, Iliad Press, 2002, Cert. of award Teacher's Tng., New Beginings Ministries, 2002—. Avocations: cooking, poetry, drawing, singing, landscaping. Home: 1101 Milbourne Ave Flint MI 48504-3367 Office: Poetess Lorraine/Inspirational Poems PO Box 4203 Flint MI 48504-3367 Office Phone: 1-810-423-2175. Home Fax: 1-810-238-9002. Personal E-mail: lmunerlyn@prodigy.net.

MUNGER, BENSON SCOTT, former professional society administrator; b. St. Johns, Mich., Jan. 21, 1942; s. Kenneth L. and Doris (Benson) M.; m. Bette Louise Johnson, June 15, 1963; children: Heidi Lynn, Chad Benson BA, Mich. State U., 1965, PhD, 1969. Tchr. Grand Ledge Pub. Schs., Mich., 1965-66; mem. staff Southwest Regional Lab, Los Angeles, 1969-70; dir. negotiations Mich. Edn. Assn., East Lansing, 1970-75; vis. asst.prof. Indsl. Relations Ctr., U. Minn., Mpls., 1975-76; dep. exec. dir. Am. Coll. Emergency Physicians, 1976-80; exec. dir. Am. Bd. Emergency Medicine, East Lansing, Mich., 1980-2000, chmn. com. bd. execs., 1991; exec. dir. Am. Bd. Vascular Surgery, 2002—. Commr. City of St. Johns, 1983—; bd. dirs. Old Kent Bank, St. Johns; cons. in field; chmn. com. bd. reps. and execs. Am. Bd. Med. Specialties, 1995—. Contbr. articles in field Mich. State U. fellow, 1966-69 Mem. Am. Soc. Assn. Execs., Am. Assn. Med. Soc. Execs. Office: Am Bd Vascular Surgery 221 W Walton Chicago IL 60610

MUNGER, BRYCE LEON, physician, educator; b. Everett, Wash., May 20, 1933; s. Leon C. and Lina (Eaton) M.; m. Donna Grace Bingham, July 20, 1957; children: Ailene, D'Arcy, Gareth Torrey, Bryce Kirtley. Student. U. Wash., 1951-54; MD magna cum laude, Wash. U., 1958. Intern in pathology Johns Hopkins U., 1958-59; investigator Armed Forces Inst. Pathology USAF, Washington, 1959—61; asst. prof. anatomy Washington U., St. Louis, 1961-65; assoc. prof. U. Chgo., 1965-66; prof. Milton S. Hershey Med. Ctr., Pa. State U., 1966-91, chmn. dept. anatomy, 1966-87; prof., head dept. anatomy U. Tasmania, Hobart, and Tasmania, Australia, 1992-96; adj. prof. anatomy Ariz. Coll. Osteo. Medicine, Midwestern U., Glendale, 1999. Bd. dirs. Pa. Spl. Olympics Inc. Mem. AAAS, Am. Assn. Anatomists, Am. Soc. Cell Biology, Phi Beta Kappa, Sigma Xi, Alpha Omega Alpha.

MUNGER, CHARLES T. diversified company executive; b. 1924; married. Ptnr. Wheeler Munger & Co., 1961-76; chmn., CEO, Blue Chip Stamps, 1976-78; vice chmn. Berkshire Hathaway, Inc., Omaha, 1978—, also chmn., CEO Wesco Fin. subs. Office: Berkshire Hathaway Inc 1440 Kiewit Plz Omaha NE 68131-3302

MUNGER, EDWIN STANTON, political geography educator; b. LaGrange, Ill., Nov. 19, 1921; s. Royal Freeman and Mia (Stanton) M.; m. Ann Boyer, May 2, 1970; 1 child, Elizabeth Stanton Gibson. B.Sc., U. Chgo., 1948, M.Sc., 1949, PhD, 1951. Fulbright fellow Makerere U., 1949-50; research fellow U. Chgo.; field assoc. Am. Univs. Field Staff, 1950-60; faculty Calif. Inst. Tech., Pasadena, 1961—, prof. polit. geography, 1960—. Research fellow Stellen-

bosch U., 1955-56; vis. prof. U. Warsaw, 1973 Author books including Afrikaner and African Nationalsim, 1968, The Afrikaners, 1979, Touched by Africa: An Autobiography, 1983, Cultures, Chess and Art: A Collector's Odyssey Across Seven Continents, Vol. 1 Sub Saharan Africa, 1996, Vol. 2, Americas, 1997, Pacific Islands and the Asian Rim, Vol. 3, 1999, 10 short stories for kids--L.A. Times on Africa, 2001-02; editor books including Munger Africana Library Notes, 1969-82; contbr. chpts. to books and numerous articles to profl. jours. Evaluator Peace Corps, Uganda, 1966, Botswana, 1967; chmn. State Dept. Evalustion Team South Africa, 1971; trustee African-Am. Inst., 1956-62; acting pres. Pasadena Playhouse, 1966; chmn. bd. trustees Crane Rogers Found., 1979-82, fellow, 1950-54; mem. exec. com. NAACP, Pasadena, 1979—, nat. del., 1984, 85; trustee Leakey Found., 1968—, pres., 1971-84; pres. Cape of Good Hope Found., 1985—; pres. Internat. Vis. Coun., L.A., 1991-93, bd. dirs., 1979-93. Recipient Alumni Citation award for pub. svc. U. Chgo., 1993, Gandhi Martin Luther King-Ikeda award Morehouse U., 2002. Fellow South African Royal Soc., Royal Soc. Arts, African Studies Assn. (founding bd. dirs. 1963-66, Martin L. King Ikeda-Mahatma Gandhi award 2002); mem. PEN USA West (v.p.), Coun. Fgn. Rels., Cosmos Club, Athenaeum Club, Twilight Club, Chess Collectors Internat. (bd. dirs. 1998—). Office: Calif Inst Tech Divsn Humanities & Social Scis 1201 E California Blvd Pasadena CA 91125-0001 E-mail: munger@hss.caltech.edu.

MUNGER, ELMER LEWIS, civil engineer, educator; b. Manhattan, Kans., Jan. 4, 1915; s. Harold Hawley and Jane (Green) M.; m. Vivian Marie Bloomfield, Dec. 28, 1939; children: John Thomas, Harold Hawley II, Jane Marie. BS, Kans. State U., 1936, MS, 1938, PhD, Iowa State U., 1957. Registered profl. engr., Nebr., Kans., Iowa, Vt.; registered pvt. land surveyor Republic of The Philippines. Rodman St. Louis-Southwestern Ry., Ark., Mo., 1937-38; engr. U.S. Engr. Dept., Ohio, Nebr., 1938-46; missionary engr. Philippine Episcopal Ch., 1946-48; engr. Wilson & Co., Salina, Kans., 1948; tchr. Iowa State U., 1948-51, 54-58; engr. C.E., U.S. Army, Alaska, 1951-54; from tchr. to dean Norwich U., Northfield, Vt., 1958-69; prof. gen. engring. U. P.R., Mayagüez, 1969-75; prof. civil engring. Mich. Tech. U., 1975-80; ret. Mem. spl. com. on engring. Inter-Am. Devel. Bank, U. W.I., 1971. Author: (with Clarence J. Douglas) Construction Management, 1970. Fellow ASCE; mem NSPE, Vt. Soc. Profl. Engrs., Am. Soc. Engring. Edn., Phi Kappa Phi, Sigma Tau, Tau Beta Pi, Chi Epsilon. Clubs: Masons, Shriners. Episcopalian.

MUNGER, PAUL DAVID, company executive, educational administrator; b. Selma, Ala., Oct. 12, 1945; s. Paul Francis and Arlene Lorraine (McFillen) M.; m. Paula Jean Dominici, May 30, 1969; children: Kimberley Beth, Christopher David. AB in Philosophy, Kenyon Coll., 1967; MA in Govt., Ind. U., 1969. Commd. 2d lt. USAF, 1969, advanced through grades to capt., resigned, 1978; asst. dir. faculty devel. Ind. U., Bloomington, 1974-77; from asst. dean to dean continuing studies Am. U., Washington, 1980-83, asst. provost acad. devel., 1983-84; dir. Commn. on Future Acad. Leadership, Washington, 1984-86; v.p. Acad. Strategies, Washington, 1986-88; pres. Strategic Edn. Svcs. Inc., Sterling, Va., 1988—. Bd. dirs. Munger Acad., 1989—. Bd. advisors Madeira Sch., McLean, Va., 1993-96; treas. Bus.-Higher Edn. Fedn., Washington, 1992-2000; asst. scoutmaster Boy Scouts Am., 1991-93, scoutmaster, 1994-97; dir. Czech-Am. Lacrosse Found., 1996—; bd. dirs. Thomas Jefferson H.S. for Sci. and Tech. Found., 1999-2001, PTSA, 1996-98, chair bus. rels. com., 1996-98. Mem. Am. Soc. Tng. & Devel. (chmn. strategic planning com. 1993-95, continuing profl. edn. electronic forum coord. 1995-97), Assn. Continuing Higher Edn., Am. Soc. Curriculum Devel. Office: Strat Edn Svs 624 W Church Rd Sterling VA 20164-4608 Office Phone: 703-430-5759. Business E-Mail: pdmunger@strategicedservices.com.

MUNGER, PAUL R. civil engineering educator; b. Hannibal, Mo, Jan. 14, 1932; s. Paul O and Anne M.; m. Frieda Anna Mette, Nov. 26, 1954; children: Amelia Ann Munger Fortmeyer, Paul David, Mark James, Martha Jane Munger Cox. BSCE, Mo. Sch. Mines and Metallurgy, 1958, MSCE, 1961; PhD in Engring. Sci., U. Ark., 1972. Registered profl. engr., Mo., Ill., Ark. Instr. civil engring Mo. Sch. Mines and Metallurgy, Rolla, 1958-61, asst. prof., 1961-65; assoc. prof. U. Mo., Rolla, 1965-73, prof., 1973-99; dir. Inst. River Studies, U. Mo., Rolla, 1976-93; exec. dir. Internat. Inst. River and Lake Systems, U. Mo., Rolla, 1984-93, interim chmn. CE dept., 1998-99, prof. emeritics of CE, 2000—. Mem. NSPE, Mo. Soc. Profl. Engr., Am. Soc. Engring. Edn., ASCE, Nat. Coun. Engring. Examiners (pres. 1983-84), Mo. Bd. Architects, Profl. Engr. and Land Surveyors (chmn. 1978-84, 95-2002).

MUNGER, SHARON, market research firm executive; m. Robert Munger; 3 children: Shawn, Shane, Blair. Grad. Vanderbilt U. Sec., data processor, acct. exec. M/A/R/C, Inc., Irving, Tex., from 1973; now pres., chief operating officer Irving, Tex. Office: M-A-R-C Inc 7850 N Belt Line Rd Irving TX 75063-6098

MUNGIA, SALVADOR ALEJO, lawyer; b. Tacoma, Feb. 19, 1959; s. Salvador Alejo Sr. and Susie (Tamaki) M. BA, Pacific Luth. U., 1981; JD, Georgetown U., 1984. Bar: Wash. 1984, U.S. Dist. Ct. (we. dist.) Wash. 1985, U.S. Ct. Appeals (9th cir.) 1986, U.S. Supreme Ct. 1992. Law clk. to Justice Fred Dore Wash. State Supreme Ct., Olympia, 1984-85; law clk. to Hon. Carolyn R. Dimmick U.S. Dist. Ct. (we. dist.) Wash., Seattle, 1985-86; assoc. Gordon, Thomas, Honeywell, Malanca, Peterson & Daheim, Tacoma, 1986-91, ptnr., 1991—. Adj. prof. Pacific Luth. U., 1993-94. Vol. atty. ACLU, Tacoma, 1986—, bd. dirs., 1987-92; commr. Tacoma Human Rights Commn., 1990-96; bd. dirs. Legal Aid for Washington, 1992-96, life bd. dirs., 1997—, pres., 2002-03; dir. bd. dirs. Grand Cinema, Tacoma, 2002-04. Recipient Am. Leadership Forum fellowship, 2001—02. Mem.: ABA, Pierce County Young Lawyers Assn. (trustee 1988—90), Tacoma-Pierce County Bar Assn. (pres. 1999), Fed. Bar Assn. Western Wash., Wash. State Bar Assn., Tacoma Club, Tacoma Lawn Tennis Club. Avocations: mountain climbing, skiing, tennis, running. Home: 2804 N McCarver St Tacoma WA 98403 Office: Gordon Thomas Honeywell Malance Peterson & Daheim PO Box 1157 Tacoma WA 98401-1157 E-mail: mungs@gth-law.com.

MUNHALL, RUTH BEATRICE, business and financial consultant; b. Mendon, Mass., Feb. 8, 1929; d. Lawrence B. and Elsie B. (Gaskill) Munhall. Grad., Salvation Army Officers Coll., Bronx, 1951; MBA, Calif. Coast U., 1980, PhD, DBA, 1981. Civilian supr. U.S. Army and VA Hosp., Framingham, Mass., 1946—50; officer, ordained clergywoman Salvation Army, various locations Mass., N.Y., N.J., 1951—64; owner, operator acctg. and real estate firm N.Y.C., 1964—68; supr. fiduciary and individual taxation Bank of N.Y., N.Y.C., 1968—79; cons. nonprofit orgns., founder R.M. Scholarship Info. Svcs., Ark., N.Y., Mass., Israel, 1981—89; pres., CEO Mu7nhall, Monahan, Chapman Fiduciary Animal Charities, Inc., 1984—; pres. Munhall Rsch. Sci. Corp., 1985—97. Cons. in field. Author: (booklet) Enlish, French, Hebrew, Spanish for the Traveler, 1990. Recipient 5 Yr. Civil Def. award, Gov. N.Y. State. Mem.: DAR, Alumni Assn. Calif. Coast U. Republican.

MUNIC, RACHELLE ETHEL, health services administrator; b. Hartford, Conn., Apr. 15, 1953; d. Abe and Sara (Levenberg) M. BS in Med. Tech. summa cum laude, U. Bridgeport, 1975; physician asst. cert., Yale U., 1979; MBA in Health & Med. Svcs. Adminstrn., Widener U., 1991. Med. technologist St. Francis Hosp., Hartford, 1975-77; physician asst. Fox Chase Cancer Ctr., Phila., 1979-85; clin. dir. Fox Chase Network, Phila., 1986-92; adminstrv. dir., oncology Cooper Hosp., U. Med. Ctr., Camden, N.J., 1992-96, healthcare cons., 1996—; corp. mgr. cancer svcs. Grad. Health Sys., Phila., 1996—; cancer svc. line adminstr. Albert Einstein Med. Ctr., Phila., 1996-99; adminstrv. dir. divsn. med. oncology, hematology & genetics Jefferson U., Phila., 1999-2001; asst. v.p. Cooper Health Sys., 2001—. Mem. Cancer Prevention and Control Adv. Group to N.J. Commn. on Cancer Rsch., New Brunswick, N.J., 1993-96; mem. program com. Greater Phila. Health Assembly, 1996; presenter in field. Dana scholar U. Bridgeport, 1972; recipient Foster G. McGaw Scholarship award Assn. Univ. Programs in Health Adminstrn., 1990, Student award Hosp. Assn. Pa., 1992; Breast Cancer project grantee The Susan G. Komen Breast Cancer Found., Dallas, 1995. Mem. Am. Hosp. Assn., Am. Cancer Soc. (Camden County), Assn. Cancer Execs., Soc. Radiation Oncology Adminstrs., Assn. Cmty. Cancer Ctrs. (del.), Widener Alumni Assn. (pres. 1995), U. Bridgeport Asteria Honor Soc. Avocations: softball, golf, swimming, cross country skiing, reading.

MUNIER, WILLIAM BOSS, medical service executive; b. Corning, N.Y., Dec. 8, 1942; s. John Hammond and Marguerite (Boss) M.; m. Sandra Lorraine Koerber, 1965 (div. 1976); m. Ann Elizabeth Wessel, 1980; children: Michael, Andrew, Laura. BA, U. Pa., 1964; MD, Columbia U., 1968; MBA, Harvard U., 1973. Diplomate Nat. Bd. Med. Examiners; lic. physician, surgeon, N.Y. Surg. intern Roosevelt Hosp., N.Y.C., 1968-69; profl. staff HEW, Washington, 1969-71, 73-75, dir. Office Quality Standards, 1975-77, dir. Office Health Practice Assessment, 1977-79; exec. v.p. Mass. Med. Soc., Boston, 1979-84; prin. Ernst & Whinney, Boston, 1984-85; pvt. practice mgmt. cons. Wellesley, Mass., 1985-86; dir. program for civilian peer rev. Commn. on Profl. and Hosp. Activities/Dept. Def., 1986-87; pres. Quality Standards in Medicine, Inc., Boston, 1986-99; chief med. officer Health Mgmt. Sys., Inc., Waltham, Mass., 1996-99; pres., CEO Wang Healthcare Info. Sys., Inc., Billerica, Mass., 1999—. Vis. prof. Harvard Sch. Pub. Health, Boston, 1980-90. Contbr. articles to profl. jours. Mem. human services com. Town of Wellesley, 1984-85. Served with USPHS, 1969-79. Mem. AMA, Mass. Med. Soc., St. Botolph Club, Capitol Hill Club. Republican. Episcopalian. Avocations: golf, skiing, music. Office Phone: 617-510-8165.

MUNIO, DAVID J. bank executive; B of Mktg., MBA, UCLA, U. Calif, 2003. With 1st Interstate Bank; exec. v.p. loan supv. Wells Fargo & Co., 1996—99, exec. v.p., dep. chief credit officer, 1999—2001, exec. v.p., CEO, 2001—. Office: Wells Fargo & Co 420 Montgomery St San Francisco CA 94163

MUNISTERI, JOSEPH GEORGE, construction executive; b. Rome, Sept. 24, 1930; s. Peter P. and Inez Gertrude (Ziniti) Munisteri; m. Theresa Grasso, June 7, 1952 (div. Dec. 2000); children: Joanne, Robert, Laura, Stephen, James, Richard; m. Barbra Coffman, Nov. 30, 2001. BE, Yale U., 1952. With Bechtel Corp., San Francisco, 1952-59; with The Lummus Co., N.Y.C., London and Houston, 1959-67, gen. mgr., 1967—70; sr. v.p. sales Brown & Root, Inc., Houston, 1970—75, group v.p. power div., 1975-80, group v.p. corp. devel., 1980-81, also bd. dirs.; pres. Enserch Engrs. & Constructors, Inc., Houston, 1981-85; exec. v.p. Ford, Bacon & Davis, Inc., Dallas, 1985-87; chmn., pres., CEO Comstock Group, Inc., Danbury, Conn., 1987-88; pres. Joseph G. Munisteri Co., Houston, 1989—. Former chmn. bd. Pine-O-Pine. Former mem. Bd. dirs. Atomic Indsl. Forum; Bd. dirs. Am. Nuclear Energy Council. Mem. Atomic Indsl. Forum, Am. Inst. Chem. Engrs., Am. Nuclear Soc., Atomic Indsl. Forum, ASTM, Council Engring. Law, ASCE, Assn. Iron and Steel Engring., Assoc. Builders and Contractors (dir.), Yale Club of Houston, Yale Club of N.Y. Office: 4265 San Felipe St Ste 1100 Houston TX 77027-2998 Office Phone: 713-960-1272. E-mail: jmunisteri@houston.rr.com.

MUNITZ, BARRY, arts and foundation administrator; b. Bklyn., July 26, 1941; m. Anne Tomfohrde. BA, Bklyn. Coll., 1963; MA, Princeton U., 1965, PhD, 1968; cert., U. Leiden, Netherlands, 1962; hon. doctorate, Claremont U., Calif. State Univ. Sys., Whittier Coll., U. Notre Dame. Asst. prof. lit. and drama U. Calif., Berkeley, 1966-68; staff assoc. Carnegie Commn. Higher Edn., 1968-70; acad. v.p. U. Ill. System, 1971—76; v.p., dean faculties Central campus U. Houston, 1976-77, chancellor, 1977-82; pres., COO Federated Devel. Co., 1982-91; vice chmn. Maxxam Inc., L.A., 1982-91; chancellor Calif. State U. System, Long Beach, Calif., 1991-98; prof. English lit. Calif. State U., L.A., 1991—; pres., CEO, trustee J.Paul Getty Trust, L.A., 1998—. Bd. dirs. KCET-TV, SLM Holdings, KB Home; cons. in presdl. evaluation and univ. governance; trustee Princeton U. Author: The Assessment of Institutional Leadership, also articles, monographs. Mem. art mus. vis. com. Princeton and Harvard; former chair bd. dirs. ACE; former co-chair trustees planning com. Gardner Mus.; former chair Calif. Gov. Transition Team. Recipient Disting. Alumnus award Bklyn. Coll., 1979, U. Houston Alumni Pres.'s medal, 1981; Woodrow Wilson fellow. Fellow Am. Acad. Arts and Scis.; mem. Phi Beta Kappa. Office: J Paul Getty Trust 1200 Getty Center Dr Ste 400 Los Angeles CA 90049-1681 E-mail: bmunitz@getty.edu.

MUNIZ, FRANKIE (FRANCISCO JAMES MUNIZ IV), actor; b. Ridgewood, N.J., Dec. 5, 1985; s. Frank and Denise Muniz. Actor: (films) Lost & Found, 1999, Little Man, 1999, My Dog Skip, 2000, It Had to Be You, 2000, (voice) Dr. Dolittle 2, 2001, Big Fat Liar, 2002, Deuces Wild, 2002, Agent Cody Banks, 2003, Agent Cody Banks 2: Destination London, 2004; (TV films) To Dance with Olivia, 1997, What the Deaf Man Heard, 1997, Miracle in Lane 2, 2000; (TV series) Malcolm in the Middle, 2000— (Young Star award for Best Young Actor/Performance in a Comedy TV Series, 2000, Young Star award for Best Young Ensemble Cast - TV, 2000, Young Artist award for Best Ensemble in a Feature Film, 2001, Young Artist award for Best Performance in a TV Comedy Series - Leading Young Actor, 2002, Young Artist award for Best Ensemble in a TV Series (Comedy or Drama), 2003, Emmy nomination for Outstanding Lead Actor in a Comedy Series, 2001), (voice) The Fairly Odd Parents[], 2001—03, Moville Mysteries, 2002. Office: United Talent Agy Ste 500 9560 Wilshire Blvd Beverly Hills CA 90212*

MUNIZ, MARCO ANTONIO See ANTHONY, MARC

MUNK, PETER, mining executive; b. Budapest, Hungary, Nov. 8, 1927; arrived in Can., 1948; s. Louis L. and Katherine (Adler) M.; m. Linda Gutterson; children: Anthony, Nina; m. Melanie Jane Bosanquet, 1973; children: Natalie, Cheyne, Marc David. BASc in Elec. Engring., U. Toronto Ont., Can., 1953, LLD, 1995, Upsala Coll., N.J., 1991, U. Toronto, Que., Can., 1995, Bishops Coll., 1995, Concordia U., Montreal, Que., 1999. Chmn., chief exec. officer So. Pacific Hotel Corp., Sydney, Australia, 1969-81; chmn. Barrick Resources, Toronto, 1981-83, Am. Barrick Resources Corp. (now Barrick Gold Corp.), Toronto, 1983—, The Horsham Corp., Toronto, 1987-96; CEO Trizec Hahn Corp., Toronto, 1996—2000, chmn., 2001—; chmn., pres., CEO, Trizec Can. Inc., Toronto, 2002—. Chmn. Trizec Properties, Inc., 2001—. Decorated officer Order of Can. Office: Barrick Gold Corp 161 Bay St # 3700 Toronto ON Canada M5J 2S1

MUNK, WALTER HEINRICH, geophysics educator; b. Vienna, Oct. 19, 1917; arrived in U.S., 1933; m. Edith Kendall Horton, June 20, 1953; children: Edith, Kendall. BS, Calif. Inst. Tech., 1939, MS, 1940; PhD in Oceanography, U. Calif., 1947; PhD (hon.), U. Bergen, Norway, 1975; PhD (hon.), Cambridge (Eng.) U., 1986; PhD (hon.), U. Crete, 1996. Asst. prof. geophysics Scripps Inst. Oceanography, U. Calif., San Diego, 1947—54, prof., 1954—; dir. Inst. Geophysics and Planetary Physics, U. Calif., La Jolla, 1960—82; prof. geophysics, dir. heard island expt. Scripps Inst., U. Calif. Author (with MacDonald): The Rotation of the Earth: A Geophysical Discussion, 1960; author: (with Worcester and Wunsch) Ocean Acoustic Tomography, 1995; contbr. over 200 articles to profl. jours. Named Calif. Scientist of Yr., Calif. Mus. Sci. and Industry, 1969; recipient Albatross award, Am. Misc. Soc., 1959, Gold medal, Royal Astron. Soc., 1968, Nat. Medal of Sci., 1985, Marine Tech. Soc. award, 1969, Capt. Robert Dexter Conrad award, Dept. Navy, 1978, G. Unger Vetlesen prize, Columbia U., 1993, Presdl. award, N.Y. Acad. Scis., 1993, Rolex Lifetime Achievement award, 1997, Kyoto prize, 1999, Prince Albert I medal, 2001, Albert A. Michelson award, Navy League of the U.S., 2001; fellow Guggenheim Found., 1948, 1955, 1962, Overseas Found., 1962, 1981—82, Fulbright Found., 1981—82, sr. Queen's, 1978. Fellow: AAAS, Marine Tech. Soc. (Compass award 1991), Acoustical Soc. Am., Am. Meteorol. Soc. (Sverdrup Gold medal 1966), Am. Geophys. Union (Maurice Ewing medal 1976, William Bowie medal 1989); mem.: N.Y. Acad. Scis. (Presdl. award 1994), Am. Geol. Soc., Am. Acad. Arts and Scis. (Arthur L. Day medal 1965), Deutsche Akademie der Naturforscher Leopoldina, Russian Acad. Sci., Royal Soc. London (fgn. mem.), Am. Philos. Soc., NAS (chmn. ocean studies bd. 1985—88, Agassiz medal 1976). Office: U Calif San Diego Scripps Inst Oceanography 0225 La Jolla CA 92093 E-mail: wmunk@ucsd.edu.

MUNN, CECIL EDWIN, lawyer; b. Enid, Okla., Aug. 8, 1923; s. Cecil Edwin and Margaret (Kittrell) M.; m. Carolyn Taylor Culver, May 8, 1948; children: Franklin Culver, Charlotte Munn Forswall. BA, U. Okla., 1945; JD cum laude, Harvard U., 1947. Bar: Okla. 1948, Tex. 1956. Practice in, Enid, 1947-54, Ft. Worth, 1954—; partner firm Cantey & Hanger, Ft. Worth, 1960-91, of counsel, 1992—. With Champlin Petroleum Co., 1954-60, v.p., atty., 1958-60, dir., 1962-75. Fellow Am. Coll. Trial Lawyers, Am. Bar Found.; mem. ABA (chmn. natural resources law sect. 1970-71), Southwestern Legal Found. (past dir.), Tex. Bar Found., Phi Delta Theta, Phi Delta Phi. Presbyterian. Office: 2100 Burnett Plz 801 Cherry St Fort Worth TX 76102-6803 Home: 1725 Hulen St Fort Worth TX 76107-3828 *Some things in life are better decided wrong than left undecided. It is amazing how much one can accomplish if unconcerned with who gets the credit.*

MUNN, JANET TERESA, lawyer; b. De Funiak Springs, Fla., Nov. 7, 1952; d. Willard Ernest and Olive Pauline (Wilkinson) M.; m. Michael E. Fass, Sept. 27, 1975. BA in Anthropology, Fla. State U., 1975, MA in Social Scis., 1977; JD with high honors, Nova U., 1985. Bar: Fla. 1985, U.S. Dist. Ct. (so. dist.) Fla. 1986, U.S. Dist. Ct. (mid. dist.) Fla. 1988, U.S. Ct. Appeals (11th cir.) 1989, U.S. Supreme Ct. 1990. Jud. clerk for Judge Jose A. Gonzalez Jr. U.S. Dist. Ct. (so. dist.) Fla., Ft. Lauderdale, 1985-87; litigation assoc. Steel Hector & Davis, Miami, Fla., 1987-91, litigation ptnr., 1992—. Editor: Southern District Digest, 1987-88. Leo S. Goodwin fellow Nova U., 1983-84. Mem. ABA (co-chmn. intellectual properties litigation com. litigation sect. 1991-94, chmn. trade regulation/intellectual property com. gen. practice sect. 1990-91, vice chmn. 1989-90), Fed. Bar Assn., Fla. Bar (Pro Bono award 1988), Phi Kappa Phi. Office: 200 S Biscayne Blvd Ste 4000 Miami FL 33131-2362

MUNN, STEPHEN P. manufacturing executive; Pres., chief exec. officer Carlisle Cos. Inc., Cin., also bd. dirs. Bd. dirs. Carrier Corp. N.Y. Office: Carlisle Cos Inc 13925 Ballantyne Corpo Pl Charlotte NC 28277

MUNN, WILLIAM CHARLES, II, psychiatrist; b. Flint, Mich., Aug. 9, 1938; s. Elton Albert and Rita May (Coykendall) Munn; m. Sandra Lynn Munn; children from previous marriage: Jude Michael, Rachel Marie, Alexander Winston. Student, Flint Jr. Coll., 1958—59, U. Detroit, 1959—61; MD, Wayne State U., 1965. Diplomate Am. Bd. Psychiatry and Neurology (examiner). Intern David Grant USAF Med. Ctr., Travis AFB, Calif., 1965—66; resident in psychiatry Letterman Army Hosp., San Francisco, 1967—70; practice medicine, specializing in psychiatry Fairfield, Calif., 1972—. Flight surgeon, chief public health, chief phys. exam ctr. McGuire AFB, NJ, 1966—67; chief in-patient psychiatry David Grant Med. Ctr., 1970—71, chmn. dept. mental health, 1971—72; psychiat. cons. Fairfield-Suisan Unified Sch. Dist., 1971—, N. Bay Med. Ctr. (formerly Intercommunity Hosp.), Fairfield, 1971—, Casey Family Program, 1980—, Solano County Coroner's Office, 1981; asst. clin. prof. psychiatry U. Calif., San Francisco, 1976—; cons. Vaca Valley Hosp., Vacaville, Calif., 1988—, VA Hosp., San Francisco, 1976, David Grant USAF Hosp., 1976. Served to maj. M.C. USAF, 1964—72. Mem.: E. Bay Psychiat. Assn., No. Calif. Psychiat. Soc., Am. Psychiat. Assn. Office: 1245 Travis Blvd Ste E Fairfield CA 94533-4842 Office Phone: 707-422-8919.

MUNNEKE, GARY ARTHUR, law educator, consultant; b. Dec. 29, 1947; s. Leslie Earl and Margaret Frances (Fortsch) M.; children: Richard Arthur, Matthew Frederick. BA in Psychology, U. Tex., 1970, JD, 1973. Bar: Tex. 1973, Pa. 1987. Asst. dean, dir. placement U. Tex., Austin, 1978-80; asst. prof., asst. dean Del. Law Sch. Widener U., Wilmington, 1980-84, assoc. prof., 1984-87; pres. Legal Info. Sys., 1987-92; prof. Sch. Law Pace U., 1988—. Contbr. articles to profl. jours. Fellow Am. Bar Found., Coll. Law Practice Mgmt.; mem. ABA (chmn. standing com. on profl. utilization and career devel. 1981-85, articles editor Legal Econs. mag. 1984-86, chmn. law practice mgmt. sect. pub. bd. 1992-95, chmn. law practice mgmt. sect. 1998-99, ho. of dels 2000—), State Bar Tex. Office: Pace U Sch Law 78 N Broadway White Plains NY 10603-3710 Business E-Mail: gmunneke@law.pace.edu.

MUNNELL, ALICIA HAYDOCK, economist; b. N.Y.C., Dec. 6, 1942; d. Walter Howe Haydock and Alicia (Wildman) Haydock Roux; m. Thomas Clark Munnell (div.); children: Thomas Clark Jr., Hamilton Haydock; m. Henry Scanlon Healy, Feb. 2, 1980. BA in Econs., Wellesley, 1964; MA in Econs., Boston U., 1966; PhD in Econs., Harvard U., 1973. Staff asst. bus. rsch. div. New Eng. Tel. Co., Boston, 1964-65; teaching fellow econs. dept. Boston U., 1965-66; rsch. asst. for dir. econ. studies program Brookings Instn., Washington, 1966-68; teaching fellow Harvard U., Cambridge, Mass., 1971-73; asst. prof. econs. Wellesley Coll., Mass., 1974; economist Fed. Res. Bank Boston, 1973-76, asst. v.p., economist, 1976-78, v.p., economist, 1979-84, sr. v.p., dir. rsch., 1984-93; asst. sec. for econ. policy Dept. Treasury, Washington, 1993-95; mem. Coun. of Econ. Advisors, 1995—. Mem. Gov.'s Task Force on Unemployment Compensation, Mass., 1975; mem. spl. funding adv. com. for Mass. pensions, 1976; mem. Mass. Retirement Law Commn., 1976-82; staff dir. joint com. on pub. pensions Nat. Planning Assn., 1978; mem. adv. com. for urban inst. HUD grant on state-local pensions, 1978-81; mem. pension rsch. council Wharton Sch. Fin. and Commerce, U. Pa., 1979—; mem. adv. group Nat. Commn. for Employment Policy, 1980-81; mem. adv. bd. Nat. Aging Policy Ctr. in Income Maintenance, Brandeis U., 1980-84; participant pvt. sector retirement security and U.S. tax policy roundtable discussions Govt. Rsch. Corp., 1984; mem. supervisory panel Forum Inst. of Villers Found., 1984; mem. Medicare working group, div. of health policy rsch. and edn. Harvard U., 1984-87; mem. Commn. on Coll. Retirement, 1984-86; mem. com. to plan major study of nat. long term care policies Inst. Medicine, Nat. Acad. Scis., 1984-87; mem. steering com. Am. Assn. Ret. Persons, 1987—; mem. adv. council Am. Enterprise Inst., 1987—; com. mem. Inst. Medicine, Nat. Acad. Scis. Human Rights Com., 1987—; co-founder, pres. Nat. Acad. Social Ins., 1986—; bd. dirs. Pension Rights Ctr.; mem. program rev. com. Brigham and Women's Hosp., 1988—; mem. Commn. to Rev. Mass. Anti-Takeover Laws, 1988-89, econs. vis. com. MIT, 1989—. Author: The Impact of Social Security on Personal Saving, 1974, Future of Social Security, 1977 (various awards), Pensions for Public Employees, 1979, The Economics of Private Pensions, 1982; co-author: Options for Fiscal Structure Reform in Massachusetts, 1975; editor: Lessons from the Income Maintenance Experiments, 1987, Is There a Shortfall in Public Capital Investment?, 1991, (conf. proc.) Retirement and Public Policy, 1991, Pensions and the Economy: Sources, Uses, and Limitations of Data, 1992, co-editor: Pensions and the Economy: Sources, Uses, and Limitations of Data; contbr. articles to profl. jours., chpts. to books. Mem. Inst. Medicine of NAS, Nat. Acad. Pub. Adminstrn. Office: Council of Econ Advisers Old EOB Exec Office Of The Pres Washington DC 20502-0001

MUNOZ, ALFREDO NECTARIO, emergency medicine physician, pediatrician; b. Quito, Ecuador, Feb. 28, 1944; s. Nectario and Fanny Munoz; m. Linda Marie Schlereth, May 22, 1972; children: Stephen, Mark, Kathy, Eric, Amy. MD, Ctrl. U. Ecuador, 1974. Diplomate Am. Bd. Emergency Medicine, Am. Bd. Pediatrics. Intern Allegheny Gen. Hosp., Pitts., 1970-71; resident in pediatrics Children's Hosp. Kings Daughters, Norfolk, Va., 1971-74; mem. staff Sewickley (Pa.) Valley Hosp., 1977—. Fellow Am. Acad. Pediatrics; mem. AMA. Office: Sewickley Valley Hosp Emergency Medicine Sewickley PA 15143-9117

MUNOZ, ANDREA LEE, human resources specialist; b. Inglewood, Calif., May 21, 1968; d. Lou and Alma Lou Munoz. BS in psychology, Lamar U., Beaumont, Tex., 1996, MS in indsl. orgnl. psychology, 2003. Store mgr. Merry-Go-Round, Beaumont, 1989—93; tech. svcs. cons. Helena Lab., Beaumont, 1993—2000; workforce devel. specialist Tex. Workforce Ctr., Port Arthur, Tex., 2000—02; spl. populations and disability coord. Lamar State Coll., Port Arthur, 2002—. Mem. bd. Workforce Devel. Ctr., Port Arthur, 2002—03; adv. bd. Lamar State Coll. Port Arthur, 2002—03. Bd. mem. S Tex. Hispanic Cultural and Edtl. Ctr., Inc., 2002—, bd. dirs., 20 Jefferson County Coun. on Alcohol and Drug Abuse. Grantee, Lama Dr. Harry Starr Pre-Med scholarship, 1989, Maime McFadde

Sci. scholarship, 1997. Mem.: Assn. on Higher Edn. and Disability, Disability Consotrium of SE Tex., Psi Chi. Roman Catholic. Office: Lamar State Coll Port Arthur 1500 Procter St Port Arthur TX 77641 Office Phone: 409-984-6241.

MUÑOZ, CALISE I. federal agency administrator; Grad., U. So. Calif.; JD, Georgetown U., 1995. Bar: Calif. White House intern Bush Adminstrn., Washington; law clk. Office Atty. Gen. State Wash.; legal clk., legis. asst. fed. affairs health team Am. Assn. Ret. Persons, Washington; legis. policy cons. Calif. State Senator Ken Maddy; legis. adv.; dep. dir. policy Office Intergovernmental Affairs U.S. Dept. Health and Human Svcs., 2001—04, regional rep. Region IX, 2004—. Office: US Dept HHS Fed Office Bldg Rm 431 50 United Nations Plaza San Francisco CA 94102

MUÑOZ, CARLOS RAMON, retired bank executive; b. N.Y.C., Dec. 8, 1935; s. Alejandro and Gladys Helena (Judah) Muñoz; m. Wilhelmina Elaine North, June 8, 1957 (div. 1993); children: Carla Christine, Kyle Alexander; m. Kassie Ohtaka, Sept. 23, 2000. BA, Columbia U., 1957, MA, 1961. Insp., ofcl. asst. Citibank N.A., N.Y.C., 1959-64, from asst. mgr. to mgr. Dominican Republic, P.R., 1965-70, asst. v.p., 1971-72, v.p. dept. head, 1972-78; sr. v.p., regional mgr. and dir. Citicorp USA, San Francisco, 1978-81, sr. v.p. mem. credit policy com., 1982-95; exec. v.p., chief credit and risk mgmt. officer Dime Savs. Bank, N.Y.C., 1995-2000; pres., dir. Dime Consulting Group, N.Y.C., 1999-2000. Adv. coun. Credit Rsch. Ctr., 1994-2000; bd. dirs. N. Am. Mortgage Corp., 1998-2000. Mem. Columbia U. Senate, 2001—03; chmn. bd. dirs. Grace Ch. Cmty. Ctr., 2003—; v.p. Episcopal Mission Soc., 1995—2000; trustee Episcopal Diocese of NY, 1994—2001, Cathedral of St. John the Divine, 1998—2004; bd. dir. Episcopal Mission Soc., NYC, 1974—2000, Inner City Scholarship Fund, 1984—95. 1st lt. USAR, 1958—64. Recipient Productivity award State Senator Diane Watson, L.A., 1981, John Jay award for Disting. Profl. Achievement Columbia Coll., 2001; named Fairfield County Alumnus of Yr., 1989-90. Mem. Columbia Coll. Alumni Assn. (bd. dirs., treas. 1988-92, v.p., 1992-93, 1st v.p. 1994-96, pres. 1996-98), Columbia Club, Westchester Hills Golf Club. Republican.

MUNOZ, JOSEPH MARK, education educator, consultant; b. Zamboanga, Philippines, Apr. 19, 1966; arrived in U.S., 1999; s. Jose Edgar Cabato and Charity Judith (Schuck) Munoz; m. Melanie Salazar Bragas, Oct. 18, 1995; children: Ma.Marijka, John Paolo, Ma.Markiesha, John Marko. BS, Univ. Philippines, Philippines, 1986; MBA, Univ. San Jose, Philippines, 1992, PhD mgmt., 1997. Retail market specialist Shell Group of Co., Manila, Philippines, 1990—92; internat. sales and mktg. dir. SGAC Retail Devel. Group, Manila, Philippines, 1992—96; country mgr. Asia Kerametal Co. Ltd., Bratislava, Slovakia, 1996—99; sr. cons. Asia Enzio Bus. Clin., Cebu, Philippines, 1997—99; acctg. dir. U.S. and Asia Ploq Rsch., NJ, 1999—2001; asst. prof. internat. bus. Millikin Univ., Decatur, Ill., 2001—; mng. dir. Munoz and Assoc. Internat., Cebu, Philippines, 2001—. Mem. of the bd. De Montaiqne Investment Banking, Sydney, Australia, 2001—, Monteland Group of Co., Cebu, Philippines, 1999—; presenter internat. bus. conferences, Hawaii, Greece, North Ireland, Malaysia, Philippines. Contbr. articles to profl. jour. Co-founder Breakfast for the World Found., Philippines, 2001. Comdr. Coast Guard, 1997—99, Philippines. Nominee Global Leader for Tomorrow, WEF; recipient Best Rsch., Enterprise Conf. Hawaii, 2003. Mem.: MBA Global Net-USA Internat. Coun. Small Bus., Internat. Exec. Svc. Corp., U.S. Assn. for Small Bus. and Entrepreurship. Catholic. Achievements include internat. rsch. project entitled "Travel Executives Perceptions on the Impact of Globalization on Contemporary Business", conducted among 119 sr. level travel exec; research in 35 countries. Home: 3783 Moundford Ave Decatur IL 62526 Office: Millikin U 1184 W Main St Decatur IL 62522

MUNOZ, MARIO ALEJANDRO, civil engineer, retired consultant; b. Havana, Cuba, Feb. 27, 1928; came to U.S., 1961, naturalized, 1968; s. Ramón and Concepción (Bermudo) M.; m. Julia Josephine Garrofe, Jan. 17, 1970. *Cuba-born wife Julia chose exile in 1960, and came to the U.S. in 1962, via Spain. Her volunteer and Philanthropic endeavors in Chicago are many: Board member of the Cardinal's Committee in the mid-1960's, Chicago Symphony Docent, Art Institute Docent, Board member of the Women's Association of the Chicago Symphony, Co-chair of the "Eternal Feminine" project at Ravinia Festival 2000, advisor of the "Crossing Boundaries" 2002 project for the Illinois Humanities Council. She and her husband were patrons of the St. James Steeplechase.* M.Arch., U. Havana, 1954; postgrad., City Colls., Chgo., 1974, U. Wis., 1974. Owner Muñoz Bermudo-Construcciones, Havana, 1954-61; designer various cos. Chgo., 1961-65; designer Chgo. Transit Authority, Mdse. Mart, 1965-69; civil engr. Dept. Water and Sewers, City of Chgo., 1969-79; supervising engr. Dept. of Sewers, 1979-85, coordinating engr., 1985-88, asst. chief engr., 1988-93. Mem. ctrl. area subway sys. utilities com. City of Chgo., 1974-93, mem. computer graphics com., 1977-78. Mem. Am. Pub. Works Assn., Western Soc. Engrs., Chgo. Architecture Found., Theodore Thomas Soc. Chgo. Symphony, Chgo. Coun. Fgn. Rels., Soc. of the shield of Loyola, The Overture soc. of the Lyric Opera, Ground Hog Club, Execs. Club (speaker's table com.), Oak Brook Bath and Tennis Club, Barrington Polo Club. Roman Catholic.

MUNOZ, OLIVIER, artistic director; Prin. dancer Cleve. San Jose Ballet, 1987-99; artistic dir. Ballet Ark., Little Rock, 2000—. Office: Ballet Ark 1521 Merrill Dr Little Rock AR 72201

MUNOZ, OSCAR, corporate financial executive; BS, U. So. Calif., 1982; MBA, Pepperdine U., 1986. Fin. analyst, acctg. mgr., mgr. fin. control Pepsico Inc., L.A. and Purchase, NY, 1983—86; divsn. contr., dir. fin. ops., asst. corp. contr. Coca-Cola Enterprises, L.A. and Atlanta, 1986—91, CFO, region v.p. Hollywood, Calif., 1991—96; exec. dir. Coca-Cola Co., Atlanta, 1996—97; v.p. fin., contr. USWEST Comms. Inc., Denver, 1997—99; CFO, v.p. U.S. West Retail Markets, Denver, 1999—2000; sr. v.p. fin. and adminstrn. Qwest Comms. Internat. Inc., Denver, 2000; CFO, v.p. AT&T Consumer Svcs. AT&T Corp., Basking Ridge, NJ, 2001—03; exec. v.p., CFO CSX Corp., Jacksonville, Fla., 2003—. Mem.: Fin. Execs. Inst. Office: CSX Corp 500 Water St Jacksonville FL 32202

MUÑOZ, ROMEO SOLANO, audio visual curator; b. Daraga, Philippines, July 2, 1933; s. Maximo M. and Fe (Solano) M.; m. Soledad Roselada, Jan. 2, 1964; children: Francis Vincent, Theresa Lourdes, Romualdo Romeo, Maria Cecilia, Anafe, Stephen Ignatius. BA in Psychology, Letran Coll., Manila, 1965; MS, Ea. Ill. U., 1968; MA, Gov.'s State U., 1989; EdD, No. Ill. U., 1995; postgrad., So. Ill. U. Audio visual curator Ateneo U., Quezon City, Philippines, 1962-67; audio visual dir. Olive-Harvey Coll., Chgo., 1969—. Prof. City Coll. Chgo., 1969—, prof. emeritus; cons. adminstrv. svcs., fin. City Coll. Bd. Trustees, Chgo., 1988—; v.p. Gov.'s State U., University Park, Ill. Author: Filipino Americans: From Invisibility to Empowerment, 2002. Del. AFL/CIO, Chgo., 1989, 90; deacon Archdiocese Chgo. Roman Cath. Ch., 1976—, Professed Secular Franciscan; trustee Calumet City Libr., 1993. Recipient fellowship Ea. Ill. U., Charleston, 1967-68, So. Ill. U., Carbondale, 1968-70, Gov.'s State U., Univ. Park, Ill., 1981-2000. Mem. ALA, Gov.'s State U. Alumni (bd. dirs.), Philippine Profls. Assn. (pres.), Nat. Fedn. of Filipino-Am. Orgns., Philippine Hist. Soc., Phi Delta Kappa (pres. 2000). Avocation: physical fitness. Home: 383 Hoxie Ave Calumet City IL 60409-2330 Office Phone: 708-891-9630. E-mail: munoz8@aol.com., rmunoz@ccc.edu.

MUNOZ, SHA[illegible] THOMAS, lawyer; b. New Orleans, Oct. 12, 1955; s. Scott Muni[illegible]es Isabelle Davis; m. Elizabeth Joan DeDeyn, Aug. 16, 1986; c[illegible]aret Anne, Sarah Catherine. Student, Northwe. U., 197[illegible]ci., U. N.H., 1977; JD, U. Conn., 1989. Bar: Conn. [illegible] 1990, U.S. Dist. Ct. (no., mid. and so. dists.) Fla. [illegible]th cir.); cert. expert in labor and employment law [illegible]artindale-Hubbell. Mgr. Tuttle Market Gardens, [illegible]wyer Day, Berry & Howard, Hartford, Conn., [illegible]alters, Sarasota, Fla., 1995-97, Zinober & [illegible]—. Mem. standing com. on advt. Fla. Bar, [illegible] Fla. Bar, 2002-; bd. dirs., 1998, 99, 2002, sec., 1999, v.p., 2000, pres., 2001, v.p., 2003, W. Ctrl. Fla., Indsl. Rels., Rsch. Assn. Recipient Book award Am. Jurisprudence, 1987, 88. Office: Zinober & McCrea PA 201 E Kennedy Blvd Ste 800 Tampa FL 33602-5863 E-mail: smunoz@zmlaw.com.

MUÑOZ DONES DE CARRASCAL, ELOISA, hospital administrator, pediatrician, consultant, educator; b. San Lorenzo, P.R., Oct. 25, 1922; d. Pedro and Maria (Dones) Muñoz; m. José D. Carrascal, Dec. 7, 1962; children: Lilia, Maria. BA in Edn. cum laude, BS in Chemistry cum laude, U. P.R., Rio Piedras, 1943; MD, Tulane U., 1948. Diplomate Am. Bd. Pediatrics. Intern Arecibo Charity Dist. Hosp., 1948-49; resident in pediatrics San Juan (P.R.) City Hosp., 1949-51, chief newborn svc., attending pediatrician, 1951—, dir. neonatal-perinatal medicine, 1965—, dir. fellowship tng. program, 1972—; from instr. to assoc. prof. clin. pediatrics sch. medicine U. P.R., 1951-89, prof., 1989—. Courtesy pediatrician neonatologist Tchrs. Hosp., Hato Rey, P.R., 1951-76, Ashford Presbyn. Drs. Hosp., Santurce, P.R., 1951-76, San Jorge H. H. Pavia Fernandez, Santurce, 1951-76; cons. pediatrician neonatologist Tchrs. H. Auxilio Mutuo H., Hato Rey, 1976—, Drs. H. San Jorge H. Ashford, San Juan, 1976—; mem. exec. com. San Juan City Hosp., 1976—, pres. med. faculty, 1976-77, 87-89, mem. instl. rev. bd., mem. ednl. rev. bd., mem. various coms.; lectr. in field. Contbr. articles to profl. jours. U.S. del. Care Orgn. Latin Am., 1962-63. Recipient Bronze medal Brazilian Acad. Human Scis., 1975, Hon. Cert. Internat. Yr. Women, City Mayor Lodo Carlos Romero Barceló, 1975, Hon. Cert. Disting. Svc. to Cmty., Julio Sellés Solá Elem. Sch., 1976, Pioneer Pediatrician award P.R. Pediat. Sect. Convention, 1993, Pioneer in Neonatology award P.R. Pediat. Sect. Convention, 1995, Pioneer Pidiat. Critical Care award Pediat. Critical Care Assn., 1996; grantee NIH, 1962. Fellow Am. Acad. Pediatrics (neonatal perinatal sect., mem. com. fetus and newborn P.R. chpt. 1956—, sec.-treas. 1962-64, mem. com. history perinatal sect. 1992—, Plaque in Recognition Disting. Pediatrician and Tchr. 1985), Pan Am. Pediatrics; mem. Am. Med. Women Assn., P.R. Med. Assn. (pediat. sect., mem. chamber of dels. 1962-63, Bronze plaque 1967, 91, Gold Pin 1980), P.R. Med. Women Assn. (sec.-treas. 1957-60, pres. 1962-64), Pan Am. Med. Women Assn. (pres. P.R. chpt. 1960-64, P.R. del. VIII Congress Manizales Colombia 1962), Pan Am. Med. Women Alliance (vis. lectr. 1962), Tulane Med. Alumni, London Royal Soc. Health, Colegio de Químicos, Soc. Dominicana de Pediatría (hon., vis. lectr. 1971), Dominican Rep. Soc. (hon.). Avocation: poetry.

MUÑOZ-SOLA, HAYDEÉ SOCORRO, library administrator; b. Caguas, P.R., Dec. 27, 1943; d. Gilberto Muñoz and Carmen Haydeé (Solá) de Muñoz; m. Juan M. Masini-Soler, Jan. 8, 1966 (div. 1979); children: Juan Martín Masini-Muñoz, Haydeé Milagros Masini-Muñoz. BA in Psychology, U. P.R., Río Piedras, 1965, MLS, 1970; D in Libr. Sci., Columbia U., 1985. Asst. libr. U. P.R., Río Piedras, 1964-67; dir. libr. Interam. U., Aguadilla, P.R., 1974-75; head svcs. to pub. U. P.R., Aguadilla, 1975-76; cataloguer Cath. U., Ponce, P.R., 1976-79, U. P.R., Río Piedras, 1982-84, head libr. and info. sci. libr., 1984-85, prof. grad. libr. sch., 1986, 99, dir. libr. sys., 1986-93, coord. external resources libr. sys., 1994-97, dir. of libr. Ponce, P.R., 1997, collection devel. officer Rio Piedras, 1998, sabbatical leave, 2000-01. Dir. P.R. Newspaper Project, Río Piedras, 1986-90; mem. Adv. Com. on Pub. Librs., San Juan, 1987-93; proposal reviewer NEH, 1990—; chmn. Puerto Rican Del. to Nat. White House Conf. on Libr. and Info. Svcs., 1991. Author: La Información y la Documentación Educativa/Informe Sobre la Situación Actual en Puerto Rico, 1991, Memorias: Sequnda Pre-Conferencia de Casa Blanca Sobre Bibliotecas y Servicios de Información en Puerto Rico, 1991, Lineamientos para Colecciones Bibliograficas Nacionales, 1997, Premio por Excelencia en Investigación Aplicada y Publicación, 1997; compiler, editor ann. Puerto Rican Bibliography, 1999—; contbr. articles to profl. jours. Mem. Ponce Sport Club, 1976-83, ARC, Ponce, 1978. Recipient plaque White House Pre-Conf. on Libr. and Info. Sci., 1990, others, Leccion Magistral Josefina del Toro Fulladosa, 2002; French Alps Study Tour scholar Assn. Caribbean Univ. Rsch. and Instl. Libr., 1989, Germany Study Tour scholar Fgn. Rels. Office, Germany, 1991, coord. So. area 1974, Lauro award 1989, Leccion Magistral Josefina del Toro Fulladosa award, 2002. Mem. ALA, Am. Mgmt. Assn., Grad. Sch. Libr. and Info. Sci. Alumni Assn. (pres. 1988-90), Seminar for Acquisitions L.Am. Libr. Materials, Iberoamerican Nat. Libr. Assn. (pres. 1992-93), Puerto Rican Libr. Soc., Assn. Caribbean U. Rsch. and Instnl. Libr. (Parchment award 1988), Asoc. para las Comunicaciones y Tecnología Educativa, Mid. States Assn. Coll. and Sch. (collaborator), Am. Women Assn., Nat. Commn. P.R. Women, Phi Delta Kappa (chair P.R. com. 1988-90, Kappan of Yr. 1990), Eta Gamma Delta. Roman Catholic. Avocations: reading, crewel work, embroidery, knitting, movies. Office Phone: 787-764-0000 2707. Personal E-mail: hmunoz@caribe.net. Business E-Mail: hmunoz@upracd.upr.clu.edu.

MUNRO, ALICE, author; b. Wingham, Ont., Can., July 10, 1931; d. Robert Eric and Anne Clarke (Chamney) Laidlaw; m. James Armstrong Munro, 1951 (div. 1976); children: Sheila, Jenny, Andrea; m. Gerald Fremlin, 1976 BA, U. Western Ont., 1952, DLitt (hon.), 1976. Established Munro Books, 1963; writer in residence U. of British Columbia & U. of Queensland, 1980. Author: (short stories) The Dimensions of a Shadow, 1950, Dance of the Happy Shades, 1968 (Gov.-Gen.'s Lit. award 1969), A Place for Everything, 1970, Lives of Girls and Women, 1971 (Can. Booksellers award, 1972), (short stories) Something I've Been Meaning To Tell You, 1974, Who Do You Think You Are?, 1979 (pub. in U.S. as Beggar Maid: Stories of Flo and Rose, 1984, Gov.-Gen.'s Lit. award 1978), The Moons of Jupiter, 1982, The Progress of Love, 1986 (Gov. Gens. Lit. award 1987), Friend of My Youth, 1990, (short stories) Open Secrets, 1994, A Wilderness Station, 1994, Selected Stories, 1996, The Love of a Good Woman, 1998 (Fiction prize Nat. Book Critics Circle 1999), Hateship, Friendship, Courtship, Loveship, Marriage, 2001; TV scripts: A Trip to the Coast, 1973, Thanks For The Ride, 1973, How I Met My Husband, 1974, 1847: The Irish, 1978. Recipient Can.-Australia Lit. Prize 1977, Marian Engel award, 1986, Governor General's award, 1968, 1978, 1986, Canadian Booksellers award, 1977, WH Smith award, 1995, Nat. Book Critics Circle award & Giller Prize, 1999, REA award for short story, 2001, O. Henry Prize for short stories, 2003. Office: William Morris Agy 16th Fl 1325 Avenue of the Americas New York NY 10019

MUNRO, BARBARA HAZARD, nursing educator, dean, researcher; b. Wakefield, R.I., Nov. 28, 1938; d. Robert J. and Honore (Egan) Hazard; children: Karen Aimee, Craig Michael, Stephanie Anne. BS, MS, U. R.I., Kingston; PhD, U. Conn. RN, Conn. Asst. prof. U. of R.I. Coll. of Nursing, Kingston; assoc. prof., chmn. program in nursing rsch. Yale U., New Haven, Conn.; assoc. prof., asst. dir. Ctr. for Nursing Rsch. U. Pa., Phila.; dean, prof. Boston Coll. Sch. Nursing, 1991—. Presenter and workshop leader various nursing confs. and seminars in U.S. Contbr. articles and rsch. to profl. pubs. Trustee St. Elizabeth's Med. Ctr. Boston, 1994—. Recipient Nat. Rsch. Svc. award. Fellow Am. Acad. Nursing; mem. ANA, Golden Key, Sigma Theta Tau, Pi Lambda Theta, Phi Kappa Phi. Office: Boston Coll Sch Nursing Cushing Hall Chestnut Hill MA 02467-3812 Office Phone: 617-552-1710.

MUNRO, DONALD JACQUES, b. New Brunswick, N.J., Mar. 5, 1931; s. Thomas B. and Lucile (Nadler) M.; m. Ann Maples Patterson, Mar. 3, 1956; 1 child, Sarah de la Roche. AB, Harvard U., 1953; PhD (Ford Found. fellow), Columbia U., 1964. Asst. prof. philosophy U. Mich., 1964-68, asso. prof., 1968-73, prof. philosophy, 1973-96, prof. philosophy and Asian langs., 1990-96; prof. emeritus philosophy and Chinese, 1996—; chmn. dept. Asian langs. and cultures U. Mich., 1993-95; vis. research philosopher Center for Chinese Studies, U. Calif., Berkeley, 1969-70; asso. Center for Chinese Studies, U. Mich., 1964—; chmn. com. on studies of Chinese civilization Am. Council Learned Socs., 1979-81. Mem. Com. on Scholarly Communication with People's Republic China, NAS, 1978-82, China Coun. of Asia Soc., 1977-80, Com. on Advanced Study in China, 1978-82, Nat. Faculty of Humanities, Arts and Scis., 1986—; Evans-Wentz lectr. Stanford U., 1970; Fritz lectr. U. Wash., 1980; Gilbert Ryle lectr. Trent U., Ont., 1983; John Dewey lectr. U. Vt., 1989; Ch'ien Mu lectr. Chinese U. Hong Kong, 2002-2003. Author: The Concept of Man in Early China, 1969, the Concept of Man in Contemporary China, 1977; editor: Individualism and Holism, 1985, Images of Human Nature: A Sung Portrait, 1988, The Imperial Style of Inquiry in Twentieth Century China, 1996. Mem. exec. com. Coll. Literature, Sci. and The Arts U. Mich., 1986-89. Served to lt. (j.g.) USNR, 1953-57. Recipient letter of commendation Chief Naval Ops.; Disting. Svc. award U. Mich., 1968, Excellence in Edn. award, 1992; Rice Humanities award, 1993-94; Nat. Humanities faculty fellow, 1971-72; John Simon Guggenheim Found. fellow, 1978-79; grantee Social Sci. Rsch. Coun., 1965-66, Am. Coun. Learned Socs., 1982-83, China com. grantee NAS, 1990; vis. rsch. scholar Chinese Acad. Social Scis. Inst. Philosophy, Beijing, 1983, dept. philosophy Beijing U., 1990. Mem. Assn. for Asian Studies (China and Inner Asia Council 1970-72), Soc. for Asian and Comparative Philosophy. Clubs: Ann Arbor Racquet. Home: 14 Ridgeway St Ann Arbor MI 48104-1739 Office: Dept Philosophy U Mich Ann Arbor MI 48104 *I believe that much knowledge is interrelated and that academic disciplinary boundaries are transitory conveniences. The human significance of any research task I undertake should be obvious to those inside and outside my professional group (a goal I seek but do not always achieve).*

MUNRO, DONALD WILLIAM, JR., non-profit organization executive; b. Phila., Dec. 27, 1937; s. Donald William and Emily McCoy (Graham) M.; m. Joyce Eleanor Thomas, Sept. 9, 1961; children: Deborah Joy, Mark William. BS, Wheaton Coll., 1959; MS, Pa. State U., 1963, PhD, 1966. Prof. biology Houghton (N.Y.) Coll., 1966-94; exec. dir. Am. Sci. Affiliation, Ipswich, Mass., 1994—. Adj. prof. biology Gordon Coll., Wenham, Mass., 1995—; chmn. biology dept. Houghton Coll., 1972-94. Capt. U.S. Army, 1960-69. Predoctoral fellow NIH, 1964-66. Mem. Am. Philatelic Soc., Newburyport Stamp Club, Houghton Stamp Club (pres. 1988-90). Republican. Presbyterian. Avocations: stamps, piano, hiking, bioethics. Office: Am Sci Affiliation PO Box 668 55 Market St Ipswich MA 01938-2262 E-mail: don@asa3.org.

MUNRO, JOHN HENRY ALEXANDER, economics educator, writer; b. Vancouver, B.C., Can., Mar. 14, 1938; s. Hector Gordon and Blanche (Almond) M.; m. Jeanette Roberta James, May 25, 1968; children: Robert Ryder, Valerie Marlene. BA with honors, U. B.C., Vancouver, 1960; MA in History, Yale U., 1961, PhD in History, 1965. Instr. in history U. B.C., 1964-65, asst. prof. history and econs., 1965-68; assoc. prof. econs. U. Toronto, 1968-73, prof., 1973—2003, prof. emeritus, 2003—; assoc. dir. Centre for Medieval Studies, U. Toronto, 1975-78. Cons. on coinage to pub. U. Toronto Press, 1973— Author: Wool, Cloth, and Gold, 1973, Bullion Flows and Monetary Policies in England and the Low Countries, 1350-1500, 1992, Textiles, Towns and Trade: Essays in the Economic History of Late-Medieval England and the Low Countries, 1994; contbr. articles to profl. jours., essays to books; mem. editl. bd. Textile History, 1980-97, Explorations in Economic History, 1998—, Internat. History Rev., 2000; Medieval area editor Oxford Ency. of Econ. History, 1996—2003. Can. Coun. leave fellow, Belgium, 1970-71, Social Scis. and Humanities Rsch. Coun. Can. fellow, Engl. and Holland, 1979-80, Belgium, 1986-87, Eng. and Belgium, 1992-96, 96-99, 99—, Connaught Rsch. fellow, 1993-94, 2000—01. Mem. Can. Econ. Assn., Econ. History Assn. (U.S.), Econ. History Soc. (U.K.), Medieval Acad. Am. (councillor 1990-93), Instituto Internazionale di Storia Economica (sci. com. 1999—, exec. bd. 2003—), Royal Flemish Acad. Belgium for Sci. and Arts. (fgn.). Presbyterian. Home: 9 Woodmere Ct Toronto ON Canada M9A 3J1 Office: Dept Econs U Toronto 150 St George St Toronto ON Canada M5S 3G7 Office Phone: 416-978-4552. E-mail: munro5@chass.utoronto.ca., john.munro@utoronto.ca.

MUNRO, MICHAEL DONALD, air transportation executive, retired military officer; b. Kindley AFB, Bermuda, May 6, 1953; (parents Am. citizens); s. Donald M. and Marilyn Barbara (Ravenelle) M. AAS in Criminology, U. M., 1978; BA in Sociology, SUNY, Plattsburg, 1981; MA in Aviation Mgmt., Embry-Riddle U., 1986. Cert. Project Mgmt. Profl. Commd. 2d lt. USAF, 1976, advanced through grades to capt., 1985; ICBM launch officer Grand Forks (N.D.) AFB, 1981-83, ICBM flight comdr., 1984-86; satellite officer Colorado Springs, Colo., 1986-87; chief satellite officer U.S. Space Command, Colorado Springs, 1987; chief U.S. Space Def. Ops. Ctr., Colorado Springs, 1988-91; ret., 1991; sr. aviation project mgr. Intersyss. USA, Inc., 1998—2002; program mgr. ARINC Airport Systems, 2002—. Sr. project mgr. Airport Info. Systems at worldwide locations; dir. IT constrn. of Salt Lake, Calgary, Springfield, Norfolk and Houston airports; dir. IT constrn. of Calgary, Ottawa, Bermuda and DFW airports. Contbr. articles to profl. jours. Recipient Scholastic Achievement award Boeing Aerospace, 1988. Mem. Crewmembers Assn. (pres. 1985-86), Grand Forks C. of C. Republican. Roman Catholic. Avocations: fishing, golf. Home: 5386 E 81st St # 811 Tulsa OK 74137

MUNRO, RALPH DAVIES, former state official; b. Seattle, June 25, 1943; s. George Alexander and Elizabeth (Troll) M.; m. Karen (Hansen), Feb. 17, 1973; one son, George Alexander. BA in History and edn. (scholar), Western Wash. U. Indsl. engr. Boeing Co., Wash., 1966-68; sales mgr. Continental Host, Inc., Wash.; asst. dep. dir. ACTION Agy., Wash., 1971; spl. asst. to gov. State of Wash., 1970-76; gen. mgr. Tillicum Enterprises and Food Svc. Co., Wash.; dir. Found. for Handicapped, 1976-80; pres. N.W. Highlands Tree Farm; sec. of state State of Wash., 1980—2000; bd. dir. Vote Here. Chmn. cmty. svc. com. Seattle Rotary Club 4; founder 1st pres. Rotary Youth Job Employment Ctr., Seattle. Named Man of Yr. Assn. Retarded Citizens, Seattle, 1970. Mem. Nat. Assn. Sec. State (pres.), Nat. Assn. Retarded Children, Wash. Hist. Mus. (dir.), Wash. Trust Hist. Preservation (founder), Nature Conservancy. Republican. Lutheran.

MUNRO, RODERICK ANTHONY, business improvement coach; b. Toronto, Ont., Can., Jan. 16, 1955; came to U.S., 1956; s. William George and Georgina Antoinette M.; m. Elizabeth J. Rice, 1994. BA, Adrian Coll., 1979, secondary provisional cert., 1981; MS, Eastern Mich. U., 1984; ednl. specialist, Wayne State U., 1998; PhD, Cambridge State U., 1999. Cert. quality engr., quality auditor, hypnotherapist, cert. quality mgr. Tchr. Lincoln Park H.S., Mich., 1980-82; mgmt. trainee Fabricon Automotive, River Rouge, Mich., 1982-84; statis. process control coord. ASC, Inc., Southgate, Mich., 1984-86; quality engr. container divsn. Johnson Controls, Inc., Manchester, Mich., 1987-88; program dir. Ford Motor Co., Dearborn, Mich., 1988—2001; bus. improvement coach RAM Q Universe, Inc., Reno, 2001—. Cons. in field, 1986—. Served to sgt. USMCR, 1974-80. Fellow Am. Soc. for Quality (bd. dirs., past cert. com., past chmn. Greater Detroit sect., past chair human resources divsn. Testimonial award 1988, 2002, Disting. Svc. award 1989, 96); mem. ASTD, Internat. Assn. Counselors and Therapists (cert.), Aircraft Owners and Pilots Assn., Am. Statis. Assn. (past pres. Greater Detroit chpt.), Internat. Soc. for Performance Improvement, Assn. Quality and Participation. Office: RAM Q Universe Inc 1135 Terminal Way Ste 209 Reno NV 89502-2168 Office Phone: 231-386-5071. E-mail: doctormunro@yahoo.com.

MUNROE, GEORGE BARBER, retired mining and manufacturing company executive; b. Joliet, Ill., Jan. 5, 1922; s. George Mueller and Ruth (Barber) Munroe; m. Elinor Bunin, May 30, 1968; children from previous marriage: George Taylor, Ralph W. Taylor. AB, Dartmouth Coll., 1943; LLB, Harvard U., 1949; BA (Rhodes scholar), Christ Church, Oxford (Eng.) U., 1951, MA, 1956; DHL (hon.), No. Ariz. U., 1981; LLD (hon.), Dartmouth Coll., 1993. Bar: N.Y. 1949. Assoc. Cravath, Swaine & Moore, N.Y.C., 1949; atty. Office Gen. Counsel U.S. High Commn. Germany, Frankfurt and Bonn, 1951-53; justice U.S. Ct. Restitution Appeals Allied High Commn. Germany, Nuremberg, 1953-54; assoc. Debevoise, Plimpton & McLean, N.Y.C., 1954-58; with Phelps Dodge Corp., 1958-87, v.p., 1962-66, pres., 1966-75, 80-82, chief exec. officer, 1969-87, chmn. bd., 1975-87, dir., 1966-94. Trustee emeritus Met. Mus. Art; chmn. bd. dirs. Acad. Polit. Sci. Served to lt. (j.g.) USNR, 1943—46. Mem. Mining and Metall. Soc. Am., Coun. Fgn. Rels., Century Assn., River Club, Univ. Club (N.Y.C.), Bridgehampton Club. Office: 444 Madison Ave Fl 19 New York NY 10022-6903

MUNSELL, DEBRA S. physician assistant, educator; b. Pt. Arthur, Tex., June 13, 1957; d. Rosemond B. and Bettie Lawrence Schoenberg; m. Lloyd Allen Foreman III, Feb. 16, 1985 (dec. Mar. 1991); m. William Peter Munsell, July 18, 1998. BS in Biology, Stephen F. Austin State U., 1979; BS in Health, U. Tex., Galveston, 1981; MPhysician Asst. Studies in Otolaryng., U. Nebr., 2000. Cert. phys. asst. Physician asst. Angleton (Tex.) Clinic, 1981-83, Tex. Dept. Corrections, Huntsville, 1983-84; physician asst. med. br. Galveston U. Tex., 1985-90, clin. instr. med. br. Galveston, 1985—, physician asst. M.D. Anderson Cancer Ctr., 1990—, dir. physician asst. student edn. program M.D.

Anderson Cancer Ctr., 1996—; clin. assoc. prof. physician asst. edn. We. U. Health Sci., Pomona, Calif., 1999—. Clin. instr. Baylor Coll. Medicine, Houston, 1999—. Author: (with others) Primary Care Oncology, 1998, Primary Care: A Collaborative Approach, 1999. Life mem. Brazoria County Fair Assn., Angleton, Tex., 1992—. Glaxo/Wellcome Leadership fellow Am. Acad. Physician Assts./Physician Asst. Found., 1997-98. Fellow: Assn. Physician Assts. in Oncology, Soc. Physician Assts. in Otolaryngology, Head and Neck Surgery (charter mem. 1991, bd. dirs. 1992—94, chair continuing med. edn 1994—96, pres. 1996—2000), Am. Acad. Otolaryngology, Head and Neck Surgery, Am. Acad. Physician Assts. (chair nominating com. 1998—2002, external liaison 2001—); mem.: Houston Yacht Club. Home: 9807 Williams Bend Ct Missouri City TX 77459-6279 Office: U Tex MD Anderson Cancer Ctr 1515 Holcombe Blvd Houston TX 77030-4009

MUNSELL, ELSIE LOUISE, retired lawyer; b. N.Y.C., Feb. 15, 1939; d. Elmer Stanley and Eleanor Harriet (Dickinson) M.; m. George P. Williams, July 14, 1979. AB, Marietta Coll., 1960; JD, Marshall-Wythe Coll. William and Mary, 1972. Bar: Va. 1972, U.S. Dist. Ct. (ea. dist.) Va. 1974, U.S. Ct. Appeals (4th cir.) 1976, U.S. Supreme Ct. 1980. Tchr. Norview High Sch., Norfolk, Va., 1964-69; asst. Commonwealth atty. Commonwealth Atty.'s Office, Alexandria, Va., 1972-73; asst. U.S. atty. Alexandria, 1974-79; U.S. magistrate U.S. Dist. Ct. (ea. dist.) Va., Alexandria, 1979-81; U.S. atty. Dept. Justice, Alexandria, 1981-86; sr. trial atty. Office of Gen. Counsel, Dept. Navy Washington, 1986-89, asst. gen. counsel installations and environ. law, 1989-91; dep. asst. environ. and safety Sec. Navy, 1991-2001, ret., 2001. Mem. USEPA Clean Air Act Adv. Com., 1997—; bd. dirs. BMT Designers & Planners. Active Va. Commn. on Status of Women, 1966-74; bd. vistors Coll. William and Mary, 1972-76; active Atty. Gen.'s Adv. Com. U.S. Attys., 1981-83; bd. dirs. Carpenter's Shelter, Inc., 1990-93; vestry St. Alban's Ch., Annandale, Va., 1996-99, 2003; fed. preservation officer Dept. Navy, 1999. Presdl. Meritorious Exec., 1999; recipient Spl. Achievement award Nat. Mil. Fish and Wildlife Assn., 2001, Disting. Civilian Svc. award, 2001. Mem. Sr. Execs. Assn., Chi Omega. Episcopalian.

MUNSEY, VIRDELL EVERARD, JR., retired utility executive; b. Washington, Sept. 25, 1933; s. Virdell Everard and Mildred Lovenia (Wood) M.; m. Bernice Ann Wilson, Sept. 20, 1956; children: Wanda Louise, Allan Coll, Andrew Everard, Carolyn Jane. BA magna cum laude, Yale U., 1955; M.P.A., Harvard U., 1967. Reporter Washington Post, 1957-63; legis. asst. Rep. Henry S. Reuss, Washington, 1963-68; info. dir. United Democrats for Humphrey, Washington, 1968; asst. dir. public affairs Dem. Nat. Com., 1968; with Nat. Planning Assn., Washington, 1969-77, exec. v.p., 1974-76; dep. asst. sec. for public affairs Dept. Treasury, Washington, 1977-81; cons. World Bank, 1981; with Va. Electric and Power Co., 1981-86, mgr. corp. communications, 1982-83, exec. dir. pub. policy, 1983-86, v.p. pub. policy, 1986, Dominion Resources Inc., 1986-96; cons., 1996—2002. Mem. Va. Coal and Energy Commn., 1983-95. Chmn. Arlington County Dem. Party, 1967-69; mem. Arlington County Bd., 1972-75, chmn., 1973; vice chmn. No. Va. Transp. Commn., 1973, chmn., 1974; bd. dirs. Washington Met. Area Transit Authority, 1975; mem. transp. planning bd. Met. Washington Coun. Govts., 1973-75; treas. Competitive Power Policy Forum, 1990-96. Served with U.S. Army, 1955-57. Am. Polit. Sci. Assn. fellow, 1966-67 Mem. United Ch. Christ.

MUNSON, ALEX ROBERT, judge; b. L.A., Sept. 25, 1941; s. Robert Alexander and Lillian Agnus (Hamel) M.; m. Kathleen Rae Abernathey, June 29, 1968. BA, Long Beach (Calif.) State Coll., 1964, MA, 1965; EdD, U. So. Calif., L.A., 1970; JD, Loyola U., L.A., 1975. Atty. Kirtland and Packard, L.A., 1978-82; chief justice High Ct. of The Trust Terr. of The Pacific Islands, Saipan, Commonwealth of the No. Mariana Islands, 1982-88; chief judge U.S. Dist. Ct. of No. Mariana Islands, Saipan, Commonwealth of the No. Mariana Islands, 1988—. Mem. ABA, Calif. Bar Assn. Republican. Home: PO Box 5356 Saipan MP 96950-5356 Office: US Dist Ct NMI PO Box 500687 Saipan MP 96950-0687

MUNSON, ERIC BRUCE, hospital administrator; b. Elmhurst, Ill., Mar. 11, 1943; married. B, Wabash Coll., 1965; MHA, U. Chgo., 1967. Asst. to adminstr. Swedish Covenant Hosp., Chgo., 1966-67; asst. dir. U. Chgo. Hosps., 1970-73; assoc. adminstr. U. Hosp., Denver, 1973-77, adminstr., 1977-80; exec. dir. U. N.C. Hosp., Chapel Hill, 1980-99, pres., CEO, 1999—. Home: 119 Black Oak Pl Chapel Hill NC 27517-6502 Office: Univ N C Hosps 101 Manning Dr Chapel Hill NC 27514-4226

MUNSON, HAROLD LEWIS, education educator; b. Windham, N.Y., Aug. 2, 1923; s. Esmond Lewis and Gladys (Disbrow) M.; m. Evelyn Claire Moore, Sept. 8, 1946; children: Michael Lewis, Jeffrey Charles. AB, Hobart Coll., 1947; MA, SUNY, Albany, 1948; Ed.D., NYU, 1961. Tchr. social studies, counselor Cairo (N.Y.) Central Sch., 1948-50; dir. guidance Williamson (N.Y.) Central Sch., 1950-54; supr. guidance N.Y. State Edn. Dept., Albany, 1954-59; prof. edn., chmn. Center for Counseling, Family and Worklife Studies, U. Rochester, N.Y., 1959-85, prof. emeritus, 1985—; prof. edn. Overseas Program, Boston U., 1985-87; pres. Munson Assocs., 1988—. Vocat. cons. Social Security Adminstrn., HEW, 1962-79 Author: (with H.W. Houghton) Organizing Orientation Activities, 1956, My Educational Plans, 1959, 70, Guidance Activities for Teachers of English, Social Studies, Science, Mathematics and Foreign Languages, 1965, (with Gilbert Gockley) Career Insights and Self Awareness Games, 1973; contbg. author: Ency. of Careers, 1967, Elementary School Guidance: Concepts, Dimensions and Practice, 1970, The Foundations of Developmental Guidance, 1971, Career Education for Deaf Students: An Inservice Leader's Guide, 1975, The Land In The Sky, 2004. Served with USNR, 1944-46. Mem. Am. Counseling Assn., Nat. Career Devel. Assn., Am. Sch. Counselor Assn., Phi Delta Kappa. Home: 9 Charleston Drive Mendon NY 14506 Office: U Rochester Warner Grad Sch Edn and Human Devel Rochester NY 14627 E-mail: hmunson@rochester.rr.com. *Success is whatever you want it to be. By defining it in such personal terms, everyone should be able to experience some degree of success. For me, it has been being able to feel a measure of personal fulfillment through my accomplishments in helping others to define and examine their own existence.*

MUNSON, HOWARD G. federal judge; b. Claremont, N.H., July 26, 1924; s. Walter N. and Helena (O'Halloran) M.; m. Ruth Jaynes, Sept. 17, 1949; children: Walter N., Richard J., Pamela A. BS in Economics, U. Pa., 1948; LL.B., Syracuse U., 1952. Bar: N.Y. With Employers' Assurance Corp., Ltd., White Plains, N.Y., 1949-50; mem. firm Hiscock, Lee, Rogers, Henley & Barclay, Syracuse, N.Y., 1952-76; judge U.S. Dist. Ct. No. Dist. N.Y., Syracuse, 1976—. Mem., pres. Syracuse Bd. Edn.; bd. dirs. Sta. WCNY-TV; chmn. ethics com. Onondaga County Legislature. Served with U.S. Army, 1943-45, ETO. Decorated Bronze Star, Purple Heart. Mem. Am. Coll. Trial Lawyers, Nat. Assn. R.R. Trial Counsel, Am. Arbitration Assn., Justinian Soc., Alpha Tau Omega, Phi Delta Phi. Office: US Dist Ct US Courthouse P O Box 7376 Syracuse NY 13261-7376

MUNSON, JANIS ELIZABETH TREMBLAY, engineering company executive; b. Beverly, Mass., Dec. 17, 1948; d. Louis Story Tremblay and Doroth Ellen (Burnham) Tonkin; divorced. BS in Geology summa cum laude, Boston U., 1976, M in Urban Planning, 1982. Tech. libr. United Engrs. & Constructors, Boston, 1971-73, land use planner, 1973-76, lead land use planner, 1976-80, supervising lic. engr., 1980—, environ./scientific cons., 1980-85, head mktg. analysis svcs. group power div., 1987-89, mgr. land use planning group, 1989-92, sr. ptnr., 1992—. Bd. dirs. Ctr. City Residents Assn., Phila., 1986; mem. Multiple Sclerosis Soc.; vol. for disabled. Mem. Internat. Platform Assn., Internat. Biog. Inst., Am. Planning Assn., Am. Inst. Cert. Planners (assoc.), World Affairs Coun., Smithsonian Assn. Republican. Congregationalist. Achievements include research on transmission line site selection process, on crime control through environmental design, on emotion exercise and nutrition fro those labeled chronic/progressive. Office: United Engrs and Constructors 30 S 17th St Philadelphia PA 19103-4001 Home: 2917 NW 3rd Ter Ocala FL 34475-2647

MUNSON, JAY DONALD, statistician; b. Des Moines, Apr. 9, 1950; s. Donald Louis and W. Irma Munson; m. Margaret Ann Munson, July 2, 1994; 1 child, Matthew Haubrich. BS, Iowa State U., 1972, MS, 1980. Statis. rsch. analyst Iowa Dept. Human Svcs., Des Moines, 1996-2001; fiscal policy analyst Iowa Dept. Revenue and Fin., Des Moines, 2001—. Mem. ctrl. com., Story County Rep. Party, Ames, Iowa, 1998—. Mem. Am. Statis. Assn., Am. Econ. Assn., Prodn. and Ops. Mgmt. Soc., Acad. Mgmt., First Story Investment Group (pres. 2000-01). Office: Iowa Dept Revenue and Fin 1305 E Walnut St Des Moines IA 50319

MUNSON, JOHN BACKUS, computer systems consultant, retired computer engineering company executive; b. Chgo., May 1, 1933; s. Mark Frame and Catherine Louise (Cherry) M.; m. Anne Lorraine Cooper, July 6, 1957; children: David B., Sharon A. BA, Knox Coll., 1955. With Unisys Corp., McLean, Va., 1957-93, v.p. corp. software engring., 1977-81, v.p. tech. ops., 1981-84, v.p. gen. mgr. space transp. systems, 1984-89, 89-93, v.p., gen. mgr. Space Systems divsn., 1989-94, ret., 1994. Mem. sci. adv. bd. USAF, 1981-86, mem. USN panel on F14D issues, 1987-88. Mem. bd. advisors U. Houston, Clear Lake, 1988-93, chmn. 1990-92; bd. dirs. Bay Area YMCA, 1988 93, chmn. 1992, Clear Lake Am. Heart Assn., 1989-93; co-chmn. Bay Area United Way, 1988—, chmn., 1992; Disting. visitor IEEE Computing Soc., 1981-94. Capt. U.S. Army, 1955-57. Recipient Exceptional Civilian Svc. award USAF, 1986, Superior Pub. Svc. award USN, 1988, cert. of appreciation NATO, 1984; named to Mgmt. Assn. Hall of Fame, 1994. Fellow IEEE (editor Trans. of Software Engring. 1982-84, bd. dirs. tech. com. software engring. 1982—); mem. AIAA, Am. Astronautical Soc. (bd. dirs. S.W. sect. 1989-94), Aerospace Industries Assn. (space com. 1989-94), U.S. Army Assn., Nat. Security Indsl. Assn., Armed Forces Comm. Electronics Assn. (pres. Houston chpt. 1987-90), S.W. Regional Coun. Corp. CEOs. Home and Office: 1018 Westcreek Ln Westlake Village CA 91362-5462 E-mail: JaxG3@aol.com.

MUNSON, JOHN CHRISTIAN, acoustician; b. Clinton, Iowa, Oct. 9, 1926; s. Arthur J. and Frances (Christian) M.; m. Elaine Hendershot, Sept. 2, 1950; children: John Christian, Holly Elizabeth. BS, Iowa State Coll., 1949; MS, U. Md., 1952, PhD, 1962; Navy Dept. scholar, MIT, 1956. Electronic scientist Naval Ordnance Lab., Washington, 1949-66; tech. dir. navy portion Practice Nine, Naval Air Systems Command, 1967; supt. acoustics divsn. Naval Rsch. Lab., 1968-85; v.p. Engring. & Sci. Assocs., 1985-94; chmn. bd. dirs., 1994; ret. Asst. extension prof. elec. engring. U. Md., 1964-66; mem. Underwater Sound Adv. Group, 1969-75, U.S. Sonar Team, 1971-85, Mobile Sonar Tech. Com., 1972-85; cons., 1985-. Editor U.S. Navy Jour. Underwater Acoustics, 1983-91; patentee in field. Mem. exec. bd. D.C. Bapt. Conv., 1973—, chmn. fin. com., 1973, v.p., 1996-97, pres., 1997-98; trustee Midwestern Bapt. Theol. Sem., 1970-80; trustee Bapt. Sr. Adult Ministries of Washington Met. Area, 1976-91, 92—, pres., 1981-88, CEO, 1991-92; mem. Gen. Bd. Am. Bapt. Chs. U.S.A., 1994-99; pres. Allied Silver Spring Interfaith Svcs. to Srs. Today, 1994-2000, bd. dirs. 1994-2003; bd. mgrs. Am. Bapt. Hist. Soc., 1996-2003, sec., 1997-2003; corp. mem. Am. Bapt. Homes of the West, 1999, dir., 2000-2004. Fellow IEEE, Signal Processing Soc. (mem. adminstrv. com. 1974-76, chmn. underwater acoustics com. 1973-76), Acoustical Soc. Am.; mem. Sigma Xi. Home: 3118 Chartwell Crescent Ln Adamstown MD 21710-9643 E-mail: johncmunsonsr@cs.com. *I have a positive joy for life, and I am an incurable optimist: my basic attitude is that things will work out for the best— but only if we do our very best. Each of us has a responsibility to grow to our maximum capacity and to be of reasonable service to mankind. The proper balance among family, job, service to God, service to others, and attention to yourself is essential. Whatever you are doing, do it from the right motivation and with enthusiasm.*

MUNSON, LAWRENCE SHIPLEY, management consultant; b. N.Y.C., Jan. 10, 1920; s. Lawrence J. and Anna (Lee) M.; m. Gretchen Thannhauser, May 24, 1947; children: Catherine Anne, Shipley John. AB, Harvard U., 1942, JD, 1948. Bar: N.Y. 1948. Assoc. Willkie, Owen, Farr, Gallagher & Walton, N.Y.C., 1948-51; assoc., then partner McKinsey & Co., Inc., N.Y.C., 1953-67; pres. Loral Corp., Scarsdale, N.Y., 1967-69; v.p. Allegheny Power System, Inc., N.Y.C., 1969-72; v.p., mng. prin. Louis Allen Assocs., Inc., 1972-97; self-employed cons., 1998—. Author: How To Conduct Training Seminars, 1984, 2d edit., 1992. Pres. East Hampton Village Preservation Soc., 1982—87, trustee, 1982—2001, chmn., 1993—2001; chmn. bd. Planned Parenthood N.Y.C., 1966—70; bd. dirs. Planned Parenthood Manhattan and Bronx, 1960—66, Planned Parenthood World Population, 1967—70, Gtr. N.Y. Fund., 1966—88, chmn. mgmt. assistance com., 1970—75; bd. dirs. United Way N.Y.C., 1988—89; co-founder, trustee East Hampton Healthcare Found., 1998—2000. Maj. USAAF, 1942—46, with USAF, 1951—53. Mem.: ASTD (pres. N.Y. met. chpt. 1988—89, chmn. bd. dirs. 1990—93), Harvard Club (N.Y.C.). Home: 27 Hartland Way Unit 202 Acton MA 01720-5871

MUNSON, LUCILLE MARGUERITE (MRS. ARTHUR E. MUNSON), real estate broker; b. Norwood, Ohio, Mar. 26, 1914; d. Frank and Fairy (Wicks) Wirick; m. Arthur E. Munson, Dec. 24, 1937; children: Barbara Munson Papke, Judith Munson Andrews, Edmund Arthur. RN, Lafayette (Ind.) Home Hosp., 1937; AB, San Diego State U., 1963; student, Purdue U., Kans. Wesleyan U. Staff and pvt. nurse Lafayette Home Hosp., 1937-41; indsl. nurse Lakey Foundry & Machine Co., Muskegon, Mich., 1950-51, Continental Motors Corp., Muskegon, 1951-52; nurse Girl Scout Camp, Grand Haven, Mich., 1948-49; owner, ret. Munson Realty, San Diego, 1964—2002. Mem. San Diego County Grand Jury, 1975-76, 80-81, Calif. Grand Jurors Assn. (charter). Address: 3875-18 Vista Campana S Oceanside CA 92057-8151

MUNSON, LYNNE ANN, cultural critic; b. Heidelberg, Germany, Mar. 20, 1968; came to U.S., 1969; d. Gordon Carl and Linda Jean (Guidarini) M. BA in Art History, Northwestern U., Evanston, Ill., 1990. Spl. asst. to the chmn. NEH, Washington, 1990-93; rsch. assoc. Am. Enterprise Inst., Washington, 1993—; dir. domestic policy Dole for Pres., 1996. V.p. Orwell Inst.; bd. dirs. Nat. Alumni Forum. Contbr. articles to N.Y. Times., Wall St. Jour., Pub. Interest, also profl. jours. Republican.

MUNSON, NANCY K. lawyer; b. Huntington, N.Y., June 22, 1936; d. Howard H. and Edna M. (Keenan) Munson. Student, Hofstra U., 1959—62; JD, Bklyn. Law Sch., 1965. Bar: NY 1966, U.S. Dist. Ct. (ea. and so. dists.) NY 1968, U.S. Supreme Ct. 1970, U.S. Ct. Appeals (2d cir.) 1971. Law clk. to E. Merritt Weidner, Huntington, 1959—66; pvt. practice, 1966. Mem. legal adv. bd. Chgo. Title Ins. Co., Riverhead, NY, 1981—; bd. dir. and legal officer Thomas Munson Found. Trustee Huntington Fire Dept. Death Benefit Fund; pres., trustee, chmn. bd. dirs. Bklyn. Home Aged Men Found.; bd. dirs. Huntington Rural Cemetery Assn., Inc. Mem.: DAR (trustee, treas. Ketewamoke chpt.), NRA, ABA, Bklyn. Bar Assn., Suffolk County Bar Assn., N.Y. State Bar Assn., Soroptimists (past pres.). Republican. Christian Scientist. Office: 197 New York Ave Huntington NY 11743-2711 Office Phone: 631-271-8161.

MUNSON, RICHARD HOWARD, horticulturist; b. Toledo, Dec. 20, 1948; s. Stanley Warren and Margaret Rose (Winter) M. BS, Ohio State U., 1971; MS, Cornell U., 1973, PhD, 1981. Plant propagator The Holden Arboretum, Kirtland, Ohio, 1973-76; asst. prof. Agrl. Tech. Inst., Wooster, Ohio, 1976-78, Tex. Tech U., Lubbock, 1981-84; dir. botanic garden Smith Coll., Northampton, Mass., 1984-95; exec. dir. The Holden Arboretum, Kirtland, Ohio, 1995-2000; dir. botanic garden U. Mo., Columbia, Mo., 2001—. V.p. Childs Park Found., Northampton, Mass., 1985-95. Ret. lt. col. USAR, 1971-99. Recipient Disting. Alumnus award Ohio State U. Coll. Agr., 1998. Mem. Internat. Plant Propagators Soc., Am. Assn. Bot. Gardens and Arboreta (com. chmn. 1987-92, 2001—), Internat. Assn. Plant Taxonomy, Sigma Xi, Pi Alpha Xi, Gamma Sigma Delta. Methodist. Avocations: fishing, fly-tying, golf, woodworking, gardening. Office: University of Missouri General Svcs Bldg Columbia MO 65211-3200 Office Phone: 573-884-6307. E-mail: munsonrh@missouri.edu.

MUNSON, RICHARD JAY, congressional policy analyst; b. Hollywood, Calif., Aug. 10, 1950; s. Jay S. and Grace P. (Palmer) M.; m. Diane MacEachern; children: Daniel, Dana. BA, U. Calif., Santa Barbara, 1971; MA, U. Mich., 1973. Instr. U. Mich., Ann Arbor, 1973-75; coord. Environ. Action Found., Washington, 1975-77; exec. dir. Solar Lobby, Washington, 1977-83, N.E.-Midwest Inst., Washington, 1986—. Author: The Power Makers, 1985, Cousteau, 1988, The Cardinals of Capitol Hill, 1993. Office: NE Midwest Inst 218 D St SE Ste A Washington DC 20003-1917

MUNSON, ROBERT SYDNEY, biomedical researcher; b. Waterbury, Conn., Jan. 18, 1947; s. Robert Sydney, Sr. and Lillian Marti M.; m. Barbara Bell, Nov. 22, 1966 (div.); children: Mary Ann, Kimberley; m. Lauren Opremcak Bakaletz, Sept. 16, 1994; stepchildren: Megan, Kelsey, Nicole. BA, U. Conn., Storrs, 1968; PhD, U. Conn., Farmington, 1976; postdoctoral fellow, Washington U., St. Louis, 1976-79. Rsch. asst. prof. pediatrics Washington U. Sch. of Medicine, St. Louis, 1980-82, asst. prof. of pediatrics, 1982-89, asst. prof. molecular microbiology, 1987-89, assoc. prof. pediatrics, 1989-94, assoc. prof. molecular microbiology, 1989-94; prof. pediatrics Ohio State U., Columbus, 1994—, prof. of molecular virology, immunology, and med. genetics, 1994—, prof. microbiology, 1999—. Mem. cons. group on vaccine devel. U.S. AID, 1989-90; co-chmn. steering com. molecular microbiology and microbial pathogenesis grad. program, Washington U. 1991-92, program coord. and chmn. steering com. molecular microbiology and microbial pathogenesis grad. program, 1992-94; mem. standing com. for the Can. Bacterial Diseases Network, 1992-93; dir. Core DNA Sequencing Facility, Children's Rsch. Inst., Columbus, 1996—; mem. NIH Bacteriology/Mycology Study Sect., 1997-2000. Contbg. author book chpts.; contbr. articles to profl. jours. and publs. Recipient Grad. fellowship U. Conn., 1970-76, Conn. State Fellowship for Grad. Students, 1971-73, fellowship NIH, 1976-78, Neurosci. Tng. Grant Postdoctoral fellowship, 1978-79; grantee NIH. Fellow IDSA; mem. Am. Soc. Microbiology (counselor-at-large 1997, co-organizer Mo. br. mtg. 1991). Office: Columbus Childrens Rsch Inst 700 Childrens Dr Columbus OH 43205-2664 E-mail: munsonr@pediatrics.ohio-state.edu.

MUNSON, VIRGINIA ALDRICH, interior designer, decorator; b. Evanston, Ill., Oct. 10, 1932; d. Jefferson Elliott and Catherine (Stinson) Aldrich; m. John Chester Munson, Feb. 4, 1956; children: Catherine, John Jr., Laura. AA, Bennett Junior Coll., 1952. Owner, pres. Virginia Munson Interiors, Lake Forest, Ill., 1967—. Mem. Lake Forest Ctr. Infant Welfare Soc., 1957-93, pres., 1976-78; active com. candidates caucus, Lake Forest, 1984-87; mem. women's bd. Lake Forest Hosp., 1977—, Guild of Chgo. Hist. Soc., 1990—, bd. dirs. Infant Welfare Soc. Chgo., 1967-93, Ill. Regent Gunston Hall, 1988-96, Altar Guild, Ch. of the Holy Spirit, 1980—; bd. trustees St. Mary's Svcs., 1998-2004; chmn. landscape and grounds Lake Forest Pl., 2000-02, chair dining svcs. com. 2002-2004, mem. resident adv. coun., 2001-03, fin. commn., 2004—. Mem.: Am. Soc. Interior Designers (Allied 1978—), Soc. Mayflower Descs., Nat. Soc. Colonial Dames Am. (bd. dirs. 1978—, pres. State of Ill. br. 1982—84), Winter Club, Onwentsia Club, Contemporary Club. Republican. Episcopalian. Avocations: tennis, needlepoint.

MUNSON, WILLIAM LESLIE, insurance company executive; b. Chgo., Apr. 28, 1941; s. David Curtiss and Leona Ruth (Anderson) M.; m. Marian Lee Blanton, July 16, 1966; children: Katherine, Sandra, Deborah. Student, U. Md., 1959-62; BBA cum laude, Coll. of Ins., 1968. CPCU, 1967. Asst. mgr. N.Y. Fire Ins. Rating Orgn., N.Y.C., 1959-69; br. mgr. CNA Ins. Co., N.Y.C., 1969-75; pres., dir. Commerce & Industry Ins. Co., N.Y.C., 1975-83; pres. Commerce & Industry of Can., 1980-83; sr. v.p., chief underwriting officer Am. Internat. Underwriters, 1983-87; exec. v.p. Home Ins. Co., 1987-93; pres., chief exec. officer Home Indemnity Ins. Co., 1987-93, also bd. dirs.; chmn. City Internat. Ins. Co. Ltd., 1991-93; pres., COO Merc. and Gen. Reins. Co. Am., 1993-97; chmn., pres., CEO Toa-Re-Ins. Co. Am. (now Toa Reinsurance Co. Am.), 1993—2003; dir. USF Ins. Co., 2004—. Trustee Coll. of Ins., 1985-2001; bd. overseers Sch. of Risk Mgmt., Ins. and Actuarial Sci., St. Johns Univ., 2001—; mem. bd. visitors Drew U., 2002—; bd. dirs. Nat. Coun. Compensation Ins., 1989-92, ISO Comml. Risk Svcs., 1993, Operation Link-Up, 2003—; mem. comml. lines com. Ins. Svcs. Office, 1989-92; trustee Am. Inst. for Charter Property Casualty Underwriters, 1996-2002. Pres. Wyckoff (N.J.) Bd. Edn., 1979-82; chmn. bd. lay leaders Grace United Meth. Ch., Wyckoff, 1989-92, trustee, 1999—. Past mem. Soc. CPCUs (bd. dirs. N.Y. chpt.); mem., Conf. Spl. Risk Underwriters, Reinsurance Assn. Am. (bd. dirs. 1993-2002). Clubs: John St. (N.Y.C.). Republican. Home: 762 Albemarle St Wyckoff NJ 07481-1005 Office Phone: 201-891-7834. E-mail: wlmunson@verizon.net.

MUNSTER, ANDREW MICHAEL, surgeon, educator; b. Budapest, Hungary, Dec. 10, 1935; came to U.S., 1965. s. Leopold S. and Marianne (Barcza) M.; m. Joy O'Sullivan, Dec. 7, 1963; children: Andea, Tara, Alexandra. MD, U. Sydney, Australia, 1959. Diplomate Am. Bd. Surgery. Rsch. fellow Harvard U. Med. Sch., Boston, 1966-67; asst. prof. surgery U. Tex., San Antonio, 1968-71; assoc. prof. surgery Med. U. S.C., Charleston, 1971-76, Johns Hopkins U., Balt., 1976-85, prof., 1985—2001; dir. Burn Ctr., Balt. City Hosp., 1976—2001; prof. emeritus Johns Hopkins U., 2001; med. dir. Transplant Resource Ctr. of Md., 2003—. V.p. Chesapeake Physicians, Balt., 1978-84; Hunterian prof. Royal Coll. Surgeons, 1974; chmn. Burn Sci. Pubs. Inc., 1998—; pres. ANDYPLOP Inc., LLC, 1998—. Author: Surgical Anatomy, 1971, Surgical Immunology, 1976, Burn Care for House Officers, 1980; contbr. numerous articles to med. jours. Pres. Chesapeake Ednl. Rsch. Trust, Balt., 1980-84, Charleston Symphony, 1974-75, Charleston TriCounty Arts Coun., 1975-76. Lt. col. U.S. Army, 1968-71. Recipient John Hunter prize U. Sydney, 1959. Fellow Royal Coll. Surgeons Eng., Royal Coll. Surgeons Edinburgh (Scotland), Am. Assn. Surgeons of Trauma, Colombian Coll. Surgeons; mem. Am. Burn Assn. (sec. 1990-93, 1st v.p. 1993-94, pres.-elect 1994-95, pres. 1995, found. pres. 2001), So. Surg. Assn., Soc. Univ. Surgeons, Am. Surg. Assn. E-mail: aandyplop@aol.com.

MUNT, JANET S. state legislator; b. N.Y.C., June 14, 1923; m. Plummer Coldwell Munt (dec.); 4 children. BA, Sweet Briar Coll., 1944; MS, Columbia U., 1948. Pvt. practice clin. social worker; mem., Chittenden County Vt. Senate, Montpelier, 1999—. Trustee Burlington Coll. Fellow Am. Orthopsychiat. Assn., Inc.; mem. NASW, Acad. Cert. Social Workers. Democrat. Office: Vt Legislative Coun 115 State St # 33 Montpelier VT 05633-0001

MUNTEANU, LAURA, mathematician, educator; b. N. Balcescu, Romania, Oct. 2, 1971; arrived in U.S., 1998; d. Aurel and Maria Florescu; m. Marius Ionut Munteanu, June 17, 2000. BA in Math., Al. I. Cuza U., Iasi, Romania, 1995; MA in Math., U. Okla., 2000. Tchg. asst. U. Okla., Norman, Okla., 1998—. Home: Apt G 1532 E Lindsey Norman OK 73071 Office: Univ Okla 601 Elm Ave Norman OK 73070

MÜNTER, LEILANI MAAJA, race car driver; b. Rochester, Minn. d. Manfred and Doris Munter. MS in Biology, U. Calif., San Diego; study, Sebring Internat. Raceway, Fla. Lic. stock car driver Nat. Assn. Stock Car Auto Racing. Former tchrs. asst. cellular biology U. Calif., San Diego; race car driver Nascar Dodge weekly series late model divsn., 2004—; competed in ROMCO Super Late Model Series, Allison Legacy Series. Spl. corr. Nascar-.com, 2004—. Photo double (for Catherine Zeta-Jones films) in Traffic and America's Sweethearts. Avocations: scuba diving, snowboarding. Office: PO Box 3335 Mooresville NC 28117 also: 5315 Highgate Dr Ste 204 Durham NC 27713

MUNTZ, ERIC PHILLIP, aerospace and mechanical engineering and radiology educator, consultant; b. Hamilton, Ont., Can., May 18, 1934; came to U.S., 1961, naturalized, 1985; s. Eric Percival and Marjorie Louise (Weller) M.; m. Janice Margaret Furey, Oct. 21, 1964; children: Sabrina Weller, Eric Phillip. BASc., U. Toronto, 1956, MASc., 1957, PhD, 1961. Halfback Toronto Argonauts, 1957-60; group leader Gen. Electric, Valley Forge, Pa., 1961-69; assoc. prof. aerospace engring. and radiology U. So. Calif., Los Angeles, 1969-71, prof., 1971-87, chmn. aerospace engring., 1987-97, A.B. Freeman prof. engring., 1992—, chmn. aerospace and mech. engring., 2000—03. Cons. to aerospace and med. device cos., 1967—; mem. rev. of physics (plasma and fluids) panel NRC, Washington, 1983-85 Contbr. numerous articles in gas dynamics, micromech. sys., and med. diagnostics to profl. publs., 1961—; patentee med. imaging, isotope separation, nondestructive testing, net shape

mfg., transient energy release micromachines, microscale vacuum sys., micropropulsion sys. Mem. Citizens Environ. Avc. Coun., Pasadena, Calif., 1972-76. Pilot RCAF, 1955-60. U.S. Air Force grantee, 1961-74, 82—; NSF grantee, 1970-76, 87-92; NASA grantee, 1990-94, 2001—; FDA grantee, 1980-86. Fellow AIAA (aerospace Contbn. to Soc. award 1987), Am. Phys. Soc.; mem. NAE. Episcopalian. Home: 1560 E California Blvd Pasadena CA 91106-4104 Office: U So Calif Univ Pk Los Angeles CA 90089-1191 Office Phone: 213-740-5366. Business E-Mail: muntz@spock.usc.edu.

MUNTZ, ERNEST GORDON, historian, educator; b. Buffalo, Nov. 15, 1923; s. J. Palmer and Laura Estelle (Wedekindt) M.; m. Marjorie Corinne Wilson, June 29, 1948; children— Carolyn Odell, Deborah Lynn, Howard Gordon. AB, Wheaton (Ill.) Coll., 1948; PhD, U. Rochester, N.Y., 1960. Asst. prof. social sci. Blue Mountain (Miss.) Coll., 1954-56; from asst. prof. to prof. history Union U., Jackson, Tenn., 1956-61; assoc. faculty U. Cin., 1961-91, prof. history, 1969-91, prof. emeritus, 1991—; dean Raymond Walters Coll., Cin., 1969-90, dean emeritus, 1991—. Cons.-evaluator North Ctrl. Assn. Colls. and Schs., 1974-91, mem. Commn. on Instns. of Higher Edn., 1983-87 Served as officer USAAF, 1943-46, ret., 1975; col. USAFR. So. Fellowships Fund fellow, 1955 Mem. Am. Assn. Cmty. and Jr. Colls. (bd. dirs. coun. 2 yr. colls. of 4 yr. instns. 1988-90), Phi Alpha Theta, Pi Gamma Mu. Presbyterian. Home: 91 Bristlecone Ct Augusta GA 30909

MUNTZ, J(OHN) RICHARD, clergyman; b. Buffalo, Dec. 14, 1927; s. J. Palmer and Laura Estelle (Wedekindt) M.; m. Marietta Hayden, June 22, 1951; children: Palmer Hayden, Laura Marie De Soer. BS, Wheaton (Ill.) Coll., 1949; BDiv, We. Conservative Bapt. Sem., Portland, Oreg., 1953; MA, Wayne State U., Detroit, 1964; ThM, No. Bapt. Sem., Chgo., 1964; MA in Libr., San Jose State U., 1976. Ordained to ministry Bapt. Ch. Pastor Grace Bapt. Ch., Rochelle, Ill., 1954-56, West Bloomfield Bapt Ch., Orchard Lake, Mich., 1957-62; prof., libr. San Francisco Bapt. Theol. Sem., 1964-72, Denver Bible Bapt. Sem., 1972-75; libr., prof. We. Bapt. Coll., Salem, Oreg., 1975—. Accreditation team mem. Am. Assn. Bible Colls., Fayetteville, Ark., 1977-94. Author: A Suggested Theological Bibliography for AABC Colleges, Supplement I, 1994. Deacon, shepherd, tchr. Bethany Bapt. Ch., Salem, Oreg. Mem. Assn. Christian Librs., So. Bapt. Hist. Soc., Beta Phi Mu. Republican. Baptist. Office: Western Bapt Coll 5000 Deer Park Dr SE Salem OR 97301-9330 Home: 5183 Sycan Ct SE Salem OR 97306-1668 E-mail: rmuntz@wbc.edu.

MUNYER, EDWARD A. zoologist; b. Chgo., May 8, 1936; s. G. and M. Munyer; m. Marianna J. Munyer, Dec. 12, 1981; children: Robert, William, Richard, Laura, Cheryl. BS, Ill. State U., 1958, MS, 1962. Biology tchr. MDR High Sch., Minonk, Ill., 1961-63; instr. Ill. State U., Normal, 1963-64; curator zoology Ill. State Mus., Springfield, 1964-67, asst. dir., 1981-98, asst. dir. emeritus, 1998—; assoc. prof. Vincennes (Ind.) U., 1967-70; dir. Vincennes U. Mus., 1968-70; assoc. curator Fla. Mus. Natural History, Gainesville, 1970-81. Mem. Mus. Accreditation Vis. Com. Roster, 1976—. Contbr. articles to profl. jours. Mem. Am. Assn. Mus. (bd. dirs. 1990-95), Assn. Midwest Mus. (pres. 1990-92, lifetime achievement award for disting. svc. 1998), Ill. Assn. Mus. (bd. dirs. 1981-86, lifetime profl. achievement award 1998), Wilson Ornithol. Soc. (life). Office: Ill State Mus Spring & Edward Sts Springfield IL 62706-0001

MUNYON, WILLIAM HARRY, JR., architect; b. Panama City, Panama, Feb. 20, 1945; (parents Am. citizens); s. William Harry and Ruth (Hyde) M.; m. Cheryl Lynn Guess, Dec. 31, 1986 BA, Tulane U., 1967; postgrad., U. Hawaii, 1972-73; BArch with high distinction, U. Ariz., 1978; postgrad., U.S. Naval War Coll., 1984, Armed Forces Staff Coll., 1985. Elec. designer Ohlsen-Mitchell, Inc., New Orleans, 1966-67; rsch. cons. hist. preservation U. Ariz., Tucson, 1974-75; cons. hist. preservation State of Ariz., Phoenix, 1974-75; mktg. dir., programmer, designer Architecture One, Ltd., Tucson, 1975-78; mng. prin. Artistic License II, graphics and design, 1975-86; mng. ptnr. Aardvark Graphics, 1986—; dir. mktg. Hansen Lind Meyer, P.C., Iowa City and Chgo., 1978-79; v.p. John F. Steffen Assocs., Inc. (subs. Turner Constrn.), St. Louis, 1979-80; sr. assoc., dir. corp. devel. Rees Assocs., Inc., Oklahoma City, 1980-82; mktg. dir., asst. to pres., dir. planning/interior arch. SHWC, Inc., Dallas, 1982-84; dir. justice facilities program Henningson, Durham & Richardson, Inc., Dallas, 1984-87; prin., dir. justice and security facilities Kaplan/McLaughlin/Diaz Architects, San Francisco, 1987-90; prin. Silver & Ziskind Architects, San Francisco, 1990-91; founder, mng. prin., lead designer The Resource Group (now TRG Consulting, Inc.), Palm Springs, Calif., 1991—; mktg. cons. TRG Consulting, Inc., Fresno, 1979—. Vice-chmn., CEO Program Mgmt. Assocs. subs. Kaplan/McLaughlin/Diaz, 1987-90; mem. adv. bd. Interior Design mag., 1978-79; mem. Bldg. Energy Performance Stds. Adv. Panel, 1979-81; founder ann. archtl. history prize U. Ariz., 1979—, ann. mil. leadership award Tulane U., 1985—, Naval War Coll. Found., 1999—. Active U. Ariz. Fund for Athletic Devel., 1977—; sponsor Dallas 500; mem. Naval War Coll. Found. With USN, 1967-73; capt. Res. Recipient Producer's Coun. prize for design excellence, 1977, Henry Adams award 1978, Regional Design awards. Mem. AIA (architecture for justice com. 1978—), Nat. Trust Hist. Preservation, Naval Res. Officers Assn., Soc. Archtl. Historians, Am. Planning Assn., Am. Correctional Assn., Am. Jail Assn. (stds. com. 1991-96), Am. Soc. Indsl. Security, Western States Corvette Coun., Nat. Corvette Mus. (charter), Naval Inst., Nat. Sheriffs' Assn. (life), Calif. State Sheriffs' Assn., Soc. Mktg. Profl. Svcs., Mil. Officers Assn. U.S. (life), Mensa, Lionel Collectors Club Am., Brit. Model Soldier Soc., William Britain Collector's Club, NRA, Profl. Svcs. Mgmt. Assn., Assn. Former Intelligence Officers, Navy League, Tulane U. Alumni Assn., Tulane U. "T" Club, U.S. Golf Assn., Blue Key, Scabbard and Blade, Phi Kappa Phi (life), Sigma Chi (life), 65 Roses Sports Club. Roman Catholic. Home: 74885 N Cove Dr Indian Wells CA 92210-7109 Office Phone: 559-269-3500. E-mail: whmunyon@lightspeed.net.

MUNZ, DIANA, Olympic athlete; b. Cleve., Jan. 19, 1982; d. Robert and Carol Munz. Student, John Carroll U. Profl. swimmer, 2000—. Recipient Gold medal 4 x 200-meter freestyle Sydney Olympics, 2000, Silver medal 800-meter freestyle World Championships, 1998; winner 800-meter freestyle, non-Olympic 1500-meter freestyle nat. championships, spring and summer 1998, spring 1999, 400-meter freestyle nat. championships, spring 1999 Office: USA Swimming 1 Olympic Plz Colorado Springs CO 80909-5746 Address: 4820 Chagrin River Rd Chagrin Falls OH 44022-2407

MUNZER, CYNTHIA BROWN, mezzo-soprano; b. Clarksburg, W.Va., Sept. 30, 1948; d. Ralph Emerson and Doris Marguerite (Dixon) Brown; 1 dau., Christina Marie. Student, U. Kans., 1965-69. Adj. prof. voice U. So. Calif., 1994—. Debut. Oxford (Eng.) Opera, 1969, Met. Opera debut, N.Y.C., 1973; performed 1973-96 with: Met. Opera, Phila. Opera, Wolftrap Festival, Washington Opera, Goldovsky Opera, Washington Civic Opera, St. Petersburg Opera, Dallas Opera, Metropolitan Opera-Japan, Boston Concert Opera, Dayton Opera, Chgo. Opera Theatre, Mich. Opera, Kansas City Opera, New Orleans Opera, Houston Grand Opera, Ft. Worth Opera, Florentine Opera-Milw., Minn. Opera, Central City Opera, Aspen Festival, Opera Colo., Boston Festival Orch., Ontario Opera, Salt Lake City Opera, Nev. Opera, Cleve. Opera, Opera Pacific, Des Moines Opera, Ky. Opera, Mobile Opera, Internat. Artist Series in Kuala Lumpur, Penang, Jakarta, Hong Kong Philharm., Shanghai Symphony, Singapore Symphony, Philippine Philharm., N.Y.C. Ballet, Am. Symphony, Nat. Symphany, Charleston Symphony, Phila. Orch., New Haven Symphony, Houston Symphony, Ft. Wayne Symphony, El Paso Symphony, San Antonio Symphony, Amarillo Symphany, Wichita Symphony, Milw. Symphony, Minn. Orch., L.A. Chamber Orch., Ventura Chamber Orch., Denver Symphony, Phoenix Symphony, Oreg. Bach. Festival, San Francisco Symphony, L.A. Philharm., Louisville Symphony, Rochester Philharm., Binghamton Symphony, Rode Island Symphony, Carmel Bach Festival, Anchorage Symphony, L'Opera De Montreal, Colo. Opera Festival, N.Y. Mozart Bicentennial Festival, Brattleboro Festival, Knoxville Opera, Gold Coast Opera, Hawaii Opera, Augusta Opera, Berkshire Opera, Madison Opera, Chattanooga Symphony, Shreveport Opera, New York City Opera. Recipient Frederick K. Weyerhaeuser award, Gramma Fisher Found. award, Goeran Gentele award, Sullivan Found. award, Geraldine Farrar award, Joseph Schland Opera Presentations award; Nat. Opera Inst. grantee; winner Met. Opera Nat. auditions. Office: Prima Americas Artists Mgmt 788 Columbus Ave Apt 15A New York NY 10025-5936

MUNZER, STEPHEN IRA, lawyer; b. NYC, Mar. 15, 1939; s. Harry and Edith (Isacowitz) M.; m. Patricia Eve Munzer, Aug. 10, 1965; children: John, Margaret. AB, Brown U., 1960; JD, Cornell U., 1963. Bar: N.Y. 1964, U.S. Supreme Ct. 1974, U.S. Dist. Ct. (so. and eas. dists.) N.Y., U.S. Ct. Appeals (3d cir.). Formerly ptnr. Pincus Munzer Bizar & D'Alessandro, 1978-83; atty., real estate investor Munzer & Saunders, LLP, 1984—. Pres. Simcor Mgmt. Corp., N.Y.C., 1984—. Lt. USNR, 1965-75. Mem. Assn. of Bar of City of N.Y., N.Y. State Bar Assn., Washington Club. Jewish. Avocations: golf, skiing. Home: 30 Lincoln Plz New York NY 10023 also: 170 Shearer Rd Washington CT 06793-1013 Office: 609 5th Ave New York NY 10017-1021

MUNZNER, ROBERT FREDERICK, biomedical engineer; b. Balt., July 3, 1936; s. Robert F. Munzner and Catherine E. (Appel) Gay; m. Jo Ann Goettee, Sept. 2, 1960 (div. 1980); children: Elizabeth Mae, Robert Victor, Ann Catherine; m. Karen E. Winstedt, Oct. 1, 1988. BS in Physics, Loyola Coll., Balt., 1963; PhD in Biomed. Engring., U. Va., 1976. Aerospace engr. Westinghouse Def. and Space, Balt., 1963-69; rsch. assoc. Johns Hopkins U., Balt., 1975-77; chief, neurol. devices br. U.S. FDA, Rockville, Md., 1977-97, expert sci. reviewer, 1998-99; regulatory affairs cons. Herndon, Va., 1999—. Exec. sec. neurol. device adv. panel. IEEE Standards Bd., 1999-2001. Co-author: Cerebellar Stimulation for Spasticity, 1984, The Physicians Perspective on Medical Law, 1997; contbr. articles to profl. jours. Fellow Johns Hopkins U., Balt., 1975, U. Va. fellow, Charlottesville, 1972-73, Thornton fellow, 1971. Mem. IEEE (sr., Millennium medal 2000), Biomed. Engring. Soc., Engring. in Medicine and Biology Soc. (chmn. stds. com., ad com. 1999—), Sigma Xi. Achievements include research in atrial mechanical stimulation producing vasomotor reflex. Office Phone: 434-263-8862. Business E-Mail: robert@doctordevice.com.

MURABITO, JOHN, insurance company executive; BA in Econs., Augustana Coll.; MA in Indsl. Rels., U. Iowa. With The Trane Co., Symbion, Inc., Frito-Lay divsn. PepsiCo; sr. v.p. human resources and corp. svcs. Monsanto; exec. v.p. human resources and svcs. divsn. Cigna Corp., Phila., 2003—. Office: Cigna Corp 1 Liberty Pl Philadelphia PA 19192-1552

MURAD, FERID, physician; b. Whiting, Ind., Sept. 14, 1936; s. John and Josephine (Bowman) Murad; m. Carol Ann Leopold, June 21, 1958; children: Christine, Marianne, Carrie, Julie, Joseph. BA, DePauw U., 1958; MD, PhD, Case Western Res. U., 1965. Diplomate Nat. Bd. Med. Examiners. Intern and resident Mass. Gen. Hosp., Boston, 1965—67; clin. assoc. NIH, Bethesda, Md., 1967—70; dir. clin. rsch. ctr. U. Va., Charlottesville, 1971—81, prof. internal medicine and pharmacology, 1975—81, Stanford (Calif.) U., 1981—88, acting chmn. dept. medicine, 1986—88; chief of medicine VA Med. Ctr., Palo Alto, Calif., 1981—88; v.p. pharm. divsn. Abbott Labs., 1988—92, CEO, pres. molecular geriatrics, 1993—95; prof. dept. medicine, chmn. dept. integrative biology and pharmacology U. Tex., Houston, 1997—, dir. Inst. Molecular Medicine, 1999—. Co-editor: The Pharmacological Basis of Therapeutics, 1985; contbr. articles to profl. jours. Recipient Albert and Mary Lasker Found. award, 1996, Nobel Prize for Medicine, 1998, others. Mem.: Western Assn. Physicians (Ciba award 1988, Lasker award 1996), Assn. Am. Physicians, Am. Soc. Clin. Investigation, Am. Soc. Physiology, Am. Soc. Biol. Chemists, Am. Soc. for Pharmacology and Exptl. Therapeutics, Am. Acad. Arts and Scis., Inst. of Medicine of NAS. Achievements include patents in field. Avocations: golf, carpentry. Office: U Tex Med Sch Dept Integrative Biology/Pharmacology PO Box 20708 Houston TX 77225-0708 Office Phone: 713-500-7509. E-mail: ferid.murad@uth.tmc.edu.

MURAD, SOHAIL, engineer educator; b. Rawalpindi, Panjab, Pakistan, May 4, 1953; came to U.S., 1975; s. Akram and Ruh Afza (Azim) M.; m. Penelope Ann Newland, Dec. 15, 1979; children: Adam, Anita. BSChE, U. Engring., Lahore, Pakistan, 1974; MSChE, U. Fla., 1976; PhD of Chem. Engr., Cornell U., 1979. Sr. engr. Exxon Rsch. and Engr. Co., Florham Park, N.J., 1981-82; asst. prof., assoc. prof. U. Ill., Chgo., 1979-91, prof., 1991—. Adv. bd. mem. Computer Applications in Engineering Education, N.Y.C., 1994—. Contbr. (ency.) Ency. of Fluid Mechanics, 1989, articles to profl. jours. Grantee Dept. Energy, 1987—, NSF, 1985—, NATO, 1985-98, Sun Microsystems, 2003-; fellow Ballistic Rsch. lab., 1985. Mem. AIChE, Am. Chem. Soc. (grantee 1994—), Am. Philatelic Soc. Office: Univ Ill MC 110 810 S Clinton St Chicago IL 60607-4408 Office Phone: 312-996-5593. E-mail: murad@uic.edu.

MURADIAN, VAZGEN, violist, composer; b. Ashtarak, Armenia, Oct. 17, 1921; arrived in U.S., 1950, naturalized, 1956; s. Grigor and Arusiak (Vardanian) Muradian; m. Arpi Kirkyasharian Muradian, Aug. 29, 1964; children: Vardges, Armen Morian. Professore di musica, Benedetto Marcello State Conservatory Music, Venice, 1948; studied composition with Gabriele Bianchi, studied composition with Vittoria Giannini, studied violin with Luigi Ferro, studied viola d'amore with Renzo Sabatini. Tchr. violin, solfeggio and theory of music Collegio Armeno, Venice, Italy, 1945-50. Pvt. tchr. viola d'amore. Composer numerous works including 57 symphonies, 68 concertos for all classical instruments and many non-traditional instruments, 12 suites for orch., 4 moto perpetuos for violin and orch., 7 sonatas for solo violin, 7 sonatas for violin and piano, 2 sonatas for piano, sonatas for viola d'amore, 2 quartets, 2 trios for violin, cello and piano, 56 songs with orch. and 8 songs for chorus and orch. in six languages on works of Shakespeare, Petrarch, Dante, Geothe, Hugo, others; more than 200 major works to date; compositions performed throughout the U.S. and abroad; author articles in field; debut, N.Y. Lincoln Center, 1972; violist with various U.S. orchs. including New Orleans Philharmonic, Wagner Opera Co.; appeared as viola d'amore soloist, U.S. and abroad. Recipient Tekeyan prize, 1962, Mashdots Medal for lifetime achievement, 1996, Viola D' Amore Soc. Am. award, 2000, Saint Sahak and Saint Mesrop Medal for lifetime achievement, 2001, and numerous others. Mem.: ASCAP, Viola D'amore Soc. Am. Achievements include being the only composer to write concertos for all classical instruments and many non-traditional instruments, to date 68 concertos for 38 different instruments; All major compositions are written in classical sonata form. All melodies and themes are his own originals. Home: 269 W 72nd St Apt 11A New York NY 10023-2719

MURAI, KEVIN, information technology executive; b. 1964; BSEE, U. Waterloo, Ontario. Former mgr. mgmt. info. svcs. Verifact, Inc., Ontario, Canada; joined Ingram Micro Inc., 1988, sr. v.p., 1997—2002, exec. v.p., 2000—, officer, 2000—; v.p., operations Ingram Micro Can., Canada, 1993—97, pres., 1997—2000, Ingram Micro US, 2000—01, COO, 2000—02; pres. Ingram Micro N. Am., 2002—. Office: Ingram Micro Inc 1600 E St Andrew Pl Santa Ana CA 92705-4931 Office Phone: 714-566-1000. Office Fax: 714-566-7900.*

MURANAKA, HIDEO, artist, educator; b. Mitaka, Tokyo, Japan, Feb. 4, 1946; s. Nobukichi and Hisae M. BFA, Tokyo Nat. U. of Fine Arts, 1970, MFA, 1972. Calif. Community Coll.- Instr. Cred. Drawing accepted for The Pacific Coast States Collection from the v.p. house, Washington, 1980, Nat. Mus. Art, Bklyn. Mus., Achenbach Found., Calif. Palace of Legion of Hon., Yergeau-Musee Internat. d'Art (Can.), Japanese Calligraphy Book, 2000. Mem. Democratic Nat. Comm., Wash., 1985—. Recipient second prize Iternat. Art Exhbn. Museo Hosio, Italy, 1984, V.J.'s Artist award Palm Springs Desert Mus., 1995; named to Hist. Preservation Am. Hall of Fame. Mem. Oakland Mus. Assn., The Fine Arts Mus. San Francisco, Lepidopterist's Soc. Avocations: collecting butterflies, music. Home: 179 Oak St Apt W San Francisco CA 94102-5948

MURANE, WILLIAM EDWARD, lawyer; b. Denver, Mar. 4, 1933; s. Edward E. and Theodora (Wilson) M.; m. Rosemarie Palmerone, Mar. 26, 1960; children: Edward Wheelock, Peter Davenport, Alexander Phelps. AB, Dartmouth Coll., 1954; LLB, Stanford U., 1957. Bar: Wyo. 1957, Colo. 1958, D.C. 1978, U.S. Supreme Ct. 1977. Assoc. then ptnr. Holland & Hart, Denver, 1961-69; dep. gen. counsel U.S. Dept. Commerce, Washington, 1969-71; gen. counsel FDIC, Washington, 1971-72; ptnr. Holland & Hart, Denver, 1972—2000. Pub. mem. Adminstrv. Conf. of the U.S., Washington, 1978-81. Bd. dirs. Ctr. for Law and Rsch., Denver, 1973-76, Acad. in the Wilderness, Denver, 1986—, Colo. Bus. Com. for Arts, 2002—; trustee Colo. Symphony Orch., 1994-2000; mem. bd. visitors Stanford U. Law Sch. Capt. USAF, 1958-61. Fellow Am. Coll. Trial Lawyers; mem. ABA (ho of dels. 1991-96), U. Club, Cactus Club. Republican. Avocations: fishing, classical music. Office: Holland & Hart 555 17th St Ste 2700 Denver CO 80202-3950

MURANO, ELSA A. federal agency administrator; b. Havana, Cuba; BS in Biol. Sci., Fla. Internat. U.; MS in Anaerobic Microbiology, Va. Polytechnic Inst.; PhD in Food Sci. and Tech., Va. State U. Asst. prof. Iowa State U., Ames, 1990—92, prof. in charge rsch. programs linear accelertor facility, 1992—95; various positions including dir. food safety A&M U., College Station, Tex., 1995—2001, assoc. prof. animal sci., 1995—2000, prof. dept. animal sci., 2000—01; undersec. food safety USDA, Washington, 2001—. Chair food safety state initiative com. Tex. Agr. Ext. Sta., 1999—2001; nat. adv. com. meat and poultry inspection USDA, 2001; mem. Nat. Alliance for Food Safety Ops. Com., 1998—2001, chair, 2000—01. Mem.: Intenat. Assn. Food Protection, Poultry Sci. Assn., Inst. Food Technologists, Assn. Meat Sci., Am. Soc. Microbiology. Office: USDA Food Safety 1400 Independence Ave Sw Washington DC 20250

MURARKA, SHYAM PRASAD, science and engineering educator, administrator; b. Jaynagar, Bihar, India, Mar. 13, 1940; came to U.S., 1966; s. Bihari L. and Suti Murarka; m. Saroj Murarka, May 21, 1962; children: Sumeet, Amal. BS in Chemistry with honors, Bihar U., Muzaffarpur, 1958, MS in Chemistry, 1960; PhD in Chemistry, Agra (India) U., 1970; PhD in Materials Sci. and Metals, U. Minn., 1970. Lectr., rsch. assoc. Bihar U., 1960-61; trainee Atomic Energy Est., Trombay, Maharastra, 1961-62, sci. officer, 1962-66; rsch. asst. U. Minn., Mpls., 1966-70, rsch. assoc., 1970-72; mem. tech. staff, supr. Bell Labs., Murray Hill, NJ, 1972-84; prof. Rensselaer Poly. Inst., Troy, NY, 1984—2002, dir. Ctr. for Integrated Electronics and Electronics Mfg., 1994-96, dir. Ctr. for Advanced Interconnect Sci. and Tech., 1996-2000, dir. Sematech Ctr. of Excellence, 1989-96, Elaine S. & Jack S. Parker chair engring., 1997—2002, prof. emeritus, 2002—. Cons. Bell Labs., Murray Hill, N.J., 1984-89, Applied Materials, Santa Clara, Calif., 1997-99. Author: Silicides for VLSI Applications, 1983, Metallization Theory and Practice for VLSI and ULSI, 1993; (with others) Electronic Materials Science and Technology, 1989, Chemical Mechanical Planarization of Microelectronic Materials, 1997, Copper Fundamental Mechanisms for Micorelectronic Applications, 2000, Interlayer Dielectrics for Semiconductor Technologies, 2003; co-editor: Advanced Metallizations in Microelectronics, 1990, Advanced Metallization and Processing for Semiconductor Devices and Circuits II, 1992, Interface Control of Electrical, Chemical, and Mechanical Properties, 1994, Advaned Metallization for Devices and Circuits, 1994, Microelectronics Technology and Process Integration, 1994, Low Dielectric Constant Materials Synthesis in Microelectronics, 1995, Interlayer Dielectrics for Semiconductor Technologies, 2003; contbr. book chpt. Transition Metal Silicides, 1983. Mem. Tri-City India Assn.'s Indian Comty. Support Group, Albany, 1996. Recipient Gold medal Bihar U., 1960; Univ. Grants Commn. scholar, 1961. Fellow IEEE, Am. Vacuum Soc., Am. Soc. Metals and Electrochem. Soc. (Thomas Callinan award 1987, Electronics Divsn. award 2001); mem. Materials Rsch Soc., Bihar U. Chem. Soc. (hon. life). Achievements include 15 patents in field, over 560 rsch. papers and talks.

MURARO, PAOLO A. immunologist, neurologist; b. Conegliano, Treviso, Italy, July 16, 1967; arrived in U.S., 2001; MD, U. Rome, 1993, PhD, 1998. Vis. fellow neuroimmunology br. NINDS, NIH, Bethesda, Md., 1995—98, vis. scientist neuroimmunology br., 2001—; resident in neurology U. G.D'Annunzio, Chieti, Italy, 1998—2001. Instr. immunology residency program in clin. pathology and lab. medicine U. Chieti Med. Sch., 1998—. Contbr. articles to sci. jours. Grantee Istituto Superiore di Sanita', Italian Ministry Health, 1996, Nat. Rsch. Coun., Italy, 1997, Ministry Univ. and Rsch., Italy, 1998—2002. Fellow: Italian Multiple Sclerosis Soc. (reviewer grant applications 1997—); mem.: Italian Neuroimmunology Assn., Am. Acad. Neurology. Office: NIH Bldg 10-5B16 10 Center Dr MSC1400 Bethesda MD 20892-1400

MURASE, JIRO, lawyer; b. N.Y.C., May 16, 1928; BBA, CCNY, 1955; JD, Georgetown U., 1958, LL.D. (hon.), 1982. Bar: D.C. 1958, N.Y. 1959. Sr. ptnr. Marks & Murase L.L.P., N.Y.C., 1971-97, Bingham McCutchen Murase, N.Y.C., 1997—. Legal counsel Consulate Gen. of Japan; mem. Pres.'s Adv. Com. Trade Negotiations, 1980-82; mem. Trilateral Commn., 1985—; apptd. mem. World Trade Coun., 1984-94; adv. com. internat. investment, tech. and devel. Dept. State, 1975. Editorial bd.: Law and Policy in Internat. Bus. Trustee Asia Found., 1979-83, Japanese Ednl. Inst. N.Y.; bd. dirs. Japan Soc., Japanese C. of C. in N.Y., Inc.; hon. bd. regents Georgetown U.; bd. visitors Georgetown Law Ctr.; adv. coun. Pace U., Internat. House Japan; pres. Japanese-Am. Assn. N.Y., Inc., 1996-98—, Japan Ctr. Internat. Exch., 2001—. Recipient N.Y. Gov.'s citation for contbns. to internat. trade, 1982; named to Second Order of Sacred Treasure (Japan), 1989. Mem. ABA, Assn. of Bar of City of N.Y., N.Y. State Bar Assn., N.Y. County Lawyers Assn., Maritime Law Assn., Consular Law Soc., Fed. Bar Coun., Am. Soc. Internat. Law, World Assn. Lawyers, Japanese-Am. Soc. Legal Studies, Am. Arbitration Assn., Lic. Execs. Soc., U.S. C. of C. Clubs: Nippon (dir.); Ardsley Country; N.Y. Athletic; Mid-Ocean (Bermuda). Office: Bingham McCutchen Murase 399 Park Ave New York NY 10022-4614

MURATA, NATHAN M. physical education educator, researcher; b. Honolulu, Nov. 18, 1962; s. Robert M. and Faye F. Murata. BEd, U. Hawaii, 1984, MEd, 1986, cert. in spl. edn., 1989; PhD, Ohio State U., 1995. Phys. educator St. Louis H.S., Honolulu, 1984—88, athletic dir., 1988—89; adapted phys. educator Honolulu Dist. Office, Honolulu, 1989—92; asst. prof. phys. edn. Chaminade U., Honolulu, 1995—96, U. Toledo, 1996—97; assoc. prof. U. Hawaii, Honolulu, 1997—. Propr. Murata & Assocs., CAPE, Honolulu, 2002—. Co-author: Case Studies in Adapte PE, 2003; contbr. articles to profl. jours. Office: U Hawaii at Manoa 1337 Lower Campus Rd Honolulu HI 96822 Office Phone: 808-956-4714. E-mail: nmurata@hawaii.edu.

MURATA, TADAO, engineering and computer science educator; b. Takayama, Gifu, Japan, June 26, 1938; arrived in U.S., 1962; s. Yonosuke and Ryu (Aomame) M.; m. Nellie Kit-Ha Shin, 1964; children: Patricia Emi, Theresa Terumi. BSE.E., Tokai U., 1962; MSE.E., U. Ill., 1964, PhD in Elec. Engring., 1966. Research asst. U. Ill., Urbana, 1962-66; asst. prof. U. Ill. at Chgo., 1966-68, assoc. prof., 1970-76, prof., 1977—, UIC disting. prof., 2002—; assoc. prof. Tokai U., Tokyo, 1968-70. Vis. prof. U. Calif., Berkeley, 1976-77; cons. Nat. Bur. Stds., Gaithersburg, Md., 9184-85; panel mem. NAS, Washington, 1981-82, 83-85; vis. scientist Nat. Ctr. For Sci. Rsch., France, 1981; guest rschr. Gesellschaft für Mathematik und Datenverarbeitung, Germany, 1979; Hitachi-Endowed prof. Osaka (Japan) U., 1993-94. Editor IEEE Trans. on Software Engring., 1986-92; assoc. editor Jour. of Cirs., Sysems and Computers, 1990—; contbr. articles to sci. and engring. jours. Recipient C.A. Petri Disting. Tech. Achievement award Soc. Design and Process Scis., 2000; Sr. univ. scholar award U. Ill., 1990; NSF grantee, 1978—, U.S.-Spain coop. rsch. grantee, 1985-87. Fellow IEEE (life; golden core charter mem. IEEE Computer Soc., Donald G. Fink Prize award 1991), Inst. Electronics, Info. and Comm. Engrs., IEICE; mem. Assn. Computing Machinery, Info. Processing Soc. Japan, European Assn. for Theoretical Computer Sci., Upsilon Pi Epsilon. Avocations: golf, travel. Office: U Ill Dept Computer Sci m/c 152 851 S Morgan St Chicago IL 60607-7042 E-mail: t.murata@ieee.org.

MURAYAMA, HITOSHI, physicist, educator; b. Tokyo, Mar. 21, 1964;, permanent resident; BSc in Physics, U. Tokyo, 1986, PhD in Theoretical Physics, 1991. Physics prof. U. Calif., Berkeley, 2000—; rsch. assoc. Tohoku U., 1991—95; postdoctoral fellow Lawrence Berkeley Lab.; asst. prof. physics dept. physics U. Calif., Berkeley, 1995—98, assoc. prof. physics, 1998—2000, prof. physics, 2000—. Mem. neutrino facilities assessment com.NRC; mem. physics adv. com. Fermilab; mem. high energy physics adv. panel, subpanel on

long range planning for U.S. High Energy Physics DOE/NSF; mem. organizational com. Snowmass 2001 Meeting. Recipient Nishinomiya Yukawa Commemoration prize in theoretical physics, 2002; fellow, Japan Soc. for Promotion Sci., 1990—91; Alfred P. Sloan fellow, 1996—99, rsch. grantee, NSF, 1996—2001, 2001—. Office: Dept Physics Univ Calif Berkeley CA 94720

MURAYAMA, MAKIO, biochemist; b. San Francisco, Aug. 10, 1912; s. Hakuyo and Namiye (Miyasaka) M.; children: Gibbs Soga, Alice Myra. BA, U. Calif., Berkeley, 1938, MA, 1940; PhD (NIH fellow), U. Mich., 1953; ScD honoris causa, Open Internat. U., Sri Lanka, 1994. Rsch. biochemist Children's Hosp. Mich., Detroit, 1943, 1945—48, Bellevue Hosp., N.Y.C., 1943—45, Harper Hosp., Detroit, 1949—54; rsch. fellow chemistry Calif. Inst. Tech., Pasadena, 1954—56; rsch. assoc. biochemistry Grad. Sch. Medicine U. Pa., Phila., 1956—58; spl. rsch. fellow Cavendish Lab. Nat. Cancer Inst., Cambridge, England, 1958; sr. rsch. biochemist NIH, Bethesda, Md., 1958—93. Author: (with Robert M. Nalbandian) Sickle Cell Hemoglobin, 1973; discovered DIPA (decompression-inducible platelet aggregation), 1975; discovered DIPA causes vascular occlusion in both acute mountain sickness and diver's syndrome, 1984. Fellow Am. Inst. Chemists; mem. AAAS, Am. Chem. Soc., Am. Soc. Biol. Chemists, Assn. Clin. Scientists, Undersea and Hyperbaric Med. Soc., Aerospace Med. Assn., Internat. Platform Assn., West African Soc. Pharmacology (hon.), N.Y. Acad. Sci., Sigma Xi. Achievements include patent for automatic amperometric titration apparatus, 1958; development of molecular mechanism of human red cell sickling and prevention of sickle cell crisis by oral prophylactic carbamide, 1972; discovery of decompression inducible platelet aggregation by means of simulation of decompression-inducible platelet aggregation of diving in frogs and mice that diver's disease and acute mountain sickness could be alleviated by piracetam and thymol, antiplatelet agents, 1986. Home: 5010 Benton Ave Bethesda MD 20814-2804 E-mail: mmurayama@aol.com.

MURCHISON, DAVID CLAUDIUS, lawyer; b. N.Y.C., Aug. 19, 1923; s. Claudius Temple and Constance (Waterman) M.; m. June Margaret Guilfoyle, Dec. 19, 1946 (dec. June 2001); children: David Roderick, Brian, Courtney, Bradley, Stacy; m. Janet Miller Paro, Aug. 10, 2002. AA, George Washington U., 1947, BA, JD with honors, George Washington U., 1949. Bar: D.C. 1949, Supreme Ct. 1955. Assoc. Dorr, Hand & Dawson, N.Y.C., 1949-50; founding ptnr. Howrey & Simon, Washington, 1956-90, counsel, 1990—. Legal asst. under sec. army, 1949-51; counsel motor vehicle, textile, aircraft, ordinance and shipbldg. divsns. Nat. Prodn. Authority, 1951-52; assoc. gen. counsel Small Def. Plants Adminstrn., 1952-53; legal adv. and asst. to chmn. FTC, 1953-55 Chmn. So. Africa Wildlife Trust. With AUS, 1943-45, ETO. Mem. ABA (chmn. com. internat. restrictive bus. practices sect. antitrust law 1954-55, sect. adminstrv. law, sect. litigation), FBA, D.C. Bar Assn., N.Y. State Bar Assn., Order of Coif, Met. Club, Chevy Chase Club, Talbot Country Club, Congl. Country Club, Columbia Country Club. Republican.

MURCHISON, DAVID RODERICK, lawyer; b. Washington, May 28, 1948; s. David Claudius and June Margaret (Guilfoyle) M.; m. Kathy Ann Kohn, Mar. 15, 1981; children: David Christopher, Benjamin Michael. BA cum laude, Princeton U., 1970; JD, Georgetown U., 1975. Bar: D.C. 1975, Fla. 1993. Legal asst. to vice chmn. CAB, Washington, 1975-76, enforcement atty., 1976-77; sr. atty. Air Transport Assn., Washington, 1977-80, asst. v.p., sec., 1981-85; sr. assoc. Zuckert, Scoutt and Rasenberger, Washington, 1980-81; v.p., asst. gen. counsel Piedmont Aviation, Inc., Winston-Salem, N.C., 1985-88; v.p., gen. counsel, sec. Braniff, Inc., Dallas, 1988-89, chief exec. officer Orlando, 1990-94; fed. adminstrv. law judge Office of Hearings and Appeals, Charleston, W.Va., 1994-96, chief adminstrv. law judge Mobile, Ala., 1996-99, adminstrv. law judge, 1999—. Lectr. continuing legal edn. program Wake Forest U., Winston-Salem, 1988. Contbr. articles to legal jours. Lt. USNR, 1970-72. Mem. ABA, Met. Club Washington. Republican. Roman Catholic. Office: Hearings & Appeals Office 550 Government St #200 Mobile AL 36602

MURCUTT, GLEN, architect; b. London, 1936; arrived in Australia, 1956; m. Wendy Lewin, 1997; 1 stepchild; 2 children from previous marriage. BArch, U. New S. Wales, 1961. Architect Ancher, Mortlock, Murray and Woolley, Australia, 1964—70, pvt. practice, Sydney, Australia, 1970—. Recipient Pritzker Architecture Prize, Hyatt Found., 2002; grantee travel grant, Royal Australian Inst. of Architects. Achievements include design of modern primitive homes that connect seamlessly with their environments. Office: Jensen and Walker Inc 8802 Ashcroft Ave Los Angeles CA 90048-2402

MURDEN, ROBERT A. medical administrator, physician; b. Radford, Va., May 5, 1951; s. William P. and Mabel S. Murden; children: Rob, Nick, Chelsea. BS, U. Mich., 1972; MD, U. Mo., Columbia, 1977. Diplomate Am. Bd. Internal Medicine; cert. added qualifications in geriatrics. Resident in internal medicine U. Tex., Galveston, 1977-80; fellow in geriatrics Mt. Sinai Sch. Medicine, N.Y.C., 1983-85; faculty medicine and geriatrics SUNY, Stony Brook, 1985-86, Bklyn., 1986-89, U. Kans. Med. Ctr., Kansas City, 1990-91; faculty medicine Ohio State U., Columbus, 1991—, divsn. dir. gen. medicine, 1994—. Co-dir. Alzheimer's Disease Assistance Ctr., SUNY, Bklyn., 1988-89. Contbr. articles to profl. jours. Fellow ACP; mem. Soc. Gen. Internal Medicine, Am. Geriatrics Soc., Soc. Am. Baseball Rsch. Office: Ohio State U 456 W 10th Ave Rm 4510 Columbus OH 43210-1240 Office Phone: 614-293-4953. Business E-Mail: murden_1@medctr.ohio_state.edu.

MURDOCH, BERNARD CONSTANTINE, psychology educator; b. Greensboro, N.C., Dec. 5, 1917; s. Homer Odell and Hilma Caroline (Lang) M.; m. Martha Grace Hood, June 29, 1946; children: Norma, Constance, Joyce, Diana. BS, Appalachian State Tchrs. Coll., 1938; EdM, U. Cin., 1939; PhD, Duke U., 1942; postgrad., NYU, 1942-43. Licensed applied psychologist, Ga. Math. critic tchr. Appalachian State Tchrs. Coll. demonstration sch., 1938; math. and sci. tchr. Lexington (N.C.) High Sch., 1939-40; sci. tchr. Harding High Sch., Charlotte, N.C., 1945-46; also dir. Guidance and Testing Bur., Vets. Info. Center, Charlotte; prof. edn. and psychology Presbyn. Coll., Clinton, S.C., 1946-48, acad. dean, 1947-48; also extension prof. edn. U. S.C., 1946-48; mem. research staff Am. Council on Edn., Office of Naval Rsch., Washington, 1948-50; dean Muskingum Coll., New Concord, Ohio, 1950-54; prof., head psychology dept. Wesleyan Coll., Macon, Ga., 1954-82, prof. emeritus, 1982—, chmn. dept. behavioral scis., 1973-82, also dir. testing.; pres. Fore(In)Sight Found., 1991—. Extension prof. Grad. Sch. Mercer U., Macon, Ga., 1960—64. Author: Consistency of Test Responses, 1942, Love and Problems of Living, 1992, God and Positive Christianity, 1998, A Revolutionary View of Education and Teaching for the Third Millennium, 2002; co-author: The Production of Doctorates in the Sciences, 1936-48; editor found. newsletter Truth Seekers; contbr. to sci., ednl. and religious publs. Served to capt. USAAF, 1942-45. Fellow AAAS; mem. APA (life), Southeastern Psychol. Assn., Ga. Psychol. Assn. (dir., pres. 1969-70), Ga. Mental Health Assn. (dir.), NEA, Ga. Mental Health Council (psychology rep. 1973-74), Ga. State Bd. Examiners Psychologists (pres. 1974-75), Am. Ednl. Rsch. Assn., Masons, Presbyterian. Home: 4966 Zebulon Rd Macon GA 31210-3059 *Opportunities vary widely, and the necessary perception to capitalize on such also is a distinct variable. Those of us who have achieved a measure of "success" in vocational or other ways must feel very humble as we recognize our good fortune. We have not only had opportunities come before us, but we were able to perceive them in such a way as to accomplish whatever recognition has been ours. Millions have not been so fortunate.*

MURDOCH, DAVID ARMOR, lawyer; b. Pitts., May 30, 1942; s. Armor M. and N. Edna (Jones) M.; m. Joan Wilkie, Mar. 9, 1974; children: Christina, Timothy, Deborah. AB magna cum laude, Harvard U., 1964, LLB, 1967. Bar: Pa. 1967, U.S. Dist. Ct. (we. dist.) Pa. 1967, U.S. Ct. Mil. Appeals 1968, U.S. Supreme Ct. 1990, U.S. Ct. Appeals (3d cir.) 1991. Assoc. Kirkpatrick & Lockhart, LLP, Pitts., 1971-78, ptnr., 1978—. Mem. adv. bd. Ctr. for Internat. Legal Edn., U. Pitt., 1997—. Co-author: Business Workouts Manual. V.p., bd. dirs. Avonworth Sch. Dist., 1977-83; mem. bd. dirs. Pitts. Expt., 1988-93, chmn., 1989-90; mem. Pa. Housing Fin. Agy., 1981-88, vice chmn., 1983-87; alt. del. Rep. Nat. Conv., 1980; elder The Presbyn. Ch. of Sewickley, 1986-92; past pres. Harvard Law Sch. Assn. W. Pa.; bd. advisors Geneva Coll., 1993-94, trustee, 1994-97; trustee Sewickley Pub. Libr., 1994-2002, vice chmn., 1997-2002; trustee World Learning, Inc., 1995—, vice chmn., 1998-2000, chmn., 2000—; dir. Allegheny County Libr. Assn., 1994-96; chair Czech Working Group, Presbyn. Ch. USA, 1995-2000; bd. visitors U. Ctr. Internat. Studies, U. Pitts., 1996—; bd. advisors The Ctr. for Bus., Religion, and Pub. Life, Pitts. Theol. Sem., 1997—; bd. dirs., mem. exec. com. World Affairs Coun. Pitts., 1997-98; bd. dirs. Am. Coun. Germany, 1998—; hon. consul Fed. Rep. of Germany in Pitts., 2002—. Capt. U.S. Army, 1968-71. Recipient Disting. Svc. award Allegheny County Libr. Assn., 2001. Fellow Am. Coll. Bankruptcy, Am. Bar Found.; mem. ABA (bus. bankruptcy com., chmn. subcom. on bankruptcy coms., trust indentures and claims trading 1991-97), Am. Law Inst. Office: Kirkpatrick & Lockhart LLP Henry W Oliver Bldg 535 Smithfield St Pittsburgh PA 15222-2312 E-mail: dmurdoch@kl.com.

MURDOCH, LACHLAN KEITH, publishing executive; b. Sept. 8, 1971; s. Keith Rupert Murdoch and Anna Maria Torv, m. Sarah O'Hare, 1998. Student, Princeton U. Former reporter San Antonio Express News, Tex., The Times, U.K.; former sub-editor The Sun, U.K.; gen. mgr. Queensland Newspapers Pty. Ltd., Australia, 1994-95; exec. dir. News Ltd., Australia, 1995; dir. Beijing PDN Xinren Info. Tech. Co. Ltd., China, 1995—; dep. chair Star TV, 1995—; dep. CEO News Ltd., Australia, 1995—97, chair, 1997—; CEO, chmn. News Ltd. Australian subs. News Corp., Australia; sr. v.p. News Corp., NY, 2000—; pub. NY Post, 2002—. Avocations: Greek philosophy, ancient history, rock climbing. Office: News Corp 3rd Fl 1211 Ave of the Americas New York NY 10036

MURDOCH, LAWRENCE CORLIES, JR., retired banker, economist; b. Phila., June 3, 1926; s. Lawrence C. and Barbara (Boyd) M.; children: Lawrence C. III, Anne G.; m. 2d Eleanor M. Egan, June 16, 1970. BS Wharton Sch., U. Pa. in Econs., 1948; MBA, Wharton Sch., U. Pa., 1956. With Fed. Res. Bank Phila., 1954-92; ret., 1992. Bd. dirs. Cliveden Inc., 1981, Fort Mifflin, 1990. Contbr. articles to consumer and monetary publs.; producer documentary films; spokesman (radio and TV). Lt. (j.g.) USN, 1948-54. Mem. Soc. Cin. (pres. 1990-93), Little Egg Harbor Yacht Club (Beach Haven, N.J.), Beta Gamma Sigma, Zeta Psi. Home: 115 Hilltop Rd Philadelphia PA 19118-3737

MURDOCH, (KEITH) RUPERT, publisher; b. Melbourne, Australia, Mar. 11, 1931; came to U.S., 1974, naturalized, 1985; s. Keith and Elisabeth Joy (Greene) M.; m. Anna Maria Torv, Apr. 28, 1967 (div.); children: Prudence, Elisabeth, Lachlan, James; m. Wendi Deng, June 25, 1999. MA, Worcester Coll., Oxford, Eng., 1953. Chmn. bd. dirs. News Corp., 1979—, chief exec., 1979—; dir. BSkyB, 1990—, chmn.; CEO Fox Entertainment Group, 1995—. Dir. Altria Group (formerly Phillip Morris Cos., Inc.), 1989—; owner, pub. numerous newspapers, mags. and TV stas. in U.S.A., Australia, U.K., Asia. Office: The News Corp Ltd 3rd Fl 1211 Avenue Of The Americas New York NY 10036*

MURDOCH-KITT, NORMA HOOD, clinical psychologist; b. Clinton, SC, May 16, 1947; d. Bernard Constantine and Martha Grace (Hood) Murdoch; m. Jonathan Michael Murdoch-Kitt, Mar. 23, 1974; children: Kelly, Michelle, Mark Jason, Sabrina Brittany, Laura Kristina. BA, Wake Forest U., 1969; MS, U. Pitts., 1971, PhD, 1975. Psychology intern Ea. Pa. Psychiat. Inst., 1972-73; asst. prof., therapist campus counseling ctr. William and Mary U., Williamsburg, Va., 1973-74; staff psychologist child psychiatry dept. Med. Coll. Va., 1974-75; pvt. practice psychotherapy, family, martial, individual Richmond, Va., 1975—. Clin. prof. psychiatry Med. Coll. Va., 1995—. Pres. Ginter Park Residents Assn., 1988—89, 1998—, North Richmond's Team of Civic Assn. Pres., 2001—04; mem. Richmond Human Rels. Adv. Commn., 1978—80, Richmond Mayor's Com. on Concerns of Women, 1987—93, chair, 1989—93; mem. Richmond Citizens' Crime Commn., 1985—88, co-chair police chief sect. com., 1994—95; bd. dirs. Richmond Tech. Ctr.; chair Richard Cmty. Criminal Justice Bd., 2004; mem. Richmond Dem. Com., 1978—79, 1982—85, 1988—89, 1991—97, 1999—2003; founder, 1st state chair polit. action com. ERA, 1977—78; chief lobbyist ERA Ratification Coun., 1977—79; long-range planning com. Bapt. Theol. Sem., Richmond, 1993—96, 1999—; v.p. The Women's Ctr. for Christian Leadership, Inc., 1996—99, vice chair, 1997—98; active Ginter Park Presbyn. Ch.; bd. dirs. Va. Psychol. Found., North Richmond YMCA, Homeward, 2002—. USPHS fellow, 1969—72. Mem.: APA (steering com. state leadership conf. 1986—91, chair 1991, Richmond area chair ARC/APA disaster mental health network 1993—), Internat. Soc. for Study Multiple Personality and Disassociation, Chronic Fatigue Assn., Richmond Acad. Clinical Psychologists (pres. 1995), Va. Breast Cancer Found. (rsch. chair 1992—96), Va. Acad. Clin. Psychologists (chair profl. affairs com. 1982—84), Va. Psychol. Assn. (state legis. lobbyist 1978—79, chair legis. com. 1981—83, bd. profl. affairs 1981—85, pres. 1986), Leadership Metro Richmond, Richmond First Club (chmn. edn. com. 1979—80, bd. dirs. 1980—81). Office: Murdoch-Kitt Profl Bldg 3217 Chamberlayne Ave Richmond VA 23227-4806 Office Phone: 804-321-5400. E-mail: shrinkrapper@juno.com.

MURDOCK, CHARLES WILLIAM, lawyer, educator; b. Chgo., Feb. 10, 1935; s. Charles C. and Lucille Marie (Tracy) M.; m. Mary Margaret Hennessy, May 25, 1963; children: Kathleen, Michael, Kevin, Sean. BSChemE, Ill. Inst. Tech., 1956; JD cum laude, Loyola U., Chgo., 1963. Bar: Ill. 1963, Ind. 1971. Asst. prof. law DePaul U., 1968-69; assoc. prof. law U. Notre Dame, 1969-75; prof., dean Law Sch. Loyola U., Chgo., 1975-83, 86—; dep. atty. gen. State of Ill., Chgo., 1983-86; of counsel Chadwell & Kayser, Ltd., 1986-89. Vis. prof. U. Calif., 1974; cons. Pay Bd., summer 1972, SEC, summer 1973; co-founder Loyola U. Family Bus. Program; arbitrator Chgo. Bd. Options Exch., Nat. Assn. Securities Dealers, N.Y. Stock Exch., Am. Arbitration Assn.; co-founder, mem. exec. com. Loyola Family Bus. Ctr., 1990—; bd. dirs. Plymouth Tube Co., 1993—. Author: Business Organizations, 2 vols., 1996; editor: Illinois Business Corporation Act Annotated, 2 vols., 1975; tech. editor The Business Lawyer, 1989-90. Chmn. St. Joseph County (Ind.) Air Pollution Control Bd., 1971; bd. dirs. Nat. Center for Law and the Handicapped, 1973-75, Minority Venture Capital Inc., 1973-75. Capt. USMCR. Mem. ABA, Ill. Bar Assn. (cert. of award for continuing legal edn.), Chgo. Bar Assn. (cert. of award for continuing legal edn., bd. mgrs. 1976-78), Ill. Inst. Continuing Legal Edn. (adv. com) Roman Catholic. Home: 2126 Thornwood Ave Wilmette IL 60091-1452 Office: Loyola U Sch Law 1 E Pearson St Chicago IL 60611-2055 Business E-Mail: cmurdoc@luc.edu.

MURDOCK, DAVID H. diversified company executive; b. Kansas City, Mo., Apr. 10, 1923; m. Maria Ferrer, Apr., 1992. LLD (hon.), Pepperdine U., 1978; LHD (hon.), U. Nebr., 1984, Hawaii Loa Coll., 1989. Sole proprietor, chmn., chief exec. officer Pacific Holding Co., L.A.; chmn. Dole Food Co. (formerly Castle & Cooke, Inc.), L.A., 1985—. also bd. dirs. Trustee Asia Soc., N.Y.C., L.A.; founder, bd. dirs. Found. for Advanced Brain Studies, L.A.; bd. visitors UCLA Grad. Sch. Mgmt.; bd. govs. Performing Arts Coun. of Music Ctr., L.A.; bd. govs. East-West Ctr., L.A.; patron Met. Opera, N.Y.C. With USAAC, 1943-45. Mem. Regency Club (founder, pres.) Bel-Air Bay Country Club, Sherwood Country Club (founder, pres.), Met. Club (N.Y.C.). Office: Dole Food Co Inc One Dole Dr Westlake Village CA 91361-4633 also: Pacific Holding Co 10900 Wilshire Blvd Ste 1600 Los Angeles CA 90024-6530

MURDOCK, MARY-ELIZABETH, history educator; b. Boston, Jan. 4, 1930; d. Lester Joseph and Elizabeth Rowe (Collingwood) M. AB, Tufts U., 1952; A.M., Boston U., 1958; PhD, Brown U., 1962; S.M., Simmons Coll., 1970; cert. mgmt. inst. women in higher edn., Wellesley Coll., 1985; cert. master gardener, U. Mass., 1988. Tchr. Nat. Cathedral Sch., Washington, 1954-57; assoc. prof. Trenton State Coll, N.J., 1962-66, U. R.I., Kingston, 1966-69; archivist, dir. Sophia Smith collection Smith Coll., Northampton, Mass., 1970-84, lectr. history, 1973-86, instr. Southeast Asian ESL program, 1986-88. Guest lectr. colls. and univs., 1986—; cons. N.Y.C. YWCA, 1974-75, HEN, 1976-86, Greenfield Cmty. Coll., Mass., 1983-86, Ednl. Testing Svc., Princeton, N.J., 1985—; faculty cons. Nat. Evaluation Sys., Amherst, Mass., 1984-92; bd. reviewers Hist. Jour. Mass., 1985-88; adv. bd. Ctr. Am. Studies, Concord, Mass., 1985-88; indexer Liberty Party newspaper (1845-48). Author articles, monographs, analytical catalogs. Mem. Am. Studies Assn., New Eng. Am. Studies Assn., Orgn. Am. Historians (state membership chmn. 1980-88), Am. Assn. State and Local History, Hist. Deerfield Inc., Hist. Northampton, Nat. Trust for Hist. Preservation, Phi Alpha Theta. Avocations: choral singing, piano, painting, photography, gardening. Mailing: PMB 261 4152 Meridian St Ste 105 Bellingham WA 98226-5589

MURDOCK, PAMELA ERVILLA, travel and advertising company executive; b. LA, Dec. 3, 1940; d. John James and Chloe Conger (Keefe) M.; children: Cheryl (dec.), Kim. BA, U. Colo., 1962. Pres. Dolphin Travel, Denver, 1972-87; owner, pres. Mile Hi Tours, Denver, 1973—, MH Internat., 1987—, Mile Hi Advt. Agy., 1986—. Bd. dirs. Rocky Mountain chpt. Juvenile Diabetes Found. Internat., 1994-2000; exec. bd. Rocky Mountain Father's Day Coun., 1998, 99. Named Wholesaler of Yr., Las Vegas Conv. and Visitors Authority, 1984; recipient Leadership award Nat. Multiple Sclerosis Soc., 1996. Mem.: NAFE, Nat. Fedn. Ind. Businessmen, Am. Soc. Travel Agts. Republican. Home: 5565 E Vassar Ave Denver CO 80222-6239 Office: Mile Hi Tours Inc 2160 S Clermont St Denver CO 80222-5007 Office Phone: 303-758-5533. E-mail: pamm@milehitours.com., pamelaemurdock@aol.com.

MURDOCK, ROBERT MEAD, curator; b. N.Y.C., Dec. 18, 1941; s. Robert Davidson and Elizabeth Brundage (Mead) M.; m. Ellen Rebecca Olson, Apr. 22, 1967 (div.); children: Alison Mead, Anne Davidson; m. Deborah C. Ryan, Apr. 28, 1995. BA, Trinity Coll., Conn., 1963; MA, Yale U., 1965; student, Mus. Mgmt. Inst., U. Calif., Berkeley, 1980. Ford Found. intern Walker Art Center, Mpls., 1965-67; curator Albright-Knox Art Gallery, Buffalo, 1967-70; curator contemporary art Dallas Mus. Fine Arts, 1970-78; dir. Grand Rapids (Mich.) Art Mus., 1978-83; chief curator Walker Art Ctr., Mpls., 1983-85; program dir. IBM Gallery of Sci. and Art, N.Y.C., 1985-87, 90-93; dir. exhbns. Am. Fedn. Arts, N.Y.C., 1987 88. Panelist, cons. Nat. Endowment for Arts, 1974-90. Author: (with others) Tyler Graphics: The Extended Image, 1987, A Gallery of Modern Art, 1994, Paris Modern, The Swedish Ballet 1920-1925, 1995, Works by Leland Bell, 1950's-1991, 2001; contbr. articles on David Novros, William Conlon, 1985, Bill Freeland, 1989, Nassos Daphnis, 1990, Cai Guo-Qiang, 1998, John Evans, 2004; exhbn. catalogues Early 20th Century Art from Midwestern Museums, 1981, Berlin/Hanover: The 1920's, 1977, Richard Tuttle: Books and Prints, 1996, Lesley Dill, 1998, Jim Torok, 1999, Debra Bermingham, 2002. Nat. Endowment for Arts fellow, 1973 Home and Office: 202 1st Ave Apt 14 New York NY 10009-3726

MURDOCK, TULLISSE ANTOINETTE (TONI MURDOCK), academic administrator; BS, MA, N. Mex. State U.; PhD, U. Ariz.; grad. HERS, Bryn Mawr Inst. Women in Higher Edn., 1988. Adminstr. Western Wyo. Coll., faculty; asst. dean coll. arts and scis. U. Ariz.; assoc. provost of programs Seattle U., 1989—97; pres. Antioch U., Seattle, 1997—. Office: Antioch U 2326 Sixth Ave Seattle WA 98121-1814

MURDY, WAYNE WILLIAM, mining company executive, financial officer; b. Los Angeles, July 4, 1944; s. Lee Robert and Louise Marie (Kleinemas) M.; m. Diana Yvonne DeCruse, Nov. 23, 1968; children: Dawn Marie, Christopher John, Joseph William, Elizabeth Anne. AA, El Camino Coll., 1966; BS, Calif. State U., Long Beach, 1968. C.P.A., Calif. With Atlantic Richfield Co., Los Angeles, 1969-78, gen. auditor Getty Oil Co., Los Angeles, 1978-81; group v.p. Texaco Trading & Transp. Inc., Denver, 1981-87; sr. v.p., chief fin. officer Apache Corp., Denver, 1987-92, Newmont Mining Corp. and Newmont Gold Co., Denver, 1993—. Mem. Am. Inst. C.P.A.s Clubs: University (Denver); Village (Cherry Hills Village, Colo.). Roman Catholic. Office: Newmont Mining Corp 1 Norwest Ctr 1700 Lincoln St Denver CO 80203-4500

MURDY, WILLIAM F. diversified services executive; BS, US Mil. Acad.; MBA, Harvard U. Various positions including COO Pacific Resources, Inc., 1974—81; mng. gen. ptnr. Morgan Stanley Venture Capital Fund; pres., CEO Gen. Investment and Devel. Co., 1989-97; chmn., CEO, pres. LandCare USA, 1997-99; interim pres., CEO Club Quarters; chmn., CEO Comfort Sys. USA, Inc., Houston, 2000—. Bd. vis. U.S. Mil. Acad., West Point; mem. Nat. Adv. Bd. Boy Scouts of Am., Nat. Bd. of Bus. Executives for Nat. Security. With U.S. Army, Vietnam. Office: Comfort Sys USA Inc 777 Post Oak Blvd Ste 500 Houston TX 77056 Office Phone: 713-830-9600. Office Fax: 713-830-9696.*

MUREN, DENNIS E. visual effects director; b. Glendale, Calif., Nov. 1, 1946; s. Elmer Ernest and Charline Louise (Clayton) M.; m. Zara Pinfold, Aug. 29, 1981; children: Gregory, Gwendolen. AA, Pasadena (Calif.) City Coll., 1966; student, Calif. State U., L.A. Freelance spl. effects expert, 1968-75; camera operator Cascade of Calif., Hollywood, 1975-76; visual effects dir. photography Indsl. Light & Magic, San Rafael, Calif., 1976-80, visual effects dir., 1980—. Guest speaker Berlin Film Festival, UCLA, Film Dept., U. Calif. Berkeley Film Series, Liverpool (Eng.) U. Film Program, Mill Valley Film Festival Program, Siggraph '86, Siggraph '87, Am. Film Inst., Portland Creative Conf. '89. Cameraman, photographer various films including Star Wars, 1977, Close Encounters of the Third Kind, 1977, Battlestar Galactica, 1978, The Empire Strikes Back, 1980 (Oscar award); visual effects supr. films include Dragonslayer, 1981 (Oscar nomination), ET: The Extraterrestrial, 1982 (Oscar award), Return of the Jedi, 1983 (Oscar award, Brit. Acad. of Film and TV award), Indiana Jones and the Temple of Doom, 1984 (Oscar award, Brit. Acad. of Film and TV award), Young Sherlock Holmes, 1985 (Oscar nomination), Captain Eo, 1986, Star Tours, 1986, Innerspace, 1987 (Oscar award), Empire of the Sun, 1987, Willow, 1988 (Oscar nomination), Ghostbusters II, 1989, The Abyss, 1989 (Oscar award), Terminator 2, 1991 (Oscar award, Brit. Film and TV award), Jurassic Park, 1993 (Oscar award, Brit. Film and TV award), Casper, 1995; visual effects supr. (TV program) Caravan of Courage (Emmy award); creative advisor Twister, 1995, Mission Impossible, 1995, Jurassic Park: The Lost World, 1997 (Academy award nomination), Star Wars: The Phantom Menace, 1999, (Acad. award nomination, Saturn award for best visual effects), A.I., 2001 (acad. award nomination), Star Wars: The Attack of the Clones, 2002, The Hulk, 2003, The Day After Tomorrow, 2004. Recipient Acad. Sci./Tech. Award for the devel. of a Motion Picture Figure Mover for animation photography, 1981, Edit/VES Honors award, 2003; star on Hollywood Walk of Fame, 1999. Mem. Am. Soc. Cinematographers, Acad. Motion Picture Arts and Scis.

MUREZ, JOHN, music education director, educator; b. Paterson, N.J., Feb. 14, 1943; s. John Sr. and Sophie A. Murez; m. Dorothy L. Pohlman, May 29, 1971; 1 child, Daniel C. BA in Elem. Edn., William Paterson U., 1963; MAT, Seton Hall U., 1966; MusM., Montclair State U., 1976; postgrad., Drew U. Cert. tchr., N.J. Tchr. Paterson (N.J.) Pub. Schs., 1963-68; asst. prof. William Paterson Coll., Wayne, N.J., 1968-70; tchr. Tenafly (N.J.) Pub. Schs., 1970-80; prof. Luther Coll., Teaneck, N.J., 1976-79; dir. Office of Music Edn. Newark Pub. Schs., 1988-98; dist. supr. fine and performing arts Paterson Pub. Schs., 1998—; music min. Mt. Carmel R.C. Ch., Montclair, N.J., 1998—. Organ design cons. various chs., North Jersey, 1976—; cons. music workshops Diocese of Paterson, 1984—. Mem. Newark Teen Arts Festival Com., 1988-98. Mem. N.J. Music Adminstrs., Music Educators Nat. Conf., Paterson Adminstrs. Assn. Home: 2 Berkeley Pl Montclair NJ 07042-2303 Office: Paterson Pub Schs 137 Ellison St Paterson NJ 07505-1308

MURFIN, ROSS C, university dean, English educator; b. Richmond, Ind., Nov. 14, 1948; s. Mark and Elizabeth (Crawford) M.; m. Pamela Kay Martin, Jan. 23, 1971; children: Audrey Dean, Justin Riley. AB in English cum laude, Princeton U., 1971; MA in English, U. Va., 1972, PhD with distinction, 1974. Asst. prof. English Yale U., New Haven, 1974-81, assoc. prof., 1981-82; dir. grad. studies in English U. Miami, Coral Gables, 1982-83, dir. program in honors, 1984-85, master Hecht Residential Coll., 1983-87, assoc. dean Coll. Arts and Scis., 1985-89, vice provost for undergrad. affairs, 1989-91, dean Coll. Arts and Scis., 1991—. Author: Swiburne, Hardy, Lawrence and the Burden of Belief, 1978, The Poetry of D.H. Lawrence, 1983, Sons and Lovers, A Novel of Division and Desire, 1987, Lord Jim: After the Truth, 1992; editor: Conrad Revisited: Essays for the Eighties, 1986, Heart of Darkness: A Case Study of Contemporary Criticism, 1989, The Scarlet Letter: A Case Study in Contemporary Criticism, 1991. Recipient Prof. of Yr. award Honors Students Assn., 1982-83, Panhellenic Prof. of Yr. award U. Miami, 1984-85; Am. Coun. Learned Socs. fellow, 1978-79, Summer fellow NEH, 1982. Mem. AAUP, MLA (chmn. 20th Century English session 1990), South Atlantic Modern

Lang. Assn. (chmn. Modern Brit. div. 1985-86), The Victorians Inst. Democrat. Congregationalist. Avocations: tennis, fishing, gardening. Home: 6506 Covecreek Pl Dallas TX 75240-5454 Office: U Miami 227 Ashe Bldg Coral Gables FL 33124

MURI, ANTHONY FREDERICK, lawyer; b. Providence, Dec. 29, 1948; s. Sam and Jacqueline (Perron) M.; m. Janet Patricia Hufnagel, Oct. 23, 1970; children: Nicole, Benjamin. BA, Coll. Holy Cross, Worcester, Mass., 1970; JD, Boston U., 1973. Bar: R.I. 1973, Mass. 1973, Maine 2002, U.S. Dist. Ct. R.I. 1974, U.S. Ct. Appeals (1st cir.) 1976, U.S. Supreme Ct. 1983. Assoc. Levy, Goodman, Semonoff & Gorin, Providence, 1973-78; ptnr. Licht & Semonoff, Providence, 1978-88, Goldenberg & Muri, Providence, 1988—. Mem. Fed. Bar Assn., ABA (sect. of litig.) R.I. Bar Assn. (mem. Fed. Bench/Bar Com. 1985—), Superior Ct. (bench/bar. com. 2002—), Def. Research Inst.

MURIAN, RICHARD MILLER, book company executive; b. East St. Louis, Ill., Sept. 17, 1937; s. Richard Miller Jr. and Margaret Keyes (Gregory) M.; m. Judith Lee, Aug. 11, 1961 (dec. Apr. 1992); 1 child, Jennifer Ann. BA, U. Calif., Davis, 1969; MLS, U. Calif., Berkeley, 1972; MA, Calif. State U., Sacramento, 1975; MDiv, Trinity Evang., 1977. Cert. history instr., libr. sci. instr., Calif. History reader Calif. State U., Sacramento, 1965-66, U. Calif., Davis, 1966-68, philosophy rschr., 1968-69; bibliographer Argus Books, Sacramento, 1970-71; rsch. dir. Nat. Judical Coll., Reno, 1971-72; libr. Calif. State U., Sacramento, 1972-76; tv talk show host Richard Murian Show, L.A., 1979-80; pres. Alcuin Books, Ltd., Phoenix, 1981—. Bd. dirs. Guild of Ariz. Antiquarian Books; pres. East Valley Assn. Evangs., Mesa, Ariz., 1984-86; cons. Ariz. Hist. Soc., 1993—, cons. FBI, 2000. Contbr. articles to profl. jours. Active U. Calif. Riverside Libr., 1981-83, KAET (PBS), 1988—, Ariz. State U., 1989—. Recipient Sidney B. Mitchell fellowship U. Calif., Berkeley, 1971. Mem. Antiquarian Bookseller Assn. Am., Am. Assn. Mus., Am. Soc. Appraisers, Ariz. Preservation Found., Grand Canyon Nature Assn., Internat. Platform Assn., Ariz. Publ. Book Assn. (awards com.), Phi Kappa Phi. Democrat. Presbyterian. Avocations: fgn. films, jazz. Office: Alcuin Books Ltd 4242 N Scottsdale Rd Scottsdale AZ 85251

MURILLO, CAROL ANN, secondary school educator; b. Portland, Oreg., Mar. 1, 1948; d. Carl Harvey and Frances Berniece Bryan; children: Michelle Frances, Adam Carlos Bryan. BA, Seattle Pacific U., 1970. Multiple subjects tchg. credential Calif., reading specialist credential Calif., secondary tchg. credential Calif. Exec. sec. Sybron Corp. - Heritage Laboratories, Inc., Seattle, 1971—72; elem. tchr. Highlands Acad., Daly City, Calif., 1973—74; dir. of childrens' ministries Resurrection City Ch., Berkeley and Oakland, Calif., 1980—82; interim prin. and tchr. Hilltop Christian Sch., Vallejo, Calif., 1982—93; cfo, ceo asst., event planner Mario Murillo Ministries, Inc., San Ramon, Calif., 1993—98; elem. sch. tchr. Vallejo City Unified Sch. Dist., Calif., 1998—2002. Mem. Falconette Academic Honors Club, Seattle, 1968—70. Editor (contributor): (book) Religious - Inspirational, 2000; editor: I'm the Christian the Devil Warned You About, 1996, Love Letters to Dangerous Christians, 1996; contbr. articles to religious magazines. Spkr. Lay Leadership conf.; worship leader religious retreats; corp. sec., trustee bd. mem. First Assembly of God, Inc., Ch. on the Hill, Vallejo, Calif., 1998—2002; mem. bd. dirs. Hilltop Christian Sch., Vallejo, 1997—2002. Mem.: Delta Kappa Gamma (grantee 1999). Avocation: travel. Home: 3008 Georgia St Vallejo CA 94591 Personal E-mail: carolannmurillo@msn.com.

MURILLO, MARISELA, English educator; b. Zacatecas, Mex., May 27, 1976; d. Santiago P. and Esther Murillo. BA in English, Mt. St. Mary's Coll., L.A., 1998; MA in Edn., Calif. State U., Carson, 2000. Cert. cross-cultural lang. and acad. devel. tchr. Calif. Tchr. English, James A. Garfield H.S., L.A., 1999—. Recipient award, The East L.A. Cmty. Union, 1994—98, scholarship, Nat. Hispanic Scholarship Fund, 1995—96, 1997—98, fellowship, Rockefeller Bros. Fund, 1997.

MURILLO-ROHDE, ILDAURA MARIA, marriage and family therapist, consultant, educator, dean; b. Garachine, Panama; came to U.S., 1945; d. Amalio Murillo and Ana E. (Diaz) de Murillo; m. Erling Rohde, Sept. 19, 1959. BS, Columbia U., 1951, MA, 1953, MEd, 1969; PhD, NYU, 1971; hon. diploma, Escuela Nat. de Enfermeria, Guatemala, 1964; Naturopathia diploma, Centro Estudios Naturista, Barcelona, Spain, 1992. RN; lic. marriage and family therapist, N.J.; cert. mental health-psychiat. nursing, ANA; lic. sex. therapist, N.J. Instr., supr. Bellevue Psychiat. Hosp., N.Y.C., 1950-54; asst. dir., dir. psychiat. div. Wayne County Gen. Hosp., Eloise, Mich., 1954-56; chief nurse psychiat. div. Elmhurst Gen. Hosp., Queens, N.Y., 1956-58, Met. Hosp. Med. Ctr., N.Y.C., 1961-63; psychiat. cons. to govt. of Guatemala WHO, UN, Guatemala, 1963-64; assoc. prof., chmn. psychiat. dept. N.Y. Med. Coll. Grad. Sch. Nursing, N.Y.C., 1964-69; dir. mental health-psychiatry, asst. prof. NYU, N.Y.C., 1970-72; assoc. prof. Hostos Coll., CUNY, N.Y.C., 1972-76; assoc. dean. acad. affairs, prof. U. Wash., Seattle, 1976-81; prof., dean Coll. of Nursing SUNY, Downstate Med. Ctr., Bklyn., 1981-85; dean and prof. emeritus SUNY, Bklyn., 1985—. Bd. dirs. Puerto Rican Family Inst., N.Y.C., 1983—96; dir. Latin Am. Oncological Nurses Fuld Fellowships, 1989-90; psychiat. cons. Sch. Nursing, U. Antioquia, Medellin, Colombia, 1972-73, WHO; psychiat./rsch. cons. for master program Sch. Nursing, U. Panama, Project Hope, 1986; dir., leader mental-psychiat. interdisciplinary group to study the Chinese family after 30 yrs. of communism People to People Amb. Program, 1985. Editor: National Directory of Hispanic Nurses, 1981, 2d edit., 1986, 3d edit., 1994; contbr. numerous articles to profl. nat. and internat. jours., chpts. to books in field. Bd. dirs. Nat. Coalition of Hispanic Mental Health and Human Svcs. Orgns., 1974-84, chmn. bd., 1980-84; mem. Wash. State adv. com. U.S. Commn. on Civil Rights, Seattle, 1971-81; nat. adv. com. White House Conf. on Families, Washington, D.C., 1979-81; pres. King County Health Planning Coun., Seattle, 1979-81; exec. com. Puget Sound Health Systems Agy., Seattle, 1979-81; mem. bd. advisors Marquis Who's Who, 1983-91; mem. Mosby Consumer Health's Hispanic adv. bd., 1996. Univ. Honors scholar NYU, 1972; named Citizen of the Day, Radio Sta. KIXI and N.W. Airlines, Seattle, 1979, Disting. lectr. Sigma Theta Tau, 1988-89, Woman of Yr., N.Y. Gotham Club Bus. and Profl. Women, 1989; recipient 1st Nat. Intercultural Nursing award Coun. of Intercultural Nursing, ANA, New Orleans, 1984, Women's Honors in Pub. Svc. award Minority Fellowship Programs and Cabinet Human Rights, ANA, 1986, Disting. Alumna award Divsn. Nursing, NYU Alumni Assn., 1989, 1st Nat. Dr. Hildegard Peplau award for outstanding svcs. in mental health, psychiat. nursing, edn., rsch. and practice, Las Vegas conv. ANA, 1992, Practice award Tchrs. Coll., Columbia U. Nursing Edn. Alumni, 1994; designated Living Legend for leadership in practice, edn. and rsch. Am. Acad. Nursing, 1994; inducted into Nursing Hall of Fame, Columbia U., 1999; bd. advisors Marquis Who's Who, 1991-99. Fellow Am. Assn. Marriage and Family Therapy; mem. ANA (affirmative action task force 1974-84, commn. human rights, cabinet human rights, rep. ANA at ICN Cong. Tokyo 1977, spokesperson Nat. Health Ins., conceived and designed Coun. Intercultural Nursing), Am. Orthopsychiat. Assn. (bd. dirs. 1976-79, treas. 1986-89, Presdl. nominee 1980, 93), N.Y. Assn. Marriage and Family Therapy (pres. 1973-76), Nat. Assn. Hispanic Nurses (founder, 1st pres. 1976-80), Internat. Fedn. Bus. and Profl. Women (UN rep. to UNICEF London, 1987—, del. to World UN Summit for Children N.Y.C. 1990, UN N.Y. Com. for Internat. Yr. of Family 1994, Hall of Fame for Outstanding Achievements in Field of Sci., Rsch., Mental Health-Psychiatry, 4th edit., 1995), Am. Rsch. Inst. (dep. govt. 1987), NYU Club, Gotham Bus. and Profl. Women's Club. Democrat. Avocations: travel, reading, music, stamp collecting/philately, skiing. Home: 300 W 108th St Apt 12A New York NY 10025-2704 Office: SUNY Bklyn Coll Nursing Box 22 450 Clarkson Ave Brooklyn NY 11203-2056 Office Phone: 212-865-9795. E-mail: murillorohde@aol.com.

MURINO, CLIFFORD JOHN, atmospheric and oceanic research institute executive; b. Yonkers, N.Y., Feb. 10, 1929; s. Vincent Joseph and Marie (Fuccillo) M.; m. Janet Rosalie Spallino, Dec. 28, 1954 (div. Dec. 1983); children: John Clifford, Carolyn Ruth, Kathryn Marie; m. Fryne Irene White, Jan.28, 1984. BS, St. Louis U., 1950, MA, 1954, PhD, 1957. Mem. faculty Parks Coll. Aero. Tech., Cahokia, Ill., 1954-60; prof. meteorology St. Louis U., 1960-75, v.p., 1969-75; div. dir. Nat. Ctr. Atmospheric Research, Boulder, Colo., 1975-80; pres. Deseert Research Inst., Reno, 1980-83, pres., bd. dirs. Found., 1982-83; pres. Univ. Corp. for Atmospheric Research, Boulder, 1983--, Bd. dirs. Found., 1986--. Co-author: Weather Motions from Space, 1969; contbr. numerous articles to sci. jours. Mem. Nev. Gov.'s Adv. Com., 1980-83, Reno Mayor's Adv. Com., 1982-83; trustee Nev. Devel. Authority, 1981-83. Recipient sustained superior performance award NSF, 1969; NSF research grantee, 1965-66, NOAA research grantee, 1966. Fellow Am. Meteorol. Soc. (pres. 1985); mem. Elks Club, Sigma Xi, Pi Mu Epsilon. Home: 1590 Bradley Dr Boulder CO 80305-7377 Office: Univ Corp for Atmospheric Rsch PO Box 3000 Boulder CO 80307-3000

MURIS, TIMOTHY JOSEPH, former federal agency administrator; b. Massillon, Ohio, Nov. 18, 1949; s. George William and Louise (Hood) M.; children: Matthew Allen, Paul Austin; m. Pam Harmon, June 27, 1997. BA, San. Diego State U., 1971; JD, UCLA, 1974. Bar: Calif. 1974, U.S. Supreme Ct. 1983. Asst. to dir. policy planning and evaluation FTC, Washington, 1974-76, dir. Bur. Consumer Protection, 1981-83, dir. Bur. Competition, 1983-85; exec. assoc. dir. Office Mgmt. and Budget, Washington, 1985-88, cons., 1988-89; law and econs. fellow U. Chgo. Law Sch., 1979-80; asst. prof. antitrust and consumer law U. Miami Law Sch. and Law Econs. Ctr., Fla., 1976-79, assoc. prof., 1979-81, prof., 1981-83; Found. prof. law George Mason U., Va., 1988—2001, interim dean, 1996-97; chmn. Fed. Trade Commn., Washington, 2001—04. Dep. counsel Presdl. Task Force on Regulatory Relief, Washington, 1981; cons. Coun. on Wage and Price Stability, Washington, 1981; mem. Nat. Issues Forum, Brookings Inst., 1986-88; mem. adv. bd. Antitrust and Trade Regulation Report, 1990—. Editor: The Federal Trade Commission since 1970: Regulation and Bureaucratic Behavior, 1981. Mem. Reagan-Bush transition team for FTC, Washington, 1980; sr. advisor Bush-Quayle transition team, 1988-89. Am. Bar Found. affiliated scholar, 1979 Mem. ABA (antitrust law spl. com. to study role of FTC 1988-89), Calif. Bar Assn., FTC (chmn.), Order of Coif*

MURKETT, PHILIP TILLOTSON, human resource executive; b. Chattanooga, Apr. 3, 1931; s. Philip Tillotson and Dorothy (Ingram) M.; m. Mary Jane Brewer, Dec. 10, 1960 (dec.); children: Emmette, Mary Jane Easter, Leanne. BA, Duke U., 1954; MBA, U. Pa., 1957; postgrad., Warnboro Coll., Oxford, England, 1980. Methods engr. Westinghouse Elec. Co., Staunton, Va., 1957-60; adminstrv. mgr. Vulcan Materials Co., Birmingham, Ala., 1960-68; human resources mgr. Blount, Inc., Montgomery, Ala., 1968-74; pres. Murkett Enterprises Inc., Montgomery, 1974—. Adj. instr. Auburn U., Montgomery, Ala.; with internat. affairs Yonok Coll., Lampang, Thailand; search cons. Murkett Assocs., Montgomery, 1974—; bd. advisors Digitech Inc. Author: Use & Value of References, 1957; editor (newsletter) H.R. Quar., 1983. Pres. Montgomery Mus. Fine Art, 1982, Cmty. Concert Assn., Montgomery, 1982, Montgomery Symphony Assn., 1987; pres. Am.-Thai Edn. Devel. Found. Inc., 1991, bd. dirs. 1990; bd. dirs. Ala. World Affairs Coun., 1997; jr. warden Episcopal Ch. of Ascension, 1972. Recipient Gov.'s Arts award Ala. Arts Coun., 1983, commendation from crown princess of Thailand, 1992. Mem. Montgomery C. of C. (task chair 1983), Montgomery Country Club, Capitol City Club, Kiwanis (bd. dirs. 1972), Delta Tau Delta (chpt. v.p. 1953). Avocations: gardening, swimming, music, tennis, geneology. Office: PO Box 527 Montgomery AL 36101-0527

MURKISON, EUGENE COX, finance educator; b. Donalsonville, Ga., July 2, 1936; s. Jeff and Ollie Mae (Shores) Murkison; m. Marilyn Louise Adams, July 3, 1965; children: James, David, Jennifer. Grad., U.S. Army JFK Spl. Warfare Sc., 1967, U.S. Naval War Coll., 1972, U.S. Army Command/Staff Coll., 1974; BSA, U. Ga., 1959; MBA, U. Rochester, 1970; PhD, U. Mo., 1986. Surveyor USDA, Donalsonville, Ga., 1956-59; commd. 2d lt. U.S. Army, 1959, advanced through grades to lt. col., 1974, inf. bn. leader, 1967-68; mechanized comdr. (G-3), ops. officer Brigade Exec. Officer, Korea, Europe and U.S., 1968-70; prof. leadership & psychology West Point, N.Y., 1970-73; ops. officer (J-3) Office of Chmn. Joint Chiefs of Staff, Washington, 1974-77; prof. mil. sci. and leadership Kemper Mil. Coll., 1977-81; ret. U.S. Army, 1981; instr. U. Mo., Columbia, 1981-84; asst. prof. Ga. So. U., Stateboro, 1984-89, assoc. prof., 1989-94, prof., 1995—, chair grad. curriculum & programs task force, 1996-99. Vis. prof. mgmt. and bus. U. Tirgoviste, Romania, 1994—96, 1998—2000; vis. prof. human resource mgmt. Tech. U. Romania, Cluj-Napoca, 1998—2000; chmn. grad. programs curriculum com. GSU, 1998—2002. Author (with Gheroghe Ionescu): Human Behavior in Organizations, 2000; contbr. articles to profl. jours., chapters to books. Adminstrv. bd. Pittman Pk. Meth. Ch., Statesboro, 1986—2000, trustee, 1992—99, chmn., trustee, 1995—96, mem. staff-Parish com., 2000—04. Decorated Bronze Star with oak leaf cluster; recipient Tchg. award, U. Mo., 1983, Devel. award, Ga. So. U., 1990, Albert Burke Rsch. award, 1992, Internat. Educator of the Yr. award, others; grantee, IREX, 1994, SOROS, 1995, 1996. Mem.: VFW, Ga. Hist. Soc., Bus. History Conf., Acad. Mgmt., Internat. Acad. Bus. (program chair 1994, 1995, Best Paper award 10th Ann. Conv.), Inst. Info. and Mgmt. Sci., So. Mgmt. Assn., Inst. Mgmt. Sci., Newcomen Soc., Scabbard & Blade, Blue Key, Alpha Zeta, Beta Gamma Sigma. Republican. Avocations: business history, military history, tomato production, hiking, boating. Office: Ga So U Coll Bus Adminstrn Statesboro GA 30460-8154 Office Phone: 912-681-0318. Business E-Mail: murkison@georgiasouthern.edu.

MURKOWSKI, FRANK HUGHES, governor; b. Seattle, Mar. 28, 1933; s. Frank Michael and Helen (Hughes) M.; m. Nancy R. Gore, Aug. 28, 1954; children: Carol Victoria Murkowski Sturgulewski, Lisa Ann Murkowski Martell, Frank Michael, Eileen Marie Murkowski Van Wyhe, Mary Catherine Murkowski Judson, Brian Patrick. Student, Santa Clara U., 1952—53; BA in Econs., Seattle U., 1955. With Pacific Nat. Bank of Seattle, 1957-58, Nat. Bank of Alaska, Anchorage, 1959-67; asst. v.p., mgr. Nat. Bank of Alaska (Wrangell br.), 1963-66; v.p. charge bus. devel. Nat. Bank of Alaska, Anchorage, 1966-67; commr. dept. econ. devel. State of Alaska, Juneau, 1967-70; pres. Alaska Nat. Bank, Fairbanks, 1971-80; senator from Alaska U.S. Senate, Washington, 1981—2002, ranking mem. Com. on Energy and Natural Resources, mem. Com. on Fin., Vets Affairs Com., Indian Affairs Com., Japan-US Friendship Com., mem. intelligence com. fgn. affairs; gov. State of Alaska, 2003—. Rep. nominee for U.S. Congress from Alaska, 1970; chmn. Can.-U.S. Interparliamentary Group. Former v.p. B.C. and Alaska Bd. Trade; mem. U.S. Holocaust Mus. Coun. Served with U.S. Coast Guard, 1955-57. Mem. AAA, AMVETS, NRA, Am. Legion, Ducks Unlimited, Res. Officer's Assn., Alaska World Affairs Coun., Coalition Am. Vets., Alaska Native Brotherhood, Am. Bankers Assn., Alaska Bankers Assn. (pres. 1973), Young Pres.'s Orgn., Alaska C. of C. (pres. 1977), Anchorage C. of C. (bd. dirs. 1966), Fairbanks C. of C. (bd. dirs. 1973-78), Pioneers of Alaska, Internat. Alaska Nippon Kai, Capital Hill Club, Washington Athletic Club, Elks, Lions. Republican. Office: Office of Gov State Capitol PO Box 110001 Juneau AK 99811

MURKOWSKI, LISA, senator; b. Ketchikan, Alaska, May 22, 1957; m. Verne Martell, Aug. 22, 1987; children: Nicholas, Matthew. BA, Georgetown U., 1980; JD, Willamette Coll., 1985. Dist. coun. atty., Anchorage, 1987-89; comml. atty. Hoge and Lekisch, 1989-96; atty. pvt. practice, 1997—; rep. Alaska Ho. of Reps., Anchorage, 1998—2002; U.S. senator from Alaska, 2002—. Dir. First Bank; mem. Mayor's Task Force Homeless, 1990-91; state ctrl. com. Dist. 14 Rep. chair, 1993-98; commr. Anchorage Equal Rights Commn., 1997-2002; citizens adv. bd. Joint Com. Mil. Bases in Alaska, 1998—. Trustee Cath. Svcs.; pres. Govt. Hill Elem. PTA; dir. Alaskan Drug Free Youth; mem. YWCA, Arctic Power. Mem. Alaska Bar Assn., Anchorage Bar Assn., Alaska Fedn. Rep. Women (bd. dirs.), Anchorage Rep. Womens Club, Midnight Sun Rep. Women. Republican. Roman Catholic. Address: 510 L St # 550 Anchorage AK 99501 Mailing: US Senate 322 Hart Senate Off Bldg Washington DC 20510 Office Phone: 202-224-6665.

MURMAN, SANDRA L. state legislator, community activist; b. Indpls., Aug. 9, 1950; BS in Bus. and Mktg., Ind. U., 1972. Mem. Fla. Ho. of Reps., Tallahassee, 1996—. Mem. bus. devel. and internat. trade com., fin. and taxation com., juvenile justice com., children and family empowerment com., environ. protection com., edn. commn. reform and accountability; cmty. activist. Bd. trustees Children's Home Inc.; mem. steering com. United Way Mgmt. Assistance Program; troop leader Girl Scouts Am.; dir. devel. Tampa (Fla.) Children's Mus., 1991-95. Republican. Roman Catholic. Avocations: running, tennis, golf. Office: State Capitol Rm 1102 Tallahassee FL 32399-1300

MURNANE, MARGARET MARY, engineering and physics educator; b. Limerick, Ireland, Jan. 23, 1959; d. Matthew and Helen (Bourke) M.; m. Henry Cornelius Kapteyn, Mar. 26, 1987. MSc, U. Coll. Cork, Ireland, 1983; PhD, U. Calif., Berkeley, 1989. Postdoctoral researcher U. Calif., Berkeley, 1990; asst. prof. Wash. State U., Pullman, 1990-95; assoc. prof. U. Mich., Ann Arbor, 1995—. Presdl. Young Investigator awardee NSF, 1991, Sloan Found. fellow, 1992, Presdl. faculty fellow NSF, 1993. Mem. Am. Phys. Soc. (Simon Ramo award 1990, Maria Goeppert-Mayer award 1997), Optical Soc. Am., Soc. Photo-Optical Instrumentation Engrs., Assn. for Women in Sci. Office: U Mich Ctr for Ultrafast Optics 2200 Bonisteel Blvd Ann Arbor MI 48109-2099

MURNION, WILLIAM EDWARD, philosopher; b. N.Y.C., Jan. 27, 1933; s. William Edward and Frances Annie (Canavan) M.; m. Deborah Warren Cary, June 14, 1969; children: William Cary, Gregory Thomas. BA, St. Joseph's Coll., 1954; STL, Gregorian U., Rome, 1958, PhD, 1969. Ordained priest Roman Cath. Ch., 1957. Parish priest Roman Cath. Archdiocese of N.Y., N.Y.C., 1958-66; lectr. St. John's Sem., Little Rock, 1966-67; asst. prof. Duquesne U., Pitts., 1967-68; faculty fellow Boston Coll., Chestnut Hill, Mass., 1968-69; asst. prof. Newton (Mass.) Coll., 1969-72; prof. Ramapo Coll., Mahwah, NJ, 1972-2000; lectr., counselor PhilosophyWorks, Bellvale, N.Y., 2000—. Dir. NEH summer seminar, 1992, 95. Author: St. Thomas's Theory of Understanding, 1969; contbr. articles to profl. jours., chpts. to books. Mem. Am. Philos. Assn., Am. Acad. Religion, Internat. Soc. Philosophy of Law and Social Philosophy, Am. Cath. Philos. Assn. Avocations: painting, gardening, sports. Office Phone: 845-986-5406. E-mail: wmurnion@warwick.net.

MUROFF, LAWRENCE ROSS, nuclear medicine physician, educator; b. Phila., Dec. 26, 1942; s. John M. and Carolyn (Kramer) M.; m. Carol R. Savoy, July 12, 1969; children: Michael Bruce, Julie Anne. AB cum laude, Dartmouth Coll., 1964, B of Med. Sci., 1965; MD cum laude, Harvard U., 1967. Diplomate Am. Bd. Radiology, Am. Bd. Nuclear Medicine. Intern Boston City Hosp., Harvard, 1968; resident in radiology Columbia-Presbyn. Med. Ctr., N.Y.C., 1970-73, chief resident, 1973; instr. dept. radiology, asst. radiologist Columbia U. Med. Ctr., N.Y.C., 1973-74; dir. dept. nuc. medicine, computed tomography and MRI Univ. Cmty. Hosp., Tampa, Fla., 1974-94, H. Lee Moffitt Cancer Hosp., Tampa, 1994—; pres. Edn. Symposia Inc., Tampa, 1975-2001; pres., CEO Imaging Cons. Inc., Tampa, 1994—; chmn. bd. Am. Phys. Ptnrs. Inc. (Radiologix), Dallas, 1996-98. Clin. asst. prof. radiology U. South Fla., 1974-78, clin. assoc. prof., 1978-82, clin. prof., 1982—; clin. prof. U. Fla., 1988-. Contbr. articles to profl. jours. Lt. comdr. USPHS, 1968-70. Fellow Am. Coll. Nuclear Medicine (disting. fellow., Fla. del.), Am. Coll. Nuclear Physicians (regents 1976-78, pres.-elect 1978, pres. 1979, fellow 1980), Am. Coll. Radiology (councilor 1979-80, 91-96, 2001—, chancellor 1981-87, chmn. commn. on nuclear medicine 1981-87, fellow 1981); mem. Am. Assn. Acad. Chief Residents Radiology (chmn. 1973), AMA, Boylston Soc., Fla. Assn. Nuclear Physician (pres. 1976), Fla. Med. Assn., Hillsborough County Med. Assn., Radiol. Soc. N.Am., Soc. Nuclear Medicine (coun. 1975-90, trustee 1980-84, 86-89, pres. Southeastern chpt. 1983, vice chmn. correlative imaging coun. 1983), Fla. Radiol. Soc. (exec. com. 1976-91, treas. 1984, sec. 1985, v.p. 1986, pres. elect 1987, pres. 1988, gold medal 1995), West Coast Radiol. Soc., Soc. Mag. resonance Imaging (bd. dirs. 1988-91, chmn. ednl. program 1989, chmn. membership com. 1989-93), Clinical Magnetic Resonance Soc. (pres. elect 1995-98, pres. 1998-2000), bd. dirs, 1995—). Office: 16804 Avila Blvd Tampa FL 33613-5220 Office Phone: 813-240-9390.

MURPHEY, ARTHUR GAGE, JR., law educator; b. Macon, Miss., June 16, 1927; s. Arthur Gage and Elizabeth (Crutcher) Murphey; m. Linda Chaney, May 17, 1975; 1 stepchild, Leslie Jo Pafford; children from previous marriage: Mason Alexander, Arthur Nesbit. Student, Vanderbilt U., 1947—48; AB, U. N.C., 1951; JD, U. Miss., 1953; postgrad., London Sch. Econs., U. London, 1953—54; LLM, Yale U., 1962. Assoc. Satterfield, Ewing Williams and Shell, Jackson, Miss., 1953; asst. prof. U. Ga., Athens, 1956-58, Emory U., Atlanta, 1958-61, U. Akron (Ohio), 1962-63, assoc. prof., 1963-67; prof. U. Ark., Little Rock, 1967-96, asst. dean Sch. Law, 1970-73, Ark. Bar Found. prof., 1996-97, Ark. Bar Found. prof. emeritus, 1997—. Vis. lectr. Case Western Res. U., Cleve., 1966; vis. prof. U. Miss., 1977. Faculty editor: Jour. Pub. Law, 1958—61; faculty advisor Ga. Bar Jour., 1958—61; contbr. articles to profl. jours. With USAAF, 1945—47. Fulbright scholar, 1953—54, Sterling fellow, 1961—62, Ford Found. grantee, 1964. Mem.: ABA, Phi Beta Kappa, Beta Theta Pi, Phi Delta Phi. Reformed Episcopal Ch. Home: 1918 Old Forge Dr Little Rock AR 72227-5515 Office: U Ark Sch Law 1201 McMath Ave Little Rock AR 72202-5142

MURPHEY, MURRAY GRIFFIN, history professor; b. Colorado Springs, Colo., Feb. 22, 1928; s. Bradford James and Margaret Winifred (Griffin) M.; children— Kathleen Rachel, Christopher Bradford, Jessica Lenoir. AB, Harvard U., 1949; PhD, Yale U., 1954. Asst. prof. U. Pa., Phila., 1956-61, assoc. prof., 1961-66, prof., 1966-2000, chmn. dept. Am. civilization, 1969-81, 87-94. Author: Development of Peirce's Philosophy, 1961, Our Knowledge of the Historical Past, 1973, (with E. Flower) A History of Philosophy in America, 1977, Philosophical Foundations of Historical Knowledge, 1994. Democrat. Home: 200 Rhyle Ln Bala Cynwyd PA 19004-2324

MURPHEY, ROBERT STAFFORD, pharmaceutical executive; b. Littleton, NC, Oct. 29, 1921; married; 2 children BS, U. Richmond, 1942; MS, U. Va., 1947, PhD in Organic Chemistry, 1949. Rsch. chemist in medicinal chemistry A.H. Robins & Co. Inc., Richmond, Va., 1948-53, dir. chemistry rsch., 1953-55, assoc. dir., 1955-57, dir. rsch., 1957-60, dir. internat. rsch., 1960-66, dir. sci. devel., 1966-82, asst. v.p., 1967-73, dir. sci. devel., v.p., 1973-82, v.p. sci. affairs and corp. devel., 1982-83, sr. v.p. sci. affairs and corp. devel., 1983-87, sr. v.p., dir. new bus. devel., 1983-90; sr. v.p., dir. bus. devel. E.C. Robins Internat., Inc., Glen Allen, Va., 1990—. Mem. AAAS, Am. Chem. Soc., Licensing Exec. Soc. Office: E C Robins Internat Inc 4551 Cox Rd Ste 200 Glen Allen VA 23060-6740

MURPHEY, SHEILA ANN, infectious diseases physician, educator, researcher; b. Phila., July 10, 1943; d. William Joseph and Sara Esther (Mallon) M. AB, Chestnut Hill Coll., 1965; MD, Women's Med. Coll. of Pa., 1969. Diplomate Am. Bd. Internal Medicine, Am. Bd. Infectious Diseases. Intern in internal medicine Mt. Sinai Hosp. of N.Y., 1969—70, resident in internal medicine, 1970—72, instr. internal medicine, 1971—72; fellow infectious diseases U. Pa. Sch. Medicine, Phila., 1972—74, instr. dept. medicine, 1974—75, asst. prof. dept. medicine, 1975—77; chief infectious diseases sect. Phila. Gen. Hosp., 1974—77; attending physician Hosp. U. Pa., Phila. Gen. Hosp., 1974—77; dir. divsn. infectious diseases, asst. prof. medicine Jefferson Med. Coll., Phila., 1977—80, clin. assoc. prof. medicine, 1980—2003; dir. divsn. infectious diseases Thomas Jefferson U., Phila., 1977—88; infection control officer, attending physician Thomas Jefferson U. Hosp., Phila., 1977—2003. Contbr. articles to profl. jours. Fellow Coll. Physicians Phila.; mem. ACP, Am. Soc. Microbiology, Soc. Healthcare Epidemiology of Am., Infectious Diseases Soc. Am., Alpha Omega Alpha. Democrat. Roman Catholic.

MURPHREE, A. LINN, pediatric ophthalmologist; b. Houston, Miss., June 6, 1945; d. John Alan and Maxine (Linn) M. BS, U. Miss., 1967; MD, Baylor Coll., 1972. Cert. Am. Bd. Ophthalmology. Resident affiliated hosps., 1973-76, chief resident ophthalmology, 1975-76; fellow ophthalmic genetics and pediatrics The Wilmer Inst., Johns Hopkins U. Hosp., 1976-77; asst. prof. ophthalmology and pediatrics U. So. Calif., Los Angeles, 1978-83, assoc. prof., 1983—91, prof., 1991—, dir. pediatric and devel. ophthalmology, 1978—; head, div. ophthalmology Children's Hosp. Los Angeles, 1978—, dir. Clayton Found. Ctr. Ocular Oncology, 1978—; chief med. ops. Childrens Hosp. of Los Angeles, 1986-87. Profl. adv. com. Blind Children's Ctr., Los

Angeles, 1980—; med. adv. bd. Nat. Assn. Visually Handicapped, 1980—. Contbr. numerous articles to profl. jours. Served to capt. med. corps., USAR, 1972-80. Dolly Green scholar Research to Prevent Blindness, 1984, Fulbright scholar U. Copenhagen, 1967-68; Medical Genetics fellow Baylor Coll. of Med. Affiliated Hosps., 1972-73. Mem. Calif. Assn. Ophthalmology, Calif. Med. Assn., Los Angeles County Med. Assn., Los Angeles Ophthalmol. Soc., Los Angeles Pediatric Soc., Ophthalmology Research Study Club Los Angeles, Pacific Coast Oto-Ophthalmol. Soc., Salerni Collegium, Am. Acad. Ophthalmology (honor award 1983), Am. Assn. Pediatric Ophthalmology and Strabismus, Am. Orthoptic Council, Assn. Research in Vision and Ophthalmology, Ophthalmic Genetics Study Club, Am. Bd. Ophthalmology (assoc. examiner), Internat. Soc. Genetic Eye Disease (sec. 1986—). Office: Childrens Hosp Los Angeles 4650 Sunset Blvd Mailstop 88 Los Angeles CA 90027-6016

MURPHREE, HAROLD T. retired minister; b. Saint Clair, Alabama, June 22, 1917; s. Soloman Cleveland and Sadie Lucas (Gibbs) Murphree; m. Sara Beatrice Smith, Dec. 1, 1940; children: Janice Elaine, Gary Doyle, Harold Wayne. Min. Bold Springs Meth. Ch., Walton County, Ga., 1962, Philadelphia & Ebenezer Chs., Rockdale City, Ga., 1963—68, Bellmont Meth. Ch., DeKalb County, Ga., 1969—70, Anvil Block Meth. Ch., Ellenwood, Ga., 1970—73, N. Covington Meth. Ch., Covington, Ga., 1974—77, Forsyth Circuit, 1977—82, Cokes Chapel Meth. Ch., Sharpsburg, Ga., 1982—83, Campbellton Meth. Ch., Fairburn, Ga., 1984—86; ret., 1986. Min. Carmel Meth. Ch., Gay, Ga., 1987—92. Author: Tried and Proven, 2000. Sgt. USAF, 1945—47, The Phillippines. Republican. Avocation: gardening. Home: 2532 Freemans Walk Path Dacula GA 30019-1390

MURPHREE, QUINCY CARL, physicist, educator; b. Roanoke, Ala., June 9, 1944; s. Hobart and Winnie Mae Murphree; m. Shirley Dianne Defoor, Aug. 26, 1972; children: Laura Leigh, Sonya Rachelle. BS, Auburn (Ala.) U., 1967; MS, U. of S.C., 1969, PhD, 1977. Asst. prof. of physics Auburn (Ala.) U., 1977—80; tech. dir. So. Inst. For Appropriate Tech., Lineville, Ala., 1980—89; tchr. Ky. Mountain Holiness Assn., Vancleve, Ky., 1989—. With U.S. Army, 1969—71. Nominee Gelini Medal, U.S. Army Mobility Equipment Rsch. & Devel. Ctr., 1971; grantee, Oak Ridge Associated Univs., 1973—77. Mem.: Sigma Pi Sigma. Avocation: mountain hiking. Home and Office: Kentucky Mountain Holiness Association PO Box 2 Vancleve KY 41385-0002 Office Phone: 606-666-5008. Personal E-mail: murphree@highstream.net.

MURPHREY, ELIZABETH HOBGOOD, history educator, librarian; b. Rocky Mount, N.C., Mar. 22, 1947; d. Isaac Green and Ernestine Ragsdale (Hobgood) Murphrey. BA, U. N.C., Greensboro, 1969; MA, Duke U., 1971, PhD, 1976; postgrad., U. Fla., 1984; MLS, U. N.C., Chapel Hill, 1993. Vis. instr. history Wake Forest U., Winston-Salem, NC, 1976; asst. prof. history N.C. A&T State U., Greensboro, 1977—81; intelligence rsch. specialist U.S. Army, Fayetteville, NC, 1982—89; adj. prof. history Fayetteville State U., 1989—90; adj. instr. history Fla. Met. U. South Campus, Orlando, 2000—03, rsch. libr., 1998—. Vis. asst. prof. of history Elizabeth City State U., NC, 1993—96. Editor (guidebook): Socialist Party of America Papers, microfilm edit., 2 vols., 1973—77. Recipient award, NEH, 1994, 1996, 2000. Mem.: LWV (bd. dirs. Seminole County chpt. 2001—, bd. dirs. Guilford County chpt. 1978—82), ALA, Fla. Libr. Assn., Am. Hist. Assn. Home: 424 Windmeadows St Altamonte Springs FL 32701 Office: Fla Met U South Orlando Campus 9200 Southpark Center Loop Orlando FL 32819 Office Phone: 407-851-2525. E-mail: emurphrey@hotmail.com.

MURPHY, ALMA SHIRLEY, political organization worker; b. Ashland, Ky., Feb. 13, 1941; d. Joseph Franklin Kirkpatrick and Goldie Evelyn Frazier; m. Francis Joseph Murphy Jr., June 21, 1959; children: Robin Denise, Dina Rene. Grad. high sch., Balt. Realtor assoc. Anne Arundel County, 1977—82; sales mgr. LaFontaine Bleu Catering, 1982—87; v.p. Allstate Alarm Systems, Inc., 1987—94, pub. rels. dir., 1994—98; elected to Anne Arundel County. Coun., 1998—2002; outreach coord. Congressman C.A. "Dutch" Ruppersberger, 2003—. V.p. Anne Arundel County Taxpayers Reform Com., 1970—72; mem. Anne Arundel County Com. Polit. Edn., 1970—74, North Glen P.T.A., 1968—77, North Glen Cmty. Assn., 1969—77, v.p., 1974, pres., 1975—77; mem. United Coun. Civic Assn., 1968—77; apptd. commr. Anne Arundel County Housing Authority, 1974—77; coord. Cystic Fibrosis Campaign, 1974—75; founding mem. Greater Pasadena Coun., 1977; mem., v.p. Rock View Beach./Rivera Isles Improvement Assn., 1977—2003; chair teleparty Am. Heart Assn., 1990—93; active Anne Arundel County D.A.R.E. and Take Back Our Sts. programs, 1991—. Named Citizen of Yr., Anne Arundel C. of C., 1991; recipient Outstanding Svc. award, Am. Heart Assn., 1993, JC Penny Golden Rule award, Pres. Clinton, 1994, Outstanding Cmty. Svc. award, Rotary Club, 1997. Democrat. Roman Catholic. Avocations: dance, travel. Home: 7845 June Dr Pasadena MD 21122

MURPHY, ANA ALVAREZ, obstetrician, gynecologist; b. 1954; MD, U. Mich., 1980. Diplomate Am. Bd. Subspecialty Reproductive Endocrinology and Infertilty Ob-Gyn. Resident ob-gyn. Johns Hopkins U., Balt., 1980-84, fellow reproductive endocrinology, 1984-86; dir. reproductive endocrinology and infertility Emory Clinic, Atlanta, 1993—; assoc. prof. Emory U., Atlanta, 1999—. Mem. ACOG, Am. Soc. Reproductive Medicine, Soc. Reproductive Endocrinology, Soc. for Gynecology Surgery, Soc. of Reproductive Surgeons. Office: Emory U Dept Ob-Gyn 1639 Pierce Dr Rm 4217 Atlanta GA 30322-0001

MURPHY, ANDREW J. managing news editor; Mng. editor news The Columbus (Ohio) Dispatch, mng. editor, 1990—. Office: The Columbus Dispatch 34 S 3rd St Columbus OH 43215-4241

MURPHY, ANN MARGUERITE, artist; b. Arlington, Mass., Feb. 21, 1937; d. Joseph Charles and Anna Marguerite (Lynah) Donnelly; m. Paul Hughes Murphy, June 19, 1960; children: Paul Hughes Jr., Debra Donnelly, Anna Marguerite. AS, Lasell Coll., Newton, Mass., 1957. One-woman and group exhbns. include Art for Heart, Bank of Boston, Cahoon Mus., Cape Cod, Cape Mus. Fine Arts, Chinese Cultural Ctr., Duxbury Art Complex Mus., Fed. Res. Bank, Guild of Boston Artists, JFK Bldg., Krasdale Gallery, N.Y., Landmark Bldg., Boston, Lyme Art Assn., Conn., Priscilla Hartley Gallery, Maine, Provincetown Art Mus., Sharon Art Ctr., N.H., Symphony Hall, Ventress Libr. Gallery, Whistler House Mus. Art; represented in permanent collections at Wright Gallery, Cape Porpoise, Maine, June Weare Fine Arts, Ogunquit, Maine. Gallery artist South Shore Art Ctr. Recipient Beman Purchase award Hudson Valley Art Assn., Fawcett award for humor North River Arts Soc., 1993, 1st pl. award, 1997, Simms Marine award 1999, 2d pl. award South Shore Art Ctr., 1992, Marine Painting award Ogunquit Art Ctr., Vayana Meml. award. Mem.: North River Arts Soc. (former art com. chmn.), Copley Soc. Boston (Copley Artist), Pastel Painters Soc. Cape Cod (Wallis Corp. award 1997), North Shore Art Assn. (Paul E. Goodridge Meml. award 1994, Alfred and Charlotte Movalli Meml. award 1997, Howard Curtis Marine award 2000, Walter Bollendonk Meml. award), New Eng. Watercolor Soc. (bd. dirs.), Concord Art Assn., Cape Cod Art Assn. (awards 1990, 1993, 1996, 1998, 1999, 2001, 2002), Am. Soc. Marine Artists, Acad. Artists, Allied Artists Am. (assoc.). Office: PO Box 585 Humarock MA 02047

MURPHY, ANN PLESHETTE, magazine editor-in-chief; m. Steven Murphy; children: Madeleine, Nick. B.A. in psychology, Harvard U. Editor-in-chief Parents mag., N.Y.C., 1988—98, contributing editor, 1998—2002; parenting contributor, Am. Family segment Good Morning Am., 1998—; columnist, Mom Know How Family Circle mag. Author: The 7 Stages of Motherhood: Making the Most of Your Life as a Mom. Bd. dirs. Child Care Action Campaign, Parents as Teachers, Zero to Three; chair, bd. dirs. Greyston Family Inn. Recipient Academy of Women Achievers, YWCA, 1990.

MURPHY, ARTHUR THOMAS, systems engineer; b. Hartford, Conn., Feb. 15, 1929; s. Arthur T. and Mary (Beakey) M.; m. Jane M. Gamble, Aug. 16, 1952; children: Thomas, Patricia, Mary, John, Sheila, Jane, Joseph. BEE, Syracuse U., 1951; MS, Carnegie-Mellon U., 1952, PhD, 1957. Registered profl. engr., Kans. Instr. Carnegie-Mellon U., Pitts., 1952-56; asst., assoc. prof., head. elec. engring. Wichita State U., Kans., 1956-61; vis. assoc. prof. mech. engring. MIT, Cambridge, Mass., 1961-62; prof., dean engring. Widener U., Chester, Pa., 1962-71, v.p., acad. dean, 1971-75; Brown prof., head mech. engring. dept. Carnegie-Mellon U., Pitts., 1975-79; prof. industry, mgr. computer and automated systems, sr. research fellow DuPont de Nemours Co., Camp Hill, Pa., 1979-87, DuPont fellow Wilmington, Del., 1987-96, DuPont fellow emeritus, 1996—, cons., 1996—; acting pres. Pa. Inst. Tech., Media, 1998. Vis. rsch. fellow Sony Corp. Rsch. Ctr., Yokohama, Japan, 1991-92, Internat. Superconductivity Tech. Ctr., Tokyo, 1993; vis. prof. control engring. U. Manchester, Eng., 1968-69; cons. Boeing Co., Wichita and Morton, Pa., 1957-68; bd. dirs. Rumford Pub. Co., Chgo., 1975-90; lectr. Pa. State U., 1983-87; DuPont rep. Chem. Rsch. Coun., 1994-97; cons. sci. adv. com. Parlec, Inc., 2000—; cons., chair microwave adv. com. Herley Industries., 2002—. Author: Introduction to System Dynamics, 1967; contbr. articles to profl. jours.; editor: Pergamon Press, 1966-75; patentee thick film filter connector, substrate and ceramic package, connection method for circuit bd. (ball grid array), superconducting mixer antenna array. Former mem. adv. coun. Tex. A&M U., Swarthmore Coll.; program evaluator Accreditation Bd. for Engring. and Tech., 1996—. DuPont fellow, 1987—; recipient DuPont Spl. Compensation award, 1988, Electronics Mktg. Excellence award DuPont Co., 1990. Fellow AAAS, IEEE (exec. com., treas. computer packaging), Am. Soc. Engring. Edn. (v.p. fin. 2001-, fellow chmn. grad. studies, instrumentation, awards com., DuPont rep., Corp. Mem. Coun., We. Electric Fund award 1966); mem. ASME (exec. com. control divsn.), Sigma Xi, Tau Beta Pi, Eta Kappa Nu, Sigma Pi Sigma, Pi Mu Epsilon, Phi Kappa Phi, Phi Theta Kappa (hon.). Avocations: hiking, photography, travel, genealogy. Home: 388 Spring Mill Rd Chadds Ford PA 19317-8226 Office: Du Pont Co B-10234 1007 Market St Wilmington DE 19898-0001 Office Phone: 302-773-0414. Business E-Mail: arthur.t.murphy@usa.dupont.com.

MURPHY, ARTHUR WILLIAM, lawyer, educator; b. Boston, Jan. 25, 1922; s. Arthur W. and Rose (Spillane) M.; m. Jane Marks, Dec. 21, 1948 (dec. Sept. 1951); 1 dau., Lois; m. Jean C. Marks, Sept. 30, 1954; children—Rachel, Paul. AB cum laude, Harvard, 1943; LL.B., Columbia, 1948. Bar: N.Y. State bar 1949. Asso. in law Columbia Sch. Law, N.Y.C., 1948-49; asso. dir. Legislative Drafting Research Fund, 1956, prof. law, 1963—; trial atty. U.S. Dept. Justice, 1950-52; asso. firm Hughes, Hubbard, Blair & Reed, N.Y.C., 1953-56, 57-58; partner firm Baer, Marks, Friedman & Berliner, N.Y.C., 1959-63. Mem. safety and licensing panel AEC, 1962-73; mem. spl. commn. on weather modification NSF, 1964-66; mem. Presdl. Commn. on Catastrophic Nuclear Accidents, 1988-90 Author: Financial Protection against Atomic Hazards, 1957, (with others) Cases on Gratuitous Transfers, 1968, 3d edit., 1985, The Nuclear Power Controversy, 1976. Served with AUS, 1943-46. Decorated Purple Heart. Mem. ABA, Assn. of Bar of City of N.Y. (spl. com. on sci. and law) Office: Columbia Sch of Law 435 W 116th St New York NY 10027-7297

MURPHY, AUSTIN DE LA SALLE, economist, educator, banker; b. NYC, Nov. 20, 1917; s. Daniel Joseph and Marie Cornelia (Austin) M.; m. Mary Patricia Halpin, June 12, 1948 (dec. May 1974); children: Austin Joseph, Owen Gerard; m. Lee Chilton Romero, Dec. 14, 1974; stepchildren: Thomas Romero, Robert Romero (dec.). AB, St. Francis Coll., Bklyn., NY, 1938; AM (Hayden fellow 1938-40), Fordham U., 1940, PhD, 1949, Canisius Coll., 1986. Instr. econ. Fordham U., 1938-41; Instr. econ. Georgetown U., 1941-42; asst. statistician, statis. controls Bd. Econ. Warfare, 1942; sr. econ. rsch. editor NY State Dept. Labor, NY, 1947-50; lectr. econ. Fordham U. Sch. Edn., 1946-55; instr. NYU Sch. Commerce, 1949-51; dean sch. bus. adminstrn. Seton Hall U., South Orange, NJ, 1950-55; Albert O'Neill prof. Am. enterprise, dean sch. bus. adminstrn. Canisius Coll., Buffalo, 1955-62; dir. edn. dept. NAM, 1962-63; exec. v.p. Savs. Banks Assn. NY State, 1963-70; chmn., pres. River Bank Am. (formerly East River Savs. Bank), 1970-89, vice chmn., dir., 1989-96, chmn. adv. bd., 1996-98. Charter trustee Savs. Bank Rockland County, 1965-70; dir. Bank of Charleston (SC), 1989-91; chmn. bd., trustee Savs. Bank Life Ins. Fund, 1983-87; chmn. dist. I, mem. adv. coun. Conf. State Bank Supr., 1986-93; bd. dir. MSB Fund, Inc. Author: (with Fleming Frasca, and Mannion) Social Studies Review Book, 1946, Leading Problems of New Jersey Manufacturing Industries, (with Bullock & Doerflinger), 1953, Reasons for Relocation, 1955, Forecast of Industrial Expansion in Buffalo and the Niagara Frontier, 1956, Metropolitan Buffalo Perspective, 1958; editor Handbook of New York Labor Statistics, 1950. Mem. Livingston (NJ) Charter Commn., 1954-55; mem. capital expenditures com., City of Buffalo, 1957-63; trustee Fordham U., 1973-79, NY Med. Coll., 1978-81; bd. dir. NY council Boy Scouts Am., 1974—, Jr. Achievement of Buffalo, 1958-63, Invest-in-Am. 1st lt. US Army, 1942-46. Named Knight of Malta, 1971. Mem. NAM (chmn. ednl. aids com. 1958-63), Am. Fin. Assn., Def. Transp. Assn. (life), Nat. Assn. Mut. Savs. Banks (bd. dir., treas. 1976-81), Friendly Sons St. Patrick (1st v.p., 1976-77), DownTown Lower Manhattan Assn. (dir., vice chmn. 1982-93), Union League Club (pres. 1991-93), Larchmont Yacht Club, Carolina Yacht Club, KC, Alpha Kappa Psi, Pi Gamma Mu. Office: RB Asset Corp 645 5th Ave New York NY 10022-5910 Home: 2409 103 Theall Rd Rye NY 10580-1406 *Through the various happy events and the difficult and sorrowful, loss of loved ones as well as the vagaries of business life, I have found that an ongoing prayerful relationship to God brings a certain detachment and peace that overcomes life's passing problems.*

MURPHY, BARBARA ANNE, emergency physician, surgery educator; b. Cin., Oct. 20, 1937; d. Harold August and Lorna Louise (Gabbard) Tiemeyer; m. D. Michael Murphy, Feb. 5, 1960; children: Michael Patrick, Douglas Andrew. BS cum laude, Ohio State U., 1959; MD magna cum laude, Med. Coll. Pa., 1975. Diplomate Am. Bd. Emergency Medicine. Resident in emergency medicine Geisinger Med. Ctr., Danville, Pa., 1978; staff physician Albemarle Hosp., Elizabeth City, N.C., 1978-79, Durham County Hosp., Durham, N.C., 1979-87; asst. prof. emergency medicine East Carolina U., Greenville, N.C., 1987-90; asst. prof. surgery-emergency medicine Duke U., Durham, 1990—. Dir. propsed residency emergency medicine Duke U., Durham, 1994—. Author: (book chpt.) Pediatric Emergency Medicine, rev. edit., 1992; editor: Micromedia Emergency Med. Abstracts, 1988—; book reviewer: Annals of Emergency Medicine, 1995—; contbr. articles to profl. jours. Fellow Am. Coll. Emergency Physicians (mem. clin. policies com. 1991—); mem. Soc. for Acad. Emergency Medicine, Alpha Omega Alpha, Phi Beta Kappa. Avocations: antique rose propagation, 18th-century american furniture collection, herbalism, needlework reproductions. Home: PO Box 837 Hillsborough NC 27278-0837 Office: Duke U Med Ctr PO Box 3096 Durham NC 27715-3096

MURPHY, BARRY AMES, lawyer; b. Summit, N.J., Mar. 3, 1938; s. Robert Joseph and Florence C. (Ames) M.; m. Leslie Lynn Smith, June 9, 1962; children— Karen Irene, Sean Patrick, Conor Brendan, Ilana Taraleigh. BA in English, Stanford U., 1960; MBA, Harvard U., 1963; JD, U. So. Calif., 1972. Bar: Calif. bar 1973, U.S. Supreme Ct 1976, U.S. Tax Ct 1976. Fin. analyst Office of Sec. Def., 1963-65; pres. Tech. Industries Inc., Los Angeles, 1966-72; invididual practice law San Mateo, Calif., 1972-74; corp. counsel Falstaff Brewing Co., San Francisco, 1974-77; sr. partner firm Levine & Murphy, San Francisco, 1978-81; v.p. Microvertics, Mountain View, Calif., 1981-86; pres. Murphy Law Corp., San Anselmo, 1987—. Mem. Am., Calif. bar assns., Calif. Trial Lawyers. Address: 28 Fern Ln San Anselmo CA 94960-1807 E-mail: barry@murphy.law.com.

MURPHY, BEN CARROLL, engineering company executive; b. Aug. 21, 1931; s. Benjamin Franklin and Effie (Lett) M.; m. Vivian Inez Hancock, March 3, 1950; children: Lanny Carroll, Debra Kay Murphy Soffitri, Kathy M. Murphy David, Gregory Lynn, Jon Patrick. BS, Delta State U., 1969, MBA, 1974; grad., United Electronic Inst., 1972. With U.S. Gypsum Co., Greenville, Miss., 1951-54, 55-56, Atlantic & Pacific Tea Co., Greenville, Miss., 1954-55; cost acct. Baxter Labs., Cleveland, Miss., 1966-69; project engr. mfg. U.S. Gypsum Co., Danville, Va., 1969-72; plant personnel and safety mgr. Cook Industries, Inc., Memphis, 1972-73, divsn. safety dir., plant personnel mgr., 1973-75, corp. compensation sr. analyst, 1976, div. indsl. rels. and personnel mgr., 1975-76, corp. compensation mgr., 1976-79; divsn. asst. personnel mgr. Robertson CECO Corp., Columbus, Miss., 1979-80, structural supt., 1980-82, mgr. prodn. control sys., 1982-92, divsn. prodn. control, schedule mgr., 1992-97. Ret. night instr. bus. and econs. N.W. Jr. Coll., Southaven, Miss., 1975-79, East Miss. C.C., 1980—; cons. in compensation S.E. Memphis Mental Health Center, 1978-82. Bd. dirs. Cmty. Water Assn. Mem. Mid-South Compensation and Benefits Assn. (dir. 1977-80, mem. organizing team 1976), Univ. for Women (adv. com. for extended studies of Miss. U.), Am. Compensation Soc., Soc. Mfg. Engrs. (sr., 3d v.p. chpt.), Miss. Mfg. Assn., Am. Mgmt. Compensation Soc., Carmack Cmty. Club (pres.). Baptist. Home: 2066 Attala Rd 3989 Vaiden MS 39176-9606 E-mail: bencm@pnidirect.net.

MURPHY, BENJAMIN EDWARD, actor; b. Jonesboro, Ark., Mar. 6, 1942; s. Patrick Henry and Nadine (Steele) M. Student, Loras Coll., 1960-61, Loyola U., New Orleans, 1961-62, U. Americas, 1962-63, 64-65; BA in Polit. Sci, U. Ill., 1964; student, Pasadena Playhouse, 1965-67; BA in Theatre Arts, U. So. Calif., 1968. Appeared in: TV series Name of the Game, NBC, 1968-70, Alias Smith and Jones, ABC, 1971-73, Griff, 1973-74, Gemini Man, NBC, 1976, The Chisholms, CBS, 1979-80, The Winds of War, 1983, Lottery, 1983-84, Berrenger's, NBC, 1985, The Dirty Dozen, Fox Network, 1988. Home: 2690 Rambla Pacifico St Malibu CA 90265-3423

MURPHY, BETTY JAGODA, small business owner; b. Washington, July 30, 1947; d. Harry Earl and Flory (Kabilio) Jagoda; m. Gregory James Murphy, Mar. 18, 1972; 1 child, Joshua. BA in Dance, Adelphi U., 1969. Cert. psychomotor therapy N.Y. Med. Ctr., 1970. Market research coord. Lee Creative Research, Fairfield, NJ, 1972-73; dir. new product test ctr. Lehn & Fink (Sterling Drug), Montvale, NJ, 1973-75; cons. new products Montclair, NJ, 1975-79; co-founder, pres. Creative Products Resource Assn., Fairfield, NJ, 1979—99; v.p. Jagoda Labs., Inc., Clifton, NJ, 1986—; pres., mng. mem. ReGenesis LLC, Montclair, NJ. Inventor, patentee household cleaning products and health & beauty aids. Adv. bd. Dress for Success, NY. Mem.: N.J. Assn. Women Bus. Owners, N.Y. Women in Comm. (membership com.). Democrat. Jewish. Avocation: performing ladino music in concert with family mems. Office: ReGenesis LLC 31 S Fullerton Ave Montclair NJ 07042 Office Phone: 973-233-1064. E-mail: bjm@regenesisllc.com.

MURPHY, BRIAN STUART, internist, consultant; b. N.Y.C., July 27; s. Walter Joseph and Veronica Mary (Nally) M. BA, NYU, 1979, MS, 1985; MD, MPH, N.Y. Med. Coll., Valhalla, 1990; MPH, Harvard U., 1996; postgrad., Columbia U. Diplomate Am. Bd. Internal Medicine. Resident in internal medicine Tufts-N.E. Med. Ctr., Boston, 1990-93; chief resident Boston U. Sch. Medicine, 1993-94; fellow in medicine Harvard Med. Sch., Boston, 1994-96, fellow in med. ethics, 1994-95; rsch. fellow Mass. Gen. Hosp., Boston, 1994-96; dir. clin. strategies program St. Vincent's Hosp., N.Y.C., 1996—; dir. med. affairs Hotel Trades Health Ctrs. N.Y., 1998—. Cons. Roche Pharms., N.J., 1996—, Merck and Co., Inc., N.J., 1996—, Roerig divsn., N.Y., 1997—; asst. prof. medicine N.Y. Med. Coll., Valhalla, 1996—. Contbg. author: Saunders Manual of Medical Practice, 1999. Mem. AMA, ACP, Am. Coll. Physician Execs., Mystery Writers of Am., Harvard Club of N.Y., Mensa, Alpha Omega Alpha. Roman Catholic. Office: St Vincents Hosp NY 153 W 11th St New York NY 10011-8305 Home: 1100 Gough St Apt 19C San Francisco CA 94109-6611

MURPHY, BRUCE ALLEN, government and law educator, author; b. Abington, Mass., Sept. 30, 1951; m. Carol Lynn Wright, June 14, 1975; children: Emily, Geoffrey. BA, U. Mass., 1973; PhD, U. Va., 1978. Fred Morgan Kirby prof. civil rights Lafayette Coll., Easton, Pa. Author: The Brandeis/Frankfurter Connection: The Secret Political Activities of Two Supreme Court Justices, 1982, Fortas: The Rise and Ruin of a Supreme Court Justice, 1988, (with Larry Berman) Approaching Democracy, 1996, 99, 2001, 03, Wild Bill: The Legend and Life of William O. Douglas, 2003. Avocations: fishing, reading, sports. Office: Lafayette Coll Dept Govt and Law 200 Kirby Hall Civil Rights Easton PA 18042 Office Phone: 610-330-5395. E-mail: murphyb@lafayette.edu.

MURPHY, CAROLYN, model; b. Walton Bch., Fla., Aug. 11, 1975; m. Jake Schroeder; 1 child. Model IMG Agy.; spokesperson Estee Lauder, 2001—. Actor: (films) Liberty Heights, 1999. Named Model Yr., VH1 Fashion Awards, 1998. Achievements include appeared on numerous mag. covers including Vogue, Harper's Bazaar, W, Elle, Marie Claire; one of the models to appear on the cover of Vogue's "Model of the Millennium" issue; starred in Calvin Klein's "Contradiction" comml. and print ads. Mailing: 420 W 45th ST New York NY 10036

MURPHY, CARYLE MARIE, foreign correspondent; b. Hartford, Conn., Nov. 16, 1946; d. Thomas Joseph and Muriel Kathryn (McCarthy) Murphy. BA cum laude, Trinity Coll., 1968; M in Internat. Pub. Policy, Johns Hopkins U., 1987. Tchr. English, history St. Cecilia Tchr. Tng. Coll., Nyeri, Kenya, 1968—71; reporter Brockton (Mass.) Enterprise, 1972—73; freelance corr. Washington Post, Newsweek, Sunday Times of London, et al, Luanda, Angola, 1974—76; reporter Fairfax County Washington Post, 1976—77, fgn. corr. in South Africa, 1977—82, reporter immigration issues, 1982—85, bur. chief Alexandria, Va., 1985—89, fgn. corr. Mid. East, 1989—94. Vol. ARC, Washington, 1984, Whitman-Walker Found., Washington, 1988—89. Recipient Courage in Journalism award, Internat. Women's Media Found., 1990, George Polk award, L.I. U., 1991, Edward Weintal Journalism award, Sch. Fgn. Svc., Georgetown U., 1991, Pulitzer Prize for internat. reporting, 1991, Edward R. Murrow fellow, Coun. on Fgn. Rels., N.Y., 1994—95. Roman Catholic. Avocations: foreign languages, hiking. Office: Washington Post Fgn Desk 1150 15th St NW Washington DC 20071-0002

MURPHY, CATHY, music educator; b. Warwick, R.I., May 29, 1963; d. John Peter and Betty Lue Murphy. BMus, Trinity U., San Antonio, 1991, MA in Edn., 1992. Asst. tchr. Tafolla Mid. Sch., San Antonio, 1991; instr., gen. music Oak Grove Elem. Sch., San Antonio, 1992—; instr., music edn. Tex. Lutheran U., 2001—; mem., clin. faculty Trinity U., San Antonio, 2003—. Contbr. articles to profl. jours.; singer: San Antonio Symphony Mastersingers, 1991—93, Tex. Bach Choir, 1996—98. Mem. St. Mark's Episcopal Ch., San Antonio, 1998—. Mem.: Ctrl. Tex. Orff Chpt., Tex. Music Educator's Assn. Democrat. Episcopalian. Avocations: travel, singing, sign language. Office: Oak Grove Elem Sch NE Ind Sch Dist 3250 Nacogdoches San Antonio TX 78217

MURPHY, CHARLES JOSEPH, investment banker; b. N.Y.C., Sept. 18, 1947; s. Charles Joseph and Mary V. (Vaughan) M.; m. Karen Lyn Canevari, Aug. 18, 1973; 4 children. BEE, Manhattan Coll., 1969; MBA, NYU, 1974, APC, 1975. Chartered fin. analyst. Avionics engr. Sikorsky Aircraft, Stratford, Conn., 1969-70; engr., rate/fin. analyst Am. Electric Power Co., N.Y.C., 1970-76; equity analyst First Boston Corp., N.Y.C., 1976-78, v.p. capital markets, 1982-84, mng. dir. utilities and telecommunications fin., 1984-87, head investment banking group, 1988-92, head investment banking dept., 1992-94, co-head worldwide investment banking, 1994-95, head global equities, 1995-96; mng. dir. Sextant Group Inc., N.Y.C., 1996-98, Merrill Lynch, N.Y.C., 1998—. Mem. CS First Boston operating com., 1993—, exec. bd., 1995—, co-chmn. investment banking operating com., 1994-95. Mem. N.Y. Soc. Security Analysts (sr.) Roman Catholic. Avocations: golf, field shooting, winter sports. Office: Merrill Lynch 24th Fl 250 Vesey St Fl 24 New York NY 10281-1201

MURPHY, CHRISTINE, medical facility administrator; b. Jan. 2, 1956; d. Mary. I. Jackson; m. Paul Murphy, June 19, 1976; children: Christie, Jannie-Kay. Diploma, Newport (R.I.) Hosp., 1977; BS, RWU, Bristol, R.I., 1994; MS, SRU, Newport, 1997. RN, R.I. Clin. educator Newport Hosp.; firm mgr. VAMC, Providence, R.I. Bd. dirs. Newport Hosp. Alumni, West House Housing Elderly. Mem. Assn. Oper. Rm. Nurse (cert.), Nat. Assn. Ambulatory Care Mgrs. Office: PVAMC 830 Chalkstone Ave Providence RI 02908-4734

MURPHY, CORNELIUS B., JR., (NEIL MURPHY), academic administrator; b. July 17, 1944; m. Joanne Murphy; children: Tracy, Megan, Maureen, Michael. B in Chemistry magna cum laude, St. Michael's Coll., 1966; PhD in Chemistry, Syracuse U., 1970; DSc (hon.), Clarkson U., 1997. Joined as a lab technician O'Brien & Gere Cos., East Syracuse, NY, 1970; sr. v.p. O'Brien &

Gere Engrs., Inc., East Syracuse, 1982—92, pres., 1992, chmn., chief scientist, 1998; pres. O'Brien & Gere Ltd., East Syracuse, 1996, chmn., 1999; pres. SUNY Coll. Environ. Sci. and Forestry, East Syracuse, 2000—. Mem.: AAAS, Am. Chem. Soc. Office: SUNY Coll Environ Sci and Forestry 1 Forestry Dr Syracuse NY 13210*

MURPHY, DANIEL IGNATIUS, lawyer; b. Phila., Mar. 14, 1927; s. John Anthony Murphy and Irene Cooper Thorn; m. Jeanne B. Genetti, July 28, 1956 (div. Aug. 1978); children: Jewel A., Daniel I. Jr.; m. Barbara Ann Uncles, Jan. 1, 1979. BS in Econs., U. Pa., 1950; LLB, Yale U., 1953. Bar: Pa. 1954, U.S. Dist Ct. (ea. dist.) Pa. 1954, U.S. Ct. Appeals (3d cir.) 1954, U.S. Tax Ct. 1956, U.S. Supreme Ct. 1959. Assoc. Evans, Bayard & Frick, Phila., 1953-55; asst. city solicitor City of Phila., Pa., 1956-59; ptnr. Cavanaugh, Murphy & Kalodner, Phila., 1958-64, Shapiro, Stalberg, Cook, Murphy & Kalodner, Phila., 1964-66, Takiff, Bolger & Murphy, Phila., 1966-72, Waters, Gallagher, Collins & Masterson, Phila., 1972-80, Stradley, Ronon, Stevens & Young, Phila., 1980-92, ret., of counsel, 1993. Tchr. Am. Soc. CLUs, Villanova, Pa., 1956-57; mem. exec. com. Phila. Estate Planning Coun., 1958-60; lectr. Pa. Bar Inst., Harrisburg, 1974-92, Pa. Coll. Orphans Ct. Judges, Harrisburg, 1978, Pitts., 1991; apptd. spl. master for trial mgmt. of complex litigation Phila. County Ct. Common Pleas, 1994—; judge pro tem Philadelphia County Ct. Common Pleas, 2000—; arbitrator Nat. Assn. Securities Dealers, 2001-2002. Editor: Phila. Bar Assn. Mag. The Shingle, 1958-67; contbr. chpts. to manuals and articles to profl. jours. Chmn. Phila. Chpt. Am. Cancer Soc., 1956-63; mem. Com. of 70, Phila., 1968-2003, chmn., 1972-74; trustee Hahnemann U., Phila., 1983-86; bd. dirs. Covenant Ho. Pa.; trustee Eastman Libr. and Info. Ctr., Pa. With USN, 1945-46. Fellow: Pa. Bar Found. (life); mem.: ABA, Colonial Soc. Pa. (bd. dirs. 2001), Phila. Bar Assn. (vice chmn. com. censors 1971), Pa. Bar Assn., Pa. Soc. S.R., Soc. Colonial Wars, Phila. Country Club, Union League Phila. Democrat. Roman Catholic. Avocation: U.S. Civil War history. E-mail: dmurphyesq@prodigy.net.

MURPHY, DEBORAH JANE, lawyer; b. Clinton, Tenn., Dec. 19, 1955; d. Robert C. and Mary R. (Melton) M.; m. Ashley B. Dickson, 2002. BS, U. Tenn., 1977; JD, Nashville Sch. Law, 1987. Bar: Tenn. 1987, U.S. Dist. Ct. (D.C. dist.) 1988, U.S. Dist. Ct. (6th cir.) 1988. Estate tax atty. U.S. Dept. Treasury, Knoxville, Tenn., 1987—2002, Atlanta, 2003—; mcpl. judge Lake City, Tenn., 1997—. Bd. dirs. Tenn. Lawyers Assn. Women, Nashville, 1997-01. Mem. cmty. adv. bd. East Tenn. Children's Hosp., 1998-01. Mem. ABA, Tenn. Bar Assn., Club LeConte. Dem. Methodist. Avocations: reading, golf, travel. Office: 5420 Snapfinger Dr Ste190 Decatur GA 30035

MURPHY, DENNIS L. psychiatrist; BS, Marquette U., 1958; MSc in Physiology, MD, U. Wis., 1963. Diplomate Am. Bd. Psychiatry and Neurology, 71, lic. Md., 65. Rsch. fellow Dept. Physiology Med. Coll. Wis., Milw., 1958—62; intern U. Minn. Hosp., Mpls., 1963—64; resident Johns Hopkins U. Sch. Medicine, Balt., 1964—66; from clin. assoc. Adult Psychiatry Br. to chief Lab. Clin. Sci. NIMH, Bethesda, Md., 1966—85, chief Lab. Clin. Sci., 1985—. Adj. faculty Johns Hopkins U. Sch. Medicine, Balt., 1977—86; mem. faculty Washington Sch. Psychiatry, Washington, 1983—97. Mem. editl. bd.: Progress in Neuropsychopharmacology, 1977—87, Psychopharmacology Comms., 1978—81, Psychiatry Rsch., 1980—, Anxiety and Depression, 1993—, Internat. Jour. Neuropsychopharmacology, 1998—, mem. editl. adv. bd.: Jour. Neurotransmission, 1982—, Dementia, 1991—, Human Psychopharmacology, 1996—, CNS Spectrums: The Internat. Jour. Neuropsychiat. Medicine, 1996—, assoc. editor: Neuropsychopharmacology, 1986—96. Recipient A.E. Bennett award, Soc. Biol. Psychiatry, 1970, Psychopharmacology Rsch. award, Am. Psychol. Assn., 1970, award, Internat. Anna-Monika Found., 1971, Hofheimer prize for rsch., Am. Psychiat. Assn., 1971, Meritorious Svc. award, Alcohol, Drug Abuse, and Mental Health Adminstrn., 1977, Superior Svc. award, USPHS, 1980, Disting. Svc. award, U.S. Dept. Health and Human Svcs., 1984, Presdl. Meritorious Exec. Rank award, 1985, 1991; fellow, March of Dimes, 1960, USPHS, 1961—62. Mem.: Soc. Neuroscience, Psychiat. Rsch. Soc., Internat. Soc. Neurochemistry, Found. Advanced Edn. in Scis., Collegium Internat. Neuropsychopharmacologium, Am. Coll. Neuropsychopharmacology, Latchkeyers, Alpha Sigma Nu, Alpha Omega Alpha. Office: Lab Clinical Sci NIMH NIH 10 Center Dr MSC 1264 Bldg 10 Rm 3D 41 Bethesda MD 20892-1264

MURPHY, DIANA E. federal judge; b. Faribault, Minn., Jan. 4, 1934; d. Albert W. and Adleyne (Heiker) Kuske; m. Joseph Murphy, July 24, 1958; children: Michael, John E. BA magna cum laude, U. Minn., 1954, JD magna cum laude, 1974; postgrad., Johannes Gutenberg U., Mainz, Germany, 1954—55, U. Minn., 1955—58; LLD, St. Johns U., 2000, U. St. Thomas, 2003. Bar: Minn. 1974, U.S. Supreme Ct. 1980. Assoc. Lindquist & Vennum, 1974—76; mcpl. judge Hennepin County, 1976—78, Minn. State dist. judge, 1978—80; judge U.S. Dist. Ct. for Minn., Mpls., 1980—94, chief judge, 1992—94; judge U.S. Ct. of Appeals (8th cir.), Mpls., 1994—. Chair U.S. Sentencing Commn., 1999—2004. Bd. editors: Minn. Law Rev., Georgetown U. Jour. on Cts., Health Scis. and the Law, 1989—92. Bd. dirs. Nat. Assn. Pub. Interest Law Fellowships for Equal Justice, 1992—95, Mpls. United Way, 1985—2001, treas., 1990—94, vice-chmn., 1996—97, chmn. bd. dirs., 1997—98; bd. dirs. Bush Found., 1982—, chmn. bd. dirs., 1986—91; organizer, 1st chmn. adv. coun. Amicus, bd. dirs., 1976—80; chair Mpls. Charter Commn., 1973—76; bd. dirs. Ops. De Novo, 1971—76, chmn. bd. dirs., 1974—75; mem., chmn. bill of rights com. Minn. Constl. Study Commn., 1971—73; regent St. Johns U., 1978—87, 1988—98, chmn. bd., 1985—98, bd. overseers sch. theology, 1998—2001; mem. Minn. Bicentennial Commn., 1987—88; trustee Twin Cities Pub. TV, 1985—94, chmn. bd., 1990—92; trustee U. Minn. Found., 1990—, chmn. of bd., 2003—; bd. dirs. Sci. Mus. Minn., 1988—94, vice-chmn., 1991—94; trustee U. St. Thomas, 1991—; vice chair bd. govs. U. St. Thomas Law Sch., 2001—02, chair, 2004—; bd. dirs. Spring Hill Conf. Ctr., 1978—84. Recipient Amicus Founders' award, 1980, Outstanding Achievement award, U. Minn., 1983, YWCA, 1981, Disting. Citizen award, Alpha Gamma Delta, 1985, Devitt Disting. Svc. to Justice award, 2001, Disting. Alumnus award, U. Minn. Law Sch., 2002, Woman Who Makes a Difference award, Internat. Women's Forum, 2003; scholar Fulbright. Fellow: Am. Bar Found.; mem.: ABA (mem. ethics and profl. responsibility judges adv. com. 1981—88, standing com. on jud. selection, tenure and compensation 1991—94, mem. standing com. on fed. jud. improvements 1994—97, Appellate Judges conf. exec. com. 1996—99, chmn. ethics and profl. responsibility judges adv. com. 1997—2000), Fed. Jud. Ctr. (bd. dirs. 1990—94, 8th cir. jud. coun. 1992—94, convener gender fairness task force 1993, mem. U.S. jud. conf. com. on ct. adminstrn. and case mgmt. 1994—99, chair gender fairness implementation com. 1997—98, 8th cir. jud. coun. 1997—), Hist. Soc. for 8th Cir. (bd. dirs. 1988—91), Fed. Judges Assn. (bd. dirs. 1982—2003, v.p. 1984—89, pres. 1989—91), U. Minn. Alumni Assn. (bd. dirs. 1975—83, nat. pres. 1981—82), Minn. Women Lawyers (Myra Bradwell award 1996), Nat. Assn. Women Judges (Leadership Judges Jud. Adminstrn. award 1998, Honoree of Yr. 2002), Nat. Assn. Governing Bds. Univs. Colls. (dir. 1998—), Am. Judicature Soc. (bd. dirs. 1982—93, v.p. 1985—88, treas. 1988—89, chmn. bd. 1989—91), Am. Law Inst., Hennepin County Bar Assn. (gov. coun. 1976—81), Minn. Bar Assn. (bd. govs. 1977—81), Order of Coif, Phi Beta Kappa. Office: 11 E US Courthouse 300 S 4th St Minneapolis MN 55415-1320 Office Phone: 612-664-5820.

MURPHY, DICK, mayor, former superior court judge; m. Jan Murphy; children: Brian, Shannon, Kelly. BS, U. Ill., 1965; MBA, Harvard U., 1967; JD, Stanford U., 1975. Mem. San Diego City Coun., 1981—85; San Diego mktg. dir. Bank of Am.; corp. atty. Luce, Forward, Hamilton & Scripps; mcpl. ct. judge, 1985—89; superior ct. judge, 1989—2000; mayor City of San Diego, Calif., 2000—. Chair Mission Trails Regional Park Task Force, Met. Transit Devel. Bd. Lieut. U.S. Army. Mem.: San Diego Rotary Club. Office: 202 C St San Diego CA 92101

MURPHY, DONALD B. investment company executive; Gen. ptnr. Brown Bros. Harriman & Co., N.Y.C. Office: Brown Bros Harriman & Co 140 Broadway New York NY 10005

MURPHY, DONNA, actress; b. Corona, N.Y., Mar. 7, 1959; Student, NYU Sch. of the Arts. Actor: (Broadway plays) They're Playing Our Song, The Human Comedy, The Mystery of Edwin Drood, Passion (Tony award best actress in a musical, 1994, Drama Desk award, Drama League award), The King and I, 1996 (Tony award best actress in a musical, 1996, Drama League award), Wonderful Town, 2003— (Tony nom. best actress in a musical, 2004, Drama Desk award best actress in a musical, 2004); (plays) Song of Singapore, Privates on Parade, Showing Off, Birds of Paradise, Little Shop of Horrors, A...My Name Is Alice, Twelve Dreams, 1995, Hello Again, 1994; (TV series) Murder One, 1995—96, Law & Order, 1993, 1997, 2000, The Practice, 1998, Ally McBeal, 1998, What About Joan, 2001, Hack, 2002; (TV miniseries) LIBERTY! The American Revolution, 1997; (TV films) Tales from the Hollywood Hills: A Table at Ciro's, 1987, Power, Passion and Murder, 1987, Passion, 1996, Someone Had to Be Benny, 1996, The Day Lincoln Was Shot, 1998, The Last Debate, 2000; (films) Jade, 1995, October 22, 1998, Star Trek: Insurrection, 1998, The Astronaut's Wife, 1999, Center Stage, 2000. Office: William Morris Agy 1325 Avenue Of The Americas New York NY 10019-6026*

MURPHY, EARL FINBAR, law educator; b. Indpls., Nov. 1, 1928; AB, Butler U., 1949, MA, 1954; JD, Ind. U., 1952; LLM, Yale U., 1955, JSD, 1959. Bar: Ind. 1952. Pvt. practice, Indpls., 1952-54; asst. prof. SUNY, Binghamton, 1955-57; Rockefeller fellow U. Wis. Law Sch., Madison, 1957-58; from asst. prof. to assoc. prof. Temple U., Phila., 1958—65, prof. law, 1965-69; prof. Ohio State U., Columbus, 1969-81, C. William O'Neill prof. law and jud. adminstrn., 1981-2000, prof. emeritus, 2000—. Vis. prof. U. Ariz., 1980. Author: Water Purity, 1961, Governing Nature, 1967, Man and His Environment: Law, 1971, Nature, Bureaucracy and the Rules of Property, 1977, Energy and Environmental Balance, 1980, Quantitative Groundwater Law, 1991. Chmn. Ohio Environ. Bd. Rev., 1972—74. Mem.: ABA, World Soc. Ekistics (pres. 1982—84), Am. Soc. Legal History, Fed. Bar Assn., Ind. Bar Assn., Masons. Unitarian. Home: 4475 Langport Rd Columbus OH 43220-4257 Office: Ohio State U Moritz Coll Law 55 W 12th Ave Columbus OH 43210-1306 E-mail: Murphy.14@osu.edu.

MURPHY, EDDIE, comedian, actor; b. Bklyn., Apr. 3, 1961; s. Vernon and Lillian Murphy Lynch; m. Nicole Mitchell, March 18, 1993; children: Bria, Myles, Shayne. Student pub. schs., Bklyn. Began performing Richard M. Dixon's White House, L.I., N.Y.; performed at various N.Y.C. clubs, including The Comic Strip; with Saturday Night Live, N.Y.C., 1980-84; host 35th Ann. Emmy Awards, 1983. Actor: (TV Special) Eddie Murphy Delirious, 1983, Eddie Murphy Raw, 1987; (films) 48 hrs., 1982, Trading Places, 1983, Best Defense, 1984, Beverly Hills Cop, 1984, The Distinguished Gentleman, 1992, Beverly Hills Cop III, 1994, The Nutty Professor, 1996, Metro, 1997, Mulan (voice), 1998, Dr. Dolittle, 1998, Holy Man, 1998, Bowfinger, 1999, Shrek (voice), 2001, Dr. Dolittle 2, 2001, Showtime, 2002, The Adventures of Pluto Nash, 2002, I Spy, 2002, Daddy Day Care, 2003, Shrek 4-D (voice), 2003, The Haunted Mansion, 2003, Shrek 2, 2004; actor, exec. prodr.: (films) The Golden Child, 1986, The Nutty Professor II: The Klumps, 2000, Harlem Nights, 1989; actor, prodr.: (films) Life, 1999; actor: Beverly Hills Cop II, 1987; writer: films Beverly Hills Cop II, 1987; actor: (films) Coming to America, 1988; writer: films Coming to America, 1988, Another 48 hrs., 1990; actor: (films) Another 48 hrs., 1990; writer: films Boomerang, 1992; actor: (films) Boomerang, 1992, Vampire in Brooklyn, 1995; actor, exec. prodr.: (TV series) The PJ's (voice), 1999, Harlem Nights, 1989; actor, prodr.: (films) Life, 1999.*

MURPHY, EDRIE LEE, laboratory administrator; b. Redwood Falls, Minn., Dec. 4, 1953; d. Melvin Arthur and Betty Lou (Wenholz) Timm; m. David Joseph Murphy, July 28, 1984; children: Michael David, Scott Christopher. BS in Med. Tech. summa cum laude, Mankato State U., 1976; MBA, U. St. Thomas, 1984. Registered med. technologist. Med. technologist Children's Hosps. and Clinics, St. Paul, 1976-81, chemistry supr., 1981-85, lab. mgr., 1985-95, dir. lab. sys. Mpls., St. Paul's Campus, 1995-99; lab. mgr. Fairview Health Sys., Mpls., 2000—. Contbr. articles to profl. jours. Charles H. Cooper scholar, 1975. Mem.: Minn. Soc. Clin. Lab. Mgmt. Assn. (sec.-treas. Minn. chpt. 1994—96, bd. dirs. 1996—, pres.-elect 1998—2000, pres. 2000—02), Am. Soc. Clin. Lab. Scis., Elan Vital Ski Club (v.p. membership 1981—82), Phi Kappa Phi. Avocations: photography, sailing, skiing, tennis, travel. Office: Fairview Health Sys 2512 7th St S R300D Minneapolis MN 55454 E-mail: emurphy2@fairview.org.

MURPHY, EDWARD FRANCIS, sales executive; b. Chgo., July 30, 1947; s. Edward F. and Marjorie (Mooney) M.; m. Kay A. Worcester, Apr. 17, 1970; 1 child, Dean D. BA in Mktg., No. Ill. U., 1976. Dist. mgr. Midas Internat. Corp., Chgo., 1977-85; sales mgr. Raybestos, McHenry, Ill., 1985-89, Wagner Brakes, St. Louis, 1989-99; owner Displays of Distinction, Mesa, Ariz., 1998—. V.p. Associated Roof Structures, Mesa, 1999—. Author: Vietnam Medal of Honor Heroes, 1987, Heroes of World War II, 1990, Korea's Heroes, 1990, Dak To, 1993, Semper Fi-Vietnam, 1996, Khe Sahn-The Hill Fights, 2000; hist. cons. (book) Above and Beyond, 1985. Sgt. U.S. Army, 1965-68. Recipient Dist. Svc. award Congl. Medal of Honor Soc., 1989. Mem. Medal of Honor Hist. Soc. (founder, pres. 1975—). Republican. Avocations: writing, flying. Home: 2659 E Kael St Mesa AZ 85213-2363

MURPHY, ELLIS, association management executive; b. Lincoln, Nebr. s. Ellis F. and Virgie (Olson) M.; m. Judy Neel, 1975; children by previous marriage: Sharon, Michael, Edward, Randall; stepchildren: Mary, Janet, Susan BS in Agr, Purdue U., 1947; MBA, Northwestern U., 1957; postgrad., Ill. Inst. Tech., 1969-81, U. Wash., 1950-51, Mexico City Coll., 1947, U. Chgo., 1964. Assoc. editor Pacific Builder & Engr., Seattle, 1948-51; tech. editor Portland Cement Assn., 1953-55; dir. public relations Chgo. chpt. AIA, 1955-56; account exec. Carrier & Jobson, Inc., Chgo., 1956-57; pres. Ellis Murphy, Inc., Chgo., 1957-73, Murphy, Tashjian & Assocs., Chgo., 1973-78; v.p. Lurie/Murphy Assocs., Inc., Chgo., 1979-83; pres. Murphy & Murphy Inc., Chgo., 1984—. Cons. mktg. communication to various bus. firms, 1970—; instr. (part-time) mktg. Ill. Inst. Tech., Chgo., 1977-79; instr. (part-time) assn. mgmt. DePaul U., Chgo., 1985—; cons. to various trade assns., 1970— Mem. Bd. Edn. Thornton Fractional Dist., Ill., 1961-67; trustee First Meth. Ch., Lansing, Ill., 1959-65; chmn. dirs. funds Purdue Club, Chgo., 1990-95. Major USMCR, 1943-46, 50-52. Mem. Public Relations Soc. Am. (citation 1963), Am. Mktg. Assn., Am. Soc. Assn. Execs., Chgo. Soc. Assn. Execs. (Disting. Service award 1986), Knights Templar, St. Bernard Commndery (past comdr.), Sigma Delta Chi. Home: 3100 N Sheridan Rd Chicago IL 60657-4954 E-mail: emememememem@aol.com.

MURPHY, EUGENE F. retired aerospace, communications and electronics executive; b. Flushing, N.Y., Feb. 24, 1936; s. Eugene P. and Delia M.; m. Mary Margaret Cullen, Feb. 20, 1960. BA, Queens Coll., 1956; JD, Fordham U., 1959; LLM, Georgetown U., 1964. Bar: N.Y. With RCA Global Communications Inc., N.Y.C., 1964-81, v.p. and gen. counsel, 1969-71, exec. v.p. ops., 1972-75, pres., chief operating officer, 1975-76, pres., chief exec. officer, 1976-81; chmn., chief exec. officer RCA Communications Inc., N.Y.C., 1981-86; sr. v.p. communications and info. svcs. GE, N.Y.C., 1986-91; pres., chief exec. officer GE Aerospace, King of Prussia, Pa., 1992-93; pres., CEO GE Aircraft Engines, Cin., 1993-97; vice chmn. bd., exec. officer GE Co., Fairfield, Conn., 1997-99; ret., 1999. Bd. dirs. Lockheed Martin Corp.; mem. Pres. Reagan's Nat. Sec. Telecommunications Adv. Com.; bd. govs. Aerospace Industries Assn. Bd. Served with USMCR, 1959-60. Recipient Aeronautics/Propulsion award Aviation Week and Space Tech., 1997. Mem. Armed Forces Comm. and Electronics Assn. (past nat. chmn.). Clubs: Marco Polo, Plandome Country, Plandome Field and Marine. Office: GE Co 3135 Easton Tpke Fairfield CT 06431-0001

MURPHY, EVELYN FRANCES, economist; b. Panama Canal Zone, May 14, 1940; d. Clement Bernard and Dorothy Eloise (Jackson) M. AB, Duke U., 1961, PhD, 1965; MA, Columbia U., 1963; hon. degrees, Regis Coll., 1978, Curry Coll., Northeastern U., Simmons Coll., Wheaton Coll., Anna Maria Coll., Bridgewater State Coll., Salem State Coll., Emmanuel Coll.; hon. degree, Suffolk U. Pres. Ancon Assocs., Boston, 1971-72; ptnr. Llewelyn-Davies, Weeks, Forrester-Walker & Bor, London, 1973-74; sec. environ. affairs Commonwealth of Mass., Boston, 1975-79, sec. econ. affairs, 1983-86, lt. gov., 1987-91; mng. dir. Brown Rudnick Freed and Gesmer, Boston, 1991-93; exec. v.p. Blue Cross/Blue Shield of Mass., Boston, 1994-98; also bd. dirs. Blue Cross Blue Shield Mass., Boston; resident scholar Brandeis U. Women's Studies Rsch. Ctr., 1999—; pres. The Wage Project, Inc., 2003—. Vis. pub. policy scholar Radcliffe Coll., 1991; vice-chmn., chmn. Nat. Adv. Com. on Oceans and Atmosphere, 1979-80; bd. dirs. Citizens Energy Corp., SBLI USA Mut. Life Ins., The Commonwealth Inst., Polaris Project, Nat. Ctr. on Women and Aging, chair, 1998-2002, chmn. emeritus, 2002; pres. Health Care and Policy Inst., 1997-98; resident scholar Brandeis U., 1998—; bd. trustees Regis Coll., 2003—. Recipient Dist. Svc. award New Eng. Coun., 1996, Nat. Sierra Club, 1978, Nat. Bd. Govs. Assn., 1978, Outstanding Citizen award Mass. Audobon Soc., 1978; Harvard U. fellow, 1979-80. Mem. Women Execs. in State Govt. (chair 1987), Internat. Women's Forum, 1993—. Democrat. Avocation: jogging. Personal E-mail: evmurphy1@aol.com.

MURPHY, EWELL EDWARD, JR., lawyer; b. Washington, Feb. 21, 1928; s. Ewell Edward and Lou (Phillips) M.; m. Patricia Bredell Purnell, June 26, 1954 (dec. 1964); children: Michaela, Megan Patricia, Harlan Ewell. BA, U. Tex., 1946, LLB, 1948; DPhil, Oxford U., Eng., 1951. Bar: Tex. 1948. Assoc. Baker & Botts, Houston, 1954-63, ptnr., 1964-93, head internat. dept., 1972-89. Pres. Houston World Trade Assn., 1972-74; trustee Southwestern Legal Found., 1978—2003; chmn. Houston Com. on Fgn. Rels., 1984-85, Inst. Transnat. Arbitration, 1985-89, Internat. and Comparative Law Ctr., 1986-87; mem. J. William Fulbright Fgn. Scholarship Bd., 1991-96, vice chmn., 1992-93, chmn., 1993-95; vis. prof. U. Tex. Law Sch., 1993-97; Disting. lectr., U. Houston Law Ctr., 1996—. Contbr. articles to profl. jours. Served to lt. USAF, 1952-54. Recipient Carl H. Fulda award U. Tex. Internat. Law Jour., 1980; Rhodes scholar, 1948-51 Mem. ABA (chmn. sect. internat. law 1970-71), Houston Bar Assn. (chmn. internat. law com. 1963-64, 70-71), Houston C. of C. (chmn. internat. bus. com. 1964, 65), Philos. Soc. Tex., Internat. Law Inst. (bd. dirs. 1994—), Fulbright Assn. (bd. dirs. 1999—, v.p. 2002-), Coun. on Fgn. Rels. Home and Office: 17 W Oak Dr Houston TX 77056-2117 Office Phone: 713-622-3840. E-mail: ewellmurphyjr@sbcglobal.net.

MURPHY, FRANCES M. government agency administrator; MD with honors, Georgetown U., Washington, 1979; MPH, Uniformed Svcs. U. of the Health Scis., 1993. Diplomate Am. Coll. Psychiatry and Neurology. Resident in neurology Georgetown U., Washington; staff neurologist Andrews AFB, Md., 1983—87; chief cons. occupl. and environ. medicine Dept. Vet. Affairs, Washington, dep. under-sec. for health, 1999—2002, acting under sec. for health, 2002, dep. under sec. for health policy coord., 2002—. Adj. assoc. prof. neurology Uniformed Svcs. U. of the Health Scis. Contbr. articles to profl. jours. With USAF. Office: US Dept Vets Affairs 810 Vermont Ave NW Washington DC 20420

MURPHY, FRANCIS, English language educator; b. Springfield, Mass., Mar. 13, 1932; s. Frank Edward and Sarah (O'Connor) M. BA, Am. Internat. Coll., 1953; MA, U. Conn., 1955; PhD, Harvard U., 1960; LittD (hon.), Am. Internat. Coll., 1986. Mem. faculty English lang. and lit. Smith Coll., 1959-99, assoc. prof., 1966-69, prof., 1970-99, prof. emeritus, 1999—. Vis. curator Springfield Mus. Fine Arts, 1975-76, Hudson River Mus., 1983-84. Editor: The Diary of Edward Taylor, 1964, Major Am. Poets, 1967, Form and Structure in Poetry, 1964, Edwin Arlington Robinson, 1970, Walt Whitman, 1969, The Uncollected Essays of Yvor Winters, 1973, The Complete Poems of Walt Whitman, 1975, Of Plymouth Plantation (William Bradford), 1981; author: Willard Leroy Metcalf, 1976, (with Dean Flower) A Catalogue of American Paintings, Water Colors and Drawings (to 1923) in the G.W.V. Smith Museum, 1976, The Landscape Within: J. Francis Murphy, 1982, The Book of Nature: American Painters and the Natural Sublime, 1983; co-editor: Norton Anthology of American Literature, 1979—, Mass. Rev., 1966-67.

MURPHY, FRANK, lawyer; b. Winston-Salem, N.C., Dec. 9, 1947; m. Mary Jo Petree, July 18, 1970; children: Mary Elizabeth, William Franklin, James Patrick. AB, Davidson Coll., 1969; JD, Vanderbilt U., 1972. Bar: N.C. 1972. Ptnr. Petree Stockton LLP, Winston-Salem, 1972—97; dep. mng. ptnr. Kilpatrick Stockton, Winston-Salem, 1997—2000, exec. com. mem., 1995—2002; exec. v.p., gen. counsel, sec. Krispy Kreme Doughnuts, Inc., Winston-Salem, 2002—. Adv. bd. dirs. Wachovia Bank, Winston-Salem. Former chair, mem. com. Young Life of Forsyth County, Winston-Salem, 1986—; former trustee, pres. Davidson Coll. Alumni Assn., 1987-89; mem. exec. com., chmn. Old Salem, Inc., Winston-Salem, 1998—; trustee Hospice Found., Winston-Salem, 1996—. Patrick Wilson scholar, Dana scholar; recipient Disting. Alumni award Davidson Coll. Mem. ABA (tax sect.), N.C. Bar Assn. (tax and corp. sects.), So. Employee Benefits Conf. (various coms. 1978-98), Piedmont Club, Forsyth Country Club, Best Lawyers in America. Avocations: golf, antiques, hiking. Home: 445 N Westview Dr Winston Salem NC 27104-2037 Office: Krispy Kreme Doughnuts Inc PO Box 83 Winston Salem NC 27102-2410*

MURPHY, FREDERICK AUGUSTUS, virologist, researcher; b. N.Y.C., June 14, 1934; s. Frederick A. and Louise A. (Knizak) M.; m. Irene M. Warwas, July 2, 1960; children: Frederick A., W. Timothy, John G., Terence D. BS, Cornell U., 1957, DVM, 1959; PhD, U. Calif., Davis, 1964; MD honoris causa, U. Turku, Finland, 1986. Chief viral pathology br. Ctrs. for Disease Control, Atlanta, 1964-78; assoc. dean Coll. Vet. Medicine Colo. State U., Ft. Collins, 1978-83; dir. divsn. viral diseases Ctrs. for Disease Control, Atlanta, 1983-87, dir. Nat. Ctr. for Infectious Diseases, 1987-91; dean Sch. Vet. Medicine U. Calif., Davis, 1991-96, prof., 1996—, dean emeritus. Program chair virology divsn. Internat. Union Microbiol. Socs., 1978-81, chair virology divsn., 1981-84; pres. Internat. Com. on Taxonomy of Viruses, 1990-96; mem. adv. bd. biology/biotech. divsn. Lawrence Livermore Nat. Lab., 1996—. Editor: (book) Virus Taxonomy, 1995, (book series) Advances in Virus Research, 1983—; editor-in-chief: (jour.) Archives of Virology, 1984-00; co-author: (book) Veterinary Virology, 1992. Capt. U.S. Army, 1959-62; comdr. USPHS, 1964-68. Recipient Presdl. Rank award U.S. Govt., 1992, K.F. Meyer Gold Headed Cane, Am. Vet. Epidemiology Soc., 1986. Fellow Infectious Diseases Soc. Am.; mem. Am. Soc. Virology (founding coun. mem.), Am. Soc. Tropical Medicine, German Acad. Natural Scis. (elected mem.), Inst. of Medicine, NIH (elected mem. 1999). Democrat. Roman Catholic. Office: U Calif Sch Vet Medicine Davis CA 95616

MURPHY, GEORGE, special effects expert; Computer graphics artist, visual effects supr. Indsl. Light & Magic, San Rafael, Calif. Films include: Hook, 1991, Death Becomes Her, 1992, Jurassic Park, 1993, Forrest Gump, 1994 (Acad. award best visual effects, Brit. Acad. Film and TV award for best visual effects 1994), Mission Impossible, 1995, Congo, 1995, Star Trek: First Contact, 1996, Starship Troopers, 1997, Mercury Rising, 1998, Mission to Mars, 1999, Impostor, 1999, Planet of the Apes, 2001, Matrix II and III, 2002-03; commls. include 1st Union Launch (gold Clio for visual effects 1999), 1st Union Noise (silver Clio for visual effects 1999), Hefty Gingerbread Man (bronze Clio for visual effects 1999); music videos include Will Smith Willenium. Mem. Acad. Motion Picture Arts and Scis. (visual effects br.). E-mail: george@georgemurphy.com.

MURPHY, GEORGE FRANCIS, dermatopathologist, educator; b. Natick, Mass., Feb. 12, 1950; s. George Francis and Barbara Elizabeth Murphy; m. Sharon Elizabeth Walters, Aug. 26, 1972; children: Erin Elizabeth, Emily Elise. BA, U. Pa., 1972; MD, U. Vt., 1976. Diplomate Nat. Bd. Med. Examiners, Am. Bd. Pathology, Am. Bd. Pathology and Dermatology. Resident, fellow Harvard Med. Sch., Mass. Gen. Hosp., Boston, 1977-81; assoc. prof. pathology Harvard Med. Sch., Boston, 1982-87; prof. dermatology and pathology U. Pa. Sch. Medicine, Phila., 1987-97, Herman Beerman endowed chair dermatology, 1991-97; prof. pathology Thomas Jefferson Med. Coll., Phila., 1997—2004, Harvard Med. Sch., Boston, 2004—. Vis. prof. pathology, dermatology and oncology Johns Hopkins U. Sch. Medicine, Balt., 2000—; pres., chmn. bd. dirs. Am. Soc. for Dermatopathology, 1997-98. Author: Fasicles in Skin Pathology, 1991, Dermatopathology, 1995; contbr. numerous articles to profl. jours. Mem. Am. Soc. for Clin. Investigation. Office: Brigham and Women's Hosp Dept Pathology 75 Francis St Boston MA 02115 Business E-Mail: gmurphy@rics.bwh.harvard.edu.

MURPHY, GERALD, retired government official, consultant; b. Washington, Aug. 25, 1938; s. Jeremiah T. and Jean (Curley) M.; m. Kathryn Beckman, Sept. 24, 1988; children by previous marriage: William Michael, Janet Marie, Kathleen Anne B.C.S. with honors, Benjamin Franklin U., Washington, 1960, M.C.S., 1963. C.P.A., D.C. Dep. div. dir. Dept. Treasury, Washington, 1970-71, div. dir., 1971-74, asst. commr., 1974-75, dep. commr., 1975-79, dep. fiscal asst. sec., 1979-86, fiscal asst. sec., 1986-98; sr. prin. Keane Pub. Enterprise Consulting, Washington, 1998-2000; ind. cons., 2000—. Lectr. in acctg. Southeastern U., Washington, 1965-70, Dept. Agr. Grad. Sch., Washington, 1970-76; mem. Govt. Acctg. Standards Adv. Council, 1984-89; mem. Fed. Acctg. Standards Adv. Bd., 1991-98. Served with U.S. Army, 1956 Recipient Disting. Alumni award Benjamin Franklin U., Washington, 1976. Mem. Am. Inst. C.P.A.s, Assn. Govt. Accts. (nat. pres. 1977-78, Robert W. King award 1983, Meritorious Exec. Rsch. award 1992), Sr. Execs. Assn., Fed. Exec. Inst. Alumni Assn. Roman Catholic.

MURPHY, GERARD NORRIS, trade association executive; b. Washington, July 10, 1950; s. Maurice J. and Marguerite (Norris) M.; m. Jacqueline F., May 26, 1973; children: Anne Marie, Michael Jonathan, Kathleen Elizabeth. BA, U. Md., 1972, MA, 1975; JD, George Mason U., 1980. Mgmt. trainee Washington Area New Automobile Dealers Assn., 1972-74, asst. CEO, 1974-82, pres., CEO, 1982—; prodr. Washington Auto Show, 2003—. Bd. dirs. Met. Washington BBB, chmn., 1992—97; bd. dirs. Small Bus. Legis. Coun., 2000—; mem. exec. com. Washington Workforce Investment Coun., 2000—; chmn. Nat. Capital Area Transp. Fedn., Washington, 1990—2000. Co-founder, past chmn. Washington Regional Alcohol Program, Vienna, Va., 1983-86; trustee Nat. Automobile Dealers Assn. Sales Rep. Cert. Commn., 1995-99; sec. Boys and Girls Clubs Greater Washington, Silver Spring, 1987-2002, v.p. 2002—; trustee Greater Washington Bd. Trade PACs, Va., 2000—, treas., 2003—; co-founder Montgomery Students Automotive Trades Found., Montgomery Pub. Schs., 1978, sec., 1990—. Recipient Govs. citation Gov. William Donald Schaefer, 1990, Silver medal Boys and Girls Clubs Am., 1997; named Automotive Trade Exec. of Yr., Northwood U., 1997. Fellow Am. Soc. Assn. Execs. (cert., com. chmn. 1989-90, 96-97); mem. ABA, Assn. Healthcare Coalition (sec. 1995, v.p. 1996-97, pres. 1998-2000), Automotive Trade Assn. Execs. (bd. dirs. 1987-88, sec., treas. 1996, v.p. 1997, pres. 1998), D.C. Bar Assn., Greater Washington Soc. Assn. Execs. (com. chmn. 1993-94, trustee Found. 1997-2000, chmn. award 1994), Leadership Washington (8th class 1993-94), Rotary (sec. 1998-00, v.p. 2001-2002, dist. conf. chmn. 2001, pres. 2002-2003, Paul Harris fellow 1990), Delta Theta Phi, Delta Tau Delta. Democrat. Roman Catholic. Office: Washington Area New Auto Dealers Assn Ste 210 5301 Wisconsin Ave NW Washington DC 20015-2015 Office Phone: 202-237-7200. Business E-Mail: gm@wanada.org.

MURPHY, GORDON JOHN, electrical engineer, educator; b. Milw., Feb. 16, 1927; s. Gordon M. and Cecelia A. (Knerr) M.; m. Dorothy F. Brautigam, June 26, 1948; children: Lynne, Craig. BS, Milw. Sch. Engring., 1949; MS, U. Wis., 1952; PhD, U. Minn., 1956. Asst. prof. elec. engring. Milw. Sch. Engring., 1949-51; systems engr. A C Spark Plug divsn. GM, 1951-52, cons., 1959-62; instr. U. Minn., 1952-56, asst. prof. elec. engring., 1956-57; assoc. prof. elec. engring. Northwestern U., Evanston, Ill., 1957-60, prof., 1960-97, head dept. elec. engring., 1960-69, dir. Lab. for Design of Electronic Systems, 1987-97, prof. emeritus, 1997—. Cons. numerous corps., 1959—; founder, 1st chmn. Mpls. chpt. Inst. Radio Engrs. Profl. Group on Automatic Control, 1956-57, Chgo. chpt., 1959-61; pres. IPC Systems, Inc., 1975-2003; expert witness in numerous patent suits, 1997-2004. Author: Basic Automatic Control Theory, 1957, 2d edit., 1966, Control Engineering, 1959; contbr. articles, papers to profl. jours.; patentee TV, electronic timers, periodontal instruments and motion control systems. Mem. indsl. adv. com. Milw. Sch. Engring., 1971-2001. Served with USN, 1945-46. Recipient ECE Centennial medal U. Wis., 1991, Outstanding Alumnus award Milw. Sch. Engring. Alumni Assn., 1974; named One of Chgo.'s Ten Outstanding Young Men Chgo. Jaycees, 1961. Fellow IEEE (for edn. and rsch. in automatic control 1967); mem. feedback control systems com. 1960-68, discrete systems com. 1962-68, adminstrv. com. profl. group on automatic control 1966-69, chmn. membership and nominating coms. 1966-67); mem. Am. Automatic Control Coun. (edn. com. 1967-69), Engr.'s Coun. for Profl. Devel. (guidance com. 1967-69), Nat. Electronic Conf. (bd. dirs. 1983-85), Am. Electronics Assn. (exec. com. M.W. coun. 1990-93), Sigma Xi, Eta Kappa Nu, Tau Beta Pi. Home: 638 Garden Ct Glenview IL 60025-4105 Office: Northwestern U Elec Engring Dept Evanston IL 60201 Office Phone: 847-491-7258.

MURPHY, GREGORY GERARD, lawyer; b. Helena, Mont., Feb. 3, 1954; s. Michael Anthony and Elizabeth (Cooney) M.; m. Katherine Joan Koch, Dec. 30, 1977; children: Megan, Brian, Allison. BA, U. Mont., 1976; JD, U. Notre Dame, 1979. Bar: Oreg. 1979, U.S. Dist. Ct. Oreg. 1979, U.S. Ct. Appeals (9th cir.) 1979, Mont. 1980, U.S. Dist. Ct. Mont. 1980, Crow Tribal Ct., No. Cheyenne Tribal Ct., U.S. Supreme Ct. 1996. Clk. to judge U.S. Ct. Appeals (9th cir.), Portland, 1979-80; assoc. Moulton, Bellingham, Longo & Mather P.C., Billings, Mont., 1980-84; shareholder Moulton, Bellingham, Longo & Mather, P.C., Billings, Mont., 1984—. Trustee Mont. dist. U.S. Bankruptcy Ct., 1982-85; examiner Mont. Bd. Bar Examiners, 1985-95, chmn. 1995-2002; trustee Nat. Conf. Bar Examiners, 1990-2002, chmn., 2000-2001, mem. multistate bar exam. com., 1986-94, chmn. 1994-98; vice chmn. commn. on rules of admission to the bar Mont. Supreme Ct., 1996-97. Assoc. editor Notre Dame Law Rev., 1978-79. Bd. dirs. Billings Symphony Soc., 1982-91, French hornist, 1981—. Thomas and Alberta White scholar U. Notre Dame, 1978-79; recipient Disting. Svc. award State Bar Mont., 2002. Mem. ABA (law sch. accreditation com. 2002-), Mont. Bar Assn., Oreg. Bar Assn., Am. Law Inst., Yellowstone County Bar Assn., Rotary. Roman Catholic. Avocations: French horn, golf, backpacking. Home: 5533 Gene Sarazen Dr Billings MT 59106-1121 Office: Moulton Bellingham et al PO Box 2559 Billings MT 59103-2559 Office Phone: 406-248-7731.

MURPHY, HAROLD LOYD, federal judge; b. Haralson County, Ga., Mar. 31, 1927; s. James Loyd and Georgia Gladys (McBrayer) M.; m. Jacqueline Marie Ferri, Dec. 20, 1958; children: Mark Harold, Paul Bailey. Student, West Ga. Coll., 1944-45, U. Miss., 1945-46; LL.B., U. Ga., 1949. Bar: Ga. 1949. Pvt. practice, Buchanan, Ga., from 1949; ptnr. Howe & Murphy, Buchanan and Tallapoosa, Ga., 1958-71; judge Superior Cts., Tallapoosa Circuit, 1971-77; U.S. dist. judge No. Dist. of Ga., Rome, 1977—. Rep. Gen. Assembly of Ga., 1951-61; asst. solicitor gen. Tallapoosa Jud. Circuit, 1956; mem. Jud. Qualifications Commn., State of Ga., 1977 With USNR, 1945-46. Fellow Am. Bar Found.; mem. ABA, Ga. Bar Assn., Dist. Judges Assn. for 11th Cir. Bar Assn., Am. Judicature Soc., Tallapoosa Cir. Bar Assn., Old War Horse Lawyers Club, Am. Inns Ct. (past pres. Joseph Henry Lumpkin sect.), Fed. Judges Assn. Methodist. Home: 321 Georgia Highway 120 Tallapoosa GA 30176-3114 Office: US Dist Ct PO Box 53 Rome GA 30162-0053

MURPHY, HELEN, recording industry executive; b. Glasgow, Scotland, Oct. 2, 1962; came to U.S., 1990; d. Francis and Kathleen (Gallagher) M.; m. Michael Christopher Luksha, Apr. 1, 1989. BA in Econs. with honors, U. Guelph, Can., 1982; MBA, U. Western Ontario, Can., 1984. CFA. Asst. mgr. securities rsch. Confederation Life, Toronto, Can., 1984-86; sr. analyst entertainment & merchandising Prudential Bache Securities, Toronto, Can., 1986-89; v.p. rsch. Richardson Greenshields Can., Toronto, 1989-90; v.p. investor rels. Polygram Holding, Inc., N.Y.C., 1990-91; v.p., treas. Polygram Records Inc., N.Y.C., 1991-92, sr. v.p. corp. fin., treas., 1992-95; sr. v.p. investor rels. PolyGram Internat. Ltd., N.Y.C., 1995-97; sr. v.p. mergers and acquisitions PolyGram Holding, Inc., N.Y.C., 1995-97, CFO, 1997-99, Westvaco Corp., 1999; CFO & chief adminstrv. office Martha Stewart Living Omnimedia, Inc., N.Y.C., 1999—2001; exec. v.p., CFO Warner Music Group, 2001—. Lectr. U. Guelph, 1982-90. Fellow Nat. Investor Rels. Inst., N.Y. Soc. Security Analysts, N.Y. Treas. Group. Office: Warner Music Group 75 Rockefeller Plz New York NY 10019

MURPHY, IRENE HELEN, publishing executive; b. Boston; d. Charles Leo and Irene Muriel (Finney) M. BA, Regis Coll., 1958; MA, Boston Coll., 1963, Northeastern U., Boston, 1968, Manhattanville Coll., 1969. Tchr. elem. sch., Boston; high sch. dir. guidance; ednl. adminstr.; prof. master tchr. program, 1969—; prof. N.Y.C.; dir. sch. svcs. Glencoe/McGraw Hill Pub. Co., Woodland Hills, Calif., 1969—; v.p. Glencoe Pub. Co., Mission Hills, Calif. Vis. lectr. univs., including Boston Coll., Sacred Heart U., St. John, Nfld., Regis Coll., Teachers Coll., Sidney, Australia, Teachers Coll., Melbourne, Australia, McGill U., Mont., Providence (R.I.) Coll. Author series ednl. games for children. Recipient Gold Seal Recognition award Today's Cath. Tchr., 1987, Leadership award in religious edn., 1992. Mem. AAUW, Nat. Cath. Edn. Assn., Nat. Assn. Female Execs., Jordan Hosp. Club, St. Peter Cath. Women's Club, Adminstrs. Club, Passport Club, Admirals Club. Roman Catholic. Avocations: sports, music, art work, poetry, literature. Home: 59 Summer St Plymouth MA 02360-3462 also: 2677 SW Thunderbird Trl Stuart FL 34997-8944 Office: Benziger Pub Co 21600 Oxnard St Ste 500 Woodland Hills CA 91367-4947 *In our times perhaps the greatest need of all is to return to the meaning of the Sacred in life, the importance of Presence—God's presence and the presence of others in building a true community with global implication of respect for all.*

MURPHY, JAMES BURTON, JR., lawyer; b. Mobile, Ala., July 2, 1954; s. James Burton and Sarah (McKee) M.; m. Jane Marie, June 5, 1982; children: Caroline Elizabeth, Courtney Erin, James Matthew. BA, Fla. Atlantic U., 1976; JD, U. Fla., 1979. Bar: Fla. 1979. Law clerk Hon. Wm. Terrell Hodges, U.S. Dist. Judge, Tampa, Fla., 1979—81; ptnr. Shook, Hardy, & Bacon, LLP, Tampa. Author: (with others) Discovery of Trade Secrets, 1989; contbr. articles to profl. jours. Pres. Westshore Breakfast Sertoma Club, Tampa, 1988-89, Bolesta Oral Tchg. Ctr., Inc., Tampa, 1990-92; bd. trustees, chmn. U. Tampa, 1994-95, 2002-, chmn. bd. counselors, 1994-95, 2002-2003, chmn. bd. fellows, 2002-03; mem. Leadership Tampa Program, 1991-92. Named Counselor of Yr. U. Tampa Bd. Counselors, 1991-92. Mem. Fla. Bar Assn. (chmn. bus. litig. com., chmn. bus. law sect. 2003-2004), Hillsborough County Bar Assn. (bd. dirs., trial lawyers sect., chmn. corp. banking, 1992-93), Ferguson-White Inn of Ct. (exec. coun.). Democrat. Methodist. Avocations: reading, golf. Office: Shook Hardy & Bacon LLP 100 N Tampa St Ste 2900 Tampa FL 33602 E-mail: jbmurphy@shb.com.

MURPHY, JAMES EDWARD, public relations and marketing executive; Degree in Journalism, U. Ill. Sr. corp. comms. officer Owens-Corning Fiberglas, Beatrice, Merrill Lynch; exec. v.p. Burson-Marsteller, vice chmn., 1990, chmn., CEO Ams., 1991-93; chmn., CEO Murphy & Co., 1993—; global mng. dir. mktg. and comm. Accenture (formerly known as Andersen Cons.), 1993—. Mem. bd. advisors Medill Sch. Journalism, Northwestern U., mem. adv. bd. Coll. Bus. and Commerce, U. Ill., also mem. devel. bd. Coll. Comm.; past pres., bd. dirs. Arthur Page Soc.; chmn. PR Coalition. Mem. Inst. Pub. Rels. Rsch. (trustee), Sky Club, Union League Club, Belle Haven Club, Woodway Country Club, Palmetto Golf Club, Preston Mountain Club. Office: Accenture 6th Fl 1345 Avenue of the Americas New York NY 10105 E-mail: james.e.murphy@accenture.com.

MURPHY, JAMES JEFFREY, electronics executive; b. Kenosha, Wis., Nov. 4, 1954; s. Eugene C. and Thelma M. (Jensen) M.; m. Susan M. Larson, June 10, 1978. BA in Bus. Mgmt. and Labor Econs. with honors, U. Wis., 1976. Sales rep. Inland Steel, Chgo., 1976-77, product analyst, 1977; sales rep. Joerndt & Ventura, Inc., Kenosha, 1977-78; field sales rep. Applied Power Corp., New Berlin, Wis., 1978-79; Magnavox regional mgr. Philips Consumer Electronics Co., Knoxville, Tenn., 1979-87, zone mgr., 1987-89, divsn. field sales mgr., 1989-91, natl. account dir., 1991-95, v.p. merchandising, 1995—. Mem. Lincoln Continental Owners Club (treas. 1991), Vintage Radio-Phonograph Soc. Avocations: car collecting, reading, walking. Home: 2330 Stonegate Dr Cumming GA 30041-7410 Office: Philips Consumer Electronics Co 64 Perimeter Ctr E Atlanta GA 30346-2295 Office Phone: 770-821-2922. Personal E-mail: murpho54@cs.com. Business E-Mail: jim.j.murphy@philips.com.

MURPHY, JAMES MICHAEL, retired judge, mediator, arbitrator; b. Spokane, Wash., Jan. 21, 1943; s. Harold Eugene and Helen Elizabeth (Rauschke) M.; m. Jill Jenene Giles, Aug. 31, 1968; children: Ryan Michael, Timothy Giles. BA, Ea. Wash. U., 1965; JD, Gonzaga U., 1973; cert, Nat. Jud. Coll., Reno, 1980. Bar: Wash. 1973, U.S. Dist. Ct. (ea. dist.) Wash. 1973. Law clk. U.S. Dist. Ct. (ea. dist.) Wash., Spokane, 1972-74; asst. atty. gen. State of Wash., Spokane, 1974-78; judge Spokane Dist. Ct., 1978-85; superior ct. State of Wash., Spokane, 1985—2003; mediator Judicial Mediation Group, L.L.P., Spokane, Wash., 2003—. Judge juvenile ct. State of Wash., 1988-89, 92, 95, presiding judge, 1990-91, drug ct. judge, 1996-2000; judge pro tem Ct. Appeals State of Wash.; mem. Bench Book com., Jud. Qualification Commn. State of Wash., 1984-85, Bd. for Jud. Adminstrn., 1984-85, chair Bd. Trial Ct. Edn. State of Wash., 1979-96; bd. for improvemnt of jud. adminstrn.; co-chair Wash. State Bd. for Jud. Adminstrn., 2000-01. Mem. Spokane County Programs Adminstrn. Bd., 1984, Spokane County Correction Adv. Bd., 1984, Mayor Chase Youth Awards Bd. City of Spokane, Dean's Bus. Forum Bd. Gonzaga U., Wash. State Supreme Ct. Task Force on Minority and Justice, 1987-90, exec. com., 1990—, State of Wash. Minority and Justice Commn., 1991—; mem. Trial Ct. Performance Standards Task Force, 1991-94; bd. trustees Inland Empire Bd. Athletics; counselor TAC Cultural exch. com., bd. dirs. Wash. cultural exch., del. nat. track and field conv., 1988-2000, mem. organizing com. Jr. Olympics, 1990; mem. Spokane Sports Unltd.; v.p. Spokane Limerick Sister City Assn.; official U.S. Track & Field Olympic Trials, 1992, 96, Olympic Games, 1996; bd. dirs. U.S.A. Track and Field; chair Cultural Exch. Com., 1997, law and legislation com., 1996—; counsel Youth Com.; co-chair Wash. State Bd. Jud. Adminstrn., 2000—; exec. com. Spokane Regional Sports Adminstrn., 2000—. Named one of Outstanding Young Men Am., 1979; recipient Disting. Alumnus award Ea. Wash. U. Sch. Pub. Affairs, 1986, 99. Mem. ABA (Wash. del. nat. conv. 1989-91), Am. Judges Assn., Wash. State Superior Ct. Judges Assn. (chmn. edn. com., benchbook com., improvement of jud. adminstrn. com., chmn. shorthand reporters com., pres. judge 1999-2001), Assn. Dist. and Mcpl. Ct. Judges (pres. 1985), Wash. State Bar Assn. (Outstanding Judge 2002), Spokane County Bar Assn. (pres. young lawyers 1974-75), Native Am. Legal Svcs. (pres. 1975-78), Spokane Enological Soc., Footprinters, Spokane Track Club (pres. team 1989), Friendly Sons of St. Patrick (pres. 1983, bd. dirs.), Kiwanis (bd. dirs. Spokane club 1980-84). Avocations: skiing, golf, backpacking, boating, track and field officiating. Office: Judicial Mediation Group LLP 534 E Trent Ave Spokane WA 99202 Office Phone: 509-456-6850. E-mail: jimmurphy@Qwest.net.

MURPHY, JAMES RODNEY, playwright; b. Kenton, Ohio, Mar. 23, 1933; m. Teruko Murakami, 1958; children: Cynthia, Laurel. BS in Bus. Adminstrn., U. Tenn., 1962; MS in Edn., U. So. Calif., 1967, MS in Sys. Mgmt., 1983; PhD in Aerospace Studies, Union Inst., Cin., 1990; Air Command and Staff Coll. Diploma, Air U., Maxwell AFB, Ala., 1987, Air War Coll. Diploma, 1988. Enlisted USAF, 1951, advanced through grades to capt., 1968, transp. combat adv., 1968-69; transp. analyst, def. transp. policy coun. advisor Ctr. for Studies and Analyses, Hdqrs. USAF, Washington, 1989-92; hazardous cargo and packaging policy specialist Directorate of Transp., Hdqrs. U.S. Air Force, Washington, 1992-95; ret. USAF, 1995—; playwright/poet, lyricist/librettist Plays Around, Colorado Springs, Colo., 1995—. Author: (musical) Truck Stop, 1994, (opera) Luke and Sarah, (musical) Member of the Team, 1996, (biography) Peon to Pentagon, 1999, also numerous poetry, lyrics and short stories. Founder, chmn. Am. Nat. Opera, 2000. Decorated Meritorious Svc. medal, Bronze Star medal, others. Mem. Nat. Def. Transp. Assn., Coun. Logistics Mgmt., Soc. Logistics Engrs., Nat. Panel Consumer Arbitrators, BBB, Masons, Internat. Soc. Poets, Rockford Writers Guild, Wyo. Players, Opera Am., Dramatists Guild, Writers Guild, Songwriters Assn. Washington, Washington Area Music Assn., Nashville Songwriters Assn. Internat., Am. Soc. Composers, Authors and Pubs., Drama League, Theatre Comms. Group, Colo. Opera Festival Guild, Phi Kappa Phi, Beta Gamma Sigma, Delta Nu Alpha, Delta Sigma Pi. Address: 4745 Purcell Dr Colorado Springs CO 80922-1615 E-mail: drjrmurphy@adelphia.net.

MURPHY, JANET GORMAN, college president; b. Holyoke, Mass., Jan. 10, 1937; d. Edwin Daniel and Catherine Gertrude (Hennessey) Gorman. BA, U. Mass., 1958, postgrad., 1960-61, EdD, 1974, LLD (hon.), 1984; MEd, Boston U., 1961. Tchr. English and history John J. Lynch Jr. H.S., Holyoke, 1958-60; tchr. English Chestnut Jr. H.S., Springfield, Mass., 1961-63; instr. English and journalism Our Lady of Elms Coll., Chicopee, Mass., 1963-64; mem. staff Mass. State Coll., Lyndonville, Vt., 1977-83; pres. Mo. Western State Coll., St. Joseph, 1983—. Mem. campaign staff Robert F. Kennedy Presdl. Campaign, 1967. Recipient John Gunther Tchr. award NEA, 1961, award Women's Opportunity Com., Boston Fed. Exec. Bd., 1963, Phi Delta Kappa Educator of Yr. award NAACP, 1992; named one of 10 Outstanding Young Leaders of Greater Boston Area, Boston Jr. C. of C., 1973. Office: Mo Western State Coll Office of the President 4525 Downs Dr Saint Joseph MO 64507-2246

MURPHY, JEREMIAH T. professional sports team executive/constuction services; BA, Bernard Baruch Coll. CPA, Calif. Sr. ptnr. Bowman and Co., 1971-82; CFO A.G. Spanos Companies, Stockton, Calif., 1982—. Mem. Am. Soc. CPAs (Calif. chpt.). Office: The Spanos Companies 1341 W Robinhood Dr Ste 1A Stockton CA 95207

MURPHY, JOANNE BECKER, writer; b. Detroit; d. Louis Norman and Gertrude Margaret (Kornmeier) Becker; m. Joseph A. Murphy, Jr., June 24, 1961; children: Michael Ellis, Joseph A. III. BA in Journalism, Mich. State U., 1958; MA in Humanities, Wayne State U., 1975. With pub. rels. dept. WBZ TV, Boston, 1958-60, The Jam Handy Orgn., Detroit, 1960-62, Detroit Symphony Orch., 1969-70; freelance writer, editor Detroit, 1978—90, Washington, 1990—. Contbg. writer: Affecting Change, 1986, Glass: State of the Art, 1989; editor: As Parents We Will, 1985 (1st Pl. award Pub. Svc. Nat. Found. for Alcoholism Comm.); writer, editor publs. for arts and human svcs. orgns.; contbr. articles to mage., newspapers. Program bd. Grosse Pointe (Mich.) War Meml., 1987—90; bd. dirs. Detroit Artists Market, 1982—90, Mich. Metro coun. Girl Scouts USA, 1971—78, Family Svcs. Detroit and Wayne County, 1970—76, All Hallows Guild Grounds Oversight Bd., Washington Nat. Cathedral, 1993 ; bd. canvassers Grosse Pointe Sch. Sys., 1986—90; DC regional bd. Nat. Capital Area United Way, Washington, 1999—. Mem.: Washington Ind. Writers, Am. News Women's Club (Washington, bd. dirs. 1996—2001), Kappa Alpha Theta. Home and Office: 2717 O St NW Washington DC 20007-3128 Office Phone: 202-337-7856. E-mail: murphy.joanne@verizon.net.

MURPHY, JOHN ARTHUR, tobacco, food and brewing company executive; b. N.Y.C., Dec. 15, 1929; s. John A. and Mary J. (Touhy) M.; m. Carole Ann Paul, June 28, 1952; children: John A., Kevin P., Timothy M., Kellyann, Robert D., Kathleen. BS, Villanova U., 1951; JD, Columbia U., 1954. Bar: N.Y. 1954. Since practiced in, N.Y.C.; ptnr. firm Conboy Hewitt O'Brien & Boardman, 1954-62; asst. gen. counsel Philip Morris Co. Inc., N.Y.C., 1962-66, v.p., 1967-76, exec. v.p., 1976-78, group exec. v.p., 1978-84, pres., 1984-91, vice chmn., 1991-92, also bd. dirs.; asst. to pres. Philip Morris Internat., 1966-67, exec. v.p., 1967-71; pres., chief exec. officer Miller Brewing Co., Milw., 1971-78, chmn. bd., chief exec. officer, 1978-84. Trustee North Shore Univ. Hosp., Marquette U., 1973-91; mem. exec. com. Keep Am. Beautiful, Inc.; mem. bd. consultors Sch. Law Villanova U.; mem. bus. com. Met. Mus. Art. Decorated Knight of Malta. Mem. ABA, N.Y. State Bar Assn. Office: Philip Morris Cos Inc 100 Park Ave New York NY 10017-5516

MURPHY, JOHN B. investment advisor; b. Pitts., May 30, 1947; s. John Bernard and Knolle Cordelia (Bonham) M.; m. Lauren Osa Brown, Mar. 20, 1994; 1 child, Kira Mei Li. BA, U. New Orleans, 1970; MBA, Columbia U., 1984. CFA 1987. Dir. La. Heritage Fair, New Orleans, 1974-75, 78-80; assoc. dir. New Orleans Jazz and Heritage Festival, 1978-80; exec. dir. New Orleans Jazz and Heritage Found. Inc., 1980; assoc. editor, analyst Value Line Pubs., N.Y.C., 1984-86; equity analyst, v.p. Drexel, Burnham, Lambert, N.Y.C., 1986-90; portfolio mgr., mng. dir. Guardian, N.Y.C., 1990—. Head of convertible investments, mng. dir. Family Svc. Life and other Guardian subs., 1998—; mem. alumni counseling bd. Sch. Bus. Columbia U., N.Y.C., 1996—; prodn. cons. Newport Jazz Festival, Capitol Radio Jazz Festival, Memphis Heritage Festival, 1978-80. Recipient Mayoralty Merit award City of New Orleans, 1978. Mem. Assn. Investment Mgmt. and Rsch., N.Y. Soc. Security Analysts, Beta Gamma Sigma (scholar 1983). Avocations: poetry, photography, golf. Home: PO Box 243 Ardsley On Hudson NY 10503-0243 Office: Guardian 7 Hanover Sq New York NY 10004-2616 E-mail: john_murphy@glic.com.

MURPHY, JOHN CARTER, economics professor; b. Ft. Worth, July 17, 1921; s. Joe Preston and Elsie (Carter) M.; m. Dorothy Elise Haldi, May 1, 1949 (dec. Jan. 1997); children: Douglas C., Barbara E.; m. Teiko Kanazawa, June 17, 2000. Student, Tex. Christian U., 1939-41; BA, North Tex. State U., 1943, BS, 1946; AM, U. Chgo., 1949, PhD, 1955; postgrad., U. Copenhagen, 1952-53. Instr. Ill. Inst. Tech., 1947-50; instr. to assoc. prof. Washington U., St. Louis, 1950-62; vis. prof. So. Meth. U., Dallas, 1961, prof., 1962-90, prof. emeritus, 1990—, dir. grad. studies in econs., 1963-68, chmn. dept., 1968-71, faculty summer program in Oxford, 1982-91, dir., 1991, pres. faculty senate, 1988-89, co-dir. Insts. on Internat. Fin., 1982-87. Vis. prof. Bologna (Italy) Ctr., Sch. Advanced Internat. Studies, Johns Hopkins U., 1961-62; UN tech. assistance expert, Egypt, 1964; vis. prof., spl. field staff Rockefeller Found., Thammasat U., Bangkok, 1966-67; sr. staff economist Coun. Econ. Advisers, 1971-72, U.S. dels. econ. policy com. and working part III OECD, 1971-72, U.S. del. 8th meeting Joint U.S.-Japan Econ. Com., 1971; cons. Washington U. Internat. Econs. Rsch. Project, 1950-53, U.S. Treasury, 1972, Fed. Res. Bank Dallas, 1994—; referee NSF; witness and referee congl. coms.; lectr. USIA Program, Germany, 1961-62, 84, Philippines, South Viet Nam, Thailand, 1972, France, Belgium, 1984; lectr. Southwestern and Midwestern Grad. Sch. Banking; adj. scholar Am. Enterprise Inst. for Pub. Policy Rsch., 1976—. Author: The International Monetary System: Beyond the First Stage of Reform, 1979; (with R.R. Rubottom) Spain and the U.S.: Since World War II, 1984; editor: Money in the International Order, 1964; contbr. articles to profl. books and jours. Chmn. rsch. com. on internat. conflict and peace Washington U., 1959-61; lectr. mgmt. tng. programs Southwestern Bell Telephone Co., 1961-66, St. Louis Coun. on Econ. Edn., 1958-61; mem. regional selection com. H.S. Truman Fellowships, 1976-89; pres. Dallas Economists, 1981, Town and Gown of Dallas, 1980-81; mem. Dallas Com. on Fgn. Rels. Lt. USNR, 1943-46. Decorated Silver Star; Fulbright scholar to Denmark, 1952-53; Ford Found. Faculty Research fellow, 1957-58; U.S.-Spanish Joint Com. for Cultural Affairs fellow, 1981; Sr. Fulbright lectr. Italy, 1961-62 Mem. Am. Econ. Assn., So. Econ. Assn. (bd. editors Jour. 1969-71), Midwest Econ. Assn., Am. Fin. Assn., Soc. Internat. Devel., Peace Rsch. Soc., Southwestern Social Sci. Assn. (pres. econs. sect. 1971-72), AAUP (chpt. pres. 1964-65). Home: 7831 Park Ln Apt 266-D Dallas TX 75225 Office: So Meth Univ Dept Econs Dallas TX 75275-0001

MURPHY, JOHN JOSEPH, manufacturing executive; b. Olean, N.Y., Nov. 24, 1931; s. John Joseph and Mary M.; m. Louise John; children: Kathleen A. Murphy Bell, Karen L. Murphy Rochelli, Patricia L. Murphy Smith, Michael J. AAS in Mech. Engring., Rochester Inst. Tech., 1952; MBA, So. Meth. U. Engr. Clark div. Dresser Industries, Olean, 1952-67, gen. mgr. roots blower div. Connersville, Ind., 1967-69, pres. crane, hoist and tower div. Muskegon, Mich., 1969-70, pres. machinery group Houston, 1970-75, sr. v.p. ops. Dallas, 1980, exec. v.p., 1982, pres., 1982-92, CEO, 1983—95, chmn. bd., 1983-96; mng. dir. SMG Mgmt. L.L.C., Dallas, 1997-2000. Bd. dirs. W.R. Grace & Co., CARBO Ceramics, Inc.; emeritus mem. Bus. Coun.; dir. ShawCor Ltd. With U.S. Army, 1954—56. Office: 5500 Preston Rd Ste 210 Dallas TX 75205-2699

MURPHY, JOHN JOSEPH, English literature educator, critic, editor; b. N.Y.C., Apr. 3, 1933; s. John and Margaret B. (Shadegg) M.; m. Sarah Marie McMahon, June 30, 1962; children: Sarah, Joseph, Willa, John, Emily. BA, St. John's U., N.Y.C., 1956, MA, 1961. Instr. English lit. Coll. of St. Teresa, Winona, Minn., 1960-65; asst. prof. English lit. Merrimack Coll., North Andover, Mass., 1965-68, assoc. prof., 1969-84, chmn. dept. English, 1974—76, 1979—82; prof. English lit. Brigham Young U., Provo, Utah, 1984—, chair Am. lit. sect. dept. English, 1986—89, assoc. dir. Ctr. for Study Christian Values in Lit., 1994—. Organizer and dir. Willa Cather and Nebr. 1st Internat. U. Nebr. Cather Seminar, Hastings and Red Cloud, Nebr., 1981; bd. govs. Willa Cather Meml., 1984—; mem. editl. bd. Willa Cather Scholarly Edit., U. Nebr. Press, 1986—; vis. prof. U. Leon, Spain, 2001, U. Santiago, Spain, 2003; presenter in field. Editor: Critical Essays on Willa Cather, 1984; author: (criticism) My Antonia: The Road Home, 1989; editor: Penguin My

Antonia, 1994, Death Comes for the Archbishop, 1999, Literature and Belief, 1994—, Willa Cather: Family, Community, History, 1990, Willa Cather and the Culture of Belief, 2002; contbr. profl. jours. including Am.Lit., Twentieth Century Lit., Am. Lit. Realism, Religion and Lit.; prodr.: (TV series) KTCA TV, Great ladies of the Am. Novel, 1963—, Nathaniel Hawthorne, Am. Realist, 1964—. With U.S. Army, 1958-60. Recipient R.E. Twitchell award N.Mex. Hist. Soc., 2000; NEH fellow for Coll. Tchrs, 1982. Home: 8707 Hidden Oak Dr Salt Lake City UT 84121-6128 Office: Brigham Young U English Dept 3171 JKHB Provo UT 84602 E-mail: john_murphy@byu.edu.

MURPHY, JOHN JOSEPH, JR., investment company executive; b. Elmhurst, NY, June 2, 1951; s. John Joseph and Ellen Marie (Ulrich) M.; m. Monica Marie Des Marais, 1975; children: Abigail, Dylan, Regan. AB, Coll. Holy Cross, 1973; MBA, Dartmouth Coll., 1975. V.p. Citicorp Venture Capital, Ltd., NYC, 1975-83; ptnr. Adler & Shaykin, NYC, 1983-87; mng. ptnr. Murphy & Ptnr., L.P., NYC, 1987—. Chmn. bd. Minority Equity Capital Corp., 1989-90; chmn. bd. dir. June/Calendar Broadcasting, Inc., 1989-99; chmn. bd. dir. Legend Med. Svc., Inc., 1990-94; chmn., bd. dir. Pacific Pub. Co., Inc., 1990—; vice chmn., bd. dir. Nat. Mobile TV, Inc., 1992-97. Mem. Holy Cross Leadership Coun., NYC; chmn. bd. dirs. Nativity Mission Ctr., 2000—; chmn. fin. coun. Ch. of the Epiphany, 1997—2002; hon. usher St. Pathrick's Cathedral; trustee Covenant of the Sacred Heart; bd. dirs. Good Shepherd Svcs., 1991—; chmn. bd. dirs. Am. Higher Edn. Devel. Corp., 1998—; chmn. bd. dir. Ruxton Healthcare Corp., 1998—2003; chmn. bd. dirs. Mosaica Edn., Inc., 1998—; trustee Coll. of the Holy Cross. Mem.: N.Y. Venture Capital Forum (bd. dirs. 1984—93, 1998—), Friendly Sons St. Patrick City of N.Y., Boston Coll. Wall St. Coun., Yale Club N.Y.C., The Leash, N.Y. Athletic Club. Democrat. Roman Catholic. Avocations: marathon running, theology. Home: 3 Stuyvesant Oval New York NY 10009-2122 Office: Murphy & Ptnrs Fund LP 45 Rockefeller Plz New York NY 10111-0100 E-mail: john@murphy-partners.com.

MURPHY, JOHN NOLAN, mining executive, researcher, electrical engineer; b. Pitts., July 14, 1939; s. Maurice J. and Elizabeth (McVey) M.; m. Catherine V. Schneider, Nov. 24, 1962; 1 child, Michael J. BSEE, U. Pitts., 1961; MBA, Duquesne U., 1967. With Nat. Inst. of Occupational Safety and Health (NIOSH), Pitts., 1961—, rsch. supr., 1971-78, rsch. dir., 1978-97, sr. scientist, 1997—. Contbr. numerous articles to profl. jours. Chmn. com. Boy Scouts Am., Bethel Park, Pa., 1987—. Recipient Brian Morgans Meml. Lecture award U.K., 1983, Disting. Svc. award, Gold medal Dept. Interior, 1985. Mem. IEEE (sr.), Soc. Mining, Metallurgy and Exptl. Engring. (past chmn., bd. dirs. Pitts. chpt.), Nat. Soc. Profl. Engrs., Nat. Mine Rescue Assn. (pres. 1990-91, bd. dirs. 1991—), Pitts. Coal Mine Inst. Am. (bd. dirs. 1989—). Avocation: golf. Office: Nat Inst of Occupl Safety & Health Pitts Rsch Ctr PO Box 18070 Pittsburgh PA 15236-0070

MURPHY, JOHN THOMAS, lawyer; b. Pierre, SD, July 20, 1932; s. Bernard J. and Gertrude (Loner) M.; m. Rose Marie Cogorno. LLB, U. SD, 1957. Bar: SD 1957, Calif. 1962. Pvt. practice, Stockton, Calif., 1965-75, Modesto, Calif., 1975—; atty. office gen. counsel quartermaster gen. U.S. Army, 1957-58, asst. chief counsel, 1958-63, gen. counsel, 1963-65; assoc. Short, Short, Scott & Murphy (and predecessor firm), 1965-68; ptnr. Hulsey, Beus, Wilson, Scott & Murphy, Stockton, 1968-70. Bd. dirs. Delta-Stockton Humane Soc., 1970-75, bd. dirs. Tuolumne River Preservation Trust; gov. emeritus Calif. Trout Inc.; mem. Stanislaus River Task Force, Stanislaus County Water Coord. Com. Mem. State Bar Calif., ATLA, Consumer Attys. Calif., Beta Theta Pi, Phi Delta Phi, Stockton Beagler's Club (sec., dir.), Am. Kennel Club (Beagle adv. com. 1984-86). Republican. Episcopalian. Office: 1124 11th St Modesto CA 95354-0826 Office Phone: 209-527-6242. E-mail: bigbad@inreach.com.

MURPHY, JOHN VINCENT, financial services company executive; b. Boston, July 12, 1949; s. James Gerald and Mary Lee (Dolan) M.; m. Kathleen Ryan, Nov. 17, 1973; children: Elizabeth Ryan, Christopher John, Carolyn Holmes. BS, Boston Coll., 1971. CPA, Mass. Acct. Arthur Andersen & Co., CPA's, Boston, 1972-77; controller Continental Investment Corp., Boston, 1977-81; v.p., controller Torchmark Fin. Services Co., Boston, 1981-85; sr. v.p. fin., chief fin. officer Liberty Fin. Services, Inc., Boston, 1985—; treas. Torchmark Leasing Programs, Inc., Boston, 1981-85, Liberty Real Estate Corp., 1981—, Liberty Asset Mgmt. Co., 1985—, Copley Venture Capital Inc., 1984—; bd. dirs. Fiduciary Trust Co. of N.H., Chatham Fin. Assocs., 1983-85; chmn. Boston Coll. High Sch. Alumni Capital Campaign, 1986-87. Mem. devel. adv. com. to bd. trustees Boston Coll. High Sch. Served with AUS, 1971-72. Mem. Am. Inst. CPA's, Mass. Soc. CPA's, Fin. Execs. Inst., Fides Exec. Com.; Greater Boston C. of C. Execs. Club. Clubs: Boston Coll. Varsity (pres. 1980-82), Boston Racquet, Blue Chips, Algonquin (Boston); Charitable Irish Soc.; Shriver. Office: Liberty Fin Services Inc Federal Reserve Plz Boston MA 02210-2204

MURPHY, JOSEPH ALBERT, JR., lawyer; b. Grosse Pointe, Mich., May 29, 1934; s. Joseph Albert and Isabel C. (Callahan) M.; m. Joanne Becker, June 24, 1961; children: Michael, Joseph III. BS, Georgetown U., 1956; JD, Detroit Coll. Law, Mich. State U., 1962. Bar: Mich. 1962, D.C. 1996. House counsel Blue Cross Mich., Detroit, 1964-69, gen. counsel, corp. sec., 1969-75; v.p., gen. counsel Blue Cross & Blue Shield Mich., Detroit, 1975—88; chief Washington counsel Blue Cross and Blue Shield Assn., Washington, 1989—2001; cons. eLawForum, Washington, 2002—. Chmn. Health Care Network, Southfield, Mich., 1981-85; chmn. Blue Care Inc., Southfield, 1986-88. Mem. Allocations panel United Found., Detroit, 1985-88; treas. Grosse Pointe Dem. Club, 1972-73; chmn. Health and People's Polit. Action Commn., Detroit, 1978-84. Served with U.S. Army, 1957-59. Mem. ABA, Mich. Bar Assn., Detroit Bar Assn., DC Bar Assn., Am. Health Lawyers Assn. (pres. 1981-82), Am. Corp. Counsel Assn., Am. Arbitrators Assn. (panel of arbitrators). Roman Catholic. Home: 2717 O St NW Washington DC 20007-3128 Office Phone: 202-337-9239. Personal E-mail: jamjr@verizon.net.

MURPHY, JOSEPH EDWARD, JR., broadcast executive; b. Mpls., Mar. 13, 1930; s. Joseph Edward Murphy and Ann Hynes; m. Diana Kuske, July 24, 1958; children: Michael, John. BA, Princeton U., 1952; postgrad., U. Minn., 1956-60. Chartered fin. analyst. Dir. investment rsch. Woodward-Elwood & Co., Mpls., 1961-67; v.p. Northwestern Nat. Bank, Mpls., 1967-83; chmn. Midwest Communications, Inc., Mpls., 1990-92; ret. Dir. Midwest Comm., Inc., 1956-89, vice chmn., 1985-89. Author: Adventure Beyond the Clouds: How We Climbed China's Highest Mountain and Survived, 1986 (Friends Am. Writers award 1986), With Interest: How to Profit From Interest Rate Fluctuations, 1987, Stock Market Probability, 1988, revised edit., 1994, South to the Pole by Ski, 1990, The Random Character of Interest Rates, 1990, To the Poles by Ski and Dogsled, 1996, Bond Tables of Probable Future Yields, 1996, The Random Character of Corporate Earnings, 1997, Why the Stock Market Rises, 1998. Vice chmn. Minn. Coun. on Quality Edn., 1971-77; trustee Macalester Coll., St. Paul, 1973-87, Mpls. Soc. Fine Arts, 1977-78, Voyageur Outward Bound, 1985-92; bd. dirs. Minn. Opera Co., 1971-80, Childrens Theater Co., 1975-80, Minn. Ctr. for Book Arts, 1987-93, Greater Mpls. coun. Girl Scouts U.S.A., 1987-93, Fund for Peace, 1988-92, Minn. Nature Conservancy, 1991-96. 2d lt. U.S. Army, 1952-55. Mem. Am. Alpine Club (life, v.p. and bd. dirs. 1975-81), Himalayan Club (life), Mpls. Club. Avocations: mountaineering (leader Am. expedition to Mt. Everest 1986, mem. internat. ski expedition to South Pole 1988-89), exploration. Home: 2116 W Lake Isle Minneapolis MN 55405-2425

MURPHY, JOSEPH JAMES, chiropractic physician; b. Newark, N.J., July 30, 1956; s. Joseph P. and Roberta (Nittolo) Murphy; m. Maria Elena Sileo, Feb. 17, 2002; children from previous marriage: Joseph Raymond, Alexandra Renee. BA in Biology, Rider Coll., 1978; D in Chiropratic Medicine, Palmer Coll., 1984. Diplomate Nat. Bd. Chiropractic Examiners; cert. N.J. State Bd. Med. Examiners. Rsch. chemist Mallinkrodt, Inc., Englewood, NJ, 1979-81; staff physician Mid-Island Chiropractic, Levittown, NY, 1984; dir., chief exec. officer Suburban Chiropractic Ctr., Chatham, NJ, 1984—. Apptd. mem. N.J. Bd. Chiropractic Examiners, 2000—; sec. NJBCE, 2003. Mem. editl. bd. Am. Chiropractor Mag., 2000—; editor-in-chief newsletter The Column. Advisor Chatham High Sch. Key Club, 1986-87; trustee Early Childhood Learning Ctr., Chatham, 1999—, sec. 2002; mem. spkrs. bur. Am. Heart Assn. D. D. Palmer scholar, 1981, 82, 83. Mem.: AAAS, APHA, Morris County Chiropractic Soc. (pres. 1987—), Bd. Chiropractic Examiners (apptd. mem. State of N.J.), Internat. Soc. Food Technologists, N.Y. Acad. Sci., N.J. Chiropractic Soc. (bd. dirs. 1987—, chmn. inter profl. rels. com. 1989—, 1st v.p. 1992—95, pres. 1995—, editor-in-chief Jersey Jour. 1986—, Meritorious Svc. award 1986, Disting. Svc. award 1987—97), Am. Chiropractic Assn., Am. Assn. Cereal Chemists, Chatham C. of C. (chmn. profl. rels. com. 1988—92, pres. 1989—92, Dist. Mem. Svc. award 1996), Kiwanis (bd. dirs. Chatham club 1986—89, Disting. Svc. award 1995), Tri Beta. Republican. Presbyn. Avocations: skiing, photography, model building, automobiles, bicycling. Home: 20 Squire Ct Basking Ridge NJ 07920 Office: Suburban Chiropractic Ctr 301 Main St Chatham NJ 07928-2410 Office Phone: 973-635-0036. E-mail: drmurphy@drmurphy.com.

MURPHY, JUDITH CHISHOLM, trust company executive; b. Chippewa Falls, Wis., Jan. 26, 1942; d. John David and Bernice A. (Hartman) Chisholm. BA, Manhattanville Coll., 1964; postgrad., New Sch. for Social Research, 1965-68, Nat. Grad. Trust Sch., 1975. Asst. portfolio mgr. Chase Manhattan Bank, N.A., N.Y.C., 1964-68; trust investment officer Marshall & Ilsley Bank, Milw., 1968-72, asst. v.p., 1972-74, v.p., 1974-75; v.p., treas. Marshall & Ilsley Invesmtent Mgmt. Corp., Milw., 1975-94; v.p. Marshall & Ilsley Trust Co., Phoenix, 1982—, Marshall & Ilsley Trust Co. Fla., Naples, 1985—; v.p., dir. instnl. sales Marshall & Ilsley Trust Co., Milw., 1994-97, sr. v.p., 1997-98, M&I Investment Mgmt. Corp., 1998—. Coun. mem. Am. Bankers Assn., Washington, 1984-86; govt. relations com. Wis. Bankers Assn., Madison, 1982-88. Contbr. articles to Trusts & Estates Mag., 1980, ABA Banking Jour., 1981, Maricopa Lawyer, 1983. Chmn. Milw. City Plan Commn., 1986—97; commr. Milw. County Commn. on Handicapped, 1988—90; bd. dirs. Cardinal Stritch Coll., Milw., 1980—89, Children's Hosp. Wis., Milw., 1989—98, Milw. Ballet Co., 1996—2001, Milw. Ctr. for Independence, 1999—2004, Girl Scouts Milw. Area, 2002—, Milw. Symphony Orch., 2002—. Recipient Outstanding Achievement award YWCA Greater Milw., 1985, Sacajawea award Profl. Dimensions, Milw., 1988, Pro Urbe award Mt. Mary Coll., 1988, Vol. award Milw. Found., 1992; named Disting. Woman in Banking, Comml. West Mag., 1988. Mem. Milw. Analysts Soc. (sec. 1974-77, bd. dirs. 1977-80), Fin. Women Internat. (bd. dirs., v.p. 1976-80), Am. Inst. Banking (instr. 1975-78), TEMPO (charter), Profl. Dimensions (hon.), University Club, Woman's Club Wis., Rotary. Democrat. Roman Catholic. Home: 3622 N Lake Dr Milwaukee WI 53211-2644 Office: M&I Investment Mgmt Corp 1000 N Water St Milwaukee WI 53202-3197

MURPHY, KATHLEEN ANN, diversified manufacturing company executive; BS in Math., Syracuse U., 1972; MBA, U. Pa., 1976. Rsch. asst. Chase Econometrics, Bala Cynwyd, Pa., 1972-76; treasury assoc. IV Internat., Phila., 1976-78, sr. treasury assoc., 1978-79, mgr. project fin., 1979-80; asst. treas. Fairchild Industries Inc., Chantilly, Va., 1980-86, dep. treas., 1985-86; v.p., treas. Connell Ltd. Partnership, 1986-93, v.p., CFO, 1993-2000, sr. v.p., CFO, 2000—. Dir. Entergy Corp., 2000. Office: Connell Ltd Partnership Ft Hill Sq 1 International Pl Boston MA 02110

MURPHY, KATHLEEN ANNE FOLEY, communications executive; b. Fresh Meadows, NY, Oct. 15, 1952; d. Thomas J. and Audrey L. Finn; m. Timothy Sean Murphy, Sept. 26, 1992; 1 child, G. David. BA, Marymount Coll., 1974; postgrad., Smith Coll., 1985. V.p. acct. supr., sr. v.p. mgmt. supr., sr. v.p. group dir. Ogilvy & Mather Inc., NYC, 1974-90; sr. v.p., worldwide account dir. Young & Rubicam, San Francisco, 1990-92, sr. v.p., dir. account svcs., 1992-95, exec. v.p., dir. acct. svcs., 1995-97, exec. v.p., gen. mgr., 1997—2002, COO, 2002—03; dir. network devel. WPP, San Francisco, 2003—. Mem. Family Caregivers Alliance. Roman Catholic. Home: One Brookside Ave Berkeley CA 94705 Office: WPP 303 Second St S Tower 9th Fl San Francisco CA 94107 E-mail: kmurphy@wpp.com.

MURPHY, KATHLEEN MARY, former law firm executive, alternative healing professional; b. Bklyn., Dec. 16, 1945; d. Raymond Joseph and Catherine Elizabeth (Kearney) M. BA in Edn., Molloy Coll., 1971; MS in Edn., Bklyn. Coll., 1975. Ordained minister Ch. of the Loving Servant; cert. hypnotherapist; cert. elem. sch. tchr., N.Y. Elem. sch. tchr. various parochial schs., L.I., Bklyn., Queens, N.Y., 1969-80; from asst. prin. to prin. parochial sch. Queens, 1980-82; supr.-trainer Davis, Polk, Wardwell law firm, N.Y.C., 1982-88; mgr. Schulte Roth & Zabel, N.Y.C., 1988-95; Reiki master (alternative healing profl.), 1996—. Trainer program for new employees, 1984; speaker edn. topics, Bklyn., Queens, 1979-81. Mem. NAFE, Reiki Alliance. Democrat. Roman Catholic. Avocations: psychic phenomenon, workings of mind, ancient histories, crossword puzzles, museums. Office Phone: 718-381-7354.

MURPHY, KENNETH F. human resources specialist; BS in Labor Rels., Cornell U., 1977. Mgr. human resources Gen. Foods Corp., 1981—85, mgr. human resources desserts divsn., 1985—94; v.p. human resources, mktg. and sales Philip Morris USA, N.Y.C., 1996; sr. v.p. human resources and adminstrn. Altria Group, Inc., 2003—. Office: Altria Group Inc 120 Park Ave New York NY 10017-5592

MURPHY, KENYON W. electronics executive, chemicals executive; BBA in Acctg., U. Ga.; JD, Harvard U. Assoc. Alston & Bird, Atlanta; from asst. counsel to sr. v.p., gen. counsel Nat. Svc. Industries Inc., 1985—2000, sr. v.p., 2000—01, gen. coun., 2000—01; sr. v.p. Acuity Brands Inc, Atlanta, 2001—, gen. counsel, 2001—. Office: Acuity Brands Inc 1170 Peachtree St NE Atlanta GA 30309*

MURPHY, LAURA, legal association administrator; b. Md. Grad., Wellesley Coll. Devel. dir. ACLU Found. So. Calif.; lobbyist ACLU, Washington, dir. D.C. office, 1993—. Mem.: ABA (mem. adv. commn. to the standing com. on election law 1998). Office: ACLU 1333 H St NW Washington DC 20005-4707

MURPHY, LEE ANN SONTHEIMER, writer; b. St. Joseph, Mo., Oct. 27, 1961; d. Jeremiah Reinhard Sontheimer and Carol Yvonne Neely; m. Roy Wayne Murphy, July 7, 1994; children: Emily Dian, Megan Lane, Patrick Wayne. AA, Crowder Coll., Neosho, Mo., 1981; BA, Mo. So. State U., Joplin, 1983. Copywriter, announcer KBTN Radio, Neosho, Mo., 1983—89; mental health profl. New Visions, Neosho, Mo., 1990—93; tchr. Neosho R-5 Schs., Mo., 1994—95; staff writer Neosho Post, Mo., 1997—99; columnist The Joplin Globe, Mo., 2000—. Mem.: Mo. Writers Guild, Writers of the Six Bulls (pres. 2002—03), Exchange Club. Democrat. Roman Catholic. Avocations: travel, photography, music.

MURPHY, LEWIS CURTIS, lawyer, former mayor; b. N.Y.C., Nov. 2, 1933; s. Henry Waldo and Elizabeth Wilcox (Curtis) M.; m. Carol Carney, Mar. 10, 1957; children— Grey, Timothy, Elizabeth. BSBA, U. Ariz., 1955, LLB, 1961. Bar: Ariz. 1961. Pvt. practice, Tucson, 1961-66; trust officer So. Ariz. Bank & Trust Co., 1966-70; atty. City of Tucson, 1970-71; mayor, 1971-87; ret., 1987. Mem. Schroeder & Murphy, Tucson, 1978-88; trustee U.S. Conf. Mayors, 1978-87, chmn. transp. com., 1984-87; pub. safety steering com. Nat. League Cities, 1973-87, transp. steering com., 1973-87; v.p. Ctrl. Ariz. Project Assn., 1978-87. Bd. dirs. Cmty. Food Bank, 1987-2000, United Way Greater Tucson, 1988-90. With USAF, 1955-58. Mem. Ariz. Bar Assn., Pima County Bar Assn., Ariz. Acad., Sigma Chi (Significant Sig award). Republican. Presbyterian.

MURPHY, MARGARET A. nursing educator, adult nurse practitioner; b. NYC, Apr. 4, 1934; d. William J. and Margaret (Burchill) Allen; m. Raymond L.H. Murphy, Jr., July 12, 1958; children: Raymond L.H. III, Michael W., Ann Murphy Postell, Maureen D. Murphy Olsen, Alice M., Matthew D. BSN, St. Joseph Coll., West Hartford, Conn., 1955; MS, NYU, 1957; PhD, Boston Coll., Chestnut Hill, Mass., 1987. RN Mass., cert. adult nurse practitioner. Instr. Boston U. Sch. Nursing, 1971-72; pulmonary clin. nurse specialist Pulmonary Assocs., Boston, 1972-73; pulmonary nurse clinician Tufts U., Medford, Mass., 1973-76; from instr. prof. nursing to assoc. prof. nursing Boston Coll., 1976—2001, assoc. prof. emeritus, 2001, chmn. adult health nursing, 1988-92, dir. adult nurse practitioner program, 1987—2001, dir. Kennedy Audio Visual Resource Ctr., 1991-95, coord. MBA-MSN program, 1993-99. Rschr. in lung sound patterns in health and disease, women's attitudes toward menopause. Co-editor: Pharmacotherapeutics and Advanced Nursing Practice, 1998; co-author: (CD-ROM) Learning Lung Sounds, 2002; contbr. articles to profl. jours. Fellow USPHS, 1957-58; grantee Uniformed Svcs. U. Health Scis., 1995-96. Fellow: Am. Coll. Nurse Practitioners; mem.: ANA, Mass. Thoracic Soc. (chmn. com. on nursing practice, counselor 1989—91), Am. Thoracic Soc., Mass. Nurses Assn. (co-chmn. cabinet on legis. 1985—88), Sigma Theta Tau (chmn. awards and scholarships com. Alpha Chi chpt. 1994—96, pres. 1996—98, newsletter editl. bd. 1998—2004, Alpha Chi chpt. Mentor award 2001). E-mail: murphy@bc.edu.

MURPHY, MARGARET HACKETT, US bankruptcy judge; b. Salisbury, N.C., 1948; BA, Queens Coll., Charlotte, N.C., 1970; JD, U. N.C., Chapel Hill, 1973. Bar: Ga. 1973, U. S. Dist. Ct. (no. dist.) Ga. 1973, U.S. Ct. Appeals (5th cir.) 1974, U.S. Ct. Appeals (11th cir.) 1982. Assoc. Smith, Cohen, Ringel, Kohler and Martin, Atlanta, 1973-79; ptnr. Smith, Gambrell & Russell (formerly Smith, Cohen, Ringel, Kohler and Martin), Atlanta, 1980-87; U.S. bankruptcy judge U.S. Dist. Ct. (no. dist.) Ga., Atlanta, 1987—. Office: 1290 US Courthouse 75 Spring St SW Atlanta GA 30303-3309

MURPHY, MARK JOSEPH, enterprise sales executive; b. Rockville Centre, N.Y., Aug. 5, 1960; s. John Stephen and Barbara Ann (Seeney) M.; m. Annamaria Martin, July 19, 1986; children: Dana Martine, Kelly Gabrielle. BS in Econs. and Fin., St. John's U., 1983. Sr. tech. clk. St. John's U., Jamaica, N.Y., 1979-83; sys. engr. Property and Liability Br. IBM Corp., N.Y.C., 1983-84, sys. engr. N.Y. Ins. Br., 1984-86, mktg. rep. Manhattan Ins. Br., 1986-89, adv. mktg. staff Ea. Area, 1989, mktg. mgr. N.Y. banking, 1990-93, sys. svcs. mgr., 1993-95, mgr. client server and internet sys. mktg. N.E. area, 1995-97, client exec. fin. industry sector, 1997—2001, software sales exec., 2001—04; v.p. sales Siemens AG, NY, 2004—. Bd. dirs. Make-A-Wish Found., Suffolk County, N.Y., past vice-chmn., past chmn. bd. devel. com., chmn. bylaws com.; vol. Make-A-Wish Found. Mem. Am. Mgmt. Assn. Avocations: golf, family, travel. Home: 134 Parkwood Rd West Islip NY 11795-3001 Office: IBM Corp 33 Maiden Ln Fl 3 New York NY 10038-4518 Office Phone: 212-493-2740.

MURPHY, MARTIN JOSEPH, JR., cancer research center executive; b. Colorado Springs, Dec. 29, 1942; s. Martin Joseph Sr. and Gertrude F. (Heffting) M.; m. Ann A. Flesher, May 29, 1965; children: Siobhan, Deirdre, Martin Joseph III, Sean, Brendan. BS, Regis Coll., 1964; MS, N.Y.U., 1967, PhD, 1969. Vis. fellow Inst. de Pathologie Cellulaire, Paris, 1969-71, Christie Hosp., Manchester, Eng., 1971-72; visiting fellow John Curtin Sch. of Med. Rsch., Canberra, Australia, 1972-74; asst. prof. Sch. Medicine Cornell U., N.Y.C.; dir. Bob Hipple Lab for Cancer Rsch., N.Y.C., 1977-85; dir. hematology tng. program Sloan-Kettering Inst. for Cancer Rsch., N.Y.C., 1978-79; prof. Sch. of Medicine Wright State U., Dayton, 1984—; pres., CEO Hipple Cancer Rsch. Ctr., Dayton, 1985-99. Chmn. bd. dirs. AlphaMed Press, Inc., Dayton; bd. dirs. Dayton Clin. Oncology Program. Editor: In Vitro Aspects of Erythropoleis, 1978, Blood Cell Growth Factors: Their Biology and Clinical Applications, 1990, Blood Cell Growth Factors: Their Utility in Hematology and Oncology, 1991; editor-in-chief Internat. Jour. Cell Cloning, 1982-93, Stem Cells, 1993—; exec. editor The Oncologist; contbr. articles to profl. jours. NIH postdoctoral fellow, 1969-70, Damon Runyon fellow, 1970-71, Spl. fellow Leukemia Soc. Am., 1971, Pro Am. award Dayton Exec. Club. Mem. Assn. of Am. Cancer Inst., Am. Soc. Hematology, Am. Soc. Oncology, Am. Assn. for Cancer Rsch., Internat. Soc. for Exptl. Hematology, Dayton Area Cancer Assn. (trustee). Avocation: photography. Office: Wright State U Sch Medicine 3640 Col Glenn Hwy Dayton OH 45435

MURPHY, MARY ANN, human services administrator; b. Salt Lake City, Feb. 13, 1943; d. Wallace L. and Irene (Hummer) Matlock; m. Robert A. Glatzer, Dec. 31, 1977; children: Gabriela, Jessica, Nicholas. BA, U. Wash., 1964; MS, Ea. Wash. U., 1975. House counselor Ryther Child Ctr., Seattle, 1966-67; tchr. presch. Head Start, L.A. and Seattle, 1967-70, Children's Orthopedic Hosp., Seattle, 1970-72; faculty Ea. Wash. U., Cheney, 1973-82; exec. dir. Youth Help Assn., Spokane, Wash., 1983-88; mgr. regional ctr. for child abuse and neglect Deaconess Med. Ctr., Spokane, 1988-97; dir. Casey Family Ptnrs., Spokane, 1997—. Pres. Wash. State Alliance for Children, Youth and Families, Seattle, 1985-87; chairperson Gov.'s Juvenile Justice Adv. Commn., Olympia, Wash., 1987—. Mem. Nat. Coun. on Juvenile Justice, 1994-98. Recipient Alumni Achievement award Ea. Wash. U., 1994; named Outstanding Women Leader in Health Care YWCA, 1992, Outstanding Children's Advocate, Wash. State Children's Alliance, 1996. Avocations: reading, swimming, backpacking. Home: 1950 W Clarke Ave Spokane WA 99201-1306 Office: Casey Family Ptnrs 613 S Washington St Spokane WA 99204-2535 *Personal philosophy: "Take the first step in faith. You don't have to see the whole staircase, just take the first step." Dr. Martin Luther King, Jr.*

MURPHY, MARY C. state legislator; BA, Coll. St. Scholastica; postgrad., U. Wis., Superior, Am. U., Ind. U. H.s. tchr.; mem. Minn. Ho. of Reps., 1976—. Mem. judiciary fin. com., chair ethics com., mem. capital investments com., labor-mgmt. rels. com.; active del. Duluth Central Labor Body AFL-CIO; mem., lector St. Raphael's Parish; dir. State Democratic Farmer-Labor Party, 1972-74, chmn. 8th Dist. credentials com., 1974—, chmn. St. Louis County Legis. Delegation, 1985-86. Mem. Duluth Fedn. Tchrs. (1st v.p. 1976-77, various coms.), Minn. Fedn. Tchrs. (legis. com. 1972-75), Am. Fedn. Tchrs. (del. nat. convs.), Minn. Hist. Soc., Alpha Delta Kappa. Office: 100 Constitution Ave Saint Paul MN 55155-1232

MURPHY, MARY MARGUERITE, artist; b. S.I., N.Y., Mar. 29, 1958; d. Vincent Joseph and Teresa Marie (O'Connell) M.; m. James Thomas Primosch, Apr. 5, 1986. Student, Tyler Sch. Art, 1976—78; BA cum laude, Barnard Coll., 1981; student, NY Studio Sch., 1986—87; MFA in Painting, Tyler Sch. Art, 1991; student, Skowhegan Sch. Painting/Sculp., 1990. Panel mem. Coll. New Rochelle, NY, 1985, Phila. Art Alliance, 1997; tchg. fellow Tyler Sch. Art, Phila., 1989—91, instr., 1995, Fleisher Art Meml., Phila., 1992—98; vis. artist Ohio State U., Columbus, 1993, Columbus, 97; tchg. artist Inst. for Arts in Edn., Phila., 1994, Phila., 97; sr. lectr. U. of the Arts, Phila., 1996—98, adj. asst. prof., 2000—; lectr. Washington U., St. Louis, 1998—99; panel moderator Beaver Coll., Glenside, Pa., 1995, Nat. Mus. Jewish History, 1997; vis. artist lectr. Ohio State U., 1993, 97, Tyler Sch. Art, 1994, Pa. State U., 1997, U. Alaska, 2002. One person shows include S.P.A.C.E.S., Cleve., 1994, Fleisher Art Meml., Phila., 1995, Larry Becker Contemporary Art, Phila., 1995, Schmidt/Dean Gallery, Phila., 1998, 99, U. Alaska, 2002; exhibited in group shows 80 Washington Sq. East Galleries, N.Y.C., 1985, Va. Ctr. for Creative Arts, Sweet Briar, Va., 1986, The Drawing Ctr., N.Y.C., 1989, Larry Becker Gallery, Phila., 1991, 95, Temple Univ. Gallery, Phila., 1991, State Theatre Ctr. for the Arts. Easton, Pa., 1991, Momenta Art Alternatives, Phila., 1991, Beaver Coll., Glenside, Pa., 1992, 96, 99, White Columns, N.Y.C., 1992, Moore Coll. of Art and Design, Phila., Pa., 1992, 99, 1708 E Main St. Gallery, Richmond, Va., 1992, Ohio State U., Columbus, 1993, Main Line Ctr. of the Arts, Haverford, Pa., 1993, 55 Mercer St., N.Y.C., 1994, Vox Populi, Phila., 1994, 558 Broome St., N.Y.C., 1994, Tyler Sch. Art, Phila., 1994, Larry Becker Contemporary Art, Phila., 1995, Del. Art Mus., Wilmington, 1996, Borowsky Gallery, Phila., 1996, Ohio State U., Columbus, 1997, Del. Ctr. Contemporary Art, 1997, Abington Art Ctr., 1997, Phila. Art Alliance, 1997, Fleisher Art Meml., Phila., 1998, Margaret Thatcher Projects, N.Y.C., 1998, N.J. Ctr. Visual Arts, Summit, 1998, David Beitzel Gallery, N.Y., 1998, Schmidt/Dean Gallery, 1999, U. of the Arts, Phila., 2000; permanent collections Wilmington Trust, The Brooklyn Mus., Ark. Art Ctr., Am. Express; works included in publs. Richmond Times Dispatch, Phila. City Paper, New Art Examiner, The Phila. Inquirer, The Plain Dealer, Artnews, Eyelevel; contbr. to The New Art Examiner; contbr. articles to The New Art Examiner, lectr. in field. Mem. alumni bd. Tyler Sch. Art, Elkins Park, Pa., 1994-98. Resident Va. Ctr. for Creative Arts, 1985, 86; fellow Skowhegan Sch. Painting and Sculpture, 1990, Nat. Endowment for Arts fellow in painting, 1993-94; grantee Fleisher Art Meml., Phila., 1994, Venture

Fund, U. of Arts, 2002, Pa. State Coun. on Arts, 2002; fellow Pa. State Coun. on the Arts, 1998; finalist Pew Fellowship in the Arts, 1994-95. Mem. Coll. Art Assn. Roman Catholic. Home: 20 Whitemarsh Ave Erdenheim PA 19038-8230 E-mail: mary.murphy52@verizon.net.

MURPHY, MICHAEL CARY, lawyer; b. Mt. Airy, N.C., Aug. 11, 1951; s. Ralph Bill Murphy and Jamalee (Bartlett) Nickle. BA, Carson-Newman Coll., 1973; JD, U. Memphis, 1980; postgrad., U. Tenn. Coll. Trial Advocacy, 1981. Bar: Tenn. 1980, U.S. Dist. Ct. Tenn. 1981, U.S. Ct. Appeals (6th cir.) 1982. Atty. Legal Svcs. Upper East Tenn., Morristown, 1980-81, EEO Office, TVA, Knoxville, Tenn., 1981-82; pvt. practice Morristown, 1982—. Part-time judge Mcpl. Ct., Morristown, Tenn., 1996-2000. Pres. bd. dirs. Cen. Svcs., Morristown, 1987-89; chmn. legal div. Morristown United Way, 1987, 88. Mem. ABA, Tenn. Bar Assn., Assn. Trial Lawyers Am., Tenn. Trial Lawyers Assn., Lakeway Tennis Assn., Cherokee Lake Sailing Club, Kiwanis (chmn. community svcs. com.), Phi Delta Phi. Methodist. Avocations: tennis, photography, skiing, hiking, biking. Office: PO Box 1365 Morristown TN 37816-1365

MURPHY, MICHAEL EMMETT, retired food company executive; b. Winchester, Mass., Oct. 16, 1936; s. Michael Cornelius and Bridie (Curran) M.; m. Adele Anne Kasupski, Sept. 12, 1959; children: Leslie Maura, Glenn Stephen, Christopher McNeil. BS in Bus. Adminstrn, Boston Coll., 1958; MBA, Harvard, 1962. Financial analyst Maxwell House div. Gen. Foods Corp., White Plains, N.Y., 1962-64, cost mgr. San Leandro, Calif., 1964-65, controller Jackonville, Fla., 1965-67, Hoboken, N.J., 1967-68, mgr. fin. planning and analysis, 1968-69; mgr. planning Hanes Corp., Winston-Salem, N.C., 1969-70, corp. controller, 1970-72; v.p. adminstrn. Hanes Corp. (Hanes Knitwear), Winston-Salem, N.C., 1972-74; v.p. fin. Ryder System Inc., Miami, Fla., 1974-75, exec. v.p., 1975-79; exec. v.p., dir. Sara Lee Corp., Chgo., 1979-93, vice chmn., 1993-97. Bd. dirs. GATX Corp., Payless Shoe Source, Inc., CNH Global N.V., Coach Inc., Bassett Furniture Industries, Inc., No. Funds. Mgmt. adviser Jr. Achievement, 1965-66; mem. exec. com. Hudson County Tax Rsch. Coun., 1967-68; trustee Boston Coll., 1980-88; chmn. Civic Fedn. Chgo., 1984-86; bd. dirs. Jobs for Youth, Chgo., 1983-86, Lyric Opera, 1986-2002; bd. dirs. Northwestern Meml. Hosp., Chgo., 1989-2000, Big Shoulders Fund, Chgo. Ctrl. Area Com., 1995—, Chgo. Cultural Ctr. Found., 1995—, Met. Pier and Exposition Authority, 2004—; prin. Chgo. United, 1995-98. Mem. Nat. Assn. Mfrs. (bd. dirs. 1989-96, dir. Big Shoulders Fund 1995—), Fin. Execs. Inst., Hoboken C. of C., Winson-Salem C. of C., Miami C. of C., Internat. Platform Assn., UN Assn., Ouimet Scholar Alumni Group, Beta Gamma Sigma. Roman Catholic. Home: 1242 N Lake Shore Dr Chicago IL 60610-2361 Office: Sara Lee Corp 3 First National Plz Chicago IL 60602 Personal E-mail: mebmurphy@aol.com.

MURPHY, MICHAEL JOSEPH, retired bishop; b. Cleve., July 1, 1915; s. William and Mary Bridget (Patton) M. BA in Philosophy, Gregorian U., Rome, 1938; S.T.L., Catholic U. Am., 1942. Ordained priest Roman Catholic Ch., 1942; prof. pro-tem St. Mary Sem., Cleve., 1943-45, prof., 1947-48, vice-rector, 1948-63, rector, 1963-76; Episcopal vicar Chancery Office, Cleve., 1976-78; coadjutor bishop of Erie, Chancery office (Pa.), 1978-82; bishop of Erie, 1982-90. Mem. scripture trans. com. Nat. Conf. Cath. Bishops. Recipient first Ann. Sem. Dept. award Nat. Cath. Ednl. Assn. Roman Catholic. Home and Office: St Patrick Church 130 E 4th St Erie PA 16507-1508

MURPHY, MICHAEL R. federal judge; b. Denver, Aug. 6, 1947; s. Roland and Mary Cecilia (Maloney) M.; m. Maureen Elizabeth Donnelly, Aug. 22, 1970; children: Amy Christina, Michael Donnelly. BA in History, Creighton U., 1969; JD, U. Wyo., 1972. Bar: Wyo. 1972, U.S. Ct. Appeals (10th cir.) 1972, Utah 1973, U.S. Dist. Ct. Utah 1974, U.S. Dist. Ct. Wyo. 1976, U.S. Ct. Appeals (5th cir.) 1976, U.S. Tax Ct. 1980, U.S. Ct. Appeals (9th cir.) 1981, U.S. Ct. Appeals (fed. cir.) 1984. Law clk. to chief judge U.S. Ct. Appeals (10th cir.), Salt Lake City, 1972-73; with Jones, Waldo, Holbrook & McDonough, Salt Lake City, 1973-86; judge 3d Dist. Ct., Salt Lake City, 1986-95, presiding judge, 1990-95; judge U.S. Ct. Appeals (10th cir.), Salt Lake City, 1995—. Mem. adv. com. on rules of civil procedure Utah Supreme Ct., 1985—95, mem. bd. dist. ct. judges, 1989—90; mem. Utah State Sentencing Commn., 1993—95, Utah Adv. Com. on Child Support Guidelines, 1989—95, Utah Child Sexual Abuse Task Force, 1989—93; mem. com. on fed.-state jurisdiction Jud. Conf. of U.S., 2001—. Recipient Freedom of Info. award, Soc. Profl. Journalists, 1989, Utah Minority Bar Assn. award, 1995, Alumni Achievement citation, Creighton U., 1997; named Judge of Yr., Utah State Bar, 1992. Fellow Am. Bar Found.; mem. ABA (editl. bd. Judges' Jour. 1997-99), Utah Bar Assn. (chmn. alternative dispute resolution com. 1985-88), Sutherland Inn of Ct. II (past pres.). Office: 5438 Federal Bldg 125 S State St Salt Lake City UT 84138-1102

MURPHY, MICHAEL TERRENCE, lawyer; b. Riverside, Calif., July 25, 1946; s. James Bernard and Opal (Cully) M. BS, Calif. State U., Long Beach, 1973; JD, Pepperdine U., 1976. Bar: Calif. 1976, N.Mex. 1977, U.S. Dist. Ct. N.Mex. 1977, U.S. Claims Ct. 1977, U.S. Tax Ct. 1977, U.S. Ct. Appeals (tenth cir.) 1977, U.S. Supreme Ct. 1980; bd. cert. specialist in family law. Ptnr. Shuler, Murphy & Shuler, Carlsbad, N.Mex., 1976-77, Rosenberg, Shuler & Murphy, Carlsbad, 1978-87; shareholder Weinbrenner, Richards, Paulowsky, Sandenaw & Ramirez, P.A., Las Cruces, N.Mex., 1987-95, Weinbrenner, Richards, Ramirez, McNeill & Murphy, P.A., Las Cruces, 1995, Pickett & Murphy, Las Cruces, 1995—. With USAF, 1967-73. Fellow Am. Acad. Matrimonial Lawyers; mem. ABA (chmn.), N.Mex. Bd. Bar Examiners. Episcopalian. Office: Pickett & Murphy 500 N Church St Las Cruces NM 88001-3440 Office Phone: 505-526-3338.

MURPHY, NICKIE LATRICE, writer, insurance adjuster; b. Jacksonville, Fla., May 17, 1976; d. Anthony Lamar Murphy and Jackie Renee Latson; 1 child, Devon Reshawn Reese. Verifier UJFPA, Jacksonville, 1999—2001; claims examiner Signet, Jacksonville, 2001—03; writer. Author: (novels) Trici's Deliverance, 1999, (poetry book) Poems for the Liberated Soul, 2003, Exodus, 2003. Pastor's aid, bd. dirs. 1st New Zion Missionary Bapt., 1999—. Home: 523 Alder St Jacksonville FL 32206

MURPHY, PATRICE ANN (PAT MURPHY), writer; b. Spokane, Wash., Mar. 9, 1955; m. Dave Wright, Feb. 14, 1999. BA in Biology, U. Calif., Santa Cruz, 1976. Sr. rsch. writer ednl. graphics dept. Sea World, 1978—82. Former instr. Clarion Speculative Fiction Workshop, Mich. State U.; former tchr. sci. fiction U. Calif., Santa Cruz; tchr. sci. fiction writing Creative Writing Program, Stanford U., 1995, 96, 97, 98. Author: The Shadow Hunter, 1982, The Falling Woman, 1987 (Nebula award 1987), Adventures in Time and Space with Max Merriwell, 2002, (novelette) Rachel in Love (Nebula award 1987, Isaac Asimov Reader's award 1987, Theodore Sturgeon Meml. award 1987), (short story collection) Points of Departure, 1990 (Philip K. Dick award 1990), (novella) Bones, 1991 (World Fantasy award 1991), (novelette) An American Childhood, Nadya-The Wolf Chronicles, There and Back Again, The City, Not Long After, 1984, By Nature's Design, The Color of Nature, 1996, The Science Explorer, 1996, Explorabook Bat Science, The Science Explorer, Out and About. Avocation: Karate. Office: care Tor Books 14th Fl 175 5th Ave Fl 14 New York NY 10010-7703 also: c/o Exploratorium 3601 Lyon St San Francisco CA 94123

MURPHY, PATRICK CHRISTOPHER, music educator; b. Big Rapids, Mich., Oct. 19, 1972; s. Avon Jack and Virginia Lewis Murphy; m. Susan Ann Dollinger, July 19, 1997; children: Mirabella Nicole, Jayden Carl. MusB cum laude, Wash. State U., 1994; MA, U. of Minn., 1997. Cert. tchr. Calif. Music tchr. Mickle Mid. Sch., Lincoln, Nebr., 1997—98; dir. of vocal music Talawanda HS, Oxford, Ohio, 1998—2001; choir dir. Faith Luth. Ch., Oxford, Ohio, 1999—2001; dir. of instrumental music Villa Pk. (Calif.) HS, 2001—. Scholar, Wash. State U., 1990—94, U. of Minn., 1995—97. Mem.: Soc. Calif. Sch. Band and Orch. Assn., Calif. Assn. for Music Edn., Music Educators Nat. Conf., Phi Beta Kappa, Kappa Kappa Psi (Named Outstanding Mem. 1994). Lutheran. Avocations: travel, athletics, reading, cooking. Home: 1330 Brentwood Circle A Corona CA 92882 Office: Villa Park High School 18042 Taft Ave Villa Park CA 92861 Office Phone: 714-628-4300 ext. 2161. Personal E-mail: pcmurphy@yahoo.com. E-mail: vphsband@yahoo.com.

MURPHY, PATRICK NEIL, lawyer; b. Wahoo, Nebr., Jan. 15, 1946; s. Albert S. and Alice B. (Daley) Murphy; m. Kathryn Ann Kearns, June 8, 1968; children: Megan, Mia, Michael. BA, U. Nebr., 1968; JD, Creighton U., 1972. Bar: Nebr. 1973, Iowa 1973, U.S. Dist. Ct. Nebr. 1973, U.S. Dist. Ct. (no. dist.) Iowa 1975, U.S. Supreme Ct. 1992. Asst atty. County of Plymouth, Iowa, 1973—92; ptnr. Murphy & Collins, LeMars, Iowa, 1973—. Dist. chmn. Prairie Gold coun. Boy Scouts Am., 1976—83; bd. dirs. Plains Area Mental Health Ctr., 1975—82; chmn., bd. dirs. Cath. Charities Diocese, Sioux City, 1992—98; charter dir. Plymouth County Conservation Found., 1993—; pres. LeMars Cmty. Sch. Bd. Dirs., 2000—02; pres. Plymouth County REAP Congress Plymouth County Civil Svc. Commn., 1988—2000; ctrl. committeeman Plymouth County Dems., 1974—84. Sgt. U.S. Army, 1969—71. Mem.: ATLA, ABA, Nebr. Assn. Trial Lawyers, Iowa Assn. Trial Lawyers (bd. govs. 1996—2000), Nebr. Bar Assn., Iowa Bar Assn. (mem. Am. citizenship commn. 1974—, mem. grievance commn. 1997), LeMars C. of C. (bd. dirs. 1980—83), KC, Elks, Sertoma. Roman Catholic. Home: 1517 1st Ave SW Le Mars IA 51031-2707 Office: Murphy and Collins PLC PO Box 526 Le Mars IA 51031-0526 Office Phone: 712-546-8844.

MURPHY, PETER E. corporate financial officer; BA, Dartmouth Coll.; MBA, Wharton Sch. Bus. With The Walt Disney Co., Burbank, Calif., 1988—; sr. v.p., CFO ABC, Inc., Burbank, Calif., 1997-98; exec. v.p., chief strategic officer The Walt Disney Co., Burbank, Calif., 1998-99, sr. exec. v.p., chief strategic officer, 1999—. Office: The Walt Disney Co 500 S Buena Vista St Burbank CA 91521

MURPHY, PETER GREGORY, literature educator, writer; b. Trenton, N.J., June 19, 1957; s. George Joseph and Margaret Ann Murphy. MA in Philosophy, Bowling Green U., 1987; MA in Spanish, U. Ark., 1997, MA in English, 1999, PhD in Comparative Lit., 2000. Cert. secondary tchr. Instr. philosophy Bowling Green (Ohio) State U., 1985—87; English tchr. McCurristin H.S., Trenton, 1987—91, Colegio Internat. de Carbobo, Valencia, Venezuela, 1991—93; Spanish instr. U. Ark., Fayetteville, 1994—97, master lectr., 1997—2000; asst. prof. U. S.C., Union, 2000—. Author essays. V.p. Union County Friends Libr., 2002—. Faculty Devel. grant, U. S.C., 2002—03, Sampa-Ulloa grant, Leonor Ulloa-Radnor, 2003. Mem.: Union Mental Health Assn. (bd. mem. 2002—), Union Libr. Coun. (bd. mem. 2002—), Simms Soc., Caroliniana Soc., Thomas Cooper Soc. Avocations: music, landscaping. Home: 915 Beltline Rd Union SC 29379 Office: Univ SC Union PO Drawer 729 Union SC 29379

MURPHY, RAMON JEREMIAH CASTROVIEJO, physician, pediatrician; b. N.Y.C., Feb. 12, 1944; s. William J. and Angelines (Castroviejo) M.; m. Lila, Sept. 12, 1971; children: Jessica, David. BA, U. Notre Dame, 1965; MD, Northwestern U., 1969; MPH, Columbia U., 1974. Diplomate Am. Bd. Pediats. Intern in medicine Cook County Hosp., Chgo., 1969-70; resident in pediats. Children's Meml. Hosp., Chgo., 1970-71, Babies Hosp.-Columbia-Presbyn. Med. Ctr., N.Y.C., 1971-73; resident in cmty. medicine Mt. Sinai Hosp., N.Y.C., 1973-74, clin. asst. pediatrician, 1974-75, asst. attending pediatrician, 1975-83, assoc. attending pediatrician, 1983—, assoc. instr. cmty. medicine, 1974-75, asst. prof. clin. pediats., asst. prof. cmty. medicine, 1975-83, assoc. prof. clin. pediats., 1983—; pediatrician Uptown Pediats., P.C., N.Y.C., 1976—, pres., 1990—. Co-dir. Mt. Sinai Children's Cmty. Health, 1999—; dir. Mt. Sinai Off-Site Pediatric Residency Tng. Program, 1999—; vis. clin. fellow pediats. Columbia U., Coll. Physicians and Surgeons, N.Y.C., 1971-73; pediats. cons. Oxford Health Plan, 1990-94. Contbr. articles to profl. jours. Co-med. dir. Benito Juarez People's Health Ctr., Chgo., 1970-71; dep. co-dir. Wagner Child Health Project, N.Y.C., 1973-75; sch. physician The Day Sch., 1984—, The Trinity Sch., 1992—, trustee, 1993-99. Fellow Am. Acad. Pediats; mem. N.Y. Pediat. Soc. (program chmn. 1986-89, pres. 1989-90), Soc. for Adolescent Medicine, Mt. Sinai Alumni Assn. Office: 1245 Park Ave New York NY 10128-1211

MURPHY, RANDALL KENT, management consultant; b. Laramie, Wyo., Nov. 8, 1943; s. Robert Joseph and Sally (McConnell) M.; m. Cynthia Laura Hillhouse, Dec. 29, 1978; children: Caroline, Scott, Emily. Student, U. Wyo., 1961—65; MBA, So. Meth. U., 1983. Dir. mktg. Wycoa, Inc., Denver, 1967—70; dir. Comm. Resource Inst., Dallas, 1971—72; account exec. Xerox Learning Sys., Dallas, 1973—74; regional mgr. Systema Corp., Dallas, 1975; pres. Performance Assocs.; pres., dir. Acclivus Corp., Dallas, 1976—; founder, chmn. Acclivus Inst., 1982—. Author: Performance Management of the Selling Process, 1979, Coaching and Counseling and Performance, 1980, Managing Development and Performance, 1982, Acclivus Performance Planning System, 1983, (with others) BASE For Sales Performance, 1983, Acclivus Coaching, 1984, Acclivus Sales Negotiation, 1985, R3 Service, 1997, BASE for Effective Presentations, 1987, BASE for Strategic Sales Presentatiions, 1988, The New BASE for Sales Excellence, 1988, Major Account Planning and Strategy, 1989, Strategic Management of the Selling Process, 1989, Building on the BASE, 1992, Negotiation Mastery, 1995, R3 Service, 1997, Co-creating R3 Value, 2002; co-inventor The Randy-Band multi-purpose apparel accessory, 1968. Active Dallas Mus. Fine Arts, Dallas Hist. Soc., Dallas Symphony Assn.; vice chmn. bd. trustees The Winston Sch., 1994-96, chmn. bd. trustees, 1997-2000; mem. adv. bd. The Women's Ctr. of Dallas, 1995-98. With AUS, 1966. Mem. ASTD, Inst. Mgmt. Scis., Soc. Applied Learning Tech., Nat. Soc. Performance and Instrn., Assn. Mgmt. Cons., Am. Assn. Higher Edn., World Future Soc., Soc. for Intercultural Edn., Tng. and Rsch., Internat. Fedn. Tng. and Devel. Orgns., Inst. Noetic Scis., Nat. Peace Inst., Amnesty Internat., Acad. Polit. Sci., The Nature Conservancy, Theosophical Soc. Am., Children's Arts and Ideas Found., So. Meth. U. Alumni Assn., U. Wyo. Alumni Assn. Home: 11110 Lawnhaven Rd Dallas TX 75230 Office Phone: 972-385-1277.

MURPHY, RICHARD WILLIAM, retired foreign service officer, Middle East specialist, consultant; b. Boston, July 29, 1929; s. John Deneen Murphy and Jane (Diehl) Bonner; m. Anne Herrick Cook, Aug. 25, 1955; children: Katherine Anne, Elizabeth Drew, Richard McGill. Grad., Phillips Exeter Acad., 1947; AB, Harvard U., 1951, Cambridge (Eng.) U., 1953; postgrad. Arabic studies, U.S. Fgn. Service Inst., Beirut, 1959-60; LLD (hon.), New Eng. Coll., 1989, Balt. Hebrew U., 1992. Vice consul U.S. Consulate Gen., Salisbury, So. Rhodesia, 1955-58; consul Aleppo, Syria, 1960-63; polit. officer Am. Embassy, Jedda, Saudi Arabia, 1963-66, Amman, Jordan, 1966-68; pers. officer U.S. State Dept., Washington, 1968-69, dir. Office Arabian Peninsula Affairs, 1969-71, asst. sec. state for Near Ea. and South Asian affairs, 1983-89; U.S. amb. to Mauritania, 1971-74, to Syria, 1974-78, to the Philippines, 1978-81, to Saudi Arabia, 1981-83; sr. fellow for Middle East Coun. Fgn. Rels., N.Y.C., 1989—2004; cons. Richard Murphy Assocs., N.Y.C., 1993—. Chmn. Fgn. Students Svc. Coun., Washington, 1989—93, Mid. East Inst., Washington, 1993—2001, Chatham House Found., 1993—2004; mem. bd. advisors Naval War Coll., 1991—94; bd. dirs. Harvard Med. Internat. Trustee Am. U. of Beirut, 1995—; mem. vis. com. Harvard Mid. East Ctr., 1999—, Near East Found., 2000—. Served with U.S. Army, 1953-55. Recipient Superior Honor award, U.S. Dept. State, 1969, Pres.'s Disting. Svc. award, 1986, 88, 89. Mem. Coun. Fgn. Rels., Fgn. Svc. Assn., Century Club. Republican. Episcopalian. Avocations: tennis, scuba diving. Home: 16 Sutton Pl # 9A New York NY 10022-3057 Home Fax: 212-421-7067. E-mail: richardwmurphy@earthlink.net.

MURPHY, ROBERT, executive search consultant; b. Davenport, Iowa; s. James and Patricia M.; children: Lisa, Todd, Kyle. BS, U. Ill. Med. Ctr., Chgo., 1963. Registered pharmacist, Ill. With Walgreen Co., Chgo., 1963-73; corp. mgr. Coll. Rels. & Recruiting Corp.; mgr. Human Resource Planning Corp.; dir. Orgn. and Human Resource Planning & Devel.; US ptnr.-in-charge exec. search PricewaterhouseCoopers, Chgo., 1974—93; founder, chmn. Murphy Ptnrs. Internat., global exec. search firm, 1993—. Contbr. articles to profl. jours. including Wall St. Jour., Newsweek. Mem. Internat. Human Resource Assn., Soc. Human Resource Mgrs., Internat. Cons. Assn., Am. Soc. Pers. Adminstrs., Soc. Human Resource Profls., Kappa Psi. Office: 956 Shoreline Rd Barrington IL 60010-3815 Office Phone: 847-304-1599. E-mail: bob@mpivips.com.

MURPHY, ROBERT BLAIR, management consulting company executive; b. Phila., Jan. 19, 1931; s. William Beverly and Helen Marie (Brennan) M.; children: Stephen, Emily, Julia, David, Catherine. BS, Yale, 1953. Indsl. engr. DuPont Corp., Aiken, S.C., 1953-55; mgr. sales can divsn. Reynolds Metals Co., Richmond, Va., 1955-69; gen. mgr. corrugated divsn. Continental Can Co., N.Y.C., 1969-73; v.p. and gen. mgr. beverage divsn. Am. Can Co., Greenwich, Conn., 1973-75; assoc. Heidrick & Struggles, Inc., N.Y.C., 1976-78, v.p., 1978; v.p., mng. dir. Stamford office Spencer Stuart & Assocs., 1978-84, ptnr., 1982-84; co-founder and CEO Sullivan-Murphy Assocs., 1984—. Mem. Riverside Yacht Club (Greenwich), Yale Club (N.Y.C.), Merion Cricket Club (Haverford, Pa.), Bucks Harbor Yacht Club (Brooksville, Maine). Home: 11 Indian Mill Rd Cos Cob CT 06807-1315

MURPHY, ROBERT JAMES, language educator, consultant; b. Decatur, Ind., Aug. 31, 1941; s. James William and Catherine Agnes (Schumacker) Murphy; m. Linda L. Nolan, June 28, 1975; 1 child, Christina Lyn. BS in Edn., Ball State U., 1963; MS in Edn., St. Francis U., 1967; postgrad., U. Denver, 1986, Ball State U., 1972. Cert. English, speech, drama and journalism tchr. Ind. Speech and drama tchr. Rochester (Ind.) H.S., 1976—78; chair dept. English Lawrenceburg (Ind.) H.S., 1978—81, Holy Family H.S., Denver, 1981—86; prin. Randall-Moore Sch., Denver, 1986—87; dir. edn. Mansfield Bus. Sch., Denver, 1987—89; prin. St. John the Bapt. Cath. Sch., Ft. Wayne, Ind., 1989—94; pres., founder Murphy Ednl. Consulting, Ft. Wayne, Ind., 1995—, D/B/A Alternative Edn. Curriculum and The Learning Kaleidoscope, Pensacola, Fla., 1995—. Cons. Am. Printing House for Blind, Louisville, 1999—2002; cons., writer, spkr. homeschooling groups, 1995—; exec. dir., co-founder The Kaleidoscope Edn. Ctr., Ft. Wayne, Ind., 2003, co-founder, dir., 03; tchr., supr. Aurora (Colo.) Evening H.S., 1986—87; tchr. U. St. Francis, Ft. Wayne, 2003—; edn. coord., tchr. M.A.Y.A. Unity Ctr., Ft. Wayne, 2003; dir. edn. Phoenix Youth Ctr., 2003—. Author: All in One Big Book, 1998, The Pump Man, 1998; co-author: Teaching the Student with a Visual Impairment, 2000, author reading and writing curriculum. Bd. dirs. Ft. Wayne Pub. Transp. Co., 2000—, The League for Blind and Disabled, Ft. Wayne, 2000—04; chmn. bd. dirs. The United Voice Coalition, Ft. Wayne, 2002—; chmn. bd. dirs. State Ind. Alliance Cmty. Inclusion, 2003—; site visitor U.S. Dept. Edn. Blue Ribbon Sch., 1991; founding bd. dirs., exec. asst. dir. Phoenix Youth Ctr.-Club Unified, Ft. Wayne, 2003—. Named Advocate of Yr., League for the Blind and Disabled, 2002, recipient Disting. Graduate award, Decatur (Ind.) Cath. Elem. and HS, 2003. Avocations: gardening, hiking, swimming.

MURPHY, ROSEMARY, actress; b. Munich; came to U.S., 1939; d. Robert D. and Mildred (Taylor) M. Ed. in, Paris, France and Kansas City, Mo. Broadway appearances include Look Homeward Angel, 1958, Night of the Iguana, World premier at Spoleto (Italy) Festival of Two Worlds, 1959, Period of Adjustment, 1961, King Lear, 1963, Any Wednesday, 1964-66, Delicate Balance, 1966, Weekend, 1968, Butterflies are Free, 1970, Lady Macbeth, Stratford, Conn., 1973, Ladies of the Alamo, 1977, John Gabriel Borkman, 1980, Learned Ladies, 1982, Coastal Disturbances, 1987, The Devil's Disciple, 1988, A Delicate Balance, 1996, Waiting in the Wings, 1999; motion picture appearances include To Kill a Mockingbird, 1962, Any Wednesday, 1966, Ben, 1972, Walking Tall, 1972, You'll Like My Mother, 1972, Forty Carats, 1973, Julia, 1976, September, 1987, For the Boys, 1991, And The Band Played On, 1993, The Tuskegee Airmen, 1995, Message in a Bottle, 1998, Dust, 2001; TV appearance Eleanor and Franklin, 1975 (Emmy award for best supporting actress 1976), George Washington, 1983 (Tony award nominations 1961, 64, 67, award Motion Picture Arts Club 1966), E-Z Streets, 1996, The Unicorn's Secret, 1998, Frasier, 1997, 99. Recipient Variety Poll award, 1961, 67. Address: 220 E 73rd St New York NY 10021-4319

MURPHY, SANDRA ROBISON, lawyer; b. Detroit, July 28, 1949; m. Richard Robin. BA, Northwestern U., 1971; JD, Loyola U., Chgo., 1976. Bar: U.S. Dist. Ct. (no. dist.) Ill. 1976. Assoc. Notz, Craven, Mead, Maloney & Price, Chgo., 1976-78; ptnr. McDermott, Will & Emery, Chgo., 1978—. Mem. ABA (family law sect.), Ill. Bar Assn. (chair sect. family law coun. 1987-88), Chgo. Bar Assn. (chair matrimonial law com. 1985-86), Am. Acad. Matrimonial Lawyers (sec. 1990-91, v.p. 1991-92, pres. Ill. chpt. 1992-93, pres.-elect 1994-95, pres. 1995-96), Legal Club Chgo.

MURPHY, SHARON MARGARET, communications educator; b. Milw., Aug. 2, 1940; d. Adolph Leonard and Margaret Ann (Hirtz) Feyen; m. James Emmett Murphy, June 28, 1969 (dec. May 1983); children: Shannon Lynn, Erin Ann; m. Bradley B. Niemcek, Aug. 7, 1999. BA, Marquette U., 1965; MA, U. Iowa, 1970, PhD, 1973. Cert. K-14 tchr., Iowa. Tchr. elem. and secondary schs., Wis., 1959-69; dir. publs. Kirkwood C.C., Cedar Rapids, Iowa, 1969-71; instr. journalism U. Iowa, Iowa City, 1971-73; asst. prof. U. Wis., Milw., 1973-79; assoc. prof. So. Ill. U., Carbondale, 1979-84; dean, prof. Marquette U., Milw., 1984-94; prof. Bradley U., Peoria, Ill., 1994—, provost, v.p. acad. affairs, 1994-97, pres. Cmty. Career and Tech. Ctr., 1997-98. Pub. rels. dir., editor Worldwide mag., Milw., 1965—68; reporter Milw. Sentinel, 1967; Fulbright sr. lectr. U. Nigeria, Nsukka, 1977—78; Fulbright sr. scholar U. Ljubljana, Slovenia, 2002. Author: Other Voices: Black, Chicano & American Indian Press, 1971; (with Wigal) Screen Experience: An Approach to Film, 1968; (with Murphy) Let My People Know: American Indian Journalism, 1981; (with Schilpp) Great Women of the Press, 1983; editor: (with others) International Perspectives on News, 1982. Mem. Peoria Riverfront Commn., 1995—2000; co-chair Peoria Race Rels. Com., 1999—2000; bd. dirs. Dirksen Congl. Leadership Ctr., 1994—2000, Dow Jones Newspaper Fund, NY, 1986—95, Peoria Symphony, 1996—2002. Recipient Medal of Merit, Journalism Edn. Assn., 1976, Amoco Award for Teaching Excellence, 1977, Outstanding Achievement award Greater Milw. YWCA, 1989; named Knight of Golden Quill, Milw. Press Club, 1977; Nat. headliner Women in Communication, Inc., 1985. Mem. Assn. Edn. in Journalism and Mass Comm. (pres. 1986-87), Soc. Profl. Journalists, Nat. Press Club, Accrediting Coun.on Edn. in Journalism and Mass Comm. (v.p. 1983-86). Democrat. Roman Catholic. Office: Bradley U Global Comm Ctr Peoria IL 61625-0001 Office Phone: 309-677-3621. E-mail: smm@bradley.edu.

MURPHY, STACIA, health service association executive; BA, Talladega Coll. With Cmty. Service Soc., N.Y. City Mission Soc., N.Y. State Divsn. Youth, Alcoholism Coun. of N.Y.; exec. dir. N.Y.C. affiliate Nat. Coun. on Alcoholism and Drug Dependence, Inc., 1990-99, pres., 1999—. Office: Nat Coun Alcoholism & Drug Dependence 20 Exchange Pl Ste 2902 New York NY 10005 Office Phone: 212-269-7797.

MURPHY, S(USAN) (JANE MURPHY), small business owner; b. Williamsport, Pa., Dec. 26, 1950; d. Jack W. and Edythe J. (Grier) M.; m. Michael J. Sanchez, Dec. 30, 1979. BBA, Pa. State U., 1978. Gen. mgr. Murphy Swift Homes, Hummelstown, Pa., 1970-75; owner, operator Murphy's Home Ctr., Hummelstown, 1975-79, 85-91; mgr. Builder's Emporium, San Diego, 1979-80; entrepreneur Castle in the Sand, San Diego, 1980-83; adminstr. Sohio Constrn., Prudhoe Bay, Alaska, 1983-85; fin. systems analyst Blue Shield, San Francisco, 1991-93; pres. San Francisco Mgmt. Svcs., Inc., San Francisco, 1993-99; entrepreneur Blue Skies Inn and Island Place of Olde Key West, Key West, Fla., 1999—. Cons. in field; dealer Servistar Home Ctrs. Photographs displayed at San Diego Art Inst. Vol. Hershey (Pa.) Free Ch. Donald MacIntyre scholar, 1979, Class of 1920 scholar, 1979, Congressman Kunkel scholar, 1979. Mem. Pa. Hardware Assn., Hummelstown C. of C., Better Bus. Bur. Evangelical Christian. Avocations: sailing, scuba diving, photography. Office: Blue Skies Inn 630 South St Key West FL 33045 Office Phone: 305-797-5228. Personal E-mail: suzyqq@earthlink.net.

MURPHY, TERENCE MARTIN, biology professor; b. Seattle, July 1, 1942; s. Norman Walter and Dorothy Louise (Smith) M.; m. Judith Baron, July 12, 1969; 1 child, Shannon Elaine. BS, Calif. Inst. Tech., 1964; PhD, U. Calif. San Diego, La Jolla, 1968. Sr. fellow dept. biochemistry U. Wash., Seattle, 1969-70; asst. prof. botany U. Calif., Davis, 1971-76, assoc. prof., 1976-82, prof. plant biology, 1982—, chmn. dept. botany, 1986-90. Author: Plant Molecular Development, 1988; co-author: Plant Biology, 1998; N.Am. exec. editor, N.Am. office, Physiologia Plantarum, 1988-98; contbr. articles to profl. jours. Mem. AAAS, Am. Soc. Plant Biologists, Am. Soc. Photobiology,

Scandinavian Soc. Plant Physiology. Home: 725 N Campus Way Davis CA 95616-3518 Office: U Calif Sect Plant Biology Davis CA 95616 Office Phone: 530-752-2413. E-mail: tmmurphy@ucdavis.edu.

MURPHY, TERENCE ROCHE, lawyer; b. Oct. 20, 1937; s. M. Leonard and Alice Lenore (Roche) Murphy; m. Suzanne Kathryn Dupré, Oct. 14, 1967 (div. Apr. 1980); children: Braden Mathias, Fiona Elizabeth Dupré; m. Patricia Ann Sherman, May 21, 1983. AB, Harvard Coll., 1959; JD with distinction, U. Mich., 1966. Bar: D.C. 1967, U.S. Supreme Ct. 1971. Trial atty. Dept. Justice, Washington, 1966-68; assoc. Wald, Harkrader & Ross, Washington, 1968-72, ptnr., 1972-83, McDermott, Will & Emery, Washington, 1983-84, Adams, Duque & Hazeltine, Washington, 1984-86; founding ptnr. Murphy Ellis Weber and predecessors, Washington, 1986—2003; mng. dir. and gen. counsel MK Technology, Washington, 2003—; sr. assoc. Ctr. Strategic and Internat. Studies, 2004—. Bd. dirs. Am. Assn. Exporters and Importers; founding chmn. Brit.-Am. Bus. Coun., 1989-90, legal counsel, 1993-96; officer, bd. dirs. Industry Coalition of Tech. Transfer; lectr. North and South Am., Asia, Europe and Mediterranean on internat. and bus. law and on strategic trade, Harvard Coll., U. Mich. Law Sch., 2004; chmn. and lectr. ann. Globalization of Export Controls Conf., London; bd. advisors European Inst., 1993—; advisor on munitions export policy, Ctr. for Strategic and Internat. Studies, 2000—, U.S. Dept. Def., 2003—; advisor on export regulation, U.S. Dept. Commerce, 2001—. Author, lectr. on internat. trade, antitrust and administrv. law.; co-editor: Coping With U.S. Export Controls, ann. edits., 1986, 87, 88; contbr. articles to European and Am. legal and policy publs. Mem. com. visitors U. Mich. Law Sch., 1975—; trustee Lawyer's Com. for Civil Rights Under Law, 1975-89; mem. adv. com. Pine Mountain Music Festival, Houghton, Mich.; councilor RSC Am., 2003—. Lt. USN, 1959-63. Decorated hon. officer Order Brit. Empire; recipient U.S. Navy commendation Cuban Missile Crisis, 1962; fellow Royal Soc. Arts. Mem. ABA (coun. adminstrv. law sect. 1980-83, co-chmn. com. on internat. and comparative adminstrv. law 1994-97, internat. liaison officer 2001—), Am. Law Inst., Internat. Bar Assn. (sec. antitrust and monopolies com. 1981-83), Am. Soc. Internat. law, Brit.-Am. Bus. Assn. (Washington, founding dir. 1987—, chmn. 1989-92, legal adv. 1992-95), Royal Inst. Internat. Affairs (London), Am. Coun. on Germany, Atlantic Coun. of U.S., Met. Club (Washington), Harvard Club (N.Y.C.), Miscowaubik Club (Calumet, Mich.). Home: 4425 Boxwood Rd Bethesda MD 20816-1817 Office: MK Tech 1823 Jefferson Pl Washington DC 20036 Office Phone: 202-213-7377. E-mail: tmurphy@mktechnology.com.

MURPHY, THEODORE R., II, utilities executive; BA in Econs., Trinity Coll., 1980; MBA in Fin., Columbia U., 1986. Chartered fin. analyst. Asst. v.p., comml. loan officer Conn. Bank and Trust; dir. credit risk mgmt. Philbro Energy; v.p. power mktg. and trading AIG Trading; various positions Enron; sr. v.p. Cinergy Corp., Cin., 2002—, chief risk officer, 2002—. Mem. com. chief risk officers Cinergy Corp. Office: Cinergy Corp 139 E 4th St Cincinnati OH 45202

MURPHY, THOMAS E. communications executive; BA in History and Polit. Sci., U. Kans. With Jasculca Termin and Assocs., 1988; various acct. exec. pos. Bozell Inc. and Edelman Worldwide Pub. Rels.; acct. supr. Barkley Evergreen and Ptnrs. Pub. Rels.; dir. media rels. and fin. comm., PCS divsn. Sprint Corp., 1996—2000, v.p. comm. and pub. rels., PCS divsn., 2000—03, sr. v.p. corp. comm. and brand mgmt., 2003—. Mem.: Cellular Telecomm. and Internet Assn. (bd. dirs. Wireless Found.). Office: Sprint Corp 6200 Sprint Parkway Overland Park KS 66251

MURPHY, THOMAS J., JR., mayor; b. Aug. 15, 1944; m. Mona McMahon; children Shannon, Molly, and T.J. BS in Biology and Chemistry, John Carroll U., 1967; MS in Urban Affairs/Planning summa cum laude, Hunter Coll., 1973. Vol. Peace Corps., Paraguay, 1970-72; exec. dir. Perry Hilltop Citizen's Coun., 1973-76; chem. sales rep. Alcoa, 1967-70; exec. dir. North Side Civic Devel. Coun., 1976-78; state rep. 20th Legis. Dist., 1979-94; mayor City of Pitts., 1994—. Democrat. Office: Office of the Mayor City-County Bldg 414 Grant St Rm 512 Pittsburgh PA 15219-2409 Office Phone: 412-255-2626. Office Fax: 412-255-2687.

MURPHY, THOMAS JOHN, publishing executive; b. Lockport, N.Y., Mar. 29, 1931; s. Matthew J. and Mary Frances (Tracy) M.; m. Maryanne Elizabeth Stadnicki, Dec. 29, 1956; children: Kevin, Janine, Peter, Thomas. BS, SUNY-Brockport, 1952; postgrad., Boston U., 1955-57, Northwestern U., 1976. Sales rep., asst. dir. advt., mgr. sales services, dir. tng., asst. dir. mktg., dir. mktg. McGraw-Hill Co., St. Louis, N.Y.C., 1954-73; v.p., gen. mgr. sch. dept. Holt, Rinehart & Winston pub. CBS, Inc., N.Y.C., 1973-78; sr. v.p. CBS Sch. Pub., 1978-80, pres., 1980-82; v.p. AICPA, 1982-88; ptnr. Profl. Pub. Svcs. Co., Westport, Conn., 1988—; pres. World Book Pubs., 1991. Contbr. articles to profl. jours. Bd. dirs. Brockport Found., 1977-83, Rec. for Blind, 1980-89, Inter-Faith Housing Assn., 1991-94; mem. social concerns com. Ch. of Assumption, Westport, 2000—. Named to Heritage Hall of Fame, SUNY. Democrat. Roman Catholic. Home and Office: 4 Ivanhoe Ln Westport CT 06880-5038 Office Phone: 203-227-7266.

MURPHY, THOMAS MICHAEL, civil engineer; b. Hubbard, Ohio, Mar. 26, 1963; s. Michael F. Jr. and Gratia Marie (Henry) M.; m. Regina Marie Quinn, Mar. 28, 1992; 1 child, Caitlin Marie. BS, Youngstown State U., 1988. Cert. asst. team leader N.Y.C. Dept. Transp., N.Y. State Dept. Transp., N.Y. State Thruway Authority. Structural engr. Marsico & Assocs., Youngstown, Ohio, 1987; constrn. inspector Adlaka & Assocs., Boardman, Ohio, 1987, Marsico & Assocs., Youngstown, 1987; structural engr. Hardesty & Hanover, N.Y.C., 1988-94, A&H Engrs., N.Y.C., 1994, Ammann & Whitney, N.Y.C., 1995-96, M.S. Cons., Youngstown, 1996; quality assurance/quality control engr. Star Aluminum Extrusions, Canfield, Ohio, 1997-99; civil engr. PSI Inc., Pitts., 1999-2000, Youngstown, Ohio, 2000—01, ACA Engring., 2001—. Mem. ASCE (affiliate mem. N.Y. met. chpt. and Youngstown State U. chpt.) Am. Soc. Cert. Engring. Technicians (mem., sec.-tres. Youngstown State U. Steel Valley chpt. 1985-86), KC (3d and 4th degree). Democrat. Roman Catholic. Avocations: photography, new technology in bridge design and construction. Office: ACA Bldg 10B 590 Western Reserve Rd Poland OH 44514 Home: PO Box 31 Hubbard OH 44425-0031

MURPHY, THOMAS MILES, pediatrician, educator; m. Priscilla Rollin Coit. AB in Math., Harvard Coll., 1969; MD, U. Rochester, 1973. Diplomate Am. Bd. Med. Examiners, Am. Bd. Internal Medicine, Am. Bd. Pediatrics, subbd. pulmonology; lic. physician, N.C. Intern Georgetown U. Med. Divsn., D.C. Gen. Hosp., Washington, 1973-74; resident in internal medicine Georgetown U. Med. Ctr., Washington, 1974-76, fellow pediat. pulmonary medicine, 1976-78; asst. prof. pediat. Georgetown U. Sch. Medicine, Washington, 1979-80, asst. prof. clin. pediat., 1980-85, U. Chgo., 1985-87, asst. prof. pediat. and medicine, 1990-93; asst. prof. pediat. U. Chgo. Pritzker Sch. Medicine, 1987-90, chief sect. pulmonary medicine dept. pediat., 1992-93; assoc. prof., chief divsn. pediat. pulmonary diseases Duke U., Durham, N.C., 1993—. Assoc. dir. Pediatric Pulmonary and Cystic Fibrosis Ctr., Georgetown U., 1978-80; asst. prof. child health and devel. George Washington U. Sch. Medicine and Health Scis., Washington, 1980-85; assoc. chmn. dept. pulmonary medicine, co-dir. Cystic Fibrosis Ctr. for Care, Teaching and Rsch., Children's Hosp. Nat. Med. Ctr., Washington, 1980-85; dir. pediatric pulmonary fellowship tng. program U. Chgo., 1990-93, dir. Cystic Fibrosis Ctr., 1991-93, assoc. chief sect. allergy, immunology and pulmonology, dept. pediatrics, 1991-92; editor ATS Pediat. Assembly Website, 2000—; ad hoc mem. lung biology and pathology study sect. NIH, 2002. Contbr. articles to profl. jours., chpts. to books; cons. referee editor New Eng. Jour. Medicine, 1989, Am. Rev. Respiratory Disease, 1989—, Am. Jour. Physiology: Lung Cellular and Molecular Physiology, 1990—, Pediatric Rsch., 1991—, Jour. Applied Physiology, 1991—, Pediat. Pulmonology, 1993—, mem. editl. bd., 1996—; contbg. editor The Hudson Monitor. Mem. ctr. com. Cystic Fibrosis Found., 1992-97, 2000-2002; chmn. childhood lung disease com. D.C. Lung Assn., 1980-83, lung disease com., 1984; mem. adv. coun. D.C. Sudden Infant Death Syndrome, 1981-83, chmn. med. adv. com., 1982-83. Recipient Cmty. Svc. award So. Md. Lung Assn., 1980, Media award Am. Acad. Pediatrics, 1980, Svc. award homicide br. Met. Police Dept. D.C., 1983, Svc. award Met. D.C. chpt. Cystic Fibrosis Foun., Washington, 1985, Nat. Cystic Fibrosis Found., 1997; Rsch. grantee Am. Lung Assn., N.Y.C., 1992, NIH, Bethesda, Md., 1993, 98. Mem.: AAAS, European Respiratory Soc., Am. Thoracic Soc. (program com. assembly on respiratory structure and function 1993—96, chair long range planning com. 2000—02, chair subcom. on physician scientists, pediat. assembly 1997—, liaison officer pediat. assembly 2000—), N.Y. Acad. Scis., Am. Physiol. Soc., Soc. Pediatric Rsch. Avocations: refereeing soccer, jazz. Office: Duke U Med Ctr PO Box 2994 Durham NC 27710-2994

MURPHY, THOMAS PATRICK, lawyer; b. Syracuse, N.Y., Feb. 12, 1952; s. George Edward and Sara Eileen (Murphy) M.; m. Susan Hollis Francher, Oct. 19, 1976 (div. Oct. 1992); m. Lise M. Adkins, Aug. 6, 1994; children: Casey Marie, Matthew Thomas. BS, Clarkson U., 1974; JD, Vermont Law Sch., 1978. Bar: N.Y. 1978, D.C. 1981, Md. 1988, Va. 1989. Asst. U.S. atty. U.S. Atty.'s Office, Washington, 1982-85; assoc. Highsaw & Mahoney, Washington, 1985-87, McGuire, Woods, Battle & Boothe, Washington, 1987-90; ptnr. Reed Smith Shaw & McClay, McLean, Va., 1990-99, Hunton & Williams, McLean, 1999—. Contbr. articles to profl. jours. Chmn. bd. profl. responsibility D.C. Ct. Appeals. With USN, 1978-82, USNR, 1978-90. Recipient Spl. Achievement Award U.S. Dept. Justice, 1984; named one of Best Lawyers in Am. for employment law. Mem. ABA, Fed. Bar Assn., N.Y. State Bar Assn., D.C. Bar Assn. (chmn. pro se litigants com.), Md. Bar Assn., Asst. U.S. Attys., Bd. Profl. Responsibility D.C. Ct. Appeals (hearing com.). Office: Hunton & Williams 1751 Pinnacle Dr Ste 1700 Mc Lean VA 22102-3836

MURPHY, TIMOTHY F. congressman; b. Cleve., Sept. 11, 1952; s. John and Florence Murphy; m. Nanette Missign, Aug. 23, 1975; 1 child, Bevin. BS, Wheeling Jesuit U., 1974; MA, Cleve. State U., 1976; PhD, U. Pitts., 1979. Mem. Pa. Senate, Dist. 37, Harrisburg, 1996—2002, U.S. Ho. Reps. from 18th Pa. dist., 2003—. Chmn. aging and youth com. Pa. State Senate, chmn. pub. health and welfare com., comm. and high tech. com., cmty. and econ. devel. com., edn. com., health care task force; asst. prof. U. Pitts. Sch. Medicine. Mem. bd. dirs. Head Start, Alliance for Infants, Parents Helping Parents, Korean War Vets. Western Pa. Meml. Fund; founding dir. St. Aides Employment Svc.; mem. St. Thomas More Ch., Bethel Park, Pa.; mem. adv. bd. Allegheny Co. Ct. of Common Pleas Family Ct. Divsn., steering com. on children's issues roundtable; mem. U.S. Mil. Acad. Review Bd. Mem. Pa. Peerinatal Assn. (bd. dirs.), Bethel Park C. of C., South Park C. of C., Brentwood-Baldwin-Whitehall C. of C., Greater Bridgeville C. of C. Republican. Office: 226 Cannon House Off Bldg Washington DC 20515-3818 E-mail: tmurphy@pasen.gov.

MURPHY, TIMOTHY JAMES, lawyer; b. Topeka, Sept. 30, 1946; s. Miles J. and Norine D. Murphy; m. Patricia MacKinnon, Apr. 7, 1990. BA, U. Ga., 1968; JD with honors, Washington & Lee U., 1970; LLM, Harvard U., 1976. Bar: Va. 1970, Fla. 1972. Atty. Anderson, Mori & Rabinowitz, Tokyo, 1970—71, Shutts & Bowen, Miami, Fla., 1976—. Contbr. articles to profl. jours. Mem. Fla. Ho. of Reps., 1982-84; bd. dirs. Cath. Charities, Inc., 1982-97, Cath. Charities Legal Svcs., Inc., Miami, 2000—, The Barnacle soc., 1991-2002, pres. 2000-02; mem. adv. bd. Miami-Dade County Pub. Libr., 1988-2002. Col. JAG Corps USAFR, 1971-95. Mem.: Internat. Bar Assn., Biscayne Bay Yacht Club, Army and Navy Club (Washington). Democrat. Roman Catholic. Avocation: sailing. Office: Shutts & Bowen 201 S Biscayne Blvd Ste 1500 Miami FL 33131-4308

MURPHY, WILLIAM ALEXANDER, JR., diagnostic radiologist, educator; b. Pitts., Apr. 26, 1945; s. William Alexander and LaRue (Eshbaugh); m. Judy Marie Lang, June 18, 1977; children: Abigail Norris, William Lawrence, Joseph Ryan. BS, U. Pitts., 1967; MD, Pa. State U., 1971. Diplomate Am. Bd. Radiology. Intern Barnes Hosp., St. Louis, 1971-72, staff radiologist, 1975-93; radiology resident Washington U., St. Louis, 1972-75, prof. radiology, 1983-93; sec. chief Mallinckrodt Inst. Radiology, St. Louis, 1975-93; cons. Office Med. Examiner City and County St. Louis, 1993—. Radiologist, prof. radiology, John S. Dunn Sr. prof., disting. chair MD Anderson Cancer Ctr. U. Tex., 1993—, v.p. hosp. and clinics, 1996-97, COO, 1997; chmn. bd. dirs. MD Anderson Physicians Network Corp., 2001—. Fellow Am. Acad. Forensic Scis., Am. Coll. Radiology; mem. Radiol. Soc. N.Am. (1st. v.p. 1997-98), Am. Roentgen Ray Soc., Am. Soc. Bone and Mineral Rsch., Internat. Skeletal Soc., Assn. Univ. Radiologists. Methodist. Home: 4808 Bellview St Bellaire TX 77401-5306 Office: U Texas Anderson Cancer Ctr Div Dx Imaging 057 1515 Holcombe Blvd Houston TX 77030-4009 Office Phone: 713-792-4916. Business E-Mail: wmurphy@di.mdacc.tmc.edu.

MURPHY, WILLIAM F. priest, monsignor, religion educator; b. Boston, May 14, 1940; s. Cornelius John and Norma (Duggan) M. AB, St. John Sem., Brighton, Mass., 1961; S.T. Lic., Pontifical Gregorian U., Rome, 1965, S.T.D., 1974. Ordained priest in Roman Cath. Ch. Asst. pastor Archdiocese of Boston, 1965-70; asst. prof. theology Emmanuel Coll., Boston, 1968-74, Pope John XXIII Sem., Weston, Mass., 1974; under-sec. Pontifical Coun., Justice and Peace, Rome, 1974-87; sec. for community rels. Archdiocese of Boston, Brighton, 1987—; lectr. social ethics St. John Sem., Brighton, 1987—. Author: Social Ethics, 1978, 80, International Politics, 1983, Theology, 1985. Mem. Tavern Club (Boston). Office: Roman Cath Archdiocese of Boston 2121 Commonwealth Ave Brighton MA 02135-3101

MURPHY, WILLIAM J. state legislator; b. West Warwick, R.I., Jan. 4, 1963; BA, U. Hartford, 1985; JD, Franklin Pierce Law Ctr., 1989. Mem. Dist. 39 R.I. Ho. of Reps., Providence, 1992—, mem. jud. com., spkr. of the house, 2003—; pvt. practice law West Warwick. Mem. West Warwick Dem. Town Com. Mem. K.C. Gibson Coun. Address: 323 State House Providence RI 02903 Office Phone: 401-222-2466.

MURPHY, WILLIAM PATRICK, lawyer, editor, writer; b. Scranton, Pa., Feb. 17, 1952; s. William James and Mildred Mary (Ferguson) M. AB, U. Scranton, 1973; JD, U. Pa., 1976. Jud. law clk. U.S. Dist. Ct. (ea. dist.) Pa., U.S. Ct. Appeals (3rd cir.), Pa. Supreme Ct., Phila., Erie, 1976-79; from asst. to assoc. prof. law St. John's U., Queens, N.Y., 1979-81, 83; atty. Beasley, Casey, Colleran, Erbstein, Thistle, Kline & Murphy, Phila., 1982, 84-89; pvt. practice Phila., 1989-94; legal editor Pa. Law Weekly, Phila., 1994-95, editor-in-chief, 1995-96; legal editor Pa. Dist. & County Reports, Phila., 1994-96; pvt. practice Phila., 1996—. Instr. Temple U., Phila., 1987-88; mem. faculty continuing legal edn. Pa. Bar Inst., Harrisburg, 1989—. Author: White Dogs, 1996, columnist, 1999—. U. Pa. scholar, 1977. Mem. Pa. Bar Assn. Roman Catholic. Avocations: running, wolves. Office: Two Penn Ctr Plz Ste 200 Philadelphia PA 19102

MURPHY-DANIELS, KAREN ILENE, environmental, safety and health professional; b. Oak Ridge, Tenn., May 20, 1955; d. Charles Everett and Charlotte Wilson Murphy; m. Richard C. Daniels, Dec. 5, 1997. BS in Transp. and Mktg., U. Tenn, 1977; MS in Occupl. Safety & Health, U. Tenn., 1982. CSP BSCP, REM & CEA Nat. Registry Environ. Profls., CHMM Inst. Hazardous Material Mgmt., ISO 14001 environ. mgmt. systems provisional auditor, cert. AHERA asbestos bldg. inspector, fall protection component person, 501 OSHA industry instr. Project mgr., comml. market mgr. Analysas Corp./DPRA, Oak Ridge, 1988—96; owner, mgmt. cons. SAFE Systems, Seattle, 1996—97; ESH specialist Boeing, Seattle, 1997—. Vol. cons. Wash. Dept. Ecology, Lacey, 1997; chair Boeing Nat. Safety Tech. Com., Seattle. Vol. Habitat for Humanity; bd. dirs. Puget Sound IHMM, Puget Sound Habitat for Humanity, 2002—. Mem.: Am. Soc. Quality, Am. Indsl. Hygiene Assn., Am. Soc. Safety Engrs. (treas., sec. East Tenn. chpt. 1988—90, v.p. Puget Sound 2003—04, bd. dir.). Democrat. Avocations: kayaking, snowshoeing, horse training, dog training. Home: 1976 McDonald Ave DuPont WA 98327 Office: Boeing PO Box 3707 MC Seattle WA 98124-2207 Business E-Mail: karen.i.murphy-daniels@boeing.com. E-mail: eshanalysis@aol.com.

MURPHY HERNLY, BETTY SOUTHARD (MRS. CORNELIUS F. MURPHY), lawyer; b. East Orange, N.J. d. Floyd Theodore and Thelma (Casto) Southard; m. Cornelius F. Murphy, May 1, 1965; children: Ann Southard Murphy, Cornelius Francis Jr.; m. H. Leland Hernly, Apr. 26, 2003. AB, Ohio State U.; student, Alliance Française and U. Sorbonne, Paris; JD, Am. U.; LLD (hon.), Eastern Mich. U., 1975, Capital U., 1976, U. Puget Sound, 1986; LHD, Tusculum coll., 1987. Bar: D.C. Corr., free lance journalist, Europe and Asia, UPI, Washington; practiced in Washington, 1960—74; mem. firm McInnis, Wilson, Munson & Woods (and predecessor firm); dep. asst. sec., adminstr. Wage and Hour Divsn. Dept. Labor, 1974-75; chmn. and mem. NLRB, 1975-79; ptnr. firm Baker & Hostetler, LLP, 1980—. Adj. prof. law Am. U., 1972-80, 99—; mem. adv. com. on rights and responsibilities of women to Sec. HHS; mem. panel conciliators Internat. Ctr. Settlement Investment Disputes, 1974-85; mem. Adminstrv. Conf. U.S., 1976-80, Pub. Svc. Adv. Bd., 1976-79; mem. human resouces com. Nat. Ctr. for Productivity and Quality of Working Life, 1976-80; mem. Presdl. Commn. on Exec. Exch., 1981-85. Trustee Mary Baldwin Coll., 1977-85, Am. U., 1980-99, 2001-, George Mason U. Found., Inc., 1990-2000, 2002-, George Mason U. Edn. Found., 1993-2000, 01-; nat. bd. dirs. Med. Coll. Pa., bd. corporators, 1976-85; bd. dirs. Ctr. for Women in Medicine, 1980-86; bd. govs. St. Agnes Sch., 1981-87; mem. exec. com. Commn. on Bicentennial of U.S. Constn., chmn. internat. adv. com., 1985-92; vice chmn. James Madison Meml. Fellowship Found., 1989-96; bd. dirs. Meridian Internat. Ctr., 1992-98; trustee Friends of Congl. Law Libr., 1992-, Friends of Dept. of Labor, 1984-; mediator World Intellectual Property Orgn., 1996-. Recipient Ohio Gov.'s award, 1980, fellow award, 1981, Outstanding Pub. Service award U.S. Info. Service, 1987; named Disting. Fellow John Sherman Myers Soc., 1986, 96; fellow Nat. Acad. Human Resources, 1998. Mem.: Nat. Assn. Women Lawyers, Women's Bar Assn., Internat Bar Assn., Am. U. Alumni Assn. (bd. dirs. 2002—, Women's Leadership Award 2004), Supreme Ct. Hist. Soc., Union Internat. des Advocats (gov. bd. 1997—2000, 2003—), Rep. Nat. Lawyers Assn. (nat. v.p. 1990—95, nat. vice chmn. 1996—2000, 2001—03, co-chmn. 2003—, memb. bd. 2003—), Am. Arbitration Assn. (bd. dirs. 1985—2000, 2000—, mem. editl. bd. 1992, mem. exec. com. 1995—2000, mem. internat. arbitration com. 1997—, steering com. lawyers for Bush 2000), Bar Assn. D.C., Inter-Am. Bar Assn. (co-chmn. labor law com. 1975—83, editor newsletter, Silver medal 1967), FBA, ABA (chmn. labor law com. 1980—83, chmn. internat. and comparative law adminstrv. law sect. 1983—88, chmn. customs, tariff and trade com. 1988—90, employment law sect. 1990—2004, chmn. internat. com. dispute resolution sect. 1995—, adminstrv. law sect.), World Peace Through Law Ctr., Mortar Bd., Kappa Beta Pi. Republican. Office: Baker & Hostetler LLP Ste 1100 1050 Connecticut Ave NW Washington DC 20036-5304 Office Phone: 202-861-1500. E-mail: bsmurphy@bakerlaw.com.

MURPHY-PILON, MONICA, cultural organization administrator; BA in Sociology, Iona Coll., 1993. Spl. events mgr. N.Y. U. Downtown Hosp., 1994—98; dir. fund devel. Northside Ctr. Child Devel., 1998—2000; dir. instl. giving Cmty. Svc. Soc., 2001—. Scholar, USMC, 1989—92. Mem.: Women In Devel., Assn. Fundraising Profls. Conservative-R.

MURR, JAMES COLEMAN, retired federal government official; b. Lake Charles, La., Oct. 29, 1944; m. Connie Paige Chadwell, Sept. 21, 1968; children: Christopher David, Richard Reno. BA, Tex. Tech U., 1966; MPA, Am. U., 1974. With Sears, Roebuck & Co., Tex., 1971-72, Dept. Labor, Washington, 1972-74, U.S. Customs Svc., Treasury, Washington, 1975-76; legis. analyst Office Mgmt. and Budget, Washington, 1977-81, br. chief, 1982-89, assoc. dir. administrn., 1990-93, asst. dir. legis. reference, 1994-98. Capt. USAF, 1967-70. Roman Catholic. E-mail: jcmurr@ktc.com.

MURRAH, ANN RALLS FREEMAN, historical association executive; b. Gadsden, Ala., June 23, 1932; d. Oscar William Freeman, Sr. and Annie Collier (Ralls) Freeman; m. Robert Leland Murrah, Aug. 9, 1952; children: Frances Ralls Murrah Lovett, Robert Leland Murrah Jr. Grad., Brenau U., 1954. Pres. Gen. Descendants of the Signers of the Constn., Orlando, Fla., 1991—. Rep. Fla. 8th congl. dist. Congl. Sr. Intern Program, Wash., 1998; keynote spkr. Feminist Summit for Global Peace, Taipei, Taiwan, 1995; mem. protocol & hospitality coms. for equestrian events 1996 Olympics; mem. Am. com. Ball des Rosenkavaliers, Vienna, 1989—90; bd. dir. Arnold Palmer Hosp. Bd., Orlando, Fla.; founder Nat. Constn. Ctr., Phila., 2003—; spkr. in field. Mem. women's com. N.Y. U. Downtown Hosp., 1996—99; gala chmn. Winter Pk. Health Found., Winter Pk., Fla., 1996; ball chmn. Arnold Palmer Hosp. for Women & Children, Orlando, Fla., 1997—99, 2001; mem. Orlando Regional Healthcare Found., Orlando; active Coun. of 101-Orlando Mus. Art; v. chmn. dinner com. fundraiser March of Dimes, 1998. Named First Woman Knighted in her own right, Order of St. John of Jerusalem, 1992; named to Brenau U. Alumni Hall of Fame, 2001; recipient Meritorious Svc. award, Sons of the Am. Revolution, 1986, Martha Washington medal, 1988, The Rallye Saintogeais Hunt award, Foret De La Coubre, France, 1988. Mem.: Nat. Soc. So. Dames Am., Plantagenet Soc., Fla. Opera Guild, Met. Opera Guild, Washington Soc., Gavel Soc., Nat. Steeplechase Assn., Shakerag Hunt Club (awarded colors), Daughters of the Am. Revolution (first vice-regent), Sovereign Colonial Soc. Am. of Royal Descent, Magna Charta Dames (herald and courier), Colonial Order of the Crown, Daughters of the Cin., Colonial Dames of Am., Descendants of Knights of the Garter, Sons & Daughters of the Pilgrims (gov. in Ga. 1992—94, historian gen. of the U.S. 1994—97, first vice-gov.), Alpha Delta Pi (province pres., dir. ritual and paraphernalia). Home and Office: Soc of Descendants of Signers of Constitiution 903 Sussex Close Orlando FL 32804

MURRAY, ALAN STEWART, publishing executive; b. Akron, Ohio, Nov. 16, 1954; s. John and Catherine (Case) M.; m. Lori Esposito, Sept. 8, 1984; children: Lucy Ann, Amanda. BA in English, U. N.C.; MS in Econs., London Sch. Econs. Editor bus. and econs. Chattanooga Times, 1977-79; reporter Congl. Quarterly, Washington, 1980-81, 82-83, Nihon Keizai Shimbun, Tokyo, 1981-82; reporter econs. Wall Street Jour., Washington, 1983-92, dep. bur. chief, 1992-93, bur. chief, 1993—. Co-author: Showdown At Gucci Gulch, 1987 (Carey McWilliams award 1988); panelist Sta. PBS, Washington in Rev.; commentary Sta. NBC, News at Sunrise. Bd. dirs., exec. com. Small Enterprise Assistance Fund, Washington, 1992—. Recipient Overseas Press Club award, 1991, Gerald Loeb award, 1992, Excellence in Bus./Fin. Journalsim award John Hancock Fin. Svcs., 1992; John Motley Morehaed scholar; Luce fellow, Tokyo, 1981-82. Mem. U. N.C. Gen. Alumnus Assn. (bd. dirs. 1993—, Disting. Young Alumnus award), Gridiron Club, Phi Beta Kappa. Office: Wall St Jour 1025 Connecticut Ave NW Washington DC 20036-5405

MURRAY, ALBERT LEE, writer, educator; b. Nokomis, Ala., May 12, 1916; s. John Lee and Sudie (Graham) Young; m. Mozelle Menefee, May 31, 1941; 1 child, Michele. BS in Edn., Tuskegee Inst., 1939; MA in English, NYU, 1948; postgrad., U. Mich., 1940, Northwestern U., 1941, U. Paris, 1950; LittD (hon.), Colgate U., 1975, Tuskegee U., 1999, SUNY, Stony Brook, 2000. Tchr. undergrad. composition and lit. Tuskegee Inst., 1940-43, 46-51, also dir. Coll. Little Theatre, cons. on jazz; lectr. Grad. Sch. Journalism, Columbia U., N.Y.C., 1968; O'Connor prof. lit. Colgate U., 1970, O'Connor lectr., 1973, prof. humanities, 1982; vis. prof. lit. U. Mass., Boston, 1971; Paul Anthony Brick lectr. U. Mo., 1972; writer-in-residence Emory U., 1978; adj. assoc. prof. creative writing Barnard Coll., N.Y.C., 1981-83; lectr., participant symposia in field. DuPont vis. scholar Washington and Lee U., 1993. Author: The Omni Americans, 1970, South to a Very Old Place, 1972, The Hero and the Blues, 1973, Train Whistle Guitar, 1974 (Lillian Smith award for fiction), Stomping the Blues, 1976 (ASCAP Deems Taylor award for music criticism), Good Morning Blues: The Autobiography of Count Basie as told to Albert Murray, 1985, The Spyglass Tree, 1991, The Seven League Boots, 1996, The Blue Devils of Nada, 1996, From the Briarpatch File, 2001, (poems) Conjugations and Reiterations, 2001; also numerous articles. Served to maj. USAAF, World War II; ret. USAAF. Woodrow Wilson fellow Drew U., 1983; recipient Lincoln Ctr. Dirs. Emeriti award, 1991, Nat. Book Critic's Cir. Lifetime Achievement award, 1996, Doctor of Humane Letters Spring Hill Coll., 1996, Doctor Letters Hamilton Coll., 1997, Harper Lee award Ala. Writer's Forum, 1998, Clarence Cason award for non-fiction U. Ala., 2001. Mem.: Am. Acad. Arts ans Scis., Am. Acad. Arts and Letters.

MURRAY, ALICE PEARL, data processing company executive; b. Clearfield, Pa., Aug. 4, 1932; d. James Clifford and Leah Mae (Williams) M.; BS, Pa. State U., 1954. With IBM, 1954—, systems svc. rep., Pitts., 1954-56, computer test ctr. rep., Endicott, N.Y., 1956-58, edn. devel. coord., Endicott,

1958-59, adv. instr., L.A., 1959-63, staff instr., L.A., 1963-68, exec. edn. coord., 1968-74, sr. instr. Info. Systems Mgmt. Inst., L.A., 1974-84, sr. edn. rep. IBM Americas Far East Corp., 1984-87; sr. staff mem. customer exec. edn., 1989; cons., 1990-95; ind. cons., 1995—; coord. exhibit Calif. State Mus. Sci. and Industry; guest speaker before civic and profl. groups; guest instr. various univs. and colls.; profl. lectr. Recipient Distinguished Educator award IBM, 1974, also Outstanding Professionalism award, 1975; hon. citizen Tex., Alaska. Mem. Los Angeles County Art Mus., Pa. State Alumni Assn., Wilshire Country Club, Assistance League of So. Calif., L.A. Libr. Found., Delta Delta Delta. Republican. Home and Office: 514 S Gramercy Pl Los Angeles CA 90020-4969

MURRAY, ANDY, professional hockey coach; Coach Phila. Flyers, 1988-90, Minn. North Stars, 1990-92, Winnipeg Jets, 1993-95; head coach Can. Nat. Team, 1996-98, L.A. Kings, 1999—. Office: Staples Ctr 111 S Figueroa St Los Angeles CA 90012-2465

MURRAY, ANNE, singer; b. Springhill, N.S., Can., June 20, 1945; d. Carson and Marion (Burke) M.; m. William M. Langstroth, June 20, 1975; children: William Stewart, Dawn Joanne. B.Phys. Edn., U. N.B., 1966, D.Litt. (hon.), 1978, St. Mary's U., 1982. Rec. artist for Arc Records, Canada, 1968, Capital/EMI Records, 1969—. Appeared on series of TV spls. CBC, 1970—81, 1988—93; star CBS spls., 1981—85; toured N. Am., Japan, Englan, Germany, Holland, Ireland, Sweden, Australia and New Zealand, 1977—82. Singer: (31 albums including) A Little Good News, 1984, (albums) As I Am, 1988, Greatest Hits, vol. I, 1981, vol. II, 1989, Harmony, 1987, You Will, 1990, Yes I Do, 1991, Croonin', 1993, The Best So Far, 1994, Now and Forever, Anne Murray, 1996, An Intimate Evening with Anne Murray-Live, 1997, What A Wonderful World, 1999, What A Wonderful Christmas, 2001, Country Croonin', 2002. Hon. chmn. Can. Save the Children Fund, 1978-80. Recipient Juno awards as Can.'s top female vocalist, 1970-81; Can.'s Top Country Female Vocalist, 1970-86; Grammy award as top female vocalist-country, 1974; Grammy award as top female vocalist-pop, 1978; Grammy award as top female vocalist-country, 1980, 83; Country Music Assn. awards, 1983-84; named Female Rec. Artist of Decade, Can. Rec. Industry Assn., 1980, Top Female Vocalist 1970-86; star inserted in Hollywood Walkway of Stars, 1980; Country Music Hall of Fame Nashville; decorated companion Order of Can.; inducted Juno Hall of Fame, 1993. Mem. AFTRA, Assn. Canadian TV and Radio Artists, Am. Fedn. Musicians. Office: Bruce Allen Talent No 500 425 Carrall St Vancouver BC Canada V6B6E3 also: EMI Music Distbn 21700 Oxnard St Ste 700 Woodland Hills CA 91367-3617

MURRAY, BARBARA OLIVIA, writer, retired psychologist; b. Summit, N.J., July 8, 1947; d. Archibald and Anna Cutler (Mattison) M. Student, Inst. d'Etudes Francaises Pour Estrangers, France, 1965, U. de Grenoble, 1968; BA in Psychology, Lake Erie Coll., 1969; MA in Clin. Psychology, Cleve. State U., 1971; postgrad., Gestalt Inst. Cleve., 1971-73; PhD in Clin. Psychology, Calif. Sch. Profl. Psychology, Fresno, 1976. Lic. psychologist, Calif. Mental health worker Cleve. Clinic Hosp., 1970—71, assoc. psychologist, 1971—73; psychiat. intake worker Cleve. Free Clinic, 1971, group leader, 1972; cons. St. John's Coll., Cleve., 1972—73; psychology intern Fresno County Dept. Health, 1973—75, student profl. worker, 1974; faculty Calif. Sch. Profl. Psychology, Fresno, 1974, psychology intern, 1974, Calif. State U., Fresno, lectr., 1976—77; dir. treatment program E. Ross Clark Home for Children, Inc., Modesto, Calif., 1976—77; clin. psychologist Santa Cruz County Cmty. Mental Health Svcs., Santa Cruz County, Calif., 1977—79, dir. psychol. svcs., 1979—83; pvt. practice Soquel, Calif., 1979—96; oral commr. Calif. State Psychology Licensing Exam, 1988—96; ret., 1996. Designated expert Calif. Med. Bd., 1991—96; mem. med. staff Dominican Hosp., 1983—93, vice chmn dept. psychiatry/psychology, 1985—87, chair dept. psychiatry/psychology, 1987—88; mem. Citizens' Involvement Assocs., 1984—87; adj. faculty Pacific Grad. Sch. Psychology, 1984—89; mem. faculty San Francisco State U., 1987; cons. NOW, 1973—76, Cmty. Hosp., Fresno, 1974; expert witness Santa Cruz, Monterey, Santa Clara and San Francisco counties, 1979—96; participant Law and Ethics Workshop, 1984, CPI-MMPI workshop, 1986, Child Sexual Assault Workshop, 1986; presenter The Role of the Profl. in Complex Custody Disputes, 1993. Contbr. articles to jours. in psychology. Mem. Women's Studies Adv. Bd., Fresno, 1975-76. Recipient Disting. Psychologist award Calif. State Psychol. Assn., 1982, recognition for contbns. to the field of psychology and Mid-Coast Psychol. Assn., 1996; Hill scholar, 1968, Smith scholar, 1969, Fritz Perls scholar, 1970. Mem. APA, Calif. Psychol. Assn. (bd. dirs. Observer 1981-83), Mid-Coast Psychol. Assn. (pres. 1981, forensic chmn. 1983-96), Psychol. Inst., Forensic Mental Health Assn., No. Calif. Psychologists for Social Responsibility, Laurel Soc., Psi Chi (v.p. 1968-69), Kappa Alpha Sigma, Cotuit Mosquito Yacht Club, Mt. Women Investment Club. Home and Office: 4595 Fairway Dr Soquel CA 95073-3010

MURRAY, BARRY WAYNE, economics educator; b. Dublin, Ga., June 1, 1946; s. Archie Guy and Helen Avis (Smith) M.; m. Laurie Lee Yoder, Sept. 11, 1976; children: Elisabeth Hope, Jonathan Guy, Caitlin Anna. BS in Econs., Auburn U., 1968; MEd in Econs. Edn., West Ga. Coll., 1978, EdS in Econs. Edn., 1980. Tchr. social studies Cobb County Bd. Edn., Marietta, Ga., 1968-85; dir. gifted program Osborne H.S., Marietta, 1985—, tchr. econs., 1989—. Coach, advisor stock market game Ga. Coun. Econ. Edn., Atlanta, 1987—, advisor 8th State Stock Market Game Championship, 1996; coord. gov.'s honors selection Gov.'s Honors Program, Atlanta, 1985—. Author: (periodical) Level of Economic Understanding of Teachers, 1980 (Student Rsch. award 1980, 7 Star Tchr. awards). Active Citizenship Coun. Cobb County, Marietta, 1985-86, Ga. Coun. Econ. Edn., Atlanta, 1987—. Mem. Ga. Acad. Team Assn., Ga. Assn. Educators. Office: 1065 Polo Club Dr NW Marietta GA 30064-1283

MURRAY, BILL, actor, writer; b. Evanston, Ill., Sept. 21, 1950; s. Edward and Lucille Murray; m. Margaret Kelly, 1980 (div. 1994); children: Homer, Luke; m. Jennifer Butler, 1997; children: Jackson, Cal, Cooper. Grad., Loyola Acad.; attended, Regis Coll., Denver; student, Second City Workshop, Chgo. Formerly with improvisational theater group Second City, Chgo.; writer; performer off-broadway National Lampoon Radio Hour; regular on TV series Saturday Night Live, 1977-80, also writer; featured in 3 prodns. of, TVTV co.; played Johnny Storm, the Human Torch in radio series Marvel Comics' Fantastic Four; appeared in movies Meatballs, 1979, Mr. Mike's Mondo Video, 1979, Where the Buffalo Roam, 1980, Caddyshack, 1980, Loose Shoes, 1980, Stripes, 1981, Tootsie, 1982, Ghostbusters, 1984, The Razor's Edge, 1984, Nothing Lasts Forever, 1984, Little Shop of Horrors, 1986, Scrooged, 1988, Ghostbusters II, 1989, What About Bob?, 1991, Groundhog Day, 1993, Mad Dog and Glory, 1993, Ed Wood, 1994, Kingpin, 1996, Larger Than Life, 1996, Space Jam, 1996, The Man Who Knew Too Little, 1997, With Friends Like These, 1998, Veeck As In Wreck, 1998, Rushmore, 1998, Wild Things, 1998, The Cradle Will Rock, 1999, Scout's Honor, 1999, Hamlet, 1999, Company Man, 1999, Charlie's Angels, 2000, Speaking of Sex, 2001, The Royal Tenenbaums, 2001, Osmosis Jones, 2001, Coffee and Cigarettes, 2003, Lost in Translation, 2003 (Golden Globe for best actor in a musical or comedy, 2004, Acad. Award nomination for best actor, 2004, Screen Actors Guild Award nomination for best actor, 2004), Garfield: The Movie (voice), 2004; (TV series) The Sweet Spot, 2002; co-prodr., co-dir., actor film Quick Change, 1990; other TV appearances include Things We Did Last Summer; prodn. asst. (TV movies) Cry for Help: The Tracey Thurman Story, 1989. Recipient Emmy award for best writing for comedy series, 1977, Sons of the Desert Comedy Performer award, 1997. Office: Creative Artists Agy care Jessica Tuchinsky 9830 Wilshire Blvd Beverly Hills CA 90212-1825*

MURRAY, BRIAN, publishing executive; Cons. media practice Booz Allen & Hamilton; dir. finance and analysis, adult book trade HarperCollins Publishers, 1997—98, v.p., finance and publishing operations, 1998—99, sr. v.p., mng. dir. gen. books group, 1999—2001; CEO HarperCollins Australia/New Zealand, 2001—04; group pres. HarperCollins Publishers, 2004—. Office: HarperCollins 10 E 53rd St New York NY 10022

MURRAY, BRIAN VICTOR, investment banker; b. Teaneck, N.J., Oct. 17, 1947; s. Harry Lawrence and Marie Antoinette (Brizzi) M.; m. Dec. 14, 1974; children: B. Patrick, Megan, Sean, Matthew. BS in Econs., Villanova U., 1970; MBA with hons., U. Chgo., 1975. Ptnr. H.C. Wainwright & Co., N.Y.C., Boston, 1974-78; sr. mng. dir. Bear, Stearns & Co., N.Y.C., 1978-96; pres. B.V. Murray & Co., Englewood Cliffs, N.J., 1996—. Chmn. First Hungary Fund, Isle of Jersey, 1996—, Carlson Bolivia Fund, 1997—; bd. dirs. 4 Front Tech., Del., U.S., 1996—, Renal Tech. DVT. N.Y.C., 1998—; founder, bd. dirs. Ascent/Meredith Asset Mgmt., N.Y.C., 1998—. Trustee, mem. exec. com. Elizabeth Morrow Sch., Englewood, N.J., 1991—. Lt. U.S. Navy, 1970. Named Internat. Dealer of Yr., Instnl. Investment Mag., 1989. Mem. Union League (N.Y.), Inst. of Chartered Fin. Analysts (chartered). Avocation: judging horses (recognized judge Am. Horse Show Assn.). Office: BV Murray & Co Inc 560 Sylvan Ave Englewood Cliffs NJ 07632 E-mail: Bvm@bvmurray.com.

MURRAY, BRYAN CLARENCE, professional sports team executive; b. Shawville, Que., Can., Dec. 5, 1942; came to U.S., 1980; s. Clarence Herbert and Rhoda (Schwartz) M.; m. Geraldine Frances Sutton, July 8, 1967; 1 dau., Heide Alicia. Grad., McGill U., 1964. Former athletic dir., hockey coach McGill U.; athletic dir. MacDonald Coll., Ste. Anne de Bellevue, Que., 1968-72; coach, tchr. Rockland Nat.-Pontiac High Sch., Rockland, Ont., 1974-76; coach Pembroke-Kings, Pembroke, Ont., 1976-79, Regina Pats, Sask., 1979-80, Hershey (Pa.) Bears, 1980-81; former coach Washington Capitals, Landover, Md., from 1981; coach, gen. mgr. Detroit Red Wings, 1990-94; gen. manager Florida Panthers, Fort Lauderdale, Fla., 1994—2001, head coach Mighty Ducks Anaheim, 2001—02, sr. v.p., gen. mgr., 2002—04; head coach Ottawa Senators, 2004—. Recipient Jack Adams award as NHL Coach of Yr., 1983-84. Office: c/o OTtawa Senators 1000 Palladium Dr K2V 1A5 Kanata ON Canada*

MURRAY, CHERRY ANN, physicist, researcher; b. Ft. Riley, Kans., Feb. 6, 1952; d. John Lewis and Cherry Mary (Roberts) M.; m. Dirk Joachim Muehlner, Feb. 18, 1977; children: James Joachim, Sara Hester. BS in Physics, MIT, 1973, PhD in Physics, 1978. Rsch. asst. physics dept. MIT, Cambridge, 1969-78; rsch. assoc. Bell Labs., Murray Hill, N.J., 1976-77; mem. tech. staff AT&T Bell Labs., Murray Hill, 1978-85, disting. mem. tech. staff, 1985-87, dept. head low-temperature and solid-state physics rsch., 1987-90, dept. head condensed matter physics rsch., 1990-93, dept. head semicond. physics rsch., 1993-97, dir. phys. rsch. lab., 1997—. Co-chair Gordon Rsch., Wolfeboro, N.H., 1982, chair, 1984. Contbr. numerous articles to profl. jours. and chpts. to books. NSF fellow, 1969; IBM fellow MIT, 1974-76. Fellow AAAS, Am. Phys. Soc. (Maria Goeppart-Mayer award 1989), Nat. Acad. Scis., Sigma Xi. Office: Bell Labs Lucent Techs 700 Mountain Ave Rm Id-269 New Providence NJ 07974-1208

MURRAY, CHRISTOPHER CHARLES, III, architect; b. Bklyn., July 6, 1950; s. Christopher Charles and Gertrude Rose (Marr) M.; m. Ann Herring, Nov. 16, 1974. BArch, U. Notre Dame, 1973. Registered arch., N.Y., Md., D.C., Va., Ga. Project arch. Hibner Archs., Garden City, NY, 1973-76; project mgr. BBM Archs., N.Y.C., 1976-79; project dir. Gensler & Assocs., N.Y.C., 1979-84; office dir., v.p., mem. nat. mgmt. com. Gensler, Washington, 1984-96, internat. practice leader profl. svc. firms, 1996—. Prin. works include interior design Sidley & Austin Worldwide, McDermott, Will & Emery, Latham & Watkins, Baker McKenzie, Covington & Burling. Asst. scoutmaster Boy Scouts Am., also NCAC dist. commr.; active Greater Washington Bd. Trade, 1986. Mem. AIA, Md. Soc. Archs., Notre Dame Club, Club at Franklin Sq. Roman Catholic. Home: 12517 Knightsbridge Ct Rockville MD 20850-3732 Office: Gensler 2020 K St NW Washington DC 20006-1806 Office Phone: 202-721-5300. E-mail: christopher_murray@gensler.com.

MURRAY, CONNIE WIBLE, state official, former state legislator; b. Tulsa, Oct. 13, 1943; d. Carl Prince Lattimore and Jimmie Bell Henry; m. Jarrett Holland Murray, May 4, 1995. Cert. of oral hygiene, Temple U., 1965; BA, Loyola Coll., 1975; JD, U. Md., 1980. Registered dental hygienist, Bethlehem, Pa., 1965-66, Joppa, Md., 1966-77; law clk. Hon. Albert P. Close, Belair, Md., 1980-81; atty., 1981-85; realtor, 1985-90; mem. Mo. Ho. of Reps., Jefferson City, 1990-96; pub. svc. commr. State of Mo., Jefferson City, 1997—. House mgr. Articles ot Impeachment of Judith Moriarty, Mo. Sec. of State, 1994; mem. budget com. Mo. Ho. of Reps., also mem. appropriations social svcs. and corrections com., judiciary and ethics com., civil and criminal law and accounts, opers. and fin. com., interim com. for fed. funds and block grants, commn. on intergovtl. affairs, commn. on mgmt. and productivity, legis. oversight com. for ct. automation, ho. automation com. Bd. dirs. North Springfield Betterment Assn., 1989; vocat. adv. bd., dir. house intern programs Nat. Conf. State Legislators. Named Outstanding Freshman Legis. on Health Care Issues, Mo. Rep. Caucus, 1992; recipient Jud. Conf. Legis. award Mo. Jud. Conf., 1994, Outstanding Woman Legis. award Assn. Probate and Assoc. Cir. Judges, 1995. Mem. LWV (bd. dirs. Springfield 1989, treas.), Nat. Order Women Legis., Nat. Conf. State Legis., Nat. Women's Polit. Caucus, Women Legis. Mo., Mo. Bar Assn. (Adminstr. for Justice award), Am. Legis. Exch. Counsel, Ctr. for Am. Women in Politics, Greene County Bar Assn., Forum-A Women's Natwork, Women in Govt. Avocations: golf, bicycling, jogging, travel. Office: Mo Gen Assembly State Capitol Office Bldg Jefferson City MO 65101-6806

MURRAY, DANIEL RICHARD, lawyer; b. Mar. 23, 1946; s. Alfred W. and Gloria D. Murray. AB, U. Notre Dame, 1967; JD, Harvard U., 1970. Bar: Ill. 1970, U.S. Dist. Ct. (no. dist.) Ill. 1970, U.S. Ct. Appeals (7th cir.) 1971, U.S. Supreme Ct. 1974. Ptnr. Jenner & Block, Chgo., 1970—. Trustee Chgo. Mo. and Western Rlwy. Co., 1988-97; adj. prof. U. Notre Dame, 1997—. Co-author: Secured Transactions, 1978, Illinois Practice: Uniform Commercial Code with Illinois Code Comments, 2003, Uniform Laws Annotated—Uniform Commercial Code Forms, 2001, Illinois Practice: Uniform Commercial Code Forms, 2002. Bd. regents Big Shoulders Fund, Archdiocese of Chgo., Bernardin Ctr., Cath. Theol. Union. Mem.: Assn. Transp. Practitioners, Transp. Lawyers Assn., Am. Coll. Comml. Fin. Lawyers, Am. Bankruptcy Coll., Am. Law Inst., Am. Bankruptcy Inst., Cath. Lawyers Guild (bd. dirs.), Lawyers' Club Chgo. Roman Catholic. Home: 1307 N Sutton Pl Chicago IL 60610-2007 Office: Jenner & Block One IBM Plz Chicago IL 60611-3605 Office Phone: 312-923-2953. Business E-Mail: dmurray@jenner.com.

MURRAY, DAVE, marketing professional, editor; V.p. fin. comm. Wells Fargo Bank; city editor major daily newspaper San Francisco Bay area; exec. v.p., prin. Neale-May & Ptnrs. Inc., 1987—. Cons. with AboveNet, Amdahl Corp., A.T. Kearney, Borland, Brobeck, Phleger & Harrison, Business-land, Cheyenne Software, Concentric Network Corp, Ernst & Young, others. Office: Neale May & Ptnrs Inc 409 Sherman Ave Palo Alto CA 94306

MURRAY, DAVID GEORGE, architect; b. Tulsa, Nov. 9, 1919; s. Lee Cloyd and Marion (Bennett) M.; m. Margaret Elizabeth Oldham, Sept. 23, 1944; children: Michael Allen, Lucy Margaret (Mrs. Norman Scheer), Patrick David. BArch, Okla. State U., 1942. Registered architect, Okla. Ptnr. Atkinson & Murray, Tulsa, 1949-52; prin. David G. Murray & Assocs., Tulsa, 1952-56; pres. Murray, Jones, Murray, Inc., Tulsa, 1957-85, chmn., 1986-89. Chmn., bd. govs. Licensed Architects, Oklahoma City, 1964-74. Prin. works include Cities Service Technology Ctr., Broken Arrow, Okla., Terminal Bldg. Tulsa Internat. Airport, St. Patrick's Ch., Oklahoma City, Coll. of Osteopathic Medicine and Surgery, Tulsa, First Nat. Tower, Tulsa, Hillcrest Med. Ctr., Tulsa, Thomas Gilcrease Mus., Tulsa, Tulsa Civic Ctr. Bldgs. Chmn., dir. Goodwill Industries of Tulsa, 1966-87; chmn., exec. com. Downtown Tulsa Unltd., 1975-87; v.p., exec. com., dir. Met. Tulsa C. of C., 1979-85. Served to 1st lt. USAF, 1942-45. Named to Hall of Fame Coll. Engring. Okla. State U., 1969. Fellow AIA (pres. Tulsa chpt. 1964, mem. com. office practice 1983-87); mem. Southern Hills Country Club (dir. 1977-80). Republican. Methodist. Avocations: travel, golf.

MURRAY, DIANE ELIZABETH, librarian; b. Detroit, Oct. 15, 1942; d. Gordon Lisle and Dorothy Anne (Steketee) LaBoueff; m. Donald Edgar Murray, Apr. 22, 1968. AB, Hope Coll., 1964; postgrad., Mich. State U., East Lansing, 1964-66; MLS, Western Mich. U., 1968; MM, Aquinas Coll., 1982. Catalog libr., asst. head acquisitions sect. Mich. State U. Librs., East Lansing, 1968-77; libr. tech. and automated svcs. Hope Coll., Holland, Mich., 1977-88; dir. librs. DePauw U., Greencastle, Ind., 1988-91; acquisitions libr. Grand Valley State U., Allendale, Mich., 1991—. Sec., vice chair, chairperson bd. trustees Mich. Libr. Consortium, Lansing, 1981—85. V.p. Humane Soc. Putnam County, Greencastle, 1990—91; bd. dirs. Loutit Dist. Libr., 1999—. Mem.: ALA. Methodist. Avocations: dog breeding and showing, handbell ringing. Office: Grand Valley State U Zumberge Libr Allendale MI 49401 Business E-Mail: murrayd@gvsu.edu.

MURRAY, EDDIE CLARENCE, baseball batting coach; b. L.A., Feb. 24, 1956; Student, Calif. State U., L.A. Player minor league teams, Bluefield, Miami, Asheville, Charlotte, Rochester, 1973-76; player Balt. Orioles, 1973-88, 96, L.A. Dodgers, 1988-91, N.Y. Mets, 1991-93, Cleveland Indians, 1993-96, Anaheim Angels, 1997; coach Baltimore Orioles, 1998—. Named to All-Star Team, 1978, 81-86, 91; named Appalachian League Player of Yr., 1973, Am. League Rookie of Yr., Baseball Writers Assn. Am., 1977, First Baseman, Sporting News Am. League All-Star Team, 1983, 90,; recipient Gold Glove award, 1982-84, Silver Slugger award, 1983-84, 90. Office: Baltimore Orioles Oriole Pk at Camden Yards 333 W Camden St Baltimore MD 21201-2435

MURRAY, EDWARD ROCK, insurance broker; b. Bklyn., Jan. 31, 1947; s. Garrett Francis and Anne M. (Rock) M.; m. Barbara Marie Robotti; children: Pamela Jean, Stephanie Elise. BA in Bus. Adminstrn., St. Bonaventure U., 1968. Claims examiner N.Y.C., 1970-72; agt. and mgr. John Hancock Life Ins., Albany, N.Y., 1972-76; regional dir. Colonial Life Insur, Albany, 1976-80; ptnr. Murray & Zuckerman, Inc., Schenectady, N.Y., 1980—. Bd. dirs. Northeast Mgmt. Forum, 1990—; treas. The Mktg. Alliance. 1st lt. U.S. Army, 1968-70, Vietnam. Mem. Mohawk Club (past chmn.), Nat. Assn. of Ind. Life Brokerage Agys. (bd. dirs., past chmn. bd.), Edison Club. Roman Catholic. Avocation: golf. Office: Murray & Zuckerman Inc 128 Erie Blvd Ste 2 Schenectady NY 12305-2283 Office Phone: 518-382-5483.

MURRAY, EILEEN K. investment company executive; BSC in acctg., Manhattan Coll., 1980. Formerly with Peat Marwick; with Morgan Stanley, 1984—2002; v.p. Morgan Stanley Group Inc., 1988—91, prin., 1991—94, mng. dir., 1994, controller and treas.; chief adminstrv. officer, instl. securities group Morgan Stanley Dean Witter & Co., 1999—2002; head of global tech, ops. & product control Credit Suisse First Boston, NYC, 2002—. Bd. dirs. Omgeo LLC, 2001—. Office: Credit Suisse First Boston 11 Madison Ave New York NY 10010

MURRAY, ELIZABETH, artist; b. Chgo., 1940; married; 1 child, Dakota Sunseri. B.F.A., Art Inst., Chgo., 1962; M.F.A., Mills Coll., Oakland, Calif., 1964. Vis. instr. Wayne State U., 1975, Calif. Inst. Arts, 1975-76, Chgo. Art Inst., 1975-76; instr. Bard Coll., Annandale on Hudson, N.Y., 1974-75, 76-77, Princeton U., 1977, Yale U., 1978-79. One-woman shows, Jacobs Ladder Gallery, Washington, 1974, Paula Cooper Gallery, N.Y.C., 1975, 76, 78, 81, 83, 88, 89, Jared Sable Gallery, 1975, Ohio State U., Columbus, 1978, Phyllis Kind Gallery, Chgo., 1978, Galerie Mukai, Tokyo, 1980, Susanne Hilberry Gallery, Birmingham, Mich., 1980, Smith Coll. Art Gallery, Northampton, Mass., 1982, Daniel Weinberg Gallery, Los Angeles, 1982, Portland Ctr. Visual Arts, Oreg., 1983, Knight Gallery, Charlotte, N.C., 1984, Mayor Rowen Gallery, London, 1989, Barbara Krakow Gallery, Boston, 1990, Gallery Mukai, Tokyo, 1990, John Berggruen Gallery, San Francisco, 1990; group shows include, Whitney Mus. Am. Art, N.Y.C., 1972, 73, 77, 79, 81, 82, 84, John Doyle Gallery Cologne, Ger., 1974, Paula Cooper Gallery, 1974, 76, 77, 78, 79, 81, 82, 83, 84, Michael Walls Gallery, N.Y., 1975, Middlebury (Vt.) Coll., 1976, Gallery of July and August, Brockport, N.Y., 1976, Susanne Hilberry Gallery, Detroit, 1976, Guggenheim Mus., N.Y.C., 1977, Sarah Lawrence Coll. Gallery, Bronxville, N.Y., 1977, Lowe Art Gallery Syracuse U., 1977, Mus. Contemporary Art, Chgo., 1977, Inst. Contemporary Art, U. Pa., 1978, Tampa Bay Art Center, Fla., 1978, Phyllis Kind Gallery, Chgo., 1979, William Patterson Coll., Wayne, N.J., 1979, Susan Caldwell Gallery, N.Y., 1979, U. N.C. Weatherspoon Art Gallery, Greensboro, 1979, Galerie Yvon Lambert, Paris, 1980, Bklyn. Mus., 1980, Dart Gallery, Chgo., 1981, Contemporary Arts Center, Cin., 1981, High Mus. Art, Atlanta, 1981, 82, Galerie Mukai, Tokyo, 1981, Va. Mus., Richmond, 1981, Boston Mus. Fine Arts, 1982, Milw. Art Mus., 1982, Art Inst. Chgo., 1982, Daniel Weinberg Gallery, Los Angeles and San Francisco, 1983, Hirshhorn Mus., Washington, 1983, Hobart and William Smith Colls., Geneva, N.Y., 1983, Mus. Art, Ft. Lauderdale, Fla., 1986, 40th Biennial Exhbn. Comtemp. Am. Paintings Corcoran Gallery of Art, 1988, numerous others; represented in permanent collections: Whitney Mus. Am. Art, N.Y.C., Guggenheim Mus., Hirshhorn Mus. and Sculpture Garden, Washington, H.H.K. Found., Milw., St. Louis Art Mus., Detroit Inst. Arts. Recipient Walter M. Campana award Art Inst. of Chgo., 1982, Am. Academy & Inst. of Arts & Letters award, 1984, Skowhegan prize for painting, 1986, Larry Aldrich prize in contemporary art, 1993, John D. & Catherine T. MacArthur Found. award, 1999, Nat. Artist award Anderson Ranch Art Ctr., 2002; honored by Artists Space, NYC, 2001. Mem. Am. Acad and Inst. of Arts and Letters, 1992. Office: Pace Wildenstein Gallery 32 E 57 St New York NY 10001*

MURRAY, ERNEST DON, artist, educator; b. Asheville, N.C., Apr. 21, 1930; s. Ernest Burgin and Daisy Ann (Bishop) M.; m. Katherine H. Shakeshaft, 1997. Student, Asheville-Biltmore Jr. Coll., 1950; AA, BA, U. Tenn., 1952; student, Art Students League, 1953; MFA, U. Fla., 1957, MEd, 1958. Instr. art Chipola Jr. Coll., Marianna, Fla., 1958, head div. humanities, 1964-68; instr. humanities U. Fla., Gainesville, 1969-72, prof. humanities, asso. chmn. dept. humanities, 1974-78, prof. fine art and humanities dept. fine art, 1978-96, prof. emeritus, 1997—; co-owner Round Earth Studio, Gainesville, 1996—. Cons. Holt, Rinehart & Winston, Inc., N.Y.C., 1963-76, Harcourt Brace, Jovanovich, Inc., N.Y.C., 1964-76 One-man shows in Knoxville, Tenn., 1952, N.Y.C., 1953, Gainesville, 1968, 71, 72, 75, 90, 93, Pub. Sculpture Commns., 1989, 90, 91, 93, 95, Fla. Mus. Natural History, Fla. State Fire Coll., Mathieson Hist. Ctr.; exhibited in group shows Asheville, 1949, Knoxville, 1951, 65, N.Y.C., 1953, 61, 67, Gainesville, Miami, Tallahassee, 1979—; represented in pvt. collections. With C.E. U.S. Army, 1954-56, USNR, 1949-54. Mem. So. Highlands Craftsman's Guild, Fla. Artists Assn., Phi Theta Kappa, Phi Kappa Phi, Phi Beta Kappa, Omicron Delta Kappa. Unitarian Universalist. E-mail: roundear@mindspring.com.

MURRAY, FRANK, former heating, air conditioning manufacturing executive; CEO Goodman Mfg., Houston, 1999. Office: Goodman Mfg 2550 N Loop W Ste 400 Houston TX 77092-8908

MURRAY, GORDON FRANKLIN, medical educator; b. Muskegon, Mich., 1939; MD, U. Mich., 1963. Intern Johns Hopkins Hosp., Balt., 1963-64, resident, 1964-66, 67-70; with W.Va. U. Hosps., Morgantown; prof. W.Va. U. Office: WVa U Dept Surgery 4061 Health Scis Ctr Morgantown WV 26506

MURRAY, JAMES ALAN, urban and environmental consultant, investor; b. Evansville, Ind., Oct. 2, 1942; s. William Dewey and Dorothy Marie (Gleason) M.; children: Heidi Lynn, Paul Alan, Kendra Leigh. BS, U. N.Mex., 1964; MBA, Harvard U., 1969; MA (NDEA fellow), U. Oreg., 1971, PhD, 1972. Dir. fin. City of Boulder (Colo.), 1972-73, dir. adminstrv. svcs., 1973-74; v.p. Briscoe, Maphis, Murray & Lamont, Inc., Boulder, 1974-78, pres., 1978-84, also dir.; dir. fin. City and County of Denver, 1984-86, CEO, 1986-87, asst. to mayor, 1987-89; pres., dir. Murray Lamont & Assocs., Inc., 1990-98, Colo. Scientific Investments, Inc., 1993-96; chmn. Lanzhou Murray Clothing Co., China, 1994-95, Lanzhou Murray Electronics Co., Ltd., China, 1995—. Adj. assoc. prof. Grad. Sch. Public Affairs, U. Colo., Boulder, 1972-80, Denver, 1985-91; dir. regional/urban design assistance team program of AIA, 1994—. Mem. open space adv. com. City of Boulder, 1972-74; bd. dirs. Met. Denver Sewage Authority, 1984-85, Colo. Baseball Commn., 1989-93. Mem. ASPA,

Am. Econ. Assn., Western Econ. Assn., Water Pollution Control Fedn., Denver Athletic Club, Kappa Mu Epsilon, Pi Alpha Alpha. Home: 2186 Woodruff DR Germantown TN 38138-4024 E-mail: Jim99s@earthlink.net.

MURRAY, JAMES DICKSON, mathematical biology educator; b. Moffat, Scotland, Jan. 2, 1931; m. Sheila Todd Campbell, Oct. 1959; children: Mark Woodeaton, Sarah Corinne. BSc in Math. with 1st class honors, U. St. Andrews, Scotland, 1953, PhD in Applied Math., 1956; MA, U. Oxford, Eng., 1961, DSc in Math., 1968; DSc (hon.), U. St. Andrews, 1994, U. Strathclyde, 1999. Lectr. applied math. King's Coll. Durham U., Newcastle, Eng., 1955-56; Gordon McKay lectr. and rsch. fellow Harvard U., Cambridge, Mass., 1956-59, rsch. assoc. engring., applied physics, 1963-64; prof. engring. mechanics U. Mich., Ann Arbor, 1965-67; prof. math. NYU, N.Y.C., 1967-70; lectr. Univ. Coll., London, 1959-61; fellow in math. Hertford Coll. U. Oxford, 1961-63, reader, 1972-86, prof. math. biology, 1986-92, fellow Corpus Christi Coll., 1970-92, dir. Ctr. Math. Biology, 1983-92, emeritus prof., 1992—, hon. fellow, 2001—. Vis. prof. applied math. MIT, 1979, U. Utah, Salt Lake City, 1979, 85, Calif. Tech. U., 1983; vis. rsch. prof. Nat. Tsing Hua U., Taiwan, 1975, U. Florence, Italy, 1976, Winegard Guelph U., 1980; guest prof. U. Heidelberg, Fed. Republic Germany, 1980; disting. vis. prof., Scott Hawkins lectr. So. Meth. U., Dallas, 1984; adj. prof. zoology U. Wash., 1988-2000, prof. applied math., 1988-2000, emeritus, 2000—, Robert F. Philip prof., 1988-94, Boeing prof., 1997-2000; ULAM scholar Los Alamos Nat. Lab., 1985; Lansdowne lectr. U. Victoria, 1990, Ostram lectr. Wash. State U. Author: Asymptotic Analysis, 1974, Nonlinear Differential Equation Models in Biology, 1977, Russian translation, 1983, Mathematical Biology, 1989, 3d edit., 2 vols., 2002, 03; co-author: (with L. Wolpert and S. Brenner) Theories of Biological Pattern Formation, 1981, (with W. Jäger) Modelling Patterns in Space and Time, 1983, (with H.G. Othmer and P.K. Maini) Experimental and Theoretical Advances in Biological Pattern Formation, 1993, (with J. Gottman et al.) The Mathematics of Marriage, 2002; contbr. over 200 articles to profl. jours. Recipient Naylor prize for applied math. London Math. Soc., 1989; vis. fellow St. Catherine's Coll., U. Oxford, 1967, Guggenheim fellow, 1967-68; La Chaire Européene, U. Paris, 1994, 95, 96. Fellow Royal Soc., Royal Soc. Edinburgh, European Soc. for Math. and Theoretical Biology (pres. 1991-94); mem. Acad. Scis. Paris (fgn. mem.). Office: U Wash Dept Applied Math PO Box 352420 Seattle WA 98195-2420 E-mail: murrayjd@amath.washington.edu.

MURRAY, JAMES DOYLE, accountant, educator; b. Rochester, N.Y., July 24, 1938; s. William Herbert and Mildred Frances (Becker) M.; m. Mary Louise Goodyear, June 22, 1962; children: William Doyle, Robert Goodyear. BS, U. Rochester, 1961. CPA, N.Y. With Ernst & Whinney, Rochester, N.Y., 1963—, ptnr., 1977-86; pvt. practice Rochester, 1986—; former mem. faculty NYSCPA. Contbr. articles to profl. jours. Treas. William Warfield Scholarship Fund, Inc.; bd. dirs. March of Dimes, Rochester chpt.; trustee B. Thomas Golisano Found.; active fund raising Boy Scouts Am., Rochester Philharm., Rochester Mus. and Sci. Ctr., U. Rochester; former bd. dirs., treas. Downstairs Cabaret; mem. Eagle bd. of rev. Boy Scouts Am.; elder Presbyn. Ch.; pres. Egypt Vol. Fire Dept. Lt. (j.g.) USN, 1961-63. Named Acct. Adv. of Yr. for region II, SBA, 1996. Mem. AICPA, N.Y. State Soc. CPAs (pres. Rochester chpt. 1982-83), Inst. Mgmt. Accts. (bd. dirs. 1978-80). Republican. Home: 42 Black Watch Trail Fairport NY 14450-3702 Office: 349 W Commercial St Ste 3000 East Rochester NY 14445-2407

MURRAY, JAMES E. managed health care company executive; Ptnr. Coopers & Lybrand, Louisville; joined Humana Inc., Louisville, 1989, interim CFO, until 1997, CFO, 1997-2000, COO Health Plan Div., 2000—01, COO svc. ops., 2001—02, COO Market and Bus. Segments Ops., 2002—. Office: Humana Inc PO Box 1438 Louisville KY 40201-1438

MURRAY, JAMES J. textiles executive; b. 1961; CPA. Tax acct. pvt. industry; mng. dir. KPMG Corp. Trans. Svc. Practice; exec. v.p., CFO, sec. Johnston Industries, Inc., 1997—. Office: Johnston Industries Inc 2401 Brookstone Centre Pkwy #200 Columbus GA 31904 Fax: 706-641-3159.

MURRAY, JAMES JOSEPH, III, association executive; b. Boston, Dec. 31, 1933; s. James Joseph Jr. and Anne Louise (Gurvin) M.; children: James Arthur, Paul, Douglas Joseph, Laura Anne. AB, Harvard U., 1955. Regional editor Prentice Hall, Inc., 1957-60, editor, 1960-64, v.p., exec. editor, 1964-69; pres. Winthrop Pubs., Inc. subs. Prentice Hall, Cambridge, Mass., 1969-82, also bd. dirs.; spl. mng. cons. Am. Coun. Edn., Washington, 1983-84, dir. external affairs, 1984—, v.p., 1997—. Chmn. N.J. Heart Fund; spl. cons. NEH, 1975—. Mem. editorial bd. Capitol Pub., 1992—; author, editor: American Colleges and Universities, 2000. Mem. Dem. Nat. Com. from N.J., 1968; del. Dem. Nat. Conv., 1968; mem. gov. bd. Marine Mil. Acad., 1995—. 1st lt. USMCR, 1955-57. Mem. Am. Polit. Sci. Assn., Assn. Physical Plant Adminstrs. (bd. dirs.), Am. Assn. of Higher Edn., Harvard Club, Harvard Varsity Club, Pi Eta. Office: One DuPont Circle Ste 800 Washington DC 20036

MURRAY, JOHN EINAR, lawyer, retired military officer, federal official; b. Clifton, N.J., Nov. 22, 1918; s. Joseph Michael and Maru Elizabeth (Liljeros) M.; m. Elaine Claire Riehlmann (dec. 1970); 1 dau., Valerie Anne; m. Phyllis Irene Harris (div. 1989). Student, St. Johns U., 1938-41; LLB, N.Y. Law Sch., 1949, LLD, 1975; MA, George Washington U., 1961. lectr. U.S. Marine Corps Nat. Def. U.; mem. sci. panel of White House Agent Orange Working Group, Def. Intelligence Agy. Task Force on POWS and MIAS; participant Georgetown U. Panel on Crisis Mgmt. Drafted pvt. U.S. Army, 1941, advanced through grades to maj. gen., 1972; comdr. truck group Europe Mil. Ports, Vietnam and maj. logistic units, 1968; dir. Army Transp., 1969-70; chief logistics Pacific Command, 1970-72, Mil. Assistance Command, Vietnam, 1972-73; def. attache Vietnam, 1973-74; ret., 1974; v.p. Assn. Am. Railroads, Washington, 1974-84; spl. counsel Am. Internat. Underwriters, 1985; prin. dep. asst. sec. of def. for spl. ops. and low intensity conflict, 1988-89; with Am. Internat. Group Cos., Washington, 1989; spl. counsel Snavely, King & Assocs., Inc. (econ. cons.), Washington, 1990—. Adv. bd. U.S. Army Transp. Mus.; lectr. Nat. Def. U.; mem. sci. panel of White House Agent Orange Working Group, Def. Intelligence Agy. Task Force on POWs and MIAs; participant Georgetown U. Panel on Crisis Mgmt. Author: (with A.M. Chester) Orders and Directive, 1952, (with V.F. Caputo) Quick on the Vigor, 1966, The Myths of Business and the Business of Myths, 1975, The Third Curse of Moses, 1975, The Military Mind and the New Mindlessness, 1976, Lawyers, Computers and Power, 1977, Pothole Plague and Knothole Outlook, 1978, Railroads, Terrorism and the Pinkerton Legacy, 1978, Raising Corn and Beans and Hell, 1979, Remembering Who You Are, 1979, Running A Muck— The Folly of Coal Slurry, 1979, The Railroads and the Energy Crisis, 1980, U.S. Security Assistance— The Vietnam Experience, 1980, Hopeless Cause or Cause of Hope, 1980, War, Transport and Show Biz, 1981, Forget Everything You Ever Knew About the Japanese Railroads, 1981, Sweet Adversity: The U.S. Army-How It Motivates, 1982, Random Danger: The Railroad Response, 1983, Vietnam Logistics: An American Debacle, 1984, Dead Headheads and Warheads, 1987; Operation Desert Shield: The Smart Way to War, 1991; He Was There, 1992, The Logistics of Limited Wars, 1992, The United Nations: Sizing Up Consultant Prospects, 1992, How to Win a Lost War, 1997; contbr.: book revs. to Nat. Def. Transp. Mag., Time-Life books., Vietnam mag. Decorated D.S.M., Legion of Merit with 4 oak leaf clusters, Bronze Star medal, Joint Services Commendation medal with oak leaf cluster, Army Commendation medal with 2 oak leaf clusters, Sec. of Def. medal for Outstanding Pub. Svc., Italian Cross of War, Knight Order of Crown of Italy, Korean Chung Mu with gold star, Vietnamese Kim Khanh medal 1st class, Vietnamese Army Distinguished Service Order 1st class, Vietnamese Navy Distinguished Service Order 1st class, Vietnamese Air Force Distinguished Service Order 1st class, Vietnamese Gallantry Cross with palm, 1998, US Army Transportation Corps Hall of Fame. Mem. Spl. Forces Assn., Nat. Def. Transp. Assn., Army War Coll. Grad. Assn., Army and Navy Club, WWII Meml. Soc. (charter).

MURRAY, JOHN MICHAEL, lawyer; b. Birmingham, Ala., Aug. 20, 1946; s. Leon Benton and Zena (Griffith) M.; m. Dona Pounds, Aug. 24, 1968 (div. 1979); m. Nancy Simon, Apr. 11, 1986 (div. 2000). BS in Aviation Mgmt., Auburn U., 1968; JD, Memphis State U., 1972. Bar: Fla. 1973, U.S. Dist. Ct. (so. dist.) Fla. 1973, U.S. Dist. Ct. (mid. dist.) Fla. 1978, U.S. Dist. Ct. (no. dist.) Fla. 1983, U.S. Dist. Ct. (mid. dist.) Ala. 1999, U.S. Dist. Ct. (so. dist.) Ala. 2003, U.S. Ct. Appeals (5th cir.) 1973, U.S. Ct. Appeals (11th cir.) 1981, U.S. Supreme Ct. 1976; bd. cert. trial lawyer, aviation lawyer. Airport planner R. Dixon Speas Assocs., Manhasset, N.Y., 1968-70; assoc., ptnr. Walton Lantaff Schroeder & Carson, Miami, Fla., 1973-81; ptnr. Thornton David & Murray, P.A., Miami, 1981-2000, Murray, Marin & Herman, P.A., Tampa, Fla., 2000—. Mem. Fla. Bar, Ala. State Bar. Office: Murray Marin & Herman PA 101 E Kennedy Blvd Ste 1810 Tampa FL 33602 E-mail: jmurray@mmhlaw.com.

MURRAY, JOHN PATRICK, psychologist, educator, researcher; b. Cleve., Sept. 14, 1943; s. John Augustine and Helen Marie (Lynch) M.; m. Ann Coke Dennison, Apr. 17, 1971; children: Jonathan Coke, Ian Patrick. PhD, Cath. U. Am., 1970. Rsch. dir. Office U.S. Surgeon Gen. NIMH, Bethesda, Md., 1969-72; asst. to assoc. prof. psychology Macquarie U., Sydney, Australia, 1973-79; vis. assoc. prof. U. Mich., Ann Arbor, 1979-80; dir. youth and family policy Boys Town Ctr., Boys Town, Nebr., 1980-85; prof., dir. Sch. Family Studies and Human Svcs. Kans. State U., Manhattan, 1985-98, interim assoc. vice provost rsch., 1998—2000, disting. prof., 2003—. Scholar-in-residence Mind Sci. Found., San Antonio, 1996-97; mem. children's TV com. CBS, 1996-99. Author: Television and Youth: 25 Years of Research and Controversy, 1980, The Future of Children's TV, 1984, (with H.T. Rubin) Status Offenders: A Sourcebook, 1983, (with E.A. Rubenstein, G.A. Comstock) Television and Social Behavior, 3 vols., 1972, (with A. Huston and others) Big World, Small Screen: The Role of Television in American Society, 1992, (with C. Fisher and others) Applied Developmental Science, 1996, Children and Television: 50 Years of Research (with N. Pecora and E. Wartella), 2004; contbr. numerous articles to profl. jours. Mem. Nebr. Foster Care Rev. Bd., 1982-84; mem. Advocacy Office for Children and Youth, 1980-85; mem. Nat. Coun. Children and TV, 1982-87; trustee The Villages Children's Homes, 1986—, Menninger Found., 1996—; mem. children's TV adv. bd. CBS-TV, 1996-99. Fellow Am. Psychol. Assn. (pres. div. child youth and family svcs. 1990); mem. Internat. Comm. Assn., Soc. Rsch. in Child Devel., Royal Commonwealth Soc. (London), Manhattan Country Club. Home: 1731 Humboldt St Manhattan KS 66502-4140 Office: Kans State U Office Vice Provost Rsch 101 Fairchild Hall Manhattan KS 66506-1100 Office Phone: 785-532-1456. E-mail: jpm@ksu.edu.

MURRAY, JOHN WILLIAM, JR., writer, legal investigator; b. Apr. 8, 1934; s. John William and Frances (Bryan) M.; m. Norma Sousa, Oct. 30, 1959 (div. Apr. 1989); children: John William III, James Patrick, Jeffrey Dean, Jerome Bryan, Jay Joseph. BS, U. Hartford, 1968; MBA, U. Conn., 1971. Cert. fraud examiner, legal investigator, criminal def. investigator. Legal investigator, Dallas, 1974—. Author: Accident Investigation in the Private Sector, 1994 (Best New Investigative Book of Yr., 1994), Accident Investigation in the Private Sector, vol. 2, 1997, Accident Investigation in the Private Sector, vol. 3, 2003 (Internat. Writer of Yr., 2003), Forensic Photography in the Private Sector, 1995, Sex Crimes, 1995, Photographing Vehicles for Litigation, 1995, Guide to Depositions and Trials for Police Officer and Accident Reconstructionists, 1999, Guide to the Internet for Accident Investigators, 2001. 1st lt. USMC, 1957-60. Named One of Top 5 Investigators in Am. PI Mag., 1998, One of Top 25 Investigators of the Century, Nat. Assn. Investigative Specialists. Mem. Nat. Assn. Legal Investigators (cert., chmn. nat. cert. 1987-89, nat. chmn. editor-pub. awards com. 1992-96, regional dir. 1999-2000, Editor-Pub. award Legal Investigator mag. 1989, 91, Nat. Dirs. award 1997, Author of Yr. award 2002), Evidence Photographers Internat. Coun., Nat. Assn. Investigative Specialists (cert. expert in investigative photography, expert in accident investigation, Outstanding Spkr. of Yr. award 1995, Lifetime Achievement award 1996, named Author of Yr. 2002), Nat. Acad. for Continuing Edn. (co-founder), North Tex. Pvt. Investigators Assn. (pres. 2000). Avocations: photography, stamp collecting/philately. Office: 3942 Rochelle Dr Dallas TX 75220-1814 E-mail: jwmpi@aol.com.

MURRAY, JOSEPH EDWARD, retired plastic surgeon; b. Milford, Mass., Apr. 1, 1919; s. William Andrew and Mary (DePasquale) Murray; m. Virginia Link, June 2, 1945; children: Virginia, Margaret, Joseph Link, Katharine, Thomas, Richard. AB, Holy Cross Coll., 1940, DSc, 1965; MD, Harvard, 1943; DSc, Rockford (Ill.) Coll., 1966, Roger Williams Coll., 1986; PhD (hon.), Anna Marie Coll., 1993, SUNY, Albany, 1993, U. Suffolk, 1993, Magill U., Montreal, 1996. Diplomate Am. Bd. Surgery, Am. Bd. Plastic Surgery. Chief plastic surgeon Peter Bent Brigham Hosp., Boston, 1951—86; chief plastic surgeon Children's Hosp. Med. Center, Boston, 1972—85; prof. surgery Harvard Med. Sch., 1970—86; ret., 1986. Chmn. Am. Bd. Plastic Surgery, 1969. Maj. M.C. U.S. Army, 1944—47. Recipient Gold medal, Internat. Soc. Surgeons, 1963, Nobel prize for medicine or physiology, 1990, Sabin award, 1994, Lifetime Achievement award, Mass. Med. Soc., 1988. Fellow: AMA, AAAS (hon.), Royal Coll. Surgeons Edinburgh, Royal Coll. Surgeons Ireland, Royal Coll. Surgeons of Eng., Royal Australasian Coll. Surgeons; mem.: NAS, ACS (regent 1970—79, v.p. 1983), Am. Acad. Arts and Scis. (Hon. award 1962), Am. Assn. Plastic Surgeons (pres. 1964—65, Hon. award 1969), Soc. U. Surgeons, Boston Surg. Soc. (pres. 1975), New Eng. Surg. Assn. (pres. 1986—87), Am. Surg. Assn. (v.p. 1979), Harvard Med. Sch. Alumni Coun. (pres. 1984), Tavern Club, Badminton and Tennis Club, Wellesley Country Club, Alpha Omega Alpha. Home: 108 Abbott Rd Wellesley MA 02481-6104

MURRAY, JOSEPH JAMES, JR., zoologist; b. Lexington, Va., Mar. 13, 1930; s. Joseph James and Jane Dickson (Vardell) M.; m. Elizabeth Hickson, Aug. 24, 1957; children: Joseph James III, Alison Joan, William Lister BS, Davidson Coll., 1951; BA, Oxford U., Eng., 1954, MA, 1957, D.Phil., 1962. Instr. biology Washington & Lee U., Lexington, Va., 1956-58; asst. prof. biology U. Va., Charlottesville, 1962-67, assoc. prof., 1967-73, prof., 1973-77, Samuel Miller prof. biology, 1977-98, prof. emeritus, 1998, chmn. dept. biology, 1984-87. Co-dir. Mountain Lake Biol. Sta., Pembroke, Va., 1963-91. Author: Genetic Diversity and Natural Selection, 1972; contbr. articles to profl. jours. Served with U.S. Army, 1955-56 Rhodes scholar, 1951-54 Fellow AAAS, Va. Acad. Sci.; mem. Am. Soc. Naturalists, Genetics Soc. Am., Soc. Study Evolution, Am. Soc. Ichthyologists and Herpetologists, Va. Acad. Sci. (pres. 1986-87), Va. Soc. Ornithology (pres. 1976-79) Avocations: walking, mountain climbing. E-mail: jjm5a@virginia.edu.

MURRAY, JOSEPH WILLIAM, banker; b. Alamosa, Colo., July 20, 1944; s. Joseph A. and Virginia (Wood) M.; m. Helen Hoberg, Jan. 20, 1970; children: Brian, Beth, Meghan. BS in Bus. with hon., U. Colo., 1966; MBA with hon., Northwestern U., 1967. Various positions with Continental Ill. Nat. Bank, Chgo., 1967-82; sr. v.p. AllFirst Bank, Balt., 1982—. Bd. dirs. Politzer & Haney, Clarity Incentive Systems; faculty mem. U. N.C. Exec. Programs on Cash Mgmt., Chapel Hill, 1982—; lectr. cash mgmt.; mem. corp. svcs. commn. Bank Adminstrn. Inst., 1992-94. Assoc. editor: Essentials of Cash Management, 4th edit., 1992, 5th edit., 1995. Pres. Wakefield Improvement Assn., Timonium, Md., 1987, 96, bd. dirs., 1996—; pres. Glen Ellyn (Ill.) Libr., 1978-82, trustee; pres. Glen Ellyn Tennis Assn., 1981, bd. dirs.; bd. trustees, sec. Ctr. Stage, 1987—; bd. dirs., Baltimore Chamber Jazz Soc., 2001. Mem. Treasury Mgmt. Assn. (editl. adv. bd., payments adv. grp., 1999), L'Hirondelle Club (Ruxton, Md.), Beta Gamma Sigma. Avocations: tennis, jazz piano, reading, racewalking. Office: AllFirst Bank PO Box 1596 Baltimore MD 21203-1596

MURRAY, JULIA KAORU (MRS. JOSEPH E. MURRAY), occupational therapist; b. Wahiawa, Oahu, Hawaii, 1934; d. Gijun and Edna Tsuruko (Taba) Funakoshi; m. Joseph Edward Murray, 1961; children: Michael, Susan, Leslie. BA, U. Hawaii, 1956; cert. occupational therapy, U. Puget Sound, 1958. Therapist Inst. Logopedics, Wichita, Kans., 1958; sr. therapist Hawaii State Hosp., Kaneohe, 1959; part-time therapist Centre County Ctr. for Crippled Children and Adults, State College, Pa., 1963; vice chmn. adv. bd. Hosp. Improvement Program East Oreg. State Hosp., Pendleton, 1974; v.p. Ind. Living, Inc., 1976-79; job search instr.; mem. adv. com. Oreg. Ednl. Coordinating Commn., 1979-82; mem. Oreg. Bd. Engring. Examiners, 1979-87; supr., occupational therapist Fairview Tng. Ctr., Salem, Oreg., 1984-94; occupational therapist U.S. Naval Hosp., Okinawa, Japan, 1994-99, Yokosuka, Japan, 1999—. Rep. from Umatilla County Commrs. to Blue Mountain Econ. Devel. Council, 1976-78; mem. Ashland Park and Recreation Bd., 1972-73; vice chmn. adv. bd. LINC, 1978; mem. exec. bd. Liberty-Boone Neighborhood Assn., 1979-83. Mem. Am. Occupational Therapy Assn., Oreg. Occupational Therapy Assn., Hawaii Occupational Therapy Assn. (sec. 1960, LWV (bd. dirs. Pendleton 1974, 77-78, pres. 1975-77; bd. dirs. Oreg. 1979-81, Ashland, Wis., 1967-71, Wis. v.p. 1970). Office: Ednl & Developmental Svcs US Naval Hosp APO AP Tokyo 96326 Japan also: Ednl & Develmntl Intervention Svcs Naval Hosp Yokosuka Japan E-mail: jkfmurray@hotmail.com.

MURRAY, JULIA KILLIN, art history educator; b. Washington, Dec. 14, 1951; d. Heslett Killin and Lucie Clark (Killin) M.; m. Andrew Michael Reschovsky, July 27, 1985; 1 child, Nina Michelle. BA, MA, Yale U., 1974, Princeton U., 1977, PhD, 1981. Researcher Asian art Met. Mus. Art, N.Y.C., 1977-79; mus. specialist Freer Gallery Art, Washington, 1979-83; curator Asian art Harvard U. Art Museums, Cambridge, Mass., 1983-86; vis. prof. Mt. Holyoke Coll., South Hadley, Mass., 1988-89; prof. art history U. Wis., Madison, 1989—. Cons. exhbn. N.C. Mus. Art, Raleigh, 1988-91; curatorial cons. East Asian legal studies Harvard Law Sch., Cambridge, 1988-89; founder, organizer New Eng. East Asian Art History Forum, Cambridge, 1987-89; assoc. Fairbank Ctr. for East Asian Rsch., Harvard U. Author: A Decade of Discovery, 1979, Last of the Mandarins, 1987, Ma Hezhi and the Illustration of the Book of Odes, 1993; art editor Jour. Sung-Yuan Studies, Albany, N.Y., 1986—. Wang Inst. Chinese Studies fellow, Lowell, Mass., 1986-87, Andrew Mellon fellow Met. Mus. Art, N.Y.C., 1979-80. Mem. Coll. Art Assn., Assn. Asian Studies. Avocation: squash. Office: Elvehjem Mus U Wis Dept Art History 800 University Ave Madison WI 53706-1414

MURRAY, KATHLEEN, municipal official; b. Phillipsburg, N.J., Nov. 1, 1960; d. Joseph A. and Joann P. (Sepple) M. BS, Rosemont Coll., 1983. Legis. asst. Office of Anna C. Verna, Phila., 1983-86, aide to fin. com., 1989-94, chief of staff, 1994—; head of circulation Haverford (Pa.) Coll., 1987-88; asst. dir. Outreach Coord. Ctr., Phila., 1988-89. Staff mem. select com. of fiscal stability, Phila., 1992-94; mem. pub. affairs com. Local Emergency Planning Commn., Phila., 1995-98; staff Mayor's Commn. of Phila. Naval Base, 1997; mem. Mayor's Commn. on Homelessness, Phila., 1993-96. Mem. Police Commrs. Gay and Lesbian Liaison Com., 1998—2001; bd. dirs. Southwest Task Force, Inc., Phila., 1983—86, Voyage House Inc., Phila., 1991—96, PrideFest Am., 1998—2001, Pride of Phila. Election Com., 1999—2001, Phila. Housing Devel. Corp., 2001—, Phila. Reinvestment Commn., 2001—, Eighteenth St. Devel. Corp., 2001—. Democrat. Episcopalian. Avocations: tennis, golf, reading, U.S. history. Office: Office of Pres 494 City Hall Philadelphia PA 19107-3201

MURRAY, KATHLEEN ANNE, lawyer; b. LA, Feb. 14, 1946; d. Francis Albert and Dorothy (Thompson) M.; 1 child, Anne Murray Ladd; m. Arthur T. Perkins Jr., June 29, 1991. BA, U. Mich., 1967; JD, Hastings Coll. of Law, 1973. Bar: Calif. 1973, U.S. Dist. Ct. (no. dist.) Calif. 1973, U.S. Ct. Appeals (9th cir.) 1973. Sr. staff atty Child Care Law Ctr., San Francisco, 1979-84, cons. child day care law and regulation, 1984-86; atty Epstein & Harris, San Francisco, 1985-86; gen. counsel Fisher Friedman Assocs., San Francisco, 1986-89; assoc. gen. counsel Calif. State Automobile Assn., San Francisco, 1989-98; sr. counsel Firemen's Fund Ins. Co., San Francisco, 1998—2002; prin. Mercer HR Cons., San Francisco, 2003—. Exec. dir., editl. adv. bd. Parenting Mag., 1985-87; chair Labor and Employment Law Com., Am. Corp. Coun. Assn., 2001-03. Editor: Child Care Center Legal Handbook; Tax Guide for California Child Care Providers; contbr. articles to profl. jours. Mem. adv. coun. Humanities West, Inc., 1986-96; vestry Episcopal Ch. of St. Mary the Virgin, 1990-92; pres. Parents' Assn., Lick-Wilmerding High Sch., 1993-94; Personnel Practices Com. of Episcopal Diocese of Calif., 1998-. Democrat. Episcopalian. Office: Mercer HR Cons Three Embarcadeo Ctr Ste 1500 San Francisco CA 94111-4015 Business E-Mail: kathleen.murray@mercer.com.

MURRAY, KEVIN DENNIS, surgeon; b. Paterson, N.J., June 22, 1953; s. Robert Emmet and Florence Sophie (Nordman) M. BS in Chemistry, Mt. St. Mary's Coll., 1974; MD, U. Md., 1978. Cert. Am. Bd. of Surgery, 1995, Am. Bd. of Thoracic Surgery, 1997. Intern U. Chgo.-Pritzker Med. Sch., 1978-79; resident in surgery U. Chgo.-Pritzker Med. Sch. Hosps. and Clinics, 1979-82; Cardiothor resident Yale-New Haven (Conn.) Hosp.-Yale U. Sch. Medicine, 1984-86; fellow in bioengring. U. Utah, 1982-84; asst. prof. Ohio State U., 1986-93; staff Arthur James Cancer Inst., Columbus, Ohio, 1990-93; staff cardiothoracic surgery Barnes-Jewish Hosp., St. Louis, 1996-97; faculty cardiothoracic surgery Washington U., St. Louis, 1996-97; assoc. prof., chief cardiothoracic surgery U. Nev. Sch. of Medicine, Las Vegas, 1997—2002; chief thoracic surgery So. Nev. VA Sys., 1998—2002; cardiothoracic surgeon Kaiser Permanenti Moanalua Hosp., Honolulu, 2003—. Med. dir. dept. circulation tech. Sch. Allied Health, Ohio State U., 1988-93; cons. Inst. Bioengring., Salt Lake City, 1995—; dir. The Heart and Lung Inst., U. Nev. Sch. Medicine, 1999-2002. Fellow Am. Coll. Surgery, Am. Coll. Cardiology, Am. Coll. Chest Physicians, Internat. Soc. Heart and Lung Transplantation, Soc. Thoracic Surgeons; mem. Am. Soc. Artificial Internal Organs, Assn. Thoracic Surgeons, Alpha Omega Alpha. Home: 1517 Makiki St Honolulu HI 96822 Office: Kaiser Permanente Moanalua Hosp 3288 Moanalua Rd Honolulu HI 96819 Office Phone: 808-432-8354. Business E-Mail: Kevin.D.Murray@KP.org.

MURRAY, LARRY, government agency administrator; b. Stratford, Ont., Can., June 6, 1947; s. William Alexander and Ethel May (Mulholland) M.; children: Wendi, Kimberly, Jeffrey, Sean. BA in History, Carleton U., Ottawa, 1968; Cert., Casn. Forces Staff Coll., 1980. Commd. Can. Forces, advanced through grades to vice admiral., 1993; comdr. can. Destroyer Squadron Maritime Command, Halifax, N.S., 1987-88; dir. gen. maritime doctrine and ops. Nat. Defence Hdqs., Ottawa, 1989-91, assoc. asst. dep. min. policy and comm., 1991-93, dep. chief def. staff, 1993—94, vice chief def. staff, 1995-97; comdr. Maritime Command, Halifax, 1994-95; acting chief def. staff Nat. Defence Hdqrs., Ottawa, 1997; assoc. dep. minister Min. Fisheries and Oceans, Ottawa, Canada, 1997—99, dep. min., 2004—, dep. minister vet. affairs Charlottetown, Canada, 1999—2004. Decorated Can. 125 medal, NATO Spl. Svc. medal, Order of Mil. Merit. Office: Fisheries & Oceans Can 200 Kent St Ottawa ON Canada K1A 0E6*

MURRAY, LAWRENCE, management consultant; b. NYC, May 10, 1939; s. Gilbert and Edna (Blatt) M.; children: Robert, Stacy, David, Daniel, Abigail. BA, Cornell U., 1961; MBA, U. Okla., 1966; PhD, Pacific Western U., 1993. Cert. Pa. Food Mgmt. Account exec. Merrill Lynch, Paramus, NJ, 1965-69; chmn., pres. Murray, Lind & Co., Inc., Jersey City, 1969-72; dir. investor rels. IU Internat. Corp., Phila., 1972-73, dir. spl. projects, 1974-75; dir. fin. comm., mem. exec. staff, chmn. bd. ARA Svcs., Inc., Phila., 1975-78; chmn., chief exec. officer Century Mgmt. and affiliated cos., West Chester, Pa., 1976-82; chmn. bd., CEO Creative Mgmt. Corp., Bala Cynwyd and West Chester, Pa., 1982-87, Fin. Mgmt. Profl. Corp., West Chester, 1983-89; chmn. bd. dirs. Venture Frontiers Co., Denver, 1984-89; chmn. bd., CEO Fin. Intelligence Corp., West Chester, 1989-95; CEO, chmn. bd. dirs. Healthy Living Ctrs., West Chester, 1993—, Tax Dr. Corp., West Chester, 2002—. Lectr. bus. orgn. and mgmt. Bergen C.C., 1971-72; chmn. bd. dirs. Med. Intelligence Corp., West Chester, 1993-95; CEO, chmn. bd. dirs. Miramax Corp.; chmn. bd. dirs., CEO, Tax Doctor Corp., West Chester, 2002-. Author: The Organized Stockbroker, 1970; A New Era in Mergers and Acquisitions, 1974; Communications: Management's Newest Marketing Skill, 1976, Powerful Tax-Saving Strategies for Honest People, 1992, Teach Your Children How to Eat Properly and Add 20 Years to Their Lives, 1999; contbr. articles to profl. jours. Pres., Congregation Beth Israel, Media, Pa., 1977-78, Parents Without Ptnrs., Valley Forge, Pa., 1982-83; v.p. Cornell U. Class of 1961, 1981-86; mem. White House Conf. on Bus. Ethics in Am., 1986; active Beth Chaim Reform Synagogue. Served to 1st lt. arty./intelligence, U.S. Army, 1963-64. Decorated U.S. Army Commendation medal. Mem. Nat. Investor Rels. Inst. (pres. Phila. chpt. 1976-78), Internat. Coun. Shopping Ctrs., Am. Health Info. Mgmt. Assn., C. of C. Greater West Chester. Home: 924 Hollyview Ln West Chester PA 19380-1376 E-mail: lmurray761@aol.com.

MURRAY, LOWELL, Canadian senator; b. New Waterford, N.S., Can., Sept. 26, 1936; s. Daniel and Evelyn (Young) M.; m. Colleen Elaine MacDonald; children: William, Colin. BA, St. Francis Xavier U., Antigonish, N.S., Can.; MA in Pub. Adminstrn., Queen's U., Kingston, Ont., Can. Chief of staff Minister of Justice and Minister of Pub. Works Can., Ottawa, Ont., Senator M. Wallace McCutcheon, Ottawa, Ont.; leader of opposition Can., Ottawa, Ont.; dep. minister Premier N.B. (Can.); mem. Senate of Can., Ottawa, Ont., 1979—, co-chmn. joint Senate-House of Commons com. ofcl. langs., 1980-84, chmn. standing Senate com. on banking, trade and commerce, 1984-86, chmn. standing senate com. on nat. fin., 1995, 99—, chmn. standing senate com. on social affairs, sci. and tech., 1997-99. Bd. dirs. SONY Can. Inc.; trustee Inst. Rsch. Pub. Policy, 1984-86, mem. Trilateral Commn., 1985-86. Sworn of the privy coun., appointed leader of Govt. in the Senate, 1986—93; Min. of State Fed.-Provincial Rels., 1986—91; min. responsible for Atlantic Can. Opportunities Agy., 1987—88, acting min. comms., 1988—89; nat. campaign chmn. gen. election Progressive Conservative Party Can., 1977—79, 1981—83. Progressive Conservative. Roman Catholic. Office: The Senate Ottawa ON Canada K1A 0A4

MURRAY, MICHAEL DENNIS, pharmacist; b. Blairsville, Pa., Apr. 13, 1952; s. Howard Jacob and Elizabeth Murray; m. Jennifer Jayne Chumbler, Aug. 4, 1979; children: Ryan Michael, Kristin Elizabeth. BSc in Pharmacy, Duquesne U., 1975, D of Pharmacy, 1977; M of Pub. Health, Ind. U., 1992. Registered pharmacist, Ind., Pa. Asst. prof. Purdue U. Sch. of Pharmacy, West Lafayette, Ind., 1982-88, assoc. prof., 1988-99, prof., 1999—2001, Bucke prof. pharmacy, 2002—. Adj. asst. prof. Purdue U. Sch. of Pharmacy, West Lafayette, 1977—82; adj. assoc. prof. Ind. U. Sch. Medicine, 1992—2001, adj. prof., 2001—; dir. rsch. Ind. Drug Evaluation and Analysis Ctr., Indpls., 1995—98; faculty Health Svcs. R&D, Indpls., 1995—98; dir. healthcare data and epidemiology Regenstrief Inst., Indpls., 1996—; faculty scholar Purdue U., 1999. Commr. Saints Football Club, Lawrence, Ind., 1996-97; v.p. Ind. Soccer League, Carmel, Ind., 1996-97. Fellow: Internat. Soc. Pharmacoepiemiology (sci. programs 1989—2004, membership chair 1990—93, bd. dirs. 1991—94); mem.: U.S. Pharmacopia (safe medicine use and therapeutic decision expert panels 2000—), Am. Soc. Clin. Pharmacology and therapeutics (pharmacoepidemiology chair 1998—2001, chair com. on coordination of sci. sects. 2001—04, bd. dirs.). Democrat. Roman Catholic. Avocations: stained glass crafts, arts, hiking, bicycling. Home: 3526 Stonegate Dr Chapel Hill NC 27516 Office: U NC Campus Box 7360 205-R Beard Hall Chapel Hill NC 27599-7360 E-mail: mick@unc.edu.

MURRAY, MICHAEL J. bank executive; b. Dubuque, Iowa, June 23, 1944; m. Christine Scribner; children: Sarah, David. BBA, U. Notre Dame, 1966; MBA, U. Wis., 1968. V.p. in charge east coast regional offices Continental Bank, Chgo., 1981-84, v.p., 1981-84, sr. v.p., 1984-85, exec. v.p., 1985—; pres. global corp. investment banking Bank of Am., San Francisco. Mem. devel. bd. subcom. export fin. Ill. Dept. Commerce and Community Affairs, Chgo., 1984; chmn. employee campaign United Way Chgo., 1986; bd. dirs. Chgo. Maternity Ctr., Northwestern Meml. Hosp., 1987—. Mem.: Chgo., Bankers of Chgo., Econ. of Chgo.; Sky (N.Y.C.). Roman Catholic. Office: Bank of America 555 California St San Francisco CA 94104-1590

MURRAY, PATRICIA, electronics company executive; b. Detroit; BA, Michigan St. U.; BS, St. Louis U.; JD, U. Mich., 1986. Employment litigator Morrison & Foerster, Palo Alto, Calif., until 1990; atty. human resource's legal staff Intel Corp., 1990-91, mgr. human resoure's legal staff, 1992-95, dir., v.p. human resources, 1996—, sr. v.p., 1997—. Office: Intel Corp PO Box 58119 2200 Mission College Blvd Santa Clara CA 95052-8119 E-mail: patricia.murray@intel.com.

MURRAY, PATRICK M. oilfield service company executive; b. New Malden, Surrey, Eng., Nov. 11, 1942; came to U.S., 1948; s. Thomas I. and Kathleen (McWeeney) M.; m. Mary Ann Pfaff, May 4, 1968; 1 child, Suzanne J. BS in Acctg., MBA, Seton Hall U. Project mgr. NL Industries, Inc., Hightstown, N.J., 1974-75, applications mgr., 1975-76; asst. controller NL Metals Corp., Hightstown, N.J., 1976-79, Shaffer div. NL Corp., Houston, 1980-81; controller Atlas Bradford div. NL Corp., Houston, 1981-82; pres. Sperry Sun Drilling Svcs., Houston, 1988—97; sr. v.p. strategic initiatives Dresser, Inc., Addison, Tex., 1994—98, CEO, 2001—. Bd. dirs. Russell Attitude Systems, Cheltonham, Eng. Served to 1st lt. U.S. Army, 1964-66. Roman Catholic. Avocations: tennis, golf, reading. Office: Dresser Inc Ste 1100 15455 Dallas Parkway Addison TX 75001

MURRAY, PATRICK ROBERT, microbiologist, educator; b. L.A., Jan. 15, 1948; married, 1970; 3 children. BS, St. Mary's Coll., Calif., 1969; MS, U. Calif., L.A., 1972, PhD in Microbiology, 1974. Rsch. fellow clinical microbiology Mayo Clinic & Mayo Found., 1974-76; asst. prof. medicine Wash. U. Sch. Med., 1976-82, assoc. dir., 1976; dir. clinical microbiology Barnes Hosp., St. Louis, 1977—, dir. postdoctoral training program, 1982—; assoc. prof. medicine Wash. U. Sch. Medicine, 1983—. Cons. St. Luke's Hosp., 1985—; mem. Nat. Com. Clinical Lab. Standards, 1980—; chmn. exam com. Am. Bd. Medical Microbiologist, 1982—, mem. joint standards and exam com., 1985—; bd. dirs. Southwestern Assn. Clinical Microbiologist; chmn. Clinical Microbiologist Divsn. Am. Soc. Microbiologist. Becton Dickinson Co. Clinical Microbiology award Am. Soc. Microbiology, 1993. Fellow Am. Acad. Med. Microbiologist, Infectious Disease Soc; mem. Am. Assn. Pathologist, Am. Soc. Microbiologist, Med. Mycol Soc. Am., Am. Federation Clinical Rsch., Sigma Xi. Achievements include research in new diagnostic and therapeutic tests for clinical microbiology. Office: Washington Univ Div of Lab Medicine 660 S Euclid Ave Saint Louis MO 63110-1093

MURRAY, PATTY, senator; b. Bothell, Wash., Oct. 10, 1950; d. David L. and Beverly A. (McLaughlin) Johns; m. Robert R. Murray, June 2, 1972; children: Randy P., Sara A. BA, Wash. State U., 1972. Sec. various cos., Seattle, 1972-76; citizen lobbyist various ednl. groups, Seattle, 1983-88; legis. lobbyist Orgn. for Parent Edn., Seattle, 1977-84; instr. Shoreline Community Coll., Seattle, 1984-88; mem. Wash. State Senate, Seattle, 1989-92; U.S. senator from Wash., 1993—. Mem. Appropriations Com. ranking minority mem. subcom. mil. constrn.; vice chmn. Dem. Senatorial Campaign Com.; mem. Com. on Labor and Human Resources, Budget Com., Health, Edn., Labor and Pensions Com., Com. on Vets. Affairs. Mem. bd. Shoreline Sch., Seattle, 1985-89; mem. steering com. Demonstration for Edn., Seattle, 1987; founder, chmn. Orgn. for Parent Edn., Wash., 1981-85; lst Congl. rep. Wash. Women United, 1983-85. Recipient Recognition of Svc. to Children award Shoreline PTA Coun., 1986, Golden Acorn Svc. award, 1989; Outstanding Svc. award Wash. Women United, 1986, Outstanding Svc. to Pub. Edn. award Citizens Ednl. Ctr. NW, Seattle, 1987. Democrat. Office: US Senate 173 Russell Senate Office Bldg Washington DC 20510-0001

MURRAY, PETER, metallurgist, manufacturing company executive; b. Rotherham, Yorkshire, Eng., Mar. 13, 1920; came to U.S., 1967, naturalized, 1974; s. Michael and Ann (Hamstead) M.; m. Frances Josephine Glaisher, Sept. 8, 1947; children: Jane, Paul, Alexander. BSc in Chemistry with honors, Sheffield (Eng.) U., 1941, postgrad., 1946-49; PhD in Metallurgy, Brit. Iron and Steel Research Bursar, Sheffield, 1948. Research chemist Steetley Co., Ltd., Worksop, Notts, Eng., 1941-45; with Atomic Energy Research Establishment, Harwell, Eng., 1949-67, head div. metallurgy, 1960-64, asst. dir., 1964-67; tech. dir., mgr. fuels and materials, advanced reactors div. Westinghouse Electric Corp., Madison, Pa., 1967-74; dir. research Westinghouse Electric Europe (S.A.), Brussels, 1974-75; chief scientist advanced power systems divs. Westinghouse Electric Corp., Madison, Pa., 1975-81, dir. nuclear programs Washington, 1981-92; sr. cons. Nuc. Programs, 1992—2001. Mem. divisional rev. coms. Argonne Nat. Lab., 1968-73; Mellor Meml. lectr. Inst. Ceramics, 1963 Contbr. numerous articles to profl. jours.; editorial adv. bd.: Jour. Less Common Metals, 1968—. Recipient Holland Meml. Research prize Sheffield U., 1949 Fellow Royal Inst. Chemistry (Newton Chambers Research prize 1954), Inst. Ceramics, Am. Nuclear Soc.; mem. Brit. Ceramics Soc. (pres. 1965), Am. Ceramic Soc., Nat. Acad. Engring. Roman Catholic. Home: 20308 Canby Ct Montgomery Village MD 20886-4014

MURRAY, PETER CARLISLE, historian, educator; b. Orangeburg, S.C., Oct. 20, 1953; s. John Vincent Murray and Sara King Fridy Murray Purser, David Purser (Stepfather); m. Mary Cathryn Murray, Sept. 16, 1950; children: Nathaniel Carlisle, Adam Scott. PhD, Ind. U., 1985. Asst. prof. Ind. State U., Terre Haute, 1985—88; prof. Meth. Coll., Fayetteville, NC, 1988—. Author: (book) Methodists and the Crucible of Race, 1930-1975, 2004. Adult leader Boy Scouts of Am., Fayetteville, NC, 1994—2004, United Meth. Ch., Fayetteville, NC, 1999—2004. Fellow Cultural Exch., Rotary Internat., 1996. Mem.: Orgn. of Am. Historians. Methodist. Avocations: racquetball, golf, camping. Office: Methodist College Dept History 5400 Ramsey St Fayetteville NC 28311 Office Phone: 910-630-7075. Office Fax: 910-630-7679. E-mail: pcmurray@methodist.edu.

MURRAY, RAYMOND LEE, retired clothing designer, writer; b. Decatur, Tenn., July 27, 1920; s. Floyd Lester and Ida Mae (McClure) M.; m. Melba Lee Murray, Dec. 21, 1947; 1 child, Alice Marie. Cert. indsl. engring., U. Tenn., 1946; cert. clothing designer, Am. Gentlemen Sch. Design, N.Y.C., 1947. Foreman, designer Hardwick Clothes, Cleveland, Tenn., 1938-55; designer Sears Roebuck Plant, Rutherford, Tenn., 1956-59; designer, plant mgr. McGregor Sportswear, Corinth, Miss., 1960-67; plant mgr. Cable Industries, Tuskegee, Ala., 1968-69; gen. mgr. T&W Mfg. Co., Bremen, Ga., 1969; mem. R&D staff Hardwick Clothes, Cleveland, Tenn., 1970-86; pres. Murray-Wright Protection Clothing, Cleveland, Tenn., 1985-95. Cons. textiles and bullet-proof fabric Murray Textile Anaylsts, Cleveland, Tenn., 1985-95. Author: Grandpa Saw it Happen WWII Normandy Beach, To Elbe, 1993, How We Uprooted Our Roots and What We Found, 1996, Bradley Divided: During Civil War, 1992, contbr. articles to profl. jours. Bd. dirs. ARC, Cleveland chpt., 1980-83, Cleveland YMCA, 1950-54. With U.S. Army, ETO. Decorated 5 Bronze Stars. Mem. VFW, Internat. Assn. Clothing Designers (pres. 1977; pres. So. chpt. 1972), Am. Soc. Quality Control (chair Tenn. chpt. 1952), Am. Legion, Elks, Vets. Battle of the Bulge, Kiwanis. Presbyterian. Avocations: fishing, hunting. Home: 102 Ridley Howard Ct Decatur GA 30030-2374 E-mail: raymurray102@mac.com.

MURRAY, RICHARD BENNETT, physics educator; b. Marietta, Ga., Dec. 5, 1928; s. William Moore and Ruth (Mozley) M.; m. Clella Bay, Apr. 1, 1956; children: Ada, Annette. BA, Emory U., 1947; MS, Ohio State U., 1950; PhD, U. Tenn., 1955. Rsch. asst. Gaseous Diffusion Plant, Oak Ridge, Tenn., 1947-48; rsch. physicist Oak Ridge Nat. Lab., 1955-66; vis. assoc. prof. physics U. Del, Newark, 1962-63, assoc. prof., 1966-69, prof., 1969-98, prof. emeritus, 1999—, acting chmn. dept. physics, 1975-76, univ. coord. for grad. studies, 1979-85, assoc. provost grad. studies, 1986-88, acting provost, v.p. acad. affairs, 1988-91, provost, 1993-94. Lectr. physics U. Tenn., Knoxville, 1963-66; vis. rsch. physicist U.S. Naval Rsch. Lab., 1991-92; vis. scientist Clarendon Lab., Oxford U., 1992; cons. to industry, 1957-93; councillor Oak Ridge Associated Univs., 1979-88, bd. dirs., 1983-94, vice chmn. coun., 1983-85, chmn. coun., 1985-88; sec.-treas. NE Assn. Grad. Schs., 1982-84; dir. U. Del. Press, 1979-82. Contbr. numerous articles on exptl. nuclear and solid state physics to profl. publs., 1948-85. Trustee Sanford Sch., Hockessin, Del., 1981-85; chmn. bd. dirs. Oak Ridge Associated Univs. Found., 1989-94; bd. dirs. Del. Inst. for Med. Edn. and Rsch., 1989-91. Predoctoral fellow Oak Ridge Inst. Nuclear Studies, 1953-55; grantee AEC, NSF, Dept. Energy, 1967-84. Fellow AAAS, Am. Phys. Soc.; mem. Southeastern Univs. Rsch. Assn. (bd. dirs. 1989-97), Phi Beta Kappa, Sigma Xi, Sigma Pi Sigma, Phi Kappa Phi, Cosmos Club. Home: 4 Bridlebrook Ln Newark DE 19711-2058 Office: U Del Dept Physics & Astronomy Newark DE 19716 E-mail: rmurray@udel.edu.

MURRAY, RICHARD MAXIMILIAN, insurance executive; b. Vienna, Nov. 21, 1922; came to U.S., 1955, naturalized, 1961; s. and Elizabeth Helen Peiker. Grad. in world commerce studies, U. Vienna; postgrad., Columbia U. Asst. sec. Sterling Offices Ltd. (reins. intermediaries), London, Toronto, N.Y.C., 1951-59; v.p. Guy Carpenter, Inc. (reins. intermediaries), N.Y.C., 1959-68, Travelers Ins. Cos., 1968-87, ret., 1987. Mng. dir. La Metropole Ins. Co., Brussels, ret., 1987; chmn. bd. Nippon Mgmt. Corp., N.Y.C., ret., 1991; chmn. bd. Travelers Marine Corp., ret., 1987; pres. Travelers Reins Co. Bermuda Ltd., ret., 1987; pres. Travelers of Asia Ltd., Hong Kong, ret., 1987; vice-chmn. bd. La Prov Corp., N.Y.C.; bd. electors Ins. Hall of Fame; bd. dirs. United Am. Inst. Co., United Am. Holdings Co., Inc.; mem. adv. bd. Firemark Global Ins. Fund, L.P.; dir. emeritus Davis Internat. Total Return Fund.; guest prof. Donau U., Krems, Austria. Contbr. articles to profl. publs. Decorated for promotion of pvt. ins. (Peru); Knight Order of St. John, Knights of Malta (ambassador at large). Mem. Internat. Ins. Coun. (chmn. 1979-81, award 1990). Home: 60 Remsen St Apt 10C Brooklyn NY 11201-3453 Office: 1 Penn Plz Ste 3600 New York NY 10119-2108

MURRAY, ROBERT FULTON, JR., physician; b. Newburgh, N.Y., Oct. 19, 1931; s. Robert Fulton and Henrietta Frances (Judd) Murray; m. Isobel Ann Parks, Aug. 26, 1956; children: Conin Charles(dec.), Robert Fulton III, Suzanne Frances, Dianne Akwe. BS, Union Coll., Schenectady, 1953; MD, U. Rochester, N.Y., 1958; MS, U. Wash., Seattle, 1968. Diplomate Am. Bd. Internal Medicine, Am. Bd. Med. Genetics. Intern Denver Gen. Hosp., 1958—59; resident in internal medicine U. Colo. Med. Ctr., 1959—62; staff investigator (service with USPHS) Nat. Inst. Arthritis and Metabolic Diseases, NIH, Bethesda, Md., 1962—65; NIH spl. fellow med. genetics U. Wash., 1965—67; faculty Howard U. Coll. Medicine, Washington, 1967—74, prof. pediatrics and medicine, 1974—, grad. prof., 1976, prof. oncology, 1976, chief divsn. med. genetics, 1968—; chmn. dept. genetics and human genetics Howard U. Coll. Medicine Grad. Sch., 1976—. Nat. adv. gen. med. scis. coun. NIH, 1971—75, recombinant DNA adv. com., 1988—92; ethics adv. bd. to sec. HEW, 1978—80; chmn. Washington Mayor's Adv. Com. on Metabolic Disorders, 1980—89; mem. Med. Com. Human Rights. Co-author: Genetic Variation and Disorders in Peoples of African Origin, 1990; co-editor: Genetic, Metabolic and Developmental Aspects of Mental Retardation, 1972, Genetic Counseling: Facts, Values and Norms, 1979, The Human Genome Project and the Future of Health Care, 1996; mem. editl. bd.: Am. Jour. Clin. Genetics, 1977—93, Ency. Bioethics, 1975—77, 1993—95, Jour. Clin. Ethics, 1990. Sci. adv. bd. Nat. Sickle Cell Anemia Found.; trustee Union Coll., 1972—80. Fellow Rotary Found. fellow, 1955—56; grantee Rsch. grantee, NIH, 1969—75. Fellow: AAAS, ACP, Am. Coll. Med. Genetics, Inst. Soc., Ethics and Life Scis., Inst. Medicine; mem.: Acad. Medicine Washington, Genetics Soc. Am., Am. Soc. Human Genetics, Assn. Acad. Minority Physicians, AAUP, Neighbors Inc. D.C., Alpha Omega Alpha, Sigma Xi. Unitarian Universalist. Home: 510 Aspen St NW Washington DC 20012-2740 Office: Howard U Coll Medicine PO Box 75 Washington DC 20059-0001

MURRAY, ROBERT GRAY, sculptor; b. Vancouver, B.C., Can., Mar. 2, 1936; U.S. citizen; s. John Gray and Vera (Meakin) M.; m. Cintra Wetherill Lofting, Jan. 23, 1971; children: Rebecca and Megan (twins), Claire, Hillary. Student, U. Sask., Can., 1956-58. One man shows Betty Parsons Gallery, N.Y.C., 1965, 66, 68, David Mirvish Gallery, Toronto, 1967, 68, 72, 73, 74, 75, Jewish Mus., N.Y.C., 1967, Hammarskjold Plaza, N.Y.C., 1971, Paula Cooper Gallery, N.Y.C., 1974, Janie Lee Gallery, Houston, 1977, Hamilton Gallery, N.Y.C., 1977, 79, 80, Klonaridis Inc., Toronto, 1979, 81, 82, Rice U., 1978, Dayton Mus., 1979, Columbus Mus., 1979, Lamont Gallery, Phillips Acad., Exeter, N.H., 1983, Art Gallery Greater Victoria, 1983, Gallery One, Toronto, 1985, Culturale Canadese Roma, 1985, Gallery 291, Atlanta, 1986, Richard Greene Gallery, N.Y.C.,1986, L.A., 1987, Del. Art Mus., Wilmington, 1990, Muhlenberg Coll., Allentown, Pa., 1992, Mira Godard Gallery, Toronto, Reading (Pa.) Pub. Mus., 1994, 96, Andre Zarre Gallery, N.Y.C., 1994, spl. showing Hillary Ground for Sculpture, Trenton N.J., 1997, Moore Gallery, Toronto, 1999, 2001, 03, Ericson Gallery, Phila., 1999, McLaren Gallery, Barrie, 2001, retrospective, Grounds for Sculpture, Trenton, 1997, Nat. Gallery of Can., Ottawa, 1999, Winchester Galleries, Victoria, 2004, Freedman Gallery, Reading, 2004, Andre Zarre Gallery, N.Y.C., 2004; exhibited in group shows at Whitney Mus. 1996— Am., Art, N.Y.C., 1964-66, Tibor de Nagy Gallery, N.Y.C., 1965, Musée cantonal des Beaux Arts, Lausanne, Switzerland, 1966, World House Gallery, N.Y.C., 1966, Betty Parsons Gallery, 1966, Sch. Visual Arts, N.Y.C., 1967, Los Angeles County Mus., 1967, Nat. Gallery Can., Toronto, 1967, Inst. Contemporary Art, Boston, 1967, U. Toronto, 1967, Guggenheim Mus., N.Y.C., 1967, Inst. Torcuato Di Tella, Buenos Aires, 1967, Musée d'Art Moderne, Paris, 1968, Whitney Mus., 1967, Walker Art Gallery, 1969, X Sao Paulo Biennial, Brazil, 1969, Boston City Hall, 1971, Artist and Fabricator, Amherst, Mass., 1975, Met. Mus., N.Y.C., 1983, Del. Art Mus., 1990, GrandRapids (Mich.) Mus., 1994; represented in permanent collections, Montreal Mus. Fine Arts, Nat. Gallery Can., Joseph Hirshhorn Collection, Art Gallery Ont., Larry Aldrich Mus., Ridgefield, Conn., New Brunswick Mus., Whitney Mus. Am. Art, Met. Mus., N.Y.C., Columbus Mus., Dayton Art Inst., Storm King Art Centre, Del. Art. Mus., Wilmington, Muhlenberg Coll., Allentown, Pa., others; major commns. include, Everson Mus., Syracuse, N.Y., Fredonia (N.Y.) State Coll., Canadian Dept. External Affairs, Ottawa, Ont., U. Mass., U. Toronto, Ont., State Mus., Juneau, Alaska, Honeywell Corp., Mpls., CNIB, Toronto, also others. Decorated Order of Can. Fax: 610-869-4403. Office Phone: 610-869-4636. E-mail: rmurray601@earthlink.net.

MURRAY, ROBERT JOHN, think-tank executive; Grad., Suffolk Coll., Harvard U. Under sec. Navy U.S. Govt., dep. asst. sec. defense, asst. to the sec., dep. sec. defense; pol. mil. attaché Am. Embassy, London; dean Naval War Coll., 1981-83; dir. Ctr. Naval Warfare Studies, 1981-83; mem. faculty, dir. nat. security program John F. Kennedy Sch. Govt. Harvard U., 1983-90; pres., CEO, trustee CNA Corp., 1990—. Pres. Ctr. Naval Analyses; mem. bd. advisors Naval War Coll., Nat. War Coll., Washington. Served USMC. Recipient numerous awards for pub. svc. Fellow Nat. Inst. Pub. Affairs; mem. Internat. Inst. Strategic Studies, In and Out Club (London). Office: CNA Corp 4401 Ford Ave Alexandria VA 22302-1432

MURRAY, ROBERT WALLACE, chemistry professor; b. Brockton, Mass., June 20, 1928; s. Wallace James and Rose Elizabeth (Harper) M.; m. Claire K. Murphy, June 10, 1951; children: Kathleen A., Lynn E., Robert Wallace, Elizabeth A., Daniel J., William M., Padraic O'D. AB, Brown U., 1951; MA, Wesleyan U., Middletown, Conn., 1956; PhD, Yale U., 1960. Mem. tech. staff Bell Labs., Murray Hill, N.J., 1959-68; prof. chemistry U. Mo., St. Louis, 1968-81, chmn. dept., 1975-80, Curators' prof., 1981-2000, Curators' prof. emeritus, 2001—. Vis. prof. Engler-Bunte Inst. U. Karlsruhe, Fed. Republic Germany, 1982, dept. chemistry Univ. Coll., Cork, Ireland, 1989; cons. to govt. and industry. Co-editor: Singlet Oxygen, 1979; contbr. articles to profl. jours. Mem. Warren (N.J.) Twp. Com., 1962-63, mayor, 1963; mem. Planning Com. and Bd. Health, 1962-64, Bd. Edn., 1966-68. Served with USN, 1951-54; Lt. comdr. USNR. Grantee EPA, NSF, NIH, Office of Naval Research. Fellow AAAS, Am. Inst. Chemists, N.Y. Acad. Scis.; mem. Am. Soc. Photobiology, Am. Chem. Soc., The Oxygen Soc., Sigma Xi. Home: 1810 Walnutway Dr Saint Louis MO 63146-3659 Office: Univ Mo Dept Chemistry Saint Louis MO 63121

MURRAY, RUSSELL, II, aeronautical engineer, security consultant; b. Woodmere, N.Y., Dec. 5, 1925; s. Herman Stump and Susanne Elizabeth (Warren) M.; m. Sally Tingue Gardiner, May 22, 1954; children: Ann Tingue, Prudence Warren, Alexandria Gardiner. BS in Aero. Engring, MIT, 1949, MS, 1950. Guided missile flight test engr. Grumman Aircraft Engring. Corp., Bethpage, N.Y., 1950-53, asst. chief operations analysis, 1953-62; prin. dep. asst. sec. of def. for systems analysis The Pentagon, Washington, 1962-69; dir. long range planning Pfizer Internat., N.Y.C., 1969-73; dir. review Center for Naval Analyses, Arlington, Va., 1973-77; asst. sec. of def. for program analysis and evaluation Dept. of Def., The Pentagon, Washington, 1977-81; prin. Systems Research & Applications Corp., Arlington, Va., 1981-85; spl. counsellor Com. on Armed Services U.S. Ho. of Reps., 1985-89, nat. security cons., 1989—. Served with USAAF, 1944-45. Recipient Sec. of Def. Medal for meritorious civilian service, 1968; Disting. Public Service medal Dept. Def., 1981 Home: 210 Wilkes St Alexandria VA 22314-3839

MURRAY, SABINA, writer; BA, Mt. Holyoke Coll., Mass.; MA, U. of Tex. Writer-in-residence Phillips Acad., Andover, Mass., 2000—. Tchr. creative fiction and poetry. Author: (novels) Slow Burn, The Caprices, 2002 (PEN/Faulkner award for fiction, 2003), A Carnivore's Inquiry, 2004. Address: Sabina Murray c/o Houghton Mifflin Co Trade Divsn Adult Editl 8th Fl 222 Berkeley St Boston MA 02116-3764 Office: Phillips Acad 180 Main St Andover MA 01810 E-mail: smurray@andover.edu.*

MURRAY, STEPHEN JAMES, lawyer; b. Phila., Jan. 27, 1943; s. Paul Martin and Hannah (Smith) M.; m. Linda Sanders, June 20, 1970; children: Gordon Joshua, Cara Sanders. AB cum laude, Brown U., 1963; JD, Harvard U., 1966; LLM, George Washington U., 1967. Bar: N.Y. 1968, U.S. Ct. Appeals (2nd cir.) 1971, U.S. Ct. Appeals (fed. cir.) 1998, U.S. Dist. Ct. (so. and ea. dists.) N.Y. 1972, U.S. Ct. Claims 1974, U.S. Supreme Ct. 1975, Conn. 1988, U.S. Dist. Ct. Conn. 1988, U.S. Ct. Internat. Trade 1998. Spl. asst. SEC, Washington, 1966-67, Maritime Adminstrn., Washington, 1967-68; assoc. Hill, Betts & Nash, N.Y.C., 1970-76; transp. atty. Union Carbide Corp., N.Y.C., 1976-78, sr. transp. atty., 1978-85, chief transp. counsel Danbury, Conn., 1985—2001, group counsel, 1986—2001, chief real estate counsel, 1992—2001, comml. counsel, 1993—2001, customs and internat. trade counsel, 1997—2001; of counsel Mahoney & Keane, New York City, 2001—. Spkr. in field. Contbr. articles to profl. jours. Lt. JAGC, USN, 1968-70. Mem. ABA, Conn. State Bar Assn., U.S. Naval Inst., Navy League of U.S., Maritime Law Assn., U.S. Transp. Lawyers Assn., N.Y. State Bar Assn., Am. Corp. Counsel Assn. (co-chair real estate com. Westchester-So. Conn. chpt.), Conn. Maritime Assn., Harvard Club, Brown Club (co-pres.), Brown Faculty Club, Brown Alumni Schs. Commn. (chmn. Fairfield County), Brown Alumni Assn. (bd. govs.). Home: 14 Pilgrim Ln Weston CT 06883-2412 Office: Mahoney & Keane 14 Pilgrim Ln Weston CT 06883 Office Phone: 203-222-1019. E-mail: sjmurray@snet.net.

MURRAY, TERRENCE, bank executive; b. Woonsocket, R.I., July 11, 1939; s. Joseph W. and Florence (Blackburn) M.; m. Suzanne Young, Jan. 24, 1960; children: Colleen, Paula, Terrence, Christopher, Megan. BA, Harvard U., 1962. With Fleet Nat. Bank, Providence, 1962—, pres., 1978-86; with Fleet Fin. Group Inc., Providence, 1969—, pres., 1978—, chmn., pres., chief exec. officer, 1982-88, pres., 1988, chmn., pres., CEO, 1988-97, also bd. dirs. Boston; chmn. & CEO FleetBoston Fin. Corp., Boston. Bd. dirs. Fleet Nat. Bank, A.T. Cross Co., Lincoln, R.I., Allmerica Fin. Corp., Worcester, Mass., CVS Corp., Woonsocket, R.I.; bd. govs. Red. Res. Bank Boston; dir. Fin. Svcs. Roundtable, Ptnrs. HealthCare Sys., Inc., Boston, Assocs. Harvard Bus. Sch.; mem. Fin. Svcs. Forum; bd. overseers' com. Harvard Coll.; mem. Gov.'s Bd. Econ. Advisors. Trustee R.I. Sch. of Design, Brown U., trustee emeritus; bd. trustees Brigham and Women's Hosp., Mus. Fine Arts, Boston; former chmn. exec. com. Coalition of Northeastern Govs.; former chmn. R.I. Strategic Devel. Commn. Recipient Outstanding Bus. Leader award Northwood Inst., 1986, Humanitarian award Nat. Jewish Ctr. for Immunology and Respiratory Medicine, 1988, Never Again award Jewish Fedn., 1989, New Englander of Yr. award New England Coun., 1990, New England Businessperson of Yr. award New England Bus. Mag., 1991, Humanitarian award Fogarty Found., 1991. Mem. Am. Bankers Assn. (bd. dirs.), Assn. of Res. City Bankers (bd. dirs.), Harvard Alumni Assn. (bd. dirs.), Alfalfa Club (Washington). Office: FleetBoston Fin Corp 100 Federal St Boston MA 02110

MURRAY, TERRY (TERENCE RODNEY MURRAY), former professional hockey team coach; b. Shawville, Que., Can., July 20, 1950; m. Linda Murray; children: Megan, Lindsey. Hockey player Calif. Golden Seals, 1972-75, Phila. Flyers, 1975-77, 78-81, Detroit Red Wings, 1977, Washington Capitals, 1981-82, asst. coach, 1982-88, head coach, 1990-94, Balt. Skipjacks, 1988-90, Philadelphia Flyers, 1994-97, Florida Panthers, Sunrise, Fla., 1998—2000; asst. coach Phila. Flyers, 2002—. Named to 3 Am. Hockey League all-star teams; named most valuable defenseman Am. Hockey League, 1978, 79.

MURRAY, THERESE, state legislator; one child. Student, El Camino Coll., Northeastern U., U. Mass., Midwest Acad., IL. Mitigation mgr. Mass. Hwy. Dept., 1984-91; mem. Mass. Senate, Boston, 1993—; chair. Joint Comm on Insurance, 2001—02; chair Ways and Means Com., 2003. Chmn. joint com. on human svcs. & elderly affairs Mass. State Senate, 1993-99, transp. com., 1993-2002; past market assoc. Coldwell Banker, Plymouth Port, Mass.;

former cmty. rels. & coord. Am. Cablesys. Dir. Mcpl. Women's Project Inc., Boston; mem. Dem. State Com. Named among Ten Women Who Make Things Happen in Mass., Redbook Mag. Mem. Vis. Nurses Assn. (bd. dirs.), Women's Transp. Seminar, Plymouth County Dem. League, LWV. Democrat. Address: Rm 212 State House Boston MA 02133

MURRAY, THOMAS HENRY, bioethics educator, writer; b. Phila., July 30, 1946; s. Thomas Henry and Colombia Rita (Lucci) M.; m. Sharon Marie Engelkraut, Jan. 1968 (div. Sept. 1975); children: Kathleen Elizabeth, Dominique Maria, Peter Albert; m. Cynthia Sarah Aberle, Apr. 1, 1978; 1 child, Emily Sarah Aberle. BA in Psychology, Temple U., 1968; PhD in Social Psychology, Princeton U., 1976; MD (hon.), Uppsala U., 2004. Instr. New Coll., Sarasota, Fla., 1971-75; asst. prof. Interdisciplinary Studies Miami U., Oxford, Ohio, 1975-80, assoc. prof., 1980; assoc. social behavioral studies The Hastings Ctr., Hastings-on Hudson, NY, 1980-84; assoc. prof. Inst. Med. Humanities U. Tex. Med. Br., Galveston, 1984-86, prof., 1986-87; prof., dir. Ctr. Biomed. Ethics Case We. Res. U., Cleve., 1987-99, Susan E. Watson prof. bioethics, 1998—99; pres. The Hastings Ctr., Garrison, NY, 1999—. Mem. Nat. Bioethics Adv. Commn., 1996-2001; mem. ethical, legal and social issues working group Human Genome Project NIH/Dept. Energy, 1989-95. Author: The Worth of a Child, 1996; founder, editor Med. Humanities Rev.; mem. editl. bd. Human Gene Therapy, Cloning, Politics and the Life Scis., Hastings Cetr. Report, Jour. of Law, Medicine and Ethics; editor: Encyclopedia of Ethical, Legal, and Policy Issues in Biotechnology, (with K.W.M. Fulford and D.L. Dickenson) Healthcare Ethics and Human Values: An Introductory Text with Readings and Case Studies, 2002, (with Carol Levine) The Cultures of Caregiving: Conflict and Common Ground Among Families, Health Professionals and Policy Makers, 2004. Fellow NEH, 1977-78, 1979-80, Aspen Inst., 1989. Fellow Hastings Ctr.; mem. APHA, Assn. Practical and Profl. Ethics, Am. Soc. Law Medicine and Ethics (bd. dirs. 1993-97), Assn. Integrative Studies (bd. dirs. 1980-87, pres. 1983), Soc. Health and Human Values (chair program dirs. sect. 1989-90, faculty assn. 1989-90, SHHV program com. 1990, pres.-elect 1992-93, pres. 1993-94), Am. Soc. Human Genetics (chair social issues com. 1998-99), Am. Coll. Ob-Gyn. (com. on ethics 1996-2001), Am. Soc. Bioethics and Humanities (pres.-elect 1998-99, pres. 1999-2000), Human Genome Orgn. (ethics com.), World Anti-Doping Agy. (ethics and edn. com.). Office: The Hastings Ctr 21 Malcolm Gordon Rd Garrison NY 10524-5555

MURRAY, THOMAS J. advertising executive; b. Bridgeport, Conn., Mar. 12, 1924; s. Thomas and Mary (Diskin) M.; m. Mary Elizabeth Cull, Feb. 22, 1945; children: Joshua Francis, Mary Elizabeth, Katherine Diskin. AB, Dartmouth Coll., 1947. Instr., Dartmouth Coll., 1947-48; with Warwick & Legler, N.Y.C., 1948-68, sr. v.p., mgmt. account supr., 1964-68; sr. v.p. group supr. Gaynor & Ducas, Inc., 1968-74, exec. v.p., 1974—, chief fin. officer and gen. mgr., 1978-87; pres. TJM & Assn., 1987—. Pres., trustee Hillcrest Gen. Hosp., N.Y.C.; Westchester Inst. for tng. in Psychoanalysis and Psychotheraphy, Mt. Kisco, N.Y. Served as 1st lt. USAAF, 1942-45. Decorated D.F.C., Air medal with 4 oak leaf clusters. Mem. Nat. Wholesale Druggists Assn., Propriety Assn., Nat. Assn. Chain Drug Stores, Am. Mktg. Assn. Home and Office: 65 Norfield Rd Weston CT 06883-2213

MURRAY, THOMAS JOHN (JOCK MURRAY), medical humanities educator, medical researcher, neurologist; b. Halifax, N.S., Can., May 30, 1938; m. Janet Kathleen Pottie; children: Shannon, Bruce, Suellen, Brian. Grad. pre-med, St. Francis Xavier U., 1958, LLD (hon.), 1989; MD, Dalhousie U., 1963; DSc (hon.), Acadia U., 1991; LittD (hon.), St. Thomas U., 2003. Family physician, Nashwaaksis, 1963-65; chief of medicine Camp Hill Hosp., Halifax, 1974-79; chief of neurology Dalhousie U., Halifax, 1979-85, dir. multiple sclerosis rsch. unit, 1980—2003, dean of medicine, 1985-92, prof. med. humanities, 1992—2003. Mem. working group on Diability in U.S. Pres., 1994-96. Co-author: (textbook) Essential Neurology; author over 200 pub. works, including 7 books and contbns. to 14 textbooks. Bd. dirs. St. Francis Xavier U., Pictou Acad. Found., Robert Pope Found., Nat. Coun. on Bioethics and Health Rsch. Decorated officer Order Can.; recipient Neilson award Hannah Inst. for Med. History, 81 rsch. grants. Fellow Royal Coll. Physicians (Can. and London, Mentor of Yr. award 2002), ACP (master; gov. 1985-90, chmn. bd. govs. 1990-91, chair bd. regents 1995-97, emeritus chair, Dr. Nicholas Davies award, Laureate award); mem. Can. Neurol. Soc. (pres. 1982-84), Am. Acad. Neurology (v.p. 1981-83, Dr. A.B. Baker award), Can. Med. Assn., N.S. Med. Soc., Assn. Can. Med. Colls. (pres. 1991-92), Can. Med. Forum (chmn. 1992-95), Consortium of Multiple Sclerosis Ctrs. (pres. 1997-99), Can. Soc. for History of Medicine (pres. 1997-99), Rotary Internat. (Paul Harris fellow). Avocations: medical history, piano, windsurfing. Home: 16 Bobolink St Halifax NS Canada B3M 1W3 Office: Dalhousie Med Sch Clin Rsch Ctr Halifax NS Canada B3H 4H7 Office Phone: 902-494-2514. E-mail: jock.murray@dal.ca.

MURRAY, THOMAS VEATCH, lawyer; b. Phoenix, July 17, 1947; s. Robert Morrison Jr. and Jane Veatch (Murray) Barber and Richard A. Barber; m. Cynthia Ann Burnett, June 2, 1971; children: Anne Caroline, Thomas Veatch Jr. BA, U. Kans., 1969; JD, U. Mich., 1972. Bar: Kans. 1972, U.S. Dist. Ct. Kans. 1972, U.S. Ct. Appeals (10th cir.) 1983, U.S. Supreme Ct. 1976. Assoc. Barber, Emerson, Six, Springer & Zinn, Lawrence, Kans., 1972-76; mem. Barber, Emerson, Springer, Zinn & Murray, L.C., Lawrence, Kans., 1976—2003; of counsel Lathrop & Gage L.C., Overland Park, Kans., 2004—. Adj. prof. western civilization U. Kans., 1975-77, Sch. Law., 1990-91, instr. bar rev. course, 1975-82; dir. The First Nat. Bank of Lawrence, Kans., 1980-91, The Reuter Organ Co., 1991-, Hall Ctr. for the Humanities, Lawrence, Kans., 1988-. Contbr. articles to profl. jours. Mem. adv. bd. Lawrence Consumer Affairs Assn., 1974—77, Sta. KANU, Lawrence, 1975—80; mem. Bd. Edn. Unified Sch. Dist. 497, Lawrence, 1991—95; mem. Kans. Bd. Law Examiners, 1995—, Lawrence Emergency Svcs. Coun., 1998—2002; dir. Lawrence C. of C., 1993—95; treas. Louie Holcom Baseball Assn., 1972—73; trustee First Presbyn. Ch., 1975—76. Mem. ABA, Fedn. Def. and Corp. Counsel (regional v.p. 1994-97, dir. 1997-99), Kans. Assn. Def. Counsel (dir. 1993-97), Kans. Bar Assn. (pres. corporation, banking and bus. law sect. 1983), Kans. Bar Found. (trustee 1999—), Douglas Co. Bar Assn., Coaches' Corner (Lawrence), Lawrence Lions Alumni Assn., Kansas City Club, Lawrence Rotary Club, Lawrence Country Club, The Fortnightly Club (Lawrence). Republican. Presbyterian. Avocation: classical and operatic music. Office: Lathrop & Gage LC 10851 Mastin Blvd Bldg 82 Ste 1000 Overland Park KS 66210-1669 Business E-Mail: tmurray@lathropgage.com.

MURRAY, TIMOTHY GARRETT, ophthalmologist; b. Biloxi, Miss., Sept. 19, 1959; s. Robert Maurice and Lynn (Lindner) M. BA, Johns Hopkins U., 1981, MD, 1985. Diplomate Am. Bd. Ophthalmology. Intern Union Meml. Hosp., Balt., 1985-86; resident ophthalmology U. Calif., San Francisco, 1986-89, chief resident ophthalmology, 1988-89; fellow ophthalmology Med. Coll. Wis., Milw., 1989-90, fellow vitreoretinal surgery, 1990-91; asst. prof. ophthalmology Bascom Palmer Eye Inst., Miami, Fla., 1991—. Contbr. chpt. to book and articles to profl. jours. Guest spkr. Mus. of Discovery and Sci., Miami, 1994; chmn. bd. Nat. Retinoblastoma Rsch. and Support Found., Miami, 1996. Grantee NIH, 1991—, 92—, Stanley J. Glaser Found., 1992-93, Am. Cancer Soc., 1993-94, Fight for Sight, Inc., 1994-95. Mem. AMA, Am. Acad. Ophthalmology, Am. Assn. for Cancer Rsch., Am. Diabetes Assn., Assn. for Rsch. in Vision & Ophthalmology, N.Am. Hyperthermia Soc. Avocations: sailing, reading, scuba diving, cooking. Office: Bascom Palmer Eye Inst 900 NW 17th St Rm 254 Miami FL 33136-1134

MURRAY, TIMOTHY P. mayor; m. Tammy L. Sullivan. BA in Am. Studies, Fordham U.; JD, Western New England Sch. Law. Pvt. law practice State of Mass., Worcester, Mass., councillor-at-large, mayor, 2002—. Office: 455 Main St, Rm 305 Worcester MA 01608-1821 E-mail: mayor@ci.worcester.ma.us.

MURRAY, WALLACE SHORDON, publisher, educator; b. Dorchester, Mass., May 9, 1921; s. Wallace Jennings and Ina (Shordon) M.; m. Eleanor Muriel Grandy, Oct. 30, 1948; children: Patricia Ann, William Howard. BS, MIT, 1942; M.Ed., Boston U., 1949; Litt.D. (hon.), Western New Eng. Coll., 1965. Tchr. Bolles Sch., Jacksonville, Fla., 1945-46, head math. dept., asst. prin., 1946-49; headmaster Berwick Acad., South Berwick, Maine, 1949-50; sales rep. D.C. Heath & Co., Boston, 1950-52, editor, 1952-53, head elementary editorial dept., 1953-55, editor in chief, 1955-66, v.p., 1962-66, dir., 1956-66, sec. of corp., 1957-66; dir. Erica Corp., 1956-66; exec. v.p. Heath de Rochemont Corp., 1960-66, dir., 1960-66; editor-in-chief, mgr. materials devel. dept. Raytheon Edn. Co., 1966-68; v.p., editorial dir. domestic and internat. ops. Grolier Inc., 1968-80, dir., 1969-82, cons., 1980-82; dir. Grolier Edn. Corp., 1968-80, Scarecrow Press Inc., 1969-80. Chmn. elementary and high sch. research com. Am. Ednl. Pubs. Inst., 1966-68, chmn. elem. and high sch. sect., 1968-69 Lay leader Boston dist. Meth. Ch., 1952-56; mem. adv. bd. Boston U. Student Christian Assn., 1954-62, treas., 1957-59, chmn., 1959-61; mem. president's adv. council St. Joseph's Coll., North Windham, Maine, 1973-88; mem. corp. New Eng. Deaconess Assn., 1965-95, exec. com., 1965-68; mem. corp. New Eng. Deaconess Hosp., 1967-93; dir. Japan America Soc. of Maine, 1981-91, pres., 1984-86; merit badge counselor Pine Tree Coun., Boy Scouts Am., 1984-95; dir. Children's Mus. of Maine, 1987-89; dir. Leisure Ctr. for the Handicapped, Inc., Portland, Maine, 1987-93, treas. 1988-93; mem. adv. council So. Maine Retired Sr. Vol. Program, 1987-90, chmn. fin. com., 1987-89; mem. Foster Care Case Review Panel Maine Dept. Human Services, 1987-91; dir. Foreside Common Condominium Assn., Falmouth, Maine, 1986-89, 1991-92, pres., 1987-89; vol. staff mem. Vol. Lawyers Project of Maine, 1987-90; vol. math. instr. Adult Basic Learning Exchange, Portland, 1987-91. Served to capt. AUS, 1942-46, to maj. USAR. Mem. Newcomen Soc., Masons, Shriners, Phi Delta Kappa. Republican. Episcopalian. Home: PO Box 17 Sebago Lake ME 04075-0017

MURRAY, WARREN JAMES, philosophy educator; b. St. Paul, Dec. 3, 1936; s. James Bernard and Louise (Robertson) M.; m. Mary Ann McAulay, July 18, 1959; children: Mark, Anne, Kathleen. Student, St. Thomas Coll., 1954-55; BA in Chemistry, Wis. State Coll., River Falls, 1962; B.Ph. in Philosophy, Universite Laval, Que., Can., 1964, Ph.L., 1965, scolarite PhD, 1966. Analytical chemist 3M Co., St. Paul, 1957-61, research chemist, 1961-63; prof. philos. sci. U. Laval, Sainte-Foy, 1966—2002, vice dean, 1979—. Invited prof. Faculte de philosophie Comparee, Paris, 1969, 72, Universite libre des sciences de l'homme, Paris, 1975—, Ecole des Hautes Etudes, Paris, 1976, Universidad Nacional de Tucuman, Argentina, 1991. Fgn. exchange teaching grantee Province Que., 1969; named to D'Alzon Chair for the Humanities, Assumption Coll., Worcester, Mass., 2002—. Mem. Soc. Aristotelian Studies (pres.), Can. Soc. History and Philosophy Sci., Soc. Ancient Greek Philosophy. Office: Faculte De Philosophie Universite Laval Sainte-Foy QC Canada G1K 7P4 Office Phone: 418-656-2131 5966. E-mail: warren.murray@fp.ulaval.ca.

MURRAY, WILLIAM BRUCE, opera singer; b. Schenectady, N.Y., Mar. 13, 1935; s. John Allison and Jessie Chrystal (Gray) M.; m. Nancy Lee Adams, Mar. 1, 1958; children: John Horton, Christopher Andrew, Judith Leora. BA in Music Edn., Adelphi U., 1956; Cert di Studio, U. Perugia, Italy, 1957; grad., Goethe Inst., 1960. Opera singer Landestheater Detmold, Germany, 1960-61, Staatstheater Braunschweig, Germany, 1961-64, Nat. Theater Mannheim, Germany, 1964-66, Staatsoper München, Germany, 1966-78, Deutsche Opera Berlin, Germany, 1969—, Houston Grand Opera, 1994—. Opera singer numerous other theaters including N.Y. State Opera, Catania, Italy, Marseille, France, L.A. Opera, Teatro Reggio Torino (Italia), 1992; prof. voice Shepherd Sch. Music Rice U., Houston. Recordings include Salome, Die Bassariden, Hochzeit des Camacho, Schöne Müllerin, Die Totestadt. With U.S. Army, 1958-60. Named Kammersänger Senate Berlin Germany, 1980; Fulbright fellow, 1956. Mem. Lions Club. Avocations: hiking, cooking, swimming. Home: 113 Homeyer Rd Sparrow Bush NY 12780-8302 E-mail: wbmurray@ruf.rice.edu.

MURRAY-KOLB, LAURA ELAINE, nutritionist, researcher; b. Abington, Pa., Mar. 27, 1973; d. George William and Annette Brice Murray; m. Philip John Kolb, May 9, 1998. BS, Pa. State U., 1995, MS, 1998, PhD, 2003. Lab. mgr. Pa. State U., University Park, 1995—96, grad. tchg. asst., 1996—98, 1998—2003; project mgr. Pa. State U./U. Philippines, 2001—. Spkr. and presenter in field. Contbr. articles to profl. jours. Recipient Grad. Program Nutrition Competitive Rsch. award, Dept. Nutritional Scis., Pa. State U., 1999—2000, Hintz Grad. Edn. Enhancement award, Health and Human Devel. Dean's Office, Pa. Sate U., 2002—03; fellow Kligman Grad. fellow, Pa. State U., 2002—03. Mem.: Golden Key Nat., Alpha Epsilon Delta, Phi Upsilon Omicron, Kappa Omicron Nu. Avocations: hiking, reading, travel. Home: 210 W Pine Grove Rd Pine Grove Mills PA 16868 Office: The Pa State U S-132 Henderson Bldg University Park PA 16802 Personal E-mail: lem118@psu.edu. E-mail: lem118@psu.edu.

MURRELL, ADRIAN BRYAN, professional football player; b. Lafayette, La., Oct. 16, 1970; Student, U. W.Va. Running back N.Y. Jets, Hempstead, NY, 1993—97, Ariz. Cardinals, Phoenix, 1998—2000; mem. NFC wildcard team, 1998—99; running back Washington Redskins, 2000—. Office: Washington Redskins 21300 Redskin Park Dr Ashburn VA 20147-6100

MURRELL, GARY, historian, educator; b. Portland, Oreg., Jan. 28, 1947; s. Evans L. and Idris Aileen Murrell; life ptnr. Michael Taylor Gyde, Aug. 15, 1979. BS, So. Oreg. State Coll., 1987; MA in History, U. Oreg., 1992, PhD, 1994. Prof. So. Oreg. State Coll., Ashland, Oreg., 1992—93, Grays Harbor Coll., Aberdeen, Wash., 1993—. Contbr. essays to profl. jours.; author: Iron Pants: Oregon's Anti-New Deal Governor, Charles Henry Martin, 2000. With USAF, 1966—70, Eng. and Germany. Mem.: ACLU (chmn. Grays Harbor chpt. 1998—, bd. dirs. Wash. chpt. 1999—2003), Orgn. Am. Historians, Mid-Atlantic Radical History Orgn., Am. Hist. Assn. (Rsch. award 2002). Avocations: gardening, music, theater. Home: 717 Lincoln Hoquiam WA 98550 Office: Grays Harbor College EP Smith Drive Aberdeen WA 98520 Office Phone: 360-538-4139.

MURRELL, KENNETH DARWIN, microbiologist, parasitologist; b. Burley, Idaho, Jan. 19, 1940; s. Kenneth Leland and Margaret (Manning) M.; m. Joyce Voyce, July 10, 1965; children: Duncan, Amy. BA, Chico (Calif.) State Coll., 1957; MSPH, U. N.C., 1963, PhD, 1969. Rsch. assoc. U. Chgo., 1967-71; rsch. scientist Naval Med. Rsch. Inst., Bethesda, Md., 1971-78, USDA Agrl. Rsch. Svc., Beltsville, Md., 1978-87; assoc. area dir. Agrl. Rsch. Svc., Beltsville, Md., 1987-89; area dir. midwest area USDA Agrl. Rsch. Svc., Beltsville, 1989-92, dir. Beltsville area, 1992-97; dep. adminstr. USDA-Agrl. Rsch. Svc., Beltsville, 1997—. Bd. dirs. Internat. Trichinell Comm., 1994—. Fulbright fellow Royal Vet. Agrl. U., Copenhagen, 1996, Presdl. Disting. Presdl. Rank award, 1997. Mem. AAAS, Am. Soc. Parasitologists (pres. 1993), Am. Assn. Vet. parasitology (pres. 1986-87, Disting. Parasitologist 1987), Internat. Trichinosis Commn. (pres. 1998—, Disting. Presdl. Exec. award 1998). Office: BARC-West Bldg 005 Agrl Rsch Svc NPS Beltsville MD 20705

MURRELL, ROBERT GEORGE, lawyer; b. Jan. 27, 1932; s. Samuel Edwin and Myrtle Josephine (Hailey) M.; m. Bonnie Bird Robinson, Nov. 11, 1961; children: Robert George, Michele Grace, Bonnie Melissa. BA, U. Fla., 1951, JD, 1953. Bar: Fla. 1953, N.Y. 1981, U.S. Dist. Ct. (so. dist.) Fla. 1953, U.S. Dist. Ct. (mid. dist.) Fla. 1980, U.S. Ct. Appeals (5th cir.) 1953, U.S. Ct. Appeals (11th cir.) 1981, U.S. Ct. Mil. Appeals 1958, U.S. Supreme Ct. 1958, U.S. Ct. Claims 1975, U.S. Tax Ct. 1975, U.S. Ct. Customs and Patent Appeals 1975, U.S. Ct. Appeals (D.C. cir.) 1989, U.S. Ct. Appeals (3rd, 4th, 6th, 7th, 8th, 9th, 10th cirs.) 1989, U.S. Ct. Appeals (2nd cir.) 1990, U.S. Ct. Vet. Appeals 1992; arbitrator Am. Arbitration Assn. Atty. Sam E. Murrell & Sons., Orlando, Fla., 1953—. Mem. Ctirus Assocs. of N.Y. Stock Exch.; pres. Colonial Mortgage Co. Fla., Inc.; dir. Weiss Realty Corp., Lake Margaret Co. With U.S. Army, 1953—55. Mem.: ATLA, ABA, Acad. Fla. Trial Lawyers, Orange County Bar Assn., Univ. Winter Park, Elks (Orlando), Shriners, Masons. Republican. Baptist. Office: Sam E Murrell & Sons 1 N Rosalind Ave Orlando FL 32801-1682 Home: 1212 Ayrshire St Orlando FL 32803 Office Phone: 407-843-8500.

MURRELL, SUSAN DEBRECHT, librarian; b. St. Louis, Aug. 10, 1951; d. Edward August and Edith (Keeney) DeB.; children: Brian, Katherine. BA in History, U. Ky., 1973; MLS, U. Mo., 1976. Children's libr. Louisville Free Pub. Libr., 1974-76, talking book libr. head, 1976-83; lower/mid. sch. libr. Ky. Country Day Sch., Louisville, 1983-84; children's libr. Emmet O'Neal Libr., Mountain Brook, Ala., 1984-86, asst. dir., 1986-89, dir., 1989—. Active Jefferson County Pub. Libr.; mem. allocations com. United Way, mem. admissions com.; bd. dirs. Mountain Brook Libr. Found., 1993—, Ala. Ctr. for Book. Mem. ALA, Ala. Libr. Assn. (mem. publicity com. 1992-93, pub. libr. chair 1995-96), Rotary Internat. Roman Catholic. Office: Emmet O'Neal Libr 50 Oak St Birmingham AL 35213-4295 Office Phone: 205-879-0492.

MURRELLE, RONALD KEMP, architectural firm executive; b. Greensboro, N.C., Aug. 14, 1940; s. George Kemp and Marian (Lewis) M.; Betsy Blackburn Stevens, Oct. 1960 (div. Aug. 1982); children: Brett Stevens, Mary Anna. Student, N.C. State Sch. Design, 1958-60. Dept. mgr. Kirkman and Koury, Inc., Greensboro, 1961-70; v.p. Wm. B. Owen Constrn. Co. Inc., Banner Elk, N.C., 1970-76, M and B Constrn. Inc., Vansant, Va., 1976-77; multifamily dept. mgr. Harmon Assoc., Greensboro, 1978-80; pres. Diversified Residential Svcs., Inc., Banner Elk, 1980-82; project designer Harmn Assoc., Greensboro, 1984-85; with Hotel Designs, 1986-88, Nu-Stone Surfacing, Orlando, Fla., 1989, Fellowship Facilities Designs, Orlando, Myrtle Beach, 1990; founder Fulfilled Mansions, Greensboro, 1997—. Noahhite Orgn.; pres. Diversified Residential Svcs., Greensboro, 1998. Author: His Father's Temple, 1994, God Experience, 1996, Recovery Words with Definitions, 1996. Avocations: chess, golf. Address: PO Box 7178 Greensboro NC 27417-0178 E-mail: ronm-drs@triad.rr.com.

MURREN, JAMES JOSEPH, recreational facility executive, hotel executive; Various positions Deutsche Morgan Grenfell, 1984—98; exec. v.p. MGM Mirage, Las Vegas, 1998—, CFO, 1998—, pres., 1999—, treas., 2001—. Office: MGM MIrage 3600 Las Vegas Blvd South Las Vegas NV 89109

MURRIAN, ROBERT PHILLIP, retired federal judge, educator; b. Knoxville, Tenn., Apr. 1, 1945; s. Albert Kinzel and Mary Gilbert (Eppes) M.; m. Jerrilyn Sue Boone, Oct. 29, 1983; children: Kimberley Ann, Jennifer Rebecca, Albert Boone, Samuel Robert. BS, U.S. Naval Acad., 1967; JD, U. Tenn., 1974. Bar: Tenn. 1974, U.S. Dist. Ct. (ea. dist.) Tenn. 1975, U.S. Ct. Appeals (6th cir.) 1982. Law clk. to judge U.S. Dist. Ct. (ea. dist.) Tenn., 1974-76; assoc. Butler, Vines, Babb & Threadgill, Knoxville, 1976-78; magistrate judge U.S. Dist. (ea. dist.) Tenn., Knoxville, 1978—2002; ptnr. Kramer, Rayson, Leake, Rodgers & Morgan, LLP, Knoxville, 2002—. Adj. prof. U. Tenn. Coll. Law, 1990-93, 95-96, 2002; arbitrator, mediator, spl. master litigation. Lt. USN, 1967-71. Green scholar, 1973-74, Nat. Moot Ct. scholar, 1974. Fellow Tenn. Bar Found.; mem. ABA, Tenn. Bar Assn., Knoxville Bar Assn. (bd. govs. 1994, 2002—), Sixth Cir. Jud. Conf. (life), Order of Coif, Am. Inn of Ct. (master of the bench, pres. 1997-98), Phi Kappa Phi. Presbyterian (Elder). Office: Kramer Rayson Leake Rodgers & Morgan LLP PO Box 629 Knoxville TN 37901-0629 Address: First Tennessee Plz 800 S Gay St Ste 2500 Knoxville TN 37929 Office Phone: 865-525-5134. E-mail: rpmurrian@kramer-rayson.com.

MURRISH, CHARLES HOWARD, oil and gas exploration company executive, geologist; b. Rochester, Mich., Dec. 27, 1940; s. Richard John and Emily Louise (Marsh) M.; m. Brigitte Marie Furlotte, Oct. 23, 1965; children: Stephanie, Stephen, Brian. Student, Mexico City Coll., 1962; BS, Mich. State U., 1963, MS, 1966. Exploration geologist and geophysicist Chevron, New Orleans, 1966-71; mgr. exploration Odeco, New Orleans, 1971-77; v.p. McMoRan Offshore Exploration Co., Metairie, La., 1977-79, sr. v.p., 1979-81; pres. McMoRan-Freeport Oil Co., Metairie, 1981-83, McMoRan Exploration Co., Metairie, 1983-86; exec. v.p. McMoRan Oil & Gas Co., 1986, sr. exec. v.p., 1986-90, Freeport-McMoRan Oil & Gas Co., 1990-92; ptnr. CLK Co., 1992-94; pres., COO McMoRan Oil & Gas Co., New Orleans, 1994—2001, McMoRan Oil & Gas LLC, New Orleans, 1998-2001; exec. v.p. McMoRan Exploration Co., New Orleans, 1998—, vice-chmn., 2001—. Chmn. bd. Hysell Ballet Arts, Inc., New Orleans, 1982-83; chmn. petroleum majors campaign United Way, 1996, 98; bd. dirs. Lenpac, Metairie, 1983; chmn. citizenship com. McMoRan Exploration Co., 2000—. Mem. New Orleans Geol. Soc., Geol. Soc. Am., Am. Assn. Petroleum Geologists, Petroleum Club of New Orleans (bd. dirs. 1988, 89, 90), Houston Geol. Soc., La. Assn. Ind. Producers, Mid-Continent Oil and Gas Assn. also: PO Box 60004 New Orleans LA 70160-0004 Office: McMoran Exploration Co 1615 Poydras St New Orleans LA 70112-1254

MURROW, WAYNE LEE, retired communications educator, dean; b. Alva, Okla., Jan. 23, 1935; s. Everett Emmet Murrow and Stella Jean McGlothlin; m. Marti L. Rogers, Aug. 19, 1956 (dec. Sept. 1966); children: Sherri, Randal, Cynthia, Jeffrey; m. Nila Arlene West, Jan. 19, 1968. BA, Bethany Nazarene Coll., 1956; M of Tchg., Ctrl. State U., 1968; PhD, U. Okla., 1972. Min. Ch. of the Nazarene, Tex.; prof. So. Nazarene U., Bethany, Okla., 1968-80, dean, prof., 1980—2002; ret. emeritus prof., adj. prof., 2002—. Evaluation team mem. Okla. State Dept. Edn., Oklahoma City, 1980-94. Mem. Nat. Comm. Assn, Ctrl. States Comm. Assn. (adv. coun. 1977-90), Okla. Theatre Speech Comm. Assn. (pres. 1976-77, Outstanding Tchr. award 1980), Christian Adult Higher Edn. Assn. (coun. mem. 1994-2000, pres. 1997-98), North Ctrl. Assn. (evaluation team mem. 1968-80, cons.-evaluator for colls. and univs. 1994—). Avocation: family history. Home: 8105 Bridgeport Ln Bethany OK 73008 Office: So Nazarene Univ 6729 NW 39th Exp Bethany OK 73008 E-mail: murrow@cox.net.

MURRY, CHARLES EMERSON, lawyer, official; b. Hope, N.D., June 23, 1924; s. Raymond Henry and Estelle Margarete (Skeim) M.; m. Donna Deane Kleve, June 20, 1948; children: Barbara, Karla, Susan, Bruce, Charles. BS, U. N.D., 1948, JD, 1950. Bar: N.D. 1950. Mem. firm Nelson and Heringer, Rugby, N.D., 1950-51; dir. N.D. Legis. Council, 1951-75; adj. gen. with rank of maj. gen. State of N.D., Bismarck, 1975-84; mgr. Garrison Diversion Conservancy Dist., 1985-93. Cons. Council State Govts.; mem. res. forces policy bd. Sec. of Def. Vice-pres. Mo. Slope Luth. Home of Bismarck, 1965-66. Served with AUS, 1942-45. Decorated D.S.M., Legion of Merit, Meritorious Service medal, Bronze Star, Army Commendation medal; Fourragere Belgium; Orange Lanyard Netherlands; recipient Sioux award U. N.D., 1970; Gov.'s award of excellence, 1971; Nat. Leadership award Bismarck C. of C., 1971 Mem. Adjs. Gen. Assn. (exec. com., sec. 1983-84), Nat. Legis. Conf. (past chmn.), N.G. Assn., Am. Bar Assn., N.D. Bar Assn., Commrs. Uniform State Laws. Lodges: Elks, Masons. Lutheran. Office: 5505 Ponderosa Ave Bismarck ND 58503-9159

MURRY, HAROLD DAVID, JR., lawyer; b. Holdenville, Okla., June 30, 1943; s. Harold David Sr. and Willie Elizabeth (Dees) M.; m. Ann Moore Earnhardt, Nov. 1, 1975; children: Elizabeth Ann, Sarah Bryant. BA, Okla. U., 1965, JD, 1968. Bar: Okla. 1968, D.C. 1974. Asst. to v.p. U. Okla., Norman, 1968-71, legal counsel Research Inst., 1969-71; atty. U.S. Dept. Justice, Washington, 1971-74; spl. asst. U.S. Atty., Washington, 1972; assoc. Clifford & Warnke, Washington, 1974-78, ptnr., 1978-91, Howrey & Simon, Washington, 1991-98, Baker Botts LLP, Washington, 1998—. Mem. ABA, Okla. Bar Assn., D.C. Bar Assn., Fed. Bar Assn., Met. Club (Washington), Chevy Chase Club (Md.), Phi Alpha Delta. Democrat. Home: 8931 Bel Air Pl Potomac MD 20854-1606 Office: Baker Botts LLP Ste 1300 1299 Pennsylvania Ave NW Washington DC 20004-2408

MURTAGH, JAMES PATRICK, finance educator, consultant; BS in Engring., West Point Acad., 1982; MBA, U. No. Colo., 1987; PhD in Fin., Rensselaer Poly. Inst., 1998. V.p., sr. cons. Exec. Systems Planning, Albany, NY, 1990—2001; asst. prof. Lally Sch. Mgmt. and Tech., Troy, NY, 1999—. Pres. Watervliet (N.Y.) Youth Soccer. Capt. U.S. Army, 1982—87. Office: Lally Sch Mgmt & Tech 110 8th St Troy NY 12180-3590 Office Phone: 518-276-2758. E-mail: murtaj@rpi.edu.

MURTAGH, MICHAEL PAUL, psychologist; b. Washington, Sept. 23, 1959; s. Hugh Hunter and Margaret (Payne) M.; m. Anne Marie Murtagh, Nov. 30, 1985. BS magna cum laude, James Madison U., 1981; MS, Villanova U., 1983; PhD, U. Mont., Missoula, 1991. Lic. psychologist, N.Y. Staff psychologist Eagleville (Pa.) Hosp., 1984-87; dir. psychol. svcs. Mont. State Prison,

Deer Lodge, 1991-94; staff psychologist, coord. forensic svcs. Madison County Dept. Mental Health, Wampsville, N.Y., 1994-2000; asst. prof. Bridgewater State Coll., 2000—. Part-time faculty Salish-Kootenai Coll., Pablo, Mont., 1988; vis. prof. U. Mont., Missoula, 1992; adj. faculty Onondaga C.C., Syracuse, N.Y., 1998-2000; coord. graduate program in psychology Bridgewater (Mass.) State Coll., 2000—; consultant sex offender treatment program Madison County Dept. Mental Health, 2000—; lectr., presenter in field. Contbr. articles to profl. jours. Vol. crisis counselor Listening Ear Svc., Harrisonburg, Va., 1980-81. Recipient Disting. Svc. award Southea. Pa. Mental Health Assn., 1985. Mem. Am. Psychol. Assn. Avocation: baseball. Home: 57 Seymour St Berkley MA 02779 Business E-Mail: mmurtagh@bridgew.edu.

MURTAUGH, CHRISTOPHER DAVID, lawyer; b. Darby, Pa., Oct. 25, 1945; s. John Michael and Rita (Sullivan) M.; m. Nancy R. Hanauer, Nov. 30, 1968; children: Jason C., Colin M., Alison M. AB, U. Ill., 1967, JD, 1970. Bar: Ill. 1970, Fla. 1973, U.S. Dist. Ct. (no. dist.) Ill. 1975. Ptnr. Winston & Strawn, Chgo., 1974—, capital ptnr., 1987—, real estate dept. chmn., 1994—. Mem. Glen Ellyn (Ill.) Capital Improvements Com., 1985-89, Glen Ellyn Plan Com., 1989-96, Met. Planning Coun., 1995—; bd. visitors U. Ill. Coll. of Law, 1998-2001. Lt. USNR, 1971-74. Mem. ABA, Am. Coll. Real Estate Lawyers, Fla. Bar Assn., Ill. State Bar Assn., Chgo. Bar Assn., Internat. Coun. Shopping Ctrs., Order of Coif. Office: Winston & Strawn 35 W Wacker Dr Ste 4200 Chicago IL 60601-1695 Office Phone: 312-558-5600. E-mail: cmurtaugh@winston.com.

MURTAUGH, PHILLIP F. automotive executive; B, Kettering U.; M in Indsl. Mgmt., Stanford U. Exec. v.p. Shanghai GM; gen. mgr. GM China; dir. mfg. GM Overseas Corp./Japan; exec. asst. to exec. dir. product planning Isuzu Motors; pres. IBC Vehicles Co., Ltd., Luton, England; chmn., mng. dir. GM China, 2000—. Mem. Asia Pacific Strategy bd. GM. Office: GM Corp Box 300 300 Renaissance Ctr Detroit MI 48265-3000

MURTHA, J. GARVAN, federal judge; b. Hartford, Conn., Mar. 3, 1941; s. John Stephen and Emily Winifred (Garvan) Murtha; m. Margaret Munro McDonald, May 24, 1969; 3 children. BA, Yale U., 1963; LLB, U. Conn., 1968; LLM, Georgetown U., 1972. Bar: Conn. 1968, DC 1968, Vt. 1968. Vol. coord. Peace Corps, Columbia, 1963—65; pub. defender Washington, 1968—70; dep. state's atty. for Windham County Dept. Justice, Vt., 1970—73; ptnr. Kristensen, Cummings and Murtha, 1973—95; chief judge U.S. Dist. Ct. Vt., Brattleboro, 1995—2002, judge, 2002—. Mem. Second Cir. Task Force on Gender, Racial and Ethnic Fairness, 1980—86, Second Cir. Com. on Fed. Rules, 1980—86, Vt. Jud. Nominating Bd., 1980—86, Vt. Profl. Conduct Bd., 1993—95; chair Vt. Commn. on Low-Level Nuc. Waste, 1987—90. Mem.: ABA, Am. Bd. Trial Advocates, Windham County Bar Assn., Vt. Bar Assn., Jud. Coun. 2nd Cir., Am. Inns of Ct. (so. Vt. chpt., bencher). Roman Catholic. Office: US Dist Ct Vt US Post Office & Courthouse PO Box 760 Brattleboro VT 05302-0760

MURTHA, JOHN PATRICK, congressman; b. New Martinsville, W.Va., June 17, 1932; s. John Patrick and Mary Edna (Ray) M.; m. Joyce Bell; three children. BA in Econs., U. Pitts., 1961; postgrad., Indiana U. of Pa., 1962-65; H.H.D. (hon.), Mt. Aloysius Jr. Coll. Mem. Pa. Ho. of Reps., 1969-73, 93rd-108th Congresses from 12th Pa. dist., Washington, 1974—; mem. appropriations com. Served to lt. USMC, 1952-55, as maj. 1966-67, Vietnam; ret. col. Res. Decorated Bronze Star, Purple Heart (2); Cross of Gallantry Vietnam; Pa. Disting. Svc. award, 1978, Pa. Meritorious Svc. medal, numerous service awards for work during Johnstown flood, 1977, Iron Mike award Marine Corps League, 1988, Disting. Am. award Nation's Capital chpt. Air Force Assn., 1989, Outstanding Veteran award Vets. Caucus of Am. Acad. Physician Assts., 1989, Man of Steel award Cold Finished Steel Bar Inst., 1989; named Man of Yr. Johnstown Jaycees, 1978 Democrat. Office: US Ho of Reps 2423 Rayburn Ho Office Bldg Washington DC 20515-0001 also: PO Box 780 Johnstown PA 15907-0780

MURTHA, JOHN STEPHEN, lawyer; b. Hartford, Conn., Apr. 30, 1913; s. John J. and Agnes E. (Hennessey) M.; m. Winifred Garvan, July 7, 1939; children— John Garvan, Leslie A., Brenda A. BA, Yale, 1935, LL.B., 1938. Bar: Conn. bar 1938. Ptnr. Murtha, Cullina, Richter & Pinney, Hartford, 1946-88, of counsel, 1989—. Asst. states atty., Hartford County, 1946-51; dir. Kaman Corp. Pres. Greater Hartford Cmty. Chest, 1968-70, Oxford Sch., Hartford, 1960-62; chmn. distbn. com. Hartford Found. for Pub. Giving, 1983-86; bd. dirs. emeritus Blue Cross and Blue Shield Conn., Boys Clubs Hartford; trustee emeritus St. Joseph Coll., West Hartford, Conn., St. Thomas More Corp., New Haven, pres., 1962-64, Loomis Chaffe Sch. Served to lt. (j.g.) USNR, 1943-46. Fellow Am. Coll. Trial Lawyers; mem. ABA, Greater Hartford C. of C., Conn. Bus. and Industry Assn., Hartford Golf Club (pres. 1961-63). Republican. Roman Catholic. Office: City Place Hartford CT 06103 Home: Apt T514 20 Loeffler Rd Bloomfield CT 06002-2289

MUSA, JOHN DAVIS, computer and infosystems executive, software reliability engineering researcher and expert, independent consultant, educator; b. Amityville, N.Y., June 11, 1933; s. Khan Hussein and Ione Geraldine (Ryan) M.; m. Marilyn Laurene Allred, June 24, 1959. BA, Dartmouth Coll., 1954, MSEE, 1955. With AT&T Bell Labs., Murray Hill, N.J., 1958-96, mem. tech. staff, 1958-63, supr. guidance program devel., 1963-68, supr. command and control program devel., 1968-69, supr. mgmt. control and new software tech., 1969-72, supr. human factors test, 1972-74, supr. computer graphics, 1974-80, supr. computer measurements, 1980-85, supr. software quality, 1985-90, tech. mgr. software reliability engring., 1991-96. Mem. N.J. Coun. R&D; lectr., spkr. in field. Author: Software Reliability: Measurement, Prediction, Application, 1987, Software Reliability Engineering: More Reliable Software, Faster Development and Testing, 1998; editor: (book series) Software Quality Institute; contbr. numerous articles to prof. jours. and books. Lt. USN, 1955-58. Fellow IEEE (Third Millenium medal for outstanding achievements and contbns.); mem. IEEE Computer Soc. (2d v.p. 1986, v.p. publs. 1984-85, v.p. tech. activities 1986, chair tech com. software engring. 1982-84, founding mem. editl. bd. IEEE Software Mag., Disting. lectr. 1980-83, Meritorious Svc. award 1984, 85, 87, Golden Core award, founding officer com. on software reliability engring., mem. editl. bds. Spectrum mag., 1984-86, Proc. of the IEEE 1983-90, Technique et Science Informatiques jour., sr. editor Software Engring. Inst. book series, sr. founding editor Software Quality Inst. book series, chair steering com. Internat. Conf. on Software Engring.), IEEE Reliability Soc. (Engr. of Yr. 2004), Assn. for Computing Machinery. Achievements include internat. leader in software engring. and in creation new tech. software reliability engring.; created two software reliability models; developed concepts and practice of operational profile, software-reliability engineered testing, concept of execution time; reduced operation software (ROS), and operational development; created concept of fault exposure ratio; developed approach for choosing software development strategies to meet different reliability objectives; international leader in reducing software reliability engineering to practice. Office: 39 Hamilton Rd Morristown NJ 07960-5341 Office Phone: 973-267-5284. E-mail: j.musa@ieee.org.

MUSA, SAMUEL ALBERT, university executive; m. Judith Friedman; children: Gregory, Jeffrey. BA, BSEE, Rutgers U., 1961; MS in Applied Physics, Harvard U., 1962, PhD in Applied Physics, 1965. Rsch. scientist Gen. Precision Inc., Little Falls, N.J., 1965-66; asst. prof. elec. engring. U. Pa., Phila., 1966-71; project leader Inst. for Def. Analyses, Arlington, Va., 1971-78; dep. dir. Office of Under Sec. Def., Washington, 1978-83; dir. rsch. and advanced tech. E-Systems, Inc., Dallas, 1983-86, v.p. rsch. and advanced tech., 1986-95; exec. dir. Ctr. Display Tech. and Mfg. U. Mich., 1995-99; assoc. v.p. for strategic initiative Northwestern U., Evanston, Ill., 1999—. Mem. sci. adv. bd. USAF, 1987-91; mem. adv. bd. Def. Intelligence Agy., Army Sci. Bd. Contbr. articles to profl. jours. Recipient Exceptional Civilian Svc. award, Sec. of Air Force, cert. of appreciation, Sec. Def. Fellow IEEE; mem. AIA (tech. and ops. coun. 1986-95, vice chmn. 1993, chmn. 1994), Sigma Xi, Tau Beta Pi, Pi Mu Epsilon. Office: 1801 Maple Ave Evanston IL 60208-0001

MUSACCHIA, X(AVIER) J(OSEPH), physiology and biophysics educator; b. Bklyn., Feb. 11, 1923; s. Castrense and Orsolina (Mazzola) M.; m. Betty Cook, Nov. 23, 1950; children: Joseph, Mary, Thomas, Laura Ann. BS, St. Francis Coll., Bklyn., 1944; MS, Fordham U., 1947, PhD, 1949. Instr. biology Marymount (N.Y.) Coll., 1948-49; from instr. to prof. biology St. Louis U., 1949-65; prof. physiology U. Mo., Columbia, 1965-78; prof. physiology and biophysics U. Louisville, 1978-91, prof. emeritus, 1991—, dean Grad. Sch., 1978-89, assoc. provost for rsch., 1985-89. Bd. dirs. Coun. Grad. Schs., 1986-89. Author: Depressed Metabolism, 1969, Regulation of Depressed Metabolism and Thermogenesis, 1976, Survival in Cold, 1981; also articles. Bd. govs. J. Graham Brown Cancer Ctr., Louisville, 1978-83; bd. dirs. Oak Ridge Associated Univs. Served with AUS, 1943-45. Research grantee NIH; Research grantee NASA. Fellow AAAS; mem. Am. Physiol. Soc., Am. Soc. Zoologists, Am. Soc. for Space and Gravitational Biology (v.p. 1988-89, pres. 1989-90), Soc. Exptl. Biology and Medicine, Corp. Marine Biol. Lab., Sigma Xi. (past chpt. pres.) Address: 1770 East Overland Dr Fayetteville AR 72703-5202

MUSACCHIO, ROBERT A. medical association administrator; B of Econs., SUNY; D of Econs., U. Wis. Sr. v.p. membership & info., chief info. officer AMA, Chgo. Bus. dir., mng. editor AMA's Health Insight, AMA's Website; mem. bd. advisors Intel. Contbr. articles to profl. jours. Office: Jour Am Med Assn 515 N State St Chicago IL 60610-4325

MUSANTE, TONY (ANTHONY PETER MUSANTE JR.), actor; b. Bridgeport, Conn.; s. Anthony Peter and Natalie Anne (Salerno) M.; m. Jane Ashley Sparkes, June 2, 1962. BA (Baker scholar), Oberlin Coll., 1958; postgrad., Northwestern U., 1957; student, HB Studios, N.Y.C., 1961-65. Appearances include: (off Broadway prodns.) Borak, 1960, Zoo Story, Night of the Dunce, The Collection, Match-Play, Kiss Mama, L'Histoire du Soldat, A Gun Play, Falling Man, Cassatt, Grand Magic, The Big Knife, The Taming of the Shrew, Two Brothers, The Archbishop's Ceiling, Souvenir, A Streetcar Named Desire, Double Play, Dancing in the End Zone, Snow Orchid, Wait until Dark, Widows, Anthony Rose, Mount Allegro, Frankie and Johnny in the Clair de Lune, Breaking Legs, The Flip Side, Love Letters, The Sisters, Italian Funerals and Other Festive Occasions (Broadway prodns.) PS Your Cat is Dead, 1975 (N.Y. Drama Desk nomination), Memory of Two Mondays, 27 Wagons Full of Cotton, The Lady from Dubuque; films: Once a Thief, 1964, The Incident (Best Actor award Mar del Plata Internat. Film Festival), 1967, The Detective, The Mercenary, One Night at Dinner, Bird with the Crystal Plumage, Grissom Gang, Anonymous Venetian, The Last Run, Pisciotta Case, Goodbye and Amen, Break-Up, Collector's Item, The Repenter, Devil's Hill, Appointment in Trieste, Nocturne, The Pope of Greenwich Village, The Deep End of the Ocean, The Yards, Life As It Comes; TV appearances include Ride with Terror, 1963, star series Toma, 1973-74 (Photoplay Gold medal award 1974), scriptwriter several episodes; star HBO series Oz, A&E series 100 Centre Street; also starred in TV miniseries and movies: Traffic, Exiled, The Seventh Scroll, Deep Family Secrets, A Kiss In the Dark, High Ice, Breaking Up is Hard to Do, The Baron, Legend of the Black Hand, The Story of Esther, My Husband is Missing, Nowhere to Hide, The Quality of Mercy (Emmy nominee 1975), Court Martial of Lt. William Calley, Night Heat, Rearview Mirror, Nutcracker: Money, Madness and Murder, Acapulco HEAT, Nothing Sacred, American Playhouse: Weekend, Last Waltz on a Tightrope; daytime TV (guest star): Loving, ABC, 1993, As The World Turns, CBS, 2000. Mem. SAG, AFTRA, ATAS, Actors Equity Assn., Writers Guild Am. West, Acad. Motion Picture Arts and Scis.

MUSCARELLA, CHRISTOPHER JAMES, finance educator; b. New Brunswick, N.J., Aug. 30, 1952; s. Mark Benjamin and Virginia (Pickert) M.; m. Bobbie Jean Weidner, June 1, 1985; children: Sarah Anne, Aaron Matthew BSEE, U. Notre Dame, 1974, MBA, 1976; PhD, Purdue U., 1983. Asst. prof. So. Meth. U., Dallas, 1984-90; sr. fin. economist U.S. Securities & Exch. Commn., Washington, 1990-91; prof., L.W. Roy and Mary Lois Clark tchg. fellow Pa. State U., University Park, 1991—. Vis. asst. prof. U. Notre Dame, Ind., 1979, U. Oreg., Eugene, 1980—82, U. Utah, Salt Lake City, 1982—84; Dale S. Coenen vis. prof. free enterprise Darden Grad. Sch. Bus. Adminstrn. U. Va., 2000; J. William Fulbright Disting. Chair Portugese Cath. U., Lisbon, 2001. Editor (assoc.): Jour. Fin. Rsch., 1993—99. Mem.: European Fin. Assn., Fin. Mgmt. Assn. (northeast regional dir. 1994—96, v.p. program 2002, assoc. editor Survey and Synthesis Soc. 2001—), Am. Fin. Assn. Avocation: genealogy. Office: Coll Bus Adminstrn 609 BAB University Park PA 16802 E-mail: cmuscarella@psu.edu.

MUSCATINE, CHARLES, English educator, author; b. Bklyn., Nov. 28, 1920; m. Doris Corn, July 21, 1945; children: Jeffrey, Alison. BA, Yale U., 1941, MA, 1942, PhD, 1948; L.H.D. (hon.), New Sch. for Social Research, 1982; Litt.D., SUNY, 1989, Rosary Coll., 1991. Mem. faculty dept. English U. Calif., Berkeley, 1948—, prof., 1960-91, prof. emeritus, 1991—, dir. Collegiate Seminar Program, 1974-80. Vis. prof. Wesleyan U., 1951-53; Ward Phillips lectr. U. Notre Dame, 1969; mem. com. of selection J.S. Guggenheim Found., 1969-89, chmn. 1985-89. Author: Chaucer and the French Tradition, 1957, The Book of Geoffrey Chaucer, 1963, Poetry and Crisis in the Age of Chaucer, 1972, The Old French Fabliaux, 1986, Medieval Literature, Style, and Culture, 1999; co-author, editor: Education at Berkeley, 1966, (with M. Griffith) The Borzoi College Reader, 1966, 7th edit., 1992, First Person Singular, 1973; co-editor Integrity in the Coll. Curriculum, 1985. Bd. dirs. No. Calif. chpt. ACLU, 1959-62, 63-66, Assn. Am. Colls., 1979-82, Ctr. for the Common Good, 1994-99; bd. dirs. Fedn. State Humanities Couns., 1989-94, chair, 1991-93; mem. Commn. on Humanities, Rockefeller Found., 1978-79, Calif. Coun. Humanities, 1986-94. With USNR, 1942-45. Recipient Navy Commendation ribbon, 1945, Berkeley citation, 1991; Fulbright fellow, 1958, 62, ACLS Rsch. fellow, 1958, Guggenheim fellow, 1962, NEH Sr. fellow, 1968. Fellow Am. Acad. Arts and Scis., Medieval Acad. of Am.; mem. MLA, New Chaucer Soc. (pres. 1980-81), Aircraft Owners and Pilots Assn., Phi Beta Kappa. Home: 2812 Buena Vista Way Berkeley CA 94708-2016 Personal E-mail: chasm@berkeley.edu.

MUSCATO, ANDREW, lawyer; b. Newark, Aug. 28, 1953; s. Salvatore and Bertha (Kubilus) M.; m. Ann Marie Hughes, Aug. 19, 1978; children: Amy, Andrew Joseph, Amanda. AB magna cum laude, Brown U., 1975; JD, Seton Hall U., 1978. Bar: N.J. 1978, U.S. Dist. Ct. N.J. 1978, U.S. Ct. Appeals (3d cir.) 1981, N.Y. 1984, U.S. Dist. Ct. (so. and ea. dists.) N.Y. 1984, U.S. Dist. Ct. (no. dist.) N.Y. 1998. Law clk. to presiding judge, appellate div. N.J. Superior Ct., Somerville, 1978-79; staff atty. Adminstrv. Office of Cts., Trenton, N.J., 1979-80; assoc. Simon & Allen, Newark, 1980-86; ptnr. Kirsten & Simon, Newark, 1987-89, Whitman & Ransom, Newark, 1989-93, Whitman Breed Abbott & Morgan, LLP, Newark, 1993-99; counsel Skadden, Arps, Slate, Meagher & Flom LLP, Newark, 1999—; commr. N.J. Pub. Employee Rels. Commn., 1999—2002; mem. N.J. Banking Adv. Bd., 2002—. Atty. Irvington (N.J.) Rent Leveling Bd., 1980—. Author: Executing on a Debtor's Interest in a Tenancy by the Entirety, 1986. Mem. ABA, Essex County Bar Assn., Trial Attys. N.J., N.J. Inst. Mcpl. Attys., Def. Rsch. Inst. Republican. Roman Catholic. Home: 66 Addison Dr Basking Ridge NJ 07920-2202 Office: Skadden Arps Slate Meagher & Flom LLP 4 Times Sq New York NY 10036

MUSCH, DAVID C. epidemiologist; BS, Calvin Coll., Grand Rapids, Mich., 1976; MPH, U. Mich., 1978, PhD, 1981. Rsch. investigator U. Mich., Ann Arbor, 1981—86, asst. rsch. scientist, 1986—89, assoc. rsch. scientist, 1989—96, rsch. scientist, 1996—97, sr. rsch. scientist, 1997—2003, prof., 2003—. Cornea panel methodologist Am. Acad. Ophthalmology, 1995—; mem. data and safety monitoring bd. Nat. Eye Inst./NIH, Bethesda, Md., 1999—. Mem. editl. bd. Ophthalmology Jour., 1987—. Bd. dirs. Ann Arbor Christian Sch., 1996—99. Recipient Honor award, Am. Acad. Ophthalmology, 1992. Fellow: Am. Coll. Epidemiology; mem.: Soc. for Clin. Trials, Assn. for Rsch. in Vision and Ophthalmology. Office: Univ of Michigan Kellogg Eye Ctr 1000 Wall St Ann Arbor MI 48105 Office Phone: 734-763-8175. E-mail: dmusch@umich.edu.

MUSCHENHEIM, FREDERICK, retired pathologist; b. NYC, July 9, 1932; s. Carl and Haroldine (Humphreys) M.; m. Linda Alexander, Mar. 29, 1958; children: Alexandra Lydia, Carl William, David Henry. AB, Harvard U., 1953; MDCM, McGill U., Montreal, Can., 1963. Intern Santa Clara County Hosp., San Jose, Calif., 1963-64; resident in pathology U. Colo. Med. Ctr., Denver, 1964-68, chief resident in clin. pathology, 1968-69; pathologist Freeman, Hanske, Munkittrick & Foley PA, Mpls., 1969-77; clin. pathologist Union-Truesdale Hosp., Fall River, Mass., 1977-78; chief pathologist St. Clare's Hosp., Denville, N.J., 1978-83, Oneida Healthcare Ctr., 1984-99, ret., 1999; cons. pathologist St. Jude Hosp., Vieux Fort, St. Lucia, West Indies, 1999—2002. Clin. asst. prof. SUNY Health Sci. Ctr., Syracuse, 1984-90, clin. assoc. prof., 1990-97, clin. prof., 1998-99, clin. prof. emeritus, 1999-2001; chief med. staff Oneida City Hosps., 1991; pres. Sunderman Fund, Bermuda Biol. Sta. for Rsch., v.p. Madison County (NY) bd. health, 1995-96, pres., 1997-2000. Choir 1st Presbyn. Ch. of Cazenovia, NY, 1984-2000, trustee, 1985-89; choir Wayzata (Minn.) Cmty. Ch., 2001—. Mem.: Syracuse ARC Blood Svcs. (chmn. med. adv. coun. 1995—99), Minn. Soc. Pathologists (sec. 2002—), N.Y. State Soc. Pathologists (councilor 2nd dist. 1991—2000, chmn. legis. com. 1991—2000, del. to MSSNY 1998—99), N.Y. State Assn. Pub. Health Labs. (v.p. 1992—93, pres. 1993—94, edn. chmn. 1994—95), Med. Soc. Madison County (v.p. 1990—91, pres. 1991—93), Med. Soc. State of N.Y. (legis. com. 1991—2000), Coll. Am. Pathologists (govt. affairs com. 1994—97, nominating com. 1995, steering com. ho. dels. 1999—2002), Assn. Clin. Scientists (v.p. 1989, pres. 1990, rec. sec. 1995—, del. Intersoc. Pathology Coun. 2004—, Diploma of Honor 1991). Home: 1159 Hollybrook Dr Wayzata MN 55391-1364

MUSCO, LYNN ANN, music educator; b. Reedsburg, Wis., Aug. 6, 1959; d. Lewis Alan and Geraldine Ann Schmidt; m. Enrico Musco III, Dec. 31, 1999; m. Bruce John Cholka, Sept. 16, 1981 (div. Nov. 1997); 1 child, Alexander Blaine Cholka. BFA, U Wis., 1984; MusM, N.Mex State U, 1986; Mus D Fla. State U, 1994. Freelance music, Fla., 1981—, 1981—; grad. asst. tchr. N.Mex State U, Las Cruces, N.Mex., 1983—86, Fla. State U, Tallahassee, 1986—88; prof. music Stetson U Sch. of Music, Deland, Fla., 1988—. Prin. clarinent Bach Festival Orch., Winter Park, Fla., 1996—. Contbr. Tres Vientos - Music of Am. Composers. Mem.: Am. Federation of Musicians, Fla. Bandmasters Assoc. (assoc.). Democrat. Meth. Avocations: reading, remodeling old homes, sewing, gardening. Office: Stetson Univeristy School of Music 421 North Woodland Blvd Deland FL 32720

MUSE, GAR, architectural firm executive; b. Newark, N.J. MArch, U. Fla. Registered Ga., cert. NCARB. From retail group dir. to prin. Cooper Carry Inc., Atlanta, 1990—92, prin., 1992—. Awards juror Superior Achievement Design and Imaging. Bd. dir. Sandy Springs Revitalization Inc. Mem.: Internat. Coun. Shopping Ctrs. Office: Cooper Carry Inc 3520 Piedmont Rd NE Ste 200 Atlanta GA 30305-1595*

MUSE, WILLIAM VAN, academic administrator; b. Marks, Miss., Apr. 7, 1939; s. Mose Lee and Mary Elizabeth (Hisaw) M.; m. Anna Marlene Munden, Aug. 22, 1964; children: Amy Marlene, Ellen Elizabeth, William Van. BS (T.H. Harris scholar), Northwestern La. State U., 1960; MBA (Nat. Def. Grad. fellow), U. Ark., 1961, PhD (Nat. Def. Grad. fellow), 1966. Instr. U. Ark., 1962-63; field supr. Tau Kappa Epsilon Fraternity, 1963-64; asst. prof. Ga. Tech., 1964-65; assoc. prof., chmn., dir. rsch. Ohio U., 1965-70; dean Coll. Bus. Appalachian State U., Boone, N.C., 1970-73; dean Coll. Bus. Adminstrn. U. Nebr., Omaha, 1973-79, Tex. A&M U., College Station, 1979-82, vice chancellor, 1983-84; pres. U. Akron, Ohio, 1984-92, Auburn U., Ala., 1992-2001; chancellor East Carolina U., 2001—. Author: Business and Economic Problems in Appalachia, 1969, Management Practices in Fraternities, 1965; Contbr. articles to profl. jours. Found. for Econ. Edn. fellow, 1967. Mem. Blue Key, Omicron Delta Kappa, Phi Kappa Phi, Delta Sigma Pi, Beta Gamma Sigma, Pi Omega Pi, Tau Kappa Epsilon, Phi Beta Kappa. Clubs: Rotarian. Office: Chancellors Office East Carolina Univ 103 Spilman Bldg Greenville NC 27858-4353 E-mail: musew@mail.ecu.edu.

MUSER, TONY, former manager professional athletics; b. L.A., Aug. 1, 1947; m. Nancy Muser; children: Tony Jr., Michael, Kristi. Student, San Diego Mesa Jr. Coll. Maj. league baseball player Boston, 1969, White Sox, 1971-75, Balt., 1975-77, Milw. Brewers, 1978; profl. baseball player Seibu Lions, Japanese Pacific League, 1979; mgr. Stockton A, Calif. League, 1980, El Paso AA then Vancouver AAA, 1983; 3rd base coach Milw. Big League Staff, 1985-88, hitting instr., 1987-89; amateur, maj. league crosschecker Milw. West Coast, 1991; mgr. Denver AAA, Am. Assn., 1991-92, Milw. Brewers; bullpen coach Chgo. Cubs, 1993, 3rd base coach then hitting coach, 1994-97; mgr. Kansas City Royals, 1997—2002. Named Calif. League Champions, 1980, Mgr. of Yr., Am. Assn., 1991. Office: Kansas City Royals Baseball Club PO Box 419969 Kansas City MO 64141-6969

MUSFELT, DUANE CLARK, lawyer; b. Stockton, Calif., Sept. 14, 1951; s. Robert H. and Doris E. (Roth) M.; m. Linh T. To, Sept. 6, 1980. Student, U. Calif., Davis, 1969-71; BA in Econs., U. Calif., Berkeley, 1973; JD, UCLA, 1976. Bar: Calif. 1976, U.S. Dist. Ct. (cen. dist.) Calif. 1977, U.S. Ct. Appeals (9th cir.) 1980, U.S. Dist. Ct. (no. dist.) Calif. 1982, U.S. Dist. Ct. (ea. and so. dists.) Calif. 1983, U.S. Supreme Ct. 1987. Assoc. Haight, Dickson, Brown & Bonesteel, L.A., 1976-77, Mori & Ota, L.A., 1977-79, Lewis, D'Amato, Brisbois & Bisgaard, L.A., 1979-82; ptnr. Lewis, Brisbois, Bisgaard & Smith, San Francisco, 1982—. Mem. State Bar Calif., Bar Assn. San Francisco. Democrat. Presbyterian. Avocations: tennis, skiing, bridge. Office: Lewis Brisbois Bisgaard & Smith One Sansome St Ste 1400 San Francisco CA 94104-4431 Office Phone: 415-362-2580. Business E-Mail: Musfelt@lbbslaw.com.

MUSGRAVE, FRANKLYN GARFIELD, obstetrician, gynecologist; b. Basseterre, St. Kitts, 1942; s. William Franklin and Inez Lucina (Clarke) M.; children: Ian K., Franklyn G. BA in Psychology and Zoology, Sir George Williams U., Montreal, 1968; MD, Howard U., 1975. Adminstrv. asst. office of the dean of students Sir George Williams U., 1968—69; biochemistry tech. Montreal Children's Hosp., 1969—70; tchg. asst. dept. zoology Howard U., 1970—71, summer fellow, 1972—73; extern in emergency care and family practice clinic Howard U. Hosp., 1973—75; intern, resident Georgetown U. Hosp., Wash., DC, 1975—78; pvt. practice ob-gyn. Washington, 1979—; clinician Pub. Benefit Corp., 1979—2001; gynecologist Comn. Pub. Health, DC, 2002—. Past v.p. DC Dr.'s Coun. Mem. Physicians for DC Youth Orchestra Program. Mem.: Assn. Clin. Physicians DC (past pres.), Med. Chrirugical Soc. DC, DC Med. Soc. (mem. judiciary com., spkr.'s bur.), Nat. Med. Assn. Office: 1808 Connecticut Ave NW Ste 104 Washington DC

MUSGRAVE, MARILYN N. congresswoman; b. Greeley, Colo., Jan. 27, 1949; m. Steven Musgrave, 4 children BA, Colo. State U. Co-owner Musgrave Bale Stacking; mem. Colo. Ho. of Reps., 1995—99, Colo. Senate, Dist. 1, Denver, 1998—2003; chmn. transp. com.; mem. health, environment, welfare and instns. com.; mem. state, vets. and mil. affairs com.; mem. U.S. Ho. Reps. from 4th Colo. dist., 2003—. Past pres. Morgan County Rep. Women; former bd. mem. RE-3 Sch. Dist. Republican. Office: 1208 Longworth HOB Washington DC 20515-0604

MUSGRAVE, MICHAEL G. musicologist, musician; b. London, Aug. 26, 1942; came to U.S., 1997; s. Albert Henry and Phillis Mary Musgrave; m. Celia Helen Terrington, July 31, 1965 (div. Mar. 1983); children: Stephen Michael, Jonathan Mark; m. Janie Elizabeth Bailey. Grad. diploma, Royal Schs. of Music, 1963; cert. music tchr., U. London, 1964, MusB with 1st class honors, 1973, PhD, 1980. Dir. music Eltham Hill Sch., London, 1964-74; lectr. in music U. London, 1974-80, prin. lectr., 1980-89, reader in music, 1989-94, prof. music, 1994-98, prof. emeritus, 1998—. Vis. rsch. fellow Royal Coll. Music, 1998—; acad. adv. coun. Manhattan Sch. Music, N.Y.C., 1999. Author: (book) The Music of Brahms, 1985, The Music of Brahms, 2d edit., 1994, The Musical Life of the Crystal Palace, 1994, Brahms: A German Requiem, 1996, A Brahms Reader, 2000; editor (contbr.): Brahms 2: Biographical, Documentary and Analytical Studies, 1987, The Cambridge Companion to Brahms, 1999, Performing Brahms, 2003; editor: (contbr.) George Grove, Music and Victorian Culture, 2003; rev. editor Music Analysis jour., 1982—93, mem.

adv. bd., 1993—; editor: articles to profl. jours., —. Fellow Royal Coll. Organists, Royal Soc. Arts; mem. Royal Coll. Music (assoc.), Trägerverein, Johannes Brahms Gesamtausgabe. Avocations: musical performance, literature, theater, travel.

MUSGRAVE, R. KENTON, federal judge; b. 1927; Student, Ga. Inst. Tech., 1945-46, U. Fla., 1946-47; BA, U. Wash., 1948; JD with distinction, Emory U., 1953. Asst. gen. counsel Lockheed Internat., 1953-62; v.p., gen. counsel Mattel, Inc., 1963-71; mem. firm Musgrave, Welbourn and Fertman, 1972-75; asst. gen. counsel Pacific Enterprises, 1975-81; v.p., gen. counsel Vivitar Corp, 1981-85; v.p., dir. Santa Barbara Applied Rsch., 1982-87; judge U.S. Ct. Internat. Trade, N.Y.C., 1987—. Trustee The Dian Fossey Gorilla Fund, Dolphins of Sharks Bay (Australia); hon. trustee Pet Protection Soc.; mem. United Way, Save the Redwoods League; active Palos Verdes Community Assn. Mem. Internat. Bar Assn., Pan Am. Bar Assn., State Bar Calif. (chmn. corp. law sect. 1965-66, del. 1966-67), L.A. County Bar Assn., Fng. Trade Assn. So. Calif. (bd. dirs.). Office: US Ct Internat Trade 1 Federal Plz New York NY 10278-0001

MUSGRAVE, STORY, astronaut, surgeon, pilot, physiologist, educator; b. Boston, Aug. 19, 1935; children: Lorelei Lisa, Bradley Scott, Holly Kay, Christopher Todd, Jeffrey Paul, Lane Linwood. BS in Math. and Stats., Syracuse U., 1958; MBA, UCLA, 1959; BA in Chemistry, Marietta Coll., 1960; MD, Columbia U., 1964; MS in Biophysics, U. Ky., 1966; MA in Lit., U. Houston, 1987, MA in Humanities, 1989. Surg. intern U. Ky. Med. Ctr., Lexington, 1964-65; scientist-astronaut NASA, Houston, 1967-97, backup sci.-pilot 1st Skylab mission, 1973, flew on first Challenger flight, STS-6, 1983, flew on Spacelab 2, 1985, flew on space shuttle mission STS-33, 1989, flew on STS-44, 1991, flew as payload comdr. STS61 Hubble Telescope Repair Mission, 1993, flew on STS-80 last flight, 1996; concept artist Walt Disney Imagineering, 1997—; innovator, inventor Applied Minds Inc., 2000—; performing artist, 1997—; poet and writer, 1997—; designer Tupperware Inc., 2003—; innovator, inventor Applied Minds Inc., 2000—; designer Tupperware, 2003—. Contbr. articles to profl. jours. With USMC, 1953-56. Recipient Reese AFB Comdr.'s trophy, 1969, NASA exceptional svc. medal, 1974, 83, 90, NASA disting. svc. medal, 1992, 94, 97, NASA spaceflight medal, 1983, 85, 89, 91, 93, 96, Space award Aviation Week and Space Tech., 1997; USAF postdoctoral fellow, 1965-66, Nat. Heart Inst. postdoctoral fellow, 1966-67. Mem. AAAS, AAS, AIAA, Flying Physicians Assn. (Airman of Yr. award 1974, 83), Civil Aviation Med. Assn., N.Y. Acad. Sci., Nat. Geog. Soc., Soaring Soc. Am., U.S. Parachute Assn., Marine Corps Assn., Alpha Kappa Psi, Phi Delta Theta, Omicron Delta Kappa, Beta Gamma Sigma. E-mail: storymusgrave@hotmail.com. *From subatomic particles, to the stardust from which I was created, from the forming galaxies, to the universes beyond our own, I live to participate physically and spiritually in every aspect of this cosmic creation and evolution.*

MUSGRAVE, THEA, composer, conductor; b. Edinburgh, Scotland, May 27, 1928; m. Peter Mark, 1971. student, Mus D, Paris Conservatory. Composer: (opera) The Abbot of Drimock, 1955, The Decision, 1964-65, The Voice of Ariadne, 1972-73, Mary, Queen of Scots, 1975-77, (first performed Scottish Opera) A Christmas Carol, 1978-79 (first performed Va. Opera Assn., 1979), An Occurrence at Owl Creek Bridge, 1981, Harriet, The Woman Called Moses, 1981-84 (first performed Va. Opera 1985), Simon Bolivar, Pontalba, New Orleans Opera, 2001-03, (ballet) Beauty and the Beast, 1969, (symphony and orchestral music) Obliques, 1958, Nocturnes and Arias, 1966, Concerto for Orch., 1967, Clarinet Concerto, 1968, Night Music, 1969, Scottish Dance Suite, 1969, Memento Vitae, 1969-70, Orfeo II, 1975, Soliloquy II and III, 1980, From One to Another, 1980, Peripeteia, 1981, The Seasons, 1988, (marimba concerto) Journey through a Japanese Landscape, (bass-clarinet concerto) Autumn Sonata, (oboe concerto) Helios, Phoenix Rising, 1997, (orchestral work) Turbulent Landscapes, (chamber and instrumental music) String Quartet, 1958, Trio for flute, oboe and piano, 1960, Monologue, 1960, Serenade, 1961, Chamber concerto No. 1, 1962, Chamber Concerto No. 2, 1966, Chamber Concerto No. 3, 1966, Music for horn and piano, 1967, Impromptu No. 1, 1967, Soliloquy I, 1969, Elegy, 1970, Impromptu No. 2, 1970, Space Play, 1974, Orfeo I, 1975, Fanfare, 1982, Pierrot, 1985, Narcissus, 1987, Niobe, 1987, (vocal and choral music) Two Songs, 1951, Four Madrigals, 1953, Six Songs: Two Early English Poems, 1953, A Suite O'Bairnsangs, 1953, Cantata for a Summer's Day, 1954, Song of the Burn, 1954, Five Love Songs, 1955, Four Portraits, 1956, A Song for Christmas, 1958, Triptych, 1959, Sir Patrick Spens, 1961, Make Ye Merry for Him That Is to Come, 1962, Two Christmas Carols in Traditional Style, 1963, John Cook, 1963, Five Ages of Man, 1963-64, Memento Creatoris, 1967, Primavera, 1971, Rorate Coeli, 1973, Monologues of Mary, Queen of Scots, 1977-86, O Caro M'e Il Sonno, 1978, The Last Twilight, 1980, Black Tambourine, 1985, For the Time Being, 1986, Echoes Through Time, 1988, Wild Winter for Viols & Voices, 1993, On the Underground Sets 1, 2 & 3, 1994, 95, (Robert Burns' poems for soprano & orch.) Songs for a Winter's Evening, 1995, (for orch.) Phoenix Rising, 1996-97, (for 3 flutes and percussion) Voices from the Ancient World, 1998, (for chorus and orch.) Celebration Day, 1998-99, (for 8 instruments) Lamenting With Ariadne, 1999, (for orch.) Turbulent Landscapes, Boston Symphony, 2004. Office: Va Opera Assn PO Box 2580 Norfolk VA 23501-2580

MUSGROVE, DAVID RONALD (RONNIE MUSGROVE), former governor; b. Sardis, Miss., July 29, 1956; s. Henry and Nina (Rogers) M.; m. Melanie Ballard, children: Jordan, Carmen, Rae. AA, Northwest Miss. C.C., 1976; BS, U. Miss., 1978, JD, 1981. Bar: Miss. Ptnr. Smith, Musgrove & McCord, Batesville, Miss., 1981—2000; lt. gov. State of Miss., 1996—2000, gov., 2001—04. State sen. Miss. State, 1988-96; chair Nat. Conf. Lt. Govs., 1998-99. Pres. Batesville Jaycees, 1982-83; chair Panola County Heart Fund, 1985-86; deacon First Bapt. Ch., Batesville, 1983-2000. Fellow Miss. Bar Found; mem. Am. Inns Ct., Panola County Bar Assn., Tri-County Bar Assn., Miss. Young Lawyers Assn. Democrat.

MUSGROVE, KAY AWALT, retired school system administrator; b. Mineral Wells, Tex., Mar. 20, 1942; d. Pat O. T. and Mary Lee Morse; m. Robert Musgrove; children: Stacy (dec.), Bradley. BS, Tex. Wesleyan Coll., 1966; MS in Edn., Baylor U., 1972; PhD, Vanderbilt U., 1988. Cert. tchr., prin., supr. Elem. tchr. San Antonio Pub. Schs., 1966, LaVega Pub. Schs., Waco, Tex., 1966-68; with reading clinic Baylor U., Waco, 1969-70; thcr. reading Franklin Spl. Schs., Tenn., 1970-71, first grade tchr., 1971-80, asst. prin., 1980-84, prin., 1984-90, Moore Elem. Sch., Franklin, 1990-97, assoc. supt., 1997—2002; ret., 2002. Adv. coun. for tchr. cert. and edn. Tenn. State Sch. Bd., 1977-86; adminstr. career level III State of Tenn., 1987—; chmn. for revision elem. cert. State of Tenn.; cons. in field. Co-author Religious Christian Day Sch. Curriculum, 1978; author: Study Book for 6-8 Year Olds, 1980. Tenn. spl. scholar, 1983-84; named Tenn. Elem. Prin. of Yr., 1994, Nat. Disting. Prin. Tenn., 1996, So. Assn. Disting. Educator, 2002. Mem. ASCD (bd. dirs. 1992-95, exec. coun. 1995-98, internat. pres.-elect 2000-01, pres. 2001-2002), Internat. Reading Assn., Mid. Tenn. Coun. Internat. Reading Assn., Tenn. Assn. Supervision and Curriculum Devel. (pres. 1986-87, 92-93, exec. sec. 1993—), Tenn. Bd. Examiners for State for Approval of Tchr. Edn., Delta Kappa Gamma (pres. Rho chpt.). Baptist.

MUSHAK, PAUL, toxicologist, consultant; b. Dunmore, Pa., Dec. 9, 1935; s. Steven and Mary Mushak; m. Elizabeth Orr Walker, June 30, 1973. BS in Chemistry (magna cum laude), U. Scranton, 1961; PhD, U. Fla., 1969; postgrad., Yale U., 1969-71. Diplomate Am. Bd. Forensic Medicine, Am. Coll. Forensic Examiners, 1996. Asst. prof. U. N.C. Sch. Medicine, Chapel Hill, 1971-77, assoc. prof., 1977-85; prin. PB Assocs., Durham, N.C., 1992—. Adj. prof. U. N.C. Sch. medicine, 1986-93; vis. prof. Albert Einstein Coll. of Medicine, Bronx, N.Y., 1995—; mem. com., cons. EPA Sci. Adv. Bd., Washington, 1989-97; mem. com. Nat. Acad. of Sci., Washington, 1989-93, 85-87, 73-75. Author and co-author chpts. to books and 175 sci. publs. in field. Mem. Environ. Affairs Bd., Durham, NC, 1990—92, Durham Housing Appeals Bd., NC, 1990—93. Recipient Pre-doctoral fellowship, NIH, 1961-67, Post-doctoral fellowship, Yale U., 1969-71; recipient Meritorious Svc. award U.S. EPA, Cin., 1981; grantee NIH, 1971-85; Hon. Mention in Colloid Chemistry Rsch., U. of S.C., 1961 Fellow Am. Coll. Forensic Examiners; mem. Soc. for Risk Analysis, Soc. of Toxicology. Achievements include Lab. methods for testing constituents of antique textiles; research in major studies on lead poisoning in children: lead vs. IQ, lead levels in remote peoples, physical chemical and biochemical determinants of metal toxicity, paths of exposure. Office: PB Assocs 714 9th St Ste 204 Durham NC 27705-4849 Office Phone: 919-286-7193. Personal E-mail: pandbmushak@cs.com.

MUSHAM, BETTYE MARTIN, consumer products executive; m. William C. Musham. Diploma, Duke U. Mgr. U.S. Louis Vuitton; owner, pres. GEAR Holdings, Inc., NYC, 1977-99, chmn., CEO, 1999—. Established internship program with GEAR and R.I. Sch. Design, Cornell U., U. Va., Auburn U.; bd. dirs. Brunswick Corp., IO Electric, Peace Links, World Svc. Council of the YWCA; adv. bd. N.Y.C. Partnership, Bus. Council United Nations, Duke U. Sch. Environment, Duke U. Hosp., 1986-91; Commr. Del. and Lehigh Navigation Canal Nat. Heritage Corridor, 1989; trustee Marymount Manhattan Coll., R.I. Sch. Design, 1983-91. Recipient Nat. Entrepreneurial award Nat. Assn. Women Bus. Owners N.Y., 1983, 1994. Mem. Nat. Home Fashions, Am. Nurses Assn., Am. Women's Econ. Dev. Corp., Women's Forum, Com. of 200, Catalyst, The Fashion Group, Sierra Club, Women's City Club N.Y. Office: GEAR Holdings Inc Radio City Sta PO Box 2236 New York NY 10101-2236 Office Phone: 212-459-0050. Office Fax: 212-459-0060. Business E-Mail: gearhome@aol.com.

MUSHEN, ROBERT LINTON, ophthalmologist, consultant; b. Klamath Falls, Oreg., Mar. 4, 1943; s. Samuel Albert and Beulah (Gore) Mushen; m. Deborah Campbell, July 5, 1969 (div. 1987); children: Melanie, Gregory, Timothy; m. Geraldine Kay Geise, Apr. 29, 1988. BSChemE (Nat. Merit scholar), Stanford U., 1964; MD, U. Oreg., 1968. Intern Santa Clara Valley Med. Ctr., San Jose, Calif., 1968—69; resident in ophthalmology Brooke Army Med. Ctr., San Antonio, 1972—75; chief svc. Kerrville (Tex.) VA Hosp., 1975—76; mem. staff Madigan Army Med. Ctr., Tacoma, 1976—77; chief of staff and eye svc. Kadlec Hosp., Richland, Wash., 1977—. Pres. Richland Eye Clinic, 1977—; cons. in field. Co-author: (book) Neuroanatomy Guide, 1967; contbr. articles to med. jours. Served with USMC, 1969—75. Recipient award, Oreg. Mus. Sci. and Industry, 1960; Nat. Eye Found. fellow, 1974—75. Mem.: AMA, Benton-Franklin County Med. Soc., Wash. Acad. Ophthalmology, Wash. Med. Assn., Soc. Eye Surgeons, Am. Intraocular Implant Soc., Am. Acad. Ophthalmology, A.C.S., Alpha Omega Alpha. Republican. Achievements include invention of bifocal trial lens. Office: Richland Eye Clinic 948 Stevens Dr Richland WA 99352-3547

MUSHINSKY, MARY M. state legislator; b. New Haven; m. Martin J. Waters; children: Martin Waters, Edward Waters. BA, So. Conn. State U., 1973; postgrad., Fla. Atlantic U.; MA, Wesleyan U., Middletown, Conn., 1993. Mem. Conn. Ho. of Reps., Hartford, 1981—, mem. environ., fin., revenue and bonding com., chmn., select com. on children. Democrat. Home: 188 S Cherry St Wallingford CT 06492-4016 Office: Conn House of Reps Capitol Ave Hartford CT 06106

MUSIAL, STAN(LEY) (FRANK MUSIAL), hotel and restaurant executive, former baseball team executive, former baseball player; b. Donora, Pa., Nov. 21, 1920; s. Lukasz M.; m. Lillian Labash, 1939; children: Richard, Geraldine, Janet, Jean. Ed. high sch., Donora. Baseball player St. Louis Cardinals Farm Team, 1938-41; 1st baseman, outfielder St. Louis Cardinals, Nat. League, 1941-63; sr. v.p. St. Louis Cardinals, 1963-91; pres. Stan Musial & Biggies, Inc., St. Louis. Author: Stan Musial: The Man's Own Story, 1964. Served with USNR, World War II. Voted Nat. League Rookie of Yr., 1943; named most valuable player Nat. League, 1943, 46, 48; mem. Nat. League All-Star Team, 1943-44, 46-63; voted most valuable player Baseball Writers Com., 1946; Maj. League Player of Year Sporting News, 1946, 51; Sid Mercer award N.Y. Baseball Writers, 1947; Kenesaw Mountain Landis Meml. plaque, 1948; Sports Illus. Sportsman of Yr., 1957; recipient Freedom Leadership medal, 1968; named to Baseball Hall of Fame, 1969; holder .331 lifetime batting average. Office: Stan the Man Inc 1650 Des Peres Rd Ste 125 Saint Louis MO 63131-1899

MUSICH, ROBERT LORIN, motivational speaker; b. Glendale, Calif., Feb. 15, 1969; s. Richard and Zola (Nickel) M. MBA, M, La Salle U. Sr. asst. mgr. Am. Gen. Fin., Upland, Calif., 1988-89; mgmt./corp. trainer Mortgage Link, Pasadena, 1989-94; mgr. AT&T, L.A., 1994-96; owner Musich & Assocs., West Covina, Calif., 1989—. Singer (tenor) So. Calif. Mormon Choir, 1994—; cand. Calif. State Assembly, 59th Dist., 1995; vol. Am. Cancer Soc., 1994-96; coach Youth League Football, 1987-92; elder's quorum pres. LDS Ch., sec., 1992-93, 2d and 1st counselor, 1995-96, mem. stake single adult com., 1993-95, mem. regional single adult com. bi-regional chmn., 1993-95. Republican. Avocations: singing, dance, theater, volleyball, football. Office: Musich and Associates 3447 E Hillhaven Dr West Covina CA 91791-1718

MUSICH, SHIRLEY ANN, research and development company executive; b. Atkinson, Nebr., Sept. 25, 1946; d. Donald John and Johanna Skrdla; children: Brian Matthew, Lisa Marie. BA, Mt. Marty Coll., Yankton, S.D., 1968; MS, U. of Minn., 1970; PhD, U. of Mich., 1998. Rsch. assoc., data analyst U. of Mich., Ann Arbor, 1995—. Contbr. articles to profl. jours. Recipient Mount Marty Professional Achievement award. Office: U Mich 1027 E Huron St Ann Arbor MI 48104

MUSICK, ANTHONY, financial executive; b. Sept. 8, 1945; BA, U. Md., 1972; MBA, George Washington U., 1990. CPA; cert. govt. fin. mgr. Various positions including dir. fin. mgmt. EPA, Washington, dep. dir. fin. mgmt.; auditor Ernst and Ernst, GAO, EPA Insp. Gen.; budget dir. Va. Commonwealth U., Richmond; CFO IRS, Washington; dep. CFO, dir. fin. mgmt. U.S. Dept. of Commerce, Washington, from 1998; CFO, Corp. Nat. Svcs., Washington. Mem. V.P. Gore's Nat. Performance Review, 1993. Office: Corp Nat Svcs 1201 New York Ave NW Washington DC 20525-0001

MUSICK, GERALD JOE, retired entomology educator; b. Ponca City, Okla., May 24, 1940; s. Arlie A. and Leona (Beier) M.; m. Florene Ione Thompson, May 11, 1962; children: Linda Kaye, Mary Louise. BS, Okla. State U., 1962; MS, Iowa State U., 1964; PhD, U. Mo., 1969. Grad. asst. Iowa State U., 1962-64; instr. U. Mo., 1964-69; asst. prof. Ohio State U., Wooster, 1969-71, assoc. prof., 1971-76; dept. head U. Ga., Tifton, 1976-79; prof., dept. head U. Ark., Fayetteville, 1979-86, interium dir. agrl. exptl. sta., 1986-87, dean, assoc. v.p. agrl. rsch., 1987-93, univ. prof. entomology, 1993—2002, chmn.-elect faculty coun. Dale Bumpers Coll. Agrl., Food and Life Scis., 1997, chmn., 1998, prof. emeritus, 2002—, ret., 2002—; chmn. faculty coun. Dale Bumpers Coll. of Agrl. Food and Life Scis., 1998. Author and co-author numerous publs. Vice-chairperson com. Coop. States Rsch. Svc., 1993, So. Expt. Sta.; chairperson steering com. Midwest Food Safety Consortium, 1991-93; mem. U. Ark. Faculty Senate, 1994—, chair campus faculty, 1998-99, chair faculty sentate 1999-2000, faculty exec. com., 1999—; coord. Pest Mgmt. Programs, 1998—. Mem. Entomol. Soc. Am. (pres. S.E. br. 1983-84), Ark. Acad. Sci., Ctrl. States Entomol. Soc. (v.p. 1995-96, pres. 1996-97), Sigma Xi, Gamma Sigma Delta. Lutheran. Avocation: golf. Office: Razorback Park Golf Course Fayetteville AR 72704 E-mail: gjmfim@cox-internet.com.

MUSICO, ANN J. executive secretary, writer; b. N.Y.C., N.Y., June 4, 1954; d. Poturi G. and Elizabeth Costos; m. Alexander Musico, July 16, 1983; children: Christopher James, Matthew Alexander, Elizabeth Grace. Secretarial course, Katharine Gibbs Secretarial Sch., N.Y.C., 1971—72; children's mag. writers course, Inst. Children's Lit., West Redding, Conn., 2002—03. Sec. Durkee Famous Foods, Englewood Cliffs, NJ, 1973—78, Okin Pressler & Shapiro, Esqs., Ft. Lee, NJ, 1978—83; 21st Century Properties, Wallkill, NY, 2002—. Author: (book) The King's Daughter, 2001. Mem. Concerned Women for Am., 2001—. Office Phone: 845-564-9600. Personal E-mail: amusico44@hotmail.com.

MUSIHIN, KONSTANTIN K. electrical engineer; b. Harbin, China, June 17, 1927; came to U.S., 1967, naturalized, 1973; s. Konstantin N. and Alexandra A. (Lapitsky) M.; m. Natalia Krilova, Oct. 18, 1964; 1 child, Nicholas. Student, YMCA Inst., 1942, North Manchurian U., 1945, Harbin Poly. Inst., 1948. Registered profl. engr., Calif., N.Y., Pa., Wash. Asst. prof. Harbin Poly. Inst., 1950-53; elec. engr. Moinho Santista, Sao Paulo, Brazil, 1955-60; constrn. project mgr. Caterpillar-Brazil, Santo Amaro, 1960-61; mech. engr. Matarazzo Industries, Sao Paulo, 1961-62; chief of works Vidrobras, St. Gobain, Brazil, 1962-64; project engr. Brown Boveri, Sao Paulo, 1965-67; sr. engr. Kaiser Engrs., Oakland, Calif., 1967-73, Bechtel Power Corp., San Francisco, 1973-75; supr. power and control San Francisco Bay Area Rapid Transit, Oakland, 1976-78; chief elec. engr. L.K. Comstock Engring. Co., San Francisco, 1978-79; prin. engr. Morrison Knudsen Co., San Francisco, 1979-84, Brown & Caldwell, Cons. Engrs., Pleasant Hill, Calif., 1984-85; cons. engr. Pacific Gas and Electric Co., San Francisco, 1986-89; sr. engr. Bechtel Corp., San Francisco, 1989. Mem. IEEE (life, sr.), NSPE, Calif. Soc. Profl. Engrs. Mem. Christian Orthodox Ch. Home: 5666 Ocean View Dr Oakland CA 94618-1533

MUSIL, ROBERT KIRKLAND, professional society administrator; b. N.Y.C., Oct. 27, 1943; s. Ralph A. and Margaret Hooker (Kirkland) M.; m. Caryn Lynne McTighe, June 15, 1968; children: Rebecca McTighe, Emily Kirkland. BA, Yale U., 1964; MA, Northwestern U., 1966, PhD, 1970; MPH, Johns Hopkins U., 2001. Instr. Def. Info. Sch., Ft. Benjamin Harrison, Ind., 1969-71; co-dir. CCCO/An Agy. for Mil. and Draft Counseling, Phila., 1971-74; dir. mil. affairs project Ctr. for Nat. Security Studies, Washington, 1974-75; asst. prof. English and Am. studies Temple U., Phila., 1976-78; prodr., host Consider the Alternatives Radio, Phila., 1978-92; exec. dir. SANE Edn. Fund, Phila. and Washington, 1984-88, Profls. Coalition for Nuclear Arms Control, Washington, 1988-92; dir. policy and programs Physicians for Social Responsibility, Washington, 1992-95, exec. dir., CEO, 1995—. Adj. prof. Sch. Internat. Svc., Am. U., 1997—. Prodr.: (documentary series) Shadows of the Nuclear Age: American Culture and the Bomb, 1980 (NEH grantee). Bd. dirs. Scoville Fellowships, Washington, 1989-92, 95—, SANE, 1978-84. Capt. U.S. Army, 1969-71. Recipient Maj. Armstrong award for radio Armstrong Found., Columbia U., N.Y.C., 1988, 89. Mem. United Ch. of Christ. Home: 8600 Irvington Ave Bethesda MD 20817-3604 Office: Physicians for Social Resp Ste 1012 1875 Connecticut Ave NW Washington DC 20009 E-mail: bmusil@psr.org.

MUSK, ELON, aerospace transportation executive; b. South Africa; married. Student, Queen's U., Kingston, Ont.; BS in Physics, U. Pa.; BS in bus., U. Pa. Wharton Sch. Bus. With Pinnacle Rsch.; software devel. Rocket Science, Microsoft; co-founder, chmn., CEO, chief tech. officer Zip2 Corp. (sold to Compaq for $307 million), 1995—99; co-founder, chmn. CEO PayPal (acquired by eBay for $1.5 billion), 1999—2002; founder, CEO, chief tech. officer Space Exploration Tech. Corp., 2002—. Bd. dirs. The Planetary Society, 2003—. Office: SpaceX 1310 E Grand Ave El Segundo CA 90245*

MUSKIN, VICTOR PHILIP, lawyer; b. N.Y.C., Mar. 1, 1942; s. Jacob Cecil and Fanya (Solomonoff) M.; m. Odette Cheryl Spreier, June 10, 1979; children: Adam James, Liana Jeanne. BA, Oberlin Coll., 1963; JD, NYU, 1966. Bar: N.Y. 1969, U.S. Dist. Ct. (so. and ea. dists.) N.Y. 1972, U.S. Ct. Appeals (2d cir.) 1974, U.S. Supreme Ct. 1974, U.S. Ct. Appeals (9th and 10th cirs.) 1978, U.S. Ct. Appeals (3d cir.) 1987. Asst. corp. counsel divsn. gen. litigation City of N.Y., 1969-73; assoc. Wolf, Popper, Ross, Wolf & Jones, N.Y.C., 1973-74, Reavis and McGrath, N.Y.C., 1974-78; pvt. practice N.Y.C., 1979, 1992—2003; ptnr. Gruen & Muskin, N.Y.C., 1980-81, Gruen, Muskin & Thau, N.Y.C., 1981-89, Munves, Tanenhaus & Storch, N.Y.C., 1989-90, Solin & Breimdel, N.Y.C., 1991-92; of counsel Scheichet & Davis, P.C., 2003—. Served with Peace Corps, 1966—68; pres. Brotherhood, Ctrl. Synagogue, N.Y.C., 1998—2002. Mem. N.Y.C. Bar Assn. (com. computer law 1982-84, com. internat. law 1996-99). Home: 529 E 84th St New York NY 10028-7330 Office: 800 Third Ave New York NY 10022 E-mail: vp.muskin@verizon.net.

MUSMANN, LOIS S. conductor, music educator; d. Myron Roger and Lois MacNary Steele; m. Ronald Clapp, Sept. 6, 1959 (div. 1983); children: Mark Douglass Steele, Debra Clapp Walter, Holly Clapp Rogers; m. Klaus Musmann, Dec. 27, 1986. MusB, New Eng. Conservatory Music, 1984; MusM, U. Redlands, 1986; D in Musical Arts, U. So. Calif., 1989. Condr., founder Musica Viva, Redlands and Riverside, Calif., 1990—95; condr., artistic dir. Euterpe Opera Theatre, L.A., 1993—; condr., founder Pacifica Chamber Orch., Redlands and Palm Springs, Calif., 1995—2001; condr. U. Calif. Choral Soc., Riverside, 1997—2000; prof. Notre Dame de Namur U., Belmont, Calif., 2001—; vis. scholar U. Calif. Beatrice Bain Rsch. Group, Berkeley, 2002—; prof. San Francisco Conservatory Music, 2003—. Lectr., founder lectr. series Redlands Symphony Orch., 1991—92, 1997—2001; chair Internat. Conf. Coll. Music Soc., Vienna, 1997; chair edn. com. San Diego Chamber Orch., La Jolla, Calif., 1997—99; mem. adv. bd. Inland Empire Chamber Music, San Bernardino, 1998—2001. Contbr. articles to profl. jours.; composer: Closing Prayer, 1987; condr.: world premier opera Serafina y Arcangela. Exec. advisor Am. Coun. N.Am. Indians, Haywood, Calif., 2001—02. Recipient Fulbright Scholar, Sr. Specialist in Music, 2004, Baroque Concerto Competition Winner, New Eng. Conservatory Music, 1984; grantee, Riverside Arts Found., 1991, 1992; Postdoctoral Fellow, U. So. Calif., 1996—2001, Disting. Accomplishments award, Goodwill Industries, 1994. Mem.: Nat. League Am. Pen Women, Assn. Calif. Symphony Orchs., Pi Kappa Lambda. Avocations: travel, reading, gardening. Home: 975 Pizarro Ln Foster City CA 94404 Office: Notre Dame de Namur Univ 1500 Ralston Ave Belmont CA 94002

MUSOLF, LLOYD DARYL, political science educator, institute administrator; b. Yale, SD, Oct. 14, 1919; s. William Ferdinand and Emma Marie (Pautz) M.; m. Berdyne Peet, June 30, 1944; children: Stephanie, Michael, Laura. BA, Huron Coll., 1941; MA, U. SD, 1946; PhD, Johns Hopkins U., 1950. Mem. faculty Vassar Coll., Poughkeepsie, NY, 1949-59, assoc. prof. polit. sci., 1955-59; chief of party adv. group Mich. State U., East Lansing, 1959-61, prof. polit. sci., 1961-63, U. Calif.-Davis, 1963-87, prof. emeritus, 1988—, dir. Inst. Govtl. Affairs, 1963-84. Vis. prof. Johns Hopkins U., Balt., 1953, U. Del., 1954, U. Mich., 1955-56; U.S. Nat. rapporteur for Internat. Congress Adminstrv. Scis., Berlin, 1983; cons., lectr. in field. Author: Federal Examiners and the Conflict of Law and Administration, 1953, Public Ownership and Accountability: The Canadian Experience, 1959, Promoting the General Welfare, Government and the Economy, 1965, (with others) American National Government-Policies and Politics, 1971, Mixed Enterprise-A Developmental Perspective, 1972, (with Springer) Malaysia's Parliamentary System-Representative Politics and Policymaking in a Divided Society, 1979, Uncle Sam's Private Profitseeking Corporations-Comsat, Fannie Mae, Amtrak and Conrail, 1983; editor: (with Krislov) The Politics of Regulation, 1964, Communications Satellites in Political Orbit, 1968, (with Kornberg) Legislatures in Developmental Perspective, 1970, (with Joel Smith) Legislatures in Development-Dynamics of Change in New and Old States, 1979; contbr. monographs, chpts. to books, articles to profl. jours. Served to lt. USNR, 1942-45. Johnston scholar Johns Hopkins U., 1946-48; Faculty fellow Vassar Coll., 1954-55; sr. assoc. East-West Ctr., Honolulu, 1968-69; vis. scholar Brookings Instn., Washington, 1980. Mem. ASPA (exec. coun. 1967-70), Nat. Assn. Schs. Pub. Affairs and Adminstrn. (exec. coun. 1972-75), Western Govtl. Rsch. Assn. (exec. bd. 1966-68), Am. Polit. Sci. Assn., Nat. Assn. State Univs. and Land Grant Colls. (rsch. com. divsn. urban affairs 1980-81). Home: 844 Lake Blvd Davis CA 95616-2611 Office: U Calif Dept Polit Sci Davis CA 95616

MUSON, HOWARD HENRY, writer, consultant; b. Mt. Vernon, N.Y., Mar. 19, 1935; s. Joseph Ernest and Beatrice (Hakmaier) M.; m. Dorothy Regina Tyor, May 21, 1967; children: Eve, Stephanie, Nickolas, Alice. AB magna cum laude, Harvard U., Cambridge, Mass., 1956; cert., Johns Hopkins Sch. Advanced Internat. Studies, Bologna, Italy, 1956-57; postgrad., U. Calif., Berkeley, 1957-58. Dir. program research CARE Inc., N.Y.C., 1960-62; bur. chief Hartford Courant, Conn., 1962; newsman, columnist AP, Boston, 1963-66; contbg. editor Time mag., N.Y.C., 1966-70; articles editor N.Y. Times mag., N.Y.C., 1970-77; exec. editor Psychology Today mag., N.Y.C., 1977-82; editor Across The Board, N.Y.C., 1983-89; editor, pub. Family Bus. mag., Phila., 1992-2000; rsch. assoc. Lansberg Gersick & Assocs., New Haven, 1998—. Vis. lectr. in residential colls. Yale U., New Haven, 1982-83;

instr. in sci. and environ. reporting program NYU, 1992. Author: Triumph of the American Spirit: Johnstown, Pennsylvania, 1989, Managing Growth: Smart Strategies for Smaller and Midsize Companies, 2000, Valuing Experience: How to Motivate and Retain Mature Workers, 2002, The Family Business Growth Handbook, 2002; co-author: Generations of Giving: Leadership and Continuity in Family Foundations, 2004; contbr. articles to profl. jours., popular mags. Dir. Project Concern/No. Westchester Walk for Mankind, Mt. Kisco, N.Y., 1986-90; media rels. Westchester Walk for Diabetes, 2002-03. Mem. Nat. Assn. Sci. Writers Office Phone: 914-941-1881. Personal E-mail: hmuson@earthlink.net.

MUSSALLEM, MICHAEL A. healthcare company executive; BChemE, Rose-Hulman Inst. Tech., 1974. With Union Carbide, Baxter Healthcare, Deerfield, Ill., 1979—, various positions in mfg., engring. and product devel., gen. mgr. Access products, v.p. product devel. Parenterals, gen. mgr. Pharms. divsn., pres. Bentley divsn., group v.p. Baxter Surg. Group, chmn. Baxter Asia-Pacific Bd., group v.p. Baxter cardiovascular and biopharms.; chmn., CEO Edwards Life Sci. Corp., Irvine, Calif., 2000—. Bd. dirs. Calif. Health Care Inst., Advanced Med. Optics, Adva Med, UCI CEO Roundtable, Octane, Keck Grad. Inst. Office: Edwards Lifesciences 1 Edwards Way Irvine CA 92614

MUSSANO, THEODORE ANTHONY, court services supervisor; b. Paterson, N.J., Dec. 15, 1943; s. Theodore Anthony, Sr. and Theresa Marie Mussano; m. Susan Fay Janusewski, May 24, 1980; 1 child, Theodore Edward. BA cum laude, Seton Hall U., 1965; MA, St. John's U., 1967. Probation officer Passaic County Probation Dept., Paterson, N.J., 1971-77, sr. probation officer, 1977-83; ct. svcs. supr. Superior Ct. N.J., Paterson, 1873—. Tchg. fellow, 1965—67, 1967—68, Weaver fellow, 1967. Mem.: Probation Assn. N.J. (pres. 1977), Soc. Ancient Numismatists, Am. Numis. Assn., KC. Roman Catholic. Avocations: ancient and medieval studies, reading. Home: 17 Fenner Pl Wayne NJ 07470-2809 Office: Passaic County Probation Divsn 63-65 Hamilton St Paterson NJ 07505 E-mail: emwardo@aol.com.

MUSSEHL, ROBERT CLARENCE, lawyer; b. Washington, May 1, 1936; s. Chester Carl and Clara Cecelia (Greenwalt) Mussehl; children: Debra Lee (dec.), David Lee, m. Misook Chung, Mar. 22, 1987, 1 child, Omar. BA, Am. U., 1964, JD, 1966. Bar: Wash. 1967, U.S. Dist. Ct. (we. dist.) Wash. 1967, U.S. Ct. Appeals (9th cir.) 1968, U.S Supreme Ct. 1971. Sr. ptnr. Thom, Mussehl, Navoni, Hoff, Pierson & Ryder, Seattle, 1967-78, Neubauer & Mussehl, Seattle, 1978-80, Mussehl & Rosenberg, Seattle, 1980—2001. Spkr. law convs. and other profl. orgns.; moot ct. judge Nat. Appelate Advocacy Competition, San Francisco, 1987; panel mem. ABA Symposium on Compulsory Jurisdiction of World Ct., San Francisco, 1987; chmn. bd., CEO The Seattle Smashers profl. volleyball club, 1976-80. Contbr. numerous articles to legal publs. Mem. Wash. Vol. Lawyers for Arts, 1976-80; statewide chair Lawyers for Durning for Gov., 1976; mem. task force on the single adult and ch. Ch. Coun. Greater Seattle, 1976-78; bd. dirs. Wash. State Pub. Interest Law Ctr., 1976-81; founder, past chair Lawyers Helping Hungry Children campaign, bd. dirs., 1991-2004; founder, past chair Wash. State Lawyers Campaign for Hunger Relief, 1991-. Recipient Jefferson award for cmty. and pub. svc. State of Wash., Am. Inst. for Pub. Svc., 1997. Fellow Am. Bar Found. (life), Am. Acad. Matrimonial Lawyers; mem. ABA (ho. of dels. 1979-91, 2003—, spl. adv. com. on internat. activities 1989-91, chair marriage and family counseling and conciliation com. family law sect. 1981-83, world order under law standing com. 1983-89, chair, 1986-89, chair ad hoc com. on the assembly 1986-89, assembly resolutions com. 1979-91, blue ribbon com. for world ct. 1987-88, standing com. on dispute resolution, 1992-93; exec. coun. sect. dispute resolution 1993-95, asst. budget officer, 1995-97, budget officer 1997-99, vice-chair 1999-, chair 2001-02, sect. liaison commn. on racial and ethnic diversity 2002-04), Wash. State Bar Assn. (exec. com. family law sect. 1973-75, chmn. internat. law com. 1974-76, sec.-treas., exec. com. world peace through law sect. 1980-, chair 1981-82, mem. edit. bd. Family Law Deskbook 1987-89), Wash. State Trial Lawyers Assn., Seattle-King County Bar Assn. (family law sect. 1971-90, other coms. 1970—, chmn. young lawyers sect. 1971-72, sec. 1972-73, trustee), Am. Arbitration Assn. (panel arbitrators), World Assn. Lawyers of World Peace Through Law Ctr. (founding mem.), Heritage Club YMCA Greater Seattle (charter 1977-), UN Assn. USA (bd. dirs. Seattle chpt. 1989-91). Avocations: squash, biking, tennis, weight training, painting, religious studies. Home: One Pacific Tower 2000 1st Ave Apt 902 Seattle WA 98121-2167 Office: Ste 3000 1000 2nd Ave Seattle WA 98104-1093 Office Phone: 206-386-7200. E-mail: bobmussehl@earthlink.net.

MUSSELMAN, ERIC, professional basketball coach; b. Ashland, Ohio, Nov. 19, 1964; m. Wendy Musselman; children: Michael, Matthew. BS, U. San Diego, 1987. Asst. dir. scouting L.A. Clippers, 1987—90; asst. coach Minn. Timberwolves, 1990—91; gen. mgr. Fla. Beach Dogs, Continental Basketball Assn., 1990—98, head coach, 1991—98, Fla. Sharks. U.S. Basketball League, 1995—96; asst. coach Orlando Magic, 1998—2000, Atlanta Hawks, 2000—02; head coach Golden State Warriors, 2002—04.

MUSSELMAN, LARRY L. chemical engineer; b. Erie, Pa., Aug. 16, 1947; s. Lloyd H. and Lyda Musselman; m. Susan E., Nov. 25, 1966; children: Cheri A., Jason L., Lucy A., Gavin A., Lauren A. BSChemE magna cum laude, Akron U., 1971, MS in Engring., 1972. Rsch. engr. Timken Co., 1971-77; sr. rsch. engr. Alcoa Co., Alcoa Center, Pa., 1977-79, sr. scientist, 1979-81, staff engr., 1981-83, tech. svc. mgr., 1983-86, tech. mgr., 1986-89; dir. tech. and ops. Polymer Additives Group, Apollo, Pa., 1989-93, v.p. tech. and ops. polymer additives group, 1993—. Mem. tech. adv. com. Ohio Legislature. Author: Handbooks of Science and Technology of Alumna Chemicals, Plastics Additives; contbr. over 50 articles on polymers and fire retardants to profl. jours.; numerous patents in field. Akron U. scholar. Mem. ASME (sect. dir.), ASTM (fire testing coms.), Am. Soc. Lubrication Engrs., Soc. Plastics Engrs., Fire Retardant Chems. Assn., Soc. Plastics Industry Coms., Sigma Xi, Sigma Tau, Alpha Chi Sigma. Office: Polymer Additives Group 321 Markle Rd Apollo PA 15613-8703 Office Phone: 724-335-1120.

MUSSENDEN, GERALD, psychologist; b. N.Y.C., June 1, 1941; s. Geraldo and Adele (Gimenez) M.; m. Iris Manuela Prado, Aug. 11, 1967; children: Gerald, Ricardo-Antonio, Gina. BA, Tarkio Coll., 1968; MS, Brigham Young U., 1971, PhD, 1974. Diplomate Am. Bd. Profl. Disability Cons., Am. Bd. Forensic Examiners, Am. Bd. Forensic Clin. Psychology. Dir. child program Albert Einstein Coll. Medicine, N.Y.C., 1974-76; psychologist Mental Health Ctr., Bartow, Fla., 1976-77, Norside Community Mentala Health Ctr., Tampa, Fla., 1977-80; pvt. practice Brandon (Fla.) Counseling Ctr., 1980—. Criminal ct. psychologist Fla. Cts., Hillsborough, Fla., 1978—; with children's svcs. State Rehab., Hillsborough, 1977—; rehab. psychologist Vocat. Rehab., Hillsborough; psychologist Div. Blind Svcs., Hillsborough. Fellow Ford Found., 1972-73. Mem. APA, Fla. Psychol. Assn., Bay Area Psychol. Assn., Soc. Personality Assessment. Home: 317 Cactus Rd Seffner FL 33584-6105 Office: Brandon Counseling Ctr 134 N Moon Ave Brandon FL 33510-4420 Office Phone: 813-681-5958.

MUSSEY, JOSEPH ARTHUR, health and medical product executive; b. Cleve., July 17, 1948; s. Arthur Glenn and Mary Jane (Silvaroli) M.; m. Mary Elizabeth Stone, July 11, 1975; 1 child, Joanna Lee. BS in Indsl. Engring. with distinction, Cornell U., 1970; MBA, Harvard U., 1976. Engring. mgmt. officer U.S. Navy Pub. Works Ctr., Pearl Harbor, Hawaii, 1971-75; mktg. exec. B.F. Goodrich, Akron, Ohio, 1976-80, fin. exec., 1980-84; v.p. fin. Combustion Engring., Stamford, Conn., 1984-85, v.p. ops., 1985-86; exec. v.p. Process Automation Bus. Combustion Engring., Columbus, Ohio, 1987-90; pres., CEO Danninger Med. Tech., Inc., Columbus, 1990—98; pres., CEO, dir. Interpore Cross Internat., Irvine, Calif., 1998—. Served as lt. U.S. Navy, 1971-75. Decorated Disting. Naval Grad. (USN), 1971, Disting. Grad. U.S. Navy Civil Engring. Corps., 1971. Mem. Alpha Pi Mu, Tau Beta Pi, Phi Eta Sigma. Clubs: Skull & Daggar. Republican. Roman Catholic. Home: 27662 Pinestrap Cir Laguna Hills CA 92653-7810 Office: Interpore Cross International 181 Technology Dr Irvine CA 92618

MUSSINA, MICHAEL COLE, professional baseball player; b. Williamsport, Pa., Dec. 8, 1968; BA Econs., Stanford U., 1990. Pitcher Balt. Orioles, 1990-2000, N.Y. Yankees, 2001—. Player Am. League All-Star Team, 1992-94. Named Internat. League Most Valuable Pitcher, 1991, recipient 5 Am. League Gold Gloves, 5-time Am. League All-Star. Office: The Ashton Group 5 Shawan Rd Ste 2 Hunt Valley MD 21030 also: The New York Yankees Yankee Stadium 161st Street and River Avenue Bronx NY 10451 E-mail: csmd12000@aol.com.

MUSSON, WARREN R. investment banker; s. Richard W. and Victoria L. Musson; m. Ann Marie Flemming, May 21, 1982; children: Kelly, Kate. BA, Alma Coll., Alma, Mich., 1978. 2nd v.p. Nat. Bank of Detriot, Mich., 1978—90; pres. Massey Holdings Inc., Plymouth, Mich., 1990—92; v.p. Great Lakes Bancorp, Ann Harbor, Mich., 1992—93; sr. v.p. Peoples State Bank, Hamtramck, Mich., 1993—99; sr. v.p., head of lending Cmty. Bank of Dearborn, Dearborn, Mich., 1999—. Mem.: Colony Swim Club (treas., pres. 1992—94), Western Golf & C.C. Avocations: boating, skiing, golf, landscape design. Home: 8900 Quail Cir Plymouth MI 48170 Office: Cmty Bank of Dearborn 22290 Mich Ave Dearborn MI 48123

MUSTACCHI, PIERO, preventive medicine physician, educator; b. Cairo, May 29, 1920; came to U.S., 1947; naturalized, 1962; s. Gino and Gilda (Rieti) M.; m. Dora Lisa Ancona, Sept. 26, 1948; children: Roberto, Michael. BS in Humanities, U. Florence, Italy, 1938; postgrad. in anatomy, Eleve Interne, U. Lausanne, Switzerland, 1938-39; MB, ChB, Fouad I U., Cairo, Egypt, 1944, grad. in Arabic lang. and lit., 1946; D Medicine and Surgery, U. Pisa, 1986; D Honoris Causa, U. Aix-Marseilles, France, 1988; hon. degree, U. Alexandria, Egypt, 1985. Qualified med. examiner, Calif. Indsl. Accident Commn., 1994. House officer English Hosp., Ch. Missionary Soc., Cairo, 1945-47; clin. affiliate U. Calif., San Francisco, 1947-48; intern Franklin Hosp., San Francisco, 1948-49; resident in pathology U. Calif., San Francisco, 1949-51; resident in medicine Meml. Ctr. Cancer and Allied Diseases, N.Y.C., 1951-53; rsch. epidemiologist Dept. HEW, Nat. Cancer Inst., Bethesda, Md., 1955-57; cons. allergy clinic U. Calif., San Francisco, 1957-70, clin. prof. medicine and preventive medicine, 1970-90, clin. prof. medicine and epidemiology, 1990-96, head occupl. epidemiology, 1975-90, head divsn. internat. health edn. dept. epidemiology and internat. health, 1985-90; médecin agréé, official physician Consulate Gen. of France, San Fransisco, 1995—; sr. cons. internat. health care U. Calif., San Francisco. Med. cons., vis. prof. numerous ednl. & profl. instns., U. Marseilles, 1981—82, U. Pisa, Italy, 1983, U. Gabon, 1984, U. Siena, Italy, 1985; cons U. Calif., 1975—, sr. cons. internat. med. care, 2000—. Contbr. chpts. to books, articles to profl. jours. Editorial bd. Medecine d'Afrique Noire, Ospedali d'Italia. Served with USN, USPHS, 1953-55 Decorated comdr. Order of Merit (Italy), officer Ordre de la Legion d'Honneur (France), Medal of St. John of Jerusalem, Sovereign Order of Malta, Order of the Republic (Egypt); Scroll, Leonardo da Vinci Soc., San Francisco, 1965; award Internat. Inst. Oakland, 1964; Hon. Vice Consul. Italy, 1971-90. Fellow ACP, Am. Soc. Environ. and Occupational Health; mem. AAAS, Am. Assn. Cancer Rsch., Calif. Soc. Allergy and Immunology, Calif. Med. Assn., San Francisco Med. Soc., West Coast Allergy Soc. (founding), Mex. Congress on Hypertension (corr.), Internat. Assn. Med. Rsch. and Continuing Edn. (U.S. rep.), Acad. Italiana della Cucina. Democrat. Avocations: music, math, languages. Home: 3344 Laguna St San Francisco CA 94123-2208 Office: U Calif Parnassus Ave San Francisco CA 94143-0560 also: 3838 California St San Francisco CA 94118-1522

MUSTAFA, SHAKIR, English and Arabic educator; b. Baghdad, Iraq, June 15, 1952; came to U.S., 1990; s. Mahmoud Mustafa and Zakiya Mahdi; m. Nawal Nasrallah, Apr. 15, 1979. BA in English Lit., Baghdad U., 1974, MA in English Lit., 1977; PhD, Ind. U., 1999. Vice chmn. English dept. Mosul (Iraq) U., 1988-90; vis. asst. prof. Ind. U., 1999-2000; asst. prof. Boston U., 2000—. Author: To the Promised Land through Gas Chambers: Zionism and the Jewish Novel in America, 1980, Literary Translation, 2 vols., 1984, 85, Seventeenth-Century English Poetry, 1988; contbr. articles to profl. jours.; co-editor: A Century of Irish Drama, 2000; translator Arabic lit. Mem. Modern Fgn. Langs., Union of Writers in Iraq. Moslem. Office: Boston U 718 Commonwealth Ave Boston MA 02215 E-mail: mustafa@bu.edu.

MUSTAIN, DOUGLAS DEE, lawyer; b. Shreveport, La., Nov. 2, 1945; s. Reginald K. and Dorothy J. (Green) M.; m. Sharon L. Tegarden, Aug. 19, 1967; children: Kristi Kaye, Kari Dee, Kenton Douglas, Kyle Robert, Kirk Stephen, Kali Elizabeth. Student Knox Coll., 1963-64, Murray State U., 1964-66; BS, U. Ill., 1971; JD, U. Iowa, 1974. Bar: Iowa 1974, Ill. 1974; U.S. Dist. Ct. (cen. dist.) Ill. 1974, U.S. Ct. Appeals (7th cir.) 1980, U.S. Supreme Ct. 1986. Law clk. Shulman, Phelan, Tucker, Boyle & Mullin, Iowa City, 1972-74; assoc. Stuart, Neagle & West, Galesburg, Ill., 1974-76; ptnr. West, Neagle & Williamson, Galesburg, 1977-89, Mustain & Lindstrom, Galesburg, 1989—; instr. real estate law Carl Sandburg Coll., Galesburg, 1977-81. Chmn. Citizens Referendum Com., Galesburg, 1983, 1987-88; bd. dirs. YMCA, Galesburg, 1983—, Cottage Hosp. Care Corp., Galesburg, 1984—; trustee 1st Presbyn. Ch., Galesburg, 1984; commr. Galesburg Pub. Transp. Commn., 1985—; pres., founder Galesburg Pub. Sch. Found., 1987-94. Served to SP5 U.S. Army, 1966-69, Vietnam. Decorated Army Commendation with oak leaf cluster. Mem. Knox County Bar Assn. (pres. 1980-82), ABA (comml. litigation com. 1981—), Assn. Trial Lawyers Am., Ill. Trial Lawyers Assn. Republican. Home: 1234 N Prairie St Galesburg IL 61401-1852 Office: Mustain Lindstrom & Henson 1865 N Henderson St Ste 11B Galesburg IL 61401-1377

MUSTAPHA, TAMTON, gastroenterologist; b. Calicut, Kerala, India, Oct. 17, 1941; s. Mahamood and Asmabi (Tamton) Thoosikannan; m. Rahma Marikar, June 15, 1969; children: Monisha, Mumtaz, Nigel. Student, Malabar Christian Coll., India, 1958; MD, Calicut Med. Coll., 1963. Diplomate Am. Bd. Internal Medicine, Am. Bd. Gastroenterology. Resident in internal medicine VA Hosp., Bklyn., 1967-68, Grasslands Hosp., Valhalla, N.Y., 1968-70; resident in gastroenterology Montefiore Hosp., Bronx, 1970-72; practice medicine, specializing in gastroenterology Hudson, 1972—; attending physician Columbia Meml. Hosp., Hudson, 1972—; chief dept. medicine Columbia Greene Med. Ctr., 1989-91; instr. Albany Med. Ctr., 1972—. Mem. med. adv. com. N.Y. State Health Dept.; bd. dirs., chmn. auditing assurance Hudson Valley PSRO; pres. No. Columbia Assocs., Columbia Greene Med. Assocs., Cairo Med. Realty, Prime Med. Assocs., Hudson, 1997—; bd. Greene Health Care Assocs.; bd. dirs. Regional Heart Assn. Mem. town planning bd. kinderhook, 1987-96; chmn. bd. trustees Columbia Greene C.C., 1995-97. Fellow Am. Coll. Gastroenterologists; mem. AMA, ACP, Columbia County Med. Soc., N.Y. State Med. Soc. (med. adv. com.), Am. Gastroent. Assn., Am. Soc. Internat. Medicine, Acad. Scis., Am. Heart Assn. (bd. dirs.), Am. Coll. Physician Execs., Columbia and Dutchess Lung Assn., Assn. for Mentally Retarded, Am. Assn. Physicians and Dentists of India (pres. Capital Dist. 1986), Rotary (dir. 1976-78, pres.-elect 1986-87, pres. 1987—, Paul Harris fellow, gov. dist. 7210 1999—), Mason (master), Shriners, Cypres Temple. Republican. Home: 2575 Rte 21 Valatie NY 12184 Office: Prime Med Assocs 949 Columbia St Hudson NY 12534-2624 E-mail: mustapha@mhmline.net.

MUSTARD, DAVID BRENDAN MACDOUGAL, economist, educator; b. Buffalo, N.Y., Sept. 18, 1968; s. E. David and Joan R. Mustard; m. Elizabeth J. Mustard, Aug. 15, 1992; children: David A., Stephen E. BA in History and Econ., U. Rochester, N.Y., 1990; MSc in Internat. and European Politics, U. Edinburgh, Scotland, 1992; PhD in Econ., U. Chgo., 1997. Mkt. analyst Scott Aviation, Lancaster, NY, 1987—91; lectr. U. Chgo., 1995—97; asst. prof. U. Ga., Athens, 1997—2003, assoc. prof., 2003—; rsch. fellow Inst. for the Study of Labor, Bonn, Germany, 2003—. Contbr. articles to profl. jours. Grantee, NSF, 2000—04, Am. Ednl. Assn., 2003—04. Mem.: Am. Ednl. Fin. Assn., Soc. of Labor Econ., Am. Law & Econ. Assn., Am. Econ. Assn. Office: Terry Coll of Bus Univ Ga Athens GA 30602 Office Phone: 706-542-3624. Business E-Mail: mustard@uga.edu.

MUSTARD, LEWIS WILLIAMS, management consultant, educator, legal consultant; b. Durham, N.C., Sept. 4, 1942; s. Harry S. and Elizabeth (Williams) M.; divorced; children: Juliana Janice, Lewis Williams Jr. AB in English, U. N.C., 1966; cert. in hosp. adminstrn., Duke U., 1970; LLB, La Salle U., Chgo., 1974; D Bus. Adminstrn., Western Coll. U., 1976; PhD in Health Adminstrn., Union Grad. Sch., Cin., 1992; MA in Humanities, Calif. State U., Dominguez Hills, 1995. Hosp. adminstr. Woodruff (S.C.) Hosp., 1968-70; exec. dir. AID, Inc., Bryn Mawr, Pa., 1970-73; sr. hosp. cons. Summerour & Assocs., Atlanta, 1975-76; regional adminstr. Qualicare, Inc., New Orleans, 1976-78, Triage Corp., Clearwater, Fla., 1978-80; pres. Health-care Mgmt. Cons., Atlanta, 1980-88; mem. continuing edn. faculty Duke U., Durham, N.C., 1994—; with Mgmt. Cons., Chapel Hill, N.C., 1993—. Adj. prof. Cen. Mich. U., Mt. Pleasant, 1993—, So. Ill. U., Carbondale, 1993—, Webster U., St. Louis, 1994—; expert witness, solo practitioner, 1992—. Served with USNR Res., 1959-68. Episcopalian. Office Phone: 919-929-1885.

MUSTELIER, ALINA OLGA, travel consultant, music educator; b. Havana, Cuba, Sept. 28, 1949; d. Carlos Enrique and Olga Castellanos Mustelier; children: Antonio Freire, Ana Freire. MusB, U. Miami, 1971; MS, Fla. Internat. U., 1982. Cert. ednl. leadership. Customer care rep. So. Bell, Miami, Fla., 1973—74; music tchr. Shenandoah Elem., Miami, Fla., 1974—75; music tchr. Coral Way Elem., Miami, Fla., 1975—78, Fairlawn Elem., Miami, Fla., 1979—88; tchr. Whispering Pines Elem., Miami, Fla., 1988—93; music tchr. Claude Pepper Elem. Sch., Miami, Fla., 1998—2001. Singer: Miami Opera Guild Chorus, 1970, Church By the Sea Choir, 1979. Recipient Sword of Honor, Sigma Alpha Iota, 1968-1971. Office: Claude Pepper Elem Sch 14550 SW 96 St Miami FL 33186 Office Phone: (305) 386-5244. Office Fax: (305) 382-7150. Personal E-mail: musteliera@aol.com.

MUSTION, ALAN LEE, pharmacist; b. Oklahoma City, Feb. 6, 1947; s. Granville E. and Iris E. (Graham) Mustion; m. Mary Jane Bozek, Dec. 4, 1982; children from previous marriage: Jeffrey Alan, Jennifer Chere. BS in Pharmacy, Southwestern Okla. State U., 1970. Staff pharmacist VA Med. Ctr., Oklahoma City, 1970—74, dir. pharmacy Richmond, Va., 1976—77, Iowa City, 1977—90; dir. pharmacy svcs. VA Hosp., Houston, 1990—2002; pharmacy mgr. Integris Bapt. Med. Ctr., Oklahoma City, 2002—. Clin. instr. clin./hosp. divsn. U. Iowa, 1977—90; adj. asst. prof. pharmacy practice U. Houston, 1990—2002. Contbr. articles to profl. jours. Served to lt. col. USAR. Grantee Rsch., Travenol Labs., 1980—87, VA HSR&D, 1984, 1988. Mem.: Okla. Soc. Health Sys. Pharmacists, Am. Soc. Health Sys. Pharmacists, Kappa Psi. Methodist. Office: 3300 NW Expressway Oklahoma City OK 73112 Home: 513 Winding Creek Rd Yukon OK 73099-4471 E-mail: alan.mustion@integris-health.com.

MUSTO, DAVID FRANKLIN, medical researcher, educator, historian, consultant; b. Tacoma, Jan. 8, 1936; s. Charles Hiram and Hilda Marie (Hanson) Mustoe; m. Emma Jean Baudendistel, June 2, 1961; children: Jeanne Marie, David Kyle, John Baird, Christopher Edward. BA, U. Wash., 1956, MD, 1963; MA, Yale U., 1961. Lic. physician, Conn., Pa. Clerk Nat. Hosp. for Nervous Disease, London, 1961; intern Pa. Hosp., Phila., 1963-64; resident Yale U. Med. Ctr., New Haven, 1964-67; spl. asst. to dir. NIMH, Bethesda, Md., 1967-69; vis. asst. prof. Johns Hopkins U., 1968-69; asst. prof. Yale U., 1969-73, assoc. prof., 1973-78, sr. rsch. scientist, 1978-81, prof., 1981—, exec. fellow Davenport Coll., 1983-88; mem. adv. editorial com. Yale Edits. Private Papers James Boswell, 1975—; cons. Exec. Office of Pres., 1973-75; mem. White House Strategy Coun., 1978-81; mem. panel on alcohol policy NAS, Washington, 1978-82; cons. White House Conf. on Families, 1979-80. Vis. fellow Clare Coll., Cambridge U., 1994; mem. alcohol adv. com. Nat. Assn. Broadcasters, 1994—; DuMez lectr. U. Md.; Walter Reed meml. lectr. Richmond Acad. Medicine; Galdston lectr. N.Y. Acad. Medicine; Sirridge lectr. U. Mo. Med. Sch.; Clendening lectr. U. Kans. Med. Sch. Author: The American Disease: Origins of Narcotic Control, 1973, expanded edit., 1987, 3rd edit., 1999; co-author: (with P. Korsmeyer) The Quest for Drug Control: Politics and Federal Policy in a Period of Increasing Drug Use, 1963-1981, 2002; editor: One Hundred Years of Heroin, 2002, Drugs in America: A Documentary History, 2002. Historian Pres.'s Commn. on Mental Health, 1977-78; adv. U.S. Del. to UN Commn. Narcotic Drugs, Geneva, 1978-79; mem. nat. coun. Smithsonian Instn., Washington, 1981-90, hon. mem., 1991—; hist. cons. Presdl. Commn. Human Immuno-deficiency Virus Epidemic, 1988; mem. nat. adv. com. on anti-drug program Robert Wood Johnson Found., 1989-2002; mem. nat. adv. com. on internat. narcotic policy UN Assn. of U.S.A., 1991; mem. adv. com. causes drug abuse Office Tech. Assessment, Congress U.S., 1992-94; commr. Conn. Alcohol and Drug Abuse Commn., 1992-93; bd. dirs. Coll. on Problems of Drug Dependence, 1990-94; trustee Assocs. of Cushing-Whitney Med. Libr., 1994—. With USPHS, 1967-69. Fellow: Coll. Problems of Drug Dependence, Am. Psychiat. Assn. (disting.); mem.: Soc. of Cin. in the State of Conn. (pres. 1998—2001), English-Speaking Union (pres. New Haven br. 1995—98), Am. Assn. History of Medicine (William Osler medal 1961), Am. Hist. Assn., Am. Inst. History of Pharmacy (Kraemers award 1974), New Haven County Med. Assn. (chmn. bicentennial com. 1983), Century Assn., Athenaeum Club (London), Cosmos Club. Office: Yale U PO Box 207900 New Haven CT 06520-7900

MUSTOE, THOMAS ANTHONY, physician, plastic surgeon; b. Columbia, Mo., June 29, 1951; s. Robert Moore and Carolyn (Swett) M.; m. Kathryn Claire Stallcup, Aug. 13, 1977; children: Anthony, Lisa. BA cum laude in biology, Harvard Coll., 1973, MD cum laude, 1978. Diplomate Am. Bd. Otolaryngology, Am. Bd. Plastic Surgery. Rsch. assoc. dept. microbiology Harvard Med. Sch., Cambridge, Mass., 1976-77; intern in medicine Mass. Gen. Hosp., Boston, 1978-79; resident in surgery Peter Bent Brigham Hosp., Boston, 1979-80; resident in otolaryngology Mass. Eye and Ear Infirmary, Boston, 1980-82, chief resident, 1982-83; resident in plastic surgery Brigham and Women;s Hosp., Children's Hosp., Boston, 1983-84, chief resident, 1984-85; asst. prof. in surgery Wash. U. Sch. Medicine, St. Louis, 1985-89, assoc. prof., 1989-91; prof., chief divsn. plastic surgery Northwestern U. Med. Sch., Chgo., 1991—; plastic surgeon Northwestern Meml. Hosp., 1991—, Evanston Hosp., 1991—, Children's Meml. Hosp., 1992—, Shriner's Hosp. Chgo., 1994—. Co-chmn. Gorden Rsch. Conf., 1995; spl. cons. FDA, 1994—98; mem. sci. adv. panel Biologies, 1997, NCI, 1998; lectr. seminars, 2001. Editl. bd. Archives of Surgery, 1992—, Plastic and Reconstructive Surgery, 1993-2001, Wound Repair and Regeneration, 1992—, Jour. Surg. Rsch., 1997—; contbr. articles to profl. jours., more than 200 publs., book chpts.; book reviewer. Harvard Nat. scholar, 1969-73; Rhodes scholar candidate, Harvard Coll., 1973. Fellow: ACS (adv. coun. plastic surgery 1999—2002, surg. forum com. 1999—2002, surg. biology club III); mem.: AMA, Coun. Plastic Surger Org., Double Boarded Soc. (pres. 1995—98), Chgo. Surg. Soc., Chgo. Plastic Surg. Soc. (sec. 1996—97), Wound Healing Soc. (program com. 1990, audit com. 1992, program com. 1992, bd. dir. 1993—96, program com. 1994, fin. com. 1994—96, program com. 1997, pres. 1997—99), Assn. Acad. Chmn. Plastic Surgery (matching program and ctrl. application svc. com. 1994), Soc. U. Surgeons, Soc. Head and Neck Surgeons (membership com. 1993—95), Plastic Surgery Rsch. Coun. (rep. coun. acad. surgeons 1991—94, com. indsl. rels. 1992, program com. 1992—94, 1995, Judge Snyder & Crikelair awards 1991), Midwest Assn. Plastic Surgeons, Lipoplasty Soc. N.Am. (lipoplasty ednl. rsch. found. 1998—2000), Am. Assn. Plastic Surgery (rsch. and edn. com. 1994—96, chmn. 1996, mem. com. 1998—, co-chmn.ASPRS-ASAPS task force on emerging trends 1999—2000, chmn. instl. coun. com. 1999—), Am. Soc. Plastic and Reconstructive Surgery (rsch. fund proposal com. 1987—92, plastic surgery device com. 1989—93, resource book for plastic surgery residents com. 1991—93, socioecon. 1992—94, sci. program com. 1993—95, chmn. device and tecyhnique assessment com. 1994—96, co-chmn. gen. reconstruction subcom. 1995, ultrasonic lipectomy task force 1995—96, task force for outcomes and guidelines 1995—98, devices and tech. com. 1995—98, chmn. instrnl. com. 1999—2002, chmn. edn. com. 1999—, chmn. resource book com.), Aesculapian Club, Sigma Xi. Avocations: reading, golf, gardening, sports. Home: 144 Greenwood St Evanston IL 60201-4712

MUSZYNSKI, JANE, interior designer, colorist, space planner; BA in Interior Design and Home Econs., Calif. State U., 1973. Profl. status Nat. Coun. Interior Design Qualification, 1986; cert. Calif. Coun. Interior Design, 1993. Graphic designer Stewart Woodard Arch., Irvine, Calif., 1973-74; interior designer Interior Space Design, Newport Beach, Calif., 1974-76; office mgr. purchasing Lockheed Marine Lab., Diablo Canyon, Calif., 1976-77; realtor assoc. Century 21 Real Estate, Los Osos, Calif., 1977-79, Sierra

Madre, Calif., 1979-80; v.p. mktg., designer S.K. Young Assocs., Tustin, Calif., 1979-88; sales acct. exec. Entouch Bus. Interiors, Rancho Cucamonga, Calif., 1988-89; sr. interior designer Walt Disney Imagineering - Disneyland, Anaheim, Calif., 1989-98; interior designer Universal Studios, Hollywood, Calif., 1998-2000; mktg. exec., owner Staffease & Advance Concepts, Walnut, Calif., 1991—2001; owner, interior designer Snow Creek Resources, 2001—; interior designer Interiors, Big Bear Lake, Calif. Realtor, sales assoc. Anthony Real Estate, Santa Maria, Calif., 1977—; instr. Mt. San Antonio Coll., Walnut, 1985, Walnut, 87, Walnut, 2001—, FIDM, Irvine, 2003, Calif. Poly. U., Pomona, 1988—89, adv. bd. interior design, 1988—90; chmn. nominating com. Bus. Devel. Assn. Orange County, Irvine, 1988—89; dir. pub. rels. NEWH-So. Countries, 2001—02. Mem. host program Bear Mountain Ski Resort, Big Bear, Calif., 1993, 94; cookie chmn. Girl Scouts Am., Walnut, 1993; vol. Nat. Ski Patrol, 2003—. Mem. Am. Soc. Interior Designers, Network Exec. Women in Hospitality. Avocations: golf, skiing. Office: Snow Creek Resources 385 S Lemon #E 253 Walnut CA 91789-3038 Business E-Mail: jane_muszynski@hotmail.com.

MUTALIPASSI, LOUIS RICHARD, psychologist, educator; b. Kansas City, Kans., Jan. 23, 1937; s. Louie R. Mutalipassi and Cleda E. (Miller) Wolverton; m. Edalee Kenworthy, July 14, 1962 (div. 1970); 1 child, Annemarie; m. Laura Ruth Posner, July 17, 1976; 2 children: Michael and Anthony. BA in Psychology, U. Calif., Santa Barbara, 1962; MA in Psychology, UCLA, 1965, PhD in Psychology, 1969. Lic. psychologist, Calif. Staff psychologist VA Med. Ctr., LA, 1969—76, chief psychology svc. Albany, NY, 1976—80; clin. assoc. prof. psychology UCLA and U. So. Calif., LA, 1980—; chief psychology svc. VA Med. Ctr., Long Beach, 1980—97; ret., 1997; clin. psychologist in pvt. practice, 1982—. Oral commr. State Bd. Med. Examiners, Calif., 1996—. Contbr. articles to profl. jour.; presenter in field. With USAF, 1954-58. Mem. APA. Avocations: golf, photography. E-mail: lrmteetime@aol.com.

MUTERS, MICHAEL C. printmaker; b. Alsip, Ill., Mar. 26, 1965; s. Noreen A. and Alfred J. Leubner(Stepfather); m. Kelly A. Holmes, May 5, 1969; children: Joshua M., Earnest A. Holmes III, Dustin M. Holmes, Morgan R., Dylan T. Cert. svc. tech. Hamada Am., 1988. Pressman Quartier Printing, Syracuse, NY, 1985—87; svc. technician Onondaga Litho Supply, 1987—91; pressman Grabowski Film and Printing, 1991—97, UpState Printing, 1997—. Author: The Journal Book Adventures: The Search for Dewba. With U.S. Army, 1984. Home: 302 Golfcrest Circle Baldwinsville NY 13027 Office: UpState Printing 212 West Division ST Syracuse NY 13204 Personal E-mail: mmuters@yahoo.com.

MUTH, ERIC PETER, ophthalmic optician; b. Munich, July 25, 1940; came to U.S., 1948, naturalized 1955; s. Erich Walter and Anna Lisa (Pentenrieder) M.; m. Rachel Hubbard, Apr. 4, 1971; children: Eric Van, Karl George, Ellen Anna. BS, Charter Oak Coll., 1978; degree (hon.), Anoka-Hennipen Tech. Coll., 1995. Sr. rsch. fellow Internat. Soc. for Philosophical Inquiry, 1991—96, pers. cons., 1996; cons. Nat. Acad. Opthamology Found. Mus., San Francisco, 1982—88, Nat. Mus. Hist. Smithsonian Inst., 1983—94, Gesell Inst. Human Devel., 1984—89; mem. adv. com. South. Cen. Cmty. Coll., Seattle, 1984—89; mem. adv. bd. internat. Scientific Inst., PR, 1989; adv. bd. Middlesex C.C. (vice chmn.), 1989; vol. VA, West Haven, Conn., 2001—. Mem. editl. bd. Dispensing Opticians, Butterworths Heinmann, 1998, co-author 2nd edit., 1998; contbr. the Social History of Eyeglasses in Japan, 1991, die Brille, Leipzig, 1989, Thinking on the Edge Agamennon, 1993; contbr. over 250 articles to profl. jours.; contbg. editor Optical Mgmt., 1979-80, OpticScan Canada, 1981-82, Indian Optician, 1982, Prism Mag., Can., 1988, 92; tech. editor Optical Index, 1980-82; book reviewer in field. Presdl. appointment U.S. Selective Svc. Sys., 1991-92; scoutmaster Boy Scouts Am., 1960-62; bd. dirs. ARC Conn. chpt., 1988; advisor Tri Hi-Y YMCA, 1964; founder, chmn. Korea-Vietnam Meml. com., Milford, 1985-86; organizer WWII Monument Com. 1991; trustee Conn. Visual Health Ctr., 1982-84; commr. Nat. Commn. on Opticianry Edn., 1989-93; life mem. Soc. 3d. U.S. Inf. Div., 1987; hon. Capt. 25th Bn. Royal Fusiliers, 1999; trooper Ct. State Militia, 2d co. gov.'s horse guard, 2003. Served with AUS, 1957-59, Conn. Army N.G., 1960-69. Decorated Roman Cath. Knight Malta, Equestrian Knight of The Order of the Holy Sepulchre, Knight Comdr.; recipient Eng. Nelson/Wingate prize, 1983, Service Above Self award, Rotary, 1986, Optician of the Yr., Guild of Prescription Opticians Am., 1993, Senate Citation, State of Conn., 1993, German-Am. Friendship award, Germany, 1995, State of Conn. Justice of the Peace, 1995, cert. of appreciation, Nat. Libr. Medicine, Bethesda, Md., 1995, Med. Scis. Divsn. Nat. Mus. History, 1995, NRA Legion of Honor, 1996, Mayoral Proclamation, Milford, Conn., 1998, Bronze medal of merit, Austrian Albert Schweitzer Soc., 1998, Chemical Corps Regimental Assn. Order of the Dragon, 1999, Oeuvre Humanitaire Croix d'Honneur, 1999, medal of merit, El Salvador Red Cross, 1999, Award of Merit, Army and Navy Union of USA, 2000, Vol. award, VA, 2003. Fellow: Conn. Opticians Assn. (pres. 1974, amb., chmn. membership and ethics coms., Optician of Yr. 1975), Opticians Assn. Am. (honored fellow, historian citation 1993, advancing opticianry award 1994, disting. svc. award 2000, diploma in refractometry 1995), Nat. Acad. Opticianry (regional membership chmn., faculty speakers bur., citation 1988), Internat. Acad. Opticianry; mem.: Nat. Contact Lens Examiners (cert.), Guild Prescription Opticians Am. (councilor 2001—02), Royal Lifesaving Soc. Can. (hon. assoc. 1998), Soc. Am. Mil. Engrs., Calif. Soc. Dispensing Opticians (hon.), Ari. Soc. Dispensing Opticians (hon.), Am. Bd. of Opticianry (master of ophthalmic optics 1972), Internat. Platform Assn., Contact Lens Soc. Am., Contact Lens Soc. Conn., Internat. Found. in Ophthalmics Optics, Conn. Guild Dispensing Opticians (pres. 1980, Optician of Yr. 1981), Charter Oak Coll. Alumni Assn. (bd. dirs. 1987, alumni citation 1995), Milford C. of C. (chmn. law and safety com. 1975, Cmty. Svc. award 1986), Disabled Am. Vets. (life), Am. Legion Post 196 (life; parade marshal 1998, citation 1986). Avocations: skydiving, parasailing, ballooning, motorcycling, Tae Kwon Do. Home: 25 Parkland Pl Milford CT 06460-7723 Personal E-mail: muth@nyc.com.

MUTH, JOHN FRASER, economics professor; b. Chgo., Sept. 27, 1930; s. Merlin Arthur and Margaret Fraser (Ferris) M. BSI.E., Washington U., St. Louis, 1952; MS, Carnegie-Mellon U., 1954, PhD, 1962. Research fellow Carnegie-Mellon U., 1956-59, asst. prof. econs., 1959-62, assoc. prof., 1962-64; prof. Mich. State U., 1964-69, Ind. U., 1969-94; ret., 1994. Author: (with others) Planning Production, Inventories, and Work Force, 1960, (with G. K. Groff) Operations Management: Analysis for Decision, 1972; editor: (with G. L. Thompson) Industrial Scheduling, 1963, (with G. K. Groff) Operations Management: Selected Readings, 1969; contbr. articles to profl. jours. Fellow Econometric Soc. Home: 21028 4th Ave Summerland Key FL 33042-4033 E-mail: muthjohn@aol.com.

MUTH, RICHARD FERRIS, economics professor; b. Chgo., May 14, 1927; s. Merlin Arthur and Margaret Ferris Muth; m. Helene Louise Martin, Dec. 23, 1955; children: Lisa Helene, Laurianne Martin Love. Student, USCG Acad., 1945-47; AB, Washington U., St. Louis, 1949, MA, 1950; PhD, U. Chgo., 1958; M of Theol. Studies, Emory U., 1995. Lectr. polit. economy Johns Hopkins U., Balt., 1955-56; economist Resources for Future, Washington, 1956-58; assoc. prof. urban econs. U. Chgo., 1959-64; economist Inst. Def. Analyses, Arlington, Va., 1964-66, cons., 1966-69; prof. econs. Washington U., St. Louis, 1966-70, Stanford U., (Calif.), 1970-83; Callaway prof. econs. Emory U., Atlanta, 1983—2001, chmn. dept., 1983-90, prof. emeritus, 2001—. Vis. assoc. prof. econs. Vanderbilt U., 1958—59; vis. sr. fellow Urban Inst., Washington, 1976—77; vis. prof. Sch. Bus. U. Calif., Berkeley, 1991. Author (with others): Regions, Resources and Economic Growth, 1960, Cities and Housing, 1969, Public Housing, 1974, Urban Economic Problems, 1975; co-author (with Allen C. Goodman): The Economics of Housing Markets, 1989. Mem. Presdl. Task on Urban Renewal, 1969, Presdl. Task Forces on Urban Affairs and Housing, 1980—81, Presdl. Commn. on Housing, 1981—82. With USCG, 1951—52. Libertarian. Methodist. Office: Emory U Dept Econs Atlanta GA 30322-2240 Business E-Mail: rmuth@emory.edu.

MUTMANSKY, JAN M. retired engineering educator; b. New Rochelle, N.Y., Apr. 26, 1941; s. Pete Martin and Veronica Vangor Mutmansky; m. Diane Elaine Huckabee, Nov. 25, 1965; children: Maria, Christine, Michael, Carin. BS in Mining Engring., Pa. State U., 1964, MS in Mining Engring., 1966, PhD in Mining Engring., 1968. Profl. engr., Utah, Pa. Sys. analyst Kennecott Copper Corp., Salt Lake City, 1968—69; asst. prof. U. Utah, Salt Lake City, 1969—73; assoc. prof. W.Va. U., Morgantown, 1973—77; assoc. to prof. Pa. State U., University Park, 1977—2001, prof. emeritus, 2001—. Co-author: MineVentilation and Air Conditioning, 3d edit., 1997, Introductory Mining Engineerring, 2d edit., 2002; assoc. editor: SME Mining Engineering Handbook, 2d edit., 1992. Recipient Stephen McCann Ednl. Excellence award, Pitts. Coal Mining Inst., 1994, Old Timer's Faculty award, 2003. Mem.: Soc. Mining, Metallurgy and Exploration (chair M&E divsn. 1985, bd. dirs. 1984—92, disting. mem.). Avocations: woodworking, fly fishing. Home: 647 Franklin St State College PA 16803 E-mail: j93@psu.edu.

MUTOMBO, DIKEMBE (DIKEMBE MUTOMBO MPOLONDO MUKAMBA JEAN JACQUE WAMUTOMBO), professional basketball player; b. Kinshasa, Zaire, June 25, 1966; Grad., Georgetown U., 1991. Ctr. Denver Nuggets, 1991—96, Atlanta Hawks, 1996—2001, Phila. 76ers, 2001—02, New Jersey Nets, 2002—03, New York Knicks, 2003—04, Chicago Bulls, 2004, Houston Rockets, 2004—. Named NBA Defensive Player of Yr., 1995, 1997, 1998, 2001; named to 8 NBA All-star teams, NBA All-Rookie team, 1992. Office: c/o Houston Rockets 1510 Polk St Houston TX 77002*

MUTTER, JOHN J., JR., writer, researcher; s. John J. Mutter, Sr. and Burnette V. Mutter; m. Karen L. Boerst, Aug. 21, 1982. Grad., Shawano Sr. H.S., Wis., 1961. Power plant operator State of Wis., Madison, Winnebago, Green Bay, Wis., 1982—2001, ret., 2001. Author: (book) To Slay a Giant; co-editor (book) Shawano County Sesquicentennial 1853-2003. E-4 USN, 1961—64, East Coast. Decorated The Vietnam Svc. Bar US Dept. of Commerce; recipient Outdoor Writing Award, Coun. for Wis. Writers, 1990, Buzzard Buster Award, Wolf Watershed Ednl. Project, 2000, 50th Bo Carter Meml., Waukesha Writers Group, 2002, 2d Pl., Al P. Nelson Feature Writing Contest, 2004. Mem.: Coun. for Wis. Writers, Wis. Regional Writers Assoc., Shawno County Hist. Soc. (life), Shawano Area Writers (pres. 2002). Avocations: writing, fishing, hunting, reading, managing woods for nature. Office: Burstone LLC N2787 McDonald Rd Shawano WI 54166-6956 Office Phone: 715-526-9277.

MUTTERPERL, WILLIAM CHARLES, lawyer, corporate financial executive; b. N.Y.C., July 15, 1946; s. Martin and Muriel (Wurtzel) M.; m. Nancy Fay Borson, July 2, 1968; children: Matthew, Adam. BA, Dartmouth Coll., 1968; JD, Columbia U., N.Y.C., 1971. Bar: N.Y. 1972, R.I. 1978, U.S. Dist. Ct. (so. and ea. dists.) N.Y. 1973, U.S. Dist. Ct. R.I. 1979. Assoc. atty. Cleary, Gottleib, Steen and Hamilton, N.Y.C., 1971-77; asst. gen. counsel Fleet Nat. Bank, Providence, 1977-79, gen. counsel, 1979-85; v.p., gen. counsel, sec. Fleet Fin. Group, Inc. (now Fleet Boston Fin Inc.), Providence, 1985-89, sr. v.p., gen. counsel, sec., 1989—2001; exec. dir. ind. oversight bd. Arthur Andersen LLP, 2002; ptnr. bus. law divsn. Brown, Rudnick, Berlack, Israels, LLP, 2002; vice chmn. PNC Fin. Svcs. Group, Pitts., 2002—. Bd. mem. Black Rock, Inc., NY, Beth Israel Deaconess Hosp., Boston; former pres. Boston Bar Found. Mem. Phi Beta Kappa. Democrat. Jewish. Office: PNC Fin Svcs Group One PNC Plaza 249 Fifth Ave Pittsburgh PA 15222-2707*

MUTTI, ALBERT FREDERICK, retired minister; b. Hopkins, Mo., Feb. 13, 1938; s. Albert Frederick and Phyllis Margaret (Turner) M.; m. Etta Mae McClurg, June 7, 1959; children: Timothy Allen, John Frederick, Martin Kent. AB, Cen. Meth. Coll., 1960; MDiv., Garrett-Evang. Theol. Sem., 1963; DMin., St. Paul Sch. Theology, 1975; DD, Baker U., 1993, Ctrl. Meth. Coll., 2000. Civ pastor Union Star Charge, Mo., 1963-65; sr. pastor Crossroads Parish, Savannah, Mo., 1965-74; assoc. coun. dir. Mo. West Conf. UMC, Kansas City, 1974-80, coun. dir., 1980-82; sr. pastor First United Meth. Ch., Blue Springs, Mo., 1982-87; dist. supt. Cen. Dist. UMC, Mo., 1987-89; dist. supr. Kansas City N. Dist., 1989-92; bishop Kans. Area United Meth. Ch., Topeka, 1992—2004; ret., 2004. Author: Breath of New Life. Chair Savannah Cmty. Betterment, 1971; bd. mem. St. Mary's Hosp., Blue Springs, 1986; dir. ARC, Savannah, 1968; bd. Discipleship, Nashville, bd. Global Ministries, N.Y.; pres. Mo. Coun. Chs., Jefferson City, Gen. Commn. on Christian Unity, Dean Mo. Area Ministers Sch., Curator, Ctrl. Meth. Coll.; trustee St. Paul Sch. Theology; organizer Rural, Religion and labor Coun. Kans. Named Disting. Alumni Ctrl. Meth. Coll.; recipient Grad. award St. Paul Sch. Theology. Methodist. Home: 7909 NE 75th Terr Kansas City MO 64158

MUTUNAYAGAM, N. BRITO, architecture and planning educator; b. Quilon, Kerala, India; came to U.S., 1976; BSc in Engring., Kerala U., Trivandrum, India, 1963; D.T.C.P., Sch. Planning, New Delhi, 1967; M Engring., Asian Inst. Tech., Bangkok, 1974; D.E.D.P., Va. Tech., Blacksburg, 1981. Jr. engr. Kerala Govt., 1963-64, town planner, 1964-77; instr. Va. Tech., Blacksburg, 1977-81; assoc. prof. Coll. Architecture, U. Nebr., Lincoln, 1981-90, prof., 1990—, assoc. dean, 1994—99, 2000—02, interim dean, 2000. Cons. several archtl. firms, Nebr., Iowa, Tex., Mass., Mo., Ariz., Wash., Calif., 1984—; mem. Speakers Bur., U. Nebr., Lincoln, 1996, 2002, 03. Co-author: Cartography and Site Analysis, 1985, Designing With Solid Models Study Guide, 1995, Dimensions Reference Guide, 1995, Command Reference Manual, 1995. Fellow Ctr. for Great Plains Studies, 1985—; grad. fellow U. Nebr., 1988—. Mem. Am. Planning Assn., Nat. Geog. Soc. Avocations: computer graphics, music, television, video recording, model ships. Office: U Nebr 307 Architecture Hall Lincoln NE 68588-0105

MUTZ, GREGORY THOMAS, insurance company executive; b. Indpls., Dec. 19, 1945; BA, DePauw U., 1967; JD, U. Mich., 1973. Chmn. bd. dir. AMLI Realty Co. subs. UICI, Chgo., 1980—; chmn. bd. trustees AMLI Residential Properties Trust, Chgo.; pres., CEO UICI, Dallas, 1999—. Bd. dirs. Nat. Multifamiy Housing Coun., Chgo., 1995—, Alleghany/Chgo. Trust, 1996—. Lt. U.S. Army, 1968-69, Vietnam. Office: UICI 9151 Grapevine Hwy North Richland Hills TX 76180

MUTZ, OSCAR ULYSSES, manufacturing and distribution executive; b. Edinburg, Ind., Feb. 12, 1928; s. Harold Winterberg and Laura Belle (Sawin) M.; m. Jean Greiling, Aug. 22, 1948; children: Marcia, H. William. BS, Ind. U., 1949. Vice pres. Peerless Corp., Indpls., 1954-63; v.p., gen. mgr. Space Conditioning, Inc., Harrisonburg, Va., 1964-66; v.p., treas. Cosco, Inc., Columbus, Ind., 1966-67; exec. v.p., 1967-69; pres., 1969-71; chmn. bd. Court Manor Corp., Columbus, 1971-73; pres. Jenn Air Corp., Indpls., 1973-75; pres., CEO Mutz Corp., 1975-81; pres., dir. Haag Drug Co., 1977-78; pres. Forum Group, Inc. (merger Mutz Corp. and Excepticon, Inc.), Indpls., 1981-91; chmn., CEO, bd. dirs. Capital Industries, Inc., Indpls., 1991-96; chmn. Lakeland Auto Mall, 1996—. Pres. Ct. Manor Corp., co-chmn. bd. dirs. Sargent & Greenleaf, Safemasters; pres. Security Group, Inc., 1991—, also bd. dirs. Nat. trustee Fellowship Christian Athletes, 1985-91, chmn. nat. conf. ctr., 1994-96; mem. pres. coun. and dean's adv. coun. Ind. U. Mem. Ind. Mfrs. Assn. (chmn. 1980), Acad. Alumnae Fellows Ind. U. Sch. Bus., Lakeland Yacht Club, Port Royal Club, Grasslands Country Club, Lone Palm Country Club. Republican. Baptist. Office: Mutz Corporation 5119 Lake in the Woods Blvd Lakeland FL 33813-2942

MUUSS, ROLF EDUARD, retired psychologist, author; b. Tating, Germany, Sept. 26, 1924; came to U.S., 1953, naturalized, 1992. s. Rudolf A. and Else M.; m. Gertrude Louise Kremser, Dec. 22, 1953 (dec. April 1999); children: Michael John (dec.), Gretchen Elise. Diploma, Tchr. Coll., Flensburg, Germany, 1951; student, U. Hamburg, Germany, 1951, Ctrl. Mo. State Coll., 1951-52, Columbia Tchrs. Coll., 1952; MEd, Western Md. Coll., 1954; PhD, U. Ill., 1957. Tchr. pub. sch., Germany, 1945-46, 51, 52-53; substitute prin., 1952-53; tchr. trainee U.S. Office Edn., 1951-52; houseparent Child Study Ctr., Balt., 1953; grad. asst. U. Ill., 1954-57; rsch. assoc. prof. Iowa Child Welfare Rsch. Sta., State U. Iowa, 1957-59; rsch. cons., 1960, 61; mem. faculty Goucher Coll., 1959-95, prof. edn., 1964-95, chmn. dept., 1972-75, dir. spl. edn., 1977-92, Elizabeth C. Todd disting. prof., 1980-85, chmn. dept. sociology and anthropology, 1983-85, prof. emeritus, 1995—. Rsch. assoc. edn. Johns Hopkins, 1962-63; part-time or summer tchr. U. B.C., 1962, Johns Hopkins U., 1962, 65, U. Del., 1965, Towson U., 1967, U. Ill., 1967; tchg. assoc. Sheppard and Enoch Pratt Hosp., 1969-80; guest lectr. Tchrs. Coll., Kiel, Fed. Republic Germany, 1977-78; hearing officer spl. edn. cases State of Md., 1980-96. Author: First-Aid for Classroom Discipline Problems, 1962, Theories of Adolescence, 1962, 5th edit., 1988, 6th edit., 1996, Grundlagen der Jugendpsychologie, 1982; also numerous articles; editor: Adolescent Behavior and Society: A Book of Readings, 1971, 4th edit., 1990, 5th edit., 1998. Served with German Air Force, 1942-45. Recipient award for disting. scholarship Goucher Coll., 1979; grantee Andrew W. Mellon Found., 1976-77. Fellow Am. Psychol. Soc., Am. Psychol. Assn., Md. Psychol. Assn. (treas. 1971-73); mem. Balt. Psychol. Assn. (chmn. membership com. 1966, v.p. 1970-71), Soc. Rsch. Child Devel., Soc. Rsch. on Adolescence, Kappa Delta Pi (v.p. Alpha chpt. 1956-57), Phi Delta Kappa. Home: 1540 Pickett Rd Lutherville Timonium MD 21093-5822 E-mail: rmuuss@goucher.edu.

MUYRES, DAVID ALLEN, industrial designer; b. Mpls., June 3, 1964; s. Duane and Judy Muyres; m. Stephanie Muyres, Nov. 21, 1998; 1 child, Annika. BS in Indsl. Design, Art Ctr. Coll. Design, 1988; postgrad., Inst. Mech. Engring., 1982—84. Staff designer, Holland, Mich., 1988—90; sr. designer, 1991—92; media resources mgr., 1993—94; design mgr., 1995—97; design dir. Burscheid, Germany, 1997—99; v.p. design consumer rsch., 2000—02; v.p., gen. mgr. product and bus. devel. Johnson Controls, Holland, 2002—. Mem. awards rev. bd. Nat. Endowment Arts, Washington, 1995. Scholar, Internat. Telephone, 1982—86, Soc. Plastics Engrs., L.A., 1987. Mem.: Design Mgmt. Inst., Indsl. Designers Soc. Am. Avocations: motorsports, writing. Home: 3255 160th Ave Holland MI 49424 Office: Johnson Controls Inc 915 E 32d St Holland MI 49423 E-mail: david.a.muyres@jci.com.

MUZYKA, RAY, application developer; MD, U. Alta., Can. Joint CEO BioWare Corp., Edmonton, Canada, 1995—. Software developer (electronic game) Baldur's Gate. Office: BioWare Corp 302 10508 82d Ave Edmonton AB T6E 6HZ Canada

MUZYKA-MCGUIRE, AMY, marketing professional, nutrition consultant; b. Chgo., Sept. 24, 1953; d. Basil Bohdan and Amelia (Rand) Muzyka; m. Patrick J. McGuire, June 3, 1977; children: Jonathan, Elizabeth. BS, Iowa State U., 1975, postgrad., 1978—; registered dietitian, St. Louis U., 1980. Cert. dietitian. Home economist Nat. Livestock and Meat Bd., Chgo., 1975-77; dietary cons. various hosps. and nursing homes, Iowa, 1978-79; supr. foodsvc. Am. Egg Bd., Park Ridge, Ill., 1980-83; assoc. dir., mgr. foodsvc. Cole & Weber Advt., Seattle, 1984-85; prin., owner Food and Nutrition Comms., Federal Way, Wash., 1986—. Co-author: Turkey Foodservice Manual, 1987; editor: (newsletter) Home Economists in Business, 1975-77, Dietitians in Business and Industry, 1982-85; Food Net on Internet, 1995, Food and Culinary Profls. Newsletter, 1999-2001; contbr. articles to profl. jours. Named Outstanding Dietitian of Yr. North Suburban Dietetic Assn., 1983, Tastemaker of the Month, 2001, 02, 03. Mem. Am. Dietetic Assn., Internat. Foodsvc. Editl. Coun., Cons. Nutritionists, Internat. Assn. Culinary Profls. Avocations: gardening, travel, music, food and beverage tastings. Home: 5340 SW 315th St Federal Way WA 98023-2034

MWENDA, KENNETH KAOMA, legal consultant, advisor, educator; LLB, U. Zambia, 1990; Gr.Dip, LCCI, U.K, 1991; DMS, IoC, U.K, 1992; BCL, U. Oxford, U.K., 1994; MBA, U. Hull, U.K, 1995; DBA, Pacific Western U., L.A., 1996, PhD in Publs., 1999; PhD, U. Warwick, U.K., 2000. Cert. Bar, Zambia, 1991; cert. cumpolsory edn., devels. in comml. securities, intellectual property law. With trust funds and co-financing dept. Vice-Presidency of World Bank, Washington, 1998—99, with poverty reduction, mgmt. and pub. sector reform unit, 1999; counsel legal dept. World Bank, Washington, 1999—2000, projects officer, 2000—03, sr. projects officer, 2003—. Vis. prof. U. Miskolc Sch. Law, Hungary, 1996; lectr. U. Zambia Law Sch., 1991—95, vis. prof., 2001; lectr. Warwick U. Law Sch., 1995—98; spkr. and presenter in field. Author: Legal Aspects of Corporate Capital and Finance, 1999, Contemporary Issues In Corporate Finance and Investment Law, 2000, Banking Supervision and Systemic Bank Restructuring, 2000, Zambia's Stock Exchange and Privatization Programme, 2001, The Dynamics of Market Integration: African Stock Exchange's in the New Millennium, 2000, Banking Supervision and Microfinance Regulation: Lessons from Zambia, 2002, Principles of Arbitration Law, 2003, Frontiers of Legal Knowledge: Business and Economic Law in Context, 2003. Tutor U. Zambia Law Sch., 1991-95. Staff Devel. fellow in law U. Zambia, 1991, U. Yale Law Faculty fellow, 1998; Rhodes scholar U. Zambia, 1992, U. Oxford, 1992-94, U. Hull, 1994-95. Fellow Royal Soc. Arts. of England, Inst. Commerce of England; mem. Internat. Bar Assn., Law Assn. of Zambia, Brit. Assn. Lawyers for Def. of Unborn. Office: The World Bank 1818 H St NW Washington DC 20433-0001 Personal E-mail: kmwenda@yahoo.com. Business E-Mail: kmwenda@worldbank.org.

MYATT, DOTTIE WOODARD, education educator; b. Nashville, Tenn., Dec. 12, 1951; d. James Edward and Dorothy Carter Woodard; m. Samuel Joseph Myatt, Aug. 27, 1972; children: Bill, Lili, Janie. BS, Lambuth U., 1974; MEd, Union U., 1991; EdD, U. Memphis, 1999. Kindergarten tchr. Haywood Elem., Brownsville, Tenn., 1974—75; preschool tchr. Parents' Coop. Preschool, Springfield, Mo., 1983—87; elem. tchr. Anderson Grammar Sch., Brownsville, 1987—92, East Elem., Jackson, Tenn., 1992—94; dir. field experience Union U., Jackson, 1994—96, instr., 1994—96, dir. tchr. edn., 1996—2004, assoc. prof., 1996—, asst. dean tchr. edn. and accreditation, 2004—. Mem. bd. of examiners Tenn. Dept. Edn., Nashville, 1998—. Mem. Englewood Bapt. Ch., Jackson, Tenn., 1987—. Mem.: Alpha Delta Kappa (pres. 1988—). Office: Union Univ 1050 Union Univ Dr Jackson TN 38305

MYATT, WILLIAM HOWARD, theater educator, director, actor; b. Maquoketa, Iowa, Mar. 1, 1961; s. Robert Bruce and Adabelle Marie Myatt; m. Christina Marie Schnock, Aug. 10, 2002; children: Anna Marie, Alexander Ashton, Zachary Leonard. BA, U. No. Iowa, Cedar Falls, 1979—84, MA, 1985—90. Cert. 7 - 12 Libr./Media Specialist Dept. of Edn., Iowa, 2001, k - 12 Talented and Gifted Educator Dept. of Edn., Iowa, 1995. Dir., actor Meml. Union Summer Resident Theatre, Ames, Iowa, 1982—83; drama dir., tchr. Burlington HS, Wis., 1984—85, No. U. HS, Cedar Falls, Iowa, 1985—87, Clinton HS, Iowa, 1987—90, Pleasant Valley Cmty. HS, Pleasant Valley, Iowa, 1990—. Workshop presenter Tenn. Thespian Conf., Nashville, 1991, Va. Thespian Conf., 1991—94, Ednl. Theatre Assn., Regional Conf., Minneapolis, Minn., 1991, Kans. Thespian Conf., 1992; workshop presenter, adjudicator Fla. Thespian Conf., Tampa Bay, 1992; workshop presenter Iowa HS Speech Assn., Des Moines, 1997—; mainstage adjudicator Ednl. Theatre Assn., Cincinnati, Ohio, 1994—, trustee, 1996—99. Contbr. articles. Aids quilt display com. Scholar Hazel B. Strayer award, U. No. Iowa Theatre Dept., 1982. Mem.: Ednl. Theatre Assn. (pres., v.p. 2001—). Avocations: theater, reading, science fiction. Office: Pleasant Valley Comm HS PO Box 332 Pleasant Valley IA 52767-0332 Office Phone: 563-332-5151. Business E-Mail: myattw@pleasval.k12.ia.us.

MYCIELSKI, JAN, mathematician, educator; b. Wisniowa, Poland, Feb. 7, 1932; s. Jan and Helena (Bal) M.; m. Emilia Przezdziecka, Apr. 25, 1959. MS, U. Wroclaw, Poland, 1955, PhD, 1957. With Inst. Math., Polish Acad. Scis., Wroclaw, 1956-68; prof. math. U. Colo., Boulder, 1969—. Vis. prof. Case Western Res. U., Cleve., 1967, U. Colo., 1967, Inst. des Hautes Etudes Scientifiques, Bures-sur-Yvette, 1978-79, dept. math. U. Hawaii, 1987; attache de recherche Centre National de la Recherche Scientifique, Paris, 1957-58; asst. prof. U. Calif., Berkeley, 1961-62, 70; long-term vis. staff mem. Los Alamos Nat. Lab., 1989-90. Author over 150 rsch. papers. Recipient Stefan Banach prize, 1965, Alfred Jurzykowski award, 1977, Waclaw Sierpinski medal, 1990. Mem. Am. Math. Soc., Polish Math. Soc., Assn. for Symbolic Logic. Office: U Colo Dept Math Boulder CO 80309-0395

MYDLAND, GORDON JAMES, judge; b. nr. Hetland, S.D., May 12, 1922; s. Jacob and Anna (Hetl) M.; m. Lorrie Grange, May 29, 1958; 1 child, Gabriel. BS, S.D. State U., 1947; JD, U. S.D., 1956. Bar: S.D. 1956. Pvt. practice law, Brookings, S.D., 1956-69, Lake Preston, S.D., 1973; S.D. circuit judge, 1973-87; presiding judge (3d Jud. Circuit), 1975, 79-80; S.D. state's atty. Brookings County, 1959-62; mem. S.D. State Senate, 1963-68; atty. gen.

S.D., 1968-72; ret., 1987. Part-time instr. constl. and bus. law S.D. State U., 1956-65 Mem. S.D. Code Compilation Commn., 1964-68. Served with USNR, 1943-46. Mem. Am. Legion. Lutheran.

MYER, DONALD BEEKMAN, architect; b. Cleve., Aug. 25, 1937; s. Beekman Walter and Jennie Helen (Gimpel) M.; m. Ellen Jane Schwartz, June 10, 1970; 1 child, Jamie Beekman. BArch, U. Ill., 1961, MArch, 1962. Registered architect Va., D.C. Supervisory architect Nat. Park Svc., Phila., Washington, Cape, Mass., 1962-65; asst. sec. Commn. Fine Arts, Washington, 1965-97; adminstrn., budget and grants cons. Keyes, Lethbridge & Condon, Architects, Washington, 1968-70; clk. of works Washington Nat. Cathedral, 1998-2001; curator bldg. and grounds Tudor Place, Georgetown, 2001—02; strategic counsel cons., 2002—. Cons. Preservation Galveston (Tex.) History Found., 1968-69, Joint Com. on Landmarks, Washington, 1969; faculty cons. Sch. of Arch., Cath. U. of Am., 1990—; apptd. bldgs. and grounds com. Protestant Episcopal Cathedral, 2003—. Author: Bridges and the City of Washington, 1974, Building Potomac Aqueduct, 1975; editor: Centennial History of Washington AIA, 1987. Mem. faculty Smithsonian Resident Assocs., Washington, 1973-81; pres. Washington Archtl. Found., 1998-2000; trustee Com. of 100 on the Fed. City, 1997-2000; mem. bldgs. and grounds com., Protestant Episc. Cathedral, 2003—. Grantee Europa-Nostra Seminar Smithsonian Fgn. Currency Program, Poland, 1974; named one of 77 People to Watch award, Washingtonian Mag., 1987. Fellow AIA (chair hist. resources 1976, v.p. found. 1980, chpt. pres. 1987, fellows selection jury 1998-2000); mem. Woodley Park Men's Club (pres. 1979-82), Lambda Alpha (hon.). Republican. Avocations: bridge history, travel, photography, furniture and clock restoration. Personal E-mail: emyer@erols.com.

MYER, WARREN HITESH, mortgage broker, internet advertising executive; b. New Delhi, Sept. 8, 1961; s. Hana N.S. and Veena Myer; m. Suki Myer, Aug. 15, 1991. MS, U. Del., 1986; MBA, U. Chgo., 1990. Instr. U. Del., Newark, 1984-86; mem. tech. staff Lachman Assoc., Naperville, Ill., 1986-88; sys. mgr. Pyramid Tech., San Jose, Calif., 1988-91; pres. Loan World Inc., San Jose, Calif., 1991—, Bestrate.com, Inc., San Jose, Calif., 1995—. Inventor in field. Avocation: windsurfing. Home: 1421 Old Piedmont Rd San Jose CA 95132-2417 Office: Myers Internet Inc 2160 Lundy Ave Ste 128 San Jose CA 95131

MYERBERG, MARCIA, investment banker; b. Boston, Mar. 25, 1945; d. George and Evelyn (Lewis) Katz; m. Jonathan Gene Myerberg, June 4, 1967 (div. Mar. 1994); 1 child, Gillian Michelle. BS, U. Wis., 1966. Corp. trust adminstr. Chase Manhattan Bank, N.Y.C., 1966-67; asst. cashier Glore Forgan, Wm. R. Staats, Phoenix, 1967-68; bond portfolio analyst Trust Co. of Ga., Atlanta, 1969-72; asst. v.p. 1st Union Nat. Bank, Charlotte, N.C., 1973-78; dir. cash mgmt. Carolina Power & Light Co., Raleigh, N.C., 1978-79; sr. v.p., treas. Fed Home Loan Mortgage Corp., Washington, 1979-85; dir. Salomon Bros. Inc., N.Y.C., 1985-89; sr. mng. dir. Bear, Stearns & Co. Inc., N.Y.C., 1989-93; mng. dir. Bear, Stearns Home Loans, London, 1989-93; chief exec. Myerberg & Co., L.P., N.Y.C., 1994—. Home: 37 W 12th St Apt 6K New York NY 10011-3205 Office: 780 3rd Ave New York NY 10017-2024

MYERNICK, GLENN, professional soccer coach; b. Dec. 29, 1954; Student, Hartwick Coll. Professional soccer player Dallas Tornado, 1977-79, Portland, 1980-82, Tampa Bay, Fla., 1983-84; asst. coach U. Tampa, 1985-86, Hartwick Coll., 1986-89; nat. coaching coord. US Soccer Team, 1989-96; asst. coach US Olympic Team, 1996; head coach Colo. Rapids, Denver, 1997—2000; asst. coach US Men's Nat. Team, 2002; head coach US Nat. Under-23 Men's Team, 2004—. Capt. U.S. Pan Am. Team, 1975, U.S. Olympic Team, 1976. Recipient Hermann Trophy as College Player of the Yr., 1976; named U.S. Soccer Fedn. Coach of the Yr. by U.S. Olympic Com., 1998. Office: US Soccer Federation 1801 S Prairie Ave Chicago IL 60616*

MYEROWITZ, P(AUL) DAVID, cardiac surgeon, educator; b. Balt., Jan. 18, 1947; s. Joseph Robert and Merry (Brown) M.; m. Susan Karen Macks, June 28, 1967 (div.); children: Morris Brown, Elissa Suzanne, Ian Matthew. BS, U. Md., 1966; MD, 1970; MS, U. Minn., 1977. Intern in surgery U. Minn., Mpls., 1970-71, resident in surgery, 1971-72, 74-77; resident in cardiothoracic surgery U. Chgo., 1977-79; practice medicine specializing in cardiovascular surgery Madison, Wis., 1979—; asst. prof. thoracic and cardiovascular surgery U. Wis., Madison, 1979-85; assoc. prof., 1985; chief sect. cardiac transplantation, 1984-85; Karl P. Klassen prof., 1985-97; chief thoracic and cardiovascular surgery Ohio State U. and Hosps., Columbus, 1985-97. Author: Heart Transplantation; contbr. articles to profl. jours. Served with USPHS, 1972-74. Mem.: ACS, Am. Assn. Thoracic Surgeons, Am. Coll. Cardiology. Jewish. E-mail: hrttx1@aol.com.

MYERS, A. MAURICE, waste management executive; b. Long Beach, Calif., May 20, 1940; s. Walter Ray and H. Priscilla (Larsen) M.; m. Elizabeth Jean Ashburn, July 16, 1960; children: Michele, Tracy, Leanne. BA, Calif. State U., Fullerton, 1964; MBA, Calif. State U., Long Beach, 1972. Fin. mgr. Ford Motor Co., Newport Beach, Calif., 1964-72; fin. cons. Merrill Lynch, Newport Beach, 1972-75; mktg. dir. Continental Airlines, L.A., 1975-82; v.p. ops. On TV, L.A., 1982-83; pres., CEO Aloha Airgroup, Honolulu, 1983-93; pres. Am. West Airlines, Phoenix, 1993-95; chmn., pres., CEO, bd. dirs. Yellow Corp., Overland Park, Kans., 1996-99; pres., CEO Waste Mgmt., Inc., Houston, 1999—2004; chmn. Waste Mgmt. Inc., Houston, 1999—. Bd. dirs. Hawaiian Elec. Industries, Honolulu, Tesoro Petroleum Inc., San Antonio, Pleasant Holidays, West Lake Village, Calif. Bd. dirs. Greater Houston Partnership, Keep Am. Beautiful. Mem. Nat. Assn. Mfrs., Waialae Country Club (Honolulu). Avocations: reading, golf, travel. Office: Waste Management 1001 Fannin St Ste 4000 Houston TX 77002-6711*

MYERS, ADELE ANNA, artist, educator, nun; b. Bklyn., Oct. 4, 1925; d. Everett Ecil and Anna Maria (Menig) M. Student, U. Notre Dame; BS in Edn., Fordham U., 1956; MA in Fine Arts, Villa Schifanoia, Florence, Italy, 1962; postgrad., NYU, Pratt Graphics Ctr., Columbia U. Cert. permanent tchr. art, grades K-12, N.Y.; joined Sparkill Dominican Sisters, Roman Cath. Ch., 1944. Tchr. art Monsignor Scanlon H.S., Bronx, N.Y., 1956-60, Albertus Magnus H.S., Bardonia, N.Y., 1961-62; founder, dir. Thorpe Intermedia Gallery, Sparkill, N.Y., 1976-91; prof., chairperson art dept. St. Thomas Aquinas Coll., Sparkill, 1962-78, adj. prof., 1978-99. Design cons. sr. housing devels. Thorpe Village and Dowling Gardens, Sparkill, N.Y., 1981—; mem. adv. bd. Bogliasco Found., N.Y.C. and Italy, 1997—; freelance curator contemporary art exhbns., 1986—. Commd. works include cross in fresco and cement St. Peter's Ch., Yonkers, N.Y., 1990, outdoor sidewalk mosaic Thorpe Village, 1997, stained glass windows for meditation rm. Dowling Gardens, 1996, outdoor mosaic, meditation garden Dominican Sisters, Sparkill, 2001, stained glass windows Our Lady of Rosary Chapel, Dominican Convent, 2001, Way of the Cross in fresco and cement, Chapel at St. Thomas Aquinas Coll., Sparkill, N.Y., 2002; exhibited sculpture in fresco and cement, most recently at ArtBldrs. Gallery, Jersey City, 1994-95, Rockland Ctr. for Arts, 1995, 96, 99, St. John's Chapel Gallery, Newark, 1996, Piermont Flywheel Gallery, N.Y., 2002, Azarian-McCullough Gallery, Sparkill, N.Y., 2001, Visions Gallery, Albany, N.Y., 2001; one-woman shows include Hopper Ho. Art Ctr., Nyack, 1992, Piermont Flywheel Gallery, 1996, 98, 2000, 01, 02, ArtBuilders Gallery, 1996, 2003, Old Ch. Cultural Ctr. Gallery, Demarest, N.J., 1997; represented in pub. and pvt. collections; works and exhibits reviewed in various publs., including N.Y. Times, Star Ledger, Suburban People, Arts Happenings; featured on cable TV program, N.J., 1988. Apptd. art in pub. places com. Rockland County, 1987-92; founding bd. dirs. Arts Fund Rockland, 1989-91. Villa Schifanoia scholar, 1960; Sister Adele Myers Scholarship established in her name St. Thomas Aquinas Coll., 1986; recipient award for Outstanding Contbn. in Field of Art, Rockland County Women's Network, Rockland C.C., Suffern, N.Y., 1980, 1st Ann. Arts award Rockland County Execs., 1987. Mem. Nat. Mus. Women in Arts, Internat. Sculpture Ctr., Christians in Visual Arts. Democrat. Avocations: reading, travel, visiting places of historical interest. Home: Dominican Convent 175 Route 340 Sparkill NY 10976-1041

MYERS, ALBERT F. aerospace executive; b. New Orleans, La., Jan. 11, 1946; BS in Mech. Engring., U. Idaho, 1969, MS in Mech. Engring., 1971; MS in Indl. Mgmt., MIT, 1992. Active duty U.S. Army, 1972-75; various positions Dryden Flight Rsch. Ctr., 1975-81; mgr. flight controls engring. Northrop Grumman, 1981, corp. v.p., Bus. Stategy, 1992-94, corp. v.p., treas., 1994—2003, corp. v.p., Strategy and Technology, 2003—. Office: Northrop Grumman Corp 1840 Century Park E Los Angeles CA 90067-2101

MYERS, ALLEN RICHARD, rheumatologist; b. Balt., Jan. 14, 1935; s. Ellis Benjamin and Rosina (Blumberg) M.; m. Ellen Patz, Nov. 26, 1960; children: David Joseph, Robert Todd, Scott Patz. BA, U. Pa., 1956; MD, U. Md., 1960. Diplomate Am. Bd. Internal Medicine, Am. Bd. Rheumatology. Intern Univ. Hosp., Balt., 1960-61, resident in medicine Ann Arbor, Mich., 1961-64; fellow in rheumatology Mass. Gen. Hosp. and Harvard Med. Sch., Boston, 1966-69; dir. clin. tng. rheumatology U. Pa. Sch. Medicine, Phila., 1969-72, chief rheumatology sect., 1972-78; dep. chair medicine Temple U. Sch. Medicine, Phila., 1978-84, acting chmn. medicine, 1984-86, dean, 1991-95, prof. medicine, 1978—, assoc. v.p. Health Scis. Ctr., 1988-95. Vis. prof. Cardiothoracic Inst., U. London, 1988; mem. med. adv. bd. Scleroderma Rsch. Found., Santa Barbara, Calif., 1986. Mem. editl. bd. Arthritis & Rheumatism, 1985—90, Brit. Jour. Rheumatology, 1989—94; editor: Systemic Sclerosis, 1985, Medicine, 1986, 1993, 1996, 2000. Pres. Phila. Health Care Congress, 1994—; adv. com. Pa. Lupus Found., 1976—; bd. dirs. Phila. Conv. and Visitors Bur., 1994—. With USPHS, 1964-66. Recipient Margaret Whitaker prize U. Md. Sch. Medicine, 1960, Lindback Found. award Temple, 1981; named Physician of Yr. Temple U. Hosp., 1986. Master: Am. Coll. Rheumatology, fellow: ACP, Phila. Coll. Physicians (pres. 2000), mem.: Am. Fedn. Clin. Rsch. Avocations: walking, classical music, reading. Office: Temple U Sch Medicine 3400 N Broad St Philadelphia PA 19140-5104 Office Phone: 215-707-1758.

MYERS, ANNE M. developer; Sec., pub. rels. adminstr. Ch. of the Brethren, 1987-97; dir. devel. Timbercrest Retirement Cmty., North Manchester, Ind., 1990—. Office: Timbercrest Retirement Cmty 2201 East St North Manchester IN 46962-9654

MYERS, ARTHUR B. journalist; b. Buffalo, Oct. 24, 1917; s. Edward A. and Isabelle (Baker) M.; m. Irma H. Ashley, 1972. BA, Hobart Coll., 1939. Journalist Rochester (N.Y.) Times Union, 1948-52, Washington Post, 1956-57, Berkshire (Mass.) Eagle, 1957-64; contbg. editor Coronet mag., 1965-68; columnist Bergen Record, Hackensack, N.J., 1969-71; exec. editor Berkshire Sampler, Pittsfield, Mass., 1971-77; tchr. writing Mass. U. extension program and Berkshire Community Coll., Pittsfield, 1958-62, Fairleigh Dickinson U., Teaneck, N.J., 1970, Cambridge (Mass.) Coll., 1989. Author: (with J. O'Connell) Safety Last: An Indictment of Auto Industry, 1966, Journalism Careers for the 70's, 1971, Analysis: The Short Story, 1975, Analysis: The Personal Profile Magazine Article, 1976, Kids Do Amazing Things, 1980, The Ghost Hunters, 1980, Sea Creatures Do Amazing Things, 1981; (with Irma Myers) Why You Feel Down and What You Can Do About It, 1982, The Ghostly Register, 1986, Ghosts of the Rich and Famous, 1988, The Ghostly Gazetteer, 1990, Ghost Hunter's Guide, 1993, The Cheyenne, 1992, The Pawnee, 1993, The First Movies, 1993, The First Baseball Game, 1993, The First Football Game, 1993, Drugs and Peer Pressure, 1995, Communicating with Animals, 1997; also short stories, articles. Mem. PEN, Nat. Writers Union, Mensa, Boston Authors Club. Home: 60 Grove St Apt 6202 Wellesley MA 02482-7716 E-mail: artmyers17@aol.com.

MYERS, BARRY LEE, lawyer; b. Phila., July 20, 1943; s. Martin Henry and Doris Alfreda (Schwartz) M.; m. Leta Franklin, June 21, 1967; children: Carla Franklin, Joseph Franklin, Rebekah Franklin. BS in Bus. Adminstrn. and Econs., Pa. State U., 1967; JD, Boston U., 1970; MS in Bus. Adminstrn., ABD, Pa. State U., 1972. Bar: Mass. 1970, Pa. 1975, U.S. Supreme Ct. 1976. Fellow Pa. State U., Univ. Park, 1970-72, lectr., 1972-73, asst. prof., 1973-78, assoc. prof., 1978-90; pvt. practice State Coll., Pa., 1970-93; gen. counsel Accu-Weather, Inc., State Coll., 1970—, exec. v.p., 1976—, bd. dirs., 1981—. Spl. cons. Nat. Sci. Found., Washington, 1973-74; program evaluator U.S. Dept. of Interior, Washington, 1976; mem. grad. sch. faculty Pa. State U., 1974-90. Author: Legal Environment of Business, 1977; staff editor Am. Bus. Law Jour, 1976-80; contbr. 22 articles, 16 monographs and published proceedings to profl. jours. Mem. task force Pa. Dept. Environ. Resources, 1973-78. Mem. ABA, Am. Arbitration Assn. (nat. panel arbitrators 1977-92), Pa. Bar Assn., Centre County Bar Assn. Avocation: tennis. Office: Accu-Weather Inc 385 Science Park Rd State College PA 16803-2215*

MYERS, BARTON, architect; b. Norfolk, Va., Nov. 6, 1934; s. Barton and Meeta Hamilton (Burrage) M.; m. Victoria George, Mar. 7, 1959; 1 child, Suzanne Lewis. BS, U.S. Naval Acad., 1956; MArch with honors, U. Pa., 1964. Commd. 2d lt. USAF, 1956, resigned, 1961; architect Louis I. Kahn, Phila., 1964-65, Bower, Fradley, Phila., 1967-68; architect, prin. A.J. Diamond & Barton Myers, Toronto, Ont., Can., 1968-75, Barton Myers Assocs., Toronto, 1975-96, architect, pres. Los Angeles, 1981—. Disting. vis. prof. Ariz. State U., Tempe, 1986; sr. prof. UCLA, 1981—; Thomas Jefferson Prof. U. Va., Charlottesville, 1982; vis. prof., lectr., Harvard U., U. Pa., other univs. U.S. and Can., 1968—. Prin. works include Myers Residence, Toronto (Ont. Assn. Architects Toronto Chpt. Annual Design award, 1971, Can. Housing Design Coun. award, 1971), Wolf Residence, Toronto (Archtl. Record: Record Houses of 1977, Twenty-five Yrs. of Record Houses, 1981), Housing Union Bldg., Edmonton (Can. Housing Design Coun. award, 1974, Design in Steel award, 1975), Citadel Theatre, Edmonton (City of Edmonton Design award, 1978, Stelco Design award, 1978), Seagram Mus., Waterloo, Ont. (Gov. Gen.'s Medal for Architecture, 1986), Howard Hughes Ctr. Master Plan and Wang Tower, L.A., 1986, Phoenix Mcpl. Govt. Ctr. (Winning Competition Entry, 1985), Portland Ctr. for the Performing Arts, Portland (Progressive Architecture Design award, 1984, USITT Merit award, 1994), Art Gallery Ont. expansion (Winning Competition Entry, 1987), Film and Drama Facility York U., Toronto, 1987, Cerritos (Calif.) Ctr. Performing Arts, 1987 (USITT Honor Award, 1994), N.J. Performing Arts Ctr., Newark, 1991, Ivan Reitman Prodn. Studio, 1994, Scripps Ocean Atmosphere Rsch. Facility, 1995; others. Recipient Gov. Gen.'s award for Architecture Woodsworth Coll., 1992, RAIC Gold Medal, 1994, Royal Archtl. Inst. Canada Fellow AIA, Royal Archtl. Inst. Can.; mem. Soc. Archtl. Historians, Royal Can. Acad. Art, Tau Sigma Delta. Avocations: travel, reading. Office: U Calif Dept Architecture Los Angeles CA 90095-0001

MYERS, C. DAVID, manufacturing executive; BS, Pa. State U. CPA. Sr. mgr. KPMG L.L.P.; dir. fin. Airside Products Group, 1994-95; corp. contr. York (Pa.) Internat. Corp., 1995-98, v.p., fin. engineered systems group, 1998-2000, v.p., CFO, 2000—03, pres., 2003—, CEO, 2004—, also bd. dirs. Office: York Internat Corp 631 S Richland Ave York PA 17403 also: York Internat Corp PO Box 1592 York PA 17405-1592*

MYERS, CAROL MCCLARY, retired sales administrator, editor; b. Dawson, N.Mex. d. Joseph Franklin and Alberta Lenore (McGarvey) McClary; m. Dwight Andrew Myers, Sept. 16, 1950 (dec. Sept. 1995); children: Robert Andrew, Debra Ann, James Allen. MusB, U. Redlands, 1950. Cert. tchr., Calif. Tchr. music Barstow (Calif.) Pub. Schs., 1950-52; sec., acct. U.S. Army, Columbus, Ga., 1952-54; part-time sec. Robert Lafollette, Atty., Albuquerque, 1954-57; sec., acct. Midland Specialty Co., Albuquerque, 1957-60; pvt. tchr. piano Oakland, N.J., 1960-70; organist, choir dir., ch. sec. Ramapo Valley Bapt., Oakland, N.J., 1965-70; order fulfillment/invoicing U. N.Mex. Press, Albuquerque, 1974-76, sales mgr., 1976-88, ret., 1988. Editor (mag.) Book Talk, 1971-2001; (7 books) In Celebration of the Book: Literary New Mexico, 1982, Literary New Mexico: Essays From Book Talk, 1998. Recipient Edgar Lee Hewett award Hist. Soc. N.Mex., 1985, Paso Por Aquí award Rio Grande Hist. Collections, 1990. Mem. N.Mex. Libr. Assn. (hon. life, treas. 1989-91, bd. dirs. 1992-94), Rocky Mountain Book Pubs. Assn. (Jack D. Rittenhouse award 1994), Mountains and Plains Booksellers Assn. Republican. Avocations: piano playing, New Mexico Book League (vol. editor). Home: 8632 Horacio Pl NE Albuquerque NM 87111-3218

MYERS, CLARK EVERETT, retired business administration educator; b. Rossville, Kans., Oct. 19, 1915; s. Thad James and Rose I (Page) M.; m. Cora Henley Hepworth, May 7, 1942; children— Clark Everett, Richard G. Hepworth. BS, U. Kans., 1939, MBA, 1946; D.C.S., Harvard, 1956. Tchr. Auburn (Kans.) Sch., 1932-34, prin., 1934-36; instr. U. Kans., 1939-41; asst. prof. U. Tex., 1947-49, asso. prof., 1949-53, chmn. dept. mgmt., 1950-53; lectr. Harvard Grad. Sch. Bus. Adminstrn., 1953-54; dean Coll. of Commerce, prof. bus. adminstrn. Ohio U., 1954-57; dir. mgmt. devel. inst. Lausanne, Switzerland, 1957-60; lectr. Harvard Grad. Sch. Bus., 1960-61; dean Sch. Bus. Adminstrn., prof. mgmt. U. Miami, Coral Gables, Fla., 1961-68; dean Grad. Sch. Bus. Adminstrn., Emory U., Atlanta, 1968-75, prof. bus. adminstrn., 1975-85, prof. emeritus, 1985—. Editor: (with William R. Spriegel) The Writings of the Gilbreths, 1953. Served as lt. USNR, 1942-45. Fellow Acad. Mgmt.; mem. Am. Assn. Collegiate Schs. Bus. (exec. com. 1965-68, 1969-70, pres. 1970-71), Phi Kappa Phi, Sigma Iota Epsilon, Delta Sigma Pi, Beta Gamma Sigma, Phi Gamma Delta, Beta Alpha Psi. Home: 1082 Vistavia Cir Decatur GA 30033-3413

MYERS, CLAY, retired investment management company executive; b. Portland, Oreg., May 27, 1927; s. Henry Clay and Helen (Mackey) M.; m. Elizabeth Lex Arndt, Oct. 1, 1955; children: Richard Clay (dec.), Carolyn Elizabeth, David Hobson. BS, U. Oreg., 1949; postgrad., Northwestern Coll. Law, 1950-52; LHD (hon.), Ch. Div. Sch. of the Pacific, 1992. With 1st. Nat. Bank, Portland, 1949-53; with Conn. Gen. Life Ins. Co., Hartford and Portland, 1953-62, state mgr., 1960-62; v.p. Ins. Co. Oreg., Portland, 1962-65; asst. sec. state State of Oreg., Salem, 1965-67, sec. state, 1967-77, state treas., 1977-84, v.p. J.P. Morgan Investment Mgmt. Co., N.Y.C., 1984-89, Capital Cons. Inc., Portland, Oreg., 1989-92. Chmn. Oreg. House Adv. Com. Legis. Reapportionment, 1961; chmn. Oreg. Gov.'s Commn. on Youth, 1969-74 Author: (with others) Population Reapportionment Initiative Constitutional Amendment, 1952. Bd. dirs., treas. Ch. Divinity Sch. of Pacific, 1977-83; trustee Pacific U., 1989-92; vestryman Trinity Parish, Wall St., 1986-93; pres. Nat. Interfrat. Conf., 1986-87; mem. social responsibility in investing com. Nat. Episcopal Ch., 1983-87; trustee Ch. Pension Fund; bd. dirs. Ch. Life Ins. Co., 1991-97; sr. warden St. Andrew's, Nogales, Az., 2002-04. Mem. Nat. Assn. State Treas. (past pres.), Multnomah Athletic Club (Portland), DeMolay Club (Legion of Honor), Lambda Chi Alpha (nat. pres. 1974-78), Sigma Nu Phi. Episcopalian. Home: PO Box 237 Tumacacori AZ 85640-0237

MYERS, CONNIE, assemblywoman; b. Staten Island, N.Y., Nov. 14, 1944; BA in English, Montclair State Coll.; MA in Pub. Adminstrn., Rider Coll. Alt. del. Rep. Nat. Conv., 1988; mem. Hunterdon County Bd. of Elections, 1989—95, Hunterdon County Planning Bd., 1992—97; county coord., local media coord. Whitman for Gov., 1993; county coord. Haytaian for U.S. Senate, 1994; assemblywoman N.J. Gen. Assembly, 1996—. Mem. Holland Twp. Rep. Com.; mem., vice chair Hunterdon County Rep. Com. Mem. Moravian Coll. Parents Coun. Mem.: N.J. Hist. Soc., Descendants of the Founders of N.J. (scholarship chair), N.J. Farm Bureau, N.J. Daughters of the Am. Revolution (geneal. records chair), North East Organic Farmers Assn. Republican. E-mail: AswMyers@njleg.org.

MYERS, DANE JACOB, lawyer, podiatrist; b. Murray, Utah, June 20, 1948; s. Lorin LaVar Myers and Irma Lee (Bell) Willette; m. Mary Jo Jackson, June 22, 1970; children: Troy, Chad, Melissa, Apryll, Tristan, Remington. DPM, Pa. Coll. Podiatric Medicine, 1977; BA, U. Utah, 1983; JD, U. Ark., 1986. Bar: Ark 1986. Pres. Tooele (Utah) Foot Clinic, 1977-83; owner N.W. Ark. Foot Clinic, Rogers, Ark., 1983—; pvt. practice law Fayetteville, 1986-97. Served to maj med serv corps USAR, 1977—94. Mem.: APHA, ABA, Ark. Podiatric Medicine Assn., Am. Podiatric Medicine Assn., Am. Soc. Law and Medicine, Ark. Bar Assn., Am. Diabetes Assn., Am. Coll. Foot and Ankle Surgeons (assoc.), Delta Theta Phi. Republican. Mem. Lds Ch. Avocations: golf, computers, history. Home: 2005 Oakhill Dr Springdale AR 72762 Office: NW Ark Foot Clinic 700 N 13th St Rogers AR 72756-3436 Office Phone: 479-636-1411. E-mail: danejmyers@hotmail.com.

MYERS, DANIEL, lawyer; b. Celina, Ohio, Jan. 27, 1950; s. David M. and Ruth E. (Henderson) Myers; m. Terry L. Noel, Oct. 25, 1975 (div. Apr. 1982); m. Jill E. Snyder, July 21, 1988. BS, U. Tenn., 1972; JD, Ohio No. U., 1975. Bar: Ohio 1976, Fla. 1976, Pa. 1977. Assoc. Myers & Myers, Celina, Ohio, 1975-77, ptnr., 1978—79; sole practice Myers Law Office, Celina, Ohio, 1996—. Pros. atty. Mercer County, Celina, 1980-92. Mem. Lions (bd. dirs. 1982-95), Elks (exalted knight 1976-77). Office: PO Box 230 90 N Ash St Celina OH 45822-1702 Office Phone: 419-586-2396.

MYERS, DANIEL N. lawyer, association executive; b. Independence, Kans., Sept. 17, 1942; s. James Kenneth and Evalyn Clair Petty (Feather) M.; m. Eileen Carruthers, Dec. 14, 1966; children: Yvette Christine, John Joseph. AA, Coffeyville Coll., 1961; BA, U. Okla., 1963; JD, Georgetown U., 1975. Bar: Va. 1976, U.S. Ct. Customs and Patent Appeals 1977, Ill. 1991. Asst. to pres. J.V. Hurson Assoc., Inc., Washington, 1968-74; mgr. fed. legis. affairs AICPA, Washington, 1974-77; dir. legis. svcs., assoc. counsel Nat. LP-Gas Assn., Arlington, Va., 1977-79; gen. counsel, v.p. govt. relations Nat. Propane Gas Assn., Arlington, Va., 1979-88, exec. v.p. Lisle, Ill., 1989—2003; exec. dir. Churchill Ctr., Washington, 2003—. Contbr. articles on good samaritan laws and genealogy to various publs. Bd. dirs. Washington Area State Rels. Group, 1980-82, mem. energy task force White House Conf. on Small Bus., 1980; chmn. good samaritan coaliton hazardous materials Adv. Coun., Washington, 1982-88; mem. motor carrier adv. com. Fed. Hwy. Adminstrn., Washington, 1982-88. Sgt. U.S. Army, 1964-68. Mem. Am. Soc. Assn. Execs. (legal sect. coun. 1980—, chmn. legal sect. 1991-92, bd. dirs. 1991-92), Spl. Indsl. Radio Svc. Assn. (bd. dirs. 1979-88), Indsl. Telecomm. Assn. (bd. dirs. 1995-97), Chgo. Soc. Assn. Execs., Nat. Vol. Firefighters Coun. Found. (bd. dirs. 1995-97). Avocations: golf, genealogy, racquetball, woodworking. Office: 4901 Forest Ave Downers Grove IL 60515 E-mail: dmyers@winstonchurchill.org.

MYERS, DANIEL WILLIAM, II, lawyer; b. Camden, N.J., Mar. 21, 1931; s. Charles Rudolph II and Myrtle Henrietta (Kress) M.; m. Eileen Ethel Kohn, Nov. 22, 1959; children: Susan Leigh, Meredith Ann Myers Winner, Kathryn Kress. BS in Commerce, U. Va., 1952, LLB, 1957. Bar: Va. 1957, N.J. 1958, U.S. Dist. Ct. N.J. 1958, U.S. Supreme Ct. 1980. Assoc. Lewis & Hutchinson, Camden, 1958-60; ptnr. Myers, Matteo, Rabii, Norcross & Landgraf and predecessors, Camden, Cherry Hill, NJ, 1960-89, Montgomery, McCracken, Walker & Rhoads, 1989-94, of counsel, 1994-98, Steven J. Jozwiak, Cherry Hill, N.J., 1998—. 1st lt. U.S. Army, 1952-54. Mem. N.J. Bar Assn., Va. Bar Assn., Camden County Bar Assn., Am. Arbitration Assn., Exch. Club (pres. Cherry Hill chpt. 1969). Republican. Lutheran. Home: 1 E Atlantic Ave Harvey Cedars NJ 08008 Office: 532 Hollywood Ave at Rte 38 Cherry Hill NJ 08002

MYERS, DARYL RONALD, engineer; b. Denver, July 12, 1948; s. James Elmer Myers and Betty Mae (Gannon) Welborn; m. Donna Lee Olsen, Oct. 3, 1990 (dec. Oct. 1995); m. Barbara Jane Bowker, Sept. 5, 1997. BS in Applied Math., U. Colo., 1970, postgrad., 1974-75. Staff physicist Smithsonian Radiation Biology Lab., Rockville, Md., 1974-78; metrology engr. Solar Energy Rsch. Inst. (now Nat. Renewable Energy Lab.), Golden, Colo., 1978-93; sr. scientist, team leader Photovoltaic Radiometric Measurements & Evaluation, 1993—. Project leader Joint U.S.-Saudi Arabian Solar Radiation Resource Assessment, 1997-2000, Joint Saudi Arabian/NASA Remote Sensing Validation Project, 1998-2001. Editor Optical Radiation News; contbr. articles to profl. jours. including Solar Energy, Solar Cells, ASME Jour. Solar Energy Engring. Russian and German interpreter, Cultural Diversity Com., Arvada, Colo., 1992. With U.S. Army, 1970-74. Mem. ASTM, Precision Measurement Assn. (John Quincy Adams award 1979-80), Am. Solar Energy Soc., Coun. Optical Radiation Measurement (v.p. 2004—), Math. Assn. Am. Democrat. Achievements include rsch. in algorithms for interpolation and corrections to measured precipitable water, aerosol optical depth, and radiometric data used in developing national solar radiation data base and international projects to establish global climate change trends via ground and satellite based instrumentation; development of revised terrestrial spectral

solar radiation reference and improved solar radiometric instrument calibration standards. Office: Nat Renewable Energy Lab 1617 Cole Blvd Golden CO 80401-3305 Business E-Mail: daryl_myers@nrel.gov.

MYERS, DAVID WAYNE, legal assistant; b. Lancaster, Ohio, Nov. 30, 1956; s. Carroll Wayne and Charlotte Idabelle Myers; m. Diane Marie Conrad, Nov. 6, 1976 (div. Mar. 1982); children: Jennifer Marie Myers-McMahan, Jeremy Wayne 1 stepchild, Braden Christian Beisse; m. Diana Lynn Pace, Feb. 29, 1988 (dec. May 1993). Student, Ohio U., 1980, Park U., 1992; BSBA, Hamilton U., 2002; legal asst., paralegal, Blackstone Paralegal Studies, Emmaus, Pa., 2002; cert. gen. office clk. supr. aide, Mid. Ga. Tech. Coll., 2003; cert property mgr., Sch. Property Mgmt., 2004. Cert. title examiner Land Title Inst. Sr. sgt. Spl. Forces U.S. Army, 1974—94; tchr. aide (prisoner) Lee State Prison Ga. Dept. Corrections, Leesburg, 1996—2001, law clk. (prisoner) Lee State Prison, 2001—. Recipient Meritorious Svc. medal (3), U.S. Army, Commendation medal (5), Achievement medal (5). Mem.: Inst. Real Estate Mgmt. (assoc.), KAIROS Internat. Prison Ministry (sec. 1997—99). Republican. Roman Catholic. Avocations: reading, Croatian language studies, corresponding. Home: 335 Lincoln Ave Pleasantville OH 43148 Office: 789787 Lee State Prison E-1 153 Pinewood Rd Leesburg GA 31763

MYERS, DONALD EARL, mathematics professor; b. Chanute, Kans., Dec. 29, 1931; s. Frank Jasper and Electa Bell (Blackburn) M.; m. Ruth Louise Pettit, June 6, 1954; children: Jill Elizabeth, Douglas Lee. BS, Kans. State U., 1953, MS, 1955; PhD, U. Ill., 1960. Assoc. prof. math. Millikin U., Decatur, Ill., 1958—60; asst. prof. math. U. Ariz., Tucson, 1960—64, assoc. prof. math., 1964—68, prof. math., 1968—, faculty chmn., 1977—79; prof. math. U. Paris, 1986; mathematician USGS, Denver, 1982—85; maitre de recherche Ecole des Mines, Paris, 1987. Cons. UN Project, China, 1991; referee NSF on math., geology and water resources rsch.; cons. NURE project, OakRidge Nat. Lab, 1980—82, NAS/NRC Com. on Assessment of Ctrs. for Disease Control and Prevention Radiation Studies from DOE contractor sites, 1997—98, 1999—2005. Co-author (with J. Carr): (paper) Computers & Geosciences (Best Paper award, 1985); contbr. articles to profl. jours. Squadron comdr. U.S. Power Squadron, 1972, dist. comdr., 1989-90. Named Disting. Alumnus, Dept. Math. Kans. State U., 1991; recipient Disting. Achievement award, Sect. on Statistics and Environment, Am. Statis. Assn., 1993; grantee, EPA, 1984—91. Mem.: AAUP (chpt. pres. 1972—74, 1992), Internat. Assn. Math. Geology, Am. Statis. Assn., Inst. Math. Statistics, Am. Math. Soc., Math. Assn. Am. Avocations: sailing, travel. Office: Univ of Ariz Dept Mathematics Tucson AZ 85721-0089 Office Phone: 520-621-6859. Business E-Mail: myers@math.arizona.edu.

MYERS, DOUGLAS GEORGE, zoological society administrator; b. L.A., Aug. 30, 1949; s. George Walter and Daydeen (Schroeder) Myers; m. Barbara Firestone Myers, Nov. 30, 1980; children: Amy, Andrew. BA, Christopher Newport Coll., 1981. Tour and show supr. Anneheuser-Busch (Bird Sanctuary), Van Nuys, Calif., 1970-74, mgr. zool. ops., 1974-75, asst. mgr. ops., 1975-77, mgr. ops., 1977-78; gen. services mgr. Anneheuser-Busch (Old Country), Williamsburg, Va., 1978-80, park ops. dir., 1980-81; gen. mgr. wild animal park Zool. Soc. San Diego, 1981-83, dep. dir. ops., 1983-85, exec. dir., 1985—; chief exec. ofcr. San Diego Wild Animal Park, Escondido, Calif. Cons. in field. Mem. adv. com. of pres.' assn. Am. Mgmt. Assn. Fellow Am. Assn. Zool. Parks and Aquariums (profl., bd. dirs.), Internat. Union Dirs. Zool. Gardens; mem. Internat. Assn. Amusement Parks and Attractions, Am. Mgmt. Assn. (adv. com. pres. assn.), Calif. Assn. Zoos and Aquariums, Rotary. Office: San Diego Zoo PO Box 120551 San Diego CA 92112-0551

MYERS, EDDIE EARL, clinical psychologist; b. Ardmore, Okla., Nov. 24, 1937; s. Finis Weldon and Fern Durrell (Johnson) M.; m. Ineta June Moore, July 2, 1955 (div. Mar. 1988); children: Richard Weldon, Ronald Leland, Marilyn June, Rebecca Jean; m. Ann Clymer Taylor, July 15, 1988 (div. May 1996); Clark Clymer Taylor, Katy Ann Taylor; m. Katherine Call Emch, Dec. 28, 1996. BSEd, Tex. Christian U., 1958; MEd, U. N. Tex., 1967, EdD, 1969. Lic. psychologist, Ohio; Nat. Drug Edn. Leadership Tng. Adlephi U., 1970. Machinist Chance Vaught Aircraft, Grand Prairie, Tex., 1957-58; 5th grade tchr., jr. high coach Ft. Worth Christian Schs., 1958-59; 6th grade tchr., jr. high coach Corpus Christi (Tex.) Ind. Sch. Dist., 1959-60; youth, music, ednl. min. Norton St. Ch. Christ, Corpus Christi, 1960-61, Procter St. Ch. Christ, Port Arthur, Tex., 1963-65; min. Cameron (Tex.) Ch. Christ, 1961-63; high sch. English tchr. Christian Schs., Inc., Dallas, 1965-66; psychology instr. Tex. Women's U., Denton, 1968-69; sr. rsch. assoc., dir. psychology dept. Ednl. Rsch. Coun. Am., Cleve., 1969-78; clin. psychologist pvt. practice Cleve., 1978—. Faculty dept. guidance anc counseling U. Oreg. Workshop, Frankfurt, German, 1972; Ea. U.S. drug abuse task force Am. Soc. Health Assn., N.Y.C., 1971-73; chmn. drug abuse and alcoholism task force Fedn. Cmty. Planning, Cleve., 1970-71; adv. bd. Freedom House Rehab. Ctr., Cleve., 1993—; adj. assoc. prof. ednl. specialists Cleve. State U., 1970-74; mem. med. staff St. John Westshore Hosp., West Lake, Ohio, Fairview Hosp., Cleve. Author: Social Isolation and Personality, 1973, Handy Asks the Psychologist, 1974, (tchr. manual) Human Persons and Use of Psychoactive Agents, 1974; co-author: (tchr. manual) New Model Me: Operator's Guide to Coping with Aggression, 1974; contbr. articles to profl. jours. R & D grantee NIMH, Washington, 1974-78, Nat. Def. Edn. Rsch. Tng. grantee U.S. Dept. Edn., Washington, 1965-69. Mem. APA, Cleve. Psychol. Assn. (bd. trustees 1981-85), Cleve. Acad. Consulting Psychologists (pres. 1984-86), Ohio Psychol. Assn. (bd. trustees 1978—), Phi Delta Kappa. Avocations: computers, golf, jet boating. Office: 3865 Rocky River Dr Ste 2 Cleveland OH 44111-4114

MYERS, ELMER, psychiatric social worker; b. Blackwell, Ark., Nov. 12, 1926; s. Chester Elmer Myers and Irene Lewis; widowed; children: Elmer Jr., Keith, Kevin. BA, U. Kans., 1951, MA, 1962; student, U. Calif., Santa Barbara, 1977-78. Lic. clin. social worker; C.C. counselor credentials. Psychiat. social worker Hastings (Nebr.) State Hosp., 1960-62, State of Calif. Bur. Social Tng. Com., Sacramento, 1962-75; supr. psychiat. social worker State of Calif., Sacramento, 1975-80, Alta Calif. Regional Ctr., Sacramento, 1980-85. Exec. dir. Tri-County Family Svcs., Yuba City, Calif., 1966-69; cons. to four convalescent Hosps., Marysville and Willows, Calif., 1969-71; lectr. Yuba Coll., Marysville, 1971-76; assoc. prof. Calif. State U., Chico, 1972-73; cons. in field, Marysville, 1985—; group therapist Depot Homeless Shelter, 1996—, facilitator HIV support group, 1993-2002, counselor, 1995—; cons., therapist New Millennium Group Home, 2000. Bd. dirs. Habitat for Humanity, 1993; juror Yuba County Grand Jury, Marysville, 1965, 1987—88; sec. Y's Men's Club, Yuba City, 1964—65; chmn. Tri-County Home Health Agy., Yuba City, 1974—76; vice-chmn. Gateway Projects, Inc., Yuba City, 1974—75; bd. dirs. Yuba County Truancy Bd., Marysville, 1964—67; asst. dir. Marysville Adult Activity Ctr., 1990—; active Yuba-Sutter United Way, 1971—73, 1991—92; active, sec. Tri-County Ethnic Forum, 1991—93; steering com. Yuba County Sr. Ctr. Assn., 1992, 1995—; chmn. Yuba County Cmty. Svcs. Commn., 1997—99, Yuba-Sutter Gleaners, 1997—, bd. dirs., 1998, 2001; chmn. Yuba-Sutter Commn. on Aging, 1996, bd. dirs., 1998, 2001; chmn. H.E.L.P. Working Group, HIV Prevention, 2000; bd. dirs. Christian Assistance Network, 1993, Golden Empire Health Sys. Agy., Sacramento, 1972—76, Youth Svcs. Bur., Yuba City, 1967, Bi-County Mental Retardation Planning Bd., Yuba City, 1972, Yuba County Juvenile Justice Commn., Marysville, 1982—90, Am. Cancer Soc., Marysville, 1985—92, Yuba County Rep. Ctrl. Com., 1983—90, Salvation Army, 1990—, facilitator care proj., 1992—2002. Recipient Cert. Spl. Recognition, Calif. Rehab. Planning Project, 1969, Cert. Spl. Recognition, State of Calif., 1967, Cert. Spl. Recognition, Alta Calif. Regional Ctrs., 1985; named Vol. of Week, Appeal Dem. newspaper, 1999. Mem. Nat. Assn. Social Workers (cert.), Kern County Mental Health Assn. (chmn. 1978-79). Lodges: Rotary (bd. dirs. Marysville club 1975-76). Avocations: gardening, reading, computers. Home and Office: 3920 State Hwy 20 Marysville CA 95901-9003 E-mail: elm@syix.com.

MYERS, EUGENE NICHOLAS, otolaryngologist, educator; b. Phila, Pa, Nov. 27, 1933; s. David and Rosalind (Nicholas) Myers; m. Barbara Labov, June 10, 1956; children: Marjorie Rose, Jeffrey N. BS in Econs., U. Pa., 1954; MD, Temple U., 1960. Diplomate Am. Bd. Otolaryngology. Intern Mt. Sinai Hosp., NYC, 1960—61; resident Mass. Eye and Ear Infirmary, Boston, 1963—65; asst. prof. clin. otolaryngology U. Pa., 1968—72; prof. clin. oncology dept. oral pathology U. Pitts. Sch. Dental Medicine, 1975—82, prof. dept. diagnostic svcs., 1982—2000, prof. dept. oral and maxillofacial surgery, 2000—; prof., chmn./chief dept. otolaryngology U. Pitts. Med. Ctr., 1972—. Cons. VA Med. Ctr., Pitts., 1972—, Children's Hosp., Pitts., 1972—. Editor: Cancer of the Head and Neck, 1981, 4th edit., 2003, Tracheotomy, 1985, 2d edit., 1998; mem. editl. bd. Laryngoscope, 1973—95, exec. editl. bd., 1995—, mem. editl. bd. Head and Neck Surgery, 1978—92, 1998—, AMA Archives of Otolaryngology, 1981—, Annals of Otology Rhinology and Laryngology, 1984—, Oncology, 1986—, European Archives of Oto-Rhino-Laryngology, 1990—97, Auris Nasus Larynx, 1996—, editor-in-chief (book) Advances in Orolaryngology, 1985—2001; co-editor: Butterworth's Intern Med. Revs., 1981—82; internat. editor Otolaryngology-Head and Neck Surgery, 1996—. Mem. adv. bd. Pa. Lion Hearing Rsch. Found., Pitts., 1983—99. Capt. M.C. U.S. Army, 1965—67. Recipient Cert. of Merit Com. Rsch., Am. Acad. Otolaryngology-Salicylate Otoxicity, 1965, Award of Merit, Am. Acad. Otolaryngology-Head and Neck Surgery Inc., 1978, Robert E. Shoemaker Rsch. award, Pa. Acad. Ophthalmology and Otolaryngology, 1979, Disting. Svc. award, Am. Acad. Oto-HNS, 2001. Fellow: Am. Acad. Otolaryngology (chmn. com. on head and neck surgery 1981—83, bd. dirs. 1985—88, 1990—2003, pres. 1994—95, internat. coord. 1996—2003), Am. Laryngol. Assn. (sec. 1982—88, pres. 1989—90, mem. coun. 1990—93, James Newcomb award 1993, DeRoaldes award 2001, ALA award 2001), ACS (bd. govs. 1981—87, mem. adv. coun. 1985—87); mem.: Triological Soc. (mem. coun. 1989—92, v.p. Ea. sect. 1994—95), Am. Soc. Head and Neck Surgery (mem. coun. 1977—93, pres. 1988—90), Nat. Cancer Inst. (chmn. upper aerodigestive tract working group 1986—89), Assn. Acad. Depts. Otolaryngology (mem. coun. 1978—80), Am. Bd. Otolaryngology (bd. dirs. 1981—99, pres.-elect 1994—96, pres. 1996—98), Pitts. Athletic Assn. Republican. Jewish. Office: U Pitts Sch Med Eye and Ear Inst Ste 500 200 Lothrop St Pittsburgh PA 15213-2546 Office Phone: 412-647-2111. Business E-Mail: myersen@upmc.edu.

MYERS, FRANKLIN LEWIS, II, ophthalmologist; b. Wichita, Kans., Mar. 20, 1933; s. Kermit Whitney and Bertha Alice (Perkins) M.; m. Gloria Joyce Johnston, Sept. 2, 1955 (div. 1993); children: Jeffrey, Jennifer; m. Helen Elizabeth Lyngaas, July 23, 1994. BA, U. Iowa, 1954, MD, 1957. Diplomate Am. Bd. Ophthalmology. Intern Highland-Alameda County Hosp., Oakland, Calif., 1957-58; resident in ophthalmology U. Wis., Madison, 1964-67, fellow, 1967-68, from instr. to prof. dept. ophthalmology, 1968-97, prof. emeritus, 1997—. Ophthalmologist, dir. Davis Duehr Eye Assn., Madison, 1968-95. Lt. comdr. USNR, 1959-61. Mem. Retina Soc., Vitreous Soc., Phi Beta Kappa, Omicron Delta Kappa, Alpha Omega Alpha. Avocations: gardening, photography, sailing, lapidary. Home: 4946 Lake Mendota Dr Madison WI 53705-1376 Office: U Wis Dept Ophthalmology 2870 University Ave Ste 206 Madison WI 53705-3611 E-mail: flmyers@wisc.edu.

MYERS, GARY, public relations executive; BS, U. Mo., 1971. Pres., CEO Morgan & Myers, Jefferson, Wis., 1997—. Recipient Founder award Agrl. Rels. Coun., 1984. Mem. Pub. Rels. Soc. Am., Coun. Pub. Rels. Firms, Nat. Agrl. Mktg. Assn. Office: Morgan & Myers 146 E Milwaukee St Jefferson WI 53549-1696

MYERS, GERALD C. music educator; b. Alton, Ill., Aug. 7, 1974; s. Gerald R. and Kathleen L. Myers; m. Laura C. Werry, June 17, 2000. MusB in Vocal Performance, Ill. State U., 1997; MA in Music/Choral Conducting, Western Ill. U., 1999. Asst. to exec. dir. Ill. Summer Sch. for the Arts, Normal, 1994—95, dean of students, 1997, 2000; musical dir. Stagefright Theatre Co., Normal, 1994—97; grad. choral asst., vocal jazz ensemble dir. Western Ill. U., Macomb, 1997—99, interim dir. of choral activities, 1999; assoc. dir. choral activities Washington and Lee U., Lexington, Va., 1999—; dir. music 1st Ch. of the Brethren, Roanoke, 2003. Choral music adjudicator Music in the Parks/Festivals of Music, Williamsburg, Va., 1999—; mem. faculty, chorus condr. Washington and Lee U. Summer Scholars, 1999—; guest choral condr. Various chs., choirs and orchs. in the Mid-Atlantic region, 1999—; music dir., condr. Eurydice Cmty. Orch., Roanoke, Va., 2002—03; adjudicator Va. Music Educators Assn., Va., 2003—; choral music festival adjudicator North Am. Music Festivals, 2004—. Scenic designer Evita, vocal dir. Hair, Little Shop of Horrors, musical dir. Grease, Stagefright Theatre Co., Normal, Ill., tenor soloist W.A. Mozart's Requiem, K. 626; singer: An Evening of Schubert. Mem.: Coll. Music Soc., Nat. Assn. Tchrs. of Singing (hon. mention 1994), Am. Choral Dirs. Assn., Phi Eta Sigma, Phi Kappa Phi, Phi Mu Alpha Sinfonia. Republican. Presbyterian. Avocation: travel. Office: Washington and Lee U Music Dept Lexington VA 24450-0303 Office Phone: 540-458-8697. E-mail: myersg@wlu.edu.

MYERS, GERALD E. humanities educator; b. Central City, Nebr., June 19, 1923; s. Harold W. and Mary (Ferguson) M.; m. Martha Coleman, Aug. 7, 1948; 1 son, Curt. BA, Haverford Coll., 1947; MA, Brown U., 1949, PhD, 1954. Instr. Smith Coll., 1950-52; asst. prof. Williams Coll., 1952-61; assoc. prof. Kenyon Coll., 1961-65; prof. C.W. Post Coll., L.I. U., 1965-67, Queens Coll. and Grad. Center, City U. N.Y., 1967—; also dep. exec. officer Ph.D. program Queens Coll. and Grad. Center, City U. N.Y. (Grad. Center); dir. intro. philosophy into N.Y.C. High Schs. project.; emeritus CUNY. Dir. humanities-and-dance projects, philosopher-in-residence Am. Dance Festival, Durham, N.C., 1979; project dir. African-Am. Perspectives in Am. Modern Dance, Am. Dance Festival/NEH. Author: Self, Religion and Metaphysics, 1961, Self: An Introduction to Philosophical Psychology, 1969, The Spirit of American Philosophy, 1970, William James: His Life and Thought, 1986; editor: The Black Tradition in American Modern Dance, 1988, African American Genius in Modern Dance, 1992; co-editor: Emotion Philos. Studies, 1983, Echoes from the Holocaust, 1988; cons. Free to Dancd PBS documentary, 2001; contbr. articles to profl. jours. NEH fellow, 1981-82. Mem. Am. Philos. Assn. (past sec.-treas. Western div.), Metaphys. Soc. Am., Soc. Phenomenology and Existential Philosophy, Phi Beta Kappa. Home: 36 Gardner Ave New London CT 06320-4313 Office: 33 W 42nd St New York NY 10036-8003

MYERS, HARDY, state attorney general, lawyer; b. Electric Mills, Miss., Oct. 25, 1939; m. Mary Ann Thalhofer, 1962; children: Hardy III, Christopher, Jonathan. AB with distinction, U. Miss., 1961; LLB, U. Oreg., 1964. Bar: Oreg., U.S. Ct. of Appeals (9th cir.), U.S. Dist. Ct. Law clerk U.S. Dist. Judge William G. East, 1964—65; pvt. practice Stoel Rives LLP, 1965—96; atty. gen. State of Oreg., 1997—. Mem. Oreg Ho. of Reps., 1975—85, spkr. of the ho., 1979—83. Pres. Portland City Planning Commn., 1973—74; chair Oreg. Jail Project, 1984—86, Citizen's Task Force on Mass Transit Policy, 1985—86, Oreg. Criminal Justice Coun., 1987—91, Portland Future Focus, 1990—91, Metro Charter com., 1991—92, task force on state employee benefits, 1994; co-chair gov. task force on state employee compensation, 1995. Democrat. Office: Oreg Atty Gen Justice Dept 1162 Court St NE Salem OR 97310-1320

MYERS, HAROLD MATHEWS, academic administrator; b. Doylestown, Pa., Apr. 13, 1915; s. Carl and Alice W. Myers; m. Margaret F. Smith, July 19, 1946 (dec. Sept. 1963); children: Donald Smith, Dean Chappell, Deborah Kay; m. L. Marjorie Bellau, Nov. 28, 1964. BS in Commerce, Drexel Inst. Tech., 1938, DSc in Commerce (hon.), 1983; postgrad., Temple U., 1940-41, U. Omaha, summer 1957. Instr. coop. edn., dir. grad. placement Drexel U., Phila., 1938-46, asst. dean men, dir. student bldgs., adj. instr. labor econs., 1946-52, dean of men, 1952-55, treas., 1955-57, v.p., treas., 1957-80, sr. v.p., 1980-82, sr. v.p. emeritus, 1982-87, interim pres., 1987-88, pres. emeritus, 1988—, life trustee, 1986—. Regional dir. First Pa. Banking and Trust Co., 1959-76; dir. Sadtler Rsch. Labs., Inc., 1963-69, Almo Indsl. Elecs., Inc., 1966-68; dir., treas. Uni-Coll Corp., 1974-81; bd. dirs. Beulah Cemetary Assn., asst. treas., 1984-89, treas., 1989-90, v.p. and treas., 1980—; bd. dirs., mem. exec. com. Univ. City Sci. Ctr., 1974-90, dir. emeritus, 1991—, chmn. fin. com., 1976-88, vice chmn., 1988-90. Contbr. articles to profl. jours. Bd. dirs. Internat. House of Phila. Inc., 1954-81, exec. com., 1972-81; active Phila. coun. Boy Scouts Am., 1953—, hon. chmn., 1985-97, pres., 1982-83; citizens fire prevention com. Phila. Fire Dept., 1970-86; bd. dirs. United Fund Greater Phila., 1983-87, Luth. Ch. of Am. Common Investing Fund, 1976-82, NCCJ, Inc., Phila. and South Jersey region NCCJ, 1959-65; dir. Phila. Coun. of Chs., 1954-61, pres. jr. coun., 1950-51; bd. dirs., pres. Ea. Assn. Coll. and Univ. Bus. Officers, 1967-68; pres. Nat. Assn. Coll. and Univ. Bus. Officers, 1971-72; treas. Lambda Chi Alpha Found., 1970-84, dir. emeritus, 1984—; pres. Broadmoor Pines Home Owners Assn., 1993-94; dir. PalmAire Cmty., Inc., 1993-95, chmn. security com., 1995—. Comdr. USNR, ret. Recipient Silver Beaver award Boy Scouts Am., 1963, Mary M. Hart award Phila. coun. Boy Scouts Am., 1986, Drexel Alumni Varsity Club award, 1966, Drexel U. Evening Coll. Alumni Assn. award, 1973, Drexel U. Anthony J. Drexel Paul award, 1988, Dept. of Army Cert. of Appreciation for Patriotic Civilian Svc., 1979, Disting. Bus. Officer award Nat. Assn. Coll. and Bus. Officers, 1989, Disting. Svc. in Trusteeship award Assn. Governing Bd. Univs. and Colls., 1989; named Educator of Yr., Phila. coun. Boy Scouts Am., 1989; named to Legion of Honor, Chapel of Four Chaplins; Drexel U. student dormitory named Myers Hall in his honor, 1984; 1 of 100 alumni honored Centennial of Drexel U., 1992. Mem. AARP, Am. Legion (life), Mil. Order World Wars (perpetual, comdr. Phila. chpt. 1958-59), Ret. Officers Assn. (life), Swedish Colonial Soc. Phila. (sec. 1968), Welsh Soc. Phila. (life), Internat. Frat. Lambda Chi Alpha (pres. 1966-70), Vet. Corps 1st Regiment Infantry, N.G.P. (hon.), Penn Club, Union League Phila. (pres. 1980-81), Sarasota Yacht Club, Masons, Rotary (Paul Harris fellow), Gulf Coast Corvair Club.

MYERS, HARRY J., JR., retired publisher; b. Denver, Aug. 7, 1931; s. Harry J. and Edith M. (Reed) M.; m. Mary Kay Racine, June 21, 1958; children: Harry J., Hans R. (dec.), Peter C. BA, Colo. U., 1957; postgrad., U. Mo., 1959-60. Pub., or pub. dir. Meredith Corp., 1962-82, Geo, Archtl. Digest, Bon Appetit, Home, Sci. Am., Cowles Mag, 1982-95. Served with USMC, 1953-56. Mem. Kappa Tau Alpha, Phi Gamma Delta. Home: 46 W Ranch Trl Morrison CO 80465-9504

MYERS, IRA LEE, physician; b. Monrovia, Ala., Feb. 9, 1924; s. Ira W. and Azelea Juanita (Cobbs) Myers; m. Dorothy Will Foust, Sept. 4, 1943 (dec. June 6, 2003); children: Martha Crystal(dec.), Ira Grady, Stephen Allen, Joanna Lynn; m. Woodard H. Luker, Dec. 7, 2003. BS, Howard Coll., Birmingham, Ala., 1945; MD, U. Ala., 1949; postgrad., Harvard U. Sch. Public Health, 1953. Diplomate: Am. Bd. Preventive Medicine. Commd. officer USPHS, 1949-55; intern USPHS Marine Hosp., Seattle, 1949-50; epidemic intelligence officer Charleston, W.Va., 1950-52, Erie County Health Dept., Buffalo, 1952, Center Communicable Disease, Atlanta, 1952-55; resigned, 1955; adminstrv. health officer Ala. Dept. Health, Montgomery, 1955-63, state health officer, 1963-86. Sec. Ala. Bd. Med. Examiners, 1962-73; chmn. Ala. Bd. Registration Sanitarians, 1964-81, Ala. Air Pollution Control Commn., 1969-82; v.p. Ala. Pollution Control Fin. Authority, 1971-81; assoc. clin. prof. preventive medicine and pub. health U. Ala. Med. Sch.; mem. Ala. vol. med. adv. com. SSS, 1968-86; chmn. Ala. Health Care Hall of Fame, 1998—. Pres. Ala. div. Am. Cancer Soc., 1991-93; chmn. bd. dirs. Dalraida Health Ctr., 1992-98; chmn. Ala. Sr. Citizens Hall of Fame, 1997—. Recipient Ala. Sr. Citizens Hall of Fame Golden Eagle award, 1986, St. George medal Nat. Divisional award Am. Cancer Soc., 1989, 1st Ann. Vol. award Montgomery Bapt. Assn., 1993. Mem. AMA, Med. Assn. Ala. (William Henry Saunders award 1968, 1st annual Ira L. Myers Service award, 1986), Montgomery County Med. Soc., Ala. Pub. Health Assn. (D.G. Gill award 1967, established Ira L. Myers Scholarship Endowment), Am. Assn. Pub. Health Physicians, Assn. State and Territorial Health Officers (Arthur N. McCormick award 1976), Ala. Hosp. Assn. (hon.), State. Ala. Acad. Honor, Tuberculosis Assn. (Heacock Gold medal 1986), Montgomery Coun. of Aging (Srs. of Achievement award 1998, Gov.'s Lifetime Achievement award 1998). Lodges: Montgomery Kiwanis. Republican. Baptist. Achievements include initiating state narcotic control program, 1967, state hosp. service for indigent, 1958. Home and Office: 925 Green Forest Dr Montgomery AL 36109-1515

MYERS, JACK FREDRICK, artist, educator, author; b. Lima, Ohio, Feb. 17, 1927; s. Harold Frank and Lesta Arvilla (Ross) M.; m. Frances Dydek, Apr. 30, 1949; children: Steven Ross, David Gene, Kevin Douglas. Student, Cleve. Inst. Art, 1947-49; MFA, Kent State U., 1980. Staff artist Bill Ripley & Assocs., Cleve., 1951-57; art dir. Premier Indsl. Corp., Cleve., 1957-70; instr. Cooper Sch. Art, Cleve., 1970-80; assoc. prof. art U. Dayton, Ohio, 1982-87; ret., 1992. Author: The Language of Visual Art, 1989, Windy Side of Care, 2002, The Greatest Gift, 2002. With USNR, 1945-46, PTO. Recipient First prize in art Newsweek/Paillard S.A., 1969. Home and Office: 22269 Country Meadows Ln Strongsville OH 44149-2000 Personal E-mail: jackms@adelphia.net.

MYERS, JAMES CLARK, advertising and public relations executive; b. Chgo., Aug. 26, 1941; s. Herbert George Myers and Lenore (Goldberg) Levi; m. Judy Anne Schnitzer, Feb. 9, 1964; children: Jeffrey Stephan, Jeremy H. BA, Washington U., St. Louis, 1964. Acct. exec. Nahas, Blumberg, Zelikow, Houston, 1967-69; mgr. spl. events Houston Post, 1969-73; pres., creative dir. Motivators, Inc., Houston, 1973—. Vice-chmn. Internat. Sci. and Engring. Fair Coun., Washington, 1972-73; bd. dirs. Sci. Engring. Fair of Houston, 1969-73; spl. corrs. Navy Times Newspaper; pres. S.W. Houston 2000, Inc., 1999—. Contbr. articles to newspapers. Chmn. Houston chpt. Boy Scouts Am. Served to capt. USNR, 1964-96. Recipient Wood Badge award, Boy Scouts Am., 1979, Shofar award, 1981; named Fondren SW Citizen of Yr., 2002. Mem. Pub. Relations Soc. Am. (Silver Anvil award 1983, 87, Excalibur 2001). Jewish. Avocations: model railroading, square dancing, photography. Home: 8006 Duffield Ln Houston TX 77071-2017 Office: Motivators Inc PO Box 710541 Houston TX 77271-0541 Personal E-mail: motivators.inc@juno.com.

MYERS, JAMES R. lawyer; b. Valdosta, Ga., Aug. 29, 1952; s. J. Walter Jr. and Mary (Gallion) M.; m. Monica Faeth Myers, Sept. 19, 1992. BA cum laude, Harvard U., 1972, JD, 1975. Bar: Mass. 1975, U.S. Dist. Ct. (D.C. dist.) 1976, D.C. 1977, U.S. Ct. Appeals (D.C. cir.) 1977, U.S. Supreme Ct. 1983, U.S. Ct. Appeals (fed. cir.) 1991, Va. 1992, U.S. Ct. Appeals (4th cir.) 1992. Assoc. Wald, Harkrader & Ross, Washington, 1976-77; assoc. solicitor U.S. Dept. Energy, Washington, 1977-79; assoc. Andrews & Kurth, Washington, 1980-85; ptnr. Steele, Simmons & Fornaciari, Washington, 1985-86, Robbins & Laramie, Washington, 1986-89, Venable, Baetjer, Howard & Civiletti, Washington, 1990-97, Kilpatrick Stockton LLP, 1997—2004, Ropes & Gray LLP, 2004—. Master Giles S. Rich Am. Inn Court for intellectual property litigators; mem. editl. bd. Practical Lawyer; spkr. in field. Contbr. articles to jour. Mem.: ABA (mem. ALI-ABA com. on continuing profl. edn.). Office: Ropes & Gray LLP 700 12th St NW Ste 900 Washington DC 20005 Office Fax: 202-508-4647. E-mail: jmyers@ropesgray.com.

MYERS, JEFFREY DANIEL, concert pianist, music educator; b. Erie, Pa., June 7, 1970; s. Neal Anthony and Beryl Diane Myers. MusB, Mercyhurst Coll., Erie, Pa., 1993; MusM, Manhattan Sch. Music, N.Y.C., 1999. Dir. Erie Piano Acad., Erie, Pa., 1999—. Soloist: piano recital Hubbard Hall, 1999, piano soloist: Erie Chamber Orch., 2000, debut piano and violin concert: Classical Concert Series, Kent State U., 2002; Classical Concert Series, Kent State U., Ashtabula, Ohio, 2003. Avocations: painting, art history, travel, world history. Home and Office: Erie Piano Acad 5522 Niemeyer Rd Erie PA 16509

MYERS, JESSE JEROME, lawyer; b. Anthony, Kans., Sept. 30, 1940; s. Claud Lewis and Lucille S. (Robertson) M.; m. Claire H. Conni, Nov., 1966; children: Timothy Todd, Jessica Joy. BS, McPherson Coll., 1963; JD, Washburn U., 1970. Bar: Kans. 1970, Mo.1996, U.S. Dist. Ct. Kans. 1970. Law clk. U.S. Dist. Ct. Judge Frank Theis, Wichita, Kans., 1970—72; individual practice law Wichita, Kans., 1972—74, 1995—; lawyer Cessna Aircraft Co., Wichita, Kans., 1974—75; v.p., dir., gen. counsel Martin K. Eby Constrn. Co., Wichita, Kans., 1975—95. Served with USN, 1963-67. Mem. Am. Bar Assn., Kans. Bar Assn.

MYERS, JOHN JOSEPH, bishop; b. Ottawa, Ill., July 26, 1941; s. M.W. and Margaret Louise (Donahue) M. BA maxima cum laude, Loras Coll., 1963; Licentiate in Sacred Theology, Gregorian U., Rome, 1967; Doctor of Canon Law, Cath. U. Am., 1977; DD (hon.), Apostolic See, Vatican City, 1987. Ordained priest Roman Cath. Ch., 1966, bishop, 1987. Asst. pastor Holy Family Parish, Peoria, Ill., 1967-70; asst. dept. internat. affairs US Cath. Conf., Washington, 1970-71; assoc. pastor St. Matthew Parish, Champaign, Ill.,

1971-74; adminstr. St. Mary's Cathedral, Diocese Peoria, 1977—78, 1984; vice chancellor Cath. Diocese Peoria, 1977-78, vocation dir., 1977-87, chancellor, 1978-87, vicar gen., 1982-90, mem. Prebyteral Coun., 1968—70, 1984—90, bd. Consultors, 1978—90, co-adjutor bishop, 1987-90; bishop of Peoria, Ill., 1990—2001; appointed Archbishop of Newark, NJ, 2001; appointed Superior of Turks and Caicos Antilles, 2001; Archbishop of Newark, NJ, 2001—. Bd. govs. Canon Law Soc. Am., Washington, 1985-87; bd. dirs. Nat. Cath. Bio Ethics Ctr., Boston, 1999—, bd. gov.; mem. sem. com. Mt. St. Mary's Sem., Md., 1989-94; bd. trustees Cath. U. Am., Washington, 1999-, Papal Found.; seminary com., fin. com., Ad Hoc Com. for By-Laws., Cat. U. Am., Washington; seminary bd. Kenrick-Glennon of the Archdiocese of St. Louis. Author: (commentary) Book V of the Code of Canon Law, 1983; contbr. numerous articles to religious publs. Mem. Canon Law Soc. Am., Nat. Conf. Cath. Bishops. (Canonical Affairs Com., 1988-2002, Com. on Shrines and Pilgrimages, 1990-, Com. on Vocations, 1995-1998, Ad Hoc Com. on Sexual Abuse, 2002, Com. on Hispanic Affiars, 2002-, and Com. on Aid to Eastern Europe, 1999-) Roman Catholic. Office: Archdiocese of Newark 171 Clifton Ave Newark NJ 07104-0500*

MYERS, JOHN THOMAS, retired congressman; b. Covington, Ind., Feb. 8, 1927; m. Carol Carruthers; children: Carol Ann, Lori Jan. BS, Ind. State U., 1951. Cashier, trust officer Fountain Trust Co.; owner, operator farm; mem. 90th-104th Congresses from 7th Dist. Ind., 1967-96; former chmn. subcom. on energy & water, appropriations com.; ret., 1997. Served with AUS, World War II, ETO. Mem. Am. Legion, VFW, Wabash Valley Assn., Res. Officers Assn., C. of C., Sigma Pi. Clubs: Mason, Elk, Lion. Republican. Episcopalian.

MYERS, JOHN WESCOTT, aviation executive; b. L.A., June 13, 1911; s. Louis Wescott and Blanche (Brown) M.; m. Lucia Raymond, Mar. 21, 1941 (dec. Mar. 1999); children: Louis W. (dec.), Lucia E. AB, Stanford U., 1933; JD, Harvard U., 1936. Bar: Calif. 1936. Ptnr. law firm O'Melveny & Myers, L.A., 1936-42; from test pilot to sr. v.p., dir. Northrop Corp., 1942-54, 1954-79; chmn. bd. Pacific Airmotive Corp., 1954-79, Airflite, Long Beach, Calif., 1970-89, Flying M Assocs., Long Beach, 1989—. Owner Flying M Ranches, Merced, Calif., 1959—. Dir. Smithsonian Nat. Air and Space Dulles Ctr. Project. Fellow Soc. Exptl. Test Pilots; mem. Calif. Bar Assn., Los Angeles Bar Assn., Inst. Aerospace Scis., Order of Daedalians (hon.). Clubs: Bohemian, California, Los Angeles Country, Los Angeles Yacht, Sunset, Aviation Country, Conquistadores del Cielo. Republican. Home: 718 N Rodeo Dr Beverly Hills CA 90210-3210 Office: 3200 Airflite Way Long Beach CA 90807-5312

MYERS, JOHN WILLIAM, lawyer; b. Aug. 8, 1941; s. Fred L. and Dossie (Huddleston) Myers; m. Jane Sutton, July 29, 1995; children: John William II, James Bryan. BS, U. Tenn., 1963, JD, 1965. Bar: Tenn. 1965. Ptnr. Myers & Bell, Attys., Newport, Tenn., 1966—. Dir. Newport Fed. Bank, 1975—, chmn., 1981—. Mem.: Tenn. Bar Assn. Republican. Episcopalian. Home: 404 6th St Newport TN 37821-3712 Office: Myers & Bell Attys PO Box 160 Newport TN 37822-0160 Office Phone: 423-623-3091.

MYERS, JOHNNIE DUMAS, law educator; b. Macon, Ga., Dec. 18, 1948; d. Ella Pearl Bryant and Johnny Dumas; children: Badru, Akii. BA, Clark Atlanta U., 1970, PhD, 1995; MS, Ga. State U., 1976; cert., Hers Women Higher Edn. Adminstrn., 1997. Parole supr. Ga. Pardons and Paroles, Atlanta, 1973—76; instr. Kennesaw (Ga.) State U., 1977—83; asst. prof. criminal justice Albany (Ga.) State U., 1983—88; chairperson criminal justice dept. Morris Brown Coll., Atlanta, 1988—. Advisor to Beta Chi chpt. Alpha Phi Sigma Morris Brown Coll., Atlanta, 1993—, faculty athletics rep. to NCAA, 1992—, former pres. faculty coun., 1997—98; presenter United Negro Coll. Fund PEJER Project, Augusta, Ga.; panelist substance abuse edn. in instns. higher learning Lonnie Mitchell Conf. Substance Abuse, Balt., 2002. Mem. personnel com. Rainbow Pk. Bapt. Ch., Decatur, Ga., 1999—2001, mem. nomination com., 2000—02; exec. bd. Nat. Historically Black Colls. and Univs. Substance Abuse Consortium, Atlanta, 1999—2002; governance coun. CORK Inst., Morehouse Sch. Medicine, Atlanta, 1989—2002; participant selection com. Ga. Police Corps, Forsyth, 2002. Recipient Outstand Svc. and Dedication to Orgn., National HBCU Substance Abuse Consortium, 2001; fellow Particia Robert Harris, U. S. Dept. Edn. through Clark Atlanta U., 1990-1993. Mem.: Nat. Assn. Blacks in Criminal Justice, Acad. Criminal Justice Scis., Am. Correctional Assn., Nat. Conf. Black Polit. Scientist (2002 conv. local arrangements com. 2001—02), Delta Sigma Theta (life; chairperson career day com. 1995—97). Baptist. Avocations: reading, bowling, travel. Home: 4925 Thames Ct Lithonia GA 30038 Office: Morris Brown Coll 643 Martin Luther King Jr Dr Atlanta GA 30314 Personal E-mail: jdmyers6@juno.com. Business E-Mail: johnnie.myers@morrisbrown.edu.

MYERS, JULIE L. federal agency administrator; b. Shawnee, KS; BA, Baylor U.; JD, Cornell U. Assoc. Mayer, Brown & Platt, Chgo., 1993—97; assoc. ind. counsel Office of Ind. Counsel Kenneth Starr, Washington, 1998—99; asst. U.S. atty. U.S. Atty.'s Office, Ea. Dist. N.Y., Bklyn., 1999—2001; dept. asst. sec. for money laundering and fin. crimes Office of Enforcement, Dept. Treasury, Washington, 2001—03; chief of staff to asst. atty. gen. criminal divsn. U.S. Dept. Justice, Washington, 2003; asst. sec. for export enforcement U.S. Dept. Commerce, Washington, 2003—. Office: Herbert Clark Hoover Bldg Rm 3721 14th St and Constitution Ave NW Washington DC 20230

MYERS, KENNETH ELLIS, hospital administrator; b. Battle Creek, Mich., Jan. 1, 1932; s. Orlow J. and Kathryn (Brown) M.; m. Nancy Lee Lindgren, June 9, 1956; children— Cynthia Lynn, Anne Lisa, Thomas Scot, Susan Elaine. BBA, U. Mich., 1956, MBA, 1957. Research analyst Bur. Bus. Research, U. Mich., 1956-57; in financial mgmt. Burroughs Corp., Detroit, 1957-66; controller William Beaumont Hosp., Royal Oak, Mich., 1966-68, asso. dir., 1968-69, hosp. dir., 1969-80, exec. v.p., 1976-80, pres., 1981-97; retired. Pres. Trinity Loss Prevention Systems, 1980-81. Elder Bloomfield Hills Christian Ch., 1979-82, Grace Chapel, 1988-92, 1995-99, 2001—; bd. visitors Oakland Sch. Bus. Adminstrn., 1978-92; adv. bd. Salvation Army, 1985-99; bd. dirs. William Tyndale Coll., 1992-2003, West Bloomfield Bldg. Authority, 1978—, William Beaumont Hosp., 1971—; trustee St. Mary's Hosp., 1992-97. Mem. Mich. Hosp. Assn. (past chmn.), Vol. Hosps. Am. Enterprises (bd. dirs. 1984-87), Full Gospel Businessmen's Fellowship, Bloomfield Hills Country Club, Belleair Country Club, Old Club, Phi Delta Theta, Beta Gamma Sigma. Home: 6085 Simsbury Ct West Bloomfield MI 48322-3567

MYERS, LINDA K. retired editor, state representative; b. Nanty Glo, Pa., Aug. 18, 1940; m. Martin J. Myers (dec.); children: Robyn, Kasey. B in Journalism, B in Polit. Sci., Kent State U. Cert. safety certifier cheerleading coaches, Vt., certified cheerleading judge Vt., N.Y., N.H. Ret. newspaper editor; state rep. State of Vt., 2001—, mem. loint legis. oversight com. corrections, 2002—. Mem. Essex Selectboard, Essex Bd. Civil Authority; justice of peace; bd. dirs. Essex Town Rep. Com. Named Contbr. of Yr., Vt. Cheerleading Coaches Assn., 2003. Mem.: Nat. Fedn. Intersch. Spirit Assn., Nat. Assn. Female Exec. (adv. bd.), Women in Comm. Inc., Am. Assn. Cheerleading Coaches and Advisors (founding mem.), Vt. Prin. Assn. Cheerleading Com. (adv. mem.). Republican. Office: 51 Forest Rd Essex Junction VT 05452 E-mail: themyers@attglobal.net., lmyers@leg.state.vt.us.

MYERS, LONN WILLIAM, lawyer; b. Rockford, Ill., Nov. 14, 1946; s. William H. and Leona V. (Janvrin) M.; m. Janet L. Forbes, May 14, 1968; children: Andrew, Hillary, Corwin. BA, Mich. State U., 1968; MBA, Ind. U., 1973; JD, Harvard U., 1976. Bar: Ill. 1976, U.S. Ct. of Fed. Claims 1977, U.S. Tax Ct. 1977, U.S. Ct. Appeals (7th cir.) 1977. Ptnr. McDermott, Will & Emery, Chgo., 1976—. Served to maj. USAR, 1968-80. Mem. ABA (capital recovery and leasing com. tax sect., tax exempt fin. com. tax sect.). Episcopalian. Home: 1711 Highland Ter Glenview IL 60025-2284 Office: McDermott Will & Emery 227 W Monroe St Chicago IL 60606-5096 Office Phone: 312-984-7537. E-mail: lmyers@mwe.com.

MYERS, MARGARET JANE (DEE DEE MYERS), television personality, editor; b. Quonset Pt., R.I., Sept. 1, 1961; d. Stephen George and Judith Ann (Burleigh) M. BS, U. Santa Clara, 1983. Press asst. Mondale for Pres., L.A., 1984; deputy Senator Art Torres, L.A., 1985; dep. press sec. to press sec. Mayor Tom Bradley, L.A., 1985-87; deputy press sec. Tom Bradley For Gov., L.A., 1986; Calif. press sec. Dukakis for Pres., L.A., 1988; press sec. Feinstein for Gov., L.A. and San Francisco, 1989-90; campaign dir. Jordan for Mayor, San Francisco, 1991; comm. cons. DeeDee Myers Assocs., Valencia, Calif., 1991—; press sec. Clinton for Pres., Little Rock, 1991-92, White House, Washington, 1993-94; co-host Equal Time, CNBC, Washington, 1995-97; contbg. editor Vanity Fair, Washington, 1995—. Mem. bd. of trustees, Calif. State U.,1999— Recipient Robert F. Kennedy award Emerson Coll., Boston, 1993. Democrat. Roman Catholic. Avocations: running, bicycling, music, major league baseball.

MYERS, MARILYN GLADYS, pediatric hematologist and oncologist; b. Lyons, Nebr., July 17, 1930; d. Leonard Clarence and Marian N. (Manning) M.; m. Paul Frederick Motzkus, July 24, 1957 (dec. Aug. 1982). BA cum laude, U. Omaha, 1954; MD, U. Nebr., 1959. Diplomate Am. Bd. Pediatrics. Intern Orange County Gen. Hosp., Orange, Calif., 1959-60, resident, 1960-62; fellow in hematology/oncology Orange County Gen. Hosp./Children's Hosp. L.A., 1962-64; assoc. in rsch., chief dept. hematology/oncology Children's Hosp., Orange, 1964-80, dir. outpatient dept., 1964-73, assoc. dir. leukapheresis unit, 1971-80; clin. practice hematology, oncology, rheumatology Orange, 1964-80; instr. Coll. Medicine U. Calif., Irvine, 1968-71, asst. clin. prof. pediatrics, 1971—; pvt. practice hematology, oncology, rheumatology Santa Ana, Calif., 1980—. Clin. rschr. exptl. drugs. Contbr. articles to med. jours. Mem. med. adv. com. Orange County Blood Bank Hemophiliac Found. Grantee Am. Leukemia Soc., 1963, Am. Heart Assn., 1964. Fellow Am. Acad. Pediatrics; mem. AMA, Calif. Med. Assn., L.A. County Med. Assn., Orange County Med. Assn., Orange County Pediatric Soc., Southwestern Pediatric Soc., L.A. Pediatric Soc., Internat. Coll. Pediatrics, Orange County Oncologic Soc., Am. Heart Assn. (Cardiopulmonary Coun.). Republican. Methodist. Avocation: reading. Office: 2220 E Fruit St Ste 217 Santa Ana CA 92701-4459 Office Phone: 714-541-3393.

MYERS, MARY A. public relations consultant; b. Waukesha, Wis., July 28, 1936; d. Willard R. and Ruth Hardaker Evans; m. Ralph Payton Myers, June 14, 1958 (dec. Sept. 1969); children: Marsha Ruth, Evan Scott. BS, Northwestern U., Evanston, Ill., 1957; MBA, De Paul U., Chgo., 1984. Mng. editor Pioneer Press, Wilmette, Ill., 1969-73; dep. bus. editor Chgo. Sun-Times, 1973-84; v.p. Hill & Knowlton, Chgo., 1984-86; dep. bus. editor The Washington Post, 1986-88; sr. v.p. Hill & Knowlton, 1988-92; dir. Burson-Marsteller, Chgo., 1992-96, mng. dir., chair Midwest corp. practice, 1996-2001. Mem.: Nat. Investor Rels. Inst., Soc. Profl. Journalists, Univ. Club, Exec. Club Chgo., Chgo. Headline Club. Presbyterian. E-mail: maryamyers@earthlink.net.

MYERS, MARY KATHLEEN, publishing executive; b. Cedar Rapids, Iowa, Aug. 19, 1945; d. Joseph Bernard and Marjorie Helen (Huntsman) Weaver; m. David F. Myers, Dec. 30, 1967; children: Mindy, James. BA in English and Psychology, U. Iowa, 1967. Tchr. Lincoln H.S., Des Moines, 1967-80; editor Perfection Learning Corp., Des Moines, 1980-87, v.p., editor-in-chief, 1987-93; pres., founding ptnr. orgn. to promote Edward de Bono Advanced Practical Thinking Tng., Des Moines, 1992—; founder Myers House LLC, 2002. Pres. Innova Tng. & Cons., Inc., 2000—. Editor: Six Thinking Hats, 1991, Lateral Thinking, 1993, Direct Attention Thinking Tools, 1997, Total Creativity, 1997; pub. A Disgrace to The Profession, 2004. Adv. bd. Sch. Bus., Econs. and Acctg., Simpson Coll., 1998—. Mem. ASTD, Am. Creativity Assn. (bd. dirs. 1997—, pres. 1999), Instrnl. Systems Assn. (mem. bd. dirs. 2002-2004). Home: 813 56th St West Des Moines IA 50266-6314 Office: APTT 2882 106th St # 200 Des Moines IA 50322-3771 E-mail: kymers@aptt.com.

MYERS, MICHELE TOLELA, academic administrator; b. Rabat, Morocco, Sept. 25, 1941; arrived in U.S., 1964; d. Albert and Lillie (Abecassis) Tolela; m. Pierre Vajda, Sept. 12, 1962 (div. Jan. 1965); m. Gail E. Myers, Dec. 20, 1968 (div. Oct. 2003); children: Erika, David. Diploma, Inst. Polit. Studies, U. Paris, 1962; MA, U. Denver, 1966, PhD, 1967; MA, Trinity U., 1977; LHD, Wittenberg U., 1994, Denison U., 1998, U. Denver, 1999. Asst. prof. speech Manchester Coll., North Manchester, Ind., 1967—68; asst. prof. speech and sociology Monticello Coll., Godfrey, Ill., 1968—71; asst. prof. communication Trinity U., San Antonio, 1975—80, assoc. prof., 1980—86, asst. v.p. for acad. affairs, 1982—85, assoc. v.p., 1985—86; assoc. prof. sociology, dean Undergrad. Coll. Bryn Mawr Coll., Pa., 1986—89; pres. Denison U., Granville, Ohio, 1989—98, Sarah Lawrence Coll., Bronxville, NY, 1998—. Comm. analyst Psychology and Commn., San Antonio, 1974—83; bd. dirs. Sherman Fairchild Found., 1992—; mem. Fed. Res. Bank Cleve., 1995—98; pres.'s commn. Nat. Collegiate Athletic Assn., 1993—97, JSTOR, 1999—, ARTSTOR, 2003—. Co-author (with Gail Myers): The Dynamics of Human Communication, 1973, The Dynamics of Human Communication, 6th and internat. edits., 1992, The Dynamics of Human Communication, French transl., 1984, Communicating When We Speak, 1975, Communicating When We Speak, 2d edit., 1978, Communication for the Urban Professional, 1977, Managing by Communicaton: An Organizational Approach, 1982, Managing by Communicaton: An Organizational Approach, Spanish transl., 1983, Managing by Communicaton: An Organizational Approach, internat. edit., 1982. Trustee Phila. Child Guidance Clinic, 1988—89; trustee assoc. The Bryn Mawr Sch., Balt., 1987—89; v.p., bd. dirs. San Antonio Cmty. Guidance Ctr., 1979—83. Bank One Columbus fellow, 1990—94, fellow in acad. adminstrn., Am. Coun. Edn., 1981—82. Mem.: Am. Coun. Edn. (commn. on women in higher edn. 1990—92, bd. dirs. 1993—99, chmn. 1997—98). Home: 935 Kimball Ave Bronxville NY 10708-5507 Office: Sarah Lawrence Coll One Mead Way Bronxville NY 10708 Office Phone: 914-395-2201. Business E-Mail: mmyers@sarahlawrence.edu.

MYERS, MICHELLE, publishing executive; Group advt. mgr. Mode mag., Girl mag.; advt. dir. Shape mag., 1999—2000, v.p., assoc. pub., 2000—01, Allure mag., 2001—04; v.p., pub. Star mag., 2004—. Office: Star Mag 1000 American Media Way Boca Raton FL 33464-1000

MYERS, MIKE, actor, writer, producer; b. Toronto, Ont., Can., May 25, 1963; s. Eric and Bunny (Hind) M.; m. Robin Ruzan, 1993. Stage appearances: The Second City, Toronto, 1986-88, Chgo., 1988-89; actor, writer: Mullarkey & Myers, Can., 1984-86, (TV show) Saturday Night Live, 1989-94 (Emmy award for outstanding writing in a comedy or variety series 1989), (film) Wayne's World, 1992, So I Married an Axe Murderer, 1993, Wayne's World II (also screenwriter, prodr.), 1993, Austin Powers: International Man Of Mystery (also screenwriter, prodr.), 1997, Pete's Meteor, 1998, It's a Dog's Life, 1998, 54, 1998, Austin Powers: The Spy Who Shagged Me (also screenwriter, prodr.), 1999, Austin Powers: The Animated Series, 1999, Shrek (voice), 2001, Austin Powers Goldmember (also writer, prodr.), 2002, View from the Top, 2003, Shrek 4-D (voice), 2003, The Cat in the Hat, 2003, Shrek 2 (voice), 2004; actor: (TV movie) John and Yoko, 1985, Elvis Stories, 1989, Saturday Night Live: The Best of Phil Hartman, 1998, Saturday Night Live: the Best of Mike Myers, 1998, Saturday Night Live: 25th Anniversary, 1999, Madonna: The Video Collection 93.99, 1999; screenwriter: (tv movie) Murderers Among Us: The Simon Wiesenthal Story, 1989, Saturday Night Live: The Best of Mike Myers, 1998; TV appearances The Littlest Hobo, 1979, Russell Gilbert Show, 1998; dir. (film) The Bacchae, 1999. Recipient Can. comedy award, 2000.*

MYERS, MILES ALVIN, educational association administrator, educator; b. Newton, Kans., Feb. 4, 1931; s. Alvin F. and Katheryn P. (Miles) M.; m. Celeste Myers; children: Royce, Brant, Roslyn. BA in Rhetoric, U. Calif., Berkeley, 1953, MAT in English, 1979, MA in English, PhD in Lang. and Literacy, U. Calif., Berkeley, 1982. Cert. secondary tchr. English. Tchr. English Washington Union High Sch., Fremont, Calif., 1957-59, Oakland (Calif.) High Sch., 1959-67, 69-74, Concord High Sch., Mt. Diablo, Calif., 1967-69; chmn. bd. dirs. Alpha Plus Corp. Preschs., Piedmont, Calif., 1968—; dir. All City High, 1973-74; tchr. English Castlemont High Sch., Oakland, 1974-75; mem. faculty U. Calif., Berkeley, 1975-85; adminstrv. dir. Bay Area writing project Sch. Edn. U. Calif., Berkeley, 1976-85; adminstrv. dir. nat. writing project Sch. Edn. U. Calif., Berkeley, 1979-85; pres., CEO Calif. Fedn. Tchrs., 1985-90; exec. dir. Nat. Coun. Tchrs. of English, Urbana, Ill., 1990-97, Edschool.com of Edvantage/Riverdeep, 1999—2001, Calif. Subject Matter Projects, U. Calif., 1997—98; dir. Inst. Rsch. on Learning and Tchg., Berkeley, Calif., 2001—; bd. dirs. Bay Area Sch. Reform Collabortive, 2000—. Co-dir. Nat. Standards Project for English Language Arts, 1992-96; adj. prof. English U. Ill., Champaign-Urbana, 1991-94; vis. lectr. at numerous colleges and Univs.; rschr. in field. Author: The Meaning of Literature, 1973; co-author: Writing: Unit Lessons in Composition, Book III, 1965, The English Book-Composition Skills, 1980; author: A Procedure for Holistic Scoring, 1980, Changing our Minds, 1996; co-author: Exemplars of Standards for English Language Arts, 3 vols., 1997, Asilomar Testing Report, 2001; editor Calif. Tchr., 1966-81; contbr. articles to profl. jours.; pub. monographs. Sgt. U.S. Army, 1953—55. Recipient cert. of Merit, Ctrl. Calif. Coun. Tchrs. of English, 1969, Commendation award Oakland Fedn. Tchrs., 1970, First Place award Internat. Labor Assn., 1971, Disting. Svc. award Calif. Coun. Classified Employees, 1991, Svc. award Nat. Writing Project, 1996. Fellow Nat. Conf. Rsch. in English; mem. Nat. Coun. Tchrs. of English, Nat. Conf. on Rsch. in English, Am. Fedn. of Tchrs. (legis. dir. Calif. Fedn. of Tchrs. 1971-72, Union Tchr. Press awards 1969-75, 86-89, 91, Ben Rust award Calif. Fedn. of Tchrs. 1994), Am. Edn. Rsch. Assn., Calif. Assn. Tchrs. of English (Disting. Svc. award 86), U. Calif./Berkeley Alumni Assn. Home: 5823 Scarborough Dr Oakland CA 94611-2721 Office: Dir Inst Rsch on Learning & Tchg Berkeley CA 94704 Home Fax: 510-531-0409. Personal E-mail: milesmye@pacbell.net.

MYERS, NORMAN ALLAN, marketing professional; b. Beeville, Tex., Dec. 10, 1935; s. Floyd Charles and Ruby (Lee) Myers; m. Suzanne Carlile, Oct. 11, 1935; children: Lisa Leigh Myers Nowlin, Matthew Scott. BS in Banking and Fin., Okla. State U., 1958. Salesman Jones and Laughlin Steel Corp., Houston, 1958-64; agt. Acacia Mutual Life Ins., Houston, 1964-69; from staff to exec v.p. Browning-Ferris Industries, Houston, 1969-81, vice-chmn., chief mktg. officer, 1982-97, exec. v.p., chief devel. officer, 1997-99, also bd. dirs. Mem. bd. SITA, subs. Suez Lyonaise des Eaux group, 1998-99. Bd. dirs. My Friends-A Neuenschwander Found. for Children in Crisis; mem. bd. govs. and assocs. Okla. State U., Okla. State U. Found. Bd. Trustees. 2d lt. U.S. Army, 1958-59. Named to Okla. State Univ. Coll. of Bus. Adminstrn. Hall of Fame, 1996. Mem. Lakeside Country Club, Hills of Lakeway Club, Red Sky Golf Club, Austin Golf Club, Shriners, Holland. Republican. Avocation: golf. Office: 2500 Citywest Blvd Ste 1050 Houston TX 77042-3000

MYERS, NORMAN LEWIS, fund development consultant; b. Xenia, Ohio, Oct. 21, 1932; s. Norman Theodore and Effie Marie (DeLawder) M.; m. Sue Anne Hanlon, Nov. 7, 1953; children: John Norman, Jeffrey Alan, Joseph Brian. Stuent, U.S. Armed Forces Inst., 1956. Chief dep. clk. Ohio Supreme Ct., Columbus, 1957-66; divsn. dir. United Way, Columbus, 1966-69; sr. assoc. dir. Children's Hosp. Found., Columbus, 1970-94. Cons. Arnold Palmer Children's Hosp., Orlando, Fla., 1995, Orland Amateur Athletic Assn., Orlando, 1996. Author: The Buck Starts Here, 1999. Bd. dirs. various ch. and civic assns.; trustee Children's Miracle Network, 1983-85. Served with USN and USNR, 1952-76, comdg. Naval Res. unit, Zanesville, Ohio. Recipient Best Total Devel. award Nat. Assn. for Hosp. Devel., 1977; Norman L. Myers Staff award for support of devel. of volunteerism named in his honor, 1994. Fellow Assn. Healthcare Philanthropy (Harold J. Seymour honors award 1991); mem. Univ. Club (Winter Park, Fla.) (2d vice chair 1998—), Sigma Phi Epsilon (hon.) Methodist. Avocations: golf, genealogy. Home: 1500 Gay Rd Apt 20B Winter Park FL 32789-2962

MYERS, PHILLIP FENTON, financial services and technology company executive; b. Cleve., June 24, 1935; s. Max I. and Rebecca (Rosenblum) M.; m. Hope Gail Strum, Aug. 13, 1961 B in Indsl. Engring., Ohio State U., 1958, MBA, 1960; D in Bus. Adminstrn., Harvard U., 1966. Staff indsl. engr. Procter & Gamble Co., Cin., 1958; sr. cons. Cresap, McCormack & Paget, N.Y.C., 1960—61; staff assoc. Mitre Corp., Bedford, Mass., 1961; cons. Sys. Devel. Corp., Santa Monica, Calif., 1963—64; dir. long range planning Electronic Splty. Co., L.A., 1966—68; chmn. Atek Industries, 1968—72; pres. Myers Fin. Corp., 1973—82; chmn. Amvid Comm. Svcs., Inc., 1975—79, Omni Resources Devel. Corp., 1979—83; chmn., pres. Am. Internat. Mining Co., Inc., 1979—83; pres. Advent Internat. Mgmt. Co., Inc., 1982—; chmn. Global Bond Mktg. Svcs., Inc., 1987—90; pres., CEO Whitehall Container Mfg. Corp., 1988—91; pres. Whitehall Motors Co., 1989—97, Allied Metamatter Tech. Corp., 1994—96; chmn. U.S. Water Resources, Inc., 1994—96; pres. Am. Tech. Venture Fund Mgmt., Inc., Advent Internat. Realty Corp., 1996—98, First Internat. Capital Corp., 1996—2000. Pres. Turbogen, Inc., 1995-98, Blue Star Material Techs. Inc., 1997-2000, founding dir. Warner Ctr. Bank, 1980-83; bd. dirs., pres. Cyber Security Systems, Inc., 2000—; lectr. bus. adminstrn. U. So. Calif., L.A., 1967-74; prof. Grad. Sch. Bus. Adminstrn. Pepperdine U., 1974-81. Trustee, treas. Chamber Symphony Soc. Calif., 1971-78; mem. campaign issues com. Reagan for Pres., 1976, 80; pub. safety commr. City of Hidden Hills, Calif., 1976-83, chmn., 1982-83; co-chmn. budget adv. com. Las Virgenes Sch. Dist., 1983-86; mem. Mayor's Blue Ribbon Fin. Com., 1981-82; mem. dean's select adv. com. Coll. Engring., Ohio State U., 1984-94; mem. state exec. com. Calif. Libertarian Party, chmn. region 61, 1989-90, chmn. strategic planning com.; dep. chmn. Los Angeles County Libertarian Party, 1991-92; chairperson campaign issues com. Marrou for Pres., 1991-92; chmn. bd. trustees WWII Hist. Soc., 1992—; first v.p. Armed Forces Cmty. Rels. Coun. Ctrl. Ohio, 2001—. Capt. USAF, 1958-60. Ford Found. fellow, 1961-64 Mem. Soc. Automotive Engrs., Harvard Bus. Sch. Assn., Ohio State Alumni Assn., Harvard Bus. Club Columbus (bd. dirs. 1998—, pres. 1996-98), Ohio State Alumni Club (pres. 1998-99), Harvard Club Ctrl. Ohio (bd. dirs.). E-mail: philmyers@wowway.com. *Personal philosophy: All out all the time. I stand for the creation of a new system of global governance which stresses individual liberty, freedom and responsibility, and which leads to a world that works for everyone with no one left out. In business, I stand for exceptional vision, creativity, innovation, and contribution.*

MYERS, PHILLIP SAMUEL, mechanical engineering educator; b. Webber, Kans., May 8, 1916; s. Earl Rufus and Sarah Katharine (Breon) M.; m. Jean Frances Alford, May 26, 1943; children: Katharine Myers Muirhead, Elizabeth Myers Baird, Phyllis Myers Rathbone, John, Mark. BS in Math. and Commerce, McPherson Coll., 1940; BSME, Kans. State Coll., 1942; PhDME, U. Wis., 1947. Registered profl. engr., Wis. Instr. mech. engring. Ind. Tech. Coll., Ft. Wayne, summer 1942; instr. U. Wis., Madison, 1942-47, asst. prof., 1947-50, assoc. prof., 1950-55, prof., 1955-86, emeritus prof., 1986—, chmn. dept. mech. engring., 1979-83. Cons. Diesel Engine Mfrs. Assn., U.S. Army, various oil and ins. cos. Contbr. articles to profl. jours. Chmn. Pine Lake com. We. Wis. Conf. Meth. Ch., 1955-60; Mem. Village Bd., Shorewood Hills, 1962-67. Recipient B.S. Reynolds Teaching award, 1964, McPherson Coll. Alumni citation of merit, 1971; Dugald Clerk award, 1971 Fellow ASME (Diesel Gas Power award 1971, Soichiro Honda award 1993), Soc. Automotive Engrs. (Colwell award 1966, 79, Horning award 1968, nat. pres. 1969, hon. mem.), AAAS; mem. NAE, Am. Soc. for Engring. Edn., Blue Key, Sigma Xi, Phi Kappa Phi, Sigma Tau, Pi Tau Sigma (Gold medal 1949), Tau Beta Pi (Ragnar Onstad Svc. to Soc. award 1978). Mem. Brethren Ch. Achievements include patents in field.

MYERS, PHILLIP WARD, otolaryngologist; b. Evanston, Ill., Nov. 11, 1939; s. R. Maurice and Vivian (Ward) M.; m. Lynetta Sargent, Dec. 22, 1963; children: Andrea, Ward, Alycia, Amanda, Andrew. BS, Western Ill. U., 1961; MD, U. Ill., 1965. Diplomate: Am. Bd. Otolaryngology. Intern St. Paul-Ramsey Hosp., 1965-66; resident in otolaryngology U. Louisville, 1966-68; resident Northwestern U., 1968-70, fellow, 1970-71; practice medicine specializing in otolaryngology Springfield, Ill., 1973—; clin. prof. otolaryngology So. Ill. U., Springfield, 1973—. Served to maj. M.C. AUS, 1971-73. Fellow Am. Soc. for Head and Neck Surgery, Am. Acad. Facial Plastic and Reconstructive Surgery; ACS, Am. Acad. Otolaryngology-Head and Neck Surgery. Achievements include research in perilymphatic fistulas. Home: 3423 N Oak Hill Rd Rochester IL 62563-9273 Office: So Ill Sch Medicine PO Box 19662 Springfield IL 62794-9662

MYERS, PRISCILLA A. insurance company executive; BS in Polit. Sci. and Econs., U. Mass., 1973; MBA, Suffolk U., 1978. Staff auditor The Prudential Ins. Co. Am., Boston, 1976-95, sr. v.p. and auditor, 1995-98, sr. v.p. demutualization, 1998—2002; sr. v.p., chief mktg. officer Prudential Fin., Inc., Newark, 2002—. Mem. Auditing Com. Mcpl. Excess Liability Joint Ins. Fund; trustee Inst. Internal Auditors Profl. Rsch. Found. Trustee St. Peter's Coll. Office: Prudential Fin Inc Chief Mktg Officer 213 Washington St 18th Fl Newark NJ 07102-2992

MYERS, R. DAVID, library director, dean; b. Hutchinson, Kans., Mar. 27, 1949; s. William Raymond and Elizabeth (Haas) M.; m. Barbara Jean Burridge, Sept. 15, 1973; 1 child, John David. BA, U. No. Colo., 1972, MA, 1974; ABD, U. Mich., 1976; MA, U. Denver, 1979. Manuscript curator Western History Collection, Denver, 1976-79; rsch. assoc. Colo. Legis. Coun., Denver, 1979-81; reference specialist Libr. of Congress, Washington, 1981-84, reference supr., 1984-88; libr. dir. State Hist. Soc. of Wis., Madison, 1988-94; assoc. dean univ. libr. N.Mex. State U., Las Cruces, 1994-2001; dir. librs., prof. history Coll. Santa Fe, 2001—. Editor Am. history Macmillan Pub., N.Y.C., 1991-94; cons. history of medicine dept. U. Wis., Madison, 1993-94. Author bibliographies for Libr. of Congress, 1987, 88. Mem. ALA, Am. Hist. Assn., Orgn. Am. Historians, Labor and Working Class History Assn. (bd. dirs.). Avocations: research, writing, baseball, mysteries. Office: Fogelson Libr Coll Santa Fe 1600 St Michaels Dr Santa Fe NM 87505 Office Phone: 505-473-6576. Business E-Mail: myers@csf.edu.

MYERS, R(ALPH) CHANDLER, lawyer; b. L.A., Jan. 9, 1933; s. Ralph Cather and Winifred (Chandler) M.; m. Rebecca Blythe Borkgren, Jan. 11, 1963. BA, Stanford U., 1954, JD, 1958; LLD (hon.), Whittier Coll., 1988. Bar: Calif. 1959, U.S. Dist. Ct. (ctrl. dist.) Calif. 1959, U.S. Supreme Ct. 1971. Law clk., then assoc. Parker, Stanbury, Reese & McGee, L.A., 1958-63; assoc. Nicholas, Kolliner & Van Tassel, L.A., 1963-65; ptnr. Myers & D'Angelo and predecessors, L.A. and Pasadena, Calif., 1965—. Nat. panelist Am. Arbitration Assn., L.A., 1964-2000; bd. visitors Stanford U. Law Sch., Calif., 1970-73; mem. judge pro tem panel L.A. Mcpl. Ct., 1971-81; mem. L.A. County Dist. Atty.'s Adv. Coun., 1976-83. Nat. vice chmn. Keystone Gifts, Stanford Centennial Campaign, 1987—92; trustee Whittier Coll., Calif., 1973—2001, chmn. bd. trustees, 1981—87, trustee emeritus, 2001—; trustee Flintridge Prep. Sch., LaCanada-Flintridge, Calif., 1981—88, chmn. bd. trustees, 1985—88; co-founder Whittier Law Sch., 1975, trustee, 1975—2001, chmn. bd. trustees, 1981—87, trustee emeritus, 2001—; bd. dirs. Opera Guild So. Calif., L.A., 1971—83, pres., 1980—82; bd. dirs. Guild Opera Co. L.A., 1974—83, pres., 1975—77; bd. dirs. Western Justice Ctr. Found., 1993—, treas., 1996—99, 2d v.p., 1999—2001, 1st v.p., 2001—03, pres., 2003—; bd. dirs. L.A. Child Guidance Clinic, 1972—83, pres., 1977—79; bd. dirs. Opera Assocs. of the Music Ctr., L.A., 1976—78. Recipient Stanford Assocs. award, 1984, Centennial Medallion award, 1991, Gold Spike award Stanford U., 1989, Disting. Svc. award Whittier Law Sch., 1993, Outstanding Achievement award Stanford Assocs., 1998. Mem. Wilshire Bar Assn. (bd. govs. 1972-81, pres. 1979-80), L.A. County Bar Assn. (trustee 1979-81), Stanford Law Soc. So. Calif. (bd. dirs. 1967-72, pres. 1970-71), Stanford Assocs. (bd. govs. 1992-97, treas. 1995-97), Jonathan Club, Univ. Club (Pasadena), Stanford Club of L.A. (bd. dirs. 1963-70, pres. 1968-69). Home: La Canada 5623 Burning Tree Dr La Canada Flintridge CA 91011-2861 Office: Myers & D'Angelo 301 N Lake Ave Ste 800 Pasadena CA 91101-4108 Office Phone: 626-792-0007.

MYERS, R(ALPH) THOMAS, chemist, educator; b. Maidsville, W.Va., Mar. 28, 1921; s. Harrison Lonzo and Martha Jane (Nuce) M.; m. Dorothy Kraus (div.); m. Evelyn Lightfoot (div.); children: Paul, Alice, Mary; m. Dorothy Amelia VanWert, Mar. 22, 1986. AB in Chemistry, W.Va. U., 1941, PhD in Chemistry, 1949. Rsch. assoc. Manhattan Project Columbia U., N.Y.C., 1944-45; assoc. prof. Waynesburg Coll., Waynesburg, Pa., 1948-51; asst. prof. chemistry Colo. Sch. Mines, Golden, 1951-56; prof. chemistry Kent (Ohio) State U., 1956-87, prof. emeritus, 1987—. Co-author: Holt Chemistry, 2004. Bd. edn., Kent, 1990-93, pres., 1993. Mem. AAAS, Am. Chem. Soc., Ohio Acad. Sci., Sigma Xi. Democrat. Unitarian-Universalist. Avocations: enviroment, skiing. Home: 1641 S Lincoln St Kent OH 44240-4448 Office: Kent State U Dept Chemistry Kent OH 44242-0001

MYERS, REX CHARLES, history educator, retired college dean; b. Cleve., July 1, 1945; s. Charles F. and Merial W. (Jones) M.; m. Susan L. Richards, Jan. 10, 1987; children: Gary W., Laura M. BA, Western State Coll., 1967; MA, U. Mont., 1970, PhD, 1972; postgrad., U. Wash., 1983, Harvard U., 1990. Instr. Palo Verde Coll., Blythe, Calif., 1972-75; reference librarian Mont. Hist. Soc., Helena, 1975-78; prof., divsn. chmn., dean Western Mont. Coll., Dillon, 1979-86; dean S.D. State U., Brookings, 1986-91; acad. dean Lyndon State Coll., Lyndonville, Vt., 1991-95; lectr. Western State Coll., Gunnison, Colo., 1995-98, Mesa State Coll., 1998-99, Lawrence U., 1999—. Author: Montana Symbols, 1976, Montana Trolleys, 1970, Lizzie, 1989; co-author: Marble Colorado, 1970, Montana: Our Land and People, 1978, Montana and the West, 1984; contbr. articles to profl. jours. Bd. dirs. Ctr. for Western Studies, Sioux Falls, SD, 1990—, Gunnison Arts Ctr., Gunnison County Libr., Fox Valley Arts Alliance, Meml. Park Arboretum and Gardens. Summer stipend NEH, 1973; fellow James J. Hill Library, 1985. Mem.: AAUW, Mont. Oral History Assn. (chmn. 1980—83), Am. Conf. Acad. Deans, Western History Assn. (chmn. membership com. 1980—83), N.E. Kingdom C. of C. (bd. dirs.), Masons (master 1984), Kiwanis (pres. Dillon 1983, lt. gov. 1984, 1997, 2003), Phi Alpha Theta, Phi Kappa Phi. Unitarian Universalist. Home: PO Box 783 Appleton WI 54912-0783 Office: Lawrence Univ PO Box 599 Appleton WI 54912 Office Phone: 920-832-7043.

MYERS, RICHARD B. Chairman of the Joint Chiefs of Staff; b. Kansas City, Mo., Mar. 1, 1942; m. Mary Jo Myers; 3 children. BSME, Kans. State U., 1965; MBA, Auburn U., 1977; Diploma, Air Command/Staff Coll., Maxwell AFB, Ala., 1977, U.S. Army War Coll., 1981; postgrad., Harvard U., 1991. Commd. 2d lt. USAF, 1965, advanced through ranks to gen., 1997; various assignments to comdr. U.S. Forces Japan and 5th Air Force, Yokota Air Base, Japan, 1993-96; asst. to chmn. of Joint Chiefs of Staff The Pentagon, Washington, 1996-97; comdr. Pacific Air Forces, Hickam AFB, Hawaii, 1997-98; comdr.-in-chief N.Am. Aerospace Def. Comm./U.S. Space Command, Peterson AFB, Colo., 1998—2000; vice chmn. of the Joint Chiefs of Staff U.S. Dept. of Def., Washington, 2000—01, chmn. of the Joint Chiefs of Staff, 2001—. Decorated Def. Disting. Svc. medal with two bronze oak leaf cluster, Disting. Svc. medal, Legion of Merit, Disting. Flying Cross with oak leaf cluster, Meritorious Svc. medal with three oak leaf clusters, Air medal with 18 oak leaf clusters, Air Force Commendation medal, others. Mailing: Chmn of the Joint Chiefs Dept of Defense Pentagon Washington DC 20318-9999

MYERS, RICHARD HEPWORTH, medical geneticist, educator; b. Austin, Nov. 1, 1947; s. Clark E. and Cora Henley (Hepworth) M.; m. Carol Anne Smith, Sept. 3, 1978; children: Margaret Anne, Madelyn Claire. BA, U. Kans., 1969; MEd, Ga. State U., 1973, MA, 1976, PhD, 1979. Diplomate Am. Bd. Med. Genetics; lic. psychologist. Asst. prof. in psychiatry Emory U., Atlanta, 1979-80; asst. prof. neurology Boston U. Sch. Medicine, 1980-87, assoc. prof. neurology, 1987—94, prof. neurology, 1994—; lectr. in neurology Harvard U. Med. Sch., Boston, 1980—; assoc. in neurology Mass. Gen. Hosp., Boston, 1980—; psychologist Univ. Hosp., Boston, 1980—. Vis. prof. MIT, Cambridge, Mass., 1993—. Contbr. articles to profl. jours. Fellow Am. Coll. Med. Genetics (founding); mem. APA, AAAS, Am. Soc. Human Genetics (mem. com. ethics of genome project 1992-94), Internat. Genetic Epidemiology Soc. Avocations: blues guitar, skiing. Office: Boston U Med Sch Dept Neurology 715 Albany St Boston MA 02118-2526

MYERS, ROBERT DAVID, judge; b. Springfield, Mass., Nov. 20, 1937; s. William and Pearl (Weiss) M.; m. Judith G. Dickenman, July 1, 1962; children— Mandy Susan, Jay Brandt, Seth William. AB, U. Mass., 1959; JD, Boston U., 1962. Bar: Ariz. 1963. Practice in, Phoenix, 1963-89; presiding judge civil dept. Superior Ct. of Arizona in Maricopa County, 1991-92; presiding judge probate and mental health dept. Superior Ct. of Ariz., Maricopa County, Ariz., 1992-95, presiding judge, 1995-2000; pro tem judge Ariz. Ct. Appeals; judge Ariz. Superior Ct., 1989—2002; chief dep. Ariz. Atty. Gen., 2003—04; gen. counsel Ariz. Dept. Corrections, Phoenix, 2004—. Adj. prof. Ariz. State U. Sch. Law, 1997—; chmn. com. on exams and admissions Ariz. Supreme Ct., 1974-75, chmn. com. on character and fitness, 1975-76, mem. multi-state bar exam. com., 1976-85; bd. dirs. Nat. Conf. Met. Judges, 1997—, pres., 1998-99. Pres. Valley of Sun chpt. City of Hope, 1965-66, Cmty. Orgn. for Drug Abuse Control, 1972-73, Valley Big Bros., 1975; chmn. Mayors Ad Hoc Com. on Drug Abuse, 1974-75; bd. dirs. Maricopa County Legal Aid Soc., 1978. Recipient award for outstanding svc. and dedication to improving the legal profession and professionalism of the bar and bench Maricopa County Bar Assn., 1999, Superior Svc. award Ariz. chpt. ASPA, 2000, Justice Tom C. Clark award Nat. Conf. Metro. Cts., 2000. Mem. ATLA (nat. chmn. gov.), Ariz. Bar Assn. (gov., com. chmn., sect. pres.), Maricopa County Bar Assn. (dir., pres. 1979-80,Judge of yr., 1999, Henry S. Steven award 2000), Ariz. Trial Lawyers Assn. (pres., dir., co-editor newsletter), Phoenix Trial Lawyers Assn. (pres., dir.), Western Trial Lawyers Assn. (pres. 1977), Am. Judicature Soc. (spl. merit citation outstanding svc. improvement of adminstrn. justice 1986), Am. Bd. Trial Advocates (Phoenix chpt. Judicial Officer of Yr. award 2001), Sandra Day O'Connor Inn of Ct. (pres. 1991-92). Office: Ariz Dept Corrections 1601 W Jefferson Phoenix AZ 85007-2205 Office Phone: 602-542-1532.

MYERS, ROBERT EUGENE, writer, educator; b. L.A., Jan. 15, 1924; s. Harold Eugene and Margaret (Anawalt) M.; m. Joyce E. Daily, 1946 (div. 1949); 1 child, Kathleen; m. Patricia A. Tazer, Aug. 17, 1956; children: Edward E., Margaret A., Hal R., Karen I. AB, U. Calif., Berkeley, 1955; MA (Crown-Zellerbach fellow), Reed Coll., 1960; EdD, U. Ga., 1968. Employed in phonograph record bus., 1946-54; tchr. elem. sch., 1954-61; rsch. asst. U. Minn., 1961-62; asst. prof. Augsburg Coll., 1962-63, U. Oreg., 1963-66; elem. tchr. Eugene, Oreg., 1966-67; assoc. prof. U. Victoria, 1968-70; assoc. rsch. prof. Oreg. System of Higher Edn., 1970-73; film maker, producer ednl. filmstrips, books, recs., 1973-77; learning resources specialist Oreg. Dept. Edn., Salem, 1977-81; with Linn-Benton Edn. Svc. Dist., Albany, Oreg., 1982-87; ret., 1987. Author: (with E. Paul Torrance) Creative Learning and Teaching (Pi Lambda Theta award 1971), 1970, La Ensenanza Creativa, 1970, Can You Imagine?, 1965, Invitations to Thinking and Doing, 1964, Invitations to Speaking and Writing Creatively, 1965, Plots, Puzzles, and Ploys, 1966, For Those Who Wonder, 1966, Timberwood Tales, Vol. II, 1977, Wondering, 1984, Imagining, 1985, What Next?, 1994, Facing the Issues, 1995, Cognitive Connections, 1996, Mind Sparklers, 1997, Multiple Ways of Thinking with Social Studies, 1997, Character Matters, 1999, A Matter of Respect, 2000, It's Your Attitude That Counts, 2000, Mind Stretchers, 2001, Stories That Build Character, 2001, Think and Write, 2002, Now What, 2002, Spurs to Creative Thinking, 2002, Word Play, 2002, Developing Creative Thinking Skills, 2003; films: Feather (CINE Golden Eagle award), 1972, The Magic Net, 1972, Elephants, 1973. Mem. exec. bd. Nat. Assn. Gifted Children, 1974-77. With U.S. Mcht. Marine, 1944-45. Recipient CINE Golden Eagle award Coun. Internat. Non-theatrical Events, 1973. Mem. Internat. Reading Assn. Democrat. Home: 1357 Meadow Ct Healdsburg CA 95448-3347

MYERS, ROBERT JAY, retired aerospace company executive; b. Bklyn., Oct. 15, 1934; s. John J. and Clara S. (Martinsen) M.; m. Carolyn Erland, Aug. 10, 1963; children: Susan, Kenneth. BCE, NYU, 1955, postgrad., 1957-65; P.MD, Harvard U., 1972. With Grumman Corp., Bethpage, N.Y., 1964-94, v.p. resources, 1980-83, sr. v.p. bus. and resource mgmt., 1983-85, sr. v.p. corp. svcs., 1985-86; pres. Grumman Data Systems Corp., Bethpage, 1986-90; pres., chief operating officer, bd. dirs. Grumman Corp., 1991-94, ret., 1994. Sci. adv. coun. Ala. Space and Rocket Ctr., 1986-91. Adv. panel on econ. devel. N.Y. State Project 2000, 1985-86; mem. L.I. Project 2000; adv. bd. L.I. Youth Guidance, 1986-91; bd. dirs. Poly. U., 1991-98, North Shore Health System, 1994—, L.I. Mus. of Sci. and Tech., 1994-96; chmn. Huntington Hosp., 1996—. 1st lt. U.S. Army, 1955-57. Fellow Poly. U., 1987, Disting. Alumni award, 1989. Mem. Am. Def. Preparedness Assn. (dir. 1992-94), Navy League, Industry Exec. Bd., Nat. Space Club (bd. govs. 1986-89), Huntington Country Club (N.Y.), Audubon Country Club (Naples, Fla.). Presbyterian. Home: 200 Cheshire Way Naples FL 34110 Personal E-mail: rjm34@aol.com.

MYERS, ROBERT LUTHER, architect, artist; b. Macon, Ga., May 29, 1926; s. John Henry and Ada (Leake) M. BArch, Cornell U., 1950; MArch, Harvard U., 1951. Registered architect, NY, cert. Nat. Coun. Archl. Registration Bds. Project designer The Architects Collaborative, Cambridge, Mass., 1951-53; instr. archtl. design Cornell U., Ithaca, N.Y., 1954-56; project designer Lashmit, James, Brown & Pollack, Winston-Salem, N.C., 1956-60, Charles Luckman Assocs., N.Y.C., 1962-67, Eggers Group Architects, N.Y.C., 1970-72; asst. head design dept. Russell, Gibson, Von Dohlen, Architects, Farmington, Conn., 1977-88; artist New Preston, Conn., 1988—. Co-founder S.E. Ctr. Contemporary Art, Winston-Salem; mem. nat. adv. bd. Ackland Art Mus. U. N.C., Chapel Hill, 1983-2002, now emeritus mem. With. inf. U.S. Army, 1944-45, M.C., 1945-46. Prix de Rome in architecture Am. Acad. Rome, 1954; Eidlitz travel fellow Cornell U., 1950. Mem. Washington-Conn. Art Assn., Chancellor's Club U. N.C., Gerrard Soc. U. N.C. Avocations: art collecting, gardening, painting, drawing. Home: 144 Curtiss Rd New Preston Marble Dale CT 06777-1007

MYERS, ROBERT MANSON, English educator, author; b. Charlottesville, Va., May 29, 1921; s. Horwood Prettyman and Matilda Manson (Wynn) M. BA summa cum laude, Vanderbilt U., 1941; MA, Columbia, 1942, Harvard, 1943; PhD, Columbia, 1948. Instr. English Yale, 1945-47; asst. prof. Coll. William and Mary, 1947-48, Tulane U., 1948-54; tchr. English Brearley Sch., N.Y.C., 1954-56; chmn. dept. English Osbourn High Sch., Manassas, Va., 1956-59; mem. faculty U. Md., College Park, 1959—, prof. English, 1968-86, prof. emeritus, 1986—. Author: Handel's Messiah, 1948, From Beowulf to Virginia Woolf, 1952, rev., 1984, Handel, Dryden, and Milton, 1956, Restoration Comedy, 1961, The Children of Pride, 1972, abridged edit., 1984 (Carey-Thomas award 1972, Nat. Book award 1973), A Georgian at Princeton, 1976, Quintet: Five Plays, 1991, Sixes and Sevens: Three Plays, 2004. Fulbright Postdoctoral Research fellow U. London, 1953-54; Fulbright lectr. Rotterdam, Netherlands, 1958-59. Mem. Modern Lang. Assn. Am., Am. Soc. 18th Century Studies, Jane Austen Soc. N.Am., Phi Beta Kappa. Home: 3804 Deckford Pl Charlotte NC 28211-3408

MYERS, ROBERTA, editor-in-chief; MA, U. Edinburgh (Scotland), 1982; MLitt, Oxford U., 1984. Sr. editor Elle mag. Hachette Filipacchi Mags., N.Y.C.; editor-in-chief Elle mag., 2000—; editor-in-chief Mirabella mag., 1997—2000; editor in chief Tell Tale; mng. editor Seventeen. Office: Hachette-Filipacchi Mags Inc 1633 Broadway 44th Fl New York NY 10019

MYERS, RODMAN NATHANIEL, lawyer; b. Detroit, Oct. 27, 1920; s. Isaac Rodman and Fredericka (Hirschman) Myers; m. Jeanette Polisei, Mar. 19, 1957 (dec. 1996); children: Jennifer Myers Grabenstein, Rodman Jay. BA, Wayne State U., 1941; LLB, U. Mich., 1943. Bar: Mich. 1943, U.S. Supreme Ct. 1962. Agt. IRS, Detroit, 1943; from assoc. to ptnr. Butzel, Keidan, Simon, Myers & Graham, Detroit, 1943-90; of counsel Honigman Miller Schwartz and Cohn, Detroit, 1991—. Mem. blue ribbon task force Mich. Dept. Edn., 1988—90; founding mem., trustee Mich. chpt. Leukemia and Lymphoma Soc., founding pres., 1984—86, nat. trustee, 1984—; founding mem., trustee Detroit Sci. Ctr.; commr. Detroit Mcpl. Parking Authority, 1963—71; pres., trustee Bloomfield Twp. Pub. Libr.; trustee Temple Beth El, Bloomfield Hills, Mich.; bd. dirs. United Cmty. Svcs. of Met. Detroit, 1978—85, v.p., 1981—85, chmn. social svcs. divsn., 1982—85; bd. dirs. Children's Ctr. of Wayne County, Mich., 1963—88, pres., 1969—72. Mem. ABA, State Bar Mich. (chmn. atty. discipline panel, past vice chmn. unauthorized practice of law com., past mem. character and fitness com.). Home: 3833 Lakeland Ln Bloomfield Hills MI 48302-1328 Office: 2290 1st National Bldg Detroit MI 48226

MYERS, ROGER PAUL, writer, playwright, actor; b. Boothbay Harbor, Maine, Dec. 22, 1932; s. Harry Marcus and Muriel Maude (Barter) Myers. BA, Wayne State U., Detroit, 1963. Co-founder The Stables Theatre, Detroit; actor Totem Pole Playhouse, 1965—70. Author: (collection) Puns and Witticisms, (musical plays) Silas: The Musical, Wonderful Alice, (novels) Hamptons Grotesque, 2000, Death By Murder, 2000; author: (with Albert E. Herbert, Jr.) The Last Survivor, 2000, The Killer Pack, 2000, The Skytower Disaster, 2000, The Quest, 2000, composer for piano, author poems. With USN, 1951—53. Mem.: Actor's Equity Assn. Episcopalian. Avocations: travel, writing, music. Home: 104 Baltusrol Williamsburg VA 23188 E-mail: rpm104@verizon.net.

MYERS, ROLLAND GRAHAM, investment counselor; b. St. Louis, Aug. 30, 1945; s. Rolland Everett and Lurilien (Graham) M. Diploma, St. Louis Country Day Sch., 1963; AB cum laude in History and Lit., Harvard U., 1966; postgrad. Faculties of Social Scis. and Law, U. Edinburgh, Scotland, 1966-67; postgrad. Fondation Nationale des Sciences Politiques and Faculte de Lettres et des Sciences Humaines, U. Paris, 1967-68. Trainee global credit dept. The Chase Manhattan Bank, N.A., N.Y.C., 1968-69, mem. 32nd spl. devel. program, 1969, strategic planner internat. dept., 1969-70, securities analyst, mktg. rep., fiduciary investment dept., 1970; assoc. Smith, Barney & Co., Inc., N.Y.C., 1971, account exec. N.Y. sales dept., 1971-72, instl. account exec. N.Y. internat. sales dept., 1972-74, 2nd v.p., stockholder, 1975-76; v.p., stockholder Smith Barney, Harris Upham & Co., Inc. (subs. SBHU Holdings, Inc.), N.Y.C., 1976-78; prin. W.H. Graham & Sons, family investment office, 1977-82, investment counsel, 1982—. Ltd. ptnr. Croke Patterson Campbell, Ltd., Denver, 1975—; joint founder, gen. ptnr. Mansion Disbursements, Denver, 1979—; pres., chmn. exec. com., bd. dirs. Fifty-Five Residents Corp., N.Y.C., 1980-84; bd. dirs. Fifty-Six Danbury Rd. Assn., Inc., New Milford, Conn. Trustee, mem. corp. Bishop Rhinelander Found. (Episcopal Chaplaincy at Harvard and Radcliffe Colls.), Cambridge, 1973-75; v.p., treas., bd. dirs. The Whitehill Graham Found., St. Louis, 1976—; bd. dirs., fin. com., bylaws com., mem. corp. Eliot Pratt Edn. Ctr., Inc. (The Pratt Ctr.: Your Connection with the Natural World), New Milford, 1987-94; mem. corp. Kent (Conn.) Land Trust, Inc., 1989—, treas., 1989-93, bd. dirs., 1989-2003, adv. bd., 2003-; project financier Restoration of 1851 Samuel Curtiss Hosford House, Nat. Register Historic Dist., Falls Village, Conn., 1984-86; commr. Housatonic River Commn., Warren, Conn., 1985-93, vice chmn., 1986-87, chmn., 1988-92; commr. Conservation, Inland Wetlands and Watercourses Commn., Kent, 1988-93, vice chmn., 1988-92; mem. schs. and scholarships com., Office of Admissions and Fin. Aid, Harvard and Radcliffe Colls., 1991—. Mem. Cum Laude Soc., Mary Inst. and St. Louis Country Day Sch. Alumni Assn., Harvard Alumni Assn., Capitol Hill Club (Washington), Harvard Club (N.Y.C.), Hasty Pudding-Inst. of 1770 (Cambridge), Wyo. Bus. Alliance, Wyo. Heritage Found., St. Andrew's Soc., New Eng. Soc. in City N.Y. Republican. Episcopalian. Office: W H Graham & Sons Investment Counsel 1818 Evans Ave Ste 207 Cheyenne WY 82001-4664

MYERS, SHARON DIANE, auditor; b. Lawrence, Kans., Sept. 18, 1955; d. Richard Paul and Helen Carol (Overbey) M. AA, Mt. San Antonio Coll., Walnut, Calif., 1981; BSBA, Calif. State U., Pomona, 1983, MBA, 1986. Cert. fraud examiner; cert. govt. fin. mgr. Revenue agt. IRS, Glendale, Calif., 1984-85; auditor Def. Contract Audit Agy., L.A., 1985-92; auditor Office Inspector Gen. FDIC, Newport Beach, 1992—2002; auditor officer Inspector Gen., USPS, Portland, Oreg., 2002—. Instr. Azusa (Calif.) Pacific U., 1987, 88, West Coast U., San Diego, 1992. Musician, Sunday sch. supt. Covina (Calif.) Bapt. Temple, 1975-95, Liberty Bapt. Ch., Irvine, Calif., 1995-2002, Landmark Bapt. Ch., Olympia, Wash., 2002—. Mem. Assn. Govt. Accts. Republican. Avocations: piano, travel. Home: 2702 44th Ave NW Olympia WA 98502-3692

MYERS, SHIRLEY DIANA, art book editor; b. N.Y.C., Jan. 6, 1916; d. Samuel Archibald and Regina (Edelstein) Levene; m. Bernard Samuel Myers, Aug. 11, 1938 (dec. Feb. 1993); children: Peter Lewis, Lucie Ellen. BA, NYU, 1936, MA, 1938. Editorial asst. Am. Dancer mag., N.Y.C., 1936-38; asst. to dir. Nat. Art Soc., N.Y.C., 1938-42; freelance, art book editor N.Y.C. and Austin, Tex., 1947—. Editor: Modern Art in the Making, 1950, 59, Mexican Painting in Our Time, 1956, The German Expressionists, 1957, 63, Understanding the Arts, 1958, 63, Bruegel, 1976, Manet, 1977, (with B.S. Myers) Dictionary of 20th Century Art, 1974; asst. editor Ency. of Painting, 1955, 70, 79; asst. editor, contbr. McGraw-Hill Dictionary of Art, 5 vols., 1960-69; contbg. editor: Art and Civilization, 1956, 67; coord., picture editor Ency. World Art: Supplement, Vol. XVI, 1982, 83. Vol. archives New Sch. for Social Rsch. Libr., 1993-95. Mem. NOW, Older Women's League (rec. sec. Greater N.Y. chpt. 1993-95, co-chair 1995-97, mem. steering com. 1997—), Quest (assoc. editor newsletter 1997-2000, mem. coun. 1997-2001, co-chair curriculum com. 1998-2001, pres. 2002—).

MYERS, THOMAS EVERETT, lawyer; b. Lubbock, Tex., Aug. 26, 1954; s. Edward Nelson and Mary Elizabeth (Worrell) M.; m. Cynthia Kay Ridlehoover, Aug. 4, 1979; children: Holly Elizabeth, Paige Michelle. BS, Baylor U., 1976, JD, 1979. Bar: Tex. 1979, U.S. Dist. Ct. (no. dist.) Tex. 1979, U.S. Dist. Ct. (we. dist.) Tex. 1988, U.S. Ct. Appeals (5th cir.) 1980, U.S. Supreme Ct. 1983; cert. in consumer law and criminal law, Tex. Bd. Legal Specialization. Asst. dist. atty. Tarrant County, Ft. Worth, 1979—84; shareholder Rohne Hoodenpyle Lobert Myers P.C., Arlington, Tex., 1984—98, Brackett & Ellis, P.C., Arlington, Tex., 1998—. Deacon 1st Bapt. Ch. Arlington, 1985—. Mem. ABA, Tex. Bar Assn., Tarrant County Bar Assn., Tex. Criminal Def. Lawyers Assn., Baylor U. Alumni Assn. (pres. Arlington chpt. 1983-84), Kiwanis (pres. Arlington chpt. 1989-90). Baptist. Avocations: music, movies, golf, reading. Office: 100 Main St Fort Worth TX 76102-3009 Office Phone: 817-338-1700. Business E-Mail: tmyers@belaw.com.

MYERS, TIMOTHY JAMES, chemical engineer, consultant; b. Green Bay, Wis., July 13, 1971; s. Gerald and Rita Myers. BS in Forest Resources, U. Wash., Seattle, 1993; PhD of Chem. Engring., U. Calif. Berkeley, 1999. Rschr. Lawrence Berkeley Nat. Lab., 1993—99; engr. Exponent, Inc., Natick, Mass., 1999—2001, sr. engr., 2001—03, mng. engr., 2003—. Scholar, Tech. Assn. of the Pulp and Paper Industry, 1992. Mem.: AIChE (sr.). Office: Exponent Inc 21 Strathmore Rd Natick MA 01760 E-mail: tmyers@exponent.com.

MYERS, VIRGINIA ANNE, art educator; b. Greencastle, Ind., May 8, 1927; d. Everett Clark Myers and Hurst (McKann) Bessie. BA in Fine Arts, George Washington U., Corcoran Sch. Art, 1949; MFA in Drawing and Painting, Calif. Coll. of Arts & Crafts, Oakland, 1951; postgrad. in print making, U. Ill., 1953-55, U. Iowa, 1955-61; studied with Stanley William Hayter, Paris, 1961-62. Rsch. asst. Sch. Art and Art History U. Iowa, Iowa City, 1958-61; instr. arts and crafts, phys. edn. Tucson Indian Tng. Sch., 1949-50; teaching asst. dept. art and architecture U. Ill., Champaign-Urbana, 1954-55; instr. printmaking U. Iowa, Iowa City, 1962-69, asst. prof. printmaking, 1969-74, assoc. prof., 1974-82, prof., 1982—. Bd. dirs., treas. Elizabeth Found. for Fellowships in the Visual Arts, N.Y.; pres. Iowa Foil Printer Corp. Author: (hardbound) Foil Imaging...A New Art Form, 2001, (manual) Creating Original Prints with Hot-Stamped foil, 1993; A Time of Malfeasance (21 engravings and drypoints), 1976, The Views from Tenacre: The Seasons (66 paintings and drawings), 1979, Landscape in Iowa (36 paintings and drawings), 1986; contbr. articles to profl. jours. Recipient Fulbright fellowship, Paris, 1961-62; grantee U. Iowa, 1973, 78, 84, 89, 93, 98-99, Iowa Arts Coun., 1974-77, 80, 85, Stanley Found., 1984-88, Thorson Found., 1984, 86. Mem. Foil Stamping and Embossing Assn. (charter), Nat. Mus. of Women in Arts (charter). Achievements include patents for Iowa Foil Printer, 1992; Underwriters Laboratories, 1997. Avocations: gardening, reading, swimming. Home: Tenacre Print 4244 210th St NE Solon IA 52333-9657 Office: Univ Iowa Sch Arts & Art History Iowa City IA 52242

MYERS, WARREN POWERS LAIRD, physician, educator; b. Phila., May 2, 1921; s. John Dashiell and Mary Hall (Laird) M.; m. Katharine Van Vechten, July 1, 1944; children: Warren Powers Laird, Jr., Anne Van Vechten Myers Evans, Duncan McNeir, Sara Myers Gormley. Grad., Episcopal Acad., 1939; BS, Yale U., 1943; MD, Columbia U., 1945; MS in Medicine, U. Minn., 1952; postgrad. (Eleanor Roosevelt Found. fellow), U. Cambridge, Eng., 1962-63. Diplomate: Am. Bd. Internal Medicine. Rotating intern Phila. Gen. Hosp., 1945-46; intern medicine Maimonides Hosp., N.Y.C., 1948-49; resident fellow in medicine Mayo Clinic, Rochester, Minn., 1949-52; clin. asst. Meml. Hosp., N.Y.C., 1952-54, asst. attending physician, 1954-58, assoc. attending physician, 1959, attending physician, 1959-90; instr. Cornell U. Med. Coll.,

1955-56, asst. prof., 1956-59, asso. prof., 1959-68, prof. medicine, 1968-86, prof. emeritus, 1986—, assoc. dean, 1977-86; chmn. dept. medicine Meml. Sloan-Kettering Cancer Ctr., N.Y.C., 1967-77; v.p. for ednl. affairs Meml. Hosp., 1977-81, Eugene W. Kettering prof., 1979-86; attending physician N.Y. Hosp., N.Y.C., 1968-86; mem. Sloan-Kettering Inst. Cancer Rsch., N.Y.C., 1969-90; mem. emeritus Meml. Sloan-Kettering Cancer Ctr., N.Y.C., 1990—; cons. Rockefeller U. Hosp., N.Y.C., 1977-86. Mem. clin. cancer tng. com. Nat. Cancer Inst., 1970-73, chmn., 1971-73, chmn. clin. cancer edn. com., 1975-78; adj. prof. medicine Dartmouth Med. Sch., 1987-96, prof. medicine emeritus, 1996—; cons. staff Mary Hitchcock Meml. Hosp., Hanover, N.H., 1987-96. Contbr. articles on cancer, bone metabolism, internal medicine, and med. edn. to med. jours. Bd. dirs. Rye (N.Y.) United Fund, 1969-72, chmn. budget com., 1968-69; bd. dirs. Damon Runyon-Walter Winchell Cancer Fund, 1976-86, pres., 1985-86; trustee Hitchcock Clinic, Lebanon, N.H., 1983-96, Dartmouth-Hitchcock Med. Ctr., Lebanon, 1983-95, chmn. exec. com., 1992-95, tchr.'s coll. Columbia U., 1980-86; trustee Friends of Norris Cotton Cancer Ctr., Dartmouth-Hitchcock Med. Ctr., Lebanon, 1997-2000, v.p., 1999-2000—; elder Presbyn. Ch., 1969-86, Norwich Congregational Ch., deacon, 1998-2002. With M.C., USNR, 1946-47. Recipient Alumni award for research Mayo Clinic, 1952, Margaret Hay Edwards Achievement medal Am. Assn. Cancer Edn., 1993. Fellow ACP, N.Y. Acad. Medicine (v.p. 1983-85); mem. Am. Clin. and Climatological Assn., Am. Assn. Cancer Research, Endocrine Soc., Harvey Soc., Am. Fedn. Clin. Research, Practioners' Soc. of N.Y., AMA, Am. Assn. Cancer Edn. (pres. 1984-85), Am. Soc. Clin. Oncology, Founders and Patriots Pa., Yale Club, Charaka Club, Century Assn. (N.Y.C.), Alpha Omega Alpha. Presbyterian (elder 1969-86). Clubs: Yale, Charaka, Century Assn. (N.Y.C.). Address: 436 Joshua Rd White River Junction VT 05001-9028

MYERS, WILLIAM, food container manufacturing executive, CFO, treas. Dart Container, Mason, Mich., now treas. Office: Dart Container 500 Hogsback Rd Mason MI 48854-9547

MYERS, WILLIAM GERRY GERRY, III, lawyer; b. Roanoke, Va., July 13, 1955; AB, Coll. of William and Mary, 1977; JD, U. Denver, 1981. Bar: Colo. 1981, Wyo. 1982, D.C. 1987, U.S. Supreme Ct. 1990, Idaho 1997. Assoc. Davis & Cannon, Sheridan, Wyo., 1981-85; legis. counsel U.S. Sen. Alan K. Simpson, Wyo., 1985-89; asst. to atty. gen. U.S. Dept. Justice, Washington, 1989-92; dep. gen. counsel for programs U.S. Dept. Energy, Washington, 1992-93, dir. fed. lands Nat. Cattlemen's Assn., 1993-97, exec. dir. Pub. Lands Coun., Washington, 1993-97; atty. Holland and Hart, Boise, Idaho, 1997—2001, 2003—; solicitor U.S. Dept. of Interior, 2001—03. Office: Holland and Hart 101 S Capitol Blvd Ste 1400 Boise ID 83702-7714 Office Phone: 208-342-5000. E-mail: wmyers@hollandhart.com.

MYERS, WILLIAM OSGOOD, thoracic and cardiovascular surgeon; b. Hastings, Nebr., Aug. 19, 1929; s. Joy Uberto and Lena C. (Osgood) M.; m. Lois Mae Payne, Dec. 26, 1952; children: Jessica, Wendell, Inez, John, Michael. BA, Hastings Coll., 1951; MD, Northwestern U., 1955. Diplomate Am. Bd. Surgery, Am. Bd. Thoracic Surgery. Intern City Detroit Receiving Hosp., 1955—56, resident in anesthesiology, 1956—57; gen. practice medicine Blue Hill, Nebr., 1959—62; surg. resident Sacred Heart Hosp., Yankton, SD, 1962—65; instr. anatomy U. S.D. Med. Sch., Vermillion, SD, 1963—65; resident in gen. surgery U. Kans. Med. Ctr., Kansas City, 1965—66, resident in thoracic and cardiovasc. surgery, 1966—68; cardiovasc. surgeon Marshfield Clinic, Marshfield, Wis.; and St. Joseph's Hosp., Marshfield, 1968—2000, chmn. sect. thoracic and cardiovascular surgery, 1972—76, chmn. dept. surgery, 1974—79; clin. prof. surgery U. Wis., 1996—; chmn. instl. rev. bd. Marshfield Rsch. Found., 2000—. Prin. investigator Coronary Artery Surgery Study, Nat. Heart, Lung and Blood Inst., 1973—; bd. dirs. Marshfield Med. Found., 1978-84. Contbr. articles to profl. jours. Chmn. rsch. com. Marshfield Med. Found., 1985-94, mem. 1996-2000; coun. on Cardiovascular Surgery AHA. Served with USAF, 1957-59. Mem.: ACS (pres. Wis. chpt. 1986, credentials com. 1988—2000), AMA, Western Surg. Assn., Ctrl. Surg. Assn., Frederick A. Coller Surgery Soc. (pres. 1998—99), Soc. Thoracic Surgeons, Am. Assn. for Thoracic Surgery, Am. Thoracic Soc., Am. Coll. Cardiology, Wis. Heart Assn. (bd. dirs. 1988—94), Wis. Surg. Soc. (pres. 1993, mem. coun.), Wis., Wood County Med. Socs. Home: 1704 Woodsview Drive Marshfield WI 54449-3418 Office: 1000 N Oak Ave Marshfield WI 54449-5703 E-mail: lmpm@tznet.com., myersw@mmrf.mfldclin.edu.

MYERS, WOODROW AUGUSTUS, JR., physician, health care management director; b. Indpls., Feb. 14, 1954; s. Woodrow Augustus Sr. and Charlotte T. (Tyler) M.; m. Debra Jackson, June 23, 1973; children: Kimberly Leilani, Zachary Augustus. BS, Stanford (Calif.) U., 1973, MBA, 1982; MD, Harvard U., 1977. Intern in internal medicine Stanford U. Med. Ctr., 1977-78, resident in internal medicine, 1978-80, fellow, critical care medicine, 1980-81; asst. prof. critical care medicine San Francisco Gen. Hosp., 1982-84; physician health advisor com. on labor and human resources U.S. Senate, Washington, 1984; commr. Ind. Dept. of Health, Indpls., 1985-90; health commr. N.Y.C. Dept. of Health, 1990-91; corp. med. dir. Assoc. Group, Indpls., 1991-95; dir. health care mgmt. Ford Motor Co., Dearborn, Mich., 1996—. Asst. prof. medicine Cornell Med. Coll., N.Y.C., 1990-91; trustee Stanford U., 1987-92; assoc. prof. medicine Ind. U. Sch. Medicine, 1992-95; assoc. clin. prof. medicine Wayne State U., 1997—; adj. assoc. prof. internal medicine U. Mich., 1998—; bd. dirs. Somnus Med. Techs. Bd. dirs. Stanford Health Systems, 1994-97, U. Calif.-San Francisco/Stanford Health Care, 1997; bd. overseers Harvard U., 1996—; mem. Medicare Payment Adv. Commn., 1997—; vice-chmn. vis. com. Harvard Med. Sch., 1997—. Robert Wood Johnson clin. scholar, Stanford U., 1980-82. Fellow ACP; mem. AMA, Inst. Medicine of NAS, Nat. Med. Assn. Office: Ford Motor Co The American Rd WHQ-500 Dearborn MI 48121-1899

MYERS BROWN, JOAN, dance company executive, consultant; b. Phila., Dec. 25, 1931; d. Julius Thomas Myers and Nellie (Woods) Lewis Myers; m. Frederick Johnson, 1951 (div.); m. Max Brown, Nov. 18, 1967 (div.); children— Dannielle C. Brown, Marlisa J. Brown. D (hon.) U. Arts, 1994. Dancer various prodns. U.S., Can., Caribbean, 1950-61, Pearl Bailey Prodns., nat. tour, 1961-66; choreographer Harlem Prodns., Atlantic City, N.J., 1958-67; dir., choreographer, tchr. Phila. Sch. of Dance Arts, 1960—; exec. dir. Phila. Dance Co., 1970—; cons. Nat. Endowment for Arts, 1970-84, panelist, 1970-82; panelist Ohio State Arts Council, 1981-84, Mich. State Arts Council, 1981-84; dance panel Pa. State Arts Council, 1987, Md. State Arts Coun., 1990, Arts Presenters, 1995, NJ/Del. State Coun. on The Arts, 1994, The Kennedy Ctr. AAEP, 1996; dir. Wade Communications, 1983— . Bd. dirs. Spruce Family Planning Clinic; mem. Mayor's Cultural Adv. Council, 1984—; bd. dirs. Greater Phila. Cultural Alliance; bd. dirs. Dance/USA, Citizens for Arts in Pa., Coalition of African-Am. Culture Inst. Recipient awards Nat. Council Negro Women, 1983, Award of Merit, West Phila. C. of C., 1983, Arts and Humanities Cultural award Phila. chpt. Continentals Socs., 1979, Philadelphians for Pub. Awareness award, 1984, Nat. Endowment Arts Choreographic fellow, 1979, Womens Way award, 1986, Theodore L. Hazlett Meml. award for excellence in the arts in Pa., 1986, Kool Achiever award, 1989, Black United Fund Arts award, 1989, Phila. Arts and Cultural award, 1989, Stella Moore Dance award, 1990, Black Unite Fund award, 1990, UNCF award, 1990, YWCA-Pioneer award, 1990, Excellence in Arts award, 1995, 50 Most Influential Women award, 1995, Arts and Business Coun. award, 1996, Chisolm award NPCBW, 1996. Democrat. Office: Phila Dance Co 9 N Preston St Philadelphia PA 19104-2299 Office Phone: 215-387-8200. Business E-Mail: jmb@philadanco.org.

MYERSON, ALAN, film and television director; b. Cleve., Aug. 8, 1936; s. Seymour A. and Vivien I. (Caplin) M.; m. Irene Ryan, June 2, 1962; 1 son, Lincoln; m. Leigh French, May 15, 1977; children: Sierra French-Myerson, Darcy French-Myerson. Student, Pepperdine Coll., 1956-57, UCLA, 1957. Mem. drama faculty U. Calif., Berkeley, 1966, San Francisco State U., 1967, Internat. Film and TV Workshops, 2002. Dir. Broadway, Off Broadway Prodns., 1958-64, including This Music Crept By Me Upon the Waters, The Committee; dir.: Second City, N.Y.C. and Chgo., 1961, 62; founder, prodr., dir. The Committee, San Francisco, L.A. and N.Y., 1963-74; dir.: (films) Steelyard Blues, 1972, Private Lessons, 1981, Police Academy 5, 1988, It's Showtime, 1976; numerous TV shows, 1975—, including Ally McBeal, Judging Amy, Joan of Arcadia, Larry Sanders Show, Friends, Frazier, Picket Fences, Miami Vice, Dynasty, Laverne and Shirley, Ed, Boston Public, Gilmore Girls, Lizzie McGuire; TV films The Love Boat, 1976, Hi, Honey, I'm Dead, 1991, Bad Attitudes, 1991, Holiday Affair, 1996. Active in civil rights, peace, anti-nuclear power movements, 1957-. Recipient Emmy nomination 1997, Cable ACE award nominations, 1995, 96, 97, TV Comedy award nomination Dirs. Guild, 1997. Mem. ASCAP, Acad. Motion Picture Arts and Scis., Acad. TV Arts and Scis., Dirs. Guild Am.

MYERSON, ALLAN STUART, chemical engineering educator, university dean; b. Bklyn., Nov. 17, 1952; s. Jules Myerson and Tilda (Rogalsky) Herman; m. Nancy Winget, June 15, 1979; 1 child, Megan. BS, Columbia U., 1973; MS, U. Va., 1975, PhD, 1977. Asst. prof. chem. engrng. U. Dayton, Ohio, 1977-79, Ga. Inst. Tech., Atlanta, 1979-83, assoc. prof., 1983-85, Polytech. U., Bklyn., 1985-88, prof., 1988-90, Joseph J. and Violet J. Jacobs prof., 1990—, head dept., 1985-92, dean Sch. Chem. and Materials Scis., 1992—. Cons. E.I Du Pont de Nemours & Co., Wilmington, Del., 1988—, Ajinomoto, Inc., Tokyo, 1990—, Molecular Simulations, Cambridge, Eng., 1992—. Editor: Crystallization as a Separation Process, 1990, Handbook of Industrial Crystallization, 1992; also over 60 articles. Mem. AICE, Am. Chem. Soc., Sigma Xi (faculty disting. rsch. award Poly. U. chpt. 1992), Tau Beta Pi. Achievements include patents on Purification of Terephthalic Acid by Supercritical Fluid Extraction, (with W. Ernst) Removal of Inorganic Contaminants from Catalysts and Regeneration of HDS Catalysts; research on area of crystallization from solution, metastable solution structure and impurity crystal interactions.

MYERSON, JACOB MYER, retired diplomat; b. Rock Hill, SC, June 11, 1926; s. Solomon and Lena (Clein) Myerson; m. Nicole Neuray, June 10, 1965 (dec. Oct. 1968); 1 child, Sylvie Anne; m. Helen Hayashi, Mar. 9, 1974 (dec. Jan. 1995). Student, Pa. State Coll., 1944; BA with distinction, George Washington U., 1949, MA, 1950; grad., Fgn. Service Inst., 1953. Joined U.S. Fgn. Svc., 1950; 3d sec. Office U.S. High Commr. Germany, Berlin, 1950-52; 2d sec. U.S. Mission to NATO and European Regional Orgn., Paris, 1953-55; also mem. U.S. permanent del. to coordinating com. InterGovtl. Consultative Group on EastWest Trade; internat. economist, internat. rels. officer State Dept., 1956-60, spl. asst. to under sec. state, 1965-66; adviser U.S. del. GATT session, Geneva, 1958; ministerial session OEEC, Paris, 1958; 1st sec., chief polit. sect. U.S. Mission to European Communities, Brussels, 1960-65; officer-in-charge NATO Polit. Affairs, Dept. State, 1966-68; adviser U.S. delegation ministerial sessions North Atlantic Council, 1966-67; dep. polit. adviser, counselor U.S. Mission to NATO, Brussels, 1968-70; counselor econ. affairs U.S. Mission to European Communities, Brussels, 1970-74, minister counselor, from 1974; U.S. rep. to UN Econ. and Social Council with rank of ambassador, 1975-77; alt. U.S. del. UN Gen. Assembly, 1975—76; alt. U.S. rep. UN Conf. on Trade and Devel., 1976; minister-counselor econ. and comml. affairs Am. Embassy, Paris, 1977-80; ret., 1980; dep. sec. gen. OECD, Paris, 1980-88. With U.S. Army, 1944—46, ETO. Decorated Bronze Star, Order of the Sacred treasure Gold and Silver medal Japan; recipient Meritorious Svc. award, State Dept., 1960. Mem.: Am. Fgn. Svc. Assn. (Rivkin award 1969), Artus, Phi Beta Kappa, Phi Eta Sigma, Pi Gamma Mu. Address: 2 rue Lucien Gaulard 75018 Paris France

MYERSON, ROBERT J. radiation oncologist, educator; b. Boston, May 12, 1947; s. Richard Louis and Rosemarie M.; m. Carla Wheatley, Aug. 8, 1970; 1 child, Jacob Wheatley. BA, Princeton U., 1969; PhD, U. Calif., Berkeley, 1974; MD, U. Miami, 1980. Diplomate Am. Bd. Radiology. Asst. prof. dept. physics Pa. State U., State Coll., 1974-76; fellow Inst. Advanced Studies, Princeton, N.J., 1976-78; resident U. Pa. Hosp., Phila., 1981-84; assoc. prof. radiology Washington U. Sch. Medicine, St. Louis, 1984-97, prof. radiology, 1997—. Contbr. articles to profl. jours. Recipient Career Devel. award Am. Cancer Soc., 1985. Fellow Am. Coll. Radiology; mem. Am. Coll. Radiation, Am. Soc. Therapeutic Radiologists, Am. Phys. Soc. Democrat. Jewish. Avocation: bicycling. Office: Washington U Radiation Oncology Ctr Box 8224 4921 Parkview Pl Saint Louis MO 63110-1001 Business E-Mail: myerson@radonc.wustl.edu.

MYERSON, ROGER BRUCE, economist, game theorist, educator; b. Boston, Mar. 29, 1951; s. Richard L. and Rosemarie (Farkas) M.; m. Regina M. Weber, Aug. 29, 1982; children: Daniel, Rebecca. AB summa cum laude, SM, Harvard U., 1973, PhD, 1976. Asst. prof. decision scis. Northwestern U., Evanston, Ill., 1976-78, assoc. prof., 1979-82, prof., 1982-2001, Harold Stuart prof. decision scis., 1986-2001, prof. econs., 1987-2001; W.C. Norby prof. econs. U. Chgo., 2001—. Guest researcher U. Bielefeld, Federal Republic of Germany, 1978-79; vis. prof. econs. U. Chgo., 1985-86, 2000-01. Author: Game Theory: Analysis of Conflict, 1991; mem. editorial bd. Internat. Jour. Game Theory, 1982-92, Games and Econ. Behavior, 1988-97; assoc. editor Jour. Econ. Theory, 1983-93; also articles. Guggenheim fellow, 1983-84; Sloan rsch. fellow, 1984-86. Fellow Econometric Soc., Am. Acad. Arts and Scis. (Midwest v.p. 1999-2002). Office: U Chgo Dept Econs 1126 E 59th St Chicago IL 60637 E-mail: myerson@uchicago.edu.

MYERS-RAMI, MASEQUA, theatrical company executive, theater producer; m. Pemon Rami, 1975. CEO, founder Masequa Myers & Assoc., 1992; co-founder Lamont Zeno Theatre and Cultural Arts Program, Chgo., 1973; appeared in, provided casting svcs. for 14 films and TV movies including Mahogany, The Spook Who Sat By the Door, 1975; co-prodr., co-dir., co-host series of radio dramas A Taste of Culture, WBMX Radio, Chgo., 1980; co-mgr. Phoenix Black Theatre Troupe, 1982; acad. dir., acting instr. Maria Gibbs' Crossroads Nat. Edn. and Arts. Ctr. of L.A., 1990. Prodr.: (romantic comedy) Miss Dessa (9 Beverly Hills/Hollywood NAACP Theatre awards), (recruitment video) Take a Close Look; dir.: (TV talk shows for series) Getting It Right; prodr., dir., creative cons., costume designer: (video) It's OK to Say No Way; Follow Your Dream; cons., prodr., dir., co-writer (touring prodn. and video) Give Life a Chance. Named one of Top 100 Prodrs. in Nation, AV Video Multimedia Prodr. mag.; recipient award, Joseph Jefferson Com. Chgo., Chgo. Black Theatre Alliance, Ariz. Commn. on Arts, Ariz. Health Edn. Media Makers award, award, Am. Advt. Fedn., Nat. Assn. Audio Visual Communicators, Key to City of Detroit. Mem.: SAG, Women in Entertainment, Phoenix Arts Commn. (mem. grant panel), Ill. Arts Coun. (mem. grant panel), Ariz. Commn. on Arts (mem. grant panel), Women in Film. Office: Masequa Myers & Assocs 6100 S Dorchester 1 West Chicago IL 60637

MYHRE, BYRON ARNOLD, pathologist, educator; b. Fargo, N.D., Oct. 22, 1928; s. Ben Arnold and Amy Lillian (Gilbertson) M.; m. Eileen Marguerite Scherling, June 16, 1953; children: Patricia Ann, Bruce Allen. BS, U. Ill., 1950; MS, Northwestern U., 1952, MD, 1953; PhD, U. Wis., 1962. Intern Evanston (Ill.) Hosp., 1953-54; resident Children's Meml. Hosp., Chgo., 1956-57, U. Wis. Hosp., Madison, 1957-60; assoc. med. dir. Milw. Blood Ctr., 1962-66; sci. dir. L.A. Red Cross Blood Ctr., 1966-72; dir. Blood Bank Harbor-UCLA Med. Ctr., Torrance, Calif., 1972-85, chief clin. pathology, 1985-2000; prof. pathology UCLA, 1972-2000, prof. emeritus, 2000—. Author: Quality Control on Blood Banking, 1974, (with others) Textbook of Clinical Pathology, 1972, Paternity Testing, 1975; editor seminar procs.; contbr. articles to med. jours., chpts. to books. Served with USAF, 1954-56. Mem.: AMA, Harbor-UCLA Faculty Soc. (past pres.), Wis. Blood Bank Assn. (past pres.), L.A. Acad. Medicine (past pres.), Calif. Blood Bank Sys. (past pres.), Calif. Med. Assn., Assn. Clin. Scientists, Coll. Am. Pathologists (chmn. blood bank survey com.), Am. Assn. Blood Banks (pres. 1978—79), Am. Soc. Clin. Pathology (dep. commr. commn. on continuing edn.), Palos Verdes Breakfast Club (past pres.). Home: 4004 Via Larga Vista Palos Verdes Estates CA 90274-1122 Office: Harbor UCLA Med Ctr 1000 W Carson St Torrance CA 90502-2004

MYHRE, JANET, mathematician, educator; b. Tacoma, Wash., Sept. 24, 1932; d. Leif Christian Klippen, Thelma Gladys Klippen; m. Philip Cushman Myhre, June 12, 1954 (div. Dec. 1984); 1 child, Karin Elizabeth; m. Leon Hollerman, May 29, 1988; 1 child, Jeremy Hollerman. BA summa cum laude, Pacific Luth. U., 1954; MA, U. Wash., 1956; PhD in Math. Stats (with highest hons.), U. Stockholm, 1968. Prof. math. Claremont McKenna Coll., Claremont, Calif., 1962—. Vis. prof. U. Stockholm, 1971—72, Swiss Fed. Inst. Tech., Zurich, 1971—72, Wash. State U., Pullman, 1978; prof. math. Claremont Grad. U., 1968—; founder, pres. Math. Analysis Rsch. Corp., Claremont, 1973—; dir. Reed Inst. for Decision Sci. Claremont McKenna Coll., Claremont, 1975—; cons. Strategic Sys. Programs USN, Washington, 1968—; cons. EPA, Washington, 1976—77. Contbr. chpts. in books, articles to profl. jours. Bd. trustees mem. The Webb Schs., Claremont, 1984—88; officer Padua Hills Homeowners Assn., Claremont, 1988—94. Recipient Austin Bonis award, Am. Soc. Quality Control, 1984; Rsch. grant, Office Naval Rsch., 1973—83. Mem.: Inst. Math. Stats., Am. Statis. Assn. (assoc. editor Technometrics 1969—75, coun. rep. 2001—03, pres. So. Calif. chpt. 2003—), Padua Hills Mus. Com., Phi Beta Kappa (pres. cmc chpt. 2004). Achievements include development of models/statistical theory used since 1972 by USN Ballistic Missile Program for reliability assessments; software/theory used by Fleet Ballistic Missile Program since 1990 for safety and risk assessment. Avocations: gardening, cooking, hiking, weaving. Office: Claremont McKenna Coll Adams Hall 9th St Claremont CA 91711

MYHREN, TRYGVE EDWARD, communications company executive; b. Palmerton, Pa., Jan. 3, 1937; s. Arne Johannes and Anita (Blatz) M.; m. Carol Jane Enman, Aug. 8, 1964; children: Erik, Kirsten, Tor; m. 2d Victoria Hamilton, Nov. 14, 1981; 1 stepchild, Paige. BA in Philosophy and Polit. Sci., Dartmouth Coll., 1958, MBA, 1959. Sales mgr., unit mgr. Procter and Gamble, Cin., 1963-65; sr. cons. Glendinning Cos., Westport, Conn., 1965-69; pres. Auberge Vintners, 1970-73; exec. v.p. Mktg. Continental, Westport, 1969-73; v.p., gen. mgr. CRM, Inc., Del Mar, Calif., 1973-75; from v.p. mktg. to pres. Am. TV and Comm. Corp., Englewood, Colo., 1975-80, chmn. bd., CEO, 1981-88; pres. Myhren Media Inc., Denver, 1989—. V.p., then exec. v.p. Time Inc., N.Y.C., 1981-88; mem. exec. com., treas., vice chmn., then chmn. bd. dirs. Nat. Cable TV Assn., Washington, 1982 91; mem. adv. com. on HDTV, FCC, 1987-89, pres. Providence Jour. Co.; bd. dirs. Advanced Mktg. Svcs., Inc., La Jolla, Calif.; Dreyfus Founders Funds, Inc., J. D. Edwards, Inc., Verio, Inc., Nat. Cable TV Ctr., Denver, Cable Labs, Inc., Boulder, Colo., Peapod, Inc., Skokie, Ill.; pres. Myhren Media, 1989—; pres., CEO King Broadcast Co., 1991-96. Mem. Colo. Forum, 1984—, chmn. higher edn. com., 1986; bd. dirs., co-founder Colo. Bus. Com. for the Arts, 1985-91; mem. exec. coun. Found. for Commemoration U.S. Constn., 1987-90; mem. Nat. GED Task Force, 1987-90, Colo. Baseball Commn., 1989-91, Colo. Film Commn., 1989-91; trustee Nat. Jewish Hosp., 1989— (Humanitarian award 1996), R.I. Hosp., 1991-95, Lifespan Health Sys., 1994-97, U.S. Ski and Snowboard Team Found., 1998—; chmn. Local Organizing Commn. 1995 NCAA Hockey Championship; trustee, exec. com., chmn. fin. com. U. Denver, 1997—. Lt. (j.g.) USNR, 1959-63. Recipient Disting. Leader award Nat. Cable TV Assn., 1988. Mem. Cable TV Adminstrn. and Mktg. Soc. (pres. 1978-79, Grand Tam award 1985, One of A Kind award 1994), Cable Adv. Bur. (co-founder 1978), Cable TV Pioneers. Episcopalian. Address: Myhren Media Inc 280 Detroit St # 200 Denver CO 80206-4807 E-mail: trygm@earthlink.net.

MYHRVOLD, NATHAN, technology executive; B in Math., M in Geophysics and Space Physics, U. Calif., 1979; M in Math. Econs., Princeton U., 1981; D in Theoretical and Math. Physics, 1983. Fellow dept. applied math. and theoretical physics Cambridge U., 1981-83; founder, pres., CEO Dynamical Sys., 1984-86; dir. spl. projects Microsoft Corp., Redmond, Wash., 1986, v.p. applications and content; chief tech. officer Advanced Tech. and Rsch., Redmond, Wash., Microsoft Corp., Redmond, Wash.; founder, mgr. Microsoft Rsch., chief tech. officer; CEO Intellectual Ventures, Bellevue, Wash. Bd. trustees Inst. Advanced Study, Princeton, N.J.; mem. Nat. Info. Infrastructure Adv. Coun.; adv. bd. Princeton U. dept. physics. Office: Intellectual Ventures 1756 114th Ave SE Ste 110 Bellevue WA 98004

MYKLEBY, KATHY, newscaster, reporter; Degree, U. Iowa, 1976. With KRNA-FM Radio, Iowa City, 1976, WKY-Radio, Oklahoma City, 1976—80, WVTV-TV Channel 18, Milw., 1980; reporter, anchor WISN, Milw., 1980—. Active telethon Children's Miracle Network; co-chmn. Briggs and Stratton Run/Walk for Children's Hosp. of Wis. Recipient Regional award for best TV feature, UP Internat., 1984, Best Single Report Contbg. to Cmty. Welfare award, Milw. Press Club, 1987, Press Club award, 1992, Best Spot News award, Wis. Broadcasters Assn., 1997. Office: WISN PO Box 402 Milwaukee WI 53201-0402

MYLNECHUK, LARRY HERBERT, financial executive; b. Littlefork, Minn., Mar. 9, 1948; s. William and Marjorie (Raco) M.; m. Sandy L. Henderson, Mar. 14, 1970; children: Kendra Elizabeth, Scott William. BA, Lewis & Clark Coll., Portland, 1970; JD, Lewis & Clark Coll., 1974. Legal specialist Oreg. Dept. Edn., Salem, 1976-82; sr. v.p., dir. Morley Capital Mgmt. Inc., Portland, 1982-89; founder, pres. Integra Assocs., Inc., Lake Oswego, Oreg., 1989—; exec. dir. The Stable Value Assn., Inc., Lake Oswego, 1990-96; co-founder, prin. Residential Capital Mgmt., LLC, 2000. Cons. Hueler Analytics, Inc., Mpls., 1989—; conf. chmn. GIC Nat. Forum Conf., Washington, 1993-95; arbitrator NASD, NY Stock Exch.; guest lectr. Portland State U., 1978, U. Oreg., 1980; bd. dirs. SAR Found. Contbr. articles to profl. jours. Founder Woodstock Neighborhood Assn., 1975; mem. Multnomah County (Oreg.) Charter Rev. Commn., 1978; mem. Tualatin (Oreg.) City Coun., 1980—84, Portland Com. on Fgn. Rels., 1976—98, bd. dirs., 1993—96; mem. Gov.'s Commn. on Adminstrv. Hearings, State of Oreg., 1988—89, Tchrs. Standards and Practices Commn., State of Oreg., 2000—02; mem. vestry, lay eucharistic min., del. State Episcopal Conv., 1996; mem. Diocesan Coun., 1996—98; mem. vestry Christ Ch. Parish, 1995—2000, Christ Episcopal Ch., 1998—2000; founding mem. St. Margaret's Ch., 2000—; trustee St. Francis of Assisi Endowment Fund, 1993; bd. dirs. Patriot Found., 2002—. Fellow NEH, 1979, ednl. policy fellow George Washington U., 1980. Mem. SAR (pres. Lewis and Clark chpt.,pres. Oreg. State Soc. 1997, nat. trustee, 1997-98, v.p. Gen.-Pacific dist. 1999-2001), Western Pension Conf., Assn. Soc. Execs., World Affairs Coun. Oreg., Citizen Amb. Program to Western Europe, Gen. Soc. The War of 1812, Soc. Colonial Wars, Sons and Daus. of Pilgrims, Oregon Soc. Sons of the Revolution (co-founder, treas. 1996), Internat. Bus. Forum (mem. adv. bd. 1996), Sons of the Bench and Bar (charter), N. Am. Soc. Securities Adminstrs. (profl. stds. com. 1998), Oreg. Assn. Adminstrv. Law Judges, Soc. Magna Charta Barons, Crown of Charlemagne Soc., Soc. Charlemagne's Descendants, Col. George Middleton Hist. Soc. (bd. dirs.) Democrat. Episcopalian. Avocations: hiking, diving. Office: Residential Capital Mgt LLC PO Box 1594 Lake Oswego OR 97035-0013 Office Phone: 503-697-8697.

MYLONAKIS, STAMATIOS GREGORY, patent agent, polymer science consultant; b. Athens, Aug. 18, 1937; s. Gregory S. and Vassiliki (Charalambopoulos) Mylonakis; m. Pamela H. Morton, May 5, 1965 (dec. Mar. 1978); 1 child, Gregory (dec.). BS, Nat. U. of Athens, 1961; MS, Ill. Inst. of Tech., 1964; PhD, Mich. State U., 1970. Rsch. assoc. Ill. Inst. of Tech., Chgo., 1964—65; rsch. scientist Brookhaven Nat. Lab., Upton, NY, 1965—68; instr. U. Calif., Berkeley, 1971—73; group leader Rohm and Haas Co., Springhouse, Pa., 1973—76; supr. DeSoto, Inc., Des Plaines, Ill., 1976—79; staff scientist Borg-Warner Corp., Des Plaines, 1979—82, mgr., 1982—87; dept. head Enichem Am., Monmouth Junction, NJ, 1988—94; tech. advisor, registered patent agt. law firm Oblon, Spivak, Arlington, Va., 1994—2000; cons., patent law practitioner, 2000—; sci. fellow Nuc. Rsch. Ctr. Democritos, Athens, 1960—62. Tech. adv. bd. Ctr. Applied Polymer Rsch. Case Western Res. U., Cleve.; adv. bd. NSF Ctr. Polymer Interfaces Lehigh U. Assoc. editor: Jour. Applied Polymer Sci.; contbr. articles to profl. jours. Lt. Greek Army. Fellow Sci., Nuc. Rsch. Ctr. Democritos, Athens, Greece, 1960—62, NSF, Mich. State U., 1968—70, U. Calif., 1971—73. Mem.: AAAS, Am. Chem. Soc., N.Y. Acad. Scis., Sigma Xi. Greek Orthodox. Achievements include patents in field of polymer sci. tech. Avocations: photography, painting, travel. Home and Office: 7009 Cashell Manor Ct Derwood MD 20855-1201 Personal E-mail: mylonakis@msn.com.

MYLOTTE, JOHN ARNOLD, writer, educator; b. Phila., Pa., Aug. 26, 1942; s. Thomas Joseph and Pauline Ellen (Arnold) Mylotte; m. Eva Benda, Sept. 20, 1997; 1 stepchild, Ilya; m. Florence Ellen Noonan, Aug. 14, 1977 (div. Nov. 1992). BA in english, Villanova U., 1964; MA in english, Lehigh U., 1967; JD, Suffolk U. Law Sch., 1980; post grad, MIT, 1981. Bar: Mass. 1981. Tech. editor Naval Air Engrng. Ctr., Phila., 1967—68; sr. tech. editor Navy

Clothing & Textile Rsch. Lab., 1968—72; dir. tech. publ. Navy Clothing & Textile Rsch., 1973—91; dir. pub. rels. Navy Clothing & Textile Rsch. Lab., 1974—91; pres. TechWrite Assoc., 1987—. Adj. prof.,sr. lectr. Northeastern U., Boston, 1981—. Author: (book) Guide to Writing the Formal Technical Report, 1985, The Art of Technical Writing, 1987; contbr. articles to jours. Elected mem. Framingham Town Mtg., 1975—78; Relay for Life Vol. Am. Cancer Society, 1995—; bd. mem. Big Brother-Big Sister Assn., Framingham, Mass., 1975—78, bd. pres., 1977—78. Recipient Command Hist. award, U.S. Navy Hist., 1981, Outstanding Performance award, U.S. Navy Dept., 1980—85. Mem.: Worcester County Poetry Soc., Longfellow Soc., Soc. for Tech. Commn. (5 commpetitive tech. writing awards 1984—86). Independent. Unitarian Universalist. Avocation: writing. Office: TechWrite Assoc 11 Clemmons St Southborough MA 01772

MYMIT, CHUCK W. music educator, musician; b. N.Y.C., Dec. 15, 1948; s. Jack Mymit, Gloria Epstein; m. Maria Laura Asuaje, Aug. 16, 1993. BMus in Composition, Berklee Coll. of Music, Boston, 1971; MA in Composition, NYU, 1982. Asst. prof. Five Towns Coll., Seaford, NY, 1973—87, prof. jazz studies Dix Hills, NY, 1973—87, 2000—; tchr. music N.Y.C. Bd. Edn., 1987—97; coord. music Peninsula Counceling Ctr., L.I., NY, 1997—2000; house pianist Nordstroms Dept. Store, L.I., 1997—2000. Jazz comml. pianist AF of M, Local 802, N.Y.C., 1973—; freelance arranger/composer, N.Y.C., 1973—; editor FTC Press Five Towns Coll., 2000—; guest condr. NMEA All State Jazz Ensemble, NY, 2002. Author: (book) A Beginner's Approach to Jazz Improvisation, 1973, Contemporary Harmony I and Workbook, 1977, Contemporary Harmony II and Workbook, 1979, Arranging for Small Band, 1980, Club Date Pianist, 1981, Voicing Techniques for the Arranger, 1997, Contemporary Concepts in Jazz Harmony, 2001; composer, pianist, arranger: CD's Tú Eras Mi Corazon, 1995; composer (pianist, arranger): The Romantic Pianist, 1995 (X-Tisch Sch. of Arts award for film composition, 95), Reflections, 1998, Ambience, 2001, music score, music performed at Carnegie Hall and Tilles Ctr. Named Most Valuable Player, Nordstroms Dept. Store, N.Y., 1997. Mem.: ASCAP, Internat. Assn. Jazz Educators. Avocation: sports. Office: Five Towns College 305 N Service Rd Dix Hills NY 11746

MYNATT, CECIL FERRELL, psychiatrist; b. Knoxville, Tenn., May 10, 1920; s. Cecil Ferrell and Ethel (May) Mynatt; m. Minnie Lee Rouser, Dec. 8, 1945 (div. Nov. 1988); children: Matthew, Cecilia, Melissa, Martha, Richard; m. Yong Cha Lee, Oct. 10, 1990; children: Katherine, John. BS, U. Tenn., 1950, MD, 1951. Pvt. practice in gen. medicine, Morristown, Tenn., 1952-61; resident Menninger Sch. Psychiatry, 1961-65; suprt. Ea. State Hosp., Knoxville, 1965-67; pvt. practice Wright Ferry Hosp., Knoxville, 1967-68; pvt. practice, co-owner Pvt. Hosp., Knoxville, 1968-73, Las Vegas, 1973-84; dir. Taliferro Mental Health Ctr., Lawton, Okla., 1984-89; supt. Western State Hosp., Woodword, Okla., 1989-91; med. dir. Rolling Hills Psychiat. Hosp., Ada, Okla., 1991-96; med. dir. behavioral medicine Mercy Meml. Hosp., Ardmore, Okla., 1996—. CEO Sun Enterprises, Inc., Ada, 1987—; cons. Pononotoc County Mental Health Assn., Ada, 1992-96, Valley View Meml. Hosp., Ada, 1992-96. Editor, pub. Voice of Experience, 1993—; contbr. articles to profl. jours. Maj. OSS, 1941-45. Decorated Silver star, Bronze star, (2) Purple Hearts. Mem. VFW, AMA, Okla. Med. Assn., Pononotoc County Med. Assn. Republican. Baptist. Avocations: motocycling, bowling, walking with wife. Home: 126 Kings Rd Ada OK 74820

MYRDAL, ROSEMARIE CARYLE, state official, former state legislator; b. Minot, North Dakota, May 20, 1929; d. Harry Dirk and Olga Jean (Dragge) Lohse; m. B. John Myrdal, (dec.) June 21, 1952; children: Jan, Mark, Harold, Paul, Amy. BS, N.D. State U., 1951. first grade tchr., N.D. Tchr., ND, 1951-71; bus. mgr. Edinburg Sch. Dist., ND, 1974-81; mem. N.D. Ho. of Reps., Bismarck, ND, 1984-92, mem. appropriations com., 1991-92; lt. gov. State of N.D., Bismarck, 1993—2001. Sch. evaluator Walsh County Sch. Bd. Assn., Grafton, N.D., 1983-84; evaluator, work presenter N.D. Sch. Bd. Assn., Bismarck, 1983-84; mem. sch. bd. Edinburg Sch. Dist., 1981-90; adv. com. Red River Trade Corridor, Inc., 1989-2001. Co-editor: Heritage '76, 1976, Heritage '89, 1989. Precinct committeewoman Gardar Twp. Rep. Com., 1980-86; leader Hummingbirds 4-H Club, Edinburg, 1980-83; bd. dir. Camp Sioux Diabetic Children, Grand Forks, N.D., 1980-90; N.D. affiliate Am. Diabetes Assn., Families First-Child Welfare Reform Initiative, Region IV, 1989-92; dir. N.D. Diabetes Assn., 1989-91; chmn. N.D. Ednl. Telecom. Coun., 1989-90; vice chmn. N.D. Legis. Interim Jobs Devel. Commn., 1989-90. Mem. AAUW (pres. 1982-84 Pembina County area), Pembina County Hist. Soc. (historian 1976-84); Northeastern N.D. Heritage Assn. (pres. 1986-92), Red River Valley Heritage Soc. (bd. dir. 1985-92); N.D. Sch. to Work Mgmt. Team chair-person Clubs: Agassiz Garden (Park River) (pres. 1968-69). Republican. Lutheran. Avocations: gardening, architecture, ethnic foods, history, cultural preservation. Home: 12987 80th St NE Edinburg ND 58227-9635

MYREN, ALLEN W(ILLIAM), retired music educator; s. Rolland H. and Marie E.E. Myren; m. Kathleen P. Nicoline; children: Scott A., Trista N., Laura A.C. BS in Music Edn. (cum laude), BS in Math Edn. (cum laude), U. Wis., LaCrosse, 1970; MS in Music Edn. (cum laude), U. Ill., 1977. Choral dir. LaCrescent (Minn.) Pub. Schs., 1970—71, Warren Twp. H.S., Gurnee, Ill., 1971—2004, Coll. Lake County, Grayslake, Ill., 1983—90; ret., 2004. Golf coach Warren Twp. H.S., Gurnee, 1974—; choral dir. concert Disneyland, 1986, 2002, Knott's Berry Farm, 1986, Sea World Fla., 1988, 90, Disneyworld, 1988, 90, 96, 2004, Ravinia Winterfest, 1990—2000, Carnegie Hall, 1998; guest condr. Lake County Children's Choral Festival, 1991, Midwest Luth. Choral Festival, 1993, Lakes Summer Choir, 1996, Nat. Luth. Choral Festival, 1992. Bd. dirs. Lake County (Ill.) Arts Coun., 1987—90; musician, arranger St. Paul Luth. Ch., Round Lake Beach, Ill., 1985—2003. Mem.: NARAS (clinician 1996, 1997, 1999), Am. Choral Dirs. Assn. (clinician 1996, 1997), Music Educators Nat. Conf. (assoc.; dist. chairperson 1983—88, clinician 1984, 2000). Independent. Lutheran. Achievements include choral dir. award winning choruses. Avocations: golf, travel. Home: 196 Southridge Dr Gurnee IL 60031 Personal E-mail: amyren@lightfirst.com.

MYRICK, BISMARCK, diplomat; b. Portsmouth, Va., Dec. 23, 1940; m. Marie Pierre Mbaye; children: Bismarck Jr., Wesley Todd, Allison Elizabeth. BA, U. Tampa, 1972; MA, Syracuse U., 1973, postgrad., 1979-80; LHD (hon.), Spelman Coll., 2002. Enlisted U.S. Army, 1959; desk officer for Somalia, U.S. Dept. State, Washington, 1980-82; advanced through grades to maj., 1975; ret., 1979; polit. officer Am. Embassy, Monrovia, Liberia, 1982-84; action officer office strategic nuclear policy bur. politico-milit. affairs U.S. Dept. State, 1985-87, dep. dir. policy plans and coordination bur. inter-Am. affairs, 1987-89, Una Chapman Cox fellow US-African Policy, 1988-90; consul gen. Am. Consulate Gen., Durban, South Africa, 1990-93, Capetown, South Africa, 1993-95; amb. to Lesotho, Am. Embassy, Maseru, 1995-98; diplomat-in-residence Atlanta U. Ctr. at Spelman Coll., 1998-99; U.S. amb. to Liberia Dept. of State, Monrovia, Liberia, 1999—2002; univ. lectr. internat. affairs Old Dominion U., 2002—; sr. fellow Joint Forces Staff Coll., Norfolk, Va., 2002—. Author: Three Aspects of Crisis in Colonial Kenya, 1975. Decorated Silver Star, Purple Heart, 4 Bronze Stars; named to U.S. Army Hall of Fame, 1996; named Ambassador Bismarck Myrick Days, City of Portsmouth, Va., 2000, Bismarck Myrick St. and Bismarck Myrick Crescent St. named in his honor, 2002. Mem.: World Affairs Coun. Hampton Rds. (bd. dirs. 2004—). Address: 1200 Mill Run Chesapeake VA 23322

MYRICK, CECILIA JANE, education educator, consultant; b. Atlanta, Ga., Aug. 31, 1951; d. James Manuel and Mattie Lean Myrick; 1 child, Celia Nicole. BA in English, Ga. State U., 1979, Med in Reading Instrn., 1983, PhD in Reading Instrn., 1996. Tchr. Cert. in Reading and Language Arts(T-7) Ga. Profl. Sds. Commn., 2002. Prof. in reading and lang. arts Governors State U., Univ. Pk., Ill., 1995—96; owner, instr. Home Study Program and Tutoring Svc., Atlanta, 1996—97; reading specialist SW Dekalb HS, Dekalb County Schs., Atlanta, 1997—98; asst. prof. reading and English Bethune-Cookman Coll., Daytona Beach, 1998—2000; chairperson, asst. prof., dir. of student tchg. dept. of edn. Morris Brown Coll., Atlanta, 2000—03; lit. coach Atlanta Pub. Schs., 2003—04. Copy editor Khepera Inst., Atlanta, 1990—97; ednl. cons. African Am. Acad., Cin., 1994—96; ednl. cons., assoc. One World Archives, Atlanta, 1998—; cons. in reading and African Am. curriculum U. Charter Acad., Atlanta U. Ctr. sponsored sch., 2002—03; mem. bd. dirs. U. Charter Acad., Atlanta, 2002—03; adj. prof. reading Ga. State U., Atlanta, 2004—. Author: (ednl. multimedia textbook) African Legacy, 1999, (website) Cultural Diversity Based on Cultural Grounding: A Cross-Cultural Literacy Curriculum, 2000. Grantee Creative tchg. Mini-grant, Bethune-Cookman Rsch. Found., 1999. Mem.: AAUP, Nat. Coun. for Black Studies, Assn. of Supervision and Curriculum Devel., Nat. Coun. of Tchr.s of English, Internat. Reading Assn. Avocations: reading, collecting african artifacts, interior decorating. Office: PO Box 42538 Atlanta GA 30311

MYRICK, SUE, congresswoman, former mayor; b. Tiffin, Ohio, Aug. 1, 1941; d. William Henry and Margaret Ellen (Roby) Wilkins; m. Jim Forest (div.); children: Greg, Dan; m. Wilbur Edward Myrick Jr., Sept. 11, 1977. Student, Heidelberg Coll., 1959-60, LLD (hon.), 1995. Exec. sec. to mayor and city mgr. City of Alliance, Ohio, 1962-63; dir. br. office Stark County Ct. of Juvenile and Domestic Rels., Alliance, 1963-65; pres. Myrick Agy., Charlotte, N.C., 1971-95; mayor City of Charlotte, 1987-91; pres. Myrick Enterprises, 1992—94; mem. 104th-108th Congress from 9th N.C. Dist., Washington, 1995—. Candidate for U.S. Senate from N.C., 1992. Active Heart Fund, Multiple Sclerosis, March of Dimes, Arts and Scis. Fund Dr.; past mem. adv. bd. Uptown Shelter, Uptown Homeless Task Force, bd. dirs. N.C. Inst. Politics; v.p. Sister Cities Internat.; mem. Pres. Bush's Affordable Housing Commn.; founder, coord. Charlotte vol. tornado relief effort; former bd. dirs. Learning How; former mem. adv. bd. U.S. Conf. Mayors; mem.-at-large Charlotte City Coun., 1983-85, Strengthening Am. Commn.; lay leader, Sunday sch. tchr. 1st United Meth. Ch.; treas. Mecklenburg Ministries; former trustee U.S. Conf. of Mayors. Recipient Woman of Yr. award Harrisonburg, Va., 1968; named one of Outstanding Young Women of Am., 1968. Mem. Women's Polit. Caucus, Beta Sigma Phi. Republican. Home and Office: Myrick Enterprises 9169 Bonnie Briar Cir Charlotte NC 28277-1576 also: US House Reps 230 Cannon Hob Washington DC 20515-0001

MYRRDIN, TERRY A. state agency administrator; b. San Diego, Aug. 31, 1950; d. Bernard O. Wallen, Jr. and Mary Ann Snyder; children: Sherilyn Ann Pillsbury, Gina Marie Pillsbury. AA, Am. River Coll., Sacramento, CA, 1970. Cert. clinical hypnotherapist Am. Coun. Hypnotists Examiners. Asst. govtl. program analyst Dept. Indsl. Rels., Sacramento, 1994—2000; spl. asst. Gov. Gray Davis, Sacramento, 2000—03, Sec. of State, Sacramento, 2003—. Owner, wedding cons. Social Graces, 1985—87. Avocations: feng shui, travel, gardening, reading. Office: Sec of State 1500 11th St 6th Fl Sacramento CA 95814

MYRSIADES, KOSTAS YANNIS, literature educator; b. Vourliotes, Samos, Greece, May 21, 1940; came to U.S., 1948; s. John and Mary (Lagos) M.; m. Linda Suny, June 6, 1965; children: Yani, Leni. BA in English, Iowa U., 1963; MA in Comparative Lit., Ind. U., 1965, PhD in Comparative Lit., 1972; cert. in modern and classical Greek, U. Athens, Greece, 1966. Instr. English Greek-Am. Cultural Inst., Athens, 1965-66, 69; asst. prof. modern Greek, dir. Ctr. for Hellenic Studies Deree Coll., Athens, 1973-74; asst. prof. English West Chester (Pa.) U., 1969-73, assoc. prof., 1974-77, prof., 1977—, chair dept. English, 1985-90. Coord. grad. English studies West Chester U., 1983-85, coord. comparative lit. studies, 1983—, assoc. dean. faculty of arts and scis., 1982-83, active numerous coms., 1972—; conf. organizer Balch Inst. Ethnic Studies, Phila., 1985; participant Delaware Valley Faculty Exch. at U. Pa., 1984; editorial cons. Centrum Phila. Pub. Co., 1981-83, G.K. Hall, Boston, 1974-81, N.J. Dept. Higher Edn.; Greek examiner Temple U., Phila., 1977—, U. Md., 1978—, Albright Coll., Reading, Pa., 1980-83; presenter numerous profl. confs., 1969—. Author: Takis Paptsonis, 1974, Approaches to Teaching Homer's Iliad and Odyssey, 1987, (with Kimon Friar) Yannis Ritsos: Scripture of the Blind, 1979, Yannis Ritsos: Monovasis and the Women of Monemvasia, 1987, Takis Papatsonis, Ursa Minor and Other Poems, 1988, Cultural Representation in Historical Resistance, 1999, (with Linda S. Myrsiades) The Karagiozis Heroic Performance in Greek Shadow Theater, 1988, Karagiozis: Culture and Comedy in Greek Puppet Theater, 1992, (with Kimon Friar) Yannis Ritsos: Selected Poems, 1938-88, 1989, Others Must Dance for the Lord Dionysus Now, 1993, Margins in the Classroom: Teaching Literature, 1994; editor: (with Jerry McGuire) Order and Partialities; Theory, Pedagogy, and the "Postcolonial," 1995, Racing Representation, 1998, Un-Disciplining Literature, 1999, (with Henry Giroux) Beyond the Corporate University, 2001, The Beat Generation, 2002; editor Coll. Lit., 1990—, Jour. Hellenic Diaspora, 1991—; contbr. book revs. to World Lit. Today, Coll. Lit. Planning grantee Phila. Coun. Humanities, 1983; dissertation grantee Ind. U., 1967; Lily fellow U. Pa., 1981; honorarium recipient G.K. Hall, 1976-81, Temple U. Press, 1979—, Ohio State U. Press, 1982—, Holt, Reinhart and Winston, 1982—, Centrum Phila., 1983—. Mem. Am. Lit. Translators Assn., Am. Comparative Lit. Assn., Assn. of Depts. of English, Assn. for Computers and the Humanities, Modern Lang. Assn. (honorarium 1982—), Nat. Assn. Self-Instructional Programs, Modern Greek Studies Assn., Assn. Pa. State Coll. and Univ. Faculty (chmn. com. of departmental chairs 1986—), English Assn. of Pa. State Univs., Greek-Turkish Univ. Alliance (co-dir. 1984—), Hellenic-Am. League of Phila., Hellenic Univ. Club of Phila. Home: 370 Malin Rd Newtown Square PA 19073-4271 Office: West Chester U Dept English 210 E Rosedale Ave West Chester PA 19380

MYSAK, LAWRENCE ALEXANDER, oceanographer, climatologist, mathematician, educator; b. Saskatoon, Sask., Can., Jan. 22, 1940; s. Stephen and Nettie Mysak; m. Diane Mary Eeles, Aug. 15, 1974; children: Paul Alexander, Claire Anastasia. BSc, U. Alta., Can., 1961; MSc, U. Adelaide, Australia, 1963; AM, Harvard U., 1964, PhD, 1967. Rsch. fellow Harvard U., 1966-67; mem. faculty U. B.C., Vancouver, 1967-86, prof. math. and oceanography, 1976-86; Atmospheric Environ. Svc./Natural Scis. Engring. Rsch. Coun.; sr. indsl. rsch. prof. climatology McGill U., Montreal, Que., Can., 1986-96, dir. Climate Rsch Group, 1986-90, Can. Steamship Lines prof. meteorology, 1989—, founding dir. Ctr. for Climate and Global Change Rsch., 1990-96. Vis. rsch. assoc. Oreg. State U., summer 1968; sr. visitor Cambridge (Eng.) U., 1971-72; vis. scientist Inst. Ocean Sci., Sidney, B.C., fall 1976, Nat. Ctr. Atmospheric Rsch., Boulder, Colo., 1977; vis. prof. U.S. Naval Postgrad. Sch., Monterey, Calif., summer 1981, Swiss Fed. Inst., Tech., Zurich, 1982-83, 2000-2001; George's Lemaître vis. prof. Cath. U. Louvain, Belgium, 1995; invitation fellowship for rsch. in Japan, Japan Soc. for Promotion of Scis., 1997; supr. 70 grad. and postdoctoral students, 1967—; vis. prof. Italian Nat. Inst. Geophysics and Volcanology, Bologna, 2001; exch. lectr. Royal Soc. Can. Nat. Acad. Scis. of Ukraine, 2002. Co-author: Waves in the Ocean, 1978; also articles in profl. jours.; assoc. editor Jour. Phys. Oceanography, 1977-92, Atmospheric-Ocean, 1988-91, Climatol. Bull., 1992-93; contbg. editor Am. Geophys. Union books on coastal and esturaine studies, 1987-2000; mem. editl. bd. Geophys. and Astrophys. Fluid Dynamics, 1983-96; series editor: Kluwer Acad. Pubs. Atmospheric and Oceanographic Scis. Libr., 2001-. Recipient Patterson Disting. Svc. medal Environ. Can. Atmospheric Environment Svc., 1997; appt. Order of Can., 1996. Fellow Acad. of Sci. of Royal Soc. Can. (v.p. Acad. of Sci. 1991-93, pres. 1993-96), Am. Meteorol. Soc., Am. Geophys. Union; mem. Can. Applied Math. Soc., Can. Meteorol. and Oceanog. Soc. (co-recipient Pres.'s prize 1980, J.P. Tully medal Oceanography 1997, inaugural fellow 1999), Royal Soc. Can. (life), European Geophys. Union, Academia Europaea (fgn.), Internat. Assn. for Phys. Scis. of Ocean (v.p. 2003—). Office: McGill U 805 Sherbrooke St W Montreal QC Canada H3A 2K6 E-mail: lawrence.mysak@mcgill.ca.

MYSKO, WILLIAM KIEFER, emergency physician, educator; b. Orange, N.J., Nov. 7, 1943; s. William J. and June O. (Kiefer) Mysko; m. Madeleine R. Seipp, June 16, 1969 (div. Feb. 2001); children: Claire, Joseph, Luke, Martha. BS, Rutgers U., 1966; DO, Phila. Coll. Osteo. Medicine, 1975. Bd. cert. diplomate Am. Bd. Emergency Medicine. Intern Walter Reed Army Med. Ctr., Washington, 1975-76; gen. med. officer U.S. Army Health Clinic, Ft. Monroe, Va., 1976-78; emergency physician St. Joseph Hosp., Towson, Md., 1979-83; dir. emergency medicine Mercy Hosp., Balt., 1983-89, Church Hosp., Balt., 1989-90; emergency physician John Hopkins Bayview Med. Ctr., Balt., 1990-91; asst. prof., clin. dir. Johns Hopkins Hosp., Balt., 1991-96, sr. attending emergency physician, 1996—. Contbr. articles to profl. jours. Capt. U.S. Army, 1975-78. Fellow Am. Coll. Emergency Physicians. Avocations: sports, music, travel, art. Office: Johns Hopkins Hosp Dept Emergency Medicine Baltimore MD 21287-0001

MYSLINSKI, NORBERT RAYMOND, medical educator; b. Buffalo, Apr. 14, 1947; s. Bernard and Amelia Joan (Lesniak) M.; m. Patricia Ann Byrne, June 19, 1970 (dec. 1980); m. René Carter, Nov. 21, 1993; children: Matthew Ryan, Kelly Lynn. BS in Biology, Canisius Coll., Buffalo, 1965-69; PhD in Pharmacology, U. Ill., Chgo., 1973. Rsch. assoc. Tufts U., Boston, 1973-75; asst. prof. U. Md., Balt., 1975-80, assoc. prof. physiology, 1980—, co-dir. Facial Pain Clinic, 1980-84, instr. nursing, 1982-84; rsch. fellow U. Bristol, Eng., 1984-85; adj. assoc. prof. U. Md. Sch. Nursing, 1997—. Instr. C.C. Balt., 1980—82; dir. grad. program dept. physiology U. Md., 1981—97, dir. HS biomedical rsch. program, 2000—, mem. faculty Marine-Estuarine Environ. Scis. grad. program, 1988—97; founder, dir. Patricia Byrne Nursing Scholarship Fund Trocaire Coll., Buffalo, 1985; dir. NIH Minority Rsch. Apprentice Program Balt. Coll. Dental Surgery, 1988—99; mem. grant rev. com. Nat. Inst. Nursing Rsch., 1993—94; grant reviewer Dept. Health and Human Svcs., 1993—94; cons. in field; appeared on more than 20 live TV and radio programs; founder, dir. Internat. Brain Bee, 1999—; chmn. Neuroscience Edn. Workshop, Prague, Czech Republic, 2003—; mem. com. Md. Higher Edn. Commn., 2003—. Editor newsletters Med. Soc. Md. Rsch., 1977-82, Brain Storm, 1999—; author book chpts., revs. and numerous abstracts on pharmacology and neurosci.; inventor in field; reviewer 7 jours. Rep. task force on aging U. Md., 1979—84; instr. Am. Heart Assn., Balt., 1978, ARC, Balt., 1977—83; Internat. Co. Md. chpt. ARC, 2003—; com. mem. Md. Higher Edn. Commn., 2003—; mem. Pres. Bush's Sec. of Edn. Summit on Sci., Washington, 2004; eucharistic min., pastoral visitor Cath. Ch., 1983—93; bd. dirs. Md. Brain Awareness Week, Md., 1996—, Balt. Brains Rule!, 2002—, Md. Brain Lit. Competition, 2000—, Md. Brain Art Competition, 2000—. Capt. U.S. Army, 1969—77. Grantee NIH, various drug cos. and founds.; USPHS fellow, 1969-73; recipient Alumni of Yr. award St. Mary's HS, Lancaster, NY, 1996, Disting. Alumni award outstanding career Canisius Coll., Buffalo, 1997, Time to Care Cmty. Svc. award U. Md., 1998, Founders Day Pub. Svc. award U. Md., 2000. Mem.: HS Neuroscience (founder 2003), Am. Soc. Pharmacology Exptl. Therapeutics, Soc. Neuroscience (pres. Balt. chpt. 1990—92, editor newsletter 1990—97, neuroscience literacy com. 1997—2001), Am. Physiol. Soc., Internat. Assn. Dental Rsch. (adv. 1980—81), Md. Soc. Med. Rsch. (exec. com. 1978—86, bd. dir. 1978—86), Internat. Brain Rsch. Orgn., European Brain Behavior Soc. (hon.). Republican. Home: 9395 Carrie Way Ellicott City MD 21042-1701 Office: U Md Sch Dentistry Dept Biomed Scis 666 W Baltimore St Baltimore MD 21201-1510 Office Phone: 410-706-7258. Office Fax: 410-706-0193. Business E-Mail: nrm001@dental.umaryland.edu.

MYSORE, SHRIKANTH BHASKAR, operations research specialist; b. Bangalore, Karnataka, India, Dec. 25, 1977; s. Bhaskar Ramarao and Gayathri Mysore. Grad. studies, U. of Ala., Tuscaloosa, 2001—. Rsch. asst. R. V. Coll. of Engring., Bangalore, India, 1995—99; grad. rsch. asst. Wichita State U., Kans., 2000—01. Rsch. cons. Ala. Productivity Ctr., Tuscaloosa, Ala., 2001—. Contbr. developed ergonomic chair design Ergonomic chair for Wiring harness (Second Prize, Am. Soc. Safety, 2001). Helped in blood donation camps Rotract, Bangalore, India, 1995—99. Mem.: Soc. Indsl. and Applied Math., Inst. for Ops. Rsch. and Mgmt. Sci. Hindu. Achievements include development of genetic algorithm based heuristic for scheduling Job Shops with Distinct Due Date Constraints on jobs. Avocations: jogging, driving, films. Home: 417 Reed St #4A Tuscaloosa AL 35401 Office: Ala Productivity Ctr 249 Bidgood Hall Box 870318 Tuscaloosa AL 35487-0318 E-mail: mbshrikanth@hotmail.com.

MYTELKA, ARNOLD KRIEGER, lawyer; b. Jersey City, July 24, 1937; s. Herman Donald and Jeannette (Krieger) M.; m. Rosalind Marcia Kaplan, Dec. 17, 1961; children: Andrew Charles, Daniel Sommer. AB, Princeton U., 1958; LLB cum laude, Harvard U., 1961; postgrad., London Sch. Econs., 1961—62. Bar: N.J. 1961, U.S. Dist. Ct. N.J. 1963, U.S. Supreme Ct. 1970, U.S. Ct. Appeals (3d cir.) 1978, U.S. Dist. Ct. (so. and ea. dist.) N.Y. 1983. Law sec. Chief Justice N.J. Supreme Ct., Newark, 1962-63; assoc. Clapp & Eisenberg, Newark, 1963-68, ptnr., 1968-94; prin. Kraemer, Burns, Mytelka, Lovell & Kulka, Springfield, N.J., 1994—. Lectr. Rutgers Law Sch., Newark, 1973; mem. Am. Law Inst., Phila., 1989—; mem. cons. group The Law Governing Lawyers, 1990-99; founding trustee Newark Legal Svcs. Project, 1965-68; trustee Edn. Law Ctr., 1974-75; chmn. dist. V ethics com. Supreme Ct. N.J., 1983-84, mem. 1981-84; trustee Legal Svcs. Found. Essex County, 1982—, pres., 1990-92; lectr. in land use law. Mem. editorial bd. N.J. Law Jour., 1991—; contbr. legal articles to profl. jours. Chmn. bd. trustees Ramapo Coll. NJ, 1979-80; mediator chancery divsn. NJ Superior Ct., 1990—, trustee, 1998-2000, 2003—, spl. fiscal agt., 1997, 2003, spl. master, 1999-2000. Frank Knox Meml. fellow Harvard U., London Sch. Econs. and Polit. Sci., 1961-62. Mem. ABA (mem. litigation sect.), N.J. State Bar Assn. (chmn. appellate practices study com. 1977-79, chmn. land use sect. 1984-85). Home: 56 Hall Rd Chatham NJ 07928-1723 Office: Kraemer Burns Mytelka Lovell & Kulka 675 Morris Ave Springfield NJ 07081-1523 E-mail: amytelka@kraemerburns.com.

NA, TSUNG SHUN (TERRY NA), Chinese studies educator, writer; b. Beijing, Nov. 3, 1932; came to U.S., 1964; s. Chi-L and Hui (Hu) N.; m. Yen Yen Chao, 1964. BA, Taiwan Normal U., 1956; MA, U. B.C., 1970; PhD, U. Minn., 1978. Assoc. prof. Taipei Normal Coll., Taiwan, Republic of China, 1956-64; vis. lectr. Ind. U., Bloomington, 1964-66; asst. prof. U. Minn., Mpls., 1970-80; vis. prof. Sun Yat-sen U., Taiwan, 1981-84; prof., dir. Am. Inst. Chinese Studies, Charles Town, W.Va., 1985—. Author: (English books) A Linguistic Study of P'i-pa Chi, 1969, Studies on Dream of the Red Chamber: A Selected and Classified Bibliography, 1979, Supplement, 1981, Taiwan Studies on Dream of the Red Chamber: A Selected and Classified Bibliography, 1983, Chinese Studies in English: A Selected Bibliography, 1991, (Chinese) Mandarin Pronunciation, 1966, Teaching Chinese in the U.S.A., 1983, Studies on Chinese Classical Novels, 1985, A Collection of Short Stories, 1987; contbr. numerous articles, short stories, and research essays to jours. and newspapers in U.S., Taiwan, ROC, and China. Mem. MLA, Assn. Asian Studies. Office: Am Inst Chinese Studies PO Box 453 Charles Town WV 25414-0453

NABEL, ELIZABETH G. medical researcher, cardiologist; BA summa cum laude, St. Olaf Coll., 1974; postgrad., Union Theol. Sem., 1974-75, Columbia U., 1975-77; MD, Cornell U., 1981; DHC (hon.), Katholik U. Leuven, 2001. Diplomate Am. Bd. Internal Medicine and cardiovascular diseases. Intern & resident in internal medicine Brigham and Women's Hosp.-Harvard Med. Sch., Boston, 1981—84, clin. and rsch. fellow cardiovasc. divsn., 1984-87; asst. prof. internal medicine U. Mich., Ann Arbor, 1987-91, assoc. prof. internal medicine, 1991-94, prof. internal medicine, 1994—, dir. Cardiovasc. Rsch. Ctr., 1992—, prof. physiology, 1995—, chief divsn. cardiology, 1997-99; sci. dir. clin. rsch. NIH/NHLBI, Bethesda, Md., 1999—. Mem. sci. adv. bd. Vical Inc., San Diego, 1992—; mem. arteriosclerosis, hypertension, and lipid metabolism adv. com. NHLBI, NIH, 1991-93, parent program project grant rev. com., 1995—, mem. task force on human gene therapy, 1992, mem. cardiology adv. com., 1993-94, mem. spl. emphasis panel arterial thrombosis, 1996; chair sci. pub. com. Am. Heart Assn., 1996-98, bd. of dir, 1996-98; chair Atherosluosis Thrombosis and Vascular Biology Coun., 2002—, Gordon Conf. on Vascular Cell Biology, 1996; pres. N.Am. Vascular Biology Orgn., 1996-97; sci. adv.bd. Keystone Symposia, 1999—, bd. of dir. 2001—; mem. com. on space medicine Inst. of Medicine, 1991-2001; councilor and sec.-treas. Am. Soc. of Clin. Investigation, 2001—; lectr. Mayo Clinic, 1996, Yale Univ., 1997, Univ. of Texas, 1997, Womens Hosp., 1997, 2001, Univ. of Hawaii, 1980, Temple Univ., 1999, John Hopkins, 1999, 2000, 2002, Am. Heart Assn., 1999, Univ. of Mich., 2001, Vanderbilt Univ., 2001, Univ, of Va., 2002, among many others. Assoc. editor Jour. of Clin. Investigation, 1997—2002, mem. editl. bd., 2002—, mem. bd. reviewing editors Science, 1998—, mem. editl. bd. New Eng. Jour. Medicine, 2001—; editor: Trends in Cardiovascular Medicine, 2001; cons. editor Circulation, Circulation Rsch., Atherial Thrombosis and Vascular Biology, 2000—. Fellow Am. Coll.

Cardiology, Am. Heart Assn. (basic sci. coun., clin. cardiology coun., circulation coun., atherosclerosis coun., bd. dirs. 1996-97, sci. adv. and coord. com. 1996-97, chair sci. pub. com. 1996-97, sci. pub. com. 1994-96, sci. sessions program com. 1994-95; rsch. fellowship com. Mich. chpt. 1993-95, rsch. grant-in-aid com. 1994-96, vice chair rsch. grant-in-aid com. 1995-96, rsch. exec. com. 1995-96, rsch. com. 1995-96, chair peer rev. rsch. com. 1996-97); mem. AAAS, ACP, Am. Soc. for Biochemistry and Molecular Biology (Amgen Sci. award 1996), Am. Fedn. Clin. Rsch., Am. Soc. Investigative Pathology, Am. Soc. Clin. Investigation, N.Y. Acad. Scis., Am. Soc. Gene Therapy (bd. dirs. 1996), Assn. Am. Physicians, N.Am. Vascular Biology Orgn. (councillor 1994-95, sec., treas. 1994-95, pres. 1996-97), Inst. of Medicine, Ctrl. Soc. Clin. Rsch., Phi Beta Kappa, Alpha Omega Alpha. Office: NIH/NHLBI Bldg 10 Rm 8C103 10 Center Dr Bethesda MD 20892

NABEL, GARY J. internal medicine and biological chemistry educator; BA in Biochemistry magna cum laude, Harvard Coll., 1975; PhD in Cell and Devel. Biology, Harvard U., 1980, MD, 1982. Instr. biology Harvard U., Boston, 1980-81, resident tutor in biology, 1980-83, clin. fellow medicine, 1983-85; intern and resident in internal medicine Brigham and Women's Hosp., Boston, 1983-85; instr. Harvard med. Sch., Boston, 1984-87; assoc. Howard Hughes Med. Inst., Whitehead Inst., MIT, Lab. David Baltimore, 1985-87; assoc. physician Brigham and Women's Hosp., 1985-87; asst. prof. internal medicine and biol. chemistry U. Mich., Ann Arbor, 1987-90, asst. investigator Howard Hughes Med. Inst., 1987-91, assoc. prof. internal medicine and biol. chemistry, 1990-93, assoc. investigator Howard Hughes Med. Inst., 1991-94, prof. internal medicine and biol. chemistry, 1993—, investigator Howard Hughes Med. Inst., 1994—, Henry Sewall prof., 1995—. Mem. AIDS rsch. adv. com. Nat. Inst. Allergy and Infectious Diseases, NIH. Contbr. articles to profl. jours. Fellow Dana-Farber Cancer Inst., Harvard U., 1980-84; Harvard Nat. scholar, 1971-75, Harvard Grad. Nat. scholar, 1976-82; recipient Mallinkrodt Book prize, 1975, James Tolbert Shipley prize for rsch. Harvard Med. Sch., 1982, Ofcl. citation Conn. State Gen. Assembly for Contbns. to Human Gene Therapy, 1992, Young Investigator award Midwest Am. Fedn. for Clin. Rsch., 1992, Amgen award Am. Soc. Biochemistry and Molecular Biology, 1996. Mem. Am. Soc. Clin. Investigation, Assn. Am. Physicians. Office: Univ Mich 4520 MSRBI 1150 W Medical Center Dr Ann Arbor MI 48109-0726

NABERS, CLAUDE LOWREY, retired periodontist, writer; b. Vernon, Tex., Mar. 29, 1924; s. John Bradford and Mae (Moore) N.; m. Blanche Lillian Eaton, Sept. 28, 1951; children: Marquis Eaton, Bradford Claude. DDS, U. Tex., 1946; MS in Dentistry, Northwestern U., Chgo., 1949. Diplomate Am. Bd. Periodontology (bd. dirs. 1965-71, chmn. 1971). Civilian cons. Brook Army Hosp., 1958—84, Lackland Air Force Hosp., 1958—75, Sch. Aerospace Medicine, 1975—80. Pres. Nabers Eaton Properties, San Antonio, 1983—; nat. cons. Surgeon Gen. USAF, 1969-71; mem. ADA Coun. on Dental Rsch., Chgo., 1983-87; lectr. in field worldwide. Author: (in Japanese) Periodontal Therapy, 1980; co-author: Periodontal Therapy, 1990; originator procedures in field. Mem. devel. bd. U. Tex. Health Sci. Ctr., San Antonio, 1989-94, pres. coun., 1994—, co-chmn., 1996, chancellor's coun. Littlefied Soc., Hermes Soc., U. Tex., Austin; trustee Cancer Therapy and Rsch. Ctr. Found. Bd., San Antonio, 1998—; elder 1st Presbyn. Ch., San Antonio, 1960; v.p. Alamo Kiwanis, San Antonio, 1990-91; bd. dirs. The 100 Club, San Antonio, 1993-96, McFarland Tennis Found., San Antonio, 1994-97, San Antonio Salvation Army, 1998—2004; bd. govs. Cancer Therapy and Rsch. Ctr., San Antonio, 1999-2003. Capt. U.S. Army, 1946-48. Recipient 1st Holler's Disting. Lectureship award, San Antonio, 1984, 1st Meml. Jack Lyon Lectureship, Pa., 1984; recipient Outstanding Civilian Svc. medal Dept. of the Army, 1978, 1st Meml. G.R. Landquist Lectureship Northwestern U., 1979, Outstanding Alumnus award U. Tex. Dental Br., Houston, 1980. Fellow Am. Coll. Dentists, Am. Acad. Periodontology (pres. 1972-73, exec. coun. 1962-74, Gold medal 1978, Master Clinician award 1990), Acad. Internat. Dentistry; mem. S.W. Soc. Periodontists (pres. 1961), San Antonio Country Club, Town Club, Conopus Club, Argyle, European Acad. Dentistry (hon.), South African Soc. Periodontology (hon.), Omicron Kappa Upsilon (hon.), Xi Psi Phi (life). Republican. Avocations: tennis, golf, hunting, bridge, travel.

NABHOLZ, JOSEPH VINCENT, biologist, ecologist; b. Memphis, Nov. 3, 1945; s. Martin Peter and Helen Kathleen (Garbacz) N.; m. Sue Ann Winterburn, Aug. 12, 1972; children: Karen Stacey, Pamela Michelle. BS, Christian Bros. U., Memphis, 1968; MS, U. Ga., 1973, PHD, 1978. Sr. biologist EPA, Washington, 1979—. Reviewer NSF and profl. jours., 1973—, Standards Methods Com., Am. Water Works Assn., Denver 18th through 21st edits.; evaluator Office Exptl. Learning U. Md., College Park, Md., 1984-86. Author: ECOSAR computer program to predict aquatic toxicity of chemicals, 2002; co-author: Methods of Ecological Toxicology, 1981, Testing for Effects of Chemicals on Ecosystems, 1981; author: Estimating Toxicity of Industrial Chemicals to Aquatic Organisms Using Structure Activity Relationships, 1988, 94; contbr. articles to profl. jours. Bd. dirs. Comty. Assn. Rollingwood Village (4th sect.), Woodbridge, Va., 1981-90, v.p. 1981-82, pres. 1983-90, maintainence chmn. 1990—. Decorated Army Commendation medal with oak leaf cluster, U.S. Army, Vietnam, 1969, '70. Mem. AAAS, Am. Inst. Biol. Scis. (life), Assn. Southeastern Biologists (life), Internat. Assn. Ecology, Ecol. Soc. Am. (life), Soc. Environ. Toxicology and Chemistry, Phi Kappa Phi (life). Roman Catholic. Achievements include pragmatic application of theory of chemical structure activity relationships for routine risk assessment of industrial chemicals for environmental toxicity. Home: 13627 Bentley Cir Woodbridge VA 22192-4340 Office: EPA 7403 1200 Pennsylvania Ave NW Washington DC 20460-0001 Office Fax: 202-564-9063. Business E-Mail: nabholz.joe@epa.gov.

NABI, GABRIELLE MONIQUE, publishing executive; b. Honolulu, July 22, 1972; d. Bruce Theodore Chosney and Michele Madeleine Evans; m. Fahmun Nabi, Aug. 17, 2002. BA, U. Chgo., 1994; MSW, Washington U., St. Louis, 1999. Family aide specialist Ctrl. Bapt. Family Svcs., Champaign-Urbana, Ill., 1995—97; behavior therapist Barnes Jewish Hosp., St. Louis, 1999—2000; prodn. editor Wiley Pub., Inc., Indpls., 2000—. Mem.: Ctrl. Ind. Writer's Assn.

NABI, STANLEY ANDREW, investment executive; b. Baghdad, Iraq, Sept. 17, 1930; arrived in U.S., 1947; s. Moshi S. and Victoria T. (Mukamal) N.; m. Bette E. Miller, Mar. 31, 1968; children: Deborah Susan, Lisa Meryl. BA, Columbia U., 1952; postgrad., NYU, 1954—58. Gen. ptnr. Schweickart & Co., N.Y.C., 1954-72; gen. ptnr., chief investment officer Lazard Freres & Co., N.Y.C., 1973-84; exec. v.p. Bessemer Trust Co., N.A., 1985-95; pres., CEO Bessemer Investors Svcs., 1985-95; vice chmn., chmn. investment policy com. Wood, Struthers & Winthrop, N.Y.C., 1995-2000; chief investment officer DLJ Asset Mgmt. Corp., N.Y.C., 1996-2000; mng. dir., sr. advisor Credit Suisse Asset Mgmt., 2000—03; vice chmn. Silvercrest Asset Mgmt. Group, 2004—. Lectr. New Sch. Social Rsch., N.Y.C., 1963-68; investment cons. U.S. Steel and Carnegie Pension Fund, N.Y.C., 1979—; dir. Bargain Town U.S.A., N.Y.C., 1962-69; mem. pres.'s coun. New Sch. U., N.Y.C., 1989—; adj. prof. fin. Grad. Sch. Bus., Fordham U., N.Y.C., 1992-97. Editor: weekly jour. The Analyst, 1957-72; assoc. editor: jour. The Fin. Analysts Jour., 1971-83. Trustee NABI Found., 1964—. Served with U.S. Army, 1952-54. Mem. N.Y. Soc. Security Analysts (pres. 1971-72), Inst. Chartered Fin. Analysts, Assn. for Investment Mgmt. and Rsch. Office: 1330 Ave of the Americas New York NY 10019 Home: 1 Kensington Gate (PH-1) Great Neck NY 11021-1202 Office Phone: 212-649-0702. E-mail: snabi@silvercrestgroup.com.

NABORS, DAVID, health facility executive; COO Pediat. Svcs. Am., Inc., Norcross, Ga., 1999—. Office: Pediat Svcs Am Inc 310 Technology Pkwy Norcross GA 30092-2932

NABORS, ROBERT L. military officer; b. Boston; married; children: Robert, Richard, Jonathan. BS in Systems Engring., U. Ariz.; MS in Systems Mgmt., U. So. Calif.; grad. Sr. Officials in Nat. Security, Harvard U.; grad., Armed Forces Staff Coll. Commd. 2d lt. U.S. Army, advanced through grades to maj. gen., with 67th Signal Battalion, overseas tours in Vietnam and Worms, Germany, also active duty tours, Aberdeen Proving Grounds, Md., aide-de-Camp for Comdg. Gen., VII Corps, 1979-81; with Office of Dir. of Plans, Programs and Policy U.S. Army Readiness Command, 1983; then comdr. 509th signal Battalion U.S. Army, Italy; spl. asst. to U.S. Army's Dir. of Info. Sys. for Command Control. Comm. and Computers; chief Integration div. Architecture Directorate U.S. Army, dep. comdr. White House Comm. Agy., comdr. 2d Signal Brigade, 1990, comdr. 5th Signal Command, 1995-98, comdr. Comm.-Electronics Command and comdr. Ft. Monmouth, 1998-2001. Decorated DSM, Def. Superior Svc. medal, Legion of Merit with 4 oak leaf clusters, Bronze Star, Meritorious Svc. medal with 4 oak leaf clusters, others; recipient Roy Wilkins award of Reknown, NAACP, 2000, Fed. Asian-Pacific Am. Coun. award, 2000, others. Mem. Mensa.

NACE, BARRY JOHN, lawyer; b. York, Pa., Nov. 28, 1944; s. John Harrison and Mildred Louise (Orwig) N.; m. Andrea Marcia Giardini. Apr. 28, 1973; children: Christopher Thomas, Jonathan Barry, Matthew Andrew. BS, Dickinson Coll., 1965, JD, 1969, LLD (hon.), 1994. Bar: Md. 1970, D.C. 1971, Pa. 1972, W.Va. 1997, U.S. Ct. Appeals (3d, 4th and D.C. cirs.), U.S. Supreme Ct. Ptnr. Davis & Nace, Washington, 1972-78, Paulson & Nace, Bethesda, Md., 1978-85, 98—; sr. ptnr. Paulson, Nace & Norwind, Washington, 1986-97. Fellow Roscoe Pound Found. (trustee); mem. Nat. Bd. Trial Advocacy in Civil Litigation (bd. govs. 2001—), D.C. Bar Assn., Montgomery County Bar Assn., Assn. Trial Lawyers Am. (gov. 1976-87, pres. 1993-94), Met. D.C. Trial Attys. (pres. 1977-78, 87-88, Atty. of Yr. 1976), Trial Lawyers for Pub. Justice (found. bd. govs. 2003—), Internat. Acad. Trial Lawyers (bd. govs. 2003—), Lambert Soc., Am. Inns of Ct., Am. Law Inst. Am. Bd. Profl. Liability Attys. Avocations: golf, tennis, reading, racquetball. Home: 6208 Garnett Dr Bethesda MD 20815-6618 Office: Paulson & Nace 1814 N St NW Washington DC 20036-2404 E-mail: BJN@Lawtort.com.

NACE, DONALD M. retired chemist; b. Hanover, Pa., Nov. 28, 1924; s. LeRoy S. and Anna M. Nace; m. Mae L. Bennett, Aug. 24, 1945; children: Allen C., David K. BSChE, Lehigh U., 1947, MS in Chemistry, 1949; PhD of Chemistry, Pa. State U., 1956. Sr. rsch. chemist Mobil R&D Corp., Paulsboro, NJ, 1958—74, rsch. assoc., 1974—87; ret., 1988. Electronics tech. 3 USN, 1944—46, WWII, Pacific and Atlantic. Recipient ACS S. Jersey Sci. Award, Am. Chem. Soc. So. Jersey Sect., 1971; fellow Mobil Incentive Fellowship, Mobil Rsch. & Develop. Corp., 1953. Mem.: Catalysis Club of Phila. (Chmn. 1972), Am. Chem. Soc. (Chmn. of So. NJ Sect. 1968). Achievements include patents for 15 US patents in field of catalytic processes; sci. publ. in fields of thermodynamics, kinetics, chemical mechanisms, catalysis. Avocation: concert clarinetist, pianist, dance band saxaphonist. Home: 4 Oak Rd Woodbury NJ 08096

NACE, MORTON OLIVER, JR., human resources professional, performance consultant; b. Tampa, Fla., June 30, 1937; s. Morton Oliver and Penelope Adele (Holland) N.; m. Eleanor Hart Moslow, June 27, 1964; children: Morton Oliver III, Jennifer Ann. BS, Boston U., 1964; MS, Syracuse U., 1974. Cert. literacy tutor Laubach Literacy Internat., Syracuse, N.Y. Exec. dir. Episcopal Diocese Chgo., 1964-70; dir. comm. Laubach Literacy Internat., Syracuse, N.Y., 1970-80; tng. and devel. specialist Rochester (N.Y.) Inst. Tech., 1980-96; adminstrv. asst., cons. City of Rochester, 1997—. Cons. tng. and orgn. devel., Rochester, 1982-98; facilitator retreats/tng. for new parish model The Apostle, 1990—; designer/presenter formats on discernment and daily ministry, 2000; asst. prof. Rochester Inst. Tech., Henrietta, N.Y., 1994; sales and consulting staff Human Resource Svcs., Rochester, 1995-97. Facilitator planning retreat City Coun. of Rochester, 1993; regional planning cons. Mayor-elect City Coun., Rochester, 1997, performance cons. and trainer, 1998—. With USAF, 1957-61. Mem. ASTD (Genesee Valley chpt., conf. presenter 1981-96), Profl. and Orgn. Devel. in Higher Edn. (nat. presenter on faculty/staff devel. 1993-96). Episcopalian. Avocations: photography, piano, physical exercise, history, travel. Home and Office: 2271 Westfall Rd Rochester NY 14618-3126

NACHMAN, GERALD WEIL, columnist, critic, author; b. Oakland, Calif., Jan. 13, 1938; s. Leonard Calvert and Isabel (Weil) N.; m. Mary Campbell McGeachy, Sept. 3, 1966 (div. 1979). Student, Merritt Coll., 1955-57; BA in Journalism, San Jose State U., 1960. TV and humor columnist San Jose (Calif.) Mercury, 1960-63; feature writer N.Y. Post, N.Y.C., 1963-66; drama critic Oakland (Calif.) Tribune, 1966-71; syndicated humor columnist N.Y. Daily News, 1973-79; critic and columnist San Francisco Chronicle, 1979-93. Juror Pulitzer Prize Com. to choose best play, 1991. Author: The Portable Nachman, 1960, Playing House, 1978, Out on a Whim, 1983, The Fragile Bachelor, 1989; contbr. to (book) Snooze, 1986, Raised on Radio, 1998, Seriously Funny: The Rebel Comedians of the 1950's and 1960's, 2003; contbr. articles to newspapers, mag.; author, co-lyricist (revues) Quirks, 1979, Aftershocks, 1992, New Wrinkles, 1999. Recipient Page One award N.Y. Newspaper Guild, 1965, Deems Taylor award ASCAP, 1989. E-mail: nachnach@aol.com.

NACHMAN, JOSEPH FRANK, retired metallurgical consultant; b. Toledo, Jan. 22, 1918; s. Frank and Jane (Wujciak) N.; m. Rosemary Anderson, May 4, 1943; children: Richard Joseph, Ronald James. BS in Chemistry, U. Toledo, 1940; MS in Metallurgy, Ohio State U., 1947. Registered profl. engr., Calif., Colo., Md. Chief metallurgy branch U.S. Naval Ordnance Lab., Silver Spring, Md., 1948-56; mgr. alloy devel. U. Denver Research Inst., 1956-63; group leader Atomics Internat., Canoga Park, CA, 1963-66; chief applied scis. Solar Turbines, San Diego, 1966-77, research staff specialist, 1977-81; pres. Metall. Cons. Services, Inc., San Diego, 1981—, ret. Editor: Rare Earth Research, 1961, Proceeding of 7th Conference on Rare-Earth Research vols. I & II., 1968; patentee in field; contbr. articles to profl. jours. Served to lt. commdr. USNR, 1943-46. Recipient Meritorious Civilian Service award, USN Ordnance Lab., 1953; spl. commendation for improvement of ordnance equipment, 1945. Mem. Am. Soc. Metals (life), AAAS, Nat. Assn. Corrosion Engrs., Sigma Xi, Alpha Sigma Phi (v.p. 1939-40). Republican. Methodist. Avocations: travel, photography, genealogy. Home: Metall Cons Services Inc The Woodlands 123 Robindale Cir Conroe TX 77384-4654

NACHMAN, MERTON ROLAND, JR., lawyer; b. Montgomery, Ala., Dec. 21, 1923; s. Merton Roland and Maxine (Mayer) N.; m. Martha Street, June 8, 1968; children: Nancy Nachman Yardley, Linda Nachman Connelly, Betsy Wild, Amy N. DeRoche, Karen Vann. AB cum laude, Harvard U., 1943, JD, 1948. Bar: Ala. 1949, U.S. Supreme Ct. 1953, U.S. Ct. Appeals (5th and 11th cirs.), U.S. Ct. Claims, U.S. Tax Ct. Asst. atty. gen. State of Ala., 1949-54; ptnr. Knabe & Nachman, Montgomery, 1954-59; adminstrv. asst. to Senator John Sparkman, Ala., 1956; ptnr. Steiner, Crum & Baker, Montgomery, 1959-86, counsel mem., 2000—; from ptnr. to coun. mem. Balch & Bingham, Montgomery, 1986-2000. Chmn. human rights com. Ala. Prison System, 1976-78. With USN, 1943-46. Recipient Merit award Ala. State Bar, 1974; cert. of appreciation Supreme Ct. of Ala., 1974. Fellow Am. Coll. Trial Lawyers; mem. ABA (com. on fed. judiciary 1982-88, bd. govs. 1978-81), Ala. State Bar (pres. 1973-74), Am. Judicature Soc. (dir. 1976-80, Herbert Lincoln Harley award 1974), Am. Law Inst., Ala. Law Inst., Unity club (Montgomery), Am. Acad. Appellate Lawyers. Episcopalian. Office: PO Box 668 8 Commerce St Ste 8 Montgomery AL 36101-0668 Office Phone: 334-823-3288. E-mail: rnachman@steinercrum.com.

NACHMAN, RALPH LOUIS, physician, educator; b. Bayonne, N.J., June 29, 1931; s. Samuel Nachman and Ethel Nelson; m. Nancy Rubin; children: Susan, Steve. BA, Vanderbilt U., 1953, MD, 1956. Lic. physician N.Y., diplomate Am. Bd. Internal Medicine, subsplty. hematology, med. oncology. Intern in medicine Vanderbilt U. Hosp., 1956—57; asst. resident in medicine Montefiore Hosp., 1960—62; asst. resident in pathology N.Y. Hosp.-Cornell U. Med. Ctr., N.Y.C., 1957—58, rsch. fellow in medicine, 1962—63; dir. labs. for clin. pathology N.Y. Hosp., 1963—69, assoc. attending physician, 1968—72, attending physician, 1972—; from instr. to asst. prof. to assoc. prof. medicine Cornell Med. Ctr., 1963—72, chief divns. hematology, 1968—93, prof. medicine, 1972—; vice chmn. dept. medicine Cornell U. Med. Coll., 1974—78, acting chmn. dept. medicine, 1974—75, dir. Specialized Ctr. Rsch. in Thrombosis, 1976—97, acting co-chmn. dept. medicine, 1980—81, bd. overseers, 1987—89, chmn. dept. medicine, 1990; physician-in-chief N.Y.-Presbyn. Hosp./Cornell Campus, 1990. Guest investigator Rockefeller U., 1969—70; Wiessberg lectr. Case Western Res. U., 1978; Aggeler lectr. U. Calif., San Francisco, 1981; Patek lectr. Boston U., 1981; Rosenthal lectr. Mt. Sinai, 1982; Beaumont lectr. Wash. U., 1983; Wiener lectr. N.Y. Blood Ctr., 1983; chmn. Gordon Conf. on Hemostasis, 1984; Alpha Omega Alpha lectr. N.Y. Med. Coll., 1985; Sharp lectr. Wayne State U., 1986; Roon lectr. Scripps Rsch. Inst., 1987; Johnson lectr. Internat. Soc. on Thrombosis, 1987; Merck lectr. Cleve. Clinic, 1987; vis. prof. Harvard U., 1991; E. Stanley Emery Jr. Meml. lectr., physician-in-chief pro tempore, 91; chief resident's vis. prof. Baylor Coll. Medicine, 1991; Samuel S. Riven vis. prof. Vanderbilt U., 1992; Hymie Nossel Meml. lectr. Columbia U., 1992; Pfizer vis. prof. Royal Soc. Medicine, 1992; disting. lectr. Am. Heart Assn., 1994; Seckler lectr. Mt. Sinai Med. Ctr., 1994; Runme Shaw Meml. lectr. Acad. Medicine, Singapore, 1994; chmn. hematology study panel Health Rsch. Coun., N.Y.C., 1973—75; mem. NIH-Program Project Com. Heart and Lung Inst., 1975—79; bd. govs. Am. Bd. Internal Medicine, 1985—88; cons. Manhattan VA Hosp.; vis. physician Rockefeller U. Hosp. Author: Genetics of Coronary Heart Disease, 1992, Systemic Lupus Erythematosus, 1993, (jours.) Blood, 1994, Ann. Internal Medicine, 1993; assoc. editor: Beeson McDermott Textbook of Medicine, XIV edit., 1975, Beeson McDermott Textbook of Medicine, XV edit., 1979, Blood, 1976—82, Am. Jour. Medicine, 1978, adv. editor: Jour. Exptl. Medicine, 1976, editl. bd.: Arteriosclerosis, 1983; contbr. articles to med. jours. With USN, 1958—60. Fellow: ACP; mem.: AAAS, N.Y. Acad. Medicine, Inst. Medicine NAS, Am. Soc. Biol. Chemists, Soc. Exptl. Biology and Medicine, Internat. Soc. Thrombosis and Hemostasis (coun. 1986—92), Am. Physiol. Assn., Harvey Soc. (coun. 1980), Am. Soc. Hematology (exec. coun. 1978—79), N.Y. Soc. for Study of Blood (pres. 1975), N.Y. Acad. Sci., Am. Clin. and Climatol. Assn., Am. Fedn. Clin. Rsch., Am. Soc. Clin. Investigation, Assn. Am. Physicians, Cornell Med. Alumni (hon.), Peripatetic Club, Nat. Blood Club (pres. 1981—82), Phi Beta Kappa, Alpha Omega Alpha. Office: NY Presbyn Hosp Weill Med Coll Cornell U 525 E 68th St # M 52 Box 130 New York NY 10021-4870

NACHMAN, RONALD JAMES, research chemist; b. Takoma Park, Md., Feb. 1, 1954; s. Joseph Frank and Rosemary (Anderson) N.; m. Lita Rose Wilson, Dec. 18, 1976 (div. 1987); m. Isidora Austria Panis, May 6, 1989. BS in Chemistry, U. Calif., San Diego, 1976; PhD in Organic Chemistry, Stanford U., 1981. Rsch. asst. Scripps Inst. Oceanography, La Jolla, Calif., 1974-76; chemist Western Regional Rsch. Ctr., USDA, Berkeley, Calif., 1981-89, Vet. Toxicology and Entomology Rsch. Lab., College Station, Tex., 1989—. Vis. scientist dept. molecular biology Salk Inst., La Jolla, 1985, Scripps Rsch. Inst., La Jolla, 1988-89. Mem. editl. adv. bd. The Jour. Peptides, guest editor, 2001, 02, 03, 04; mem. organizing com. Ann. Invertebrate Neuropeptide Conf.; contbr. sci. articles to profl. jours. Recipient USDA Cert. of Merit, 1988, 91, 94-2001, Arthur S. Flemming award for sci. achievement, 1994. Fellow Internat. Neoropeptide Soc. (bd. dirs. 2000—); mem. AAAS, Internat. Neuropeptide Soc., Am. Chem. Soc., N.Y. Acad. Scis., Sigma Xi. Avocations: travel, photography, jogging, racketball. Home: 14891 Pollux Dr Willis TX 77318-5079 Office: USDA Southern Plains Agrl Rsch Ctr 2881 F And B Rd College Station TX 77845-4988

NACHMIAS, JACOB, psychologist, educator; Prof. psychology dept. U. Pa., Phila., prof. emeritus, 1995—. Recipient Edward D. Tillyer award Optical Soc. Am., 1994. Office: U Pa Dept Psychology Philadelphia PA 19104

NACHT, SERGIO, biochemist; b. Buenos Aires, Apr. 13, 1934; came to U.S., 1965; s. Oscar and Carmen (Scheiner) N.; m. Beatriz Kahan, Dec. 21, 1958; children: Marcelo H., Gabriel A., Mariana S., Sandra M. BA in Chemistry, U. Buenos Aires, 1958, MS in Biochemistry, 1960, PhD in Biochemistry, 1964. Asst. prof. biochemistry U. Buenos Aires, 1960-64; asst. prof. medicine U. Utah, Salt Lake City, 1965-70; rsch. scientist Alza Corp., Palo Alto, Calif., 1970-73; sr. investigator Richardson-Vicks Inc., Mt. Vernon, N.Y., 1973-76, asst. dir., dir. rsch., 1976-83, dir. biomed. rsch. Shelton, Conn., 1983-87; sr. v.p. rsch. and devel. Advanced Polymer Sys., Redwood City, Calif., 1987-93, sr. v.p. sci. and tech., 1993-98, sr. v.p. dermatology and skin care, 1998-2000, Enhanced Derm Techs., Redwood City, 2000—02; chief sci. officer, ptnr. Riley-Nacht, LLC, Las Vegas, 2002—. Lectr. dermatology dept. SUNY Downstate Med. Ctr., Blkyn., 1977-87. Contbr. articles to profl. jours.; patentee in field. Mem. Soc. Cosmetic Chemists (award 1981), Dermatology Found., Am. Acad. Dermatology. Democrat. Jewish. Office Phone: 702-547-1611. Personal E-mail: sernacht@aol.com.

NACHTIGAL, PATRICIA, lawyer; b. 1946; BA, Montclair State U.; JD, Rutgers U.; LLM, NYU. Tax atty. Ingersoll-Rand Co., Ltd., Hamilton, Bermuda, 1979—83, dir. taxes and legal, 1983—88, sec., mng. atty., 1988—91, v.p., gen. counsel, 1991—2000, sr. v.p., gen. counsel, 2000—, bd. dirs., 2002—. Gov., trustee Rutgers, State U. N.J., 1996—, chair, 2003—04. Office: Ingersoll-Rand Co Ltd 200 Chestnut Ridge Rd Woodcliff Lake NJ 07677 Office Phone: 201-573-0123.

NACHUM, LILACH, international business educator; b. Afula, Israel; d. Yitchak Mayran and Malca Mayran-Abbas; m. Kurt Uri Nachum, 1986; children: David, Ruth, Philippe. BA, Tel Aviv U., 1983, MBA, 1990; PhD, Copenhagen (Denmark) Bus. Sch., 1994. Vis. prof. bus., vis. rsch. fellow Uppsala (Sweden) U., 1994; vis. rsch. fellow, dept. econs. Reading (Eng.) U., 1994—95; sr. rschr. divsn. transnational corp. and fgn. investment UN, 1994—97; vis. rsch. fellow, Sch. Bus. Stockholm U., 1996; rsch. assoc. Internat. Inst. Mgmt. Devel., Lausanne, Switzerland, 1996; vis. prof. Webster U. (affiliate Am. U .), Geneva, 1996—97; sr. rsch. fellow, Ctr. Bus. Rsch. Cambridge (Eng.) U., 1997—2002; assoc. prof. internat. bus. Baruch Coll., CUNY, N.Y.C., 2002—. Bd. advisors fgn. direct investment Devel. Gateway Cmty., MIGA, World Bank; cons. in field; spkr. Nat. Conf. State Legislators Seminar, Capitol Hills, Wash., DC, 2003; vis. prof. exec. edn. program Baruch Coll., Taiwan, 2004, Singapore, 04. Author: (novels) (book) books in field, 1999—2000; contbr. articles to profl. jours., including Jour. of Internat. Bus. Studies and Strategic Mgmt. Jour. Recipient numerous awards in excellence in tchg. and rsch. Mem.: Strategic Mgmt. Soc., Acad. Mgmt., Assn. Internat. Bus. Avocations: music, dance, travel. Office: Baruch Coll City Univ Box B12-240 55 Lexington Ave New York NY 10010 Office Phone: 646-312-3276.

NACHWALTER, MICHAEL, lawyer; b. N.Y.C., Aug. 31, 1940; s. Samuel J. Nachwalter; m. Irene, Aug. 15, 1965; children: Helynn, Robert. BS, Bucknell U., 1962; MS, L.I. U., 1967; JD cum laude, U. Miami, 1967; LLM, Yale U., 1968. Bar: Fla. 1967, D.C. 1979, U.S. Dist. Ct. (so. dist.) Fla. 1967, U.S. Dist. Ct. (mid. dist.) Fla. 1982, U.S. Ct. Appeals (5th and 11th cirs.) 1967, U.S. Supreme Ct. 1975. Law clk. to judge U.S. Dist. Ct. (so. dist.) Fla.; shareholder Kelly, Black, Black & Kenny; now shareholder Kenny Nachwalter Seymour Critchlow & Spector, P.A., Miami. Lectr. Law Sch. U. Miami. Editor-in-chief U. Miami Law Rev., 1966-67. Fellow Am. Coll. Trial Lawyers; mem. ABA, FBA, Am. Bd. Trial Advs., Fla. Bar Assn. (bd. govs. 1982-90), Internat. Soc. Barristers (dir.), Dade County Bar Assn., Jud. Qualifications Commn. (vice chmn. 1995-2000), Iron Arrow, Soc. Wig and Robe, Omicron Delta Kappa, Phi Kappa Phi, Phi Delta Phi. Office: Kenny Nachwalter Seymour Arnold Critchlow & Spector PA 201 S Biscayne Blvd Ste 1100 Miami FL 33131-4327

NACK, CLAIRE DURANI, artist, author; b. N.Y.C., NY, Dec. 02; d. Myron Irving and Rachel Rita Adele (Feldman) N. Student, NYU, 1975, Sculpture Ctr., N.Y.C., 1975, Arts Student League. Pres., owner, founder Claire Durani Nack Corp. subs. Princess Enterprs./Durani Co., N.Y.C., 1993; pres. Books of Poetry by Claire Durani Nack, Mystery Stories by Claire Durani Nack, Books of Science Fiction by Claire Durani Nack, Works of Art by Claire Durani Nack, C.D.N. Co. Prof. N.Y. State Mus., Albany, 1992, Hudson Valley C.C., 1986-92, Schenectady (N.Y.) Mus.; lectr. Troy Arts League, 1989. Artist sketchbooks; author (plays for theater); author/artist: Something Happened in the Kitchen, 1981, European Journey, Book II, 1981, Cat Book, 1994, Diary, 2, 1980, Diary, Vol. 4, 1994, Vol. 5, 1994, The Journals of Claire Durani Nack, 1994, Art Book 1, 1982, Art Book 2, 1982, My World, 1999, Blue Book, Upwards Bent (books 1-5), 1993-94, Spiders Web Unspun, 1994, An Unfamiliar Place, 1993, The Adventures of Cora, 1994 (books 1-5), Cahiers de Dessins de Paris, 1994, Big City Lights, 1991, Something Happened in the Bathroom, 1981, Something Happened in the Living Room, 1981, Children's Coloring Books, 1995, Animal Book, 1995, The Adventures of Cora, Plot,

Counterplot, Plot, 1997, All About Life, Sorrow and Joy, Essays and Soliliquies, Stoolie the Ghoulie, The Small Book of Art, The Gold Book, 1997, The Book of Art, 1997, Conversations with Myself, 2003, Facts, Fools and Ghools, 1997, All About Life, 1997, Sorrow and Joy, 1997, The Silver Book, 1997, A Light's Work, 1997, (play) The Agenda, 1997, 2003, Being C, 1997, (play) Not the Marrying Kind, Liz Muller, Alive, 1998, The Cheerful Book, 1998, Essays and Soliloquies, 1998, Questions and Answers, 1998, The Prosecuting Lawyer, 1998, Life's a Theatre, 1999, (short story)The Cheetah, 1999, Toulouse Lautrec and Claire Durani Nack, 1999, The Scrapbook of Claire Durani Nack, 1998, The Album of Claire Durani Nack, 1999, Life's a Theatre, 1999, The Portfolio of Claire Durani Nack in Paris, 1999, Conversations with Myself, Garden of the Orient, 2001, Dating, Waiting & Mating, The Orange Book, Excavations and Illuminations, Elizabeth Getty, The BroRon Doll and Elizabeth Getty Repaired. Recipient poetry award Nat. Libr. of Poetry, Calif., 1991; scholar Art Students League, 1985. Mem. Nat. Mus. of Women in the Arts (charter mem.), Art Students League (life), N.Y. State Mus. Avocations: travel, collecting model airplanes, collecting hats, art and art books, Am. and European real estate. Office: 416 East St Rensselaer NY 12144-2303

NACKEL, JOHN GEORGE, technology executive; b. Medford, Mass., Nov. 4, 1951; s. Michael and Josephine (Maria) N.; m. Gail Helen Becker, Oct. 30, 1976; children: Melissa Anne, Allison Elizabeth. BS, Tufts U., 1973; MS in Pub. Health and Indsl. Engring., U. Mo., 1975, PhD, 1977. Sr. mgr. Ernst & Young, Chgo., 1977—83; nat. dir. health care cons. Cleve., 1983—87; regional dir. health industry svcs., 1987—91; mng. dir. health care Ernst & Young, Cleve., 1991—93; mng. dir. Health Consulting, LA, 1993—99, New Ventures, 1999—2000; CEO Sogeti USA, LLC, 2000—01; chmn., CEO Sértan Corp., Santa Fe Springs, Calif., 2002—03; exec. v.p. US Tech., Aliso Viejo, Calif., 2003—. Author: Cost Management for Hospitals, 1987 (Am. Hosp. Assn. book award 1988); mem. editl bd. Jour. Med. Systems, 1983-; contbr. articles to profl. jours. Grantee Dept. Health Edn. Welfare, Washington, 1973-76. Fellow Am. Coll. Healthcare Execs., Healthcare Info. and Mgmt. Systems Soc. (articles award); mem. Inst. Indsl. Engrs. (sr.), U. Mo. Health Svcs. Mgmt. Alumni Assn. (pres.), L.A. Country Club, Annandale Golf Club. Republican. Avocations: golf, tennis, squash, paddle, photography. Home: 666 Linda Vista Ave Pasadena CA 91105-1145 Business E-Mail: john.nackel@ustri.com.

NACKNOUCK, JAMES DOMINIC, management executive; b. Newark, May 7, 1950; BS, Montclair State U., 1972; MBA, Fairleigh Dickinson U., 1984. Asst. art dir. Markal Corp., Montclair, NJ, 1972-75; art educator Phillipsburg (N.J.) Pub. Sch., 1975; prodn. mgr. Landmark Assocs. Ltd., Orange, 1975-77; graphic designer Exxon Rsch. and Engring. Co., Florham Park, 1977-81, supr. graphic design, 1981-88; unit head accounts payable Exxon Central Svcs., 1988-92; process leader Exxon Rsch. and Engring. Co., 1992-93, acctg. group head, 1993-95, acctg. leader, 1995-97, fin. govt. and tax reporting process leader, 1997-98; earnings reporting process leader Exxon Co., Internat., Fla., 1998-2000; controls and planning adv. Exxon Mobil, 2000—04; payable controls advisor ExxonMobil Global Svcs., Houston, 2004—. Pres. The Users Group, N.J., 1986-88. Home: 3750 Ottawa Ln Hollywood FL 33026-4619 Office: ExxonMobil Global Svcs 4500 Dacoma Houston TX 77092

NACLERIO, ROBERT MICHAEL, otolaryngologist, educator; b. N.Y.C., Mar. 30, 1950; s. Albert Paul and Lee Ann (Rabinowitz) N.; m. Sharon Ann Silhan, Mar. 30, 1983; children: Jessica, Daniel. BA, Cornell U., 1972; MD with honors, Baylor U., 1976. Diplomate Am. Bd. Otolaryngology. Intern in surgery Johns Hopkins Hosp., Balt., 1976-77, resident in surgery, 1977-78; resident in otolaryngology Baylor Coll. Medicine, Houston, 1978-80, chief resident in otolaryngology, 1982-83; fellow in clin. immunology divsn. Johns Hopkins U. Sch. Medicine, Balt., 1980-82, asst. prof. medicine and otolaryngology, 1983-87, asst. prof. pediat., 1986-87, dir. divsn. pediat. otolaryngology, 1986-94, assoc. prof. otolargyngology, medicine and pediat., 1987-92, prof. otolaryngology, medicine and pediat., 1992-94; chief of otolaryngology, head and neck surgery U. Chgo., Chgo., 1994—. Cons. Richardson-Vicks Inc., 1986-89, 90, NIH, 1987, Proctor & Gamble, 1987, 94, Sandoz Rsch. Inst., 1988, Schering Rsch., 1988, Wallace Labs., 1989, Joint Rhinologic Conf., 1989, Internat. Congress Rhinology, 1991, Norwich-Eaton Pharm. Inc., 1991-92, Ciba-Geigy Corp., 1991-92, Mktg. Corp. Am., 1993—, Astra, others; mem. med. bd. Children's Ctr., 1991-94, other local comms.; reviewer Am. Jour. Rhinology, others; lectr. in field. Editor: Rhinoconjunctivitis: New Perspectives in Topical Treatment, 1988; asst. editor: Am. Jour. Rhinology, 1986—, Rhinology, 1988—; mem. editl. bd. Otolaryngology-Head and Neck Surgery, 1990-97, Laryngoscope, 1990—, Jour. Allergy and Clin. Immunology, 1992-97; contbr. numerous chpts. to books, papers and abstracts to profl. jours. and procs. Fellow ACS, Am. Acad. Otolaryngology-Head and Neck Surgery (mem. com. 1985-90, 90-92, subcom. 1987-92), Am. Laryngol., Rhinol. and Otol. Soc., Inc.; mem. Am. Acad. Allergy and Immunology (mem. com. 1983-88, 88-89, 88-95, chmn. com. 1990-91, 91—, Jerome Glazer Meml. lectureship), Am. Fedn. Clin. Rsch., Am. Soc. Pediat. Otolaryngology (mem. rsch. com. 1990-94, chmn. subcom. 1990), Soc. Univ. Otolaryngologists-Head and Neck Surgeons, Pan-Am. Assn. Otorhinolaryngology, Internat. Symposium on Infection and Allergy of the Nose (v.p.). Office: U Chgo Sect O-HNS 5841 S Maryland Ave # 1035 Chicago IL 60637-1463 E-mail: rnacleri@surgery.bsd.uchicago.edu.

NACOL, MAE, lawyer; b. Beaumont, Tex., June 15, 1944; d. William Samuel and Ethel (Bowman) N.; children: Shawn Alexander Nacol, Catherine Regina Nacol. BA, Rice U., 1965; postgrad., South Tex. Coll. Law, 1966. Bar: Tex. 1969, U.S. Dist. Ct. (so. dist.) Tex. 1969. Pvt. practice law, Houston, 1969—; escrow officer Land Am./Commonwealth Land Title Co., Houston; mem. bd. devel. Prosperity Bank, Houston. Author, editor ednl. materials on multiple sclerosis, 1981-85. Nat. dir. A.R.M.S. of Am. Ltd., Houston, 1984-85. Recipient Mayor's Recognition award City of Houston, 1972. Mem. Fed. Bar Assn., Houston Bar Assn. (chmn. candidate com. 1970, membership com. 1971, chmn. lawyers referral com. 1972), Assn. Trial Lawyers Am., Tex. Trial Lawyers Assn., Am. Judicature Soc. (sustaining), Houston Fin. Coun. Women, Houston Trial Lawyers Assn. Presbyterian. Office: 600 Jefferson St Ste 750 Houston TX 77002 also: 2600 S Gessner Ste 120 Houston TX 77063 Office Phone: 713-655-7055.

NADADUR, SRIKANTH S, molecular biologist; s. Srinivasa Chari and Lakshmi S Nadadur; m. Anupama Mudipalli, July 13, 1987; 1 child, Saikrishna Srikanth. PhD, S. V. U., Tirupathi, AP, India, 1985; MSc, S. V. U., 1980. Biologist Us Epa, Durham, NC, 2000—, vis. scientist, 1998—2000; cancer rsch. scientist 1 Roswell Pk. Cancer Inst., Buffalo, 1994—98, rsch. assoc., 1992—94. Mem.: Soc. of Toxicology. Achievements include patents for As lead molecular biologist involved in the isolation and partial characterization of a novel cytosolic protein that protects the cell lysis caused by TNF. A patent was issued for this work; research in Isolated a novel cDNA with putative growth suppressor function. Its role in cancer and angiogenesis is currently being investigated; Isolated 27 novel cDNA fragments from human and mouse cells and they are currently part of EST database in GenBank. Office: Us Epa 4930 Page Rd Mail Drop B-143-02 Durham NC 27703 E-mail: nadadur.srikanth@epa.gov.

NADAS, JOHN ADALBERT, psychiatrist, educator; b. Innsbruck, Austria, Mar. 14, 1949; arrived in U.S., 1950; s. Julius Zoltan and Ibolya Erzsebet (Szöllösy) Nadas; m. Gabriella Ilona Ormay, Apr. 11, 1981; children: János, Miklós, István. BA, Case Western Res. U., Cleve., 1970; MD, Duke U., Durham, NC, 1974. Resident in psychiatry U. Chgo., 1974-77; pvt. practice Munster, Ind., 1977-84, Canton, Ohio, 1984—; instr. psychiatry Northeastern Ohio U. Coll. Medicine, Rootstown, 1985-86, asst. prof., 1986—; coord. psychiat. edn. Mercy Med. Ctr., Canton, 1985-87, clin. dir. psychiat. svcs., 1990-91. Cons. Crisis Ctr., Canton, 1985—92. Author: Philosophical Basis of Depth Psychotherapy, 1983, Journey Toward Energy, 1995, Transformation, 1999. Trustee Sisters of Charity Found., Canton, 1996—2003. Named NCAA nat. collegiate epee champion, 1970; named to All-Am. Fencing Team, 1969, 1970. Mem.: AMA, Am. Psychiat. Assn., Hungarian Assn. (pres. 2000—03). Roman Catholic. Avocations: basketball, computer programming. Office: 1330 Mercy Dr NW Ste 320 Canton OH 44708-2624

NADASKAY, RAYMOND, architect; b. Newark, Aug. 26, 1938; s. Charles and Marie (Roncskevitz) Nadaskay; m. Nancy Searle, 1962; 1 child, Cathy. BArch, Washington U., St. Louis, 1962. Registered architect, N.J., Conn., Vt., Mass., Ill., Ohio, S.C., Vt., Del.; registered planner; cert. NCARB. Designer Rotwein and Blake, Architects, Union, N.J., 1962-63, I.M. Pei, N.Y.C., 1963-64; designer, assoc. McDowell Goldstein, Morristown, N.J., 1964-72; pres. Nadaskay Kopelson Architects, P.A., Morristown, 1972—. Chair Mendham (N.J.) Twp. Hist. Preservation Commn.; mem. Mendham Twp. Roadscape Commn., Mendham Twp. Facilities Com., Mendham Twp. Open Space Com., Morristown Streetscape Com.; mem. Blue Ribbon adv. com. Morris County Hist. Preservation Trust Fund; trustee Ralston Cider Mill. Recipient numerous spl. commendations, awards of merit for variety of works. Mem.: NJ Soc. Archs. (conv. chmn. 1985—86, past pres. Newark Suburban chpt. 1984, Herman Litwak award AIA Newark Suburban chpt. 2001), Porsche Club (No. NJ). Avocations: woodworking, sailing, auto rally events, swimming. Office: Nadaskay Kopelson Architects 95 Washington St Morristown NJ 07960-6816 E-mail: nadaskayr@nkarchitects.com.

NADEAU, BERTIN FELIX, diversified financial services company executive; b. May 26, 1940; s. J.-D. and Irene (Daigle) N.; m. Juliette Angell, July 24, 1971; children: Eric, Shahn, Stephanie. BA, Coll. St-Louis, 1961; grad., Ecole des Hautes Etudes Commerciales de Montreal, 1964; postgrad., Harvard U.; DBA, Ind. U., 1969; LLD (hon.), Queen's U.; D in Fin. (hon.), Moncton U.; DBA (hon.), Sainte-Anne U.; D in Civil Law (hon.), Bishop's U. Chmn., CEO Unigesco Inc., 1982-94, Provigo Inc., 1989-93; chmn., CEO, Gescolynx Inc., Montreal, 1994—. Bd. dirs. Sun Life Fin., Inc., Sun Life Assurance Co. Can., Lafarge N.Am. Inc. Bd. dirs. Montreal Gen. Hosp. Found. Office: GescoLynx Inc 606 Cathcart Ste 1035 Montreal QC Canada H3B 1K9

NADEAU, JACQUES O. brokerage house executive; Chmn. bd. Montréal Exch., Canada, 2000—; vice chmn. bd. Yorkton Securities Inc., Montréal, Canada, 2001—. Office: Bourse de Montréal Inc Tour de la Bourse PO Box 61 800 Victoria Sq Montreal QC Canada H4Z 1A9

NADEAU, JERRY, race car driver; b. Danbury, Conn., Sept. 9, 1970; m. Jada Nadeau. Racecar driver Richard Jackson, 1997, Hendrick Motorsports. Named winner, NAPA 500, 2000, Rookie of the Yr., Skip Barber Ea. Series, 1991; recipient 4th pl., European Formula Ford Festival, 1993, Silver medal, Nations Cub VII, Eng., 1996. Avocations: skiing, golf. Office: c/o Hendrick Motorsports 4400 Papa Joe Hendrick Blvd Charlotte NC 28262

NADEAU, JOHN, marketing and corporate communications consultant; b. NYC, Apr. 22, 1934; m. Beryl Green, July 11, 1962; children: Louise, Philip. BA, Emerson Coll., 1956; MA, Harvard U., 1957. Announcer WGBH-TV-FM, Boston, 1954-57; English tchr. Lynnfield (Mass.) H.S., 1957-60; announcer WBCN-FM, Boston, 1960; English tchr. Whitman H.S., South Huntington, N.Y., 1961-64; pub. rels. dir. Dutchess Coll., Poughkeepsie, NY, 1964-69; editor Berkshire Life, Pittsfield, Mass., 1969-76; mgr. advt., pub. rels. Gen. Am. Life, St. Louis, 1976-86, dir. corp. comm., 1986-92, dir. comm. svcs., 1993-98, GenAm. Mgmt. Co., St. Louis, 1999. Editor Gen. Am. Solutions mag., 1994-99; contbr. articles to profl. jours. Reader Wash. Talking Book and Braille Libr., Seattle, 2002—; bd. advisors Creative Retirement Inst., Edmonds, Wash., 2003—; bd. dirs. Mo. Concert Ballet, St. Louis, 1978—85. Recipient Telly award for corp. video, 1990, 97, 98, Golden Reel award for script writing 1998 Internat. TV Assn., Spl. Appreciation award Mathews-Dickey Boys Club, St. Louis, 2001; Fulbright fellow, Padiham, Eng., 1960-61. Mem.: Life Ins. Communicators Assn. (exec. com. 1985—87, faculty and dir. comm. workshop and ann. meeting, Excellence awards, Best of Show awards 1996, 1997, Spl. Recognition for Outstanding Contbns. award 1987), Harvard Club of Western Wash. Unitarian Universalist. Avocations: reading, travel, French language and literature, bicycling. Office Phone: 360-435-2662. Personal E-mail: nadeaujandb@msn.com.

NADEAU, JOSEPH EUGENE, health care management consultant, information systems consultant; b. Portland, Maine, Sept. 23, 1937; s. Edwin Tustin and Beatrice Margaret (Spiller) N.; m. Mary Lou Prendible, Dec. 2, 1961; children: Laura, Keith, Michael. BS in Math., Boston Coll., 1960. Cert. computer profl. Dir. sys. devel. Mass. Hosp. Assn., Burlington, 1967-72; S.E. regional mgr. Automatic Data Processing, Miami, Fla., 1972-73; S.E. regional mktg. mgr. Space Age Computer Sys., Louisville, 1973-74; prin. COMPUTERx Cons., Miami, 1974—. Asst. scoutmaster South Fla. coun. Boy Scouts Am., 1972-81. 1st lt. U.S. Army, 1960-64, Germany. Mem. Am. Hosp. Assn., Soc. Computer Medicine, Data Processing Mgmt. Assn., Hosp. Mgmt. Sys. Soc., Assn. Sys. Mgmt. (pres. 1971-72), Hosp. Fin. Mgmt. Assn. (chmn. data processing com. 1967-84), Am. Arbitration Assn. (arbitrator 1980—). Home: 10260 SW 144th St Miami FL 33176-7034 Office: COMPUTERx Consulting 9719 S Dixie Hwy Ste 1 Miami FL 33156-2834

NADEAU, JOSEPH P. state supreme court justice; AB, Dartmouth Coll.; LLB, Boston U., 1962. Pvt. practice trial atty., 1962—81; justice Durham Dist. Ct., 1968-81; judge N.H. Superior Ct., 1981-92, chief justice, 1992; assoc. justice N.H. Supreme Ct., 2000—. Mem. Jud. Br. Adminstrv. Coun., Supreme Ct. Jud.Ednl. Svcs. Com., Supreme Ct. Accreditation Commn.; pres. Am. Acad. Jud. Edn., 1990-92; participant ct. study program former Soviet Union, faculty jud. edn. program, Latvia, study programs in Russia, Georgia, Armenia; involved in jud. edn. seminars and legis. activities in Albania, Bulgaria, Kazakhstan, Poland. Mem. Gov.'s Commn. on Domestic Violence. Office: Supreme Ct Bldg One Noble Dr Concord NH 03301-6160

NADEAU, MICHAEL JOSEPH, staff assistant; b. Glens Falls, NY, Dec. 19, 1949; s. John Long and Mary Catherine (Cimo) N. Student of Eli Siegel's Aesthetic Realism, N.Y.C., 1977-81; AA in English with honors, Borough of Manhattan C.C., N.Y.C., 1992. Orderly Glens Falls (N.Y.) Hosp., 1969-72; record storage clk. Continental Ins. Co., Glens Falls, 1972-75; purchasing agt. Maersk Inc., Madison, N.J., 1975-93; coll. svc. asst. Passaic County C.C., Paterson, N.J., 1993-99, staff asst. Wanaque Acad. Ctr., 1999—. Author: The Adventures of Prudence Longface, 1993. Actor, singer Elbee Audio Players, N.Y.C., 1979-81. With USN, 1969-70. Mem. Am. Legion. Democrat. Roman Catholic. Avocations: bowling, swimming, boating, woodworking, singing. Home: 15 Overlook Ave Mine Hill NJ 07803-3100 Office Phone: 973-248-3000. Business E-Mail: mnadeau@pccc.edu.

NADEAU, REGINALD ANTOINE, medical educator; b. St. Leonard, N.B., Can., Dec. 18, 1932; married, 1957; 2 children. BA, Loyola Coll., Montreal, 1952; MD, U. Montreal, 1957. From asst. prof. to assoc. prof. Faculty Medicine, U. Montreal, 1964-70, prof. physiology, 1972-75, prof. medicine, 1975-99; cardiologist Hopital Sacre Coeur, Montreal, 1972—2002. Career investigator Med. Rsch. Coun. Can., 1965. Fellow Royal Coll. Physicians (Can.); mem. Can. Physiol. Soc., Can. Cardiovasc. Soc., Am. Coll. Cardiology. Achievements include research in basic and clinical cardiology. Office: Sacre Coeur Hosp Montreal 5400 Gouin Blvd W Montreal QC Canada H4J 1C5 E-mail: r-nadeau@crhsc.umontreal.ca.

NADEAU, ROBERT BERTRAND, JR., lawyer; b. Miami Beach, Fla., July 15, 1950; s. Robert B. and Ernestine Inez (Nicholson) N. BBA magna cum laude, U. Notre Dame, 1972; JD with honors, U. Fla., 1975. Bar: Fla. 1975, U.S. Dist. Ct. (mid. dist.) Fla. 1976, U.S. Dist. Ct. (so. dist.) Fla. 1982, U.S. Ct. Appeals (11th cir.) 1982. Asst. to pres. The Fla. Bar, Tampa, 1975-76; ptnr. Akerman, Senterfitt & Eidson, P.A., Orlando, Fla., 1976—. Arbitrator Am. Arbitration Assn., Orlando, 1987—. Mem. ABA, The Fla. Bar (chmn. student edn. and admission to bar com., vice chmn. 9th cir. grievance com.), Notre Dame Club Greater Orlando (pres. 1979-80). Avocations: golf, running. Office: Akerman Senterfitt & Eidson PA 255 S Orange Ave Orlando FL 32801-3445 Office Phone: 407-843-7860.

NADEAU, STEVEN C. lawyer; b. Schenectady, N.Y., July 6, 1954; AB magna cum laude, Boston Coll., 1974, JD cum laude, 1977. Bar: Mich. 1977. Mediator Wayne County Cir. Ct., 1983-88; mem., chair environ. law dept. Honigman Miller Schwartz and Cohn LLP, Detroit. Coord. dir. Sediment Mgmt. Work Group, 1998—. Mem. ABA (sect. natural resources), State Bar Mich. (sect. environ. law). Office: Honigman Miller Schwartz and Cohn LLP 660 Woodward Ave Ste 2290 Detroit MI 48226-3506 E-mail: snadeau@honigman.com.

NADEINE, VLADIMIR, journalist, editor; b. Donetzk, Ukraine, USSR, Apr. 19, 1938; s. Dimitri and Sofia Nadeine; m. Olga Krassouska; 1 child, Olga. MA, Lviv State U., Ukraine, 1960, journalist degere, 1961, Moscow State U., 1961, MA, 1963. Mng. editor Crocodile mag., Moscow, 1963-71; satire columnist Izvestia, Moscow, 1971-89, bur. chief Washington, 1989-97; dir. programming Ethnic Am. Broadcasting Co., Ft. Lee, N.J., 1997—. Author: (short stories) How To Sell Rams, 1965, Non-Dimenional Pants, 1967, Three Carats for You Only, 1976, You Will Be Surprised, 1978. Recipient award for best Moscow journalist Union Journalists, 1968, for best Russian satire writer, 1974, for best journalist of USSR, 1988. Avocations: gardening, fishing. Home: 188 Hiawatha Blvd Oakland NJ 07436-3643 Office: EABC One Bridge Plz Fort Lee NJ 07024

NADEL, ELLIOTT, investment firm executive; b. NYC, Nov. 23, 1945; s. Archie and Faye (Braverman) N.; children: Lindsey, Amanda. BBA, Baruch Coll., 1969, MBA, 1971. Portfolio mgr. SwissRe Advisors, N.Y.C., 1973-74; v.p., stockbroker E. F. Hutton, N.Y.C., 1975-84, Shearson Lehman Bros., N.Y.C., 1984-85, Oppenheimer & Co., N.Y.C., 1985, Rooney Pace Inc., N.Y.C., 1986-87, Philips Appel & Walden, N.Y.C., 1987-88; sr. v.p. investments Moore, Schley & Cameron, N.Y.C., 1988-90, Prudential-Securities, N.Y.C., 1990-94; sr. v.p. Gilford Securities, N.Y.C., 1994—96, SFY Investments, 1996—97, Westrock Advisor, 1997—99, Tarpon Scurry Investments, 1999—2000, Chgo. Investments Group, 2001, EN Investments, 2001—; prin. Hedge Fund. With U.S. Army, 1969-74. Jewish. Avocations: jogging, reading, cars, golf, travel. Office Phone: 917-301-7600.

NADEL, MONROE STANLEY, retired architect, landscape architect; b. The Bronx, N.Y., July 24, 1922; s. Joseph Paurice Nadel and Rae Ruth (Gross); m. Evelyn Feldman, Sept. 6, 1953; children: Jonathan Oren, Jeremy Adam. Journeyman shipfitter, N.Y. Naval Shipyard Sch., 1943; BS in Social Sci., CCNY, 1949; BArch, Columbia U., 1956, MArch, 1975. Registered architect, N.Y.; registered landscape architect, N.Y. Shipfitter, estimator N.Y. Naval Shipyard, Bklyn., 1940—46; estimator M.W. Kellogg Co. Oil Refinery Engrs., N.Y.C., 1946—49, Nat. Supply Export Corp., Oil Well Supplies, N.Y.C., 1949—51; draftsman Seelye, Stevenson, Value & Knecht, Engrs., N.Y.C., 1951—52, Coffin & Coffin, Architects, N.Y.C., 1953, Alfred Hopkins & Assocs., N.Y.C., 1953-55; designer, draftsman York & Sawyer Architects, N.Y.C., 1955-60; architect Associated Archs. & Engrs., N.Y.C., 1960; architect, site planner Viola, Bernhard and Philips, Architects and Engrs., N.Y.C., 1960-65; architect Divsn. of Sch. Bldgs./N.Y. Bd. Edn. Bur. of Design, Long Island City, N.Y.C., NY, 1965-69, chief archtl. design sect., sr. arch. to adminstrv. arch., 1969-76, chief archtl. sect., contracts sect., cons. rev. sect., 1976-92; ret., 1992. Mem. AIA (emeritus, corp. mem.), Am. Soc. Landscape Architects (emeritus). Avocations: genealogy, stamp collecting/philately, gardening, yoga exercises. Home (Winter): 25 Plaza St W Apt 2D Brooklyn NY 11217 Home (Summer): PO Box 2183 Bridgehampton NY 11932-2183

NADEL, NORMAN ALLEN, civil engineer; b. N.Y.C., Apr. 10, 1927; s. Louis and Bertha (Julius) N.; m. Cynthia Esther Jereski, July 6, 1952; children: Nancy Sarah Frank, Lawrence Bruce. B.C.E., CCNY, 1949; postgrad., Columbia U., 1949-50. Registered profl. engr., N.Y., Conn. Engr. Arthur A. Johnson Corp., N.Y.C., 1950-53; engr. Slattery Contracting Corp., N.Y.C., 1953-56; mgr., estimator Hartsdale Constrn. Corp., Hartsdale, N.Y., 1956-59; engr. MacLean Grove & Co., Inc., Greenwich, Conn., 1959-63, project mgr., 1963-66, v.p., 1966-70, pres., 1970-94; chmn. Nadel Assocs., Inc., Brewster, N.Y., 1988—. Cons. tunnel and underground constrn.; mem. com. on tunneling Transp. Rsch. Bd., Washington, 1974-75; mem. U.S. Nat. Com. on Tunneling Tech., Washington, 1976-82, chmn., 1980-81; chmn. adv. com. Superconducting Super Collider Underground Tech., 1992-94. Trustee Tunnel Workers Welfare Fund, N.Y.C., 1976-88; mem. adv bd. CCNY Engring. Sch., 1992—. With USNR, 1945-46 Named Heavy Constrn. Man of Yr., United Jewish Appeal, 1984; Benjamin Wright award Conn. Soc. Civil Engrs., 1984, Townsend Harris medal City Coll. of N.Y. Alumni Assn., 1987. Fellow ASCE (Constrn. Mgmt. award 1986); mem. NAE, Conn. Acad. Sci. and Engring., The Moles (pres. 1982-83, Outstanding Achievement in Constrn. award 1985), Am. Arbitration Assn., Tau Beta Pi, Chi Epsilon. Office: Nadel Assocs Inc 420 Clock Tower Commons Brewster NY 10509-4060

NADELBERG, ERIC PAUL, brokerage house executive; b. Providence, Dec. 14, 1947; s. Arnold and Sandra (Schwartz) N.; m. Evelynne Luberoff, Dec. 12, 1968; children: Amanda, Ariel. BA, Bklyn. Coll., 1973; MA, Sch. of Journalism, N.Y.U., 1994. Registered commodities rep. News analyst The Wall Street Jour., N.Y.C., 1973-76; reporter Reuters Ltd., N.Y.C., 1976-77; sr. analyst E.F. Hutton & Co., Inc., N.Y.C., 1977-79, v.p., 1983-85, Gill & Duffus Svcs., Inc., N.Y.C., 1979-81, Rudolf Wolff Futures, Inc., N.Y.C., 1981-83; pres. Tropical Trader, Inc., Hoboken, N.J., 1985-90; 1st v.p. Merrill Lynch Inc., N.Y.C., N.J., 1990-96; sr. v.p. Latin Am. divsn. ABN-AMRO, N.Y.C., 1996-98; mng. dir. ADM Investor Svcs. Inc., N.Y.C., 1998—2004; sr. v.p. investments Prudential Fian. Derivatives, LLC, 2004—. Dir. Futures Rsch. co., 1991—; cons. UNCTAD, 1993—, World Bank, 1993—. Contbr. Barrons Fin. Mag., 1976-79; contbg. editor Commodity Rsch. Bur., 1986-93; columnist Cotton Mag., Memphis, 1977-88. With U.S. Army, 1968-71. Mem.: Market Technicians Assn. Democrat. Avocations: fishing, walking, writing. Office: ADM Invesor Svcs Inc 140 Broadway New York NY 10005-1101

NADELLA, SATYA, information technology executive; MS in Computer Sci., U. Wis.; MBA, U. Chgo. Software devel. engr. Sun Microsystems Inc.; from group product mgr. to leader bCentral mktg. & bus. devel. Microsoft, Redmond, Wash., leader bCentral mktg. & bus. devel. Office: One Microsoft Way Redmond WA 98052-6399

NADELSON, CAROL COOPERMAN, psychiatrist, educator; b. Bklyn., Oct. 13, 1936; m. Theodore Nadelson, July 16, 1965; children: Robert, Jennifer. BA magna cum laude, Bklyn. Coll., 1957; MD with honors, U. Rochester, N.Y., 1961. Dir. med. student edn. Beth Israel Hosp., Boston, 1974-79, psychiatrist, 1977; assoc. prof. psychiatry Harvard U. Med. Sch., Boston, 1976-79; rsch. scholar Radcliffe Coll., Cambridge, Mass., 1979-80; prof. psychiatry Tufts Med. Sch., Boston, 1979-95; vice-chmn., dir. tng. and edn. dept. psychiatry Tufts-New Eng. Med. Ctr., Boston, 1979-93; clin. prof. psychiatry Harvard Med. Sch., Boston, 1995—; psychiatrist dept. medicine, divsn. psychiatry Brigham and Women's Hosp., Boston, 1998, dir., ptnr. office for women's careers, 1998. Cons. Peace Corps, 2000. Editor: The Woman Patient, Vols. 1, 2 and 3, 1978, 82; Treatment Interventions in Human Sexuality, 1983; Marriage and Divorce: A Contemporary Perspective, 1984, Women Physicians in Leadership Roles, 1986, Training Psychiatrists for the '90s, 1987, Treating Chronically Mentally Ill Women, 1988, Family Violence, 1988, Women and Men: New Perspectives on Gender Differences, 1990, International Review of Psychiatry Vols. 1 & 2, 1993, 96, Major Psychiatric Disorders, 1982, The Challenge of Change: Perspectives on Family, Work and Education, 1983; editor-in-chief Am. Psychiatric Press, Inc., 1986—, pres., CEO, 1995—; contbr. over 217 articles to profl. jours. Trustee Menninger Found., 1988—. Recipient Gold Medal award Mt. Airy Psychiat. Ctr., 1981, award Case Western Res. U., 1983, Elizabeth Blackwell award Am. Med. Women's Assn., 1985, Women in Medicine Leadership Devel. award Am. Assn. Med. Colls., 1999, Alexandra Symonds award 2002; Picker Found. grant, 1982-83. Fellow: Am. Psychiat. Assn. (pres. 1985—86, Seymour D. Vestermark award 1992, Disting. Svc. award 1995), Ctr. Advanced Study Behavioral Scos.; mem.: AMA (impaired physicians com. 1984, Sidney Cohen award 1988), Group for Advancement of Psychiatry (bd. dirs. 1984), Am. Coll. Psychiatrists (bd. regents 1991—94, Disting. Svc. award 1989), Phi Beta

Kappa, Alpha Omega Alpha. Avocation: travel. Office: Brigham and Women's Hosp 75 Francis St PB502 Boston MA 02119- Home: 30 Amory St Brookline MA 02446 E-mail: carol_nadelson@hms.harvard.edu.

NADER, LAURA, anthropology educator; b. Winsted, Conn., Sept. 30, 1930; m. Norman Milleron, Sept. 1, 1962; 3 children BA, Wells Coll., 1952; PhD, Radcliffe Coll., 1962. Mem. faculty U. Calif.-Berkeley, 1960—, now prof. anthropology; vis. prof. Yale Law Sch., New Haven, fall 1971; Henry R. Luce prof. Wellesley Coll., Mass., 1983-84; Henry R. Luce prof. Sch. Law Harvard U., 1987-89, Stanford U., 1987-89. Field work in Mex., Lebanon, Morocco; mem. adv. com. NSF, 1971-75; mem. cultural anthropology com. NIMH, 1968—, chmn. to 1971, chmn. social scis. research tng. rev. com., 1976-78; mem. NAS-NRC assembly behavioral and social scis., 1969-71, 73-75, 75—; mem. com. Nuclear and Alternative Energy Forms, NAS, 1976-77. Editor: Law in Culture and Society, 1969, The Disputing Process, 1978, No Access to Law-Alternatives to the American Judicial System, 1980, Harmony Ideology, 1990, Naked Science, 1996, The Life of the Law, 2002; contbr. articles to profl. jours.; author ednl. films, mem. editl. com. Law and Soc. Rev., 1967—. Mem. Calif. Coun. for the Humanities, 1975-79; mem. Carnegie Coun. on Children, 1972-77; active Coun. Librs. at Libr. of Congress, Washington, 1988—. Radcliffe Coll. grantee, 1954-59; Thaw fellow Harvard U., 1955-56, 58-59; Peabody Mus. grantee, 1954-59; Am. Philos. Assn. grantee, 1955; Mexican Govt. grantee, 1957-58; Milton Fund grantee, 1959-60, Wellness Found. grantee, 1993-96; fellow Ctr. Advanced Study in Behavioral Scis., Stanford, Calif., 1963-64; NSF grantee, 1966-68; Wenner Gren Found. grantee, 1964, 66, 73; Carnegie Corp. grantee, 1975; Woodrow Wilson fellow, 1979-80; Wells Coll. Alumnae award, 1980; Radcliffe Coll. Alumnae award, 1984 Mem.: AAAS, Soc. Women Geographers, Am. Acad. Arts and Scis., Ctr. for Study of Responsive Law (trustee 1968—), Law and Soc. Assn. (trustee 1967—72, Harry Kalven prize 1995), Social Sci. Rsch. Coun., Am. Anthrop. Assn. (planning and devel. com. 1968—71, 1975—76), Am. Acad. Arts and Scis. Office: U Calif Dept Anthropology 313 Kroeber Hl Berkeley CA 94720-0001 Office Phone: 510-642-1218., 510-642-3391.

NADER, RALPH, consumer advocate, lawyer, author; b. Winsted, Conn., Feb. 27, 1934; s. Nadra and Rose (Bouziane) N. AB magna cum laude, Princeton U., 1955; LLB with distinction, Harvard U., 1958. Bar: Conn. 1958, Mass. 1959, U.S. Supreme Ct. 1959. Practiced law in, Hartford, Conn., from 1959; lectr. history and govt. U. Hartford, 1961-63; founder Essential Info., 1982, The Multinational Monitor Mag., 1980. Founder Center for Responsive Law, Pub. Interest Research Group, Center for Auto Safety, Pub. Citizen, Clean Water Action Project, Disability Rights Ctr., Pension Rights Ctr., Project for Corporate Responsibility; lectr. to colls. and univs.; lectr. Princeton U., 1967-68; co-founder Princeton Project 55, 1989. Author: Unsafe at Any Speed, 1965, rev., 1972; sponsor: Working on the System: A Manual for Citizen's Access to Federal Agencies, 1972; co-author: Action for a Change, 1972, You and Your Pension, 1973, Taming the Giant Corporation, 1976, Menace of Atomic Energy, 1977, The Lemon Book, 1980, The Big Boys, 1986, Winning The Insurance Game, 1990, The Ralph Nader Reader, 2000; editor: Whistle Blowing: The Report on the Conference on Professional Responsibility, 1972, The Consumer and Corporate Accountability, 1973; co-editor: Corporate Power in America, 1973, Verdicts on Lawyers, 1976, Who's Poisoning America, 1981; contbg. editor: Ladies Home Jour., 1973—, also articles. Presdl. candidate, 2000, 2004. With U.S. Army, 1959. Recipient Nieman Fellows award, 1965-66; named One of 10 Outstanding Young Men of Year U.S. Jr. C. of C., 1967 Mem. ABA, AAAS, Phi Beta Kappa. Green party. Address: Ctr for Study of Responsive Law PO Box 19367 Washington DC 20036-9367*

NADER, ROBERT ALEXANDER, judge, lawyer; b. Warren, Ohio, Mar. 31, 1928; s. Nassef J. and Emily (Nader) N.; m. Nancy M. Veauthier. BA, Western Res. U., 1950, LL.B., 1953. Bar: Ohio 1953. Ptnr. Paul G. Nader, Warren, 1953-83. Pres. Warren City Police and Fire Pension Bds., 1960-66; trustee Office Econ. Opportunity, 1970-72; mem. Warren City Coun., 1960-66, pres. pro tem, 1964-66; mem. Ohio Ho. of Reps., 1971-83, chmn. reference com., 1977-81, chmn. judiciary com., 1981-83; presiding judge Trumbull County Ct. Common Pleas, 1983-91; judge Ohio 11th Dist. Ct. Appeals, 1991-2003; trustee Family Svc. Assn., 1959-65. With AUS, 1946-48. Recipient Outstanding Young Man of Yr. award, 1964, award Am. Arbitration Assn., 1965, Community Action award Warren Area Bd. Realtors, 1967, Outstanding Svc. award Kent State U., Trumbull campus. 1978, Outstanding Svc. award Children's Rehab. Ctr., 1980; named to Warren H.S. Disting. Alumni Hall of Fame, 1993, Sports Hall of Fame, 2003. Mem. Ohio State Bar Assn., Trumbull County Bar Assn. (past pres., Pres.'s award for disting. svc. 2003), Ct. Appeals Judges Assn. (chmn. legis. com. 1995-98), Trumbull County Law Libr. Assn. (trustee 1958-72), Trumbull New Theatre (past pres.), KC, Elks, Lambda Chi Alpha. Roman Catholic. Home: 798 Wildwood Dr NE Warren OH 44483-4458 Office: 11th Dist Ct # Appeals 111 High St NE Warren OH 44481 *My parents provided me with a strong moral background and the inspiration to improve. I will never feel that I have achieved success and thus may continue to improve.*

NADICH, JUDAH, rabbi; b. Balt., May 13, 1912; s. Isaac and Lena (Nathanson) N.; m. Martha Hadassah Ribalow, Jan. 26, 1947; children: Leah N. (Mrs. Aryeh Meir), Shira A. (Mrs. James L. Levin), Nahma M. Nadich (Mrs. David Belcourt). BA, CCNY, 1932; MA, Columbia U., 1936; rabbi, M.H.L., Jewish Theol. Sem. Am., 1936, D.H.L., 1953, D.D. (hon), 1966. Rabbi Temple Beth David, Buffalo, 1936-40; co-rabbi Anshe Emet Synagogue, Chgo., 1940-42; lecture tour U.S., South Africa and Rhodesia, 1946-47; rabbi Kehillath Israel Congregation, Brookline, Mass., 1947-57, Park Ave. Synagogue, N.Y.C., 1957-87, rabbi emeritus, 1987—. Conducted first Bat Mitzvah in People's Republic of China, 1990. Author: Eisenhower and the Jews, 1953, Jewish Legends of the Second Commonwealth, 1983, Legends of the Rabbis, 2 vols., 1994, Rabbi Akiba and His Contemporaries, 1998; editor, translator: (Menachem Ribalow) The Flowering of Modern Hebrew Literature, 1959; editor: (Louis Ginzberg) Al Halakha v'Aggada, 1960. Pres. Rabbinical Assembly, 1972-74; pres. Jewish Book Coun. Am., 1968-72; hon. bd. dirs. Jewish Theol. Sem. Am.; past bd. dirs., mem. exec. com. Nat. Jewish Welfare Bd., Fedn. Jewish Philanthropies N.Y.; former mem. hospice com. Beth Israel Med. Ctr.; past mem. N.Y.C. Holocaust Meml.; hon. v.p. bd. dirs. Jewish Braille Inst.; bd. dirs. Friends of Jewish Hist. Mus., Warsaw; past pres. Assn. Jewish Chaplains Armed Forces; adv. to Gen. Eisenhower on Jewish affairs, ETO, 1945; com. 50th anniversary World War II U.S. Dept. Defense. Lt. col., chaplain AUS, 1942-46, ETO. Assimilated rank of Maj. Gen. South Vietnam, 1971. Decorated Order Brit. Empire, 1943, ETO with battle star medal, 1944, Croix de Guerre (France), 1945, Occupation of Germany medal, 1945, Victory medal, 1945, Ittur Lohamai Hamedinah (Israel), 1975; fellow Herbert Lehman Inst. Talmudic Ethics, 1958; Jewish Theol. Sem. Am. honoree, 1997. Mem. Mil. Chaplains Assn., Phi Beta Kappa. Lodges: Masons. Home: 1040 Park Ave New York NY 10028-1032 Office: Park Ave Synagogue 50 E 87th St New York NY 10128-1099 *Live so that your life will make a difference for the better in the lives of other people.*

NADIG, GERALD GEORGE, manufacturing executive; b. Astoria, N.Y., May 9, 1945; s. Charles Edwin and Louise (Hahn) N.; m. Nancy Hanford Stewart, June 20, 1970; children: Sara Hanford, Jennifer Stewart. AB cum laude, Harvard Coll., 1967, MBA, 1974. Fin. mgr. Rockwell Internat., Hopedale, Mass., 1974-76, materials mgr. Oshkosh, Wis., 1976-78, Marysville, Ohio, 1978-79, ops. mgr., 1979-80, plant mgr., 1980-82, regional mgr. Atlanta, 1984-85; mng. dir. Rockwell Maudslay Ltd., Great Alne, Eng., 1982-84; dir. mfg. Toyoda Machinery USA, Arlington Heights, Ill., 1985-87, v.p., gen. mgr., 1987-88; v.p., gen. mgr. Littell div. Allied Products Corp., Chgo., 1988-89; exec. v.p. pre finish metals Material Scis. Corp., 1989-90; pres. Pre Finish Metals Material Scis. Corp., 1990-91; pres., chief oper. officer Material Scis. Corp., Chgo., 1991-96, pres., CEO, 1997—2003, chmn. bd. dirs., 1998—2003; bd. dirs. Tokheim Corp., 2000—03. Mem. adv. bd. Masters in Mgmt. Program Northwestern U. Trustee Village of Lake Barrington, 1989-91. With U.S. Army, 1966-70. Mem. Soc. Mfg. Engrs. (sr.), Nat. Assn. Corp. Dirs. (bd. dirs. Chgo. chpt. 2002—), Biltmore Country Club (bd. dirs.). Avocations: golf, tennis, game theory. Home: 24354 N Grandview Dr Barrington IL 60010-6218 Office Phone: 847-381-3464. Personal E-mail: gerrynadig@aol.com.

NADIRI, M. ISHAQ, economics educator, researcher, lecturer, consultant; b. Kabul, Afghanistan, Oct. 16, 1936; s. M. Alam and Gul-Nasa N.; m. Tahira Homayun, Sept. 9, 1978; children: Youssof, Khalid. BS with highest distinction, U. Nebr., 1958; MA, U. Calif.-Berkeley, 1960, PhD, 1965; postgrad., Yale U., 1962-63. Asst. prof. Northwestern U., Evanston, Ill., 1964-66, U. Chgo. Bus. Sch., 1966-67; research fellow Nat. Bur. Econ. Research, N.Y.C., 1968-70, research assoc., 1969—; full prof. econs. NYU, 1970—, Jay Gould prof. econs., 1975—, chmn. dept. econs., 1972-78; Disting. vis. prof. Am. U. Cairo, 1993. Cons. in field; participant seminars NSF Ctr. Strategic Studies, UN Assn.; adviser to Afghanistan Interim Govt. and Pres. Hamid Karzai; CEO, Global Partnership for Afghanistan; mem. Pvt. Sector Devel. Task Force for Afghanistan; mem. Aid Coord. Com. of Afghanistan, Afghanistan-Am. Found. Author: books, including A Disequilibrium Model of Demand for Factors of Production, 1974; research, numerous publs. in field; editor books including The Importance of Technology and the Permanence of Structure in Industrial Growth, 1978, Commodity Markets and Latin American Development: A Modeling Approach, 1980; editorial bd.: Annals of Econs. and Social Measurement. Mem. Com. to Upgrade Central Park, N.Y.C.; mem. Com. to Help Afghan Refugees in the U.S. C. Miller fellow, 1958-59; U. Calif. fellow, 1959-60; Earnhart fellow, 1962-63, 63-64; grantee NSF, Ford Found., IBM Corp., AT&T. Mem. Am. Econs. Assn., Econometrica Soc., Univs.-Nat. Bur. Econ. Research, Internat. Assn. Research in Income and Wealth; mem. AAAS, Am. Statis. Assn., Council Fgn. Relations, Phi Beta Kappa, Pi Sigma Alpha, Beta Gamma Sigma Office: NYU Dept Econs 269 Mercer St Fl 7 New York NY 10003-6633 E-mail: min1@nyu.edu.

NADLER, GERALD, management consultant, educator; b. Cin., Mar. 12, 1924; s. Samuel and Minnie (Krumbein) N.; m. Elaine Muriel Dubin, June 22, 1947; children: Burton Alan, Janice Susan, Robert Daniel. Student, U. Cin., 1942-43; BSME, Purdue U., 1945, MS in Indsl. Engring, 1946, PhD, 1949. Instr. Purdue U., 1948-49; asst. prof. indsl. engring. Washington U., St. Louis, 1949-52, assoc. prof., 1952-55, prof., head dept. indsl. engring., 1955-61, prof. U. Wis., Madison, 1964-83, chmn. dept. indsl. engring., 1964-67, 71-75; prof., chmn. dept. indsl. and sys. engring. U. So. Calif., L.A., 1983-93, IBM chair engring. mgmt., 1986-93, IBM chair emeritus, prof. emeritus, 1993—; v.p. Artcraft Mfg. Co., St. Louis, 1956-57; dir. Intertherm Inc., St. Louis, 1969-85. Pres. Ctr. for Breakthrough Thinking Inc., L.A., 1989—; vis. prof. U. Birmingham, Eng., 1959, Waseda U., Tokyo, 1963-64, Ind. U., 1964, U. Louvain, Belgium, 1975, Technion-Israel Inst. Tech., Haifa, 1975-76; spkr. in field. Author: The Planning and Design Approach, 1981; (with S. Hibino) Breakthrough Thinking, 1990, 2d edit., 1994, Creative Solution Finding, 1995; (with G. Hoffherr, J. Moran) Breakthrough Thinking in Total Quality Management, 1994, (with W. Chandon) Ask the Right Questions, 2003, Smart Questions, 2004; contbr. articles to profl. jours.; reviewer books, papers, proposals. Mem. Ladue Bd. Edn., St. Louis County, 1960-63, L.A. County Quality and Productivity Commn., 1997—; chmn. planning com. Wis. Regional Med. Program, 1966-69; bd. dirs. USC Credit Union, 1994—. Served with USN, 1943-45. Gilbreth medal Soc. Advancement Mgmt., 1961, Editl. award Hosp. Mgmt. Mag., 1966, Disting. Engring. Alumnus award Purdue U., 1975, Outstanding Indsl. Engr. award, 1997; Book of Yr. award Inst. Indsl. Engrs., 1983, Frank and Lillian Gilbreth award, 1992; Phi Kappa Phi Faculty Recognition award U. So. Calif., 1990, Engring. Disting. Svc. award U. Wis. Madison, 2000. Fellow AAAS, Inst. Indsl. Engrs. (pres. 1989-90), Inst. Operations Rsch. and Mgmt. Scis., Inst. for Advancement Engrs., Am. Soc. Engring. Edn.; mem. NAE, Japan Work Design Soc. (hon. adv. 1968—), World Future Soc., Acad. Mgmt., Engring. Mgmt. Soc., Sigma Xi, Alpha Pi Mu (nat. officer), Pi Tau Sigma, Omega Rho, Tau Beta Pi. Office: Univ Park GER 240 Dept Of I&se Los Angeles CA 90089-0193 Office Phone: 213-740-6415. Business E-Mail: nadler@usc.edu. E-mail: gnadler@breakthroughthinking.com.

NADLER, HENRY LOUIS, pediatrician, geneticist, medical educator; b. N.Y.C., Apr. 15, 1936; s. Herbert and Mary (Kartiganer) N.; m. Benita Weinhard, June 16, 1957; children: Karen, Gary, Debra, Amy. AB, Colgate U., 1957; MD, Northwestern U., 1961; MS, U. Wis., 1965. Diplomate: Am. Bd. Pediatrics, Am. Bd. Med. Genetics. Intern NYU Med. Ctr., 1961-62, sr. resident pediatrics, 1962-63, chief resident, 1963-64; teaching asst. NYU Sch. Medicine, 1962-63, clin. instr., 1963-64, U. Wis. Sch. Medicine, 1964-65; practice medicine specializing in pediatrics Chgo., 1965—; fellow Children's Meml. Hosp. dept. pediatrics Northwestern U., 1964-65; assoc. in pediatrics Northwestern U. Med. Sch., 1965-66, asst. prof., 1967-68, assoc. prof., 1968-70, prof., 1970-81, chmn. dept. pediatrics, 1970-81; prof. Northwestern U. Med. Sch. (Grad. Sch.), 1971-80; mem. staff Children's Meml. Hosp., 1965-81, head div. genetics, 1969-81, chief of staff, 1970-81; dean, prof. pediatrics, ob-gyn Wayne State U. Med. Sch., Detroit, 1981-88; prof. U. Chgo., 1988-89, U. Ill., 1989—; pres. Michael Reese Hosp. and Med. Ctr., Chgo., 1988-91; market med. dir. Aetna Health Plans, Phoenix, 1993-94, mktg. v.p., CEO, 1994-95; v.p. managed care/physician integration, med. dir. Am. Healthcare Sys., San Diego, 1995. Mem. vis. staff, div. medicine Northwestern Meml. Hosp., 1972-81; staff Children's Hosp. of Mich., 1981-88. Mem. editorial bd. Comprehensive Therapy, 1973-84, Am. Jour. Human Genetics, 1979-83, Pediatrics in Rev., 1980-83, Am. Jour. Diseases of Children, 1983-91; contbr. articles to profl. jours. Recipient E. Mead Johnson award for pediatric rsch., 1973, Meyer O. Cantor award for Disting. Svc. Internat. Coll. Surgeons, 1987; Irene Heinz Given and John La Porte Given rsch. prof. pediatrics, 1970-81. Fellow Am. Acad. Pediatrics; mem. Am. Soc. for Clin. Investigation, Am. Soc. Human Genetics, Am. Pediatric Soc., Soc. for Pediatric Rsch., Midwest Soc. for Pediatric Rsch., Pan Am. Med. Assn., Alpha Omega Alpha. Home and Office: 25150 N Windy Walk Dr Unit 23 Scottsdale AZ 85255-8105 E-mail: hlnadler@aol.com.

NADLER, JERROLD LEWIS, congressman, lawyer; b. Brooklyn, N.Y., June 13, 1947; m. Joyce L. Miller, 1976; 1 child, Michael. JD, Fordham U., 1978; AB, Columbia Coll., 1969. Mem. Community Planning Bd. No. 7, Manhattan, 1967-71; Dem. leader 67th Assembly Dist. Part C, 1969-71; exec. dir. Community Free Dem., 1972; law clerk Morgan, Finnegan, Pine, Foley & Lee, 1976; Dem. dist. leader 69th Assembly dist. Part A, 1973-77; assemblyman N.Y. State 69th dist., 1977-82, 67th dist., 1983-92; mem. 102d Congress from 17th N.Y. dist., Washington, 1992, 103d-108th Congress from 8th N.Y. Dist., Washington, 1993—; subcoms. comml./adminstrv. law, cts. intellectual property 103d-105th Congress from 8th N.Y. Dist., 1995-96, ranking Dem. subcom. on comml./adminstrv. law, 1997-2000, mem. subcom. on constn., 1997—, mem. subcoms. on surftace transp., water resources, environ., 1993-94, mem. subcoms. on railroads/aviation, 1995—, mem. subcoms. on surface transp. and railroads, 1997-2000; mem. Judiciary com., transp. infrastructure com., Regional Whip 106th Congress from 8th N.Y. Dist., 1999—2002, asst. whip, 2003—. Mem. coms. on judiciary and pub. works and transp. U.S. Ho. Reps., 1995—, subcom. on constl. law and immigration, 1993-94, jud. com., ranking mem. comml. and adminstr. law subcom., transp. and infrastructure com., chmn. Assembly Com. on Corps, Authorities and Commn., 1991-92, Assembly Consumer Affairs and Protection Com., 1987-90, Assembly Com. on Ethics and Guidance, 1985-86, Assembly Subcom. on Mass Transit and Rail Freight, 1979-86, mem. Assembly Com. on Judiciary, Gov. Ops., Legis. Tax Study Commn.; mem. Assembly Com. Ways and Means, Housing, Real Property Tax, Health, Election Law, Ins., ranking mem. subcom. on constn., subcom. on comml. and admintrv. law, subcom. on hwys. and transit, subcom. on railroads. Founder, chmn. West Side Peace Com., 1969-71; former mem. exec. coun. N.Y. State New Dem. Coalition; pres. Zionist Orgn. Am. dist. 7A; active Common Cause, Met. Coun. on Housing, West Side Tenants Union, Community Free Dems.; mem. nat. governing coun. Am. Jewish Congress; former bd. dirs. N.Y. State Nat. Abortion Rights Action League, Women's InterArts Ctr. Recipient hon. recognition award N.Y. State Nurses Assn., 1982, Disting. Svc. award Coalition on Domestic Violence, 1989; named Assembly Mem. of Yr. N.Y. chpt. NOW, 1980; Pulitzer scholar Columbia U. Mem. NOW, NAACP, N.Y. Bar Assn., N.Y. Civil Liberties Union (honor roll), Citizens Union, League Conservation Voters, New Dem. Coalition, Ams. for Dem. Action (bd. dirs., nat. v.p.). Democrat. Office: US Ho of Reps 2334 Hob Washington DC 20515-3208 E-mail: jerrold.nadler@mail.house.gov.

NADLER, LEE M. research scientist; MD, Harvard U., 1973. Resident Columbia-Presbyn.; trainee tumor immunology Nat. Cancer Inst.; med. oncology fellow Dana-Farber Cancer Inst., staff, 1980—, sr. v.p. exptl. medicine. Prof. medicine Harvard Med. Sch. Office: Dana Farber Cancer Inst 44 Binney St Boston MA 02115

NADLER, MYRON JAY, lawyer, director; b. Youngstown, Ohio, July 22, 1923; s. Murray A. and Jean (Davis) N.; m. Alice Blue, Nov. 4, 1951; children: Jed M., Wendy D., John M.S. Student, N.Mex. State Coll., 1943-44; BS in Econs. Wharton Sch., U. Pa., 1947; JD with distinction, U. Mich., 1949. Bar: Ohio 1950. Pres., shareholder Nadler, Nadler & Burdman Co., L.P.A., Youngstown, 1950-95, pres., 1950-95; ret., 1996. Asst. editor Mich. Law Rev., 1949; instr. Youngstown U. Law Sch., 1952-59. Author: (with Saul Nadler) Nadler on Bankruptcy, 1965, April's Bankruptcy Forms and Practice, 1964; contbr. articles to profl. jours. Chmn. exec. budget com. United Appeal, Youngstown, 1964-66, v.p., 1967-70; co-chmn. Mayor's Commn. Human Rights, 1957; mem. Mahoning County Planning Commn., 1965-71, Nat. Budget and Consultation Com., 1967-70; trustee Cmty. Corp., Youngstown, v.p., 1977-82, chmn. pers. com., 1974-92; bd. dirs. Ctr. for Learning, Villa Maria, Pa., 1969-95, pres., 1981-89, chmn. bd., 1989-94. With AUS, 1943-45. Decorated Purple Heart with oak leaf cluster. Mem. Fellows of Ohio Bar Assn. Found., ABA, Ohio Bar Assn., Mahoning County Bar Assn., Scribes Assn. Legal Writers, Comml. Law League Am., Squaw Creek Country Club (pres. 1966-68), Hamlet Country Club. Home: 601 Pine Lake Dr Delray Beach FL 33445-9042 Office: 20 Federal Plz W Ste 600 Youngstown OH 44503-1423

NADLER, NONA JEAN, social worker; b. Greensboro, N.C., Feb. 13, 1945; d. Quincy and Beulah (Snipes) Campbell; m. David Henegan, Feb. 7, 1963 (div. Sept. 1992); children: Shrella Henegan, David Jr. Henegan, Sheila Henegan, Tyrone Henegan, Sherry Henegan; m. Jerold Nadler, Nov. 22, 1992. AA, Boricua Coll., Bklyn., 1988; BS, Boricua Coll., 1990. Registered dental technician N.Y., 1996, cert. arrhythmia technologist N.Y., 1989. Legal dept. adminstrv. asst. N.Y. Property Underwriting Inc., N.Y.C., 1971—86; child life specialist Interfaith Hosp., Bklyn., 1990—92; nursery dir. Rose Kennedy Family Ctr., Bklyn., 1992—93; borough dir. MHRA, Bklyn., 1993—95; bd. adminstr. Good Samaritan Devel. Ctr., Bklyn., 1995—99; client svcs. adminstr. Toddlers & Infant Program, Spl. Edn., Inc., Bklyn., 1999—. Child care cons., Bklyn., 1995—; Reiki cons. Metamorphiss Healing Ctr., Bklyn., 1996—; infancy parenting cons. Bank St. Coll., N.Y.C., 1991. Mem. N.Y.C. Children's Coun., Bklyn., 1995—. Named Bronze Leader, DAV, 2002—03, Silver Leader, 2003. Mem.: Nat. Geog. Soc., N.Y. Acad. Scis. Avocations: sponge art painting, writing, new age crafts, collecting DVD movies. Office: Toddlers & Infants Program Ste 5 401 Bloomingdale Rd Staten Island NY 10309

NADLER, ROBERT B. medical educator; AB, Dartmouth Coll., 1985; MD, Northwestern U., 1989. Cert. Nat. Bd. Med. Examiners, 1990, Am. Bd. Urology, 1998. Instr. urologic surgery Wash. U. Sch. Medicine, St. Louis, 1995—96; asst. prof. urologic surgery, head sect. endourology, laparoscopy and stone disease Northwestern U. Feinberg Sch. Medicine, Chgo., 1996—2001, assoc. prof. urologic surgery, endourology fellowship dir., 2001—. Lectr., urology clerkship for 3rd yr. students Northwestern U. Feinberg Sch. Medicine, Chgo., 1996—2002, facilitator problem based learning, 1999—. Editor: Urology, 1999—. Grantee, Am. Found. for Urol. Disease, 1992—93, NIH; Nat. Kidney Found. fellow, Am. Found. for Urologic Disease, 1992—93, Clin. Oncology fellow, Am. Cancer Soc., 1992—93, Targeted Rsch. Project grantee. Mem.: ACS, AMA, Ill. Urol. Assn., Endourological Assn. (exec. com.), Chgo. Urol. Soc., Am. Urol. Assn. (North Ctrl. sect.). Office: Northwestern Univ Galter 20-150 675 North St Clair St Chicago IL 60611

NADLER, SIGMOND HAROLD, physician, surgeon; b. Bklyn., May 16, 1932; s. Morris and Rose (Levine) N.; m. Beverly Melcher, June 20, 1954; children: Geoffrey, Shail, Tamara, Kimberly. BA, State U. Iowa, 1955, MD, 1957. Intern Menorah Med. Ctr., Kansas City, Mo., 1957-58, resident in surgery, 1958-61, Roswell Park Meml. Inst., 1961-63, mem. staff, 1962-68, clin. coord. Ea. region clin. drug evaluation program, 1966-68, project dir. nat. adj. studies, 1966-68, assoc. chief cancer rsch. surgery, 1966-68; assoc. prof. surgery Jefferson Med. Coll., Phila., 1968-70; also dir. clin. cancer tng., asst. clin. prof. surgery SUNY, Buffalo, 1970-94, prof. emeritus, 1994—. Mem. Am. Soc. Clin. Oncology. Achievements include research in human tumor immunotherapy.

NADLER-HURVICH, HEDDA CAROL, public relations executive; b. Bronx, N.Y., June 15, 1944; d. Julius Louis and Julia Cohen; m. David George Nadler, Oct. 3, 1965 (div. 1979); 1 child, Laura Lee Nadler; m. Burton Earl Hurvich, Dec. 8, 1984. BBA, Baruch Coll., 1965. V.p., sec. Irving L. Straus Assocs., Inc., N.Y.C., 1965-80; pres. Mount & Nadler Inc., N.Y.C., 1999—. Avocations: aerobics, yoga. Office: Mount & Nadler 425 Madison Ave New York NY 10017-1110 Office Phone: 212-759-4440. E-mail: Hedda615@aol.com.

NADOLSKI, DORA J. social sciences educator, researcher; d. Harold V. and Dora H. Glidewell; m. Thomas P. Nadolski (div.); 1 child, Christopher A. MA in Social Sci., Antioch U., Yellow Springs, OH, 1965; PhD in polit. social sci., U. Mo., Kansas City, 2000. Assoc. prof. polit. sci. Northwest Nazarene Coll., Nampa, Idaho, 1966—68; lectr. Rockhurst U., Kansas City, 1995—97; prof., lectr. Park U., Kansas City, 1997—. Instr. Bedai U., Kanazawa, Japan, Kanazawa U., Peace Corps, Turkey. Co-author: Survey of U.S. Econometric Modeling Organizations; author: Special Curriculum Methods for Teaching Foreign Students; editor: Social Science Consortium Newsletter; author: The Etatist Turkish Republic and Its Political and SocioEconomic Performance from 1980-1999: A Developing State Impacted by International Organizations and Interdependence, Ottoman and Secular Civil Law International Journal of Middle East Studies, 1977. Chair Cub Scouts Am., Reston, Va., 1982—88; donor, supporter Disabled Am. Vets., Washington, 1995—. Fellow, NDEA, Soc. Sci. Rsch. Coun., U.Erfurt; grantee, NEH; scholar Fulbright, Sophia U.; Chancellor's Interdisciplinary Fellowship, U. Mo. Mem.: Am. Polit. Sci. Assn., Soc. Advancement Socio-Economics, Pi Sigma Alpha. Catholic. Avocations: cross country skiing, swimming, church choir.

NADZICK, JUDITH ANN, accountant; b. Paterson, N.J., Mar. 6, 1948; d. John and Ethel (McDonald) N. BBA in Acctg., U. Miami, 1971. CPA, N.J. Staff acct., mgr. Ernst & Whinney, C.P.A.s, N.Y.C., 1971-78; asst. treas. Gulf & We. Industries, Inc., N.Y.C., 1979-83; asst. v.p., 1980-82; v.p., 1982-83; v.p., corp. contr. United Mchts. and Mfrs. Inc., N.Y.C., 1983-85; sr. v.p., 1985-86; exec. v.p., CFO, 1986-97; pres., 1997—; also bd. dir. Mem. U. Miami Alumni Assn., Delta Delta Delta. Roman Catholic. Home: 280 Lincoln Ave Elmwood Park NJ 07407-2824 E-mail: judenadz@aol.com.

NAEGELE, CARL JOSEPH, university academic administrator, educator; b. Newark, Jan. 1, 1939; s. Carl Joseph Sr. and Mabel (Flood) N.; m. Elizabeth C. McVey, June 19, 1971; children: Jennifer, Erin. BS, Kean Coll., 1965; MS, Syracuse U., 1969; PhD, Cornell U., 1974. Tchr. physics Summit (N.J.) High Sch., 1965-68; instr. physics Kean Coll., Union, N.J., 1968-70; physics instr. Cornell U., Ithaca, N.Y., 1973-75; prof. Mich. State U., East Lansing, 1975-79; program dir. NSF, Washington, 1979-81, 91-92; dean coll. arts and scis. U. San Francisco, 1981-91; dir. Sci. Inst., 1984—; prof. physics and computer sci. U. San Francisco, 1981—; pres. Lucas Valley Cable, Inc., 2001—. Computer cons., San Rafael, Calif., 1981—. Author: Physics for the Life and Health Sciences, 1974, Laboratory Experiment in General Physics, 1976, Electronic Mail and Communications Networks, 1984, Computer Systems and Applications, 1998, Experiments in Physical Science, 1998; contbr. articles to profl. jours. Served with U.S. Army, 1959-61, Korea. Recipient Outstanding Tchg. award Mich. State U., 1978, Leadership award U. San Francisco, 1985;

grantee NSF, 1968, 78, 94-99, Coun. for Basic Edn., 1984-89. Mem. Am. Phys. Soc., Am. Assn. Physics Tchrs., Am. Assn. Univ. Adminstrs., Assn. for Computing Machinery. Avocations: flying, boating, skiing, tennis, running. Office: U San Francisco Coll Arts & Scis Ignatian Heights San Francisco CA 94117-1080

NAEGELE, ELIZABETH MARIE, musician, educator; b. Minot, N.D., July 17, 1951; d. George Eugene and Margaret Lenora (Wiens) Faul; m. Michael Dean Naegele, June 17, 1972; children: Heidi Marie, Nicholas Michael. Diploma, Moody Bible Inst., 1972; MusB, Mich. State U., 1975, MusM, 1976; MusD, Northwestern U., Evanston, Ill., 1989. Prof. music Moody Bible Inst., Chgo., 1976—. Organ recitalist, Ill., Mich., Ind. Dir. music Eastminster Presbyn. Ch., East Lansing, Mich., 1975-76, Carter Westminster Presbyn., Skokie, Ill., 1976-82, 1st Presbyn. Ch., Waukegan, Ill., 1990—; organist Winnetka (Ill.) Bible Ch., 1982-89. Mem. Assn. Am. Guild Organists (bd. dirs. Chgo. chpt. 1977-79, 88-91, 96—), Chgo. Club Woman Organists (bd. dirs. 1986-94), Phi Kappa Phi. Avocation: word games. Home: 2516 Edina Blvd Zion IL 60099-2702 Office: Moody Bible Inst 820 N La Salle Dr Chicago IL 60610-3263 E-mail: SocratesNaegele@att.net., enaegele@moody.edu.

NAEGELE, JOSEPH LOYOLA, SR., lawyer; b. San Francisco, July 19, 1955; s. Charles Frederick and Rosemary Cecilia (Ledogar) N.; children: Joseph Loyola Jr., Elizabeth Anne. BA, U. Calif., Davis, 1977; JD, Hastings Law Sch., San Francisco, 1981. Bar: Calif. 1982. Legal intern U.S. Congress, Washington, 1976; legal extern Calif. Ct. Appeals, San Francisco, 1980; law clk. U.S. Dist. Ct., San Francisco, 1981, Sacramento Dist. Atty.'s Office, Sacramento, 1982; tchr. St. Francis High Sch., Sacramento, 1982; atty. Law Offices of Jack Komar, San Jose, Calif., 1983-85, Law Offices of Joseph L. Naegele & Loyola Medration Ctr., 1983-; prof. Lincoln Law Sch., San Jose, 1983-85. Mem. Santa Clara County Bar Assn., Calif. Trial Lawyers Assn., Santa Clara County Trial Lawyers Assn., St. Thomas Moore Soc., Barristers Club. Roman Catholic. Office: 1530 The Alameda Ste 205 San Jose CA 95126-2303 E-mail: josephnaegele@hotmail.com.

NAEGELE, PHILIPP OTTO, violinist, violist, music educator; b. Stuttgart, Fed. Republic Germany, Jan. 22, 1928; came to U.S., 1940; s. Reinhold and Alice (Nordlinger) N.; m. Susanne Russin (div. 1980); 1 child, Matthias Dominic; m. Barbara Wright, Mar. 1992. BA, Queens Coll., 1949; MFA, Princeton U., 1950, PhD, 1955. Violinist, violist Marlboro (Vt.) Music Festival, 1950—; violinist Cleve. Orch., 1956-64; from asst. prof. to assoc. prof. to prof. violin dept. music Smith Coll., Northampton, Mass., 1964-78, William R. Kenan Jr. prof. music, 1978-2000, William R. Kenan Jr. prof. music emeritus, 2000—; violist Cantilena Piano Quartet, 1980-96; mem. Boccherini Ensemble, 1980-84; adj. prof. violin Amherst Coll., 2002—. Mem. resident string quartet Kent (Ohio) State U., 1960-64; mem. violin faculty Cleve. Inst. Music, 1961-64, Vegh String Quartet, 1977-79; rec. artist Columbia Mus. Heritage Soc., Pro Arte, Nonesuch Records, Bis Records, Marlboro Rec. Soc., Arabesque Records, Da Camera, Spectrum Records, Bayer Records, Sony Classical, Philomusica, Qualitone Records. Contbr. to New Groves Dictionary of Music, also articles to profl. jours. With U.S. Army, 1955-56. Fellow Am. Council Learned Socs., 1949-50, Proctor fellow, 1952-53, Fulbright fellow, 1953-54. Mem. Phi Beta Kappa. Home: 57 Prospect St Northampton MA 01060-2130 E-mail: pnaegele@smith.edu.

NAEGELE, TOBIAS, editor; Editor Times News Svc., Springfield, Va., 1992—. Office: Times News Svc 6883 Commercial Dr Springfield VA 22159-0001

NAEGLE, MADELINE ANNE, mental health nurse, educator; b. Penn Yan, N.Y., Feb. 2, 1942; d. Lester Lawrence and Nona Caroline (Muir) N.; m. James Michael McGowan, Aug. 6, 1966 (div. 1984); children: Amanda Allen, Benjamin Logan. BS, Nazareth Coll. Rochester, 1964; MA, NYU, 1967, PhD, 1980. Staff nurse Syracuse (N.Y.) Meml. Hosp., summer 1964; staff nurse, asst. head nurse Payne Whitney Clinic, N.Y.C., 1964-65; instr. nursing Herbert H. Lehman Coll., Bronx, N.Y., 1972-75, part-time instr. nursing, 1975-78; asst. clin. prof. Sch. Nursing U. Pa., Phila., 1979-83; pvt. practice N.Y.C., 1980—; assoc. prof. Leinhardt Sch. Nursing Pace U., Pleasantville, N.Y., 1983-85; prof. div. nursing NYU, N.Y.C., 1985—2003, prof., 2003—. Cons. The Day Sch., 1980-84; mem. N.Y. State Gov.'s Health Care Adv. Bd., 1991-94. Author: Nursing Process with Clients Using Drugs, 1993, Patterns of Substance Abuse, 1996; author, editor: (model curriculum) Substance Abuse Education in Nursing, 1991; editor Addictions Nursing, 1988-98, Addictions and Substance Abuse: Stratgies for Advanced Nursing Practice, 2000; contbr. articles to profl. jours. Recipient Presdl. Citation award N.Y. County RN Assn., 1986, Amanda Silver Disting. Svc. award N.Y. County RN Assn., 1994; named Outstanding Alumna, Nazareth Coll. of Rochester, 2000; inducted into Acad. Women Achievers, YWCA, 1991; USPHS fellow, 1978-79, Pres.'s award Nat. Nurses Soc. on Addiction; grantee Nat. Inst. Alcohol Abuse and Alcoholism, Nat. Inst. Drug Abuse, 1989-90, Ctr. for Substance Abuse Prevention, 1990-95, U.S. Human Resources Adminstrn., 1999; Fulbright scholar U. Malta, 1995. Fellow: Am. Acad. Nursing; mem.: ANA (com. chair 1987—89, com. on addiction 1999, nominating com. 1996—2000, pres.-elect 1987—89, pres. 1989—91, Hildegard Peplau award 2002), Assn. Med. Educators and Rschrs. in Substance Abuse, N.Y. State Nurses Assn. (chair com. on impaired nursing practice 1986—88), Sigma Theta Tau. Democrat. Avocations: hiking, running, dance, theater, music. Office: NYU Div Nursing 246 Greene St New York NY 10003-6677 Business E-Mail: MAN1@nyu.edu.

NAESER, NANCY DEARIEN, geologist, researcher; b. Morgantown, W.Va., Apr. 15, 1944; d. William Harold and Katherine Elizabeth (Dearien) Cozad; m. Charles Wilbur Naeser, Feb. 6, 1982. BS, U. Ariz., 1966; PhD, Victoria U., Wellington, New Zealand, 1973. Geol. field asst. U.S. Geol. Survey, Flagstaff, Ariz., 1966; sci. editor New Zealand Jour. Geology and Geophysics, New Zealand Dept. Sci. and Indsl. Rsch., Wellington, 1974-76; postdoctoral rsch. assoc. U. Toronto, 1976-79, U.S. Geol. Survey, Denver, 1979-81, geologist, 1981—. Adj. prof. Dartmouth Coll., Hanover, NH, 1985—97, U. Wyo., Laramie, 1984—91. Editor: Thermal History of Sedimentary Basins--Methods and Case Histories, 1989, Debris-Flow Hazards - Mechanics, Prediction and Assessment, 2000; contbr. articles on fission-track analysis to profl. jours. Docent, Denver Zoo, 1991-99. Fulbright fellow, New Zealand, 1967-68. Fellow Geol. Soc. Am.; mem. Am. Assn. Petroleum Geologists, Geol. Soc. New Zealand, Mortar Board, Phi Kappa Phi. Methodist. Office: US Geol Survey Mail Stop 926 A 12201 Sunrise Valley Dr Reston VA 20192-0002 Office Phone: 703-648-5328. Business E-Mail: nnaeser@usgs.gov.

NAEVE, MILO MERLE, curator, director; b. nr. Arnold, Kans., Oct. 9, 1931; s. Bernhardt and Fern (Yasmer) N.; m. Nancy Jammer, July 18, 1954. BFA, U. Colo., 1953; MA, U. Del., 1955. Curatorial asst. Henry Francis duPont Winterthur Mus., 1957, asst. curator, 1958, sec. of mus., 1959-63, registrar, 1963-65; editor Winterthur Portfolio, 1965-66; asst. dir. dept. collections Colonial Williamsburg, Va., 1967-69, curator, dir. dept. collections, 1970; dir. Colorado Springs (Colo.) Fine Arts Ctr., 1971-74; curator Am. arts Art Inst. Chgo., 1975-91; ret. Am. Arts, Art Inst. Chgo., 1991. Curator emeritus Field McCormick. Author: The Classical Presence in American Art, 1978, Identifying American Furniture: A Pictorial Guide to Styles and Terms, Colonial to Contemporary, 1981, 3rd edit., 1998, John Lewis Krimmel: An Artist in Federal America, 1987, 150 Years of Philadelphia Painters and Painting: Selections from the Sewell C. Biggs Museum of American Art, 1999; mem. editl. bd. Am. Art Jour.; contbr. articles to profl. jours. Trustee Skowhegan Sch. Painting and Sculpture, Libr. Co. of Phila., Nat. Coun. of the Fine Arts Mus. of San Francisco, Calif. Recipient Robert C. Smith award for most disting. article pub. in field in U.S., Decorative Arts Soc., 1996. Fellow Royal Soc. Arts; mem. Coll. Art Assn. Am., Nat. Trust Hist. Preservation, Am. Assn. Museums, Museums Assn. (Eng.), Ill. Acad. Fine Arts (Lifetime Achievement award 1991), Grolier Club.

NAEVE, STEPHEN W. electric power industry executive; b. Rapid City, S.D., 1947; B in Mech. Engring., M in Environ. Health Engring., U. Tex. With Houston Light & Power Co., 1972-93, gen. mgr. planning and strategic mgmt., v.p., treas.; v.p. strategic planning and adminstrn. Houston Industries, Inc., 1993-96, sr. v.p., CFO, 1996-97; exec. v.p., CFO Reliant Resources, Inc. (formerly Houston Industries, Inc.), 1997—2002, pres., COO, 2002—. Mem.: Fin. Execs. Inst., Advisory Council, Coll. of Bus. Admin, U. of Texas. Office: Reliant Resources PO Box 4567 Houston TX 77210-4567

NAEYE, RICHARD L. pathologist, educator; b. Rochester, N.Y., Nov. 27, 1929; s. Peter John and Gertrude Ellen (Lookup) N.; m. Patricia Ann Dahl, June 4, 1955; children: Nancy Ellen, Susan Amy, Robert Peter. AB, Colgate U., 1951; MD, Columbia U., 1955. Diplomate: Am. Bd. Pathology. Intern N.Y. Hosp., N.Y.C., 1955-56; resident Columbia-Presbyn. Med. Ctr., 1956-58, Mary Fletcher Hosp., Burlington, Vt., 1958-60; practice medicine, specializing in pathology Burlington, 1960-67, Hershey, Pa., 1967—; asst. attending pathologist Mary Fletcher Hosp., 1960-63; assoc. prof. U. Vt., 1963-67, prof. pathology, 1967; prof. dept. pathology M.S. Hershey Med. Ctr., Pa. State U. Coll. Medicine, 1967—, chmn. dept. pathology, 1967-97. Mem. NIH study sect. USPHS, 1968-72. Mem. editl. bd. Human Pathology, 1982-96, Pediatric Pathology, 1983-96, Pediatric and Perinatal Epidemiology, 1987-94, Modern Pathology, 1993-96; contbr. articles to med. jours. Markle scholar in acad. medicine, 1960-65. Mem. Am. Soc. Exptl. Pathology, U.S. Can. Acad. Pathology, Am. Soc. Pathologists, Am. Soc. Clin. Pathologists, Coll. Am. Pathologists, Pediatric Pathology Soc., Pa. Soc. Clin. Pathologists, Investigative Pathology. Home: 50 Laurel Ridge Rd Hershey PA 17033-2513 Office: Pa State U Coll Medicine Dept Pathology 500 University Dr Hershey PA 17033 Office Phone: 717-531-8352.

NAFISI, AZAR, humanities educator; b. 1950; PhD in English Lit., Okla. U. Prof. Tehran U., Allemeh Tabatabai U.; vis. fellow Oxford U.; prof. Johns Hopkins U., Sch. Advanced Internat. Studies, Washington. Author: Reading Lolita in Tehran: A Memoir in Books, 2003. Home: 12026 Gatewater Dr Potomac MD 20854-2875 Office: c/o Random House 1745 Broadway New York NY 10019*

NAFTALIS, GARY PHILIP, lawyer, educator; b. Newark, Nov. 23, 1941; s. Gilbert and Bertha Beatrice Naftalis; m. Donna Arditi, June 30, 1974; children: Benjamin, Joshua, Daniel, Sarah. AB, Rutgers U., 1963; AM, Brown U., 1965; LLB, Columbia U., 1967. Bar: N.Y. 1967, U.S. Dist. Ct. (so. dist.) N.Y. 1969, U.S. Ct. Appeals (2d cir.) 1968, U.S. Ct. Appeals (3d cir.) 1973, U.S. Ct. Appeals (D.C. cir.) 1993, U.S. Supreme Ct. 1974. Law clk. to judge U.S. Dist. Ct. So. Dist. N.Y., 1967-68; asst. U.S. atty. So. Dist. N.Y., 1968-74, asst. chief criminal divsn., 1972-74; spl. asst. U.S. atty. for V.I., 1972-73; spl. counsel U.S. Senate Subcom. on Long Term Care, 1975, N.Y. State Temp. Commn. on Living Costs and the Economy, 1975; ptnr. Orans, Elsen, Polstein & Naftalis, N.Y.C., 1974-81, Kramer, Levin, Naftalis & Frankel, N.Y.C., 1981—. Lectr. Law Sch. Columbia U., 1976-88; vis. lectr. Law Sch. Harvard U., 1979; mem. deptl. disciplinary com. Appellate div. 1st Dept., 1980-86. Author: (with Marvin E. Frankel) The Grand Jury: An Institution on Trial, 1977, Considerations in Representing Attorneys in Civil and Criminal Enforcement Proceedings, 1981, Sentencing: Helping Judges Do Their Jobs, 1986, SEC Actions Seeking to Bar Securities Professionals, 1995, SEC Cease and Desist Powers Limited, 1997, The Foreign Corrupt Practices Act, 1997, Prosecuting Lawyers Who Defend Clients in SEC Actions, 1998, Obtaining Reports from a Credit Bureau for Litigation May be a Crime, 1999, Encouraging Cooperation by Individual Respondents in SEC Enforcement Investigations, 2002, Navigating the Foreign Corrupt Practices Act, 2002, Fugitive Disentitlement in Civil Forfeiture Proceedings, 2002; editor: White Collar Crimes, 1980. Trustee Boys Brotherhood Rep., 1978—, Blueberry Treatment Ctr., 1981-91, Joseph Haggerty Children's Fund, 1991—; bd. dirs. The Legal Aid Soc., 2000—. Fellow: Am. Coll. Trial Lawyers; mem.: ABA (white collar crime com. criminal justice sect. 1985—, coun. criminal justice sect. 2002—), N.Y. Coun. Def. Lawyers (bd. dirs. 2000—01), Internat. Bar Assn. (bus. crimes com. 1988—), N.Y. Bar Assn. (com. state legis. 1974—76, exec. com. comml. and fed. litigation sect.), Fed. Bar. Coun. (com. cts. 2d cir. 1974—77), Assn. of Bar of City of N.Y. (com. criminal cts. 1980—83, com. judiciary 1984—87, coun. criminal justice 1985—88, com. on criminal law 1987—90, 1997—2001). Home: 1125 Park Ave Apt 7B New York NY 10128-1243 Office: Kramer Levin Naftalis & Frankel 919 3rd Ave New York NY 10022-3902

NAFTOLIN, FREDERICK, physician, reproductive biologist educator; b. Bronx, N.Y., Apr. 7, 1936; s. Nathan and Jean (Pesacov) N.; children: Michael Eugene, Joshua Joseph; m. Marcie Myerson, Nov. 1, 1987. AA, UCLA, 1957; BA with honors, U. Calif., Berkeley, 1958; MD with honors, U. Calif., San Francisco, 1961; DPhil, U. Oxford, 1970. Intern King County Hosp., Seattle, 1961-62; resident in ob-gyn UCLA, 1962-66; asst. chief gynecology, reproductive endocrine fellow USPHS, Seattle, 1966-68; NIH fellow Oxford (Eng.) U., 1968-70; asst. prof. ob-gyn U. Calif., San Diego Sch. Medicine, 1970-73; asso. prof. ob-gyn Harvard Med. Sch., 1973-75; prof., chmn. ob-gyn dept. McGill Faculty Medicine, Montreal, 1975-78; prof., chmn. dept. ob-gyn Yale Med. Sch., New Haven, 1978-2000, prof. dept. biology, 1983—; dir. Yale U. Ctr. for Research in Reproductive Biology, 1986—, head reproductive neuroscience unit, 2000—. Vis. prof. U. Geneva, 1982-83, Weizmann Inst., 1991-92, Complutense U., Spain, 1999; prof extraordinaire Complutense U., 1999. Author: 15 books including: Subcellular Mechanisms in Reproductive Neuroendocrinology, 1976, Abnormal Fetal Growth, 1978, Clinical Neuroendocrinology, 1979, Dilation of the Uterine Cervix, 1980, 2-vol. series Basic Reproductive Medicine, Vol. I, Basis of Normal Reproduction, Vol. II, 1981, Male Reproduction, Vol. III, Metabolism of Steroids by Neuroendocrine Tissues, Follicle Stimulation and Ovulation Induction, 1986; mem. editl. bd.: Jour. Soc. Gynecologic Investigation, Menopause, Gynecol. Endocrinology, African Jour. Reproductive Medicine, sect. editor: Reproductive Biology, jour. Exptl. Zoology, 2002—; editor: Reproductive Divsn. Am. Jour. Zoology; contbr. more than 600 articles to med. jours. Named Fogarty Internat. fellow, 1982, John Simon Guggenheim fellow, 1983, Berlex Internat. scholar, 1991; recipient Arnaldo Bruno prize, Acad. Di Lincei, Italy, 2002; fellow ad eundem, Royal Coll. Ob-Gyn. Mem. Am. Gynecol. and Obstet. Soc., Soc. Gynecol. Investigation (pres. 1991-92, Disting. Scientist award 2003), Endocrine Soc., Internat. Soc. Neuroendocrinology, New Haven Ob-Gyn. Soc., Can. Fertility Soc., Soc. for Neurosci., N.Am. Menopause Soc. (pres. 1998-99). Office: Yale Med Sch Dept Ob-Gyn FMB 331 333 Cedar St Dept Ob New Haven CT 06520-8063

NAFZIGER, JAMES ALBERT RICHMOND, lawyer, educator; b. Mpls., Sept. 24, 1940; s. Ralph Otto and Charlotte Monona (Hamilton) N. BA, U. Wis., 1962, MA, 1969; JD, Harvard U., 1967. Bar: Wis. 1967. Law clk. to chief judge U.S. Dist. Ct. (ea. dist.) Wis., 1967-69; fellow Am. Soc. Internat. Law, Washington, 1969-70, adminstrv. dir., 1970-74; exec. sec. Assn. Student Internat. Law Socs., 1969-70; lectr. Sch. Law Cath. U. Am., Washington, 1970-74; assoc. prof. law Coll. Law Willamette U., Salem, Oreg., 1977-80, prof., 1980-95, Thomas B. Stoel prof., 1995—, assoc. dean, 1985-86, dir. internat. programs, 1984—. Scholar-in-residence Rockefeller Found. Ctr., Bellagio, Italy, 1985; vis. assoc. prof. Sch. Law, U. Oreg. 1974-77; vis. prof. Nat. Autonomous U. Mex., 1978; hon. prof. East China U. of Politics and Law, 1999—; lectr. tutor Inst. Pub. Internat. Law and Internat. Rels., Thessaloniki, Greece, 1982; cons. Adminstrv. Conf. U.S., 1988-90, Internat. Com. Migration, 1997—; mem. bd. advisors Denver Jour. Internat. Law and Policy, Am. Jour. Comparative Law (bd. dirs. 1985—). Author: Conflict of Laws: A Northwest Perspective, 1985, Internat. Sports Law, 1988; editor: Procs. of Am. Soc. Internat. Law, 1977; co-editor: Law and Justice in a Multistate World, 2002; contbr. articles to profl. jours. Adv. com. on internat. law U.S. Dept. of State, 2001—; bd. dirs. N.W. Regional China Coun., 1987—89. 1st lt. U.S. Army, 1962—64. Recipient Burlington No. Faculty Achievement award, 1988, Willamette U. Pres.'s award for excellence in scholarship, 2000. Mem.: ACLU (pres. chpt. 1980—81, mem. state bd. 1982—88, sec. 1983—87), ABA (legal special ctrl. and east European law initiative 1992—), Internat. Law Assn. Am. Br. (chmn. human rights com. 1983—88, exec. com. 1986—, co-dir. studies 1991—95, v.p. 1994—2000, pres. 2000—), Nat. Sports Law Inst. (bd. advisors 2002—), Internat. Sports Law Assn. (v.p. 1992—), Oreg. Internat. Coun. (pres. 1990—92), Am. Law Inst., Assn. Am. Law Schs. (chmn. law and arts sect. 1981—83, chmn. internat. law sect. 1984—85, chmn. law and arts sect. 1989—91, chmn. immigration law sect. 1990—91, chmn. internat. law workshop 1995, com. on sects. and ann. meeting 1995—98, chmn. internat. exchs. sect. 1999—2000, U.S. Dept. of State adv. com. internat. law 2001—, chmn. conflict of laws sect. 2003—04), Am. Coun. Learned Socs. (exec. com. 2002—, conf. adminstrv. officers), Internat. Studies Assn. (exec. bd. 1974—77, internat. law sect.), Washington Fgn. Law Soc. (v.p. 1973—74), UNA-USA (pres. Oreg. divsn. 1987—90, v.p. 1990—94, bd. dirs. 1990—, exec. com. coun. chpt. and divsn. prof.), Internat. Law Assn. (cultural heritage law com. 1990—2001, rapporteur 1990—2001, exec. coun. 2000—, U.S. dept. state adv. coun. 2001—, chmn. 2001—), Internat. Acad. Comparative Law, Am. Soc. Comparative Law (bd. dirs. 1985—, treas. 1997—), Am. Soc. Internat. Law (exec. coun. 1983—86, chmn. ann. meeting 1988, chmn. nominating com. 1989, exec. coun. 1992—95, exec. com. 1994—95), Phi Kappa Phi, Phi Beta Kappa. Home: 3775 Saxon Dr S Salem OR 97302-6041 Office: Willamette U Coll Law Salem OR 97301

NAGABHUSHANA, NAGENDRA, materials scientist, educator; PhD, Indian Inst Sci., Bangalore, 1998. Rsch. fellow Sch. of Mineral Engring., U. Alaska, Fairbanks, 2000—03; rsch. asst. prof. Petroleum Devel. Lab., U. Alaska, Fairbanks, 2003—. Office: Petroleum Devel Lab Univ Alaska Fairbanks AK 99775 E-mail: ffnn@uaf.edu.

NAGANO, KENT GEORGE, conductor; b. Morro Bay, Calif. BA in Sociology & Music (high honors), U of Calif., Santa Cruz; MA in Composition, San Francisco State U.; studied with, Laszlo Varga. Former asst. Opera Co. Boston; former prin. guest condr. Ensemble InterContemporain & the Dutch Radio Orch.; mus. dir. & condr. Berkeley Symphony, 1978—; mus. dir. Opéra de Lyon, 1989—; assoc. prin. & guest condr. LSO, London, England, 1990; mus. dir., prin. condr. designate Hallé Orch., England, 1991-94, mus. dir., prin. condr., 1994-2000, Deutsche Symphonie, Berlin, 2000—. Has performed with numerous orchestras around the world; recordings include: Songs of the Auvergne, Peter and the Wolf, Turandot and Arlecchino (Grammy nom.), La Boheme, Dialogues of the Carelites, The Death of Klinghoffer (Grammy nom.), Love for Three Oranges (Grammy nom.), Susannah (Grammy award), La damnation de Faust, The Rite of Spring, Rodrgue et chimene. Recipient Seaver/NEA Conducting award, 1985; Record of Yr. award Gramophone; named "officer" of France's Order of Arts and Letters, 1993. Office: Vincent Farrell & Assocs 157 W 57th St New York NY 10019-2210 also: Berkeley Symphony Berkeley CA 94704

NAGATA, AKIRA, publishing executive; b. Tokyo, Aug. 8, 1929; s. Koichi and Mikiko (Minami) N.; m. Tomoko Iida, Apr. 21, 1958; children: Junko, Hidehiko, Kazuhiko. BS in Econs., Jiyu-Gakuen Coll., Tokyo, 1953. Gen. mgr. for N.Am. Nihon Keizai Shimbun, Inc., Tokyo, 1973-77, spl. asst. to pres., 1977-80; dir. Nikkei-McGraw-Hill, Inc., Tokyo, 1980-88; sr. exec. dir. Nikkei Bus. Publs., Inc., Tokyo, 1988-90, pres., CEO, 1990-94, chmn., 1994-98, spl. advisor, 1998—; pres., CEO Nikkei Nat. Geog. Inc., 1994-96. Pres./CEO Nikkei Nat. Geographic Inc., 1994-96; dep. chmn. Internat. Fedn. Periodical Press, London, 1995-97, vice chmn., 1997-99; chmn. Postal Coop. Assn. of Shin-Tokyo, 1992-98, Postal Coop. Assn. of Harumi, Tokyo, 1983-90; chmn. bd. Jiyu Gakuen, 2001—. Co-author: Japanese Agriculturl Industry Off for a New Start, 1961, Revaluation of the Japanese Yen, 1971, Business Culture in the U.S., 1978, The Nine Years in New Delhi, London and New York, 1980. Mem. Japan Mag. Pubs. Assn. (exec. dir. 1993-99), Rotary (Tokyo Club). Avocations: golf, tennis, opera. E-mail. Office: Nikkei Bus Publs Inc 2-7-6 Hirakawa cho Tokyo 102-8622 Japan E-mail: nagata@nikkeibp.co.jp.

NAGEL, BRUCE H. lawyer; b. Paterson, N.J., Aug. 28, 1952; s. David A. and Norma N.; m. Marla Nagel, July 15, 1978; children: Arielle, Emma, Molly. BS in Indsl. and Labor Rels., Cornell U., 1974; JD, NYU, 1977. Bar: N.J. 1977, U.S. Dist. Ct. N.J. 1977, U.S. Ct. Appeals (3rd cir.) 1977, U.S. Ct. Appeals (3d, 1st and 4th cir.) 1995; cert. civil trial atty. Sr. ptnr. Nagel, Rice & Mazie, Livingston, NJ, 1983—. Adj. prof. Seton Hall Law Sch.; lectr. Inst. Continuing Legal Edn.; chmn. bd. trustees Kairos Inst., Madison, N.J., 1998—; bd. dirs. Teardrop Golf Co., Morton Grove, Ill.; moderator and lectr. in field. Contbr. articles to profl. jours. Mem. ATLA, N.J. Bar Assn., Essex County Bar Assn., Million Dollar Advocate Forum. Office: Nagel Rice & Mazie 301 S Livingston Ave Ste 201 Livingston NJ 07039-3991 Office Phone: 973-535-3100.

NAGEL, EDWARD MCCAUL, lawyer, former utilities executive; b. Geneva, N.Y., Sept. 6, 1926; s. Edward Samuel and Helen Veronica (McCaul) N.; m. Mary Elizabeth Klein, Sept. 11, 1950; children: Christopher, Linda, Michael, Jeffrey, Ellen. AB, Harvard, 1949; LL.B., U. Pa., 1952; postgrad., Cornell U. Bus. Sch., 1962. Bar: Pa. 1953. Assoc. Simpson, Thacher & Bartlett, N.Y.C., 1953-54; atty. Pa. Power & Light Co., Allentown, 1952, 54-62, asst. counsel, 1962-68, asst. gen. counsel, 1968-71, gen. counsel, 1971-85, sec., 1971-89, v.p., 1973-91; prin. Edward M. Nagel Atty. at Law, 1991—. Dir. Exec. Svc. Corps of Lehigh Valley. Chmn. Mayor's Citizens Adv. Com., Allentown, 1968-72; assoc. counsel, bd. dirs. Minsi Trails council Boy Scouts Am. Served with USNR, 1945-46. Mem. Pa. Bar Assn., Lehigh County Bar Assn. Home: 417 N 28th St Allentown PA 18104-4838

NAGEL, MECHTHILD EUPHROSYNE, philosopher, educator, sociologist; b. Fulda, Hessen, Germany, June 8, 1966; d. Hans Fritz and Irene Helene Nagel; life ptnr. Philip Rodi Otieno. BA, Freiburg U., Germany, 1987; MA, U. Mass., Amherst, 1991; PhD, U. Mass, Amherst, 1996. Asst. prof. Mankato State U., Minn., 1996—99; assoc. prof. SUNY, Cortland, NY, 1999—. Sr. vis. fellow Cornell U., Ithaca, NY, 2003—04. Editor: (anthology) Race, Class, Community Identity; author: (monograph) Masking the abject: A genealogy of play. Grantee Study grant, Labor/Mgmt. Com., SUNY, 2002-2003. Mem.: Am. Philosophy Assn. (assoc.; co-chair radical philosophy assn. 2002). Office: SUNY Cortland Philosophy Dept POB 2000 Cortland NY 13045 Office Phone: 607-753-2013. E-mail: nagelm@cortland.edu.

NAGEL, PAUL B. geography and social studies educator; b. Libertyville, Ill., Apr. 25, 1969; s. Marilyn Nagel; m. KimberLeigh G. Nagel, Oct. 10, 1992. BA, U. Minn., 1991; MA, U. Guam, 1997; PhD, Tex. State U., San Marcos, 2003. Cert. tchr. Tex., Guam. Geography tchr. Dept. Edn., Agana, 1994—98, Inarajan, 1994—98; social studies tchr. Austin (Tex.) Ind. Sch. Dist., 1998—99, NYOS Charter Sch., Austin, 1999—2000; asst. prof. geography and social studies edn. Northwestern State U., Natchitoches, La., 2003—. Mem.: Nat. Coun. for the Social Studies (conf. com. 2003—, elem. awards com. 2003—), Tex. Coun. for the Social Studies (webmaster/tech. chair 2001—, tech. chair 2000—, grantee), Nat. Coun. for Geog. Edn. (corr. grantee). Republican. Avocations: baseball, travel. Office: Northwestern State U Coll of Edn Natchitoches LA 71459

NAGEL, SIDNEY ROBERT, physics educator; b. NYC, Sept. 28, 1948; s. Ernest and Edith (Haggstrom) Nagel. BA, Columbia U., 1969; MA, Princeton U., 1972, PhD, 1974. Rsch. assoc. Brown U., Providence, 1974-76; asst. prof. physics U. Chgo., 1976-81, assoc. prof., 1981-84, prof., 1984—, assoc. dean divsn. phy. scis., 1997-2000, Louis Block prof., 1998-2000, assoc. dean divsn. phy. scis., 1997-2000, Stein-Freiler disting. svc. prof., 2001—. Contbr. articles to profl. jours. Recipient Klopsteg Meml. Lecture award Am. Assn. Physics Tchrs., 1998; Alfred Sloan Found. fellow, 1978-82. Fellow AAAS, Am. Phys. Soc. (Oliver E. Buckley prize 1999), Am. Acad. Arts and Scis.; mem. NAS. Home: 4919 S Blackstone Ave Chicago IL 60615-3003 Office: U Chgo 5640 S Ellis Ave Chicago IL 60637-1433

NAGEL, THOMAS, philosopher, educator, lawyer, educator; b. Belgrade, Yugoslavia, July 4, 1937; came to U.S., 1939, naturalized, 1944; s. Walter and Carolyn (Baer) N.; m. Doris Blum, June 18, 1958 (div. 1973); m. Anne Hollander, June 26, 1979. BA, Cornell U., 1958; B.Phil., Oxford (Eng.) U., 1960; PhD, Harvard, 1963. Asst. prof. philosophy U. Calif., Berkeley, 1963-66; asst. prof. Princeton U., 1966-69, assoc., 1969-72, prof., 1972-80, NYU, 1980—. prof. philosophy and law, 1986—, Fiorello LaGuardia prof.

law, 2001—03, Univ. prof., 2002—. Vis. prof. Rockefeller U., 1973, U. Mex., 1977, U. Witwatersrand, 1982, UCLA, 1986, U. Calif., Berkeley, 2004. Author: The Possibility of Altruism, 1970, Mortal Questions, 1979, The View from Nowhere, 1986, What Does It All Mean?, 1987, Equality and Partiality, 1991, Other Minds, 1995, The Last Word, 1997; author: (with Liam Murphy) The Myth of Ownership, 2002; author: Concealment and Exposure, 2002; assoc. editor: Philosophy and Public Affairs, 1970—82. Guggenheim fellow, 1966, NSF fellow, 1967-69, NEH fellow, 1978, 84-85, vis. fellow All Souls Coll., Oxford, Eng., 1990. Mem. Am. Philos. Assn., Am. Acad. Arts and Scis., Brit. Acad.

NAGEL, VERNON J. chemicals executive, electronics executive; BBA, U. Mich. V.p. fin., CFO, treas., sec. Stericycle Inc.; exec. v.p., CFO, treas. Kuhlman Corp., 1993—99; prin. Jepson Assocs., Inc., 1999—2001; CFO Acuity Brands, Inc., Atlanta, 2001—, vice chmn., 2004—. Office: Acuity Brands Inc 1170 Peachtree St NE Atlanta GA 30309*

NAGEOTTE, MICHAEL PATRICK, obstetrician; b. Berea, Ohio, Nov. 1, 1951; s. Francis Louis Nageotte and Kathleen Marie Sweeney; m. Monica Pearl Leff, July 25, 1982; children: Ryan Joseph, Stephen Jeffrey, Zoë Anne. BA, Stanford U., 1973; MD, Loyola Stritch Sch. Medicine, 1976. Diplomate Am. Bd. Ob-Gyn. Resident ob-gyn. Harbor-UCLA Med. Ctr., Torrance, 1976—80; fellow Maternal/Fetal Medicine U. Calif. Irvine, 1980—82; dir. perinatology Hoag Meml. Hosp., Newport Beach, Calif., 1982—90; med. dir. Women's Health Long Beach Meml. Hosp., Long Beach, Calif., 1990—. Bd. dirs. Soc. Maternal-Fetal Medicine, Washington, 1998—2001, Long Beach Meml. Hosp. Co-author: Fetal Heart Rate Monitoring, 2d edit., 1990, Fetal Heart Rate Monitoring, 3d edit., 2003. Recipient Rsch. award, Soc. Maternal-Fetal Medicine, 1996. Fellow: Am. Coll. Ob-Gyn. Office: Long Beach Meml Hosp 2801 Atlantic Ave Long Beach CA 90801

NAGERA, HUMBERTO, psychiatrist, psychoanalyst, educator, author; b. Havana, Cuba, May 23, 1927; m. Gloria Maria Hernandez, Sept. 8, 1952; children: Lisette Maria, Humberto Felipe, Daniel. B.Sc., U. Havana, 1945; MD, Havana Med. Sch., 1952. Intern, resident in psychiatry Havana U. Hosp., 1950-55; sr. staff, chmn. research Anna Freud's Clinic, London, 1958-68; prof. psychiatry U. Mich., Ann Arbor, 1968-87, chief youth services, 1973-79, prof. emeritus, 1987; prof. psychiatry U. South Fla., 1987—, dir. adolescent inpatient unit and children's inpatient unit, 1987-97, dir. Carter Jenkin Ctr., 2002—. Author: Early Childhood Disturbances, Problems of Developmental Psychoanalytic Psychology, 1966, Vincent Van Gogh, 1966, Basic Psychoanalytic Concepts on the Libido Theory, 1969, Basic Psychoanalytic Concepts on the Theory of Instincts, 1970, Basic Psychoanalytic Concepts of Metapsychology Conflicts, Anxiety, and Other Subjects, 1970, Female Sexuality and the Oedipus Complex, 1975, Obsessional Neurosis: Developmental Psychopathology, 1977, 2nd edit., 1993, The Developmental Approach in Child Psychopathology, 1981; Contbr. articles to profl. jours. Mem. Am. Psychiat. Assn., Internat. Psychoanalytic Assn., Mich. Psychoanalytic Inst. (pres. 1975-77), Am. Assn. Child Psychoanalysis, Cuba Med. Assn. in Exile, South Fla. Tampa Bay Psychoanalytic Soc. (pres. 1992-93). Home: 5202 Dwire Ct Tampa FL 33647-1016 Office: U South Fla Dept Psychiatry 3515 E Fletcher Ave Tampa FL 33613-4706 Office Phone: 813-974-8900. E-mail: hnagera@hcs.usf.edu.

NAGI, CATHERINE RASEH, retired educational administrator, financial planner; b. Bklyn., Oct. 13, 1940; d. Massed and Catherine (Irato) N. BS, Bklyn. Coll., 1962, MS, 1964, postgrad., 1965-67, 76, Hofstra U., 1967-76, St. Johns U., Queens, N.Y., 1976-78. Cert. dist. sch. adminstr., supr., prin., asst. prin., tchr. health/phys. edn., N.Y.; CFP. Tchr. health/phys. edn. Jr. High Sch. 211-Dist. 18, Bklyn., 1962, Bay Ridge High Sch., Bklyn., 1962-63; tchr., acting chair Jr. High Sch. 78-Dist. 22, Bklyn., 1963-70; acting asst. prin. Intermediate Sch. 302-Dist. 19, Bklyn., 1970-71; narcotics edn. tchr. trainer Dist. 19 Bd. of Edn., Bklyn., 1971-73, supr. health/drug edn./svcs., 1973-75; supr. reimbursable programs Dist. 22 Bd. of Edn., Bklyn., 1975-79, supr. comprehensive planning, 1979-84, dep. supt., 1984-90; acting prin. Pub. Sch. 217-Dist. 22, Bklyn., 1980; sch. supt. Dist. 28 Bd. of Edn., Queens, N.Y., 1990-97; ret., 1997. Tchr. Adult Edn./Community Ctrs., N.Y.C., 1959-65; presenter N.Y.C. and N.Y. State Ednl. Confs., Univs.; grant writer N.Y.C. Bd. Edn., 1973—. Co-author, cons. (math. workbook) Get Ahead in Math, 1985; creator, editor (ednl. mag.) Gateways to Learning, 1977-90; creator, developer ednl. data system, 1976; developer first N.Y.C./N.Y. State early identification learning disabilities program, 1975. Named Educator of Yr. Assn. Tchrs. N.Y., 1980; recipient City Coun. Proclamation N.Y.C. Coun., 1991, 97, Legis. resolution N.Y. State Assembly/Senate, 1991, 97, Congl. Record recognition U.S. Congress, 1991, 97, Recognition award Forestdale Foster and Adoptive Parents Assn., Queens, 1992, Queensboro Pres. Proclamation, Supts.' Network Recognition, Fordham U., N.Y.C., Recognition, 112 Pct. Cmty. Coun. Mem. ASCD, Am. Assn. Sch. Adminstrs., N.Y.C. Assn. Supts., N.Y.C. Adminstrv. Women in Edn., Bklyn./N.Y. State Reading Coun./Assn., Thomas Jefferson Dem. Club, Kings County Dem. Com. Avocations: travel, languages, sports, singing, gourmet cooking, collecting stamps, coins and pens. Office: 122 Crispell Rd Krumville NY 12461-5408

NAGIN, C. RAY, mayor; m. Seletha Nagin; children: Jeremy, Jarin, Tianna. BSc in Acctg., Tuskegee U., 1978; MBA, Tulane U., 1994. V.p., gen. mgr. Cox Comm. S.E. La. cable sys.; mayor City of New Orleans, 2002—. Mem. bd. dirs. United Way, Convenant Ho.; chmn. United Negro Coll. Fund Walkathon fundraising campaign; pres. 100 Black Men Metro New Orleans. Recipient La. State Bd. Edn. Disting. Bus. Ptnr. award, 1994, Young Leadership Coun. Diversity and Role Model award, 1995, Gambit weekly New Orleanian of Yr. award, 1998. Office: 1300 Perdido St Rm 2E04 New Orleans LA 70112 Office Phone: 504-565-7793. Office Fax: 504-565-6423.

NAGIN, STEPHEN ELIAS, lawyer, educator; b. Phila., Nov. 7, 1946; s. Harry S. and Dorothy R. (Pearlman) N.; m. Marjorie Riley, Sept. 4, 1983. BBA, U. Miami, 1969; JD, 1974. Bar: Fla. 1974, D.C. 1976, U.S. Supreme Ct. 1978. Asst. atty. gen. State of Fla., Miami, 1974-75; atty. FTC, 1975-80; spl. asst. U.S. Atty., Washington, 1980-81; ptnr. Nagin, Gallop & Figuerdo, P.A., 1987—. Adj. prof. St. Thomas U. Sch. Law, 1984-94; instr. Nat. Inst. Trial Advocacy, 1992—. Mem. ABA (editor, trial lawyers sect. 1983-84, spl. antitrust task force 1983—, chmn. editl. bd., Florida Bar Jour. 1982-83, chmn. antitrust com. 1996-98, chmn. intellectual property com. 2001-03, chmn. antitrust and trade regulation cert. com. 2000-03), Patent Lawyers Assn. South Fla. (sec., 2000), Coral Gables Bar Assn. (bd. dirs. 1983-87). Office: Nagin Gallop & Figueredo PA 3225 Aviation Ave Fl 3D Miami FL 33133-4741

NAGLE, JEAN SUSAN KARABACZ, sociologist, psychologist; b. Detroit, 1936; d. Peter and Hedy (Grusczynski) Karabacz; m. Robert D. Nagle, Nov. 20, 1956; children: Carl A., Sonya L., Paula E. BS in Sociology, Wayne State U., 1956; postgrad., U. Chgo., 1953-55; MA, N.Mex. Highlands U., 1960; PhD, Union Grad. Sch., 1977; postgrad., Bryn Mawr. Inst., 1981. Diagnostic technician Vocat. Counseling Inst., Detroit, 1952; rsch. technician United Auto Workers-CIO, Detroit, 1958; clin. psychology intern N.Mex. State Hosp., Las Vegas, 1962-63; clin. psychology trainee VA Hosp., Omah and Lincoln, Nebr., 1963-64; instr. sociology N.W. Mo. State U., Maryville, 1965-70, prof. sociology and psychology, 1971-92, ret., 1992. Bd. dirs. Inst. Discourse. Grantee N.W. Mo. State U., 1981, 82. Mem. APA, Am. Sociol. Assn., Am. Psychol. Soc., Midwest Sociol. Soc., Psychology/Sociology Club, Mo. Psychol. Assn., World Federalists, Psi Chi, Pi Gamma Mu. also: 3106 E 80th St Kansas City MO 64132-3638

NAGLE, JEFFREY KARL, chemist, educator; b. Marietta, Ohio, Mar. 12, 1953; s. Kenneth Lee and Hope (Wells) Nagle; m. Constance Ruth Eaton, June 12, 1976; children: Eric Kenneth, Hannah Allyn. BA, Earlham Coll., 1975; PhD, U. N.C., 1979. Vis. asst. prof. Bucknell U., Lewisburg, Pa., 1979-80; asst. prof. chemistry Bowdoin Coll., Brunswick, Maine, 1980-86; vis. assoc. prof. chemistry U. Calif., Davis, 1986-87; assoc. prof. Bowdoin Coll., Brunswick, 1986-92, prof., 1992—. Fulbright vis. prof. U. Regensburg, Germany, 1993-94; vis. prof. Free U., Amsterdam, The Netherlands, 2000-01. Contbr. articles to profl. jours. Mem.: Am. Chem. Soc. Office: Bowdoin Coll Dept Chemistry 6600 College Sta Brunswick ME 04011-8466 Office Phone: 207-725-3167. Business E-Mail: jnagle@bowdoin.edu.

NAGLE, JOHN FREDERICK, physicist; b. Easton, Pa., Sept. 29, 1939; s. Edgar Eugene and Julia Elizabeth (Meeder) N. BA, Yale U., 1960, MS, 1962, PhD, 1965. Asst. prof. physics Carnegie-Mellon U., 1967-72, asso. prof. physics and biol. scis., 1972-78, prof., 1978—. NATO Fellow, 1965—66, Alfred P. Sloan fellow, 1969—71, Guggenheim fellow, 1979—80. Fellow Am. Phys. Soc. (chair divsn. biol. physics 1992-93); mem. AAUP, Biophys. Soc. (Avanti prize in lipids 2003), Phi Beta Kappa, Sigma Xi. Office: Physics Dept Carnegie-Mellon U Pittsburgh PA 15213 Office Phone: 412-268-2764. Business E-Mail: nagle@cmu.edu.

NAGLE, ROBERT OWEN, lawyer; b. Watertown, S.D., Feb. 10, 1929; s. John Raymond and Kathleen Margaret (McQuillen) N.; m. Louise Emerson H'Doubler, Mar. 14, 1954; children— Robert Owen Jr., Charles Francis, Margaret Louise. BS in Econs., U. Wis., 1951; LLB, U. Calif., 1957. Bar: Calif. 1957. Asso. firm Morrison, Foerster, Holloway, Clinton and Clark, San Francisco, 1957-62, ptnr., 1962-64; gen. atty. Spreckels Sugar div. Amstar Corp., San Francisco, 1964-66, v.p., 1966-68, exec. v.p., 1968-71, v.p. parent co., 1971-76; exec. v.p. Am. Sugar div. Amstar Corp., N.Y.C., 1975-76; pres., chief exec. officer Calif. and Hawaiian Sugar Co., San Francisco, 1976-82, also dir.; ptnr. Brobeck, Phleger & Harrison, 1982-86; pvt. investor Piedmont, Calif., 1986—. Bd. dirs. Providence Hosp., Oakland, Calif. Mem. Law Rev. Bd. dirs. San Francisco Bay Area coun. Boy Scouts Am.; trustee U. Calif. Berkeley Found., Wis. Alumni Rsch. Found., Pacific Vascular Rsch. Found., San Francisco. Served to lt. j.g. USN, 1951-54, Korea. Decorated Bronze Star with V, Air medal. Mem. ABA, State Bar Calif., Bar Assn. San Francisco, Order of Coif. Clubs: Claremont Country, Pacific Union.

NAGLER, ARNOLD LEON, pathologist, research scientist, educator; b. N.Y.C., 1935; s. Max and Esther (Finkel) N.; m. Rosalie Groden, Feb. 18, 1961; children: Stephen Marc, Melissa Sue. BS, CCNY, 1953; MD, NYU, 1958, PhD, 1960. Lic. dir. labs., N.Y. Postgrad. tng. NYU-Bellevue Med. Ctr., 1958-61; research assoc. Mt. Sinai Hosp., N.Y.C., 1960-61; mem. faculty Albert Einstein Coll. Medicine, Bronx, N.Y., 1961— assoc. prof. pathology surgery, 1975—; sr. assoc. dean, prof. and chmn. pathology N.Y. Coll. Osteo. Medicine, Old Westbury, 1978—, chmn. dept. biomed. scis., sr. assoc. dean emeritus. Trustee Robert Chambers Microsurgery Research Labs., 1978—; founder, trustee Esther Nagler Dystrophy Research Fund, N.Y. Coll. Osteo. Medicine Mem. editorial bd.: Circulatory Shock; contbr. articles to profl. jours. Chmn. Jericho council Boy Scouts Am., 1971-73; mem. Pres.'s Task Force, 1981—, Nat. Republican Congressional Com., U.S. Senatorial Club; trustee Liberal Jewish Day Sch., N.Y.C.; corp. mem. Nassau-Suffolk Health Systems Agy., mem. Primary Care Task Force. Served with U.S. Army, 1953-55. NIH grantee, 1961— Fellow Am. Soc. Clin. Pathologists; mem. N.Y. Acad. Sci., N.Y. Acad. Medicine, AAAS, Am. Trauma Soc. (founder), Sigma Xi Jewish. Home: 72 Hazelwood Dr Jericho NY 11753-1704 Office: Albert Einstein Coll Medicine 1300 Morris Park Ave Bronx NY 10461-1926 *I was guided by my parents when they were alive and directed by their teachings and precepts after their death to strive to do the best that I possibly may, in any and every endeavor that I undertake. They provided the armoury: Do no harm to anyone— achieve by dedicating yourself to excellence/performance. Do not rally in relegating someone to a lesser state; this is only relative success and is neither satisfying nor worthwhile to the soul, nor is it real.*

NAGLER, BARRY, lawyer; b. N.Y.C., Feb. 21, 1957; s. Charles and Toby (Freyman) N.; m. Laurie Beth Carter, Aug. 23, 1981; children: Daniel, Alyssa. BA magna cum laude, Franklin & Marshall Coll., 1978; JD cum laude, Harvard U., 1981. Bar: Mass. 1981. Assoc. Foley, Hoag & Eliot, Boston, 1981-87; v.p., asst. gen. coun. Reebok Internat., Stoughton, Mass., 1987-95, v.p., gen. counsel, 1995-98, sr. v.p., gen. counsel, 1998-99, Hasbro Corp., Pawtucket, R.I., 2000—. Author: Reebok Rules for Litigation Management, 1997; contbr. articles to profl. jours. Mem. Am. Corp. Counsel Assn. (dir. N.E. chpt. 1993—), Mass. Bar Assn. (vice-chmn. in-house subcom. litigation com. 1993—), New Eng. Legal Found. (steering com.), Coun. Chief Legal Officers.*

NAGLER, HARRIS M. urologic surgeon; b. Bklyn., Dec. 23, 1949; s. Simon H. and Thelma N.; m. Freema Gluck, May 25, 1978; children: Arielle Rachel, Gabrielle Marin. BS, Union Coll., 1971; MD, Temple U., 1975. Diplomate Nat. Bd. Med. Examiners, 1975, Am. Bd. Urology, 1982; lic. physician N.Y., 1976, N.J., 1993. Intern in gen. surgery Columbia-Presbyn. Med. Ctr., N.Y.C., 1975-76, resident in urology, 1976—79, fellow in reproductive medicine, 1979—80; instr. urology Columbia U. Coll. Physicians and Surgeons, N.Y.C., 1980—81, asst. prof. urology, 1982-87, assoc. prof. urology, 1987-89; dir. dept. urology Beth Israel Med. Ctr., N.Y.C., 1989-94, chmn. dept. urology, 1995—, lab. dir., 1996—, chief grad. med. edn. and acad. affairs, 1999. Co-dir. N.Y. Male Reproductive Ctr., 1981-84, dir., 1984-89; chief Vanderbilt Urology Clinic, 1982-87; asst. attending urologist Presbyn. Hosp., N.Y.C., 1982-87, assoc. attending urologist, 1987-89; chmn. dept. urology Beth Israel Med. Ctr., N.Y.C., 1989—, com. of surgery, 1989—, med. bd. com., 1989—, adminstrv. adv. com., 1989—, faculty practice plan adv. coun., 1989-92, chmn. faculty practice plan adv. coun., 1992—; mem. devel. com., Beth Israel Med. Ctr., 1995-, Cancer Com., 1997-, Dept. of Surgery Chmn. Search Com., 1998-, Surgical Svcs. Oversight Com., 1998-, Faculty Practice Plan Com. (chmn.), 1998-, chief of acad. affairs, 1998-, chair, Philips Ambulatory Care Mgmt. Com., 2002-; prof. urology Mt. Sinai Sch. Medicine, 1989-94, Albert Einstein Coll. Medicine, 1995—. Editl bd. Molecular Andrology, 1989, Investigative Urology, 1989-93, Gynecologic and Obstetric Investigation, 1992, Fertility and Sterility, 1993-2001, Assisted Reproductive Reviews, 1991; reviewer Fertility and Sterility, 1986-93, Investigative Urology, 1986-89 Bd. dirs. Coalition to Save City & Suburban Housing, N.Y.C., 1993-94. Ferdinand C. Valentine fellow, 1981. Fellow ACS, N.Y. Acad. Medicine (pres. sect. urology); mem. AMA, Am. Assn. Med. Colls. (task force inegrating edn. and patient care 1999—), Kidney and Urology Found. of Am. (bd. mem.), 2002-, Am. Urol. Assn. (1st prize in clin. rsch. 1982), Am. Soc. Andrology, Soc. Productive Surgeons (sec. 1993, treas. 1993-94, v.p. 1995, pres. 1996), Soc. for Study of Male Reprodn. (pres. 1993), N.Y. County Med. Soc., Harvey Soc., Am. Fertility Soc. (Pacific Coast chpt., urology com. 1984, urology-andrology com. 1985, movies com. 1987—, co-chmn. male reproduction/urology com. 1986-88, award selection com. 1987-88, program com. 1988-90, co-chmn. male reproduction/urology com. 1988-90, program chair N.Y. sect. annual meeting 1991, exec. com. N.Y. chpt., 2000—, urology prize 1985), Am. Cystoscope Makers Inc. (urology prize 1982), Alpha Omega Alpha. Office: Beth Israel Med Ctr 1st Ave at 16th St New York NY 10003

NAGLER, MICHAEL NICHOLAS, peace and conflict studies educator; b. N.Y.C., Jan. 20, 1937; s. Harold and Dorothy Judith (Nocks) N.; m. Roberta Ann Robbins (div. May 1983); children: Jessica, Joshua. BA, NYU, 1960; MA, U. Calif., Berkeley, 1962, PhD, 1966. Instr. San Francisco State U., 1963-65; prof. classics, peace studies and comparative lit. U. Calif., Berkeley, 1966-91, prof. emeritus, 1991—. Author: Spontaneity and Tradition, 1974, America Without Violence, 1982, Is There No Other Way: The Search for a Nonviolent Future, 2001, Am. Book award, 2002; co-author: The Upanishads, 1987; contbr. articles to profl. publs. Pres. bd. dirs. METTA Ctrs. for Nonviolence Edn. Fellow Am. Coun. Learned Socs., NIH; MacArthur Found. grantee, 1988. Mem. Am. Philolog. Soc. Office: U Calif Peace and Conflict Studies Berkeley CA 94720-0001 E-mail: mnagler@igc.org.

NAGLER, STEWART GORDON, insurance company executive; b. Bklyn., Jan. 30, 1943; s. Henry and Mary Nagler; m. Bonnie Lawrence, Aug. 9, 1964 (dec.); children: David, Ellen; m. Ronnie Hendler, Jan. 9, 2000. BS summa cum laude, Poly. U., 1963. With Met. Life Ins. Co., N.Y.C., 1963—, exec. v.p., 1983-85, sr. exec. v.p., 1985-93, sr. exec. v.p., CFO, 1993-98, vice chmn. bd., 1998—, CFO, 1998—2003. Fellow Soc. Actuaries, Acad. Actuaries. Office: Met Life Ins Co 1 Madison Ave New York NY 10010-3603

NAGORSKI, ZYGMUNT, political scientist, writer; b. Warsaw, Sept. 27, 1912; came to U.S., 1948, naturalized, 1953; s. Zygmunt Julian and Maria Nagorski; m. Marie Bogdaszewski, Nov. 22, 1938; children: Maria, Andrew, Teresa. MA, U. Cracow (Poland), 1935; postgrad., U. Geneva, 1937-38, Internat. Inst. Trade and, Berne, Switzerland, 1937-38. Reporter Chattanooga Times, 1948; editor-in-chief Fgn. News Svc., Inc., N.Y.C., 1949-56; chief Internat. Br. Office Rsch. USIA, Washington, 1956-59; fgn. svc. officer Cairo, 1959-61, Seoul, 1961-64, Paris, 1964-66; spl. asst. to pres. Fgn. Policy Assn., Inc., N.Y.C., 1966-68; mem. profl. staff Hudson Inst., Inc., 1968-69; dir. members meetings program Coun. Fgn. Rels., N.Y.C., 1969-78; v.p. Lehrman Inst., 1978-80; spl. advisor Aspen Inst. Adj. asst. prof. polit. sci. dept. Queens Coll., 1974-75; v.p. Human Resource Svcs., Inc., 1980-81; guest lectr. Wilton Park, Sussex, Eng., Fgn. Svc. Inst., Ctr. Study Human Values, Tanglewood, N.C., Experiment in Internat. Living (Vt.), also nummerous univs.; v.p., dir. exec. seminars programs Aspen Inst. Humanistic Studies, 1981-85; pres. Ctr. Internat. Leadership, N.Y.C., 1986—. Author: Armed Unemployment, 1945, The Psychology of East-West Trade, 1975; co-author U.S.-Japan Economic Relations, 1979; contbr. articles to newspapers and mags. Pres. Am. Friends Wilton Park, 1967-70, 94-96, Mid-Atlantic Club N.Y., 1972-90; bd. dirs. Scarsdale Adult Sch., 1968-72, Internat. U. Found. Served with Polish Army, 1939-45, under French and Brit. command. Decorated Brit. War medal, officer's cross Order of Merit (W. Germany); comdr. Order of Leopold II (Belgium); recipient Meritorious Svc. award USIA, 1965, Outstanding Fgn. Born Am. award Internat. Ctr. N.Y., 1988. Mem. Coun. Fgn. Rels., Am. Polit. Sci. Assn., Internat. Studies Assn., Polish Inst. Arts and Scis., Am. Fgn. Svc. Assn., Fgn. Svc. club, Nat. Press Club (Washington). Democrat. Roman Catholic. Home: Ctr for Internat Leadership Inc 3050 Military Rd NW 624 Washington DC 20015 Fax: (202) 686-3769. Office Phone: 202-686-3767. E-mail: znagorski@aol.com.

NAGOURNEY, HERBERT, publishing company executive; b. N.Y.C., Jan. 30, 1926; s. Isidor and Tillie (Burstein) N.; children: Adam, Beth, Eric, Sam. BS, Columbia U., 1946, MS, 1947. Pres. Profl. and Tech. Programs, N.Y.C., 1951-65; v.p. Macmillan Co., N.Y.C., 1965-69; pres. Quadrangle/New York Times Book Co., N.Y.C., 1969-76, New York Times Book Co., N.Y.C., 1971-76, Quartet Books, Inc., N.Y.C. and London, 1976-81, Knowledge Tree Group Inc., 1979-89; v.p., dir. Sci. DataLink, 1981-88, Comtex Sci., 1981-90; pres. Profl. and Tech. Pub. Inc., 1989—, Sci. Datalink, 1990—. Served with AUS, 1944. Home: 320 Joshuatown Rd Lyme CT 06371-3000 Office: 45 Christopher St New York NY 10014-3533 E-mail: hnagourney@rcn.com.

NAGPAL, MADAN LAL, biochemist, educator, researcher; b. Kurram, Pakistan, Dec. 15, 1939; m. Raman Verma, Oct. 14, 1943; 1 child, Manish. PhD, Panjab Agrl. U., 1968. Asst. prof. Panjab Agrl. U., Ludhiana, India, 1968-75; rsch. assoc. prof. U. S.C., Columbia, 1987—. Scientist, chemist Dorn Vets. Hosp., Columbia, 1990-95. Rsch. grant U. S.C., 1989-91. Fellow Linnean Soc. of London. Achievements include contributions to the effects of cytokines in Leydig cell function/steroidogenesis in the field of endocrinology and biochemistry. Avocations: golf, fishing, travel, photography, hiking. Home: 709 Skylane Dr Hopkins SC 29061 Office: U SC Sch Medicine Garner's Ferry Rd Columbia SC 29209 E-mail: madan@med.sc.edu.

NAGRA, PARMINDER, actress; b. Leicester, England, Oct. 5, 1975; Actor: (films) Bend It Like Beckham, 2002, Ella Enchanted, 2004; (TV series) Turning World, 1996, Always and Everyone, 1999, ER, 2003—; (TV films) King Girl, 1996, Donovan Quick, 1999, Twelfth Night, 2003, Second Generation, 2003. Office: NBC/ER 4000 Warner Blvd Burbank CA 91522

NAGTALON-MILLER, HELEN ROSETE, humanities educator; b. Honolulu, June 27, 1928; d. Dionicio Reyes and Fausta Dumrigue (Rosete) Nagtalon; m. Robert Lee Ruley Miller, June 15, 1952. BEd, U. Hawaii, 1951; Diplôme, The Sorbonne, Paris, 1962; MA, U. Hawaii, 1967; PhD, Ohio State U., 1972. Cert. secondary education educator. Tchr. humanities Hawaii State Dept. Edn., Honolulu, 1951-63; supr. student tchrs. French lab. sch. Coll. of Edn. U. Hawaii, Honolulu, 1963-66, instr. French, coord. French courses Coll. Arts and Scis., 1966-69; teaching asst. Coll. Edn. Ohio State U., Columbus, 1970-72; instr. French lab. sch. Coll. Edn. U. Hawaii, Honolulu, 1974-76; adminstr. bilingual-bicultural edn. project Hawaii State Dept. Edn., Honolulu, 1975—76; coord. disadvantaged minority recruitment program Sch. Social Work, U. Hawaii, Honolulu, 1976—83; coord. tutor tng. program U. Hawaii, Honolulu, 1983—85; program dir. Multicultural Multifunctional Resource Ctr., Honolulu, 1985—86; vis. prof. Sch. Pub. Health, ret. U. Hawaii, Honolulu, 1986—91. Bd. dirs. Hawaii Assn. Lang. Tchrs., Honolulu, 1963-66, Hawaii Com. for the Humanities, 1977-83; mem. statewide adv. coun. State Mental Health Adv. Com., Honolulu, 1977-82; task force mem. Underrepresentation of Filipinos in Higher Edn., Honolulu, 1984-86. Author: (with others) Notable Women in Hawaii, 1984; contbr. articles to profl. jours. Chairperson edn. and counseling subcom. First Gov.'s Commn. on Status of Women, Honolulu, 1964; vice chairperson Honolulu County Com. on the Status of Women, 1975—76, Hawaii State Dr. Martin Luther King Jr. Commn., Honolulu, 1982—85; pres. Filipino-Am. Hist. Soc. of Hawaii, 1980—2000; mem. Hawaii State Adv. Com. to U.S. Commn. on Civil Rights, 1981—, chairperson, 1982—85; bd. dirs. Japanese Am. Citizens League Honolulu chpt., 1990—2001, mem. Hawaiian Sovereignty com., 1994—98, Protect Our Constitution; mem. Pro-Choice Polit. Action Com., 1989—92. Women of Distinction, Honolulu County Com. on Status of Women, 1982; recipient Nat. Edn. Assn. award for Leadership in Asian and Pacific Island Affairs, NEA, 1985, Alan F. Saunders award ACLU in Hawaii, 1986, Disting. Alumni award U. Hawaii Alumni Affairs Office, 1994. Mem. Filipino Am. Nat. Hist. Soc., Filipino Coalition for Solidarity, Gabriela Network (Hawaii chpt.), Filipino Cmty. Ctr., Philippine Centennial Coordinating Com./Hawaii, NOW, Alliance Française of Hawaii, Rainbow Peace Fund. Democrat. Avocations: social-political advocacy, reading, classical music, theater, literary presentations. Home and Office: 47-543 Halemanu St Kaneohe HI 96744-4604 E-mail: rlrmiller@earthlink.net.

NAGY, BOB, editor; Exec. editor Motor Trend, L.A., 1983—. Office: Motor Trend 6420 Wilshire Blvd Fl 7 Los Angeles CA 90048-5502

NAGY, GEORGE, education educator; b. Budapest, Hungary, July 7, 1937; s. Stephen and Helen Nagy; m. Jill Beckoff Nagy, July 20, 1963; children: Naomi, Edwin. B in Engring Physics, McGill U., Montreal, 1959, M in Engring EE, 1960; PhD, Cornell U., Ithaca, NY, 1962. Tech. staff IBM T.J. Watson Rsch. Ctr., Yorktown, NY, 1963—73; dept. chair computer sci. U. Nebr., Lincoln, 1972—81, prof. computer sci., 1981—85; prof. computer engrng. Rensselaer Polytech. Inst., Troy, NY, 1985—. Co-author: (book) Optical Character Recognition, 1989; contbr. articles to profl. jours. Recipient Lifetime Rsch. award, Internat. Conf. Document Analysis and Recognition, 2001. Fellow: IEEE (life), Internat. Assn. Pattern Recognition. Avocations: skiing, hiking, sailing. Office: Rensselaer Polytech Inst 110 8th St Troy NY 12180

NAGY, LOUIS LEONARD, engineering executive, researcher; b. Detroit, Jan. 15, 1942; s. Alex and Helen Nagy; m. Dianna M. Skarjune, Aug. 5, 1961; children: Tammy, Kimberly, Kristine, Amanda. BSEE, U. Mich., Dearborn, 1965; MSEE, U. Mich., Ann Arbor, 1969, PhDEE, 1974. Registered profl. engr. Rsch. engr. U. Mich., Ann Arbor, 1962-69; staff rsch. engr. GM R & D Ctr., Warren, Mich., 1969-98; sr. staff rsch. engr. Delphi Rsch. Labs., Warren, 1999—. Contbr. articles to profl. jours.; patentee in field. Bd. dirs. Convergence Ednl. Found., Birmingham, Mich., 1990-97, Convergence Transp. Electronics Assn., Birmingham, 1990-97. Recipient 1998 R&D 100 award R&D Mag. Fellow IEEE; mem. Convergence Fellowship (bd. dirs. 1988-96), Vehicular Tech. Soc. (Spl. Recognition award 1979, Avant Garde award 1986, Paper of Yr. 1975), Soc. Automotive Engrs., Tau Beta Pi, Eta Kappa Nu. Avocations: electronics, antennas, radar, automotive radar, microwaves. Office: Delphi Rsch Labs MC 483-478-105 51786 Shelby Pkwy Shelby Township MI 48315 E-mail: Louis.L.Nagy@delphi.com.

NAGY, STEPHEN MEARS, JR., physician, allergist; b. Yonkers, N.Y., Apr. 1, 1939; s. Stephen Mears and Olga (Zahoruiko) N.; m. Brenda Yu Nagy, 1966; children: Catherine, Stephen III. BA, Princeton U., 1960; MD, Tufts U., 1964. Diplomate Am. Bd. Internal Medicine, Am. Bd. Allergy and Immunology. Pvt. practice, Sacramento, Calif., 1971-2000; prof. Sch. Medicine U. Calif., Davis, 1974—. Author, editor Evaluation & Management of Allergic and Asthmatic Diseases, 1981; mem. editl. bd. Clinical Reviews in Allergy; creator Famous Teachings in Modern Medicine-Allergy Series slide collection. Capt. U.S. Army, 1966-68, Vietnam. Fellow Am. Acad. Allergy, Am. Coll. Allergy; mem. CMA, Sacramento-El Dorado Med. Soc. (bd. dirs. 1971-95, 1989-95). Avocations: bicycling, book collecting, opera, fencing. Office: 4801 J St Ste A Sacramento CA 95819-3746 Office Phone: 916-456-4782.

NAHAI, FOAD, plastic surgery educator; b. Teheran, Iran, Sept. 23, 1943; came to U.S., 1970; m. Shahnaz Mossanen, Aug. 4, 1969; children: Farzad R., Fariba R. BSc with honors, U. Bristol, Eng., 1966, MB ChB, 1969. Diplomate Am. Bd. Surgery, Am. Bd. Plastic Surgery. Med. and surg. intern United Bristol Hosps., 1969-70; intern in surgery Balt. City Hosps., 1970-71; resident in surgery Johns Hopkins Hosp., Balt., 1971-72; resident in gen. surgery Emory U. Affiliated Hosps., Atlanta, 1972-74, chief resident, 1974-75, fellow in hand surgery and microsurgery, 1975-76, resident in plastic surgery, 1976-77; instr. in surgery Emory U., Atlanta, 1975-76, 78, from asst. to assoc. prof., 1978-91, prof., 1991-98; pvt. practice Paces Plastic Surgery, Atlanta. Author: (with S.J. Mathes) Clinical Atlas of Muscle and Musculocutaneous Flaps, 1979, Clinical Applications for Muscle and Musculocutaneous Flaps, 1982, (with others) Microvascular Surgery in Reconstruction of the Head and Neck, 1989, Plastic and Reconstructive Breast Surgery, 1990, Grabb's Encyclopedia of Flaps, 1990, (with Bostwick Eaves) Endoscopic Plastic Surgery, 1994, (with S.J. Mathes) Reconstructive Surgery, 1996, others; mem. editl. bd. Annals Plastic Surgery, 1984, Outlook Plastic Surgery, 1988; contbr. articles to profl. jours.; co-prodr. (movies) Breast Reconstruction After a Radical Mastectomy with Latissimus Dorsi Musculocutaneous Flap, 1978, The Tensor Fascia Lata Free Flap, 1979; prodr. (videotapes) TFL Neurosensory Flap for Coverage of Greater Trochanteric and Ischium, Rectus Abdominis Flap for Sternal Coverage, Gastrocnemius Muscle Flap for Coverage of Tibia, others. Recipient Gold Medal Paper Presentation Southeastern Surg. Conf., 1976, Best Paper award Atlanta Clin. Soc., 1980, award Am. Med. Writers Assn., 1983. Fellow ACS (3d Ann. Residents Competition award Ga. chpt. 1977); mem. AMA, Am. Assn. Plastic Surgeons (James Barrett Brown award 1982), Am. Soc. Aesthetic Plastic Surgery, Am. Soc. Plastic and Reconstructive Surgeons (rsch. grantee ednl. found.), Ga. Soc. Plastic Surgeons, Med. Assn. Ga., Ga. Surg. Soc., Med. Assn. Atlanta, Southeastern Soc. Plastic and Reconstructive Surgeons (Outstanding Resident award 1977), Internat. Assn. Univ. Plastic Surgeons, Plastic Surgery Rsch. Coun. (program chmn. 1988, chmn. 1989), Brazilian Coll. Surgeons (corr.), Brazilian Soc. Plastic Surgeons, Italian Soc. Plastic, Reconstructive and Aesthetic Surgery, Soc. Residents and Ex Residents of Inst. Reconstructive Surgery (hon.), Sociedad Jaime Planas de Cirurgia Plastica, Internat. Soc. Aesthetic Plastic Surgery (sec. gen.), Am. Soc. Aestetic Plastic Surgery (sec.). Office: Paces Plastic Surgery 3200 Downwood Cir NW Ste 640 Atlanta GA 30327-1624 Office Phone: 404-351-0051.

NAHAS, GABRIEL GEORGES, pharmacologist, educator, writer; b. Alexandria, Egypt, Mar. 4, 1920; came to U.S., 1947, naturalized, 1962; s. Bishara and Gabrielle (Wolff) N.; m. Marilyn Cashman, Feb. 13, 1954; children: Michele, Anthony, Christiane. BA, U. Toulouse, France, 1937, MD, 1944; MS, U. Rochester, 1949; PhD, U. Minn., 1953; DSc (hon.), U. Uppsala, 1988. Rockefeller Found. fellow U. Rochester, 1947-48; Mayo Found. fellow Mayo Clinic, 1949-50; rsch. fellow U. Minn., 1950-53, mem. faculty, 1955-57; mem. staff Walter Reed Army Inst. Rsch., 1957-59; faculty George Washington U. Med. Sch., 1957-59; mem. faculty Columbia U. Coll. Physicians and Surgeons, N.Y.C., 1959-92, prof. anesthesiology, 1962-92; prof. emeritus, 1992; rsch. prof. anesthesiology NYU Med. Sch., N.Y.C., 1992—. Disting. vis. scientist Addiction Rsch. Ctr., NIDA, 1987; adj. rsch. prof. anesthesiology U. Paris, 1968-71; fellow Coun. Circulation and Basic Sci., Am. Heart Assn., 1961—; mem. com. on trauma NRC, 1964-66; mem. adv. bd. Cousteau Soc.; cons. commn. on narcotics, drug control program UN. Author 700 sci. publs. and 40 books and monographs in English and French. Decorated Presdl. Medal of Freedom with gold palm Govt. of U.S.; comdr. Legion of Honor, Croix de Guerre with 3 palms (France), Order Brit. Empire, Order Orange Nassau Netherlands, Silver medal City of Paris; recipient Medal of Honor, Statue of Liberty Centennial, 1986; Fulbright scholar, 1966. Fellow AAAS, N.Y. Acad. Sci.; mem. Am. Physiol. Soc., Harvey Soc., Am. Soc. Pharmacology and Exptl. Therapeutics, Soc. Physiol. Langue Française, French Acad. Medicine (laureate 1995, 96), Brit. Pharm. Soc., Sigma Xi. Achievements include research on med. instrumentation, pharmacology Tham, acid-base regulation, pharmacology of cannabis and cocaine, drug dependence, consciousness, college problem on drug dependence. Home: 40 E 74th St New York NY 10021-2732 Office: NYU Med Ctr Dept Anesthesiology 550 1st Ave New York NY 10016-6402 *Courage is to stand by one's own conviction unheeding the trends of fashion or pressure groups. It is to suffer alone and be scorned for a lifetime. But, in the end, one will hear "he was right!".*

NAHASS, RONALD G(EORGE), internist, educator; b. Belle Mead, N.J., Mar. 2, 1957; s. George Fred and Margaret Hannah (Kattine) N.; m. Rosanne Vita, Aug. 15, 1982; children: Ronald George Jr., Thomas Andrew, Meghan Marie. BS, Rennselaer Poly. Inst., 1978; MD, U. Medicine and Dentistry N.J., 1982. Diplomate Am. Bd. Internal Medicine, Am. Bd. Infectious Disease. Intern, then resident Robert Wood Johnson Sch., U. Medicine and Dentristry N.J., Piscataway, 1982-85, chief resident, 1985-86, fellow, 1986-88, clin. instr., 1983-86, asst. prof., 1988-95, assoc. prof., 1995—2002; prof. Robert Wood Johnson Sch., 2003—; attending physician Robert Wood Johnson Sch., U. Medicine and Dentristry N.J., Piscataway, 1988—, Somerset (N.J.) Med. Ctr., 1990—, Med. Ctr. at Princeton, Robert Wood Johnson U. Hosp., 1990—. Active Dept. Health, Montgomery Twp., N.J., 1996-00. Recipient Physician Recognition award AMA, 1996, 2001. Fellow ACP, Am. Coll. Medicine, Infectious Disease Soc. Am., Acad. Medicine N.J.; mem. Infectious Disease Assn. (pres. 1991—). Office: 411 Courtyard Dr Hillsborough NJ 08844-4254 E-mail: rnahass@idcare.com.

NAHAT, DENNIS F. performing company executive, choreographer; b. Detroit, Feb. 20, 1946; s. Fred H. and Linda M. (Haddad) N. Hon. degree, Juilliard Sch. Music, 1965. Prin. dancer Joffrey Ballet, N.Y.C., 1965-66; prin. dancer Am. Ballet Theatre, N.Y.C., 1968-79; co-founder Cleve. Ballet, 1976, Sch. of Cleve. Ballet, 1972; founder, artistic dir. San Jose Cleve. Ballet, 1985, Sch. Cleve. San Jose Ballet, 1996; founder New Sch. of Cleve. San Jose Ballet, 1996—. Co-chair Artists Round Table Dance USA, 1991; trustee Cecchetti Coun. Am., 1991; mem. adv. bd. Ohio Dance Regional Dance Am. Prin. performer Broadway show Sweet Charity, 1966-67; choreographer Two Gentlemen of Verona (Tony award 1972), 1969-70; (ballet) Celebrations and Ode (resolution award 1985), 1985, Green Table, Three Virgins and a Devil (Isadora Duncan award 1985); conceived, directed, choreographed Blue Suede Shoes, PBS, 1997-98. Grantee Nat. Endowment Arts, 1978, Andrew Mellow Found., 1985; recipient Outstanding Achievement award Am. Dance Guild, 1995, 96, 2000—. Avocation: master chef. Office: Cleve San Jose Ballet 3615 Euclid Ave Ste 1A Cleveland OH 44115-2527 also: Cleve San Jose Ballet PO Box 1666 San Jose CA 95109-1666 also: San Jose Cleve Ballet 40 N 1st St San Jose CA 95113-1200

NAHAVANDI, AMIR NEZAMEDDIN, retired engineering firm executive; b. Tehran, Iran, Apr. 6, 1924; came to U.S., 1956, naturalized, 1970; s. Ahmad and Fatima (Razaghi) N. Electromech. Engring. degree, Tehran U., 1947; MS in Mech. Engring, Carnegie Inst. Tech., 1957, PhD, 1960. Registered profl. engr., Pa. Engr. Tehran U., 1948-50; head design group Nat. Iranian Oil Co., Tehran, 1950-56; adv. engr. Westinghouse Electric Corp., Pitts., 1957-66; prof., chmn. dept. mech. engring. U. Vt., 1967-68; research prof. N.J. Inst. Tech., 1969-77; prof. engring. and applied Sci. Columbia U., N.Y.C., 1977-81; chief scientist Electronic Assocs., Inc., West Long Branch, N.J., 1981-82; pres. Mazen, Inc., Long Branch, N.J., 1982-92. Decorated Sci. medal 1st degree Iran). Fellow ASME; mem. N.Y. Acad. Scis., Phi Kappa Phi, Sigma Xi, Tau Beta Pi. Achievements include research and devel. in dynamics of steam generators and boiling systems, dynamic and accident analysis of conventional and nuclear power plants, vibration of reactor structures, thermal pollution of lakes and rivers, solid-fluid interaction, development of analytical models for stock market forecasting. Home: 532 Meridian Way Carlsbad CA 92009-5400

NAHIGIAN, ROBERT JOHN, real estate development broker; b. Boston, Feb. 24, 1956; s. John Moses and Theresa (Zeytoundjian) N.; m. Donna P. Dewar, Oct. 23, 1993; children: Jessica Lee, Kimberly Patricia. BA cum laude, Lehigh U., 1978; MS in Urban Planning, Columbia U., 1980. Cert. real estate mediator Mass. Property mgr. Auburndale (Mass.) Realty Co., 1972-77; jr. planner Bethlehem (Pa.) Redevel. Authority, 1978; planner, tech. analyst Perkins & Will Archtl. Firm, N.Y.C., 1978-80; city planner, econ. developer City of Bowie, Md., 1980-81; v.p. The Norwood Group, Inc., Burlington, Mass., 1981-88; v.p., dir. The Robbins Group, Cambridge, Mass., 1988-89; pres. Auburndale Realty Co., Newton, Mass., 1989—. Dir., lectr. real estate studies Northeastern U., Boston, 1982—93; instr. real estate Boston U., 1994—; lectr., spkr. at convs. in field; Boston U. lectr. U. of Hong Kong Polytech.; 1st SIOR spkr. at Latin America's First Real Estate Conf., Bogota, Colombia, 1998; invited lectr. Czech Republic, Poland; mem. Greater Boston Real Estate Bd. Comml. Broker Assn., Govt. and Agy. Law Task Force Affairs rep., bd. dirs., 2002—; mem. Comml. Overlay State Task Force; apptd. by Gov. Romney Mass. Hwy. Real Estate Rev. Bd., 2004. Co-author: Master Office Leasing, 1993, rev. edit., 2000; contbr. articles to profl. jours. Mem. Wang Ctr. for the Performing Arts, Boston, 1985. Recipient Cert. of Appreciation, Exch. Club, 1991, Alumni award Lehigh U., 1993, N.E. Constrn. Show, So. Calif. Constrn. Show, Mex. Nat. Bd. Realtors, 1997, Disting. Achievement in cml. leasing Greater Boston Real Estate Bd., 1999; First Mass. Comml. Broker as Cert. Instr., Banker and Tradesman Top 125 Bus. Leaders in Mass. for 1999, 1st Comml Broker as Cert. Mass. Real Estate Mediator, 2001. Mem.: Worcester Regional Assn. Realtors (edn. task force, nominated 2003 Educator of Yr. 2004), Comml. Brokers Assn. (govt. affairs rep., agy. law task force to Mass. Assn. Realtors 2002—03, bd. dirs. 2002—, coml. overlay state task force study, Broker Achievement Bronze award 2000, Broker Achievement Gold award 2001, Indsl. Deal of Yr. award 2001, Comml. Leasing Achievement Gold award 2001, adv. assignment 2003, nominated Broker of Yr. 2003), Nat. Assn. Indsl. and Office Parks (New Eng. chpt. membership com. 1993—96, membership com. chmn. 1996, exec. com. 1996, cert. appreciation Mass. chpt.), Am. Soc. Real Estate (counselors of real estate 1996, nat. conv. spkr. 1997, com. mem. nat. edn. com., nat. presdl. task force 1998—2000, vice chmn. pub. rels. com. 1998—2000, nat. spl. task force 2001, nat. chmn. pub. rels. and comm. 2001—02, nat. bd. dirs. 2001—), Soc. Indsl. and Office Realtors (nat. vice chmn. office courses 1993—94, edn. exec. com. 1993—94, nat. regional v.p. 1994—96, nat. exec. com. 1994—96, nat. bd. dir. 1994—96, nat. chmn. instrs. com. 1994—97, nat. chmn. edn. com. 1994—98, ex officio edn. fund 1995—97, nat. chmn. edn. exec. com. 1995—97, nat. nominating com. 1995—98, Presdl. edn. task force 1995—99, bd. dir. New Eng. chpt. 1995—, pres. New Eng. chpt. 1998—99, spl. adv. and immediate past pres. 2000, nat. budget and fin. com. 2000—02, spl. advisor 2000—, v.p. nat. com. programs, nat. convention co-chmn., nat. bd. dirs. 2001, nat. vice chmn. designation courses edn. com., nat. nominating com. 2002, nat. vice chmn faculty com. 2003—, sr. instr., instrs. com. and office mktg. forum, task force indsl. office leasing handbook, property evaluation forum, expert roundtable com., Nat. Real Estate Instr. of Yr. 1994, medal of appreciation New Eng. chpt. 1998—99, Appreciation medal New Eng. chpt. 1998—99, Nat. Real Estate Instr. of Yr. 2002, cert. appreciation, cert. profl. edn. com., cert. appreciation as outgoing nat. ednl. chair, Nat. Real Estate Instr. of Yr. 2003), Mass. Assn. Realtors (com. mem. 2001—, agy. law task force 2003—04, comml. bd. overlay task force 2004—, govt. affairs com. for CBA), Nat. Assn. Realtors (cert. of appreciation 1992, Mass. mediation officer award 2001), Counselors of Real Estate (nat. bd. dirs. 2002—), Algonquin Club, Lehigh Club (class '78 pres. 1993—98), Lambda Alpha. Republican. Mem. Armenian Apostolic Ch. Home: 365 Highland St Weston MA 02493-2624 Office: Auburndale Realty Co PO Box 66125 335 Auburn St Newton MA 02466-1902 Office Phone: 617-332-6900. E-mail: rob@siorcre.com.

NAHMAD, ALBERT H. manufacturing executive, United States federal commissioner; b. Oct. 15, 1940; m. Jane Davis; 2 children. BS in Mech. Engring., U. N. Mex., 1962; MS in Indsl. Adminstrn., Purdue U., 1963. Mgmt. cons. Arthur Young, N.Y.C.; group v.p. W.R. Grace & Co.; chmn. pres., CEO Watsco, Inc., Coconut Grove, Fla.; commr. Panama Canal Commission, Washington. Bd. dirs. Am. Bankers Ins. Group, Mayor's Jewelers. Mem. Fla. Coun. 100; chmn. bd. of trustees Miami Children's Hosp.; past chmn. Fla. chpt Young Presidents' Org. Office: Watsco Inc 2665 S Bayshore Dr Ste 901 Coconut Grove FL 33133-5436

NAHMAN, NORRIS STANLEY, electrical engineer; b. San Francisco, Nov. 9, 1925; s. Hyman Cohen and Rae (Levin) N.; m. Shirley D. Maxwell, July 20, 1968; children: Norris Stanley, Vicki L., Vance W., Scott T. BS in Electronics Engring, Calif. Poly. State U., 1951; MSE.E., Stanford U., 1952; PhD in Elec. Engring, U. Kans., 1961. Registered profl. engr., Colo. Electronic scientist Nat. Security Agy., Washington, 1952-55; prof. elec. engring., dir. electronics rsch. lab. U. Kans., Lawrence, 1955-66; sci. cons., chief pulse and time domain sect. Nat. Bur. Standards, Boulder, Colo., 1966-73, chief time domain metrology, sr. scientist, 1975-83, group leader field characterization group, 1984-85; v.p. Picosecond Pulse Labs, Inc., Boulder, 1986-90, scientific advisor, co-chair tech. adv. bd., 1990—; cons. elec. engr., 1990—; prof., chmn. dept. elec. engring. U. Toledo, 1973-75; prof. elec. engring. U. Colo., Boulder, 1966—; affiliate staff Los Alamos (N.Mex.) Nat. Lab., 1990—. Disting. lectr., prin. prof. Ctr. Nat. d' Etude des Telecomm. Summer Sch., Lannion France, 1978; disting. lectr. Harbin Inst. Tech., Peoples Republic China, summer 1982; mem. faculty NATO Advanced Study Inst., Castelvecchio, Italy, 1983, Internat. Radio Sci. Union/NRC; chmn. Internat. Intercomm. Group Waveform Measurements, 1981-90, chmn. Commn. A, 1985-86. Contbr. rsch. articles profl. jours.; patentee in field. Asst. scoutmaster Longs Peak coun. Boy Scouts Am., 1970-73, 75-89. With U.S. Mcht. Marine, 1943-46, U.S. Army, 1952-55. Ford Found. faculty fellow MIT, 1962; Nat. Bur. Standards sr. staff fellow, 1978-79; recipient Disting. Alumnus award Calif. Poly. State U., 1972, Order of Arrow Boy Scouts Am., 1976. Fellow IEEE (life), Internat. Sci. Radio Union; mem. Instrumentation and Measurement Soc. of IEEE (admstrv. com. 1982-84, editorial bd. Trans., 1982-86, Andrew H. chi Best Tech. Paper award 1984, Tech. Leadership and Achievement award 1987), Am. Assn. Engring. Edn. (life), U.S. Mcht. Marine Veterans World War II, Am. Legion, Calif. Poly. State U. Alumni Assn. (life), Stanford U. (life), U. Kans. (life), Am. Radio Relay League Club (life), Sigma Pi Sigma, Tau Beta Pi, Eta Kappa Nu, Sigma Tau, Sigma Xi. E-mail: nsnahman@ieee.org.

NAHRWOLD, DAVID LANGE, surgeon, educator; b. St. Louis, Dec. 21, 1935; s. Elmer William and Magdalen Louise (Lange) N.; m. Carolyn Louise Hoffman, June 14, 1958; children: Stephen Michael, Susan Alane, Thomas James, Anne Elizabeth. AB, Ind. U., 1957, MD, 1960. Diplomate Am. Bd. Surgery, Am. Bd. Thoracic Surgery. Intern, then resident in surgery Ind. U. Med. Ctr., Indpls., 1960-65; postdoctoral scholar in gastrointestinal physiology VA Ctr., UCLA, 1965; asst. prof. surgery Ind. U. Med. Sch., 1968-70; assoc. prof. Coll. Medicine Pa. State U., 1970-73; vice-chmn. dept. surgery Pa. State U., 1971-82, assoc. provost, dean health affairs, 1981-82, prof., chief divsn. gen. surgery, 1974-82; Loyal and Edith Davis prof., chmn. dept. surgery Northwestern U. Med. Sch., Chgo., 1982-97; surgeon-in-chief Northwestern Meml. Hosp., Chgo., 1982-97; pres., CEO Northwestern Med. Faculty Found., Inc., 1996-99; prof. surgery, exec. assoc. dean clin. affairs Northwestern U. Med. Sch., 1997-99, prof. emeritus, 1999—. Mem. Nat. Digestive Disease Adv. Bd., 1985—89; bd. dirs. Am. Bd. Surgery, vice chmn., 1994—95, chmn., 1995—96; bd. dirs. Northwestern Healthcare Network; former mem. exec. bd. Am. Bd. Med. Spltys., 1997—, pres., 2002—04; mem. exec. com. Accreditation Coun. for Grad. Med. Edn., 1999—2000; bd. commrs. Joint Commn. Accreditation Healthcare Orgns., 2002—. Editor emeritus Jour. Laparoendoscopic Surgery, 1997-2004; mem. editl. bd. Surgery, 1981-94, Archives of Surgery, 1983-93, Digestive Surgery, 1986-99, Am. Jour. Surgery, 1994-2000, Jour. Gastrointestinal Surgery, 1996-2000, Current Opinion in Gen. Surgery, Jour. Lithotripsy and Stone Disease, 1988-92; contbr. articles to profl. jours. With MC U.S. Army, 1966—68. Recipient John P. Hubbard award, Nat. Bd. Med. Examiners, 2003. Fellow: ACS (bd. govs. 1992—98, vice chmn. 1994—96, chmn. bd. govs. exec. com. 1996—98, interim dir. 1999—2000, bd. regents, Disting. Svc. award 2001), Philippine Coll. Surgeons (hon.); mem.: AMA, Chgo. Surg. Soc. (pres. 1993—94), Chgo. Med. Soc., We. Surg. Assn., Soc. Univ. Surgeons, Soc. Surgery Alimentary Tract (pres. 1989—90, trustee), Soc. Clin. Surgery (sec. 1984—88), Internat. Biliary Assn., Ill. Surg. Soc., Ill. State Med. Soc., Internat. Fedn. Surg. Colls. (hon.; treas. 1999—2002), Gastroenterology Rsch. Group, Collegium Internat. Chirurgiae Digestive (pres. U.S. chpt. 1988—90), Ctrl. Surg. Assn. (sec. 1994—97, pres.-elect 1997—98, pres. 1998—99, pres. Found. 2002—03), Assn. Surg. Edn., Assn. Acad. Surgery, Am. Surg. Assn. (2d v.p. 1993—94), Am. Phys. Soc., Alpha Omega Alpha, Sigma Xi. Office: Dept Surgery Galter 10-105 251 E Huron St Chicago IL 60611-2908 Office Phone: 312-695-4908. E-mail: dnahrwol@nmh.org.

NAIDES, STANLEY J. physician, educator, researcher; b. Phila. BA, Princeton U., 1974; MD, Hahnemann U., Phila., 1978. Diplomate Nat. Bd. of Med. Examiners, 1979, Medicine Diplomate Am. Bd. of Internal Medicine, 1981, Rheumatology Diplomate Am. Bd. of Internal Medicine, 1983. Asst. prof. Divsn. of Rheumatology, Dept. of Internal Medicine, U. of Iowa, 1986—92, assoc. prof., 1992—99; dir. Helen C. Levitt Ctr., U. of Iowa, 1997—99; hallowell prof. rheumatology Pa. State Hershey Med. Ctr., 1999—, prof. medicine, microbiology & immunology, 1999—, prof. pharmacology, 2000—, chief divsn. of rheumatology, 1999—2004. Co-dir. immunobiology option, integrative biosciences grad. program Pa. State Hershey Med. Ctr., 2001—. Grantee Rsch., NIH, Arthritis Found., Veterans Affairs Med. Ctr., Nat. Mar. of Dimes Found., Lupus Found., Am. Philosophy. Soc., Schwartz Found., 1984—2004, Burroughs-Wellcome Fund Young Investigator award;, Baxter Healthcare Corp., Gull Labs., Inc., Ctrl. Pa. Arthritis Assn. Fellow: ACP, Am. Coll. of Rheumatology; mem.: AAAS, Ctrl. Soc. for Clin. Rsch. (chair, rheumatology coun. 1996—99), Am. Soc. Microbiology, Am. Assn. Immunology, Phila. Rheumatism Soc., Am. Soc. Virology. Office: Pa State Hershey Med Ctr H038 BMR C5840 500 Univ Dr Hershey PA 17033-0850 E-mail: snaides@psu.edu.

NAIDICH, THOMAS PAUL, neuroradiologist, educator; b. Bklyn., Apr. 8, 1944; s. James and Rose (Bitko) N.; m. Rochele Miriam Pudlowksi, Feb. 2, 1975 (div. Nov. 1981); children: 1 child, Sandra Rebecca; m. Michele W. Levin, Dec. 29, 1990. BA, Cornell U., 1965; MD, NYU, NY, 1969. Diplomate in radiology and in neuroradiology Am. Bd. Radiology. Intern Bronx Mcpl. Hosp. Ctr., NY, 1969-70; resident in radiology Montefiore Hosp., Bronx, NY, 1970-73; fellow in neuroradiology NYU Sch. Medicine, NY, 1973-75; prof. radiology and neurosurgery Mt. Sinai Med. Ctr. NYU, NY, 1998—, dir. neuroradiology, 1998—, vice chmn. radiology for acad. affairs, 2001—, Irving and Dorothy Regenstreif Rsch. prof. of neurosci., 2002—; asst. prof. Albert Einstein Coll. Medicine, Bronx, NY, 1975-77; from asst. prof. to assoc. prof. Mallinckrodt Inst. Radiology, St. Louis, 1978-80; from assoc. prof. to prof. Northwestern U. Sch. Medicine, Chgo., 1980-88; clin. prof. neuroradiology U. Miami Sch. Med., Fla., 1988-98; dir. neuroradiology Bapt. Hosp. Miami, Fla., 1988-98; dir Clin. Imaging Rsch. Core, Mt. Sinai Med. Ctr., Mt. Sinai, NY, 2001—. Author: (with R. M. Quencer) Clinical Neurosonography, 1987; (with Valavanis, Schubiger) Clinical Imaging of the Cerebello-Pontine Angle, 1987; (with Daniels, Haughton) Cranial and Spinal Magnetic Ressonance Imaging, 1987; editor-in-chief Neuroradiology, 1980-91, chmn. editl. bd., 1991-93; assoc. editor Surg. and Radiol. Anatomy, 1991-97; founding editor Internat. Jour. Neuroradiology, 1994-00; contbr. articles to profl. jour. Recipient John Caffey award Soc. Pediatric Radiology, 1983. Mem. Am. Soc. Neuroradiology (treas. 1991-93, Cornelius Dyke award 1975), Am. Soc. Pediatric Neuroradiology (pres. 1994-95), gold medal Sociedad dbero-latino Americana de Neurorradiology (SILAN), European Soc. Neuroradiology (hon.), Brit. Soc. Neuroradiologists (hon.), Swiss Soc. Neuroradiology (hon.). Avocation: antique furniture. Office: Mt Sinai Med Ctr Dept Radiology Box 1234 1 Gustave Levy Pl New York NY 10029 E-mail: thomas.naidich@mountsinai.org.

NAIDORF, LOUIS MURRAY, architect; b. Los Angeles, Aug. 15, 1928; s. Jack and Meriam (Abbott) N.; m. Dorise D. Roberts, June 1948 (div.); children: Victoria Beth Naidorf-Slifer; m. Patricia Ann Shea, June 1, 1968 (div.); m. Patricia Ruth Allen, Dec. 6, 1992 (dec.). BA, U. Calif., Berkeley, 1949, MA, 1950; Doctorate (hon.), Woodbury U., 2000. Registered architect, Calif. Designer Welton Becket Assocs., L.A., 1950-51, Pereira and Luckman, L.A., 1951-52; project designer Welton Becket Assocs., L.A., 1952-55, sr. project designer, 1955-59, v.p. asst., dir. design, 1959-70, sr. v.p., dir. rsch., 1970-73; sr. v.p., design prin. Ellerbe Becket Assocs., L.A., 1973-95; dean Sch. Architecture and Design Woodbury U., L.A., 1990-2000; prin. Allen Naidorf Design Cons., 1995—. Mem. peer rev. panel Nat. Endowment Arts, 1995—; vis. lectr. Calif. Poly. Sch. Architecture, San Luis Obispo, 1975-82; instr. UCLA Sch. Architecture, 1985, UCLA Landscape Archtl. Program, 1980-85, Otis-Parsons, L.A., 1986-92. Prin. works include Capitol Records Bldg., Century City, Los Angeles, Hyatt Regency, Dallas, Restoration Calif. State Capitol Bldg. Bd. dirs. Inst. for Garden Studies, L.A., 1986—, ARC, 2000; trustee Woodbury U., 2000. Recipient Honor award Nat. Trust for Hist. Preservation, 1985. Fellow AIA (bd. dirs. Los Angeles chpt. 1977-79, Silver Medal 1950, Nat. Honor award 1985, Educator of Yr. 1997). E-mail: naidorf@msn.com. *Leadership often requires decisions based on limited information. Course corrections can be made but only after action is taken because you can't steer a car that isn't moving.*

NAIFEH, JAMES O. (JIMMY NAIFEH), state legislator, speaker of the house; b. Covington, TN, June 16, 1939; m., three children., U. Tennessee, Knoxville, TN. Pres. Covington Wholesale Comp., Inc., Covington, TN; partner Naifeh Realty Comp., Covington, TN; congressman TN General Assembly, Dist.-81, Nashville, 1978—; majority floor leader TN General Assembly, Nashville, 1979-83, majority leader, 1983-85, speaker of the house, 1986—. Formerly chrm., Rural West TN Dem. Caucus, House Ethics Comm., House Rules Comm.; former v-chrm., Select Oversight Comm. on Corrections; mem., House/Senate Joint Managment Comm. Former pres., mem., Bd. Dirs. Covington-Tipton County Chamber of Comm., mem., South Tipton Chamber of Comm., Bd. Dirs. TN Wholesale Grocers' Assn.; former pres., Covington Rotary Club, Tipton County U. TN Alumni Assn.; bd. mem., First State Bank - Covington, TN; bd. govnrs. dirs., ALSAC - St. Jude Childrens' Research Hosp. Recipient of NCSL Leadership Awd, 1990; TN State Employees Assn, 1990; Legislator of the Year Awd, by TN Assn. of Human Resource Agencies, TN Dist. Attr. Generals' Conf., TN School Bds. Assn., and TN Court Clerks' Assn. Am. Legion Post # 67. Democrat. Episcopalian. Home: PO Box 97 Covington TN 38019-0097 Office: 19 Legislative Plz Nashville TN 37243

NAIFEH, STEVEN WOODWARD, writer; b. Tehran, Iran, June 19, 1952; s. George Amel and Marion (Lamphear) N. AB, Princeton U., 1974; JD, Harvard U., 1977, MA, 1978. Staff lectr. Nat. Gallery Art, Washington, 1976; assoc. Milbank, Tweed, Hadley & McCloy, N.Y.C., 1976; v.p. Sabbagh, Naifeh and Assocs., Washington, 1980; pres. Woodward/White, Inc., 1981; chmn. Best Doctors, Inc., 1998—. Author: Culture Making: Money, Success and the New York Art World, 1976; (with Gregory White Smith) Moving Up in Style, 1980, Gene Davis, 1981, How to Make Love to a Woman, 1982, What Every Client Needs to Know About Using a Lawyer, 1982, The Bargain Hunter's Guide to Art Collecting, 1982, Why Can't Men Open Up?: Overcoming Men's Fear of Intimacy, 1984, The Mormon Murders: A True Story of Greed, Forgery, Deceit, and Death, 1988, Jackson Pollack: An American Saga, 1989 (Nat. Book award nomination for nonfiction 1990, Pulitzer Prize for biography 1991), Final Justice: The True Story of the Richest Man Ever Tried for Murder, 1993, A Stranger in the Family: A True Story of Murder, Madness, and Unconditional Love, 1995, On a Street Called Easy, In a Cottage Called Joye, 1996, Making Miracles Happen, 1997; editor: (with Smith) The Best Lawyers in America series, The Best Doctors in America series. Office: Woodward White Inc 129 First Ave SW Aiken SC 29801

NAIMARK, ARNOLD, medical educator, physiologist, internist; b. Winnipeg, Man., Can., Aug. 24, 1933; s. Harvey and Lisa N.; m. Barbara Jean Alder, Feb. 28, 1960; children: David, Mila. MD, BSc in Medicine, U. Man., Winnipeg, 1957, MSc, 1960; postgrad., U. London, 1962-63, U. Calif.,

1960-62; LLD (hon.), Mt. Allison U., 1986, U. Toronto, 1997. Registrar in medicine Hammersmith Hosp., London, 1962-63; asst. prof. physiology U. Man., 1963-64, assoc. prof., 1965-66, prof., 1967-71, acting head dept. physiology, 1966-67, head dept., 1967-71, dean Faculty Medicine, 1971-81, pres. and vice chancellor, 1981-96, prof. medicine and physiology, 1971—, dir. Ctr. for Advancement Medicine, 1996—. Dir. Health Scis. Ctr., 1971-99; cons. to govt. agys. and founds.; chmn. Can. Health Svcs. Rsch. Found., Can. Biotech. Adv. Com.; dir. Can. Imperial Bank of Commerce, Urban Idea Ctr., Inspiraplex Ltd.; mem. adv. coun. Order of Can., 1988-89; v.p., Can., Inter-Am. Orgn. for Higher Edn., 1993-95. Contbr. articles to profl. jours. Mem. nat. hon. bd. dirs. Juvenile Diabetes Fedn. Internat. Can. Lt. Royal Can. Arty., 1950-53. Decorated officer Order of Can.; recipient Queen Elizabeth Silver Jubilee medal; Symons medal Commonwealth Univs.; medal in physiology U. Man., 1955; Stefansson Meml. prize, 1957; Prowse prize in clin. rsch., 1959; Isbister scholar, 1950-53, 54-56 Fellow Royal Coll. Physicians, AAAS, Royal Soc. Can. (G. Malcolm Brown award 1987, com. univ. rsch. 1989-91); mem. Can. Med. Assn., Can. Physiol. Soc., Am. Physiol. Soc., Can. Soc. Clin. Investigation, Med. Rsch. Soc. Gt. BRit., Assn. Chairmen Depts. Physiology, Can. Tb and Respiratory Disease Assn., Assn. Commmonwealth Univs. (coun. 1985-91), Assn. Univs. and Colls. Can. (pres. 1986-88), Am. Heart Assn., Assn. Commonwealth Univs. (chmn. 1988), Can. Soc. for Acad. Medicine. Office: U Man Ctr for Adv Medicine 730 William Ave Ste 230 Winnipeg MB Canada R3E 3J7

NAIMARK, GEORGE MODELL, marketing and management consultant; b. NYC, Feb. 5, 1925; s. Myron S. and Mary (Modell) N.; m. Helen Anne Wythes, June 24, 1946; children: Ann, Richard, Jane. BS, Bucknell U., 1947, MS, 1948; PhD, U. Del., 1951. Rsch. biochemist Brush Devel. Co., Cleve., 1951; dir. quality control Strong, Cobb & Co., Inc., Cleve., 1951-54; dir. sci. svcs. White Labs., Inc., Kenilworth, N.J., 1954-60; v.p. Burdick Assocs., Inc., N.Y.C., 1960-66; pres. Rajah Press, Summit, N.J., 1963—, Naimark and Barba, Inc., Florham Park, N.J., 1966—, Naimark & Assocs., Inc., Florham Park, N.J., 1994—; dir. Alteon, Inc., 2000—. Bd. dirs. Alteon Inc., Ramsey, N.J. Author: A Patent Manual for Scientists and Engineers, 1961, Communications on Communication, 1971, 3d edit., 1987, A Man Called Skeeter, 1996; patentee in field; contbr. articles in profl. jours. With USNR, 1944-46. Fellow AAAS, Am. Inst. Chemists; mem. Am. Chem. Soc., N.Y. Acad. Scis., Am. Mktg. Assn. Home: 87 Canoe Brook Pky Summit NJ 07901-1404 Office: Naimark & Barba Inc 248 Columbia Tpke Ste 1 Florham Park NJ 07932-1210 Office Phone: 973-377-0816.

NAIMARK, NORMAN M. academic administrator; b. N.Y.C. BA, Stanford U., 1966, PhD, 1972. Prof. History Boston U.; fellow Russian Rsch. Ctr. Harvard U., 1994-97; former vis. Catherine Wasserman Davis chair of Slavic Studies Wellesley Coll.; Robert and Florence McDonnell chair in East European Studies Stanford U. Chmn. dept. History, sr. fellow Hoover Instn.; dir. Stanford's Ctr. Russian and East European Studies; joint com. Am. Coun. Learned Soc.; program com. Internat. Rsch. and Exchange Corp.; exec. com. Am. Assn. Advancement Slavic Studies. Author: The Russians in Germany, 1995, Terrorists and Social Democrats, 1983; lectr., author, co-editor in field. Grantee IREX, ACLS, Alexander von Humbolt Found, Fulbright-Hays, Nat. Coun. Soviet and East European Studies, Hist. Commn. in Berlin; recipient Officer's Cross of Order of merit, Fed. Republic of Germany, 1996, Richard W. Lyman award, 1995. Office: Stanford U Dept History Stanford CA 94305

NAIMI, SHAPUR, cardiologist, educator; b. Tehran, Iran, Mar. 28, 1928; came to U.S., 1959; s. Mohsen and Mahbuba (Naim) n.; m. Amy Cabot Simonds, May 11, 1963; children: Timothy Simonds, Susan Lyman, Cameron Lowell. MB, ChB, Birmingham (Eng.) U., 1953. Diplomate Royal Coll. Physicians (London), Royal Coll. Physicians (Edinburgh), Am. Bd. Internal Medicine (subsplty. bd.cardiovascular disease). House physician Royal Postgrad. Med. Sch. London, 1955; sr. house officer Inst. Diseases of the Chest, London, 1956; fellow in grad. tng. New Eng. Med. Ctr. and MIT, 1961-64; cardiologist Tufts New Eng. Med. Ctr., Boston, 1966—, dir. intensive CCU, 1973—2001, assoc. prof., 1970-93, prof., 1993—. Contbr. articles to profl. jours. Fellow royal Coll. Physicians (Edinburgh), ACP, Am. Coll. Cardiology; mem. Am. Soc. Exptl. Biology and Medicine, AHA, Mass. Med. Soc., Country Brookline, Cohaset Yacht. Home: 265 Woodland Rd Chestnut Hill MA 02467-2204 also: 55 Lothrop Ln Cohasset MA 02025-1425 Office: 750 Washington St Boston MA 02111-1526

NAIMI-TAJDAR, REZA, petroleum engineer; b. Mashhad, Khorasan, Iran, Mar. 21, 1967; arrived in U.S., 1996; s. Hosein Naimi-Tajdar and Batool Saeri-Baghal; m. Susan Rabi-Yousefi, Oct. 12, 1962. BSc, U. Tehran, Iran, 1990; MSc, U. Petroleum Industry, Ahvaz, Iran, 1993; PhD, U. Tex., 2004. Rsch. engr. Rsch. Inst. Petroleum Industry, Tehran, 1991—93; instr. Ferdowsi U. Mashhad, 1993—96; tchg. and rsch. asst. U. Tex., Austin, 1997—2001; reservoir engring. advisor Petrotel Inc., Plano, Tex., 2001—03; rsch. asst. U. Tex., Austin, 2004—. Mem.: Iranian Oil Assn., Soc. Petroleum Engrs. Office: U Tex PGE Dept 26th St Austin TX 78712 Office Phone: 512-471-1240. Business E-Mail: naimi@mail.utexas.edu.

NAIMOLI, VINCENT JOSEPH, diversified operating and holding company executive; b. Paterson, N.J., Sept. 16, 1937; s. Ralph A. and Margaret R. (Calabrese) N.; children— Christine, Tory Ann, Alyson, Lindsey. BSM.E., U. Notre Dame, 1959; MSM.E., N.J. Inst. Tech., 1962; MBA, Fairleigh Dickinson U., 1964; grad. Advanced Mgmt. Program, Harvard Bus. Sch., 1974. With Continental Group, 1965-77, v.p., gen. mgr. ops., 1975-77; pres., chief oper. officer Allegheny Beverage Corp., Balt., 1977-78; sr. v.p., group exec. Jim Walter Corp., Tampa, Fla., 1978-81; group v.p. packaging Anchor Hocking Corp., Lancaster, Ohio, 1981-83; chmn. bd., pres., chief exec. officer Anchor Glass Container Corp., Lancaster, 1983-89; chmn., pres., CEO Anchor Industries Internat., Tampa, Fla., 1990—; chmn., chief exec. officer Electrolux Corp., Atlanta, 1990-91; chmn., CEO Doehler Jarvis Corp., Toledo, 1991-95; CEO Ladish, Inc., Milw., 1992-95; chmn., pres., CEO Harvard Industries, 1993-97; mng. gen. ptnr., CEO Tampa Bay Devil Rays, 1992—. Roman Catholic. Office: Anchor Industries Internat 1 Tropicana Dr Saint Petersburg FL 33705-1703

NAIPAUL, VIDIADHAR SURAJPRASAD, author; b. Chaguanas, Trinidad, Aug. 17, 1932; s. Seepersad Naipaul; m. Patricia Ann Hale, 1955 (dec. 1966); m. Nadira Khannum Alvi, 1966. Student, Queen's Royal Coll., Trinidad, 1943-48; BA, University Coll., Oxford, Eng., 1953; D.Litt. (hon.), St. Andrews Coll., Scotland, 1979, Columbia U., 1981, Cambridge U., 1983, London U., 1988; DLitt (hon.), Oxford U., 1992. Broadcaster BBC's Caribbean Voices, 1954—56; regular fiction reviewer New Statesman, 1957—61. Author: The Mystic Masseur, 1957, The Suffrage of Elvira, 1958, Miguel Street, 1959, A House for Mr. Biswas, 1961, The Middle Passage: Impressions of Five Societies - British, French and Dutch in the West Indies and South America, 1962, Mr. Stone and the Knights Companion, 1963, An Area of Darkness, 1964, A Flag on the Island, 1967, The Loss of El Dorado: A History, 1969, In a Free State, 1971, The Overcrowded Barracoon and Other Articles, 1972, Guerrillas, 1975, India: A Wounded Civilization, 1977, A Bend in the River, 1979, A Congo Diary, 1980, The Return of Eva Peron, 1980, Among the Believers: An Islamic Journey, 1981, Finding the Centre, 1984, The Enigma of Arrival, 1987, A Turn in the South, 1989, India: A Million Mutinies Now, 1990, (with R. Jhabvala and S. Rushdie) Homeless By Choice, 1992, Bombay, 1994, A Way in the World, 1994, Beyond Belief, 1997, Between Father and Son: Family Letters, 2000, Reading & Writing: A Personal Account, 2000, Half Life, 2001, The Writer and the World, 2002. Recipient David Cohen British Literature prize, 1993, The Nobel Prize in Literature, 2001. Office: Aitken & Stone Ltd 29 Fernshaw Rd London SW10 0TG England

NAIR, BALA RADHAKRISHNAN, engineer; b. Belgaum, Mysore, India, Feb. 14, 1936; came to U.S., 1967; s. Cherukatt Balakrishnan and Malamal Parvathy Nair; m. Indira Rajagopal Menon, Dec. 9, 1963; children: Nandita, Sarita. BS in Mech. Engring., U. Madras, 1959; MS in Indsl. Engring., Kansas State U., 1969. Jr. engr. Larsen & Toubro, Ltd., Bombay, 1959-60; trainee AEC, Bombay, 1960-61, scientific officer, 1961-64; asst. engr. Voltas Ltd., Bombay, 1964-67; sr. engr. Crane Co., Chgo., 1969-72; design engr. Rockwell Internat., Pitts., 1972-74; sr. prin. engr. Westinghouse Electric Corp., Pitts., 1978—85, engring. mgr., 1986—. Patentee in field; contbr. articles to profl. jours. Recipient grand prize Excellence in Design, Design News Mag., Chgo., 1988, R & D Mag. award, 1993. Mem. ASME, Am. Nuclear Soc., Laser Inst. Am., Titanium Devel. Assn. Republican. Hindu. Avocations: reading, travel. Home: 5556 Forbes Ave Pittsburgh PA 15217 Office: Curtiss Wright Electromechanical Corp Cheswick PA 15024

NAIR, MIRA, film producer, film director; b. Bhubaneshwar, Orissa, India; Student, U. New Delhi, Harvard U. Prodr., dir., co-writer (films) Salaam Bombay, 1988 (Camera d'Or and Prix du Publique, Cannes Film Festival, Acad. Award nominee for Best Fgn. Lang. Film), So Far From India, 1982, Mississippi Masala, 1991, The Perez Family, 1993, Monsoon Wedding, 2001; dir. (TV) India Cabaret, 1985, Hysterical Blindness, 2002 (TV documentary) Children of a Desired Sex, 1987

NAIR, VELAYUDHAN, pharmacologist, medical educator, academic administrator; arrived in U.S., 1956, naturalized, 1963; m. Jo Ann Burke, Nov. 30, 1957; children: David, Larry, Sharon. PhD in Medicine, U. London, 1956, DSc, 1976, LHD (hon.) h.c., 2003. Rsch. assoc. U. Ill. Coll. Medicine, 1956-58; asst. prof. U. Chgo. Sch. Medicine, 1958-63; dir. lab. neuropharmacology and biochemistry Michael Reese Hosp. and Med. Ctr., Chgo., 1963-68, dir. therapeutic rsch., 1968-71; prof. pharmacology FUHS/Chgo. Med. Sch., 1971—, disting. prof., 2001, vice chmn. dept. pharmacology and therapeutics, 1971—76, dean Sch. Grad. and Postdoctoral Studies, 1976—2003, v.p. rsch., 1999—2003, v.p., dean emeritus, 2003—, disting. prof., 2001. Vis. assoc. prof. pharmacology FUHS/Chgo. Med. Sch., 1963—68, vis. prof., 1968—71, Harvard U., 1994, Johns Hopkins Sch. Medicine, 1995. Contbr. articles to profl. jours. Recipient Morris Parker award, U. Health Scis./Chgo. Med. Sch., 1972. Fellow: AAAS, Am. Coll. Clin. Pharmacology, N.Y. Acad. Scis.; mem.: AAUP, Internat. Soc. Devel. Neurosci., Am. Coll. Toxicology, Internat. Soc. Chronobiology, Soc. Neurosci., Soc. Exptl. Biology & Medicine, Pan Am. Med. Assn. (coun. on toxicology), Royal Inst. Chemistry (London), Brit. Chem. Soc., Am. Chem. Soc., Soc. Toxicology, Radiation Rsch. Soc., Am. Soc. Clin. Pharmacology & Therapeutics, Am. Soc. Pharmacology & Exptl. Therapeutics, Internat. Soc. Biochem. Pharmacology, Internat. Brain Rsch. Orgn., Cosmos Club (Washington), Alpha Omega Alpha, Sigma Xi. Office: Rosalind Franklin Univ Medicine and Sci 3333 Green Bay Rd North Chicago IL 60064-3037 *Success like happiness is relative and can only be gauged by one's own standards and ideals. There is probably no universal formula for either of them, but I have been guided by the following tenets: Dedication and committment to one's responsibilities and in the conduct of everyday life, honesty and sincerity in personal relations. One must have tolerance for those in less fortunate situations. As one grows older, one recognizes that no one makes it alone. As for me, I have received help from many; some of whom I can never repay except by passing on the gift which I was privileged to share. Above all, a faith that looks beyond the immediate helps to bear the inevitable ups and downs in life.*

NAIR, VELUPILLAI KRISHNAN, cardiologist; b. Kerala, India, Dec. 30, 1941; came to U.S., 1973; s. Veupillai and Bharathy Nair; m. Sathy C. Nair, Apr. 22, 1971; children: Parvathy, Pradeep. BSc, Kerala U., Trivandum, India, 1961, MB BS, 1965, MD, 1971. Diplomate Am. Bd. Internal Medicine, Am. Bd. Cardiology. Intern, resident, fellow in cardiology Bergen Pines County Hosp., Paramus, N.J.; asst. prof. N.Y. Med. Coll. Lincoln Hosp., Bronx, 1979-80; cardiologist, dir. cardiology svc. Somerset (Pa.) Hosp., 1980—, chief of med. dental staff, 1990-93. V.p. bd. dirs. Somerset Hosp., 1997, Somerset Health Svcs., 2000—; clin. asst. prof. Drexel U. Coll. Medicine, 1996—; bd. dirs. Somerset Hosp., 1993—99, 2000—. Former pres. Somerset County divsn. Am. Heart Assn.; bd. dirs. Somerset Hosp. Fellow ACP, Am. Coll. Cardiology; mem. AMA, Pa. Med. Soc., Somerset County Med. Soc. (former pres.), Soc. Hypertension, Soc. Echocardiography, Cardiac Club (advisor). Avocations: reading, tennis, travel. Office: 223 S Pleasant Ave Somerset PA 15501-2188 E-mail: vknair@pol.net.

NAIRN, RODERICK, immunologist, educator, biochemist; b. Dumbarton, Scotland, Mar. 25, 1951; came to U.S., 1976; s. James Bell and Muriel Elizabeth (Hyde) N.; m. Morag Gilhooly, Dec. 29, 1971; 1 child, Carolyn Mhairi. BS, U. Strathclyde, Glasgow, Scotland, 1973; PhD, U. London, 1976. Postdoctoral fellow Albert Einstein Sch. Medicine, N.Y.C., 1976-81; asst. prof. U. Mich. Med. Sch., Ann Arbor, 1981-87, assoc. prof., 1987-95, dir. student biomed. rsch. programs, 1989-92, dir. med. scientist tng. program, 1992-95; prof., chair dept. med. microbiology and immunology Sch. Medicine, Creighton U., Omaha, 1995—, interim dean, 1997-98, sr. assoc. dean academic affairs, 1998—. Contbr. chpts. to books, articles to profl. jours. Grantee NIH, Am. Cancer Soc. Mem. AAAS, Am. Che. Soc., Soc. for Microbiology, Am. Assn. Immunologists. Presbyterian. Office: Creighton U Sch Medicine Dept Med Microbiology & Immu Omaha NE 68178-0001 E-mail: rnairn@creighton.edu.

NAITO, AKEMI, composer; b. Tokyo, Jan. 24, 1956; d. Schunzo and Chizuko Naito. BA, Toho Gakuen Sch. Music, Tokyo, 1974—78, MFA, 1978—80. Lectr. Toho Gakuen Sch. Music, Tokyo, 1980—91. Lectr. Marymount Manhattan Coll., N.Y.C., 2002; mem. music panel N.Y. State Coun. on the Arts, N.Y.C., 2003. Composer: (albums) Strings and Time, 1997, (score) Memory of the Woods, 2000. Recipient Aaron Copland Award, 1999; fellow, N.Y. Found. for the Arts, 1998, 2002, Bellagio Ctr., 2003, Macdowell Colony, 2001, Yaddo, 2000, 2002, Millay Colony for Arts, 2001; grantee, Chamber Music Am., 2001, Asian Cultural Coun., 1991. Mem.: ASCAP. Home: 22 Cornelia St #4 New York NY 10014

NAJARIAN, JACK GEORGE, investment banker; b. Beirut, Jan. 11, 1956; came to U.S., 1970, naturalized, 1976; s. George O. Najarian and Marie Keuftejian; m. Victoria A. Dickson, Oct. 6, 1984; 1 child, Emily Jane Marie. BBA in Pub. Acctg., Bernard Baruch Coll., 1976; JD, Hofstra U., 1979. Internat. tax cons. Arthur Andersen & Co., N.Y.C., 1979-81; internat. banking cons. Deloitte & Touche, N.Y.C., 1981-82; v.p. internat. treasury and capital markets Societe Generale, N.Y.C., 1982-94; acting treas. treasury and capital markets Nat. Australia Bank, N.Y.C., 1994-96; chmn. Griffin Securities, Inc., N.Y.C., 1997-99; pres. Weatherly Securities Corp., N.Y.C., 1999—. Chmn. acctg., fin. and taxation dept. World Trade Inst.; mem. Securities Ins. Protection Corp.; bd. dirs. Uni-Marts, Inc., Weatherly Internat. Plc. Mem. Securities Industry Assn. (bd. dirs. 1997—), Nat. Assn. Securities Dealers.

NAJARIAN, JOHN SARKIS, surgeon, educator; b. Oakland, Calif., Dec. 22, 1927; s. Garabed L. and Siranoush T. (Demirjian) N.; m. Arlys Viola Mignette Anderson, Apr. 27, 1952; children: Jon, David, Paul, Peter. AB with honors, U. Calif., Berkeley, 1948; MD, U. Calif., San Francisco, 1952; LHD (hon.), Univ. Athens, 1980; DSc (hon.), Gustavus Adolphus Coll., 1981; LHD (hon.), Calif. Luth. Coll., 1983. Diplomate Am. Bd. Surgery. Surg. intern U. Calif., San Francisco, 1952-53, surg. resident, 1955-60, asst. prof. surgery, dir. surg. research labs., chief transplant service dept. surgery, 1963-66, prof., vice chmn., 1966-67; spl. research fellow in immunopathology U. Pitts. Med. Sch., 1960-61; NIH sr. fellow and assoc. in tissue transplantation immunology Scripps Clinic and Research Found., La Jolla, Calif., 1961-63; Markle scholar Acad. Medicine, 1964-69; prof., chmn. dept. surgery U. Minn. Hosp., Mpls., 1967-93; med. dir. Transplant Ctr., clin. chief surgery Univ. Hosp., 1967-94; chief hosp. staff U. Minn. Hosp., Mpls., 1970-71, Regents' prof., 1985-95, Jay Phillips Disting. Chair in Surgery, 1986-95, prof. emeritus, prof. surgery, 1995—. Spl. cons. USPHS, NIH Clin. Rsch. Tng. Com., Inst. Gen. Med. Scis., 1965-69; cons. U.S. Bur. Budget, 1966-68; mem. sci. adv. bd. Nat. Kidney Found., 1968; mem. surg. study sect. A div. rsch. grants NIH, 1970; chmn. renal transplant adv. group VA Hosps., 1971; mem. bd. sci. cons. Sloan-Kettering Inst. Cancer Rsch., 1971-78; mem. screening com. Dernham Postdoctoral Fellowships in Oncology, Calif. div. Am. Cancer Soc. Editor: (with Richard L. Simmons) Transplantation, 1972; co-editor: Manual of Vascular Access, Organ Donation, and Transplantation, 1984; mem. editorial bd. Jour. Surg. Rsch., 1968—, Minn. Medicine, 1968—, Jour. Surg. Oncology, 1968—, Am. Jour. Surgery, 1967—, assoc. editor, 1982—; mem. editorial bd. Year Book of Surgery, 1970-85, Transplantation, 1970—, Transplantation Procs, 1970—, Bd. Clin. Editors, 1981-84, Annals of Surgery, 1972—, World Jour. Surgery, 1976—, Hippocrates, 1986—, Jour. Transplant Coordination, 1990—; assoc. editor: Surgery, 1971; editor-in-chief: Clin. Transplantation, 1986—. Bd. dirs., v.p. Variety Club Heart Hosp., U. Minn.; trustee, v.p. Minn. Med. Found. Served with USAF, 1953-55. Hon. fellow Royal Coll. Surgeons of Eng., 1987; hon. prof. U. Madrid, 1990; named Alumnus of Yr., U. Calif. Med. Sch., San Francisco, 1977; recipient award Calif. Trudeau Soc., 1962, Ann. Brotherhood award NCCJ, 1978, Disting. Achievement award Modern Medicine, 1978, Internat. Gt. Am. award B'nai B'rith Found., 1982, Uncommon Citizen award, 1985, Sir James Carreras award Variety Clubs Internat., 1987, Silver medal IXth Centenary, U. Bologna, 1988, Humanitarian of Yr. award, U. Minn., 1992, Najarian Festschrift award Am. Jour. Surgery, 1993, Jubilee medal Swedish Soc. Medicine, 1994. Fellow ACS; mem. Internat. Pediat. Transplantation Assn. (pres. 1998-2000), Soc. Univ. Surgeons, Soc. Exptl. Biology and Medicine, AAAS, Am. Soc. Exptl. Pathology, Am. Surg. Assn. (pres. 1988-89), Am. Assn. Immunologists, AMA, Transplantation Soc. (v.p. western hemisphere 1984-86, pres. 1994-96), Am. Soc. Nephrology, Internat. Soc. Nephrology, Am. Assn. Lab. Animal Sci., Assn. Acad. Surgery (pres. 1969), Internat Soc. Surgery, Soc. Surg. Chairmen, Soc. Clin. Surgery, Central Surg. Assn., Minn., Hennepin County med. socs., Mpls., St. Paul, Minn., Howard C. Naffziger, Portland, Halsted surg. socs., Am. Heart Assn., Am. Soc. Transplant Surgeons (pres. 1977-78), Council on Kidney in Cardiovascular Disease, Hagfish Soc., Italian Research Soc., Minn. Acad. Medicine, Minn. Med. Assn., Minn. Med. Found., Surg. Biology Club, Sigma Xi, Alpha Omega Alpha, others. Office: U Minn Surgery Dept Mayo Mail Code 195 420 Delaware St SE Minneapolis MN 55455-0374 Business E-Mail: najar001@umn.edu.

NAJIMY, KATHY, actress; Actress theater The Kathy and Mo Show, 1985-89 (also writer)(Obie award, 1989), Afterbirth: Kathy and Mo's Greatest Hits, 2004; Broadway shows Dirty Blonde, 2001; films Topsy and Bunker, Other People's Money, 1991, The Hard Way, 1991, The Fisher King, 1991, Soapdish, 1991, This Is My Life, 1992, Sister Act, 1992, Hocus Pocus, 1993, Sister Act 2: Back in the Habit, 1993, It's Pat, 1994, Jeffrey, 1995, Cats Dont' Dance, 1997, Nevada, 1997, Woman Without Implants, 1997, Hope Floats, 1998, Zack and Reba, 1998, Bride of Chucky, 1998, Attention Shoppers, 2000, Leaving Peoria, 2000, The Wedding Planner, 2001, Rat Race, 2001; TV: King of the Hill (voice), 1997-, Veronica's Closet, 1997-2001; TV movies: If These Walls Could Talk II, 2000, The Scream Team, 2002. Office: Creative Arts Agy 9830 Wilshire Blvd Beverly Hills CA 90212-1804

NAJITA, KIYOSHI YOUNG, education educator; b. Northfield, Minn., June 5, 1966; s. Tetsuo and Elinor Najita; m. Gillian Gilman Culff, Aug. 14, 1991; children: Kieran, Sivan. BA, Sarah Lawrence, Bronxville, NY, 1988. After sch. program supr. U. Chgo. Lab. Schools, 1989—93; tchr. in residence U. Chgo., 1994—95; tchr./adv. Parker Sch., Kamuela, Hawaii, 1995—. Author: (short stories) The Sounds of the Surface Return in an Explosion, 1996. Site supr. Parker Sch., 1995—. Avocations: music, surfing, bicycling. Office: Parker Sch 65-1224 Lindsey Rd Kamuela HI 96743

NAJITA, TETSUO, history educator; b. Honokaa, Hawaii, Mar. 30, 1936; s. Niichi and Kikuno (Manpuku) N.; m. Elinor Moon, Aug. 2, 1958; children: Mie Kim, Kiyoshi Young. BA, Grinnell Coll., 1958; MA, Harvard U., 1960, PhD, 1965; LLD, Grinnell Coll., 1989. Asst. prof. Carleton Coll., Northfield, Minn., 1964-66, Washington U., St. Louis, 1966-68; assoc. prof. U. Wis., Madison, 1968-69; Robert S. Ingersoll disting. prof. history/Japanese studies U. Chgo., 1969—2002, prof. emeritus, 2002—, dir. Ctr. for East Asian Studies, 1974-80, assoc. dean, 1983-87, master collegiate div. social scis., 1983-87. John A. Burns disting. visiting chair U. Hawaii, Manoa, 1994; chair dept. history U. Chgo., 1994-97; Ena H. Thompson lectr. Pomona Coll., 1996; Catherine Gould Chism vis. prof. U. Puget Sound, Tacoma; Maruyame Masao lectr. U. Calif., Berkeley, 2000. Author: Hara Kei in the Politics of Compromise, 1969 (J.K. Fairbank prize Am. Hist. Assn.), Intellectual Foundations of Modern Japanese Politics, 1974, Visions of Virtue in Tokugawa Japan, 1987, Tokugawa Political Writings, 1998. Recipient Yamagata Banto prize Prefecture of Osaka, 1989; grantee NEH 1973-74, 1980-81; Fulbright fellow 1961-63, 68, Guggenheim fellow 1980-81. Fellow Am. Acad. Arts and Scis.; mem. Am. Hist. Assn., Assn. for Asian Studies (v.p., pres. 1991-93), Phi Beta Kappa. Office: U Chgo Dept History 1126 E 59th St Chicago IL 60637-1580

NAKA, YOSHIFUMI, surgeon, researcher; b. Aug. 9, 1959; arrived in U.S., 1993; s. Yasushi and Eiko Naka; m. Kayoko Tomoda Naka, Dec. 24, 1988; 1 child, Ryoko. Completion of premed. course, Osaka (Japan) U., 1980; MD, Osaka U., 1984, PhD, 1988. Cert. Japanese Bd. Surgery, lic. physician N.Y., Japan. Resident Osaka U. Hosp., 1984—86; rsch. and clin. fellow Osaka U. Med. Sch., 1986—89; resident Osaka Police Hosp., 1989—93; postdoctoral rsch. fellow dept. physiology Columbia U., N.Y.C., 1993—96, instr. clin. dept. surgery, 1996—99, asst. prof. surgery, 1999—. Dir. cardiac transplantation and mech. circulatory support program N.Y.-Presbyn. Hosp., N.Y.C., 2003—. Guest editor: Annals of Thoracic Surgery, 2001; author: Atherosclerosis and Coronary/Artery Disease, 1996; contbr. to profl. jours. including Jour. of Clin. Investment, Nat. Sci., Proc. Nat. Acad. Sci., 2003; author: Cardiac Surgery in the Adult, 2003. Named Herbert Irving asst. prof. surg. treatment of atrial fibrillation, Columbia U. Physicians and Surgeons, 2001—; recipient grant, Found. for Advanced of Cardiac Therapies, 2002—; grantee KO-8 grant, Vein Graft Preservation Thrombosis, and Neointimal Disease/NIH, 2001—05. Mem.: ASAIO, Soc. Univ. Surgeons, Internat. Soc. for Heart and Lung Transplantation, N.Y. Soc. Thoracic Surgeons, Am. Heart Assn. Avocations: tennis, downhill skiing, reading, cooking. Office: Milstein Hosp Bldg 7-435 177 Ft Washington Ave New York NY 10032

NAKAGAWA, ALLEN DONALD, radiologic technologist; b. N.Y.C., Mar. 14, 1955; s. Walter Tsunehiko and Alyce Tsuneko (Kinoshita) N. BS in Environ. Studies, St. John's U., Jamaica, N.Y., 1977; MS in Marine Biology, C.W. Post Coll., 1980. Cert. radiologic technologist, in fluoroscopy, Calif.; cert. Am. Registry Radiol. Technologists. Research asst. environ. studies St. John's U., 1976-78; lab. asst. Bur. Water Surveillance, Nassau Co. of Health Dept., Wantaugh, N.Y., 1978; clin. endocrinology asst. U. Calif. VA Hosp., San Francisco, 1981-83; student technologist St. Mary's Hosp., San Francisco, 1985-86; radiologic technologist Mt. Zion Hosp., San Francisco, 1986-88; sr. radiologic technologist U. Calif., San Francisco, 1989—, urosurg. radiologic technologist, 1988-89, sr. radiologic technologist, 1989—, sr. surg. radiologic technologist, 2003—. Attendee U. Calif. San Francisco Trauma and Emergency Radiology Conf., 1995, U. Calif. San Francisco Musculoskeletal MRI Conf., 1996, PACS for Hour Hosp., 1998, Breast Imaging for Technologists and Health Care Providers, U. Calif. Stanford Health Care, 1999, Clinical MRI 2000, U. Calif., San Francisco, 2000, Resident Rev. Diagnostic Imaging, U. Calif., San Francisco, 2001, Digital X-ray & PACs: An Ednl. Forum, 2002. Mem. ACLU, Am. Soc. Radiologic Technologists, Calif. Soc. Radiologic Technologists, Calif. Acad. Scis., Japanese-Am. Nat. Mus., Sigma Xi. Democrat. Methodist. Avocations: photography, music, environmentalist, volunteering, studying advanced technology. E-mail: datarover@onebox.com. *If you know, believe and have faith in yourself first, only then can you endeavor to assist someone else. Otherwise, you have wasted your efforts and may have even caused a loss of life.*

NAKAGAWA, KOJI, endocrinologist, educator; b. Sapporo, Hokkaido, Japan, June 5, 1932; s. Satosu and Michi (Yokoyama) N.; m. Keiko Hirato, Oct. 20, 1962; children: Shin, Tamao Yamaguchi. MD, Hokkaido U., 1957, PhD, 1962. Lic. endocrinologist, Japan. Staff scientist Worcester Found. for Exptl. Biology, Shrewsbury, Mass., 1964-65; rsch. staff Syntex Rsch. Ctr., Palo Alto, Calif., 1965; rsch. fellow U. Utah Med. Ctr., Salt Lake City, 1965-66; rsch. assoc. 2d dept. medicine Hokkaido U. Sch. Medicine, Sapporo, 1967-83, asst. prof., 1983-89; prof. Health Adminstrn. Ctr., Hokkaido U. Edn., Sapporo, 1989-96, dir. Health Adminstrn. Ctr., 1990-96; prof. dept. nutrition Tenshi Coll., Sapporo, 2000—. Contbr. articles to profl. jours. Fellow Japan Endocrine Soc.; mem. Endocrine Soc., Japanese Soc. Internal Medicine, Japan Diabetes Soc. Home: 2-8 4-chome Yamanote 1-jo Nishi-ku Sapporo 063-0001 Japan Office: Tenshi Coll North 13 East 3 Higashi-Ku Sapporo 065-0013 Japan

NAKAGAWARA, VAN B. optometrist, researcher; b. Honolulu, Hawaii, Mar. 8, 1947; s. Barney Hiromi and Sue Miyako Nakagawara; m. Janice Elizabeth Varner, July 29, 1979; children: Anna Elizabeth Miyako, Esther Malia Hiromi. BS in Biology, Gonzaga U., 1969; OD in Optometry, Pacific U., 1973. Lic. Bd. Examiners in Optometry, Hawaii and S.C. Optometry officer U.S. Army, Columbia, SC, 1973—76; clin. optometrist USAF, Honolulu, 1976—81; indsl. optometrist USN, Honolulu, 1981—86; rsch. optometrist FAA/Civil Aerospace Med. Inst., Oklahoma City, 1986—. Nat. adv. bd. Nat. Eye Rsch. Found., Chgo., 1992—94; mem. study group Internat. Civil Aviation Orgn., Montreal, Canada, 1999—; med. ops. cons. NASA, Houston, 1998—99. Contbr. scientific papers to profl. jours. Capt. U.S. Army, 1972—76. Named Boss of Yr., Am. Bus. Women of Hawaii, 1982. Fellow: Am. Acad. Optometry; mem.: Armed Forces Optometric Soc., Aerospace Med. Assn., Am. Optometric Assn. (mem. aviation com. 1999—), Mike Monroney Aero. Ctr. (Asian Pacific Am. com. 1996—99), Okla. Optometric Assn. (interprofl. rels. com. 1990—95), Am. Nat. Stds. Inst. Avocations: running, stamp collecting/philately, coin collecting/numismatics, golf. Home: 11313 Lakeridge Run Oklahoma City OK 73170 Office: FAA/Civil Aerospace Med Inst PO Box 25082 Oklahoma City OK 73125 Office Phone: 405-954-6235. E-mail: van.nakagawara@faa.gov.

NAKAJIMA, HIROSHI, education educator; b. Hiroshima, Japan, June 12, 1923; s. Iwao and Tamae (Takenaka) N.; m. Sei Sakao, May 2, 1966; children: Akihiko, Takehiko. Student, Nishogakusha Coll., 1942-44; BA, Waseda U., 1950; MA, 1954, EdD (hon.), 1989. Asst. prof. Japan women's Coll. Econs., 1954-59; lectr. Waseda U., 1954-63; asst. prof., 1963-68; prof. comparative and internat. edn., 1968-94; prof. emeritus, 1994—. Vis. prof. U. Helsinki, 1962-63; advisor Japanese Inst. Social Studies on Sweden, 1989—; vice-chmn. youth com. Higashikurumeshi, 1978-83; mem. bd. edn. Higashikurumeshi, 1983-91. Served with Japanese Army, 1943-46. Recipient Acad. Hon. Medal U. Helsinki, 1963; decorated Nat. 3rd Order, 2000. Mem.: Comparative and Internat. Edn. Soc. (mem. 1963), Finnish Acad. Sci. and Letters (fgn. 1984). Home: 1-4-37 Minamisawa Higashikurume-shi Tokyo 203-0023 Japan Office Phone: 81-3-5606-4311.

NAKAJIMA, YASUKO, medical educator; b. Osaka, Japan, Jan. 8, 1932; came to U.S., 1962, 69; m. Shigehiro Nakajima; children: Hikeko H., Gene A. MD, U. Tokyo, 1955, PhD, 1962. Intern U. Tokyo Sch. Medicine, 1955-56, resident, 1956-57, instr., 1962-67; assoc. prof. Purdue U., West Lafayette, Ind., 1969-76, prof., 1976-88; prof. anatomy and cell biology U. Ill. Coll. Medicine, Chgo., 1988—. Vis. rsch. fellow Coll. Physicians and Surgeons, Columbia U., N.Y.C., 1962-64; asst. rsch. anatomist UCLA Sch. Medicine, 1964-65; vis. rsch. fellow Cambridge U., 1967-69; mem. study sect. NIH, 1996-98. Contbr. articles to sci. jours. Fulbright travel grantee, 1962-65; Univ. scholar U. Ill., 1997—. Mem. AAAS, Am. Physiol. Soc., Soc. Neurosci., Am. Soc. Cell Biology, Am. Assn. Anatomists, Biophys. Soc., Marine Biol. Lab. Corp. Office: U Ill Coll Medicine Dept Anatomy m/c 512 808 S Wood St Chicago IL 60612-7300

NAKAMURA, HIDEO, law educator; b. Tokyo, Mar. 2, 1926; s. Muneo and Fumiko (Mitani) N.; m. Mitsuko Terai, Feb. 25, 1958; children: Eri, Akiyoshi. LLB, Waseda U., Tokyo, 1947, LLD, 1980; Dr. honoris causa, Athens U., 1995. Assoc. prof. Faculty of Law Waseda U., tokyo, 1955-60, prof., 1960, dean Grad. Sch. Law, 1980-82, dir. Inst. Comparative Law, 1984-88, pres. Law Assn., 1990-94; dir. Inst. Comparative Civil Law, tokyo, 1975—; ret. hon prof. Waseda U., 1996. Author: (in German) The Japanese Criminal Procedure Code, 1970, Japan and German Civil Procedure, 1995, (in Japanese) Collected Works on Civil Procedure, Vols., 1-5, 1975-86; Civil Procedure, 1987; co-author: (in German) The Japanese Civil Procedure Code, 1978; editor: Family Law Litigation, 1984. Recepient Honor of Freedom award City of Athens, 1998. Mem. Japanese Assn. of Law of Civil Procedure (exec. com. 1960-80, hon.), Japanese Assn. of Law of Pub. Notary (coun. 1978—), Japan Fedn. of Bar Assn. (commr. disciplinary com. 1984-87), Acad. Assn. of Law of Internat. Procedure. Avocation: photography. Home: 2-6-6 Kamitakata Nakano-ku Tokyo 164-0002 Japan Office: Inst Comparative Civil Law 43 Waseda-Minamicho Shinjuku-ku Tokyo 162-0043 Japan

NAKAMURA, HIROSHI, urology educator; b. Tokyo, Mar. 22, 1933; s. Yataroh and Hideko (Tanaka) N.; m. Miyoko Kodachi, Aug. 13, 1966. MD, Keio U., Tokyo, 1960; PhD, Grad. Sch. Medicine, Keio U., 1966. Med. diplomate. Asst. resident Mt. Sinai Hosp., N.Y.C., 1962—63; rsch. fellow Cornell U. Med. Coll., N.Y.C., 1966—68; asst. Sch. Medicine Keio U., Tokyo, 1968—70; chmn. urology dept. Tokyo Elec. Power Hosp., Tokyo, 1970—73; vis. asst. prof. surgery Cornell U. Med. Coll., N.Y.C., 1973; chmn. urology Kitasato Inst. Hosp., Tokyo, 1973—77; chmn. dept., prof. urology Nat. Def. Med. Coll., Tokorozawa, Japan, 1977—98, dir. dept. acad. affairs, 1994—96, prof. emeritus, 1999—; emeritus dir. Tokorozawa Ishikawa Clinic, 1998—. Author: Bedside Urology, 1983, Modern Clinical Point-Urology, 1993; editor: Up-to-Date Urology, 1983, Caveats & Pitfalls in Clinical Urology, 1999, Medical Ethics Q&A, 2002. Recipient Tamura award, Keio U. Sch. Medicine, 1967, All-around Med. award, Igaku-Shoin, Ltd., Tokyo, 1967, The Order of the Sacred Treasure, Emperor of Japan, 2003. Buddhist. Avocations: jazz, audiophile, travel, fishing, baseball. Home: 11-1-1204 Higashicho Tokorozawa Saitama 359-1116 Japan Office: Tokorozawa Ishikawa Clin Iseki Bldg 4F 9-22 Hiyoshicho Tokorozawa 359-1123 Japan Office Phone: 04-2925-7355.

NAKAMURA, JAMES I. economics educator; b. Toppenish, Wash., Mar. 16, 1919; s. Ichihei and Suya (Hirayama) N.; m. Tetsuko Fujii; children— Richard Ken, Leonard Isamu AA, Santa Maria Jr. Coll., 1939; BS, Columbia U., 1952, PhD, 1964. Asst. prof. Columbia U., N.Y.C., 1964-68, assoc. prof., 1968-80, prof. econs., 1980-89, prof. emeritus, 1989—; vis. research scholar Kobe U., Japan, 1971-72; co-founder, co-dir., sec.-treas. Japan Econ. Seminar (supported by Columbia U., Harvard U., George Washington U.), 1965-90. Author: Agricultural Production and Economic Development of Japan, 1966, Nihon no Keizai Hatten to Nogyo, 1968; mem. editorial bd. Japan Econ. Studies, 1972-90; contbr. numerous articles to profl. jours. Editor newspaper War Relocation Ctr., Gila River, Ariz., 1943-44; legal researcher Shanks Village Com. to Fight Closure, Orangeburg, N.Y., 1952. Served to lt. U.S. Army, 1945-48, PTO. Ford Found. fellow 1952-55, 62-63; Fulbright-Hays fellow, 1967. Mem. Econ. History Assn., Am. Econ. Assn., Assn. for Asian Studies, Japan Econ. Research Ctr., Phi Beta Kappa. Buddhist. Home: 35 Claremont Ave New York NY 10027-6802 E-mail: jinl@columbia.edu.

NAKAMURA, KIMIKO, language educator; b. Fukui-Ken, Japan, Feb. 11, 1945; arrived in USA, 1966; d. Toshiji and Emiko Matsumura; m. Takamitsu Nakamura, Jan. 22, 1966; children: Takashi, Yoko. BM, Osaka Coll. Music, Japan, 1966; MusB, DePaul U., 1993; MusM, Valparaiso U., 1996. Japanese tchr. Inland/EastPack Co., Ea. Chgo., 1987—. Piano instr. O'Day Music Sch., Highland, Ind., 1999—. Mem.: Nat. Guild Piano Tchrs., Japan-Am. Soc. (Japanese lang. tchr. 1996—). Office: Japan America Soc Chgo 20 N Clark St Ste 750 Chicago IL 60602

NAKAMURA, RICHARD, mental health research professional; BA Psychology, Earlham Coll.; MA Psychology, NYU; PhD Psychology, SUNY, Stony Brook. Postdoctoral fellow intramural lab. neuropsychology Nat. Inst. Mental Health, 1976, chief behavioral and integrative neurosci., 1990, dir. sci. policy and program planning, 1990, acting dir., 2001—02. Mem. info. tech. bd. dirs. NIH. Recipient Disting. Svc. award, Dept. Health and Human Svcs. Sec., 2000, 2004, Outstanding Achievement award, NIH Asian/Pacific Am. Orgn.'s, 2001, Pres. Meritorious Exec. award, 2002. Office: Rm 235 6001 Executive Blvd Bethesda MD 20892-9669

NAKAMURA, ROBERT MOTOHARU, pathologist; b. Montebello, Calif., June 10, 1927; s. Mosaburo and Haru (Suematsu) N.; m. Shigeyo Jane Hayashi, July 29, 1957; children: Mary, Nancy. AB, Whittier Coll., 1949; MD, Temple U., 1954. Cert. of spl. qualification in pathologic anatomy, clin pathology, immunopathology, Am. Bd. Pathology. Prof. pathology U. Calif., Irvine, 1971-74, adj. prof. pathology, 1974-75; chmn. dept. pathology Scripps Clinic and Rsch. Found., La Jolla, Calif., 1974-92; sr. cons., 1992—; pres. Scripps Clinic Med. Group, La Jolla, 1981-91; prof. dept. immunology and exptl. and molecular medicine Scripps Rsch. Inst., 1997—; chmn. pathology Scripps Clinic, 1998-99, chmn. emeritus pathology, 1999—. Adj. prof. pathology U. Calif., San Diego, 1975-93. Author, editor profl. publs.; co-editor Jr. Clin. Lab. Analysis, 1989—. Fellow: Coll. Am. Pathologists, Am. Soc. Clin. Pathologists, Assn. Clin. Scientists, Am. Coll. Nutrition; mem. Internat. Acad. Pathology. Avocation: reading. Home: 8841 Nottingham Pl La Jolla CA 92037-2131 Office Phone: 858-554-8166.

NAKAMURA, SHUJI, engineering educator; B in Electronic Engring., U. Tokushima, Japan, 1977; M in Electronic Engring., U. Tokushima, 1979, D in Engring., 1994. R&D staff Nichia Chem. Industry, Ltd., 1979—84, group head R&D 1st sect., 1985—88, group head R&D 2nd sect., 1989—93, sr. rschr. dept. R&D, 1993—99; prof. materials dept. U. Calif., Santa Barbara, 1999—. Vis. rsch. assoc. electronic engring. U. Fla., 1988—89. Mem. editl. bd.: Applied Physics Soc., 1998—2000. Recipient Nikkei BP Engring. award, 1994, 1996, Best Paper award, Japanese Applied Physics Soc., 1994, 1997, Sakurai award, 1995, Nishina Meml. award, 1996, IEEE Lasers and Electro-0ptics Soc. Engring. Achievement award, 1996, Spl. Recognition award, Soc. for Info. Display, 1996, Okochi Meml. award, 1997, medal award, Materials Rsch. Soc., 1997, Innovation in Real Materials award, 1998, C&C award, Jack A. Morton award, IEEE, 1998, Brit. Rank prize, 1998, Julius-Springer prize for applied physics, 1999, Takayanagi award, 2000, Carl Zeiss Rsch. award, 2000, Honda award, 2000, Crystal Growth and Crystal Tech. award, 2000, Asahi award, 2001, OSA Nick Holonyak award, 2001, LEOS Disting. Lectr. award, 2001, medal in engring., Franklin Inst., 2002. Achievements include development of first group-III nitride-based blue/green LEDs; design of first group-III nitride-based violet laser diodes. Office: Materials Dept Univ Calif Santa Barbara CA 93106-5050

NAKANISHI, ALAN, ophthalmologist; b. Sacramento, Mar. 21, 1940; BA, Pacific Union Coll., 1962; MD, Loma Linda U.; MS in Health Adminstrn., Va. Commonwealth U., 1991. Intern, L.A. Coutny Med. Ctr. L.A. County Med. Ctr. U. So. Calif., 1965-66; resident, L.A. County Med. Ctr. Delta Eye Med. Group, 1966-69, ophthalmologist; mem. Lodi City Council, 1998—2001; mayor Lodi, Calif., 2001; mem. Calif. Ho. of Reps., 2002—. Maj. M.C., U.S. Army, 1969-71. Office: Delta Eye Med Group 1617 Saint Marks Plz Stockton CA 95207-6423 also: State Capital PO Box 942849 Sacramento CA 94249

NAKANISHI, DON TOSHIAKI, Asian American studies educator, writer; b. L.A., Aug. 14, 1949; m. Marsha Hirano; 1 child, Thomas. BA in Polit Sci. cum laude, Yale U., 1971; PhD in Polit. Sci., Harvard U., 1978. Instr. dept. urban studies Yale U., 1971; lectr. Coun. on Ednl. Devel. UCLA, 1973, instr. Asian Am. Studies Ctr., 1974, acting asst. prof. dept. polit. sci., 1975-78; vis. scholar Sophia U., Inst. Internat. Relations, Tokyo, 1978-89; adj. asst. prof. dept. polit. sci. UCLA, 1979-82, asst. rschr. Asian Am. Studies Ctr., 1979-82, from asst. prof. to full prof. Grad. Sch. Edn., 1982—, assoc. dir. Asian Am. Studies Ctr., 1985-87, chair interdepartmental program Asian Am. studies, 1989-90, dir. Asian Am. Studies Ctr., 1990—. Co-founder and publr. Amerasia Jour., 1970-75, edtl. bd., 1975—; researcher Social Sci. Rsch. Coun. of N.Y. and the Japan Soc. for the Promotion of Sci. of Tokyo Joint-Project on Am.-Japanese Mut. Images, 1971-73; mem. Asian Am. task force for social studies guideline evaluation, Calif. State Dept. Edn., 1973; guest spkr. Ctr. for the Study of Ednl. Policy, Grad. Sch. Edn., Harvard U., 1974, Metropathways, Ethni-City Sch. Desegregation Program, Boston, 1974; researcher, co-project chair Hispanic Urban Ctr., Project Sch. Desegregation, L.A., 1974; numerous coms. UCLA; numerous conf. chmns.; cons., rschr., speaker, presenter in field. Co-editor: (with Marsha J. Hirano-Nakanishi) The Education of Asian and Pacific Americans: Historical Perspectives and Prescriptions for the Future, 1983, (with Halford H. Fairchild, Luis Ortiz-Franco, Lenore A. Stiffarm) Discrimination and Prejudice: An Annotated Bibliography, 1991, (with Tina Yamano Nishida) The Asian Pacific American Educational Experience: A Sourcebook for Teachers and Students, 1995, (with James Lai) National Asian Pacific American Political Almanac, 1996, 98, 2000; contbr. numerous articles to profl. jours., monographs, book reviews and reports. Chair Yale U. Alumni Schs. Com. of So. Calif., 1978—; bd. dirs. Altamed and La Clinica Familiar Del Barrio of East L.A., 1982—; commr. Bd. Transp. Commrs., City of L.A., 1984-90; v.p. Friends of the Little Tokyo Pub. Libr., 1986-88; co-chair nat. scholars adv. com. Japanese Am. Nat. Mus., 1987—; mem., bd. govs. Assn. of Yale Alumni, 1988-91; mem. exec. coun. Mayor's LA's Best Aftersch. Program, City of Los Angeles, 1988-90. Rsch. fellow Japan Soc. for the Promotion of Sci., 1978; recipient Nat. Scholars awrd for Outstanding Rsch. Article on Asian Pacific Am. Edn., Nat. Assn. for Asian and Pacific Am. Edn., 1985, Civil Rights Impace award Asian Am. Legal Ctr. of So. Calif., 1989; grantee Chancellors' Challenge in the Arts and Humanities, 1991, Calif. Policy Seminar, 1992, U. Calif. Pacific Rim Studies, 1992; recepient numerous other research and conference grants. Mem. Nat. Assn. for Interdisciplinary Ethnic Studies (bd. dirs. 1976-79), Assn. Asian Am. Studies (nat. pres. 1983-85), Nat. Assn. for Asian and Pacific Am. Edn. (exec. bd. dirs., v.p. 1983—). Home: 4501 N Berkshire Ave Los Angeles CA 90032 Office: UCLA Asian Am Studies Ctr 3230 Campbell Ave Los Angeles CA 90024-1546 E-mail: dtn@ucla.edu.

NAKANISHI, KOJI, chemistry educator, research institute administrator; b. Hong Kong, May 11, 1925; came to U.S., 1969; s. Yuzo and Yoshiko (Sakata) N.; m. Yasuko Abe, Oct. 25, 1947; children: Keiko, Jun. BSc, Nagoya U., Japan, 1947; PhD, Nagoya U., 1954; DSc (hon.), Williams Coll., 1987, Georgetown U., 1992. Asst. prof. Nagoya U., 1955-58; prof. Tokyo Kyoiku U., 1958-63, Tohoku U., Sendai, Japan, 1963-69; prof. chemistry Columbia U., N.Y.C., 1969-80, Centennial prof. chemistry, 1980—; dir. research Internat. Ctr. Insect Physiology and Ecology, Nairobi, Kenya, 1969-77; dir. Suntory Inst. for Bioorganic Research, Osaka, Japan, 1979-91. Hon. prof. Shanghai Inst. Materia Medica, 1995. Author: Infrared Spectroscopy-Practical, 1962, rev. edit., 1977, Circular Dichroic Spectroscopy-Exciton Coupling in Organic Stereochemistry, 1983, A Wandering Natural Products Chemist, 1991; co-editor, contbr. chpt. Comprehensive Natural Products Chemistry, vol. 1-9, 1999; contbr. chpts. to books. Recipient Asahi cultural prize, 1968, Sci. Workers Union medal, Bulgaria, 1978, E.E. Smissman medal U. Kan., 1979, H.C. Urey award Columbia U., 1980, Alcon ophthalmology award, 1986, Paul Karrer gold medal U. Zurich, 1986, E. Havinga medal Havinga Found., Leiden, 1989, Imperial prize Japan Acad., 1990, Japan Acad. prize, 1990, R.T. Major medal U. Conn., 1991, L.E. Harris award U. Nebr., 1991, award in chem. scis. NAS, 1994, J. Heyrovsky hon. gold medal Czech Acad. Scis., 1995, Robert A. Welch award in chemistry, 1996, Person of Cultural Merit award Japanese Govt., 1999, T. Wang Bioorganic lectureship award, 2001, King Faisal Internat. prize for sci. King Faisal Found., Riyadh, 2003. Fellow N.Y. Acad. Scis., Nat. Acad. Sci. Italy (fgn.); mem. Chem. Soc. Japan (hon., award in pure chemistry 1954, award 1979, Nakanishi prize established 1996), Am. Chem. Soc. (E. Guenther award 1978, Remsen award Md. sect. 1981, A.C. Cope award 1990, Nichols medal N.Y. sect. 1992, Mosher award Santa Clara Valley sect. 1995, internat. award in agrochems. 1995), Biochem. Soc. Japan, Chem. Soc. Japan, Brit. Chem. Soc. (Centenary medal 1979), Swedish Acad. Pharm. Scis. (Scheele award 1992), Am. Acad. Arts and Scis., Am. Soc. Pharmacognosy (rsch. achievement award 1985), Internat. Chirality Symposium (Chirality gold medal 1995), Pharm. Sc. Japan (hon.), Am. Mus. Soc. Natural History (1st environ. award 2000, King Faisal Internat. prize in sci. 2003). Home: 560 Riverside Dr New York NY 10027-3202 Office: Columbia U Dept Chemistry Mail Code 3114 3000 Broadway New York NY 10027-6941

NAKANISHI, YUKO JULIE, engineering educator, consultant; b. Westland, Mich. d. Ukyo Stanley and Tatsuko Ann Nakanishi; life ptnr. Larry Lifschultz. BA in English Lit., Harvard U., 1987; MBA, Columbia U., 1993; MSCE, CCNY, 1997; PhD in Civil Engring., Polytech U., 2004. Chair NY Area Data Coun., NYC, 1997-99; sr. tchg. assoc., cons. Rensselaer Poly. Inst., Troy, NY, 1999-2000; program mgr. Urban ITS Ctr. Poly. U., Bklyn., 2000—; chair subcommittee on tng., ed., and tech. transfer, 2003—. Chair Freight and Intermodal Transp. Data Com., NY, 1997-2000; asst. dir. Univ. Transp. Rsch. Ctr., NYC, 1996-99; info. svc. com. Transp. Rsch. Bd., 1998—, critical transp. infrastructure protection com., chair edn., tng. and tech. transfer subcom. Contbr. articles to profl. jours. Fellow Eisenhower fellow, 1997—2000, Eno fellow, 2001. Mem. IEEE, ASCE, Inst. Transp. Engr., Intelligent Transp. Soc. NY (bd. dir.), NY Data Coun. Bd. of Dir. Office: Poly U 6 Metrotech Ctr Brooklyn NY 11201 Home: 93-40 Queens Blvd 6A Rego Park NY 11374 Office Phone: 718-260-3349. Business E-Mail: ynakanis@poly.edu. E-mail: orynakan@aol.com.

NAKARAI, CHARLES FREDERICK TOYOZO, music educator, adjudicator; b. Indpls., Apr. 25, 1936; s. Toyozo Wada and Frances Aileen N. BA cum laude, Butler U., 1958, Mus.M., 1967; postgrad., U. N.C., 1967-70. Organist, dir. choirs Northwood Christian Ch., Indpls., 1954-57; min. music Allisonville Christian Ch., Indpls., 1957-58; asst. prof. music Milligan Coll., Tenn., 1970-72; pvt. instr. organ, piano Durham, NC, 1972—. Mem. faculty piano camp U. N.C.-Greensboro, 1996, 97, 2000, 01; adjudicator N.C. Music Tchrs. Assn., N.C. Fedn. Music Clubs, Raleigh Music Tchrs. Assn., Charlotte Piano Tchrs. Forum, Chapel Hill Music Tchrs. Assn. Composer: Three Movements for Chorus, 1971, Bluesy, 1979. Served with USAF, 1958-64. Mem. Am. Musicol. Soc., Coll. Music Soc., Am. Guild Organists, Music Tchrs. Nat. Assn., Music Libr. Assn., N.C. Music Tchrs. Assn., Organ Hist. Soc., Durham Music Tchrs. Assn., Triangle Guitar Soc. Address: 2312 Anthony Drive Durham NC 27705

NAKASHIMA, TADAYOSHI, retired biochemist, researcher; b. Yokkaichi, Mie-ken, Japan, Dec. 1, 1922; s. Chunosuke and Hina Nakashima; m. Fukuko Kondo, Nov. 15, 1947; 1 child, Rieko. BP, Nagoya Pharm. Coll., Aichi-ken, 1941—43; BS, Taihoku Imperial U., Taihoku, 1943—46; PhD, Kyushu U., Fukuoka, 1960—61. Rsch. Scientist U. of Miami, 1964. Acting chief, rsch. lab. Sanyo Penicillin Co., 1946—50; assoc. prof. Kwassui Coll., 1951—62; post doctoral U. of Hawaii, 1962—64; vis. rsch. scientist U. of Bonn, Germany, 1966—69; rsch. prof. Inst. for Molecular and Cellular Evolution, U. of Miami, 1964—89. Author: (molecular evolution) Journals, (protoribosomes) In Molecular Evolution and Protobiology, 1984, (genetic code) Proc. Nat. Acad. Sci., 1972, (amino acid sequence) J. Biol. Chem.1966. Mem.: Am. Chem. Soc. Home: 7400 SW 159th Ter Palmetto Bay FL 33157-2452

NAKATA, GARY KENJI, lawyer; b. Okinawa, Japan, Nov. 13, 1964; arrived in U.S., 1971; s. Hiroshi Nakata and Miwako Kin; m. Jo Ann Akiko Tengan, Aug. 22, 1998. BBA in Fin., U. Hawaii, 1988; JD with distinction, U. of the Pacific, 1995. Bar: Hawaii 1996, Calif. 1996, U.S. Dist. Ct. Hawaii, 1996; cert. mgmt. acct.; cert. fin. mgr.; cert. grad. Am. Banker's Assn. Nat. Sch. Regulatory Compliance. Credit analyst Bank of Hawaii, Honolulu, 1988-90, sr. credit analyst, 1990-92; law clk. Hawaii Atty. Gen. Tax Divsn., Honolulu, 1994; sr. assoc. Kobayashi, Sugita & Goda, Honolulu, 1995—2003; dep. corp. counsel City and County of Honolulu, 2003—04; CFO Honolulu City & County Employees Fed. Credit Union, 2004—. Mem. new product devel. adv. bd. Warren Gorham & Lamont, N.Y.C., 1997-98. Editor-in-chief: The Transnational Lawyer, 1994, 95. Pres., enlisted adv. coun. Hawaii Air Nat. Guard, Honolulu, 1986-92; mem. ex officio alumni coun., mem. membership com., mem. membership benefits subcom. U. Hawaii Alumni Assn., Honolulu, 1990-91; mem. fin. com. and bylaws subcom. Soc. Coll. Bus. Alumni and Friends, U. Hawaii Coll. Bus. Adminstrn. Alumni Affairs, Honolulu, 1990-91, founding mem., treas., 1990-91, mem. steering com. to form alumni orgn., 1997-98, pres., 1998-2000; at-large rep., treas., legis. liaison Neighborhood Bd., Kaneohe, Hawaii, 1991-92. Mem.: ABA (bus. law sect., comml. fin. svcs. com., consumer fin. svcs. com.), Hawaii Fin. Regulatory Compliance Assn. (bd. dirs. 1997—2003, chairperson fair credit reporting act regulatory update com. 1998—2003), Inst. Cert. Mgmt. Accts. (bd. dirs. 1998—2000, dir. mem. acquisition 1998—2000), Calif. State Bar Assn., Hawaii State Bar Assn. (mem. real property and fin. svcs. sect. 1997—), Hawaii Jaycees (legal counsel 2000—01, exec. v.p. 2002, pres. 2003), Hawaii Bus. Jaycees (charter pres. 1991—92, chmn. bd. 1992—93, charter mem.). Office: Dept Corp Counsel City and County of Honolulu 530 S King St Rm 110 Honolulu HI 96813

NAKAYAMA, PAULA AIKO, state supreme court justice; b. Honolulu, Oct. 19, 1953; m. Charles W. Totto; children: Elizabeth Murakami, Alexander Totto. BS, U. Calif., Davis, 1975; JD, U. Calif., 1979. Bar: Hawaii 1979. Dep. pros. atty. City and County of Honolulu, 1979-82; ptnr. Shim, Tam & Kirimitsu, Honolulu, 1982-92; judge 1st Cir. Ct. State of Hawaii, Oahu, 1992-93; justice State of Hawaii Supreme Ct., Honolulu, 1993—. Mem. Am. Judicature Soc., Hawaii Bar Assn., Sons and Daughters of 442. Office: Hawaii Supreme Ct Ali'iolani Hale 417 S King St Honolulu HI 96813-2902

NAKAYAMA, WATARU, engineering educator, consultant; b. Kamakura, Kanagawa, Japan, Jan. 7, 1936; s. Shiroh and Haru N.; m. Michiko Aoyagi, Jan. 8, 1967. BS, Defense Acad., Yokosuka, Japan, 1958; MS, Tokyo Inst. Tech., 1963, DEng, 1966. Lectr. U. Sherbrooke, Que., 1969-70; rschr. Hitachi, Ltd., Tokyo, 1970-71, chief rschr. Tsuchiura, Japan, 1971-78, sr. rschr., 1978-88, sr. chief rschr., 1988-91, hon. engr., 1991-92; Hitachi chair prof. Tokyo Inst. Tech., 1989-92, prof., 1992-96; vis. prof. U. Md., 1996-98; pres. ThermTech Internat., 1998—. Lectr. in field. Author: (with others) Heat Transfer in Electronic and Microelectronic Equipment, 1990, High Performance Computing in Japan, 1992, Computers and Computing in Heat Transfer Science and Engineering, 1993; contbr. articles to profl. jours. Recipient New Tech. Innovation award Ichimura Found., 1978, best paper award Gas Turbine Soc. of Japan, 1984. Fellow IEEE, ASME (K-16 com. 1981—, chmn. Japanese chpt. 1990-92, Best Paper award 1981, Heat Transfer Meml. award 1992, Electronic Packaging award 1996, Achievement award 2001), InterPack (Achievement award 2000); mem. Japanese Soc. Mech. Engrs. (vice chmn. thermal engring. divsn. 1989-90, chmn. 1990-91, Best Paper award 1965, 80, Tech. award 1978), Heat Transfer Soc. Japan (pres. 1994). Achievements include patents for industrial application of heat transfer enhancement techniques to heat exchangers, rotating machinery, cooling systems of computers. E-mail: watnakayama@aol.com.

NAKONECZNY, MICHAEL MARTIN, artist; b. Detroit, Oct. 30, 1952; s. Michael and Edithe (Pheil) N.; 1 child, Alysha. Student, Kent State U., 1972-74; BA, Cleve. State U., 1979; MFA, Univ. Cin., 1981. Artist in residence Pub. Sch. 1, Long Island City, N.Y., 1986; instr. Cuyahoga C.C., Cleve., 1987, Cleve. Inst. of Art, 1988; vis. artist Herron Sch. of Art Ind. U., Indpls., 1990, Kansas City (Mo.) Art Inst., 1991; artist in residence Bemis Found., Omaha, 1992; vis. artist Tamarind Inst., Albuquerque, N. Mex., 1995, Ill. State U., 1997; asst. prof. U. Alaska, Fairbanks, 2002—. Vis. artist Mont. State U., 1998. One-man shows include south Bend Regional Mus. of Art, Graham Modern Gallery, NYC, 1988, Cleve. Ctr. for Contemporary Art, 1993, Zolla Lieberman Gallery, Chgo. 1991-93, 96-2003, Horwitch LewAllen Gallery, Santa Fe, 1995, Purdue U., West Lafayette, Ind., 1995, Clark Gallery, Boston, 1999, Anchorage Mus. of History and Art, South Bend Regional Mus. Art, 2003; exhibited in group shows at Corcoran Gallery Art, Washington, 1985, Alternative Mus., NY, 1986, LA County Mus. Art, 1987, Graham Modern Gallery, NYC, 1989, Machida City Mus. Graphic Arts, Tokyo, 1993, Galleria Art, Sao Paulo, Brazil, 1994, Weatherspoon Art Gallery, U. NC, 1995, Chgo. Ctr. Book & Paper Arts, Columbia Coll., 1996, Banco Ctrl., Cuenca, Ecuador, 1996, Calif. Mus. Art, Santa Rosa, 1997, U. Alaska Mus., Fairbanks. Fellow, U. Cin., 1979—81, Ohio Arts Coun., 1990, Arts Midwest NEA Regional fellow, 1994—95, Ill. Arts Coun., 1995, Visual Arts 7, 1987. Address: 660 Rebecca St Apt 16 Fairbanks AK 99709-3563 Office Phone: 901-474-6545. E-mail: ffmmn@uaf.edu.

NAKU, ROLF D. gas industry executive; BS, NYU, 1973; MBA, Rensselaer Poly., 1974. With human resources and telecom. AMF, Inc.; joined Ultramar, 1983; v.p. human resources Ultramar Corp.; dir. compensation, benefits and human resources sys. Sunoco, Inc., 1998—2000, v.p. uman resources and pub. affairs, 2000—03, sr. v.p. human resources and pub. affairs, 2003—. Office: Sunoco Inc Ten Penn Ctr 1801 Market St Philadelphia PA 19103-1699

NALCIOGLU, ORHAN, physics educator, radiological sciences educator; b. Istanbul, Turkey, Feb. 2, 1944; came to U.S., 1966, naturalized, 1974; s. Mustafa and Meliha Nalcioglu. BS, Robert Coll., Istanbul, 1966; MS, Case Western Res. U., 1968; PhD, U. Oreg., 1970. Postdoctoral fellow dept. physics U. Calif., Davis, 1970-71; rsch. assoc. dept. physics U. Rochester, N.Y., 1971-74, U. Wis., Madison, 1974-76; sr. physicist EMI Med. Inc., Northbrook,

Ill., 1976-77; prof. depts. radiol. scis., elec. engring., medicine and physics U. Calif., Irvine, 1977—, head divsn. physics and engring., 1985—, dir. biomed. magnetic resonance rsch., 1987—2002, dir. Rsch. Imaging Ctr., 1992—, vice chair dept. radiology, 2000—. Cons. UN, 1980-86; gen. chmn. IEEE Nuclear Sci. Symposium and Med. Imaging Conf., 1996, 99. Editor several books; guest editor IEEE Nuclear Sci. Symposium and Med. Imaging Conf., 1997; contbr. articles to profl. jours. Mobil scholar, 1961-66; recipient Athalie Clarke award for rsch. excellence, 2001, Outstanding Achievement in the Arts and Scis. award ATAA, 2002, Outstanding Scientist award Assembly of Turkish-Am. Assns., Washington, 2002. Fellow IEEE (pres. Nuclear and Plasma Scis. Soc. 1993-94, Millennium medal 2000, NPSS Richard Shea award 2000), Am. Assn. Physicists in Medicine, Internat. Soc. Magnetic Resonance in Medicine; mem. Nuclear and Plasma Scis. Soc., Internat. Soc. Maj. Rsch. in Medicine. Office: Univ Calif Rsch Imaging Ctr Irvine CA 92697-0001 Business E-Mail: nalci@uci.edu.

NALDER, ERIC CHRISTOPHER, investigative reporter; b. Coulee Dam, Wash., Mar. 2, 1946; s. Philip Richard and Mibs Dorothy (Aurdal) Nalder; m. Jan Christiansen, Dec. 20, 1968; 1 child, Britt Hillary. BA in Comms., U. Wash., 1968. News editor Whidbey News-Times, Oak Harbor, Wash., 1971; reporter Lynnwood (Wash.) Enterprise, 1972, Everett Herald, Lynnwood, 1972—75; gen. assignment reporter Seattle Post-Intelligencer, 1975—78, edn. writer, 1977—78, investigative reporter, 1978—83; chief investigative reporter Seattle Times, 1983—2001; investigative reporter San Jose Mercury News, 2001—. Author: (book) Tankers Full of Trouble, 1994. Recipient Edn. Writers Assn. award, Charles Stewart Mott Found., 1978, Hearst Cmty. Svc. award, 1978, C.B. Blethen award (13), Outstanding Govt. Reporting award, Seattle Mcpl. League, Pub. Svc. in Journalism award, Sigma Delta Chi, 1987, Edward J. Meeman award, Scripps Howard Found., 1987, Thomas Stokes award, Washington Journalism Ctr., 1990, Pulitzer Prize for nat. reporting, 1990, Nat. Headline award, 1991, AP Sports Editors Investigative Reporting award, 1992, Pub. Svc. award, AP Mag. Editors Assn., 1992, Goldsmith prize for investigative reporting, 1992, Worth Bingham prize for investigative reporting, 1992, Headliner award, 1992, Investigative Reporters and Editors award, 1992, 1995, Silver Gavel award, ABA, 1995, Pulitzer prize for investigative reporting, 1997, John B. Oakes award for disting. environ. journalism, 1998, Edward J. Meeman award, Scripps Howard Found., 1999, Robert L. Kozik award, Nat. Press Club, 1999, Susan Hutchinson Bosch award, Soc. for Profl. Journalism, 2000, Headliner award and Best of the West in Investigative Reporting, 2000, Clarion award for investigative series, Headliner award, 2000. Mem.: Pacific N.W. Newspaper Guild, Investigative Reports and Editors Assn. Avocation: downhill skiing. Office: Seattle Times 1120 John St Seattle WA 98109-5321 Address: PO Box 70 Seattle WA 98111-0070

NALE, ROBERT D. finance educator; s. Frederick E and Dorothea G Nale; m. Julia A Nale, Feb. 27, 1971; children: Daniel A, Kerry E. BBA, Western Ill. U., Macomb, 1973; MBA, Roosevelt U., Chgo., 1977; PhD, U. of Miss., 1984. Asst. prof. Monmouth Coll., Ill., 1978—85, Coastal Carolina U., Conway, SC, 1985—88, asst./assoc. dean, 1988—98, interim dean, 2000—02, dept. chair/prof., 1998—. Sgt. USAF, 1966—69. Mem.: SE InfORMS (treas. 1998—2000, v.p. 2000—01, pres. 2001—02), Phi Kappa Phi, Beta Gamma Sigm. Avocations: reading, music. Office: Coastal Carolina Univ PO Box 261954 Conway SC 29528 Personal E-mail: bob@coastal.edu.

NALEN, CRAIG ANTHONY, government official; b. Montclair, NJ, Apr. 17, 1930; s. Paul Anthony and Mildred A. (Tucker) N.; m. Katherine Andrews, Dec. 30, 1953; children: Katherine M., David A., Peter H. BA, Princeton U., 1952; MBA, Stanford U., 1957. Mktg. exec. Procter & Gamble, Cin., 1957-62, Foremost-McKesson, San Francisco, 1962-64; divisional gen. mgr., corp. v.p. Gen. Mills Inc., Mpls., 1964-72; pres., also bd. dirs. Am. Photograph Corp., Great Neck, N.Y., 1972-75; pres., chmn. bd. dirs. STP Corp., Ft. Lauderdale, Fla., 1975-80; pres., chief exec. officer Overseas Pvt. Investment Corp. (govt. agy.), Washington, 1981-89, also bd. dirs.; chmn. AES Transpower, Washington, 1989-92. Bd. dirs. Glendale Internat. Corp., Ont., Canada, Sonex Corp. Bd. dirs., founder Children's World, Denver. Lt. USNR, 1952-55. Mem. Chevy Chase (Md.) Club, Gulf Stream Golf Club (Fla.), Gulf Stream Bath & Tennis Club (Delray Beach, Fla.), Valley Golf Club (Sun Valley, Idaho). Republican. Home: 532 Banyan Rd Gulf Stream FL 33483-7404 also: 3101 New Mexico Ave NW Apt 844 Washington DC 20016-5917 also: PO Box 2423 Ketchum ID 83340-2439

NALIN, DAVID ROBERT, retired pharmaceutical executive; b. N.Y.C., Apr. 22, 1941; s. Edward Murray Nalin and Hilda (Cumsky) Mehlman. BA, Cornell U., 1961; MD, Albany Med. Coll., 1965. Intern, resident Montefiore Hosp., Bronx, N.Y., 1965-67; rsch. assoc. internat. rsch. NIH, Bethesda, Md., 1967-70; sr. resident medicine Harvard U., Boston, 1970-71; rsch. assoc. pathobiology, instr. medicine Johns Hopkins U. Med. Coll., Balt., 1971-73, asst. prof. medicine and pathobiology, 1973-76; ass. prof. medicine Med. Coll. U. Md., Balt., 1976-79, chief physiology sect. ctr. vaccine devel., 1978-79, assoc. prof. internat. medicine, dir. Pakistan Med. Ctr., 1979-82, clin. assoc. prof. epidemiology and preventive medicine, 1981-82; dir. clin. rsch. Merck Rsch. Lab., West Point, Pa., 1983-98; dir. vaccine sci. affairs Merck Vaccine Divsn., West Point, Pa., 1998—2002; ret., 2002. Cons. WHO, Geneva, 1969—90, USAID, Washington, 1970—82; sr. asst. surgeon USPHS, 1965—70. Contbr. Co-founder Bangladesh Info. Ctr., Washington, 1970—72. Recipient medals and plaques, Govts. of Bangladesh and Pakistan, Internat. Ctr. for Diarrheal Diseases Rsch., Bangladesh, 1972, 1981, 1992, Pollin prize for Pediatric Rsch., Columbia U., 2002. Mem.: ACP, Royal Soc. Tropical Medicine & Hygiene, Am. Soc. Microbiology, Am. Soc. Tropical Medicine & Hygiene. Avocation: art collector.

NALLE, PETER DEVEREUX, publishing company executive; b. N.Y.C., July 26, 1947; s. Peter Borie and Margaret Graham (Josephs) N.; m. Eleanor Jo Graham, June 14, 1969; 1 child, Graham Devereux. BA, Brown U., 1969. Salesman and mem. sales mgmt. dept. McGraw-Hill Book Co., N.Y.C., 1970-76, editor, mem. editorial mgmt. dept., 1976-81, mktg. dir., 1981-82, gen. mgr., 1982-84, group v.p., 1984-87; pres., chief exec. officer J.B. Lippincott Co., Phila., 1987-90; pres. Simon and Schuster Profl. Info. Group, Englewood Cliffs, N.J., 1990-93; COO Grolier, Inc., Danbury, Conn., 1994-97; investor Various Cos., 1997—. Bd. dirs. Trudy Corp., Nichols Pub., Market Access Internat. Bd. dirs. Schuylkill River Devel. Coun. Mem.: Info. Industry Assn., Am. Med. Pubs. Assn. (bd. dirs.), Washington Square Assn. (bd. dirs.), Soc. Scholarly Pub., Assn. Am. Pubs. (exec. council profl. and scholarly div. 1985-87, bd. dirs. 1995-96), Athenaeum of Phila., Friends of Schuylkill River Park (v.p.). Home: 2113 Delancey St Philadelphia PA 19103-6511

NALLE, SARA TILGHMAN, historian, educator; d. Peter Borie and Margaret Graham Nalle. PhD, Johns Hopkins U., Balt., 1982. Prof. history William Paterson U., Wayne, NJ, 2001—. Author: God in La Mancha: Religious Reform and the People of Cuenca, 1500-1650 (Roland Bainton prize, 1993), Mad for God: Bartolome Sanchez, the Secret Messiah of Cardenete. Grantee, NEH; Fulbright-Hays Rsch. grant. Mem.: Am. Hist. Assn. (mem. nominating com. 1999—2001). Office: William Paterson Univ 300 Pompton Rd Wayne NJ 07470 Personal E-mail: nalles@wpunj.edu.

NALLEY, ELIZABETH ANN, chemistry professor; b. Catron, Mo., July 8, 1942; d. Arthur E. and Thelma L. (King) Frazier; m. Robert L. Mullican, Jan. 2, 1986; 1 child, George L. BS, Northeastern Okla. State U., 1965; MS, Okla. State U., 1969; PhD, Tex. Woman's U., 1975. High sch. tchr. Muskogee (Okla.) Ctrl. High Sch., 1964-65; instr. Cameron U., Lawton, Okla., 1969-72, asst. prof., 1972-75, assoc. prof., 1975-78, prof., 1978—. Contbr. articles to profl. jours. Recipient Disting. Svc. award Cameron U., 1995, Alumni Hall of Fame award, 1996; named Okla. Sci. Tchr. of Yr., Okla. Sci. Tchrs. Assn., 1999, S.W. Tech. Disting. Rsch. award, 2001, Disting. Alumnus Tex. Woman's U., 2001. Mem. AAAS, Assn. for Advancement of Computers in Edn., Am. Chem. Soc. (councilor 1980-97, sec. div. profl. rels. 1987-, sec. divsn. profl. rel. 1987-96, chair-elect divsn. profl. rels. 1996, chair divsn. profl. rels. 1997, nat. bd. dirs. 1997-2003, Okla. Chemist award 1992, divsn. profl. rels. Henry Hill award, 1996), Am. Inst. Chemists (nat. bd. dirs.), Phi Kappa Phi (regent 1981-89, nat. v.p. 1989-92, nat. pres.-elect 1992-95, nat. pres. 1995-98, Disting. Faculty award 1978), Sigma Xi, Sigma Pi Sigma, Iota Sigma Pi. Home: RR 3 Box 176-1 Chickasha OK 73018-9544 Office: Cameron U Dept of Chemistry 2800 W Gore Blvd Lawton OK 73505-6320 E-mail: annn@cameron.edu.

NALLEY, JAMES H., II, music educator, musician; b. Kyonggi-do, Republic of Korea, July 28, 1968; s. James H. and Kyu Cha Nalley. MusB, Temple U., 1992, MusM, 1994; D of Musical Arts, Eastman Sch. Music, 1998. Dir. keyboard studies George Mason U., Fairfax, Va., 1999—2002; asst. prof. piano Fla. State U., Tallahassee, 2003—. Vis. asst. prof. Sweet Briar (Va.) Coll., 1998—99. Performer: (albums) James Nalley Plays Ives and Copland, 2002. Scholar, Fulbright Found., 2002—. Mem.: MTNA, Coll. Music Soc., Phi Kappa Lambda. Home: 2305 Killearn Center Blvd B 48 Tallahassee FL 32309 E-mail: james.nalley@music.fsu.edu.

NALLI, NICHOLAS ROCCO, physical scientist; s. Rocco and Marlene Nalli; m. Christine Nez, June 28, 2003. PhD, U. of Wisconsin-Madison, 1996—2000, MS, 1992—95; MS in Edn., SUNY, Coll. at Oneonta, 1988—90, BS, 1983—87. Postdoctoral fellow Colo. State U., Ft. Collins, 2000—; grad. rsch. asst. U. of Wisconsin-Madison, 1992—2000, grad. tchg. asst., 1997—97; math. tchr. grades 3 - 8 Canajoharie Ctrl. Sch., NY, 1991—91; eighth grade phys. sci. tchr. Ft. Plain Ctrl. Sch., 1988—89. Author: (articles) Journal of Atmospheric and Oceanic Technology, Journal of Geophysical Research, Bulletin of the American Meteorological Society, (article) Applied Optics, Journal of Climate, (PhD dissertation) A Physical Multispectral Method for the Retrieval of Ocean and Lake Surface Temperatures via Scanning Spectrometer, (master's thesis) Sea Surface Skin Temperature Retrieval Using the High-Resolution Interferometer Sounder (Lettau Award for an Excellent MS Rsch. Thesis, 1996). Pres., young adults fellowship Our Lady of Lourdes Cath. Ch., Arlington, Va., 2000—03. Recipient Recognition of Outstanding Achievement, Nat. Space Grant Coll. and Fellowship Program, 1995-1996, Empire Challenger Award, NY State, 1990; fellow Grad. Rsch. Assistantship, Wis. Space Grant Consortium, 1995-2000, Global Change Fellowship, Am. Meteorol. Soc., 1996. Mem.: Am. Geophys. Union, Am. Meteorol. Soc., SUNY-Oneonta Meteorology Club (vice-president 1989—90). R-Consevative. Roman Catholic. Achievements include research in infrared remote sensing of water bodies; development of algorithms for the remote sensing of sea surface temperatures from NOAA environmental satellites; satellite-based sea surface temperature climatologies. Avocations: church & community volunteer work, weight training, hiking, biking, reading. Office: Noaa/Nesdis/Ora 5200 Auth Road Camp Springs MD 20746 E-mail: nick.nalli@noaa.gov.

NALLY, DENNIS MATHEW, accountant, finance company executive; b. Washington, Oct. 11, 1952; s. Thomas J. and Margaret (Allen) N.; m. Karen L. Kidder, June 18, 1977; children: Brian, Lindsay, Kathryn, Lauren. BBA, Western Mich. U., 1974; completed, Columbia U. Exec. Program, Penn State U. Exec. Programs. CPA, Mich., Ohio. Staff acct. Price Waterhouse, Detroit, 1974-77, audit sr., 1977-78, audit mgr., 1978-85, audit ptnr., 1985, NYC, 1985 88, ptnr. in charge Dayton, Ohio, 1988—92, nat. dir. of strategic planning, 1992—95, mem., US firm policy com. US mgmt. com., gen. coun. of the worldwide org., vice chmn for fin. and key client svcs. support, 1995—97; nat. dir., strategic planning PricewaterhouseCoopers, 1992—95, leader for assurance and bus. adv. svcs. for Am. Theatre, 1996—2000, mng. ptnr., US Firm, 2000—01, mem., policy com., US Firm, 2000—01; chmn., sr. ptnr. PricewaterhouseCoopers, LLP, 2002—, mem. US bd. of partners and principals, mem., US mgmt. com. Spkr., guest lectr. in field. Treas., pres.-elect The Muse Machine, Dayton, 1989; mem. exec. com. Dayton Contemporary Dance, 1988-90; bd. dirs. Dayton Urban League, 1990, US C. of C., US-Japan Bus. Coun.; bd. trustee St. Michael's Coll., Colchester, VT, NY POPs, Fin. Com. of Diocese, Bridgeport, Conn. Mem. AICPA, Ohio Soc. CPAs, Mich. Soc. CPAs, NY State Soc. CPAs, Beta Alpha Psi (hon. mem. Dayton chpt.) Avocations: golf, sailing, jogging, computers. Office: PricewaterhouseCoopers LLP 1177 Ave of the Americas New York NY 10036 Office Phone: 646-471-4000. Office Fax: 646-471-3188.

NAM, BYUNG-HO, statistician, educator; b. Seoul, Republic of Korea, Oct. 6, 1961; s. Kyu-Chul Nam and Jae-Sun Jung; m. Heejae Im, July 11, 1964; children: Henie, Jenie, Annie. BA, Seoul Nat. U., 1980—84; MBA, Ea. Mich. U., Ypsilanti, 1986—90; MS, U. Mich., Ann Arbor, 1990—93; PhD, Boston U., 1994—2000. Rsch. asst. prof. Boston U., 2000—; biostatistitian Framingham Heart Study, Mass., 1996—; tchg. fellow Boston U., 1996—99, rsch. fellow, 1995—2000. Author: (book) Goodness-of-fit Tests and Model Validity. Deacon, group study leader Evergreen Ch. of Boston, Brookline, 1997—2002. Mem.: Am. Statis. Assn. Achievements include research in Performance measures of mathematical prediction models. Home: 185 Freeman St Brookline MA 02446 Office: Boston Univ 111 Cummington St Boston MA 02215 E-mail: byungho@bu.edu.

NAM, CHARLES BENJAMIN, demographer, sociologist, educator, writer; b. Lynbrook, NY, Mar. 25, 1926; s. Samuel and Yetta (Huff) N.; m. Marjorie Lee Tallant, Jan. 1, 1956; children: David Wallace, Rebecca Jane. BA, NYU, 1950; MA, U. N.C., 1957, PhD, 1959. Statistician U.S. Bur. Census, Washington, 1950-53, chief edn. and social stratification br., 1957-64; statistician USAF, Montgomery, Ala., 1953-54; rsch. asst. U. N.C., Chapel Hill, 1954-57; prof. sociology Fla. State U., Tallahassee, 1964—96, chmn. dept. sociology, 1968—71, disting. rsch. prof., 1994—96, disting. rsch. prof. emeritus, 1996—; rsch. assoc. Ctr. for Demography and Population Health, 1967—, dir., 1967—82; mem. population adv. com. U.S. Bur. Census, 1978-81. Cons. population divsn. Orgn. for Econ. Coop. and Devel., 1968-70, UNESCO, 1978-83, Indonesian Ministry of Population and Environment, Jakarta, 1988-90; Social Sci. Rsch. Coun., 1981-88. Author: (with John K. Folger) Education of the American Population, 1967, Population and Society, 1968, (with Susan Gustavus) Population: The Dynamics of Demographic Change, 1976, Nationality Groups and Social Stratification, 1981; (with Susan Philliber) Population: A Basic Orientation, 1983; (with Mary Powers) The Socioeconomic Approach to Status Measurement, 1983, Our Population: The Face of America, 1988, Understanding Population Change, 1994; (with Richard Rogers and Robert Hummer) Living and Dying in the USA, 2000; (with Janusz Balicki and Ewa Fratczak) Mechanisms of Population Changes and Population Policy (in Polish), 2003; editor: Demography, 1972-75; co-editor: (with David Sly, William Serow) International Handbook of Internal Migration, 1990, Handbook of International Migration, 1990; mem. editl. bd. Population Research and Policy Review, 1993-94. Fellow AAAS (rep. sect. K 1999-); mem. Am. Sociol. Assn. (chmn. sect. on population 1976-78), Population Assn. Am. (pres. 1979), Internat. Union for Sci. Study Population, Am. Statis. Assn. (chmn. social statistics sect. 1974), So. Sociol. Soc. (pres. 1981-82), So. Demographic Assn. (vice chmn. 1974-75; fellow 2001), Soc. Study Social Biology (bd. dirs. 1996—, exec. com. 1998-99). Home: 820 Live Oak Plantation Rd Tallahassee FL 32312-2413 E-mail: charlesnam2@earthlink.net.

NAMBOODIRI, KRISHNAN, sociology educator; b. Valavoor, Ind., Nov. 13, 1929; s. Narayanan and Parvathy (Kutty) N.; m. Kadambari Kumari, Sept. 7, 1954; children: Unni (dec.), Sally. B.Sc., U. Kerala, 1950, M.Sc., 1953; MA, U. Mich., 1962, PhD, 1963. Lectr. U. Kerala, India, 1953-55, 58-59; tech. asst. Indian Statis. Inst., Calcutta, 1955-58; reader demography U. Kerala, 1963-66; asst. prof. sociology U. N.C., Chapel Hill, 1966-67, asso. prof., 1967-73, prof., 1973-84, chmn. dept., 1975-80; Robert Lazarus prof. population studies Ohio State U., Columbus, 1984—2000, chmn. dept. sociology, 1989-93, prof. emeritus, 2000—. Author: (with L.F. Carter and H.M. Blalock) Applied Multivariate Analysis and Experimental Designs, 1975; editor: Demography, 1975-78, Survey Sampling and Measurement, 1978, Auth. Matrix Algebra: An Introduction, 1984, (with C.M. Suchindran) Life Table Techniques and Their Applications, 1987, (with R.G. Corwin) Research in Sociology of Education and Socialization: Selected Methodological Issues, 1989, Demographic Analysis: A Stochastic Approach, 1991, (with R.G. Corwin) The Logic and Method of Macrosociology, 1993, Methods for Macrosociological Research, 1994, A Primer of Population Dynamics, 1996; contbr. articles to profl. jours. Fellow Am. Statis. Assn.; mem. Population Assn. Am. (dir. 1975-76), Internat. Union Sci. Study Population, Am. Sociol. Assn., Indian Sociol. Assn., Am. Statis. Assn., Sociol. Research Assn. Home: 3107 N Star Rd Columbus OH 43221-2366 E-mail: namboodiri.2@osu.edu.

NAMBU, YOICHIRO, physics educator; b. Toyko, Jan. 18, 1921; arrived in U.S., 1952; m. Chieko Hida Nambu, Nov. 3, 1945; 1 child, Jun-ichi. Research asst. U. Tokyo, 1945—49; prof. physics Osaka City U., Japan, 1950—56; mem. Inst. Advanced Study, 1952—54; research assoc. U. Chgo., 1954—56, mem. faculty, 1956—, prof. physics, 1958, Disting. prof., 1971—; emeritus, 1991—. Contbr. articles to profl. jours. Recipient J.J. Sakurai prize, Am. Phys. Soc., 1994, Wolf prize in Physics, 1994. Mem.: NAS, Am. Phys. Soc., Am. Acad. Arts and Scis. Office: Univ of Chicago Enrico Fermi Inst 5740 S Ellis Ave Chicago IL 60637-1434

NAMDARI, BAHRAM, surgeon; b. Oct. 26, 1939; s. Rostam and Sarvar Namdari; m. Kathleen Wilmore, Jan. 5, 1976; children: Mondona, Mietra, Ariana. MD, 1966. Diplomate Am. Bd. Surgery. Resident in gen. surgery St. John's Mercy Med. Ctr., St. Louis, 1969-73; practice medicine specializing in gen. and vascular surgery Milw., 1976—. Mem. staff St. Mary's Hosp., Milw., St. Luke's Hosp., Milw., St. Michael Hosp., Milw.; founder, pres. Famous Mealwaukee Foods Enterprises. Contbr. articles to med. jours.; patentee med. instruments and other devices. Cardiovascular Surgery fellow with Michael DeBakey, Baylor Coll. Medicine, Houston, 1974-75. Fellow ACS, Internat. Surgeons; mem. AMA, Med. Soc. Milwaukee County, Milw. Acad. Surgery, Wis. Med. Soc., Wis. Surg. Soc., Royal Soc. Medicine Eng. (affiliate), Am. Soc. Bariatric Surgery, World Med. Assn., Internat. Acad. Bariatric Medicine (founding mem.), Am. Acad. Cosmetic Surgery, Michael DeBakey Internat. Cardiovascular Soc. Office: Great Lakes Med and Surg Ctr 6000 S 27th St Milwaukee WI 53221-4805

NAMEROW, DAVID MARK, pediatrician; b. N.Y.C., Dec. 12, 1947; s. Nathan and Claire (Goodstein) N.; m. Pearila Brickner, June 14, 1981; children: Jordan Ilana, Evan Gabrielle, Zoe Alexandra. BS, CCNY, 1968; MD, U. Louisville, 1972. Pediatric intern Children's Hosp. Med. Ctr., Cin., 1972-73, resident in pediatrics, 1973-75; fellow in adolescent medicine U. Md. Hosps., Balt., 1975-77; pediatrician Plaza Med. Assocs., Flanders, N.J., 1977-79; dir. adolescent medicine St. Joseph's Hosp. Med. Ctr., Paterson, N.J., 1977-81; founder, pediatrician PediatriCare Assocs., Fair Lawn, N.J., 1979—. Attending pediatrician, assoc. dir. dept. pediatrics Valley Hosp., Ridgewood, N.J., 1979—; adj. asst. clin. prof. pediatrics N.Y. Hosp.-Cornell Med. Ctr., N.Y.C., 1979—. Fellow Am. Acad. Pediatrics; mem. Soc. for Adolescent Medicine, Ambulatory Pediatric Assn. Office: PediatriCare Assocs 20-20 Fair Lawn Ave Fair Lawn NJ 07410-2319 also: 400 Franklin Tpke Mahwah NJ 07430-3516

NAMFUA, JACQUELINE VETTA, broadcast executive; b. Machame, Tanzania, Jan. 17, 1975; d. Marcel William and Salome Maria Namfua. Diploma in broadcast journalism, Loyalist Coll., 1994; BA in Mass Comm. (hon.), Carleton U., 1998; MA in Broadcast Journalism, Syracuse U. Newhouse, 2001. Assignment editor asst. CBS Network Radio, N.Y.C., 2001—02; outreach coord. CBNS, Flushing, 2002. Author: (collection of poetry) A Rivers Journey to the Sea.

NANAGAS, MARIA TERESITA CRUZ, pediatrician, educator; b. Manila, Jan. 21, 1946; came to U.S., 1970; d. Ambrosio and Maria (Pasamonte) Cruz; m. Victor N. Nanagas, Jr.; children: Victor III, Valerie, Vivian. BS, U. of the Philippines, 1965, MD, 1970. Diplomate Am. Bd. Pediat. Intern, resident St. Elizabeth's Hosp., Boston, 1971-74; fellow in ambulatory pediat. North Shore Children's Hosp., Salem, Mass., 1974-75; active staff medicine Children's Med. Ctr., Dayton, Ohio, 1976—, head divsn. gen. pediat., 1988-90, 95-97, co-interim head ambulatory pediat., 1989-90, med. dir. ambulatory pediat., 1990—. Clin. asst. prof. pediat. Wright State U., Dayton, 1977-83, clin. assoc. prof. pediat., 1983—, selective dir., 1989—, assoc. prof. pediat., 2000—; clin. asst. prof. family practice Wright State U., Dayton, 1999—; dir., preceptor Wright State U. residents continuing clinic Children's Med. Ctr., 1989—, attending physician family practice programs, 1978—. Active Miami Valley Lead Poisoning Prevention Coalition, 19926. Fellow Am. Acad. Pediat.; mem. Western Ohio Pediat. Soc., Ambulatory Pediat. Assn. Office: Children's Med Ctr Health Clinic 1 Childrens Plz Dayton OH 45404-1898 Office Phone: 937-641-3500.

NANANUKUL, SORACHA, electrical engineer; b. Bangkok, Mar. 2, 1968; arrived in U.S.A., 1989; s. Kasem and Chuancheun Nananukul; m. Veronica Atlantis Femia, Nov. 8, 2000. B Engring., Chulalongkorn U., Bangkok, 1988; MS, PhD, U. Mass., 1996. Sr. performance engr. Ascend Comm., Westford, Mass., 1996—97; sr. rsch. engr. Nokia Rsch. Ctr., Burlington, Mass., 1997—2000, asst. rsch. mgr., 2000—03, prin. scientist, 2003—. Recipient George S. Axelby Outstanding Paper Award, Control Systems Soc., IEEE, 1997; Grad. Sch. fellow, U. Mass., 1993—94. Mem.: IEEE (George S. Axelby Outstanding Paper award 1997). Office: Nokia 5 Wayside Rd Burlington MA 01803 E-mail: soracha.nananukul@nokia.com.

NANCE, ALLAN TAYLOR, retired lawyer; b. Dallas, Jan. 31, 1933; s. A.Q. and Lois Rebecca (Taylor) N. BA, So. Meth. U., 1954, LLB, 1957; LLM, NYU, 1978. Bar: Tex. 1957, N.Y. 1961. With Simpson Thacher & Bartlett, N.Y.C., 1960-65; asst. counsel J.P. Stevens & Co., Inc., N.Y.C., 1965-70, sec., 1970-78, asst. gen. counsel, 1970-89; counsel J.P. Stevens & Co. Inc. and WestPoint-Pepperell Inc., 1989-93; asst. gen. counsel WestPoint Stevens Inc., N.Y.C., 1993-98, ret., 1998. With USNR, 1957-59. Woodrow Wilson fellow Columbia U., 1959-60. Mem. Phi Beta Kappa. Home: 201 E 66th St New York NY 10021-6451

NANCE, BETTY LOVE, librarian; b. Nashville, Oct. 29, 1923; d. Granville Scott and Clara (Mills) N. BA in English magna cum laude, Trinity U., 1957; MLS, U. Mich., 1958. Head dept. acquisitions Stephen F. Austin U. Libr., Nacogdoches, Tex., 1958-59; libr. 1st Nat. Bank, Ft. Worth, 1959-61; head catalog dept. Trinity U., San Antonio, 1961-63; head tech. processes U. Tex. Law Libr., Austin, 1963-66; head catalog dept. Tex. A&M U. Libr., College Station, 1966-69; chief bibliographic svcs. Washington U. Libr., St. Louis, 1970; head dept. acquisitions Va. Commonwealth U. Libr., Richmond, 1971-73; head tech. processes Howard Payne U. Libr., Brownwood, Tex., 1974-79; libr. dir. Edinburg (Tex.) Pub. Libr., 1980-91. Pres. Edinburg Com. Salvation Army. Mem. ALA, Pub. Libr. Assn., Tex. Libr. Assn., Hidalgo County Libr. Assn. (v.p. 1980-81, pres. 1981-82), Pan Am. Round Table Edinburg (corr. sec. 1986-88, assoc. dir. 1989-90), Edinburg Bus. and Profl. Womens Club (founding bd. dirs., pres. 1986-87, bd. dirs. 1987-88), Zonta (bd. dirs. West Hidalgo Club, 1986-88, San Antonio 1996-97), Alpha Lambda Delta, Alpha Chi. Methodist. Home: 5359 Fredericksburg Rd # 806 San Antonio TX 78229-3549 E-mail: bettynance@webtv.net.

NANCE, CYNTHIA ELEANOR, law educator; b. Chgo., Sept. 3, 1958; d. Eual Dean and Fern Elizabeth Nance. BS in Econs. magna cum laude, Chgo. State U., 1986; JD with distinction, U. Iowa, 1990, MA in Fin., 1991, ABD in Indsl. Rels., 1993. Lic.: Iowa Supreme Ct. 1990. Law clk. Glasson, Grove, Sole & McMannus, Cedar Rapids, Iowa, 1989; program coord. U. Iowa Labor Ctr., 1989—91; tchg. asst. U. Iowa Coll. Bus., 1991—93; faculty fellow U. Iowa Coll. Law, 1993—94; asst. prof. law U. Ark. Sch. Law, Fayetteville, 1994—99, assoc. prof. law, 1999—. Bd. dirs. Sources for Ind. Living, Fayetteville, Ark., 1994—97; mem. audit com. Law Sch. Admissions Coun., Newtown, Pa., 1994—98, fin. and legal affairs com., Newton, Pa., 1998—, chair fin. and legal affairs com., Newtown, Pa., 2003—; women of the elca anti-racism trainer Evang. Luther Ch. in Am., Chgo., 1996—2002; mem., adv. com. on corp. social responsibility Evang. Luth. Ch. of Am., Chgo., 1999—; bd. dirs. ACLU, Little Rock, 1998—99; pres. Ozark Mountain Masters Swim Team, Springdale, Ark., 1999—2001; bd. mem. Nat. Interfaith Com. for Worker Justice, Chgo., 1999—; mem. sect. on minorities in the law Am. Assn. of Law Schools, Washington, 1994—; chair labor and employment law sect. Am. Assn. of Law Schs., Washington, 2000—01, chair employment discrimination sect., 2001—02; co-chair Greensboro Massacre Truth and Reconciliation Commn. Adv. Com., NC, 2001—; mem. ch. coun. Good Shepherd Luth.

Ch., Fayetteville, Ark., 2002—03. Recipient Martin Luther King Jr. Individual Achievement award, 2004, Woman of Distinction award, Girl Scouts N.W. Ark.; fellow Grad. Opportunities for Advanced Level Studies Found., U. of Iowa Coll. of Bus., 1990—92; Tchg. Fellow, U. of Iowa, Coll. of Law, 1993—94. Mem.: ABA (co-chair labor and employmentlaw sect. ethics and professionalism com. 2001—, mem. pro bono com. labor and employment law sect. 2003—), Indsl. Rels. Rsch. Assn., Ark. Bar Assn. (jurisprudence and law reform com. 1995—, lawyer assistance program com. 1999—, com. on diversity 2000—, labor law sect.), W. B. Putman Am. Inn of Ct., Nat. Bar Assn., Alpha Kappa Alpha (chpt. pres. 1999—2002, faculty advisor 2001—03, Outstanding Svc. award 2000), Beta Gamma Sigma, Phi Delta Phi. Liberal. Evangelical Lutheran. Avocations: swimming, travel, cooking. Home: 1653 Applebury Dr Fayetteville AR 72701 Office: U of Ark Sch of Law 225 Waterman Hall Fayetteville AR 72701 Office Phone: 479-575-2403. Personal E-mail: cnance@uark.edu.

NANCE, JOHN JOSEPH, lawyer, writer, air safety analyst, broadcaster, consultant; b. Dallas, July 5, 1946; s. Joseph Turner and Margrette (Grubbs) N.; m. Benita Ann Priest, July 26, 1968; children: Dawn Michelle, Bridgitte Cathleen, Christopher-Sean. BA, So. Meth. U., 1968, JD, 1969; grad., USAF Undergrad. Pilot Tng., Williams AFB, Ariz., 1971. Bar: Tex. 1970, U.S. Ct. Appeals (fed. cir.) 1994. News reporter, broadcaster, newsman various papers and stas, Honolulu and Dallas, 1957-66; news anchorman Sta. WFAA-AM, Dallas, 1966-70; newsman including on camera Sta. WFAA-TV, Dallas; pvt. practice Dallas, 1970—; news dir. Newscom Network, Dallas, 1970; airline pilot Braniff Internat. Airways, Dallas, 1975-82, Alaska Airlines, Inc., Seattle, 1985—; chmn., pres. Exec. Transport, Inc., Tacoma, 1979-85; chmn., CEO EMEX Corp., Kent, Wash., 1987—; mng. ptnr. Phoenix Ptnrs., Ltd., Tacoma, Wash., 1995—; project devel. assoc. Columbia Tristar TV, 1997—; with Nance & Carmichael, PLLC, Austin, Tex., 1997—. Spkr. Human Mgmt., 1984—, Teamwork and Comms. in the Med. Profession; airline safety, advocate Ind. Cons., earthquake preparedness spokesman Ind. Cons.; dir. steering com. Found. for Issues Resolution in Sci. Tech., Seattle, 1987-89; speaker Northwestern Transp. Ctr. Deregulation and Safety Conf., 1987; cons. NOVA Why Planes Crash, PBS, 1987, ABC World News Tonight Crash of US AIR 427, 1994; aviation analyst ABC-TV and radio, 1995—; aviation editor: ABC Good Morning Am., 1995—; broadcast analyst, 1986—; spkr. in field. Author: Scorpion Strike, 1982, Splash of Colors, 1984, Blind Trust, 1986, On Shaky Ground, 1988, Final Approach, 1990, What Goes Up, 1991, Operating Handbook USAF Air Carrier Safety and Inspection, 1991, Phoenix Rising, 1994, Medusa's Child, 1997, The Last Hostage, 1998, Blackout, 2000, Headwind, 2001, Turbulence, 2002, Skyhook, 2003, Fireflight, 2003; contbr. Transportation Deregulatio in the U.S., 1988; actor: appeared in Sheep on the Runway, 1975; (TV series) Pandora's Clock, 1996; tech. advisor (TV series) Pandora's Clock, 1996; actor: (TV series) Medusa's Child, 1997; prodr.: USAF SOC CRM Program, 1992; author: USAF SOC CRM Program, 1992, USF Video Prodns.: ANG Introduction to CRM, 1992, The Teamwork Connection, 1996; dir.: The Teamwork Connection, 1996. Pres. Fox Glen Homeowners Assn., Tacoma, 1974-77; cons. Congl. Office Tech. Assessment, Tacoma, 1987; witness air safety hearings U.S. Congress, Washington, 1986-88; bd. dirs. St. Charles Borromeo Sch., Tacoma, 1975-78, Nat. Patient Safety Found. of AMA, 1997—; mem. Mayor's Vets. Task Force, Tacoma, 1991; bd. advisors Jour. Air Law and Commerce So. Meth. Sch. Law, 1995—, exec. bd. Sch. of Law, 1998—; bd. advisors Pacific Northwest Writer's Conf., 1994—; adv. bd. supply and logistics mgmt. program Portland State U., 1997-98. Capt. USAFR, 1975-94; lt. col. Persian Gulf. Decorated Merit Svc. medal; named Airline Safety Man of Year Wash. State Div. of Aeronautics, 1987; recipient Disting. Alumni award So. Meth. U., 2002. Fellow Chartered Inst. Transport (Canberra, Australia); mem. ABA, SAG, Tex. Bar Assn., Author's Guild Am., Res. Officers Assn. (life), Aircraft Owners' and Pilots' Assn., Phi Alpha Delta, Delta Chi. Home and Office: John Nance Prodns 4512 87th Ave W Tacoma WA 98466-1920 Office: Phoenix Ptnrs Ltd PO Box 24465 Federal Way WA 98093-1465

NANCE, ROBERT LEWIS, oil company executive; b. Dallas, July 10, 1936; s. Melvin Renfro Nance and Ruth Natlie (Seibert) Nowlin; m. Penni Jane Warfel; children: Robert Scott, Amy Louise, Catherine Leslie. BS, So. Meth. U., 1959; LLD (hon.), Rocky Mountain Coll., 1989. V.p. geology Oliver & West Cons., Dallas, 1960-66; ptnr. Nance & Larue Cons., Dallas, 1966-69; pres., CEO Nance Petroleum Corp., Billings, Mont., 1969—. Bd. dirs. First Interstate Bank, Mont., MDU Resources, Rocky Mountain Coll., Billings, chmn., 1986—91; mem. Nat. Petroleum Coun., 1992—94; chmn. Petroleum Tech. Transfer Coun., 1996—99. Coun. pres. Am. Luth. Ch., Billings, 1980; trustee, chmn. Deaconess Med. Ctr., Billings; chmn. Deaconess Billings Clinic Healty Sys. Recipient Hall of Fame award Rocky Mountain Coll. Alumni, 1987, Disting. Svc. Trusteeship, Assn. Governing Bds. Univs. Colls., 1988. Mem. Am. Assn. Petroleum Geologists, Ind. Petroleum Assn. Am. (exec. com., nat. bd. govs., Roughneck of Yr. 2002), Ind. Petroleum Assn. Mountain States (v.p. Mont. 1977-79, Wildcatter of Yr. 1999), Mont. Petroleum Assn., Hilands Golf Club, Billings Petroleum Club. Avocations: fly fishing, scuba diving, skiing. Office: Nance Petroleum Corp PO Box 7168 550 N 31st St Billings MT 59103

NANCE, TONY MAX-PERRY, designer, illustrator; b. Montclair, NJ, Feb. 25, 1955; s. Perry Hedgeman and Ida Delea (King) N.; m. June Anne Percival, Oct. 31, 1986 (div. May 1994); children: Jack Anthony, Jacqlene Angela, Jihad Conan. Student, U. Denver, 1975; BA, NY Sch. Visual Arts, 1976, postgrad., 1980-81, NJ Inst. Tech., 1977-78, Rutgers U., 1980-82. Design engr. Automation Controls, Montclair, 1975-77; artist, designer Greg Copeland, Inc., Fairfield, NJ, 1976-79; owner, designer Stalhaus, Inc., Montclair, 1976-80; editor contemporary ads Graphics Mag., NYC, 1977-79; illustrator, artist L.C. Graphics, Inc., Clifton, NJ, 1979-80; carrier supr. Montclair Post Office, 1980-93; owner, design engr. Decotech Alternations, Orange, NJ, 1984—, Electronics Tech-Atlas Soundolier, 1992-95, Machine Tech-Atlas Soudolier, 1995-98; illustrator, designer, artist Magic Circle Printine, NY, NJ, 1998—; owner NANCEart NANCEtech, Montclair. Editor Graphis mag.; artist, art dir. (album covers) Bhang, 1984 Ron Smyth I, 1986; artist, illustrator (album cover, tour and advt. promotion) Passport Greatest Hits/Doldinger, 1977 (album cover, internat. poster) Zap and the Wires-The Saga of the Black Silk Jetmen; producer, illustrator (album cover) The Little Things by Dogs Eating Glass with Loren Tindall; one man shows include Discovery Galleries, Montclair, 1978, The Gallery, Fairfield, 1979, Broghton Galleries, Bloomfield, NJ, 1983, Scotland Galleries, Laurinburg, NC, 1993; contbr. artist mags. Verotika, 1996, Hard Core, 1996; various musical and graphic copyrights; mem. Southern Ambition band, 1993-97, Southern Fried Dogs band, 1996-98; creator comic strip Appliances, 1995-97, Just Buggin', 1998; head guitarist, writer, keyboarder, vocalist Walsh-Nancy Band, 1999—. Art dir. Montclair Coalition for Performing Arts, Montclair, 1982, patron, 1998—. Mem. Soc. for Creative Anachronism (founding assoc.), Local Musicians Union, Nat. Rifle Assn., Mensa, Scotland County Art Guild, Scotland County Chamber Music Soc., Porsche Club Am., NC SCCA. Avocations: music, prop and special effect design, collecting plastic toys, computer software design, collecting guitars. Home: 138 Walnut St Apt B2 Montclair NJ 07042-3854 E-mail: rhjiuun@yahoo.com.

NANCE, WELDON BAILEY, petroleum engineer; b. Alice, Tex. s. Weldon Bailey and Viola (Freeman) N.; m. Frances Kay Bourriague, June 20, 1969 (div. Oct. 1987); 1 child, David Wayne; m. Donna Marie Villarrubia, Aug. 3, 1989; 1 child, Olivia Eleanor. BS, U. Southwestern La., 1968; MS, Australian Nat. U., Canberra, 1976. Product devel. supr. Milchem Inc., Houston, 1975-79; drilling engr. Tenneco Oil Co., Lafayette, La., 1979-84, engring. cons., 1984-86, chem. svcs. mgr., 1986-87; drilling engring. supr. Brit. Gas, Houston, 1989-92; gen. mgr. Brit. Gas Gabon, Port Gentil, 1992-94, Amerada Hess Gabon, Libreville, 1994—, also bd. dirs. Contbr. articles to sci. publs. With USMCR, 1961-67. Mem. Soc. Petroleum Engrs. Roman Catholic. Achievements include 2 patents in field. Home: 2131 Watts Rd Houston TX 77030 Office: Amerada Hess PO Box 2040 Houston TX 77252

NAND, SUCHA, medical educator; b. Thiriewal, Punjab, India, Feb. 3, 1948; d. Narsingh Dass and Swaran Devi; m. Surinder S. Nand, June 15, 1973; children: Ranveer, Rahul. Pre-med. student, Dayanand Ayur Vedic Coll., Amritsar, India, 1966; MB, BS, Med. Coll., Amritsar, India, 1971. Diplomate Am. Bd. Internal Medicine, Am. Bd. Hemotology, Am. Bd. Med. Oncology. Asst. prof. Stritch Sch. Medicine Loyola U., Maywood, Ill., 1981-88, assoc. prof. Stritch Sch. Medicine, 1989-95; prof. medicine, 1996—. Editor Jour. of Med. Coll., 1969-71; contbr. articles to profl. jours. Clin. fellow Am. Cancer Soc., 1981; Brilliant Student scholarships, 1962-71. Mem. Am. Soc. Hematology, Am. Soc. Clin. Oncology, S.W. Oncology Group (mem. leukemia com. 1988—). Avocations: chess, reading, running. Office: Loyola Univ Med Ctr 2160 S 1st Ave Maywood IL 60153-3304 Office Phone: 708-327-3182.

NANDA, AJAYA KUMAR, chemist, educator; b. Orissa, India, May 8, 1972; arrived in U.S., 2000; s. Udayanath and Bichitrabala Nanda; m. Sagarika Nanda. BS in Chemistry, India, 1993; MS in Organic Chemistry, Utkal U., Orissa, India, 1995; PhD, Indian Inst. Sci., Bangalore, 2000. Rsch. scholar Indian Inst. Sci., 1995—2000; postdoctoral rsch. scientist U. Mass., Amherst, 2000—01, Carnegie Mellon U., Pitts., 2001—03; vis. rsch. sci. U. So. Miss., Polymer Sci. Dept., 2004—. Leader Indian Inst. Sci., India. Recipient Best ACS Chemist award, 2004, Chemist of Yr. award, Am. Chem. Soc., 2004;, Coun. Sci. and Indsl. Rsch. scholar, 1995—2000. Mem.: Am. Chem. Soc. (hon.). Achievements include research in Bio-mimetic, Thermal responsive and Controlled architecture; anaerobic adhesives; energitic polymeric materials, polyperoxides; thermal labile polymers; atom transfer radical polymerization; bio-degradable polymers; mini emulsion polymerization; hybrid materials; polyurethane nano composities; good barrier plastics. Office: U So Miss PO Box 10076 118 Coll Dr Hattiesburg MS 39406 Office Phone: 601-266-6884. Personal E-mail: ajayananda@yahoo.com. E-mail: ajaya.nanda@usm.edu.

NANDA, VED PRAKASH, law educator, university official; b. Gujranwala, India, Nov. 20, 1934; arrived in U.S., 1960; s. Jagan Nath and Attar (Kaur) N.; m. Katharine Kunz, Dec. 18, 1982; 1 child, Anjali. MA, Punjab U., 1952; LLB, U. Delhi, 1955, LLM, 1958, Northwestern U., 1962; postgrad., Yale U., 1962-65; LLD, Soka U., Tokyo, 1997, Bundelkhand U., Jhansi, India, 2000. Asst. prof. law U. Denver, 1965—68, assoc. prof. law, 1968—70, prof. law, dir. Internat. Legal Studies Program, 1970—, Thompson G. Marsh prof. law, 1987—, Evans U. prof., 1992—, asst. provost, 1993—94, vice provost, 1994—. Vis. prof. Coll. Law U. Iowa, Iowa City, 1974—75; vis. prof. Fla. State U., 1973, U. San Diego, 1979, U. Colo., 1992; disting. vis. prof. internat. law Kent Coll. Law, 1981, Calif. We. Sch. Law, San Diego, 1983—84; disting. vis. scholar Sch. Law U. Hawaii, Honolulu, 1986—87; cons. Solar Energy Rsch. Inst., 1978—81, Dept. Energy, 1980—81. Co-author (with David Pansius): Litigation of International Disputes in U.S. Courts, 1987; co-editor (with M. Cherif Bassiouni): A Treatise on International Criminal Law, 1973, Water Needs for the Future, 1977; co-editor: (with George Shepherd) Human Rights and Third World Development, 1985; co-editor: (with others) Global Human Rights, 1981, The Law of Transnational Business Transactions, 1981, World Climate Change, 1983, Breach and Adaption of International Contracts, 1992, World Debt and Human Conditions, 1993, Europe Community Law After 1992, 1993, International Environmental Law and Policy, 1995, European Union Law After Maastricht, 1996; co-editor: (with William M. Evan) Nuclear Proliferation and the Legality of Nuclear Weapons, 1995; co-editor: (with S.P. Sinha) Hindu Law and Legal Theory, 1996; co-editor: (with D. Krieger) Nuclear Weapons and the World Court, 1998; co-editor: (with George Prins) International Environmental Law and Policy for the 21st Century, 2003; editor, contbr. Refugee Law and Policy, 1989, mem. editl. bd. Jour. Am. Comparative Law, Indian Jour. Internat. Law, Transnational Pubs. O-chmn. Colo. Pub. Broadcasting Fedn., 1977—78; mem. Gov.'s Commn. on Pub. Telecomm., 1980—82. Mem. World Jurist Assn. (v.p. 1991—, pres. 1998-2000, hon. pres. 2000—), World Assn. Law Profs. (pres. 1987-93), UN Assn. (v.p. Colo. divsn. 1973-76, pres. 1986-88, 93-96, nat. coun. UNA-USA 1990—, mem. governing bd. UNA-USA 1995—), World Fedn. UN Assns. (vice-chmn. 1995-2001), Am. Assn. Comparative Study Law (bd. dirs.), Am. Soc. Internat. Law (v.p. 1987-88, exec. coun. 1969-72, 81-84, bd. rev. and devel. 1988-91, hon. v.p. 1995-96, counselor 2000—), Assn. Am. Law Schs., U.S. Inst. Human Rights, Internat. Law Assn. (exec. com. 1986—, hon. pres. 2001—), Colo. Coun. Internat. Orgns. (pres. 1988-90), Assn. U.S. Mems. Internat. Inst. Space Law (bd. dirs., exec. com. 1980-88), Internat. Acad. Comparative Law (assoc.), Order St. Ives (pres.), Rotary, Cactus Club, Univ. Club, Colo. Athletic Club. E-mail: vnanda@mail.law.du.edu.

NANDEDKAR, SANJEEV DATTATRAYA, medical researcher, educator; b. Pune, India, Dec. 28, 1955; s. Dattatraya Yadav and Madhumalti Dattatraya Nandedkar; m. Anjali Sanjeev Dadhe, Dec. 27, 1978; children: Desh Sanjeev, Vishesh Sanjeev. PhD, U. of Va., 1977—83. Med. rsch. asst. prof. Duke U. Med. Ctr., 1986—90; clin. applications mgr. Oxford Instruments Med. Systems, Hawthorne, NY, 1990—. Editor: emg on cd CASA Engring., Hopewell Junction, NY, 1997—. Author (editor): (multi-media text books) EMG on CD: Volumes I - III; author: (researcher) (sci. articles) Engring. and Med. Journals; author: (section editor) (rev. chapters) Textbooks on Clin. Neurophysiology. Recipient Disting. Svc., Am. Assn. of Electrodiagnostic Medicine, 2002, Excellence in Rsch. Writing, Assn. of Academic Physiatrists, 1997. Achievements include development of The Synergy Electromyograph; Multi Motor unit analysis and Median averaging; research in Computer simulations in Electromyography. Office: Oxford Instruments 12 Skyline Dr Hawthorne NY 10532 Personal E-mail: sanjeev@nandedkar.com.

NANGLE, JOHN FRANCIS, federal judge; b. St. Louis, June 8, 1922; s. Sylvester Austin and Thelma (Bank) N.; m. Jane Adams, June 7, 1986; 1 child, John Francis Jr. AA, Harris Tchrs. Coll., 1941; BS, U. Mo., 1943; JD, Washington U., St. Louis, 1948. Bar: Mo. 1948. Pvt. practice law, Clayton, 1948-73; judge U.S. Dist. Ct., 1973—, chief judge, 1983-90, sr. judge, 1990—91, Ga., 1991—. Mem. 8th Cir. Jud. Coun.; mem. exec. com. Jud. Conf. U.S.; chmn. Jud. Panel on Multidist. Litigation, mem. working group on mass torts, mem. jud. resources working group. Mem. Ad Hoc Comm. on Abestos. Mem. Mo. Rep. Com., 1958-73; mem. St. Louis County Rep. Cen. Com., 1958-73, chmn., 1960-61; pres. Mo. Assn. Reps., 1961, Reps. Vets. League, 1960; mem. Rep. Nat. Com., 1972-73; Grand Orator and bd. dirs. Masonic Home Mo. With AUS, 1943-46. First Sgt. USAR. Named Mo. Republican of Year John Marshall Club, 1970, Mo. Republican of Year Mo. Assn. Reps., 1971; recipient Most Disting. Alumnus award Harris-Stowe Coll., Most Disting. Alumnus award Washington U. Sch. Law, 1986. Mem. ABA, Legion of Honor DeMolay, Mo. Bar Assn., St. Louis Bar Assn., St. Louis County Bar Assn. (mem. com.). Office Phone: 912-650-4014.

NANNE, LOUIS VINCENT, professional hockey team executive; b. Sault Ste. Marie, Ont., Can., June 2, 1941; s. Michael and Evelyn N.; m. Francine Yvette Potvin, Aug. 27, 1962; children: Michelle, Michael, Marc, Marty. BS in Mktg., U. Minn., 1963. Mem. Minn. North Stars hockey club, 1967-78, v.p., gen. mgr., 1978-88, pres., 1988-91; sr. v.p. Piper Capital Mgmt., Mpls., 1991-95; exec. v.p. Voyageur Asset Mgmt., Mpls., 1995—. Bd. govs. Nat. Hockey League, 1981-91; mem. internat. com. USA Hockey. Bd. dirs. Mpls. C.C. Found., 1986-90, Children's Home Soc., 1998—. Recipient Lester Patrick award NHL, 1989; named among Top 50 Coll. Players in 50 Yrs.; inducted into U. Minn. Hall of Fame, U.S. Hockey Heritage Hall of Fame award, Sault St. Marie Hall of Fame, U.S. Hockey Hall of Fame, Internat. Ice Hockey Hall of Fame. Mem. Interlachen Country Club (bd. dirs. 1992-95), Spring Hill Golf Club (bd. dirs. 1996-2004). Roman Catholic. Office: Voyageur Asset Mgmt 90 S 7th St Minneapolis MN 55402-3903

NANNEY, DAVID LEDBETTER, geneticist, educator; b. Abingdon, Va., Oct. 10, 1925; s. Thomas Grady and Pearl (Ledbetter) Nanney; m. Jean Kelley, June 15, 1951; children: Douglas Paul, Ruth Elizabeth Beshears. AB, Okla. Bapt. U., 1946; PhD, Ind. U., 1951; Laurea honoris causa (hon.), U. Pisa, Italy, 1994. Asst. prof. zoology U. Mich., Ann Arbor, 1951-56, assoc. prof., 1956-58; prof. U. Ill., Urbana-Champaign, 1959-76, prof. genetics and devel., 1976-86, prof. ecology, ethology and evolution, 1987-91, prof. emeritus, 1991—. NIH sr. postdoctoral fellow Ind. U., 1949—51. Author (with Herbert Stern): (book) The Biology of Cells, 1965, Experimental Ciliatology, 1980. Named Disting. Lectr., Sch. Life Scis., U. Ill., 1981; recipient Disting. Alumnus award, Okla. Bapt. U., 1972, Preisträger, Alexander von Humboldt Stiftung, Germany, 1984. Fellow: AAAS, Am. Acad. Arts and Scis.; mem.: Soc. Protozoologists, Am. Genetic Assn. (pres. 1982), Genetics Soc. Am. Home: 703 W Indiana Ave Urbana IL 61801-4835 Office: U Ill Dept Animal Biology 505 S Gregory St Urbana IL 61801 E-mail: d-nanney@life.uiuc.edu.

NANOS, GEORGE PETER, JR., science administrator, military officer, physicist; b. Torrington, Conn., Apr. 11, 1945; s. George N.; m. Joanne Louise Knowles, July 5, 1969; 1 child, George. Grad., U.S. Naval Acad., 1967; PhD in Physics, Princeton U., 1974; attended, U.S. Naval Destroyer Sch., Newport, R.I., 1974, Def. Sys. Mgmt. Coll., Ft. Belvoir, Va., 1991. Commd. ensign USN; advanced through grades to vice admiral; antisub warfare gunnery officer USS Glennon (DD-840), 1967-69; engr. officer USS Forrest Sherman (DD-931), 1974-76; material officer mem. staff destroyer squadron 10, 1976-78; mgr. tech. devel. high energy laser program office (NAVSEA PMS-405), 1978-82; engring. duty officer, 1980; combat sys. officer Norfolk Naval Shipyard, 1982-84; engr. officer USS America (CV-66); dep. dir. warfare sys. engring. space and naval warfare sys. cmd., 1984-86; head navigation br., 1988-90; head missile br. devel., prodn., operational support missile subsys., 1990-92; dir. tech. divsn. strategic syss. program, 1992-94; dir. strategic sys. program, 1994-98; commr. naval sea sys. command, 1998—2002, retired, 2002; prin. dep. assoc. dir. Threat Reduction Directorate Los Alamos Nat. Lab., N.Mex., 2002—03, interim dir., 2003, dir., 2003—. Decorated Legion of Merit, Meritorious Svc. medal, Navy Achievement medal. Office: Los Alamos Nat Lab PO Box 1663 Los Alamos NM 87545*

NANTO, ROXANNA LYNN, marketing professional, management consultant; b. Hanford, Calif., Dec. 17, 1952; d. Lawson Gene Brooks and Bernice (Page) Jackson; m. Harvey Ken Nanto, Mar. 23, 1970; 1 child, Shea Kiyoshi. AA, Chemeketa Community Coll., 1976; BSBA, Idaho State U., 1978. PBX operator Telephone Answer Bus. Svc., Moses Lake, Wash., 1965-75; edn. coord. MimiCassia Community Edn., Rupert, Idaho, 1976-77; office mgr. Lockwood Corp., Rupert, Idaho, 1977-78; cost acct. Keyes Fibre Co., Wenatchee, Wash., 1978-80; acctg. office mgr. Armstrong & Armstrong, Wenatchee, Wash., 1980-81; office mgr. Cascade Cable Constrn. Inc., East Wenatchee, Wash., 1981-83; interviewer, counselor Wash. Employment Security, Wenatchee, 1983-84; pres. chief exec. officer Regional Health Care Plus, East Wenatchee, 1986-88; dist. career coord. Eastmont Sch. Dist., East Wenatchee, 1984-90; prin. Career Cons., 1988-90; exec. dir. Wenatchee Valley Coll. Found., 1990-91; ednl. cons. Sunbelt Consortium, East Wenatchee, 1991-93; cons. CC Cons. Assocs., 1993—; ptnr. Cmty. Devel. Mktg. and Mgmt. Resource Group, Wenatchee, Wash., 1994—, also bd. dirs.; ptnr. Bus. Consulting and Rsch., Malaga, Wash., 1997-99. Speaker North Cen. Washington Profl. Women, Wenatche, 1987, Wen Career Women's Network, Wenatchee, 1990, Wenatchee Valley Rotary, 1990, Meeting the Challenge of Workforce 2000, Seattle, 1993; cons., speaker Wash. State Sch. Dirs., Seattle, 1987; speaker Wenatchee C. of C., 1989; sec. Constrn. Coun. of North Cen. Washington, Wenatchee, 1981-83; bd. dirs. Gen. Vocat. Adv. Bd., Wenatchee, 1986-88, Washington Family Ind. Program, Olympia, 1989-91; mem. econ. devel. coun. Grant County, 1992—; ptnr. low income housing devel. Bus. Cons. & Rsch., Wenatchee, 1996-99. Mem. at large career Women's Network, 1984—, mem. Econ. Devel. Coun. of No. Cen. Washington; mem. Steering Com. to Retain Judge Small. Recipient Nat. Paragon award, 1991, Wash. State Gov.'s award for achievement in farmworker housing, 2001; grantee Nat. Career Devel. Guidelines Wash. State, 1989; named Wenatchee Valley Coll. Vocat. Contbr. of Yr., 1991. Fellow Dem. Women's Club; mem. Nat. Assn. Career Counselors, Nat. Assn. Pvt. Career Counselors, Nat. Coun. Resource Devel., NCW Estate Planning Coun. Avocations: self improvement books, staff and organizational development, cmty. improvements advocate, housing development for elderly and special needs individuals. Home and Office: 2961 Riviera Blvd Malaga WA 98828-9733

NANTUS, SHERYL, writer; b. Montreal, Quebec, Canada, Apr. 29, 1964; d. Jolan and Arthur John Martin; m. Martin Andrew Nantus, June 23, 2000. Ont. Secondary Sch. Diploma, Streetsville Secondary Sch., 1980—82; media arts writing elective diploma, Sheridan Coll., 1982. Author: (novels) The Dragon Who Was Bored, (book) The Pacific South States of Mexico. Home: 137 East End Rd Brownsville PA 15417 Personal E-mail: xfdragon@zoominternet.net.

NANULA, RICHARD, health products executive; BA in economics, U. Calif., Santa Barbara; MBA, Harvard Bus. Sch. Chmn. and CEO Broadband Sports; pres. and COO Starwood Hotels; various positions Walt Disney Co.; exec. v.p. - fin., strategy and comm. Amgen, 2001—. Office: Amgen Amgen Ctr Thousand Oaks CA 91320

NAN YU, XIAO, dancer; b. Dalian, China; Trained at, Shen Yang Sch. of Dance, Beijing Dance Acad., China, Nat. Ballet Sch. Can., 1995—96. Apprentice ballerina Nat. Ballet Can., Toronto, Canada, 1996—2000, first soloist, 2000—. Office: Walter Carsen Ctr for Nat Ballet Canada 470 Queens Quay West Toronto ON M5V 3K4 Canada

NANZ, ROBERT HAMILTON, petroleum consultant; b. Shelbyville, Ky., Sept. 14, 1923; s. Robert Hamilton and Willie Virginia (O'Brien) N.; m. Norma Lee Peters, Dec. 21, 1944; children— Robert H., Loren P. BA in Geology, Miami U., Oxford, Ohio, 1944; PhD, U. Chgo., 1952. With Shell Oil Co., 1947-83, exploration mgr., 1964-66, exploration mgr. Pacific Coast area Los Angeles, 1966-67, dir. exploration research Houston, 1959-64, v.p. exploration and prodn. research center, 1967-70, v.p. exploration N.Y.C., Houston, 1970-75, v.p. Western exploration and prodn. ops. Houston, 1975-81, v.p. tech., 1982-83. Fellow Geol. Soc. Am.; mem. Am. Petroleum Inst. (past chmn. gen. com. exploration affairs, chmn. public lands task force), Am. Assn. Petroleum Geologists (select com. on OCS). Clubs: Lakeside Country (Houston). Presbyterian. Home: 10102 Briar Dr Houston TX 77042-1209

NAOR, DANIEL, food products executive; b. Paris, July 1, 1960; s. Shlomo and Sarah (Puderbeutel) N.; 1 child, Nathalie. BS in Elec. Engring., MS in Elec. Engring. and Computer Sci., MIT, 1981; MBA, INSEAD, 1990. Cert. engr. Project mgr. ELOP, Rehovot, Israel, 1985-87, mktg. mgr., 1988-89; assoc. McKinsey & Co., Paris, 1990-95, prin., 1995-98, Dallas, 1998—2002; v.p. strategy, planning and bus. devel. Frito Lay N.Am., Plano, Tex., 2002—. Contbr. articles to profl. jours. Mem. bd. dirs. Dallas Theater Ctr. Bd., 1999-2002, Variety, 1997—. Capt. Israeli Air Force, 1981-85. Mem. IEEE, Tau Beta Pi, Sigma Xi (assoc.). Jewish. Avocations: ballroom dancing, cinema, theater, stamp collecting/philately. Office: Frito Lay N Am 7701 Legacy Dr 3A-254 Plano TX 75024 Business E-Mail: Daniel.Naor@FritoLay.com.

NAPADENSKY, HYLA SARANE, engineering consultant; b. Chgo., Nov. 12, 1929; d. Morris and Minnie (Litz) Siegel; m. Arnaldo I. Napadensky; children: Lita, Yafa. BS in Math., MS in Math., U. Chgo. Design analysis engineer Internat. Harvester Co., Chgo., 1952-57; dir. rsch. Ill. Inst. Tech. Rsch. Inst., Chgo., 1957-88; v.p. Napadensky Energetics Inc., Evanston, Ill., 1988-94; engring. cons., Lutsen, Minn., 1994-98. Contbr. numerous articles to profl. jours. Bd. overseers Armour Coll. Engring. Ill. Inst. Tech., 1988-93. Mem. NAE, Sigma Xi. Home and Office: 3284 W Highway 61 Grand Marais MN 55604-7537

NAPIER, CAMERON MAYSON FREEMAN, historic preservationist; b. Shanghai, Dec. 5, 1931; d. Hamner Garland and Cameron Middleton (Brame) Freeman; m. John Hawkins Napier III, Sept. 11, 1964. Student, L'Ecole des Artes Municipale, Paris, 1950-51; BA, U. Ala., 1955. Photographer's asst. Scott, Demott & Perry, Montgomery, Ala., 1951; art dir. WCOV-TV, Montgomery, 1955; self-employed graphic designer Dallas, 1956-64; self-employed designer Alexandria, Va., 1965-71; restoration chmn. White House Assn. Ala., Montgomery, 1973-76, 1st vice regent, 1976-80, regent, 1980—. Co-founder Friends of Stratford Hall for No. Va., Alexandria, late 1960s; docent chmn. Lee's Boyhood Home, Alexandria, late 1960s; bd. dirs. Landmarks Found., Montgomery, 1971-75; advisor Conde Charlotte House, Mobile, Ala., 1994-95. Author, designer booklet: The First White House of the Confederacy, 1978 (nat. printers award 1979). Bd. dirs. English Speaking Union, Montgomery, 1980-83. Named Hon. First Lady, by the Gov.'s wife, Montgomery, Ala., 1985; recipient Awards of Excellence, Advt. Artists Assn., Dallas, 1960, 1961,

1962, disting. svc. award, Ala. Hist. Commn., Montgomery, 1977, Cert. of Commendation, Gov. Ala., 1986, So. Patriot award, 1997, Lifetime Achievement award, Ala. Preservation Alliance, 2001, Jefferson Davis award, 1984, Winnie Davis award, United Daus. of Confederacy, 1985. Mem.: Antiquarian Soc. (pres. 1981—82), Sojourners Lit. Club (pres.), Order of the Crown in Am., Soc. Desc. of Colonial Clergy, Sovereign Mil. Order Temple of Jerusalem (aumoniere 1995, dame comdr. 1996), Nat. Soc. Colonial Dames in Am. (hist. properties com. 1994—95, state bd. mgrs. 1998—2000, ctr. vice chmn. 1998—2000), Am. Soc. Most Venerable Order of the Hosp. St. John of Jerusalem (assoc. officer sister 1995—2002, named Comdr. Sister 2002), Daus. of Barons Runnymede, Militi Templi Scotia (dame 1993), Kappa Delta. Episcopalian. Avocations: jumbles, cryptoquotes, crossword puzzles, afternoon tea. Office: First White House Confed 644 Washington St Montgomery AL 36130-3057 Office Phone: 334-242-1861.

NAPIER, DOUGLAS WILLIAM, lawyer; b. Alexandria, Va., Sept. 11, 1951; s. William Wilson and Leo Elizabeth (Moore) Napier; m. Kathy Gwen Talbert, Aug. 24, 1974; children: Brian Douglas, Adam Scott, Brooke Elizabeth. BS, Va. Poly. Inst. and State U., 1973; JD, Wake Forest U., 1976. Bar: Va. 1976, U.S. Ct. (ea. and we. dist.) Va. 1978, U.S. Ct. Appeals (4th cir.) 1983. Assoc. Ambrogi, Mote & Ritter, Winchester, Va., 1976—77; ptner. Napier & Napier, Front Royal, Va., 1977—98; county atty. Warren County (Va.), Va., 1978—; atty. Chem. Abuse Task Force, 1983—. Author: The Cross, 1982; mem. staff, contbr.: Wake Forest Law Rev. Del. People to People Citizen Amb. Program's Legal Del. to China, 1987; parliamentarian Warren County Rep. Com., 1981; active Rep. Nat. Com.; bd. dirs. United Way, Front Royal, 1978; cons. Coun. Domestic Violence, 1984. Mem.: ABA, Blue Ridge Arts Coun. (bd. dirs. 1992—), Front Royal C. of C. (v.p. 1986—88, pres. 1988—89, bd. dirs.), Nature Conservancy, Va. Trial Lawyers Assn., Va. Bar Assn., Warren County Bar Assn. (v.p., pres.), Warren Workshop (bd. dirs. 1992—), Internat. Platform Assn., Isaac Walton League, Optimist Internat. (sec. 1980—81, Achievement award 1980), Rotary Internat., Front Royal Rotary Club (bd. dirs. 2001—). Baptist. Home: 195 Park Ridge Ct Front Royal VA 22630-5142

NAPIER, JOHN HAWKINS, III, historian; b. Berkeley, Calif., Feb. 6, 1925; s. John Hawkins and Lena Mae (Tate) Napier; m. Harriet Elizabeth McGehee, Aug. 30, 1950 (dec.), m. Z. Cameron Mayson Freeman, Sept. 11, 1964. BA, U. Miss., 1949; MA, Auburn U., 1967; postgrad., Georgetown U., 1971; D (hon.), Napier U., Edinburgh, 2000. Journalist, tchr. Picayune (Miss.) H.S., 1946; commd. 2d lt. U.S. Air Force, 1949, advanced through grades to lt. col., 1966; ret., 1977. Staff dir. Congressional Com. on S.E. Asia, 1970; faculty Air War Coll., 1971-74; Air U. Command historian, 1974-77; asst. to exec. dir. Ala. Commn. on Higher Edn., Montgomery, 1977-78; adj. history faculty Auburn U., Montgomery, 1980-85; columnist Montgomery Advertiser, 1980-87; lectr. in field. Author: Lower Pearl River's Piney Woods: Its Land and People, 1985; The Air Force Officers Guide, 30th edit., 1995, Dr. Patrick Napier: His Ancestors and Some Descendants, 1991; contbr. articles to profl. jours. With USMC, 1943-46, col. Ala. State Defense Force, 1991-97, brig. gen., dep. comdr., 1997-99. Decorated Legion of Merit; Order of St. John of Jerusalem, Milit. and Hospitaller Order of St. Lazarus of Jerusalem, Sovereign Mil. Order of Temple of Jerusalem; recipient award of merit Ala. Hist. Commn., 1976, Ala. Disting. Svc. medal, 1999, merit award English-Speaking Union U.S., 1983; Taylor medal and grad. fellow U. Miss., 1949; Storrs scholar Pomona Coll., 1942-43. Fellow: Soc. Antiquaries Scotland; mem.: S.R. SAR (pres. 1974—75), Sons of Confederate Vets. (vice comdr. Ala. 1979—80), Ala. Hist. Assn. (pres. 1979—80), Royal Order Scotland, English-Speaking Union (pres. 1978—87, nat. dir. 1980—86, 1987—90, 1991—94), Scabbard and Blade, Royal Scots (Edinburgh), Mil. Order Carabao, Soc. Colonial Wars, Soc. War of 1812 (pres. Ala. 1980—82), St. Andrews Soc., Clan Napier in N.Am. (lt. to chief 1985—), Order 1st Families Va., Jamestowne Soc., Soc. Cincinnati, Ala. Assn. (pres. 1998—2001), Aztec 1847, Soc. Pioneers Montgomery (pres. 1979—80), Montgomery Country Club, Masons (32d degree), Pi Sigma Alpha, Phi Alpha Theta, Omicron Delta Kappa, Phi Kappa Phi, Sigma Chi. Democrat. Episcopalian. Home: Kilmahew 158 Mt Zion Rd Ramer AL 36069-6505

NAPIER, WILLIAM JAMES, JR., marine oil and gas construction consultant; b. Dallas, July 19, 1952; s. William James and Frankie (Hanchey) N.; m. Christine Ann Douget, June 18, 1977; children: Jay, Stephanie, George, Catherine. BS in Marine Biology, U. So. Miss., 1974; BS in Civil Engring., La. Tech. U., 1976. Project engr., field engr. inland svcs. divsn. McDermott Internat. Inc., Harvey, La., 1976-80, project coord. New Orleans and Houston, 1982-86, sr. project coord./project coord. worldwide bus. devel. New Orleans, 1986-89; project engr. McDermott Nigeria, Ltd., Warri, 1980-82; mgr. marine sales/dir. marine sales, nat. accounts mgr. Bailey Controls Co., New Orleans, 1989-92; pres. COO Balehi Marine, Inc., Lacombe, La., 1992-94; pres., owner Fairwinds Internat. Inc., Covington, La., 1994—. Elder Lakeview Christian Ctr., New Orleans, 1985-92. Mem. Soc. Naval Architects and Marine Engrs., Franco's Athletic Club. Republican. Baptist. Avocations: weightlifting, racquetball, bicycling. Home: 913 Beau Chene Dr Mandeville LA 70471-1505 Office: Fairwinds Internat Inc 128 Northpark Blvd Covington LA 70433 Office Phone: 985-809-3808. E-mail: bnapier@fairwindsintl.com.

NAPLES, CAESAR JOSEPH, law and public policy educator, lawyer, consultant; b. Buffalo, Sept. 4, 1938; s. Caesar M. and Fannie A. (Occhipinti) N.; children: Jennifer, Caesar; m. Sandra L. Harrison, July 16, 1983. AB, Yale U., 1960; JD, SUNY, 1963. Bar: N.Y. 1963, Fla. 1977, Calif. 1988, U.S. Supreme Ct. 1965. With Moot & Sprague, Buffalo, 1965-69; asst. dir., employee rels. N.Y. Gov. Office, Albany, 1969-71; asst. v. chancellor SUNY, Albany, 1971-75; vice chancellor and gen. counsel Fla. State U. System, 1975-82; vice chancellor Calif. State U. System, 1983-92, vice chancellor emeritus, 1992—, prof. law and fin. emeritus, 1983—; bd. dirs., gen. counsel, corp. sec. Open U., Denver and Wilmington, Del., 1999—2003; gen. counsel Walden U., 1989—2003. Cons. Govt. of Australia, U. Nev. Sys., Assn. Can. Colls. and Univs., Que., also other univs. and colls. Contbr. articles to profl. jours.; co-author: Romanov Succession, 1989 with J. Victor Baldridge. Mem. Metlife Resources Adv. Bd., 1986-2002, chmn., 1992-2002; mem. Meml. Heart Inst. Long Beach Meml. Hosp., 1993—, bd. dirs., chmn. 1998—, found. bd., 1996—; bd. dirs. Calif. Acad. Math. and Scis., 1995—. Capt. U.S. Army, 1963-65. Mem. Acad Pers. Adminstrn. (founder), Nat. Ctr. for Study Collective Bargaining Higher Edn. (bd. dirs.). Avocations: opera, tennis. Fax: 310-798-0065. E-mail: cjnaples@csulb.edu.

NAPLES, RONALD JAMES, manufacturing executive; b. Passaic, N.J., Sept. 10, 1945; s. James V. and Lee A. Naples; m. Suzanne Lorraine Shoudy, June 17, 1967; children: Regen Jeffrey, Marcus Jamison, Tiffany Marie. BS, U.S. Mil. Acad., 1967; MA, Fletcher Sch. Law, 1972; MBA with distinction, Harvard U., 1974. Assoc. in corp. fin. Loeb Rhoades Co., 1973; fellow, spl. asst. to counselor to Pres. The White House, 1974; spl. asst. to adminstr. Fed. Energy Adminstrn., 1975; exec. dir. Presdl. Task Force on Energy, Washington, 1975-76; v.p. internat. Hunt Mfg. Co., Phila., 1976, exec. v.p., 1980-81, vice chmn., pres., CEO, 1981-86, chmn., CEO, 1987-95; also dir.; pres. Hunt Internat. Co., 1977-82; pres., CEO Quaker Chem. Corp., 1995-97, chmn., pres., CEO, 1997—. Bd. dirs. Glatfelter Paper Co.; chmn. Fed. Res. Bank, Phila., U. of Arts. Bd. dirs. Rock Sch. Pa. Ballet, ARC, Fgn. Policy Rsch. Inst., Phila., Phila. Mus. Art, Franklin Inst. With U.S. Army, 1967—71. Decorated Bronze star with oak leaf cluster, Army Commindation medal with oak leaf cluster, Air medal, Cross of Gallantry Vietnam; named Outstanding Young Man Am., U.S. Jaycees, 1977, CEO of Decade Bus. Equipment, Fin. World Mag., 1989; recipient Mil. Order Wars medal, U.S. Mil. Acad., 1967, Phila. Inc. Cmty. Leadership award, 1990, Human Rels. Civic Achievement award, Am. Jewish Coun., 1989, Semper Fidelis award, Marine Corps Scholarship Fedn., 1991, Stephen Girard award, Phila. Fin. Assn., 1992, Touching a Life award, Boys and Girls Club Am., 1994, Torch of Liberty award, Anti-Defamation League, 2002; Walter Heller fellow, Harvard U., 1974, White Ho. fellow, 1974—75. Mem.: Assn. Grad. U.S. Mil. Acad., Chief Execs. Orgn., World Pres.' Orgn., White Ho. Fellows Assn., Harvard Bus. Sch. Alumni Assn., Phila. Country Club, Harvard Bus. Sch. Club Phila., Pyramid Club, Racquet Club. Office: Quaker Chem Corp One Quaker Park 901 Hector St Conshohocken PA 19428

NAPOLES, VERONICA, graphic designer, consultant; b. N.Y.C., July 9, 1951; d. Florencio Andres and Elena (Colomar) N.; 1 child, Samuel Andres. BA, U. Miami, 1972; BArch, U. Calif., Berkeley, 1979. Account supr. Marsh & McLennan, Miami, Fla., 1974-76; designer Mus. of Anthropology, San Francisco, 1977-79; project dir. Landor & Assocs., San Francisco, 1979-81; prin. Communications Planning, Kentfield, Calif., 1981—. Bd. dirs. Mind Fitness, Mill Valley, Calif., Main Arts Coun., Mykytyn Cons. Group; instr. U. Calif.-Berkeley, San Francisco, 1983—, Sonoma State U., Santa Rosa, Calif., 1983-84; tchr. Dynamic Graphics Ednl. Found., San Francisco. Author: Corporate Identity Design, 1987; exhibited at San Francisco Airport, 1992. Bd. dirs. Marin Arts Coun. Recipient Bay Area Hispanic Bus. Achiever award, 1988, Design award PRINT, 1988, Excellence award Am. Corp. Identity, 1989, 90, 91, 92, 93, 94, 95, 96, Excellence award N.Y. Art Dirs. Show, 1989; finalist Sundance Inst., 1991. Mem. Am. Inst. Graphic Arts, Women in Communications. Avocations: painting, writing. Office: Napoles Design 189 Madrone Ave Larkspur CA 94939-2113

NAPOLITANO, GRACE F. congresswoman; b. Brownsville, Tex., Dec. 4, 1936; d. Miguel and Maria Alicia Ledezma Flores; m. Frank Napolitano, 1982; 1 child, Yolando M., Fred Musquiz Jr., Edward M., Michael M., Cynthia M. Student, Cerritos Coll., L.A. Trade Tech, Tec Southwest Coll. Mem. Calif. Assembly, 1993-98, U.S. Congress from 38th Calif. dist., Washington, 1999—; mem. resources com., sml. bus. com. U.S. Ho. Reps.; mem. Ho. Com. on Internat. Relations. Councilwoman City of Norwalk, Calif., 1986-92, mayor, 1989-90; active Cmty. Family Guidance. Mem. Cerritos Coll. Found., Lions Club. Democrat. Roman Catholic. Office: US Ho Reps 1609 Longworth Ho Office Bldg Washington DC 20515-0001 also: PO Box 408 Sacramento CA 95812-0408

NAPOLITANO, JANET ANN, governor; b. N.Y.C., Nov. 29, 1957; d. Leonard Michael and Jane Marie (Winer) Napolitano. BS summa cum laude, U. Santa Clara, Calif., 1979; JD, U. Va., 1983. Bar: Ariz. 1984, U.S. Dist. Ct. Ariz. 1984, U.S. Ct. Appeals (9th cir.) 1984, U.S. Ct. Appeals (10th cir.) 1988, U.S. Ct. Appeals (5th cir.), U.S. Ct. Appeals, U.S. Ct. Appeals (7th cir.), U.S. Ct. Appeals (8th cir.). Law clk. to Hon. Mary Schroeder U.S Ct. Appeals 9th Cir., 1983—84; assoc. Lewis & Roca, Phoenix, 1984—89, ptnr., 1989—93; U.S. atty. Dist. Ariz., Phoenix, 1993—97; atty. Lewis and Roca, Phoenix, 1997—98; atty. gen. State of Ariz., Phoenix, 1999—2002, gov., 2003—. Mem. Atty. Gen.'s Adv. Com., 1983—, chair, 1995—96; chair victims rights subcom. Ariz. Criminal Justice Commn.; chair Ariz. High Intensity Drug Traficking Area; mem. Ariz. Peace Officer Stds. and Tng. Bd., Ariz. Pros. Attys.' Adv. Coun.; past com. to study civil litigation abuse, cost and delay Ariz. Supreme Ct.; past pres. Ariz. Cmty. Legal Svcs. Corp.; past judge pro tem Ariz. Ct. Appeals. Contbr. articles to profl. jours. Chmn. Nucleus, 1989—91; active Phoenix Design Stds. Rev. Com., 1989—91, Ariz. Women's Forum, Charter 100; hon. chmn. Camp Fire Boys and Girls, 1999; 1st vice-chmn. Ariz. Dem. Com., 1990—92; active Dem. Nat. Com., 1990—92; chmn. Ariz. del. Dem. Nat. Conv., 1992, chmn., 2000; active Ariz. Bd. Tech. Registration, 1989—92; bd. dirs. Ariz. Fire Fighters and Emergency Paramedics Meml., Phoenix Children's Hosp., Actors' Lab Ariz., Inc., Ariz. Peace Officers Meml.; bd. regents Santa Clara U., 1992—. Named Ariz. Dem. of Yr., 1989; recipient Leader of Distinction award, Anti-Defamation League, Human Betterment award, Roots and Wings, Golden Apple award, West Valley NOW, Nat. Network To End Domestic Violence award, Woman of Distinction award, Crohns and Colitis Disease Found., Women Making History award, Nat. Mus. Women's History, Tribute to Women award, YWCA; fellow Dillard fellow; scholar, Truman Scholarship Found, 1977. Fellow: Ariz. Bar Found.; mem.: ABA, Raven Soc., Sandra Day O'Connor Inn of Ct. (barrister), Ariz. Women Lawyers Assn., Ariz. State Bar (chmn. civil practice and procedure com. 1991—92), Am. Judicature Soc., Maricopa County Bar Assn. (past long range planning com.), Ariz. Bar Assn. (past com. on minorities in law, past chmn. civil practice and procedure com.), Nat. Assn. Attys. Gen. (exec. com., tobacco bankruptcy working group, health care fraud group, co-chmn. civil rights com., stop underage smoking com., exec. working group on prosecutorial rels.), Am. Law Inst., Alpha Sigma Nu, Phi Beta Kappa. Democrat. Avocations: hiking, walking, travel, reading, film. Office: Office of Gov 1700 W Washington Phoenix AZ 85007

NAPP, GUDRUN F. artist; b. Kiel, Germany, Aug. 14, 1929; arrived in U.S., 1956; d. Walter Alexander and Erika Elisabeth (Burchard) Rode; m. Edmund Carl Napp, Dec. 29, 1951 (dec. Dec. 2001; children: Helenita F., Johann Christian, Anneke J., Florian D. Student, Art Sch., Kiel, 1949, Escuela Artes Plastias, Caracas, Venezuela, 1950, Toronto (Can.) Coll. Art, 1950—51. Assoc. dir. One Ear Soc., 1999—2001. Exhibited in group shows at Miami Beach Conv. Ctr., 1997, Art Expo L.A., 1997, 98, Art Expo N.Y., 1998, Art Expo Fla., 2000, FIA Caracas Internat. Art Fair, 2003; one-woman shows include Art Am., 1997. Recipient cert. of excellence Art Horizon, N.Y.C., 1988, hon. mention Royal Poinciana Fiesta, Miami, 1993, The Fla. Mus. of Hispanic and L.Am. Art, Miami, 1994, Miami Watercolor Soc. exhibit, 1999, One Ear Soc. exhibit. Mem. Nat. Collage Soc., Internat. Soc. Exptl. Artists (signature mem.), Miami Watercolor Soc. (signature mem., pres. 1995-96, trustee 1997, publicity chair 1998-99, 3rd place 1990), Art Expo Fla. Lutheran. Avocation: painting. Home: 1586 Passion Vine Cir Weston FL 33326 Studio: Studio Gallery Napp Inc 1388 Weston Rd Weston FL 33326 E-mail: art1100@aol.com.

NAPPI, JAMES FRANCIS, hand surgeon, educator; b. Ashtabula, Ohio, June 3, 1951; s. Samuel and Caroline Rose Nappi; children: Justin, Veronica, Celia, Samuel. BS cum laude, John Carroll U., 1973; MD, Ohio State U., 1976. Diplomate Am. Bd. Plastic Surgery C.A.Q. Hand Surgery. Instr. surgery Ohio State U., Columbus, 1980-82, asst. prof. surgery, 1983-86, clin. asst. prof. surgery, 1987—; mem. provisional staff Curtis Hand Ctr., Balt., 1982-83; founder Hand and Microsurgery Assocs., Columbus, 1987—; instr. Agee Endoscopic Carpal Tunnel Release Sys., 1993—. Sect. head plastic surgery Grant/Riverside Hosps., Columbus, 1994-98, sect. head hand surgery Grant/Riverside Meth. Hosps., 1999—. Contbr. chpts. to books, articles to profl. jours. Active Animal Rsch. vs. Animal Rights, Ohio State U., 1990—. Recipient Edwin Ellison award Dept. Surgery Ohio State U., 1982. Mem.: Am. Soc. Peripheral Nerve, Assn. Acad. Surgery, Plastic Surgery Rsch. Coun., Am. Soc. Reconstructive Microsurgery (edn. com. 1994—96), Am. Soc. Surgery of the Hand (self assessment exam com. 1991—, vice chair 2000), Sigma Xi. Avocations: golf, sailing, woodworking, children. Office: Hand & Microsurgery Assocs 3400 Olentangy River Rd Columbus OH 43202-1576

NAPPIER, DENISE L. state official; BA, Va. State U., 1973; MA in Cmty. Planning, U. Cin., 1975. Analyst Office Hartford (Conn.) City Mgr.; cons. Conn. Office of Policy and Mgmt.; dir. instnl. rels. U. Conn. Health Ctr.; city treas. City of Hartford, 1989—98; treas. State of Conn., Hartford, 1999—. Exec. dir. Riverfront Recapture, Inc. Office: Office of State Treas 55 Elm St Hartford CT 06106-1746

NAQVI, TASNEEM ZEHRA, cardiologist, researcher, consultant; b. Karachi, Sind, Pakistan, Jan. 19, 1960; came to U.S., 1991; d. Shaiq Hussain and Laila (Rajabali) Zaidi; m. Syed Shujat A. Naqvi, June 30, 1985; children: Ali A., Kazim A. BS, St. Joseph's Coll., Karachi, 1976; MBBS, Dow Med. Coll., Karachi, 1984. Diplomate in internal medicine and cardiovasc. disease Am. Bd. Internal Medicine, Nat. Bd. Echocardiography, Am. Bd. Vascular Tech. House officer internal medicine & gen. surgery Civil Hosp., Karachi, 1984—85; resident med. officer internal medicine Aga Khan U. Hosp., Karachi, 1985—86; registrar, instr. Civil Hosp., Karachi, 1986—87; sr. house officer Lister Hosp., Stevenage, England, 1988—89; registrar Queen Elizabeth U. Hosp., Birmingham, England, 1989—91; asst. clin. instr. in medicine Stony Brook U. Hosp., NY, 1991—93; fellow in clin. cardiology Cedars Sinai Med. Ctr., L.A., Calif., 1993—96, staff cardiologist, 1996—, assoc. dir. cardiac non-invasive lab, 1996—, dir. interventional echocardiography, 2003. Asst. prof. medicine UCLA Sch. Medicine, 1997-2004, assoc. prof. cardiology, 2004-; mem. instl. review bd. Cedars-Sinai Med. Ctr.; spkr. in field. Reviewer Jour. Am. Coll. Cardiology, Am. Jour. Cardiology, Jour. Am. Soc. Echocardiography, Am. Jour. Med. Scis., Archives of Internal Medicine, Echocardiography. Co-recipient Young Investigator award Am. Heart Assn., 1995; recipient Laverna Titus Young Investigators award Am. Heart Assn., 1995; fellow Am. Coll. Cardiology/Merck, 1996-97, L.A.Echo Soc., 1997. Fellow Am. Coll. Cardiology (cardiovasc. imaging com. 2003-, edn. com. 2003-, Merck Rsch. Fellowship award 1996-97, Jr. Faculty award), Am. Soc. Echocardiography (vascular task force, women's health adv. group 2003-), L.A. Soc. Echocardiography (bd. dirs. 1997-, mem. adv. bd.); mem. Royal Coll. Physicians U.K., Am. Heart Assn., Pakistan Med. and Dental Coun. Office: Cedars Sinai Med Ctr 8700 Beverly Blvd Rm 5341 Los Angeles CA 90048 Office Phone: 310-423-6889. Business E-Mail: tasneem.naqvi@cchs.org.

NARAD, JOAN STERN, psychiatrist; b. N.Y.C., June 21, 1943; d. Victor and Grete (Metzger) S.; m. Richard M. Narad; children: Christine, Laurie, Michael. BA, NYU, 1964; MD, Woman's Med. Coll., Pa., 1968. Diplomate Am. Bd. Psychiatry, Am. Bd Child Psychiatry. Intern pediatrics Stanford (Calif.) U. Hosp., 1968-69; resident adult psychiat. Med. Coll., Phila., 1969-71, chief resident in child psychiatry, 1971-73; grad. in psychoanalysis and child psychoanalysis Phila. Psychoanalytic Inst., 1978; practice medicine specializing in child and adolescent psychiatry Westport, Conn., 1973-98; chief Adolescent and Young Adult Svc., Silver Hill Found., New Canaan, Conn., 1980-84, 89-93, sr. adolescent cons., 1993-94; unit chief Riverview Hosp. for Children and Youth, Middletown, Conn., 1994—, assoc. med. dir., 1998—. Cons. Cath. Home Girls, Phila., 1971-78, Germantown Friends Sch., 1973-79; asst. prof. Child Psychiat. Med. Coll. Pa., 1975-79; asst. clin. prof. Yale Child Study Ctr., 1979-92, assoc. clin. prof., 1992—. Fellow NIMH, 1968. Fellow Am. Acad. Child and Adolescent Psychiat., Am. Acad. Pediats.; mem. Am. Psychiat. Assn., AMA, Alumnae Assn. Med. Coll. Pa., Western New Eng. Psychoanalytic Soc., Conn. Coun. Child Psychiatry. Home: 7 N Cove Rd Old Saybrook CT 06475-2538 Office: Riverview Hosp Middletown CT 06457 Office Phone: 860-704-4182.

NARAHASHI, TOSHIO, pharmacology educator; b. Fukuoka, Japan, Jan. 30, 1927; arrived in U.S., 1961; s. Asahachi and Itoko (Yamasaki) Ishii; m. Kyoko Narahashi, Apr. 21, 1956; children: Keiko, Taro. BS, U. Tokyo, 1948, PhD, 1960. Instr. U. Tokyo, 1951-65; research assoc. U. Chgo., 1961, asst. prof., 1962, Duke U., Durham, N.C., 1962-63, 65-67, assoc. prof., 1967-69, prof., 1969-77, head pharmacology div., 1970-73, vice chmn. dept. physiology and pharmacology, 1973-75; prof., chmn. dept. pharmacology Northwestern U. Med. Sch., Chgo., 1977-94; Alfred Newton Richards prof. Med. Sch. Northwestern U., Chgo., Ill., 1983—, John Evans prof. Evanston, Ill., 1986—. Mem. pharmacology study sect. NIH, 1976-80; mem. rsch. rev. com. Chgo. Heart Assn., 1977-82, vice chmn. rsch. coun., 1986-87, chmn., 1988-90; mem. Nat. Environ. Health Scis. Coun., 1982-86; rev. com. Nat. Inst. Environ. Health Scis., 1991-95. Editor: Cellular Pharmacology of Insecticides and Pheromones, 1979, Cellular and Molecular Neurotoxicology, 1984, Insecticide Action: From Molecule to Organism, 1989, Ion Channels, 1988—; specific field editor Jour. Pharmacology and Exptl. Therapeutics, 1972-97; assoc. editor Neurotoxicology, 1994—; contbr. articles to profl. jours. Recipient Javits Neurosci. Investigator award, NIH, 1986. Fellow AAAS; mem. Am. Soc. for Pharmacology and Exptl. Therapeutics (Otto Krayer award 2000), Am. Physiol. Soc., Soc. for Neurosci., Biophys. Soc. (Cole award 1981), Soc. Toxicology (DuBois award 1988, Merit award 1991, 1st Ann. Disting. Investigator Lifetime Achievement award 2001), Agrochem. Divsn. Am. Chem. Soc. (Burdick L. Jackson Internat. award 1989). Home: 175 E Delaware Pl Apt 7911 Chicago IL 60611-7745 Office: Northwestern U Med Sch Dept Mol Pharmaco Biol Chem 303 E Chicago Ave Chicago IL 60611-3008 Office Phone: 312-503-8284. Business E-Mail: narahashi@northwestern.edu.

NARAIN, PREM, agricultural scientist, educator, researcher; b. Lucknow, India, Jan. 3, 1934; s. Govind Narain Verma and Lalli Devi; m. Krishna Srivastava, June 14, 1955; 1 child, Dhirendra Verma. BSc (hons.), Lucknow U., 1953, MSc, 1954; PhD, Edinburgh (Scotland) U., 1969, DSc, 1984. Stats. investigator Ministry of Transport, New Delhi, 1955-58; asst. rsch. officer Indian Vet. Rsch. Inst., Izatnagar, 1958-61; asst. prof. Indian Agrl. Rsch. Stats., New Delhi, 1961-70, from prof. to sr. prof., 1970-78; joint dir. Indian Agrl. Stats. Rsch. Inst., New Delhi, 1978-81, dir., 1981-92; prin. scientist Indian Agrl. Rsch. Inst., New Delhi, 1992-93, dean, joint dir., 1993-94, prof. emeritus, 1994—99. Author: Statistical Genetics, 1990; editor, chair Indian Soc. Agrl. Stats. Jour., 1983, Impact Of P.V. Sukhatme On Agricultural Statistics And Nutrition, 1984. Recipient Rafi Ahmad Kidwai prize Indian Coun. Agrl. Rsch., 1977, Sankhyiki Bhushan award Indian Soc. Agrl. Stats., 1991, O.P. Bhasin Found. award, 1992, Dr. M.S. Randhawa Meml. medal, Nat. Acad. Agrl. Sci., 1999, Nat. award in states. Govt. of INdia, 2003. Fellow Indian Nat. Sci. Acad. (G.P. Chatterji Meml. prize 1987), Indian Acad. Sci.; mem. Nat. Acad. Agrl. Sci. (founding), Internat. Statis. Inst. (mem. coun. 1989-93), Internat. Biometric Soc. (mem. coun. 1988-91). Home: B-3/27 A Lawrence Rd Keshav Puram New Delhi 110035 India E-mail: naraimprem@hotmail.com.

NARANG, DEBORAH LYNN, education educator; b. Columbus, Ohio, Aug. 31, 1961; d. Gerald R. and Alice M. Haas; m. Kamal Narang, Sept. 14, 1985; 1 child, Maya Noelle. BA in Math., Capital U., 1983; MS in Math., Ohio State U., 1987; PhD in Math., U. N.H., 1994. Vis. asst. prof. SUNY, Potsdam, 1994—95, U. of Alaska, Anchorage, 1995—2001, assoc. prof., 2001—. Pres. faculty senate U. Alaska, Anchorage, 2002—. Mem.: Math. Edn. Reform Forum, Assn. Women in Math., Am. Math. Soc., Math. Assn. Am. Avocations: oriental brush painting, water aerobics, birdwatching. Office: U Alaska Anchorage 3211 Providence Dr Anchorage AK 99508 E-mail: afdln@uaa.alaska.edu.

NARANJA, ROGELIO DARUSIN, SR., psychiatrist; b. Manila, Philippines, Feb. 1, 1939; came to U.S., 1964; s. Maximo and Consolacion (Darusin) N.; m. Antonietta Tobias, June 12, 1965 (dec. Jan. 1971); children: Rogelio Jr., Anthony; m. Imelda Tanada, Sept. 15, 1973. AA, U. Santo Tomas, Manila, 1958, MD, 1963. Diplomate in gen. psychiatry, child and adolescent psychiatry, forensic and geriatric psychiatry Am. Bd. Psychiatry and Neurology. Intern Meth. Hosp., Peoria, Ill., 1964-65; resident in gen. psychiatry Medfield State Hosp., Mass., 1965-68; spl. fellow in legal psychiatry Boston U. Medicine Inst., 1967-68; fellow in child psychiatry Kans. City Gen. Hosp. Med. Ctr. U. Mo. Sch. Medicine, 1968-70; med. dir. N.D. State Hosp. Children's Ctr., Jamestown, 1970-77; chief psychiat. svcs., chief med. svcs. USAF, Phoenix, also Minot, N.D., 1977-84; med. dir. forensic unit N.D. State Hosp., Jamestown, 1984-89; med. dir. mental health unit Mercy Hosp., Williston, N.D., 1989-95, N.W. Human Svc. Ctr., Williston, 1989—; pvt. practice. Cons. N.D. State Penitentiary, Bismarck, 1986-89, USAF, Minot AFB, N.D., 1984—, Good Samaritan Nursing Home, Crosby, N.D., 1990—. Col. USAF, 1977-99, ret. Mem. Am. Psychiat. Assn. Roman Catholic. Avocations: gardening, sightseeing, travel, reading, listening to music. Home: 2304 14th Ave W Williston ND 58801-3106 Office: Mercy Med Ctr and NW Human Svc Ctr 1301 15th Ave W Williston ND 58801-3821

NARASIMHAN, PADMA MANDYAM, physician; b. Bangalore, India; came to U.S., 1976; d. Alasingracher Mandyam and Alamela Mandyam Narasimhan; 1 child, Ravi. MD, Maulana Azad Med. Coll., New Delhi, 1970. Diplomate Am. Bd. Internal Medicine. Intern in internal medicine Flushing Hosp., N.Y.C., 1976-77; resident in internal medicine Luth. Med. Ctr., N.Y.C., 1977-79; fellow hematology, oncology Beth-Israel Med. Ctr., N.Y.C., 1979-81; asst. prof. King Drew Med. Ctr., L.A., 1983-87, Harbor UCLA, Torrance, 1987—. Mem. editorial bd. Jour. Internal Medicine, 1986—. Mem. ACP, AAPI, Am. Soc. Clin. Oncology, So. Calif. Acad. Clin. Oncology. Hindu. Avocations: travel, reading, meeting people, music, walking. Home: 6604 Madeline Cove Dr Palos Verdes Peninsula CA 90275-4608 Personal E-mail: padmanarasim@yahoo.com.

NARASIMHAN, PARTHASARATHY, physician; b. Cuddapah, India, June 15, 1935; Grad., Govt. Coll. Kumbakpnam, India, 1952; MD, Madras Med. Coll., India, 1956. Diplomate Am. Bd. Oncology, 1979, Am. Bd. Hematology, 1980, Am. Bd. Internal Medicine, Am. Bd. Medicine. Intern Knickerbocker Hosp., N.Y.C., 1959, resident, 1960, Luth. Med. Ctr., Bklyn., 1961-62; fellow hematology Meth. Hosp., Bklyn., 1969-71; pvt. practice Managed Care-HMO; dir. hematology, oncology, assoc. dir. medicine Northshore U. Hosp., Forest

Hills, N.Y. Clin. asst. prof. Cornell U. Med. Sch. Fellow ACCP, ACP, RCPCan. Office: GLIMG 96-10 Metropolitan Ave Forest Hills NY 11375 Fax: 718-286-3922. E-mail: narasu@aol.com.

NARASIMHAN, RAVI, electrical engineer; b. Newport Beach, Calif., Feb. 5, 1974; BSEE, U. Calif., Berkeley, 1995; PhD, Stanford U., 2000. Sr. engring. design mgr. Marvell Semiconductor, Sunnyvale, Calif., 2000—04; cons. asst. prof. Stanford U., 2003—; asst. prof. U. Calif., Santa Cruz, 2004—. Contbr. articles to profl. jours. (best student paper award IEEE, 1998). Fellow, NSF, 1995—99. Mem.: IEEE, Golden Key Nat. Honor Soc., Phi Beta Kappa, Sigma Xi. Achievements include patents for method and apparatus for handoff in wireless communication systems using pattern recognition.

NARASIMHAN, THIRUPPUDAIMARUDHUR NARAYANAIYER, science educator, research scientist; b. Madras, Tamil Nadu, India, Oct. 6, 1935; arrived in US, 1970; s. Lakshminarayana Iyer and Lakshmi Narayanaiyer; m. Vijayalakshmi Krishnamurthy, Nov. 14, 1962; 1 child, Lakshminarayanan Ravi. BSc with honors, U. Madras, Chennai, 1956; MS, U. Calif., Berkeley, 1971, PhD, 1975. Geol. asst. to geologist Geol. Survey India, Hyderabad, India, 1956—70; from staff scientist to staff sr. scientist Lawrence Berkeley Nat. Lab., 1975—90; from lectr. to prof. in residence U. Calif., 1977—90, prof., 1990—. Authored and edited (numerous tech. and spl. papers). Recipient Oscar Meinzer award, Geol. Soc. Am., 1986. Fellow: Geol. Soc. Am. (Oscar E. Meinzer award 1986), Geol. Soc. India; mem.: Am. Geophys. Union (chmn. soil water com. 1984—86). Hindu. Avocations: philosophy, science. Office: U Calif Berkeley 210 Hearst Mining Bldg Berkeley CA 94720-1760 Home Fax: None. E-mail: tnnarasimhan@lbl.gov.

NARAYAN, RAMESH, astronomy educator; b. Bombay, Sept. 25, 1950; came to U.S., 1983; s. G.N. and Rajalakshmi (Sankaran) Ramachandran; m. G.V. Vani, June 6, 1977. BS in Physics, Madras U., 1971; MS in Physics, Bangalore U., 1973, PhD in Physics, 1979. Rsch. scientist Raman Rsch. Inst., Bangalore, India, 1978-83; postdoctoral fellow Calif. Inst. Tech., 1983-84, sr. rsch. fellow, 1984-85; assoc. prof. astronomy U. Ariz., Tucson, 1985-90, prof., 1990-91; prof. astronomy Harvard U., Cambridge, Mass., 1991—2003, chmn. dept., 1997-2001, Thomas Dudley Cabot prof. natural scis., 2003—. Sr. astronomer Harvard-Smithsonian Ctr. for Astrophysics, 1991—, assoc. dir., 1996-97; adv. bd. Inst. Theoretical Physics U. Calif., Santa Barbara, 1994-98, chmn., 1996-97; com. gravitational physics NRC, 1997-99; chmn. adv. bd. Ctr. for Gravitational Wave Physics, Pa. State U., 2001—; mem. adv. bd. Max Planck Inst. for Astrophysics, 2002—, chmn., 2003—. Contbr. articles to profl. jours. Named NSF Presdl. Young Investigator, 1989, George Darwin lectr. Royal Astron. Soc., 2002. Mem.: AAAS, Internat. Astron. Union (mem. U.S. nat. com. 2000—03), Am. Astron. Soc. (mem. exec. com. High Energy Astrophys. Divsn. 2002—04). Achievements include research in the general area of theoretical astrophysics, specializing in accretion disks, black holes, gravitational lenses, gamma-ray bursts, radio pulsars, image processing and scintillation. Office: Harvard-Smithsonian Ctr Astrophysics 60 Garden St # 51 Cambridge MA 02138-1516

NARAYAN, VADUVUR SRINIVASAN, preventive medicine physician; b. Tanjore, India, Aug. 8, 1944; came to U.S., 1977; BS, U. Bombay, 1963, MB, BS, 1969; diploma in pub. health, U. Liverpool, Eng., 1974; MS, U. Cin., 1979. Diplomate Am. Bd. Preventive Medicine, Am. Bd. Occupl. Medicine. Intern Sir J.J. Group, Bombay, 1968-69; provincial officer medicine Zambia, 1970-76; resident in preventive medicine U. Cin. Med. Ctr., 1977-79; staff physician GE, Cin., 1979-81; asst. corp. dir. medicine Atlantic Richfield Co., Louisville and Phila., 1981-84; med. dir. Monsanto Co., Pensacola, Fla., 1993-95; pvt. practice, 1996—. Cons. in preventive medicine. Address: 6830 Madrid Ave Jacksonville FL 32217-2680

NARAYANAMURTI, VENKATESH, research administrator; b. Bangalore, Karnataka, India, Sept. 9, 1939; came to U.S., 1961; s. Duraiswami and Janaki (Subramaniam) N.; m. Jayalakshmi Krishnayya, Aug. 23, 1961; children: Arjun, Ranjini, Krishna. BSc, MSc, St. Stephen's Coll., Delhi, India, 1958; PhD, Cornell U., 1965. Instr., rsch. assoc. Cornell U., Ithaca, N.Y., 1965-68; mem. tech. staff AT&T Bell Labs., Murray Hill, N.J., 1968-76, dept.head, 1976-81, dir., 1981-87; v.p. rsch. Sandia Nat. Labs., Albuquerque, 1987-92; dean engring. U. Calif., Santa Barbara, 1992-98; dean engring. and applied scis., dean phys. scis. Harvard U., Cambridge, Mass., 1998—. Chmn. condensed matter and materials phys. panel NRC, 1996-99; mem. U. Calif. Pres.' Coun. for Nat. Labs., 1995-98; mem. NAE Pub. Info. Adv. Bd., 1993-94, NSF Dir.'s Strategic Planning Bd., 1994-98; mem. adv. bd. Miller Inst. for Basic Sci., U. Calif. Berkeley, 1999—. Author more than 180 publs.; patentee in field. Fellow IEEE, AAAS, Am. Phys. Soc., Indian Acad. Scis.; mem. NAE, Royal Swedish Acad. Engring. Scis. (fgn.). Avocations: long distance running, squash. Office: Harvard Univ DEAS Pierce Hall 217 29 Oxford St Cambridge MA 02138-2901

NARAYANAN, MOHANRAM, health facility administrator, medical educator; BS, Loyola Coll., 1978; MBBS, Christian Med. Coll., Ludhiana, India, 1982. Diplomate Am. Bd. Internal Medicine, Am. Bd. Nephrology, Am. Bd. Geriatric Medicine. Resident in internal medicine Cook County Hosp., Chgo., 1986-89; clin. fellow nephrology U. Ill. Coll. Medicine, 1989-90, U. Tex. Southwestern Med. Ctr., 1990-91; med. dir. dialysis unit, asst. prof. internal medicine Scott & White Reg Clinics, Temple, Tex. Fellow ACP, Royal Coll. Physicians and Surgeons Can.

NARAYANAN, VADAKE K. management educator, consultant; b. Cohin, Kerala, India, June 20, 1949; arrived in U.S., 1974; s. Thadavillil Madhava Menon and Kalyanikutty Amma; m. Sunanda Rajagopal Narayanan, July 15, 1984; 1 child, Shriram. BTech, Indian Inst. of Tech., Madras, 1971; postgrad. diploma in bus. adminstrn., Indian Inst. of Mgmt., Ahmedabad, India, 1973; PhD, U. Pitts., 1979. Prof. U. Kans., 1978—2000; assoc. prof. Rutgers U., Newark, 1988—90; Stubbs prof. strategy and entrepreneurship Drexel U., Phila., 2000—. Chair strategy process interest group Strategic Mgmt. Soc. Author: Managing Technology, 2000. Office: 9 Bailey Dr Princeton NJ 08540-7956

NARBONI, LILIAN, writer; b. Marroco, Nov. 9, 1957; children: Roi, Reut, Anat, Kineret. Author: Avodat Habirurim-The Vital Connection Between Psychology and Spirituality, 2002. Jewish. Achievements include patents for safe ear clean button and protection with attachment device. E-mail: Liliannarboni@aol.com.

NARDELLI, ROBERT L. consumer home products executive; b. Old Forge, PA, May 17, 1948; m. Sue Nardelli; 4 children. BS in Bus., Western Ill. U., 1971; MBA, U. Louisville, 1975. With GE, 1971-88; exec. v.p., gen. mgr. worldwide parts and components Case Corp., Racine, Wis., 1988-91; pres., CEO Can. Appliance Mfg. Co. subs. GE, Toronto, Ont., Can., 1991-92, GE Transp. Sys., Erie, Pa., 1992-95, GE Power Sys., 1995-2000, The Home Depot, Atlanta, 2000—, chmn., 2002—. Recipient Disting. Pennsylvanian Award, Gannon U., 1995, Disting. Alumni Award, Western Ill. U., 1998, Alumnus of the Year, U. Louisville, 2001. Mem.: bd. directors, The Coca-Cola Co., 2002-, President's Coun. on Service and Civic Participation, 2003. Office: The Home Depot 2455 Paces Ferry Rd Atlanta GA 30339*

NARDI, GLEN, publishing executive; Grad., US Naval Acad.; M in Personnel Mgmt., George Wash. U. Joined Knight Ridder, 1980; production mgr. Miami Herald, 1980—84; with Philadelphia newspapers Knight Ridder, 1984—87; various positions to v.p. ops. The State, Columbia, SC, 1987—2004; sr. v.p. ops., IT and circulation San Jose Mercury News, San Jose, 2004—. Office: San Jose Mercury News 750 Ridder Park Drive San Jose CA 95190*

NARDINI, LUISA, music educator; b. Paolisi, Italy, Apr. 22, 1967; d. Guilio Nardini and Rita Piscitelli; m. Guido Olivieri, Oct. 12, 1996; 1 child, Elena. Diploma in piano performance, Conservatory, Italy, 1991; BA, MA, U. Federico II, Italy, 1995; PhD, U. La Sapienza, Italy, 2001; postdoctral lic. in Med. Studies, Pontifical Inst. of Med. Studies, Toronto, Can., 2004. Tchr. Pub. Schs., Napoli, Italy, 1996—97; vis. scholar U. Calif., 2001—; instr. Ventura (Calif.) Coll., 2002—03; lectr. U. Calif, 2002—03; postdoctoral fellow Pontifical Inst. Medieval Studies, U. Toronto, Canada, 2003—, Halian Acad. for Advanced Studies in Am., Columbia Univ., N.Y., 2004—. Cons. Teatro San Carlo, Napoli, Italy, 1997; contbr. Found. Franceschini, Firenze, Italy, 1998—2001; music cons. U. Calif., 2002. Grant, Assoc. Vice Chancelor for Academic Progress, 2002, Andrew Mellon fellow, 2003—. Mem.: Soc. Italian Musicology, Am. Musicological Soc.

NARDI RIDDLE, CLARINE, legislative staff member; b. Clinton, Ind., Apr. 23, 1949; d. Frank Jr. and Alice (Mattioda) Nardi; children: Carl Nardi, Julia Nardi. AB in Math with honors, Ind. U., 1971, JD, 1974; LHD (hon.), St. Joseph Coll., 1991. Bar: Ind. 1974, U.S. Dist. Ct. (so. dist.) Ind. 1974, Conn. 1979, Fed. Dist. Ct. Conn. 1980, U.S. Supreme Ct. 1980, U.S. Ct. Appeals (2d cir.) 1986, U.S. Ct. Appeals (D.C. cir.) 1994. Staff atty. Ind. Legis. Svc. Agy., Indpls., 1974-78, legal counsel, 1978-79; dep. corp. counsel City of New Haven, 1980-83; counsel to atty. gen. State of Conn., Hartford, 1983-86, dep. atty. gen., 1986-89, acting atty. gen., 1989, atty. gen., 1989-91, judge Superior Ct., 1991-93; assn. exec., sr. v.p., gen. counsel Nat. Multi-Housing Coun., Nat. Apartment Assn., 1995—2003; chief of staff Senator Joseph I. Lieberman, Washington, 2003—. Asst. counsel state majority Conn. Gen. Assembly, Hartford, 1979, legal rsch. asst. to prof. Yale U., New Haven, 1979; legal counsel com. on law revision Indpls. State Bar Assn., 1979; mem. Chief Justice's Task Force on Gender Bias, Hartford, 1988-90; mem. ethics and values com. Ind. Sector, Washington, 1988-90; co-organizer Ind. Continuing Legal Edn. Forum Inst. Legal Drafting Legislature and Pvt. Practice; Internat. Women's Yr. panelist Credit Laws and Their Enforcement; mem. Atty. Gen.'s Blue Ribbon Commn., Chief Justice's Com. Study Publs. Policy Conn. Law. Jour., Law Revision Commn. Adminstrv. Law Study, Chief Justice's Task Force Gender, Justice and Cts., Gov.'s Task Force Fed. Revenue Enhancements; mem. exec. com. Jud. Dept.; mem. panel arbitrators Am. Arbitration Assn., 1994; gen. counsel Nat. Multi Housing Coun.; lectr. in field. Author: (with F.R. Rembusch) Drafting Manual for the Indiana General Assembly, 1976; sr. editor Ind. U. Law Sch. Interdisciplinary Law Jour.; contbr. articles to profl. jours. Bd. visitors Ind. U., Bloomington, 1974-92; mem. Gov.'s Missing Children Com., Hartford, Conn. Child Support Guidelines Com., Gov.'s Task Force on Justice for Abused Children, Hartford, 1988-90; mem. Mayor's City of New Haven Task Force Reorganization Corp. Counsel's Office, Gov.'s Child Support Commn., Mayor of New Haven's Blue Ribbon Commn.; former bd. dirs. New Haven Neighborhood Music Sch.; bd. dirs., mem. youth adv. com. Gov.'s Partnership Prevent Substance Abuse Workforce-Drugs Don't Work. Recipient Women in Leadership Recognition award Hartford Region YWCA, 1986, Award of Merit, Women & Law Sect. Conn. Bar Assn., 1989, Fellowship award South End Ladies Dem. Club, 1989, Woman of Yr. award Greater Hartford Fedn. of Bus. & Profl. Women's Clubs, 1990, Conn. Original award Somers-Mabelle B. Avery Sch., 1990, Cert. of Recognition, Consortium Law-Related Edn., 1990, Citizen award Conn. Task Force Children's Constl. Rights, 1991, Ann. award Hartford Assn. Women Attys., 1993; named Conn. History Maker, U.S. Dept. Labor, Women's Bur. & Permanent Commn. Status Women, 1989, Impact Player, The Conn. Law Tribune, 1992; inductee Ind. U. Sch. Law Alumni Acad. Fellow, 1999. Mem. ABA, Conn. Bar Assn. (chair com. on gender bias, Citation of Merit women and law sect. 1989), Nat. Assn. Attys. Gen. (chair charitable trusts and solicitation 1988-90), New Haven Neighborhood Music Sch. (bd. dirs.), Am. Arbitration Assn. (arbitration panel 1994), Ind. Bar Assn., Conn. Bar Assn. (chair com. gender bias legal profession), Indpls. Bar Assn., Ind. Civil Liberties Union (bd. dirs., mem. exec. com., chair long range planning com., mem. women's rights project, membership v.p., Disting. Svc. award), Conn. Consortium Law and Citizenship Edn., Inc. (bd. dirs.), Conn. Judges Assn. (mem. legislation com.), Ind. U. Law Sch. Alumni Assn. (bd. dirs.), Enomene Hon. Soc., Pleiades Hon. Soc., Mortar Bd. (nat. fellow), Alpha Lambda Delta. Democrat. Presbyterian. Office: Nat Multi Housing Coun 1850 M St NW Ste 450 Washington DC 20036-5803

NARDONE, DENNIS M. protective services official, radio personality; b. New Rochelle, NY, July 17, 1951; s. Anthony and Esther Nardone. Attended, Ft. Lauderdale Coll., 1970, LaGuardia Cmty. Coll., 1971; cert., Inst. Relational Mgmt., 1972. Cmty. svc. officer New Rochelle Police Dept., NY, 1976—81, emergency response tech., 1976; law enforcement official Westchester County Dept. Correction, Valhalla, NY, 1981—; radio personality/DJ Whitney Radio, New Rochelle, 1996—, radio host talk radio show, 1996—, radio host oldies music show, 2002—. Equal employment opportunity counselor, Westchester County, 2000; New Penitentiary Transition Team, Westchester County, 02. Chmn. Westchester County Alliance Against Crime, 1996—, Westchester County Crimestoppers, 1996—; mem. cmty. rels. adv. bd. Dist. Atty. Office on Crime, 1996—; pres. C. of C., Harrison, NY, 1998—, CEO, 1998—; exec. bd. Conservative Party, Harrison, 1995—2001. Named Citizen Yr., Town of Harrison, 1999; recipient Cert. for Post-Incident Trauma, NY State Police, 1985, Cert. award - Stress Behind the Walls, Mediplex Group, Westchester County, 1985, Honor Bar award, Tri-County Fedn. Police, Hawthorne, NY, 1986, Cert. Outstanding Union Leadership, Westchester County Correction Officers Benevolent Assn., 1986, Commendation Key Free Program, Harrison Police Dept., NY, 1994, Disting. Svc. Citation, Harrison Rotary, 1998, Outstanding Work for Veterans, Harrison Veterans Com., 1999, Cmty. Svc. award, Westchester County Clerk, 2001. Mem.: Westchester County Coalition Against Bigotry, United Fedn. Police Officers, Police Columbia Assn. of Westchester County, NY State Fraternal Order of Police, Westchester County Correction Emerald Soc., United Correction Officers Coalition, Environ. Protection Assn., Harrison for the Coun. and Arts, NAACP, Coalition for Mutual Respect, New Rochelle Italian-Am. Club. Achievements include created the Key Free Program for keeping youth from jail by providing lectures and materials; honored by Westchester Irish Com., 2000, Great Hunger Found., 2000, Columbus Day Soc., 2001. Avocations: running, swimming, golf, music. Home: 470 Halstead Ave Harrison NY 10528

NARDONE, WILLIAM ANDREW, lawyer; b. Groton, Conn., June 16, 1954; s. Henry Joseph and Mary Frances (Herley) N.; m. Diane Ruth Hall, July 1, 1988; children: Madison Catherine, William Chase. BA, U. R.I., 1976; JD, Suffolk U., 1980. Bar: R.I. 1981, U.S. Dist. Ct. R.I. 1981, U.S. Supreme Ct. 1991. Assoc. Law Office of M.L. Lewiss, Westerly, R. I., 1980-83; ptnr. Orsinger & Nardone Law Offices, Westerly, 1983—. Solicitor Westerly Sch. Dept., 1984-90, 94-96, 98-2000, 02—. Mem. com. Westerly YMCA, 1980, bd. dirs., 1991—, exec. com., 1994—; bd. dirs., pres. Westerly Adult Day Care Ctr., 1985-93; trustee Westerly Hosp., 1993—, sec., asst. treas., 1999-2001, treas. and v.p., 2002—; trustee SNEPHO, 1994—. Mem. Nat. Coun. Sch. Attys., R.I. Bar Assn. (rep. Ho. of Dels. 1984-90), Nat. Assn. Legal Problems in Edn. Republican. Roman Catholic. Home: 38 Wicklow Rd Westerly RI 02891-3644 Office: Orsinger & Nardone 53 High St Westerly RI 02891-6001

NARDOZZI, PETER MICHAEL, pharmacist, clinical educator, lecturer, entrepreneur; b. Brockton, Mass., Nov. 6, 1937; s. Michael John Nardozzi and Doris M. (MacLea) Worthington; m. Sandra Scott Boyatsis (div. 1975); 1 child, Mark; m. Sandra Scafani, Dec. 31, 1984; 1 child, Cody Abernathy. BS in Pharmacy, Northeastern U., 1960; MS in Nutrition, Hawaii Inst. for Health, Diet and Nutrition, 1982; PharmD, Southeastern Coll. Pharm. Scis., Miami, Fla., 1992. Registered pharmacist, Fla., Maine, Mass.; lic. cons. pharmacist, Fla. Exec. v.p. Nardozzi Rexall Drug and other firms, Fla. and Mass., 1960-77; propr. Bonnie & Clyde's Tavern, Brockton, Mass., 1974—76; treas. Columbian Enterprises Importing/Emeralds, Caribbean Salvage Diving Co., Boston, 1975-77; ptnr., v.p., pharmacist Oceanside Drug, Pompano Beach, Fla., 1965-87; pharmacist mgr. Grand Union Pharmacy Dept., Hialeah, Fla., 1977-78; chief pharmacist Shoppers Drug Mart, Ft. Lauderdale, Fla., 1978-80; pres. Carribean Salvage, Inc., Pompano Beach; dir. pharm. services Bodee Med. Facilities, Pompano Beach, 1981; founder, exec. v.p. Hawaii Diet Plan, Honolulu, 1982-84; founder, pres. Innovative Bus. Devel. Group, Albuquerque, 1984-85; pharmacist, mgr. Cunningham Drug, Singer Island, Fla., 1986-87, Popular Pharmacy, Miami, 1987—89, Pharmor Drug, Miami, 1989—93; pharmacist, clin. educator Rite Aid Corp., Bath, Maine, 1994—. Mem. Rite Aid Adv. Coun. Region 66, 2004; assoc. Achievement Research & Verification Systems, Albuquerque, 1984-85; bd. dirs. Alliance Enterprises, Albuquerque, Zyne Design, Taos, N.Mex.; founder, pres. ITOCAM-Alternative Medicine Cons. Co.; mem. Pharmacy in the Amazon Rainforest, Pharmacy on the Belize Reef, Internat. Expdns.; lectr. continuing edn. alternative complementary therapies. Author weight loss booklet, 1985; editor Nat. Nutrition Newsletter, 1982-84; health columnist; co-patentee nutritional diet supplement. Youth counselor Hawaii Supreme Ct., Honolulu, 1982; lectr. drug abuse Nat. Assn. Retail Druggists. Fellow Am. Soc. Cons. Pharmacists; mem. Am. Pharm. Assn., Am. Mktg. Assn., Nat. Small Bus. Assoc., Maine Pharmacy Assn., Fla. Pharm. Assn., Hawaii Soc. Corp. Planners, Ctr. for Entrpreneurial Mgmt., Soc. Integrative Medicine, Soc. Natural Pharmacy, Venture Founders, Mortar and Pestle Soc. E-mail: docn@gwi.net.

NARENDRA, KUMPATI SUBRAHMANYA, electrical engineer, educator; b. Madras, India, Apr. 14, 1933; came to U.S., 1954, naturalized, 1974; s. Subrahmanya and Sarada (Alladi) Kumpati; m. Barbara Lamb, Nov. 3, 1961. BEE with honors, U. Madras, 1954; MS, Harvard U., 1955, PhD, 1959; MA (hon.), Yale U., 1968; DSc (hon.), Anna U., Madras, 1995. Lectr., postdoctoral asst. Harvard U., Cambridge, Mass., 1959-61, asst. prof., 1961-65; assoc. prof. Yale U., New Haven, 1965-68, prof. elec. engring., 1968—, Harold W. Cheel prof. elec. engring., 2003—, chmn. dept. elec. engring., 1984-87, dir. Neuroengring. and Neurosci. Ctr., 1995-96. Cons. to comml. firms, 1961—; dir. Ctr. for Systems Sci., 1981—; disting. lectr. Tex. A&M Coll., 1997; disting. vis. scientist Jet Propulsion Lab., 1994—95; hon. vis. prof. Anna U., Madras, India, 1993—; mem. adv. bd. Inst. Advanced Engring., Republic of Korea; disting. lectr. U. N.Mex., 1999, U. Va., 2001; plenary spkr. Am. Control Conf., 2000; keynote spkr. Conf. on Intelligent Control, U. Va., 2001, Internat. Conf. of Soc. of Indsl. and Control Engring., Osaka, Japan, 2002; Hamilton lectr. Hamilton Inst., Ireland, 2003. Author: Frequency Domain Criteria for Absolute Stability, 1973, Stable Adaptive Systems, 1989, Learning Automata-An Introduction, 1989; editor: Applications of Adaptive Control, 1980, Adaptive and Learning Systems: Theory and Applications, 1987, Advances in Adaptive Control, 1991; editor issue on learning automata Jour. Cybernetics and Info. Sci., vol. I, 1977. Recipient John R. Ragazzini Edn. award Am. Automatic Control Coun., 1990, Leadership award Neural Network Soc., 1994, Hendrik W. Bode prize/Lectr. award Control Sys. Soc., 1995, Richard E. Bellman Control Heritage award 2003. Fellow AAAS, IEEE (life, Franklin V. Taylor award 1973, George S. Axelby award 1988, Outstanding Paper of neural network coun. 1991), Inst. Elec. Engrs. (U.K.); mem. Conn. Acad. Sci. and Engring., Sigma Xi. Home: 35 Old Mill Rd Woodbridge CT 06525-1523 Office: Yale U Ctr Systems Sci PO Box 2157 New Haven CT 06520-2157 E-mail: kumpati.narendra@yale.edu.

NARIN, STEPHEN B. lawyer; b. Phila., Nov. 23, 1929; s. Bernard E. and Anne (Lipsius) N.; m. Sandra C. Goldberg, Sept. 29, 1963; children: Howard Glen, Brenda Teri. BS, Temple U., 1951, LL.B., 1953; LL.M. in Taxation, NYU, 1960. Bar: Pa. 1954, U.S. Supreme Ct. 1958; CPA, Pa. Dep. atty. gen. Commonwealth of Pa., Harrisburg, 1955-57; instr. acctg. Temple U., Phila., 1954-55; lectr. in law grad. legal studies div. Temple U. Sch. Law, Phila., 1976-85; lectr. Practicing Law Inst., 1967-69; ptnr. Narin & Chait, Phila., 1970-89, Predecessor Ptnrships., Phila., 1955-70; v.p., gen. counsel Travelco Assocs., Phila., 1989-90; of counsel Krekstein, Wolfson & Krekstein, Phila., 1989-92; v.p., gen. counsel Eagle Nat. Bank, 1990-91; counsel Schachtel, Gerstley, Levine & Koplin, Phila., 1993-98; pvt. practice, Ardmore, Pa., 1998—. Mem. Phila. County Bd. Law Examiners, 1961-65. Mem. nat. governing council Am. Jewish Congress, 1963-84, nat. exec. com., 1978-84, pres. Greater Phila. council, 1965-67; mem. Nat. Commn. on Law and Social Action, 1964-84. Mem. Phila. Bar Assn., Phi Alpha Delta. Office: 631 Kenilworth Rd Ardmore PA 19003-2914 Office Phone: 610-645-5772.

NARITA, HIRO, cinematographer; b. Seoul, Republic of Korea, June 26, 1941; arrived in Japan, 1945,arrived in U.S., 1957; s. Masao and Masako (Kojima) Morikawa; m. Barbara Parker, Sept. 8, 1971. BFA in Design, San Francisco Art Inst., 1964. Lectr. Mill Valley Film Festival, 1984, Hawaii Internat. Film Festival, 1984. Dir. photography: (films) Farewell to Manzanar, 1976 (Emmy nomination, 1976); Never Cry Wolf, 1983 (Best Cinematography award Nat. Soc. Film Critics, 1983); Solomon Northrup's Odyssey, 1984; Go Tell It on the Mountain, 1985; Amerika, 1987; Honey, I Shrunk the Kids, 1989; The Rocketeer, 1991; Star Trek VI, 1992; Hocus Pocus, 1993; White Fang II, 1994; James & The Giant Peach, 1995; The Arrival, 1995; Stones & Paper, 1997; Conceiving Ada, 1998; Shadrach, 1998; I'll Be Home for Christmas, 1998; Dirty Pictures, 1999 (Emmy nomination, 2000); Half Past Autumn, 2001 (Emmy nomination, 2001); Technolust, 2002. With U.S. Army, 1964—66. Mem.: Acad. TV Arts and Scis., Acad. Motion Picture Arts and Scis., Am. Soc. Cinematographers, Internat. Photographers Guild. Personal E-mail: bphnarita@earthlink.net.

NARKIEWICZ-LAINE, CHRISTIAN K. GF. museum director, painter, poet; Student, U. de Strasbourg, France, 1970—72, Athens, Greece, 1972—73; grad., Lake Forest (Ill.) Coll., 1975. Arch. critic Chgo. Sun-Times, 1978—81; editor Inland Arch., 1979—81; pub. Met. Press Ltd., 1983; dir., pres. Chgo. Athenaeum, 1988—. Arch. cons.; tchr. arch. history and aesthetics Ill. Inst. Tech. Author: Helmut John, 1984, Landmark Springfield, 1985; author: (anthology of poetry) Distant Fires, 1997; author: Inspiration: Nature and the Poet (The Collected Poems of the Chicago architect, Louis H. Sullivan), 1999, Baltic Hours, 1999, Greenland, 2002. Office: c/o Chicago Athenaeum 190 S Roselle Rd #I Schaumburg IL 60193-1647

NARULA, SUBHASH CHANDER, management science and statistics educator; b. Bannu, India, Jan. 20, 1944; came to U.S., 1968, naturalized; s. Har Dial and Sumitra Devi Narula. B Engring. in Mech. Engring., U. Delhi, India, 1964; MS in Indsl. and Mgmt. Engring., U. Iowa, 1969, PhD in Indsl. and Mgmt. Engring., 1971. Supr. Hindustan Machine Tools Ltd., Pinjore, India, 1965-68; asst. prof. dept. indsl. engring. SUNY, Buffalo, 1971-77; assoc. prof. Rensselaer Poly. Inst. Sch. Mgmt., Troy, N.Y., 1977-83; prof. mgmt. sci. and stats. Va. Commonwealth U., Richmond, 1983—. Chair optimization dept. math. Linkoping (Sweden) Inst. Tech., 1991—93; mem. organizing com. Internat. Symposium on Locational Decision VI, Chios, Greece, 1993; mem. organizing com. founding meeting Mid. East Forum, Chios, 1995; mem. adminstrv. com. Inst. Mid. East Studies Al-Mamun, 1994—; presenter numerous profl. meetings, univs. and confs. including Aarhus (Denmark) U., Asian Inst. Tech., Bangkok, Charles U., Prague, Czech Republic, Swiss Fed. Inst. Tech., Zurich, Helsinki U. Econs., U. Lisbon, Bulgarian and Polish Acad. Scis., Nat. U. Singapore, Tech. U., Sofia, Bulgaria, U. Brasilia, Brazil, Univs. Bergen, Norway, Bielefeld, Germany, Birmingham, England, Bremen, Germany, Hong Kong, Ioannina, Greece, Liverpool, England, Nanjing, China, Seville, Spain, Sao Paulo, Stockholm, Zurich; participant numerous regional, nat. and internat. confs., latest being 16th Internat. Conf. of Internat. Fedn. Ops. Rsch., Edinburgh, Scotland, 2002. Author: (with G. Stangenhaus) Analise de Regessao L, 1988; assoc. editor Jour. Quality Tech., 1989-91, Studies in Locational Analysis, 1992—, Zimbabwe Jour. Sci. and Tech., 1999—; editor Internat. Jour. Math. and Statis. Scis., 1991—; assoc. editor, mem. adv. bd. Mid. East Forum-Jour. Inst. Mid. East Studies, 1995—; contbr. over 125 articles to stats., ops. rsch. and mgmt. sci. jours. and procs., chpts. to books. Scholar, Va. Commonwealth U., 2000. Fellow Am. Statis. Assn. (com. on internat. rels. in stats. 1989-94, vice chmn. 1994; sec.-treas. Buffalo-Niagara chpt. 1974-75, v.p. 1975-76, pres. 1976-77), Am. Soc. for Quality, Royal Statis. Soc.; mem. Constantine Porphyrogenetus Internat. Assn. (chmn. sci. com. 1995—, award 1994), Decision Scis. Inst., Inst. for Ops. Rsch. and Mgmt. Scis., Internat. Soc. on Multiple Criteria Decision Making, Internat. Statis. Inst. (life), Internat. Working Group on Environ., Locational Decision Scis. and Regional Planning (founding), Math. Programming Soc., Sigma Xi, Tau Beta Pi, Beta Gamma Sigma, Omega Rho (regional dir. 1988-98, treas. 1998—2003, sec. 2004-). Office: Va Commonwealth U Sch Bus 1015 Floyd Ave # 844000 Richmond VA 23284-4000

NARVER, JOHN COLIN, business administration educator emeritus; b. Portland, Oreg., Aug. 5, 1935; s. Ursel Colin and Merle (Wells) N.; children: Gregory, Allison Ann, Colin. BS, Oreg. State U., 1957; MBA, U. Calif.-Berkeley, 1960; PhD, 1965. With Boise Cascade Corp., Portland, 1960-61; asst. prof. U. B.C., Can., 1964-66; asst. prof. dept. mktg. and internat. bus. U. Wash., Seattle, 1966-68, assoc. prof., 1968-71, prof., 1971-99, chmn. dept., 1974-78. Vis. prof. Norwegian Sch. Econs., 1973, Bogazici U., Istanbul,

Turkey, 1974, U. Helsinki, 1995; cons. in field. Author: Conglomerate Mergers and Market Competition, 1967, (with R. Savitt) The Marketing Economy: An Analytical Approach, 1971, (with S. Slater) The Effect of a Market Orientation on Business Profitability, 1990., Responsive and Proactive Market Orientation and New Product Sucess, 2004 (with S. Slater and D. MacLachlan). Served to lt. U.S. Army, 1957-59. Mem. Phi Delta Theta. Democrat. Episcopalian. Home: 2015 Federal Ave E Seattle WA 98102-4141

NARWOLD, LEWIS LAMMERS, JR., paper products manufacturer; b. Cleve., Sept. 4, 1921; s. Lewis Lammers and Dorothy Marie (Andrus) N.; m. Marilyn Ebner, Oct. 26, 1944; 1 dau., Christine. BBA, Western Res. U., 1942; MBA, Harvard, 1947. Salesman Hoerner Boxes, Inc., 1950-54, gen. sales mgr., 1954-57, v.p., gen. mgr., 1957-62; v.p. So. div. Hoerner Waldorf Corp., St. Paul, 1962-70; sr. v.p., container div. Hoerner Waldorf Corp., 1970-72; CEO, founder, pres. SouthWest Packaging Inc., Tulsa, 1972—. Dir. UNCA Bankshares, Utica Nat. Bank & Trust, Thermo Chem. Corp., Sooner Box Corp., Hoerner Boxes, Inc., So. Mo. Container Corp.; organizer 1st Bank & Trust Co. of Okla. Chmn. United Fund of Sand Springs, Okla.; pres., trustee Tulsa Charity Horse Show.; Trustee Children's Med. Center of Tulsa, Tulsa Psychiat. Clinic, U. of the Ozarks. Capt. USMC, 1943-45. Decorated Purple Hearts; recipient Presdl. Citation. Mem. Sand Springs C. of C. (dir.), Tulsa C. of C. (dir.), N.A.M., Tulsa Mfg. Club, Mason Club, Summit Club (dir. and organizer), So. Hills Country Club, Union League Club (Chgo.), Coves Golf Club. Home: 7116 S College Ave Tulsa OK 74136-5601 Office: 6106 W 68th St Tulsa OK 74131-2429

NASCA, THOMAS JOSEPH, dean; b. Bklyn., June 1, 1949; m. Jean S. Styslinger; children: Patrick T., Brian J. children: Thomas J, Andrew J. BS, U. of Notre Dame, Ind., 1971; MD, Jefferson Med. Coll., Philla., 1975. Diplomate Am. Bd. Internal Medicine 1978, Am. Bd. Nephrology 1982. Intern Mercy Hosp. of Pitts., 1975—76, resident in internal medicine, 1976—79; fellow in nephrology RI Hosp.-Brown U., Providence, 1979—81; coord. of clin. services, dept. of medicine Mercy Hosp. of Pitts., 1981—85, chmn. and residency program dir., dept. of medicine, 1985—92; vice chmn., dept. of medicine Jefferson Med. Coll., Phila., 1992—97, assoc. dean for edn. and rsch., 1997—2000, acting dean, 2000—01, dean, 2001—; sr. v.p. Thomas Jefferson U., Phila., 2001—; pres. Jefferson U. Physicians, Phila., 2001—. Chmn. Residency Rev. Com. for Internal Medicine, Chgo., 2001—. Contbr. over 40 articles to profl. jours. Named White Plains H.S. Citizen of the Yr., Nat. Exch. Club, 1967; recipient Caduceus Award for Exemplary Leadership, Mercy Hosp. of Pitts., 1986, W.W.G. Mclauchlan Award for Exemplary Contbns. in Edn., 1993, The Christian R. and Mary F. Lindback Award for Disting. Tchg., Jefferson Med. Coll., 1994, Presentation of Portrait to Thomas Jefferson U., Class of 2000, Jefferson Med. Coll., 2000, Sister M. Ferdinand Clark Outstanding Alumnus Achievement Award, Mercy Hosp. of Pitts., 2001. Fellow: ACP, Coll. of Physicians of Phila.; mem.: Myasthena Gravis Assn. Western Pa. (bd. dirs. 1990—92), Assn. of Program Dirs. in Internal Medicine (mem. coun. 1990—2001, sec.-treas. 1995—99, pres. 2000—01), Chester Valley Golf Club, Pyramid Club, Alpha Omega Alpha. Avocations: golf, photography, basketball, marine aquarist, rugby. Office: Jefferson Med Coll 1025 Walnut St Philadelphia PA 19107 E mail: thomas.nasca@jefferson.edu.*

NASCHAK, BRUCE STEPHEN, education educator, consultant; b. San Diego, Calif., Sept. 5, 1951; s. John and Katherine Naschak; m. Mary Alice Ashley Wysong, Apr. 13, 1974 (div. May 1979); 1 child, Anya; 1 child, Tiffany. AA, Grossmont Coll., 1971; BA with highest honors and distinction in English, San Diego State U., 1975, MA, 1978. Adj. prof. Grossmont Coll., El Cajun, Calif., 1979—88, San Diego Cmty. Coll., 1980—88; prof. San Diego Mesa Coll., 1988—. Bus. adv. Shukra Corp., San Diego, 2003. Author: (novels) Lal: The Beloved, 1999, (poetry) The Mirror and the Flame, 1979, The Circle of Love, 1979, Celebration of Life, 1980, The Unicorn and Other Realities, 1980. Pres. Student Internat. Meditation Soc., San Diego, 1972—78. Mem.: San Diego Transcendental Meditaiton Ctr., Phi Beta Kappa. Avocation: mythology. Office: San Diego Mesa Coll 7250 Mesa College Dr San Diego CA 92111 Office Phone: 619-388-2309.

NASGAARD, ROALD, museum curator; b. Denmark, Oct. 14, 1941; s. Jens Larsen and Petra (Guldbaek) N. BA, U. B.C., 1965, MA, 1967; PhD, Inst. Fine Arts, N.Y. U., 1973. Lectr., asst. prof. U. Guelph, 1971-75; curator contemporary art Art Gallery of Ont., Toronto, 1975-78, chief curator, 1978-89, deputy dir., chief curator, 1989-93, sr. curator rsch., 1993; chair dept. art Fla. State U., Tallahassee, 1995—; co-dir. programming Inst. of Modern and Contemporary Art, Calgary, Alta., Can. Vis. lectr. U. Guelph, York U.; vis. lectr., adj. prof. U. Toronto; rsch. fellow Nat. Gallery Phila. Libr. and Archives (summer), 2002. Author, curator: Ron Martin: World Paintings, 1976, Structures for Behavior, 1977, Garry Neill Kennedy: Recent Work, 1978, Ten Canadian Artists in the 1970's, 1980, Yves Gaucher: A Fifteen Year Perspective, 1978, The Mystic North: Symbolist Landscape Painting in Northern Europe and North America, 1890-1940, 1984, Gerhard Richter: Paintings, 1988, Individualites: 14 Contemporary Artists from France, 1991, Free Worlds: Metaphors and Realities in Contemporary Hungarian Art, 1991, Concealing/Revealing: Voices from the Canadian Foothills, 1997, Pleasures of Sight and States of Being: Radical Abstract Painting, 2001, co-organizer: The European Iceberg: Creativity in Germany and Italy Today, 1985. Mem. Toronto Pub. Art Commn., Gershon Iskowitz Found. Can. Council fellow, 1967-68, 70-71 Mem. Coll. Art Assn., Univ. Art Assn. Can., Internat. Art Critics Assn. Office Phone: 850-644-8254. E-mail: rnasgaar@mailer.fsu.edu.

NASH, ALICIA, computer programmer, physicist; b. San Salvador, Jan. 1, 1933; came to U.S., 1944; d. Carlos Roberto and Alicia (Lopez-Harrison) Larde; m. John Forbes Nash, Jr., Feb. 16, 1957; children: John Charles Martin. BS in Physics, MIT, 1955, postgrad., 1959. Physicist Nuclear Devel. Corp. of Am., White Plains, N.Y., 1956-57, Tech. Ops., Burlington, Mass., 1957-58; rsch. assoc. MIT Computation Ctr., Cambridge, Mass., 1958-59; physicist, aerospace engr. R.C.A. Astro Divsn., Hightstown, N.J., 1960-66; programmer, analyst Mgmt. Data Processing, N.Y.C., 1972-74, Con Edison, N.Y.C., 1974-80, Blue Cross Blue Shield of N.Y., N.Y.C., 1980-82; systems/analyst programmer specialist N.J. Transit, Newark, 1983—. Mem. AAUW, MIT Club of Princeton (past pres., bd. dirs.), Soc. of Women Engring. Home: 932 Alexander Rd Princeton Junction NJ 08550-1002 Office: NJ Transit One Penn Plaza East Newark NJ 07105

NASH, CAROL, minister, director; d. Willie Hiram and Juanita Johnson Nash. MA in Religion, Iliff Sch. of Theology, Denver, 1987. Sr. pastor Bethel Apostolic Temple, Miami, Fla., 2000—; dir. new student ctr. Miami Dade Coll., Fla., 2001—03. Author: (book) From Chaos to Clarity: Calling Your Life to Order, 2004. Mem. Potters Ho. Internat. Pastoral Alliance, Dallas, 2002—03; chaplain Delta Sigma Theta Sorority, Miami Alumnae Chpt., Fla., 1999—2003. Recipient Disting. Educator award, Delta Sigma Theta Sorority, 2000. Mem.: Fla. Assn. of C.C. (assoc.; chair membership com. 1998—2001, Disting. Svc. award 1999). Democrat. Pentecostal. Office: Bethel Apostolic Temple 1855 NW 119th St Miami FL 33167 Office Phone: 305-688-8830. Business E-Mail: pastornash@bethelapostolictemple.org.

NASH, CHARLES D. investment banker; b. Atlanta, Feb. 8, 1943; s. Floyd Johnson and Ida Lee (Camp) N.; m. Augusta Horsey; 1 child, Paren J. BBA in Fin., Ga. State U., 1968. V.p. Courts & Co., Atlanta, 1961-70, The Dornbush Co., Atlanta, 1970-76; pres., chief exec. officer So. Turf Nurseries, Inc., Tifton, Ga., 1976-83, Neville & Gladstone, Inc., Atlanta, 1984-86; sr. v.p. Wheat First Securities, Atlanta, 1987-91, Interstate/Johnson Lane, Atlanta, 1991-97; investment banker Nash Equity Capital, Atlanta, 1997—. Mem. Ansley Golf club. Republican. Episcopalian. Avocations: tennis, boating, travel, golf.

NASH, CHARLES PRESLEY, chemistry professor; b. Sacramento, Calif., Mar. 15, 1932; s. Clarence and Mildred Vida (Johnson) N.; m. Lois Olive Brown, May 29, 1955 (dec. May 1999); children: Nancy Caroline, Sandra Lee, James Roy, m. D.Clinton Congdon, June 3, 2002. BS, U. Calif., Berkeley, 1952; PhD, UCLA, 1958. Instr. chemistry UCLA, 1956-57; from instr. to assoc. prof. U. Calif., Davis, 1957-70, prof., 1970-93, prof. emeritus, 1993—, chmn. acad. senate, 1987-90, chmn. faculty assn., 1993-97; v.p. external rels. Coun. U. Calif. Faculty Assns., 1997—. Vis. sr. lectr. Imperial Coll., London, 1968-69; disting. vis. prof. USAF Acad., Colorado Springs, 1979-80. Contbr. articles to profl. jours. Bd. pres. Explorit Sci. Ctr., 1995-97. Recipient Disting. Teaching award U. Calif. Davis, 1978; named Disting. Alumnus of Yr. Sacramento City Coll., 2000. Mem. Sigma Xi, Phi Lambda Upsilon. Office: U Calif at Davis Dept Chemistry Davis CA 95616

NASH, CYNTHIA JEANNE, journalist; b. Detroit, Dec. 24, 1947; d. Frederick Copp and Carolyn (Coffin) N.; 1 child, Lydia Anne Maza; m. Richard Zahler, July 22, 1994. BA, U. Mich., 1969. Reporter Detroit News, 1970-75, sports columnist, 1975-77, Life Style columnist, Life Style editor, 1979-82; news features editor Seattle Times, 1983; asst. mng. editor Sunday Seattle Times, 1983-86, assoc. mng. editor, 1986-97, dir. content devel., 1986-2000, dir., brand and content devel., 2000—. Mem. Harbor Sq. Club. Office: Seattle Times PO Box 70 Fairview Ave N & John St Seattle WA 98111-0070 E-mail: cnash@seattletimes.com.

NASH, DAVID BRET, physician; b. N.Y.C., Nov. 15, 1955; s. Albert J. and Charlotte Nash; m. Esther Jean Nash; children: Rachel and Leah (twins), Jacob. BA, Vassar Coll., 1977; MD, U. Rochester, 1981; MBA, U. Pa., 1986. Internship The Graduate Hosp., U. Pa., 1981-82, residency, 1982-84; med. dir. Health Evaluation Ctr., Hosp. U. Pa., Phila., 1988-90; dir. health policy and clin. outcomes Thomas Jefferson U. Hosp., Phila., 1990—; assoc. dean Jefferson Med. Coll., Phila., 1996—. Editor: Future Practice Alternatives, 1987, Providing Quality Care, 1989. Fellow ACP; mem. Phi Beta Kappa. Office: Thomas Jefferson U 115 Curtis Bldg 1015 Walnut St Philadelphia PA 19107-5005

NASH, DONALD GENE, commodity investigator; b. Paris, Ill., July 20, 1945; s. Lelan and Mildred (Washburn) N.; m. Jo Ann Bellew, Aug. 29, 1964; children— Stacey Alan, Ryan Christopher, Shaun Christian BS, So. Ill. U., 1967, MS, 1969; postgrad., DePaul U., 1970-71. Farm mgr., test farms So. Ill. U., Carbondale, 1968-69; economist Commodity Futures Trading Commn., Chgo., 1969-77; v.p.-ops. Mid. Am. Commodity Exch., Chgo., 1977-86; sr. investigator divsn. enforcement Commodity Futures Trading Commn., Chgo., 1986—. Bd. trustees Friends of Danada, Wheaton, Ill., 2001—. With N.G. U.S. Army, 1968—71. Recipient Outstanding Mktg. award Wall St. Jour., 1966, award of merit Am. Farm Econ. Assn., 1967, cert. of merit Commodity Exch. Authority, merit award Naperville Art League, 1994, Honorable Mention award Danada Nature Show, 1995, 2002. Methodist. Avocations: photography, woodworking, sketching. Home: 923 Bainbridge Dr Naperville IL 60563-2002 Office: Commodity Futures Trading Commn 525 W Monroe St Ste 1100 Chicago IL 60661 Business E-Mail: dnash@cftc.gov.

NASH, EDWARD L. advertising agency executive; b. N.Y.C., Nov. 8, 1936; s. Irving and Mina (Koppel) N.; m. Diana R. Kithcart, June 2, 1968; 1 child, Amelia. BA, CCNY, 1953. Dir. advt. Crowell, Collier, Macmillan, Inc., N.Y.C., 1961-62; v.p. mktg. LaSalle Extension U., Chgo., 1962-64; pres. Capitol Record Club, Inc., Los Angeles, 1964-69; founder, pres. Nash Pub., Los Angeles, 1969-74; exec. v.p. Rapp & Collins, N.Y.C., 1975-82; pres., chief exec. officer BBDO Direct, N.Y.C., 1982-86; owner, pres. Nash Direct Inc., N.Y.C., 1986-91; chmn. Nash, Wakeman & de Forrest, Inc., 1991-92; exec. v.p. Bozell, Jacobs, Kenyon & Eckhardt, N.Y.C., 1992-95; CEO, mng. ptnr. Team Nash, Inc., N.Y.C., 1996—. Lectr. in field; chmn. Direct Mktg. Day, N.Y.C., 1985, Internat. Direct Mktg. Conf., 1996; instr. NYU, 1998—, Va. Commonwealth U., 1998—. Author: Direct Marketing: Strategy/Planning/Execution, 1982, 2d edit., 1986, 3d edit., 1995, 4th edit., 2000; editor: The Direct Marketing Handbook, 1984, 2d edit., 1991, Database Marketing, 1993. Mem. Direct Mktg. Assn. (chmn. mktg. coun. 1980-82, Silver Apple award 1999). Office: Team Nash Inc 245 E 58th St #21E New York NY 10022-1356 Office Phone: 646-497-0297.

NASH, GORDON BERNARD, JR., lawyer; b. Evergreen, Ill., Feb. 24, 1944; s. Gordon Bernard and Lilyan (Grafft) N.; m. Roseanne Joan Burke, Aug. 24, 1968; children: Caroline, Brian, Terry, Maureen. BA, Notre Dame U., 1966; JD, Loyola U., Chgo., 1969. Bar: Ill., U.S. Dist. Ct. (no. dist.) Ill. Atty. Office U.S. Atty. No. Dist. Ill., Chgo., 1971-78; prin. Gardner Carton & Douglas, LLC, Chgo., 1978—. Chmn. Ill. Bd. Ethics, Springfield, 1980-85. Served to capt. U.S. Army, 1969-71. Recipient John Marshall award U.S. Dept. Justice, 1978, Spl. Commendation award, 1975, Disting. Achievement award Internat. Acad. Trial Lawyers, 1969. Mem. ABA, Ill. Bar Assn., Chgo. Bar Found. Local Chpt. (bd. dirs. 1983-85, 87-89), Fed. Bar Assn. (bd. govs. 1986-91), Chgo. Bar Assn. (bd. mgrs. 1983-85, pres. 1990-91), Constl. Rights Found. Com. (bd. dirs. 1993—, chmn., 1998-2001), Am. Coll. Trial Lawyers, Ctr. for Conflict Resolution (bd. 1992-2000, v.p. 1995-2000), Chgo. Inn of Ct. (pres. 1996-97), Olympia Fields Country Club. Democrat. Roman Catholic. Home: 5101 Harvey Ave Western Springs IL 60558-2042 Office: Gardner Carton & Douglas LLC 191 N Wacker Dr Ste 3700 Chicago IL 60606-1698 E-mail: gnash@gcd.com.

NASH, GRAHAM WILLIAM, singer, composer; b. Blackpool, Lancashire, Eng., 1942; Mem.: Brit. group The Hollies, 1963-68; joined David Crosby and Stephen Stills to form group Brit. group, Crosby, Stills & Nash, 1969, then with Neil Young, to 1971, now soloist and duo (with David Crosby), then regrouped (with Stephen Stills), 1977; (with Hollies) albums include Bus Stop, 1966, Stop, Stop, Stop, 1967, Hollies' Greatest Hits, 1967, Evolution, 1967, Dear Eloise/King Midas in Reverse, 1967, (with Crosby and Stills) Crosby, Stills & Nash, 1969, CSN, 1977, (with Crosby, Stills and Young) Deja Vu, 1970, 4 Way Street, 1971, (with Crosby) Graham Nash and David Crosby, 1972, Wind on the Water, 1975, Whistling Down the Wire, 1976, Crosby/Nash Live, 1977, American Dream, 1988, The Best Vol. 1, 1988, Vol. 2, 1988, Epic Anthology, 1990, All Time Greatest Hits, 1990, Magic Touch, 1992, 30th Anniversary Collection, 1993, After The Storm, 1994, Crosby, Stills & Nash, 1994, Best of the Hollies, 1995, Archive Alive!, 1997, Looking Forward, 1999; solo albums Songs for Beginners, 1971, Wild Tales, 1974, Earth & Sky, Innocent Eyes, 1986; appeared in film Woodstock, 1970, Journey Throught the Past, 1972, No Nukes, 1980, (video) Deja View, 1986, The Return of Bruno, 1988, Flashing on the Sixties: A Tribal Document, 1990, (video) Crosby, Stills & Nash: Long Time Comin', 1990, The History of Rock 'N' Roll, Vol. 3, 1995, Elvis Meets Nixon, 1997; host (TV documentary) Rock 'n' Roll Revolution: The British Invade America, 1995. Recipient Grammy award (with Crosby and Stills) for Best New Artist of Year, 1969; inducted into Rock and Roll Hall of Fame, 1997. Office: Atlantic Records 1290 Avenue Of The Americas New York NY 10104-0184

NASH, HENRY WARREN, marketing educator; b. Tampa, Fla., Sept. 19, 1927; s. Leslie Dikeman and Mildred (Johnson) N.; m. Frances Lora Venters, Aug. 20, 1950; children: Warren Leslie, Richard Dale. BS in Bus. Adminstrn, U. Fla., 1950, MBA, 1951; postgrad., Ind. U., 1951-53; PhD, U. Ala., 1965. Student asst. U. Fla., 1948-50, grad. asst., 1950-51, Ind. U., 1951-53; salesman Field Enterprises, Inc., Chgo., 1953; assoc. prof. bus. and econs. Miss. Coll., 1953-57; assoc. prof. marketing Miss. State U., 1957-66, prof., head dept., 1966-96; emeritus prof. mktg.; emeritus head dept. mktg., quantitative analysis, bus. law; dir. Coll. Bus. and Industry Acad. Advising Ctr., 1995-2000; ptnr. Southland Cons. Assos., 1968-84; bd. dirs. Govt. Employees Credit Union, 1969-92, v.p., 1969-73, pres., 1973-78. Author: (with others) Principles of Marketing, 1961. Served with USNR, 1945-46. Loveman's Merchandising fellow U. Ala., 1961-62 Mem. Am. Mktg. Assn., Am. Acad. Advt., Acad. Internat. Bus., So. Econ. Assn., So. Mktg. Assn. (sec. 1974-75, pres. 1976-77), Sales and Mktg. Execs. (internat. chmn. educators com. 1967-70), Miss. Retail Mchts. Assn. (bd. dirs.), Pi Sigma Epsilon (Nat. educator, v.p. 1967-69, nat. pres. 1967-71), Kiwanis (treas. Starkville club 1969-70, v.p. 1973-74, pres. 1974-75, lt. gov. 1977-78, gov. 1982-83), Blue Key, Beta Gamma Sigma, Omicron Delta Kappa, Mu Kappa Tau (nat. v.p. 1977-79, 86-88, pres. 1979-81, 88-90), Alpha Kappa Psi, Phi Kappa Phi (v.p. Miss. State U. 1990-91, pres. 1991-92). Baptist (tchr., deacon). Home: 2800 W Main St Cottage 302B Tupelo MS 38801-3027

NASH, HOWARD ALLEN, geneticist, researcher; b. N.Y.C., Nov. 5, 1937; s. Harvey and Harriet (Ratner) N.; m. Dominie Maria Shortino, Aug. 31, 1963; children: Janet Elisabeth, Emily Julia. BS, Tufts U., 1957; MD, U. Chgo., 1961, PhD, 1963. Intern U. Chgo. Clinics, 1963-64; rsch. assoc. NIMH, Bethesda, Md., 1964-68, med. officer (res), 1968-84, chief, sec. molecular genetics, 1984—. Chmn. Gordon Conf. on Nucleic Acids, 1988; vice-chair FASEB Conf. on Genetic Recombination, 1993, chair, 1995. Assoc. editor Cell Jour., 1985-91; editl. bd. Current Biology Jour., 1993—, Genes to Cells, 1996—, Jour. Neurogenetics, 1998—. Lt. comdr. USPHS, 1964-68. Recipient Superior Svc. award USPHS, 1985, Disting. Svc. award HHS, 1990, Alumni award for Disting. Svc., U. Chgo., 1994. Fellow Am. Acad. Arts and Sci.; mem. NAS. Office: Lab Molecular Biology NIMH 36 Convent Dr Bethesda MD 20892-0001 Office Phone: 301-402-1041. Business E-Mail: howardnash@mail.nih.gov.

NASH, JAMES LEE, poet, security official; b. Lynchburg, Va., Oct. 1, 1957; s. James Belvy and Marjorie Lea Gilden (Campbell) N. Grad., Brookville H.S., Lynchburg, 1977. VIP transp.-info. aide de camp Greater Ft. Lauderdale Broward County Conv. Ctr.; with Brookville H.S., Lynchburg, 1977. Author: (poetry) Casus Belli, 1993, Enduring Significance, 1996; contbg. author: T.P.O.A., 1994, Treasure the Moment, 1996, A Shadow in the Light, 1999, Love and Other Observations, 1999, Melodies and Madness, 1999, Explanations, 2000, Other Planets are Places Too, 2000, The Erotic Adventures of a White Trash Southern Boy, 2002, Faces and Places on Capitol Hill, 2004. Mem. at large Dem. Exec. Com., Broward County, Fla., 1997-2000; mem. Croissant Park Civic Assn., Ft. Lauderdale, Fla., 1997-2000. Mem. Titanic Hist. Soc., Soc. Am. Magicians. Avocations: playing piano, juggling. Home: 1114 F St NE # 108 Washington DC 20002 Office: Trover 221 Pennsylvania Ave SE Washington DC 20003 E-mail: jlnashpoet@aol.com.

NASH, JAN R. OLIVE, historian, consultant; b. Virginia, Minn., Apr. 3, 1951; d. Gail Maxine Nelson and Robert Eugene Olive, Robert Joseph Thornton (Stepfather); m. Jerome Frederick Full, June 22, 2002; m. John Alexander Nash, Dec. 22, 1980 (div.); m. Alan Lee Thomae, Dec. 27, 1969 (div.); 1 child, Eric Joseph Thomae. Bachelors, U. of Iowa, 1976, JD, 1979, MA, 1989; ABD for PhD in progress, Loyola U. of Chgo., 1997—2003. Cert.: Supreme Ct. of Iowa (Admission) 1979. Corp. legal counsel Life Investors Inc./AEGON, Cedar Rapids, Iowa, 1979—86; archtl. history cons. Iowa City, 1989—93; mng. mem. Tallgrass Historians L.C., Iowa City, 1993—. Participant Victorian Soc. in Am., London, 1988; founding bd. mem., exec. dir. Iowa Hist. Preservation Alliance, Iowa City, 1990—92; participant Preservation Leadership Tng. Workshop, Ft. Wayne, Ind., 1991; co-dir. Ft. Atkinson Area Cultural Resources Field Sch., Ft. Atkinson, Iowa, 2001. Author: (essay) Dictionary of Am. History, 75 cultural resource reports and papers. Mem. Iowa Heritage Tourism Adv. Com. - Iowa Dept. of Econ. Devel., Des Moines, 1995—96; historian advisor Englert Civic Theatre Inc., Iowa City, 2000—02; commn. mem. Johnson County Hist. Preservation Commn., Iowa City, 1996; preservation advisor Old Brick Episcopal Luth. Corp., Iowa City, 1999—2003; historian advisor Iowa State Preserves Bd. - Iowa Dept. of Natural Resources, Des Moines, 1996—2000. Recipient Margaret Nowysz Preservation Person of the Yr. award, City of Iowa City - Hist. Preservation Commn., 1994; scholar Merit award Tuition Scholarship, Loyola U. of Chgo., 1997—98. Mem.: Soc. for Comml. Archeology, Orgn. of Am. Historians, Nat. Trust for Hist. Preservation-Preservation Forum, Nat. Coun. on Pub. History, Iowa State Bar Assn., Iowa Hist. Preservation Alliance (bd. mem. 1990—92), Phi Alpha Theta. Democrat. Avocation: gardening. Office: Tallgrass Historians LC 2460 S Riverside Dr Iowa City IA 52246 E-mail: jolivenash@aol.com.

NASH, JOHN DAVIDSON, JR., economist; b. Houston, Apr. 12, 1953; s. John Davidson and Virginia (Bryant) N.; m. Sarah Hendrickson, June 26, 1982; children: Scott, Rachel. BS, Tex. A&M U., 1975; MA, U. Chgo., 1978, PhD, 1982. Asst. prof. econs. Tex. A&M U., College Station, 1980-83; economist Bur. Econs., FTC, Washington, 1982-83, dep. asst. dir. consumer protection, 1983-84, asst. dir. trade regulation rules, 1984-86, advisor to chmn., 1986; agrl. sector economist Latin Am. and Caribbean Agrl. Projects divsn. The World Bank, Washington, 1986—, economist trade policy divsn., 1987-96; prin. economist/lead economist Environmentally and Socially Sustainable Devel. Dept. of Europe and Ctrl. Asia, 1996-2001, advisor for commodities and trade, 2001—. Author: (with others) Strategic Minerals for Defense Needs, 1979, Colombia: External Sector and Agriculture Policies for Adjustment and Growth, 1985, Best Practices in Trade Policy Reform, 1991, Trade Policy and Exchange Rate Reform in Sub-Saharan Africa, 1997, Trade Policy Reform: Lessons and Implications, 1998, Food and Agricultural Policy in Russia: Progress to Date and The Road Forward, 2002, Agriculture and the WTO: Creating a Trading System for Development, Liberalizing Agricultural Trade: Issues and Options for Sub-Saharan Africa in the WTO, 2003; contbr. articles to profl. jours. Mem. Am. Econs. Assn., We. Econs. Assn., So. Econs. Assn., Phi Kappa Phi, Omicron Delta Epsilon, Phi Eta Sigma, Libertarian. Avocations: scuba diving, tennis, running. Home: 3307 Brandy Ct Falls Church VA 22042-3705 Office: The World Bank 18th And H Sts NW Washington DC 20433-0001 E-mail: jnash1@worldbank.org.

NASH, JOHN FORBES, JR., research mathematician; b. Bluefield, W.Va., 1928; BS in Math., MS in Math., Carnegie-Mellon U., 1948, ScD (hon.), 1999; PhD, Princeton U., 1950, U. Athens, 2000, U. Naples, 2003, U. Charleston, W.Va., 2003. Rsch. asst., instr. Princeton (N.J.) U., 1950—51; Moore instr. MIT, 1951—53, asst. prof., 1953—57, assoc. prof., 1957—59; sr. rsch. mathematician Princeton U. Cons. RAND Corp., 1950, 52, 54; vis. mem. Inst. Advanced Study Princeton U., 1956—57, 1961—62, 1963—64; rsch. assoc. math. MIT, 1966—67. Co-recipient Nobel Prize in Econ. Scis., 1994, Bus. Week award, Erasmus U., Rotterdam, 1998, Leroy P. Steele prize in math., 1999; recipient von Neumann Theory prize, Ops. Rsch. Soc. Am., Pres.'s award, Nat. Alliance for the Mentally Ill, 1999; Sloan fellow, NSF fellow, Westinghouse scholar. Fellow: Am. Acad. Arts and Scis., Econometric Soc.; mem.: NAS. Office: Princeton U Fine Hall Math Dept Princeton NJ 08544-0001

NASH, KAREN MARSTELLER MYERS, sculptor, designer, systems analyst; b. Washington, Aug. 30, 1943; d. Frederick Arell and Ruth Mary (Quinn) Marsteller; m. Christian W. Myers, Oct. 4, 1963 (div. 1973); children: Christian W. Myers III, Meredith Kennedy. Student, U. Va., Fredericksburg, 1961-63. Boatbuilder Solna Corp., Newport, RI, 1974-75; boatbuilder, purchasing agt. Coddington Yachts, Jamestown, RI, 1975-77, Williams & Manchester Shipyard, Newport, 1983-87; boatbuilder, dir. purchasing Shannon Boat Co., Bristol, RI, 1987-89, Aries Powercraft Ltd., Fall River, Mass., 1989-90; systems designer, mgr. Ronaco Internat. Inc., New Bedford, Mass., 1990-96, 1990—96; programmer, analyst, designer Wildcat Cons. & Design, Newport, 1996—. Designer, cons. Grand Design, Newport, 1975—; design and sys. cons. Blue Pelican Jazz Club, Newport, 1983—91; artist, mem. Newport Art Mus., 1995—, DeBlois Gallery, Newport, 2003—. Costume designer R.I. Shakespeare Theatre, Newport, 1978—90, bd. dirs., 1981—84; costume designer Am. Renaissance Theatre, N.Y.C., 1982—84; bd. dirs. Cultural Affairs Commn., Newport, 1982—84, Hill Assn., Newport, 1983—85. Recipient Rhody award, Providence Jour., 1984; U.S. Dept. Interior grantee, 1978. Episcopalian. Avocations: computers, sailing, fishing, camping, parrots. Home: The Gothic Cottage 104 John St Newport RI 02840-3108 Office: Wildcat Consulting & Design 104 John St Newport RI 02840-3108

NASH, LEONARD KOLLENDER, retired chemistry professor; b. N.Y.C., Oct. 27, 1918; s. Adolph and Carol (Kollender) N.; m. Ava Byer, Mar. 3, 1945; children— Vivian C., David B. BS, Harvard, 1939, MA, 1941, PhD, 1944. Rsch. asst. Harvard U., Cambridge, Mass., 1943-44, instr., 1946-48, asst. prof., 1948-53, assoc. prof., 1953-59, prof. chemistry, 1959-86, chmn. dept., 1971-74; rsch. assoc. Columbia, 1944-45; instr. U. Ill., 1945-46; ret. Staff Manhattan Project, 1944-45 Author: Elements of Chemical Thermodynamics, 1962, The Nature of the Natural Sciences, 1963, Stoichiometry, 1966, Elements of Statistical Thermodynamics, 1968, ChemThermo, 1972. Recipient Mfg. Chemists' award, 1966; James Flack Norris award, 1975 Home: 11 Field Rd Lexington MA 02421-8014

NASH, MARY HARRIET, artist, educator; b. Washington, May 8, 1951; d. Richard Harvey and Janet Rose (Nivinski) Nash; m. Richard Day, 1980. BA, George Washington U., 1973; MFA, Wsh. State U., 1976. Guest lectr. Mus. Art, Wash. State U., Pullman., 1976, 2d St. Gallery, Charlottesville, Va., 1980, U. Ala., Tuscaloosa, 1981, SEWSA Conf., Charlottesville, 1983; artist-in-residence Va. Mus. Fine Arts, Richmond, 1984—; guest juror Twinbrook Art Show, Fairfax, Va., 1978; tchg. asst. Wash. State U., 1975-76 vis. artist, lectr. Johnson (Vt.) State Coll., 1995; guest lectr. Julian Scott Meml. Gallery, 1995, Stetson U., DeLand, Fla., 1997, Emerson Gallery, McLean (Va.) Project for the Arts, 1997, 2001; guest co-curator New Orleans Mus. Art, 2001. Author: (artist's book) Skulls Are Forever, 1986; contbr. articles to profl. jours.; painting commd. by Nat. Hockey League, 2001; painting commd. Prince George's Co., Md., 2003. Recipient cert. for outstanding achievement Women in Design Internat., 1983, 5 gubernatorial citations Gov. of Va., Richmond, 1995-96; named Jinx Hazel Arts Citizen of Yr., Arts Coun. Fairfax County, 2001. Mem. Southeastern Ctr. for Contemporary Art (hon. mention 1979), MacDowell Colony Fellows, Phi Kappa Phi.

NASH, MELVIN SAMUEL, lawyer; b. Atlanta, Aug. 26, 1949; s. Ralph Samuel and Mary Pauline (Quarles) N.; m. Cynthia Joanna Hamrick, Aug. 21, 1980 (div.); m. Kristine Marie Clark, Nov. 22, 1997. A.B., Ga. State U., 1974; J.D., U. Fla., 1976. Bar: Ga. 1978, U.S. Ct. Claims 1983, U.S. Ct. Internat. Trade 1983, U.S. Tax Ct. 1982, U.S. Ct. Appeals (5th cir.) 1978, U.S. Ct. Appeals (11th cir.) 1981, U.S. Supreme Ct. 1985. Asst. solicitor State Ct., Cobb County, Marietta, Ga., 1977-78; assoc. Milam & Smith, Austell, Ga., 1978; ptnr. Milam, Smith & Nash, Austell, 1978-79; sole practice, Marietta, 1979—; spl. master Cobb Superior Ct., 1982—; dir. Nash Trucking Co., Inc., Marietta, Security Fiedelity Mortgage, Marietta, Nash Properties, Marietta. Magistrate Prohac Vice State Ct. Cobb County, Marietta, 1980-82; candidate state rep. State of Ga. Dist. 21, Marietta, 1982. Served with USAF, 1967-71. Mem. ABA, Acad. Fla. Trial Lawyers, Assn. Trial Lawyers Am., Nat. Assn. Criminal Def. Lawyers, Ga. Assn. Criminal Def. Lawyers, Cobb County Bar Assn. (com. 1983-84), Cobb Criminal Def. Bar Assn. (sec., Seminar award 1984), State Bar Ga. (fee arbitrator 1982—). Democrat. Presbyterian. Clubs: Atlanta Ski, Atlanta Track (Marathon finisher). E-mail: melvinsnash@msn.com.

NASH, NICHOLAS DAVID, retail executive; b. Mpls., June 11, 1939; s. Edgar Vanderhoef and Nancy (Van Slyke) N. AB, Harvard U., 1962; MEd, Bowling Green State U., 1970; PhD, U. Minn., 1975. Head lower sch. Maumee Valley (Ohio) Country Day Sch., 1965-71; assoc. dir. Univ. Council for Ednl. Adminstrn.; adj. asst. prof. Ohio State U., 1975-78; v.p. programming Minn. Public Radio, St. Paul, 1978-82, Am. Pub. Radio, St. Paul, 1982-85; pres. The Nash Co., 1985—. Bd. dirs. Artspace Projects, Inc. Author works in field. Bd. dirs. Nash Found., 1975—, Humane Soc. for Companion Animals, 2002-04. Mem. Univ. Club St. Paul. Episcopalian. Home: 1340 N Birch Lake Blvd Saint Paul MN 55110-6716 Office: 2179 4th St Ste 2H Saint Paul MN 55110-3041

NASH, PAUL LENOIR, lawyer; b. Poughkeepsie, N.Y., Jan. 29, 1931; s. George Matthew and Winifred (LeNoir) N.; m. Nancy Allyn Thouron, Dec. 30, 1961; children: Andrew Gray, Laurie L., Daphne Thouron. BA, Yale U., 1953; LLB, Harvard U., 1958. Bar: N.Y. 1959. Assoc. Dewey Ballantine, N.Y.C., 1958-66, ptnr., 1966—. Pres. bd. trustees Peck Sch., Morristown, N.J., 1978-82. Served to capt. USMC, 1953-55; Japan. Mem. Assn. of Bar of City of N.Y. Republican. Home: 4 Westminster Pl Morristown NJ 07960-5810 Office: Dewey Ballantine LLP 1301 Avenue Of The Americas New York NY 10019-6022 Office Phone: 212-259-7100. E-mail: pnash@deweyballantine.com., pnash65131@aol.com.

NASH, RICHARD EUGENE, aerospace engineer; b. San Diego, Feb. 18, 1954; s. Clifford Arthur Jr. and Dorothy Fay (Johnson) N.; m. Lynn Elora Martin, Aug. 5, 1978. BSCE, U. Ky., 1981; MSCE, U. So. Calif., 1988; MSEM, West Coast U., 1995; EMBA, U. LaVerne, 2001. Registered profl. civil engr., Calif.; cert. profl. mgr. Mem. tech. staff Boeing, Huntington Beach, Calif., 1982—, lead engr. space shuttle propulsion systems Downey, Calif., 1986-88; engr. Nat. Aero-Space Plane, Long Beach, Calif., 1988-89, space shuttle orbiter project engr., 1989-95; project mgr. problem action ctr., product mgr., problem reporting and corrective action, orbiter shuttle program Boeing, Huntington Beach, Calif., 1995—2001, sys. engring. staff on Future Shuttle between space launch initiative and future shuttle, project mgr. future shuttle program, tech. liaison Huntington, Calif., 2001—03, sr. staff engr. GPS IIF control segment, project mgr. GPS ctr., 2003—. Pvt. practice civil engring., Calif., 1985-87. Scoutmaster Boy Scouts Am., Covington, Ky., 1972-74, Williamstown, Ky., 1976-82, asst. scoutmaster, Ft. Hood, Tex., 1975-76. Sgt. U.S. Army, 1976, Korea. Recipient Quality Spotlight award, 1971, Space Flight Awareness award, 1992, 95, Manned Space Flight Awareness award 1996, NASA Group Achievement award, 1997, Sustained Superior Performance award, 1985, Divsn. Quality award, 1997; named to Hon. Order of Ky. Cols., 1985. Mem. Nat. Mgmt. Assn. (series facilities), Nat. Eagle Scout Asst. (advisor 1983), Masons (32 degree, sr. warden), Chi Epsilon. Republican. Avocations: backpacking, scouting. Office: Boeing Human Space Flight and Exploration 5301 Bolsa Ave MC H017-D414 Huntington Beach CA 92647-2099 *Personal philosophy: If you want to be a doctor; talk to a doctor, she has already done it. If you want to be an engineer; talk to an engineer, he has already done it. If you want to be a success; talk to yourself, for only you know how to define success.*

NASH, SEYMOUR CY, surgeon, urologist; b. N.Y.C., Nov. 18, 1931; s. Annette (Gersten) Cook; m. Sally Anne Kugler, Aug. 6, 1958; children: Allison, Elizabeth, Gregory. BS, U. Fla., 1952; MD, Washington U., St. Louis, 1956. Diplomate Am. Bd. Urology. Surg. intern Yale Med. Ctr., New Haven, Conn., 1956-57, surg. resident, 1957-59; clin. assoc. Nat. Cancer Inst., Bethesda, Md., 1959-61; urology resident Georgetown U. Hosp., Washington, 1961-64; pvt. practice in urology Miami Beach, Fla., 1964—; assoc. clin. prof. U. Miami Med. Sch., 1964-94; chmn. dept. urology Mt. Sinai Hosp., Miami Beach. Co-author: Prostate Cancer Making Survival Decisions, 1994. Capt. USPHS, 1959-61. Fellow Am. Coll. Surgeons; mem. AMA, Am. Assn. Clin. Urologists, Fla. Med. Assn., Dade County Med. Assn. Republican. Jewish. Avocation: tennis. Office: 4302 Alton Rd Ste 670 Miami Beach FL 33140-2877 Office Phone: 305-531-7671.

NASH, SYLVIA DOTSETH, consultant; b. Montevedio, Minn., Apr. 25, 1945; d. Owen Donald and Selma A. (Tollefson) Dotseth; married; 1 child, Elizabeth Louise. Grad., Calif. Luth. Bible Sch., 1965; doctorate (hon.), Pilgrims Theol. Seminary, 1994. Office mgr. First Congl. Ch., Pasadena, Calif., 1968-75; pastoral asst. Pasadena Presbyn. Ch., 1975-78; dir. adminstrv. svcs. Fuller Theol. Sem., Pasadena, 1978-81; CEO Christian Mgmt. Assn., Diamond Bar, Calif., 1981-94; pres. Christian Healthcare Network, La Mirada, Calif., 1994-95; sr. cons. Lillestrand and Assocs., Chino Hills, Calif., 1996—. Cons. various orgns., 1985—. Author: Inspirational Management, 1992 (Your Church Mag. award 1992); editor: The Clarion, 1975-78, The Christian Mgmt. Report, 1981-94; mem. editl./adv. bd. Your Church Mag.; mem. editl. bd. Jour. Ministry Mktg. and Mtmg.; contbr. articles to profl. jours. Bd. dirs. Nat. Network of Youth Ministries, The Mustard Seed, Inc., Nat. Assn. of Ch. Bus. Adminstrn., Found. for His Ministry, Lamb's Players, Gospel Lit. Internat., Evang. Coun. for Fin. Accountability, Campus Crusade for Christ Internat. Sch. Theology. Mem. NAFE, Nat. Assn. Ch. Adminstrs. (sec. 1979-81), Am. Soc. Assn. Execs., So. Calif. Soc. Assn. Execs. Office: Lillestrand & Assocs 2729 Brookside Drive Chino Hills CA 91709

NASH, WARREN LESLIE, banker; b. Jackson, Miss., Aug. 26, 1955; s. Henry Warren and Frances Lora (Venters) N.; m. Valerie Ann Roberts, Nov. 22, 1980; children: John Wilson, Warren Graham, William Dixon. Student, U.S. Naval Acad., 1973-75; BS in Banking and Fin., Miss. State U., Starkville, 1978; MBA, U. Ala., Birmingham, 1982; profl. cert., Stonier Grad. Sch. Banking, Newark, Del., 1987. Asst. br. mgr. 1st Nat. Bank of Birmingham, Ala., 1978-80, br. officer, 1980-81, asst. v.p., 1981-84; v.p. AmSouth Bank, N.A., Birmingham, 1984-86, v.p., regional retail banking mgr. Montgomery, Ala., 1986-89; sr. v.p. AmSouth Bank, Montgomery, 1989-91; sr. v.p. consumer banking AmSouth Bank, N.A., Birmingham, 1991-93; v.p. productivity AmSouth Bank, Birmingham, 1993-94, sr. v.p. tech., 1994-95, sr. v.p. retail delivery, 1995-98; pres. Retail BancAssocs., LLC, Birmingham, 1998—2001; exec. dir. Canterbury United Meth. Ch., 2001—. Instr. fin. Samford U., Birmingham, 1982-84; v.p., Ala. Automated Clearing house, 1983-84. Counselor Jr. Achievement, Birmingham, 1980-82; loaned exec. United Way, Birmingham, 1980; com. chmn. Birmingham Festival Arts, 1985-86. Named one of Outstanding Young Men of Am., 1984, 85, 86. Mem. Am. Mktg. Assn. (bd. dirs. 1983-84), Am. Inst. Banking, Birmingham C. of C. (dept. coord. 1985), Newcomen Soc., Young Montgomerians Bus. Club, Summit Club, Kiwanis (local pres. 1985-86), Alpha Kappa Psi, Beta Gamma Sigma. Independent. Methodist. Office: Canterbury United Meth Ch 350 Overlook Rd Birmingham AL 35213 Home: 3824 Spring Valley Rd Birmingham AL 35223-1568 Office Phone: 205-874-1555.

NASH, WILLIAM ARTHUR, civil engineer, educator; b. Chgo., Sept. 15, 1922; s. William A. and Rose (Keck) N.; m. Verna Lucile Baer, Aug. 8, 1953; children: Rebecca Ann, Phillip Arthur. BSCE, Ill. Inst. Tech., 1944, MS, 1946; PhD, U. Mich., 1949. Rsch. engr. David W. Taylor Model Basin, Navy Dept., Washington, 1949-54; mem. faculty U. Fla., Gainesville, 1954-67, head dept. engring. mechanics, 1964-67; prof. civil engring. U. Mass., Amherst, 1967—. Cons. to govt. and industry; hon. prof. Shanghai Inst. Tech., 1985; pres. Cons. Engring., Amherst, 1992—. Author: Theory and Outline of Strength of Materials, 4th edit., 1998, Statics and Mechanics of Materials, 1991, Hydrostatically Loaded Structures, 1995; contbr. over 100 articles to profl. jours.; editor Internat. Jour. Nonlinear Mechanics. Recipient Humboldt U.S. Sr. Scientist award to Fed. Republic Germany, 1986. Fellow ASME; mem. Internat. Assn. Shell and Spatial Structures, Am. Soc. Engring. Edn. (Curtis W. McGraw Rsch. award 1961), AIAA, Earthquake Engring. Rsch. Inst. Congregationalist. Office: 235 Marston Hall U Mass Amherst MA 01003

NASHAT, GUITY, historian, education educator, researcher; b. Bagdad, Iraq, July 28, 1937; arrived in U.S., 1956; d. Muhammad Sadegh Nashat-Mirdamad and Qamar Afshar; m. Gary S. Becker, Oct. 31, 1979; children: Michael, Cryus Claffey stepchildren: Judy, Catherine. BA, Barnard Coll., N.Y., 1958; MS journalism, Columbia Univ., N.Y., 1959; PhD hist., Univ. Chgo., Chgo., 1974. Vis. asst. prof. Loyola Univ., Chgo., 1974—75; asst. prof. Univ. Ill., Chgo., 1975—83, assoc. prof., 1983—. Rsch. fellow Hoover Inst., Stanford Univ., 1995—. Author: The Origins of Modern Reform in Iran 1870-1880, 1982, Middle Eastern History Selected Reading Lists and Course Outlines from American Colleges and Universities, 1988; editor: Women and Revolution in Iran, 1984; co-author: Women in the Middle East and North Africa, 1999; co-editor: The Economics of Life, 1996, Women in Iran From the Rise of Islam to 1800, 2003, Women in Iran from 1800 to the Islamic Republic, 2003. Grantee Ford Found. Grant, Univ. Chgo., 1968—69, Soc. Sci. Rsch. Coun. summer grant, 1978, Soc. Sci. Rsch. Coun. grant, 1976—77; Ford Found. fellowship, Columbia Sch. of Journalism, 1958—59. Mem.: Mont Pelerin Soc., Qajar Studies Assn., Iranian Studies (exec. bd. mem. 1986—89), Middle Eastern Studies Assn. Office: Univ Ill at Chgo 601 S Morgan St Chicago IL 60607-7109

NASHIF, TAYSIR N. researcher; b. Tayyiba, near Jerusalem, Mar. 22, 1940; came to U.S., 1969; s. Najm A. and Aisha A. Nashif; m. Mayyada I. Nashif, Apr. 15, 1968; children: Fawz, Fayruz, Hanin. BA in Polit. Sci./Arabic Lang. & Lit., Hebrew U., Jerusalem, 1964, MA in Internat. Rels., 1968; MA in Islamic Studies, U. Toronto, 1969; PhD in Polit. Sci., SUNY, Binghamton, 1974. Prof. U. Oran, Algeria, 1974—76, UN, N.Y.C., 1976—77, polit. affairs officer, 1980—81, reviser, editor, 1982—96; prof. Essex County Coll., Newark, 1985—93; chief Arabic verbatim reporting sect. UN, N.Y.C., 1996—2002. Author: The Palestine Arab and Jewish Political Leaderships, 1979, Nuclear Warfare in the Middle East, 1984, Nuclear Weapons in Israel, 1996, The Arabs and the World in the Next Century, 1999, Authority, Intellectual Freedom and Society, Palestinian Thinkers in the Twentieth Century; contbr. articles on strategic and polit. issues to profl. jours. Grantee SUNY, 1971-73. Mem.: Third World Studies Assn., Am. Translators Assn., Mid. East Studies Assn., Am. Polit. Sci. Assn. Avocations: sea cruising, fishing, mountain climbing. E-mail: tnnashif@aol.com.

NASHMAN, ALVIN ELI, computer company executive; b. N.Y.C., Dec. 16, 1926; s. Joseph and Fay (Portnoy) N.; m. Honey Weinstein, May 29, 1960; children: Jessica Rachel, Pamela Wynne, Stephanie Paige. BEE, CUNY, 1948; MEE, NYU, 1951; ScD (hon.), Pacific U., 1968, George Washington U., 1986. With Ketay Mfg. Corp., N.Y.C., 1951-52; dir. missile systems lab, dir. rsch. and devel. programs ITT Fed. Labs., Nutley, N.J., 1952-62; dir. ops., systems engring. and tech. advisor Defense Comms. Agency ITT Intelcom, Inc., Falls Church, Va., 1962-65; pres. Computer Scis. Corp., Falls Church, 1965-67, bd. dir., 1968-95, v.p., 1969-92. Patentee in field; contbr. articles to profl. jours. Trustee Inova Hosp. System Found. With USN, 1944-46. Fellow IEEE; mem. Armed Forces Communications and Electronics Assn. (dir., internat. v.p. 1976-79, chpt. pres. 1979-80, exec. com. 1980-84, chmn. bd. 1984-86), AIAA, Nat. Space Club, Nat. Security Indsl. Assn., Tau Beta Pi, Eta Kappa Nu. Republican. Jewish. Home: 3609 Ridgeway Ter Falls Church VA 22044-1308

NASKY, H(AROLD) GREGORY, lawyer; b. Titusville, Pa., June 9, 1942; s. Harold G. and Majella Marie (Beck) N.; m. Rosanne Guson, July 22, 1967. AB, St. Bonaventure U., 1964; JD, U. Notre Dame, 1967. Bar: Pa. 1967, Nev. 1972, Hawaii, 2003. Assoc. Eaton & Hill, Warren, Pa., 1967-68, Vargas, Bartlett & Dixon, Reno, 1972-73; ptnr. Vargas & Bartlett, Las Vegas, Nev., 1974-94, mng. ptnr., 1981-91; of counsel Kummer, Kaempfer, Bonner & Renshaw, Las Vegas, 1994—; prin. Resort Devel. Cons., 1998—. Corp. sec. Showboat, Inc. (NYSE-SBO), Las Vegas, 1978-98, bd. dirs., 1983-98, exec. v.p., 1995-98; bd. dirs. U. Notre Dame Law Assn., 1990-2000; mem. adv. bd. U. Nev. Sch. Medicine.; chmn. 1993, bd. dirs. Author: Inter Alia Jour. of State Bar of Nevada, A Glimpse of China, 1986; Nev. contbg. author: Real Property, Probate & Trust Law Jour., Disposition of Rents, 1981. Legal advisor Nev. Dance Theatre, Las Vegas, 1977-94, bd. dirs. 1988-2000; legal com. Nev. Resort Assn., Las Vegas, gaming regulations com. 1990-93; bd. dirs. Boulder Dam coun. Boy Scouts Am., Las Vegas, 1986-93; del. People to People Citizen Ambassador Program, People's Republic China, 1985, New Zealand/Australia, 1987, Hungary, Czechoslovakia and Poland, 1990, Russia and Estonia, 1992. Served to capt. JAGC, U.S. Army, 1968-72, Vietnam. Decorated Bronze Star, 1970. Mem. ABA (bus. sect. task force conflicts interest com. 1993-95), State Bar Nev. (chmn. fee dispute com. 1983-89, exec. com. mem. Gaming Law Sect. 1985-93), Am. Soc. Corp. Secs., Internat. Assn. Gaming Attys., Notre Dame Club Las Vegas (past pres. 1978-79), U. Nev. Las Vegas Found. (president's assocs. 1993, chmn.). Office: Kummer Kaempfer Bonner & Renshaw 3800 Howard Hughes Pky Fl 7 Las Vegas NV 89109-0925 also: Resort Devel Cons PMB A14 9101 W Sahara Ave Ste 105 Las Vegas NV 89117 Office Phone: 702-792-7000. Business E-Mail: gnasky@kkbr.com.

NASLUND, ERIC, architectural firm executive; B in Architecture (hons.), Calif. Polytechnic State U. Lic. Calif., N.Mex. Prin., ptnr. Studio E Archs., 1986—. Adj. faculty mem. Woodbury U., San Diego. Fellow: Am. Inst. of Architecture. Office: Studio E Architects 1262 Kettner Blvd San Diego CA 92101-3308

NASLUND, HOWARD RICHARD, geological science educator; b. Green Hills, Ohio, Nov. 25, 1950; married, 1979; 5 children. BS, U. Ill., 1972; MS, U. Oreg., 1977, PhD, 1980. Leader East Greenland Expeditions, 1985, 1986, 1988, 1989; igneous petrologist Ocean Drilling Program, 1991, 97; asst. prof. Dartmouth Coll., 1979-87; assoc. prof. dept. geol. scis. and environ. studies SUNY, Binghamton, 1987-95, assoc. chmn. geol. scis. and environ. studies, 1987-88, dir. grad. studies geol. scis., 1988-92, prof. dept. geol. scis. and environ. studies, 1995—, chmn. geol. scis. and environ. studies, 1992-95,97-2000. Vis. prof. Departamento de Geologia, U. Chile, 1995-96, vis. prof. Departamento de Ingenieriá en Minas, U. de Santiago,Chile, 2001-02; outside rev. com. dept. geology SUNY, New Paltz, 1995, sponsored programs adv. coun., 1994-97, grad. coun., 1994-97, chair adv. com. on scholarship and rsch., 1994-97, material rsch. inst., 1991—, faculty senate, 1988-90, 96-98; trustee Glenn G. Bartle Meml. Fund, 1988-90, 96-98; exec. com. of faculty Dartmouth Coll., 1982-85, com. on stds., 1981-86. Contbr. articles to profl. jours. J. William Fulbright scholar, 1995-96; rsch. grant USSAC, 1991, 92, 97, 98, NSF, 1982, 88, 90, 99, equipment grant NSF, 1990, 91. Mem. Geol. Soc. of Am. (Penrose Rsch. award 1974, 76), Mineralogical Soc. of Am., Am. Geophys. Union, Soc. for Mining, Metallurgy and Exploration of AIME, Sociedad Geologica de Chile, N.Y. State Geol. Assn. (pres. 1997-98), Internat. Assn. Volcanic Chemistry Earty Interior. Office: Geol Scis SUNY Binghamton NY 13902-6000 Office Phone: 607-777-4313. Business E-Mail: Naslund@Binghamton.edu.

NASO, VALERIE JOAN, automobile dealership executive, travel company operator, artist, photographer, writer; b. Stockton, Calif., Aug. 19, 1941; d. Alan Robert and Natalie Grace (Gardner) McKittrick Naso; m. Peter Joralemon, May 31, 1971 (div.). Student pub. schs., Piedmont, Calif. Cert. graphoanalyst. Pres., Naso Motor Co. (formerly Broadway Cadillacs, Oakland, Calif.) Bishop, Calif., 1964—; freelance artist, 1965—; owner, operator Wooden Horse Antiques, Bishop, 1970-82; editor, writer, photographer Sierra Life Mag., Bishop, 1980-83; freelance writer, photographer, 1972—; owner, operator Boredom Tours, Bishop, 1981—; owner, sole photographer, Renaissance Photography, N.Y.C. and Bishop, Calif., 1982—, Keyboard Colors, 1986; cons. graphoanalyst, 1976—. Fiction, non-fiction work pub. in Horse and Horseman, Am. Horseman, Horse & Rider Mag., Cameo Mag., Desert Mag., Sierra Life Mag. Mem. Nat. Assn. Female Execs., Authors Guild, Inc., Authors League Am., Am. Film Inst., Archives of Am. Art, Lalique Soc. Am., Musical Box Soc. Internat., Alliance Francaise (N.Y. chpt.), Bishop C. of C., Victorian Soc. Am., Nat. Trust for Hist. Preservation, Am. Craft Coun., Nat. Rifle Assn. Clubs: Cadillac LaSalle (nat. and so. calif. chpts.); Wagner Soc. (N.Y.C.). Office: 783 N Main St Bishop CA 93514-2427 also: PO Box 1625 Bishop CA 93515-1625

NASON, BARRY MARK, systems engineer, mathematician, educator; b. Newton, Mass., Jan. 24, 1948; s. Louis and Muriel Rose Nason; m. Diane Elizabeth Bowman, Aug. 26, 1974; 1 child, Elizabeth Anne. BS in Sys. Engring., U. Fla., 1973; MS in Stats., Wright State U., 1994; MS in Math., Tenn. State U., 2000. Cert. quality engr., Am. Soc. for Quality, 1993, reliability engr., Am. Soc. for Quality, 1994; CPIM Am. Prodn. and Inventory Control Soc., 1994. Systems analyst Combustion Engring., Chattanooga, 1973—76, performance analyst Windsor, Conn., 1976—78; sys. analyst divsn. Ingersoll Rand Torrington (Conn.) Co., 1978—82; project leader Colt Firearms, Hartford, Conn., 1982—88; mgr. devel. Garden Way, Inc., Troy, NY, 1988—90; sr. sys. designer Grumman Data Sys., Dayton, Ohio, 1990—94; sr. sys. engr. EDS-Mil. Sys., Dayton, 1994—96, EDS-TennCare, Nashville, 1996—2002; sys. arch. EDS-Kans. XIX, Topeka, 2002—. Contbr. articles to profl. jours. With U.S. Army, 1971—72. Mem.: Am. Math. Soc. (assoc.), Math. Assn. Am. (assoc.), Am. Statis. Assn. (assoc.), Phi Kappa Phi (assoc.), Beta Theta Pi (life). Avocations: reading, mathematics. Home: 821 Justin St Lawrence KS 66049 Office: EDS Ste 204 3600 South Topeka Blvd Topeka KS 66611 E-mail: barry.nason@eds.com.

NASON, CHARLES TUCKEY, diversified financial services company executive; b. Apr. 22, 1946; s. Raymond W. and Helen (Tuckey) Nason; m. Elizabeth Lucille Rabun, May 1, 1999; children: Rebecca Ann, Jill Nicole. BA, Washington and Jefferson Coll., 1968; MBA, U. Pitts., 1969. Cert. fin. planner, chartered fin. cons. Dist. sales mgr. Met. Life Ins. Co., Pitts., 1971-77; mng. dir. Acacia Group Co., Pitts., 1977-88; founder, pres. Coordinated Capital Ltd., Pitts., 1982-85; chmn., pres., CEO Acacia Life Ins. Co., Washington, 1988—2003. Chmn. devel. coun. exec. com. Washington and Jefferson Coll., 1982—85, trustee, 1988—, chmn. Nat. Ann. Giving Fund, 1992—96; trustee Washington Fed. City Coun., 1988—; bd. dirs. Greater Washington Bd. Trade, chmn.-elect, 1993, chmn., 1994; bd. dirs. Washington Real Estate Investment Trust, Medstar Inc., Blue Cross Blue Shield Washington, 1991—93, Greater Washington Boys and Girls clubs, Am. Coun. Life Ins., 1993—2000, Medlantic Healthcare Group, 1997—98. Lt. USAF, 1970—71. Mem.: Ins. Mktg. Stds. Assn. (bd. dirs. 1999—, chmn.-elect 2001, chmn. 2002), Inst. Cert. Fin. Planners (bd. dirs.), Nat. Assn. Securities Dealers, Estate Planning Coun. (bd. dirs.), Am. Soc. CLUS (pres. 1981—82), Gen. Agts. and Mgrs. Assn. (pres. 1984—85), Fiddlesticks Golf and Country Club, Talbout Country Club, Congl. Country Club, Burning Tree Club. Republican. Roman Catholic. Home: 8015 Quarry Ridge Way Bethesda MD 20817 Office: Acacia Group 7315 Wisconsin Ave Fl 10W Bethesda MD 20814-3202

NASON, DOLORES IRENE, computer company executive, social services administrator, eucharistic minister; b. Seattle; d. William Joseph Lockinger and Ruby Irene; m. George Malcolm Nason, Jr.; children: George Malcolm III, Scott James, Lance William, Natalie Joan. Student, Long Beach (Calif.) City Coll.; cert. in Religious Edn. for elem tchrs., cert. teaching, cert. secondary teaching, Immaculate Heart Coll.; attended, Salesian Sem. Buyer J. C. Penney Co., Barstow, Calif.; prin. St. Cyprian Confraternity of Christian Doctrine Elem. Sch., Long Beach; prin. summer sch. St. Cyprian Confraternity of Christian Doctrine Elem. Sch., Long Beach; pres. St. Cyprian Confraternity Orgn., Long Beach; dist. co-chmn. L.A. Diocese; v.p. Nason & Assocs., Inc., Long Beach, 1978—; pres. L.A. County Commn. on Obscenity & Pornography, 1984—; eucharistic minister St. Cyprian Ch., Long Beach, 1985—; bd. dirs. L.A. County Children's Svcs., 1988—; assoc. dir. social svcs. Disabled Resources Ctr., Inc., Long Beach, 1992—. Vol. Meml. Children's Hosp., Long Beach, 1977—; mem. scholarship com. Long Beach City Coll., 1984-90, Calif. State U., Long Beach, 1984-90; bd. dirs. L.A. County Access Svc. Inc. Pres. St. Cyprian's Parish Coun., 1962—; mem. Long Beach Civic Light Opera, 1973-96, Assistance League of Long Beach, 1976—. Mem.: KC (Family of Month award 1988), U. of Pacific Club. Roman Catholic. Avocations: physical fitness, theater, choir, travel.

NASON, NICOLE, federal agency administrator; married; 1 child, Alexandra. Grad., Am. U., Washington, 1992; JD, Case Western Res. U., Cleve. Counsel House Judiciary Subcom. on Crime, Washington; govt. affairs counsel Met. Life Ins. Co., 1999—2000; comm. dir., counsel U.S. Rep. Porter J. Goss, 2000—02; asst. commr. Office of Congl. Affairs, U.S. Customs Svc., Washington, 2002—03; asst. sec. for govtl. affairs U.S. Dept. Transp., Washington, 2003—. Office: US Dept Transportation 400 7th St Washington DC 20590

NASON, ROCHELLE, conservation organization administrator; b. Oakland, Calif., May 21, 1959; d. Milton and Ann Frances (Reed) Nason. BA, U. Calif., Berkeley, 1984; JD, U. Calif., San Francisco, 1987. Bar: Calif. 1987. Law clk. to Chief Justice Malcolm Lucas Supreme Ct. of Calif., San Francisco, 1987-88; litigation assoc. Morrison & Foerster, San Francisco, 1988-92; staff lawyer League to Save Lake Tahoe, South Lake Tahoe, Calif., 1992-93, exec. dir., 1993—. Adj. instr. Sierra Nev. Coll., Incline Village, 1992—94, Lake Tahoe C.C., 1992—96. Editor: The Traynor Reader, 1987; sr. rev. editor: Hastings Law Jour., 1986—87; editor: (jour.) Keep Tahoe Blue, 1992—; columnist: newspaper Tahoe Daily Tribune; contbr. articles to profl. jours. Mem. leadership coun. Tahoe-Truckee Regional Econ. Coalition, Stateline, Nev., 1992—94; v.p., bd. dirs. Jewish Cmty. South Lake Tahoe/Temple Bat Yam, 1992—99; bd. dirs. Tahoe Ctr. Sustainable Future, Glenbrook, Nev., 1995—98, Earthshare Calif., 2002—. Mem.: Thurston Soc., Order of Coif. Jewish. Avocations: backpacking, skiing. Office: League to Save Lake Tahoe 955 Emerald Bay Rd South Lake Tahoe CA 96150-6410

NASON, SCOTT D. airline company executive; V.p. ops. planning and performance AMR Corp., Fort Worth, Tex., 1991—. Office: AMR Corp 4333 Amon Carter Blvd Fort Worth TX 76155

NASR, GEORGE ELIAS, electrical engineer, consultant, computer engineer, educator; s. Elias Mikhael and Noha Nasr; m. Roula Elias Kandalaft, Aug. 29, 1998; children: Leah George, Lynn George. PhD EE, U of KY, Lexington, KY, 1985—88; MS EE, U of KY, Lexington, KY, 1983—85; BS EE, U of KY, Lexington, KY, 1981—83; BS gen. sci., Beirut U. Coll., Beirut, Lebanon, 1978—81. Asst. prof. of EE U of KY, Lexington, Ky., 1988—91; asst. prof. of engring. Valdosta State U., Valdosta, Ga., 1991—93; asst. prof. of elec. and computer engring. Lebanese Am. U., Byblos, Lebanon, 1994—96, coord. of engring. programs, 1994—95, assoc. prof. of elec. and computer engring., 1996—, chairperson, dept. of elec., computer, indsl., and mech. engring.,

1995—. Author over 30 internat. jour. and conf. papers. Recipient The outstanding Tchr. in EE, Coll. of Engring. at U of KY, 1991; grantee Pi, U of KY Info. Svc., 1988, CO-Investigator on PREP Grant, Dept. of Energy, 1993, Pi, Nat. Coun. for Sci. Rsch., 1995, CO-Investigator in the Workshop on Water Resources Quality and Mgmt. in the Mid. East and North Africa Grant - $10,000, USAID, 1997; scholar Grad. Assistantship, U of KY, 1983—88. Mem.: Am. Soc. Elec. Engineers, IEEE, Ga. Acad. of Sci., Sigma Pi Sigma, Eta Kappa Nu, Tau Beta Pi. Achievements include research in Energy Modeling and Forecasting; Neural Networks; Parallel Processing; Mathematical Modeling, Optimization and System Theory. Office: Lebanese Am U 475 Riverside Dr Ste 1846 New York NY 10115-0033 Personal E-mail: genasr@lau.edu.lb. E-mail: genasr@lau.edu.lb.

NASR, NABIL ZAKI, national center executive; b. Cairo, Apr. 6, 1954; came to U.S., 1981; s. Zaki and Monera (Sherbini) N.; m. Gwendolyn Susan Breon, June 15, 1986; children: Laura, Amy. BS, Helwan U., Cairo, 1978; MS, Rutgers U., 1983, PhD, 1990; M Engring., Pa. State U., 1985. Instr. Helwan U., Cairo, 1978-81; design engr. Uni-Peak Cons., Cairo, 1978-81; teaching asst. Rutgers U., New Brunswick, N.J., 1985-89; asst. prof. indsl. engring. Rochester (N.Y.) Inst. Tech., 1989-95, Earl W. Brinkman prof., 1996—, dir. Nat. Ctr. for Remfg. and Resource Recovery, 1997—. Ind. cons. Piscataway, N.J., 1985-89; cons. Advanced Mfg. Systems, Pittsford, N.Y., 1989—. AMIDEAST fellow, Washington, 1981. Sr. mem. Inst. Indsl. Engring., Soc. Mfg. Engrs. (chpt. chair 1985-87, Outstanding Student Svc. award 1987), Computer and Automated Systems Assn. Avocations: reading, tennis, swimming, soccer. Office: Rochester Inst Tech Nat Ctr Remfg 133 Lomb Memorial Dr Rochester NY 14623-5608 E-mail: nzneie@rit.edu.

NASRALLAH, HENRY ATA, psychiatry researcher, educator; b. Apr. 30, 1947; came to U.S., 1972; s. Ata George and Rose G. (Yameen) N.; m. Amelia C. Tebsherani, June 9, 1972; children: Ramzy George, Rima Alice. BS in Biology, Am. U. of Beirut, 1967; MD, Am. U. Coll Medicine, Beirut-Lebanon, 1971. Intern Am. U. Med. Ctr., Beirut, 1972, resident in psychiatry U. Rochester, N.Y., 1972-75; rsch. assoc. NIMH, Washington, 1975-77; asst. prof. psychiatry U. Calif., San Diego, 1977-79; from assoc. prof. to prof. psychiatry U. Iowa, Iowa City, 1979-85; prof., chair psychiatry Ohio State U., Columbus, 1985-98; prof. psychiatry U. Miss. Med. Ctr., Jackson, 1998—2002, assoc. dean U. Cin. Coll. Medicine, 2003—. Staff psychiatrist VA Med. Ctr., La Jolla, Calif., 1977—79, chief psychiatry svc., Iowa City, 1979—85. Editor: (5 vol. book series) Handbook of Schizophrenia, 1986-90; co-editor: NMR Spectroscopy in Psychiatric Brain Disorders, 1995; editor-in-chief Schizophrenia Rsch., 1987—, Jour. Psychiatry Disorders, 1996—; author and co-author over 200 published articles, 1976—. Pres. Psychiat. Rsch. Found. of Columbus, 1985—; mem. Alliance for the Mentally Ill, Columbus, 1987—. Recipient VA grants, 1979-84, NIMH, 1983—. Fellow Am. Psychiat. Assn. (coun. on rsch.), Am. Coll. Neuropsychopharmacology (chmn. pubs. com. 1992-95), Am. Coll. Psychiatrists (Deans Award com. 1996—), Am. Acad. Clin. Psychiatrists (pres. 1989-90), Soc. Biol. Psychiatry (awards com. 1988-90). Avocations: photography, tennis, poetry. Office: U Cin Med Ctr Dept Psychiatry 231 Albert Sabin Way Cincinnati OH 45267-0559

NASRALLAH, JUNE, plant pathologist, department chairman; PhD in Genetics, Cornell U. Prof. plant biology, chair plant genomics Cornell U., Ithaca, NY. Contbr. articles to profl. jours. Mem.: NAS. Office: Cornell U 218 Plant Sciences Ithaca NY 14853 Business E-Mail: jbn2@cornell.edu.

NASS, CONNIE KAY, state auditor; m. Alan Nass; 3 children. V.p. Nass & Son, Inc., 1974—; auditor State of Ind., 1999—. Bd. Senator Richard Lugar's Excellence in Pub. Svc. Program. Bd. mem. Huntingburg Utility Bd., 1975—; city coun. mem., Huntingburg, 1979-88, mayor, 1988-96; mgr. municipally owned utility cos., Huntingburg, 1988-96; candidate for lt. gov. State of Ind., 1995-96; mem. GOP Platform Com., 1992; del. Rep. Nat. Conv., 1996; bd. dirs. Welborn Found. Evansville, S.W. Ind. Regional Health Care Ctr., Inc.; adv. bd. AAA, Evansville, 1990—; mem. fin. com. and emergency svcs. com. ARC Greater Indpls., 1999—; nat. gen. synod del. Ind.-Ky. Conf. United Ch. of Christ, 1981, com. on planning and evaluation, 1990—, bd. dirs., 1996—; Sunday sch. tchr., music dir. Salem United Ch. of Christ. Recipient Protect Our Woods Environtl. award, 1995; named Outstanding Rep. Woman Ind. Reps Mayor's Assn., 1995. Mem. Nat. Automated Clearing House Assn. (internet coun., electronic benefits coun., strategic expansion bd.), Nat. Assn. State Auditors, Comptrs. and Treas., Network Women in Bus., Women Execs. in State Govt., Ind. State Auditor Adv. Coun., Ind. Farm Bur., Ind. Assn. of Cities and Towns (bd. dirs.), Dubois County GOP Women's Club (pres. 1996-98), Marion County GOP Women's Club, Huntingburg C. of C. Republican. Office: State House Rm 240 200 W Washington St Indianapolis IN 46204-2728

NASS, LEONARD IRA, chemist, consultant; b. N.Y.C., Apr. 23, 1927; s. Irving and Sylvia Nass; m. Irene Shirley Wurman, June 3, 1950; children: Meryl, Hillary Atzori, Laura. BS in Chemistry, Syracuse U., 1949; postgrad., Poly. Inst., N.Y.C., 1950—54. Quality control chemist Consolidated Film Industries, Ft. Lee, NJ, 1949—51, Cineque Color Film Labs, N.Y.C., 1951—53; synthetic rsch. chemist Advance Solvents and Chems. Corp., N.Y.C., 1953—65; mgr. specialty chems. Nat. Starch & Chem. Corp., Plainfield, NJ, 1965—68; pvt. cons. Warren, NJ, 1968—; founder, pres. Tech. Info. Exch., Gouldsboro, 1983—. Contbr. articles to profl. jours.; editor, author: Encyclopedia of PVC, 3 vols., 1975;; editor: (rev. edit.) Encyclopedia of PVC, 4 vols., 1986; author: Modern Vinyl Compounding and Stabilization, 1964. Pharmacist mate 3d class USN, 1945—47. Fellow: Soc. Plastics Engrs. (pres. Palisades sect. 1965—66, founder, councilor polymer modifiers and additives divsn. 1984—87, councilor Palisades sect. 1980—83, Outstanding Achievements award Polymer Modifiers and Additives Divsn. 1987, Contbns. to Vinyl award Vinyl Plastics Divsn. 1997); mem.: ASTM, Plastics Inst. Am., Am. Chem. Soc. Achievements include patents for polyurethane foam and benzotriazole u.v. absorbing monomers and polymers. Avocations: jazz, photography. Home: PO Box 242 Gouldsboro PA 18424 Office: Tech Info Exch 156 Mountainside Dr Gouldsboro PA 18424 E-mail: l.nass@att.net.

NASS, MERYL J. physician, writer, research scientist; b. Rockville Ctr., N.Y., Apr. 6, 1951; d. Leonard Ira and Irene Shirley Nass; m. John Duncan Abernethy, Aug. 13, 1977 (div. 1987); children: Abraham David Abernethy, Jacob Duncan Abernethy. BS biology, Mass. Inst. of Tech., Cambridge, Mass., 1974; MD, Univ. Miss. Med. Sch., Jackson, Miss., 1980. Diplomate Am. Bd. of Internal Medicine, 1986. Physician hosp. and health care ctrs., 1985—98; self-employed, 1999—. Mem. adv. bd. Alliance for Human Rsch. Protection, N.Y., 2001—, Nat. Vaccine Info. Ctr., Vienna, 2000—, Inst. for Molecular Medicine, Huntington Beach, Calif., 2000—; cons. Interamerican Devel. Bank, Washington, 2001—; presenter testimony on anthrax vaccine reaction NAS Inst. Medicine, U.S. Congress, major mass media, 1998—. Contbr. scientific papers to profl. jour., articles over 30 to profl. jour. Achievements include development of assessment and treatment strategies for fibromyalgia, Gulf War syndrome, chronic fatigue sydrome; discovery of first use of biological weapons in modern times-anthrax in Rhodesia; high rate of severe reactions to anthrax vaccine; research in establishing long-term safety and efficacy for vaccines and drugs before licensure and widespread use; improving criteria to distinguish naturally occurring from deliberate outbreaks of disease; development of comprehensive epidemiologic surveillance to identify questionable disease outbreaks; research in mitigation of bioterrorism events. Office: Mount Desert Island Hosp 10 Wayman Lane Bar Harbor ME 04609 Office Phone: 207-288-5082 220. E-mail: mnass@anthraxvaccine.org.

NASSAR, A.J. retail executive; V.p., chief oper. officer Kenny Carpet & Linoleum, Inc., 1986-90; pres., CEO The Maxim Group, Inc., Kennesaw, Ga., 1990—. Bd. dirs. millionaire.com. Office: The Mexim Group Inc 210 Townpark St Kennesaw GA 30144

NASSAR, JAFET M. plant animal specialist, researcher; b. Caracas, Venezuela, Apr. 25, 1966; s. Hofez H. Nassar and Eutimia Hernández; m. Beatriz Janet Castro, Oct. 30, 1991. PhD, U. Miami, 1999. Cert. Tropical Biology U. Miami, 1999, lic. biology U. Ctrl. de Venezue. Tech. dir. Provita, Caracas, Venezuela, 1993—94; asst. prof. U. Miami, Coral Gables, Fla., 1999; assoc. rschr. Instituto Venezolano de Investigaciones Científicas, Caracas, Venezuela, 2000—. Contbr. articles various profl. jours. Mem.: Sociedad Latinoamericana de Cactáceas y Suculentas, Am. Soc. of Mammalogists, Bot. Soc. of Am., The Assn. for Tropical Biology and Conservation. Office: Ivic Carretera Panamericana Km 11 Miranda/DF Caracas 1020-A Venezuela Office Phone: +58(212)5041631. Home Fax: +58(212)5041088; Office Fax: +58(212)5041088. Personal E-mail: jnassar@oikos.ivic.ve. E-mail: jnassar@oikos.ivic.ve.

NASSAU, MICHAEL JAY, lawyer; b. NYC, June 3, 1935; s. Benjamin and Belle (Nassau) N.; m. Roberta Bluma Herzlich, June 26, 1971; children: Stephanie Ellen, William Michael. BA summa cum laude, Yale U., 1956, LLB cum laude, 1960. Bar: NY 1960, US Ct. Appeals (2d cir.) 1963, US Tax Ct. 1963, US Supreme Ct. 1965, US Dist. Ct. (so. dist.) NY 1978. Asst. instr. in constl. law Yale U., 1959-60; law clk. judge US Ct. Appeals 2d Cir., 1960-61; assoc. tax dept. Paul, Weiss, Rifkind, Wharton & Garrison, NYC, 1961-73; ptnr. Kramer Levin Naftails & Frankel LLP, and predecessor, NYC, 1974—. Mem. adv. bd. Matthew Bender Fed. Pension Law Service, 1975-76; mem. adv. com. NYU Ann. Inst. Employee Plans Exec. Compensation, 1976 79; mem. steering com. Am. Pension Conf., 1981-83; lectr. field; panelist various seminars employee benefits; panelist Pension Video Seminar, 1983; mem. N.E. region pension liaison group IRS. Mem. editl. bd. Bank Corp. Governance Law Reporter, 1989—; contbr. chpts. to books and articles to profl. jours. Recipient Excellence Benefits award achievement benefits svc., Worldwide Employee Benefits Network, 2003. Charter fellow Am. Coll. Employee Benefits Counsel; mem. ABA (sect. taxation, employee benefits com. 1993), NY State Bar Assn. (co-chmn. employee benefits sect. taxation 1976 78, mem. exec. com. sect. taxation 1976-79), Assn. Bar City NY (chmn. subcom. pension legis. of com. taxation 1975-76, employee benefits com. 1987-92), WEB (NY chpt. bd. dirs. 1990—, pres. 1993-94), Phi Beta Kappa. Office: Kramer Levin Naftalis & Frankel LLP 919 3rd Ave New York NY 10022-3902 Office Phone: 212-715-9416. Business E-Mail: mnassau@kramerlevin.com.

NASSER, JACQUES, automotive executive; b. Australia, Dec. 12, 1947; Degree in Bus. studies, Royal Melbourne Inst. Tech. With Ford of Australia, 1968-73; mem. fin. staff N. Am. truck ops. Ford Motor Co., Australia, 1973, mgr. profit analysis, product programming, 1973-75, various positions internat. automotive ops., from 1975, with Asia-Pacific and Latin-Am. ops., 1970—80; dir., v.p. fin. and adminstrn., Autolatina joint venture, 1987-90; pres., CEO Ford of Australia, 1990-93; chmn. Ford of Europe Ford Motor Co., 1993-96, v.p., 1993-96, chmn. Ford of Europe, pres. Ford automotive ops., exec. v.p., 1996—99, pres., CEO, 1999—2001. Chmn. Polaroid Corp., 2002.

NASSETTA, CHRISTOPHER J. hotel facility executive; Various positions Oliver Carr Co., 1984-91, chief devel. officer; pres. Bailey Realty Corp., 1991-95; exec. v.p. Host Marriott Corp., 1995-97, COO, 1997-2000, pres., CEO, 2000—. Office: Host Marriott Corp 10400 Fernwood Rd Bethesda MD 20817-1118

NASSIF, GARY TANNUS, singer and entertainer, art and special education educator, sculptor; b. Cedar Rapids, Iowa, June 11, 1941; s. Elias Joseph and Adele Helen Nassif. BFA in art, Drake U., 1964. Cert. teaching 1969. Mgr. family bus. Tony's Charcoal Steak House, Cedar Rapids, Iowa; NBC and CBS scenic art, 1964—69; artist and designer JC's, Cedar Rapids, Iowa, 1971—76, Mercy Hosp., sculptures and healing music, Cedar Rapids, Iowa, 1976; headliner and entertainer Shrine Auditorium, LA, Century Plaza, LA, St. Jude Children's Rsch. Hosp., M.G.M. Grand, Las Vegas, and other major hotels and Hollywood, Calif., 1982—94; sculptor St. Jude Children's Rsch. Hosp. for Danny Thomas and the Children, Memphis, 1986. Spkr. in field. Writer (inspirational biog. manuscript) Stop Crying and Listen to the Music, Cedar Rapids, Iowa, 1994—2001. Entertainer U. of Iowa Hosp., Iowa City, 1994; singer for Sisters of Mercy Convent, Cedar Rapids, Iowa, 1994—2002; motivational spkr. various schs. and orgns. Greek Orthodox. Achievements include statue "The Christ", statue nun.& adminstrn. inspired "Jeremiah Children", St. Jude Children's Rsch. Hosp., Memphis. Avocations: painting, sculpting, writing, mentor, equestrian. Home and Office: 2503 Bever Ave SE Cedar Rapids IA 52403-2944 Office Phone: 319-651-7440. E-mail: garytnassif@hotmail.com.

NASSIF, THOMAS ANTHONY, business executive, former ambassador; b. Cedar Rapids, Iowa, July 22, 1941; s. George Joseph and Clara Christine (Nofal) N.; m. Zinetta Marie Meherg, Sept. 14, 1968; children— Jaisa Diane, Matthew Christian BS, Calif. State U.-Los Angeles, 1965; JD, Calif. Western Sch. Law, 1969, LLD (hon.), 1988. Ptnr. Gray, Cary, Ames & Frye, El Centro, Calif., 1980-81; dep. and acting chief of protocol Dept. State, Washington, 1981-83; dep. asst. sec. Bur. Near Eastern and South Asian Affairs, Dept State, Washington, 1983-85; U.S. ambassador to Morocco, 1985-88; chmn. bd. Gulf Interstate Internat. Corp., San Diego, 1988-95; chmn. of bd. Gulf Intern. Inc., Houston, 1988-95, Gulf Internat. Consulting Inc., San Diego, 1992—. Chmn. Am. Task Force for Lebanon, Washington, 1991—; pres. Los Alamos Internat., Inc., San Diego, 1988—; mng. ptnr. Aequintas Internat. Cons., 2001—. Active campaign Reagan for Pres., 1980; mem. Calif. State Rep. Cen. Com. Served with U.S. Army and USNG, 1960-67. Recipient disting. alumnus award Calif. State U., L.A., Ellis Island Medal of Honor, 1993. Office: Gulf Internat Consulting Inc Ste 1025 4660 La Jolla Village Dr San Diego CA 92122-4608

NASSOS, GEORGE P. chemical engineer, educator; s. Peter and Mary Nassos; m. Patricia Limperis Nassos, June 30, 1968; children: Nicholas, Maria. BS in Chem. Engring., U. Ill., 1961; MS in Chem. Engring., Northwestern U., 1963, PhD in Chem. Engring., 1965, MBA, 1972. Various positions Internat. Minerals and Chem., Northbrook, Ill., 1965—81, Chem. Waste Mgmt., Oak Brook, Ill., 1981—95; program dir., prof. Ill. Inst. Tech., Chgo., 1997—. Bd. dirs. Extract Inc., Escondido, Calif., Am. Quality Schs., Chgo. Mem.: Air and Waste Mgmt. Assn. (dir. 2000—). Greek Orthodox. Home: 1412 Elizabeth Ln Glenview IL 60025 Office: Ill Inst Tech 565 W Adams Chicago IL 60661

NASSTROM, ROY RICHARD, retired education educator; b. Oakland, Calif., Oct. 28, 1930; s. Roy Richard and Edith Dolores (Spilman) N.; m. Sally Louise Shaw, Aug. 29, 1964; children: Karen, Eric. AA, U. Calif., Berkeley, 1955, BA, 1956, MA, 1964, PhD, 1971. Asst. to supt. Ravenswood Sch. Dist., East Palo Alto, Calif., 1964-65; acting instr. edn. U. Calif., Berkeley, 1965-68; asst. prof. ednl. adminstrn. U. Ky., Lexington, 1969-70; asst. prof. edn. Purdue U., West Lafayette, Ind., 1971-76; mediator, fact finder Ind. Edn. Employment Rels. Bd., 1974-76; asst. grad. dean Winona (Minn.) State U., 1976-77, chmn. ednl. adminstrn. dept., 1976-88, prof., 1976-01, prof. emeritus, 2001—, chmn. ednl. leadership dept., 1998-01; ednl. polit. cons. R. Nasstrom, 2002—. Cons., spkr. various orgns. and schs., 1969—; mem. bd. abstractors Ednl. Adminstrn. Abstracts, 1976-83; dir. post-masters studies, Winona State U., 1992-99. Editor Ravenswood Report, 1964-65, U. Calif.-Berkeley Sch. Edn. Newsletter, 1965-68; bd of editors AASA Prof., 1979-82; manuscript reviewer various jours. and pubs, 1983-87; contbr. articles and revs. to profl. jours., chpts. to books. Mem. steering com. Winona On-line Democracy, 2003—. With U.S. Army, 1952—54. Recipient numerous grants, 1969-98. Mem.Am. Ednl. Rsch. Assn. (paper reviewer 1983-2000), Calif. Alumni Assn., Am. Assn. Colls. for Tchr. Edn. (instnl. rep., paper reviewer), Nat. Assn. Scholars, Phi Delta Kappa, Pi Sigma Alpha . Avocation: photography. Home: 1702 Edgewood Rd Winona MN 55987-2149 E-mail: nasstrom@cal.berkeley.edu., rrn@hbci.com.

NAST, DIANNE MARTHA, lawyer; b. Mount Holly, N.J., Jan. 30, 1948; d. Henry Daniel and Anastasia (Lovenduski) N.; m. Joseph Francis Roda, Aug. 23, 1980; children: Michael, Daniel, Joseph, Joshua, Anastasia. BA, Pa. State U.; JD, Rutgers U., 1976. Bar: Pa. 1976, U.S. Dist. Ct. Pa. 1976, N.J. 1976, U.S. Dist. Ct. N.J. 1976, U.S. Ct. Appeals (3d, 5th, 6th, 7th, 8th and 11th cirs.) 1976, U.S. Supreme Ct. 1982, U.S. Dist. Ct. Ariz. 1985. Dir., v.p. Kohn, Nast & Graf, P.C., Phila., 1976-95, Roda & Nast, P.C., Lancaster, Pa., 1995—. Mem. lawyers adv. com. U.S. Ct. Appeals (3d cir.), 1982-84, chmn., 1983-84, mem. com. on revision jud. conf. conduct rules, 1982-84; mem. Third Cir. Task Force on Selection of Class Clunsel, 2001-02mem. U.S. Ct. Appeals for the 3d Cir. Jud. Conf. Permanent Planning Com., 1983-90; bd. dirs. 3d Cir. Hist. Soc., Phila. Pub. Def., 1980-89, Fed. Jud. Ctr. Found., 1992-2002, chmn. 1997-2002; chmn. lawyers adv. com. U.S. Dist. Ct. (ea. dist.) Pa., 1982-90. Pres. Hist. Soc., 1988-91. Fellow ABA (coun. litigation sect. 1986-89, co-chmn. anti-trust com. litigation sect. 1984-86, div. dir. 1990-91, practical litigation editl. bd. 1989—, ho. of dels. 1992-94, mem. task force state justice initiatives, mem. task force state of justice system, 1993, mem. task force long range planning com. 1994), Am. Law Inst. (chair internat. professionalism com. 1991-94, civil justice task force 1993-95), Am. Arbitration Assn. (bd. dirs., mem. alt. dispute resolution and mass torts task force), Am. Judicature Soc., Pa. Bar Assn. (bd. of dels. 1983-95), N.J. Bar Assn., Pa. Trial Lawyers Assn., Phila. Bar Assn. (bd. govs. 1985-87, chmn., bicentennial com. 1986-87, chmn. bench bar conf. 1988-89), Lancaster Bar Assn. (co-chair civil litigation and rules com. trial law sect.), Rutgers Law Sch. Alumni Assn. Home: 1059 Sylvan Rd Lancaster PA 17601-1923 Office: Roda & Nast PC 801 Estelle Dr Lancaster PA 17601-2130 E-mail: dnast@rodanast.com.

NAST, EDWARD PAUL, cardiac surgeon; b. Balt., Dec. 13, 1958; s. Richard Cecil and Lenora (Heilig) N.; 1 child, Bennett Ross. BS, Emory U., 1979; MD, U. Md., 1984. Diplomate Am. Bd. Thoracic Surgery, Am. Bd. Surgery. Intern Georgetown U. Med. Ctr., Washington, 1984-85, resident in gen. surgery, 1985-86, 88-91; resident in thoracic and cardiovascular surgery U. Md. Med. Sys., Balt., 1991-93; fellow in cardiac surgery NIH, Bethesda, Md., 1986-88; cardiac surgeon Arnot Ogden Med. Ctr., Elmira, NY, 2001—. Contbr. articles to profl. jours. Named one of Outstanding Young Men of Am., 1996, 98. Fellow ACS, Am. Coll. Cardiology, Am. Coll. Chest Physicians; mem. AMA, Med. Soc. State N.Y., Soc. Thoracic Surgeons, Phi Beta Kappa. Home: 670 Euclid Ave Elmira NY 14901-1948 Office: 600 Ivy St Ste 201 Elmira NY 14905 Personal E-mail: enast@stny.rr.com. Business E-Mail: enast@aomc.org.

NASTASI, ALDO A. judge; b. N.Y.C., Sept. 18, 1932; s. Anthony and Santina N.; m. Marie A. Nastasi, Dec. 26, 1954; children: Aldo, Robert, Marc, Anthony, David. B in Social Sci., Fordham U., 1954, LLD, 1959. Bar: N.Y. 1960, U.S. Supreme Ct. 1974. City ct. judge, Yonkers, N.Y., 1975-79; judge Westchester County Ct., N.Y., 1980-83, N.Y. State Supreme Ct., 1984-97, 98—. Councilman City of Yonkers, 1972-75, selected coun. majority leader. 1st lt. USMC, 1954-56. Mem. N.Y. State Lawyers Trial Assn., Westchester County Bar Assn., Columbia Lawyers Assn. (bd. dirs. 1992-98). Republican. Roman Catholic. Avocations: reading historical novels, accouts and biographies, golf. Office: 9th Jud Dist Ct NY Westchester County Ct House 111 MLK Jr Blvd White Plains NY 10601

NASTEK, THOMAS EDWARD, engineer, researcher, writer; b. Chgo., Mar. 22, 1965; s. Edward David and Joan Eleanor Nastek; m. Donna Mae Lucarz, Aug. 14, 1957; children: Lori Lee Sciarrone, Kevin John, Shane Thomas. Technician LIttelfuse, Des Plaines, Ill., 1986—88; sr. rsch. & devel. engr. Watlow, Winona, Minn., 1988—. Author: While in Pursuit of the Perfect Ballad, (short stories) 2121 Lake Street - Journey Anthology, (poem) Pages Turning. Chair, founder Pages Turning Found., Winona, Minn., 2003—04. Achievements include patents for Graphical Interface for programming ramping controls; patents pending for Asset Management system for kitchen equipment. Office: Watlow 1241 Bundy Blvd Winona MN 55987 Personal E-mail: edward@emotketsan.com. E-mail: tnastek@watlow.com.

NASTRI, WAYNE, government agency administrator; BS in Biol. Sci., U. Calif., Irvine. Dir. Calif. office Jefferson Group; founder, pres. Environ. Mediation Inc., 1995—2001; adminstr. region 9 US EPA, San Francisco, 2001—. Pro bono legis. dir. Calif. Environ. Bus. Coun.; implementation adv. com. Calif. Air Resources Bd. Zero Emission Vehicle; governing bd. South Coast Air Quality Mgmt. Dist. Mem.: Nat. Assn. Environ. Profls. (Editor-in-chief newsletter). Office: US EPA Region 9 75 Hawthorne St Kansas City KS 66101

NATALICIO, DIANA SIEDHOFF, academic administrator; b. St. Louis, Aug. 25, 1939; d. William and Eleanor J. (Biermann) Siedhoff. BS in Spanish summa cum laude, St. Louis U., 1961; MA in Portuguese lang., U. Tex., 1964, PhD in Linguistics, 1969. Chmn. dept. modern langs. U. Tex., El Paso, 1973-77, assoc. dean liberal arts, 1977-79; acting dean liberal arts, 1979-80; dean Coll. Liberal Arts U. Tex., El Paso, 1980-84, v.p. acad. affairs, 1984-88, pres., 1988—. Bd. dirs. El Paso br. Fed. Res. Bd. Dallas, chmn., 1989; mem. Presdl. Adv. Commn. on Ednl. Excellence for Hispanic Ams., 1991; bd. dirs. Sandia Corp., Trinity Industries; bd. dirs. Nat. Action Coun. for Minorities in Engring., 1993—; mem. Nat. Sci. Bd. 1994-2000; mem. NASA Adv. Coun., 1994-96; bd. mem. Fund for Improvement of Post-Secondary Edn., 1993-97; bd. dirs. Fogarty Internat. Ctr. of NIH, 1993-96; bd. chair Am. Assn. Higher Edn., 1995-96; bd. dirs. U.S.-Mexico Commn. for Ednl. and Cultural Exch., 1994—. Co-author: Sounds of Children, 1977; contbr. articles to profl. jours. Bd. dirs. United Way El Paso, 1990-93, chmn. needs survey com., 1990-91, chmn. edn. divsn., 1989; chmn. Quality Edn. for Minorities Network in Math. Sci. and Engring., 1991-92; chairperson Leadership El Paso, Class 12, 1989-90, mem. adv. coun., 1987-90, participant, 1980-81; mem. Historically Black Colls. and Univs./Minority Instns. Consortium on Environ. Tech. chairperson, 1991-93. Recipient Harold W. McGraw. Jr. prize in edn., 1997, Torch of Liberty award Anti-Defamation League B'nai B'rith, 1991, Conquistador award City of El Paso, 1990, Humanitarian award El Paso chpt. NCCJ, 1990; mem. El Paso Women's Hall of Fame, 1990. Mem. Philos. Soc. Tex. Avocations: hiking, bicycling, skiing, skating. Home: 711 Cincinnati Ave El Paso TX 79902-2616 Office: U Tex at El Paso Office Of President El Paso TX 79968-0001

NATANI, KIRMACH, forensic psychologist; b. Milw., June 5, 1935; s. Whit Baer Naabane and Natasha Rucoss Nabona. MSc in Clin. Psychology, Okla. U., 1970; PhD in Biopsychology, Okla. U. Health Sci. Ctr., 1977; postgrad., USAF Sch. Aerospace Medicine, San Antonio, 1977—79. Lic. clin. psychologist, health svc. provider, cert. forensic neuropsychologist, sr. disabiloty analyst, divorce mediator. Physics tech./profl. Lawrence Berkeley Lab., Berkeley, Calif., 1958—63; vol. Peace Corps, Thailand, 1963—65; clin. rschr. Okla. City VA Hosp., 1966—77; human factors engr. McDonnell-Douglas, St. Louis, 1980—92; postodoctoral resident/cons. St. Mary's Hosp., East St. Louis, Ill., 1992—97; pvt. practice clin. neuropsychologist, cons. Bi-State Neurometric Svcs., various cities, 1998—. Clin. mgr. Mo. Dept. Corrections, Farmington, Mo., 1999—2001; sr. care mgr. Magellan Behavior Health, St. Louis, 2001—02; ad hoc peer reviewer profl. psychology, rsch., practice, 2001; mem. adv. com. NRC, 1978—83. Contbr. numerous articles to profl. jours., chpts. to books. With USAF, 1955—63. Recipient, Roche Labs. awards, 1973; grantee Rsch. grantee, Divsn. Polar Programs, NSF, 1966—75. Fellow: Am. Coll. Forensic Examiners; mem.: Am. Bd. Disability Analysts, Am. Bd. Psychol. Specialities, Internat. Orgn. Psychophysiology, APA Internat., Soc. for Neuronal Regulation. Avocations: computer graphics, digital photographic restoration. E-mail: knat3@juno.com.

NATARUS, BURTON F. lawyer, municipal legislator; b. Wausau, Wis., Nov. 7, 1933; BS in Polit. Sci., U. Wis., 1956, JD, 1960; postgrad., John F. Kennedy Sch. Govt., 1993. Chair qualified arbitrator: Cir. Ct. Cook County, Ill. Pvt. practice law, Chgo.; elected alderman 42d Ward, Chgo., 1971; chmn. Chgo. City Coun. Com. Traffic Control and Safety, 1997—; mem. Chgo. Plan Com. State St. Com., 1997—. Mem. Mayor's Zoning Reform Commn.; mem. Ctrl. Area Planning Task Force, Ill. Regional Transp. Task Force, State Street Coun. Mem. 2000 Yr. Chgo. Trade Del. to China. Capt. USAR, ret. Fellow Acad. Polit. Sci.; mem. Internat. Soc. Poets, City Club, Greater North Michigan Ave. Assn., Streeterville C. of C., River North Assn., North Dearborn Assn., North State, Astor, Lake Shore Dr. Assn., Streeterville Orgn. Active Residents, Ctrl. Mich. Ave. Assn. Address: 30 N La Salle St Ste 2900 Chicago IL 60602-2584 Office: City Hall Rm 306 121 N Lasalle St Chicago IL 60602-1202

NATCHER, STEPHEN DARLINGTON, retired lawyer, business executive; b. San Francisco, Nov. 19, 1940; s. Stanlus Zoch and Robena Lenore Collie (Goldring) N.; m. Carolyn Anne Bowman, Aug. 23, 1969; children: Tanya Michelle, Stephanie Elizabeth. AB in Polit. Sci., Stanford U., 1962; JD,

U. Calif., San Francisco, 1965. Bar: Calif. 1966. Assoc. firm Pillsbury, Madison & Sutro, San Francisco, 1966-68; counsel Douglas Aircraft div. McDonnell Douglas Corp., Long Beach, Calif., 1968-70; v.p., sec. Security Pacific Nat. Bank, 1971-79; asst. gen. counsel Security Pacific Corp., 1979-80; v.p., sec., gen. counsel Lear Siegler, Inc., Santa Monica, Calif., 1980-87; v.p., gen. counsel Computer Sci. Corp., El Segundo, Calif., 1987-88; exec. v.p., gen. counsel, sec. CalFed Inc., 1989-90; sr. v.p. adminstrn., gen. counsel, sec. Wyle Electronics, Irvine, Calif., 1991-98; gen. counsel VEBA Electronics LLC, Santa Clara, Calif., 1998—2002, ret., 2002. With USCG, 1965-71. Mem.: St. Francis Yacht Club (San Francisco). Republican. E-mail: snatcher@starstream.net.

NATH, JOGINDER, genetics and biology educator, researcher; b. Joginder Nagar, Panjab, India, May 12, 1932; arrived in U.S., 1957; s. Moti Ram and Vira Wali (Khorana) N.; m. Charlotte Lynn Reese, Apr. 5, 1969; children— Pravene, Brian BS with honors, Panjab U, Amritsar, India, 1953, MS with honors, 1955; PhD, U. Wis., 1960. Research assoc. Am. Inst. Biol. Research, Madison, Wis., 1960-63; asst. prof. So. Ill. U., Carbondale, Ill., 1964-66; from asst. to assoc. prof. W.Va. U., Morgantown, 1966-72, prof., chmn. dept. genetics and devel. biology, 1972—. Contbr. articles on cytogenetics, mutagenesis, biochem. genetics and cryobiology to profl. jours. Chmn. bd. Morgantown Day Sch., 1977—79. Recipient Alexander Hollaender award, Environ. Mutagen Soc., 1997, Edn. and Student Mems. Com. award, 2000, Mehra Meml. award, Panjab U., 2000; grantee, NSF, 1967—68, DOE, 1992—95, Nat. Inst. Occupl. Safety and Health, 1985—95, NIH, 2002—. Mem. Soc. Cryobiology, Environ. Mutagen Soc., Sigma Xi. Office: WVa U Coll Agr Dept Genetics & Devel Biology Morgantown WV 26506 E-mail: jnath@wvu.edu.

NATH, SHYAMAL K. research scientist; s. Krishna Nath and Maya Devi; m. Protiti Sarker, May 3, 1999. BS, Mechanical Engring., Bangladesh Engring. U., 1991; MS, N. Mex Tech., 1993; PhD, N.Mex Inst. Mining and Tech., 1996. Rsch. fellow U. Wis., Madison, 1996—99; sci. software developer Accelrys Inc., San Diego, 1999—2004; Sr. Rsch. Scientist N. Mex. Tech., Socorro, 2004—; Sr. rsch. scientist N. Mex Tech., Socorro, Calif., 2004—. Recipient Ashman award, N.Mex Inst. Mining and Tech., 1995. Mem.: Am. Phys. Soc. Achievements include first to force field and methodology development for vapor-liquid phase equilibria simulation of industrially important systems.

NATHAN, DAVID GORDON, pediatrician, educator; b. Boston, May 25, 1929; s. E. Geoffrey and Ruth (Gordon) Nathan; m. Jean Louise Friedman, Sept. 1, 1951; children: Deborah, Linda, Geoffrey. BA, Harvard U., 1951; MD, Harvard Med. Sch., 1955. Diplomate Am. Bd. Internal Medicine, Am. Bd. Pediat. Intern dept. medicine Peter Bent Brigham Hosp., Boston, 1955—56, sr. resident, 1958—59; jr. assoc. in medicine Brigham and Women's Hosp., Boston, 1961—67, sr. assoc. in medicine, 1967—; assoc. in medicine, hematology Childrens Hosp., Boston, 1963—68, chief, divsn. hematology, 1968—73, chief divsn. hematology and oncology, 1974—84; pediatrician-in-chief Dana Farber Cancer Inst., Boston, 1974—85; Robert A. Stranahan prof. pediat. Harvard Med. Sch., Boston, 1977—95; physician-in-chief Childrens Hosp., Boston, 1985—95; pres. Dana-Farber Cancer Inst., Boston, 1995—2000; Richard and Susan Smith prof. medicine Harvard Med. Sch., Boston, 1996—2000, prof. pediat., 1996—2000, Robert A. Stranahan Disting. prof. pediat., 2001—. Chair NIH Panel on Clin. Rsch., 1995—98; pres. emeritus Dana Farber Cancer Inst., 2001—. Author: Genes, Blood and Courage, 1994; editor: Hematology in Infancy and Childhood, 1993, 1997. With USMC, 1948—49. Recipient Nat. medal Sci., NSF, 1990. Fellow: AAAS; mem.: Am. Philos. Soc., Am. Soc. Hematology (pres. 1986), Am. Soc. Clin. Investigators, Assn. Am. Physicians, Soc. Pediatric Rsch., Am. Pediatric Soc., Am. Acad. Arts and Scis., Inst. Medicine NAS, Phi Beta Kappa (hon.). Avocations: tennis, hiking, sailing. Office: Dana-Farber Cancer Inst 44 Binney St Boston MA 02115-6084 E-mail: david_nathan@dfci.harvard.edu.*

NATHAN, FREDERIC SOLIS, lawyer; b. N.Y.C., June 24, 1922; s. Edgar Joshua and Mabel (Unterberg) N.; m. Frances E., Oct. 28, 1956; children: Jean E., Frederic S. Jr., William E. BA, Williams Coll., Williamstown, Mass., 1943; LLD, Yale U., 1948. Bar: N.Y. 1948, U.S. Dist. Ct. (so. and ea. dists) N.Y. 1948, U.S. Ct. Appeals (2d cir.) 1953, U.S. Supreme Ct. 1968. Instr. Williams Coll., Williamstown, 1948; assoc. Rathbone Perry Kelley & Drye, N.Y.C., 1948-53; asst. U.S. atty. U.S. Attys.' Office (so. dist.), N.Y.C., 1953-56; assoc. Greenbaum, Wolff & Ernst, N.Y.C., 1956-58, ptnr., 1959-65, 70-82; 1st asst. corp. counsel N.Y.C. Law Dept., N.Y.C., 1966-69; ptnr. Kelley, Drye & Warren, N.Y.C., 1982—. Mem. N.Y. Rep. County Com., N.Y.C., 1948-66; trustee Mt. Sinai Hosp., N.Y.C., 1970—; chmn. bd. FOJP Svc. Corp., N.Y.C., 1977-85, bd. dirs., 1979—; bd. dirs., v.p. Am. Jewish Soc. for Svc., N.Y.C., 1950—; bd. dirs. Everybody Wins Found., Inc., 1992—. With U.S. Army, 1943-45, ETO. Fellow Am. Coll. Trial Lawyers; mem. ABA, Assn. of Bar of City of N.Y. (exec. com. 1979-81), Fed. Bar Council (pres. 1975-76), N.Y. State Bar Assn. Clubs: Century Assn., Yale of N.Y.C.; Sunningdale Country. Republican. Jewish. Home: 180 East End Ave New York NY 10128-7763 Office: Kelley Drye & Warren 101 Park Ave New York NY 10178-0062 Office Phone: 212-808-7840. E-mail: fnathan@kelleydrye.com.

NATHAN, LAURA E. sociology educator; b. L.A., Oct. 28, 1951; d. Monroe and Sheila (Solomon) Engelberg; m. Mark D. Nathan, April 9, 1978; children: Justin, Michael. BA in Sociology, U. Calif., Santa Barbara, 1973; MA in Sociology, U. Calif., L.A., 1975, PhD in Sociology, 1981. Tchg. assoc. in sociology Univ. Calif., L.A., 1975—76; acting asst. prof. sociology Calif. State Univ., Fullerton, 1977-81; coord., instr. Univ. Calif., L.A., 1979-80; assoc. prof. sociology and psychology Antelope Valley Coll., Lancaster, Calif., 1981-82; asst. prof. sociology Mills Coll., Oakland, Calif., 1982-87, assoc. prof. sociology, 1987-93, prof. of sociology, 1993—, Robert J. and Ann B. Wert prof. of sociology, 1993-96, head dept. sociology and anthropology, 2000—01, dean social sci., 2001—02. Lectr. in sociology and womens studies Calif. State Univ., Long Beach, 1978; program evaluator U.S. Dept. Health, Edn. and Welfare, L.A., 1974-75, program dir. 1975-76; mem. conf. planning com. Womens Leadership Conf., Mills Coll., also com. chair, 1992-93; bd. dirs. Am. Cancer Soc., East Bay Region, Calif., 1985-96, Calif. divsn., 2001-; bd. dirs. Am. Cancer Soc. East Bay Metro Unit, 1996—, pres., 1999-2001, bd. dirs. Am. Cancer Soc. Calif. Divsn. Author: (with others) Secondary Analysis of Survey Data, 1985; contbr. chpts. to books. Regents Rsch. grantee, 1979, Mellon Found. grantee, 1983, Faculty Devel. Rsch. grantee Mills. Coll., 1985, 86, 87, 90, 91, 94, 95, 99, 2002, Barratt Found. grantee, 2002, W.K. Kellogg Nat. fellow, 1988, Thornton Bradshaw Humanities fellow Claremont Grad. Sch., 1990, Graduate Leadership Am., 1997; recipient Disting. Leadership award Am. Cancer Soc., 1995, Unit and Region Lifetime Achievement award, 2000, ten Broek Soc. award for Excellence in Teaching, 1996. Mem. Pacific Sociol. Assn. (mem. nominating com. 1985-88, mem. program com. 1995-96, exec. coun., 1997-99), Am. Sociol. Assn. (membership com. 1988-92, com. soc. and persons with disabilities 1997-2000, chair), Soc. for the Study of Social Problems (chmn. poverty, class inequality div. 1987-88). Jewish. Avocations: traveling, mysteries, vol. work, beading, pilates. Office: Mills Coll 5000 Macarthur Blvd Oakland CA 94613-1301 E-mail: laura@mills.edu.

NATHAN, PAUL S. editor, writer; b. Oakland, Calif., Apr. 2, 1913; s. Alfred Jacobs and Frances (Strause) N.; m. Dorothy Goldeen, July 14, 1935 (dec. Dec. 1966); children: Andrew J., Carl F., Janet D. Souza; m. Ruth Wilk Notkins, May 26, 1972. BA, U. Calif., Berkeley, 1934. Reporter Oakland Post-Enquirer, 1929-36; asst. play editor Paramount Pictures, NYC, 1937-48; Hosp. pub. rels. Will, Folsom & Smith, NYC, 1948-61; sci. editor Nat. Cystic Fibrosis Rsch. Found., NYC and Atlanta, 1963—73; columnist Rights and Permissions (subsequently Rights) Pubs. Weekly, NYC, 1946-98. US liaison Jerusalem Internat. Book Fair, 1976-77 Author: (play) Ricochet, 1980 (Edgar Allan Poe award of Mystery Writers Am. for best play of 1980), Texas Collects: Fine Arts, Furniture, Windmills & Whimseys, 1988; co-editor: (anthology) View: Parade of the Avant-Garde, 1991; author: (novels) Protocol for Murder, 1994, No Good Deed, 1995, Count Your Enemies, 1997; columnist Pub. News, London, 1998-2003; contbr. fiction and articles to Story, NY Times mag., Saturday Evening Post, Saturday Rev., others. Mem.: PEN, Mystery Writers Am., Authors League, Authors Guild, Dramatists Guild, Phi Beta Kappa. Home and Office: 141 E 33rd St New York NY 10016-4606 Office Phone: 212-683-4162. E-mail: paulnathanny@aol.com.

NATHAN, PETER E. psychologist, educator; b. St. Louis, Apr. 18, 1935; s. Emil and Kathryn (Kline) N.; m. Florence I. Baker, Nov. 26, 1959; children: David Edward, Anne Miller, Laura Carol, Mark Andrew. AB, Harvard U., 1957; PhD, Washington U., 1962. Research fellow psychology Harvard U., 1962-64, research asso., 1964-68, asst. prof. psychology, 1968-69; research psychologist Boston City Hosp., 1964-68, dir. alcohol study unit, 1967-70; prof. Rutgers U., New Brunswick, N.J., 1969-89, dir. clin. psychology tng., 1969-87, dir. Alcohol Behavior Research Lab., 1970-87, chmn. dept. clin. psychology, 1976-87, dir. Ctr. Alcohol Studies, 1983-89, Henry and Anna Starr prof. psychology, 1983-89; sr. program officer, health program MacArthur Found., 1987-89; v.p. acad. affairs, found. disting. prof. psychology U. Iowa, 1990—, dean faculties, 1990-93, provost, 1993-95, acting pres., 1995. Mem. advisory council VA, 1972-76; chmn. alcoholism com. Nat. Inst. on Alcohol Abuse and Alcoholism, 1973-76, co-chmn. spl. rev. com., 1985, mem. nat. adv. coun., 1990-94; mem. psychol. scis. fellowship rev. com. NIMH, 1977-79; chmn. N.J. State Community Mental Health Bd., 1981-84; mem. working group substance use disorders, DSM-IV. Author: Cues, Decisions, and Diagnoses, 1967, Psychopathology and Society, 1975, 2d edit., 1980, Experimental and Behavioral Approaches to Alcoholism, 1978, Alcoholism: New Directions in Behavioral Treatment and Research, 1978, Clinical Case Studies in the Behavioral Treatment of Alcoholism, 1982, Professionals in Distress, 1987, Neuropsychological Deficits in Alcoholism, 1987, Introduction to Psychology, 1987, 2d edit., 1990, Abnormal Psychology, 1992, 2d edit., 1996, A Guide to Treatments that Work, 1998, 2d edit., 2002; exec. editor: Jour. Studies Alcohol, 1983—90; assoc. editor Am. Psychologist, 1977—85, Contemporary Psychology, 1991—97, Prevention and Treatment, 1998—2001, Psychol. Bull., 2002—, mem. editl. bd. Jour. Clin. Psychology, 1969—95, Jour. Cons. Clin. Psychology, 1973—95, Profl. Psychology, 1976—89. Fellow Am. Psychol. Assn. (chmn. sect. 3 div. 12 1976-77, rep. to council 1976-79, 82-85, pres. div. 12 1984-85; Disting. Contbns. to Knowledge award 1999). Democrat. Jewish. Home: 248 Black Springs Cir Iowa City IA 52246-3800 Office: Univ Iowa E119 Seashore Hall Iowa City IA 52242-1316 Office Phone: 319-384-5390. Business E-Mail: peter-nathan@uiowa.edu.

NATHANSON, HARVEY CHARLES, electrical engineer; b. Pitts., Oct. 22, 1936; s. David Benjamin and Ella (Sachs) N.; m. Esther Janet Mishelevich, Oct. 13, 1963; children: Marc Elliot, Elinor Sharon. BSEE, Carnegie Inst. Tech., 1958, MSEE, 1959, PhD, 1962. Sr. engr. Junction Device Physics, Westinghouse, Research/Devel. Center, Pitts., 1962-67, fellow engr., 1968-72, mgr. silicon junction physics, 1972-77, mgr. microelectronics dept., 1978-90, chief scientist electronic div., 1990-95; chief scientist Northrop Grumman Sci. Tech. Ctr., 1996—2001; cons. Northrop Grumman, 2002—. Instr. Carnegie Inst. Tech., Pitts., 1959-60; chmn. Westinghouse Sat. Sci. Honors Inst. for High Sch. Students, 1970-76; mem. adv. group on electron devices U.S. Dept. Def., 1976-86; adviser to Nat. Materials Bd., 1986-87. Contbr. articles to profl. jours.; mem. editorial bd. Solid State Electronics, 1985—; patentee in field. Bd. dirs. Temple Sinai, 1981-83, 95-97; pres. Brotherhood, 1993-95. Recipient IR100 award, 1965, hon. mention Outstanding Young Engr. award Eta Kappa Nu, 1967, Best Display Paper award Soc. Info. Display, 1972, Carnegie-Mellon Alumni award, 1982, Westinghouse Top Corp. Patent award, 1990; named to Westinghouse Order of Merit, Westinghouse Electric Corp., 1987. Fellow IEEE (editl. bd. Spectrum mag. 1989-91, 3e Millennium medal 2000, Pitts. Inventor of Yr. 2002); mem. IEEE Electron Device Soc. (pres. 1978-80), Fedn. Materials Socs. (bd. dirs. 1987-90), Sigma Xi, Eta Kappa Nu. Democrat. Jewish. Home: 5635 Marlborough Rd Pittsburgh PA 15217-1404 Office: Northrop Grumman Sci-Tech Ctr Advanced Tech Lab PO Box 1521-MS 3B10 Baltimore MD 21203 E-mail: harvey.c.nathanson@ngc.com.

NATHANSON, LARRY, medical educator, physician; b. Boston, Dec. 23, 1928; s. Robert Bernard and Leah (Rabin) N.; m. Anna Bloch, May 27, 1962; children: Andrew, Aran, Nicholas. AB, Harvard Coll., 1950; MD, U. Chgo., 1955. Diplomate Am. Bd. Internal Medicine, Am. Bd. Med. Oncology. Instr. medicine Harvard Med. Sch., Boston, 1966-68; from asst. to prof. Tufts U. Sch. Medicine, Boston, 1968-79; prof. medicine SUNY Stony Brook Sch. of Medicine, 1980-96, prof. emeritus, 1996—. Pres., CEO Oncology Cons., Cambridge, Mass., 1996—; cons. John Wayne Cancer Inst., Santa Monica, Calif., 1996—; councilor Cambridge Hist. Soc.; bd. dirs. Mass. Soc. for Med. Rsch. Editl. bd. Cancer, 1977—, Jour. Clin. Oncology, 1995-98, Seminars in Oncology, 1979-83, Med. & Pediat. Oncology, 1977-96, Jour. Cancer Edn., 1986-92; editor 6 books; contbr. over 280 articles to profl. jours. Trustee Cold Spring Harbor Lab., 1990-94, Soc. Preservation L.I. Antiquities, Setauket, N.Y., 1982-92, Cambridge Sch. of Weston, 1997—, Mass. Soc. Med. Rsch., 2002-. Capt. U.S. Army Med. Corps., 1956-58. Nat. Cancer Inst. fellow, 1964-66; recipient Disting Svc. award Vet. Affairs Rev. Bd. in Cancer Rsch., 1974-78, Winthrop U. Hosp., 1993. Fellow ACP; mem. Mass. Soc. Med. Rsch. (trustee 2002—), Harvard Club (Boston, N.Y.), Seawanhaka Corinthian Yacht Club (race com. 1990-96), Harvard Faculty Club. Avocations: sailing, squash, tennis, history. Office: Oncology Cons 3 Gray Gdns E Cambridge MA 02138-1401 Office Fax: 617-441-0043. Personal E-mail: larrymd@ix.netcom.com.

NATHANSON, LINDA SUE, publisher, author, technical writer; b. Washington, Aug. 11, 1946; d. Nat and Edith (Weinstein) N.; m. James F. Barrett. BS, U. Md., 1969; MA, UCLA, 1970, PhD, 1975. Tng. dir. Rockland Research Inst., Orangeburg, N.Y., 1975-77; asst. prof. psychology SUNY, 1978-79; pres. Cabri Prodns., Inc., Ft. Lee, N.J., 1979-81; rsch. supr. Darcy, McManus & Masius, St. Louis, 1981-83; mgr. software tng., documentation On-Line Software Internat., Ft. Lee, 1983-85; pvt. practice Ft. Lee, 1985-87; founder, exec. dir. The Edin. Group, Inc., Gillette, N.J., 1987-98; founder, pres. Edin Books, Inc., Gillette, N.J., 1994—. Author: (with others) Psychological Testing: An Introduction to Tests and Measurements, 1988; (with S.J. Thayer) Interview with an Angel, 1997; (with S.J. Thayer) The Heart of Interview with an Angel, 1998; publ. A Funny Thing Happened at the Interview (G.F. Farrell), 1996, Angel Talk (R. Crystal), 1996; (audiobook with W. Barnes) I Built the Titanic: Past-Life Memories of a Master Shipbuilder, 1999, Thomas Andrews, Voyage into History, 2000; (audio book with W. Barnes and F. Baranowski) A Past-Life Interview with Titanic's Designer, 1999. Recipient Rsch. Svc. award 1978; Albert Einstein Coll. Medicine Research fellow, 1978-79. Jewish. Home and Office: 102 Sunrise Dr Gillette NJ 07933-1944 Office Phone: 908-361-3535. Business E-Mail: edinbooks@patmedia.net.

NATHANSON, NEAL, virologist, epidemiologist, educator; b. Boston, Sept. 1, 1927; s. Robert B. and Leah (Rabinowitch) N.; m. Constance Allen, June 8, 1954; children: Katherine L., John A., Daniel R.; m. Phoebe Starfield, Oct. 7, 1984. BA, Harvard U., 1949, MD, 1953. Chief polio surveillance unit USPHS, 1955-57; rsch. assoc., asst. prof. anatomy Johns Hopkins U., Balt., 1957-63, assoc. prof. epidemiology, 1963-68, prof., 1968-79; chmn. dept. microbiology U. Pa., Phila., 1979-93, vice dean rsch., 1993-95, dir. Office of AIDS Rsch., 1998-2000, vice provost rsch., 2000—. Editor-in-chief: Am. Jour. Epidemiology, 1964-79, Microbial Pathogenesis, 1985-88. Achievements include research in pathogenesis, immunology, and epidemiology of viral infections. Home: 1600 Hagys Ford Rd Apt 9W Narberth PA 19072-1049 Office Phone: 215-898-0848. E-mail: nathanson@mail.med.upenn.edu.

NATHMAN, JOHN B. career military officer; b. San Antonio; m. Sue Wooddell; children: Amy, Ryan. Graduate, U.S. Naval Acad., 1970; MS in Aero Engring. Enlisted USN, 1972, advanced through grades to adm., 2004; various assignments Fighter Squadron 213; topgun tng. officer Navy Fighter Weapons Sch.; pilot Fighter Squadron 51, 1980; sr. naval test pilot Nellis AFB, Nev.; comdr. Strike Fighter Squadron 132; stationed on USS LaSalle, 1987; various assignments Asst. Chief of Naval Ops.; comdr. USS Nimitz, 1992—94; various assignments Allied Forces So. Europe; comdr. Carrier Group 7 and Nimitz Battle Group; dep. comdr. Joint Task Force-Southwest Asia; comdr. UN Special Commn., Iraq; dir. air warfare Chief Naval Ops., 1998—2000; comdr. Naval Air Force US Pacific Fleet, 2000—01; comdr., Naval Air Forces US Navy, 2001—02, dep. chief naval ops. (warfare requirements & programs), 2002—04, vice chief naval ops., 2004—. Decorated Legions of Merit, Bronze Star (combat V). Office: 2000 Navy Pentagon Washington DC 20350-2000*

NATHWANI, BHARAT N. pathologist, consultant; b. Bombay, Jan. 20, 1945; came to U.S., 1972; MBBS, Grant Med. Coll., Bombay, 1969, MD in Pathology, 1972. Intern Grant Med. Coll., Bombay U., 1968-69; asst. prof. pathology Grant Med. Coll., 1972; fellow in hematology Cook County Hosp., Chgo., 1972-73; resident in pathology Rush U., Chgo., 1973-74; fellow in hematopathology City of Hope Med. Ctr., Duarte, Calif., 1975-76, pathologist, 1977-84; prof. pathology, chief hematopathology U. So. Calif., L.A., 1984—. Contbr. numerous articles to profl. jours. Recipient Grant awards Nat. Libr. Medicine, Bethesda, Md., Nat. Cancer Inst., 1991. Mem. Internat. Acad. Pathology, Am. Soc. Clin. Pathology, Am. Soc. Hematology, Am. Soc. Oncology. Office: Hmr 209 2011 Zonal Ave Los Angeles CA 90033

NATION, EARL F. retired urologist, educator; b. Zephyr, Tex., Jan. 16, 1910; s. Joseph Madison and Alma Emily (Johnson) N.; m. Evelyn Stapp Poynter, Aug. 11, 1936; children: William Earl, Robert Joseph. BA, San Diego State U., 1931; MD, Western Res. U., 1935. Lic. urologist, Calif.; diplomate Am. Bd. Urology. Internship, resident in urology Los Angeles County Gen. Hosp., 1935-39; pvt. practice Pasadena, Calif., 1941-90; ret., 1990. Instr., assoc. prof. urology U. So. Calif., L.A., 1941-55; sr. attending staff Huntington Meml. Hosp., Pasadena, 1941—, St. Luke Hosp., Pasadena, 1941—, also past pres.; pres. Pasadena Dispensary, 1946; lectr. Coll. Med. Evangelists (now Loma Linda U.), 1941-48. Mem. editorial bd. Jour. of Urology, 1958-66, Calif. Medicine, 1965-69, Forum on Medicine; contbr. articles to profl. jours., contbg. author to numerous books. Sec.-treas. Pasadena Breakfast Forum, 1970-73, pres. 1974-75. Crile rsch. scholar Western Res. U., 1931. Mem. ACS, AMA, Am. Urol. Assn. (past pres., Ramon Guiteras award 2002), Am. Osler Soc. (past pres.), L.A. County Med. Assn., Calif. Med. Assn., Pasadena Hist. Soc., So. Calif. Hist. Soc., Am. Soc. Clin. Urologists, Pasadena U. Club, Zamorano Club (v.p. L.A. chpt. 1991), Twilight Club, Alpha Omega Alpha. Republican. Avocations: book collecting, reading, writing, gardening, fishing. Home: # E 311 E Sierra Madre Blvd Apt E Sierra Madre CA 91024-2669 E-mail: enoitan@gte.net.

NATION, PHILIP DAVID, financial planner; b. London, May 31, 1962; came to U.S., 1965; s. John A. and Sally G. (Leeds) N.; m. Cynthia Anne Bateman, Apr. 19, 1986. BA in Econs., Cornell U., 1984; M in Estate Planning, Coll. Fin. Planning, 1993. CFP. Sr. fin. advisor Am. Express Fin. Advisors, Raleigh, N.C., 1987—. Mem. Fin. Planning Assn., Cornell Alumni Club. Avocations: exercise, theater. Office: Am Express Fin Advisors Inc 3720 Benson Dr Raleigh NC 27609-7321 Home: 1401 Ballyclare Ct Raleigh NC 27614-7168

NATIONS, BILL, dentist, state representative; b. Greenville, Tex., June 28, 1942; m. Teena Nations; 1 child. DDS, Baylor Coll. Dentistry, 1968. Pvt. practice in dentistry, 1970—; mayor City of Norman, Okla., 1992—98; rep. Ho. of Reps., State of Okla., 1998—. Chmn. higher edn. com. Okla. Ho. Reps., Okla. City, 2002—; mem. appropriations and budget com., 2002—; vice chmn. subcom. on health and social svcs. Okla. Ho. Reps., Okla. City, 2002—; co-chmn. joint com. on accountability in govt. Okla. Ho. Reps-Okla. Senate, Okla. City; mem. banking and fin., human svcs. coms., 2002—. World Affairs Coun. Ctrl. Okla.; mem. Norman City Coun., Okla., 1986—92; U. Okla. Higher Edn. Almni Coun.; mem. Norman Downtown Revitalization Com.; Link Norman Assn.; mem. Norman Sister City Com. With USAR, 1957—63. Mem.: Norman C. of C., Am. Dental Assn., Okla. Dental Assn., Norman Bus. Assn., Okla. Sooner Club. Democrat. Presbyn. Office: Capitol Bldg 2300 N Lincoln Ave rm 410 Oklahoma City OK 73105 Home and Office: 2328 Parkland Way Norman OK 73069 E-mail: nationsbi@lsb.state.ok.us.

NATIONS, HOWARD LYNN, lawyer; b. Dalton, Ga., Jan. 9, 1938; s. Howard Lynn and Eva Earline (Armstrong) Lamb; m. Ella Lois Johnson, June 4, 1960 (div. Nov. 1976); children: Cynthia Lynn Nations Garcia, Angela Jean Gordon Hernandez. BA, Fla. State U., 1963, JD, 1966. Bar: Tex. 1966; cert. trial atty. Tex. Bd. Legal Specialization. Assoc. Butler, Rice Cook & Knapp, Houston, 1966-71; pres. Nations & Cross, Houston, 1971—; v.p., dir., co-founder Ins. Corp. Am., Houston, 1972—; pres. Caplinger & Nations Galleries, Houston, 1973—, Nations Investment Corp., Houston, 1975—, NCM Trade Corp., Houston, 1975; v.p. Delher Am. Inc., Houston, 1975—; pres. Howard L. Nations, PC, Houston, 1971—, Trial Focus, Inc., 1995—. Founder Nations Found.; adj. prof. So. Tex. Coll. Law, Houston, 1967—; speaker in field. Author: Structuring Settlements, 1987; co-author: Texas Workers' Compensation, 1988, (with others) The Anatomy of a Personal Injury Lawsuit, 3rd rev. edit. 1991; editor: Maximizing Damages in Wrongful Death and Personal Injury Litigation, 1985; contbr. articles to profl. jours. Chmn., trustee Nat. Coll. Advocacy, Washington, 1985-92. With M.I. Corps, U.S. Army, 1957-60. Recipient Gene Cavin Excellence award State Bar Tex., 2000. Fellow Tex. Bar Found., Houston Bar Found. (life); mem. ATLA (exec. com. 1991-95), Nat. Bd. Trial Advocacy (diplomate civil trial advocacy), So. Trial Lawyers Assn. (pres. 1994-95), Tex. Trial Lawyers Assn. (pres. 1992-93). Office: The Sterling Mansion 4515 Yoakum Blvd Houston TX 77006-5821 Office Phone: 713-807-8400.

NATKIN, ROBERT, painter; b. Chgo., Nov. 7, 1930; s. Phillip and Betty Natkin; m. Judith Dolnick; children: Joshua, Leda. BA, Art Inst. Chgo., 1952. Exhibited paintings in numerous one-man shows, including Andrè Emmerich Gallery, N.Y.C., Holburne of Menstrie Mus., Bath, Eng., Art Inst. Chgo., Moore Coll. Art, The Reele Galleries, N.Y.C., Phila., Ivory/Kimpton Gallery, San Francisco, Gimpel Fils Gallery, London, Gimpel & Weitzenhoffer Gallery, N.Y.C., A.B.C.D. Gallery, Paris, Tortue Gallery, Santa Monica, Calif., Butler Inst. Am. Art, Ohio, Galerie Brusberg, Hannover, Fed. Republic Germany, Hirshhorn Mus. and Sculpture Garden, Washington, Okla. Art Ctr., Oklahoma City, 1982, Gloria Luria Gallery, Miami, 1984, Klonarides Gallery, Toronto, 1985; group shows include Mus. Art, Pa. State U., 1973, Poindexter Gallery, N.Y.C., 1976; represented in permanent collections, including Art Inst. Chgo., Mus. Modern Art, N.Y.C., Solomon R. Guggenheim Mus., N.Y.C., Whitney Mus. Am. Art, Hirshhorn Mus. and Sculpture Garden, Smithsonian Instn., Washington, Mus. Fine Arts, Houston, Mus. Art, R.I. Sch. Design, San Francisco Mus. Art, Mus. Art, Carnegie Inst., Duke U. Mus. Art, Centre Georges Pompidou (Beaubourg), Paris, Milw. Art Ctr., Fogg Mus. Harvard U., Met. Mus. Art, N.Y.C., Akron (Ohio) Inst., Albright-Knox Art Gallery, N.Y.C., Butler Inst. Am. Art, L.A. County Mus. Art, Mint Mus. Art, N.C., Wadsworth Atheneum, Conn.

NATOLI, JOESEPH T. (JOE), newspaper publishing executive; Pres. The Miami Herald, Fla., 1994—2001; pres., pub. San Jose Mercury News, 2001—03; pub., chmn. Phila. Inquirer, Pa., 2003—. Mem., bd. dir. United Way-Silicon Valley. Office: Publisher Phila Inquirer PO Box 8263 Philadelphia PA 19101

NATOLI, JOSEPH, English language educator; b. Brooklyn, N.Y., Aug. 24, 1943; m. Elaine Tuminelli, June 6, 1970; children: Amelia, Brenda. BA, Bklyn. Coll., 1965, MA, 1968; PhD, SUNY, Albany, 1973. Asst. prof. English New Eng. Coll., Henniker, N.H., 1971-73, 1973-75; acting dir. libr., adj. lectr. English Bluefield (W.Va.) State Coll., 1975-77; head reference and bibliography libr. Wake Forest U., Winston Salem, N.C., 1977-81; bibliographer, adj. lectr. humanities U. Calif., Irvine, 1981-83, Mich. State U., East Lansing, 1983—, dir. study abroad program Europe, 1996—. Series editor SUNY Press Postmodern Culture, Albany, 1990—. Author: Mots D'Ordre, 1992, Hauntings, 1994, Primer to Postmodernity, 1997, Speeding to the Millenium, 1998, Postmodern Journeys, 2000, Memory's Orbit, 2003; editor: Twentieth Century Blake Criticism, 1982, Psychological Perspectives on Literature, 1984, Psychocriticism, 1984, Tracing Literary Theory, 1987, Literary Theory's Future(s), 1989, A Postmodern Reader, 1993, Postmodernism: The Key Figures, 2002. Mem. MLA. Office: Ctr Integrative Studies 304 Linton Hall Mich State U East Lansing MI 48824 E-mail: natoli@pilot.msu.edu.

NATORI, JOSIE CRUZ, apparel executive; b. Manila, May 9, 1947; came to U.S., 1964; d. Felipe F. and Angelita A. (Almeda) Cruz; m. Kenneth R. Natori, May 20, 1972; 1 child, Kenneth E.F. BA in Econs., Manhattanville Coll., 1968; Degree (hon.), Acad. Art Coll., San Francisco, 2003. With Bache Securities, N.Y.C.; joined Merrill-Lynch Co. as an investment banker, 1971; v.p., 1976—77; owner, CEO The Natori Co., N.Y.C., 1977—. Bd. dirs. The Alltel Corp., 1995—. Bd. dirs. Philippine Am. Found., Jr. Achievement, Inc., 1992, Ednl. Found. for Fashion Industries; trustee Manhattanville Coll., Asian Cultural Coun.; commr. White House Conf. on Small Bus., 1993. Recipient Human Relations award Am. Jewish Com., N.Y.C., 1986, Harriet Alger award Working Woman, N.Y., 1987, Castle award Manhattanville Coll., Purchase, 1988, Galleon award Pres. Philippines, 1988, N.Y.C. Asian-Am. award, Friendship award Philippine-Am. Found., Hall of Fame award Mega Mags., Salute to Am. Fashion Designers award Dept. of Commerce, Ellis Island medal of Honor, 1994, Presdl. Awards for Filipino Individuals and Orgns. Overseas, Pamana ng Pilipino award Philippine Consulate Gen., 2002; named Bus. Woman of Yr. N.Y.C. Partnership and C. of C., 1998. Mem. CFDA, Young Pres.'s Orgn., Fashion Group, Com. of 200. Avocations: pianist, tennis player. Home: 45 E 62nd St New York NY 10021-8025 Office: Natori Co 40 E 34th St Fl 18 New York NY 10016-4563

NATOWITZ, JOSEPH B. chemistry educator, research administrator; b. Saranac Lake, N.Y., Dec. 24, 1936; BS in Chemistry, U. Fla., 1958; Cert. in Meteorology, UCLA, 1959; PhD in Nuc. Chemistry, U. Pitts., 1965. Staff meteorologist, 1st lt. USAF, 1958-61; grad. teaching asst. U. Pitts., 1961-62, grad. rsch. asst., 1962-65; postdoctoral rsch. assoc. SUNY, Stony Brook, 1965-67; rsch. collaborator Brookhaven Nat. Lab., 1965-67; asst. prof. Tex. A&M U., College Station, 1967 72, assoc. prof., 1972 76, prof., 1976 2004, Disting. prof., 2004—, head dept. chemistry, 1981-85, dir. Cyclotron Inst., 1991—2003, Bright chair in nuc. sci., 2002—. Part-time instr. SUNY-Stony Brook, 1966-67; rsch. collaborator Lawrence Radiation Lab., Berkeley, Calif., 1966, Los Alamos (N.Mex.) Nat. Lab., 1973-74; Alexander Von Humboldt sr. scientist Max Planck Inst. für Kernphysik, Heidelberg, Germany, 1978; vis. prof. Inst. for Nuc. Studies, U. Tokyo, 1979, U. Claude Bernard, Inst. de Physique Nucleaire, 1983, U. de Caen, 1985, Ctr. des Etudes Nucleaires de Saclay, 1986, U. Cath. de Louvain, 1987; former mem. accelerator review com. TASCC, Chalk River, Can.; former mem. adv. com. LBL Superhilac, ORNL Cyclotron, Nat. Superconducting Cyclotron Lab.; mem. program adv. com. Ganil Lab; mem. nuc. sci. vis. com. Lawrence Berkeley Nat. Lab. Contbr. over 200 articles to profl. jours., also to approx. 40 books and procs. Chmn. Cub Scout Pack 802, 1973-75; v.p. College Hills PTO, 1974-75; mem. A&M Consol. Sch. Bd., 1975-78, pres., 1977-78; pres. A&M Consol. Band Boosters, 1980-81. NSF summer fellow, 1962; NASA predoctoral fellow, 1964-65; recipient Disting. Achievment award-rsch. Tex. A&M U., 1988, Am. Chem Soc. award for Nuc. Chemistry, 1995. Fellow Am. Phys. Soc.; mem. Am. Chem. Soc. (vice chmn. div. nuc. chemistry and tech. 1993, chmn. 1994, award in nuc. chemistry 1995, S.W. Regional award 2000), Sigma Xi, Phi Lambda Upsilon. Office: Tex A&M U Cyclotron Inst College Station TX 77843-0001

NATSIOS, ANDREW, federal agency administrator; b. Mass. m. Elizabeth Natsios; children: Emily, Alexander, Phillip. BA, Georgetown U., 1971; MPA, Harvard U., 1979. State rep. Mass. Ho. Reps.; exec. dir. Northeast Pub. Power Assn.; chief fin. and adminstrv. officer Commonwealth of Mass.; v.p. World Vision U.S., 1993—98; chmn. Mass. Turnpike Authoruty; adminstr. U.S. AID, Washington. Author book. Lt. col. USAR. Fellow, U.S. Inst. Peace, 1998—99. Office: AID 1300 Pennsylvania Ave NW Washington DC 20523

NATSIOS, NICHOLAS ANDREW, retired foreign service officer; b. Lowell, Mass., July 31, 1920; s. Andrew and Fanny (Papageorgiou) N.; m. Mitzi Peterson, Sept. 2, 1951; children: Christine Daphne, Deborah Diane, Valerie Sophia, Alexandra Roxanne. Student, Lowell Technol. Inst., 1939-40; BA cum laude, Ohio State U., 1948; MAL.D., Fletcher Sch. Law and Diplomacy, 1983. Civilian spl. adviser polit. problems U.S. Mil. Mission, Salonika, Greece, 1948-50, polit. adviser mil. secretariat Athens, Greece, 1951-56; polit. officer, 1st sec. embassy, spl. asst. to ambassador Am. embassy, Saigon, Viet Nam, 1956-60, attache Paris, 1960-62, spl. asst. to ambassador Seoul, Korea, 1962-65; 1st sec. American embassy, Buenos Aires, Argentina, 1965-69; spl. asst. to ambassador Am. embassy, The Hague, The Netherlands, 1969-72, regional affairs officer. Tehran, Iran, 1972-74; mgmt. cons., 1977—. Served to capt. AUS, 1942-47; comdg. officer Italian Frontier Control Detachment, U.S. Occupation Forces, 1945-47, Milan, Italy. Decorated Medal of Merit; decorated Bronze Star U.S.; knight comdr. of Italy; Knight comdr. Order of St. George; Cross of Mil. Valor, Cross of Mil. Merit (Italy); D.S.C. 1st class Knights of Malta; Order of Eagle Yugoslavia; Disting. Svc. medal Greece; Order of Svc. Merit Korea); recipient Ellis Island medal of honor, 2002. Mem. Phi Beta Kappa, Phi Eta Sigma. Address: 77 Lincoln Pky Lowell MA 01851-3405

NATTEL, STANLEY, cardiologist, research scientist; b. Haifa, Israel, Jan. 28, 1951; arrived in Can., 1952; s. William and Julie (Zwirek) N.; m. Celia Anne Reich, Sept. 25, 1973; children: Jonathan, Ilana, Daniel, Sarah. BSc magna cum laude, McGill U., 1972, MD, 1974. Diplomate Am. Bd. Internal Medicine, Am. Bd. Cardiology. Intern in medicine Royal Victoria Hosp., 1974-75, resident in internal medicine, 1975-76; resident in clin. pharmacology Montreal (Que., Can.) Gen. Hosp., 1976-78, cardiologist, clin. pharmacologist, 1981-87, dir. coronary care unit, 1983-87; fellow in cardiology Ind. U., 1978-80; fellow in physiology U. Pa., 1980-81; asst. prof. pharmacology, medicine McGill U., Montreal, 1981-87, assoc. prof., 1987—; cardiologist Montreal Heart Inst., 1987—, dir. rsch. ctr., 1990—2004; prof. dept. medicine U. Montreal, 1995—, Paul-David chair in cardiovasc. electrophysiology, 2003—. External reviewer Med. Rsch. Coun., 1981—, Ont. Health Ministry, 1983-84, NSF, 1992, others; chmn. libr. com. dept. pharmacology McGill U., 1982-86, mem. grad. com., 1984-89, chmn. grad. tng. com., 1986-89, departmental rep. grad. faculty coun., 1989-91, coord. grad. tchg. pharmacology, 1989-91; mem. oper. grants com. Can. Heart Found., 1983-86; chmn. clin. trials com. Montreal Gen. Hosp., 1983-87, chmn. pharmacy and therapeutics com., 1984-87, sec. clin. chemistry rev. com., 1984, course dir. drug therapy, 1984-87, acting dir. divsn. clin. pharmacology, 1984-85, mem. various coms., 1985-87; mem. fellowship awards com. FRSQ, 1988-90, mem. ctr. grants pharmacology/pharmacy com., 1989-90; chmn. pharmacology com. Montreal Heart Inst., 1988-90, mem. search com. pharmacist-in-chief, 1989-90, mem. ethics com., 1991-2004, chmn. internal rsch. com., 1991-2004, mem. consultative com. exec. dir., 1991-2004, chmn. consultative com. rsch. ctr., 1991-2004; cons. coun. pharmacology Province of Quebec, 1989-90; mem. safety monitoring com. CAMIAT Study, 1990-95; assoc. prof. medicine U. Montreal, 1991-95, prof. 1995—, chmn. search com. dir. rsch. Sacré-Coeur Hosp., 1991, mem. rsch. com. Cormes faculty medicine, 1991—2002, mem. rsch. com. dept. medicine, 1991-2004; chmn. search com., dir. rsch. Maisonneuve Rosemont Hosp., 1996; mem. site visit team program project grant NIH, 1991, cons. program project grant, 1993, spl. reviewer cardiovascular study sect., 1993, 95, 97, 98; mem. oper. grants com. Med. Rsch. Coun. Can., 1988-93, (chmn. 2002-); mem. sr. pers. awards com. Can. Heart Found., 1994-96; lectr. in field. Assoc. editor Can. Jour. Physiology and Pharmacology, 1990-95, Br. Jour. Pharmacology, 2000--; mem. editl. bd. Jour. Cardiovasc. Electrophysiology, 1991—, Drugs, 1993—, Cardiovasc. Drugs and Therapy, 1993-2001, Circulation Rsch., 1995—, JACC, 1995—2000, Cardiovascular Rsch., 1999-2002, others; manuscript reviewer Am. Jour. Cardiology, Can. Med. Assn. Jour., 1999-2003, New Eng. Jour. Medicine, PNAS, Science, others; contbr. chpts. to books and articles to profl. jours. Chmn. edn. com. Hebrew Acad. Sch., Montreal, 1991-92. Grantee Que. Heart Found., 1981—, Nordic Pharms., 1985-87, Knoll Pharms., 1991-93, others; fellow Med. Rsch. Coun. Can., 1979-81; McGill U. scholar, 1967-74, Sir Edward Beatty scholar McGill U., 1967-70, Rsch. scholar Med. Rsch. Coun., 1982-87, Sr. Rsch. scholar Fonds de la Recherche en Santé du Quebec, 1990-93; recipient Rsch. Achievement award Can. Cardiovasc. Soc., 2001. Fellow Am. Coll. Cardiology, Royal Coll. Physicians Can. (cert. medicine, cardiology); mem. Am. Heart Assn. (coun. basic sci.), Am. Soc. Pharmacology and Exptl. Therapeutics, Can. Cardiovasc. Soc. (councilor 1992-95), Can. Soc. Clin. Pharmacology (Kenneth M. Piafsky Young Investigator award 1985), Pharm. Soc. Can. Biophys. Soc., Comm. Sci. Sessions Planning Am. Heart Assn., 2000-2002. Avocations: studying jewish religious works, sports. Home: 5609 Alpine Ave Côte Saint Luc QC Canada H4V 2X6 Office: Montreal Heart Inst 5000 Belanger St E Montreal QC Canada H1T 1C8 Office Phone: 514-376-3330. Personal E-mail: stanleynattel@aol.com. Business E-Mail: stanley.nattel@icm-mhi.org.

NAUERT, CHARLES GARFIELD, history educator; b. Quincy, Ill., July 26, 1928; s. Charles G. and Helen C. (Frazer) N.; m. Jean Grace Porter, June 21, 1964; children: Paul, Jonathan. AB, Quincy (Ill.) Coll., 1950; AM, U. Ill., 1951, PhD in History, 1955. Instr. Bowdoin Coll., Brunswick, Maine, 1955-56; asst. prof. Williams Coll., Williamstown, Mass., 1956-61; prof. history U. Mo., Columbia, 1961—, chair dept., 1965-68. Exec. sec.-treas. Mo. Conf. on History, Columbia, 1980-93; hist. annotator Erasmus in English, Toronto, Ont., 1984—; sr. rsch. fellow Am. Coun. Learned Socs., London, 1975-76. Author: Agrippa and the Crisis of Renaissance Thought, 1965, Age of Renaissance and Reformation, 1977, rev. edit., 1992, Humanism and the Culture of Renaissance Europe, 1995, Historical Dictionary of the Renaissance, 2004; mem. editl. bd.: Sixteenth Century Jour., 1972—, gen. editor: 16th Century Essays and Studies, 1980—96. Bd. dirs. Columbia Soccer Club, 1969-73. Recipient Middlebush Chair, U. Mo., Columbia, 1982-85, Thomas Jefferson award U. Mo. Ctrl. System, 1991. Mem. Am. Hist. Assn. (chair Adams prize 1978-81), Renaissance Soc. Am. (coun. 1991-94), 16th Century Studies Conf. (pres. 1978), Ctrl. Renaissance Conf. (pres. 1974, 91), Soc. Reformation Rsch. (coun. 1985-88). Democrat. Episcopalian. Home: 1009 Falcon Dr Columbia MO 65201-6235 Office: U Mo Dept History 101 Read Hall Dept History Columbia MO 65211-7500 Office Phone: 573-882-2481. Business E-Mail: nauertc@missouri.edu.

NAUGHTON, ANN ELSIE, primary school educator; b. N.Y.C., Apr. 27, 1942; d. George and Wilma (Lubitz) Bruning; m. Gerald Richard Naughton, Dec. 26, 1965 (dec. Apr. 1983); 1 child, Jonathan. BA, CUNY, 1963; MA, Columbia U., 1965; postgrad., Greenburgh Inst. Tchrs.; ESL Cert., Long Island (N.Y.) U., 1990. Social worker div. child and family welfare Westchester County, Yonkers, N.Y., 1963-64; tchr. Hastings On Hudson (N.Y.) Pub. Schs., 1965—. Tchr. Lincoln Ctr. Inst., N.Y.C., 1986—. Mem. Hastings Tchrs. Union (mem.-at-large exec. com. 1982—, state facilitator and trainer N.Y. parent tchrs. confs. 1988—, exec. com. 1982-88, corr. sec. 1989—), N.Y. Zool. and Ecol. Habitat (trainer 1991—), Impact II Grant Winner 1993-94, Scarsdale (N.Y.) Woman's Club (v.p.), Investment Club, Montauk Art Assn. Avocations: gardening, horseback riding, swimming, painting, art history. Home: 31 Walbrooke Rd Scarsdale NY 10583-2743 E-mail: anaug67171@aol.com.

NAUGHTON, JAMES LEE, internist; b. 1946; AB, Dartmouth Coll., 1968; MD, Harvard U., 1972. Intern U. Calif. Moffitt Hosp., San Francisco, 1972-73; resident in medicine U. Calif. Affiliated Hosps., San Francisco, 1973-75, San Francisco Gen. Hosp., 1975-76; fellow in nephrology U. Calif., San Francisco, 1976-77, assoc. clin. prof. medicine, 1982—; pvt. practice internal medicine, ptnr. Alliance Med. Group, Pinole, Calif., 1982—. Mem. Am. Bd. Internal Medicine (bd. dirs. 1995-2002, exec. com. 1997-2002, trustee found. 2000—). Office: Alliance Med Group 2160 Appian Way Ste 200 Pinole CA 94564-2524

NAUGHTON, JAMES MARTIN, journalist; b. Pitts., Aug. 13, 1938; s. Francis Patrick and Martha Ann (Clear) N.; m. Diana Marie Thomas, Sept. 5, 1964; children: Jenifer Mary Naughton Genovesi, Lara Marie, Michael Thomas, Kerry Marie. BA cum laude, U. Notre Dame, 1960. Reporter, photographer Painesville (Ohio) Telegraph, summer, 1955-60; reporter Cleve. Plain Dealer, 1962-69; Washington corr. N.Y. Times, 1969-77; nat. editor Phila. Inquirer, 1977-79, met. editor, 1979-83, assoc. mng. editor, 1980-86, dep. mng. editor, 1986-90, mng. editor, 1990-91, exec. editor, 1991-96; pres. The Poynter Inst. for Media Studies, St. Petersburg, Fla., 1996—2003, pres. emeritus, 2003—. Marsh prof. U. Mich., 1977 Served with USMC, 1960-62. Recipient Disting. Service award Sigma Delta Chi, 1973 Roman Catholic. Home: 2500 Coffee Pot Blvd NE Saint Petersburg FL 33704-3466 E-mail: swami@poynter.org.

NAUGHTON, JOHN PATRICK, cardiologist, medical educator; b. West Nanticoke, Pa., May 20, 1933; s. John Patrick and Anne Frances (McCormick) N.; children: Bruce, Marcia, Lisa, George, Michael, Thomas. AA, Cameron State U., Lawton, Okla., 1952; BS, St. Louis U., 1954; MD, Okla. U., 1958; MD (hon.), Kosin U., 1995. Intern George Washington U. Hosp., Washington, 1958-59; resident U. Okla. Med. Center, 1959-64; asst. prof. medicine U. Okla., 1966-68; assoc. prof. medicine U. Ill., 1968-70; prof. medicine George Washington U., 1970-75, dean acad. affairs, 1973-75, dir. div. rehab. medicine and Regional Rehab. Research and Tng. Center, 1970-75; dean Sch. Medicine SUNY, Buffalo, 1975-96, prof. medicine, physiology, social, preventive and rehab. medicine Sch. Medicine, 1975—, acting v.p. for health scis., 1983-84, v.p. clin. affairs, 1984-96, interim chmn. rehab. medicine, 2003—. Dir. Nat. Exercise and Heart Disease Project, 1972-83; chmn. policy adv. bd. Beta-blocker Heart Attack Trial Nat. Heart, Lung and Blood Inst., 1977-82; pres. Western N.Y. chpt. Am. Heart Assn., 1983-85, v.p. N.Y. State affiliate, 1985, pres. N.Y. State affiliate, 1988-90; chmn. clin. applications and preventions adv. com. Nat. Heart, Lung and Blood Inst., 1984; mem. Fed. COGME working group on consortia, 1996-97, N.Y. Gov.'s Commn. on Grad. Med. Edn., 1985, N.Y. State Coun. on Grad. Med. Edn., 1988-90, chmn. 1996—; pres. Assoc. Med. Schs. N.Y., 1982-84, mem. adminstrv. com. Coun. of Deans, 1983-89; mem. N.Y. State Dept. of Health Adv. Com. on Physician Recredentialing; mem. exec. coun. Nat. Inst. on Disability and Rehab. Rsch. 1991-92; v.p. James H. Cummings Found. Author: Exercise Testing and Exercise Training in Coronary Heart Disease, 1973, Exercise Testing: Physiological, Biomechanical, and Clinical Principles, 1988 Career devel. awardee Nat. Heart Inst., 1966-71; recipient Brotherhood-Sisterhood award in medicine NCCJ, N.E. Minority Educators award, 1990, Acad. Alumnus of Yr. award Okla. U., 1990, award for svc. to minorities in med. edn., 1991, Frank Sindelar award N.Y. State Am. Heart Assn., 1995, James Platt White Soc. award, 1995, Outstanding Contbns. in the field of Health Care award Sheehan Meml. Hosp., 1995, Chancellor Charles P. Norton medal, SUNY, Buffalo, 1997, AMS Disting. Svc. award, 2001. Fellow ACP, Am. Coll. Cardiology, Am. Coll. Sports Medicine (pres. 1970-71, Citation award 2000), Am. Coll. Chest Physicians; Am. Coll. Preventive Medicine, Am. Heart Assn. (epidemiology coun. 2000—, coun. on nutrition, phys. activity and metabolism), Acad. Health Profls. Ins. Assn. (hon.). Office: SUNY Buffalo 128 Farber Hall 3435 Main St Buffalo NY 14214-3099 Office Phone: 716-829-3092. Business E-Mail: jpn@buffalo.edu.

NAUGHTON, LORRAINE RIFFLE, oil industry administrator; b. Hagerstown, Md., Feb. 20, 1976; d. John Edward and Barbara M. Riffle; 1 child, Connor McGowan. BA in Journalism, U. Ga., Athens, 1994—98. Mktg. Chevron Products Co., Atlanta, Ga., 1999—2000, promotions assoc., 1999—2000; office mgr. ChevronTexaco, Washington, 2002—. Mem.: Jr. League (life), Hesperia Soc. (life Top Ten Greek Women 1998), Delta Epsilon Iota (life), Order of Omega (life), Rho Lambda (life), Omicron Delta Kappa (life; sec. 1998—99), Alpha Chi Omega (life; pres. 1998—99). Catholic. Office: ChevronTexaco 1401 I St NW Washington DC 20005 Business E-Mail: llri@chevrontexaco.com.

NAULT, BRIAN A. entomologist, researcher, education educator; b. Wooster, Ohio, July 22, 1966; s. Lowell R. and Loretta A. Nault; m. Melissa Nault, Oct. 26, 1996; children: Nicolette E., Julian B. BS Entomology, Ohio State Univ., Columbus, Ohio, 1988; MS Entomology, Univ. Ga., Athens, Ga., 1990; PhD Entomology, N.C. State Univ., Raleigh, N.C., 1994. Post doc. rsch. assoc. entomology N.C. State Univ., Raleigh, NC, 1994—97; asst. prof. entomology Va. Tech, Eastern Shore Agrl. Rsch. Extension Ctr., Painter, Va., 1997—2001, Cornell Univ., Geneva, NY, 2001—. Mem.: Ga. Entomol. Soc., Entomol. Soc. of Am. (governing bd. mem. 2001—03, J.H. Comstock award 1994), Phi Kappa Phi. Avocations: tennis, running, fishing, hiking. Office: Cornell Univ Dept Entomology NY State Agrl Expt Station 630 W North St Geneva NY 14456 Office Phone: 315-787-2354.

NAULT, ROBERT DANIEL, legislator; b. Ste.-Anne, Manitoba, Can., Nov. 9, 1955; married. Student, U. Alta., Winnipeg, Can. Trainman CP Rail, 1980-86; chmn. Local 431 United Transp. Union, 1986; head Kenora Dist. Liberal Assn., 1984-86; elected House of Commons, 1988—; parliamentary sec. Min. Labour (Human Resources Devel.), 1995—96, Min. Employment & Immigration (Human Resources Devel.), 1996, Min. Human Resources Devel., 1997—98; min. Indian affairs & no. devel. Govt. of Can., 1999—2003. Mem. several parliamentary coms. including chair standing com. natural resources, chair govt. task force CN Commercialization. Liberal. Office: House of Commons West Confederation Bldg Rm 707 Ottawa ON Canada K1A OA6 also: 81 Duke St P8N1G2 Dryden ON Canada Office Phone: 613-996-1161.

NAULT, WILLIAM HENRY, publishing executive; b. Ishpeming, Mich., June 9, 1926; s. Henry J. and Eva (Perrault) N.; m. Helen E. Matthews, Nov. 28, 1946; children: William Henry, Rebecca Nault Marks, Ronald, George, Peter, Julia Nault Doyle, Robert, David. AB, No. Mich. U., 1948, LittD (hon.), 1988; MA, U. Mich., 1949; EdD, Columbia U., 1953, LHD (hon.), 1980, LLD (hon.), 1986, LittD (hon.), 1988. Dir. adult edn., Battle Creek, Mich., 1948—49; guidance counselor, 1949-50; prin. W.K. Kellogg High Sch., Battle Creek, 1950-53; research assoc. Columbia U., 1953-54; asst. supt. Ridgewood, N.J., 1954-55; adj. prof. William Patterson U. N.J., 1954—55; dir. research World Book, Inc. (formerly Field Enterprises Edn. Corp.), Chgo., 1955-63, v.p., 1963-66, sr. v.p., editorial dir., 1966-68, exec. v.p. and editorial dir., 1968-83; pres., pub., chief operating officer World Book, Inc., 1983-84, gen. chmn. editorial adv. bds., 1968-99, pub., 1983-95, pub. emeritus, 1995—. Past vice chmn. Govt. Adv. Com. on Internat. Library and Book Programs, U.S. Dept. State; past mem. nat. adv. bd. Ctr. on Ednl. Media and Materials for Handicapped; past mem. exec. bd. Commn. Instns. Higher Edn., North Central Assn. Colls. and Secondary Schs.; mem. dean's adv. council Coll. Bus. and Pub. Adminstrn., U. Mo., Columbia; mem. nat. council Inst. Internat. Edn. Author material on courses of study. Mem. alumni com. Columbia Tchrs. Coll. Capital Campaign; mem. White House Conf. on Youth, White House Conf. on Librs., White House Conf. on Edn.; pres. Oak Park (Ill.) Bd. Edn., 1960 63; v.p. LaGrange (Ill.) Libr. Bd.; bd. regents Lincoln Acad., Ill.; past trustee Adler Planetarium, De Paul U., Chgo. Geol. Soc.; bd. dirs. H.V. Phalin Found. Grad. Study, World Book, Inc., A.J. Nystrom Co., Field Edn. Co., Libr. Movens, Inc.; mem. adv. bd. Rosary Coll.; mem. liberal arts and scis. adv. council De Paul U. Served with F.A., AUS, 1944-45. Recipient Columbia U. Tchrs. Coll. medal for disting. svc. in edn.; named Disting. Alumnus No. Mich. U., U. Mich., Columbia U. Fellow AAAS; mem. ALA, Chgo. Planetarium Soc. (trustee), Chgo. Geog. Soc. (dir.), Am. Acad. Polit. and Social Sci., Am. Edn. Rsch. Assn., Am. Assn. Sch. Adminstrs., ASCD, Chgo. Pubs. Assn. (past pres.), Ill. Assn. Sch. Adminstrs., Ill. Acad. Sci., NSTA, Nat. Council Tchrs. English, Assn. Am. Geographers, Assn. Childhood Edn. Internat., NAESP, Nat. Assn. Secondary Sch. Prins., Council for Advancement Sci. Writing, Internat. Platform Assn., Nat. Council Social Studies, Nat. Soc. Study Edn. Clubs: Mid-Am, Mchts. and Mfrs. Roman Catholic. Office: World Book Inc 525 W Monroe St Chicago IL 60661-3629 Personal E-mail: naultwh@aol.com., naultwh@comcast.net.

NAULTY, SUSAN LOUISE, archivist, b. Abington, Pa., May 28, 1944, d. Charles J. and Ruth E. (Schick) N. BA, Whittier Coll., 1967; MA, Loyola U., L.A., 1972. Tchr. history and English, Whittier (Calif.) H.S., 1968-70; from libr. asst. to asst. curator Huntington Libr., San Marino, Calif., 1972-91; archivist Richard Nixon Libr. and Birthplace, Yorba Linda, Calif., 1991—. Office: Richard Nixon Libr and Birthplace 18001 Yorba Linda Blvd Yorba Linda CA 92886-3903

NAUMAN, ANN KEITH, education educator, department chairman; b. Greensboro, N.C., Aug. 2, 1931; d. Erle Almon and Santa Maria Keith; m. William Logan Nauman, Sept. 15, 1951; children: Richard Logan, Gerald Keith. BA, La. State U., 1961, MA, 1965, BS, 1966, MS, 1969, PhD, 1974; postgrad., Southeastern La. U., 1976-78, Cath. U., Santiago, Chile. Sch. libr. Parish Sch. Sys., Baton Rouge, 1966-76; asst. prof. ednl. founds. Southeastern La. U., Hammond, 1976-80, assoc. prof., 1986-89, prof., 1989—; prof., head dept. St. Joseph Sem. Coll., St. Benedict, La., 1980—. Author: Biographic Handbook of Educators, 1981, Guide to Latin American Archives, 1982, Time Management for Librarians, 1991, Inés de Suarez, Conquistadora, 2000. Fellow La. State U., 1972, OAS, Santiago de Chile, 1973; Mellon grantee Tulane U. Office: Southeastern La U PO Box 659 Hammond LA 70402-0001 Office Phone: 504-549-5203.

NAUMAN, SPENCER GILBERT, JR., lawyer, director; b. Bryn Mawr, Pa., Mar. 4, 1933; s. Spencer Gilbert and Gertrude Howard (Olmsted) Nauman; m. Helen Gibbon Trimble, Oct. 19, 1963; children: Spencer G., Helen G., John T. AB, Princeton U., 1955; LLB, U. Pa., 1961. Bar: Pa. 1962, US Dist. Ct. (mid. dist.) Pa. 1968. Assoc. Nauman, Smith, Shissler & Hall, Harrisburg, Pa., 1962—66, ptnr., 1966—. Asst. city solicitor City of Harrisburg, 1962-69, 1962—69; bd. dirs. Wagner Bros. Containers, Inc., Balt. Past pres., trustee emeritus Harrisburg Acad.; bd. dirs. Harrisburg chpt. ARC; bd. mgrs. Harrisburg Cemetery Assn., Harrisburg Hosp., 1973—79. With U.S. Army, 1955—58. Mem.: ABA, Dauphin County Bar Assn., Pa. Bar Assn., West. Shore Country Club (Camp Hill, Pa.), Princeton Club (NYC), Racquet Club (Phila.). Republican. Episcopalian. Home: Creek Farm Bowmansdale PA 17008 Office: 200 N 3d St 18th Fl Harrisburg PA 17108-0840 Office Phone: 717-236-3010.

NAUMANN, HANS J. manufacturing executive; b. Germany, May 5, 1935; arrived in U.S., 1960; s. Herbert and Elfriede (Heydenreich) N.; m. Edith Huempel; children: Irene, Michelle, Jacqueline, John. MME, U. Hamburg, Fed. Rep. Germany, 1960; MBA, Rochester (N.Y.) U., 1965; D of engring. (hon.), Tech. U. Chemnitz, 2003. Registered profl. engr., NY. Mgr. engring. Farrell Corp., Rochester, 1961-66; exec. v.p. Hegenscheidt Corp., Troy, Mich., 1966-70; pres., CEO, stockholder Hegenscheidt GmbH, Erkelenz, Germany, 1970—82; chmn., CEO Internat. Knife Corp., Erlanger, Ky., 1982—84; chmn. bd., CEO, stockholder Simmons Machine Tool Corp., Albany, NY, 1984—; chmn., CEO, stockholder Niles-Simmons Industrieanlagen, GmbH, Chemnitz, Germany, 1992—; chmn., CEO Niles-Simmons-Hegenscheidt Gmbh, Chemnitz, Germany, 2001. Author: Tool and Manufacturing Engineering Handbook, 1976; patentee roller finishing and deep rolling. Bd. dirs. U. Albany Fund, Inc., 1986—. Decorated Bundesverdienstkreuz Germany. Mem. ASME, SAE, Am. Inst. Mgmt. (pres.'s coun.), Am. Mgmt. Assn., Am. Pub. Transit Assn., Verein Deutscher Ingenieure, Soc. Mech. Engrs., Capital Region Tech. Devel. Coun., Capital Region World Trade Coun., Assn. for Mfg. Tech., Albany Colonie Regional C. of C., Rwy. Supply Assn., N.Y. R.R. Club Inc., Lions (past pres.). Avocations: sailing, tennis, golf, skiing. Home: 26 Folmsbee Dr Albany NY 12204-1206 Office: Simmons Machine Tool Corp 1700 Broadway Albany NY 12204-2701 also: Niles-Simmons Industrieanlagen Zwickauer Str 355 09117 Chemnitz Germany Office: Niles-Simmons Hegenscheidt Hegenscheidt Pl Erkelenz 41812 Germany E-mail: hnaumann@smtgroup.com., hj.naumann@niles-simmons.de.

NAUMANN, JOSEPH F. bishop; b. St. Louis, June 4, 1949; BA, Cardinal Glennon Coll., St. Louis, 1971; degree in theology, Kenrick Sem., St. Louis, 1975. Transitional deacon St. Christopher's Parish, Florissant, Mo., 1974-75; assoc. pastor St. Dominic Savio Parish, Affton, Mo., 1975-79, Our Lady of Sorrows Parish, St. Louis, 1979-84; part-time assoc. pastor Most Blessed Sacrament Parish, St. Louis, 1984-89; pastor Ascension Parish, Normandy, Mo., 1989-94; apptd. Vicar Gen. with responsibilities for finances of the Archdiocese of St. Louis, 1994—; Aux. Bishop of St. Louis/Titular Bishop of Caput Cilla, 1997—. Office: 4445 Lindell Blvd Saint Louis MO 63108-2403

NAUMANN, ROBERT BRUNO ALEXANDER, chemistry and physics educator; b. Dresden, Germany, June 7, 1929; came to U.S., 1932, naturalized, 1951; s. Eberhard Bruno and Elsa Henriette (Haege) N.; m. Marina Grot Turkevich, Sept. 16, 1961; children: Kristin Ragnhild Naumann Juros, Andrew John Bruno. BS, U. Calif., Berkeley, 1949; MA, Princeton U., 1951, PhD, 1953. Faculty Princeton U., 1953—, prof. chemistry and physics, 1973-92, prof. emeritus, 1992—. Mem. vis. staff Los Alamos Nat. Lab., 1970-86; rsch. collaborator Brookhaven Nat. Lab., 1984-87; sci. assoc. CERN, Geneva,

1985-96; vis. prof. physics dept. Tech. U. Munich, 1988; vis. scholar physics Dartmouth Coll., 1992-96, adj. prof. physics and astronomy, 1996—; adj. prof. chemistry, 2003—. Author articles electromagnetic isotope separation, nuclear structure via radioactive and charged particle nuclear spectroscopy, implantation radioactive isotopes into solids, formation and properties of muonic atoms. Recipient Alexander von Humboldt Stiftung Sr. U.S. Scientist award, 1978, 83; Allied Chem. and Dye Corp. fellow, 1951-52, Procter and Gamble faculty fellow, 1959-60; Deutsche Forschungsgemeinschaft grantee, 1988. Fellow Am. Phys. Soc., AAAS; mem. Am. Chem. Soc. (chmn. Princeton U. sect. 1975, Chmn. Div. Nuclear Chemistry and Technology 1984), Sierra Club, Phi Beta Kappa, Sigma Xi (chmn. Princeton, N.J. sect. 1986-87). Episcopalian. Home: 387 Hawk Pine Rd Norwich VT 05055-9631

NAUMANN, WILLIAM CARL, consumer products company executive; b. Peoria, Ill., Mar. 25, 1938; s. William Louis and Emma (Bottin) N.; m. Polly Roby, May 20, 1962 (div. 1980); children: Jeff, Heather, Derek; m. Patricia Gallagher, Sept. 9, 1993. BSCE, Purdue U., 1960; MBA, U. Chgo., 1975. With Inland Steel Products Co., Chgo., 1960-74, N.Y. dist. mgr., 1968-70, div. gen. mgr., 1971-74; group v.p., bd. dirs. Inryco, Melrose Park, Ill., 1974-81; asst. chief engr. Inland Steel Co., Chgo., 1981-82, asst. gen. mgr. corp. planning, 1982-83, asst. gen. mgr. sales, 1983-85, gen. mgr. sales and mktg., 1985-87; exec. v.p. internat. ops. Hussmann Corp., Bridgeton, Mo., 1987, exec. v.p. sales and mktg., 1987; pres. Hussmann Food Svc. Co., Bridgeton, 1987-89; corp. v.p., chief quality officer Whitman Corp., Chgo., 1990-91; COO Ranger Industries, 1992; sr. v.p., COO Pexco Holdings, Inc., Tulsa, 1993-96; chmn. bd. dirs., CEO Sports Holdings Corp., Montreal, Can., 1996-97; pres., CEO Hatteras Yachts, Inc., New Bern, N.C., 1997—. Past chmn., bd. dir. New Bern Mil. Alliance. Mem. N.C. Mfrs. Assn. (bd. dirs.), Nat. Assn. Boat Mfrs. (bd. dir.), U. Chgo. Exec. Program Club (past pres.), U. Chgo. Alumni Assn. (past pres., bd. govs. 1986-95), Eastern Carolina Yacht Club, New Bern C. of C. (past chmn.), Ocean Reef Club, New Bern Golf and Country Club, Beta Gamma Sigma. Avocations: boating, travel, cooking. Home: 406 Wexford Pl Trent Woods NC 28562-7105 Office: Hatteras Yachts Inc 110 N Glenburnie Rd New Bern NC 28560-2703 E-mail: bnaumann@hatterasyachts.com.

NAURATH, DAVID ALLISON, engineering psychologist, researcher; b. Houston, Mar. 11, 1927; s. Walter Arthur and Joy Frances (Bradbury) N.; m. Barbara Ellen Coverdell; children: Kathleen Ann, David Allen, Cynthia Ellyn, Randall Austin. BA, Simpson Coll., Indianola, Iowa, 1948; MA, Southern Meth. U., 1949; postgrad., U. Denver, 1955-57. Job analyst U.S. Air Force, San Antonio and Denver, 1951-55, rsch. psychologist Lowry AFB, Colo., 1955-60, Navy, Life Scis. & Systems div., Point Mugu, Calif., 1960-76; engring. psychologist Navy Systems Engring., Point Mugu, 1976-83; ret. Presenter at profl. socs. and orgns. in field. Contbr. articles to Jour. Engring. Psychology, jour. Soc. for Info. Display, jour. Soc. Photo-optical Instrument Engrs. With USAAF, 1944-46. Mem. AAAS (life), IEEE (sr.), Am. Psychol. Assn., N.Y. Acad. Sci. (emeritus), Human Factors Soc. (panel mem. Certification of Human Factors Engrs. 1976), Soc. Engring. Psychologists, Soc. for Info. Display (life). Methodist. Home: 5633 Pembroke St Ventura CA 93003-2200

NAVA, CARMEN P. communications executive; Degree in Bus. Adminstrn., U. So. Calif., 1984. Joined gen. mgmt. devel. program Pacific Bell, 1984, v.p., gen. mgr. Diverse Markets Group; regional pres. L.A. SBC Comm., L.A., 1997—99, pres. SBC Ctr. for Learning, 1999, pres. SBC West Consumer Markets, 1999—. Bd. govs. U. So. Calif. Alumni Assn. Office: SBC Comm Inc 175 E Houston San Antonio TX 78205-2233

NAVA, CYNTHIA L. state legislator; b. Dona Ana, N. Mex., 1953; BS, Western Ill. U.; MA, Ea. Ill. U. Dep. supt. Gadsden Schools; mem. N.Mex. Senate, Dist. 31, Santa Fe, 1992—; mem. rules com., fin. com. N.Mex. Senate, chair legis. edn. study com., excellence in higher edn. com., health & human svcs. com., 1997—. Home: 3002 Broadmoor Dr Las Cruces NM 88001-7501 Office: N Mex Senate State Capitol Rm 301 Santa Fe NM 87503-0001

NAVA, ELOY LUIS, financial planner, financial consultant; b. N.Y.C., May 19, 1942; s. Eloy and Dolores Nava; m. Diane Margret Binder, Dec. 21, 1968; children: Alyson Beth, David Eloy. BMgmt Engring., Rensselaer Poly. Inst., 1964, BMech. Engring., 1965, MSMgmt., 1970. Cert. fund specialist, CFP. Indsl. engr. Johnson & Johnson Inc., Troy, N.Y., 1965-66; nuclear project engr. and chief nuclear test engr. to ops. analysis project mgr. Electric Boat Div., Gen. Dynamics Corp., Groton, Conn., 1966-78; ptnr., chief fin. officer Collado Ozamiz Co., N.Y.C., 1978-88; pres., chmn. bd. JB Apparel Corp., N.Y.C., 1984-93; v.p., sr. fin. cons. Cruice Investment Advisors, Ltd., 1994-97; sr. assoc. Fleming, Relyea & Cox, Inc., Stamford, Conn., 1996-2000; pres. Nava Investment & Fin. Svcs., LLC, Stamford, Conn., 2000—. Bd. dirs. Jose Blanco Inc., Santo Domingo, Dominican Republic; mgmt., fin. cons. various orgns. in Dominican Republic. Chmn. water, sewer com. City of Waterford, Conn., 1975-77; mem. Rep. Nat. Com.; swimming ofcl. YMCA, USS. Mem. NRA, Am. Philatelic Soc., Internat. Assn. Fin. Planners, Inst. CFPs (Fairfield County chpt. trustee), Western Conn. Estate and Tax Planning Coun., Midwest Decoy Collectors Assn. Roman Catholic. Avocations: fishing, golf, skiing, stamp and antique decoy collecting. Home: 15 Pasture Ln Darien CT 06820-5618

NAVA, GREGORY, film director, screenwriter, producer; b. San Diego, Calif., Apr. 10, 1949; Dir. (films) The Confessions of Amans, 1976, El Norte, 1984, A Time of Destiny, 1988, My Family, Mi Familia, 1995, Selena, 1997, Why Do Fools Fall in Love, 1998 (TV film) The 20th Century: In the Melting Pot, 1999; dir., writer, exec. prodr. (TV series) American Family, 2002; dir., prodr. (film) Killing Pablo, 2002; screenwriter: (film) Frida, 2002, My Family, Salina. Office: ICM c/o Martha Luttrell 8942 Wilshire Blvd Beverly Hills CA 90211-1934

NAVA, PATRICIA ANN, electrical engineering educator, researcher; b. Las Cruces, N.Mex., Oct. 17, 1958; d. Jose Encarnacion Nava and Margarita Renteria; children: Marcela Osorno, Ileana Osorno. BSEE, N.Mex. State U., 1980, MSEE, 1982, PhD, 1995. Registered profl. engr., Tex. Design engr. office products divsn. IBM, Boulder, Colo., 1979-80; electronics engr. Office Advanced Tech. White Sands (N.Mex.) Missile Rsch., 1982-84; mem. computer engring. faculty No. Ariz. U., Flagstaff, 1984-88; asst. prof. elec. and computer engring. Calif. State U., L.A., 1988-91; coll. asst. prof. N.Mex. State U., Las Cruces, 1995-96; asst. prof. elec. and computer engring. U. Tex., El Paso, 1996—, Forrest and Henrietta Lewis prof. elec. engring., 1998-2000. Rschr. in fuzzy neural networks. Contbr. articles to sci. jours. Recipient Ariz. Educator of Yr. award collegiate divsn. LULAC, 1987; Crimson scholar N.Mex. State U., 1980; fellow N.Mex. Commn. on Higher Edn., 1992-95; grantee NSF, 1996, U. Tex., 1996-97, NASA-Jet Propulsion Lab., 1999-2002. Mem. IEEE (faculty counselor student sect. U. Tex. 1996—, treas. El Paso-Las Cruces sect. 1998—, svc. award 2000), Phi Kappa Phi (life), Tau Beta Pi (faculty co-advisor to student chpt. 1998—). Democrat. Avocations: classical music, martial arts. Office: U Tex at El Paso 500 W University St El Paso TX 79968-0523 Fax: 915-747-7871. E-mail: pnava@ece.utep.edu.

NAVA, ROXANNE, state agency administrator; BS in Fin., DePaul U. Formerly with Citibank FSB, Bank One/First Chgo.; former comml. banking relationship mgr. Logan Sq. Fin. Ctr., former v.p. No. Trust Co.; dir. Ill. Dept. Fin. Instns., Chgo., 2003—. Mem. Cordi Marian Women's Aux. Bd., Holy Cross Scholarship Bd.; Inter-Am. Magnet Schs. Local Sch. Coun.; trustee, mem. bd. com. on fin. adminstrv. svcs., com. on human resource svcs., chair acad. and student svcs. com. City Colls. of Chgo.; bd. dirs. Mex.-Am. C. of C., Eighteen St. Devel. Corp., Family Focus. Mem.: Hispanic Bankers Assn. Office: Dept Fin Instns 10 W Randolph St Ste 15-700 Chicago IL 60601 Office Fax: 312-814-8672. Business E-Mail: roxanne_nava@dfi.state.il.us.

NAVAR, LUIS GABRIEL, physiology educator, researcher; b. El Paso, Tex., Mar. 24, 1941; s. Luis and Concepcion (Najera) N.; m. Randa Ann Bumgarner, Oct. 15, 1965; children: Tonia, Tess, Gabriel, Daniel. BS, Tex. A&M U., 1962; PhD, U. Miss., 1966, postdoctoral study, 1966-69. Instr. dept. physiology/biophysics U. Miss., Jackson, 1966-67, asst. prof., 1967-71, assoc. prof., 1971-74, U. Ala., Birmingham, 1974-76, prof., 1976-88, assoc. prof. Nephrology Rsch. and Tng. Ctr., 1979-83, prof., 1983-88; prof., chmn. dept. physiology Tulane U. Med. Sch., New Orleans, 1988—, co-dir. Hypertension and Renal Ctr. of Excellence, 2001—. Vis. scientist Duke U. Med. Ctr., Durham, N.C., 1972-73; adv. bd. NIH Ctr. Sci. Rev., 1998-99; bd. dirs. Fedn. Am. Socs. Exptl. Biology, 1997—. Assoc. editor News in Physiol. Scis., 1994—, Am. Jour. Physiology, 1983-89, mem. editl. bd., 1982-83, 97—; mem. editl. bd. Kidney Internat., 1976-87, Jour. Am. Soc. Nephrology, 1996-2001, Am. Jour. Kidney Disease, 1997-2001; mem. editl. bd. Hypertension, 1980-83, assoc. editor, 1993-2000; mem. editl. bd. Kidney, 1992—, Clin. Sci., 1994-99, Jour. Am. Soc. Nephrology, 1996-2001, Am. Jour. Kidney Diseases, 1997-2001, Am. Jour. Hypertension, 1999—; contbr. sci. papers and book chpts. to profl. publs. Chmn. cardiorenal rsch. study com. Am. Heart Assn., 1994—95, mem. nat. rsch. com., 1994—99; mem. cardiovascular and renal study sects. NIH, 1998—, chmn., 2000—; bd. dirs. Consortium for Southeastern Hypertension Control, 1998—2000. Recipient Rsch. Career Devel. award, Nat. Heart, Lung and Blood Inst., 1974—79, Merit award, 1988—97; vis. scholar Pfizer/ACCF, 2002. Fellow: AAAS; mem.: Assn. Chmn. Depts. Physiology (councillor 1993—95, pres.-elect 1995—96, pres. 1996—97, Disting. Svc. award 2003), Interam. Soc. Hypertension (chair awards com. 2003—), Am. Soc. Hypertension (coun. 1992—94, chmn. basic. sci. com. 1997, treas. 1997—2001, Richard Bright award 2001), Internat. Soc. Nephrology, Am. Soc. Nephrology, Am. Heart Assn. (Lewis K. Dahl Lectr. 1997, profl. and pub. edn. com. 1999—, kidney, high blood pressure couns., Sci. Coun. Disting. Achievement award 1999, Corcoran Lectr. award 2001), Am. Physiol. Soc. (coun. 1991—94, Gottschalk Disting. Lectr. Renal Physiology 1997, pres.-elect 1997—98, pres. 1998—99). Democrat. Roman Catholic. Home: 10020 Hyde Pl New Orleans LA 70123-1522 Office: Tulane U Med Sch Dept Physiology 1430 Tulane Ave New Orleans LA 70112-2699 Office Phone: 504-988-2594. Business E-Mail: navar@tulane.edu.

NAVARRA, TOVA, writer; b. Newark, July 10, 1948; d. Joe and Rose Leslie Treihart; m. John G. Navarra Jr., Aug. 26, 1967 (div. 1998); children: Yolanda, John G. III; m. Robert B. Kern, July 10, 2004. BA magna cum laude, Seton Hall Univ., 1974; AAS with honors, Brookdale C.C., Lincroft, N.J., 1984; postgrad., Fairleigh Dickinson U. Elem. sch. tchr., Jersey City, 1967-69; corr. Village Times, Long Island, N.Y., 1974-75; tchr. music, humanities, German, art, art history Seton Hall Prep. Sch., South Orange, N.J., 1975-78; entertainment, feature writer, press corr. Asbury Park Press, Neptune, N.J., 1978-85, feature writer, art critic, family writer, 1985-92; feature writer, art columnist Two River Times, Red Bank, N.J., 1993-94. Psychiatric charge nurse, 1985; supr. grant rsch. Vis. Nurse Assn. Ctrl. Jersey, Red Bank, N.J., 1993-94; art coord. Monmouth Players, Navesink, N.J.; lectr. at writing confs. Author: The New Jersey Shore: A Vanishing Splendor, 1985, Jim Gary: His Life and Art, 1987, Your Body: Highlights of Human Anatomy, 1990, Playing It Smart: What to Do When You're on Your Own, 1989, also, pub. On My Own: Helping Kids Help Themselves, (translated into Italian, Portuguese and Hebrew) 1994, 2d edit., 2003, An Insider's Guide to Home Health Care: An Interdisciplinary Approach (with Margaret Lundrigan), 1995, Wisdom for Caregivers, 1995; (staged readings) Through the Kunai Grass with Dad, 1988, Don't Cry, Pandora, 1989; (with Myron A. Lipkowitz and John G. Navarra) Therapeutic Communication: A Guide to Effective Interpersonal Skills for Health Care Professionals, 1990, Encyclopedia of Vitamins, Minerals, and Supplements, 1995, 2d edit., 2004; (with Lipkowitz), Allergies A-Z, 1994; Images of America: Howell and Farmingdale 1996; (with Lundrigan) Image of America: Levittown: The First Fifty Years, 1997, Staten Island, 1997, Staten Island II, 1998, Levittown II, 1998; Toward Painless Writing, 1998; The American Century: Staten Island (with Lundrigan), 1999; Seton Hall University: A Photographic History, 1999, Monmouth University, 2001, Encyclopedia of Asthma and Respiratory Disorders, 2003, Young People/Tough Problems, 2003, Encyclopedia of Allergies 2d edit., 2004, Encyclopedia of Complementary and Alternative Medicine, 2004; illustrator Drugs and Man, 1973; editor in chief Shore Affinity, 1979-81; contbg. editor Am. Jour. Nursing, 1990-94; staff writer, illustrator, photographer N.J. Music and Arts, 1978-81; editor Associated Univ. Presses, 1981-82; copywriter, photographer Jersey Shore Med. Ctr., 1985; feature writer, columnist Copley News Svc., 1988-93; health trend columnist Personal Fitness, 1989-90; assoc. editor The Courier, Middletown, N.J., May-Dec. 1998; lifestyle editor The Two River Times, Red Bank, N.G. May 1999-2000; contr. to Nursing Spectrum Magazine; photography exhbns. in N.Y., N.J., Pa.; guest various radio and TV programs; contbr. photographs to books, articles and photogs. to mags., newspapers; solo exhibits include Atlantic City Art Ctr., 1982, O.K. Harris Works of Art, N.Y.C., 1990, Gallery Axiom, Phila., 1991, Monmouth U., 1991, M. Thomson Kravetz Gallery, Bay Head, N.J., Oceanic Pub. Libr., 2000, Novesink Libr. Theater, 2004; group shows at Art Forms, Red Bank, 1991, Moravian Coll., Bethlehem, Pa., 1992. Mem. Gov.'s Coun. on Alcoholism and Drug Abuse Prevention, co-chair Later Childhood subcom., 1992 Mem. N.J. Playwrights Workshop (charter), N.J. State Nurses Assn. Avocations: singing, guitar, piano, dance, crafts. Office: Sanford J Greenburger Assocs care Faith H Hamlin 55 5th Ave New York NY 10003-4301

NAVARRE, RICHARD A. mining executive; Dir. fin. planning Peabody Group, St. Louis, 1993, v.p., CFO, exec. v.p., CFO, 2001—. Pres., v.p. fin., controller Peabody COALSALES; bd. advisors Coll. Bus. and Adminstrn. and Sch. Acct. So. Ill. U., Carbondale Office: Peabody Group 701 Market St Saint Louis MO 63101 E-mail: publicrelations@peabodygroup.com.

NAVARRETE, JORGE EDUARDO, ambassador; b. Mexico City, Apr. 29, 1940; s. Gabriel and Lucrecia (Lopez) N.; m. Marie Bolaños, 1965 (dec. Sept. 1985); 1 child, Federico Navarrete Linares; m. Angeles Salceda, July 31, 1986. BA in Econs., U. Mexico, 1970. Head econ. studies Nat. Fgn. Trade Bank, Mexico City, 1967-72; Mexican ambassador to Venezuela, 1972-75, 1976, 1977-78, UN, 1979; undersec. econ. affaiirs Ministry Fgn. Affairs, Mexico City, 1979-85; ambassador to Eng. London, 1986—. Author: Latin American External Debt, 1987. Avocation: chess. Office: Embassy of Mexico 8 Halkin St London SW1X 7DW England

NAVARRO, BRUCE CHARLES, lawyer; b. West Lafayette, Ind., Oct. 30, 1954; s. Joseph Anthony and Dorothy Gloria (Gnazzo) N.; children: Philip Joseph, Joanna Christina; m. Andrea Fox; children: Christi Renee, Karina Michelle. BA, Duke U., 1976; JD, Ind. U., 1980. Bar: D.C. 1980. Asst. counsel U.S. Senate Labor Subcom., Washington, 1981-84; acting dep. undersec. for legis. affairs Dept. Labor, Washington, 1984-85; atty. advisor EEOC, Washington, 1985-86; dir. Office of Congl. Rels. Office of Pers. Mgmt., Washington, 1986-89; prin. dep. asst. atty. gen. for legis. U.S. Dept. of Justice, Washington, 1989-91; spl. asst. to gen. counsel U.S. Dept. HHS, Washington, 1991; expert cons. U.S. Dept. Def., Washington, 1992; counsel to the vice chmn. U.S. Consumer Product Safety Commn., Bethesda, Md., 1992-95; prin. Navarro Regulatory and Legis. Affairs, Washington, 1995—. Mem. Arlington County (Va.) Rep. Com., 1983; bd. dirs. Prince William Cmty. Safe Kids Coalition, 1997-99. Mem. D.C. Bar Assn. Roman Catholic. Avocations: music, golf. Home: 12631 Magic Springs Way Bristow VA 20136 Office: Ste 800 2121 K St NW Washington DC 20037 Business E-Mail: nlra@erols.com.

NAVARRO, JOSEPH ANTHONY, statistician, consultant; b. New Britain, Conn., July 6, 1927; s. Charles C. and Josephine V. (Bianco) N.; m. Dorothy G. Gnazzo; children: Kenneth M., Bruce C., Joseph S. BS, Cen. Conn. State U., 1950; MS, Purdue U., 1952, PhD, 1955. Rsch. staff, cons. GE, 1955-59; rsch. staff mgmt. IBM, 1962-64; sr. staff mem., asst. dir. Inst. Def. Analyses, Alexandria, Va., 1964-72; pres., chief oper. officer System Planning Corp., Arlington, Va., 1972-86; dep. undersec. test and evaluation Dept. Defense, Washington, 1986-87; now pvt. practice cons., 1987—; pres. Wackenhut Applied Technologies Ctr., Fairfax, Va., 1989-90. Contbr. articles to profl. jours. Mem. Bd. Trade, Washington, 1983-85. Mem. Internat. Test and Evaluation Assn. Clubs: COSMOS (Washington). Republican. Roman Catholic. Home: 8010 Grand Teton Dr Potomac MD 20854-4074 E-mail: jadgnav@aol.com.

NAVARRO, LETICIA, Mexican government official; b. Colima, Mex., Nov. 10, 1953; Student bus. adminstrn., Nat. Autonomous U. Mex.; student, Simmons Coll., Boston. Various positions including supr. trademark group, mktg. coord. Lat. Am. Gillette, dir. sales and svcs.; comml. dir., gen. mgr., World pres. Jafra, Mexico; gen. mgr. Alegro internat. divsn. PepsiCo; gen. mgr. Grupo Panificador Azteca; secretary of tourism Govt. of Mexico, 2000—. Lectr. in field. Office: Ave Presidente Masaryk 172 11587 Mexico City Mexico

NAVAS, WILLIAM ANTONIO, JR., federal agency administrator, retired military officer; b. Mayaguez, P.R., Dec. 15, 1942; s. William Antonio Sr. and Ethel Ines (Marin) N.; m. Wilda Margarita Cordova Navas, Aug. 7, 1965; children: William Antonio III, Gretchen Maria. BSCE, U. P.R., 1965; MS in Engring. Mgmt., U. Bridgeport, 1979. Registered profl. engr., P.R. Commd. 2d. lt. U.S. Army, 1966, advanced through grades to maj. gen., 1990; served in U.S. Army Corps of Engrs., 1966-70; project engr. Empresas Navas, Inc., Mayaguez, P.R., 1970-72; ptnr., prin. W.A. Navas Jr. & Assocs., Mayaguez, 1972-80; dir. Navas & Moreda, Inc., Mayaguez, 1973-81; with Interamerican Def. Coll., Washington, 1981-82; dir. ops. P.R. Army Nat. Guard, San Juan, 1982-84, 84-87; comdr. Engr. Task Force, Panama, 1984; dep. dir. Army Nat. Guard Bur., Washington, 1987-97; vice chief Nat. Guard Bur., 1990; mil. exec. res. forces policy bd. Office of Sec. of Def., 1992-94, dep. asst. sec. of def., 1994-95; dir. Army Nat. Guard, 1995-97, ret., 1997; asst. secy. navy manpower reserve affairs U.S. Dept. Defense, Washington, 2001—. Chmn. Dept. of Army Hispanic Employment Commn., Washington, 1988. Decorated Knight Eq. Order of Holy Sepulchre. Mem. Nat. Guard Assn. of the U.S. (del. 1980-86), Nat. Guard Assn. of P.R., Soc. of Am. Mil. Engrs. Roman Catholic. Avocations: militaria collection, reading, running, travel, tennis. Office: US Dept Defense Manpower Reserve Affairs 1000 Navy Pentagon Washington DC 20350-1000 E-mail: bnavas@aol.com.

NAVASKY, VICTOR SAUL, magazine editor, publisher; b. N.Y.C., July 5, 1932; s. Macy and Esther Blanche (Goldberg) N.; m. Anne Landey Strongin, Mar. 27, 1966; children: Bruno, Miri, Jenny. AB, Swarthmore Coll., 1954; LL.B., Yale U., 1959. Spl. asst. to Gov. G. Mennen Williams, Mich., 1959-60; editor, pub. Monocle Mag., 1961-65; editor N.Y. Times mag., 1970-72, The Nation mag., N.Y.C., 1978-94; editl. dir. and pub. The Nation, N.Y.C., 1995—; Delacorte prof. of mag. journalism Columbia U., 1999—. Vis. scholarRussell Sage Found., 1975—76; Ferris prof. journalism Princeton U., 1976—77. Author: Kennedy Justice, 1971 (Nat. Book Award nominee), Naming Names, 1980 (Am. Book award 1981), rev. edit., 1991, 2003; editor: (with C. Cerf) The Experts Speak, 1984; playwright: (with Richard R. Lingeman) Starr's Last Tape, 1999. Mem. bd. mgrs. Swarthmore Coll., 1991-94. Served with U.S. Army, 1954-56. Guggenheim fellow, 1974-75; fellow Inst. of Politics, Harvard U., 1994; Sr. fellow Freedom Forum, 1994. Mem. Author's Guild (coun.), Com. To Protect Journalists (exec. com.), Phi Beta Kappa. Democrat. Jewish. Office: The Nation 33 Irving Pl Fl 8 New York NY 10003-2332 E-mail: vic@thenation.com.

NAVATTA, ANNA PAULA, lawyer; b. Hackensack, N.J., Jan. 7, 1956; d. Jack Anthony and Natalie (Pretto) N. BA, Rutgers U., 1978, MA, 1979; JD, Seton Hall U., 1982. Bar: N.J. 1983, U.S. Dist. Ct. N.J. 1983, U.S. Ct. Appeals (3d cir.) 1986. Law clk. to presiding justice Superior Ct. N.J., Hackensack, 1982-83; staff atty. Bergen County Legal Svcs., Hackensack, 1983—. Instr. Am. Inst. Paralegal Studies, Mahwah, N.J., 1986-95; atty. Lyndhurst (N.J.) Planning Bd., 1987-89. Mem. ABA, Fed. Bar Assn., N.J. State Bar Assn., Bergen County Bar Assn., Emblem Club. Democrat. Roman Catholic. Office: Northeast NJ Legal Svcs 61 Kansas St Hackensack NJ 07601-5351

NAVON, ROBERT, real estate investor, former book publisher; b. N.Y.C., May 18, 1954; s. Jack and Estelle N. AB, CUNY, Bronx, 1975; MLS, SUNY, Geneseo, 1978; MA, PhD, U. Kans., 1987; postgrad., U. N.Mex., 1991-93. Coll. libr. N.Y. Inst. Tech., N.Y.C., 1978-79; tchr. history and English N.Y.C. Schs., 1983-86; pub. Selene Books, N.Y.C., 1984-86, Lawrence, Kans., 1986-88, El Paso, Tex., 1988-93, Marianna, Fla., 1996-99; tchr. ESL, Evergreen Inst., Korea, 1993-94; real estate investor, Panama City, Fla., 1995—. Author: Patterns of the Universe, 1977, Autumn Songs, 1983, The Harmony of the Spheres, 1991, Cosmic Patterns, 1993, Tales of the Future, 1999. Mem. Internat. Soc. for Comparative Study of Civilizations, Phi Beta Kappa. Avocations: chess, international travel, collecting movies. Home: PO Box 634 Panama City FL 32402

NAVONE, EDWARD WILLIAM, artist, educator; b. Richmond, Calif., Oct. 5, 1937; s. Julio Mario and Helen Marie (Gianelli) N. BA in art, San Jose (Calif.) State Coll., 1959, MA in art, 1961; postgrad., U. Calif., Berkeley, 1961-62. Vis. instr. Ea. Wash. State Coll., Cheney, 1962-63; from instr. to prof. Washburn U., Topeka, 1964—. Asst. dir. Mulvane Art Mus., Topeka, 1964-79; taught and conducted course on Italian Renaissance Art History including 20-day trip to Italy, 1972, 73, 90-94, 2000, 04; cons. Salina Arts and Humanities Commn., 1989; mem. various coms. including acad. policy com., 1981-84, athletic com., 1978-79, spl. instructional program com., 1974-81, libr. com., 1966-81. One-person shows include Topeka/ Shawnee County Pub. Libr. Gallery, 1993, Art Gallery Univ. No. Iowa, 1998, Benedictine Coll., Atchinson, Kans., 1965, Sheldon Art Gallery, Lincoln, Nebr., 1969, U. Calif. Davis Gallery, 1971, U. Mo., Kansas City, 1976, Mabee-Gerrer Mus., Shawnee Okla., 1987, Swarthmore Coll., 1988, Mulvane Art Ctr. Gallery, 1989, U. No. Iowa, 1998, Mulvane Art Mus., 1999; group exhbns. Ancestral Legacy, Drury Coll., Springfield, Mo., 1992, Mulvane Art Mus., 1997, Shafer Gallery Barton County Comty. Coll., 1998; murals commd. for White Concert Hall/Washburn U., 1997, Lawrence Art Ctr., 2002, E. Cen. Univ., Ada, Okla., 2002, Birger Sandzen Gallery, 2002. Recipient numerous grants including Sweet Summer Sabbatical Italy, France, 1994, Sweet Sabbatical Italy, Austria, 1999, Italy, Belgium, France, 2002, Univ. Rsch. Com. joint project to design, execute and install a ceramic mural in corridor of Garvey Fine Arts Ctr., 1990, Summer Sweet Sabbatical N.Y., 1970, 40th Anniversary Retrospective, Mulvane Art Mus., 2003. Mem. Coll. Art Assn., Kansas City Artists Coalition, Phi Kappa Phi, Phi Beta Delta. Roman Catholic. Avocations: travel, classical music, photography. Home: 1325 SW Jewell Ave Topeka KS 66604-2731 Office: Washburn U 1700 SW College Ave Topeka KS 66621-0001 Office Phone: 785-231-1010 2243.

NAVRATILOVA, MARTINA, professional tennis player; b. Prague, Czech Republic, Oct. 18, 1956; came to U.S., 1975, naturalized, 1981; d. Miroslav Navratil and Jana Navratilova. Student, schs. in Czechoslovakia; Hon. doctorate, George Washington U., 1996. Tennis commentator/broadcaster HBO Sports, 1995-99; Profl. tennis player, 1973-94, 2003—. Player U.S. Fed Cup Team, 1982—86, 1989, 95, 2003; mem. World Team Tennis, 1990—. Author: (with George Vecsey) Martina, 1985, (with Liz Nickles) The Total Zone, 1995, (with Liz Nickels) The Breaking Point, (with Liz Nickles) 1996, Killer Instinct, 1997; columnist. Co-founder Rainbow Card. Winner Czechoslovak Nat. singles, 1972-74, U.S. Open singles, 1983, 84, 86, 87, U.S. Open doubles, 1977, 78, 80, 83, 84, 87, 90, U.S. Open mixed doubles, 1987, Va. Slims Tournament, 1978, 83, 84, 85, 86, Va. Slims doubles, 1991, Wimbledon singles, 1978, 79, 82, 83, 84, 85, 86, 87, 90, Wimbledon women's doubles, 1976, 79, 81, 82, 83, 84, 86, Wimbledon mixed doubles, 1985, 93, 95, 2003, French Open singles, 1982, 84, Australian Open singles, 1981, 83, 85, Australian Doubles (with Nagelsen) 1980, (with Shriver), 1982, 84, 85, 87, 88, 89, Australian Mixed Doubles, 2003, Roland Garros (with Shriver), 1985, 87, 89, Italian Open doubles (with Sabatini), 1987, (with Shriver) COREL WTA Tour doubles team of yr., 1981-89, triple Crown at U.S. Open, 1987; recipient Women's Sports Found. Flo Hyman award, 1987; named Female Athlete of the Decade (1980s) The Nat. Sports Review, UPI, and AP, WTA Player of Yr., 1978-79, 82-86, Women's Sports Found. Sportswoman of Yr., 1982-84, Hon. Citizen of Dallas, AP Female Athlete of Yr., 1983, Chgo. Hall of Fame, 1994; Martina Navratilova Day proclaimed in Chgo., 1992; recipient BBC Lifetime Achievement Award, 2003. Mem. Women's Tennis Assn. (dir., exec. com., pres.), Women's Tennis Assn. Tour Player's Assn. (pres. 1979-80, 83-84, 94-95). Achievements include being the holder of 167 singles titles and 173 doubles titles; holder of record of singles-match wins (1,309), 1991; holds record for 109 consecutive doubles matches won; 3rd women in history to win singles, doubles and mixed doubles titles at all four Grand Slam Tournaments; oldest women (43 years) to become a Wimbledon Champion (mixed doubles, 2003).*

NAWY, EDWARD GEORGE, civil engineer, educator; b. Baghdad, Iraq, Dec. 21, 1926; arrived in U.S., 1957, naturalized, 1966; s. George M. and Ava (Marshall) Nawy; m. Rachel E. Shebbath, Mar. 23, 1949; children: Ava Margaret, Robert M. DIC, Imperial Coll. Sci. and Tech., London, 1951; CE, MIT, 1959; D of Engring., U. Pisa, Italy, 1967. Registered profl. engr., N.J., N.Y., Pa., Calif., Fla. Head structures Israel Water Planning Authority, Tel-Aviv, 1952-57; faculty Rutgers U., New Brunswick, N.J., 1959—, grad. faculty, 1961—, prof. civil engring., 1966-72, Disting. prof. (prof. II), 1972—, chmn. dept. civil and environ. engring., dir. grad. programs, 1980-86. Chmn. Coll. Engring. Del. Assembly, 1969—72; mem. Univ. Senate, 1973—80, mem. exec. com., faculty rep., bd. govs., trustee; guest prof. Nat. U. Tucaman, Argentina, 1963, Imperial Coll. Sci. and Tech., 1964; mem. Civil Engring. Tech. Adv. Coun. N.J., 1966—72, N.J. Chancellor Higher Edn. for Higher Edn. Master Plan; vis. prof. Stevens Inst. Tech., Hoboken, NJ, 1968—72; gen. chmn. Internat. Symposium Slabs and Plates, 1971; mem. Rutgers U. rep. Transp. Rsch. Bd., 1974—2001, mem. bridge com., chmn. com. concrete materials; hon. prof. Nanjing Inst. Tech., China, 1987; U.S. mem. commn. cracking Comitè EuroInternational du Beton; concrete sys. cons. FAA, Washington; cons. energy divsn. U.S. Gen. Acctg. Office, Washington; hon. presidium internat. conf. Reunion Internat. des Lab. d'Essais et de Rsch. sur Les Materiaux et les Constructions, Budapest, 1977; mem. Accreditation Bd. Engring. and Tech. Author: Simplified Reinforced Concrete, 1986, Fundamentals of High Performance Concrete, 2d edit., 2001, Reinforced Concrete, 5th edit., 2003, Prestressed Concrete, 4th edit., 2003; author, editor-in-chief: Concrete Construction Engineering Handbook, 1998; contbr. articles to profl. jours. V.p. Berkeley Twp. Taxpayers Assn., Ocean City, NJ, 1966—70. Recipient Merit citation and award, N.J. Concrete Assn., 1966; C. Gulbenkian Found. fellow, 1972. Fellow. ASCE (mem. joint com. slabs), Instn. Civil Engrs. (London); mem.: AAUP (chmn. budget and priorities com. Rutgers U. chpt. 1972), NSPE, ACI (hon.), N.J. Contractors Assn. (cons. ednl. com., mem. tall bldgs. coun.), Tall Bldgs. Coun., N.Y. Acad. Scis., Am. Concrete Inst. (hon.; pres. N.J. chpt. 1966, chmn. nat. com. cracking 1966—73, bd. com. chpts. 1969—72, pres. N.J. chpt. 1977—78, chmn. nat. com. deflection 1989—96, ACI rep. internat. commn. fractures, H. L. Kenneday award 1972, award of recognition N.J. chpt. 1972, chpt. activities award 1978, Concrete Rsch. Coun. Philleo award 2001, Design Practice award 2003), Prestressed Concrete Inst. (mem. tech. activities com., Bridge Competition award 1971), Am. Soc. Engring. Edn., Rotary, Sigma Xi, Tau Beta Pi, Chi Epsilon (hon.). *Success is normally the result of honesty and continuous setting and updating of high goals which have to be perseverely pursued.*

NAYAK, NIHAR RANJAN, reproductive physiologist; arrived in U.S., 1998; s. Rama Chandra and Basanti Nayak; m. Sabita Dhal, Apr. 28, 1998; children: Neha, Sanket. B of Vet. Sci. and Animal Husbandry, Orissa U. Agr. and Tech., India, 1986, DVM, 1989; PhD, All India Inst. Med. Scis., New Delhi, 1998. Asst. prof. Orissa U. Agr. and Tech., Bhubaneswar, India, 1989—98; postdoctoral fellow Oreg. Health Scis. U., Beaverton, 1998—2000; staff scientist Oreg. Nat. Primate Rsch. Ctr./Oreg. Health Scis. U., Beaverton, 2000—02; rsch. scientist dept. ob-gyn. Stanford (Calif.) U. Med. Ctr., 2002—. Grantee, Mellon Found., 2000—03; Jr. fellow, Indian Coun. Agrl. Rsch., 1987—89, Rsch. Associateship, Indian Coun. Med. Rsch., 1995—97, Postdoctoral fellow, Lalor Found., 1998—2000, Travel grantee, Endocrine Soc., 1999. Mem.: Am. Soc. for Reproductive Medicine, The Endocrine Soc., Soc. for the Study of Reproduction (Burroughs Wellcome Fund Travel fellow 1999), Indian Soc. for Study of Reproduction and Fertility (life), Soc. Animal Physiologist India (life), Indian Poultry Sci. Assn. (life), Assn. Physiologists and Pharmacologists India (life A.V. Tilak Parvathi Devi award 1996). Achievements include research in endometrial physiology in primates with emphasis on endometrial growth, angiogenesis, and development of new contraceptive strategies. Home: 1600 Villa St #118 Mountain View CA 94041 Office: Stanford Univ Med Ctr 300 Pasteur Drive HH-333 Stanford CA 94305-5317 E-mail: nayakn@stanford.edu.

NAYAK, SUBHADARSHI, research scientist; b. Cuttack, Orissa, India, Apr. 2, 1972; arrived in U.S.A., 2000; s. Gangadhar and Satyabhama Nayak; m. Jyoti Agrawal, Aug. 15, 2003. B in tech with honours, Indian Inst. Tech., Kharagpur, India, 1991—95; PhD, U. Tenn., Knoxville, 2000—03. Rsch. asst. Indian Inst. Tech., Kharagpur, 1995—95; engr., metallurgist Tractor Engrs. Ltd., Bombay, 1995—2000; sys. analyst, quality Infosys Techs. Ltd., Bangalore, 2000; grad. rsch. asst. U. Tenn., Knoxville, 2000—; summer intern Ford Motor Co., Dearborn, Mich., 2001. Contbr. articles, columns in newspapers, articles, scientific papers, (Second Prize, Outstanding Student Paper, Minerals, Metals, and Materials Soc., 2002). Sponsor and vol. Save the Children Fund, Cuttack, India, 1990—2004. Recipient Materials Quiz, Nat. Level, Indian Inst. Tech., 1995, Citation Extraordinary Profl. Promise in Rsch., U. Tenn., 2002; fellow Merit Scholarship, Indian Inst. Tech., 1991-92, Grad. Fellowship, Tenn. Advanced Materials Lab., 2003; grantee High Temperature Materials Lab. User Program Grant, Oak Ridge Nat. Lab., 2000, 2001, Shared Rsch. Equipment User Program Grant, 2002. Mem.: Am. Ceramics Soc., Materials Rsch. Soc., Am. Physics Soc., ASM Internat. (membership coord. 1999—2000), Minerals, Metals, and Materials Soc. Office: Dept Materials Sci & Enrng Dougherty Enrng UT Knoxville TN 37996 Office Phone: 865-974-5160. Business E-Mail: snayak@utk.edu.

NAYAR, BALDEV RAJ, political science educator; b. Gujrat Dist., India, Oct. 26, 1931; emigrated to Can., 1964; s. Jamna Das and Durga Devi (Marwah) N.; m. Nancy Ann Skinner, Aug. 27, 1961; children— Sheila Jane, Kamala Elizabeth, Sunita Maria. BA, Punjab U., 1953; MA, 1956, U. Chgo., 1959, PhD, 1963. Asst. prof. Calif. State Coll., Hayward, 1963-64; mem. faculty dept. polit. sci. McGill U., 1964-94, assoc. prof., 1966-71, prof., 1971-94, prof. emeritus, 1996—, assoc. chmn., 1990-93. Rsch. assoc. Internat. Devel. Rsch. Centre, 1978 Author: Minority Politics in the Punjab, 1966, National Communication and Language Policy, 1969, The Modernization Imperative and Indian Planning, 1972, American Geopolitics and India, 1976, India's Quest for Technological Independence, 1983, India's Mixed Economy, 1989, The Political Economy of India's Public Sector, 1990, Superpower Dominance and Military Aid, 1991, The State and International Aviation in India, 1994, The State and Market in India's Shipping, 1996, Globalization and Nationalism, 2001, India and the Major Powers After Pokhran II, 2001; co-author: India in the World Order, 2003. Bd. dirs. Shastri Indo-Canadian Inst., 1970-72, sr. fellow, 1978, 86. Recipient Watumull prize Am. Hist. Assn., 1966; Charles E. Merriam fellow, 1957; Carnegie Study New Nations fellow, 1962; Can. Council sr. fellow, 1967, 74; SSHRC leave fellow, 1982 Mem. Can. Asian Studies Assn. Office: McGill Univ Dept Polit Sci Montreal QC Canada H3A 2T7 E-mail: bnayar@po-box.mcgill.ca.

NAYDAN, MICHAEL M. foreign language educator; b. Trenton, N.J., Oct. 20, 1952; s. William and Anna (Yaremko) N.; m. Roxanne Robak; 1 child Liliana Marika. BA magna cum laude, The American U., Washington, 1973, MA, 1975; MPh, Columbia U., 1980, PhD, 1984. Asst. prof. Yale U., New Haven, Conn., 1982-86; vis. asst. prof. Rutgers U., New Brunswick, N.J., 1986-88; asst. prof. Pa. State U., Univ. Park, 1988-90, assoc. prof., 1990—. Gen. asst. Columbia U. Bakhmeteff Archive of Russian and East European History and Culture, 1979-81; adj. instr. Russian Rutgers U., Newark, 1982; preceptor and instr. Russian, Columbia Univ., 1980-82; acting instr. Russian Yale U., 1982-84; head of instruction Yale Russian and Slavic Summer Lang. Inst., 1984-86; panelist, lectr. on Russian and Slavic poets at convs. and meetings of nat. and internat. orgns. Translator: (books) The Poetry of Lina Kostenko: Wanderings of the Heart, 1990, Marina Tsvetaeva's After Russia, 1992, From Three Worlds: New Writing from Ukraine, 1996, Yuri Vynnyohuk's The Windows of Time Frozen and other Stories, 2000, Parlo Tychyna's The Complete Early Poetry Collections of Paulo Tychyna, 2000, A Hundred Years of Youth: A Bilingual Anthology of Ukranian Poetry, 2000, Landscapes of Memory: Selected Later Poetry of Lina Kostenko, 2002, Olga Sedakova's Poems and Elogies, 2003, Igor Klekh's A Country the Size of Binoculars, 2003, Yuri Andrukhovych's Perversion, 2003; contbr. articles and reviews to profl. jours. and encyclopedias, translations in book chpts., journals and periodicals; contbr. poetry to Monmouth Review, 1975, Poet Lore, 1977, Bitterroot, 1979; editor-in-chief Slavic and East European Journal, 1993-98; assoc. editor Comparative Literature Studies, 1990—; assoc. editor and co-founder Ulbandus Review: A Jour. of Slavic Langs. and Lits., 1977-84. Recipient Pushkin prize, 1975, 76, 81, Columbia U., Eugene Kayden Meritorious Achievement award in translation, U. Colo., 1993, Mihaly-Mogilat fellowship, Columbia U., 1979; grantee Schevchenko Scholarly Soc., 1980, Moore Fund, 1983-84, N.J. Dept Higher Edn., 1987-88 (2), Woskob Fellow in Humanities, Nat. Endowment for the Humanities, 1991-92, 95. Mem. Am. Assn. for Advancement of Slavic Studies, Am. Assn. Tchrs. of Slavic and East European Langs., Am. Assn. Ukranian Studies (v.p.), Phi Kappa Phi. Ukranian Catholic. Avocations: tennis, squash. Office: Pa State Univ Germanic andSlavic Studies Dept 311 Burrowes Bldg University Park PA 16802-5201

NAYLON, BETSY ZIMMERMANN, artist; b. Buffalo, Jan. 27, 1934; d. Gerard M. and Marion G. (McDonald) Zimmermann; m. Bernard M. Naylon, Aug. 11, 1956; children: Lisa, Bernard, Claire. BA, Rosary Hill Coll., 1955; postgrad., Daeman Coll., 1976; studied with, William Paden, N.Y.C., 1986. Instr. Daeman Coll., Buffalo, 1969-70, SUNY, Buffalo, 1974-79, Niagara U., 1981-83, Trinity Ch., 1990-91. Tchr. tutorial studio classes, 1999-2004; art exhbn. judge Niagara Arts Guild Spring Exhibit, 1997, Internat. Children's Art Exhibit, Niagara Falls, Ont., Can., 1991, Lewiston Art Festival, 1982, 86, Castellani Art Gallery, Niagara U., 1982, 85, 89, Niagara Falls Soc. Artists, 1992-94; Am. judge for internat. art exhibit Niagara on the Lake, Ont., 1977; judge ann. group show Grand Island Art Group Exhibit, 1982, 88. One-woman shows include O'Keefe Ctr., Toronto, 1981, Rainbow Ctr., Niagara Falls, 1983, EW Brydges Libr., Niagara Falls, 1983, 84, Occidental Hooker Bldg., Niagara Falls, 1984, Buffalo Forge Co., 1984, Chautauqua Inst. Art Gallery, 1986, Capen Hall, SUNY, Buffalo, 1986, Carnegie Cultural Ctr., Tonawanda, NY, 1987, CP Chelsea Gallery, 1988, Kenan Gallery, Lockport, NY, 1989-90, Stella Niagara, 1994-97, Wilhelmenia Gallery, Seneca Falls, NY, 1997-98, exhibited in group shows at Albright-Knox Gallery, Buffalo, 1980-2004, Burchfield Art Ctr., Buffalo, 1980-2003, O'Keefe Ctr., 1982, AAO Galleries, Buffalo, 1984, A-K WNY exhbn, 1984, Nat. Assn. Women Artists, NYC, 1997-98, Sarasota, Fla., 2000, 02, Nat. League Am. Penwomen, Washington, 1996, NFWS, Lockport, NY, 1996, 2001, ALMC Internat. Fine Arts Exhbn., Fla., 1997, U. Wis., 1987, Western NY Artists Group, Art Dialogue Gallery, 1998-2000, D'Youville Coll. Art Gallery, 2001, Art Loft Gallery, Buffalo Soc. Artists, 2001-04, Impact Gallery, 2004; executed mural Niagara Falls Meml. Med. Ctr., 1995, Peller & Mure Co., Buffalo, 1985, JNW Ent., Lewiston, NY, 1997, Woman Free, Seneca Falls, NY, 1998; artwork and articles about artwork entered into the Women's History Collection, U. Buffalo Archives, 1998-2000, LCTV Channel 21 interviews. Recipient Grumbacher Gold Medal award, 1996. Mem. Nat. Assn. Women Artists (traveling printmaking exhibit U.S. 1987-89, 2002, India 1989-90), Nat. League Am. Penwomen (1st Place award 1991, Merit award 1989), Nat. Mus. Women in Arts, Nat. Women's Caucus for Art, Niagara Coun. Arts (bd. dirs. 1983-84), Niagara Frontier Watercolor Soc. (painting award 1989, 1st prize 1994), Buffalo Soc. Artists. Home: 25 Melbourne Pl Buffalo NY 14222-1455 Studio: Our Lady of Loretto 172 15th St Buffalo NY 14213-2606

NAYLON, MICHAEL EDWARD, retired army officer; b. Rochester, N.Y., Jan. 15, 1943; s. Edward M. and Patricia (Brennan) N.; m. Beverly Marzano, Mar. 27, 1965; children: Michelle A. Faber, Colleen M. Burgos. BA, John Carroll U., 1965; MBA, Marymount U., 1986; grad., U.S. Army War Coll., 1989. Indsl. rels. specialist Gen. Ry. Signal Co., Rochester, Farrell Co., Rochester; manpower adminstr. City of Rochester; employment mgr. U. Rochester; pers. dir. Interstate Brands Corp., Rochester; office mgr., dir. adminstrn., regional tng. coord. Nat. Machine Tool Builders Assn., McLean, Va.; chief U.S Army Res. Hdqs. Dept. of Army, Washington; staff officer Joint Chiefs of Staff, col., sr. res. advisor Dept. Def., Washington; with U.S. So. Command, Panama City, Panama; col. U.S. Army, ret. Dir. ops. Nat. Assn. Ret. Fed. Employees; nat. exec. dir. AMVETS; exec. dir. Presdl. Spl. Oversight Bd., Dept. Def. investigations of Gulf War chem. and biol. incidents; chief of staff Nat. Com. Employer Support of Guard and Res., Arlington, Va.; dep. dir. Office of Asst. Sec. of Def. for Res. Affairs, Pentagon, Washington. Mem. VFW, AMVETS, U.S. Army War Coll. Alumni Assn., John Carroll U. Alumni Assn., Res. Officers Assn. USA, Ret. Officers Assn., Am. Legion, Vietnam Vets. Home: 1434 Aldenham Ln Reston VA 20190-3901 E-mail: naylonmike@juno.com.

NAYLOR, AUBREY WILLARD, botany educator; b. Union City, Tenn., Feb. 5, 1915; s. Harry Joseph and Clara Mae (Isbell) N.; m. Frances Valentine Lloyd, Dec. 26, 1940 (dec. May 1998); children: Virginia Dawson Naylor Kirby, Edith-Margaret Naylor DeWitt. BS, U. Chgo., 1937, MS, 1938, PhD, 1940. Mem. staff, bur. plant industry U.S. Dept. Agr., Chgo., 1938-40; instr. botany U. Chgo., 1940-44, Northwestern U., Evanston, Ill., 1944-45; asst. prof. U. Wash., Seattle, 1946-47, Yale U., 1947-52; assoc. prof. Duke U., 1952-59, prof., 1959-72, James B. Duke prof., 1972-85, James B. Duke prof. emeritus, 1985—. Program dir. for metabolic biology NSF, Washington, 1961-62, cons., 1960-63; chmn. com. examiners for Grad. (Sch.) Record Examination on Biology, Edn. Testing Svc., Princeton, N.J., 1966-72; cons. Oak Ridge Nat. Lab., 1957-58, Rsch. Triangle Inst., N.C., 1968—, TVA, 1969-75, Schaper and Brümmer Pharm. Co., Salzgitter, Fed. Republic of Germany, 1986-92, Akzo Salt Co., 1991-96; mem. summer faculties U. N.C., Chapel Hill, 1960-61, Greensboro, 1964-65; mem. summer faculties Bennett Coll., Greensboro, N.C.; vis. prof. U. Bristol, Eng., 1958-59, U. Tex., Austin, 1977 Contbr. chpts. to books, articles and book revs. to profl. jours. NRC fellow Boyce Thompson Inst. for Plant Rsch., Yonkers, N.Y., 1945-46, Guggenheim fellow, 1958-59; NSF sr. fellow, 1958-59; grantee, 1956-86, Am. Cancer Soc. grantee, 1953-57, Herman Frasch Found. grantee, 1957-72. Fellow AAAS (life mem.); mem. Am. Soc. Plant Physiologists (life, chmn. bd. trustees 1962-74, pres. 1961, exec. com. 1959-60, 62-74, 81-82, Disting. Svc. award So. sect. 1981, Charles Reid Barnes life membership 1981, archivist 1987—), Am. Inst. Biol. Scis., Am. Soc. Cell Biologists, Bot. Soc. Am. (life, cert. of merit 1988), Scandinavian Soc. Plant Physiologists, Japanese Soc. Plant Physiologists, Australian Soc. Plant Physiologists, Cosmos Club (Washington), Sigma Xi (life, pres. chpt. 1968-69). Home: Ste 400 3211 Shannon Rd Durham NC 27707-6323 E-mail: anaylor1@nc.rr.com. *Almost everything interests me. For this reason, I am seldom bored. Channeling my curiosity has been best achieved through a burning desire to learn how living things grow from a single cell, differentiate into a distinct multicellular organism and reproduce. The joy of discovery feeds upon itself and motivates me to work, work, and work some more.*

NAYLOR, CRAIG G. engineering company executive; b. Media, Pa., Nov. 24, 1948; m. Sharon Jamison (dec.); 2 children. B of Engring. in Chem. Engring., Stevens Inst. Tech. Various chem. engring. positions Dupont, 1970—74, area supt. Teflon, 1977—79, project mgr. Teflon, 1979—81, product mgr. Teflon, 1981—83, customer svc. mgr. Polymer Products dept., 1983—84, devel. mgr. engring. polymer, 1984—85, devel. mgr. engring. polymers automotive, 1985—87, Asia Pacific regional dir. Tokyo, 1987—91, products dir. engring. polymers Wilmington, Del., 1991—92, Nylon resins bus. dir. Geneva, 1992—96, v.p., gen. mgr. engring. polymers, 1996—2000, group v.p., gen. mgr. engring. polymers, fluoroporucts and packagaing and indsl. polymers, 2000—02, group v.p. Performance Materials, 2002—. Office: DuPont DuPont Bldg 1007 Market St Wilmington DE 19898

NAYLOR, JAMES CHARLES, psychologist, educator; b. Chgo., Feb. 8, 1932; s. Joseph Sewell and Berniece (Berg) N.; m. Georgia Lou Mason, Feb. 14, 1953; children— Mary Denise, Diana Darice, Shari Dalice. BS, Purdue U., 1957, MS, 1958, PhD, 1960. Asst. prof. Ohio State U., 1960-63, asso. prof., 1963-67, prof. vice chmn. dept. psychology, 1967-68; prof. Purdue U., Lafayette, Ind., 1968-86, head dept. psychol. scis., 1968-79; prof., chmn. dept. psychology Ohio State U., Columbus, 1986-98, prof. emeritus, 1999—. Fulbright rsch. scholar, Umea, Sweden, 1976; Disting. scholar, vis. scientist Flinders U., South Australia, 1982-83, UNESCO ednl. cons. to Hangzhou U., Peoples Republic of China, 1984; chmn. Coun. Grad. Depts. Psychology, 1993-94; lead reviewer Psychology Program Rev., State U. Sys. Fla., 1996. Author: Industrial Psychology, 1968, A Theory of Behavior in Organizations, 1980; founder, editor: Organizational Behavior and Human Decision Processes; mem. editorial bd.: Prof. Psychology; Contbr. articles to profl. jours. Served with USN, 1950-54. Fellow AAAS, Am. Psychol. Soc., Am. Psychol. Assn.; mem. Psychonomic Soc., Psychmetric Soc., Internat. Assn. Applied Psychology, Soc. Organizational Behavior (founder), Midwestern Psychol. Assn. (coun. 1994-97), Phi Beta Kappa, Sigma Xi. Home: 176 Tucker Dr Columbus OH 43085-3064 Office: Ohio State U Dept Psychology Columbus OH 43210 E mail: naylor.2@osu.edu.

NAYLOR, JEFFREY GORDON, consumer products company executive; b. Montreal, Que., Can., Nov. 15, 1958; s. Gordon Charles and Patricia Grace (Pryde) N.; m. Shawn Elizabeth Baker, Oct. 6, 1984; 1 child, Madeleine Baker Naylor. BA in econs., Northwestern U., 1980, MBA, 1982. CPA, Ill. Pub. acct. Deloitte, Haskins & Sells, Chgo., 1982-86; assoc. N.Am. Venture Capital, Chgo., 1986-88; mgr. mergers and acquisitions A.C. Nielsen, Northbrook, Ill., 1988-90, dir. fin. analysis, 1990-91; dir. finance Kraft Foods Sales, Northfield, Ill., 1991-93, Kraft Foods Corp., Northfield, 1993-95; v.p. credit divsn. Sears Roebuck & Co., Hoffman Estates, Ill., 1995—; v.p., contr The LimitedInc; CFO, sen. v.p. fin. Dade Behring, Dearfield, Ill, 2000—. Prof. acctg. Keller Grad. Sch. Mgmt., Chgo., 1987-91. Treas. Episcopal Ch. of Northwestern U., Evanston, 1996—; mem. Brookfield Zoo, 1995—, Northwestern U. "N" Club, 1980—. Mem. AICPA, Ill. CPA Soc. Episcopalian. Avocations: competitive swimming, Sunday Sch. tchr., gourmet cooking, reading, ice skating.

NAYLOR, PAUL DONALD, lawyer; b. St. Bernard, Ohio, May 28, 1925; s. David Frederick and Erna Helen (Miller) N.; m. Geraldine L. Lacy, Jan. 20, 1945; children: Linda S., Paul Scott, Todd L. JD, U. Cin., 1948. Bar: Ohio 1948. Ptnr. Pulse & Naylor, Cin., 1949-65; pvt. practice Cin., 1965—. Mem. Nat. Rep. Com. Lt. (j.g.) USN, 1943-46. Recipient Svc. to Mankind award Sertoma Internat. Mem. Cin. Bar Assn. (real property com. 1966-86), Ohio Bar Assn., Cin. Lawyers Club (pres. 1955), Order of the Coif.

NAYLOR, PHYLLIS REYNOLDS, writer; b. Anderson, Ind., Jan. 4, 1933; d. Eugene Spencer and Lura Mae (Schield) Reynolds; m. Thomas A. Tedesco, Jr., Sept. 9, 1951 (div. 1960); m. Rex V. Naylor, May 26, 1960; children: Jeffrey, Michael. Diploma, Joliet Jr. Coll., 1953; BA, Am. U., 1963. Author more than 120 books including Crazy Love: An Autobiographical Account of Marriage and Madness, 1977, Revelations, 1979, A String of Chances, 1982 (ALA notable book), The Agony of Alice, 1985 (ALA notable book), The Keeper, 1986 (ALA notable book), Unexpected Pleasures, 1986, Send No Blessings, 1990 (YASD best book for young adults), Shiloh, 1991 (ALA notable book, John Newbery medal 1992), The Fear of Place, 1994, Sang Spell, 1998, Walker's Crossing, 1999, Blizzard's Wake, 2002, After, 2003. Recipient Golden Kite award Soc. Children's Book Writers Am., 1985, Child Study award Bank St. Coll., 1983, Edgar Allan Poe award Mystery Writers Am., 1985, 2004, Internat. book award Soc. Sch. Librs., 1988, Christopher award, 1989, Newbery award ALA, 1992, Nat. Endowment of Arts Creative Writing fellow, 1987. Mem. Children's Book Guild of Washington (pres. 1974-75, 83-84), Soc. Children's Book Writers, Authors Guild, PEN, Council for a Livable World, Physicians for Social Responsibility, Amnesty Internat. Unitarian Universalist. Avocations: theater, swimming. Home and Office: 9910 Holmhurst Rd Bethesda MD 20817-1618 Office Phone: 301-530-2340.

NAYLOR, THOMAS HERBERT, economist, educator, consultant; b. Jackson, Miss., May 30, 1936; s. Thomas Hector and Martha (Watkins) N.; m. Magdalena Raczkowska, Dec. 14, 1985; children: Susanne, Alexander. BS in Math., Millsaps Coll., 1958; BS in Indsl. Engring., Columbia U., 1959; MBA in Quantitative Bus. Analysis, Ind. U., 1961; PhD in Econs., Tulane U., 1964. Instr. Sch. Bus. Adminstrn. Tulane U., 1961-63; asst. prof. econs. Duke U., 1964-66, assoc. prof. econs., 1966-68, prof. econs., 1968-93, prof. emeritus econs., 1994—. Vis. prof. U. Wis., 1969-70, Middlebury Coll., 1993-94, U. Vt., 1994-96; pres. Social Systems, Inc., 1971-80; mng. dir. Naylor Group, 1980; cons., lectr. in over 30 countries. Co-author: (with Eugene Byrne) Linear Programming, 1963, (with Joseph L. Balintfy, Donald S. Burdick and Kong Chu) Computer Simulation Techniques, 1966, translated into Japanese, Portuguese and Spanish, (with John Vernon) Microeconomics and Decision Models of the Firm, 1969, translated into Spanish, (with James Clotfelter) Strategies for Change in the South, 1975, (with John M. Vernon and Kenneth Wertz) Managerial Economics: Corporate Economics and Strategy, 1983, (with William H. Willimon) The Abandoned Generation: Rethinking Higher Education, 1995, Downsizing the U.S.A., 1997, (with Rolf Österberg and William H. Willimon) The Search for Meaning in the Workplace, 1996, others; author or co-author of 30 books including: Computer Simulation Experiments with Models of Economic Systems, 1971, translated into Spanish, Polish, and Russian, Corporate Planning Models, 1979, Strategic Planning Management, 1980, The Corporate Strategy Matrix, 1986, translated into Hungarian, The Gorbachev Strategy, 1988, The Cold War Legacy, 1991, (with William H. Willimon and Magdalena R. Naylor), The Search for Meaning, 1994; editor: The Impact of the Computer on Society, 1967, The Design of Computer Simulation Experiments, 1969, The Politics of Corporate Planning and Modeling, 1978, Simulation Models in Corporate Planning, 1979, Simulation in Business Planning and Decision Making, 1981, others; co-editor: (with H. Brandt Ayers) You Can't Eat Magnolias, 1972, (with Michele H. Mann) Portfolio Planning and Corporate Strategy, 1983, (with Celia Thomas) Optimization Models for Strategic Planning, 1984, (with John DeGraff and David Wann), Affluenza, 2001, translated into French, German and Japanese, The Vermont Manifesto, 2003, others; contbr. numerous articles to profl. publs.; mem. editl. bd. jours. Exec. dir., founder. L.Q.C. Lamar Soc., Washington, 1969-73; founder Second Vt. Republic, 2003. Named to Lambda Chi Alpha Alumni Hall of Fame, 1996. Mem.: Beta Gamma Sigma, Omicron Delta Kappa. Home: 202 Stockbridge Rd Charlotte VT 05445-9358 Office Phone: 802-425-4133.

NAYLOR-JACKSON, JERRY, public relations consultant, retired, entertainer, broadcaster; b. Chalk Mountain, Tex., Mar. 6, 1939; s. William Guy and Mary Bernice (Lummus) Jackson; m. Pamela Ann Robinson, Jan. 30, 1966; children: Geoffrey K. Naylor, Kelli A. Naylor-Dobrzynski, Gregory K. Naylor. Grad., Elkins Electronics Inst., Dallas, 1957. Life first class radio/TV engring. lic. FCC. Broadcaster various local TV and AM radio stas., San Angelo, Texas, 1955-57; lead singer Buddy Holly and the Crickets, 1960-65; solo entertainer, performer, recording artist and producer, 1965-87; sr. v.p. corp. devel. Newslink Internat. Satellite Broadcast Comms. Co., Inc., Washington, 1986-88; pres. Internat. Syndications, Inc. subs. Newslink, Inc., Washington, 1986-88; pres., CEO, owner The Jerry Naylor Co./Nayco Entertainment, Inc., McMinnville, Oreg., 1984—; v.p. capital programs, sr. cons. Calif. Luth. Univ., Thousand Oaks, 1990-92. Sr. cons., dir. ann. fund Calif. Luth. U., 1989-90; polit./media cons. various Rep. candidates and orgns., 1968-93; spl. cons. to Violeta Barrios de Chamarro, Pres. of Republic of Nicaragua, 1990-92; disc jockey Sta. KHEY-AM, Sta. KINT-AM, El Paso, Tex., 1959; on-air personality Sta. KRLA-AM, Sta. KDAY-AM, L.A., 1960; on-air disc jockey, air personality, celebrity host KLAC-AM, L.A., 1974-83; on-camera and voice-over spokesman for Safeway Stores, Inc., Avis Rent-a-Car, Mut. of Omaha, Wrigley Co., 1968-83; U.S. presdl. appointee, chmn. Job Tng. Partnership Act work group/youth at risk subcom. Nat. Commn. for Employment Policy, 1985-91; nat. dir. spl. events Reagan for Pres., 1979-81; apptd. mem. commn. for employment policy Pres. Ronald Reagan, 1985-91. Rec. artist maj. labels including Capitol/Tower Records, Mercury/Smash Records, CBS/Columbia Records, Mike Club Prodns., Warner/Curb Records, Motown Records, Warner Bros. Records, EMI Records, 1965-84; solo rec. artist, prodr. Phonograph Records and TV Documentaries; host weekly nat. and internat. syndicated radio program Continental Country (Number 1 syndicated country music radio show in Am., Billboard Mag., Country Music Assn., 1974), weekly syndicated TV variety show Music City, USA, 1966-67. Nat. dir. spl. events Reagan for Pres., 1975-76, 79-80; sr. cons. to White House, 1981-88, 89-92. With U.S. Army, 1957-58, Germany. Named to Top 40 Male Vocalists of Yr., Cashbox Mag., 1970, named #1 Rock Group (Crickets), New Musical Express Mag., U.K., 1962. Mem. NARAS, Country Music Assn., Acad. Country Music (Telly award for TV documentary 1991, 92), Pi Kappa Phi (alumni). Avocation: writing prose and poetry. Home and Office: Jerry Naylor Co/Nayco Entertainment Inc 1279 SW Russ Ln Mcminnville OR 97128-5699 E-mail: j.naylor@comcast.net. *Know no boundaries. Experience the world and become enriched from its varied inhabitants.*

NAYMARK, SHERMAN, consulting nuclear engineer; b. Duluth, Minn., May 12, 1920; s. David N. and Lena (Naymark); children by previous marriage: Ronald L., Janet Naymark Stone. BS in Engring., U.S. Naval Acad., 1941; MS in Engring. and Constrn., MIT, 1946. Sr. scientist Argonne Nat. Lab., (Ill.), 1948-52; dir. reactor div. project, engring. mgr. Schenectady office AEC, 1952-56; with Gen. Electric Co., 1956-70; engring. mgr. nuclear turnkey plants San Jose, 1967-69; pres. Quadrex Corp., Campbell, Calif., 1970-86, chmn., 1986. Lectr. U. Va., MIT, U.S. Naval Res. Officer tng. Schs.; adviser to U.S. del. 3d Internat. Conf. on Peaceful Uses of Atomic Energy, Geneva, 1964; sr. examiner Profl. Engrs. State of Calif., 1960-70; mem. fusion power coordinating com. Dept. Energy Contbr. numerous articles on nuclear research, devel., engring. to profl. jours. Served to capt. USN, 1941-54. Fellow Am. Nuclear Soc. (gen. chmn. ann. meeting, nat. treas. 1978-80), nat. treas. (mem. governing bd. Nuclear Tech. 1979-81); mem. AAAS, Am. Pub. Power Assn. (assoc.), U.S. Naval Inst. (hon. life) Democrat. Jewish. Home: 218 Forrester Rd Los Gatos CA 95032-6509 E-mail: snaymark@aol.com.

NAZAIRE, MICHEL HARRY, physician; b. Jérémie, Haiti, Sept. 29, 1939; s. Joseph and Hermance N.; m. Nicole Lamarque, Dec. 28, 1968 (div.); children: Hannick and Carline (twins). BS, DOE, Port-Au-Prince, Haiti, 1959; MD Faculty of Medicine and Pharmacology, State U. Haiti, 1966. Intern State U. Hosp., Port-Au-Prince, Haiti, 1965-66; resident physician Sanitarium, Port-Au-Prince, Haiti, 1966-68; physician pneumology, 1966-68; physician pneumo-phtisiology, 1966—; fellow Klinik Havelhohe and Heckeshorn, Berlin, 1969-70, 89-91; attending physician Sanitarium, Port-Au-Prince, 1976-91. Dep. mem. Internat. Parliament for Safety and Peace, envoy-at-large Internat. State Parliament, mem. global environ. technol. network WHO. Contbr. articles to profl. jours. including Jour. Indsl. Hygiene, Pneumology and Respiratory Protection. Recipient Physician's Recognition award, Am. Med. Assn., 2002, AMA, 2002. Fellow Internat. Soc. for Respiratory Protection, Am. Coll. Chest Physicians (assoc.); mem. AMA (Physician's Recognition award 2002), Am. Pub. Health Assn., Am. Conf. Govtl. Indsl. Hygienists, Internat. Union Against Tuberculosis, Internat. Platform Assn., Physicians for Social Responsibility. Address: 12 B St NE Apt 103 Auburn WA 98002 Home Fax: 253-333-6520.

NAZARIAN, JOHN, academic administrator, mathematics educator; b. Pawtucket, R.I., Sept. 6, 1932; s. Zakie and Amenia (Nahas) N. EdB, R.I. Coll., 1954; AM, Brown U., 1956; MA, U. Ill., 1961; PhD, NYU, 1967. Instr. math. R.I. Coll., Providence, 1954-58, asst. prof., 1958-67, assoc. prof., 1967-71, prof., 1971—, assoc. dean Arts and Scis., 1970-72, spl. asst. to pres., 1971-77, v.p. adminstrn. and fin., 1977-90, pres., 1990—. Chmn., vice-chmn. Arabic Ednl. Found., Pawtucket, 1966-72; chmn. Sargeant Rehab. Ctr, Providence, 1983-86, Diocesan Pastoral Coun., West Newton, Mass., 1974-78; chmn. Diocesan Fin. Coun., 1996-. Recipient Cross of Jerusalem, Patriarch of Melkite Ch., 1976; inducted into R.I. Island Heritage Hall of Fame, 2003. Avocations: music, golf, reading. Office: RI Coll Roberts Hall 404 600 Mount Pleasant Ave Providence RI 02908-1924 E-mail: jnazarian@ric.edu.

NAZARIAN, LAWRENCE FRED, pediatrician; b. N.Y.C., May 17, 1940; s. Samuel George and Winifred Lucia (Zotian) N.; m. Sharon Louise Carlson, June 22, 1963; children: Douglas, Stephen, Sarah. BA, Yale U., 1960; MD, U. Rochester, 1964. Pediatrician Panorama Pediatric Group, Rochester, NY, 1969—2004; clin. prof. pediatrics U. Rochester Sch. Medicine and Dentistry, 1969—. Bd. dirs. James P. Wilmot Found., Rochester. Assoc. editor Pediatrics in Rev. Jour., 1990—; contbr. articles to profl. jours. Mem. troop com. Boy Scouts Am., Penfield, N.Y., 1978-88; mem. coun. com. Luth. Ch. of Reformation, Rochester, 1969—. Maj. USAR, 1967-69. Fellow Am. Acad. Pediatrics; mem. Med. Soc. State of N.Y., Ctrl. N.Y. Pediatric Club, Monroe County Med. Soc., Rochester Acad. Medicine, Rochester Pediatric Soc. Avocations: hiking, camping, canoeing, gardening, cross country skiing. Office: U Rochester Med Ctr 601 Elmwood Ave Box 777 Rochester NY 14642 Office Phone: 585-275-0170.

NAZARIO, SONIA, reporter; b. Madison, Wis., Sept. 8, 1960; m. William Regensburger. BA in History, Williams Coll., Williamstown, Mass., 1982; MA in Latin Am. Studies, U. Calif., Berkeley, 1988. Freelance reporter El Pais, Madrid, 1980; staff reporter Wall St. Jour., Atlanta, 1982—84, Miami, 1984—86, LA, 1988—93; urban affairs writer L.A. Times, 1993—94, projects and urban affairs reporter, 1994—. Recipient Pulitzer prize for feature writing, 2003, Pulitzer prize finalist for pub. svc., 1998, Nat. Coun. on Crime and Delinquency PASS award, 1998, Commendation for outstanding reporting on psychiat. issues, Am. Psychiat. Assn., 1998, Life-Time award, Inst. for Suicide Prevention, 1997, Guillermo Martinez-Marquez award for overall excellence, Nat. Assn. Hispanic Journalists, 1995, George Polk award for local reporting, 1994, Cameron R. Duncan World Hunger Media award, 1994, George Polk award for internat. reporting, 2003, Robert F. Kennedy Journalism award, 2003, Overseas Press Club award, 2003, award, Nat. Assn. Hispanic Journalists Guillermo Martinez-Marquez, 2003. Office: LA Times 202 W 1st St Los Angeles CA 90012

NAZEM, FEREYDOUN F. venture capitalist; b. Tehran, Iran, Dec. 29, 1940; came to U.S., 1960; naturalized, 1976; s. Hassan and Afsar N.; m. Susie Gharib, Jan. 20, 1973; children: Alexander, Taraneh. BS, Ohio State U., 1964; MSc, U. Cin., 1967; MBA, Columbia U., 1971. Sr. rsch. chemist Matheson Coleman & Bell, Norwood, Ohio, 1967-68; asst. v.p., investment analyst Irving Trust Co., N.Y.C., 1969-74; v.p., venture capital officer Charter N.Y., N.Y.C., 1974-75; mng. dir. Collier Enterprises, N.Y.C., 1976-81; mng. ptnr. Nazem & Co. I, II, III and IV, N.Y.C., 1981—, Explorer Fund, N.Y.C., 1997—, Transatlantic Venture Fund, 1998—, Hedgeworth, L.L.C., N.Y.C., 2003. Bd. dirs. Genetix Corp., Boston, ETRIALS, Carey, N.C., Cradle Corp., Mt. View, Calif., U.S. Open Health, N.Y.C. Author: The Chemical Industry and Energy Shortage, Hedgeworth Market Letter. Office: Nazem & Co 645 Madison Ave New York NY 10022-1010 Office Phone: 212-371-7900. E-mail: fnazem@nazem.com. *You can have success and serenity at the same time. Become a possibilitarian- spend time solving problems, not worrying about them.*

NDEGWA, STEPHEN N. political scientist, educator; b. Trans Nzoia, Kenya, Jan. 12, 1969; s. Ephraim Muthungu and Mary Wangare Ndegwa; m. Dorothy W. Mwawasi; 1 child, Faith Wangare. BA, Coll. of Wooster, 1990; PhD, Ind. U., 1993. Asst. prof. Coll. of William and Mary, Williamsburg, Va., 1994—2000, assoc. prof., 2000—04; goverance specialist The World Bank, Washington, 2002—. Cons. U.S, AID, Washington, 1995—2000; young profl. World Bank, Washington, 2002—. Author: (book) The Two Faces of Civil Society; editor: The Uncertain Promise of Southern Africa, (jour. spl. edition) Rethinking Citizenship in Africa, A Decade of Democracy in Africa; contbr. articles to profl. jours. (Runner Up Best Article in Discipline award Am. Polit. Sci. Rev., 1997). Recipient Rsch. fellowship, Am. Coun. of Learned Societies, 1997, Borgenicht Peace Scholarship award, Reves Ctr. for Internat. Studies, 2000. Mem.: Am. Polit. Sci. Assn. (grantee 1996), African Studies Assn. (life; bd. dirs 1998—2001). Office: The World Bank 1818H St NW Washington DC 20433-8795 Office Phone: 202-473-1510. Business E-Mail: sndegwa@worldbank.org.

NEAGLE, DENNIS EDWARD (DENNY NEAGLE), professional baseball player; b. Gambrills, Md., Oct. 13, 1968; Grad. high sch., Gambrills, Md.; student, U. Minn. With Minn. Twins, 1991; pitcher Pitts. Pirates, 1992-96, Atlanta Braves, 1996-98, Cin. Reds, 1999—. Selected to N.L. All-Star Team, 1995. Achievements include being a mem. Pitts. Pirates N.L. East Champions, 1992. Office: Cin Reds Cinergy Field 100 Cinergy Fld Cincinnati OH 45202-3543

NEAL, A. MICHAEL, utilities executive; BS, Ga. Inst. Tech., 1975. V.p., gen. mgr., Vendor Fin. Svcs. G.E. Capital, 1987—90, gen. mgr., Comml. Equip. Financing, 1990—94; sr. v.p. G.E. Co., 1993—; exec. v.p. G.E. Captial, 1994—2000; pres., COO G.E. Capital, 2000—02; pres., CEO G.E. Comml. Fin., 2002—. Mem. adv. bd. European Inst. Bus. Adminstrn. Bd. trustees Fairfiled U.; trustee Ga. Tech. Found.; chmn. GE Captial United Way campaign. Office: GE Commercial Fin 260 Long Ridge Rd Stamford CT 06927

NEAL, CHARLES D., JR., lawyer; b. McAlester, Okla., Jan. 4, 1949; BSBA, Okla. State U., 1972; JD Okla. City U., 1975. Bar: Okla. 1975, U.S. Dist. Ct. Okla. (ea., we., no. dists.), U.S. Dist. Ct. Ark. (ea. and we. dists.), U.S. Ct. Appeals (10th, 8th and 5th cirs.), U.S. Supreme Ct. Ptnr. Steidley & Neal, McAlester, 1976—; mcpl. judge Kiowa, Okla., 1981—88, Krebs, Okla., 1981—. Fellow: Okla. Bar Found. (trustee 1998—2001), Am. Bar Found.; mem.: Okla. Assn. Def. Counsel, Def. Rsch. Inst., Pittsburg County Bar Assn. (pres. 1980—81), Okla. Bar Assn. (pres. 2001—02), ABA (ho. dels. 2000—01). Office: Steidley & Neal 100 E Carl Albert Pkwy PO Box 1165 Mcalester OK 74502

NEAL, DARWINA LEE, government official; b. Mansfield, Pa., Mar. 31, 1942; d. Darwin Leonard and Ina Belle (Cooke) N. BS, Pa. State U., 1965; postgrad., Cath. U. 1968-70. Registered landscape architect. Landscape architect nat. capital region Nat. Pk. Svc., 1965-69, office of White House liaison, 1969-71, office of profl. services, 1971-74, div. design svcs., 1974-89, chief design svcs., 1989-95, chief landscape arch. office of stewardship and partnership, 1996-98, chief cultural resource preservation svcs. nat. capital reg., 1998—. Judge numerous award juries. Contbr. articles to profl. jours.; co-author sects. of profl. bull., mag.; author introduction to book Women, Design and the Cambridge School; columnist: Land monthly, 1975-79. Recipient Merit award Landscape Contractors Met. Washington; recipient hon. mention Les Floralies Internat. Montreal, 1980 Alumni Achievement award Pa. State U. Arts and Architecture Alumni Soc., 1981 Fellow Am. Soc. Landscape Architects (v.p. 1979-81, pres. elect 1982-83, pres. 1983-84, trustee 1976-77, nat. treas. 1977-79, legis. coord. 1975-79, sec. Coun. Fellows 1988-90, del. to Internat. Fedn. Landscape Architects 1989-92, 2000-03, ex-officio rep. to U.S./internat. coun. on monuments and sites 1985-98, liaison to historically black coll. and univ. program Dept. Interior, chair internat. task force 1999-2000, Pres.' medal 1987); Treas. U.S. Internat. coun. on Monuments and Sites, 1998-2004, sec. Internat. Fed. Landscape Architects, W. Region, 2003-; mem. Landscape Archtl. Accreditation Bd. (roster vis. evaluators), Nat. Recreation and Parks Assn., Nat. Soc. Park Resources (bd. dirs. 1978-80), Nat. Trust Hist. Preservation, Pa. State U. Alumni Assn. (Washington met. chpt. trustee 1972-74), Am. Arbitration Assn. (nat. panel arbitrators), Com. 100 for the Fed. City, Preservation Action, Nat. Assn. Olmsted Parks, Beekman Pl. Condominium Assn. (bd. dirs. 1985-91, archtl. control com. 1977-2000, landscape com. 2000-02), Alliance for Historic Preservation, Garden Conservancy, Scenic Am., Preservation Action, Preservation Roundtable, Hist. Soc. Washington. Office: Nat Park Svc/Nat Capital Region Off Lands Resources & Plan 1100 Ohio Dr SW Washington DC 20242-0001

NEAL, DENNIS MELTON, middle school administrator; b. Lakeland, Fla., Feb. 7, 1966; s. M. H. and Alice Marie (Twiddy) N.; m. Christine Anne Rufo, Oct. 21, 1989; children: Lauren Elizabeth, Waverly Rose, Emma Katherine. AA, Polk C.C., Winter Haven, Fla., 1987; BS, Fla. So. Coll., 1991; MEd, Stetson U., 1995. Cert. elem. tchr., ednl. leader, prin., Fla. Guest svcs. Cypress gardens, Winter Haven, 1985-86; entertainer Boardwalk and Baseball, Baseball City, Fla., 1986-88; guest svcs. Hilton Walt Disney World, Orlando, Fla., 1988-91; tchr. Deltona (Fla.) Middle Sch., 1991-95, asst. prin., 1995-99, Heritage Middle Sch., Deltona, Fla., 1999-2000; prin. intern Pine Ridge H.S., 2000—. Chair correlate com., team leader Deltona Middle Sch., sch. adv. coun. Tchr. Lith. Ch. of Providence, Orange City, Fla., 1992-93; active Parent, Tchr., Student Assn. Named One of Top 100 Beginning Tchrs. in Nation, Sallie Mae Student Loan Assn., 1992. Avocations: soccer, racquetball, drawing, painting.

NEAL, HOMER ALFRED, physics educator, researcher, university administrator; b. Franklin, Ky., June 13, 1942; s. Homer and Margaret Elizabeth (Holland) Neal; m. Donna Jean Daniels, June 16, 1962; children: Sharon Denise, Homer Alfred. BS in Physics with honors, Ind. U., 1961; MS in Physics (John Hay Whitney fellow), U. Mich., 1963, PhD in Physics, 1966. Asst. prof. physics Ind. U., 1967—70, assoc. prof., 1970—72, prof., 1972—81, dean research and grad. devel., 1976—81; prof. physics SUNY, Stony Brook, 1981—87, provost, 1981—86; prof. physics, chmn. U. Mich., Ann Arbor, 1987—93, v.p. rsch., 1993—97, interim pres., 1996—97, prof. of physics, 1987—2000, Samuel A. Goudsmit disting. prof. physics, 2000—, dir. of atlas project, 1997—. Bd. dirs. Ford Motor Co., Covanta Corp.; mem. Nat. Sci. Bd., 1980—86; mem. adv. coun. Oak Ridge Nat. Lab., 1993—99; mem. external adv. coun. Nat. Computational Sci. Alliance, 1997—; mem. applications strategy coun. Univ. Corp. for Advanced Internet Devel., 2000—; chmn. Argonne Zero Gradient Synchrotron Users Group, 1970—72; trustee Argonne Univs. Assn., 1971—74, 1977—80; physics adv. panel NSF, 1976—79, chmn. physics adv. panel, 1987—89; high energy physics adv. panel U.S. Dept. Energy, 1977—81. Contbr. articles to profl. jours. Mem. bd. regents Smithsonian Instn., 1989—2001; trustee Ctr. for Strategic and Internat. Studies, 1990—2000; Oak Ridge (Tenn.) Nat. Lab., 1993—; mem. bd. overseers Superconducting Super Collider, 1989—93; trustee Environ. Rsch. Inst. of Mich., 1994—96; N.Y. Sea Grant Inst., 1982—86. Recipient Stony Brook medal, 1986, Ind. U. Disting. Alumni award, 1994; fellow NSF, 1966—67, Sloan, 1968, Guggenheim, 1980—81. Fellow: AAAS, Am. Acad. Arts and Scis., Am. Phys. Soc.; mem.: Univs. Rsch. Assn. (trustee), Sigma Xi. Office: Dept of Physics Rm 2477 Randall Lab 500 East University Ann Arbor MI 48109-1120

NEAL, IRENE COLLINS, artist, educator; b. Greensburg, Pa., May 14, 1936; d. Oliver Shupe and Betsey Cowap (Mann) Collins; m. Paul Whitaker Neal, Nov. 24, 1960; children: Paul Collins Gordon, Betsey Whitaker. BA, Wilson Coll., 1958; student, Sch. Visual Arts, Rio de Janeiro, 1976-77, Memphis Sate U., 1979-80, U. Bridgeport, 1982-83; participant, Triangle Art Workshop, Pine Plains, N.Y., 1985. Guest spkr. Coll. Santa Fe, Albuquerque, N.Mex., 1994. One-woman shows include Allied Chem. Corp., Morristown, N.J., 1975, Planetarium Rio de Janeiro, 1977, Pat Ackerman Gallery, Memphis, 1980, Westmoreland Mus. Art, Greensburg, 1986, Wilson Coll., 1993, Cooper Classics Collections, N.Y.C., 2001, 02, Trans-Lux Cocteau Corp., Irene Neal Recent Paintings, Santa Fe, N.M., 2003; group exhbns. include Jersey City Mus., 1975, N.J. State Mus., 1975, Somerset (N.J.) Tri-State Mus., 1975, Nat. Arts Club, N.Y.C., 1975, Garden State Watercolor Soc., 1975, Salao de Marinhas, Rio de Janeiro, 1977, Stamford Mus., 1984, 85, 89, Branchville Soho Gallery, Ridgefield, Conn., 1984, Silvermine Guild, New Canaan, Conn., 1984, Stamford Libr., 1985, Shippee Gallery, N.Y.C., 1986, 110 Greene St., N.Y.C., 1986, Wilton (Conn.) Libr., 1986, Aldrich Mus. Contemporary Art, Ridgefield, 1987, Visual Arts Festival, Edmonton, Alta., Can., 1989, Mus. Art., Ft. Lauderdale, Fla., 1991-92, Salander-O'Reilly Galleries, Inc., N.Y., 1994, Vanderleelie Gallery, Edmonton, 1996, Galerie Piltzer, Paris, 1996, Fine Art 2000 Gallery, Stamford, 1996, 97, York Coll., Queens, N.Y., 1997, Ctr. for Performing Arts, Stamford, 1997, Mus. Contemporary Art, Palm Beach, Fla., 1997, Griffis Art Ctr., New London, 1997, Vero Beach (Fla.) Mus., 1998, Flint (Mich.) Inst. Art, 1999, Mus. Contemporary Art, Denver, 1999, Gelabert Studios Gallery, N.Y.C., 2000, Hotel de Ville, Brussels, 2000, 69th Regiment Armory, N.Y.C., New New Painters, The Real Avant Garde, 2000, Nat. Gallery, Prague, The Czech Repub., 2001, 2002 Galerie Anne-Lettrie, Paris, 2001, The Durst Orgn., N.Y.C., 2002, 03, Musee du Bas-Saint Laurant Riviere de Lupe, Que., Can., 2002-03, Scope N.Y. Stevenson Fine Art, Dylan Hotel, N.Y.C., 2003, Mus. au Bus, St. Laurant, Quebec, 2003, Elfsar Collection, Ltd., Vancouver, BC, 2003, Juten Gallery, Toronto, Ont., 2003, Anew Found., Ft. Lauderdale, Fla., 2004; represented in permanent collections Planetarium Rio de Janeiro, Internat. Paper, N.Y.C., Westmoreland Mus. Art, Greensburg, Pa., Pepperdine U., Malibu, Calif., Newport Harbor Art Mus., Newport Beach, Calif., Hoover Instn. Stanford U., St. Matthew's Episcopal Ch., Wilton, Columbia U., Ctr. Arts, Vero Beach, Fla., Mus. Art, Ft. Lauderdale, Alamo Rent A Car, Ft. Lauderdale, Denver Ctr. Performing Arts, Flint (Mich.) Inst. Art, The Nat. Gallery, Prague, The Czech Rep., Wilson Coll., Chambersburg, Pa., The Appleton Mus. of Art, Ocala, Fla.; pub., contbr. art to book New New Painting, 1996, catalog, 2000, Cooper Classics Collection, 2001, 2002. Recipient Tift award, Wilson Coll., Chambersburg, Pa., 2003. Republican. Episcopalian. Avocations: ocean diving, tennis, golf, gardening. Home: 700 River Rd Cos Cob CT 06807-1907 Office Phone: 203-325-8927.

NEAL, JAMES AUSTIN, architect; b. Nov. 23, 1935; s. Charles Albert Neal and Jane (Anderson) Cole; m. Leonette Dedmond, April 13, 1963; 1 child, Heather. B in Arch., Clemson U., 1959. Registered architect, S.C. Designer McMillan Architects, Greenville, S.C., 1960-62; project mgr. W.E. Freeman Architects, Greenville, S.C., 1963-64; project architect J.E. Sirrine Co., Greenville, S.C., 1964-68; prin., owner Neal, Prince & Ptnrs. Architects Inc., Greenville, S.C., 1969—. Vis. prof. Clemson U. Coll. Architecture, 1974-75; mem. bd. advisors Wachovia Nat. Bank. Pres. Leslie Meyer Devel. Ctr., Greenville, 1980-82. Recipient Leadership award Greenville C. of C., 1983. Fellow AIA (Merit Design award 1978, pres. S.C. chpt. 1991, regional dir. S.C., Ga., N.C., mem. nat. bd. 1994-96, co-recipient Twenty-five Yr. award 1997, medal of distinction S.C. chpt. 1999); mem. Greenville Coun. Architects (past pres.), Interfaith Forum of Religious Art and Architecture (nat. bd.), Poinsett Club (pres. 1985-86). Baptist. Avocations: jogging, flying. Office: Neal Prince & Ptnrs 110 W North St Greenville SC 29601-2757

NEAL, JAMES PRESTON, state senator, project engineer; b. Cin., July 1, 1935; s. James Preston and Desha Frank (Thompson) N.; m. Nancy Joan Tyner, June 11, 1961; children: Leslie Neal Driscoll, Karen Desha, James P. BSME, U. Ill., 1960. Registered profl. engr., Del. Project engr. DuPont Co., 1960-92; dir. Tetra Tech Inc., Christiana, Del., 1992-95; pres. Tech. Mgmt., 1994—2001. Mem. Del. Ho. of Reps., 1978-80; mem. Del. Senate, 1980-94; bd. trustees U. Del., 2002—. Patentee in field. Councilman City of Newark, 1973-78; elder Presbyn. Ch. With U.S. Army, 1954-56. Recipient Disting. Svc. award Forum to Advance Minorities in Engring., 1989, Disting. Svc. citation Del. Libr. Assn., 1994, Appreciation award Del. Autistic Program, 1999. Mem. Am. Legis. Exch. Coun. (sr. fellow, nat. officer 1991-94, Outstanding Leader 1989, Outstanding Legis. mem. 1994), Conf. World Regions (sr. fellow), IEEE (sr.), Del. Engring. Soc. (Engr. of Yr. 1989), Instrument Soc. Am. Republican. Presbyterian. Avocations: photography, reading. Home and Office: 50 Bridlebrook Ln Newark DE 19711-2061

NEAL, JOAN BURKES, librarian; b. Phenix City, Ala., Feb. 27, 1928; d. George Ashby and Maybelle Ethel (Barnes) Burkes; m. Charles A. Land, May 25, 1944 (dec. Sept. 1947); 1 child, Jo Sandra Land; m. Ray Verlin Neal, Dec. 25, 1952 (dec. May 8, 1996); children: Jo Griffeth, J. Kim, Roger Verlin, Kathy Brown. BS in Edn., U. Ga., 1951, postgrad., 1966. Dir. kindergarten Fayetteville (Ga.) First Bapt. Ch., 1958-63; tchr. 3d grade Fayetteville Elem. Sch., 1964-67, libr., 1967—91. Bd. dirs. Atlanta PTA, 1977—80; spkr. Silver Haired Legis. Mem. Ga. State Dem. Party, Atlanta, 1977—; sec. ARC, Fayetteville, 1979-83; pres. Band and Athletic Boosters, Fayetteville, 1968-70. Mem. Fayette County Assn. Educators (pres., v.p., sec. 1963—), Ga. Assn. Educators (governing bd. Atlanta chpt. 1976-79, legis. chair 1981, 83), Fayette County Bus. and Profl. Women (pres. 1976-78, treas., sec.), Kappa Kappa Iota (pres. Fayetteville chpt. 1970-72). Avocations: reading, golf, politics, walking. Home: 432 Forrest Ave Fayetteville GA 30214-1327

NEAL, JOSEPH LEE, vocational school educator; b. Memphis, Feb. 17, 1948; s. James Henry and Minnie Rue (Waldrop) N.; children: Janice Celeste Neal, Mary Joanne; m. Lou Alice Smith, Apr. 10, 1999. AAS, N.W. C.C., Senatobia, Miss., 1979, AS in Bus., 1980; BS, U. S. Miss., 1984, MS, 1986. Cert. tchr. Miss. Police officer City of W. Memphis, Ark., 1970-72; customer svc. rep. Biomed. Labs., Little Rock, Ark., 1972-75; sales, svc. rep Moore Ford Co., N. Little Rock, 1975-77; electronics technician N.W. Miss. C.C., Senatobia, 1979-82; electronics inst., 1982-83; electronics engr. U. So. Miss., Hattiesburg, 1983-85; electronics instr. Tex. State Tech. Inst., Sweetwater, 1985-87, De Soto County Vo-Tech. Ctr., Southaven, Miss., 1988-97, South Panola H.S., Batesville, Miss., 1997—. Cons. engr. various radio ops., Hattiesburg, 1982-85; mem. curriculum com. De Soto County Schs., 1990-95; steering com. N.W. Miss. Tech. Prep., Senatobia, 1992-95, participant in Learn to Work Workshop Miss. St. U. and Pealey Electronics, 1997, tchr. trainer for Tech. Discovery, 1998, 99. Bd. dirs. Optimist Club, Sweetwater, Tex., 1987. Named Outstanding Tchr., Horn Lake So. C. of C., 1992. Mem. Am. Vocat. Assn., Miss. Trade and Tech. Assn. (v.p. 1994-95, pres. 1995-96), Miss. Assn. Vocat. Educators (pres. dist. 1 1991-92, 95-96, bd. dirs. 1991-92, 95-96, sec. dist. 1 1993-94, v.p. 1994-95), Vocat.-Indsl. Clubs of Am. (100% Advisor 1990, 91, 92, VICA state advisor of yr. 1993), N.Am. Hunting Club (life). Baptist. Avocations: hunting, fishing, pub. speaking. Home: PO Box 172 1578 Freeman Rd Como MS 38619 Office: South Panola HS Batesville MS 38606

NEAL, LEORA LOUISE HASKETT, social services administrator; b. N.Y.C., Feb. 23, 1943; d. Melvin Elias and Miriam Emily (Johnson) Haskett; m. Robert A. Neal, Apr. 23, 1966; children: Marla Patrice, Johnathan Robert. BA in Psychology and Sociology, City Coll. N.Y., 1965; MS in Social Work, Columbia U., 1970, cert. adoption specialist, 1977; IBM cert. community exec. tng. program, N.Y., 1982. Cert. social worker N.Y. Caseworker N.Y.C. Dept. Social Service, 1965-67, Windham Child Care, N.Y.C., 1967-73; exec. dir., founder Assn. Black Social Workers Child Adoption Counseling and Referral Service, N.Y.C., 1975-96; adoption tng. specialist Ctr. for Devel. Human Svcs., SUNY-N.Y. State Office Children and Family Svcs., Yonkers, 1996—. Cons. in field; founder Haskett-Neal Publs., Bronx, N.Y., 1993. Co-author: Transracial Adoptive Parenting: A Black/White Community Issue, 1993; contbr. articles to profl. jours. Pres. bd. dirs. Fountain Ave. Cmty. Devel. Corp. Child Welfare League Am. fellow, 1976; recipient cert. No Time to Lose cert. N.Y. State Dept. Social Svcs., 1989. Mem. NAFE, Nat. Assn. Black Social Workers, Columbia U. Alumni Assn., CCNY Alumni Assn., Missionary Com. Revival Team (outreach chair 1982-88). Democrat. Avocations: writing, history and religious studies, travel, cultural activities. Office: NY State Office of Children and Family Svcs SUNY 525 Nepperhan Ave Yonkers NY 10703-2857

NEAL, MARGARET SHERRILL, writer, editor, graphics designer, web designer; b. Memphis, Apr. 13, 1950; d. Wilburn Franklin and Merle Aileen (Willis) N. BA, Memphis State U., 1972, postgrad., 1973; MS, Columbia Pacific U., 1984. Cert. internet webmaster. Air traffic contr. FAA, Memphis, 1974-76, New Bern, N.C., 1976-81, Vero Beach, Fla., 1981-83; detection sys. specialist U.S. Customs Svc., Miami, 1983-87, intelligence rsch. specialist, 1987-89; ret., 1989. Editor newsletter Highlands Neighborhood Watch. Sec. Pompano Beach Highlands Civic Improvement Assn., 1998; mem. Highlands Neighborhood Watch. Mem. NOW, Smithsonian Instn., Mensa, Nat. Trust Hist. Preservation, Greenpeace, Clan Macneil Soc., Environ. Def., Nature Conservancy, Lighthouse Point Writers' Workshops, Save the Manatee Club. Democrat. Presbyterian. Avocations: genealogy, growing orchids. Office Phone: 954-943-2276. Personal E-mail: sayitwithstyle@care2.com.

NEAL, MARY DARLIN', writer, education educator; d. James Farrell and Virginia Neal; life ptnr. Brian Craft; 1 child, Sara Floyd. MA in English, N.Mex State U., Las Cruces, N. Mex., 1990; MFA in Creative Writing, U. Ariz., Tucson, Ariz., 1993; PhD, U. So. Miss., Hattiesburg, Miss., 2001. Writer-in-residence Miss. Arts Commn. All Write Program for Literacy, Jackson, Miss., 2001—03; instr. English U. Miss., Oxford, Miss., 2001—04. Author: (short stories) A Man Wrapped In Gold, Liddy, Ghosts, Things She Can Hear, Blue Star, A Man Wrapped In Gold, Honey, Don't, Lafayette, (novels) Blessed Are, Farewell, Angelina, Open House. Advisor Miss. Arts Commission's and NEA's AllWrite Program for Literacy, Jackson, Miss., 2003—03. Recipient Frank Waters Fiction Fellowship, N.Mex State Univ. English Dept., 1990, Finalist, Chesterfield Film Co. Writer's Project, 1994, Joan Johnson Short Story Award, Ctr. for Writers at U. So. Miss., 1999, Semifinalist for The William Faulkner Creative Writing Award, William Faulkner Creative Writing Awards, 2003, Semifinalist in The Gt. Am. Novel Contest, Meridian and Tupelo Press, 2003, Henfield Transatlantic Rev. Award, Henfield Found., 1993, Semifinalist Playboy's Coll. Fiction Award, Playboy Mag., 1998, Semifinalist in Zoetrope's Samuel Adams Short Story Contest, Zoetrope, 2000, Zoetrope All-Story Short Story Contest, 2000, Finalist Mo. Review's Editors' Prize, Mo. Rev., 1993. Mem.: Associated Writer's Program, Phi Beta Phi. Liberal. Avocations: travel, gardening, reading, nieces. Office: English Dept Univ Miss Oxford MS Business E-Mail: mneal@olemiss.edu.

NEAL, PHIL HUDSON, JR., manufacturing executive; b. Birmingham, Ala., Nov. 17, 1926; s. Phil Hudson and Amy (Gross) N.; m. Sarah Swift Britton, Sept. 19, 1959; children: Amy Neal Ager, Phil Hudson, III, Samuel Abney Britton. AB, Duke U., 1950; MBA, Harvard U., 1952. Investment analyst First Nat. Bank, Birmingham, 1952-55; procedures analyst Gen. Electric Co., Hendersonville, N.C., 1955-58; with Ala. By-Products Corp., Birmingham, 1958-79, asst. treas., 1964-68, treas., 1968-79; dir., v.p. Utility Tool Co., Birmingham, 1979-86; dir., pres. Nutec Metal Finishing Inc., Birmingham, 1986-92, chmn., 1992—. Trustee Advent Episcopal Sch., 1967—, pres., 1968-89, trustee charitable endowment trust, 1981—; treas. Cathedral Ch. of Advent, 1981-82, mem. chpt., 1983-85, 86-89; bd. dirs. Greater Birmingham Ministries, 1975-77, Advent Episcopal Assn. for Edn., 1968-89, Jefferson County chpt. Ala. Soc. Crippled Children and Adults, Inc., 1977-79; trustee Ala. Found. for Hearing and Speech, 1967-74, v.p., 1968-69, pres., 1969-71. Served with USNR, 1945-46. Mem. Newcomen Soc. N.Am., Birmingham Country Club, The Club, The Summit Club, Phi Beta Kappa, Sigma Nu, Phi Eta Sigma. Episcopalian (vestryman, sr. warden). Home: 3336 Hermitage Rd Birmingham AL 35223-2004 also: 81 Old Duck Hole Rd East Orleans MA 02643 Office: 3669 Indsl Pkwy PO Box 170746 Birmingham AL 35217-0746

NEAL, PHILIP MARK, diversified manufacturing executive; b. San Diego, Aug. 28, 1940; s. Philip Mark and Florence Elizabeth (Anderson) N.; children: Brian, Kevin. BA, Pomona Coll., 1962; MBA, Stanford U., 1964. Mgr. financial planning and analysis CBS, Hollywood, 1964-66; cons. McKinsey & Co., L.A., 1966-73; v.p., contr. Avery Internat. Corp., L.A., 1974-78, sr. v.p. fin. Pasadena, Calif., 1979-88, group v.p. materials group, 1988-90, exec. pres., 1990, pres., COO, 1990-98, pres., CEO, 1998-2000, chmn., CEO, 2000—. Bd. dirs. L.A. Bus. Advisors, Edwards Lifescis. Corp. Trustee Pomona Coll.; bd. govs. Town Hall of Calif., bd. dirs. Calif. Inst. Tech., Pacific Basin Inst., L.A. World Affairs Coun., Music Ctr. Los Angeles County. Mem.: Calif. Bus. Roundtable (bd. dirs.). Republican. Episcopalian. Office: Avery Dennison Corp 150 N Orange Grove Blvd Pasadena CA 91103-3534

NEAL, RICHARD EDMUND, congressman, former mayor; b. Worcester, Mass., Feb. 14, 1949; s. Edmund J. and Mary H. (Garvey) N.; m. Maureen Conway, Dec. 20, 1975; children— Rory, Brendan, Maura, Sean BS, Am. Internat. Coll., Springfield, Mass., 1972; M.P.A., U. Hartford, Conn., 1976; postgrad., U. Mass., Amherst, 1982. Adminstrv. aide to Mayor City of Springfield, Mass., 1973-78, mem. city council, 1978-83, mayor, 1984-88, mem. U.S. Congress from 2nd. Mass. dist., 1989—; mem. ways and means com., budget com. Lectr. history and politics Springfield Tech. Community Coll., Mass., 1973-83; lectr. bus. and govt. Western New Eng. Coll., Springfield, 1979-82; project dir. Springfield Tech. Community Coll., 1979-82 Trustee ARC, YMCA, Springfield Named to Outstanding Young Men in Am., U.S. Jr. C. of C., Springfield Mem. Am. Internat. Coll. Alumni Assn. (pres. 1980, Alumni Achievement award 1985). Springfield Library and Mus. Assn. (trustee) Clubs: Valley Press. John Boyle O'Reilly (Springfield). Democrat. Roman Catholic. Office: US House of Reps 2133 Rayburn House Ofc Bldg Washington DC 20515-0001

NEAL, ROBERT LEE, JR., government official; m. Beverly N.; 1 child, Aja. BS in bus. mgmt., U. Md., Coll. Pk., 1976; MBA in fin., Am. U., Washington, D.C., 1992; postgrad., Am. U. Mgr. analyst, chemist Def. Mapping Agy.; various positions Mgmt. and Budget office; assoc. dep. administr. Govt. Contracting/Minority Enterprise; assoc. Adminstr. Gen. Svcs. Adminstr.; dir. Under Sec. of Def. Office, 1996—. Recipient Outstanding and Disting. Pub. Svc. medals, Outstanding Achievement award Sec. of Def., Spl. Performance awards, EEO award, Hammer award, Spl. Performance Divsnl. awards Office of Mgmt. and Budget.

NEAL, STU M. finance educator, writer; b. Portland, Maine, Aug. 18, 1952; s. Paul Millard and Barbara Neal; m. Pamela Acker, Dec. 1, 1983 (div. June 28, 2003); children: Nerissa Rene, Miesha Acker. Student, So. Maine Vocat. Tech. Inst., 1970—72. Prin., owner Neal-Godsoe Corp., Windham, Maine, 1978—93, Nealco Inc., Windham, 1989—92; regional sales mgr. Accu Industries, Inc., Ashland, Va., 1993—95; dist. bus. mgr. Matco Tools, Inc., Stow, Ohio, 1995—97; prin., owner SMN Group, Mechanicsville, Va., 1997—2003; dir. Ctr. Entrepreneurial Devel. C.C. Workforce Alliance, Richmond, Va., 1999—; pres. Fliprack, Mechanicsville, Va., 2003—. Co-chmn. Bus. Edn. Adv. Com. Maine Dept. Edn., Augusta, Maine, 1988—90; mem. econ. coun. Key Bank Maine, 1992. Author: Disc, 2002; contbr. columns in newspapers. Vice chmn. Windham (Maine) Town Coun., 1989—93; town rep. Greater Portland (Maine) Coun., 1989—93; del. White House Conf. Small Bus., Washington, 1986; bd. dir. Windham (Maine) C. of C., 1978—92; adv. bd. Retail U. Career Ctr., Richmond, Va., 2004, Asian Am. Bus. Assistance Ctr., Ashland, Va., 2004. Mem.: Nat. Spkrs. Assn., Bull and Bear Club, Rotary (Paul Harris fellow 1988). Republican. Avocations: writing, fly fishing, scuba diving, camping, antique toys. Home: 10137 Spring Ivy Lane Mechanicsville VA 23116 Office: Ctr Entrepreneurial Devel Cmty Coll Workforce Alliance 501 East Franklin St Richmond VA 23219

NEAL, THOMAS FREDERICK, lawyer; b. Orlando, Fla., Jan. 18, 1960; s. Thomas Earl and Nina Delores (Tomarelli) N. BGS, U. Mich., 1982; JD, U. Fla., 1985. Bar: Fla. 1986, U.S. Dist. Ct. (mid. dist.) Fla. 1987, U.S. Ct. Appeals (11th cir.) 1987, U.S. Supreme Ct. 1991. Assoc. Sam E. Murrell & Sons, Orlando, 1986-87, Drage, de Beaubien, Knight & Simmons, Orlando, 1987-90, ptnr., 1990-92, Drage, deBeaubien, Knight Simmons, Mantzaris and Neal, Orlando, 1992—2002, de Beaubien, Knight, Simmons, Mantzaris & Neal, 2002—. Bd. dirs., chmn. govt. rels. com. Lakeside Alternatives, Inc. Mem. Orange County Bar Assn., Touchdown Club (bd. dirs., past pres.). Democrat. Roman Catholic. Home: 4126 Shorecrest Dr Orlando FL 32804-2227 Office: de Beaubien Knight Simmons Mantzaris and Neal 332 N Magnolia Ave Orlando FL 32801-1609 Office Phone: 407-422-2454. Business E-Mail: tneal@dbksmn.com.

NEAL-BARNETT, ANGELA MARIE, psychology educator; b. Youngstown, Ohio, Feb. 13, 1960; d. Andrew Lee and Doris Lucille Neal; m. Edgar J. Barnett Jr., July 17, 1995; 1 child, Reece. BA, Mt. Union Coll., 1982; MA, DePaul U., 1985, PhD, 1988. Lic. psychologist, Ohio. Clin. therapist ECHO Community Health Orgn., Chgo., 1985-87; post-doctoral fellow U. Pitts. (Pa.), Western Psychiat. Inst., 1988-89; asst. prof. Kent (Ohio) State U., 1989—, 1989-95, assoc. prof., 1995—. Pres., founder Rise Sally Rise Prodn.; founder, CEO Rise, Sally, Rise, Inc.; bd. dirs. King-Kennedy Ctr., Ravenna, Ohio, 1989—95; rsch. fellow Inst. African Am. Affairs, Kent, 1991—; co-chair Allied Health Edn. Com., 1994—; mem. NIMH Child Psychopathology and Treatment Rev. Panel, 1996—99; spkr. in field. Author: Forging Limits: African American Children Clinical Developmental Perspectives; contbr. articles to profl. jours.; author: Soothe Your Nerves: The Black Women's Guide to Understanding and Overcoming Anxiety, Panic and Fear; author, prodr.: CD Believe and Succeed. Mem. alumni coun. Mt. Union Coll.; mem. governing bd. Ida B. Wells Cmty. Acad., 1998-2000. Urban Rsch. grantee Ohio Bd. Regents, 1990, biomed. support grantee NIH, 1991, small grantee NIMH, 1994-96; recipient Minority Career Advancement award NSF. Mem. APA (, mem. adv. com. minority fellowship program, Kenneth & Marie Clark award), Ohio Pscyhol. Assn., Assn. Advancement Behavior Therapy, Assn. Black Psychologists, African Am. Lit. Guild Kent. Methodist. Avocations: tennis, reading. Office: Kent State U Dept Psychology 118 Kent Hl Kent OH 44242-0001 also: Rise Sally Rise Inc 361 Starr Line Dr Tallmadge OH 44278 E-mail: aneal@kent.edu.

NEALE, E(RNEST) R(ICHARD) WARD, retired university official, consultant; b. Montreal, Que., Can., July 3, 1923; s. Ernest John and Mabel Elizabeth (McNamee) N.; m. Roxie Eveline Anderson, June 3, 1950; children: Richard Ward, Owen Curtis. B.Sc., McGill U., Montreal, 1949; MS, Yale U., 1950, PhD, 1952; LL.D. (hon.), Calgary U., Alta., Can., 1977; DSc (hon.), Meml. U., Nfld., Can., 1989. Asst. prof. geology U. Rochester, N.Y., 1952-54; sect. chief Geol. Survey Can., Ottawa, Ont., 1954-63, div. chief, 1965-68, 1976-81; commonwealth geol. liaison officer London, 1963-65; prof., head geology Meml. U., St. John's, Nfld., Can., 1968-76, v.p. acad., 1982-87; cons., Calgary, Alta., Can., 1987—. Chmn. nat. adv. bd. on sci. publs. NRC-Natural Scis. and Engring. Rsch. Coun., Ottawa, 1982-88. Author: Geology and Geophysics in Canadian Universities, 1980. Editor: Some Guides to Mineral Exploration, 1967, Geology of the Atlantic Region, 1968, The Geosciences in Canada, 1968; Editor: Can. Jour. of Earth Science, 1974-79, Science and the Public, 1988. Bd. dirs. Unitarian Ch. Calgary, 1993—, pres., 1995-96. Petty officer Royal Can. Navy, 1943-45. Decorated officer Order of Can., 1990; recipient Queen's Jubilee medal Govt. of Can., 1977, Can. 125 medal, 1992, Golden Jubilee medal, 2002, Integrity award, Calgary Rotary, 2003. Fellow Royal Soc. Can. (coun. 1972-75, chmn. com. pub. awareness of sci. 1987-91, Bancroft medal 1975), Geol. Assn. Can. (pres. 1973-74, Ambrose medal 1986, 1st E.R. Ward Neale medal 1995), Can. Geosci. Coun. (pres. 1975-76, R.T. Bell medal Can. Mining Jour. 1977), Geol. Soc. Am.; mem. Assn. Earth Sci. Editors, Nat. Def. (chmn. biol. and chem. def. rev. com. 1990-93), Univ. Club Calgary, Chancellor's Club, Crows Nest Club, Calgary Sci. Network (pres. 1989), Sigma Xi (nat. lectr. New Haven 1976, chmn. Avalon chpt. 1986). Avocations: golf, cross country skiing, hiking, canoeing. Home and Office: 5108 Carney Rd NW Calgary AB Canada T2L 1G2

NEALE, GAIL LOVEJOY, non-profit organization management consultant; b. Detroit, Feb. 8, 1935; d. Elijah Parish and Jane Appleton (Howell) Lovejoy; m. Richard Potter (div.); m. Anthony Astrachan (div.); children: Owen Lovejoy Astrachan, Joshua Howell Astrachan; m. Robert Edward Neale, June 23, 1984. Student, Vassar Coll., 1952-54. Rsch. aide, dir. devel., corp. sec., v.p. Hudson Inst., Inc., Croton on Hudson, N.Y., 1962-76; v.p. Aspen Inst., N.Y.C., 1976-78; dir. external affairs Middlebury (Vt.) Coll., 1978-80; pres. Hudson Inst., Croton on Hudson, 1980-82; corp. sec. Commonwealth Fund, N.Y.C., 1983-86; project adminstr. Mt. Holyoke Coll., South Hadley, Mass., 1986-88; dir. devel. Hampshire Coll., Amherst, Mass., 1988-91; exec. v.p., COO Salzburg Seminar, Middlebury, Vt., 1991-96; pres., founder The Lovejoy Consulting Group, Inc., Burlington, Vt., 1997—. Trustee JL Found., L.A.; bd. dirs. Capital Income Builder, L.A., Capital World Growth and Income Fund, L.A., Fundamental Investors, L.A., Growth Fund Am., Vera Inst. for Justice, N.Y.C.; trustee Endowments, Inc., L.A.; dir., chair campaign Shelburne Farms, 1997-2000; dir. Circus Smirkus. Bd. dirs. Conern for Dying, N.Y.C., 1986-90; dir. Frances Clark Ctr. for Keyboard Pedagogy, 1997-2000, mem. Preservation Land Trust Vt., Mozart Festival Vt., Flynn Theatre. Mem. Origami U.S.A. Democrat. Episcopalian. Avocations: reading, cooking, knitting, origami, magic. Office: The Lovejoy Consulting Group Inc 154 Prospect Pkwy Burlington VT 05401-4148 Fax: 802-658-6189. E-mail: neale@together.net.

NEALE, GARY LEE, utilities executive; b. Lead, S.D., Mar. 3, 1940; s. Vearl J. and Gladys M. (Trenkle) N.; m. Sandra C. Lovell, June 16, 1962; children: David G., Julie C. BA in Econs., U. Wash., 1962, MBA, 1965. Loan examiner Wells Fargo, 1966-69; sr. fin. analyst Kaiser Industries, 1969-70; chmn., pres., chief exec. officer Planmetrics, Chgo., 1970-89; pres., chief oper. officer No. Ind. Pub. Svc. Co., Hammond, 1989-93; chmn., pres., CEO Ni Source Inc. (formerly No. Ind. Pub. Svc. Co.), Hammond, 1993—. Bd. dirs. Modine Mfg., Racine, Wis., Am. Gas Assn., Arlington, Va., Ind. Gas Assn./Ind. Electric Assn., Indpls., Nipsco Industries Inc., Hammond. Bd. dirs. N.W. Ind. Symphony, 1990; mem. Ind. Energy Policy Forum, 1991. Lt. (j.g.) USN, 1962-64. Mem. Econ. Club Chgo., Chgo. Univ. Club, NYU Club. Office: NiSource Inc 801 E 86th Ave Merrillville IN 46410-6272

NEALE, HENRY WHITEHEAD, plastic surgery educator; b. Richmond, Va., July 18, 1940; s. Richard C. and Eva W. Neale; m. Margaret C. Neale, June 20, 1964; children: Leigh, Jennifer, Henry Whitehead Neale Jr., William. BS, Davidson Coll., 1960; MD, Med. Coll. Va., 1964. Diplomate Am. Bd. Surgery, Am. Bd. Plastic Surgery . Intern Mercy Med. Ctr., Springfield, Ohio, 1964—65; resident in gen. surgery U. Cin. Med. Ctr., 1965—71, dir. divsn. plastic, reconstructive and hand surgery, 1974—; resident in plastic surgery Duke U. Med. Ctr., Durham, NC, 1971—74; fellow in hand surgery, Christine Kleinert hand fellow U. Louisville, 1973; asst. prof. surgery U. Cin. Coll. Medicine, 1974—77, assoc. prof., 1977—82, prof., 1982—; active staff, dir. hand surgery and plastic surgery clinics U. Cin. Med. Ctr. Hosp. Group, 1974—, prof., chmn. divsn. plastic surgery, 1974—. Guest examiner Am. Bd. Plastic Surgery, 1986—90, dir., 1990—96, com. on plans and qualifying exam. com., liaison to Am. Bd. Surgery, 1993—96, exec. com., 1993—, chmn. certifying examing com., 1993—95, ethics com., 1993, chmn.-elect, 1995—96; dir. burn reconstructive and plastic surgery, co-dir. hand surgery svc. Shriners Burns Inst., Cin., 1983—; dir. divsn. plastic, reconstructive and hand surgery and plastic surgery clinic Childrens Hosp. Med. Ctr., Cin., 1983—; assoc. attending staff Good Samaritan Hosp.; courtesy staff Christ Hosp., Jewish Hosp.; presenter in field. Mem. editl. bd.: Jour. Plastic and Reconstructive Surgery, 1989—; contbr. articles to profl. jours. Grantee Rsch. grant, Eli Lilly Co., 1979—91. Fellow: ACS; mem.: AMA, Plastic Surgery Rsch. Coun., Ohio Valley Soc. Plaastic and Reconstructive Surgery (pres. 1985—86), Ohio Med. Assn., Greater Cin. Soc. Plastic and Reconstructive Surgeons (pres. 1988—89), Grad. Surg. Soc. Cin., Cin. Surg. Soc., Assn. Acad. Chairmen in Plastic Surgery, Acad. Medicine Cin., Am. Soc. for Surgery of Hand, Am. Soc. Plastic and Reconstructive Surgeons, Am. Soc. for Aesthetic Plastic Surgery, Am. Cleft Palate Assn., Am. Burn Assn., Am. Assn. Plastic Surgeons. Home: 2970 Alpine Ter Cincinnati OH 45208-3408 Office: U Cin Coll Medicine Plastic Reconst and Hand Su 231 Bethesda Ave Cincinnati OH 45267-0001

NEALE, ZAHIDI SAHAJ, artist, educator; b. Bakersfield, Calif., Jan. 19, 1953; d. Harold Jess Wilson and Beryl Kathleen Heaney; m. Michael Daniel Luttrell (div. Aug. 1, 1986); m. Michael John Neale, Oct. 12, 1986; children: Daya Darshan Luttrell, Ian Robert. AA, Bakersfield Coll., 1976. Lic. Massage Therapist CA, 1979; cert. Instructor Drawing on the Right Side of the Brain DRSB-CA, 2000, Talented Arts Evaluator-Visual La. Med. asst., recovery rm. tech Family Planning Assocs. Med. Group, Bakersfield, 1974—81; med. asst. Cmty. Health Ctrs. Kern County, Bakersfield, 1975—76; massage therapist Elder Chiropractic, Bakersfield, Calif., 1982—86, Pleasanton, Calif., 1987—91; artist, instr. cmty. edn. program Zahidi Neale Studios, Slidell, La., 2000—; talented arts evaluator St. Tammany Parish Sch. Dist., St. Tammany Parish, La., 2000—. Evaluation panel La. Decentralized Arts Funding Grants, Slidell, 1999. Sculptural ceramics, Geologic (Parish Permanent Collection Purchase award, 2001). Founder Kern Bodyworkers Guild, Bakersfield, 1990—92. Airman first USAF, 1971—73. Recipient Vol. of Yr., Boys and Girls Club of Southea. La.-Slidell Club, 2000—01, Silvestri Internat. award, 2000; grantee, City of Slidell, 2001. Mem.: St. Tammany Art Assn., Am. Bodyworkers Massage Profls., Anaheim Art Assn. (newsletter com. 1996), Bakersfield Art Assn. (sec., scholarship chair, permanent collection com. 1992—94), Slidell Art League (treas. 1999—2002, Artist of Month 2000). Surat Shabd. Avocation: gardening. Home and Office: Zahidi Neale Studios 113 Palm Swift Dr Slidell LA 70461 Personal E-mail: zahidi@zeeartist.com.

NEALE-MAY, DONOVAN, marketing professional; Degree in journalism, Rhodes U., South Africa. Leader pub. rels. ops. Ogilvy & Mather, Calif.; pvt. practice as pres., founder, 1987—. Mem. adv. bd. pub. rels. degree program San Jose State U., Calif.; cons. with various clients; several acct. mgmt., sr. exec. positions comm. agys., England. Mem. bd. Travelzoo.com; mem. bd. Rhodes U. Charitable Trust. Scholar Cape Times . Office: Donovan Neale-May 409 Sherman Ave Palo Alto CA 94306

NEALIS, JAMES GARRY THOMAS, III, pediatric neurologist, educator, author; b. N.Y.C., Mar. 7, 1945; s. James and Catherine N.; m. Arlene Dee Kramer, Feb. 6, 1981; children— Peyton Colleen, Douglas Andrew, Gregory Haynes, James Garry Thomas IV, Patrick Ryan. B.A., Fordham U., 1966; M.D., U. Miami, 1971. Diplomate Am. Bd. Psychiatry and Neurology, Am. Bd. Electroencephalography. Intern in pediatrics Babies Hosp., Columbia Presbyn. Med. Ctr., Columbia U. Sch. Medicine, N.Y.C., 1971-72, resident, 1972-73; resident in neurology Boston U. Sch. Medicine, 1973-74, 75-76, resident in neurology Harvard U. Sch. Medicine, Boston, 1975-76, instr. pediatric neurology, 1976-78; chief resident Boston City Hosp., 1975-76; asst. in neurophysiology Boston Children's Hosp., 1976-78; founder Neuro-Ednl. Evaluation Clinic, 1977-78; asst. prof. clin. neurology U. Fla., Jacksonville; chief pediatric neurology Jacksonville Children's Hosp., 1979—; lctr. U. N. Fla.; clin. instr. neurology cons. Naval Regional Med. Ctr., Jacksonville, 1979—; adviser Pres.'s Com. Med. Ethics, Washington, 1980; sec. Fla. Neurol. Inst., 1985; lectr. in field. Contbg. author: Physical Disabilities and Health Impairments. Contbr. chpts. to med. books, articles to med. jours. Trustee Epilepsy Found.; bd. dirs. Speech and Hearing Clinic; founder, bd. dirs. Northeast Fla. League Against Reye's Syndrome; founder, bd. dirs. Jacksonville Parents Assn. Against Gilles de la Tourette Syndrome; mem. Jacksonville Police Council, 1981—; founder Jacksonville Alzheimer's Ctr.; profl. adviser Parents in Action Against Drugs and Substance Abuse, 1983—; multiple TV appearances including (host) To Your Health, WJXT, 1983, The Brain, WJXT, 1985, Drugs and Your Brain, 1986; (guest) Alzheimers Disease, 1984, The 700 Club, CBN, 1985. Named Outstanding Young Man of Yr., Bold City Jr. C. of C., 1980. Mem. Am. Acad. Neurology, Eastern Assn. EEG, Am. Med. Electroencephalographic Assn. (pres. 1984), Jacksonville Assn. Children with Learning Disabilities (bd. advisers), Am. Epilepsy Soc., Duval County Med. Soc., (trustee) Child Neurology Soc. (mem. nat. com. med. ethics 1984-85, adv. 1985-86, nat. adv. pediatric brain death 1985, practice com.), Fla. Soc. Neurology (sec. 1980, v.p. 1981, pres. 1983), Fla. Med. Assn. (del. 1983-84), Council Exceptional Children, Jacksonville C. of C.

NEALON, WILLIAM JOSEPH, JR., federal judge; b. Scranton, Pa., July 31, 1923; s. William Joseph and Ann Cannon (McNally) N.; m. Jean Sullivan, Nov. 15, 1947; children: Ann, Robert, William, John, Jean, Patricia, Kathleen, Terrence, Thomas, Timothy. Student, U. Miami, Fla., 1942-43; BS in Econs, Villanova U., 1947; LL.B., Cath. U. Am., 1950; LL.D. (hon.), U. Scranton, 1975. Bar: Pa. 1951. With firm Kennedy, O'Brien & O'Brien (and predecessor), Scranton, 1951-60; mem. Lackawanna County Ct. Common Pleas, 1960-62; U.S. dist. judge Middle Dist. Pa., 1962—, chief judge, 1976-88, sr. judge, 1989—. Mem. com. on adminstrn. of criminal law Jud. Conf. U.S., 1979—, lectr. bus. law and labor law U. Scranton, 1951-59, mem. jud. council 3d Cir. Ct. Appeals, 1984—; dist. judge rep. from 3d Cir. Jud. Conf. of U.S., 1987—. Mem. Scranton Registration Commn., 1953-55; hearing examiner Pa. Liquor Control Bd., 1955-59; campaign dir. Lackawanna County chpt. Nat. Found., 1961-63; mem. Scranton-Lackawanna Health and Welfare Authority, 1963—; assoc. bd. Marywood Coll., Scranton; pres. bd. dirs. Cath. Youth Center; pres. Father's Club Scranton Prep. Sch., 1966; chmn. bd. dirs. Mercy Hosp., 1991-95; chmn. bd. trustees U. Scranton; vice chmn. bd. trustees Lackawanna Jr. Coll., Scranton; bd. dirs. St. Joseph's Children's and Maternity Hosp., 1963-66, Lackawanna County unit Am. Cancer Soc., Lackawanna County Heart Assn., Lackawanna County chpt. Pa. Assn. Retarded Children, Scranton chpt. ARC, Lackawanna United Fund, Mercy Hosp., Scranton, 1975—; trustee St. Michael's Sch. Boys, Hoban Heights; adv. com. Hosp. Service Assn. Northeastern Pa. Served to 1st lt. USMCR, 1942-45. Recipient Americanism award Amos Lodge B'nai B'rith, 1975; Cyrano award U. Scranton Grad. Sch., 1977; Disting. Service award Pa. Trial Lawyers Assn., 1979; named one of 50 Disting. Pennsylvanians Greater Phila. C. of C., 1980, Outstanding Fed. Trial Judge Assn. Trial Lawyers Am., 1983 Mem. Pa. Bar Assn., Lackawanna County Bar Assn. (Chief Justice Michael J. Eagen award 1987), Friendly Sons St. Patrick (pres. Lackawanna County 1963-64), Pi Sigma Alpha. Clubs: Scranton Country (Clarks Summit, Pa.) (bd. dirs.). Lodges: K.C. Office: US Courthouse PO Box 1146 Scranton PA 18501-1146

NEAMAN, MARK ROBERT, hospital administrator; b. Buffalo, Oct. 22, 1950; married. B, Ohio State U., 1972, MHA, 1974. Adminstrv. asst. Evanston (Ill.) Hosp., 1974-76, asst. to v.p., 1976-78, asst. v.p., 1978-80, v.p., 1980-84, sr. v.p., 1984-85, pres., exec. v.p., 1985-90, pres., 1990-92, pres., CEO, 1992—. Bd. dir. Healthcare Leadership Coun. Fellow Am. Coll. Healthcare Execs. (chmn., RS Hudgens award 1988). Home: 263 W Onwentsia Rd Lake Forest IL 60045-2826 Office: Evanston Northwestern Healthcare 1301 Central St Evanston IL 60201-1781

NEAME, RONALD, director, producer; b. Hendon, Middlesex, Eng., Apr. 23, 1911; s. Stuart Elwin and Ivy Lillian (Close) N.; m. Beryl Yolanda Heanly, Oct. 15, 1933; 1 son, Christopher Elwyn; m. Dona Friedberg, Sept. 12, 1993. Student pvt. schs., London and Sussex, Eng. Asst. cameraman Brit. Internat. Pictures, Estree, Eng., 1928-35, chief cameraman, 1935-45. Dir.: photography, prodn. supr. various films, including In Which We Serve, 1942, This Happy Breed, 1943, Blithe Spirit, 1944; co-writer, producer: films Brief Encounter, 1945, Great Expectations, 1946; producer: film Oliver Twist, 1947; dir.: films Take My Life, 1948, Golden Salamander, 1949, The Promoter, 1952, Man with a Million, 1953, The Man Who Never Was, 1954, Windom's Way, 1957, The Horse's Mouth, 1958, Tunes of Glory, 1960, I Could Go On Singing, 1962, The Chalk Garden, 1963, Mr. Moses, 1964, Gambit, 1966, The Prime of Miss Jean Brodie, 1968, Scrooge, 1970, The Poseidon Adventure, 1972, The Odessa File, 1974, Meteor, 1978, Hopscotch, 1979, First Monday in October, 1980-81, Foreign Body, 1985, The Magic Baloon, 1989; co-founder film co. Cineguild Co., Denham, Eng., 1943-44. Decorated Comdr. of the Order of the Brit. Empire, 1996. Mem. Dirs. Guild Am., Am. Film Inst., Acad. Motion Picture Arts and Scis. (gov. 1977-79), Brit. Acad. Film and TV Arts (London and Los Angeles), Savile Club (London). *When I am asked which film I consider to be my best, I reply, "I haven't made it yet. Perhaps next time.".*

NEAR, TIMOTHY, theater director; Grad., San Francisco State U., Acad. Music and Dramatic Art, London. Artistic dir. San Jose Repertory Theatre, 1987—. Past actress, dir. with numerous prestigious theaters including The Guthrie Theatre, Berkeley (Calif.) Repertory Theater, La Jolla (Calif.) Playhouse, The Alliance Theatre, Atlanta, The Mark Taper Forum, L.A., Ford's Theatre, Washington, Repertory Theatre of St. Louis, N.Y. Shakespeare Festival, Stage West, Mass., A.C.T., Seattle. Dir. Ghosts on Fire, La Jolla Playhouse (Drama League award), Singer in the Storm, Mark Taper Forum (Drama League award), Thunder Knocking on the Door (Drama League award). Recipient 1997 Woman of Achievement in the Arts, San Jose Mercury News and The Woman's Fund. Office: San Jose Repertory Theatre 101 Paseo De San Antonio San Jose CA 95113-2603

NEARING, VIVIENNE W. lawyer; b. N.Y.C. d. Abraham M. and Edith Eunice (Webster) N. BA, Queens Coll.; MA, JD, Columbia U. Bar: N.Y., D.C., U.S. Dist. Ct. (so. and ea. dists.) N.Y., U.S. Ct. Appeals (2d cir.), U.S. Claims Ct. Ptnr. Stroock & Stroock & Lavan, N.Y.C. Gen. counsel Plays for Living, 1998—2002, gen. co-counsel, 2002—. Mem. editorial bd. Communications and the Law, 1978-82, adv. bd. 1982—; mem. editorial bd. U.S. Trademark Reporter, 1982-86. Bd. dirs. Light Opera of Manhattan, 1981-82, Lyric Opera N.Y., 1984-90, Concert Artists Guild, 1989-91, Plays for Living, 1998—. Mem. ABA, Fed. Bar Coun., N.Y. State Bar Assn., U.S. Trademark Assn., Copyright Soc. U.S.A., N.Y. Lawyers for Pub. Interest (bd. dirs. 1983-87), Am. Arbitration Assn., Commn. for Law and Social Justice, Carnegie Coun., Women's City Club, Respect for Law Alliance. Office: Stroock Stroock & Lavan 180 Maiden Ln New York NY 10038-4982 E-mail: vnearing@stroock.com.

NEARY, DANIEL, insurance company executive; b. Carroll, Iowa, 1952; Degree, U. Iowa, 1974. With Mut. of Omaha, 1975—, exec. v.p. group benefit svcs., 1999—2003; pres., bd. dirs. Mut. of Omaha and United of Omaha, 2003—. Bd. dirs. United Way, Midlands and Am. Red Cross. Mem.: Soc. Actuaries. Office: Mut of OMaha Mutual of Omaha Plz Omaha NE 68175

NEARY, PATRICIA ELINOR, ballet director; b. Miami; d. James Elliott and Elinor (Mitsitz) N. Corps de ballet Nat. Ballet of Can., Toronto, Ont., 1957-60; prin. dancer N.Y.C. Ballet, 1960-68; ballerina Geneva Ballet, Switzerland, 1968-70, ballet dir., 1973-78; guest artist Stuttgart Ballet, Germany, 1968-70; asst. ballet dir., ballerina West Berlin Ballet, 1970-73; ballet dir. Zurich Ballet, Switzerland, 1978-86, La Scala di Milano ballet co., Italy, 1986-88; tchr. Balanchine ballets, Balanchine Trust, 1987—.

NEARY, THOMAS H. career officer; b. Idaho; B in Geography, U. Idaho, 1968, M in Statis. Geography, 1969; disting. grad., Squadron Officer Sch., 1974, Air Command and Staff Coll., 1978; student, Nat. War Coll., 1986; student program sr. execs. nat. and internat. security, John F. Kennedy Sch., 1995. Commd. 2d lt. USAF, 1969, advanced through grades to maj. gen., 1997; cartographic officer 15th Reconnaissance Tech. Squadron, March AFB, Calif., 1969-72; missile combat crew comdr. 341st Strategic Missile Wing, Malmstrom AFB, Mont., 1972-77, wing sr. standardization crew comdr. and wing plans officer, 1972-77; vice comdr. 341st Missile Wing, Malmstron AFB,

1992-93; missile ops. staff officer, chief missile tactics div. Hdqs. Strategic Air Command/Joint Strategic Target Planning, Offutt AFB, Nebr., 1978-81; planning/programming officer, asst. chief strategic forces Hdqs. USAF, Washington, 1981-85; dep. comdr. ops. 485th Tactical Missile Wing, Florennes Air Base, Belgium, 1986-87; spl. asst. to chief of staff Supreme Hdqs. Allied Powers Europe, Mons, Belgium, 1987-89; sr. Air Force fellow Coun. Fgn. Rels., N.Y.C., 1989-90; asst. dep. comdr. maintenance 351st Strategic Missile Wing, Whiteman AFB, Mo., 1990-91; comdr. 90th Missile Wing, Francis E. Warren AFB, Wyo., 1993-94; stationed at U.S. Strategic Command, Offutt AFB, 1994-97; dir. nuc. and counterproliferation, dep. chief of staff air and space ops. Pentagon, Washington, 1997-98. Decorated Legion of Merit. Office: 20 AF CC 6610 Headquarters Dr Ste 1 Fe Warren Afb WY 82005-3943

NEAS, JOHN THEODORE, investment company executive; b. Tulsa, May 1, 1940; s. George and Lillian J. (Kaspar) N.; m. Sally Jane McPherson, June 10, 1966; children: Stephen, Gregory, Matthew. BS, Okla. State U., 1967, MS, 1968. With acctg. dept. Rockwell Internat., 1965; with contr.'s dept. Amoco Prodn. Co., 1966—67; mem. audit and tax staf Deloitte, Haskins & Sells, 1968—75; pres. Nat. Petroleum Sales, Inc., Tulsa, 1975—, John Neas Tank Lines, Inc., 1986—, McPherson Fuels & Asphalts, Inc., 1981—88, sec., 1989—; prin. Neas Investments Ltd. Partnership, 1997—, Sebring Investments Ltd. Partnership, 1997—. Stockholder N-H Dealership Investments, Inc., 1996—; mem. coun. Oak Bldg. Mgmt., LLC, 1997—; mem. Brad Noe Autoplex, LLC, 1997—; mem. Vet. Properties, LLC, 1994—; asst. instr. U. Tulsa, 1974; bd. dirs. Summit Bank; former mem. bd. dirs. Waterways Bd. Okla. Dept. Transp., 1989-96. Mem. AICPA, Inst. Mgmt. Accts. (v.p. membership 1976-77), Okla. Soc. CPAs, McClellan-Kerr Arkansas River Nav. Sys. Hist. Soc., Okla. Heritage Assn., Okla. State U. Pres.'s Club, Okla. State U. Coll. Bus. Adminstrn. Assocs. (v.p. memberships 1989-91, Hall of Fame 1991, Acctg. Dept. Hall of Fame 1993), Oaks Country Club, The Gol Club Okla. Republican. Lutheran. Office: Nat Petroleum Sales Inc 5401 S Harvard Ave Ste 200 Tulsa OK 74135-3861

NEASE, JUDITH ALLGOOD, marriage and family therapist; b. Arlington, Mass., Nov. 15, 1930; d. Dwight Maurice Allgood and Sophie (Wolf) Allgood Morris; m. Theron Stanford Nease, Sept. 1, 1962; children: Susan Elizabeth, Alison Allgood. Student, Rockford Coll., 1949-50; BA, NYU, 1953, MA, 1954; MS, Columbia U. Sch. Social Work, 1956. Psychiat. social worker Bellevue Psychiat. Hosp., N.Y.C., 1956-59, St. Luke's Hosp., N.Y.C., 1959-62; asst. psychiat. social work supr. N.J. Neuropsychiat. Inst., Princeton, 1962-64; group co-leader Ctr. for Advancement of Personal and Social Growth, Atlanta, 1973-76; asst. dir., social work supr., group co-leader Druid Hills Counseling Ctr., Columbia Theol. Sem., 1973-82; marriage and family therapist Cath. Social Svcs., Atlanta, 1978-87; chief Cmty. Mental Health Svc., Ft. McPherson, Atlanta, 1987-92; master's level clinician Ctr. for Psychiatry, Smyrna, Ga., 1990-92; pvt. practice Grayson, Ga., 1992—. Democrat. Episcopalian. Home and Office: 1557 Bennett Rd Grayson GA 30017-1046 Office Phone: 770-982-9590.

NEASE, STEPHEN WESLEY, college president; b. Everett, Mass., Jan. 15, 1925; s. Floyd William and Madeline Anzelette (Nostrand) N.; m. Dorothy Christine Hardy, June 17, 1946; children: Linda Carol Nease Scott, Floyd William II, Stephen Wesley Jr., David Wayne, Melissa Jo Nease Wallace. AB, Brown U., 1946; Th.B., Eastern Nazarene Coll., 1947, D.D., 1966; Ed.M., Boston U., 1956; postgrad., Harvard Div. Sch., 1946-48. Ordained to ministry Ch. of the Nazarene, 1951; pastor East Side Ch. of the Nazarene, Newark, Ohio, 1948-50; dean men, instr. religion Ea. Nazarene Coll., Wollaston, Mass., 1950-53, dir. devel., 1953-66, pres. emeritus; founding pres. Mt. Vernon (Ohio) Nazarene Coll., 1966-72, pres. emeritus; pres. Bethany (Okla.) Nazarene Coll., 1973-76, Nazarene Theol. Sem., Kansas City, Mo., 1976-80, Eastern Nazarene Coll., Wollaston, Mass., 1981-89; edn. commr. Ch. of the Nazarene, 1989-94; exec. dir. Capital and Endowment Devel., Mt. Vernon, Ohio, 1994—. Served with USNR, 1943-46. Office: 51 Haverhill Rd Windham NH 03087-1515

NEATON, MARCIA LYNNE, accountant, financial analyst; b. Troy, NY, May 21, 1960; d. Ronald A. and Barbara Westcott Neaton. BS, Russell Sage Coll., 1982. Acctg. mgr. U.S. Sprint, Atlanta, 1988—89; contr. L.J. Hooker Corp. Inc., Atlanta, 1989—91; owner Fin. Mechanics, Duluth, Ga., 1991—99; sr. fin. analyst Arris Interactive, Duluth, 1999—2000; elected Gwinnett County Commr. Dist. 1, 2001—. Vice chmn. Bd. of Health, Lawrenceville, Ga., 2001—; mem. Gwinnett Conv. and Visitors Bur., Duluth, 2002—. Vol. Peachtree Christian Hospice, Duluth, 2001; mem. Gt. Day of Svc. - Foster Children, Gwinnett, 2002; grad. Atlanta Regional Planning Commn./Com. Planning Acad.; mem. Greater Gwinnett Rep. Women, 2000—03; elder Pleasant Hill Presbyn. Ch. Recipient Lt. Col. Aid de Camp Gov. Staff award, Gov. Sonny Perdue, Atlanta, 2003; Marcia Neaton Day proclaimed in her honor, City of Duluth, 2000. Republican. Presbyterian. Avocations: reading, volleyball, travel. Office: Gwinnett County Bd Commrs 75 Langley Dr Lawrenceville GA 30045 Office Phone: 770-822-7000. Personal E-mail: marcia.neaton@gwinnettcounty.com. E-mail: neatonma@co.gwinnett.ga.us.

NEAVES, WILLIAM BARLOW, cell biologist, educator; b. Spur, Tex., Dec. 25, 1943; s. William Fred and Revvie Lee (Hefner) N.; m. Priscilla Wood, Jan. 28, 1965; children: William Barlow, Clarissa D'laine. AB magna cum laude, Harvard U., 1966; postgrad., Med. Sch., 1966-67, PhD, 1969. Lectr. vet. anatomy U. Nairobi, 1970-71, vis. prof., 1978; lectr. anatomy Harvard U., 1972; asst. prof. cell biology U. Tex. Health Sci. Ctr., Dallas, 1972-74, assoc. prof., 1974-77, prof., 1977—. Doris and Brian Wildenthal Prof. of Biomed. Sci., 1993—, dean Grad. Sch. Biomed. Scis., 1980-88, interim dean Southwestern Med. Sch., 1986-88, dean Southwestern Med. Sch., 1989-98, exec. v.p. acad. affairs, 1998—. Rsch. assoc. herpetology Los Angeles County Mus., 1970-73; vis. lectr. U. Chgo., 1976-77. Assoc. editor Anat. Record, 1975-87; mem. editl. bd. Biology of Reprodn., 1983-86, Jour. Andrology, 1987-89; contbr. chpts. to books, articles to profl. jours. Bd. dirs. Dallas Zool. Soc., 1989-94, Dallas Mus. Natural History, 1993-95, Damon Runyan-Walter Winchell Cancer Fund, 1986-92, v.p., 1990-92, Sarnoff Endowment, 1998—. Rockefeller Found. fellow, 1970-71; Milton Fund grantee, 1970-71; Population Council grantee, 1973-75; NIH grantee, 1973-89; Ford. Found. grantee, 1976-78. Fellow AAAS; mem. Am. Assn. Anatomists, Am. Soc. Andrology (Young Andrologist award 1983), Dallas Assembly, N.Y. Acad. Scis., Soc. Study of Reprodn., Liaison Com. on Med. Edn. (joint com. of AMA and Assn. Am. Med. Colls.), Sigma Xi, Alpha Omega Alpha. Methodist.

NEAVOLL, GEORGE FRANKLIN, writer; b. Lebanon, Oreg., Aug. 20, 1938; s. Jesse Hunter and Mazie Maude (Meyer) N.; m. Laney Lila Hunter Hough, June 21, 1969 (dec. Nov. 2000); m. Joanne Darlen MacRoberts, May 4, 2002. BS, U. Oreg., 1965. Reporter, photographer Lebanon (Oreg.) Express, 1969-70; state editor Idaho State Jour., Pocatello, 1970-72; editorial writer The Jour.-Gazette, Ft. Wayne, Ind., 1972-75, Detroit Free Press, 1975-78; editorial page editor The Wichita (Kans.) Eagle, 1978-91, Portland (Maine) Press Herald, Maine Sunday Telegram, 1991-99. Vol. Peace Corps, India, 1967-69; bd. councilors Save-the-Redwoods League, 1980—; bd. dirs. Population Inst., 2002—. Recipient Edward J. Meeman award Scripps-Howard Found., 1973, Honor Roll award Izaak Walton League Am., 1974, Jamaica Daily Gleaner award Inter Am. Press Assn., 1985, Global Media award Population Inst.,1996, Henri A. Benoit award for leadership in pvt. sector Greater Portland (Maine) C. of C., 1999; named Hon. Pk. Ranger, Nat. Pk. Svc., 1988. Mem.: NAACP, Nat. Press Club, Portland C. of C. Home: 151 North St No 204 Portland ME 04101-2794 E-mail: gneavoll@maine.rr.com.

NEBEL, SARA DROUGHT, artist, poet; b. Norwalk, Conn., Oct. 25, 1961; d. James William and Lorna Beryl (Carlson) Drought; m. Emil B. Nebel, May 5, 1984; children: James Blakely, Corrado Carlson, Franceska Nereise. Student, Bennington Coll., 1979-80; Fine Arts Cert., Silvermine Guild Sch. Arts, New Canaan, Conn., 1982. Commercial artist, illustrator, 1980—; owner Earthspirit Gallery, Westport, 1996—. One-woman exhibns. include The Inn at Longshore, Westport, Conn., 1982, Carmen's Country Homes, Westport, Conn., 1982; group shows include Westport Downtown Art Show, 1981, 91, 94, 96, 97, Kent (Conn.) Art Assn. Gallery, Town Hall, Westport, 1986, Earthspirit Art Gallery, Westport, 1996, 98; illustrator Christmas card, 1980, (book cover, design) So Long Chicago, 1982, Queen of Spades, 1982, (cover, interior) Mexamerica Mag., 1980, Writer in Exile, Centennial issue; commd. portraits, mural, landscapes; designer billboard; creator, designer backdrops Sesame St. Children's TV Workshop, 1996. Recipient award The Madison Art Soc., 2000. Mem. Shoreline Arts Alliance, Kent Art Assn. Home: 101 Fort Path Rd Madison CT 06443 Studio: Earthspirit Art Studio 101 Fort Path Rd Madison CT 06443

NEBENZAHL, KENNETH, rare book and map dealer, author; b. Far Rockaway, N.Y., Sept. 16, 1927; s. Meyer and Ethel (Levin) N.; m. Jocelyn Hart Spitz, Feb. 7, 1953; children: Kenneth (dec.), Patricia Suzanne Nebenzahl Frish, Margaret Spitz Nebenzahl Quintong, Suzanne Spitz Nebenzahl Nichol. Student, Columbia U., 1947-48; L.H.D. (hon.), Coll. William and Mary, 1983. Solicitor new bus. United Factors Corp., N.Y.C., 1947-50; sales rep. Fromm & Sichel, Inc., N.Y.C., 1950-52; v.p. Cricketeer, Inc., Chgo., 1953-58; pres. Kenneth Nebenzahl, Inc., Chgo., 1957—. Bd. dirs. Imago Mundi, Ltd., London, 1976-; cons. Rand McNally and Co., 1966-97. Author: Atlas of the American Revolution, 1974, Bibliography of Printed Battle Plans of the American Revolution, 1975, Maps of the Holy Land, 1986 (German edit. 1995), Atlas of Columbus and the Great Discoveries, 1990, also edits. in Spanish, German, Italian, Portugese and French langs., Mapping Asia: The Silk Road and Beyond, 2,000 Years of Exploring the East; contbr. articles to profl. jours. and monographs. Trustee Glencoe Pub. Libr., 1963-69, pres., 1966-69; bd. dirs. North Suburban Libr. System, 1966-69, Beverly Farm Found., Godfrey, Ill., 1961-67, Nature Conservancy of Ill., 1980-88; trustee Adler Planetarium, 1969—, chmn., 1977-81; mem. exec. com. Northwestern U. Libr. Coun., 1973-75; sponsor Kenneth Nebenzahl Jr. lectures history cartography Newberry Libr., Chgo., 1965—; mem. assoc. coun. John Crear Libr., Chgo., 1972-99, trustee, 1976-84; trustee U. Chgo., 1982—, mem. vis. com. to libr., 1978-96, chmn., 1987-95; co-chair Phillips Soc.-Libr. of Congress, Washington, 1995-98; bd. dirs. Evanston Hosp. Corp., 1978-85, Am. Himalayan Found., 1994—; mem. U.S. nat. adv. coun. World Wildlife Fund, 1993—; founding pres. Ill. Ctr. for Book, 1986-88. With USMCR, 1945-46. Recipient IMCoS-Tooley award (London), 1984. Fellow Royal Geog. Soc., Royal Soc. for Asian Affairs; mem. Manuscript Soc. (dir. 1965-71), Am. Library Trustees Assn. (nat. chmn. com. intellectual freedom 1967-68), Bibliog. Soc. Am., Newberry Library Assocs. (bd. govs. 1965-78, chmn. 1976-78), Newberry Library (trustee 1978-2003, vice chmn. 1994-2003, life trustee 2003—), Antiquarian Booksellers Assn. Am. (bd. govs. 1965-67, v.p. 1975-77), Am. Antiquarian Soc. (gov. 1981-85), Soc. History Discoveries (dir. 1974-76), Chgo. Map Soc. (dir. 1976-86), Ill. Ctr. for the Book (pres. 1986-88), N.Am. Elk Breeders Assn., Caxton Club (Chgo.) (bd. govs. 1961-68, 74-80, pres. 1964-66), Wayfarers Club (Chgo.) (pres. 1970-80), Lake Shore Country Club, Century Club (N.Y.C.), Grolier Club (N.Y.C.) (bd. govs. 1998-99). Office: PO Box 370 Glencoe IL 60022-0370

NEBERGALL, DONALD CHARLES, management consultant; b. Davenport, Iowa, Aug. 12, 1928; s. Ellis W. and Hilda (Bruhn) N.; m. Shirley Elaine Williams, Apr. 12, 1952; children: Robert W., Nancy L. Nebergall Bosma. BS, Iowa State U., 1951. With Poweshiek County Nat. Bank, 1957-72, sr. v.p., to 1972; founding pres., CEO Brenton Bank and Trust Co., Cedar Rapids, Iowa, 1972-82, chmn. bd., 1982-86; v.p. Chapman Co., 1986-88. Bd. dirs. Telephone & Data Systems, Inc.; bd. dirs. Guaranty Bank and Trust, Barlow Investment Co.; former vice chmn. bd. Iowa Transfer Svc. V.p., bd. dirs. Iowa 4-H Found., 1972-76; divsn. campaign chmn. United Way; former bd. dirs., past pres. Methwick Retirement cmty.; founding trustee Cedar Rapids Cmty. Sch. Dist. Found.; past pres. Cedar Rapids Greater Downtown Assn. With AUS, 1946-48. Recipient Ptnr. in 4-H award Iowa 4-H, 1983, charter 4-H Found. Ct. of Honor, 1989. Mem. Rotary, Alpha Zeta, Gamma Sigma Delta, Delta Upsilon. Republican. Methodist. Office: 2919 Applewood Pl NE Cedar Rapids IA 52402-3323 Office Phone: 319-634-8386. E-mail: dneber@worldnet.att.net.

NEBERT, DANIEL WALTER, molecular geneticist, research administrator; b. Portland, Oreg., Sept. 26, 1938; s. Walter Francis Nebert and Marie Sophie (Schick) Kirk; m. Myrna Sisk, Mar. 12, 1960 (div. 1975); children: Douglas Daniel, Dietrich Andrew; m. Kathleen Dixon, Aug. 15, 1981 (div. 1997); children: Rosemarie Dixon, Rebecca Frances, David Porter, Lucas Daniel; m. Lucia Jorge Fung, Mar. 6, 2000. BA, Wesleyan U., 1959; BS and MS in Biochemistry, U. Oreg., MD, 1964. Lic. physician, Ohio; bd. qualified in pediats. and human genetics; Am. Bd. Pediat. and Human Genetics. Pediat. intern UCLA Hosps., 1964-65, resident in pediat., 1965-66; postdoctoral fellow Nat. Cancer Inst., NIH, Bethesda, Md., 1966-68; sr. investigator Nat. Inst. Child Health and Human Devel., Bethesda, 1968-71, sect. head, 1971-74, lab. chief, 1974-89; prof. dept. environ. health U. Cin. Med. Ctr., 1989—, prof. dept. pediatrics, 1991—; dir. Ctr. Environ. Genetics, 1992-97. Mem. faculty bd. cert. in human genetics NIH, 1981-89; coord. med. genetics program U.S.-China Coop. Med. Health Protocol, 1982-89; Pfizer lectr. U. Vt., Burlington, 1978, Stanford U., 1979; Wellcome vis. prof. biochemistry and molecular biology U. S.D., Vermillion, 1991; assoc. dir. physician scientist tng. program MD/PhD, U. Cin. Med. Ctr., 1994-98; mem. nomenclature com., joint commn. on bichem. nomenclature, Internat. Union Biochem. Molecular Biology, Internat. Union of Pure and Appied Chemistry; mem. internat. adv. com. Human Genome Orgn., gene nomenclature com., 1999-; mem. nat. adv. Environ. Health Scis. Coun., 2000-04; mem. expert sci. coun. protein info. resource Nat. Biomed. Rsch. Found. Georgetown U., Wash., 2000-; mem. external adv. bd. Howard U. Cancer Ctr., Wash., 1998-, U. Lisbon, 1998-, Inst. DNA and Human Genomics U. Panama, 1999-2004. Mem. editl. bd.: Molecular Pharmacology, 1972-1984, Archives Biochemistry and Biophysics, 1973-76, Archieves Internationales de Pharmacodynamie et de Therapie, 1975-81, Jour. Environ. Scis. and Health, 1976-81, Teratogenesis, Carcinogenesis and Mutagenesis, 1980-86, Anticancer Research, 1981-83, Chemico-Biol. Interactions, 1977-83, DNA and Cell Biology, 1986—, Endocrinology, 1989—, Pharmacogenetics, 1991—, N.Am. Assoc. Ed. for Biochem. Pharmacology, 1994—, European Jour. Pharmacology, 2002, Human Geonmics, 2003, others; assoc. editor DNA+ Cell Biology, 1994—, Mut. Rsch., 1996—, Environ. Health Perspectives, 1997—; contbr. more than 530 articles to profl. jours. Capt. USPHS, 1966-89. Recipient Meritorious Svc. medal USPHS, 1978, Frank Ayrey fellow award in clin. pharmacology, U.K., 1984, Bernard B. Brodie award, 1986, Ernst A. Sommer Meml. award, 1988; GM scholar, 1956-59, Lawrence Selling scholar, 1961, 63. Fellow AAAS; mem. Am. Soc. Human Genetics, Am. Soc. Pharmacology and Exptl. Therapeutics, Am. Soc. Biochemistry and Molecular Biology, Am. Soc. Clin. Investigation (emeritus 1984-), Soc. Toxicology, Human Genome Variation Soc. (founding mem.), Sigma Xi. Republican. Episcopalian. Avocations: gardening, golf, piano, skiing, squash, art. Home: 20 Oliver Rd Cincinnati OH 45215-2631 Office: U Cin Med Ctr Dept Environ Health PO Box 670056 Cincinnati OH 45267-0001

NEBLETT, CAROL, soprano; b. Modesto, Calif., Feb. 1, 1946; m. Philip R. Akre; 3 children. Studies with, William Vennard, Roger Wagner, Esther Andreas, Ernest St. John Metz, Lotte Lehmann, Pierre Bernac, Rosa Ponselle, George London, Jascha Heifetz, Norman Treigle, Sol Hurak, Dorothy Kirsten, Maestros Julius Rudel, Claudio Abbado, Daniel Barenboin, Erich Leinsdorf, James Levine, others. Soloist with Roger Wagner Chorale; performed in U.S. and abroad with various symphonies; debut with Carnegie Hall, 1966, N.Y.C. Opera, 1969, Met. Opera, 1979; sung with maj. opera cos. including Met. Opera, N.Y.C., Lyric Opera Chgo., Balt. Opera, Pitts. Opera, Houston Grand Opera, San Francisco Opera, Boston Opera Co., Milw. Florentine Opera, Washington Opera Soc., Covent Garden, Cologne Opera, Vienna (Austria) Staatsoper, Paris Opera, Teatro Regio, Turin, Italy, Teatro San Carlo, Naples, Italy, Teatro Massimo, Palermo, Italy, Gran Teatro del Liceo, Barcelona, Spain, Kirov Opera Theatre, Leningrad, USSR, Dubrovnik (Yugoslavia) Summer Festival, Salzberg Festival, others; rec. artist RCA, DGG, EMI; appearances with symphony orchs., also solo recitals, (film) La Clemenza di Tito; filmed and recorded live performance with Placido Domingo, La Fancuilla del West; numerous TV appearances. Office: 622 Glorietta Blvd Coronado CA 92118-2304

NECARSULMER, HENRY, investment banker; b. N.Y.C., Mar. 6, 1914; s. Edward and Manuela Fortlouis (Maas) N.; m. Elizabeth Louise Borden, Mar. 21, 1946; children: Susan N. Goldsmith, John B., Peter B. AB, Dartmouth Coll., 1934. With Kuhn, Loeb & Co., N.Y.C., 1935-77, gen. partner, 1956-77, mng. partner, 1969-77; vice chmn. Kuhn, Loeb & Co., Inc., 1977; mng. dir. Lehman Bros. Kuhn Loeb Inc., 1977-81, adv. dir., 1981-84, Shearson Lehman Bros. Inc., 1984-85, mng. dir., 1986-88, adv. dir., 1988-90, cons., 1990-93, Lehman Bros., Inc., 1993-96. Past dir. various corps. Mem. Am. Stock Exchange, 1973-78; mem. governing council Securities Industry Assn., 1972-75; mem. State of N.Y. Judiciary Relations Com., Appellate Div., 1st Jud. Dept., 1973-77; Trustee Jewish Child Care Assn. N.Y. Served to capt. AUS, 1942-46. Office: 590 5th Ave New York NY 10036-4702

NECCO, E(DNA) JOANNE, school psychologist; b. Klamath Falls, Oreg., June 23, 1941; d. Joseph Rogers and Lillian Laura (Owings) Painter; m. Jon F. Puryear, Aug. 25, 1963 (div. Oct. 1987); children: Laura L., Douglas F.; m. A. David Necco, July 1, 1989. BS, Ctrl. State U., 1978, MEd, 1985; PhD in Applied Behavioral Studies, Okla. State U., 1993. Med.-surg. asst. Oklahoma City Clinic, 1961-68; spl. edn. tchr. Oklahoma City Pub. Schs., 1978-79, Edmond (Okla.) Pub. Schs., 1979-83; co-founder, owner Learning Devel. Clinic, Edmond, 1983-93; asst. prof. profl. tchr. edn. U. Ctrl. Okla., Edmond, 1993-97, assoc. prof., 1998—2001, prof. profl. tchr. edn., 2002—. Adj. instr. Ctrl. State U., Edmond, 1989-93, Oklahoma City U., 1991-93; mem. rsch. group Okla. State U., Stillwater, 1991-93; faculty senator U. Ctrl. Okla., 1998-2000; Coll. Edn. rep. AAUP, 2000-01; presenter in field. Contbr. articles to profl. jours. Com. mem. Boy Scouts Am., SCUBA Post 604, Oklahoma City, 1981-86; mem. Edmon Task Force for Youth, 1983-87, Edmond C. of C., 1984-87; presenter internat. conf. Okla. Ctr. for Neurosci., 1996; evaluator for Even Start Literacy Program, 1994-96, reviewer Okla. Even Start applicants, 1997, presenter internat. conf., Singapore, 1996, Alta., Can., 1996, 98; tri-coord. U. Ctrl. Okla. Am. Democracy Project, 2003—. Named to State of Okla. Outstanding Profs.' Acad., 2003, Am. Registry of Outstanding Prof., 2001—02. Mem. AAUP, ASCD, PEO, Am. Psychol. Soc., Nat. Assn. for Sch. Psychologists, Am. Bus Women's Assn., Coun. for Exceptional Children, Learning Disabilities Assn., Am. Assn. for Gifted Underachieving Students, Am. Tchr. Educators, Okla. Learning Disabilities Assn., Okla. Ctr. Neurosci., Okla. Assn. for Counseling and Devel., Okla. Psychol. Soc., U. Ctrl. Okla. Golden Key Nat. Honor Soc., Internat. Soc. for Sci. Study of Subjectivity, Am. Coun. on Rural Spl. Edn., Ctrl. State U. (Okla., life), Phi Delta Kappa. Republican. Avocations: scuba diving, underwater photography, water-skiing, travel, golf. Home: 3624 Equestrian Ct Edmond OK 73034-5871 Office: U Ctrl Okla Coll Edn 100 N University Dr Edmond OK 73034-5207 Office Phone: 405-974-5413. Business E-Mail: jnecco@ucok.edu.

NECHEMIAS, STEPHEN MURRAY, lawyer; b. St. Louis, July 27, 1944; s. Herbert Bernard and Toby Helen (Wax) N.; m. Marcia Rosenstein, June 19, 1966 (div. Dec. 1981); children: Daniel Jay, Scott Michael; m. Linda Adams, Aug. 20, 1983. BS, Ohio State U., 1966; JD, U. Cin., 1969. Bar: Ohio 1969. Ptnr. Taft, Stettinius & Hollister, Cin., 1969—. Adj. prof. law No. Ky. U., Chase Coll. Law. Tax comment author: Couse's Ohio Form Book, 6th edit., 1984. Mem. Ohio State Bar Assn. (chmn. taxation com.), Cin. Bar Assn. (chmn. taxation sect. 1985), Legal Aid Soc. Cin. (pres., trustee). Democrat. Jewish. Home: 2490 Royalview Ct Cincinnati OH 45244 Office: 1800 US Bank Tower 425 Walnut St Cincinnati OH 45202-3923

NECHIN, HERBERT BENJAMIN, lawyer; b. Chgo., Oct. 25, 1935; s. Abraham and Zelda (Benjamin) Nechin; m. Susan Zimmerman (div.); 1 child, Jill Rebecca; m. Roberta Fishman, Oct. 24, 1976; 1 child, Stefan. BA in History with distinction, honors, Northwestern U., 1956; JD, Harvard U., 1959. Bar: Ill. 1960. From assoc. to ptnr. Brown Fox & Blumberg, Chgo., 1960-75; ptnr. Taussig Wexler & Shaw, Chgo., 1975-79, Fink Coff Stern, Chgo., 1979-81, Holleb & Coff, Chgo., 1981-2000; of counsel Levin & Schreder, Ltd., Chgo., 2000—. Contbr. articles to profl. jours. Pres. Emanuel Congregation, Chgo., 1994—97. Staff sgt. USAR, 1960—66. Mem.: ABA, Am. Coll. Trust and Estate Counsel, Chgo. Bar Assn. (chmn. trust law com. 1990—91), Ill. Bar Assn., Cliff Dwellers Club, Phi Beta Kappa. Office: Levin & Schreder Ltd 120 N Lasalle St Ste 3800 Chicago IL 60602-2417 Office Phone: 312-332-6300. E-mail: Herb@LevinSchreder.com.

NECKERS, BRUCE WARREN, lawyer; b. Jamestown, N.Y., May 13, 1943; s. Carlyle and Doris (Van Lente) N.; m. Susan E. Sonnevelot, June 17, 1967; children: Matthew, Melissa, Allison. BA, Hope Coll., Holland, Mich., 1965; JD, Ohio State U., 1968. Bar: Mich. 1968, Ohio 1968, U.S. Dist. Ct. (we. dist.) Mich. 1968. Assoc., ptnr. Mohey, Goodrich & Titta, Grand Rapids, Mich., 1968-87; ptnr. Rhoades McKee, Grand Rapids, 1987—, chmn. exec. com., 1994—. Chmn. gen. program coun., mem. gen. synod exec. com., mem., officer Exec. Found., Ref. Ch. in Am. Fellow Mich. Bar Found.; mem. Fed. Bar Assn. (pres. Western Mich. chpt. 1980-81), State Bar Mich. (pres. 2001-02), Grand Rapids Bar Assn. (pres. 1991-92). Avocations: all sports, golf, skiing. Office: Rhoades McKee 161 Ottawa Ave NW Ste 600 Grand Rapids MI 49503-2766

NEDELKOFF, RICHARD R. former federal agency administrator; b. Ohio; BS in Criminal Justice, Bowling Green State U., 1980; MS in Adminstrn. of Justice with high honors, U. Louisville; JD, Capital U., 1986. Dir. Bur. Justice Assistance U.S. Dept. Justice, Washington, 2001—03. Instr. criminal justice and juvenile justice Capital U.

NEDELMAN, ADAM, entrepreneur; b. Los Angeles, Calif., Dec. 6, 1966; s. Naomi and Charles Irving Nedelman. BA, San Francisco State U., 1990—94. Founder, chmn. of the bd. Psychology Online, Inc. Contbr. software. Ednl. Achievement, Vista Del Mar, 1986—90. Office: Psychology Online Inc 65 Hallam St San Francisco CA 94103 Personal E-mail: admin@psyline.com. E-mail: admin@psyline.com.

NEDERLANDER, JAMES LAURENCE, theater owner, producer; b. Detroit, Jan. 23, 1960; s. James Morton and Barbara (Smith) N. Student, Cranbrook Prep, Boston U. Asst. mgr. Pineknob, Clarkston, Mich., producer N.Y.C.; v.p. Nederlander, N.Y.C., now pres. Bd. trustees Comprehensive Cancer Ctr. Wake Forest U. Assoc. producer (plays) including The Tragedy of Carmen, 1984 (Tony award 1984), Starlight Express, 1989, Cafe Crown, 1989, (musicals) On Your Toes, 1987, Barry Manilow on Broadway, 1989; producer show Mort Sahl on Broadway, 1988, Kenny Loggins on Broadway, 1988, Billy Joel and Twyla Tharp's Movin Out, 2002, Thoroughly Modern Millie, 2002 (Tony award), (with Alfred Molina) Fiddler on the Roof, 2004; co-producer Billy Joel at Yankee Stadium, 1990, Harry Connick Jr. on Broadway, 1990, Yanni on Broadway, 1993, Pink Floyd at Yankee Stadium, 1994, Basia on Broadway, 1994, Shari Lewis and Lambchop on Broadway, 1994, Laurie Anderson on Broadway, 1995, A Midsummer Night's Dream, 1996, Ray Davies-20th Century Man, 1996, The Capeman, 1997. Mem. Com. Am. Candlelite Vigil, 1990; bd. trustees Intrepid Museum, 1990, Fizher Ctr. for Alzheimer's Rsch. Found.; bd. dirs. Midtown Mgmt. Group, 1996, Berkshire Theatre Festival, 1994; exec. com. N.Y.C. Vis. Bur.; bd. dirs. ASPCA. Mem. Exec. League N.Y. Theatres.

NEDERLANDER, JAMES MORTON, theater executive; b. Detroit, Mar. 31, 1922; s. David T. and Sarah L. (Applebaum) N.; m. Charlene Saunders, Feb. 12, 1969; children: James Laurence, Sharon, Kristina. Student, Detroit Inst. Tech. Chmn. Nederlander Orgn., Inc. (formerly Nederlander Producing Co. Am., Inc., N.Y.C., 1966—. Owner and operator of numerous theaters including Palace Theatre, Lunt-Fontanne Theatre, Nederlander Theatre, Brooks Atkinson Theatre, Gershwin Theatre, Neil Simon Theatre, Marquis Theatre, Minskoff Theatre, Richard Rodgers Theatre, N.Y.C., Greek Theatre, Pantages Theatre, Henry Fonda Theatre, L.A., Shubert Theatre, Chgo., Fisher Theatre, Masonic Temple, Detroit, Aldwych Theatre, Adelphi Theatre, Dominion Theatre, London; producer numerous shows for Broadway including She Loves Me, Will Rogers Follies, Me and My Girl, Orpheus Descending, Les Liaisons Dangereuses, Nicholas Nickleby, Annie, La Cage aux Folles, Nine, Applause, Not Now Darling, See Saw, Oliver, Abelard and Heloise, Sherlock Holmes, Treemonisha, Habeus Corpus, Otherwise Engaged, Whose Life is it Anyway?, Betrayal, Woman of the Year, Lena Horne: The Lady and Her Music, The Dresser, Noises Off, Merlin, Night and Day, My Fat Friend, Shirley MacLaine on Broadway, Sweet Charity, Benefactors, Breaking the

Code; numerous road show prodns.; revivals: Peter Pan, She Loves Me, Hello Dolly, Porgy and Bess, The Music Man, I Do! I Do!, Oklahoma, On a Clear Day You Can See Forever, Fiddler on the Roof. Office: Nederlander Orgn Inc 1450 Broadway Fl 6 New York NY 10018 2201

NEDERLANDER, ROBERT E. entertainment and television executive, lawyer; b. Detroit, Apr. 10, 1933; s. David T. and Sarah (Applebaum) N.; m. Caren Berman (div.); children: Robert E. Jr., Eric; Gladys Rackmil, Jan. 1, 1988. BA in Econs., U. Mich., 1955, JD, 1958, LLD (hon.), 1990. Ptnr. Nederlander, Dodge & Rollins, Detroit, 1960-90; pres. Nederlander Co. LLC (formerly Nederlander Orgn. Inc.), N.Y.C., 1981—, Nederlander TV & Film Prodns., N.Y.C., 1985—. Mng. gen. ptnr. N.Y. Yankees, 1990-91. Regent U. Mich., Ann Arbor, 1969-84; trustee Am. Health Found., 1989—; chmn. Gateway Am., 1991—. Recipient Disting. Alumni Svc. award U. Mich., 1985; named Man of Yr. by Gov.'s Com. on Scholastic Achievement, N.Y.C., 1991. Fellow ABA, Mich. Bar Assn. Avocations: tennis, baseball. Office: Nederlander Co LLC 1450 Broadway Ste 2000 New York NY 10018

NEDERMAN, CARY JOSEPH, political scientist, director; b. Pitts., May 6, 1957; s. Harold Joseph and Rena May Nederman; m. Donnalee Dox. BA in Philosophy cum laude, Columbia U., 1978; MA in Social and Polit. Thought, York U., Toronto, 1979, PhD in Social and Polit. Thought, 1983. Tch. asst. faculty of arts York U., Toronto, Canada, 1978—80, instr. Glendale Coll., 1980—84, instr. Atkinson Coll., 1980—84, instr. faculty of arts, 1980—84; vis. asst. U. Alta., Canada, 1984—86, prof., 1984—86, Mactaggart rsch. fellow, 1984—86; lectr. U. Canterbury, Christchurch, New Zealand, 1986—91; vis. assoc. prof. Siena Coll., Loudonville, NY, 1991—92; asst. prof. U. Ariz., Tucson, 1992—95, assoc. prof., 1995—2000; prof. Tex. A&M U., 2000—. Rsch. affiliate Ctr. for History of European Discourses, U. Queensland. Author: (monograph) Comm. and Consent: The Secular Polit. Theory of Marsiglio of Padua's Defensor Pacis, 1995, Medieval Aristotelianism and its Limits: Classical Traditions in Moral and Polit. Philosophy, 1997, Worlds of Difference: European Discourses of Toleration c. 1100-c. 1500, 2000, John of Salisbury, 2004. Fellow, York U., 1978—79; Ont. grad. fellow, 1980—83, Tchg. fellow, Cambridge U, 1997, Hon. fellow, Siena Coll., 1999, Faculty fellow, Tex. A&M U., 2001—02. Mem.: So. Polit. Sci. Assn., Midwest Polit. Sci. Assn., Conf. for the study of Polit. Thought, Medieval Acad. of Am., Am. Polit. Sci. Assoc. Achievements include published various articles in jours., chapters in books, and lectures on the history and political principles; acted as asst. editor, cons. editor, editor, advisor and referee on various professional activities. Home: 1409 Clement Court College Station TX 77840 Office: TX A&M Univ Political Sci Mail Stop 4348 College Station TX 77840 Office Phone: 979-845-8594.

NEDIMOVIC, MLADEN, geophysicist; b. Belgrade, Serbia, Serbia-Monteneg (Yugoslavia), Feb. 18, 1965; s. Radenko and Ruzica Nedimovic; m. Jennifer Helen Dell, June 22, 2002; 1 child, Forde Kovan. M.Sc., U.Toronto, Can., Ph.D., 2000. Geophysicist Geophys. Inst., Belgrade, Serbia and Montenegro, 1991—93; vis. fellow Pacific Geosci Ctr., Sidney, Canada, 2000—02; post doctoral rsch. scientist Lamont-Doherty Earth Obs. Columbia U., Palisades, NY, 2002—. Contbr. articles to profl. jours. Fellow Open Doctoral Fellowship, U. of Toronto, 1997-98, 1996-97, 1995-96, Vis. Fellow, Geol. Survey of Can., 2000-2002; grantee Hart Ho. Film Bd. Prodn. Grant, Hart Ho. Film Bd., 1997, Hart Ho. Film Bd. Post Prodn. Grant; scholar Grad. Scholarship, Ont. Govt., 1994-95, Scholarship, Can. Soc. of Exploration Geophysicists, 1997-98, 1995-96, State Oil and Gas Co. of Yugoslavia Grad. Scholarship, NIS-NAFTAGAS, Yugoslavia, 1992-93. Mem.: Geol. Soc. of Am., Am. Geophys. Union, Soc. of Exploration Geophysicists. Achievements include research in Method for reflection mapping of great earthquake rupture area; Methods for swath 3D imaging of feathered 2D marine and crooked-line 2D land seismic reflection data. Home: 56 Central Ave 2nd Fl Englewood NJ 07631 Office: LDEO of Columbia University 61 Route 9W PO Box 1000 Palisades NY 10964-8000 E-mail: mladen@ldeo.columbia.edu.

NEDOM, H. ARTHUR, petroleum consultant; b. Lincoln, Nebr., Aug. 19, 1925; s. Henry Arthur and Pearle Bertrick (Swan) N.; m. Patricia Margaret Rankin, July 4, 1974; children: Richard A., Robert L., Nicole C. BS, U. Tulsa, 1949, MS, 1950; postgrad. in bus. adminstrn., Northwestern U., Evanston, Ill., 1968. Chief engr. Amerada Petroleum Corp., Tulsa, 1961-65, v.p., 1965-70, Natomas Co., San Francisco, 1971-74; also dir.; pres. Norwegian Oil Co., Houston, 1974-75; pres., mng. dir. Weeks Petroleum Ltd., Westport, Conn., 1975-82; cons., 1982—; chmn. bd. arbitration Prudhoe Bay Unit, 1983-85. Chmn. Offshore Tech. Conf., 1971; bd. dirs. Engrs. Joint Council, 1978 Contbr. articles to profl. jours. Served with inf. U.S. Army, 1943-45, ETO. Decorated Bronze Star; named Disting. Alumnus U. Tulsa, 1972 Mem. Soc. Petroleum Engrs. (dir. 1965-68, pres. 1967, Disting. Lectr. 1973, Disting Svc. award 1978, DeGolyer Disting. Svc. medal 1981, Disting. mem. 1983, Disting. lectr. emeritus 1989, Legion of Honor 1998, v.p. SPE Found. 1988-89), AIME (dir. 1966-69, 76-79, pres. 1977, hon. mem. 1982, Disting. Svc. award 1993), Am. Assn. Engring. Soc. (dir. 1980-82, chmn. 1981, Spl. award 1979, Engring. Svc. award 1980). Home: 21 Deerwood Ln Westport CT 06880-2648 Personal E-mail: artnedom@aol.com.

NEDWEK, BRIAN, academic administrator; b. Milw., Wis., Sept. 1, 1941; s. Thomas and Josephine Nedwek; m. Judith Ann Weber, June 16, 1966; children: Elizabeth, Sarah. BA, Marquette Univ., Milw., Wis., 1965, MA, 1967; PhD, Univ. Wisc.-Milw., Milw., Wis., 1974. Prof. St. Louis Univ., 1976—85, assoc. v.p. for acad. affairs, 1985—88, acad. v.p., 1988—89, assoc. provost, 1989—97; dean, coll. of liberal arts Univ. Detroit, Mercy, Detroit, 1998—2001; vice provost St. John's Univ., Jamaica, NY, 2001—04; v.p. acad. affairs Maryville U., 2004—. Editl. com. CAUSE, 1993—96; cons. N. Ctrl. Assn., Chgo., 1996—2001; com. on substantive change Mid. States Commn., Phila., 2002—. Author, editor: Doing Academic Planning, 1996; co-author: Measuring Up, 1994; contbr. chapters to books, 1999. Bd. mem. N.W. Detroit Neighborhood, Detroit, 2000—01, Citizens Adv. Com., St. Louis, 1982, St. Louis Pub. Sch. Mem.: Soc. for Coll. & Univ. Planning (pres. 1996—97, Disting. Svc. award 2002). Cath. Avocations: golf, photography. Office: Maryville U 13550 Conway Rd Saint Louis MO 63141 Office Phone: 314-529-9400.

NEE, LINDA ELIZABETH, social science analyst; b. Boston, Dec. 29, 1938; d. Thomas Markham and Ellen Thomas (Jamieson) Nee. BA, Russell Sage Coll., 1961; MS in Social Work, Va. Commonwealth U., 1968. Social worker, social svc. dept., N.Y. Neurol. Inst., Columbia Presbyn. Med. Ctr., N.Y.C., 1961-66; med. social worker Tb San., Med. Coll. Va., Richmond, summer 1967; clin. social worker social work dept. Clin. Center, NIH, Bethesda, Md., 1968-74, clin. rsch. social worker sect. exptl. therapeutics, lab. clin. sci., NIMH, Bethesda, 1974-84, clin. genetics rsch. assoc. Nat. Inst. Neurol. Disorders and Stroke, 1984, social sci. analyst, 1984—; mem. ethics com. Md. State Bd. Social Work Examiners, 1979—. Adv., organizer, bd. dirs. Met. D.C. chpt. Alzheimer's and Related Diseases Assn., 1979-88, pres., 1982-86; mem. sci. bd. Familial Alzheimer's Disease Rsch. Found., Tulsa, 1987—; bd. dirs. Friends of Clin. Ctr., Bethesda, 1989—, pres., 1992; trustes The Sage Colls., Troy, N.Y., 1993—. Mem. NASW (chmn. ethics and grievances 1977-79; pres. Met. Washington 1975-77). Editor: Jour. Social Work Met. Washington, 1975-77; columnist: The Bulletin newsletter Nat. Assn. Social Workers, 1975-77; contbr. articles to profl. jours. Office: Clin Ctr Ninds Bethesda MD 20892-0001

NEE, SISTER MARY COLEMAN, college president emeritus; b. Taylor, Pa., Nov. 14, 1917; d. Coleman James and Nora Ann (Hopkins) N. AB, Marywood Coll., 1939, MA, 1943; MS, Notre Dame U., 1959; DHL (hon.), U. Scranton; Dr.Humanities (hon.), King's Coll.; DHL (hon.), Marywood U., 2003. Joined Order of Sisters, Servants of Immaculate Heart of Mary, 1941; assoc. prof. math. Marywood Coll., Scranton, Pa., 1959-68, pres., 1970-88, pres. emerita, 1988—. Apostolic coord. Sisters, Servants Immaculate Heart of Mary, Scranton, Pa., 1968-70. Home and Office: Cathedral Convent 333 Wyoming Ave Scranton PA 18503-1223 Office Phone: 570-344-9725.

NEECE, OLIVIA HELENE ERNST, investment company executive, consultant; b. LA, Jan. 3, 1948; d. Robert and Beatrice Pearl Ernst; m. Huntley Lee Bluestein, 1967 (div. 1974); children: Melissa Dawn, Brendon Wade; m. Anthony Ray Neece, Mar. 20, 1976. Cert. interior design, UCLA, 1975, MBA, 1993; BSBA, U. So. Calif., 1990; postgrad., Claremont U., 1998—. Cert. interior designer Calif. Coun. for Interior Design; lic. gen. contractor, real estate broker, Calif. Staff designer Frances Lux Designs, LA, 1974; project designer Yates Silverman Inc., LA, 1974-77; owner Olivia Neece Planning & Design, Tarzana, Calif., 1977-86; v.p. project devel. Design Svc. /Aircoa, Englewood, Colo., 1986-87; v.p. project adminstrn. Hirsch-Bedner Assoc., Santa Monica, Calif., 1987-88; treas.-sec. EON Corp., LA, 1980—; owner Olivia Neece Planning & Design, Tarzana, 1988-93; dir. ops. The Ernst Group, LA, 1980—85. Instr. ext. program UCLA, 1981—83; part-time prof. Calif. State U., Northridge, 1994—99; acad. rschr. Jet Propulsion Lab., 2000—02; spkr. in field. Co-author: A Step by Step Approach to Hotel Devel., 1988; contbr. chapters to books, articles to profl. jours. Co-chair LA Master Chorale Gala; mem. Hollywood Bowl Soc.; charter mem. L.A. County Mus. Art; vol. restoration of San Diego R.R. Mus., 1985—92; patron LA Philharm.; gold patron LA Opera Soc.; Found. of Music Ctr. of Los Angels; fellow circle Ctr. Theatre Group; Patron and charter mem. of LA Country Mus. of Art; bd. dir.,historian Master Choral Assoc. Recipient Holiday Inn Devel. award, Foster City, Calif., 1986, Warwick, R.I., 1988, 1st and 2d pl. awards, Lodging Hospitality Designers Cir., 1987, Gold Key award, Russell St. Inn, 1986, Best Paper award, Am. Conf. on Info. Systems, 2002. Mem. Am. Soc. Interior Designers (1st pl. portfolio competition 1974), Acad. of Mgmt. (Best Paper award 2002), Fin. Mgmt. Assn., Internat. Inst. Designers & Arch. (profl., v.p., bd. dir.), We. Acad. Mgmt., Assn. Info. Sys., Inst. Ops. Rsch. and Mgmt. Sci, Beta Gamma Sigma. Office: Neece Assoc 18200 Rosita St Tarzana CA 91356-4622

NEEDELL, JEFFREY DAVID, historian, educator; b. N.Y.C., Dec. 24, 1951; s. Burton Peter Needell and Novella Cecilia Belden, Charles Belden (Stepfather); m. Fatima Lima Maia de Maia, Sept. 5, 1980; children: Gabriel Burton Maia de, Renata Jurandy Maia de, Ethan Lucas Maia de. AB, U. of Calif. at Berkeley, 1974; MA, Yale U., New Haven, 1978; PhD, Stanford U., Calif., 1982. Asst. prof. of history U. of Oreg., Eugene, 1982—87; program assoc. Latin Am. Program, Woodrow Wilson Internat. Ctr. for Scholars, Washington, 1985—87; asst. prof. of history U. of Fla., Gainesville, 1987—89, assoc. prof. of history, 1990—. Vis. prof. history Cath. U. Am., 1986—87, Royal U. of Leiden, Netherlands, 1994, Fed. Fluminense U., Brazil, 1997. Author: (history monograph) A Tropical Belle Epoque: Elite Culture and Society in Turn-of-the-Century Rio de Janeiro.; contbr. articles to profl. jours. Recipient Travel award, Am. Philos. Soc., 1988, 1996; fellow Danforth fellow, Danforth Found., 1976—82, Dissertation fellow, Social Sci. Rsch. Coun., 1979—82, Fulbright Dissertation fellow, Fulbright Commn., 1978—80, Postdoctoral fellow, NEH, 1989—90, Social Sci. Rsch. Coun., 1996—97, Lectr. Rsch. fellow, Fulbright Commn. Brazil, 1997. Mem.: Brazilian Studies Assn., Latin Am. Studies Assn., Conf. on Latin Am. History, Am. Hist. Assn. Office: Univ of Florida Dept of History PO Box 117320 Gainesville FL 32611-7320 E-mail: jneedell@history.ufl.edu.

NEEDHAM, CAROL ANN, lawyer, educator; b. Chgo., Nov. 1, 1957; d. Robert Michael and Loretta Ann Needham; m. Thomas Joseph Timmermann, July 23, 1994; 1 child, Genevieve Timmermann. BA in English, Northwestern U., 1979, JD, 1985; MA in English, U. Va., 1982. Bar: Calif. 1987, D.C. 1989, Ill. 1985. Jud. law clk. U.S. Dist. Ct., Honolulu, 1985-86; atty. Gibson, Dunn & Crutcher, L.A., 1986-90, Chadbourne & Parke, L.A., 1990-91; prof. law St. Louis U. Sch. Law, 1992—. Mem. corp. ethics com. St. Mary's Health Sys. Bd. Co-author: Lawyers and the Legal Profession; contbr. numerous articles to profl. jours. Chair scholarship com. Verbum Dei H.S., L.A., 1987—92. Mem.: ABA, Mo. Bar Assn. (vice chmn. com. on lawyers' advt. 1995—98, com. on multidisciplinary practice 2000, professionalism com. 2000—, com. on multijurisdictional practice 2001—), Am. Assn. Law Schs. (profl. responsibility exec. com. 1995—98, 2004—), Ctrl. States Law Assn. (treas. 1995—96, v.p. 1996—98, pres. 1998—99). Office: St Louis U Sch Law 3700 Lindell Blvd Saint Louis MO 63108-3412

NEEDHAM, ED, editor; Degree in Am. Lit., Sussex (Eng.) U., 1986. Freelance translator, Spain; freelance journalist, 1996; dep. editor FHM, 1996—97, editor, 1997—2000, editor-in-chief Am. edit., 2000—02; mng. editor Rolling Stone, 2002—04; editor-in-chief Maxim, 2004—. Office: Maxim 1040 Ave of the Americas New York NY 10018*

NEEDHAM, GEORGE AUSTIN, investment banker; b. Beverly, Mass., Jan. 27, 1943; s. Everett Austin and Edith Strode (Walton) N.; m. Ellen Ann Levin, July 9, 1978; children: Michael Austin, Sarah Elisabeth, Paul Everett. BS in Bus. Adminstrn., Bucknell U., 1965; MBA, Stanford U., 1971. Portfolio mgr. Bankers Trust Co., N.Y.C., 1967-69; mng. dir. First Boston Corp., N.Y.C., 1971-84; chmn., CEO Needham & Co. Inc., N.Y.C., 1985—. Trustee Stanford Bus. Sch. Trust, Palo Alto, Calif., 1983-89. Served to 1st lt. U.S. Army, 1965-67. Mem. Fin. Analysts Fedn., Bond Club N.Y., The Links, Univ. Club, Sleepy Hollow Country Club, Coral Beach Club. Republican. Home: 79 E 79th St New York NY 10021-0202 Office: Needham & Co Inc 445 Park Ave New York NY 10022-2606 Business E-Mail: gneedham@needhamco.com.

NEEDHAM, GEORGE MICHAEL, association executive; b. Buffalo, July 3, 1955; s. Paul James and Dolores Ann (Duffy) N.; m. Joyce Elaine Leahy, Nov. 28, 1992; 1 stepchild, Katherine Callison. BA in English, SUNY, Buffalo, 1976, MLS, 1977. Various profl. positions Charleston (S.C.) County Libr., 1977-84; dir. Fairfield County Dist. Libr., Lancaster, Ohio, 1984-89; mem. svcs. dir. Ohio Libr. Assn., Columbus, 1990-92; exec. dir. Pub. Libr. Assn., Chgo., 1993-96; state librarian State of Mich., Lansing, 1996-99; v.p. mem. svcs. OCLC Online Computer libr. Ctr., Dublin, Ohio, 1999—. Mem. adv. bd. Libr. Video Project, 1996—. Co-author: A Director's Checklist for Connecting Public Libraries to the Internet, 1995; author (book revs.) Booklist, 1994-2002 (video revs.), Libr. Jours., 1979-94. Bd. dirs. Fairfield County chpt. ARC, Lancaster, 1984-88, Mt. Prospect Theatre Soc., Mt. Prospect, Ill., 1993-96, Lib. Media Project, 1997—. Mem. ALA, Pub. Libr. Assn., Ohio Libr. Assn. Achievements include 2 time Jeparody champion. Avocations: acting, traditional folk music, writing. Office: OCLC Online Computer Libr Ctr 6565 Frantz Rd Dublin OH 43017-3395 Office Phone: 614-761-5173. E-mail: needhamg@oclc.org.

NEEDHAM, JAMES JOSEPH, retired financial services executive, consultant; b. Woodhaven, N.Y., Aug. 18, 1926; s. James Joseph and Amelia (Pasta) N.; m. Dolores A. Habick, July 1, 1950 (dec. Feb. 1993); children: James, Robert, Ravenna, Michael, Catherine; m. Patricia Henry Campo, May 24, 1995. Student, Cornell U., 1946; BBA, St. John's U., 1951, LLD (hon.), 1972. CPA, N.Y. Acct. Price Waterhouse & Co., N.Y.C, 1947-54; ptnr. R. T. Hyer & Co., Port Washington, N.Y., 1954-57; ptnr., mem. exec. com. A. M. Pullen & Co., N.Y.C., 1957-69; commr. SEC, Washington, 1969-72; chmn., chief exec. officer N.Y. Stock Exch., 1972-76; v.p. Internat. Fedn. Stock Exchs., 1973-75, pres., 1990—94; amb. of U.S. com. gen. to EXPO in Japan, 1984—85; councilman Town of Southampton, N.Y., 1986—. Disting. prof., grad. div. Coll. Bus. Adminstrn., St. John's U., Jamaica, N.Y.; U.S. amb. to Japan Expo '85, 1982—; bd. dirs. Mut. of Am. Mut. Funds. Treas. Central Sch. Dist. 4, 1951-52, mem. budget and finance com., 1951, 63, chmn. high sch. planning com., 1947; active local Boy Scouts Am., 1962-65; mem. bishop's com. of laity Catholic Charities, Rockville Center, N.Y., 1960-68; mem. lay adv. bd. Cath. Youth Orgn., 1964-67; bd. advs. Coll. Bus. Adminstrn., St. John's U.; mem. hon. com. Am. Cancer Soc.; N.Y. State co-chmn. fin. Reagan for Pres. Campaign, 1980; Past dir., auditor Plainview (N.Y.) Republican Club.; Bd. govs. Fed. Hall Meml. Assos.; trustee N.Y. Foundling Hosp. Served with USNR, 1944-46. Recipient Disting. Citizen award N.Y. U. Law Sch., Disting. Service award in investment edn. Nat. Assn. Investment Clubs; named Bus. Person of Year Bus. Adminstrn. Soc. St. John's U., 1975; fellow Aspen Inst. for Humanistic Studies. Mem.: AICPA (past mem. coun.), Accts. Club Am., Cath. Accts. Guild (past pres.), N.Y. Credit and Fin. Mgmt. Assn. (Laurel award), N.Y. Soc. CPA's (past dir., treas., past pres. Nassau-Suffolk chpt., recognition award), Downtown-Lower Manhattan Assn. (dir., exec. com.), N.Y. Chamber Commerce and Industry, L.I. Assn., Internat. C. of C. (U.S. coun.), Burning Tree Club, Wheatley Hills Golf Club (past treas.), Cornell Club of Nassau County, Serra Club (Nassau) (past pres.). Home: 97 Coopers Farm Rd Unit 1 Southampton NY 11968-4066

NEEDHAM, RICHARD LEE, magazine editor; b. Cleve., Jan. 16, 1939; s. Lester Hayes and Helen (Bender) N.; m. Irene Juechter, Aug. 7, 1965; children: Margaret, Richard, Trevor. BA, Denison U., 1961; MA, U. Mo., 1967. Copy editor Sat. Rev., N.Y.C., 1967-68; editor-in-chief Preview Internat., N.Y.C., 1968-69; financial and N.Y. editor Instns. mag.; also editor Service World Internat., N.Y.C., 1969-70; copy dir. American Home mag., N.Y.C., 1970-71; exec. editor Ski Mag., N.Y.C., 1971-74, editor, 1974-92, editor-in-chief, 1992-94, sr. contbg. editor, 1994—; contbg. editor Yachting Mag., N.Y.C., 1996; editor Ency. of Skiing, 1978, Ski Fever, 1995; editl. dir. Times Mirror Mags. Conservation Coun., 1994-96; editor-in-chief Inside Tracks, 1996—2002; automotive writer Gannett Suburban Newspapers, 1995—; editor Arthritis Advisor, 2002—, Skiing Heritage, 2002—. Broadcaster: Ski Spot, CBS Radio, N.Y.C., 1978-83, On the Slopes, Audio Features Syndicate, 1984-87; author: Ski--50 Years in North America, 1992, Ski Fever!, 1995. Served to lt. USNR, 1961-65. Recipient Lowell Thomas award, 1985 Mem. N.Am. Ski Journalists Assn., Ea. Ski Writers Assn., Internat. Assn. Ski Journalists, Internat. Motor Press Assn. Home and Office: 481 Sandy Point Ave Portsmouth RI 02871-3515 E-mail: richardneedham@cox.net.

NEEDLEMAN, ALAN, mechanical engineering educator; b. Phila., Sept. 2, 1944; s. Herman and Hannah (Goodman) N.; m. Wanda Sapolsky, Apr. 12, 1970; children: Deborah, Daniel BS, U. Pa., 1966; MS, Harvard U., 1967, PhD, 1970. Instr. applied math. MIT, Cambridge, 1970-72, asst. prof., 1972 75; asst. prof. engring. Brown U., Providence, 1975 78, assoc. prof., 1978-81, prof., 1981—, dean engring., 1988-91, Florence Pirce Grant Univ. prof. Vis. asst. prof. Tech. U. Denmark, Lyngby, 1973; vis. fellow Clare Hall, U. Cambridge, Eng., 1978; vis. prof. MIT, Cambridge, 1991. Contbr. articles to profl. jours. Guggenheim fellow, 1977. Fellow ASME, Am. Acad. Mechanics, Danish Ctr. for Applied Math. and Mechanics (fgn.), Groupe Francais de Macanique des Matèriaux (hon.); mem. NAE. Home: 24 Elton St Providence RI 02906-4106 Office: Brown U Div Engring Providence RI 02912-0001 E-mail: Alan_Needleman@brown.edu.

NEEDLEMAN, BARBARA, newspaper executive; BS in Eng., Northwestern Univ., 1994. V.p. Tribune Media Svcs., Chgo., 1993—. Office: Tribune Media Svcs 435 N Michigan Ave Ste 1500 Chicago IL 60611-4012

NEEDLEMAN, HERBERT LEROY, psychiatrist, pediatrician; b. Phila., Dec. 13, 1927; s. J. Joseph and Sonia Rita (Shupak) Needleman; m. Shirley Weinstein, Sept. 12, 1948 (div. 1957); 1 child, Samuel; m. Roberta Pizor, June 2, 1963; children: Joshua, Sara. BS, Muhlenberg Coll., Allentown, Pa., 1948; MD, U. Pa., 1952. Intern Phila. Gen. Hosp., 1952—54; resident in pediat. Children's Hosp. of Phila., 1957—58, chief resident in pediat., 1958—59; resident in psychiatry Temple U. Med. Ctr., Phila., 1962—65, asst. prof. psychiatry, 1967—71; spl. fellow in psychiatry NIMH, Bethesda, Md., 1965—67; assoc. prof. psychiatry Harvard Med. Sch., Boston, 1971—81; prof. psychiatry and pediat. U. Pitts. Sch. Medicine, 1981—. Cons. air lead criteria document EPA, Washington, 1977; editor Ctrs. for Disease Control, Atlanta, 1978; mem. adv. com. on childhood lead poisoning prevention, 90; chmn. devel. toxicology subpanel NAS, 1986. Editor: Low Level Lead Exposure: The Clinical Implications of Current Research, 1980; contbr. articles to profl. jours. Chmn. Alliance to End Childhood Lead Poisoning, Washington, 1991—92, Com. of Responsibility, Boston, 1966—75; bd. dirs. Mass. Advocacy Ctr., Boston, 1972—80. Capt. U.S. Army, 1955—57. Recipient Sarah L. Poiley Meml. award, N.Y. Acad. Scis., 1985, The Charles A. Dana award, 1989, NAS IOM, 1990, H. John Heinz award, 1995, Edward Barsky award, Physicians' Forum, 1997, Disting. Grad. award, U. Pa. Sch. Medicine, 1999, Prince Mahidol award in pub. health, Bangkok, 2003, Vernon Houk award, Soc. Occupl. Environ. Health. Fellow: Am. Acad. Pediat.; mem.: Am. Acad. Pediat. Com. on Environ. Hazards, Am. Acad. Child and Adolescent Psychiatry, Am. Pediat. Soc., Soc. of Toxicology, Sigma Xi, Phi Beta Kappa. Democrat. Jewish. Avocations: trout fishing, carpentry. Office: Univ Pitts Sch Medicine 3520 5th Ave Pittsburgh PA 15213-3320

NEEDLEMAN, JACOB, philosophy educator, writer; b. Phila., Oct. 6, 1934; s. Bemjamin and Ida (Seltzer) Needleman; m. Carla Satzman, Aug. 30, 1959 (div. 1989); children: Raphael, Eve; m. Gail Anderson, Dec. 1989. BA, Harvard U., 1956; grad., U. Freiburg, 1957-58; PhD, Yale U., 1961. Clin. psychology trainee West Haven (Conn.) Veterans Hosp. Adminstrn., 1960-61; rsch. assoc. Rockefeller Inst., N.Y., 1961-62; from asst. prof. to assoc. prof. philosophy San Francisco State U., 1962-66, prof philosophy, 1967—, chair dept. philosophy, 1968-69. Vis. scholar Union Theol. Seminary, 1967-68; dir. Ctr. Study New Religions, 1977-83; lectr. psychiatry, cons. med. ethics U. Calif., 1981-84. Author: Being-in-the-World, 1963, The New Religions, 1970, Religion for a New Generation, 1973, A Sense of the Cosmos, 1975, On the Way to Self-Knowledge: Sacred Tradition and Psychotherapy, 1976, Lost Christianity, 1980, Consciousness and Tradition, 1982, The Heart of Philosophy, 1982, Sorcerers, 1986, Sin and Scientism, 1986, Lost Christianity: A Journey of Rediscovery to the Centre of Christian Experience, 1990, Money and the Meaning of Life, 1991, Modern Esoteric Spirituality, 1992, The Way of the Physician, 1993, The Indestructible Question, 1994, A Little Book on Love, 1996, Time and the Soul, 1998; The American Soul, 2002; (trans.) The Primary World of Senses, 1963, Essays on Ego Psychology, 1964; editor Care of Patients with Fatal Illness, 1969, The Sword of Gnosis, 1973, Sacred Tradition and Present Need, 1974, Understanding the New Religions, 1978, Speaking of My Life: The Art of Living in the Cultural Revolution, 1979, Real Philosophy: An Anthology of the Universal Search for Meaning, 1991, The American Soul, 2002; contbr. Death and Bereavement, 1969, To Live Within, 1971, My Life with a Brahmin Family, 1972, The New Man, 1972, The Universal Meaning of the Kabbalah, 1973, The Phenomenon of Death. Grantee Religion in Higher Edn., Marsden Found., 1967—68, Ella Lymna Cabot Trust, 1969, Far West Inst., 1975. Office: San Francisco State U Dept Philosophy 1600 Holloway Ave San Francisco CA 94132-1722 Office Phone: 415-338-2216. Business E-Mail: jneedle@sfsu.edu.

NEEDLEMAN, PHILIP, cardiologist, pharmacologist; b. Bklyn., Feb. 10, 1939; BS, Phila. Coll. Pharm. & Sci., 1960; MS, U. Md. Med. Sch., 1962, PhD in Pharmacology, 1964. Fellow Sch. Medicine Washington U., St. Louis, 1965—67, from asst. prof. to prof. Sch. Medicine, 1967—75, prof. Sch. Medicine, 1975—, adj. prof., 1976—, chief scientist, 1991—; co-pres. Searle. Contbr. numerous articles to profl. jours. Recipient Rsch. Career Devel. award, NIH, 1974, 1976, Wellcome Creesy award in clin. pharmacology, 1977, 1978, 1980, 1987, Cochems Thrombosis Rsch. prize, 1980. Office: Wash Univ Sch of Med McDonnell Medic 3901 63 S Euclid Ave Saint Louis MO 63110

NEEDLES, BELVERD EARL, JR., accountant, educator; b. Lubbock, Tex., Sept. 16, 1942; s. Belverd Earl and Billie (Anderson) N.; m. Marian Powers, May 23, 1976; children: Jennifer Helen, Jeffrey Scott, Annabelle Marian, Abigail Marian. BBA, Tex. Tech. U., 1964, MBA, 1965; PhD, U. Ill., 1969. CPA, Ill.; cert mgmt. acct. Asst. prof., assoc. prof. acctg. Tex. Tech. U., Lubbock, 1968-72; dean Coll. Bus. and Adminstrn., Chgo. State U., 1972-76; prof. acctg. U. Ill., Urbana, 1976-78; dir. Sch. Accountancy DePaul U., Chgo., 1978-86, prof. acctg., 1976-88, Arthur Andersen & Co. alumni disting. prof. acctg., 1988—2002, Ernst & Young dist. prof. acctg., 2003—. Author: Accounting and Organizational Control, 1973, Modern Business, 2d edit., 1977, Principles of Accounting, 1980, 8th edit., 2002, Financial Accounting, 1982, 8th edit., 2004, The CPA Examination: A Complete Review, 7th edit., 1986, Comparative International Auditing Standards, 1985, Financial and Managerial Accounting, 5th edit., 2002; editor Accounting Instructor's Report, 1981—, The Accounting Profession and the Middle Market, 1986, Creating and Enhancing The Value of Post-Baccalareate Accounting Education, 1988, A Profession in Transition: The Ethical and Responsibilities of Accountants, 1989, Comparative International Accounting Educational Standards, 1990, Accounting Education for the 21st Century: The Global Challenges, 1994, Financial Acctg.: A Global Approach, 1999. Treas., bd. dirs. CPAs for Pub. Interest, 1978-86. Gen. Electric fellow, 1965-66, Deloitte Haskins and Sells fellow, 1966-68; named Disting. Alumnus Tex. Tech. U., 1986; recipient

Award of Merit DePaul U., 1986, Faculty Award of Merit Fedn. of Schs. of Accountancy, 1990, Excellence in Tchg. Award DePaul U., 1998; named among 100 most influential accts. Acctg. Today, 2001. Fellow Am. Acctg. Assn. (sec. internat. sect. 1984-86, vice chmn. 1986-87, chmn. 1987-88, named outstanding internat. acctg. educator 1996); mem. AICPA (named Outstanding Educator 1992), Fedn. Schs. Accountancy (bd. dirs. 1980-87, pres. 1986), Acad. Internat. Bus., Ill. CPA Soc. (bd. dirs. 1994-96, vice chair 2001-02, sr. vice chair 2002-2003, chmn., 2003-04, Outstanding Acctg. Educator 1990), European Acctg. Assn. (exec. com. 1986-89), Intenrat. Assn. for Edn. & Rsch. in Acctg. (v.p. 1989-92, sec.-treas. 1992-97, pres. 1997-2002), Phi Delta Kappa, Phi Kappa Phi, Beta Alpha Psi (named Acct. of Yr. for Edn. 1992), Beta Gamma Sigma. E-mail: bneedles@needles-powers.com.

NEEL, C. WARREN, state finance department commissioner; b. Mobile, Ala., Dec. 6, 1938; s. Check and Ena Neel; m. Annelle Neel; children: Todd, Eric, Anna. BS, Miss. State U., 1960; MBA, U. Ala., 1966, PhD, 1969. Asst. mgr. engring. adminstrn. Internat. Paper Co., 1962-65; instr. U. Ala., 1968-89; from asst. prof. to assoc. prof. U. Tenn., Knoxville, 1969-74; dean U. Tenn. Coll. Bus. Adminstrn., Knoxville, 1977—2000; commr. fin. and adm. dept. of Tenn., Nashville, 2000. Vis. lectr. U. So. Calif., summer, 1969; bd. dirs. Am. HealthCorp., O'Charley's, Inc., Saks, Inc., Clayton Homes, Inc. With U.S. Army. Mem. Soc. Internat. Bus. Fellows, Beta Gamma Sigma, Phi Kappa Phi, Chi Alpha Phi. Office: Tenn Finance and Administration Department 1st Fl State Capitol Nashville TN 37243 Fax: 423-974-1766.

NEEL, HARRY BRYAN, III, surgeon, scientist, educator; b. Rochester, Minn., Oct. 28, 1939; s. Harry Bryan and May Birgitta (Bjornsson) N.; m. Ingrid Helene Vaga, Aug. 29, 1964; children: Carlton Bryan, Harry Bryan IV, Roger Clifton. BS, Cornell U., 1962; MD, SUNY-Bklyn., 1966; PhD, U. Minn., 1976. Diplomate Am. Bd. Otolaryngology. Intern Kings County Hosp., Bklyn., 1966-67; resident in gen. surgery U. Minn. Hosps., Mpls., 1967-68; resident in otolaryngology Mayo Grad. Sch. Medicine Mayo Clinic, Rochester, Minn., 1970-74, cons. in otorhinolaryngology, 1974—, cons. in cell biology, 1981—, assoc. prof. otolaryngology and microbiology Med. Sch., 1979-84, prof., 1984—, also chmn. dept. otolaryngology. Mem. sci. adv. com. Pitts. Eye and Ear Found.; lifetime vis. prof. Hunan U., China, 2003—. Author: Cryosurgery for Cancer, 1976; contbr. chpts. to books, articles to profl. jours. V.p. bd. dirs. Minn. Orch. in Rochester, Inc., 1982, pres., chmn., 1983—84; mem. devel. com. Minn. Orchestral Assn., 1983, Mayo Found., 1983—86; bd. dirs. Mayo Health Plan, 1986—92, chmn., 1990—92; mem. bd. Mayo Mgmt. Svcs., Inc., 1992—94; mem. bd. regents U. Minn., 1991—2003, chair faculty staff, student affairs com., 1993—95, 1999, vice chmn. bd., 1995—97, chmn. fin. and ops. com., 1999, mem. audit com., 1995—2000, chair litigation review com., 2001—03, chair facilities com., 2001—03; bd. dirs. Greater Rochester Area Univ. Ctr., 1993—; trustee U. Minn. Found., 1996—, mem. fin. com., 1999—2001; chmn. U. Minn. Investment Adv. Com., 1999—2002; mem. State Commn. on U. Minn. Excellence, 2002; founder U. Minn. Neel Scholarship Fund, Rochester, 2003. With USPHS, 1968—70. Recipient travel award Soc. Acad. Chmn. Otolaryngology, 1974, Ira J. Tresley rsch. award Am. Acad. Facial and Reconstructive Surgery, 1982, Master Tchr. award in surgery Alumni Assn. Coll. Medicine, SUNY, Health Sci. Ctr., Bklyn., 1991, Notable award Nat. Assn. Collegiate Women Athletic Adminstrs., 1992, The Best Doctors in Am. award Woodward/White, 1992—. Mem. AMA, ACS (bd. govs. 1985-90, devel. bd. 1988—, treas. 1990-98, sec.-treas. Minn. chpt. 1983-85, pres. 1988-89), Am. Acad. Otolaryngology-Head and Neck Surgery (prize for basic rsch. in otolaryngology 1972, bd. dirs. 1988-91, established Neel Disting. Rsch. Lectureship Endowment Fund 1994, audit com. 1998-2000, chair investment adv. com. 1995—, chmn. audit com. 1999-2000), Minn. Med. Assn. (com. on adminstrn. and fin. 2003—, Pub. Svc. Achievement award 2003), Zumbro Valley Med. Soc., Am. Broncho-Esophagological Assn. (pres.-elect 1988, pres. 1989-90), Am. Laryngological, Rhinological and Oto. Soc. (Mosher award 1980, pres.-elect 1995-96, centennial pres. 1996-97, investment com. 1994—, historian, 2001—), Am. Laryngological Assn. (Casselberry award 1985, sec. 1988-93, v.p. 1994, pres. 1994—, Newcomb award 1996, Baker lectr. 1998), Assn. for Rsch. in Otolaryngology, Assn. Acad. Depts. in Otolaryngology (sec.-treas. 1984-86, pres.-elect 1986, pres. 1988-9), Alumni Assn. Cornell U. (Outstanding Alumni award 1985), Collegium ORL Amicitiae Sacrum (bd. dirs. 2000—), Am. Bd. Otolaryngology (bd. dirs. 1986—, treas. 1998—), Am Laryngol. Voice Rsch. and Edn. Found. (charter bd. dirs. 1996—), Rochester Golf and Country Club. Republican. Presbyterian. Home: 828 8th St SW Rochester MN 55902-6310 Office: Mayo Clinic 200 1st St SW Rochester MN 55905-0002

NEEL, JOHN DODD, cemetery executive; b. McKeesport, Pa., Aug. 7, 1923; s. Harry Campbell and Anna (Dodd) N.; m. Jean Wyatt, Feb. 11, 1948; children: Harry C., John Dodd II, W. Wyatt (dec.), Jeffrey J. BA, Pa. State U., 1946. From salesman to pres. Jefferson Meml. Park, Pitts., 1946-88, chmn. bd. dirs., 1988—; chmn. Jefferson Meml. Funeral Home. Former mem., and chmn now alt. Zoning Hearing Bd., Pleasant Hills, Pa., 1970—. Mem. adv. bd. Pa. State U., McKeesport; former mem. Pa. State Real Estate Commn. 1st lt. USAAF, 1943-45. Decorated Air medal with 4 clusters, D.F.C.; recipient George Washington cert. Freedom Found., 1974. Mem. Pa. Cemetery Fun. Assn. (pres. 1963-65), Internat. Cemetery and Funeral Assn. (pres. 1973-74), West Jefferson Hills C. of C. (pres. 1984), VFW, Am. Legion 57th Bomb Wing Assn., South Hills Country Club, Indian Lake Golf Club, Aero Club, OX-5CLUB, Kiwanis (pres. 1959), Masons, Shriners, Tau Kappa Epsilon, Delta Sigma Pi. Presbyterian. Office: 401 Curry Hollow Rd Pittsburgh PA 15236-4636 Office Phone: 412-655-4500.

NEEL, JUDY MURPHY, association executive; b. Rhome, Tex. d. James W. and Linna B. (Vess) Neel; m. Ellis F. Murphy, Jr., Dec. 30, 1975; children from previous marriage: Mary B. Schmidt, Janet E. Hollingsworth, Susan E. Salinas. BS, Northwestern U., 1977; MBA, Roosevelt U., 1983. V.p. Murphy, Tashjian & Assocs., Chgo., 1960-73; exec. dir. Automotive Affiliated Rep. Assn., Chgo., 1973-78; mgr. Automotive Svc. Ind. Assn., Chgo., 1978-80; exec. dir. Am. Soc. Safety Engrs., Des Plaines, Ill., 1980-98, Am. Assn. Diabetes Educators, 1999—2003. Recipient Assn. Leadership Award Bus. Women's Network/Assn. Trends Mag., 1998. Mem. Chgo. Soc. Assn. Execs. (bd. dirs. 1979—, pres. 1985—, Shapiro award 1991), Am. Soc. Assn. Execs. (sec.-treas. 1994, found. dir. 1986-90, bd. dirs. 1990-95, Key award 1986). Republican.

NEEL, RICHARD EUGENE, economics and business educator; b. Bluefield, Va., Jan. 7, 1932; s. Charles Richard and Zell LaVerne (Bowling) Neel; m. Binnie Jo LeFever, June 10, 1961; children: Jeffrey Richard, Cynthia Jo. BS, U. Tenn., 1954, MS, 1955; PhD, Ohio State U., 1960. Instr. econs. Ohio State U., 1958-60; asst. prof. econs. Coll. William and Mary, 1960-61; asst. prof. U. South Fla., 1961-63, assoc. prof., 1963-66, chmn. econs. and fin. programs, 1964-66, acting chmn. grad. program Coll. Bus Adminstrn., 1965-66; dir. instl. planning Fla. Tech. U., 1966-68, chmn. dept. econs., prof. econs., 1968-69; assoc. dean Sch. Bus. Adminstrn. Ga. State U., 1969-77, dean grad. studies Sch. Bus. Adminstrn., 1973-77, prof. econs. Sch. Bus. Adminstrn., 1969-78; dean Coll. Bus. Adminstrn. U. N.C., Charlotte, 1978-93, prof. econs., 1978-97, dean emeritus Belk Coll. Bus. Adminstrn., 1997—, prof. econs. emeritus, 1997—. Author (contbg auth): (book) The Case Study of Off-Campus Postsecondary Education on Military Bases, 1980; contbr. articles, monographs to profl publs; editor: (book) Readings in Price Theory, 1973. Bd dirs Charlotte Foreign Trade Zone. Mem.: Beta Gamma Sigma, Phi Kappa Phi. Presbyterian. Office: U NC at Charlotte Dept Economics Charlotte NC 28223 Office Phone: 704-687-4122. Business E-Mail: reneel@email.uncc.edu.

NEEL, SPURGEON HART, JR., physician, retired army officer; b. Memphis, Sept. 24, 1919; s. Spurgeon Hart and Pyrle (Womble) N.; m. Alice Glidewell Torti, Nov. 18, 1939; children: Spurgeon Hart III, Alice Leah Neel Zartarian. Student pre-med., Memphis State U., 1939; MD, U. Tenn., 1942; MPH, Harvard U., 1958; MSBA, George Washington U., 1965. Diplomate: Am. Bd. Preventive Medicine. Intern Meth. Hosp., Memphis, 1943; resident x-ray Santa Ana (Calif.) AFB, 1944; resident aviation medicine USAF Sch. Aerospace Medicine, 1960; commd. 2d lt. U.S. Army, 1942, advanced through grades to maj. gen., 1970; various assignments U.S., 1943-44, 47-48, WWII European Theater, ETO, 1944-47; chief surgeon service Ft. McPherson, Ga., 1949; med. service Ft. McPherson Army Hosp., Ft. McPherson, Ga., 1949; div. surgeon (82d Airborne Div.), Ft. Bragg, NC, 1949-51; comdr. (30th Med. Group), Korea, 1953-54; dep. dir. div. physiology and pharmacology (WRAIR, WRAMC), 1956; chief aviation br. (OTSG), 1957; chief aviation medicine Ft. Rucker, Ala., 1960; comdg. officer U.S. Army Hosp., post surgeon, 1961-64; stationed in Vietnam, 1965-66, 68-69; dep. surgeon gen. U.S. Army, Washington, 1969-73; comdr. (U.S. Army Health Services Command), 1973-77. Clin. assoc. prof. family practice U. Tex. Health Sci. Ctr., San Antonio, now prof. emeritus occupl. and aerospace medicine U. Tex. Sch. Pub. Health; med. cons. U.S. Automobile Assn., other industries, San Antonio. Contbr. articles med. jours. Decorated D.S.M. with oak leaf cluster, Legion of Merit with 4 clusters, Bronze Star with oak leaf cluster, Air medal with 3 oak leaf clusters, Joint Service Commendation medal, USAF Commendation medal, Purple Heart, others.; recipient Seaman award Assn. Mil. Surgeons U.S., 1950, Gary Wratten award, 1967; McClelland award Army Aviation Assn. Am., 1962; named to U.S. Army Aviation Hall Fame, 1976; recipient Lyster award Aerospace Med. Assn., 1977, Nat. Soc. DAR medal of honor, 1999. Fellow ACP, Am. Coll. Preventive Medicine (past v.p.), Royal Soc. Health, Aerospace Med. Assn. (past pres., Louis H. Bauer Founders award 2003), Internat. Acad. Aviation and Space Medicine, Am. Acad. Med. Adminstrs., Am. Coll. Health Care Execs.; mem. AMA (past-sec. sect. mil. medicine), Assn. Mil. Surgeons U.S., Assn. U.S. Army, Army Aviation Assn. Am., Dustoff (Hall of Fame 2001), Phi Chi (assoc.). Home: 4106 Tarlac Dr San Antonio TX 78239-3072

NEELEMAN, DAVID, air transportation executive; b. 1959; m. Vicki Neeleman; 9 children. Student, U. Utah. With Southwest Airlines; exec. v.p. Morris Air Corp., 1984—88, co-founer, pres., 1988—94; CEO Open Skies, 1995—98; co-founder WestJet; CEO JetBlue Airways Corp., Forest Hills, NY, 1998—, also bd. dirs. Named Travel Industry Innovator, Time mag., 2000; named one of Top Ten Entrepreneurs of 2000, Bus. Week Mag., Most Influential Bus. Travel Execs., Bus. Travel News, 2000. Office: JetBlue Airways Corp 118-29 Queens Blvd Forest Hills NY 11415

NEELEY, BEVERLY EVON, sociologist, consultant; b. Oakland, Calif., June 14, 1947; d. Chester Arthur Neeley Jr. and Thalia Evon Littlefield; m. Niles Bruce, Sept. 13, 1970 (div. Aug. 1977); children: Autumn Yvonne, Bruce Curd, Thalia Evon Neeley-Littlefield. BA, U. Calif., Berkeley, 1970, MPH, 1972; PhD, U. Calif., San Diego, 1983. Eligibility supr. W. Oakland Health Ctr., 1970-72; health edn. supr. San Diego County Drug Edn., 1972-74; proposal writer, cons. Cmty. Crisis Ctr., San Diego, 1974-77; sociologist, dir., sec., treas. Image Mind, Inc., Oakland, 1993—. Instr. Calif. State U., San Diego, 1976; health planner Health Sys. Agy., San Diego, 1978; mem. adv. bd. Help Other People Evole Inst., Oakland, 2000—; sr. acad. cons. Hercules NAACP Saturday Sch., 2002; tchrs., rschr. Oakland Pub. Schs., 1983—. Author: The Ethiopian Grail, 1994, Ancient Ethiopian Egyptian Cultural Excellence, 2003. Founder S.E. Drug Coalition, San Diego, 1974, Nu-Way Youth Svc. Ctr., San Diego, 1976. Mem. NAACP, Sojourner Truth Tenants Assn. Avocations: reading, walking, cooking. Home and Office: 5915 Martin Luther King Jr Way B10 Oakland CA 94609 E-mail: drbneeley3@hotmail.com.

NEELEY, DELMAR GEORGE, mediator, pastoral counselor; b. Charleston, Ill., June 4, 1937; s. Glenn Truman and Gladys Bernice (Dittman) N.; m. Terry Anne Barbour, Aug. 28, 1971; children: Robert James, Stephen Edward. BA in Philosophy, Olivet Nazarene U., 1965, MA in Bibl. Lit., 1969; EdD, U. Sarasota, 1996. Cert.: Fla. Bar Assn. (mediator); cert. clinical paster, cert. profl. corp. chaplain. Mgr. mgmt. devel. Rauland Divsn. Zenith Corp., Chgo., 1967-70; sr. personnel cons. Mid. West Svc. Co., Chgo., 1971-73; dir. human resources Nichols-Homeshield Inc., West Chicago, Ill., 1974-76, Gould Inc./Ind. Battery Divsn., Langhorne, Pa., 1976-81; pres., owner Barbour-Neeley Inc., Sarasota, Fla., 1982-91. Stephen Ministries leader. Min. of Visitation United Ch. of Christ. Recipient Meritorious Svc. award Chgo. Boys Club, 1970, Svc. award Chgo. Jaycees, 1967-71. Mem.: Nat. Conservative Christian Ch. (ordained min. pastoral counseling), Fla. Assn. Christian Counselors (cert.), Fla. Acad. Profl. Mediators, Fla. Assn. Profl. Chaplains, Nat. Christian Counselors Assn. United Ch. Of Christ. Home: 3778 Bonaventure Ct Sarasota FL 34243-4862

NEELEY, JAMES KAME, credit agency executive; b. Visalia, Calif., Dec. 4, 1955; s. James M. and Dorothy Neeley; m. Lynn Travioli, Aug. 13, 1977; children: Janessa, Jimmy. BS in Bus. Adminstrn., Calif. State U., Fresno, 1978. Lic. personal property appraiser. Loan officer Visalia Prodn. Credit Assn., Tipton, Calif., 1978-82; asst. br. mgr. Visalia (Calif.) Prodn. Credit Assn., 1982-83; v.p., br. mgr. Valley Prodn. Credit Assn., Visalia, 1983-91, FarmCreditWest, Visalia, 1991—2003; v.p. Capitol Markets Farm Credit West, 2003—. Advisor Redwood Future Farmers of Am., Visalia, 1988-90; advisor computer software devel. Western Farm Credit Bank, Sacramento, 1990-91; mem., advisor Kit Fox Adv. Com., Visalia, 1995-96. Mem. Ctrl. Dem. Com., Visalia, 1975-77; soccer coach Am. Youth Soccer Orgn., Tulare, Calif., 1990-96, 99; coach Tulare Little League, 1996-97; parent vol. St. Alyosios Sch., Tulare, 1993-96; mem. coun. on fin., head audit com. Calif./Nev. United Meth., 1990-96; layleader Tulare United Meth. Ch., 1994-96, mem. adminstrv. bd., 1996-97. Scholar So. Calif. Edn., 1974. Mem. Tulare Host Lions Club (pres. 1982-83, ag leader alumni com. 1999—), Phi Kappa Phi. Avocations: collecting old and rare books, soccer, basketball, skiing. Office: FarmCreditWest PO Box 4379 Visalia CA 93278-4379 E-mail: james.neeley@farmcreditwest.com.

NEELEY, STEVEN G. lawyer, educator, psychotherapist; s. G.W. and Mildred Neeley. BS, Xavier Univ., Ohio, 1980; JD, Univ. Cin. Coll.; MA, Univ. Cin., Cin., 1987, PhD, 1989. Law clk. Law Offices of T.D. Shackleford, Ohio, 1982—84; adj. prof. Union Inst., 1989; vis. asst. prof. Xavier Univ., Ohio, 1989—92; atty. pvt. practice, Loretto, Pa., 1985—; adj. prof. Coll. Mt. St. Joseph, 1992—93; philol. psychotherapist pvt. practice, Loretto, Pa., 1997—; prof. St. Francis Univ., Loretto, Pa., 1997—. Assoc. editor Contemporary Philosophy; mem. Pre law Adv. Bd. St. Francis, 1999; advisor Philosophy Club St. Francis. Author: The Constitutional Right to Suicide, 1994, Schopenhauer: A Consistant Reading, 2003. Mem.: A.P.A. Sarte Cir., AMINTAPHIL, Am. Philol. Assn. (Excellence in Tchg. 1998).

NEELEY, VERNON DEAN, music educator; b. Lima, Ohio, Feb. 6, 1970; s. Robert Lee Mosley and Coleen Elva Neeley; m. Stacey Renee Ward, June 29, 1996. MusB in Performance, Ohio No. U., 1993; MusM in Performance, U. Toledo, 2001. Lectr. music and applied saxophone Ohio No. U., Ada, 1997—. Tenor saxophonist Hepcat Revival, Toledo, 2000—. Scholar, U. Toledo, 1999—2001. Mem.: North Am. Saxophone Alliance, Tau Beta Sigma (Dist. Svc. award), Theta Chi. Avocations: performing, golf, travel. Home: 530 N Main Street Ada OH 45810 Office: Ohio Northern Univ 525 S Main St Ada OH 45810 Personal E-mail: vsneeley@earthlink.net. E-mail: v-neeley@onu.edu.

NEELIN, J. DAVID, meteorologist, educator; arrived in U.S., 1983; BS with honors, U. Toronto, 1981, MS, 1983; PhD, Princeton U., N.J., 1987. Postdoctoral assoc. MIT, Cambridge, Mass., 1987—88, vis. assoc. prof., 1994—95; asst. prof. UCLA, 1988—92, assoc. prof., 1992—95, prof., 1995—. Mem. Inst. Geophysics and Planetary Physics, L.A., 1996—; assoc. editor Jour. of Climate, Boston, 1996—. Contbr. articles to profl. jours. Recipient Presdl. Young Investigator Award, 1991—96, Spl. Creativity Award, NSF, 1999—2000, C. L. Meisinger Award, Am. Meteorol. Soc., 1996; fellow, 2002. Fellow: Royal Meteorol. Soc.; mem.: AAAS, Can. Meteorol. and Oceanog. Soc., Am. Geophys. Union. Office: UCLA 7127 Math Sci Bldg 405 Hilgard Ave Los Angeles CA 90090-1565

NEELY, CAMERON MICHAEL, former professional hockey player; b. Comox, B.C., Can., June 6, 1965; Hockey player Vancouver Canucks, 1983-86, Boston Bruins, 1986-96. Player NHL All-Star Game, 1988-91. Recipient Bill Masterton Meml. trophy, 1993-94; named to Sporting News All-Star Team, 1987-88, 93-94. Office: Cam Neely Found Neely House 30 Winter St Ste 2D Boston MA 02108-4720

NEELY, CHARLES B., JR., lawyer; b. Raleigh, N.C., Dec. 11, 1943; AB with honors, U. N.C., 1965; JD, Duke U., 1970. Bar: N.C. 1970. Lawyer Maupin Taylor P.A., Raleigh. Mem. 4th Cir. Jud. Conf. Mem. N.C. Ho. of Reps., 1995-99. Capt. USNR, JAGC, 1965-89. Fellow Am. Bar Found.; mem. ABA (taxation sect.), N.C. Bar Assn. (chmn. law office mgmt. sect. 1986-88, bd. govs. 1995-98), Inst. for Profls. in Taxation. Address: Maupin Taylor PA PO Drawer 19764 Ste 500 3200 Beechleaf Ct Raleigh NC 27619 E-mail: cneely@maupintaylor.com.

NEELY, JOHN GAIL, otolaryngologist; b. Oklahoma City, Dec. 10, 1939; MD, U. Okla., 1965. Intern U. Oreg. Med. Ctr., Portland, 1965-66; resident in surgery Baylor Hosp., Houston, 1968-69, resident in otolaryngology, 1969-72; fellow Otologic Med. Group, L.A., 1972-73; staff Barnes Hosp., St. Louis, 1992—, Jewish Hosp., St. Louis, 1992—; prof., dir. rsch. Washington U., St. Louis, 1992—. Mem. ACS, Am. Neurotology Soc., Am. Otol. Soc., Am. Acad. Otolaryngology, Head and Neck Surgery, Soc. Univ. Otolaryngologists, Triologic Soc. Office: Washington U Sch Medicine Dept Oto Head-Neck Surgrey 660 S Euclid Ave Rm 8115 Saint Louis MO 63110-1010 Office Phone: 314-362-7344. Business E-Mail: neelyg@ent.wustl.edu.

NEELY, RICHARD, lawyer; b. Aug. 2, 1941; s. John Champ and Elinore (Forlani) N.; m. Carolyn Elaine Elmore, 1979; children: John Champ, Charles Whittaker. AB, Dartmouth Coll., 1964; LLB, Yale U., 1967. Bar: W.Va. 1967. Practiced in, Fairmont, W.Va., 1969-73; chmn. Marion County Bd. Pub. Health, 1971-72; mem. W.Va. Ho. of Dels., 1971-73; justice, chief justice W.Va. Supreme Ct. of Appeals, Charleston, 1973-95; ptnr. Neely & Hunter, Charleston, 1995—. Chmn. bd. Kane & Keyser Co., Belington, W.Va., 1970-88. Author: How Courts Govern America, 1980, Why Courts Don't Work, 1983, The Divorce Decision, 1984, Judicial Jeopardy: When Business Collides with the Courts, 1986, The Product Liability Mess: How Business Can Be Rescued from State Court Politics, 1988, Take Back Your Neighborhood: A Case for Modern-Day Vigilantism, 1990, Tragedies of our Own Making: How Private Choices have Created Public Bankruptcy, 1994; contbr. articles to nat. mags. Mem. bd. advisors BNA Class Action Litigation Report. Capt. U.S. Army, 1967-69. Decorated Bronze Star, Vietnam Honor medal 1st Class. Mem.: Am. Legion, VFW, Internat. Brotherhood Elec. Workers, W.Va. Bar Assn., Fourth Cir. Jud. Conf. (life), Moose, Phi Sigma Kappa, Phi Delta Phi. Episcopalian. Office: Neely & Hunter 159 Summers St Charleston WV 25301-2134 Office Phone: 304-343-6500. E-mail: rneely@neelyhunter.com.

NEELY, ROBERT ALLEN, retired ophthalmologist; b. Temple, Tex., Mar. 1, 1921; s. Jubal A. and Almeida (Fordtran) N.; m. Eleanor V. Stein, June 29, 1944 (dec.); m. Joy S. Brown, Aug. 24, 1990; children: Byron D., Warren F. BA, U. Tex., 1942, MD, 1944; postgrad., Washington U., St. Louis, 1951-52. Intern, then resident Hermann Hosp., Houston, 1944-45, 55-57; gen. practice medicine, 1946—51; specializing in ophthalmology, 1955—92; ret., 1992. Trustee, staff mem. Bellville Hosp., Inc.; pres. Mid-Tex. Nursing Homes, Inc.; ret., 1992. Mem. Bellville Ind. Sch. Dist. Sch. Bd., 1948-53; past pres. Bellville Area United Fund; mem. adv. bd. Sam Houston Area coun. Boy Scouts Am., also past mem. Nat. coun.; mem. chancellor's coun. U. Tex. Sys.; pres. Bellville Econ. Devel. Corp., 2000-01. With USNR, 1943-46, 53-55. Recipient Silver Beaver award Boy Scouts Am. Fellow Am. Acad. Ophthalmology; mem. AMA, Austin-Grimes-Waller Counties Med. Soc. (past pres.), 9th Dist. Med. Soc. (psst pres.), Tex. Med. Assn., Tex. Ophthal. Assn., Tex. Soc. Ophthalmology and Otolaryngology, Belleville C. of C., Littlefield Soc. (U. Tex., Austin), VFW, Bellville Golf Club (past pres.), Doctors Club, LIons (past pres.). Republican. Lutheran. Home: 105 E Hacienda St Bellville TX 77418-3103

NEELY, SALLY SCHULTZ, lawyer; b. L.A., Mar. 2, 1948; BA, Stanford U., 1970, JD, 1971. Bar: Ariz. 1972, Calif. 1977. Law clk. to judge U.S. Ct. Appeals (9th cir.), Phoenix, 1971-72; assoc. Lewis and Roca, Phoenix, 1972-75; asst. prof. Law Sch. Harvard U., Cambridge, Mass., 1975-77; assoc. Shutan & Trost, P.C., L.A., 1977-79; ptnr., sr. counsel Sidley & Austin, L.A., 1980—. Co-chair Am. Law Inst.-ABA Chpt. 11 Bus. Reorgns., 1989-95, 97—, Banking and Comml. Lending Law, 1997-99, Nat. Conf. Bankruptcy Judges, 1988, 90, 95, 96, 97, 99, 2002, Fed. Jud. Ctr., 1989, 90, 94-95, Southeast Bankruptcy Law Inst., 2002, Workshop Bankruptcy and Bus. Reorgn. NYU, 1992—; rep. 9th cir. jud. conf., 1989-91; mem. Nat. Bankruptcy Conf., 1993—, chair com. on legislation, 2001—, mem. exec. com. Chair Stanford U. Law Sch. Reunion Giving, 1996; bd. vis. Stanford U. Law Sch., 1990-92. Mem.: ABA, Calif. Bar Assn., Am. Coll. Bankruptcy (mem. bd. regents 1998—2003, chair ednl. programs com. 2003—, bd. dirs. 2003—). Office: Sidley Austin Brown & Wood LLP 555 W 5th St Ste 4000 Los Angeles CA 90013-3000 Office Phone: 213-896-6024. E-mail: sneely@sidley.com.

NEELY, WILLIAM CHARLES, chemistry educator, consultant, research scientist; b. Cave City, Ark., Nov. 22, 1931; s. Kenneth Andrew and Sara Virginia Neely; m. Betty Jean Tibi, Dec. 7, 1956; children: Virginia Stringfellow, William(dec.). D, La. State U., 1962. Rsch. chemist Chemstrand Rsch. Ctr. Inc., Research Triangle Park, NC, 1962—66; prof. Auburn (Ala.) U., 1962—. Cons. Auburn Chem. Co. Inc., 1986—, Sci. Applications Internat., San Diego, 1995—. Contbr. articles to profl. jours.; inventor in field. Chmn. Bd. Zoning Adjustment, Auburn, 1986—96. Served with U.S. Army, 1955—66, Germany. Mem.: Sigma Xi (life). Home: 415 Hare Ave Auburn AL 36830 Office: Auburn U Dept Chemistry 257 Chemistry Bldg Auburn AL 36849 E-mail: neelywc@auburn.edu.

NEENAN, PETER ANTHONY, state agency administrator; b. Sioux City, Iowa, Dec. 12, 1946; s. Edward W. and Margaret B. Neenan; m. Linda J. Fisher, Feb. 5, 1947. BA, Creighton U., 1969; MA, U. Iowa, 1972; PhD, U. Wis., 1982. Asst. prof. Simmons Coll., Boston, 1978—82, U. of NC, Chapel Hill, 1982—86, sr. rsch. assoc., 1987—97; rsch. scientist Rsch. Triangle Inst., Research Triangle Park, NC, 2000—01; dir., labor market info. Employment Security Commn. of NC, Raleigh, 2002—. Contbr. articles to profl. jours. Precinct chair Dem. Party of NC, 1985—86. Mem.: ALA, Nat. Assn. State Workforce Agys., Nat. Assn. Welfare Rsch. and Stats., Am. Assn. Pub. Opinion Rsch., Am. Evaluation Assn. (co-chair human services tig 2001—02). Democrat. Roman Catholic. Avocations: travel, history, stamp collecting/philately. Office: Employment Security Commission of North 700 Wade Ave Raleigh NC 27611

NEER, CHARLES SUMNER, II, orthopedic surgeon, educator; b. Vinita, Okla., Nov. 10, 1917; s. Charles Sumner and Pearl Victoria (Brooke) N.; m. Eileen Meyer, June 12, 1990; children: Charlotte Marguerite, Sydney Victoria, Charles Henry. BA, Dartmouth Coll., 1939; MD, U. Pa., 1942. Diplomate Am. Bd. Orthopaedic Surgery (bd. dirs. 1970-75). Intern U. Pa. Hosp., Phila., 1942-43; asso. in surgery N.Y. Orthopedic-Columbia-Presbyn. Med. Center, N.Y.C., 1943-44; instr. in surgery Coll. Physicians and Surgeons, Columbia U., N.Y.C., 1946-47, instr. orthopaedic surgery, 1947-57, asst. prof. clin. orthopaedic surgery, 1957-64, asso. prof., 1964-68, prof. clin. orthopaedic surgery, 1968-90, prof. clin. orthopaedic surgery emeritus, spl. lectr. orthopaedic surgery, 1990—. Attending orthopaedic surgeon Columbia-Presbyn. Med. Ctr., N.Y.C.; chief adult reconstructive svc. N.Y. Orthopaedic Hosp.; chief shoulder and elbow clinic Presbyn. Hosp.; cons. orthopaedic surgeon emeritus N.Y. Orthopaedic-Columbia-Presbyn. Med. Ctr., 1991—; chmn. 4th Internat. Congress Shoulder Surgeons; chmn. Internat. Bd. Shoulder Surgery, 1992—. Founder, chmn. bd. trustees Jour. Shoulder and Elbow Surgery, 1990—; contbr. articles to books, tech. films, sound slides. Served with U.S. Army, 1944-46. Recipient Disting. Svc. award Am. Bd. Orthopaedic Surgeons 1975. Fellow ACS (sr. mem. nat. com. on trauma), Am. Acad. Orthop. Surgeons (com. on upper extremity, shoulder com.); mem. AMA, ACS (mem. com. trauma), Am. Bd. Orthop. Surgeons (bd. dirs. 1970-75, Disting. Svc. award 1975), Am. Shoulder and Elbow Surgeons (inaugural pres.), Am. Assn. Surgery Trauma, Am. Orthop. Assn., Mid-Am. Orthop. Assn. (hon.), N.Y. Acad. Medicine, Allen O. Whipple Surg. Soc., N.Y. State Med. Soc., N.Y.

County Med. Soc., Pan Am. Med. Assn., Am. Trauma Soc., Soc. Latino Am. Orthop. y Traumatology, Internat. Soc. Orthop. Surgery and Traumatology, Va. Orthop. Soc. (hon.), Carolina Orthop. Alumni Assn. (hon.), Conn. Orthop. Club (hon.), Houston Orthop. Assn. (hon.), Soc. Française de Chirurgie Orthop. et Traumatology (hon.), Soc. Italiana Orthop. Etravmatologia e Traumatologia; patron, Shoulder and Elbow Soc. Australia, South African Shoulder Soc., Giraffe Club, Internat. Bd. Shoulder Surgery (chmn. 1992—), Alpha Omega Alpha, Phi Chi. Home and Office: 231 S Miller St Vinita OK 74301-3625 E-mail: elmcreekacres@junct.com. *Forever grateful I could be a doctor and especially to work in the exciting area of shoulder surgery.*

NEESON, LIAM, actor; b. Ballymena, No. Ireland, June 7, 1952; s. Barney and Kitty N.; m. Natasha Richardson, July 3, 1994; children: Michael Richard Antonio, Daniel Jack. Theatrical appearances include (Broadway) The Judas Kiss, 1998, Anna Christie, 1993 (Theatre World award, 1993); films include Excalibur, 1981, Krull, 1983, The Bounty, 1984, The Innocent, 1984, Lamb, 1986, Duet for One, 1986, The Mission, 1986, A Prayer for the Dying, 1987, Suspect, 1987, Satisfaction, 1988, The Good Mother, 1988, Next of Kin, 1989, Darkman, 1990, Crossing the Line, 1990, Ruby Cairo, 1991, Shining Through, 1992, Under Suspicion, 1992, Husbands and Wives, 1992, Leap of Faith, 1992, Ethan Fromme, 1992, Schindler's List, 1993 (Best Actor Acad. award nominee 1994), Nell, 1994, Rob Roy, 1995, Before and After, 1996, Michael Collins, 1996, Les Miserables, 1998, Star Wars: Episode I-The Phantom Menace, 1999, The Haunting, 1999, Gun Shy, 2000, K-19: The Widowmaker, 2002, Gangs of New York, 2002, Love Actually, 2003. Officer of the Order of the British Empire, 1999. Office: ICM 8942 Wilshire Blvd # D Beverly Hills CA 90211-1934 also: Ed Limato ICM 8942 Wilshire Blvd Beverly Hills CA 90211*

NEEWOOR, ANUND PRIYAY, ambassador; b. Mauritius, June 26, 1940; married; 3 children. BA in English with honors, Delhi U.; attended, Makerere U., Uganda, UN Inst. Tng. and Rsch. Tchr., prin. secondary sch.; in charge UN affairs, West Asia Fgn. Ministry, Mauritius, 1970-73; served Mauritius High Commn., London; 1st sec. Mauritian Embassy, New Delhi, min. counselor Washington, 1982; high commr. for Mauritius India, Sri Lanka, Bangladesh, 1983-93; amb. to Russia, Myanmar, Nepal, Thailand, 1983-93; amb. to U.S Govt. of the Rep. of Mauritius, Washington, 1993—; sec. fgn. affairs Govt. of Mauritius, 1996-98; amb., permanent rep. to UN, 1999—. Fellow Carnegie Endowment for Internat. Peace. Office: Permanent Mission of Mauritius to UN 211 E 43rd St Fl 15 New York NY 10017-4707 Home: Apt 108 7420 Lakeview Dr Bethesda MD 20817-6450

NEFF, A. GUY, lawyer; b. Calcutta, India, Mar. 24, 1951; BA, Vanderbilt U., 1972; JD, U. Fla., 1975. Bar: Fla. 1975. Lawyer Holland & Knight, LLP, Orlando, Fla. Mem. ABA, Fla. Bar Assn., Phi Delta Phi (magister 1975). Office: Holland & Knight LLP 200 S Orange Ave Ste 2600 Orlando FL 32801-3453

NEFF, BONITA DOSTAL, communication development facilitator; b. Grinnell, Iowa, Aug. 16, 1942; d. Lester Ernest and Mary Margaret (Hudnut) Dostal; m. Gregory Pall Neff, Apr. 27, 1974; 1 child, Kristiana. BA, U. N. Iowa, 1964, MA, 1966; PhD, U. Mich., 1973; AA cum laude, Lansing (Mich.) C.C., 1980. Edn. leadership fellow George Washington U., Washington, 1976-77; specialist Mich. State U., East Lansing, 1977-80, co-investigator family and child inst. energy rsch. team, 1980-82; asst. prof. comm. Purdue U., Hammond, Ind., 1982-87; pres. Pub. Comm. Assocs., Munster, Ind., 1986—; assoc. prof. comm. Valparaiso (Ind.) U., 1991—. Co-organizer European Comm. Conf., Dubrovnik, Croatia, 2002—; vis. prof. grad. comm. program U. Kadar, Croatia, 2003; co-founding mem. Internat. Interdisciplinary and Intercultural Annual Conf. in Pub. Rels.; presenter, cons. in field. Mem. adv. bd., reviewer Jour. Applied Comm. Rsch.; mem. editl. bd. Jour. Promotional Mgmt., Jour. Pub. Rels. Rsch., on-line jour. multicultural comm. from Cyprus; reviewer Mgmt. Comm. Quar.: An Internat. Jour.; editor procs. on accreditation for nat. conf.; contbr. chpts. in books, profl. articles and poetry to jours. Mem. Nat. Steering Commn. for Revision of Pub. Rels. Curriculum, 1996—; chair nat. benchmark study on pub. rels. edn.; mem. Nat. Task Force Pub. Rels. Conf. 1998; mem. Lake County (Ind.) Cmty. Devel. Bd., 1984—; bd. dirs. Big Bros. and Big Sisters N.W. Ind., 1984, 87; pres., chmn. bd. dirs. N.W. Ind. Youth Chorus, 1985—; bd. dirs., mem. mktg. com. N.W. Ind. Symphony, bd. dirs. PBS56-Ind., sec. exec. com., 2000—. Faculty rsch. grantee U. Mich., 1971, Consumer Product Safety Coun. grantee, 1976-77, Ind. Arts Commn./Nat. Endowment for Arts grantee, 1990-92, Valparaiso U. Diversity grantee, 1996; recipient top rsch. honors regional confs. Mem.: Nat. Commn. on Undergrad. and Grad. Pub. Rels. Curriculum (nat. task force for conf. 1998), Pub. Rels. Soc. Am. (advisor 2001, established student chpt.), Internat. Acad. Bus. Disciplines (co-chair pub. rels. divsn.), World Comm. Assn., Assn. Educators in Journalism Mass Comm. (chair internat. com. 1994—96, scholarly liaison com. 1995—), Ctrl. States Comm. Assn. (founder and chmn. 1988—89, pub. rels. officer 1989—92), Nat. Comm. Assn. (founder and twice chair of pub. rels. divsn. 1988, chmn. nat. Pub. Rels. Rsch. awards com. PRIDE 1988, nat. legis. coun. rep. 1993—, nat. com. on convs. allied orgns., task force on nat. policy), Internat. Pub. Rels. Assn., Internat. Comm. Assn. (chmn. task force on accreditation 1988, newsletter editor 1997, chair planning pub. rels. divsn. internat. conf. South Korea, chair dissertation thesis award com. pub. rels. divsn.), Assn. Women in Comm. (assoc.; pres. Calumet chpt. 1985—90, advisor Valparaiso Student AWC, Inc. 1994—, Outstanding Communicator 1990, Nat. Outstanding chpt. advisor 1999). Democrat. Roman Catholic. Avocations: ballet, tap, piano, reading, professional clown. Home: 8320 Greenwood Ave Munster IN 46321-1813 Office: Pub Comm Assocs 8320 Greenwood Ave Munster IN 46321-1813 Office Phone: 219-464-6827. E-mail: bonita.neff@valpo.edu.

NEFF, CAROLE CUKELL, lawyer; b. Geneva, N.Y., Aug. 3, 1951; d. Samuel and Hannah (Schoenfeld) C.; m. Richard Theodore Neff, Dec. 28, 1976; children: Alex Ryan, Hilary Shayna. BS magna cum laude, SUNY, Buffalo, 1973; JD, Tulane U., 1977. Bar: La. 1977. Law clk. La. State Supreme Ct., New Orleans, 1977—78; assoc. Session & Fishman, New Orleans, 1978—83; ptnr. Session, Fishman & Nathan, LLP, New Orleans, 1983—. Co-author: (with Max Nathan) Louisiana Estate Planning, Will Drafting and Estate Administration 2nd ed., 2000; mem. bd. editors Tulane U. Law Rev. Bd. dirs., 1st v.p., sec., chmn. devel. com. Jewish Endowment Found., New Orleans, 1983—. Named Achiever, Am. Coun. for Career Women, 1990, Woman of Yr., New Orleans Bus. and Profl. Women, 1991, YWCA Role Model, 1992; recipient Young Family award for profl. excellence Jewish Endowment Found., 1999. Fellow Am. Coll. Trust and Estate Counsel; mem. NCJW, La. Bar Assn., New Orleans Bar Assn. (CLE chair 1987-89, 3d v.p. 1989-90, probate chair 1991-2000), Women's Profl. Coun. (bd. dirs., 1st v.p. 1989-90, pres. 1990-91), Profl. Fin. Planners of Greater New Orleans (sec. 1982-83, pres. 1983-84), New Orleans Estate Planning Coun. (pres. 2002-03), Order of Coif, Rotary Internat. (bd. dirs. 1994-96), Hadassah, Sisterhood Shir Chadesh (v.p. 2004—). Democrat. Jewish. Avocations: cooking, piano playing, travel. Office: Session Fishman & Nathan LLP 201 Saint Charles Ave Ste 3500 New Orleans LA 70170-3500 Office Phone: 504-582-1500. Business E-Mail: cneff@sessions-law.com.

NEFF, DONALD LLOYD, news correspondent, writer; b. York, Pa., Oct. 15, 1930; s. Harry William and Gertrude Marie N.; m. Abigail Trafford; 1 son, Gregory Harry. Student, Trinity Coll., San Antonio, 1949, York Coll., 1950-52, N.Y. U., 1953. Reporter York Dispatch, 1954-56, L.A. Mirror-News, 1956-57, UPI, L.A., 1957-61; with L.A. Times, 1961-64, bur. chief, 1964; with Time mag., 1965-81, corr., 1965-66, writer, 1966-68, bur. chief Houston, 1968-70, L.A., 1970-73, Jerusalem, 1975-78, N.Y.C., 1978-79, sr. editor, 1973-75; news svcs. editor Washington Star, 1979-80. Author: Warriors at Suez: Eisenhower Takes America into the Middle East, 1981, Warriors for Jerusalem, The Six Days That Changed the Middle East, 1984; Warriors Against Israel, 1988, Fallen Pillars; U.S. Policy Toward Palestine and Israel since 1945, 1995, 2d edit., 2002, Fifty Years of Israel, 1998. Served with AUS, 1948-50. Recipient Theta Sigma Phi Matrix award, 1962, Calif.-Nev. AP Writing Contest best met. spot news story award, 1962, Overseas Press Club award for best fgn. article in a mag., 1979; finalist Am. Book Award History category, 1982. Mem. Fgn. Press Assn. (Israel pres. 1977, v.p. 1978)

NEFF, FRED LEONARD, lawyer; b. St. Paul, Nov. 1, 1948; s. Elliott Ira and Mollie (Poboisk) N.; m. Christa Ruth Powell, Sept. 10, 1989; 1 child, Lena. BS with high distinction, U. Minn., 1970; JD, William Mitchell Coll. Law, 1976. Bar: Minn. 1976, N.D. 1994, U.S. Dist. Ct. Minn. 1977, U.S. Ct. Appeals (8th cir.) 1985, U.S. Supreme Ct. 1985, Wis. 1986, U.S. Dist. Ct. (ea. and we. dists.) Wis. 1992. Tchr. Hopkins (Minn.) Pub. Schs., 1970-72; instr. U. Minn., Mpls., 1974-76; pvt. practice Mpls., 1976-79; asst. county atty. Sibley County, Gaylord, Minn., 1979-80; mng. atty. Hyatt Legal Svcs., St. Paul, 1981-83, regional ptnr., 1983-85, profl. devel. ptnr., 1985-86; pres. Neff Law Firm, PA, Mpls., 1986—; CEO Profl. Devel. Inst. Inc., Edina, Minn., 1994—, also bd. dirs. Instr. Inver Hills Coll., 1973-77; counsel Am. Tool Supply Co., St. Paul, 1976-78; cons. Nat. Detective Agy., Inc., St. Paul, 1980-83; CEO A Basic Legal Svc., Bloomington, 1990—; CEO, bd. dirs. Profl. Devel. Inst., Inc., Edina, Minn., 1994—; lectr., guest instr. U. Wis., River Falls, 1976-77; spl. instr. Hamline U., St. Paul, 1977; vis. lectr. Coll. St. Scholastica, Duluth, Minn., 1977; program. faculty, cons. Employment Law Seminar for Colo., Fla., La., Oreg., Employment and Labor Law Seminar for Ala., Alaska, Calif., Conn., Ind., N.C., Ohio, Va., N.C. Safety and Health at the Workplace, S.C. Labor Law, Ohio Safety at the Workplace; bd. dirs. Acceptance Ins. Holdings, Inc., Omaha; active Internat. Confederation Jurists, 1993; mem. faculty sem. Ariz. Safety at Workplace, Hawaii Employment & Labor, Miss. Employment & Labor Law, Del. Employment & Labor, Alaska Employment and Labor Law, Ga. Employment & Labor Law, N.J. Employment & Labor, Wash. Employment Law, Mass. Employment & Labor Law, 1995—, Ark. Employment and Labor Law, Mo. Employment and Labor Law, Iowa Employment and Labor Law, Utah Employment and Labor Law; pres. Martial Arts Bookstore Internat., Inc., 1998; pres. Endless Fist Soc., Inc., 1998. Author: Fred Neff's Self-Defense Library, 1976, Everybody's Self-Defense Book, 1978, Karate Is for Me, 1980, Running Is for Me, 1980, Lessons from the Samurai, 1986, Lessons from the Art of Kempo, 1986, Lessons from the Western Warriors, 1986, Lessons from the Fighting Commandos, 1990, Lessons from the Ancient Japanese Masters of Self-Defense, 1990, Lessons from the Eastern Warrors, 1990, Mysterious Persons of the Past, 1991, Great Mysteries of Crime, 1991; host TV series Great Puzzles In History; co-host TV series Great Unsolved Crimes, Minn.; asst. editor: Hennepic County Lawyer, 1992—. Advisor to bd. Sibley County Commrs., 1979-80; speaker civic groups, 1976-82; mem. Hennepin County Juvenile Justice Panel, 1980-82, Hennepin County (Minn.) Pub. Def. Conflict Panel, 1980-82, 86—, Hennepin County Bar Assn. Advice Panel Law Day, 1987, mem. dist. ethics com., 1990—; mem. Panel Union Privilege Legal Svcs. div. AFL-CIO, 1986—, Montgomery Wards Legal Svcs. Panel, 1986—, Edina Hist. Soc., Decathlon Athletic Club; charter mem. Commn. for the Battle of Normandy Mus.; founding sponsor Civil Justice Found., 1986—; mem. com. for publ. Hennepin County Lawyer, 1992; pres. Endless Fist Soc., Inc., 1998. Recipient Outstanding Tchr. award Inver Hills Coll. Student Body, 1973, St. Paul Citizen of Month award Citizens Group, 1975, Kempo Club award U. Minn., 1975, U. Minn. Student Appreciation award Kempo Club, 1978, Sibley County Atty. Commendation award, 1980, Good Neighbor award WCCO Radio, 1985, Lamp of Knowledge award Twin Cities Lawyers Guild, 1986, N.W. Cmty. TV Commendation award, 1989-91, Presdl. Merit medal Pres. George Bush, 1990, N.W. Cmty. TV award, 1991, HLS Leadership award, 1984, Mng. Attys. Guidance award, 1985, Creative Thinker award Regional Staff, 1986, HLS Justice award, 1986, Honors cert. for Authors, Childrens Reading Round Table of Chgo., 1988, Wisdom Soc. Wisdom award, 1998. Fellow Roscoe Pound Found., Nat. Dist. Attys. Assn.; mem. ABA, ATLA, Minn. Bar Assn. (com. on ethics 1994—, com. on alternative dispute resolution 1994—), Minn. Trial Lawyers Assn., Hennepin County Bar Assn. (dist. ethics com. 1990—), Wis. Bar Assn., Ramsey County Bar Assn., Am. Judicature Soc., Internat. Platform Assn., Am. Arbitration Assn. (panel of arbitrators 1992), Minn. Martial Arts Assn. (pres. 1974-78, Outstanding Instr. award 1973), Nippon Kobudo Rengokai (bd. dirs. North Ctrl. States 1972-76, regional dir. 1972-76), Endless Fist Soc. (pres. 1998), Internat. Confedn. Jurists, Edina C. of C., Southview Country Club, Masons, Kiwanis, Scottish Rite, Sigma Alpha Mu. Avocations: reading, far eastern and oriental studies, civic activities, physical conditioning, gardening. Home: 4515 Andover Rd Minneapolis MN 55435-4031 also: 1711 County Road B W Ste 340N Roseville MN 55113-4077 Office: 7400 Metro Blvd Ste 390 Edina MN 55439 Office Phone: 952-831-6555.

NEFF, JACK KENNETH, apparel manufacturing company executive; b. N.Y.C., Feb. 23, 1938; s. William K. and Rose T. N.; m. Barbara Joan Neff, Nov. 4, 1961; 1 son, Craig William. AAS., Queens Coll., 1968; postgrad., Stanford Advanced Mgmt. Coll., 1973. Gen. mdse. mgr. youthwear Levi Strauss & Co., 1973-78, v.p. mktg., 1978-80; pres. Salant & Salant Co., N.Y.C., 1980-81; exec. v.p. Salant Corp., N.Y.C., 1981-84; pres., CEO Thomson Co., N.Y.C., 1984-87; exec. v.p., COO Stanley Blacker Co., N.Y.C., 1987-90; with Inside Mgmt. Assocs., N.Y.C., 1991-93; v.p., gen. mgr. Reebok Worldwide Apparel Divsn., 1993-94; sr. v.p., 1994-96; ptnr. The Muller Sports Group, NYC, 1996—2002; COO Atletica, San Antonio, Guadalajara, Mexico, 2002—04; ptnr. Asia Pacific Initiatives, 2004—. Served in USN, 1956-59.

NEFF, JEANNE HENRY, academic administrator; b. Fairmont, W. Va., Oct. 5, 1942; d. Percy Byron Henry and Rebecca Jacqueline Ridgely; m. Richard E. Kammer, Aug. 6, 1966 (div. July 1978); 1 child, Brian S. Kammer; m. Edward W.S. Neff II, Dec. 19, 1982; stepchildren: Larrie A., Edward W.S. III. BA, Wheeling Coll., 1964; MA, Rice U., 1966; ArtsD, Carnegie-Mellon U., 1976; postdoct., Harvard U., 1984. Instr. English Carlow Coll., Pitts., 1966-69; from asst. prof. to assoc. prof. English Wheeling (W. Va.) Coll., 1970-77, from assoc. dean to dean, 1977-80, academic v.p., 1980-86; v.p. academic affairs Susquehanna U., Selingsgrove, Pa., 1986-95; pres. The Sage Colls., Troy and Albany, N.Y., 1995—. Bd. dirs. Capital Bank & Trust Co., Albany. Trustee Albany Acad., 1996—; mem. Waterfront Commn., Troy, N.Y., 1996—; dir., v.p. Troy Redevel. Found., 1996—. Mem. Am. Coun. Edn. (fellow 1978-79, mem. commn. leadership devel. 1995—), Assn. New Am. Colls. (mem. pres.'s coun. 1997—), Assn. Am. Colls. and Univs. (dir. 1984-88, chair Am. Conf. Academic Deans, 1987), Univ. Heights Assn. (dir., v.p. 1996—). Home: 46 1st St Troy NY 12180-3811 Office: The Sage Colls 45 Ferry St Troy NY 12180-4115

NEFF, JOHN BROWN, financial portfolio manager; b. Wauseon, Ohio, Sept. 19, 1931; s. John Franklin Neff and Barbara (Brown) Hutton; m. Lillian Elizabeth Tulak, Oct. 4, 1935; children: Lisa, Stephen. BBA summa cum laude, U. Toledo, 1955; MBA, Case Western Reserve U., 1958; MA (hon.), U. Pa., 1984. Chartered fin. analyst. Asst. v.p. security analysis Nat. City Bank of Cleve., 1955-63; mng. ptnr., sr. v.p., portfolio mgr. Wellington Mgmt. Co., Valley Forge, Pa., 1963—95. Bd. dirs. Gen. Accident Ins., Crown Holdings, Inc., Amkor Tech., Inc., Chrysler Corp., Assn. Investment Mgmt. and Rsch. Author (with S.L. Mintz): John Neff on Investing. Charter trustee U. Pa., Phila.; trustee Case Western U. Served with USN, 1951-53. Recipient Giving Forward award, Phil. Edn. Fund, 1995. Mem. Chartered Fin. Analysts Fedn., Fin. Analysts of Phila. Avocations: tennis, golf, travel, history.

NEFF, MARILYN LEE, nursing consultant; b. Lancaster, Pa., Nov. 12, 1942; d. Norman Booth and F. Irene (Fridy) N. RN, U. Pa., 1963, BA, 1974; MBA, Widener U., 1988. Cert. nephrology nurse, nurse adminstr. advanced. Staff nurse Hosp. of U. Pa., Phila., 1963-64, asst. head nurse, 1964-68, staff nurse, 1968-71, asst. head nurse, 1971-75, head nurse, 1975-77, nursing supr., 1977-84; adminstr. Out-patient Dialysis Unit U. Pa., Phila., 1984-86; v.p. ops. Renal Care Cts. Corp., Wilmington, Del., 1986-88, Renal Treatment Ctrs., Inc., Berwyn, Pa., 1988-91; cons. MLN Cons., Wallingford, Pa., 1991-92; v.p. bus. devel. Healthdyne Home Nutritional Svcs., Inc., Marietta, Ga., 1992-94; cons. MLN Enterprises, Marietta, Ga., 1994—. Contbr. articles to profl. jours. Pres. Women's Fellowship, Calvary Presbyn. Ch., Media, Pa., 1982-86. Mem. ANA, Nat. Renal Adminstrs. Assn., Nat. Kidney Found. (del. 1990-91, Disting. Vol. Svc. award, 1990), Am. Nephrology Nurses Assn. (pres. 1991-92, Shiley Mgmt. award 1988, rsch. grant 1989). Avocations: Sunday sch. tchr., choir mem., reading, motorsports spectator. Home and Office: 5222 Pikes Peak Ct Marietta GA 30062-6550

NEFF, MICHAEL ALAN, lawyer; b. Springfield, Ill., Sept. 4, 1940; s. Benjamin Ezra and Ann (Alpert) N.; m. Lin Laghi, Mar. 26, 1977; 1 son, Aaron Benjamin. Student, U. Ill., 1958-61; BA, U. Calif., Berkeley, 1963, postgrad., 1963-64; JD, Columbia U., 1967. Bar: NY 1967, US Dist. Ct. (so. and ea. dists.) NY 1969, US Ct. Appeals (2d cir.) 1988, US Supreme Ct. 1988. Congl. intern US Ho. of Reps., 1965; assoc. Sage, Gray, Todd & Sims, NYC, 1967-74, Fellner & Rovins, NYC, 1974-75; ptnr. Poier, Tulin, Clark & Neff, NYC, 1976-77; pvt. practice NYC, 1977-83; pres. private practice, 1983—. Counsel St. Dominic's Home, 1971-74, Louise Wise Svcs., 1976-77, Edwin Gould Svc. for Children, 1969-79, 76—, Family Svc.of Westchester, Inc., 1977-87, The Children's Village, 1977-84, Brookwood Child Care, 1980—, Forestdale, 1988—, Fam. Support Sys. Unlimited, 1990—, Ednl. Assistance Corp., 1990-95, Coalition for Hispanic Family Svcs., 1992-93, Soc. Children and Families, 1996—, Pius XII Youth and Family Svcs., 2000—, Child Devel. Support Corp, 2001—, Hale House Ctr., Inc., 2001—; tchg. asst. U. Calif., 1963-64; instr. Social Welfare Policy and Law, Marymount Manhattan Coll., 1973; mem. Indigent Defendant's Legal Panel, Appellate Div., First Dept., 1974-84; participant NY State Conf. on Children's Rights, 1974; asst. sec. Edwin Gould Svcs. for Children, 1977—; cons. NY Task Force on Permanency Planning For Children in Foster Care, 1985-90, NY State Foster and Adoptive Parent Assn., Inc., 1988—, NY Spaulding for Children, 1988-90, Ct. Appointed Spl. Advs., 1988-91; instr. adoption law in NY, City Bar Ctr. for CLE, 2001—; mem. Adoption Adv. Com. NY State Dept. Social Svcs., 1997-98; advisor Nat. Resource Ctr. for Foster Care and Permanency Planning, 2000—; trainer Inst. for Families and Children, 1992-95, NYC Adminstrn. for Children's Svcs., 1996-97; facilitator Parenting Journey, 2000—; group leader Model Approach to Partnerships in Parenting, 2001—. Author: Freeing Foster Children for Adoption, A Child's Right to a Plan of Permanency, 1972, Permanent Neglect Proceedings, 1980, Adoption Proceedings, Basic Matrimonial Practice in New York, 1980, Foster Parenting Handbook, 1997 Adopting Foster Children: A Handbook for Foster Parents, 1999, Permanency Planning ASFA, Best Practices: A Handbook for Caseworkers, 2000; Contbr. articles to profl. jours. Mem. Protestant Bd. of Guardians, 2001—. Mem. ABA, Am. Acad. Adoption Attys., Assn. Bar City of NY (mem. com. on children and law, family law sect.). Home: 5 W 86th St Apt 6B New York NY 10024-3664 E-mail: manpc@aol.com.

NEFF, PATRICK LEE (PAT NEFF), music educator; b. Oklahoma City, Apr. 29, 1959; s. Raymond Michael and Jeannette (Bunny) Claire Neff; m. Antoinette Norine Burks, Sept. 20, 1966; children: Zandra Jeannette, Joseph Michael. MusM in Edn., Southwestern Okla. State U., 1983. Dir. bands, guitar Wingate H.S., Fort Wingate, N.Mex., 1989—; instr. music ed. elem. teachers U. N.Mex, Gallup, 1999—2004. Composer: Please Color Me Human (award, 2000); performer: (songs) Albuquerque Folk Festival, Silverton Jubilee, Santa Fe Bluegrass Festival Red Mesa Rounders, Rusty Strings & the Flat Tones, Roswell Cheese Festival, Bluff Utah Jubilee, Wickenburg Bluegrass Festival, Kerrvill Folk Festival. Home: 507 Vandenbosch Parkway Gallup NM 87301 Office: Wingate High School PO Box 2 Fort Wingate NM 87316 Personal E-mail: pneff@cia-g.com. E-mail: pneff@whs.bia.edu.

NEFF, P(AUL) SHERRILL, venture capitalist; b. Balt., Dec. 18, 1951; s. Paul Heston and Mary (Poulnot) N.; m. Sarah B. Barrett, June 20, 1976 (div. 1985); 1 child, Jacob Colin; m. Alicia Phyll Felton, May 26, 1988; children: Michael Felton, Jonathan Felton. BA, Wesleyan U., 1974; JD magna cum laude, U. Mich., 1980. Bar: Pa. 1980. Atty. Morgan Lewis & Bockius, Phila., 1980—84; investment banker Alex Brown & Sons, Inc., Balt., 1984—93, mng. dir., 1992—93; sr. v.p. corp. devel. U.S. Healthcare, Blue Bell, Pa., 1993—94; pres., CFO Neose Techs., Inc., Horsham, 1994—2000, pres., COO, 2000—02; mng. ptnr. Quaker Bio Ventures, Phila., 2002—. Bd. dirs. Resource Am., Inc., Phila., Biolex, Inc., Medmark, Inc., BioRexis Pharms., Inc.; bd. dirs., v.p., pres. Greater Phila. Venture Group; policy bd. WXPN-FM. Trustee Zero Moving Dance Co., Phila., 1984-93; bd. dirs. Univ. City Sci. Ctr., 1998—. Mem. Pa. Biotech. Assn. (bd. dirs. 1996-2002, pres.-elect 1997-98, pres. 1998-99). Democrat. Jewish. Home: 619 Revere Rd Merion Station PA 19066-1007 Office: Quaker Bio Ventures 1811 Chestnut St Philadelphia PA 19103

NEFF, RICHARD B. consumer products company executive; b. 1948; BS, Fairleigh Dickinson U., 1970. CPA. With Arthur Andersen & Co., 1970-73; various exec. positions including exec. v.p., CFO and dir. Transco Group, Inc., 1973-86; mng. ptnr. Greenwood Meadows Devel. Co., 1988—; exec. v.p., CFO, dir. Di Giorgio Corp., 1990—; pres. Las Plumas Lumber, 1991—; officer White Rose Foods, Inc., 1992—, CEO, co-chmn, 2000—. Office: Di Giorgio Corp 380 Middlesex Ave Carteret NJ 07008-3446

NEFF, ROBERT CAREY, lawyer; b. Orange, NJ, Nov. 9, 1935; s. Walter Holt and Nan Carey Neff; m. Shirley Ruth Fitzeram, May 6, 1961; children: Robert C. Jr., Sandra Wilichowski, Carl J., Thomas H. BA, Yale U., 1957; LLB, Georgetown U., 1964. Cert. N.J. 1965, U.S. Dist. Ct. N.J. 1965, U.S. Supreme Ct. 1965. Assoc. Carey & Jardine, Newark, 1965-67; ptnr. Meth, Wood Neff & Cooper, Newark, 1967-76, Shanley & Fisher, Newark, 1976-82, Kraft & Hughes, Newark, 1982-87, Pitney, Hardin, Kipp & Szuch, Morristown, N.J., 1987—. Trustee NJ Cmty. Found., Morristown, 1990-97, Riverview Hosp. Found., 2002—; commr. NJ State Racing Commn., 1986-90; active Rumson Fair Haven Regional Bd. Edn., 1985-86; councilman Borrough of Shrewsbury, NJ, 1969-71. Capt. USMCR, 1957-61. Fellow Am. Coll. of Trust and Estate Counsel; mem. ABA (chmn. com. legal svcs. for elderly 1989-91), NJ Bar Assn. Republican. Roman Catholic. Home: 85 Grange Ave Fair Haven NJ 07704-3039 Office: Pitney Hardin Kipp & Szuch 125 Halfmile Rd Red Bank NJ 07701

NEFF, ROBERT CLARK, SR., lawyer; b. St. Marys, Ohio, Feb. 11, 1921; s. Homer Armstrong and Irene (McCulloch) N.; m. Betty Baker, July 3, 1954 (dec.); children: Cynthia Lee Neff Schifer, Robert Clark Jr., Abigail Lynn (dec.); m. Helen Picking, July 24, 1975. BA, Coll. Wooster, 1943; postgrad., U. Mich., 1946-47; LLB, Ohio No. U., 1950. Bar: Ohio 1950, U.S. Dist. Ct. (no. dist.) Ohio, 1978. Pvt. practice, Bucyrus, Ohio, 1950—; ptnr. Neff Law Firm Ltd.; law dir. City of Bucyrus, 1962-95. Chmn. blood program Crawford County (Ohio) unit ARC, 1955-89; life mem. adv. bd. Salvation Army, 1962—; clk. of session 1st Presbyn. Ch., Bucyrus, 1958-96; bd. dirs. Bucyrus Area Cmty. Found., Crawford County Bd. Mental Retardation and Devel. Disabilities, 1977-82. With USNR, WWII; comdr. Res. ret. Recipient "Others" plaque for 30 yrs. adv. bd. svc. Salvation Army, Ohio No. U. Coll. Law Alumni award for cmty. svc., 1996; inducted Ohio Vets. Hall Fame, Columbus, 1996. Mem. Ohio Bar Assn., Crawford County Bar Assn., Naval Res. Assn., Ret. Officers Assn., Am. Legion, Bucyrus Area C. of C. (past bd. dirs., Outstanding Citizen award, 1973, Bucyrus Citizen of Yr. 1981), Kiwanis (life mem., past pres.), Masons. Republican. Home: 1085 Mary Ann Ln Bucyrus OH 44820-3145 Office: 840 S Sandusky Ave PO Box 406 Bucyrus OH 44820-0406 Fax: 419-562-1660. E-mail: nefflaw@cybrtown.com.

NEFF, ROBERT MATTHEW, lawyer, financial services executive; b. Huntington, Ind., Mar. 26, 1955; s. Robert Eugene and Ann (Bash) N.; m. Lee Ann Loving, Aug. 23, 1980; children: Alexandra, Graydon, Philip. BA in English, DePauw U., 1977; JD, Ind. U., Indpls., 1980. Bar: Ind. 1980, U.S. Dist. Ct. (so. dist.) Ind. 1980, U.S. Supreme Ct., 1993. Assoc. Krieg, DeVault, Alexander & Capehart, Indpls., 1980-85, ptnr., 1986-88; ptnr. Baker & Daniels, Indpls., 1988-92; of counsel, 1993-96; dept. to chmn. Fed. Housing Fin. Bd., Washington, 1992-93; pres., CEO Circle Investors, Inc., Indpls., 1993-97, also bd. dirs.; chmn., CEO Senex Fin. Corp., Indpls., 1998—. Mem. faculty Grad. Sch. of Banking of South, 1988—90; chmn. Liberty Bankers Life Ins. Co., 1995—98, Am. Founders Life Ins. Co., Laurel Life Ins. Co., Aztek Life Assurance Co., 1996—97; bd. dirs. Quanta Surplus Lines Ins. Co., CH Assurance Ltd., Unified Fin. Svcs., Inc. Exec. editor Ind. Law Rev., 1979-80. Participant Lacy Exec. Leadership Conf., Indpls., 1985-86; trustee DePauw U., 1977-80; bd. govs. Riley Children's Found., 1999—. Mem. ABA (chmn. bus. law com. young lawyers divsn. 1988-90, banking law com. 1990-92), Ind. Bar Assn. (chmn. corps. banking and bus. law sect. 1987-88), DePauw Alumni Assn. (bd. dirs. 1982-88), Phi Kappa Psi, Phi Beta Kappa. Avocations: Tae Kwon Do, golf. Home: 7202 Merriam Rd Indianapolis IN 46240 Office: Senex Fin Corp 3500 DePauw Blvd # 3050 Indianapolis IN 46268 Office Phone: 317-613-3000.

NEFF, ROBERT WILBUR, academic administrator, educator, minister; b. Lancaster, Pa., June 16, 1936; s. Wilbur Hildebr and Hazel Margaret (Martin) N.; m. Dorothy Rosewarne, Aug. 16, 1959; children: Charles Scott, Heather Lynn. BS, Pa. State U., 1958; BD, Yale Div. Sch., 1961, MA, 1963, PhD, 1969; DD, Juniata Coll., 1978, Manchester Coll., 1979; DHL, Bridgewater Coll., 1979. Asst. prof. Bridgewater Coll., 1964-65; mem. faculty dept. Bibl. studies Bethany Theol. Sem., 1965-77, prof., 1973-77; gen. sec. Ch. of the Brethren, Elgin, Ill., 1978-86; pres. Juniata Coll., 1986-98, pres. emeritus, 1998—. Vis. prof. Pa. State U., 1998-2003; assoc. for resource devel. The Village at Morrison's Cove, 1999-; mem. faculty North Park Sem., No. Bapt. Sem., Theol. Coll. No. Nigeria; bd. dirs. Mellon Bank (Ctrl.) Nat. Assn., exec. com., 1989, chair exec. com., 1993, chair CRA com., 1994-2001; mem. pres.'s com. NCAA, 1996-99; bd. dirs. Susquehanna Valley Satellite, 2002-; adj. faculty Bethany Theol. Sem., 1999—; cons. Archdiocese (Altoona/Johnstown), 2003-; lectr. Young Ctr. at Elizabethtown Coll., 2002; mem. USDA Del. to Baltic States, 2000. Mem. governing bd. Nat. Coun. Chs. of Christ, 1976-86, mem. exec. com., 1979-86; mem. Mid-East panel, 1980, 2d v.p., 1985-86; mem. ctrl. com. World Coun. Chs., 1983-92; rep. Assembly of World Coun. Chs., 1983, mem. exec. com. on interch. rels., 1980-84, mem. del. to China, 1981, chmn. presdl. panel, 1982-84; bd. dirs. Bethany Theol. Sem., 1978-86; campaign chmn. United Way, Huntington County, 1989; chair higher edn. com. Ch. of Brethren, 1993-98. Danforth fellow, 1958-69. Mem. Soc. Bibl. Lit., Soc. Old Testament Study, Chgo. Soc. Bibl. Rsch., Soc. Values in Higher Edn., Coun. Ind. Colls. (nat. bd. dirs. 1991-94, treas. 1995-98), Pa. Coun. Ind. Colls. and Univs. (exec. com. 1988-90, 92-96, chair ann. conf. nominating com. 1993-94), Mid Atlantic Athletic Conf. (sec., mem. exec. com. 1994-97). Democrat. Home: 7889 River Hill Ln Alexandria PA 16611 Office: Village at Morrisons Cove 429 Market St Martinsburg PA 16866 Office Phone: 814-793-5207. E-mail: rneff@pennswoods.net.

NEFF, SEVERINE, music educator; b. Waterbury, Conn., Dec. 17, 1949; d. Victor and Evangeline Josephine Neff; m. Joel Stanley Feigin, June 7, 1986. AB, Barnard Coll., 1971; MA, Yale U., 1972; MFA, Princeton (N.J.) U., PhD, 1979. Asst. prof. Bates Coll., Lewiston, Maine, 1979—80, U. Hawaii, Honolulu, 1980—81; fellow Cornell U., Ithaca, NY, 1981—83; asst. prof. Barnard Coll., N.Y., NY, 1983—91; assoc. prof. Cin. (Ohio) Coll.-Conservatory, 1991—92, prof., 1993—95; prof. music U. N.C., Chapel Hill, NC, 1995—2003, Eugene Falk disting. prof., 2004—. Author: Coherence, Counterpoint, Instrumentation, Theory of Form, 1994, The Musical Idea, 1995; editor: Theory and Practice, 1991—93; editor: (reviews) Music Theory Spectrum, 1999—2002. Fellow, Mellon Found., 1981; grantee, NEH, 1993; scholar, Fulbright Found., 1998—99. Mem.: Soc. Music Theory (sec. 1991—94, bd.dirs., revs. editor 2000—02), Coll. Music Soc. (theory rep. 2001—, bd.dirs.). Achievements include discovery of unknown work of Arnold Schoenberg. Avocation: antiques. Office: University North Carolina CB 3320 Chapel Hill NC 27599

NEFF, THOMAS JOSEPH, executive search firm executive; b. Easton, Pa., Oct. 2, 1937; s. John Wallace and Elizabeth Ann (Dougherty) N.; m. Susan Culver Paull, Nov. 26, 1971 (dec.); children: David Andrew, Mark Gregory, Scott Dougherty; m. Sarah Brown Hallingby, Jan. 20, 1989; stepchildren: Brooke, Bailey BS in Indsl. Engring., Lafayette Coll., 1959; MBA, Lehigh U., 1961. Assoc. McKinsey & Co., Inc., N.Y.C. and Australia, 1963-66; dir. mktg. planning Trans-World Airlines, N.Y.C., 1966-69; pres. Hosp. Data Scis., Inc., N.Y.C., 1969-74; prin. Booz, Allen & Hamilton, Inc., N.Y.C., 1974-76; regional ptnr. Spencer Stuart, Inc., N.Y.C., N.Am., 1976-79; bd. dirs. Spencer Stuart & Assocs., N.Y.C., 1976-79, pres., 1979-96, also bd. dirs., chmn. U.S., 1996—. Bd. dirs. Lord Abbett Mut. Funds, Ace Ltd., Exult, Inc.; chmn. Brunswick Sch., 1991-95. Trustee, exec. com. Lafayette Coll., 1992—. 1st lt. U.S. Army, 1961-63. Mem. Links Club, Sky Club, Blind Brook Club, Quogue (N.Y.) Beach Club, Quogue Field Club, Round Hill Club, Coral Beach Club, Quantuck Beach Club, Nat. Golf Links, Lost Tree Club, McArthur Golf Club. Republican. Roman Catholic. Office: Spencer Stuart & Assocs 277 Park Ave 29th Fl New York NY 10172-2998 Home: 6 Sherwood Farm Ln Greenwich CT 06831

NEFF BALCH, BETTY MARIE, retired nursing educator; b. Durkee, Oreg., Oct. 9, 1925; d. Charles F. and Blanche O. (Hickerson) Schuck; m. William F. Neff, Oct. 6, 1946 (div.); children: Charles, Susan, Doris Ann, William Jr.; m. George E. Balch, Jr., Sept. 1998. Diploma, St. Elizabeth Hosp., 1946; BS, St. Joseph's Coll., 1981; MEd, Northern Mont. Coll., 1986; M in Career Guidance and Planning, No. Mont. Coll., 1989; EdD, Mont. State U., 1995. RN Mont., cert. tchr. Mont. Staff nurse De Paul Hosp., Cheyenne, Wyo., 1963—65, USAF Hosp., Wiesbaden, Germany, 1965—71, Great Falls, Mont., 1971—76; ind. contractor Great Falls Vo-Tech Ctr./Mont. State U., 1976—93; headmaster cert. nurse aides Distance Learning Instrn. by Computer, Helena, Mont., 1993—98; ret., 1998. Presenter Motivational Workshop, Mont. Health Care Assn., 1989; speaker and piloting nurse's aides program in field. Contbr. articles to profl. jours. Named Tchr. of Yr., Mont. Health Occupation, 1986, grantee 5 Carl Perkins grants, Am. Medal of Honor, Am. Bio. Inst., 2003, Woman of the Yr. award for outstanding cmty. and profl. achievement, Am. Bio. Inst., 2003 Mem. Mt. Voc. Assn. (am. voc. assn. nat. bylaws com., speaker N. Mex. convention, 1988), Sons of Norway, Friendship Force, Elks, Beta Sigma Phi. Home: 8002-68 Ave SW Tacoma WA 98499

NEFISSI, SAMI, mathematician, educator; s. Ali Bou Menjel Nefissi and Rebbah Ben Ammar; m. Laura Stepanski, 2001; 1 child, Lilia Ferrielle. BS in Math., U.Sci.,Tunis II, Tunisia, 1994; MS, George Mason U., Fairfax, Va., 2000; Grad. Cert. in Computational Techniques and Applications, George Mason U., Va., 2001. Adj. prof. George Mason U., Fairfax, Va., 1999—; math instr. Islamic Saudi Acad., Alexandria, Va., 2002—. Computer cons., pvt. tutor, Fairfax, Va., 1997—. Home: 3329 Willow Crescent Dr #23 Fairfax VA 22030 Office: George Mason Univ 4400 University Dr Fairfax VA 22030-4444 Personal E-mail: snefissi@gmu.edu. E-mail: snefiss@gmu.edu.

NEFSKE, DONALD JOSEPH, engineer; b. Detroit, Dec. 18, 1938; s. Frank J. and Esther M. N.; m. Susan Sung, Dec. 10, 1983. BS magna cum laude, U. Detroit, 1962; MS, U. Mich., 1964, PhD, 1969. Engr. Ford Motor Co., Dearborn, Mich., 1960-61; rsch. engr. GM, Warren, Mich., 1969-70, sr. rsch. engr., 1970-85, sr. staff engr., 1985-93; prin. engr., 1993—. Contbr. articles profl. jour., chapters to books. Mem. ASME, AIAA, Acoustical Soc. Am., Soc. Automotive Engr., Sigma Xi. Roman Catholic. Achievements include research in rsch./interests: Automotive vehicle noise and vibration, airbag safety systems. Office: Gen Motors R&D Ctr Engring Mechs Dept 30500 Mound Rd Warren MI 48092-2031

NEFT, SUZI TERRY, television producer, marketing, public relations executive, advertising executive; b. Pitts., Sept. 17, 1957; d. Harris Rosenberg and Fannie Rachel Neft; m. Paul Alan Byers, June 14, 1986 (div. 2002); 1 child, Charles Alexander II Byers. BA in Journalism and Comm., Point Park Coll., 1979. Announcer, writer WNUF-FM, Millvale, Pa., 1979-80; news reporter WESA-AM, Charleroi, Pa., 1980-81; ops. coord. WQED-TV, WQEX-TV, WQED-FM, Pitts., 1981-87; location prodn. mgr. You TV Cable Network, Pitts., 1988; tv prodr. The Mercy Hosp., Pitts., 1992-93; dir. internship devel., sr. tv prodr. Reliance Tng. Networks, Pitts., 1996-2000; freelance TV prodr., writer, pub. rels./mktg. profl., 1977—. Assoc. prodr. KDKA/Children's Hospital Free Care Fund Benefit Show, 1994, 95, Lucille's Car Care Clinic, 1994; prodr. HealthVision, 1998-99. Pub. rels., mktg. Jewish Assn. Aging; mem. publicity com., intergenerational choir Temple Sinai, trustee. Recipient Emmy Mid-Atlantic Region Best Live Show, Acad. TV Arts and Scis., 1991, 1st pl. best tv comml. Women in Comm., 1994, 1st pl. spl. events promo under $20,000 Women in Comm., 1995, 1st pl. spl. events budgets under $20,000 Women in Comm., 1996. Mem.: Press Club Western Pa. (bd. dirs. 1994—95), Am. Women in Radio and TV (pres. chpt. 1995—97). Home and Office: 44 Rosemont Ln Pittsburgh PA 15217-3161

NEGI, DEVENDRA S. communications services company administrator; b. Varanasi, Uttar Pradesh, India, Aug. 8, 1953; s. Vidya Wati and (Deceased) Balwant S Negi. B of Mech. Engring., Indian Inst. Tech., 1974; MS in Indsl. Engring, Kans. State U., 1981, PhD in Indsl. Engring, 1989. Engr. trainee Bharat Heavy Electricals Ltd., Hardwar, India, 1975—76, engr., 1976—79; grad. rsch. asst. Kans. State U., Manhattan, 1980, 1986—89; systems analyst Patso Co., Inc, Houston, 1981—82; indsl. engr. Millar Instruments, Inc., 1882—1984; ops. rsch. analyst Phillips Petroleum Co., Bartlesville, Okla., 1990—97; sr. tech. staff mem. AT&T, Florham Park and Murray Hill, NJ, 1997—2001, dist. mgr. Florham Park, 2001—04, group mgr. Middletown and Florham Park, 2004—. Vis. asst. prof. Ohio U., Athens, 1989—90. Mem.: Inst. Ops. Rsch. and Mgmt. Scis., Inst. Indsl. Engrs. Avocations: travel, movies, tennis. Home: 1428-1432 South Ave Apt 1-H Plainfield NJ 07062 Office: AT&T 180 Park Ave Florham Park NJ 07932 Office Phone: 732-420-0370. Personal E-mail: dsnegi@worldnet.att.net. E-mail: dsnegi@homer.att.com.

NEGISHI, EI-ICHI, chemistry professor; arrived in U.S., 1960; BS in Organic Chemistry, U. Tokyo, 1958; PhD in Organic Chemistry, U. Pa., 1963. Rsch. chemist Teijin Ltd., 1958-65; postdoctoral assoc. Purdue U., 1966-68, asst. to H.C. Brown, 1968-72; asst. prof. Syracuse (N.Y.) U., 1972-76, assoc. prof., 1976-79; prof. Purdue U., West Lafayette, Ind., 1979-99, Herbert C. Brown disting. prof., 1999—. Lectr. in field. Recipient A. von Humboldt Rschr. award 1998—; Fulbright scholar, 1960-63. Mem.: Royal Soc. Chemistry (Sir E. Frankland Prize lectureship 2000), Japan Chem. Soc. (award 1997), Am. Chem. Soc. (Organometallic Chemistry award 1998), Sigma Xi, Phi Lambda Epsilon. Office: Purdue U Chem Dept 1393 Brown Labs West Lafayette IN 47907-1393 Office Phone: 765-494-5301. Business E-Mail: negishi@purdue.edu.

NEGRETE MCLEOD, GLORIA, state official; married. Pres., mem. governing bd. Chaffey C.C., 1995—2000; candidate Dist. 61 Calif. State Assembly, 1998, state assembly mem. Dist. 61, 2000—. Mem. appropriations com.; mem. govtl. orgn. com.; mem. health com.; mem. higher edn. com.; mem. labor and employment com.; chair pub. employees, retirement and social security com. Democrat. Mailing: Rm 5016 PO Box 942849 Sacramento CA 95814 Office: Ste 100B 4959 Palo Verde St Montclair CA 91763

NEGRON-GARCIA, ANTONIO S. law educator, former territory supreme court justice; b. Rio Piedras, P.R., Dec. 31, 1940; s. Luis Negron-Fernandez and Rosa M. Garcia-Saldana; m. Gloria Villardefrancos-Vergara, May 26, 1962; 1 son, Antonio Rogelio. BA, U. P.R., 1962, LL.B., 1964. Bar: P.R. bar 1964. Law aide and lawyer legal div. Water Resources Authority, 1962-64; judge Dist. Ct., 1964-69, Superior Ct., 1969-74; justice P.R. Supreme Ct., San Juan, 1974—2001; administrating judge, 1969-71; exec. officer Constl. Bd. for Revision Senatorial and Rep. Dists., 1971-72; mem. Jud. Conf., 1974—2000; first exec. sec. Council for Reform of System of Justice in P.R., 1973-74; prof. InterAmerican U. Puerto Rico, 2001—. Chmn. Gov.'s Advisory Com. for Jud. Appointments, 1973-74; lectr. U. P.R. Law Sch., 1973-74 Mem. P.R. Bar Assn., Am. Judicature Soc. Roman Catholic. Office: Univ InterAmericana de Puerto Rico Apartado 70351 San Juan PR 00936-8351

NEGROPONTE, JOHN DIMITRI, ambassador; b. London, July 21, 1939; s. Dimitri John and Catherine (Coumantaros) Negroponte; m. Diana Mary Villiers, Dec. 14, 1976; children: Marina, Alexandra, John, George, Sophia. BA, Yale U., 1960. Commd. fgn. svc. officer U.S. Dept. of State, 1960; vice consul Hong Kong, 1961—63; 2nd sec. Saigon, 1964—68; mem. U.S. Del. to Paris Peace Talks on Viet-Nam, 1968—69; mem. staff NSC, 1970—73; polit. counselor Quito, Ecuador, 1973—75; consul gen. Thessaloniki, Greece, 1975—77; dep. asst. sec. of state for oceans and fisheries affairs Washington, 1977—79; dep. asst. sec. for East Asian and Pacific affairs U.S. Dept. State, Washington, 1980—81; U.S. amb. to Honduras, 1981—85; asst. sec. for oceans and internat. environ. and sci. affairs, 1985—87; dep. asst. Pres. for Nat. Security Affairs, 1987—89; U.S. amb. to Mex., 1989—93; U.S. amb. to The Philippines, 1993—96; spl. coord. for post-1999 U.S. presence in Panama, 1996—97; exec. v.p. global markets McGraw-Hill Cos., N.Y.C., 1997—2001; permanent U.S. rep. UN, N.Y.C., 2001—04; U.S. amb. to Iraq U.S. Dept. State, Baghdad, 2004—. Co-pres. U.S./Mex. Commn. for Ednl. and Cultural Exch., 1997—2001; chmn. The French-Am. Found., 1998—2001; mem. exec. com. U.S. Coun. for Internat. Bus., 1998—2001. Mem.: Fgn. Policy Assn., Am. Acad. Diplomacy, Coun. on Fgn. Rels., Am. Fgn. Svc. Assn. Greek Orthodox. Office: Coalition Provisional Authority APO AE 09335 Baghdad Iraq

NEHAMAS, ALEXANDER, philosophy educator; b. Athens, Greece, Mar. 22, 1946; came to U.S., 1964; s. Albert and Christine (Yannuli) N.; m. Susan Glimcher, June 22, 1983; 1 child, Nicholas Albert Glimcher. BA, Swarthmore Coll., 1967; PhD, Princeton U., 1971; D in Philosophy (hon.), Athens, 1993. Asst. then assoc. prof. philosophy U. Pitts., 1971-81, prof., 1981-86; prof. philosophy U. Pa., 1986-90; vis. prof. Princeton (N.J.) U., 1978-79, 89, Edmund Carpenter prof. humanities, 1990—, prof. philosophy and comparative lit., 1990—, chair humanities coun., 1994—2002, chmn. program in Hellenic studies, 1994—2002. Dir. Princeton Soc. Fellow in Liberal Arts, 1999-2002; Mills vis. prof. U. Calif., Berkeley, 1983; Sather vis. prof., 1993; vis. prof. U. Calif., Santa Cruz, 1988; bd. dirs. Princeton U. Press; trustee Nat. Humanities Ctr., 1996-99, Athens Coll., 1996--. Author: Nietzche: Life as Literature, 1985, The Art of Living: Socratic Reflectionsfrom Plato to Foucault, 1998, Virtues of Authenticity: Essays on Plato and Socrates, 1999; translator Plato's Symposium, 1989, Plato's Phaedrus, 1995; co-editor: Aristotle's Rhetoric: Philosophical Essays, 1994; contbr. articles to profl. jours.; mem. editl. bd. Am. Philos. Quar., 1981-86, History of Philosophy Quar., 1983-88, Ancient Philosophy, 1984—, Jour. Modern Greek Studies, 1986—, Arion, 1989—, Philosophy and Lit., 1989—, Philosophy and Phenomenological Rsch., 1990—. Recipient Lindback Found. Tchg. award, U. Pa., 1989, Behrman award in humanities, Princeton U., 1999, Ann. prize in Hellenic Studies Acad., Athens, 2000, Internat. Nietsche prize, 2001, Mellon Disting. Achievement award, 2001; grantee Guggenheim fellow, 1983, NEH, 1978. Mem. MLA, Am. Philos. Assn. (chmn. program 1982-83, exec. com. 1990-92, v.p. ea. divsn. 2002, pres. 2003), Modern Greek Studies Assn. (exec. com. 1983-89), Am. Soc. Aesthetics, N.Am. Nietzche Soc. (exec. com. 1988-91), Phi Beta Kappa (vis. prof. 1989, vis. scholar 1995). Office: Princeton U Dept Philosophy Princeton NJ 08544-0001

NEHER, ROBERT TROSTLE, biology professor; b. Mt. Morris, Ill., Nov. 1, 1930; s. Oscar Warner and Etha Mae (Trostle) N.; m. Mary Rebecca Timmons, June 12, 1954; children: Kenneth, Jon, Daniel. BA in Sci., Manchester Coll., Ind., 1953; MAT in Biology, Ind. U., 1955, PhD in Botany, 1963; MRE in Counseling, Bethany Sem., Chgo., 1957. Assoc. Christian edn. Ch. of Brethren, Elgin, Ill., 1956; asst. prof., then assoc. prof. biology U. LaVerne, Calif., 1958-62, prof. biology, 1966—, chmn. nat. sci. divsn., 1978—, provost, v.p. acad. affairs, 2000-01; dir. U. LaVerne Field Sta. Magpie Ranch, Drummond, Mont., 1994—. Dep. dir. Nat. Energy Rsch. and Info. Inst., 1982-88, chair pre-health sci. com., program dir., academic coun., 1985—; aquaculture cons. Bolsa Aquaculture Consortium, 1973-76, AM China Corp., 1981; cons. devel. of in-svc. tchg. tng. in environ. edn. L.A. Pub. Schs.; dir. coll. level curriculum program Montclair High Sch., Van Nuys, Calif. Co-editor: Energy from Biomass, 1979; contbr. articles to profl. jours. City councilman LaVerne City Coun., 1976-84, mayor pro tem, 1980-84; commr. L.A. County Watershed Commn., 1976-91; bd. dirs. Pomona Valley Youth Svcs.; juvenile divsn. chmn. 1978-79; chmn. San Gabriel Valley Get-About Transp. Bd., 1980-84; mem. L.A. County Solid Waste Curbside Recycling Task Force, 1980-82; chmn. La Verne City Commn. on Environ. Quality, 1972-75; mem. La Verne City Planning Commn., 1966-72; moderator La Verne Ch. of Brethren, 1966-75, chmn. bd. 1977-80, mem. ch. bd. dirs., 1966-84; trustee, officer San Gabriel Valley Mosquito and Vector Control Dist., 1991—. Named Outstanding Tchr. of Yr., La Verne Coll., 1969—70; recipient Els Johnson Cmty. Svc. award, U. La Verne, 2003; grantee, NSF, 1960—61; NSF faculty fellow, Ind. U., Bloomington, 1961—62. Mem. AAAS (life mem), Am. Soc. Plant Taxonomists, Calif. Bot. Soc., San Bernardino County Mus. Assn., Audubon Soc., Sierra Club, Nat. Geog. Soc., Sigma Xi. Office: U La Verne Natural Science Divsn 1950 3rd St La Verne CA 91750-4401 Office Phone: 909-593-3511. E-mail: neherr@ulv.edu.

NEHRA, GERALD PETER, lawyer; b. Detroit, Mar. 25, 1940; s. Joseph P. and Jeanette M. (Bauer) N.; m. children: Teresa, Patricia; m. Peggy Jensen, Sept. 12, 1987. B.I.E., Gen. Motors Inst., Flint, Mich., 1962; JD, Detroit Coll. Law, 1970. Bar: Mich. 1970, N.Y. 1972, Colo. 1992, U.S. Dist. Ct. (ea. dist.) Mich. 1970, U.S. Dist. Ct. (so. dist.) N.Y. 1972, U.S. Dist. Ct. (no. dist.) N.Y. 1976, U.S. Ct. Appeals (6th cir.) 1978. Successively engr., supr., gen. supr. Gen. Motors Corp., 1958-67; mktg. rep. to regional counsel IBM Corp., 1967-79; v.p. gen. counsel Church & Dwight Co., Inc., 1979-82; dep. chief atty. Amway Corp., 1982-83; dep. gen. counsel, 1983-92; dir. legal div., 1989-91; sec., dir. corp. law, 1991-92; v.p. gen. cousnel Fuller Brush, Boulder, Colo., 1991-92; pvt. practice, 1992—. Adj. instr. Dale Carnegie Courses, 1983-91. Recipient Outstanding Contbn. award Am. Cancer Soc., 1976. Mem. ABA, Mich. Bar Assn., Colo. Bar Assn., N.Y. State Bar Assn. Home and Office: 1710 Beach St Muskegon MI 49441-1008 Office Phone: 231-755-3800. Business E-Mail: gnehra@mlmatty.com.

NEHRBASS, SETH MARTIN, patent lawyer; b. Lafayette, La., Nov. 10, 1960; s. Neil Martin and Janet (Himbert) N.; m. Mary Elizabeth Dennis, Aug. 12, 2000; children: Gabriel, Fabian. Student, U. Catholique de l'Ouest, Angers, France, 1980, U. Paul Valéry, Montpellier, France, 1981; BS in Physics summa cum laude, U. Southwe. La., 1982; JD cum laude, Loyola U., 1990. Bar: U.S. Patent & Trademark Office 1984, La. 1990, U.S. Dist. Ct. (ea., mid., and we. dists.) La. 1990, U.S. Ct. Appeals (5th and fed. cirs.) 1990; cert. notary public, La. Patent examiner U.S. Patent & Trademark Office, 1982-84; patent agt. with law firm New Orleans, 1986-87; assoc. Pravel, Hewitt, Kimball & Krieger, New Orleans, 1987-97, shareholder, 1997-98, Garvey, Smith, Nehrbass & Doody, L.L.C., Metairie, La., 1998—. Adj. law faculty Tulane Law Sch., 1997—; judge practice round moot ct. teams Loyola Law Sch., 1992—; preparer questions patent bar exam PTO Q & A Bd., 1992-93; presenter in field. Contbr. articles to profl. jours. Den leader 2d grade Cub Scouts, Boy Scouts Am., Lusher Sch., Audubon Dist., 1991-92, 3d grade, 1994-95, asst. den leader 3d grade, 1992-93, 4th grade, 1993-94; soccer coach Carrollton Booster Club, New Orleans, 1993-95, Lakeview Soccer Club, New Orleans, 1995-96; adv. mem. La. Ctr. for Law and Civic Edn., 1996-98. Recipient Hornbook award West Pub. Co., 1986-87, 87-88, Corpus Juris Secundum award, 1986-87, Am. Jurisprudence awards (2), 1986; scholar La. State U. Alumni Fedn., 1978, Coun. Devel. French La./French Govt., 1980-81, Loyola Law Sch., 1986. Mem. ABA (sect. law, sci., tech. 1988-91, law student divsn. liaison patent trademark and copyright law 1988-90, intellectual property law sect. 1988—, chmn. law student com. 1996-98, chmn. spl. com. drug crisis 1990-93, co-chmn. ann. meeting arrangements com. 1993-94, internat. treaties and laws com. 1994—, co-chmn. young lawyers com. 1998-99), Am. Intellectual Property Law Assn. (ADR com., internat. and fgn. law com., patent law com. 1994-2000), La. Bar Assn. (internat. law sect. 1992—, intellectual property law sect. 1996—, vice chmn. 1997-98, chair-elect 1998-99, chair 1999-2000), New Orleans Bar Assn. (interim chmn. ad hoc com. drug crisis 1991-92, chmn. intellectual property law com. 1991-95, chmn. law related edn. com. 1995-97), Loyola Law Sch. Moot Ct. Alumni Assn., Sigma Pi Sigma, Pi Delta Phi, Alpha Sigma Nu. Democrat. Roman Catholic. Avocations: gardening, dance, travel, hunting, fishing. Home: 453 Audubon Blvd New Orleans LA 70125-3503 Office Phone: 504-835-2000. E-mail: Nehrbass@aol.com., nehrbass@gsnd.com.

NEHRING, RONALD E. judge; Degree, Cornell U., 1976; JD, U. Utah, 1978. Atty. Utah Legal Svcs.; shareholder Prince, Yeates and Geldzahler, Salt Lake City; judge U.S. Dist. Ct. (3d dist.) Utah, 1995—2003, Utah Supreme Ct., Salt Lake City, 2003—. Chmn. Bd. Dist. Ct. Judges; mem. adv. com. rules profl. conduct Utah Supreme Ct. Fellow: ABA. Office: Utah Supreme Ct PO Box 140210 Salt Lake City UT 84114-0210*

NEHRIR, M. HASHEM, electrical engineer, educator; b. Shiraz, Fars, Iran, Aug. 16, 1946; s. Mohammad Hossein Nehrir; m. Maryam Nehrir, Oct. 15, 1970; children: Ali Reza, Sara, Amin Reza. BSEE, Oreg. State U., 1969, MSEE, 1971, PhD, 1978. Instr. Shiraz U., 1971—75, asst./assoc. prof., 1978—86; vis. scholar Univ. Idaho, 1986—87; asst./assoc. prof. Mont. State U., Bozeman, 1987—96, prof., 1996—. Author: (textbooks) Basic Electric Circuits, 1981, Hybrid Simulation of Engineering Systems, 1986 (Mont. State U. Alumini Assn. and Bozeman Area C. of C. award of excellence, 2001); contbr. numerous articles to profl. jours. Fellow Rsch., Kumamoto U., Japan, 1998, Curtin U. Tech., 2001—04; grantee Rsch., NSF, 1992, 1997, 2002—05, U.S. Dept. Energy, 1994—2000, 2002—, Mont. State U., 1997, 2000. Mem.: IEEE (vice chair 1997, chair Mont. sect. 1998). Avocations: travel, hiking. Office: Mont State U Elec and Computer Engring Dept Bozeman MT 59717 Business E-Mail: hnehrir@ece.montana.edu.

NEHRT, CHADWICK C. business educator; s. Lee C. and Ardith A. Nehrt; m. Ursula F. Mathers, July 20, 1985; children: Ross M., Spenser S. BA, U. Pa., 1976; MBA, Columbia U., 1981; PhD, U. Mich., 1993. Gen. mgr. Wichita (Kans.) Stamp & Seal, 1977—79; analyst Internat. Paper Co., N.Y.C., 1981—82; sr. analyst Philip Morris Internat., N.Y.C., 1982—85, asst. to v.p. Africa Switzerland, 1985—88; asst. prof. U. Tex. at Dallas, Richardson, 1993—97; assoc. prof. internat. bus. Quinnipiac U., Hamden, Conn., 1997—2003, prof. internat. bus., 2003—. Chair undergrad. com. Quinnipiac U. Sch. Bus., 2000—, dir. freshman program, 2001—. Contbr. articles to profl. jours. Mem.: Acad. Mgmt., Acad. Internat. Bus. Avocations: hiking, reading, martial arts, squash. Office: Quinnipiac U Hamden CT 06518

NEHRT, LEE CHARLES, management educator; b. Baldwin, Ill., Sept. 12, 1926; s. Martin William and Amanda Fredarika (Tillock) N.; m. Ardith Ann Saltzman, Mar. 26, 1952; children: Chadwick Charles, Philip Lee, Dana Ann. BS, USCG Acad., 1949; cert. d'etudes politiques, U. Paris, 1955; MBA, Columbia U., 1956, PhD, 1962. Fgn. ops. supr. Atomics Internat., Canoga Park, Calif., 1956-60; prof. internat. bus. Ind. U., 1962-65, 67-69, 71-74; Ford Found. adv. to minister planning, economy and industry, 1965-67; chief adv. group U. Dacca, E. Pakistan, 1969-71; R.P. Clinton prof. internat. mgmt. Wichita (Kans.) State U., 1974-78; pres. World Trade Inst., N.Y.C., 1978-81; Owens-Ill. prof. internat. mgmt. Ohio State U., Columbus, 1981-86. Cons. UN, World Bank, advisor Ministry Planning Govt. Indonesia, 1987-89; dir., curator The Blacksmith Mus., 1991-92. Author: Education in International Business, 1963, Foreign Marketing of Nuclear Power Plants, 1965, Financing Capital Equipment Exports, 1966, International Finance for Multinational Business, 1967, 2d rev. edit. 1972, International Business Research: Past, Present and Future, 1969, The Political Climate for Private Investment in North Africa, 1970, Managerial Policy and Strategy for Developing Countries, 1973, Managerial Policy, Strategy and Planning for South-East Asia, 1974, Managerial Policy and Strategy for the Philippines, 1976, 3d rev. edit. 1989, Business and International Education, 1977, The Internationalization of the Business School Curriculum, 1979, Case Studies in the Internationalization of the Business School Curriculum, 1981, The Politico-Economic Analysis of Countries, 1981; contbr. articles to profl. jours. Chmn. bd. dirs. Monroe County ARC, 1996-98. Lt. (j.g.) USCG, 1949-53. Mem. Acad. Internat. Bus. (pres. 1972-74, dean fellows 1978-81), Soc. Internat. Devel. (gov. 1968-71)

NEI, MASATOSHI, biology professor; b. Miyazaki, Japan, Jan. 2, 1931; came to U.S., 1969; s. Tadashi and Masae (Kawasaki) N.; m. Nobuko Hara, April 25, 1963; children: Keitaro, Maromi. BS in Genetics, Miyazaki U., Japan, 1953; MS in Genetics, Kyoto U., Japan, 1955, PhD in Quantitative Genetics, 1959; D (hon.), Miyazaki U., 2002. Asst. prof. Kyoto (Japan) U., 1960; geneticist Nat. Inst. Radio. Scis., Japan, 1962-65, head population genetics lab., 1965-69; assoc. prof. biology Brown U., Providence, 1969-71, prof. biology, 1971-72; prof. population genetics U. Tex., Houston, 1972-80, acting dir. population genetics, 1978-80, 86-87; disting. prof. biology Pa. State U., University Park, 1990-94, dir. Inst. Molecular Evolutionary Genetics, 1990—, Evan Pugh prof. biology, 1994—. Staff population genetics dept. Univ. Calif., Davis, 1960, N.C. State Univ., Raleigh, 1961; mem. overseers com. Harvard Univ., Cambridge, Mass., 1988-94; mem. working group FAO, Rome, 1994; mem. DNA Forensic Sci., NRC, NAS, 1994-95. Author: Molecular Evolution and Phylogenetics, 2000, Molecular Population Genetics & Evolution, 1975, Molecular Evolutionary Genetics, 1987; editor Molecular Biology & Evolution, 1983-92. Recipient Japan Soc. of Human Genetics award, Ube, 1977, Kihara prize Genetics Soc. of Japan, Tokyo, 1990, Internat. prize for Biology, Tokyo. Fellow AAAA, Am. Acad. Arts. and Sci. (Internat. prize 2002); mem. NAS, Genetics Soc. Am. (editl. bd.), Soc. Molecular

Biology and Evolution (pres. 1994), Internat. Soc. Molecular Evolution; Am. Genetic Assoc. (pres. 1999). Office: Penn State Univ 327 Mueller Lab University Park PA 16802-5303 E-mail: nxm2@psu.edu.

NEIBERG, MICHAEL SCOTT, history professor; b. Pitts., Aug. 2, 1969; s. Laurence and Phyllis S Neiberg; m. Barbara L. Lockley, Dec. 17, 1994; children: Claire JiangHuang, Maya XinFen. PhD, Carnegie Mellon U., 1996. Prof. history USAF Acad., Colo., 1997—. Author: (nonfiction book) Warfare and Society in Europe, 1898 to the Present, 2003. Mem.: Soc. for Mil. History. Office: Hqrs USAF Acad/Dfh 2354 Fairchild Dr Ste 6F101 U S A F Academy CO 80840 Personal E-mail: mbneiberg@aol.com. Business E-Mail: mike.neiberg@usafa.af.mil.

NEIDERT, DAVID LYNN, administrator; b. Akron, Ohio, Nov. 4, 1954; s. William K. and Violet P. (Barker) N.; married; children: Sarah, David, Mariah. BA, Anderson U., 1977, MA, 1987. Dir. human resources Anderson (Ind.) U., 1978-85, dir. aux. svcs., 1985-2000; dir. Ctr. Christian Leadership, 2000—. Author: (book) Four Seasons of Leadership, 1999; co-author: A New Paradigm of Leadership, 1997; contbr. articles to profl. jours. Chair Jr. Achievement, Anderson, 1995-96. Mem.: Inst. Cert. Profl. Mgrs. (bd. govs., chair bd. dirs. 2000—01), Anderson Area Leadership Acad. (Disting. Svc. award 1987, 1995, Servant Leadership award 2002), Internat. Mgmt. Coun. (nat. pres. 1994—95, program chair 1996—, Nat. Disting. Svc. award 1999, Wilbur McFeely award 2003). Republican. Avocations: writing, public speaking, facilitation, consulting. Office: Anderson U 1100 E 5th St Anderson IN 46012-3495 Office Phone: 765-641-4526. E-mail: dlneidert@anderson.edu.

NEIDERT, KALO EDWARD, accountant, educator; b. Safe, Mo., Sept. 1, 1918; s. Edward Robert and Margaret Emma (Kinsey) N.; m. Stella Mae Vest, June 22, 1952; children— Edward, Karl, David, Wayne, Margaret. BS in Bus. Adminstrn. with honors, Washington U., St. Louis, 1949, MS in Bus. Adminstrn, 1950; postgrad., U. Minn., 1950-54. CPA, Nev. Mem. faculty U. Minn., 1950-54; mem. faculty U. Miss., 1954-57, U. Tex., Austin, 1957-61, Gustavus Adolphus Coll., St. Peter, Minn., 1961-62; prof. acctg. and info. systems U. Nev., 1962-90, prof. emeritus, 1990—; auditor Washoe County Employee Fed. Credit Union, 1969-82, dir., treas., 1982-86. Author: Statement on Auditing Procedure in Decision Tree Form, 1974. Asst. scoutmaster local Boy Scouts Am., asst. dist. commr. New Area coun.; bd. dirs. Tahoe Timber Trails, 1980-82, treas., 1981-82, v.p. fin., 1982-84; Bd. dirs. St. Johns Child Care Center, 1982-84; cen. com. mem. Washoe County Rep. Party, Reno, 1986-88, 90—. Mem. AICPA, Assn. System Mgmt. (treas. Reno chpt. 1984—), Am. Acctg. Assn., Am. Econ. Assn., Am. Fin. Assn., Fin. Mgmt. Assn., Nev. Soc. CPAs, Western Fin. Assn., Oddfellows, Beta Alpha Psi, Beta Gamma Sigma. Presbyterian. Office: U Nev Coll Bus Adminstrn Reno NV 89557-0001 E-mail: kneidert@osardtcak.net. *I am the descendent of a second generation American. In addition I was raised on a farm in rural America. Early in life, I learned that achievements come only with hard work and taking advantage of each opportunity that comes along, not waiting to see if there was a better opportunity around the corner. All through life this has been my philosophy; take advantage of each opportunity and work hard to make it succeed.*

NEIDHARDT, FREDERICK CARL, microbiologist, educator; b. Phila., May 12, 1931; s. Adam Fred and Carrie (Fry) N.; m. Elizabeth Robinson, June 9, 1956 (div. Sept. 1977); children: Richard Frederick, Jane Elizabeth; m. Germaine Chipault, Dec. 3, 1977; 1 son, Marc Frederick. BA, Kenyon Coll., 1952, DSc (hon.), 1976; PhD, Harvard U., 1956; DSc (hon.), Purdue U., 1988, Umea U., 1994. Research fellow Pasteur Inst., Paris, 1956-57; H.C. Ernst research fellow Harvard Med. Sch., 1957-58, instr., then assoc., 1958-61; mem. faculty Purdue U., 1961-70, assoc. prof, then prof., assoc. head dept. biol. scis., 1965-70; mem. faculty U. Mich., Ann Arbor, 1970—, chmn. dept. microbiology and immunology, 1970-82, F.G. Novy disting. univ. prof., 1989-99, F.G. Novy disting. univ. prof. emeritus, 2000—, assoc. dean faculty affairs, 1990-93, assoc. v.p. for rsch., 1993-96, acting v.p. for rsch., 1996-97, interim v.p. for rsch., 1997, v.p. for rsch., 1998. Cons. Dept. Agr., 1964-65; mem. grant study panel NIH, 1965-69, 88-92; mem. commn. scholars Ill. Bd. Higher Edn., 1973-79; mem. test com. for microbiology Nat. Bd. Med. Examiners, 1975-79, chmn., 1979-83; mem. sci. adv. com. Neogen Corp., 1982-92; mem. basic energy scis. adv. com. U.S. Dept. Energy, 1994-98; Wellcome vis. prof. in microbiology U. Ky., 1986. Author books and papers in field; mem. editorial bd. profl. jours. Recipient award bacteriology and immunology Eli Lilly and Co., 1966; Alexander von Humboldt Found. award for U.S. sr. scientist, 1979; NSF sr. fellow U. Copenhagen, 1968-69 Mem. Am. Soc. Microbiology (pres. 1981-82), Am. Acad. Arts and Scis., Am. Soc. Biochemistry and Molecular Biology, Am. Inst. Biol. Scis., Genetics Soc. Am., Bavarian Acad. Sci., Soc. Gen. Physiology, Waksman Found. for Microbiology (bd. dirs. 1996—, pres. 2001—), Phi Beta Kappa, Sigma Xi. Office: U Mich Med Sch Dept Microbiology and Immunology Ann Arbor MI 48109-0620 E-mail: fcneid@umich.edu.

NEIDHART, JAMES ALLEN, oncologist, educator; b. Steubenville, Ohio, Aug. 30, 1940; s. James Leonard and Mary Jane (Daniels) N.; m. Patricia Irene Harpkamp, Aug. 16, 1966 (div. Apr. 1985); children— James, Jeffrey, Jennifer; m. Mary Gagen, Feb. 1986; children: Andrew, Rae Ann. BS, Union Coll., Alliance, Ohio, 1962; MD, Ohio State U., 1966. Diplomate Am. Bd. Internal Medicine, Am. Bd. Hematology and Oncology. Intern Bronson Hosp., Kalamazoo, Mich., 1966-67; resident Ohio State U., Columbus, Ohio, 1969-71; postdoctoral fellow Coll. Medicine, Ohio State U., Columbus, 1972-74, asst. prof. medicine, 1974-78, assoc. prof., 1978-84, dir. interdisciplinary oncology unit Comprehensive Cancer Ctr., 1975-80, dep. dir. Comprehensive Cancer Ctr., 1980-84; prof. medicine U. Tex.-Houston-M.D. Anderson Hosp. and Tumor Inst., 1984-86, Hubert L. and Olive Stringer prof. oncology, 1984-86, dep. head div. medicine, 1984-86, chmn. dept. med. oncology, 1984-86; dir. Cancer Rsch. and Treatment Ctr., U. N.Mex., Albuquerque, 1986-96, chief hematology and oncology, 1986-91; dir. Cancer Rsch. and Treatment Ctr. San Juan Regional Cancer Ctr., 1996—. Contbr. chpts. to Recent Advances in Clinical Therapeutics, Clinical Immunotherapy Former mem. bd. dirs. Am. Cancer Soc., Columbus; former v.p. Ohio Cancer Research Assocs. Served to lt. USN, 1967-69, Vietnam Mem. Am. Soc. Hematology, Am. Soc. Clin. Oncology, Am. Assn. Cancer Research, ACP, S.W. Oncology Group, Wilderness Soc., Sierra Club Home: 66 Road 2577 Aztec NM 87410-1020 Office: San Juan Regional Cancer Ctr Farmington NM 87401

NEIDICH, GEORGE ARTHUR, lawyer; b. N.Y.C., Feb. 22, 1950; s. Hyman and Rosalyn N.; m. Alene Wendrow, Jan. 10, 1982; 1 child, Hannah Lauren. BA, SUNY, Binghamton, 1971; JD magna cum laude, SUNY, Buffalo, 1974; MLT, Georgetown U., 1981. Bar: N.Y. 1975, D.C. 1979, Va. 1996, Conn. 1990. Assoc. Runfola & Birzon, Buffalo, 1973-75, Duke, Holzman, Yaeger & Radlin, Buffalo, 1975-77; gen. counsel subcom. on capital, investments and bus. opportunity, com. on small bus. U.S. Ho. of Reps., Washington, 1977-79, subcom. on gen. oversight, 1979-80; sr. legal advisor Task Force Product Liability and Accident Compensation Office of Gen. Counsel, Dept. Commerce, Washington, 1980-81; assoc. Steptoe & Johnson, Washington, 1981-86, of counsel, 1986-89; gen. counsel, sr. v.p. Preferred Health Care, Ltd., Wilton, Conn., 1989-93; COO Value Behavioral Health, Inc., Falls Church, Va., 1993-95; counsellor at law, 1995—; gen. counsel CareAdvantage, Inc., Iselin, NJ, 1999—. Adj. prof. Georgetown U. Law Ctr., 1985-87. Office: 9301 Morison Ln Great Falls VA 22066-4153 Personal E-mail: gneidich@aol.com.

NEIDITCH, H. MICHAEL, historian; b. N.Y.C., May 17, 1946; BA, U. Pa., 1968; PhD, Cambridge U., 1978. Supr. history Cambridge U., 1969—71; lectr. U. Pa., 1972—80, asst. to the provost, 1972—80; legis. dir. on fgn. policy Congressman Benjamin S. Rosenthal (Dem.-N.Y.), 1980—83; dir. programs B'nai B'rith Internat., 1984—94; pub. B'nai B'rith Books, 1986—94; pres. Jerusalem Found. Inc. U.S., 1994—98; dir. devel. and endowment U.S. Holocaust Meml. Mus., 1998—2001; v.p. for leadership giving Am. Com. for the Weizmann Inst. Sci., Israel, 2001—; prin. cons. Nat. Slavery Mus., Fredericksburg, Va., 2000—02; chmn. bd. B'nai B'rith Klutznick Nat. Jewish Mus., Washington, 2002—04; series editor Jewish History, Life and Culture U. Tex. Press, 2004—. Adj. prof. history Am. U. Sch. Internat. Svc., Washington, 1988—2000. Trustee Wolgin Prizes, Israel. Recipient Sara Norton prize, 1971; U. Pa. Thouron scholar, St. John's Coll., Cambridge, 1968—71. Office: Am Com for the Weizmann Inst Sci #409 1730 Rhode Island Ave NW Washington DC 20036*

NEIDLE, CAROL, language educator, researcher; b. N.Y.C., May 31, 1956; d. Amos and Estelle Laura Neidle. BA, Yale U., 1978; MA, Middlebury French Sch., Vt., 1973—76; PhD, MIT, 1982. Faculty mem. Middlebury Coll., Vt., 1983, 1985—88; dir. PhD program in applied linguistics Boston U., 1988—94, prof. linguistics, 1982—. Dir. Am. Sign Lang. Linguistic Rsch. Project, Boston, 1994—. Author: The Role of Case in Russian Syntax, 1988; co-author: The Syntax of American Sign Language, 2000; prin. designer SignStream (software). Grantee, NSF, 1994—. Office: Boston Univ 718 Commonwealth Ave Boston MA 02215

NEIDLINGER, SHERI KIM, music educator; b. Indpls., Feb. 17, 1958; d. William Howard Branum and Carol Sue Boyer; m. Craig N. Neidlinger, Jr., Dec. 19, 1997. BS in Music Edn., U. Tenn., 1980, MusM in Choral Conducting, 1981; cert. in edn. specialist music edn., Ga. So. U., 1996. Cert. SC. State Bd. Edn., 1998, educator Ga. Profl. Stds. Commn., 2001, Nat. Bd. Profl. Tchrs. Orgn., 2003. Tchr. Allendale (S.C.) County Schs., 1982—83, Griffin-Spalding County Schs., Griffin, 1983—84, Cobb County Schs., Marietta, Ga., 1985—86, Atlanta Speech Sch., 1986—87, Savannah-Chatham County Schs., Savannah, Ga., 1988—98, Newberry (S.C.) County Schs., 1998—2001, Morgan County Schs., Madison, Ga., 2001—. Instr. Armstrong Atlantic State U., Savannah Inst. Edn. Arts, Savannah, Ga., 1994—97; adjudicator, cons. Ga. Governor's Honors Program, Atlanta, 1994—. Musician: Atlanta Symphony Orchestra Chorus, Warwick International Choral Festival, Savannah Symphony Chorale, A Tribute To Oscar Hammerstein II, Forsyth Park Festival, I Cantori. Mem. Madison Artist Guild, 2002—03, Ashburn Chorale, Madison, Ga., 2003. Recipient Excellence In Tchg., Savannah News Press and Carolina Morning News, 1999. Mem.: Pa. Ga. Educators, Am. Choral Dirs. Assn., Music Educators Nat. Conf., Ga. Music Educators Assn. (all-state chorus organizing chair 1997—98, clinician conf. 2003), Sigma Alpha Iota Music Frat. (life Sword of Honor 1977). Achievements include research in a study of the relationship between participation in music courses and selected achievement measures. Home: 546 Poplar St Madison GA 30650 Office: Morgan County Mid Sch 920 Pearl St Madison GA 30650 Personal E-mail: kneidlinger@morgan.k12.ga.us. E-mail: kneidlinger@morgan.k12.ga.us.

NEIGHBORS, IRA ARTHELL, social work educator; b. L.A., Oct. 10, 1946; s. Richard Neighbors and Eliza Beaviory Peyton. BA in Psychology, Calif. State U., Dominguez Hills, 1973; MSW in Social Welfare Adminstrn., UCLA, 1983; D of Social Work, Howard U., 1994. Diplomate Am. Bd. Clin. Social Work; lic. clin. social worker, Calif.; adult edn. credential, Calif. Dept. Edn. Psychiat./clin. social worker Dept. Devel. Svcs. State of Calif., Pomona and Porterville, 1984-90; adult correctional tchr. County of Riverside (Calif.) Dept. Edn., 1987-90; grad. tchg. asst. Howard U., Washington, 1991-93; social worker-adoption and quality assurance Dist. Govt., Washington, 1992-94; asst. prof. dept. social work Calif. State U., San Bernardino, 1995-99; assoc. prof. So. U., New Orleans, 1991—. Tchr. ESL Porterville Adult Schs., 1984-86, Moreno Valley (Calif.) Schs., 1997-98; cons. Option Ho., San Bernardino, 1998; social work counselor Vasquez Mgmt. Consulting, Redlands, Calif., 1999; mem. faculty forensic social work Tulane Sch. Social Work Ctr. for Lifelong Learning, New Orleans, 2000. Contbr. articles to profl. jours., chpts. to books. Bd. dirs. Inland Behavioral Svcs., San Bernardino, 1995-98, L.A. Inst. Black Parenting, 1997-2000. Mem. NASW, Nat. Orgn. Forensic Social Work (bd. dirs., pres. 2000-01), Inst. for Black Parenting (bd. dirs., adv. bd.), Inland Area Assn. Black Social Workers (pres. 1995-2001), Calif. Assn. Black Social Work (pres. 1998-2000), Coun. on Social Work Edn. Avocations: reading, jazz, swimming, walking, gymnastics. Home: 1122 W 56th St San Bernardino CA 92407-5346 E-mail: ineighbo@csusb.edu.

NEIKIRK, WILLIAM ROBERT, journalist; b. Irvine, Ky., Jan. 6, 1938; s. Lewis Byron and Nancy Elizabeth (Green) N.; m. Ruth Ann Clary, Sept. 10, 1960; children: Paul Gregory, John Stuart, Christa Lynn. BA in Journalism, U. Ky., 1960. Reporter Lexington (Ky.) Herald, 1959-60; state capital corr. AP, Frankfort, Ky., 1961-66, Baton Rouge, 1966-69; econ. corr. AP (Washington Bur.), 1970-74; nat. econ. writer Chgo. Tribune, Washington, 1974-83, White House corr., 1977, 94-98—, econ. columnist, 1980—, news editor Washington bur., 1983, fin. editor, 1988-91, sr. writer, 1991—, chief Washington corr., 1998—. Author: The Work Revolution, 1983, Volcker: The Money Man, 1987. Recipient Beck award Chgo. Tribune, 1975, Bus. Writing award U. Mo., 1978, 80, Bus. Writing award Amos Tuck Grad. Sch. Bus., Dartmouth Coll., 1980, John Hancock Bus. Writing award Wharton Sch. Fin., U. Pa., 1979, finalist, 1990, 91, John Hancock Bus. Writing award U. Houston, 1980, Loeb Bus. Writing award UCLA Grad. Sch. Mgmt., 1979, Chgo. Headliner Club award, 1979, 84, Raymond Clapper Meml. award, 1981, Barnet Nover award, 1994, Merriman Smith award, 1995, White House Correspondents Assn.; named to Ky. Journalism Hall of Fame, 1998, One of Top 100 Bus. News Luminaries of the Century, TJFR mag., 2000; co-recipient Pulitzer Prize, 2001. Mem. Gridiron Club. Mem. United Ch. of Christ Home: 5121 38th St N Arlington VA 22207-1827 Business E-Mail: wneikirk@tribune.com. E-mail: Billnei@aol.com.

NEIL, DANIEL, journalist; b. Jan. 12, 1960; married; 1 child. BA in creative writing, E. Carolina U., 1982; MA in English lit., N. Carolina U., 1986. Lectr. NC Wesleyan Coll., 1986—87; copy editor, arts columnist Spectator Mag., 1987—89; copy editor, arts reporter News & Observer, Raleigh, NC, 1989—91, automotive section editor, 1991—96; sr. contbg. editor Autoweek mag., 1994—97; automotive reviewer NY Times, 1995—2003; contbg. editor Attache Mag., 1997—99, Car & Driver mag., 1997—2003; sr. travel editor Expedia Travels Mag., 1993—2003; contbg. editor Worth Mag., 2001—03; automotive columnist LA Times, 2003—. Freelance columnist Conde Nast Traveler, Travel and Leisure, Baltimore Sun mag., Atlanta Jour.-Constn., Art Forum, Robb Report, numerous other newspapers and mag. Named to Houghton Mifilin's Best Am. Sports Writing, 2002; recipient Golden Wheel award, Detroit Free Press Club Found., 1992, Ken Purdy award, Internat. Motor Press Assn., 2001, Pulitzer Prize for criticism, 2004. Home: LA Times 202 W First St Los Angeles CA 90012*

NEIL, FRED APPLESTEIN, public relations executive; b. Balt., Nov. 26, 1933; s. Frank and Mollie (Schapiro) Applestein; m. Sheila Tilles, Aug. 30, 1959 (div. May 1980); children: Jay Alan, Brian Mark Applestein, Gail Renee Murphy; m. Dawn Francis Fisher, July 6, 1986. BA, U. Md., 1959. News and sports editor Sta. WITH, Balt., 1959-60; dir. news and sports Sta. WCBM, Metromedia, Balt., 1960-69; press officer Mayor William Donald Schaefer, Balt., 1970-71; gen. mgr. Balt. Banners World Team Tennis League, 1971-72; pres. Fred Neil Assocs., Pub. Rels., Balt., 1972—. Staff specialist pub. info. Md. Rehab. Ctr., Balt., 1980-91; owner Cruising for Mems., 1987—, P.I.O. Office of Comm. and Cmty. Rels., Divsn. Rehab. Svcs., Balt., 1980-2003. Author: It's a Very Simple Game!, The Life and Times of Charles Eckman, 1995, A Funny Thing Happened on the Way to the Health Fair, 2002; editor, contbr. Lafayette Sq. Newsletter, 1974-82, Fed. Hill Newsletter, 1974-82, Greater Penn Ave. Newsletter, 1974-82, MPCA News Letter, 1982—, Md. Rehab. Assn. News Letter, 1985—, Front and Center newsletter, 1980-92, Rehab Digest, 1992—; contbr. articles to mags., newspapers, and newsletters. Bd. dirs. Liberty Showcase Theater, 1985-87, Howard County Summer Theatre, 1992-99, pres. 1995-99; mem. consumer adv. bd., Jewish Vocational Svc., Balt., 2002. With U.S. Army, 1956-58. Recipient award for spot reporting Chesapeake AP, 1967, award for in-depth sports reporting, 1967, 69, Media Appreciation award U.S. Intercollegiate Lacrosse Assn., 1970, Humanitarian award Md. Rehab. Assn., 1982, Appreciation award 1986, Profl. Svc. award Md. Rehab. Counseling Assn., 1985, Ams. with Disabilities Act award The Task Force on the Rights and Empowerment of Ams. with Disabilities, 1991, Outstanding Contbns. award, 1994, Md. Gov.'s Com. on Employment of People with Disabilities Print Media award, 1996, Golden Radio Buffs' Golden Mike award, 1996. Mem. Md. Rehab. Assn. (pres. 1985, 87), Md. Press Club (pres. 1988-89, 97-98, bd. dirs. 1990-91), Md. State Pest Control Assn. (sec. 1981—, exec. sec. 2003-, editor newsletter 1981), Balt. Sports Reporters Assn. (pres. 1964), Balt. Press Reporters Assn. (pres. 1965), Mid-Atlantic Rehab. Adminstrs. Assn. (pres. 1990). Home: PO Box 117 Marydel MD 21649-0117

NEIL, ROBERT F. broadcast executive; Pres., CEO Cox Radio Inc., Atlanta, 1986—. Office: Cox Radio Inc 6205 Peachtree Dunwoody Rd Atlanta GA 30328

NEIL, SANDRA EILLEEN SILVERBERG, psychologist; b. NYC, Sept. 30, 1945; d. Marcus and Pearl (Bloom) Glickfeld; m. Robert Silverberg; children: Gerard David, Simonne Elizabeth, Julien Richard, Shari Beth Silverberg. BE in Counseling, LaTrobe U., Melbourne, Australia, 1976; MA in Clin. Psychology, U. Melbourne, 1985; BA, LaTrobe U., Melbourne, Australia, 1986; PhD in Medicine, U. Melbourne, 1993. Registered clin. and forensic psychologist 1979, cert. family therapist Avanta Virginia Satir Network, 1987. Rsch. asst. dept. ednl. psychology U. Melbourne, 1965—68; clin. psychologist Janefield Hosp., Melbourne, 1975—77, Prince Henry Hosp., Melbourne, 1977—79, Cairnmillar Inst., Melbourne, 1979—83; pvt. practice Melbourne, 1983—; clin. psychologist St. Vincent's Hosp., Melbourne, 1986—93; clin. psychologist and family therapist, founding dir. Satir Centre Australia, Armadale, Australia, 1993—. Forensic psychologist Supreme Ct., Melbourne, 1976—87; media psychologist, 1977—; sworn marriage counsellor Atty. Gen.'s Dept., Melbourne, 1978—. Author: The Persistence of Obesity, 1986, The Psychodynamics of Obesity, 1993, The Family Chessboard, 1995; editor: A Matter Of Life: Psychological Theory, Research And Practice, 1999; author: A Journey Through Three Continents And Four Generations: A Family Reconstruction, 2001. Active Opera Australia. Mem.: APA, Internat. Coun. Psychologists (pres. 1997—2000, named World Area Chair 2000—), Internat. Acad. Family Psychology (Australian nat. rep. 1997—2002), Australian Psychol. Soc. (chmn. pub. and media rels. Victorian Br. 1983—), Patron Opera Australia, Avanta, The Virginia Satir Internat. Network, Lyceum Club. Office: Satir Centre of Australia Suite 2 1051 A/B High Street Victoria Armadale 3143 Australia Office Phone: +613 9824 7755. Office Fax: +61 (0)3 98247865. Business E-Mail: icp@netspace.net.au.

NEILL, DENIS MICHAEL, international consultant; b. Grand Rapids, Mich., Apr. 27, 1943; s. Thomas Patrick and Agnes Josephine (Weber) N.; m. Mary Kathleen Golden, June 11, 1966; children: Mark, Erin. AB cum laude, St. Louis U., 1964, JD cum laude, 1967. Bar: Mo. 1967, D.C. 1969. Gen. atty. Office of Asst. Regional Counsel IRS, Newark, 1967-68; assoc. Arent, Fox, Kintner, Plotkin & Kahn, Washington, 1969-71, Morgan, Lewis & Bockius, Washington, 1971-72; atty. advisor office gen. counsel AID, Washington, 1972-73, asst. gen. counsel legis. and policy coordination, 1973-75, asst. adminstr. legis. affairs, 1975-77; sr. v.p., gen. counsel Aeromaritime Internat. Corp., Washington, 1977-80; counsel Surrey & Morse, Washington, 1980-81; sr. ptnr. Neill & Shaw, Washington, 1981-92; sr. law ptnr. Dalley, Neill, Assevero, Carroll & Nealer, Washington, 1992-93; pres. Neill & Co., Inc., Washington, 1981—; counsel Fin. Markets Internat., Inc., 1998—. Bd. dirs. Barker Found., 1981-86, Fed. City Nat. Bank, Washington, 1987. Lt. USCG, 1968-71. Recipient Superior Unit Citation AID, 1976, Disting. Honor award, 1977. Mem. ABA, FBA, D.C. Bar Assn., Mo. Bar Assn., Nat. Security Indsl. Assn. (bd. dirs. 1982-90), Capitol Hill Club, Columbia Country Club (Chevy Chase, Md.), Jefferson Islands Club. Democrat. Home: 5945 Searl Ter Bethesda MD 20816-2022 Office: Neill & Co 5945 Searl Ter Bethesda MD 20816-2022 E-mail: denisneill@aol.com.

NEILL, RICHARD ROBERT, retired publishing company executive; b. N.Y.C., June 20, 1925; s. Robert Irving and Mildred Mary (Hall) N.; m. Patricia Mae Robinson, Dec. 27, 1952; 1 son, Robert Kenneth. AB summa cum laude, Princeton U., 1948; MA, N.Y. U., 1953. With Prentice-Hall, Inc., N.Y.C. and Englewood Cliffs, N.J., 1948-85, advt. mgr., 1953-58, v.p. advt., 1958-62; pres. Executive Reports Corporation, 1962-85, ret., 1985. Regional chmn. Princeton Alumni Giving, Yonkers, N.Y., 1960-63, Tarrytown-Irvington, N.Y., 1977-80 Pres. Tarrytown (N.Y.) Jr. High Sch. PTA, 1971-72; bd. dirs. Martling Owners, Tarrytown, 1980-84, 89-93. Lt. (j.g.) USNR, 1943-46, PTO. Mem. USN Meml. Found., Princeton Terrace Club (bd. govs. 1986-92), Phi Beta Kappa. Republican. Mem. Reform Ch. Home: Apt 6E 222 Martling Ave Tarrytown NY 10591-4756 *A thought acquired from one of my first bosses: "Everything happens for the best - or can be made to do so." This has been a lifelong help.*

NEILL, ROLFE, retired newspaper executive; b. Mount Airy, N.C., Dec. 4, 1932; s. Kenneth A. and Carmen (Goforth) N.; m. Rosemary Clifford Boney, July 20, 1952 (div.); children: Clifford Randolph, Sabrina Ashley, Dana Catlin, Jessica Rosemary Ingrid, Quentin Roark Robinson; m. Ann Marshall Snider, Sept. 24, 1988. AB in History, U. N.C., 1954. Reporter Franklin (N.C.) Press, 1956-57; reporter Charlotte (N.C.) Observer, 1957-58, bus. editor, 1958-61; editor, pub. Coral Gables (Fla.) Times and The Guide, 1961-63, Miami Beach (Fla.) Daily Sun, 1963-65; asst. to pub. N.Y. Daily News, 1965-67, suburban editor, 1967-68, asst. mng. editor, 1968-70; editor Phila. Daily News, 1970-75; v.p., dir. Phila. Newspapers Inc., 1970-75; chmn., pub. Charlotte (N.C.) Observer, 1975-98. Served with AUS, 1954-56. Office: Knight Pub Co 600 S Tryon St PO Box 32188 Charlotte NC 28232-2188

NEILL, VE, make-up artist; b. Riverside, Calif., May 13, 1951; d. Charles and Eileen Anne (Bernasco) Flores. Grad., Louisville H.S., Woodland Hills, Calif. Credits include (TV movies) Cry for Help, 1978, The London Affair, 1978, Sultan and the Rock Star, 1979, Muppets Go to the Movies, 1981, First Lady of the World, 1982, Money on the Side, 1982, Jane Doe, 1986; (TV Spls.) Sold Out-Lily Tomlin, 1981, Lily for President, 1982, Comedy Store 15th Yr. Reunion, 1988; (TV pilots) One Night Band, 1981, T.J. Hooker, 1981, Madeline (Madeline Kahn), 1982, Girls Life, 1982, A-Team, 1982, Rock & Roll Mom, 1987, Kowalski Loves, 1987, Stephen King's The Shining, 1996 (Emmy award Best Make Up), From the Earth to the Moon, 1997 (Emmy award nomination); (TV show) Pee Wee's Playhouse (Emmy award 1988, Emmy award nominee 1989); (feature films) Star Trek: The Motion Picture (Saturn award 1981), The Incredible Shrinking Woman, 9 to 5, Monty Python at the Hollywood Bowl, Sword and the Sorcerer, The Last Star Fighter, All of Me, The Lost Boys, 1986 (Saturn award 1987), Beetlejuice, 1987 (Acad. award 1987, Saturn award 1988, Brit. Acad. award nominee 1988), Cocoon II, 1988, Big Top Pee Wee, 1988, Dick Tracy, 1989, Flatliners, 1989, Edward Scissorhands, 1990 (Acad. award nominee 1989, Brit. Acad. award nominee 1990), Curly Sue, 1990, Hook, 1991, Batman Returns, 1991 (Saturn award 1992, Acad. award nominee 1992, Brit. Acad. award nominee 1992), Hoffa, 1992 (Acad. award nominee 1992), Rising Sun, 1992, Mrs. Doubtfire, 1993 (Acad. award 1993), Ed Wood, 1993 (Acad. award 1994), Cobb, 1994, Junior, 1994, Batman Forever, 1995, Matilda, 1995, Evening Star, 1996, Mars Attack, 1996, Gattaca, 1996, Batman and Robin, 1996, Amistad, 1997, Stigmata, 1998, Man on the Moon, 1998, Galaxy Quest, 1999, How the Grinch Stole Christmas, 1999, Blow, 2000, A.I., 2000, Death to Smochy, 2001, Duplex, 2002, Blackout, 2002, Pirates of the Caribbean, 2002, (commercial) Sony Mini Disc, 1997, (mag.) Vanity Fair Hollywood Issue, 1998. Mem.: Brit. Acad. Film and TV, Acad. Motion Picture Arts and Scis. Avocations: collecting antiques, beading with antique Am. trade beads, hiking, traveling the U.S. Office: IATSE Local 706 828 N Hollywood Way Burbank CA 91505

NEILL, WILLIAM HAROLD, JR., biological science educator, researcher; b. Wynne, Ark., Oct. 21, 1943; s. William H., Sr. and Shirley A. (Ellis) N.; m. Charlotte A. Jackson, Dec. 20, 1964; 1 child, Amanda K. BS in Zoology, U. Ark., 1965, MS in Zoology, 1967; PhD in Zoology/Statis., U. Wis., 1971. Rsch. fishery biologist Southwest Fisheries Ctr. Nat. Marine Fisheries Svc., Honolulu, 1971-74; assoc. prof. Tex. A&M U./Tex. Agrl. Expt. Sta., College Station, 1975-83; prof. Tex. A&M U./TAES, College Station, 1983—; interim head Dept. Wildlife and Fisheries Sci., College Station, 1992-93; faculty assoc. Bush Inst. Sci., Tech. and Pub. Policy, Tex. A&M U., College Station, 1999—. Mem. organizing com. Advanced Rsch. Inst. on Mechanisms Fish Migration, NATO, 1980-82; mem. tech. com. So. Regional Aquaculture Ctr., USDA, 1987-89; mem. sci.-tech. adv. com. Corpus Christi Bay Nat. Estuary Program, 1994-97; mem. Tex. Sea Grant adv. bd., 1998—. Editor Tex. Jour. Sci., 1983-85; mem. editl. adv. bd. Critical Revs. in Aquatic Sci., 1986-90;

assoc. editor Transactions of the Am. Fisheries Soc., 1995-97; contbr. numerous articles to sci. jours. and books. Grantee numerous orgns., 1975—. Fellow Tex. Acad. Sci.; mem. Am. Fisheries Soc. (life, Award of Excellence com. 1987, 89, chair Publ. Awards com. 1993, editl. bd. 1995), Am. Inst. Fishery Rsch. Biologists, Phi Beta Kappa, Sigma Xi, Phi Sigma, Gamma Sigma Delta. Office: Texas A&M U Dept Wildlife & Fisheries Scis 2258 TAMUS College Station TX 77843-2258 Business E-Mail: w-neill@tamu.edu.

NEILON, PATRICK DANIEL, special education educator; s. John Joseph and Brenda May Neilon; m. Hsin-Yen Sunny Kuo, July 26, 1997; children: John, Brenda. BA, San Francisco State U., 1985. Tchr. L.A. United Sch. Dist., 1996, tchr. spl. edn., 1997—99, San Bernardino City Unified Sch. Dist., 1999—. Pub. Pat and Sunny Press, Fontana, Calif., 2002—. Author (illustrator): The Day My Brain Ran Away, 2002, Super Duper Baby, 2003, I Want to Play, 2003. Mem.: NEA (nat. conv. del. 2000, natino conv. del. 2003), San Bernardino Tchrs. Assn. (union rep. 2003—). Republican. Avocations: songwriting, skiing.

NEILSEN, CRAIG H. hotel executive; b. 1942; Pres. Cactus Pete, Inc., Jackpot, Nev., 1984—, Ameristar Casino Vicksburg, Miss., 1993—. Office: Ameristar Casinos Inc 3773 Howard Hughes Pkwy Las Vegas NV 89109

NEILSON, ERIC GRANT, physician, educator, health facility administrator; b. Bklyn., Sept. 14, 1949; s. Jack Drew and Lynette Elsie (Lundquist) N.; m. Linda Rae Apolzon, May 27, 1972; children: Tinsley, Sigrid. BS magna cum laude, Denison U., 1971; MD magna cum laude, U. Ala., 1975; MD (hon.), U. Pa., 1987. Asst. prof. U. Pa., Phila., 1980-87, assoc. prof., 1987-91, prof., 1991-98, C. Mahlon Kline prof., 1993-98, chief renal-electrolyte & hypertension divsn. dept. medicine, 1988-98; Hugh Jackson Morgan prof., chmn. dept. medicine Vanderbilt U. Med. Ctr., Nashville, 1998—. Attending physician Hosp. of U. Pa., 1980-98; physician-in-chief Vanderbilt U. Hosp., 1998—; cons. in field. Med. editl. bds. on sci. jours.; assoc. editor Kidney Internat., 1997—; contbr. numerous articles to profl. jours. Chmn. med. adv. bd. Lupus Found. of Phila., 1985-95; chmn. pathology A study sect. NIH, Bethesda, Md., 1990-92; chmn. grant rev. com. Nat. Kidney Found. of Delaware Valley; mem. adv. coun. NIDDK, NIH; mem. bd. sci. advisors Polycystic Kidney Found., 1997-2000; mem. postdoctoral fellowship com. Howard Hughes Med. Inst., 1997-2000. Recipient Clin. Scientist award Am. Heart Assn., 1980, Young Investigator award Am. Soc. Nephrology/Am. Heart Assn., 1985, Established Investigator award Am. Heart Assn., 1985-90, President's medal Am. Soc. Nephrology, 1994, AN Richard Disting. Achievement award, 1998. Fellow: ACP; mem.: Internat. Soc. Nephrology (treas. 2003—), Assn. Prof. Medicine (chmn. rsch. com. 2000—), Assn. Subsplty. Profs. (pres. 1994—96, Disting. Prof. award 2003), Am. Assn. Immunologists, Am. Clin. Climatol. Assn., Am. Soc. Nephrology, Assn. Am. Physicians, Am. Soc. Clin. investigation. Mem. Soc. Of Friends. Office: Vanderbilt U Med Ctr Dept Medicine D3100 Med Ctr N Nashville TN 37232-0001 Office Phone: 615-322-3146. Business E-Mail: eric.neilson@vanderbilt.edu.

NEILSON, LINDA EMERSON, theater educator, writer; b. Louisville, Ky., Oct. 3, 1943; d. Charles Castro and Bessie Merle Emerson; m. George Lockhart II Neilson, Oct. 10, 1965 (div.); 1 child, George Lockhart III. BA, Georgetown Coll., 1961—64; MA, U. Ga., 1964—66. Adj. prof. U. Windsor, Canada, 1967—84, Pepperdine U., Malibu, Calif., 1986—96; artistic dir./founder Ont. Kaleidoscope Theatre, Windsor, Canada, 1974—78; prodr. Windsor Dinner Theatre, Windsor, Canada, 1979—80; producer-documentary series Storer Cable TV, Sarasota, Fla., 1983—84; instr. Sr. Acad. at U. South Fla., 1999—. Bd. of directors, v.p. Sr. Acad., Sarasota, Fla., 2000—; consulting/edn. St. Clair C.C., Windsor, Canada, 1976—79; playwright Family Services Bur., Windsor, Canada, 1980—81; cons. & dir. Windsor Sr. Theatre, Windsor, Canada, 1981—83; host of tv show, in the pub. interest Storer Cable TV, Sarasota, Fla., 1982—84. Actor: (shakespeare in central park) Othello and Midsummer Night's Dream; host (television program) In the Public Interest; author: (plays) Men OH! Pause (Finalist in West Coast Playwright Competition, 2003); actor: (industrial show) General Motors, (tv commercials); co-prodr.: (historical drama) Frontier of Freedom; author (voice overs): Hist. Pub. Svc. Spots; author: (director) (television documentary series) Florida Phenomenon; author: (plays) One Acts commissioned to dramatize Social Problems, Communication Gap; actor(director): (television special program) Christmas Memories; author: (plays) Creativity in the Classroom Series; author: (director) infomercials, commercials; author: (films) Habitat For Humanity. Social & program chair U. of Windsor Women's Club, Windsor, Canada, 1967—80; chair, speaker's bur. & pub. rels. Habitat For Humanity, Ventura, Calif., 1995—98; pres. Windsor Theatre for Young People, Windsor, Canada, 1975—80. Recipient Co-Winner of Playwright Competition, West Coast Playwrights Play's The Thing Competition, 2003; grant, Province of Ont., 1975—77. Mem.: Profl. Sarasota Writers (pres. 2002—04), Am. PEN Women, Sarasota Film Soc., West Coast Women Writers, Sarasota Fiction Writers, Info. Forum (founding mem. 2000—04). Liberal. Avocations: travel, tennis, reading, swimming, theater. Personal E-mail: emersonlinda@yahoo.com.

NEILSON, WINTHROP CUNNINGHAM, III, communications executive, financial communications consultant, photographer; b. N.Y.C., Jan. 7, 1934; s. Winthrop Cunningham, Jr. and Frances Fullerton (Jones) N.; m. Ilse Rossenbeck, Jan. 4, 1957; children: Luise R., Victoria F.; m. Demaris King Hetrick, July 5, 1985; 1 child, Whitney C. C.; stepchildren: Norman P. Hetrick Jr., D. Page Hetrick BA, Harvard U., 1956; grad. in security analysis, N.Y. Inst. Finance, 1963. Asst. prodr., asst. dir. Rangley Lakes Theater, 1955; gen. assignment reporter Albany (N.Y.) Times-Union, 1959—60; pub. info. writer, spkr. Consol. Edison, 1960—61; asst. dir. pub. rels. Union Svc. Corp., 1962; with Georgeson & Co., N.Y.C., 1962—81, prin., 1969—81; sr. v.p. D.F. King & Co. Inc., N.Y.C., 1982—86; founder, mng. dir. Krone Comm., Harrisburg, Pa., 1986—87; pres. Krone Group Inc., Harrisburg, 1987—89; mng. dir. Neilson/Hetrick Group, Montclair, NJ, 1990—93, Harrisburg, Pa., 1993—97, chmn. Chambersburg, Pa., 1987—; mng. dir. Corp. Investor Comm., Carlstadt, NJ, 1991—93; guest lectr. NYU, 1991; profl. nature photographer, 2001—. Author: series Aunt Jane, 1971, 73, The Reluctant Marriage, 1978, Investorism, 1981, Annual Reports, The Agony and the Ecstasy, 1985, Individual Investors, a Counterbalance to Institutional Investors, 1986; writer, assoc. editor: Trends, 1965-81; contbr. articles to profl. jours. Mem. Mountain Lakes (N.J.) Econ. Devel. Council, 1974-79, chmn., 1977-79; pres. Robert A. Taft Republican Club, Queens, N.Y., 1964-65, chmn., 1966-67; treas. 23d Assembly Dist. Rep. Party, 1966-67; county committeeman, 1964-67; del. N.Y. State Nominating Conv., 1966; campaign mgr. for 2 assemblymen and state senator; mem. exec. com. Chambersburg Cmty. Theater, Inc., 2002-03. Served with AUS, 1956-59. Recipient Investor Edn. Disting. Service award Nat. Assn. Investors Clubs, 1986. Mem. Nat. Investor Rels. Inst. (charter dir. 1980-84, v.p. manpower 1980-81, v.p. long-range planning 1981-84), Pub. Rels. Soc. Am. (charter, exec. com. investor rels. 1982-90, chmn. 1987, Pres. award 1987, charter inductee into Hall of Fame for Investor Rels.), Corp. Rels. Soc. Ctrl. Pa. (v.p. 1986-89, pres. 1994-95), Ctrl. Pa. Entrepreneurial Assn. (bd. dirs. 1988-89, adv. bd. tech. coun. Ctrl. Pa. 1994-96), Chambersburg Country Club, DU Club, Hasty Pudding Club, Ausable Club. Lutheran. Home and Office: 3333 Carnoustie Dr Chambersburg PA 17201-8116 Home (Summer): Ausable Club 14 Neilson Way Saint Huberts NY 12943 E-mail: neil@pa.net.

NEIMAN, DONALD FLINT, lawyer; b. Hammond, Ind., Oct. 17, 1944; s. John Hammond and Madeline Clare (Flint) N.; m. Susan Maher, July 25, 1969; children: Amy Maher, Donald Flint II. BBA, U. Iowa, 1966; JD, Drake U., 1969. Bar: Iowa 1969, U.S. Dist. Ct. (no. and so. dists.) Iowa, Ct. Appeals (8th cir.). Pres., shareholder Neiman, Neiman, Stone & Spellman, PC, Des Moines, 1972-90, Bradshaw, Fowler, Proctor & Fairgrave PC, Des Moines, 1991—. Trustee U.S. Bankruptcy Ct., Des Moines, 1972—. Chmn. tax assessment com. West Des Moines, 1998-99, chmn. capital planning com., 1990-95. Capt. USAF, 1969-72. Mem.: Natl. Assn. of Bankruptcy Trustees, Federal Bar Assn., Iowa State Bar Assn. Republican. Roman Catholic. Avocations: handball, skiing, hunting. Office: Bradshaw Fowler Proctor et al 801 Grand Ave Ste 3700 Des Moines IA 50309-2727 E-mail: neiman.donald@bradshawlaw.com.

NEIMAN, GARY S. university administrator; b. Chgo., Oct. 2, 1947; s. David J. and Miriam (Factor) N.; m. Margalit C. Buchsbaum, June 11, 1972; children: Emily R., Lisa R. BS, U. Ill., MA, 1971, PhD, 1973. Cert. of clin. competence Am. Speech-Lang.-Hearing Assn. Rsch. and clin. assoc. Ctr. for Craniofacial Anomalies U. Ill./Abraham Lincoln Sch. of Medicine, Chgo., 1972; speech, pathologist, facial deformity team Carle Found. Hosp., Urbana, 1972-73; asst. prof. speech Kans. State U., Manhattan, 1973-77, dir. Speech and Hearing Clinic, 1974-77; assoc. prof. Sch. of Speech Pathology and Audiology Kent (Ohio) State U., 1977-92, dir. Sch. of Speech Pathology and Audiology, 1979-90; assoc. dean for grad. affairs and health-related programs Kent State U., 1990-99, prof., speech pathology and audiology, 1992-99. Co-dir. and speech pathologist Akron Craniofacial Ctr., Children's Hosp. Med. Ctr. of Akron, 1977-99; mem. med. adv. bd. Kent Vis. Nurse Assn., 1979-85; dean Coll. Health and Human Svcs. Ohio U., 1999—, prof. Sch. Hearing and Speech Scis., 1999—. Author: (book) A Parent's Guide: Cleft Lip and Palate and Other Craniofacial Problems, 1985; contbr. articles to profl. jours.; presenter in field. Vice-pres. bd. dirs. Portage County Unit, Am. Cancer Soc., Kent, 1980-85; pres. Temple Beth Shalom, Hudson, Ohio, 1992-94; pres., bd. trustees Orgn. for Health Improvement in Appalachia, 2002-. Mem. Am. Cleft Palate-Craniofacial Assn., Am. Speech Lang. Hearing Assn., Internat. Assn. of Logopedics and Phoniatrics, Internat. Soc. for the Study of Behaviour Devel., Phi Beta Delta. Office: Coll Health and Human Svcs Ohio U W 381 Grover Ctr Athens OH 45701-1711 E-mail: neiman@ohio.edu.

NEIMAN, KENNETH PAUL, judge; b. N.Y.C., July 4, 1945; s. Julius and Gertrude (Fox) N.; m. Jan Dumond, May 24, 1987; children: Jennifer Gottlieb, Anna L. Neiman, J. Matthew Gowdy, Kerri Escudero. BA, Tufts U., 1967; JD, Harvard Law Sch., 1971. Bar: N.Y. 1972, Mass. 1974, U.S. Dist. Ct. Mass. 1974, U.S. Ct. Appeals (1st cir.) 1981, U.S. Supreme Ct. 1978. Staff atty. Mental Health Info. Svcs., N.Y.C., 1971, Ctr. Social Welfare, Policy & Law, N.Y.C., 1971-73; rsch. fellow Legal Svcs. Corp. Rsch. Inst., Washington, 1978; mng. atty. Western Mass. Legal Svcs., Holyoke, 1973-81; ptnr. Fierst & Neiman, Northampton, Mass., 1981-94; U.S. magistrate judge Dist. Mass., Springfield, 1995—. Mem. ABA, Mass. Bar Assn., Mass. Bar Found., Hampshire County Bar Assn. Office: US Dist Ct 1550 Main St Springfield MA 01103-1422

NEIMAN, LEROY, artist; b. St. Paul, June 8, 1927; s. Charles and Lydia (Serline) Runquist; m. Janet Byrne, June 22, 1957. Student, Sch. Art Inst., Chgo., 1946-50, U. Ill., 1951, DePaul U., 1951; LittD (hon.), Franklin Pierce Coll., 1976; D (hon.), St. John's U., 1980, Iona Coll., 1985, Hofstra U., 1997, St. Francis Coll., 1998, St. Bonaventure U., 1999. Instr. Sch. Art Inst. Chgo., 1950-60, Saugatuck (Mich.) Summer Sch. Painting, 1957-58, 63, Sch. Arts and Crafts, Winston-Salem, N.C., 1963; instr. painting Atlanta Youth Council, 1968-69; printmaker-graphics, 1971—; artist Olympics, ABC-TV, Munich, 1972, ofcl. artist Montreal, 1976, U.S. Olympics, 1980, 84; computer artist CBS-TV (Superbowl), New Orleans, 1978; ofcl. artist Goodwill Games CNN-TV, Moscow, USSR, 1986; 1st ofcl. artist Ky. Derby, Louisville, 1997; ofcl. artist Mardi Gras, New Orleans, 2002. Mem. adv. com. LeRoy Neiman Ctr. for Print Studies Sch. of the Arts Columbia U., 1995; mem. adv. com. for N.Y.C. Commn. for Cultural Affairs, 1995, UCLA LeRoy Neiman Ctr. for Study of Am. Soc. and Culture, 1998; established LeRoy Neiman Art Ctr. for Youth, San Francisco, 2000, Watsonville, Calif., 2002. One-man shows include Oehlschlaeger Gallery, Chgo., 1959, 61; O'Hana Gallery, London, Gallerie O. Bosc, Paris, 1962, Hammer Gallery, N.Y.C., 1963, 65, 67, 70, 72, 76, 78-79, 81-83, 85-87, 89, 92, 94, 97, 2000, 03, Huntington-Hartford Gallery Modern Art, N.Y.C., 1967, Heath Gallery, Atlanta, 1969, Abbey Theatre, Dublin, Ireland, 1970, Museo de Bellas Artes, Caracas, Indpls. Inst. Arts, 1972, Hermitage Mus., Leningrad, Tobu Gallery, Tokyo, 1974, Springfield (Mass.) Mus. Fine Arts, 1974, 84, Knoedler Gallery, London, 1976, Casa gratica, Helsinki, 1977, Renée Victor, Stockholm, 1977, Okla. Art Ctr., Oklahoma City, 1981, Harrod's, London, 1982; retrospective show, Minn. Mus. Art, St. Paul, 1975, Meredith Long Galleries, Houston, 1978, Hanae Mori Gallery, Tokyo, 1988, New State Tretyakov Mus., 1988, Butler Inst., Youngstown, Ohio, 1990, Galerie Marcel Bernheim, Paris, 1993, Ky. Derby Mus., Louisville, 1995, 1997, Marlborough Gallery, NYC, 2000, The Fairfield, Sturgeon Bay, Wis., 2001, Nat. Art Mus. Sport, Ind. U.-Purdue U., 2001, Wildlife Experience, Parker, Colo., 2003; two-man show, Neiman-Warhol, Los Angeles Inst. Contemporary Art, 1981; exhibited in group shows at Art Inst. Chgo., 1954-60, Carnegie Internat., 1956, Corcoran Gallery Am., Washington, Walker Art Center, Mpls., 1957, Ringling Mus., Sarasota, Fla., 1959, Salon d'Art Mus., Paris, 1961, Nat. Gallery Portraiture, Smithsonian Instn., Washington, Minn. Mus. Art, 1969, Rotunda Della Basana, Milan, Italy, 1971, Royal Coll. Art, London, 1971, Minn. Mus. Art Nat. Tour, 1976-77, Whitney Mus., 1985; Master Prints of 19th and 20th Centuries, Hammer Gallery, N.Y., 1987, Salon d'Automne, Paris, 1992-93, Newport Art Mus., 2004; represented in permanent collections Mpls. Inst. Arts, Ill. State Mus., Springfield, Joslyn Mus., Omaha, Wodham Coll., Oxford, Eng., Nat. Art Mus. Sport, NYC, Museo De Ballas Artes Caracas, Hermitage Mus., Indpls. Inst. Arts, U. Ill., Balt. Mus. Fine Art, The Armand Hammer Collection, Los Angeles, Edwin & Ruth Kennedy Mus. Am. Art at Ohio U., Midwest Mus. Am. Art, Elkhart, Ind., Nat. Art Mus. Sport, Indpls.; executed murals at Merc. Nat. Bank, Hammond, Ind., Continental Hotel, Chgo., Swedish Lloyd Ship S.S. Patricia, Stockholm, ceramic tile mural, Sportsmans Park, Chgo.; author: LeRoy Neiman—Art and Life Style, 1974, Horses, 1979, LeRoy Neiman. Posters, 1980, LeRoy Neiman. Catalogue Raisonné, 1980, Carnaval, 1981, LeRoy Neiman: Winners, 1983, Japanese translation, 1985, LeRoy Neiman, Monte Carlo Chase, 1988, The Prints of LeRoy Neiman, 1980-90, Big Time Golf, 1992, LeRoy Neiman, An American in Paris, 1994, LeRoy Neiman on Safari, 1997, The Prints of LeRoy Neiman 1991-2000, LeRoy Neiman, Five Decades, 2003, The LeRoy Neiman Sketchbook, 2004; illustrator: 12 paintings deluxe edit. Moby Dick, 1975, 35 charcoal drawings deluxe edit. Casey at the Bat, 2000, trade edit., 2002. Served with AUS, 1942-46. Recipient 1st prize Twin City Show, 1953, 2d prize Minn. State Show, 1954, Clark Meml. prize Chgo. Show, 1957, Hamilton-Graham prize Ball State Coll., 1958, Municipal prize Chgo. Show, 1958, Purchase prize Miss. Valley Show, 1959, Gold medal Salon d'Art Modern Paris, 1961; award of merit as nation's outstanding sports artist AAU, 1976; Olympic Artist of Century award, 1979, Gold Medal award St. John's U., 1985. Address: 1 W 67th St New York NY 10023-6200

NEIMAN, MARCUS LAWRENCE, educational consultant; b. Akron, Ohio, Feb. 22, 1948; s. Eli and Mildred Pauline Neiman; m. Mary Ann Grof, Aug. 10, 1991; children: Nancy Elizabeth Schneider, Jennifer Ann Smith; m. Margaret Brown, May 9, 1970 (div. May 10, 1990). BS in Music Edn., U. Akron, 1970; MusM Edn., U. Mich., 1971. Ednl. Supervision State of Ohio, 1980. Fine arts cons. Medina County Schs. Ednl. Svc. Ctr., Medina, Ohio, 1980—2000, dir. of fine arts tours and festivals, 2001—. Condr. of bands Medina Cmty. Band, Medina, Ohio, 1972—; artistic dir./owner Marcus Neiman & The Sounds of Sousa Band, Medina, Ohio, 1981—. Home: Medina County Performing Arts Found. (v.p. 2001—02, pres. 2003). Home: 4756 Gateway Dr Medina OH 44256 Personal E-mail: mneiman312@aol.com. E-mail: mneiman312@aol.com.

NEIMS, ALLEN HOWARD, pediatrician, educator, dean, researcher; b. Chgo., Oct. 24, 1938; s. Irving Morris and Ruth (Geller) N.; m. Myrna Gay Robins, June 18, 1961; children: Daniel Mark, Susan Roberta, Nancy Elizabeth. BA, BS, U. Chgo., 1957; MD, Johns Hopkins U., 1961, PhD, 1966. Intern, resident in pediatrics Johns Hopkins Hosp., 1961-62, 66-68; research assoc. Lab. Neurochemistry, NIH, 1968-70; asst. prof. physiol. chemistry and pediatrics Johns Hopkins Med. Sch., 70-72; assoc. prof. McGill U., 1972-77, prof. pharmacology and pediatrics, 1977-78; dir. Roche developmental pharmacology unit, 1972-78; prof., chmn. dept. pharmacology and therapeutics, prof. pediatrics U. Fla., Gainesville, 1978-89, dean Coll. Medicine, 1989-96, prof. pharmacology, pediat., 1996—; dir. Ctr. for Spirituality and Health, 2002—. Dir. Ctr. Spirituality and Health; Fulton Bequest prof. U. Melbourne, Australia, 1974; mem. human embryology and devel. study sect. NIH, 1979-83; sci. cons. Can. Found. for Study of Sudden Infant Death, 1974-77, Nat. Soft Drink Assn., 1976-78, Internat. Life Scis. Inst., 1978-89; bd. sci. counsellors Nat. Inst. Child Health and Human Devel., 1984-89. Contbr. chpts. to books, articles to med. jours. Served to comdr. USPHS, 1968-70. NIH, Can. Med. Research Council grantee. Mem. Can. Assn. Research in Toxicology (pres. 1976-78), Am. Soc. Pharmacology and Exptl. Therapeutics (past mem. exec. coms. clin. pharmacology and drug metabolism), Am. Pediatric Soc., Am. Acad. Pediatrs. Office: U Fla Coll Medicine PO Box 100267 Gainesville FL 32610-0267 Office Phone: 352-392-0687. E-mail: ahneims@ufl.edu.

NEINAS, CHARLES MERRILL, economist, consultant, sports association executive; b. Marshfield, Wis., Jan. 18, 1932; s. Arthur Oscar and Blanche Amelia (Reeder) N.; children: Andrew, Toby. BS, U. Wis., 1957. Asst. exec. dir. Nat. Collegiate Athletic Assn., Kansas City, Mo., 1961-71; commr. Big Eight Conf., Kansas City, 1971-81; exec. dir. Coll. Football Assn., 1981—97; Dr. Patricia L. Pacey prof. econs. U. Colo., Boulder, 1981—, econ. cons., 1981—. Adviser Am. Football Coaches Assn., 1997—; cons. NCAA Football, 1997—. Served with USNR, 1952-54. Office: Neinas Sports Svcs 6630 Gunpark Dr Boulder CO 80301-3372 Home: 5344 Westridge DR Boulder CO 80301-6501

NEIS, ARNOLD HAYWARD, pharmaceutical company executive; b. NYC, Feb. 13, 1938; s. Harry H. and Mary Ruth (Bishop) N.; children: Nancy R., Robert C. BS cum laude, Columbia U., 1959; MBA, NYU, 1967. With Scott Chem. Co., 1959-64; v.p. mktg., then v.p. Odell, Inc., N.Y.C., 1964-71, pres. Thayer Knomark div., 1969-71; pres., chief exec. officer E.T. Browne Drug Co., Inc., Englewood Cliffs, N.J., 1971—, chmn., 2000—. Dir. Esquire A.B. Stockholm, Knomark Can. Ltd., E.T. Browne Internat. Fellow Royal Soc. Chemists, Royal Geog. Soc., Am. Inst. Chemists, N.Y. Acad. Scis.; mem. AAAS, Am. Chem. Soc., Am. Pharm. Assn., New Eng. Soc. (pres., bd. dirs.), Explorers Club (v.p., bd. dirs., Sweeney medal 1997), Chemists Club, Lotos Club, Soldiers, Sailors and Airmans Club (bd. dirs.), St. Georges Soc., Ch. Club, Pilgrims of the U.S., Order St. John. Episcopalian. Home: 898 Park Ave New York NY 10021-0234 Office: PO Box 1613 440 Sylvan Ave Englewood Cliffs NJ 07632-2700

NEIS, ARTHUR VERAL, healthcare and development company executive; b. Lawrence, Kans., May 30, 1940; s. Veral Herbert and Louise (Schlegel) N.; m. Fleeta Weigel, Apr. 12, 1969 (dec. 1999); children: Frederich Arthur, Benjamin Jason, Sarah Louise. BS in Bus., U. Kans., 1962, MS in Acctg., 1963. CPA, Kans., Iowa. Mgmt. cons. Arthur Andersen & Co., Kansas City, Mo. and Mpls., 1963-74; chief corp. acctg. Carlson Co., Mpls., 1974-76; contr. The Fullerton Cos., Mpls., 1976-78; asst. treas. Fru-Con Corp., St. Louis, 1978-80, asst. contr., 1981, contr., 1982-86; corp. contr. LCS Holdings, Inc. (Weitz Corp. and Subsidaries), Des Moines, 1986-87, v.p., treas., CFO, 1987—; treas., CFO Weitz Co., Des Moines, 1987-93, Life Care Services LLC, Des Moines, 1987—; v.p., treas., CFO, mem. exec. com. LCS Holdings and Subs., Inc., 1995—, also trustee retirement plan, bd. dirs. Adv. group Nat. Assn. Ins. Com., 1990—93; mem. task force pvt. co. reporting GAAP, 2004; treas., exec. com. bd. Villa de Maria Montessori Sch., St. Louis, 1984—86; trustee Fin. Execs. Rsch. Found., 1994—2000, chair audit com., 1997—98, vice chair rsch., 1998—2000, chmn., 2000—01; trustee Plymouth Congl. Ch., 1997—97, found. trustee, 1998—2001, chair, 2000—01; active Des Moines Poetry Festival, 2000—04, treas. bd. dirs., 2003—04; bd. dirs. Inst. Humane Studies, George Mason U., Fairfax, Va., 1971—, exec. com., 1975—83, chmn., 1978—83; bd. dirs. Lake Country Sch., Mpls., 1973—78, Alliance for Arts and Understanding, co-chair, 1993—96, bd. trustees, 1993—2002, chair, 1996—2002. Mem. AICPA (pvt. co. fin. registry task force 2004), Kans. Soc. CPAs, Iowa Soc. CPAs, Fin. Execs. Inst. (bd. dirs. Iowa chpt. 1986, 88-94, sec. 1988-90, v.p. 1990-91, pres. 1991-92). Avocation: history. Home: 1575 NW 106th St Clive IA 50325-6604 Office: 1575 NW 106th St Clive IA 50325

NEIS, JAMES MICHAEL, lawyer; b. Chgo., Mar. 3, 1946; BA, DePaul U., 1969, JD, 1973. Bar: Ill. 1973, U.S. Tax Ct. 1974. Ptnr. Winston & Strawn, Chgo., 1977-93, mng. ptnr., 1993—. Adj. prof. law DePaul U., 1979-86. Mem. ABA, Ill. State Bar Assn., Chgo. Bar Assn. Office: Winston & Strawn 35 W Wacker Dr Ste 4200 Chicago IL 60601-1695

NEISER, BRENT ALLEN, foundation executive, public affairs and personal finance consultant, speaker; b. Cin., Sept. 16, 1954; s. Rodger and Hazel Neiser; m. Marion, Apr. 1, 1978; children: Christy Jean, Steven José, April Reneé. BA in Pub. Affairs, George Washington U., 1976; MA in Urban Studies, Occidental Coll., 1978; MBA, U. Louisville, 1979; postgrad. in internat. affairs and homeland security, U. Denver, 2003—. Cert. fin. planner, 1985; cert. assn. exec., 1994; chartered mut. fund counselor, 1996; accredited asset mgmt. specialist, 1998; cert. sr. advisor, 2004. Project mgr., analyst Legis. Research Com., Frankfort, Ky., 1978-84; pres. Moneyminder, Denver and Frankfort, 1983-91; dir. edn., govt. affairs Inst. Cert. Fin. Planners, Denver, 1985-91, exec. dir., 1991-94; pub. affairs, govt. rels. bus. strategies cons. The Brent Neiser Co., Englewood, Colo., 1994—; dir. collaborative programs Nat. Endowment for Fin. Edn., 1995—. Mng. dir. Fin. Products Stds. Bd., Denver, 1985-91; co-creator Personal Econ. Summit '93, Washington. Author: EPCOT/World Showcase External Directions, Walt Disney Imagineering, 1977, Personal Management, 1996, 2000, 03; co-inventor: Trivia Express (game) Denver, 1986; developer over 100 publs. for disaster victims, low income families and children. Vol., v.p. Big Bros./Big Sisters, Frankfort, 1982; del. Colo. Model Constn. Conv., 1987; mem. citizens budget rev. com. Greenwood Village; mem. long range planning com. Adoption Exch., Denver, 1992-93, bd. dirs., 1993-99; polit. action dir. Frankfort NAACP, 1983, legis. chmn. state conf., 1984; troop com. mem., asst. scoutmaster Boy Scouts Am., Englewood, 1993-99; bd. dirs. Young Ams. Bank Edn. Found., 1993-99, chair edn. coun.; mem. Leadership Denver, 1994; vol. host com. Denver Summit of the Eight, 1997; nat. spokesperson Protect our Children Campaign, 1996; active Annie E. Casey Found.: Nat. Foster Care Awareness Project, 1999-2002; citizen's panelist News Hour with Jim Lehrer (PBS), 1998—; founding ptnr. Social Venture Ptnrs., Denver, 2000-04, Colo. Coun. of Advisors on Consumer Credit, 2000—; mem. CFP bd. Consumer Adv. Coun. on Fin. Planning, 2001-03; bd. advisors Coll. Visual and Performing Arts, Winthrop U., 2002—. Lt. (j.g.) USNR, 1985-92. Recipient Assn. Advance Am. award Excellence, 1996, 1998; Pub. Affairs fellow Coro Found., 1976-77; fellow Ctr. for Social Innovation Stanford U., 2003. Mem. Investors Edn. Assn. Colo. (bd. dirs. 1995-2001), Nat. Assns. in Colo., Denver C. of C. (pub. affairs coun.), N.Am. Securities Adminstrs. Assn. (investment adviser and fin. planner adv. com.), Nat. Soc. Compliance Profls. (bd. dirs. 1987-89), Am. Film Inst. (writers workshop), Am. Polit. Items Collectors, Fin. Planning Assn., Snowboard Outreach Soc. Avocations: snowboarding, drums (jazz) and latin percussion music, golf, swimming, modern design. Office: 5860 Big Canyon Dr Englewood CO 80111-3516 Office Phone: 303-224-3501. E-mail: ban@nefe.org.

NEISSER, HORST, library director; b. Nuernberg, Germany, July 30, 1943; s. Heinrich and Eleonore (Mergner) Neisser; m. Barbara Friedrich. Student, U. Frankfurt, Germany, 1965-68; DPhil, U. Tuebingen, Germany, 1973. Subject specialist EKZ, Reutlingen, Germany, 1973-76; dir. City Libr. Saarbrücken, Germany, 1976-86, City Libr. Cologne, Germany, 1986—. Lectr Fochhochschule für Sozialwesen, Esslingen, Germany, 1973—76, Fachhochschule für Bibliotheken, Cologne, Germany, 1987—; mem various library communications, Berlin, 1982—; mem various adv comts, 1974—. Author: (book) Die Jugendzeitschrift, 1975, Diskotheken in Deutschland, 1979, Traumzeiten, 1984, Der Gott der Ameise, 1993, Centratur, 1996, Centratur II, 1997. Mem.: Deutschen Gesellschaft fuer Informationswissenschaft und Informationspraxis (pres 1999), Verband Deutscher Schriftsteller. Avocations: painting, music. Home: Katharinental 13 51467 Bergisch-Gladbach Germany Office: City Libr Cologne Josef-Haubrich-Hof 1 50676 Cologne Germany E-mail: horst@neisser.info.

NEITER, GERALD IRVING, lawyer; b. L.A., Nov. 11, 1933; s. Harry and Ida Florence (Alperin) N.; m. Margaret P. Rowe, Mar. 5, 1961; children: David, Karen, Michael. BSL, JD, U. So. Calif., 1957. Bar: Calif. 1958. Judge pro tem Mcpl. Cts., L.A. and Beverly Hills, 1970-94, Calif. Superior Ct., L.A. County, 1974-94, family law mediator, 1976—; prin. Gerald I. Neiter, P.C., L.A., 1981—. Lectr. State Bar of Calif., 1968, 76, 79, 81; former referee State Bar Ct.; arbitrator Am. Arbitration Assn.; mediator L.A. Superior Ct. Mem.

ABA, Los Angeles County Bar Assn. (arbitrator), Beverly Hills Bar Assn., State Bar Calif. Office: 1925 Century Park E Ste 2000 Los Angeles CA 90067-2701 Office Phone: 310-277-2236. E-mail: Neitlaw@aol.com.

NEITHERCUT, DAVID J. real estate executive; CFO Equity Residential Properties Trust, Chgo. Office: Equity Residential Properties Trust 2 N Riverside Plz Ste 450 Chicago IL 60606-2600

NEITHERCUT, MARK EDWARD, foundation executive; b. Flint, Mich., June 26, 1951; s. Edward John and Elizabeth Koegel Neithercut; m. Helen Patrick Lownie, Oct. 6, 1990. BA with high honors in history, U. Mich., 1974; MA, Mich. State U., 1977; PhD, U. B.C., Vancouver, Can., 1984. From instr. to asst. prof. U. Ala., Tuscaloosa, 1982-85; dir. Mich. Met. Info. Ctr. Wayne State U., Detroit, 1985-93, assoc. prof. rsch., 1993; program officer Kresge Found., Troy, Mich., 1993-95; v.p. program Cmty. Found. for Southeastern Mich., Detroit, 1995—. Adj. prof. urban planning Wayne State U., Detroit, 1990—95; chmn. Mich. Nonprofit Rsch. Program, Aspen Inst., Washington, 2003—; membership com. Coun. on Founds., Washington, 1999—; bd. dirs. Detroit Local Initiatives Support Corp. Author: (monographs) Status of Detroit Youth, 1993, Patterns of Mortgage Lending in the City of Detroit, 1990. Bd. dirs. Mich. Housing Trust Fund, Lansing, 1994-98, Detroit Inst. Arts, 1993-94, Detroit Artists Market, 1993-95; membership com. Detroit Inst. Arts, 1995—; pres. Founders Jr. Coun., Detroit Inst. Arts, 1993-94; chmn. Detroit Area Grantmakers, 2001-2003; mem. cmty. found. leadership team Coun. of Found., 2001—; mem. adv. com. John S. and James L. Knight Found., Detroit, 2002—; mem. bd. govs. Cranbrook Schs., 2003—. Named NSFRE Vol. of Yr., Detroit Inst. Arts, 1994; grantee Kresge Found., 1998—2004; James B. Angell scholar, U. Mich., 1974, Internat. Schoolboy fellow, English Spkg. Union, 1969—70, doctoral fellow, U. B.C., 1978—80. Mem. Grosse Pointe Club, Flint Rainbow Club, Phi Beta Kappa. Avocations: steelhead fly fishing, tennis. Office: Cmty Found for Southeastern Mich Ste 2010 333 W Fort St Detroit MI 48226

NEITZKE, ERIC KARL, lawyer; b. Mobile, Ala., Dec. 10, 1955; s. Howard and Otti S. Neitzke; m. Kathryn Sloan; children: Kyle, Blake, Blaire. BA, U. Fla., 1979, JD, 1982. Bar: Fla. 1982, U.S. Dist. Ct. (mid. dist.) Fla. 1987. Asst. state atty. 7th Jud. Cir., State Atty., Daytona Beach, Fla., 1982; atty. Dunn, Smith & Withers, Daytona Beach, 1982-88, Monaco, Smith, Hood and Perkins, Daytona Beach, 1988—2003, Eric K. Neitzke, P.A., Daytona Beach, 2003—. Adj. faculty family law and criminal law Daytona C.C.; chmn. adv. com. Juvenile Detention Ctr. Contbr. articles to profl. jours. Mem. Fla. Acad. Trial Lawyers, Assn. Trial Lawyers Am., Volusia Bar Assn., Fla. Assn. Criminal Def. Lawyers, Phi Beta Kappa. Avocations: water sports, shooting, travel. Home: 19 Lost Creek Ln Ormond Beach FL 32174-4840 Office: Eric K Neitzke PA 412 N Wild Olive Ave Daytona Beach FL 32118 Office Phone: 386-323-1900. Personal E-mail: knightmas@aol.com.

NEJELSKI, PAUL ARTHUR, retired judge, freelance writer; b. Chgo., Feb. 24, 1938; s. Leo Lawrence and Rena Grace (Martin) N.; m. Marilyn Ray Mills, Oct. 2, 1965; children: Nicole Rena, Stephen Downing. BA magna cum laude, Yale U., 1959, LLB, 1962; MPA, Am. U., 1969; cert. of theol. studies, Georgetown U., 1989. Bar: N.J. 1963. Law clk. appellate div. N.J. Superior Ct., 1962-63; asst. U.S. atty. U.S. Dist. Ct. N.J., 1964-65; atty., later chief immigration unit Dept. Justice, Washington, 1965-69; chief cts. desk Nat. Inst. Justice, Washington, 1969-70; asst. dir. Criminal Justice Ctr., Harvard U., 1970-71; dir. planning phase Inst. Jud. Adminstrn.-ABA Juvenile Justice Standards Project, N.Y.C., 1971-73; dir. Inst. Jud. Adminstrn., NYU, 1973-76; dep. ct. adminstrn. Conn. Jud. Dept., Hartford, 1976-77; dep. asst. atty. gen. Office for Improvements in Adminstrn. Justice, Dept. Justice, Washington, 1977-79; dir. Action Commn. to Reduce Ct. Costs and Delay, ABA, Washington, 1979-81; cir. exec. 3rd Cir., Phila., 1981-84; ct. adminstr. U.S. Tax Ct., 1984-89; immigration judge Dept. Justice, Arlington, Va., 1989-98. Mem. faculty law NYU, 1972-74, U. Conn., 1976-77, U. Md., 1981-82; cons. Author: (with C.O. Philip) Where Do Judges Come From?, 1976; editor: Social Research in Conflict With Law and Ethics, 1976; contbr. articles to profl. and popular jours. With U.S. Army, 1963-64. Home: 4628 Western Ave Bethesda MD 20816-2749

NEKRITZ, ELAINE, state representative; b. Wichita, Kan., Dec. 11, 1957; m. Barry Nekritz. BA, Trinity Univ., 1979; JD, Univ. of Mich., 1982. State Rep. House of Rep., Dist. 57, 2002—; atty., 1982—; former ptnr. Altheimer & Gray Law Firm. Mem.: Local Gov. Comm., Judiciary I - Civil Law Comm., Housing & Urban Develop. Comm., Elections & Campaign Reform Comm., Appropriations Comm.- pub. health, Trail Users Rights Found. Bd. Mem.- 1995-present, Chgo. Bar Assoc.-1982-1989, Am. Bar Assoc.-1982-1989, Ill. State Bar Assoc., 1982-present, Comty. Rels. Commn. (chair), Chgo. and Bicycle Fed. Democrat. Office: Capitol 244-W Stratton Office Bldg Springfield IL 62706 also: District 24 So Des Plaines River Suite 200 Des Plaines IL 60016

NELIGAN, PETER C. plastic surgeon; b. July 20, 1952; married; 2 children. BA, U. Dublin, Trinity Coll., 1973, MBBCh, 1975. Cert. Ont., 1985. Clin. fellow, plastic surgery The Hosp. for Sick Children, Toronto, Canada, 1983—84, rsch. fellow, plastic surgery, 1984—85, assoc. staff surgeon, 1995—, rsch. project dir., rsch. inst., 1995—; clin. fellow, microvascular surgery Toronto Gen. Hosp., Canada, 1985; clin. burn fellow The Ross Tilley Burn Ctr., Wellesley Hosp., Toronto, Canada, 1986; dir. The Ross Tilley Burn Ctr., The Wellesley Hosp., Toronto, Canada, 1992—93; attending plastic surgeon Laurentian Hosp., Sudbury, Canada, 1987—91, Sudbury Gen. Hosp., Canada, 1987—91, Sudbury Meml. Hosp., Canada, 1987—91, The Wellesley Hosp., Toronto, Canada, 1991—93, assoc. staff, 1993—2000; asst. prof., dept. surgery U. Toronto, Canada, 1991—97, chair, divsn. plastic surgery, 1996—, assoc. prof., dept. surgery, 1997—2002, prof., dept. surgery, 2002—; attending plastic surgeon The Toronto Hosp., Canada, 1993—, dep. head, divsn. plastic surgery, 1994—96, head, divsn. plastic surgery, 1996—; assoc. staff surgeon Mt. Sinai Hosp., Toronto, Canada, 1993—; cons., dept. surg. oncology Princess Margaret Hosp., Toronto, Canada, 1995—, Wharton chair in reconstructive plastic surgery, 1999—. Mem. editl. bd. Can. Jour. of Plastic Surgery, 1996—, Annals of Plastic Surgery, 2002—, Jour. of Reconstructive Microsurgery, 2002—, Brit. Jour. of Plastic Surgery, 2003—. Fellow: Royal Coll. Physicians and Surgeons of Can., Am. Coll. Surgeons (mem., adv. com. on plastic and maxillofacial surgery 2000—03), Royal Coll. Surgeons Ireland; mem.: Plastic Surgery Edn. Found. (nominating com. mem. 2002—, joint outcomes com. mem. 2002—), Ontario Soc. Plastic Surgery, Am. Burn Assn., Can. Med. Protective Assn., Irish Assn. Plastic Surgeons, Internat. Soc. for Burn Injuries, Can. Med. Assn., World Soc. Reconstructive Microsurgery (adv. coun. mem. 2001—), Plastic Surgery Rsch. Coun. (Snyder Award 1998, Hardesty Award 2000), Internat. Confederation for Plastic Reconstructive and Aesthetic Surgery, Internat. Microsurg. Soc., Ontario Med. Assn., N.Am. Skull Base Soc. (program com. mem. 2003—), Can. Soc. Plastic Surgeons, Am. Soc. Plastic and Reconstructive Surgeons (mktg. com. mem. 1999—2002, scientific program com. mem. 1999—, bd. dirs. 2001—, ethics com. mem. 2003—, Certificate of Merit, Investigator award 1984), Am. Soc. for Reconstructive Microsurgery (membership com. mem. 1999—, nominating com. mem. 1999—2001, program com. mem. 2001—), Am. Assn. Plastic Surgeons (comm. com. mem. 1999—), Inst. Med. Sci. Office: Toronto Gen Hosp Eaton North 7-229 200 Elizabeth St Toronto ON M5G 2C4 Canada*

NELIPOVICH, SANDRA GRASSI, artist; b. Oak Park, Ill., Nov. 22, 1939; d. Alessandro and Lena Mary (Ascareggi) Grassi; m. John Nelipovich Jr., Aug. 19, 1973. BFA in Art Edn., U. Ill., 1961; postgrad., Northwestern U., 1963, Gonzaga U., Florence, Italy, 1966, Art Inst. Chgo., 1968; diploma (hon.), Accademia Universale Alessandro Magno, Prato, Italy, 1983. Tchr. art Edgewood Jr. High Sch., Highland Park, Ill., 1961-62, Emerson Sch. Jr. High Sch., Oak Park, 1962-77; batik artist Calif., 1977—; illustrator Jolly Robin Publ. Co., Anaheim, Calif., 1988—2001, Assistance League of Anaheim, Calif., 2000—. Supr. student tchrs., Oak Park, 1970-75; adult edn. tchr. ESL, ceramics, Medinah, Ill., 1974; mem. curriculum action group on human dignity, EEO workshop demonstration, Oak Park, 1975-76; guest lectr. Muckenthaler Ctr., Fullerton, Calif., 1980, 92, Niguel Art Group, Dana Point, Calif., 1989, Carlsbad A.A., 1990, ARt League, Oceanside Art Group, 1992; 2d v.p. Anaheim Hills Women's Club, 1990-91, rec. sec. 1991-92; fabric designer for fashion designer Barbara Jax, 1987; illustrator Assistance League Anaheim (Calif.), 2000—. One-Woman shows include Lawry's Calif. Ctr., L.A., 1981-83, Whittier (Calif.) Mus., 1985-86, Anaheim Cultural Ctr., 1986-88, Ill. Inst. Tech., Chgo., 1989, Muckenthaler Cultural Ctr., Fullerton, 1990; also gallery exhibits in Oak Brook, 1982, La Habra, Calif., 1983, Millard Sheets Gallery, Pomona, Calif., 1996; represented in permanent collections McDonald's Corp., Oak Brook, Glenkirk Sch., Deerfield, Ill., Emerson Sch., Oak Park, Calif.; poster designer Saratoga Fine Arts. Active Assistance League, Anaheim, Calif., 1992—, 2d v.p. ways and means com., 1995—96, 1997—98, historian, 2002—03, Anaheim Arts Coun., 2002—. Recipient numerous awards, purchase prizes, 1979—; featured in Calif. Art Rev., Artists of So. Calif., Vol. II, Nat. Artists' Network, 1992, Batik for Artists and Quilters, 2001. Mem. AAUW (hospitality chmn. 1984-85), Soc. Children's Book Writers and Illustrators, Assistance League Anaheim, Orange Art Assn. (jury chmn. 1980). Roman Catholic. Avocations: cooking, gardening, travel. Home and Office: 5922 E Calle Cedro Anaheim CA 92807-3207

NELLAS, LOUIS SPIRO, secondary school educator; b. Athens, Greece, Jan. 18, 1964; arrived in U.S., 1964; s. Spiro Louis and Victoria Nellas; m. Marilyn Jane Newberry-Nellas, June 6, 1999; 1 child, Spiro Louis. BA, Hiram (Ohio) Coll., 1986; MA, Kent (Ohio) State U., 1991; tchg. cert., Robert Morris Coll., 1997. Permanent secondary tchg. cert. Mktg. mgr. Adelphia Cable, Rochester, Pa., 1987—90; group sales Pitts. Pirates, 1991; dir. video pub. Ryno Prodns., Bridgewater, Pa., 1992—95; mktg. cons. Integra Mktg., Beaver Falls, Pa., 1996; bar mgr. Boots Texas Roadhouse, Bridgeville, Pa., 1996—97; tchr. Deer Lakes Sch. Dist., Russellton, Pa., 1998—. Head track and field coach Deer Lakes H.S., Russellton, 2000—. Author: Ashland (pseudonym Plato Stratus), 1995; playwright: Six Nights and a Bed, 2000. Mem.: Pa. State Edn. Assn., Omicron Delta Kappa, Phi Gamma Epsilon (pres. 1985—86). Democrat. Greek Orthodox. Avocations: running, weightlifting, travel, writing, art.

NELLER, TODD W. computer science educator; b. Wilmington, Del., Dec. 18, 1970; s. Alvin Louis and Wildred Louise Neller; m. Johanna Ruth Taylor, June 29, 1996; children: Grace Elizabeth children: Taylor Christian. BS Computer Sci. with distinction, Cornell U., 1993; MS Computer Sci., Stanford U., 1996, PhD, 2000. Asst. prof. computer sci. Gettysburg Coll., 2000—. Growth group leader Gettysburg Bapt. Ch., Pa., 2002. Recipient Cum Laude Soc., Phillips Exeter Acad., 1989; Stanford Lieberman Fellowship, Stanford U. Dept. of Computer Sci., 1998. Mem.: Assn. for Computing Machinery, Am. Assn. for Artificial Intelligence (life), Tau Beta Pi (life). Achievements include extensions of artificial intelligence search techniques to hybrid dynamical systems; design of various puzzles and games (e.g. the Word Maze); computation of solution to a simple jeopardy dice game called Pig; development of a reinforcement learning approach to the control of simulated annealing for combinatorial optimization; artificial intelligence rsch. iterative refinement for action timing discretization.

NELLERMOE, LESLIE CAROL, lawyer; b. Oakland, Calif., Jan. 26, 1954; d. Carroll Wandell and Nora Ann (Conway) N.; m. Darrell Ray McKissic, Aug. 9, 1986; 1 child, Devin Anne. BS cum laude, Wash. State U., 1975; JD cum laude, Willamette U., 1978. Bar: Wash. 1978, U.S. Dist. Ct. (ea. dist.) Wash. 1979, U.S. Dist. Ct. (we. dist.) Wash. 1983. Staff atty. Wash. Ct. Appeals, Spokane, 1978-79; asst. atty. gen. Wash. Atty. Gen. Office, Spokane, 1979-83, Olympia, 1983-85; assoc. Syrdal, Danelo, Klein, Myre & Woods, Seattle, 1985-88; ptnr. Heller Ehrman White & McAuliffe, Seattle, 1990—. Bd. dirs. N.W. Environ. Bus. Coun., 1996—, Campfire Boys & Girls, Seattle, 1991-97. Mem. ABA, Wash. State Bar Assn., King County Bar Assn., Wash. Environ. Industry Assn. (bd. dirs.). Office: Heller Ehrman White & McAuliffe 701 5th Ave 6100 Columbia Ctr Seattle WA 98104-7043

NELLHAUS, TOBIN, librarian, theater educator; s. Gerhard and Arlynn Nellhaus. BA, U. Mich., Ann Arbor, Mich., 1977; MA, U. Iowa, Iowa City, 1980; PhD, Northwestern U., Evanston, Ill., 1991; MLS, Simmons Coll., Boston, Mass., 2000. Lectr. dept. theater Ohio State U., 1992—94; vis. scholar, sch. of drama U. Wash., 1995; vis. lectr., dept. drama and dance Tufts U., 1996; libr. for drama, film and theater studies Yale U., New Haven, 2000—. Co-editor (with Susan Haedicke): (collection) Performing Democracy: International Perspectives on Urban Community-Based Performance; contbr. articles pub. to profl. jour. Fulbright Lectureship, U. Helsinki, Fulbright Comm., 1997-1998, Rsch. fellowship, Am. Coun. of Learned Societies, 1996-1997. Mem.: Am. Soc. for Theater Rsch., Theater Libr. Assn. (bd. mem. 2004—). Office: Yale Univ SML 130 Wall St PO Box 208240 New Haven CT 06520-8240 Business E-Mail: tobin.nellhaus@yale.edu.

NELLI, HUMBERT STEVEN, historian, researcher, retired social studies educator; b. Chgo., Jan. 12, 1930; s. Humbert Orazio and Florence Purcell Nelli; m. Elizabeth Rolfe Thomson, Nov. 21, 1961; children: Steven Humbert, Christopher Rolfe, William Richard. BCS, U. Ga., Atlanta, 1951; MA, Columbia U., N.Y.C., 1956; PhD, U. Chgo., Ill., 1965. Instr. history U. Ill., Chgo., 1964—65; asst. prof. history Fordham U., Bronx, NY, 1965—67; asst. prof. to full prof. history U. Ky., Lexington, 1967—95. Participant Nat. Consultation on Ethnic Am., N.Y.C., 1967—68; mem. Marraro prize com. Am. Hist. Assoc.-Am. Cath. Hist. Assoc., Washington, 1974—76; dir, bicentennial conf. Am. Italian Hist. Assn., Washington, 1975—76, exec. bd., N.Y.C., NY, 1970—78; mem. com. of historians Am. Mus. of Immigration, N.Y.C., NY, 1975—78; cons. organized crime in Am. Thames TV, London, 1983—84; mem. interview panel Fulbright Tchr. Exch. Program., Chgo., 1986—90; consulting editor Criminal Organizations: Int'l Jour., N.Y.C., 1988—92. Author: Italians in Chgo.: A Study in Ethnic Mobility, 1971, The Bus. of Crime: Italians and Syndicate Crime in the U.S., 1976, From Immigrants to Ethnics: The Italian Americans, 1983 (Anisfield-Wolf award in Race Rels., 1984), The Winning Tradition: A History of Ky. Wildcat Basketball (2 editions), 1984, 1998; editor: The United States and Italy: the First Two Hundred Years, 1976; contbr. articles to ency., to profl. jours. Dir. Ky. History Day, Lexington, Ky., 1978—79; spkr. local orgns., media Louisville and Lexington, 1966—95. With U.S. Army, 1951—53, Germany. Grantee, NEH, 1973—75. Mem.: Orgn. of Am. Historians (life), Navy League of the U.S. (life).

NELLIGAN, ANNETTE FRANCES, clinical coordinator; b. Bangor, Maine, Sept. 20, 1954; d. Paul James and Laura Jenny (Sumner) N.; m. Peter Jamie Smith, June 22, 1985 (dec. June, 1997); children: Angelica Grace Nelligan-Smith, Acatia Faith Nelligan-Smith. AA, U. Maine, Bangor, 1974; BS, U. Maine, 1977, MEd, 1978, EdD, 1995. Lic. clin. profl. counselor; lic. marriage and family counselor; lic. social worker; cert. secondary sch. tchr., Maine, sch. counselor, Maine. Tchr. Bangor H.S., 1978, Etna (Maine)-Dixmont Sch., 1979-80; residential advisor Penobscot Job Corps, Bangor, 1980-84; group life worker St. Andre's Home, Bangor, 1984; caseworker, supr. Maine Dept. Human Svcs., Bangor, 1984-96; clin. coord. Old Town Regional Program, Bangor, 1996—. Mem. Homeless Edn. Adv. Bd., Bangor, 1992-95; instr. counselor edn. U. Maine, 1996—. Mem. ACA, Assn. for Specialists in Group Work. Roman Catholic. Avocations: doll collecting, camping, downhill skiing, sailing. Home: 24 Albert Lane GL Enburn ME 04401-5505 Office: Main St Old Town ME 04468

NELLIGAN, KATE (PATRICIA COLLEEN NELLIGAN), actress; b. London, Ont., Can., Mar. 16, 1951; d. Patrick Joseph and Alice (Dier) N. Attended, York U., Toronto, Ctrl. Sch. Speech and Drama, London. Appeared in plays in Bristol, London, and New York: Barefoot in the Park, 1972, Misalliance, A Streetcar Named Desire, The Playboy of the Western World, London Assurance, Lulu, Private Lives, Knuckle, 1974, Heartbreak House, 1975, Plenty, 1975, As You Like It, A Moon for the Misbegotten, 1984, Virginia, 1985, Serious Money, 1988, Spoils of War, 1988, Bad Habits; films include: The Count of Monte Cristo, 1979, The Romantic Englishwoman, 1979, Dracula, 1979, Mr. Patman, 1980, Eye of the Needle, 1980, Agent, 1980, Without a Trace, 1983, Eleni, 1985, White Room, 1990, Bethune: The Making of a Hero, 1990, Frankie and Johnnie, 1991 (BAFTA Film award, 1992), The Prince of Tides, 1991, Shadows and Fog, 1992, Fatal Instinct, 1993, Wolf, 1994, Into the Deep, 1994, How to Make an American Quilt, 1995, Margaret's Museum, 1995, Up Close and Personal, 1996, U.S. Marshals, 1998, (voice) Stolen Moments, 1998 Boy Meets Girl, 1998, The Cider House Rules, 1999; TV appearances include: The Arcata Promise, 1974, The Onedin Line, The Lady of the Camellias, Licking Hitler, Measure for Measure, Therese Raquin, 1980, Forgive Our Foolish Ways, 1980, Kojak: The Price of Justice, 1987, Control, 1987, Love and Hate: A Marriage Made in Hell, 1990, Terror Strikes the Class Reunion, 1992, The Diamond Fleece, 1992, Liar Liar, 1993, Shattered Trust: The Shari Karney Story, 1993, Spoils of War, 1994, Million Dollar Babies, 1994, A Mother's Prayer, 1995, Captive Heart: The James Mink Story, 1996, Calm at Sunset, Calm at Dawn, 1996, Love Is Strange, 1998, Swing Vote, 1999, Blessed Stranger: After Flight 111, 2000, Walter and Henry, 2001, A Wrinkle in Time, 2002; TV guest appearance Road to Avonlea, 1990. Recipient Best Actress award Evening Standard, 1978. Avocations: reading, cooking. Office: Innovative Artists Ste 2850 1999 Avenue Of The Stars Los Angeles CA 90067-4612

NELLIGAN, WILLIAM DAVID, III, professional association executive; b. Halstead, Kans., Aug. 10, 1926; s. William D. and Katherine (Roberts) N.; m. Dorothy Meyer, Aug. 17, 1952; children: Richard, Arthur, Mark. Student, U. Wichita, 1944-46; BS, U. Kans., 1949. Display advt. salesman Kansas City Star and Times, Mo., 1949-51; mgr. SW Kans. Extension Ctr. U. Kans., Garden City, 1951-55, exec. dir. dept. postgrad. med. edn. Sch. Medicine Kansas City, Kans., 1955-64; asst. to pres. Med. Coll. Ga., Augusta, 1964-65; exec. v.p. Am. Coll. Cardiology, Bethesda, Md., 1965-92; v.p. Marion Merrell DOW, Inc., Kansas City, Mo., 1992-94; exec. dir. Am. Soc. Nuc. Cardiology, Bethesda, 1994-2001, Cert. Bd. Nuclear Cardiology, Damascus, Md., 1996—. Mem. Nat. Commn. Diabetes, 1975-76, adv. council Nat. Diabetes and Digestive and Kidney Diseases, 1987-88; bd. dirs. Arthur E. Hertzler Research Found., Halstead, Kans., 1961—2004. Recipient Man with a Heart award N.Y. Cardiol. Soc., 1970, Presdl. citation Am. Coll. Cardiology, 1975, Disting. Service award Am. Coll. Cardiology, 1986, CLC Hall of Leaders award, 1986. Fellow Am. Coll. Cardiology; mem. AMA (citation of layman for disting. svc. 1993), Profl. Conv. Mgmt. Assn. (pres. 1974-75, Disting. Svc. award 1990), Am. Med. Writers Assn. (dir., exec. com., treas. 1970-78, Harold Swanberg Disting. Svc. award), Am. Soc. Assn. Execs. (cert., dir. 1975-78, sec.-treas. 1987-88, Key award 1984), Am. Assn. Med. Soc. Execs. (pres. 1986-87), Brit. Cardiac Soc. (hon.), Alliance for Continuing Med. Edn. (Pres.'s award 1994), Masons. Office: 9929 C Main St Damascus MD 20872-2068

NELLIS, M. DUANE, dean; b. Spokane, Wash., July 26, 1954; s. Marvin B. and Sophie Ann Nellis; m. C. Ruth Nellis, June 21, 1975; children: Jonathan Duane, Jason Scott. BS, Mont. State U., 1976; MS, Oreg. State U., 1977, PhD, 1980. Asst. prof. dept. geography Kans. State U., Manhattan, 1980-86, assoc. prof. dept. geography, 1986-90, prof. dept. geography, 1990-97, dept. head dept. geography, 1987-94, dir. Inst. for Social and Behavioral Rsch., 1990-94, assoc. dean Coll. Arts and Scis., 1994-97; dean Eberly Coll. Arts and Scis. W.Va. U., Morgantown, 1997—2004; provost Kans. State U., Manhattan, 2004—. Bd. dirs. W.Va. U. Rsch. Corp., Morgantown, 1997—, Snowshoe Inst., Charleston, W.Va. Co-author: Perspective on Applied Physical Geography, 1997, co-editor: Contemporary Rural Systems in Transition, 1993; co-editor Geocarto Internat. Jour., 1999—; contbr. chpts. to books and articles to profl. jours. Pres. Kans. Acad. Sci., Emporia, 1990. Recipient Outstanding Contbns. award Assn. Am. Geographers Remote Sensing Specialty Bd., 1995; grantee NASA, NSF, U.S. Agy. for Internat. Devel., 1985—. Mem. Coun. Colls. Arts and Scis. (rsch. univs. com. mem. 1999-2002), Assn. Am. Geographers (nat. councilor 1996-99, pres. 2002-2003, John Fraser Hart award for rsch. excellence contemporary agr. and rural land use splty. group 1991, Honors award 2001), Nat. Coun. for Geog. Edn. (pres. 1994), Am. Soc. Photogrammetry and Remote Sensing, Gamma Theta Upsilon (pres. 1999-2000), Phi Kappa Phi, Phi Beta Kappa. Avocations: travel, running, reading. Office: Kans State U 106 Anderson Hall Manhattan KS 66506

NELLIS, NOEL, thoracic surgeon, educator; b. Cheyenne, Wyo., Sept. 9, 1935; s. Leon Irving and Jessie Letitia Nellis; m. Helen Kay Nellis, July 1, 1959; children: Kathleen, James, Diana, David. BS with honors, U. Utah, 1957, MD, 1960. Diplomate Am. Bd. Surgery, Am. Bd. Thoracic Surgery. Intern U. Utah Affiliated Hosp., 1961; resident in surgery U. Colo., Denver, 1961—65; chief surgery Bassett Army Hosp., Fairbanks, Alaska, 1965—68; resident in thoracic surgery U. Utah Med. Ctr., Salt Lake City, 1968—70; pvt. practice Ogden, Utah, 1970—85, Ashtabula, Ohio, 1985—91; chief surgery VA Med. Ctr., Dublin, Ga., 1992—2002; ret., 2002. Assoc. prof. surgery Mercer U. Sch. Medicine, Macon, Ga., 1992—; clin. assoc. prof. Weber State U., Ogden, 1970—85, U. Utah, Salt Lake City, 1970—85; cons. Portsmouth (Va.) Naval Hosp., 1990—92; presenter in field. Contbr. articles to profl. jours. Sr. patrolman Nat. Ski Patrol Sys.; active Found. for Ancient Rsch. & Mormon Studies; med. chmn. March of Dimes, Weber County, 1971—75; pres. Am. Cancer Soc., Weber County, 1976—78, bd. dirs. Utah chpt., 1978—85, co-chmn. profl. edn. com., 1983—85; med. adv. Alaska divsn. Nat. Ski Patrol Sys., 1965—68, med. adv. snow basin intermountain divsn., 1970—82; active Boy Scouts Am.; elders quorum pres., high priest group leader, young men's pres., Gospel doctrine tchr. bishopric, high coun., scholar Atlanta Temple, med. advisor S.E. No. Am. Med. LDS Ch. Capt. USAR, 1961—65, Maj. M.C. U.S. Army, 1965—70, Col. USAFR, Col. USAF, 1990—91. Fellow: ACS, Am. Coll. Chest Physicians (gov. 1982—85); mem.: AMA (life), Ohio State Med. Assn., Utah State Med. Assn. (del. 1975—78), Ashtabula County Med. Soc., Weber County Med. Soc., Will C. Sealy Surg. Soc., Western Thoracic Surg. Assn., Soc. Thoracic Surgeons, Soc. Laparoendoscopic Surgeons, Res. Officers Assn., Ogden Surg. Soc. (treas. 1975—80, pres. 1981—82, program dir. winter meeting 1984—85), Nat. Assn. VA Physicians and Dentists, Macon Surg. Soc., Intermountain Thoracic Soc. (pres. 1977—78), Assn. VA Surgeons, Assn. Air Force Res. Flight Surgeons, Am. Thoracic Soc., Am. Heart Assn., Am. Coll. Physician Exec., Collegium Aesculapium, Rotary. Republican. Mem. Lds Ch. Avocations: music, skiing, photography, hiking. Home: 338 Regency Cir Dublin GA 31021

NELLUMS, ROBERT O. retired chemical engineer; b. Nashville, Sept. 19, 1921; s. Marcus E. and Elizabeth Overman Nellums; m. Elizabeth Alexander Nellums, June 20, 1947; children: Mary Youman, Robert Jr., Richard, Margaret Carter. BE, Vanderbilt U., Nashville, Tenn., 1942; postgrad., Washington U., St. Louis, 1943—44, U. Minn., Mpls., 1946; adv. mgmt., Syracuse U., 1968. Profl. engr., Mo. Prodn. supr. Monsanto Co., St. Louis, 1942—44, rsch. engr., 1947—56, rsch, sect. leader, 1957, asst. dir. rsch., 1957—59, asst. dir. engring., 1959—62, dir. of purchasing oper., 1963—71, bus. dir. fiber intermediates, 1971—85; project dir. McNeil Splty. Products Co., Swords, Ireland, 1986—87; cons. Noramco, Athens, Ga., 1988—2002, Wilmington, Del., 1988—2002; ret., 2002. Cons. v.p. Exec. Svc. Corp., St. Louis, 1986—92; mem. emeritus Am. Chem. Soc. Sr. warden, vestryman Grace Episcopal Ch. Lt.(j.g.) USNR, 1944—52, PTO. Avocations: travel, fly fishing, gardening, golf.

NELLY, (CORNELL HAYNES JR.), rap artist; b. Austin, Tex., Nov. 02; s. Cornell Haynes and Rhonda Mack; children: Chanel, Cornell III. Formed St. Lunatics, 1993; co-owner, co-founder, spokesperson Vokal Clothing Co., St. Louis, 1997—; co-owner, founder Apple Bottoms, 2003—; co-owner Billy Ballew Motersports, NASCAR racing team, 2003—; CEO Derrty Entertainment, 2003—; co-owner Charlotte Bobcats, 2004—. Performer: (albums) Country Grammar, 2000 (Album of Yr., Source Hip-Hop Music awards, 2001), Nellyville, 2002 (Grammy award for best make rap solo performance, 2002, Grammy award best rap/sung collaboration for "Dilemma," featuring Kelly Rowland, 2002), Da Derrty Versions: The Reinvention, 2003, Iz U, 2004, (with St. Lunatics) Free City, 2001, (singles) E.I., 2001, Ride With Me, 2001, (songs) Shake Ya Tailfeather (with P. Diddy and Murphy Lee), Bad Boys II soundtrack, 2003 (Grammy award best rap performance by a duo or group, 2003); actor: (films) Snipes, 2001. Founder 4sho4kids. Recipient New Artist of Yr., Source Hip-Hop Music Awards, 2001, Best New Artist, BET awards, 2001, Best R&B/Soul or Rap New Artist, Soul Train Music Awards, 2001, Favorite Artist-Rap/Hip-Hop, Am. Music Awards, 2002, Source Found. Image Award, Source Hip-Hop Music Awards, 2003, Artist of Yr., 2003, Sammy Davis Jr. Entertainer of Yr., Soul Train Music Awards. Office: Vokal

Jack Thompson Square 1204 Washington Ave 3rd Fl Saint Louis MO 63103 also: Uptown/Universal Records 1755 Broadway New York NY 10019 also: The 4Sho4Kids Found Inc 9648 Olive Blvd Ste 230 Saint Louis MO 63132 Office Phone: 314-531-3346.*

NELON, ROBERT DALE, lawyer; b. Shawnee, Okla., Aug. 8, 1946; s. Cecil Eugene and Neata Madelyn (Fox) N.; m. Freddie Anne Tipton, Aug. 2, 1975; children: Lindsay Anne, Gregory Tipton. BA, Northwestern U., 1968; JD, U. Okla., 1971. Bar: Okla. 1971, U.S. Dist. Ct. (we., no. and ea. dists) Okla. 1971, U.S. Ct. Appeals (10th cir.) 1971, (8th cir.) 1992, (2d cir.) 1993, U.S. Mil. Ct. Appeals 1972, U.S. Supreme Ct. 1989. Law clk. Okla. Atty. Gen., Oklahoma City, 1966-70; mem. Andrews, Davis, Legg, Bixler, Milsten & Price, Oklahoma City, 1971-95, Hall Estill Hardwick Gable Golden & Nelson, Oklahoma City, 1995—. Served to capt. USMCR, 1972-74. Mem. ABA, Okla. Bar Assn., Am. Judicature Soc. Democrat. Methodist. Office: Hall Estill Hardwick Gable Golden & Nelson Bank One Center, Suite 2900 100 N Broadway Ave Oklahoma City OK 73102-8865 Office Phone: 405-553-2805. E-mail: bnelon@hallestill.com.

NELP, WIL B. physician, medical educator; s. Wil B. and Olive E. (Edwards) Nelp; m. Barbara M. Monroe; children: Todd, Nancy, Paige, Blaine. BA cum laude, Franklin Coll.of Ind., 1951; MD, Johns Hopkins U., 1955; DSc (hon.), Franklin Coll., Ind., 1967. Lic. Md., 1955, Wash., 1962, cert. Am. Bd. Nuc. Medicine, 1972, Am. Bd. Internal Medicine. Intern asst. resident Johns Hopkins Hosp., Osler Med. Svc., Md., 1955—60; rsch. fellow Johns Hopkins Hosp., Dept. Medicine and Radiology, Divsn. Nuc. Med., Md., 1960—62; instr. Johns Hopkins U., Medicine and Radiology Dept., Md., 1961—62; asst. prof., assoc. prof., and prof. U. Wash., Dept. Medicine and Radiology, 1962—95; head dept. U. Wash., Nuc. Medicine, 1962—95; co-dir. U. Hosp., Thyroid Clin., Wash., 1978—83; attending physician Endocrine Thyroid Clin., Wash., 1983—; prof. emeritus U. Wash., Dept. Medicine and Radiology, 1996; assoc. staff Veterans Adminstrn. Hosp., Wash., Harborview Med., Seattle; cons. in nuc. medicine Group Health Coop. of Puget Sound, Providence Hosp., Northwest Hosp., Children's Orthopedic Hosp., Seattle, Madigan Army Hosp., Tacoma. Cons. Nat. Heart and Lung Inst., 1968—74; cons. to commr. FDA Radiopharmaceuticals, 1970—74, usp adv. panel, 1970—80; adv. to Romanian govt. UN Nuc. Medicine, IAEA, 1971—72; diagnostic rsch. adv. group Nat. Cancer Inst., 1977—81; usp adv. panel Radiopharmaceuticals, 1982—86; sec. coun. for nuc. medicine AMA, 1982—88; mem. adv. com. Elecromagnetic Isotope Enrichment Facility, Oak Ridge Nat. Lab., Oak Ridge, 1986, Nuc. Regulatory Commn., Med. Uses of Isotopes, 1993—99. Dir. U. Wash. residency Nuc. Medicine Tng. Program, 1964—96; chrmn., organizer U. Wash. Med. Ethics, Human Use, Review Sys. in Exptl. Rsch., 1967—71; mem. Med. Staff Exec. Com., 1973—80; com. mem. Los Alamos Sci. Lab., N.Mex., 1976—80; coun. mem. AMA, Nuc. Med. Sect., 1976—79; affiliate mem. Assn. of Governing Bd. of U. and Coll., 1996—. Capt., acting chief med. svc. Offult AFB USAF, 1957—59, Nebr. Named Outstanding Young Man of Am. Award, 1964; recipient NIH rsch. fellow, 1960—62, Disting. Scientist Award, Soc. of Nuc. Medicine, Western Region, 1980, Creative Devel. Award, NASA, 1980, Korean Soc. of Nuc. Medicine Honoree, 1990. Fellow: ACP, Am. Coll. Nuc. Physicians; mem.: Seattle Acad. Internal Med., Soc. Nuc. Med. (v.p. 1970—71, nat. pres. 1973—74), Am. Bd. of Nuc. Medicine (life; dir. 1984, treas. 1986, vice chmn. 1987), Johns Hopkins Med. Surg. Assn. Office: U Wash Med Ctr Pacific Ave Seattle WA 98195

NELSEN, HART MICHAEL, sociologist, educator; b. Pipestone, Minn., Aug. 3, 1938; s. Noah I. and Nova (Ziegler) N.; m. Anne Kusener, June 13, 1964; 1 dau., Jennifer. BA, U. No. Iowa, 1959, MA, 1963; M.Div., Princeton Theol. Sem., 1963; PhD (NSF faculty fellow), Vanderbilt U., 1972. Asst. prof. sociology Western Ky. U., Bowling Green, 1965-70, assoc. prof., 1970-73, Catholic U. Am., 1973-74, prof., 1974-81, chmn. dept. sociology, 1974-77, mem. Boys Town Ctr. for Study Youth Devel., 1974-81; prof. sociology La. State U., Baton Rouge, 1981-84, chmn. dept. sociology, head dept. rural sociology, 1981-84, coordinator rural sociology research, 1981-84; dean Coll. Liberal Arts Pa. State U., 1984-90, prof. sociology, 1984—2004, prof. emeritus, 2004—. Author: (with Anne K. Nelsen) Black Church in the Sixties, 1975; co-author: The Religion of Children, 1977, Religion and American Youth, 1976; editor: (with others) The Black Church in America, 1971; adv. editor: Sociol. Quar, 1976-82; assoc. editor: Sociol. Analysis, 1977-80, Rev. Religious Research, 1977-80, 84—, editor, 1980-84; mem. editorial bd.: Social Forces, 1983-86. Co-rec. sec. Capitol Hill Restoration Soc., 1979-80, v.p., 1980-81; mem. exec. bd. Lafitte Hills Assn., 1983-84; pres. Midtown Sq. Condo. Assn., 1996-99, treas., 1999-2001. Presbyterian Chs. grantee, 1966-69; NIMH co-grantee, 1969-72; Russell Sage Found. co-grantee, 1972-73; La. Gov.'s Commn. on Alcoholism and Drug Abuse grantee, 1982 Mem. Assn. Sociology Religion (exec. coun. 1974-76, 78-82, v.p. 1978-79, pres. 1980-81), Religious Rsch. Assn. (dir. 1977-80, pres.-elect 1985-86, pres. 1987-88), Soc. Sci. Study Religion (coun. 1981-83, exec. sec. 1984-87), Am. Sociol. Assn., So. Sociol. Soc. (chmn. membership com. 1983-85), AAAS (rep. 1984-2000). Mem. United Ch. Of Christ. Home: Residence 1121 Market Sq Residences 801 Pennsylvania Ave NW Washington DC 20004-2615

NELSEN, WILLIAM CAMERON, retired not-for-profit developer; b. Omaha, Oct. 18, 1941; s. William Peter and Ellen Lucella (Cameron) N.; m. Margaret Leone Rossow, May 30, 1981; children by previous marriage: William Norris, Shawna Lynn; 1 adopted dau., Sarah Ruth. BA, Midland Luth. Coll., Fremont, Nebr., 1963; MA, Columbia U., 1966; PhD, U. Pa., 1971; Fulbright scholar, U. Erlangen, W. Ger., 1964; D (hon.), Midland Luth. Coll., 1995. Program exec. Danforth Found., St. Louis, 1970-73; asst. dean, then v.p., dean coll. St. Olaf Coll., Northfield, Minn., 1973-80; dir. Project on Faculty Devel. Assn. of Am. Colls., 1979; pres. Augustana Coll., Sioux Falls, S.D., 1980-86, Scholarship Am., St. Peter, Minn., 1986—2004, ret., 2004. Bd. dirs. 1st Nat. Bank and Bancommunity Svc. Corp., St. Peter, Minn. Author: Effective Approaches to Faculty Development, 1980, Renewal of the Teacher Scholar, 1981, also articles. Bd. dirs. S.D. Symphony, 1980-85, Sioux Falls YMCA, 1980-86, Luth. Ednl. Conf. N.Am., 1982-86, Sioux Falls United Way, 1983-86; nat. bd. advisors Coun. Aid to Edn.; mem. nat. coun. Connect Am., Points of Light Found., 1998-2003; chmn. bd. U.S. Dream Acad., 1999-2004; mem. exec. bd. Nat. Assembly; bd. dirs. Nat. Scholarship Providers Assn., 1999-2004, chmn. bd., 2003-04. Recipient McKee award Nat. Assn. Ptnrs. in Edn., 1999, award Freedoms Found., 2003; Danforth Grad. fellow, 1963, Woodrow Wilson fellow, 1963. Mem. Assn. Am. Colls. (bd. dirs. 1984-86), Shoreland Country Club (pres. 1996-99), Consortium for Advancement of Pvt. Higher Edn., Coun. of Ind. Colls., Nat. Dollars for Scholars, Rotary Club. Republican. Lutheran. Home: 804 Spruce Pl Saint Peter MN 56082-1598

NELSON, ALAN RAY, internist, medical association administrator; b. Logan, Utah, June 11, 1933; s. Ray J. and Leah B. (Olson) Nelson; m. Gwen L. Sparrow, Jan. 2, 1959; children: John R., Shannon, Alan L. Student, Utah State U., 1951—54; MD, Northwestern U., 1958. Diplomate Am. Bd. Internal Medicine, Am. Bd. Endocrinology and Metabolism. Intern Highland Alameda County Hosp., Oakland, Calif., 1958—59; resident in internal medicine U. Utah, Salt Lake City, 1959—62, assoc. clin. prof., 1964—89, clin. prof., 1989—92; practice medicine specializing in internal medicine and endocrinology Salt Lake City, 1964—91; assoc. Meml. Med. Ctr., Salt Lake City, 1964—91; exec. v.p. Am. Soc. Internal Medicine, Washington, 1992—98; assoc. exec. v.p. Am. Coll. Physicians Am. Soc. Internal Medicine, Washington, 1998—2000, spl. advisor to exec. v.p., 2000—. Mem. Nat. Profl. Std. Rev. Coun., 1973—77; pres. Utah Profl. Rev. Orgn., 1971—75; mem. AMA Coun. on Legis., 1977—80, trustee, 1980—, chmn., 1986—88, pres.-elect, 1988—89, pres., 1989—90; commr. Joint Commn. on Accreditation of Hosps., 1982—86, sec.-treas., 1985—86. Chair Health Care Quality Alliance, 1992—96. With M.C. USAF, 1962—64. Recipient Spl. Recognition award, Am. Soc. Internal Medicine, 1973, Disting. Internist award, 1989, Coble award, Am. Assn. Clin. Endocrinology, 1999. Master: ACP; mem.: World Med. Assn. (pres.-elect 1990—91, pres. 1992), Med. Payment Adv. Commn., Inst. Medicine of NAS (governing coun. 1984—87), Utah Med. Assn. (pres. from 1976, award 1973, 1979). Home: 11905 Parkside Dr Fairfax VA 22033-2648 Office: ACP 2011 Pennsylvania Ave NW Washington DC 20006-1813 Office Phone: 703-385-3360. Business E-Mail: anelson@mail.acponline.org.

NELSON, ALLEN F. proxy solicitation company executive; b. Portland, Oreg., Oct. 17, 1943; s. Roy August and Mildred Mary (Jensen) N.; m. Johanna Molenaar, Dec. 8, 1973. BS, U. Iowa, 1965, MA, 1968. V.p. Shareholder Comm. Corp., N.Y.C., 1970-72; v.p. Trafalgar Capital Corp., N.Y.C., 1973; pres. Nelson, Lasky & Co., Inc., N.Y.C., 1974-76; account exec. Corp. Comm., Inc., Seattle, 1976-77; pres. Allen Nelson & Co., Inc., Seattle, 1977—. Mem. Fin. Analysts Fedn., Nat. Investor Rels. Inst., Nat. Security Traders Assn., Practicing Law Inst. (U.S. Presdl. rank rev. bd.), Pub. Rels. Soc. Am., Am. Soc. Corp. Secs., Can. Corp. Secs., Ranier Club, Montana Club, Vancouver Club. Home: 4400 Beach Dr SW Seattle WA 98116-3937 Office: Allen Nelson & Co Inc PO Box 16157 Seattle WA 98116-0157 Office Phone: 206-938-5783. E-mail: anelson@worldproxy.com.

NELSON, ANTONYA, writer; b. Wichita, Kans., 1961; m. Robert Boswell; children: Jade, Noah. BA, U. Kans., 1984; MFA, U. Ariz., 1986. Prof. Warren Wilson MFA program, N.Mex. State U. Author: The Expendables (Flannery O'Connor award, 1990), In the Land of Men, Family Terrorists, Talking in Bed (Heartland award, 1996), Nobody's Girl, Living to Tell; contbr. stories to mags. Named one of N.Y. Times Notable Books, 1992, 1996, 1998, 2000; fellow, Guggenheim Found., 2000—01; grantee, NEA, 2000—01. Office: New Mexico State Univ Dept English Dept 3E Las Cruces NM 88003

NELSON, ARTHUR HUNT, real estate company executive; b. Kansas City, Mo., May 21, 1923; s. Carl Ferdinand and Hearty (Brown) N.; m. Eleanor Thomas, Dec. 27, 1954; children: Carl F., Frances, Pamela. AB, U. Kans., 1943; JD, Harvard U., 1949. Bar: Mass. 1949. Staff radiation lab. MIT, 1943-44; sr. engr., cons. Raytheon Mfg. Co., Boston, 1948-52; pvt. practice Boston, 1949; v.p., treas., dir. Gen. Electronic Labs., Inc., Cambridge, Mass., 1951-64, chmn. bd., 1959-63; treas., dir. Sci. Electronics, Inc., Cambridge, 1955-64, Assocs. for Internat. Rsch., Inc., Cambridge, 1954—, pres., 1968—; treas., dir. Victor Realty Devel., Inc., Cambridge, 1959-76, pres., 1972-76, gen. ptnr., 1976—, Prospect Hill Exec. Office Park, Waltham, Mass., 1977—; chmn. Nelson Cos., 1990—, Cambridge Devel. Lab., Cambridge, 1994—2001. Bd. dirs. Internat. Data Group, Inc., Sterling Bank. Pres., trustee Tech. Edn. Rsch. Ctrs., Inc., 1965—; trustee Winsor Sch., Boston, 1978-88, treas., 1978-82; bd. dirs. Charles River Mus. Industry, Waltham, 1986—, pres. 1994—, pres., dir. 128 Bus. Coun. Inc., 1987—, Hist. Waltham Inc., 1996—, Am. Computer Fedn. Inc., 1996—, Charles River Pub. Internet Ctr. Inc., 1996—. Ensign USNR, 1944-46. Recipient Ernst & Young New Eng. Master Entrepreneur of Yr. award, 1999. Mem. ABA, Mass. Bar Assn., Boston Bar Assn., Boston Computer Soc. (bd. dirs. 1985-97, chmn. 1994-97), Greater Boston C. of C., Harvard Club Boston, Beta Theta Pi, Phi Beta Kappa, Sigma Xi. Home: 75 Robin Rd Weston MA 02493-2436 Office: care The Nelson Cos Prospect Place 230 3rd Ave Waltham MA 02451-7528

NELSON, AUDREY MAY, physician; b. Austin, Minn., Apr. 1, 1940; d. Glen Stanley and Clara May (Torgerson) N. BA, U. Minn., 1962, BS, 1963, MD, 1965. Diplomate in internal medicine and rheumatology Am. Bd. Internal Medicine. Assoc. cons. Mayo Clinic, Rochester, Minn., 1972, cons. in internal medicine and rheumatology, 1972—2002; instr. medicine Mayo Med. Sch., Rochester, 1973-76, from asst. prof. to assoc. prof. medicine, 1976-2000, prof., 2000—02, prof. emeritus, 2002—, chair pediat. rheumatology, 1993-2001; cons. staff Shriners Hosp. for Children, Mpls., 1985—. Bd. govs. Mayo Clinic, 1982-89; trustee Mayo Found., 1982-93, v.p., 1989-92; cons. staff mem. Shriners Hosp. Children, Mpls., 1985—. Trustee Christ United Meth. Ch., Rochester, 1995—2002, vice chair, 1999—2001, chair, 2001—02. Recipient Woman of Achievement award YWCA, Alumni Recognition award U. Minn. Alumni Med. Soc., 2002; named Woman Physician of Yr., Alpha Epsilon Iota. Fellow: ACP, Am. Coll. Pediat., Am. Coll. Rheumatology (bd. dirs. 1995—99, Disting. Svc. award 2002); mem.: AMA (del. 1984—2002), Am. Med. Group Assn. (chair elect 1996—97, bd. dirs. 1996—99, chair bd. dirs. 1997—98), Am. Group Practice Assn. (assoc.; trustee 1991—96, v.p. 1995, pres.-elect 1996), Minn. Med. Assn. (trustee 1985—2002, bd. dirs. 1996—99, Disting. Svc. award 1999), Phi Beta Kappa, Alpha Omega Alpha. Avocation: sailing. Office: Mayo Clinic 200 1st St SW Rochester MN 55905-0002

NELSON, BARRY, actor; b. San Francisco; s. Trygve and Betsy (Chritophison) Neilsen. BA, U. Calif., Berkeley. Broadway appearances include Light Up the Sky, 1949, The Rat Race, 1950, The Moon is Blue, 1951-53, No Time For Sergents, London, Eng., 1956, Mary-Mary, 1960-61, Cactus Flower, 1965-67, Everything in the Garden, 1967, The Only Game in Town, 1970, Seascape, 1975, The Norman Conquest, 1975, The Act, 1978 (nominated for Tony award); nat. co. 42d Street, 1983-86, Broadway co., 1986-87; motion pictures appearances in Mary-Mary, 1963, Airport, 1970, Pete and Tillie, 1972, The Shining, 1979; TV series The Hunter, 1953, My Favorite Husband, 1954-55. Office: Fifi Oscard Agency Inc Rm 1601 110 W 40th St New York NY 10018-8512

NELSON, BEN, JR., retired air force officer; b. Ft. Lewis, Wash., Jan. 31, 1942; s. Ben and Marie (Warn) N.; m. Suzanne Wiseman, Dec. 22, 1963; 1 child, William Bryant. BBA, U. Tex., 1964; MPA, Golden Gate U., 1976. Commd. 2d lt. USAF, 1964, advanced through grades to brig. gen., 1988; instr. pilot 3525th Fighter Tng. Squadron, Williams AFB, Ariz., 1965-70; flight comdr. 390th Tactical Fighter Squadron, DaNang, Vietnam, 1970-71, Sheppard AFB, Tex., 1971-74; chief pers. tng. br. Office Dep. Chief of Staff for Pers., Hdqrs. Tactical Air Command, Langley AFB, Va., 1974-77; ops. officer, comdr. 428th Tactical Fighter Squadron, Nellis AFB, Nev., 1977-81; student Naval War Coll., Newport, R.I., 1981-82; chief fighter plans br. Office Dep. Chief of Staff Plans, Hdqrs. USAF, Washington, 1982-84; vice comdr. 32d Tactical Fighter Group, Soesterberg Air Base, The Netherlands, 1984-85; vice comdr., then comdr. 50th Tactical Fighter Wing, Hahn Air Base, Fed. Republic Germany, 1985-88; asst. dep. chief of staff for plans Hdqrs. Tactical Air Command, Langley AFB, 1988-89; comdr. 56th Fighter Wing, MacDill AFB, Fla., 1989-92; dep. comdr. 5th Allied Tactical Air Forces (NATO), Vicenza, Italy, 1992-94; CEO regional office ARC, Tampa Bay, Fla., 1994—. Bd. dirs. CMS, Inc., Tampa, Fla.; COO, Skylynx Comm., Inc., San Jose, Calif., 1998—99; ptnr. Harrod Properties, Inc., 1999—; 0044. Recipient Phoenix award Dept. Def., 1987, O'Malley award Dept. Air Force. Mem. Air Force Assn., Tampa C. of C. (bd. dirs. 1989-92), Order of Daedalians. Episcopalian. Avocation: golf.

NELSON, BENJAMIN, senator, former governor, lawyer; b. McCook, Nebr., May 17, 1941; s. Benjamin Earl and Birdella Ruby (Henderson) N.; m. Diane C. Gleason, Feb. 22, 1980; children from a previous marriage: Sarah Jane, Patrick James; stepchildren: Kevin Michael Gleason, Christine Marie Gleason. BA, U. Nebr., 1963; MA, 1966, JD, 1970; LLD (hon.), Creighton U., 1992, Peru State Coll., 1993. Bar: Nebr. 1970. Instr. dept. philosophy U. Nebr., 1963-65; supr. Dept. Ins. State of Nebr., Lincoln, 1965-72; dir. ins., 1975-76; asst. gen. counsel, gen. counsel, sec., v.p. The Ctrl. Nat. Ins. Group Omaha, 1972-75; exec. v.p., 1976-77; pres., 1978-81; CEO, 1980-81; of counsel Kennedy, Holland, DeLacy & Svoboda, Omaha, 1985-90; gov. State of Nebr., Lincoln, 1991-98; of counsel Lumson, Dugan and Murray, Omaha, 1999—2001; U.S. Senator from Nebr., 2001—. Co-chmn. Carter/Mondale re-election campaign, Nebr., 1980; chair Nat. Edn. Goals Panel, 1992-94; co-founder Gov.'s Ethanol Coalition, chair, 1991, 94; pres. Coun. of State Govs., 1994. Recipient Disting. Eagle award Nat. Eagle Scout Assn., 1994; named Amb. Plenipotentiary, 1993. Mem. ABA, Nat. Assn. Ind. Insurers, Nat. Assn. Ins. Commrs. (exec. v.p. 1982-85), Nebr. Bar Assn., Consumer Credit Ins. Assn., Midwestern Govs. Assn. (chair 1994), Western Govs. Assn. (vice chair 1994, chair 1995), Happy Hollow Club, Omaha Club, Hillcrest Country Club. Democrat. Methodist. Avocations: reading, hunting, fishing. Office: US Senate 720 Hart Senate Office Bldg Washington DC 20510

NELSON, BERNARD WILLIAM, foundation executive, educator, physician; b. San Diego, Sept. 15, 1935; s. Arnold B. and Helene Christina (Falck) N.; m. Frances Davison, Aug. 9, 1958; children— Harry, Kate, Anne, Daniel AB, Stanford U., 1957, MD, 1961. Asst. prof., asst. dean medicine Stanford U., Palo Alto, Calif., 1965-67, assoc. dean medicine, 1968-71, cons. assoc. prof., 1980-86; assoc. dean U. Wis., Madison, 1974-77, acting vice chancellor, 1978-79; exec. v.p. Kaiser Family Found., Menlo Park, Calif., 1979-81, 1981-86; prof., chancellor U. Colo. Health Sci. Ctr., Denver, 1986-95, prof. dept. preventive med. and biometrics, 1995—. Mem., v.p., pres. Nat. Med. Fellowships, 1969-77 Trustee Morehouse Med. Sch., 1981-83 Fellow Inst. Medicine; mem. Calif. Acad. Sci., Alpha Omega Alpha (bd. dirs. 1978—) Avocations: fishing, photography, gardening, carpentry. Office: U Colo Health Sci Ctr Box C245 4200 E 9th Ave Denver CO 80262-3706

NELSON, BILL, senator, former state treasurer; b. Miami, Fla., Sept. 29, 1942; s. C.W. and Nannie (Merle) N.; m. Grace H. Cavert, Feb. 19, 1972; children: C. William, Nan Ellen. BA, Yale U., 1965; JD, U. Va., 1968. Bar: Fla. 1968. Practice law, Melbourne, Fla., 1970-79; mem. Fla. Ho. of Reps., 1972-78, U.S. Congress, 1979-91; flew on 24th Flight of Space Shuttle, 1986; treas. State of Fla., Tallahassee, 1995—2000; U.S. senator from Fla., 2000—; vice chmn. Dem. Senatorial Campaign com., 2000—. Served to capt. USAR, 1965-75, with U.S. Army, 1968-70. Democrat. Office: US Senate 716 Hart Sen Office Bldg Washington DC 20510 Address: 225 E Robinson St Ste 410 Orlando FL 32801

NELSON, BRUCE, consumer products company executive; Sr. mgmt. positions Boise Cascade, 1968-90; pres., CEO BT Office Products USA, 1991-94, Viking, 1995—98; pres. Office Depot Internat., 1998—2000, CEO, 2000—, chmn., 2001—. Office: Office Depot 2200 Old Germantown Rd Delray Beach FL 33445-8299*

NELSON, BRYCE EAMES, journalist, educator; b. Reno, Nev., Dec. 16, 1937; s. H.V. and Jennie Nelson; m. Martha Streiff, Sept. 23, 1961 (dec. Dec. 2002); children: Kristin, Matthew. BA, Harvard Coll., 1959; MPhil (Rhodes Scholar), U. Oxford, Eng., 1962. Instr. U. Pitts., 1962-63; fgn. affairs asst. Senator Frank Church, Washington, 1963-65; reporter Washington Post, 1965-66, Sci. Mag., Washington, 1966-69; midwest bur. chief, corr. L.A. Times, Chgo., Washington, 1969-82; writer human behavior N.Y. Times, 1982-84; prof. journalism U. So. Calif., L.A., 1984—. Dir. U. So. Calif. Sch. Journalism, 1984-88. Mem. editl. bd. Am. Oxonian, Claremont, Calif., 1996—; contbr. articles to publs. Recipient award Calif. Assoc. Press Contest for Investigative Reporting, 1980, Disting. Contbr. award APA, 1983, Deutsch award for Disting. Journalism Am. Orthopsychiat. Assn., 1970. Mem. Assn. Am. Rhodes Scholars, Soc. Profl. Journalists, Assn. Edn. in Journalism and Mass Comm., Am. Hist. Assn., We. History Assn. Episcopalian. Avocations: history and literature of Western America, hiking, biking, music. Office: Univ So Calif Sch Journalism Annenberg Sch Los Angeles CA 90089-0281 Fax: 213-740-8036.

NELSON, CARL ROGER, retired lawyer; b. Gowrie, Ia., Dec. 26, 1915; s. Carl Helge and Inez Olivia (West) N.; m. Elizabeth Boswell Campbell, Apr. 27, 1946; children: Thomas C., Nancy L. AB, Grinnell Coll., 1937; MA, Columbia, 1938, LLB, 1941. Bar: N.Y. 1941, D.C. 1947, U.S. Supreme Ct. 1947. Law clk. to Chief Justice Stone, 1941-42; Washington asso. firm Root, Ballantine, Harlan, Bushby & Palmer, 1946-51; mem. firm Purcell & Nelson, Washington, 1951-80, Reavis & McGrath, 1980-83, Nelson Thurston Jones & Blouch, 1984-86. Mem. Adminstrv. Conf. U.S., 1967-73 Served to capt. AUS, 1942-46. Fellow Am. Bar Found.; mem. ABA (mem. ho. dels. 1964-66, mem. coun. 1960-66, chmn. sect. adminstrv. law 1963-64), Mediation Panel U.S. Ct. Appeals (D.C. cir.), Chevy Chase (Md.) Club, Lawyers Club (Washington), Met. Club (Washington), Phi Beta Kappa. Mem. United Ch. of Christ.

NELSON, CAROL KOBUKE, bank executive; m. Ken Nelson; 2 children. BA in fin. magna cum laude, Seattle U., Wash., 1978, MBA, 1984; attended grad. sch. Credit & Fin. Mgmt., Santa Clara U., Calif. With SeaFirst Bank (now Bank of Am.); sr. v.p., No. regional consumer exec. Bank of Am.; pres., COO Cascade Fin. Corp., Everett, Wash., 2001—02, pres., CEO, 2002—, Cascade Bank, Everett, Wash., 2001—. Exec. adv. bd. Albers Sch. Bus. and Economics Seattle U. Chair bd. dirs. United Way, Snohomish County; bd. dirs. Boys and Girls Club, Snohomish County, Econ. Devel. Coun., Snohomish County; adv. bd. Leadership Snohomish County. Named One of 25 Women to Watch, U.S. Banker Mag., 2003. Mem.: Wash. Bankers Assn. (bd. dirs.), Wash. Fin. League (bd. dirs.). Office: Cascade Financial Corp 2828 Colby Ave Everett WA 98201

NELSON, CAROLYN, state legislator; b. Madison, Wis., Oct. 8, 1937; m. Gilbert W. Nelson; children: Paul, John, Karla. BS, N.D. State U., 1959, MS, 1960. Sr. lectr. emeritus N.D. State U., 1968—; mem. N.D. Ho. of Reps., 1986-88, 92-94, N.D. Senate from 21st dist., 1994—; mem. judiciary com., vet. affairs com. N.D. Senate, minority caucus leader, 2000—. Mem. N.D. State Investment Bd., 1989-92. Mem. Bd. Edn., Fargo, N.D., 1985-91, pres., 1989-90; trustee N.D. Tchrs. Fund for Retirement, 1985-92, pres., 1990-92; mem. N.D. PTA, pres., 1978-81, N.D. Women's and Children's Caucus. Recipient Merit Svc. award Gamma Phi Beta, 1978, 90, Legis. Voices award Children's Caucus, 1995; named Legislator of Yr., N.D. Bar Assn., 2000, N.D. Student Assn., 2001. Mem. LWV, Am. Guild English Handbell Ringers (area chmn. 1982-84, nat. bd. dirs. 1982-90), N.D. Fedn. Music Clubs (life; pres. 1997-2001, Rose Fay Thomas fellow 2001), Gamma Phi Beta, Phi Kappa Phi, Sigma Alpha Iota. Address: 1125 College St Fargo ND 58102-3433 Office: ND Senate State Capitol Bismarck ND 58505

NELSON, CHARLES A. physicist, educator; b. Chadron, Nebr., Oct. 11, 1943; s. Arnold W. and Martha J. (Brackman) Nelson; m. Nancy Kneller, May 21, 1988; 4 children. BS in Engring. Physics, U. Colo., 1965; PhD in Theoretical Physics, U. Md., 1969. Rsch. assoc. City Coll. CUNY, N.Y.C., 1968-70; cons. Ctr. Particle Theory, U. Tex., Austin, 1970-72; rsch. assoc. La. State U., Baton Rouge, 1970-72, Nat. Bur. Stds., Gaithersburg, Md., 1972-73; prof. physics SUNY, Binghamton, 1973—. Vis. scientist Fermilab, Batavia, Ill., 1980—81, Kyoto (Japan) U., 1981. Contbr. scientific papers to confs. and jours. Grantee, NSF, 1978—81, U.S. Dept. Energy, 1982—. Mem.: Am. Phys. Soc. Office: SUNY Dept Physics Binghamton NY 13902 Business E-Mail: cnelson@binghamton.edu.

NELSON, CHARLES ARTHUR, publishing executive, writer; b. Berwyn, Ill., Dec. 21, 1922; s. Arthur A. R. and Florence Dorothy (Lagergren) Nelson; m. Anne Ballou Higgins, July 1946; children: Christopher, Janet, Colin, Edward. BA, St. John's Coll., Annapolis, Md., 1947. Dir. liberal arts program, humanities lectr. U. Chgo., 1947-52; exec. dir. Am. Found. For Polit. Edn., Chgo., 1947-56; sr. cons. Cresap, McCormick & Paget, N.Y.C., 1956-58; pres. Nelson Assocs., N.Y.C., 1958-68; prin. Peat Marwick Mitchell & co., N.Y.C., 1968-83; pub. Croton-Cortlandt Gazette, Croton-on-Hudson, 1986—. Author: Developing Responsible Public Leaders, 1963; co-author: The University, The Citizen & World Affairs, 1956, Financial Management for the Arts, 1975, Ratio Analysis in Higher Education, 1980, Ethics, Leadership and the Bottom Line, 1991, Scott Buchanan: A Centennial Appreciation of His Life and Word, 1995, Stringfellow Barr: A Centennial Appreciation of His Life and Work, 1997, Radical Visions, 2001; contbr. articles to profl. jours. Chmn. bd. dirs. Exec. Coun. Fgn. Diplomats, N.Y.C.; trustee St. John's Coll., Annapolis, Md., Santa Fe, 1952—91, chmn. bd. trustees, 1978—83. Mem.: Asian and Western Studies Initiative (pres. 1997—99), New Providence Club. Democrat. Home and Office: 7101 Bay Front Dr Annapolis MD 21403

NELSON, CHARLOTTE BOWERS, public administrator; b. Bristol, Va., June 28, 1931; d. Thaddeus Ray and Ruth Nelson (Moore) Bowers; m. Gustav Carl Nelson, June 1, 1957; children: Ruth Elizabeth, David Carl, Thomas Gustav. BA summa cum laude, Duke U., 1954; MA, Columbia U., 1961; MPA, Drake U., 1983. Instr. Beaver Coll., 1957-58, Drake U., Des Moines, 1975-82; office mgr. LWV of Iowa, Des Moines, 1975-82; exec. asst. Iowa Dept. Human Svcs., Des Moines, 1983-85; exec. dir. Iowa Commn. on Status of Women Dept. Human Rights, Des Moines, 1985—. Bd. dirs., pres. LWV, Beloit, Wis., 1960-74; bd. dirs. LWV, Des Moines, 1974-82, Westminster House, Des Moines, 1988-97, pres. 1996-97. Recipient Gov.'s Golden Dome award as Leader of the Yr., 2002; named Visionary Woman, Young Women's Resource Ctr., 1994. Mem. Am. Soc. Pub. Adminstrn. (mem. exec. coun. 1984-92, 98-99, past pres., Mem. of Yr. 1993), Phi Beta Kappa, Pi Alpha Alpha. Home:

1141 Cummins Cir Des Moines IA 50311-2113 Office: Human Rights Dept Lucas State Office Bldg Des Moines IA 50319-0001 Office Phone: 515-281-4467. E-mail: charlotte.nelson@iowa.gov., nelson514@aol.com.

NELSON, CHRIS A. secretary of state; b. Mitchell, SD, Aug. 18, 1964; married; 1 child. BS, SD State Univ., 1987. Farmer/rancher self-employed, 1981—; UCC supr. State of SD, 1987—89, state election supr., 1989—2002, sec. of state, 2003—. Republican. Christian. Office: 500 E Capitol Ave Ste 204 Pierre SD 57501

NELSON, CHRISTOPHER GRANT, dermatologist; b. Peoria, Ill., Feb. 11, 1946; s. Grant Leonard and Shirlee Ann (Brunnenmeyer) N.; m. Mary Jo Donnelly, June 30, 1972; children: Christopher Jr., Andrew Anthony. BS, U. Iowa, 1968, MD, 1971. Diplomate Am. Bd. Dermatology. Intern Ball Meml. Hosp., Muncie, Ind., 1971-72; resident in dermatology U. Tex. Med. Br., Galveston, 1974-77; staff Bayfront Med. Ctr., St. Petersburg, 1977—, St. Anthony's Hosp., St. Petersburg, 1977—; tchr. Bayfront Med. Ctr., 1977—; affiliate assoc. prof. U. South Fla. Coll. Medicine, 1977—; staff Tampa Gen. Hosp., 2001—. Contbr. articles to profl. jours. Vol. Am. Cancer Soc. Mem. ACP, So. Med. Assn., Fla. Med. Assn., Am. Acad. Dermatology, Am. Soc. Dermatologic Surgery, Soc. Investigative Dermatology, Pinellas County Med. Soc., Fla. West Coast Soc. Dermatology (sec.-treas. 1982-84, pres. 1984-87), Fla. Soc. Dermatologic Surgery, St. Petersburg Yacht Club (bd. dirs. 1989-95, entertainment chmn. 1989-92, house and grounds com. 1987-95), Dragon Club, Masons, Royal Order of Jesters. Presbyterian. Avocations: sailing, scuba diving, photography, amateur ham radio. Office Phone: 727-895-8131.

NELSON, CLARA SINGLETON, human resources consultant; b. Union Ridge, Tenn., Apr. 10, 1935; d. Ernest Caldwell and Willie Emma (Hord) Singleton; m. Joe Edward Nelson, July 26, 1953; children: Drexel Edward, Dorissia Lynett. Student, Tenn. State U., 1961-62, Middle Tenn. State U., 1984; AS, Motlow Coll., 1978; BS in Edn. with highest honors, U. Tenn., Knoxville, 1991. Sec., adminstrv. asst. Bedford County Sch., Shelbyville, Tenn., 1957-64; sec., personnel asst. Aro, Inc., Arnold Air Force Sta., Tenn., 1964-71; mem. pub. rels. staff, job interviewer Employment Security, Shelbyville, 1971-81; mgr. employment EEO Calspan Corp., Arnold Air Force Sta., 1981-94; with Micro Craft Tech., 1994-95; employment and recruiting mgr. Sverdrup Tech., 1995-97; pvt. practice human resource cons., 1998—. Cons. dir. Career Devel. Workshops, Shelbyville. Mem. adv. bd. Tenn. Area Vocat. Sch., Shelbyville, 1979-2001; chmn. adv. commn. Equal Employment Opportunity, 1983—, chmn. employer com. Tullahoma Job Svc., Tenn., 1985—; mem. Patrons Coun. Argie Cooper Libr., Shelbyville; trustee Motlow Coll. Found.; former mem. Shelbyville Regional Planning Commn.; mem. Shelbyville Power, Water and Sewerage Bd. Recipient cert. of appreciation ARC, 1985. Mem.: Soc. of Human Resource Mgmt. (state diversity chair 2000—, cert.), Nat. Assn. Bus. and Profl. Women's Clubs, Inc. (chair membership 1991—93, charter mem.), Nat. Mgmt. Assn., Nat. Assn. Female Execs. (network dir. 1985, charter mem.), Highland Rim Human Resources Mgmt. Assn. (treas. 1983—84, 1987, sec. 1988, chair program com. 1989, sec. 1994, SHRM affiliate), Am. Mgmt. Assn. (chair program com. 1994—, pres. 1998—2000), Am. Assn. Affirmative Action Tenn. State U. Cluster (chmn. 1984—2000), Better Homes and Gardens Shelbyville Club. Methodist. Avocations: reading, gardening, writing. Home and Office: 105 Sun Cir Shelbyville TN 37160-2519 Office Phone: 931-684-4184.

NELSON, CLAUDIA B. literature educator, writer; b. Ft. Belvoir, Va., Nov. 2, 1960; d. David Aldrich and Mary (Dickson) Nelson; 1 child, Mary Isabel. AB, Bryn Mawr Coll., 1980; PhD, Ind. U., 1989. Copy editor Book-of-the-Month Club, N.Y.C., 1980—84; mng. editor Coll. Lit. West Chester (Pa.) U., 1990—91; assoc. prof. English Tex. State U., San Marcos, 1993—2003, Tex. A&M U., College Station, 2003—. Mem. exec. bd. dirs. Children's Lit. Assn., Battle Creek, Mich., 1997—2000. Editor (with Lynne Vallone): The Girl's Own: Cultural Histories of the Anglo-American Girl, 1830-1915, 1994; editor: (with Ann Sumner Holmes) Maternal Instincts: Visions of Motherhood and Sexuality in Britain, 1875-1925, 1997; editor: (with Michelle H. Martin) Sexual Pedagogies: Sex Education in Britain, Australia, and America 1879-2000, 2004; contbr. articles to profl. jours. Fellow, NEH, 1999; Charlotte W. Newcombe fellow, Woodrow Wilson Found., 1988.

NELSON, CRAIG ALAN, management consultant; b. San Rafael, Calif., July 11, 1961; s. Kenneth Alfred and Anne Catherine (Laurie) N. BS in Fin., San Diego State U., 1984. Loan assoc. Union Bank, San Diego, 1984-85, comml. loan officer, 1985-86, corp. banking officer, 1986-87, asst. v.p., 1987-89, v.p. corp. banking, 1989-93; v.p. Alexander & Alexander, San Diego, 1993-95; sr. assoc. Goreham-Moore & Assocs., San Diego, 1995-98; v.p. Sedgwick Tech. Group Sedgwick of Calif., Inc., San Diego, 1998; v.p., dir. tech. Marsh Inc., La Jolla, Calif., 1998—; regional v.p. Comerica Tech. Banking Group, San Diego; regional v.p., sr. mgr. Bank of the West, San Diego, 2002—. V.p. Sedgwick Tech. Group, 1997. Community group chair San Diego chpt. Am. Cancer Soc., 1989; mem. com. Juvenile Diabetes Assn.; bd. dirs. San Diego State Found., 1989—; pres. Am. Lung Assn., San Diego and Imperial counties, San Diego State U. Athletic Found., 2004-. Mem. San Diego State U. Young Alumni Assn. (pres. 1988-89, bd. dirs. emeritus 1989). Home: 1233 San Dieguito Dr Encinitas CA 92024-5116 Office: Bank of the West 1280 4th Ave San Diego CA 92101

NELSON, DARRELL WAYNE, university administrator, scientist; b. Aledo, Ill., Nov. 28, 1939; s. Wayne Edward and Olive Elvina (Peterson) N.; m. Nancyann Hyer, Aug. 27, 1961; children: Christina Lynne, Craig Douglas. BS in Agriculture, U. Ill., 1961, MS in Agronomy, 1963; PhD in Agronomy, Iowa State U., 1967. Cert. profl. soil scientist. Div. chief U.S. Army Chem. Corps., Denver, 1967-68; asst. prof. Purdue U., West Lafayette, Ind., 1968-73, assoc. prof., 1973-77, prof. agronomy, 1977-84; dept. head U. Nebr., Lincoln, 1984-88, dean for agr. rsch. and dir. Nebr. Agrl. Experiment Sta., 1988—. Cons. U.S. EPA, Washington, 1977-79, Ind. Bd. of Health, Indpls., 1977-83, Eli Lilly Co., Indpls., 1976. Editor: Chemical Mobility and Reactivity in Soils, 1983. Served to capt. U.S. Army, 1967-68. Fellow AAAS, Am. Soc. Agronomy (bd. dirs., pres.-elect, pres. 2001, past pres. 2002, CIBA-Geigy award 1975, Agronomic Achievement award 1983, Environ. Quality Rsch. award 1985), Soil Sci. Soc. Am. (bd. dirs., pres. elect 1992, pres. 1993, past. pres. 1994); mem. Internat. Soil Sci. Soc., Lions Lodge (treas. 1980-83, Lafayette, Ind. chpt.). Presbyterian. Avocations: fishing, skiing, jogging. Office: Univ of Nebr Agrl Rsch Divsn Lincoln NE 68583-0704 Office Phone: 402-472-2045. Business E-Mail: dnelson1@unl.edu.

NELSON, DAVID ALDRICH, judge; b. Watertown, N.Y., Aug. 14, 1932; s. Carlton Low and Irene Demetria (Aldrich) Nelson; m. Mary Dickson, Aug. 25, 1956; 3 children. AB, Hamilton Coll., 1954; postgrad., Cambridge U., Eng., 1954—55; LLB, Harvard U., 1958. Bar: Ohio 1958, N.Y. 1982. Atty.-advisor Office of the Gen. Counsel, Dept. of the Air Force, 1959—62; assoc. Squire, Sanders & Dempsey, Cleve., 1958—67, ptnr., 1967—69, 1972—85; judge U.S. Ct. Appeals (6th cir.), Cin., 1985—99, sr. judge, 1999—. Gen. counsel U.S. Post Office Dept., Washington, 1969—71; sr. asst. postmaster gen., gen. counsel U.S. Postal Svc., Washington, 1971; nat. coun. Ohio State U. Coll. Law, 1988—98. Trustee Hamilton Coll., 1984—88. Served to maj. USAFR, 1959—73. Recipient Benjamin Franklin award, U.S. Post Office Dept., 1969; Fulbright scholar, 1954—55. Fellow: Am. Coll. Trial Lawyers; mem.: Cin. Bar Assn., Ohio Bar Assn., Fed. Bar Assn., Emerson Lit. Soc., Ct. of Nisi Prius (sgt. emeritus), Phi Beta Kappa. Office: US Ct Appeals 6th Cir Potter Stewart US Ct House 5th and Walnut St Cincinnati OH 45202-3988 Office Phone: 513-564-7414.

NELSON, DAVID LEONARD, process management systems company executive; b. Omaha, May 8, 1930; s. Leonard A. and Cecelia (Steinert) N.; m. Jacqueline J. Zerbe, Dec. 26, 1952; 1 child, Nancy Jo. BS, Iowa State U., 1952. Mktg. adminstr. Ingersoll Rand, Chgo., 1954-56; with Accuray Corp., Columbus, Ohio, 1956-87, exec. v.p., gen. mgr., 1967, pres., 1967-87, chief exec. officer, 1970-87; pres. process automation bus. unit Combustion Engring., Inc., Columbus, 1987-90; pres. bus. area process automation Asea Brown Boveri, Stamford, Conn., 1990-91, v.p. customer satisfaction Ams. region, 1991-93, v.p. customer support Ams. region, 1994-95; chmn. bd. dirs. Herman Miller Inc., Zeeland, Mich., 1995-2000, counsel, 2000—. Patentee in field. Served to capt. USMCR, 1952-54. Mem. IEEE, Instrument Soc. Am., Newcomen Soc. N.Am., Tau Beta Pi, Phi Kappa Phi, Phi Eta Sigma, Delta Upsilon. Home: 1113 Roundhouse Ln Alexandria VA 22314-5935 Office Phone: 703-299-4588.

NELSON, DAVID LOREN, geneticist, educator; b. Washington, June 25, 1956; s. Erling Walter and Marlys Joan (Jorgenson) N.; m. Claudia Jane Hackbarth, July 31, 1982; children: Jorgen William, Erik Alexander. BA, U. Va., 1978; PhD, MIT, 1984. Staff fellow NIH, Bethesda, Md., 1985-86; sr. assoc. Baylor Coll. Medicine, Houston, 1986-89, instr., 1989-90, asst. prof., 1990-94, assoc. prof., 1994-99, prof., 1999—. Dir. Human Genome Ctr., 1995-96. Editor: Genome Data Base, 1992-2000; assoc. editor Genomics, 1994-2002. Achievements include development of Alu PCR; discovery of fragile X syndrome gene (FMR-1), new form of genetic mutation (simple repeat expansion); identification of gene defects in Lowe Syndrome and Incontinentia Pigmenti. Office: Baylor Coll Dept Medicine Molecular & Human Genetics 1 Baylor Plz Houston TX 77030-3411 E-mail: nelson@bcm.tmc.edu.

NELSON, DAVID ROBERT, physics educator; b. Stuttgart, Federal Republic of Germany, May 9, 1951; came to U.S., 1953; s. Robert Charles and Faye Scott (Abernethy) N.; m. Patricia Schneider, Dec. 30, 1975; children: Meredith, Leigh, Christopher David, Peter Charles. AB, Cornell U., 1972, MS, 1974, PhD, 1975; MA (hon.), Harvard U., 1980. Jr. fellow Harvard Soc. Fellows, Cambridge, Mass., 1975-78; assoc. prof. physics Harvard U., Cambridge, 1978-80, prof., 1980-91, Mallinckrodt prof. physics, 1992-97, prof. applied physics, 1997—. Cons. IBM, Yorktown Heights, N.Y., 1976-82, Mitre Corp., Bedford, Mass., 1985—, AT&T Bell Labs., Murray Hill, N.J., 1988—, Exxon Rsch. & Engring., 1994-95. Author: Defects and Geometry in Condensed Matter Physics, 2002; co-author: Phase Transitions and Critical Phenomena, Vol. 7, 1983; co-author, editor: Statistical Mechanics of Membranes and Interfaces, 1989. A.P. Sloan Found. fellow, 1979-83, MacArthur Found. Prize fellow, 1984-89, Guggenheim fellow, 1993-94; recipient award for initiatives in rsch. NAS, 1986, Ledlie prize, 1995. Fellow Am. Phys. Soc., Harvard Soc. Fellows (sr.); mem. APS, AAAS, NAS, Am. Acad. Arts and Scis. Office: Harvard U Dept Physics Cambridge MA 02138

NELSON, DENNIS LEE, finance educator; b. Randall, Minn., Nov. 4, 1929; s. George Otto and Emma Ida (Schwanke) N.; m. Joyce Marie Prozinski, Aug. 25, 1956; children: Constance, Kristin, Norma Joan. BS, St. Cloud State U., 1954; MA, U. Minn., 1964, PhD in Econs., 1970. Prof. econs. U. Minn., Duluth, 1964—, dir. ctr. for econ. edn., 1967-71, grad. faculty, 1970—, head dept. econs., 1971-77, assoc. chancellor, 1977-88, vice chancellor fin. ops., 1987-88. Mem. faculty Westhill Coll., U. Birmingham, Eng., 1996-97; instnl. rep. for adminstrs. on Nat. Collegiate Athletic Assn., 1978-87; adminstr., vis. faculty Oxford U., Eng., 1997, Yonsei U., Seoul, 1988, Moscow U., 1978, 84. Recipient Disting. Alumnus award U. Minn. Mem. Duluth Blueline Club, Duluth Quarterback Club, UMD Rasmussen Fund, UMD Hoop Club, Pres. Club U. Minn. Lutheran. Avocations: gardening, writing, reading, woodworking, bridge. Home: On the Lake 21190 Forest Rd Little Falls MN 56345-4065 Office: U Minn 10 University Dr Duluth MN 55812-2403

NELSON, DON HARRIS, gas and oil industry executive; b. Phila., Mar. 18, 1932; s. Morris Daniel and Catherine (Kaplan) N.; m. Ruth Kaiser Nelson, Aug. 31, 1959 (div. 1981); children: Michael Stewart, Pamela Blair, Randolph Miles, Timothy Blake; m. Karen Fulton, Feb. 12, 1982 (div. 1998); m. Sara Louise Rothman, July 10, 1998. BA, Yale U., 1953; MBA, U. Pa., 1957. Project engr. GE, Phila., 1957-60; mgr. exploration Kaiser Francis Oil Co., Tulsa, 1960-77; CEO Sanguine, Ltd., Greenwich, Conn., 1977—. Mem. Yale Devel. Bd., 1988—; chmn. Mus. African Art, N.Y.C., 1991-94. Pres. Family and Childrens Svc. Agy., Tulsa, 1975. Capt. USMC, Korea. Mem. Am. Assn. Petroleum Geologists, Stanwich Club, Yale Club (N.Y.C.), Tulsa Tennis Club. Avocations: post-impressionistic and african art, tennis, skiing, scuba diving, golf. Home: 1121 Lake Ave Greenwich CT 06831-2748 Office: Sanguine Ltd 95 E Putnam Ave Greenwich CT 06830-5611

NELSON, DONALD ARVID (NELLIE NELSON), professional basketball coach; b. Muskegon, Mich., May 15, 1940; Student, U. Iowa. Player NBA teams, Chgo. Zephyrs, 1962-63, Los Angeles Lakers, 1963-65, Boston Celtics, 1965-76; from asst. to head coach Milw. Bucks NBA, 1976-87, also dir. player personnel; exec. v.p., part owner Golden State Warriors, NBA, Oakland, Calif., 1987-95; mem. Nat. Basketball championship teams, 1966, 68, 69, 74, 76; head coach Golden State Warriors, 1988-95, New York Knicks, 1995-96; coach Dream Team II, 1994; coach, gen. mgr. Dallas Mavericks, Dallas, 1996—. Named Coach of Yr. NBA, 1983, 85, 92. Office: Dallas Mavericks 2909 Taylor St Dallas TX 75207-4411

NELSON, DONNA GAYLE, state representative; b. Paducah, Tex., June 13, 1943; d. Jack Harold Williams and Hazel Louise (Cooper Moss) Stephens; m. Douglas Caldwell Nelson, June 24, 1966 (div. 1976); children: Kellye Lou Fetters, Robert Kreg Nelson, J. Graigory. AB, South Plains Coll., Levelland, Tex., 1963; BBA, West Tex. A&M U., Canyon, 1965, MBA, 1967. Founder Evergreen Mut., McMinnville, Oreg., 1975; co-founder Evergreen Life Line, McMinnville, 1978—; founder, corp. dir. AAA Profl. Promotions, McMinnville, 1977—; pres. Evergreen Bus. Mgmt. Co., McMinnville, 1978—; sr. v.p. Evergreen Helicopters, Inc., McMinnville, 1978—, Evergreen Internat. Aviation, Inc., McMinnville, 1978—; mem. Oreg. State Ho. of Reps., 2000—, vice chair govt. com., vice chair agr. com. Bd. dirs. Evergreen Air Ctr., Inc., Marana, Ariz., Evergreen Aircraft Sales & Leasing Co., Evergreen Aviation Ground Logistics Enterprises, Inc.; sr. v.p., bd. dirs. Evergreen Internat. Aviation, Inc., McMinnville; speaker Nat. Speakers' Assn., Phoenix, 1986—; mem. adv. bd. Chemeketa Community Coll., McMinnville, 1984-85; owner 3N & Assocs. Inc., Donna G. Nelson Auctions, LLC; founder Yamhill Co. Market; teacher Tex., Calif., and Oregon; author, journalist. Poet World's Most Beloved Poetry, 1985 (Silver poet); writer Aviation/Space Writers' Assn., 1989-90; columnist It Takes Grit. Mem. Team 100 Rep. party, Washington, 1989; co-founder Poyama Land Treatment Ctr., Independence, Oreg., 1973; den mother, sustained membership chmn. Boy Scouts Am., McMinnville, 1977-79; dr. mem. March of Dimes, Heart Fund, McMinnville, 1973-75; sr. transportation com., Yamhill Co. Budget Parks, Elks Lions, Red Cross, NRA, N1IB Farm Bur.; founder Newcomers Club, Fund for Hope, Free Enterprise Fund for Kids; bd. dirs. Humane Soc., Linfield Chamber Orch., Salvation Army. Named Woman of Excellence, Portland, Oreg., 1985. Mem. DAR, C. of C., McMinnville Duplicate Bridge Assn. (founder), Soroptimists Club, Elks, Lions, Beta Sigma Phi (pres. 1974-75, Woman of Yr. 1990). Republican. Baptist. Avocations: music, sports, bridge, writing, fishing, speaking, travel, fishing, computers, charity auctioneer. Home and Office: 2150 St Andrews Dr # 1252 Mcminnville OR 97128-2436 Office Phone: 503-472-7446.

NELSON, DONNA JEAN, chemistry educator, researcher; b. Eufaula, Okla., Aug. 29, 1952; d. John Howard Jr. and Dorotha (Eckelkamp) Baker; 1 child, Christopher Brammer. BS in Chemistry, U. Okla., 1974; postgrad., Auburn (Ala.) U., 1974-76; PhD, U. Tex., 1979; postgrad., Purdue U., 1980-83. Robert A. Welch pre-doctoral fellow, 1977, 78, 79; Robert A. Welch postdoctoral fellow, 1980; asst. prof. U. Okla., Norman, 1983-89, assoc. prof., faculty adminstrv. fellow Provost's Office, 1989—. Jr. faculty rsch. fellow Okla. U., 1984, assocs. disting. lectr., 1985-86; vis. prof. MIT, 2003. Asst. editor: Progress Mag., 2002—, assoc editor: AWIS Mag., 2002—03. Recipient Sooner Spotlight award U. Okla., 1986, Sequoyah medal Am. Indians in Sci. and Engring. Soc., 2003; named Woman of Achievement, USBE and Info. Tech. Mag., 2003; Robert A. Welch grantee, 1979; A.P. Sloan Found. travel awardee, 2003; Ford Found. fellow, 2003-04; Guggenheim awardee, 2003-04. Mem. Am. Chem. Soc. (women chemists com. 1988—, James Flack award com. 1987-90), Phi Lambda Upsilon, Alpha Chi Sigma, Iota Sigma Pi, Sigma Xi (nat. diversity com. 2001—). Home: 1700 Winding Ridge Rd Norman OK 73072-3149 Office: U Okla Dept of Chemistry Norman OK 73072 E-mail: djnelson@ou.edu.

NELSON, DOROTHY WRIGHT (MRS. JAMES F. NELSON), federal judge; b. San Pedro, Calif., Sept. 30, 1928; d. Harry Earl and Lorna Amy Wright; m. James Frank Nelson, Dec. 27, 1950; children: Franklin Wright, Lorna Jean. BA, UCLA, 1950, JD, 1953; LLM, U. So. Calif., 1956; LLD (hon.), U. San Diego, 1997, U. So. Calif., 1983, Georgetown U., 1988, Whittier U., 1989, U. Santa Clara, 1990, Whittier U., 1989, Pepperdine U. Sch. of Law, 2003. Bar: Calif. 1954. Rsch. assoc. fellow U. So. Calif., 1953—56, instr., 1957, asst. prof., 1958—61, assoc. prof., 1961—67, prof., 1967—, assoc. dean., 1965—67, dean., 1967—80; judge U.S. Ct. Appeals 9th Cir., 1979—95, sr. judge, 1995—. Com. to consider stds. for admission to practice in fed. cts. Jud. Conf. U.S., 1976—79; cons. project STAR Law Enforcement Assistance Adminstrn.; select com. on internal procedures Calif. Supreme Ct., 1987—; co-chair Sino-Am. Seminar on Mediation and Arbitration, Beijing, 1992. Contbr. articles to profl. jours.; author: Judicial Adminstration and The Administration of Justice, 1973; author: (with Christopher Goelz and Meredith Watts) Federal Ninth Circuit Civil Appellate Practice, 1995. Co-chair Confronting Myths in Edn. for Pres. Nixon's White House Conf. on Children, Pres. Carter's Commn. for Pension Policy, 1974—80; pres. Reagon's Madison Trust; mem. Nat. Spiritual Assembly of Bahais of U.S., 1967—; bd. dirs. Dialogue on Transition to a Global Soc., Weinacht, Switzerland, 1992; bd. vis. U.S. Air Force Acad., 1978; bd. dirs. Coun. on Legal Edn. for Profl. Responsibility, 1971—80, Constl. Right Found., Am. Nat. Inst. for Social Advancement; adv. bd. Nat. Ctr. for State Cts., 1971—76; adv. com. to promote equality for woman and men in cts. Nat. Jud. Edn. Program; bd. dirs. Pacific Oaks Coll., Childrens Sch. & Rsch. Ctr., 1996—98; adv. bd. World Law Inst., 1997—, Tahirih Justice Inst., Washington, 1998—; chmn. bd. Western Justice Ctr., 1986—; chair 9th Cir. Standing Com. on Alternative Dispute Resolution, 1998—. Named Law Alumnus of Yr., UCLA, 1967, Woman of Yr., Times, 1968, Disting. Jurist, Ind. U. Law, 1994; recipient Profl. Achievement award, 1969, AWARE Internat. award, 1970, Humanitarian award, U. Judaism, 1973, Ernestine Stalhut Outstanding Woman Lawyer award, 1972, Pub. Svc. award, Coro Found., 1978, Pax Orbis ex Jure medal, World Peace thru Law Ctr., 1975, Hollzer Human Rights award, Jewish Fedn. Coun., 1988, Medal of Honor, UCLA, 1993, Emil Gumpert Jud. ADR Recognition award, L.A. County Bar Assn., 1996, Julia Morgan award, YWCA, 1997, Samuel E. Gates Litigation award, Am. Coll. Trial Lawyers, 1999, Bernard E. Witkin award, State Bar Assn. Calif., 2000, Judge of the Year award, Pasadena Bar Assn., 2002; fellow, Davenport Coll.; Lustman fellow, Yale U., 1977. Fellow: Davenport Coll., Am. Bar Found.; mem.: ABA (sect. on jud. adminstrn., chmn. com. on edn. in jud. adminstrn. 1973—89, D'Alemberte/Raven award 2000), Assn. Am. Law Schs. (chmn. com. edn. in jud. adminstrn.), Am. Judicature Soc. (bd. dirs., Justice award 1985), Bar Calif. (bd. dirs. continuing edn. bar commn. 1967—74), Order of Coif (nat. v.p. 1974—76), Phi Beta Kappa. Office: US Ct Appeals Cir 125 S Grand Ave Ste 303 Pasadena CA 91105-1621

NELSON, EDITH ELLEN, dietitian; b. Vicksburg, Mich., Sept. 26, 1940; d. Edward Kenneth and Anna (McManus) Rolffs; m. Douglas Keith Nelson; children: Daniel Lee, Jennifer Lynn. BS, Mich. State U., 1962; MEd in Applied Nutrition, U. Cin., 1979. Lic. dietitian, Fla. Clin. dietitian Macon (Ga.) Gen. Hosp., Blodgett Meml. Hosp., Grand Rapids, Mich.; grad. teaching asst. U. Cin., 1978-79; dir. nutrition svcs. Dialysis Clinic, Inc., Cin., 1979-88; cons. dietitian Panama City Devel. Ctr., Ft. Walton Beach Devel. Ctr., Fla., 1988-94; renal dietitian Dialysis Svcs. Fla., Ft. Walton Beach, 1989-92; cons. dietitian N.W. Fla. Community Hosp., Chipley, Fla., 1993-94, Beverly Enterprises, Panama City Beach, 1994-96, pvt. practice, Panama City, Fla., 1996—. Mich. Edn. Assn. scholar, 1958; Nat. Kidney Found. grantee, 1986. Mem. Am. Dietetic Assn., Fla. Dietetic Assn., Panhandle Dist. Dietetic Assn., Nat. Kidney Found. (coun. on renal nutrition, Fla. coun. on renal nutrition), Omicron Nu. Home and Office: 3522 Fox Run Blvd Panama City Beach FL 32408-7151

NELSON, EDWARD GAGE, merchant banking investment company executive; b. Nashville, May 17, 1931; s. Charles and Polly (Prentiss) N.; m. Carole Olivia Frances Minton, Sept. 17, 1960; children— Carole Gervais, Emily Minton, Ellen Prentiss BA in Polit. Sci., U. of South, Sewanee, Tenn., 1952. Exec. v.p. Clark, Landstreet & Kirkpatrick, Inc., Nashville, 1955-64, Commerce Union Bank, Nashville, 1968-72, pres., 1972-82, cons., 1985—, chmn., CEO, 1982-84; chmn., pres. Nelson Capital Corp., Nashville, 1985—. Hon. consul gen. Japan; bd. dirs. Werthan Packaging, Consumers Ins., Franklin Industries, Trans Arabian Investment Bank, Berlitz Internat., Inc. Ctrl. Parking Sys., Ohio Star Forge; mem. 1st adv. coun. Japan/Tenn. Soc. Trustee Vanderbilt U., Nashville, 1979—, chmn. med. ctr. bd., 1984-2003. Spl. agt. U.S. Army, 1955, Japan. Mem. Belle Meade Country Club, River Club (N.Y.C.). Republican. Episcopalian. Home: 1305 Chickering Rd Nashville TN 37215-4521 Office: Nelson Capital Corp 3401 W End Ave Ste 300 Nashville TN 37203-1085

NELSON, EDWARD HUMPHREY, architect; b. Winchester, Mass., Sept. 2, 1918; s. Richard MacDonald and Evelyn Miller (Humphrey) N.; m. Lois Whitaker Renouf, Sept. 24, 1948 (dec.); children: Susan, David, Sarah; m. Miriam P. Ketcham, Jan. 2, 1988. Grad., Lenox Sch., 1936; B.Arch., Yale, 1950. Pvt. archtl. practice, Tucson, 1953-61; sr. v.p. CNWC Architects, Tucson, 1961-88, pres., 1989-94; ret., 1994. Mem. adv. com. U. Ariz. Coll. Architecture, 1984-93. Works include: design for Tucson Community Ctr. Pres. Tucson Cmty. Coun., 1969-71, Tucson Art Ctr., 1960; bd. dirs. Tucson Housing Found., 1969-, Estes Gardens Low Rent Sr. Housing, 2004-, Tucson Symphony, 1977-84, Tucson United Way, 1980, NBA Tucson Housing, 2002-, Tucson Art Mus., 1960-74, Tucson Trade Bur., 1976-91, pres., 1984; trustee Green Fields Sch., 1960-74; vestry St. Philips Episc. Ch., 1967-69, sr. warden, 1987-90, parish warden, 1993-94; convenor Episcopal Interparish Coun., 1990-92; mem. Episcopal Diocese of Ariz., S.W. Regional Parish; 1st Phila. City Troop, 1940—, horse cavalry, 1940-42. Served to capt. AUS, 1940-41, WWII, ETO. Decorated Bronze Star with oak leaf cluster, Purple Heart; recipient Disting. Citizen award U. Ariz., 1981, St. Philips medal St. Philips Episc. Ch., 2000. Fellow: AIA (pres. So. Ariz. chpt. 1962, emeritus 1994, chmn. Ariz. Fellows 1986—94); mem.: Ariz. Soc. Archs. (pres. 1963), U. Ariz. Pres.'s Club, Yale Club (pres. Tucson chpt. 1962, 1983, dir. 1979—). Home: 2020 E 4th St Tucson AZ 85719-5114 E-mail: miriamned@cox.net.

NELSON, EDWARD SHEFFIELD, lawyer, retired utilities executive; b. Keevil, Ark., Feb. 23, 1941; s. Robert Ford and Thelma Jo (Mayberry) N.; m. Mary Lynn McCastlain, Oct. 12, 1962; children: Cynthia, Lynn (dec.), Laura. BS, U. Cen. Ark., 1963; LLB, Ark. Law Sch., 1968; JD, U. Ark., 1969. Mgmt. trainee Ark. La. Gas Co., Little Rock, 1963-64, sales engr., 1964-67, sales coordinator, 1967-69, gen. sales mgr., 1969-71, v.p., gen. sales mgr., 1971-73, pres., dir., 1973-79, pres., chmn., chief exec. officer, 1979-85; ptnr., chmn. bd., chief exec. officer House, Wallace, Nelson & Jewel, Little Rock, 1985-86; pvt. practice law Little Rock, 1986—; of counsel Jack, Lyon & Jones, P.A., 1991—. Bd. dirs. Fed. Res. Mem. N.G., 1957-63, Fellowship Bible Ch.; bd. dirs. U. Ark., Little Rock, vice chmn. bd. visitors, 1981; bd. dirs. Philander Smith Coll., 1981; chmn. Ark. Indsl. Devel. Commn., 1987, 88; past chmn. Little Rock br. Fed. Res. Bd. St. Louis; chmn. Econ. Expansion Study Commn., 1987—; bd. dirs. Ark. Ednl. TV Found., Ark. Game and Fish Commn. Found.; founder, 1st pres. Jr. Achievement Ark., 1987-88; Rep. nominee for Gov. of Ark., 1990, 94; co-state chmn. Ark. Reps., 1991-92, nat. committeeman Ark. GOP, 1993-2000; mem. Ark. Higher Edn. Coord. Bd., 1997-99; apptd. commr. Ark. Game and Fish Commn., 2000—. Named Ark.'s Outstanding Young Man Ark. J. C. of C., 1973; One of Am.'s Ten Outstanding Young Men U.S. Jr. C. of C., 1974; Citizen of Yr. Ark. chpt. March of Dimes, 1983; Humanitarian of Yr. NCCJ, 1983; Best Chief Exec. Officer in Natural Gas Industry Wall Street Transcript, 1983; recipient 1st Disting. Alumnus award U. Cen. Ark., 1987. Mem. Am., Ark., Pulaski County Bar Assns., Ark. C. of C. (dir.), Little Rock C. of C. (dir., pres. 1981), Sales and Mktg. Execs. Assn. (pres. 1975, Top Mgmt. award 1977), U. Ark. Law Sch. Alumni Assn. (pres. 1980), Sigma Tau Gamma (Ben T. Laney Leadership award for leadership and achievement 2000), Ark. Wildlife Fedn. (Conservationist of Yr. 2002), Am. Lung Assn. (Philanthropist of Yr. 2003). Fellowship Bible Ch. Office: 6th and Broadway 3400 TCBY Bldg Little Rock AR 72201 Office Phone: 501-375-1122. Personal E-mail: esn@jlj.com.

NELSON, EDWIN STAFFORD, actor, educator; b. New Orleans, Dec. 21, 1928; s. William Jackson and Aimee (Robelot) N.; m. Patricia Amelia Miller, June 9, 1951; children— Gregory, Christopher, Cynthia, Elizabeth, Mary, Anne. BA in Media Arts, Tulane U., 2000; degree, Sch. Radio Technique, N.Y.C., 1953. Asst. dir. WDSU-TV, New Orleans, 1953-56. Adj. prof. Tulane U., 2001—, U. New Orleans, 2002—. Free-lance actor, 1956-62, actor, under contract to, Universal Studios, Cal., 1962-64, 72, contract with, 20th Century Fox, Calif., 1964-69; starred on TV series Peyton Place, 1965-70, Silent Force; series, 1971-72, ABC's Ed Nelson show, 1976, daytime series Capital, 1982-87. Mem. L.A. County Sheriff's Res., 1968-73, Mountain Rescue Unit, 1968-71; Pres. Univ. Calif. Polytech. Inst. Pomona Assocs., 1973-75. Served with USN, 1946-49. Named TV Father of Year, 1968; presented George award, 1968; inducted New Orleans Walk of Fame, 2003. Mem. AFTRA, SAG, Equity, Acad. Motion Picture Arts and Scis. Office: care Marvin Josephson 16 W 22nd St Fl 3 New York NY 10010-5803 E-mail: edpaedpactor@aol.com. *Consider your critics more accurate than your complimentors. Success is building on attempts that failed.*

NELSON, ELAINE EDWARDS, lawyer; b. Waco, Tex., Sept. 16, 1947; d. Bedford Duncan and Joyce (Harlan) Edwards; m. David A. Nelson, Apr. 12, 1969; children: Carol Christine, Harlan Claire. BA, Baylor U., 1969, JD, 1978. Bar: Tex. 1978. Gen. counsel Austin Industries, Inc., Dallas, 1978—. Office: Austin Industries Inc 3535 Travis St Ste 300 Dallas TX 75204-1466 also: PO Box 2879 Dallas TX 75221-2879

NELSON, ELIZABETH HAWKINS, public association administrator; b. Rockville Centre, NY, Jan. 27, 1931; arrived in Eng., 1951; d. Harry Dadmun and Gretchen (Hawkins) N.; m. Ivan Piercy, Dec. 7, 1960 (div. 1972); children: Catherine, Christopher, Nicholas; m. Claude Jacob Esterson, July 26, 1975 (div. 1998). BA, Middlebury Coll., 1951; PhD, U. London, 1953; DSc (hon.), City London U., 1993; PhD (hon.), Open U., 2003. Rsch. psychologist Mars Ltd., London, 1954-55; dir., mng. dir. rsch. unit Benton & Bowles, London, 1955-64; dir. Mass Observation Ltd., London, 1964-65; founder dir., chmn. Taylor Nelson/Sofres plc, London, 1965-92; chief exec. The Princess Royal Trust for Carers, London, 1992-95; chair coun. U. Surrey Roehampton, 1995—2001; chmn. South West London Cmty. NHS Trust, 1997—2002. Chair exec. com. WellBeing Royal Coll. Ob-Gyns., 2002—04; chair Stargate Capital Investment Group Ltd; non-exec. dir. Royal Bank Scotland, Edinburgh, 1988—97; chmn. bd. UK Ecolabelling, 1992—98; pres. World Assn. Pub. Opinion Rsch., 1990—92; coun. mem. City & Guilds, 1998—; mem. adv. com. on degree awarding powers Quality Assurance Agy., 1998—; chmn. Stargate Capital Investment Group Ltd., 2004—. Vice chair coun. Open U., Milton Keynes, England, 1991—2001; dir. U.S. Open U., 1998—2001; Mem. Doctors and Dentists Pay Rev. Bd., London, England, 1992—97. Decorated Order Brit. Empire; hon. fellow City & Guilds, 1994, U. Surrey, Roehampton, 2003. Fellow: Market Rsch. Soc., Royal Soc. Arts; mem.: Freedom City of London, Internat. Women's Forum (bd. mem. 2001—), First Forum U.K. Avocations: choral singing, opera, bridge. Home: 57 Home Park Rd London SW19 7HS England Office Phone: 44 0 207236 4001. E-mail: liznlson53@aol.com.

NELSON, ELMER KINGSHOLM, JR., (KIM NELSON), educator, writer, mediator, consultant; b. Laramie, Wyo., Sept. 14, 1922; s. Elmer Kingsholm and Alice (Downey) N.; m. Jane Beckwith Oliver, Aug. 4, 1945; 1 son, Elmer Kingsholm III (Kirk). BA, U. Wyo., 1943, JD, 1948, MA, 1949; Dr. Pub. Adminstrn., U. So. Calif., 1959. Instr. psychology U. Wyo., 1947-49; psychologist, staff psychologist dept. probation Contra Costa County, Calif., 1949-51; sr. psychologist Cal. State Dept. Corrections, San Quentin and Chino Prisons, 1951-52; asst. prof. criminology U. B.C., Can., 1952-54, assoc. prof., 1954-56, head criminology div., 1953-56; warden Haney Correctional Instn., B.C., 1956-58; assoc. dir. Youth Studies Ctr. U. So. Calif., 1958-59, dir. Youth Studies Ctr., 1959-64, assoc. prof. pub. adminstrn., 1958-61, prof., 1961—, dean Sch. Pub. Adminstrn., 1971-76, prof., co-dir. Sacramento Pub. Affairs Ctr.; head Bay Area Research Center, Berkeley, 1979—; prof. emeritus U. So. Calif. Dep. adminstr. Youth and Adult Corrections Agy., State of Calif., Sacramento, 1964-65; interim exec. dir. Office Criminal Justice Planning, spring 1975; dir. Nat. Study Probation and Parole, 1976-77; chmn. task force on corrections, asso. dir. Pres.'s Commn. on Law Enforcement and Adminstrn. of Justice, Washington, 1966-67; dir. nat. study of correctional adminstrn. U. So. Calif. for Joint Commn. on Correctional Manpower and Tng., 1967-69 Co-author: Corrections in America, 1975; contbr. articles, monographs, research reports to profl. jours. Advisor on mgmt. Boys Republic, Chino, Calif., 1967—; bd. dirs., v.p. Am. Justice Inst., Sacramento; bd. dirs. Human Interaction Rsch. Inst., L.A. Recipient Disting. Alumnus award U. Wyo., 1975, Exemplary Alumni award U. Wyo. Coll. Arts and Scis., 1994; Ford Found. Travel Study grantee, 1970-71; E. Kim Nelson endowed doctoral fellowship established at U. So. Calif., 1987. Sr. fellow Nat. Acad. Pub. Adminstrn.; mem. Wyo. Bar Assn., Alpha Tau Omega, Phi Beta Kappa, Phi Kappa Phi, Psi Chi. Home: 355 St Augustine Ct Benicia CA 94510-2866 E-mail: eknscarq@aol.com.

NELSON, FLORENCE ELY, civic leader; b. N.Y.C., June 3, 1931; d. Albert H. and Constance (Jennings) Ely; m. Jerry Nelson, Nov. 21, 1964; children: Nicolas Jennings, Thomas Burr, James Pollock. DHL(hon.), Ariz. State U., 1995. Stage, screen technician various theaters, 1949-64. Design cons. Oaxaca Rest/Le Relais, Scottsdale, Ariz., 1986, Corp. Bldg. of Pinnacle Paradise Inc., 1986, pvt. residences, Scottsdale, 1986. Bd. dirs. Ariz. Mus. Sci. and Tech., Phoenix, 1984—, Ballet Ariz., Phoenix, 1985—, Scottsdale Prevention Inst., 1987—; coord. Boy Scouts Am., Ariz., 1977—; mem. Ariz. Opera, 1985; learning leader Paradise Valley Sch. Dist., Ariz., 1987—; mem. Ariz. Astronomy Bd. Recipient Disting. Achievement award Ariz. State U., 1990; mamed Woman of Achievement Jr. League of Ariz., 1987; named to Scottsdale's History Hall of Fame, 2000. Mem. Charter 100 (program chair 1985-86, membership com. 1986-87, v.p. 1987-88), Scottsdale Chairwomen (co-founder), Phoenix Com. Fgn. Relations (founder), Ariz. Assn. Gifted and Talented (hon. bd. dirs. 1986, pres. 1987—), Nat. Space Soc. (bd. dirs. 1984—). Clubs: Troon Golf and Country (Scottsdale), Skyline Golf and Country (Tucson), Pinnacle Peak Golf and Country (Scottsdale). Democrat. Episcopalian. Avocations: scuba diving, bicycling, cross country skiing, joint rehab., cooking. Home: 8711 E Pinnacle Peak Rd Scottsdale AZ 85255-3517

NELSON, FRANKLIN W. commissioner, retired banker; B, Fort Hays State U.; attended, U. Wis. Pres. pvt. investment firm; commr. Kans. Bank Commr.'s Office, Topeka, 1999—. Office: Kans Bank Commrs Office 700 SW Jackson St Ste 300 Topeka KS 66603-3757

NELSON, FREDA NELL HEIN, librarian; b. Trenton, Mo., Dec. 16, 1929; d. Fred Albert and Mable Carman (Doan) Hein; m. Robert John Nelson, Nov. 1, 1957 (div. Apr. 1984); children: Thor, Hope. Nursing diploma, Trinity Luth. Hosp., Kansas City, Mo., 1950; B. Philosophy, Northwestern U., 1961; MS in Info. and Libr. Sci., U. Ill., 1986. RN. Operating rm. nurse Trinity Luth. Hosp., Kansas City, Mo., 1950-52, Johns Hopkins Hosp., Balt., 1952, Wesley Meml. Hosp., Chgo., 1952-58, Tacoma Gen. Hosp., 1958-59, Chgo. Wesley Hosp., 1959-61; libr. asst. Maple Woods Campus Met. Community Colls., Kansas City, 1987-89, libr., libr. mgr. Blue Springs Campus, 1989-96; ret., 1996. Co-founder Coll. for Kids, Knox Coll., Galesburg, Ill., 1982. Nurses scholar Edgar Bergen Found., 1947; recipient Award of Merit, Chgo. Bd. Health, 1952. Avocations: swimming, walking, cross-word puzzles. Home: 7000 N Elm St Pleasant Valley MO 64068-9571

NELSON, FREDERICK CARL, mechanical engineering educator; b. Braintree, Mass., Aug. 8, 1932; s. Carl Edwin and Marjorie May (Miller) N.; m. Delia Ann Dwaresky; children: Jeffrey, Karen, Richard (dec.), Christine. BSME, Tufts U., 1954; MS, Harvard U., 1955, PhD, 1961. Registered profl. engr., Mass. Instr. Tufts U., Medford, Mass., 1955-57, asst. prof. mech. engring., 1957-64; assoc. prof. mech. engring., 1964-71; prof. mech. engring. Tufts U., Medford, 1971—, dean engring., 1980-94. Cons. SAVIAC, 2003—. Translator: Mechanical Vibrations for Engineers, 1983. Recipient Career Achievement award Tufts U. Dept. Mech. Engring., 1996. Fellow ASME (centennial medal award 1980), AAAS, ASA, Nat. Inst. Applied Scis. of Lyon (medal 1988), Korea Advanced Inst. Sci. and Tech. (medal 1988, partnership award 2003), Tufts U. Alumni Assn. (medal 1991), The Vibration Inst. (bd. dirs. 1999—). Office: Tufts U Sch Engring Medford MA 02155-5555 E-mail: frederick.nelson@tufts.edu.

NELSON, FREDERICK DICKSON, judge; b. Cleve., Oct. 19, 1958; s. David Aldrich and Mary Ellen (Dickson) N. AB, Hamilton Coll., 1980; JD, Harvard U., 1983. Bar: Ohio 1984, D.C. 1985. Majority counsel subcom. on criminal law U.S. Senate Judiciary Com., Washington, 1983-85; spl. asst. to asst. atty. gen., Office of Legal Policy U.S. Dept. Justice, Washington, 1985-86, dep. asst. atty. gen., Office of Legal Policy, 1986-87; assoc. Taft, Stettinius & Hollister, Cin., 1988-89, of counsel, 1991-93; assoc. counsel to Pres. of U.S. The White House, Washington, 1989-90. Advisor to govts. of Ukraine and Russia, ABA Ctrl. and East European Law Initiative, 1992-93; adj. prof. constl. law Salmon P. Chase Coll. Law, U. No. Ky., 1994; chief of staff, legal coun. U.S. Rep. Steve Chabot, 1995-97; cons. Constnl. Commn. Albania, per Internat. Rep. Inst., 1998; pres. Civic Solutions, LLC, Cin., 1998-2002; co-creator, panelist Hotseat, Sta. WCPO-TV, (Cin. Channel 9), 2000-02; judge Hamilton County Ct. of Common Pleas, 2003—. Exec. editor Harvard Jour. of Law and Pub. Policy, 1982-83. Mem. Hamilton County Rep. Policy and Appts. Coms., 1999-2002; cons. Chabot for Congress Campaign, Cin., 1994, 98; mem. Ohio Bd. Uniform State Laws, Nat. Conf. Commrs. on Unifort State Laws, 2001—. Harry S. Truman Found. scholar, 1978-81. Mem. NATAS (Ohio Valley chpt.), Federalist Soc., Harvard Club. of Cin. (bd. dirs. 1989, 2001—), Phi Beta Kappa. Republican. Office: Hamilton County Ct House Rm 380 Cincinnati OH 45202-1217 Office Phone: 513-946-5840.

NELSON, GARY MICHAEL, lawyer; b. Mpls., July 12, 1951; s. Emery Marshal and Henrietta Margaret (Flategraff) Nelson; m. Deb Snyder; 1 child, Courtney Snyder; children: Rachel Mary, Amy Margaret. BA, Gustavus Adolphus Coll., St. Peter, Minn., 1973; JD, Harvard U., 1976. Bar: Minn. 1976, U.S. Dist. Ct. Minn. 1976. Ptnr., CEO Oppenheimer Wolff & Donnelly, Mpls., 1976-97; exec. v.p., gen. counsel, corp. sec. Ceridian Corp., Mpls., 1997—. Chair corp. practice inst. Minn. Inst. Legal Edn., Mpls., 1978-93. Sec., v.p. Mpls. Girls' Club, 1978-83. Recipient Significant Contbns. award Am. Girls' Clubs Am., 1982. Mem. ABA. Lutheran. Avocations: fishing, hunting, hiking, reading. Home: 2685 Maplewood Rd Wayzata MN 55391 Office: Ceridian Corp 3311 E Old Shakopee Rd Minneapolis MN 55425-1640

NELSON, GAYLORD ANTON, former senator, association executive; b. Clear-Lake, Wis., June 4, 1916; s. Anton and Mary (Bradt) N.; m. Carrie Lee Dotson, Nov. 14, 1947; children— Gaylord, Cynthia, Jeffrey. Grad., San Jose State Coll., Calif., 1939, U. Wis. Law Sch., 1942. Bar: Admitted Wis. bar 1942. Practiced in, Madison, 1946-58; mem. Wis. Senate, 1949-58, Democratic leader, 1948-52; gov. Wis., 1958-62; U.S. senator from Wis., 1963-81. Mem. finance com., chmn. subcom. on Social Security; chmn. employment, poverty and migratory labor subcom. of human resources com.; chmn. select com. on small bus., chmn. monopoly subcom. Author: Environmental Education Act, 1970, Nat. Environmental Education Act, 1972; co-author: The National Teacher Corps, 1965. Counselor Wilderness Soc., Washington, 1981—; founder Earth Day. 1st lt. AUS, World War II. Recipient Conservationist of the Year Award, Nat. Wildlife Fedn., 1989, Only One Earth Award, Environmental Leadership Award, UN Environment Prog., 1992, 95, Presdl. Freedom medal, 1995. Mem. State Bar Assn. Wis. Democrat. Home: 3611 Calvend Ln Kensington MD 20895-3154 Office: Wilderness Soc 1615 M St NW Washington DC 20036

NELSON, GEORGE DALMAN, JR., banker; b. Shreveport, La., May 28, 1950; s. George Dalman and Nell Carolyn (Querbes) N.; m. Clare deNelle Morgan, May 8, 1982; children: George D. III, Catherine, Morgan, Spencer. BA, Tulane U., 1972; MBA, Harvard U., 1974; JD, Georgetown U., 1977, LLM, 1980. CPCU. V.p., mng. dir. Querbes & Nelson, Shreveport, 1979-95; chmn. Bank One, Shreveport, 1995-2000, chmn. adv. bd., 2000—. Dir. La. Cos. Inc., Baton Rouge, 1980-95, Premier Bancorp Inc., Baton Rouge, 1990-95. Pres., dir. Shreveport Symphony, 1985-87; chmn. campaign United Way of N.W. La., Shreveport, 1988; chmn. Downtown Devel. Authority, Shreveport, 1988. Named Rising Young Bus. Leader Shreveport C. of C., 1987. Mem. Shreveport Club (dir. 1997-99), Shreveport Country Club, Boston Club, Cambridge Club, Rotary Club of Shreveport (pres.). Episcopalian. Avocations: golf, baseball, football, children. Home: 3315 Fairfield Ave Shreveport LA 71104-4103 Office: PO Box 5 Shreveport LA 71161-0005

NELSON, GEORGE DRIVER, astronomy and education educator, former astronaut; b. Charles City, Iowa, July 13, 1950; s. George Vernon and Evelyn Elenor (Driver) N.; m. Susan Lynn Howard, June 19, 1971; children: Aimee Tess, Marti Ann. BS, Harvey Mudd Coll., 1972; MS, U. Wash., 1974, PhD, 1978; DSc (hon.), U. Colo., 2000; LHD (hon.), Towson U., 2001. Astronaut NASA, Houston, 1978-89; mission specialist Space Shuttle flight, 1984, 86, 88; assoc. vice provost for rsch., assoc. prof. astronomy U. Wash., Seattle, 1989-96; dir. project 2061 AAAS, Washington, 1996—2000; dir. sci., math., and tech. edn. Western Wash. U., Bellingham, 2002—. Adj. assoc. prof. edn. U. Wash., 1989-96. Recipient Haley Space Flight award AIAA, 1989. Unitarian Universalist. Avocations: reading, athletics, guitar. Office: SMATE Western Wash Univ 516 High St Bellingham WA 98225-9155 Office Phone: 360-650-3637. Business E-Mail: george.nelson@wwu.edu.

NELSON, GLEN DAVID, medical products executive, physician; b. Mpls., Mar. 28, 1937; s. Ralph and Edna S. Nelson; m. Marilyn Carlson, June 30, 1961; children: Diana, Curtis, Wendy. AB, Harvard U., 1959; MD, U. Minn., 1963. Diplomate Am. Bd. Surgery, also sub-bd. bariatric and peripheral vascular surgery; cert. Am. Bd. Surgery, 1970. Intern Hennepin County Gen. Hosp., Mpls., 1963—64, resident in gen. surgery, 1964—69; staff surgeon Park Nicollet Med. Ctr. (formerly St. Louis Park Med. Ctr.), Mpls.; practiced surgery, 1969—86; chmn., pres. and CEO Park Nicollet Med. Ctr., 1975—86; chmn. and CEO Am. MedCenters, Inc., 1984—86; vice chmn. Medtronic, Inc., 1982—2002; chmn., prin. owner GDN Holdings, LLC, Minnetonka, Minn., 2002—. Current bd. dirs. Advanced BioSurfaces, Inc., Cardiovascular Systems, Inc., Carlson Holdings, Inc., Carlson Sch. Mgmt., DexCom, Inc., Harvard Univ. Dean's Coun., Itamar, Inc., Jackson Hole Group, Johns Hopkins Medicine Bd. of Visitors, LifeLinkMD, Minn. Public Radio, Minute-Clinic (QuickMedx); dir. & chmn. The Perth Corp., Regent Aviation, Stanford Radiology Med. Imaging Adv. Bd., The St. Paul Co., Inc., Transneuronix, Inc., Univ.; Emeritus clinical prof. surgery, U. Minn.

NELSON, GORDON LEIGH, chemist, educator; b. Palo Alto, Calif., May 27, 1943; s. Nels Folke and Alice Virginia (Fredrickson) N. BS in Chemistry, U. Nev., 1965; MS, Yale U., 1967, PhD, 1970; DSc (hon.), William Carey Coll., 1988. Staff research chemist corp. research and devel. Gen. Electric Co., Schenectady, N.Y., 1970-74, mgr. combustibility tech. plastics div. Pittsfield, Mass., 1974-79, mgr. environ. protection plastics div., 1979-82; v.p. materials sci. and tech. Springborn Labs. Inc., Enfield, Conn., 1982-83; prof., chmn. dept. polymer sci. U. So. Miss., Hattiesburg, 1983-89; dean Coll. Sci. and Liberal Arts, prof. chemistry Fla. Inst. Tech., Melbourne, 1989—, mem. coun. sci., soc. pres., sec., 1989-90, chair-elect, 1991, chair, 1992. Cons. in field. Author: Carbon-13 Nuclear Magnetic Resonance for Organic Chemists, 1972, Carbon-13 Nuclear Magnetic Resonance for Organic Chemists, 2d edit., 1980; co-author: Polymeric Materials-Chemistry for the Future, 1989, Carbon Monoxide and Human Lethality, 1993; editor: Fire and Polymers-Materials and Tests for Hazard Prevention, 1990, 1995; co-editor: Fire and Polymers-Materials and Solutions for Hazard Prevention, 2001, editor books on coating sci. tech.; contbr. articles to profl. jours. Mem.: ASTM (E5 cert. of appreciation 1985, D1 1997), Soc. Advancement of Scandinavian Study, Coun. Colls Arts and Scis., Soc. Plastics Industry (structural plastics divsn., Man of Yr. 1979), Internat. Electrotech. Commn. (U.S. tech. adv. group on info. processing equipment), So. Soc. for Coatings Tech., Ctr. Sci. Tech. and the Media (bd. dir. 1991—94), Info. Tech. Industry Coun. (chmn. plastics task group), Am. Chem. Soc. (bd. dirs. 1977—85, 1987—89, pres. 1988, bd. dirs. 1992—94, 1st Nelson award Orlando sect. 1996, Charles Holmes Herty medal Ga. sect. 1998), Am. Inst. Chemists, Nev. Hist. Soc., Yale Chemists Assn. (pres. 1981—), Sigma Xi. Republican. Presbyterian. Avocations: travel, western U.S. history. Office: Fla Inst Tech Coll Sci & Liberal Arts 150 W University Blvd Melbourne FL 32901-6975 Office Phone: 321-674-7260.

NELSON, GRANT STEEL, lawyer, educator; b. Mitchell, S.D., Apr. 18, 1939; s. Howard Steel and Clara Marie (Winandy) N.; m. Judith Ann Haugen, Sept. 22, 1962; children: Mary Elizabeth, Rebekah Anne, John Adam. BA magna cum laude, U. Minn., 1960; JD cum laude, 1963. Bar: Minn. 1963, Mo. 1971. Assoc. Faegre & Benson, Mpls., 1963-67; mem. law faculty U. Mo., Columbia, 1967-91, assoc. prof., 1970-72, prof., 1972-91, Enoch H. Crowder prof. law, 1974-91; prof. UCLA, 1991—. Mem. bd. legal advisors Gt. Plains Legal Found., 1978-85; vis. asst. prof. U. Mich., Ann Arbor, 1969-70, Brigham Young U., Provo, Utah, summer 1976; vis. prof. U. Minn., Mpls., 1981-82, UCLA, 1989-90; disting. vis. prof. Pepperdine U., 1987-88; vis. endowed Campbell prof. U. Mo., Columbia, 1996-98; commr. Nat. Conf. Commrs. Uniform State Laws, 1983-91; mem. West Pub. Law Sch. Adv. Bd. Author: (with Van Hecke and Leavell) Cases and Materials on Equitable Remedies and Restitution, 1973, (with Whitman) Cases and Materials on Real Estate Finance and Development, 1976, Cases and Materials on Real Estate Transfer, Finance and Development, 1981, (with Osborne and Whitman) Real Estate Finance Law, 1979, (with Leavell and Love) Cases and Materials on Equitable Remedies and Restitution, 1980, (with Whitman) Land Transactions and Finance, 1983, 3d edit., 2004, (with Whitman) Real Estate Finance Law, 1985, 3d edit., 2001, (with Leavell and Love) Cases and Materials on Equitable Remedies, Restitution and Damages, 1986, rev. edit., 1994, rev. edit., 2000, (with Browder, Cunningham, Stoebuck and Whitman) Basic Property Law, 1989, (with Stoebuck and Whitman) Contemporary Property, 1996, rev. edit., 2002, (with Whitman) Cases and Materials on Real Estate Transfer, Finance and Development, 1987, 4th edit., 2003; co-reporter ALI Restatement of Property-Mortgages; contbr. articles to profl. jours. 1st lt. AUS, 1964-65. Recipient award for meritorious service and achievement U. Mo. Law Sch. Found., 1974; recipient Disting. Faculty Service award U. Mo.-Columbia Alumni Assn., 1978, Disting. Faculty award, 1986, Disting. Non-Alumnus award, 1991, Rutter award for excellence in tchg. UCLA Law Sch., 2000, Disting. Tchg. award UCLA Alumni Assn., 2002. Mem. Am. Law Inst., Assn. Am. Law Schs. (sect. chmn. 1976-77), Am. Coll. Real Estate Lawyers, Mo. Bar Assn. (vice chmn. property law com. 1974-75, chmn. 1975-77), Order of Coif, Phi Beta Kappa, Phi Delta Phi. Office: UCLA Sch Law Hilgard Ave PO Box 951476 Los Angeles CA 90095-1476

NELSON, HAROLD BERNHARD, museum director; b. Providence, R.I., May 14, 1947; s. Harold B. and Eleanor (Lavina) N. BA, Bowdoin Coll., 1969; MA, U. Del., 1972. Rsch. fellow NMAA Smithsonian Inst., Washington, 1976-77; curator Am. art Mus. Art & Archeol., U. Mo., Columbia, 1977-79; registrar Solomon R. Guggenheim Mus., N.Y.C., 1979-83; exhibition program dir. Am. Fedn. Arts, N.Y.C., 1983-89; dir. Long Beach (Calif.) Mus. of Art, 1989—. Juror Annual Art Exhibition Mus. Art, Sci. & Industry, Bridgeport, Conn., 1988, Annual Art Exhibition, Clark County Dist. Libr., Las Vegas, Nev., 1984; speaker Am. Assn. Mus. Annual Conf., Detroit, 1985, annual meeting Western Mus. Conf., Portland, Oreg., 1987, Grantmakers in Art Symposium, N.Y.C., 1986, annual meeting Western Mus. Conf., Salt Lake City, 1985; mem. adv. com. APA, Assn. Sci. and Tech. Ctrs.; panelist Aid to Spl. Exhibitions, NEA, Washington, 1986; participant Am. Legal Assn., ABA Conf., San Francisco, 1986; observer, respondent Mus. Symposium, NEA, Dallas, 1985. Author: Sounding the Depths: 150 Years of American Seascape, 1989, New Visions: Selina Trieff, 1997, Bountiful Harvest: American Decorative Arts from the Gail-Oxford Collection, 1997, For a New Nation: American Decorative Arts from the Gail-Oxford Collection, 1998, In Ye Grandest Manner and After Ye Newest Fashion, 2000, Conjunction: The Melba and Al Langman Collection, 2000, Tulips, Pomegranates and Kings: Delftware from the Collection of Benjamin F. Edwards III, 2000, Imps on a Bridge: Wedgwood Fairyland and Other Lustres, 2001, The Enamels of Annemarie Davidson, 2004, For the people: American Folf Art From the Collection of Thomas H. Oxford and Victor Gail, 2004. Office: Long Beach Mus Art 2300 E Ocean Blvd Long Beach CA 90803-2442

NELSON, HARRY DONALD, telecommunications executive; b. Chgo., Nov. 23, 1933; s. Harry E. and Elsie I. (Liljedahl) N.; m. Carol J. Stewart, Mar. 31, 1957; children: Donald S., David S., Sharon J. Arnold. BS, Northwestern U., Evanston, Ill., 1955, MBA, 1959. Sales rep., sales trainer Procter & Gamble, Chgo., 1955-58; sales adminstr. internat. products GE, N.Y., Ky., 1959-70, 1959-72, product mgr., 1978-81; mgr. mktg. Tex. Instruments, Dallas, 1972-74; v.p. mktg. Rockwell Internat., Anaheim, Calif., 1975, HMW-Pulsar, Lancaster, Pa., 1976-78, Genesco, Nashville, 1981-83; v.p. cellular ops. Tel. and Data Systems, Chgo., 1983-85; pres., CEO U.S. Cellular, Chgo., 1985—. Mem. Dean's Adv. Bd. Kellogg Sch. Mgmt. Northwestern U., Evanston, 1994—, Alumni Adv. Bd., 1991—. With U.S. Army, 1956-57. Recipient Dean's Alumni award Kellogg Sch. Mgmt., 1996. Mem. Cellular Telecomm. Industry Assn. (treas., bd. dirs., exec. com. 1986—, Pres.'s award 1996). Republican. Baptist. Avocations: paperweight collecting, antique sales, stamp and coin collecting. Office: US Cellular 8410 W Bryn Mawr Ave Ste 700 Chicago IL 60631-3486

NELSON, HOWARD JOSEPH, geographer, educator; b. Gowrie, Iowa, Jan. 12, 1919; s. Joseph A. and Hannah (Swanson) N.; m. Betty Marie Garlick, June 18, 1944; children: Linda Ann, James Allan. BA with high honors, Iowa State Tchrs. Coll., 1942; MA, U. Chgo., 1947, PhD, 1949. Mem. faculty UCLA, 1949—, prof. geography, 1963-86, prof. emeritus, 1986—, chmn. dept., 1966-71. Author: (with W.A.V. Clark) Los Angeles, The Metropolitan Experience, 1976, The Los Angeles Metropolis, 1983. Served with AUS, 1943-46. Mem. Assn. Am. Geographers (regional councillor 1968-71), Sigma Xi. Home: 3939 Walnut Ave #162 Carmichael CA 95608 Office: Univ Calif Dept Geography Los Angeles CA 90024

NELSON, IRIS DOROTHY, retired guidance and rehabilitation counselor; b. N.Y.C., July 5, 1937; d. Simon and Bertha (Rapkine) N. BA, Barnard Coll., 1959; MA, Columbia U., 1964, Ed.M., 1980; postgrad., Inst. Rehab. Medicine, 1983-84, NYU, 1983-84. Cert. tchr., guidance and rehab. counselor, N.Y. Rsch. asst. to chmn. zoology dept. Columbia U., N.Y.C., 1959-64; tchr., activity therapist Psychiat. Treatment Ctr., N.Y.C., 1964-67; tchr., guidance counselor gen., spl. edn. programs N.Y.C. Pub. Schs., 1967-77; assoc. chmn. com. on handicapped Cmty. Sch. Dist. Divsn. Spl. Edn. and Pupil Personnel Svcs., 1977-78; sch. and rehab. counselor youth employment and tng. program N.Y.C. Bd. Edn. Office Career Edn., 1978-82; Bronx Ctr. for Career and Occupl. Svcs. Office f Career Edn., 1982-83; sch. and rehab. counselor divsn. spl. edn. N.Y.C. Bd. Edn., 1984-90; sch. and rehab. counselor citiwide programs spl. edn. dist. # 75 P.S. 186, Bronx, N.Y., 1990-95; ret., 1995. Vocat. rehab. counselor Internat. Ctr. for the Disabled, N.Y.C., 1988-89. Annual cmty. sponsor West Side Cmty. Conf.; mem. alumnae adv. vocat. com. Barnard Coll., 1974-76. Mem.: ACA, ACLU, N.Y.C. Assn. Counseling and Devel. (bd. dirs.), N.Y. State Career Devel. Assn. (past v.p.), N.Y. State Rehab. Counselors Assn., N.Y. State Sch. Counselors Assn., Assn. Profl. Sch. Counselors N.Y., N.Y. State Mental Health Counselors Assn., N.Y. Counseling Assn. (v.p. profl. rels. 2000—01), Women's Am. Orgn. Rehab. Through Tng. (educators chpt.), United Fedn. Tchrs. Guidance Counselors (del. to del. assembly retiree chpt.), Jewish Labor Com. (educators chpt.), Nat. Rehab. Counseling Assn. (divsn. mem., N.Y.C. Metro chpt. pres.), Nat. Rehab. Assn., Assn. Adult Devel. and Aging (divsn. mem.), Assn. Religious and Values Issues in Counseling (divsn. mem.), Am. Rehab. Counselors Assn. (divsn. mem.), Am. Sch. Counselor Assn. (divsn. mem.), Joint Coun. for Mental Health Svcs. (life), Kappa Delta Pi (bd. dirs. Kappa chpt.), Chi Sigma Iota (life). Home: 235 W 102d St #7B New York NY 10025-8400

NELSON, IVORY VANCE, academic administrator; b. Curtis, La., June 11, 1934; s. Elijah H. and Mattie (White) N.; m. Patricia Robbins, Dec. 27, 1985; children: Cherlyn, Karyn, Eric Beatty, Kim Beatty. BS with distinction, Grambling (La.) State U., 1959; PhD with distinction, U. Kans., 1963. Assoc. prof. chemistry So. U., Baton Rouge, 1963-67, head div. sci., 1966-68; prof. chemistry Prairie View (Tex.) A&M U., 1968-83, asst. acad. dean, 1968-72, v.p. rsch., 1972-82, acting pres., 1982-83; exec. asst. Tex. A&M U. System, College Station, 1983-86; chancellor Alamo C.C. Dist., San Antonio, 1986-92;

pres. Cen. Wash. U., Ellensburg, 1992-99, Lincoln U., Pa., 1999—. DuPont teaching fellow U. Kans., 1959; rsch. chemist Am. Oil Co., 1962; sr. rsch. chemist Union Carbide Co., 1969; vis. prof. U. Autonomous Guadalajara, Mex., 1966, Loyola U., 1967; Fulbright lectr., 1966; cons. evaluation coms. Oak Ridge (Tenn.) Assoc. Univs., NSF, Nat. Coun. for Accreditation Tchr. Edn., So. Assn. Colls. and Schs.; mem. regional policy coms. on minorities Western Interstate Com. on Higher Edn., 1986-88; mem. exec. com. Nat. Assn. State Univs. and Land Grant Colls., 1980-82. Contbr. articles to profl. jours. Bd. dirs. Target 90, Goals San Antonio, 1987-89, coun. of pres.NAIDA,(1993-96) Commn. on Student Learning, Wash., 1992—, United Way San Antonio, 1987-89, Alamo Area coun. Boy Scouts Am., 1987-89, San Antonio Symphony Soc., 1987-91, Key Bank of Wash.; mem. bd. dirs. assn. Western U., (1995—) mem. com. for jud. reform State of Tex., 1991; mem. edn. adv. bd. Tex. Rsch. Park, 1987-89; bd. givs. Am. Inst. for character Edn., Inc., 1988-91; mem. adv. com. Tex. Ho. of Reps., 1978; chmn. United Way Campaign Tex. A&M U. System, 1984, others. Staff sgt. USAF, 1951-55, Korea. T.H. Harris scholar Grambling State U., 1959; fellow Nat. Urban League, 1969. Mem. AAAS, Am. Chem. Soc., Tex. Acad. Sci., NAACP, Phi Beta Kappa, Sigma Xi, Phi Lambda Upsilon, Beta Kappa Chi, Alpha Mu Gamma, Kappa Delta Pi, Sigma Pi Sigma, Omega Psi Phi, Sigma Pi Phi, Phi Kappa Phi. Avocations: fishing, photography, sports. Office: Lincoln U Office of Pres PO Box 179 Lincoln University PA 19352-0999 Office Phone: 610-932-8300. E-mail: inelson@lincoln.edu.

NELSON, J. GORDON, geography educator; Adj. prof. planning and geography, disting. prof. emeritus U. Waterloo, Ont., Can., 1998—. Recipient Massey medal Royal Can. Geog. Soc., 1993. Office: U Waterloo Dept Geography Waterloo ON Canada N2L 3G1 Office Phone: 519-888-4567.

NELSON, JACK LEE, education educator; b. Cheyenne, Wyo., Nov. 2, 1932; s. Myron Alfred and Mary Elizabeth (Baker) N.; m. Gwen Margret Names, Mar. 13, 1953; children: Barbara Louise Nelson Vollmer, Steven Lee. BA, U. Denver, 1954; MA, Calif. State U.-Los Angeles, 1958; Ed.D., U. So. Calif., 1961. Tchr. pub. schs., Riverside, Calif., 1956-58; instr. Calif. State U., Los Angeles, 1958-59, asst. prof., 1959-63; instr. Citrus Community Coll., Glendora, Calif., 1959-63; assoc. prof. SUNY, Buffalo, 1963-68, chmn. dept., 1966-68; prof. edn. Rutgers U., New Brunswick, NJ, 1968—, Disting. prof., 1975; dean, prof. Sch. Edn. San Jose (Calif.) State U., 1986-87. Chmn. dept. sci. and humanities edn. Rutgers U., 1972-75; vis. prof. Cambridge U., Eng., 1974, 75, 79, 80, 83, 84, 85; vis. scholar U. Calif., Berkeley, 1975-76, Stanford U., 1982-83, Western Australia Inst. Tech., 1985, U. Colo., 1989, U. Wash., 1993, U. Sydney, Australia, 1994-95, 2003, Edith Cowan U., Australia, 1997; cons. editor Random House Inc., McGraw-Hill Inc., Primis Pubs.; cons. author Scott, Foresman Publs.; mem. adv. coun. New World Dictionary; mem. San Diego County Supt. Com. on Tchr. Quality, 2000—. Author: (with J. Michaelis) Secondary Social Studies, 1980, (with V. Green) International Human Rights, 1980, (with Frank Besag) Foundations of Education, 1984, (with S. Palonsky and K. Carlson) Critical Issues in Education, 1990, 5th edit., 2004; contbr. numerous articles to profl. jours.; editor: Social Sci. Rsch., 1964-68, Theory and Rsch. in Social Edn., 1982-85. Mem. exec. bd. ACLU, Middlesex County, N.J., 1968-83; mem. Erie County Dem. Com., 1967-68, N.J. Gov.'s Task Force on Rehab. Edn. for Prisoners, 1970-74, mem. Highland Park Bd. Edn., N.J., 1972-75, pres., 1974-75; mem. Highland Park Hist. Commn., 1980-86; mem. nat. panel Project Censored, 1976—; mem. N.J. Rural Adv. Commn., 1992—, Carlsbad Sister Cities Commn., 2002-05. Robert Taft Found. grantee Inst. in Govt., 1970, 86; Inst. for World Order grantee Rutgers U., 1973; Rutgers U. grantee; SUNY-Buffalo grantee, 1967-68; ACLU of N.J. grantee, 1972-73; U.S. Office Edn. grantee, 1967-68; N.J. Dept. Higher Edn. grantee, 1985-86 Mem. Am. Acad. Polit. and Social Sci., AAUP (editorial bd. 1977-80, rep. nat. council 1982-85, com. on acad. freedom and tenure 1983-86, com. on legis. affairs 1992-95, 96—, exec. bd., state confs. 1996—), Am. Ednl. Research Assn., Internat. Studies Assn., Nat. Council for Social Studies, Social Sci. Edn. Consortium (bd. dirs. 1983-85), Phi Delta Kappa Home: 1360 Las Flores Dr Carlsbad CA 92008-1031 Office: Rutgers U Grad Sch Edn Rutgers U Grad Sch Edn New Brunswick NJ 08903 E-mail: junelson@rci.rutgers.edu.

NELSON, JACQUELINE DUNHAM, elementary school educator; b. Catawba, S.C., Jan. 20, 1937; d. John Ervin and Jessie Gazree (Walker) D.; m. Raymond Talmadge Nelson, Nov. 20, 1967 (div. June 1970); 1 child: Ouinette Michelle Willingham. BS, Morgan State U., 1960; MA, George Washington U., 1977, EdD, 1991. Kindergarten tchr. Dept. Def., Kaneohe, Hawaii, 1962-64; tchr. reading, health educator Cleveland County Pub. Schs., Shelby, N.C., 1964-66; tchr. health and phys. edn. Prince Edward County Schs., Cumberland, Va., 1966-67; tchr. health and phys. edn., curriculum writer D.C. Pub. Schs., Washington, 1967—. Advisor Montgomery Elem. Sch., Washington, 1993-94. Author: Teacher/Student Behavior, 1991. Named Coach of Yr., Va. Intercollegiate Assn., 1966. Avocations: photography, skiing, fishing, antique collecting. Office: Maury Elem Sch 13th & Constitution Ave NE Washington DC 20002 Home: 1907 Savannah Pl SE Washington DC 20020-2105

NELSON, JAMES, wholesale food distribution executive; CFO Grovers Supply, Houston. Office: Grocers Supply 3131 E Holcombe Blvd Houston TX 77021 Office Fax: (713) 746-5797.

NELSON, JAMES ALONZO, radiologist, educator; b. Cherokee, Iowa, Oct. 20, 1938; s. Joe George and Ruth Geraldine (Jones) N.; m. Katherine Metcalf, July 16, 1966; children: John Metcalf, Julie Heaps. AB, Harvard U., 1961, MD, 1965. Asst. prof. radiology U. Calif., San Francisco, 1972-74; assoc. prof. U. Utah, Salt Lake City, 1974-79, prof., 1979-86, U. Wash., Seattle, 1986-2000, prof. emeritus, 2000—. Dir. radiol. rsch. U. Calif./Ft. Miley VA Hosp., 1973—74, U. Utah, 1974—85, U. Wash., 1986—98; mem. bd. sci. advisors NeoVision, 1995—96, Oreg. Life Scis., 1995—; co-founder Circulation, Inc., 1996; mem. adv. panel on non-radioactive diagnostic agts. USP, 1984—96; mem. NIH RSN study sect., 1998—. Contbr. chpts. to books, articles to Am. Jour. Roentgenology, Radiology, Investigative Radiology, others. Capt. USAF, 1967-69. John Harvard scholar, 1957-61, James Picker Found. scholar, 1973-77; recipient Mallinckrodt prize Soc. Body Computerized Tomography, 1990, Roscoe Miller award Soc. Gastrointestinal Radiology, 1991. Fellow Am. Coll. Radiology (diplomate); mem. Radiol. Soc. N.Am., Assn. Univ. Radiology. Achievements include patents (with others) for Non-Surgical Peritoneal Lavage, Recursive Band-Pass Filter for Digital Angiography, for Unsharp Masking for Chest Films, Oral Hepatobiliary MRI Contrast Agent, non-surgical myocardial revascularization magnetic gut motility monitor. Office: U Wash Dept Radiology Diagnostic Imaging Sci Ctr PO Box 357115 Seattle WA 98195-7115 Personal E-mail: jalonzonel@comcast.net.

NELSON, JAMES C, state supreme court justice; b. Idaho, Feb. 20, 1944; m. Chari Werner; 2 children. BS, U. Idaho, 1966; JD cum laude, George Washington U., 1974. Fin. analyst SEC, Washington; pvt. practice Cut Bank; county atty. Glacier County; assoc. judge Mont. Supreme Ct., 1993—. Former mem. State Bd. Oil and Gas Conservation, also chmn.; former mem. State Gaming Adv. Counsel, Gov. Adv. Coun. on Corrections and Criminal Justice Policy; liaison to Commn. of Cts. of Ltd. Jurisdiction, mem. adv. com. Ct. Assessment Program. Served U.S. Army. Office: Supreme Ct PO Box 203001 Helena MT 59620

NELSON, JAMES CARMER, JR., writer, editor, advertising executive; b. Denver, Nov. 10, 1921; s. James Carmer and Helen (McClelland) N.; m. Mary-Armour Ransom, Sept. 9, 1950; children: James Carmer III, Marie-Louise Nelson Graves, Jeffrey Armour, Sophia McClelland (dec.), Rebecca McClelland Nelson Sylla. AB, Yale, 1943. Mktg. editor Bus. Week mag., N.Y.C., 1946-48, illustration editor, 1948-52; freelance author Sonoma, Calif., 1952-57; copy chief Hoefer, Dieterich & Brown, Inc., San Francisco, 1957-59, v.p., creative dir., 1959-66, exec. v.p., 1966-76, pres., 1976-79, vice chmn., 1979-80; ptnr. John H. Hoefer & Assocs., 1972—82; vice chmn. Chiat/Day/Hoefer, 1980; pvt. advt. cons., 1980—87. Bd. dirs. McKinney, Inc., Phila.; instr. Golden Gate Coll., San Francisco, 1958-59, Nat. Advt. Rev. Bd., 1971-75. Author: The Trouble With Gumballs, 1957, Great Cheap Wines: A Poorperson's Guide, 1977, Great Wines Under $5, 1983, Killing Dave Henderson, etc., 2004; contbr. articles and fiction to popular mags. Mem. Harold Brunn Soc. for Med. Research, Mt. Zion Hosp., San Francisco; bd. assos. Linus Pauling Inst. Sci. and Medicine, Palo Alto, Calif.; mem. Colony Found., New Haven; trustee Coro Found., 1965-75, Marin Art Complex; bd. mgrs. Marin County YMCA. Served with USNR, 1942-46. Mem. ASCAP. Clubs: Villa Taverna (San Francisco). Home: 649 Idylberry Rd San Rafael CA 94903-1231

NELSON, JAMES HAROLD, health sciences administrator; b. Gosnell, Ark., Apr. 26, 1936; s. J.D. and Louise (Gann) N.; m. Betty Sue Leonard, Sept. 21, 1974; children: Amelia Rebecca, Rachel Louise. BS, Ark. State U., 1961, MS, 1969; PhD, Okla. State U., 1972. Br. chief U.S. Army Environ. Hygiene Agy., Edgewood, Md., 1972-76; from rsch. area mgr. to div. chief U.S. Army Biomed. R & D Lab., Fort Detrick, Md., 1976-92; project mgr. applied med. systems U.S. Army Med. Materiel Devel. Activity, Fort Detrick, Md., 1992-96, dir., 1996-2000; chief liaison office U.S. Army Med. Rsch. & Materiel Command, U.S. Army Med. Dept. Ctr. and Sch., Fort Sam Houston, Tex., 2000—. Mem. Fed. Work Group Pest Mgmt., Washington, 1977-81; chmn. equipment com. Armed Forces Pest Mgmt. Bd., Washington, 1979-83; cons. dir. engrs. Ft. Detrick, 1976-2000; guest lectr. Acad. Health Scis., U.S. Army, Ft. Sam Houston, Tex., 1986-88. Contbr. articles to profl. jours.; assoc. editor: Jour. Am. Mosquito Control Assn., 1982-88; chmn. editorial bd.: Equipment & Insecticides-Mosquito Control, 1989. With USN, 1954-58. Recipient numerous commendations U.S. Army, Ft. Detrick, 1981-2000, R&D Achievement award Asst. Sec. of the Army, 1988, Order of Mil. Med. Merit, 1992. Mem. AAAS, AMVETS, Am. Pub. Health Assn., Assn. Mil. Surgeons U.S., Am. Legion, N.Y. Acad. Scis., Sigma Xi (pres. 1987-88). Presbyterian. Achievements include patent for far-forward surgical table. Home: 1315 Brook Bluff San Antonio TX 78248-2632 Office: US Army Med Res & Materiel Command US Army Med Dept Ctr & Sch 1400 E Grayson St Ste 303E Fort Sam Houston TX 78234-6100 E-mail: james.nelson@amedd.army.mil., jhnelson@prodigy.net.

NELSON, JAMES LARS, writer; b. Lewiston, Maine, Apr. 5, 1962; s. David Arthur and Selma Arlene Nelson; m. Lisa Maria Nelson, Apr. 11, 1993; children: Elizabeth, Nathaniel, Jonathan. BA, U. Calif., motion picture,T.V., L.A., 1986. Third mate HMS Rose - sailing ship, Bridgeport, Conn., 1991—92; writer, 1996—. Author (The Revolution at Sea Saga): (pocket book) By Force of Arms, 1996; author: The Maddest Idea, 1997, The Continental Risque, 1998, Lords of the Ocean, 1999, All the Brave Fellows, 2000; author: (The Brethren of the Coast Trilogy) (book) The Guardship, 2000; author: The Blackbirder, 2001, The Pirate Round, 2002. Bd. dir. firefighter and rescue driver Harpswell Neck Fire and Rescue, Harpswell, Maine, 2002—. E-mail: jlnelson@suscom-maine.net.

NELSON, JAMES LINDEMANN, philosophy educator, bioethicist; b. Williamsport, Pa., Apr. 2, 1954; s. David C. and Jeanne Gormley Nelson; m. Hilde Lindemann, Jan. 18, 1986; children: Eric, Laura, Melissa, Elise Robinson, Ellen Robinson, Paul Robinson. PhD, SUNY, Buffalo, 1980; BA, Canisius Coll., 1974. Assoc. for ethical studies The Hastings Ctr., Garrison, N.Y., 1990-95; prof. philosophy U. Tenn., Knoxville, 1995-2000, Mich. State U., East Lansing, 2000—. Vis. prof. philosophy Duke U., 2001-02. Co-author: Alzheimer's: Answers to Hard Questions, 1996, The Patient in the Family, 1995; author: Hippocrates' Maze, 2003; contbr. articles to profl. jours. Fellow The Hastings Ctr.; mem. Am. Philos. Assn., Am. Soc. Bioethics and Humanities, Assn. Feminist Ethics and Social Theory, Brit. Soc. Ethical Theory (assoc.). Home: 1117 Wildwood Dr East Lansing MI 48823 Office: Philosophy Dept Mich State U 503 S Kedzie Hall East Lansing MI 48824 E-mail: jlnelson@msu.edu.

NELSON, JAMES SMITH, pathologist, educator; b. St. Louis, Mar. 19, 1933; s. Victor Paul and Dorothy Gertrude (Smith) N.; children: Paul F., Andrew S. BS, St. Louis U., 1950-53, MD, 1957. Pathology intern, resident St. Louis U. Hosps., 1957-59, 60-61; neuropathology fellow Columbia U. Coll. Phys. & Surgery, N.Y.C., 1959-60; neurochemistry fellow Washington U. Med. Sch., St. Louis, 1961-63, instr. in pathology, 1963-64, assoc. prof., prof. pathology & pediatrics, 1973-87; asst. prof., assoc. prof. pathology St. Louis U. Med. Sch., 1964-73; head divsn. neuropathology Henry Ford Hosp., Detroit, 1987-89; clin. prof. neuropathology U. Mich. Med. Sch., Ann Arbor, 1988-89; prof. pathology La. State U. Med. Ctr., New Orleans, 1989—; chmn. dept. neuropathology Armed Forces Inst. Pathology, Washington, 1990-94. Ad hoc cons. NIH, Washington, 1973-92; mem. Nat. Cancer Inst. CNS Oncology Working Group, Washington, 1986-89; mem. neuropathology test com. Am. Bd. Pathology, Tampa, Fla., 1984-90; mem. WHO Brain Tumor Working Group, Zurich, Switzerland, 1990—; adv. mem. neuropathology com. Coll. Am. Pathologists, Chgo., 1992-99. Author: Medical School Admission: A Systematic Guide, 1974; author, editor: Principles and Practice of Neuropathology, 1993; contbr. over 150 articles to profl. jours. Col. M.C., U.S. Army, 1990-94. Decorated Legion of Merit; recipient U.S. Sr. Scientist award Alexander von Humboldt Found., Free U. Berlin, 1979-80, Cert. of Achievement, U.S. Surgeon Gen., 1985, Res. Components Achievement medal U.S. Army, 1986; NIH spl. rsch. fellow in neurochemistry, 1961-63; NIH grantee, 1966-87, 95—. Mem. AMA, Coll. Am. Pathologists (com. mem.), Am. Soc. Clin. Pathologists, Am. Assn. Neuropathologists, U.S. & Can. Acad. Pathology, Am. Inst. Nutrition. Roman Catholic. Avocations: sailing, fishing, photography. Office: Dept of Pathology La State Univ Med Ctr 1901 Perdido St New Orleans LA 70112-1328 Home: 31 Palione Pl Kailua HI 96734-2118

NELSON, JANE GRAY, state legislator, small business owner, educator; b. Hamilton, Ohio, Oct. 5, 1951; d. Robert Allen and Edna Mae (Allen) Gray; m. James Michael Nelson, Sept. 27, 1978; children: Brian, Elizabeth, Christina, Michelle, Jennifer. Student, U. Tex., Arlington, 1969-70; BS in Edn. and Linguistics, N. Tex. State U., 1972, postgrad., 1973-75, So. Meth. U., 1973-75. Cert. tchr. Tchr. Arlington (Tex.) Ind. Sch. Dist., 1973-78; instr. community edn. Lewisville (Tex.) Ind. Sch. Dist., 1980—; owner, pres. Connections, Lewisville, 1987-92; owner Mayday Mfg., 1992—; mem. Tex. State Senate, 1993—. Chmn. Lewisville Community Edn. Adv. Coun., 1986-89; mem. steering com. Tex. Coummunity Edn. Counel of Couns., 1986; pres. Tex. Community Edn. Adv. Coun. Assn., 1986-88; bd. dirs., founder INFOHELP, Lewisville; mem. Tex. Bd. Edn., 1988-90; mem. adv. com. Tex. Ctr. for Ednl. Rsch.; mem. Nat. Com. for Tech. Edn. Excellence; vice chmn. TPC Task Force on Family; chmn. Tex. Rep. Women Leaders Forum Author: Drill Team, 1985; mem. editorial adv. bd. Tex. Researcher. Chmn. cultural arts Lewisville Ind. Sch. Dist. Community Edn. Adv. Council, 1984-89, ticket sales fundraiser, 1984-85, nominating com., 1986, sci. fair, 1985, ednl. com. Congressman Armey's Drug Abuse Task Force, Denton County, Tex., 1986-89, communications Lewisville Bond Election Steering Com., 1986, talent com. Red Stockings Follies Prodn., Lewisville, 1985, student com. Tex. State Bd. Edn., 1988-90; adv. com. Tex. Ctr. Ednl. Rsch.; nat. com. Tech. Edn. Excellence; editorial adv. bd. Tex. Researcher; founder, charter mem. Community Against Substance Abuse, Lewisville, 1987-89; mem. Lewiston Ind. Sch. Dist. Drug and Alcohol Abuse Task Force, 1986-89, Community Action League Lewisville, 1979—, v.p., 1980-81; active Lewisville Ind. Sch. Dist. Council PTA's, Highland Village Elem. PTA, (PTA Tex. Life Membership award 1987), Am. Cancer Soc.; bd. dirs. Dist.-Wide Drill Team and Baton Twirling Corps, 1980-86, edn. work com. 1st United Meth. Ch., Parent Support, Friends of Hospice, Denton, Tex., 1986—; mem. Tex. Cancer Coun., 1995—, Tex. Conservative Coalition Bd., 1993-96. Mem. Nat. Community Edn. Assn. (Citizen Leadership award 1986), Tex. Community Edn. Assn. (Citizen Leadership award 1987), Tex. Community Edn. Adv. Coun. Assn. (pres. 1986-88), Tex. Tchrs. Assn. (chmn. textbook adoption com. 1975-76), North Tex. State U. Alumnae Assn., Delta Zeta (founder Lewisville-Lake Cities chpt., bd. dirs. Province XVII 1975-81). Republican. Avocations: reading, travel. Office: PO Box 12068 Capitol Sta Austin TX 75028-7871 also: Senator Jane Nelson 1235 S Main St #280 Grapevine TX 76051-7546

NELSON, JANIE RISH, hospital executive; b. Mar. 1, 1941; d. William Hubert and Essie Dell (Davis) Rish; m. John Preston Nelson, Aug. 19, 1984. Student, S.W. Miss. Jr. Coll., 1959—61, Stephens Coll., 1981—. Accredited record tech. Admissions clk. Field Hosp., Centreville, Miss., 1963—68, asst. dir. med. records, 1968—73; dir. med. records West Feliciana Parish Hosp., St. Francisville, La., 1976—2000; ret., 2000. Med. records cons. Beverly Enterprises & Centreville Health Care, 1983—84. Mem. U.S. Congl. Adv. Bd. for La., 1985; fund raiser Rep. Com., 1984; mem. nat. adv. bd. Am. Security Coun., 1984—85. Mem.: NAFE, Tumor Registration Assn. La., La. Med. Records Assn., Am. Med. Records Assn., Miss. Sheriffs Assn. (hon.), Civic Club. Republican. Presbyterian. Avocations: reading, public speaking, gardening. Home: PO Box 374 Centreville MS 39631-0374

NELSON, JASON CRAIG, company executive; b. Houston, Tex., Feb. 4, 1971; s. James Craig Nelson and Jessica Darlene Nichols. BS in Fin., U. Houston, 1993; MBA, Tulane U., 1997; AM in Sociology, Stanford U., 2001, AM in Bus. Rsch., 2002. Analyst Bankers Trust Corp., Houston, 1993—95; deal mgr. Chase Bank, Houston, 1998; deal devel. assoc. Enron Energy Svcs., Houston, 1998—99; dept. mgr. First Union Securities, Charlotte, Tex., 1999—2000; dir. Valenzcura, LLC, Plano, Tex., 2000—. Bd. dirs. Envisien Phuket (Thailand) Co. Ltd., Valenzcura, LLC, Plano. Tribal mem. Tex. Cherokee. Recipient Cmty. Svc. award, City of New Orleans, 1997. Mem.: Coastal Conservation Assn. Avocations: snorkeling, diving. Home: PO Box 3041 Ann Arbor MI 48106

NELSON, JERRY R. food company executive; Pres. Con Agra Turkey Co., El Dorado, Ark. Office: ConAgra Turkey Co 422 N Washington Ave El Dorado AR 71730-5616

NELSON, JOANN, secondary school educator, educational consultant; b. Little Rock, Arkansas, July 11, 1943; d. Lucinda Nelson. BA cum laude(hon.), Philander Smith Coll., Little Rock, 1962—66; EdM, Cleveland State U., 1977—79. Cert. tchg. Ark., 1966, Ohio, 1966, 1987. English tchr. Cleve. Pub. Sch., 1966—78, dept. chmn., English, reading, and language arts, 1978—96. Cons., Cleve., 1996—. Rec. sec. Neighborhood St. Club, Cleve., 1978—96. Mem.: Greater Cleve. Roundtable, Metro Cleve. Alliance of Black Sch. Educators, Nat. Coun. of Negro Women, Nat. Coun. of Teachers of English. Democrat. Baptist. Achievements include city wide lesson plans, Cleve. Pub. Sch., 1982; students' performance and reading tests, Cleve. Pub. Sch., 1986; proficiency test coord.,Cleve. Pub. Sch., 1994. Avocations: reading, theater, photography, travel, collecting brass and crystal. E-mail: njoannn1@aol.com.

NELSON, JOHN C. obstetrician/gynecologist; b. 1944; m. Linda Nelson, 8 children. MPH, U. Utah, 1993, MD. Diplomate Am. Bd. Ob-Gyn. Intern Providence Hosp., Portland, Oreg.; resident U. Utah Sch. of Medicine. Charter mem. Prospective Payment Assessment Commn.; dep. dir. Utah's Dept. of Health; leader govs. task force on child abuse and neglect, teenage pregnancy prevention. Com. mem. Utah Domestic Violence adv. com.; former bd. mem. Salt Lake City Boys and Girls Club. Served in U.S. Army. Recipient Light of Learning award Utah State Office of Edn. Fellow Am. Coll. of Ob-Gyn.; mem. AMA (bd. trustees 1994-, sec-treas. 2002-04, pres-elect 2004), Utah Med. Assn. (former pres.), Salt Lake County Med. Soc. (past pres.), Motion Picture Assn. Am. TV Parental Guidelines Monitoring Bd. Office: 370 9th Ave Ste 101 Salt Lake City UT 84103-3186 also: AMA 515 N State St Chicago IL 60610-4325

NELSON, JOHN HOWARD (JACK HOWARD NELSON), journalist; b. Talladega, Ala., Oct. 11, 1929; s. Howard Alonzo and Barbara Lena (O'Donnell) N.; m. Virginia Dare Dickinson, Aug. 4, 1951 (div. Nov. 1974); children: Karen Dare, John Michael, Steven Howard; m. Barbara Joan Matusow, Dec. 7, 1974. Student, Ga. State Coll., 1953—57. Reporter Biloxi (Miss.) Daily Herald, 1947-51, Atlanta Constitution, 1952-65; so. bur. chief L.A. Times, Atlanta, 1965-70, with Washington bur., 1970—, Washington bur. chief, 1975-96, chief Washington corr., 1996—2002. Author: (with Gene Roberts, Jr.) The Censors and the Schools, 1963, (with Jack Bass) The Orangeburg Massacre, 1970, (with R.J. Ostrow) The FBI and the Berrigans, 1972, Captive Voices, Shocken Books, 1974, Terror in the Night, 1993. Mem. vis. com. U. Miami Sch. Comm. With AUS, 1951-52. Recipient Pulitzer prize for local reporting under deadline pressure, 1960; Drew Pearson award for gen. excellence in investigative reporting, 1974; Nieman fellow Harvard U., 1961-62, Shorenstein fellow Harvard U., 2002. Mem. The Gridiron Club. Home: 4 Wynkoop Ct Bethesda MD 20817-5936 Office Phone: 301-320-2058.

NELSON, JOHN KEITH, electrical engineer, educator; b. Oldham, Lancashire, Eng., July 3, 1943; s. John Collins and Joyce Palfrey (Simmons) N.; m. Christine Anne Baker, Feb. 10, 1968; children: David John, Peter Mark. BS in Engring., U. London, 1965, PhD, 1969. Chartered profl. engr., Inst. Elec. Engrs. (U.K.). Rsch. fellow U. London, 1966-69, lectr., 1969-78, reader, 1978-79; rsch. mgr. GE, Schenectady, NY, 1979-82; prof. elec. power engring. Rensselaer Poly. Inst., Troy, NY, 1982—, Philip Sporn prof., 2001—, head dept., 1987—2001. Examiner U. Sri Lanka, 1970—85; cons. in field. Contbr. articles to profl. jours.; patentee in field. Recipient Snell premium, IEE, London, 1972, J.R. Beard award, 1976, Rsch. award, Brit. Coun., 1974, 76, Travel award, Royal Soc., London, 1976, Power Engring. Educator award Edison Elec. Inst., 1994, Fellowship award Am. Soc. Nondestructive Testing, 1997. Fellow: IEEE (tech. v.p. Dielectrics and Elec. Insulation Soc. 1991—92, Whitehead Meml. lectr. 1993, adminstrv. v.p. 1993—94, pres. 1995—96, tech. activities bd. 1995—96, membership devel. com. 1997—, Hans Tropper meml. lectr. 2002, Forster Disting. Svc. award 1998), Inst. Elec. Engrs. (U.K.). Episcopalian. Avocations: squash, sailing, scuba diving, flying. Office: Rensselaer Poly Inst Dept Elec Comp and Sys Engring Troy NY 12180-3590 Office Phone: 518-276-6329. E-mail: r.nelson@ieee.org.

NELSON, JOHN MARTIN, corporate executive; b. N.Y.C., Aug. 9, 1931; s. Martin H. and Margaret (Larkin) N.; m. Linda Crocker Moore, Aug. 30, 1992; children: Murrey E., Christopher L. AB, Wesleyan U., 1953; MBA, Harvard U., 1959. With Norton Co., Worcester, Mass., 1959-90; pres., chief exec. officer Norton Christensen Inc. subs. Norton Co., Salt Lake City, 1978-86; pres., chief operating officer Norton Co., Worcester, 1986-88, chmn., chief exec. officer, 1988-90; chmn., CEO Wyman-Gordon Co., Worcester, 1991-94, chmn., 1995-97, The TJX Cos., Inc., Framingham, Mass., 1995-99, Brown & Sharpe Mfg. Co., Kingstown, RI, 2000—01, Commonwealth Nat. Bank, 2001—03. Bd. dirs. Brown & Sharpe Mfg. Co., Kingston, RI, 2000-20001, Eaton Vance Corp., Boston, Commerce Holdings, Inc., Webster, Mass; chmn. Commonwealth Nat. Bank, Worcester, Mass., 2001-. Trustee Wesleyan U., 1978-81, Worcester Poly. Inst., 1986—, chmn. 1995-2000; bd. dirs. Worcester Mcpl. Rsch. Bur., 1989—, pres., 1998-99; bd. dirs. Greater Worcester Cmty. Found., 1990-98, pres., 1990-94; bd. dirs. Alliance for Edn., 1991—, United Way Ctrl. Mass., 1993-98, chmn., 1993; trustee Worcester Found. for Biomed. Rsch., 1993-2000, Worcester Art Mus., 1988-99, chmn., 1996-99; trustee Worcester Area C. of C., 1992-97, chmn., 1994; trustee Meml. Hosp. Med. Ctr., 1991-98. Home: Ritz Carlton Towers S Tower 27E Two Avery St Boston MA 02111 Office: Office J Nelson 446 Main St Worcester MA 01608-2359

NELSON, K. BONITA, literary agent; b. Austin, Minn., July 5, 1945; d. Wallace Arthur and Opal Rebecca (Lastine) N. BA, Hunter Coll., 1969; B in laws, LaSalle U., 1982. Lit. agt. Am. Play Co., Inc., N.Y.C., 1970-75; legal sec., reviewer Eastman & DaSilva, Esqs., N.Y.C., 1975-79; founder, pres. BK Nelson Literary Agy., N.Y.C., 1983—, BK Nelson Lect. Bureau, N.Y.C., 1988—, BK Nelson Wordprocessing, Pleasantville, NY, 1994—; pres., publ. Internat. Media Comm., Inc., 1998. Bd. dirs. Dynaray, N.Y.; founder BK Nelson, Inc., 1995; founder Literacy Inst. for Edn. (Life) Inc., 1996. Collaborator: Looking for Canterbury, 1994; author: My Literary Agent, 1998; co-prodr. (movie) Beyond Forever, 2003. Mem. Authors Guild (assoc.), NAFE (assoc.), Nat. Assn. Campus Activities (assoc.), AAUW, (assoc.), Dramatists Guild (assoc.), Minority and Woman Owned Businesses. Avocations: aerobics, yoga, needlepoint, stamp collecting/philately. Home and Office: 1565 Paseo Vida Palm Springs CA 92264 Office: NY Office 84 Woodland Rd Pleasantville NY 10570 E-mail: bknelson4@cs.com.

NELSON, KEITH MILTON, lawyer; b. Ft. Worth, May 10, 1957; s. Paul Milton and Betty Pauline (Martin) N.; m. Terry Gayle Beaver, Apr. 11, 1987; children: Staley, Ashley, Chad, Caroline, Erin, Katelyn. BA, Baylor U., 1979; JD, Baylor U., 1983. Bar: Tex. 1983, U.S. Dist. Ct. (no. dist.) Tex. Ptnr. Ashley, Nelson & Leake, Irving, Tex., 1987-88; assoc. Koons, Fuller,

McCurley and Vanden Eykel, Dallas, 1988-92; ptnr. McCurley, Orsinger, McCurley, Nelson & Downing, Dallas, 1992—. Speaker in field. Contbr. articles to profl. jours. Cons. Lawyers Against Domestic Violence; mem. visitation subcom. Supreme Ct. Adv. Com. on Child Support and Visitation Guidelines. Mem. ABA (family law sect.), Am. Acad. Matrimonial Lawyers, Tex. Acad. Family Law Specialists, Tex. Trial Lawyers Assn., State Bar Tex., Dallas Bar Assn. (family law sect., bd. dirs.), Irving Bar Assn. (pres. 1991-92), Nat. Assn. Counsel for Children. Baptist. Avocations: racquetball, skiing, spectator sports. Office: McCurley Orsinger McCurley Nelson & Downing 5950 Sherry Ln # 800 Dallas TX 75225-6533 Office Phone: 214-273-2400. Business E-Mail: keith@momnd.com.

NELSON, KELLY EDWARD, actor, writer; b. Manhattan, Kans., Feb. 23, 1960; s. Lon Edward Nelson and Nancy Byrne McCracken. Grad., Sanford Meisner, Hollywood, 1992. Co-founder Sanford Meisner Ctr. Arts, Hollywood, 1995—; chmn. bd. Meisner Ctr. Players, 2004—. Actor: Social Suicide, 1991, Columbo, 1992, Children of Corn III, 1995, Melrose Place, 1999, Which Way to Oz, 1996, Dark Secrets, 1998, Garden of Evil, 1998, The Story Tellers, 1999, Sabretooth, 2002; author: (screenplays) Redheaded Stepchild, 2003, (plays) Niagara Falls, 2000, Bimbo and Brick, 2000. Mem.: Screen Actors Guild. Avocations: films, theater, sports, singing. Office Phone: 800-601-3543.

NELSON, KIMBERLY TERESE, federal agency administrator; B, Shippensburg U.; M, U. Pa. Spl. asst. to sec., spl. asst. to deputy sec. adminstrn., spl. asst. deputy sec. field ops. Pa. Dept. Environ. Resources, 1987—95; dir. program integration and effectiveness then chief info. officer Pa. Dept. Environ. Protection, 1999—2001; asst. adminstr. environ. info. EPA, Washington, 2001—. Office: EPA 1200 Pennsylvania Ave NW MC 2810A Washington DC 20460

NELSON, LARRY A. statistics educator, consultant; b. Omaha, Oct. 28, 1932; s. Rudolph Lawrence and Elizabeth Coleman (Lewis) N. BS in Agronomy, Iowa State U., 1954; MS in Soil Sci., Tex. A&M U., 1958; PhD in Soil Sci.-Stats., N.C. State U., 1961. Soil scientist Iowa Agrl. Exptl. Sta., Ames, 1954-55; soils instr. Tex. A&I Coll., Kingsville, 1955; rsch. soil scientist Tex. A&M Rsch. Found., College Station, 1956; soils lab. instr. Tex. A&M U., College Station, 1956-58; rsch. asst. N.C. State U., Raleigh, 1959-61; asst. specialist in land classification Land Study Bur., U. Hawaii, Honolulu, 1961-64; asst. prof. exptl. stats. N.C. State U., Raleigh, 1964-66, assoc. prof. exptl. stats., 1966-71, prof. stats., 1971-89, prof. emeritus stats., 1989—, coord. Concade Project (Bolivia), 1999—2003, interim coord. internat. programs Coll. Agr. and Life Scis., 2002—03, asst. dean for internat. programs Coll. Agr. and Life Scis., 2003—. Lectr., tchr., cons. in field; spl. advisor head dep. stats. Kasetsart U., Bangkok, Thailand, 1973; evaluator quantitative skills IADS, Bangladesh, 1984; mem. rev. team Ctr. for Agrl. Econs. and Ctr. for Data Processing, Winrock Internat., Indonesia, 1985; statis. cons. PROCAFE, El Salvador, 1993-96, ICRAF, Nairobi, Kenya, 1991—; cons. Potash and Phosphate Inst. Can., China and India, 1990, 94, 96; ptnr. Statis. Rsch. Assocs., Honolulu, 1962-63. Assoc. editor Geoderma, 1976-84, Agronomy Jour., 1981-87; contbr. numerous articles to profl. publs. NATO fellow Data Analysis Lab., Lyngby, Denmark, 1978. Fellow AAAS, Am. Statis. Assn. (mem. biometrics sect. com. 1989-90, mem. com. on internat. rels. in stats. 1996-98), Am. Soc. Agronomy, Soil Sci. Soc. Am.; mem. Statis. Assn. Thailand (life), Internat. Biometric Soc. (bus. mgr. and treas. 1969-79, awards com. 1987-94, chmn. 1990-93, com. on edn. 1997-99), Internat. Statis. Inst., Sigma Xi, Gamma Sigma Delta (internat. pres. 1984-86, award of merit 1973-74, rep. to AAAS 1978-86), Phi Kappa Phi, Sigma Iota Rho. Baptist. Avocations: music, genealogy, diving, bicycling, travel. Home: 2816 Wycliff Rd Raleigh NC 27607-3035 Office: NC State U Office Internat Programs PO Box 7608 Raleigh NC 27695-7608 Office Phone: 919-515-2665. E-mail: lan@unity.ncsu.edu., lnelson460@worldnet.att.net.

NELSON, LARRY DEAN, telecommunications and computer systems company executive, consultant; b. Newton, Kans., Aug. 5, 1937; s. Carl Aaron and Leta V. (Van Eaton) N.; m. Linda Hawkins, June 2, 1972. BA, Phillips U., 1959; MS, Kans. State U., 1962; PhD, Ohio State U., 1965. From rsch. asst. to rsch. assoc. Rsch. Found., Ohio State U., Columbus, 1962—65; mathematician II Batelle Meml. Inst., Columbus, 1962—65; from mem. tech. staff to supr. math. dept., data sys. devel. Bellcomm, Inc., Washington, 1965—72; supr. mgmt. info. sys. dept. Bell Telephone Labs., Murray Hill, NJ, 1972—77; supr. rate and tariff planning divsn. AT&T, N.Y.C., 1977—79; dep. adminstr. rsch. and spl. programs adminstrn. U.S. Dept. Transp., Washington, 1979—81; pres. MCS, Inc., Washington, 1981—; supr. govt. comm. ctr. AT&T Bell Labs., 1985—89; mgr. govt. mktg. AT&T Network Sys., 1989—90, supr. secure info. sys. engring., 1990—94, disting. mem. tech. staff, secure sys. engring., 1995—96; tech. cons. AT&T Labs, Info. Security Ctr., AT&T, 1996—98; prin. network security engr., cons. mem. tech. staff Lucent Tech. Government Solutions, Inc., 2003—. Cons. Contel Info. Sys., Denver, 1982-85, Martin Marietta Corp., Denver, 1982-85; mem. info. assurance task force, info infrastructure group, intrusion detection task force, cybercrime subgroup Nat. Security Telecomms. Advisory Com. Contbr. articles to profl. jours. Organizer, sponsor Odd Jobs Club, Washington, 1967-72; pres. Mountain County Condominiums Assn., Dillon, Colo., 1975-83, 85—; treas. Chris' Landing Condominium Assn., 1986-90; mem. am. del. 5th Meeting of US-USSR Working Group on Transp., Moscow, 1979; head Am. del. 5th Meeting of US-USSR Working Group on Transport of Future, Moscow, 1979; head meeting Am. Del. to ISO/IEC TCI/SC27 Working Group 1 of Info. Tech., Security Methodology Std., editor Intrusion Detection Project, Germany 1997, Kista, Sweden, 1998, Rio De Janeiro, 1998, Spain, 1999, US, 1999, Eng. and Tokyo, 2000, Oslo, Norway, 2001, Berlin Germany, 2002; internat. rep. Am. Std. Inst.-Tech. Com. on Info. Tech. Security Methodology, 1999-2002. Mem. ABA (assoc., info. security com.), Am. Nat. Stds. Inst. (info. tech. security tech. stds. com., internat. rep. tech. com. on info. tech. security mgmt.), IEEE (sec. D.C. sect. 1982, cert. appreciation 1968), Sys., Man and Cybernetics Soc. (sec. 1981, v.p. 1982-83), Math. Programming Soc, Am. Math Soc., N.Y. Acad. Scis., Assn. Computing Machinery, Sigma Xi, Phi Kappa Phi, Pi Mu Epsilon. Democrat. Mem. Disciples of Christ. Current work: information systems, networks and network management, digital signature, public key infrastructure, and electronic commerce technology. Subspecialties: secure information technology systems and networks; systems engineering. Office: 440 New Jersey Ave SE Washington DC 20003-4008 E-mail: ldcnelson@att.net.

NELSON, LAWRENCE EVAN, business consultant; b. Chgo., Dec. 3, 1932; s. Evan Thomas and Elizabeth Marie (Stettka) N.; m. Jean H. Clayton, July 11, 1953; children: Lori Jean, Lawrence Evan. BS with honors, So. Ill. U., 1959; MBA, U. Chgo., 1969. CPA, Ill. Sr. acct. Price Waterhouse & Co., CPA's, Chgo., 1959-65; sec.-treas. Bradner Cen. Co., Chgo., 1965-73; pres. Protectoseal Co., Bensenville, Ill., 1973-84, Plan Ahead Inc., Palos Park, Ill, 1984—. Author: (book) Personal Financial Planning, 1985. Treas. City of Palos Heights, Ill., 1964-68, alderman, 1970-71; trustee Palos Heights FPD, 1977-1995. Served with USNR, 1952-56. Mem. Am. Inst. CPA's, Ill. Soc. CPA's. Office: Plan Ahead Inc PO Box 164 Palos Park IL 60464-0164 Office Phone: 708-448-8569.

NELSON, LEONARD JOHN, III, lawyer, educator; b. Spokane, Wash., July 31, 1949; s. Leonard John Jr. and Lois Marian (McCuaig) N.; m. Janice Helen Linebarger, Aug. 15, 1970; children: Leonard John IV, Mary Beth, Monica Teresa. Student, Whitman Coll., 1967-68; BA magna cum laude, U. Wash., 1970; JD cum laude, Gonzaga U., 1974; LLM, Yale U., 1984. Bar: Wash. 1974, Okla. 1979. Asst. prof. Gonzaga U. Law Sch., 1974; law clk. Wash. Supreme Ct., Olympia, 1975-76; ct. clk. Wash. Ct. Appeals, Spokane, 1976-78; from asst. to assoc. prof. O.W. Coburn Sch. Law, Tulsa, 1979-83; assoc. prof. Cumberland Sch. Law, Birmingham, Ala., 1984-87, prof., 1987—. Contbr. editor: The Death Decision, 1984; contbr. articles to law revs. Mem. instl. rev. bd. Samford U., 1986-2001. Mem. Fellowship Cath. Scholars, Phi Beta Kappa. Roman Catholic. Home: 1817 Parkside Cir Birmingham AL 35209-6960 Office: Cumberland Sch of Law 800 Lakeshore Dr Birmingham AL 35229-0001 Office Phone: 205-726-2410. E-mail: ljnelson@samford.cdi.

NELSON, LESTER, lawyer; b. N.Y.C., Dec. 23, 1928; s. Samuel and Celia (Plotkin) N.; m. Vita Reiner, Aug. 27, 1961; children: Lee Reiner, Clifford Samuel, Cara Ritchie. BSS, CCNY, 1950; LLM, NYU, 1959; JD, Havard U., 1953. Bar: N.Y. 1953. Ptnr. Gerdes & Montgomery, N.Y.C., 1955-83, Golenbock & Barell, N.Y.C., 1983-85, Rabinovich, Nelson, Gordon & Burstein, N.Y.C., 1985-95, Nelson & Nelson, N.Y.C., 1995—. Adj. prof. N.Y. Law Sch., N.Y.C., 1972-87; internat. adv. bd. Oceana Publs., Inc., 1988-92. Author: Credit Manual of Commercial Laws, 1972-92; editor Digest of Comml. Laws of the World, 1972-98, Digest of Intellectual Property Laws of the World, 1972-98, N.Y. Internat. Law Rev., 1992— Sec. The Spanish Inst., N.Y.C., 1975; bd. dirs. Am. Jewish Com., Westchester Co., 1983-89, 96—, Inst. for Continuing Edn. in Law and Librarianship, 1980-92. With U.S. Army, 1953-55. Mem. ABA, N.Y. Co. Lawyers Assn. (chmn. fgn. and internat. law com. 1985-89), N.Y. State Bar Assn. Jewish. Avocations: tennis, skiing, reading, music. Home: Pleasant Ridge Rd Harrison NY 10528 Office: Nelson & Nelson 60 E 42nd St Rm 565 New York NY 10165-0565 Office Phone: 212-983-1950.

NELSON, LINDA J. state legislator; b. Plentywood, Mont., June 12, 1942; m. Roger Nelson. Grad., Medicine Lake H.S. Farmer, rancher; mem. Mont. Ho. of Reps., 1989-94, Mont. Senate, Dist. 49, Helena, 1994—2004; mem. ethics com., mem. rules com., mem. fin. and claims com.; mem. agr., livestock and irrigation com.; mem. jt. appropriations subcom. natural resources/commerce; minority whip Mont. Senate, 1999—2002, dean of senate, 2003—04. Mem. Medicine Lake (Mont.) Sch. Bd., 1981-88, chair, 1984-88; active Mont. Dem. Party. Mem. Women Involved in Farm Econs., Nat. Order Legis. Women, N.E. Mont. Land and Mineral Owners Assn., Mont. Grain Growers, Sheridan County Dem. Women. Democrat. Lutheran. Home: 469 Griffin Medicine Lake MT 59247-9708

NELSON, LUTHER SULLIVAN, radiologist; b. Lasker, N.C., 1926; s. Charles Wesley and Maggie Virginia (Collier) N.; m. Thelma Olivia Joyner, June 23, 1951 (dec. Feb. 2002); children: James Elliott, Stuart Edward, Glenda Ann Nelson Rogers. BA, BS, East Carolina U., 1950; MD, U. N.C., 1958. Diploamte Am. Bd. Radiology. Intern U. Mich., Ann Arbor, 1958-59; resident U. N.C., Chapel Hill, 1965-68; pvt. practice; radiologist St. Anthony's Hosp., Amarillo, Tex., 1968—. Mem. AMA, Am. Coll. Radiologists. Republican. Methodist.

NELSON, MARILYN (MARILYN NELSON WANIEK), education educator, poet; b. Cleve., Apr. 26, 1946; d. Melvin Moton and Johnnie Edwina (Mitchell) Nelson; m. Erdmann Waniek, 1970 (div. 1979); m. Roger B. Wilkenfeld, 1979 (div. 1998); children: Jacob, Dora. BA, U. Calif., Davis, 1968; MA, U. Pa., 1970; PhD, U. Minn., 1979. With Lane C.C., Eugene, Oreg., 1970-72; vis. prof. Reed Coll., Portland, Oreg., 1971-72, Nr. Nissum Seminarium, Denmark, 1972-73, St. Olaf Coll., Northfield, Minn., 1973-78, Universitat Hamburg, Fed. Republic of Germany, spring 1977, U. Conn., Storrs, 1978—2002, Trinity Coll., Hartford, Conn., 1982-83; adj. prof. NYU, 1986—87, 1994—95; instr. MFA program Vt. Coll., 1988-89; Fulbright tchg. fellow France, 1995; vis. prof. U.S. Mil. Acad., West Point, NY, 2000, U. Del., 2002—04; faculty low residency MFA program New Eng. Coll., 2004—; spl. emerita faculty Univ. Conn., 2004—. Resident faculty Frost Place, Franconia, N.H., 1986. Author: For the Body, 1978, The Cat Walked Through the Casserole, 1984, Mama's Promises, 1985, The Homeplace, 1990, Partial Truth, 1992, Magnificat, 1994, The Fields of Praise: New and Selected Poems, 1997, Carver: A LIfe in Poems, 2001, Triolets for Triolet, 2001, She-Devil Circus, 2001, Fortune's Bones: The Manumission Requiem, 2004; translator: Literary Sex Roles, 1975, Hundreds of Hens and Other Poems, 1983, "Hecuba" in Euripides I of Penn Greek Drama Series, The Thirteenth Month, 2005, The Ladder, 2004, Selected Verse of Halfdan Rasmussen, 2004. Recipient Annisfield-Wolf award, 1992, The Poets prize, 1998, The Boston Globe-Horn Book award, 2001; Kent fellow, 1976, NEA fellow, 1981, 90; Danish Ministry of Culture grantee, 1984; Guggenheim fellow, 2001; nominee Pulitzer prize, 1985, 91, Nat. Book award finalist, 1991, 97, 2001. Mem. AAUP, Associated Writing Programs, Soc. for the Study of Multi-Ethnic Lit. of the U.S., Soc. for Values in Higher Edn., Third World Villanelle Soc., Phi Kappa Phi. Avocations: quilting, travel, contemplation.

NELSON, MARILYN C. hotel executive, travel company executive, food service executive, marketing professional; b. Mpls. m. Glen Nelson; children: Diana, Curtis C., Wendy. Student, U. Sorbonne, Paris, Inst. Hautes Etudes Econ., Geneva; degree in internat. econs. with honors, Smith Coll., 1961; DBA (hon.), Johnson & Wales U.; DHL (hon.), Coll. St. Catherine, Gustavus Adolphus Coll. Securities analyst Paine Webber, Mpls.; pres., COO Carlson Cos., Inc., Mpls., 1997—2003, CEO, 1998—, chmn., 1999—, also bd. dirs. Co-chair Carlson Holdings, Inc., 1991—; dep. chair Thomas Cook Holdings; co-chair Carlson Wagonlit Travel, 1994—; disting. vis. prof. Johnson & Wales U.; bd. dirs. Exxonmobil Corp.; chmn. Nat. Women's Bus. Coun., 2002—. Pres. United Way Mpls., campaign chair, 1984; bd. dirs. United Way Am., 1988-90, U.S. Nat. Tourism Orgn., 1996-98, Ctr. for Internat. Leadership, 1990—; mem. Internat. Adv. Coun., 1996—; mem. disting. adv. coun. Coll. of St. Catherine, 1989—; mem. Bretton Woods Com., 1986—; hon. bd. dirs. Svenska Inst., Stockholm, 1993—; mem. adv. bd. Hubert H. Humphrey Inst. Pub. Affairs, 1992-96; co-founder Minn. Women's Econ. Roundtable, 1974—; chair Minn. Super Bowl Task Force, 1984-92; chair, founder Midsummer Internat. Festival of Music; co-chair New Sweden '88; past bd. dirs. Guthrie Theatre, Greater Mpls. Girl Scout Coun., Jr. Achievement, Jr. League Mpls., KTCA Pub. TV, Minn. Congl. Award, Minn. Opera Co., Women's' Assn. Minn. Symphony Orch.; trustee Smith Coll., Northampton, Mass., 1980-85, Macalester Coll., St. Paul, 1974-80. Named Woman of Yr., Minn. Exec. Women in Tourism, Sales Exec. of Yr., Sales and Mktg. Exec. of Mpls., Woman of Yr. Roundtable for Women in Foodsvc., 1995, Outstanding Individual in Tourism, Minn. Office of Tourism, 1992, Woman of Yr., Minn. Exec. Women in Tourism, 1991-92, The Top 25 Execs. Yr. Bus. Week, 1999, Exec. Yr. Corp. Report Minn., 1999; recipient Minn. Congl. award for initiative and svc. to cmty., cert. of commendation State of Minn., Cmty. Svc. award YWCA, Independence award Vinland Nat. Ctr., Cmty. Svc. award Park-Nicollet Med. Ctr., Outstanding Mktg. Exec. of Yr. award, Minn. Distributive Edn. Club Am., Career Achievement award Sales and Mktg. Execs. Mpls., Outstanding Achievement award United Way Mpls., Extraordinary Leadership award Greater Mpls. C. of C., Disting. Svc. award United Way of Am., 1984-90, Nat. Caring award Caring Inst., 1995, Outstanding Bus. Leader award Northwood U., 1995, The 50 Most Powerful Women award in Am. Bus. Fortune, 1998-2003, United Way Minn. Disting. Svc. award United Way's highest vol. honor, 1998, Good Neighbor award WCCO Radio, 1999, Caring Heart award charitable contbns. by Larry King Cardiac Found., 1999, Am.'s 100 Most Important Women award Ladies' Home Jr., 1999, The 50 Most Powerful Women in Bus. Fortune 1999-2001, The Most Powerful Women in Travel #1 Travel Agent Mag., 1997-2003, Svc. Above Self award The Rotary Club Downtown, Minn., 1999, The Top 500 Women-Owned Bus.'s award Working Woman, 1999-2001, The 25 Most Influential Executives award Leisure Travel News, 2000, Northwest Airlines Disting. World Traveler award Hospitality Sales and Mktg. Assn. Internat., 2000, Responsible Capitalism award FIRST mag., 2001, Businesswoman of World, Bus. Women's Network, 2001, Glass Ceiling award Minn. Women's Consortium, 2001, Great Swedish Heritage award Swedish Coun. Am., 2002, Lifetime Achievement award Internat. Investment Forum, 2002; named Swedish Am. of Yr., 2003, Minnesotan of Yr., 2003; named to Sales and Mktg. Execs. Hall of Fame, 2003, Lifetime Achievement award Hospitality Sales and Mktg. Assn. Internat., 2004. Mem. Hennepin County Med. Soc. Aux., Jr. League Mpls., Minn. Meetings, Smith Coll. Alumni Assn., Smith Club Mpls., Woodhill Country Club, Mpls. Club, N.W. Tennis Club, Nat. Ctr. Social Entrepreneurs, Com. of 200, Hospitality Sales and Mktg. Assn. Internat. (Lifetime Achievement award 2004), Minn. Orchestral Assn., Orphei Dranger, Alpha Kappa Psi. Office: Carlson Cos Inc PO Box 59159 Minneapolis MN 55459-8212 Office Phone: 763-212-5000.

NELSON, MARK A. music educator; b. Mpls., May 20, 1957; s. Dennis Darrell Nelson and Nancy Jean Wilson; m. Monica T. Nelson, Aug. 18, 1984; children: Jude, Luke. BA, Point Loma Nazarene U., San Diego, 1980; MMus, Ariz. State U., 1982, DMA, 1985; MEd, U. Vt., 1991. Instrumental music tchr. Scottsdale (Ariz.) Pub. Schs., 1982—84, 1998—2000; assoc. prof. music U. Vt., Burlington, Vt., 1984—93; prin. tuba Vt. Symphony Orch., Burlington, Vt., 1984—93; prof. music Millikin U., Decatur, Ill., 1993—98; chair performing arts Pima C.C., Tucson, 2000—. Performer: (CD) Aboriginal Voices, 1996, New England Reveries, 1991; author: The Tuba as a Solo Instrument: Composer Biographies, 1995. Mem.: Music Educators Nat. Conf., Internat. Tuba and Euphonium Assn. Office: Pima Cmty Coll 2202 W Anklam Rd Tucson AZ 85709 Office Phone: 520-206-6826. E-mail: mark.nelson@pima.edu.

NELSON, MARTHA JANE, magazine editor; b. Pierre, SD, Aug. 13, 1952; d. Bernard Anton and Pauline Isabel (Noren) Nelson. BA, Barnard Coll., 1976. Mng. editor Signs: Jour. of Women in Culture, NYC, 1976—80; staff editor Ms. Mag., NYC, 1980—85; editor-in-chief Women's Sports and Fitness Mag., San Francisco, 1985—87; exec. editor Savvy, NYC, 1988—89, editor-in-chief, 1989—91; asst. mng. editor People, 1993; founding editor In Style Mag., NYC, 1993—2002, exec. prodr. TV program Celebrity Weddings, 1997—2002, exec. prodr. TV programs Celebrity Moms, Celebrity Homes, 2001; mng. editor People Mag., NYC, 2002—. Editor: Women in the American City, 1980; editor: (cons. editor) Who Weekly, 1992; contbr. articles to profl. jours. Bd. dirs. Painting Space 122, N.Y.C., 1982—85, 1995—96, Urban Athletic Assn., 1986, ACRIA, Comm. Rsch. Inst. on AIDS, Am. Soc. Mag Editors; adv. bd. Accessories Coun., 1999—2001, NYU Grad. Sch., 2000—03. Recipient Child Victimization in the News award, Nat. Ctr. for Missing and Exploited Children, 2003. Mem.: N.Y. Women in Comm., Women in Film, Am. Soc. Mag. Editors, Athletic and Swim Club (bd. dirs. 2000—).

NELSON, MARVIN DALE, JR., radiologist, educator; b. Hastings, Nebr., June 16, 1954; s. Marvin Dale Sr. and Patricia J. (Pingenot) N.; m. Mary C. Baron, Sep. 30, 1990; children: Kevin James, Andrew John. BS, MD, Loma Linda U., 1978; MBA, U. So. Calif., 1999. Diplomate Am. Bd. Radiology, Am. Bd. Daignostic Radiology, Am. Bd. Pediat. Radiology, Am. Bd. Neuroradiology. Intern, resident in radiology Loma Linda U. Med. Ctr., 1978-82; fellow in neuroradiology Nat. Hosp. for Nervous Disease, London, 1985-86, Rothschild Founds., Paris, 1986; fellow in pediat. neuroradiology Children's Mem. Hosp., Chgo., 1986-87; asst. prof. radiology Children's Hosp.-USC Sch. Med., 1987-93, assoc. prof., 1993-2001; chmn. dept. radiology Children' Hosp., L.A., 1998—, prof., 2001—, John L. Gwinn prof. pediat. radiology, 2002—. Maj. USAF, 1982-85. Recipient Cornelius Dyke award for original rsch. Am. Soc. Radiology, 1990, Gabriel Wilson award for best paper Western Neuroradiol. Soc., 1997. Fellow Am. Coll. Radiology; mem. Am. Soc. Neurol. Radiology, Am. Soc. Pediat. Neuroradiology (pres. 2004-05), Western Neuroradiog. Soc. (pres. 2001). Office: Children's Hosp 4650 W Sunset Blvd Los Angeles CA 90027-6062 Office Phone: 323-669-4572. E-mail: mdnelson@chla.usc.edu.

NELSON, MARVIN RAY, retired life insurance company executive; b. Thornton, Iowa, Aug. 29, 1926; s. Clarence Anton and Rose Bessie (Nicolet) N.; m. Juanita Mae Brown, May 26, 1951; children: Nancy, Kenneth. BS, Drake U, 1951. Actuary Security Mut. Life Ins. Co., Lincoln, Nebr., 1951-58; assoc. actuary Life Ins. Co. N.Am., Phila., 1958-59; group actuary Bankers Life of Nebr., Lincoln, 1959-66; actuary Mut. Service Life Ins. Co., St. Paul, 1966-68; sr. v.p. Horace Mann Educators Corp., Springfield, Ill., 1968-77, Security Life of Denver, 1977-83, exec. v.p., 1988-91; pres., chief oper. officer, dir., mem. investment com. Midwestern United Life Ins. Co., Ft. Wayne, Ind., 1983-89; ret., 1991. Bd. dirs., treas. Ft. Wayne Urban League, 1983-87; bd. dirs. Taxpayers Research Assn., Ft. Wayne, 1984-88. Served with U.S. Army, 1946-47. Fellow Soc. Actuaries; mem. Am. Acad. Actuaries, Pi Kappa Phi. Home: 5224 S Shalom Pk Cir Aurora CO 80015-2263

NELSON, MARY CARROLL, artist, writer; b. Bryan, Tex., Apr. 24, 1929; d. James Vincent and Mary Elizabeth (Langton) Carroll; m. Edwin Blakeley Nelson, June 27, 1950; children: Patricia Ann, Edwin Blakely. BA in Fine Arts, Barnard Coll., 1950; MA, U. N.Mex., 1963. Juror Am. Artist Golden Anniversary Competition, 1987. Guest instr. continuing edn. U. N.Mex., 1991; conf. co-organizer Affirming Wholeness, The Art and Healing Experience, San Antonio, 1992, Artists of the Spirit Symposium, 1994. Group shows include N.Mex. Mus., 1987, Art is for Healing, The Universal Link, San Antonio, 1992, Fuller Lodge Art Ctr. Los Alamos, N.Mex., 1993, Layering, Albuquerque, 1993, Crossings, Bradford, Mass., 1994, The Layered Perspective, Fayetteville, Ark., 1994, Tree of Life, San Miguel de Allende, Mex., 1996, (honoree Magnifico, Albuquerque, 1997, Bravo award Excellence in Arts 2004), Guardian Spirits, Marlborough, Eng., 1997, Memories in Multi-Media, Columbus, Ohio, 1998, Agora Gallery, NYC, 1998, Celtic Connections, Mass., 1998, Bridging Time and Space, Calif., 1999, Musings on the Millennium, Ohio, 2000, Layerists in Multi-Media/Affirming Wholeness, Albuquerque, 2000, The Birth of Wisdom, N. Mand Gordes, France, 2000, Tides of Change, Tex., 2001, EarthSpirit, Ohio, 2001, Shadow & Light, Albuquerque, 2001, Landscape and Memory, Sedona, Ariz., 2002, dsg Gallery, Albuquerque, 2002, Albuquerque Mus., 2003, Fire in the Heart, Ashland, Oreg., 2003, Layered Images, Albuquerque, 2003, Masterworks Miniatures, 2004 (Lot award Mixed Media), others; represented in pvt. collections in U.S., Germany, Eng. and Australia; author: American Indian Biography Series, 1971-76, (with Robert E. Wood) Watercolor Workshop, 1974; (with Ramon Kelley) Ramon Kelley Paints Portraits and Figures, 1977, The Legendary Artists of Taos, 1980, (catalog) American Art in Peking, 1981, Masters of Western Art, 1982, Connecting, The Art of Beth Ames Swartz, 1984, Artists of the Spirit, 1994, Doris Steider, A Vision of Silence, 1997, Beyond Fear, A Toltec's Guide to Freedom and Joy, 1997, Layering, An Art of Time and Space, 1985, (catalog) Layering/Connecting, 1987; contbg. editor Am. Artist, 1976-91, Southwestern Art, 1987-91; editor (video) Layering, 1990; arts corr. Albuquerque Jour., 1991-93; contbr. One Source Sacred Journeys, 1997, Bridging Time and Space, Essays on Layered Art, 1998, Lightstream, 2003; co-author: Bridging Time and Space, Essays on Layered Art, 1998, Toltec Prophecies of Don Miguel Ruiz, 2003; co-editor The Art of Layering: Making Connections, 2004. Mem. Albuquerque Arts Bd., 1984-88. Mem. Soc. Layerists in Multi-Media (founder 1982). Home: 1408 Georgia St NE Albuquerque NM 87110-6861 E-mail: mcn50@comcast.net.

NELSON, MARY ELLEN DICKSON, retired actuary; b. Mpls., Mar. 24, 1933; d. William Alexander and Laura Winona (Baxter) Dickson; m. David Aldrich Nelson, Aug. 25, 1956; children: Frederick Dickson, Claudia Baxter, Caleb Edward. BA, Vassar Coll., 1954; postgrad., Cambridge (Eng.) U., 1954-55. Rsch. assoc. N.Am. Life & Casualty Co., Mpls., 1955-56; actuarial asst. John Hancock Mut. Life Ins. Co., Boston, 1956-58; actuary David R. Kass & Assocs., Cleve., 1973-74; pres. Nelson & Co., Cleve., 1975, Conrad, Nelson & Co., Cleve., 1975-81, Nelson & Co., Cleve./Cin., 1981-99; ret., 1999. Bd. dirs. Union Ctrl. Life Ins. Co., Cin. Fulbright scholar, 1954—55. Fellow: Soc. Actuaries, Phi Beta Kappa; mem.: Am. Acad. Actuaries, Midwest Benefits Conf. (chair 1991), Cin. Actuaries Club. Republican.

NELSON, MAURICE S., JR., metal products company executive; CEO Earle M Jorgensen Co., Brea, Calif. Office: Earle M Jorgensen Co 10650 Alameda St Lynwood CA 90262-1754

NELSON, MERLIN EDWARD, international business consultant, company director, lawyer; b. Fargo, N.D., Jan. 30, 1922; s. Theodore G. and Eva C. (Hultgren) N.; m. Nancy Ellen Craig, June 1952 (div. June 1962); children: Craig Edward, Brian Anthony; m. Janet April Pope, Aug. 30, 1963; children: Claudia Jane, Rolf Merlin. BS in Polit. Sci., U. Oreg., 1943; postgrad., Fordham U., 1943-44; JD, Yale U., 1948. Bar: Oreg. 1948, N.Y. 1954, U.S. Dist. Ct. D.C. 1954. Atty. Office Gen. Counsel, ECA, Washington and Paris, 1949-52; assoc. Davis, Polk, Wardwell, Sunderland & Kiendl, 1952-59; exec. asst. to v.p. AMF, Inc., N.Y.C., 1960-62; chmn., mng. dir. AMF Internat., Ltd., London, 1962-63; v.p., group exec. AMF, Inc., 1963-70, exec. v.p., vice chmn., dir., 1970-84, now cons., 1984—; ret., 1984. Bd. dirs. Mitsui Found., Mizuho Found.; chmn., pres. Tuckernuck Land Trust. Mem. Coun. Fgn. Rels.; mem. nat. leadership coun. Trust for Pub. Land. Decorated Purple Heart WWII. Mem. Phi Beta Kappa. Home and Office: 16 W 77th St Apt 12E New York NY 10024-5126 E-mail: nelsonmj@earthlink.net.

NELSON, MICHAEL UNDERHILL, association executive; b. Balt., May 5, 1932; s. Cyril Arthur and Elise (Macy) N.; m. Barbara Gail Hutchins, June 25, 1960; children: Kevin Underhill, Bronwyn Hastings, Gayle Hutchins, Corey Williams. AB, Rutgers U., 1957, EdM, 1968. Salesman J & N Distbg. Co., New Brunswick, N.J., 1957-59; extension assoc. Univ. Coll., Rutgers U., New Brunswick, 1959-61; asst. dir. summer session Rutgers U., 1961-68; asst. dean sch. continuing edn., dir. summer sch. Washington U., St. Louis, 1969-81, dir. div. of profl. and community programs sch. continuing edn., 1975-78; exec. sec. N.Am. Assn. Summer Sessions, 1979—; account exec. Trio Printing Co., 1982-84; sr. procedures analyst McDonnell Douglas Corp, St. Louis, 1984-96. Bd. dirs. Adult Edn. Council of Greater St. Louis, 1975-78. Served with USMC, 1951-54. Mem. North Ctrl. Conf. Summer Schs. (pres. 1974-75), Am. Assn. Univ. Adminstrs., Assn. Univ. Summer Sessions, Am. Summer Sessions Senate, N.Am. Assn. Summer Sessions (pres. 1978), Alpha Sigma Lambda, Phi Delta Kappa. Episcopalian. Home and Office: 43 Belanger Dr Dover NH 03820-4602 Office Phone: 603-740-9880. Personal E-mail: NAASS@aol.com.

NELSON, NANCY ELEANOR, pediatrician, educator; b. El Paso, Apr. 4, 1933; d. Harry Hamilton and Helen Maude (Murphy) N. BA magna cum laude, U. Colo., 1955, MD, 1959. Intern, Case Western Res. U. Hosp., 1959-60, resident, 1960-63; pvt. practice medicine specializing in pediats., Denver, 1963-70; clin. prof. U. Colo. Sch. Medicine, Denver, 1988-2002, assoc. dean student affairs U. Colo. Sch. Medicine, 1988—. Mem. Am. Acad. Pediats., AMA (sect. med. schs. governing coun. 1994-96), Denver Med. Soc. (pres. 1983-84), Colo. Med. Soc. (bd. dirs. 1985-88, mem. jud. coun. 1992—, mem. liason com. med. edn. 1993—).

NELSON, NEVIN MARY, interior designer; b. Cleve., Nov. 5, 1941; d. Arthur George Reinker and Barbara Phyllis (Gunn) Parks; m. Wayne Nelson (div. 1969); children: Doug, Brian. BA in Interior Design, U. Colo., 1964. Prin. Nevin Nelson Design, Boulder, Colo., 1966-70, Vail, Colo., 1970—, Denver, 2002—. Program chmn. Questers Antique Study Group, Boulder, 1969. Coord. Bob Kirscht for Gov. campaign, Eagle County, Colo., 1986; state del. Rep. Nat. Conv., 1986-88; county coord. George Bush for U.S. Pres. campaign, 1988, 92; chmn. Eagle County Reps., 1989-93; v.p. bd. dirs. Park Lane Condo Assn., Denver, 1995-96; pres. Save Our Imperiled Land, Vail, 1998. Mem. Am. Soc. Interior Designers, City Club of Denver, Chaine des Rotisseurs; Fndr. Denver Dollies Red Hat Soc., 2001. Episcopalian. Avocations: gardening, party planning, cooking, reading, travel. Home: 1440 S Dahlia St Denver CO 80222

NELSON, NORMAN DANIEL, government official; b. Dec. 30, 1968; married; 1 child. BSBA, U. Fla., 1991; MBA, U. Miami, 1997; MA, Georgetown U., 2000. Intern corp. fin. divsn. mergers and acquisitions Commerzbank AG, Frankfurt, 1992; intern corp. fin. divsn. internat. leasing and new stock issues Deutsche Bank AG, Frankfurt, 1992; commd. 2d lt. disting. mil. grad. USAR, 1991; advanced through grades to maj. USAR, C.E. and Civil Affairs, 2002; econ. plans and program officer U.S. Dept. of State, 1997—2001; pres., CEO Nelson Systems Internat. Corp., 1998—2000; fgn. svc. officer U.S. Dept. State, 2001—. Decorated Army Commendation medal (3); recipient Meritorious Honor award U.S. Dept. State, 2003; Fed. Chancellor scholar Alexander-von-Humboldt Found., 1991-92. Mem. Sigma Chi. E-mail: nelsonnd@state.gov.

NELSON, PAUL JAMES, educator; b. Porter County, Ind., Dec. 1, 1932; s. Forrest Ross and Bessie Marie (Kline) N.; m. Judith Ann Benda, Feb. 14, 1956; children: Douglas Ross, Paula Ann, Daniel Forrest. Grad. high sch., Chesterton, Ind. Lic. comml. pilot; cert. tchr., Ind. With U.S. Steel Co., Gary, Ind., 1951-54, 59-83; pilot, instr. Phillips Airlines, Michigan City, Ind., 1983-85; tchr. Gary Cmty. Sch. Corp., 1985-95; profl. grant writer for edn. Employed Bethlehem Steel, Chesterton, Ind., 1997—. Author: (text book) Machinist Study Guides, 1980. Trustee Town of Pines, 1970; pres. Pines Planning Commn., Inc., 1973, v.p., 1991—; Pines Bd. Zoning Appeals, 1978; mem. Ind. Dunes Nat. Lakeshore Task Forces, 1980, Gary Regional Airport Task Force, 1988; cert. airlift vol. Am. Cancer Soc., 1981; Dem. precinct com. person Pine Twsp., Ind.; treas. Porter County Dem. Ctrl. Com., 1997—. With USAF, 1954-56. Democrat. Avocations: restoration old aircraft, building scale locomotives. Home: 1545 Ash St Michigan City IN 46360-6652 Office: Burns Harber Divsn PO Box 248 Chesterton IN 46304-0248

NELSON, PAUL WILLIAM, real estate broker; b. Mpls., Mar. 7, 1952; s. William H. and Jean (Darrington) N.; m. Jill Brownson, Oct. 18, 1986 (dec. Nov. 1990); children: Emily J., Joshua C.; m. Robin K. Carpenter, Aug. 14, 1993. BS, U. Colo., 1974. Lic. real estate broker, Colo. Advt. dir. Denver Beechcraft, 1976-77; real estate broker Coldwell Banker, Grand Junction, Colo., 1977—. Bd. dirs. Colo. Assn. Realtors, Denver, 1981-83. Mem. Grand Junction City Coun., 1985-93, also mayor pro tem; mem. Downtown Devel. Authority, Grand Junction, 1985-91; bd. dirs. Mesa County Planning Commn., Grand Junction, 1980-85, Colo. Nat. Monument Assn., 1989-91, Grand Junction Visitors and Conv. Bur., 1993-96; Lobbying Group; mem. Mesa County Uranium Mill Tailings Removal Citizens Com.; mem. co-chmn. Mesa County Riverfront Commn., 1993-99; mem. dist. resource adv. coun. Bur. Land Mgmt., 1990-92, Grand Junction Visitors and Conv. Bur. bd. dirs., 1992-96; mem. Colo. Juvenile Parole Bd., 2000—; trustee Colo. Riverfront Found., 1999—. Recipient Citizen Svc. award Mesa County, 1985, winner Parade Mag. MIllennium Photo Contest. Mem. Mesa County Assn. Realtors (bd. dirs. 1981-83, treas. 1999—), Rotary, Club 20 (bd. dirs. 1994-96). Republican. Avocations: pvt. pilot, skiing. Office: Coldwell Banker PO Box 3117 Grand Junction CO 81502-3117 E-mail: pablonelsoni@yahoo.com.

NELSON, PAULA MORRISON BRONSON, gifted and talented educator, consultant; b. Memphis, Mar. 26, 1944; d. Fred Ford and Julia (Morrison) Bronson; m. Jack Marvin Nelson, July 13, 1968; children: Eric Allen, Kelly Susan. BS, U. N.Mex., 1967; MA, U. Colo., Denver, 1985. Physical edn. tchr. Grant Union Sch. Dist., Sacramento, 1967-68, Denver Pub. Schs., 1968-74, with program for pupil assistance, 1974-80; tchr. ESL Douglas County Pub. Schs., Parker, Colo., 1982-83; chpt. 1 reading specialist Denver Pub. Schs., 1983-96, computer/reading specialist, 1996-98, reading specialist, gifted and talented tchr., 1998-99, lead tchr. in charge instrn., 1999-2001, edn. cons., 2001—02. Demonstration tchr. Colo. Edn. Assn., 1970-72; mem. curriculum com. Denver Pub. Schs., 1970-72; mem. Douglas County Accountability Com., Castle Rock, Colo., 1986-92; mem. educators rev. panel Edn. for Freedom; computer trainer Denver Pub. Schs. Tech. Team, 1992-02. Co-author: Gymnastics Teacher's Guide Elementary Physical Education, 1973, Applauding Our Constitution, 1989; editorial reviewer G is for Geography, Children's Literature and the Five Themes. 1993; producer slide shows Brotherhood, 1986, We the People...Our Dream Lives On, 1987, Celebration of Cultures, 1988. Named Pub. Edn. Coalition grantee, Denver, 1987, 88, 89, 90, grantee Rocky Mountain Global Edn. Project, 1987, Wake Forest Law Sch., Winston-Salem, N.C., 1988, 89, 90, 92, Read to Achieve grantee Colo. State Dept. Edn., 2000; recipient chpt. II grant, 1991, Tech. grant, 1993, Title VI Reading grant, 1999, 2000, Three R's of Freedom award State Dept. Edn., 1987, Nat. Recognition award Commn. on Bicentennial of Constitution., 1987, Distinguished Tchr. award City of Denver, 1994. Mem.: Denver Fedn. Tchrs., Am. Fedn. Tchrs., Tech. in Edn. Republican. Methodist. Avocations: snow and water skiing, tennis. Home: 18 Covewood Dr Norwalk CT 06853

NELSON, PHILIP FRANCIS, musicology educator, consultant, choral conductor; b. Waseca, Minn., Feb. 17, 1928; s. Elmer Philip and Frances (Bretzke) N.; m. Georgia Ann Yelland, June 5, 1950; children: Curtis Ann, Philip Francis Jr. AB, Grinnell Coll., 1950; AM, U. N.C., 1956, PhD, 1958; Diplome (Fulbright scholar), U. Paris, 1957; student, Conservatoire Nat. de Paris, 1956-57; MA (hon.), Yale U., 1971; LHD (hon.), Grinnell Coll., 1981. Asst. prof. Ariz. State U., 1958-62, assoc. prof., 1962-63; prof., chmn. dept. music SUNY, Binghamton, 1963-70; prof., dean Sch. Music, Yale U., 1970-81; prof., provost, dean U. Calif., Santa Cruz, 1981-83; chmn. trustee com. Curtis Inst., 1982-83; sr. v.p. AED, N.Y.C., 1984-87; v.p. Aspen Inst. for Humanistic Studies, 1987-89; interim chancellor Sch. Arts, U. N.C., 1989-90; assoc. fellow Nat. Humanities Ctr., 1990-91; interim vice chancellor U. N.C., Chapel Hill, 1991; cons. edn., arts, 1992-93; chmn. grad. sch. adv. coun. U. N.C., Chapel Hill, 1993-96, cons. arts and humanities, 1996—; interim dir. N.C. Sch. Sci. and Math., 1999-2000; sr. cons. U. N.C. and Nat. Humanities Ctr., 2000—. Music critic Phoenix Gazette, 1959-62; music cons. Taliesin West, 1959-63; chmn. Nat. Screening Com. for Fulbright Awards in Musicology, 1965-68; cons. Nat. Endowment for Arts, 1984-90; vis. lectr. Duke U., 1992—. Contbg. editor: College and Adult Reading List, 1962, Nicolas Bernier, Principles of Composition, 1964, Recherches sur la musique Française classique, 1979, 80; contbr. to Groves Dictionary of Music, 6th edit.; editor publs. in the arts for The Aspen Inst. for the Humanities, 1987-89. Bd. dirs. various symphonies, chamber music socs., arts groups; trustee Curtis Inst. Music, Phila., 1980-83; mem. exec. com. Conn. State Golf Assn., 1975-81; founder Seven Springs Soc., 1975; bd. dirs. Conn. Hospice, 1983-87, Nat. Soc. to Prevent Blindness, 1987-93;, bd. dirs., v.p., 1987-93; mem. Chapel Hill Arts Ctr., 1992—; mem. Triangle J. Coun. Govt., 1992-95. Served from ensign to lt. comdr. USCGR, 1952-72. Found. grantee. Mem. Am. Musicol. Soc., Internat. Musicol. Soc., Coll. Music Soc. (nat. coun., editor jour. 1966-69), Société Française de Musicologie, Soc. Ethnomusicology, U.S. Srs. Golf Assn., Mory's Club (New Haven), Yale Club (N.Y.C.), Elizabethan Grads.Club, Carolina Club, Yale Golf Club, Finley Golf Club, Chapel Hill Country Club. Home: 621 Greenwood Rd Chapel Hill NC 27514-5921 *Keep casting bread on the waters-it may come back as French toast.*

NELSON, PRINCE ROGERS See PRINCE

NELSON, R. DAVID, electronics executive; Various mfg., quality control metallurgy, materials, sales and mktg., and purchasing pos. TRW Inc., 1957—87; v.p. purchasing to sr. v.p. purchasing and corp. affairs Honda of Am. Mfg., Marysville, Ohio, 1987—97, bd. dirs.; v.p. worldwide supply mgmt. Deere & Co., Moline, Ill., 1997—2001; v.p. global supply mgmt. Delphi Corp., Troy, Mich., 2002—. Founding mem. Nat. Initiative Supply Chain Integration, Ltd.; bd. dirs. Purchasing Round Table. Co-author: 2 books. Recipient medal of profl. excellence, Purchasing Mag., 2001. Mem.: CAPS Rsch. (bd. trustees), Inst. Supply Mgmt. (chmn.). Office: World Hdqrs Delphi Corp 5725 Delphi Dr Troy MI 58098-2815

NELSON, RALPH ALFRED, physician; b. Mpls., June 19, 1927; s. Alfred W. and Lydia (Johnson) N.; m. Rosemary Pokela, Aug. 7, 1954; children—Edward Ancher, Audrey Anne, Elizabeth Marie, Andrew William, Evan Robert. BA, U. Minn., 1949, MD, 1953, PhD, 1961. Diplomate Am. Bd. Internal Medicine. Intern Cook County (Ill.) Hosp., 1953-54; resident U. Minn. Hosps., Mpls., 1954-55, U. Minn., Mpls., 1955-56; fellow in physiology Mayo Grad. Sch., Rochester, Minn., 1957-60, resident in internal medicine, 1976-78; practice medicine specializing in internal medicine and clin. nutrition Sioux Falls, S.D., 1978-79, Urbana, Ill., 1979—. Bd. dirs. Scott Research Lab., Fairview Park Hosp., Cleve., 1962-67; assoc. in physiology Western Res. U., Cleve., 1962-67; asst. prof. physiology Mayo Grad. Sch., 1967-73, Mayo Med. Sch., 1973, assoc. prof. nutrition, 1974; cons. in nutrition Mayo Clinic, 1967-76; assoc. prof. medicine U. S.D. Sch. Medicine, Sioux Falls, 1978-79; prof. nutrition U. Ill. Coll. Medicine, Urbana-Champaign, 1979—2002, chmn. dept. medicine prof. nutritional sci., physiology, biophysics dept. food sci. Sch. Agr., 1979-2002, also prof. medicine, exec. head dept. internal medicine, 1989-2002, exec. head four sites of Coll. Medicine, 2002, emeritus prof. internal medicine, emeritus prof. nutritional scis.; dir. med.research Carle Found. Hosp., Urbana, 1979—; cons. nutritional support service Danville (Ill.) VA Hosp., 1980—. Co-author: The Mayo Clinic Renal Diet Cookbook, 1974; contbr. articles on nutrition, physiology, and hibernation to sci. jours.; editor: Geriatrics, 1980—2002, The Physician and Sportsmedicine, 1980-88, Am. Jour. Clin. Nutrition, 1980-83. Cons. in nutrition Nat. Cancer Inst., 1976; cons. in nutrition HEW, 1976, 79, 89, Nat. Heart and Lung Inst., 1976. Served with USAF, 1945-47. Fulbright scholar, Morocco, 1988. Fellow ACP; mem. Am. Physiol. Soc., Am. Inst. Nutrition, Am. Soc. Clin. Nutrition, Central Soc. Clin. Research, Am. Gastroent. Assn. Lutheran. Home: 2 Illini Cir Urbana IL 61801-5813 Office: Carle Foundation Hospital 611 W Park St Urbana IL 61801-2529 Office Phone: 217-383-3036. Business E-Mail: r-nelson@staff.UIUC.edu.

NELSON, RALPH ERWIN, investment company executive, coin dealer; b. Chgo., July 30, 1946; s. Vernon Leslie and Astrid Lorene (Seagren) N.; BS, McPherson Coll., 1971; MBA, U. Sarasota, 1980, MFM, 1981; MHS, U. Sarasota, 1983; PhD, Columbia Pacific U., 1984; m. Elarie Marie Fletcher, Oct. 14, 1967; 1 child, Anne Marie. Chief planning dept. Roberts & Zoller Inc., Bradenton, Fla., 1971-76; v.p., supr. planning div. Dan Zoller Engring. Inc., Bradenton, 1976-78; pres. Ralph Nelson & Assocs., Inc., Landscape Architects, Planners, Architects and Engrs., Bradenton, 1978-88, Nelson Investments, Inc., 1981—. Baptist. Address: PO Box 14777 Bradenton FL 34280-4777

NELSON, RALPH STANLEY, lawyer; b. Mpls., Mar. 15, 1943; s. Stanley L. and Louise M. Nelson; m. Judy E. Nelson, July 8, 1867; children: Sara C., Amy E., David A. BS in Bus. Adminstrn., U. Minn., 1966; JD with honors, Drake U., 1972. Bar: Minn. 1973, Wash. 1982, Tex. 1985. Assoc. Wiese and Cox, Ltd., Mpls., 1973-76; atty. Burlington No. R.R., St. Paul, 1976-81; sr. corp. counsel Burlington No. Inc., Seattle, 1981-85; v.p. law and adminstrn. Burlington Motor Carriers Inc., Ft. Worth, 1985-88, exec. v.p. and gen. counsel, 1988-93, sr. v.p., gen. counsel Daleville (Indpls.), Ind., 1993-96, Trism Inc., Kennesaw, Ga., 1996-2001, exec. v.p., gen. counsel, 2001—, pres., CEO, 2001—03; sr. v.p., gen. counsel Tango Transport Inc., Shreveport, La., 2003—. Mem. law rev. Drake U. Mem. Order of the Coif. Office: 6009 Financial Plz Shreveport LA 71129-2615 E-mail: ralphneslo@yahoo.com.

NELSON, RICHARD A. military career officer; b. Perkins, Okla. m. Alice Faudree; two children. BS, Okla. State U., 1963; MD, U. Okla., 1966. Diplomate in occupl. medicine Am. Bd. Preventive Medicine. Commd. lt. USN, 1967, advanced through grades to vice adm., 1998; intern Bapt. Meml. Hosp., Oklahoma City; resident occupl. medicine U. Cin.; with Naval Hosp., Corpus Christi, Tex.; med. officer Naval Ammunition Depot, McAlester, Okla., Naval Hosp., Bremerton, Wash.; head occupl. med. br. Bur. Medicine and Surgery, Washington; with Navy Environ. Health Ctr., Cin.; dir. occupl. and environ. health svcs. Fleet Liaison Team, Naval Regional Med. Ctr., Bremerton, Wash., coord.; head Med. Dept. Naval Submarine Base, Bangor, Wash.; med. dept. head Puget Sound Naval Shipyard, Bremerton, Wash.; commdg. officer Navy Environ. Health Ctr., Norfolk, Va.; dir. occupl. health and preventive medicine divsn., Fleet Readiness and Support, Naval Med. Command, Washington; commdg. officer Naval Hosp., Bremerton, 1989-91; fleet surgeon U.S. Atlantic Fleet, 1991-93; cmdr. Naval Med. Ctr., San Diego; lead agent Mil. Health Sys. So. Calif., 1993—98; surgeon gen. USN, 1998—2001; cons. Silverdale, Wash., 2001—. Decorated Def. Superior Svc. medal, 3 Legion of Merit medals, Meritorious Svc. medal, Navy Achievement medal, Navy Disting. Svc. medal, Def. Disting. Svc. medal. Mem.: AMA, Assn. Mil. Surgeons U.S. Personal E-mail: rnelson863@aol.com.

NELSON, RICHARD ARTHUR, lawyer; b. Fosston, Minn., Apr. 8, 1947; BS in Math., U. Minn., 1969, JD, 1974. Bar: Minn. 1974, U.S. Ct. Appeals (D.C. cir.) 1975, U.S. Dist. Ct. Minn. 1975. Law clk. U.S. Ct. Appeals (D.C. cir.), Washington, 1974-75; ptnr. Faegre and Benson, Mpls., 1975—, group head employee benefits group, 2002—. Seminar lectr. in employee benefits and labor laws, 1983—. Note and articles editor Minn. Law Rev., 1973-74. Active Dem.-Farmer-Labor Party State Cen. Com., Minn., 1976—, del. dist. and local coms. and convs., 1970—, state exec. com., 1990—; student rep. bd. regents U. Minn., Mpls., 1973-74; mem. adv. coun. IRS Mid-States Key Dist. EP/EO, 1996-2000, IRS Ctrl. Mountains Region TE/GE, 2001—; chair Mpls. Pension Coun., 1999-2000. Served with U.S. Army, 1970-72. Mem. ABA, Minn. Bar Assn. (chair employee benefits sect. 1997-98), Order of Coif, Tau Beta Pi. Lutheran. Office: Faegre and Benson 90 S 7th St Ste 2200 Minneapolis MN 55402-3901 Office Phone: 612-766-7321. E-mail: rnelson@faegre.com.

NELSON, RICHARD DAVID, lawyer; b. Chgo., Jan. 29, 1940; s. Irving E. and Dorothy (Apolsky) N.; m. Davida Distenfield, Dec. 17, 1960; children: Cheryl, Laurel. BS in Acctg., U. Ill., 1961, LLB, 1964. Bar: Ill. 1964. Ptnr. Defrees & Fiske Law Offices, Chgo., 1964-81; ptnr., counsel, chief adminstrv. officer Heidrick & Struggles, Inc., Chgo., 1981—2001; pres. Galrk Sheridan, Inc., Highland Park, Ill., 2001—. Bd. dirs., exec. com. Heidrick & Struggles, Inc., Chgo., 1981-99. Pres. Jewish Cmty. Ctrs. of Chgo., 1987-89; chmn. Sign Graphics Task Force, Highland Park, Ill., 1986-88, Bus. and Econ. Devel. Commn., Highland Park, 1993-96, 2004—, Ft. Sheridan Joint Plan Commn., 1997-2000. Mem. Ill. State Bar Assn., Chgo. Bar Assn., Standard Club, Northmoor Country Club. Office: Galrk Sheridan Inc 1896 Sheridan Rd Ste 200 Highland Park IL 60035-4635 Office Phone: 847-926-9191.

NELSON, RICHARD JOHN, playwright, film director, screenwriter; b. Chgo., 1950; s. Richard Finis and Viola (Gabriel) Nelson; m. Cynthia Blair Bacon; 2 children. BA, Hamilton Coll., 1972. Literary mgr. BAM Theatre Co., Bklyn., 1979-81; assoc. dir. Goodman Theatre, Chgo., 1980-83; dramaturg Guthrie Theatre, Mpls., 1981-82. Author: (plays and screenplays) The Killing of Yablonski: Scenes of Involvement in a Current Event, 1975, Conjuring an Event, 1976, Scooping, 1977, The Vienna Notes, 1978 (OBIE award playwriting 1978-79), Jungle Coup, 1978, Bal, 1980, Rip Van Winkle, 1981, Chess, 1988, Principia Scriptoriae, 1987 (ABC-TV Playwriting award, London Theatre award, 1987), Roots in Water, 1988, Some Americans Abroad, 1989, The End of a Sentence, 1991, Two Shakespearean Actors, 1991 (Tony nomination, 1992, Antoinette Perry award nomination best play, 1992), Columbus and the Discovery of Japan, 1992, Life Sentences, 1993, Ethan Frome, 1993, Misha's Party, 1993, New England, 1994, The General From America, 1996; dir.: (plays and screenplays) The General From America, 2001; author: (plays and screenplays) Goodnight Children Everywhere, 1997; dir.: (plays and screenplays) Goodnight Children Everywhere, 2001 (Laurence Olivier award best new play, 2000, BBC award best new play, 2000), author, co-dir.: Between East and West, 1984, author, dir. Franny's Way, 2001; author: (adaptations) Moliere's Don Juan, 1979, Erdman's The Suicide, 1980, Brecht's Jungle of Cities, 1981, Goldoni's Il Campiello, 1981, de Beaumarchais's The Marriage of Figaro, 1982, The Return of Pinocchio, 1983, Chekhov's The Three Sisters, 1984, Fo's The Accidental Death of an Anarchist, 1984, Jitterbugging, 1989, Sensibility and Sense, 1990, and staging, The Three Sisters, 1995, Moliere's The Imaginary Cuckold and The School for Husbands, 1995, Strindberg's The Father, 1996, Pirandello's Enrico IV, 2001; author, dir.: (adaptations) James Joyce's The Dead, 1999 (N.Y. Drama Critics Circle award 1999-2000, Tony nominations book adaptation and lyrics, 1999, Tony award best book for a musical, 2000, Lucille Lortel award best new musical, 2000, Outer Critics Circle award nomination outstanding musical dir., 2000, FANY award nomination outstanding book of a musical and outstanding dir. of a musical, 2000); Isherwood's Madame Melville, 2000—01; author: (radio plays) Languages Spoken Here, 1987 (Giles Cooper award best radio play, 1988), Eating Words, 1989, Roots in Water, 1989, Advice to Eastern Europe, 1989, The American Wife, 1994, The Fall of Agnew, Hank Aaron's 715th, The Unrequited Lovers' Manual, Watergate: An Audio Memory; translator: The Wedding as The Marriage Dance: An Evening of Farce, 1980. Named hon. assoc. artist, Royal Shakespeare Co.; recipient OBIE citation innovative programming, BAM Theatre Co., 1979—80, Playwrights USA award, 1986, Lila Wallace Writers award, 1991—93, Lannan Literary award, 1995; fellow, Nat. Endowment for the Arts, 1979, 1986, 1987; grantee, Office for Advanced Drama Rsch., 1976, Rockefeller Found., 1979, 1988; Thomas J. Watson Travel fellow, 1972, Guggenheim fellow, 1983. Office: William Morris Agy 1350 Avenue Of The Americas New York NY 10019-4702*

NELSON, RICHARD LAWRENCE, surgeon, educator; b. Evanston, Ill., Oct. 11, 1946; s. Richard Lawrence and Mary Jane Nelson; m. Susan Jane Berryman, June 17, 1972; children: Cicely Adams, Joseph Lawrence, Moira Louise, Eric James, Patrick Matthew. BA, Stanford U., 1968; MD, U. Chgo., 1972. General Surgery Am. Bd. of Surgery, 1980, Colorectal Surgery Am. Bd. of Colon & Rectal Surgery, 1980. Prof. of surgery U. Ill., Chgo., 1980—; asst. prof., epidemiology & biometry U. Ill., Sch. of Pub. Health, Chgo., 1987—. Cons. Nat. Inst. Health, Bethesda, Md., 1991—2004. Musician: (cd & musical competitions) Championship Brass (Champions, NABBA, 1996, 1997, 1998, 2000, 2001, 2002, 2000). Recipient Order of Brass Band World - New Years Honors List, Brass Band World, 2000. Mem. Am. Coll. Surgeons. Roman Catholic. Achievements include patents for intestinal tubes. Avocations: bicycling, brass banding, hiking. Home: 2224 Lincolnwood Dr Evanston IL 60201-2020 Office: U Ill at Chgo 1740 W Taylor m/c 957 Chicago IL 60612 Office Phone: 312-996-5162. Home Fax: 1 312 996 2704; Office Fax: 312-996-2704. Personal E-mail: shadow881@aol.com. E-mail: shadow881@aol.com.

NELSON, ROBERT ARTHUR, civil engineer; b. Davis, SD, Sept. 9, 1939; s. Kermit George and Georgia Alice Nelson; m. Mary Jean Ellsworth, Aug. 5, 1960 (dec. 2003); children: David, Michael, Karen, Chris. BSCE, S.D. Sch. Mines, 1961; cert. bus. mgmt., U. Calif. Riverside, 1971; MPA, U. So. Calif. LA, 1974. Project engr. S.D. Highway Dept., Vermillion, 1961-62; from jr. engr. to assoc. engr. Riverside (Calif.) County Flood Control Dist., 1965-67; sr. engr. Pub. Utilities City of Riverside, 1967—69; planning engr. Riverside County Flood Control Dist., 1969-77, asst. chief flood control engr., 1977-88; gen. mgr., chief engr. Riverside County Waste Mgmt. Dept., 1988—2002; ret., 2002; cons. engr., 2003—. Bd. trustees First United Meth. Ch. of Riverside, chmn. 2000-01. 1st lt. U.S. Army, 1962-65. Mem. ASCE (Young Engr. of Yr. 1974), Solid Waste Assn. N.Am., So. Calif. Waste Mgmt. Forum (pres. 1998-99), Riverside County/San Bernardino City Engrs. (pres. 1992), Kiwanis (pres. Uptown Riverside chpt. 1980-81, Golden Rule award 1979). E-mail: rnelson01@earthlink.net.

NELSON, ROBERT CHARLES, retired publishing executive; b. Phila., Dec. 10, 1924; s. Charles Emil and Florence E. (Kelly) N.; m. Jeanne H. Wallace, Mar. 10, 1945; children— John R., Barbara J., Nancy A. Student, The Citadel, 1942-43; ME, Stevens Inst. Tech., 1949. Asst. mech. supt. N.Y. News, N.Y.C., 1949-52; with Detroit News, 1952—, prodn. mgr., 1952-69, ops. mgr., 1969-75, v.p., 1973-79, gen. mgr., 1975-81, pres., 1981-87, pres., pub., 1982-87, spl. asst. to chmn., 1987—90; exec. v.p. newspaper div. Evening News Assn., Detroit, 1978-87; ret., 1990. Bd. dirs., sec. Greater Detroit Safety Council, 1973—; bd. dirs. Engring. Sci. Fair, Detroit, 1975—; bd. dirs., mem. exec. com. Better Bus. Bur., Detroit, 1976— Vol. All Children's Hosp., 1997—; trustee New Detroit, 1980—. With USNR, 1943-46, PTO. Mem. Engring. Soc. Detroit, Greater Detroit C. of C. (bd. dirs. 1980—, vice chmn. 1985—), Acad. Sr. Profls. at Eckerd Coll., Detroit Club, Orchard Lake Country Club, Adcraft Club of Detroit, Econ. Club, St. Petersburg Yacht Club, St. Anthony's Hosp. Aux., Brookwood, SCORE; vol. All Children's Hosp.

NELSON, ROBERT EDDINGER, retired management consultant; b. Mentone, Ind., Mar. 2, 1928; s. Arthur Irven and Tural Cecile (Eddinger) N.; m. Carol J., Nov. 24, 1951; children: Janet K., Eric P. BA, Northwestern U., 1949; LHD, Iowa Wesleyan Coll., 1969, North Ctrl. Coll., 1987. Asst. dir. alumni rels. Northwestern U., Evanston, Ill., 1950-51; v.p., dir. pub. rels. Iowa Wesleyan Coll., Mt. Pleasant, 1955-58; vice chancellor for devel. U. Kansas City, 1959—61; v.p. instl. devel. Ill. Inst. Tech., Chgo., 1961-68; pres. Robert Johnston Corp., Oak Brook, Ill., 1968-69, Robert E. Nelson Assocs., Inc., Oak Brook, 1969—2004; ret., 2004. Bd. dirs. Chautauqua Workshop in Fund Raising and Instl. Relations, Continental Bank of Oak Brook Terr., The Sun Cos.; nat. conf. chmn. and program dir. Am. Coll. Pub. Relations Assn., 1961; trustee, Iowa Wesleyan Coll., 1962-68; faculty mem. Ind. U. Workshops on Coll. and Univ. Devel., 1963-65, Loretto Heights Summer Inst. for Fund Raising and Pub. Relations, 1964-68; mem. Pub. Review Panel for Grants Programs, Lilly Endowment, Inc., 1975. Contbr. chpt. to Handbook of College and University Administration, 1970. With U.S. Army, 1951-54. Mem.: Chgo. Soc. Fundraising Execs., Nat. Small Bus. Assn., Nat. Soc. Fundraisers, Pub. Rels. Soc. Am., Coun. Fin. Aid to Edn. (bd. dirs. 1957—63), Union League, Internat. Club (Chgo.), Blue Key, Execs. Club, Club Internat., DuPage Club, Econ. Club, Masons, Delta Tau Delta. Methodist. Home: 5 Oakbrook Club Dr N101 Oak Brook IL 60523-1348

NELSON, ROBERT LOUIS, lawyer; b. Dover, NH, Aug. 10, 1931; s. Albert Louis and Alice (Rogers) N.; m. Rita Jean Hutchins, June 11, 1955; children: Karen, Robin Andrea. BA, Bates Coll., Lewiston, Maine, 1956; LLB, Georgetown U., 1959. Bar: D.C. 1960. With U.S. Commn. Civil Rights,

1958-63, AID, 1963-66; program sec. U.S. Mission to Brazil, 1965-66; exec. dir. Lawyers Com. Civil Rights Under Law, 1966-70; dep. campaign mgr. Muskie for Pres., 1970-72; v.p. Perpetual Corp., Houston, 1972-74; sr. v.p., gen. counsel Washington Star, 1974-76; pres. broadcast div. Washington Star Communications, Inc., 1976-77; asst. sec. of army U.S. Dept. Def., 1977-79; spl. advisor to chief N.G. Bur., Dept. Def., 1980-85; pres., dir. Mid-Md. Communications Corp., 1981-85; ptnr. Verner, Liipfert, Bernhard, McPherson and Hand, 1979-87; gen. counsel Paralyzed Vets. Am., 1988-99, sr. counsel, 2000—. Vice chmn. D.C. Redevel. Land Agy., 1976-77; bd. dirs. Friends of Nat. Zoo, 1975—89, pres., 1982-84; bd. dirs. Downtown Progress, 1976-77, Fed. City Coun., 1976-77, 83-87, Pennsylvania Ave. Devel. Corp., 1976-77, Cmty. Found. Greater Washington, 1977-78, Pep Direct, 2003—; trustee Wolfe's Neck Farm Found., 2001—. Served with AUS, 1953-54. Mem. ABA, D.C. Bar Assn., Army Navy Club (Washington). Democrat. Episcopalian. Home (Summer): Robins Nest Orrs Island ME 04066 Home (Winter): 11 Zeitler Farm Rd Brunswick ME 04011

NELSON, RODERICK D. communications executive; BSEE, U. Minn., 1982. From mem. staff to chief tech. officer, exec. v.p. AT&T Wireless Svcs., Inc., Redmond, Wash., 1985—98, chief tech. officer, 1998—. exec. v.p., 1998—. Bd. dir. Tropian, Inc. Office: AT&T Wireless Services Inc 7277 164th Ave NE Bldg 1 Redmond WA 98052

NELSON, ROGER HUGH, management educator, corporate consultant, business executive; b. Spring City, Utah, Mar. 7, 1931; s. Hugh Devere and Maudella Sarah (Larsen) N.; m. DeEtte Munk, Aug. 26, 1955 (dec. Sept. 1998); children— Steven R., Deanne, Mark L. BS, U. Utah, 53, MS, 1953; Ed.D., Columbia U., 1958. Mem. faculty U. Utah Coll. Bus., 1953-97, prof. mgmt., 1970-97, prof. emeritus, 1997—, dir. programs in emerging bus., 1989-97, chmn. mgmt. dept., 1976-82, asst. dean, 1969-74; dir. MBA integrative field studies, 1993-96; pres. David Eccles Sch. of Bus. Faculty, 1995-96; mem. faculty Utah Mgmt. Inst., 1968-75; v.p. Computer Logic Corp., 1970-73; pres. Am. Leisure & Sports Investment Corp., 1973-75, Oil Resources, Inc., 1980-88, Puma Energy Corp., 1981-88, The Ultimate Choice Catalog Co., 1986—. Fin. and mgmt. cons., 1965—; founder Utah Small Bus. Devel. Ctr., U. Utah, 1979; trustee Utah Tech. Fin. Corp., 1998-2003; chmn. Am. Recreation and Sports, Inc., 1996—. Author: Personal Money Management, 1973, The Utah Entrepreneur's Guide, 1995, also articles, reports, manuals. Active local Am. Heart Assn., Am. Cancer Soc. campaigns; mem. exec. bd. Utah Opera Co., 1981-85, gen. bd., 1985-89. Danforth Teaching fellow, 1957 Mem. Acad. Mgmt., Adminstrv. Mgmt. Soc., NEA, AAUP, Phi Kappa Phi, Beta Gamma Sigma, Phi Delta Kappa, Delta Phi Epsilon. Inventor comml. color separation camera and related dye-transfer processes. Home: 2662 Skyline Dr Salt Lake City UT 84108-2855

NELSON, RON, composer, conductor, educator; b. Joliet, Ill., Dec. 14, 1929; s. Walter E. and Lois (Fulton) N.; m. Helen Mitchell, 1954 (dec. 1967); children: Marc W., Kristen R. Mus.B., Eastman Sch. Music, 1952, Mus.M., 1953, Mus.D., 1956; postgrad., L'École Normale, Normale, Paris, 1954-55; MA, Brown U., 1959. Prof. Brown U., Providence, chmn. dept. music, 1963-73, Acuff chair of excellence in creative arts, 1991, prof. emeritus, 1993—. Film composer, HEW, Eastman Kodak, ARC, Columbia Pictures, commns. from, Cin. Symphony, Lima Symphony, Rochester Philharmonic, R.I. Philharm., Am. Bapt. Soc., U. Minn., Dartmouth Coll., Brown U., New Music Ensemble, LaSalle Coll., Western Mich. U., Classic Chorale, U.S. Air Force Band, Nat. Symphony Orch.; composer (for orch.) Savannah River Holiday, 1954, Sarabande: For Katherine in April, 1954, (opera) The Birthday of the Infanta, 1956; (cantata) The Christmas Story, 1958: (for orch.) Tocatta for Orchestra, 1963; (oratorio) What is Man?, 1964; (orch./wind ensemble) Rocky Point Holiday, 1968-69; This is the Orchestra; (orch. and tape trilogy) Trilogy: JFK-MLK-RFK, 1969; (choral) Prayer of Emperor of China, 1973; (choral) Thy Truth is Great, 1973; (choral) Psalm 95, 1974; (orch.) Five Pieces for Orchestra after Paintings by Andrew Wyeth, 1975; (choral) Prayer of St. Francis of Assisi, 1976; (orch.) Meditation and Dance for Orch., 1976; (choral) Six Pieces for Chamber Ensemble, 1977, Four Choral Pieces After the Seasons, 1978, Three Autumnal Sketches, 1979, Here We Come As in The Beginning, 1979, Mass in Honor of St. LaSalle, 1981, Three Nocturnal Pieces, 1982, Three Seasonal Reflections, 1982; composer: Fanfare for a Celebration, 1982; (choral) On Christmas Night, 1982; Medieval Suite, 1983; (choral) Dreams, 1982; (band) Fanfare for a Celebration, 1983; (cello-piano) And the Moon Rose Golden, 1983; (band) Medieval Suite, 1983; composer: Aspen Jubilee, 1984; (organ-brass) Pebble Beach Sojourn, 1984; (chorus-band) Te Deum Laudamus, 1985; (choral) Lost and Found, 1985, Light Years, 1985, Three Settings of the Moon, 1985, (strings-trumpet) Elegy, 1986, (brass) Brevard Fanfare, 1986, (chorus/band) Prime: The Hour of Sunrise, 1987, (choral) White, 1987, (choral) Another Spring, 1987, (choral) Miniatures from a Bestiary Parts I and II, 1988, (saxophone-band) Danza Capriccio, 1988, (choral) Three Pieces after Tennyson (1988), (choral) Three Mountain Ballads, 1989, (brass-winds-percussion) Fanfare for the Hour of Sunrise, 1989, (band) Morning Alleluias for the Winter Solstice, 1989, (band) Resonances, 1990; (chorus) And This Shall Be for Music, 1990, Invoking the Powers, 1991, Songs of Praise and Reconciliation, 1991, The Meadow, 1991, (band) Lauds: Praise High Day, 1992, To the Airborne, 1991, Passacaglia (Homage on B-A-C-H), 1992, Chaconne (In Memoriam), 1994, Sonoran Desert Holiday, 1994, (band), Epiphanies (Fanfares and Chorales bands), 1995, Courtly Airs and Dances, 1995, (orch.) Resonances II, 1996, (orch., band) Resonances III, 1996,(orch.) Panels (Epiphanies II), 1996, The Music of Ron Nelson, 1996, (euphonium and winds) Night Song, 1998, (band) Fanfare for the New Millennium, 1999, Proclaim This Day for Music, 2002, The Meadow (chorus), 2004. Recipient ASCAP awards, 1962-20047, Found. award for World tour, 1965-66, Nat. Band Assn. award, 1992, John Philip Sousa medal of merit, 1994; Fulbright fellow, 1954; Ford Found. commn., 1962, NEA grantee, 1973, 76, 79; awarded Acuff Chair of Excellence on the Creative Arts, 1991; winner Am. Bandmasters Assn. Ostwald Contest, 1993, Am. Band Assn. contest, 1992, Sudler Internat. Wind Band Competition, 1993.

NELSON, RONALD ERWIN, not-for-profit fundraiser; b. Painesville, Ohio, Sept. 29, 1944; s. Everett Erwin and Betty Jane (Boehnke) Nelson; m. Paula Beth Manz, July 12, 1969; children: Jason, Kristin. BS in Edn., Concordia Coll., 1968; MEd, Memphis State U., 1973. Prin. Holy Cross Luth. Sch., Memphis, 1968—75, C.C. Hadden Sch., Painesville, 1975—80; office mgr. Alpers Ohio, Inc., North Randall, 1980—81; dir. pub. rels. Concordia Sem., Fort Wayne, Ind., 1981—87; mgr. stewardship interpretation Internat. Ctr. Luth. Ch.-Mo. Synod, St. Louis, 1987—95, assoc. dir. stewardship, 1995—2000; v.p. mktg. Luth. Ch.-Mo. Synod Found., 2000—01, dir. mission support, 2001—. Cons. WLAB-FM Radio, Fort Wayne, 1984; cons. direct mail Luth. Ch.-Mo. Synod, St. Louis, 1982—. Author (booklet): Planning School Buildings, 1974; Creator, host TV program, 1980; editor (newspaper): Called to Serve, 1981—87. Coord. voters Sen. Howard Baker Campaign, 1972; corr. sec. Young Reps. Shelby County, Memphis, 1972—75. Mem.: St. Louis Direct Mktg. Assn. (bd. dirs., treas. 1991), Internat. Assn. Bus. Communicators (chmn. edn. com., bd. dirs. 1984, Bronze Quill 1984), Auto Plate Collectors Assn. (Nat. Recognition award 1979), Fort Wayne C. of C. (pub. rels. com. 1981—87, conv. bur. 1983—87). Avocations: photography, golf, swimming, collecting license plates. Home: 9826 Affton View Ct Saint Louis MO 63123-6273 Office: Luth Ch-Mo Synod Internat Ctr 1333 S Kirkwood Rd Saint Louis MO 63122-7226 Business E-Mail: ronald.nelson@lcms.org.

NELSON, RONALD HARVEY, animal science educator, researcher; b. Union Grove, Wis., Aug. 10, 1918; s. Harvey August and Myra Frances (Sheen) N.; m. Elizabeth Jane Lappley, Apr. 13, 1940; children: David Peter, Marjorie Jean, Linda Louise, Ronda Elizabeth. BS, U. Wis., 1939; MS, Okla. A&M U., 1941; PhD, Iowa State U., 1943. Mem. faculty Mich. State U., 1946-85, prof., head, animal sci. dept., 1950-84, prof. emeritus, 1985—; chief of party Mich. State U. tech. assistance project Balcarce, Pcia, Buenos Aires, 1966-68. Recipient Grad. Distinction award Okla State U., 1987, Nat. Saddle and Sirloin Portrait award, 1990. Fellow Am. Soc. Animal Sci. (Internat. Animal Agr. award 1978, Animal Industry award 1984); mem. Am. Angus Assn. (chmn. research advisory com. 1956-60), Mich. Angus Assn. (pres. 1977-78), Animal Sci. Assn., Sigma Xi, Phi Kappa Phi, Alpha Zeta. Home: 1545 N Harrison Rd East Lansing MI 48823-1801

NELSON, RONALD L. film company executive; Exec. v.p., CFO Paramount Comm. Inc. (formerly Gulf & Western Inc), 1987-94, bd. dirs., 1992; CFO, founding mem. DreamWorks SKG, Univeral City, Calif., 1994—. Bd. dirs. Advanced Tissue Scis., Inc., 1997—. Office: DreamWorks SKG 100 Universal Plaza Universal City CA 91608

NELSON, ROY LESLIE, cardiac surgeon, researcher, educator; b. N.Y.C., May 3, 1941; s. Sam and Anna (Kaminetsky) N.; m. Anne Judith Sachs, Jan. 6, 1973; children: Samuel Phillip, Amy Joy, Jill Heather. BS, Lafayette Coll., Easton, Pa., 1963; MD magna cum laude, Free U. Brussels, Belgium, 1971. Cert. MD Am. Bd. Surgery, Am. Bd. Thoracic Surgery; cert. in laser surgery. Intern surgery Bronx Mcpl. Hosp./Albert Einstein Coll. Medicine, 1971-72; resident surgery NYU Med. Ctr. Bellevue Hosp., N.Y.C., 1972-74; thoracic rschr. UCLA Med. Ctr., L.A., Calif., 1974-76; resident surgery NYU Med. Ctr. Bellevue Hosp., 1976-78, fellow cardiothoracic surgery NYU Med. Ctr., 1978-80; asst. attending cardiothoracic surgeon dept. surgery North Shore U. Hosp., Manhasset, N.Y., 1984-90, assoc. attending cardiothoracic surgeon, 1984-90, attending cardiothoracic surgeon, 1991—, asst. dir. dept. surgery, 1990—. Rschr. Bureau Biological Rsch., New Brunswick, N.J., 1963-64, Surg. Rsch. Lab., St. Pierre Hosp., Free U. Brussels, 1969-71, Divsn. Thoracic Sugery, UCLA, 1974-76; physician-in-charge Cardiovascular Rsch. Lab., North Shore U. Hosp., 1980—; teaching asst. Dept. Surgery, Albert Einstein Coll. Medicine, 1971-72, NYU Med. Ctr., 1972-74, 76-77; clin. instr. surgery NYU Med. Ctr., 1977-80; asst. prof. surgery Cornell U. Med. Coll., 1980—. Author: (with others) Plasmapheresis, 1982, Pathophysiology and Techniques of Cardiopulmonary Bypass II, 1983; contbr. articles to profl. jours. Recipient Barnett Meml. prize NYU, 1974, Physician's Recognition award AMA, 1986. Fellow ACS, Am. Coll. Angiology, Am. Coll. Cardiology, Am. Coll. Chest Physicians (coun. critical care 1990—), Am. Soc. for Laser Medicine and Surgery, N.Y. Cardiological Soc.; mem. AAAS, Am. Heart Assn. (rsch com. 1982—, coun. cardiovascular surgery 1984—), Am. Soc. Artificial Internal Organs, Am. Soc. Extra-Corporeal Tech., Internat. Soc. for Artificial Organs (reviewer artificial organs 1984—), Internat. Soc. for Heart Transplantation, Med. Soc. State N.Y., Nassau County Med. Soc., N.Y. Acad Scis., N.Y. Soc. for Thoracic Surgery, N.Am. Society for Pacing and Electrophysiology, Soc. Critical Care Medicine, Soc. Thoracic Surgeons, Spencer Surg. Soc., Undersea Med. Soc. Achievements include research in radical transplantation of the lungs studying different experimental procedures, the importance of alkalosis in maintenance of "ideal" blood pH during hypothermia, the effects of profound topical cardiac hypothermia on myocardial blood flow, metabolism, compliance and function, myocardial preservation during cardiopulmonary bypass, citrate reperfusion of ischemic hearts on cardiopulmonary bypass, improved myocardial performance after aortic cross clamping by combining pharmacologic arrest with topical hypothermia, the effects of hypothermia on regional mycardial blood flow and metabolism during cardiopulmonary bypass, optimizing myocardial supply/demand balance with adrenergic drugs during cardiopulmonary resuscitation, hemoconcentration by ultrafiltration, following cardiopulmonary bypass, intra-aortic balloon rupture, cocaine induced acute aortic dissection, the role of cardioplegia oxygen concentration in limiting myocardial reperfusion injury, the role of morbid obesity and diabetes in the outcome of coronary bypass surgery, isolated intra-thoracic trauma following deployment of an air bag. Office: North Shore U Hosp 300 Community Dr Manhasset NY 11030-3801

NELSON, RUSSELL MARION, surgeon, educator; b. Salt Lake City, Sept. 9, 1924; s. Marion C. and Edna (Anderson) N.; m. Dantzel White, Aug. 31, 1945; children: Marsha Nelson McKellar, Wendy Nelson Maxfield, Gloria Nelson Irion, Brenda Nelson Miles, Sylvia Nelson Webster, Emily Nelson Wittwer (dec.), Laurie Nelson Marsh, Rosalie Nelson Ringwood, Marjorie Nelson Helsten, Russell Marion Jr. BA, U. Utah, 1945, MD, 1947; PhD in Surgery, U. Minn., 1954; ScD (hon.), Brigham Young U., 1970; DMS (hon.), Utah State U., 1989; LHD (hon.), Snow Coll., 1994. Diplomate: Am. Bd. Surgery, Am. Bd. Thoracic Surgery (dir. 1972-78). Intern U. Minn. Hosps., Mpls., 1947, asst. resident surgery, 1948-51; first asst. resident surgery Mass. Gen. Hosp., Boston, 1953-54; sr. resident surgery U. Minn. Hosps., Mpls., 1954-55; practice medicine (specializing in cardiovascular and thoracic surgery), Salt Lake City, 1959-84; staff surgeon LDS Hosp., Salt Lake City, 1959-84, dir. surg. research lab., 1959-72, chief cardiovascular-thoracic surg. div., 1967-72, also bd. govs., 1970-90, vice chmn., 1979-89; staff surgeon Primary Children's Hosp., Salt Lake City, 1960; attending in surgery VA Hosp., Salt Lake City, 1955-84, Univ. Hosp., Salt Lake City, 1955-84; asst. prof. surgery Med. Sch. U. Utah, Salt Lake City, 1955-59, asst. clin. prof. surgery, 1959-66, asso. clin. prof. surgery, clin. prof., 1966-69, research prof. surgery, 1970-84, clin. prof. emeritus, 1984—; staff services Utah Biomed. Test Lab., 1970-84. Dir. tng. program cardiovascular and thoracic surgery at Univ. Utah affiliated hosps., 1967-84; mem. policyholders adv. com. New Eng. Mut. Life Ins. Co., Boston, 1976-80 Contbr. articles to profl. jours. Mem. White House Conf. on Youth and Children, 1960; bd. dirs. Internat. Cardiol. Found.; bd. govs. LDS Hosp., 1970-90, Deseret Gymnasium, 1971-75, Promised Valley Playhouse, 1970-79; mem. adv. com. U.S. Sec. of State on Religious Freedom Abroad, 1996-99. 1st lt. to capt. M.C., AUS, 1951-53. Markle scholar in med. scis., 1957-59; Fellowship of Medici Publici U. Utah Coll., 1967; Gold Medal of Merit, Argentina, 1974; named Hon. Prof. Shandong Med. U., Jinan, People's Republic of China, 1985; Old People's U., Jinan, 1986; Xi-an (People's Republic of China) Med. Coll., 1986, Legacy of Life award, 1993. Fellow A.C.S. (chmn. adv. council on thoracic surgery 1973-75), Am. Coll. Cardiology, Am. Coll. Chest Physicians; mem. Am. Assn. Thoracic Surgery, Am. Soc. Artificial Internal Organs, AMA, Dirs. Thoracic Residencies (pres. 1971-72), Utah Med. Assn. (pres. 1970-71), Salt Lake County Med. Soc., Am. Heart Assn. (exec. com. cardiovascular surgery 1972, dir. 1976-78, chmn. council cardiovascular surgery 1976-78), Utah Heart Assn. (pres. 1964-65), Soc. Thoracic Surgeons, Soc. Vascular Surgery (sec. 1968-72, pres. 1974), Utah Thoracic Soc., Salt Lake Surg. Soc., Samson Thoracic Surg. Soc., Western Soc. for Clin. Research, Soc. U. Surgeons, Am., Western, Pan-Pacific surg. assns., Inter. Am. Soc. Cardiology (bd. mgrs.), Phi Beta Kappa, Sigma Xi, Alpha Omega Alpha, Phi Kappa Phi, Sigma Chi. Mem. Ch. of Jesus Christ of Latter-day Saints (pres. Bonneville Stake 1964-71, gen. pres. Sunday sch. 1971-79, regional rep. 1979-84, Quorum of the Twelve Apostles 1984—). Office: 47 E South Temple Salt Lake City UT 84150-1200 Office Phone: 801-240-3206.

NELSON, SARAH MILLEDGE, archaeology educator; b. Miami, Fla., Nov. 29, 1931; d. Stanley and Sarah Woodman (Franklin) M.; m. Harold Stanley Nelson, July 25, 1953; children: Erik Harold, Mark Milledge, Stanley Franklin. BA, Wellesley Coll., 1953; MA, U. Mich., 1969, PhD, 1973. Instr. archaeology U. Md. extension, Seoul, Republic Korea, 1970-71; asst. prof. U. Denver, 1974-79, assoc. prof., 1979-85, prof. archaeology, 1985—, chair dept. anthropology, 1985-95, dir. women's studies program, 1985-87, John Evans prof., dir. Asian studies, 1996, vice provost for rsch., 1998—2002, interim vice provost grad. studies and rsch., 2001—02. Vis. asst. prof. U. Colo., Boulder, 1974; resident Rockefeller Ctr. in Bellagio, Italy, 1996. Co-editor: Powers of Observation, 1990, Equity Issues for Women in Archaeology, 1994; author: Archaeology of Korea, 1993, Gender in Archaeology: Analyzing Power and Prestige, 1997, 2d revised edit., 2004, (novel) Spirit Bird Journey, 1999, The Goddess Temple, 2004; co-author: Denver: An Archaeological History, 2001; editor: The Archaeology of Northeast China, 1995, Ancestors for the Pigs: Pigs in Prehistory, 1998; co-editor: In Pursuit of Gender: Worldwide Archaeological Perspectives, 2001, Ancient Queens: Archaeological Perspectives, 2003. Active Earthwatch, 1989. Recipient Outstanding Scholar award U. Denver, 1989; grantee S.W. Inst. Rsch. on Women, 1981, Acad. Korean Studies, Seoul, 1983, Internat. Cultural Soc. Korea, 1986, Colo. Hist. Fund, 1995-97, Rockefeller Found. Residency, Bellagio, Italy, Wenner-Gren Found., 2000-02, Nat. Geographic Soc., 2000—. Fellow Am. Anthrop. Assn.; mem. Soc. Am. Archaeology, Assn. Asian Studies, Royal Asiatic Soc., Sigma Xi (sec.-treas. 1978-79), Phi Beta Kappa. Democrat. Avocations: skiing, gardening. Home: 5878 S Dry Creek Ct Littleton CO 80121-1709 Office: U Denver Dept Anthropology Denver CO 80208-0001 Business E-Mail: snelson@du.edu.

NELSON, SHIRLEY W. bank executive; From jr. teller to v.p., sr. mgr. Ctrl. Bank Med. Ctr. branch, Oakland, Calif., 1966—82; founder, chmn., CEO, pres. Summit Bank, Oakland, Calif., 1982—90, chmn., CEO, 1982—, Summit Bancshares Inc. Chmn. bd. Summit Bank Found., 1998—, No. Calif. Women's Leadership Forum. Co-chmn. No. Calif. Women's League Coun.; bd. dirs. Cal State Hayward Ednl. Found. Named One of 25 Most Powerful Women in Banking, U.S. Banker Mag., 2003. Office: Summit Bancshares Inc 2969 Broadway Oakland CA 94611-5710

NELSON, STANLEY, film director, writer, film producer; BFA in film, City Coll.of N.Y. Exec. prodr. Firelight Media, N.Y.C. Fellow Am. Film Inst.; Revson fellow Columbia U.; Fulbright media fellowship com.; instr. Howard U.; juror for documentary competitions Sundance Film Festival, 2002, Independent Feature Project, 2002. Exec. prodr.: (documentaries) Two Dollars and a Dream: The Story of Madame C. J. Walker and A'lelia Walker, 1989 (Best Film of the Decade, Black Filmmaker Found.), Freedom Bags, 1990; exec. prodr., exec. prodr.: (documentaries) Free Within Ourselves, 1993, Methadone: Curse or Cure, 1997, Shattering Silences: The Case for Minority Faculty, 1997, The Black Press: Soldiers without Swords, 1999 (Alfred I. Dupont-Columbia U. award, Excellence in Broadcast Journalism, Sundance Film Festival's Freedom of Expression award Black Internat. Cinema, 1999, Best Documentary, San Francisco Film Festival, 1999, Hollywood Black Film Festival 1st Place Jury Award, 1999), Marcus Garvey: Look for Me in the Whirlwind, 2001 (Best Prodn. of the Yr., Black Filmmakers' Hall of Fame, Best Prodn. of the Yr., Black Internat. Cinema Festival, Berlin, 2002), Running: the Campaign for City Coun., 2002 (Henry Hampton award, Coun. on Foundations), The Murder of Emmett Till, 2003 (Spl. Jury Prize, Sundance Film Festival, 2003), Puerto Rico: Our Right to Decide; TV prodr.: What Can We Do About Violence?; Listening to Am. with Bill Moyers; Michael Moore's TV Nation. Office: Firelight Media 324 Convent Ave New York NY 10031

NELSON, STEVEN CRAIG, lawyer; b. Oakland, Calif., May 11, 1944; s. Eskil Manfred and Florence Lucille (Boatman) N.; m. Kathryn Cassel Stoltz, Nov. 30, 1974 (div. Apr. 1997); children: Carleton Philip, Whitney Cassel. BA in Econs. with exceptional distinction, Yale U., 1966, LLB, 1969. Bar: DC 1969, Minn. Supreme Ct. 1975, U.S. Supreme Ct. 1973, Hong Kong 2000. From atty. adviser to asst. legal adviser U.S. Dept. State, Washington, 1969-74; from assoc. to ptnr. Oppenheimer, Wolff, Foster, Shepard & Donnelly, St. Paul and Mpls., 1975-85; ptnr. Dorsey & Whitney LLP, Mpls., 1985—. Mem. bd. appeals NATO, Brussels. 197702993; adj. prof. law U. Minn, 1980-86; spkr. in field. Contbr. articles to profl. jours. Mem. ABA (chmn. internat. law and practice 1988-89), Minn. Bar Assn., Am. Fgn. Law Assn., Am. Soc. Internat. Law, Internat. Bar Assn. (mem. coun. 1996-2000), Union Internat. des Avocats (1st v.p. 1991-94), Minikahda Club. Avocations: golf, tennis, skiing, sailing. Office: Dorsey & Whitney 50 S 6th St Ste 1500 Minneapolis MN 55402-1498

NELSON, STEVEN DWAYNE, lawyer; b. Austin, Minn. m. Vicky L. Staab, July 6, 1990. BA in English, SUNY, Buffalo, 1972; JD, U. Mont., 1978. Bar: Mont. 1978, U.S. Dist. Ct. Mont. 1978. Sole practice, Bozeman, Mont., 1978—; city prosecutor City of Bozeman, 1979-82; city atty. City of Ennis (Mont.), 1980-82; prof. U. Great Falls, Mont., 1990—, mediator, 1998—. Mem. Mont. State Bar Assn., Phi Delta Phi. Avocations: fishing, skiing, hiking. Home and Office: 4590 Maiden Rock Rd Bozeman MT 59715-7769 E-mail: snelson@ugf.edu.

NELSON, STEVEN LESLIE, surgeon; BA in Chemistry, Pacific Union Coll., Angwin, Calif., 1975; MD, Loma Linda U., 1978. Diplomate Am. Bd. Surgery. Intern Loma Linda U. Med. Ctr., 1979, resident in gen. surgery, 1980-83; surgeon U.M. Bryner M.D., Inc., Yreka, Calif., 1984—. Mem. staff Fairchild Med. Ctr., Yreka. Mem. Siskiyou County Pub. Health Adv. Bd., Yreka, 1990—. Fellow ACS; mem. AMA, Calif. Med. Assn., Alpha Omega Alpha. Office: U M Bryner MD Inc 814 N Main St Yreka CA 96097-2538 Office Phone: 530-842-1293.

NELSON, STEWART, computer company executive; With IBM; sr. v.p. Novell, 1994, COO, 2000—. Office: Novell Inc 122 E 1700 S Provo UT 84606-6194

NELSON, STUART OWEN, agricultural engineer, researcher, educator; b. Pilger, Nebr., Jan. 23, 1927; s. Irvin Andrew and Agnes Emilie (Nissen) N.; m. Carolyn Joye Fricke, Dec. 27, 1953 (dec. Nov. 1975); children: Richard Lynn, Jana Sue; m. Martha Ellen White Fuller, Apr. 8, 1979. BS in Agrl. Engring., U. Nebr., 1950; MS in Agrl. Engring., 1952; MA in Physics, U. Nebr., 1954; PhD in Engring., Iowa State U., 1972; DSc (hon.), U. Nebr., 1989. Grad. asst. U. Nebr., Lincoln, 1952-54, rsch. assoc., 1954-60, assoc. prof., 1960-72, prof., 1972-76. Project leader Farm Electrification Rsch., Agrl. Rsch. Svc., USDA, Lincoln, 1954-59, rsch. investigations leader, 1959-72, rsch. leader 1972-76, rsch. agrl. engr. Russell Rsch. Ctr., Athens, Ga., 1976—; adj. prof. U. Ga., 1976—; sci. adv. coun. Am. Seed Rsch. Found.; mem. CAST Task Force on Irradiation for Food Preservation and Pest Control; adv. com. grain moisture measurement Nat. Coun. Weights and Measures; mem. sci. bd. 4th Internat. Conf. on Phys. Properties Agrl. Materials, Prague, 1985. Assoc. editor Jour. Microwave Power 1975-76, 95-2000; contbr. more than 500 articles to sci. and tech. jours. With USN, 1946-48. Recipient HM Crops and Soils award Am. Soc. Agronomy, 1966, Founders Gold medal Fed. Engr. of Yr. NSPE, 1985, Superior Svc. award USDA, 1986, Profl. Achievement Citation Engring. award Iowa State U., 1987, Ga. Engring. Found. medal of honor, 1999; named to U. Nebr. Biol. Systems Engring. Hall of Fame, 1999, USDA-ARS Sci. Hall of Fame, 2002. Fellow IEEE, Am. Soc. Agrl. Engrs. (Tech. Paper award 1965, 94, Engr. of Yr. award Ga. sect. 1988, chmn. Ga. sect. 1988-89, Cyrus Hall McCormick-Jerome Increase Case Gold Medal award 2000), Internat. Microwave Power Inst. (Decade award 1981), AAAS; mem. The Electromagnetics Acad., Internat. Soc. Agromaterials Sci. and Engring., Internat. Dielectrics Soc., Ga. Soc. Profl. Engrs. (Engr. of Yr. in Govt. award 1991, Engr. of Yr. 1998), Nat. Acad. Engring., Nat. Soc. Profl. Engrs., Orgn. Profl. Employees of Dept. of Agrl. (pres. Athens area chpt. 1984-86, nat. coun. rep. 1988-95, Profl. of Yr. award 1987), Athens Optimist (pres. 1980-81, 2000-2001, lt. gov. Ga. dist. 1983-84, Optimist of Yr. award 1982, disting. and outstanding lt. gov. Ga. dist. 1985), Assn. for Microwave Power in Europe for Rsch. and Edn., Sigma Xi, Sigma Tau, Gamma Sigma Delta, Tau Beta Pi. Methodist. Home: 270 Idylwood Dr Athens GA 30605-4635 Office: USDA Agrl Rsch Svc Russell Rsch Ctr PO Box 5677 Athens GA 30604-5677

NELSON, THOMAS ADAMS, electrical engineer, transportation consultant; b. Berkeley, Calif., Aug. 26, 1921; s. Thomas Fleming and Mabel Margaretta (Adams) N.; m. Mary Anne Mares, July 12, 1958. AA, LA City Coll., 1942; BS, U. So. Calif., 1949, MS, 1953; postgrad. cert. bus. mgmt., UCLA, 1970. Registered profl. engr., Calif. Design engr. LA Dept. Water and Power, 1950—53, quality assurance engr., resident engr. factories in U.S., Europe and Japan, 1953—65, asst. chief quality assurance engr., 1965—68, chief quality assurance engr., 1968—72, sr. engr. in charge oper. engring., 1972—77, prin. engr., mgr. comm., transmission lines, sta. maintenance and distbn. trouble, 1977—80, rail transp. cons. on coal delivery to elec. generating stas. Ariz. and Nev., 1973-79, rep. to Calif. Power Pool, 1975-77; cons. engr., transp. cons. LA, 1980—. Reviewer rail transit plans So. Calif. Rapid Transit Dist., LA County Transp. Commn., LA County Met. Transp. Authority, Orange County Transit Dist., Caltrans, San Diego Met. Transit Devel. Bd., 1978—. Editor, maj. author Railroad Chronology Compendium, 1976, 50 Years of Railroading in Southern California, 2001; editor Jour. Pacific R.R. Soc., 1980-84, 87-94, cons. editor, 1994—; contbr. articles to profl. jours. Mem. Citizens Adv. Commn. for Met. Rail, Hollywood, Calif., 1982-84, Met. Rail CORE Forum, 1987; advisor Beijing ofcl. regarding rail transit, 2002, Spokane Transit Authority, 2003. Served to capt. USAAF, 1942-45, ETO. Mem. IEEE (sr.), Vehicular Tech. Soc., Pacific R.R. Soc. (bd. dirs. 1977-80, 82-83, v.p. 1986, pres. 1987-89, publs. mgr. 1981-94), Eta Kappa Nu, Tau Beta Pi, Phi Kappa Phi.

NELSON, THOMAS C. manufacturing executive; BS in Indsl. Engring., Stanford U.; MBA, Harvard U. Investment banker Morgan Stanley & Co.; spl. asst. to Sec. of Def. Richard B. Cheney U.S. Dept. Defense, Washington, 1992; gen. ptnr. Wakefield Group, 1988; CEO, pres. Nat. Gypsum, Charlotte, 1999—. Vice-chmn, policy advisory bd. Harvard U. Joint Ctr. for Housing Studies, 2003—. Office: Nat Gypsum Co 2001 Rexford Rd Charlotte NC 28211

NELSON, THOMAS G. federal judge; b. Idaho Falls, Idaho, 1936; Student, U. Idaho, 1955—59, LLB, 1962. Ptnr. Parry, Robertson, and Daly, Twin Falls, Idaho, 1965—79, Nelson, Rosholt, Robertson, Tolman and Tucker, Twin Falls, 1979; judge U.S. Ct. of Appeals (9th cir.), Boise, Idaho, 1990—. With Idaho Air N.G., 1962—65, with USAR, 1965—68. Mem.: ABA, Idaho Law Found., Am. Bd. Trial Advocates (pres. Idaho chpt.), Idaho Assn. Def. Counsel, Idaho State Bar (pres., bd. commrs.), Am. Coll. Trial Lawyers, Am. Bar Found., Phi Alpha Delta. Office: US Ct Appeals 9th Circuit 304 N Eighth St PO Box 1339 Boise ID 83701-1339

NELSON, VIRGINIA SIMSON, pediatrician, educator, physiatrist; b. L.A. d. Jerome and Virginia (Kuppler) Simson; children: Eric, Paul. AB, Stanford U., 1963, MD, 1970; MPH, U. Mich., 1974. Diplomate Am. Bd. Pediatrics, Am. Bd. Phys. Medicine and Rehab. Pediatrician Inst. Study Mental Retardation and Related Disabilities, U. Mich., Ann Arbor, 1973-80; mem. faculty phys. medicine and rehab. dept. U. Mich. Med. Ctr., Ann Arbor, 1980-83, 85—, resident in phys. medicine and rehab., 1983-85, chief pediatric phys. medicine and rehab. physician, 1985—. Contbr. articles to profl. jours. Office: Univ Mich Med Ctr F7822 Mott Hospital Ann Arbor MI 48109-0230 also: Pediat Phys Medicine and Rehab 325 E Eisenhower Dr Ste 100 U Mich Campus Zip 0744 Ann Arbor MI 48108

NELSON, VITA JOY, editor, publisher; b. N.Y.C., Dec. 9, 1937; d. Leon Abraham and Bertha (Sher) Reiner; m. Lester Nelson, Aug. 27, 1961; children: Lee Reiner, Clifford Samuel, Cara Ritchie. BA, Boston U., 1959. Promotion copywriter Street & Smith, N.Y.C., 1958-59; asst. to mng. editor Mademoiselle Mag., N.Y.C., 1959-60; mcpl. bond trader Granger & Co., N.Y.C., 1960-63; founder, editor, pub. Westchester Mag., Mamaroneck, N.Y., 1968-80, L.I. Mag., 1973-78, founder, editor, pub., pres. Moneypaper, 1981—. Pub. The Guide to Dividend Reinvestment Plans, Direct Investing; founder MP63 Fund; pres. Moneypaper Advisor Inc., 1999—. Author: (with Donald Korn) Create and Manage Your Own Mutual Fund, 1994. Bd. dirs. United Way of Westchester/Putnam County, 1998—2002; bd. govs., v.p. Am. Jewish Com., Westchester, 1979—89. Recipient citation Coun. Arts, 1972, Media award Pub. Rels. Soc. Am., 1974. Mem. Women in Comms. (Outstanding Communicator award 1983). Democrat. Home: Pleasant Ridge Rd Harrison NY 10528-1004 Office: The Moneypaper Inc 555 Theodore Frend Ave Rye NY 10580 Office Phone: 914-925-0022. E-mail: vitajoy@aol.com.

NELSON, WALDEMAR STANLEY, civil engineer, consultant; b. New Orleans, July 8, 1916; s. Bernard Stanley and Mary Lockett (Hutson) N.; widowed; children: Mary Sue Nelson Roniger, Martha Nelson Frost, Charles W., Virginia Nelson Dodge, Kenneth H. BS in Mech. and Elec. Engring., Tulane U., 1936. Registered civil, elec. and mech. engr., 43 states. Jr. engr. A. M. Lockett & Co., 1936-37; civil engr. Jeff. Lake Sulphur Co., Brazoria, Tex., 1937-38; chief survey party N.O. Pub. Belt. R.R., New Orleans, 1938; resident engr. James M. Todd, Buras, La., 1938-39; pvt. practice New Orleans, 1939-40; asst. chief engr. W. Horace Williams Co., Camp Claiborne, La., 1940-41; sr. engr. U.S. Engr. Dept., Camp Claiborne, 1941-44; prin. Waldemar S. Nelson and Co. Inc., New Orleans, 1945—, dir. emeritus, 2003—. Past chmn. La. State Bd. Registration Profl. Engrs. and Land Surveyors; founding mem., pres. bd. advisors sch. engring. Tulane U. Chmn. Tulane Alumni Fund, Mems' Coun., 1984; mem. bd. visitors Tulane U.; active The Chamber/New Orleans, Boy Scouts Am.; past chmn. Com. of 50; past pres. bd. commrs. New Orleans City Pk. Improvement Assn.; mem. exec. bd. Christmas New Orleans, 1988; past sr. warden of vestry St. Andrew's Episcopal Ch., mem. property com.; past chmn. bd. dirs. St. Andrew's Episcopal Sch.; past pres. bd. trustees St. Martin's Protestant Episcopal Sch.; trustee Tulane Engring. Found.; bd. dirs. River Region, MetroVision. Recipient Outstanding Engring. Alumnus award Tulane U., 1976, Honor award Constrn. Industry Assn. New Orleans, Inc., 1982, Role Model of Yr. award Young Leadership Coun., 1987, Vol. of Yr. award Tulane U. Alumni Affairs, 1992, George Washington Honor medal Freedom's Found. at Valley Forge New Orleans chpt., 1998, Weiss award Nat. Conf. for Cmty. and Justice, 1998, Times-Picayune Loving Cup, 2001. Fellow: NSPE (past. v.p., past chmn. bd. ethical rev.), ASME (life; past. chmn. New Orleans sect.), ASCE (life); mem.: French-Am. C. of C. (pres. La. chpt. 1992—93, chmn. 1994, pres. 1996—97, 1998, named to Bus. Hall of Fame 1997, UNO's First Citizen of the Learning Soc. award 1998), Soc. Tulane Engrs. (past pres.), La. Engring. Found. (trustee 1990, treas. 1991, sec. 1994—95, pres. 1995—96, 1997—99), Soc. Naval Archs. and Marine Engrs., La. Engring. Soc. (hon.; past pres., Charles M. Kerr Pub. Rels. award, Leo M. Odom Profl. Svcs. award, A.B. Paterson medal, Andrew M. Lockett medal), Am. Pub. Works Assn. (life), Soc. Am. Mil. Engrs., Nat. Coun. Engring. Examiners (past treas., Disting. Svc. award), Am. Acad. Environ. Engrs. (diplomate), IEEE, La. Southeast Council, Engrs. Club New Orleans (past pres.), Tulane Alumni Assn. (past. pres.), Boy Scouts of Am. (Disting. Citizen award 2001), Eta Kappa Nu, Pi Tau Sigma, Tau Beta Pi. Avocations: fishing, boating, gardening, shop work, photography. Office: Waldemar S Nelson & Co Inc 1200 Saint Charles Ave New Orleans LA 70130-4334 Business E-Mail: Waldemar.Nelson@wsnelson.com.

NELSON, WALLACE JAY, patent attorney; b. Patrick County, Va., Aug. 1, 1926; s. Willie Everitt and Mollie Jane (Tudor) N.; m. Helen Nixon Blount Nelson, Oct. 27, 1951; children: Jane Elizabeth Shuart, Wallace J. Nelson Jr. BS, Va. Tech., Blacksburg, 1951; JD, The Am. U., Washington, 1960. Patent atty., U.S. Patent Office, Va. State Bar. Chem. lab. tech., analystical chemist Dept. U.S. Army, Radford, Va., 1951-55; patent examiner U.S. Patent Office, Washington, 1955-61; patent atty. Nat. Aeronautics and Space Adminstrn., Hampton, Va., 1961-86, pvt. practice, Hampton, Va., 1986—2002. Inventor Slosh Alleviator, 1969. Mem. AF&AM #306 Masonic Lodge (past master), Scottish Rite of Freemasonry USA, Va. State bar. Methodist. Avocations: spectator sports, reading, golf, fishing. Home: 34 Salt Pond Rd Hampton VA 23664-1736 E-mail: walheln@aol.com.

NELSON, WALTER HENRY, communications consultant, author; b. Munich, Mar. 23, 1928; parents Am. citizens; m. Rose Marie Carson, Mar. 4, 1950; children: Roger Stuart, Gregory Eugene, Victoria Eugenie; 2d marriage to Rita L. Christoffersen, June 30, 1962; 1 child, Samantha Christine. Student, NYU, 1944, Norwich U., 1944-46, Columbia U., 1949-50. News editor, info. analyst Radio Free Europe, N.Y.C., Munich, 1950-53; dir. mag. info. Am. Heritage Found., N.Y.C., 1953-55; mag. pub. dir., editor quar. Am. Petroleum Inst., 1955-57; dir. pub. rels. Reach, McClinton & Co., Inc., N.Y.C., 1957-59; v.p., gen. mgr. Candygram, Inc., Chgo., 1959-60; asst. to pres. Stevens Candy Kitchens, Inc., Chgo., 1960-61; assoc. in pub. rels. Fred Rosen Assocs., Inc., 1961-62; ptnr. Prittie and Nelson Internat. Pub. Rels., London, 1975-81; chmn. Nelson Assocs. Ltd., London, 1981-93; freelance author and comms. cons., 1993—. Pub. rels. dir. William H. Rentschler for U.S. Senator, 1959-60. Author: Small Wonder: The Amazing Story of the Volkswagen Beetle, 1965, rev., 1998, German edit., 1966, Br. edit., 1967, rev., 1971, Dutch edit., 1968, Spanish edit., 1974, revised edit., 1998, The Great Discount Delusion, 1965, The Berliners: Their City and Their Saga, 1969, Br. edit., 1969, The Soldier Kings: The House of Hohenzollern, 1970, Br. and Italian edits., 1971, German edit., 1972, 98, Ernest Hemingway, 1971, Germany Rearmed, 1972, The Londoners: Life in A Civilized City, 1974, Br. edit., 1975, Japanese edit., 1976, 77, (with Terence Prittie) Economic War Against the Jews, 1977, Br. Edit., 1978, the Siege of Buckingham Palace, 1980, The Minstrel Code, 1979, Spanish edit., 1982, Gautama Buddha: His life and his Teaching, U.K. edit., 1998, Buddha: Life & Teaching, U.S. edit., 2000; contbr. articles to popular mags., newspapers. Served in U.S. Army, 1946-49. Address: 23 Clifford Ave London SW14 7BT England E-mail: walter.nelson@blueyonder.co.uk.

NELSON, WAYNE K. advertising executive; b. 1938; BS, MS in Jurisprudence, Northwestern U. With Proctor & Gamble, Cinn., 1962-66, Glendining & Co., Westport, Conn., 1966-71, Johnson & Johnson, New Brunswick, NJ, 1971-85, Lever Bros., NYC, 1986-87; founder Nelson Comm., Inc., NYC, 1987, chmn. emeritus bd. dirs. Princeton, NJ, 1988—. Office: Nelson Comm Inc 105 Madison Ave 18th Fl New York NY 10016 Address: Nelson Comm Inc 202 Carnegie Ct Ste 101 Princeton NJ 08540*

NELSON, WILLIAM EUGENE, lawyer; b. Roland, Iowa, Sept. 23, 1927; s. Sam J. and Katherine A. (Coffey) N.; m. Sherlee M. Stanford, July 11, 1959; children: Anne, Kristin, William. BA, U. Iowa, 1950; JD, Drake U., 1957. Bar: Iowa 1957, D.C. 1965, Md. 1976. Trial atty. civil divsn. U.S. Dept. Justice, 1957—65, asst. chief tort sect., 1966—70, chief r.r. reorgn. unit, 1970—71; gen. counsel Cost of Living Coun. Phase I, 1971, chief econ. stblzn. sect., 1971—74; ptnr. Nelson and Nelson, LLP, Washington, Bethesda, Md., 1975—. Gen. counsel the Communicators, Inc., Myersville, Md. Assoc. editor Drake Law Rev., 1955-57. With USN, 1945-46. Recipient Atty. Gen.'s Disting. Svc. award, 1972. Mem. Order of Coif, Omicron Delta Kappa. Home: 511 Colston Dr Falling Waters WV 25419 Office: Nelson & Nelson LLP 3 Bethesda Metro Ctr Ste 700 Bethesda MD 20814-6300 E-mail: sswen@aol.com.

NELSON, WILLIAM RANKIN, surgeon, educator; b. Charlottesville, Va., Dec. 12, 1921; s. Hugh Thomas and Edith (Rankin) N.; m. Nancy Laidley, Mar. 17, 1956 (div. 1979); children: Robin Page Nelson Russel, Susan Kimberly Nelson Wright, Anne Rankin Nelson Cron; m. Pamela Morgan Phelps, July 5, 1984. BA, U. Va., 1943, MD, 1945. Diplomate Am. Bd. Surgery. Intern Vanderbilt U. Hosp., Nashille, 1945-46; resident in surgery U. Va. Hosp., Charlottesville, 1949-51; fellow surg. oncology Meml. Sloan Kettering Cancer Ctr., N.Y.C., 1951-55; instr. U. Colo. Sch. Medicine, Denver, 1955-57, asst. clin. prof., 1962-87, clin. prof. surgery, 1987—. Asst. prof. Med. Coll. Va., Richmond, 1957-62; mem. exec. com. U. Colo. Cancer Ctr.; mem. nat. bd., nat. exec. com. Am. Cancer Soc. Contbr. articles to profl. jours. and chpts. to textbooks. Capt. USAAF, 1946-48. Recipient Nat. Div. award Am. Cancer Soc., 1979. Fellow Am. Coll. Surgeons (bd. govs. 1984-89); mem. AMA, Internat. Soc. Surgery, Brit. Assn. Surg. Oncology, Royal Soc. Medicine (U.K.), Soc. Surg. Oncology (pres. 1975-76), Soc. Head and Neck Surgeons (pres. 1986-87), Am. Cancer Soc. (pres. Colo. div. 1975-77, exec. com., nat. bd. dirs., del. dir. from Colo. div. 1985-94), Am. Soc. Clin. Oncology, Western Surg. Assn. Colo. Med. Soc., Denver Med. Soc., Denver Acad. Surgery, Rocky Mt. Oncology Soc., Univ. Club, Rotary. Republican. Episcopalian. Avocations: skiing, backpacking, travel, bicycling, fly fishing. Personal E-mail: wrn3@msn.com.

NELSON, WILLIE HUGH, musician, songwriter; b. Fort Worth, Tex., Apr. 30, 1933; children: Jacob, Lukas, Paula Carlene, Amy, Lana, Susie, Billy. Student, Baylor U. Salesman; announcer, host country music shows local Tex. stas.; bass player Ray Price's band; formed own band; personal appearances at Grand Ole Opry, Nashville, throughout U.S., 1964—; rec. artist Atlantic, Columbia and RCA records. Musician: (albums) Love & Pain, 1961, And Then I Wrote, 1962, Here's Willie Nelson, 1963, Country Willie: His Own Songs, 1965, Country Favorites: Willie Nelson Style, 1966, Live Country Music Concert, 1966, Make Way for Willie Nelson, 1967, Texas in My Soul, 1968, Good Times, 1968, My Own Peculiar Way, 1969, Both Sides Now, 1970, Laying My Burdens Down, Yesterday's Wine, 1971, Willie Nelson & Family, 1971, The Willie Way, 1972, The Words Don't Fit the Picture, 1972, Shotgun Willie, 1973, Phases and Stages, 1974, Red Headed Stranger, 1975 (Grammy award Best Country Vocal Performance for song "Blue Eyes Crying In The Rain", 1975), Willie Nelson Live, 1976, The Sound in Your Mind, 1976, The Troublemaker, 1976, To Lefty from Willie, 1977, Stardust, 1978 (Grammy award Best Country Vocal Performance for song "Georgia on My Mind", 1978), Waylon & Willie, 1978 (Grammy award Best Country Vocal Performance By A Duo Or Group for song "Mammas Don't Let Your Babies Grow Up to Be Cowboys", 1978), Willie and Family Live, 1978, The Electric Horseman, 1979, Sings Kris Kristofferson, 1979, One for the Road, 1979, Pretty Paper, 1979, San Antonio Rose, 1980, Honeysuckle Rose, 1980 (Grammy award Best Country Song for "On The Road Again", 1980), Blue Skies, 1981, Somewhere over the Rainbow, 1981, Pancho & Lefty, 1983 (Vocal Duo Yr. (with Merle Haggard) Country Music Assn. Awards, 1983), Old Friends, 1982, Always on My Mind, 1982 (Grammy award Best Country Vocal Performance for song "Always On My Mind", 1982, Country Music Assn. awards: Album Yr., 1982, Single Yr. for "Always On My Mind", 1982), Tougher Than Leather, 1983, Without a Song, 1983, Take It to the Limit, 1983, Music from "Songwriter", 1984, Portrait in Music, 1984, Angel Eyes, 1984, City of New Orleans, 1984, Me and Paul, 1985, Half Nelson, 1985 (Vocal Duo Yr. (with Julio Iglesias) Country Music Assn. Awards, 1984), Brand on My Heart, 1985, Funny How Time Slips Away, 1985, Partners, 1986, The Promiseland, 1986, Island in the Sea, 1987, Seashores of Old Mexico, 1987, What a Wonderful World, 1988, Horse Called Music, 1989, Born for Trouble, 1990, The IRS Tapes: Who'll Buy My Memories?, Willie Nelson, 1993, Across the Borderline, 1993, Moonlight Becomes You, 1994, Healing Hands of Time, 1994, Pancho, Lefty and Rudolph, 1995, Six Hours of Pedernales, 1995, Just One Love, 1996, Spirit, 1996, How Great Thou Art, 1996, Christmas with Willie Nelson, 1997, Hill Country Christmas, 1997, Teatro, 1998, Life's Railway to Heaven, 1998, Back to Back: Willie Nelson and Patsy Cline, 1998, Night and Day, 1999, Clean Shirt, 2000, Outlaws, 2000, Memories of Hank Williams, Sr., 2000, Me and the Drummer, 2000, Milk Cow Blues, 2000, Good Ol' Country Singin', 2000, Rainbow Connection, 2001, Tales Out of Luck, 2001, The Great Divide, 2002, Home is Where You're Happy, 2002, All of Me Live...in Concert, 2002, Stars & Guitars, 2002 (Grammy award (with Lee Ann Womack) Best Country Collaboration With Vocals for song "Mendocino County Line", 2002), Night Life, 2002, Country Willie, 2002, Is There Something on Your Mind, 2002, On the Road Again, 2002, Honky Tonk Heroes, 2003, Broken Promises, 2003, Reunion - Can't Get the Hell Out of Texas, 2003, Willie Nelson and Friends: Live and Kickin', 2003, Standard Time, 2003, Keepsake, 2003, Run That By Me One More Time, 2003, I Just Don't Understand, 2003, Live in Amsterdam, 2004, Music Legends: The Best of Willie Live, 2004, Live at Billy Bob's Texas, 2004; appeared on (album by Waylon Jennings) Good Hearted Woman, 1972 (Single Yr. (with Waylon Jennings) Country Music Assn. Awards, 1976), appeared with various artists (albums) Wanted: The Outlaws, 1976 (Vocal Duo Yr. (with Waylon Jennings) Country Music Assn. (CMA) Awards, 1976, Album Yr. (with Waylon Jennings, Tompall Glaser, Jessi Colter) Country Music Assn. Awards, 1976), (film appearances include) Electric Horseman, 1979, Honeysuckle Rose, 1980, Thief, 1981, Barbarosa, 1982, Anthem, 1997, Wag the Dog, 1997, Half Baked, 1998, Dill Scallion, 1999, Austin Powers: The Shy Who Shagged Me, 1999; performer: (theme song for film) Welcome Home, 1989; (TV films appearances include) Where the Hell's That Gold, 1988, Once Upon a Texas Train, 1989, A Pair of Aces, 1990, Born for Trouble, 1990, Another Pair of Aces: Three of a Kind, 1991, Big Country, 1994, Big Dreams and Broken Hearts: The Dottie West Story, 1995, The Beach Boys: Nashville Sounds, 1996, Starlight, 1996, Farm Aid '96, 1996, Outlaw Justice, 1998; author: (autobiography) I Didn't Come Here and I Ain't Leaving, 1988. Served in USAF. Named Entertainer Yr., Country Music Assn. (CMA), 1979; named to, Nashville Songwriters Assn. Hall Fame, 1973, Country Music Hall Fame, 1993; recipient citation for Top Album Artist, Billboard mag., 1976, Special Humanitarian award, Nat. Farmers Orgn., 1986, Grammy Lifetime Achievement award, 1989. Office: care Mark Rothbaum & Assocs Inc PO Box 2689 Danbury CT 06813-2689 Address: William Morris Agency 150 El Camino 90212*

NELSON-THORPE, CARLON JUSTINE, engineering and operations executive; b. Siloam Springs, Ark., May 26, 1960; d. Robert F. and Jean (Caroom) Toenges. BS in Indsl. Engring., U. Ark., 1982; MBA, Houston Bapt. U., 1988. Registered profl. engr., Tex. Supr. codes and regulatory compliance Tex. Ea., Houston, 1982-85, supr. ops. spl. projects, 1985-87, mgr. project devel., 1987-90; dir. spl. projects, tech. asst. to pres. Enron, Houston, 1990-91, dir. throughput engring., 1991-92, project dir., 1992-95; v.p. engring. So. Union Gas Co., Austin, Tex., 1995-96; v.p. ops. Mo. Gas Energy, Kansas City, Mo., 1996-99; gen. mgr. Shell Tech. Ventures, Houston, 1999—2002. Mem.: NSPE, Tex. Soc. Profl. Engrs. Home: 5334 Indian Shores Ln Houston TX 77041-4298

NELSON-WALKER, ROBERTA, management software company executive; b. N.Y.C., Sept. 1, 1936; d. Richard E. and Esther (McBride) Martin; m. Robert L. Nelson, July 20, 1957 (div.); children: Carol, Craig, Robert H.; m. Dan Walker, Nov. 1978 (div.). BA, DePaul U., 1976, MS in Mgmt. with distinction, 1977. Dir. devel. Ray Graham Assocs., Elmhurst, Ill., 1970-76; dir. human resources Nat. Easter Seal Soc., Chgo., 1979-81; v.p. Butler Walker Inc., Oak Brook, Ill., 1981-85; pres. CNR, Inc., Oak Brook, Ill., 1985-91; spl. agt. Prudential Ins., Oak Brook, Ill., 1991-95; mng. dir. Visimark L.L.C., Oak Brook, Ill., 1995—. Author: Creating Acceptance for Handicapped People, 1975, Creating, Planning, and Financial Housing for Handicapped People, 1979. Founder, organizer Found. for Handicapped, 1970-76,; pres. DuPage County Pub. Health Coun., 1974; bd. dirs. DuPage County Mental Health Assocs., 1970, Forest Found. DuPage County, 1976-86, Shakespeare Globe, London and Chgo., 1982—; mem. DuPage County Bd Health, 1975, Ill. Gov.'s Com. for Handicapped, 1976, women's coun. Chgo. Heart Assn., 1979—. Recipient Meritorious Svc. award, Chgo. Heart Assn., 1968, 70, Fond du Coer award AHA, 1968, Cursade of Mercy Achievement awards, 1974-76, State of Ill. procalmation by Gov. James Thompson, Ill. Epilepsy Assn., 1978. Home: Apt 601A 580 Arastradero Rd Palo Alto CA 94306-3947

NEMAN, EILEEN, not-for-profit organization executive; 1 child. Exec. dir. Film/Video Arts, N.Y.C., 1998—. Program officer New Visions for Pub. Schs. Mem.: The N.Y. Film/Video Coun. (bd. dirs.), N.Y. Women in Film and TV (bd. dirs., past v.p.), Educators for Social Responsibility (v.p.). Office: Film/Video Arts 462 Broadway Ste 520 New York NY 10013

NEMANIC, MARY LOU, communications educator, film producer, photographer; b. St. Paul, Minn., Sept. 17, 1950; d. William Louis and Mary Lou Kroening; m. Douglas Francis Nemanic, Dec. 30, 1988; 1 stepchild, Geoffrey (dec.). BA summa cum laude, Univ. Minn., Mpls., 1975, MA Mass Commn., 1977, PhD Am. Studies, 1996. Lectr. Univ. Minn., Mpls., 1975—77; adj. Metropolitan State U., Mpls., 1987—98; lectr. Univ. Minn., Mpls., 1991—96; asst. prof. Penn State Altoona, Pa., 2001—. Media advisor Cattleman's Days Assn., Gunnison, Colo., 1999—2001. Contbr. chapters to books, articles pub. to prof. jour.; co-dir.: (documentaries) Tamarack, 1987—98; prodr.:, 1977—98; exhibitions include City of Aurora Centennial, 2003, Cattlemen's Days 100-year, Quigley Gallery, 2000, John Mariucci, Gunnison Photo Gallery, 2000, 1999; co-dir., prodr.: (documentaries) Documentary America, 1999. Mem.: Pop Culture Assn., Kappa Tau Alpha, Phi Beta Kappa. Office: Penn State Altoona 3000 Ivyside Pk Altoona PA 16601

NEMCEK, ADRIAN R. electronics executive; BSEE, Ill. Inst. Tech.; MBA, Loyola U., Chgo. Joined Motorola, Inc., 1970, with wireless infrastructure global sales and market ops. group, 1994—2000, sr. v.p., gen. mgr. Global Telecom Solutions Sector, exec. v.p., pres., CEO Global Telecom. Solutions Sector, 2001—. Mem. bd. advisors HP Corp. Office: Motorola 1303 E Algonquin Rd Schaumburg IL 60196

NEMCOVA, EVA, professional basketball player; b. Czech Republic, Dec. 3, 1972; arrived in U.S., 1997; Guard A.S. Montferrand, France, 1993—96, Bourges, France, 1996—97, Cleveland Rockers, (WNBA), 1997—. Named Best Player European Championship, 1995, 1996. Avocations: volleyball, handball, football, mountain biking. Office: Cleve Rockers Gund Arena 1 Center Ct Cleveland OH 44115-4001

NEMEC, JOSEF, retired organic chemist, researcher; b. Ostresany, Czechoslovakia, Sept. 7, 1929; came to U.S., 1969; s. Josef Nemec and Marie (Joskova) Nemcova; m. Anna Pastush, Aug. 29, 1975; 1 child, Marketa. MS, Inst. Chem. Tech., Prague, Czechoslovakia, 1954; PhD, Czechoslovak Acad. Scis., Prague, 1958. Organic chemist Inst. Chem. Tech., Prague, 1954-61; sr. rsch. chemist Czechoslovak Acad. Scis., Prague, 1961-69; rsch. fellow in organic chemistry Wayne State U., Detroit, 1969-70; sr. rsch. scientist Squibb Inst. Med. Rsch., New Brunswick, N.J., 1970-75; staff mem. St. Jude Children's Rsch. Hosp., Memphis, 1975-84; sr. scientist Nat. Cancer Inst.-Program Resources, Inc. Cancer R&D Ctr., Frederick, Md., 1984-95; ret., 1995. Adj. prof. med. chemistry U. Tenn., Memphis, 1979-91; external examiner U. Zimbabwe, Harare, 1994—; cons. in field. Contbr. articles to scholarly and profl. jours. Grantee Nat. Cancer Inst., 1975-85. Mem. AAAS, Am. Chem. Soc., Royal Soc. Chemistry, Czechoslovak Soc. Arts and Scis. Achievements include patents in fields of anticancer agents, organic chemicals, semimicroequipment in organic chemistry; research in natural products, synthetic anticancer agents, monosaccharides, experimental semimicrotechniques in organic chemistry.

NEMECEK, ALBERT DUNCAN, JR., retail company executive, investment banker, management consultant; b. Helena, Mont., Mar. 10, 1936; s. Albert Duncan and Geneva (Reindle) N.; m. Marilyn Ann Shaughnessy, Sept. 7, 1963 (div.); children: Maureen Ann, Steven Mathew; m. Judith Eileen Swift, Sept. 18, 1981 (div.); 1 child, Jennifer Eileen. BS, U. Md., 1960, postgrad. in econs., 1961. Agt. IRS, Washington, 1961-65; tax dir. Macke Co., Washington, 1965-69; tax dir., then sec. Garfinckle, Brooks Bros., Miller & Rhoads, Inc., Washington, 1969-76, treas., 1976—, v.p., 1979—; mng. ptnr. Nemecek & Falleroni, 1987, Nemecek & Jacknis, investment bankers, mgmt. cons., Falls Church, Va., 1989; founder Nemecek & Co., Inc., Falls Church, 1990. Founder Entrepreneurial Growth Fund, Falls Church, 1990. Founder The Leadership Group, 1996. Home: PO Box 21 Occoquan VA 22125-0021 Personal E-mail: fixit00001@aol.com. *A man's success is measured by the respect he has gained from his peers, his understanding and compassion, respect for the feelings of others, appreciation of the world's beauty, and his attempts to leave the world better than he found it.*

NEMECEK, GEORGINA MARIE, molecular pharmacologist; b. Mineola, N.Y., Aug. 27, 1946; d. George and Frances Valerie (Masaryk) N. AB, Mt. Holyoke Coll., 1968; PhD, U. Pa., 1972. Rsch. assoc. dept. biochemistry U. Mass. Med. Sch., Worcester, 1972-73, postdoctoral fellow of Am. Heart Assn., dept. biochemistry, 1974, asst. prof., 1974-80, assoc. prof., 1981-83; sr. scientist platelet dept. Sandoz Pharm. Corp., East Hanover, N.J., 1983-85, mem. sr. sci. staff, platelet dept., 1986, fellow, sect. head molecular biology, 1987-91, fellow diabetes, 1991-93, study dir. regulatory toxicology, 1993-96; internat. project mgr. preclin. safety Novartis Pharm. Corp., East Hanover, 1997, assoc. dir. project mgmt., 1997-2000, dir. project mgmt., 2000—02, dir. integrative compound and product profiling, 2002—03, dir. project review, biomarker devel., 2003—. Vis. scientist dept. molecular biology, Princeton (N.J.) U., 1987, Sea Pharm. Inc., 1985, NATO, U. Libre, Brussels, 1979, biotechnology dept. Sandoz AG, Basel, Switzerland, 1988. Contbr. articles to profl. jours. Named Nat. Heart, Lung, and Blood Inst. Young Investigator, NIH, 1977-81. Mem. Am. Soc. Pharmacol. Exptl. Therapeutics, N.Y. Acad. Scis. (chmn. biochem. sect. 1992-94), Tissue Culture Assn., Soc. Toxicology, Soc. Toxicol. Pathologists, Sigma Xi. Avocations: boating, gardening, riding, needlecrafts. Office: Novartis Pharm Corp 1 Health Plz East Hanover NJ 07936-1005

NEMECHEK, JOE, race car driver; b. Lakeland, Fla., Sept. 26, 1963; m. Andrea Nemechek; 1 child, John Hunter. Student, Fla. Inst. Tech. Founder, racecar driver NEMCO Motorsports, Mooresville, NC, 1990—. Entered NASCAR driving ranks in 1990 with the family-operated NEMCO Motorsports team, competed fulltime in NASCAR Busch Series Grand Nat. Divsn. through 1993; formed own team in 1994, securing a Burger King sponsorship for the season; moved to SABCO in 1996-2000; driver with Andy Petree's No. 33, 2000, sponsored by Oakwood Homes. Career includes: NASCAR finishes between 26th and 34th in every full season of his career; won first place NASCAR Winston Cup Series, N.H., 1999; recipient All-Pro Late Model Rookie of Year, 1989, Rookie of Year award NASCAR Busch Series Grand

Nat., 1993, 3rd place in a field of candidates for NASCAR Winston Cup Rookie of the Year award 1994. Avocations: racing, skiing, fishing, boating. Office: Nemco Motorsports 128 S Iredell Indsl Park Rd Mooresville NC 28115

NEMEROFF, CHARLES BARNET, neurobiology and psychiatry educator; b. Bronx, N.Y., Sept. 7, 1949; s. Philip Peace and Sarah (Greenberg) N.; m. Melissa Ann Pilkington, May 24, 1980 (div.); children: Matthew P. (dec. 1997), Amanda P., Sarah-Frances P.; m. Gayle Applegate, June 11, 2001. BS, CCNY, 1970; MS, Northeastern U., 1973; PhD, U. N.C., 1976, MD, 1981. Diplomate Am. Bd. Psychiatry and Neurology; lic. physician, N.C., Ga. Rsch. asst. ichthyology Am. Mus. Natural History, N.Y.C., 1968-71; neurochemistry lab. McLean Hosp., Belmont, Mass., 1971-72; rsch. assoc. surgery Beth Israel Hosp., Boston, 1972-73; tchg. asst. biology Northeastern U., 1972-73; postdoctoral fellow Biol. Scis. Rsch. Ctr., U. N.C., Chapell Hill, 1976-77, rsch. fellow, 1977-83, clin. instr. psychiatry, 1983; resident psychiatry N.C. Meml. Hosp., Chapel Hill, 1981-83; asst. prof. dept. psychiatry and pharmacology Duke U., Durham, N.C., 1983-85, assoc. prof. psychiatry, 1985-89, assoc. prof. pharmacology, 1986-89, prof. depts. psychiatry and pharmacology, 1989-91, chief divsn. biol. psychiatry, 1988-91; prof., chmn. dept. psychiatry and behavioral scis. Emory U. Sch. Medicine, 1991—, Reunette W. Harris prof. psychiatry and behavioral scis., 1994—. Vis. prof. physiology Cath. U., Santiago, Chile, 1978; sci. coun. Nat. Alliance for Rsch. Schizophrenia and Depression, 1997—; mem. coun. NIMH, 1999-2002; mem. biomed. rsch. counl NASA, 2000-03; bd. dirs. George West Mental Health Found., 1999—, Cypress Bioscis. Inc., 2001—. Editor: (with A.J. Prange Jr.) Neurotensin, a Brain and Gastrointestinal Peptide, 1982, (with A.J. Dunn) Peptides, Hormones and Behavior, 1984, (with P.T. Loosen) Handbook of Clinical Psychoneuroendocrinology, Neuropeptides in Psychiatric and Neurological Disorders, 1987, Neuropeptides in Psychiatric Disorders, 1991, Neuroendocrinology, 1992, (with P. Kitabgi) The Neurobiology of Neurotensin, 1992, (with A.F. Schatzberg) Textbook of Psychopharmacology, 1995, 2nd edit., 1998, (with A. F. Schatzberg) Recognition and Treatment of Psychiatric Disorders, 1999; editor-in-chief: Depression, 1993-2000, Psychopharmacology Bull., 2001-02, Neuropsychopharmacology, 2002--; co-editor-in-chief: Critical Revs. in Neurobiology, 1992-2001; contbr. chpts. to books and articles and abstracts to profl. jours. Recipient Michiko Kuno award U. N.C., 1978, 79, Merck award for acad. excellence, 1981, Merck award for young investigators Am. Geriatrics Soc., 1985, 2nd prize Anna Monica Found. for Rsch. in Endogenous Depression, 1987, merit award NIMH, 1987, rsch. prize World Fedn. Socs. Biol. Psychiatry, 1991, Edward J. Sachar award Columbia U., 1993, Edward A. Strecker prize Instnl. Pa. Hosp., 1993, Outstanding Alumni award in health scis. Northeastern U., 1995, Disting. Alumni award U. N.C. Sch. Medicine, 1999, George Ham Alumni award dept. psychiatry U. N.C., 2000; grantee Nat. Inst. Aging, 1982-83, NIMH, 1983—, NIDA, 1996-98; predoctoral fellow Schizophrenia Rsch. Found., Soc. Scottish Rite, Lexington, Mass., 1975-76, postdoctoral fellow Nat. Inst. Neurol., Communicative Disorders and Stroke, 1977, Nanaline Duke fellow Duke U. Med. Ctr., 1985-87. Fellow Am. Coll. Neuropsychopharmacology (Mead Johnson Travel award 1982, Efron award 1987, coun. mem. 1993—, pres. 1997), Am. Coll. Psychiatrists (chmn. contbns. com. 1991-93, 95—, edn. com. 1993-96, 96—, bd. regents 1994-97, first v.p. 1999, pres.-elect 2000, pres. 2001, Mood Disorders Rsch. award 1998, Bowis award 1999); mem. AAAS, AMA, Soc. Neurosci. (program com. 1993-95), Internat. Soc. Psychoneuroendocrinology (pres. 1993-96, Curt P. Richter award 1985), Internat. Soc. Neuroendocrinology, Internat. Soc. Neurochemistry, Am. Soc. Neurochemistry (Jordi-Folch-Pi award 1987), Endocrine Soc., Soc. Neuroendocrinology, Soc. Biol. Psychiatry (A.E. Bennett award 1979, Gold medal award 1996), Am. Fedn. Clin. Rsch., Am. Pain Soc., Am. Psychiat. Assn. (coun. rsch. 1993-98, 2002-, chmn. 1994-95, bd. dirs. rsch. inst. 1999—, chair coun. rsch. subcom. on psychiat. treatments 1999—, Kempf award 1989, Samuel Hibbs award 1991, Rsch. prize 1996, 99—, Disting. Psychiatrist Lecture Ann. Meeting 1999, 2003), Am. Coll. Physicians (William C. Menninger award 2000), Anxiety Disorders Assn. Am. (chmn. adv. bd. 2001—, Charles Burlingame prize, Inst.for Living, 2002), Argentine Assn. Psychoneuroendocrinology (sci. coun.), Nat. Depressive and Manic Depressive Disorders Assn. (vice chair 1996-98, bd. dirs. 1999—, chair 1999-2000, Gerald L. Klerman Lifetime Achievement award 1997), Anxiety Disorder Assn. Am. (chmn. sci. adv. bd., 2001-03), N.Y. Acad. Scis., Am. Found. for Suicide Prevention (scientific adv. bd. 1997—, bd. dirs. 1998—, Research prize, 2001), Inst. Medicine, Sigma Xi. Democrat. Jewish. Office: Emory U Sch Medicine Dept Psychiatry 1639 Pierce Dr Atlanta GA 30322-0001

NEMEROFF, MICHAEL ALAN, lawyer; b. Feb. 16, 1946; s. Bernard Gregor and Frances (Gotleib) N.; m. Sharon Lynn Leininger, Sept. 22, 1974; children: Theodore, Patrick, James. BA, U. Chgo., 1968; JD, Columbia U., 1971. Asst. counsel Subcom. on Juvenile Delinquency of Senate Jud. Com., Washington, 1971-73; assoc. Sidley & Austin, Washington, 1973-78; ptnr. Sidley Austin Brown & Wood, Washington, 1978—. Treas. Friends of Jim Sasser, 1978-96, Andy Ireland Campaign Com., 1984-92. Office: Sidley Austin Brown & Wood LLP 1501 K St NW Washington DC 20005

NEMEROWICZ, GLORIA, academic administrator; 2 children. BA, MA, PhD in Sociology, Rutgers U. Assoc. prof. sociology Monmouth Coll., NJ, provost; exec. dir. Women's Leadership Inst. Wells Coll., Aurora, NY, 1993—96; pres. Pine Manor Coll., Chestnut Hill, Mass., 1996—. Author: (books) Children's Perceptions of Gender and Work Roles; co-author (with Eugene Rosi): Professionalism in Unpaid Work; contbr. op-ed pieces to newspapers. Office: Pine Manor Coll 400 Health St Chestnut Hill MA 02467

NEMETH, NORMAN E. sculptor, engraver; b. Newport News, Va., Nov. 23, 1942; BFA in Sculpture, U. Hartford, 1968. Designer, sculptor Franklin Mint, 1969—80; freelancer, 1980—2001; sculptor, engraver US Mint, 2001—. Exhibitions include Gallery Charve, Phila., Zarick Gallery, Farmington, Conn. With USAF, 1961—65. Office: 801 9th St NW Washington DC 20220

NEMETZ, PETER NEWMAN, economics researcher, policy analysis educator; b. Vancouver, B.C., Can., Feb. 19, 1944; s. Nathan Theodore and Bel Nemetz; m. Roma E.S. Kellock, July 16, 1994; 1 stepchild, Fiona Susan. BA in Econs. and Polit. Sci., U. B.C., 1966; AM in Econs., Harvard U., 1969, PhD in Econs., 1973. Tchg. fellow, tutor Harvard U., Cambridge, Mass., 1971-73; lectr. Sch. Planning U. B.C., Vancouver, 1973-75, asst. prof. to assoc. prof. policy analysis, 1975-96, prof., 1996—, chmn., 1984-90. Non-resident faculty Green Coll., 1993-94, 95-97, St. John's Coll., 1997-2002; vis. scientist, rschr., collaborator Dept. Health Scis. Rsch. Mayo Clinic, 1986—; cons. consumer and corp. affairs, Can., 1977-80, B.C. Hydro, 2000-02; program chmn. The Vancouver Inst., 1987—; mem. bd. advisors evidence-based practice ctr. rsch. project U. Calif., San Francisco, 2000-01; mem. sr. faculty Ctr. Health Svcs. and Policy Rsch., U. B.C., 1990-, dept. resource mgmt. and environ. studies, 1979—, Ctr. Japanese Studies, 1992—; mem. Inst. for Resources and Environment, U. B.C., 1997—, selection com. Rhodes Scholarship, 1991-99, mem. senate, 1998-2002, mgmt. com. Ctr. Southeast Asia Rsch., 1992-99, assoc. mem. Faculty Medicine dept. health care and epidemiology faculty medicine, 1995—; bd. dirs. U. B.C. Press, 1993-2002; assoc. Ctr. Pacific Basin Monetary and Econ. Studies, Econ. Rsch. Dept., Fed. Reserve Bank of San Francisco, 1991—. Editor Jour. Bus. Adminstrn., 1978—; mem. editl. bd. Jour. Internat. Bus. Edn., 2001—; contbr. articles to sci. jours. Life mem. BC-Yukon divsn. Can Nat. Inst. for Blind. Postdoctoral fellow Westwater Rsch. Ctr., Vancouver, 1973-75; grantee Natural Scis. and Engring. Rsch. Coun. of Can., 1976-92, Consumer and Corp. Affairs Can., 1978-80, Econ. Coun. of Can., 1979-80, Max Bell Found., 1982-84. Mem. Am. Econ. Assn., Internat. Epidemiol. Assn., Harvard Club of B.C. (pres. 1986-94), Vancouver Club. Jewish. Avocations: swimming, photography. Office: Sauder Sch Bus Univ BC Faculty Commerce Vancouver BC Canada V6T 1Z2 Office Phone: 604-822-8443. Business E-Mail: peter.nemetz@sauder.ubc.ca.

NEMFAKOS, CHARLES PANAGIOTIS, defense industry executive, strategic consultant; b. Athens, Greece, Oct. 21, 1942; s. Panagiotis Soterios and Mirka (Kyriakakis) N.; children: Mirka Leigh, Charles Jr.; m. Pamela Durrant; 1 child, Alexandra. BA, Pan Am. U., 1964; MA, Georgetown U., 1982. Cert. in nat. security. Health advisor USPHS, Washington, 1965-66; fed. mgmt. intern Dept. Navy, Washington, 1966-67; budget analyst Naval Ordnance Systems Command, Washington, 1967-71; supervisory budget analyst Naval Ship Systems Command, Washington, 1971-73; sr. budget analyst Office of Sec. of Def., Washington, 1973-75; divsn. dir. Office Budget and Reports Dept. Navy, Washington, 1975-76, assoc. dir., 1976-93, dep. asst. sec., 1994-95, dep. undersec., 1995—2001, sr. civilian ofcl. for fin. mgmt., comptr., 1998—2001; dir. internal programs devel. Lockheed Martin Corp., Manassas, Va., 2001—03; organizing mem. Nemfakos Ptnrs., LLC, Arlington, Va., 2003—. Bd. dirs. First Command Ednl. Found., Am. Automar and Atlantic Marine; lectr. Naval Postgrad. Sch., Monterey, Calif., 1984—, Georgetown U., Washington, 1987—, Ind. U. Grad. Sch., 1996-, Def. Acquisition U., 2001-; mem. base structure com. Dept. Navy, Washington, 1990-91, mem. sr. advisors group, 1991-92, vice-chmn. base structure com., 1992-95; gen. adminstrn. bd. USDA Grad. Sch., 2000—. Contbr. articles to profl. jours. Coach McLean (Va.) Youth Soccer, 1978-93, chmn., 1982-85; bd. dirs. McLean Youth, Inc., 1980-84; registrar Va. Youth Soccer Assn., 1984-86. Recipient Dept. Navy Superior Civilian Svc. award Asst. Sec. of Navy, 1980, Dept. Navy Disting. Civilian Svc. award Sec. of Navy, 1985, 87, 93, 2000, 01, Dept. Def. Disting. Civilian Svc. award Sec. of Def., 1990, 2000, 01, Dept. Navy Disting. Pub. Svc. award Sec. of Navy, 1995, Roger W. Jones award exec. leadership Am. U., 2000; named to Rank of Disting. Exec. Pres. of U.S., 1986, 95, to Rank of Meritorious Exec., Pres. of U.S., 1981, 91; named Career Civilian Exemplar Sec. of Def., 2004. Mem. Am. Assn. Budget and Program Analysis (dir.-at-large 1980-83), Am. Soc. Mil. Comptrs. (v.p. 1988-90), Fed. Execs. Inst. Alumni Assn., Tau Kappa Epsilon (chpt. pres. 1964-65). Greek Orthodox. Avocations: golf, tennis, coaching soccer. Office Phone: 703-362-6391. Business E-Mail: charles@nemfakospartners.com.

NEMHAUSER, GEORGE L. industrial, systems engineer, operations research educator; b. N.Y.C., July 27, 1937; s. Martin and Rose (Schwartz) N.; m. Ellen Krupsaw, Sept. 14, 1959; children: Wendy, Dennis. B.Chem.Engring., CCNY, 1958; MS, Northwestern U., 1959, PhD, 1961. Prof. ops. research Johns Hopkins U., Balt., 1961-69; prof. Cornell U., Ithaca, N.Y., 1969-84, Leon C. Welch prof. engring., 1984-85, dir. Sch. Ops. Research and Indsl. Engring., 1977-83; Chandler prof. indsl. and systems engring. Ga. Inst. Tech., 1985—, inst. prof., 1992—. Vis. prof. U. Leeds, U.K., 1963-64; vis. prof., dir. research Center for Ops. Research and Econometrics, U. Louvain, Belgium, 1975-77; cons. NSF (others.) Author: Introduction to Dynamic Programming, 1966, Integer Programming, 1972, Integer and Combinatorial Optimization, 1988; editor-in-chief: Ops. Research, 1975-78, Ops. Research Letters, 1981-2002; contbr. articles to profl. jours. NSF faculty fellow, 1969-70 Fellow INFORMS (pres. 1981-82, Lanchester prize 1977, 89, Kimball medal 1988); mem. NAE, Soc. Indsl. and Applied Math., Am. Inst. Indsl. Engrs., Math. Programming Soc. (chmn. 1989-1992). Home: 1208 Villa Dr NE Atlanta GA 30306-2567 Office Phone: 404-894-2306.

NEMIR, DONALD PHILIP, lawyer; b. Oakland, Calif., Oct. 31, 1931; s. Philip F. and Mary (Shavor) N. AB, U. Calif., Berkeley, 1957, JD, 1960. Bar: Calif. 1961, U.S. Dist. Ct. (no. dist.) Calif. 1961, U.S. Ct. Appeals (9th cir.) 1961, U.S. Dist. Ct. (ctrl. dist.) Calif. 1975, U.S. Supreme Ct. 1980. Pvt. practice, San Francisco, 1961—. Pres. World Commoditites, Ltd. Home: PO Box 1089 Mill Valley CA 94942-1089 Personal E-mail: nemir@mindspring.com.

NEMIRO, BEVERLY MIRIUM ANDERSON, author, educator; b. St. Paul, May 29, 1925; d. Martin and Anna Mae Anderson; m. Jerome Morton Nemiro, Feb. 10, 1951-75; children: Guy Samuel, Lee Anna, Dee Martin. Student, Reed Coll., 1943-44; BA, U. Colo., 1947; postgrad., U. Denver. Tchr. Seattle Pub. Sch., 1945-46; fashion coord., dir. Denver Dry Goods Co., 1948-51; fashion dir. Denver Market Week Assn., 1952-53; free-lance writer Denver, 1958—. Moderator TV program Your Presch. Child, Denver, 1955-56; instr. writing and comm. U. Colo. Denver Ctr., 1970—, U. Calif., San Diego, 1976-78, Met. State Coll., 1985; dir. pub. rels. Fairmont Hotel, Denver, 1979-80; freelance fashion and TV model. Author, co-author: The Complete Book of High Altitude Baking, 1961, Colorado a la Carte, 1963, Colorado a la Carte, Series II, 1966, (with Donna Hamilton) The High Altitude Cookbook, 1969, The Busy People's Cookbook, 1971 (Better Homes and Gardens Book Club selection 1971), Where to Eat in Colorado, 1967, Lunch Box Cookbook, 1965, Complete Book of High Altitude Baking, 1961, (under name Beverly Anderson) Single After 50, 1978, The New High Altitude Cookbook, 1980. Co-founder, pres. Jr. Symphony Guild, Denver, 1959-60; active Friends of Denver Libr., Opera Colo.; mem. Friends of Painting and Sculpture, Denver Art Mus. Recipient Top Hand award Colo. Authors' League, 1969, 72, 79-82, 100 Best Books of Yr. award NY Times, 1969, 71; named one of Colo. Women of Yr., Denver Post, 1964. Mem. Am. Soc. Journalists and Authors, Colo. Authors League (dir. 1969-79), Authors Guild, Authors League Am., Friends Denver Libr., Opera Colo. Guild, Denver Women's Press Club, Rotary, Kappa Alpha Theta. Address: Park Towers 1299 Gilpin St Apt 15W Denver CO 80218-2556

NEMIROFF, MAXINE CELIA, art educator, gallery owner, consultant; b. Chgo., Feb. 11, 1935; d. Oscar Bernard and Martha (Mann) Kessler; m. Paul Rubenstein, June 26, 1955 (div. 1974); children: Daniel, Peter, Anthony; m. Allan Nemiroff, Dec. 24, 1979. BA, U. So. Calif., 1955; MA, UCLA, 1974. Sr. instr. UCLA, 1974-92; dir., curator art gallery Doolittle Theater, Los Angeles, 1985-86; owner Nemiroff Deutsch Fine Art, Santa Monica, Calif. Leader of worldwide art tours; cons. L'Ermitage Hotel Group, Beverly Hills, Calif., 1982—, Broadway Dept. Stores, So. Calif., 1979—, Security Pacific Bank, Calif., 1978—, Am. Airlines, Calif. Pizza Kitchen Restaurants; art chmn. UCLA Thieves Market, Century City, 1960—, L.A. Music Ctr. Mercado, 1982—; lectr. in field. Apptd. bd. dirs. Dublin (Calif.) Fine Arts Found., 1989; mem. Calif. Govs. Adv. Coun. for Women, 1992; mem. art selection com. Calif. State Office Bldgs., 1997—. Named Woman of Yr. UCLA Panhellenic Council, 1982, Instr. of Yr. UCLA Dept. Arts, 1984; recipient Woman of Achievement award Friends of Sheba Med. Ctr., 2003; elected to Fashion Circle of the Costume Coun., L.A. County Mus. Art, 1997—; honoree L.A. Art Core 15th Ann. Awards Benefit, 2003. Mem. L.A. County Mus. Art Coun., UCLA Art Coun., UCLA Art Coun. Docents, Alpha Epsilon Phi (alumnus of yr. 1983). Avocations: tennis, horseback riding, skiing, piano and guitar. E-mail: mumseyart@aol.com.

NEMIROW, ARNOLD MYLES, manufacturing executive; b. Hartford, Conn., Mar. 25, 1943; s. Benjamin and Elsie (Nozik) N.; m. Barbro Sandberg, Dec. 22, 1967 (dec. Aug. 1983); children: Matthew, Adam; m. Sharon Green, April 23, 1988. AB cum laude, Harvard U., 1966; JD, U. Mich., 1969. Bar: N.Y. Atty. Carter, Ledyard & Milburn, N.Y.C., 1969-73; asst. gen. counsel Coleco Industries Inc., Hartford, 1973-74; atty., asst. gen. counsel Gt. No. Nekoosa Corp., Stamford, Conn., 1974-80, dir. indsl. rels., 1981-83, v.p., 1984-90; pres. Gt. Southern Paper Co., Cedar Springs, Ga., 1984-87, Nekoosa Papers Inc., Port Edwards, Wis., 1988-90; pres., CEO Wausau Papers, Wausau, Wis., 1990-94; CEO, pres. Bowater Inc., 1995—; chmn. Bowater, 1996—. Office: 55 E Camperdown Way Greenville SC 29601-3511

NEMIROW, LAWRENCE H. lawyer; b. Bklyn., Dec. 4, 1948; s. Hyman W. Nemirow and Irma Carver; m. Shari Dee Nemirow; children: Jennifer, Adam, Jaime, Aaron. JD, Western State U., Fullerton, Calif., 1995; BBA, U. Detroit, 1978, MBA, 1980. V.p., ins. mgr. Ford Motor Co., Dearborn, Mich., 1973-80; dir. ins. and benefits John Morrell & Co., Northfield, Ill., 1980-84; dir. risk mgmt. Honda North Am., Torrance, Calif., 1985-88; prin., risk mgmt. Windes & McClaughry, Long Beach, Calif., 1988-89; risk mgmt. cons. The Nemirow Group, Los Alamitos, Calif., 1989-95; pvt. practice Los Alamitos, 1995—. Amb. Cypress Chamber, Calif., 1988-98. Mem. ATLA, ABA, Orange County Bar Assn. Office: 5242 Katella Ave Ste 104 Los Alamitos CA 90720-2862 E-mail: nemirow@aol.com.

NEMMERS, JOSEPH M., JR., pharmaceutical executive; b. Dec. 22, 1954; B in History, Ariz. State U. Numerous positions in comml. ops., mfg. and materials mgmt. Abbott Labs., Abbott Park, Ill., 1980—99, v.p., exec. dir. Clara Abbott Found., 1999—2000, divisional v.p. Acquisition Integration Mgmt., 2001—02, corp. v.p., 2001—02, v.p. hosp. products bus. sector, 2002, v.p. global comml. ops., 2002—03, sr. v.p. diagnostic ops., 2003—. Mem. supervisory bd. Abbott Mgmt. GmbH and Abbott Holding GmbH. Chmn. bd. dirs. United Way Lake County, Carmel H.S.; bd. dirs. Ct. Appointed Spl. Advs., Boys and Girls Club Waukegan. With USAR. Office: Abbott Labs 100 Abbott Park Rd Abbott Park IL 60064-6400

NEMPHOS, SPEROS P. chemist, consultant; b. N.Y.C., July 9, 1930; s. William S. Nemphos and Philanthe Exar; m. Ann Chakalis-Nemphos, Dec. 23, 1989; children: Phyllis-Ann, George, Stephen. BS in Chemistry, Ursinus Coll., 1953; MS in Phys. Chemistry, U. Del., 1955, PhD in Polymer Chemistry, 1957. Chemist, group leader, mgr. R&D Monsanto Co., Springfield, Mass., 1956—85, St. Louis, 1956—85; mgr. R&D Nova Chem. Co., Leominster, Mass., 1986—92, Chem. Rsch. and Licensing, Houston, 1992—2000; cons. in field Houston, 2000—. Contbr. articles to profl. jours. Recipient Kirpatric award, AIChE, 1981. Mem.: Am. Chem. Soc. (emeritus). Greek Orthodox. Achievements include patents for new ABS type graft copolymers; suspension polymerization; polymer stabilization; new/improved copolymers; antistatic agents; plastic foams; improved fire resistance plastics; polymer alloys; patents in field. Avocations: tennis, chess, gardening, 20th century world history. Office: PO Box 58362 Houston TX 77258

NEMSER, EARL HAROLD, lawyer; b. N.Y.C., Jan. 17, 1947; s. Harold Summers and Eleanor Patricia (Beckerman) N.; m. Randy Lynn Lehrer, June 17, 1974 (div.); children: Eliza Sarah, Maggie Lehrer. BA, NYU, 1967; JD magna cum laude, Boston U., 1970. Bar: N.Y. 1970, U.S. Supreme Ct. 1975, U.S. Claims Ct. 1979, U.S. Tax Ct. 1985. Law clk. hon. Collins J. Seitz chief judge U.S. Ct. Appeals 3rd Cir., 1970-71; ptnr. Cadwalader, Wickersham & Taft, N.Y.C., 1971-95, Swidler Berlin Shereff Friedman, LLP, N.Y.C., 1996—2001, sr. of counsel, 2002—; pres. Park and 76th Street Co., Inc., N.Y.C., 1998—. Vice chmn. Interactive Brokers Group, LLC, Greenwich, Conn., 1995—; dir. Timber Hill, LLC, Greenwich, Caribbean Cellular Telephone Ltd., Tortola, BVI, 1997-2002. Spl. town atty. Town of Southampton, NY, 2002—; mem. bd. advisors Lenox Hill Hosp. Mem. ABA, Nat. Assn. Criminal Def. Lawyers, Assn. Bar City N.Y.; dir. The Quiogue Assn. Office: Swidler Berlin Shereff Friedman LLP 405 Lexington Ave New York NY 10174-0002 E-mail: ehnemser@swidlaw.com.

NEMSER, ROBERT SOLOMON, visual communications consultant, art director, creative director, designer, writer, educator; b. Bklyn., May 30, 1938; s. Leo Lewis Nemser and Mae (Silver) Wolf; m. Fredda Carol Siegel, Oct. 15, 1960; children: Lori, Adam, Alec, Ian. AAS, N.Y. Coll. Arts and Scis., 1960; MFA, Syracuse U., 1990. Designer Inst. Life Ins., N.Y.C., 1960, Dell Pub. Co., N.Y.C., 1962-65; art. dir. Universal Pub. Co., N.Y.C., 1965-67; v.p. Corp. Ann. Reports, N.Y.C., 1967-73; pres., owner Robert S. Nemser Assocs., N.J. and N.Y., 1974—. Mem. adj. faculty Rutgers U. Mason Gross Sch. Arts, 1987-91; asst. prof. art Trenton (N.J.) State Coll., 1993-94, Baruch/SUNY, 1996-98, Gibbs Coll., 2000—; spkr. on Psychodelic Art in the '60s and the San Francisco Music Scene, The Art of Seeing: Creating with Your Camera, The Psychology and Design of Coffee-Table Books, Photoluminescence: Painting with the Camera; prin. in marquee music and entertainment Home of the Cleftones and Class Act Enterprises, 2003—. Designer, photo editor (books) Martin Luther King Jr., 1976 (Gold medal 1977), The Eternal Sea (Gold medal 1977), Your Future in Space, 1986, King Remembered, 1986, He Had a Dream: Martin Luther King Jr. and the Civil Rights Movement, 1995 (Silver medal 1995); designer Ctrl. N.J. Jewish Home for Aged logo, 1975, East Brunswick (N.J.) Libr. logo, 1976; work exhibited at Art Dirs. Club N.J., 1970—, Rutgers U., 1990; prodr.: (concerts) From the Heart, 1996, 97, 99, 2000—. Bd. dirs. East Brunswick Jewish Ctr., 1975-77, publicity chmn., 1976; TV photo show host East Brunswick Channel 8 Cable TV, 1986. Served to sgt. U.S. Army, 1960-66. Recipient numerous design awards from various profl. orgns.; invited to White House to present Portrait of a President to Pres. Gerald Ford, 1976. Mem. Art Dirs. Club N.J. (life, pres. 1976-77, chmn. edn. coun. 1987-92, numerous awards), Advt. Club N.Y. (Andy award 1973). Avocations: collecting military medals and paraphernalia, collecting elephants, eagles, patriotic and police badges, racquetball, paddleball, noted authority on rock and roll and doo wop music of 1950's and 1960's. Office: PO Box 2229 Fort Lee NJ 07024-0497 E-mail: resmen@aol.com.

NEMYIER, MARGARET GERTRUDE, sales executive; b. Herkimer, NY, Dec. 23, 1930; d. Frank Clark and Reba Louise (Jones) Culver; m. Charles Henry Nemyier, July 22, 1978. BS, SUNY Oneonta, 1953; MS in Edn., SUNY Geneseo, 1973. Cert. elem. tchr. N.Y. Elem. tchr. Richfield Springs Ctrl. Sch., NY, 1953—54, Ilion Ctrl. Sch., NY, 1954—57, Webster Ctrl. Sch., NY, 1957—76; sales rep. Equitable Ins. Co., Perfield, NY, 1976—77; sales clk. Fuelihan's Dress Store, East Rochester, NY, 1977—79; with Projansky Furier & Dress Shop, Victor, NY, 1979—81; sales rep. Avon Products, 1977—. Sec.-treas. Webster Plank North PTA, 1959; vol. cemetery tours Mt. Hope Cemetery Orgn., Rochester, NY, 1978—83; vol. fundraiser at various PBA's, 1977—79; reach for recovery vol. Am. Cancer Soc., Rochester, 1981—86; vol. Gen. Herkimer's Homesite, Ilion Little Theatre Club, 2004; election insp. Monroe & Herkimer Counties, NY, 1990—2003; coord. Ilion HS Mega Reunion Com., 2002. Recipient Cert. of Appreciation, Dept. of Recreation and Parks, Rochester, 1980. Mem.: NEA (life). Democrat. Methodist. Avocations: latch hook rugs, embroidery, traveling to hist. places, collectibles. Home: 236 E Main St Ilion NY 13357

NEN, ROBERT ALLEN (ROBB NEN), professional baseball player; b. San Pedro, Calif., Nov. 28, 1969; s. Dick Nen. Grad. high sch., Los Alamitos, Calif. With Tex. Rangers, 1993; pitcher Fla. Marlins, 1993-97, San Francisco Giants, 1997—. Office: San Francisco Giants 3 Com Park 24 Willie Mays Plz San Francisco CA 94107-2199

NENE, VISHVANATH, research scientist; BSc in Physiology and Biochemistry, U. Southampton, Eng., 1977; PhD in Biochemistry, U. Nottingham, Eng., 1980. Postdoctoral rsch. fellow dept. biochemistry Queen's Med. Ctr., U. Nottingham, 1980—83; postdoctoral rsch. fellow dept. pathology U. Cambridge, England, 1983—86; scientist Internat. Livestock Rsch. Inst., Nairobi, Kenya, 1986—2001; investigator Inst. for Genomic Rsch., Rockville, Md., 2001—. Contbr. articles to profl. jours. Achievements include research in genomics research of eukaryotic protozoan pathogens as a means of understanding their biology and their interactions with mammalian hosts. Office: Inst for Genomic Rsch 9712 Medical Center Dr Rockville MD 20850

NENNEMAN, RICHARD ARTHUR, retired publishing executive; b. Chgo., Oct. 13, 1929; s. William T. and Fannie (Peterson) N.; m. Katherine Ann LaBrunerie, June 29, 1954; children: Ann Walker, Mary Lisa, Katherine Conley. AB magna cum laude, Harvard U., 1951, MA in Internat. Affairs, 1953. With No. Trust Co., Chgo., 1957-58; v.p., treas., dir. First Fed. Savs. & Loan Assn., St. Joseph, Mo., 1958-60; with Valley Nat. Bank, Phoenix, 1960-65; asst. v.p., 1963-65; bus. and fin. editor Christian Sci. Monitor, Boston, 1965-74; v.p., dir. investment rsch. Girard Bank, Phila., 1974-77, sr. v.p., chmn. trust investment policy com., 1977-82; mng. editor Christian Sci. Monitor, Boston, 1983-86; editor, exec. prodr., TV broadcasting Christian Sci. Pub. Soc., Boston, 1987; editor-in-chief Christian Sci. Monitor, 1988-93; ret., 1993. Mem. investment com. Gen. Accident Ins. Group., until 1982; dir. DLB Fund Group, 1994—. Contbr. to Understanding Our Century, 1984; editor: (with Earl Foell) How Peace Came to the World, 1986, The New Birth of Christianity, 1992, Persistent Pilgrim: The Life of Mary Baker Eddy, 1997. Trustee Barnes Found., until 1982; selectman Town of Weston, Mass., 1973-74. Served with AUS, 1954-57. Mem.: Coun. on Fgn. Rels. Home: 314 Hemlock Cir Lincoln MA 01773-4923

NENNER, VICTORIA CORICH, nurse, educator; b. Marshall, Tex., Mar. 17, 1945; d. Bernard Paul and Mary DeLayne (Bowen) Corich; m. Paul Edwin Nenner, Aug. 12, 1970. BSN, Tex. Women's U., 1966; cert., U. Paris, summer 1966; MSN, U. San Diego, 1984. Mem. nursing staff St. Thomas Hosp., London, 1966-67, Parkland Meml. Hosp., Dallas, 1967-68; coord. nursing continuing edn. Scripps Meml. Hosp., La Jolla, Calif., 1974-85; owner, pres. Marvik Ednl. Svcs., Inc., 1985—. Mem. part-time faculty U. Calif., San Diego; mem. vis. faculty U. B.C.; mem. Inservice Coun. San Diego and Imperial Counties, 1974-80, pres., 1976-77; mem. San Diego C.C. Health Edn. Adv. Bd., 1976-84. Contbg. author in healthcare software; prodr. oncology

nursing ednl. videotapes; contbr. articles to profl. jours. Bd. dirs. San Diego Performing Arts League, 1990-92; chair Star Awards Luncheon, 1995; mem. Puente de Oro com. Girl Scouts, 1998—; bd. dirs. Vietnam Vets. San Diego, 1998—. Capt. Nurse Corps, USAF, 1968-77. Named Tex. Student Nurse of Yr., 1966; Regents scholar, Krost-Freeman scholar, Mary Gibbs Jones Nursing scholar. Mem. ANA, Am. Soc. Health Edn. and Tng., Nat. League Nursing (Leadership award 1995), Calif. League for Nursing (pres. 1993-94), Sigma Theta Tau. Office: 1677 1/2 Los Altos Rd San Diego CA 92109-1322 E-mail: vcnenner@cs.com.

NENOV, IVO P. mathematical and software researcher; b. Nikolaevo, Bulgaria, May 5, 1964; arrived in U.S., 1995; s. Panayot Nenov Ivanov and Maria Todorova Ivanova; m. Albena Dragomirova Stoilova-Nenova, Aug. 16, 1987 (div. Apr. 7, 1994); 1 child, Lubomir Ivov. MS, Tech. U. Sofia, Bulgaria, 1990, PhD (hon.), 2003; cert. in internat. bus. mgmt., U. Del., 1992. Rschr. Microprocessor Control Lab., Sofia, Bulgaria, 1986—86; rschr., developer CAD R&D Ctr. Ltd., Sofia, 1990—92; developer, technologist DataMap-Europe Ltd., Sofia, 1993—94; self-employed rschr., developer, cons. Calif., 1995—. Participated, set up European br. Frontline Sys., Inc., Incline Village, Nev., 2003; presenter in field. Contbr. articles to profl. jours. Capt. arty. Bulgarian armed forces, 1982—84. Recipient prize, Nat. Olympiad of Math., 1985, prize for tech., Nat. Competition for Tech., Sofia, 1989, award for extraordinaty ability in sci., INS, 2000. Mem.: Soc. Indsl. and Applied Math. Bulgarian Orthodox. Avocation: flying. Home and Office: 337 Saxonville Way Antelope CA 95843 Office Phone: 415-305-2440. E-mail: ivo_nenov@msn.com.

NENSTIEL, SUSAN KISTHART, fundraising professional; b. Hazleton, Pa., Aug. 21, 1951; d. Frank W. and Mary A. (Price) Kisthart. BS, Pa. State U., 1973; MBA, Wilkes (Pa.) Coll., 1982. Cert. fund raising exec. Control mgr. Barrett, Haentjens & Co., Hazleton, 1973-79, export mgr., 1979-86; exec. dir. Leadership Hazleton, 1986 87; devel. officer Planned Parenthood of NE Pa., Wilkes-Barre, 1986-87; ins. broker, office mgr. Nenstiel & Nenstiel, West Hazleton, Pa., 1988-96; assoc. dir. devel. Hospice St. John, 1996-97; devel. assoc. Luth. Svcs. N.E., 1997-98, reg. dir. devel., 1998-2000; exec. dir. LWV of Pa., 2000-01; sr. v.p. devel. Easter Seals Ea. Pa., 2001—03; dir. major gifts Albright Coll., 2003—. Pres. YWCA, Hazleton, 1983-85, Women's Coalition of Greater Hazleton, 1989-91; sec. Govt. Study Commn., Hazleton, 1986; trustee Hazleton Area Pub. Libr., sec., 1987-89, v.p., 1990-91, pres., 1991-93; chmn. Luzerne County Commn. for Women, 1988-91; mem., chmn. Hazleton City Zoning Bd., 1988-92; treas. Pa. Women's Campaign Fund, 1987-91, pres., 1991-92; mem. Leadership Hazleton Adv. Coun., 1988-92; mem. Pa. Pub. Libr. Project, 1992-94; bd. dirs. Hazleton Health Care Found., 1992-2000, chairperson, 1994-99, Cmty. Banks, Inc., 1996-2001; mem. Greater Hazleton Health Alliance Bd., 1995-2000, sec., 2000; mem. Luzerne County Regional Bd. Cmty. Banks, N.A., 1993-2000, YWCA adv. coun., 1998-2000. Named one of Outstanding Women Penns Woods Coun. Girl Scouts USA, 1977, Outstanding Young Women in Am., 1985, Woman of Yr. Soroptimist Internat., 1984, Greater Hazleton Jaycee Disting. Svc. award, 1990; recipient Luzerne County Pathfinder's award, 1990, Hon. P.E.A.R.L. award YWCA, 1996; named to Pa. Honor Roll of Women, 1996. Mem. AAUW (br. pres. 1977-79, 97-2000, state sec. 1981-83, state treas. 1983-85, state pres. 1992-96, Br. Outstanding Woman of Yr. 1980, assn. program com. 1995-97, ednl. found. bd. dirs. 1999—2003, ednl. found. devel. v.p. 2001-2003), Assn. Fund Raising Profls. (chpt. v.p. 2003—), Greater Hazleton C. of C. (bd. dirs. 1995-2000, treas. 1998-2000). Home: 318 Oxford Pl Macungie PA 18062-1817 E-mail: s.nenstiel@worldnet.att.net.

NENTWICH, MICHAEL ANDREAS ERHART, educator, consultant; b. Prague, Czech Republic, Sept. 6, 1941; came to U.S., 1994; s. Walter Joseph and Charlotte Rosina (Hawle) N. Student, schs. in Linz, Schörfling, Austria, Wellingborough, Eng., Karlsruhe, Germany, Nuremberg (Germany) U., Heidelberg (Germany) U., 1960-64, 65-69, PhD, 1973. German tchr. St. Olave's and St. Saviour's Grammar Sch., London, 1964-65; English lectr. Mannheim (Germany) U., 1969-75; vis. lectr. in German, Chinese U. Hong Kong, 1975-80; rsch. scholar in English Tech. U. Berlin, 1980-81; educator, cons. Goethe-Inst., Bremen, Germany, 1982, Madrid, 1983-85, Düsseldorf, Germany, 1985-88, São Paulo, 1988-92, Munich, 1992-94, N.Y.C., 1994-2000, exec. dir. Atlanta, 2000—. Author: Der schottische Shaw, 1973, Werbemappe—Advocacy Binder for Teachers of German in the USA, 1999; editor Modern Germany Update, Goethe News; contbr. articles to profl. jours. Recipient Sophie Bernsthen scholarship U. Heidelberg, 1968. Avocations: music, painting, travel, theater. Office: Goethe-Inst Atlanta Colony Sq Plaza Level 1197 Peachtree St NE Atlanta GA 30361-3502 Office Phone: 404-892-2388. E-mail: goetheatlanta1@mindspring.com.

NEPHEW, JULIA ANNE, language educator; d. Albert Henry and Elizabeth Anne Nephew. PhD of French Lit., U. Wis.-Madison, 1998. Prof. French Rockford Coll. Co-founder and dir. Jane Addams Tenant Resource Ctr., Rockford, Ill., 2001—03. Recipient Phi Sigma Iota Fgn. Lang. Honor Soc., Phi Sigma Iota, 1999, Pi Delta Phi French Honor Soc., Pi Delta Phi, 1988; scholar Grad., U. Mich., 1988, Whiteside Scholarship Fund, 1984—88; Cmty. Engagement grant, Ill. Campus Compact, 2001—02, Partners in Action grant, 2002—03, Summer Rsch. grant, Rockford Coll., 2001, Summer Travel grant, 1999. Mem.: Betsy-Tacy Soc. (hon. bd. mem.), Medieval Assn. of Midwest, Sixteenth Century Studies, Christine de Pizan Soc. (treas. 2003—). Avocations: travel, cross country skiing, reading, bicycling. Personal E-mail: nephewja@yahoo.com.

NEPOMUCENO, CECIL SANTOS, physician; b. The Philippines, Feb. 1, 1936; came to U.S. 1967; s. Dominador and Augustina (Santos) N.; m. Edna Manacsa, Dec. 4, 1963; children: Joy, Regina, Celeste. MD, U. Santo Tomas, Manila, The Philippines, 1962. Diplomate Am. Bd. Phys. Medicine and Rehab. Intern St. Francis Hosp., Wichita, Kans., 1963; resident Baylor U. Med. Ctr., Dallas, 1967-70; staff physician HealthSouth Lakeshore Rehab. Hosp., Birmingham, Ala., 1994-99; prof. dept. rehab. medicine U. Ala., Birmingham. Former cons. Social Security Adminstrn.; oral bd. examiner Am. Acad. Phys. Medicine and Rehab. Lt. col. USAMR, 1982-94, ret. Mem. Ala. Soc. Phys. Medicine and Rehab.(past pres.), So. Soc. Phys. Medicine and Rehab. (past pres.). Roman Catholic. Home: 1070 Country Club Cir Birmingham AL 35244-1478 E-mail: nepomuceno@charter.net.

NEPPL, WALTER JOSEPH, retired retail store executive; b. Halbur, Iowa, June 15, 1922; s. Frank and Anna (Halbur) N.; m. Marian Maher, Oct. 15, 1945; children: Eugenie Neppl Kauffman, Marilee Neppl Cumming, Deborah Neppl Johnson, John, Thomas (dec.), Christina Neppl Totino, Nancy Neppl Tripucka. With J.C. Penney Co., Inc., 1940—, mgr. store, 1954-55, dist. mgr. Pitts., 1955-61, store coordination mgr. N.Y.C., 1961-64, asst. to dir. dist. mgmt. dept., 1964-65, gen. mdse. mgr. hard lines, 1965-67, v.p., 1967-68, gen. sales and mdse. mgr., 1968-71, dir. merchandising, 1971-72, exec. v.p., 1972-76, pres., chief operating officer, 1976-81, vice-chmn. bd., 1981-82, ret., 1982, dir., 1968-85. Bd. dirs. emeritus J.C. Penney Co. Inc. Trustee emeritus Geraldine R. Dodge Found. Served to capt. USAAF, 1943-45. Decorated D.F.C. Roman Catholic. Home: The Enclave 5345 Annabel Ln Plano TX 75093-3428

NEPTUNE, JOHN ADDISON, retired chemistry educator, consultant; b. Barnesville, Ohio, Nov. 27, 1919; s. George Addison and Lola Mae (Skinner) N.; m. Ruth Elizabeth Dorsey, Aug. 24, 1947; 1 child, Benjamin BS summa cum laude, Muskingum Coll., 1942; MS, U. Wis., 1949, PhD, 1952. Instr. chemistry Muskingum Coll., New Concord, Ohio, 1943-44, 45-48; foreman Tenn. Eastman Corp., Manhattan Project, 1944-45; asst. prof. chemistry Bowling Green State U., Ohio, 1949-50; instr. pharm. chemistry U. Wis.-Madison, 1952-55; asst. prof. chemistry San Jose State U., Calif., 1955-58, assoc. prof., 1958-61, prof., 1961-90, chmn. dept., 1973-86. Mem. Am. Chem. Soc., AAUP. Methodist. Home: 50 Cherokee Ln San Jose CA 95127-2513 Office: San Jose State U Dept Chemistry San Jose CA 95192-0001 Office Phone: 408-924-4941.

NEREM, ROBERT MICHAEL, engineering educator, consultant; b. Chgo., July 20, 1937; s. Robert and Borghild Guneva (Bakken) Nerem; m. Jill Ann Thomson, Dec. 21, 1958 (div. 1977); children: Robert Steven, Nancy Ann Nerem Chambers; m. Marilyn Reed, Oct. 7, 1978; stepchildren: Christina Lynn Maser, Carol Marie Maser. BS, U. Okla., 1959; MS, Ohio State U., 1961, PhD, 1964; D (hon.), U. Paris, 1990. Asst. prof. Ohio State U., Columbus, 1964-68, assoc. prof., 1968-72, prof., 1972-79, assoc. dean Grad. Sch., 1975-79; prof. mech. engring., chmn. dept. U. Houston, 1979-86; Parker H. Petit prof. Ga. Inst. Tech., Atlanta, 1987—, Inst. prof., 1991—, dir. Inst. for Bioengring. and Biosci., 1995—; dir. Ga. Tech/Emory Ctr. for the Engring. of Living Tissues NSF Engring. Rsch. Ctr., Atlanta, 1998—. Mem. Ga. Gov.'s Adv. Coun. on Sci. and Tech. Devel., Atlanta, 1992—95; Alza disting. lectr. Biomed. Engring. Soc., 1991; ASME Thurston lectr., 94; mem. sci. bd. FDA, 2000—03; sr. adv. for bioengring. Nat. Inst. Biomed. Imaging and Bioengring., 2003—. Contbr. articles to profl. jours. Fellow: AAAS, ASME, Am. Inst. Med. and Biol. Engring. (founding pres. 1992—94), Instn. Mech. Engrs., U.K. (hon.); mem.: NAE, Polish Acad. Scis., U.S. Nat. Com. on Biomechanics (chmn. 1988—91), Internat. Fedn. for Med. and Biol. Engring. (pres. 1988—91), Japanese Soc. for Med. & Biol. Engring. (hon.), Internat. Union for Phys. and Engring. Scis. in Medicine (pres. 1991—94), Inst. Medicine, Biomed. Engring. Soc., Am. Acad. Arts and Scis. Home: 2950 Waverly Ct SE Atlanta GA 30339-4200 Office Phone: 404-894-2768. Business E-Mail: robert.nerem@ibb.gatech.edu.

NERHOOD, ROBERT CLARKE, obstetrician and gynecologist; b. Altoona, Pa., Aug. 27, 1944; s. Albert and Jeanne (VanOrmer) N.; m. Carolyn Haught, Aug. 27, 1965, children. Robert, Timothy; m. Deborah Brooks, Nov. 30, 1984. Student, W.Va. U., 1962-65, MD, 1969. Diplomate Am. Bd. Ob-Gyn. Intern Polyclinic Hosp., Harrisburg, Pa., 1969-70; resident in ob-gyn. W.Va. Hosp., Morgantown, 1970-73, Kessler Air Force Med. Ctr., 1973-75; clin. assoc. prof. Sch. Medicine Marshall U., Huntington, 1977-87; dir. resident edn. Allegheny Gen. Hosp./Med. Coll. Pa.; assoc. prof. ob-gyn. Med. Coll. Pa., 1989-92; chief ob-gyn. Berkshire Health Sys.; assoc. prof. Med. Sch. U. Mass.; with Mass. Bd. Perinatal Medicine; chmn. bd. Cabell Huntington Hosp., 2002—; prof. chmn. ob-gyn. divsn. Sch. Medicine Marshall U., Huntington, W.Va., 1992—. Mem. W.Va. Bd. Perinatal Medicine, 1977-87. Ob-gyn. editor Postgraduate Medicine, 1997—. Maj. USAF, 1973-75. Mem. Am. Coll. Ob-Gyn (vice chair W.Va. sect. 1992-95, chair W.Va. sect. 1995-98, 2001-, mem. adv. coun. dist. IV 1992-98, 2001-). Office: Marshall U Sch Medicine Ob-Gyn 1600 Medical Center Dr Huntington WV 25701-3655 Office Fax: 304-691-1453.

NERLINGER, JOHN WILLIAM, retired trade association administrator; b. Detroit, June 22, 1920; s. John W. and Bessie Prudence (Beith) N.; m. Pearl Pauline Procup, Nov. 4, 1943; children: John Charles, Ruth Marie Nerlinger Blazevich. Grad., Detroit Bus. Inst., 1939; BA, Detroit Inst. Tech., 1950; LLD (hon.), Northwood U., Midland, Mich., 1990. Bus. mgr. Retail Gasoline Dealers Assn. Mich., Detroit, 1939-51, exec. sec., 1951-63, Nat. Congress Petroleum Retailers, Detroit, 1951-63; asst. exec. v.p. Automotive Service Industry Assn., Chgo., 1963-73, exec. v.p., 1973-80, pres., 1981-91; ret., 1991. Vice chmn. Automotive Hall of Fame; advisor Nat. Hwy. Users Fedn. Served with AUS, 1942-45, PTO. Recipient Petroleum Man of Yr. award Gasoline News, 1961, Automotive Replacement Edn. award Northwood U., Midland, Mich., 1975, Disting. Svc. citation Automotive Hall of Fame, 1978, Industry Leadership award Automotive Svc. Industry Assn., 1978. Mem. Am. Soc. Assn. Execs. (mem. edn. com.), Chgo. Soc. Assn. Execs., Automotive Old Timers, Automotive Info. Council (dir.), Automotive Boosters Clubs Internat., Chgo. Assn. Commerce and Industry (mem. govt. relations com.), Nat. Assn. Wholesalers-Distbrs. (exec. com., dir. distbn. research and edn. found), Automotive Acad. Clubs: Mid-America, Inverness Golf. Lodges: Masons (32 deg.), Shriners. Lutheran. Home: 601 E Fairview St Arlington Heights IL 60005-2770

NERLOVE, MARC LEON, economics professor; b. Chgo., Oct. 12, 1933; s. Samuel Henry and Evelyn (Andelman) N.; children: Susan, Miriam. BA, U. Chgo., 1952; MA, Johns Hopkins U., 1955, PhD, 1956. Analytical statistician USDA, Washington, 1956-57; assoc. prof. U. Minn., Mpls., 1959-60; prof. Stanford (Calif.) U., 1960-65, Yale U., 1965-69; prof. econs. U. Chgo., 1969-74; F.W. Taussig rsch. prof. Harvard Coll., Cambridge, Mass., 1967-68; vis. Cook prof. Northwestern U., Evanston, Ill., 1973-74, Cook prof., 1974-82; prof. econs. U. Pa., Phila., 1982-86, Univ. prof., 1986-93; prof. agr. and resource econs. U. Md., College Park, 1993—. Author: Dynamics of Supply, 1958, Distributed Lags and Demand Analysis, 1958, Estimation and Identification of Cobb-Douglas Production Functions, 1965, Analysis of Economic Time Series: A Synthesis, 1979, Household and Economy: Welfare Economics of Endogenous Fertility, 1987, Essays on Panel Data Econometrics, 2002; contbr. numerous articles to profl. jours. 1st lt. AUS, 1957-59. Recipient award Am. Farm Econ. Assn., 1956, 58, 61, 79, P.S. Mahalanobis medal Indian Econ. Soc., 1975. Fellow Am. Statis. Assn., Econometric Soc. (v.p. 1980, pres. 1981), Am. Acad. Arts and Scis., Am. Agrl. Econ. Assn.; mem. NAS, Am. Econ. Assn. (mem. exec. com. 1977-79, John Bates Clark medal 1969), Royal Econ. Soc., Phi Beta Kappa, others. Achievements include research on economics of agriculture with particular reference to developing countries, population and economic growth; analysis of categorical data, particularly business and household surveys. Office: U Md Dept Agr and Resource Econs College Park MD 20742-0001 E-mail: mnerlove@arec.umd.edu.

NERN, CHRISTOPHER CARL, lawyer; b. N.Y.C., Sept. 30, 1944; s. William Francis and Jule Anne (Allison) N.; m. Kathleen Jean Brogan, Aug. 24, 1974 (div. Nov. 1985). BA, Mich. State U., 1967; JD, Wayne State U., 1972. Bar: Mich. 1973, U.S. Dist. Ct. (ea. and we. dists.) Mich. 1973, U.S. Ct. Appeals (6th cir.) 1974, U.S. Supreme Ct. 1979. Asst. atty. gen. State of Mich., Lansing, 1972-73; staff atty. corp. affairs div. Detroit Edison Co., 1973-74, sr.atty. rates and regulatory div., 1975-78, gen. atty. regulatory affairs div., 1978-82, assoc. gen. counsel, mgr., 1982-89, asst. v.p., asst. gen. counsel, 1989-93, v.p., gen. counsel, 1993-2000, DTE Energy, 1993-2000; adj. prof. St. Mary's Coll., 2001—. Adj. prof. Lawrence Tech. U., 2002—. Mem. allocation com. United Found., Detroit, 1983, 86-87; bd. dirs. Oakland Parks Found., Oakland County, Mich., 1985, Mich. Opera Theatre, 1996—; trustee Music Hall Ctr. for the Performing Arts, 1987-93. Served with USAF, 1967-69. Mem. ABA (bd. trustees), Detroit Met. Bar Assn. (trustee found.), Am. Corp. Counsel Assn. (pres. Mich chpt. 1986-88), Econs. Club (Detroit), Detroit Golf Club, Detroit Athletic Club. Roman Catholic. Home: 1052 Stratford Ln Bloomfield Hills MI 48304-2930 E-mail: nernchris@aol.com.

NERODE, ANIL, mathematician, educator; b. L.A., June 4, 1932; s. Nirad Ranjan and Agnes (Spencer) N.; m. Sondra Raines, Feb. 12, 1955 (div. 1968); children: Christopher Curtis, Gregory Daniel; m. Sally Riedel Sievers, May 16, 1970; 1 child, Nathanael Caldwell. BA, U. Chgo., 1949, BS, 1952, MS, 1953, PhD, 1956. Group leader automata and weapons systems Lab. Applied Sci., U. Chgo., 1954-57; mem. Inst. for Advanced Study, Princeton, 1957-58, 62-63; vis. asst. prof. math. U. Calif. at Berkeley, 1958-59; mem. faculty Cornell U., 1959—, prof. math., 1965—, Goldwin Smith prof. math., 1990—, chmn. dept. math., 1982-87, dir. Math. Sci. Inst., 1986-97; acting dir. Center for Applied Math., 1965-66; vis. prof. Monash U., Melbourne, Australia, 1970, 74, 78, 79, U. Chgo., 1976, M.I.T., 1980, U. Calif., San Diego, 1981; disting. vis. scientist EPA, 1985-87; dir. Ctr. for Found. of Intelligent Sys. Cornell U., 1997—2001. Prin. investigator numerous grants; mem. sci. adv. bd. EPA, 1988-93, chair tech. adv. panel Global Change, 1990-92; mem. sci. adv. bd. Ctr. for Intelligent Control, Harvard-MIT-Brown U., 1988-94; cons. to govt. and industry; co-founder Hynomics Corp., 1995. Author: (with John Crossley) Combinatorial Functors, 1974, (with Richard Shore) Logic for Applications, 2d edit., 1996, (with G.A. Metakides) Principles of Logic and Logic Programming, 1996, (with B. Khoussainov) Automata Theory and its Applications, 2001; editor Advances in Mathematics, 1967-70, Jour. Symbolic Logic, 1967-82, Annals of Pure and Applied Logic, 1983-96, Future Generation Computing Systems, 1983-97, Jour. Pure & Applied Algebra, 1988—, Annals of Math. and Artificial Intelligence, 1989—, Logical Methods in Computer Sci., 1991-94, Computer Modelling and Simulation, 1991—, Constraints, 1995-2001, Grammers, 1997-2001, (with J. Remmel, S. Goncharov, Y. Ershov) Handbook of Recursive Algebra, 1998. Mem. AIII, IEEE, Assn. Computing Machinery, Am. Math. Soc. (assoc. editor procs. 1962-65, v.p. 1992-95), Soc. Indsl. and Applied Math., Math. Assn. Am., Assn. Symbolic Logic, European Assn. for Theoretical Computer Sci. Home: 406 Cayuga Heights Rd Ithaca NY 14850-1402 Office: Cornell U 545 Mallott Hall Dept Math Ithaca NY 14853-4201 E-mail: anil@math.cornell.edu.

NERY, EDMUNDO BARBIN, periodontist, researcher; b. Daet, Camarines Norte, Philippines, Apr. 6, 1930; came to U.S., 1953; naturalized, 1973; s. Jose Robel and Paula (Barbin) N.; m. Teresita Lacorte, July 2, 1966; children—Jose, Melissa. D.M.D., Nat. U., Manila, Philippines, 1951. Intern, then resident in oral surgery Balt. City Hosp., 1953-55; resident in gen. dentistry Albert Einstein Med. Ctr., Phila., 1956-57; postdoctoral fellow Temple U., Phila., 1957-58; rsch. assoc. U. Pa., Phila., 1963-65, U. Pitts., 1965-68; assoc. clin. prof. Marquette U., Milw., 1974—; chief dental rsch. VA Med. Ctr., Milw., 1973—; rsch. cons. Elwyn Inst., Pa., 1969-71; chmn. VA Coop. Study Program, Milw., 1981—. Contbr. articles to profl. jours. Guggenheim Found. fellow, 1955-56; Am. Cancer Soc. fellow, 1964-65. Mem. ADA, Am. Acad. Periodontology, Internat. Assn. for Dental Research, Wis. Soc. Periodontists, Filipino-Am. Assn. Wis., Omicron Kappa Upsilon. Roman Catholic.

NES, DAVID GULICK, retired diplomat; b. York, Pa., Feb. 17, 1917; s. Charles Motier and Ethel (Billmeyer) N.; m. Elizabeth Taylor Houghton, Dec. 7, 1946; children: Victoria, Nancy, Margaret, Audrey, Wendy. AB in History with hons., Princeton U., 1939; postgrad., Harvard U., 1939-40. With Balt. Sun, 1940-41; div. asst. Dept. State, Washington, 1941-42, fgn. svc. officer, 1946-68, assigned to Washington, 1952-54, 56-59; vice consul Am. Consulate, Glasgow, Scotland, 1946-49; 2d sec. Am. Embassy, Paris, 1949-52; dep. chief mission, counselor Tripoli, 1954-56, Rabat, 1959-62; dep. chief mission min. Saigon, Vietnam, 1963-64, Cairo, 1965-67; ret., 1968. Columnist, lectr. in field, 1968—. Capt. AUS, 1942-46, CBI. Decorated Bronze Star. Mem. Chevy Chase Golf Club, Green Spring Valley Hunt Club, West River Sailing Club, N.Y. Yacht Club. Home: 15 Crestline Ct Owings Mills MD 21117-4336

NES, SHERMAN J. academic administrator, management educator, investment executive; b. Newport News, Va., Jan. 12, 1946; s. Sherman Edward and Leola Mae (Pryor) J.; children: Kimberly, Sherman Edward. BA in Am. Studies with honors, Williams Coll., 1968; MBA, Harvard U., 1970, EdD, 1978. Woodrow Wilson adminstrv. intern, asst. to pres. Cen. State U., Ohio, 1970-71; asst. dir. Office Coop. Acad. Planning Inst. for Svc. to Edn., Washington, 1971-72; mgmt. cons. Cresap, McCormick & Paget, Inc., Washington, 1972-75; mgmt. cons. mgmt. div. Acad. for Ednl. Devel., Inc., Washington, 1975-77; v.p. for adminstrn. Fisk U., Nashville, 1977-80, v.p., acting dean, 1980-82; exec. v.p., prof. mgmt. Tuskegee (Ala.) U., 1982-84, prof. mgmt., exec. v.p., provost, 1984-91; prof. mgmt., provost, v.p. for acad. affairs Clark Atlanta U., 1991-93; pres., headmaster So. Normal Sch., Brewton, Ala., 1993-96; investment rep. Edward D. Jones & Co., 1996-99; fin. advisor Prudential Securities, Inc., Atlanta, 1999—2002; v.p. devel. Knoxville (Tenn.) Coll., 2000—03; prin., owner Jones Fin. Svcs., 2004. Bd. dirs. Better Bus. Bur. Nashville/Middle Tenn., 1978-82; mgmt. bd. John A. Andrew Community Hosp., 1982-85; adv. bd. St. Andrews Sewanee Sch., Tenn., 1986-92, bd. trustees, 1993-97; mem. Nashville Coun. on Fgn. Rels.; bd. trustees YMCA, Brewton, Ala., 1995—. Harvard Grad. Sch. Edn. teaching fellow in edn., 1976-77. Mem. Alumni Coun. Harvard Grad. Sch. Edn., Williams Coll. Exec. Coun. Alumni Soc, Kiwanis. Republican. Unitarian Universalist. Avocations: sports, reading, tennis, weightlifting, cooking. Home: PO Box 11222 Knoxville TN 37939 Office: Raymond James 6555 Chapman Hwy Knoxville TN 37920 Office Phone: 865-579-2776. Business E-Mail: sherman.jones@raymondjames.com.

NESBETH-TONG, SERENA BRIDGET, finance educator, consultant; d. Austin Nesbeth and Doris May Cassie-Nesbeth; m. Keith Tong, Sept. 25, 1999. BA, Bklyn. Coll., 1996; MBA (hon.), LI U., 2003. Paralegal: ABA. Tng. coord. JP Morgan Chase & Co., N.Y.C., 1991—2001; lead instr. bus. mgmt. LI Bus. Inst., Flushing, NY, 2002—. Mem.: Decision Scis. Soc., Orgn. of Mgmt., Sigma Beta Delta. Office: LI Bus Inst 37-12 Prince St Flushing NY 11354 Personal E-mail: renabet@aol.com. E-mail: stong@libi.edu.

NESBIT, LYNN, literary agent; BA in speech, Northwestern U. Asst. to agent Sterling Lord; head literary dept. Internat. Creative Mgmt.; ptnr. Janklow & Nesbit Assocs., N.Y.C., 1989—. Achievements include representing leading authors, among others, Tom Wolfe, Toni Morrison. John LeCarre, Jimmy and Rosalynn Carter, Anne Rice, Nora Ephron, Michael Crichton and Gail Sheehy. Office: Janklow & Nesbit Assocs 598 Madison Ave New York NY 10023

NESBIT, PHYLLIS SCHNEIDER, judge; b. Newkirk, Okla., Sept. 21, 1919; d. Vernon Lee and Irma Mae (Biddle) Schneider; m. Peter Nicholas Nesbit, Sept. 14, 1939. BS in Chemistry, U. Ala., 1948, BS in Law, 1958, JD, 1969. Bar: Ala. 1958. Ptnr. Wilters, Brantley and Nesbit, Robertsdale, Ala., 1958-74; pvt. practice Robertsdale, 1974-76; dist. judge Baldwin County Juvenile Ct., 1977-88; supernumerary dist. judge and juvenile ct. judge Baldwin County, 1989—. Bd. dirs. Baldwin Youth Svcs.; bd. dirs., v.p. women's activities So. Ala. chpt. Nat. Safety Coun., 1978-83; chmn. quality assurance com. The Homestead Retirement Village, 1992-95. Mem. Nat. Assn. Women Lawyers, Nat. Assn. Women Judges, N.Am. Judges Assn., Ala. Dist. Judges Assn., Ala. Coun. Juvenile Judges, Am. Judicature Soc., Baldwin County Bar Assn., Baldwin Sr. Travelers (sec. 1994-98), Spanish Fort, Fairhope Bus. and Profl. Women's, Phi Alpha Delta. Methodist.

NESBIT, ROBERT GROVER, management consultant; b. Scranton, Pa., Feb. 8, 1932; s. George Archibald and Mildred Maude (Bohl) N.; m. Nancy Elizabeth Wilson, June 17, 1961; children: Robert, Jonathan. BS, U. Scranton, 1957; MS, NYU, 1958. Asst. to dean NYU, N.Y.C., 1960-64; mdse. mgr. Associated Merchandising Corp., N.Y.C., 1964-67; dir. corp. mktg. Genesco, Inc., Nashville, 1968-77; v.p., div. gen. mgr. Levi Straus & Co., San Francisco, 1977-79; sr. partner Korn/Ferry Internat., N.Y.C., 1979—. Trustee Rollins Coll., 1992-95, U. Scranton, 1995—. With U.S. Army, 1953-55. Mem. Orchid Island Golf and Tennis Club, Sigma Nu. Clubs: N.Y. Athletic. Presbyterian. Home: 939 Orchid Pt Way Vero Beach FL 32963

NESBIT, ROBERT RAYMOND, JR., surgeon; b. New Haven, Apr. 1, 1939; BA, Harvard U., 1961; MD, U. Rochester, 1965. Diplomate Am. Bd. Surgery. Intern Strong Meml. Hosp., Rochester, 1965-66, resident in surgery, 1966-67, 69-74; chief vascular surgery Med. Coll. Ga. Hosps., Augusta, 1994-2000; prof. surgery Med. Coll. Ga., 1994 2000, prof. surgery emeritus, 2000—, dir. med. student edn. dept. surgery, 2002—. Fellow ACS; mem. Am. Assn. for Vascular Surgery, So. Surg. Assn., Assn. VA Surgeons, So. Assn. Vascular Surgery, Augusta-Richmond County Hist. Soc. (pres. 2003—), Am. Osler Soc., Atlanta Vascular Soc., (pres. 2004—), Phi Beta Kappa, Alpha Omega Alpha. Office: Med Coll Ga Dept Surgery Augusta GA 30912 Office Phone: 706-721-1967. E-mail: rnesbit@mail.mcg.edu.

NESBIT, SANDI MICHELLE, personnel director; b. Marietta, Ga., Aug. 30, 1963; d. Walter DeForest (Stepfather) and Linda S. Van Fleet, William E. Ray; m. Eric James E Nesbit, Oct. 11, 1998; 1 child, Cora Helene. Title Insurance Agent Tenn., 2002; Notary Public at Large Tenn., 2000. Ceo/founder NNBS, Inc., Anytime Services.com, Knoxville, Tenn., 1999—; mgr. Nationwide Homes, Alcoa, Tenn., 1998—2000. Author: (educational workbook) The Title Searchers Handbook. Hon. chmn. Nat. Rep. Congl. Com., 2003. Pentacostal. Avocations: travel, reading, music, animals. Office: NNBS Inc PO Box 50666 Knoxville TN 37950 Office Phone: 865-633-5079.

NESBIT, WILLIAM TERRY, small business owner, consultant; b. Pitts., Jan. 30, 1945; s. William Frank and Glenna (Cleeton) N.; divorced. Owner, CEO Narrow Gauge Car Shop, Evergreen Outdoor Ctr., Shiremanstown, Pa., 1972—; mem. faculty Millersville (Pa.) U., 1976-81, Temple U., Phila., 1979, Nat. Aquatic and Small Craft Sch., Bemis Point, N.Y., 1980, Harrisburg (Pa.) Area C. C., 1981-82, 91, Dickinson Coll., Carlisle, Pa., 1982-83. Judge 32d Capital Area Sci., Engring. Fair, Dickinson Coll., Carlisle, Pa., 1989; mem. tech. briefs reader adv. panel NASA, 2000—. Co-developer ARC basic and whitewater canoeing programs for instrn., 1977-79; inventor, developer The Z

Drag for Boat Rescues, 1980; developer, mfr. first HOn3 ready-to-run plastic rolling stock having NMRA warrant; contbg. author: The Brown Book, 2d edit., 1982. Vol. ARC, 1961—; contbr. A.C. Kalmbach Meml. Libr., Chattanooga; benefactor Carlyton Sch. Dist. Libr., Carnegie, Pa. Recipient award for Humanity ARC, 1967, award for 30 Yrs. Vol. Svc., 1991; named Class I Radiol. Protection Officer, U.S. Dept. Def. and NRC, 1993. Mem. Math. Assn. Am., Nat. Assn. Canoe Liveries and Outfitters (founding), Nat. Model Railroad Assn. (life, mid-eastern region bd. dirs. 1997-2001, supt. Susquehanna divsn. 1996-2000, edn. chair 2002-), Conewago Canoe Club (canoe tng. officer 1999—). Episcopalian. Avocation: ferroequinology. Office: Evergreen Outdoor Ctr PO Box 3081 Shiremanstown PA 17011-3081 E-mail: william.nesbit@dla.mil.

NESBITT, CHARLES RUDOLPH, lawyer, energy consultant; b. Miami, Okla., Aug. 30, 1921; s. Charles Rudolph and Irma Louise (Wilhelmi) N.; m. Margot Dorothy Lord, June 6, 1948; children: Nancy Margot Nesbitt Nagle, Douglas Charles, Carolyn Jane Nesbitt Gresham-Fiegel. BA, U. Okla., 1942; JD, Yale U., 1947. Bar: Okla. 1947, U.S. Supreme Ct. 1957. Pvt. practice, Oklahoma City, 1948-62, 67-69, 75-91, 95—; atty. gen., 1963-67; mem. Okla. Corp. Commn., 1968-75, chmn., 1969-75; sec. of energy State of Okla., 1991-95; pvt. practice Oklahoma City, 1995—. Okla. rep., v.p. Interstate Oil and Gas Compact. Trustee endowment fund St. Gregory's Coll.; pres. Hist. Preservation, Inc.; pres. bd. trustees Okla. Mus. Art; v.p., bd. dirs. Western History Collections Assocs., U. Okla. Librs.; mem. panel arbitrators Am. Arbitration Assn., NASD, NYSE. With AUS, 1942-46. Mem. ABA, Okla. Bar Assn., Oklahoma City C. of C., Phi Beta Kappa, Phi Delta Phi. Episcopalian. Home: 1703 N Hudson Ave Oklahoma City OK 73103-3428 Office: 125 NW 6th St Oklahoma City OK 73102-6014 Office Phone: 405-235-5333.

NESBITT, GREGORY LEON, utility executive, mechanical engineer; b. Albany, Oreg., Feb. 20, 1938; s. John Wesley and Eleanor Mae (Porter) N.; m. Jennylee Sandberg, June 15, 1958; children: Denise Lynn, Staci Lynn, Gregory Leon. BSM.E., Oreg. State U., 1958. Diplomate: registered profl. engr. Calif. Engr. San Diego Gas & Electric Co., Calif., 1961-64, staff engr., 1964-68, supr. mech. engring., 1968-70, mgr. resource planning, 1970-76, mgr. fuel supply, 1976-80; sr. v.p. Central La. Electric Co., Pineville, 1980—. Asst. v.p. energy San Diego C. of C., 1978-80; dir. Alexandria, Pineville C. of C., 1983. Served to lt. (j.g.) U.S. Navy, 1958-61. Mem. ASME (chmn. San Diego sect. 1967-68), Electric Power Research Inst., Nat. Acad. Engring., Pi Kappa Phi Office: CLECO Corporation PO Box 5000 Pineville LA 71361-5000 Home: 936 Manzanita Ave Eureka CA 95503-5466 *Seek out the unknown! From my earliest days I have been driven by a powerful curiosity to learn about what I do not know. The world is full of wonder. I hope I never stop searching it out.*

NESBITT, JOHN ARTHUR, recreational therapist, writer, educator, researcher; b. Detroit, Mar. 29, 1933; s. John Jackson and Anna Maye (Hartley) N.; children: John Arthur, and Victoria Bowen. Attended, Howe Mil. Sch., 1945-51, Olivet Coll., 1952-53; BA, Mich. State U., 1955; MA, Columbia Univ., 1961, EdD, 1968. Registered hosp. recreation dir.; cert. therapeutic recreation splty. Program dir. Jaycees Internat., Miami, Fla., 1957-60; therapeutic recreation specialist Rusk Inst. Rehab. Medicine, N.Y.U., Bellevue Med. Ctr., 1960-61; dir. World Commn. on Vocat. Rehab., Rehab. Internat., N.Y.C., 1963—65; dep. dir. gen. World Leisure and Recreation Assn., N.Y.C., 1964—66; asst. sec. gen. Rehab. Internat., N.Y.C., 1966-68; asst. prof., coord. rehab. svc., leisure studies San Jose State U., Calif., 1968-69; prof., chmn. recreation edn. program U. Iowa, Iowa City, 1972-76, prof. therapeutic recreation, 1977—91, prof. emeritus, 1991—. Pres., CEO Spl. Recreation disABLED Internat., Inc., 1978—; dir., vice chair People to People Com. Disability, 1964-2000; chmn. sub com. recreation and leisure U.S. President's Com. on Employment of Handicapped, 1972-81; dir. Internat. Ctr. on Spl. Recreation, 1978—. Author, editor books in field; editor Alert Mag., 1956; Jaycees Internat. World, 1957-60; Internat. Rehab. of Disabled Rev., 1965-68; Therapeutic Recreation Jour., 1968-70; Jour. Iowa Parks and Recreation, 1974-76; Play, Recreation, and Leisure for People Who Are Disabled, 1977; Fed. Funding for Spl. Recreation, 1978; New Concepts and New Processes in Spl. Recreation, 1978; New Horizons in Profl. Tng. in Recreation Svc. for Handicapped Children and Youth, 1983; Nisbet, Nesbitt Family Surname Assn. Newsletter, 1983-86; Spl. Recreation for DisABLED Digest, 1983-89; U.S.A. Ban Fireworks and Fireworks Safety Campaign Bull., 1988—; UNAGRAM, 1997-99; sr. editor Recreation and Leisure Svc. for Disadvantaged, 1969 (Nat. Recreation Lit. award); editor, compiler Spl. Recreation Compendium of 1,500 Resources for Disabled People, 3d edit., 1989; Special Recreation for Disabled Press, University Heights, Iowa, 1989; webmaster Global Vision Rehab. and Recreation for People with Disabilities, American Stop Fireworks Victimization Campaign, Eric Collection. Bd. dir., treas. United Cerebral Palsy Assn., San Mateo and Santa Clara County, 1970-72; bd. dir. Harold Russell Found., 1971-73; Goodwill Industries Santa Clara County, 1969-72; rehab. counselor, master therapeutic recreation specialist; bd. dir. Hawkeye Area Poverty Cmty. Action Program, Iowa; Iowa Pk. and Recreation Assn., Am. Leisure and Recreation Assn., Washington, others; bd. dir., state v.p. Iowa Aging Coalition, Iowa; bd. dir., founding pres. Santa Clara County Assn. on Recreation Handicapped, Iowa; bd. dir., tech. adv. Disability Internat. Found., 1997—. Served in USAFR, 1955-57; maj. Ret. Recreation Svc. Ill. and Handicapped fellow; recipient numerous awards and citations for work with handicapped, including Torch of Gold Award, Nat. Boy Scouts Am.; Appreciation Award Philippines Found. Mem. Nat. Therapeutic Recreation Soc. (pres. 1970-71, Disting. Svc. Award), Nat. Rehab. Assn.; Am. Assn. Leisure and Recreation (bd. dir. 1977-80, with Tommy Wilson svc. Handicapped Youth); Nat. Consortium on Phys. Edn. and Recreation for Handicapped (pres. 1976-77, Nat. Scholarship award); Nat. Forum Comml. Recreation and Handicapped (chmn. 1979); Iowa Parks and Recreation Assn. (bd.dir. 1973-75, 89-90); Nat. Rehab. Counseling Assn.; Council Exceptional Children; Pi Sigma Epsilon. Presbyterian. Avocations: art, gardening, travel, genealogy, cmty. svc. Office: Spl Recreation disABLED Internat 701 Oaknoll Dr Iowa City IA 52246-5168 E-mail: john-nesbitt@uiowa.edu.

NESBITT, LLOYD IVAN, podiatrist; b. Toronto, Ont., Can., Sept. 24, 1951; s. Allan Jay and Rose (Shuster) N.; m. Marlene Cindy Wegler, May 13, 1984; children: Hilary Liza, Andrea Eve, Jeffrey Ryan. D in Podiatric Medicine, Calif. Coll. Podiatric Medicine, San Francisco, 1975. Diplomate Internat. Soc. Podiatric Laser Surgery. Residency program Vancouver (B.C.) Gen. Hosp., Can., 1975-76; pvt. practice podiatric medicine Toronto. Lectr. numerous colls., fitness ctrs. and sports medicine confs., Ont., 1979—; bd. dirs. Cumba Ins. Co., Toronto. Contbr. numerous articles to sports medicine books and jours; editor Canadian Podiatrist Jour., 1979-88. Bd. dirs. Cumba Charitable Found. Fellow: Am. Acad. Podiatric Sports Medicine, Can. Podiatric Sports Medicine Acad. (pres. 1979—89, editor newsletter 1977—89); mem.: Ont. Podiatric Med. Assn. (past pres.), Am. Podiatric Med. Assn., Am. Soc. Laser Medicine & Surgery (diplomate), Sierra Club. Avocations: skiing, in-line skating, hockey, sailing, bicycling, gardening. Home: 122 Argonne Crescent Willowdale ON Canada M2K 2K1 Office: Madison Ctr Office Tower 4950 Yonge St Ste 2414 Toronto ON Canada M2N 6K1 Office Phone: 416-733-8533.

NESBITT, LOIS ELLEN, personal trainer, writer; d. George Davis and Maureen White Nesbitt. Student, Stanford U., 1977—79; BA magna cum laude, Harvard U., 1981; PhD, Princeton U., 1988. Registered yoga tchr. Yoga Alliance. Freelance writer/critic, 1977—; editor Princeton U. Press., MIT Press, N.Y.C., 1987—96; yoga instr., tchr. trainer Blue Sky Yoga, N.Y.C. and East Hampton, 1997—. Lectr./tchr. in field, 1988—94. Author: Brodsky & Utkin, 1991; New Mus. of Contemporary Art, N.Y., Vienna Scussion, Austria, 1989—99. Mem.: Phi Beta Kappa. Home: Apt 4E 95 Christopher St New York NY 10014

NESBITT, MARK, management consultant; b. Ottawa, Ont., Can., Dec. 31, 1952; s. William Alonzo and Barbara (Ellis) N.; 1 child, Karen Elizabeth. BSc, Carleton U., Ottawa, 1973, BA, 1974; MBA, Harvard U., 1978. Cert. Mgmt. Cons. Cons. Peat Marwick & Ptnrs., Ottawa, 1978; assoc./ mgr. Veritas Cons. Inc., Toronto, Ont., Can., 1978-86, pres., 1986-93; pres., CEO Vertex Cons. Inc., Toronto, 1993—. IS com. mem. YMCA Metro Toronto, 1992-93; bd. dirs. Inst. Cert. Mgmt. Cons. Can. Mem. Am. Mktg. Assn., Inst. Cert. Mgmt. Cons. Ont., Inst. Cert. Mgmt. Cons. Can. (pres. 1997-98, chmn. 1998), Assn. for Creative Change, Internat. Mgmt. Devel.: Internat. Consulting (1st v.p., sec.-treas. 1995-98, pres. 1998—). Anglican. Avocations: bicycling, photography, programming. Office: Vertex Cons Inc 14 Dundonald St Toronto ON Canada M4Y 1K2

NESBITT, ROBERT EDWARD LEE, JR., physician, educator, scientific researcher, writer, poet; b. Albany, Ga., Aug. 21, 1924; s. Robert E.L. and Anne Louise (Hill) N.; m. Ellen Therese Morrissey. BA, Vanderbilt U., 1944, MD, 1947. Diplomate: Am. Bd. Ob-Gyn (asso. examiner). Asst. prof. Johns Hopkins U., 1954-56, chief obstetric pathology lab., acting chief obstetrics, 1955-56; prof., chmn. dept. ob-gyn Albany (N.Y.) Med. Coll., Union U., 1956-61, SUNY Health Sci. Ctr., Syracuse, 1961-81, dir. gen. gynecology service, 1982-84, prof. and chmn. emeritus dept. ob-gyn; obstetrician-gynecologist-in-chief Albany Hosp., 1956-61; obstetrician, gynecologist-in-chief Syracuse Meml. Hosp., 1961-65; obstetrician-gynecologist-in-chief Crouse-Irving Hosp., 1963-70, attending staff, 1970-84; prof. surgery U. South Fla., Tampa, 1988-92, prof. ob.-gyn., 1988-92. Chief ob-gyn State U. Hosp., 1964-81, chmn. med. staff and med. bd., 1964-66; attending staff St. Joseph's Hosp.; cons., chief gynecology sect. surg. service Syracuse VA Hosp., 1984-88; chief gynecology sect., asst. chief surgery, dir. uro-gynecology VA Med. Ctr., Bay Pines, Fla., 1988-92, acting chief of staff, 1990, interim chief surgery, 1991-92, chmn. O.R. com. surg. svc., 1988-92, chmn. patient care evaluation com., 1989-90, chmn. clin. exec. bd., 1990, chmn. drug usage evaluation com., 1990-91, chmn. profl. standards bd., 1990; cons. Syracuse Psychiat. Inst.; mem. cancer tng. grants and edn. com. Nat. Cancer Insts.; mem. adv. com. Bur. Maternal and Child Health, N.Y. State Dept. Health, 1957-61; nat. adviser to Children, publ. of Children's Bur., HEW, 1959-63; cons. Children's Bur., 1959-62; mem. prenatal care guide subcom. Am. Pub. Health Assn., 1962-64; cons. to regional adviser in maternal and child health Pan Am. San. Bur., WHO, 1963-65; numerous guest professorships including univs. in Mex., Chile, Uruguay, Colombia, St. Vincent (W.I.), Venezuela, People's Republic of China, Western Europe, Panama, Australia, Canada. Author: Perinatal Loss in Modern Obstetrics, 1957, Last Twig on the Bush?, 1999, In the Fullness of Time, 1999, Hearts of Flesh, 2001, (poetry collections) Chorales for Arid Souls, 1999, The Fullness Search, 2000, Visions Shared, 2000, Daily Relevance, 2000, Glimpses, 2002, Marked Off from Pagans, 2000, Puppet or Saint, 2001, Latent Harvest, 2002, Dry River Beds, 2003, Language of the Soul, 2003, over 530 published poems, also poems in numerous anthologies (15 Editor's Choice awards, Best Poems and Poets, 2000-2003, Internat. Who's Who in Poetry, 2004), sect. on ob-gyn in Rypin's Med. Licensure Exams, over 300 nuggets of spiritual discernment; co-author: Infant, Perinatal, Maternal and Childhood Mortality in U.S, 1968; editor: sect. on obstetrics and gynecology Stedman's Medical Dictionary, 1958—64, sect. on fetus Funk and Wagnalls Universal Std. Ency., 1959; 1st guest editor: sect. on fetus Clinics in Perinatology, 1974; 1st editor sect. on fetus Clinical Diagnosis Quiz for Obstetrics and Gynecology, 1976, Clini-Pearls in Obstetrics and Gynecology, 1977; contbr.: sect. on fetus Attorneys' Textbook of Medicine. Capt. M.C., U.S. Army, 1952-54. Named One of Ten Outstanding Young Men in Am., U.S. Jr. C. of C., 1957; Robert E.L. Nesbitt Jr. scholarship, Sr. Resident in Ob-Gyn, and Robert E.L. Nesbitt Jr. student scholarship established in his honor, SUNY Health Sci. Ctr. at Syracuse, 1987; recipient Wisdom award, 2001, named to Hall of Fame, Wisdom Soc., 2001, Winston Churchill medal of wisdom, 2002. Fellow: A.C.S. (com. forum fundamental surg. problems 1962—67), N.Y. Acad. Scis., Am. Coll. Obstetricians and Gynecologists (chmn. com. mental retardation and perinatal health 1966), Am. Assn. Maternal and Child Health, Venezuelan Obstetrics-Gynecol. Soc. (hon.); mem.: AMA (mem. residency accreditation com., site visit team mem.), Internat. Soc. Poets (disting.), Pub. Health Council N.Y. State, Am. Soc. Cytology, Onondaga County Med. Soc., Med. Soc. N.Y. State (regional obstetrics chmn., subcom. Maternal and Child Welfare), Pan Am. Med. Assn. (med. ambassador goodwill, life mem. sect. on cancer), Soc. for Gynecol. Investigation (coun.), Alpha Omega Alpha, Southwest, Fla. obstet. and gynecol. socs. (hon.). Achievements include research and 230 publications on cytologic, cytochemical and histochemical study of early cervical cancer, perinatal and placental pathology, cytologic and hormonal studies in normal and high-risk obstetrics patients, experimental production of abruptio placentae, reproductive endocrinology, animal experimentation, induced endocrine insults upon pregnant and nonpregnant ewes and hormonal influence on placentation, invitro placenta perfusion, fetal growth and development, female urology, surgical techniques for restoration of female pelvic floor integrity; human spirituality; inspirational poetry. Home: 3743 Roscommon North Martinez GA 30907

NESBITT, WANDA L. ambassador; b. Phila., Dec. 1956; married. BA in Internat. Rels. and French, U. Pa., 1978; postgrad., Nat. War Coll., 1996—97. Vice-consul Dept. State, Port-au-Prince, Haiti, 1982—83, Paris, 1983—85, with Bur. L.Am., 1986—88, regional consular officer, 1990—92, with consular affairs Kinshasa, Zaire, 1992—93, with legis. affairs, 1995—96, dep. chief of mission, 1997—99, Dar es Salaam, Tanzania, 1999—2001, U.S. amb. to Madagascar, 2002—. Office: DOS Amb 2040 Antananarivo Pl Washington DC 20521 E-mail: nesbittwl@state.gov.

NESCI, MARK A. retail executive; Exec. v.p., COO Burlington (N.J.) Coat Factory. Office: Burlington Coat Factory 1830 Route 130 N Burlington NJ 08016-3020

NESCI, VINCENT PETER, lawyer; b. New Rochelle, N.Y., Feb. 27, 1947; s. Vincent S. and Carmela (DeMasi) N.; m. Donna M. Dahlgren, July 21, 1968; children: Vincent P. Jr., Joseph E., Patricia A. BA, Sacred Heart U., 1969; JD, St. John's U., 1971. Bar: N.Y. 1972, U.S. Dist. Ct. (ea. dist.) N.Y. 1973, U.S. Dist. Ct. (so. dist.) N.Y. 1978), U.S. Supreme Ct. 1976. Assoc. Campbell, Hyman & Lang, New Rochelle, 1972-76; ptnr. Lang & Nesci, P.C., New Rochelle, 1976-79; pvt. practice Yonkers, N.Y., 1980-93. Gen. counsel Liberty Lines, Yonkers, 1979-93; CEO Specialized Risk Mgmt., White Plains, N.Y., 1993—; mgr. ptnr. Nesci Keane Piekarski Keogh & Corrigan, White Plains, 1993—; cons. Summit Investment, Queensland, Australia, 1992—. Avocation: auto racing. Home: RR 2 Bedford NY 10506-9802 Office: 245 Main St Ste 600 White Plains NY 10601 E-mail: vnesci@nesci-keane.com.

NESHEIM, MALDEN C. academic administrator, nutrition educator; Provost emeritus Cornell U., Ithaca, N.Y., prof. emeritus nutrition, 1997—. Office: Cornell U 311 Savage Hall Ithaca NY 14853-7601 E-mail: mcn2@cornell.edu.

NESHEIM, ROBERT OLAF, retired food products executive; b. Monroe Center, Ill., Sept. 13, 1921; s. Olaf M. and Sena M. (Willms) Nesheim; m. Emogene P. Sullivan, July 13, 1946 (div.); children: Barbara Mowry, Susan Yost(dec.), Sandra Rankin; m. Doris Howes Calloway, July 4, 1981 (dec.). BS, U. Ill., 1943, MS, 1950, PhD, 1951; postgrad. in advanced mgmt. program, Harvard U., 1971. Farm mgr. Halderman Farm Mgmt. Svc., Wabash, Ind., 1946-48; instr. U. Ill., 1951; mgr. feed rsch. The Quaker Oats Co., Barrington, Ill., 1952-64; prof., head of dept. animal sci. U. Ill., 1964-67; dir. nutrition rsch. The Quaker Oats Co., Barrington, Ill., 1967-69, v.p. R & D, 1969-78, v.p. sci. & tech. Chgo., 1978-83; sr. v.p. sci. & tech. Avadyne, Inc., Monterey, Calif., 1983-85; pres. Advanced Healthcare, Monterey, 1985-91; ret., 1991. Food and nutrition bd. NAS, 1972—78, chmn. com. in mil. nutrition rsch. FNB, 1982—97; chmn. Bioscis. Info. Svcs., 1982—84. Capt. U.S. Army, 1943-46, South Pacific. Fellow Am. Inst. Nutrition (treas. 1983-86), AAAS; mem. Inst. Food Technologists, Fed. Socs. Exptl. Biologists (treas. 1973-79), APHA, Corral de Tierra Club (Salinas, Calif.). Avocations: gardening, golf.

NESIN, JEFFREY DAVID, academic administrator; b. N.Y.C. m. Diane Garvey, 1968; children: Kate Dillon, Sarah Grace. BA in Eng. Lit., Hobart Coll., 1966; MA in Eng. Lit, SUNY, Buffalo, 1971, MA in Am. Studies, 1973. Faculty dept. humanities & scis. Sch. Visual Arts, N.Y.C., 1974-91; pres. Memphis Coll. Art, 1991—. Asst. to pres. Sch. Visual Arts, 1982-91; cons. Smithsonian Instn., IBM, 1st Tenn. Bank; panelist, speaker in field. Contbg. editor: High Fidelity, Creem; contbr. reviews, interviews, essays to mags.; adv. editor Jour. Popular Music and Society. Recipient Thomas W. Briggs Found. Cmty. Svc. award, 1998. Mem. Am. Studies Assn., Met. Am. Studies Assn. (past pres.), Assn. Ind. Colls. Art & Design (bd. dirs. 1991—), Nat. Assn. Schs. Art & Design (chair commn. on accreditation, exec. com. and bd. 1999—), Ctr. for So. Folklore (bd. and exec. com. 2000—), Memphis Rotary. Avocations: mystery novels, barbecue, baseball, american music. Office: Memphis Coll Art Office of President 1930 Poplar Ave Memphis TN 38104-2756 Home: 1545 Vinton Ave Memphis TN 38104-4923

NESLAGE, JOHN EDWARD, lawyer; b. Pampa, Tex., Aug. 13, 1946; AA cum laude, N.Mex. Milit. Inst., 1966; BBA magna cum laude, Tex. Tech. U., 1969; JD cum laude, U. Houston, 1972. Bar: Tex. 1972. Mem. Baker Botts L.L.P., Houston. Mem. ABA, State Bar Tex., Houston Bar Assn., Phi Kappa Phi, Phi Alpha Delta, Order of the Barons. Office: Baker Botts LLP One Shell Plz 910 Louisiana Houston TX 77002-4995 Office Phone: 713-229-1342.

NESMITH, JEFF, journalist; b. Hillsborough County, Fla. m. Achsah Posey; children: Susannah, Jeff. BS in Journalism, U. Fla., 1963. Tchr. English Howey Acad., Fla.; reporter The Atlanta Constitution, 1964; investigative reporter Phila. Bull., 1975—77; feature writer nat. reporting health, sci., environ, issues Cox Newspapers/Washington Bur., 1977—. Author: No Higher Honor, 1999. Recipient Gold medal Investigative Reporters and Editors, Goldsmith award, Harvard U., 1997, Pulitzer Prize for nat. reporting for series: Unncesssary Danger: Military Medicine, 1998. Office: c/o cox Newspapers Washington Bur 400 N Capitol St NW Ste 750 Washington DC 20001-1536

NESMITH, RICHARD A. education educator, consultant; b. Lakeland, Fla., Jan. 13, 1959; s. Wendell B. and Patricia A. NeSmith; m. Melissa M. NeSmith; children: Ricky A., Wendell C. BS, Hyles-Anderson Coll., 1983, MRE, 1984; D in Ministry, Bethany Theol. Sem., 1986; BS, USC, 1991, MEd, 1993; specialists in edn., Augusta State U., 1997; EdD, Curtin U. Tech., 2003. Tchg. cert. biology SC. State Dept. Edn., 1991, educator cert. biology, ednl. leadership, mid. grade Ga. State Dept. Edn., 1995, curriculum validator Western Australia Curriculum Coun., 2000. Secondary sci. tchr. SC. Dept. Edn., Lexingington, 1992—93; sch. prin. Winfield Heights Christian Sch., Williston, SC, 1994—95; secondary sci. tchr. Ga. Pub. Schs., Ga., 1995—98; head sci. and math dept. Marannatha Christian Coll., Perth, Australia, 1999—2001; asst. prof. edn. Ea. Ill. U., Charleston, 2003—; asst. prof. of edn. Lake Erie Coll., Painsville, Ohio, 2002—03. Bd. examiners Ohio State Dept. Edn., Columbus, 2002—03. Author: (textbook) Human Biology I: Entering the 21st Century; sci. author, cons.: BioSci. Edn., 1996—. Mem.: Assn. Childhood Edn. Internat. (assoc.), Am. Rsch. Ednl. Assn. (assoc.), NSTA (assoc.), Nat. Mid. Sch. Assn. (assoc.), Phi Delta Kappa (assoc.). R-Consevative. Baptist. Achievements include research in middle school students perception of effective teaching and learning; various approaches to improving the curriculum and teaching of science in secondary schools. Avocations: hiking, travel, computers, writing. Office: Ea Ill Univ 600 Lincoln Avenue Charleston IL 61920 Business E-Mail: bioscience_ed@yahoo.com.

NESMITH, STEVEN B. congressional and intergovernment relations secretary; BA, Am. Univ.; grad, Georgetown Univ. Law Ctr. Dep. asst. Sec. for Congl. and Intergovtl. Affairs US Dept. of Comm.; sr. counsel Legis. Strategies Group; dir. of op. Mayor's Office of Comm. Svc./Dept. of Housing and Urban Devel. Empowerment Zone, Phila., 1997—98. Achievements include nomination by Pres. George W. Bush as Asst. Sec. of Housing and Urban Devel. for Congl. and Intergovtl. Affairs at the US Dept. of Commerce. Office: Dept of Housing and Urban Devel 451 Seventh St SW, Rm 10120 Washington DC 20410

NESOFF, IRWIN, social work educator, management consultant; b. Mexico City, Jan. 28, 1948; s. Hyman and Sally Leah Nesoff; m. Paula Moszenberg, Feb. 1, 1970; 1 child, Jeremy. BA in Sociology, CUNY, 1970; MSW, Hunter Coll. Sch. Social Work, 1978; D of Social Welfare, CUNY, 1998. Cert. social worker, social work mgr. Exec. dir. Sunnyside (N.Y.) Cmty. Svcs., 1983-90; dir. Bur. Cmty. Svcs., N.Y.C. Dept. for Aging, 1990-92; assoc. exec. dir. Ednl. Alliance, N.Y.C., 1992-94; assoc. prof. social work Kean U., Union, NJ, 1995—. Mgmt. cons. Nesoff Assocs., Mgmt. Support for Non-profits, Congers, N.Y., 1994—. Author: Reaching Out to Older New Yorkers: A Handbook for Service Providers, 1998; contbr. articles to profl. jours. Pres. Nat. Ctr. for Creative Aging, Bklyn., 1996-2002, Park Slope Geriatric Day Ctr., Bklyn., 1999-2002; mem. commn. on racial, ethnic and cultural minorities, Council on Social Work Edn. Mem. NASW (chair nominating com. 1994-96, N.Y.C. chpt. exec. bd. polit. action for candidate election 1995-98), Nat. Network for Social Work Mgrs., Coun. on Social Work Edn., CUNY Grad. Ctr. Alumni Assn. Jewish. Avocations: tai chi, bicycling, scuba diving, travel. Office: Kean Univ 1000 Morris Ave Union NJ 07083 E-mail: INAssoc@aol.com.

NESOFF, ROBERT (BOB NESOFF), newspaper publisher; b. Bronx, N.Y., July 6, 1938; s. Hyman and Sally Leah (Reznikoff) N.; m. Sandra Roberta Levine, June 27, 1965; children: Wendy Naimaister, Barbara Thorson, Karen Nesoff. Editor Country Wide Publs., N.Y.C., 1964-65; reporter The Record, Hackensack, N.J., 1965-66, Newark News, 1966-72; pub. Metro Publs. Group/Metro Feature Syndicate, Oradell, N.J., 1972—, Palisadian Newspaper, East Bergen, N.J., 1984—. Pub. rels. cons. U.S. Homes Corp., 1973, Best Western Internat. Hotels, 1979, tourism ministries Republics of Guatemala, 1979-80, Panama, 1979-81, Kenya, 1985; former N.Y. State pub. rels. dir. Common Cause, N.Y.C. Mcpl. Svcs. Adminstrn., 1974-75; pub. rels. dir. N.J. State Assn. Chiefs of Police, Bergen County Police Chiefs Assn.; com. dir. Bergen County Sheriff's Dept., 2000-01; instr. police-press rels. Bergen County Police Acad., 1970-75; nat. rep., spokesman Fed. Criminal Investigators Assn., 1974-85; mem. Stein Commn., N.Y. State Commn., dir. info. and investigations.; dir. investigations into funeral home abuses; expert witness FTC, 1975; appeared on numerous radio and TV shows including 20/20, Sta. KABC, L.A., Sta. WABC Radio, N.Y., Eleanor Guggenheim Consumer show on Channel 5, Richard Bey, Jackie Mason shows on Sta. WWOR-TV; capt., exec. officer Bergen County SPCA Law Enforcement Divsn., 1997—. Contbg. editor Lifestyles mag., 1997—; columnist Metro Feature Svc., 1972—; radio and TV appearances. Pres. sch. bd. New Milford, N.J., 1983-90, Ctrl. Bergen Crime Stoppers Orgn.; councilman City of New Milford, 1990-99, pres. coun., 1996-98, 99; pres. New Milford Jewish Ctr., 1991-92, past bd. dirs.; past trustee New Milford Swim Club, past sec., v.p., 1980-83; former coach Princess League Softball, 1983; scoutmaster Boy Scouts Am., New Milford; mem. N.J. Dem. State Com., 1997—, Dem. County Com., 1998-2002, Bergen County Task Force on Youth Violence, Bias Crimes sub-com., 1994, Bergen County Bicentennial Com., 1976, Family Life Curriculum Com.; commr. New Bridge Landing Pk. Commn., 1996-98; pres. Bergen County SPCA, 2004—. Sgt. U.S. Army 11th Spl. Forces Group (Green Berets), 1962-64. Recipient Heroism award N.Y.C. Police Dept., cert. of recognition Newark Police Dept., Voice of Democracy award VFW, cert. of appreciation NCCJ, Citizenship award Am. Legion, cert. of appreciation Kiwanis, Pax Et Justicia plaque Royal St. Vincent Police Force, Grenadine Islands, 30 awards from various press assns.; named hon. mem. Fed. Criminal Investigators Assn., Leonia (N.J.) Police Dept. SWAT Team. Mem. N.Am. Travel Journalists Assn. (pres. 1989-96, Best Profile Feature, 1996, other awards), Working Press Assn. N.J. (pres. 1987-90, Best Edtl. Writer 1985-86, 90-91, 93, 95, Best Column 1990, Best Critical Rev. 1991-95, Gold Medal award), North Jersey Press Assn. (pres. 1972-73, 76-77, 81-83), N. Am. Ski Journalists Assn., Ea. Ski Writers Assn. (bd. dirs. 1998-2001), Jewish War Vets. (comdr. Wallch-Gold-Moses Post #773 1996-97). Democrat. Jewish. Avocations: skiing, scuba diving. Office: Metro Publs Group/Metro Feature Syndicate 626 McCarthy Dr New Milford NJ 07646-1029

NESS, ANDREW DAVID, lawyer; b. San Francisco, Oct. 29, 1952; s. Orville Arne and Muriel Ruth (Trendt) N.; m. Rita M. Kobylenski, May 25, 1980; children: Katherine, Austin, Emily. BS, Stanford U., 1974; JD, Harvard U., 1977. Bar: Calif. 1977, D.C. 1979, Va. 1986, U.S. Dist. Ct. (no. dist.) Calif. 1977, U.S. Dist. Ct. D.C. 1983, U.S. Dist. Ct. (ea. dist.) Va. 1988, U.S. Ct. Appeals (4th cir.) 1989. Law clk. U.S. Dist. Ct., San Francisco, 1977-78; assoc. Lewis, Mitchell & Moore, Vienna, Va., 1979-82, ptnr., 1982-87, Morgan, Lewis & Bockius LLP, Washington, 1987-2000, Thelen Reid & Priest LLP, Washington, 2000—, mng. ptnr. D.C. office, 2001—, mem. partnership coun. and exec. com., 2003—. Instr. U. Md., College Park, 1987-90; mem.

faculty constrn. exec. program Stanford (Calif.) U., 1984-87. Co-editor Fed. Govt. Construction Contracts, 2003; contbr. chpts. to books, articles to profl. jours. Mem. ABA (forum on constrn. industry, pub. contract law sect.). Avocations: hiking, bicycling. Office: Thelen Reid & Priest LLP 701 Pennsylvania Ave NW Washington DC 20004-2608 Office Phone: 202-508-4368. Business E-Mail: adness@thelenreid.com.

NESS, ARTHUR JOSEPH, musicologist; b. Chgo., Jan. 27, 1936; s. Martin J. and Rosetta Ness; m. Charlotte A. Kolczynski, Dec. 29, 1982. MusB in Music Theory, U. So. Calif., L.A., 1958; AM in Music, Harvard U., 1961; PhD in Musicology, NYU, 1984. Asst. prof. U. So. Calif., L.A., 1963-76; prof., dept. chmn. Daemen Coll., Buffalo, 1976-84; faculty SUNY, Buffalo, 1984-86, State U. Coll. N.Y., Fredonia, 1984-86. Editor: Lute Works of Francesco Canova da Milano, 1970, Lute Works of Marco dall'Aquila, 2003; contbr. New Grove Dictionary, 1970, New Harvard Dictionary of Music, 1980; contbr. articles to profl. jours. With USNR, 1954-62. Fulbright fellow, Munich, 1965-68. Mem. Am. Musicol. Soc. (chpt. sec.-treas. 1964-66), Lute Soc. Am., Lute Soc. U.K., Lute Soc. Germany, Lute Soc. The Netherlands, Internat. Assn. Music Librs., Internat. Musicol. Soc. Home and Office: 2039 Commonwealth Ave Apt 10 Boston MA 02135-5163 Office Phone: 617-254-6509. E-mail: 71162.751@compuserve.com.

NESS, EVALINE (MRS. ARNOLD A. BAYARD), illustrator, writer; b. Union City, Ohio, Apr. 24, 1911; d. Albert and Myrtle Woods (Carter) Michelow; m. Arnold A. Bayard, Nov. 1959. Student, Muncie (Ind.) State Tchrs. Coll., 1931, Chgo. Art Inst., 1933, Corcoran Art Sch., 1945, Art Students League, N.Y.C., 1947, Accademia de Belle Arti, Rome, Italy, 1950. Tchr. children's art classes Corcoran Sch. Art, Washington, 1945-46, Parsons Sch. Design, N.Y.C., 1959-60; fashion illustrator Saks Fifth Ave., N.Y.C., 1946-49; mag. and advt. illustrator, 1946-49; illustrator numerous books, from 1959. (Recipient 1st prize painting Corcoran Sch. Art 1945, Caldecott medal childrens books 1967), Author, illustrator: Josefina February, 1963, Gift for Sula Sula, 1963, Pavo and the Princess, 1964, Exactly Alike, 1964, A Double Discovery, 1965, Sam Bangs and Moonshine, 1966, The Girl and the Goatherd, 1969, Do You Have the Time, Lydia, 1971, Yeck Eck, 1973, Marcella's Guardian Angel; author, designer: Fierce: The Lion, 1980, American Colonial Paper House, Paper Palace, Four Rooms from the Metropolitan Museum, Victorian Paper House, Shaker Paper House. Home: Palm Beach, Fla. *I depend on my instincts rather than on rationalization.* Deceased.

NESS, NORMAN FREDERICK, astrophysicist, educator, administrator; b. Springfield, Mass., Apr. 15, 1933; s. Herman Hugo and Eva (Carlson) N.; children: Elizabeth Ann, Stephen Andrew. BS, Mass. Inst. Tech., 1955, PhD, 1959. Space physicist, asst. prof. geophysics UCLA, 1959-61; NAS-NRC postdoctoral rsch. assoc. NASA, 1960-61; rsch. physicist in space scis. Goddard Space Flight Center, Greenbelt, Md., 1961-86, head extraterrestrial physics br., 1968-69, chief Lab. for Extraterrestrial Physics, 1969-86; prof. Bartol Rsch. Inst., U. Del., Newark, 1987—, pres. Bartol Rsch. Inst., 1987-2000; dir. NASA Space Grant Coll. Consortium, Del., 1991—. Lectr. math. U. Md., 1962-64, assoc. research prof., 1965-67 Contbr. articles profl. jours. Recipient Exceptional Sci. Achievement award NASA, 1966, 81, 86, Arthur S. Flemming award, 1968, Space Sci. award AIAA, 1970, Disting. Svc. medal NASA, 1986, Nat. Space Club Sci. award, 1993, Emil Wiechert medal German Geophys. Soc., 1993, Space Sci. award COSPAR, 1996. Fellow Am. Geophys. Union (John Adam Fleming award 1965); mem. NAS, Academia Nazionale dei Lincei, Royal Ocean Racing Club. Achievements include research, experimental studies of interplanetary and planetary magnetic fields by satellites and space probes. Home: 9 Wilkinson Dr Landenberg PA 19350-9359 Office: U Del Bartol Rsch Inst 215 Sharp Lab Newark DE 19716-4793 E-mail: nfness@bartol.udel.edu.

NESS, SUSAN, federal official; married; 2 children. BA, Douglass Coll., Rutgers U., 1970; JD cum laude, Boston Coll.; MBA, U. Pa. Asst. counsel com. banking, currency and housing U.S. House of Reps.; founder, dir. jud. appointments project Nat. Women's Polit. Caucus; commr. FCC, Washington, 1994—2001. Chair Charter Rev. Commn., Montgomery County, Md.; vice chair Montgomery County Task Force on Cmty. Access TV; pres. Montgomery County Commn. for Women. Named one of 12 to Watch, Electronic Media, 1997. Mem. Nat. Assn. Regulatory Utility Commrs. (com. comm.), Leadership Washington, Fed. Comm. Bar Assn. Office: FCC 1919 M St NW Washington DC 20554-0001

NESSAN, CRAIG LEE, minister, educator; b. Lansing, Mich., June 9, 1952; s. Lee A. and Lucy E. (Welford) N.; m. Cathy Sue Gee, Dec. 16, 1972; children: Benjamin, Nathaniel, Sarah, Andrew, Jessica, Mary Catherine. BA, Mich. State U., 1974; M. Div., Wartburg Theol. Sem., 1978; S.T.M., 1978; ThD., U. Munich, 1986. Ordained to ministry Am. Luth. Ch., 1978. Pastor Trinity Luth. Ch., Phila., 1978-82, St. Mark Luth. Ch., Cape Girardeau, Mo., 1987-94; univ. asst. U. Regensburg, Germany, 1982—86; prof. contextual theology Wartburg Theol. Sem. (E.L.C.A.), Dubuque, Iowa, 1994—, acad. dean, 1999—. Author: Orthopraxis or Heresy, 1989, Wer bist du Christus?, 1998, Beyond Maintenance to Mission, 1999, Who is Christ for Us?, 2002, Give Us This Day, 2003, The Air I Breathe Is Wartburg Air, 2003, Many Members, Yet One Body, 2004; contbr. articles to profl. jours. Mem. Bread for the World, Fellowship of Reconciliation, Am. Acad. of Religion, Luth., Peace Fellowship, Phi Beta Kappa. Office: 333 Wartburg Pl Dubuque IA 52003-7769 Office Phone: 563-589-0207. Business E-Mail: cnessan@wartburgseminary.edu.

NESSEL, EDWARD HARRY, swimming coach; b. Roselle, New Jersey, 1945; s. Irving Meyer Nessel and Ruth Elliott; m. Eileen Robin (Berstein), 1973; children: Lee Allyson, Jason Eric (dec.), Matthew Scott (dec.). BS in Chemistry, Rutgers U., 1967, degree in Pharmacy Chemistry, 1968; post grad., Jersey City State, 1970, Rutgers U., 1971; MS in Bacteriology, MPH, Wagner Coll., 1978. Registered pharmacist, Calif., N.J., Fla.; cert. U.S. Swimming Coach. Rschr., product developer Mennen Co., Morris Plains, NJ, 1967; pharmacist supr. Pathmark Pharmacies, NJ, 1968—79; pharmacist, mgr. Roxy Drug Co., Inc., Irvington, NJ, 1979—90. Diet and nutrition cons. Fanwood Scotch Plaines YMCA, 1985-91, masters swim coach, 1984-91, swimming and racing cons., head age group coach, asst. sr. coach, 1989-91; head swim coach Jewish Cmty. Ctr. Metrowest, West Orange, 1991-2001; head masters swim coach Rutgers U., New Brunswick, N.J., 2000-04; head swim coach Maccabi, 1990-91, 92, 93, 94, head coach swimming USA Nat. Team World Maccabi Games, Israel, 1997; coach N.J. Masters Swimming, 1981-2004; physiology and sports medicine cons. Nat. Health and Fitness; health and fitness chmn. N.J. Masters Swimming; nat. masters swimming coaches com. Nat. Com. for Sports Medicine; nat. libr. U.S. Masters Swimming; chair N.J. Masters Swimming Com.; pres. Jersey Masters Swimming Inc.; sports chair age group and masters swimming Garden State Games; summer coord. long-course 50 meter swim season Rayway YMCA, 1987-2004. Contbg. articles on swimming, self def., and physiology to profl. journals.; two patents adjustable hand-swim paddle. Athletic and swimming cons. N.J. Spl. Olympics, 1986; cons. Essex County Narcotic Strike Force; Garden State Games ofcl.; chair gov. coun. phys. fitness for swimming events Garden State Games, 1989-96. Recipient Presdl. Series Award 1986; winner N.J. State Pentathlon champion Masters Swimming, 1986-87, YMCA Masters Nat. Swim Champion, 1988, 91, 95, 98, 2000-04, Masters All Am. Relay, 1998-99, 2002-03, Nat. Svc. Award U.S. Masters Swimming, 1999; apptd. head swim coach U.S. Jr. Nat. Swim Team, World Maccabi Games, Israel, 1997; named Coach of Yr., U.S. Masters Swimming, Inc., 1998, mentor coach, 2000, 2003; USMS Nat. Champion 100 meter breast stroke, 2003. Mem. NRA (disting. expert rating pistol shooting), Am. Assn. Microbiologists, N.J. Pharm. Assn., N.J. Guild Pharmacists, Internat. Practical Shooters Confedn. (N.J. State Champion 1982, 83), Am. Swimming Coaches Assn. (life mem., master level cert. level five coach, cert.level four, YMCA; Am. Masters Aquatic Coaches Assn. (pres. 1999-2003), U.S. Swimming Coaches Assn. (cert. level five, masters swimming coaches and sports medicine coms.), Master Swim Coaches Assn. Am., Rutgers Coll. Pharmacy Alumni Assn., Am. Med. Athletic Assn. (life mem., clin. cons., contbg. editor quar. 1993—, clin. advisor 1996-2004), Masters Aquatic Coaches Assn. Am. (pres.), N.J. Masters Swimming Inc. (chmn. 1999-2003), Willow Grove Swim Club (bd. dir. 1986-90), South River Pistol Club. Avocations: clarinet, saxophone, flute, mus. quality ship builder. Home: 10 Irene Ct Edison NJ 08820-1024 Personal E-mail: Ednessel@aol.com.

NESSMITH, H(ERBERT) ALVA, dentist; b. Miami, Fla., Nov. 27, 1935; s. William Boyd and Florence Editha (Lowe) N.; m. Paula Ann Fox, Oct. 1, 1960 (div. 1984); children: Amy Susan, Lynn Margaret, Mark Alva. Student, U. Miami, Fla., 1953-56; DDS, Northwestern U., 1960. Gen. practice dentistry, Tequesta, Fla., 1963—; dental cons. Palm Beach-Martin County Med. Ctr., Jupiter, Fla., 1970—; rsch. assoc. Colgate Palmolive Co., 1997—. Calibrated caries examiner, cons. Colgate Dental Rsch., 1997—. Mem. advminstrv. bd. United Meth. Ch. Tequesta, Jupiter, 1970—, chmn., 1988-90; pres. Meth. Men, 1982; chmn. Coun. on Ministries, 1992-94, mem. staff parish rels. com. 1999—; pres. Jupiter Elem. PTO, 1972; clarinetist Symphonic Band of Palm Beaches, Fla. Concert Band; pianist and clarinetist United Meth. Ch.; active Village of Tequesta Hist. Commn., 1992-96, Jupiter (Fla.) Cmty. Resource Ctr., 1994—; mem. adminstrv. bd., v.p. Christian Dental Soc., 1994—, v.p., 1995—, Andean Rural Health Care, 1999—. Mem. ADA, North Palm Beach County Dental Soc., Fla. Dental Assn., Jupiter-Tequesta-Juno Beach C. of C. Lodges: Kiwanis (pres. Jupiter/Tequesta chpt. 1980-81). Democrat. Avocations: mission dentistry, latin american studies, gardening, music, travel. Home: 196 River Dr Tequesta FL 33469-1934 Office: Inlet Profl Bldg 175 Tequesta Dr Jupiter FL 33469-2733

NESTER, EUGENE WILLIAM, microbiology educator; b. Johnson City, N.Y., Sept. 15, 1930; married, 1959; 2 children. BS, Cornell U., 1952; PhD, Western Reserve U., 1959. Am. Cancer Soc. rsch. fellow genetics Stanford U., 1959-62, instr. microbiology, 1962-63, from asst. to assoc. prof. microbiology and genetics, 1963-72; prof. microbiology U. Wash., Seattle, 1972—, chmn. microbiology, 1982-96. Recipient Chiron Corp. Biotechnology Rsch. award, Australia prize, 1990. Fellow NAS, AAAS, Am. Acad. Microbiology; mem. Am. Soc. Microbiology Achievements include bacterial-plant relationships. Office: U Wash Microbiology Dept Box 357242 Seattle WA 98195-7242

NESTER, WILLIAM RAYMOND, JR., retired academic administrator and educator; b. Cin., Feb. 19, 1928; s. William Raymond and Evelyn (Blettner) N.; m. Mary Jane Grossman; children: William Raymond, Mark Patrick, Brian Philip, Stephen Christopher. BS, U. Cin., 1950, EdM, 1953, EdD, 1965; DHL (hon.), No. Ky. U., 2001, U. Nebr., 2002. Dir. student union U. Cin., 1952-53, asst. dean of men, 1953-60, dean of men, 1960-67, assoc. prof. edn., 1965-70, dean of students, 1967-69, vice provost student and univ. affairs, 1969-76, prof. edn., 1970-78, assoc. sr. v.p., assoc. provost, 1976-78; v.p. student svcs. Ohio State U., Columbus, 1978-83, prof. edn., 1978-83; pres. Kearney State Coll., Nebr., 1983-91, prof. edn., 1983-93; chancellor U. Nebr., Kearney, 1991-93, prof. emeritus, chancellor emeritus, 1993—; v.p. univ. rels. devel. No. Ky. U., 1996-99. Pres. emeritus Mus. Nebr. Art, 1991—; cons. on higher edn., 1993—. Pres. Metro-Six Athletic Conf., 1975-76. Mem. Am. Assn. State Colls. and Univs. (bd. dirs.), Ctrl. States Intercollegiate Conf. (pres. 1986-89), Nat. Assn. Student Pers. Adminstrs. (past regional v.p., mem. exec. com.), Am. Assn. Higher Edn., Ohio Assn. Student Pers. Adminstrs. (past pres.), Nat. Intrafrat. Conf. (pres. 1991-92), Frat. Scholarship Officers Assn. (past pres.), Mortar Bd., Pi Kappa Alpha (nat. pres. 1978-80, pres. nat. interfrat. conf. 1988-89, past pres. Pi Kappa Alpha Edn1. Found.), Omicron Delta Kappa, Phi Delta Kappa, Phi Alpha Theta, Phi Eta Sigma, Sigma Sigma. Episcopalian. Home: 7674 Coldstream Dr Cincinnati OH 45255-3932 E-mail: wrnchanem@cs.com.

NESTLER, ERIC J. psychiatry educator; BA, MS, Yale U., 1976, PhD, 1982, MD, 1983. Resident psychiatry McLean Hosp., Yale U.; joined Yale U., 1987, dir. Abraham Ribicoff Rsch. Facilities, 1992—, Elizabeth Mears and House Jameson prof. psychiatry, prof. pharmacology. Bd. sci. counselors Nat. Inst. on Drug Abuse; mem. sci. adv. bd. Nat. Alliance for Rsch. in Schizophrenia and Depression, Nat. Alliance for Autism Rsch. Recipient Jordi Folch-Pi Young Investigator award Am. Soc. for Neurochemistry, 1990, Judith Silver Young Investigator award, 1993, Efron award Am. Coll. Neuropsychopharmacology, 1994, Pasarow Found. award for neuropsychiat. rsch., 1998; Pfizer scholar ACNP, 1987-89, McKnight scholar, 1989-92; Alfred P. Sloan Rsch. fellow, 1987-89. Mem.: Am. Bd. Psychiatric Neurology, Am. Psychiatric Assn., Acad. of Sci. Inst. of Medicine. Office: Yale U Sch Medicine Abraham Ribicoff Rsch Facs 34 Park St New Haven CT 06508 E-mail: Eric.Nestler@Yale.edu.

NESTLER, ERIC M. music educator; b. Sellersville, Pa., Oct. 19, 1964; s. Paul R. Jr. and June J. Nestler. MusB, Susquehanna U., Selinsgrove, Pa., 1986; MusM, Ind. U., 1988, Dr.Mus., 1993. Prof. music U. North Tex., Denton, 1992—. Host N.Am. Saxophone Alliance Biennial Conf., 2002; Carnegie Hall recital, 03. Mem.: World Saxophone Congress (exec. v.p. organizing com. 2003—). Office: Univ of North Texas Coll of Music Ave C Denton TX 76203

NESTOR, LARRY, songwriter, musician; b. Chgo., Jan. 29, 1940; s. John Louis and Theresa Inez Nestor; children: Thomas John, Anne Marie. Author: Foursome the Spider, Tune Up the Banjo (winner Bicentennial Folk Song Contest, Loyola U., 1976), The Kettle (theme song of the Salvation Army); songwriter (musicals) Lumberjacks & Weddingbelles, Seven Brides for Dracula, The Brementown Musicians, Stone Soup, Androcles & the Lion, The Velveteen Rabbit, Pinnochio, God's Faithful Messenger, Triple Play, Don't Rock the Boat, It's a Howl!, Nashville Dreams, Conecticut Yankee, A Tale of Two Cities, Sincerely, Samantha, Midsummer Night's Dream, Unhappily Ever After, The Shoemaker & the Elves, Tangerine Dusk, 2003 (Seahorse award for best libretto Moondance Film Festival, Boulder, Colo., 2003); contbr. articles to jours., mags. Mem.: ASCAP, Chgo. Fedn. Musicians. Roman Catholic. Address: PO Box 226 River Grove IL 60171 E-mail: nofoesent@cs.com.

NESTOR CASTELLANO, BRENDA DIANA, real estate company executive; b. Palm Beach, Fla., Nov. 10, 1948; d. John Joseph and Marion O'Connor Nestor; m. Robert Castellano. Student, U. Miami, Fla., 1978. Lic. real estate broker, Fla. Salesman Oscar E Dooley, Inc., Miami, Fla., 1978-80; prin. Brenda Nestor Assocs, Inc., Miami Beach, Fla., 1980—. Exec. v.p., bd. dirs. D.W.G. Corp., 1988-94, N.V.F. Corp., Salem Corp., 1988-97, Southeastern Pub. Svc., Graniteville Corp., 1988-94, Essex Ins., Chesapeake Ins.; exec. v.p., dir. Security Mgmt. Bd. dirs. Vizcayan Mus.; dir. Miami's Jackson Meml. Found. Named Ms. Charity, City of Miami, 1985, Lady Comdr., State of Fla. Mem. Miami Beach Bd. Realtors (bd. dirs. 1984—), Real Estate Securities and Exch. Com., Knights of Malta, Doubles Club (N.Y.C.), La Gorce Country Club, Fisher Island Club, Surf Club. Episcopal. Avocations: golf, tennis, boating. Home and Office: 39 Palm Ave Miami FL 33139-3263 Office Phone: 954-455-5954. Personal E-mail: LadyBNestor@aol.com.

NETHERCUTT, GEORGE RECTOR, JR., congressman, lawyer; b. Spokane, Wash., Oct. 7, 1944; s. George Rector and Nancy N.; m. Mary Beth Socha Nethercutt, Apr. 2., 1977; children: Meredith, Elliott. BA in English, Wash. State U., 1967; JD, Gonzaga U., 1971. Bar: D.C. 1972. Law clk. to Hon. Raymond Plummer U.S. Dist. Ct. Alaska, Anchorage, 1971; staff counsel to U.S. Senator Ted Stevens Washington, 1972; chief of staff to U.S. Senator Ted Stevens, 1972-76; pvt. practice Spokane, Wash., 1977-94; mem. 104th-108th Congresses from 5th Wash. dist., Washington, 1995—. Mem. house appropriations and sci. coms. Chmn. Spokane County Rep. Party, 1990-94, co-founder Vanessa Behan Crisis Nursery, pres. Spokane Juvenile Diabetes Found., 1993-94. Mem. Masons (lodge #34), Lions Club (Spokane Ctrl.), Sigma Nu. Republican. Presbyterian. Avocations: running, handball, squash. Office: US House Reps 2443 Rayburn HOB Washington DC 20515-4705

NETHERLAND, JOSEPH H. manufacturing executive; BS in Indsl. Engring., Ga. Inst. Tech.; MBA, U. Pa. Bus. planner machinery group FMC Corp., 1973-78, ops. mgr. ordnance divsn., 1978-83, mgr. fluid control divsn., 1983-84, mgr. wellhead divsn., 1984-85, gen mgr. wellhead divsn., 1985-89, gen. mgr. specialized machinery group, 1989-99, pres., 1999—. Bd. dirs. Am. Petroleum Inst. Office: FMC Corp 200 E Randolph St Ste 5200 Chicago IL 60601-6662

NETHERY, JOHN JAY, government official; b. Mpls., June 4, 1941; s. Ronald Jay and Mary Vesta (McVeety) N.; m. Sonya Elisabeth Magin, July 27, 1968; children: William Jay, Mary Elisabeth (dec.), Sarah Ann. BA, U. Denver, 1963, MPA, 1968. Mgmt. intern USAF Logistics Command, San Antonio, 1969-71, budget analyst Dayton, Ohio, 1971-72; chief, fiscal analysis USAF Hdqrs., Washington, 1973-80, chief, investment div., 1980-81, chief budget mgmt., 1981-85; dep. asst. sec. programs and budget Dept. of USAF, Washington, 1986-88, asst. to undersecretary, 1988-89, dep. asst. sec. fin. ops., 1989—. Mem. Air Force bd. for the correction of mil. records, Washington, 1980—. Recipient Gov.'s Scholastic award Gov. of Colo., 1968, Presdl. Rank award, 1988. Mem. Sr. Execs. Assn., Air Force Assn. Presbyterian. Avocations: history, military minatures. Home: 12349 Coleraine Ct Reston VA 20191-1627 Office: Dept USAF SAF/FM The Pentagon Washington DC 20330-1130 E-mail: Jnethery@aol.com.

NETHERY, VINCENT MICHAEL, adult education educator; b. Grafton, New South Wales, Australia, Aug. 27, 1955; s. Francis George and Eunice Nola Nethery; children: Michael Andrew, Jacqueline Renee, Sara Michelle. PhD, U. of Oreg., 1989. Cert. tchr. N.S.W. Dept. of Edn., 1977. Prof. - health sciences The U. of Wollongong, Australia, 1983—87; prof. - exercise sci. Ctrl. Wash. U., Ellensburg, 1988—. Cons. Sound Health Solutions Bariatric Clinic, Bellevue. Bd. of directors Whisky Dick Triathlon, Ellensburg. Recipient Young Investigator, Assn. for Fitness in Bus., 1990. Mem.: NAASO, Am. Coll. of Sports Medicine. Home: 804 C St Ellensburg WA 98926 Office: CWU: Exercise Science Laboratory 400 E 8th Ave Ellensburg WA 98926 Business E-Mail: netheryv@cwu.edu.

NETI, CHALAPATHY, computer scientist, researcher; s. Narayana Murthy and Seetha Devi Neti; m. Vishalakshi Bhagavatula; children: Akhil Narayana, Nikhil Narayana. PhD, Johns Hopkins U., Balt., 1990. Rsch. staff IBM T.J. Watson Rsch. Ctr, Yorktown Heights, NY, 1996—2000, rsch. mgr., 2001—. Assoc. editor Trans. on Multimedia IEEE, NJ, 2001—, mem. multimedia signal processing tech. com., NY, 2001—. Recipient Rsch. Divsn. Award, IBM, 2002. Achievements include patents in field. Office: IBM T J Watson Rsch Ctr Rte 134 Yorktown Heights NY 10598

NETI, SUDHAKAR, mechanical engineering educator; b. Bapatla, India, Sept. 27, 1947; came to U.S., 1968; naturalized, 1977. s. Chiranjeeva Rao and Meenakshi Neti; m. Kathy Gibson, Jan. 11, 1974. BME, Osmania U., 1968; MS, U. Ky., 1970, PhD, 1977. Research asst. U. Ky., 1968-77; asst. prof. mech. engring. Lehigh U., Bethlehem, Pa., 1978-83, assoc. prof., 1983-92, prof., 1992—. Vis. fellow Wolfson Coll., Oxford U., Eng.; vis. rsch. assoc. U.K. Atomic Energy Rsch. Establishment, Harwell, Eng.; fallout shelter analyst Fed. Emergency Mgmt. Adminstrn.; chair Mech. Engring. Thermal-Fluids Divsn., 1996—, dir. Lehigh U. Indsl. Assessment Ctr., 2000—, mem. Asian studies program, 2001-, Lehigh Valley Planning Commn., 1996, 97; bd. dirs. ANS, PANE; cons. to industry. Contbr. articles to profl. jours. Summer faculty fellow NASA-Am. Soc. Engring. Edn., 1978; grantee electric Power Research Inst., Dept. Energy, NSF, NRC. Mem. ASME, AAAS, Sigma Xi (chpt. treas. 1997-2002), Phi Beta Delta. Office: Lehigh U Mech Engring Dept 19 Memorial Dr W Bethlehem PA 18015-3085 E-mail. sn01@lchigh.cdu.

NETRAVALI, ARUN N. communications executive; b. Bombay, May 26, 1946; m. Chitra Netravali; 2 children. BS in Tech. with honors, Indian Inst. Tech., Bombay, 1967; MS, Rice U., 1969, PhD, 1970; PhD (hon.), Ecole Polytechnique Federale, Lausanne, Switzerland, 1994. With NASA, Orlando, Fla., 1970-72; mem. tech. staff AT&T Bell Labs., Holmdel, N.J., 1972-78, head visual comm. rsch. dept. Murray Hill, N.J., 1978-83, dir. computing systems rsch., 1983-92, exec. dir. rsch., comm. scis. divsn., 1992-94; exec. v.p. rsch. Lucent Techs., 1994—; pres. Bell Labs. Adj. prof. media lab. MIT, Cambridge, Mass., 1984—; lectr. City Coll. N.Y., Columbia U., MIT, Rutgers U.; advisor Ctr. for Telecomm. Rsch. of Columbia U., 1987—, EPFL Swiss Fed. Inst. Tech., Lausanne, 1986—, Beckman Inst. of U. Ill. Co-author: Digital Pictures: Representation and Compression, 1987, Visual Communication Systems, 1989; contbr. 100 tech. papers to sci. jours.; patentee for 64 inventions. Mem. N.J. Govs. Com. on Schs. Program. Recipient Journal award Soc. of Motion Pictures and TV Engrs., 1982, Ann. Asian Am. Corp. Employees award Orgn. Chinese Ams., 1991, Engr. of Yr. award Assn. Engrs. of India, 1992. Fellow IEEE (editor Communications 1984—, mem. editorial bd. Proceedsings of IEEE 1980-84, Fink prize 1980, L.G. Abraham prize 1985, 91, Alexander Graham Bell medal 1991, mem. digitals TV com.), AAAS; mem. NAE, Tau Beta Pi, Sigma Xi. Avocation: tennis. Home: 10 Byron Ct Westfield NJ 07090-2250 Office: Lucent Techs 600 Mountain Ave Rm 6A412 New Providence NJ 07974-2008

NETSIRI, CHAIYAPOJ, academic administrator, researcher; b. Bangkok, Thailand, May 29, 1964; s. Patcharin Netsiri. BSEE, King Mongkut's Inst. Tech., Bangkok, 1986; MS in Computer Sci., Chiba U., Japan, 1996; PhD, U. Tokyo, 1999. Prodn. engr. Kang Yang Electric MFG Co., Ltd., Samutprakarn, Thailand, 1987—89; elec. engr. Tom Tech Co., Ltd., Bangkok, 1990—92; R&D engr. Yamada Kikai Kogyo Co., Ltd., Chiba, Japan, 1992—94; rsch. assoc. U. Cambridge, England, 1999—2001, Albert Einstein Coll. Medicine, Bronx, NY, 2001—03; sr. staff assoc. Columbia U., N.Y.C., 2003—04. Rsch. scientist Rice U., Japan, 2004—. Fellow, U. Cambridge, 1999—2001; grantee, Royal Soc., 2000—01; scholar, Nagai Found., 1994—95, Japanese Govt., 1995—99. Mem.: Soc. Neurosci. (assoc.), IEEE (assoc.). Office: Rice Univ Dept Psychology MS25 6100 Main St Sewall Hall Houston TX 77005 Office Phone: 212-543-5103., 713-348-3052. E-mail: cn2113@columbia.edu., cnetsiri@rice.edu.

NETTELBECK, FRED ARTHUR, poet; b. Chgo., Nov. 9, 1950; s. Manfred Emil Nettelbeck and Thelma Anderson; m. Billy Joe Nettelbeck, July 17, 1999; children: James, Danny, Amandla. Student, El Camino Coll., 1969—71. Author: The Quick and The Dead, 1970, Spectator, 1977, Large Talk, 1983, Americruiser, 1983, The Kiss Off, 1984, Hands on a Mirror, 1987, Albert Ayler Disappeared, 1989, Ecosystems Collapsing, 1992, Hurting Music, 1998, All Fell Down, 2003, Everything Written Exists, 2004; others; editor: This is Important mag., 1980—. Democrat. Avocations: angling, marksmanship, entheogenic plants. Home and Office: PO Box 69 Beatty OR 97621 Office Phone: 541-533-2486.

NETTELHORST, ROBIN PAUL, academic administrator, writer; b. Ohio, Mar. 14, 1957; s. Paul Merrit and Naomi Jean (Saylor) N.; m. Ruth Williamson, June 25, 1983; children: Vanessa Rachel, Nichole Antoinette, Sarah Brittany. BA, L.A. Bapt. Coll., 1979; MA, UCLA, 1983. Lectr. Christian Heritage Coll., El Cajon, Calif., 1984; lectr. old testament and bibl. langs. L.A. Bapt. Coll., 1984-87; novelist, 1987—; v.p. Quartz Hill (Calif.) Sch. Theology, 1992—. Webmaster Quartz Hill Sch. Theology, 1996—. Editor Quartz Hill Jour. Theology, 1994-99; author short stories; contbr. articles to mags.; host (internet and FM Radio broadcast) Beyond the Box, 1999—; author: What Dreamers Be These Rocks: Tableland, Book I, 2000, Dreams of Nothingness: Tableland, Book II, 2000, Awakens the Dreamer: Tableland, Book III, 2000, The Wrong Side of Morning, 2000, With a Rod of Iron, 2000, Antediluvian, 2000, Somewhere Obscurely, 2000, Does God Have a Long Nose? vol. I, 2001, Does God Have a Long Nose? vol. 2, 2001. Ordained deacon Quartz Hill Cmty. Ch., 1989—. Mem. Am. Acad. Religion, Soc. Bibl. Lit. Baptist. Avocations: camping, reading, stamp collecting/philately, coin collecting/numismatics. Office: Quartz Hill Sch Theology 43543 51st St W Quartz Hill CA 93536-5608 E-mail: robin@theology.edu. *To hold the hand of God, to listen to his heart, to feel his pain, to taste his joys, to long for his happiness—that is to love God.*

NETTELS, ELSA, English language educator; b. Madison, Wis., May 25, 1931; d. Curtis Putnam and Elsie (Patterson) N. BA, Cornell U., 1953; MA, U. Wis., 1955, PhD, 1960. From instr. to asst. prof. English Mt. Holyoke Coll., South Hadley, Mass., 1959-67; from asst. prof. to prof. English Coll. William and Mary, Williamsburg, Va., 1967-97, prof. emeritus, 1997—. Author: James and Conrad, 1977 (South Atlantic Modern Lang. Assn. award 1975), Language, Race and Social Class in Howells' America, 1988, Language and Gender in American Fiction: Howells, James, Wharton, and Cather, 1997;

contbr. articles to profl. jours. NEH fellow, 1984-85. Mem. MLA, South Atlantic MLA (edit. bd. 1977-83), Henry James Soc. (editl. bd. 1983—). Office: Coll William and Mary Dept English Williamsburg VA 23187 Office Phone: 757-221-3905. Business E-Mail: exnett@wm.edu.

NETTELS, GEORGE EDWARD, JR., retired mining executive; b. Pittsburg, Kans., Oct. 20, 1927; s. George Edward and Mathilde A. (Wulke) N.; m. Mary Joanne Myers, July 19, 1952; children: Christopher Bryan, Margaret Anne, Katherine Anne, Rebecca Jane. BSCE, U. Kans., Lawrence, 1950. With Black & Veatch Engrs., Kansas City, Mo., 1950-51, Spencer Chem. Co., Kansas City, Mo., 1951-55, Freeto Constrn. Co., Pittsburg, 1955-57; pres. Midwest Minerals, Inc., Pittsburg, 1957—; chmn. bd. McNally Pittsburg Mfg. Corp., 1970-76, pres., CEO, 1976-87, ret., 1987. Past chmn. bd. Nat. Limestone Inst.; bd. dirs. Pitts. Indsl. Devel. Com. Mem. bd. advisors U. Kans. Endowment Assn.; mem. Kans. U. Chancellor's Club, Kans., Inc.; past pres. Bd. Edn. 250, Pittsburg; past chmn. bd. trustees Mt. Carmel Hosp.; past mem. Kans. Commn. Civil Rights; chmn. Kans. Republican Com., 1966-68; Kans. del. Rep. Nat. Conv., 1968, Kans. Bus. and Industry Com. for Re-election of Pres., 1972. With AUS, 1946-47. Recipient Disting. Svc. citation U. Kans., 1980, Disting. Engring. citation U. Kans., 1985; named Kansan of Yr. Natives Sons and Daus. Kans., 1986. Mem. ASCE, NAM (past. dir.), Kans. C. of C. and Industry (dir., chmn. 1983-84), Kans. Right to Work (dir.), Pittsburg C. of C. (past dir.), Kans. U. Alumni Assn. (pres. 1977), Kans. Leadership Com., Crestwood Country Club, Wolf Creek Golf Club (Olathe), Tau Beta Pi, Omicron Delta Kappa, Beta Theta Pi. Office: Midwest Minerals Inc 509 W Quincy St Pittsburg KS 66762-5689 Business E-Mail: george@midwestminerals.com.

NETTL, BRUNO, anthropology and musicology educator; b. Prague, Czechoslovakia, Mar. 14, 1930; s. Paul and Gertrud (Hutter) N.; m. Wanda Maria White, Sept. 15, 1952; children: Rebecca, Gloria. AB, Ind. U., 1950, PhD, 1953; MA in L.S, U. Mich., 1960; LHD (hon.), U. Chgo., 1993; LHD (hon.), U. Ill., 1996, Carleton Coll., 2000, Kenyon Coll., 2002. Mem. faculty Wayne State U., Detroit, 1953-64, asst. prof., 1954-64, music librarian, 1958-64; mem. faculty U. Ill., Urbana, 1964—, prof. music and anthropology, 1967—, chmn. div. musicology, 1967-72, 75-77, 82-85. Vis. lectr., Fulbright grantee U. Kiel, Fed. Republic of Germany, 1956-58; cons. Ency. Britannica, 1969—, also on ethnomusicology to various univs.; vis. prof. Williams Coll., 1971, Wash. U., 1978, U. Louisville, 1983, U. Wash., 1985, 88, 89, 93, 95, 98, 2000, Fla. State U., 1988, Harvard U., 1989, U. Alta., 1991, Colo. Coll., 1992, Northwestern U., 1993, U. Minn., 1994, U. Chgo., 1996, Carleton Coll., 1996, U. So. Calif., 2002. Author: Theory and Method in Ethnomusicology, 1964, Music in Primitive Culture, 1956, Folk and Traditional Music of the Western Continents, 1965, 2nd edit., 1973, Eight Urban Musical Cultures, 1978, The Study of Ethnomusicology, 1983, The Western Impact on World Music, 1985, The Radif of Persian Music, 1987, rev. edit., 1992, Blackfoot Musical Thought, 1989, Comparative Musicology and Anthropology of Music, 1991, Heartland Excursions, 1995, In the course of Performance, 1998, Encounters in Ethnomusicology, a Memoir, 2002; co-author Excursions in World Music, 1992, 3rd edit., 2000, 4th edit., 2003; editor Ethnomusicology, 1961-65, 98-2002, Yearbook of the International Folk Music Council, 1975-77; sr. adv. editor Garland Ency. of World Music; contbr. articles to profl. jours. Recipient Koizumi prize in ethnomusicology, Tokyo, 1994. Fellow Am. Acad. of Arts and Scis.; mem. Soc. Ethnomusicology (pres. 1969-71), Am., Internat. musicol. socs., Internat. Coun. for Traditional Music, Coll. Music Soc, Am. Musicological Soc. (hon.), Soc. for Ethnomusicology (hon.) Home: 1423 Cambridge Dr Champaign IL 61821-4958 Office: U Ill Sch Music Urbana IL 61801 Office Phone: 217-333-9617.

NETTLES, JOHN BARNWELL, obstetrics and gynecology educator; b. Dover, N.C., May 19, 1922; s. Stephen A. and Estelle (Hendrix) N.; m. Eunice Anita Saugstad, Apr. 28, 1956; children: Eric, Robert, John Barnwell; m. 2d, Sandra Williams, Sept. 14, 1991; stepchildren: Steven Williams, Clayton Williams. BS, U. S.C., 1941; MD, Med. Coll. S.C., 1944. Diplomate: Am. Bd. Obstetrics and Gynecology. Intern Garfield Meml. Hosp., Washington, 1944-45; research fellow in pathology Med. Coll. Ga., Augusta, 1946-47; resident in ob-gyn. U. Ill. Rsch. and Ednl. Hosps., Chgo., 1947-51; instr. to asst. prof. ob-gyn. U. Ill. Coll. Medicine, Chgo., 1951-57; asst. prof., assoc. prof., prof. ob-gyn. U. Ark. Med. Ctr., Little Rock, 1957-69; dir. grad. edn. Hillcrest Med. Ctr., Tulsa, 1969-73; prof. ob-gyn Coll. Medicine, U. Okla., Oklahoma City, 1969-78; chmn. dept. ob-gyn. U. Okla.-Tulsa Med. Coll., 1975-80, prof., 1980—, mem. coun. on residency edn. in ob-gyn., 1974-79. Dir. Tulsa Obstet. and Gynecol. Edn. Found., 1969-80; Coordinator med. edn. Nat. Def., Ark., 1961-69; mem. S.W. regional med. adv. com. Planned Parenthood Fedn. Am., 1974-78; mem. adv. com. Health Policy Agenda Am. People, 1982-85, rev. com. Accrediation Coun. for Continuing Med. Edn., 1987-92. Contbr. articles on uterine malignancy, kidney biopsy in pregnancy, perinatal morbidity and mortality, human sexuality sch. age pregnancy to profl. jours. Served as lt. (j.g.) M.C. USNR, 1945-46; as lt. 1953-54. Recipient Nat. Faculty award. Fellow Am. Coll. Obstetricians and Gynecologists (dist. sec.-treas. 1964-70, dist. chmn. exec. bd. 1970-73, v.p. 1977-78, Disting. Svc. award 1998, Dist. VIII Outstanding Clin. Prof. award 1989, Nat. Tchr. award 1992), ACS (bd. govs. 1969-71, program com. 1970-71, Surg. forum 1977-84, adv. com. gyn/ob 1985-92), Royal Soc. Health, Royal Soc. Medicine; mem. Ark. Obstet. and Gynecol. Soc. (exec. sec. 1959-69), Ctrl. Assn. Obstetrics and Gynecology (exec. com. 1966-69, pres. 1978-79), Internat. Soc. Advancement Humanistic Studies in Gynecology, Assn. Mil. Surgeons U.S., AMA (sect. coun. on obstetrics and gynecology 1975-96, chmn. 1982-96, del. from Am. Coll. Obstetricians and Gynecologists 1987-96, governing coun. sr. physicians group 2003—, Young at Heart award Young Physicians sect. 1994), Nurses Assn. Am. Coll. Obstetricians and Gynecologists (exec. bd. 1970-73, assoc. 1980-95), So. Med. Assn. (chmn. obstetrics 1973-74), Okla. Med. Soc. (Ed L. Calhoun Leadership in Organized Medicine award, 2004), Tulsa County Med. Soc., Chgo. Med. Soc., Am. Assn. for Maternal and Infant Health, Assn. Am. Med. Colls., Am. Public Health Assn., Am. Assn. Sex Edn. Counselors and Therapists (S.W. regional bd. 1976-79), Soc. for Gynecol. Investigation, AAAS, Am. Soc. for Study Fertility and Sterility, Internat. Soc. Gen. Semantics, So. Gynecol. and Obstet. Soc. (pres. 1981-82), Am. Cancer Soc. (pres. Okla. div. 1979-83, St. George's medal 1991), Com. on In-Tng. Exam. in Obstetrics and Gynecology, Am. Coll. Nurse Midwives (governing bd. examiners 1979-83), Sigma Xi (pres. Tulsa chpt. 1992-93), Phi Rho Sigma. Lutheran. Office: U Okla Health Sci Ctr 1145 S Utica Ave Ste 600 Tulsa OK 74104-4070 Office Phone: 918-582-0955. *To live life fully, with faith and trust in God and his people, working with others to make our world a little better, and willing to fill the gaps wherever they are.*

NETZEL, PAUL ARTHUR, fund raising management executive, consultant; b. Tacoma, Sept. 11, 1941; s. Marden Arthur and Audrey Rose (Jones) Netzel; m. Diane Viscount, Mar. 21, 1963; children: Paul M., Shari Ann. BS in Group Work Edn., George Williams Coll., 1963. Program dir. S. Pasadena-San Marino (Calif.) YMCA, 1963—66; exec. dir. camp and youth programs Wenatchee (Wash.) YMCA, 1966—67; exec. dir. Culver-Palms Family YMCA, Culver City, Calif., 1967—73; v.p. met. fin. devel. YMCA Met. Los Angeles, 1978—78, exec. v.p. devel., 1979—85; pres. bd. dirs. YMCA Employees Credit Union, 1977—80; chmn. N. Am. Fellowship of YMCA Devel. Orricers, 1980—83; chmn., CEO Netzel Assocs., Inc., 1985—; pvt. practice cons., fund raiser. Adj. faculty U. So. Calif. Coll. Continuing Edn., 1983—86, Loyola Marymount U., 1986—90, Calif. State U., 1991—92, UCLA Extension, 1991—. Bd. mgrs. Culver-Palms YMCA, Culver City, 1985—, chmn., 1989—91, 1991—93; mem. Culver City Bd. Edn., 1975—79, pres., 1977—78; mem. Culver City Edn. Found., 1982—91, Culver City Redevel. Agy., 1980—88, chmn., 1983—84, 1987—88, vice chmn., 1985—86; chmn. bd. dirs. Calif. Youth Model Legislature, 1987—92; mem. World Affairs Coun., 1989—92; mem. adv. bd. Automobile Club So. Calif., 1996—2002; mem. Culver City City Coun., 1980—88, vice mayor, 1980—82, 1984—85, mayor, 1983, 1986—87; bd. dirs. L.A. Psychiat. Svc., 1971—74, Goodwill Industries of So. Calif., 1993—97, L.A. County Sanitation Dists., 1982—83, 1985—87, Western United Way, 1986—93, vice chmn., 1991—92. Recipient Man of Yr. award, Culver City C. of C., 1972. Mem.: Nat. Soc. Fund Raising Execs. (nat. bd. dirs. 1989—91, vice chmn. 1994, v.p. bd. dirs. Greater L.A. chpt. 1986—88, pres. bd. dirs. 1989—90, Profl. of Yr. 1983), Mountain Gate Country Club, Rotary Internat. (L.A. # 5 pres. 1992—93, treas. L.A. found. 1995—96, gov. dist. 5280 1997—98, chmn. L.A. conv.), Calif. Club. Address: Netzel Assocs Inc 9696 Culver Blvd Ste 105 Culver City CA 90232-2753 E-mail: pretzel@earthlink.net.

NETZER, DICK, economics professor; b. N.Y.C., May 14, 1928; s. Solomon and Sue (Dick) Netzer; m. Carol Risika, Dec. 30, 1945; children: Jenny, Katherine. BA, U. Wis., 1946; MA, M.P.A., Harvard U., 1948, PhD, 1952. Successively economist, sr. economist, asst. v.p. Fed. Res. Bank Chgo., 1948-60; econ. cons. Regional Plan Assn., N.Y.C., 1960-80; assoc. prof. N.Y. U., 1961-64, prof. econs., 1964—, dean Grad. Sch. Pub. Adminstrn., 1969-82, dir. Urban Research Center, 1981-86. Cons. in field, 1960—. Author: Economics of the Property Tax, 1966, The Economics of Public Finance, 1974, The Subsidized Muse, 1978, Urban Politics New York Style, 1990; editor: N.Y. Affairs, 1973—88. Mem. Mayor N.Y.C. Fiscal Adv. Com., 1969—73; treas. Colony-South Bklyn. Houses, 1968—73; mem. Mcpl. Securities Rulemaking Bd., 1978—81, vice chmn., 1980—81; bd. dirs. Mcpl. Assistance Corp., N.Y.C., 1975—97, Citizens Union Found.; bd. dirs., treas. Adolph and Esther Gottlieb Found., 1975—, v.p., 1979—88, pres., 1989—. Fellow: Am. Inst. Cert. Planners; mem.: Nat. Tax Assn., Regional Sci. Assn., Am. Econs. Assn., Assn. Cultural Econs. Internat. (pres. 1993—94). Home: 41 Huckleberry Ln East Hampton NY 11937-2830 Office: 295 Lafayette St New York NY 10012 Office Phone: 212-998-7510. Business E-Mail: dick.netzer@nyu.edu.

NETZLY, DWIGHT H. lawyer; b. Navarre, Ohio, May 7, 1919; s. Harry E. Netzly and Lillian N. Ramsey; m. Martha L. Emerick, Jan. 29, 1949; children: Duane, Dwight K., Doyle, Derek. BSBA, Kent State U., 1948; LLB, William McKinley Law Sch., 1952. Bar: Ohio 1952. Acct. H.C. Schwitzgebul, Canton, Ohio, 1948-52; pvt. practice law and acctg. Massillon, Ohio, 1952—. Sgt. U.S. Army, 1941-45. Mem. Am. Assn. Atty. CPAs, Ohio State Bar Assn., Ohio Soc. CPAs, Am. Legion (state treas. 1993-94). Republican. Home: 6179 Pigeon Run Rd SW Navarre OH 44662-8738 Office: 1237 Lincoln Way E Massillon OH 44646-6954 E-mail: dhnetz@aol.com.

NEU, CHARLES ERIC, historian, educator; b. Carroll, Iowa, Apr. 10, 1936; s. Arthur Nicholas and Martha Margaret (Frandsen) N.; m. Deborah Dunning, Sept. 2, 1961 (div. 1978); children: Hilary Adams, Douglas Bancroft.; m. Sabina deWerth Tuck, Mar. 27, 1999. BA, Northwestern U., 1958; PhD, Harvard U., 1964. Instr. history Rice U., 1963-64, asst. prof., 1964-67, asso. prof., 1968-70; asso. prof. history Brown U., Providence, 1970-76, prof., 1976—2003, prof. emeritus, 2003—, chmn. dept. history, 1995—98, 1999—2002. Dir. summer seminar NEH, 1979, 1986—87, 1989, 92; adj. prof. history U. Miami, 2004—. Author: An Uncertain Friendship: Theodore Roosevelt and Japan, 1906-1909, 1967, The Troubled Encounter: The United States and Japan, 1975, America's Lost War: Vietnam, 1945-1975, 2004; co-editor: The Wilson Era: Essays in Honor of Arthur S. Link, 1991; editor: After Vietnam: Legacies of a Lost War, 2000. Recipient, Woodrow Wilson Found. fellowship, 1958—59, Am. Coun. Learned Socs. fellowship, 1975—76, Charles Warren Ctr. fellowship, 1971—72, Howard Found. fellowship, 1976—77, Guggenheim fellowship, 1981—82, NEH scholarship, 1968—69, guest scholarship, Woodrow Wilson Ctr., 1988, Barrett Hazeltine citation for disting. undergrad. tchg., 1998. Mem. Am. Hist. Assn., Orgn. Am. Historians, Soc. Historians of Am. Fgn. Policy, Phi Beta Kappa. Democrat. Home: 4929 SW 71st Place Miami FL 33155 E-mail: cneu@bellsouth.net.

NEU, JIM A, playwright; b. Brooklyn, NY, Nov. 18, 1943; s. Frederick Albert Theodore Neu and Johanna Jacoba Kruidenier; m. Carol Mullins, Feb. 24, 1998. BS in edn., SUNY Oneonta, 1961—65. Actor, writer Robert Wilson's Byrd Hoffman Sch. of Byrds, 1970—75, 1978—80, Napa Valley Theater Co., 1975—80. Playwright member Andy's Summer Playhouse, Wilto, NH. Playwright (plays) Kiss Shot, Situation Room, Chance's Place, An Evening With Jesse James, Duet For Spies, Basic Behavior, Him Or Me, AEROBIA, Undercurrent Incorporated, Mondo Beyondo, The Floatones, Dark Pocket, The Wrong Mistake, Live Witness, screenwriter (film) The Big Blue, Doomed Love. Spec 5 U.S. Army, 1965—67, Korea. Recipient ArtsLink Collaborative Projects award, ArtsLink, 2000; New Works grant, NY State Coun. on the Arts, 1994, Playwrights Incentive Commn., Howard and Mimi Steinberg Found., 1993, Playwriting fellowship, NY Found. for the Arts, 1987, fellowship, Nat. Endowment for the Arts, 1985. Avocations: jazz, pool, singing. Home: 161 President St Brooklyn NY 11231 Personal E-mail: jimneu1@aol.com.

NEU, RICHARD W. credit agency executive; B of Acctg., Ea. Mich. U., 1977. Sr. audit mgr. KMPG Peat Marwick; sr. v.p., chief fin. officer FirstFed Mich. Corp., 1985—89, chief fin. officer, 1989—95; exec. v.p., chief fin. officer Charter One Fin., Inc., 1995—. Past chmn. Thrift Industry Acctg. Com. Office: Charter One Fin Inc 1215 Superior Ave Cleveland OH 44114

NEUBAUER, CHARLES FREDERICK, investigative reporter; b. Berkeley, Ill., Feb. 13, 1950; s. Fred Charles and Dolores Jeanne (Pries) N.; m. Sandra Carol Bergo, Oct. 4, 1975; 1 child, Michael Frederick. BSJ., Northwestern U., 1972, MSJ., 1973. Investigator Better Govt. Assn., Chgo., 1971-73; investigative reporter Chgo. Today, 1973-74, Chgo. Tribune, 1974-83, Chgo. Sun Times, 1983—2001; investigative reporter Washington bur. L.A. Times, 2001—. Recipient Pulitzer prize local reporting, 1976; Edward Scott Beck award for domestic reporting Chgo. Tribune, 1980 Office: 401 N Wabash Ave Chicago IL 60611-5642

NEUBAUER, DEANE, academic administrator; PhD, Yale U. Interim chancellor U. Hawaii, interim v.p. acad. affairs; adj. prof. U. Hawaii, U. Sydney; dean coll. social sci. U. Hawaii, 1980—88. Served Western Assn Sch. & Coll., 1983—, mem. sr. commn., 1995—2001. Recipient Robert W. Clopton award, 1997. Office: U Hawaii-Manoa 2444 Dole St Honolulu HI 96822

NEUBAUER, HUGO DUANE, JR., computer network engineer; b. Mankato, Minn., Oct. 31, 1959; s. Hugo Duane and Joan Marie (Habinger) N.; m. Susan A. May, July 7, 1990. Student, U. Miami, 1978-80; AA, U. Fla., 1981; AS, Santa Fe C.C., 1984; student, U. Fla., 1984—. Microsoft cert. profl. Aquaculture specialist, technician Aqualife Rsch. Inc., 1979-80; automotive dept. K-Mart, 1981-82; electronic technician Synergetics, Inc., 1983-84; water resources equipment technician Environ. Sci. and Engring., Inc., Gainesville, Fla., 1984-89, tech. ops. equipment mgr., 1990-91, geosciences divsn. equipment mgr., 1992-93, ctr. 3 equipment mgr., 1994-95; office mgr. Keck Instruments, Inc., Newberry, Fla., 1996-98; founder, owner, web master and designer Innovative Computer and Instrument Svcs., Alachua, Fla., 1996—; co-founder, co-owner Dances with Hooves Farm, Alachua, Fla., 1997—; info. tech. systems adminstr. CPAmerica Internat. (formerly Acctg. Firms Associated Inc.), 1999—2002; MIS mgr. Hunter Marine, Inc., Luhrs Marine Group, Alachua, Fla., 2002—. Cons. in field. Mem. IEEE, IEEE Computer Soc., NRA, Internat. Webmasters Assn., HTML Writers Guild. Avocations: computer programming and Internet, horses, gun collecting and shooting, videography and photography, scuba diving. Home and Office: 14108 NW 195th St Alachua FL 32615-8023 Fax: 253-276-5435. E-mail: hdneubauer@ieee.org, hdneubauer@Luhrs.com.

NEUBAUER, NICKOLAS J. brokerage house executive; BA, U. Minn., 1967; JD, Stanford U. Law Sch.; MBA, Stanford U. Bus. Sch. Co-founder and pres. Tradelink Corp., 1979—87; mgmt. cons. McKinsey and Co.; corp. and tax lawyer Sidley & Austin, Chgo.; vice chmn. arbitration com. Chgo. Bd. Trade, 1993—97, chmn. bd. dirs., 2000—; pres. Sano Corp., 1991—. Office: Chgo Bd Trade 141 W Jackson Blvd Chicago IL 60604-2994

NEUBAUER, PETER BELA, psychoanalyst; b. Krems, Austria, July 5, 1913; came to US, 1941, naturalized, 1946; s. Samuel and Rose (Blau) N.; m. Susan Rachlin, Nov. 25, 1953 (dec.); children: Joshua Rachlin, Alexander Lewis. MD, U. Berne, 1938. Intern Lawrence Meml. Hosp., New London, Conn., 1941, Beth-El Hosp., Bklyn., 1942; resident in psychiatry Bellevue Hosp., NYC, 1943-45; dir. Child Devel. Ctr., Jewish Bd. Family Children's Svcs., NYC, 1951-83; clin. prof. psychiatry Psychoanalytic Inst., NYU, 1979—. Lectr. child psychoanalysis Psychoanalytic Inst. Tng. Research Columbia U., 1973 Author: Children in Collectives: Child Rearing Aims and Practices in Kibbutzim, 1965, Early Child Day Car, 1974, Process of Child Development, 1976, (with Alexander Neubauer) Nature's Thumbprint, 1990; contbg. author: Fathers and Their Families, 1989; mem. editorial bd. Psychoanalytic Study of the Child, 1978. Recipient Hulse award NY Council Child Psychiatry, 1975, Heinz Hartmann award NY Psychoanalytic Soc., 1981, Mary S. Sigourney award, 1994. Mem. Am. Psychoanalytic Assn., Am. Acad. Child Psychiatry, Assn. Child Psychoanalysis, Internat. Assn. Child and Adolescent Psychiatry, Assn. Child Psychoanalysis (pres. 1974-76). Office: 33 E 70th St New York NY 10021-4941 Office Phone: 212-288-2348.

NEUBAUER, RICHARD A. library science educator, consultant; b. Meadville, Pa., Oct. 9, 1933; s. Carl Gustave and Velma Winston (Watson) N.; m. Janice Ernest; children: David, Lynda, Karl, Jennifer; m. Carol Barton. BS, Clarion U., 1955; MLS, SUNY, Geneseo, 1966; attended, Kent St. U., 1966-68, Simmons Coll., 1970-72. Cert. profl. libr., sch. libr., tchr. Tchr. geography Franklin (Pa.) Sch. Dept., 1957-58, N. Bedford County Schs., Woodbury, Mass., 1958-60; tchr. history Hornell (N.Y.) Jr. High Sch., 1960-62, sch. libr., 1962-65; prof. libr. sci. Edinboro (Pa.) U., 1965-68, assoc. libr. Hamilton Libr., 1965-68; dir. sch. librs. Duxbury (Mass.) Sch. Dept., 1968-69; dir., cons. Pub. Libr., Lincoln, Mass., 1969-70; prof. libr. sci. Bridgewater (Mass.) State Coll., 1969-78, chair dept. libr. sci., 1978-80, prof. libr. sci., 1980-91, coord. libr. media program, 1991-95; prof. emeritus libr. sci., 1996—. Adj. prof. libr. sci. U. R.I., Kingston, 1975-88; cons. Tabor Acad., Marion, Mass., 1970-71, Abington (Mass.) Pub. Libr. Trustees, 1973-76, Duxbury Free Libr., 1968-72. Author: Planning the Elementary School Library, 1968; author, editor Exploring the U.S.-Northeast, 1994. Chmn. Mass. Dept. Edn. Cert., Quincy, 1989-90; resource cons. Project Contemporary Competitiveness, Bridgewater, Mass., 1973-83. 1st lt. USMC, 1955-57. Inst. grantee HEA of 1965 Edinboro U., 1968. Mem. NEA, Am. Libr. Assn., Intellectual Freedom Found., Mass. Assn. of Edn. Media, Mass. Sch. Libr. Media Assn., Mass. Tchrs. Assn. Democrat. Avocations: gardening, woodworking, reading. Home: 22 Pleasant St Carver MA 02330-1013

NEUBERG, HANS W. internist, educator; b. Hannover, Germany, Mar. 26, 1921; came to U.S., 1937, naturalized, 1943. s. Georg and Gertrud (Dux) N.; m. Birgit Aron, Apr. 8, 1949; children: Peter G., Gerald W. BS, Wagner Coll., 1941; MD, Columbia U., 1950. Diplomate Am. Bd. Internal Medicine. Intern Presbyn. Hosp., N.Y.C., 1950-53, asst. resident, NRC fellow in medicine, 1953-54, asst. attending physician, 1966-80, assoc. attending physician, 1980-91, attending physician, 1992—; pvt. practice, 1954-83. Instr. medicine Columbia U. Coll. Phys. and Surg., N.Y.C., 1954-63, assoc. in medicine, 1963-67, asst. prof. clin. medicine, 1967-80, assoc. clin. prof. medicine, 1980-91, clin. prof. medicine, 1992—, mem. Instnl. Rev. Bd. With AUS, 1943-46. Fellow ACP; mem. Alpha Omega Alpha. Mem. Am. Diabetes Assn. Home: 85 Erledon Rd Tenafly NJ 07670-2503 Office: 620 W 168th St New York NY 10032-3702 E-mail: NeubergH@aol.com.

NEUBERGER, EGON, economics professor; b. Zagreb, Croatia, Yugoslavia, Feb. 27, 1925; came to U.S., 1940; s. Paul and Ann (Freund) N.; m. Florence Perlmutter, Dec. 22, 1949; children: Leah Ruth, Marc Joseph. BA, Cornell U., 1947; MA, Harvard U., 1949, PhD, 1958. Econ. analyst State Dept., Washington, 1949-54; asst. prof. econ. Amherst (Mass.) Coll., 1957-60; economist RAND Corp., Santa Monica, Calif., 1960-67; prof. econ. SUNY, Stony Brook, 1967-81, leading prof. econs., 1982-97, emeritus, 1998—, dean social and behavioral scis., 1982-88, vice provost for undergraduate studies, 1989-90. Econ. officer Am. Embassy, Moscow, 1952-53; vis. prof. U. Mich., Ann Arbor, 1965-66, U. Konstanz, Germany, 1995, U. Tuebingen, Germany, 1996. Served with U.S. Army, 1943-46, ETO. Mem. Assn. Comparative Econ. Studies (mem. exec. com. 1974-76, pres. 1990-91), Am. Econ. Assn., Assn. Study of Grants Economy (adv. bd.), Omicron Delta Epsilon (pres. 1979-81, exec. bd., Disting. Ser. award 1981). Democrat. Jewish. Home: 5 Somerset Ct East Setauket NY 11733 Office: SUNY Dept Econs Stony Brook NY 11794-4384 E-mail: eneuberger@notes.cc.sunysb.edu.

NEUBERGER, JOHN STEPHEN, preventive medicine and epidemiology educator; b. NYC, June 29, 1938; s. Seymour Neuberger and Norma (Endel) Greenspan; m. Geri Cox, July 13, 1980; 1 child. BME, Cornell U., 1961; MBA, Columbia U., 1967; MPH, Johns Hopkins U., 1974, DrPH, 1977. Asst. prof. U. Kans. Sch. Medicine, Kansas City, 1978—84, assoc. prof., 1984—2003, prof., 2003—. Cons. region VII, EPA, Kansas City, 1979-81; toxicology adv. com. Kans. Dept. Health and Environ., Topeka, 1982-86. Contbr. articles to profl. jours. Bd. dirs. Coalition for Environment, Kansas City, 1987-91, pres., 1990-91; adv. bd. Kansas City Earth Week, 1990; mem. Cherokee County Task Force, 1986-94, Oak Grove Sch. Task Force, Kansas City, 1989-90; air quality forum, 1991-93; mem. Kansas City Pub. TV Cmty. Adv. Bd., 1991-92. 1st lt. U.S. Army, 1961-63. Grantee EPA, 1979-80, Kans. Dept. Health and Environ., 1982-86, US Dept. Energy, 1988-89. Mem. AAAS, Am. Assn. Cancer Rsch., Am. Coll. Epidemiology, Am. Coun. on Sci. and Health (scientific bd., policy advisor 1986—), Am. Pub. Health Assn. (epidemiology and environ. health sects.). Avocations: travel, swimming, hiking. Office: U Kans Sch Medicine 3901 Rainbow Blvd Mail Stop 1008 Kansas City KS 66160 Office Phone: 913-588-2745. Business E-Mail: jneuberg@kumc.edu.

NEUBURGER, KAREN, apparel executive; Retail buyer Maurice's, Emporium, San Francisco; v.p. merchandising Eber Internat., 1980-91; founder, pres., design dir. Karen Neuburger Sleepwear, San Rafael, Calif., 1991—. Guest appearence Oprah Winfrey TV show. Office: 2505 Kerner BLVD San Rafael CA 94901-5571

NEUENSCHWANDER, PIERRE FERNAND, medical educator; BS in Chemistry, 1985; PhD in Biochemistry & Molecular Biology, SUNY, Stony Brook, 1990. Lab. tchg. asst. SUNY, Stony Brook, 1985-86, lecture tchg. asst. in biochemistry, 1986, 87; assoc. rsch. scientist Cardiovascular Biology Rsch. Program Okla. Med. Rsch. Found., Oklahoma City, 1990-93, sr. rsch. scientist, 1993-94, found. rsch. scientist, 1994-95, asst. mem., 1995-2001; assoc. prof. biochemistry U. Tex. Health Ctr., Tyler, 2001—. Co-editor Trigger newsletter; rev. Jour. Biol. Chemistry; contbr. articles to profl. jours. Recipient Am. Heart Assn. Travel stipend, 1994, Internat. Soc. Haematology Travel award, 1992, Am. Soc. Hematology Travel award, 1989, 90. Mem. Am. Heart Assn. (coun. on thrombosis), Am. Chem Soc. (divsn. biol. chemistry), Internat. Soc. Thrombosis and Haemostasis, Sigma Xi, Alpha Chi Sigma. Office: Univ Tex Health Ctr Biomed Rsch Lab C7 11937 US Hwy 271 Tyler TX 75708 E-mail: Pierre.Neuenschwander@uthct.edu.

NEUENSCHWANDER, ROGER, architectural firm executive; MBA, Wharton Sch., Univ. of Pa., Pa., 1976; BA arch., Sch. of Arch., Ball State Univ., Muncie, In. Pres. Thompson Ventulett Stainback & Assoc., Atlanta, 1994—, employed, 1973. Mem.: AIA, constn. ind. groups (spkr.), Am. Inst. of Arch. (Chair of the Risk Mgmt. Comm. 2003). Office: TVS 2700 Promenade Two 1230 Peachtree St NE Atlanta GA 30309-3591

NEUER, PHILIP DAVID, lawyer, real estate consultant; b. Bklyn., May 31, 1946; s. Murray and Adele (Jacobs) Neuer; m. Rena Donna Levine, July 30, 1972 (div. 1987); children: Jeremy Evan, Linzy Michelle, Sari Faith. BBA, CCNY, 1968; postgrad., Boston U., 1968-69; JD, Seton Hall U., 1976. Bar: N.J. 1976, U.S. Dist. Ct. N.J. 1977, U.S. Supreme Ct. 1980. Asst. town atty. Town of West Orange, NJ, 1976-77; assoc. Margolis and Bergstein, Verona, 1979-80; ptnr. Slavitt and Slavitt, West Orange, 1980-81; assoc. Mandelbaum and Targan, West Orange, 1981-83; ptnr. Margolis Neuer, Verona, 1984-91; of counsel Slavitt Simon & Neuer, Parsippany, 1991-2000; exec. v.p., gen. counsel Safer Textiles Group, Safer Devel. and Mgmt. Co., Newark, 1993—; of counsel Lum, Danzis, Drasco, Positan & Kleinberg, LLC, Roseland, 2000—02. Faculty mem. NYU Grad. Sch. Real Estate, N.Y.C., 2004—. Mem. editl. bd. Internat. Jour. Corp. Real Estate, 1998—2004. With USN, 1969—73. Named to, Internat. Corp. Real Estate Hall of Fame, 2002. Mem.: ABA, Urban Land Inst., Inst. Corp. Real Estate (bd. dirs., pres. 1998—2002), Internat. Assn. Corp. Real Estate Execs. (pres., bd. dirs., gen. counsel N.J. chpt.,

designated internat. assoc., internat. bd. dirs., Mem. of the Yr. 1993, N.J. Corp. Real Exec. of the Yr. 1993), Essex County Bar Assn., N.J. State Bar Assn., Mensa. Office: 1875 McCarter Hwy Newark NJ 07104-4211 Office Phone: 973-482-0840. Business E Mail: philneuer@safertextiles.com E-mail: pdneuer@aol.com.

NEUERBURG-DENZER, URSULA, theater director, educator, actress; b. Bonn, Germany, May 18, 1962;, U.S., 1990; d. Helmut Neuerburg, Doris Neuerburg-Heusler; m. Ralph Denzer; children: Clara Louise Denzer, Emil Jakob Denzer. Acting cert., Arne Baur-Worch Acting Sch., Berlin, 1987; BA, Freie U. Berlin, 1990; MA, NYU, 1992; postgrad., Freie U., 2003. Cert. midwife. Vis. asst. prof. U. Calif., Santa Cruz, Calif., 1996—99; resident dir. Swarthmore (Pa.) Coll., 1999—. V.p. Theater Zerbrochene Fenster, Berlin, 1985—90; pres. East Coast Artists, N.Y.C., 1992—96. Dir.: (Shakespeare) Macbeth, 1995, (Seneca) Trojan Women, 1997, (Brecht) Mother Courage, 1998, (Tretyakov) I Want a Baby, 2002. Named Outstanding Artist Visa, Internal Naturalization Svs., 1994, 1995; grantee, Arts Internat., 1992, Goethe Inst., 1992—94. Mem.: Theatre Comm. Group.

NEUFELD, ELIZABETH FONDAL, biochemist, educator; b. Paris, Sept. 27, 1928; married, 1951. PhD, U. Calif., Berkeley, 1956; DHc (hon.), U. Rene Descartes, Paris, 1978; DSc (hon.), Russell Sage Coll., Troy, N.Y., 1981; DSc (hon.), Hahnemann U. Sch. Medicine, 1984; DSc (hon.), Queens Coll., 1996. Asst. rsch. biochemist U. Calif., Berkeley, 1957—63; with Nat. Inst. Arthritis, Metabolism and Digestive Diseases, Bethesda, Md., 1963—84, research biochemist, 1963—73, chief sect. human biochem. genetics, 1973—79, chief genetics and biochem. br., 1979—84; prof. Dept. Biol. Chemistry Sch. Medicine U. Calif., 1984—, chmn. Dept. Biol. Chemistry Sch. Medicine, 1984—2004. Named Passano Found. sr. laureate, 1982, Calif. Scientist of Yr., 1990; recipient Dickson prize, U. Pitts., 1974, Hillenbrand award, 1975, Gairdner Found. award, 1981, Albert Lasker Clin. Med. Rsch. award, 1982, William Allan award, 1982, Elliott Cresson medal, 1984, Wolf Found. prize, 1988, Christopher Columbus Discovery award for biomed. rsch., 1992, Nat. Medal of Sci., 1994. Fellow: Fellow AAAS; mem.: NAS, Am. Soc. Gene Therapy, Am. Soc. Clin. Investigation, Am. Soc. Cell Biology, Am. Soc. Biochemistry and Molecular Biology (pres. 1992—93), Am. Chem. Soc., Am. Soc. Human Genetics, Am. Philos. Soc., Am. Acad. Arts and Scis, Inst. Medicine of NAS. Office: UCLA David Geffen Sch Medicine Dept Biol Chemistry 33-257 CHS 33-355 CH Box 951737 Los Angeles CA 90095-1737 Business E-Mail: eneufeld@mednet.ucla.edu.

NEUFELD, JACOB A. pediatrician, physiatrist, physical medicine and rehabilitation; b. Phila. BA, Drew U., Madison, N.J., 1984; MS in Pub. Health, U. N.C., 1988; MD, Wake Forest U., Winston-Salem, 1993. Diplomate Am. Bd. Pediats., Am. Bd. Phys. Medicine and Rehab., lic. physician Va., N.Y., Mich., diplomate Nat. Bd. Med. Examiners. Intern Wayne State U., Detroit, 1993—94; and phys. medicine and rehab. Detroit Med. Ctr., Children's Hosp. of Mich./Rehab. Inst. Mich., 1994—98; asst. prof. dept. phys. medicine & rehab. NYU Sch. Medicine, N.Y.C., 1996—98; attending in pediats. and phys. medicine and rehab. Hosp. Joint Diseases Orthop. Inst., 1998—2002; chmn. divsn. pediats. rehab. Va. Commonwealth U., Richmond, 2002—; dir. pediat. rehab. Children's Hosp., Richmond, 2002—; assoc. prof. phys. medicine and rehab., divsn. pediat. rehab. Va. Commonwealth U./Med. Coll. Va., 2002—. Grad. asst. dept. health policy and adminstrn. U. N.C., Chapel Hill, 1988; rsch. assoc. N.C. Divsn. of Health Svcs., AIDS Control Br., 1987; grad. asst. program on aging U. N.C. Sch. Pub. Health, 1987. Contbr. articles to profl. jours. Mem. N.Y.C. Pub. Sch. health Commn., 2000—02; vol. physician Muscular Dystrophy Camp; vol. med. dir., classifier Nat. Disability Sports Festival, Conn.; vol. physician 1996 Paralympics, Atlanta; team physician Warren Consol. Sch. Football Program, 1994—96; chmn. Trek for Health, Bowman Gray Sch. Medicine, 1989—90, advisor, 1990—93; asst. scoutmaster Troop 44, Boy Scouts Am., Moorestown, NJ, 1985—86; numerous other civic activities; bd. dirs. Concepts of Independence, 2002—. Recipient Bronze Palm award, Boy Scouts Am.; AMA grantee, 1991, AMSA grantee, 1991, Dept. Edn. grantee, 1992, Rsch. grantee, Nat. Inst. for Disability and Rehab., 1998, Rotary scholar, 1983, 1980, Paul Harris fellow, 1985. Mem.: Am. Acad. Phys. Medicine and Rehab., Am. Assn. Physiatrists, Am. Acad. Pediats. Office: Children's Hospital 2924 Brook Rd Richmond VA 23220

NEUFELD, MACE, film company executive; b. N.Y.C., July 13, 1928; s. Philip M. and Margaret Ruth (Braun) N.; Feb. 28, 1954; children: Bradley David, Glenn Jeremy, Nancy Ann. BA, Yale U., 1948; postgrad., NYU, 1958-60. Photographer various N.Y. pubs., 1943-45; prodn. asst. Raymond E. Nelson, 1949-50; founder, owner Ray Bloch Assos., Inc., N.Y.C., 1951-59; ptnr. BNB Prodns., N.Y.C., 1959-70, Neufeld-Davis Prodns., Inc., Beverly Hills, Calif., 1981—. Trustee Am. Film Inst., 1978—; chmn. life achievement award nominating com. and scholarship fund. Producer in assn. with Harvey Bernhard The Omen, 1976, Damien - Omen II, 1977, Omen III - The Final Conflict, 1980; producer: The Frisco Kid, 1979, Angel on My Shoulder, 1980, The American Dream, 1980; ABC-TV mini-series East of Eden, 1981; CBS-TV series Cagney and Lacey, 1984; MGM film The Aviator, 1984, ABC-TV A Death in California, 1985; producer films Transylvania 6-5000, 1985, No Way Out, 1987, The Hunt for Red October, 1989, Flight of the Intruder, 1990, Necessary Roughness, 1991, Patriot Games, 1992, Clear and Present Danger, 1994, Gettysburg, 1994, Beverly Hills Cop 3, 1994, The Saint, 1996, The General's Daughter, 1998. Photograph entitled Sammy's Home voted Picture of Yr. N.Y. World Telegram-Sun, 1955; recipient Grand prize Eastman Kodak's First Nat. Salon of Photography, 1945; named N.A.T.O./Showest Producer of the Yr., 1993. Mem. Acad. TV Arts and Scis., Acad. Motion Picture Arts and Scis., ASCAP, Am. Film Inst. Clubs: Friars, Yale of N.Y. Democrat. Office: Sony Pictures Ste 220 10202 W Washington Blvd Culver City CA 90232

NEUFELD, MICHAEL JOHN, curator, historian; b. Edmonton, Alta., Can., July 7, 1951; s. Henry John and Isabel Grace (Mitchell) N.; m. Sheila Faith Weiss, May 29, 1983 (div. Dec. 1992); m. Karen Lee Levenback, June 14, 1994. BA with 1st class honors, U. Calgary, Alta., 1974; MA, U. B.C., Vancouver, Can., 1976, Johns Hopkins U., 1980, PhD in History, 1984. Hist. rschr. Dept. Supply and Svcs., Ottawa, Ont., Can., summer 1973, 74; teaching asst. Johns Hopkins U., Balt., 1979-80; instr. Clarkson U., Potsdam, N.Y., 1983-84, from part-time instr. to part-time asst. prof., 1983-85; vis. asst. prof. SUNY, Oswego, 1985-86, Colgate U., Hamilton, N.Y., 1986-88; Verville fellow Nat. Air and Space Mus., Washington, 1988-89, Smithsonian postdoctoral fellow, 1989-90, curator aeronautics, 1990-99, curator space history, 1999—. Curator Air Power in WWII series, 1991-94; sr. lectr. Johns Hopkins U., 2001. Author: The Skilled Metalworkers of Nuremberg, 1989, The Rocket and the Reich, 1995; editor: Planet Dora, 1997; co-editor: The Bombing of Auschwitz, 2000; contbr. articles and book revs. to profl. jours. Recipient History Manuscript award AIAA, 1995, Dexter Prize SHOT, 1997, NSF Scholar's award History of Sci. and Tech. Program, 1989-90. Mem. German Studies Assn., Soc. Mil. History, Soc. for History Tech., History of Sci. Soc. Avocation: amateur astronomy. Office: Nat Air & Space Mus Divsn Space History Smithsonian Instn PO Box 37012 Washington DC 20013-7012 E-mail: neufeldm@nasm.si.edu.

NEUFELD, PETER, lawyer; b. Bklyn. BA, U. Wis.; degree (hon.), Northeastern U. Sch. Law; LLD (hon.), Gonzaga U. Ptnr. Cochran, Neufeld & Scheck LLP, N.Y.C. Co-founder, dir. The Innocence Project, Benjamin Cardoza Sch. Law, Yeshiva U., N.Y.C., 1992—; mem. N.Y. State's Commn. Forensic Sci. Co-author (with Barry Scheck and Jim Dwyer): Actual Innocence: Five Days to Execution and Other Dispatches from the Wrongly Convicted, 2000. Named one of the Top 100 Influential Lawyers in Am., Nat. Law Jour., 2000. Office: Cochran Neufeld & Scheck LLP 99 Hudson St 8th fl New York NY 10013 Address: Benjamin N Cardozo Sch Law Yeshiva Univ Brookdale Ctr 55 Fifth Ave (at 12th St) New York NY 10003*

NEUFELD, TIMOTHY LEE, lawyer; b. Glendale, Calif., Apr. 23, 1947; s. Stanley and Marie E. (Scott) Neufeld; m. Naomi Das, Nov. 27, 1971; children: Pamela, Katherine. AB, Brown U., 1969; JD, Boston U., 1975. Bar: Calif. 1975. Assoc. Richards, Watson & Gershon, LA, 1975—80, ptnr., 1980—2001, Neufeld Jaffe, LLP, LA, 2001—. Lt. (j.g.) USN, 1969—72. Mem.: Los Angeles County Bar Assn., State Bar Calif. Avocation: competitive running. Office: Neufeld Jaffe LLP 30th Fl 555 W Fifth St Los Angeles CA 90013 Office Phone: 213-533-4141.

NEUGEBAUER, GERRY, retired astrophysicist, educator; b. Göttingen, Germany, Sept. 3, 1932; came to U.S., 1939; s. Otto E. and Grete (Brück) N.; m. Marcia MacDonald, Aug. 26, 1956; children: Carol, Lee. BS, Cornell U., 1954; PhD, Calif. Inst. Tech., 1960. Mem. faculty Calif. Inst. Tech., Pasadena, 1962—, prof. physics, 1970—, Howard Hughes Prof. Physics, 1985—, chmn. divsn. physics, math and astronomy, 1988-93; mem. staff Hale Obs., 1970-80; acting dir. Palomar Obs., 1980-81, dir., 1981; prof. physics Calif. Inst. Tech., Pasadena, now ret. Served with AUS, 1961-63. Recipient Except. Sci. Achievement medal NASA, 1972, 1984, Richtmyer Lectr. award, 1985, Space Sci. award Am. Inst. Aeronaut and Astronaut, 1985, Rumford Premium Am. Acad. Arts & Sci., 1986, Henry Norris Russell Lectureship Am. Astron. Soc., 1996. Fellow Am. Acad. Arts and Scis.; mem. NAS, Am. Philos. Soc., Am. Astron. Soc., Royal Astron. Soc., Internat. AStron. Union. Office: Calif Inst Tech Down Lab Physics 320 47 Pasadena CA 91125-0001

NEUGEBAUER, MARCIA, physicist, administrator; b. N.Y.C., Sept. 27, 1932; d. Howard Graeme MacDonald and Frances (Townsend) Marshall; m. Gerry Neugebauer, Aug. 25, 1956; children: Carol, Lee. BS, Cornell U., 1954; MS, U. Ill., 1956; D of Physics (hon.), U. New Hampshire, 1998. Grad. asst. U. Ill., Urbana, 1954-56; vis. fellow Clare Hall Coll., Cambridge, Eng., 1975; sr. research scientist Jet Propulsion Lab. Calif. Inst. Tech., Pasadena, 1956-96, disting. vis. scientist, 1996—2003; vis. prof. planetary sci. Calif. Inst. Tech., Pasadena, 1986-87. Mem. com. NASA, Washington, 1960-96, NAS, Washington, 1981-94; Regents lectr. UCLA, 1990-91; adj. sr. rsch. sci. Lunar & Planetary Lab., U. Ariz., 2002-; bd. dirs. Acad. Svcs. Corp., Ariz. Sr. Acad. Contbr. numerous articles on physics to profl. jours. Named Calif. Woman Scientist of Yr. Calif., Mus. Sci. and Industry, 1967, to Women in Tech. Internat. Hall of Fame, 1997; recipient Exceptional Sci. Achievement medal NASA, 1970, Outstanding Leadership medal NASA, 1993, Disting. Svc. medal NASA, 1997, COSPAR award for space sci., 1998. Fellow Am. Geophys. Union (sec., pres. solar planetary relationships sect. 1979-84, editor-in-chief Rev. Geophysics 1988-92, pres.-elect 1992-94, pres. 1994-96) mem. governing bd. Amer. Inst. Physics, 1995-97. Democrat. Home: 7519 S Eliot Ln Tucson AZ 85747-9627 Office: U Ariz Lunar & Planetary Lab 1629 E Univ Blvd Tucson AZ 85721

NEUGEBAUER, RANDY, congressman; b. Dec. 24, 1949; m. Dana Collins. BBA, Tex. Tech Univ., 1972. Mgr. Sentry Property Mgmt., Lubbock, Tex., 1972—75; instr. S. Plains Coll., Lubbock, 1975—78; v.p. First Nat. Bank, Lubbock, 1975—82; pres. Prestige Homes, Lubbock, 1983—87, Lubbock Land Co., 1987—2003; mem. 108th Congress from 19th Tex. dist., 2003—. Councilman City of Lubbock, 1992—98, mayor pro tempore, 1994—96. Republican. Office: 1026 Longworth House Office Bldg Washington DC 20515-4319

NEUGEBAUER, VOLKER EGDAR, biomedical scientist, neuroscientist, physician; b. Werneck, Bavaria, Germany, June 11, 1964; came to U.S., 1995; s. Erich Karl and Rosemarie (Gehring) N.; 1 child, Benjamin David. MD, U. Würzburg, Germany, 1991, PhD equivalent, 1992. Med. lic., Germany. Intern U. Würzburg, 1991-92, postdoctoral fellow, 1992-95; rsch. scientist U. Tex. Med. Br., Galveston, 1995-97, asst. prof. dept. anatomy and neuroscis., 1998—2002, clin. asst. prof. dept. anesthesiology, 1996-99, mem. Marine Biomed. Inst., 1999—, assoc. prof. neurosci. and cell biology, 2002—. Instr. Acad. Phys. Therapy, Schweinfurt, Germany, 1993-95; invited lectr. nationally and internationally. Author 10 book chpts. and revs.; contbr. over 30 rsch. articles to biomed. jours. including Jour. Neurosci., European Jour. Neurosci. Jour., Neurophysiology, Jour. Pharmacology and Exptl. Therapeutics. Recipient 1st award Lower Franconia Meml. Endowment for Sci., Würzburg, 1993, Rsch. Career Devel. award German Rsch. Coun., Bonn, 1995, Pain Rsch. award German Soc. for Study of Pain, Heidelberg, 1995. Mem. Internat. Assn. for Study of Pain, German Neurosci. Assn., Soc. for Neurosci., Sigma Xi. Roman Catholic. Achievements include development of animal (rat) model for acute arthritis; discovery of antinociceptive and analgesic potencies of drugs acting on spinal neurotransmitter and neuropeptide receptors; discovery of antiepileptogenic potency of metabotropic glutamate receptor agonists (presynaptic) as novel anticonvulsants; definition of the role of neuropeptides and glutamate receptors in cocaine sensitization; discovery of metabotropic glutamate receptors as novel targets for pain relief; identification of the amygdala as a key player in the emotional component of pain. Office: Marine Biomed Inst Dept Neurosci and Cell Biology U Tex Med Rsch Bldg 2 138 Galveston TX 77555-1069 Office Phone: 409-772-2124. Business E-Mail: voneugeb@utmb.edu.

NEUGEBOREN, JAY, author; b. Bklyn., May 30, 1938; s. David and Anne (Nassofer) N.; m. Betsey Bendorf, June 7, 1964 (div. Oct. 1982); children: Miriam, Aaron, Eli. BA, Columbia U., 1959; MA, Ind. U., 1963. Preceptor Columbia U., N.Y.C., 1964-66; vis. prof. Stanford (Calif.) U., 1966-67; prof. SUNY, Old Westbury, 1969-71; prof., writer-in-residence U. Mass., Amherst, 1971-2001. Author: Big Man, 1966, Corky's Brother, 1969, Sam's Legacy, 1977, An Orphan's Tale, 1976, The Stolen Jew, 1981, Before My Life Began, 1985, Poli, 1989, Imagining Robert, 1997, Don't Worry About the Kids, 1997/Transforming Madness, 1999, Open Heart, 2003; editor: Story of Story Magazine, 1980. Pres. Cong. Bnai Israel, Northampton, Mass., 1978-80; exec. com. Fifth Ave. Peace Parade, N.Y.C., 1963-66; bd. dirs. Pathways to Housing, N.Y.C., Art in Edn., others. Recipient Ken award Nat. Alliance for Mentally Ill, 1999, Best Novel of Yr. award, 1981, 85; Guggenheim fellow, 1978, NEA fellow. Democrat. Jewish. Avocations: swimming, tennis, guitar, piano. Office: care Richard Parks Agy 138 E 16th St New York NY 10025-1945

NEUGER, SANFORD, orthodontics educator; b. Cleve., Aug. 17, 1925; s. Samuel and Ethel (Manheim) N.; m. Marjorie Odess, Sept. 8, 1963; 1 child, Howard Michael. BS, Western Res. U., 1947, DDS, 1953; MS in Orthodontics, Ind. U., 1957. Diplomate Am. Bd. Orthodontics. Orthodontics demonstrator Western Res. U., Cleve., 1957-58; asst. prof., assoc. prof. orthodontics Western Res. U./Case Western Res. U., Cleve., 1958-75; clin. prof. orthodontics Case Western Res. U., Cleve., 1975—, acting chmn. Orthodontics Dept., 1969-71. Asst. dental surgeon U. Hosp., Cleve., 1967—. Author: (syllabus) Contemporary Edgewise Mechanics-Sliding Mechanics, 1973, Limited Tooth Movement, 1970; author-presenter: (videotape) Orthodontics Soldering, 1970. Vol. United Way, 1988, Case Western Res. U. Alumni Assn., Jewish Nat. Fund. Comdr. USNR (ret. 1972). Named Man of Yr. Case Western Res. U. Orthodontics alumni, 1982. Fellow Am. Coll. Dentists; mem. Am. Dental Soc., Cleve. Dental Soc. (bd. dirs. 11965-90), Cleve. Soc. Orthodontists (pres. 1969)., Great Lakes Assn. Orthodontists Assn., Am. Assn. Orthodontists, Pierre Fauchard Soc., Alpha Omega (pres. Cleve. chpt. 1984-85), Omicron Kappa Upsilon. Jewish. Avocation: replicar building. Home: 24850 Hilltop Dr Cleveland OH 44122-1350 Office: Neuger Sanford DDS Inc 24850 Hilltop Dr Cleveland OH 44122-1350

NEUGER, WIN J. insurance company executive; m. Christie Cozad Neuger. AB, MBA, Dartmouth Coll. With Northwestern Nat. Bank Mpls., 1973—82; chief investment officer Western Asset Mgmt. Co., L.A., 1982—84; mng. dir. global investment mgmt.-equity Bankers Trust Co., N.Y.C., 1984—95; sr. v.p., chief investment officer Am. Internat. Group, 1995—2002, exec. v.p., chief investment officer, 2002—, chmn., CEO, Global Investment Group. Mem.: Am. Investment Mgmt. and Rsch., N.Y. Soc. Security Analysts. Office: Am Internat Group 175 Water St 24th Fl New York NY 10038 also: Am Internat Group 70 Pine St New York NY 10270

NEUHARTH, ALLEN HAROLD, newspaper publisher; b. Eureka, S.D., Mar. 22, 1924; s. Daniel J. and Christina (Neuharth) N.; m. Loretta Fay Helgeland, June 16, 1946 (div. 1972), m. Lori Wilson, Dec. 31, 1973 (div. 1982), m. Rachel Fornes, March 21, 1993; children: Daniel J. II, Jan, Alexis Rae Fornes-Neuharth. BA cum laude, U. S.D., 1950. Reporter Rapid City (S.D.) Jour., 1948; sports writer Mitchell (S.D.) Daily Republic, 1949; staff writer AP, Sioux Falls, S.D., 1950-52; editor, pub. SoDak Sports, Sioux Falls, 1952-54; from staff to asst. mng. editor Miami (Fla.) Herald, 1954-60, asst. mng. editor, 1958-60; asst. exec. editor Detroit Free Press, 1960-63; gen. mgr. Times-Union and Democrat and Chronicle, Rochester, N.Y., 1963-66; exec. v.p. Gannett Co., Inc., Washington, 1966-70, pres., COO, 1970-73, pres., CEO, 1973-79, chmn., CEO, 1979-86; founder, chmn. USA Today, 1982; chmn. Gannett Co., Inc., Washington, 1986-89, Gannett Found., Arlington, Va., 1989-91; founder Freedom Forum, 1991—. Author: Confessions of an S.O.B., 1989. Trustee, chmn. Gannett Found. Inf. AUS, 1943-46, ETO, PTO. Decorated Bronze Star; recipient Horatio Alger award, 1975; named Outstanding Chief Exec. of Yr. in Pub. and Printing Industry for 3 consecutive yrs. Mem. Am. Newspaper Pubs. Assn. (bd. dirs. 1968-82, chmn., pres. 1979-80), Jockey Club (Miami), Ocean Reef Club (Key Largo, Fla.), Sky Club, Sigma Delta Chi (past nat. region I dir.). Office: Freedom Forum 1101 Wilson Blvd Ste 2300 Arlington VA 22209-2265

NEUHARTH, DANIEL J., II, psychotherapist; b. Sioux Falls, South Dakota, Nov. 10, 1953; s. Allen Harold and Loretta Faye (Helgeland) N. BA, Duke U., 1975; MS in journalism, Northwestern U., 1978; MA, John F. Kennedy U., 1988; PhD in clin. psychology, Calif. Sch. Profl. Psychology, 1992. Lic. marriage, family, and child counselor. Reporter USA Today, Washington, 1982-83; lectr. San Diego State U., 1983-84; talk show host KSDO-AM, San Diego, 1983-84; pres. Dialogues, San Francisco, 1987—; psychotherapist pvt. practice, San Francisco, 1992—. Vis. prof. U. Fla., Gainesville, 1980-81; U. Hawaii, 1981-82; adj. faculty U. San Francisco, 1989-92. Host, prodr. radio talk show Saturday Night People, 1984; Author: If You Had Controlling Parents, 1998, Secrets You Keep from Yourself, 2004, (with others) Confessions of an S.O.B., 1989. Office: 900 S Eliseo Dr Ste 101 Greenbrae CA 94904

NEUHAUS, PHILIP ROSS, investment banker; b. Houston, Dec. 25, 1919; s. Hugo Victor and Kate Padgitt (Rice) N.; m. Elizabeth Lacey Thompson, Oct. 31, 1942 (div. 1967); children: Philip Ross (dec.), Lacey Neuhaus Dorn, Elizabeth Neuhaus Armstrong, Joan Neuhaus Schaan; m. Barbara R. Haden, Aug. 14, 1968; 5 stepchildren. Grad., St. Mark's Sch., Southborough, Mass., 1938; BA, Yale, 1942. With Nat. City Bank of Cleve., 1946-47, McDonald & Co., Cleve., 1947; with Neuhaus & Co., 1947; chmn. Underwood, Neuhaus & Co., Inc., Houston, 1948-89; hon. chmn. Lovett Underwood Neuhaus & Webb, Houston, 1989-92; sr. v.p. Kemper Securities Inc., Houston, 1992-95, Everen Securities, Inc., Houston, 1995-99, Wachovia Securities Inc. (formerly First Union Securities, Inc.), Houston, 1999—. Chmn. bd. Voss-Woodway, Inc., 1994—. Mem. adv. bd. Tex. Children's Hosp., 1973-; assoc. Rice U.; advisory bd. Salvation Army, Houston, 1969-91. Served to capt., cav. AUS, 1942-45. Mem. Securities Industry Assn. Am. (bd. govs., chmn. Tex. dist. 1973, exec. com. 1975), Houston Soc. Financial Analysts (pres. 1959), Stock and Bond Club Houston (past pres.), Nat. Fedn. Financial Analysts (v.p. 1963, dir.) Clubs: Bayou, Houston Country, Houston, Eagle Lake Rod and Gun. Home: 407 Thamer Ln Houston TX 77024-6939 Office: Wachovia Securities Inc 909 Fannin Ste 2100 Houston TX 77010-1001

NEUHAUS, WILLIAM OSCAR, III, architect; b. Houston, Mar. 16, 1944; s. W. Oscar and Betty Palmer (Bosworth) N.; m. Kay Ficklen; children: Kimberly Sautelle, Sara Palmer. BArch, Ga. Inst. Tech., 1967. Registered architect, Tex., N.Mex. Intern architect Caudill Rowlett Scott, Houston, 1967-69; assoc. Charles Tapley Assocs., Houston, 1969-72; prin. W.O. Neuhaus Architecture/Planning, Houston, 1972-83; owner, mgr. W.O. Neuhaus Assocs., Houston, 1984—. Co-author trading Toilets: The Subterranean Zoning of Houston, 1982; author Foreward, 1992. Pres. Rice Design Alliance, Houston, 1982-83, bd. dirs. 1978-84; pres. Armand Bayou Nature Ctr. Found., 1986-90, Stages Repertory Theatre, Houston, 1988-89; mem. Mayor's Land Use Strategy com., Houston, 1990, Arts Task Force, Houston, 1992; exec. com. Cultural Arts Coun. Houston/Harris City, 1997—. Fellow Am. Leadership Forum, AIA (pres. 1990-91, chair design com. 1988-89); mem. Tex. Soc. Architects (mem. design com. 1989-90). Office: WO Neuhaus Assocs 4100 Montrose Blvd Ste D Houston TX 77006-4938

NEUHAUSER, DUNCAN VONBRIESEN, medical educator; b. Phila., June 20, 1939; s. Edward Blaine Duncan and Gernda (vonBriesen) Neuhauser; m. Elinor Toaz, Mar. 6, 1965; children: Steven, Ann. BA, Harvard U., 1961; MHA, U. Mich., 1963; MBA, U. Chgo., 1966, PhD, 1971. Rsch. assoc. U. Chgo., 1965—70; asst. prof. Sch. Pub. Health, Harvard U., Boston, 1970—74, assoc. prof., 1974—79; cons. in medicine Mass. Gen. Hosp., Boston, 1975—80; assoc. dir. Health Systems Mgmt. Ctr. Case Western Res. U., Cleve., 1979—85, prof. epidemiology, biostats., orgnl. behavior, 1979—, prof. medicine, 1981—, prof. family medicine, 1990—, Charles Elton Blanchard prof. health mgmt., 1995—, co-dir. Health Systems Mgmt. Ctr., 1985—. Mem. biomed. staff Metrohealth Med. Ctr., 1981—; adj. mem. med. staff Cleve. Clinic Found., 1984—99; vis. prof. Vanderbilt U. Sch. Nursing, 1998—, Karolinska Med. Sch., Stockholm, 2002—. Author: numerous books, sci. papers; editor (jours.): Health Matrix, 1982—90, Med. Care, 1983—97. Vice chmn. bd. dirs. Vis. Nurse Assn. Greater Cleve., 1983—84, chmn., 1984—85; bd. dirs. New Eng. Grenfell Assn., Boston, 1972—, Braintree (Mass.) Hosp., 1975—86; trustee Internat. Grenfell Assn., St. Anthony, Canada, 1975—83, Blue Hill (Maine) Hosp., 1983—94, Hough Norwood Health Ctr., 1983—94, chmn., 1993—94; mem. vis. com. Columbia U. Sch. Nursing, 2000—. Recipient E.F. Meyers Trustee award, Cleve. Hosp. Assn., 1987, Hope award, Nat. Multiple Sclerosis Soc., 1992, Neuhauser lectr., Soc. Pediatric Radiology, 1982, Freedlander lectr., Ohio Permanente Med. Group, 1986, Univ. medal, Tohoku Med. U., Sendi, Japan, 2001; scholar Keck Found., 1982—; Kellogg fellow, U. Chgo., 1963—65. Mem.: Soc. for Clin. Decision Making, Inst. Medicine NAS, Cleve. Skating Club, Kollegewidgwok Yacht Club (Blue Hill) (commodore 1991—93), St. Botolph Club (Boston), Beta Gamma Sigma. Home: 2655 N Park Blvd Cleveland Heights OH 44106-3622 Office: Case Western Reserve U Med Sch 10900 Euclid Ave Cleveland OH 44106-4945 Office Fax: 216-368-3970 216-368-3970. E-mail: duncan.neuhauser@case.edu.

NEUKIRCHEN, KAJO, industry executive; Dr.rer.pol, Bonn U., 1973. With Kabelwerke Reinshagen GmbH, Wuppertal, 1973-77, Felten & Guilleaume Carlswerke AG, Cologne, 1977-81, SKF Kugellagerfabriken GmbH, Schweinfurt, 1981-87, KHD Aktiengesellschaft, Cologne, 1987-91; CEO Hoesch AG, Dortmund, 1991-92, mg technologics ag, Frankfurt, Germany, 1993—. Office: mg technologies ag 60325 Frankfurt Germany E-mail: info@mg-technologies.com.

NEUKOM, WILLIAM H. lawyer; b. Chgo., Nov. 7, 1941; s. John Goudey and Ruth (Horlick) N.; m. Diane McMakin, Dec. 28, 1963 (div. Jun. 1977); children: Josselyn, Samantha, Gillian, John. BA, Dartmouth Coll., 1964; LLB, Stanford U., 1967. Bar: Calif., Wash., U.S. Dist. Ct. (we. dist.) Wash., U.S. Dist. Ct. (no. dist.) Calif., U.S. Ct. Appeals (9th cir.) 1968, U.S. Supreme Court 1974. Atty. MacDonald, Hoague & Bayless, Seattle, 1968—77; ptnr. Preston, Gates & Lucas (formerly Shidler, McBroom, Gates & Lucas), Seattle, 1978—85; v.p., law, corp. affairs Microsoft Corp., Redmond, Wash., 1985—93, exec. v.p. law & corp. affairs, sec., 1994—. Trustee Seattle Art Mus., 1993-99; mem. Assn. Gen. Counsel, 1994—; bd. dirs. Greater Seattle C. of C., 1987—, exec. com. 1988—, YMCA Greater Seattle, 1988—, Corporate Coun. Arts, 1988—, exec. com. 1993—, Nature Conservance (Wash. chpt.), 1991-99, Oreg. Shakespeare Festival, 1993-99. Fellow ABA (bd. editors ABA Jour. 1987-93, alternate dispute resolution com. 1987-91, exec. coun. sect. individual rights and responsibilities 1972-75, 87-92, sec. 1983-87, asst. sec. 1979-83, chmn. young lawyers divsn. 1977-78); mem. Seattle-King County Bar Assn. (long range planning com. 1972-75, 88-91, mgmt., orgn. and planning com. 1986-87, indigent defense svcs. task force 1981-83, trustee legal aid bur. 1974-77, chmn. young lawyers sect. 1972-73), Wash. State Bar Assn., (sec. 1983, pres., chmn., 1977-78, task force professionalism 1986-89, judicial recommendation com. 1985-88, planning com., faculty mem. Pacific Rim Computer Law Inst. 1984-91, orgn. and govt. of bar com. 1973-75, trustee young lawyers sect. 1973-76), Wash. State Trial Lawyers Assn. Avocations: fly-fishing, skiing, running, golf, jazz. Office: Microsoft Corp 1 Microsoft Way Redmond WA 98052-8300

NEUMAIER, GERHARD JOHN, environment consulting company executive; b. Covington, Ky., July 27, 1937; s. John Edward and Elli Anna (Raudies) N.; m. Ellen Elaine Klepper, Oct. 24, 1959; children: Kevin Scott, Kirsten Lynn. BME, Gen. Motors Inst., 1960; MA in Biophysics, U. Buffalo, 1963. Research ecologist, project mgr. Cornell Aero. Lab., Buffalo, 1963-70; pres., chief exec., chmn. bd. Ecology and Environment Inc., Buffalo, 1970—. Recipient Theodore Roosevelt Citizen of Yr. award City of Buffalo, 1990, Paul McClennan Environ. Citizen of Yr. award Erie County, 2000. Mem. APHA, Air Pollution Control Assn., Internat. Assn. Gt. Lakes Research, Inst. Environ. Scis., Ecol. Soc. Am., Am. Inst. Biol. Scis., Urban Land Inst., Arctic Inst. N.Am., Nat. Parks and Conservation Assn., Defenders of Wildlife, Nat. Wildlife Fedn., Wilderness Soc., Am. Hort. Soc., Smithsonian Assocs., Nat. Audubon Soc. Home: 284 Mill Rd East Aurora NY 14052-2805 Office: Ecology & Environment Inc 368 Pleasant View Dr Lancaster NY 14086-1316

NEUMAN, CHARLES P. electrical and computer engineering educator; b. Pitts., July 26, 1940; s. Daniel and Frances G. Neuman; m. Susan G. Neuman, Sept. 4, 1967 BS in Elec. Engring. with honors, Carnegie Inst. Tech., 1962; S.M., Harvard U., 1963, PhD in Applied Math., 1968. Tchg. fellow Harvard U., Cambridge, Mass., 1962-64, rsch. asst., 1964-67; mem. tech. staff Bell Telephone Labs., Whippany, N.J., 1967-69; asst. prof. elec. engring. Carnegie-Mellon U., Pitts., 1969-71, assoc. prof., 1971-78, prof. elec. engring., 1978-83, prof. elec. and computer engring., 1983—, undergrad. advisor, 1994—. Mem. editorial bd. Internat. Jour. Modelling and Simulation, Control and Computers; contbr. numerous articles to profl. jours. Mem. IEEE (sr., assoc. editor Trans. on Systems, Man and Cybernetics), Inst. Mgmt. Scis., AAAS, Instrument Soc. Am. (sr.), Soc. Harvard Engrs. and Scientists, Soc. Indsl. and Applied Math., Sigma Xi, Phi Kappa Phi, Tau Beta Pi, Eta Kappa Nu Office: Carnegie-Mellon U Dept Elec & Computer Engring Pittsburgh PA 15213 Office Phone: 412-268-2460. Business E-Mail: cpn@ece.cmu.edu.

NEUMAN, CLIFFORD, computer scientist, educator; s. Peter H-X. Neuman and Barbara Diane (Allen) Gordon; m. Grace Ruth (Kwok) Neuman. BS in Computer Sci. and Engring., MIT, 1985; MS in Computer Sci., U. of Wash., 1988, PhD in Computer Sci., 1992. With MIT Project Athena, Cambridge, Mass., 1985—86; sr. rsch. scientist U. of So. Calif., Info. Scis. Inst., Marina del Rey, Calif., 1991—; rsch. assoc. prof. U. of So. Calif., Dept. of Computer Sci., LA, 1992—; chief scientist CyberSafe Corp., Issaquah, 1992—2001; dir. U. of So. Calif., Ctr. for Computer Sys. Security, Marina del Rey, Calif., 2002—. Participant Internet Rsch. Task Force, 1991—, Internet Engring. Task Force, 1991—. Co-designer Kerberos computer security system, designer Prospero distributed computer system, NetCheque elec. payment system; contbr. articles to profl. jours. Mem. King County (Wash.) Search and Rescue, 1987-91. Recipient Top ten tech. innovators, InfoWorld Mag., 2002. Mem. IEEE (sr.), Assn. for Computing Machinery, Internet Soc., Usenix Assn., Am. Radio Relay League, Aircraft Owners and Pilots Assn. Achievements include development of Kerberos authentication sys; NetCheque electronic payment sys; Prospero Directory Svc. Avocations: flying, hiking, skiing, photography, cooking, amateur radio. Office: U So Calif Information Scis Inst 4676 Admiralty Way Marina Del Rey CA 90292 Office Phone: 310-822-1511. E-mail: ww05@clifford.neuman.name.

NEUMAN, EDWARD GEORGE, mathematician, educator; b. Rydultowy, Katowice, Poland, Sept. 19, 1943; arrived in U.S., 1984; s. Emanuel and Matylda Neuman; m. Barbara Warszawa, Sept. 21, 1974; children: Emanuel Karol, Magdalena Natalia. Undergrad., grad., U. Wroclaw, Poland, 1962—67, PhD in Math., 1972. Asst. prof. U. Wroclaw, 1976—84; assoc. prof. So. Ill. U., Carbondale, 1986—89, prof. math., 1989—. Chmn. numerical analysis dept. U. Wroclaw, 1981—84. Contbr. articles to profl. jours. Fellow Summer Undergrad. Tchg. fellow, So. Ill. U., Carbondale, 1999; grantee, Polish Acad. Scis., 1974—84. Mem.: Rsch. Group on Math. Inequalities and Applications (assoc.), Soc. for Indsl. and Applied Math. (assoc.). Achievements include research in spline theory, special functions and mathematical inequalities. Office: So Ill Univ Carbondale Dept Math Neckers 373 Carbondale IL 62901-4408

NEUMAN, JOEL H. psychologist, educator; b. N.Y.C., Jan. 26, 1948; s. Samuel Neuman and Shirley Goldstein, Frieda Litman (Stepmother); m. Mildred Hoisch, Dec. 17, 1940; children: Jeffrey Scott, Keri Michelle. BA, SUNY - New Paltz, 1984, MA, 1986; PhD, U. at Albany, SUNY, 1990. Nat. svc. mgr. United Audio Products, Inc., Mt. Vernon, NY, 1971—83; assoc. prof. of mgmt. & orgnl. behavior SUNY - New Paltz, 1989—. Contbr. articles to profl. jours., chpts. to books. With USN, 1967—71. Decorated Republic of Vietnam Campaign Medal USN, Vietnam Svc. Medal, Nat. Def. Svc. Medal; recipient Chancellor's Recognition award for scholarship and rsch., SUNY-New Paltz, 2001. Mem.: APA, Soc. for Indsl. and Orgnl. Psychology, Am. Mgmt. Assn., Acad. of Mgmt. Avocations: writing, reading, travel. Office: State University of New York - New Paltz 75 S Manheim Blvd New Paltz NY 12561-2443 Office Phone: 845-257-2928. Business E-Mail: neumanj@newpaltz.edu.

NEUMAN, LINDA KINNEY, retired state supreme court justice, lawyer; b. Chgo., June 18, 1948; d. Harold S. and Mary E. Kinney; m. Henry G. Neuman; children: Emily, Lindsey. BA, U. Colo., 1970, JD, 1973; LLM, U. Va., 1998. Ptnr. Betty, Neuman, McMahon, Hellstrom & Bittner, 1973-79; v.p., trust officer Bettendorf Bank & Trust Co., 1979-80; dist. ct. judge, 1982-86; supreme ct. justice State of Iowa, 1986—2003; ptnr. Betty Neuman & McMahon. L.L.P., Davenport, Iowa. Mem. adj. faculty U. Iowa Law Sch., 2003—; part-time jud. magistrate Scott County, 1980-82; mem. Supreme Ct. continuing legal edn. commn.; chair Iowa Supreme Ct. commn. planning 21st Century; mem. bd. counselors Drake Law Sch., time on appeal adv. com. Nat. Ctr. State Cts.; mem. Uniform State Laws Commn., 2004. Trustee St. Ambrose U. Recipient Regents scholarship, U. Colo. award for disting. svc. Fellow ABA (life; chair appellate judges conf., mem. appellate standards com., JAD exec. coun.); mem. Am. Judicature Soc., Iowa Bar Assn., Iowa Judges Assn., Scott County Bar Assn., Nat. Assn. Woman Judges (bd. dirs.), Dillon Am. Inn of Ct. (pres. 2003-04), U.S. Assn. Constl. Law, Am. Acad. ADR Attys, Nat. Uniform Laws Comm. (commnr., 2004). E-mail: lkn@bettylawfirm.com.

NEUMAN, NANCY ADAMS MOSSHAMMER, civic leader; b. Greenwich, Conn., July 24, 1936; d. Alden Smith and Margaret (Mevis) Mosshammer; m. Mark Donald Neuman, Dec. 23, 1958; children: Deborah Adams, Jennifer Fuller, Jeffrey Abbott. BA, Pomona Coll., 1957; LLD, 1983; MA, U. Calif., Berkeley, 1961; LHD, Westminster Coll., 1987. Disting. lectr. Am. govt. Pomona Coll., 1990; disting. vis. prof. Washington and Jefferson Coll., 1991, 94, Bucknell U., 1992. Editor: A Voice of Our Own: Leading American Women Celebrate the Right to Vote, 1996, True to Ourselves: A Celebration of Women Making a Difference, 1998. Pres. Lewisburg (Pa.) LWV, 1967-70; bd. dirs. LWV Pa., 1970-77, pres., 1975-77; bd. dirs. LWV U.S., 1977-90, 2nd v.p., 1978-80, 1st v.p., 1982-84, pres., 1986-90; mem. Pa. Gov.'s Commn. on Mortgage and Interest Rates, 1973, Pa. Commonwealth Child Devel. com., 1974-75, Nat. Commn. on Pub. Svc., 1987-90; bd. dirs. Housing Assistance Coun., Inc., Washington, 1974—2003, pres., 1978-80; bd. dirs. Nat. Coun. Agrl. Life and Labor, 1974-79, Nat. Rural Housing Coalition, 1975-95, Pa. Housing Fin. Agy., 1975-80, Jud. Inquiry and Rev. Bd. Pa., 1989-93; disciplinary bd. Supreme Ct. Pa., 1980-85; mem. Pa. Gov.'s Task Force on Voter Registration, 1975-76, Nat. Task Force for Implementation Equal Rights Amendment, 1975-77; mem. adv. com. Pa. Gov.'s Interdepartmental Coun. on Seasonal Farmworkers, 1975-77; mem. Appellate Ct. Nominating Commn. Pa., 1976-79; mem. Fed. Jud. Nominating Commn. Pa., 1977-85, chmn., 1978-81, 82-83; mem. Pa. Gov.'s Study Commn. on Pub. Employee rels., 1976-78; del. Internat. Women's Yr. Conf., 1977; bd. dirs. ERAmerica, Inc., 1st v.p., 1977-79, Nat. Low Income Housing Coalition, 1979-82; Rural Am., 1979-81, Fed. Home Loan Bank Pitts., 1979-82; mem. Nat. adv. Com. Women, 1978-79; mem. nat. adv. com. Pa. Neighborhood Preservation Support Sys., 1976-77; bd. dirs. Pa. Women's Campaign fund, 1984-86, 92-2002, pres., 1992-96, 2001-02, Rural coalition, Washington, 1984-90, Com. on the Constitutional Sys., 1988-90, Am. Judicature Soc., 1989-93; exec. com. Leadership Conf. Civil Rights, 1986-90; bd. dirs. Pennsylvanians for Modern Cts., 1986—; trustee Citizen's Rsch. Found., 1989-99; mem. mid. dist. Pa. adv. com. judicial and U.S. atty. nominations, 1993-94; bd. dirs. Pathmakers, 1993-97, pres. 1993-95; bd. dirs. Capital Concerts, 1997—. Virginia Travis lectureship Bucknell U., 1982; Woodrow Wilson vis. fellow, 1993-2000; recipient Disting. Alumna Award MacDuffle Sch. Girls, 1979, Liberty Bell award Pa. Bar Assn., 1983, Barrows Alumni Award Pomona Coll., 1987, Thomas P. O'Neill Jr. award for Exemplary Pub. Svc., 1989; Disting. Daughter of Pa., 1987. Mem. ABA (com. election law and voter participation 1986-90, accreditation com. 1990-96, coun. sect. of legal edn. 1997-2003, sec. 2000-03), Cosmos Club. Home: 190 Verna Rd Lewisburg PA 17837-8747

NEUMAN, ROBERT HAROLD, communication executive; b. Phila. s. Otto and Bessie Neuman; m. Joan Elizabeth Huhn, June 3, 1978 (dec. Feb. 1996). BA, U. Md., 1972; MLA, Johns Hopkins U., 1983. Cert. sys. application U. So. Calif., 1981, advanced study Johns Hopkins U., 1983, Nat. Conservatory of Dramatic Arts, Washington, DC, 1988. Photographer Photo Corp. Am., Rockville, Md., 1973; retail mgr. various firms, 1974-77; acct. rep. Kastle Security Inc., Arlington, Va., 1977-80; sr. data technician Mantech Internat. Corp., Rockville, 1981-82; computer programmer Harry Diamond Lab., Adelphi, Md., 1982-86; program analyst Lab. Command, Adelphi, 1986-88; analyst internat. programs Army Rsch. Lab., Adelphi, 1988-93; owner, mgr. Neu-Enterprise Prodns., Potomac, Md., 1993—. Prodr., program dir. Laurel Cable Network, Md., 1990—98, bd. dirs. Bd. dirs. Vistas Condominium, Laurel, 1993—95, Ebay Internet Bus., 1999—; vol. Hospice Caring, Inc., Gaithersburg, Md., 2000—02, The Sr. Connection, Silver Spring, Md., 2004—. With U.S. Army, 1960—63. Mem.: Internat. TV Assn., Alliance for Cmty. Media. Avocations: videography, travel. E-mail: robh4life@aol.com.

NEUMAN, ROBERT STERLING, art educator, artist; b. Kellogg, Idaho, Sept. 9, 1926; s. Oscar C. and Katherine (Samuelson) N.; m. Helen Patricia Feddersen, Apr. 6, 1947 (div. 1971); children— Ingrid Alexandra, Elizabeth Catherine; m. Sunne Savage, June 3, 1979; 1 dau., Christina Mary. Student, U. Idaho, 1944-46; BAA., M.F.A., Calif. Coll. Arts and Crafts, 1947-51; student, San Francisco Sch. Fine Arts, 1950-51, Mills Coll., 1951. Assoc. prof. art Brown U., 1962-63; lectr. drawing Carpenter Center for Visual Arts, Harvard, 1963-72; prof. art, chmn. dept. Keene (N.H.) State Coll., 1972-90. Exhbns. include, Mus. Modern Art, Whitney Mus. Am. Art, Carnegie Internat., Fogg Mus. Art, Harvard U., San Francisco Mus. Art, Boston Mus. Fine Arts, Worcester (Mass.) Art Mus., also, Japan and Europe. Served with AUS and USAAF, 1945-46. Recipient Howard Found. award for painting, 1967; Fulbright grantee, 1953-54; Guggenheim fellow, 1956-57; Bender grantee San Francisco Art Assn., 1952. Home: 135 Cambridge St Winchester MA 01890-2411

NEUMAN, SHLOMO P. hydrology educator; b. Zilina, Czechoslovakia, Oct. 26, 1938; came to U.S., 1963, naturalized, 1970; s. Alexander Neumann and Klara (Pikler) Lesny; m. Yael B. Neuman, Jan. 30, 1965; children: Gil, Michal, Ariel. BSc in Geology, Hebrew U., Jerusalem, 1963; MS in Engring. Sci., U. Calif., Berkeley, 1966, PhD in Engring. Sci., 1968. Cert. profl. hydrogeologist. Acting asst. prof., asst. rsch. engr. dept. civil engring. U. Calif., Berkeley, 1968-70, vis. assoc. prof. dept. civil engring., 1974-75; sr. scientist, assoc. rsch. prof. Inst. Soil and Water Agrl. Rsch. Orgn., Bet-Dagan, Israel, 1970-74; prof. hydrology dept. hydrology and water resources U. Ariz., Tucson, 1975-88, Regents' prof. dept. hydrology and water resources, 1988—. Cons. to U.S., Can. and Swedish govts. on hydrologic issues concerning nuc. waste disposal; vis. scientist dept. isotope Weizmann Inst. Sci., Rehovot, Israel, 1976; maitre de rsch. Ctr. d'Informatique Geologique, Ecole Mines Paris, Fountainebleau, France, 1978, dir. rsch., 1981; vis. prof. dept. fluid mechanics and heat transfer Tel-Aviv U., 1981; hon. appointment concurrent prof. Nanjing U., China; disting. lectr. in field; hon. prof. Nanjing Hydraulic Rsch. Inst., China, 1998—. Mem. editl. bd. Jour. Hydrology, 1977—84, Water Sci. and Tech. Libr. (The Netherlands), 1983—86, Stochastic Environmental Research and Risk Assessment, 1992—, Water Resources Rsch. Jour., 1987—93, Hydrogeology Jour., 1999—, guest editor spl. issue in memory of Eugene S. Simpson, 1997—98; contbr. over 270 articles to profl. publs., chapters to books. Hebrew U. scholar, 1962-63, Edwin Letts Oliver scholar, 1965-66; Jane Lewis fellow, 1966-68; recipient Cert. of Appreciation award USDA, 1975, C.V. Theis award Am. Inst. Hydrology, 1990. Fellow Geol. Soc. Am. (O.E. Meinzer award 1976, Birdsal Disting. Lectr. 1987), Am. Geophys. Union (4th Walter B. Langbein lectr. hydrology 1996, Robert E. Horton award 1969, Robert E. Horton medal, 2003), mem. ISI highly cited rschrs. database, Soc. Petroleum Engrs. of AIME, NAE, Assn. Groundwater Scientists and Engrs. of Nat. Well Water Assn. (Sci. award 1989), Ariz. Hydrol. Soc., Internat. Assn. Hydrogeologists. Jewish. Office: U Ariz Dept Hydrology & Water Resou Tucson AZ 85721-0001 Business E-Mail: neuman@hwr.arizona.edu.

NEUMAN, SUSAN B. federal agency administrator; Grad., Am. U.; master's, Calif. State U., Hayward; doctorate, U. Pacific. Reading specialist; tchr. elem. sch.; instr. Boston Coll., U. Mass., Yale U.; prof. Temple U., Phila.; dir. Ctr. Improvement Early Reading Achievement U. Mich., Ann Arbor, prof.; asst. sec. elem. and secondary edn. Dept. Edn., Washington, 2001—. Office: Dept Edn Office Elem and Secondary Edn 400 Maryland Ave SW FOB 6 Washington DC 20202-6100

NEUMAN, SUSAN CATHERINE, public relations and marketing consultant; b. Detroit, Jan. 29, 1942; d. Paul Edmund and Elsie (Goetz) N. AB, U. Miami, Fla., 1964; MBA, Barry U., Miami Shores, Fla., 1985. Journalist, writer The Miami Herald, 1962-65; editor Miamian Mag., 1965-69; pres. Susan Neuman Inc., Miami, 1969—; ptnr. Neuman Enterprises Unltd., 1994—. Mem. Fla. Gov.'s Pub. Rels. Adv. Coun., 1978-86. Mem. Pub. Rels. Soc. Am. (accredited, past officer, bd. dirs.), Miami C. of C., Counselors Acad., Miami City Club (founder, bd. govs.), Miami Internat. Press Club (charter, founder, pres. 1985-86), Com. of One Hundred (bd. dirs., sec.). Democrat. Roman Catholic. Home: 13540 NE Miami Ct Miami FL 33161-2739 Office: Susan Neuman Inc Venetia 25th Fl 555 NE 15th St Ste 25K Miami FL 33132-1404 Office Phone: 305-372-9966. E-mail: s_neuman@hotmail.com., susan@miamipr.net.

NEUMAN, TOM S. emergency medical physician, educator; b. N.Y.C., July 23, 1946; s. Otto and Susan Ann (Baltaxe) N.; m. Doris Rubin, Aug. 24, 1969; children: Allison Rachel, Russell Solomon. AB, Cornell U., 1967; MD, NYU, 1971. Diplomate Nat. Bd. Med. Examiners, Am. Bd. Internal Medicine, Am. Bd. Pulmonary Diseases, Am. Bd. Preventive Medicine in Occupl. Medicine and Underseas and Hyperbaric Medicine), Am. Bd. Emergency Medicine. Intern Bellevue Hosp., N.Y.C., 1971-72, resident, 1972-73; commd. med. officer USN, 1973; advanced through grades to capt. USNR, 1990; instr. Naval Undersea Med. Inst., New London, Conn., 1973-74; staff med. officer Submarine Devel. Group One, San Diego, 1974-76, 78-80; emergency room physician Chula Vista (Calif.) Community Hosp., 1975-80; attending physician VA Med. Ctr., La Jolla, Calif., 1976-78; fellow in pulmonary medicine and physiology U. Calif. Sch. Medicine at San Diego, 1976-78, clin. instr., 1978-80, asst. clin. prof., 1980-84, flight physician Life Flight Aeromed. Program, 1980-86, asst. dir. dept. emergency medicine, 1980-94, assoc. dir. dept. emergency medicine, 1994—, attending physician pulmonary divsn., 1980-99, assoc. clin. prof. medicine and surgery, 1984-87, base hosp. physician, 1984—, dir. Hyperbaric Med. Ctr., 1984—; med. officer UDT/SEAL Res. Unit 119, San Diego, 1980-84, Mobile Diving and Salvage Unit One, USNR, San Diego, 1984-86, PRIMUS Unit 1942-A, U. Calif. at San Diego, 1988-90; sr. med. officer Seal Teams 1/3/5, USNR, Coronado, Calif., 1986-87; asst. officer in charge Med. Unit 1942-A U. Calif. Sch. Medicine, San Diego, 1990-95, prof. clin. medicine, 1996—. Mem. med. adv. bd. western regional underwater lab. program U. So. Calif. Marine Sci. Ctr., Catalina, 1982—85; assoc. adj. prof. medicine and surgery U. Calif. Sch. Medicine at San Diego, 1987—90, adj. prof. medicine and surgery, 1990—96, prof. clin. medicine and adj. prof. surgery, 1996—; mem. San Diego Coroner's com. for investigation of diving fatalities, 1974—; mem. diving cons. Vocat. Diver Tng. Facility, Calif. Inst. Med., Chino, 1967; mem. task force City Mgr. on Carbon Monoxide Poisoning, San Diego, 1991; mem. com. for minimal course content for recreational scuba instr. cert. Am. Nat. Stds. Inst., 1992—94, chmn. emergency med. physician quality improvement com., 1992—94; mem. undersea and hyperbaric medicine exam subcom. Am. Bd. Preventative Medicine, 1999—; mem. com. on creating vision for space medicine beyond earth orbit, mem. com. on extreme environments NAS; mem. com. longitudinal study of astronaut health NAS-IOM; cons. NASA. Author: book chpts.; contbr. articles to profl. jours.; editor: textbooks. Fellow ACP, Am. Coll. Preventive Medicine; mem. Am. Thoracic Soc., Am. Lung Assn., Undersea and Hyperbaric Med. Soc. (program com. 1981-82, nominations com. 1982-83, chmn. 1988-89, mem. edn. com. 1982-87, chmn. awards com. 1983-84, v.p. exec. com. 1983-84, co-chmn. credentials com. 1984-85, editor-in-chief Undersea and Hyperbaric Medicine 1995—2002), Profl. Assn. Diving Instrs. (emeritus), NAS-IOM (com. on extreme environment, com. on longitudinal study of astronaut health, com. on bioastronautics critical path roadmap). Avocations: scuba diving, fishing, photography. Office: U Calif Med Ctr Dept Emergency Medicine 200 W Arbor Dr Dept 8676 San Diego CA 92103-8676 E-mail: tneuman@ucsd.edu.

NEUMANN, ALFRED JOHN, music director; b. Bklyn., Dec. 15, 1928; s. Erich Paul and Elsa (Kleiber) N. BS, Davidson Coll., 1951; MMus, U. Mich., 1954. Asst. to music dir. Brevard (N.C.) Music Ctr., 1948-52; dir. of bands Furman U., Greenville, S.C., 1951-52; asst. instr. in music U. Mich., Ann Arbor, 1952-54; music dir. Nat. Conv. of United Ch. of Christ, Washington, 1976, Christ Congregational Ch., Silver Spring, Md., 1958-94; accompanist Washington Performing Arts Soc. Concerts in Schs., Washington, 1972-97, Todd Duncan Voice Studio, Washington, 1992-98. Mem. adv. bd. to select the Bicentennial hymn, U.S. Army, Washington, 1976; student condr. U. Mich. Choirs, Ann Arbor, 1952-54; accompanist U. Mich. Opera Dept., Ann Arbor, 1952-54, The Mozart Trio, Washington, 1958-68. Composer: (church anthems) Truly, We Shall Be in Paradise, 1970, I Sing to Thee, 1983, (sacred opera) An Opera for Christmas, 1961, An Opera for Easter (both premeired on NBC-TV, Washington); contbr. articles to profl. jours. Organizer, dir. concerts to benefit AMA Colls., Washington, 1974, 75; music dir. Nat. Conv. of the United Ch. of Christ, Washington, 1976. Recipient Cert. commendation Can. Internat. Exhbn., Montreal, Can., 1967, Performance award WGMS Good Music Sta., Washington, 1980, 1981. Democrat. United Ch. of Christ. Home: Ste 1515 1400 E West Hwy Apt 1515 Silver Spring MD 20910-3264 Office Phone: 301-588-6950.

NEUMANN, ANDREW CONRAD, geological oceanography educator; b. Oak Bluffs, Mass., Dec. 21, 1933; s. Andrew Conrad Neumann and Faye Watson (Gilmore) Gilmour; m. Jane Spaeth, July 7, 1962; children: Jennifer, Christopher, Jonathan. BS in Geology, Bklyn. Coll., 1955; MS in Oceanography, Tex. A&M U., 1958; PhD in Geology, Lehigh U., 1963. Asst. prof. marine geology Lehigh U., Bethlehem, Pa., 1963-65; asst. prof. marine sci. U. Miami, Fla., 1965-69, assoc. prof. marine sci., 1969-72; prof. marine sci. U. N.C., Chapel Hill, 1972-85, Bowman and Gordon Gray prof. geol. oceanography, 1985—. Program dir. NSF, Washington, 1969-70; Kenan prof. U. Edinburgh, Scotland, 1978; summer vis. investigator U.S. Geol. Survey, Woods Hole, Mass., 1981—, Woods Hole Oceanographic Inst., 1981—; vis. prof. U. Naples, Italy, 1984, 92, 95, Eötvös U., Budapest, Hungary, 1991. Contbr. articles to profl. jours. Trustee Bermuda Biol. Sta. for Research Inc., 1972-76. Recipient Disting. Alumni award Bklyn. Coll., 1987. Fellow Geol. Soc. Am.; mem. Soc. Econ. Paleontologists and Mineralogists, N.C. Acad. Sci. Avocations: fishing, gardening, sailing. Office: U NC Dept Marine Scis 12-7 Venable Hl Chapel Hill NC 27599-0001

NEUMANN, CHARLES HENRY, mathematician, educator; b. Washington, Jan. 30, 1943; s. Bernhardt Walter and Emma (Habitz) Neumann; m. Cheryl Elaine Girard, June 18, 1965; children: Matthew Roy, Kristen Elizabeth. AS, Alpena (Mich.) CC, 1962; BS in Math., Mich. State U., 1964, MAT. in Math., 1965. Sci. tchr. Alpena (Mich.) Pub. Schs., 1965-66; instr. math. Alpena CC, 1966-84, math. sci. dept. chair, 1969-84; prof. Oakland CC, Bloomfield Hills, Mich., 1984—. Scoutmaster troop 92 Boy Scouts Am., Alpena, 1981—84; bd. dirs. Luth. Social Svcs. Mich., 1996—, vice chair of bd., 1999—2003, chmn. bd., 2004; trustee Mich. Edn. Spl. Svcs., 1975—93, 2002—, pres., 1976—93; mem. exec. com. Oakland County Dem. Com., Mich., 1995—96; bd. dirs. Mich. Vision Svc. Assn., Columbus, 1985—89, Ohio Vision Svc. Assn., 1988—89, Blue Cross Blue Shield Mich., 1986—94. Mem.: NEA (del. 1974—80, mem. adv. com. membership 1993—96), Oakland CC Faculty Assn. (v.p. 1994—95, pres. 1995—98, v.p. 1998—2001), Mich. Assn. Higher Edn. (v.p. two-yr. colls. 1970—96, 2002—04), Mich. Math. Assn. Two-Yr. Colls., Mich. Edn. Assn. (bd. dirs. 1974—80), Am. Math. Assn. Two-Yr. Colls., Math. Assn. Am., Phi Kappa Phi. Lutheran. Avocations: collecting antique books, racquetball, cross country skiing. Home: 5871 Warbler Clarkston MI 48346-2973 Office: Oakland CC 2900 Featherstone Rd Auburn Hills MI 48326-2817

NEUMANN, DEBORAH BROCHI, not-for-profit fundraiser; b. Boston, June 9, 1965; d. John E. and Catherine A. (Cunneen) Brochi; m. Benjamin J. Neumann, July 8, 1995; 1 child, Renee stepchildren: Casey, Sara, Paige. BA, U. Mass., Boston, 1989; Cert. in Corp. and Promotional Comm., U. Mass., 1994. Sec. Gray Gray & Gray, Boston, 1989—91; adminstrv. asst. Alternative Concepts, Inc., Boston, 1991—94; jr. account exec., officer mgr. KCSA Comms., Boston, 1994—98; devel. assoc. Children's Hosp. Trust, Brookline, Mass., 1998—2000, prospect rschr., 2000—01, sr. prospect rschr., 2001—. Author: Hedge Fund Basics, 2003; contbr. articles to profl. jours. Mem.: New Eng. Devel. Rsch. Assn., Assn. for Profl. Rschrs. for Advancement. Avocations: reading, painting, hiking.

NEUMANN, ED, human resource executive; BS in Acctg., West Chester U. CPA, Pa. Audit mgr. Ernst & Young LLP, Phila.; sr. mgr. corp. audit Crown, Cork & Seal Co., Inc., 1996-97; various positions HR Logic, Waltham, Mass., 1997-2000, CFO, 2000-2001, sr. v.p., CAO, 2001—. Office: HR Logic Inc 1050 Winter St Ste 1000 Waltham MA 02451-1402

NEUMANN, EDWARD SCHREIBER, transportation engineering educator; b. Harvey, Ill., Mar. 6, 1942; s. Arthur Edward Schreiber and Adeline Ruth (Spenks) N.; m. Carole Ann Dunkelberger, Apr. 19, 1969; children: Edward Schreiber, Jonathan David. MS, Mich. Technol. U., 1964, Northwestern U., 1967, PhD, 1969, Cert. in Prosthetics, 2000. Registered profl. engr., W.Va., Nev.; cert. prosthetist Am. Bd. Certification. Mem. faculty W.Va. U., Morgantown, 1970-90, prof. transp. engring., 1980-90, interim dir. Harley O. Staggers Nat. Transp. Ctr., 1982-95, dir., 1985-90; prof. U. Nev., Las Vegas, 1991—, chmn. dept., 1991-99, dir. Transp. Rsch. Ctr., 1991-98. Editor numerous conf. procs.; contbr. articles and rsch. reports to profl. lit. Bd. dirs. Mason Dixon Hist. Park Assn., 1978-90; chmn. new transp. systems and tech. com. TRB, 1998—. Capt., C.E., AUS, 1969-70. Resources for Future fellow, 1969. Fellow Inst. Transp. Engrs.; mem. ASCE (chmn. com. on automated people movers, chmn. exec. com. urban planning and devel. divsn., chmn. exec. com. urban transp. divsn., James Laurie prize 1996), Nat. Soc. Profl. Engrs., Am. Soc. Engring. Edn., OITAF-NACS, Advanced Transit Assn. (bd. dirs., pres. 1988-90), Sigma Xi, Tau Beta Pi, Phi Kappa Phi, Phi Eta Sigma, Chi Epsilon. Presbyterian. Home: 935 E Eldorado Ln Las Vegas NV 89123-0515 Office: UNLV Dept Civil Environ Engring Las Vegas NV 89154-4015 E-mail: neumann@ce.unlv.edu.

NEUMANN, FORREST KARL, retired health facility administrator; b. St. Louis, Oct. 7, 1930; s. Metz Earl and Ruth (McGhee) N.; m. Erika Stefanie Turkl, Feb. 11, 1955; children: Tracey Neumann Liberson, Karen Neumann Kruger, Scott, Lisa BS, Roosevelt U., 1953; MS in Hosp. Adminstrn., Northwestern U., 1955. Adminstrv. resident Louis A. Weiss Hosp., Chgo., 1954-55; mem. staff Sparrow Hosp., Lansing, Mich., 1958-90; CEO, pres., dir. Edward W. Sparrow Hosp., Lansing, 1962-90; pres., chief exec. officer, dir. Mason Gen. Hosp., Mich., 1973-85; chmn. bd. Caymich Ins. Co. Ltd., Cayman Islands, 1979-91, emeritus dir., 1991—; chmn. bd. Caymich Ins. Co. (Barbados) Ltd., 1986-91; pres., CEO, Mich. Hosp. Assn. Ins. Co., 1990-96; dir. Mich. Hosp. Assocs. Ins. Co., 1976-98; pres., CEO, Sparrow, Inc., 1984-90. Chmn. bd. Mich. Hosp. Assn. Ins. Co., 1979-90; dir. First of Am. Bank Corp., 1980-95, Auto Owners Ins. Co., 1980-90. Chmn. hosp. div. United Community Chest, 1965-68, chmn. budget steering com., 1970-71, bd. dirs., mem. exec. com., 1969-75; mem. adv. com. Capitol Area Comprehensive Health Planning Assn., 1969, bd. dirs., 1971-75, treas., 1974-75; mem., vice chmn. Mich. Arbitration Adv. Com., 1975-80; bd. dirs. Grad. Med. Edn.,

Inc., 1971-80, pres., 1972-73, treas. 1973 Fellow Am. Coll. Hosp. Adminstrs. (life); mem. Southwestern Mich. Hosp. Council (trustee 1968-73, pres. 1970-71), Am. Hosp. Assn. (del. 1979-87), Mich. Hosp. Assn. (1st v.p. 1972-73, bd. dirs., exec. com., treas. 1974-75, chmn. 1976-77, Meritorious Key award 1979), Rotary.

NEUMANN, HARRY, philosophy educator; b. Dormoschel, Germany, Oct. 10, 1930; came to U.S., 1937, naturalized, 1948; s. Siegfried and Frieda (Lion) N.; m. Christina Sopher, Sept. 25, 1959. BA, St. John's Coll., 1952; MA, U. Chgo., 1954; PhD, Johns Hopkins U., 1962; postgrad., U. Heidelberg, Germany, 1956-58. Mem. faculty Mich. State U., 1962-63, Lake Forest Coll., 1963-65; prof. philosophy, and govt. Claremont Grad. U. Scripps Coll., Claremont (Calif.) Grad. Univ., 1966—. Research assoc. Rockefeller Inst., N.Y.C., 1963 Author: Liberalism, 1991; contbr. articles profl. jours. With AUS, 1954-56. Classical Philosophy fellow Ctr. Hellenic Studies, Dumbarton Oaks, Washington, 1965-66, rsch. fellow Salvatori Ctr. for Study of Individual Freedom in the Modern World, 1970; rsch. fellow Earhart Found., 1973-74, 78, 82, 86, 90, 94, 98. Mem. John Brown Cook Assn. for Freedom (advisor). Office: Claremont Grad U Dept Politics & Policy Claremont CA 91711

NEUMANN, HERSCHEL, physics educator; b. San Bernardino, Calif., Feb. 3, 1930; s. Arthur and Dorothy (Greenhood) N.; m. Julia Black, June 15, 1951; 1 child, Keith. BA, U. Calif., Berkeley, 1951; MS, U. Oreg., 1959; PhD, U. Nebr., 1965. Theoretical physicist GE, Richland, Wash., 1951—57; instr. physics U. Nebr., Lincoln, 1964—65; asst. prof. physics U. Denver, 1965—71, assoc. prof. physics, 1971—85, prof. physics, 1985—, chmn. physics and astronomy, 1985—97, assoc. chmn. physics and astronomy, 2001—04, interim chmn. physics and astronomy, 2004—. Contbr. over 20 articles to profl. jours. Dir. numerous pub. outreach programs in physics. Mem. Am. Assn. Physics Tchrs. Home: 964 Salem Aurora CO 80011-6344 Office: U Denver Dept Physics Astronomy Denver CO 80208-2238 Office Phone: 303-871-3544. E-mail: hneumann@du.edu.

NEUMANN, JEFFREY JAY, photographer, minister; b. Cleve., Aug. 6, 1948; s. Fred and LaVerne (Vavra) N.; m. Charlene Rose Sparrow, Apr. 21, 1968 (dec.); children: Stephan, Corene, Lara; m. Carolyn Hannah, Nov. 4, 1972; 1 son, Jeffrey. Ordained to ministry 1962. Lithographer, camera operator Advertype, Inc., Cleve., 1972; lab. technician Vista Color Lab., Cleve., 1972-73; prodn. mgr. Mort Tucker Photography, Cleve., 1973-78; owner, photographer Photography by Jeffrey Neumann, Wadsworth, OH, 1978—. Lectr. in field. Author: Thirty Years as Jehovah's Slave, 1999, Forty Years as Jehovah's Willing Slave, 2002., 120 Years Preaching the Good News of the Kingdom, 2002, To Have and Remember the Perfect Wedding, 2003. Mem. Sm. Bus. Mgmt. Adv. Com., 1980-83. Mem. Internat. Platform Assn., Profl. Photographers Am. (awards), Wedding and Portrait Photographers Internat. (awards), Profl. Photographers Ohio (awards). Jehovah'S Witness. Home and Office: 9960 Mount Eaton Rd Wadsworth OH 44281-9028 E-mail: jneumann@neo.rr.com.

NEUMANN, LINDA KAY, marketing professional; b. Wyandotte, Mich., Feb. 5, 1959; d. Michael and Raelene Fern (Bongart) Goldman; m. David Dewain Neumann, Mar. 31, 1980; children: Rachel Anne, Kyle Wayne. Student, Mesa CC, San Diego, 1976-86; grad. with honors, Bank Mktg. Sch., 1991. Mail clk., securities clk. Hawaiian Trust Co. Ltd., Honolulu, 1977-78, supr., 1979-81; securities vault clk., bank card clk. Union Bank Calif., San Diego, 1981-82, sales adminstrv. asst., 1983-86, mktg. adminstrv. asst., mktg. officer, 1986-88, from mktg. asst. v.p. to mktg. v.p., 1992-94, mktg. v.p., mgr., 1994-96, bus. and sales planning mgr., v.p., 1996—2002; pres. Brilliant Mktg. Ideas, Inc., San Diego, 2002—. Chmn. San Diego Ednl. Coun., Am. Banking Assn., Am. Inst. Banking, 1996—97. Pres. Rolling Hills Elem. PTA, 1995—96; parliamentarian Deer Canyon Elem. PTA; nat. del. San Diego Imperial Coun. Girl Scouts, 2002—; chmn. bd. dirs. San Diego Safety Coun., Pacific Safety Coun.; bd. dir., pres. Westview Found. Mem.: San Diego Employers Assn., Nat. Soc. Fundraising Execs., Advt. Splty. Inst. Promotional Products Assns., Bank Mktg. Assn., San Diego Direct Mktg. Assn., Advt. Club San Diego, Direct Mktg. Assn., Am. Soc. Autism. Office: Brilliant Marketing Ideas PO Box 721419 San Diego CA 92172-1419 Business E-Mail: linda@brilliantmarketingideas.com. E-mail: ideas@adexec.com.

NEUMANN, LISELOTTE, professional golfer; b. Finspang, Sweden, May 20, 1966; With LPGA, 1987—. Mem. European Solheim Cup Team, 1990, 92, 94, 96, 98. Named Golf Digest Rolex Rookie of Year, 1988, Swedish Golfer of Year, 1994, GolfWorld's Most Improved Golfer, 1994. Achievements in LPGA victories include: U.S. Women's Open, 1988, Mazda Japan Classic, 1991, Minn. LPGA Classic, 1994, Weetabix Women's Brit. Open, 1994, GHP Heartland Classic, 1994, Chrysler-Plymouth Tournament of Champions, 1996, PING/Welch's Championship, 1996, First Bank-Edina Realty Classic, 1996, Welch's Champsionship, 1997, Toray Japan Queens Cup, 1997, Standard Register Ping, 1998, Chick-fil-A Charity Championship, 1998; other victories include: European Open, 1985, German Open, 1986-88, French Open, 1987, Solheim Cup, 1998. Office: LPGA 100 International Golf Dr Daytona Beach FL 32124-1092

NEUMANN, MARK W. former congressman, real estate developer; b. Waukesha, Wis., Feb. 27, 1954; m. Sue; 3 children. BS, U. Wis., Whtiewater, 1975; MS, U. Wis., River Falls, 1977. Real estate developer Neumann Devels. (now Neumann Corp.), 1980—; mem. 104th and 105th Congresses from 1st Wis. dist., 1994-97. Mem. appropriations, nat. security, vets. affairs, HUD and ind. agys., budget coms. Address: W330 N6233 Hasslinger Dr Nashotah WI 53058-9432

NEUMANN, NANCY RUTH, studio educator; b. L.A., Feb. 1, 1948; d. Robert Thomas and Frances Andersen; m. Bernd Fritz Dietmar Neumann, June 26, 1971; children: Peter, Christina, Linda, Christoph, Karin. BA, U. Calif., Riverside, 1969; MA, Sorbonne U., Paris, 1971; credentials, Calif. State U., San Bernardino, 1985. Cert. community coll. tchr., various subjects, Calif., studio tchr., Calif. Missionary, reading instr., Maroua, Cameroon, Africa, 1971-73; instr. Pasadena (Calif.) City Coll., 1974-75; secondary tchr. Riverside (Calif.) Christian Sch., 1985-86; studio tchr. Vista Films, Culver City, 1986, Hollywood (Calif.) Studios, 1986-88, Paramount Studios, Hollywood, Calif., 1986-93, MGM - Lorimar Prodns., Culver City, Calif., 1986-91, Universal Studios, Universal City, Calif., 1986-90, R.J. Louis Prodns., Burbank, Calif., 1987, Michael Landon Prodns., Culver City, 1987-88, Carsey-Werner Prodns., L.A., 1988; instr. Riverside Community Coll., 1988; studio tchr. Bob Booker Prodns., Hollywood, 1988-90, Walt Disney Prodns., Burbank, 1992—; exec. producer Am. Pictures, Riverside, 1989—; studio tchr. NBC Prodns., Burbank, 1990—2003, 20th Century Fox, 1993—2004, Warner Bros., 1996—2004. Pvt. tutor, Riverside, L.A., 1987—; drama coach Grace Ch., Riverside, 1981-82, Magnolia Ave. Bapt. Ch. Riverside, 1986-89. Author: several plays, 1981-89; writer 70 songs, 1968—; pub. access TV prodr. Nancy Norway Presents: Windmills, L.A. and Riverside, 1994-2004. Coach mock trial Riverside Christian H.S., 1985-86; choir dir. Riverside Christian Sch., 1985-86; Sunday Sch. tchr. Grace Bapt. Ch., Harvest Christian Fellowship, Riverside, Magnolia Ave. Bapt. Ch., 1968-92, Wheat, Oil and Wine Christian Fellowship, Riverside, Sunday sch. supt., 1992-93; children's choir dir. Grace Bapt. Ch., 1981-82; Christian edn. coord., Sunday sch. tchr., and vacation Bible sch. dir. First United Meth. Ch., Riverside, 2002-03. Recipient Golden Star Halo award, Star Sapphire Halo award, Jeanie Golden Halo award for acting and teaching So. Calif. Motion Picture Coun., 1994. Mem. Nat. Assn. Christian Educators, Internat. Alliance of Theatre and Stage Employees, Internat. Platform Assn., Greater L.A. World Trade Ctr. Assn., Sons of Norway (study scholar 1967), Delta Phi Alpha. Democrat. Avocations: photography, music, travel, production of films and videos. Home: 1787 Prince Albert Dr Riverside CA 92507-5852 Office: Walt Disney Studios 500 S Buena Vista St Burbank CA 91521-0006 E-mail: nneumann@earthlink.net.

NEUMANN, PETER GABRIEL, computer scientist; b. N.Y.C., Sept. 21, 1932; s. J.B. and Elsa (Schmid) N.; m. Elizabeth Susan Neumann; 1 child, Helen K. AB, Harvard U., 1954, SM, 1955; Dr rerum naturarum, Technische Hochschule, Darmstadt, Fed. Republic Germany, 1960; PhD, Harvard U., 1961. Mem. tech. staff Bell Labs, Murray Hill, N.J., 1960-70; Mackay lectr. Stanford U., 1964, U. Calif., Berkeley, 1970-71; prin. scientist SRI Internat., Menlo Park, Calif., 1971—. Adj. prof. U. Md., 1999. Author: Computer-Related Risks, 1995. Recipient Nat. Computer Sys. Security award, 2002; Fulbright grantee, 1958—60. Fellow AAAS, IEEE, Assn. for Computing Machinery (editor jour. 1976-93, chmn. com. on computers and pub. policy 1985—). Avocations: music, tai chi, holistic health. Office: SRI Internat EL-243 333 Ravenswood Ave Menlo Park CA 94025-3493 Business E-Mail: pneumann@acm.org.

NEUMANN, RITA NUNEZ, lawyer; b. New Brunswick, N.J., Apr. 23, 1944; d. Arno Otto and Florence (Alligier) N. BA in Math., Trenton State Coll., 1965; MS in Math., Stevens Inst. Tech., 1970; JD, Seton Hall U., 1976; LLM in Tax Law, U. San Diego, 1983. Bar: D.C. 1984, U.S. Tax Ct. 1984, N.Y. 1985, N.J. 1986, U.S. Supreme Ct. 1989, Mont. 1990, U.S. Ct. Appeals (9th cir.) 1991. Instr. math. Middlesex County Coll., Edison, N.J., 1971-74; tax cons. Evan Morris Esq. Offices, Woodland Hills, Calif., 1975-85; asst. to editor Jour. Taxation, N.Y.C., 1985-86; pvt. practice law New Brunswick, 1986-94, Las Cruces, N.Mex., 1994—; mcpl. prosecutor Manville, N.J., 1987. Adj. instr. bus. law and fin. L.A. C.C. Dist., 1976-82; adj. instr. law and bus. calculus Ventura (Calif.) C.C. Dist., 1977-82; adj. prof. bus. calculus Calif. State U., Northridge, 1981-83; adj. instr. internat. law Laverne U. and San Fernando Valley Coll. Law, 1983-85; disting. lectr. in law and mgmt. Troy State U., Holloman AFB/White Sands Missile Range.; atty. Ability Ctr. of Las Cruces; candidate Ct. of Appeals of N.Mex., 2000. Author: Doing Business in North America, 1994, 95, 96, Legal Aspects of Doing Business in North America, 1995-2003; contbr. articles to profl. pubis. Vol. to farm workers ctr., Moorpark, Calif., 1979; instr. community extension ctr. for women, Calif., 1980; vol. atty. for N.J. Vietnam Vets., 1986; organizer 10-kilometer run to benefit ill children, Manville, N.J., 1986; guest lectr. taxes Second Ann. Bus. Seminar for Vets. and Non-Vet. Am. Indians of N.W. U.S., Billings, Mont., 1988; candidate for freeholder, Middlesex County, 1988; active with numerous Am. Indian tribes thoughout the U.S. in bus. devel. and Indian rights. Fellow Nat. Sci. Found., 1968-71. Mem. Kappa Delta Phi. Avocation: 10-kilometer runs (recipient several medals). Office: 1850 N Solano Dr Las Cruces NM 88001-1851

NEUMANN, RONALD DANIEL, nuclear medicine physician, educator; b. Watertown, Wis., Oct. 10, 1947; BS summa cum laude, Carroll Coll., 1970; MD with highest honors, Yale U., 1974. Diplomate Nat. Bd. Med. Examiners, Am. Bd. Nuclear Medicine; lic. physician, Md., D.C. Resident in pathology Yale-New Haven Hosp., 1974-77, resident in nuclear medicine, 1977-79, chief resident in nuclear medicine, 1978-79, attending physician, 1979-85; asst. prof. diagnostic radiology Sch. Medicine Yale U., 1979-83, assoc. prof. diagnostic radiology and pathology, 1983-86; dep. chief dept. nuclear medicine NIH, Bethesda, Md., 1985-88, chief. dept. nuclear medicine, 1988—, dir. nuclear medicine residency tng. program, 1986-92; clin. prof. diagnostic radiology and nuclear medicine Sch. Medicine George Washington U., Washington, 1986—. Chmn. med. isotopes and radiation safety com. West Haven VA Med. Ctr., 1979-85; mem. clin. rsch. panel Nat. Inst. Diabetes and Digestive and Kidney Diseases, 1987-88; mem. radiation safety com. NIH and Nat. Ctr. for Health Stats., 1987-89. Patentee Antigen-specific composition and in-vivo methods for detecting and localizing an antigenic site and for radiotherapy; contbr. over 200 articles and abstracts to med. and sci. jours., 30 chpts. to books and conf. proceedings. Nat. Merit scholar; NASA summer fellow. Fellow Am. Coll. Chest Physicians; mem. AAAS, Am. Soc. for Investigative Pathology, Soc. Nuclear Medicine (co-chmn. C.M.E. program 1995-96, pres.-elect 1997, pres. Mid.-Atlantic chpt. 1998), Internat. Acad. Pathology (U.S. and Can. divsns.), European Assn. Nuclear Medicine, Sigma Xi., Delta Sigma Nu. Office: NIH-CC Dept Nuclear Medicine 10 Center Dr Ms 1180 Bethesda MD 20892-0001

NEUMANN, RONALD ELDREDGE, former ambassador; b. Washington, Sept. 30, 1944; s. Robert G. N. and Marlen Eldredge; m. Margaret Elaine Grimm, Jan 23, 1966; children: Helen, Brian. BA, U. Calif., Riverside, 1966, MA, 1967; student, Nat. War Coll., 1991. Joined Fgn. Svc., 1970; vice-consul Am. Embassy, Dakar, Senegal, 1971—73; from vice-consul to consul Am. Consulate, Tabriz, Iran, 1973-76; desk officer office of so. European affairs Dept. State, Washington, 1976-77, aide to asst. sec. Near East and South Asian Affairs, 1977-78, desk officer Jordanian Affairs, 1978-81, dep. dir. Arabian Peninsula Affairs, 1983-86, dir. No. Gulf affairs, 1991-94; dep. chief mission Am. Embassy, Sana'a, North Yemen, 1981-83; with Arabic Lang. Tng., Washington, 1986-87; dep. chief mission Am. Embassy, Abu Dhabi, United Arab Emirates, 1987-90; amb. to Algeria, 1994-97; dep. asst. sec. of state for Mid. East Dept. State, 1997-2000, amb. to Bahrain, 2001—04; spl. negotiator with Spain, 2000—01; counselor for polit. mil. affairs Embassy Baghdad, 2004—. 1st. lt. US Army, 1969-70, Vietnam. Decorated Bronze Star, Combat Infantry Badge, Army Commendation medal, State Dept. Superior Honor medal. Mem. Am. Fgn. Svc. Assn., U. Calif. Riverside Alumni Assn., Officer Candidate Sch. Alumni Assn., Assn. of 5th Divsn. Nat. War Coll. Alumni, Phi Beta Kappa. Avocations: reading, backpacking, bicycling, hiking.

NEUMANN, ROY COVERT, architect; b. Columbus, Nebr., Mar. 1, 1921; s. LeRoy Franklin and Clara Louise (Covert) N.; children: Tali, Scott; m. Donna Corwin, Oct. 11, 2003. Student, Midland Coll., 1939-40, U. Calif.-Berkeley Armed Forces Inst., overseas, 1942-43; AB, U. Nebr., 1948, BArch, 1949; MA, Harvard U., 1952; postgrad., U. Wis., Iowa State U. Registered profl. architect, Iowa, Nebr., Kans., Minn., S.D., N.Y., Mass., Ohio, Pa., Tenn., Ky., Va., W.Va., Ga., Mich., Mo., Ill., Wis., Tex., Colo. Ptnr., architect R. Neumann Assocs., Lincoln, Nebr., 1952-55; officer mgr. Sargent, Webster, Crenshaw & Folley, Schenectady, N.Y., 1955-59; dir. architecture, ptnr. A.M. Kinney Assocs., Cin., 1959-65; officer mgr. Hunter, Campbell & Rea, Johnstown, Pa., 1965-66; dir. architecture, ptnr. Stanley Cons., Muscatine, Iowa, 1966-76; pres., chmn. bd. Neumann Monson P.C., Iowa City, 1976—. Ptnr. Clinton St. Ptnrs., Iowa City, 1983—, Iris City Devel. Co. Mt. Pleasant, Iowa, 1986, Linn Mar Elem./Mid. Sch., Marion, Iowa. Prin. works include Harbour Facilities, Antigua, W.I., S.C. Johnson Office Bldg., Racine, Wis., Iowa City Transit Facility Bldg., addition to Davenport Ctrl. High Sch., V.A. Adminstrv. Office Bldg., Iowa City, Johnson County Office Bldg., Iowa City Mercer Park Aquatic Ctr., Iowa City, Coll. Bus. U. Iowa, Iowa City, renovation Lawrence County Courthouse, Deadwood, S.D., H.S. and Elem. Schs., Mt. Pleasant, Iowa. Mem. bd. edn. Muscatine Community Sch. Dist., 1974-76. Served with USN, 1942-46, PTO. Recipient Honor award Portland Cement Assn., 1949, Lorraine D. Wright award for outstanding constrn. Camanche (Iowa) H.S., 1998-99. Mem. AIA (Honor award 1975), Constrn. Specifications Inst. (pres. 1974-76, Honor award 1983, 84, 85, 86), Soc. Archtl. Historians, Archtl. Assn. London, U. Nebr. Alumni Assn., Harvard U. Alumni Assn., Iowa City C. of C., Phi Kappa Psi, Univ. Athletic Club (Iowa City), Masons, Ea. Star, Elks Republican. Presbyterian. Avocations: golf, fishing, medieval history, big band music. Home: 312 Locust St Muscatine IA 52761-3510 Office: Neumann Monson Architects 111 E College St Iowa City IA 52240-4012 Office Phone: 319-338-7878.

NEUMANN, WILLIAM ALLEN, state supreme court justice; b. Minot, N.D., Feb. 11, 1944; s. Albert W. and Opal Olive (Whitlock) N.; m. Jaqueline Denise Buechler, Aug. 9, 1980; children: Andrew, Emily. BSBA, U. N.D., 1965; JD, Stanford U., 1968. Bar: N.D. 1969, U.S. Dist. Ct. N.D. 1969. Pvt. practice law, Williston, N.D., 1969-70, Bottineau, N.D., 1970-79; former judge N.D. Judicial Dist. Ct., N.E. Judicial Dist., Rugby and Bottineau, 1979-92; justice N.D. Supreme Ct., Bismarck, 1993—. Chmn. elect N.D. Jud. Conf., 1985-87, chmn. 1987-89. Mem. ABA, State Bar Assn. N.D., Am. Judicature Soc. (bd. dirs. 1998—2004). Lutheran. Office: ND Supreme Ct Jud Wing 1st Fl Dept 180 600 E Boulevard Ave Bismarck ND 58505-0530 Office Phone: 701-328-2221.

NEUMARK, GERTRUDE FANNY, materials science educator; b. Nuremberg, Germany, Apr. 29, 1927; came to U.S., 1939; d. Siegmund and Bertha (Forchheimer) N.; m. Henry Rothschild, Mar. 18, 1950. BA, Barnard Coll., 1948; MA, Radcliffe Coll., 1949; PhD, Columbia U., 1951. Advanced rsch. physicist Sylvania Rsch. Labs., Bayside, N.Y., 1952-60; sr. mem. tech. staff Philips Labs., Briarcliff Manor, N.Y., 1960-85; prof. materials sci. Columbia U., N.Y.C., 1985-99, Howe prof. materials sci. and engring., 1999—. Cons. Am. Inst. Physics, N.Y.C., 1968-69; NSF vis. prof., 1982; panelist NRC; panelist, reviewer NSF. Contbr. Encyclopedia of Advanced Materials, numerous articles to sci. jours., chpt. to books; inventor in field. Rice fellow, 1948, Dana fellow, 1948, AAUW Anderson fellow, 1951. Fellow Am. Phys. Soc. (Goeppert-Meyer award com. 1987-89); mem. Materials Rsch. Soc., Soc. Women Engrs. (sr.), Am. Chem. Soc.

NEUMARK, MICHAEL HARRY, lawyer; b. Cin., Oct. 28, 1945; s. Jacob H. and Bertha (Zubor) N.; m. Sue Daly, June 5, 1971; children: Julie Rebecca, John Adam. BS in Bus., Ind. U., 1967; JD, U. Cin., 1970. Bar: Ohio 1970, D.C. 1972. Atty. chief counsel's office IRS, Washington, 1970-74, acting br. chief, 1974-75, sr. atty. regional counsel's office, 1975-77; assoc. Paxton & Seasongood Legal Profl. Assn., Cin., 1977-80; ptnr. Thompson, Hine & Flory, 1980—, mem. mgmt. com., 1993—. Chmn. So. Ohio Tax Inst., 1987; mem. IRS and Bar Liaison Com., 1991-93; spkr. at profl. confs. Contbr. articles to profl. jours. Bd. dirs. 1987 World Figure Skating Championship, Cin., 1986-89; precinct exec. Hamilton County Rep. Orgn., 1980-86; vol. referee Hamilton County Juvenile Ct., 1980-86; trustee Cin. Contemporary Arts Ctr., St. Rita Sch. for Deaf, 1991-97, Legal Aid Soc. Cin., 1997—, v.p., 2002—; bd. visitors U. Cin. Coll. Law. Recipient Commendation Resolution Sycamore Twp., 1987. Mem. ABA (ho. of dels. 1998-2002), Ohio State Bar Assn., Cin. Bar Assn. (pres. 1996-97, recognition award 1985, treas., bd. trustees 1988-91, trustee 1992—, chair tax sect., 1990-91), Leadership Cin., Ohio Met. Bar Assn. (pres. 1996-97), Kenwood Country Club, Indian Hill Club, Ohio Met. Bar (pres. 1996-97), Cin. Acad. of Leadership for Lawyers (founder, chair). Republican. Avocations: golf, travel. Office: Thompson Hine & Flory 312 Walnut St Ste 1400 Cincinnati OH 45202-4089 Home: 7715 Shawnee Run Rd Cincinnati OH 45243-3119

NEUMEIER, JOHN, choreographer, ballet company director; b. Milw., Feb. 24, 1942; s. Albert and Lucille N. BA, Marquette U., 1961, DFA (hon.), 1987; student, Stone-Camryn Ballet Sch., Chgo., 1957-62, Royal Ballet Sch., London, 1962-63; student of Vera Volkova, Copenhagen, 1962-63. Dancer Sybil Shearer Co., Chgo., 1960-62, Stuttgart (Fed. Republic Germany) Ballet, 1963-69; artistic dir. Frankfurt (Fed. Republic Germany) Opera Ballet, 1969-73, Hamburg (Fed. Republic Germany) State Opera Ballet, 1973—; prof. City of Hamburg, 1987; dir. Hamburg Ballet, 1996, ballettintendant, 1997—. Found. ballet sch. Hamburg State Opera, 1978; found. ballet ctr. John Neumeier, ballet sch., Hamburg State Opera co. tng. under one roof., 1989. Guest choreographer for various cos. including Am. Ballet Theatre, Royal Ballet London, Royal Danish Ballet, Nat. Ballet Can., Royal Winnipeg Ballet, Stuttgart Ballet, Munich Opera, Vienna Opera, Ballet du XX siecle, Brussels, Opera de Paris, Opera of Stockholm, Mariinsky Theatre, St. Petersburg; guest opera dir. Otello, Munich Opera, Hamburg State Opera; ballet dir. (films) Rondo, 1971 (Prix Italia 1972), Third Symphony of Gustav Mahler (Golden Camera award 1978), Legend of Joseph, Wendungen (String Quintet in C major by Schubert), 1979, Scenes of Childhood, The Lady of the Camellias, 1986, Othello, 1987; choreographer Romeo and Juliet, The Nutcracker, 1971, Daphnis and Chloé, 1972, Third Symphony of Gustav Mahler, 1975, Illusions-Like Swan Lake, 1976, A Midsummer Night's Dream, 1977, Sleeping Beauty, The Lady of the Camelias, 1978, Matthaeus-Passion, 1981, Giselle, 1983, Sixth Symphony of G. Mahler, 1984, Peer Gynt, 1989, Fifth Symphony of G. Mahler, 1989, Requiem, 1991, A Cinderella Story, 1992, Odyssee, 1995, Vivaldi Or What You Will, 1996, Sylvia, 1997, Images from Bartók, 1998, Messias, 1999 (Danza Danza award 2001), Nijinsky, 2000, Giselle, 2000, Sounds of Empty Pages, 2001. Decorated knight's cross Danebrog Order (Denmark); recipient Dance mag. award, 1983, Fed. German Cross of Merit, 1987, German Dance prize, 1988; title of Prof. conferred by City of Hamburg, 1987, Deutscher Tanzpreis, Fed. Republic of Germany, 1988; recipient Prix Diaghilev award, France, 1988, Order Des Arts et des Lettres award French Minister Culture, 1991, Carina Ari award, Stockholm, 1994, Nijinsky medal Polish Minister Culture, 1996, Danebrog Order in Gold, Denmark, 2000, First prize for best contemporary choreography, Vasva 2002, Dilhelm Hanser prize, 2002, Medal for Art and Science, 2003; named Hon. Mem. Semper Opera, 2002. Mem. Acad. der Kuenste Hamburg, Acad. der Kuenste Berlin, Golden Mask. Roman Catholic. Office: Ballettzentrum Hamburg Caspar-Voght-Strasse 54 D-20535 Hamburg Germany E-mail: intendanz@hamburgballett.de.

NEUMEIER, MATTHEW MICHAEL, lawyer, educator; b. Racine, Wis., Sept. 13, 1954; s. Frank Edward and Ruth Irene (Effenberger) N.; m. Annmarie Prine, Jan. 31, 1987; children: Ruthann Marie, Emilie Irene, Matthew Charles. B in Gen. Studies with distinction, U. Mich., 1981; JD magna cum laude, Harvard U., 1984. Bar: NY 1987, Mich. 1988, Ill. 1991, US Dist. Ct. (ea. dist.) Mich. 1988, US Dist. Ct. (ea. dist. and trial bar) Ill. 1991, US Ct. Appeals (7th cir.) 1992, US Ct. Appeals (fed. cir.) 1998, US Supreme Ct. 1991. Sec.-treas. Ind. Roofing & Siding Co., Escanaba, Mich., 1973-78; mng. ptnr. Ind. Roofing Co., Menominee, Mich., 1977-78; law clk. to presiding justice US Ct. Appeals (9th cir.), San Diego, 1984-85; law clk. to chief justice Warren E. Burger US Supreme Ct., Washington, 1985-86; spl. asst. to chmn. US Constn. Bicentennial Comm., Washington, 1986; assoc. Cravath, Swaine & Moore, NYC, 1986-88; spl. counsel Burnham & Ritchie, Ann Arbor, Mich., 1988; assoc. Schlussel, Lifton, Simon, Rands, Galvin & Jackier, P.C., Ann Arbor, Mich., 1988-90, Skadden, Arps, Slate, Meagher & Flom, Chgo., 1990-96; ptnr. Jenner & Block, Chgo., 1996—. Adj. prof. computer law and high tech. litig. John Marshall Law Sch., Chgo., 1999—. Editor: Harvard Law Rev., 1982—84. Pres., bd. dirs. Univ. Cellar Inc., Ann Arbor, 1979-81; bd. dirs. Econ. Devel. Corp., Menominee, 1978-79, Midwestern divsn. Am. Suicide Found., sec., 1992-97, Commonwealth Plaza Condominium Assn., dir., 1999—, pres., 2000—, Harvard Law Soc. Ill., 2003—; mem. vestry Ch. Our Savior, 1997-2000; bd. dirs. Chgo. Children's Mus., 1999—, sec., 2003-; chmn. Harvard Law Sch. 15 Yr. Reunion Gift Fund, 1999; vice chair Harvard Law Sch. 20 Yr. Reunion Gift Fund, 2003-. Mem. ABA, State Bar Mich., Assn. of Bar of City of NY, Chgo. Bar Assn., Ill. State Bar Assn., Def. Rsch. Inst., The 410 Club, Econ. Club Chgo., City Club of Chgo. Republican. Avocations: classic automobiles, piano, choir. Office: Jenner & Block Ste 4200 One IBM Plz Chicago IL 60611 Office Phone: 312-222-9350. E-mail: mneumeier@jenner.com.

NEUMEYER, JOHN LEOPOLD, research company administrator, chemistry educator; b. Munich, July 19, 1930; came to U.S., 1945, naturalized, 1950; s. Albert and Martha (Stern) N.; m. Evelyn Friedman, June 24, 1956; children: Ann Martha, David Alexander, Elizabeth Jean. BS, Columbia U., 1952; PhD, U. Wis., 1961. Rsch. chemist Ethicon Inc., New Brunswick, N.J., 1952-57, FMC Corp., Princeton, N.J., 1961-63; sr. staff chemist Arthur D. Little, Inc., Cambridge, Mass., 1963-69; prof. medicinal chemistry, chemistry Northeastern U., Boston, 1969-91, dir. grad. sch., 1978-85, univ. disting. prof., 1982—92, univ. disting. prof. emeritus, 1992—; chmn. bd., chief sci. officer, co-founder Rsch. Biochem. Internat., Natick, 1981-97; pres., co-founder Brain Rsch. Labs., Inc., 1999—2002. Mem. com. of revision U.S. Pharmacopeia, 1970-85; lectr. in psychiatry dept. psychiatry Harvard Med. Sch., 1996—; Boudewijn Tieboel vis. prof., Groningen-Utrecht Inst. for Drug Exploration, Holland, 1997, dir. medicinal chemistry program Alcohol and Drug Abuse Rsch. Ctr. McLean Hosp., Belmont, Mass., 1996—; vis. prof. chemistry U. Konstanz, Germany, 1975-77cons. in field. Contbr. articles to profl. jours., chpts. to books; patentee in field. Mem. Bd. Health, Wayland, Mass., 1968-75, Pesticide Bd., Mass., 1972-75; mem. panel to sec. HEW Commn. on Pesticides and their Relationship to Environ. Health, 1969; mem. Mass. Tech. Collaborative, 1996-2002. Served to cpl. U.S. Army, 1953-55. Recipient Lunsford Richardson award, 1961, Marie Curie award in Nuclear Medicine, 1992; sr. Hayes Fulbright fellow, 1975-76, Henry A. Hill award for Outstanding Svc. to the Northeastern Sect., Am. Chem. Soc., 1998. Fellow: AAAS (mem. at large 1983—87, chmn. pharm. sci. sec. 1992—93), Am. Assn. Pharm. Scis. (Rsch. Achievement award in medicinal chemistry 1982); mem.: Am. Chem. Soc. (bd. editors Jour. Medicinal Chemistry 1974—88, chmn. divsn. med. chem. 1982, councilor 1985—, trustee 1989—93, N.E. sect. chmn.-elect 2002, chmn. 2003), Am. Soc. Exptl. Pharm. and Exptl. Therapeutics, Am. Soc. Neurosci., Acad. Pharm. Scis. Office: Harvard Med Sch/McLean Hosp ADARC 115 Mill St Belmont MA 02478-1041 E-mail: neumeyer@mclean.harvard.edu.

NEUMEYER, ZACHARY T. hotel executive; Pres., CEO Sage Hospitality Resources LP, Denver. Office: Sage Hospitality Resources LLC 1512 Larimer St Ste 800 Denver CO 80202-1623

NEUNER, JEROME LAWRENCE, academic administrator, educator; b. Buffalo, N.Y., Aug. 5, 1947; s. Clarence Lawrence and Theresa Barbara Neuner; m. Barbara Ann Bork; children: Jennifer Leah, Sarah Beth. BA, Canisius Coll., Buffalo, 1965—69; MA, SUNY, Binghamton, 1969—73; PhD, SUNY, Buffalo, 1977—83. Cert. in reading edn. N.Y. State Bd. Regents, 1978. Assoc. dean continuing studies Canisius Coll., Buffalo, 1980—83, assoc. v.p., 1986—, acting v.p., 1990—92. Bd., trustees Christ the King Sem., E. Aurora, NY, 1996—2004; pres. Am. Assn. of U. Adminstrs., Providence, 2000—01. Specialist 4th class U.S. Army, 1970—72, Frankfurt, Germany. Fellow, Nat. Endowment for the Humanities, 1985. Liberal. Roman Catholic. Avocations: literature, travel, running, bicycling. Office: Canisius Coll 2001 Main St Buffalo NY 14208 Office Phone: 716-888-2120. E-mail: neuner@canisius.edu.

NEUNER, ROBERT, lawyer; b. N.Y.C., Dec. 11, 1938; s. John G. R. and Helen C. (Shanley) Neuner; m. Claire A. Cavaliere, Jan. 27, 1961; children: Kristine Lynne, Karen Elizabeth, Christopher Michael, Christopher Michael. BEE, Manhattan Coll., 1960; LLB, Fordham U., 1965. Bar: U.S. Dist. Ct. (so. dist.) N.Y. 1967, U.S. Ct. Appeals (1st cir.) 1971, U.S. Ct. Appeals (3d cir.) 1972, U.S. Ct. Appeals (2d cir.) 1975, U.S. Dist. Ct. (ea. dist.) N.Y. 1978, U.S. Ct. Customs and Patent Appeals 1979, U.S. Supreme Ct. 1980, U.S. Ct. Appeals (DC cir.) 1982, U.S. Ct. Appeals (4th cir.) 1983, U.S. Ct. Appeals (7th cir.) 1984. Ptnr. Brumbaugh, Graves, Donohue & Raymond, then Baker Botts, N.Y.C., 1965—2004; sr. counsel Baker Botts, N.Y.C., 2004—. Lectr. on patent litig. techniques and practice before U.S. Internat. Trade Commn. Practicing Law Inst., 1974—. Columnist: N.Y. Law Jour.; contbr. articles to profl. jours. Mem. bd. edn., Teaneck, NJ, 1969—72. Mem.: Assn. Bar City of N.Y. (mem. com. profl. and jud. ethics 1976—78, mem. com. fed. cts. 1982—85, mem. com. antitrust and trade regulation 1985—88), N.Y. Intellectual Property Law Assn. (pres. 2001—02). Office: Baker Botts LLP 30 Rockefeller Plz New York NY 10112-0002 E-mail: robert.neuner@bakerbotts.com.

NEUNZIG, CAROLYN MILLER, elementary, middle and high school educator; b. L.I., May 5, 1930; kd. Stanley and Grace (Walsh) Miller; m. Herbert Neunzig, May 28, 1955; children: Kurt Miller, Keith Weidler. BA, Beaver Coll., Glen Side, Pa., 1953; MSSc, Syracuse U., 1989; postgrad., Adelphi U.; Cert., N.C. State U., Raleigh. Cert. in elem. edn., reading, history and English, N.C., permanent cert. in secondary English, N.Y. Reading tchr. grades K-6 St. Timothy's Sch., Raleigh, N.C., 1971-83, 5th grade tchr., 1983-88, 5th grade lead tchr., 1986-88; tchr. English and geography 7th grade St. Timothy's Mid. Sch., Raleigh, 1991—; tchr Am. govt. 12th grade St. Timothy's Mid. Sch./Hale H.S., Raleigh, 1991-93. Instr. continuing edn. program history Meredith Coll., Raleigh, 1990-91, spl. high sch. registration commr., 1991-93, instr. presdl. classroom, 1998, 99; mem. Ctr. for Study of Presidency, 1998-2003. Asst. election ofcl. Wake County, N.C., 2003. Mem. AAUW, Am. Acad. Polit. and Social Sci., Acad. Polit. Sci., Ctr. for Study of the Presidency, Churchill Ctr. E-mail: c.neunzig@gte.net.

NEUSEL, MARA DICLE, mathematician, educator; b. Stuttgart, Germany, May 14, 1964; d. Günter and Ayla Neusel. Diploma in math., U. Göttingen, Germany, 1988, Dr. rer. nat., 1992, Privatdozentin, 2001. Lectr. Yale U., New Haven, 1995—95, Otto von Guericke U., Magdeburg, Germany, 1995—97, Yale U., 1998—99; assoc. prof. Tex. Tech U., Lubbock, 2002—. Visitor Queens U., Kingston, Ont., Canada, 1997; vis. asst. prof. U. Minn., Mpls., 1998, U. Notre Dame, Ind., 1999—2002; reviewer in field. Mem.: Ctr. Rsch. Math., Text and Acad. Author, Assn. Women in Math., Math. Assn. Am., Am. Math. Soc. Achievements include research in inverse invariant theory and steenrod ops. Office Phone: +1/806/742-2566.

NEUSTEIN, ROBIN, investment company executive; Attended, Mt. Holyoke Coll., 1971—73; AB in anthropology, Brown U., 1975; JD, MBA, Northwestern U., 1979. Atty. Altheimer & Gray, Chgo.; with Goldman Sachs & Co., N.Y.C., 1982—, ptnr. Investment Banking Divsn., 1990-95, chief of staff to sr. ptnrs., 1992—99, mng. dir., 1996—, co-head Pvt. Equity Group, 1999—, past mem. mgmt. com. Trustee Rockefeller U., Brown U., Mount Holyoke U., Mount Sinai Med. Ctr.; pres. bd. trustees Am. Ballet Theatre, 2002—. Mem.: Am. Women's Econ. Devel. Corp. (bd. mem., vice chmn.). Office: Goldman Sachs & Co 85 Broad St New York NY 10004-2456

NEUTRA, DION, architect; b. Los Angeles, Oct. 8, 1926; s. Richard Joseph and Dione (Niedermann) N.; children: Gregory, Wendy, Haig, Nicholas. Student, Swiss Inst. Tech., 1947-48; B.Arch. cum laude, U. So. Calif., 1950. With Richard J. Neutra (architect), Los Angeles, 1942-55; assoc. Neutra & Alexander, Los Angeles, 1955-60; assoc. Robert E. Alexander, Los Angeles, 1960-62; prin. Richard & Dion Neutra, Architects and Assos., Los Angeles, 1962—; pres. Richard J. Neutra, Inc., 1970—. Exec. cons. Inst. for Survival Through Design, L.A.; lectr. Calif. State U., L.A., Sacramento City Coll., Mira Costa State U., Cabrillo State U., Soka U., Tokyo, San Diego City Coll., Germany, Switzerland, England, Austria; vis. prof. Calif. State U., Pomona, 1970, 1985—86, Va. Commonwealth U., 1998; vis. lectr. U. Minn., 2000, Fullerton U., 2001, Nat. Bldg. Mus., 2002, SHPO, Puerto Rico, 2003, U. So. Calif. Prin. works include various residential, ednl., religious and instnl. facilities including Am. Embassy Karachi, Pakistan, Gettysburg Meml., Simpson Coll. Libr., Adelphi Univ. Libr., Libr. and Resource Ctr. for City of Huntington Beach, Calif., Treetops Townhouses, 1980; exhbns. "View from Inside", 1984, 86, 92, 98, 99, travelling show, 2000, Visions & Exiles", Vienna, 1995, Am. Century Art and Culture, Whitney Mus., N.Y.C., 1999. Mem. Silver Lake-Echo Park Dist. Plan Adv. Com., Master Plan City of Los Angeles, 1970-71; mem. Citizens to Save Silver Lake, 1973-76; dir. Child Care and Devel. Services, 1970-71, Preservation and Maintenance of Existing Neutra Projects. Served with USNR, 1944-46. Street named Neutra Pl. in firm's honor, Silverlake, 1992; Neutra Centennial, 1992, Firm's 75th Anniversary Celebration, 2001. Mem. AIA, Nat. Council Archtl. Registration Bds., Alpha Rho Chi. Studio: Richard & Dion Neutra 2440 Neutra Pl Los Angeles CA 90039-4400 Office Phone: 323-666-1806. E-mail: dionN@aol.com.

NEUWIRTH, ALAN JAMES, lawyer; b. N.Y.C., July 4, 1943; s. Bernard and Audrey (Hattenbach) N.; m. Patricia E. Neuwirth, Sept. 4, 1966; children: John A., Daniel P. BA, Lehigh U., 1965; JD, NYU, 1969. Bar: N.Y. 1970, U.S. Dist. Ct. (so. and ea. dists.) N.Y. 1972, U.S. Ct. Appeals (2d cir.) 1972, U.S. Ct. Internat. Trade 1983, U.S. Ct. Appeals (Fed. cir.) 1984, U.S. Supreme Ct. 1988. Assoc. Miller & Summit, N.Y.C., 1970-72, Ratheim, Hoffman, Kassel & Silverman, N.Y.C., 1973-75; ptnr. Kassel, Neuwirth & Geiger, N.Y.C., 1976-86, Webster & Sheffield, N.Y.C., 1987-90; sr. ptnr. Morgan, Lewis & Bockius LLP, N.Y.C., 1990—. Bd. dirs. various cos. With U.S. Army, 1969-74, USAR. Mem. ABA, Assn. of Bar of City of N.Y., Internat. Trade Commn., Trial Lawyers Assn. Office: Morgan Lewis & Bockius LLP 101 Park Ave New York NY 10178-0060

NEUWIRTH, BEBE (BEATRICE NEUWIRTH), dancer, actress; b. Newark, Dec. 31, 1958; d. Lee Paul and Sydney Anne Neuwirth; m. Paul Dorman, 1984 (div.); m. Michael Danek. Student, Juilliard Sch., 1976-77. Appeared: (on Broadway) A Chorus Line (as Sheila), 1975-90, Dancin', 1978-82, Little Me, 1982, Sweet Charity, 1986-87 (Tony award for best featured actress in a musical, 1986), Damn Yankees, 1994-95, Chicago, 1996 (Tony award for best actress in a musical, 1997, Outer Critics Circle award for best actress in a musical, 1997, Drama League Award for disting. performance, 1997, Drama Desk Award for outstanding actress in a musical, 1997, Astaire Award for best female dancer, 1997), Fosse, 1999-2001, Funny Girl, 2002, Here Lies Jenny, 2004; (off Broadway) include West Side Story, 1981, Upstairs at O'Neal's, 1982-83, The Road to Hollywood, 1984, Just So, 1985, Waiting in the Wings: The Night the Understudies Take the Stage, 1986, Showing Off, 1989, Kiss of the Spider Woman (London), 1993, Pal Joey, 1995, Here Lies Jenny, 2004. Prin. dancer on Broadway Dancin', 1982; leading dance role Kicks, 1984. Actor: (TV series) The Edge of Night, 1981, Cheers, 1986-93 (Emmy award for Best Supporting Actress in a Comedy Series 1990, 91), (voice) Aladdin, 1993, (voice) All Dogs Go to Heaven: The Series, 1996, Deadline, 2000-01; (TV series guest appearances) Frasier, 1994-2003; (TV miniseries) Wild Palms, 1993; (TV films) Without Her Consent, 1990, Unspeakable Acts, 1990, Dash and Lilly, 1999, Cupid & Cate, 2000, Sounds From a Town I Love, 2001; (films) Say Anything, 1989, Green Card, 1990, Bugsy, 1991, The Paint Job, 1992, Malice, 1993, Jumanji, 1995, (voice) All Dogs Go to Heaven 2, 1996, The Adventures of Pinocchio, 1996, The Associate, 1996, Dear Diary, 1996, Celebrity, 1998, The Faculty, 1998, (voice) An All Dogs Christmas Carol, 1998, Summer of Sam, 1999, Liberty Heights, 1999, Getting to Know You, 1999, Tadpole, 2002, How to Lose a Guy in 10 Days, 2003, Le Divorce, 2003, The Big Bounce, 2004. Vol. performances for March of Dimes Telethon, 1986, Cystic Fibrosis Benefit Children's Ball, 1986, Ensemble Studio Theater Benefit, 1986, Circle Repertory Co. Benefit, 1986, all in N.Y.C. Democrat. Office: Internat Creative Mgmt 8942 Wilshire Blvd Beverly Hills CA 90211-1934*

NEUWIRTH, GLORIA S. lawyer; b. N.Y.C., Aug. 16, 1934; d. Nathan and Jennie (Leff) Salob; m. Robert S. Neuwirth, June 9, 1957; children: Susan Madeleine Guerra, Jessica Anne, Laura Helaine, Michael Jonathan. BA, Hunter Coll., 1955; JD, Yale U., 1958. Bar: N.Y. 1959, Fla. 1979, U.S. Supreme Ct. 1976, U.S. Dist. Ct. (so. and ea. dists.) N.Y. 1976. Assoc. dir. Joint Rsch. Project on Ct. Calendar Congestion Columbia U., N.Y.C., 1958-61; assoc. Kridel & Friou, N.Y.C., 1974-76; ptnr. Kridel, Slater and Neuwirth, N.Y.C., 1976-82, 87-94; assoc. Kaye, Scholer, Fierman, Hays and Handler, N.Y.C., 1982-84, Graubard Moskovitz McGoldrick Dannett & Horowitz, N.Y.C., 1984-86; ptnr. Davidson, Dawson & Clark, N.Y.C., 1995—. Vol. arbitrator Better Bus. Bur. Author: (with R.B. Hunting) Who Sues in New York City: A Study of Automobile Accident Claims, 1962; contbr. articles to profl. jours. Trustee Blueberry Inc., 1962-70, Riverdale Country Sch., 1981-86; trustee, v.p., sec. Nat. Kidney Found., Inc., N.Y./N.J., 1980-2002, trustee nat. office, 1980-90; dir. Estate Planning Coun. N.Y.C., Riverdale Mental Health Assn., Bronx Opera Co., The Ruth Turner Fund, The Associated Blind, Riverdale Sr. Svcs.; sec. Kidney & Urology Found. Am., 2002-. Recipient C. LaRue Munson prize, Yale Law Sch., 1958. Fellow Am. Coll. Trust and Estate Counsel; mem. ABA, N.Y. State Bar Assn. (vice chmn. com. on law of the elderly), Assn. Bar City N.Y., Fin. Women's Assn., Estate Planning Coun. N.Y., Nat. Elder Law Attys., Appalachian Mtn. Club. Office: Davidson Dawson & Clark LLP 330 Madison Ave Fl 35 New York NY 10017-5094 Fax: 212-286-8513. Office Phone: 212-557-7720. E-mail: gsneuwirth@davidsondawson.com.

NEUWIRTH, ROBERT SAMUEL, obstetrician, gynecologist; b. NYC, July 11, 1933; s. Abraham Alexander and Phyllis Neuwirth; children from previous marriage: Susan, Jessica, Laura, Michael, Alexander. BS, Yale U., 1955, MD, 1958. Intern Presbyn. Hosp., NYC, 1958-59, resident, 1959-64; asst. prof. ob-gyn. Columbia U., NYC, 1964-68, assoc. prof., 1968-71, prof., 1972-2001, Babcock prof., 1977-2001, Babcock prof. emeritus, 2001—. Dir. ob-gyn. Bronx Lebanon Hosp., NYC, 1967-72, Woman's Hosp., NYC, St. Luke's Hosp. Ctr., 1974—, St. Luke's Roosevelt Hosp., 1981-91; prof. Albert Einstein Coll. Medicine, 1971-72; cons. WHO, NIH, AID, FDA; interim dir. St. Luke's Roosevelt Hosp., 1998-2000. Author: Hysteroscopy, 1975; contbr. articles to profl. jours. Mem.: ACOG, Assn. Vol. Sterilization (chmn. biomed. com. 1971—), Am. Assn. Profs. Ob-Gyn., NY Obstet. Soc., Soc. Gynecol. Investigation, Am. Gynecol. and Obstet. Soc. Office: St Lukes Roosevelt Hosp 1000 10th Ave Dept Ob New York NY 10019-1147

NEUZIL, DENNIS R. civil engineer; b. Berwyn, Ill., 1937; s. Florian and Mildred Neuzil; m. Donna Joy Neuzil, 1961; 1 child, Gregory. BSCE, U. Wash., 1961, MSCE, 1962; DrEngring., U. Calif., 1965. Registered profl. engr., Wash., Colo. Asst. prof. U. Colo., Boulder, 1965—67, U. Del., Newark, 1967—70; cons. engr. Tippetts Abbett McCarthy Stratton, Boston, 1970—72, various cons. firms, Seattle, 1972—78, Entranco Engrs., Bellevue, 1978—96, Harding Engrs., 1996—2001, Perteet Engrs., Everett, 2002—. Fellow: Inst. Transp. Engrs. (Wash. state pres. 1982—83), ASCE. Home: 2307 94 Ave NE Bellevue WA 98004

NEVAI, LUCIA, writer; b. Des Moines, Iowa, Sept. 11, 1945; d. Darwin Thomas and Ruth Marcella (Courson) Lynner; m. Andrew Nevai, July 6, 1968 (div. Sept. 1984); children: Nandor, Matthew. BA, New Sch. for Social Rsch., 1967. Author: (novels) Seriously, (short stories) Normal, Star Game (Winner of The Iowa Short Fiction Award 1987); contbr. articles in numerous profl. jours.; author: (short stories) (anthologies) New Stories from The South 2002, The Year's Best, Francis Ford Coppola's Zoetrope: All Story, Fault Lines: Stories of Divorce, The Algonkian, The Way We Write Now: Short Stories from the AIDS Crisis, Closing: An Anthology of American Short Fiction on The Art of Selling, American Fiction Award Anthology No. 4, The Iowa Award: The Best Stories from Twenty Years. Recipient Iowa Award For Lit. 2001, The Iowa Review, 2001, Winner PEN Syndicated Fiction Award, The Chgo. Tribune Mag., Am. Fiction Award, American Fiction No. 4, Best Fiction, The Newsday Mag., The State Mag. Home and Office: 579 Totem Lodge Averill Park NY 12018

NEVANS, LAUREL S. rehabilitation counselor; b. N.Y.C., Aug. 1, 1964; d. Roy N. and Virginia (Place) Nevans; m. Russell Baird Palmer III, Oct. 12, 1991 (div. Jan. 2001). BA in English, Secondary Edn. cum laude, U. Richmond, 1986, postgrad., 1989-92; MA in Edn. and Human Devel., George Washington U., 1991, cert. in job devel. and placement, 1992. Group leader S.E. Consortium for Spl. Svcs., Larchmont, NY, 1980—85; vocat. instr. Assn. for Retarded Citizens Montgomery County, Rockville, Md., 1986—89; edn. specialist George Washington U. Out of Sch. Work Experience Program, Washington, 1989—90; rsch. asst. George Washington U. Dept. Tchr. Prep. & Spl. Edn., Washington, 1989—91; employability skills tchr., rsch. intern Nat. Rehab. Hosp. Rehab. Engring. Dept., Washington, 1991; vocat./ind. living skills specialist The Independence Ctr., Rockville, Md., 1991—93; leadership team mgr. Career Choice project The Endependence Ctr. of No. Va., Arlington, 1993—94; program dir. United Cerebral Palsy of D.C. and No. Va., Washington, 1994—97; sr. assistive tech. specialist Tech., Automation & Mgmt., Inc., Greenbelt, Md., 1997—98; owner WebLaurels Designs, Silver Spring, Md., 1998—, ArtistCrafts, 2001—, Clayers with Disabilities Listserv (electronic discussion list), 2002—, Artist Crafts, Silver Spring, 2001—. Teaching asst. Rehab. Counseling Program, George Washington U., 1991; moderator FPList Electronic Discussion List, 2000—; owner Clayers with Disabilities Electronic Discussion List, 2002- . Bd. mem., newsletter editor Cameron Hill Owners Assn., 2002—. Recipient traineeship GWU Counseling Dept., 1990, 91. Mem. Nat. Rehab. Assn., Nat. Rehab. Counselors Assn., D.C. Met. Area Assn. Person's in Supported Employment (editor newsletter 1995-97), Nat. Career Devel. Assn., Nat. Employment Counseling Assn., Nat. Assn. Ind. Living, Am. Assn. Counseling and Devel., Am. Rehab. Counseling Assn., Nat. Polymer Clay Guild. Democrat. Avocations: writing, photography, music, travel, jewelry making. Home: 8501 Cameron St Silver Spring MD 20910-3466 E-mail: laurel@artistcrafts.com.

NEVANS, ROY NORMAN, food products executive, producer; b. N.Y.C., July 1, 1931; s. Al Nevans and Lillian (Schiff) Margolis; m. Virginia Place, Dec. 31, 1961; children: Lisa Ann, Laurel Sue, Judith Lynn. BS, U. Pa., 1953; MBA, Columbia U., 1957. Mgmt. trainee Henningsen Foods, Inc., N.Y.C., 1958-60, mgr. export sales div., 1960-65, mgr. nat. sales div., 1965-70, v.p. mktg. White Plains, N.Y., 1970-90; mng. dir. Henningsen Van Den Burg, Waalyk, Holland, 1979-90, Henningsen Nederland B.V., Waalyk, 1984-90, Henningsen Foods, Ltd., London, 1977-90; pres. Royco Internat. Inc., Stamford, Conn., 1991—. Pres Royal Productions, Ltd, New York, NY, 1966, New York, 73, Int TV Productions, Ltd, London, 1978—; exec producer NCM Entertainment, Inc, New York, NY, 1982—; bd dirs Global Educ Mgt, Wall St Inst, World Trade Club. Prodr.: (Broadway plays) Gandhi, 1969, Solitaire Double Solitaire, 1972; (TV series) Juke Box, 1978—79; exec. prodr.: (TV miniseries) Roots of Rock and Roll, 1981. Lt comdr USN, 1953—56. Mem.: NATAS, US Naval Order, US Naval War Col, Univ Pa Club, Jaguar Touring Club, River Club. Avocations: classic cars collector, boating, theater. Home: 74 Greenwich Hills Dr Greenwich CT 06831 also: 1945 Gulf of Mexico Dr #108 Longboat Key FL 34228 also: 302 W 12th St New York NY 10014 Office: Royco Internat Inc 1177 High Ridge Rd Stamford CT 06905-1203 E-mail: roycointl@att.net.

NEVAREZ, MIGUEL A. academic administrator; Pres. U. Tex.-Pan Am., Edinburg, 1981—. Office: U Tex-Pan Am 1201 W University Dr Edinburg TX 78539-2909 E-mail: info@www.panam.edu.

NEVE, VICTORIA J. music educator; b. Watseka, Ill., Apr. 25, 1950; d. Frank J and Florence M Rider; m. Patrick M Neve, Aug. 30, 1970; 1 child, Branwyn. B in music, Ill. Wesleyan, 1972; M in music, U. of Kans., 1975, Mus D, 1979. Prof. of music San Francisco State U., 1975—; dir. San Francisco Young Pianists Competition, 1983—. Adj. MTNA, MTAC et al., 1984—. Office: San Francisco State U Dept of Music 1600 Holloway Ave San Francisco CA 94132 Business E-Mail: docvic@sfsu.edu.

NEVELOFF, JAY A. lawyer; b. Bklyn., Oct. 11, 1950; m. Arlene Sillman, Aug. 26, 1972; children: David, Kevin. BA, Bklyn. Coll., 1971; JD, NYU, 1974. Bar: N.Y. 1975, D.C. 1992, U.S. Dist. Ct. (so. and ea. dists.) N.Y. 1975, U.S. Ct. Appeals (2d cir.) 1975, U.S. Supreme Ct. 1982. Assoc. Marshall, Bratter, Greene, Allison & Tucker, N.Y.C., 1974-82, Rosenman, Colin, Freund, Lewis & Cohen, N.Y.C., 1982-83, ptnr., 1983-88, Kramer, Levin, Naftalis, Nessen, Kamin & Frankel, N.Y.C., 1988—98. Editor N.Y. Real Property Service. Mem. planning bd. Briarcliff Manor, 1995—. Mem. ABA (vice chmn. com. partnerships, joint ventures and other investment vehicles 1988-95), Am. Law Inst., Am. Coll. Real Estate Attys., N.Y. State Bar Assn. (financing com.), Practising Law Inst. (lectr. 1988—, mem. adv. bd. 1991—), N.Y. County Lawyers Assn. (lectr. 1984-94), Assn. Bar City N.Y. (real property law com., lectr. 1984-88), Cmty. Assns. Inst. (lectr. 1986), Law Jours. Seminars (lectr. 1987—), Strategic Resources Inst. (lectr. 1994-98), Internat. Health Network Soc. (vice chmn. 1995-2000), Inst. Internat. Rsch. (lectr. 1994—). Home: 134 Alder Dr Briarcliff Manor NY 10510-2218 Office: Kramer Levin Naftalis & Frankel LLP 919 3rd Ave New York NY 10022-3902 Office Phone: 212-715-9290. E-mail: jneveloff@kramerlevin.com.

NEVERSON, NORMAN CARL, political organization administrator; BA, George Washington U., 1967, MA, 1971. Chair D.C. Dem. Com., Washington; CEO Neverson & Assocs., Washington. Office: Democratic Com Chmn 499 S Capitol St SE Fairchild Blfg Ste 100 Washington DC 20003 Home: 2136 Sudbury Pl NW Washington DC 20012

NEVEU, JEAN, printing company executive; Contr., mgr. Quebecor, Inc., Montreal, 1969—79; in mag. pub. and distbn., 1979—88; chmn., CEO, Quebecor Printing Inc., 1989—2002; pres., CEO Quebecor World Inc., 2003—; pres., CEO, Quebecor Inc., 1999—, chmn., 1999—. Chmn. Groupe TVA Inc.; bd Quebecor Media Inc. Chmn. Fondation du centre Hospitalier PierreBoucher; active Mutins de Longueuil; bd. dirs. Internationaux du sport de Montreal. Office: Quebecor Inc 612 Saint Jacques St Montreal QC Canada H3C 4M8

NEVIASER, ROBERT JON, orthopaedic surgeon, educator; b. Washington, Nov. 21, 1936; s. Julius Salem and Jane Frances (Gibbons) N.; m. Anne Maclean Shedden, Dec. 3, 1966; children: Jeanne Nicole, Robert Jon Jr., Ian Maclean, Andrew Shedden. Grad., Phillips Acad., Andover, Mass., 1954; AB, Princeton U., 1958; MD, Jefferson Med. Coll., 1962. Diplomate Am. Bd. Orthop. Surgery with cert. of added qualification in surgery of hand. Intern N.Y. Hosp., Cornell Med. Ctr., N.Y.C., 1962-63, asst. resident, 1963-64; asst. resident in orthopaedic surgery N.Y. Orthop. Hosp., Columbia-Presbyn. Med. Ctr., N.Y.C., 1964-66, jr. Annie C. Kane fellow, resident, 1966-67; fellow in surgery of the hand Orthop. Hosp., L.A., 1969-70; asst. prof. divsn. orthop. and hand surgery, chmn. dept. U. Conn., Hartford, 1970-71; assoc. prof. orthop. surgery George Washington U., Washington, 1971-76, prof., 1976—, dir. orthop. edn., assoc. chmn. dept. orthop. surgery, 1984-87, chmn. dept. orthop. surgery, 1987—; chmn. governing bd. Med. Faculty Assocs. George Washington U. Med. Ctr., 1995-98, trustee, 2000—03. Editor-in-chief Jour. of Shoulder and Elbow Surgery, 1997—; contbr. articles in field to profl. jours. Lt. comdr. USNR, 1967-69. Fellow Am. Soc. Surgery of the Hand, Am. Acad. Orthop. Surgeons, Ea. Orthop. Assn., Am. Shoulder and Elbow Surgeons, Am. Orthop. Assn., Princeton Club (N.Y.), Manor Country Club, Cosmos Club, Alpha Kappa Kappa, Alpha Omega Alpha. Republican. Office: 2150 Pennsylvania Ave NW Washington DC 20037-3201 Office Phone: 202-741-3301.

NEVILL, WILLIAM ALBERT, chemistry professor; b. Indpls., Jan. 1, 1929; s. Irwin Lowell and Mary Marie (Barker) N.; m. Nancy Neiman (Roll), May 19, 1979; children: Paul David, John Michael, Steven Joseph, Anne Marie, Deborah Ruth. BS, Butler U., 1951; PhD, Calif. Inst. of Tech., 1954. Rsch. chemist Procter and Gamble, Cin., 1954; chemistry prof., chmn. dept. Grinnell Coll., 1956-67; prof. chemistry Ind. U., Purdue, Indpls., 1967-83, chmn. dept., 1967-72, dean sch. sci., 1972-79, dir. grad. studies, 1979-83; pres. B and N Cons. Co., 1972-93; vice chancellor acad. affairs La. State U., Shreveport, La., 1983-85, prof., 1983-94; pres. Catoctin Assoc., 1993—. Arbitrator, mediator, Ind. Employment Rels. Bd., 1975-83. Author: Gen. Chemistry, 1967, Expt. in Gen. Chemistry, 1968. Bd. dir. Indpls. Sci. and Engring. Found., 1972-75, 79-82, Westminster Found., Lafayette, Ind., 1972-74, Am. Chem. Soc., 1986-92. With U.S. Army, 1954-56; col., USAR, 1956-84. Grantee NSF, 1959-74; Grantee NIH, 1963-70; Grantee Office Naval Rsch., 1953 Mem. Ind. Acad. Sci., Am. Chem. Soc., chmn. sect. 1972, counselor 1973-92. Presbyterian.

NEVILLE, CARA LEE T. judge; JD, William Mitchell Coll. Law, 1975. Lawyer felony divsn. Hennepin County Attys. Office, 1972; asst. pub. defender Hennepin County, 1978; judge Hennepin County Mcpl. Ct., 1983, Hennepin County Dist. Ct., 1986; dist. ct. judge 4th Jud. Dist., Mpls., 1986—. Mem.: ABA (bd. govs. 9th dist. 2000—03). Office: Hennepin County Dist Ct 1859-C Govt Ctr 300 S 6th St Minneapolis MN 55487-0999

NEVILLE, GWEN KENNEDY, anthropology educator; b. Taylor, Tex., Mar. 23, 1938; d. Matthew Ranken and Gwendolyn (Harrison) Kennedy; m. William Gordon Neville (div.); children: Katherine, Mary Grace, William Kennedy; m. Jack Gregory Hunnicutt, Jr., 1975. BA, Mary Baldwin Coll., Staunton, Va., 1959; MA, U. Fla., 1968, PhD, 1971. Asst. prof. Emory U., Atlanta, 1971-78, assoc. prof., 1978-79; from assoc. prof. to prof. emeritus Southwestern U., Georgetown, Tex., 1979—98, prof. emeritus, Elizabeth Root Paden chair, 1998—. Cons. Wenner-Gren Conf., Mt. Kisco, N.Y., 1983; grant holder NEH, Washington, 1972, 89; researcher, writer Lilly Endowment, Indpls., 1988—. Author: Kinship and Pilgrimage, 1987, The Mother Town, 1994; co-author: Generation to Generation, 1973, Learning Through Liturgy, 1978; contbr. articles to profl. jours. Fellow Am. Anthropol. Assn.; mem. Am. Ethnological Soc., Soc. for Anthropology of Europe (bd. dirs. 1989-92), Assn. for Scottish Ethnography, Coun. on Anthropology and Edn. (bd. dirs. 1971-74), So. Anthropol. Soc. (editor 1974-77), Phi Beta Kappa. Office: 26 Meadows End Georgetown TX 78628

NEVILLE, JAMES MORTON, retired lawyer, consumer products company executive; b. Mpls., May 28, 1939; s. Philip and Maurene (Morton) N.; m. Judie Martha Proctor, Sept. 9, 1961; children: Stephen Warren, Martha Maurene Hereford. BA, U. Minn., JD magna cum laude, 1964. Bar: Minn. 1964, Mo. 1984. Assoc. Neville, Johnson & Thompson, Mpls., 1964-69, ptnr., 1969-70; assoc. counsel Gen. Mills, Inc., Mpls., 1970-77, sr. assoc. counsel, 1977-83, corp. sec., 1976-83; v.p., sec., asst. gen. counsel Ralston Purina Co., St. Louis, 1983-84, v.p., gen. counsel, sec., 1984-96, v.p., gen. counsel, 1996-2000, v.p., sr. counsel, 2000-01; ret., 2001; chmn. The Thompson Ctr., 2002. Lectr. bus. law. U. Minn., 1967-71. Named Man of Yr., Edina Jaycees, 1967. Mem. ABA, Mo. Bar Assn., U.S. Supreme Ct. Bar Assn., St. Louis Bar Assn., U. Minn. Law Sch. Alumni Assn., Old Warson Country Club, Ladue Racquet Club, Order of Coif, Phi Delta Phi, Psi Upsilon. Episcopalian. Home: 9810 Log Cabin Ct Saint Louis MO 63124-1133 E-mail: jnev57@aol.com.

NEVILLE, PHOEBE, choreographer, dancer, educator; b. Swarthmore, Pa., Sept. 28, 1941; d. Kennith R. and Marion (Eberbach) Balsley; m. Philip E. Hipwell, June 21, 1969 (dissolved Sept. 1978); m. Philip Corner, Nov. 3, 1996. Student, Wilson Coll., 1959-61. Cert. practitioner body mind centering, registered somatic movement therapist. Instr. Bennington (Vt.) Coll., 1981-84, 87-88; vis. lectr. UCLA, 1984-86. Dancer, choreographer Judson Meml. Ch., N.Y.C., 1966—70, Dance Uptown Series, 1969, Cubiculo Theatre, 1972—75, Delacorte Dance Festival, 1976, Dance Umbrella Series, 1977, Riverside Dance Festival, 1976, 1978, N.Y. Seasons, 1979—, dancer, artistic dir. Phoebe Neville Dance Co., N.Y.C., 1975—, Jacob's Pillow Splash! Festival, 1988—, Dance Theater Workshop Winter Events, 1988—, performances with Philip Corner: Venice, Genoa San Michele al' Adige, 1966—, BBB Festival, Thailand, Genoa, Salso Maggiore, Terme, 1997—, Seoul NY Max Festival, N.Y.C., 1998, Malpartida de Caseras, Spain, Caserano, Italy, 1998, Besancon, France, 1998, Paris, Lyon, 1999, Saluggia, Italy, 1999, Performance Festival, Odense, Denmark, 1999, 2001, Bassano del Grappa, Genoa, Italy, 2000, 2001, 2002, Novarra, Italy, 2002—; performances with, Ghent, Belgium, 2002—; performances with: Castelvetro di Modena, 2003; Argos Festival, 2003. Recipient Creative Artist Public Svc. award, 1975; Nat. Endowment for Arts fellow, 1975, 79, 80, 85-87, 92-94, Choreographic fellow N.Y. Found. for Arts, 1989. Mem.: Internat. Assn. Healthcare Practitioners, Internat. Somatic Movement Edn. and Therapy Assn. (registered), Body-Mind Centering Assn. (cert. practitioner and tchr.). Buddhist. E-mail: phphcn@tin.it.

NEVILLE, ROY GERALD, scientist, chemical management and environmental consultant; b. Bournemouth, Dorsetshire, Eng., Oct. 15, 1926; came to U.S., 1951, naturalized, 1957; s. Percy Herbert and Georgina Lallie (Jenkins) N.; m. Jeanne Frances Russ, July 26, 1952; children: Laura Jean, Janet Marilyn. BSc with honors, U. London, 1951; MSc, U. Oreg., 1952, PhD, 1954, FRIC, Royal Inst. Chemistry, London, 1963, DSc (hon.), 1973. Research chemist Monsanto Chem. co., Seattle, 1955-57; sr. chem. engr. Boeing Co., Seattle, 1957-58; sr. research scientist Lockheed Missiles & Space Co., Palo Alto, Calif., 1958-61; sr. staff scientist Aerospace Corp., El Segundo, Calif., 1961-63; prin. scientist Rockwell Internat. Corp., Los Angeles, 1963-67; head dept. materials Scis. Lab., Boeing Sci. Research Labs. Boeing Co., Seattle, 1967-69; sr. environ. engring. specialist Bechtel Corp., San Francisco, 1969-73; pres. Engring. & Tech. Cons., Inc., Redwood City, Calif., 1973—. Contbr. numerous sci. articles on inorganic and organic synthesis, thermally stable polymers, pollution control processes to profl. jours. and books; many U.S. and fgn. patents in field; associateship Southampton U., England, 1951. Founder R.G. Neville Hist. Chem. Libr. The Chem. Heritage Found., Phila.; dir. Sequoia Hosp. Found., Redwood City, Calif. Fulbright scholar to U.S., 1951; USPHS fellowship, 1951-52, Research Corp. fellow, 1952-54; chartered chemist, London. Fellow Royal Soc. Chemistry (London), Am. Inst. Chemists, AAAS; mem. Am. Chem. Soc., Am. Inst. Chem. Engrs., History Sci. Soc., Soc. Study Early Chemistry, Royal Instn. Great Britain, Research Soc. Am., Soc. Mining Engrs. of AIME, Calif. Mining Assn., Sigma Xi. Office: ETC Inc 1552 Viscaino Rd Pebble Beach CA 93953-3303

NEVILLE, THOMAS LEE, food service company executive; b. Columbus, Ind., Jan. 1, 1947; s. Frank Thomas and Esquline Coons (Davis) N.; m. Shavona Rose Lagneau, Aug. 10, 1966; children: Timothy David, Sherry Lynn. AAS, Austin Peay State U., Clarksville, Tenn., 1994. Cert. exec. chef; cert. food exec. Enlisted U.S. Army, 1966, apptd. WO1, 1976, commd. CW3, 1986; food advisor Army Food Rsch., Devel. and Engring. Ctr., Natick, Mass.; ret. U.S. Army, 1990; regional mgr. KCA Corp., Hopkinsville, Ky., 1990—. Mem. Warrant Officers Assn., 1976-90. Mem. Ret. Officers Assn., Am. Soc. Quality Control, Am. Culinary Fedn., Am. Mgmt. Assn., Internat. Food Svc. Execs. Assn., Masons. Home: 1728 Clara Ct Clarksville TN 37040-7823 Office: KCA Corp PO Box 641 Hopkinsville KY 42241-0641 Office Phone: 270-886-5551. Business E-Mail: tneville@kcacorp.com.

NEVIN, CROCKER, investment banker; b. Tulsa, Mar. 14, 1923; s. Ethelbert Paul and Jennie Crocker (Fassett) N.; m. Mary Elizabeth Sherwin, Apr. 24, 1952 (div. 1984); children: Anne, Paul, Elizabeth, Crocker; m. Marilyn Elizabeth English, Nov. 3, 1984; 1 child, Jennie Fassett. Grad. with high honors, St. Paul's Sch., 1942; AB with high honors, Princeton U., 1946. With Vick Chem. Co., 1949-50, John Roberts Powers Cosmetic Co., 1950-52; with Marine Midland Grace Trust Co. of N.Y., 1952—, exec. v.p., 1964-66, pres., 1966-70, chmn. bd., chief exec. officer, 1968-73; also dir.; vice chmn. bd. Evans Products Co., N.Y.C., 1974-76, Drexel Burnam Lambert Co., investment bankers, N.Y.C., 1976-88; chmn. bd., chief exec. officer CF & I Steel Corp., Pueblo, Colo., 1985-93. Dir. Magnatek, Inc. Chmn. exec. com. ACCION Internat. Lt. (j.g.) AC USN, 1942-46. Mem. Riverside Yacht Club, N.Y. Yacht Club (N.Y.C.), Blind Brook Club. Home: 526 W Lyon Farm Greenwich CT 06831

NEVIN, DAVID WRIGHT, real estate broker, mortgage broker; b. Culver City, Calif., July 27, 1947; s. Wilbur D. and Anita J. (Hulderman) N.; m. Shirley Grimes, Nov. 12, 1977; children: Jenny, David Wright Jr. BA, Calif. State Poly. U., 1974. Rural manpower asst. employment devel. State Calif., Riverside, 1970-74; pers. mgr. Lindsay Olive Growers, 1974-79; employee rels. mgr. Morton Salt Co., Newark, 1979-80; real estate salesman Valley Realty, Fremont, 1980-85; owner Nevin & Nevin Inc., Fremont, 1984-88, CitiDesign, Fremont, 1989—. Co-owner Brokers Exch., Inc., 1985-86; dir., officer CitiBrokers Real Estate, Inc., 1986-94; owner Nevin Fin/Mortgage Exchange 1992—; br. mgr. Brandt Property Mgmt. Group, 1994-95; mgr. Internat. Trade Corp., Saigon, Vietnam, 1997. Sustaining mem. Rep. Nat. Com., Washington, 1984; mem. Presdl. Task Force, Washington, 1984, Calvary Chapel, Visalia. With U.S. Army, 1967-69. Mem. Realtors Nat. Internat. Real Estate Fedn., So. Alameda County Bd. Realtors (local govt. rels. com. 1983-86). Address: 18755 Ave 314 Visalia CA 93292 E-mail: davidwnevin@yahoo.com.

NEVIN, JEAN SHAW, artist; b. Bklyn., Dec. 21, 1934; d. Marshall Robert and Dorothy Frances (Brown) Shaw; m. Robert Stephen Nevin, Dec. 9, l955. BA in English, SUNY, Albany, l956. Textbook and freelance editor, 1959—74; printmaker, papermaker Jean Nevin Graphics, Indpls., 1969—84; owner, mgr., knitwear designer Chameleon, Indpls., 1985—88; pres., knitwear designer Knitting Machine Shop, Inc., Indpls., 1988—91; owner Knitwearables, Albuquerque, 1991—97; painter Albuquerque, 1995—. Instr. print and paper making Indpls. Art League, 1974-83, exhibits coord., 1969, 73, edn. coord., 1979-80, editor Artifacts, 1968-69, 72-73; editor, pub. Swatchnotes, 1987-91; owner, gallery dir. Kokopelli Gallery, 2000-01. Exhibited to nat. group shows and galleries prints and handmade paper, 1970-84, garments and jewelry, 1992-97, Florence Biennale, Florence, Italy, 2003; painter, sculptor, mixed media artist, 1998-2001; digital painter, 2001—. Mem.: Digital Fine Art Soc. N.Mex. (co-founder), Soc. Layerists in MultiMedia. (signature mem.). Home and Studio: 9641 Mendoza Ave NE Albuquerque NM 87109-6614 Office Phone: 505-288-2044. E-mail: jean@nevinart.com.

NEVIN, JOHN ROBERT, business educator, consultant; b. Joliet, Ill., Jan. 27, 1943; s. Robert Charles and Rita Alice (Roder) N.; m. Jeanne M. Conroy, June 10, 1967; children: Erin, Michael. BS, So. Ill. U., 1965; MS, U. Ill., 1968, PhD, 1972. Asst. prof. bus. U. Wis., Madison, 1970—77, assoc. prof. bus., 1977—83, prof. bus., 1983—, Wis. disting. prof. bus., 1988—89, Grainger Wis. disting. prof. bus., 1989—, exec. dir. Grainger Ctr. for Supply Chain Mgmt., 1992—, assoc. dean masters program, 1999—2002, exec. dir., Ctr. Product Mgmt., 2003—. Mem. investment adv. com. Venture Investors of Wis., Inc., Madison, 1986-99. Author: International Marketing: An Annotated Bibliography, 1983; mem. editl. bd. Jour. of Mtg. Channels, The Haworth Press, Inc., 1991—; contbr. articles to profl. jours. Bd. dirs. Madison civic Ctr., 1983-99. Mem. Am. Mktg. Assn. (bd. dirs. PhD consortium 1979, editorial bd. Jour. of Mktg. Chgo. chpt. 1983-97), Assn. for Consumer Rsch. Avocations: golf, skiing, running. Home: 7514 Red Fox Trl Madison WI 53717-1860 Office: U Wis Grainger Ctr Supply Chain Mgmt 975 University Ave Madison WI 53706-1324 Office Phone: 608-262-8912. E-mail: jnevin@bus.wisc.edu.

NEVIN, JOSEPH FRANCIS, computer systems engineer; b. Washington, Mar. 20, 1947; s. John Joseph and Mary Frances (O'Donnell) N.; m. Kathleen Cecelia Ridgell, Mar. 16, 1991; children: Christopher, Andrew, Amy, Megan. BA, Georgetown U., 1969; MS, Am. U., 1977. Dir. applications devel. U.S. Dept. HHS/Health Resources and Svc. Adminstrn., Rockville, Md., 1997—. Historian Smithsonian Assocs., Washington, 1982—. Dir. Balt. and Ohio RR Hist. Soc., 1979—, pres., 1982-83, 94-97, v.p., 1984-94. Recipient Adminstrs. award Health Resources and Svcs., 1983; Pub. Health Spl. Recognition award USPHS, 1984. Avocation: railroad and transportation history. Office: 5600 Fishers Ln Rockville MD 20852-1750

NEVIN, PHILLIP, professional baseball player; b. Fullerton, Calif., Jan. 19, 1971; First baseman San Diego Padres, 1999—, Anaheim Angles, 1998—99, Detroit Tigers, 1995—97, Houston Astros, 1995—95. Office: 100 Park BLVD San Diego CA 92101-7405

NEVIN, ROBERT CHARLES, information systems executive; b. Dayton, Ohio, Nov. 4, 1940; s. Robert Steely and Virginia (Boehme) N.; m. Linda Sharon Fox, Apr. 16, 1966; children: Heather, Andrew. BA, Williams Coll., 1962; MBA, U. Pa., 1970. Fin. planning mgr. Huffy Corp., Dayton, Ohio, 1971-72, asst. treas., 1972-73, treas., 1973-75, v.p. fin., 1975-79, exec. v.p., 1982-85; pres., gen. mgr. Frabill Sporting Good, Milw., 1979-82; exec. v.p. Reynolds & Reynolds, Dayton, Ohio, 1985-88, pres. bus. forms divsn., 1988-97; pres. automotive group, 1997—. Bd. dirs. Reynolds & Reynolds, Olympic Title Ins. Co. Bd. dirs., pres. Camp Fire Girls, Dayton, 1975; bd. dirs. ARC, 1977; participant, then trustee Leadership Dayton, 1986-95; vice chmn. Med. Am. Corp.; trustee, treas. Victory Theater Assn., 1985-91, Dayton Mus. Natural History, 1982-96; trustee, chmn. Alliance for Edn., Dayton Art Inst. 1st lt. USN, 1962-70. Mem. Beta Gamma Sigma, Racquet (Dayton), Dayton Country, Country Club of the North. Republican. Episcopalian

NEVINNY-STICKEL, HANS BORIS, oncologist; b. Jan. 12, 1927; MD, Leopold Franzen's U., Innsbruck, Austria, 1951; SM in Hygiene, Harvard U., 1961. Rsch. fellow, assoc. Harvard Med. Sch., 1958-70; rsch. assoc. Children's Cancer Rsch. Found. and Peter Bent Brigham Hosp., Boston, 1963-70; clin. asst., assoc. prof. U. Ill., Chgo., 1970-87; assoc. prof. hematology/oncology sect. U. Chgo., 1988-89; dir. Alfred Strauss Tumor Inst. L.A. Weiss Meml. Hosp., Chgo., 1970-89; chief med. oncology Cancer Treatment of Tulsa, 1990—. Contbr. articles to profl. publs. and chpts. to books, including Cancer Rsch., Cancer Chemotherapy Reports, Jour. of AMA, Am. Jour. Surgery. Bd. dirs. Uptown br. Am. Cancer Soc., 1970-89. Mem. Am. Assn. for Cancer Rsch., Am. Soc. Oncology, Am. Assn. for Cancer Edn. Office: Meml Med Ctr and Cancer Inst 2408 E 81st St Ste 100 Tulsa OK 74137-4222 E-mail: hans.nevinny@ctcoftulsa.com.

NEVINS, ARTHUR GERARD, JR., lawyer; b. Bklyn., Dec. 23, 1948; s. Arthur Gerard Sr. and Gertrude Anna May (Schlueter) N.; m. Reine T. Hughes, June 26, 1982; m. Amanda Mitchell, May 16, 1989. BS, Cornell U., 1971; JD, Fordham U., 1974. Bar: N.Y. 1975, N.J. 1976. Assoc. Lester, Schwab, Katz & Dwer, N.Y.C., 1975-77, Law Offices of Peter De Blasio, N.Y.C., 1977-80, Law Offices of Robert Ginsberg, N.Y.C., 1980-82; pvt. practice N.Y.C., 1982—. Mem. ABA, N.Y. State Bar Assn., N.J. Bar Assn., N.Y. County Bar Assn., Hudson County Bar Assn., Phi Gamma Delta. Roman Catholic. Home: 41 Charlestown Rd Hampton NJ 08827-2781 Office: 138 Central Ave Jersey City NJ 07306-2119 also: 225 Broadway Ste 3111 New York NY 10007-3001

NEVINS, JOHN J. bishop; b. New Rochelle, N.Y., Jan. 19, 1932; Student, Iona Coll., N.Y., Cath. U. Washington, Tulane U. Ordained priest Roman Cath. Ch., 1959. Ordained titular bishop of Rusticana and aux. bishop Diocese of Miami, 1979—84; first bishop Diocese of Venice, Fla., 1984—. Office: PO Box 2006 1000 Pinebrook Rd Venice FL 34292

NEVINS, LYN (CAROLYN A. NEVINS), educational supervisor, trainer, consultant; b. Chelsea, Mass., June 9, 1948; d. Samuel Joseph and Stella Theresa (Maronski) N.; m. John Edward Herbert, Jr., May 1, 1979; children: Chrissy, Johnny. BA in Sociology, Edn., U. Mass., 1970; MA in Women's Studies, George Washington U., 1975. Cert. tchr., trainer. Tchr. social studies Greenwich (Conn.) Pub. Schs., 1970-74; rschr. career/vocat. edn. Conn. State Dept. Edn., Hartford, 1975-76; rschr., career/vocat. edn. Area Coop. Edn. Svcs., Hamden, Conn., 1976-77; program mgr., trainer career edn. and gender equity Coop. Ednl. Svcs., Norwalk, Conn., 1977-83, trainer, mgr., devel., Beginning Educator Support and Tng. program Fairfield, Conn., 1987—; state coord. career edn. Conn. State Dept. Edn., Hartford, 1982-83; supr. Sacred Heart U., Fairfield, 1992—. Bias com. Conn. State Dept. Edn., Hartford, 1981—; vision com. Middlesex Mid. Sch., Darien, Conn., 1993-95; mem. ednl. quality and diversity com. Town of Darien, 1993-95; cons., trainer career devel./pre-retirement planning Cohen and Assocs., Fairfield, 1981—, Farren Assocs., Annandale, Va., 1992—, Tracey Robert Assocs., Fairfield, 1994—; freelance cons., trainer, Darien, 1983-87; presenter Nat. Conf. GE, 1980, Career Edn., 1983, Am. Edn. Rsch. Assn., 1991; lectr. in field. Tennis coach Spl. Olympics, 1993—, Darien (Conn.) Girls' Softball League, 1992-96, tennis coord. Spl. Olympics Summer Games, 1997—; mem. bldg. com. Darien (Conn.) High Sch., 1999—. Mem. NOW (founder, state coord. edn. 1972-74), ASCD. Avocations: tennis, running, walking, golf, travel. Home: 4 Hollister Ln Darien CT 06820-5404 Office: Coop Ednl Svcs 40 Lindeman Drive Trumbull CT 06611-4723

NEVINS, SHEILA, television programmer and producer; b. N.Y.C. d. Benjamin and Stella Nevins; m. Sidney Koch; 1 child, David Andrew. BA, Barnard Coll.; MFA, Yale U. TV prodr. Great Am. Dream Machine, NET, 1971-73, The Reasoner Report, ABC, 1973, Feeling Good, Children's TV Workshop, 1975-76, Who's Who, CBS, 1977-78; dir. documentary and family programming HBO, N.Y.C., 1978-82; v.p. documentary programming Home Box Office, N.Y.C., 1986-95, sr. v.p. original programming, 1998-99; exec. v.p. original programming HBO, N.Y.C., 1999—2003, pres. documentary and family, 2004—. Bd. dirs. Film Forum, Creative Capital, Ind. Feature Project. Bd. dirs. Women's Action Alliance. Named Woman of Achievement YMCA, 1991, Top 25 Women in TV, Emmy mag., 1996, Top 25 Smartest Women Am., Mirabella Mag., 1999; named one of Top 50 Women in TV, Hollywood Reporter Mag.; named to Broadcasting and Cable Hall of Fame, 2000; recipient Peabody award, 1986, 1992, 1995, 1996, 1997, 1999, 2000, 2003, Glaad Media award, 1989, Acad. Award for Documentary, 1993, 1996, 1998, 1999, 2000, 2001, 2003, Emmy award, 1994, 1995, 1996, 1997, 1998, 1999, 2000, 2002, 2003, Media award Mental Health Assn. N.Y.C., 1996, Personal Peabody award, 1999, NATAS Silver Cir., 2000, Wellness Cmty. award, 2001, Humanitarian award, Nat. Bd. Rev., 2002, Lucy award, Women in Film, 2003, Three Arts award. Mem.: Internt. Documentary Assn. (Vision award 1998), N.Y. Women in Film (Muse award 1998), Writers Guild Am.

NEVINS, WILLIAM J. oil and gas brokerage executive, consultant; b. Yonkers, N.Y., Sept. 16, 1952; s. Francis Robert and Alice Frances (Stager) N.; m. Joan Evelyn Leach, June 8, 1975 (div. June, 1980). BA in English Lit. and Fin., U. Miami, Coral Gables, Fla., 1974; postgrad. studies in Law, Western State U., Fullerton, Calif., 1974-75. CEO Nevins Enterprises Ltd., various cities, U.S., 1976—; CEO, pres. Century 21, Heritage Realty, Inc., North Miami, Fla., 1985-87, N&Z, Heritage Realty, Inc., Miami, 1987-96; sr. assoc., registered rep. Texakoma Fin. Oil and Gas, 1996-98; oil and gas broker Western Am. Securities, Reef Exploration, Inc., 1998—2001, v.p., 1998-2001, sr. v.p., 2001—, Geo Cos. of N.A. Inc., 2002—; oil and gas broker, sr. v.p. GeoSecurities Inc., 2002—, Geo Natural Resources, Inc., 2002—; sr. v.p. Geo Cos. of N.Am., Inc., 2002—03, Prolific Energy, LLC, 2003; exec. dir. Am. Landmark Securities, Inc./ Prodigy Oil & Gas, LLC, 2004—. V.p., bd. dirs. Pyramid Fin. Svcs., Inc., North Miami Beach, Fla., 1982; cons. Park West Overtown Devel. Com., Miami, 1984—85, Miami Beach Developers and Investors Conf., 1985—90. Author: Oil Patch and Oilmen. Vol. asst. mgr. John V. Lindsay Miami Dem. Primary Campaign. 1972; founder Universal Children's Found. Inc., 1995. Mem. Nat. Assn. Security Dealers (registered rep.), Security Investment Protection Corp. Orgn., Nu Beta Epsilon. Roman Catholic. Avocations: game fishing, antique autos, coin collecting/numismatics, travel, yachting. Office: Nevins Enterprises Ltd 13237 Montfort Dr Ste 438 Dallas TX 75240-1117 Office Phone: 800-655-0606 ext. 107. E-mail: wjnevins@yahoo.com.

NEVLING, HARRY REED, human resources consultant; b. Rochester, Minn., Sept. 15, 1946; s. Edwin Reid and Ruth Margaret (Mulvihill) N.; m. Joanne Carol Meyer, Nov. 26, 1976; 1 son, Terry John. AA, Rochester C.C., 1973; BA cum laude, U. Winona, 1974; MBA, U. Colo., 1990. Pers. rep. Rochester Meth. Hosp., 1974-75, dist. mgr. Internat. Dairy Queen Corp., 1975-76; with David Realty Corp., Littleton, Colo., 1976-83, v.p., 1979-83, gen. mgr., 1981-83, Longmont (Colo.) United Hosp., 1977-99, pers. dir., 1977-87, dir. human resources, 1988-95, v.p. human resources, 1995-99; prin. HR Cons., Rochester, Minn., 1999—. Cons. Front Range C.C. Denver, 1983-85; prin. Harry R. Nevling-Broker, 1983-85, 95-97; v.p. Realty Mart Internat., Inc., 1985-93, Dist. chmn. Am. party, 1973-74, St. Vrain Valley Sch. Dist., Health Occupations Adv. Com. 1977-99, chmn. 1979-85, Vocat. Edn. Adv. Coun. 1986-91, pres. 1986-91; with Citizen Amb. People to People Program, Hungary, Czech Republic, Germany, 1991; mem. exec. com. Nat. Health Care Skills Stds. Project, 1993-95; spkr., presenter in field. Co-author: Healthcare Reform: The Human Resources Cornerstone to Successful Reform, 1992. Served to capt. U.S. Army, 1965-72; Vietnam. Decorated D.F.C., Bronze Star with oakleaf cluster, Air medal (22, valor device). Recipient Rescue citation for lifesaving Boeing Co., 1969, Helping Hand award United Way, 1974, Outstanding Svc. award, 1979, cert. of appreciation, 1982, Disting. Young Alumni award Winona State U., 1989. Mem. VFW (past post comdr.), Longmont Area Human Resources Assn., 1980-89, Boulder Area Human Resource Assn., 1978-2000, Mountain States VHA (pers. com. 1989-96, chmn. 1989-93), Colo. Healthcare Assn. for Human Resource Mgmt. (sec. 1980, pres. elect 1981, pres. 1981-82, exec. com. 1986-2000), Am. Soc. for Healthcare Human Resources Adminstrn. (ann. meeting chmn. 1985-86, regional dir. 1986-90, legis. and labor liaison 1988-90, chpt. rels. com. 1990-91, pres. elect 1991-92, pres. 1992-93, immediate past pres. 1993-95, exec. com. 1991-95, chmn. nominating com. 1994-95, chmn. conflict of interest com., 1994-95, nat. nominating com. 1996, Bylaws com. 1992-93, 96-99, Disting. Svc. award 1996), Soc. Human Resource Mgmt., Human Resource Cert. Inst. (sr. profl. in human resources), Vietnam Helicopter Pilots Assn., Bus. Dependent Care Assn. 1995-99, (pres. 1996) (chmn. inequities subcom. 2003- Region 10 Stakeholders, 2002— QAT mbr 2003-, mentor, 2003—, VOICE ref. com., 2003—, leader brain injury subgroup, 2003—, brain injury cmty. coun. mem. 2003-). Home and Office: 1916 Century Hills Dr NE Rochester MN 55906-7623

NEW, ANNE LATROBE, retired public relations executive; b. Evanston, Ill., May 10, 1910; d. Charles Edward and Agnes (Bateman) N.; m. John C. Timmerman, Sept. 30, 1933; 1 child, Jan LaTrobe. AB, U. S.C., 1930; postgrad., Hunter Coll., 1930-31, NYU, 1932-33. APR (Accredited Pub. Relations Practitioner). Editl. asst. Pictorial Review Mag., N.Y.C., 1930—32; copy asst. J. Walter Thompson Co., N.Y.C., 1932—33; sub editor Cosmopolitan Mag., N.Y.C., 1933—37; with Girl Scouts of the U.S., N.Y.C., 1937—57, chief pub. rels. officer, 1945—57; dir. pub. info. edn. Nat. Recreation and Park Assn., 1957—66; special asst. gen. dir. Internat. Social Svc. Am. Branch, N.Y.C., 1966—68; dir. devel. Nat. Accreditation Coun. for Agys. Serving Blind and Visually Handicapped, N.Y.C., 1969—78; pres. Timmerman & New Inc., Mamaroneck, NY, 1980—2001; ret., 2001. Cons. dept. pub. adminstrn. Baruch Coll., CUNY, 1987-94, Sch. Pub. Affairs, 1994-99. Author: Service For Givers, The Story of the National Information Bureau, 1983, Raise More Money for Your Nonprofit Organization, 1991; contbr. articles to profl. jours. Bd. dirs. Mamaroneck (N.Y.) United Fund, 1963-64; chair nominating com. LWV, Mamaroneck, 1988; warden emerita St. Thomas' Episc. Ch., Mamaroneck. Recipient Marzella Garland award for outstanding achievement in promotion of improved housing conditions in Mamaroneck Village, 1995. Mem. Pub. Rels. Soc. Am. (bd. dirs. N.Y. chpt. 1958-72), Women Execs. Pub. Rels. (sec. 1962-63), Assn. Fundraising Profls. (bd. dirs. Greater N.Y. chpt. 1978-84), Phi Beta Kappa. Democrat.

NEW, MARIA IANDOLO, pediatrician, educator; b. N.Y.C. d. Loris J. and Esther B. (Giglio) Iandolo; m. Bertrand L. New, 1949 (dec. 1990); children: Erica, Daniel, Antonia. BA, Cornell U., 1950; MD, U. Pa., 1954; degree in medicine (hon.), U. degli Studi di Roma, Rome, 1999, U. di Parma, Italy, 2000. Diplomate Am. Bd. Pediat. Med. intern Bellevue Hosp., N.Y.C., 1954-55; resident in pediat. N.Y. Hosp., 1955-57; fellow NIH, 1957-58, 61-64; practice medicine specializing in pediat. N.Y.C., 1955—; mem. staff N.Y. Hosp., dir. Pediatric Endocrine and Metabolism Clinic, 1964—, attending pediatrician, 1971-80; pediatrician-in-chief N.Y.-Presbyn. Hosp., 1980—2002, dir. pediatric endocrinology, 1998—2002; prof. pediat. Mt. Sinai Sch. Medicine, N.Y.C. Asst. prof. dept. pediat. Joan and Sanford Weill Med. Coll. of Cornell U., N.Y.C., 1963-68, assoc. prof., 1968-71, prof., 1971—, Harold and Percy Uris prof. pediatric endocrinology, 1978-2004, prof., 1980-, chmn. dept. pediat., 1980-2002; program dir. Childrens Clin. Rsch. Ctr., 1996-2002; assoc. dir. Pediatric Clin. Rsch. Ctr., 1980-88; adj. faculty prof. Rockefeller U., 1981—; career scientist N.Y.C. Health Rsch. Coun., 1966-75; adj. attending pediatrician dept. pediat. Meml. Sloan-Kettering Cancer Ctr., 1979-93; cons. United Hosp., Port Chester, N.Y., 1977—, North Shore Univ. Hosp., 1982-97, dept. pediat. Cath. Med. Ctr. Bklyn. and Queens, N.Y., 1987—; vis. physician Rockefeller U. Hosp., N.Y.C., 1973-87; mem. endocrine study sect. NIH, 1977-80, Gen. Clin. Rsch. Ctrs. Adv. Com.; chmn. Divsn. Rsch. Resources Gen. Clin. Rsch. Ctrs. Com. NIH, 1987-88; bd. dirs. Robert Wood Johnson Clin. Scholars Program; mem. N.Y. State Gov.'s Task Force on Life and Law, 1985—; mem. NIH Reviewers Res.; mem. FDA endocrinology and metabolism drug adv. com., 1994—; panelist ACGME bd. appeals, 1994—; cons. Meml. Sloan-Kettering Cancer Ctr., 1993—, Meml. Hosp. for the Cancer and Allied Diseases, 1993—; hon. mem. pediat. dept. Blythedale Children's Hosp., Valhalla, N.Y., 1992—; mem. rsch. adv. com. Population Coun. Ctr. for Biomed. Rsch., 1991-97. Editor-in-chief Jour. Clin. Endocrinology and Metabolism, 1994-99; mem. editl. adv. coun. Jour. Endocrinological Investigation, 1995—; mem. editl. bd. Jour. Women's Health, 1993, Endotext; corr. editor Jour. Steroid Biochemistry, 1985; mem. adv. bd. pediatric anns., assoc. editor Metabolism. Trustee Irma T. Hirschl Trust. Recipient Mary Jane Kugel award Juvenile Diabetes Found., 1977, Katharine D. McCormick Disting. Lectureship, 1981, Robert H. Williams Disting. Leadership award, 1988, Albion O. Bernstein award Med. Soc. State N.Y., 1988, medal N.Y. Acad. Medicine, 1991, Disting. Grad. award U. Pa. Sch. Medicine, 1991, Optimate Recognition award Assn. Student-Profl. Italian-Ams., 1991, Outstanding Woman Scientist award N.Y. chpt. Am. Women in Sci., 1986, Maurice R. Greenberg Disting. Svc. award, 1994, Humanitarian award Juvenile Diabetes Found., 1994, Rhône Poulenc Rorer Clin. Investigator Lecture award, 1994, Dale medal Brit. Endocrine Soc., 1996, MERIT award USPHS, NIHCHD, 1998, 11th Ann. award for excellence in clin. rsch. USPHS, NIH, 1998; grantee; named to Hall of Honor, NICHD, 2003. Fellow AAAS, Italian Soc. Endocrinology (hon.); mem. NAS (sr. mem. Inst. Medicine), AAAS, APHA, Am. Soc. Human Genetics, Am. Acad. Pediat., Soc. for Pediatric Rsch., Harvey Soc., Endocrine Soc. (mem. coun. 1981-84, pres. 1991-92, Fred Conrad Koch award), Lawson Wilkins Pediatric Endocrine Soc. (pres. 1985-86), Am. Soc. Nephrology, Am. Soc. Pediatric Nephrology, Am. Pediatric Soc., Am. Fedn. Clin. Rsch., Am. Diabetes Assn., European Soc. Pediatric Endocrinology, Soc. for the Advancement of Women's Health Rsch. (basic sci. award 1996), Am. Coll. Clin. Pharmacology, Am. Clin. and Climatol. Assn., N.Y. Acad. Scis., Pan Am. Med. Assn., Assn. Am. Physicians, Am. Fertility Soc., U.S. Pharmacopeial Conv. (elected), Am. Acad. of Arts and Scis. (elected 1992), Alpha Omega Alpha. Office: Mt Sinai Sch Medicine Box 1198 1 Gustav L Levy Pl New York NY 10029 Office Phone: 212-241-7847. E-mail: maria.new@mssm.edu.

NEW, ROSETTA HOLBROCK, home economics educator, nutrition consultant; b. Aug. 26, 1921; d. Edward F. and Mabel (Kohler) Holbrock; m. John Lorton New, Sept. 3, 1943; 1 child, John Lorton Jr. BS, Miami U., Oxford, Ohio, 1943; MA, U. No. Colo., 1971; PhD, Ohio State U., 1974; student, Kantcentrum, Brugge, Belgium, 1992, Lesage Sch. Embroidery, Paris, 1995, Kent State U., 1998. Cert. tchr. Colo. Tchr. English and sci. Monahans (Tex.) H.S., 1943—54; emergency war food asst. USDA, College Station, Tex., 1945—46; dept. chmn. home econs., adult edn. Hamilton (Ohio) Pub. Schs., 1946—47; tchr., dept. chmn. home econs. East H.S., Denver, 1948—59, Thomas Jefferson H.S., Denver, 1959—83. Exec. bd. Denver Pub. Schs.; lectr. in field; exec. dir. Ctr. Nutrition Info. U.S. Office Edn. Grantee, Ohio State U., 1971—73. Mem.: Internat. Platform Assn., Fairfield (Ohio) Hist. Soc., Ohio State Home Econs. Alumni Assn., Ohio State U. Assn., Hamilton Hist. Soc.,

Am. Vocat. Assn., Am. Home Econs. Assn., Nat. Trust for Hist. Preservation, Cin. Art Mus., Internat. Old Lacers, Embroiders Guild Am., Rep. Club Denver, Order White Shrine of Jerusalem, Daus. of the Nile, Masons, Order of Ea. Star, Phi Upsilon Omicron. Presbyterian. Home and Office: 615 Crescent Rd Hamilton OH 45013-3432 Office Phone: 513-858-2411.

NEW, THOMAS L. public affairs, consultant; b. Greenfield, Ind., Apr. 4, 1951; m. Deborah R. New; 1 child, Emily R. BA cum laude, Harvard U., 1973; MAT, U. Chgo., 1974; M of Pub. Policy, Harvard U., 1984. Tchr. social scis. and humanities Maine Twp. H.S. South, Park Ridge, Ill., 1974-81; spl. asst. U.S. Senator Alan J. Dixon, Washington, 1982; tchg. fellow Johns F. Kennedy Sch. Govt./Harvard U., Cambridge, Mass., 1983-84; fiscal policy adivosr Ind. Senate Dem. Caucus, Indpls., 1984-88; exec. asst. for policy devel. Office of Lt. Gov. of Ind., Indpls., 1989-92, chief of staff, 1992-95, Office of Gov. of Ind., Indpls., 1997—2000; exec. dir. govt. affairs Krieg DeVault LLP, 2000—. Dem. candidate Ind. State Treas., 1997—2000; campaign mgr. Gov. Frank O'Bannon, 1996, 2000.

NEW, WILLIAM NEIL, physician, retired naval officer; b. Atoka, Okla., Oct. 24, 1908; s. Robert Calvin and Nommar Bell (Willmore) N.; m. Ruth Anderson Pride, Mar. 30, 1940. BA, Central State Tchrs. Coll., Edmond, Okla., 1931; BS in Medicine, U. Okla., 1932, MD, 1934; postgrad., Northwestern U. Med. Sch., 1947-48. Diplomate: Am. Bd. Dermatology and Syphilology. Intern So. Pacific R.R. Hosp., San Francisco, 1934-35; commd. lt. (j.g.), M.C. U.S. Navy, 1935, advanced through grades to rear adm., 1963; resident dermatology and syphilology Naval Hosp., Phila., 1946-47; med. officer on gunboat and USMC Hosp., Shanghai, 1937-39; regtl. surgeon 7th Marines in Guadalcanal; later div. surgeon 5th Marine Div. (Japanese occupation), 1945; established Naval Med. Field Research Lab., Camp Lejeune, 1943; chief dermatology services naval hosps. Great Lakes, Ill., 1948-51, Phila., 1951-53, San Diego, 1956-59; force surgeon Fleet Marine Force, Pacific, 1954-56; comdg. officer U.S. Naval Hosp., Yokusuka, Japan, 1959-62; dir. staff Office Dep. Asst. Sec. Def. for Health and Med., 1962-66; pvt. practice dermatology Dallas Med. and Surg. clinic, 1968-91; ret., 1991. Clin. assoc. prof. dermatology Southwestern Med. Sch., U. Tex., Dallas, 1966-92. Mem. ACP (life), Am. Acad. Dermatology (life), Pacific Dermatol. Assn. (life), Assn. Mil. Dermatologists (past pres.), N.Am. Clin. Dermatol. Soc. (co-founder, life), Space Dermatol. Found. (co-founder), Cutaneous Therapy Soc. (co-founder, life). Home: 5826 Walnut Hill Lane Dallas TX 75230 *Love and live today as we plan a rewarding tomorrow.*

NEWACHECK, PAUL W. medical educator, researcher; s. Franklin William Newacheck and Lois Elaine Abrahamson. AB in Econs., U. Calif., Berkeley, 1974, M in Pub. Policy, 1976, DPH, 1989. Prof. of health policy Inst. for Health Policy Studies, UCSF, San Francisco, 1992—; prof. of pediat. Dept. of Pediat., UCSF, San Francisco, 1992—. Mem. editl. adv. bd. The Future of Children, 1990—, mem. editl. bd. Health Services Rsch., 1998—, Ambulatory Pediatrics, 1999—, Children's Services: Social Policy, Rsch. and Practice, 1999—, contbr. articles to profl. jours. including The New England Jour. of Medicine. Adv. com. mem. Nat. Com. of Vital and Health Stats., US HHS, 1997—2002; bd. mem. Nat. Acad. of Sci., Washington, 1993—99, Am. Acad. of Pediat., Elk Grove Village, Ill., 1998—2000, Ctr. on Children's Health Rsch., Washington, 1998. Recipient Health Services Rsch. award for excellence in health services rsch. on behalf of children, The Am. Acad. of Pediatric Dentistry Found., 2001, Friend of Children award, for improving the lives of children with spl. health care needs, Family Voices, 2001, Disting. Tchg. award, Divsn. of Health and Med. Sciences, Sch. of Pub. Health, UC Berkeley, 1994, 1996; Fellow, Acad. for Health Svc. Rsch. and Health Policy, 1997. Fellow: Ambulatory Pediat. Assn., Acad. of Health Services Rsch. and Health Policy; mem.: APHA. Achievements include work contributing to changes in federal health care policies for children with special health care needs. Avocation: nature photography. Office: University of California San Francisco 3333 California Street #265 San Francisco CA 94118 Office Phone: 415-476-3896. Business E-Mail: pauln@itsa.ucsf.edu.

NEWBAUER, JOHN ARTHUR, editor; b. Newport, R.I., Apr. 24, 1928; s. John Arthur and Theo Caroline (Trewhella) N.; m. Marilyn Mahler, Oct. 14, 1956; children: April, Dana, Miranda. BA, U. Calif., Berkeley, 1951. Sr. editor and writer sci. and engring., rocket devel. dept. U.S. Naval Ordnance Test Sta., China Lake, Calif., 1951-56; editor in chief Astronautics and Aeronautics jour., N.Y.C., 1963-83; adminstr. sci. publs. AIAA, 1983-91, cons. editor, 1991—; editor in chief Aerospace Am., 1983-87, aquisitions editor, 1987-89. Fellow AIAA (assoc.), Brit. Interplanetary Soc. Home: 356 Bay Ridge Ave Brooklyn NY 11220-5315

NEWBERG, DOROTHY BECK (MRS. WILLIAM C. NEWBERG), portrait artist; b. Detroit, May 30, 1919; d. Charles William and Mary (Labedz) Beck; student Detroit Conservatory Music, 1938; m. William C. Newberg, Nov. 3, 1939; children: Judith Bookwalter Bracken, Robert Charles, James William, William Charles. Trustee Detroit Adventure, 1967-71, originator A Drop in Bucket Program for artistically talented inner-city children. Cmty. outreach coord. Reno Police Dept.; bd. dirs. Bloomfield Art Assn., 1960-62, trustee 1965-67; bd. dirs. Your Heritage House, 1972-75, Franklin Wright Settlement, 1972-75, Meadowbrook Art Gallery, Oakland U., 1973-75, Sierra Nevada Mus. Art, 1978-80, NCCJ; mem. adv. bd. Gang Alternatives Partnership Adv. Bd. Recipient Heart of Gold award, 1969; Mich. vol. leadership award, 1969, Outstanding Vol. award City of Reno, 1989-90. Mem. Nevada Mus. Art, No. Nev. Black Cultural Awareness Soc. (bd. dirs.), Hispanic 500 C. of C. No. Nev. Roman Catholic. Home: PO Box 18527 Reno NV 89511-0527

NEWBERG, ESTHER, literary agent; d. Marion Newberg. MA, Wheaton Coll., Norton, Mass., 1963, hon. degree, 2003. Worked with Gov. Ella Grasso, Conn., Robert F. Kennedy, Bella Abzug, Morris Udall Presdl. Campaign, 1976; joined Internat. Creative Mgmt., N.Y.C., 1976, v.p., co-dir. lit. dept., 1988, sr. v.p., co-dir. lit. dept. Recipient Matrix Award, N.Y. Women in Comm., 1997. Office: Internat Creative Mgmt 40 W 57th St New York NY 10019*

NEWBERG, WILLIAM CHARLES, stock broker, real estate broker, automotive engineer; b. Seattle, Dec. 17, 1910; s. Charles John and Anna Elizabeth (Anderson) N.; BSME, U. Wash., 1933; MME, Chrysler Inst. Engring., 1935; LLB (hon.), Parsons Coll., 1958; m. Dorothy Beck, Nov. 3, 1939; children: Judith N. Newberg Bookwalter, Robert Charles, James William, William Charles. Salesman, Am. Auto Co., Seattle, 1932-33; student engr. Chrysler Corp., Detroit, 1933-35, exptl. engr., 1935-42, chief engr. Chgo. plant, 1942-45, mem. subs. ops. staff, Detroit, 1945-47, pres. airtemp. divsn., Dayton, Ohio, 1947-50, v.p., dir. Dodge divsn., Detroit, 1950-51, pres. Dodge divsn., 1951-56, group v.p., Detroit, 1956-58, exec. v.p., 1958-60, pres., 1960; corp. dir. Detroit Bank & Trust, Detroit, 1955-60; corp. cons., Detroit, 1960-76; realtor Myers Realty, Inc., Reno, 1976-79; owner Bill Newberg Realty, 1979—; account exec. Allied Capital Corp., Reno, 1980—; chmn. Newberg Corp., 1982; treas. Perfect "10" Industries. Elder, St. John's Presbyn. Ch., Reno, 1976—; mem. exec. bd. Detroit Area coun. Boy Scouts Am., 1955-74, Nev. Area coun. Boy Scouts Am., 1976—; Mich. state chmn. March of Dimes, 1967-68. Mem. Soc. Automotive Engrs., Am. Def. Preparedness Assn. (life), Automotive Orgn. Team (life), U. Wash. Alumni Assn. (life), Newcomen Soc., Franklin Inst., Alpha Tau Omega. Clubs: Prospectors, Harley Owners Group.

NEWBERN, WILLIAM DAVID, retired state supreme court justice; b. Oklahoma City, May 28, 1937; s. Charles Banks and Mary Frances (Harding) N.; m. Barbara Lee Rigsby, Aug. 19, 1961 (div. 1968); 1 child, Laura Harding; m. Carolyn Lewis, July 30, 1970; 1 child, Alistair Elizabeth. BA, U. Ark., 1959, JD, 1961; LL.M., George Washington U., 1963; MA, Tufts U., 1967. Bar: Ark. 1961, U.S. Dist. Ct. (we. dist.) Ark. 1961, U.S. Supreme Ct. 1968, U.S. Ct. Appeals (8th cir.) 1983. Commd. 1st lt. advanced to maj. U.S. Army JAGC, 1961-70; Prof. law U. Ark., Fayetteville, 1970-84; adminstr. Ozark Folk Ctr., Mountain View, Ark., 1973; judge Ark. Ct. Appeals, Little Rock, 1979-80; assoc. justice Ark. Supreme Ct., Little Rock, 1985-99. Mem. faculty sr. appellate judges seminar NYU, 1987-91; panel chmn. com. on profl. conduct Ark. Supreme Ct., 2001—. Editor Ark. Law Rev., 1961; author: Arkansas Civil Practice and Procedure, 1985, (with John J. Watkins) 3d edit., 2003. Mem. Fayetteville Bd. Adjustment, 1972-79; bd. dirs. Decision Point, Inc., Springdale, Ark., 1980-85, Hot Springs Music Festival, 2000—03; bd. dirs. Little Rock Wind Symphony, 1993-2001, pres. 1993-95. Fellow Ark. Bar Found.; mem. Ark. Bar Assn., Am. Judicature Soc. (bd. dirs. 1985-89), Inst. Jud. Adminstrn., Ark. IOLTA Found. (bd. dirs. 1985-87). Democrat. Avocations: string band-guitar, mandolin, banjo and brass quintet-tuba. Personal E-mail: dnewbern@aristotle.net.

NEWBERRY, CONRAD FLOYDE, aerospace engineering educator; b. Neodesha, Kans., Nov. 10, 1931; s. Ragan McGregor and Audra Anitia (Newmaster) N.; m. Sarah Louise Thonn, Jan. 26, 1958; children: Conrad Floyde Jr., Thomas Edwin, Susan Louise. AA, Independence Jr. Coll., 1951; BEME with aero. sequence, U. So. Calif., 1957; MSME, Calif. State U., Los Angeles, 1971, MA in Edn., 1974; D.Environ. Sci. and Engring., UCLA, 1985. Registered profl. engr., Calif., Kans., N.C., Tex.; chartered engr., U.K. Mathematician L.A. divsn. N.Am. Aviation Inc., 1951-53, jr. engr., 1953-54, engr., 1954-57, sr. engr., 1957-64; asst. prof. aerospace engring. Calif. State Poly. U., Pomona, 1964-70, assoc. prof. aerospace engring., 1970-75, prof. aerospace engring., 1975-90, prof. emeritus, 1990—; staff engr. EPA, 1980-82; engring. specialist space transp. systems div. Rockwell Internat. Corp., 1984-90; prof. aeronautics and astronautics Naval Postgrad. Sch., Monterey, Calif., 1990—2002, prof. emeritus, 2002—, acad. assoc. space systems engring., 1992-94. Recipient John Leland Atwood award as outstanding aerospace engring. educator AIAA/Am. Soc. Engring. Edn., 1986, Fred Merryfield Design award ASEE, 1997. Fellow: AIAA (dep. dir. edn. region VI 1976—79, dep. dir. career enhancement 1982—91, chmn. L.A. sect. 1989—90, chmn. acad. affairs com. 1990—93, dir.tech. aircraft sys. 1990—93, chmn. Point Lobos sect. 1990—91, 1999—2001); mem.: IEEE, ASME, AAAS, NSPE, Am. Soc. Naval Engrs., Nat. Assn. Environ. Profls., Calif. Water Pollution Control Assn., Assn. Unmanned Vehicle Sys. Internat., Soc. Allied Weight Engrs., Soc. Automotive Engr., Water Environ. Fedn., Exptl. Aircraft Assn., Inst. Environ. Scis., Air and Waste Mgmt. Assn., Soc. Naval Architects and Marine Engrs., Am. Helicopter Soc., U.S. Naval Inst., Am. Meteorol. Soc., Am. Soc. Pub. Adminstrn., Am. Soc. Engring. Edn. (divsn. exec. com. 1976—80, chmn. aerospace divsn. 1979—80, exec. com. ocean, marine engring. divsn. 1982—85, newsletter editor 1982—87, divsn. exec. com. 1989—94, exec. com. ocean, marine engring. divsn. 1990—97, program chmn. 1991—93, chmn. 1993—95, chmn. Profl Interest Coun. 1995—97, bd. dirs. 1995—97, trustee 1999—2002), Am. Acad. Environ. Engrs. (cert. air pollution control engr.), Calif. Soc. Profl. Engrs., Royal Aero. Soc., Inst. Advancement Engring., Brit. Interplanetary Soc., Planetary Soc., SAFE, SID, Kappa Delta Pi, Sigma Gamma Tau, Tau Beta Pi. Democrat. Achievements include research on aircraft, spacecraft, missiles, and engine design, waveriders, aircrew centered system design and related impacts on exergy, quality, concurrent engineering, cost and environmental controls. Home: 9463 Willow Oak Rd Salinas CA 93907-1037 Office: Naval Postgrad Sch Dept Aeronautics Astronautics AA/Ne 699 Dyer Rd Monterey CA 93943-5106

NEWBLATT, STEWART ALBERT, federal judge; b. Detroit, Dec. 23, 1927; s. Robert Abraham and Fanny Ida (Grinberg) N.; m. Flora Irene Sandweiss, Mar. 5, 1965; children: David Jacob, Robert Abraham, Joshua Isaac. BA with distinction, U. Mich., 1950, JD with distinction, 1952. Bar: Mich. 1953. Ptnr. White & Newblatt, Flint, Mich., 1953-62; judge 7th Jud. Cir. Mich., 1962-70; ptnr. Newblatt & Grossman (and predecessor), Flint, 1970-79; judge U.S. Dist. Ct. (ea. dist.) Mich., Flint, 1979-93, sr. judge, 1993—. Adj. instr. U. Mich.-Flint, 1977-78, 86. Mem. Internat. Bridge Authority Mich., 1960-62. Served with AUS, 1946-47. Mem. Fed. Bar Assn., State Bar Mich., Dist. Judges Assn. 6th Circuit. Jewish. Office: PO Box 522 Glen Arbor MI 49636-0522

NEWBOLD, JOHN LOWE, retired banker, financial consultant; b. Washington, Dec. 26, 1935; s. John Lowe and Katharine Emily (Wilkins) N.; m. Judith Allen Bourne, June 20, 1959; children: Jennifer Hathaway, Timothy Bourne, Michael Fleming. BS, Yale U., 1957; MBA, NYU, 1963; sr. execs. program cert., MIT, 1970. Asst. v.p., credit instr. Citibank, N.A., N.Y.C., 1968-69, v.p. retail trade unit, 1969-70, v.p. info. svcs. dept., 1970-72, v.p., corp. bank head Tokyo, 1972-73, v.p., country head Singapore, 1974-76, sr. v.p., shipping dept. head N.Y.C., 1976-85, divsn. exec., Global Shipping Divsn., 1985—97, divsn. exec., Global Transp. Divsn., 1989—93; ret., 1997; chmn., dir. Mchts. Fund, Inc., Bethesda, Md., 1981—2003. Bd. dirs. Timex B.V., Netherlands, Castalia Ptnrs. Ltd., Grupo TMM S.A. de C.V. Mex., 1997-2003. Trustee Reeves Reed Arboretum, Summit, N.J., 1999-2002, Summit Area Cmty. Coun., 1983-86, United Way, Summit, 1984-92; pres. PTA Presidents' Coun., Summit, 1981-83; pres., dir. One Fifth Ave. Apt. Corp., 2001—; dir., v.p. Friends of Chilmark Public Libr., Mass, 2003—; vice chmn. Friends of Chilmark Libr., 2003—. Served as lt. (j.g.) USNR, 1957-63. Mem. Yale Club of Ctrl. N.J. (trustee 1980-85). Home: 1 Fifth Ave 11J New York NY 10003 Office Phone: 212-674-5881. Personal E-mail: jocknewb@aol.com.

NEWBORG, GERALD GORDON, state archives administrator; b. Ada, Minn., Dec. 13, 1942; s. George Harold and Olea (Halstad) N.; m. Jean Annette Gruhl, Aug. 14, 1964; children: Erica, Annette. BA, Concordia Coll., Moorhead, Minn., 1964; MA, U. N.D., 1969; MBA, Ohio State U., 1978. Cert. archivist. Tutor, preceptor Parsons Coll., Fairfield, Iowa, 1964-67; state archivist Ohio Hist. Soc., Columbus, 1968-76; v.p. Archival Systems Inc., Columbus, 1978-81; state archivist State Hist. Soc. of N.D., Bismarck, 1981—. Instr. Franklin U., Columbus, 1974; adj. prof. Bismarck State Coll., 1985-86. Co-author: North Dakota: A Pictorial History, 1988. Recipient Resolution of Commendation Ohio Ho. of Reps., Columbus, 1976. Mem. Soc. Am. Archivists, Nat. Assn. Govt. Archives & Records Adminstrs. (bd. dirs. 1984-86, sec. 1994-99), Midwest Archives Conf., N.D. Libr. Assn. (exec. bd. 1985-86). Home: 1327 N 18th St Bismarck ND 58501-2827 Office: State Hist Soc 612 E Boulevard Ave Bismarck ND 58505-0660

NEWBORN, JUD, anthropologist, writer, curator, educator, historian; b. NYC, Nov. 8, 1952; s. Solomon and Rita Newborn. BA magna cum laude in Anthropology and English, NYU, 1974; postgrad., Clare Hall, Cambridge U., 1974-75; MA in Anthropology, U. Chgo., 1977, PhD with distinction, 1994. Free-lance writer, N.Y.C., Munich, Chgo., 1974—; publicist Oxford U. Press, N.Y.C., 1975-76; founding historian Mus. Jewish Heritage (N.Y. Holocaust Meml. Commn.), N.Y.C., 1986-92, 96-00. Cons., spkr., lectr. in field. Author: Shattering the German Night: The Story of the White Rose Anti-Nazi Resistance, 1986, Herder Verlag, 2002; contbg. editor Diplomatic World Obs., UN, 1999-2000; freelance writer, lyricist. Bd. dirs. B'na B'rith United Nations Adv. Coun. Fulbright fellow, 1980-82; Newcombe fellow, 1984-85. Mem. ASCAP, Am. Anthrop. Assn., Am. Hist. Assn., Authors Guild, Assn. Holocaust Orgns., NY Old Growth Forest Assn., Phi Beta Kappa.

NEWBRUN, ERNEST, oral biology and periodontology educator; b. Vienna, Dec. 1, 1932; came to U.S., 1955; s. Victor and Elizabeth (Reichl) N; m. Eva Miriam, June 17, 1956; children: Deborah Anne, Daniel Eric, Karen Ruth. BDS, U. Sydney (New South Wales), 1954; MS, U. Rochester, 1957; DMD, U. Ala., 1959; PhD, U. Calif., San Francisco, 1965; Odont. Dr. (hon.), U. Lund, Sweden, 1988; DDSc (hon.), U. Sydney, 1997. Cert. periodontology, 1983. Rsch. assoc. Eastman Dental Ctr., Rochester, N.Y., 1955-57, U. Ala. Med. Ctr., Birmingham, 1957-59; rsch. fellow Inst. Dental Rsch., Sydney, Australia, 1960-61; rsch. tchr. trainee U. Calif., San Francisco, 1961-63, postdoctoral fellow, 1963-65, assoc. prof., 1965-70, prof. oral biology, 1970-83, prof. oral biology and periodontology, 1983-94, prof. emeritus, 1994—. Cons. FDA, 1983—. Author: Cariology, 1989, Pharmacology and Therapeutic Dentistry, 1989, (with others) Pediatrics, 1991; editor: Fluorides and Dental Caries, 1986; mem. editorial bd. Jour. Periodontal Rsch., 1985-90, Jour. Periodontology, 1990—. Bd. dirs. Raoul Wallenberg Dem. Club, San Francisco, 1987-92. Fellow AAAS (chmn. dental section, 1988-89), Internat. Assn. Dental Rsch. (pres. 1989-90); mem. Dental Health Foun. (chmn. bd. dirs., 1985-92). Jewish. Avocations: gardening, hiking, skiing, opera, theater. Office Phone: 415-476-1004. Business E-Mail: newbrun@itsa.ucff.edu.

NEWBURGER, BETH WEINSTEIN, historical association administrator; b. Schenectady, July 8, 1937; d. H. Edward and Shirley (Diamond) Weinstein; m. Alan C. Newburger, Jan. 23, 1963 (dec. Oct. 1980); children: Mark, Lori, Eric, Jill; m. Richard Schwartz, May 26, 1989. BA, Cornell U., 1959. Dir. advt. New Republic, Washington, 1974-77; mktg. mgr. Washington Post, 1977-84; pres. Owlcat/Digital Rsch., Inc., Monterey, Calif., 1984-86; pres., CEO Corabi Internat. Telemetrics, Inc., Alexandria, Va., 1986-95; assoc. adminstr. Gen. Svcs. Adminstrn., Washington, 1996—2001; dir. comm. Nat. Trust for Hist. Preservation, 2001—. Chmn. bd. Health Street, Inc., Bethesda, Md., 1985—95; mem. NASA adv. coun. Tech. Commercialization Adv. Com., 1995—98; co-chmn. President's Comm. on Celebration of Women in Am. History, 1998—2000; commr., exec. dir. Women's Progress Commemorative Commn., 2000—01; bd. dirs. Nat. Women's History Project, 2000—02; adv. bd. Eleanor Roosevelt Papers, 2000—; bd. dirs. Nat. Women's Hall of Fame, 2001—04; trustee Jewish Women's Archives, 2002—. Chmn. bd. Capital Children's Mus., Washington, 1994—98, trustee, 1984—; bd. dirs. Arena Stage, Washington, 1993—, BOAT/U.S., 1990—. Named Woman of Yr., Svc. Guild, Washington, 1972, 73. Mem. Women in Advt. and Mktg. (bd. dirs. 1986-89). Home: 1401 N Oak St Arlington VA 22209-3648

NEWBURGER, CARYN LASON, English educator; b. Chgo., Aug. 28, 1960; d. Marvin Mitchell and Sandra Woolman Lason; m. Manuel Harry Newburger, Aug. 14, 1983; children: Michael Jonathon, Joshua Ian. BA in English, U. Tex., 1982, postgrad., 1996-97, MEd in Ednl. Psychology, 1989. Cert. counselor; cert. tchr. Tex. Tchr. lang. arts Bastrop (Tex.) Ind. Sch. Dist., 1982-89; assoc. prof. Austin C.C., 2001—. Adj. instr., writing Austin C.C., 1989-2001, assoc. prof. devel. writing, 2001—; adj. rep. Austin C.C., Austin, 1996-2001; ednl. cons., writer Comms. Cons., Norman, Okla., 1989—. Student coun. advisor Bastrop Ind. Sch. Dist., 1983-86, mid. sch. gifted program coord., 1988-89; room parent St. Francis Sch., Austin, 1998-2000; ballet docent Ballet Austin, 1989-90. Recipient Tchg. Excellence award Nat. Inst. for Staff and Orgnl. Devel., 2000. Mem. MLA, Nat. Coun. of Tchrs. of English. Avocations: ballet dancing, writing, gardening. Office: Austin CC 5930 Middle Fiskville Rd Austin TX 78752-4341 E-mail: carynn@austin.cc.tx.us.

NEWBURGER, HOWARD MARTIN, psychoanalyst; b. N.Y.C., May 16, 1924; s. Bernhard and Bertha (Travers) N.; m. Doris Schekter, July 3, 1949; children: Amy, Barry, Cary. BA, NYU, 1948, MA, 1950, PhD, 1952; tng. in Jungian, Neo-Freudian and Horneyian psychoanalysis. Cert. in group psychotherapy and psychodrama. Rotating intern N.J. Dept. Instns. and Agys., 1948-49; chief psychologist N.J. State Instn., Annandale, 1949-52; dir. psychoanalysis Div. Social Def. UN, 1952; pvt. practice in psychoanalysis and group psychotherapy, 1952—; dir. rsch. HEW, 1958; rsch. assoc. Beth Israel Hosp., 1958-69. Staff mem. St. Agnes Hosp., White Plains, 1991-93; lectr., adj. assoc. prof. NYU, 1951-60, chmn. dept. exceptional child and youth, 1954-62; chmn. faculty and supr. treatment Inst. Applied Human Dynamics, 1960-99; prelect prof. psychology John Jay Coll. Criminal Justice, 1969-72; chmn. bd. dirs. Inst. Applied Human Dynamics, N.Y.C. and Westchester, N.Y., 1960-81, exec. v.p., 1983-85; dean faculty IAHD, 1999-2002; lectr., cons. in field. Co-author: Winners and Losers. Assoc. editor: Excerpta Medica, 1951-62. Contbr. articles and papers to tech. jours. Trustee Acad. Jewish Religion, 1991-96. Served with AUS, World War II, ETO; with AUS, MTO. Recipient Outstanding Service to Humanity award Inst. Applied Human Dynamics for Handicapped, 1970 Mem. Am. Psychol. Assn., Am. Soc. Group Psychotherapy and Psychodrama (sec.-treas. 1954-55). Office: 4 Timber Trl Rye NY 10580-1935 *Our country affords tremendous opportunity. Through the development of our inner resources, and their assertion, we can all have happy and effective lives.*

NEWBURY, KIRSTEN RAE, computer scientist, educator; b. Inglewood, Calif., July 20, 1946; d. Ray Selmer and Ella Louise (Carter) Newbury. BS, U. Wis., Oshkosh, 1971; MS, U. Colo., 1980; postgrad., Army War Coll., 1987; EdD in Adult and Higher Edn., EdD, Mont. State U., 1998. Cert. flight instr. FAA. Chief info. svc. Mont. State Dept. Labor and Industry, Helena; dir., personal property and bus. lic. div. County of Fairfax, Va.; analyst officer U.S. Army Pentagon, Washington; battalion commdr. U.S. Army, Frankfurt, Germany, assoc. prof. West Point, NY; adj. tchr. computer tech. Helena Coll. Tech., U. Mont., chmn. computer electronics tech. dept., 2002—03; computer cons., 2004—. Adj. prof. Western Mont. Coll., U. Mont.; del. People-to-People Women Computer Sci. Profls. program, China; coord. 1st statewide program for instrs. new to 2-yr. coll. sys.; faculty practitioner U. Phoenix; faculty fellow for svc. learning Mont. Campus Compact, 1999—2000, mentoring fellow, 2001—03. Del. to China Citizen's Amb. Program, 1993. Lt. col. U.S. Army, 1964—88. Faculty fellow, Mont. Campus Compact, 1999—2000, Mentoring fellow, 2001—02. Mem.: Am. Fedn. Tchrs., Assn. Computing Machinery.

NEWBY, EARL FERNANDO, educator; b. Louisville, Apr. 14, 1948; BS, Tenn. State U., 1970; MA, U. Louisville, 1972; EdD, Spalding U., 1998; MA, Vanderbilt U., 2002. Cons., tchr. edn. Ky. Dept. Edn., Frankfort, 1970; tchr., prin. Jefferson County Schs., Louisville, 1971-75, Greater Clark County Schs., Jeffersonville, Ind., 1975-98; cons., computer tech. Newby & Assocs., Louisville, 1996—; asst. prof. Morehead (Ky.) State U., 1998—. Adj. prof. Western Ky. U., Bowling Green, 1998; prof. Eastern Ky. U., 1999-2004; assoc. prof. Austin Peay State U., Clarksville, Tenn., 2004-2006; apptd. to serve on many scholastic audit sch. rev. teams, 2002—; presenter So. Regional Coun. Ednl. Adminstrs., 2004, Nat. Coun. Profs. of Ednl. Adminstrs., 2004, Internat. Conf. Profs. of Black Sch. Educators, 2004. Author: Leadership Perspectives, 2004; contbr. articles to profl. publs. Named to Order Ky. Cols. Mem. Am. Assn. Sch. Adminstrs. (presenter ann. internat. conf. Orlando, Fla. 2001), NAESP (presenter ann. internat. conf. San Diego, Calif. 2001), So. Regional Coun. Ednl. Adminstrs., Nat. Coun. Profs. Ednl. Adminstrn. (presenter nat. conf. Houston 2001, Sedona, Ariz. 2003), Nat. Assn. Black Sch. Educators, Ky. Assn. Sch. Adminstrs., Ky. Assn. Black Sch. Educators, Lexington Assn. Black Sch. Educators, Kappa Alpha Psi, Phi Delta Kappa, Pi Lambda Theta (presenter profl. assn. in edn. ann. conf. Mpls. 2001), Sigma Rho Sigma. Democrat. Methodist. Avocations: tennis, basketball, reading, bowling, golf. Home: PO Box 211 Harrods Creek KY 40027-0211 Office: Austin Peay State U Educational Leadership Studies Coll Profl Programs and Social Scis Clarksville TN 37044 Fax: 859-622-1126. Office Phone: 502-523-9565.

NEWBY, JOHN ROBERT, metallurgical engineer; b. Kansas City, Mo., Nov. 17, 1923; s. Merritt Owen and Gladys Mary (McCleery) N.; m. Audry Marie Loniker, Sept. 21, 1963 (div. 1980); children: Deborah A., Walter J., William F., Matthew O., Robert J. BA, U. Mo., Kansas City, 1947; BS in Metall. Engring., Colo. Sch. Mines, 1949; MS, U. Cin., 1963. Cert. profl. engr. Chemist Bar Rusto Plating Corp., Kansas City, 1949; supr. United Chromium, Ferndale, Mich., 1949-52; prin. rsch. metallurgist Armco Inc., Middletown, Ohio, 1952-85; prin. John Newby Cons., Middletown, 1985—. Cons. Phoenix Cons., Inc., Cin., 1988—. Author, editor: Formability 2000, 1982, Metallic Materials, 1978, Sheet Metal Forming, 1976; editor: Mechanical Testing, Vol. 8, 9th edit., 1985. Scoutmaster Boy Scouts Am., Middletown, 1952-86, now asst. dist. commr.; chmn. Safety Coun., Middletown, 1978-80. Staff sgt. USAF, 1943-46, PTO. Fellow ASTM (chmn. 1963—, chmn. E-28 com. on mech. testing 1998-2002, Award of Merit 1984), ASM (sustaining mem., chpt. chmn. 1970, Award of Merit 1980); mem. SAE (sect. chmn. 1984). Democrat. Achievements include patent for high strength formable steel sheet; development of interstitial free steel, strain analysis process for metallic sheet formability. Home and Office: 100 Marymont Ct Middletown OH 45042-3735

NEWCOM, JENNINGS JAY, lawyer; b. St. Joseph, Mo., Oct. 18, 1941; s. Arden Henderson and Loyal Beatrice (Winans) N.; m. Cherry Ann Phelps, Apr. 4, 1964; children: Shandra Karine, J. Derek Arden. BA, Graceland U., Lamoni, Iowa, 1964; JD, Harvard U., 1968; LLD (hon.), Graceland U., 1999. Bar: Ill. 1968, Calif. 1973, Mo. 1979, Kans. 1981, Colo. 1999. Atty. McDermott, Will & Emery, Chgo., 1968-73; ptnr. Rifkind, Sterling & Lockwood, Beverly Hills, Calif., 1973-79, Shook, Hardy & Bacon L.L.P., Kansas City, Mo., 1979-99, Davis, Graham & Stubbs, LLP, Denver, 1999—; gen. counsel Lovell Minnick Ptnrs. LLC, LA, 1999—; dir. Skillpath Seminars, Overland Park, Kans.; bd. dirs. Duff & Phelps Holdings LLC, Chgo., Atlantic

Asset Mgmt. LLC, Stamford, Conn., Stanford, Conn., Berkeley Capital Mgmt., LLC, San Francisco. Trustee Hubbard Found., Linde Found. Mem. Denver Bar Assn., State Bar Assn. Calif. Office: Davis Graham & Stubbs LLP 1550 17th St Ste 500 Denver CO 80202-1500

NEWCOMB, BRUCE, state legislator, farmer, rancher; b. Burley, Idaho, Mar. 2, 1940; m. Celia Gould; 5 children. Student, N.W. Christian Coll., Stanford; BS, U. Oreg. Mem. Idaho Ho. of Reps., Boise, 1987, past majority leader, caucus chmn., house spkr., 1999—. Methodist. Avocations: fly fishing, hunting, family. Office: State Capitol Boise ID 83720-0001 Fax: 208-334-2491. E-mail: infocenter@lso.state.id.us.

NEWCOMB, ELDON HENRY, retired botany educator; b. Columbia, Mo., Jan. 19, 1919; s. Ernest Henry and Ruby Josephine (Anderson) N.; m. Joyce Bright Rieling, June 21, 1949; children— Norman Robert, Barbara Pauline, Cynthia Irma. Student, U. Kansas City, 1936-38; AB, U. Mo., 1940, A.M., 1942; PhD, U. Wis., 1949; DS honoris causa, U. Mo., Columbia, 1993. Asst. prof. botany U. Wis.-Madison, 1949-54, assoc. prof., 1954-58, prof., 1958-90, prof. emeritus, 1990—; dir. Inst. Plant Devel., 1979-88; chmn. dept. botany U. Wis.-Madison, 1982-88, Folke Skoog prof. botany, 1987—. Cons. Shell Devel. Co., 1954-59 Sr. author: Plants in Perspective, 1963; mng. editor Protoplasma, 1969-73; mem. editorial bd. Ann. Rev. Plant Physiology, 1965-69, Protoplasma, 1973-99, Planta, 1981-90; contbr. articles to profl. jours. Served with AUS, 1942-45. NRC predoctoral fellow U. Wis., 1946-49; Guggenheim Found. fellow U. Calif. at Berkeley, 1951-52; Sci. Faculty fellow Harvard, 1963-64; Fulbright Sr. Research scholar Australian Nat. U., Canberra, 1976 Mem. NAS, Am. Soc. Cell Biologists, Am. Acad. Arts and Scis., Bot. Soc. Am., Am. Soc. Plant Physiologists, Soc. Devel. Biology, Phi Beta Kappa (pres. Wis. Alpha chpt. 1978-79), Sigma Xi. Achievements include being a mem. expdn. to Great Barrier Reef, 1973. Home: 52 Oak Creek Trl Madison WI 53717-1510 Business E-Mail: enewcomb@facstaff.wisc.edu.

NEWCOMB, HELENE E, retired research scientist; b. New York, N.Y. d. Otto Wilhelm Post and Hella (Drexler) Walburga; m. Frederick J Newcomb, Aug. 15, 1953; children: J Mark, Paula Marie. Author: (books of poetry) Echoes in the Wind, 2002, On the Wings of Thought, 2002. Mil. case worker ARC Mountain Valley Chpt., Provo, Utah, 1978—; Telecare ARC Mountain Valley Chpt., 1980—. With U.S. Army, 1951—53. Recipient Vol. of the Yr. award, ARC, 1981, Roberta Drissler Disting. Svc. award, 1986, Mil. Social Svc. Caseworker award, Clara Barton award, 1999, Portrait of Character award, Farm Bur. Mut. Ins. Co., Merit Silver award Bowl, Internat. Soc. of Poets, 2002, Editors Choice awards, 2000, 2003, Silver cup, Internat. Soc. of Poets, 2003. Latter Day Saint. Avocations: stamp collecting/philately, crocheting. Home: 942 N 800 E Genola UT 84655

NEWCOMB, JONATHAN, publishing executive; b. Chappaqua, N.Y., June 12, 1946; s. Russell L. and Louise B. Newcomb; m. Deborah Small, Dec. 11, 1970; 2 children, Zachary. AB in Econs., Dartmouth Coll., 1968; MBA, Columbia U., 1970. Mgr. Dun & Bradstreet, N.Y.C., 1972—74, Standard & Poor's Corp, N.Y.C., 1974—75, dir., 1976—79, v.p., 1979—80, sr. v.p., 1980—82, group v.p., 1982—84, exec. v.p., 1984—85; pres. McGraw-Hill Fin. & Econ. Info. Co., N.Y.C., 1985—88, Simon & Schuster Profl. Info. Group, N.Y.C., 1989—91; pres., CEO, Simon & Schuster, N.Y.C., 1991—94, chmn., CEO, 1994—. Bd. dirs. CorpTech, Boston, Teltech, Mpls. Bd. dirs. Bklyn. Acad. of Music; bd. overseers Amos Tuck Sch. Bus., Dartmouth Coll. 1st lt. U.S. Army, 1969—71, Vietnam. Mem.: Heights Casino (Bklyn.). Home: 35 Pierrepont St Brooklyn NY 11201-3359 Office: Simon & Schuster Inc 1230 Ave of Americas New York NY 10020-1513

NEWCOMB, ROBERT DOUGLAS, optometrist, clinician, educator; b. Middletown, Ohio, Jan. 8, 1947; s. Huber Charles and Betty Marie (Martz) N.; m. Pamela Kristine Yerian, June 16, 1984; 1 child, Nicholas Scott. BS in Physiol. Optics, Ohio State U., 1970, OD, 1971; MPH, U. Ala., Birmingham, 1975. Diplomate Nat. Bd. Examiners in Optometry; lic. optometrist, Ohio, Fla. Chief optometry svc. VA Med. Ctr., Birmingham, Ala., 1976-80, VA Outpatient Clinic, Columbus, Ohio, 1980-97; assoc. prof. optometry U. Ala., Birmingham, 1976-80; clin. prof. optometry, endowed chair Vision Svc. Plan Ohio State U., Columbus, 1997—. Cons. Nat. Bd. Examiners in Optometry, 1981-89, Ohio State Bd. Optometry, Coun. on Optometric Edn., Coun. on Clin. Optometric Care; invited lectr. profl. orgns. in field. Co-editor: (textbook) Public Health and Community Optometry, 1980, 2d edit., 1990; contbr. articles to profl. jours. Fellow Am. Acad. Optometry (program com. 1982-86, bd. dirs. 1986—); mem. APHA (Outstanding Paper/Project award 1982), Am. Optometric Assn. (editl. bd. 1977-83, Optometric Recognition award 1980), Nat. Assn. VA Optometrists (treas. 1976-87, prs. 1976-83), Ohio Optometric Assn. (chair continuing edn. 1992-98, chair new technology 1995-97, Optometrists of Yr 2002), Assn. Mil. Surgeons U.S. (Outstanding Svc. and Recognition award 1997), Nat. Acad. Practice Optometry (chair 2001—). Independent. Avocations: tennis, music. Business E-Mail: newcomb.2@osu.edu.

NEWCOMB, ROBERT WAYNE, electrical engineer educator; b. Glendale, Calif., June 27, 1933; s. Robert Dobson and Dorothy Opal (Bissinger) N.; m. Sarah Eleanor Fritz, May 22, 1954; children: Gail E., Robert. W. BSEE, Purdue U., 1955; MS, Stanford U., 1957; PhD, U. Calif., Berkeley, 1960. Registered profl. engr., Calif. Rsch. intern Stanford Rsch. Inst., Menlo Park, Calif., 1957-60; tchg. assoc. U. Calif., Berkeley, 1957-60; asst. and tenured assoc. prof. Stanford U., 1960—70; prof. elec. engring. U. Md., College Park, 1970—. Bd. dirs. PARCOR Rsch. program, Universidad Politecnica de Madrid, Spain. Author: Linear Multisport Synthesis, 1966, Active Integrated Circuit Synthesis, 1968, Concepts of Linear Systems and Control, 1968, Network Theory, 1967; editor: Neurocomputing Letters, 2002—. Recipient IEEE CAS Edn. awrd, 2001; Fulbright fellow, 1963; Fulbright-Hays fellow, 1976; Robert Wayne Newcomb Lab. opened at U. Politecnica Madrid, 1995. Fellow IEEE (life, golden jubilee medal 1999), Am. Inst. Med. and Biol. Engrs.; mem. Soc. Indsl. and Applied Math., Math. Assn. Am., Acad. Am. Poets. Avocations: film, literature, poetry, guitar. Home: 13120 Two Farm Dr Silver Spring MD 20904-3418 Office: U Md Microsystems Lab Elec/Computer Engring College Park MD 20742-0001 Office Phone: 301-405-3662. E-mail: newcomb@eng.umd.edu.

NEWCOMBE, HOWARD BORDEN, biologist, consultant; b. Kentville, N.S., Can., Sept. 19, 1914; s. Edward Borden and Mabel Elsie (Outerbridge) N.; m. Beryl Honor Callaway, Feb. 14, 1942; children— Kenneth Donald, Charles Philip, Richard William B.Sc., Acadia U., Wolfville, N.S., 1935; Assoc., Imperial Coll. Tropical Agr., Trinidad, 1938; PhD, McGill U., Montreal, P.Q., Can., 1939; D.Sc. (hon.), McGill U., 1966, Acadia U., 1970. Sci. officer Brit. Ministry of Supply, London, 1940-41; rsch. assoc. Carnegie Instn. Washington, 1946-47; rsch. sci. Atomic Energy of Can. Ltd., Chalk River, 1947-79, head biology br., 1949-70, head population rsch. br., 1970-79. Vis. prof. genetics Ind. U., Bloomington, 1963; mem. Internat. Commn. on Radiol. Protection, 1965-77, chmn. com. on biol. effects, 1965-72 Contbr. articles to profl. jours. Served to lt. Brit. Royal Naval Vol. Res., 1941-46 Fellow Royal Soc. Can.; mem. Genetics Soc. Am. (sec. 1956-58), Am. Soc. Human Genetics (pres. 1965), Genetics Soc. Can. (pres. 1964-65) Home: 67 Hillcrest Ave PO Box 135 Deep River ON Canada K0J 1P0

NEWCOMER, CLARENCE CHARLES, federal judge; b. Mount Joy, Pa., Jan. 18, 1923; s. Clarence S. and Marion Clara (Charles) N.; m. Jane Moyer Martin, Oct. 2, 1948; children: Judy (Mrs. Kenneth N. Birkett Jr.), Nancy Jane Newcomer (Mrs. Edward H. Vick), Peggy Jo Pollack (dec.). AB, Franklin and Marshall Coll., 1944; LL.B., Dickinson Sch. Law, 1948. Bar: Pa. 1950, U.S. Dist. Ct. Pa., U.S. Ct. Appeals (3rd cir.), U.S. Supreme Ct. Pvt. practice, Lancaster, 1950-52; spl. dep. atty. gen. Dept. Justice, Commonwealth of Pa., 1952-54; partner firm Rohrer, Honaman, Newcomer & Musser, Lancaster, 1957-60; with Office of Dist. Atty., Lancaster, 1960-64, 1st asst. dist. atty., 1964-68, dist. atty., 1968-72; partner Newcomer, Roda & Morgan, 1968-72; fed. dist. judge Eastern Dist. Pa., Phila., 1972-88, sr. judge, 1988—. Served to lt. (j.g.) USNR, 1943-46, PTO. Office: US Dist Ct 13614 US Courthouse 601 Market St Philadelphia PA 19106-1713

NEWCOMER, JAMES HENRY, retired federal agency administrator; b. Waterloo, Iowa, Sept. 11, 1920; s. Henry Raymond and Nettie (Logston) Newcomer; m. Esther Laura Reinhardt, July 29, 1941; children: James Ralph, Edward Reinhardt, Henry Lewis, Carolyn Ruth. Warehouseman Cutler Wholesale Hardware, Waterloo, 1939-42; electrician Cedar Falls (Iowa) Electric & Hardware, 1946-51; quality assurance rep. Def. Contract Adminstrn. Svcs., St. Louis, 1951-78; trail ranger Black Hawk County Conservation Bd., Cedar Falls, 1990-96; tchr. computers Waterloo Sr. Activity Ctr., 1996. Compiler geneology: Newcomer and Related Families. With U.S. Army, 1942—46, ETO. Decorated Purple Heart, Bronze Star; recipient Disting. Career award, Dept. Def., 1978, cert. of Appreciation, Hawkeye Valley Area Agy. Aging, 1996, Gov.'s Vol. award, 1997. Mem.: VFW, DAV, Am. Legion. Republican. Presbyterian. Avocations: photography, boating, woodworking, metalworking, cooking. Home: 5051 Foulk Rd Waterloo IA 50702-4825 E-mail: jhander@mchsi.com.

NEWCOMER, KERMIT LEE, retired internist, kidney specialist; b. Bryan, Ohio, Nov. 15, 1930; MD, Case Western Res U., 1959. Intern Walter Reed Gen. Hosp., Washington, 1959—60, resident, 1960—63; internal medicine physician Gundersen /Luth. Hosp., LaCrosse, Wis., 1967—95; ret. Past pres. World Svc. La Crosse, Inc., med. cons., bd. mem., 1995—. Recipient Benjamin Rush award for citizenship and cmty. svc., AMA, 2003, Presdl. Citation award, Wis. Med. Soc., 2004. Achievements include development of specialized health ctr. in Russia, China, Ukraine. Office: World Svc La Crosse Inc 1601 Caledonia St Ste B La Crosse WI 54603 Office Phone: 608-781-4194. Office Fax: 608-781-4197. E-mail: knew3213@aol.com.

NEWELL, BARBARA ANN, coatings company executive; b. Portland, Oreg., Mar. 20, 1945; d. John Wesley and Marion Josephine (Hill) Clausen; children: Shamaz, Hukam (dec.), Mardana. BA, Lindenwood Coll. for Women, 1968; MA, Portland State U., 1972; PhD, Summit U., 2000. Owner Shamaz Trading Co., Ukiah, Calif., 1974-77; mgr. small bus. dept. Ernst & Ernst, Portland, 1977-78; CFO All Heart Lumber Co., Ukiah, 1978-83; CFO, CEO Performance Coatings Inc., Ukiah, 1983—, chmn. bd. dirs., 1992—. Chmn. bd. dirs. Rural Visions Found.; treas. chmn. fin. com. Mendocino County Health Clinic, chmn. bd. dirs., 2001-03; CEO, chmn. bd. dirs. Dusky Rose & Assoc., Botanics of Calif.; founder Potter Valley Cafe, 2000; owner Hukam Maj Arabian Horse Ranch, 1998—. Founder, chair Penofin Jazz Festival; chmn. bd. dirs. Mendocino Ballet Co.; bd. dirs. Potter Valley Youth and Cmty. Ctr. Mem. Nat. Paint and Coatings Assn., Golden State Paint and Coatings Assn., Ukiah C. of C. (mem. econ. devel. com. 1993-94), Women in Coatings (Leadership award 1994), Leadership Mendocino. Avocations: showing Arabian horses, reading, children, organic gardening, dance. Office: Penofin-Performance Coatings Inc PO Box 1569 Ukiah CA 95482-1569 Office Phone: 707-462-3023. E-mail: ceo@penofin.com.

NEWELL, BYRON BRUCE, JR., pastor; b. Long Beach, Calif., July 31, 1932; s. Byron Bruce and Eleanor Whitaker (Davis) N.; m. Ingrid Charlotte Asche, June 11, 1955 (dec. July 1989); children: Thomas, Susan, Robert, Michael; m. Theresa Ann Troncale, Sept. 1, 1990. Student, Wesleyan U., 1950-51; BS, U.S. Naval Acad., 1955; MSEE, U.S. Naval Postgrad. Sch. Monterey, 1962; postgrad. nuclear power tng., 1964-65; MDiv, Va. Theol. Sem., 1987. Ordained priest, Episcopal Ch., 1988. Commd. ensign U.S. Navy, 1955, advanced through grades to rear adm., 1980; weapons officer U.S.S. Lowry, Hull (destroyers), 1955-58; comdg. officer salvage ship, 1962-64; exec., comdg. officer nuclear cruisers, 1968-77; manpower/tng. surface ship personnel, 1977-79; with Nat. Mil. Command Center, Washington, 1979-80, chief navy info., 1980-82, chief navy legis. affairs, 1982-84; assoc. dean Trinity Episcopal Sch. for Ministry, Ambridge, Pa., 1990-96. Chmn., trustee Breakthrough, Inc. Decorated Legion of Merit, D.S.M. Mem. Naval Inst., Naval Hist. Soc., Met. Club. Home: 256 Thorn St Sewickley PA 15143-1204

NEWELL, CHARLDEAN, public administration educator; b. Ft. Worth, Oct. 14, 1939; d. Charles Thurlow and Mildren Dean (Looney) Newell. BA, U. North Tex., 1960, MA, 1962; PhD, U. Tex., 1968; cert., Harvard U., 1988. Instr. U. North Tex., Denton, 1965-68, asst. prof., 1968-72; assoc. prof., dir. Fedn. North Tex. Area Univs., Denton, Dallas, 1972-74; assoc. prof., assoc. v.p. acad. affairs U. North Tex., Denton, 1974-76, assoc. prof., chair dept. polit. sci., 1976-80, prof. polit. sci., 1980-92, assoc. v.p., spl. asst. to chancellor, 1982-92, regents prof. pub. adminstrn., 1992—2002, prof. emeritus, 2002—. Cons. Miss. Bd. Trustees State Instns. Higher Learning, Jackson, 1983—84, Ednl. Testing Svc., Princeton, NJ, 1980, Princeton, 82, Princeton, 85, Spear Down & Judin, Dallas, 1994—95, North Tex. Inst. Edn. Visual Arts, Denton, 1993—94; bd. regents Internat. City/County Mgmt. Assn., Washington, 1994—98, vol. credentialing adv. bd., 2002—. Author (with others): (book) City Executives: Leadership Roles, Work Characteristics and Time Management, 1989, Texas Politics, 2002, The Effective Local Govt. Mgr., 2004, Essentials of Tex. Politics, 2004; contbr. articles to profl. jours. Chmn. Denton Charter Rev. Com., 1978—79; mem. Denton CSC, 1989—97, chmn., 1992—97; active Denton Blue Ribbon Capital Improvements Com., 1995—96; mem. Denton Devel. Plan Com., 1996—97, Denton Pub. Utilities Bd., 1997—, chmn., 2002—; v.p. Denton Christian Pre-Sch. Bd., 2001—02, pres., 2002—; mem. Cit Council Ethics Com., 2004; mem. exec. coun. Episcopal Diocese Dallas, 1985—88. Recipient Elmer Staats Career Pub. Svc. award, Nat. Assn. Sch. Pub. Affairs Adminstrn., 1993. Fellow: Nat. Acad. Pub. Adminstrn.; mem.: Am. Soc. for Pub. Adminstrn. (sect. chmn. 1982—83, mem. editl. bd. 1985—88, Donald C. Stone award 2004), Internat. City/County Mgmt. Assn. (hon.), Pi Alpha Alpha (exec. coun. 1995—99), Pi Sigma Alpha (exec. coun. 1988—92). Democrat. Avocations: spectator sports, reading. Home: 2008 Tremont Cir Denton TX 76205-7408 Business E-Mail: cn0003@unt.edu.

NEWELL, CHARLES ANSEL, JR., social studies educator; b. Newport News, Va., June 6, 1947; s. Charles Ansel and Jane Goodwin Newell; m. Alice Elizabeth Wilson, June 21, 1969; children: Adam Christopher, James Grayson, Charles Ansel Newell, III. BA in hist., Campbell U., 1971; MA in hist., U. North Carolina-Greensboro, 1975. Cert. tchr. NC, 1981. Hist. instr. Old Dominion U., Norfolk, Va., 1976—78; social studies tchr. Guilford County Schools, Greensboro, NC, 1978—98; ins. rep. Woodmen of the World Life Ins. Soc., Greensboro, 1998—2000; social studies tchr. Am. Hebrew Acad., Greensboro, 2001—. Debate coach Guilford County Schools, Greensboro, 1987—2000. Author: North Carolina Dictionary of Biography. Adv. Human Rels. Commn., Greensboro, 1984—87; mem. Hist. Dist. Commn., Greensboro, 1992—98, United Day Care Svcs., Greensboro, 1980—83. Recipient Time Honored Debate Coaches award, Burford Forum, 1996, Diamond Coaches' award, Nat. Forensic League, 1998. Mem.: Am. Acad. of Polit. Sci. (assoc.), Am. Hist. Assn. (assoc.), Phi Alpha Theta (assoc.). Democrat. Achievements include first to started the Aycock Neighborhood Assn. and achieved Historic District status for the neighborhood. Avocations: bicycling, sailing, nature photography. Home: 704 Cypress St Greensboro NC 27405 Office: Am Hebrew Acad 4334 Hobbs Rd Greensboro NC 27410 Office Phone: 336-217-7000.

NEWELL, DANIEL K. utilities company executive; CFO, sr. v.p. fin. Northwestern Corp., Sioux Falls, S.D., mng. dir., CEO. Office: Northwestern Corp 125 S Dakota Ave Sioux Falls SD 57104

NEWELL, ERIC JAMES, financial planner, tax consultant, former insurance executive; b. Toronto, Ont., Can., Sept. 24, 1930; came to U.S., 1959, naturalized, 1970; s. James and Anne (Brown) N.; m. Essie Miskelly, Sept. 30, 1950; 1 son, Eric Wayne. Student, U. Toronto, 1951-53. Pub. acct. W.J. Wilcox & Co., Toronto, 1949-53; chief acct. Toronto Mut. Life Ins. Co., 1953-57; asst. sec. Holland Life Ins. Co., Toronto, 1957-59; with Penn Mut. Life Ins. Co., Phila., 1959-86, assoc. controller, 1965-70, 2d v.p., controller, 1970-84, v.p., controller, 1984-86, ret., 1986; fin., tax cons., 1986—; dir. Hotel Brunswick, Lancaster, Pa., 1982-85. Mem. Traffic and Transp. Bd., Cherry Hill, N.J., 1971-73, Zoning Bd., 1975-78; vice chmn. Cherry Hill Econ. Devel. Bd., 1973-75; pres. Greater Kingston Civic Assn., Cherry Hill, 1970-76; Democratic committeeman, Camden County, 1976-79; vice chmn. Dem. Party, Cherry Hill, 1976. Fellow Life Mgmt. Inst., Royal Commonwealth Soc.; mem. Fin. Execs. Inst., Am. Inst. Corp. Contrs., N.Y. Ins. Accts. Club (chmn. 1984), Nat. Soc. Tax Profls., Royal Black Knights of Ireland, Loyal Orange Assn. (past master), Scotch-Irish Soc. of U.S. (mem. coun., pres. 1999), Am. Legion. Presbyterian (deacon 1969-72). Home and Office: 137 E Partridge Ln Cherry Hill NJ 08003-4407

NEWELL, MICHAEL ALFRED, electrical engineer; b. L.A., May 26, 1963; s. Paul Eugene and Clare Fritzsche Newell; m. Thuy Lam Newell. BSEE, Calif. Poly. State U., 1990. Electronics design engr. Space Payloads Group, Pasadena, Calif., 1983—86; software engr. Qualitel Svcs., Pomona, Calif., 1986—88; sr. mem. tech. staff Jet Propulsion Lab., Pasadena, 1988—. ASIC designer Cassini Spacecraft Jet Propulsion Lab., Pasadena, 1992—94, electronics lead APEX reconfigurable hardware Flight Experiment, Pasadena, 1994—97, Muses CN electronics cognizant engr., Pasadena, 1998—2001, Deep Impact avionics lead, 2001—; Gilgamesh Supercomputer electronics cognizant engr. Caltech, Pasadena, 2000—; task mgr. extreme electronics, Electronics Parts Program NASA, Pasadena, 2001—. Contbr. articles to profl. jours.; patentee in field. Exec. advisor JPL Explorer Post, Pasadena, 1993—2001. Mem.: IEEE. Avocations: bicycling, reading. Home: 3545 N Glenrose Ave Altadena CA 91001 Office: Jet Propulsion Lab 4800 Oak Grove Dr Pasadena CA 91109 Personal E-mail: mikenewell@earthlink.net. Business E-Mail: Michael.A.Newell@jpl.nasa.gov.

NEWELL, MIKE, film director; b. St. Albans, England, Mar. 28, 1942; Films include: The Awakening, 1980, Bad Blood, 1983, Dance With a Stranger, 1985, The Good Father, 1986, Amazing Grace and Chuck, 1987, Soursweet, 1988, Enchanted April, 1991, Into the West, 1992, Four Weddings and a Funeral, 1994, An Awfully Big Adventure, 1995, Donnie Brasco, 1997, Pushing Tin, 1999,; exec. prodr. (films) Photographing Fairies, 1997, 200 Cigarettes, 1999, Best Laid Plans, 1999, High Fidelity, 2000, Traffic, 2000; TV films include: Big Soft Nellie, Mrs. Mouse, Baa Baa Blacksheep, The Melancholy Hussar, Ready When You Are Mr. McGill, Destiny, The Man in the Iron Mask, 1977, The Gift of Friendship, Blood Feud, 1983, Common Ground, 1990; exec. prodr., dir. (TV series) The Branch, 2003, dir. (TV movie) Jo, 2002. Office: Dogstar UK 5 Sherwood St London W1V 7RA England Address: ICM Ste 219 8942 Wilshire Blvd Beverly Hills CA 90211

NEWELL, NORMAN DENNIS, paleontologist, geologist, museum curator, educator; b. Chgo., Jan. 27, 1909; s. Virgil Bingham and Nellie (Clark) N.; m. Valerie Zirkle, Feb. 25, 1928 (dec. 1972); m. Gillian Wendy Wormall, Apr. 28, 1973 BS, U. Kans., 1929, MA, 1931; PhD in Geology, Yale U., 1933. Faculty mem. U. Kans., Lawrence, 1934-37; assoc. prof. geology U. Wis.-Madison, 1937-45; prof. geology Columbia U., N.Y.C., 1945-77, prof. emeritus, 1977—; curator Am. Mus. Nat. History, N.Y.C., 1945-77, curator emeritus, 1977—. Geologist Kans. Geol. Survey, Lawrence, 1929-37; cons. on petroleum geology Peruvian Govt., 1942-45 Author: Permian Reef Complex of the Guadalupe Mountains Region, Texas and New Mexico, 1953, Creation and Evolution: Myth or Reality?, 1982, also numerous sci. articles and papers. Recipient Disting. Svc. Alumni award Kans. U., 1961, Hayden award Phila. Acad. Sci., 1965, Verrill medal Yale U., 1966, Gold medal for achievment in sci. Am. Mus. Natural History, 1978, Raymond C. Moore medal Soc. Econ. Paleontologists and Mineralogists, 1980, Scientific Freedom and Responsibility award AAAS, 1987, Geol. Soc. Peru medal, 1997, Internat. Symposium on the Paleobiology and Evolution of the Bivalvia Festschrift, 1998, The Royal Tyrrell Mus. Palaeontology, Drumheller. Mem. Nat. Acad. Scis. (Mary Clark Thompson medal 1960), Am. Philos. Soc., Am. Acad. Arts and Scis., Am. Assn. Petroleum Geolologists (spl. award 1996), Geol. Soc. Am. (Penrose medal 1990), Soc. Study Evolution (pres. 1949), Soc. Systematic Zoology (pres. 1972-73), Paleontol. Soc. (pres. 1960-61, medal 1979), Can. Soc. Petroleum Geologists (hon.). Avocation: geologic field expeditions. Home: 135 Knapp Ter Leonia NJ 07605-1216 Office: Am Mus Natural History Central Park W and 79 St New York NY 10024 E-mail: newell@amnh.org.

NEWELL, PAUL HAYNES, JR., engineering educator, former college president; b. Nashville, July 1, 1933; s. Paul Haynes Newell; m. Martha A. Newell; children: Paul Haynes III, Mike, Nan. B.M.E., U. Tenn., 1958, M.M.E., 1961; Mech.E., Mass. Inst. Tech., 1964, PhD, 1966. Registered profl. engr., Ala., Tenn., Tex., N.J. Student asst. mech. engring. U. Tenn., 1957, instr. mech. engring., 1958-62; NSF Sci. faculty fellow Mass. Inst. Tech., 1962-65; asso. prof. mech. engring. U. Ala. Coll. Engring., 1966-69; prof. mech. engring. Tex. A. and M. U., 1969-72, asso. dean engring., 1972; prof. biomed. engring., dept. phys. medicine Baylor Coll. Medicine, 1969-74, prof. biomed. engring., dept. physiology, 1970-74, prof. biomed. engring., dept. community medicine, 1972-74, prof. biomed. engring., dept. rehab., 1972—, mem. grad. faculty, 1970-74; prof., head indsl. engring. dept. Tex. A. & M. U., 1972-74, prof., head combined programs of behavioral engring., bioengring., cybernetic engring., hygiene and safety engring., indsl. engring., 1972-74; pres., prof. Newark Coll. Engring., N.J. Inst. Tech., 1974-78; prof. Adminstrn. Prosthetics Ctr., N.Y., 1973-75, VA Hosp., Houston, 1972-75, Baylor Coll. Medicine, Houston, from 1971; pres. Newell Engring., Greenbrier, Tenn., 1979—. Dir. N.J. Bell Telephone Co., Mid Atlantic Nat. Bank, Thomas-Betts Corp. Contbr. articles to profl. jours., chpts. to books. Mem. NSF liaison com., Newark Transp. Council, N.J. Safety Council; sec. exec. com. council Boy Scouts Am., Birmingham, Ala., 1966-68; bd. dirs. N.J. State Opera, United Hosps. Newark. Served with USMCR, Korean Conflict. Recipient NSF Sci. Faculty fellowship. Mem. Am. Soc. Tool and Mfg. Engrs., N.Y., Ala. acads. scis., AAAS, Am. Congress Rehab. Medicine, Am. Heart Assn., Am. Inst. Indsl. Engrs., Am. Soc. Artificial Internal Organs, Am. Soc. Engring. Edn., ASME, Biomed. Engring. Soc., Inst. Engring. Deans, Internat. Soc. Prosthetics and Orthotics, Nat. Soc. Profl. Engrs., Soc. Advanced Med. Systems, Soc. Engring. Sci., Pres.'s Assn., Am. Fluid Power Soc., N.J. Soc. Engrs., Sigma Xi, Tau Beta Pi, Phi Kappa Phi, Pi Tau Sigma. Clubs: Rotary. Address: 1855 Lake Rd Greenbrier TN 37073-4619 Office: Newell Engring Greenbrier TN 37073-4619 Office Phone: 615-859-5873.

NEWELL, REGINALD EDWARD, physics educator; b. Peterborough, Eng., Apr. 9, 1931; came to U.S., 1954, naturalized, 1969; s. Harold Aubrey and Edith (Swiffin) N.; m. Maireen W. Lees, Sept. 6, 1954; children: Madeleine, Elizabeth, Oliver, Nicholas. BS in Physics, U. Birmingham, Eng., 1954; MS, Mass. Inst. Tech., 1956, Sc.D., 1960. With Brit. Meteorol. Office, 1947-50; successively research staff asst., asst. prof., asso. prof., prof. MIT, Cambridge, 1954—; mem IUGG Internat. Commn. Meteorology Upper Atmosphere, 1967-75; mem. Internat. Commn. Atmospheric Chemistry and Global Pollution, 1971-83; pres. Internat. Commn. on Climate, 1977-83. Joint author: The General Circulation of the Tropical Atmosphere, Vol. I, 1972, Vol. 2, 1974, Global Ocean Surface Temperature Atlas, 1990; contbr. articles to profl. jours. Served with RAF, 1950-51. Fellow Royal Meteorol. Soc., Am. Meteorol. Soc.; mem. Am. Geophys. Union. Home: 45 Jason St Arlington MA 02476-6446 Office: MIT 54-1824 77 Massachusetts Ave Cambridge MA 02139-4307

NEWELL, RUSSELL ANDERSON, financial planner; b. N.Y.C., Mar. 16, 1921; s. William Anderson and Ethel Rogers N.; m. Carol Byrnes, July 29, 1943; 1 child, Karen Newell Tiburzl. BSME, Rensselaer Poly Tech Inst., 1949; MS, MIT, 1957. CFP; comml. pilot. Design engr. Eastman Kodak Co., Rochester, N.Y., 1949-52; engring. mgr., chief engr., project mgr. RCA, Moorestown, N.J., 1952-67; exec. v.p. United tech. Norden Group, Norwalk, Conn., 1967-69; pres. Ranco Co., Haddonfield, N.J., 1969-76; 1st v.p. Smith Barney, Phila., 1976-97; retired. Fin. advisor Smith Barney, Phila., 1977-97; pres. Buy & Sell Mag., Westmont, N.J., 1972-75, Ranco Co., Haddonfield, N.J., 1970—. Chmn. West Jersey Health & Hosp. Found., Vorhees, N.J., 1986-97; mem., pres. Wedgewood Swim Club, Haddonfield, 1951-57. 1st lt. U.S. Army Air Corps, 1942-46; pilot instr. Aircorp. Sloan fellow MIT, 1957. Mem. Jonathan's Landing Golf Club, Palm Valley Country Club, Tavistock County Country Club, Sigma Xi, Pi Tau Sigma, Tau Beta Pi. Avocations: gardening, travel, computers, financial and management. Home: 425 Queensboro Ln Haddonfield NJ 08033-4014

NEWFIELD, PHILIPPA, anesthesiologist; b. Bklyn., Nov. 9, 1945; d. Joseph and Ruth Newfield; m. Phillip Gordon; children: Ethan Glaubiger, David Glaubiger. AB, Hunter Coll., 1969; MD, NYU Sch. of Medicine, 1973. Bd. cert. diplomate Am. Bd. Anesthesiology. Internship Manhattan VA Hosp.,

1973—74; fellowship U. of Pitts., 1976—77; asst. prof. anesthesiology U. Calif., San Francisco, 1977—82; attending anesthesiologist Children's Hosp., San Francisco, 1982—90, Los Angeles, 1990—91, Calif. Pac. Med. Ctr., 1991—. Pres. Soc. of Neuroanesthesia and Critical Care, 1980; sec. Calif. Soc. of Anesthesiology, 1985—95; mem. bd. dirs. San Francisco Med. Soc., 1993—95. Editor: (book) Handbook of Neuroanesthesia, 2000. Avocations: travel, hiking, photography. Office: Calif Pacific Med Ctr 3700 California San Francisco CA 94118

NEWHALL, DAVID, III, former government official; b. Phila., Dec. 6, 1937; s. David Jr. and Jane Martyn (Dunn) N. AB in Politics, Princeton U., 1961. Mgr. Bell Tel. Co. of Pa., Norristown, 1961-63; adminstrv. asst. U.S. Rep. R.S. Schweiker, Washington, 1963-69; chief of staff U.S. Senator R.S. Schweiker, Washington, 1969-81, HHS, Washington, 1981-83; pres. Marmion Plantation Co., King George, Va., 1983—85; prin. dep. asst. sec. def.(health affairs) U.S. Dept. Def., Washington, 1985-90, acting asst. sec. def. (health affairs), 1989-90; gen. ptnr. Marmion Partnership Restorations, 1990—. Bd. dirs. We. Healthcare Alliance, Phoenix, 1995-97; chmn. compliance com. and lead dir. TrailBlazer Health Enterprises, LLC, Dallas, 1997—. Mem. Princeton Tower Club. Republican. Episcopalian. Home and Office: 7382M Marmion Ln King George VA 22485-7300

NEWHALL, ERIC LUTHER, American literature educator; b. Reno, Nev., July 3, 1945; s. David Havens and Geraldine (Gilbert) N.; m. Sylvia Kurtovich, July 21, 1971 (div. June 1988); children: David K., Katherine H.; m. Jaclyn Toni Rodriguez, Apr. 7, 1990; chldren: Andrea Rodriguez-Scheel, Amanda Rodriguez-Newhall. BA, Occidental Coll., L.A., 1967; PhD, UCLA, 1975. Prof. Am. lit. Occidental Coll., L.A., 1975—, assoc. dean, 2000—. Contbr. articles to profl. jours. Liaison Hispanic Urban Ctr./Occidental Coll., 1976-82; mem. Learn coun. Eagle Rock Elem. Sch., L.A., 1998-2000. Recipient Oreg. Peace award Coun. of Chs., Portland, 1971, Loftsgordon award for outstanding tchg., 1979, 85, 93, 99, 2000; Danforth Assoc., 1981-85. Mem. MLA (regional del.), Am. Studies Assn., Phi Beta Kappa. Democrat. Avocations: tennis, chess. Home: 2037 Escarpa Dr Los Angeles CA 90041-3016 Office: Occidental Coll 1600 Campus Rd Los Angeles CA 90041-3314 E-mail: newhall@oxy.edu.

NEWHALL, JOHN HARRISON, retired non profit company executive; b. Phila., Sept. 29, 1933; s. Blackwell and Mary Large (Harrison) N.; m. Jane Carol Ward, July 15, 1961; children: Carol Newhall Neilson, Thomas Blackwell, Daniel Ward. BA, Williams Coll., 1955; MBA, Harvard U., 1960. Product mktg. mgr. Campbell Soup Co., Camden, NJ, 1960—67; product group mgr. Gen. Foods Corp. (now Kraft Corp.), White Plains, NY, 1967—70; dir. corp. planning, gen. mgr. Europe H.J. Heinz Co., Pitts., 1970—77; v.p. mktg. Sunoco Corp., Phila., 1977—81; chmn., CEO Aitkin-Kynett Co. (subs. Foote Cone & Belding), Phila., 1981—84; mng. dir., exec. v.p. Campbell-Ewald Co., N.Y.C., 1984—86; prin. mgmt. cons. SRI Internat., Menlo Park, Calif., 1987—90; mng. dir. Strategic Directions, Narberth, Pa., 1990—99; pres. Advanced Promotion Techs., Deerfield Beach, Fla., 1992—93; CEO The Newcomen Soc. of the U.S., Exton, Pa., 1999—2003; ret., 2003. Mem. devel. coun. Williams Coll., Williamstown, Mass., 1977-87, regional vice chmn. capital campaign, 1991-93; mem. Com. of 70, Phila., 1981-84; bd. dirs. Bryn Mawr (Pa.) Hosp., 1982-88, The Haverford (Pa.) Sch., 1980-86, mem. headmaster selection com., 1992, mem. strategic planning com., 1994; bd. dirs. World Affairs Coun., Phila., 1982-86, Found. for Vascular Hypertension Rsch., Phila., 1982-2001, chmn., 1987; bd. dirs. Jr. Achievement, Phila., 1977-81, vice chmn., 1981; bd. dirs. SE chpt. ARC, Phila., 1981-84, Pa. Economy League, 1981-84; vestryman, lay reader Episcopal Ch., 1964-70, chmn. ann. campaign, 1992, vice chmn. capital campaign, 1994; mem. bd. overseers Hospitality Hall of Honor, 2000-2003. Lt. USN, 1955-58. Recipient Cert. of Merit Chapel of Four Chaplains, 1983, 85. Mem. Assn. Nat. Advertisers (exec. com. 1977-81), Harvard Bus. Sch. Club Phila. (pres. 1994-96, chmn. 1986-98), Union League (Phila.) Club, Merion Cricket (Haverford) Club, Gulph Mills (Pa.) Golf Club, Harbor (Seal Harbor, Maine) Club. Republican. Episcopalian. Avocations: skiing, golf, sailing. Home: 414 Righters Mill Rd Penn Valley PA 19072-1423 E-mail: janejohn6@earthlink.net.

NEWHART, BOB, entertainer; b. Oak Park, Ill., Sept. 5, 1929; m. Virginia Quinn, Jan. 12, 1963; 4 children. BS, Loyola U., Chgo., 1952. Acct. U.S. Gypsum Co.; copywriter Fred Niles Film Co.; appeared on Jack Paar Show, 1960; TV performer numerous guest appearances, 1961—; star TV series The Bob Newhart Show, 1972—78, Newhart, 1982-90. Rec. artist (album) The Button Down Mind of Bob Newhart; royal command performance, London, 1964, appeared in films Hell is for Heroes, 1962, Hot Millions, 1968, Catch 22, 1970, On a Clear Day You Can See Forever, 1970, Cold Turkey, 1971, First Family, 1980, Little Miss Marker, 1980, In and Out, 1997; TV films include Thursday's Game, 1974, Marathon, 1980. Grand marshall Tournament Roses Parade, 1991. With U.S. Army, 1952-54. Recipient Emmy award, 1961, Peabody award, 1961, Sword of Loyola award, 1976, Legend to Legend award, 1993, three Grammy awards 1960, The Sports Pages/How Doc Waddems Finally Broke 100, 2001, Kennedy Ctr. Mark Twain award, 2002; named to Acad. Hall of Fame, 1993. Office: c/o Capell Rudolph 11601 Wilshire Blvd Ste 1840 Los Angeles CA 90025-1759

NEWHOUSE, ALAN RUSSELL, federal government executive; b. N.Y.C., Feb. 27, 1938; s. Russell Conwell and Clara Lucille (Scovell) N.; m. Margo Stiles Hicks, Feb. 3, 1960; children: Daryl, Jeffrey, William. BEE, Cornell U., 1960. Engr. Bur. of Ships, Washington, 1964-66; nuc. power engr., chief West Milton field office AEC, Schenectady, NY, 1966-69; sr. exec. AEC, ERDA, U.S. Dept. Energy, Washington, 1969-92; dep. asst. sec. Space and Def. Power Systems Office Nuc. Energy, Washington, 1992-93; dir. Office Space and Def. Power Systems, 1993-95; ind. cons., 1995—2002; dir. Project Prometheus Office of Exploration, NASA, 2003—. Composer numerous musical works. Mem. Cmty. Orchestra So. Md. in Concert, Friday Morning Music Club. Lt. USN, 1960-64. Mem.: AIAA, IEEE, Am. Soc. Naval Engrs., Am. Nuc. Soc. Unitarian Universalist. Home: 24670 Greenview Dr Hollywood MD 20636-4823 Office: 3274 400 E St NW Washington DC Business E-Mail: anewhous@hq.nasa.gov. E-mail: arn6@cornell.edu.

NEWHOUSE, DONALD E. newspaper publishing executive; b. 1930; s. Samuel Newhouse. Student, Syracuse U. With Advance Publs. Inc., Staten Island, NY, 1951—, pres., 1979—; chmn. The Associated Press, N.Y.C., 1997—2002. Treas. Herald Am., Syracuse, 1960—, The Post Standard, Syracuse, 1960—, The Syracuse Herald Jour., 1960—, The Herald Co. Inc., 1960—; co-founder Metro-Suburbia, Inc., N.Y.C., 1963; prin. The Trenton (N.J.) Times, Times of Trenton Pub. Corp.; pres. The Star Ledger, Newark. Office: Advance Publications Inc 950 Fingerboard Rd Staten Island NY 10305-1453

NEWHOUSE, JOSEPH PAUL, economist, educator; b. Waterloo, Iowa, Feb. 24, 1942; s. Joseph Alexander and Ruth Linnea (Johnson) Newhouse; m. Margaret Louise Locke, June 22, 1968; children: Eric Joseph, David Locke. BA, Harvard U., 1963, PhD, 1969; postgrad (Fulbright scholar), Goethe U., Frankfort, Germany, 1963—64. Staff economist Rand Corp., Santa Monica, Calif., 1968—72, dep. program mgr., health and biosci. rsch., 1971—88, sr. staff economist, 1972—81, head econs. dept., 1981—85, sr. corp. fellow, 1985—2001; John D. MacArthur prof. health policy and mgmt., dir. div. Health Policy Rsch. and Edn., Harvard U., 1988—. Lectr. UCLA, 1970—83, adj. prof., 1983—88; mem. faculty Rand Grad. Sch., 1972—88; dir. Rand-UCLA Ctr. for Study Health Care Fin. Policy, 1984—88, co-dir., 1988—92; prin. investigator health ins. study grant HHS, 1971—86; chmn. health svcs. rsch. study sect. HHS-Agy. for Health Care Policy and Rsch., 1989—93; mem. Nat. Commn. Cost Med. Care, 1976—77; mem. health svcs. devel. grants study sect. HEW, 1978—82, Inst. Medicine of NAS, 1978—, mem. coun., 1991—97; mem. Physician Payment Rev. Commn., 1993—96; chmn. Prospective Payment Assessment Com., 1996—97; vice chair Medicare Payment Assessment Commn., 1997—2001, mem., 2001—; bd. regents Nat. Libr. Medicine, 1999—; bd. dirs. Aetna, ABT Assocs., Nat. Com. Quality Assurance. Author: The Economics of Medical Care, 1978, The Cost of Poor Health Habits, 1991, A Measure of Malpractice, 1993, Free for All?, 1993, Pricing the Priceless, 2002; editor: Jour. Health Econs., 1981—; assoc. editor: Jour. Econ. Perspectives, 1992—98, mem. editl. bd.: New Eng. Jour. Medicine, 2003—; contbr. articles to profl. jours. Recipient David Kershaw award and prize, Assn. Pub. Policy and Mgmt., 1983, Baxter Am. Found. prize, 1988, Adminstr.'s citation, Health Care Fin. Adminstrn., 1988, Hans Sigrist Found. prize, 1995, Elizur Wright award, 1995, Zvi Griliches award, 2000, Kenneth Arrow award, 2001. Fellow: AAAS, Am. Acad. Arts and Scis.; mem.: Am. Soc. Health Economists (pres. 2002—), Internat. Health Econs. Assn. (pres. 1996—98, bd. dirs. 1996—), Econometric Soc., Royal Econ. Soc., Am. Econ. Assn., Assn. for Health Svcs. Rsch. (bd. dirs. 1991—, pres. 1993—94, Article of Yr. award 1989). Office: Harvard U Health Policy Rsch and Edn 180 Longwood Ave Boston MA 02115-5821

NEWHOUSE, MARK WILLIAM, publishing executive; b. N.Y.C., Oct. 14, 1948; s. Norman Nathan and Alice (Gross) Newhouse; m. Lorry A. Whitehead, June 1, 1974; children: Jesse Louis, Charlotte Ann. BA, Yale U., 1969. V.p., gen. mgr. The Star-Ledger, Newark, 1980—. Bd. dirs. N.Y.C. Opera, 1992—, pres., 1993—; bd. dirs. Audit Bur. Circulations, 1995—, Glimmerglass Opera, 1997—. Office: Newark Morning Star Ledger Co One Star Ledger Plz Newark NJ 07102-1200

NEWHOUSE, NANCY RILEY, newspaper editor; b. Bellingham, Wash. d. Fenwick Charles and Elizabeth (Grace) Riley; m. John Newhouse, Sept. 27, 1961 (div. 1970); m. Michael Iovenko, Mar. 6, 1983. BA, Vassar Coll., 1958. Sr. editor N.Y. Mag., N.Y.C., 1970-75, House & Garden Mag., N.Y.C., 1976; successively home editor, style editor and travel editor N.Y. Times, N.Y.C., 1976—. Editor: Hers: Through Women's Eyes, 1985; editor Hers column N.Y. Times, 1976-92; mem. adv. bd. Vassar Quar., Poughkeepsie, N.Y., 1985—. Decorated chevalier Nat. Order Merit; recipient Penney-Mo. Newspaper award U. Mo. Sch. Journalism, 1982-83. Mem. The Century Assn., Women's Forum N.Y. Office: NY Times Co 229 W 43rd St New York NY 10036-3959

NEWHOUSE, ROBERT J., JR., insurance executive; Ret. vice chmn. bd. Marsh & McLennan Cos., Inc. Chmn. bd. Mid Ocean Reins. Co. Ltd., Bermuda; dir., chm. exec. comm. ACE. Ltd., Bermuda, dir., Trident Corp., Bermuda. Office: 55 Madison Ave Ste 450 Morristown NJ 07960-7397

NEWHOUSE, SAMUEL I., JR., publishing executive; b. 1928; m. Victoria Newhouse. Pub. Vogue mag., 1964; chmn. Condé Nast Publs. Inc., N.Y.C., 1975—; also chmn. bd. dirs., CEO Advance Publs. Inc., S.I., NY, 1979—. Recipient Henry Johnson Fisher award, Mag. Pubs. Assn., 1985. Address: Advance Pubs Inc 950 Fingerboard Rd Staten Island NY 10305-1453

NEWHOUSE, STEPHAN F. securities company executive; b. 1948; Joined Morgan Stanley & Co. Inc., NYC, 1979, mng. dir., 1988, officer, 1987—, named to mgmt. com., 1998, dep. head, institutional securities, 1997—2000, co-pres., COO, institutional securities, 2000—03, pres., 2003—; chmn. Morgan Stanley & Co. Internat. Ltd., 2000—03. Office: Morgan Stanley & Co Inc 1585 Broadway New York NY 10036 Office Phone: 212-761-4000.

NEWICK, CRAIG DAVID, architect; b. Orange, N.J., Feb. 14, 1960; s. Russel Forester and Helen (Welch) N.; m. Linda Hammer Lindroth, June 6, 1987; 1 child, Zachary Eran. BA in Architecture, Lehigh U., 1982; MArch, Yale U., 1987. Registered architect, Conn. Designer, draftsman The Archtl. Studio, Easton, Pa., 1983-84; job capt., project designer Svigals & Assocs., New Haven, 1985; designer, draftsman Centerbrook (Conn.) Architects, 1986; job capt., project designer Allan Dehar Assocs., Architects & Planners, New Haven, 1988-90; ptnr. Lindroth & Newick, New Haven, 1991—; designer Cesar Pelli & Assocs., Inc., New Haven, 1992; project arch. Tai Soo Kim Ptnrs., Hartford, Conn., 1995—2001; prin. Newick Archs., New Haven, 2001—. Vis. faculty Vis. Critics Studio, Lehigh U., 1993; vis. critic Wesleyan U., 1990-93, R.I. Sch. Design, 1988; faculty Creative Arts Workshop, New Haven, 1991, 92. Exhibitions include Out Of Bounds; author: Simultaneous Space (first prize artists books, 1994). Recipient 1st place award Am. Visionary Set Design Competition, 1989, 3d place award Astronauts Meml. Design Competition, 1988, ID Mag. Ann. Design Rev. award, 1990, 2d prize African Burial Ground Competition Mcpl. Arts Soc. N.Y., 1994, 1st place drawing award Conn. Soc. Architects, 1997, AIA Conn. honor award, 2000; grantee New Eng. Found. for Arts, 1992, NEA Interarts grantee Rockefeller Found., 1989-90, Found. for Contemporary Performance Art, 1989, 90, Humanities Coun. of Fairfield U., 1995; New Eng. Found. for Arts Regional fellow, 1993, Conn. Commn. on the Arts fellow, 1998, others. Mem. Architecture League N.Y. (young architects forum 1991, emerging voices, 1996). Office: Newick Archs 85 Willow St New Haven CT 06511

NEWIRTH, RICHARD SCOTT, cultural organization administrator; b. N.Y.C. BA in Maths. magna cum laude, Brown U., 1980; MBA, U. Calif., Berkeley, 1990. Dividend analyst, actuarial asst. Met. Life Ins. Co., San Francisco, 1980-83, sr. underwriter, 1983-85, mgr. renewal svcs., 1985-87, dir. fin. analysis, 1988; benefits and ins. adminstr. San Francisco Symphony, 1990-92; asst. dir. San Francisco Art Commn., 1993-95, dir. cultural affairs, 1995—. Cons. Berkeley (Calif.) Repertory Theatre, 1990; spkr. Nat. Conf. State Legislators, 1997, Far W. Region Cultural Tourism Leadership Forum, 1997; dist. chair Calif. Assembly of Local Arts Agys.; v.p. Urban Arts Fedn., 1998-99, pres., 2000. Mem. mktg. com., vol. Under One Roof. Recipient Pub. Managerial Excellence award, 2001, Ca. Arts Coun. Exemplary Leadership award, 2001. Office: City San Francisco San Francisco Art Commn 25 Van Ness Ave Ste 240 San Francisco CA 94102-6053 Fax: 415-252-2595.

NEWITT, JAY, construction management educator; PhD, Colo. State U., 1981. Tchr. Brigham Young U., Provo, Utah. Recipient John Trimmer Merit Shop Tchg. award Excellence Edn. Construction Found., 1992. Office: Brigham Young U PO Box 24206 Provo UT 84602

NEWKIRK, JOHN BURT, retired metallurgical engineer, administrator; b. Mpls., Mar. 24, 1920; s. Burt Leroy and Mary Louise (Leavenworth) N.; m. Carolyn Mae Jordan, Aug. 4, 1951; children: Jeffrey Burt (dec.), John Jordan, Victoria Louise Lierheimer, Christina Newkirk Seldomridge. B. Metall. Engring, Rensselaer Poly. Inst., Troy, N.Y., 1941; MS, Carnegie Inst. Tech., 1947, Sc.D., 1950. Metall. investigator Bethlehem Steel Co., Pa., 1941-42; Fulbright postdoctoral fellow Cambridge (Eng.) U., 1950-51; research metallurgist research lab. Gen. Electric Co., Schenectady, 1951-59; prof. Cornell U., 1959-65; Phillipson prof. U. Denver, 1965-74, prof. phys. chemistry, 1975-84, Phillipson prof. emeritus, 1984—; pres. Denver Biomaterials, Inc., 1969-86, Colo. Biomed., Inc., 1987-2000, ret. Editor Rews. on High Temperature Materials, 1973-78; co-editor: 16 ann. volumes Advances in X-Ray Analysis; contbr. over 75 articles profl. jours. Lt. USNR, 1942-46. Fellow Am. Soc. Metals (life); mem. Sigma Xi, Tau Beta Pi, Phi Kappa Phi, Alpha Sigma Mu (internat. pres. 1950), Alpha Tau Omega. Republican. Baptist. E-mail: jbn@snowvalley.org.

NEWKIRK, THOMAS CHARLES, lawyer; b. NYC, June 6, 1942; s. Rudolph H. and Ruth H. (Wilson) N.; m. Nancy W., Dec. 23, 1965; children: Jennifer L., Christopher T. BA, Cornell U., 1964, LLB with distinction, 1966. Bar: N.Y. 1966, D.C. 1976, U.S. Ct. Appeals (2d cir.) 1968, U.S. Ct. Appeals (D.C. cir.) 1974. Assoc. Donovan Leisure Newton & Irvine, N.Y., 1966-72; asst. chief counsel Securities Industry Study, U.S. Senate, Washington, 1972; assoc. Donovan Leisure Newton & Irvine, Washington, 1973-75; sr. atty. Office of Legal Counsel, Dept. Justice, Washington, 1975-78; asst. gen. counsel Dept. Energy, Washington, 1978-79, dep. gen. counsel, 1979-85, chief counsel for jud. litigation, 1985; chief litigation counsel SEC, Washington, 1986-93, assoc. dir. div. of enforcement, 1993—. Lectr. in field. Contbr. articles to profl. jours. Recipient Presdl. Meritorious Exec. award Pres. of U.S., 1980, 92, Exceptional Svc. award Sec. of Energy, 1985, Outstanding Svc. medal Sec. of Energy, 1981. Mem. ABA, Assn. Bar City of N.Y. Office: SEC 450 5th St NW Washington DC 20549-0801 Office Phone: 202-942-4550. E-mail: newkirkt@sec.gov.

NEWLAND, CHESTER ALBERT, public administration educator; b. Kansas City, Kans., June 18, 1930; s. Guy Wesley and Mary Virginia (Yoakum) N. BA, U. N. Tex., Denton, 1954; MA, U. Kans., 1955, PhD, 1958. Social Sci. Rsch. Coun. fellow U. Wis. and U.S. Supreme Ct., 1958-59; instr. polit. sci. Idaho State U., Pocatello, 1959-60; mem. faculty U. North Tex., Denton, 1960-66, prof. govt., 1963-66, dir. dept. govt., 1963-66; prof. polit. sci. U. Houston, 1967-68; dir. Lyndon Baines Johnson Libr., Austin, Tex., 1968-70; prof. pub. adminstrn. U. So. Calif., 1966-67, 68-71, 76-82, 84-92, Duggan disting. prof. pub. adminstrn., 1992—; prof. George Mason U., Fairfax, Va., 1982-84. Mem. faculty Fed. Exec. Inst., 1971-76, dir. 1973-76, 80-81; mgr. task force on fed. labor-mgmt. rels. U.S. Pers. Mgmt. Project, Pres.'s Reorgn., Washington, 1977-78. Editor in chief Pub. Adminstrn. Rev., 1984-90; contbr. articles to profl. jours. Chmn. Mcpl. Rsch. Coun., Denton, 1963-64; city councilman, Denton, 1964-66; mem. Pub. Sector Commn. on Productivity and Work Quality, 1974-78; trustee Sacramento (Calif.) Mus. History, Sci. and Tech., 1993-95; mem. UN Devel. Program Kazakhstan, 1997-2000, strategy review program, 2002, Moldova, 1994, Kuwait, 1991, 95-96; cons. Poland, 1990-91, Hungary, 1991, Czech and Slovak Republics, 1992, Bank of Greece, 1999-2002, 04, Taiwan, 2001. Mem. Nat. Acad. Pub. Adminstrn., Southwestern Social Sci. Assn. (chmn. govt. sect. 1964-65), Am. Soc. Pub. Adminstrn. (pres. Dallas-Ft. Worth chpt. 1964-65, nat. coun. 1976, 78-81, editorial bd. jour. 1972-76, chmn. publ. com. 1975-79, program chmn. 1977, nat. pres. 1981-82, Dimock award 1984, Van Riper award 2002), Am. Polit. Sci. Assn., Internat. Pers. Mgmt. Assn. (program chmn. 1978, Stockberger award 1979), Am. Acad. Polit. and Social Sci., Internat. City Mgmt. Assn. (hon., mem. bd. Calif. chpt., 2003-04), Nat. Assn. Schs Pub. Affairs and Adminstrn. (Staats Pub. Svc. award 1989). Office: Univ Southern California 1800 I St Sacramento CA 95814-3004

NEWLAND, RUTH LAURA, small business owner; b. Ellensburg, Wash., June 4, 1949; d. George J. and Ruth Marjorie (Porter) N. BA, Cen. Wash. State Coll., 1970, MEd, 1972; EdS, Vanderbilt U., 1973; PhD, Columbia Pacific U., 1981. Tchr. Union Gap (Wash.) Sch., 1970-71; owner Newland Ranch Gravel Co., Yakima, Wash., 1998; ptnr. Arnold Artificial Limb, Yakima, 1981-86, owner, pres. Yakima and Richland, Wash., 1986—. Owner Newland Ranch, Yakima, 1969—. Contbg. mem. Nat. Dem. Com., Irish Nat. Caucus Found.; mem. Pub. Citizen, We The People, Nat. Humane Edn. Soc.; charter mem. Nat. Mus. Am. Indian. George Washington scholar Masons, Yakima, 1967. Mem. NAFE, NOW, Am. Orthotic and Prosthetic Assn., Internat. Platform Assn., Nat. Antivisection Soc. (life), Vanderbilt U. Alumni Assn., Peabody Coll. Alumni Assn., Columbia Pacific U. Alumni Assn., World Wildlife Fund, Nat. Audubon Soc., Greenpeace, Mus. Fine Arts, Humane Soc. U.S., Wilderness Soc., Nature Conservancy, People for Ethical Treatment of Animals, Amnesty Internat., The Windstar Found., Rodale Inst., Sierra Club (life), Emily's List. Democrat. Avocations: reading, gardening, sewing, handcrafts, people. Home: 2004 Riverside Rd Yakima WA 98901-8540 Office: Arnold Artificial Limb 9 S 12th Ave Yakima WA 98902-3106 *Personal philosophy: God first. Then be politically and socially conservative but liberal in your concern for others.*

NEWLER, JEROME MARC, accountant; b. Irvington, N.J., Dec. 3, 1947; s. Leon and Lola Lee (Warner) N.; m. Holly Ann Ogust, Mar. 13, 1977 (div.); children: Jonathan Lane, Andrea Meryl. BBA, Marquette U., 1969; postgrad., NYU, 1970-74. CPA, N.J. Fgn. tax specialist, supr. ops. Bankers Trust Co., N.Y.C., 1970-74; pub. acct. Howard Kuperman, Newler & Tracy Co., East Orange, N.J., 1974-77; ptnr. Newler & Co. CPAs, Union, N.J., 1977-84; owner J.M. Newler & Co. CPAs, Springfield, N.J., 1984—; prin., dir. litig. support svcs. Zeller, Weiss & Kahn LLP CPAs, Mountainside, N.J., 1998-2000. Ind. trustee First Fidelity Bank Collective Investment Trust, 1987-90; treas., instr. N.J. Chung Do Kwan Inc., 1997—; lectr. N.J. Jud. Coll., Adminstrv. Office of Supreme Ct., N.J. Inst. for Legal Edn., others; cons. N.Y. Minority Enterprises. With Army N.G., 1969-75. Mem. AICPA, N.J. Soc. CPAs (com. to confer with bench and bar, chmn. com. matrimonial acctg., chmn. jud. edn., profl. conduct com., chmn. Union County chpt. com. to confer with bench and bar, trustee Union County chpt.), Nat. Soc. Pub. Accts., Inst. Bus. Appraisers, Marquette U. Alumni Assn. (alumni admissions asst., class agt.), B'nai B'rith, Alpha Epsilon Pi. Avocation: chung do kwan tae kwan do (black belt 1st degree). Home: 580 Patten Ave unit 77 Long Branch NJ 07740-7881 Office: JM Newler & Co PO Box 522 Springfield NJ 07081-0522 Business E-Mail: jnewlercpa@cpadivure.com.

NEWLIN, GEORGE CHRISTIAN, writer; b. Bklyn., Feb. 14, 1931; s. Albert Chauncey and Janet Bethell Newlin; m. Janine Jordan, Dec. 23, 1967 (div. Apr. 1991); children: Jennifer Williams, Pamela Bowen, Ian Williams, Elizabeth Coker, Colin. AB, Princeton U., 1952; postgrad., Salzburg Mozarteum, 1954, Vienna Acad. Music, 1955-56; LLB, Yale U., 1955; MA in History, Trinity U., San Antonio, 1958. Legal assoc. Milbank, Tweed, Hadley & McCloy, N.Y.C., 1958-65; vp. corp. fin. Dominick & Dominick, Inc., N.Y.C., 1965-71; v.p. corp. fin. G. H. Walker & Co. Inc., N.Y.C., 1971-72; v.p., gen. counsel Faxon Comm. Inc., White Plains, N.Y., 1972-76; pres. Braintree Mgmt. Ltd., N.Y.C., 1976-88, Windows into Fiction, Somers, N.Y., 1988—. Presenter, lectr. in field English lit., U.S., Can., Eng.; vis. lectr. Lucyle Hook series Barnard Coll., Calif. State U., Fullerton; lectr. Dickens Conf., U. Calif., Santa Cruz. Author, editor: (anthologies) Everyone in Dickens, 3 vols., 1995, Every Thing in Dickens, 1996, Everyone and Everything in Trollope, 4 vols., 2004, (reference) Understanding A Tale of Two Cities, 1998, Understanding Great Expectations, 2000, (collections) The Book of Our History, 2002, Fifty Years at Home and Abroad, 2002; concert pianist N.Y. met. area; stage actor; trained with Shakespeare & Co., Lenox, Mass.; interviewee Can. Pub. Radio, ABC Radio, N.Y.; appeared in spl. TV broadcast on Great Expectations, Learning Channel. Past mem. planning bd., past chmn. conservation bd., New Castle, N.Y.; founder New Castle Glazier Arboretum; treas., bd. dirs. Koussevitzky Found. for Music, Robert Miller Fund for Music; past pres., past chmn. bd. dirs. Westchester Conservatory of Music; trustee, mem. fin. com. Bagby Found. for Music; founding pres. then chmn. Coun. for Arts in Westchester (now Westchester Arts Coun.); trustee, asst. treas. Composers Conf. Wellesley Coll. Mem. The Century Assn. N.Y.C. Home and Office: 310 Jefferson Rd Princeton NJ 08540 E-mail: gcnewlin@aol.com.

NEWLIN, L. MAX, parks and recreation director; b. June 4, 1942; BS, Wilmington Coll., 1968. Mgr. Massacre Rocks State Pk., American Falls, Idaho, 1996—. Exec. dir. Friends Massacre Rocks Inc.; v.p. S.E. Idaho Travel Coun. Idaho Parks and Recreation Assn. fellow, 1990. Mem. Power County/Am. Falls Hist. Soc. (chmn.). Office: Massacre Rocks State Pk 3592 Park Ln American Falls ID 83211-5556

NEWLIN, LYMAN WILBUR, bookseller, consultant; b. Buda, Ill., May 26, 1910; s. Fred Matheny and Maude Lillian (Potter) N.; m. Evy Ottonia Magnusson, 1966; children: Fred M. II, Erik B.M. Student, Coll. Emporia, Kans., 1928-30, U. Chgo., 1930-32. Buyer, bus. mgr. Follett Book Co., Chgo., 1934-44; mgr. Minn. Book Store and Macalester Coll. Book Store, Mpls. and St. Paul, 1944-48; co-owner Broadwater Lodge, Hackensack, Minn., 1948-65; founder, owner Broadwater Books, Lewiston, N.Y., 1948—; buyer, dept. mgr. Kroch's & Brentano's Book Store, Chgo., 1951-65; regional mgr. Richard Abel and Co., Portland, Oreg. and Zion, Ill., 1966-69, asst. to pres., 1969-75; founder, prin. counselor Lyman W. Newlin Book Trade Counselors, Lewiston, N.Y., 1975—; mdse. mgr. Coutts Library Services, Inc., Lewiston, 1976-90; pub. rels. advisor The Charleston (Coll. Libr.) Conf., 1985—; pub. liaison Book News, Inc., Portland, 1989—; v.p. Zenaida Pub., Amherst, Mass., 2004—. Program coord. Acad. of Scholarly Pub. seminar Coll. of Charleston, 1995—; cons. Rutgers U. Press, New Brunswick, N.J., 1975-81; panelist and lectr. to acad. librs. and schs., booksellers; v.p. Zenaida Pub., Amherst, Mass., 2004—. Pub. Rev. Index Quar. Guide to Profl. Revs., 1941-43; co-editor: Scholarly Publishing, Books, Journals, Publishers and Libraries in the Twentieth Century, 2002; pub. rels. advisor, contbr. Bi-Monthly Publ. Against the Grain, 1985—; contbr. articles to profl. jours. Founder, 1st pres. Boy River Chain of Lakes Improvement Assn., Cass County, Minn., 1961-65, Concerned Parents Orgn., Freehold, 1976-79; trustee, v.p., sec., chmn. new libr. bldg. com. Lewiston Pub. Libr., 1985-98, pres. bd. trustees, 1998-2002; committeeman Niagara County Dem. Party, 1987—, sec., 1988-90; mem. coun. Luth. Ch. Messiah, Lewiston, 1982-93, deacon, 1992-97; mem. Town of Lewiston

Sr. Citizens Adv. Bd., 1992—; mem., com. person Zion Luth. Ch., Niagara Falls, N.Y., 1995—. Named Dem. of Yr., Town of Lewiston, 2003. Mem. ALA, Assn. Book Travelers (50 Yr. award 1984), Am. Booksellers Assn. (50 yr. bronze plaque 1998), Soc. Scholarly Pub. (program com. 1985), Am. Assn. Pubs. (emeritus), Pi Kappa Delta. Lutheran. Democrat. Avocations: amateur ornithology, Am. folk music, New Orleans jazz, book collecting. Office: PO Box 278 Lewiston NY 14092-0278 Office Phone: 716-754-2031. *If the Golden Rule is truly one's rule in living, no other rule is needed.*

NEWLIN, WILLIAM RANKIN, lawyer; b. Pitts., Dec. 1, 1940; s. Theodore F. Newlin and Elizabeth Crooks; m. Ann Kleinschmidt, Aug. 25, 1962; children: Steffler Ann, Shelley Kay, William Rankin II. AB, Princeton U., 1962; JD, U. Pitts., 1965; DBA (hon.), Robert Morris Coll., 1997. Bar: Pa. 1965. Assoc. Buchanan Ingersoll, Pitts., 1965-71, ptnr., 1971—, mng. dir., 1980—; mng. gen. ptnr. CEO Venture Fund, Pitts., 1985—; chmn. bd. Kennametal Inc., Latrobe, Pa., 1996—. Bd. dirs. bd. Nat. City Bank Pa., Pitts., Parker/Hunter, Pitts., Black Box Corp., Pitts., Pitts. Regional Alliance, (hon.) British Consul, Pitts. Editor in chief U. Pitts. Law Rev., 1963; contbr. articles to profl. jours. Chmn., Gov. Thornburgh's Corp. Adv. Com., 1980-82; bd. dirs. Mfr. Studies Bd. nat. Rsch. Coun., Washington, 1988-89, Pitts. High Tech. Coun., 1982—, Pa. Tech. Coun. Recipient Entrepreneur of Yr. award Ernst & Young, Inc. Mag./ Merrill Lynch, 1991. Fellow Am. Bar Found., Pa. Bar Found.; mem. ABA (corp. banking, bus. law sect.), Pa. Bar Assn. (mem. coun. corp. banking and bus. law sect. 1973-82, chmn. sect. 1979-81, Spl. Achievement award 1982), Allegheny County Bar Assn., Assn. of Bar of City of N.Y., Am. Law Inst., Pa. S.W. Assn. (trustee), Greater Pitts. C. of C. (bd. dirs.), Duquesne Club (dir. 1982-85), Rivers Club (bd. dirs. 1983—), Laurel Valley Golf Club, Allegheny Country Club (bd. dirs. 1988—). Office: Buchanan Ingersoll One Oxford Centre 301 Grant St Fl 20 Pittsburgh PA 15219-1410 E-mail: newlinwr@bipc.com.

NEWMAN, ALYSE MAXINE, artist, writer, lyricist; d. Leonard and Evelyn Newman; m. Eliot Loshak. BFA with honors, Pratt Inst., Bklyn. Author (artist): (cartoon strip) First Date, Newman, Maxine, over forty flip books; exhibitions include; author (artist): (children's books) Every Saturday, It's Me, Claudia!, Albert and the Chairman; children's books, Margery Williams' The Velveteen Rabbit, exhibitions include NY Arsenal Gallery, NY Pub. Libr. Vocalist, guitarist The NY Foundling Hosp. Mem.: Graphic Artists Guild, NY Artists Cir. Avocations: playwright, poetry.

NEWMAN, ANDREA FISCHER, air transportation executive; AB, U. Mich., 1979; JD, George Washington U., 1983. Sr. v.p. govt. affairs Northwest Airlines, Detroit. Bd. regents U. Mich., Ann Arbor, 1994—; vice chmn. George W. Bush for Pres. Campaign, co-chmn. fin. com., 2000; bd. dirs. Mich. Econ. Devel. Corp. Found., Mich. Thanksgiving Day Parade Found., Isiah Thomas Found. Mem.: Detroit Econ. Club (v.p.). Office: Northwest Airlines Detroit Met Airport North Terminal Mezzanine Level Detroit MI 48242

NEWMAN, ANDREW, physician; b. Phila., Mar. 29, 1938; s. Louis M. and Ruth (Auerbach) N.; m. Sandra S. Mislove, June 18, 1960; children: Kenneth T., Marjorie F., Pamela B. BA summa cum laude, Temple U., 1959, MD, 1963; JD, Rutgers U., 1987; LLM in Health Law, Widener U., 2001. Bar: Pa. 1987, N.J. 1987, D.C. 1988; bd. cert. Am. Bd. Legal Medicine, 1988, bd. cert. Am. Acad. Pain Mgmt., 1989, bd. cert. Am. Bd. Orthopedic Surgery, 1971, recert., 1995. Intern Lower Bucks County Hosp., Bristol, Pa., 1963-64; resident East Orange (N.J.) V.A. Hosp., 1964-65, Phila. (Pa.) Gen. Hosp., 1967-69, Shriners Hosp., Phila., 1969-70; pvt. practice in orthopedic surgery Phila., 1970—; clin. asst. prof. Hahnemann Med. Univ., Dept. Orthopedics, 1970—; attending physician, Dept. Orthopedics Rolling Hill Hosp., Elkins Park, Pa., 1970-84, Parkview Hosp.-Tenet, 1971—. Adj. prof. med. ethics Arcadia U., Glenside, Pa., 1996; cons. in orthopedics to Pa. Blue Shield; mem. Osteopathic Med. Bd., Pa.; team physician Lower Moreland H.S. Football Team, Huntingdon Valley, Pa.; cons. Bd. Med. Licensure and Discipline, RI; prof. legal medicine Temple U. Sch. Podiatric Medicine. Contbg. editor (textbook) Legal Medicine Update, 1988-89; asst. editor Legal Aspects Medical Practice; assoc. editor Bulletin of the Am. Acad. of Orthopedic Surgery; contbr. articles to profl. jours. Lt. col. USAFR. Named Man of Yr., Am. Podiatry Assn., Chgo., 1982; recipient pres.'achievement award Am. Coll. Legal Medicine, Palm Springs, Colo. 1988. Fellow Am. Acad. Orthopedic Surgery, Am. Coll. Legal Medicine; mem. AMA, Am. Assn. Hand Surgery (assoc.), Am. Soc. Law and Medicine, Pa. Med. Soc., Phila. County Med. Soc., Am. Orthopedic Foot Soc., Phila. Orthopedic Soc., Nat. Bd. Podiatric Med. Examiners. Avocations: gardening, Am. history (Civil War).

NEWMAN, ANDREW EDISON, restaurant executive; b. St. Louis, Aug. 14, 1944; s. Eric Pfeiffer and Evelyn Frances (Edison) N.; m. Peggy Gregory, Feb. 14, 1984; children: Daniel Mark, Anthony Edison. BA, Harvard U., 1966, MBA, 1968. With Office of Sec. Def., Washington, 1968-70; with Edison Bros. Stores, Inc., St. Louis, 1970-95, v.p. ops. and adminstrn., 1975-80, dir., 1978-96, exec. v.p., 1980-86, chmn., 1987-95; chmn., CEO Race Rock Internat., St. Louis, 1995—. Bd. dirs. Lee Enterprises, Davenport, Iowa. Trustee Washington U. Office: 8000 Maryland Ave Saint Louis MO 63105-3752

NEWMAN, ANITA NADINE, surgeon; b. Honolulu, June 13, 1949; d. William Reece Elton and Margie Ruth (Pollard) Newman; children: Justin Ellis, Chelsea Newman, Andrew Frank, Tyler William. BA, Stanford U., 1971; MD, Dartmouth Coll., 1975. Diplomate Am. Bd. Otolaryngology. From intern to resident in gen. surgery Northwestern Meml. Hosp., Chgo., 1975-77, resident in otolaryngology, 1977-78; resident UCLA Hosp. and Clinics, 1979-82; assoc. prof. UCLA, 1982-96; staff surgeon Wadsworth VA Hosp., LA, 1982-84; rsch. fellow in neurotology, 1984-88; surgeon USC Head and Neck Group, 1997-2000; pvt. practice LA, 2000—. Contbr. articles to profl. jours. Mem. alumni admissions support com. Dartmouth Med. Sch. Alumni Coun., 1983-87. Fellow ACS; mem. Am. Acad. Otolaryngology, Am. Med. Women's Assn., LA County Med. Women's Assn., Assn. Rsch. Otolaryngology, Stanford Women's Honor Soc. Democrat. Office: 8631 W 3d St Ste 625E Los Angeles CA 90048 Office Phone: 310-657-6420. E-mail: entdoc49@aol.com.

NEWMAN, ARNOLD, photographer; b. N.Y.C., Mar. 3, 1918; s. Isidore and Freda (Perell) N.; m. Augusta Rubenstein, Mar. 6, 1949; children— Eric Allan, David Saul. Student, U. Miami, Coral Gables, Fla., 1937-38, DFA (hon.), 1981; DHL (hon.), Art Ctr. Coll. Design, Pasadena, Calif., 1987; hon. univ. doctorate, U. Bradford, Eng., 1989; DFA (hon.), New Sch. Social Rsch./Parson Sch. Design, 1990; DHL (hon.), Acad. Art Coll., San Francisco, 1996; DFA (hon.), U. Arts, Phila., 1999, Newbury Coll., Brookline, Mass., 1999, Corcoran Coll. Art Design, Washington, 2000, U. Hartford, 2003. Began photography, 1938; exptl. portraiture, 1941; opened N.Y.C. studio, 1946; adj. prof. photography Cooper Union, N.Y.C., NY, 1968—75. Resident dirs. visitor/lectr. Inst. for Advanced Study, Princeton, N.J., 1991; lectr. U.S. and abroad. Exhibited and represented in collections, Mus. Modern Art, NYC, Met. Mus. Art, NYC, Art Inst. Chgo., Smithsonian Instn., Washington, Phila. Mus. Art, Internat. Mus. Photography at George Eastman House, Rochester, NY, Photography Gallery, London, Israel Mus., Jerusalem, Victoria and Albert Mus., London, Moderna Museet, Stockholm, Australia Nat. Gallery, Camberra, Nat. Portrait Gallery, London, Nihon U. Coll. Art, Tokyo, Odakyu Gallery, Tokyo, Japan, Nat. Gallery Can., Ottawa, Tel Aviv Mus., Israel, Stedelijk Mus., Amsterdam, Internat. Ctr. Photography, NYC, Ctr. Creative Photography, Univ. Ariz., Tucson, others; traveling retrospective exhbn., Arnold Newman-Five Decades, Mus. of Photographic Arts, San, Diego, 1986, Art Inst. of Chgo., 1986, Mpls. Inst. Art, 1987, Norton Gallery & Sch. Art, MIT Mus., Cambridge, 1988, Modern Art Mus., Ft. Worth, 1988-89, Cin. Art Mus., 1989, De Nieuwe Kerk, Amsterdam, The Netherlands, 1989, The Joan Miró Fedn., Barcelona, Spain, 1990, Frankfurter Kunstverein, Germany, Musee de l'Elysee, Lausanne, Switzerland, 1992, Mus. Modern Art, Oxford, England, 1992, Arnold Newman's Ams., Nat. Portrait Gallery, Washington, 1992, One World, One People, originated Portland Jewish Mus., 1999, Arnold Newman: Breaking Ground, Internat. Ctr. Photography, NYC, 1999, Mpls. Inst. Art, 2000, Corcoran Gallery, Washington, 2000, Denver Mizel Mus., 2001, Hotel Sully, Paris, 2002, Glerie Chateau Eau, Toulouse, France, 2003, La. Mus. Modern Art, Humlebaek, Denmark, 2003, Jewish Mus. Fla., 2003; author: Bravo Stravinsky, 1967, One Mind's Eye: The Portraits and Other Photographs of Arnold Newman, 1974, Faces USA, 1978, The Great British, 1979, Artists: Portraits from Four Decades, 1980, I Grandi Fotographi Arnold Newman, 1983, Arnold Newman-Five Decades, 1986, Arnold Newman in Florida, 1987, Arnold Newman's Americans, Portrait Gallery, Washington, 1992, Arnold Newman's Americans, 1992; Arnold Newman, 1992, The Detroit Inst. Arts, 1993, LBJ Libr. & Mus., Austin, Tex., 1993, Columbus (Ga.) Mus. Art, 1993-94, Greenville (S.C.) County Mus. Art, 1994, Worcester (Mass.) Art Mus., 1994, Arnold Newman's Gift, George Eastman House, Rochester, N.Y., 1994, Arnold Newman-Selected Photographs, 1999; Arnold Newman, 2000; contbr. to Travel and Leisure, Life, Look, Holiday, Fortune, Esquire, Town & Country, Vanity Fair, Scientific American, Harper's Bazaar, The New Yorker, 1946—; subject of Nebr. Ednl. TV program The Image Makers: The Environment of Arnold Newman, 1977; invited exhbn. and lecture tour throughout country Czechoslovakian govt., 1989, Mus. Contemporary History, Budapest, Hungary, 1990. Bd. dirs., founder photography dept. Israel Mus., Jerusalem, 1965. Recipient Photokina award, Cologne, Germany 1951, Newhouse citation Syracuse (N.Y.) U. 1961, Gold medal 4th Biennale Internazionale della Fotagrafic, Venice, Italy 1963, Andy award Advt. Club N.Y., 1983, Mo. Honor medal for journalism U. Mo., 1985, Medal of Merit, 1986, Medal of Merit Lotos Club, 1986, Lifetime Achievement in Photography award Photographic Adminstrs., 1988, Joseph Sudek Commemorative medal, 1989, Honor award Am. Soc. Media Photographers, 1996, Master of Photography award Internat. Ctr. Photography, 1999, Master Photography award Internat. Ctr. Photography, 1999, Lifetime Achievement award WPPI, 2000, Profl. Photographers Am., 2002, Nat. Treasure award Seasoned Citizen Theatre Co., 2003, Commandeur Ordre Arts des Lettres award French Min. Culture and Comm., 2003, others; named Hon. Fellow of Israel Mus. of Jerusalem, 1986, Commemorative medal in hon. 150th anniversary photography Ministry of Culture Czechoslovakia, 1989, Disting. Alumnus award U. Miami, 1993; named N.Y. Alumnus of Yr. U. Miami, 1993; World Image award and Arnold Newman Scholarship Fund named in honor Parsons Sch. Design, N.Y.C., 1993. Mem. Bd. of Israel Mus., Jerusalem and founded photography dept., 1965, Am. Soc. Mag. Photographers (Life Achievement in Photography award 1975, honor award 1996), Inst. for Advanced Study (bd. dirs. visitor Princeton chpt. 1991). Office: 39 W 67th St New York NY 10023-6244

NEWMAN, BARBARA MILLER, psychologist, educator; b. Chgo., Sept. 6, 1944; d. Irving George and Florence (Levy) Miller; m. Philip r. Newman, June 12, 1966; children: Samuel Asher, Abraham Levy, Rachel Florence. Student, Bryn Mawr Coll.; AB with honors in Psychology, U. Mich., 1966, PhD in Devel. Psychology, 1971. Undergrad. research asst. in psychology U. Mich., 1963-64, research asst. in psychology, 1964-69, teaching fellow, 1965-71, asst. project dir. Inst. for Social Research, 1971-72, univ. lectr. in psychology and research assoc., 1971-72; asst. prof. psychology Russell Sage Coll., 1972-76, assoc. prof., 1977-78; assoc. prof. and chair dept. family rels. and human devel. Ohio State U., 1978-83, prof. and chair, 1983-86, assoc. provost for faculty recruitment and devel., 1987-92, prof., 1992-2000; prof. and chair dept. human devel. and family studies U. R.I., 2000—. Author: Development Through Life, 1975, 8th edit., 2003; author: (with P. Newman) Living: The Process of Adjustment, 1981, Understanding Adulthood, 1983; author: Adolescent Development, 1986, When Kids Go to College, 1992, Childhood and Adolescence, 1997; author: (with P. Newman, L. Landry-Meyer and B. Lohman) Life Span Development: A Case Book, 2003; contbr. articles to profl. jours. Mem. AAAS, APA, Soc. Rsch. in Child Devel., Am. Psychol. Soc., Nat. Coun. Family Rels., Groves Conf. on Marriage and Family, Soc. for Rsch. on Adolescence. Office: U RI Human Devel and Family Studies 112 Transition Ctr Kingston RI 02881 Office Phone: 401-874-7135. Business E-Mail: bnewman@uri.edu.

NEWMAN, BARRY INGALLS, retired banker, lawyer; b. N.Y.C., Mar. 19, 1932; s. M.A. and T.C. (Weitman) N.; m. Jean Short, Mar. 6, 1965; children: Suzanne, Cathy, David. BA, Alfred U., 1952; JD, NYU, 1955. Bar: N.Y. 1957, Ohio 1958, U.S. Supreme Ct. 1967, Calif. 1990; practice in N.Y.C., 1957. Assoc., then ptnr. firm Shapiro Persky Marken & Newman, Cleve., 1957-63; asst. v.p. Meinhard & Co. (now Meinhard Comml. Corp.), N.Y.C., 1963-65; v.p. Amsterdam Overseas Corp., N.Y.C., 1966-68; pres. No. Fin. Corp., L.A., 1968-72; sr. v.p. Aetna Bus. Credit, Inc., Hartford, Conn., 1972-78; exec. v.p. Security Pacific Fin. Group, San Diego, 1978-81, chmn., pres., CEO, 1981-82; sr. exec. v.p. Gt. Am. First Savs. Bank, 1982-88, ret., 1988. Chmn. bd. dirs. San Diego County Capital Asset Leasing Corp., 1984-2000. Past pres. U. Club of San Diego; past chmn. bd. trustees Calif. Ctr. for the Arts, Escondido; past pres. San Diego County Taxpayers Assn.; dep. foreman San Diego County Grand Jury, 1999-2000; chmn. San Diego County Treasury Oversight com., 1995—; mem. bd. govs. San Diego Found.; active San Diego County Civil Svc. Commn.; treas. The Episcopal Diocese of San Diego, 1993-2001; mem. planning commn., City of Escondido. Recipient Disting. Svc. award Cleve. Jr. C. of C., 1961. Mem. ABA, N.Y. State Bar Assn., Ohio Bar Assn., Calif. Bar Assn., San Diego Bar Assn., Masons. Republican. Home: 3308 Avenida Sierra Escondido CA 92029-7937 Office Phone: 760-743-5005. E-mail: BNewmanlaw@aol.com.

NEWMAN, BARRY MARC, pediatric surgeon; b. N.Y.C., Dec. 13, 1951; s. Sheldon and Miriam (Jasphy) N.; m. Jane Post, July 2, 1989; 1 child, Alexander Ross. BA, U. Pa., 1973; MD, SUNY, Stony Brook, 1976. Diplomate Nat. Bd. Med. Examiners, Am. Bd. Surgery, Am. Bd. Pediatric Surgery. Resident in surgery N.Y. Med. Coll., N.Y.C., 1976-78; sr. resident in surgery SUNY, Stony Brook, 1978-81; chief resident pediatric surgery Childrens Hosp. of Buffalo, 1981-83, fellow pediatric surgery and gastroenterology, 1983-84; asst. prof. surgery U. Va., Charlottesville, 1984-88, U. Ill., Chgo., 1988-93; dir. pediatric surgery Luth. Gen. Children's Hosp., Park Ridge, Ill., 1991-96; clin. assoc. prof. surgery U. Chgo., 1993-95; dir. pediatric surg. svcs. Loyola U. Med. Ctr., Maywood, Ill., 1996—, co-dir. surg. laparoscopy lab., 1996-97, assoc. prof. surgery and pediatrics, 1996—2004, prof. surgery and pediatrics, 2004—. Instr. Adv. Trauma and Life Support, ACS, Chgo., 1984—. Contbr. articles to profl. jours., chpts. to books. NIH grantee, 1982-83, 87-88. Fellow ACS, Am. Coll. Chest Physicians, Am. Acad. Pediatrics; mem. Am. Gastroenterol. Assn., Am. Pediatric Surg. Assn., Am. Coll. Physician Execs. Democrat. Jewish. Avocations: wine collecting, scuba diving, underwater photography, personal computing. Office: Loyola U Med Ctr Dept Surgery 2160 S 1st Ave Dept Surgery Maywood IL 60153-3304 Office Phone: 708-327-2782.

NEWMAN, BOB, radio personality, security consultant; b. Washington, Jan. 24, 1958; s. William Robert and Mary Jane Newman; m. Susan C. Roiger, Jan. 9, 1958; 1 child, Britta Sue. Student, U. Maine, 1975—77. Commd. 2d lt. U.S. Marines, 1977, advanced through grades to gunnery sgt., ret., 1997; mil. sci. & terrorism analyst Clear Channel, Inc., Denver, 2001—; dir. counterterrorism svcs. Geoscope Group, Greeley, Colo., 2002—03; co-host Radio Sta. KHOW, Denver, 2003—. Spkr. on terrorism, guerrilla warfare, spl. ops., survial and security. Author: (military science manual) Guerrillas in the Mist: A Battlefield Guide to Clandestine Warfare, (novel) Trenches & Hard-Points: A Gulf War Novel, (military science manual) Marine Special Warfare & Elite Unit Tactics, (survival manual) Wilderness Wayfinding: How to Survive in the Wilderness as You Travel; contbr. news radio (Edward R. Murrow award (Nat.), 2002, AP/Colo. Broadcasters Assn. award, 2001); editor: Hunting the Dangerous Game of Africa (Best of 1997, 1997). Mem.: VFW. Office: Clear Channel Inc 4695 S Monaco St Denver CO 80237 Office Phone: 303-713-8473. E-mail: bobnewman@clearchannel.com.

NEWMAN, BRUCE MURRAY, antiques dealer; b. N.Y.C., N.Y., Jan. 27, 1930; s. Meyer and Evelyn (Kantor) Newman; m. Judith S Brandus, June 26, 1965; 1 child, Emily Rachel. BA, Pratt Inst., 1953, D (hon.), 1997, BFA (hon.), 1998, degree in fine arts (hon.), 1997. Pres. Newel Art Galleries Inc., N.Y.C., 1975—2001. Lectr mus and univs; mem regional adv bd Chase Manhattan Bank; mem regional adv bd J P Morgan Chase Bank. Author: (book) Fantasy Furniture, 1989; featured numerous TV & radio programs, mags, and other publs, guest CBS Morning Show, 1988. Assoc mem Mt Sinia Med Ctr, 1988—; bd dirs New York City Ctr, 1988—90; trustee Pratt Inst, Brooklyn, NY, 1983—. Named Man of the Yr., Pratt Inst., 1993; recipient Designer Award, Art Dirs. Club, 1984. Mem.: Victorian Soc Am, Am Soc Interior Designers (bd dirs 1989—). Avocations: golf, reading, jogging, travel.

NEWMAN, CAROL L. lawyer; b. Yonkers, N.Y., Aug. 7, 1949; d. Richard J. and Pauline Frances (Stoll) N. AB/MA summa cum laude, Brown U., 1971; postgrad., Harvard U. Law Sch., 1972-73; JD cum laude, George Washington U., 1977. Bar: D.C. 1977, Calif. 1979. With antitrust divsn. U.S. Dept. Justice, Washington and L.A., 1977-80; assoc. Alschuler, Grossman & Pines, L.A., 1980-82, Costello & Walcher, L.A., 1982-85, Rosen, Wachtell & Gilbert, L.A., 1985-88, ptnr., 1988-90, Keck, Mahin & Cate, L.A., 1990-94; pvt. practice L.A., 1994—. Adj. prof. Sch. Bus., Golden Gate U., spring 1982. Commr. L.A. Bd. Transp. Commrs., 1993—98, v.p., 1995—96; pres. Bd. Taxicab Commrs., 1999—2001; candidate for State Atty. Gen., 1986; bd. dirs. Women's Progress Alliance, 1996—98. Mem. ABA, State Bar Calif., L.A. County Bar Assn., Ventura County Bar Assn., L.A. Lawyers for Human Rights (co. pres. 1991-92), Log Cabin (bd. dirs. 1992-97, 2003—, pres. 1996-97), Calif. Women Lawyers (bd. govs. 1991-94), Order of Coif, Phi Beta Kappa. Office Phone: 818-225-0056. E-mail: cnewman540@aol.com.

NEWMAN, CHARLES A. lawyer; b. L.A., Mar. 18, 1949; s. Arthur and Gladys Newman; m. Elizabeth F.; children: Anne R., Elyse S. BA magna cum laude, U. Calif., 1970; JD, Washington U., 1973. Bar: Mo. 1973, U.S. Dist. Ct. (ea. dist.) Mo. 1973, U.S. Dist. Ct. (so. dist.) Ill. 2001, U.S. Dist. Ct. (ea. dist.) Mich. 2002, U.S. Ct. Appeals (8th cir.) 1975, U.S. Supreme Ct. 1976, D.C. 1981, U.S. Tax Ct. 1981, U.S. Claims Ct. 1981, U.S. Ct. Appeals (11th cir.) 1994, U.S. Ct. Appeals (9th cir.) 1995, U.S. Ct. Appeals (3d, 5th, 7th and 10th cirs.) 1996, U.S. Ct. Appeals (6th cir.) 1997. From assoc. to ptnr. Thompson & Mitchell, St. Louis, 1973-96; ptnr. Thompson Coburn, St. Louis, 1996-97, Bryan Cave LLP, St. Louis, 1997—. Lectr. law Washington U., St. Louis, 1976-78. Bd. dirs. Hawthorn Found., 1997-2000; trustee Mo. Bar Found., 1990-96, mem. Mo. Bar Bd. Govs, 1980-84; bd. dirs. United Israel Appeal, N.Y.C., 1990-93, Coun. Jewish Fedns., N.Y.C., 1992-95, United Jewish Appeal Young Leadership Cabinet, N.Y.C., 1985-88, Ctr. for Study of Dispute Resolution, 1985-88, Legal Svcs. Ea. Mo., 1985-94, St. Louis Community Found., 1992-2001, vice-chmn. 1997-99, St. Louis chpt. Young Audiences 1993-95, Planned Parenthood St. Louis, 1986-89, Jewish Fedn., St. Louis, 1986-98, asst. treas., 1989-90, v.p. fin. planning, 1990-93, asst. sec., 1994-95; v.p. Repertory Theatre, St. Louis, 1986 89, sr. v.p., 1990 91; pres. St. Louis Opportunity Clearinghouse, 1974-78. Recipient Lon O. Hocker Meml. Trial award Mo. Bar Found., 1984. Mem. Bar Assn. Met. St. Louis (Merit award 1976). Democrat. Avocations: golf, reading, music, sailing. Office: Bryan Cave LLP One Metropolitan Square Saint Louis MO 63102-2750 Office Phone: 314-259-2000. E-mail: canewman@bryancave.com.

NEWMAN, CLAIRE POE, private investor; b. Jacksonville, Fla., Dec. 12, 1926; d. Leslie Ralph and Gertrude (Criswell) Poe; m. Robert Jacob Newman, July 3, 1948 (dec. 1994); children: Leslie Claire, Robert, Christopher David. Student, Fla. State Coll. for Women, 1944-45, Tulane U., 1971-73. Co-owner Vineyards in Burgundy, France. Com. mem. New Orleans Mus. Art; women's com. New Orleans Philharmonic Symphony Assn., 1961—, chmn. orch. rels. com., 1961-63; chmn. New Orleans Easter Seal Drive, 1963; La. trustee Nat. Soc. Crippled Children and Adults, 1963-65. Featured on cover of Life mag., Sept. 25, 1944. Mem. Women's Aus. C. of C., New Orleans Soc. Archeol., Inst. Am. (v.p. 1972-74), Confrèrie des Chevaliers du Tastevin, Sigma Kappa, Eichenheim Golf Club, Golden Skibook Club (Austria), Ski Club (Arlberg), Eichenheim Golf and Country Club. Address: Timberg 6370 Kitzbuehel Austria

NEWMAN, CONSTANCE BERRY, federal agency administrator; b. Chgo., July 8, 1935; d. Joseph Alonzo and Ernestine (Siggers) B.; m. Theodore Roosevelt Newman, July 25, 1959 (div. 1980). AB, Bates Coll., 1956; BSL, U. Minn., 1959; JD (hon.), Bates Coll., 1972, Amherst Coll., 1980; LHD (hon.), Central State U., 1991. Dir. VISTA, Washington, 1971-73; commr. Consumer Product Safety Commn., Washington, 1973-76; asst. sec. U.S. HUD, Washington, 1976-77; pres. The Newman & Hermanson Co., Washington, 1977-82; cons. Govt. of Lesotho, 1987-88; dir. nat. voter coalition Bush-Quayle '88, Washington, 1988; dir. Office Pers. Mgmt., Washington, 1989-92; under sec. Smithsonian Instn., Washington, 1992-2000; vice chair D.C. Fin. Responsibility and Mgmt. Assistance Authority, 1994—2000; ptnr. Upstart Ptnrs., 2000—01; asst. adminr. bur. for Africa USAID, Washington, 2001—04; asst. sec. for African affairs US Dept. State, 2004—. Mem. adj. faculty John F. Kennedy Sch. Govt., Harvard U., Cambridge, Mass., 1979-82. Contbr. articles to profl. jours. Mem. Adminstrn. Conf. U.S., Washington, 1973-76, 1989—; commr. M.L. King Fed. Holiday Commn., Washington, 1989; chmn. Def. Adv. Com. on Women in the Svcs., Washington, 1985-86; trustee Community Coll. Balt., 1985-89; adv. to chmn. 1988 Rep. Nat. Conv., New Orleans, 1988; bd. overseers Morehouse Coll. Sch. Medicine, Atlanta, 1976-77; bd. dirs. Brookings Instn., Aspen Inst., Coun. for Excellence in Govt. Recipient Pub. Svc. award Ohio State U., 1991. Mem. NAACP, Exec. Women in Govt. (founding mem.), Internat. Repub. Inst., 1998-2000. Republican. Avocation: photography. Office: US Dept State 2201 C St NW Washington DC 20520

NEWMAN, DEAN GORDON, business consultant; b. North Branch, Iowa, Mar. 17, 1929; s. Floyd William and Hazel Jane (Covault) N.; m. Maggie Newman; children: Gary Dean, Craig William. BA, Simpson Coll., 1950; MBA, Stanford U., 1952. Trainee GE, Schenectady, N.Y., 1952, Syracuse, N.Y., 1955-56, Chgo., 1956-58, mem. employee and cmty. rels. staff, 1958-62, mgr. employee and cmty. rels. Milw., 1962-67, DeKalb, Ill., 1967-69; v.p. employee and pub. rels. United Nuclear Corp., Elmsford, NY, 1969—71; v.p. employee and indsl. rels. Apache Corp., Mpls., 1971-83, v.p. human resources and comm., 1983-87; v.p. mktg. Nelson Cons. Group, Mpls., 1989-92; chmn., CFO Linear Fitness Systems, Inc., Allenspark, Colo., 1998—. Pres. Apache Found., 1973—87; v.p., bd. dirs. Boys Clubs, Mpls., 1978—85; chmn. Boys and Girls Club Mpls., 1985—88, exec. com., 1988—89; v.p. fin., bd. Boys and Girls Club Larimer County, 1993—96; vice chmn. Bus. Econs. Edn. Found., 1986—88, chmn. fin. com., 1988—89; com. mem., treas. Allenspark Sr. Adv. Com., 1999—2003; treas. Allenspark Fire Protection Dist., 2000—, bd. dirs., 2000—. With USNR, 1952—55, Korea. Nat. Meth. scholar, 1946—50. Mem.: Nat. Assn. Mfrs. (dir. 1981—87), Allenspark Area Club (bd. dirs., treas. 2000—03, Founder's award 2002, Boulder County Honoring Our Elders award 2003), Pi Gamma Mu, Sigma Tau Delta, Epsilon Sigma, Alpha Tau Omega. Republican. Methodist. Home and Office: 125 County Road 84 W Allenspark CO 80510-9713 Office Phone: 303-747-2825. E-mail: mdnewman85@earthlink.net.

NEWMAN, DENNIS NATHAN, lawyer; b. N.Y.C., Aug. 16, 1946; s. Isidor and Dorothy (Siegel) Newman; m. Ronna Susan Smith, July 31, 1971; 1 child, Abigail. BA, Brandeis U., 1969; JD, U. Mich., 1972. Bar: Ill. 1972, U.S. Dist. Ct. (no. dist.) Ill. 1972, U.S. Ct. Appeals (7th cir.) 1973. Assoc. Sonnenschein Carlin Nath & Rosenthal, Chgo., 1972-79, ptnr., 1979-88, Sonnenschein Nath & Rosenthal LLP, Chgo., 1989—. Adj. prof. Chgo.-Kent Coll. Law, 2000, 01. Mem.: ABA. Jewish. Office: Sonnenschein Nath Rosenthal LLP 8000 Sears Tower 233 S Wacker Dr Ste 8000 Chicago IL 60606-6491 Office Phone: 312-876-8179.

NEWMAN, DIANA S. development consultant; b. Toledo, June 15, 1943; d. Fred Andrew and Thelma Elizabeth (Hewitt) Smith; m. Dennis Ryan Newman, Feb. 15, 1964; children: Barbara Lynn Newman LaBine, John Ryan, Elizabeth Anne. Student, Oberlin Coll., 1961-64. Asst. treas. Marble Cliff Quarries Co., 1964-68; cmty. vol., 1968-83; dir. Ohio Hist. Found., Columbus, 1983-90; v.p. advancement The Columbus (Ohio) Found., 1990-95; pres. Philanthropic Resource Group, Columbus, 1995—. Author: Opening Doors: Pathways to Diverse Donors, 2002 (AFP/Skystone Ryan prize for rsch., 2003). Bd. dirs. Leader Inst., Inc., 2001-04; mem. governing bd. First Cmty. Ch., 1983-88, chair, 1987-88; bd. dirs. LWV Ctrl. Ohio, 1968-72, Ohio Mus. Assn., 1985-90, Crittenton Family Svcs., Columbus, 1992-95; founder Franklin County Com. on Criminal Justice, Columbus, 1972; pres. Jr. League Columbus, 1980-81. Recipient Skystone Ryan Prize for Rsch. on Fundraising and Philanthropy, Assn. Fundraising Profls., 2003. Mem. Assn. Fundraising Profls. (bd. dirs. Ctrl. Ohio chpt. 1985-88, 2004-, nat. rsch. coun. 2003—), Ctrl. Ohio Planned

Giving Coun. (bd. dirs. 1990-2001, pres. 1998), Columbus Female Benevolent Soc. (bd. dirs. 1984—). Home: 1944 Chatfield Rd Columbus OH 43221-3702 Office: Philanthropic Resource Group 1944 Chatfield Rd Columbus OH 43221-3702 Office Phone: 614-486-4787. Business E-Mail: diana.newman@columbus.rr.com.

NEWMAN, FRANCINE M. healthcare company executive; b. 1954; BA, St. Lawrence U. With group ins. ops. CIGNA Co., 1970-73, with human res., mgmt. svcs., 1973-81, dir. underwriting for life and health reinsurance ops., 1981-82; 2d v.p. CIGNA Reinsurance, 1982-84, pres., 1984—. Bd. dirs. Lyme Borelleosis Found. Mem. Greater Hartford C. of C. Edn. Task Force on Strategic Planning (mem. women execs. subcom.). Named among America's Top 50 Women Executives Business Week Magazine, 1987; co-recipient Partners in Leadership award Soc. of Info. Mgmt. Mem. Home Office Life Underwriters Assn. (exec. com.), Health Ins. Assn. Am. (group ins. com.), Am. Coun. Life Ins. (reinsurance subcom.). Office: CIGNA Corp CIGNA Reinsurance 1 Liberty Pl Philadelphia PA 19192-0001

NEWMAN, FRANCIS A. medical device company executive; b. 1947; Sr. v.p. merchandising F.W. Woolworth, 1980-84, exec. v.p. household merchandising, 1984-85; pres., CEO, dir. F&M Distributors, Inc., 1986-93; pres., COO Eckerd Fleet, Inc., Largo, Fla., 1993-98, pres., COO, chmn., 1998-2000; pres., CEO More.com, San Francisco, 2000—. Address: PO Box 4689 Clearwater FL 33758-4689 Office: More com 520 3rd St Fl 2 San Francisco CA 94107

NEWMAN, FRANK NEIL, retired bank executive; b. Quincy, Mass., Apr. 20, 1942; m. Lizabeth Newman. BA in Econs. magna cum laude, Harvard U., 1963. Exec. v.p., CFO Wells Fargo & Co. and Wells Fargo Bank, San Francisco, 1980-86; CFO, vice-chmn. bd. dirs. Bank Am. Corp, Bank of Am., San Francisco, 1986-93; under sec. domestic fin. Dept. Treasury, Washington, 1993-94, dep. sec., 1994-95; sr. vice chmn. Bankers Trust, 1995—96, pres., 1996—99, CEO, chmn., 1996—99, chmn. emeritus, 1999. Bd. dirs. Dow Jones & Co., Inc. Office: 200 Liberty St New York NY 10281

NEWMAN, FREDRIC SAMUEL, lawyer, business executive; b. York, Pa., June 22, 1945; s. Nat. Howard and Josephine (Farkas) N.; m. Mary E. Kiley, May 19, 1973; children: Lydia Ann, Anne Marie, Pauline. AB cum laude, Harvard U., 1967; JD, Columbia U., 1970; cert. the exec. program, U. Va., 1984. Bar: N.Y. 1971, U.S. Dist. Ct. (so. and ea. dists.) N.Y. 1972, U.S. Ct. Appeals (2d cir.) 1974, U.S. Ct. Claims 1993. Assoc. White & Case, N.Y.C., 1970-80; asst. gen. counsel Philip Morris Cos., N.Y.C., 1981-87; gen. counsel, v.p., sec. Philip Morris, Inc., N.Y.C., 1987-90; chief exec. officer TeamTennis, Inc., 1991; prin. Law Office of Fredric S. Newman, N.Y.C., 1992-95; founding ptnr. Hoguet Newman & Regal, LLP, 1996—; pres., CEO, Pathe Comm. Corp., N.Y.C., 1993-97. Bd. dirs. Exel Ins. Co., Bermuda. Trustee Calhoun Sch., N.Y.C., 1985-88; bd. dirs. N.Y. Fire Safety Found., N.Y.C., 1985-88; treas. Clean Water/Clean Air Bond Act Com., 1996. Fellow Am. Bar Found.; mem. Columbia Law Sch. Assn. (bd. dirs. 1999-2001). Office: 10 E 40th St New York NY 10016-0200

NEWMAN, GEORGIA A. literature educator; b. Sylacauga, Ala., Mar. 10, 1946; d. James Frederick and Lora B. (McPhaul) Newman; m. Arthur James Powell, May 17, 1975; stepchildren: Craig Powell, Scott Powell, Diana Powell Cuillo, Laura Powell Young. AB, Woman's Coll. of Ga., Milledgeville, 1967; MA, Fla. State U., 1970, EdS, 1977; PhD, U. South Fla., 1999. Tchr. English, speech Warner Robins H.S., Warner Robins, Ga., 1967—68; prof. English Polk C.C., Winter Haven, Fla., 1970—2000; assoc. prof. English Ga. Coll. and State U., Milledgeville, 2000—03; vis. prof. O'Connor Studies Brigham Young U., Idaho, 2003. Author: poetry, children's dramas, essays, speeches; contbr. articles to profl. jours.; performer: (poetic theater) The Double Entendre, 1973—. Founding mem. Winter Haven Human Rels. Com. Named Thelma Raley Endowed Chair, Polk C.C., 1997, Outstanding Young Educator of the Yr., Winter Haven Jaycees, 1976. Mem.: MLA, Conf. on Christianity and Lit., Soc. So. Lit., Soc. Bibl. Lit., Conf. on Coll. Composition and Comm. (exec. com. 1998—2001), Fla. Coll. English Assn. (pres. 1995), Nat. Two-Yr. Coll. English Assn. (chair 2000), Nat. Coun. Tchrs. English (exec. com. 1999—2001), Phi Kappa Phi. Democrat. Episcopalian. Avocations: travel, writing, harp, football, collecting art and antiques.

NEWMAN, GERALDINE ANNE, advertising executive; b. Boston, Apr. 01; d. Joseph M. and Clara (Bistry) N. BS, UCLA; postgrad., Alliance Francaise, Paris, Los Angeles Sch. Fine Arts, NYU. Writer Tinker Dodge and Delano, N.Y.C., 1970-72, Ketchum Advt., N.Y.C., 1972-75, Advt. to Women, N.Y.C., 1975-78; v.p., creative supr. Young and Rubicam, N.Y.C., 1978-83; v.p., assoc. creative dir. Backer Spielvogel Bates Worldwide Internat. Div., N.Y.C., 1983-90; pres. Geraldine Newman Comm., Inc., N.Y.C., 1990—. County committeewoman Dem. Party, N.Y.C., 1972; advt. adviser Youth at Risk, Breakthrough Found., Food Bank, Food for All, Gifts that Give Back. Featured in Adweek Mag., 1986, Response Mag., 2004; winner Andy award 1975, 78, 82, 84, Clio award 1982, ERA award, 1998, Astrid award Mercomm Internat., 2002, numerous others. Mem.: Ad Club N.Y., Electronic Retailing Assn., Ad-net (bd. dirs. 1984—89, creative dir. 1986—89, Pres.'s award 1988), N.Y. Women in Film. Avocations: travel, painting. Home and Office: 315 E 72nd St New York NY 10021-4625 Office Phone: 212-988-3395.

NEWMAN, JAY HARTLEY, finance company executive; b. N.Y.C., Dec. 20, 1951; life ptnr. Elissa L. Kramer; children: David Timothy, Daniel James. BA, Yale U., 1973; JD, Columbia U., 1976; LLM, NYU, 1981. Bar: N.J. 1976, N.Y. 1977, DC 1978. Assoc. Cravath Swaine & Moore, N.Y.C., 1977-79, Hughes Hubbard & Reed, N.Y.C., 1979-83; v.p. Lehman Bros., N.Y.C., 1983-85; sr. v.p. Shearson Lehman Hutton, Inc., N.Y.C., 1985-88, mng. dir., 1988—89, Dillon Read & Co., 1989—90, Morgan Stanley & Co., Inc., N.Y. C., 1990-93, Emerging Market Strategies, Inc., N.Y.C., 1993-98; vice chmn. Lease Holding B.V., Amsterdam, Netherlands, 1996-98; sr. portfolio mgr. Elliott Assocs., LP, N.Y.C., 1996—. Editor: Columbia Law Rev., 1974—76. Trustee N.Y.C. Police Found., 1997—, Coun. Fgn. Rels., 2000—, JINSA, 2002—.

NEWMAN, JOAN MESKIEL, lawyer; b. Youngstown, Ohio, Dec. 12, 1947; d. John F. and Rosemary (Scarmuzzi) Meskiel; children: Anne R., Elyse S. BA in Polit. Sci., Case-Western Reserve U., 1969; JD, Washington U., St. Louis, 1972, LLM in Taxation, 1973. Bar: Mo. 1972. Assoc. Lewis & Rice, St. Louis, 1973-80, ptnr., 1981-90, Thompson Coburn, St. Louis, 1990—. Adj. prof. law Washington U. Sch. Law, St. Louis, 1975-92; past pres. St. Louis chpt., mem. Midwest Pension Conf. Mem. nat. coun. Washington U. Sch. Law, 1988—91; chmn. bd. dir. Great St. Louis coun. Girl Scouts USA, 1975—92, officer, 1978—92; mem. cmty. wide youth svcs. panel United Way Greater St. Louis, 1992—96; fin. futures task force Kiwanis Camp Wyman, 1992—93; chmn. staff blue ribbon fin. com. Sch. Dist., Clayton, 1986—87; vol. Women's Self Help Ctr.; bd. dirs. Parents as Teachers, 2001—; bd. dir., exec. com. Girl Scouts USA, 1993—99, nat. treas., 1996—99; bd. dirs. Met. Employment and Rehab. Svcs., 1980—2001, chmn. bd. dir., 1994—96; bd. dirs. Jewish Ctr. Aged, 1990—92, bd. dir., 1999—2001, Jewish Fedn. St. Louis, 1991—96, City Mus., 1998—2001, Parents as Tchrs., 2000—; chmn. bd. dir. Women of Achievement, 1993—96; bd. dir. United Way Greater St. Louis, 2000—, Oasis, 1999—2001; bd. dirs. MERS/Goodwill Industries, 2001—, Walker Scottish Rite Ctr., 2002—. Named Woman of Achievement St. Louis, 1991. Mem. Mo. Bar Assn. (staff pension and benefits com. 1991—), Bar Met. St. Louis (past chmn. taxation sect.), St. Louis Forum, Order of Coif (hon.). Office: Thompson Coburn LLP Ste 3300 One US Bank Plz Saint Louis MO 63101-1643

NEWMAN, JOHN M., JR., lawyer; b. Youngstown, Ohio, Aug. 15, 1944; BA, Georgetown U., 1966; JD, Harvard U., 1969. BAr: Ill. 1970, Calif. 1972, Ohio 1976. Law clerk ctrl. dist. U.S. Dist. Ct., Calif., 1969-70, asst. U.S. Atty. ctrl. dist., 1970-75; ptnr. Jones, Day, Cleve. Fellow Am. Coll. Trial Lawyers; mem. Phi Beta Kappa. Office: Jones Day North Point 901 Lakeside Ave E Cleveland OH 44114-1190 Business E-Mail: jmnewman@jonesday.com.

NEWMAN, JOHN MERLE, lawyer; b. Cleve., June 25, 1934; s. Emanuel Robert and Theresa Esther (Dreissinger) N.; 1 child, Thomas Edward; m. Thelma Aitken, July 10, 1992; 1 child, Jennifer Ann Newman-Brazil. AB, Miami U., Oxford, Ohio, 1957; LLB, Cornell U., 1957. Bar: N.J. 1971, U.S. Ct. Appeals (3d cir.) 1961, U.S. Dist. Ct. N.J. 1983, U.S. Dist. Ct. (so. and ea. dists.) N.Y. 1983; cert. civil atty. Supreme Ct. of N.J. Assoc. Bertram Polow, Morristown, N.J., 1960-62; ptnr. Porzio Bromberg & Newman P.C., Morristown, 1962-76, 80—; presiding judge chancery/family divsn. Superior Ct. of N.J., Morristown, 1976-80. Trustee, officer Cmty. Med. Ctr., Randolph Libr., Morristown, 1970-74, Hist. Speedwell Mus., Morristown, 1991—, Family Svc., Morristown, 1988-91; trustee Occupational Tng. Ctr., Morristown, 1965-69. Recipient Cert. of Acad. Performance U. Edinburgh, Scotland, 1956, Trial Bar award N.J. Trial Lawyers Assn., 1997, various certs. for bar and cmty. svcs. Fellow Internat. Soc. Barristers; mem. ABA (litigation sect., environ. subcom., environ. law sect. corp. counsel subcom., vice chair various coms.), N.J. State Bar Assn., Morris County Bar Assn., Omicron Delta Kappa. Avocations: bicycling, tennis. Office: Porzio Bromberg & Newman 163 Madison Ave Ste 6 Morristown NJ 07960-7323

NEWMAN, JOHN NICHOLAS, naval architect educator; b. New Haven, Mar. 10, 1935; s. Richard and Daisy (Neumann) N.; m. Kathleen Smedley Kirk, June 16, 1956; children— James Bartram, Nancy Kirk, Carol Ann. BS Mass. Inst. Tech, 1956, MS, 1957, Sc.D., 1960; postgrad., Cambridge (Eng.) U., 1958-59; D.Tech honoris causa, U. Trondheim, Norway, 1992. Research naval architect David Taylor Model Basin, Navy Dept., Washington, 1959-67; assoc. prof. naval architecture MIT, Cambridge, 1967-70, prof., 1970—, prof. emeritus. Vis. prof. U. New South Wales, Australia, 1973, U. Adelaide, Australia, 1974, Tech. U. Norway, 1981-82; cons. Navy Dept., Dept. Justice, pvt. firms. Author: Marine Hydrodynamics, 1977; Contbr.: articles to profl. jours., including Sci. Am. Recipient prize Am. Bur. Shipping, 1956; Walter Atkinson prize Royal Instn. Naval Architects, 1973, also Bronze medal, 1976; Guggenheim fellow, 1973-74; research grantee Office Naval Research; NSF. Mem. AAAS, NAE, Soc. Naval Architects and Marine Engrs. (Davidson medal 1988), Norwegian Acad. Sci. Home: 1 Bowditch Rd Woods Hole MA 02543-1201 Business E-Mail: jnn@mit.edu.

NEWMAN, JOHN SCOTT, chemical engineer, educator; b. Richmond, Va., Nov. 17, 1938; s. Clarence William and Marjorie Lenore (Saucerman) Newman; m. Nguyen Thanh Lan, June 30, 1973; children: Natalie Diane, Michael Alexander. BS, Northwestern U., 1960; MS, U. Calif., Berkeley, 1962, PhD, 1963. Asst. prof. chem. engring. U. Calif., Berkeley, 1963-67, assoc. prof., 1967-70, prof., 1970—; prin. investigator environ. energy tech. divsn. Lawrence Berkeley Nat. Lab., 1963—. Vis. prof. U. Wis., Madison, 1973; Onsager prof. Norwegian U. Sci. and Tech., 2002; summer participant Oak Ridge Nat. Lab., 1965, 66. Author: Electrochemical Systems, 1973, 3d edit., 2004; assoc. editor Jour. Electrochem. Soc., 1990—2000; contbr. articles to profl. jours. Fellow: Electrochem. Soc. (Young Author's prize 1966, 1969, David C. Grahame award 1985, Henry B. Linford award 1990, Olin Palladium medal 1991, Rsch. award Battery Divsn. 2004); mem.: AIChE (Excellence in Indsl. Rsch. award No. Calif. sect. 2000), NAE. Home: 114 York Ave Kensington CA 94708-1045 Office: U Calif Dept Chem Enging Berkeley CA 94720-1462 Business E-Mail: newman@newman.cchem.berkeley.edu.

NEWMAN, JON O. federal judge; b. N.Y.C., May 2, 1932; s. Harold W. Jr. and Estelle L. (Ormond) Newman; m. Martha G. Silberman, June 19, 1953; children: Leigh, Scott, David. Grad., Hotchkiss Sch., 1949; AB magna cum laude, Princeton U., 1953; LLB, Yale U., 1956; LLD (hon.), U. Hartford, 1975, U. Bridgeport, 1980, Bklyn. Law Sch., 1995, N.Y. Law Sch., 1996. Bar: Conn. 1956, D.C. 1956. Law clk. to Hon. George T. Washington U.S. Ct. Appeals, 1956—57; sr. law clk. to Hon. Earl Warren U.S. Supreme Ct., 1957—58; ptnr. Ritter, Satter & Newman, Hartford, Conn., 1958—60; counsel to majority Conn. Gen. Assembly, 1959; spl. counsel to gov. Conn., 1959—61; asst. to sec. HEW, 1961—62; adminstrv. asst. to U.S. senator, 1963—64; U.S. atty. Dist. of Conn., 1964—69, U.S. dist. judge, 1972—79; pvt. practice, 1969—71; U.S. cir. judge, 1979—93; chief judge U.S. Ct. of Appeals 2d Cir., Hartford, 1993—97, sr. judge, 1997—. Co-author: Politics: The American Way, 1964, A Genealogical Chart of Greek Mythology, 2003. With USAR, 1954—62. Recipient Learned Hand medal, Fed. Bar Coun., 1987. Fellow: Am. Bar Found.; mem.: ABA, Am. Judicature Soc., Conn. Bar Assn., Am. Law Inst. Democrat. Office: US Ct Appeals 2d Cir 450 Main St Hartford CT 06103-3022

NEWMAN, JOSEPH HERZL, advertising consultant; b. N.Y.C., Dec. 1, 1928; s. Max A. and Tillie C. (Weitzman) N.; m. Ruth Zita Marcus, Dec. 19, 1954 (div. Feb. 1987); children: Deborah Lynn, David Alan, Mark Jonathan; m. Nancy Kramer Deutschman, Aug. 19, 1990; stepchildren: Pamela Sue Deutschman, Douglas Hayes Deutschman, Cindi Elaine Deutschman-Ruiz. AB, Bethany Coll., W.Va., 1949; MS Grad. Sch. Bus., Columbia U., 1956. With 20th Century Fox Film Corp., NYC, 1949—53; media supr. Fred Wittner Advt. Agy., NYC, 1953—56; media dir. O.S. Tyson & Co., NYC, 1956—64; v.p., media dir. Marsteller Inc., NYC, 1965—85; v.p., assoc. media dir. HBM/Creamer, NYC, 1985—87, Della Femina, McNamee, Inc., NYC, 1987—89; pres. Newman And Assocs., Cleve., 1989—. Mem. faculty Advt. Age Media Workshop, 1972; past chmn. media mgrs. adv. com. Bus. Publs. Audit of Circulation Inc., N.Y.C.; condr. profl. media planning seminars, 1989-99. Contbr. articles to profl. jours. Past chmn. bus.-to-bus. media com. Am. Assn. Advt. Agys.; vice chmn. tax incentive rev. coun. City of Mayfield Heights, Ohio, 1994-97, chmn., 1997—; mem. master plan adv. com. City of Mayfield Heights, 2003-04; rep. Mayfield Heights to Euclid Creek Watershed Coun., 2003-. With U.S. Army, 1950-52. Mem. Bus. Mktg. Assn. (past mem. media comparability coun., media data form com. and rsch. resource com., Agy. Exec. of Yr., N.Y. chpt. 1960, 66, 71, 73, cert. bus. communicator). Home and Office: 6338 Woodhawk Dr Mayfield Heights OH 44124-4153 Office Phone: 440-449-1804. E-mail: nknewmansion@aol.com.

NEWMAN, JOYCE A. obstetrician/gynecologist; b. N.Y.C., 1940; MD, NYU, 1975. Diplomate Am. Bd. Ob/gyn. Resident in ob/gyn. Mt. Sinai Hosp., N.Y.C., 1975-79; asst. attendant Beth. Israel Hosp., N.Y.C., 1980—, N.Y. Downtown Hosp.; pvt. practice N.Y.C. Fellow Am. Coll. Ob/gyn.; mem. N.Y. Med. Soc. Home: 5261 Fieldston Rd Bronx NY 10471-2911 Office: 233 E 69th St New York NY 10021-5414

NEWMAN, LAWRENCE WALKER, lawyer; b. Boston, July 1, 1935; s. Leon Bettoney and Hazel W. (Walker) N.; children: Timothy D., Isabel B., Thomas H. AB, Harvard U., 1957, LL.B., 1960. Bar: D.C. 1961, N.Y. 1965. Atty. U.S. Dept. Justice, 1960-61, Spl. Study of Securities Markets and Office Spl. Counsel on Investment Co. Act Matters, U.S. SEC, 1961-64; asst. U.S. atty. So. Dist. N.Y., 1964-69; assoc. Baker & McKenzie, N.Y.C., 1969-71, ptnr., 1971—. Mem. internat. adv. coun. World Arbitration Inst., 1984-87; mem. adv. com. Asia Pacific Ctr. for Resolution of Internat. Trade Disputes, 1987—; mem. adv. bd. Inst. for Transnat. Arbitration, 1988—; chmn. U.S. Iranian Claimants Com., 1982—; mem. adv. bd. World Arbitration and Mediation Report, 1993-2002, co-chmn., 2002—; mem. bd. adv. to Corporate Counsel's Internat. Adviser, 1995—. Co-author: The Practice of Internat. Litigation, 1992, 93, 2d edit. 1998, Litigating Internat. Commercial Disputes, 1996; columnist N.Y. Law Jour., 1982—; bd. advisors Corp. Counsel's Internat. Adviser; contbr. articles to profl. jours. and books on litigation and internat. arbitration; editor: Enforcement of Money Judgments, Attachment of Assets, Internat. Arbitration Checklists; chmn. editl. bd. Juris Pub., Inc.; co-editor: Revolutionary Days: The Iran Hostage Crisis and the Hague Claims Tribunal, A Look Back, 1999, Leading Arbitrator's Guide to International Arbitration, International Arbitration Checklists, Take the Witness: Essays on Cross-Examination. Mem. Internat. Bar Assn. (com. dispute resolution, com. constrn. litigation), Inter-Am. Bar Assn., Fed. Bar Coun., Am. Fgn. Law Assn., Maritime Law Assn. U.S., Assn. Bar City N.Y. (com. on arbitration and alternative dispute resolution 1991-94, com. internat. comml. dispute resolution, 2000—, chmn. 2003—), Am. Arbitration Assn. (corp. counsel com. 1987—, panel internat. arbitrators), U.S. Coun. Internat. Bus., Ct. Arbitration of Polish Chamber Fgn. Trade (panel of arbitrators), Brit. Col. Internat. Comml. Arbitration Ctr., Am. Law Inst., Bar Assn. City N.Y. (inaugural mem. com. on internat. comml. dispute resolution, chmn. 2003—). Office: Baker & McKenzie 805 3rd Ave New York NY 10022-7513 Office Phone: 212-891-3970. E-mail: lwn@bakernet.com.

NEWMAN, LAWRENCE WILLIAM, financial executive; b. Chgo., Jan. 14, 1939; s. Eskil William and Adele Diane (Lawnicki) N.; m. Christine Harriet Jaronski, Sept. 22, 1962; children: Paul, Scott, Ron. BBS, U. Ill., 1965; MBA, Northwestern U., 1970. CPA, Ill. Auditor Price Waterhouse, Chgo., 1965-66; controller ECM Corp., Schaumburg, Ill., 1966-70, Nachman Corp., Des Plaines, Ill., 1970-76, v.p., treas., controller, 1976-79; v.p. fin. P & S Mgmt. Inc., Schiller Park, Ill., 1979-83; controller Underwriters Labs., Northbrook, Ill., 1983-86, asst. treas., 1986-89, v.p., 1990-98, treas., 1990-97, CFO, 1997—; sr. v.p. Underwriters Labs., Northbrook, 1998—. Mem. Fin. Execs. Inst., Am. Inst. CPA's. Clubs: Exec. of Chgo. Office: Underwriters Labs 333 Pfingsten Rd Northbrook IL 60062-2002

NEWMAN, LEONARD JAY, retail jewel merchant, gemologist; b. Milw., Oct. 25, 1927; s. David and Pia Goldie (Smith) N.; m. Louise Shainberg, Jan. 14, 1951; children: Shelley, Marty, Alan, Heidi, Dee. BS, Purdue U.; postgrad., Washington U., St. Louis. Owner, mgr. Newman's Diamond Ctr., Jasper, Ind., 1951—; tchr. The Jasper Ctr., Ind., 1970-80. Bd. dirs. Sta. WFIU Pub. Radio, VUJC Found., State Bd. Health Systems Agy., sub area Health Systems Agy., Internat. Harp Competition, Bloomington United Way, Ind. U. Hillel Found.; consellor Sr. corps Re. Execs.; 1st v.p. Vincennes Univ. Found.; past pres. Jasper Community Arts Commn.; pres. Friends of Arts; commnr. Boy Scouts Am.; mem. Dubois County Mental Health Assn.; lay adv. bd. Convent Immaculate Conception Sisters of St. Benedict, Ferdinand, Ind,; adv. bd. Jasper Hist. Soc., German Club, Young Abe Lincoln Soc., WFIU pub. radio; bd. dirs. Dubois County Crippled Children's Soc., Bloomington (Ind.) Symphony, Patoka Valley Vocat. Coop., Patoka Valley Rehab., Beth Shalom, Monroe County Purdue Alumni, Camerata Orch., Ind. U. Friends of Music, Ind. Jewish Hist. Soc., Hillel Found.; pres. Jasper Edn. Fund; mem., chmn. nominee com. Raintree Coun. Girl Scouts U.S.A., bd. dirs.; Midwest bd. dirs. Anti-Defamation League. Recipient Outstanding Citizenship award Purdue U. Alumni Assn., 1980 Outstanding Alumni award Jasper High Sch., Outstanding Community Svc. award Bloomington, Ind. C. of C., 2000, 01, Gov.'s award Sagamore of the Wabash, 2001. Mem. Nat. Assn. Jewelry Appraisers (sr.), Ind. Jewelers Orgn. Am., Retail Jewelers Am., Jasper C. of C., Jaycees (Rooster, past pres., past nat. bd. dirs., Disting. Svc. award 1957), Monroe County Purdue Alumni Club (bd. dirs.), Nat. Soc. Arts and Letters (bd. mem.), Svc. Corp. Ret. Execs. (pres.), Purdue Agrl. Alumni Assn. (hon.), Skull and Crescent (hon.), Hadassah, Sigma Alpha Mu, Alpha Phi Omega, Lions, Masons, Shriners (past pres.), B'nai Brith, Temple Beth Shalom (pres.). Office: Newman's Diamond Ctr 3 D Pl Jasper IN 47546 Home: 3754 Villa Glen Ct Bloomington IN 47401 E-mail: newmangem@insightbb.com.

NEWMAN, LOIS MAE, marketing executive; b. Phoenix, Aug. 16, 1942; d. Harold Orville and Agnes Louise (Rindos) Little; children: Annette James, Tyler Katonak. BA, Hamilton Coll., Utica, N.Y., 1964; MA, Hamilton Coll., 1968; postgrad., U. Ariz., 1969, Ariz. State U., 1970. Office mgr. Dunes Hotel and Country Club, Phoenix, 1962-83; prin., treas. Sincere Press, Inc., Phoenix, 1982-90; pres., CEO Euneek, Phoenix, 1983—; staff Ridd Assocs., Inc., Phoenix, 1986-89; reg. mktg. exec. Golden Nugget, Phoenix, 1988-89; adminstr. James F. O'Toole Co., Inc., Phoenix, 1991-94, Western Promotions, Inc., Phoenix, 1994—. Bd. dirs. Sincere Press, Inc., Internat. Wines & Spirits Ltd., Encino, Calif., Euneek, Inc. Bd. dirs. Sml. Bus. Coun., Phoenix, Congl. Action Com., Phoenix, Israel Bonds, Phoenix; active Better Bus. Bur., Arizonians for Jobs & Energy, Valley Leadership, others; chmn. Phoenix Childrens Hosp. Peregrinations; original founder, endorser Maimonides Day Sch.; chmn. Anti-Defamation League; adv. com. vice chmn. Nat. Coun. Christians and Jews; arrangements chmn. City of Hope. Mem. Phoenix Met. C. of C., Ariz. World Trade Assn., Internat. Wine and Food Soc. of Scottsdale (bd. dirs. local chpt., founder). Home: 6808 N 26th St Phoenix AZ 85016-1208 Office: Euneek 6808 N 26th St Phoenix AZ 85016 Office Phone: 602-912-8520. E-mail: lnewman@westernpromotions.com.

NEWMAN, MALCOLM, mechanical and civil engineering consultant; b. N.Y.C., June 29, 1931; m. Estelle Ruth Glotzer, June 11, 1955. BSCE, CCNY, 1952; MSCE, Columbia U., 1957; D in Engring. Sci., NYU, 1962. Registered profl. engr., N.Y. Chief structural mechanics Republic-Fairchild Hiller Corp., Farmingdale, N.Y., 1962-65, staff cons., 1970-71; dir. structural mechanics Harry Belock Assocs. Inc., Great Neck, N.Y., 1965-69; dir. structural mechanics and design Analytical Mechanics Assn., Jericho, N.Y., 1969-70; prof. mech. engring. Tel Aviv U., 1972-75; pres., tech. dir. Inter-City Testing and Cons., Mineola, N.Y., 1976—. Pres. Athletic Safety Products Inc., Mineola, 1985—; adj. prof. engring. Cooper Union. Contbr. over 80 articles to profl. jours.; patentee in field. Bd. dirs. Cinema Arts Ctr., Huntington, N.Y., 1989—. Mem. NSPE, Am. Soc. Safety Engrs., Nat. Assn. Profl. Accident Reconstruction Specialists, Soc. Automotive Engrs., System Safety Soc. (pres. 1983-85). Office: Inter-City Testing & Cons 167 Willis Ave Ste 2 Mineola NY 11501-2680

NEWMAN, MARIE STEFANINI, law librarian, educator; b. Boston, Aug. 30, 1951; d. Mario and Elizabeth (Just) S.; m. Gary Nathaniel Newman, Sept. 30, 1978; children: Alexander, Elizabeth. AB, Smith Coll., 1973; MS, Columbia U., 1974; JD, Rutgers U., 1983. Bar: N.Y. 1984. Jr. librarian Bayonne (N.J.) Pub. Library, 1974-75; editor Microfilming Corp. Am., Glen Rock, N.J., 1975-78; circulation librarian SUNY Downstate Med. Ctr, Bklyn., 1979-80; head reference svcs. N.Y. Law Sch., N.Y.C., 1984-90, adj. assoc. prof. law, 1985-90; assoc. dir. Pub. Svcs., lectr. U. Pa. Law Sch., 1991-93; dep. libr. dir. and adj. prof. law Pace U. Sch. Law, White Plains, N.Y., 1993-99, libr. dir., assoc. prof. law, 1999—. Database mgr. Inst. Internat. Comml. Law, 1994—. Mem. Am. Assn. Law Libraries. Office: Pace Law Libr 78 N Broadway White Plains NY 10603-3710 Business E-Mail: mnewman@law.pace.edu.

NEWMAN, MARJORIE YOSPIN, psychiatrist; b. N.Y.C., July 8, 1945; d. Toby and Audrey (Kreinik) Yospin; children: Eric, David. Student, Smith Coll., 1963-64; AB, Barnard Coll./Columbia U., 1967; MD, Med. Coll. Pa., 1971. Diplomate Am. Bd. Psychiatry and Neurology. Psychiatry intern, resident Albert Einstein Coll. Medicine, N.Y.C., 1971-75; asst. prof. psychiatry U. Tex. Health Sci. Ctr., San Antonio, 1975-77, UCLA Sch. Medicine, 1977-80; dir. residency tng. in psychiatry Harbor-UCLA Med. Ctr., 1977-79; asst. clin. prof. psychiatry UCLA Sch. Medicine, 1980—; pvt. practice Pasadena, Calif., 1983—. Mem. admissions com. UCLA Med. Sch., 1995—. NSF grantee, London, Eng., 1969; Am. Field Svc. Internat. scholar, Argentina, 63. Fellow Am. Psychiat. Assn. (disting.), Smith Coll. Alumna Assn., Barnard Coll. Alumnae Assn., Columbia U. Alumni Assn., Calif, L.A. Acad. Medicine (bd. govs. 2000—, sec. 2002-03, v.p. 2003-04, pres. 2004—); mem. So. Calif. Psychiat. Soc. (regional coun. 2001-04). Avocations: travel, music, art, swimming, bicycling. Office: Cotton Med Ctr South 50 Alessandro Pl Ste 340 Pasadena CA 91105-3149 Office Phone: 626-564-1750.

NEWMAN, MARK S. electronics company executive; With Diagnostic/Retrieval Systems Inc., Oakdale, N.J., 1974—, pres., CEO, 1994—. Office: DRS Technologies Inc Five Sylvan Way Parsippany NJ 07054

NEWMAN, MICHAEL D. retail executive; b. 1957; Degree, Amherst (Mass.) Coll. With Gen. Electric, 1978—96; v.p., CFO Hussmann Internat., Inc., 1996—2000, Intimate Brands, Inc., 2000; sr. v.p. RadioShack Corp., Ft. Worth, 2001—, CFO, 2001—. Office: RadioShack Corp 100 Throckmorton Ste 1900 Fort Worth TX 76102

NEWMAN, MICHAEL RODNEY, lawyer; b. N.Y.C., Oct. 2, 1945; s. Morris and Helen Gloria (Hendler) N.; m. Cheryl Jeanne Anker, June 11, 1967; children: Hillary Abra, Nicole Brooke. Student NASA Inst. Space Physics, Columbia U., 1964; BA, U. Denver, 1967; JD, U. Chgo., 1970. Bar: Calif. 1971, U.S. Dist. Ct. (cen. dist.) Calif. 1972, U.S. Ct. Appeals (9th cir.) 1974, U.S. Dist. Ct. (no. dist.) Calif. 1975, U.S. Supreme Ct. 1978, U.S. Dist.

Ct. (so. dist.) Calif. 1979, U.S. Tax Ct. 1979, U.S. Dist. Ct. (ea. dist.) Calif. 1983. Assoc. David Daar, 1971-76; ptnr. Daar & Newman, 1976-78, Miller & Daar, 1978-88, Miller, Daar & Newman, 1988-89, Daar & Newman, 1989—; judge pro-tem L.A. Mcpl. Ct., 1982—, L.A. Superior Ct., 1988—. Vice chmn., bd. dirs. German-Am. C. of C.; bd. govs. U. Haifa, Israel, mem. fin. and phys. devel. com.; bd. dirs. Consulegis EEIG; mem. bd. dirs. Ctr. Study Emerging Markets (Grad. Coll. Bus. and Econs. Calif. State U. Fullerton); founder, facilitator First, Second and Third Ann. German-Am. Strategic Partnership Conf.; lectr. in field. Mem. L.A. Citizens Organizing Com. for Olympic Summer Games, 1984, mem. govtl. liaison adv. commn., 1984; mem. So. Calif. Com. for Olympic Summer Games, 1984; cert. ofcl. Athletics Congress of U.S., co-chmn. legal com. S.P.A.-T.A.C., chief finish judge; trustee Massada lodge B'nai Brith; bd. dirs. Ctr. for the Study of Emerging Markets, Calif. State U. Fullerton Grad. Sch. Bus. and Econs. Recipient NYU Bronze medal in Physics, 1962, Maths. award USN Sci., 1963. Mem.: TAC (bd. dirs., Disting. Svc. award 1988), ABA (multi-dist. litigation subcom., com. on class actions), Lawyers Profl. Liability Bar Assn., German Am. C. of C. (vice chmn.), So. Pacific Assn., Conf. Ins. Counsel, Los Angeles County Bar Assn. (chmn. attys. errors and omissions prevention com., mem. cts. com., mem. internat. law com., state cts. coord. com. litigation sect.), City Club on Bunker Hill, Breakfast Club, Porter Valley Country Club. Office: 865 S Figueroa St Ste 2300 Los Angeles CA 90017-2567 Office Phone: 213-892-0999. Business E-Mail: mnewman@daarnewman.com.

NEWMAN, MONROE, retired economist, educator; b. Bklyn., Jan. 31, 1929; s. David A. and Ida Mary (Leight) N.; m. Ruth Zielinski, Feb. 6, 1951. BA, Antioch Coll., 1950; MA, U. Ill., 1953, PhD, 1954. Mem. rsch. staff AFL, 1947-48; examiner NLRB, 1949-50; asst. rsch. analyst U. Ill., 1950-54; research analyst Assn. Casualty and Surety Cos., 1954-55; mem. faculty Pa. State U., University Park, 1955—, prof. econs., 1961-86, prof. emeritus, 1986—, head dept., 1958-62, 78-85, chmn. grad. program regional planning, 1971-72, dir. Ctr. for Study of Environ. Policy, 1972-73. Vis. rsch. prof. econs. U. Pitts., 1964-65; economist Appalachian Regional Commn., Washington, 1964-65, rsch. dir., 1965-66, spl. cons., 1966-86, sr. econ. advisor, 1986-93. Co-author: Insurance and Risk, 1964, Acid Mine Drainage in Appalachia, 1969, Experiment in Appalachia, 1973; author: Political Economy of Appalachia, 1972, also articles. Mem. So. Regional Sci. Assn. (pres.), Am. Econ. Assn., Regional Sci. Assn. Home: 4101 Cathedral Ave NW Washington DC 20016-3585

NEWMAN, MORRIS, mathematician, educator; b. N.Y.C., Feb. 25, 1924; s. Isaac and Sarah (Cohen) N.; m. Mary Aileen Lenk, Sept. 18, 1948; children: Sally Ann, Carl Lenk. AB, N.Y.U., 1945; MA, Columbia U., 1946; PhD, U. Pa., 1952. Mathematician applied math div. Nat. Bur. Standards, Washington, 1951-63, chief numerical analysis sect., 1963-70, sr. rsch. mathematician, 1970-76; prof. math. U. Calif., Santa Barbara, 1976-94, prof. emeritus, 1994—; dir. Inst. Interdisciplinary Applications of Algebra and Combinatorics, 1976-80. Lectr. U. B.C., 1960, U. Calif.-Santa Barbara, 1965, Am. U., Cath. U., U. Md. Author: Matrix Representations of Groups, 1968, Integral Matrices, 1972; editor: Jour. Research Nat. Bur. Standards, 1966-76, Math. of Computation, 1975-86; assoc. editor: Jour. Linear and Multilinear Algebra, 1973—, Letters in Linear Algebra, 1979—; contbr. articles to profl. jours. Recipient Gold medal U.S. Dept. Commerce, 1966 Mem. Am. Math. Soc. (council 1980-86), London Math. Soc., Math. Assn. Am., Washington Acad. Scis., AAAS, sigma Xi Home: 5350 2B Calle Real Santa Barbara CA 93111 Office: U Calif Dept Math Santa Barbara CA 93106-1686 E-mail: newman@math.ucsb.edu.

NEWMAN, MURIEL KALLIS STEINBERG, art collector; b. Chgo., Feb. 25, 1914; d. Maurice and Ida (Nudelman) Kallis; m. Albert H. Newman, May 14, 1955; 1 son by previous marriage, Glenn D. Steinberg. Student, Art Inst. Chgo., 1932-36, Ill. Inst. Tech., 1947-50, U. Chgo., 1958-65. Hon. life trustee, benefactor Met. Mus. Art, N.Y.C., vis. com. dept. 20th Century Art, acquisitions com., 1981—, decorative arts com., 1989; also Costume Inst. Dir., 20th Century Painting and Sculpture Com., Art Inst. Chgo., 1955-80, governing mem. inst., 1955—, disting. benefactor, 1979—; pioneer collector Am. abstract expressionist art, 1949—, major show of collection, Met. Mus. Art, N.Y.C., 1981, personal collection of costumes and jewelry, 1981. Bd. govs. Landmarks Preservation Council, Chgo., 1966-78; woman's bd. U. Chgo., 1960-81, Art Inst. Chgo., 1953—, 20th century com., Asian com.; trustee Mus. Contemporary Art, 1970, benefactor, 1970; trustee Chgo. Sch. of Architecture Found., 1971, Archives Am. Art, 1976; bd. dirs. Bright New City Urban Affairs Lecture Series, 1966—; trustee Art Inst. Chgo., mem. African and American art com. Recipient Scroll Recognition of Pub. Svc., U.S. Dept. State, 1958; named Disting. Benefactor, Art Inst. Chgo., 1998. Mem. Antiquarian Soc. of Art Inst. Chgo., Chgo. Hist. Soc. (mem. guild 1958—), Arts Club Chgo., Casino Club Chgo. Clubs: Arts (Chgo.), Casino (Chgo.). *Searching for truth is a given for a life of value. For me visual art ontologically reveals the truth of the search. Striving for excellence is the spearhead with which to proceed.*

NEWMAN, MURRAY ARTHUR, aquarium administrator; b. Chgo., Mar. 6, 1924; emigrated to Can., 1953, naturalized, 1970; s. Paul Jones and Virginia (Murray) N.; m. Katherine Greene Rose, Aug. 8, 1952; 1 child, Susan. BSc, U. Chgo., 1949; postgrad., U. Hawaii, 1950; MA, U. Calif., Berkeley, 1951; PhD, U. B.C., Vancouver, Can., 1960. Curator fisheries UCLA, 1951-53; curator fisheries Ichthyology Mus. U. B.C., 1953-56; curator Vancouver Pub. Aquarium, 1956-66, dir., 1966-93; pres. Mana Aquarium Cons. Fgn. adv. Nat. Mus./Aquarium Project, Taiwan; past chmn. adv. com. Western Can. Univs. Marine Biol. Soc.; co-chmn. Enoshima (Japan) Internat. Aquarium Symposium, 1997; spl. advisor Enoshima Aquarium, 1998, Port of Nagoya Pub. Aquarium, 1999, 2000; hon. com. Fifth Internat. Congress, Monaco, 2000, grand opening new Enoshima Aquarium, 2004. Author: Life in a Fishbowl: Confessions of an Aquarium Director, 1994. Served with USN, 1943-46. Decorated Order of Can.; recipient Man of Yr. award City of Vancouver, 1964; Centennial award Govt. Can., 1967, cert. of merit, 1988; Harold J. Merilees award Vancouver Visitors Bur., 1976, 75 Achievers award, 1987, Silver Bravery medal Royal Soc. Can., 1992, Can. 125 medal, 1992, Golden Jubilee medal, 2002. Mem. Am. Assn. Zool. Parks and Aquariums, Internat. Union Dirs. Zool. Gardens, Can. Assn. Zool. Parks and Aquariums (pres. 1978-79), Vancouver Club, Round Table Club. Office: Vancouver Pub Aquarium PO Box 3232 Vancouver BC Canada V6B 3X8

NEWMAN, NANCY, publishing executive; Sr. v.p. & publ. dir. Ziff Davis Pub. Co., N.Y.C. Office: Ziff Davis Pub Co 28 E 28th St Fl 12 New York NY 10016-7930

NEWMAN, OSCAR, architect, city planner, sculptor; b. Montreal, Sept. 30, 1935; m. Irene Kopper; children: Paul, Jon, Hinde. BArch, McGill U., Montreal, 1959. Cert. arch., city planner. Assoc. prof. arch., city planning Washington U., St. Louis, 1964-68, Columbia U., N.Y.C., 1968-70, NYU, 1970-72, dir. Inst. Planning and Housing, 1970-72; exec. dir., founder Inst. Cmty. Design Analysis, N.Y.C., 1972—. Keynote spkr. Internat. Crime Prevention Conf., New Zealand, Australia, 2001, Environ. Design Rsch. Conf. Harvard U., 1995; participant numerous confs.; feature writer The Mountain Eagle, 2000; spkr. in field. Author: Defensible Space, 1972, Community of Interest, 1976, Unmasking a King, 1981, Issues in Housing Discrimination, 1985, Creating Defensible Space, 1996, Visualizing Myth, 1999, Secret Stories in the Art of the Northwest Indian, 2003; contbr. articles to profl. jours.; sculptor Native Am. masks, totem poles; work featured in documentary; featured in Nat. Pub. Radio NBC Nightly News, Dateline NBC TV, other radio and tv shows; subject of articles in Miami Herald, Time, U.S. News and World Report, Readers Digest, Chgo. Tribune, N.Y. Times, The Oregonian, Newsweek, San Francisco Examiner, L.A. Times, numerous other publs. Exec. dir. Interdenominational Housing Program, N.Y., 1978—; mem. bd. rev., bd. dirs. Greene Co. Coun. on the Arts, 1998—; fed. ct. master Yonkers (N.Y.) housing discrimination case, 1986-94 Named Man of Yr. Law Enforcement News, 1995; recipient Achievement award Environ. Design Rsch. Conf., 1997, Annual Award of Achievement Environ. Design Rsch. Assn., 1998. Office: Inst Cmty Design Analysis 672 Round Hill Rd Hensonville NY 12439

NEWMAN, PAUL, actor, professional race-car driver, food company executive; b. Cleve., Jan. 26, 1925; s. Arthur S. and Theresa (Fetzer) N.; m. Jacqueline Witte, Dec. 1949 (div. 1958); children: Scott (dec.), Susan, Stephanie; m. Joanne Woodward, Jan. 1958; children: Elinor, Melissa, Clea. BA, Kenyon Coll., 1949; postgrad., Yale U. Sch. Drama, 1951; studied with Lee Strasberg, Actor's Studio; LHD (hon.), Yale U., 1988. Founder, pres. Newman's Own Found., Inc., Westport, Conn., 1982—. Appeared on Broadway in: Picnic, 1953-54, Desperate Hours, 1955, Sweet Bird of Youth, 1959, Baby Want a Kiss, 1964; TV movies Come Along With Me, 1982, Our Town, 2003; TV series Tales of Tomorrow, 1951, The Aldritch Family, 1952-53; motion pictures include Somebody Up There Likes Me, 1956, The Long Hot Summer, 1958 (Best Actor award Cannes Internat. Film Festival, 1958), Cat on a Hot Tin Roof, 1958, From the Terrace, 1960, Exodus, 1960, The Hustler, 1961 (British Film Acad. award for best foreign actor, 1961), Sweet Bird of Youth, 1962, Hud, 1963, The Outrage, 1964, The Prize, 1964, Lady L, 1965, Harper, 1966, Hombre, 1967, Cool Hand Luke, 1967, Winning, 1969, Butch Cassidy and the Sundance Kid, 1969, WUSA, Sometimes a Great Notion, 1971, Pocket Money, 1972, The Life and Times of Judge Roy Bean, 1972, The MacIntosh Man, 1973, The Sting, 1973, The Towering Inferno, 1974, Drowning Pool, 1975, Buffalo Bill and the Indians, 1976, Slap Shot, 1977, Quintet, 1979, Fort Apache, The Bronx, 1980, When Time Ran Out, 1980, Absence of Malice, 1981, The Verdict, 1982, The Color of Money, 1986 (Acad. award for best actor, 1987, Nat. Bd. of Review award for best actor, 1987), Blaze, 1989, Mr. and Mrs. Bridge, 1989, The Hudsucker Proxy, 1994, Nobody's Fool, 1994 (NY Film Critics Circle award for best actor, Nat. Soc. of Film Critics award for best actor, 1994, Berlin Film Fest. Silver Bear for best actor, 1995), Super Speedway, 1997, Twilight, 1998, Message in a Bottle, 1999, Where the Money Is, 2000, Sweet Dreams, 2001, The Road to Perdition, 2002; dir. motion pictures including: Rachel, Rachel, 1968 (Golden Globe Award for best dir., Prodrs. Guild of Am. Award for best motion picture prodr., NY Film Critics Circle award for best dir., 1968), Sometimes a Great Notion, 1971, The Effect of Gamma Rays on Man-in-the-Moon Marigolds, 1973,, The Shadow Box, 1980, Glass Menagerie, 1987; dir., screenwriter, actor in film Harry and Son, 1984; appeared in TV documentary Baseball, 1994. Served with AC USNR, 1943-46. Recipient Theatre World Award, 1953, Man of Yr. award Hasty Pudding Theater, Harvard U., 1968, Cecil B. DeMille award, 1984, Acad. award for lifetime achievement, 1985, SAG lifetime achievement award, 1985, D.W. Griffith Best Actor award Nat Bd. Rev. Motion Pictures, 1986, Kennedy Center Honors lifetime achievement award, 1992, Jean Hersholt Humanitarian award Acad. Motion Pictures Arts and Scis., 1993; named World Film Favorite, Hollywood Foreign Press, 1963, 65, 67. Best Motion Picture Prodr. of Yr., Prodrs. Guild of Am., 1968. Address: Newman's Own Inc 246 Post Rd E Westport CT 06880-3615*

NEWMAN, PAULINE, federal judge; b. N.Y.C., N.Y., June 20, 1927; d. Maxwell Henry and Rosella Newman. BA, Vassar Coll., 1947; MA, Columbia U., 1948; PhD, Yale U., 1952; LLB, NYU, 1958. Bar: N.Y. 1958, U.S. Supreme Ct. 1972, U.S. Ct. Customs and Patent Appeals 1978, Pa. 1979, U.S. Ct. Appeals (3d cir.) 1981, U.S. Ct. Appeals (fed. cir.) 1982. Research chemist Am. Cyanamid Co., Bound Brook, NJ, 1951—54; mem. patent staff FMC Corp., N.Y.C., 1954—75, Phila., 1975—84, dir. dept. patent and licensing, 1969—84; judge U.S. Ct. Appeals (fed. cir.), Washington, 1984—; Disting. prof. George Mason Law Sch., 1995—. Program specialist Dept. Natural Scis. UNESCO, Paris, 1961—62; mem. State Dept. Adv. Com. on Internat. Indsl. Property, 1974—84; lectr. in field. Contbr. articles to profl. jours. Trustee Phila. Coll. Pharmacy and Sci., 1983—84; bd. dirs. Med. Coll. Pa., 1975—84, Midgard Found., 1973—84. Mem.: ABA (coun. sect. patent trademark and copyright 1983—84), Coun. Fgn. Rels., U.S. Trademark Assn. (bd. dirs. 1975—79, v.p. 1978—79), Pacific Indsl. Property Assn. (pres. 1979—80), Am. Inst. Chemists (bd. dirs. 1960—66, 1970—76), Am. Chem. Soc. (bd. dirs. 1972—81), Am. Patent Law Assn. (bd. dirs. 1981—84), Yale Club, Vassar Club, Cosmos Club. Office: US Ct Appeals Nat Cts Bldg 717 Madison Pl Washington DC 20439-0002*

NEWMAN, PHILIP ROBERT, psychologist; b. Dec. 17, 1942; s. Samuel M. and Sara Rose (Dumain) N.; m. Barbara Miller, June 12, 1966; children: Samuel Asher, Abraham Levy, Rachel Florence. AB with high distinction, U. Mich., 1964, PhD, 1971. Asst. prof. psychology U. Mich., Ann Arbor, 1971-72, Union Coll., Schenectady, N.Y., 1972-76; dir. human behavior curriculum project APA, Washington, 1977-81; pvt. practice psychology Columbus, Ohio, 1978-2000, South Kingston, R.I., 2000—. Adj. prof., sr. rschr. young scholars program Ohio State U., 1990-98; adj. prof. human devel. and family studies U. R.I., 2000—; cons. Agy. Instrnl. TV, 1979. Author: (with B. Newman) Development through Life: A Psychosocial Approach, 1975, 8th edit., 2003; Infancy and Childhood Development and Its Context, 1978, An Introduction to the Psychology of Adolescence, 1979, Personality Development through the Life Span, 1980, Living: The Process of Adjustment, 1981, Understanding Adulthood, 1983, Principles of Psychology, 1983, Adolescent Development, 1986, When Kids Go to College: A Parents Guide to Changing Relationships, 1992, Childhood and Adolescence, 1997, (with B. Newman, L. Landry-Meyer, B. Lohman) Life Span Development: A Case Book, 2003; editor: (with B. Newman) Development Through Life: A Case Study Approach, 1976. Woodrow Wilson fellow U. Mich., 1964, Univ. fellow, 1964-66, Horace H. Rackham Rsch. scholar, 1969-71. Mem. APA, APHA, Internat. Assn. Applied Psychology, Internat. Sociol. Assn., Soc. Psychol. Study Social Issues, Am. Sociol. Assn., Nat. Coun. Family Rels., Groves Conf. Marriage and Family, Ea. Psychol. Assn., N.Y. Acad. Sci., Gerontol. Soc. Am., Am. Orthopsychiat. Assn., Am. Statis. Assn., Soc. for Rsch. on Child Devel., Soc. for Rsch. on Adolescence, Phi Beta Kappa, Sigma Xi, Phi Kappa Phi. Home and Office: 240 Broad Rock Rd Wakefield RI 02879 Office Phone: 401-559-1245. Personal E-mail: prn10@yahoo.com.

NEWMAN, PHYLLIS, adult education educator, psychologist; b. N.Y.C., June 23, 1931; d. Arthur and Augusta (Cohen) Deutsch; m. Stan Newman, Dec. 10, 1967; 1 child, Allen. BS in Indsl. Labor Rels., Cornell U., 1952; MS in Edn.-Psychology, profl. diploma, St. John's U., Jamaica, N.Y., 1976. Tchr. N.Y.C. Bd. Edn., 1963-83, psychologist, 1983-86; instr. adult edn. Pima C.C., Green Valley, Ariz., 1988—92, Pima County Adult Edn., Tucson, 1989—95. Psychologist, counselor, N.Y.C., 1978-86; owner, mgr. Transitions Assocs., seminar condrs., N.Y.C. Tucson and Green Valley, 1991-99. Author: Transitions: A Woman's Guide to Successful Retirement, 1991. Home and Office: 420 E 55th St Apt 4D New York NY 10022-5140

NEWMAN, R. DONALD, paper company executive; V.p., resident mgr. Bowater, Inc., Calhoun, Tenn., 1987; v.p. Bowater, Inc., Canadian Newsprint Oper., 1998—2001; v.p., strategic planning Bowater, Inc., 2001—02, exec. v.p., COO, 2002—. Office: Bowater Inc 55 E Camperdown Way Greenville SC 29602

NEWMAN, RACHEL, editor; b. Malden, Mass., May 1, 1938; d. Maurice and Edythe Brenda (Tichell) Newman; m. Herbert Bleiweiss, Apr. 6, 1973 (div. Apr. 1989); m. Michael Lucas, Feb. 24, 2004. BA, Pa. State U., 1960; cert., N.Y. Sch. Interior Design, 1963. Accessories editor Women's Wear Daily, N.Y.C., 1964—65; designer, publicist Grandoe Glove Corp., N.Y.C., 1965—67; assoc. editor McCall's Sportswear and Dress Merchandiser mag., N.Y.C., 1967; mng. editor McCall's You-Do-It Home Decorating, 1968—70, Ladies Home Jour. Needle and Craft mag., N.Y.C., 1970—72; editor-in-chief Am. Home Crafts mag., N.Y.C., 1972—77; fashion dir. Good Housekeeping mag., N.Y.C., 1977—78, home bldg. and decorating dir., 1978—82; editor-in-chief Country Living mag., N.Y.C., 1978—98; founding editor Country Cooking mag., 1985—90, Dream Homes mag., 1989—2000, Country Kitchens mag., 1990—93, Country Living Gardener Mag., 1993—2000, Healthy Living mag., 1996—2000. Bd. dirs. Mothers and Others for a Livable Planet. Named Disting. Alumna, Pa. State U., 1988; recipient Cir. of Excellence award, Internat. Furnishings and Design Assn., 1992, YMCA Hall of Fame, 1992; Pa. State U. Alumni fellow, 1986. Mem.: Am. Soc. Mag. Editors, Am. Soc. Interior Designers, Nat. Home Fashions League, N.Y. Fashion Group. E-mail: Rachelsfree@aol.com.

NEWMAN, RANDY, singer, songwriter, musician; b. Los Angeles, Calif., Nov. 28, 1943; s. Irving and Adele N.; m. Gretchen Newman; children: Amos, Eric, John, Patrick, Alice. Degree, U. Calif. Arranger, singer, songwriter, musician various record firms; singer-composer: (albums) including Randy Newman, 1968, Twelve Songs, 1969, Live, 1971, Sail Away, 1972, Good Old Boys, 1974, Little Criminals, 1977, Born Again, 1979, Trouble In Paradise, 1983, Land of Dreams, 1988, Bad Love, 1999; (with others) Randy Newman's Faust, 1995; appeared in film: Ragtime, 1981; also TV and concert engagements; music composer for films: Performance, 1970, Pursuit of Happiness, 1971, Cold Turkey, 1971, Ragtime, 1981, The Natural, 1984, Three Amigos (also co-wrote screenplay), 1986, Parenthood, 1989, Avalon, 1990, Awakenings, 1990, Toy Story, 1995 (Acad. award nominee for best original score 1996, Acad. award nominee for best original song 1996); composer (films) Michael, 1996, James and the Giant Peach, 1996 (Acad. award nomination), Cat's Don't Dance, 1997, A Bug's Life, 1998, Pleasantville, 1998, Toy Story 2, 1999 (Best Song Written for a Motion Picture, TV or other Visual Media Grammy award 2001), Meet the Parents, 2000 (nominee Best Music Acad. award 2001), Monsters, Inc., 2001 (Top Box Office Film ASCAP award 2001, Best Music Acad. award 2002); recorded 30 Years of Randy Newman (4 CD set), 1998. Recipient Grammy award for best instrumental composition, 1984 Office: care Cathy Kerr Mgmt 9079 Nemo St Los Angeles CA 90069-5511

NEWMAN, REBECCA K. principal; BA, Mich. State U., 1968; MEd, U. Kans., 1975, EdD, 1978. Cert. spl. edn. grades K-12 Md., secondary prin. and supr. Md., supt. Md., elem. edn. K-8 Mich., spl. edn. K-12 Mich., English 9-12 Mich., social studies 7-9 Mich. Head tchr. adolescent unit Lafayette Clinic, Detroit, 1968—70; asst. prin., tchr. Island View Adolescent Ctr., Detroit, 1970—71; head tchr. children's unit Lafayette Clinic, Detroit, 1971—73; ednl. dir. Mid-Continent Psychiat. Hosp., Olathe, Kans., 1973—75; program mgr. Severe Personal Adjustment Program, Kansas City, Kans., 1975—78; asst. prin. Rock Terrace H.S. Montgomery County Pub. Schs., 1978—80, prin. Regional Inst. for Children and Adolescents, 1980—86, prin. Mark Twain Mid.-Sr. H.S., 1986—90, supr. secondary instrn. Area 3, 1990—91, acting asst. prin. Wootton H.S., 1991—92, prin. Paint Branch H.S., 1992—95, prin. Wootton H.S., 1995—. Mem. Corp. Partnerships Task Force, Montgomery County, 1996; participant prin.'s view Montgomery County Pub. Schs. Pub. TV, 1989; mem. adv. bd. multidisciplinary master's degree tng. program for tchrs. of the behaviorally disordered/emotionally disturbed U. Md., College Park, 1985—86. Mem. editl. bd.: Focus on Autistic Behavior, 1990—91. Mem.: Montgomery County Assn. Adminstrv. and Supr. Pers. (mem. negotiations team 1993—96).

NEWMAN, RICHARD AUGUST, psychiatrist, educator; b. Oak Park, Ill., May 27, 1931; s. Henry Adolph and Mildred Kathyn (Haaker) N.; m. Nancy Jane Werdelin, Aug. 28, 1954; children: John Henry, Kurt Alan, Richard Steven, Scott David. BS, U. Ill., 1953, MD, 1956. Diplomate Am. Bd. Psychiatry and Neurology. Intern Swedish-Am. Hosp., Rockford, Ill., 1956-57; resident in psychiatry Walter Reed Gen. Hosp., Washington, 1958-61; rschr. Walter Reed Army Inst., 1961; chief psychiat. svc. Valley Forge Gen. Hosp., Phoenixville, Pa., 1962-64, also asst. chief dept. psychiatry and neurology, 1962-64; practice medicine, specializing in psychiatry Paoli, 1962-96; dir. milieu therapy Phila. Gen. Hosp., 1968-69; dir. residency tng., dept. mental health scis. Hahnemann Med. Coll., 1969-73, assoc. prof., 1970-79; prof. psychiatry Med. Coll. Pa., 1979—. Dir. continuing mental health edn., 1983—87, 1983—87; dir. continuing med. edn., 1985—87; regional med. dir. for mental health Intracorp/Cigna, 1989—93; assoc. med. dir. for mental health U.S. Healthcare, 1993—95; vis. prof. psychiatry U. Alta., 1975; chief cons. psychotherapy Chester County Cmty. Mental Health Clinic, 1967—68; psychiatrist Chester County Commr.'s Bd. for Mental Health/Mental Retardation, 1971—77; instr. Phila. Psychoanalytic Soc. Extension Sch., 1972—90; mem. faculty Inst. of Phila. Psychoanalytic Soc.; chmn. psychiatric sect. Paoli Meml. Hosp., 1974—83, med. dir. psychiatry svc., 1977—83; psychiat. cons. St. Judes Hosp., St. Lucia, West Indies, 1983—89, St. Jones Ctr. for Behavioral Health, 1999, Kent Gen. Hosp., Dover, Del., 1999, Fairbanks (Alaska) Health Ctr., Alaska, 1999—2000; interim med. dir. Connections CSP, Wilmington, Del., 1995—96; staff psychiatrist Philhaven Hosp., Mt. Gretna, Pa., 1996—97; cons. St. Joseph's Hosp., Reading, Pa., 2000—. Contbr. articles to profl. jours. Maj. M.C., AUS, 1958-64. Fellow APA (disting. life fellow) Pa. Psychiat. Assn. (chmn. ethics com.); mem. AMA, Phila. Psychoanlaytic Soc., Am. Psychoanalytic Assn. (cert. psychoanalyst), Christian Med. Soc., Soc. Med. Coll. Dirs. Continuing Med. Edn., Pa., Chester County Med. Socs., Dirs. of Residency Tng. in Psychiatry of Del. Valley (past pres.). Lutheran. Home: 600 Nancy Jane Ln Downingtown PA 19335-1670 Office Phone: 610-208-8860.

NEWMAN, RICHARD G. engineering company executive; BSCE, Bucknell U.; MSCE, Columbia U.; grad. Exec. Mgmt. Program, UCLA. Chmn., CEO AECOM Tech. Corp., LA, 2002—. Bd. dirs. Southwest Water Co., 13 mutual funds under Capital Rsch. and Mgmt. Co., Sempra Energy, San Diego, 2002—, mem. audit and corp. governance coms. Fellow: Inst. for Advancement of Engring.; mem.: NSPE, Am. Soc. Civil Engrs., Chief Executives Orgn. Office: AECOM Tech Corp 555 S Flower St Ste 3700 Los Angeles CA 90071-2300 Office Phone: 215-593-8000. Office Fax: 213-593-8729.*

NEWMAN, ROBERT GABRIEL, physician; b. The Netherlands, Oct. 26, 1937; came to U.S., 1939; s. Randolph H. and Eva E. (Feilchenfeld) N.; m. Seiko Kusuba, Oct. 26, 1968; children— Henry Seiji, Hana Marie. BA, NYU, 1958; MD with honors, U. Rochester, 1963; MPH, U. Calif.-Berkeley, 1969. Intern and resident in surgery Univ. Hosps., Cleve., 1963-65; dist. health officer N.Y.C. Health Dept., 1968; dir. Nat. Nutrition Survey of N.Y.C., 1969-70; asst. commr. N.Y.C. Health Dept., 1970-74; health cons., 1974-76; assoc. gen. dir. Beth Israel Med. Ctr., N.Y.C., 1976-78, CEO, pres., 1978-97; prof. dept. community medicine Mt. Sinai Sch. Medicine, N.Y.C., 1982-94; prof. depts. epidemiology and social medicine/psychiatry Albert Einstein Coll. of Medicine, 1994—; CEO, pres. Continuum Health Ptnrs. Inc. (formerly Greater Met. Health), N.Y.C., 1997—2000, pres. emeritus; dir. Baron Edmond de Rothschild Chem. Dependency Inst., N.Y.C., 2000—. Cons. addiction problems Govt. of Hong Kong, 1975-85 Author book in field of methadone treatment; contbr. articles to profl. jours. Trustee U. Rochester, NY, 1994—2002. With USAF, 1965—67. WHO fellow, 1972 Fellow N.Y. Acad. Medicine, Am. Coll. Preventive Medicine; mem. Public Health Assn. N.Y.C., Hosp. Assn. N.Y. State (past chmn. 1992), Greater N.Y. Hosp. Assn. (past chmn. bd.), Am. Public Health Assn. Office: Continuum Health Ptnrs Inc 555 W 57th St Fl 18 New York NY 10019-2925 E-mail: rgnewmanmd@hotmail.com.

NEWMAN, RYAN, race car driver; b. South Bend, Ind. Degree in vehicle structure engring., Purdue U., 2001. Racecar driver Penske Racing, 2001—. Named winner, All-Am. Midget Series, 1993, Rookie of the Yr., USAC Nat. Midget Series, 1995, USAC Silver Crown Series, 1996, Sprint Car, 1999, winner, USAC Coors Light Silver Bullet Series, 1999, Pepsi Automobile Racing Club Am. 200, 2000, Automobile Racing Club Am. Ky. Speedway, 2000, Automobile Racing Club Am. Lowe's Motor Speedway, 2000; scholar Rich Vogler Meml. scholar, 2001. Office: c/o Penske Racing 136 Knob Hill Rd Mooresville NC 28117

NEWMAN, SAMUEL, retired trust company executive; b. N.Y.C., Mar. 12, 1938; s. Aaron and Rachel (Hershkowitz) N.; m. Carolyn Gropper, Oct. 27, 1963; children: Marci Ann, Jodi Robin, Michael David. BBA, CUNY, 1971; grad. Advanced Mgmt. Program, Harvard U., 1982. Methods analyst Bankers Trust Co., N.Y.C., 1960-67; project leader Clark O'Neill SVC Corp., Fairview, N.J., 1967-68; sr. v.p. Irving Trust Co., N.Y.C., 1968-85; sr. v.p., gen. mgr. trade svcs. and GEOSERVE legal and regulatory support Mfrs. Hanover Trust (merger with Chem. Bank 1992), N.Y.C., 1985-92; sr. v.p., gen. mgr. funds transfer and trade svcs. Chem. Bank, N.Y.C., 1992-93; sr. v.p. and bus. head payment products First Fidelity Bank NA, Newark, 1993-95; head dept. project support Fleet Pa. Svcs. Inc., Scranton, Pa., 1995-98; dir. new bus. devel., mgr. customer svc., internat. fin. instns. Fleet Bank, N.Y.C., 1998—2001; dir. float mgmt. Fleet Nat. Bank, Melville, NY, 2001—03. Past chmn. bd. dirs. S.W.I.F.T. Terminal Svcs.; past chmn. N.Y. Clearing House funds transfer com.; speaker industry confs. Contbr. articles to profl. jours.

Advisor Nat. Conf. of Commrs. on Uniform State Laws; former mem. U.S. coun. Internat. Banking Exec. Com., U.S. del. to Uncitral Working Group on Internat. Payments; former chief U.S. del. to tech. com. 168 Internat. Standards Orgn. Mem. Soc. Worldwide Fin. Telecom. (bd. dirs. 1978-92, dep. chmn 1989-92), Internat. Fin. Svcs. Assn. (bd. dirs. 2001—03). Avocation: foreign currency note collection. Office: PO Box 887 Melville NY 11747 Personal E-mail: wallstrbkr@aol.com.

NEWMAN, SANDRA SCHULTZ, state supreme court justice; BS, Drexel U., 1959; MA, Temple U., 1969; JD, Villanova U., 1972; D (hon.) (hon.), Gannon U., 1996, Widener U., 1996, Clarion U., 2000. Bar: Pa., U.S. Dist. Ct. (ea. dist.) Pa., U.S. Ct. Appeals (3d cir.), U.S. Supreme Ct. Asst. dist. atty. Montgomery County, Pa.; pvt. practice; judge Commonwealth Ct. of Pa., 1993—95; justice Supreme Ct. of Pa., 1995—. Past chair bd. consultors Villanova U. Law Sch.; mem. jud. coun. Supreme Ct. of Pa., liaison to the 3rd cir. task force on mgmt. of death penalty litigation, liaison to Pa. lawyers fund for client security bd., liaison to domestic rels. procedural rules com.; liaison Pa. Bar Inst.; jud. work group HHS; mem. adv. com. Nat. Ctr. for State Cts., Am. Law Inst.; mem. Drexel U. Coll. Bus. and Adminstrn.; lectr. and spkr. in field. Author: Alimony, Child Support and Counsel Fees, 1988; contbr. articles to profl. jours. Named named Disting. Daughter of Pa.; recipient Phila. award for Super Achiever, Pediatric Juvenile Colitis Found. Jefferson Med. Coll. and Hosp, 1979, award for Dedicated Leadership and Outstanding Contbns. to the Cmty. and Law Employment, Drexel 100 award, Police Chiefs Assn. of Southeastern Pa., 1993, Medallion of Achievement award, Villanova U., 1993, Susan B. Anthony award, Women's Bar Assn. Western Pa., 1996, award, Justinian Soc., 1996, Tau Epsilon Law Soc., 1996, Legion of Honor Gold Medallion award, Chapel of Four Chaplain, 1997, honored by, Women of Greater Phila., 1996. Fellow: Pa. Bar Found., Am. Bar Found.; mem.: Montgomery Bar Assn., Nat. Assn. Women Judges, Am. Law Inst. Office: Supreme Ct Pa Ste 400 100 Four Falls Corporate Ctr West Conshohocken PA 19428-2950

NEWMAN, SHERRYL A. HOBBS, secretary of the district; BA in Chemistry, Rutgers Coll.-Rutgers Univ., New Brunswick, NJ, 1986; BA in Economics, Rutgers Coll.-Rutgers Univ., 1986; MBA in Management, Lubin Graduate Sch. of Bus. Pace Univ., White Plains, NY, 1992. Exec. sec.-Tax Operation Bureau NYC-Dept. of Finance, 1986, special projects coordinator-Program Devel. Divsn., 1986—87, special property coordinator-Program Devel. Divsn., 1986—87, asst. to dir.-Taxpayer Assistance Divsn., 1987—89, unit mgr.-Taxpayer Corr., 1989—90, unit mgr.-Real Estate Tax Assistance, 1990—92, acting dep. dir.-Taxpayer Assistance Divsn., 1992—93, city collector-Property Bureau, 1993—96; dir. Customer Svc. Adminstrn.-Office of Tax and Revenue, DC, 1997—99, Citywide Customer Svc. Adminstrn.-Office of the City Adminstr., DC, 1999, Dept. of Motor Vehicles, DC, 1999—2003; sec. of dist. DC Govt., 2003—. Office: John A Wilson Bldg 1350 Pennsylvania Ave NW Rm 419 Washington DC 20004

NEWMAN, SLATER EDMUND, psychologist, educator; b. Boston, Sept. 8, 1924; s. Max and Gertrude (Raphael) N.; m. Corrine Lois Silfen, June 18, 1950 (div. 1968); children: Kurt Douglas, Jonathan Mark, Eric Bruce; m. Patricia Ellen Christopher Thomas, July 2, 1969; 1 stepchild, Arthur C. Thomas III. BS, U. Pa., 1947; MA, Boston U., 1948; PhD, Northwestern U., 1951. Research psychologist U.S. Air Force, 1951-57; mem. faculty N.C. State U., Raleigh, 1957—2003, prof. emeritus psychology, 2003—. Vis. fgn. mem. Exptl. Psychology Soc. U.K., 1973-74, 82-83, 90. Contbr. chpts. to books, articles to profl. publs. Bd. dirs. ACLU, 1992-97, mem. biennial conf. com., 1994-97, mem. task force internat. human rights, 1994—, mem. spl. nominating com, 1996, mem. constn. com., 1996-97, youth affairs com., 1997, mem. nat. adv. coun., 1998—; pres. N.C. Civil Liberties Union, 1980-82, organizing com., 1965, exec. com., 1986-87, bd. dirs., 1969-73, 76-82, 84-90, 91-97; chmn. Com. on Internat. Human Rights, 1988—; chair founding com. Wake County Chpt. ACLU, 1969, pres., 1969-72, 84-86, bd. dirs., 1969-73, 76-82, 84-90, 91-97, 99—; mem. steering com. ACLU-Affiliate Leadership Network, 1991-95; founding mem. North Carolinians Against the Death Penalty, 1967, bd. govs., 1967-73; mem. Mayor's Com. UN Week, Raleigh, 1986-95; active Amnesty Internat.; co-founder, coord. Com. to Reverse Arms Race, 1982—; co-founder, mem. steering com. North Carolinians Against Apartheid, 1985-87; mem. Wake County Com. Bicentennial U.S. Constn., 1987-89; co-founder, co-chair N.C. Com. for Celebration of Human Rights, 1989-97; mem. Human Rights Week Com. N.C. State U., 1993-99, founder, 1993, chair, 1993-96; co-founder, co-chmn. Human Rights Coalition N.C., 1997—; co-founder North Carolinians for Ratification, Conv. on Elimination of All Forms of Discrimination Against Women, 1997, chmn., 1998—; mem. civil rights adv. bd. N.C. Mus. History, 2001—. USAF, 1943-46 (2nd lt., 1952-53). USPHS spl. rsch. fellow U. Calif.-Berkeley, 1965-66; U. London hon. rsch. fellow, 1973-74, 82-83, 90; recipient W.W. Finlator award ACLU of Wake County, 1997, Norman Smith award ACLU of N.C., 1998; recipient Frank Porter Graham Award, ACLU of N.C., 2004. Fellow: APA, AAAS, Am. Psychol. Soc.; mem.: AAUP (pres. N.C. State U. chpt. 1968—69), Carolinas Conf. for Undergrad. Rsch. in Psychology (co-founder 1976, co-advisor), Ea. Psychol. Assn., N.C. Cognition Group (founder 1972), Southea. Psychol. Assn. (exec. com. 2001—04, sec.-treas. 2004—), Southea. Workers in Memory (founder 1969), So. Soc. Philosophy and Psychology, Psychonomic Soc., UN Assn. (bd. dirs. Wake County chpt. 1991—95), Psi Chi (v.p. southea. region 1990—94, nat. coun. 1990—94, nat. pres.-elect 1996—97, nat. coun. 1996—99, nat. pres. 1997—98, nat. past pres. 1998—99), Sigma Xi. Home: 315 Shepherd St Raleigh NC 27607-4031 Office: NC State U Dept Psychology Raleigh NC 27695-7650 Office Phone: 919-515-1728. E-mail: slater_newman@ncsu.edu., slaterpat@mindspring.com.

NEWMAN, STACEY CLARFIELD, artist, curator; b. N.Y.C., July 21, 1956; d. Wallace J. Clarfield and Elinor (Kandel) Clarfield-Toberoff; m. Fredric Alan Newman, Nov. 27, 1983; children: Benjamin Clarfield, Marissa Paige, Alexandra Brooke. Student, Franklin & Marshall, 1974-76; BS in Labor Rels. and Mgmt., U. Bridgeport, 1978. Dir. ops. Nat. Rec. and Video Studios, N.Y.C., 1978-80; dir. tech. ops. VCA/Teletronics, N.Y.C., 1980-82, cons., client rep./MTV, 1981-83, exec. prodr., 1982-85; artist, art curator Stacey Clarfield Newman Studios, Scarsdale, N.Y., 1986—; mem. faculty Young at Art, Scarsdale Art Enrichment Ctr., 2002—; dir. tech ops. prodr. VCA/Teletronics, N.Y.C. Merchandise dir. Tahari Fashions, N.Y.C., 1985-86; artist mem., jury com. You Gotta Have Art program White Plains Hosp. Ctr., 1990-92; art tchr. collage Scarsdale (N.Y.) Adult Edn. Program, 1993-95; artist in residence Scarsdale Elem. Schs., 1995-97; art cons., curator Manhattan Transfer, Inc., N.Y.C., 1997-2000; faculty mem. Young at Art Enrichment Sch., Scarsdale, 2002-03; artist in residence Scarsdale Elem. Sch., 1995-2003; juror The Figure & Form, Edward Hopper House Mus., N.Y., 2004 One-person shows include Quogue (N.Y.) Gallery, 1986, Piermont (N.Y.) Fine Arts Gallery, 1997-98, Manhattan Transfer, Inc., 1997, Piermont Fine Arts Gallery, 2001, J&W Gallery, New Hope, Pa., 1999, Studio 4 West, 1999, 93 South Gallery, 2000, Adele Greenberg Salon, Cambridge, Mass., 2000, Amb. Galleries, Palm Beach, Fla., 2001, Viridian Gallery, N.Y.C., 2001, 02, Piermont Fine Arts Gallery, 2001, Viridian Gallery @ Chelsea, 2002, 04; exhibited in juried group shows: Piermont Fine Art Gallery, 1995, 96, 98, 2000, 01, Anaya Gallery, Scarsdale, 1986, Katonah (N.Y.) Gallery, 1986, Gallery at Jamaica, Stratton Mountain, Vt., 1987, CDS Contemporary Art, Albuquerque, 1989, Mari Galleries, Mamaroneck, N.Y., 1992, Manhattan Transfer, Inc., 1993, 98, 93 South Gallery, Nyack, N.Y., 1998-99, Bibro Fine Arts Gallery, Chelsea, N.Y., 1998, Weber Fine Art, Scarsdale, N.Y., 1998, 2000, 93 South Gallery, Nyack, N.Y., 1998, J&W Gallery, New Hope, Pa., 1998, 99, 2001, Studio 4 West, Piermont, N.Y., 1999, Hewlett Mus., 2000, Ambassador Gallery, Palm Beach, Fla., 2000, Viridian Gallery, N.Y.C., 2000-04, Hewlett Mus., 2000, Adele Greenberg Salon, 2000, 01, A Pirate Space, Denver, 2001, Contemporary Art Oasis, Denver, 2001, J&W Gallery, 2001, 2002, Manhattanville Coll. Gallery, 2002, Nat. Assn. Women Artists, N.Y.C., 2003, Chgo. Fine Arts Bldg. Gallery, 2003, Chgo. Fine Arts Bldg. Gallery, 2003; commd. Am. Soc. Plastic and Reconstructive Surgeons, L.A. Conv. Ctr., 1988, White Plains Hosp. Ctr., 1989, 90, Cystic Fibrosis Found., N.Y.C., 1990, Joan Kroc Found., Calif., 1989-91. 1st v.p., bd. dirs. Internat. Coll. Surgeons aux., Chgo., 1988—90; mem. Juvenile Diabetes Found., Gala, 2000; Regional v.p. Am. Cancer soc., White Plains, 1986—88; bd. dirs. White Plains Hosp. Ctr. Aux., 1995—; fund raiser, event planner Holocaust Commn., N.Y.C., 1998; mem. J&W Gallery, 2000—, Viridian Artists, Inc., 2001—; active Scarsdale Tremont Synagogue Gala, 2001, 2002; mem. Nat. Assn. Women Artists; fund-raiser Alternative Arts and Music Events, Scarsdale Teen Ctr., 2003—; liaison Scarsdale HS PTA, Alternative Art and Music Events, Scarsdale Teen Ctr., 2003—05. Mem. Internat. Platform Assn., Nat. Mus. Women in Contemporary Arts, Nat. Assn. Women Artists, Inc., Katonah Mus., Nat. Mus. Women in the Arts (artist mem.), Nat. Arts Club. Avocations: piano, photography, tennis, kayaking, skiing. Studio: 21 Wayside Ln Scarsdale NY 10583-2911 Office Phone: 914-725-1174. Personal E-mail: StaceySCN21@aol.com.

NEWMAN, STANLEY RAY, oil industry executive; b. Milo, Idaho, Mar. 5, 1923; s. Franklin Hughes and Ethel Amelda (Crowley) Newman; m. Rosa Klein, May 27, 1961 (div. Mar. 1980); children: Trudy Lynn, Susan Louise, Karen Elizabeth, Paul Daniel, Phillip John; m. Madelyn Wycherly, Jan. 10, 1991; children: Heidi, Heather, Amy. Student, Tex A&M U., 1944-45; BS, U. Utah, 1947; PhD, 1952. With Texaco Rsch. Ctr., Beacon, NY, 1951-82, technologist, 1973-77, sr. technologist rsch. mfg.-fuels, 1977—82; profl. cons. on fuels and chems., 1983-91. Chmn. planning bd. Village of Fishkill, NY, 1973—77, trustee, 1990—92; mem. Dutchess County Solid Waste Mgmt. Bd., 1974—76. With Signal Corps U.S. Army, 1944—46. Mem.: AAAS, N.Y. Fruit Testing Assn., Dutchess County Geneal. Soc. (pres. 1981—87, exec. v.p. 1987—88), N.Y. Acad. Scis., Sigma Xi (pres. Texaco Rsch. Ctr. br. 1980—81). Republican. Mem. Lds Ch. Achievements include patents in field. Home: 285 Plantation Cir Idaho Falls ID 83404-7990 E-mail: stamad39@aol.com. *I was born of humble parents in Idaho. Life was hard and difficult so early in my life at considerable sacrifice I went the extra distance to go to a good high school to prepare for college. By working at night and weekends, I was able to complete college with a Ph.D. Blessed with an inquiring mind, a strong will to work, and a desire to learn, I moved to the east coast, worked hard both at my job and in the community, always retaining the honesty, integrity and strong religious values taught by my humble parents. At retirement, I had numerous patents, publications, and had world wide responsibility for fuels for Texaco.*

NEWMAN, STEPHEN ALEXANDER, chemical engineer, thermodynamicist; b. Auburn, N.Y., Apr. 12, 1938; s. Solomon and Anna (Reich) N.; m. Mary Ellen Lassow, July 26, 1964; children: Sharon Rose, Lori Suzanne. BSChemE, Rensselaer Poly. Inst., 1960; MSChemE, MIT, 1962; PhD, Rutgers U., 1976. Registered profl. engr., N.J. Rsch. engr. M.W. Kellogg Co., Piscataway, N.J., 1962-67; tech. mgr. Foster Wheeler Energy Corp., Clinton, NJ, 1967—96; prin. engr. Kvaerner Process, Bridgewater, NJ, 1996—99, cons. engr., 1999—, clients have included ABB Lummus Global (Bloomfield, NJ) and Kvaerner Process (Bridgewater, NJ). Frequent speaker nat. and internat. sci. meetings; organizer, conf./symposium chmn. Nat. Thermodynamics Conf., 1978, World Congress Chem. Engring., Montreal, 1981, CODATA Congress, Jerusalem, 1984; panel NAS, 1980-82; cons. Nat. Bur. Standards, Washington, 1979; chmn. various project coms. U.S. Dept. Energy, 1977-84. Editor: Thermodynamics of Aqueous Systems with Industrial Applications, 1980, Chemical Engineering Thermodynamics, 1983, Shale Oil Upgrading and Refining, 1983, Acid and Sour Gas Treating Processes, 1985; book and article reviewer Chem. Engring. mag., Gulf Publs., 1980—; contbr. numerous articles to profl. jours. Pres. Mens' Club Temple Israel, Union, N.J., 1980-81. AEC fellow, 1961-62; grantee NSF, 1978, 84. Fellow AIChE (chmn. nat. rsch. com. 1984-85, co-founder Design Inst. Phys. Property Data 1977, vice chmn. 1979-85, award 1989); mem. Am. Petroleum Inst. (chair contractors com. on tech. data 1978-96), Gas Processors Assn. (project monitor 1976-85, tech. com.), Am. Assn. Engring. Socs. Jewish. Home: 941 Douglas Ter Union NJ 07083-6523 Office Phone: 908-688-5167.

NEWMAN, STEPHEN MICHAEL, lawyer; b. Buffalo, Jan. 12, 1945; s. Howard A. and Mildred (Ballow) N.; m. Gayle Mallon, May 24, 1969; children: Holly, Deborah. AB, Princeton U., 1966; JD, U. Mich., 1969. Bar: N.Y. 1969, Fla. 1976. Assoc. Hodgson, Russ, Andrews, Woods & Goodyear, Buffalo, 1969-73; ptnr. Hodgson Russ, LLP (formerly Hodgson, Russ, Andrews, Woods), Buffalo, 1973—. Lectr. in field. Bd. dirs. Leukemia Soc., United Jewish Fedn. Buffalo Inc., Jewish Ctr. Greater Buffalo Inc., Temple Beth Zion; bd. dirs., chpt. chmn., exec. com. Am. Jewish Com., Buffalo chpt.; bd. advisors Am. Lung Assn., Southeast Fla. chpt. Fellow Am. Coll. Trusts and Estates Coun.; mem. ABA (personal svc. corps. com. tax sect.), N.Y. State Bar Assn. (chair trusts and estates law sect. 2001), Princeton Club of Fla. Office: Hodgson Russ LLP 2000 1 M&T Plz Buffalo NY 14203 Office Phone: 716-856-4000. Business E-Mail: snewman@hodgsonruss.com.

NEWMAN, STEVEN E. neurologist; b. Detroit, July 1, 1945; children: Nathan, Rachel, Emily, Benjamin, Daniel. BA, Albion Coll., 1966; MD, U. Mich., 1970. Diplomate Am. Bd. Psychiatry & Neurology, Am. Bd. Forensic Examiners, Am. Bd. Forensic Medicine, Am. Bd. of Clin. Neurophysiology, Am. Bd. of EEG. With dept. neurology Dept. Internal Medicine, Dept. Psychiatry U. Mich., 1971-77; with NIH, 1977-79, Detroit Inst. PM&R, 1979—. Mem. Mich. Spinal Cord/Traumatic Brain Injury Adv. Com., 1994-97; mem. State of Mich. Adv. Coun. Traumatic Brain Injury Grant Com., 1999—; med. dir. Fedn. for Spinal Cord Injury Prevention; bd. dirs. Mich. Neurol. Assn. Author: Legal Medicine, 1995; contbr. articles to profl. jours. Recipient Palatucci Advocacy Leader Award. Fellow Am. Acad. Neurology; mem. Am. Coll. of Forensic Examiners, Mich. State Med. Soc. (bd. dirs.), Oakland County Med. Soc. (pres. 2000-2001), Nat. Assn. Disability Evaluating Physicians, Am. Acad. Clin. Neurophysiology. Office: Detroit Inst Phys Med & Rehab 25811 W 12 Mile Rd Southfield MI 48034-1896

NEWMAN, STEVEN HARVEY, insurance company executive, director; b. Bklyn., Apr. 26, 1943; s. Charlotte Newman Bart; m. Lenore Blaustein, June 14, 1964; children: Richard, Michael, Stephanie. BS, Bklyn. Coll., 1963. Actuarial asst. Royal Globe Ins. Co., N.Y.C., 1963-65; asst. sec. Ins. Rating Bd., N.Y.C., 1965-69; v.p., sr. casualty actuary Am. Internat. Group, N.Y.C., 1969-82; exec. v.p. Home Ins. Co., N.Y.C., 1982-85, pres., 1985-86, also bd. dirs.; chmn., CEO Underwriters Reinsurance Co., Woodland Hills, Calif., 1987—2001; now chmn. Platinum Underwriters Holdings, Ltd., Bermuda, 2002—. Chmn. GCR Holdings, 1993-97, Reins. Assn. Am., 1995-96. Fellow Casualty Actuarial Soc. (pres. 1981-82); mem. Am. Acad. Actuaries, Internat. Actuarial Assn.

NEWMAN, SUZANNE DINKES, web site development executive; b. Bklyn., Apr. 28, 1949; d. Philip and Natalie (Hollander) Dinkes; m. Ralph Michael Newman, Mar. 9, 1975. Student, Cooper Union, 1967—71, Sch. Visual Arts, NYC, 1971—72. Asst. art dir. Lincoln Ctr. Art Programs, NYC, 1973-74; art dir. BimBamBoom Mag., Yonkers, NY, 1974; with Fairfax Advt., NYC, 1974-75; dir. ops. TBE Advt., NYC, 1975-87, CEO Yonkers, NY, 1987-94; art dir. Timer Barrier Express, Yonkers, 1975-80; CEO R.S. Newman Assocs., Yonkers, 1994-98; ptnr. WWW.Dott-Comm.com, 1997—. Concert coord. Classic Harmony Prodns., NYC, 1975; apl. event planner, The Left Bank, Mt. Vernon, NY, 1980-81; apl. event cons. Glen Island Casino, New Rochelle, NY, 1984-85; event coord., Top Brass, Yonkers, 1986-87; art dir., cons. various music publs., 1974-80. Editor: Rockin' in the Fourth Estate, 1979-80, Chamber News, 1998—; art dir.: White and Still All Right!, 1977, Sun Records, 1980, The Buddy Holly Story, 1979. Mem. Yonkers Citizen's Adv. Grp., Yonkers Mayorial Transition Com., 1991-92, Alliance Devel. Com., Yonkers Sch. and Bus. Alliance, 1991-94, program com., 1991-94; mem. Yonkers Coun. Pres.'s Citizens Adv., Group, 1992, Yonkers Dem. Com., dist. leader, 1991-93; jour. chair gala com. Hudson River Mus., 1992; mem. Yonkers Local Bus. Adv. Coun., 1992-94; mem. Yonkers Pvt. Industry Coun., 1992-94, sec. 1993-94; promotion chair Yonkers Hudson Riverfest, 1992-93; bus. adv. com. Yonkers Econ. Devel. Zone, 1993-94; active Yonkers Waterfront Task Force, 1993-94; bd. dirs. Youth Theater Interaction, 1994—; bd. dirs. Westchester divsn. Jewish Guild for Blind, 1994-97, gala chair, 1994; events coord. Mayor's Inaugural Ball, 1996; leader Jr. Girl Scouts, Southwest Yonkers, 1996—. Recipient Disting. Leadership and Svc. award, Westchester County C. of C., 1985, Westchester award, Westchester Small Bus. Coun., 1989, Outstanding Leader award Girl Scouts U.S., 2000. Mem. Westchester Small Bus. Coun. (comm. chmn. 1984-85, Westchester winner, 1989), Yonkers C. of C. (bd. dirs. 1996—, comm. chair 1996-97), Coun. for Arts Westchester. Democrat. Jewish. Avocations: reading, antiques, gardening. E-mail: snewman@dott-comm.com.

NEWMAN, THEODORE ROOSEVELT, JR., judge; b. Birmingham, Ala., July 5, 1934; s. Theodore R. and Ruth L. (Oliver) N. AB, Brown U., 1955, LL.D., 1980; JD, Harvard U., 1958. Bar: D.C. 1958, Ala. 1959. Atty. civil rights div. Dept. Justice, Washington, 1961-62; practiced law in Washington, 1962-70; assoc. judge D.C. Superior Ct., 1970-76; judge D.C. Ct. Appeals, 1976-91, chief judge, 1976-84, sr. judge, 1991—; bd. dirs. Nat. Center for State Cts., v.p., 1980-81, pres., 1981-82. Trustee Brown U. With USAF, 1958-61. Fellow Am. Bar Found.; mem. Nat. Bar Assn. (past pres. jud. coun., C. Francis Stradford award 1984, William H. Hastie award 1988). E-mail: tnewman@dcca.state.dc.us.

NEWMAN, THOMAS DANIEL, minister, school administrator, archaeologist; b. London, Eng., May 12, 1922; s. Frederick and Margaret (O'Leary) N.; m. Louise Johannah Albertano, Apr. 1, 1963; 1 dau., Susan (Mrs. Alan J. Rennie). Student, Glasgow Sch. Accounting, 1946, Unity Sch. Christianity, 1962-66, Harvard Div. Sch., 1967—; DSc, Alma Coll., 1975. Ordained to ministry Ch. of Christ, 1966. Mng. dir. Thomas Newman (Printers) Ltd., 1945-49; mng. dir. H. & M.J. Pubs. Ltd., 1947-49, Forget-Me-Not Greeting Cards Ltd., 1949-61, Diplomat Greetings Ltd., 1957-61, Nevill's Ltd., 1955-57; pastor Christ's Ch., Springfield, Mo., 1966-67, Longwood, Brookline, Mass., 1967-99; adminstrv. dir. Am. Schs. Oriental Rsch., 1968, treas., 1970—, trustee, 1972—. Pastor Jefferson (N.H.) Cmty. Chapel, 2000—; founder Carthage Rsch. Inst., Khereddine, Tunisia, 1975, Cyprus Archaeol. Rsch. Inst., Nicosia, 1977; cons. Joint Archeol. Expdns. to, Ai, 1969-73, to; Tell-El-Hesi, 1970-73, to, Idalion, 1970-73; mem. Joint Archeol. Expdn. to, Caesarea Maritima, 1971, to; Carthage, 1975; dir. Logistics Survey Qu'Rayyah, Saudi Arabia, 1973; pub. cons. (Dead Sea Scrolls Com.), 1968-73; Trustee Allbright Inst. Archeol. Rsch., Jerusalem.; Am. Center Oriental Rsch., Amman, Jordan. Served with RAF, 1940-45. Mem. Archeol. Inst. Am., Soc. Bibl. Lit., Soc. O.T. Studies, Masons, Harvard Faculty Club, Univ. Club Boston. Home: 359 Ivy Terrace Dahlonega GA 30533 Office Phone: 706-864-5853. E-mail: revtomn@alltel.net.

NEWMAN, URSULA IRENE, music educator; b. Toledo, May 24, 1954; d. Lowell Cauffiel and Ursula Irene Zulka; m. Bruce Lee Newman, Nov. 15, 1986; children: Joanna, Betsy; m. Larry Spieldenner (div.); 1 child, Larry Spieldenner. Attended, Mary Manse Coll., Toledo, Columbia U., N.Y. Owner Ursula Cauffiel Sch of Music, Toledo, 1980—90. Adv. Ursula Cauffiel Sch. of Music, Toledo, 1990—; music dir. Temple Beth Israel, Phoenix, 1999—2001. Founder PracticeAthon, 2004—. Mem.: Desert Valley Music Teachers Assn., Music Tchr. Nat. Assn. Avocations: swimming, acting. Home: 10201 N 109th Pl Scottsdale AZ 85259-4809 Personal E-mail: grandpiano2002@aol.com.

NEWMAN, WILLIAM, real estate executive; b. N.Y.C., July 6, 1926; s. Morris B. and Ida (Singer) N.; m. Anita Eagle, Dec. 12, 1948; children: Steven (dec.), Sharon (dec.), Debra Newman Bernstein. BBA, CCNY, 1947. CPA, N.Y. Ptnr. Morris B. Newman & Co., N.Y.C., 1947-61; pres. New Plan Realty Corp., N.Y.C., 1961-72; chief exec. officer New Plan Realty Trust, N.Y.C., 1972—, also chmn. bd. trustees. Trustee Baruch Coll. Fund.; founder Steven L. Newman Real Estate Inst. at Baruch Coll., 1996. Recipient Gold award Wall St. Transcript, 1986, Bronze award, 1989, Silver award, 1990, 91, Outstanding Achievement award Baruch Coll. Alumni Assn., 1991; Baruch Coll. Libr. designated William and Anita Newman Libr. Mem. Nat. Assn. Real Estate Investment Trusts (chmn. 1990-92, Industry Leadership award 1995, Entrepreneur of Yr. 1998), Chief Execs. Orgn., Met. Pres.'s Orgn., Colony Club (London), Brae Burn Country Club, Boca Rio Golf Club, Princeton Club. Office: New Plan Realty Trust Ste 2200 1120 Avenue Of The Americas Fl 12 New York NY 10036-6711*

NEWMAN-GORDON, PAULINE, French language and literature educator; b. N.Y.C., Aug. 5, 1925; d. Bernard and Eva Newman; m. Sydney A. Gordon, Sept. 13, 1959 (dec.); m. Richard Yellin, Feb. 9, 1997. BA, Hunter Coll., 1947; MA, Columbia U., 1948; PhD, Sorbonne U., Paris, 1951. Instr. French Wellesley (Mass.) Coll., 1952-53; mem. faculty Stanford (Calif.) U., 1953—, prof. French lit., 1969-93, prof. emerita, 1994—. Author: Marcel Proust, 1953, Eugene Le Roy, 1957, Corbiere, Laforgue and Apollinaire, 1964, Helen of Troy Myth, 1968, (poetry) Mooring to France, (prose poem) Sydney: editor: Dictionary of Ideas in Marcel Proust, 1968, also articles in field; contbr. articles to profl. jours. Scholar Internat. Inst. Edn., 1948-51, MLA, 1956-57, AAUW, 1962-63, Am. Philos. Soc., 1970-71, NEH, 1989; elected to Hall of Fame, Alumni Assn. Hunter Coll. of CUNY, 1990 Mem. MLA, Am. Assn. Tchrs. French, Soc. Friends Marcel Proust. Office: Stanford U Dept French Italian Stanford CA 94305

NEWMAR, JULIE CHALANE, actress, dancer, real estate businesswoman; b. Hollywood, Calif. d. Donald Charles and Helene (Jesmer) Newmeyer; m. J. Holt Smith, Aug. 5, 1977 (div. Apr. 1986); 1 child, John Jewl Smith. Student, UCLA. Actress TV series, plays, movies. Mem. Actors Studio, N.Y. and Los Angeles. Appeared on Broadway in Marriage Go Round (Tony award), Damn Yankees, Guys and Dolls, Irma La Douce, Stop the World, L'il Abner, Dames At Sea; films: Seven Brides for Seven Brothers, Marriage Go Round, Mackenna's Gold, The Maltese Bippy, Streetwalkin', 1985, Dance Academy, 1987, Ghosts Can't Do It, Oblivion I and II, To Wong Foo, Thanks for Everything, Julie Newmar; TV: Rhoda the Robot in My Living Doll, Catwoman on Batman, guest starred on Get Smart, The Monkees, Bewitched, Route 66, Hart to Hart, Love American Style, Star Trek, Twilight Zone, Beverly Hillbillies, Columbo, Fantasy Island, Melrose Place, Hope & Gloria, The Making of Seven Brides for Seven Brothers, 1997; prima ballerina with L.A. Opera Co.; video: Too Funky (George Michael); Thierry Mugler high fashion shows, Paris. Recipient Antoinette Perry award. Avocations: gardening, piano.

NEWMARK, EMANUEL, ophthalmologist; b. Newark, May 25, 1936; s. Charles Meyer and Bella (Yoskowitz) Newmark; m. Tina Steinberg, Aug. 25, 1957; children: Karen Beth, Heidi Ellen, Stuart Jeffrey. BS in Pharmacy, Rutgers U., 1959; postgrad., U. Amsterdam, The Netherlands, 1960-63, Armed Forces Inst. Pathology, Washington, 1971; MD, Duke U., 1966; postgrad., Harvard U., 1967. Diplomate Am. Bd. Ophthalmology. Intern George Washington U. Hosp., Washington, 1966; trainee NIH rsch. U. Fla., Gainesville, 1967-70; resident ophthalmology U. Fla. Hosp., 1967-70; instr. dept. ophthalmology U. Fla., 1970; cons. ophthalmology Gainesville VA Hosp., 1970; clin. instr. ophthalmology U. Tex. Med. Sch., San Antonio, 1971-72; cons. ophthalmology Kerrville (Tex.) VA Hosp., 1971-72; asst. chief ophthalmology svc. Brooke Army Gen. Hosp., Fort Sam, Tex., 1971-72. Clin. asst. prof. ophthalmology Bexar County Hosp. and Clinics, San Antonio, 1971—72; tchg. faculty Joint Commn. Allied Health Pers. in Ophthalmology, commr., 2004—; sec., treas. Palm Beach Eye Assocs., Atlantis, Fla., 1973—98; pharm. adv. com. Agy. Health Care Adminstrn. Bd. Optometry, 1991—; mem. adv. bd. Fla. east coast chpt. Nat. Sjorgren's Syndrome. Contbr. chapters to books, articles to profl. jours.; editor: Ophthalmic Medical Assisting An Independent Study Course. Alumni assoc. Rutgers Coll. Pharmacy, 1990—, chmn. reunion, 1986, 2001, Duke U. Med. Alumni Assn., NC, 1967—; centurian Davison Club-Duke U. Med. Sch., NC, 1982—; campaign chmn., nat. vice chmn. Israel Bonds, Palm Beach County, Fla., 1988—; participant charitable orgns.; v.p. Palm Beach Liturgical Culture Found., 1994—2000, pres., 2000—01. Decorated Lion of Judea State of Israel; recipient Gates of Jerusalem medal, 1991, Jerusalem medal, 1996, Recognition award, Joint Commn. Allied Health Personnel in Ophthalmology, 2001. Fellow: ACS, Am. Acad. Ophthalmology (del. to coun. 1996—2001, allied health edn. com. 1997—2002, editor Refinements 1998—2000, rep. to joint com. allied health pers. in ophthalmology 2004, Fla. state chmn. ednl. trust, Achievement award 2001, Councillors award 2001); mem.: AMA, Fla. Soc. Ophthalmology (ethics chmn. 1985—90, pres. 1990—91, James W. Clower Jr. Cmty. Svc. award 1995), Palm Beach County Ophthal. Soc. (pres. 1984—85), Palm Beach County Med. Soc. (chair ethics com. 1997—2000, vice chair ethics com. 2002, bd. dirs. 2003, bd. dirs. mem.-at-large 2003—, coun. on ethical and jud. affairs 2004), Fla. Med. Assn.

(ho. dels. 1993—95, 2001—04), Am. Orgn. for Rehab. Through Tng. Fedn. (nat. exec. com.-campaign cabinet 1987, pres. 1987—90, Palm Beach Men's Achievement award 1988, Pres. award 1989), Founder's Soc. Duke U. Jewish. Avocations: travel, organizational medicine, teaching. Home: 180 Palm Cir Atlantis FL 33462-6627 Office: Regional Eye Inst 1920 Palm Beach Lakes Blvd West Palm Beach FL 33409-3512 also: Florida Eye 1717 Woolbright Rd Boynton Beach FL 33436 Office Phone: 561-689-9100., 561-737-5500. Personal E-mail: mannynewmark@msn.com.

NEWMARK, LEONARD DANIEL, linguistics educator; b. Attica, Ind., Apr. 8, 1929; s. Max Jacob and Sophie (Glusker) N.; m. Ruth Broessler, Sept. 16, 1951; children: Katya, Mark. AB, U. Chgo., 1947; MA, Ind. U., 1951, PhD, 1955. Instr. English U. Ill., Urbana, 1951; vis. asst. prof. linguistics U. Mich., Ann Arbor, 1961; assoc. prof. English Ohio State U., 1954-62; assoc. prof. linguistics Ind. U., Bloomington, 1962-63; prof. linguistics U. Calif., San Diego, 1963-91, prof. emeritus, 1992—, chmn. dept., 1963-71, 79-85, head program in Am. lang. and culture, 1979-84, rsch. linguist Ctr. for Rsch. in Lang., 1992—. Author: Linguistic History of English, 1963, Spoken Albanian, 1997, Standard Albanian, 1982, Albanian-English Dictionary, 1998, Albanian Handbook, 1999; editor UCSD Emeriti Newsletter: Chronicles, 2001-2004; inventor memory aid device. Mem. Linguistics Soc. Am., Dictionary Soc. N.Am., Phi Beta Kappa. Home: 2643 St Tropez Pl La Jolla CA 92037-3541 Office: U Calif San Diego Dept Linguistics La Jolla CA 92093 Business E-Mail: ldnewmark@ucsd.edu.

NEWMARK, MARILYN, sculptor; b. NYC, July 20, 1928; d. Edward Ellis and Mabel (Davies) Newmark; m. Leonard J. Meiselman, Mar. 15, 1952. Student, Adelphi Coll., 1945—47, Alfred U., 1949. Sculpture specializing in horses, equestrian figures, dogs, foxes. Exhibited in group shows; sculpture exhbn. Ky. Derby Mus., Fleischer Mus., Scottsdale, Leigh Yawkey Woodson Art Mus., Wis., Bennington Ctr. for Arts, Vt., NAD, NYC, Nat. Arts Club, NYC, Smithsonian Instn., Washington, Mus. of Horse, Ky., Port of History Mus., Pa., Marietta/Cobb Mus. Art, Wildlife Experience, Denver, Brookgreen Gardens, SC, Nat. Geog. Soc., Washington, Allegheny Colls. Galleries, Butler Inst. Am. Art; represented in permanent collections Nat. Mus. Racing, Saratoga, NY, Internat. Mus. Horse, Ky. Horse Park, also in pvt. collections. Recipient Anna Hyatt Huntington award, 1970, 71, 72, 75, 78, 80, 81, 82, 83, 86, 88, 90, 97, 2002, Gold medal, 1973, award Coun. Am. Artists Socs., 1972, 73, 79, 80, Hudson Valley John Newington award, 1973, 77, Gold medal, 1979, Elliot Liskin Meml. award, 1989, 96, Academician NAD Ellin P. Speyer award, 1974, 93, 99, Artist Fund award, 1982. Fellow Nat. Sculpture Soc. (coun. 1973-75, rec. sec. 1976, sec. 1977-79, coun. 1981-83, 92-97, Bronze medal 1986, Mildred Victor Meml. award 1996, Leonard Meiselman Meml. award 2003), Audubon Artists (Elliott Liskin Meml. award 2000, 02), Am. Artists Profl. League (Gold medal 1974, 77, medal of hon. 1987), Allied Artists Am. (Gold medal 1981, 93, In Memorium award 1994), Pen & Brush Club (Gold medal 1977, Salmagundi Club award 1982, 83, 91, C. Dunwiddie Meml. award 1999, 2004), Soc. Animal Artists (jury of admissions 1972-75, 90—, bd. dirs. 1991—, v.p. 1998—, Legacy award 2002), Am. Acad. Equine Art (founding mem., dir. sculpture 1980—), Nassau Suffolk Horsemans Assn. (dir. 1968-82), Catherine Lorillard Wolfe Art Club, Smithtown Hunt Club, Meadowbrook Hunt Club. Address: 22 Woodhollow Rd Roslyn Heights NY 11577-2217 Office Phone: 516-621-5914.

NEWMARK, RICHARD ALAN, chemist; b. Urbana, Ill., Nov. 11, 1940; s. Nathan M. and Anne Mae (Cohen) N.; m. Joan Friedman, July 4, 1965; children: David, Merel. AB, Harvard Coll., 1961; PhD, U. Calif., Berkeley, 1964. Postgrad. fellow Mass. Inst. Tech., Cambridge, 1964-66; asst. prof. U. Colo., Boulder, 1966-69; rsch. chemist 3M, St. Paul, 1969-72, rsch. specialist, 1972-76, sr. rsch. specialist, 1976-81, staff scientist, 1981-92, corp. scientist, 1992—2001; cons., 2002—. Councilor Minn. section Am. Chem. Soc., Washington, 1992-94. Contbr. articles to profl. jours. Chair Dist. 1 Community Coun., St. Paul, 1984-88; co-chair St. Paul Sch. Bd. Commn. of Gifted and Talented, 1986-88. Recipient award 3M Carlton Soc., 1993, Minn. award Am. Chem. Soc., 2000. Mem.: Sigma Xi, Phi Beta Kappa. Avocations: skiing, bicycling. Office: 3M 201-bs 05 Saint Paul MN 55144-0001 Office Phone: 651-270-9345. E-mail: neumarque@comcast.com.

NEWPORT, L. JOAN, clinical social worker, retired psychotherapist; b. Newkirk, Okla., July 5, 1932; d. Crawford Earl and Lillian Pearl (Peden) Irvine; m. Don E. Newport, July 9, 1954 (div. 1971, dec. 1999); children: Alan Keith, Lili Kim. BA cum laude, Wichita State U., 1955; MSW, U. Okla., 1977. Bd. cert. diplomate in clin. social work Acad. Cert. Social Workers; lic. clin. social worker, Okla. Dir. children's work Wesley United Meth. Ch., Oklahoma City, 1969-71; social worker Dept. Human Svcs., Newkirk, Okla., 1972-77; in-sch. suspension counselor Kay County Youth Svcs., Ponca City, Okla., 1977; med. social worker St. Joseph Med. Ctr., Ponca City, 1977-78, dir. social work, 1978-83; pvt. practice, Ponca City, 1979-97; med. social worker Healthcare Svcs., Ponca City, 1983-84; pvt. practice home studies, cons., supervision, Newkirk, 1997—. Cons. Blackwell, Perry, Pawhuska, O'Keene Hosps., 1978-85; cons. social work Bass Meml. Hosp., Enid, Okla., 1985; sponsor, organizer Kay County Parents Anonymous, Ponca City, 1976-83; vice chair Okla. State Bd. Lic. Social Workers, Oklahoma City, 1988-90; presentor, lectr. in field; supr. students Okla. U. Sch. Social Work, Okla. State U., No. Okla. Coll., Okla. Christian Coll., 1977-85; supr. for clin. social workers working toward lic. in Okla., 1985—. Mem. Okla. Women's Network, 1989-96; mem. adv. bd. Displaced Homemakers, Ponca City, 1985-89; mem. adv. bd. Kay County Home Health, 1979-83, chair, 1979-81; Sunday sch. tchr. Newkirk United Meth. Ch.; mem. Newkirk Main St., 1999-2000. Named Hon. State Life Mem. Burbank PTA, Oklahoma City, 1971; scholar Wichita (Kans.) Press and Radio Women, 1953, Conoco, Inc., Houston, 1951-54. Mem. NASW (Okla. del. Del. Assembly Washington 1987, chmn. vendorship com. 1985-87, pres. Okla. chpt. 1988-90, Social Worker of Yr. 1987), Child Abuse Prevention Task Force (pres. dist. 17 1986-88, mem. grant evaluation com. 1986-96), Zeta Phi Eta. Democrat. Methodist. Office: PO Box 74 Newkirk OK 74647-0074

NEWSOM, CAROLYN CARDALL, management consultant; b. South Weymouth, Mass., Feb. 27, 1941; d. Alfred James and Bertha Virginia (Roy) Cardall; m. John Harlan Newsom, Feb. 4, 1967; children: John Cardall, James Harlan. AB, Brown U., 1962; MBA, Wharton Sch., 1978; PhD, U. Pa., 1985. Systems engr. IBM, Seattle, 1964-70, Newsom S.E. Services, Seattle, 1970-76; instr. U. Pa. Wharton Sch., Phila., 1978-81; v.p., prin. sr. cons. PA Cons. Group, Princeton, N.J., 1981-88; pres. Newsom Assocs., Yardley, Pa., 1988; ptnr. Bus. Strategy Implementation, Princeton, N.J., 1989-90; pres. Strategy Implementation Solutions, Yardley, Pa., 1990—. Examiner N.J. Gov.'s Performance Excellence Award, 1993, sr. examiner, 1994—2002; judge N.J. Gov.'s Performance Excellence award, 2003—04; examiner Malcolm Baldrige Nat. Quality award, 2003. Bd. dirs. Chandler Hall, 1980-87; trustee St. Mary Hosp., Langhorne, Pa., 1986-94; sec. bd. dirs. Gordonstown Am. Found., 1999—. Mem.: Quality N.J. (vice chair 1998—99), Am. Soc. for Quality, Am. Acad. Mgmt., Brown Alumni Assn. (pres.-elect 1993—95, pres. 1995—97). Office: Strategy Implementation Solutions 1588 Woodside Rd Yardley PA 19067-2611

NEWSOM, DAVID DUNLOP, foreign service officer, educator; b. Richmond, Calif., Jan. 6, 1918; s. Fred Stoddard and Ivy Elizabeth (Dunlop) N.; m. Jean Frances Craig, Nov. 17, 1942; children: John, Daniel, Nancy, David, Catherine. AB, U. Calif., 1938; MS, Columbia U., 1940; LLD, U. Pacific, 1979. Pulitzer traveling scholar, 1940-41; pub. Walnut Creek (Calif.) Courier-Jour., 1946-47; 3d sec., info. officer Am. embassy, Karachi, Pakistan, 1948-50; 2d sec., vice consul Oslo, 1950-51; pub. affairs officer Baghdad, Iraq, 1952-55; officer-in-charge Arabian peninsula affairs Dept. State, Washington, 1955-59; with Nat. War Coll., 1959-60; 1st sec. Am. embassy, London, 1960-62; dep. dir. Office No. African Affairs, Dept. State, Washington, 1962-63, dir., 1963-65; U.S. ambassador Libya, 1965-69; asst. sec. state for African affairs, 1969-74; U.S. ambassador, 1974-77, 1977-78; undersec. state of polit. affairs, 1978-81; dir. Inst. Study of Diplomacy, Sch. Fgn. Svc., Georgetown U., 1981-90, Marshall Coyne rsch. prof. diplomacy, 1989-91; interim dean Sch. Fgn. Svc. Georgetown U., 1995-96; Cumming Meml. prof. internat. rels. U. Va., 1991-98; spl. adviser U.S. del. UN Gen. Assembly, 1972, 78, 79, 80. Sr. fellow The Miller Ctr., U. Va., 1999-2003; mem. com. on sci., tech. and health aspects of fgn. policy Nat. Rsch. Coun., 1999. Author: (book) Soviet Brigade in Cuba, Diplomacy and The American Democracy, The Public Dimension of Foreign Policy, The Imperial Mantle. Served to lt. USNR, 1942-46. Recipient Commendable Service award USIS, 1955; Dept. State Meritorious Service award, 1958; Nat. Civil Service League award, 1972; Rockefeller Pub. Service award, 1973; Lifetime award Am. Fgn. Svc. Assn., 2000. Mem. U.S. Fgn. Svc. Assn., Coun. Fgn. Rels., Cosmos Club. Presbyterian. Home: 2409 Angus Rd Charlottesville VA 22901-2631

NEWSOM, GAVIN, mayor; b. San Francisco, Calif., Oct. 10, 1967; m. Kimberly Guilfoyle Newsom, Dec. 8, 2001. BA in Polit. Sci., Santa Clara U., 1989. Founder PlumpJack Wines Mgmt. Group, San Francisco, 1992—; pres. Pkg. and Traffic Commn., San Francisco, 1996—97; supr. Office of Bd. Suprs., San Francisco, 1997—2003; mayor City of San Francisco, 2003—. Office: City Hall Room 200 1 Dr Carlton B Goodlett Place San Francisco CA 94102*

NEWSOM, GERALD HIGLEY, astronomy educator; b. Albuquerque, Feb. 11, 1939; s. Carroll Vincent and Frances Jeanne (Higley) N.; m. Ann Catherine Bricker, June 17, 1972; children: Christine Ann, Elizabeth Ann. BA, U. Mich., 1961; MA, Harvard U., 1963, PhD, 1968. Research asst. McMath-Hulbert Obs., Pontiac, Mich., summers 1959, 61; research asst. astronomy dept. U. Mich., Ann Arbor, 1959-61; research asst. Shock Tube Lab. Harvard U., Cambridge, Mass., 1962, 64-68; research asst. dept. physics Imperial Coll., London, 1968-69; asst. prof. astronomy Ohio State U., Columbus, 1969-73, assoc. prof., 1973-82, prof., 1982—, acting chmn. dept. astronomy, 1991-93, vice chmn. dept. astronomy, 1993—, acting asst. dean, 1985-86; sr. post-doctoral research asst. Physikalisches Institut, Bonn, Fed. Republic of Germany, 1978. Author: Astronomy, 1976, Exploring the Universe, 1979; contbr. articles to profl. jours. Fellow Woodrow Wilson Found., 1961-62, NSF, 1961-63; grantee Noble Found., 1961-64. Mem. Internat. Astron. Union, Am. Astron. Soc. Home: 46 W Weisheimer Rd Columbus OH 43214-2545 Office: Ohio State U Dept Astronomy 140 W 18th Ave Columbus OH 43210-1173 Office Phone: 614-292-2632. Business E-Mail: gnewsom@astronomy.ohio-state.edu.

NEWSOM, JAMES THOMAS, lawyer; b. Carrollton, Mo., Oct. 6, 1944; s. Thomas Edward and Hazel Love (Mitchell) N.; m. Sherry Elaine Retzloff, Aug. 9, 1986; stepchildren: Benjamin A. Bawden, Holly K. Bawden. AB, U. Mo., 1966, JD, 1968. Bar: Mo. 1968, U.S. Supreme Ct. 1971. Assoc. Shook, Hardy & Bacon, London and Kansas City, Mo., 1972, ptnr., 1976—. Mem. Mo. Law Rev., 1966-68. Lt. comdr. JAGC, USNR, 1968-72. Mem. ABA, Kansas City Met. Bar Assn., U. Mo. Law Sch. Law Soc., U. Mo. Jefferson Club, Order of Coif, Perry (Kans.) Yacht Club, Stone Horse Yacht Club (Harwich Port, Mass.). Avocations: skiing, sailing, car racing. Office: Shook Hardy & Bacon 2555 Grand Blvd Kansas City MO 64108-2613 Office Phone: 816-474-6550. E-mail: jnewsom@shb.com.

NEWSOM, JOHN HARLAN, family physician; b. Worland, Wyo., May 6, 1940; s. John Cecil and Arlene Zelda (Finch) N.; m. Carolyn Cardall, Feb. 4, 1967; children: John Cardall, James Harlan. BS, U.S. Naval Acad., 1963; MD, U. Wash., 1971. Diplomate Am. Bd. Family Practice. Intern Doctors Hosp., Seattle, 1971-72; physician in pvt. practice, Newport, Oreg., 1972-73; physician Group Health, Seattle, 1973-74; physician in solo pvt. practice, Yardley, Pa., 1974—; mem. med. staff St. Mary Med. Ctr., 1974—, chmn. family practice dept., 1978-80, pres. med. staff, 1980-81, pres.-elect, med. staff, 2004—, v.p. med. affairs, 1983—85, 1999—2004. Trustee St. Mary Hosp., Langhorne, Pa., 1981-83; bd. dirs. Pennswood Village, Newtown, Pa., 1978-81; clin. asst. prof. Temple U. Sch. Medicine, 1978-91; clin. instr. Pa. State Med. Sch., 2000-01. Contbr. articles to profl. jours. Pres. Parents at Lawrenceville, N.J., 1989-90. Lt. USN, 1963-67. Decorated Bronze Star; named a Top Doc, Phila. Mag., 2002. Fellow Am. Acad. Family Physicians; mem. U. Washington Alumni Assn. (pres. Del. Valley chpt. 1989-90), Pa. Med. Soc. (del. 1985), Coll. Physicians Phila., Union League Phila., Bucks County Med. Soc. (pres. 1985). Office: 1588 Woodside Rd Yardley PA 19067-2611

NEWSOM, JON W. musicologist; b. N.Y.C. AB in Music magna cum laude, Columbia Coll., N.Y.C., 1963; MFA in Musicology, Princeton U., 1965, PhD, 1966. Music reference and music acquisition libr. Libr. of Congress, Washington, 1966—74, head, reference sect., 1974—78, asst. chief, music divsn., 1978—97, acting chief, music divsn., 1985—87, 1995—97, chief, music divsn., 1997—. Contbr. articles to profl. music pubs.; editor: Musical Quarterly, Music Libr. Assn. Notes. Mem.: Music Libr. Assn., Am. Musicological Soc., Soc. for the Preservation of Film Music (Award for Oustanding Work in Documenting and Preserving Film Music 1994), Nat. Artistic Directorate, Am. Classical Music Hall of Fame. Office: Libr of Congress Music Divsn 101 Independence Ave SE Washington DC 20540*

NEWSOM, MELVIN MAX, retired research company executive; b. El Paso, Tex., Dec. 27, 1931; s. Melvin William and Dorthy Maxine (Kinnison) N.; m. Rose Marie Neill, June 5, 1953; children— Terri Laine, Cherri Leigh, Michael Dirk, Thomas Cody. BS in Elec. Engring, Tex. A. and M. U., 1955, MS in Elec. Engring. (Tex. Power & Light fellow), 1956. Mem. tech. staff Sandia Lab., Albuquerque, 1956—, sect. supr., 1961-64, div. supr., 1964-77, dept. mgr., 1977-92, dir. Ctr. for Applied Def. Tech., 1992-94. Cons. Dept. Energy; mem. U.S. group on petroleum tech. Joint U.S./USSR Energy Program; participant several programs Nat. Acad. Engring. Contbr. numerous articles to profl. jours. Dist. chmn. Rep. Party, 1960-61, asst., 1963-64; pres. Scenic Hills Cmty. Assn., 2000—; bd. dirs. The Dunes Condominiums, Port Aransas, Tex., 1998- . With USN, 1951-53. Decorated Am. Spirit Honor medal; Dept. Energy grantee. Mem. Am. Inst. Mining Engrs., Am. Rose Soc., Tau Beta Pi, Etta Kappa Nu. Clubs: Coronado (chmn. bd. 1965-66, 69-70, 73-74, 76-79, dir.). Presbyterian. Achievements include research in improved drilling tech. for petroleum, geothermal and sci. drilling, and on high temperature well logging. Home: 3628 Scenic Dr Cibolo TX 78108-2227 E-mail: mnewsom53@aol.com.

NEWSOME, HEBER H. academic administrator; Dean Va. Commonwealth U. Med. Coll., 2000—. Office: Deans Office PO Box 980565 Sanger Hall Richmond VA 23298

NEWSOME, JAMES E. commodity futures exchange executive; m. Mei Mei Newsome; children: Molly, Riley. BS in Econ., U. Fla., 1982; MS in Agr., Miss. State U., 1985, PhD in Animal Sci./Agrl. Econs., 2001. Mem. U.S. Commodity Futures Trading Commn., Washington, 1998-01; chmn. Commodity Futures Trading Commn., Washington, 2001—04; pres. NY Mercantile Exchange, Inc., NYC, 2004—. Mem. Pres. Working Group on Fin. Markets; mem. U.S. Corp. Fraud Task Force; exec. v.p. Miss. Cattlemen's Assn. and Beef Coun., chmn. Miss. Agribus. Coun., mem. Gov's. Task Force on Future Miss. Agrl., pres. Fla. Future Farmers Am., pres. U. Fla. Agrl. Coun. Mem. Assn. Miss. Agrl. Orgns. (pres.). Office: NYMEX World Financial Ctr One N End Ave New York NY 10282-1101*

NEWSOME, LEE ANN, anthropologist, educator; BA, U. of Fla., 1982, MA, 1986, PhD, 1993. Curator of collections So. Ill. U. Ctr. for Archaeological Investigations, Carbondale, 1993—2001; assoc. prof. Pa. State U., U. Pk., 2002—. Contbr. articles in Jour. of Ethnobiology, Am. Antiquity, Southeastern Geology. Office: Dept of Anthropology Pa State U 316 Carpenter Bldg University Park PA 16802-3404

NEWSOME, OZZIE, manager professional athletics; b. Muscle Shoals, Ala., Mar. 16, 1956; s. Ethel Newsome and Ozzie Newsome Sr.; m. Gloria Jenkins. BS, U. Ala. Tight end Cleveland Browns, 1978-90; v.p., player personnel Baltimore Ravens, 1996—99, sr. v.p., football ops., 1999—2002, gen. mgr., 2002—. Active Big Bros., Athletes in Action; bd. dirs. Police Athletic League. Named Ala. Amateur Athlete of Yr., Ala. Sportswriters Assn., 1977; named to AFC Pro-Squad, 1981, Outstanding Team Player, 1981, All Pro, Pro-Football Writers Assn. and Sporting News, 1979; Cleveland Browns All-Time Leading Receiver, MVP on Offense, Cleve. TD Club (three times); ranked among NFL's top 10 in receptions; became 14th player in NFL history to make over 500 receptions; all-time leading tight end in NFL history; leading receiver in AFC, 1984; inducted into Coll. Football Hall of Fame, 1994; Inductee Pro Football Hall of Fame, 1999, Canton Ohio. Mem. Fellowship of Christian Athletes. Office: 11001 Owings Mills Blvd Owings Mills MD 21117-2857

NEWSOME, RANDALL JACKSON, judge; b. Dayton, Ohio, July 13, 1950; s. Harold I. and Sultana S. (Stone) N. BA summa cum laude, Boston U., 1972; JD, U. Cin., 1975. Bar: Ohio 1975, U.S. Dist. Ct. (so. dist.) Ohio 1977, U.S. Ct. Appeals (6th cir.) 1979, U.S. Supreme Ct. 1981. Law clk. to chief judge U.S. Dist. Ct. (so. dist.) Ohio, 1975-77; assoc. Dinsmore & Shohl, Cin., 1978-82; judge U.S. Bankruptcy Ct. (so. dist.) Ohio, 1982-88, U.S. Bankruptcy Ct. (no. dist.) Calif., Oakland, 1988—2004, chief judge, 2004—. Faculty mem. Fed. Jud. Ctr., ALI-ABA, 1987—; mem. Nat. Conf. of Bankruptcy Judges, 1983—, mem. bd. govs., 1987-88, pres., 1998-99. Contbg. author: Chapter 11 Theory and Practice, 1994—, Collier on Bankruptcy, 1997—. Fellow Am. Coll. Bankruptcy; mem. Am. Law Inst., Phi Beta Kappa. Democrat. Office: US Bankruptcy Ct PO Box 2070 Oakland CA 94604-2070

NEWSOME, STEVEN CAMERON, former museum director; b. Norfolk, Va., Sept. 11, 1952; BA, Trinity Coll., Hartford, Conn., 1974; MLS, Emory U., 1975. Reference libr. black studies Northwestern U. Libr., Evanston, Ill., 1975-78; asst. refernce libr. The Univ. Libr., U. Ill., Chgo., 1980-83, acting refernce libr., 1982-83; curator Vivian G. Harsh Collection Afro-Am. Lit. and History Chgo. Pub. Libr., 1983-86; exec. dir. Md. Commn. on Afro-Am. History and Culture, Annapolis, 1986-91; chief office of cultural and ednl. svcs. divsn. hist. & cultural programs Dept Housing, Cmty. Devel., Annapolis, 1989-91; dir. Anacostia Mus. Smithsonian Instn., Washington, 1991-95; dir. Anacostia Mus./Ctr. for Afro-Am. History & Culture, Washington, 1995—2004. Workshop leader, panelist, speaker at hist. and cultural confs., 1987—; mem. planning com. Black Expressions/Am. Tradition, Chgo. collaboration Art Inst., Office Fine Arts and Pub. Libr., 1985; mem. vis. faculty Smithsonian Instn., Office of Mus. Programs; participant seminar on exhibition critiques, Smithsonian Instn. Nat. Mus. Am. History, 1989, chmn. coun. of bur. dirs., 1993, mem. 150th anniversary steering com., 1993, arts cons. Republic S. Africa, through U.S. Info. Svc., 1994. Advisor N.Y. State Arts Coun. Minority Fellows Program,, 1990; mem. outreach com., steering com., chair pub. rels. and mktg. com. Balt. Symphony Orch., 1990; judge Congrl. Arts Caucus U.S. Competition, 1992, 93, 94; exhibitor, developer Congrl. Black Caucus Found. legis. weekend, 1992, 93; mem. comty. and friends bd. John F. Kennedy Ctr. for the Performing Arts; bd. dirs. Md. Humanities Coun., Cultural Alliance of Greater Washington. Mem. Internat. Coun. Mus., Am. Assn. Mus., African Am. Mus. Assn.*

NEWTON, A. RICHARD, engineering educator; B of Engring., U. Melbourne, Australia, 1973, M of Engring. Sci., 1975; PhD in Elec. Engring. and Computer Sci., U. Calif., Berkeley, 1978. Mem. faculty U. Calif., Berkeley, 1979, chair dept. elec. engring. and computer scis., dean Coll. Engring., Roy w. Carlson prof. engring., 1979—. Founding dir. MARCO/DARPA Gigascale Silicon Rsch. Ctr. for Design and Test, rschr., 2002; leader establishment Ctr. for Info. Tech. Rsch. in Interest of a Soc.; bd. dirs. Crossbow, Synopsys, Tensilica; cofounder SDA Sys. (now Cadence Design Sys.), Synopsys; tech. coun. ST Microelectronics; tech. adv. bd. Form Factor, Lightspeed, Semiconductor, Pharmix, Sonics, Woodside Networks, Microsoft Rsch. Labs.; pres., CEO Silicon Light Machine, 1994—95; founding mem. tech. and steering coms. EDIF; advisor CAD Framework Initiative; founding mem. EDAC; mem. adminstrv. com. IEEE Cirs. and Sys. Soc., 1985—88; tech. program chair ACM/IEEE Design Automation Confs., 1988, 89; vice chair ACM/IEEE Design Automation Conf., 1990, gen. chair, 91. Assoc. editor: IEEE Transactions on Computer-Aided Design for Integrated Cirs., 1984—88. Recipient C. Holmes McDonald Outstanding Young Prof. award, Eta Kappa Nu, 1987, Best Paper award, European Solid State Cirs. Conf., 1998, ACM/IEEE Design Automation Confs., 1987, 1989, Internat. Conf. on Computer Design. Fellow: IEEE; mem.: ACM. Office: U Calif Coll Engring 320 McLaughlin Hall # 1700 Berkeley CA 94720-1700

NEWTON, BALDWIN CHARLES, artist, educator; b. Lucknow, India, Jan. 24, 1936;, US; s. Harry Charles and Kathren Georgina (Gardner) N.; m. Shirley Hatfield (dec. Sept. 23, 1992); children: Beverly, Richard, Michelle, Dawn. Diploma in fine arts, Coll. Arts, India, 1962; BA, Meerut U., India, 1971. Art tchr. Woodstock Sch., Mussoorie, India, 1962; art tchr. Mil. Sch., Tilya Dam, India, 1963-64, Wynberg Allen Sch., India, 1965-74, Mt. Hermon Coll., Darjeeling, India, 1977-78, Barnes Sch., Develali, India, 1978-86, 1993, New Creative Enterprise, Milford, Ohio, 1999—2002. One-man show at Carnegie Visual Art Ctr., Ky., 1999 (award), Exposition of 20th Century Art Consortium, 2000, Louisville Visual Art Assn. (award 2003), Rosewood Gallery, Kettering, Ohio, 2004, Filton Ctr. Creative Arts, 2004; works include Roller Coaster, a painting for Louisville Art Assn., 1996 (merit award 1997), Hidden Odyssey, a painting for Arts Consortium, 1996 (merit award 1996), Master Works 53, a painting for Cin. Art Club, 1995 (1st pl. award 1995). Recipient Manhattan Internat. award of excellence, 1995, honorable mention Can. Water Color Soc., Courtnay, B.C., 1996, Art Crowd Internat. award, 2001, Norman Kohlhepp award, Louisville Visual Art Assn., 2001. Home: 320 Hanna Ave Bldg 2 Apt 11 Loveland OH 45140-3074 E-mail: bnewton6@earthlink.net.

NEWTON, DEAN, state representative; m. Anita Newton. Grad., Kans. U.; degree in Law, NYU. Atty. Sonnenschein, Nath & Rosenthal; mem. Kans. Ho. of Reps., 2001—. Founder Kids for Brighter Future, 1998—, Project Smile, 1999—. Republican. Office: 112-S State Capitol 300 SW 10th Ave Topeka KS 66612 Address: 4808 W 77th Terr Prairie Village KS 66208

NEWTON, DON ALLEN, real estate broker, economic development consultant; b. Laurel, Miss., Oct. 19, 1934; s. Wilfred L. and Mary (McMullan) N.; m. Coleta Farrell, Oct. 11, 1958; children: Don Jr., Coleta Midge Rast. AA, Meridian (Miss.) C.C., 1954; BA, U. Ala., 1956; postgrad. in Assn. Mgmt., U. N.C.; postgrad. in Econ. Devel., U. Okla. Asst. mgr. Meridian C. of C., 1956; mgr. Winston County C. of C., Louisville, Miss., 1960—61; asst. dir. Delta Coun. Indsl. and Cmty. Devel. Bd., Stoneville, Miss., 1961—62, dir., 1963—70; exec. v.p. Met. Devel. Bd., Birmingham, Ala., 1970—74; pres. Birmingham Area C. of C., 1974—99; pub. Birmingham Mag., Birmingham Bus. Mag., 1974—99; pres. Birmingham Area C. of C. Found., Inc., 1988-99, Devel. Assocs. Real Estate, Econ. Devel. and Pub. Cons., 1999. Contbr. articles to profl. jours., newspapers. Former appointee Ala. Export Coun.; bd. dirs. Birmingham Met. Devel. Bd., Ala. Sports Found. Lt. USNR, 1957-60. Named Ala. Mktg. Man of Yr., 1972. Mem.: Sigma Chi. Home: 4156 Glenbrook Dr Birmingham AL 35213 Office: Development Assocs PO Box 530093 Birmingham AL 35253-0093 Office Phone: 205-542-8997.

NEWTON, ELIZABETH PURCELL, counselor, consultant, author; b. Madison, N.C., June 3, 1925; d. Charles Augustus and Anna Meta (Buchanan) P.; m. William Edward Newton, June 11, 1949; children— James Purcell, Betsy Newton Hein, Christina Newton Harwood. A.A., Peace Coll., 1944; B.A., U. N.C., 1946; M.Ed., Ga. State U., 1969; Ed.S., West Ga. Coll., 1981. Tchr., counselor S. Cobb High Sch., Austell, Ga., 1965-69; counselor, dept. head Wheeler High Sch., Marietta, Ga., 1969-76; counselor, div. head guidance services Walton High Sch., Marietta, Ga., 1976—90; ret., 1990; sch. rep. Coll. Bd., Princeton, N.J., 1981—90, panelist, presenter S.E. region, Atlanta, 1983-85; presenter Ga. Sch. Counselors Assn., Atlanta, 1980—90; cons. Panhandle Area Edn. Coop., Chipley, Fla., 1985. Author: Steps to College Admissions, 1978; Student's Guide to College Admissions, 1981; Student's Guide to Career Preparation, 1982. Sch. rep. Citizens Adv. Council, Marietta, 1981, 82, 85. Ga. Dept. Edn. grantee, 1981; named Outstanding Woman in Edn., Atlanta Jour., 1985. Mem. Cobb Counselor Assn. (organizer, chmn. nominations com. 1985), Ga. Sch. Counselors Assn. (Secondary Counselor of Yr. 1983), Am. Sch. Counselors Assn. (Nat. Secondary Counselor of Yr. 1984), Phi Delta Kappa. Presbyterian.

NEWTON, ESTHER MARY, anthropologist, educator; b. N.Y.C., Nov. 28, 1940; d. Saul B. and Virginia Newton. BA, U. Mich., 1962; MA, U. Chgo., 1964, PhD, 1968. Asst. prof. CUNY, Queens, 1968-71; from asst. prof. to

assoc. prof. anthropology SUNY, Purchase, 1971-92, prof. anthropology, 1992—, Kempner disting. professorship, 1999. Coord. women's studies program SUNY, Purchase, 1984-86; vis. prof. Yale U., 1970, U. Amsterdam, 1993; affiliated scholar CUNY, 1992-93; scholar in residence U. Calif., Santa Cruz, 1993; curator exhbn. Gay and Lesbian Cmty. Svcs. Ctr., 1993. Author: Mother Camp: Female Impersonators in America, 1972, reprinted with new introduction, 1979, Cherry Grove, Fire Island: Sixty years in America's First Gay and Lesbian Town, 1993, Margaret Meade May Me Gay, 2000; co-author: (with Shirley Walton) Womanfriends, 1976; contbr. to anthologies including The Lesbian Issue: Essays from Signs, 1985, Hidden from History: Reclaiming the Gay and Lesbian Past, 1989, International Gay Studies: The Amsterdam Conference, 1994, History of Homosexuality in Europe and America, 1994, Writing Lesbian and Gay Culture, 1995; mem. editl. bd. The Cutting Edge: Lesbian Life and Literature Series, Between men, Between Women: Lesbian and Gay Studies Series, GLQ: Jour. of Queer Studies, Jour. of Homosexuality, Jour. Sexuality in History; contbr. to books including Amazon Expedition, 1973, Anthropology and American Life, 1974, Symbolic Anthropology: A Reader in the Study of Symbols and Meaning, 1977, Strategies des femmes, 1984, Pleasure and Danger: Exploring Female Sexuality, 1984, Homosexuality, Which Homosexuality? Vol. 2, 1987, The Lesbian and Gay Studies Reader, 1993; contbr. articles to mags. and jours. La Verne Noyes scholar U. Chgo., 1962-63; training grantee NIH, 1963-65, faculty support grantee SUNY, Purchase, 1987, 92; pre-doctoral fellow NIMH, 1965-67; recipient experienced faculty travel award SUNY, 1987, 91; Rockefeller Humanities fellow, 1999. Mem. Am. Anthrop. Assn. (cochair commn. lesbian and gay issues, 1994-96). Avocation: dog training. Office: Divsn Social Sci SUNY Purchase NY 10577

NEWTON, FRANK GEORGE, bank executive; b. Bklyn., Oct. 2, 1936; s. Anthony and Hedwig (Borak) N.; m. Mary Soto Newton, Apr. 20, 1963; children: Kevin Francis, Andrew Francis. BS, CCNY, 1958; MA, Alexander Hamilton Inst., N.Y.C., 1960. V.p., sec. Long Island City Savings Bank, N.Y.C., 1960-75; exec. v.p. Bay Ridge Savings Bank, Bklyn., 1975-81; pvt. investor; owner Gables Inn. Bd. incorporators Lee Bank, Mass., 1999—; bd. regents Long Island Coll. Hosp., Bklyn., 1977-80; pres. Queens County Bankers, N.Y., 1972. Pres. Lenox C. of C., Mass., 1990-95; treas. Lenox Rep. Party, Mass., 1995-2000. With U.S. Army, 1959-61. Mem. Lenox Club, Montauk Club. Roman Catholic. Avocation: collecting art and music. Home: 17 Main St Lenox MA 01240 Office: The Gables Inn 81 Walker St Lenox MA 01240

NEWTON, FREDERICK J., III, utilities executive; married; 2 children. BBA in Human Resources, U. R.I.; MBA in Labor Rels. and Human Resources, San Diego State U. Mgr. human resource functions Pepsico, Tex., Kans. and Calif.; sr. dir. human resources Unilever, N.Y.C.; sr. v.p. human resources Venator Group, N.Y.C.; exec. v.p., chief adminstrv. officer Cinergy Corp., Cin., 2002—. Vis. lectr., prof. Bellarmine U. Bd. dirs. Kentuckiana Minority Supplier Devel. Coun., Greater Louisville, Inc., Louisville Orch., Lincoln Heritage coun. Boy Scouts Am., Pritchard Com. Officer USN. Mem.: Soc. Human Resource Mgmt., Human Resource Planning Soc., Conf. Bd. Office: Cynergy Corp 139 E 4th St Cincinnati OH 45202

NEWTON, HERBERT BRUCE, neuro-oncologist; b. San Diego, Nov. 8, 1956; s. Jefferson Frederick and Leona Maxine (Reese) N.; m. Cheryl Lynn Donaldson, Jul. 6, 1991; children: Alexander James, Ashley Rene. BA, SUNY, 1979, MS, 1980, MD, 1984. Diplomate Am. Bd. Psych. & Neurology. Internship SUNY Buffalo Affiliated Hosp., Buffalo, 1984-85; residency U. Mich. Medical Ctr., Ann Arbor, Mich., 1985-88; fellowship neuro oncology Meml. Sloan-Kettering Cancer Ctr., N.Y., 1988-90; asst. prof., dir. div. neuro-oncology The Ohio State U., Columbus, 1990-96, assoc. prof., dir. neuro-oncology, 1996—2004, prof. neurology, dir. neuro-oncology, 2004—, co-dir. Dardinger Neuro-oncology Ctr., Esther Dardinger chair in neuro-oncology, 2004—, grad. faculty Neurosci. Grad. Studies program, 1991—; staff physician sec. neurology dept. pediatrics Children's Hosp., Columbus, 1991—. Adv. profl. edn. com., Am. Cancer Soc., Columbus, 1991—; cons. Cen. Ohio Brain Tumor Support group, Columbus, 1990—. Contbr. articles to profl. jours. Recipient rsch. grant for treatment of malignant glioma, Amgen, 1994. Fellow Am. Acad. Neurology, Royal Soc. Medicine; mem. European Soc. Med. Oncology, Am. Acad. Neurology, Internat. Soc. Analytical Cytology, Am. Assn. Cancer Rsch., Ctrl. Soc. Neurol. Rsch. Avocations: basketball, reading science fiction, music, art. Office: Ohio State U dept Neurology 1654 Upham Dr 465 Means Hall Columbus OH 43210 Office Phone: 614-293-8930. E-mail: newton.12@osu.edu.

NEWTON, HUGH C. public relations executive; b. N.Y.C., Oct. 17, 1930; s. Avery Curtis and Ruth (Juster) N.; m. Charlotte Eloise Wallin, Nov. 3, 1956 (div. 1968); 1 child, Margaret Wren Newton Rossello; m. Joanne Elaine Harding, Dec. 27, 1969; children: Matthew Curtis, Christopher Stuart, Kimberly Kelly. BA, Washington & Lee U., 1952. Reporter Danville (Va.) Bee, 1955; mgr. news Carnegie Inst. Tech., Pitts., 1956-57; staff writer Westinghouse Elec., Pitts., 1957; acct. exec. Burson Marsteller Assocs., Pitts., 1958-59; asst. dir. pub. rels. Rockwell Mfg., Pitts., 1959-61; mgr. spl. projects Reynolds Metals Co., Richmond, Va., 1961-64; dir. pub. rels. Nat. Right to Work Com., Washington, 1964-67, Air Transport Assn., Washington, 1967-68; pres. Hugh C. Newton & Assocs., Washington, 1968—. Mem. Interstate Commn. on Potomac River Basin, Washington, 1982-89. Contbr. to Lesly's Public Relations Handbook, 1991. Bd. dirs. Friends of the Torpedo Factory Art Ctr., Alexandria, Va., 1987-91. Recipient Silver Anvil award Pub. Rels. Soc. Am., 1966, 85. Mem. Nat. Press Club. Episcopalian. Avocation: stamp collecting/philately. Home: 629 S Fairfax St Alexandria VA 22314-3833 Office: Hugh C Newton & Assocs 108 N Washington St Alexandria VA 22314

NEWTON, JOHN MILTON, academic administrator, psychologist, educator; b. Schenectady, Feb. 25, 1929; s. Harry Hazleton and Bertha A. (Lehmann) N.; m. Elizabeth Ann Slattery, Sept. 11, 1954; children: Patricia, Peter, Christopher. BS, Union Coll., Schenectady, 1951; MA, Ohio State U., 1952, PhD, 1955. Lic. psychologist, Nebr. Rsch. psychologist Electric Boat divsn. Gen. Dynamics Corp., Groton, Conn., 1957-60; mem. faculty U. Nebr., Omaha, 1960—, prof. psychology, 1966-99, chmn. dept., 1967-74, acting vice chancellor acad. affairs, 1994-95, prof. emeritus, 1999—, dean Coll. Arts and Scis., 1974-94, dean emeritus, 1999—. Cons. in field, 1960-72 Author research papers in field. Served to 1st lt. Med. Service Corps, AUS, 1955-57. Mem. Am. Psychol. Assn., Psychonomic Soc., Midwestern Psychol. Assn. Home: 5611 Jones St Omaha NE 68106-1232 Office: Univ of Nebr-Omaha Dept Psychology Omaha NE 68182-0001 Business E-Mail: jnewton@mail.unomaha.edu.

NEWTON, JOHN WHARTON, III, lawyer; b. Beaumont, Tex., Feb. 18, 1953; s. John Wharton and Katherine (King) N.; children: Martha Garrison, John Wharton IV, Stephen King. BA, U. Tex., 1975; JD, U. Houston, 1978. Bar: Tex. 1979, U.S. Dist. Ct. (ea. dist.) Tex. 1979, U.S. Ct. Appeals (5th cir.) 1981, U.S. Dist. Ct. (so. dist.) Tex. 1987. Ptnr. Orgain, Bell & Tucker, Beaumont, 1984—. Mem. ABA, Tex. State Bar Assn., Tex. Assn. Def. Counsel, Jefferson County Bar Assn., Coll. of State Bar of Tex., Beaumont Club (pres. 1988-89). Episcopalian. Office: Orgain Bell & Tucker 470 Orleans St Ste 400 Beaumont TX 77701-3076

NEWTON, JULIANNE H, education educator, photographer; b. Dallas, Tex., Apr. 11, 1949; d. Julius R and Vivian Dunn Hickerson; m. Rick Williams, May 12, 1990; children: Joshua Williams, Kathryn Williams, Matthew. BA in journalism magna cum laude, Baylor U., 1970; MA in journalism, U. Tex. at Austin, 1983, PhD in journalism, 1991. Editl. intern Ft. Worth Star-Telegram, Tex., 1969, Baylor News Sci., 1970; reporter Waco News Tribune, Times Herald, Tex., 1970—71; editor Assn. of Coll. Unions- Internat., Stanford, 1971—72; writer, news and info. svc. UT Austin, 1972—77; copy editor Austin Am. Statesman, 1985; freelance editor, photographer, designer, writer, cons., 1977—; dir. student pub. St. Edward's U., 1981—84; adj. lectr. photo commn. New Coll., St. Edwards U., 1982—84; head, photojournalism program U. Tex. at Austin, 1994—96, asst. prof., 1992—99, lectr., 1984—92, tchg. asst., 1977, 1979, 1984; assoc. prof. visual commn. Sch. of Journalism and Commn., U. Ore., 2000—. Author: (book) The Burden of Visual Truth: The Role of Photojournalism in Mediating Reality, 2001; contbr. articles, chapters to books; exhibitions include Tex. Humanities Resource Ctr., Twentieth Juried Photography Exhbn., Jewish Cmty. Ctr. of Houston, Deutser Gallery, 1992, George Eastman House Internat. Mus. Photography, 1990—91, Tex. Folklife Resources Gallery, 2001—02, Harry Ransom Humanities Rsch. Ctr., 2000, Nat. Press Photographers Assn., Albany, 1999, Barnes and Noble Opening Ceremonies, Austin, Tex., 1997—98, Laguna Gloria Art Mus., Austin, 1991, Artists League of Tex., 1988, Carver Cmty. Cultural Ctr., San Antonio, 1988, Washington Project for the Arts, 1987, Houston Ctr. for Photography, 1987; editor: Visual Commn. Quarterly, 2001—, (newsletter) ViewPoints, —. Nominee three tchg. awards, U. Oregon, 2001—03; recipient Fifth Ann. Award of Excellence in Visual Commn. Rsch., Visual Commn. Divsn., Nat. Commn. Assn., 2003, Appreciation for Svc. award, Visual Commn. Divsn., Assn. for Edn. in Jour. and Mass Commn., 1995, Tchg. Excellence award, U. of Tex. Coll. of Commn., 1993; fellow, Applied Ethics Seminar, U. Ill., 2002, Summer Rsch. grant, New Faculty award, U. Oregon, 2001, Travel grants, U. Rshc. Inst., 1992—99, Coll. fellowship, UT Coll. of Commn., 1996. Mem.: Nat. Press Photographers Assn., Visual Commn. Conf., Internat. Visual Literacy Assn., Internat. Commn. Assn., Assn. for Edn. in Jour. and Mass Commn., Nat. Commn. Assn., Internat. Assn. of Media and Commn. Rsch., Golden Key Nat. Honor Soc. Office: Sch Journalism and Communication 1275 University of Oregon Eugene OR 97403

NEWTON, KENNETH KURT, physician, educator, administrator; b. Landsberg, Germany, May 18, 1927; came to U.S., 1946; s. Arthur Neuweg and Margaret Joan (Blume) Newton. BA, U. Buffalo, 1951; MD, Western Res. U., 1955; honor grad., U.S. Army Command/Gen. Staff Coll., Ft. Leavenworth, Kans., 1972; flight surgeon tng., U.S. Army Aviation Sch., Ft. Rucker, Ala., 1974. Med. lic. Ohio, Mich. Advanced through ranks to col. U. S. Army, 1946-97; intern Henry Ford Hosp., Detroit, 1955-56, resident in internal medicine, phys. medicine and rehab., 1956-60; preceptor, dept. family medicine Wayne State U., Mich. State U., U. Mich., 1960—; clin. assoc. prof. medicine Wayne State U., Detroit, 1995—; dir. med. edn. Holy Cross Hosp., Detroit, 1976-88, chief dept. medicine, 1977-79, 91, pres. of staff, 1982-83; departmental surgeon Reserve Officers Assn. of Mich., Detroit, 1988-98; pres. EKG Assocs., P.C., Detroit, 1990—. Med. officer 107th med. battalion, Mich. Army N.G., 1955-57, divsn. artillery surgeon, 46th inf. divsn., 1957-59, command surgeon, 1959-75, state surgeon, 1975-85, post surgeon Camp Atterbury Res. Forces Tng. Area, 1985-89, divsn. surgeon 70th divsn., Livonia, Mich., 1989-92, flight surgeon U.S. Army 1993; instr., course dir. ACLS, Am. Heart Assn., 1977—, Acad. Health Scis., U.S. Army, Ft. Sam Houston, Tex., 1992—; mem. governing bd. Holy Cross Hosp. 1988-92, pres. 1990; tchr. U. Buffalo, N.Y., 1950-51, preceptor U. Essen, Germany, 1980, U. Göttingen, Germany, 1993, U. München, Germany, 1993, Humboldt U., Berlin, 1994; med. advisor to Selective Svcs. Sys., Washington, 1968-76; mem. ad hoc med. panel to Res. Forces Policy Bd., Dept. Army, Washington, 1972; mem. adv. group for Aerospace R&D, NATO, 1978; mem. med. evaluation bds. State of Mich., Lansing, 1975-85. Decorated Legion of Merit, 1977, 97; recipient cert. of pub. svc. State of N.Y., 1958, Disting. Svc. medal State of Mich. 1985, Spl. tribute State of Mich. Senate, 1985, Invitation Governing Mayor of Berlin, 1990, Conspicuous Svc. order, State of N.Y., 1997. Mem. (life) Sr. Army Reserve Comdrs. Assn., (life) Reserve Officers Assn. (nat. surgeon 1993), (life) Nat. Guard Assn. (dir. 1979-82), Am. Heart Assn. (course dir. 1980—), Soc. of Med. Consultants to the Armed Forces, Confedn. Interalliée des Officiers de Reserve NATO (del. 1973—, vice chief del. 1986). Avocations: travel, photography, music and the arts, national security. Office: 15252 Gratiot Ave Detroit MI 48205-1327 E-mail: kennethknewtonmd@aol.com.

NEWTON, LISA HAENLEIN, philosopher, educator; b. Orange, N.J., Sept. 17, 1939; d. Wallen Joseph and Carol Bigelow (Cypiot) Haenlein; m. Victor Joseph Newton, June 3, 1972; children: Tracey, Kit, Cynthia Perkins, Daniel Perkins, Laura Perkins. Student, Swarthmore Coll., 1957-59; BS in Philosophy with honors, Columbia U., 1962, PhD, 1967. Asst. prof. philosophy Hofstra U., Hempstead, NY, 1967-69; from asst. prof. to assoc. prof. Fairfield (Conn.) U., 1969—78, prof., 1978—, dir. program applied ethics, 1983—, dir. program environ. studies, 1986—; lectr. in medicine Yale U., 1984—. Lectr., cons. in field. Author: Ethics and Sustainability, 2002, Ethics in Am., Study Guide, 2d edit., 2003, Ethics in Am. Source Reader, 2d edit., 2003, Business Ethics and the National Environment, 2004; co-author: (book) Watersheds, 1994, 3d edit., 2001, Wake-Up Calls, 2d edit., 2003; co-editor: Taking Sides: Controversial Issues Bus. Ethics, 8th edit., 2004; contbr. articles to profl. jours. Mem. exec. bd. Conn. Humanities Coun., 1979—83. Mem.: Internat. Soc. Environ. Ethics (mem. exec. bd.), Assn. Practical Prof. Ethics (exec. bd.), Soc. Bus. Ethics (past pres.), Am. Soc. Bioethics and Humanities, Soc. Ethics Across Curriculum (exec. bd.), Am. Soc. Polit. and Legal Philosophy, Am. Philos. Assn., Am. Soc. Value Inquiry (past pres.), Phi Beta Kappa (local sec.). Home: 4042 Congress St Fairfield CT 06824 Office: Fairfield U Program Applied Ethics Fairfield CT 06824 Office Phone: 203-254-4128. Business E-Mail: lhnewton@mail.fairfield.edu.

NEWTON, MICHELLE MARIE, sales executive; b. Orange, Calif., May 27, 1971; d. Wayne Clair and Maria Palmar Newton; 1 child, Jazmyn Victoria Wallington. BA in Comm., Calif. State U., Fullerton, 1994; MBA, Pepperdine U., 2000. Mktg. adminstr. Ingram Micro, Santa Ana, Calif., 1994—96, internat. mktg. adminstr., 1995; sales support rep. APL, Ltd., Costa Mesa, Calif., 1996—97, inside sales rep., 1997—98, acct. exec., 1998—2000, sr. acct. exec., 2000—02; child care owner Michelle's Child Care, Rancho Santa Margarita, Calif., 2002—03; internat. sales Oakley, Inc., Foothill Ranch, Calif., 2003—. Roman Catholic. Avocations: motorcycling, skiing, rollerblading, walking, shopping. Home: 1 Spinel Ct Rancho Santa Margarita CA 92688 Office Phone: 949-829-6462.

NEWTON, NELL JESSUP, dean, law educator; b. St. Louis, Apr. 30, 1944; d. Robert Edward and Marcella (Boehm) Mier. BA, U. Calif., Berkeley, 1973; JD, U. Calif., Hastings, 1976. Bar: Calif., Washington, U.S. Ct. Appeals (9th crct.), U.S. Supreme Ct. Prof. Cath. U. Sch. Law, 1976-92; prof. Washington Coll. Law Am. U., Washington, 1992—98; dean U. Denver Law Sch., 1998—2000, U. Conn. Sch. Law, Hartford, 2000—. Lectr. Internat. Law Inst., Washington, 1984-89; prof. Pre-Law Summer Inst. for Native Am. Students, U. N.Mex. Law Sch., Albuquerque, 1990, 91, 93; panelist, speaker NEH, 1981; presenter S.W. Intertribal Ct. of Appeals, 1990; panelist Orgn. Am. Historians, 1991. Co-author: American Indian Law, 3d edit., 1991; contbr. articles to profl. jours. NEH fellow Harvard Law Sch., 1980. Mem. Assn. Am. Law Schs. (Native Am. rights sect., mem. exec. com. 1987—, chair 1987-88, oral argument newsletter editor 1987—, mem. women in legal edn. sect. 1987—, chair profl. devel. workshop com. 1992, sec. 1993), Balt.-Washington-Va. Women Law Tchrs. Group (planning com. Symposium on Scholarship I 1985, II 1986), Thurston Soc., Order of Coif. Office: U Conn Sch Law Hartranft 103 55 Elizabeth St Hartford CT 06105

NEWTON, PAUL GEORGE, musician, retired librarian; b. Syracuse, N.Y., Dec. 1, 1930; s. Wayland LeRoy and Georgia Crumrine Newton; m. Dahlia Lorraine Brazell, Dec. 24, 1961; children: Jessica Suzanne, Roy Christopher. *Wife, Dahlia Brazell Newton, prof. emeritus, Athens State U., Athens, Ala., taught in School of Business, 1985-2001. Daughter, Jessica Newton Orvis, and husband Jeffrey Orvis, PhD, teach in Department of Chemistry, Georgia Southern U., Statesboro, Ga. Son, Roy Christopher Newton, E.D.S., employee at Saturn plant, Spring Hill, Tenn.; wife, Nancy Cagle Newton, software specialist. Brother, Robert LeRoy Newton, retired; former partner, Eberstadt Chemical Fund; former mutual fund director, Marsh & McLennan. Grandchildren: Jacob Jeffrey Orvis, Jameson Christopher Orvis, Emma Belle Newton.* MusB cum laude, Syracuse U., 1952; MusM, Ind. U., 1954; PhD, U. North Tex., 1968; MLS, U. N.C., 1974. Instr. Augustana Coll., Sioux Falls, SD, 1954—56; prof. Wayland Bapt. Coll., Plainview, Tex., 1956—58, 1960—64; asst. prof. N.W. La. State Coll., Natchitoches, 1958—59, Stephen F. Austin State U., Nacogdoches, Tex., 1964—65, Ark. State U., Jonesboro, 1965—66; orch. dir. Forsyth County Schs., Winston-Salem, NC, 1968—69; music libr. Mars Hill (N.C.) Coll., 1969—83; libr. dir. Martin Meth. Coll., Pulaski, Tenn., 1983—93. Violist Asheville (N.C.) Symphony Orch., 1979—83; archivist Mars Hill Coll., 1979—83. *PhD dissertation, U. North Texas, 1968, 2 vols. (Univ. Mic. pub. 68-16645): Florence, Biblioteca del Conservatorio di Musica Luigi Cherubini, Manuscript Basevi 2439: Critical Edition and Commentary. Professors: Sidney Sukoenig, piano, Syracuse U.; Ernst Bacon, composition, Syracuse U.; Sidney Foster, piano, Indiana U.; Helen Hewitt, musicology, U. North Texas.* Recipient Merit award, Kennedy-Douglass Mus., Florence, Ala., 1994. Mem.: So. Appalachian Mineral Soc., Am. Musicol. Soc., Ark. Archaeol. Soc. Avocations: travel, art, archaeology, geology, photography. Home: 114 S Sam Davis Ave Pulaski TN 38478 Office: 94 W Ridge Rd Mars Hill NC 28754 E-mail: dbnewton@usit.net.

NEWTON, RHONWEN LEONARD, writer, microcomputer consultant, data processing executive, consultant; b. Lexington, NC, Nov. 13, 1940; d. Jacob Calvin and Mary Louise (Moffitt) Leonard; children: Blair Armistead Newton Jones, Allison Page, William Brockenbrough III. AB, Duke U., 1962; MS in Edn., Old Dominion U., 1968. French tchr. Hampton (Va.) Pub. Schs., 1962-65, Va. Beach (Va.) Pub. Schs., 1965-66; instr. foreign lang. various colls. and univs., 1967-75; foreign lang. cons. Portsmouth (Va.) Pub. Schs., 1973-75; dir. The Computer Inst., Inc., Columbia, S.C., 1983; pres., founder The Computer Experience, Inc., Columbia, 1983-88, RN Enterprises, Columbia, 1991—. Author: WordPerfect, 1988, All About Computers, 1989, Microsoft Excel for the Mac, 1989, Introduction to the Mac, 1989, Introduction to DOS, 1989, Introduction to Lotus 1-2-3, 1989, Advanced Lotus 1-2-3, 1989, Introduction to WordPerfect, 1989, Advanced WordPerfect, 1989, Introduction to Display/Write 4, 1989, WordPerfect for the Mac, 1989, Introduction to Microsoft Works for the Mac, 1990, Accountant, Inc for the Mac, 1992, Introduction to Filemaker Pro, 1992, Quicken for the MAC, 1993, Quicken for Windows, 1993, WordPerfect for Windows, 1993, Advanced WordPerfect for Windows, 1993, Lotus 1-2-3 for Windows, 1993, Introduction to Quick Books, 1994, Quick Book for Windows, 1994, Introduction to Word for Windows, 1995, Introduction to File Maker Pro 4.0, 1998, Introduction to Microsoft Word, 1999, Introduction to Microsoft Excel, 1999, Introduction to AOL, 1999, Introduction to Excel, 1999, Using America OnLine, 1999. Mem. Columbia Planning Commn., 1980-87; bd. dirs. United Way Midlands, Columbia, 1983-86, Assn. Jr. Leagues, NYC, 1980-82, SC Wildlife Fedn., 1997-98; trustee Heathwood Hall Episcopal Sch., Columbia, 1979-85; active SC Episcopal Home Bd., 1999—, chmn., 2001-2003; vestry Trinity Cathedral, 1999-02; active SC Real Estate Appraisers Bd., 2000, sec., 2002—. Mem. Investment Club (pres. 1995-97, regional coun.), Nat. Assn. Investors Corp. (dir. S.C. Midlands regional coun. 1998-02). Republican. Episcopalian. Avocations: golf, walking. Home and Office: 1635 Kathwood Dr Columbia SC 29206-4509 Business E-Mail: rnewton@sc.rr.com.

NEWTON, ROGER GERHARD, educator, physicist; b. Landsberg, Germany, Nov. 30, 1924; came to U.S., 1946, naturalized, 1949; s. Arthur and Margaret (Blume) Neuweg; m. Ruth Gordon, June 18, 1953; children: Rachel, Julie, Paul. Student, U. Berlin, Germany; AB summa cum laude, Harvard, 1949, MA, 1950, PhD, 1953. Teaching fellow Harvard, 1951-52; mem. Inst. Advanced Study, Princeton, 1953-55, 79; mem. faculty Ind. U., 1955—, prof. physics, 1960-78, disting. prof. physics, 1978—95, disting. prof. emeritus, 1995—, chmn. dept., 1973-80, chmn. math. physics program, 1965-86, dir. Inst. for Advanced Study, 1982-86. Vis. prof. U. Rome, Italy, 1962-63, U. Montpellier, France, 1971-72 Author: Scattering Theory of Waves and Particles, 1966, 2d edit., 1982, The Complex j-Plane, 1964, Inverse Schrödinger Scattering in Three Dimension, 1989, What Makes Nature Tick?, 1993, The Truth of Sci., 1997, Thinking About Physics, 2000, Quantum Physics, 2002, Galileo's Pendulum, 2004; assoc. editor: Jour. Math. Physics, 1967—70, 1973—76, 1983—86; editor, 1992—; assoc. editor: Am. Jour. Physics, 1986—88, Inverse Problems, 1985—90; internat. adv. panel, 1991—; contbr. articles to profl. jours. Pres. Bloomington Civil Liberties Union, 1968. Served with AUS, 1946-47. Recipient Bowdoin prize Harvard, 1948; Jewett fellow, 1953-55; NSF sr. postdoctoral fellow, 1962-63; C.N.R.S. fellow U. Montpellier, France, 1971-72 Fellow AAAS (coun. 1987-89), Am. Phys. Soc. (chmn. Heinemann prize com. 1991-92); mem. AAUP, N.Y. Acad. Scis., Fedn. Am. Scientists, Phi Beta Kappa (pres. Gamma chpt. 1991-92), Sigma Xi.

NEWTON, TERRY FERNANDO, health information specialist, writer; b. Miami, Fla., Dec. 10, 1956; s. Julius Lee Newton and Frances Louise Cason; children: Torrence Levine, Patrick Fernando. Student, Fla. Montanari, 1976—78. Child care specialist Montanari Clin. Sch., Hialeah, Fla., 1976—79; mental health technician Miami Variety Children's Hosp., Coral Gables, Fla., 1979—80; psychiat. nurse technician Cedars of Lebanon Hosp., Miami, Fla., 1980—82; from office asst. dir. of safety to health info. specialist II Jackson Hosp., Miami, 1982—83, health info. specialist II, 1983—. Bd. dir. Body Mind & Soul Inc., Miami; 1st v.p. Lip Tongue & Ear Prodn., Miami, 1999—. Author: A Composition in Verse, 1996, A Cascade of Memories, 1998, America at the Millenium, 2000, Earthbeat, 2002, Theatre of the Mind, 2003. Active media rep. Concern & Committed Bros. Inc., Miami, 2002; bd. dir. BMS Movement, 2001—. Named African Am. Achiever, JM Family Enterprise, Inc., 1998—2003, Cmty. Achiever, Macedonia Ch., 1999; named to Internat. Poetry Hall of Fame, 1997, Miami Dade Office of Mayor, Bd. County Commrs.; recipient Accomplishment award, Gov. Lawton Chiles, 1997. Mem.: Fla. State Poetry Hosts Coalition (promotor 2003), Concern Bros. Inc. Poetry Club (dir. 2001, Mentor award 1997). Avocations: reading, performing, basketball, birdwatching. Home: 10762 SW 145th St Miami FL 33176 Office: Lip Tongue and Ear Production 1271 NW 172nd St Miami FL 33169 Office Phone: 786-487-4859.

NEWTON, VIRGINIA, archivist, historian, librarian; d. John Walter and Reba Catherine Newton; m. Alvin E. Schmid, 2003. Student, Inst. Tecnológico y de Estudios Superiores de Monterrey, Nuevo Leon, Mex., 1957; AA in Bus. Adminstrn., Stephens Coll., 1958; BA in History, Okla. State U., 1960; M of Librarianship, U. Wash., 1963; cert. in libr. sci., U. Tex., 1968, MA in History Archives and Libr. Sci., 1975, PhD in History, Archives and Libr. Sci., 1983. Libr. Inst. Pub. Affairs U. Tex., Austin, 1963-65, libr. Art Libr., 1965-67; coord. Sr. Cmty. Svcs. Program Econ. Opportunities Devel. Corp., San Antonio, 1968-69; archivist, spl. collections libr. Trinity U., San Antonio, 1969-73; spl. collections and reference libr. Pan Am. U., Edinburg, Tex., 1974-77; archivist records analyst Alaska State Archives and Records Svc., 1983-84, dep. state archivist, 1984-87; state archivist Alaska State Archives & Records Mgmt. Svcs., 1988-93; dir. Columbus Meml. Libr. OAS, Washington, 1993—2001. Archives cons. Ford Found. for Brazilian Archivists Assn., 1976, Soc. for Ibero-Latin Thought, 1980, Project for a Notarial Archives Computerized Guide, 1980; chair Alaska State Hist. Records Adv. Bd., 1988-93, coords. steering com., 1991-93; cons. Puerto Rican Hist. Records Adv. Bd., 1997-99. Author: An Archivists' Guide to the Catholic Church in Mexico, 1979; contbr. articles to profl. publs. Founder jail libr. Bexar County Jail, San Antonio; hon. dep. sheriff Bexar County, 1972-75; mem. Dem. party; chair Dems. Abroad in Mex., 1979-81; mem. Dems. Abroad Del. The Dem. Nat. Conv., N.Y., 1980; vice- chair Bill Egan Forum Greater Juneau Dem. Precinct, 1986-88 Recipient Commendation award Gov. of Alaska William Sheffield, 1985, Disting. Alumnae award U. Tex. Sch. Libr. and Info. Sci., 1998; Masonic Scholarship for internat. rels. George Washington U., 1960-61; univ. fellow U. Tex.-Austin, 1982-83, post masters fellow U.S. Dept. Edn.-U. Tex., Austin, 1967-68; scholar Orgn. Am. States, 1980, 81, Fulbright-Hays scholar, 1979, 80, scholar Nat. Def. Fgn. Lang.-U. Tex., Austin, 1978-79, scholar Calif. State Libr., 1962-63. Mem. AAUW (bd. dirs. 1983-86, scholar 1983), Nat. Assn. Govt. Archives and Records Adminstrs. (bd. dirs. 1989-93, chair membership com. 1989-93), Alaska Hist. Soc. (bd. treas. 1988-94), Alaska Libr. Assn., Acad. Cert. Archivists (cert. 1989), Rotary, Phi Kappa Phi. Democrat. Unitarian Universalist. Avocations: skiing, dance, researching, reading, hiking. Office: 206 Laurel Heights Place San Antonio TX 78212

NEWTON, WILLIAM ALLEN, JR., pediatric pathologist; b. Traverse City, Mich., May 19, 1923; s. William Allen and Florence Emma (Brown) N.; m. Helen Patricia Goodrich, Apr. 21, 1945; children: Katherine Germaine, Elizabeth Gale, William Allen, Nancy Anne. B.Sc. cum laude, Alma (Mich.) Coll., 1943; MD, U. Mich., 1946. Diplomate: Am. Bd. Pathology, Am. Bd. Pediatrics. Intern Wayne County Gen. Hosp., Detroit, 1947; resident in pediatric pathology/oncology/hematology Children's Hosp. Mich., Detroit, 1948-50; resident in pediat. Children's Hosp. Phila., 1950; dir. labs. Children's Hosp. Columbus, Ohio, 1952-88, rsch. pathologist, 1989—; mem. faculty

Coll. Medicine, Ohio State U., 1952—, prof., 1965—, chief pediatric pathology, 1952-89, chief divsn. pediatric hematology, 1952—82, prof. emeritus, 1989—. Chmn. pathology com. Children's Cancer Study Group, 1965 91; chmn. Pathology Com. Intergroup Rhabdomyosarcoma Study Group; chmn. pathology com. Late Effects Study Group. Contbr. articles to med. jours. Trustee, mem. exec. com. Am. Cancer Soc., Ohio div., 1972-86; mem. adv. com. on childhood cancer Am. Cancer Soc.; chmn. exec. com. Consortium for Cancer Control of Ohio, 1982-86; mem. sci. adv. com. Armed Forces Inst. Pathology; pres. Internat. Consortium for Cure of Childhood Cancer in China, 2000—. Served to capt. M.C. U.S. Army, 1950-52, brig. gen. Res. ret. Mem. Ohio State Med. Assn. (com. on cancer), Midwest Soc. Pediatric Research (mem. council 1960-63, pres. 1964-65), Soc. Pediatric Research, Am. Pediatric Soc., Pediatric Pathology Club (pres. 1968-69), Am. Soc. Clin. Oncology, Internat. Soc. Pediatric Oncology, Sigma Xi, Phi Sigma Pi. Republican. Baptist. Home: 2500 Harrison Rd Johnstown OH 43031-9540 Office: PO Box 6957 Columbus OH 43205 Office Phone: 614-722-3269.

NEXSEN, JULIAN JACOBS, lawyer; b. Kingstree, S.C., Apr. 14, 1924; s. William Ivey and Barbara (Jacobs) N.; m. Mary Elizabeth McIntosh, Jan. 28, 1948; children: Louise Ivey (Mrs. Heyward Harles Bouknight, Jr.), Julian Jacobs Jr. Student, The Citadel, 1941-43; BS magna cum laude, U. S.C., 1948, JD magna cum laude, 1950. Bar: S.C. 1950, U.S. Supreme Ct. 1960. Ptnr. firm Nexsen Pruet, LLC, Columbia, SC. Trustee Richland County Pub. Libr., chmn., 1976-77; trustee Providence Hosp., chmn., 1984-86; trustee Providence Found., Providence Ministries, Sisters of Charity of St. Augustine Health Sys.; past bd. dirs. Columbia Music Festival Assn., ARC Richland-Lexington Counties, Ctrl. Carolina Cmty. Found.; mem. U.S.C. Law Sch. partnership bd.; elder Eastminster Presbyn. Ch., trustee Congaree Presbytery, 1967-87, Synod, S.C., 1969-74, mem. Trinity Presbytery Coun. Lt. inf. AUS, 1943-46, ETO, capt., 1950-51, Korea. Decorated Bronze Star with oak leaf cluster; recipient Compleat Lawyer award U. S.C. Sch. Law. Mem. ABA, S.C. Bar (treas., bd. govs. 1974-79, ho. of dels. 1980-92), Richland County Bar Assn. (pres. 1974-75, Disting. Svc. award 1987), Am. Bar Found., S.C. Bar Found. (pres. 1971-72), S.C. Law Inst. (coun., exec. com. 1986—), Am. Law Inst., Am. Coll. Trust and Estate Counsel (regent 1973-82), Am. Judicature Soc., Forest Lake Country Club, Palmetto Club, Kiwanis (bd. dirs. 1972-74, 77-79), Phi Beta Kappa. Home: 2840 Sheffield Rd Columbia SC 29204-2332 Office: Nexsen Pruet LLC Drawer 2426 1441 Main St Columbia SC 29202-2426 Office Phone: 803-253-8247. E-mail: jnexsen@nexsenpruet.com.

NEXSEN, JULIAN JACOBS, JR., lawyer; b. Columbia, S.C., Sept. 22, 1954; s. Julian J. and Mary Elizabeth (McIntosh) N.; m. Christine Spigner Johnston, Feb. 25, 1984; children: Elizabeth Kincaid, Julian J. III, Sarah Ivey. BA, Washington and Lee U., 1976; JD, U. S.C., 1979. Bar: S.C. 1979, U.S. Ct. Appeals (4th cir.) 1982. Assoc. Nexsen, Pruet, Jacobs & Pollard, Columbia, S.C., 1979-84; assoc. in house counsel, asst. sec. Greenwood (S.C.) Mills, Inc., 1984-95, exec. v.p., 1999—2001; exec. v.p., COO Greenwood Devel. Corp., 1995-99, pres., CEO, 1999—. Bd. dirs. CountyBank, Greenwood Devel. Corp., Ctrl. Trust Co., SC Biotech. Incubation Program, Partnership for a Greater Greenwood; trustee Self Family Found., Self Regional Healthcare Ctr. Bd. visitors Lander Coll., 1985-87; bd. dirs. Edn. Enrichment Found., 1986-89, Greenwood United Way, 1989-92, Greenwood Community Theatre, 1989-93, Greenwood Uptown Devel. Corp., 1991-93; bd. deacons 1st Presbyn. Ch., 1990-93, session, 1993-96; trustee Self Meml. Hosp., 1992-98, Self Family Found., Self Regional Healthcare Ctr.; bd. dirs. Greenwood County Econ. Alliance, 1999-2001. Mem. ABA, Am. Corp. Counsel Assn., S.C. Bar Assn., Forest Lake Club, Greenwood Country Club, S.C. C. of C. (bd. dirs. 1990-93). Presbyterian. Home: 512 E Henrietta Ave Greenwood SC 29649-3142 Office: Greenwood Devel Corp PO Box 1546 Greenwood SC 29648-1546 E-mail: jnexsen@greenwooddevelopment.com.

NEY, ALEXANDER, artist, sculptor; b. Leningrad, Russia, Sept. 27, 1939; arrived in U.S., 1974; m. Liz Ney; children: Yana, Hannah, Joel. Student, Acad. Fine Art, Leningrad, 1954—57, Art Sch. Surikon Inst., Moscow, 1957—58, Repin Inst. Fine Arts, Leningrad, 1960—69. Cert. artist France, Russia, U.S. One-man shows include Hansen Gallery, N.Y.C., 1974, Wingspread Gallery, Northeast Harbor, Maine, 1977, Eduard Nakhamkin Fine Arts, N.Y.C., 1979, 1979, 1980, Gallery Saireido, 1992, Chassidic Art Inst., Bklyn., 1996, Duke U. Mus. Art, 1998, sculpture, Scientist, 1986, Stargazer, 1988, Thundering Saxophonist, 1998, Windows at Tiffany & Co., N.Y.C., 1978—94, Atlanta, 1982, Boston, 1991—94, Represented in permanent collections Zimmerli Art Mus., Rutgers U., New Brunswick, C.A.S.E. Mus., Jersey City, Yeshiva Univ. Mus., N.Y.C., Mus. Beeldan aan Zee, The Netherlands. Grantee, Robert Rauschenberg's Change, Inc., 1997, Adolph & Esther Gottlieb Found., 1997. Mem.: Union Artists (young artists divsn.). Office: c/o Bill Bowler Internat Creative Mgmt 40 W 57th St New York NY 10019

NEY, EDWARD N. ambassador, advertising and public relations company executive; b. St. Paul, May 26, 1925; s. John Joseph and Marie (Noonan) N.; m. Suzanne Hayes, 1950 (div. 1974); children: Nicholas, Hilary, Michelle; m. Judith I. Lasky, May 24, 1974. BA (Lord Jeffrey Amherst scholar 1942), Amherst Coll., 1947. With Young & Rubicam, Inc., N.Y.C., 1951-86, chmn., pres. CEO, 1970-86; chmn. Paine Webber/Young & Rubicam Ventures, N.Y.C., 1987-89; vice-chmn. Paine Webber, Inc., N.Y.C., 1987-89; amb. to Can., Am. Embassy, Ottawa, 1989-92; chmn. bd. advisors Burson-Marsteller, N.Y.C., 1992-98; chmn. Marsteller Advt.; chmn. emeritus Young & Rubicam Advt., N.Y.C., 1999—. Mem. adv. bd. Coun. on Fgn. Rels., 1975—, Ctr. for Strategic and Internat. Studies (C.S.I.S.), 1986—; honorary chmn. Advt. Coun.; mem. Advt. Hall of Fame. Life Trustee Amherst Coll., 1979—; Trustee Bush Presidential Libr. Found., James A. Baker III Inst. for Public Policy, Rice U., Museum of TV/Radio (MTR), 1982—. Office: Young Rubicam Advt 285 Madison Ave New York NY 10017-6486

NEY, PETER ERNEST, mathematician, educator; b. Brno, Czech Republic, July 6, 1930; s. Paul E. and Katherine B. Ney; m. Irene Paulu Ney, July 28, 1993; children: Paul A., Christine E. BS, MIT, Cambridge, 1951; MA, Columbia U., N.Y.C., 1952, PhD, 1961. Instr., math. Cornell U., Ithaca, NY, 1958—60, asst. prof., opers. rsch., 1960—63, assoc. prof., opers. rsch., 1963—65; vis. asst. prof., stats. Stanford U., Calif., 1963—64; assoc. prof., math. U. Wis., Madison, 1965—67, prof., math., 1967—2000, chmn., dept. math., 1974—77, emeritus prof., math., 2000—. Author: Branching Processes, 1971; editor: Advances in Probability, 1971—84, Annals of Probability, 1988—90; contbr. articles to profl. jours. Fellow, Guggenheim Found., 1971—72, Fulbright Found., 1984, Humboldt Found., 1991, 1994. Fellow: Inst. Math. Stats. (coun. mem.); mem.: Internat. Stats. Soc., Am. Math. Soc. Home: 104 Riverside Dr Unit C606 Cocoa FL 32922 Office: Dept Math Univ Wis 480 Lincoln Dr Madison WI 53706 Office Phone: 608-263-3054. Business E-Mail: ney@math.wisc.edu.

NEY, ROBERT W. congressman; b. Wheeling, W. Va., July 5, 1954; m. Liz; children: Bobby, Kayla Marie. BS in Edn., Ohio State U., 1976. Am. Embassy tchr., supr. affiliate school of Shiraz (Iran), 1978; health and edn. program mgr. Ohio Office of Appalachia, 1979; safety dir. City of Bellaire, Ohio, until 1980; mem. Ohio Ho. of Reps., 1980-84, Ohio Senate, 1984-94, U.S. Congress from 18th Ohio dist., 1995—; mem. fin. svcs. com., transp. and infrastructure com., chmn. adminstrn. com. Mem. Kiwanis, Elks, Lions, Sportsmen clubs, NRA. Republican. Office: US House of Reps 2438 Rayburn Ho Office Bldg Washington DC 20515-3518 also: 146 A West Main St Saint Clairsville OH 43950

NEYER, JEROME CHARLES, consulting civil engineer; b. Cin., July 15, 1938; s. Urban Charles and Marie Helen (Hemsteger) N.; m. Judy Ann Drolet, June 17, 1961; children: Janet, Karen. BCE, U. Detroit, 1961; MCE, U. Wash., 1963. Registered profl. engr. 16 states. Facilities engr. Boeing Co., Seattle, 1961-62; found. engr. Metro Engrs., Seattle, 1962-65; project engr. Hugo N. Helpert Assocs., Detroit, 1965-70; pres. NTH Cons. Ltd., Farmington Hills, Mich., 1970—. Adj. prof. U. Detroit, 1973-79. Contbr. articles to profl. jours. Mem. mineral well adv. bd., Lansing, Mich., 1975, mem. constrn. safety stds. bd., 1982; chmn. bldg. appeals bd. City of Farmington Hills, 1983. Mem. ASTM, ASCE (br. pres. 1973-74), Engring. Soc. Dtroit, Cons. Engrs. Mich. (pres. 1981), Mich. Soc. Profl. Engrs. (bd. dirs. 1980), Assn. Engring. Firms Practicing in the Geoscis. (pres. 1991). Roman Catholic. Avocations: golf, tennis. Home: 26478 Ballantrae Ct Farmington Hills MI 48331-3528 Office: NTH Consultants Ltd 38955 Hills Tech Dr Farmington MI 48331-3434 E mail: jneyer@nthconsultants.com.

NEYLAN, JOHN FRANCIS, III, nephrologist, educator, scientist; b. Chgo., Feb. 20, 1953; s. John Francis and Mary Alice (Coogan) N.; m. Cynthia Barnes, May 17, 1980; children: John Francis IV, Elizabeth Marie, James Christopher. BS, Duke U., 1975; MD, Rush Med. Coll., Chgo., 1979. Intern in medicine Vanderbilt U., Nashville, 1979-80, resident, 1980-82; fellow in nephrology Brigham and Women's Hosp., Boston, 1983-84; fellow in immunogenetics Harvard U. Med. Sch., Boston, 1984-86, clin. preceptor, 1986; asst. prof. medicine U. Calif., Davis, 1986-88, Emory U., Atlanta, 1988-93, assoc. prof., 1993-98, prof. medicine, 1998-2000, med. dir. renal transplantation, 1988-2000; v.p. clin. rsch. and devel. Wyeth Rsch., Collegeville, Pa., 2000—. Vis. cons. Wanless Hosp., Miraj, India, 1982-83; assoc. med. dir. Lifelink of Ga. Organ Procurement Orgn., Atlanta, 1989-2000; bd. govts. Lifelink Found., Tampa, Fla., 1988-2000. Editor: Am. Soc. Transplantation Newsletter, 1994-98, contbr. articles and abstracts to med. jours., chpts. to books. Vol. Nat. Kidney Found., N.Y.C., 1990—, ARC, Atlanta, 1991, Spl. Olympics, Atlanta, 1991—, Habitat for Humanity, 1993—; chmn. Nat. Kidney Found. Coun. on Transplantation, 1995-98; bd. dirs. United Network for Organ Sharing. Recipient Physician's Recognition award AMA, 1989. Mem. ACP, Am. Fedn. Clin. Rsch. (councillor 1988), Am. Soc. Transplantation (co-chmn. patient care com. 1988-90, chmn. 1991-93, councillor-at-large exec. coun. 1993-96, sec.-treas. 1996-97, pres.-elect 1997-98, pres. 1998-99, editor newsletter), Am. Soc. Nephrology, Internat. Soc. Nephrology, Transplantation Soc., United Network for Organ Sharing, Circumnavigator Club, Alpha Omega Alpha. Avocations: bicycling, tennis, windsurfing. Office: Wyeth Rsch 500 Arcola Rd Collegeville PA 19426 Office Phone: 484-865-4283. E-mail: neylanj@wyeth.com.

NEYLAND, MALCOLM, priest; Ordained priest Roman Catholic. Ch. Dir. Vatican Mus. Exhbn. Office: 1001 Main St Ste 204 Lubbock TX 79401-3309 Fax: 806-749-2350.

NG, BETTY, electronics executive; Pres. Reliance Tech Svcs., Sunnyvale, Calif., 1981—. Office: Reliance Tech Svcs 895 Kifer Rd Sunnyvale CA 94086-5205 Fax: 408-720-0838. E-mail: info@RTSII.com.

NG, HOCK MIN, research scientist; m. Ginny Ng. BS, Boston U., 1994, MS, 1996, PhD, 1999. Tech. staff Bell Labs Lucent Technologies, Murray Hill, NJ, 1999—. Recipient Snell Premium, Inst. Elec. Engrs., UK, 2003. Mem.: Am. Phys. Soc., Electrochem. Soc., Materials Rsch. Soc., IEEE, Golden Key Nat. Honor Soc., Tau Beta Pi (sec. 1993). Achievements include research in GaN and related wide bandgap semiconductors. Office: Bell Labs Lucent Technologies 600 Mountain Ave Rm 6H-426 Murray Hill NJ 07974 Business E-Mail: hmng@lucent.com.

NG, LAWRENCE MING-LOY, pediatrician; b. Hong Kong, Mar. 21, 1940; came to U.S., 1967, naturalized, 1977; s. John Iu-cheung and Mary Wing (Wong) N.; m. Bella May Ha Kan, June 25, 1971; children: Jennifer Wing-mui, Jessica Wing-yee. MBBS in Medicine, U. Hong Kong, 1965. Diplomate Am. Bd. Pediat. House physician Queen Elizabeth Hosp., Hong Kong, 1965-66, med. officer, 1966-67; resident physician Children's Hosp. of Los Angeles, 1967-68, Children's Hosp. Med. Ctr., Oakland, Calif., 1968-70; fellow in pediatric cardiology, 1970-72; now mem. tchg. staff; practice medicine specializing in pediat. and pediatric cardiology, San Leandro, Calif., 1972—, Oakland, Calif., 1982—; mng. ptnr. Pediatric Med. Assocs. of East Bay, 1990—. Chief pediat. Oakland Hosp., 1974-77, Meml. Hosp., San Leandro, 1986-88; chief pediat. Vesper Meml. Hosp., 1977-79, sec. staff, 1984, v.p. staff, 1985; founder Pediatric Assocs. of East Bay, 1990. Active Republican Party. Recipient Small Bus. Leadership award, Oakland Chinatown C. of C., Comty. Svc. award, Ethnic Health Inst., Family Bridges Comty. Svc. award. Fellow: Am. Acad. Pediatrics; mem.: AMA, Chancellor's Assocs. U. Calif. at Berkeley, Children's First Healthcare Network (bd. dirs. 1997—), Oakland Chinatown C. of C. (bd. dirs. 1986—91, 1986—91, adv. bd. 1992—, Cmty. Spirit award 2000), Ethnic Health Inst. (bd. dirs. 1998—, Frank Stagger Sr. Cmty. svc. award 2004), Fedn. Chinese Med. Socs. (dir. 1998—), Chinese-Am. Physicians Soc. (sec. 1980, pres. 1983, exec. dir. 1997—2001, bd. dirs. 2003—), Chinese-Am. POlit. Assn. (life), Orgn. Chinese Ams. (chpt. pres. 1984), Smithsonian Assocs., L.A. Pediat. Soc., Alameda County Assn. Primary Care Practitioners (membership chmn. 1993—97, sec.-treas. 1994—97), Am. Heart Assn., Calif. Med. Assn., Family Bridges Inc. (bd. dirs. 2002—, Kenneth Hoh award for cmty. svc. 2004), Stanford U. Alumni Assn. (life), Consumer's Union (life), Hong Kong U. Alumni Assn. (sec. No. Calif. chpt. 1992—96, pres. 1997—2000, chair 2001—), Friends of Hong Kong U. (bd. dirs. 2001—, treas. 2003—), Oakland Asian Cultural Ctr. (dir. 1996—99, treas. 1996—99), U.S. Golf Assn., San Leandro Golf Club, No. Calif. Golf Assn., Commonwealth Club, PGA Tour Ptnrs. Club (life). Buddhist. Office: 345 9th St Ste 204 Oakland CA 94607-4206 also: 101 Callan Ave Ste 401 San Leandro CA 94577-4523 Office Phone: 510-839-1072.

NG, WING CHIU, accountant, educator, application developer, lawyer, educator, advocate; b. Hong Kong, Oct. 14, 1947; came to U.S., 1966; s. Bing Nuen and Oi Ying (Lee) Ng. BS, MS, Yale U., 1969; PhD, NYU, 1972; JD, U. Hawaii, 2000. Bar: Hawaii 2001; CPA, Hawaii. Rsch. assoc. SUNY, Stony Brook, 1972-74; asst. prof. U. Md., College Park, 1974-76; rsch. physicist U. Bonn, Fed. Republic of Germany, 1976-78; chartered acct. Richter, Usher & Vineberg, Montreal, Can., 1978-80; pvt. practice Honolulu, Hawaii, 1980—; pres. Bowen, Ng & Co., Honolulu, 1983-84, Asia-Am. Investment, Inc., Honolulu, 1983—, Mathematica Pacific, Inc., Honolulu, 1984—. Part-time prof. U. Hawaii, Honolulu, 1982—; ptnr. Advance Realty Investment, Honolulu, 1980—; dir. S & L Internat., Inc., Honolulu, 1987—. Creator: (computer software) Time Billing, 1984, Dbase General Ledger, 1987, Dbase Payroll, 1987, Dbase Accounts Receivable, 1989; co-author: Draft Constitution of the Federal Republic of China, 1994. Dir. Orgn. of Chinese Ams., Honolulu, 1984-86, Fedn. for a Dem. China, Honolulu, 1990—, Hong Kong, 1991—; dir. Alliance Hong Kong Chinese in U.S., 1995—. Included in Prominent People of Hawaii, Delta Pub. Co., 1988. Mem. AICPA, Hong Kong Soc. Accts., Hawaiian Trail & Mountain Club (auditor 1987—). Democrat. Buddhist. Avocations: hiking, the internet. Office: 1149 Bethel St Ste 306 Honolulu HI 96813-2210

NGAI, SZE-MAN, education educator; s. Lung Lai Ngai and Lai Wa Chung; m. Mercy Ming-See Fung, May 15, 1992; children: Stanley Hiu-On, Beverly Hiu-Wai. BSc, U. Hong Kong, 1987; MA, U. Pitts., 1989, PhD, 1995. Instr. Chinese U., Hong Kong, 1995—95, postdoctoral fellow, 1996—97; vis. asst. prof. Ga. Inst. Tech., Atlanta, 1998—2000; asst. prof. Ga. So. U., Statesboro, 2000—; vis. asst. prof. Cornell U., Ithaca, NY, 1998. Cons. in fractals Med. Coll. Ga., Augusta, 2001—. Contbr. articles to profl. jours. Mem.: Am. Math. Soc. Office: Ga Southern Univ Dept Math Sci Statesboro GA 30460-8093 Office Phone: 912-681-5839. Business E-Mail: smngai@georgiasouthern.edu.

NGANDU, PIUS NKASHAMA, education educator; b. Mbujimayi, Kasai, Zaire, Sept. 4, 1946; arrived in France, 1973; s. Prosper Kalonji and Marcelline Musuamba; m. Godelieve Ngandu-Kalenga, Sept. 28, 1968 Diploma, Lovanium-Kinshasa, 1970; LLD, U. Strasbourg, France, 1981; postgrad., Univ. Annaba-Constantine, Algeria, 1982-90, Univ. Aarhus, Denmark, 1988-90, U. Baton Rouge, 1995, Albuquerque, 1995, Portland, 1995, 96. Charge de cours Univ. Limoges, France, 1990—, maitre Confs. Invite, 1990-91; prof. Univ. Zaire, Lubumbashi, 1979—, Univ. Annaba-Constantine, 1982—, U. Paris III-Sorbonne Nouvelle, 2000, La. State U., 2000—; dir. Ctr. for French and Francophone Studies, La. State U., Baton Rouge; disting. prof. Bibliotheque: World Wide, BWW Soc./LAPGS. Dir. lit. Edits. L'Harmattan and Nouvelles du Sud, Paris, 1990—; pres. Groupe de Rsch. Interdisciplinaires about Afrique, Paris, 1992—; coord. Notre Libr., Paris, 1993-94. Author: Yakouta, 1995, Le doyen marri, 1994, Le fils du mercenaire, 1994, Citadelle d'espoir, 1995, Bidi ntwilu, bidi mpelelu, 1995, Enseigner les litteratures africaines, 2000, Dictionaire Critique des Oeuvres Littéraires, 2002, (theatrical works) May Britt de Santa Cruz, 1993, L'empire des ombres vivantes, Bonjour monsieur le Ministre, 1983, others, Mulongeshi Wanyi, 2003. Recipient Fonlon-Nichols award excellence creative writing, African Lit. Assn., Bruxelles, 2004. Office: La State U Dept French Studies Baton Rouge LA 70809 Home: 977 Elysian Dr Baton Rouge LA 70810-2615 E-mail: nngandl@lsu.edu.

NGO, KHIEM VIET, research scientist; b. Saigon, Vietnam, Sept. 23, 1973; s. Ngoan Viet Ngo and Xuan (Maria) Thi Tran. BS in Math., Va. Poly. Inst. and State U., 1997, MS in Math., 1998; MSME, U. Ill., 1999; postgrad., Stanford U., 2003—. Summer intern NASA Goddard Space Flight Ctr., Greenbelt, Md., 1999—99; mech. engr. Naval Air Warfare Ctr., China Lake, Calif., 2000—00; rsch. scientist, dept. of elec. & computer engring. U. Va., Charlottesville, 2001—03. Adj. faculty math. No. Va. C.C., Annandale, 1999. Recipient Freshman prize, Va. Tech., Dept. Math., 1995, award, Golden Key Nat. Honor Soc., 1996, Achievement award, NASA Goddard Space Flight Ctr., 1999; scholar, Va. Tech., Dept. Math., 1995. Mem.: IEEE, Soc. Indsl. and Applied Math., Eta Kappa Nu, Pi Mu Epsilon. Achievements include research in the impact of variations on 1-D flow in gas turbine engines via Monte Carlo simulations; co-development of a vehicle movement algorithm for a virtual Maglev-guideway signaling system for the discrete-event simulation of magnetically levitated trains; co-development of the failure mode scenarios for the Monte Carlo probabilistic simulation of trains; research in Analytical Derivation Related to Nonlinear Energy Pumping in Coupled Oscillators; Introduction to Eigenvalue Perturbation Theory; Eigenvalues of Infinite Mass-Spring Systems: Approximate and Exact Solutions of the Extended Timoshenko Beam Model; discovery of a formula for the area of a triangle in terms of its three medians. Home: 10501 Moonglow Ct Manassas VA 20112 Office: Dept Aeronautics and Astronautics Stanford Univ 496 Lomita Mall Durand Bldg Stanford CA 94305-4035 E-mail: khiem.ngo@stanford.edu.

NGO, TUNG THANH, writer, photographer; b. Soctrang, Vietnam, May 18, 1936; came to U.S., 1975; s. Lung The Ngo and Thui Thi Lam; m. Lan My Vu, Jan. 12, 1962; children: Peter, Vincent, Mike, Vinh. B of Law, U. Saigon, Vietnam, 1964; M of Pub. Affairs, U. Pitts., 1970. Judge advocate, corps II South Vietnam Armed Forces, Pleiku, 1964—66; assemblyman, gen. sec. Nat. Constituent Assembly, Saigon, Vietnam, 1966—67; dean, prof. Hoa Hao U., Long Xuyen, Vietnam, 1970—75; sch. tchr. Garden Grove (Calif.) Sch. Dist., 1978—86; computer operator Alta Bates Med. Ctr., Berkeley, 1987—2001; writer, photography instr. Vietnamese Photoraphy Assn., Calif., 1981—. Author: (in Vietnamese) Visiting California, 1995, Entering Photography I, 1999, Entering Photography II, 2000; editor: Vietnam's Traditional Angling, 1977, Dr. Cung or Boat People, 1987, Selection of Photgraphs, 2001. Grantee The Ford Found., 1975; hon. fellowship The Hong Kong Photography Club of L.A., 2000, The Vietnamese Artists Photography Assn., 2000. The Vietnamese Artistic Photography Assn. (v.p. 1981—, hon. fellowship 2000), The Vietnamese Artistic Photography Assn. in No. Calif. (chpt. pres.). Home: 49 Killybegs Rd Alameda CA 94502

NGUYEN, ALEX THINH, internet company executive, aerospace engineer, consultant; b. Saigon, Vietnam, Nov. 25, 1974; came to U.S., 1980; s. Chien Van Nguyen and Bich-dao Thi Trinh. BS in Aerospace Engring., U. Md., 1996, postgrad.; MS sys. engring., Univ. MD, 2001. Systems programming coord. U. Md., College Park, 1992-98; aerospace systems engr. Analytical Graphics, Inc., Lanham, Md., 1998-00; dir. bus. devel. Wonderclick.com, Inc., Washington, 1999—; v.p. bus. devel. AboveCable.com, Inc., Washington, 1999—; founder, pres. Concepts Beyond, Inc.; mng. dir. AboveCable India Pvt. Ltd., 2000—. Cons. Analytical Graphics, Inc., Lanham, 2000—. Pres. Vietnamese Cultural Soc., Falls Church, Va., 1998-99, bd. dirs. 2000—; mem. Asian Am. LEAD, Washington, 1998—. Mem.: Asia Soc., Vietnamese Cultural Soc., Nat. Air and Space Mus., Balt. Coun. for Fgn. Affairs, Omicron Delta Kappa, Sigma Gamma Tau (pres. 1995). Avocations: skiing, camping, mountain biking, photography. Office: AboveCable 2400 N St NW Washington DC 20037

NGUYEN, ANN CAC KHUE, pharmaceutical and medicinal chemist; b. Kieu Moc, Sontay, Vietnam, Nov. 12, 1949; d. Nguyen Van Soan and Luu Thi Hieu. BS, U. Saigon, 1973; MS, San Francisco State U., 1978; PhD, U. Calif., San Francisco, 1983. Tchg. and rsch. asst. U. Calif., San Francisco, 1978-83, postdoctoral fellow, 1983-86, rsch. scientist, 1987—. Contbr. articles to profl. jours. Recipient Nat. Rsch. Svc. award, NIH, 1981-83; Regents fellow U. Calif., San Francisco, 1978-81. Mem. AAAS, Am. Chem. Soc., N.Y. Acad. Scis., Bay Area Enzyme Mechanism Group, Am. Assn. Pharm. Scientists. Roman Catholic. Home: 1488 Portola Dr San Francisco CA 94127-1409 Office: U Calif PO Box 446 San Francisco CA 94143-0001 E-mail: cackhue@itsa.ucsf.edu.

NGUYEN, CHARLES CUONG, engineering educator, researcher, dean; b. Danang, Vietnam, Jan. 1, 1956; arrived in U.S., 1978, naturalized, 1978; s. Buoi and Tinh Thi Nguyen; m. Kim-Bang Pham, Aug. 5, 1989; children: Carissa Kim Thuy Duong, Olivia Quynh Duong, Dylan Nhat Khang, Parker Duy Khang. Diploma, Konstanz U., Fed. Rep. Germany, 1978; MS with distinction, George Washington U., 1980, DSc with superiour performance, 1982. Engr. Siemens Corp., Erlangen, Germany, 1977-78; lectr. George Washington U., Washington, 1978-82; asst. prof. engring. Cath. U. Am., Washington, 1982-85, assoc. prof. elec. engring., 1985-92, prof., 1992—, chmn. dept. elec. engring. and computer sci., 1997-2001, dean Sch. Engring., 2001—. Cons. Mitre Corp., Meridian Corp., Jet Propulsion Lab., others; dir. Ctr. Artificial Intelligence and Robotics, 1985—; mem. organizing coms. various robotics confs.; sr. rsch. assoc. NAS, 1990—; program vice chair IEE-Internat. Conf. Robotics 2d Automation, 1997, Internat. Symposium and Robotic Automation, 1997; chmn. organizing com. Robotics Internat., Internat. Symposium Robotics and Mfg. Founding editor, editor-in-chief: Jour. Intelligent Automation and Soft Computing; editor: (book) Robotics and Manufacturing, Vol. 5, 1994, Intelligent Automation and Soft Computing, Vol. 1, 1994, Intelligent Automation and Soft Computing, Vol. 2, 1994; mem. editl. bd.: Jour. Intelligent and Fuzzy Sys., Engring. Design and Automation, assoc. editor: Computers and Elec. Engring.: An Internat. Jour., 1992—, guest editor: Jour. Robotic Sys., —; contbr. scientific papers to profl. jours. Apptd. by Pres. Bus to bd. dirs. Vietnam Edn. Found., 2004—07. Recipient Rsch. Initiation award, Engring. Found., 1985, Lifetime Achievement award, World Automation Congress, 2004, Cmty. Svc. award, Asia Entertainment Inc., 2004; fellow, NASA-Am. Soc. Elec. Engring., 1985, 1986, NASA-Am. Soc. Elec. Engring. Summer, Goddard Space Flight Ctr., 1994. Mem.: IEEE (sr.; program v.p. Washington chpt.), Soc. Mfg. Engrs. (sr. Robotics Internat.), Internat. Soc. Mini-and Microcomputers, Tau Beta Pi (faculty advisor), Sigma Xi. Roman Catholic. Avocations: guitar, singing, tennis, skiing, ping pong/table tennis. Business E-Mail: nguyen@cua.edu.

NGUYEN, DONG, computer scientist, researcher, education educator; s. Dao Nguyen and Khau Thi Le; m. Dung Xuan Phi, Dec. 30, 1976; children: Henry Huy, Huy Tuan. BS in Computer Sci. and Engring., Calif. State U., Long Beach, 1985, MS in Computer Sci., 1988; PhD in Computer Engring. and Applied Math., Claremont Grad. U., 2000, exec. MBA, 2002, MS in Math., 1997. Software engr. Info. Internat., Inc., Culver City, Calif., 1984—86; sr. software engr. CALCOMP, Anaheim, Calif., 1986—90; sr. programmer analyst Sys. Divsn. Ball Aerospace, Huntington Beach, Calif., 1985—87; sr. firmware engr. Micro Tech., Inc., Anaheim, Calif., 1990—92; sr. software engr., sys. engr. Beckman Instruments, Brea, 1990—97, B/E Aerospace, Irvine, Calif., 1997—2001; sr. adv. engr., rschr. Kofax Image Products, Irvine, Calif., 2001—03; software engr. mgr. Celerity Group, Inc., Yorba Linda, 2003—. Lectr. Cal State Univ., Longweach, 1998—2000, in field. Prodr.(music concerts): Young Love, 1992—94. Achievements include research in reliability modeling and evaluation in real-time distributed multimedia systems; recovery blocks in real-time distributed systems; failure mode and effect analysis in software reliability; reliability modeling and evaluation in computer networks and distributed systems; development of rasterization algorithm which greatly improved the speed of converting the vector data to raster data in printers/plotters.

NGUYEN, DUOC TAN, small business owner; b. Tan Quoi, Cantho, Vietnam, Apr. 5, 1944;, U.S., 1988; s. Hay Tan Nguyen and Kiev Thi Tran; m. Luu Thi Ha, Aug. 15, 1984; 1 child, Nguyen Nghia Hieu. Law cert., Law U., Cantho, 1974. Cert. acctg., tax, notary pub. Dir. criminal investigation Rokee Hdqs., 1966—75; transl. Refugee Camp, 1988—89; pres. South Vietnam Police Forces Orgn., Calif., 1990—95; sec. Vietnamese Cmty. in So. Calif., 1996—2002; chmn. Collective Com., 2002—. Advisor South Vietnam Police Orgn., 1998—2000; sec. Vietnamese Nat. Support Assn. Editor: South Vietnamese Police Forces Orgn. Mag., 1992—. Mem. ACLU, 1998—; sec. Hungviet Orgn., Calif., 1992—. Mem.: U.S. Fed. Police Orgn. Avocations: basketball, football, fishing, music, poetry. Home: #2 7091 Trask Ave #2 Westminster CA 92683 Office: Vietnamese Cmty Svcs # 211 15355 Brookhurst St Westminster CA 92683

NGUYEN, HAN VAN, mechanical engineer; b. Danang, Vietnam, June 10, 1956; came to U.S., 1974; s. Tien Van and Dieu Anh (Khoa) N.; m. Thien-Tam Trang, Jan. 7, 1995; children: Huy, Minh. BSME with distinction, Iowa State U., 1979; MSME, Purdue U., 1981, PhD, 1986. Registered profl. engr., Calif., Wash. Grad. rsch. asst. Purdue U., West Lafayette, 1979—83; sr. engr. Westinghouse Electric Corp., Sunnyvale, Calif., 1983—87; assoc. tech. fellow The Boeing Co., Downey and Huntington Beach, Calif., 1987—. Mem. adj. faculty Calif. State Poly. U., Pomona, 1995-97. Contbr. articles to profl. jours. Bd. dirs. L.A. Coun. Engrs. and Scientists, 2000-01, Asian Am. Profl. Assn., 2002-2004 Recipient Cert. of Appreciation, Rockwell Internat. Corp., 1989, 94, Instant Compensation award Rockwell Internat. Corp., 1992, 94, NASA Group Achievement award, 1992; Iowa State U. scholar; Purdue U. fellow. Fellow: AIAA (assoc.; liquid propulsion tech. com. 2000—, conf. session chair 2002, 2003), Inst. Advancement Engring.; mem.: Sigma Xi, Golden Key, Phi Eta Sigma, Pi Mu Epsilon, Eta Kappa Nu, Pi Tau Sigma, Tau Beta Pi, Phi Kappa Phi. Achievements include development of numerous thermo-fluid models to evaluate the design and predict the performance of launch vehicle propulsion systems, and publications in space propulsion. Office: The Boeing Co MC H012-B201 5301 Bolsa Ave Huntington Beach CA 92647-2048

NGUYEN, HOA THAI, academic administrator; arrived in U.S., 1975; s. Han Van Nguyen and May Thi Trinh; m. Xuyen Ngoc Thai, Aug. 6, 1988; children: Stephanie Thai, Katherine Thai, Meisha Thai. MBA, U. Detroit, 1991. On-Line Faculty Training Mich. Virtual U., 2003. Fin. specialist Mich. Dept. Of State, Lansing, 1995—2001; asst. v.p. Lansing CC, 2001—. Adj. faculty Olivet Coll., Mich., 1995—97. Commr. Mich. Commn. On Asia In The Schools, Lansing, 2002—03. Mem.: Mich. CC Bus. Officer Assn., Nat. Assn. of Coll. and U. Bus. Officers. Office: Lansing CC PO Box 40010 Lansing MI 48901-7210 Office Phone: 517-483-1765. E-mail: nguyenh8@lcc.edu.

NGUYEN, HUONG TRAN, English language professional, federal agency official; b. Haiphong, Vietnam, Nov. 16, 1953; came to the U.S., 1971; d. Joe (Quang) Trong Tran and Therese (Nguyet-Anh) (Do) Dotran; m. Tony (Phu) The Nguyen; children: Long Tran Nguyen, Ty Tran Nguyen. B in Liberal Studies, San Diego State U., 1976, tchg. credential grades K-12, 1977; M in Curriculum Devel., Point Loma Coll., 1984; lang. devel. specialist cert., Calif. Commn. Credentialing, 1991. ESL tchr. San Diego (Calif.) Job Corps, 1978-80; resource tchr. grades K-12 San Diego (Calif.) Unified Sch. Dist., 1980-82; resource tchr. SEAL project grades K-12 Long Beach (Calif.) Unified Sch. Dist., 1982-83, ESL specialist, 1983-85, 85-92, English lang. devel. tchr., chair, 1992-95; adminstr., 1996-98; sr. fellow officer U.S. Dept. Edn., Office Bilingual & Minority Lang. Affairs, Washington, 1995-96; disting. tchr.-in-residence Calif. State U., Long Beach, 1998—. Named Outstanding Tchr. of 1994, Disney Co. Am. Tchr. Awards, Washington, 1994, Outstanding Tchr. in Fgn. Lang./ESL, Disney Co. Am. Tchr. Awards, Washington, 1994. Mem. NEA, TESOL, Calif. Lang. Tchrs. Assn., Calif. Tchr. Assn., Calif. Assn. for Bilingual Edn., Tchr. Assn. Long Beach, Assn. Curriculum and Supervision. Avocations: reading, travel, gardening, visiting museums. Home: 6262 Cherokee Dr Westminster CA 92683-2004 Office: Calif State U Coll Edn Dept Tchr Edn 1250 N Bellflower Blvd Long Beach CA 90840-0001

NGUYEN, KHUE VU, molecular biologist, researcher; b. Ha Noi, Vietnam, Sept. 24, 1952; arrived in France, 1974; s. Cang Van Nguyen and Dy Thi Vu; m. Martine Françoise Juilleret, Sept. 18, 1979; 3 children. BS in Biochemistry, U. Louis Pasteur, Strasbourg, France, 1979, MS in Molecular Biology, 1980, PhD in Macromolecular Phys. Chemistry, 1983, PhD (D d'Etat) in Phys. Scis., 1986. Postdoctoral rschr. Faculty Medicine, Strasbourg, 1986-87; rsch. scientist Anda Biols. Co., Strasbourg, 1987-97, Neurofit Co., Strasbourg, 1998-99, U. Calif. San Diego Sch. Medicine, 1999—. Contbr. articles to profl. jours.; patentee in field. Mem. AAAS, Am. Soc. Microbiology, Am. Chem. Soc., N.Y. Acad. Scis. Address: 2828 Univ Ave Apt 303 San Diego CA 92104 Office Phone: 619-543-3623. Business E-Mail: k25nguyen@ucsd.edu.

NGUYEN, LAN THI HOANG, physician, educator; b. Hai-Duong, Vietnam, July 18, 1950; came to U.S., 1975; d. Thua Nang and Niem Thi (Do) N.; m. Khanh Vinh Quoc, Oct. 15, 1981. MD, U. Kans., 1983. Intern St. Mary Med. Ctr./UCLA, Long Beach, Calif., 1983-84; resident City of Faith Med. Rsch. Ctr.-Oral Roberts Sch. Medicine, Tulsa, 1986-88; fellow VA Med. Ctr.-Wadsworth-UCLA, 1988-90; physician Santa Ana (Calif.) Med. Ctr., Doctors Hosp. Santa Ana, Fountain Valley (Calif.) Regional Med. Ctr. Clin. assoc. prof. family medicine Keck Sch. Medicine U. So. Calif., L.A., 2002—. Contbr. articles to profl. jours. V.p. Vietnamese Am. Med. Rsch. Found. Kans. Med. scholar, 1979-81. Fellow: ACP, Am. Coll. Endocrinology, Am. Coll. Nutrition; mem.: Am. Assn. Clin. Endocrinologists (charter). Office: 14971 Brookhurst St Westminster CA 92683-5556 Office Phone: 714-839-5898.

NGUYEN, NHUNG THANH, psychologist, educator; PhD, Va. Commonwealth U., 2001. Asst. prof. Lamar U., Beaumont, Tex., 2001—. Cons. Workskills First, Inc., Richmond, Va., 2001—. Contbr. articles various rsch. papers. Recipient Outstanding Paper award, So. Mgmt. Assn., 2002, Doctoral Dissertation, Wonderlic, Inc., 2001; fellow Post-doctoral, Sasakawa Found., 2003; Rsch. Enhancement grant, Lamar Grad. Sch., 2002. Mem.: Soc. for Indsl. & Orgnl. Psychology, Soc. of Human Resource Mgmt., So. Mgmt. Assn., APA, Acad. of Mgmt., Beta Gamma Sigma Assn. Home: 3340 Kipling Dr Beaumont TX 77706 Office: Lamar U 4400 Martin Luther King Pkwy Beaumont TX 77710 Office Phone: 409-880-8295. Office Fax: 409-880-8620. E-mail: nguyennt@hal.lamar.edu.

NGUYEN, PAUL DUNG QUOC, lawyer; b. Hung Yen, Vietnam, Feb. 2, 1943; came to U.S., 1975; s. Trac Trong and Do Thi (Vu) N.; m. Maria Kim-Dung T. Dang, Dec. 26, 1967; children: Theresa Thu, Catherine Bao-Chau, Jonathan Hung. LLB, Hue Law Sch., Vietnam, 1965; MA in Pub. Policy Adminstrn., U. Wis., 1973. Bar: N.Y. 1979, U.S. Dist. Ct. (so. and ea. dists.) N.Y. 1979, U.S. Tax Ct. 1979. Prof. law Hue & Can Tho Law Schs., Vietnam, 1973-75; assoc. Proskauer, Rose, Getz & Mendelsohn, N.Y.C., 1979-80; pvt. practice N.Y.C., 1980-81; corp. law specialist Office of Corp. Counsel, City of N.Y., 1981-94; counsel, country rep. Hanoi Rep. Office White & Case, Vietnam, 1994-95; sr. counsel Port Authority of N.Y. and N.J., N.Y.C., 1995—. Adj. asst. prof. NYU, 1998—. Bd. dirs. N.Y.C. Indochinese Refugees; hon. chmn. lawyers com. for human rights Vietnamese Legal Protection Fund, 1990-94; legal advisor Indochina Resource Action Ctr., 1990-94; dir. S.E. Asia Resource Action Ctr., 1995-98. Recipient Nat. Legion Honor award Office of Pres., Saigon, 1970. Mem. ABA, Assn. of Bar of City of N.Y. (Outstanding Performance award com. on mcpl. affairs 1986), Asian Am. Bar Assn. N.Y. (pres. 2000-01, bd. dirs. 1993-2001), Nat. Asian Pacific Am. Bar Assn. (N.E. regional gov. 1998-2000). Avocations: golf, reading, classical music.

NGUYEN, QUOC, mechanical engineer; b. Saigon, Vietnam, Jan. 10, 1953; came to U.S. 1976; s. Thinh V. and Oanh (Le) N.; children: Jenifer, Michelle. BSME, West Coast U., 1978. Mech. engr. Jaras, Baum & Bolles, L.A., 1976-80, asst. office mgr., 1980-83; project mgr. Store, Matakovich & Wolfberg, San Gabriel, Calif., 1983-86, v.p. El Monte, Calif., 1986-93, sr. v.p., 1993—, also dir., 1986—; prin. Antieri & Assocs., Cons. Engrs., Inc., L.A., 1998-99; pres. East West Cons. Svcs., Pomona, Calif., 1999—. Mem. ASHRAE.

NGUYEN, RU, entomologist; b. Nhatrang, Khanh Hoa, Vietnam, Dec. 12, 1944; s. Tam Nguyen and Van Thi Le; m. Kim-Dung Thi Nguyen, Jan. 28, 1981; 1 child, Kim-Anh. BS, Coll. Agr., Saigon, Vietnam, 1966; PhD, U. Fla., 1975. Asst. entomologist U. Fla., Gainesville, 1976—78; rsch. fellow Alexander von Humboldt-Stiftung/U. Bonn, Germany, 1978—79; rsch. entomologist, leader USDA-APHIS-PPQ, Ft. Lauderdale, Fla., 1980—82; rsch. entomologist divsn. plant industry Fla. Dept. Agr., Gainesville, 1982—. Mem. Caribbean fruit fly tech. com. Fla. Dept. Agr., 1983—; mem. citrus leafminer task force U. Fla., Gainesville, 1994—98; mem. nat. genetic resources adv. coun. USDA, Washington, 2000—. Contbr. articles to profl. jours.; author: (book) Catalog of Aleyrodidae on Citrus and Their Natural Enemies, 1993. Recipient Disting. Svc. to Agr. award, Gamma Sigma Delta Honor Soc. of Agr., 1995, Outstanding Achievement award in developing Fly Free Zone, Fla. Dept. Agr. and Consumer Svcs., 1984. Mem.: Fla. Entomol. Soc. (Team Rsch. award 1997, Achievement award for rsch. 2002), Internat. Orgn. for Biol. Control, Entomol. Soc. Am. Office: Divsn Plant Industry PO Box 147100 Gainesville FL 32614 Office Phone: 352-372-3505. Business E-Mail: nguyenr@doacs.state.fl.us.

NGUYEN, SAM (VAN NGUYEN), economist, researcher; b. Vinhthanh, Vietnam, Aug. 7, 1928; s. Phuoc van and Mai thi Nguyen; m. Diem Tonnu, Jan. 25, 1958; children: Hang, Huy, Khoi, Binh, Trang, Loan. BA in Law, Saigon U., 1957, MS in Econs., 1961; AA, Ohlone Coll., 1995. Officer Nat. Bank of Vietnam, Saigon, 1959-75; econs. rschr. Calif., 1990—. Author: Eph Pha Tha, 1998. Home: 41445 Millennium Ter Fremont CA 94538 E-mail: Sam_Nguyen@yahoo.com.

NGUYEN, THACH NGOC, cardiologist; b. Feb. 2, 1953; s. Sau Ngoc Nguyen and Hanh Hong Tran. Diploma, Hue Med. Sch., 1978. Diplomate Am. Bd. Internal Medicine, Am. Bd. Cardiovasc. Diseases and Interventional Cardiology. Resident internal medicine Bklyn. Hosp., 1982-85, fellow cardiology, 1985-87; clin. asst. prof. medicine Ind. U. Sch. Medicine, 1992—; dir. cardiovascular rsch. St. Mary Med. Ctr., Hobart, Ind., 1997—, dir. interventional cardiology, 2001—, pres. med. staff, 2002—; pvt. practice. Chmn. Internat. Continuing Med. Edn. Com., 1995—; course dir. Cardiology Update, Siriraj Hosp., Bangkok, 1999; editl. cons. Jour. of Interventional Cardiology, 1998, Vietnamese Med. Jour., 2001; chmn. sci. com. 11th and 12th Gt. Wall Internat. Congress Cardiology, Beijing, 2000, Beijing, 02. Editor: Cardiology Today, 1995, Advances and Challenges in Today's Cardiology, 1997, Management of Complex Cardiovascular Problems: The Consultant's Approach, 2002, 2d edit., 2001, Spanish edit., 2002, Vietnamese edit., 2002, Practical Handbook of Advanced Interventional Cardiology, 2000, 2003; co-editor: Jour. Geriatric Cardiology, 2003. Fellow: ACP, Soc. Cardiovascular Angiography and Intervention, Am. Coll. Cardiology (edn. com. 2004—). Roman Catholic. Address: 200 E 86th Pl Merrillville IN 46410-6258 Fax: 219-756-1410. Office Phone: 219-756-1400. E-mail: thachnguyen2000@yahoo.com.

NGUYEN, TUAN MANH, internist, perinatologist, obstetrician, gynecologist; b. Hanoi, Vietnam, Sept. 27, 1953; s. Dao Huu and Thi Le (Nga) Nguyen; m. Chau Ngoc-Minh Dao, Aug. 3, 1996. BA summa cum laude, San Francisco State U., 1977, BS summa cum laude, 1979; MD, Chgo. Med. Sch., 1983. Diplomate Am. Bd. Ob-Gyn. 1997, Am. Bd. Internal Medicine 1986, Nat. Bd. Med. Examiners 1984, Am. Bd. Maternal Fetal Medicine 1999. Asst. medicine U. Ill. at Chgo., 1984—86; emergency dept. physician St. Joseph Hosp., Belvidere, Ill., 1986—90; instr. ob-gyn. U. Ill. at Chgo., 1994—96, asst. prof. ob-gyn., 1996—2001; assoc. prof. ob-gyn. So. Ill. U., Springfield, 2001, dir. maternal-fetal medicine, 2001, Cook County Hosp., Chgo., 2001—. Dir. perinatal ultrasound U. Ill. at Chgo., 1998—2000. Contbr. articles to profl. jours., chpts. to books. Recipient Excellence in Undergrad. Med. Edn. award, Dept. Ob-Gyn., U. Ill., Chgo., 1995—96, Golden Apple award for Excellence in Resident Edn., 1999—2000, Nat. Faculty award for Excellence in Resident Edn., Coun. on Resident Edn. in Ob-Gyn., 1995—96, 2001—02, Faculty Devel. award, Berlex Found., 1998, APGO award for Excellence in Tchg., Assn. Profs. of Gynecology and Obstetrics, 1997—98; Galloway fellow, Sloan-Kettering Cancer Ctr., 1993. Fellow: ACOG; mem.: AMA, ACP, Assn. Profs. of Ob-Gyn., Soc. Maternal Fetal Medicine, Ill. State Med. Soc., Alpha Omega Alpha (life), Chicago Medical Society. Avocations: swimming, soccer, guitar, ping pong/table tennis. Office: Cook County Hosp Dept Ob-Gyn 1835 W Harrison St Chicago IL 60612

NGUYEN, D.O. TUAN H. cosmetic surgeon, general surgeon; b. Saigon, Vietnam, Dec. 18, 1966; s. Chau H. Nguyen and Trang X. Vu; m. Thuy-Anh P. Nguyen, Mar. 14, 1994; children: Bao-Tam Nguyen, Viet-Tien Nguyen, Duc-Toan Nguyen, Maithy Nguyen. BS, Calif. State Poly. U., 1992; D in Osteopathy, U. Health Scis.-Coll. Osteo. Medicine, Kansas City, Mo., 1996. Cert. Am. Bd. Osteo. Gen. Surgery, 2002. Intern Ohio U. Coll. Osteo. Medicine-Grandview Hosp. & Med. Ctr., 1996—97; resident gen. surgery Wright State U. Sch. Medicine, Dayton, 1997—98, Weill Med. Coll. Cornell U. (Wyckoff), Bklyn., 1998—2002. V.p. Union Vietnamese Student Assns. So. Calif., 1990—92; pres. Vietnamese Student Assn., Pomona, Calif., 1988—89; commr. of student svcs. Cerritos CC, Norwalk, Calif., 1986—87. Mem.: Am. Coll. Osteo. Surgeons, Am. Osteo. Assn.

NGUYEN-DINH, THANH, internist, geriatrician, acupuncturist; b. Saigon, Vietnam; s. Bam and Chanh (Thi Duong) Nguyen-Dinh; m. Kim-Chi Nguyen-Dinh; children: Trung, Kim-Trang, Kim-Trinh, Trong. MD, Free U. Brussels, 1974; Tropical MD, Antwerp Tropical Med. Inst., 1975. Diplomate Am. Bd. Internal Medicine, Am. Bd. Geriat. Medicine, Am. Bd. Forensic Examiners, Am. Bd. Forensic Medicine, Coll. Acupuncutre and Neuromuscular Therapy, Am. Assn. Integrative Medicine. Asst. prof. medicine Howard Med. Svc., Washington, 1981—; physician dir. St. Elizabeth Unit, D.C. Gen. Hosp., Washington, 1983-94. Co-dir. Howard U. Md. Clinics, D.C. Gen. Hosp., 1990-96. Contbr. articles to profl. jours. Fellow ACP, Am. Assn. Integrative Medicine (diplomate). Avocations: chess, swimming. Office: 611 S Carlin Springs Rd Ste 211 Arlington VA 22204-1078 E-mail: tnguyendinh@netscape.net.

NI, TING, historian, educator; b. Tianjin, China, May 15, 1952; arrived in U.S., 1987; d. Shouzheng Ni and Chengyi Pan; m. Bingzhen Han, July 16, 1982; 1 child, Lily Han. BA in history, Nankai U., China, 1982, MA in history, 1984; MA in libr. sci., U. Iowa, 1997, PhD in history, 1996. Instr. Nankai U., Tianjin, China, 1985—87; asst. prof. St. Mary's U., Winona, Minn., 1997—. Guest lectr. at U.'s China, 2002. Author: The Cultural Experience of Chinese Students who Studied in the U.S. during the 1930's and 1940's, 2002; contbr. chapters to books. Mem. 80/20, Calif., 2001. Fellow, Taiwan Gt. Alliance, 2002; scholar, Fulbright Found., 1987. Mem.: Am. Historian Assn., Hist. Soc. 20 Century China, Chinese Historians in the U.S. Inc. Avocations: movies, classical music, stamp collecting/philately. Office: St Marys U of Minn 700 Terrace Heights Winona MN 55987 Home: 334 Pleasant Hill Dr Winona MN 55987 Business E-Mail: tni@smumn.edu.

NIBERT, GREGORY JAMES, lawyer; b. Roswell, N.Mex., Jan. 3, 1958; s. James M. and Elaine (LeGrand) N.; m. Carolyn Salazar, Aug. 20, 1983; children: Gregory James Jr., Jeffrey Edward. BA, U. N.Mex., 1980; JD cum laude, Pepperdine U., 1983. Bar: N.Mex. 1983, U.S. Dist. Ct. N.Mex. 1984, U.S. Ct. Appeals (10th cir.) 1984. Assoc. Hinkle, Cox, Eaton, Cofield & Hensley, Roswell, 1983-88, ptnr., 1988—. Trustee Rocky Mountain Mineral Law Found.; rsch. fellow Southwestern Legal Fedn. Editor-in-chief Pepperdine U. Law Rev., 1983; rsch. and ann. chpt. supplement author Law of Federal Oil and Gas Leases, 1985—; contbr. articles to profl. publs. Mem. Rocky Mountain Mineral Law Found.; chmn. Rep. Party of Chaves County, 2001-03. Mem. Ind. Petroleum Assn. of N. Mex. (v.p.), Rio Hondo Dist. of Conquistador Coun. Boy Scouts Am. (chmn. 1997-2003), Am. Assn. Petroleum Landmen, N.Mex. Landmen's Assn., N.Mex. Bar Assn. (bd. dirs. sect. of natural resources, energy and environ. law 1985—, chair 1990-91), Chaves County Bar Assn., Sand Divers Scuba Club, Kiwanis (bd. dirs. Roswell chpt. 1987, pres. 1993-94). Mem. Ch. of Christ. Avocations: football, basketball, skiing, scuba diving, camping. Office: Hinkle Hensely Shanor and Martin LLP PO Box 10 400 N Pennsylvania St #700 Roswell NM 88202-0010

NIBLACK, JOHN F. pharmaceutical company executive; BS, Okla. State U.; MS, PhD, U. Ill. Molecular biologist Pfizer, Inc., Groton, 1967-80, dir. rsch. drug discovery ops., 1980-86, exec. v.p. ctrl. rsch. divsn., 1986-90, pres. ctrl. rsch. divsn., 1990-93, exec. v.p. R&D, 1993-97, exec. v.p., 1997-99; vice chmn. Pfizer Inc., N.Y.C., 1999—. Office: Pfizer Inc 235 E 42d St New York NY 10017-5755

NIBLEY, ANDREW MATHEWS, editorial executive; b. Maxwell AFB, Ala., May 25, 1951; s. Owen Smoot and Frances Elizabeth (Browder) N.; m. Mary Elizabeth Michael, Nov. 24, 1984; children: Kevin Mathews, Carlyle Gower, Leath Michael. Attended, Montgomery Coll, Rockville, Md., 1970-72, Univ. Md., 1973. Legis. corr. UPI, Hartford, Conn., 1975-78, bur. chief Concord, N.H., 1979, Treasury corr. Washington, 1980, Reuters N.Am., Washington, 1980-82, editor-in-charge, 1982, news editor, 1982-85, N.Y.C., 1985-87; news editor Europe Reuters Holdings, London, 1987-89; editor, America Reuters America Inc., N.Y.C., 1989-94, sr. v.p., news and TV, 1993-94; editor, exec. v.p., bd. dirs. Reuters New Media Inc., N.Y.C., 1994-97; pres. Digest and Media Publishing Reuters Group PLC, N.Y.C., 1998-99; exec. v.p. Reuters Am. Holdings Plc.; pres. Reuters TV Am., Inc., 1998-99; pres., CEO Get Music LLC, 1999—2001; chmn., bursar Marsteller, 2003—. Mem. Knight-Bagehot editl. panel Columbia U., 1995-99; bd. dirs. Sportsline USA, Inc., iMediation SA, Kinecta Corp.; bd. advisors Red Herring Mag., Nervestruck Media, Xlantic LLC; exec. mgmt. com. Reuters Am. Holdings, Inc., 1994-99; bd. dirs. New Directions for News, Overseas Press Club Found. Mem. Gov.'s Coun. on Alcoholism and Drug Abuse, mem. media subcom., 1991-92; trustee N.J. Ctr. for Family Studies; bd. advisors Grad. Sch. Journalism U. Calif., Berkeley, 1993-98; bd. dirs. NY chpt. Leukemia and LYmphoma Soc. Am. Recipient Meritorious Service award Nat. Press Club. Mem. Am. Soc. Newspaper Editors (editl. bd. 1992-93), Overseas Press Club (program vice chmn. 1990-93, bd. govs. 1993-96, treas. 1996-2000), Fgn. Press Assn., Internat. Platform Assn., N.Y. New Media Assn., Triathlon Fedn. Am., Montclair Golf Club (Verona, N.J.), Essex Running Club, The Athletic and Swim Club (N.Y.C.). Avocations: golf, tennis, jogging, racquetball, triathlons. Home: 53 W 94th St Apt 1G New York NY 10025-7131

NIBLOCK, LEE, recreation director; Pks. and recreation dir. Marion County Pks. and Recreation, Ocala, Fla. Office: Marion County Pks Dept 8282 SE Hwy 314 Ocala FL 34470 E-mail: nibby53@aol.com., lee.niblock@marioncountyfl.org.

NIBLOCK, ROBERT, home improvement warehouse executive; Sr. v.p. fin. Lowe Co. Inc., Wikesboro, N.C., sr. v.p., CFO, 2000—01; exec. v.p., CFO Lowe's Companies Inc., Wikesboro, 2001—. Office: 1605 Curtis Bridge Rd Wilkesboro NC 28697-2246

NICASTRO, KATHLEEN WANDA, artist, educator; d. Bartholomew Joseph Nicastro and Irene Mary Ziarko. MA, SUNY at Buffalo, 1984. Creative writing instr. North York Bd. of Edn., Toronto, Canada, 1990—97; adminstrv. asst. Ryerson Poly. U., Toronto, Canada, 1997—99; asst. to the dir. of student rels. Princeton Theol. Sem., NJ, 1999—2002; sec. IV Eastman Sch. of Music, Rochester, NY, 2002—03; instr. Monroe C.C., Rochester, NY, 2002—; owner/artist Alchemist of Sand, Webster, NY, 2003—. Adminstrv. cons. Eastman Sch. of Music, Rochester, NY, 2003—. Art glass, painting, mixed media, sculpture, Exhibit: Preparing the Light; contbr. articles to profl. jours. Mem. Arts and Cultural Coun. of Rochester; ordained elder Presbyn. Ch., Toronto, Canada, 1991—99. Recipient Senate Excellence Award in Pub., Houghton Coll., 1982; scholar Grad. Student Excellence award, SUNY at Buffalo, 1983. Mem.: Christians in the Visual Arts (CIVA), Glass Art Soc., Meml. Art Gallery of the U. of Rochester. Christian. Avocations: travel, music composition, piano, horseback riding/show jumping. Home and Office: Alchemist of Sand 264 San Ron Dr Webster NY 14580 Personal E-mail: knicastro@alchemistofsand.com. E-mail: webmaster@alchemistofsand.com.

NICASTRO, TRACEY A. lawyer; b. 1969; BA, U. Ill., 1991; JD, Valparaiso U., 1994. Bar: Ill. 1994. With Sidley Austin Brown & Wood, Chgo., 1996—, ptnr., 2002—. Mem.: ABA, Chgo. Bar Assn. Office: Sidley Austin Brown and Wood Bank One Plz 10 S Dearborn St Chicago IL 60603

NICCHI, VINCENT, JR., cardiologist; b. Bklyn., Nov. 16, 1955; s. Vincent Sr. and Rosalie (Martino) N.; m. Kathleen Mary Healy, May 26, 1985; children: Kristina Rose, Lisa Marie, Michelle Kathleen, Vincent Michael. BS in Chemistry, Bklyn. Coll., 1977; MD, U. Noreste, Tampico Tamps, Mex., 1981. Diplomate Am. Bd. Internal Medicine, Am. Bd. Cardiovasc. Diseases, Am. Bd. Nuc. Cardiology. Intern Maimonides Med. Ctr., Bklyn., 1982-83, resident, 1983-85; fellow in cardiology Deborah Heart Lung Ctr., Browns Mills, N.J., 1985-87; invasive/interventional cardiologist Ariz. Heart Inst., 1987-96; founder Cardiac Care Consultants, Sun City, Ariz., 1996—; mem. staff Boswell Hosp., Sun City. Past chmn. credential com. Del Webb Hosp., Sun City West, Ariz., past mem. med. exec. com. Fellow: Am. Coll. Cardiology; mem.: AMA. Roman Catholic. Office: Cardiac Care Consultants 13188 N 103d Dr Ste 201 Sun City AZ 85351

NICCOLINI, DIANORA, photographer; b. Florence, Italy, Oct. 3, 1936; arrived in U.S., 1945, naturalized, 1960; d. George and Elaine (Augsbury) N. Student, Hunter Coll., 1955-62, Art Students League, 1960, Germain Sch. Photography, 1962; BA magna cum laude, Marymount Manhattan Coll., 1995. Med. photographer Manhattan Eye, Ear and Throat Hosp., 1963-65; organizer med. photography dept. Lenox Hill Hosp., 1965-67, 1st chief med. photographer, 1965-67; organizer, head dept. med. and audio visual edn. St. Clare's Hosp., N.Y.C., 1967-76; mem. Third Eye Gallery, N.Y.C., 1974-76; owner Dianora Niccolini Creations, 1976—. Instr. photography Camera Club N.Y., 1978-79, Germain Sch. Photography, 1978-79, N.Y. Inst. Photography, 1981-83; instr. comml. photography N.Y. Inst. Tech., 1996-97. One-woman shows include 209 Photo Gallery, Top of the Stairs Gallery, Third Eye Gallery, 1974, 75, 77, Photographics Unltd. Gallery, N.Y.C., 1981, West Broadway Gallery, N.Y.C., 1981, Camera Club N.Y., 1982, Overseas Press Club, N.Y.C., 1983, Impulse Gallery, Provincetown, Mass., 1983, Throckmorton Fine Art Gallery, N.Y.C., 1998, 2001; exhibited in group shows at Photography Over 65, N.Y.C., 1978, Jacob Javits Fed. Bldg., N.Y.C., 1992, Neikrug Gallery, N.Y.C., 1993, Ward-Nasse Gallery, N.Y.C., 1996, Internat. Salon, N.Y.C., 1996, Curcio-Spector Gallery, N.Y.C., 1996, Throckmorton Fine Art, Inc., 1997, 2001; pub. portfolios; author: Women of Vision, 1982, Men in Focus, 1983, Big Fun with Billy, 2001; editor: P.W.P. Times, 1981-82; contbr. to photog. books; designer greeting cards Flashcards, Inc., 1988-90; contbg. editor Functional Photography, 1979-80, N.Y. Photo Dist. News, 1980. Mem. Women Photographers N.Y. (founder 1974), Biol. Photog. Assn., Internat. Ctr. Photography, Am. Soc. Mag. Photographers, Am. Soc. Picture Profls., Profl. Women Photographers (pres. 1980-84). Home: 356 E 78th St New York NY 10021-2239 Personal E-mail: dianoran@aol.com.

NICCOLLS, WESLEY OLIVER, retired electronics technician; b. Star, Idaho, Jan. 17, 1918; s. Herbert Oliver Niccolls and Hazel Katherine Gillaspy; m. Doris Louise Ball, June 1, 1946; children: James Leslie, Wesley Oliver, Douglas Eldon, Jeffry Herbert, Linda Jane, Barbara Louise, John William. Student, L.A. City Coll., 1938—39, Modesto Jr. Coll., 1940—42, U.S. Navy Electronics, Treasure Island, Calif., 1943. Radio tech. U.S. Navy Reserve, PTO, 1942—45; tech. advisor electronics supply office U.S. Navy, North Chgo., Ill., 1946—51; electronics engr. tech. Diamond Ordnance Fuze Lab., Washington, 1951—70. Achievements include design of production inspection instrumentation for Smart Bomb fuze; electronic circuit in TOW anti-tank missile pitch and yaw sensing device; patents for direct current motor for space vehicles and robotics industry; neon photoconductor ring oscillator circuit; photoelectric ring oscillator circuit with voltage doubler; low and high pressure steam whistle; patents pending in field. Home: 508 S 25th St Arlington VA 22202 Fax: 703-418-1829.

NICCUM, LARRY CURT, minister, educator; s. Edward Bert and Glenda Jean Niccum; m. Deborah C. Holt, Mar. 23, 1981; children: Jonathan, Katrina. BA, Lubbock Christian U., Tex., 1985; MDiv, Abilene Christian U., Tex., 1992; PhD, U. Notre Dame, South Bend, Ind., 2000. Assoc. min. Donmoyer

Ave. Ch. of Christ, South Bend, Ind., 1994—97; asst. to editor Dead Sea Scrolls Project, South Bend, Ind., 1995—98; assoc. prof., Bible Okla. Christian U., Oklahoma City, 1997—2004; dir., adult edn. Meml. Rd. Ch. of Christ, Oklahoma City, 2000—03. Contbr. articles to profl. jours. Foster parent Christian Svcs. Okla., Oklahoma City, 1999—2004. Mellon fellow, U. St. Louis, 1998, Heckman Scholar, St. John's U., Collegeville, Minn., 1999. Mem.: North Am. Patristics Soc., Assn. for Case Study Tchg., Soc. of Biblical Lit. Office: Coll Biblical Studies Okla Christian Univ PO Box 11000 Oklahoma City OK 73136 Office Phone: 405-425-5379.

NICE, CARTER, conductor, music director; b. Jacksonville, Fla., Apr. 5, 1940; s. Clarence Carter and Elizabeth Jane (Hintermister) N.; m. Jennifer Charlotte Smith, Apr. 4, 1983; children: Danielle, Christian, Olivia. MusB, Eastman Sch. Music, 1962; MusM, Manhattan Sch. Music, 1964. Asst. condr., concert master New Orleans Philharm., 1967-79; condr., music dir. Sacramento Symphony, 1979-92; music dir., condr. Bear Valley Music Fest., 1985—. Office: 7729 Rio Barco Way Sacramento CA 95831-4458 Personal E-mail: ccniii@aol.com.

NICELY, OLZA M. (TONY), insurance company executive; b. Va., 1943; BBA, Georgia Coll. Cert. gen. ins. Ins. Inst. Am. Endorsement clk GEICO, 1961—73, asst. v.p., 1973—80; v.p. GEICO Ins. Cos., 1980—85, sr. v.p., 1985—87, exec. v.p., 1987—89, pres., 1989—, CEO, 1991—, chmn., 1993—. Trustee Geo. Mason Univ. Found. Mem.: Ins. Inst. for Hwy Safety, Property Casualty Insurers Assn. Am. Office: GEICO One Geico Plaza Washington DC 20076-0001*

NICHOL, ALICE J. state legislator; b. Denver, Feb. 6, 1939; m. Ron Nichol; 4 children. Grad. H.S. Ret. sch. sec.; beauty cons. Mary Kay; mem. Colo. Ho. of Reps., 1992-98, Colo. Senate, Dist. 24, Denver, 1998—. Active Tri-City Bd. Health, Grassroots Adams City Dem. Party. Democrat. Roman Catholic. Office: State Capitol 200 E Colfax Ave Ste 274 Denver CO 80203-1716 also: 891 E 71st Ave Denver CO 80229-6806 Fax: 303-287-7742.

NICHOL, GENE RAY, JR., dean, department chairman; b. Dallas, May 11, 1951; s. Gene R. and Dolores (Dumas) N.; m. Janet Castle, Aug. 20, 1973 (div. 1978); m. Glenn George, Nov. 25, 1984. BA in Philosophy, Okla. State U., 1973; JD, U. Texas, 1976. Bar: Alaska 1978. Assoc. Ely, Guess and Rudd, Anchorage, 1976-78; asst. prof. W.Va. U., Morgantown, 1978-80, assoc. prof., 1980-82; prof. law U. Fla., Gainesville, 1983-84; Cutler prof. law, dir. Inst. of Bill of Rights Law Coll. William and Mary, Williamsburg, W.Va., 1984-88; dean U. Colo. Law Sch., 1988-95; dean, Burton Craige prof. law U.N.C. Sch. of Law, 1999—. Host Culture Wars, KBDI T.V., Denver, 1995-96. Author: (with M. Redish) Federal Courts; columnist: Rocky Mt. News, 1999-2000, Raleigh News and Observer, 2000-04; contbr. articles to profl. jours. Posten research grantee U. W.Va., 1980, 81, 82. Mem. Nat. Lawyers Guild (coms. 1978, vice chair Colo. reapportionment commn.), Am. Law Inst., ACLU (coms. 1978—), Am. Bar Found. Fellows, Order of Coif. Roman Catholic. Avocation: back packing. Office: U N C Sch of Law 5011 Van Hecke-Wettach Hall 100 Ridge Rd Chapel Hill NC 27599

NICHOL, NORMAN J. manufacturing executive; b. East Cleveland, Ohio, Feb. 12, 1944; s. Norman George and Irene Josephine (Peters) N.; m. Janice E. Nichol, Oct. 19, 1968; children: Gerard, Katherine. BBA, Kent State U. Mktg. trainee A.B. Dick Co., Chgo., 1968, sales rep., supr.-spl. markets mgr., 1971-75, br. mgr. Indpls. and Chgo., 1975-80, dir.-gen. mgr. internat., 1980-82, pres., 1982—; pres., CEO Rycoline Products Co., Chgo., 1982—; pres. Sun Graphic Inc., Rogersol Inc. With U.S. Army, 1968-70. Home: 1021 Dover Ct Libertyville IL 60048-3509 Office: Rycoline Products Inc 5540 N Northwest Hwy Chicago IL 60630-1134 E-mail: njnsplace@aol.com, norm.nichol@rycoline.com.

NICHOLAS, ARTHUR SOTERIOS, manufacturing executive; b. Grand Rapids, Mich., Mar. 6, 1930; s. Samuel D. and Penelope A. (Kalapodes) N.; m. Bessie Zazanis, Aug. 25, 1957; children: Niki Stephanie, Arthur S., Thomas. BS in Chem. Engring, U. Mich., 1953; BA in Indsl. Mgmt, Wayne State U., 1957. Registered profl. engr., Mich. Project engr. B.F. Goodrich Co., 1953-54; plant mgr. Cadillac Plastics and Chem. Co., 1954-69; pres., chief exec. officer Leon Chem. and Plastics, Inc., Grand Rapids, 1960-69; with U.S. Industries, Inc., 1969-73, pres., chief operating officer, 1973; now pres. The Antech Group. Bd. dirs. ERO Industries, Inc. Patentee in field. Judge Jr. Achievement, Chgo. Served with USNR, 1948-49. Recipient Distinguished Alumni award Grand Rapids Jr. Coll., 1970 Mem. Young Pres. Orgn., Soc. Plastic Engrs., Mich. Acad. Sci., Arts and Letters, Chgo. Coun. on Fgn. Rels., Pres.' Assn. Mem. Greek Orthodox Ch. Clubs: Chgo. Athletic Assn. (Chgo.), Executives (Chgo.). Home: 655 Oak Rd Barrington IL 60010-3135 Office: 2300 Barrington Rd # 411 Hoffman Estates IL 60195-2082

NICHOLAS, DAVID ROBERT, minister, college president; b. L.A., May 10, 1941; s. Robert Grant and Pearl Elizabeth (Pickard) N.; m. Donna Lynn Roberts, June 28, 1969; children: Joy Lynn, Faith Elizabeth. AB, Azusa Pacific U., 1963; MS, U. So. Calif., 1967; MDiv., L.A. Bapt. Theol. Sem., 1966; ThM, Talbot Theol. Sem., 1971; ThD, Grace Theol. Seminary, 1982. Ordained to ministry Gen. Assn. Regular Bapt. Chs., 1970. Dir. admissions, mem. faculty L.A. Bapt. Coll., Newhall, Calif., 1966-71; dean, pres. Van Nuys (Calif.) Christian Coll., 1972-76; pastor Tri-Lakes Bapt. Ch., Columbia City, Ind., 1977-78; acad. dean, assoc. prof. Southwestern Coll., Phoenix, 1978-80; sr. pastor, acad. supt. Grace Bapt. Ch., Yuba City, 1980-82; sr. pastor Placerita Bapt. Ch., Newhall, 1982-84; pres., prof. theology Shasta Bible Coll., Redding, Calif., 1985—. Chmn. Greater Redding Area Christian Edn. Conv., 1988—; mem. accreditation commn. Transnat. Assn. Christian Colls. and Schs., 1994—; trustee Regular Bapt. Conf. So. Calif., 1983-85, pres., 1963-65; dir. Bapt. Youth Assn., So. Calif., 1969-71. Author: Foundations of Biblical Inerrancy, 1978, What's A Woman to Do ... In the Church?, 1979, Church Discipline: Option or Obligation, 1991, Biblical Judgments, Dictionary of Pre-Millenial Theology, 1996; contbr. articles to religious jours.; recordings include Trombone Testimonies, 1990; Bible tchr. broadcast program Truth for Today, 1988—, Bible Answer Man, 1978-80. Trustee Christian Heritage Coll., El Cajon, Calif., 1981-85; mem. steering com. Calif. Activists Network, Los Altos, Calif., 1991; del. Conf. on the Preservation of the Family, 1991; gov. Am. Coalition for Trad. Values, Washington, 1984; chaplain Los Angeles County Bd. Suprs., 1984. Recipient Svc. award Am. Legion, 1955. Mem. Evang. Theol. Soc., Creation Rsch. Soc., Shasta County Evang. Ministerial Assn. (pres. 1992-95), Kappa Tau Epsilon. Republican. Home: 8264 Taylor Ln Redding CA 96001-9530 Office: Shasta Bible Coll 2951 Goodwater Ave Redding CA 96002-1544

NICHOLAS, FREDERICK M. lawyer; b. NYC, May 30, 1920; s. Benjamin L. and Rose F. (Nechols) N.; m. Eleanore Berman, Sept. 2, 1951 (div. 1963); children: Deborah, Jan, Tony; m. Joan Fields, Jan. 2, 1983. AB, U. So. Calif., 1947; postgrad., U. Chgo., 1949-50; JD, U. So. Calif., 1952. Bar: Calif. 1952, U.S. Dist. Ct. Calif. 1952, U.S. Ct. Appeals (9th cir.) 1952. Assoc. Loeb & Loeb, L.A., 1952-56; ptnr. Swerdlow, Glikbarg & Nicholas, Beverly Hills, Calif., 1956-62; pvt. practice Beverly Hills, 1962-80; pres., atty. Hapsmith Co., Beverly Hills, 1980—. Bd. dirs. Malibu Grand Prix, L.A., 1982-90; gen. counsel Beverly Hills Realty Bd., 1971-79; founder, pres. Pub. Counsel, L.A., 1970-73. Author: Setting Up a Shopping Center, 1960, Commercial Real Property Lease Practice, 1976. Chmn. Mus. Contemporary Art, L.A., 1987—93, life trustee, 2002—; chmn. com. Walt Disney Concert Hall, L.A., 1987—95; trustee Music Ctr. Los Angeles County, 1987—95, L.A. Philharm. Assn., 1987—95, Mus. Flying, Santa Monica, Calif., 1991—2002, Frederick R. Weisman Art Found., 2003—. Frederick R. Weisman Philanthropic Found., 2003—, Pitzer Coll., 1992—95, Art Ctr. Coll. Design, 2003—; chmn. Calif. Pub. Broadcasting Commn., Sacramento, 1972—78; pres. Maple Ctr., 1977—79; co-developer Ronald Reagan Bldg., Washington, 1998; adminstr. Estate of Sam Francis, 1996—. Named Citizen of Yr. Beverly Hills Bd. Realtors, 1978, Man of Yr. Maple Ctr., 1980, Outstanding Founder in Philanthropy, Nat. Philanthropy Day Com., 1990; recipient Pub. Svc. award Coro Found., 1988, Medici award LA C. of C., 1990, Founders award Pub. Counsel, 1990, Trustees award Calif. Inst. Arts, 1993, City of Angels award LA Ctrl. Bus. Assn., Disting. Svc. award U. So. Calif. Law Sch. Class of 1952, 2002. Mem. Beverly Hills Bar Assn. (bd. govs. 1970-76, Disting. Svc. award 1974, 81, Exceptional Svc. award 1986), Beverly Hills C. of C. (Man of Yr. 1983). Home: 1001 Maybrook Dr Beverly Hills CA 90210-2715 Office: Hapsmith Co 5440 McConnell Ave Los Angeles CA 90066

NICHOLAS, HENRY THOMPSON, III, former communications engineering executive; b. 1959; BSEE, MSEE, PhD in EE, UCLA. With TRW; dir. microelectronics PairGain Techs.; pres., CEO Broadcom Corp., Irvine, Calif., 1991—2003. Named one of Top 20 Entrepreneurs, 1997 Red Herring, 1997, World's Top Cyber Elite, 1997 Time Digital Mag., 1997; recipient Engrepreneur of the Yr. award, Ernst & Young, 1996.

NICHOLAS, JAMES A. surgeon, consultant, educator; b. Portsmouth, Va., Apr. 15, 1921; s. Harry and Julie N.; m. Kiki Chris, June 14, 1952; children: Philip Duncan, Stephen James, Nicole Hambro. BA, NYU, 1942; MD, Downstate Med. Ctr., 1945. Diplomate Am. Bd. Orthop. Surgery. Resident various hosps., N.Y.C., 1946-52; asst. dir. rsch. Hosp. Spl. Surgery, N.Y.C., 1952-60; dir. dept. orthop. surgery Lenox Hill Hosp., N.Y.C., 1970—, dir. emeritus, 1995—, James A. Nicholas chair in perpetuity, 2003; founding dir. Nicholas Inst. Sports Medicine, N.Y.C., 1973—; dir. Inst. Sports Medicine & Athletic Trauma, N.Y.C., 1973-99, dir. emeritus, 1999—; dir. Gulf & Western Corp., N.Y.C., 1983-93, Paramount Comm., Inc., N.Y.C. Orthopaedic cons. NFL, N.Y.C., 1968—97; mem. Presdl. Coun. Phys. Fitness in Sports, Washington, 1979—82, cons., 1993—98; prof. orthopaedic surgery Cornell Med. Coll., N.Y.C., 1970—2001. Editor 15 books including: Injuries to the Spine and Lower Extremity in Sports Medicine, 1986, 2nd edit., 1995, the Upper Extremity in Sports Medicine, 1990, 2nd edit., 1996; patentee manual muscle tester. Trustee ctr. coun. Cornell U. Med. Ctr. N.Y. Hosp., 1986—94; trustee Am. Jour. of Sports Medicine, 1980—2002. Capt. U.S. Army, 1945—46, capt. U.S. Army, 1952—53. Recipient Frank Babbott Disting. Alumnus award, 1985, Royal Order of Phoenix, Greek Govt. Svc., 1970, David D. Moyer award Ea. Athletic Tng. Assn., 1997; named Health Am. Fitness Leader, Jaycees, 1982; Spingold Found. grantee in sports medicine, 1976—. Fellow ACS, Am. Orthop. Assn.; mem. Orthop. Rsch. Soc. (sec. treas. 1968-69), Am. Orthop. Soc. for Sports Medicine (pres. 1980, named Mr. Sports Medicine 1982, inducted into Hall of Fame, 2003), N.Y. Acad. Medicine (pres. 1974), Acad. Orthop. Soc., Greek Orthodox, Hellenic Univ. Club, Westchester Country Club. Avocations: astronomy, golf, piano, synthesizer. Home: 22 Cayuga Rd Scarsdale NY 10583-6940 Office: 130 E 77th St New York NY 10021-1851

NICHOLAS, LAWRENCE BRUCE, advisory company executive; b. Dallas, Nov. 9, 1945; s. J. W. and Helen Elouise (Whiteacre) N.; m. Virginia Pearl Farmer, Aug. 5, 1967; children: Helen Brooke, John Lawrence, Alexis Bradlee. BBA, So. Meth. U., 1968. Mem. sales staff Nicholas Machinery Co., Dallas, 1963-69; sales mgr. Indsl. and Comml. Rsch. Corp., Dallas, 1969-74; v.p. Precision Concepts Corp., Dallas, 1974-76, gen. mgr., 1976-78, pres. Addison, Tex., 1978-86, dir., 1974-86; pres. INCOR Inc., Addison, 1974-91, dir., 1972—; pres. INCOR Internat., Dallas, 1981-91. Pres., dir. Multiple Axis Machine Corp., 1981-96, Investment Svcs. Corp., 1991-93; mem. adv. bd. Consultores Patrimoniales, Mex. City, 1992—; pres. Equity Capital Interests, Inc., San Antonio, Tex., 1993—; chmn. bd. dirs. Cross Securities Internat. Corp., San Antonio, 1993-94; pres. Worldwide Exec. Aviation, 1996—. Served as officer Ordnance Corps, U.S. Army, 1968, N.G., 1968-74. Mem. NRA, Soc. Mfg. Engrs., Nat. Shooting Sports Found., Safari Club Internat.

NICHOLAS, LYNN B. medical association administrator; b. Tenn. BS in med. tech., Tenn. Wesleyan Coll.; M in mgmt., Cent. Mich. U., 1983. Bd. cert. fellow Am. Coll. Healthcare Exec. (ACHE). Med. technologist to sr. v.p. clinical and ambulatory svc. Morristown Meml. Hosp., NJ; exec. v.p., COO NJ Hosp. Assn., 1995—2000; pres., CEO La. Hosp. Assn., 2000—04; CEO Am. Diabetes Assn., 2004—. Mem. bd. gov. Am. Coll. Healthcare Exec.; chair La. Health Works Commn.; mem. La. Health Care Commn.; rep. La. hosp. Am. Hosp. Assn. Recipient Early Career Healthcare Exec. award (first recipient in NJ), Am. Coll. Healthcare Exec. Office: Am Diabetes Assn 1701 N Beauregard St Alexandria VA 22311 Office Phone: 703-549-1500., 800-342-2383. Office Fax: 703-739-9346.

NICHOLAS, LYNN HOLMAN, historian, researcher, writer; b. New London, Conn., Nov. 11, 1939; d. William Grizzard Holman and Carol (Ackiss) Wakelin; m. Robert Carter Nicholas III, Dec. 20, 1965; children: William C., R. Carter, Philip H. Student, Radcliffe Coll., 1957-59; diploma, U. Madrid, 1960; BA, Oxford (Eng.) U., 1964. Mem. adv. panel Presdl. Commn. on Holocaust Assets in the U.S., 1999. Author: The Rape of Europa, 1994 (Nat. Book Critics Circle award 1995). Decorated chevalier Légion d'Honneur (France); named Amicus Poloniae, Govt. of Poland, 2003. E-mail: lynnick105@aol.com.

NICHOLAS, NICKIE LEE, retired industrial hygienist; b. Lake Charles, La., Jan. 19, 1938; d. Clyde Lee and Jessie Mae (Lyons) N. BS, U. Houston, 1960, MS, 1966. Tchr. sci. Pasadena (Tex.) Ind. Sch. Dist., 1960-61; chemist FDA, Dallas, 1961-62, VA Hosp., Houston, 1962-66; chief biochemist Baylor U. Coll. Medicine, 1966-68; cheist NASA Johnson Spacecraft Ctr., 1968-73; analytical chemist TVA, Muscle Shoals, Ala., 1973-75; indsl. hygienist, compliance officer OSHA, Dept. Labor, Houston, 1975-79, area dir. Tulsa, 1979-82, mgr. Austin, Tex., 1982-96, ret., 1996. Faculty VA Sch. Med. Tech., Houston, 1963—66. Recipient award for outstanding achievement German Embassy, 1958, Suggestion award VA, 1968, Group Achievement award Skylab Med. Team, NASA, 1974, Personal Achievement award Dept. Labor Fed. Women's Program, 1984, Career Achievement award Federally Employed Women, Inc., 1988, Meritorious Performance award DOL-OSHA, 1990, Disting. Career Svc. award Det. Labor, 1991, Sec.'s Exceptional Achievement award Dept. Labor, 1991, Cert. Appreciation, Osha, 1991, Asst. Sec.'s Leadership award DOL-OSHA, 1992, 96. Mem. Am. Chem. Soc. (dir. analytical group Southeastern Tex. and Brazosport sects. 1971, chmn. elect 1973), Am. Assn. Clin. Chemists, Am. Conf. Govtl. Indsl. Hygienists, Am. Indsl. Hygiene Assn., Am. Soc. Safety Engrs., Am. Harp Soc., Fed. Exec. Assn. (pres. 1984-85), Order Eastern Star, Kappa Epsilon. Home: 1002 Sundance Dr Dripping Springs TX 78620-9501

NICHOLAS, PETER M. medical products executive; married; 3 children. BS, Duke U.; MS, U. Pa. Chmn., CEO Boston Sci., Natick, Mass., 1979—99, co founder, chmn. bd. dirs., 1999—. Office: Boston Sci 1 Boston Sci Pl Natick MA 01760-1537

NICHOLAS, RALPH WALLACE W. anthropologist, educator; b. Dallas, Nov. 28, 1934; s. Ralph Wendell and Ruth Elizabeth (Oury) N.; m. Marta Ruth Weinstock, June 13, 1963. BA, Wayne U., 1957; MA, U. Chgo., 1958, PhD, 1962. From asst. prof. to prof. Mich. State U., East Lansing, 1964-71; prof. anthropology U. Chgo., 1971—, chmn. dept., 1981-82, dep. provost, 1982-87, dean of coll., 1987-92, dir. Ctr. Internat. Studies, 1984-95, William Rainey Harper prof. anthropology and social scis., 1992-2000, William Rainey Harper prof. emeritus, 2000—; pres. Internat. House of Chgo., 1993-2000. Cons. Ford Found., Dhaka, Bangladesh, 1973 Author: (with others) Kinship Bengali Culture, 1977, The Fruits of Worship, 2003; editor: Jour. Asian Studies, 1975-78. V.p. Am. Inst. Indian Studies, 1974-76, treas., 1993-2001, pres.-elect 2001-02, pres. 2002—; trustee Bangladesh Found.; dir. Indo-Am. Ctr., Chgo. Ford Found. fgn. area tng. fellow, India, 1960-61; Sch. Oriental and African Studies research fellow, London, 1962-63; sr. Fulbright fellow, West Bengal, India, 1968-69 Fellow AAAS, Am. Anthrop. Assn., Royal Anthrop. Inst. (Eng.); mem. Assn. Asian Studies, India League of Am. Found. (trustee). Office: U Chgo Dept Anthropology 1126 E 59th St Chicago IL 60637-1580 also: Am Inst Indian Studies 1130 E 59th St Chicago IL 60637

NICHOLAS, RONALD WAYDE, business consultant; b. Dallas, July 29, 1938; s. J.W. Nicholas and Helen Eloise Whiteacre Duniven; m. Wanda Elaine Hagen, Aug. 27, 1960; children: Charles Wayde, Laurence Eliot. BBA, U. Tex., 1960. Dir. instnl. sales Anderson Clayton Foods, Dallas and Sherman, Tex., 1962-84; comml. dir. Anderson, Clayton S.A. de C.V., Mexico City, 1984-86; ptnr., operator 2 retail businesses, Pittsburg, Tex., 1986-87; assoc. gen. dir. Pilgrim's Pride, S.A. de C.V., Mexico City, 1987-97; bus. cons. Ray & Berndtson, Mexico City, 1997—. Cmty. advisor Jr. League of Mexico City, 1996—. Co-founder, bd. dirs. Am. Charities, A.C., Mexico City, 1996—; co-founder, chair Am. Charities Golf and Tennis Classic, 1996—; bd. mem. Tex./Mexico Bus. Coun., 2000—. Capt. U.S. Army, 1960-62. Mem. Am. C. of C. (bd. dirs. 1993-94, procedures auditor 1995-96), U.S./Mex. C. of C. (chair agr. com., bi-nat. bd., Mexico City bd. 1992—), VFW, Am. Soc. of Mex. (bd. dirs., pres.), Am. Benevolent Soc. (sec., bd. dirs., pres.), U. Tex. Ex Students Assn. (bd. dirs., v.p.), Phi Sigma Kappa (treas., pres.). Avocations: golf, stamp collecting/philately, cooking. Office: Ray & Berndtson Palo Santo 6 Col Lomas Alta Mexico City Mexico 11950 E-mail: ronwan@aol.com.

NICHOLAS, WILLIAM RICHARD, lawyer; b. Pontiac, Mich., June 19, 1934; s. Reginald and Edna Irene (Bartlett) N.; m. Diana Lee Johnson, Aug. 20, 1960; children: Susan Lee, William Richard Jr. BS in Bus., U. Idaho, 1956; JD, U. Mich., 1962. Bar: 1963. Of counsel Latham & Watkins, Los Angeles, 1962-96. Contbr. numerous articles on taxation. Lt. (j.g.) USN, 1956-59. Mem. Calif. Bar Assn., Los Angeles County Bar Assn., Am. Coll. Tax Counsel. Home: 1808 Old Ranch Rd Los Angeles CA 90049-2207 Office: Latham & Watkins 633 W 5th St Ste 4000 Los Angeles CA 90071-2005 Office Phone: 310-485-1234.

NICHOLAS, (RICHARD G. SMISKO), bishop; b. Perth Amboy, N.J., Feb. 23, 1936; s. Andrew and Anna (Totin) S. Grad., Christ the Saviour Sem., Johnstown, Pa., 1959; student, Patriarchal Theol. Acad., Istanbul, Turkey; BA, U. Youngstown, 1961; BTh, U. Pitts. Ordained priest Am. Carpatho-Russian Orthodox Greek Cath. Diocese, 1959. Pastor Sts. Peter and Paul Ch., Windber, 1959-62; prefect of discipline, tchr. Christ the Saviour Sem., Johnstown, 1963-65; pastor Sts. Peter and Paul Ch., Homer City, 1965-71, St. Michael's Ch., Clymer, 1971-72, St. Nicholas Ch., N.Y.C., 1972-78; elevated to archimandrite Am. Carpatho-Russian Orthodox Greek Cath. Diocese, 1976; abbot Monastery of Annunciation, Tuxedo Park, N.Y., 1978-82; elected titular bishop of Amissos, aux. bishop Ukrainian Orthodox Diocese of Ecumenical Patriarchate, 1983; consecrated bishop Am. Carpatho-Russian Orthodox Greek Cath. Diocese, 1985, bishop, 1985—. Asst. Christ the Saviour Cathedral, 1963-65; chmn. XIV Diocesan Coun., New Brunswick, N.J., 1985, XV Diocesan Coun., Pitts., 1991, elevated to Met., 1998. Russian Orthodox. Office: 312 Garfield St Johnstown PA 15906-2122

NICHOLLS, PETER J. academic administrator; BS in Math., London U., 1967; PhD in Math., Cambridge (Eng.) U., 1970. Prof. math. scis. No. Ill. U., 1971—91, acting dean Coll. Liberal Arts and Scis., 1988—89, assoc. dean Coll. Liberal Arts and Scis., 1987—88, 1989—91; dean Coll. Arts and Scis. Kans. State U., 1991—2002, prof. math., 1991—2002; provost, acad. v.p. Colo. State U., Ft. Collins, 2002—. Office: Office of the Provost 108 Administration Colo State Univ Fort Collins CO 80523-1001*

NICHOLLS, RICHARD AURELIUS, obstetrician, gynecologist; b. Norfolk, Va., Aug. 12, 1941; s. Richard Beddoe and Aurelia (Gill) N.; m. Geri Bowden, Feb. 24, 1986. BS in Biology, Stetson U., 1963; MD, Med. Coll. Va., 1967. Diplomate Am. Bd. Ob-Gyn. Intern, Charity Hosp., Tulane div., New Orleans, 1967-68, resident in ob-gyn, 1968-71; asst. prof. ob-gyn Tulane Med. Sch., New Orleans, 1973-74, clin. asst. prof., 1974-83; practice medicine specializing in ob-gyn, Pascagoula, Miss., 1974-89; pvt. practice medicine, Ocean Spring, Miss., 1989—; mem. staff Singing River Hosp., chmn. surg. and ob-gyn depts., 1979-80, chmn. Ob-Gyn Dept., 1984, mem. staff Ocean Springs Hosp., laser com., pharmacy com., and theraputics com., chmn. OB-Gyn dept., mem. exec. bd., 1990-91; sec., treas. staff Ocean Springs Hosp., 1991-92, exec. bd., 1991-92, chief of staff elect, 1992-93, chief of staff, 1993-94; bd. dirs. Singing River Hosp. System, 1993-94. Bd. dirs. Miss. Racing Assn. Maj. US. Army, 1971-73. Fellow Am. Coll. Ob-Gyn, ACS; mem. Miss. State Med. Soc., Singing River Med. Soc., Am. Fertility Soc., Am. Assn. Gynecol. Laparoscopists, Am. Med. Soc., So. Med. Soc., New Orleans Grad. Med. Assembly, New Orleans Ob-Gyn Soc., Gulf Coast Ob-Gyn Soc., Conrad Collins Ob-Gyn Soc., Am. Venereal Disease Soc., Am. Cancer Soc. (bd. dirs Jackson County Br.). Contbr. articles to med. jours.

NICHOLLS, RICHARD H. lawyer; b. Toronto, Ont., Can., Oct. 27, 1938; s. Richard S. and Roberta T. Nicholls; m. Judy Carter, Apr. 15, 1963; children: Christopher T., Jamie C.; m. Anne Delaney, June 10, 1978. BA cum laude, Amherst Coll., 1960; LLB, Stamford U., 1963; LLM, NYU, 1964. Bar: Calif. 1964, N.Y. 1965, D.C. Assoc. Mudge Rose Guthrie, Alexander & Ferdon and predecessor, N.Y.C., 1964-70, ptnr., 1971-94; of counsel Orrick, Herrington & Sutcliffe, N.Y., 1995—. Mem. ABA, N.Y. State Bar Assn., Nat. Assn. Bond Lawyers, Stamford Yacht Club. Home: 159 Ocean Dr W Stamford CT 06902-8004 Office: Orrick Herrington & Sutcliffe 666 5th Ave New York NY 10103-1798 E-mail: rnicholls@orrick.com.

NICHOLLS, ROBERT LEE, civil engineer, educator; b. Lincoln, Nebr., June 11, 1929; s. Carrol C. and Claire (McDermet) N.; m. Ruth Ann Allen, Aug. 30, 1958; children: David, Jonathan, Carol. BSCE with high honors, U. Colo., 1951; MSCE, Iowa State U., 1952, PhD, 1957. Registered profl. engr., Del., Pa., Iowa, Md. Design engr., constrn. supr. U.S. Army Corps Engrs., Japan, Korea, 1953-55; chief materials engr. and hwy. design engr. Gannett & Fleming, Harrisburg, Pa., 1957-59; prof. civil engring. U. Del., Newark, 1959-93. Geotech. engring. and constrn. materials cons. DuPont, Hercules, Thiokol, others. Author: Composite Construction Materials, 1976; co-author: Civil Engineering Systems, 1972 (also Polish and Spanish edits.); author, editor: ASCE Structural Plastics Selection Manual, 1984; also articles; 7 patents in field. Dist. advance chmn. Boy Scouts Am.; vol. cons. concrete products plants Internat. Exec. Svc. Corp., 1993—, cons. airfield and hanger designs, Engring. Ministries Iternat., 1993—. Fellow (life) ASCE (pres. Del. sect. 1974-75, recipient nat. citation for sect. activities 1975), Ops. Rsch. Soc. Am., Internat. Soc. Soil Mechanics, Transp. Rsch. Bd., Am. Concrete Inst. E-mail: 04605@udel.edu.

NICHOLLS, STEPHEN CHARLES, surgeon, educator; b. New Zealand, Oct. 8, 1950; came to U.S., 1976; BS, U. Auckland, New Zealand, MD, 1975. Diplomate Am. Bd. Surgery, Am. Bd. Vascular Surgery. Intern Auckland Pub. Hosp., 1975; resident in surgery Albert Einstein Med. Ctr., N.Y.C., 1976-77, Mt. Sinai Hosp., N.Y.C., 1979-83, fellow vascular surgery, 1985-86; fellow clin. rsch. U. Wash., Seattle, 1983-85, surgeon, 1986—; chief vascular surgery, dir. vascular lab. Harborview Med. Ctr., Seattle; assoc. prof. U. Wash., Seattle, 1986—. Fellow AHA Stroke Coun., Wellcare Networks, Soc. VAscular Surgery (disting.), Internat. Soc. Cardiovascular Surgery (disting.). Home: 726 12th Ave E Seattle WA 98102-4622 Office: U Wash Dept Surgery 359796 325 9th Ave Seattle WA 98104-2499 Business E-Mail: stevenic@u.washington.edu.

NICHOLS, ALBERT L. economic consultant; b. Poughkeepsie, N.Y., Feb. 13, 1951; s. Albert and Margaret (Schaefer) N.; m. Eve Kaufman, June 16, 1973; children: Matthew, Elizabeth. AB, Stanford U., 1973; M of Pub. Policy, Harvard U., 1975, PhD, 1981. Assoc. prof. Harvard U., Cambridge, Mass., 1977-83, 85-88, dir. adminstrv. planning, 1988-89; dir. econ. analysis EPA, Washington, 1983-85; v.p. Nat. Econ. Rsch. Assocs., Cambridge, 1989—2004; prin. LECG, LLC, Cambridge, 2004—. Author: Targeting Economic Incentives for Environmental Protection, 1984; contbr. numerous articles to profl. jours. Nat. Merit scholar, 1969. Mem. ABA, AAAS, Am. Econ. Assn., Phi Beta Kappa. Avocation: woodworking. Home: 14 Baskin Rd Lexington MA 02421-6929 Office: 200 Clarendon St Boston MA 02116-5021 Office Phone: 617-761-0152. E-mail: anichols@lecg.com.

NICHOLS, ALBERT MYRON, retired minister; b. Creston, Iowa, Oct. 17, 1914; s. Albert Maurice and Lou (Myers) N.; m. Phyllis Cochran, June 28, 1939; children: Byron Albert, Phillip Garrett. AB, UCLA, 1936; BS, San Francisco Theol. Sem., 1940; DD, Occidental Coll., 1952. Ordained to ministry United Presbyn. Ch. in U.S.A., 1940. Pastor chs., North Hollywood, Calif., 1940-43; assoc. pastor Pasadena (Calif.) Presbyn. Ch., 1943-57; pastor 1st Presbyn. Ch., Pendleton, Oreg., 1957-82, ret., 1982. Chmn. gen. assembly

com. on responsible marriage and parenthood United Presbyn. Ch. in U.S.A., 1959-62, mem. Bd. Christian Edn., 1969-72; mem. 1st coun. Synod of Pacific; moderator Oreg. Synod, 1968, 69; stated clk. Ea. Oreg. Presbytery, 1975-99. Pres. Pasadena Child Guidance Clinic, 1955-57, Glen Eddy Residents Assn., 2004; trustee San Francisco Theol. Sem., 1963-84; life trustee Lewis and Clark Coll., Portland, Oreg.; active Pendleton City Recreation Commn., 1965-2001; founding bd. dirs. Presbyn. Intercommunity Hosp., Whittier, Calif.; active State of Oreg. Health Coun., 1985-88, State Trauma Adv. Bd., 1987-91; chmn. City of Pendleton Capital Improvements Commn., 1983-2001. Named 1st Citizen of Pendleton, 1984. Home: 114 Glen Eddy Dr Niskayuna NY 12309

NICHOLS, ANTHONY A., SR., trust company executive; Chmn. Brandywine Realty Trust, Newtown Square, Pa., 1996—. Office: Brandywine REalty Trust 401 Plymouth Rd #500 Plymouth Meeting PA 19462-1645

NICHOLS, AVIS B. state legislator; b. Waterbury, Vt. married; 3 children. Student, Burdett Bus. Coll., U. N.H. Mem. dist. 2 N.H. Ho. of Reps.; fin. com., adminstrv. rules com.; tchr. Burdett Bus. Coll.; pvt. sec. Mem. Merrimack County Rep. com. and exec. com., Rep. state com., state boiler adv. coun., Kearsarge Regional Sch. Bd., 1976-89, Warner budget com., 1977-83; co-chair Warner br. ARC, 1972-82, dir. swimming program; former marshal and fin. chair Rebekah Assembly N.H.; mem. Girl Scouts U.S. Mem. Welcome Rebekah Lodge (former noble grand). Avocations: painting, photography. Home: PO Box 306 Main St Warner NH 03278 Office: NH Ho of Reps State House Concord NH 03301

NICHOLS, BRENDA SUE, nursing educator; b. Henderson, Ky., Dec. 6, 1950; d. Marvin Elam and Cleona Jane (Bentley) Ashby; m. Harry David Nichols, Nov. 13, 1967; children: David Allen, Christopher Lynn, Thomas Andrew. AS in Nursing, U. Evansville, 1972, BSN, 1976, MA, 1978; DSc in Nursing, Ind. U., 1983. Staff nurse Community Meth. Hosp., Henderson, 1972-76, 81, 83; sch. nurse Evansville (Ind.)-Vandeburg Sch. Corp., 1977-78; nursing instr. Ky. Wesleyan Coll., Owensboro, 1978; asst. prof. U. Evansville, Ind., 1978-84; assoc. prof., dir. rsch. U. So. Miss., Hattiesburg, 1984-87; prof. nursing, dean sch. health sci. U. New Eng., N.Rivers, Lismore, Australia, 1987-90; assoc. prof., chair sch. nursing Old Dominion U., Norfolk, Va., 1990-97, prof., 1997—. Bd. dirs. Norfolk Neighborhood Clinic, pres., 1997-98; statis. cons. Dr. James Crumbaugh and R. Henrion, Biloxi, Miss., 1984-85; cons. Gold Coast Coll., Queensland, Australia, 1988-89, Mitchell Coll., Bathurst, Australia, 1988, Children's Hosp. of the Kings Daus., 1990-94; WHO cons. to U. Indonesia, 1995; cons. distance edn. Dept. Def., VA, Uniformed Svcs. U. Health Sci., 1995—; mem. peer evaln. bd. Coun. Baccalaureate and Higher Degrees Nat. League Nursing Accredition Commn., 1996-98. Author: Nursing Theories, 1989; contbr. chpts. to book, articles to profl. jours.; NCLEX item writer, 1993—. Vol. Am. Cancer Soc., 1983—, Drug and Alcohol Prevention, Virginia Beach, Va., 1990-92. Fellow Am. Pain Soc., Royal Coll. Nursing; mem. ANA, Nat. League for Nursing (program evaluator 1991—), Va. Assn. Colls. Nursing (sec. 1991), Va. League for Nursing (bd. dirs. 1996—), Am. Assn. Colls. Nursing (bd. dirs. 2000—). Democrat. Episcopalian. Avocations: swimming, crafts, reading. Office: Old Dominion U Sch Nursing Norfolk VA 23529-0500 Home: 5315 Greenbriar Ln Beaumont TX 77706-7348

NICHOLS, BUFORD LEE, JR., pediatrician, physiologist; b. Ft. Worth, Dec. 12, 1931; married; 3 children. BA, Baylor U., 1955, MS, 1958; MD, Yale U., 1960. Diplomate Am. Bd. Pediatrics, Am. Bd. Nutrition. Instr. pediatrics Baylor U. Coll. Medicine, Houston, 1956-57, instr. physiology and pediatrics, 1964-66, from asst. prof. to assoc. prof. pediatrics, 1966-67, instr. physiology, 1967-74, chief sect. nutrition and gastroenterology, dept. Pediatrics, 1970-78, assoc. prof. community medicine, 1975—, prof. physiology and pediatrics, 1977—, head sect. nutrition and physiology, 1979-92; intern in pediatrics Yale-New Haven Med. Ctr., 1960-61, chief resident in pediatrics, 1963-64; resident in pediatrics Johns Hopkins Hosp., 1961-63; instr. pediatrics Yale U. Sch. Medicine, 1963-64; dir. USDA Children's Nutritional Rsch. Ctr., Houston, 1979-92. Recipient award Bristol-Myers, 1984. Mem. Am. Acad. Pediatrics, Am. Soc. Clin. Nutrition, Am. Coll. Nutrition (v.p. 1975-76, pres. 1977-79). Achievements include research in environmental effects upon growth and development in the infant especially alterations in body composition and muscle physiology in malnutrition, chronic diarrhea and malnutrition; cloned and sequenced intestinal maltase-glucoamylase gene. Office: Baylor Coll Medicine Childrens Nutrition Rsch Ctr 1100 Bates Ave Houston TX 77030-2600 E-mail: bnichols@bcm.tmc.edu., blnir@aol.com.

NICHOLS, C. WALTER, III, retired trust company executive; b. N.Y.C., Aug. 25, 1937; s. Charles Walter and Marjorie (Jones) N.; m. Anne Sharp, Aug. 8, 1959 (dec. Nov. 1996); children: Blair, Sandra, Walter, Hope; m. Helga Faulenbach, Aug. 24, 2002. V.p. Citibank, N.Y.C., 1962-78, J.P. Morgan & Co., N.Y.C., 1979-93; 1st v.p. Republic Nat. Bank N.Y., N.Y.C., 1994. Bd. dirs. Nichols Found., Inc., 1959—, Greenwich House, 1969-94, Westport River Watershed Alliance, 2004—; trustee Choate Rosemary Hall, 1972-77, 82-89, Westover Sch., 1979-81, ea. N.Y. chpt. Nature Conservancy, 1978-87; Caramoor Music Festival, 1980-90, John Jay Homestead, 1980-2000, Nat. Audubon Soc., 1983-87; mem. adv. bd. Wildlife Conservation Soc. (Bronx Zoo), 1987-94. Served to 1st lt. U.S. Army, 1960-62. Decorated Army Commendation medal. Mem. Naturist Soc., Nat. Assn. Railroad Passengers (bd. dirs. 1996-98), Am. Assn. for Nude Recreation, Yale (N.Y.C.) Club. Home: 1 Bent Oak Run Westport MA 02790-5179

NICHOLS, CARL MICHAEL, venture capital executive; b. Springfield, Mass., Sept. 19, 1961; BS, Brown U., 1983; MBA, Harvard U., 1987. Mgr. Aarhus Olrefabrik, Aarhus, Denmark, 1983; project mgr. Booz Allen & Hamilton, San Francisco, 1983-85, 87-91; mgr. AT&T Internat., Morristown, N.J., 1986; v.p. strategic bus. mgmt. Scrivner Inc., Oklahoma City, 1991-94; asst. v.p. Pacific Telesis, San Francisco, 1994-96; COO Internet Fin. Network Corp., 1996-97; v.p. bus. devel. Net Channel, Inc., 1996-97; COO Epicentric Inc., 1998-99; mng. ptnr. Outlook Ventures, 1996—. Editor: Technology in Business, 1983 (award 1984). Cons. Jr. Achievement, Edmond, Okla., 1991-93; vol. Okla. Sch. Sci. and Math., Oklahoma City, 1992-94; bd. dirs. San Francisco Edn. Fund, 1996-97. Mem. Sigma Xi. Avocations: tennis, skiing, sailing.

NICHOLS, CARL WHEELER, retired advertising agency executive; b. Ottawa, Kans., Oct. 9, 1923; s. Carl Wheeler and Cora Merle (Hanks) N.; children: Christine, Carl Wheeler, Nancy, Matthew; m. Anna Norris, Apr. 18, 1992. Student, Baker U., 1940-41, U. Mo., 1941-43; BA, U. Mich., 1944. Research analyst Cunningham & Walsh, Inc. (advt. agy.), N.Y.C., 1946-49, copywriter, 1949-58, co-creative dir., v.p., 1958-59, dir. account mgmt., 1959-61, pres., 1961-69, chmn., chief exec. officer, 1969-85, chmn. emeritus, 1986. Trustee Vero Beach Mus. Art, 1996, chmn. bd. trustees, 2002—03. Capt. USMCR, 1943-46, 50-52, Korea. Named to Advt. Hall of Fame, 1986. Mem. N.Y. Advt. Coun. (bd. dirs. 1974-85), Am. Advt. Fedn. (dir. 1972—, chmn. 1975-76), Advt. Ednl. Found. (bd. dirs., sec., treas. 1983-91), Birchwood Farms Golf Club, John's Island Club, Sigma Xi. Presbyterian (elder). Home: 241 Island Creek Dr Vero Beach FL 32963-3304

NICHOLS, CLYDE RICHARD, minister, consumer products company executive; b. N.Y.C., Apr. 15, 1945; s. William and Novella Nichols; m. Marsha A. Wade, Oct. 11, 1986; children: Forest, Marvin, Anthony, Gerald. BS, Met. State Coll., Denver, 1985; ThD, Berean Bible Coll., Dallas, 1994. Ordained pastor and bishop Fellowship of Deliverance Chs., Inc. Correction officer City and County Denver, 1981-92; sr. pastor Redeeming Love Ch., Denver; sr. dir. M&C Enterprises, Inc., Denver. Dir. membership Greater Metro Denver Ministers Alliance Orgn., Denver, 1997-99. Bd. dirs. Denver Opportunities for Outreach and Reflection (D.O.O.R.), 2000—. Recipient award for outstanding cmty. work Cheyenne (Wyo.) br. NAACP, 1982, award for outstanding cmty. activities 24th Syl Morgan Acad. Arts, Denver, 1992, Juanita Gray award. Avocations: travel, reading, computers. Home and Office: PO Box 31092 Aurora CO 80041-0092 Business E-Mail: mcenterpr31092@aol.com. E-mail: rev98crn@aol.com.

NICHOLS, DAVID GREGORY, anesthesiologist, pediatrician, educator; b. Hampton, Va., Oct. 1, 1951; MD, Mt. Sinai Sch. Medicine, 1977. Diplomate Am. Bd. Anesthesiology, Am. Bd. Pediatrics, Am. Bd. Critical Care Medicine. Intern Children's Hosp., Phila., 1977-78, resident in pediatrics, 1978-80; resident in anesthesiology U. Pa. Hosp., Phila., 1981-83; fellow in anesthesiology Critical Care Children's Hosp., Phila., 1983; assoc. prof. anesthesiology, critical care & pediatric medicine Johns Hopkins U. Sch. Medicine, Balt., 1991—98, prof. anesthesiology, critical care & pediatric medicine, 1998—, vice dean edn., 2000—. Dir. Pediat. ICU, Johns Hopkins U. Hosp., Balt., 1991-97, Pediat. Anesthesiology and Critical Care Medicine, 1997—. Mem. Am. Soc. Anesthesiology, Soc. for Pediat. Rsch., Soc. Critical Care Medicine, Am. Thoracic Soc. Office: Johns Hopkins U Hosp Anesthesiology/Critical Car 600 N Wolfe St Baltimore MD 21287-0005

NICHOLS, DAVID L. retail executive; b. Toledo, Sept. 1, 1941; s. Lee Roy and Marianne (smith) N.; children: Fredericka, JoLynn, Jennifer, Laurie, Martha, Meredith; m. Lenore Grotke Nichols, Sept. 15, 1990. BA in Bus., U. Toledo, 1990. With The McAlpin Co., Cin., 1963-76; store mgr. McAlpin's Northgate, Cin., 1976-78; gen. mdse. mgr. Mercantile Stores Co., Inc., N.Y.C., 1978-82, v.p., CFO, treas., 1989-91, exec. v.p., CFO, treas., 1991-92, chmn., CEO, 1992-98; pres. Lion Store, Toledo, 1982-89, chmn., CEO, 1989; chmn. Flooring Am., Kennesaw, Ga., 2000—. Bd. dirs. Andersons, Inc., Fed. Res. Bank Cleve., Value City Dept Stores Active Cin. Bus. Com., 1992. Recipient Green Thumb award Am. Apparel Mfr. Assn., 1993. Avocations: golf, gourmet cooking.

NICHOLS, DEBRA, bank executive; Sr. v.p. and dir. women's fin. adv. svcs. Wachovia Bank, Charlotte, NC, 1997—. Office: Wachovia Corp 301 South College St Charlotte NC 28288-0570

NICHOLS, DONALD ARTHUR, economist, educator; b. Madison, Conn., Dec. 20, 1940; s. Edward Charles and Ruth (Nilson) Nichols; m. Linda Powley, Aug. 19, 1962 (dec. Oct. 1982); children: Charles Spencer, Elizabeth Clarke; m. Barbara Jakubowski Noel, May 22, 1983 (dec. Dec. 26, 2000); m. Jane Bartels, Sept. 26, 2001. BA, Yale U., 1962, MA, 1963, PhD, 1968. Mem. faculty dept. econs. U. Wis., Madison, 1966—, prof., 1977—, chmn. dept. econs., 1983-86, 88-90, mem. exec. com. faculty senate, 1987-90, chmn., 1989-90, dir. Robert M. LaFollette Sch. Pub. Affairs, 2002—, Wis. Idea fellow, 2004—; lectr. Yale U., 1970—71; sr. economist Senate Budget Com., Washington, 1975—76; dep. asst. sec. for econ. policy and rsch. Dept. Labor, Washington, 1977-79; dir. Ctr. for Rsch. on Wis. Economy. Econ. advisor to gov. State of Wis., 1983—86; exec. sec. Gov.'s Coun. Econ. Advisors, 1983—86; mem. Gov.'s Export Strategy Commn., 1994—95, Gov.'s Econ. Growth Coun., 2003—; mem. acad. adv. coun. Fed. Res. Bank of Chgo., 2004—; bd. dirs. Thompson, Plumb Funds, 1987—, Sustainable Woods Co-operative, 2001—03; dir. Ctr. for World Affairs and Global Economy, 1995—2000; affiliate Christensen Assocs., Madison, 1999—; cons. in field. Author: (with Clark Reynolds) Principles of Economics, 1970, Dollars and Sense, 1994; contbr. articles to profl. jours. Trustee U. Wis. Bookstore, 1990-95; bd. advisors Am. Players Theatre, Spring Green, Wis., 1993-2001, Taliesin Coun., 2001—. NSF fellow, 1963-66, 70-72; Nat. Commn. Employment Policy rsch. grantee, 1980-82; recipient William H. Kiekhofer Meml. Teaching prize U. Wis., 1973 Mem. Am. Econ. Assn., Econometric Soc., Royal Econ. Soc. Office: U Wis 1225 Observatory Dr Madison WI 53706

NICHOLS, DONNA MARDELL, nurse anesthetist; b. Mpls., Mar. 24, 1936; d. Donald Burma and Lucille Elvera Nichols. Diploma, Northwestern Hosp. Sch. Nursing, Mpls., 1957, Mpls. Sch. Anesthesia, 1959; BS in Nurse Anesthesia, U. Minn., 1977. RN Minn., 1957. Nurse anesthetist Hennepin County Med. Ctr., Mpls., 1959—60, Eden Twp. Hosp., Castro Valley, Calif., 1960—63, Bethesda Hosp., St. Paul, 1963—64, Meml. Bapt. Hosp., Houston, 1964—67, St. Joseph's Hosp., St. Paul, 1967—95; ret., 1995. Mem.: Minn. Assn. Nurse Anesthetists (bd. dirs. 1975—77), Am. Assn. Nurse Anesthetists (emeritus, cert. anesthetists). Avocations: golf, gardening, antiques. Home: 10427 Upton Ave S Bloomington MN 55431

NICHOLS, EDIE DIANE, executive recruiter; b. Grahamstown, Eastern Cape Province, Republic of South Africa, Mar. 28, 1939; arrived in U.S., 1963; d. Cyril Doughtry and Dorothy Ethel (Nottingham) Tyson; m. John F. Nichols, Dec. 16, 1962 (div. Dec. 1978); 1 child, Ian Tyson. Adminstrv. asst. Am. Acad. Medicine, N.Y.C., 1963-64, Jack Lenor Larsen, Inc., N.Y.C., 1964-70; v.p. John Scott Fones, Inc., N.Y.C., 1971-76, Howard J. Rubenstein Assocs. Inc., N.Y.C., 1976-80; dir. comm. Carl Byoir & Assocs., N.Y.C., 1981-83; account supr. Hill and Knowlton, N.Y.C., 1983-85; broker Cross & Brown Co., N.Y.C., 1986-88; v.p. Marc Nichols Assocs., Inc., N.Y.C., 1989-95; mng. ptnr. Nichols Brown Internat., N.Y.C., 1995—. Trustee Ctrl. Pk. Hist. Soc., N.Y.C., 1978-80. Mem. NOW, Internat. Assn. Corp. and Profl. Recruitment, N.Y. Women in Comm. (pub. rels. chair 1980-81, v.p., programs bd. dirs. 1985-87), Fin. Women's Assn. of N.Y. (bd. dirs. 1997-98), City Club of N.Y. (trustee, v.p., fin. and devel. 1987-89). Democrat. Episcopalian. Office: Nichols Brown Internat 155 W 20th St 2J New York NY 10011-3612 Home: 16 Stuyvesant Oval Apt 10F New York NY 10009

NICHOLS, ELIZABETH GRACE, nursing educator, dean; b. Feb. 1, 1943; d. Terence and Eleanor Denny (Payne) Quilliam; m. Gerald Ray Nichols, Nov. 20, 1965; children: Tina Lynn, Jeffrey David. BSN, San Francisco State U., 1969; MS, U. Calif., San Francisco, 1970, D of Nursing Sci., 1974; MA, Idaho State U., 1989. Staff nurse Peninsula Hosp., Burlingame, Calif., 1966-72; asst. prof. U. Calif.-San Francisco Sch. Nursing, 1974-82; chmn. dept. nursing Idaho State U., Pocatello, 1982-85; assoc. dean Coll. Health Scis. Sch. Nursing U. Wyo., Laramie, 1985-91, asst. to pres. for program revs., 1991-95; dean Coll. Nursing U. N.D., 1995—2004, Mont. State U., Bozeman, 2004—. Cons. U. Rochester, NY, 1979, Carroll Coll., Mont., 1980, divsn. Nursing Dept. HHS, Washington, U. Maine, Ft. Kent, 1992, Stanford Hosp. Nursing Svc., Calif., 1981—82, Ea. N.Mex. U., 1988, Met. State U., Minn., 1998, U. Nev.-Reno, 2003; cons. evaluator Higher Learning Commn., 1993—2004; site visitor CCNE, 1998—; mem. accreditation review com. The Higher Learning Commn., 2001—04. Contbr. articles to profl. jours. Mem. adv. bd. dir. Ombudsman Svc. of Contra Costa Calif., 1979—82, U. Calif. Home Care Svc., San Francisco, 1975—82, Free Clin. of Pocatello, 1984; mem. bd. of rev. coun. baccalaureate & higher degree programs, 1990—92. Fellow ACE, U. Maine Sys., 1990—91. Fellow: Am. Acad. Nursing, Gerontol. Soc. Am. (chmn. clin. medicine sect. 1987, sec. 1990—93); mem.: ANA, Western Inst. Nursing (chmn. 1990—92, bd. govs., bd. dir. mid-west alliance), Idaho Nurses Assn. (dist. 51 adv. bd. dir. 1982—84), ND Nurses Assn. (pres. 2003—04), Oakland Ski Club. (1st v.p. 1981—82), Sigma Theta Tau. Office Phone: 406-994-3784. Business E-Mail: egnichols@montana.edu.

NICHOLS, ELIZABETH LITTERER, real estate developer; b. Nashville, Sept. 24, 1953; d. William and Jean (Gray) Litterer; m. J. Donald Nichols, Dec. 7, 1985; 1 child, Mary Britt. BS, U. Tenn. Mgmt. trainee First Am. Nat. Bank, Nashville, 1975-76; mortgage loan officer Dobson's Johnson, Nashville, 1976-81; v.p. fin. JDN Ent., Nashville/Atlanta, 1981-89; pres. JDN Realty Corp., 1989—. Treas. bd. Cumberland Mus. of Sci. Ctr.; bd. dirs., exec. com. Nashville Ballet; bd. dirs. Tenn. Repertory Theatre, Mercedes Benz of Nashville; chmn. Swan Ball Auction Com.; active Jr. League of Nashville. Mem. Internat. Coun. Shopping Ctrs. Republican. Episcopalian. Avocations: skiing, tennis, reading, swimming. Home: 416 Jackson Blvd Nashville TN 37205-3426 Office: JDN Realty Corp Ste 400 359 E Paces Ferry Rd NE Atlanta GA 30305-2373

NICHOLS, EUGENE DOUGLAS, mathematics professor; b. Rovno, Poland, Feb. 6, 1923; came to U.S., 1946, naturalized, 1951; s. Alex and Anna (Radchuk) Nichiporuk; m. Alice Bissell, Mar. 31, 1951. BS, U. Chgo., 1949, postgrad., 1949-51; MEd, U. Ill., 1953, MA, 1954, PhD, 1956. Instr. math. Roberts Wesleyan Coll., North Chili, N.Y., 1950-51, U. Ill., 1951-56; assoc. prof. math. edn. Fla. State U., 1956-61, prof., head dept., 1961-73; dir. Project for Mathematical Devel. of Children, 1973-77; dir. math program NSF, 1958-61; dir. Math. Inst. Elem. Tchrs., 1961-70; pres. Nichols Schwartz Pub., 1992—; prof. math. edn. Fla. State U., 1974-90. Chmn. U. Ill. Com. on Sch. Math., 1954-55; cons. editor math McGraw-Hill Book Co., summer 1956 Co-author: Modern Elementary Algebra, 1961, Introduction to Sets, 1962, Arithmetic of Directed Numbers, 1962, Introduction to Equations and Inequalities, 1963, Introduction to Coordinate Geometry, 1963, Introduction to Exponents, 1964, Understanding Arithmetic, 1965, Elementary Mathematics Patterns and Structure, 1966, Algebra, 1966, Modern Geometry, 1968, Modern Trigonometry, 1968, Modern Intermediate Algebra, 1969, Analytic Geometry, 1973, Holt Algebra 1, 1974, 78, 82, 86, 92, Holt Algebra 2, 1974, 78, 82, 86, 92, Holt Geometry, 1974, 78, 82, 86, Holt School Mathematics, 1974, 78, 81, Holt Pre-Algebra Mathematics, 1980, 86, Holt Mathematics, 1981, 85, Elementary School Mathematics and How to Teach It, 1982, Geometry, 1991, Holt Pre-Algebra, 1992, Mathematics Dictionary and Handbook, 1993, 95, 98, 99; author: Pre-Algebra Mathematics, 1970, Introductory Algebra for College Students, 1971, Mathematics for the Elementary School Teacher, 1971, College Mathematics, 1975, College Mathematics for General Education, rev. edit., 1975. Named Fla. State U. Disting. Prof., 1968-69; recipient Disting. Alumni award U. Ill. Coll. Edn., 1970. Mem. Am. Math. Soc., Math. Assn. Am., Sch. Sci. and Math. Assn., Nat. Coun. Tchrs. Math., Coun. Basic Edn., Text and Acad. Authors Assn., Pi Mu Epsilon, Phi Delta Kappa. Home: 3386 W Lakeshore Dr Tallahassee FL 32312-1305 Office Phone: 570-253-9362. Personal E-mail: eunichols@aol.com. *Do not look for a career--look for opportunities to do kind things for others. Be honest with yourself and with those around you.*

NICHOLS, GRACE A. retail executive; b. 1946; married; 2 children. Degree, UCLA. With Weinstock's, Sacramento, 1971—78; mgr. gen. merchandise The Broadway, Calif., 1978—86; v.p., mgr. gen. merchandise Victoria's Secret Stores, 1986—88, exec. v.p., mgr. gen. merchandise, 1989—91, pres., CEO, 1991—. Office: Victorias Secret Stores Inc Four Ltd Pkwy Reynoldsburg OH 43068

NICHOLS, GREGORY A. mathematician, educator; b. Walnut Ridge, Ark., Apr. 24, 1971; s. Fred Wilbur Nichols and Judith Nanna Hazlewood; m. Melissa Ann Hill, July 13, 1974; children: Samantha Kate, Isaac Dana. BBA, U. of Okla., 1993; tchr. cert., Southwestern Okla. State U., 1995; MS, Emporia State U., 1999. Cert. secondary edn. Okla. State Bd. of Edn., Kans. State Bd. of Edn. Tchr. Ness City (Kans.) Schs., 1995—96, El Dorado (Kans.) Schs., 1996—98; grad. asst. Emporia (Kans.) State U., 1998—99; instr. of math. Cowley Coll., Arkansas City, Kans., 1999—. Adj. instr. Butler County C.C., El Dorado, 1997—99. Youth leader 1st United Meth. Ch., Arkansas City, 2000. Mem.: Math. Assn. of Am. Avocations: woodworking, remodeling. Office: Cowley Coll 125 S Second Arkansas City KS 67005 Personal E-mail: nichols@cowley.edu. E-mail: nichols@cowley.edu.

NICHOLS, GUY WARREN, retired institute executive, utilities executive; b. Colchester, Vt., Oct. 27, 1925; s. Guy W. and Gladys (Tomlinson) N.; m. Shirley Hibbard, June 21, 1947; children: Pamela, Gail, Sally. BSCE, U. Vt., 1947; postgrad., Worcester Poly. Inst. Sch. Indsl. Mgmt., 1953-56; MS in Bus. Adminstrn., MIT, 1961. With New. Eng. Electric System, Westborough, Mass., 1947-84, exec. v.p., 1968-70, pres., 1970-84, chief exec. officer, 1972-84, chmn. bd., 1978-84. Bd. dirs. Amoresco Inc. Chmn., trustee Woods Hole Oceanographic Instn., 1985-95. Sloan fellow, MIT, 1961. Fellow Am. Acad. Arts and Scis. Office: 25 Research Dr Westborough MA 01582-0001 Office Phone: 508-389-2796. Personal E-mail: looncall99@comcast.net.

NICHOLS, HAROLD JAMES, university dean; b. Mitchell Field, N.Y., July 27, 1945; s. Harold J. and Ruth (McCain) N.; m. Mary Frances Lutes, Nov. 25, 1967 (div. 1992); children: Ruth, David, Debra; m. Anna Marie Douet, July 4, 1992. BS, Iowa State U., 1967; MA, Ind. U., 1969, PhD, 1971. Assoc. instr. Ind. U., Bloomington, 1970-71; asst. prof. Kans. State U., Manhattan, 1971-75, assoc. prof., 1975-81, prof., 1981-84, prof., head speech dept., 1985-93; dean Coll. Fine Arts and Humanities, U. Nebr., Kearney, 1993-97; dean Sch. Arts and Scis., Ga. Southwestern State U., Americus, GA, 1997—. Guest scholar DePauw U. Undergrad. Honors Conf., Greencastle, Ind., 1988; cons. Commonwealth of Va. Dept. Edn., 1988, Nebr. Wesleyan U., Lincoln, 1989, So. Ill. U., 1989, U. Va., 1992, U. No. Iowa, 1992. Co-editor: Status of Theatre Research-1984, 1986; contbr. articles to profl. jours. Named Outstanding Coll. Tchr., Kans. Speech Communications Assn., 1985. Mem. Assn. Theatre in Higher Edn. (pres. 1987-88), Am. Coll. Theatre Festival (region chair 1987-88, Kennedy Ctr. medallion 1990), Mid-Am. Theatre Conf. (chief regional officer 1978-81). Home: 1923 Rose Ave Americus GA 31709-4721 Office: Ga Southwestern State Univ Sch Arts and Scis 800 Wheatley St Americus GA 31709-4376 E-mail: hjn@canes.gsw.edu.

NICHOLS, HENRY ELIOT, lawyer, savings and loan executive; b. N.Y.C. m. Frances Griffin Morrison, Aug. 12, 1950 (dec. July 1978); children: Clyde Whitney, Diane Spencer; m. Mary ann Wall, May 31, 1987. BA, Yale U., 1946; JD, U. Va., 1948. Bar: D.C. 1950, U.S. Dist. Ct. 1950, U.S. Ct. Appeals 1952, U.S. Supreme Ct. 1969. Assoc. Frederick W. Berens, Washington, 1950-52; sole practice Washington, 1952—. Real estate columnist Washington Star, 1966-81; pres., gen. counsel Hamilton Fed. Savs. & Loan Assn., 1971-74; vice chmn. bd. Columbia 1st Bank (formerly Columbia 1st Fed. Savs. & Loan Assn.), Washington, 1974-90, bd. dirs.; pres. Century Fin. Corp., 1971-90; regional v.p. Preview, Inc., 1972-78; bd. dirs., exec. com. Columbia Real Estate Title Ins. Co., Washington, 1968-78. Contbr. articles to profl. jours. Nat. adv. bd. Harker Prep. Sch., 1975-80; exec. com. Father Walter E. Schmitz Meml. Fund, Cath. U., 1982-83; bd. dirs. Vincent T. Lombardi Cancer Rsch. Ctr., 1979-84; del. Pres. Johnson's Conf. LAw and Poverty, 1967; vice chmn. Mayor's Ad Hoc Com. Housing Code Problems, Washington, 1968-71; mem. Commn. Landlord-Tenant Affairs Washington City Coun., 1970-71; vice chmn. Washington Area Realtors Coun., 1970; exec. com., dir. Downtown Progress, 1970; bd. dirs. Washington Mental Health Assn., 1973, Washington Med. Ctr., 1975. Capt. USAAF, 1942-46. Mem. Am. Land Devel. Assn., Nat. Assn. Real Estate Editors, Washington Bd. Realtors (pres. 1970, Realtor of Yr. 1970, Martin Isen award 1981), Greater Met. Washington Bs. Trade (bd. dirs. 1974-80), U.S. League Savs. Assns. (attys. com. 1971-80), Washington Savs. and Loan League, ABA, D.C. Bar Assn., Internat. Real Estate Fedn., Yale Club, Cosmos Club, Rolls Royce Club, Antique Auto Club, St. Elmo Club, Omega Tau Rho. Episcopalian. Achievements include patents in field. Home: Apt 905 4550 N Park Ave Chevy Chase MD 20815 Office: 1112 16th St NW Washington DC 20036-4823 Office Phone: 202-872-1919.

NICHOLS, HENRY LOUIS, lawyer; b. Collin County, Tex., Nov. 7, 1916; s. Jesse Cleveland and Leva (Stiff) N.; m. Elaine Guentherman, May 17, 1949; children: David Michael, Martha Marie. LL.B., So. Meth. U., 1940. Bar: Tex. 1939. Asst. city atty., Dallas, 1946-50; pvt. practice, 1951—. Mem. adv. bd. Ctr. for Legal Mcpl. Studies. Served to lt. col. AUS, 1941-46; col. USAR ret. Rsch. fellow Southwestern Legal Found., 1964. Fellow Am. Bar Found.; mem. ABA, Dallas Bar Assn. (pres. 1963), State Bar Tex., Tex. Bar Found. (charter), Lakewood Country Club. Home: 3131 Maple Ave Apt 13H Dallas TX 75201-1206 Office: 1800 Lincoln Plz Dallas TX 75201 Office Phone: 214-965-9900. *As a night-school graduate (Law School), I believe the opportunities in America are unlimited for anyone willing to work. Nowhere in the world are such opportunities available. We who live in the U.S.A. are blessed and the most fortunate of all people. We should strive to maintain that which our fathers preserved for us.*

NICHOLS, IRIS JEAN, illustrator; b. Yakima, Wash., Aug. 2, 1938; d. Charles Frederick and Velma Irene (Hacker) Beisner; (div. June 1963); children: Reid William, Amy Jo; m. David Gary Nichols, Sept. 21, 1966. BFA in Art, U. Wash., 1978. Freelance illustrator, graphic designer, Seattle, 1966—2004; med. illustrator, head dept. illustration Swedish Hosp. Med. Ctr., Seattle, 1981-86; owner, med. and sci. illustrator Art for Medicine, Seattle, 1986—2003; ret., 2003. Med. illustrator U. Wash., Seattle, 1966-67; part-time med. illustrator, graphic coord. dept. art The Mason Clinic, 1968-78; instr. advanced illustration Cornish Coll. Arts, Seattle, 1988-90; organized, coordinated and gifted the artwork of Prof. Glen E. Alps of U. Wash. after his death in 1966. Illustrator various books including Bryophytes of Pacific Northwest, 1966, Microbiology, 1973, 78, 82, 94, 98, Introduction to Human Physiology, 1980, Understanding Human Anatomy and Physiology, 1983, Human Anatomy, 1984 Regional Anesthesia, 1990, many other med. and sci. books,

and children's books on various subjects; exhibited in group shows at Seattle Pacific Sci. Ctr., summer 1979, 82, Am. Coll. Surgeons (1st prize 1974), N.W. Urology Conf. (1st prize 1974, 76, 2d prize 1975); pub. illustrations Constellation Pk. and Marine Res., City Seattle Pk., 1999. Pres. ArtsWest (formerly West Seattle Arts Coun.), 1983; active Seattle Art Mus.; chmn. West Seattle (Wash.) H.S. Art Acquisition Com., 2003—. Named to West Seattle H.S. Alumni Hall of Fame, 1986, Matrix Table, 1986-96. Mem. Assn. Med. Illustrators (Murial McLatchie Fine Arts award 1981), Nat. Mus. Women in the Arts (Wash. state com., bd. dirs. 1987-95, pres. 1993-94), Women Painters of Wash. (pres. 1987-89), U. Wash. Alumni Assn., Lambda Rho (pres. alumni assn. 1995-98, treas. 2002-04) Avocations: artwork, printmaking, small books. E-mail: artformed@aol.com., irisnichols@comcast.net.

NICHOLS, J. LARRY, energy company executive, lawyer; b. Oklahoma City, July 6, 1942; s. John Whiteman and Mary (Davis) N.; m. Polly Puckett, Oct. 16, 1971; children: Tyler, Sally. BA in Geology, Princeton U., 1964; JD, U. Mich., 1967. Bar: Okla. 1967. Law clk. to chief justice U.S. Supreme Ct., Washington, 1967-68; spl. asst. to asst. atty. gen. U.S. Dept. Justice, Washington, 1968-70; pres., CEO, Devon Energy Corp., Oklahoma City, 1970—. Dir. Am. Stock Exch. Commr. Urban Renewal Authority Bd., Oklahoma City, 1989; pres. domestic petroleum coun. Okla. Nature Conservancy. Mem. Okla. Bar Assn. (bd. dirs., v.p.), Ind. Petroleum Assn. Am. (bd. dirs.), NAM (bd. dirs.), Oklahoma City C. of C., Econ. Club (pres. 1988-89). Office: Devon Energy Corp 20 N Broadway Ave Ste 1500 Oklahoma City OK 73102-8260

NICHOLS, JAMES RICHARD, civil engineer, consultant; b. Amarillo, Tex., June 29, 1923; s. Marvin Curtis and Ethel (Nichols) N.; m. Billie Louise Smith, Dec. 24, 1944; children: Judith Ann, James Richard Jr., John M. BS in Civil Engring., Tex. A&M U., 1949, MS in Civil Engring., 1950; DHum (hon.), Tex. Wesleyan U., 1990. Registered profl. engr., Tex., Okla., N.Mex. Ptnr. Freese & Nichols, Inc., Cons. Engrs., Fort Worth, 1950-76, pres., 1977-88, chmn., 1988—. Chmn. Tex. Bd. Profl. Engrs. Former chmn. Ft. Worth Conv. and Visitors Bur.; bd. dirs. Pub. Comm. Found. North Tex., Tex. A&M Rsch. Found., Tex. Wesleyan U.; co-chmn. Metroplex Mission with Billy Graham. With U.S. Army, 1943—46. Fellow: ASCE, Am. Cons. Engrs. Coun.; mem.: NSPE, Tex. Water Conservation Assn., Ft. Worth C. of C. (bd. dirs., adv. coun.), Rotary, Ft. Worth Club, Exch. Club. Methodist. Home: 4821 Overton Woods Dr Fort Worth TX 76109-2429 Office: Freese & Nichols Inc 4055 Internat Plz Ste 200 Fort Worth TX 76109-4895 Office Phone: 817-735-7300. E-mail: jrn@freese.com.

NICHOLS, JOHN DOANE, diversified manufacturing corporation executive; b. Shanghai, 1930; m. Alexandra M. Curran, Dec. 4, 1971; children: Kendra E., John D. III. BA, Harvard U., 1953, MBA, 1955. Various operating positions Ford Motor Corp., 1958-68; dir. fin. controls ITT Corp., 1968-69; exec. v.p., COO Aerojet-Gen. Corp., 1969-79, Ill. Tool Works Inc., Chgo., 1980-81, CEO, dir., 1982-95, chmn., 1986-96; pres., CEO Marmon Group Inc., Chgo., 2002. Bd. dirs. Household Internat., Philip Morris Cos., Inc., Rockwell Internat.; overseer Harvard U., 1994-99, vis. com. Sch. Edn., com. athletics, com. univ. resources. Trustee U. Chgo., 1987-93, Lyric Opera Chgo., Mus. Sci. and Industry, Jr. Achievement Chgo., Chgo. Commerce Club Civic Com.; life trustee Chgo. Symphony Orch.; bd. dirs. Art Inst. Chgo., past chmn.; mem. bd. govs. Argonne (Ill.) Nat. Lab., 1988-93; vice chmn. exec. com. Chgo. Cmty. Trust, 1997—. Mem. Harvard Club (N.Y., Chgo.), Indian Hill Club (Winnetka, Ill.), Chgo. Club, Comml. Club, Econ. Club Chgo. Office: Marmon Group Inc 225 W Washington St Chicago IL 60606

NICHOLS, JOSEPH J., SR., surgeon; b. Atlanta, July 16, 1929; MD, Med. Coll. Ga., 1958. Diplomate Am. Bd. Surgery, Am. Bd. Colon & Rectal Surgery. Intern Ga. Bapt. Hosp., Atlanta, 1958-59, resident, 1959-61, 65-67; fellow Precept Drs. Boling-Finch, 1967-69; with Piedmont Hosp., Atlanta; asst. clin. prof. surgery Med. Coll. Ga.; clin. asst. prof. surgery Emory U. Sch. Med. Mem. AMA, ACS, Am. Soc. Colon and Rectal Surgery, Southern Med. Assn., Southeastern Surg. Congress. Office: 2001 Peachtree Rd NE Ste 540 Atlanta GA 30309-1476

NICHOLS, KAREN, academic administrator; b. Ind. m. Jim Nichols. DO, U. Health Scis., Coll. Osteo. Medicine, Kansas City. Intern and resident in internal medicine Okla. Osteo. Hosp., Tulsa; asst. dean grad. med. edn. Ariz. Coll. Osteo. Medicine; dean Chgo. Coll. Osteo. Medicine, 2002—. Contbr. articles to profl. jours. Bd. trustees Mut. Ins. Co. of Ariz.; with Mesa Symphony, Mesa United Way, Central Christian Ch. Recipient Physician of Yr., Ariz. Osteo. Med. Assn., 1996, Educator of Yr., Mesa Gen. Hosp. Mem.: Am. Osteo. Assn. (chair bur. state and govt. affairs, mem. health related and fed. health policies coms., chair adv. com. of end-of-life care). Office: Chgo Coll Osteo Medicine Midwestern U 555 31st St Downers Grove IL 60515

NICHOLS, KAREN, architect; Grad., Smith Coll., MIT. Prin. Michael Graves & Assocs., Princeton, NJ, 1977—. Fellow: AIA. Office: 341 Nassau St Princeton NJ 08540

NICHOLS, KATIE, investment company executive; b. Des Moines, May 19, 1940; d. Gardner "Mike" and Lois (Thornburg) Cowles; m. Julian Strauss, June 11, 1960 (div. 1971); children: Elizabeth Lois Strauss Grossi, Gwen Beatrix Strauss Jenkins, Kate Anne Strauss Long; m. Roger Marvin Nichols, Sept. 1, 1973 (div. 1981); m. H.E. Rummel, Mar. 27, 1983 (div. 1994). Student, Cornell U., 1957—61. Ptnr., v.p. The Rummel Group, Inc., St. Petersburg, Fla., 1985—, chmn., CEO, 2003—. Trustee Cowles Charitable Trust, NYC, 1985—. Vol. Hosp. Albert Schweitzer, Deschapelles, Haiti, 1961-63; vice chmn. Fla. Human Rels. Commn., Tallahassee, 1974-75; Dem. candidate Fla. Pub. Svc. Commn., 1976; commr. Fla. Pub. Svc. Commn., 1981-89, chmn., 1987-89; vice chmn. Fla. Corrections Commn., 1994-98; bd. dirs. Nat. Coun. on Crime and Delinquency, San Francisco, 1990—, chmn. 1997-98; bd. dirs. HAS2000 Campaign for Hosp. Albert Schweitzer, Haiti; trustee Cowles Charitable Trust, 1985—. Recipient Honor award, Fla. Human Rels. Commn., 1985. Mem. NOW, Emily's List, League of Women Voters of Fla. Democrat. Episcopalian. Avocations: reading, needlepoint. Home: 1682 Oceanview Dr Tierra Verde FL 33715-2500 Office: The Rummel Group Inc 1641 1st Ave N Saint Petersburg FL 33713-8935 Office Phone: 727-895-7804.

NICHOLS, LELAND M. retired microbiologist, counter-bioterrorism researcher; b. Fulton, Mo., July 13, 1947; s. John Shannon and Oleta May Nichols; m. Rebecca Mae Moore, Oct. 7, 1972; children: Mark Anthony, Shannon Matthew. BS, Lincoln U., Jefferson City, 1997. Virologist Mo. Dept. of Health, Jefferson City, 1977—90, environ. bacteriologist, 1990—2002. Author: (screenplays) The Thirty-First Parallel. Sgt. USAF, 1967—71. Achievements include research in Anthrax decontamination tests using a safe simular bacterium. Home: 7350 Old Highway 54 S Fulton MO 65251 Office: U Mo 349 Engring Bldg W Columbia MO 65211 Personal E-mail: nichols@socket.net.

NICHOLS, M(ARIAN) THERESA, radio station executive; b. Bowman, S.C., Feb. 15, 1947; d. Marion Carvin and Jessie Mae (Robinson) Day; m. Bobby Bernard Nichols, Aug. 2, 1969; 1 child, Yvette Rochelle. BA summa cum laude, S.C. State Coll., 1968; MA, Atlanta U., 1971; PhD, U. S.C., 1977. Cert. mediator, assessor, S.C. Assoc. prof. English, S.C. State Coll., Orangeburg, 1969-88; copy editor, asst. slot editor The State, Columbia, SC, 1988-90; edn. program cons. S.C. Dept. Edn., 1990, coord. edn. project, 1990-97; spl. asst. to CEO, NICWILD Comms., Inc., Barnwell, 1997—. Reading cons. Dorchester Sch. Dist. 4, St. George, S.C., 1971; grammar cons. S.C. State Coll., Orangeburg, 1972-82, The State, 1988; workshop presenter, motivational speaker, 1989—; cons. race/sex equity, 1990—; mem. S.C. Black History Curriculum Com. Co-editor coll. catalog, coll. self-study. Mem. Multicultural Forum, U. S.C., 1992-97; mem. multicultural/gender equity task force S.C. Dept. Edn., 1992-97, mem. civil rights compliance MOA task force, 1991-97, sch. safety task force, 1993-97; active Dem. Party, Black, 1966-67; vol. Am. Cancer Soc., Orangeburg, 1985, Leukemia Soc. Am., 1989, The Male's Place, 1991-92. Nat. Fellowship for Black Ams. fellow, 1976. Mem. NAFE, Women Impacting Pub. Policy, Nat. Mus. Women in Arts, Ga. Assn. Broadcasters, Nat. Home Gardening Club, Phi Delta Kappa, Kappa Delta Pi, Sigma Tau Delta, Alpha Kappa Alpha, Alpha Kappa Mu. Methodist. Avocations: reading, travel, fashion, interior decorating, architectural design. Home: 375 Woodlawn Dr NE Orangeburg SC 29115-2755 Office: WIIZ Radio WIZ Plz 8968 Marlboro Ave Barnwell SC 29812 E-mail: wiizard@sc.rr.com., wiizard@aol.com.

NICHOLS, MICHAEL COOPER, food products executive, lawyer; b. Birmingham, Ala., Feb. 4, 1952; s. F.W. and Jeannett (Cooper) N.; m. Marcia Couch, Sept. 23, 1976; children: Joshua, Jessica, Zachary. BA with honors, Brown U., 1974; JD, Emory U., 1977. Bar: Ga., 1977, Tex., 1981. Mem. Ga. Ho. of Reps., Atlanta, 1977-81; chief adminstrv. officer Appletree Mktg., Houston, 1988-91; gen. counsel SYSCO Corp., Houston, 1981-88, v.p., 1991—98, v.p., sec., gen. counsel, 1998—. Sec., bd. dirs. Congregation Beth Israel, Houston, 1986—; pres. Houston Food Bank, 1990-92; trustee Houston Police Officer Pension Fund. Home: 12155 Maple Rock Houston TX 77077 Office Phone: 281-584-1471. E-mail: nichols.mike@corp.sysco.com.

NICHOLS, MIKE, stage and film director; b. Berlin, Nov. 6, 1931; s. Nicholaievitch and Brigitte (Landauer) Peschowsky; m. Patricia Scott, 1957 (div.); m. Margot Callas, 1974 (div.); m. Annabel Davis-Goff (div.); m. Diane Sawyer, Apr. 29, 1988. Student, U. Chgo., 1950-53; student acting, Lee Strasberg. Ptnr. with Elaine May in comedy act; first appeared at Playwrights Theatre Club, Compass Theatre, Chgo.; N.Y. debut An Evening with Mike Nichols and Elaine May, 1960; acted in A Matter of Position, Phila., 1962; dir.: (plays) Barefoot in the Park, 1963 (Tony award best dir.), The Knack, 1964, Luv, 1964 (Tony award best dir.), The Odd Couple, 1965 (Tony award best dir.), The Apple Tree, 1966, The Little Foxes, 1967, Plaza Suite, 1968 (Tony award best dir.), The Prisoner of 2d Avenue, 1971 (Tony award best dir.), Uncle Vanya (co-adapted), 1973, Streamers, 1976, Comedians, 1976, The Gin Game, 1977, (L.A. Drama Critics award), Drink Before Dinner, 1978, Lunch Hour, 1980, Fools, 1981, The Real Thing, 1984 (Tony award 1984,), Hurlyburly, 1984, Social Security, 1984, Elliot Loves, 1990, Death and the Maiden, 1992; (films) Who's Afraid of Virginia Woolf?, 1966, (Academy award nomination best director 1966), The Graduate, 1967 (Academy award best director 1967), Catch-22, 1970, Carnal Knowledge, 1971, The Day of the Dolphin, 1973, The Fortune, 1975, Silkwood, 1983 (Academy award nomination best director 1983), Heartburn, 1986, Biloxi Blues, 1987, Working Girl, 1988 (Academy award nomination best director 1988), Postcards From the Edge, 1990, Regarding Henry, 1991, Wolf, 1994, The Bird Cage, 1995, Primary Colors, 1998; dir., prodr.: What Planet Are You From?, 2000; prodr. All the Pretty Horses, 2000; prodr.: (musical) Annie, 1977; (TV movie) dir., exec. prodr. Wit, 2001, (miniseries) dir. Angels in America, 2003; performed at N.Y. musical Pres. Johnson's Inaugural Gala, 1965.*

NICHOLS, RALPH ARTHUR, lawyer; b. Clinton, N.Y., Jan. 27, 1919; s. Arthur Britcher and Carrie Lena (Pitcher) N.; m. Pamela Crow Bermingham, May 3, 1947 (dec. Feb. 1980); children: Jeremy Nichols Pierce, Ralph A. Jr., Melinda Nichols Mayer; m. Victoria Requa Lalli, Sept. 5, 1981. AB, Hamilton Coll., 1940; LLB, Yale U., 1947. Bar: Conn. 1949, N.Y. 1947, U.S. Dist. Ct. (so. dist.) N.Y. 1949, U.S. Dist. Ct. Conn. 1950, U.S. Supreme Ct. 1959. Assoc. Burke & Burke, N.Y.C., 1947-49, Maguire, Walker & Middleton, Stamford, Ct., 1949-54; assoc., then ptnr. Cummings & Lockwood, Stamford, 1954—. Founder, former bd. dirs. Stamford Land Conservation Trust; former bd. dirs. Conservationists Stamford, Inc., Stamford YMCA; former bd. dirs., sec. Stamford Area Commerce and Industry; trustee Stamford YMCA. Lt. USNR, 1942-46, ETO, PTO. Fellow Am. Coll. Trust and Estate Counsel; mem. ABA, Woodway Country Club (Darien, Conn.), Yale Club (N.Y.C.), Phi Delta Phi. Republican. Episcopalian. Office: Cummings & Lockwood PO Box 120 4 Stamford Plz Stamford CT 06902-3834 Home: 32 Bank St New Canaan CT 06840-6238 E-mail: rnichols@cl-law.com.

NICHOLS, ROBERT HASTINGS, lawyer; b. Mpls., Aug. 12, 1941; s. James Hastings and Judith (Beach) Nichols; m. Jean Christy, Nov. 30, 1968; children: Marc O., Seth J., Ethan D., Rebecca J. AB, Yale U., 1963; JD, U. Chgo., 1967. Bar: Ill. 1967, U.S Dist. Ct. (no. dist.) Ill. 1967, U.S. Ct. Appeals (7th cir.) 1972, U.S Dist. Ct. (ea. dist.) Wis. 1975, U.S. Ct. Appeals (DC cir.) 1976, U.S. Supreme Ct. 1986, U.S. Ct. Appeals (8th cir.) 1975; cert. in Pub. Affairs Coro Found., 1964. Ptnr. Cotton, Watt, Jones and King, Chgo., 1967—95; sr. atty. and coord. United Airlines Master Exec. Coun., Air Line Pilots Assn., Internat. AFL-CIO, 1995—. Cons. Govt. of New Zealand, Auckland, 1980; mem. lawyers coord. com. AFL-CIO. Contbr. articles to legal publs. Mem.: Columbia Yacht Club. Democrat. Presbyn. Home: 1030 E 49th St Chicago IL 60615-1814 Office: Ste 700 6400 Shafer Ct Rosemont IL 60018-6198 Office Phone: 847-292-1700.

NICHOLS, ROBERT LEIGHTON, civil engineer; b. Amarillo, Tex., June 24, 1926; s. Marvin Curtis and Ethel Nichols; m. Frances Hardison, June 8, 1948; children: Eileen, William C., Michael L. BSCE, Tex. A&M U., 1947, MSCE, 1948. Grad. asst., instr. Tex. A&M U., 1947-48; assoc. Freese & Nichols (and predecessors), Ft. Worth, 1948-50, partner, 1950-77, v.p., 1977-88, pres., 1988-91, vice chmn., 1991-92, pres. emeritus, 1992—. Mem. Bldg. Stds. Commn., 1956—62; pres. Tri-State Water Resource Coalition, 2003—. Chmn. Horn Frog dist. Boy Scouts Am., pres. Longhorn coun., 1990—93, Ozark Trails coun., 1998—99; mem. City Coun., Webb City, Mo. Mem.: NSPE (pres. 1977—78, pres. Ednl. Found.), ASCE, Nat. Inst. Engring. Ethics (pres. 1995—97), Tex. Pub. Works Assn., Tex. Water Utilities Assn., Am. Pub. Works Assn., Water Environ. Assn. Tex. (pres. 1962—63), Water Environ. Fedn., Tex. Water Conservation Assn., Am. Water Works Assn., Tex. Soc. Profl. Engrs. (pres. 1965—66), C. of C. Webb City, Mo. (exec. dir. 1997—2001), Masons, Chi Epsilon, Tau Beta Pi. Methodist. Office: 1 S Main St Ste 102 Webb City MO 64870-2325 Office Phone: 417-673-7151. E-mail: rln@freese.com.

NICHOLS, ROBERT LYMAN, retired foreign service officer, lecturer; b. Milw. s. Malcolm Strong and Ruth Mary (Lyman) N.; m. Virginia Lee Straghan, Sept. 7, 1947 (dec. 1989); children: Robert Gibbs (dec.), Nancy Lee, Peter Lyman. Student, Swarthmore Coll., 1942-43; BA, Tufts U., 1949; MA, Fletcher Sch. Law & Diplomacy, Medford, Mass., 1950; diploma, U.S. Army War Coll., Carlisle, Pa., 1969. Fgn. svc. officer U.S. Dept. State, The Philippines, 1951-53, USIA, Italy, 1954—56, 1956—58, 1959—61, 1969—71, 1961—65, 1971—74; dir. Chinese divsn. Voice of America, 1966-69; dep. dir. East Asia Cultural Afairs U.S. Dept. State, Washington, 1974-76; dep. dir. East Asia USIA, Washington, 1977-79; ret., 1979; part-time faculty Cape Cod C.C., Barnstable, Mass., 1981—2004; tchr. of Chinese Light House Charter Sch., Orleans, Mass., 1997. China tour leader Chinese Ednl. Travel, Nat. Com. US-China Rels. and Smithsonian, 1980—95, 1999; tchr. Chinese Cape Cod Acad.; lectr. in field. Contbr. articles newspapers and profl. jours. Bd. dirs. Cape Cod Human Svcs., Hyannis, Mass., 1987-2004, chmn., 1990-91. Quartermaster 1st class, USN, 1943-46, Pacific. Episcopalian. Avocations: boating, fishing, theater acting, yoga. Home: 248 Kates Path Yarmouth Port MA 02675-1451 Personal E-mail: rlnichols@comcast.net.

NICHOLS, ROGER SABIN, genealogist, retired school counselor; b. Ames, Iowa, Oct. 21, 1938; s. Sabin Alfred and Margaret Pauline (Andrew) N.; m. Glendene Donna Greta, June 12, 1960; children: Margaret Emily, Charles Sabin II. BS, Iowa State U., 1960; MA in Edn., U. No. Iowa, 1965, EdS, 1976. Cert. tchr. sci., social studies, lang. arts, counselor K-12, dir. pupil svcs., Iowa. Tchr., counselor Bridgewater-Fontanelle (Iowa) Cmty. Sch. Dist., 1960-66; counselor, guidance dir. Sioux City (Iowa) Cmty. Sch. Dist., 1966-98. Human rels. cons. Western Hills Area Edn. Agy., Sioux City, 1979-82, spl. edn. transition adv. com., 1987-97, chmn. career devel. unit writing com., 1989-90; mem., chmn. spl. needs adv. com. Western Iowa Tech. Cmty. Coll., Sioux City, 1982-87, area planning coun. for vocat. edn., 1986-90; com. mem. Sioux City Cmty. Sch. Dist., 1967-89; evaluation team N. Ctrl. Assn. Colls. and Schs., 1983; brief counseling rsch. project Iowa State U., 1989-90; counselor's adv. com. office of admissions U. S.D., 1990-92; state conf. presenter Iowa Assn. Counseling and Devel., 1990, 94; local coord. Counseling for Higher Skills Rsch. Project, Kans. State U., 1994-96; primary rschr. Berning Family book project, 1999—. Contbg. author: Critical Incidents in School Counseling, 1973, Simmerman Family Record, 1995; author: William Fawcett Thompson as William Fawcett, Actor, 1999, A Mellor Family Genealogy, 2004; contbr. poetry to Lyrical Iowa, 1965, 67; contbr. articles to profl. jours. On-air friendraiser host Friends of FM-90, Sioux City, 1982-2000; mem. 4-H subcom. Woodbury County Extension Svc., Sioux City, 1984-96; 4-H departmental fair departmental supt. Woodbury County Fair Assn., Moville, Iowa, 1984-89, mem. Scholarship Com. Waitt Family Found., 1999—; voting mem. Iowa Ann. Conf., United Meth. Ch., 1999—. Named Iowa Counselor of Yr., Iowa Assn. Coll. Admissions Counselors, 1995; recipient Nat. Def. Edn. Act Stipend, U. S.D., 1968. Mem. ACA, NEA (life), Nat. Geneal. Soc., Internat. Suzuki Assn., Iowa State Edn. Assn. (del. assembly 1965), Sioux City Edn. Assn. (chmn. profl. rights and responsibilities com. 1967-68, rep. assembly 1968-69), Iowa Counseling Assn., Am. Sch. Counselors Assn., Iowa Sch. Counselors Assn. (chair ethics com. 1997-98), Nat. Career Devel. Assn. (career info. rev. svc. 1970-73), Iowa Career Devel. Assn. (state membership chmn. 1975-76), Iowa Specialists in Group Work, Am. Vocat. Assn., Iowa State Hist. Soc., Iowa State Geneal. Soc., Conn. Soc. Genealogists, Czechoslovak Geneol. Soc. Internat., N.E. Historic Geneal. Soc., Nat. Geneal. Soc. (contbg. author NGS Newsmag.), Derbyshire Family History Soc. (contbg. author Branch News 1993), Siouxland Master Chorale (pres. 1968-71, v.p. 1977-80, 88-90, treas. 1982-83), Sioux City Chamber Music Assn. (pres. 1980 81), Phi Delta Kappa (pres. Siouxland chpt. 1996-97). Republican. Methodist. Avocation: church musician. Home: 3819 Peters Ave Sioux City IA 51106-1813 E-mail: rngnichols@aol.com.

NICHOLS, RONALD LEE, surgeon, educator; b. Chgo., June 25, 1941; s. Peter Raymond and Jane Eleanor (Johnson) N.; m. Elsa Elaine Johnson, Dec. 4, 1964; children: Kimberly Jane, Matthew Bennett. MD, U. Ill., 1966, MS, 1970. Diplomate Am. Bd. Surgery (assoc. cert. examiner, New Orleans, 1991), Nat. Bd. Med. Examiners. Intern U. Ill. Hosp., Chgo., 1966-67, resident in surgery, 1967-72, instr. surgery, 1970-72, asst. prof. surgery, 1972-74, assoc. prof. surgery U. Health Scis. Chgo. Med. Sch., 1975-77, dir. surg. edn., 1975-77; William Henderson prof. surgery Tulane U. Sch. Medicine, New Orleans, 1977—2002, vice chmn. dept. surgery, 1982-91, staff surgeon, 1977—2002, prof. microbiology, immunology, 1979—, William Henderson prof. surgery emeritus, 2003—; sr. vis. surgeon Med. Ctr. La., New Orleans, 1988—. Cons. surgeon VA Hosp., Alexandria, La., 1978-93, Huey P. Long Hosp., Pineville, La., 1978-2002, Lallie Kemp Charity Hosp., Independence, La., 1977-85, Touro Infirmary, New Orleans, Monmouth Med. Ctr., Long Branch, NJ, 1979-88; sr. vis. surgeon Med. Ctr. La., New Orleans, 1988—; mem. VA Coop. Study Rev. Bd., 1978-81, VA Merit Rev. Bd. in Surgery, 1979-82; sci. program com. 3d Internat. Conf. Nosocomial Infections, Ctr. Disease Control, sci. program and fundraising com. 4th Internat. Conf.; bd. dirs. Nat. Found. Infectious Diseases, 1989-2003, v.p., 1994-97, pres.-elect., 1997-99, pres., 1999-2001, trustee, 2003—; hon. fellow faculty Kasr El Aini Cairo U. Sch. Medicine, 1989; adv. com. on infection control Ctrs. for Disease Control, 1991-97; disting. guest, vis. prof. Royal Coll. Surgeons Thailand, 1989, 1992; infectious diseases adv. bd. Roche Labs., 1988-95, Abbott Labs., 1990-92, Kimberly Clark Corp., 1990-99, SmithKline Beecham Labs., 1990-95, Fujisawa Pharm., chmn., 1990-99, Bayer Pharm., 1994-2001, Merck Sharpe Dohme, 1996, Depotech, 1996, Zeneca Pharm., 1997—, Rhone-Poulenc Rorer, 1997-99, Wyeth-Ayrest Labs., 1998—, Pfizer Pharm., 1999, Searle Pharm., 1999-2001, GlaxoWellcome, 1999, Aventis, 1999-2000, Cubist Pharm., 2000—, others; study group Prophylaxis Antibiotic Project La. Health Care Rev., Inc., 1995-2000, Nat. Com. Study Blood Borne Disease Transmission make Nat. Policy, Rockefeller Brothers Fund, 2001-03; lectr. Royal Coll. Physicians and Surgeons Can., 1998, Internat. Infectious Disease Soc. Ob-gyn., 1998, 20th NY State Surg. Symposium, 1998, dept. surgery Dept. U. Ark., 1998; apptd. by gov. La. commn. HIV and AIDS, 1999-2003; nat. policy com. study innovative surgery reg. Greenwall Found., 2003—. Author: (with Gorbach, Bartlett and Nichols) Manual of Surgical Infection, 1984; author, guest editor: (with Nichols, Hyslop Jr. and Bartlett) Decision Mking in Surgical Sepsis, 1991; guest editor, author: Surgical Sepsis and Beyond, 1993; mem. editl. bd. Current Surgery, 1977—, Hosp. Physician, 1980—, Infection Control, 1980-86, Guidelines to Antibiotic Therapy, 1976-81, Am. Jour. Infection Control, 1981-99, Internat. Medicine, 1983—, Confronting Infection, 1983-86, Current Concepts in Clin. Surgery, 1984—, Fact Line, 1984-91, Host/Pathogen News, 1984—, Infectious Diseases in Clin. Practice, 1991—, surg. sect. editor, 1992—, Surg. Infections: Index and Revs., 1991—, So. Med. Jour., 1992-97, ANAEROBE, 1994—, Surg. Infections, 1998—, Clin. Infectious Diseases, 1999—; editl. adv. bd. MD Consult Infectious Diseases, 2002-04; mem. adv. bd. Physician News Network, 1991-95; patentee (with S.G. schoenberger and W.R. Rank) Helical-Tipped Lesion Localization Needle Device; patentee in field. Elected faculty sponsor graduating class Tulane Med. Sch., 1979-80, 83, 85, 87, 88, 91-92. Maj. USAR, 1972-75. Recipient House Staff tchg. award U. Ill. Coll. Medicine, 1973, Douglas Stubbs Lectr. award Surg. Sect. Nat. Med. Assn., 1987, Prix d'Elegance award Men of Fashion, New Orleans, 1993, Ann. La. Laureate Emeritus lectureship, 2002; named Brit. Jour. of Surgery Lectr., 1997, 1st Ann. Warren Cole lectr., 2001. Fellow Infectious Disease Soc. Am. (mem. FDA subcom. to develop guidelines in surg. prophylaxis 1989-93, co-recipient Joseph Susman Meml. award 1990), Am. Acad. Microbiology, Internat. Soc. Univ. Colon and Rectal Surgeons, ACS (mem. oper. rm. environ. com. 1978-80, vice chair oper. rm. environ. com. 1980-81, chmn. oper. rm. environ. com. 1981-83, sr. mem. oper. rm. environ. com. 1983-87, mem. internat. rels. com. 1987-93, sr. mem. internat. rels. com. 1993-97); mem. AMA, Nat. Found. for Infectious Diseases (bd. dirs.), Joint Commn. on Accreditation of Health Care Orgn. (Infection Control adv. group, 1988-98, sci. program com. 3d internat. conf. nosocomial infections CDC/Nat. Found. Infectious Diseases 1990, FDA Subcom. to Develop Guidelines in Surg. Prophylaxis, 1989-93; prophylactic antibiotic study group La. Health Care Rev. Inc. 1996-2000, clin. advisor, mem., 2001—, AIDS commn. State of La. 1992-94, mem., La. Commn. HIV and AIDS, 1999—), 5th Nat. Forum on AIDS (sci. program com.), U.S. Pharmacopeial Convention Inc. (adv. panel surg. drugs and devices 1995-2000, nominating com. The Heinz Awards 1995-96), Assn. Practitioners in Infection Control (physician adv. coun. 1991-98), Internat. Soc. Anaerobic Bacteria, So. Med. Assn. (vice chmn. sect. surgery 1980-81, chmn. 1982-83), Assn. Acad. Surgery, NY Acad. Sci., Warren H. Cole Soc. (pres.-elect 1988, pres. 1989-90), Assn. VA Surgeons, Soc. Surgery Alimentary Tract, Inst. Medicine Chgo., Midwest Surg. Assn., Ctrl. Surg. Assn., Ill. Surg. Soc., European Soc. Surg. Rsch., Collegium Internationale Chirugiae Digestivae, Chgo. Surg. Soc. (hon.), New Orleans Surg. Soc. (bd. dirs. 1983-87), Soc. Univ. Surgeons, Surg. Soc. La., Southeastern Surg. Soc., Phoenix Surg. Soc. (hon.), Hellenic Surg. Soc. (hon.), Ctrl. NY Surg. Soc. (hon.), Tulane Surg. Soc., Alton Ochsner Surg. Soc., Am. Soc. Microbiology, Soc. Internat. de Chirugie, Surg. Infection Soc. (sci. study com. 1982-83, fellowship com. 1985-87, ad hoc sci. liaison com. 1986-89, program com. 1986-87, chmn. ad hoc com. rels. with industry 1990-93, mem. sci. liaison com. 1995-96), Soc. for Intestinal Microbial Ecology and Disease, Soc. Critical Care Medicine, Am. Surg. Assn., Kansas City Surg. Soc. (hon.), Bay Surg. Soc. (hon.), Cuban Surg. Soc. (hon.), Panhellenic Surg. Soc. (hon.), Tacoma Surg. Club (hon.), Sigma Xi, Alpha Omega Alpha. Episcopalian. Home: 1521 7th St New Orleans LA 70115-3322 Office: 1430 Tulane Ave New Orleans LA 70112-2699 Office Phone: 504-588-5168. E-mail: ronald.nichols@tulane.edu.

NICHOLS, SANDRA B. public health service officer; b. Little Rock, Mar. 27, 1958; m. Ronnie A. Nichols, 1985; 1 child, Marquise. BA in Chemistry, Columbia Coll., Mo., 1980; student, Meharry Med. Coll., 1979-80; MS in Biology, Tenn. State U., 1982; MD, U. Ark., 1988. With dept. physiology U. Ark. Med. Scis., Little Rock, 1984-85, with microbiology lab., 1985-88, resident dept. family and community medicine, 1988-91, chief resident dept. family and community medicine, 1990-91, fellow dept. family and community medicine, occupational and environ. medicine, 1991-92; dir. Ark. Dept. of Health, Little Rock, 1994—; med. dir. United Health Care Corp. of Ark., 1998-2000; sr. med. dir. United Healthcare Ala., Inc., 2000. Adj. prof. health adminstrn. U. Ark., Little Rock; officer dept. health and human svcs. FDA; physician Mid Delta Health Clinic, 1992-94, interim med. dir., 1993-94; med. educator Delta Area Health Agy., U. Ark. Med. Scis., 1992—; dir. Merc. Bank; bd. dirs. Nat. Cancer Policy Bd., Nat. Mamography Quality Assurance Adv. Com. Author: (with others) Family Medicine Principles and Practice, 1994, 95; contbr. articles to profl. jours. Officer HHS, FDA; mem. Pine Bluff Arsenal Citizen's Adv. Com.; chmn. Gov.'s Partnership Coun. for Children and Families, Women Execs. in State Govt.; conf. participant Am. Swiss Found. Young Leaders Conf., 1995; mem. Ark. chpt. Internat. Women's Forum, Ark.

Arts Ctr., Nat. Cancer Policy Bd., Nat. Mammography Quality Assurance Assessment Com.; bd. dirs. Mercantile Bank; spkr. Career Day, local schs.; vol. physician high schs. Recipient Nat. FBI Comty. Leadership award, 1996; named one of Ark. Bus. Top 100 Women in Ark., 1996-97, Top 10 Women in Ark., 1995, Top 100 Women in Ark., 1998, 1999, one of Outstanding Young Women in Am., 1981; Nat. Med. fellow, 1984-85; Pub. Health Leadership Inst. scholar, 1996, scholar Columbia Coll., 1976-80. Mem. AMA, Ark. Med. Assn., Am. Acad. Family Physicians, Ark. Acad. Family Physicians, Pulaski County Med. Soc., Assn. State and Territorial Health Officers (sec.-treas.), Zeta Phi Beta. Avocations: tennis, reading, speaking, bicycling, travel. Office: 3700 Colonnade Pkwy Birmingham AL 35243-2361

NICHOLS, STEVEN, apparel executive; b. 1942; With Nichols Foot Form Corp., 1962-79; pres. Stride Rite Retail Corp., 1979-82, Stride Rite Footwear, 1982-86, dir., v.p. merchandise, 1980-86; pres., chmn. bd. K-Swiss, Inc., Westlake Village, Calif., 1987—. Recipient INC 500 award, INC Mag., 2001. Office: K-Swiss Inc 31248 Oak Crest Dr Westlake Village CA 91361-4643 Fax: (818) 706-5390.

NICHOLS, STEVEN PARKS, mechanical engineer, lawyer, educator, academic administrator; b. Cody, Wyo., July 1, 1950; s. Rufus Parks Nichols and Gwen Sena (Frank) Keyes; m. Mary Ruth Barrow, Aug. 5, 1990; 1 child, Nicholas Barrow Nichols. PhD, U. Tex., Austin, 1975, JD, 1983. Assoc. dir. Tex. Space Grant Consortium, Austin, 1989-91, dir. Design Projects Program, 1989—2002; dep. dir. Ctr. for Energy Studies, U. Tex., Austin, 1988-91, dir. of Ctr., 1991-99, acting dir. Ctr. for Electromechanics, 1994-99, assoc. prof. mech. engring., 1996—2000, prof. mech. engring., 2004—, assoc. chair dept. mech. engring., 1999—2001, dir. Ctr. for Energy and Environ. Resources, 1998—99, fellow Ctr. for Nano and Molecular Scis., 1998—99, dir. Chair of Free Enterprise, 2001—, fellow, 2001—, assoc. v.p. rsch., 2002—. Bd. dirs. Assn. Mfg. Excellence; chmn. Nat. Coun. Space Grant Dirs., NASA, 1989-92; bd. dirs. So. Coalition for Advanced Transp., 1994-99, chair elect 1998-99, chair 1998-2000; bd. dirs. Nat. Inst. for Engring. Ethics, 1996-2001; chmn. mgmt. divsn. ASME Internat., 1999-2001, exec. com. engring. and tech. mgmt., 1999-. Patentee (with others) pulsed welding techniques, railgun igniter, inert burner, rail thruster, other patents pending. Fellow ASME, IC2 Inst. (sr.), Ctr. for Nano and Biotech.; mem. NSPE, ABA, Am. Soc. Engring. Edn. (Fred Merryfield Design award 2001), Nat. Inst. Engring. Ethics (bd. govs. 1987-93, 96-2001), N.Y. Acad. Scis. Home: 1400 Lorrain St Austin TX 78703-4023 Office: U Tex Dept Mech Engring Austin TX 78712

NICHOLS, VICKI ANNE, financial consultant, librarian; b. Denver, June 10, 1949; d. Glenn Warner and Loretta Irene (Chalender) Adams; m. Robert H. Nichols, Oct. 28, 1972 (div.); children: Christopher Travis, Lindsay Meredith. BA, Colo. Coll., 1972; postgrad., U. Denver, 1976-77. Treas., controller, dir. Polaris Resources, Inc., Denver, 1972-86; controller InterCap Devel. Corp., 1986-87; treas., controller, dir. Transnat. Cons., Ltd., 1986-91; web coord. Jefferson County (Colo.) Pub. Libr., 1986—. Dir., owner Nichols Bus. Services. Home: 4305 Brentwood St Wheat Ridge CO 80033-4412 Office: 10200 W 20th Ave Lakewood CO 80215 Office Phone: 303-275-2230. E-mail: vnichols@jefferson.lib.co.us.

NICHOLS, WENDALYN R. publishing executive; d. JoAnna N.S. Klein and Phillip A. Nichols, Fritz D. Schoenknecht (Stepfather) and Edgar Klein(Stepfather); m. Emanuel J. Barron, Sept. 2, 2000; m. Gary M. Hawkins, Apr. 27, 1991 (div. Aug. 1, 1995); 1 child, Veronica Grace Nichols Barron. BA, Seattle Pacific U., 1984; MPhil, Oxford U., 1989. Remedial English and ESL tchr., England, 1980—92; lexicographer Longman Dictionaries, Harlow, 1992—94, editl. mgr., 1994—97; editl. dir. Random House Reference, N.Y.C., 1998—2002; ref. pub. cons. N.Y.C., 2002—. Editor: (dictionary) Random House Webster's College Dictionary, 2001; editor: (author) RH Webster's Easy English Dictionary, 2001; dir.: (quotations collection) RH Webster's Quotationary, 1998; editor: (lang. history) Homegrown English, 2002, (vocabulary building) Verbal Advantage, 2000, (dictionary) Longman Advanced American Dictionary, 2000; editor, lexicographer: dictionary Longman Dictionary of Contemporary English, 1995, Longman Dictionary of American English, 1997. Advisor Am. Nat. Corpus Consortium, 1998—; advisor, linguistics grad. program Montclair (N.J.) State U., 1999—. Overseas Rsch. scholar, Oxford U., 1987—89. Mem.: MLA, Am. Dialect Soc., EURALEX, Dictionary Soc. N.Am. (bd. dirs. 2003—). D-Liberal. Episcopalian. Avocations: ghost writing/book doctoring, yoga, collecting children's books. Personal E-mail: wendalyn@nyc.rr.com.

NICHOLS, WILLIAM CURTIS, psychologist, family therapist, consultant; b. Fayette, Ala., Apr. 16, 1929; s. William Curtis and Eva (Hargett) N.; m. Alice Louise Mancill, May 29, 1954 (dec. 1990); children: Alice Camille, William Mancill, David Paul; m. Mary Anne Pace, Feb. 29, 1992. AB, U. Ala., 1953; EdD, Columbia U., 1960. Diplomate Am. Bd. Profl. Psychology. Asst. prof. sociology U. Ala., Birmingham, 1960-63; postdoctoral fellow Merrill-Palmer Inst., 1963-64, mem. psychotherapy faculty, 1965-69; prof. sociology Samford U., Birmingham, Ala., 1963-65; pvt. practice clin. psychology and marital and family therapy Grosse Pointe, Mich., 1969-73, 76-87; pvt. practice psychology, marital and family therapy Birmingham, Mich., 1976-87; prof. home and family life, dir. marriage and family counseling Fla. State U., 1973-76; exec. dir. Gov.'s Constituency Children, Fla., 1987-89; pvt. practice marital and family therapy S.E. Family Inst., 1989-90; pres. William Nichols Assocs., Organizational Cons., 1990-91; cons., marital and family therapist Atlanta, 1992—97; cons. in field, 1997-98; with The Nichols Group, Inc., 1998. Adj. prof. clin. psychology U. Detroit, 1976-83; adj. prof. family therapy Fla. State U., 1990-91; adj. prof., grad. faculty child and family devel. dept. U. Ga., 1992—, founder, chair adv. com. Family Therapy Archives, 1993—, The Nichols Group, Inc., 1998-99. Author: Treating People in Families: An Integrative Framework, 1996, Marital Therapy: An Integrative Approach, 1988, Treating Adult Survivors of Childhood Sexual Abuse, 1992, The AAMFT: Fifty Years of Marital and Family Therapy, 1992, Family Therapy Around the World: A Festschrif to Florence Kaslow, 2004; co-author: Systematic Family Therapy, 1986; editor: (with others) Handbook of Family Development and Intervention, 2000; editor The Family Coord., 1970-75, Jour. Marriage and Family Counseling, 1974-76, Contemporary Family Therapy: An Internat. Jour., 1986—, Family Therapy News, 1986-91, The Internat. Connection, 1996-99; mem. editl. bd. Internat. Jour. Family Therapy, 1977-85, Jour. Divorce and Remarriage, 1976-83, 85—, Sage Family Studies Abstracts, 1977—, Family Systems Medicine, 1982-96, Jour. Marital and Family Therapy, 1984—, Jour. Family Psychotherapy, 1990—, Jour. Family Psychology, 1986-90. Mem. mental health and health coms. Mayor's Commn. on Children and Youth, 1966-69; bd. dirs. Family and Children's Svc., Oakland, Mich., 1977-87, chmn., 1984-86, dir. emeritus, 1987—. With C.E., U.S. Army, 1948-49. Recipient Svc. award Ala. Assn. for Mental Health, 1962, Spl. award for Outstanding Contbns. Fla. Assn. Marriage and Family Therapy, 1977, 82, 90; NSF fellow U. Colo., 1963, Disting. Svc. to families award Southeastern Coun. on Family Rels., 1996. Fellow: Am. Assn. Marriage and Family Therapy (dir. 1969—72, founding editor Jour. Marital and Family Therapy 1974—76, co-chmn. Atlanta Multiregional Conf. 1975, chmn. accreditation com. 1976—77, co-chmn. Atlanta Multiregional Conf. 1977, pres.-elect 1979—80, dir. 1979—83, pres. 1981—82, Spl. awards 1976, 1978, Disting. Leadership awards 1982, 1983, Disting. Leadership award 1991, Orgnl. Contbns. award 1992), Am. Psychol. Soc., APA; mem.: Internat. Family Therapy Assn. (bd. dirs. ex-officio 1996—98, charter, editor Internat. Connections 1996—99, pres.-elect 1998—99, pres. 2000—01), Ga. Assn. for Marriage and Family Therapy (pres.-elect 1994—95, pres. 1996), Mich. Bd. Marriage Counselors (chmn. 1980—87), Nat. Coun. on Family Rels. (bd. dir., exec. com. 1969—78, pres. 1976—77), Mich. Assn. Marriage Counselors (pres. 1969—71, chmn. profl. liaison com. 1972—73), Mich. Inter-Profl. Assn. on Marriage, Divorce and Family (com. chmn. 1968—71, 1976—86, trustee 1977—80, Orgnl. Contbn. award 1992), Assn. Marital and Family therapy Regulation Bds. (MFT examination adv. bd. 1989—92), Am. Assn. Marriage and Family therapy Edn. and Rsch. Found. (trustee 1992—94). Home: 755 W Lake Dr Athens GA 30606 Personal E-mail: nicholsw@aol.com.

NICHOLS, WILLIAM FORD, JR., foundation executive, business executive; b. Palo Alto, Calif., July 4, 1934; s. William Ford and Elizabeth (Woodyatt) N.; m. Rosemary Peterson, 1988; children: Deborah, John, Andrew. AB, Stanford U., 1956, MBA, 1958. CPA, Calif. With Price Waterhouse, San Francisco, 1958-69, Price Waterhouse & Co., Sydney, Australia, 1966; asst. contr. Saga Corp., Menlo Park, Calif., 1969-72, contr., 1972—, asst. treas., 1981-83; assoc. prof. San Jose State U., 1983-88; treas. William and Flora Hewlett Found., Menlo Park, 1985-2000. Trustee Investment Fund for Founds., 1991-2001. Bd. dirs. Lucile Packard Found. for Children's Health, Palo Alto, Calif., 1999—. Mem. AICPA, Calif. Soc. CPA's, Inst. Mgmt. Accts. (nat. v.p. 1974-75, bd. dirs.), Fin. Execs. Inst. (pres. Santa Clara Valley chpt. 1979-80). Home: 330 August Cir Menlo Park CA 94025-5829

NICHOLS, WILLIAM J. film studies educator; b. N.Y.C., Aug. 19, 1942; s. James William and Nellie Mae Nichols; m. Catherine M. Soussloff, June 24, 1994; 1 child, Eugenia Clark. BA, Duke U., 1964; MA, UCLA, 1972, PhD, 1978. Prof. Queen's U., Kingston, Ont., Can., 1978-87, chair, 1976-85, San Francisco State U., 1987-90, prof., 1987-2001, 2002—; prof. art history, Frances Knapp Allen chair of art history U. Rochester, 2001—02. Vis. assoc. scholar U. Calif., Santa Cruz, 1990-93; legal cons., L.A. and San Francisco, 1991—; critic Sta. KUSP-NPR Radio, Santa Cruz, 1990-2001. Author: Movies and Methods, 2 vols., 1985, Representing Reality, 1991, Blurred Boundaries, 1994 (Critic's Choice award, 1994), Introduction to Documentary, 2001, Maya Deren and the American Avant-Garde, 2001. Getty rsch. assoc. Getty Mus., L.A., 1999-00. Office: Cinema Dept SFSU 1600 Holloway Ave San Francisco CA 94132 Office Phone: 415-338-6192. E-mail: wnichols@sfsu.edu.

NICHOLSON, BRITAIN W. health facility administrator, physician, educator; MD, Duke U., 1976. Diplomate Am. Bd. Internal Medicine. Resident in gen. medicine Mass. Gen. Hsop., Boston, 1980, fellow in gen. medicine, 1982, sr. v.p., chief med. officer, dir. primary care, instr. in medicine. Office: Bulfinch Med Group Founders House 3rd Fl 55 Fruit St Boston MA 02114-2622

NICHOLSON, BRUCE ALLEN, lawyer; b. Phila., Nov. 12, 1949; s. Charles Glanz and Jean (Billman) N.; m. Linda King Barton, Apr. 22, 1972; children: Jessica Ann, James Barton. BA, Cornell U., 1971; JD cum laude, Boston Coll., 1975. Bar: Pa. 1975. Staff asst. Mass Bar Assn., Boston, 1973-75; assoc. Duffy, North, Wilson, Thomas & Nicholson, LLP, Hatboro, Pa., 1975-78; ptnr., 1978—. Solicitor Mongomery County (Pa.) Redevel. Authority, 1993—. Pres. Main St. Hatboro Revitalization Com., 1995-2000; mem. Hatboro Boro Coun., 1984-88; chmn. Hatboro Hist. Commn., 1981-83; bd. mgrs. Hatboro Area YMCA, 1984-95, bd. chmn., 1990, 91; pres., Comet Class Yacht Racing Assn., 1979-80; chmn., Washington District, Cradle of Liberty Coun., Boy Scouts of Am., 2004-. Named YMCA Vol. of Yr., 1989, 92. Mem. ABA, Pa. Bar Assn., Montgomery Bar Assn., greater Hatboro C. of C. (v.p., bd. dirs.), Rotary, Yacht Club Stone Harbor (N.J.), Riverton Yacht Club (N.J.). Office: Duffy North Wilson Thomas & Nicholson PO Box 726 104 N York Rd Hatboro PA 19040-2699 E-mail: banicholson@duffynorth.com.

NICHOLSON, BRUCE J. insurance company executive; With Ministers Life Ins. Co., Mpls., 1975-1984, Towers Perrin Co, Mpls., 1984-1990; now with Lutheran Brotherhood Inc., 1990—, now sr. exec. v.p. financial svcs., CEO, 2000—. Office: Lutheran Brotherhood Inc 625 4th Ave S Ste 100 Minneapolis MN 55415-1665

NICHOLSON, DOUGLAS ROBERT, accountant; b. Avon, N.Y., Dec. 4, 1921; s. Robert William and Ruth (Neff) N.; m. Gertrude Jane Scott, Apr. 24, 1944; children— Laurie, Scott, Susan, Steven. AB, U. Rochester, 1942, MS, 1948. Baseball player St. Louis Cardinal Farm Teams, 1942, 46; staff acct. Oliver & Clapp, 1948-49; sr. acct. Charles L. Clapp & Co., 1949-51; tchr. income taxes U. Rochester, 1950-61; office mgr. Williams, Clapp & Co., 1951-53, ptnr., 1953-56; prin. Haskins & Sells, CPA's, Rochester, N.Y., 1956-59, ptnr., 1959-67, ptnr.-in-charge Rochester office, 1967-82. Author: After Reagan-Bush is it Too Late, 2002. Pres. Estate Planning Coun. Rochester; team capt. YMCA capital fund dr., 1961, Rochester Inst. Tech. new campus fund dr., 1964; chmn. spl. gifts com. U. Rochester, 1965, group leader 38 million capital fund campaign, 1966; mem. acctg. adv. bd. Syracuse U., 1968; adv. com. M.S. program Rochester Inst. Tech. Bd. Dirs.; treas. Highland Hosp., Rochester; bd. dirs. Hosp. Computer Ctr. Rochester, Rochester Regional Rsch. Libr. Coun.; mem. deferred giving adv. coun. Rochester Inst. Tech.; mem. N.Y. State Bd. Pub. Accountancy, 1977-82. Lt. USN, 1942-45, WWII. Decorated two battle stars; recipient Gannett Newspapers awards, 1956, SUNY Empire State medal for philanthropy, 1999. Mem. AICPA, N.Y. State Soc. CPAs (past pres. Rochester), Nat. Assn. Accts., Am. Acctg. Assn., Am. Mgmt. Assn., Rochester C. of C., Beta Alpha Psi. Democrat. Unitarian (trustee). Clubs: Oak Hill Country, University, Genesee Valley. Home and Office: 663 Lake Rd Webster NY 14580-1552

NICHOLSON, ELLEN ELLIS, clinical social worker; b. Boston, Apr. 1, 1940; d. George Letham and Mary Stirling (Money) McIver; divorced; 1 child, Matthew Norman Ellis. Dental Hygienist, Forsyth Coll., 1959; BS, Northeastern U., 1973, MEd in Counseling, 1974; MSW, Boston U., 1984. Registered dental hygienist, Mass. Dental hygienist, 1959-66; clin. coord., pvt. dental practice Forsyth Dental Ctr., Boston, 1966-70; dir. vol. counseling Solomon Mental Health Ctr., Lowell, Mass., 1974-75; social worker East Boston Social Ctrs., Inc., 1976-77, dir. youth family counseling, 1977-79; supr. family svc. Boston Housing Authority, 1979-81; social worker Mass. Soc. Prevention Cruelty to Children, Hyannis, 1984-86, supr., 1986-93, clinic dir., 1993-95; dir. profl. svcs. Child and Family Svc. of Cape Cod, Hyannis, 1995-98, dir., 1998—, dir. Abuse Prevention Svcs., 1995-96, dir., 1995—. Psychotherapist Riverview Sch., Sandwich, Mass., 1989-93. Advisor youth group Christ Episcopal Ch., Needham, Mass., 1960-64, St. Paul's Ch., Newburyport, Mass., 1964-65; vol. counselor Solomon Mental Health Ctr., Lowell, 1972-74; chair Barnstable County Children's Task Force, 1994-96; chmn. adv. com. Barnstable County Sexual Abuse Intervention Network, 1994-96; mem. task force Barnstable County Juvenile Firesetters, 1995-96, mem. steering com., 1996—; mem. adv. bd. Cape and Islands Child Advocacy Ctr.; mem. Cape & Islands Domestic Violence Coun. Bd., 1998—. Mem. NASW, Am. Profl. Soc. on Abuse of Children, Assn. for Treatment of Sexual Abusers, Sigma Phi Alpha, Sigma Epsilon Rho, Kappa Delta Pi. Avocations: travel, ballroom dancing, skiing. Office: Child and Family Svc Cape Cod 1019 Rt 132 Hyannis MA 02601-1839

NICHOLSON, FREDA HYAMS, museum executive, medical educator; b. Asheville, N.C., Sept. 10, 1934; d. John Fred and Thelma (Lewis) Hyams; m. Henry Hale Nicholson Jr., Sept. 24, 1956; children: Henry Hale III, T.D. Miller, J. Christie, Michael Witherspoon, Freda Amanda, Stuart. RN, St. Joseph's Hosp., 1955; BS in Nursing and Biology, Queens Coll., 1959, LHD (hon.), 1982; MEd, U. N.C., Charlotte, 1976. Surg. nurse Ochesner Clinic, New Orleans, 1955-56; nursing adminstr. Presbyn. Hosp., Charlotte, 1956-59; part-time instr. biology and nursing Ctrl. Piedmont Coll., Charlotte, 1976-81; health educator, edn. curator Discover Place, Inc. (formerly Charlotte Nature Mus.), 1971-80, pres., CEO, 1981—. Acting dir. Discovery Place, Charlotte, 1981; cons. health Health Adventure, Asheville, 1968; mem. mus. planning com. Sci. Mus. Project, Little rock, 1984; in internat. partnership NEA, Washington, 1983; mem. U.S. Cultural Commn./India, participant in seminar in India, 1984; mem. adv. panel NSF, 1988—; bd. dirs. First Union Nat. Bank N.C. Bd. dirs. United Way, Charlotte, 11983, March of Dimes, Charlotte, 1978-83, Jr. Achievement, 1983—, Mission Air, 1984—; cons. Gov.'s Com. for Econ. Growth throuth Edn., 1984; mem. exec. bd. N.C. Sch. of Math. and Sci., 1986—; active mem. local, state and nat. med. auxs., 1956—; mem. bd. visitors J.C. Smith U., Charlotte, 1983—; mem. adv. panel NSF, 1988—. Recipient Gov.'s N.C. award, 1994; named Woman of Yr., City of charlotte, 1982, Nat. Outstanding Alumna Alpha Chi Omega, 1983, Outstanding Alumna Queens Coll., 1982. Mem. AAUW, Women Execs., Assoc. Sci./Tech. Ctrs. (sec. 1984-90, pres. 1990), Internat. Coun. Mus. Execs. (commr. Semocet-Sci. 1988—), Am. Assn. Mus. (commr. for accreditation, at-large coun., mem. 1989—), S.E. Mus. Coun., Greater Charlotte C. of C. (advt. com.), Jr. Women, Guild of Nature Mus. Office: Discovery Place 301 N Tryon St Charlotte NC 28202-2138

NICHOLSON, GEOFFREY WILLIAM GREER, management consultant; b. Montreal, Quebec, Canada, Mar. 5, 1959; s. John Greer and Monique Forthomme Nicholson; m. Elizabeth Theresa Lutley, Apr. 16, 1960; children: Henry, Miranda, William, Esme, Rupert. AB, Harvard U., 1980, MBA, 1984. Ptnr. The Boston Consulting Group, N.Y.C., 1980—99; mng. dir. Goldman Sachs Internat., London, 2000—02, Mercer Oliver Wyman, 2002—. Baker scholar, Harvard Grad. Sch. Bus. Adminstrn., 1984. Mem.: Belle Haven Club. Conservative. Episcopalian. Avocations: travel, skiing, bicycling. Home: 495 Field Point Road Greenwich CT 06830 Office: Mercer Oliver Wyman 1 Neal Street London WC2H 9QL England Office Phone: +44-207 259-0839. Personal E-mail: gwgnicholson@btinternet.com. E-mail: gnicholson@mow.com.

NICHOLSON, GERALD LEE, airport administrator; b. Belleville, Ill., Dec. 30, 1944; s. Chester Lee and Bette Joan (Tarr) N.; m. Cathy Ann Sammons, May 3, 1975; children: Laura, Brianna. BA in Sociology, So. Ill. U., 1974, BS in Math., MBA, So. Ill. U., 1976. Bus. mgr. Northland Orthopedic Group, St. Louis, 1976-78; cons. AMA, Chgo., 1978-80; cons. pvt. practice Evansville, Ind., 1981-85; adminstr. Mo. Eye Inst., St. Louis, 1985-91; regional v.p. Co-Care Eye Cts., St. Louis, 1985-91; adminstr. Orthopaedic Assoc., P.C., Cape Girardeau, Mo., 1992—2001; gen. mgr. Mt. Vernon (Ill.) Airport. Tax preparer Nicholson Cons., St. Louis, 1990-92. Mem. Citizen Interaction Com., Chesterfield, Mo., 1989, Leadership Cape, 1992. Capt. USMC, 1966-72, Vietnam. Mem.: Am. Assn. Airport Execs., Aircraft Owners and Pilots Assn, Exptl. Aircraft Assn., Little Egypt Bicycle Club, Elks, Rotary Internat. (pres. local chpt.). Avocations: running, flying. Home: 3105 Jamison Blvd Mount Vernon IL 62864 Office: Mt Vernon Airport 100 Aviation Dr Mount Vernon IL 62864

NICHOLSON, HENRY HALE, JR., surgeon; b. Statesville, N.C., June 22, 1922; s. Henry Hale and Martha Haseltine (Miller) N.; m. Freda Hyams, Sept. 24, 1956; children: Henry Hale III, Thomas Dalton Miller, John Christie, Michael Witherspoon, Freda Amanda, W. Stuart Cooper. BA in Chemistry, Duke U., 1944, MD, 1947; grad., USAF Sch. Aviation Medicine, 1952. Diplomate Am. Bd. Gen. Surgery, Am. Bd. Colon and Rectal Surgery. Rotating intern U. Wis. Gen. Hosp., Madison, 1947-48; resident in gen. surgery Med. Coll. Va., Richmond, 1948-49, Alton Ochsner Hosp. and Clinic, New Orleans, 1949-51, 53-55, inaugeral resident in colon and rectal surgery, 1955-56; resident in gen. surgery Tulane U., La. Charity Hosp., New Orleans, 1949-51, 53-55; pvt. practice gen., colon and rectal surgery, aerospace medicine Charlotte, N.C., 1956—; sr. surg. staff mem. Carolinas Med. Ctr. and Mercy Hosp., Charlotte. Sr. active staff Presbyn. Hosp., Charlotte; sr. active teaching staff Carolinas Med. Ctr., 1956-85, cons. staff, 1985—. Mem. Airport Authority Charlotte/Douglas Internat. Airport, 1992—; mem. Mayor's Com. of 100 to study regional transp. and make appropriate recommendations, 1993-94; sr. examiner FAA, 1952—; mem. athletic-med. bd. N.C. Shrine Bowl, 1980—. With U.S. Army, 1943-46; flight surgeon USAF, 1951-53, Korea; col. USAFR, 1961-82; 1st air surgeon N.C. (command) Air. NG, 1970-82, surg. cons. Surgeon Gen. USAF, 1971-82, command flight surgeon 1981 (award) U.S. Air NG, 1st alternate flight surgeon 1982 (award) USAF. Decorated Legion of Merit; recipient Disting. Svc. medal N.C. Fellow ACS, Am. Soc. Colon and Rectal Surgeons; mem. Mecklenberg County Med. Soc. (pres. 1972), Charlotte Surg. Soc. (pres. 1987), Shriners (Scottish Rite), Masons (32 degree), Jesters, Alton Ochsner Surg. Soc., Hazel Creek Trout Club, Robert Burns Soc., St. Andrews Soc. of Carolina, Air Force Assn., Hound Ears Club (Blowing Rock, N.C.), Charlotte Country Club, Alpha Tau Omega, Phi Chi, Omicron Delta Kappa. Methodist. Avocations: golf, skiing, fly fishing, travel, painting. Home: 3933 Fellsway Dr Charlotte NC 28209-3417

NICHOLSON, JACK, actor; b. Neptune, NJ, Apr. 22, 1937; raised by John and Ethel May N.; m. Sandra Knight, 1961 (div. 1966); children: Jennifer, Lorraine Broussard. Acting debut: (Hollywood stage prodn.) Tea an Sympathy; actor: (films) Cry-Baby Killer, 1958, Studs Lonigen, 1960, Little Shop of Horrors, 1960, Ensign Pulver, 1964, The Trip, 1967, Easy Rider, 1969 (Acad. award nomination best supporting actor), Five Easy Pieces, 1970, Carnal Knowledge, 1971, A Safe Place, 1971, The Last Detail, 1974 (Cannes Film Festival prize, BAFTA award best actor), Chinatown, 1974 (BAFTA award best actor, Acad. award nomination, NY Film Critics Circle award, Golden Globe award best actor), Tommy, The Passenger, 1975, The Fortune, 1975, One Flew Over the Cuckoo's Nest, 1975 (Golden Globe award best actor, Acad. award best actor, NY Film Critics Circle award, BAFTA award best actor), The Missouri Breaks, 1976, The Last Tycoon, 1976, The Shining, 1980, The Postman Always Rings Twice, 1981, Reds, 1981 (BAFTA award best supporting actor, Acad. award nomination best supporting actor), The Border, 1982, Terms of Endearment, 1983 (Acad. award best supporting actor, Golden Globe award best actor), Prizzi's Honor, 1985, Heartburn, 1986, The Witches of Eastwick, 1987, Broadcast News, 1987, Ironweed, 1987 (Acad. award nomination best actor), Batman, 1989; actor, actor: (films) Man Trouble, 1991, A Few Good Men, 1992, Hoffa, 1992, Wolf, 1994, The Crossing Guard, 1995, Mars Attacks!, 1996, The Evening Star, 1996, Blood and Wine, 1996, As Good As It Gets, 1997 (Acad. award best actor, Golden Globe award best actor, SAG award best actor), The Pledge, 2001, About Schmidt, 2002 (Acad. award nomination best actor, Golden Globe award best actor), Anger Management, 2003, Something's Gotta Give, 2003; prodr.: Head, 1968, Ride the Whirlwind, The Shooting; dir.: Drive, He Said, 1971; dir., actor: (films) Goin' South, 1978, The Two Jakes, 1990. Co-recipient (with Bobby McFerrin) Grammy award for best recording for children, 1987; recipient Life Achievement award, Am. Film Inst., 1994, Cecil B. DeMille award, 1999. Office: Bresler Kelly & Assocs 11500 W Olympic Blvd Ste 510 Los Angeles CA 90064-1578

NICHOLSON, JIM, political organization administrator; m. Suzanne Nicholson; 3 children. BA, U.S. Mil. Acad. at West Point, 1961; MA, Columbia U., 1969; JD, U. Denver, 1972. Atty., Denver, 1973-78; pres. Renaissance Homes, Denver, Nicholson Enterprises, Inc.; chmn. Rep. Nat. Com., 1997—. Chmn. task force presdl. primaries and caucuses Rep. Nat. Com., 1996, chmn. rules com., 1993-97, mem. budget com. Col. U.S. Army, Vietnam. Decorated Bronze Star, Combat Infantry badge, Meritorious Svc. medal with oak leaf cluster, Vietnamese Cross for Gallantry, 2 Air medals. Office: Rep Nat Com 310 1st St SE Washington DC 20003-1885

NICHOLSON, JOHN W. federal agency administrator; BS, West Point; MPA, Shippensburg U. Under-sec. for meml. affairs Dept. VA, 2003—. Recipient Fed. Exec. fellowship in fgn. policy, Brookings Instn. Office: Rm 400 810 Vermont Ave Washington DC 20420

NICHOLSON, JOSEPH BRUCE, real estate developer; b. San Jose, Calif., Jan. 21, 1940; s. Wilmot Joseph and Ruth (Russell) N.; m. Susan Knight, Nov. 1963 (div. 1972); children: Kelsey Erin, Craig Wilmot; m. Linda Mirassou, Aug. 1992. BArch, U. Oreg., 1963. Exec. v.p. Nicholson-Brown Inc., Santa Clara, Calif., 1967-80; prin. Nicholson Assocs., Aptos, Calif., 1977—; v.p., gen. mgr. Nicholson-Wilson Co., Santa Clara, 1980-83; prin. The Nicholson Co., Campbell, Calif., 1984—; v.p. Pacific Property Ventures Inc., Campbell, 1988—; pres. Nicholson Constrn. Inc., Campbell, 1989—; v.p. Nicholson Property Mgmt. Inc., Campbell, 1989—; pres. The Nicholson Family Found., 1996—. Bd. dirs. Transmetrics Inc., San Jose. Bd. dirs. Triton Mus., Santa Clara, 1979, Hope Rehab. Svc., San Jose, 1979, United Way Ctrl. Area, San Jose, 1991. Devel. Engring. Rsch. Inst., Carmel, Calif., 1999—, Cabrillo Festival of Contemporary Music, Santa Cruz, Calif., 2002—, Tannery Art Ctr., Santa Cruz, 2003—; pres. adv. bd. de Saisset Mus., Santa Clara U., 1991; trustee Mus. of Art and History, Santa Cruz, 1993. Lt. USN, 1963-67. Mem. Rotary, Commonwealth Club (San Francisco), World Trade Club (San Francisco), Santa Cruz Yacht Club, Tennis Club Rio Del Mar. Republican. Avocations: travel, reading, art, painting, tennis. Home: 218 Shoreview Dr Aptos CA 95003-4621 Office: The Nicholson Co 75 Cristich Ln Campbell CA 95008-5403 E-mail: brucenicholson@thenicholsonco.com.

NICHOLSON, LELAND ROSS, retired utilities company executive, energy consultant; b. Carrington, ND, Feb. 21, 1924; s. Malcom and Lena May (Kerlin) N.; m. Virginia E. Blair, Mar. 16, 1946; children: Heather Le Nicholson Studebaker, Leland B., Holly Kay. Student, Northwestern U., 1940-41; BSEE, U. N.D., 1949; postgrad. in utility mgmt., U. Minn., 1952. Planning and mktg. engr. Minkota Power Coop., Grand Forks, N.D., 1949-54; dir. new bus. Kans. Power & Light Co., Topeka, 1954-64, v.p. mktg., 1964-76, sr. v.p., 1976-80, exec. v.p., 1980-83, also bd. dirs.; pres. Kans. Power & Light Gas Service, Topeka, 1985-88, ret., 1988; pres., chief operating officer The Gas Service Co., Kansas City, Mo., 1983-85. Pres. Indsl. Devel. Corp., Topeka; chmn. Kans. Coun. on Electricity and Environment; exec. com. Kansas City Labor Mgmt. Coun., 1986-89; mem. Mktg. Execs. Conf.; bd. dirs. Gas Service Energy Corp., Kansas City, Merchants Nat. Bank, Topeka. Idea innovator heat pump water heater, photo cell controlled yard light, electric grill. Bd. dirs., area relations com. Kansas City (Mo.) Area Econ. Devel. Council, 1983-89; bd. dirs. Kansas City Pvt. Industry Coun., 1986-89, Kansas City Downtown Council; trustee U. Mo., Kansas City, 1984-91; mktg. chmn. Kansas City Full Employment Council; past chmn., mem. Topeka-Shawnee County Planning Commn.; adult adv. com. Sea Scouts. Master sgt. USMC, 1942-46. Mem. Am. Gas Assn., Midwest Gas Assn. (bd. dirs. 1985-89), Mo. Valley Electric Assn. (chmn. 1979-81), Edison Electric Inst. (mktg. chmn. 1978-80), Assoc. Industries of Mo., Kans. Assn. Commerce and Industry, Greater Kansas City (Mo.) C. of C. (bd. dirs. 1979-82), Shawnee Yacht Club (Topeka) (commodore 1972-74), Lake Gaston Assn. (pres. 1993-97), Kansas City Club, Rotary. Republican. Congregationalist. Avocations: sailing, canoeing, fishing, reading, electronics.

NICHOLSON, MARILYN LEE, arts administrator; b. San Jose, Calif., Feb. 7, 1949; d. John Hart Nicholson and Betty Ann (Price) Shepardson; m. Neal Luit Evenhuis. BA in English and History, U. Ariz., 1972; BFA in Studio, MA in English, U. Hawaii-Manoa, Honolulu, 1977, AS, 1984. Edn. coord., dir. Bishop Mus. Arts and Crafts Sch., Honolulu, 1977-79; owner Fiber Arts Store, Kailua, Hawaii, 1978-82; field coord. Hawaii State Found. on Culture and Arts, Honolulu, 1981-85; exec. dir. Sedona (Ariz.) Arts Ctr., 1986-92, Volcano (Hawaii) Art Ctr., 1992—. Mem. bd. artist selection com. Ariz. Indian Living Treasures, 1988-92; bd. dirs., treas. Sedona Cultural Arts Ctr., 1987-92; conf. speaker Nat. Assembly Arts Agys., 1988. Founding Chmn. Sedona Gallery Assn., 1990-92; mem. com. Sedona Acad., 1986-92; mem. steering com. community plan City of Sedona, 1989-91, comm. Arts & Cultural Cu., Sedona, 1989-91; mem. exec. com. planning Volcano Community Assn., 1993-96. Recipient Mayor's award for Disting. Svc., Sedona City Coun., 1992. Mem. Hawaii Mus. Assn. (bd. dirs. 1995-00), Cooper Ctr. Coun. (bd. dirs. 1992—), Aloha Festivals-Hawaii Island (bd. dirs. 1992-99). Office: Volcano Art Ctr PO Box 129 Volcano HI 96785

NICHOLSON, R. STEPHEN, organization administrator; b. Radford, Va., Mar. 4, 1926; s. Roy S. and Ethel Dovie (Macy) Nicholson; m. Carol Peterson; 1 child, Suzanne Carpenter. AB, Marion Coll., 1950; MA, Syracuse U., 1956; PhD, Mich. State U., 1971. Pres. Daley Coll., Chgo., 1969-71; prof. Lansing C.C., Lansing, Mich., 1963-66, acad. dean, 1971—76; pres. Clark County C.C. (now So. Nev. C.C.), 1971—76, Mt. Hood C.C., 1976—85; chancellor Oakland C.C., 1985-90; vice chancellor Higher Colls. of Tech., United Arab Emirates, 1990-92; CEO Internat. Christian Leadership, 1992-93, Mercy Corps Internat., 1994—95, chmn. bd. dirs., 1997—2004. Pres. Creative Futures; bd. dirs. MCI. Sr. fellow for higher edn. M.J. Murdock Trust, 1993—95, 1996—99; chair bd. dirs. N.W. Autism Found., 2000—02. Mem.: World Affairs Coun., Am. Acad. Polit. and Social Scis., Am. Sociology Assn., Am. Sch. Adminstrs. Assn., N.W. Assn. Cmty. and Jr. Coll.s (pres. 1976), Am. Assn. Cmty. and Jr. Colls. (pres. Pres.'s Acad. 1982, bd. dirs. 1985—87), Am. Futurist Soc., Japan-Am. Soc., Gresham C. of C. (dir. 1977—79), Rotary Club (pres. 1983, Paul Harris fellow 1986), Phi Delta Kappa. Home: 9685 Irvine Bay Ct Las Vegas NV 89147-8365

NICHOLSON, RALPH LESTER, botanist, educator; b. Lynn, Mass., Aug. 25, 1942; s. Nathan Aaron and Muriel Spinney (Buxton) N. BA, U. Vt., 1964; MS, U. Maine, 1967; PhD, Purdue U., 1972. Prof. dept. botany and plant pathology Purdue U., West Lafayette, Ind., 1972—. Contbr. chpts. to books, more than 100 articles to profl. jours. Active Big Bros./Big Sisters, Lafayette, Ind., 1974—. Fellow Am. Phytopathol. Soc. Office: Purdue U Botany and Plant Pathology Lafayette IN 47907 E-mail: nicholson@btny.purdue.edu.

NICHOLSON, RICHARD SELINDH, educational association administrator; b. Des Moines, Apr. 5, 1938; s. George Eugene and Margaret (Selindh) N.; m. Mary Lou Weisbrod, Aug. 1, 1958 (div. 1971) 1 child, Jeffrey Richard; m. Lois Ann Karls, Aug. 15, 1976; 1 child, Gregory Michael. BS, Iowa State U., 1960; PhD, U. Wis., 1964; LHD (hon.), CUNY, 1994, CUNY-Mt. Sinai Med. Ctr., 1994. Rsch. assoc. U. Wis., Madison, 1963-64; asst. prof. Mich. State U., East Lansing, 1964-67, assoc. prof., 1967-70; program dir. NSF, Washington, 1970-77, div. dir., 1977-82, chief of staff, 1983-85, asst. dir., 1985-89; exec. dir. Nat. Sci. Bd. Commn., Washington, 1982-83; exec. officer, pub. Science AAAS, Washington, 1989—. Cons. on sci. affairs Pres. of U.S., Washington, 1978-79; exec. sec. Pres.' Com. on Nat. Medal Sci., Washington, 1976-84; mem. Pres.' Nat. Commn. on Superconductivity, 1989; vice chair Commn. on Phys. Scis., Math and Resources NRC, 1989—, Edn. Coordinating Coun., 1991—, com. on environ. rsch., 1991-92, co-chair coun. on competitiveness, 1993—; mem. statutory vis. com. Nat. Inst. of Stds. and Tech., 1990-93; vis. com. chemistry dept. Harvard U., 1989—; bd. dirs. Quality Edn. for Minorities Network, 1989—; trustee Gordon Rsch. Conf., 1989—; sci. policy adv. com. com. space, sci. and tech. U.S. Ho. Reps., 1992—; co-chair Coun. on Competitiveness, 1993—, Dept. of Energy Panel on Basic Rsch., 1995—; chmn. edn. adv. com. Genentech, 1993—. Mem. editorial bd. Analytical Chemistry, 1980-82, Chem. and Engring. News, 1985-88; contbr. articles to profl. jours. and chpts. to books. Served as seaman USN, 1956-63. Recipient Presdl. Disitng. Ranking, Pres. Reagan, 1982, Alumni Citation Merit award Iowa State U., 1983. Fellow AAAS; mem. Am. Chem. Soc. (chmn. Mich. State U. sect. 1968-70), Chem. Soc. Washington (nominations com. 1977), Cosmos Club, Nat. Press Club. Avocations: sports, tennis, reading. Home: 1020 Union Church Rd Mc Lean VA 22102-1115 Office: AAAS 1200 New York Ave NW Ste 100 Washington DC 20005-3941

NICHOLSON, ROBERT ARTHUR, college president; b. Pepin, Wis., Oct. 13, 1923; s. Arthur W. and Ethel (Weeden) N.; m. Dorothy Nelis, June 17, 1944; children: Paul, Gary. BS, Anderson U., Ind., 1944; MA, NYU, 1946, PhD, 1953. With Anderson U., 1945-90, successively instr., asst. prof., assoc. prof. music, chmn. dept., asst. to dean, 1945-58, dean, 1958-83, v.p., 1964-83, pres., 1983-90, pres. emeritus, 1990—. Author: Handbook to the Hymnal of the Church of God, 1953; Editor: Hymnal of the Church of God, 1953, 71. Interim CEO Ch. of God Ministries, Inc., 1998, cons., 1997-99; interim exec. pastor, Park Place Ch. of God, 1995; interim min. of music, 1999-2002; mem. pub. bd. Ch. of God, 1955-80, chmn. commn. higher edn., 1963-70, 83-86, vice chmn., 1970-83, cons., 1990-96; cons. Warner Pacific Coll., Oreg., 1990-98, N.Ind. United Meth. Found., Inc., 1992-95, Anderson Pub. Libr., 1994-95, United Faith Housing Corp., 1994, Hopewell Ctr., 1996, Alexandria Cmty. Ctr., Inc., 1997, Family Network Agy., Inc., 1997-2000, Wilson Boys and Girls Club, 1997, Cmty. Found. Grant County, 1998, United Way Anderson and Madison County, Ind., 1998, 2000, Anderson Area C. of C., 1998, 2001, Christian Ctr., 2001; bd. dirs. Anderson Symphony Orch., 1974-87, 93-94, United Way Madison County, 1985-89, 91-94, Minnetrista Cultural Found., 1988-2002; bd. dirs., v.p. Anderson Internat., 1990-93; bd. dirs. Cmty. Hosp. Madison County, 1986-95, vice chmn., 1988-94, interim pres., CEO, 1991; mem. Madison County Cmty. Found., Inc., 1991-2003, pres., 1991-98. Mem. Associated Colls. of Ind., Ind. Colls. and Univs. of Ind. (chmn. 1988-89), Anderson Area C. of C. (bd. dirs. 1985-90, vice chmn. and chmn. elect 1988, chmn. 1989).

NICHOLSON, WILL FAUST, JR., bank holding company executive; b. Colorado Springs, Colo., Feb. 8, 1929; s. Will Faust and Gladys Olivia (Burns) N.; m. Shirley Ann Baker, Nov. 26, 1955; children: Ann Louise Nicholson Naughton, Will Faust III. S.B., M.I.T., 1950; MBA, U. Denver, 1956. V.p. Van Schaack & Co., Denver, 1954-66; pntr. N. G. Petry Constrn. Co., Denver, 1966-70; sr. v.p. Colo. Nat. Bankshares, Inc., Denver, 1970-75, pres., 1975-95, chmn. bd., chief exec. officer, 1985-95; chmn. Rocky Mountain Bankcard Sys., Denver, 1995—2001. Bd. dirs. Boys and Girls Clubs of Metro Denver; active Downtown Denver, Inc., Colo. Assn. of Commerce and Industry, chmn. 1990-91, Denver Urban Renewal Authority, 1958-59, Denver Bd. Water Commrs., 1959-65, pres. 1964, 65; Nat. Western Stock Show; bd. Health One. With USAF, 1950-53. Mem. Assn. Bank Holding Cos. (bd. dirs. 1979-87, 89-91, exec. com. 1980-85, vice chmn. 1981-82, chmn. 1983-84), U.S. C. of C. (bd. dirs. 1990—, chmn. 1999-2000), U.S. Golf Assn. (exec. com. 1974-82, v.p. 1978, 79, pres. 1980, 81), Denver Country Club, Univ. Club Colo., Univ. Club N.Y., Castle Pines Golf Club, Royal and Ancient Golf Club (St. Andrews, Scotland), Augusta (Ga.) Nat. Golf Club. Republican. Episcopalian. Home: 37 Polo Club Cir Denver CO 80209-3307 Office: Rocky Mountain BankCard Sys Inc PO Box 5168 Denver CO 80217-5168

NICHOLSON, WILLIAM JOSEPH, forest products consultant; b. Tacoma, Aug. 24, 1938; s. Ferris Frank and Athyleen Myrtle (Fesenmaier) N.; m. Carland Elaine Crook, Oct. 10, 1964; children: Courtney, Brian, Kay, Benjamin. SB in ChemE, MIT, 1960, SM in ChemE Practice, 1961; PhD in ChemE, Cornell U., 1965; MBA, Pacific Luth. U., 1969. Registered profl. chem. engr., Wash. Sr. devel. engr. Hooker Chem. Co., Tacoma, 1964—69, Battelle N.W., Richland, Wash., 1969—70; planning assoc. Potlatch Corp., San Francisco, 1970—75, mgr. corp. energy svc., 1976—94, dir. corp. energy and environ. svcs., 1994—2002, ind. energy and environ. cons., 2002—; chair energy coun. Am. Forest and Paper Assn., Washington, 1998—2002. Chmn. electricity com. Am. Forest and Paper Assn., 1977-98, solid waste task force, 1988-91, air quality com., 1989-2002, water quality com., 2000-2002, regulatory policy com., 1994-2002, vice-chmn. life cycle analysis work group, 1994-2000, chmn. wood products environ. task force, 1994-99, chief tech. officers com. 1994-2002, climate change com., 1992-2002; U.S. expert on environ. labelling to Internat. Stds. Orgn., 1994-2000; chmn. adv. bd. Forest Products Lab., U. Calif., Richmond, 1993-95, 2003; adv. bd. Coll. of Natural Resources, U. Calif., Berkeley, 1993-95; adv. com. Fed. Biomass, 2000-, USDOE Project Peer Reviewer 2004-. Mem. AAAS, AIChE (assoc.), Am. Chem. Soc., Commonwealth Club (San Francisco), Sigma Xi. Republican. Avocations: industrial history, genealogy. Home and Office: PO Box 1114 Ross CA 94957-1114

NICHOLSON, WILLIAM NOEL, clinical neuropsychologist; b. Detroit, Dec. 24, 1936; s. James Eardly and Hazel A. (Wagner) N.; m. Nancy Ann Marshall, June 15, 1957; children: Anne Marie, Kristin, Scott. AB, Wittenberg U., 1959; MDiv, Luth. Theol. Sem., Phila., 1962; PhD, Mich. State U., 1972. Diplomate Am. Bd. Forensic Examiners, Am. Bd. Med. Psychotherapists; lic. clin. psychologist, Mich.; ordained to ministry Luth. Ch., 1962; cert. Nat. Register health Care Providers in Psychology. Parish pastor Our Saviour Luth. Ch., Saginaw, Mich., 1962-69; intern in psychology Ingham Mental Health Bd., 1971-72; resident in psychology Bay-Arenac Mental Health Bd., 1972-74; dir., psychologist Riverside Ctr., Bay City, Mich., 1974-75; pastor, psychologist Psych Studies and Clergy Consultation of Mich., 1989—2003. Pres. Bay Psychol. Assocs., P.C., Bay City, 1975—2002; cons. Gov.'s Office of Drug Abuse, 1972-74. Author: A Guttman Facet Analysis of Attitude-Behaviors Toward Drug Users by Heroin Addicts and Mental Health Therapists, 1972, An Episcopalian Guide to the Augsburg Confession, 1997; contbr. articles to profl. jours. Mem. APA, Mich. Psychol. Assn. Office: 820 Arlington Ave Ste 2 Petoskey MI 49770 Office Phone: 231-347-4700. Personal E-mail: fatherbill36@hotmail.com.

NICHOLSON-GUTHRIE, CATHERINE S. See GUTHRIE, CATHERINE

NICITA, RICK, agent; m. Paula Wagner, 1984. Agent Creative Artists Agy., co-chmn., 1995—. Chmn. Am. Cinematheque; former vice-chmn. Am. Film Inst. Office: Creative Artists Agy 9830 Wilshire Blvd Beverly Hills CA 90212-1825

NICKEL, ALBERT GEORGE, advertising agency executive; b. Pitts., July 12, 1943; s. Frank George and Dorothy (Wiefling) N.; m. Dana Cooper; children: Mark, Grace, Olivia. AB, Washington and Jefferson Coll., 1965; MBA, Ind. U., 1967. Mktg. rsch. analyst Pfizer, Inc., N.Y.C., 1967, prof. svc. rep., 1967-68, mktg. rsch. mgr., 1968-69, product mgr., 1969-70, USV Internat., Tuckahoe, NY, 1970-71; account supr. Sudler & Hennessey, N.Y.C., 1973-77; sr. v.p. mgmt. group supr. Young and Rubicam, N.Y.C., 1977-79; chmn., pres., COO Dorritie Lyons & Nickel, Inc., N.Y.C.; chmn., pres., CEO HMC Group Omnicom, Inc., 1999—; pres., chmn., CEO Lyons, Lavey, Nickel, Swift, Inc., 2000—. Trustee Wilton YMCA, Five Town Found.; bd. dirs., exec. com. Wilton LaCrosse Assn.; bd. trustees Dominican Coll., Healthcare Businesswoman's Assn., Wilton H.S. Long Range Planning Team, Am. Coun. on Sci. and Health; co-chmn. TBWA WorldHealth. Capt. USAF, 1969. Recipient Ellis Island medal of honor, 2002. Mem. Pharm. Rsch. and Mfrs. Assn. (bd. dirs.), Healthcare Mktg. and Comm. Coun. (bd. dirs.), Vis. Nurses Assn. (mem. found. bd.), Midwest Healthcare Mktg. Assn., Wilton Riding Club (pres.), Shore and Country Club, Silver Spring Country Club. Home: 65 Keelers Ridge Rd Wilton CT 06897-1608 E-mail: anickel@llns.com.

NICKEL, JANET MARLENE MILTON, geriatrics nurse; b. Manitowoc, Wis., June 9, 1940; d. Ashley and Pearl Milton; m. Curtis A. Nickel, July 29, 1961; children: Cassie, Debra, Susan. Diploma, Milw. Inst., 1961; ADN, N.D. State U., 1988. Nurse Milw. VA, Wood, Wis., 1961-62; supervising nurse Park Lawn Convalescent Hosp., Manitowoc, 1964-65; newsletter editor Fargo (N.D.) Model Cities Program, 1970-73; supervising night nurse Rosewood on Broadway, Luth. Hosps. and Homes, Fargo, 1973-92; assoc. dir. nursing Elim Care Ctr., Fargo, 1992-94, night nurse, 1994—. Mem. Phi Eta Sigma. Office: 3534 S University Dr Fargo ND 58104-6228

NICKEL, MELVIN EDWIN, metallurgical engineer; b. St. Louis, Aug. 24, 1915; s. Jacob William and Mary Anna Nickel; m. Mary Louise Breuer, Sept. 12, 1942; children: Elizabeth Ann Nickel Overleas, Mary Patricia Nickel Hepburn, Sheila Breuer Nickel Stojak, William Louis. BS in Metall. Engring., U. Mo., Rolla, 1938, degree in metall. engring., 1967. Mgmt. trainee Bethlehem (Pa.) Steel Corp., 1938-39; asst. to supt. blast furnaces Wis. Steel div. Internat. Harvester Co., Chgo., 1939-43, gen. foreman furnaces, blast furnaces, 1943-48, asst. supt. blast furnaces, 1948-49, supt. open hearths, 1949-61, supt. basic oxygen furnaces, mgr. steel prodn., 1961-68, mgr. primary ops., 1968-77; mgr. facilities planning and appropriations, works mgr. Envirodyne Industries, Inc., Wis. Steel Corp., 1977-80; pres. Melvin E. Nickel & Assocs., Inc., Chgo., 1980—. Contbr. articles to profl. jours. Trustee Iron and Steel Soc. Found., Warrendale, Pa., 1980—91. Named to Athletic Hall of Fame, Mo. Sch. Mines/U. Mo.-Rolla, 1993; recipient Disting. Merit award, U. Mo.-Rolla, 1960, Benjamin F. Fairless award, Iorn and Steel Soc., 2001. Mem.: AIME (hon.; nat. v.p., dir. 1974—76, Hon. Membership award 1978), Western States Blast Furnaces and Coke Assn., Assn. Iron and Steel Engrs., Metall. Soc. of AIME, Iron and Steel Soc. of AIME (nat. pres. 1974—75, elected disting. mem. 1975), Acad. Sch. Mines and Metallurgy U. Mo.-Rolla, U. Mo. Rolla Alumni Assn., Jackson Hole Wildlife Soc., Beverly Hills Univ. Club, Ridge Country Club Chgo., Triangle Fraternity. Republican. Roman Catholic. Achievements include development of early practices for production of special bar quality and alloy steel in top blown basic oxygen furnace. Avocations: hunting, fishing, carpentry, mineral collecting, boating. Home and Office: 10601 S Hamilton Ave Chicago IL 60643-3127

NICKELL, FRANK (NICK) T. diversified financial services company executive; m. Carol Nickell. BS in Bus. Adminstrn. and Acctg., U. N.C. CPA AICPA. With A.M. Pullen & Co., 1971—77; from mem. staff to pres., CEO Kelso & Co., L.P., N.Y., 1977—98, pres., 1998—, CEO, 1998—. Bd. dir. BlackRock Inc., Bear Stearns Cos., Earle M. Jorgensen Co. Bd. visitors U. N.C.; trustee NYU Hosps. Ctr. Avocations: bridge, golf. Office: Kelso & Co 320 Park Ave Fl 24 New York NY 10022*

NICKELL, JOE, paranormal expert; b. Lexington, Ky., Dec. 1, 1944; s. James Wendell and Ella Kathleen (Turner) Nickell; 1 child, Cherette. BA, U. Ky., 1967, MA, 1982, PhD, 1987. Profl. stage magician, Toronto, Ont., Can., 1968-73; pvt. investigator, 1973-75; mus. exhibit designer Dawson City (Yukon) Mus., 1975-76; freelance investigative writer, 1976—; tchg. asst. U. Ky., Lexington, 1980-87, instr., 1987-95; sr. rsch. fellow Com. for the Sci. Investigation of Claims of the Paranormal, Amherst, N.Y., 1995—. *Joe Nickell has been an artist and poet, inventor, and civil rights activist. He augmented his professional career with stints as a blackjack dealer, riverboat manager, carnival pitchman, movie extra, and other "roles" (including undercover jobs as a detective). Although best known as a paranormal investigator, (traveling the world to examine crop circles, "weeping" icons, allegedly haunted places, monster claims, and many other mysteries), he also has an avocation as a historical-document consultant. As such, he has exposed numerous sensational forgeries (such as the reputed Jack the Ripper diary) as well as authenticating many other rare documents and texts.* Author: Inquest on the Shroud of Turin, 1983, Secrets of the Supernatural, 1988, The Magic Detectives, 1989, Wonder-workers, 1991, Mysterious Realms, 1992, Ambrose Bierce is Missing, 1992, Looking for a Miracle, 1993, Camera Clues, 1994, Entities, 1995, Detecting Forgery, 1996; (with John F. Fischer) Crime Science, 1999, Pen, Ink & Evidence, 2000, Real-Life X-Files, 2001, The Kentucky Mint Julep, 2003, The Mystery Chronicles, 2004; mem. editl. bd. Skeptical Inquirer, 1993—, columnist, 1995—. Fellow Com. for the Sci. Investigation of Claims of the Paranormal. Home: 1992 Sheridan Dr Apt 6 Buffalo NY 14223-1249 Office: Ctr for Inquiry 3965 Rensch Rd Amherst NY 14228-2743

NICKELS, ELIZABETH ANNE, office furniture manufacturing executive; 2 children. BSBA in Acctg., Econs. and Bus. Admin., Aquinas Coll., 1983. CPA. CFO, mem. exec. and ops. coms. Universal Forest Products, Grand Rapids, Mich., 1993-2000; CFO Herman Miller, Inc., Zeeland, Mich., 2000—. Office: Herman Miller Inc 855 E Main Ave Zeeland MI 49464-0302

NICKELS, GREG, mayor; b. Chicago, Ill., Aug. 7, 1955; s. Bob and Kathie Nickels; m. Sharon Nickels; children: Jacob, Carey. Legis. asst. to Council member Norm Rice City of Seattle, 1979—87; mem. King County Coun., 1987—2002; mayor City of Seattle, 2002—. Chair Seattle/King County Bd. Health, 1996—2001; mem. exec. com. & bd. dirs. Dirs. of Sound Transit. Address: Seattle City Hall 600 Fourth Ave 7th Fl Seattle WA 98124-4749

NICKELS, JOHN L. retired state supreme court justice; m. Merita Nickels; 7 children. Bachelor's degree, No. Ill. U.; law degree, DePaul U. Pvt. practice, 20 yrs; judge Appellate Ct.; cir. judge 16th Jud. Cir.; supreme ct. justice State of Ill., 1992-98; ret., 1998. Bd. dirs. Kane County Bank & Trust Co. Bd. trustees Waubonsee Coll.; mem. Kane County Planning Commn., Zoning Bd. Appeals; mem. St. Gall's Parish, Elburn. Home: 17901 Owens Rd Maple Park IL 60151

NICKELS, RUTH ELIZABETH, band director; b. Warsaw, Ind., Nov. 21, 1955; d. Marjorie Jane Shipley; m. David Brent Nickels, July 7, 2001. MusB in Performance, DePauw U., 1978, MusM in Performance, Ithaca Coll., 1980; cert. in edn., Grace Coll., 1986; post-master credits, Ind. U., 1986. Profl. tchg. lic. music edn. Dir. bands Fairfield Jr.-Sr. H.S., Goshen, Ind., 1986—92; H.S. band dir. Yorktown (Ind.) H.S., 1992—93; dir. bands Orleans (Ind.) Jr.-Sr. H.S., 1993—97, Southwestern Jr.-Sr. H.S., Hanover, Ind., 1997—. Music judge Ind. State Music Assn., Indpls. Mem.: NEA, Ind. State Tchrs. Assn., Ind. Bandmasters Assn., Music Educator's Nat. Conf., Women Band Dirs. Assn., Nat. Band Assn. Avocations: reading, travel, cooking, walking. Home: PO Box 337 Hanover IN 47243 Office: Southwestern Mid and HS 167 S Main Cross St Hanover IN 47243 Personal E-mail: nickels@aol.com. Business E-Mail: rnickels@swjcs.k12.in.us.

NICKELS, THOM, writer, journalist; b. Darby, Pa., Oct. 12, 1947; s. Thomas Clavey Nickels and Teresa Marie Muldoon. Diploma in journalism, Charles Morris Price Sch. Advt.and Journalism, 1967; BA, Eastern Coll., Batl., 1968. Ordained priest Sts. Cyril and Methodius Ch., 2001, apptd. archpriest Anglican Cath. Byzantine Orthodox Ch., 2002. Station editor TV Guide, 1978; editor Soc. Hill Towers Newsletter, Phila., 1981—83; gay issues columnist Welcomat, Phila., 1983—94; resume and grant writer, 1990—94; cometary columnist Phila. Inquirer, 1998—2001; newspaper columnist, feature writer Weekly/Univ. City Press, Phila., 1999—. Book reviewer Lambda Books Report, Washington, 1996—, Gay and Lesbian Rev., Boston, 1999—; commentary columnist Phila. Daily News, 1999—2001; feature writer Philly Style Mag., Phila., 2000—01; weekly issues columnist PrideVisionTV, Toronto, Que., Canada, 2001—; freelance arts and entertainment writer, reviewer TPI Metro, Phila., 2001—. Author: (plays) Z for Shelter, 1967 (Hon. Mention Samuel French Young Playwrights Contest, 1968), (novels) The Cliffs of Aries, 1988, Two Novellas: Walking Water & After All This, 1989 (Nominated for a Hugo award and a Lambda Literary award), (book) Manayunk, 2001, Gay and Lesbian Philadelphia, 2002, Tropic of Libra, 2002, (anthology) The Boy on the Bicycle, 1992, The Boy on the Bicycle (reissue), 1993, Out in History, 2005; contbr. (anthology) Superstars, 2000, 2001, 2002, Tough Guys, 2002. Vol. Lyndon B. Johnson Presdl. Campaign, West Chester, Pa., 1964; founder Coalition Phila. Art, 1998—2002; mem. Boston Gay Liberation Front, 1968—69. Mem.: Nat. Lesbian and Gay Journalist Assn. Home and Office: 2643 Mercer St Philadelphia PA 19125

NICKELSON, KIM RENÉ, internist; b. Chgo., Feb. 13, 1956; d. Robert William and Carolynn Lucille (Marts) N.; m. Louis Peter Sguros; children: Brian Louis, Justin Robert Peter. BS in Chemistry, U. Ill., 1978; MD, Loyola U., Maywood, Ill., 1981. Diplomate Am. Bd. Internal Medicine. Intern and resident in internal medicine Luth. Gen. Hosp., Park Ridge, Ill., 1981-84; pvt. practice Oakbrook, Ill., 1984-87, Plantation, Fla., 1987—. Adj. attending staff Rush-Presbyn. St. Luke's Med. Ctr., Chgo., 1984-87; assoc. attending staff Hinsdale (Ill.) Hosp., 1984-87, Westside Regional Med. Ctr., Plantation, Plantation Gen. Hosp., Fla. Med. Ctr., Lauderhill, Fla. Musician Elk Grove (Ill.) Community Band, 1978-87, Hollywood (Fla.) Symphony Orch., 1987—, Sunrise (Fla.) Pops Symphony, 1987—, Deerfield (Fla.) Community Band, 1987—. Mem. ACP, Internat. Horn Soc. Office: Internal Medicine Assocs 499 NW 70th Ave Ste 200 Plantation FL 33317-7578

NICKENS, HARRY CARL, medical association administrator; b. Monterey, Tenn., June 25, 1944; s. Van B. and Martha (Winningham) N.; m. Alicia Beck, Aug. 26, 1967; children: Kimberly, Cassidee, Brad. BS, Tenn. Tech. U., 1966, MS, 1968; EdD, U. Tenn., 1972. Counselor Va. Western C.C., Roanoke, 1972-76, dir. student devel., 1977-78, dean students, 1979-84, exec. dir. community devel. and tng., 1985-89; pres. Coll. Health Scis., Roanoke, 1989—2001; v.p. cmty. rels. and devel. Ephraim McDowell Health, Danville, Ky., 2003—. Chair Roanoke Valley Chamber's Sch., originator Grad, Ctr.; pres. Ephraim McDowell Health Care Found., 2003—. Pres. Roanoke Valley Career Edn.; bd. dirs. Va. Cares, Adult Care Ctr., Am. Heart Assn., Va. Amateur Sports.; active mem. Lexington Ave. Bapt. Ch.; mem. bd. suprs. Roanoke County; trustee St. Catherine Coll. Mem. Kiwanis (pres. Roanoke chpt. 1990-2002, v.p. Danville chpt., vice chmn. cmty. devel. coun.). Avocation: gardening. Home: 107 Patrick Henry Ct Danville KY 40422 Office: Ephraim McDowell Health 217 South 3rd St Danville KY 40422 Office Phone: 859-239-2362. Business E-Mail: giving@emrmc.org.

NICKENS, PAULA, political organization administrator; b. Washington; BA, U. D.C., 1975. Chair Dem. State Com., Washington, 1998—. Mem. Assn. of State Dem. Chairs. Office: Dem State Com 499 S Capitol St SW Ste 100 Washington DC 20003-4001

NICKERSON, GREG, public relations executive; b. Iowa, Nov. 3, 1958; BS in Agrl. Journalism, Iowa State U., 981. Mkt. analyst, exec. editor Brock Assocs., Brookfield, Wis., 1981-85; with pub. rels. dept. Bader Rutter & Assocs., Brookfield, 1985-88, acctg. group supr., 1988-90, v.p., group supr., 1990-92, v.p., dir. pub. rels. group, 1992-98, exec. v.p., 1998—. Office: Bader Rutter & Associates 13845 Bishops Dr Brookfield WI 53005-6604

NICKERSON, GUY ROBERT, lumber company executive; b. Salt Lake City, May 20, 1956; s. Charles Augustus and Florence May (Fogel) N.; m. Maggie Rose McDonnell, May 30, 1992; children: Melissa Marie, Rebecca Rose. B Acctg., U. Utah, 1977, M Profl. Accountancy, 1978. CPA, Utah. Sr. mgr. Deloitte Haskins & Sells, Salt Lake City and N.Y.C., 1978-87; v.p. fin. Anderson Lumber Co., Ogden, Utah, 1987-96, v.p. ops., 1996—. Office: Anderson Lumber Co 4700 Harrison Blvd Ogden UT 84403-4305

NICKERSON, HARDY OTTO, professional football player; b. Compton, Calif., Sept. 1, 1965; m. Amy Nickerson; children: Ashleigh, Hardy, Haleigh. Degree in sociology, U. Calif. Linebacker Pitts. Steelers, 1987-92, Tampa Bay Buccaneers, 1993-98, Jacksonvilel Jaguars, 1998—2001, Green Bay Packers, 2002—. Named to 1st Team All-Pro by AP and the Sporting News, 1993, Pro Bowl, 1996. Office: 1265 Lombardi Ave Green Bay WI 54304

NICKERSON, JAMES FINDLEY, retired educator; b. Gretna, Nebr., Dec. 16, 1910; s. Elmer Samuel and Lulu Perkins (Patterson) N.; m. Juanita M. Bolin, Mar. 3, 1934; children: Ann Rogers Nickerson Lueck, Maria De Miranda. BS, Nebr. Wesleyan U., 1932; MA, Columbia Tchrs. Coll., 1940; PhD, U. Minn., 1948; ScD (hon.), Yankton (S.D.) Coll., 1971. Tchr. pub. schs., Giltner, Nebr., 1932-35; sch. music supr. Gordon, Nebr., 1936-38, Bayshore, L.I., 1939-41, Grand Island, Nebr., 1941-42; instr. Coll. Edn., music supr. high sch. U. Minn., 1942-46, vis. prof. Coll. Edn., summer 1948; asst. prof. music edn. U. Kans., 1946-48, assoc. prof., 1948-53. Rsch. assoc. dept. psychology U. So. Calif., assigned human factors div. U.S. Navy Electronics Lab., San Diego, 1953-54; dean edn., dir. summer quar., prof. psychology Mont. State U., 1954-64, head dept. psychology, 1954-56, rsch. assoc. Electronics Rsch. Lab, 1958-64; v.p. acad. affairs N.D. State U., Fargo, 1964-66; pres. Minn. State U ., Mankato, 1966-73, then pres. emeritus, disting. svc. prof., 1973-76; dir. Svc. Mems. Opportunity Colls., Am. Assn. State Colls. and Univs., Washington, 1973-81; dir. Northwestern Nat. Bank, Mankato, 1967-69; cons. publ. edn. Office Gov. Wash., 1964; exec. sec., study dir. interim com. edn. Wash. Legislature, 1959-60; chmn. regional conf. womanpower Nat. Manpower Coun. and Mont. State Coll., 1957; mem. steering com. Pacific N.W. Con. Higher Edn., 1962; mem. nat. adv. com. sci. edn. NSF, 1968-71, chmn., 1970-71; mem. vis. com. Harvard Grad. Sch. Edn., 1970-76, Schola Cantorum, N.Y.C., 1938-39, Choral Arts Soc., Washington, 1969-71. Stringbass Mont. State Coll. Symphonette, 1959-63, Mankato Symphony Orch., 1967-73, 83-93, bd. dirs., 1987-90. Recipient citation interim study Wash. Legislature and Gov., 1960, Outstanding Achievement award Bd. Regents U. Minn., 1968, Alumni award Nebr. Wesleyan U., 1968; Sec. Def. medal for outstanding pub. svc., 1981, citation Am. Coun. Edn., 1981; James F. Nickerson Medal of Merit for outstanding svc. to mil. edn. created by Am. Assn. Sr. Colls. and Univs., 1981; Danforth Found. adminstrn. grantee, 1969; named to Internat. Adult and Continuing Edn. Hall of Fame, 1999; Nickerson Conf. Rm., Student Union, Minn. State U. dedicated, 2003. Mem. Nat. Assn. State Univs. and Land Grant Colls. (senate, chmn. div. tchr. edn. 1962-65, sec. coun. acad. officers 1965), Am. Assn. State Colls. and State Univs. (bd. dirs. 1966-71), Am. Assn. Colls. Tchr. Edn. (bd. dirs. 1969-71), Am. Assn. Higher Edn. (chmn. resolutions com. 1974), Assn. Minn. Colls. (pres. 1972), Edn. Commn. States (commr. 1967-73, mem. task force on coordination, governance and structure postsecondary edn. 1973), Sigma Xi, Phi Mu Alpha Sinfonia. Home and Office: 301 S 5th St Apt 220 Mankato MN 56001-4580

NICKERSON, JERRY EDGAR ALAN, business executive; b. North Sydney, N.S., Can., Apr. 28, 1936; s. Jeremiah Beldon and Jean Frances (Innes) N.; m. Jean Frances Ritcey, Sept. 20, 1958; children: Mark Alan, Jerry Ross. B.Commerce, Dalhousie U., 1958. Chmn. bd. H.B. Nickerson & Son, Ltd., North Sydney. Bd. dirs. Gt. West Life & Annuity, Gt. West Life Assurance Co., Seaside Cable TV Ltd., Great-West Lifeco Inc., London Ins. Group, London Life Ins., Power Fin., Inc., Power Corp. Can., Can. Life Fin. Corp., Can. Life Assurance Co., Can. Life Capital Corp. Mem. Chief Execs. Orgn., Zeta Psi. Office: HB Nickerson & Sons Ltd PO Box 130 North Sydney NS Canada B2A 3M2 E-mail: jeanickerson@aol.com.

NICKERSON, JOHN MITCHELL, political science educator; b. Lewiston, Maine, July 1, 1937; s. Elmer Winfield and Marion Gertrude (Howard) N. BA, U. Maine, 1959; MA, Wash. State U., 1966; PhD, U. Idaho, 1971. Commd. 2d lt. US Army, 1959, advanced through grades to capt., resigned, 1967; rsch. assoc. Bur. Pub. Adminstrn. U. Maine, Orono, 1967—68, mem. grad. faculty, 1970—88, asst. prof., assoc. prof. polit. sci. Augusta, 1970—81, prof., 1981—, developer 10 baccalaureate degrees pub. adminstrn.; dir. New Eng. Govtl. Rsch. Inst., Inc., Waterville, Maine, 1971. Lectr. Colby Coll., Waterville, Maine, 1979, Maine State Dedimus Justice; cons. in field. Author: The Control of Civil Disturbances, 1968; Municipal Police in Maine - A Study of Selected Personnel Practices with Emphasis on Recruit Selection and Training, 1969; (with others) A Study of Policy-Making: The Dynamics and Adaptability of the United States Federal System, 1971; editor, author foreward: Is the Municipality Liable for Insufficiently Trained Police? (James P. Murphy), 1968; contbr. articles to profl. jours. Mem. Maine State Police Planning Adv. Group, 1984-87, Maine State Bd. Assessment Rev., 1981-84, Maine Hwy. Safety Com., 1984-87; vice chmn. adv. bd. Salvation Army, Augusta, 1980-85; trustee, treas. Lithgow Library, 1980-85; incorporator Kennebec Valley Med. Ctr., Augusta, 1980-97. Dept. Justice grantee, 1967. Mem. Am. Polit. Sci. Assn., New Eng. Polit. Sci. Assn., Northeastern Polit. Sci. Assn., Acad. Polit. Sci. (life), Am. Acad. Polit. and Social Sci. (life), Am. Soc. for Pub. Adminstrn., ACLU (life), Kennebec Hist. Soc. (life), Kennebec Valley Humane Soc. (life), Maine Civil Liberties Union (life, legis. com.), Pi Sigma Alpha, Pi Alpha Alpha. Home: 190 Capitol St Apt 216 Augusta ME 04330-6237 Office: U Maine at Augusta 46 University Dr Augusta ME 04330 Office Phone: 207-621-3287. Business E-Mail: john.nickerson@maine.edu.

NICKISCH, CRAIG WENDELL, language professional, educator; b. Belle Fourche, S.D., Apr. 20, 1939; s. Theodore and Fern Lucille (Olin) N.; m. Marjorie Ilene Hill, Dec. 15, 1963; children: Heidi Marlene, Curt Wendell, Kirsten Margret. BS, S.D. State U., 1961; MA, Northwestern U., 1963; grad., U.A. Army C&GS Coll., Ft. Leavenworth, Kans., 1974; PhD, U. Nebr., 1985. Commd. U.S. Army, 1964, advanced through grades to col., 1985, troop comdr. 8th cavalry, 8th inf. div., 1964-66, liaison officer 1st inf. div. Lai Khe, Vietnam, 1967-68, asst. prof. U.S. Mil. Acad. West Point, N.Y., 1968-73, permanent assoc. prof., 1982-88, student officer Command and Gen. Staff Coll. Ft. Leavenworth, 1973-74, staff officer 3rd armored div. Frankfurt, Fed. Republic Germany, 1974-78, sr. advisor 5th cavalry brigade Lincoln, Nebr., 1978-80, ret., 1988; assoc. prof., head German sect. Idaho State U., Pocatello, 1988—. Mem. Com. on Excellence in Edn., Highland Falls, N.Y., 1987-88. Co-author: John Pers, Weaver, 1985; editor book Der Leutnant und das Mädchen Tatjana, 1972; creator lang. teaching computer programs; contbr. articles to profl. jours. Trustee Friends of West Point Library, 1986—; mem. exec. bd. Hudson Del. Council Boy Scouts Am., Midletown, N.Y., 1986-88, pres. West Point troop com., 1986-88. Decorated Bronze star (3), Legion of Merit; recipient Fed. Cross of Merit Pres. of Germany, 1987; Fulbright scholar, 1961-62; army doctoral fellow U. Nebr., 1980-82. Mem. Am. Assn. Tchrs. German (pres. 1986-88, cert. of merit 1985), German Studies Assn. (exec. com. Tempe, Ariz., 1987—), Modern Lang. Assn., Am. Council on Teaching Fgn. Langs., Am. Radio Relay League, Am. Legion, Interagency Lang. Roundtable, Res. Officers' Assn., Phi Kappa Phi (Outstanding Scholar 1987, 88). Avocations: flying, amateur radio, outdoor sports. Home: Wendamin Ranch 4161 Bannock Hwy Pocatello ID 83204-4525 Office: Idaho State U Dept Of Fgn Langs Pocatello ID 83209-0001 Office Phone: 208-236-3132. Business E-Mail: nickcrai@isu.edu.

NICKLAS, THERESA ANN, nutritionist, educator, researcher; b. Elsworth, S.D., Sept. 29, 1956; d. James and Muriel (Schard) N. BS in Dietetics and Nutritional Care, Roch. Inst. Tech., 1979; MPH in Maternal and Child Health, Tulane U., 1980, DrPH in Nutrition, 1987. Lic. dietitian and nutritionist, La. Nutritionist Dept. Family and Children's Svcs., Atlanta, 1974-75; adminstrv. asst., head nutritionist Haitian Bur. Nutrition, Port-au-Prince, 1975-76; dietary technician Glen Cove (N.Y.) Community Hosp., 1977-78; instr. nutrition dept. medicine La. State U. Med. Ctr., New Orleans, 1984-87, asst. prof. sect. cardiology, 1987—, sr. rsch. nutritionist Bogalusa Heart Study, 1984-87, head nutrition Bogalusa Heart Study, 1987—. Prin. nutrition investigator Ft. Polk Heart Smart Project, 1988-91; adj. instr. nutrition sect. dept. applied health scis. Tulane U. Sch. Pub. Health and Tropical Medicine, New Orleans, 1988-97; prof., chmn. dept. food and nutrition N. D. State U., Fargo, 1997-99; prof. pediats. Children's Nutrition Rsch. Ctr., Baylor Coll. of Medicine, Houston, 1999—; presenter numerous profl. meetings, workshops and seminars for health profls.; vis. prof. Wyeth-Ayerst Labs., 1990—; referee Jour. Am. Coll. Nutrition, Preventive Medicine, Health Edn. Quar., Jour. Clin. Nutrition. Contbr. articles to sci. jours., also chpts. to books, monographs. Vol. La. Am. Heart Assn., New Orleans, 1980—, bd. dirs., 1989—, mem. tassk force com. on women and heart disease, 1990—, sec. New Orleans div. 1989-90, coord. physicians' cholesterol edn. program, 1988-91. Grantee Nestle's, Kelloggs Co., 1981, 91, Nat. Heart, Lung and Blood Inst., 1984—, AID, 1981, U.S. Army Rsch. Inst. for Environ. Medicine, 1988—, Nat. Cancer Inst., 1993, also FDA. Mem. Am. Dietetic Assn. (nutrition dietetic rsch. practive group 1987—, co-editor Digest 1989—), Am. Soc. Clin. Nutrition, Am. Inst. Nutrition, Am. Heart Assn. (fellow coun. on epidemiology), N.Y. Dietetic Assn., La. Dietetic Assn. (bd. dirs. 1989—, chmn. fundraising 1989-90), New Orleans Dietetic Assn. (pres. 1990—), La. Heart Assn., Sigma Xi (assoc.), Delta Omega (dietary guidlines com.). Roman Catholic. Avocations: tennis, cooking, collecting antique cookbooks. Office: Children's Nutrition Rsch Ctr Baylor Coll Medicine 1100 Bates Ave Houston TX 77030-2600

NICKLAUS, JACK WILLIAM, professional golfer; b. Columbus, Ohio, Jan. 21, 1940; s. Louis Charles, Jr. and Helen (Schoener) N.; m. Barbara Bash, July 23, 1960; children: Jack William II, Steven Charles, Nancy Jean, Gary Thomas, Michael Scott. Student, Ohio State U., 1957-62, D of Athletic Arts (hon.), 1972; LLD (hon.), U. St. Andrews, 1984. Chmn., chief exec. officer Golden Bear Internat., Inc. Author: My 55 Ways to Lower Your Golf Score, 1964, Take a Tip From Me, 1968, The Greatest Game of All, 1969, Jack Nicklaus' Lesson Tee, 1972, Golf My Way, 1974, Jack Nicklaus' Playing Lessons, 1976, On and Off the Fairway, 1978, Play Better Golf, Vols. 1-3, 1980, 81, 83, The Full Swing, 1982, My Most Memorable Shots in the Majors, 1988. Chmn. Ohio div. Am. Cancer Soc., 1967; chmn. sports div. Nat. Easter Seal Soc., 1967. Named PGA Player of Year, 1967, 72, 73, 75, 76, Dunlop Profl. Athlete of Yr., 1972, Golfer of Year Profl. Golfers Assn., 1973, Byron Nelson award, 1964, 65, 72, 73, Bob Jones award, 1975; named Sportsman of Year, Sports Illus. mag., 1978; named to World Golf Hall of Fame; named Athlete of the Decade for 1970-79, 1979, Golfer of the '70s, 1979, Golfer of the Century, 1988. Mem. President's Club Ohio State U., Phi Gamma Delta. Achievements include playing on over 105 golf courses on 5 continents, 12 ranked in U.S. Top 100; hosted 185 profl. tournaments 1973—; won 71 tournaments including 20 maj. championships; maj. tournaments won include Tournament of Champions, 1963, 64, 71, 73, 77, U.S. Amateur, 1959, 61, U.S. Open, 1962, 67, 72, 80, U.S. Masters, 1963, 65, 66, 72, 75, 86, Brit. Open, 1966, 70, 78, PGA Championship, 1963, 71, 73, 75, 80, Internat. Pro-Amateur, 1973, Atlanta Golf Classic, 1973, Walt Disney World Golf Classic, 1971-73, 75, Hawaiian Open, 1974, Tournament Players Championship, 1974, 76, 78, Hawaiian Open, 1974, Doral-Eastern Open, 1975, Heritage Classic, 1975, Australian Open, 1964, 68, 71, 75, 76, 78, World Series of Golf, 1962, 63, 67, 70, 76, Gleason Inverrary Classic, 1976, 77, 78, Phila. Classic, 1965, 78, Colonial Nat. Invitational, 1982, PGA Seniors Championship, 1991, U.S. Senior Open, 1991, 93, Mercedes Sr. Championship, 1994, others. Office: Golden Bear Realty Inc. 11684 US Hwy #1 North Palm Beach FL 33408

NICKLE, DENNIS EDWIN, electronics engineering consultant, deacon; b. Sioux City, Iowa, Jan. 30, 1936; s. Harold Bateman and Helen Cecilia (Killackey) H. BS in Math., Fla. State U., 1961. Ordained deacon Roman Cath. Ch., 1979. Reliability mathematician Pratt & Whitney Aircraft Co., West Palm Beach, Fla., 1961-63; br. supr. Melpar Inc., Falls Church, Va., 1963-66; prin. mem. tech. staff Xerox Data Sys., Rockville, Md., 1966-70; sr. tech. officer WHO, Washington, 1970-76; software tech. mgr. Melpar divsn. E-Sys., Inc., Falls Church, 1976-95; software process improvement mgr. Bell Atlantic, Arlington, Va., 1996-97; sr. software mgr. Litton Denro, Gaithersburg, Md., 1997—2001; cons., 2001—. Lectr. in field; coord. D.C. Software Process Improvement Network, 1995—2001, chair, 1997—2002. Author: Stress in Adolescents, 1986; co-author: Handbook for Handling Non-Productive Stress in Adolescence, Standard for Software Life Cycle Processes, IMPEESA Junior Leader Training Guide, Standard for Software Quality Assurance, 1984-91, Standard for Developing Software Life Cycle Processes, Configuration Management Procedures, Software Quality Assurance Procedures, Software Development Procedures; contbr. to profl. jours. Chief judge for computers Fairfax County Regional Sci. Fair, 1964-88; scoutmaster, commr. Boy Scouts Am., 1957-92; youth custodian Fairfax County Juvenile Ct., 1973-87; chaplain No. Va. Regional Juvenile Detention Home, 1978-88; moderator Nocturnal Adoration Soc.; parochial St. Michael's Ch., Annandale, Va., 1979-89, Christ the Redeemer, Sterling, Va., 1990-93. With U.S. Army, 1958-60. Recipient Eagle award, Silver award, Silver Beaver award, other awards Boy Scouts Am.; Ad Altare Dei, St. George Emblem, Diocese of Richmond. Mem. Assn. Computing Machinery, Computer Soc., Am. Soc. for Quality Control, CODSIA (chmn. working groups), ORLANDO II (Govt./industry working group), Old Crows Assn., Rolm Mil-Spec Computer Users Group (internat. pres.), San Antonio I (select industry coord. group), Nat. Security Indsl. Assn. (conv. com. 1985-96, software quality assurance subcom., regional membership chmn. 1981-89, nat. exec. vice-chmn. 1989-94, chmn. 1994-96), Am. Security Coun., IEEE (sr., stds. working group in computers 1983—, Outstanding Vol. award 1993, Golden Core 1996), Def. Software Devel. Stds. Adv. Bd. (chmn. 1991-96), Soc. Software Quality, Hewlett-Packard Users Group, Smithsonian Assn., Internat. Platform Assn., NRA (endowment), Nat. Eagle Scout Assn. (life), KC (4 deg.), Alpha Phi Omega (life), Sigma Phi Epsilon. Home: 43245 Preston Ct Ashburn VA 20147-5307 Office Phone: 703-729-2653.

NICKLES, DON (DONALD NICKLES), senator; b. Ponca City, Okla., Dec. 6, 1948; s. Robert C. and Coeweene (Bryan) N.; m. Linda L. Morrison, Sept. 5, 1968; children— Donald Lee II, Jennifer Lynn, Kim Elizabeth, Robyn Leigh. BA in Bus. Adminstrn., Okla. State U., 1971. Owner, operator Don Nickles Profl. Cleaning Svc., Stillwater, Okla., 1968-71; v.p., gen. mgr. Nickles Machine Corp., Ponca City, 1972—80; mem. Okla. Senate, 1979-80, U.S. Senate from Okla., 1981—. Asst. majority whip, 1996-2002; chmn. Senate Rep. policy com., mem. com. on energy and natural resources, com. on rules and adminstrn., com. on budget fin., budget com., mem. arms control observer group, rural health caucus, world climate conv. observer group, Rep. task force on nat. security and regulatory reform, senate budget com., 2003-; passed legislation to provide for econ. and employment impact statement for all new laws and regulations. Chmn. platform com. Rep. Nat. Conv., 1992; bd. dirs. Ponca City United Way; bd. advisors Close Up Found.; mem. Kay Coun. for Retarded Children, Ponca City, St. Mary's Roman Cath. Parish Coun.; mem. adv. bd. Salvation Army, Ponca City. With USNG, 1970-76. Named one of Outstanding Young Men of Am., U.S. Jaycees, 1983. Mem. Fellowship Christian Athletes, Ponca City C. of C. Clubs: Rotary. Republican. Office: US Senate 133 Hart Senate Office Bldg Washington DC 20510-0001

NICKLES, SHELLEY KAPLAN, curator, educator; b. Kingston, N.Y., Apr. 3, 1964; d. Jerome Allen and Leah (Maskowsky) Kaplan; m. John Peter Nickles, Sept. 3, 1995; 1 child, Kealani Rose. BA in History, Cornell U., 1986; MA in Early Am. Culture, U. Del., 1990; PhD in history, U. Va., 1999. Instr. Parsons Sch. Design, N.Y.C., Washington, 1996—2002; mus. curator Nat. Mus. Am. History Smithsonian Instn., Washington, 1999—. Adj. asst. prof. George Washington U., 2002—04. Editor: (exhibit rev.) Home Cultures Jour., 2003—04; contbr. articles to profl. jours. Fellow, Winterthur and Hagley Mus., Wilmington, 1993, Wolfsonian Mus., Miami Beach, 1994, Smithsonian Instn., 1995—97; Lois F. McNeil fellow, Winterthur Mus., Wilmington, 1988—90. Mem.: Am. Studies Assn., Soc. Winterthur Fellows, Orgn. Am. Historians. Business E-Mail: nickless@si.edu.

NICKLIN, GEORGE LESLIE, JR., psychoanalyst, educator, physician, author; b. Franklin, Pa., July 25, 1925; s. George Leslie and Emma (Reed) N.; m. Katherine Mildred Aronson, Sept. 30, 1950 BA, Haverford Coll., 1949; MD, Columbia U., 1951; cert. in psychoanalysis, William A. White Inst., N.Y.C., 1962. Diplomate Am. Bd. Psychiatry and Neurology. Resident, then chief resident Bellevue Psychiat. Hosp., N.Y.C., 1953-56; pvt. practice specializing in psychoanalytic psychiatry, 1956—; staff Bellevue Hosp., 1956—; assoc. clin. prof. psychiatry NYU Med. Sch., 1970—; dir. L.I. Inst. Psychoanalysis, 1978-88, dir. emeritus, 1988—, dir. emeritus. Mem. Com. to Award Martin Luther King Peace Prize. Author: Doctors In Peril, 2000. Mem. Corp. Haverford Coll., 1957-2003; trustee Westbury Friends Sch., 1957-2000; founder Friends World Coll., 1958. With AUS, 1943-46, ETO. Decorated Purple Heart with oak leaf cluster, Bronze Star with oak leaf cluster and three battle stars. Fellow Am. Acad. Psychoanalysis, Am. Psychiat. Assn. (disting. life fellow, 2003); mem. AAAS, NAACP, Soc. Med. Psychoanalysts (pres. 1986-87), White Psychoanalytic Soc., Assn. for World Edn. (charter trustee, treas. 1970-78), 9th Inf. Divsn. Assn., Vets. of the Bulge, Mil. Order of the Purple Heart. Clubs: Gardiner's Bay Country (Shelter Island, N.Y.); Penn (London). Mem. Soc. Of Friends. Home and Office: 6 Butler Pl Garden City NY 11530-4603 *Education is essential to the future evolution of human society. But education alone is not enough. Integrity, creative thinking and informed action open the path to the future.*

NICKOLAI, BEATRICE ROSE, education educator; b. St. Louis, Mo. d. Paul A and Doris Rose Beuttenmuller; m. Thomas Charles Nickolai, Aug. 14, 1976; children: John, Kevin, Daniel, Annie, Michael. MA, St. Louis U., 1974—92. Lectr. St. Louis U., St. Louis, 1975; adj. instr. Maryville U., St. Louis, 1977—89, asst. prof. English, 1989—. Chair, humanities faculty Maryville U., St. Louis, 1994—2000, faculty advisor, Delta Epsilon Sigma honors soc., 1996—, dir., inst. for leadership & values, 1998—, program dir., humanities, 2002—. Mem.: Nat. Coun. of Teachers of English. Roman Cath. Avocation: ballet and tap dancing. Office: Maryville University 13550 Conway Rd Saint Louis MO 63141

NICKOLETT, CHIP, information technology executive, consultant; s. Kay and Ronald D. Nickolett; m. Jacqueline Marie Sharak, May 7, 1988; children: Heather Marie, Jacob Matthew, Paige Marie. AS in Bus. Data Processing, Waukesha County Tech. Coll., 1984. Sys. analyst DCI Mktg., Milw., 1986—91; mgr., tech. svcs. Catalyst USA, Brown Deer, Wis., 1991—93; sr. cons. Ingres Products Divsn., ASK Group, Alameda, Calif., 1993—94; regional project mgr. Computer Assoc., Islandia, NY, 1994—97; dist. mgr. Caribou Lake Software, Mpls., 1997—99; pres. Comprehensive Solutions, Brookfield, Wis., 1999—. Mem., ingres product adv. coun. Computer Assoc., Islandia, NY, 2003—. Contbr. articles to profl. jours. Mem. Children's Cir. of Care, Milw.; mem., pres.'s coun. Children's Hosp. Wis., Milw., 2000, mem. Emelie Vogel Nunnemacher Soc.; mem. bus. adv. coun. Nat. Rep. Congl. Com., Washington, 2000. Recipient Congl. Medal of Distinction, Nat. Rep. Congl. Com., 2001. Mem.: NRA, Nat. Ctr. Employee Ownership, Project Mgmt. Inst., North Am. Ingres Users Assn. (pres. 2000—01). R-Consevative. Achievements include registered trademarks. Avocations: working with children, donating to charitable causes. Office: Comprehensive Solutions 250 N Sunny Slope Rd Ste 300 Brookfield WI 53005 Office Phone: 262-785-8101. E-mail: chipn@comp-soln.com.

NICKOLOFF, EDWARD LEE, radiology physicist; m. Diane Zambetti; children: Andrea Lee, Edward Jr Lee. BS, Lebanon Valley Coll., Annville, Pa., 1965; MS, U. of N.H., 1968; DSc, Johns Hopkins U., 1977. Lic. nuclear medicince physics and diagnostic radiology physics Am. Bd. Radiology, cert. health physicist Am. Bd. Health Physics, lic. diagnostic imaging physics Am. Coll. Med. Physics. Asst. prof. of radiology, acting dir. of physics and engring. dept. radiology Johns Hopkins Med. Instns., Balt., 1977—81; prof. of clin. radiology, chief hosp. physicist dept. radiology Columbia U. Physicians and Surgeons, N.Y.C., 1982—. Contbr., tchr., adviser Columbia U.; presenter in field. Contbr. articles and abstracts to profl. jours., chpts. to books. Fellow: Am. Coll. Radiologists (life), Am. Coll. Med. Physics (chmn.), Am. Assn. Physicists Medicine. Independent. Achievements include research in image quality and radiation dosimetry. Avocations: hiking, gardening, reading, theater. Office: Columbia U Physicians and Surgeons 177 Fort Washington Ave New York NY 10032-3784 Personal E-mail: eln1@columbia.edu. E-mail: eln1@columbia.edu.

NICKON, ALEX, chemist, educator; b. Poland, Oct. 6, 1927; came to U.S., 1955, naturalized, 1961; s. Steve and Maria (Nickon) m. Beulah Monica Godby, Aug. 22, 1950; children— Dale Beverly, Linda Cheryl, Leanne Marie. B.Sc., U. Alta., 1949; MA, Harvard U., 1951, PhD, 1953. Vis. lectr. Bryn Mawr Coll., 1953; postdoctoral fellow Birkbeck Coll., U. London, Eng., 1953-54, NRC, Ottawa, Can., 1954-55; NSF sr. fellow; Imperial Coll., London, 1963-64; U. Munich, Germany, 1971-72; mem. faculty Johns Hopkins, 1955—, prof. chemistry, 1964-94, Vernon K. Krieble prof. chemistry, 1975-94, prof. emeritus, 1994—. Vis. assoc. Am. Chem. Soc. on Profl. Tng., 1975-95; mem. medicinal chem. panel NIH, 1966-70; postdoctoral panel NRC, 1968-69. Sr. editor Jour. Organic Chemistry, 1965-71; Am. exec. editor: Tetrahedron Reports, 1978-96. Recipient Md. Chemist award, 1990; Sloan Found. fellow, 1957-61 Fellow N.Y. Acad. Scis.; mem. Am. Chem. Soc. (nat. awards com. 1974-76), Brit. Chem. Soc. Home: 1009 Painters Ln Cockeysville Hunt Valley MD 21030-1729 Office: Dept Chemistry Johns Hopkins U Baltimore MD 21218-2685

NICKS, STEVIE (STEPHANIE LYNN NICKS), singer, songwriter; b. Phoenix, May 26, 1948; Joined Fleetwood Mac, 1974. Albums include: (with Lindsey Buckingham) Buckingham Nicks, 1973, (with Fleetwood Mac) Fleetwood Mac, 1975, Rumours, 1977 (co-winner, Billboard award for Album of the Year, Group of Year 1977), Tusk, 1979, Fleetwood Mac Live, 1980, Mirage, 1982, Tango in the Night, 1987, Greatest Hits, 1989, Behind The Mask, 1990, 25 Years-The Chain, 1992, The Dance, 1997, Say You Will, 2004; (solo) Bella Donna, 1981, The Wild Heart, 1983, Rock a Little, 1985, The Other Side of the Mirror, 1989, Time Space, 1991, Street Angel, 1994, Enchanted: The Works of Stevie Nicks, 1998, Trouble in Shangri-La, 2001, The Divine, 2001; composer songs Rhiannon, 1975, Landslide, 1975 (Most Performed Country Song of the Year, BMI Awards 2003), Leather and Lace, 1975, Dreams, 1977, Sara, 1979, Edge of Seventeen, 1981, If Anyone Falls (with Sandy Stewart), 1982, Stand Back (with Prince Rogers Nelson), 1983, I Can't Wait (with others), 1985, Seven Wonders (with Sandy Stewart), and others.*

NICOL, BRIAN, publishing executive; Publisher Home & Away, Inc., Omaha. Office: Home & Away Inc 10703 J St Omaha NE 68127-1023

NICOL, DOMINIK, writer, photographer; b. nr. Oltenia, Romania, Sept. 25, 1930; came to U.S., 1969, naturalized, 1976; s. Dumitru and Valentina (Sandulescu) Nicolaescu-Stroe. Diploma in Chemistry and Tech. of Antibiotics, The Tech. Sch., Bucharest, Romania, 1954. Photo-reporter Agerpress, Bucharest, 1950-51; med. photographer Cantacuzino Hosp., Bucharest, 1955-68; ret., 1995. Author, editor: Self Encounter, 1979, Ten Oneiric Sketches, 1980, Rendes-Vous sau Intalnire cu mine insumi, 1987; (play) Vacuum (Colocviu de abis), 1979, Vacuum-Void, 1988, Pe portativul vietii, 1992. Home: 334 W 49th St Apt 4FE New York NY 10019-7308

NICOL, ROBERT DUNCAN, architect; b. La Jolla, Calif., Sept. 16, 1936; s. Duncan and Catherine (Muffly) N.; m. Susann Kay Larson; 1 child, Jennifer E. AA, Principia Coll., 1956; BArch, U. Calif., Berkeley, 1961. Registered arch., Ariz., Calif., Mont., Wash. Designer Kawneer Mfg. Co., Richmond, Calif., 1961-62, Claude Oakland, San Francisco, 1962-64; project arch. David T. Johnson, Oakland, Calif., 1964-68; pvt. practice Oakland, Calif., 1968—. Mem. bd. appeals City of Alameda, 1971-73, vice chair planning commn., 1973-77, founder, chair, vice chair design rev. bd., 1974-80, founder, chair, vice chair hist. adv. bd., 1976—, co-founder, chair, vice chair mayor's com. for handicapped, 1980-86; mem. Calif. State Access Bd., 1995—. Recipient Design award Am. Registered Archs., 1969, Harper Plz. Design award Calif. Bldg. Ofcls. Assn., 1985. Fellow AIA; mem. Soc. Am. Registered Archs., Nat. Coun. Archtl. Registration Bds. (sr.), Alexander Graham Bell Assn. for Deaf (lectr.), Oral Hearing Impaired Sec., San Leandro Hist. Railway Soc. (founder, charter mem., chair, vice-chair), Alameda Jr. C. of C. (project dir. 1969), Alameda Victorian Preservation Soc. Republican. Office: 455 17th St Ste 300 Oakland CA 94612-2101

NICOLAI, EUGENE RALPH, public relations consultant, editor, writer; b. Renton, Wash., June 26, 1911; s. Eugene George and Josephine (Heidinger) N.; student U. Wash., 1929, Whitman Coll., 1929-30; B.A., U. Wash., 1934; postgrad. Am. U., 1942; M.A., George Washington U., 1965; m. Helen Margaret Manogue, June 5, 1935; 1 son, Paul Eugene. Editor, U. Wash. Daily, Seattle, 1934; asst. city editor, writer, nat. def. editor Seattle Times, 1934-41; writer Sta. KJR, Seattle, 1937-39; writer, editor, safety edn. officer Bur. Mines, Washington, 1941-45; news dir. Grand Coulee Dam and Columbia Basin Project, Washington, 1945-50; regional info. dir. Bur. Mines, Denver and Pitts., 1950-55, asst. chief mineral reports, Washington, 1955-61, news dir. office of oil and gas, 1956-57; sr. info. officer, later sr. public info. officer Office Sec. Interior, Washington, 1961-71, staff White House Nat. Conf. on Natural Beauty, spl. detail to White House, 1971, ret.; now public relations cons., tech. editor, writer. Formerly safety policy adviser Interior Dept.; com. mem. Internat. Cooperation Year, State Dept., 1971. With George Washington U. Alumni Found.; founder, mng. dir. Josephine Nature Preserve; pres. Media Assocs. Bd. dirs. Wash. State Council on Alcoholism; adviser Pierce Transit Authority, Pierce County Growth Mgmt., Pierce County Ethics Commn. Named Disting. Alumnus, recipient Penrose award, both Whitman Coll., 1979. Mem. Nature Conservancy, Wash. Environ. Council, Nat. Audubon Soc. (Am. Belgian Tervuren dist. rep.), Crook County (Oreg.) Hist. Soc., Washington State Hist. Soc., Emerald Shores Assn, Sigma Delta Chi, Pi Kappa Alpha. Presbyn. Clubs: George Washington U., Purdy (pres.). Lodge: Masons. Author: The Middle East Emergency Committee; editor: Fed. Conservation Yearbooks.

NICOLAI, PAUL PETER, lawyer; b. Trenton, N.J., Jan. 22, 1953; s. Ernest and Preziosa E. (Cattani) N.; m. Anne Marie Elizabeth LaRochelle, May 14, 1976; children: Caroline Emma, Peter Ernest, Margaret Elizabeth, Alexandra Marie, Elizabeth Anne. BA, Am. Internat. Coll., 1975; JD, Western New Eng. Coll., 1979. Bar: Mass. 1979, U.S. Dist. Ct. Mass. 1980, U.S. Ct. Appeals (1st cir.) 1983, U.S. Supreme Ct. 1984, N.Y. 1987, Washington DC 1987, U.S. Ct. Appeals (Fed. cir.) 1990, U.S. Tax Ct. 1991, Conn. 2003. Legal asst. Friendly Ice Cream Corp., Wilbraham, Mass., 1976-79, staff counsel, 1979-81, co. counsel, 1981-88; pres. Nicolai Law Group, P.C., Springfield, Mass., 1990—. Pres., dir., chair bus. plan rev. com. WMV Forums, Inc., 2000-02. Bd. dirs. Citizens for Ltd. Taxation, Mass., 1981-84, chmn., 1984-97; mem. we. Mass. exec. com. NCCJ, mem. we. Mass. and Conn. devel. com. 1995-99, nat. trustee, 1991-99; corporator Springfield Day Nursery, Inc., 1995—, mem. mktg. com., 1995-96, Springfield Libr. Mus. Assn., Inc., 1985-2003; bd. dirs. Pioneer Valley Montessori Soc., Inc., Springfield, 1985-93, v.p., 1988-92, pres., 1992-93; bd. dirs., chmn. Citizens Econs. Rsch. Found., Inc., Boston, 1984-97; mem. adv. bd. Springfield Enterprise Ctr., 1998—. Mem. ABA, Am. Arbitration Assn. (arbitration panel 1992—), Mass. Bar Assn. (fee arbitration bd. 2000—, chmn. 2003—, fee arbitration panel 1997-, arbitration and mediation panel 1999-2002, law practice mgmt.sect. coun. 2002—), Hampden County Bar Assn. (arbitration and mediation panel 1998-2002), Assn. Bar City N.Y., D.C. Bar Assn., Fed. Cir. Ct. Appeals Bar Assn., Am. Internat. Coll. Corp. (reunion com., 2000, nat. bd. dirs., v.p. 1989-90, pres. 1990-91, corporator 2000—), Soc. Everett Barney Inc. (treas., clk. 1995-99, dir. 1995-2002, sec. 1996-99), Western Mass. Tech. Bus. Coun. (bd. dirs.), We. Mass. Software Assn. (bd. dirs. 1998-2001, treas. 2000-01), We. Mass. Venture Forums, Inc. (pres. 2001-02, bd. dirs. econ. devel. coun. western Mass.,2004—), Reg. Tech. Corp. Steering Com., 2004-. Roman Catholic. Avocation: reading. Home: 24 Venture Dr Springfield MA 01119-2727 Office: Nicolai Law Group PC 146 Chestnut St Ste 501 Springfield MA 01103-1539 Office Phone: 413-272-2000. Business E-Mail: paul.nicolai@niclawgrp.com.

NICOLAIDES, MARY, lawyer; b. N.Y.C., June 7, 1927; d. George and Dorothy Nicolaides. BCE, CUNY, 1947; MBA with distinction, DePaul U., 1975, JD, 1981. Bar: Ill. 1982, U.S. Dist. Ct. (no. dist.) Ill. 1982, U.S. Patent Office 1983. Sr. design engr. cement subs. U.S. Steel Corp., N.Y.C., then Pitts., 1948-71; sole practice Chgo., 1982—. Republican. Greek Orthodox. Address: 233 E Erie St Apt 1804 Chicago IL 60611-2903

NICOLAOU, K. C. chemistry professor; b. Karavas, Kyrenia, Cyprus, June 5, 1946; came to U.S., 1972; s. Costa and Helen (Yettimi) N.; m. Georgette Karayianni, July 15, 1973; children: Colette, Alexis, Christopher, Paul. BSc, Bedford Coll., London, 1969; PhD, U. Coll., London, 1972; DSc, U. London, 1994; PhD (hon.), U. Athens, 1995. Rsch. assoc. Columbia U., N.Y.C., 1972-73, Harvard U., Cambridge, Mass., 1973-76; from asst. prof. to Rhodes-Thompson prof. chemistry U. Pa., Phila., 1976-89; Darlene Shiley prof. chemistry, chmn. dept. The Scripps Rsch. Inst., La Jolla, Calif., 1989—; prof. chemistry U. Calif. at San Diego, La Jolla, 1989—. Vis. prof. U. Paris, 1986; mem. exec. com. Diann. Cyprus Conf. on Drug Design; mem. med. study sect. D, NIH, 1988-90; mem. internat. adv. bd. Angewandte Chemie, 1994—. Author: (with N. A. Petasis) Selenium in Natural Products Synthesis, 1984, (with E. J. Sorensen) Classics in Total Synthesis, 1996; co-editor: Synthesis, Germany, 1984-90, Chemistry and Biology, 1994; editl. bd. Prostaglandins, Leukotrienes and Medicine, 1978-88, Synthesis, 1990—, Accounts of Chem. Rsch., 1992—, Carbohydrate Letters, 1993—, Chemistry-A European Jour., 1994—, Perspectives in Drug, Discovery and Design, 1994—, Indian Jour. of Chemistry, Sect. B, 1995—; mem. bd. consulting editors Tetrahedron Publs., 1992—; mem. adv. bd. Contemporary Organic Synthesis, 1993—; mem. regional adv. bd. J. C. S. Chem. Comm., 189—, J. C. S. Perkin I, 1991—; contbr. articles to profl. jours.; patentee in field. Recipient Japan Soc. for Promotion Sci. award 1987-88, U.S. Sr. Scientist award Alexander von Humboldt Found., 1987-88, Alan R. Day award Phila. Organic Chemists Club, 1993, Pfizer Rsch. award, 1993-94, Paul Janssen Prize, 1994, Alexander the Great Award Hellenic Cultural Soc. of San Diego, 1994, Rhone-Poulenc medal Royal Soc. of Chemistry, 1995, Chem. Pioneer Am. Inst. of Chemists, 1996, Inhoffen Medal of Gesellscaft fur Biotechnologische Forschung mbH (GBF) Tech. U. of Braunschweig, 1996, Linus Pauling award, 1996; fellow A.P. Sloan Found., 1979-83, J. S. Guggenhiem Found., 1984; Camille and Henry Dreyfus scholar, 1980-84, Arthur C. Cope scholar, 1987. Fellow N.Y. Acad. Scis., AAAS; mem. Am. Chem. Soc. (Creative Work in Synthetic Organic Chemistry award 1993, William H. Nichols medal N.Y. sect. 1996, Ernest Guenther award in chemistry of natural products 1996), Chem. Soc. London, German Chem. Soc., Japanese Chem. Soc. Office: Scripps Rsch Inst Dept Chemistry 10550 N Torrey Pines Rd La Jolla CA 92037-1000

NICOLAS, JOHN SCOTT (JACK NICOLAS), benefits company executive; b. Brockton, Mass., Aug. 28, 1960; s. Alvin Perry and Rose Esther Nicolas; m. Kristin Diane Johnson, Sept. 3, 1983; children: Daniel John, Kelly Ann. BS in Polit. Sci./Pub. Adminstrn., Bridgewater State Coll., 1982; MBA, Nichols Coll., 1988. Cert. designation Health Ins. Assn. of Am. Registered rep. Prudential/Basche, Brockton, 1982-83; sales/svc. mgr. Hertz Leasing Corp., Waltham, Mass., 1984-86; mktg. mgr. Payco Am., Westboro, Mass., 1987-89; sr. account mgr. Blue Cross Blue Shield, Boston, 1990-97; pres. K D Benefits, Inc., Norton, Mass., 1997—. Bd. dirs. Old Colony United Way, Brockton, 1994—, David John Louison Child Ctr., Brockton, 1995-98, Horace Mann Ednl. Assocs., Franklin, Mass., 1997—; mem., past chmn. Town Fin. Com., Norton, 1993—; chmn. Town Mgr. Search Com., Norton, 1997; vice chair Town Charter Com., Norton, 1997-98; mem. Sch. Com., Norton. Recipient Comty. Svc. award David Jon Louison Child Ctr., 1995. Mem. The Labor Guild, Archdiocese of Boston, Foxboro Country Club (fin. com. 1995—), Tournament Players Club, Delta Mu Delta. Roman Catholic. Avocations: golf, basketball, skiing, playing with my children. Office: K D Benefits Inc PO Box D 10 W Main St Norton MA 02766-

NICOLATUS, STEPHEN JON, financial consultant; b. Salt Lake City, June 6, 1950; s. George Stephen and Viola (Kerikas) N. BS in Polit. Sci., U. Utah, 1975; MS in Agril. Econ., U. Ariz., 1977. Rsch. assoc. U. Ariz., Tucson, 1975-77; rsch. lab. asst. Utah Cooperative Assn., CENEX, Salt Lake City, 1977; rsch. assoc. Frank K. Stuart & Assocs., Salt Lake City, 1977-81, v.p., 1981-89; ptnr. Stuart, Nicolatus & Peterson, Salt Lake City, 1989-90; prin. Houlihan, Dorton, Jones, Nicolatus & Stuart, OTRA Securites, Salt Lake City, 1990-95; pres. We. Econ. and Valuation Cons., 1995—. Econs. faculty U. Phoenix, Salt Lake City, 1985—, area chair econs., 1987-95. With USAFR, 1968-74. Mem. Am. Soc. Appraisers (cert. sr. appraiser, bus. valuation), Wasatch Front Econ. Forum, SLC Chpt. of ASA (pres. 1998-99). Greek Orthodox. Avocations: golf, stock market, snorkeling, skiing. Home: 1021 Cutter Ln Park City UT 84098-7553 Office: 675 E 2100 S Ste 260 Salt Lake City UT 84106 also: 2441 Tech Ctr Ct Ste 111 Las Vegas NV 89128

NICOLETTI, PAUL LEE, retired veterinarian, educator; b. Goodman, Mo., Oct. 26, 1932; s. Felix and Clarice N.; m. Earlene Brown, June 6, 1954; children: Diana, Julie, Nancy. BS in Agr., DVM, U. Mo., 1956; MS, U. Wis., 1962. Diplomate Am. Coll. Vet. Preventative Medicine. Veterinarian U.S. Dept. Agriculture, Mo., Wis., N.Y., 1956-68, UN Food and Agr. Orgn., Tehran, Iran, 1968-72, U.S. Dept. Agriculture, Jackson, Miss., 1972-75, Gainesville, Fla., 1973-78; prof. veterinary medicine U. Fla., Gainesville, 1978—2003, prof. emeritus, 2003—. Recipient awards from Fla. Cattleman's Assn., 1978, Dairy Farmers, Inc., 1978, Borden award, 1979, Gold Star award Fla. Veterinary Medicine Assoc., 1981, 86, U. Austral, Chile, 1981, P.R. Dairy Assn., 1978, faculty alumni award U. Mo., 1987; named Basic Scis. Tchr. of Yr. Nat. Student Am. Vet. Med. Assn., 1994, Alumnus of Yr. award, U. Mo., 2000, U. Fla. Disting. Svc. award, 2003. Mem. Am. Vet. Medicine Assn. (internat. prize 1991), Fla. Vet. Medicine Assn. (pres. 1995-96, veterinarian of yr. 1994, Disting. Svc. award 1999, Lifetime Achievement award 2004), Am. Coll. Vet. Preventive Medicine (pres. 1997-98), Phi Zeta (nat. pres. 1997-99). Home: 2552 SW 14th Dr Gainesville FL 32608-2042 Office: Univ of Fla Coll Vet Medicine PO Box 110880 Gainesville FL 32611-0880 Office Phone: 352-392-4700 x5860. Business E-Mail: nicolettip@mail.vetmed.ufl.edu.

NICOLL, EDWARD J. internet financial company executive; JD, Yale U. Co-founder, pres. Waterhouse Investor Svcs., Inc. (sold to Toronto-Dominion Bank and became TD Waterhouse), 1979—96; chmn., CEO Datek Online Holdings, Corp., Iselin, NJ, 1999—2002; CEO Instinet Group, Inc., 2002—. Trustee New Cmty. Found. Fellow Yale U. Achievements include first to to attend Yale Law without a college degree. Office: 3 Times Square New York NY 10036*

NICOLS, ANGELA C. software engineer, computer consultant; b. Jamaica, N.Y., Apr. 15, 1940; d. Henry Ralph and Josephine Sadie (Zarcone) Grieco; m. Otto John Nicols, May 21, 1960; children: Annemarie Nicols-Grinenko, Elizabeth Marie, John Joseph, William Joseph, Richard Joseph. BS in Math., Hofstra U., 1979; MS in Math. and Computer Sci., Adelphi U., 1985. Supr. programs/project leader Book Clubs Info. Sys. Doubleday and Co. Inc., Garden City, N.Y., 1979-87; mgr. software engring. Martin Marietta Info. Sys., Orlando, Fla., 1987-94; chmn. tech. and grants Mus. of the Apopkans Apopka (Fla.) Hist. Soc., 1994—2002, v.p. Mus. of the Apopkans, 2002—; computer cons. and trainer, owner Nicols Cons., Apopka, 1995—. Vol. Apopka H.S. Adv. Coun., 1994-97; sec. Bd. Edn.: Bishop Moore H.S., Orlando, 1995-98. Mem. St. Francis Disabilities Com., 1995—; mem. pastoral coun. St. Francis of Assisi Ch., mem. social action commn., 2000-03. Mem. AAUW, IEEE Computer Soc., Assn. for Computing Machinery, Math. Assn. Am., Nat. Assn. Women in Computing, Am. Math. Soc., Apopka Hist. Soc., Coun. Cath. Women, Gray Panthers, Foliage Garden Club of Apopka (2d v.p. 1996-2001), Errol Estates Country Club (comms. com. 1998-2000), Golfside Village Homeowners Assn. (exec. v.p. 1999—), Kappa Mu Epsilon. Office Phone: 407-886-2057. E-mail: angenic@cfl.rr.com.

NICOLSON, DAN H. plant taxonomist; b. Kansas City, Mo., Sept. 5, 1933; s. John Whitley and LeOna Johanna (Teget) N.; m. Alice Black Crawford, Aug. 22, 1959; children: John Crawford, Sarah Whitley, David Teget. AB, Grinnell Coll., 1955; MBA, Stanford U., 1957; MSc, Cornell U., 1959, PhD, 1964. Asst. curator Smithsonian Instn., Washington, 1964-65, assoc. curator, 1965-74, curator, 1974—. Author: Flora of Dominica, 1991; co-author: An Interpretation Van Rheede's Hortus Malabaricus, 1988, The Forsters and the Botany of the Second Cook Expedition (1772-1775), 2004; co-editor: Flora of the Hassan District, 1976. Mem. Internat. Assn. Plant Taxonomy (v.p. 1987-93, pres. 1993-99), Washington Biologists Field Club (treas. 1981-97), Washington Bot. Soc. (pres. 1989-90, treas. 1997—). Office: Dept Botany MRC-166 Nat Mus Natural History Smithsonian Instn Washington DC 20013-7012

NICULESCU, FLORIN IOAN, immunology and rheumatology researcher, educator; b. Blaj, Alba, Romania, Feb. 4, 1955; came to U.S., 1990; s. Ionel and Iuliana Niculescu; m. Daniela Niculescu; 1 child, Linda. MD, U. Med. Sch., Cluj, Romania, 1981, PhD, 1992. Diplomate in internal medicine and rheumatology Am. Bd. Internal Medicine. Intern, fellow in clin. immunology Med. Clinic, Cluj, 1981-85; clin. rschr. Cantacuzino Inst., Bucharest, 1985-90; fellow in immunology U. Md., Balt., 1990-92, immunology instr., 1993, asst. prof., 1994—. Assoc. editor Jour. Immunology, 1999—; contbr. more than 65 articles to profl. jours., 5 chts. to med. textbooks; inventor in field. Recipient Fogarty Internat. award NIH, 1991, Complement Internat. award, 1992. Mem. AMA, ACP, AAAS, Am. Assn. Immunologists, Am. Coll. Rheumatology, Romanian Acad. Scis. Avocations: medical research, classical music, literature, painting. E-mail: fnicules@umaryland.edu.

NICULESCU, PETER S. mortgage company executive; Degree in Econs., Victoria U., Wellington, New Zealand; PhD in Econs., Yale U. With fixed-income rsch. and portfolio mgmt. Salomon Bros., Sanford C. Bernstein and Co.; joined Goldman Sachs, 1990, mng. dir., co-head fixed-income rsch. and strategy; sr. v.p. portfolio strategy Fannie Mae, Washington, 1999—2002, exec. v.p. mortgage portfolio bus., 2002—. Office: Fannie Mae 3900 Wisconsin Ave NW Washington DC 20016-2892

NIDES, THOMAS RICHARD, diversified financial services company executive; s. Mr. and Mrs. Arnold R. Nides BA, U. Minn. Campaign staffer, midwest region polit. and fin. div. Mondale-Ferraro presdl. campaign, 1984; polit. action com. dir. Dem. Congressional Campaign Com., 1985—86; spl. asst. Tony Coelho, House Majority, 1986—89; exec. asst. to spkr. Ho. of Reps. Thomas Foley, 1989—93; chief of staff Michael Kantor, US Trade Rep., 1993—94; v.p. housing impact Fannie Mae, 1995—96, sr. v.p. human resources, 1997—2001; prin., head of corp. affairs Morgan Stanley, NYC, 1996—97; campaign mgr., vice-presidential campaign Joe Lieberman, 2000; chief adminstrv. officer Credit Suisse First Boston LLC, NYC, 2001—, mem., oper. com. Office: Credit Suisse First Boston LLC 11 Madison Ave New York NY 10010-3629 Office Phone: 212-325-2000.

NIDETZ, MYRON PHILIP, health care delivery systems consultant; b. Chgo., Dec. 29, 1935; s. David J. and Rose Y. (Yudell) N.; m. Linda Freeman, Dec. 18, 1960; children: Julia, Allison. BS, U. Ill., 1958; M in Bus. and Commerce, Hamilton Inst., Phila., 1972; MPA, Roosevelt U., 1981. Diplomate Am. Acad. Med. Adminstrs. Dir. Union Coop. Eye Care Ctr., Chgo., 1961-65; dir. med. adminstrv. svcs. Michael Reese Hosp. and Med. Ctr., Chgo., 1965-75; assoc. dir. program to imrpove med. care and health svcs. AMA, Chgo., 1975-79; exec. dir. North Ctrl. Dialysis Ctrs., Chgo., 1979-92; pres. Myron P. Nidetz & Assocs., Inc., Chgo., 1992—. Disting. vis. lectr. health care adminstrn. Roosevelt U., Chgo., bd. govs., 1992—, pres. pub. adminstrn. coun., 1993—, mem. curriculum rev. com. pub. adminstrn., 1992—97, chair admissions com., 1992—, chair coun. and chpt. leadership com., 1998—; vis. lectr. Ind. U. N.W., 2003—; Nat. Inst. Corrections tech. cons. U.S. Dept. Justice, 1978—90; adj. prof., program chair Calumet Coll., St. Joseph U., Whiting, Ind., 1997—99. Mem. adv. bd. Inst. of Medicine, 1979—; active Health Planning Facilities Bd., Ill., 1979—93, Ill. Dept. Pub. Aid, 1992—99, Ill. Dept. Aging, 1992—99; mem. adv. bd. Am. Kidney Fund, chmn. Midwest core group, 1979—92; mem. adv. bd. Nat. Kidney Found., 1992—99; Met. area satellite group, state legis. com., 1992—99; cmty. coord. AARP, 1992—98; pres. bd. dirs. Suburban Area Agy. on Aging, 1997—99, sr. adv. cons., 1999—; mem. Munster Area Rotary Club, Humane Soc. of the Calumet Area, Friends of Theatre at the Ctr., Munster Hist. Soc., Lake County Devel. Com.; bd. dirs., mem. ethics com. Hospice of Calumet Area; counselor Svc. Core of Ret. Execs., 1992—2002; bd. dirs. Active Srs. Found., 1999—, chair bd. devel. com.; regional rev. panelist Ind. Arts Commn., 2002; bd. dirs. Lake County Pub. Libr. Found. With U.S. Army, 1959—60. Fellow: APHA, Am. Acad. Med. Adminstrs., Royal Soc. Health; mem.: AMA, Humane Soc. of Calumet Area, 21st Century Fund (trustee), Lake County Libr. Found. (bd. dirs.), Humane Soc. of the Calunet Area, Hospice of the Calunet Area, Ind. Pub. Health Assn., Ill. Pub. Health Assn., Am. Mgmt. Assn., Assn. U. Programs Health Adminstrn., Gerontol. Soc., Inst. Soc. Ethics and Life Scis., Am. Mgmt. Assn., Am. Hosp. Assn., Am. Geriatrics Soc., Am. Acad. Polit. and Social Sci., Nat. Renal Adminstrs. Assn. (govt. affairs com.), Am. Assn. Kidney Patients, Nat. Dialysis Assn. (sec.), Assn. Hosp. Med. Edn., Munster Hist. Soc., Friends of the Theatre, Ind. Regional Arts Commn. (commr.), Munster Rotary Club, Ind. U. Northwest Cultural Discovery & Learning Group (bd. dir.), Ind. U. Northwest Theatre Patron, Ind. U. Northwest (bd. dir.), Books, Brushes & Bands (bd. dir.), Munster Ednl. Found. (bd. dir.), Hammond Cmty. Concerts Assn. Soc., Hammond Cmty. Concerts Assn., No. Ind. Arts Assn. (bd. dir., devel. com.), Lyric Opera Chpt., Auditorium Bldg. Soc., NW Ind. Excellence in Theatre Found. (bd. dir.), Ill. Theatre Ctr. Guild (chmn. 1990—91), Ill. Theatre Ctr., Northwest Ind. Symphony Soc. (bd. dirs.), No. Ind. Arts Assn. (bd.dir.).

NIE, ZENON STANLEY, manufacturing executive; b. Chgo., Nov. 19, 1950; m. Carol Ann Klockowski, Mar. 27, 1970; 1 child, Andrea Nicole. BS, U Ill., Chgo., 1971; MBA, Loyola U., Chgo., 1974. Mgr. sales stats. Zenith Electronics, Chgo., 1971-74; mktg. mgr. Hollister, Inc., Chgo., 1974-79; dir. market devel. Sealy, Inc., Chgo., 1979-81; sr. v.p. Serta, Inc., Chgo., 1981-89, exec. v.p., 1988-89, pres., 1989-91, The Bibb Co., Macon, Ga., 1991-93; chmn., pres., CEO, Simmons Co., 1993—. Instr. Coll. of Lake County, Ill., 1978-81; bd. dirs. Ladd Furniture Co. Bd. dirs. Cottage Sch. Mem. Internat. Sleep Products Assn. (chmn. stats. com. 1985—), Young Presidents Orgn., Bus. Execs. for Nat. Security. Avocations: scuba diving, fishing, skiing, jogging. Office: Simmons Co One Concourse Pky Atlanta GA 30328

NIEBYL, JENNIFER ROBINSON, obstetrician, gynecologist, educator; b. Montreal, Que., Can., Dec. 5, 1942; BSc, McGill U., Mont., 1963; MD, Yale U., 1967. Diplomate Am. Bd. Ob-Gyn., Am. Bd. Maternal and Fetal Medicine. Intern in Internal Medicine N.Y. Hosp.-Cornell Med. Ctr., 1967-68, resident in ob-gyn., 1968-70, Johns Hopkins Hosp., Balt., 1970-73, fellow in maternal and fetal medicine, 1976-78, mem. staff, 1973—88, U. Iowa Hosps. and Clinics, Iowa City, 1988—; prof., head ob-gyn. dept. U. Iowa Sch. Medicine, Iowa City, 1988—. Mem. ACOG, Am. Gynecol. and Obstetrical Soc., Soc. Gynecol. Investigation, Soc. Maternal Fetal Medicine, Inst. Medicine of NAS. Office: U Iowa Hosps & Clinics 200 Hawkins Dr Iowa City IA 52242 Office Phone: 319-356-1976.

NIED, THOMAS H. media company executive; b. Queens, N.Y., May 4, 1942; s. Herman Joseph and Margaret (Jos) N.; m. Carol J. Thomas, June 6, 1964; children: Stacey, Allison. BA, Rutgers U., 1964, LLB, 1967; LLM in Taxation, NYU, 1972. CPA, N.J., Ga. Tax mgr. Ernst & Young, N.Y.C., Atlanta, Newark and Trenton, N.J., 1968-77; v.p. taxation N.Y. Times Co., N.Y.C., 1977-97; v.p. fed. tax Universal Music Group (formerly Polygram Holding Inc.), N.Y.C., 1997—. Founder Media Tax Group, 1979, mem., 1979-99. Mem. ABA, AICPA, Tax Execs. Inst. (bd. dirs. 1986-2004, pres. N.Y. chpt. 1991-92, exec. com. 1992-93), Newspaper Assn. of Am. (chmn. tax com. 1995-97, chmn. ind. contractor task force 1995-97, mem. pub. policy com. 1995-97). Avocations: travel, reading, stamp collecting/philately, birding. Home: 31 Vreeland Ct Princeton NJ 08540-6760 Personal E-mail: tomnied@aol.com.

NIEDEL, JAMES EDWARD, pharmaceuticals executive; b. Milw., Mar. 30, 1944; m. Selaine Benaim, Mar. 12, 1969; children: Ian Edward, Felisa Ann, Shira Beth. BS, U. Wis., 1965; MD, U. Miami, 1973, PhD, 1974. Diplomate Am. Bd. Internal Medicine. Scientist Burroughs-Wellcome, Research Triangle Park, N.C., 1977-80; prof. medicine Duke U., Durham, N.C., 1980-89; v.p. rsch. Glaxo Rsch. Inst., Research Triangle Park, 1989-92, sr. v.p. R & D, 1992-95; bd. dirs. Glaxo Wellcome plc, London, 1995-2001; chmn., CEO Glaxo Wellcome R & D Ltd., Greenford, U.K., 1995-2001; chief sci. and tech. officer Glaxo Smith Kline plc, Greenford, 2000—. Chmn. Affymax Tech. N.V., 1995-2001. Bd. overseers Duke Cancer Ctr., Durham, 1990—. Searle scholar, 1981-84; recipient Career Devel. award NIH, 1981-84. Fellow Royal Coll. Physicians; mem. Am. Soc. Clin. Investigation, Am. Soc. Biochemistry and Molecular Biology, Am. Soc. Immunology. Office: Glaxo Wellcome R&D PO Box 13408 Research Triangle Park NC 27709

NIEDERAUER, GEORGE H. bishop; b. L.A., June 14, 1936; s. George and Elaine N. BA Philosophy, St. John's Seminary, Camarillo, CA, 1959; BA Sacred Theology, Catholic U., Washington, DC, 1962; MA English Lit., Loyola U., L.A., 1962; PhD English Lit., USC, 1966. Ordained priest 1962, named prelate of honor (monsignor) 1984, named bishop Diocese of Salt Lake City, 1994. Asst. pastor Our Lady of the Assumption Parish, Claremont, Calif., 1962—63; priest in residence Holy Name of Jesus Parish, Los Angeles, 1963—65; instr. English Lit. St. John's Seminary Coll., Camarillo, Calif., 1965—79; instr. of English Lit. Mt. St. Mary's Coll., Los Angeles, 1967—74; English Dept. chmn. St. John's Seminary Coll., Camarillo, 1968—77, spiritual dir., 1972—79; part-time instr. of Spiritual Theology St. John's Seminary Theologate, 1976—79, full-time instr. of Spiritual Theology, 1979—87; part-time instr. of English Lit. St. John's Seminary Coll., 1979—92; rector St. John's Seminary, 1987—92, spiritual dir., 1979—95; co-dir. Cardinal Manning House of Prayer for Priests, Los Angeles, 1992—95; bishop Salt Lake City, 1995—. Mem. Nat. Fedn. of Spiritual Dirs., pres., 1975—77; mem. bd. of the Comm. of Priests' Retreat Archdiocese L.A.; mem. select comm. for revision of U.S. Cath. Conf. "Program for Priestly Formation" 3rd edit.; mem. Vatican Visitation Team for Theologates; spkr. World Vision Internat., Fuller Theol. Sem., Calif. Lutheran Coll. Mem.: Camarillo Ministerial Assn., Western Assn. of Spiritual Dirs. (pres. 1973—75), Alpha Sigma Nu (Jesuit Honor Soc. - LMU chpt.). Avocations: classical music, stamp collecting/philately, reading, film appreciation. Office: Chancery Office 27 C St Salt Lake City UT 84103-2302

NIEDERBERGER, JANE, information technology executive; m. Mark Niederberger; children: Amy, Sarah. BS in nutrition, Simmons Coll., 1982; MBA in health care adminstrn., Northeastern U. With Pilgrim Health Care, Boston, 1983—96; with IT divsn. Anthem, Inc., Indpls., 1997, acting CIO, 1998—99, CIO, 1999—. Bd. mem. Jr. Achievement, Indpls. Recipient Women and Hi Tech Leading Light award, 2002. Office: Anthem Inc 120 Monument Cir Indianapolis IN 46204

NIEDERHUBER, JOHN EDWARD, surgical oncologist and molecular immunologist, university educator and administrator; b. Steubenville, Ohio, June 21, 1938; s. William Henry and Helen (Smittle) N.; m. Tracey J. Williamson (dec. Dec. 2001); children: Elizabeth Ann, Matthew John. BS, Bethany Coll., 1960; MD, Ohio State U., 1964. Diplomate Am. Bd. Surgery. Internship, surgery Ohio State U. Hosp., Columbus, 1964-65; from resident surgery to prof. U. Mich. Med. Ctr., Ann Arbor, 1967—80, prof. surgery, prof. microbiology and immunology, 1980-87, chief divsn. surg. oncology sect. gen. surgery, 1983—86, sr. assoc. dean med. sch., 1983-86; cons. Wayne County Gen. Hosp., Mich., 1973-84; cons. surgery Ann Arbor VA Hosp., 1973-87; prof. surgery, oncology, molecular biology and genetics The Johns Hopkins U. Sch. Med., Baltimore, 1987-91; Emile Holman prof. surgery, chair, dept. surgery, head sect. surgical scis. Stanford (Calif.) U. Sch. Medicine., 1991-95, prof. microbiology and immunology, 1991-97; chief of surgery Stanford (Calif.) U. Hosp., 1991-95; dir. planning Comp. Cancer Ctr. Stanford (Calif.) Med. Ctr., 1991-95; prof. surgery and oncology Sch. Medicine U. Wis., Madison, 1997—, asst. dean oncology, dir. Comprehensive Cancer Ctr., 1997—2002. Vis. prof. Howard Hughes Med. Inst. Dept. Molecular Biology and Genetics The Johns Hopkins U. Sch. Medicine, Baltimore, 1986-87; cons. in field. Author books on cancer and surgery; mem. editl. bd. Jour. Immunology, 1981-85, Jour. Surg. Res., 1989-95, Current Opinion in Oncology, 1989—, Cure, 2002—, Annals of Surgery, 1991—, Surg. Oncology, 1991—, Jour. Clin. Oncology, 1993, Annals of Surg. Oncology, 1993—, Jour. ACS, 1994—, The Oncologist, 1995—, Surgery, 1999—; contbr. articles to profl. jours. Active bd. sci. councilors NCI divsn. Cancer Treatment, 1986-91, chmn., 1987-91, Gen. Motors Cancer Rsch. Found. Awards Assembly, 1988-92, 98-2003; chmn. nat. cancer adv. bd. NCI, 2002—; mem. Nat. Dialogue on Cancer, 2001—, mem. planning and budget com., vice chair cancer ctrs. constituency com., mem. CEO Roundtable, 2003—. Served to

capt. U.S. Army, 1965-67 Recipient USPHS Rsch. Career Devel. award Nat. Inst. Allergy and Infectious Disease, 1974-79, Disting. Faculty Svc. award U. Mich., 1978, Alumni Achievement award Ohio State U. Coll. Medicine, 1989, Alumni Achievement award in Medicine Bethany Coll., 1995; vis. rsch. fellow divsn. immunobiology Karolinska Inst., Stockholm, 1970-71, Am. Cancer Soc. Jr. Faculty Clin. fellow, 1977-79. Fellow ACS; mem. Am. Soc. Transplant Surgeons, Transplantation Soc., Am. Surg. Assn., Am. Assn. Immunologists, Am. Assn. Cancer Insts. (v.p. 1999-2001, pres. 2001-03), Coller Surg. Soc., Soc. Univ. Surgeons, Assn. Acad. Surgeons, Soc. Surg. Oncology (v.p. 1999-2001, pres. 2001-02), Ctrl. Surg. Soc., Am. Assn. Cancer Rsch., Am. Soc. Clin. Oncology, Soc. Clin. Surgery, Biology Club II, Robert M. Zollinger-Ohio State U. Surg. Soc., Pacific Coast Surg. Assn., Soc. Surgery of the Alimentary Tract. Avocations: golf, gardening. Office: U Wis Sch Medicine Dept Surgery 600 Highland Ave Madison WI 53792-0001 Office Phone: 608-263-1375. E-mail: niederhu@biostat.wisc.edu.

NIEDERMAN, JAMES CORSON, physician, educator; b. Hamilton, Ohio, Nov. 27, 1924; s. Clifford Frederick and Henrietta (Corson) N.; m. Miriam Camp, Dec. 12, 1951; children— Timothy Porter, Derrick Corson, Eliza Orton, Caroline Noble. Student, Kenyon Coll., 1942-45, D.Sc. (hon.), 1981; MD, Johns Hopkins U., 1949. Intern Osler Svc. Johns Hopkins Hosp., Balt., 1949-50; asst. resident in medicine Yale-New Haven Med. Center, 1950-51, assoc. resident, 1953-55; med. ctr. practice specializing in internal medicine, infectious disease and clin. epidemiology New Haven, 1955-97; instr. Yale U., 1955-58, asst. prof., 1958-66, assoc. prof., 1966-76, clin. prof. medicine and epidemiology, 1976-97, emeritus clin. prof. medicine and epidemiology, 1997—, clin. prof. emeritus epidemiology and pub. health, 1998; mem. Nat. Coun. for Johns Hopkins Medicine. Trustee Kenyon Coll., 1974-97, trustee emeritus, 1997—; bd. counselors Smith Coll., 1970-77. Served to 1st lt. M.C. U.S. Army, 1951-53. Fellow Silliman Coll., Yale U. Fellow Am. Coll. Epidemiology; mem. Infectious Diseases Soc. Am., Am. Epidemiol. Soc., Johns Hopkins Med. and Surg. Assn.; mem. The Kenyon Rev. Bd. Trustees, Conn. Soc. Arts and Scis. Clubs: Yale (N.Y.C.); New Haven Lawn. Democrat. Episcopalian. Achievements include research in clin. epidemiology of Epstein Barr virus infections and demonstration of its causal relationship of infectious mononucleosis. Home: 429 Sperry Rd Bethany CT 06524-3544 Office: 60 College St New Haven CT 06510-3210 Office Fax: 203-393-1902.

NIEDERMEIER, DONNA M. newswriter, lyricist; b. Detroit, Mich., Sept. 9, 1940; d. Oakley David and Mary Marie Seeley; m. James Henry Niedermeier, Sept. 1, 1964; 1 child, Steven James; m. Kenneth A. Rogers, Jan. 12, 1958 (div. Sept. 6, 1963); children: Diane Lynn, Carolyn Leslie. Freelance writer Cheboygan Tribune Daily, Cheboygan, Mich., 1982—86; writer of songs WCBY Radio Sta., Cheboygan, Mich., 1989—92. Writer ASCAP, NY, 1989. The Church Songs, 1989; author: The Virgin Mary Poems, 1996. Cath. Avocation: doll collecting.

NIEDUNG, HELEN BOVBJERG, voice educator; b. Takoma Park, Md., Apr. 17, 1937; d. Folmer and Anna Emma Bovbjerg; m. Dieter Kurt Niedung, May 3, 1968; children: Konstanze, Kirsten. MusB, U. Rochester, 1958, MusM, 1959. Cert. voice tchr. Fla. Leading soprano Opera Co., Ulm, Germany, 1961—63, Kiel, 1963—66, Wuerzburg, Germany, 1968—71; prof. voice Edison C.C., Ft. Myers, Fla., 1980—; tchr. voice Studio of Voice, Cape Coral, 1980—; dir. music T.A. Edison Congl. Ch., Ft. Myers, 1980—. Grantee, Martha Baird Rockefeller Music Fund, Munich, 1962, Martha Baird Rockefeller Music Fund, Rome, 1963, Martha Baird Rockefeller Music Fund, Hamburg, Germany, 1965. Mem.: Cape Coral Coun. Arts and Humanities, Met. Opera Guild, Alliance of Arts, Nat. Assn. Tchrs. Singing, Southwest Fla. Symphony Soc., Ft. Myers Music Tchrs. Assn. (pres. 1980—82, v.p. 1986—88), Fla. State Music Tchrs. Assn. (v.p. 1994—96), Music Tchrs. Nat. Assn., Friends of Opera Club, Calusa Musicale Music Club (v.p. 1983—85, 2003—), Fla. Fedn. Music Clubs, Nat. Fedn. Music Clubs. Lutheran. Avocations: travel, photography.

NIEFELD, JAYE SUTTER, advertising executive; b. Mpls., May 27, 1924; s. Julius and Sophia (Rosenfeld) N.; m. Piri Elizabeth Von Zabrana-Szilagy, July 5, 1947; 1 child, Peter Wendell. Cert., London U., 1945; BA, U. Minn., 1948; BS, Georgetown U., 1949; PhD, U. Vienna, 1951. Project dir. Bur. Social Sci. Research, Washington, 1952-54; research dir. McCann-Erickson, Inc., N.Y.C., 1954-57; v.p., dir. mktg. Keyes, Madden & Jones, Chgo., 1957-60; pres., dir. Niefeld, Paley & Kuhn, Inc., Chgo., 1961-71; exec. v.p. Bozell, Inc., Chgo., 1971-89; pres. The Georgetown Group, Inc., 1991—. Cons. U.S. Dept. State, Commerce, HEW, also others; lectr. Columbia U., Northwestern U., U. Chgo., 1989-94; chmn. Ctr. Advanced Comm. Rsch.; owner Glencoe Angus Farms, Glencoe Arabians; comm. adv. com. Arabian Horse Registry Am.; ptnr. Sunny Valley Farm, Talcott-Fromkin Freehold Assocs., Neptune Realty, J&J Enterprises; bd. dirs. Mktg. Decisions, Inc., E. Morris Comms., Inc. Author: The Making of an Advertising Campaign, 1989; (with others) Marketing's Role in Scientific Management, 1957, Advertising and Marketing to Young People, 1965, The Ultimate Overseas Business Guide for Growing Companies, 1990; contbr. articles to profl. jours. Mem. adv. bd. Glencoe Family Svc.; bd. dirs. Big Bros. Met. Chgo.; exec. v.p. City of Hope; mem. Theodore Thomas Soc. Chgo. Symphony Orch., Overture Soc. Lyric Opera Chgo. Capt. AUS, 1942-46. Decorated Bronze Star. Mem. Am. Assn. Pub. Opinion Rsch., Am. Film Inst., Am. Mktg. Assn., Am. Sociol. Assn., Smithsonian Instn., Internat. Arabian Horse Assn., Arabian Horse Registry (comm. com.), The Caxton Club, Chgo. Horticultural Soc. (governing bd.), Chgo. Coun. on Fgn. Rels. Home: 1011 Bluff St Glencoe IL 60022-1120 E-mail: JNiefeld@msn.com.

NIEHAUS, ED, engineering executive; Degree in engring., Duke U. Pres., CEO Neuhaus Ryan Wong, Inc., South San Francisco. Bd. dirs. Foresight Inst., Inst. Molecular Mfg., Software Forum. Office: 601 Gateway Blvd Ste 900 South San Francisco CA 94080-7006

NIEHAUS, MARY C. C. lawyer; b. 1961; BA with honors, Grinnell Coll., 1985; JD cum laude, Northwestern U., 1988. Bar: Ill. 1988, U.S. Dist. Ct. (no. dist.) Ill. 1988, U.S. Tax Ct. 1989. With Sidley & Austin, Chgo., 1988—, ptnr., 1996—. Mem. editl. staff Northwestern U. Law Rev., 1987-88. Mem. Order of Coif, Phi Beta Kappa. Office: Sidley & Austin Bank One Plz 10 S Dearborn St Chicago IL 60603 Fax: 312-83-7036. E-mail: mniehaus@sidley.com.

NIEHAUS, SHERRY M. social welfare administrator; b. Heber Springs, Ark., Dec. 12, 1946; d. Ewing W. and Fay D. Mays; m. Joseph T. Niehaus, May 27, 1972 (div.); children: Vincent E., Jessica F.; m. Stephen P. Mers, Apr. 30, 1992. Tabulating clk. Dover Elevator, Cin., 1968-71; data machine operator Little Rock Water Works, 1971-76; acctg. clk. Mays Mission for the Handicapped, Heber Springs, 1978-85, exec. dir., 1985-95, pres., 1995—. Bd. dirs., sec. Ark. State Rehab. Coun., Little Rock, 1999—, chair, 2004. Vol. Tax Income Assistance, Heber Springs, 1978; bd. sec. Cmty. Sch. Cleburne County, Heber Springs, 1987—. Mem.: Rotary (bull. editor Cleburne County chpt. 1995—, sec. 2000—01, 2003—04). Avocations: horses, reading, genealogy, computers, martial arts. Home: 2208 Misty Ln Heber Springs AR 72543 Office: Mays Mission for the Handicapped 604 Colonial Dr Heber Springs AR 72543 Office Phone: 501-362-7526. E-mail: sniehaus@maysmission.org.

NIEHM, BERNARD FRANK, retired health facility administrator; b. Sandusky, Ohio, Feb. 7, 1923; s. Bernard Frank and Hedwick (Panzer) N.; m. Eunice M. Patterson, Oct. 4, 1924; children— Julie, Patti, Bernie. BA, Ohio State U., 1951, MA, 1955, PhD in Ednl. Exceptional Children, Guidance and Couseling, Psychology, 1968. Tchr. pub. schs., Sandusky, 1951-57; chief ednl., vocat. and occupational therapy svcs. Vineland (N.J.) Tng. Sch., 1957-61; exec. dir. Franklin County Coun. Retarded Children, Columbus, Ohio, 1962-64; dir. Ohio Sheltered Workshop Planning Project Mental Retardation, 1964-66, coordinator mental retardation planning, 1966-68; project dir. Ohio Gov.'s Citizen Com. on Mental Retardation Planning, 1966-68; adminstr. Franklin County Program for Mentally Retarded, 1968-70; supt. Gallipolis (Ohio) State Inst., 1970-76; tchr. spl. edn. Ohio U., Columbus, 1975-77, dir. consultation and edn., 1977-79, dir., 1978-95; exec. dir. Woodland Ctrs. Inc., Gallipolis, 1995; ret. Woodland Farm, Gallipolis, 1995. Pres. Gallco, 1989-90. Contbr. articles to profl. jours. Active Foster Grandparents Adv. Coun., Gallia County, 1974-76, Gallipolis State Inst. Parent Vol. Assn., 1970-76, Franklin County Bd. Mental Retardation, 1967-68; chmn. MGM dist. Tri-State Boy Scout Coun.; chmn. Meigs, Gallia, Mason Counties Boy Scout Dist., 1972-94; pres. Gallipolis Girls Athletic Assn. Booster Club, 1976—, Gallia County Arthritis Unit, 1986-96, Galleo Industries Bd. to Serve Handicapped Adults, 1987-94; pres. bd. dirs. Outreach Ctr. Gallia County, 1997-99; mem. Ch. Coun., St. Paul Luth. Ch., 1994-99, pres.; bd. dirs. United Cerebral Palsy, Columbus, 1968-70, Gallco Sheltered Workshop for Mentally Handicapped, Outreach Inc., Tri-State coun. Boy Scouts of Am.; mem. gov. bd. Gallia County Coun. on Aging; bd. alcohol, drug addiction and mental health svcs. Gallia-Jackson, Meigs; pres. Gallia County Pub. Employment Retiree Inc.; mem. United Way Gallia County. With U.S. Army, 1943-46. Mem. Am. Assn. Mental Deficiency (past chmn. Ohio chpt., chmn. Great Lakes region), Am. Mental Health Adminstrs. (nat., Ohio chpts.), Nat. Rehab. Assn., Ohio Rehab. Assn., Ohio Assn. Retarded Children (2d v.p. 1974-76, dir.), Vocat. Rehab. Assn., Ohio Coun. Community Mental Health Ctrs., Gallia County Arthritis Assn. (pres. 1991—), Gallipolis Area C. of C., Gallipolis Rotary. Lutheran. Home: 1525 Mill Creek Rd Gallipolis OH 45631-8616 Office: Woodland Ctr Inc 3086 State Route 160 Gallipolis OH 45631-8418

NIEHOFF, KARL RICHARD BESUDEN, financial executive; b. Cin., May 11, 1943; s. Karl George and Jean (Besuden) N.; children: K. Richard B. Jr., Kelly B. BA, U. Cin., 1967. Corp. trust ops. officer 5th-3d Union Trust, Cin., 1968-74; v.p., gen. mgr. Sabina (Ohio) Water Co., 1974-76; v.p., sec. Weil, Roth and Irving, Inc., 1974-76; co-mgr., mcpl. fin. dept. Thomson McKinnon Securities, Cin. and N.Y.C., 1976-79; exch. rep. Consol. Quote, Consol. Tape Oper. Coms., 1979-90, alt., 1991-92; pres. Fin. Instruments Svcs. Corp., Cin., Chgo., London, 1985-90; v.p. Trading Svcs. NASDAQ, Inc., 1990—92, D.E. Shaw Securities, LLC, N.Y.C., 1992—94, D.E. Shaw & Co., N.Y.C., 1992-94; pres., mng. ptnr. Niehoff and Assocs., N.Y.C., 1994-99; mng. dir., chief of party OTC Capital Mkt. Devel. Project, Warsaw, 1994—96; dep. advisor Ministry Mass Privatization, Republic of Poland, Warsaw, 1994-96; v.p., dir. Third Market Trading Corp., Chicago, 1994-98; pres., dir. SBX Inc., Cin., Princeton, N.J., 1997-2000, VSX Techs. Inc., N.Y.C., Indpls., 1999—2000; pres., CEO Webix, Inc., N.Y.C., 2000—02; chmn. The X-Change Corp., 2002, pres., 2002; pres., CEO Mark Securities, Inc., Boston, 2002—, Pelham Manor, NY. Witness U.S. Ho. Reps. Consumers Protection and Fin. Com., 1977—, other gen. oversight, GAO com. panels and inquiries, 1987—94; v.p. Wit Capital Corp., N.Y.C., 1998—99; mem. Cin. Stock Exch., 1974—89, trustee, 1974—90, chmn. bd. trustees, 1978—79; voting mem. Inter-Market Trading Com., 1980—90, Stock Exch. Chief Execs. Com., 1988—90; mem. P.B.W. Stock Exch., Phila., 1975—77, GLOBEX Task Force Com., 1988—89, Easdaq, Brussels, 1995—96; vis. lectr. U. Cin. Coll. Bus. Adminstrn., Xavier U. Bus. Adminstrn. Coll., Cin.; long-term planning com. Chgo. Bd. Options Exch., 1987—88; pres. Digital Stock Market, N.Y.C., 1998—99; vis. com. USIA, N.Y.C., 1992—95; mng. dir. trading and tech. Unified Mgmt. Corp., Inc., Indpls. and N.Y.C., 1999—2000; pres. WEBIX, Inc., 1999—2002; dir., sec. Schuyler Park Manor Co-op, Pelham Manor, NY, 2000—; co-founder U.S. Capital Market LLC, NY, 2004. Trustee, sec. Contemporary Arts Ctr., Cin., 1975-83; mem. Young Mens Mercantile Libr. Assn., 1974-90, adv. com., 1974-77; mem. devel. com. Tangeman Gallery of Art, 1981-82; pres., dir. Bermuda Condominium High Assn., Delray Beach, Fla., 1999-2004. Mem.: Internat. Ops. Divsn. (N.Y.), Securities Traders Assn. N.Y. (chmn. listed trading com. 1993, chmn. STA trading subcom. 2002—, OTC Bull. Bd. 2002—), Nat. Acad. Design, India House, Keeneland Assn. (Lexington, Ky.), Queen City Mcpl. Bond Club (trustee 1974—80), NYAC Yacht Club (Pelham Manor, N.Y.), N.Y. Stock Exch. Luncheon Club, Univ. Club (Cin.), N.Y. Athletic Club, Cin. Stock and Bond Club (trustee and 1st v.p. 1974—90), Nat. Arts Club (N.Y.C.), Phi Alpha Theta.

NIEHUSS, JOHN MARVIN, lawyer; b. Ann Arbor, Mich., Mar. 7, 1937; s. Marvin Lemmon Niehuss and Lois Celicia Markham; m. Rosemary Juliette Neaher, June 30, 1973 (div. Mar. 1991); children: Juliette, John. BA, Amherst Coll., 1958; JD, U. Mich., 1962. Assoc. atty. Sullivan & Cromwell, N.Y.C., 1966-69; legal advisor Govt. of Zambia, Lusaka, 1969-71; loan officer, dir. World Bank, Washington, 1971-73, 90-91; dep. asst. sec. U.S. Treasury Dept., Washington, 1974-77, 89-90; v.p. Merrill Lynch, N.Y.C., 1977-89; gen. counsel Inter-Am. Devel. Bank, Washington, 1992-99, Export-Import Bank U.S., Washington, 1999-2001. Mem. adv. bd. Internat. Law Inst., Washington, 1977—. Mem. Coun. Fgn. Rels., Met. Club. Avocations: golf, hiking, fly fishing. Home: 3019 45th St NW Washington DC 20016-3523 Office Phone: 202-362-1164.

NIELSEN, ALDON LYNN, literature educator; b. Grand Island, Nebr., Oct. 22, 1950; s. Aldon Dale and Vivian L. Nielsen; m. Anna Everett, Aug. 5, 1989. BA, U. D.C., 1977; PhD, MPhil, George Washington U., 1985. Lectr. Howard U., Washington, 1985—87; prof. San Jose (Calif.) State U., 1987—97; Fletcher Jones chair lit. and writing Loyola Marymount U., L.A., 1997—2001; Kelly prof. Am. lit. Pa. State U., University Park, 2001—. Humanist in residence DC Pub. Schs., Washington, 1981—82; dir. poetry writing workshop Martin Luther King Pub. Libr., Washington, 1984—85; vis. prof. UCLA, 1996. Author: Heat Strings, 1985, Evacuation Routes: A User's Manual, 1992, Stepping Razor, 1997, VEXT, 1998, Writing Between the Lines: Race and Intertextuality, 1997, Black Chant: Languages of African American Postmodernism, 1994, C.L.R. James: A Critical Introduction, 1997, Integral Music: Languages of African American Innovation, 2004, Reading Race: White American Poets and the Racial Discourse in the 20th Century (Kayden Prize, 1988, SAMLA Studies Prize, 1988, Gustavus Myers Citation, 1988); editor: Reading Race in American Poetry: An Area of Act, 2000. Recipient Larry Neal Poetry award, DC Commn. Arts Humanities, 1983, Meritorious Performance and Profl. Promise Award, Calif. State U., 1989, Meritorious Performance and Profl. Promise award, Calif. Sate U., 2000, Gertrude Stein Poetry award, Sun and Moon Press, 1994, 1995; fellow Trustees Rsch. stipend, Calif. State U., 1988, 1992, NEA, 1991, 1996, Inst. Am. Cultures, UCLA, 1993—94, Trustees Rsch. fellow, Loyola Marymount U., 1998, 2000; grantee Individual Artist's grantee, DC Commn. Arts Humanities, 1985, 1986. Mem.: MLA, Coll. Lang. Assn., Horton Soc. African Am. Poetry, African Am. Lit. Culture Soc. Avocation: music. Office: Pennsylvania State University Dept of English - 116 Burrowes University Park PA 16802-6200 Personal E-mail: aln10@psu.edu. E-mail: aln10@psu.edu.

NIELSEN, BARBARA STOCK, state educational administrator; State supt. S.C. Dept. Edn., Columbia, 1991—99; vis. prof. sch. edn. Coll. at Charleston; sr. fellow Strom Thurmond Inst. Clemson U., 2000—; dir. Schs. Around the World. Office: Strom Thurmond Inst Govt and Pub Affairs Clemson U Perimeter Rd Clemson SC 29634-0125

NIELSEN, DANIEL C. poet; b. Norfolk, Nebr., Aug. 19, 1968; s. Daniel L. and Donna F. Nielsen; m. Svetlana A. Nielsen, Feb. 5, 2000; children: Bredan Mitchell, Emily Ann, Amber Nicole, Ashley Breann. Dipl., Childrens Inst. of Lit., Redding, Conn., 1997. Cert. ISO 9000 AQC Moody. Editor nebraskafishing.com, Norfolk, Nebr., 2000—04. Author: (poem) The Rage of Angels (Best New Poems of 1996, 1996), Shattered Season, Another Winter, Like Wind Carries Dust, (short story) Dark Waters, (poem) Dead Mans Winter, Abide not the Shadows, Dark Angel, Memories Requiem, (fantasy novel (in progress) Darksteel Destinies, (children's short story) The Ring of the Gargoyle, (poem) Barbarian Soul, The Darker Element (Inst. of Contemporary Poets, 1998), The Dead of Winter, The Adversary; contbr. articles to profl. jours. Fishing tournament coord. and weigh-in judge nebraskafishing.com, Crofton, Nebr., 2000—03. With U.S. Army, 1987—89. Mem.: N.Am. Fishing Club. Independent. Lutheran. Avocations: travel, reading, swimming, Web design, learning new languages. Home: #72 2304 Northeastwood Norfolk NE 68701 Office: #72 2304 Northeastwood Norfolk NE 68701 Personal E-mail: dnielsen@conpoint.com. E-mail: dnielsen@conpoint.com.

NIELSEN, FORREST HAROLD, research nutritionist; b. Dancy, Wis., Oct. 26, 1941; s. George Adolph and Sylvia Viola (Blood) N.; m. Emily Joanne Currie, June 13, 1964; children: Forrest Erik, Kistin Emily. BS, U. Wis., 1963, MS, 1966, PhD, 1967. NIH grad. fellow, dept. biochemistry U. Wis., Madison, 1963-67; rsch. chemist, Human Nutrition Rsch. Inst. USDA, Beltsville, Md., 1969-70, rsch. chemist Human Nutrition Rsch. Ctr. Grand Forks, N.D., 1970-86, ctr. dir. and rsch. nutritionist, 1986-2001, rsch. nutritionist, 2001—. Adj. prof. dept. biochemistry and molecular biology, U. N.D., Grand Forks, 1971—, speaker in field. Assoc. editor Magnesium and Trace Elements Jour., 1990-93; mem. editl. bd. Jour. Trace Elements in Exptl. Medicine, 1988—, Biol. Trace Element Rsch. Jour., 1979—, Jour. Nutrition, 1984-88, Biofactors, 1997—; contbr. articles to profl. jours. Capt. U.S. Army, 1967-69. Recipient Klaus Schwarz Commemorative medal and award Internat. Assn. of Bioinorganic Scientists; named Scientist of Yr. U.S. Dept. Agrl., 1993. Mem. Internat. Soc. Trace Element Rsch. in Humans (gov. bd. 1989—, pres. 1992-95), Soc. for Exptl. Biology and Medicine, Am. Soc. for Nutritional Scis., N.D. Acad. Sci. (pres. 1988-89), Internat. Bone and Mineral Soc., Sigma Xi (pres. U. N.D. chpt. 1976-77). Lutheran. Achievements include patent for use of Boron Supplements to Increase in Vivo Production of Hydroxylated Steroids; discovery of the nutritional essentiality of the trace elements boron and nickel. Office: USDA ARS GFHNRC PO Box 9034 Grand Forks ND 58202-9034 Office Phone: 701-795-8455. Business E-Mail: fnielsen@gfhnrc.ars.usda.gov.

NIELSEN, FREDRICK HENRY, historian, educator; b. Nebraska City, Nebr., June 20, 1952; s. Leo R. and Wilma L. Nielsen; m. Susan E. Epperson, Aug. 9, 1986. BA, Midland Luth. Coll., Fremont, Nebr., 1974; MPhil, U. Kans., 1980, PhD, 1997. Adj. prof. history U. of Nebr., Omaha, 1992—. Interviewer Talking History radio program (NPR), 2000—; spkr. Speakers' Bur., Nebr. Humanities Coun., Nebr., 1993—. Contbr. articles to profl. jours. and ency. Supt.'s citizen's adv. com. Omaha Pub. Schs., Omaha, 1999—2002; exec. bd. Nebr. State Coun. for the Social Studies, Nebr., 2000—03. Mem.: Thoreau Soc., Am. Studies Assn., Am. Soc. for Environ. History, Orgn. of Am. Historians, Am. Hist. Assn., Pinochle Club (life; sec. treas.). Office: U Nebr Dept History 60th and Dodge Sts Omaha NE 68182 E-mail: fnielsen@unomaha.edu.

NIELSEN, GEORGE LEE, architect; b. Ames, Iowa, Dec. 12, 1937; s. Verner Henry and Verba Lucile (Smith) N.; m. Karen Wall, Feb. 28, 1959; children: David Stuart, Kristina, Melissa. B.Arch., Iowa State U., 1961; M.Arch., M.I.T., 1962. Registered arch., Mass., Ohio, N.Y., Ill., Ind., Ky., Miss., Kans., Colo., Mich., Nat. Coun. Archtl. Registration Bds. Designer Perry, Shaw, Hepburn & Dean, Boston, 1961-64, F.A. Stahl & Assos., Cambridge, Mass., 1964-65; project architect Peirce & Pierce, Boston, 1965-70; project mgr. A.M. Kinney Assos., Cin., 1970—, partner, 1978—; sec. A.M. Kinney Assocs., Inc., Ill., 1993—, also dir.; v.p. A.M. Kinney Inc., Cin., 1992-94, pres., 1994-99, also dir.; sr. prin. A.M. Kinney Inc. Assocs., 1999—. Architect assoc. with major projects for Avco Rsch. Lab., Children's Hosp. Med. Ctr., Square D. Corp., Nalco Chem. Co., Olin Corp., Mead Johnson/Bristol Myers Squib, Cin. Gas and Elec. Co., Sandoz Pharm. Corp., Hoechst Celanese, Hoechst Marion Roussel, Martek Biosciences, Witco Corp., Sotheby's, Shell Chem. Co., Bayer Corp., Univ. Ky., Purdue U., Wright Patterson and Edwards AFB. Served with U.S. Army, 1962-64. Mem. AIA (design awards 1970-71, 74, 78, 81, 91, 94, 95). Episcopalian. Home: 3419 Ault View Ave Cincinnati OH 45208-2518 Office: A M Kinney Inc 150 E 4th St Fl 6 Cincinnati OH 45202-4131

NIELSEN, GREG ROSS, lawyer; b. Provo, Utah, Sept. 24, 1947; s. Ross T. and Carma (Peterson) N.; m. Jo Rita Beer, Sept. 3, 1971; children: Jennifer, Jerilyn, Eric Michael, Brittany Anne. BA in Polit. Sci. magna cum laude, Brigham Young U., 1971; JD cum laude, Harvard U., 1975. Bar: Ariz. 1975, U.S. Dist. Ct. Ariz. 1975, U.S. Ct. Appeals (9th cir.) 1977, Utah 1990, Nev. 2003. Assoc. Snell & Wilmer, Phoenix, 1975-80, ptnr., 1981—2004, mng. ptnr. Salt Lake City, 1991—2002, adminstrv. coord. real estate practice group Phoenix, 1988-90; gen. counsel GE Capital Franchise Fin. Corp., Scottsdale, Ariz., 2004—. Mem. dist. com. Theodore Roosevelt coun. Boy Scouts Am., 1988-90; trustee Utah Heritage Found., 1998-2000, Swaner Nature Preserve, 2002-04. Hinckley scholar Brigham Young U., 1970; fellow Ford Found., 1970. Mem. ABA. Republican. Mem. Lds Ch. Office: GE Franchise Fin Corp 17207 N Perimeter Dr Scottsdale AZ 85255 Office Phone: 480-585-2234. Business E-Mail: greg.nielsen@ge.com.

NIELSEN, GWYN ENGLISH, writer, illustrator, publishing executive; b. Plainfield, N.J., Dec. 12, 1958; d. Richard English and Valerie Victoria Youtkus; m. Christian Anthony Nielsen, June 22, 1986 (div. Nov. 1996); 1 child, Saxony Annin. BA in English/Comm. cum laude, Bucknell U., 1981. Cert. English tchr. NJ.J. Dept. Edn. State Bd. Examiners. Adminstrv. coord. Group W Satellite Comm., N.Y.C., 1981—83; dir. drama Ctrl. Bucks H.S. East, Buckingham, Pa., 1983—84; English tchr. Rahway (N.J.) H.S., 1984—85; English and drama tchr. Mother Seton Regional H.S., Clark, NJ, 1985—89; English tchr. Connackamack Sch., Piscataway, NJ, 1989—90; pres. Video Sta. CGS Inc./Overlook Video, Summit, NJ, 1990—2002, CGS Press, Scotch Plains, NJ, 1997—. English tutor Mentor Learning Group, Summit, 1989; substitute tchr. Bd. Edn., Scotch Plains, Westfield, 2000—; playwright, dir. Performing Arts Studio, Scotch Plains, 2001; tchr. Summit Cmty. Ctr., Summit, NJ, 2002—03. Author, illustrator: children's book Torey the Turkey Goes Skiing, 1998, author, pub.: poetry Teaching Love Life, 2000, children's book Serendipity and the Dream Catcher, 2003; vocalist Music for All Seasons, Scotch Plains, NJ. HEART grantee, Union County Arts Coun. bd. freeholders, 2002. Mem.: Soc. Children's Book Writers and Illustrators, Acad. Am. Poets, Publishers Mktg. Assn., Bucknell Univ. Assn. of the Arts, Alpha Lambda Delta. Presbyterian. Avocations: singing, acting. Office: CGS Press PO Box 1394 Mountainside NJ 07092

NIELSEN, HARALD CHRISTIAN, retired chemist, researcher; b. Chgo., Apr. 18, 1930; s. Svend Aage and Seena (Hansen) N.; m. Eloise Wilma Soule, Dec. 19, 1953; children: Brenda Mae, Paul Erick, Gloria Lynn, Judy Ann (dec.). BA, St. Olaf Coll., 1952; PhD, Mich. State U., 1957. Cereal grain protein chemist Nat. Ctr. for Agrl. Utilization Rsch. (formerly No. Regional Research Ctr.), Agrl. Research Service, USDA, Peoria, Ill., 1957-87. Contbr. articles to profl. jours. Mem. Peoria Area Combined Fed. Campaign Coord. Com., 1980—87; pres. local 3247 Am. Fedn. Govt. Employees, AFL-CIO, 1977—86; active Peoria Prostrate Cancer Support Group, 1996—, editor newsletter, 2000—. Mem.: Nat. Assn. Ret. Fed. Employees (officer chpt. 268 1989—92, pres. chpt. 268 1991, editor chpt. newsletter 1999—), Am. Assn. Cereal Chemists. Democrat. Lutheran. Home: 2318 N Gale Ave Peoria IL 61604-3229 Personal E-mail: nielsen425@yahoo.com. *What useful thing have I accomplished this day? What did I learn today? These two questions I ask myself at the end of each day.*

NIELSEN, JAKOB, computer interface engineer; b. Copenhagen, Oct. 5, 1957; came to U.S., 1990; s. Gerhard and Helle (Hopfner) N.; m. Hannah Kain, Feb. 18, 1984. MS in Computer Sci., Aarhus (Denmark) U., 1983; PhD in Computer Sci., T.U. of Denmark, 1988. Rsch. fellow Aarhus U., 1983-84; vis. scientist IBM User Interface Inst., Yorktown Heights, N.Y., 1985; adj. asst. prof. T.U. Denmark, Lyngby, 1986-90; mem. rsch. staff Bell Comm. Rsch., Morristown, N.J., 1990-94; disting. engr. Sun Microsystems, Mountain View, Calif., 1994-98; principal Nielsen Norman Group, Mountain View, CA, 1998—. Author: Hypertext and Hypermedia, 1990, Usability Engineering, 1993, Multimedia and Hypertext: The Internet and Beyond, 1995, Designing Web Usability: The Practice of Simplicity, 2000, Homepage Usability: 50 Websites Deconstructed, 2001; editor: Coordinating User Interfaces for Consistency, 1989, Designing User Interfaces for International Use, 1990, Usability Inspection Methods, 1994, International User Interfaces, 1996; mem. editl. bd.: Behavior and Info. Tech., 1989—, Hypermedia Jour., 1989—95, Interacting with Computers, 1989—, Internat. Jour. Human-Computer Interaction, 1989—, Internat. Jour. Man-Machine Studies, 1991—94, ACM Networker, 1997—2000, Personal Technologies, 1997—; contbr. articles to profl. jours. Mem.: Assn. for Computing Machinery (papers co-chair internat. conf. 1993, editl. bd. Networker 1997—2000, spl. interest group on computer human interaction). Achievements include holder 74 patents in field; founding of discount usability engineering approach; invention (with R. Molich) of heuristic evaluation method for cost-effective improvement of user interfaces; demonstration (with T.K. Landauer) that user testing and heuristic evaluation both follow same mathematical model; definition of the parallel design method for rapidly exploring user interface alternatives.

NIELSEN, JENNIFER LEE, molecular ecologist, researcher; b. Balt., Mar. 21, 1946; d. Leo Jay and Mary Marriott (Mules) N.; divorced; children: Nadja Ochs, Allisha Ochs. MFA, Ecole des Beaux Arts, Paris, 1968; BS, Evergreen State Coll., 1987; MS, U. Calif., Berkeley, 1990, PhD, 1994. Artist, Seattle, 1969-78; fish biologist Weyerhaeuser Co., Tacoma, Wash., 1978-89; resource cons. Berkeley, 1989-90; rsch. biologist USDA-Forest Svc., Albany, Calif., 1990-99; vis. scientist Stanford U., Pacific Grove, Calif., 1994-99; supr. fisheries Alaska Biol. Sci. Ctr., Anchorage, 1999—. Rsch. assoc. Calif. State U. Mosslanding Marie Sta., 1995-99; adj. prof. integrated biology U. Calif., Berkeley, 1998; adj. prof. U. Alaska, Fairbanks, 1999—; supervisory rsch. fishery biologist U.S. Geol. Svc., Biol. Resources Divsn., Alaska Biol. Sci. Ctr., Anchorage, 1999—. Editor-in-chief: Reviews in Fish Biology and Fisheries, 1999—; editor: Evolution and the Aquatic Ecosystem, 1995, Environ. Biology of Fishes, 1998—; contbr. over 80 articles to profl. jours.; paintings exhibited at Metro. Mus. Modern Art, 1966; represented in numerous pvt. collections, U.S. and Europe. Mem. Am. Fisheries Soc. (pres. chpt. 1993-94, genetics sect. pres. 1999—, 2d v.p. 2003), Molecular Marine Biology and Biotech. (regional editor 1995), Animal Behaviour Soc. (policy com. 1993-94). Avocations: painting, cooking, gardening, rock climbing, sailing. Office: USGS/BRD Alaska Biol Sci Ctr 1011 E Tudor Rd Anchorage AK 99503-6119

NIELSEN, JOHN A. investment company executive; Gen. ptnr. Brown Bros. Harriman & Co., N.Y.C. Office: Brown Bros Harriman & Coi 59 Wall St New York NY 10005-2808

NIELSEN, KENNETH ANDREW, chemical engineer; b. Berwyn, Ill., Oct. 10, 1949; s. Howard Andrew and La Verne Alma (Wentzer) N.; m. Linda Kay Miller, Aug. 22, 1970; children: Annette Marie, Kirsten Viola. BS in Chem. Engring., Iowa State U., 1971, MS in Chem. Engring., 1974, PhD in Chem. Engring., 1977. Sr. engr. Union Carbide Corp., Charleston, W.Va., 1976-80, project scientist, 1980-87, rsch. scientist, 1987-94, sr. rsch. scientist, 1994—. Contbr. articles to profl. jours. Co-founder Forest Hills Assns., Charleston, 1981; advisor Boy Scout Explorer Post, Charleston, 1992. Recipient Fellowships NDEA Title IV, Procter and Gamble Co., Am. Oil Co., Elias Singer award Troy Chem. Co., 1990, Kirkpatrick Chem. Engring. Achievement award Chem. Engring. mag., 1991, Profl. Progress in Engring. award Coll. Engring. Iowa State U. 1992. Mem. AIChE, Soc. Rheology, Inst. Liquid Atomization and Spraying Sys. Achievements include invention of UNICARB system for spray coating, a recognized major new pollution-prevention technology; co-inventor of SERT process for applying mold release agents in polyurethane foam manufacture; discovery of fundamentally new type of spray atomization, known as a decompressive spray; 33 U.S. patents and 5 U.S. patents pending, also foreign patents. Home: 108 Stratford Pl South Charleston WV 25303-2819 Office: Union Carbide Corp PO Box 8361 South Charleston WV 25303

NIELSEN, KENNETH RAY, academic administrator; b. Oct. 15, 1941; s. Frank and Elinor (Hansen) N.; children: Elizabeth, Mary. BEd, U. Wis., Whitewater, 1965; MS, U. Wis., Stout, 1966; EdD, U. Wyo., 1968. Dir. student activities Cornell U., Ithaca, N.Y., 1968-72; adminstr., prof. Tchr. Tng. Coll., San Juan, P.R., 1974-77; v.p. student affairs Northland Coll., Ashland, Wis., 1972-77; v.p. student life Seattle U., 1977-84; pres. Coll. St. Mary, Omaha, 1984-96, Woodbury U., Burbank, Calif., 1996—. Bd. dirs. Boy Scouts Am., Girl Scouts U.S.A., Nat. Coun. Christians and Jews, Providence Hosp. Found.; chmn. edn. sect. United Way Bd.; mem. Gov.'s Community Svcs. and Continuing Edn. Mem. Am. Coun. Edn., Am. Assn. Higher Edn., Am. Assn. Univ. Adminstrs., Coun. Ind. Colls. Roman Catholic. Avocations: reading, exercising. Office: Woodbury U 7500 N Glenoaks Blvd Burbank CA 91504-1099

NIELSEN, LESLIE, actor; b. Regina, Sask., Can., Feb. 11, 1926; s. Ingvard and Maybelle Nielsen; m. Monica Bayar, 1950 (div. 1955); m. Sandy Ullman, 1958 (div.); children: Thea, Maura; m. Brooks Nielsen, 1981 (div. 1983). Student, Neighborhood Playhouse, N.Y.C. Former announcer, disk jockey, Can. radio; feature films include The Vagabond King, 1956, Forbidden Planet, 1956, Ransom!, 1956, The Opposite Sex, 1956, Hot Summer Night, 1957, Tammy and the Bachelor, 1957, Night Train to Paris, 1964, Harlow, 1965, Dark Intruder, 1965, Beau Geste, 1965, Gunfight in Abilene, 1967, The Reluctant Astronaut, 1967, Rosie, 1967, Counterpoint, 1967, Dayton's Devils, 1969, How to Commit Marriage, 1969, Change of Mind, 1969, The Resurrection of Zachary Wheeler, 1971, The Poseidon Adventure, 1972, Viva, Knievel, 1977, City of Fire, 1979, Airplane!, 1980, Wrong is Right, 1982, Creepshow, 1983, Spaceship, 1983, Soul Man, 1986, The Patriot, 1986, Nuts, 1987, Nightstick, 1987, Home Is Where the Hart Is, 1987, The Naked Gun, 1988, Dangerous Curves, The Repossessed, The Naked Gun 2 1/2: The Smell of Fear, 1991, All I Want for Christmas, 1991, Surf Ninjas, 1993, The Naked Gun 33 1/3: The Final Insult, 1994, Rent-a-Kid, 1995, Dracula: Dead and Loving It, 1995, Spy Hard, 1996; Family Plan, 1997, Mr. Magoo, 1997, Wrongfully Accused, 1998, 2001: A Space Travesty, 1999, Camouflage, 2001, Kevin of the North, 2001, Men with Brooms, 2002, Scary Movie 3, 2003; TV films include Crime Syndicated, 1952, Man Behind The Badge, 1954, See How They Run, 1964, Shadow Over Elveron, 1968, Hawaii Five-O, 1968, Companions in Nightmare, 1968, Trial Run, 1969, Deadlock, 1969, Night Slaves, 1970, The Aquarians, 1970, Hauser's Memory, 1970, Monty Nash, 1971, They Call It Murder, 1971, Incident in San Francisco, 1972, Snatched, 1973, The Letters, 1973, Can Ellen Be Saved?, 1974, Brinks! The Great Robbery, 1976, Little Mo, 1978, miniseries Back Stairs At the White House, 1979, Institute For Revenge, 1979, Ohms, 1980, The Night The Bridge Fell Down, 1980, Murder Among Friends, 1982, Cave-In, 1983, Blade in Hong Kong, 1985, The Loner, Fatal Confession: A Father Dowling Mystery, Chance of a Lifetime, 1991, Harvey, 1996, Mr. Willowby's Christmas Tree, 1995, Safety Patrol, 1998, Santa Who?, 2000, Noël Noël, 2003; numerous other TV appearances including dramatic series Studio One, Armstrong Circle Theater, Goodyear Playhouse; TV series include The New Breed, 1961, The Bold Ones, 1963-67, Peyton Place, 1965, Bracken's World, 1969-70, Shaping Up, 1984, Police Squad, 1982, The Golden Girls, 1992, (voice) Pumper Pups, 2000, Liography, 2001, Zeroman, 2004; toured country in one man show Darrow, 1979; co-author: The Naked Truth, 1993. With Can. Air Force, WWII. Office: Bresler Kelly and Assocs Ste 510 11500 W Olympic Blvd Los Angeles CA 90064-1529*

NIELSEN, LINDA MILLER, city councilwoman; b. Cedar Falls, Iowa, Apr. 13, 1948; d. Donald Hugh and Mary I. (Hansen) Miller; m. Kenneth Andrew Nielsen, Aug. 22, 1970; children: Annette Marie, Kirsten Viola. BS in Home Econs., Iowa State U., 1970, MS in Food Sci., 1972. Rsch. asst. Iowa State U., Ames, 1970-72, rsch. assoc., 1972-74, instr., 1975-76; city councilwoman City of Charleston, W.Va., 1988—; minority leader Charleston City Coun., 2003—; asst. dir. continuing edn. and cmty. svc. W.Va. State Cmty. and Tech. Coll., 1998—. Leader Girl Scouts U.S.A., 1978-96; chair environ. and recycling com. of Charleston, 1991-2003, realignment com. of Charleston, 1992-94, 2002, mcpl. planning com., 1988—, fin. com., 1995—, storm water com., 1997-99, 2003—, parks and recreation com., 1988-95; classroom vol. Kanawha County Schs., Charleston, 1978-90; mem., officer Forest Hills Comm. Assn., Charleston, 1983-87. Contbr. articles to profl. publs. Mem. NICS (bd. dirs. 1994—), Sigma Xi, Iota Sigma Pi, Omicron Nu. Republican. Avocations: hiking, camping, reading, sewing, cooking. E-mail: nielsen413@charter.net.

NIELSEN, NANCY, publishing executive; b. Jeffersonville, Ind., 1950; BA, Univ. Calif., Berkeley, 1975; MBA, Yale U., 1979. Asst. city editor, weekend mag. editor Dallas Times Herald, 1975-77; cons. McKinsey & Co. Inc.; dir. office of comm. Capital Cities/ABC Inc., N.Y.C., 1984-86; deputy dir. corp. rels. The N.Y. Times Co., N.Y.C., 1986-88, dir. corp. rels./Pa., 1987-93, v.p. corp. comm., 1992-2000; dir. bus. and media devel. Harvard U., 2000—. Bd. dirs. Berkeley Div. Sch. Yale U. Recipient Alumni Assn. award for outstanding performance in journalism Univ. Calif. Berkeley. Mem. Coun. Fgn. Rels. Office: The New York Times Co 229 W 43rd St New York NY 10036-3959

NIELSEN, NANCY H. health organization executive; m. Don Nielsen; 5 children. BA, W.Va. U., 1964; MS in Microbiology, Cath. U., 1967, PhD in Microbiology, 1969; MD, SUNY, Buffalo, 1967. Past chief med. officer N.Y. State Dept. Health Western Region; former pres. med. staff Buffalo Gen. Hosp.; asst. dean med. edn., clin. prof. medicine U. Buffalo Sch. Medicine and Biomed. Sci., Buffalo; spkr. ho. dels. Med. Soc. State of N.Y., 1995—2000; 3 term vice spkr. AMA Ho. of Dels., 2000—03, spkr., 2003—. Former pres. Erie County (N.Y.) Med. Soc.; mem. AMA Coun. on Sci. Affairs; bd. dirs. Med. Liability Mut. Ins. Co.; assoc. med. dir. for quality Ind. Health Assn. N.Y. Bd. dirs. Nat. Patient Safety Found. Recipient Samuel P. Capen award, U. Buffalo Alumni Assn., 1996. Fellow: ACP. Office: AMA 515 N State St Chicago IL 60610 Business E-Mail: nielse@buffalo.edu.

NIELSEN, NIELS CHRISTIAN, JR., theology educator; b. Long Beach, Calif., June 2, 1921; s. Niels Hansen and Frances (Nofziger) N.; m. Erika Kreuth, May 10, 1958; children— Camilla Regina, Niels Albrecht. BA, George Pepperdine Coll., L.A., 1942; BD, Yale U., 1946, PhD, 1951. Ordained to ministry Meth. Ch., 1946. Pastor Woodbury (Conn.) Meth. Ch., 1944-46; instr. religion Yale U., New Haven, 1948-51; faculty Rice U., Houston, 1951—, J. Newton Rayzor prof. religious studies., prof. emeritus, 1991—; Amax presdl. prof. humanities Colo. Sch. Mines, Golden, 1982-83. Author: Philosophy and Religion in Contemporary Japan, 1957, Geistige Landerkunde USA, 1960, A Layman Looks at World Religions, 1962, God in Education, 1966, Solzhenitsyn's Religion, 1975, The Religion of Jimmy Carter, 1977, The Crisis of Human Rights, 1978, Religions of the World, 1982, Revolutions in Eastern Europe: The Religious Roots, 1991, Fundamentalism, Mythos and World Religions, 1993; editor: Religion After Communism in Russia, 1994; contbr. articles to profl. jours. Mem. Am. Acad. Religion, Am. Philos. Soc., Am. Soc. Study Religion (sec. 1977-89), Soc. European Culture, Soc. for Values in Higher Edn. Democrat. Home: 2424 Swift Blvd Houston TX 77030-1806 E-mail: niels@ruf.rice.edu.

NIELSEN, PAUL DOUGLAS, engineering executive, retired military officer; b. New Orleans, Apr. 18, 1951; s. Jack Alton and Shirley Mae (Gillette) N.; m. Dorothy Webb Spragins, May 3, 1975; children: Eric Douglas, Kristin Echols, Steven Spragins. BS, USAF Acad., 1972; MS, U. Calif., Davis, 1973, PhD, 1981; MBA, U. N.Mex., 1977; postgrad., Nat. War Coll., 1988-89. Mil. asst., col. Office of Asst. Sec. Def., Washington, 1989-92; comdr. Rome Lab., Griffiss AFB, N.Y., 1992-95; command dir. Cheyenne Mountain Ops. Ctr., Cheyenne Mountain Air Sta, Colo., 1995-96, chief ops., 1996-97; brig. gen., dir. plans N.Am. Aerospace Def. Command, Peterson AFB, Colo., 1997-99; vice comdr. Aero. Systems Ctr., Wright-Patterson AFB, Ohio, 1999-2000; maj. gen. Air Force Rsch. Lab., Wright-Patterson AFB, 2000—04; CEO, dir. Software Engring Inst. Carnegie Mellon U., Pitts. Fellow Hertz Found., Livermore, Calif., 1972-73, 78-81. Fellow AIAA (Hap Arnold award 2002), Armed Forces Comm. and Electronics Assn., Air Force Assn.; sr. mem., IEEE. Office: Software Eng Inst Carnegie Mellon Univ 4500 Fifth Ave Pittsburgh PA 15213-3890 Home: 30 Wedgewood Ln Pittsburgh PA 15215-1560 E-mail: paul.nielsen@wpafb.af.mil.

NIELSEN, PHILIP EDWARD, physicist, research manager; b. Chgo., July 18, 1944; s. John Edward and Doris Anne (Roessler) N.; m. Mary Jane Hill, Aug. 21, 1971; children: Aaron P., June E., David C. BS in Physics, Ill. Inst. Tech., 1966; MS in Physics, Case Western Reserve U., 1968, PhD, 1970. Commd. 2d lt. USAF, 1970, advanced through ranks to col., 1988; ret., 1996; chief, interaction physics group AF Weapons Lab., Kirtland AFB, N.Mex., 1970-74; assoc. prof. physics AF Inst. Tech., Wright-Patterson AFB, Ohio, 1974-79; dep. dir. Directorate of Aerospace Studies, Kirtland AFB, 1980-84; dep. chief, missile divsn. AF Studies and Analyses, Pentagon, Washington, 1984-86, chief, force analyses divsn., 1986-87; dir. tech. Fgn. Tech. Divsn., Wright-Patterson AFB, 1988-92; chief, tech. requirements HQ AF Materiel Command, Wright-Patterson AFB, 1992-96; dir. tech. ctr. MacAulay-Brown, Inc., Dayton, Ohio, 1996—. Author: Effects of Directed Energy Weapons, 2000. Pres. Shadowbrook Homeowners Assn., Mt. Vernon, Va., 1986-87. Recipient USAF R & D award, 1975, Supr. Rsch. award Air Command and Staff Coll., Montgomery, Ala., 1980, Disting. Govt. Svc. award Albuquerque-Santa Fe Fed. Exec. Bd., 1983, Devel. Planning cert. of merit AF Systems Command, Washington, 1983. Mem. AAAS, Am. Phys. Soc., Inst. Ops. Rsch. and Mgmt. Sci., Mil. Ops. Rsch. Soc. Achievements include co-discovery (with P.L. Taylor) of an effect in the low-temperature thermoelectric power of metals and alloys now known as the "Nielsen-Taylor" or "N-T" effect; resolution of many puzzling results in the laser-induced breakdown thresholds of clean and aerosol-laden atmospheres; analysis of solid response to laser radiation which provided insights needed to extrapolate small scale experiments to large scale applications. Home: 9138 Payne Farm Ln Dayton OH 45458-9388 Office: MacAulay-Brown Inc 4021 Executive Dr Dayton OH 45430-1062

NIELSEN, STEVEN E. telecommunications company executive; Grad. magna cum laude, Williams Coll., 1985. Pres. Fiber Cable Inc., 1993; v.p., gen. mgr. Ansco & Assocs., Inc., 1993-95, pres., 1995-96; chmn., pres., CEO Dycom Industries, Inc., Palm Beach Gardens, Fla., 1996—. Office: Dycom Industries Inc First Union Ctr Ste 600 4440 PGA Blvd Palm Beach Gardens FL 33410-6542

NIELSEN, SUZANNE RUTH, literature educator, writer; b. St. Paul, July 9, 1956; d. Morten William and Gloria LaVon Nielsen; m. John Edmund Plomondon, Sept. 6, 1997; m. Ernest William Murphy, Sept. 28, 1985 (div. June 10, 1994); children: Taylor William Murphy, Evan William Murphy. Postgrad., Hamline U., 2002—. Contbr. articles to profl. jours. Mem.: Creative Writing Adv. Bd. (assoc.). Dfl. Avocations: travel, education, reading, fiction, dogs. Home: 1747 Rockstone Ln New Brighton MN 55112 Office: Metropolitan State Univ 700 East Seventh St Saint Paul MN 55106-5000 Personal E-mail: srnielsen@earthlink.net. E-mail: suzanne.nielsen@metrostate.edu.

NIELSEN-JONES, IAN RICHARD, lottery and gaming executive, business operations consultant; b. Winchester, Eng., Jan. 24, 1950; arrived in Can., 1950; came to U.S., 1995; s. Richard and Jean-Marie (Edwards) Nielsen-J.; m. Linda Ann George, June 10, 1972; children: Christopher James, Alison Leigh, Eric Philip. BA in Econs., Loyola Coll., 1971; MA in Econs., McMaster U., 1972. From investigator to dep. dir. investigation & rsch. Competition Bur., Ottawa, Ontario, Canada, 1972-89; pres. Ont. Lottery Corp., Toronto, Sault Ste. Marie, Can., 1989-93; mng. dir. nat. lottery Rank Orgn. Plc, London, 1993-94; pres. gaming and recreation Rank Canada Ltd., Toronto, 1994-95; pres., COO CUE Network Corp., Irvine, Calif., 1995-97; pres., CEO Online Internat. Corp., Smithtown, N.Y., 1997-99, Gaming Mgmt. Corp., Del., 1999-2000, Entertainment Mgmt. Group Ltd., British Virgin Islands, 2001—. Bd. dirs. Lotto4U.com, Calif., Computer Radio Network, Ltd., Granada Empresarial, S.A., Dominican Republic, Toronto, LotCo Plc, London, Gaming Mgmt. Corp., Del., 100400 P.E.I. Inc., Can., Granada Empresorial S.A., Dominican Rep. Hon. bd. dirs. Bushplane Mus., Sault Ste. Marie, Ont.; bd. dirs. Econ. Devel. Corp., Sault Ste. Marie, 1992-93, United Way, 1990-93, Plummer Hosp., 1991-93, Algoma Univ. Coll., 1991-93. Named newsmaker of yr. Gaming and Wagering Mag., 1992. Avocations: writing, music, running, coin collecting/numismatics, travel. Home: 8 Zinfandel Ct RR2 Niagara-on-the-Lake ON Canada L0S 1J0 E-mail: iannielsenjones@sympatico.ca.

NIEMANN, WILLIAM LOVEKAMP, company executive, lawyer; b. Jacksonville, Ill., July 25, 1920; s. Otto Henry and Lila Marie (Lovekamp) N.; m. Doris Elizabeth Greenstreet, Mar. 16, 1956; children— William Learned, John Justin. B.A. in History and Social Scis., Carthage Coll., 1941, LL.D. (hon.), 1976; J.D. cum laude, Northwestern U., 1947. Bar: Ill. 1947, Calif. 1952, U.S. Supreme Ct. Assoc. Snyder, Chadwell & Faberburg, 1947-50; atty. Montgomery Ward & Co., Chgo., 1950-52, regional atty., 1952-57, gen. atty., 1957-59; gen. atty. Brunswick Corp., Skokie, Ill., 1959—, v.p. law, 1983—; pres. Brunswick Found., Inc. Served to 1st lt. U.S. Army, 1942-46, capt. USNG, 1947-52. Mem. Am. Soc. Corp. Secs., Order of Coif. Lutheran. Clubs: Law; Michigan Shores (Wilmette, Ill.). Office: Brunswick Corp 1 N Field Ct Lake Forest IL 60045-4810

NIEMCZAK, BARBARA ELAINE, retired secondary school educator; b. Bristol, Tenn., Sept. 18, 1946; d. Samuel Joseph and Ethel Elizabeth Bullock; m. Walter Eugene Niemczak, June 30, 1990. BS, East Tenn. State U., 1968, EdM, 1982. Tchr. Sullivan County Sch. Sys., Blountville, Tenn., 1968—98; ret. Mem. steering com., planner Rhythm and Roots Reunion Music Festival, Bristol, 2001—; mem., cmty. adv. Believe in Bristol Coalition, 1999—; mem., planner Bristol Design Symposium, 2001—; mem. adv. bd. Literacy Acad., 2002—; trustee Bristol Pub. Libr. Bd. Trustees, 1999—. Mem.: Master Gardeners, Arts Alliance Mountain Empire (sec. 2003—), Lost State Writers' Guild (asst. to dir. 1998—). Roman Catholic. Avocations: reading, playing lap dulcimer, writing, exercise. Personal E-mail: bbn918@aol.com.

NIEMETH, CHARLES FREDERICK, lawyer; b. Lorain, Ohio, Nov. 25, 1939; s. Charles Ambrose and Christine Cameron (Mollison) N.; m. Anne Marie Meckes, Oct. 12, 1968. BA, Harvard U., 1962; JD, U. Mich., 1965. Bar: Calif. 1966, N.Y. 1984. Assoc. O'Melveny & Myers, Los Angeles, 1965-72, ptnr., 1973—. Mem. leadership com. Consol. Corp. Fund of Lincoln Ctr. Mem. nat. com. Mich. Law Sch. Fund; trustee Challengers Boys and Girls Club, 1968-83; mem. bus. adv. coun. UCLA, 1979-83; mem. exec. com. Internat. Student Ctr., 1979-83; bd. dirs. Olympic Tower Condominium, 1986-92; bd. visitors Mich. Law Sch., mem. Tri-Bar Opinion Com. Mem. Riviera Tennis Club, Regency Club, N.Y. Athletic Club, Field Club (Greenwich, Conn.), Bel-Air Bay Club. Democrat. Roman Catholic. Home: 70 Oneida Dr Greenwich CT 06830-7131 Office: O'Melveny & Myers 1999 Avenue Of The Stars Los Angeles CA 90067-6035 also: 7 Times Square New York NY 10036 E-mail: cniemeth@omm.com.

NIEMEYER, ANTONIO BILISOLY, JR., school system administrator; b. Norfolk, Va., Apr. 13, 1928; s. Antonio Bilisoly Niemeyer and Lutie Stuart Spotts; m. Alice Virginia Berry, Nov. 20, 1965; children: William Frederic, Frank Berry, John Stuart. BS, Va. Mil. Inst., 1949; MEd, U. Va., 1955; cert. advanced study, Old Dominion U., 1973. Asst. prin. Portsmouth (Va.) Schs., 1966-67, supr. sci., 1967-77, prin. Churchland Jr., 1977-78, prin. Manor H.S., 1978-80, 86-88, dir. secondary edn., 1980-86, dir. personnel, 1988-91. Dir. Va. Jr. Acad. Sci., 1979-81. Cons. Science Far and Near, Tchrs. edit., 1973. Pres. Tidewater Heart Assn., 1968. Recipient Disting. Svc. award Jr. C. of C., 1957; named Sci. Educator of Yr., Tidewater Sci. Congress, 1975; fellow Va. Acad. Sci. Mem. SAR. Episcopalian. Avocation: historical studies. Home: 4324 Greendell Rd Chesapeake VA 23321-5504 E-mail: niemeyer@gateway.net.

NIEMEYER, ERIN JANICE, pharmaceutical sales consultant, journalist, editor; b. Torrance, Calif., July 5, 1974; d. Robert Frederick and Patricia Ann Niemeyer. BA magna cum laude, U. Nev., Las Vegas, 1998. Freelance writer-editor, Las Vegas, 1997—; substitute tchr. Clark County Sch. Dist., Las Vegas, 1998—; individual ins. sales rep. UNUMProvident, Las Vegas, 1998—. Vol. Juvenile Diabetes Found., Las Vegas, 1992-95, Big Bros. and Big Sisters, Las Vegas, 1996-97. Mem. Soc. Profl. Journalists, Phi Kappa Phi, Phi Alpha Delta, Alpha Gamma Delta. Republican. Christian. Avocations: writing, reading nonfiction, exercising, teaching, motivational speaking. Home and Office: 944 Osterville St Unit B Hendersonville NV 89052 E-mail: erin.j.niemeyer@pharmacia.com.

NIEMEYER, PAUL VICTOR, federal judge; b. Princeton, N.J., Apr. 5, 1941; s. Gerhart and Lucie (Lenzer) Niemeyer; m. Susan Kinley, Aug. 24, 1963; children: Jonathan K., Peter E., Christopher J. AB, Kenyon Coll., 1962; student, U. Munich, Federal Republic of Germany, 1962—63; JD, U. Notre Dame, 1966. Bar: Md. 1966, U.S. Dist. Ct. Md. 1967, U.S. Ct. Appeals (4th cir.) 1968, U.S. Supreme Ct. 1970, U.S. Dist. Ct. (so. dist.) Tex. 1977, U.S. Ct. Appeals (5th cir.) 1978, U.S. Ct. Appeals (3d cir.) 1980. Assoc. Piper & Marbury, Balt., 1966—74, ptnr., 1974—88; U.S. dist. judge U.S. Dist. Ct. Md., Balt., 1988—90; circuit judge U.S. Ct. Appeals (4th cir.), Balt., 1990—. Lectr. advanced bus. law Johns Hopkins U., Balt., 1971—75; lectr. Md. Jud. Conf., Md. Ct. Clks. Assn.; sr. lecturing fellow in appellate advocacy Duke U. Sch. of Law, 1994—; mem. standing com. on rules of practice and procedure cts. appeals, 1973—88; atty. grievance com.-hearing panel, 1978—81; select com.-profl. conduct, 1983—85; adv. com. on Fed. Rules of Civil Procedure, 1993—2000; chmn., 1996—2000. Co-author: Maryland Rules Commentary, 1984, Maryland Rules Commentary supplement, 1988, Maryland Rules Commentary, 3d. edit., 2003; contbr. articles to profl. jours. Recipient Spl. Merit citation, Am. Judicature Soc., 1987. Fellow: Am. Law Inst., Md. Bar Assn. (Disting. Svc. award litigation sect. 1981), Md. Bar Found., Am. Bar Found., Am. Coll. Trial Lawyers; mem.: Lawyers' Round Table, Wednesday Law Club. Republican. Episcopalian. Office: US Cir Ct Md US Courthouse 101 W Lombard St Ste 910 Baltimore MD 21201-2611

NIEMI, JANICE, retired lawyer, retired state legislator; b. Flint, Mich., Sept. 18, 1928; d. Richard Jesse and Norma (Bell) Bailey; m. Preston Niemi, Feb. 4, 1953 (div. 1987); children: Ries, Patricia. BA, U. Wash., 1950, LLB, 1967; postgrad., U. Mich., 1950-52; cert., Hague Acad. Internat. Law, The Netherlands, 1954. Bar: Wash. 1968. Assoc. firm Powell, Livengood, Dunlap & Silverdale, Kirkland, Wash., 1968; staff atty. Legal Svc. Ctr., Seattle, 1968-70; judge Seattle Dist. Ct., 1971-72, King County Superior Ct., Seattle, 1973-78; acting gen. counsel, dep. gen. counsel SBA, Washington, 1979-81; mem. Wash. State Ho. of Reps., Olympia, 1983-87, chmn. com. on state govt., 1984; mem. Wash. State Senate, 1987-95; sole practice Seattle, 1981-94; superior ct. judge King County, 1995-2000; chief criminal judge, 1997-2000; ret., 2000; mem. Wash. State Gambling Commn., 2002—. Mem. White Ho. Fellows Regional Selection Panel, Seattle, 1974—77, chmn., 1976, 77; incorporator Soudn Savs. & Loan, Seattle, 1975; bd. dirs. Artists Trust; mem. panel Am. Arbitration Assn., 2003—. Bd. visitors dept. psychology U. Wash., Seattle, 1983—87, bd. visitors dept. sociology, 1988—98; mem. adv. bd. Tacoma Art Mus., 1987—; mem. Wash. State Gender and Justice Commn., 1987—89; Bd. dirs. Allied Arts, Seattle, 1971—78, Ctr. Contemporary Art, Seattle, 1981—83, Women's Network, Seattle, 1981—84, Pub. Defender Assn., Seattle, 1982—84, Artist's Trust, 2002—. Named Woman of Yr. in Law, Past Pres.'s Assn., Seattle, 1971, Woman of Yr., Matrix Table, Seattle, 1973, Capitol Hill Bus. and Profl. Women, 1975. Mem. Wash. State Bar Assn., Wash. Women Lawyers, Am. Arbitration Assn. (panel 2003—). Democrat. Home: PO Box 20516 Seattle WA 98102-1516 E-mail: janicen@aol.com.

NIEMIEC, DAVID WALLACE, investment management executive; b. Midland, Mich., Dec. 17, 1949; s. George G. and Eleanor (Yack) N.; m. Melanie Taveau Mason, Oct. 4, 1975; children: Elizabeth Street, Margaret Johnson AB, Harvard U., 1972, MBA, 1974. Assoc. Dillon, Read & Co., Inc., N.Y.C., 1974-78, v.p., 1979-81, sr. v.p., chief adminstrv. officer, 1982-83, mng. dir., chief adminstrv. officer, 1984-97, vice chmn., 1991-97; mng. dir. Saratoga Ptnrs., N.Y.C., 1998—2001, adv., 2001—. Bd. dirs. Emeritus Corp., Seattle. Trustee Nightingale-Bamford Sch., N.Y.C., 1993-2004; bd. govs. The Mannes Coll. of Music, N.Y.C., 1996-. Mem. Union Club N.Y.C. Republican. Unitarian Universalist. Office: Saratoga Ptnrs 535 Madison Ave New York NY 10022-4212

NIEMIEC, EDWARD WALTER, retired professional association executive; b. Detroit, Nov. 1, 1936; s. Walter A. and Mary N.; m. Nancy M. Bennett, Aug. 25, 1962; children: Lisa, Julie, Brenda. BS, U. Detroit, 1959, MBA, 1961. With Paine Webber Jackson & Curtis, N.Y.C., 1959-80, exec. v.p., dir. adminstrv. divsn., to 1980; v.p., bd. dirs. Moseley, Hallgarten, Estabrook, Weeden, Inc., 1980-82; also bd. dirs. Moseley, Hallgarten, Estabrook & Weeden Holding Corp.; pres., CEO, dir., mem. exec. com. Securities Settlement Corp. (subs. The Travelers 1982), N.Y.C., 1980-87; pres., dir. Inc. Trading Co. subs. Instinet Corp., 1988-89; COO Instinet Corp. subs. Reuters Holdings Plc., 1988-89; group v.p. AICPA, N.Y.C., 1989—2001. Served with U.S. Army. Roman Catholic.

NIENHUIS, ARTHUR WESLEY, physician, researcher; b. Hudsonville, Mich., Aug. 9, 1941; s. Willard M. and Grace (Prince) Nienhuis; children: Carol Elizabeth, cragi Wesley, Kevin Robert, Heather Grae, Carol Elizabeth, Craig Wesley, Kevin Robert, Heather Grace. Student, Cornell Coll., 1959-61; MD, UCLA, 1963-68. Am. Bd. Internal Medicine, Am. Bd. Hematology. Intern Mass. Gen. Hosp., Boston, 1968-69, asst. resident, 1969-70; clin. assoc. NHLBI, NIH, Bethesda, Md., 1970-72; clin. fellow hematology Children's Hosp., Boston, 1972-73; chief. clin. svc. Molecular Hematology NIH, Bethesda, Md., 1973-77; dept. clin. dir. NHLBI, NIH, Bethesda, Md., 1976-93,

chief clin. Hematology Branch, 1976-93; dir. St. Jude Children's Rsch. Hosp., Memphis, 1993—. Editor BLOOD-J Am. Soc. Hematology, Bethesda, Md., 1988-92; chmn. Hematology Bd. Am. Bd. Internal Med., Phila., 1988-92. Editor: Molecular Basis of Blood Diseases, 1986, 93. Mem. Am. Soc. Hematology (pres. 1994), Am. Soc. Clin. Investigation, Assn. Am. Physicians, Nat. Cancer Adv. Bd. Office: St Jude Children's Rsch Hosp 332 N Lauderdale St Memphis TN 38105-2729 E-mail: Arthur.Nienhuis@stjude.org.

NIENKE, STEVEN A. construction company executive; b. 1950; Carpenter Halsey Tevis, Wichita, Kans., 1970-72; pres. Midwest Drywall Co. Inc., Wichita, Kans., 1972—. Office: Midwest Drywall Co Inc PO Box 771170 1351 S Reca Ct Wichita KS 67277-1170 Office Phone: 316-722-9559. Office Fax: 316-722-9682. Business E-Mail: dennis@mwdw.com.*

NIENSTEDT, JOHN CLAYTON, priest, educator; b. Detroit, Mar. 18, 1947; s. John and Elizabeth S. (Kennedy) N. BA, Sacred Heart Sem., 1969; BST, Pontifical Gregorian U., 1972; Licentiate in Sacred Theology, Pontifical Inst. of St. Alphonsus, 1977, DST, 1985. Ordained deacon North Am. Coll., Rome, 1972, priest Sacred Heart Ch., Dearborn, Mich., 1974. Deacon intern Sacred Heart Parish, Dearborn, Mich., 1973-74; assoc. pastor Guardian Angels Ch., Clawson, Mich., 1974-76; priest/sec. Cardinal John Dearden, Archbishop, Detroit, 1977-80; apptd. minor official of 2nd grade Vatican Secretariate of State, 1980-85; temporary assoc. pastor St. Regis Parish, Birmingham, Mich., 1986; pastor St. Patrick's Parish, Union Lake, Mich., 1986-87; former rector Sacred Heart Major Sem., Detroit, former asst. prof. moral theology; auxiliary bishop Archdiocese of Detroit, 1996—. Part-time prof. Moral Theology St. John's Sem., Plymouth, Mich., 1977-78; weekend assoc. pastor St. Fabian's Parish, Farmington HIlls, Mich., 1977, Our Lady of Sorrow's Parish, Farmington, 1978-80; mem. med. moral com. Mich. Conf. for Cath. Health Facilities, 1977-80; served as Vicar Gen. of Archdiocese of Detroit, 1979-80; asst. chaplain Baby Jesus Hosp., Rome, Italy 1980-83; chaplain Bros. of Holy Cross assigned to Notre Dame High Sch. for Boys, Rome, 1981-84; instr. religion First Eucharist Program Marymont Internat. Sch., 1980-83; temp. assoc. pastor St. Regis Parish, Birminham, 1986; adj. prof. moral theology Orchard Lake Schs., 1986; bd. trustees Madonna Coll., 1989—, trustee com. acad. affairs, 1989—; mem. Midwest/Western Rector's Conf., 1987—, Wranglers, 1986-90, Archdiocesan Med. Moral Com., 1987—; presenter in field. Apptd. a Chaplain to His Holiness by Pope John Paul II bearing title Monsignor, 1985, a Prelate of Honor by Pope John Paul II, 1990. Mem. Cath. Theol. Soc. Am., Assn. Gov. Bds. of U. and Colls. (workshop theol. sch. trustees, chief execs. Cin. chpt. 1989), Midwest Assn. Theol. Schs. (ann. participation 1988, 89, 90), Assn. Am. Colls. (ann. participation 1990). Office: Diocese of New Ulm Catholic Pastoral Ctr 1400 6th St N New Ulm MN 56073

NIEPORENT, DREW, restaurant group executive; Owner Montrachet, N.Y.C., 1985—; co-owner Tribeca Grill, N.Y.C., 1990—; pres., owner Myriad Restaurant Group, N.Y.C., 1993—. Guest lectr. Cornell U., NYU, N.Y.C., Syracuse (N.Y.) U., New Eng. Culinary Inst., N.Y.Restaurant Assn., New Sch., N.Y.C. Hon. co-chairperson, master ceremonies Starfish Found., 1995; co-chair Share Our Strength's Taste Nation, N.Y.C., 1997—99; guest honor Tourette Syndrome Assn. Dinner, 1997; culinary chair Momentum Project. Named Man of the Yr., Food Beverage Assn., 1993, Humanitarian of the Yr., James Beard Found., 2000, Restaurateur of the Yr., Bon Appetit Mag., 2000; recipient Gates Jerusalem medal, Israel Bonds, 1994, Outstanding Svc. award, James Beard Awards, 1995. Mem.: Am. Inst. Wine and Food (bd. dirs.). Office: Myriad Restaurant Group 375 Greenwich St New York NY 10013

NIERENBERG, NORMAN, urban land economist, retired state official; b. Chgo., May 8, 1919; s. Isadore Isaac and Sadie Sarah (Dorfman) N.; m. Nanette Joyce Fortgang, Feb. 9, 1950; children: Andrew Paul, Claudia Robin. AA, U. Chgo., 1939; AB, Calif. State Coll., L.A., 1952; MA, U. So. Calif., 1956. Lic. real estate broker, Calif.; cert. supr. and coll. instr., Calif. Right-of-way agt. Calif. Dept. Transp., L.A., 1951-61, 85-90, sr. agt. San Francisco, 1988-89; instr. UCLA, 1960-61, 67-75, 81-85; coord. continuing edn. in real estate U. Calif., Berkeley, 1961-64. Coord. econ. benefits study Salton Sea, Calif. Dept. Water Resources, L.A., 1968-69; regional economist L.A. dist. CE, 1970-75, chief economist, 1981-85; regional economist Bd. Engrs. for Rivers and Harbors, Ft. Belvoir, Va., 1975-81; faculty resource person Oakland Project, Ford Found., U. Calif., Berkeley, 1962-64; project reviewer EPA, Washington, 1972-73. Editor: History of 82d Fighter Control Squadron, 1945; assoc. editor Right of Way Nat. Mag., 1952-55. Capt. USAAF, 1942-46, ETO, Lt. Col. USAFR ret. Mem.: NEA, L.A. Coll. Tchrs. Assn., Calif. Tchrs. Assn., Mil. Officers Assn. Am., Omicron Delta Epsilon. Democrat. Jewish. *Personal philosophy: Strive for excellence. Honorable in all endeavors.*

NIERMAN, WILLIAM C. research scientist; BS, U.S. Naval Acad., 1968; MS, Naval Postgrad. Sch., 1969; PhD, U. Calif., Berkeley, 1979. Investigator Inst. for Genomic Rsch., Rockville, Md., 1998—; grad. fellow U. Calif., Berkeley, 1975—79; NIH postdoctoral fellow U. Calif. Med. Ctr., San Francisco, 1979—80; assoc. staff scientist bacteriology dept. Am. Type Culture Collection, Rockville, Md., 1980—87, collection scientist molecular biology program, 1987—98, program dir. molecular biology program, 1995—98; investigator Inst. for Genomic Rsch., Rockville, 1998—. Contract faculty human genetics course Johns Hopkins U., 1993—; prof. biochemistry and molecular biology George Washington U., Washington, 2000—. Contbr. articles to profl. jours. Grad. fellow, NSF, 1975—78, postdoctoral fellow, NIH, 1979—80. Achievements include research in genomic analysis of microbial pathogens. Office: Inst for Genomic Rsch 9712 Medical Center Dr Rockville MD 20850

NIESEN, JAMES LOUIS, theater director; b. St. Louis, Feb. 15, 1946; s. James Louis and Emily Elise (Brennecke) N. BFA, Ill. Wesleyan U., 1968; MFA, Ohio U., 1974. Actor Stage South, Columbia, S.C., 1974-75, Long Wharf Theatre, New Haven, 1977-78, Geva Theater, Rochester, N.Y., 1978-79; freelance dir., 1980-83; stage mgr. Roundabout Theater, N.Y., 1982-83; artistic dir. Irondale Ensemble Project, N.Y., 1983—. Panelist N.Y. Found. on the Arts, N.Y., 1988-89. Author: (book) Game Guide, 1988; contbr. articles to profl. jours.; dir. (play) St. Joan of the Stockyards, 1993, Danton's Death, 1994, You Can't Win, 1994, Andrew Carnegie Presands the Jew of Malta, 1996, The Mother, 1997, Degenerate Art, 1998, The Murals of Rockefeller Center, 2002, The Pope and the Witch, 2000, Brecht on Brecht, 2000, Jungle of Cities, 2001, Peter Pan, 2001, Seuss Centennial Tour, 2004, Outside the Law, 2004. Mem. Actors Equity Assn. Avocations: folk music, country music, tennis. Home: 419 Pacific St Brooklyn NY 11217-2204 Office: Irondale Ensemble Project PO Box 150604 Brooklyn NY 11215-0604 Office Phone: 718-488-9233.

NIETO, JUAN MANUEL, emergency medicine physician; b. Alpine, Tex., Sept. 24, 1949; s. Edmundo Miguel and Socorro (Herrera) N.; children: Ana Raquel, Cristina Marie. BS, U. Notre Dame, 1970; MD, U. Colo., 1974. Intern L.A. County, U. So. Calif. Med. Ctr., 1974-75; physician Cmty. Health Found., L.A., 1975-77; physician emergency dept. Physicians Med. Group, Marina Del Ray, Calif., 1977-78; resident in emergency medicine Denver Gen.-St. Anthony Hosp. Sys., 1978-80; mem. staff North Colo. Med. Ctr., Greeley, 1980-83; emergency physician, med. dir. emergency dept. Brackenridge Hosp., Austin, Tex., 1984-85; practice medicine Austin, 1983—. Emergency physician Emergency Physicians Affiliates, 1986-89; assoc. prof. U. Tex. Health Sci. Ctr., San Antonio, 1994—; mem. planning com. Starflight Helicopter Air Transport, 1985; instr. advanced cardiac life support, 1977; bd. dirs. Nat. Chicano Health Orgn., 1971-74; advisor East Los Angeles Hypertension Screening Program, 1978; med. advisor Weld County Ambulance Service, 1980-83; med. dir. Air Life, 1980-83; med. dir. Alamo Heights Emergency Med. Svc., 1988-90, med. dir. AMR Ambulance, 1991-98; amb. Nat. Health Svc. Corps, 2003—. Del. Colo. Med. Soc., 1983. Fellow: Nat. Hispanic Med. Assn., Am. Acad. Emergency Medicine, Am. Coll. Emergency Physicians, NYU Wagner Sch. (leadership fellow 2001); mem.: APHA, Physicians for a Nat. Healthcare Program, Nat. Hispanic Med. Assn., Travis County Med. Soc., Tex. Med. Assn., Nat. Hispanic Med. Assn. (leadership fellow, advisor, board mem. 2001—, mem. adv. bd. 2003—), Nat. Health Svc. Corps., Nat. Health Svc.Corps (ambassador 2003—, 2003—), Amnesty Internat. Office Phone: 210-358-2078. E-mail: juan.nieto@austin.rr.com.

NIETO, MICHAEL MARTIN, theoretical physicist; b. L.A., Mar. 15, 1940; s. Jose Guadeulupe and Delfina Dolores Nieto; m. Merete Henriksen Henriksen, June 1, 1973; children: Mikkel David, Katrina Maria. BA with highest honors, U. Calif., Riverside, 1961; PhD, Cornell U., 1966. Rsch. assoc. Inst. for Theoretical Physics, SUNY, Stony Book, 1966—68; vis. physicist The Niels Bohr Inst., U. Copenhagen, 1968—70; lectr./asst. prof. dept. physics U. Calif., Santa Barbara, 1970—71; vis. physicist Rsch. Inst. Fundamental Physics, Kyoto (Japan) U., 1971—71; sr. rsch. assoc. dept. physics Purdue U., West Lafayette, Ind., 1971—72; sci. staff mem. theoretical divsn. Los Alamos (N.Mex.) Nat. Lab., 1972—2003, lab. fellow, 2003—. Contbr. articles to profl. jours. Recipient Sr. Rsch. Award, Alexander von Humboldt Found., 1994—2000; fellow, Woodrow Wilson Found., 1961, NSF, 1961—66; Vis. Erskine fellow, U. Canterbury, Christchurch, New Zealand, 1989. Fellow: Am. Phys. Soc.; mem.: Phi Beta Kappa. Office: Los Alamos Nat Lab Theoretical Divsn (MS-B285) Los Alamos NM 87545

NIEUWSMA, MILTON JOHN, writer, journalist; b. Sept. 5, 1941; s. John and Jean (Potter); m. Marilee Gordon, Feb. 1, 1964; children: Jonathan, Gregory, Elizabeth. BA, Hope Coll., Holland, Mich., 1963; postgrad., Wayne State U., 1963—65; MA, U. Ill., 1978. Pres. Trans. Am. Syndicate, Inc., Chgo., 1988—97; vis. prof. Rutgers U., New Brunswick, NJ, 1990—95, St. Xavier U., Chgo., 1996—97. Author: Kinderlanger, 1998; writer, cons.: Children of The Shoah, PBS, 2004; contbg. editor: Chgo. Tribune, L.A. Times, others. Home: 2421 Central-Idlewood Beach Holland MI 49424-2277 Personal E-mail: mnieuwsma@macatawa.com.

NIEWIAROSKI, TRUDI OSMERS (GERTRUDE NIEWIAROSKI), social studies educator; b. Jersey City, Apr. 30, 1935; d. Albert John and Margaret (Niemeyer) Osmers; m. Donald H. Niewiaroski, June 8, 1957; children: Donald H., Donna, Margaret Anne, Nancy Noel. AB in History and German, Upsala Coll., East Orange, N.J., 1957; MEd, Montgomery County Pub. Schs., Rockville, Md., 1992. Cert. tchr., Md. Tchr. geography Colego Americano, Quito, Ecuador, 1964-66; bd. dirs. Cotopaxi Acad., Quito, 1964-65; tchr. speed reading Escuela Lincoln, Buenos Aires, Argentina, 1966-67; substitute thcr. Montgomery County Pub. Schs., Rockville, 1978-83, tchr. social studies, 1984—. Del. Eisenhower People to People Educators' Del. Vietnam, 1993; pres. Fulbright Meml. Fund Program, 1997; resident tchg. fellow Russia-Ukraine Excellence in Tchg. Program, 1997; resident scholar in Korea, The Korea Soc., 1999. Author curricula; contbr. chpts. to books, articles to profl. jours.; lectr. at workshops. Bd. dirs. Cotopaxi Acad., Quito, 1964-65; pres. Citizens Assn., Potomac, Md., 1977-81; leader Girl Scouts U.S., 1975-76; adv. coun. Milken Found; pres. Fulbright Meml. Fund Program Japan Alumni, 1999—. Recipient Md. Tchr. of Yr. award State of Md. Edn. Dept., 1993, finalist nat. Tchr. of Yr., 1993, Disting. Alumni award Upsala Coll., 1993, Nat. Educator award Milken Found., 1994, Summer Fellowship Korean Studies Program, 1999, Joseph Malone fellowship Sultanate of Oman, 2003, Goethe Inst. fellowship, Germany, 2003; Fulbright fellow, India, 1985, China, 1990, Japan Keizai Koho Ctr. fellow, 1992, Fulbright Meml. Fund Tchr. Program fellow, Japan, 1997, Fulbright fellow, South Africa, 2001, Malone fellow, Oman, 2003; UMBC-U. Mex. Art and Culture scholar, 1995; mem. Cuba Study Tour, 2004, Dar Al Islam Study Tour, Iran, 2004; fellow U. Pitts. and Freeman Found., China, 2004. Mem. AAUW, ASCD, Nat. Coun. Social Studies, Md. Coun. for Social Studies, Asia Soc., Smithsonian Instn., Montgomery County Hist. Soc., Spl. Interest Groups-China, Japan and Korea, Md. Bus. Roundtable for Edn., Nat. Social Studies Suprs. Assn., Kappa Delta Pi. Avocations: cake and cookie decorating, travel. Office: R Montgomery High Sch Rockville MD 20852 E-mail: trudi_niewiaroski@fc.mcps.k12.md.us.

NIGHTENGALE, ROCHELLE M. rehabilitation services professional; d. Richard W. and Mary N. Nightengale. MS, Med. Coll. of Va., Richmond, 2002; BS, Norfolk State U., 1984. Cert. rehab. counselor Commn. on Rehab. Counselor Cert., 2003. Asst. systems ops. analyst City of Richmond, Va., 1999—; supported employment supr. Rehabilitative Services, Richmond, Va., 2003; in-home therapist Wilkerson, Inc., Richmond, Va., 2004—. Vol. Salvation Army Christmas Distbn. Ctr., Richmond, Va., 1993—2003; publicity chairperson Ebenezer Bapt. Ch., Charlottesville, 1991—2004. Scholar A. D. Williams award, Med. Coll. of Va. at Va. Commonwealth U., 1999 -2002. Mem.: Richmond Tri-Cities Human Rights Com. (assoc.), Am. Mental Health Counselors Assn. (assoc.), Norfolk State U. Richmond Alumni Chpt. (assoc.; membership chairperson 2001—04), Chi Sigma Iota (assoc.). Personal E-mail: rmnight@vcu.org.

NIGHTINGALE, DEBORAH SEIFERT, systems engineer, consultant; b. Dayton, Ohio, Sept. 10, 1949; m. Tom Seifert, 1971; children: Jessica, Danielle, Jordan. BS, U. Dayton, 1970; MS, Ohio State U., 1975, PhD, 1979. Programmer U. Dayton Rsch. Inst., 1968-71; sr. engring. scientist Wright Patterson AFB, 1971-79; project leader Allied Signal Engines, 1979-80; mgr. facility planning, factory modernization, Corp CIM Com., 1980-84, mfg. sys. engr., indsl. engr., ops. support, chmn., 1984-87, sr. project mgr. mktg. svc., dir. strategic planning, 1987-96; cons. Paradise Valley, Ariz., 1996—; prof., focus lead, Lean Enterprise Team & Lean Aerospace Initiative Dept. of Aerospace & Aeronautics, MIT, Cambridge, Mass., 1997—. Contbr. articles to profl. jour. Mem. NAE (4th decade com. 1993—), Inst. Indsl. Engr. (pres. elect 1994—), Soc. Mfg. Engr., Computer and Automated Sys. Assn. Home: 43 Canterbury St Andover MA 01810-2850 Office: Dept Aerospace & Aeronautics MIT Rm 33-312 77 Mass Ave Cambridge MA 02139

NIGHTINGALE, EDMUND JOSEPH, clinical psychologist, educator; b. St. Paul, Jan. 10, 1941; s. Edmund Anthony and Lauretta Alexandria (Horejs) N.; m. Marie Arcara, Apr. 9, 1978 (dec. April 1992); 1 child, Edmund Bernard. Student, Nazarath Hall Prep. Sem., 1959—61; AB, St. Paul Sem., 1963; AB magna cum laude, Cath. U. Louvain, Belgium, 1965, MA, STB cum laude, Cath. U. Louvain, Belgium, 1967; postgrad., U. Minn., 1971; MA, Loyola U., Chgo., 1973, PhD in Clin. Psychology, 1975. Lic. clin. psychologist, Ill., Minn., cert. Nat. Registry of Health Svc. Providers in Psychology; diplomate in clin. psychology Am. Bd. Profl. Psychology. With Cath. Archdiocese of St. Paul and Mpls., 1967-73; int. in clin. psychology Michael Reese Hosp. and Med. Ctr., Chgo., 1973-74; with West Side VA Hosp., Chgo., 1974-75; staff psychologist Student Counseling Ctr., Loyola U., Chgo., 1975; staff psychologist, clin. coord. inpatient unit Drug Dependency Treatment Ctr., 1975—80; chief psychology VA Med. Ctr., Danville, Ill., 1980-86, VA Med. Ctr. Mpls., 1986—. Mem. pers. bd. Archdiocese of St. Paul and Mpls., 1968-70; lectr. psychology, Loyola U., Chgo., 1975; asst. professorial lectr. psychology, St. Paul Xavier Coll., Chgo., 1975-78; adj. asst. prof. psychology in psychology, Abraham Lincoln Sch. Med., Med. Ctr. U. Ill., Chgo., 1977-82; adj. prof. psychology Purdue U., 1981-87; asst. prof. psychology Med. Sch., U. Minn., 1987—, clin. assoc. prof. psychology Coll. Liberal Arts, 1986-90; adj. asst. prof., 1990—; clin. asst. prof. U. Ill. Sch. Med., Urbana/Champaign, 1982-87; mem. grad. faculty in counseling psychology Ind. State U., Terre Haute, 1983-86. Founding editor: Louvain Studies, 1966; editor: VA Dir. of Psychology Staffing and Svcs., 1982, 83, 84, 85, 87. Bd. dirs. Inst. Postgrad. Studies, Ill. Psychol. Assn. Fellow APA (clin. psychology, pub. svc., psychol. hypnosis, sec. treas. pub. svc. 1990-91, coun. reps. 1999-2004); mem. AAAS, Am. Psychol. Soc., Assn. for Advancement of Psychology, Ill. Psychol. Assn. (clin. psychology and acad. sects., sec. 1982-83, pres.-elect 1983-84, pres. 1984-85), Am. Group Psychotherapy Assn., Am. Soc. Clin. Hypnosis, Minn. Psychol. Assn. (pub. svc.- pres. 1997-99), Eagle Scout Assn., Assn. VA Chief Psychologists (sec., treas. 1987-90, pres.-elect 1990-91, pres. 1991-92, past pres. 1992-93, Outstanding Leadership award 1992), Minn. Soc. Clin. Hypnosis (bd. dirs. 1999-2001). Home: 2281 Ocala Ct Mendota Heights MN 55120-1646 Office: VA Med Ctr Minneapolis MN 55417

NIGHTINGALE, ELENA OTTOLENGHI, geneticist, pediatrician, academic administrator, educator; b. Livorno, Italy, Nov. 1, 1932; arrived in U.S., 1939, naturalized; d. Mario Lazzaro and Elisa Vittoria (Levi) Ottolenghi; m. Suart L. Nightingale, July 1, 1965; children: Elizabeth, Marisa. AB summa cum laude, Barnard Coll., 1954; PhD, Rockefeller U., 1961; MD, NYU, 1964. Asst. prof. Cornell U. Med. Coll., N.Y.C., 1965-70, Johns Hopkins U., Balt., 1970-73; fellow in clin. genetics and pediat. Georgetown U. Hosp., Washington, 1973-74; sr. staff officer NAS, Washington, 1975-79, sr. program officer Inst. Medicine, 1979-82, sr. scholar-in-residence, 1982-83; spl. advisor to pres. Carnegie Corp. N.Y., N.Y.C., 1983-94, sr. program officer, 1989-94; scholar-in-residence NAS, Washington, 1995—. Vis. assoc. prof. Harvard Med. Sch., Boston, 1980—84, vis. lectr., 1984—95; adj. prof. pediat. Georgetown U. Med. Ctr., 1984—, George Washington U. Med. Ctr., 1994—; mem. recombinant DNA adv. com. NIH, Bethesda, Md., 1979—83. Editor: The Breaking of Bodies and Minds: Torture, Psychiatric Abuses and the Health Professions, 1985, Prenatal Screening, Policies and Values: The Example of Neural Tube Defects, 1987, Promoting the Health of Adolescents: New Directions for the 21st Century, 1993, Adolescent Risk and Vulnerability: Concepts and Measurement, 2001; co-author: Before Birth: Prenatal Screening for Genetic Disease, 1990; contbr. numerous sci. articles to profl. publs. Bd. dirs. Amnesty Internat., U.S.A., Washington, 1989—91, Ctr. for Youth Svcs., Washington, 1980—84, Sci. Svc., Inc., Washington, 1985—96. Fellow: AAAS (chmn. com. on sci. freedom and responsibility 1985—88), Royal Soc. Medicine, N.Y. Acad. Scis.; mem.: Inst. Medicine of NAS (chmn. com. on health and human rights 1987—90), Genetics Soc. Am., Am. Soc. Human Genetics (social issues com. 1982—85), Am. Soc. Microbiology, Sigma Xi, Phi Beta Kappa. Office: NAS 2101 Constitution Ave NW Washington DC 20418-0007 Office Phone: 202-334-3882.

NIGHTINGALE, STUART LESTER, physician, public health officer; b. N.Y.C., Jan. 26, 1938; s. Lester M. Nightingale and Beatrice L. N. (Liebowitz) Helpern; m. Elena Ottolenghi, July 1, 1965; children: Elizabeth S., Marisa O. BA, Yale U., 1959; MD, NYU, 1964. Diplomate Am. Bd. Internal Medicine. Intern in medicine and surgery Montefiore Hosp. and Med. Ctr., Bronx, N.Y., 1964-65, resident in internal medicine, fellow in adolescent medicine, 1965-66, 67-69, asst. attending physician, 1969-70; resident in anatomical pathology NYU Sch. Medicine, 1966-67; med. dir. drug abuse adminstrn. Dept. Health and Mental Hygiene State of Md., Balt., 1971-72; chief treatment and rehab., office of programs, spl. action office for drug abuse prevention Exec. Office of Pres., Washington, 1972-74, chief office treatment and rehab., spl. action office for drug abuse prevention, 1974-75; dir. divsn. resource devel. Nat. Inst. on Drug Abuse, Rockville, Md., 1974-76; asst. to dir. Bur. Drugs, Food and Drug Adminstrn., Rockville, 1976-79; dep. assoc. commr. for health affairs FDA, Rockville, 1979-82, acting assoc. commr. for health affairs, 1979-82, assoc. commr. for health affairs, 1982-2000; sr. med. adv. to dir. global health affairs and chief med. officer Office of the Asst. Sec. for Planning and Evaluation Dept. of Health and Human Svcs., Washington, 2000—. Vis. physician Balt. City Hosps., 1970-72; clin. instr. dept. medicine Coll. Medicine SUNY, Bklyn., 1970; asst. physician out-patient dept., instr. dept. medicine Johns Hopkins U. Sch. Medicine, Balt., 1970-72, med. dir. drug abuse ctr., 1970-71, instr. dept. med. care and hosps. Sch. Hygiene and Pub. Health, 1971-74, rsch. program mgr. health svcs. rsch. and devel. ctr., 1970-71; chmn. rsch. involving human subjects com. FDA, 1979-84; liaison mem. Commn. on Fed. Drug Approval Process, U.S. Congress, 1980-81; mem.-at-large U.S. Pharmacopeial Conv., Inc., 1985-95; bd. trustees The Milton Helpern Libr. of Legal Medicine, N.Y.C., 1982-2000; bd. dirs. Nat. Coun. on Patient Info. and Edn., Washington; mem. forum on drug devel. and regulation Inst. Medicine, NAS, Washington, 1986-2000. Contbg. author Jour. AMA, 1985-99, Am. Family Physician, 1986-99. Capt. med. corps USAR, 1966-72; with USPHS. Recipient Disting. Svc. Spl. Action Office for Drug Abuse Prevention award Exec. Office of Pres., 1975, Pub. Health Superior Svc. award, 1983, Disting. Contbn. award Nat. Coun. Patient Info. and Edn., 1987, Achievement award Am. Assn. Physicians for Human Rights, 1990, Presdl. Meritorious Exec. Rank award, 1990, Pub. Health Svc. Spl. Recognition award, 1993, Sec.'s Recognition award Dept. HHS, 1999. Fellow ACP; mem. AMA, Sr. Execs. Assn., Cosmos Club. Office: Dept Health and Human Svcs 200 Independence Ave SW Washington DC 20201-0004 Office Phone: 202-205-8830. Business E-Mail: stuart.nightingale@hhs.gov.

NIGHTINGALE, WILLIAM JOSLYN, management consultant; b. Mpls., Sept. 16, 1929; s. William Isaac and Gladys (Joslyn) N.; children: Paul, Sara, William Joslyn, Margaret. BA, Bowdoin Coll., 1951; MBA, Harvard U., 1953. Mktg. mgr. Gen. Mills Inc., Mpls., 1957-66; sr. assoc. Booz, Allen & Hamilton Inc., N.Y.C., 1966-68; v.p. fin. Hanes Corp., Winston-Salem, N.C., 1969; pres. Bali Co. Inc., N.Y.C., 1970—95; founder, pres., chmn., sr. adviser Nightingale & Assocs. LLC, Stamford, Conn., 1975—2000. Bd. dirs. Ring's End Inc.; trustee Naragansett Tax Free Bond Fund, Churchill Tax Free Bd. Fund. Active numerous charitable orgns.; vestryman St. Luke's Episcopal Ch., 1975-78, sr. warden, 1989-91; mem. Darien Representative Town Meeting, 1971-74. Lt. (j.g.) USNR, 1953-57. Mem. Wee Burn Country Club, Noroton (Conn.) Yacht Club, Harvard Club (N.Y.C.). Republican. Home: 195 Rowayton Ave Norwalk CT 06853-1237

NIGRO, RUSSELL M. state supreme court justice; b. Mar. 23, 1946; Justice Pa. Supreme Ct., Phila., 1996—. Office: Pa Supreme Ct 1818 Market St Ste 3205 Philadelphia PA 19103-3639

NIHILL, KAREN BAILEY, nursing home executive, nurse clinician; b. Erie, Pa., Mar. 15, 1947; d. William C. and Eleanor (Danielson) Bailey; 1 son, Liam H. RN, Hamot Med. Ctr., Erie, 1968; postgrad., SUNY, Gannon U., U. S.C., U. Pa., 1974—. RN, Pa. Critical care nurse Hamot Med. Ctr., 1968-71, VA Hosp., Phila., 1974-77; dir. nursing Chapel Manor and Nursing Home, Phila., 1977—, also Phila. Protestant Home and Elmira Jeffries Nursing Home; critical care nurse coord., supr. Millcreek Community Hosp., Erie, Pa., 1991—. Active Lutheran Ch. Women's Orgn. Served to lt. Nurse Corps, USN, 1971-73. VA grantee, 1974. Mem. ACLS, Am. Assn. Critical Care Nurses, Pa. Nurses Assn. Republican. Home: 5316 Bryant St Erie PA 16509-2404

NIIMI, ATSUSHI, automotive executive; b. Aichi, Japan, 1947; m. Michiko Niimi; 2 children. Degree in Aero. Engring., Nagoya U., 1971. Joined Toyota, 1971, gen. mgr. prodn. mgmt. team, 1995, gen. mgr. prodn. control divsn., 1997, gen. mgr. prodn. engring. mgmt. divsn., 1999, dir., 2000, mng. officer, 2003. Avocations: golf, swimming, driving. Office: Toyota Motor Mfg NAm Inc 25 Atlantic Ave Erlanger KY 41018

NIJENHUIS, ALBERT, mathematician, educator; b. Eindhoven, Netherlands, Nov. 21, 1926; came to U.S., 1952, naturalized, 1959; s. Hendrik and Lijdia (Koornneef) N.; m. Marianne Dannhauser, Aug. 14, 1955; children: Erika, Karin, Sabien, Alaine. Candidaat, U. Amsterdam, Netherlands, 1947, Doctorandus, 1950, Doctor cum laude, 1952. Assoc. Math. Ctr., Amsterdam, Netherlands, 1951-52; asst. Inst. Advanced Study, Princeton, NJ, 1955, mem., 1953-55, 61-62; instr., rsch. assoc. U. Chgo., 1955-56; faculty U. Wash., Seattle, 1956-63, prof., 1961-63, affiliate prof., 1988—; prof. math. U. Pa., Phila., 1963-87, prof. emeritus, 1987—. Rschr. and author publs. on subjects including differential geometry, deformation theory in algebra, combinatorics, especially tensors, holonomy groups, graded lie algebras, algorithms; Fulbright lectr. U. Amsterdam, 1963-64; vis. prof. U. Geneva, 1967-68, Dartmouth Coll., 1977-78. Co-author: Combinatorial Algorithms, 1975, 78; editor: Jour. Algorithms, Jour. Differential Geometry. Postdoctoral fellow Princeton, 1952-53; Fulbright grantee, 1952-53, 63-64; Guggenheim fellow, 1961-62. Mem. Am. Math. Soc., Math. Assn. Am., Netherlands Math. Soc., Royal Netherlands Acad. Scis. (corr.). Office: U Wash Dept Math PO Box 354350 Seattle WA 98195-4350 E-mail: nijenhuis@math.washington.edu.

NIJENSOHN, DANIEL EDGARDO, neurosurgeon; b. Mendoza, Argentina, Nov. 8, 1946; s. Leon and Mary Bekerman N.; m. Goldie L., June 25, 1972; children; Zev D., Samuel E. BA, Nat. Coll. Mendoza, Argentina, 1962; MD summa cum laude, Nat. U. Cuyo Med. Sch., Argentina, 1970; MS in Neurosurgery, U. Minn., 1976; PhD in Neuroanatomy, Nat. U. Cuyo, 1976. Rsch. asst. dept. physiology U. Cuyo, 1964-66; intern U. Buenos Aires, 1969-70, Baylor Coll. Medicine Affiliated Hosps., Tex. Med. Ctr., Houston, 1970-71; resident Mayo Clinic, U. Minn. Sch. Medicine, 1971-76; staff mem. Gamma Knife Ctr. Yale-New Haven (Conn.) Health; courtesy staff Griffin Hosp., Derby, Conn.; sr. attending staff Bridgeport (Conn.) Hosp.; chief divsn. neurosurgery St. Vincent's Med. Ctr., Bridgeport; assoc. clin. prof. neurol.

surgery Yale U. Sch. Medicine. Presenter in field. Contbr. articles to profl. jours. Recipient Myrtle Wreath award Conn. Region Hadassah, 1981; Med. Sch. scholar. Fellow Am. Coll. Surgeons, Am. Coll. Neurosurgeons, Am. Heart Assn., Argentine Coll. Neurosurgeons; mem. AMA, Am. Assn. Neurol. Surgeons, L.Am. Neurol. Fedn. (founding), New England Neurol. Soc. (trustee), Conn. Med. Soc., Conn. Soc. Neurol. Surgeons (pres. 1997-99), Fairfield County Med. Assn., Greater Bridgeport Med. Soc., Congress Neurol. Surgeons, Interam. Coll. Physicians & Surgeons, Mayo Alumni Assn., Mayo Alumni Neurol. Soc. Office: Neurol Surgeons 340 Capitol Ave Bridgeport CT 06606-5445 Fax: 203-336-5802. E-mail: nijensohn@aol.com.

NIJINSKY, TAMARA, actress, puppeteer, author, librarian, educator; b. Vienna; came to U.S., 1961; d. Waslaw and Romola (de Pulszky) N.; widowed; 1 child, Kinga Maria Szakats-Gaspers. ed. in Europe, postgrad. studies in U.S. Mem., actress Nat. Theater of Budapest; owner, tchr. Tamara Nijinsky Performing Art Studio, Montreal; tchr. speech/drama, French and German, libr. Cath. H.S., Phoenix; established non-profit internat. orgn. The Waslaw and Romola Nijinsky Found., Inc., 1991, exec. dir., 1991—. Lectr. on Nijinsky, U.S., Can. and Europe. Author: Nijinsky and Romola, 1991. Decorated chevalier de l'Ordre des Arts et des Lettres, officier de l'Ordre des Arts et des Lettres (France); recipient Nijinsky medal, Pagart, Poland, Polish Order of Arts and Letters, 1997, La Medaille Vermeil de Paris, 2000. Roman Catholic. Avocations: reading, computer, swimming. Office: Nijinsky Foundation Inc PO Box # 15981 Phoenix AZ 85060-5981 Fax: (602) 952-7149, 602-840-9605.

NIK, NINFA, language educator; d. Joe and Micaela Verdin; m. Sam Nik, July 11, 1971; children: Andrew, Jason. MA in French, U. Tex. Arlington, 1978, MA in Spanish, 1982, PhD of Humanities, 1984. Prof. Arya Mehr U., Tehran, Iran, 1972—74; lectr. Northlake Coll., Irving, Tex., 1984—85; prof. Tarleton State U., Stephenville, Tex., 1986—89; assoc. prof. Tex. Woman's U., Denton, 1989—. Co-author: (plays) Somewhere a Voice, 1990. Mem.: Southwest Coun. Latin Am. Studies, Am. Popular Culture, Phi Sigma Iota, Sigma Delta Pi. Avocations: chess, travel, reading. Office: Tex Woman's Univ Language Dept PO Box 425829 Denton TX 76204

NIKAS, RICHARD JOHN, lawyer; b. Long Beach, Calif., Sept. 9, 1968; s. John Nikolas and Dorothy (Bernardo) N. BA in Internat. Rels., U. So. Calif., 1991, JD, 1995. Bar: Calif. Spl. projects coord. Vessel Assist Assn. Am., Newport Beach, Calif., 1989-94; ptnr. Herrick Nikas, LLP, Costa Mesa, Calif., 2003—. Guest lectr. maritime law U. So. Calif., L.A., 1998—; lectr. admiralty and maritime law Calif. Maritime Acad., Vallejo; chmn. USCG Working Group on Nat. Maritime Incident Reporting Sys., Washington, 1997—, designated proctor in admiralty, The Maritime Law Assn. of the U.S.A. Author: Benedict on Admiralty, 1998, Moore's Federal Practice, 1998, The Last Yankee, 1999, Recreational Boating Law, 2000, Admiralty Practice and Procedure, 2000. Head football coach Ocean View H.S., Huntington Beach, 1995; mentor Huntington Beach Unified Sch. Dist., 1997—; pitcher Greek Olympic Baseball Team, Atlantic City Surf Profl. Baseball Club; mng. gen. ptnr. Old Reliable Baseball, LLC; bd. govs. The Am. Mariner, Loyola U., 1999. Recipient Best Oralist award Spong Nat. Invitational Moot Ct., Williamsburg, Va., 1995, Meritorious Pub. Svc. medal USCG. Mem. Calif. State Bar Assn., Maritime Law Assn., Soc. of Naval Architects and Marine Engrs. (chmn. panel 0-38), Assn. of prof. Ball Players of Am. Avocation: baseball. Address: 17652 Wrightwood Ln Huntington Beach CA 92649-4969 Office Phone: 714-546-1400. E-mail: rnikas@herricknikas.com.

NIKODINOV, ANGELA, professional figure skater, Olympic athlete; b. Spartanburg, S.C., May 9, 1980; Competitive history includes 2d place Pacific Coast Jr., 1994, 3rd place Southwest Pacific Jr., 1994, 5th place U.S. Championships Jr., 1994, 2nd place Pacific Coast Jr., 1995, 3rd place Southwest Pacific Jr., 1995, 5th place U.S. Championships Jr., 1995, 6th place World Jr. Selections Competition, 1996, 2d place Pacific Coast Sr., 1996, 5th place U.S. Olympic Festival, 1995, 1st place Southwest Pacific Sr., 1996, 3rd place O. Nepela Meml., 1996, 1st place Pacific Coast Sr., 1997, 3rd place World Jr. Selection Competition, 1997, 2nd place Pokal Der Blauen Scwerter, 1996, 4th place U.S. Championships, 1997, 4th place Skate America, 1997, 5th place U.S. Championships, 1998, 11th place World Jr. Championships, 1998, 4th place Goodwill Games, 1998, 2nd place Keri Lotion Figure Skating Classic, 1998, 3rd place Four Continents Championships, 1999, 3rd place Skate America, 1998, 3d place U.S. Championships, 1999, 12th place World Championships, 1999, 7th place Skate America, 1999, 5th place Keri Lotion Figure Skating Classic, 1999, 4th place Cup of Russia, 1999, 4th place U.S. Championships, 2000, 1st place Four Continents, 2000, 9th place World Championships, 2000, 3d place Cup of Russia, 2001, 3rd place Nations Cup, 2001, 3rd place, U.S. Championships, 2001, 2nd place, Great American Figure Skating Challenge, 2001, 5th place Workd Championships, 2001, 4th place, U.S. Championships, 2002, 1st place, Pacific Coast Sectionals, 2004, 5th place, U.S. Championships, 2004. Avocations: water-skiing, skiing, rollerblading, jet skiing. Office: USFSA 20 1st St Colorado Springs CO 80906-3624

NIKOLAI, LOREN ALFRED, accounting educator, writer; b. Northfield, Minn., Dec. 14, 1943; s. Roman Peter and Loyola (Gertrude) N.; m. Anita Carol Baker, Jan. 15, 1966; children: Trishia, Jay. BA, St. Cloud State U., 1966, MBA, 1967; PhD, U. Minn., 1973. CPA, Mo. Asst. prof. U. N.C., Chapel Hill, 1973-76; assoc. prof. U. Mo., Columbia, 1976-80, prof., 1980-82, Ernst & Young Disting. prof. Sch. Accountancy, 1982—, dir. masters programs, 2002—. Author: Financial Accounting: Concepts and Uses, 1988, 3d edit., 1995, Intermediate Accounting, 1980, 9th edit., 2003, Accounting Information for Business Decisions, 2000, 2d edit., 2004. Recipient Faculty award of merit Fedn. Schs. of Accountancy, 1989, Disting. Alumni award St. Cloud U., 1990, Coll. of Bus. Faculty Mem. of Yr. award, 1991, Mo. Outstanding Acctg. Educators award, 1993; Kemper fellow U. Mo., 1992, Alumni award MU Faculty, 1996, UM Presdl. awd. for Outstanding Teaching, 1999; Coll. of Bus. Teacher of the Yr., 1999. Mem. AICPA, Am. Acctg. Assn., Mo. Soc. CPAs, Fedn. Schs. of Acctg. (pres. 1994). Office: U Mo Sch Accountancy 303 Cornell Hall Columbia MO 65211-0001

NIKOLIC-TIRKAS, BOJANA, aerospace engineer, researcher; b. Belgrade, Yugoslavia, Sept. 28, 1964; arrived in U.S., 1991; d. Jovan and Milica Nikolić; m. Panayiotis Tirkas, June 13, 1992; children: Stefan Tirkas, Mateja Tirkas. BS in Mech./Aero. Engring., U. Belgrade, 1988; MS, Ariz. State U., 1994, PhD, 1998. Rsch. engr./scientist JPL/Makpetrol, Belgrade, 1988—92; rsch./tchg. asst. Ariz. State U., Tempe, 1992—94, 1994—98; prof. Grossmont Coll., El Cajon, Calif., 1999; sr. aerospace engr., scientist MSE-TA, Inc., Butte, Mont., 2002—. Instr. Mont. Tech., Butte, 2003. Regents' Grad. Acad. scholar, Ariz. State U., 1992, Grad. Acad. scholar, 1993. Mem.: AIAA, The Planetary Soc., Nat. Space Soc. Avocations: astronomy, poetry, writing, bicycling, skiing. Office: MSE-TA Inc PO Box 4078 200 Technology Way Butte MT 59702

NIKOLOVA - KARAKASHIAN, MARIANA, biomedical researcher; b. Sofia, Bulgaria, June 24, 1961; arrived in U.S., 1992; d. Nikola Georgiev Nikolov and Iona Alexandrova Nikolova; m. Alexander Agop Karakashian, June 15, 1991; 1 child, Claudia Alexander Karakashian; 1 child, Anita Plamenova Gardeva. MSc, Sofia U. Snt. Clement Ohridsky, 1979—84; PhD, Bulgarian Acad. Scis., Sofia, 1987—92. Rsch. assoc. Emory U., Atlanta, 1992—97, rsch. asst. prof., 1997—98; asst. prof. U. Ky., Lexington, 1998—. Observer parlamental and presdl. elections Bulgarian Union Fair Elections, Sofia, 1990—92. Recipient Am. Fedn. Aging Rsch. award, Am. Fedn. Aging Rsch., 1997; grantee Scientist devel. grant, Am. Heart Assn., 2001, Nat. Inst. Aging, 2001, 2002. Mem.: Nat. Sci. Adv. Coun. Am. Fedn. Aging Rsch., Am. Assn. Advancement Scis., Am. Heart Assn. Democrat-Npl. Achievements include research in Cell signaling mechanisms during aging and inflammation in mammalian organisms. Avocations: travel, reading. Office: U Ky MS 508 Physiology Dept 800 Rose St Lexington KY 40536 Office Phone: 859-323-8210. Business E-Mail: mnikolo@uky.edu.

NIKOUI, HOSSEIN REZA, quality assurance professional; b. Tehran, Iran, Feb. 4, 1949; came to U.S., 1977; s. Gholam Reza and Monireh (Jahanshahi) N.; m. Niki Forouzi, Oct. 25, 1983; children: Neda Lili, Amir Reza. BSChemE, Arya-Mehr Univ., Tehran, 1971; Diploma in Ops. Rsch., U. Toronto, 1981; cert. in quality assurance, Ryerson Univ., Toronto, 1983; cert. sys. approach/quality improvement, Madonna U., Livonia, Mich., 1996; MSBA in Quality and Ops. Mgmt., Madonna U., 1998; cert. in lean mfg., U. Mich., 2001. Registered profl. engr.; cert. quality engr., quality auditor, quality systems lead auditor, quality mgr. Quality engr. Gen. Motors, Tehran, 1971-72, supt. supplier quality assurance, 1973-74, mgr. quality assurance, 1975-78, resident materials mgr. Oshawa, Ont., Can., 1978-79; mgr. quality control G.S. Woolley, Toronto, 1979-82, mgr. quality assurance, 1982-85; dir. corp. quality assurance The Progressive/Woolley Group, Toronto, 1985-88, Manchester Plastics, Troy, Mich., 1988-97; dir. quality assurance Collins & Aikman Plastics, Manchester, Mich., 1997-99; dir. corp. quality assurance Oakwood Group, Dearborn, Mich., 1999-2000, dir. ops., 2000-01; lean mfg. coach Ford Motor Co., 2001—02, paint area mfg. super., 2002—03, quality oper. system leader, 2003—. Instr. Centenial Coll., Toronto, 1984-88; cons. Can. Post Corp., Toronto, 1985-86. Contbr. articles to profl. jours. Fellow Am. Soc. for Quality; mem. ASTM, Soc. Plastic Engrs., Am. Inst. Indsl. Engrs., Soc. Automotive Engrs., Engring. Soc. Detroit, Inst. of Quality Assurance. Avocations: collecting stamps and coins, tennis, reading, classical music. Home: 5539 Pinecrest Estates Dr Ann Arbor MI 48105-9351 Home Fax: 734-668-6883. Personal E-mail: hrnikoui@aol.com.

NILES, DEBORAH OLIVE, veteran benefits coordinator; b. Port of Spain, Trinidad & Tobago, Sept. 13, 1967; d. Timothy Nathaniel and Joan Elaine Niles; children: Aundre Maurice Eugene, Jorden Kayleigh Niles-Foster. BS, Westfield State Coll., 1999. Police officer Westfield State Coll., Mass., 1994—2002; res. police officer Westfield Police Dept., 1999—2002; adminstrv. specialist Westfield State Coll., 2002—. Rape investigator Westfield State Coll., 1998—2002, domestic violence investigator, 1998—2002. Author: (poetry) Works by D.Niles. Specialist U.S. Army, 1986—89, Weisbaden, Germany, staff sgt. Nat. Guard, 2000—. Decorated Army Achievement Medal U.S. Army; recipient Editors Choice awards for Outstanding Acheivemnet in Poetry. Home: 26 St Paul Street Westfield MA 01085 Office: Westfield State College 577 Western Ave Westfield MA 01086 Personal E-mail: spoken_word03@yahoo.com. E-mail: dfailey@wsc.ma.edu.

NILES, GEDDES LEROY, private investigator; b. Haines, Alaska, Oct. 31, 1926; s. Geddes William and Gladys Bell (McCormack) N.; m. Aline Terii Tehei, June 17, 1960; children: Diana Mareva Niles-Hansen, Stephen Lloyd Teva. BA, U. Calif., Berkeley, 1949. Investigator and hearing officer U.S. Civil Service Commn., San Francicso, 1955-62, Honolulu, 1962-78; pres. Niles Realty Ltd., Honolulu, 1979—; dir. The Niles Agy., Honolulu, 1983—. Mem. Neighborhood Bd., Kailua, Hawaii, 1979-80. Mem.: Iaorana Tahiti (Honolulu) (treas. 1985-89). Avocation: mystery writer. Office: 350 Ward Ave Ste 106 Honolulu HI 96814-4004

NILES, JOHN SOUTHWORTH, III, counselor, farmer; b. Carbondale, Pa., Dec. 3, 1933; s. John S. Jr. and Helen Hemelright Niles; m. Elsie E. Axford (div. 1969); children: John S. IV, David A., Elizabeth C.; m. Dorothy L. Keill, June 12, 1999. BA, Yale U., 1956. Cert. addictions counselor, Pa. Roughneck Mim Oil Drilling Co., Victoria, Tex., 1959; mfg. mgr. KVP-Sutherland Paper Co., Kalamazoo, Mich., 1960-67; mgr. Cold Springs Farms, Pleasant Mount, Pa., 1968-79, Baccus Farms, Minneapolis, Kans., 1979-82; counselor Marworth Treatment Ctr., Waverly, Pa., 1982-93, ret., 1993. 1st lt. USMC, 1956-58. Mem. NRA, Marine Corps Assn., Countryside Convervancy, Delta Kappa Epsilon. Republican. Avocations: hunting, fishing, horses, reading, sports. Home: Crystal Lake RR 1 Box 1106 Carbondale PA 18407-9015 E-mail: jsniles@webtv.net.

NILES, KEVIN BRYAN, music educator; s. Norman Ewing and Rosalyn Marie Niles. BA in mktg., Anderson U., Ind., 1980—84; BA in mgmt., Anderson U., 1980—84, MDiv, 1989—93. Assoc. pastor New Castle First Friends Ch., New Castle, Ind., 1989—91, Hemlock Friends Ch., Kokomo, Ind., 1991—96, Sycamore Friends Ch., Greentown, Ind., 1997—2000; sales mgmt. trainee Zales Corp, Bloomington, Ill., 2000—02; choral and gen. music tchr. Cornerstone Christian Acad., Bloomington, Ill., 2001—. Musician and worship leader East White Oak Bible Ch., Carlock, Ill., 2000—03. Mem.: Ill. Music Educators Assn., MENC Nat. Assn. Music Edn. Home: 1414 Montgomery St Normal IL 61761 Office: Cornerstone Christian Acad Bloomington IL

NILES, THOMAS MICHAEL TOLLIVER, business association executive; b. Lexington, Ky., Sept. 22, 1939; s. John Jacob and Rena (Lipetz) N.; m. Carroll C. Ehringhaus, July 22, 1967; children: John Thomas, Mary Chapman. BA, Harvard U., 1960; MA, U. Ky., 1962. Commd. fgn. service officer Dept. State, Washington, 1962, U.S. ambassador to Can., 1985-1989; then permanent rep. EEC, Brussels; asst. sec. of state Europe and Can., 1991-93; amb. to Greece, 1993-97; v.p. Nat. Def. U., 1997-98; pres. U.S. Coun. Internat. Bus., 1999. Recipient Superior Honor award Dept. State, 1982, 85, Presdl. award, 1988, 89, 94. Mem. Phi Beta Kappa Office: USCIB 1212 Ave of Ams New York NY 10036

NILLES, JOHN MICHAEL, lawyer; b. Langdon, N.D., Aug. 20, 1930; s. John Joseph and Isabel Mary (O'Neil) N.; m. Barbara Ann Cook, June 22, 1957; children: Terese M., Daniel J., Marcia L., Thomas M., Margaret J. BA cum laude, St. Johns U., 1955; JD cum laude with distinction, U. N.D., 1958. Bar: N.D. 1958, U.S. Dist. Ct. N.D. 1958, U.S. Ct. Appeals (8th cir.) 1958, Minn. 1991. Shareholder, dir., pres. Nilles, Hansen and Davies, Ltd., Fargo, N.D., 1958-90, of counsel, 1990-95; exec. v.p., gen. counsel Met. Fin. Corp., Mpls., 1990-95, First Bank F.S.B., Mpls., 1995; ret., 1996. Pres., bd. dirs. Legal Aid Soc. N.D., Fargo, 1970-76, Red River Estate Planning Coun., 1980-87; vice-chmn. disciplinary bd. Supreme Ct. N.D., 1984-90. Bd. editors N.D. Law Rev., 1957-58. Mem. exec. bd. Red. River Valley coun. Boy Scouts Am., 1959-70; bd. regents U. Mary, Bismarck, N.D., 1967-77; pres., bd. dirs. Cath. Charities, Fargo, 1959-65, Southeast Mental Health Ctr., Fargo, 1972-80. Staff sgt. USAF, 1951-54. Fellow Am. Coll. Trust and Estate Counsel (state dir. 1979-90); mem. ABA, State Bar Assn. N.D., Minn. Bar Assn., Order of Coif. Republican. Roman Catholic. Avocations: tennis, downhill skiing, cross country skiing, hunting, gun collecting. Home: 10412 Fawns Way Eden Prairie MN 55347-5117

NIMER, STEPHEN, physician, leukemia researcher; b. Chgo., May 20, 1954; m. Georgia Takigawa, Oct. 18, 1987. BS, MIT, 1975; MD, U. Chgo., 1979. Diplomate Am. Bd. Internal Medicine, Am. Bd. Hematology, Am. Bd. Med. Oncology. Asst. prof. medicine UCLA Sch. Medicine, 1987-92; dir. transplantation biology Jonsson Compr. Cancer Ctr., L.A., 1991-92; assoc. mem. Sloan-Kettering Inst., N.Y.C., 1993-99, mem., 1999—; chief hematology svc. Meml. Hosp., N.Y.C., 1993—; head, divsn. hematologic oncology Meml. Sloan-Kettering Cancer Ctr., N.Y.C., 1996—; prof. medicine Weill Medical Coll., 2000—. Funded investigator NIH, 1990—. Mem. editl. bd.: Blood, 1997—2002; co-editor: Hematologic Complications of Cancer, 1996; contbr. over 120 sci. articles to profl. jours. Chmn. med. adv. bd. G&P Charitable Found., N.Y.C., 1998—. Recipient Irma T. Hirschl Career Scientist award Cornell U. Med. Sch., 1995. Fellow ACP; mem. Am. Soc. for Clin. Investigation, Am. Soc. for Hematology, Am. Soc. Clin. Oncology, Am. Assn. for Cancer Rsch., Leukemia Soc. Am. (bd. trustees NY chpt. 1998-2004), Aplastic Anemia Found. Am. (bd. med. dirs. 1996—), MDS Found. (med. bd.), Alpha Omega Alpha. Avocations: tennis, photography, gardening. Office: Meml Sloan Kettering Cancer Ctr Box 575 1275 York Ave New York NY 10021-6094

NIMETZ, MATTHEW, lawyer, investment company executive; b. Bklyn, NY, June 17, 1939; s. Joseph L. and Elsie (Botwinik) N.; m. Gloria S. Lorch, June 24, 1975; children: Alexandra Elise, Lloyd. BA, Williams Coll., 1960, LL.D. (hon.), 1979; BA (Rhodes scholar), Balliol Coll., Oxford (Eng.) U., 1962, MA, 1966; LL.B., Harvard U., 1965. Bar: NY 1966, DC 1968. Law clk. to Justice John M. Harlan, US Supreme Ct., 1965-67; staff asst. to Pres. Johnson, 1967-69; assoc. firm Simpson Thacher & Bartlett, NYC, 1969-74, ptnr., 1974-77; counselor Dept. of State, Washington, 1977-80, acting coord. refugee affairs, 1979-80, under sec. of state for security assistance, sci. and tech., 1980; ptnr. firm Paul, Weiss, Rifkind, Wharton & Garrison, NYC, 1981-2000; ptnr., mng. mem. Gen. Atlantic Ptnr. LLC, Greenwich, Conn., 2000—. Commr. Port Authority NY and NJ, 1975-77; dir. World Resources Inst., chmn., 1982-94; mem. NY State Adv. Coun. on State Productivity, 1990-92; presdl. envoy Greece-Macedonian Negotiations, 1994-95, spl. rep. UN Sec. Gen., 1999—. Trustee William Coll., 1981-96; chmn. UN Devel. Corp., 1986-94; bd. dir. Charles H. Revson Found., 1990-98, NY State Nature Conservancy, 1997—; chmn. Carnegie Forum in US, Greece and Turkey, 1996-98; chmn. Ctr. for Democracy and Reconciliation in S.E. Europe, 1998—; dir. Inst. Pub. Adminstrn., 1999—; chair internat. adv. com. Ctrl. European U., Budapest, Hungary, 2001. Mem. Assn. of Bar of City of NY, Coun. on Fgn. Rels. Clubs: Harvard (NYC). Office: Gen Atlantic Ptnrs LLC 3 Pickwick Plz Greenwich CT 06830-5538 E-mail: mnimetz@gapartners.com.

NIMIROWSKI, RAMONA FURPHY, legal administrator; b. Manchester, Conn., Mar. 10, 1952; d. John Edward and Madeline Raymond F.; m. Peter John Nimirowski, Aug. 7, 1971 (div. Jan. 1986); children: Todd Justin, Teresa Rose. Degree in acctg. and bus. adminstrn., Manchester (Conn.) C.C., 1980; BS in Bus., U. Hartford, 1987. Paralegal, clerk Travelers Ind. Co., Hartford, 1981-90, mgr., 1987-87, asst. dir. corp. law, 1990-98, 2d v.p., 1998—. Mem. Eta Mu Lambda. Home: 102 Wetherell St Unit 102 Manchester CT 06040 Office: Travelers Ins Co 1 Tower Sq Hartford CT 06183 E-mail: ramona.f.nimirowski@travelers.com.

NIMKIN, BERNARD WILLIAM, retired lawyer; b. N.Y.C., Apr. 15, 1923; s. Myron Benjamin and Anabel (Davidow) N.; m. Jean Horowitz, Feb. 9, 1947; children— David Andrew, Margaret Lee, Katherine. BS cum laude, Harvard U., 1943, LL.B. cum laude, 1949. Bar: N.Y. State bar 1949, U.S. Supreme Ct., 1999. Asso. firm Carter, Ledyard & Milburn, N.Y.C., 1949-58; asso. and partner firm Kaye Scholer, LLP, N.Y.C., 1958-91. Lectr. Practising Law Inst., Banking Law Inst.; Mem. Am. Law Inst.; vis. com. U. Miami Law Sch.; mem. adv. bd. Rev. of Securities Regulation. Contbr. articles to profl. jours. Mem. Conservation Commn., Town of Mamaroneck, N.Y., 1970-74; bd. dirs., sec. United Way of Tri-State, 1985-91. Served to 1st lt. U.S. Army, 1943-46. Mem. ABA (mem. fed. regulation of securities com. 1975—, corp. laws com. 1984-92, legal opinions com. 1989—), N.Y. State Bar Assn. (chmn. sect. banking corp. and bus. law 1979-81, ho. of dels. 1981-84, chmn. corp. law com. 1976-79), Assn. Bar City of N.Y. (chmn. uniform state laws com. 1962-65), Tribar Opinion Com. Democrat. Jewish. Home: 116 E 63rd St New York NY 10021-7325 Office: Kaye Scholer LLP 425 Park Ave New York NY 10022-3506 E-mail: bandjnimkin@earthlink.net.

NIMNI, MARCEL EPHRAIM, biochemistry educator; b. Buenos Aires, Feb. 1, 1931; came to U.S., 1955; s. Sam and Sarah Dora (Freedman) N.; children: Elizabeth, Brian Sam; m. Fabiola Cordoba, Dec. 21, 1996. BS in Pharmacy, U. Buenos Aires, 1954, PhD, 1960; MS, U. So. Calif., 1957; MD honoris causae (hon.), Maimonides U., 2002. Cert. nutrition specialist. Rsch. fellow U. So. Calif., L.A., 1960-61, asst. prof. biochemistry, 1963-66, assoc. prof., 1966-72, prof., 1972—, prof. surgery, 1990—, prof. orthop., 1980—; dir. biology Don Baxter Labs., Glendale, Calif., 1962. Cons. Hancock Labs., Glendale, Calif., 1962; cons. Hancock Labs., Anaheim, Calif., 1970-78, pathobiochemistry study sect. NIH, 1980-85, orthopaedics and biomechanics study sect., 1987-90; mem. NASA Tissue Engring. Rev. Bd., 2002—; dir. biochemistry rsch. Orthopaedic Hosp., L.A., 1980-91; cons. Tillots Pharma Labs., Basle, Switzerland, 1986-94; dir. surg. rsch. Chidlren's Hosp. of L.A., 1991-98, dir. Tissue Engring. Lab., 1998—; mem. adv. bd. Maimonides U., Buenos Aires. Editor: Collagen: Biochemistry, Biotechnology and Molecular Biology, Vols. I-V,1987-91; editor Matrix, 1980-93, Connective Tissue Rsch., 1973-91, Jour. Orthopaedic Rsch., 1989-94; patentee collagen tech., transderman drug delivery. Recipient Merit award NIH, 1987; rsch. grantee NIH Arthritis Inst., 1966-94, NIH Aging Inst., 1982-2000. Fellow AAAS, Am. Coll. Nutrition, Soc. Biomaterials (Founders award 1986); mem. Am. Inst. Nutrition, Am. Assn. Biochem. and Molecular Biology. Office: DOH-104 Health Scis Campus Los Angeles CA 90033

NIMOITYN, PHILIP, cardiologist; b. Phila., Mar. 6, 1951; s. Benjamin Solomon and Edith (Ornstein) N.; m. Hillary Rachel Saul, June 11, 1989. BS in Biology with distinction, Phila. Coll. Pharmacy and Sci., 1972; MD, Thomas Jefferson U., 1976. Cert. Nat. Bd. Med. Examiners, Am. Bd. Internal Medicine, Am. Bd. Cardiovascular Disease. Intern Hahnemann U. Hosp., Phila., 1976-77; resident in internal medicine Thomas Jefferson U. Hosp., Phila., 1977-79, cardiovascular disease fellow, 1979-81, instr. medicine, 1981-90, clin. asst. prof., 1990—; attending physician Pa. Hosp., Phila., 1995—; cons. physician Wills Eye Hosp., Phila., 1981—; attending physician Penn. Hosp., Phila., 1995—. Author: (with others) Artificial Cardiac Pacing, 1984, Quick Reference to Cardiovascular Disease, 1987, Cardiac Emergency Care, 1991; contbr. articles to profl. jours. Recipient Cert. of Merit for Sci. Exhibits AMA, 1974, 2d prize for sci. exhibits Ind. State Med. Assn., 1974. Fellow Am. Coll. Cardiology; mem. AMA, Pa. Med. Soc., Phila. County Med. Soc. Office: 1128 Walnut St Ste 401 Philadelphia PA 19107-5568 Office Phone: 215-629-1158. Business E-Mail: philip.nimoityn@mail.tju.edu.

NING, SHOUCHENG, cancer biologist, head and neck surgeon; b. Gao-Qing, Shandong, China, Aug. 1, 1951; came to U.S., 1988; s. Yun-You and Shu-Zheng (Gao) N.; m. Ling-Yi Zhang, Sept. 10, 1979; 1 child, Kevin X.B. MD, Shanghai 2d Med. U., 1978, MS, 1982, PhD, 1986. Asst. prof. Shanghai 2d Med. U., 1978-81, attending surgeon, 1982-88, assoc. prof., vice chief surgeon, 1988—; rsch. fellow Stanford (Calif.) U. Med. Sch., 1988-93, rsch. scientist, 1993—. Author: Modern Treatment in Internal Medicine, 1987, China Yearbook of Stomatology, 1988; contbr. articles to Internat. Jour. Radiation Oncology and Biol. Physics, Jour. Cellular Physiology. Recipient award for outstanding young scientists Shanghai Assn. Sci. and Tech., 1985, nat. award in cancer rsch. China Ministry Pub. Health, 1986, nat. award for advancement of sci. and tech. China. Nat. Coun. for Edn., 1994. Mem. Am. Assn. for Cancer Rsch., N.Am. Hyperthermia Soc., Chinese Med. Assn. Office: Stanford U Med Ctr A010 300 Pasteur Dr Palo Alto CA 94304-2203

NING, XUE-HAN (HSUEH-HAN NING), physiologist, researcher; b. Peng-Lai, Shandong, People's Republic of China, Apr. 15, 1936; came to U.S., 1984; s. Yi-Xing and Liu Ning; m. Jian-Xin Fan, May 28, 1967; 1 child, Di Fan. MD, Shanghai 1st Med. Coll., People's Republic of China, 1960. Rsch. fellow Shanghai Inst. Physiology, 1960-72, leader cardiovasc. rsch. group, 1973-83, head, assoc. prof. cardiovasc. rsch. unit, 1984-87, prof. and chair hypoxia dept., 1988-90, vice chairperson academic com., 1988-90; NIH internat. rsch. fellow U. Mich., Ann Arbor, 1984-87, vis. prof., hon. prof., rsch. investigator, 1990-95; prof. and dir. Hypoxia Physiology Lab. Academia Sinica, Shanghai, 1989-90. Acting leader, High Altitude Physiology Group, Chinese mountaineering and sci. expdn. team to Mt. Everest, 1975; leader High Altitude Physiology Group, Dept. Metall. Industry of China and Ry. Engring. Corps, 1979; vis. prof. dept. physiology Mich. State U., East Lansing, 1989-90; vis. prof. dept. pediat. U . Wash., Seattle, 1994-97; affiliate prof., U. Wash., 1997—; rsch. scientist Children's Hosp. and Regional Med. Ctr., Seattle, 1997—. Author: High Altitude Physiology and Medicine, 1981, Reports on Scientific Expedition to Mt. Qomolungma, High Altitude Physiology, 1980, Environment and Ecology of Qinghai-Xizang (Tibet) Plateau, 1982; mem. editl. bd. Chinese Jour. Applied Physiology, 1984—, Acta Physiologica, 1988-90; contbr. articles to profl. jours. Recipient Merit award Shanghai Sci. Congress, 1977, All-China Sci. Congress, Beijing, 1978, Super Class award Academia Sinica, Beijing, 1986, 1st Class award Nat. Natural Scis., Beijing, 1987, # 1 Best Article award Tzu-Chi Med. Jour., Taiwan, 1995. Mem. Am. Physiol. Soc., Am. Heart Assn., Internat. Soc. Heart Rsch., Royal Soc. Medicine, Shanghai Assn. Physiol. (bd. dirs. 1988-91), Chinese Assn. Physiol. (com. applied physiology 1984-93, com. blood, cardiovascular, respiratory and renal physiology 1988-93), Chinese Soc. Medicine, Chinese Soc. Biomed. Engring. Achievements include research in predictive evaluation of mountaineering performance, paradox phenomenon of cardiac pump function injury after climbing or giving oxygen, blood flow-metabolism-function relationship of heart during hypoxia and ischemia, effect of medicinal

herbs on cardiac performance, cardiovascular adaptation and resistance to hypoxia and ischemia, Hypothermic adaptation protects heart from subsequent ischemia and hypoxia; the critical temperature 30 degrees celsius "temperature threshold" for modulating myocardial energy, metabolism and gene expression to resist ischemia and hypoxia, hypothermia preserves signaling for mitochondrial biogenesis, triggers stress pathways and inactivates apoptosis in hypoxic myocardium; first electrocardiograph recording at summit of Mt. Everest. Home: 7033 43rd Ave NE Seattle WA 98115-6015 Office: U Wash Dept Pediatrics Box 356320 1959 NE Pacific St Seattle WA 98195-0001

NINNEMANN, THOMAS GEORGE, secondary school educator; b. Chgo., Apr. 13, 1950; s. Milton Charles and Bernice Helen (Sharp) N.; m. Nancy Gail Rogers, Aug. 12, 1972; children: Stephanie Christine, Peter Christopher. BA, U. No. Colo., 1972. Dir. news. Sta. KGLN, Glenwood Springs, Colo., 1972-73; program mgr. Sta. KKEP, Estes Park, Colo., 1973-74; ops. mgr. Sta. WMST-AM-FM, Mt. Sterling, Ky., 1974-75; dir. news Sta. KPIK-AM-FM, Colorado Springs, Colo., 1975-77; news stringer AP, UPI, various stas., Colorado Springs, Colo., 1977-78; mgr. driver edn., safety dept. Am. Automobile Assn., Denver, 1978-81; pres. mkt. rschr. Rampart Range Broadcasting Inc., Castle Rock, Colo., 1981-83; news editor Sta. KDEN, Denver, 1983-84; dir. news Stas. KSGT and KMTN-FM, Jackson, Wyo., 1984-94; instr. radio and TV/prodr. dist. TV programming Teton County Sch. Dist., Jackson, 1989—. Panelist Yellowstone Fire Rev., Yellowstone Nat. Pk., 1989; contract spokesperson on fire safety Bridger-Teton Nat. Forest, Jackson, 1990-97; seasonal pub. affairs specialist Grand Teton Nat. Park, summers 1995-2001; mem. broadcast curriculum adv. com. Ctrl. Wyo. Coll., 1995—. Asst. scoutmaster, then scoutmaster Boy Scouts Am., Castle Rock, Colo., 1979-84, mem. dist. com., 1984-93, 2001—; vice chair Teton County Centennial Com., Jackson, 1989; co-founder Jackson Hole Cmty. Band, 1989—; charter mem. Shepherd of the Mountains Luth. Ch., 1985-2000; active Jackson Hole Brass Quintet, 1985—; mem. local com. Christian Ministry in Nat. Parks, 1988-96; mem. pub. adv. com. Wyo. Pub. Radio, 1990—; com. mem. Jackson divsn. Am. Heart Assn., 1994-95; bd. dirs. Jackson Hole Crimestoppers, 1996-2004. Recipient Tony Bevinette Friend of Wyo. Tourism award Wyo. Travel Commn., 1993, Bronze Smokey award U.S. Forest Svc., 1998; co-recipient Wyo. News Station of Yr. award AP, 1990; named Colo. Broadcast Newsman of Yr. AP, 1976. Mem.: Broadcast Edn. Assn. Avocations: instrumental music, camping, furniture refinishing, local history. Home: PO Box 1050 Jackson WY 83001-1050 Office: Jackson Hole HS PO Box 568 Jackson WY 83001-0568 E-mail: tninn@bresnan.net., tninnemann@teton1.k12.wy.us.

NINNIS, WILLIAM RAYMOND, JR., lawyer; b. San Francisco, Aug. 23, 1932; s. William Raymond and Oda Marie (Jensen) N.; m. Mary Frances Parker; children: William Bradley, David Raymond. AB, San Francisco State U., 1958; LLB, JD, U. Calif., 1962. Bar: Calif. 1963, U.S. Dist. Ct. (no. dist.) Calif. 1963, U.S. Ct. Appeals (9th cir.) 1963, U.S. Dist. Ct. (ea. dist.) Calif. 1967, U.S. Dist. Ct. (cen. dist.) Calif. 1984. Assoc. house counsel Pacific Gas and Electric Co., San Francisco, 1962-67; trial atty., v.p. and sec. Dawson & Ninnis PLC, Fresno, Calif., 1967-84; ptnr., trial atty. Ninnis & Cribbs, Fresno, 1984—; judge pro tem Workers Compensation Appeals Bd., 1984—, arbitrator, 1994—. Mem. Calif. State Bar Assn., San Francisco County Bar Assn., Fresno County Bar Assn., Clovis Bar Assn. (v.p., bd. dir. Fresno rape coun. 1988), San Francisco Bar Assn. (chmn. worker's compensation com. 1965-67), No. Calif. Def. Atty.'s Assn. (bd. dirs. 1973-83). Republican. Methodist. Avocations: hunting, fishing. Home: 11028 El Capitan Dr Madera CA 93638-7411 Office: Ninnis & Cribbs 3106 Willow Ave Clovis CA 93612-4749 also: PO Box 5314 Fresno CA 93755-5314

NIRENBERG, LOUIS, mathematician, educator; b. Hamilton, Ont., Can., Feb. 28, 1925; arrived in U.S., 1945, naturalized, 1954; s. Zuzie and Bina (Katz) Nirenberg; m. Susan Blank, Jan. 25, 1948; children: Marc, Lisa. BSc, McGill U., Montreal, 1945, DSc (hon.), 1986; MS, NYU, 1947, PhD, 1949; DSc (hon.), U. Pisa, Italy, 1990, U. Paris Dauphine, 1990, McMaster U., Can., 2000. Mem. faculty NYU, 1949—, prof. math., 1957—, dir. Courant Inst., 1970—72. Visitor Inst. Advanced Study, 1958; hon. prof. Nannkai U., Zhejiang U. Author rsch. articles. Recipient Crafoord prize, Royal Swedish Acad., 1982, Nat. medal of Sci., 1995; fellow NRC, 1951—52, Sloan Found., 1958—60, Guggenheim Found., 1966—67, 1975—76, Fulbright, 1965. Mem.: NAS, Ukrainian Acad. Sci. (fgn.), Accademia de Scienze e Lettere (fgn.), Istituto Lombardo, Accademia dei Lincei (fgn.), French Acad. Scis. (fgn.), Am. Philos. Soc., Am. Math. Soc. (v.p. 1976—78, M. Bocher prize 1959, L.P. Steele prize 1994), Am. Acad. Arts and Scis., European Acad. Scis. (hon.). Home: 221 W 82nd St New York NY 10024-5406 Office: Courant Inst 251 Mercer St New York NY 10012-1185 E-mail: nirenl@cims.nyu.edu.

NIRENBERG, MARSHALL WARREN, biochemist; b. N.Y.C., N.Y., Apr. 10, 1927; s. Harry Edward and Minerva (Bykowsky) Nirenberg; m. Perola Zaltzman, July 14, 1961. BS in Zoology, U. Fla., 1948, MS, 1952; PhD in Biochemistry, U. Mich., 1957. Postdoctoral fellow Am. Cancer Soc. at NIH, 1957—59; postdoctoral fellow USPHS at NIH, 1959—60; mem. staff NIH, 1960—; research biochemist, chief lab. biochem. genetics Nat. Heart, Lung and Blood Inst., 1962—. Co-recipient Louisa Gross Horowitz prize Columbia, 1968, Nobel prize in physiology or medicine, 1968; recipient Molecular Biology award, NAS, 1962, award in biol. scis., Washington Acad. Scis., 1962, medal, HEW, 1964, Modern Medicine award, 1963, Harrison Howe award, Am. Chem. Soc., 1964, Nat. Medal Sci., Pres. Johnson, 1965, Hildebrand award, Am. Chem. Soc., 1966, Research Corp. award, 1966, A.C.P. award, 1967, award merit, Gairdner Found., Can, 1967, Prix Charles Leopold Meyer, French Acad. Scis., 1967, Franklin medal, Franklin Inst., 1968, Albert Lasker Med. Research award, 1968, Priestly award, 1968. Fellow: AAAS, N.Y. Acad. Scis.; mem.: NAS, Pontificial Acad. Scis., Leopoldina Deutsche Akademie der Naturforscher, Soc. Devel. Biology, Soc. for Study Devel. and Growth, Washingon Acad. Scis., Harvey Soc. (hon.), Biophys. Soc., Am. Acad. Arts and Scis., Am. Chem. Soc. (Paul Lewis award enzyme chemistry 1964), Am. Soc. Biol. Chemists. Achievements include research in mechanism protein synthesis, genetic code, nucleic acids, regulatory mechanisms in synthesis macromolecules, and neurobiology.*

NIRENSTEIN, JACK, writer; b. Poland, Dec. 25, 1928; came to U.S., 1931; s. Hyman and Frieda N.; divorced; children: Michael, Debby Bloom. Owner advt. co. Virtu Assocs., N.Y.C., 1965-86. Author: Guided Muscles for Winning Sports, 2000. With U.S. Army, 1947-49. Avocations: running, sports, computer graphics, photography. Home: # 50A 623 Canterbury Dr Myrtle Beach SC 29579 E-mail: pro8form@aol.com.

NIRO, CHERYL, lawyer; b. Feb. 19, 1950; d. Samuel James and Nancy (Canezaro) Ippolito; m. William Luciano Niro, July 1, 1979; children: Christopher William, Melissa Leigh. BS with highest honors, U. Ill., 1972; JD, No. Ill. U., 1980. Bar: Ill. 1981, U.S. Dist. Ct. (no. dist.) Ill. 1981, U.S. Ct. Appeals (7th cir.) 1990, U.S. Supreme Ct. 1999, cert.: negotiator, mediator, facilitator. Assoc. Pope Ballard Sheppard & Fowle, Chgo., 1980-81; ptnr. Partridge and Niro PC; now ptnr. Quinlan & Carroll, Chgo.; now pres. Judicial Dispute Resolution, Inc., Chgo. Spl. counsel to Atty. Gen., 1996—99; exec. dir. Com. to Commerorate U.S. Constn. in Ill., 1985—86; creator Bicentennial Law Sch. Program; tchg. asst. program instrn. lawyers mediation and negotiation workshops and guest lectr. Harvard Law Sch. Program of Instrn. for Lawyers Harvard U.; mem. appt. panel U.S. Ct. Appeals (7th cir.); found. dir. Nat. Ctr. for Conflict Resolution Edn.; mem. copyright arbitration royalty panel U.S. Libr. of Congress, 2000—05; mem. London Ct. of Internat. Arbitation. Named one of Ten Most Influential Women Lawyers in Ill, Am Lawyer Media, 2000; named to Today's Chgo. Woman Mag. Hall of Fame, 2002. Mem.: ATLA, ABA (comn multijurisdictional practice, standing comt bar servs, dispute resolution sect coun, house delegs), Internat. Ctr. for Healing the Law (mem. bd. adv.), Internat. Bar Assn., Ill. State Bar Assn. (mem assembly 1993, bd govs 1994—97, treas 1995—96, 2d vpres 1997—98, pres 1999—2000, pres. 1999—2000, standing comt legal-related educ pub), Ill Trial Lawyers Assn. Home: 633 N East Ave Oak Park IL 60302-1715 Office: Quinlan & Carroll 30 N Lasalle St Ste 2900 Chicago IL 60602-2590 Office Phone: 312-917-8839. Business E-Mail: cherylniro@qclaw.com.

NIRSCHL, ROBERT PHILLIP, orthopedic surgeon; b. South Milwaukee, Wis., Aug. 28, 1933; s. Boyd A. and Helen (Wozny) N.; m. Mary Ann Oleniczak, June 21, 1958; children: Suzanne, Robert C., Julie. Student, Coll. Holy Cross, 1951-53, Marquette U., 1953-54; MD, Med. Coll. Wis./Marquette U., 1958; MS, U. Minn., 1965. Diplomate Am. Bd. Orthop. Surgery. Intern St. Mary's Hosp., Duluth, Minn., 1958-59; resident in orthop. Mayo Clinic, Rochester, Minn., 1959-63; lt. comdr. USN, Washington, 1963-65; pvt. practice Arlington, Va., 1965—. Attending orthop. surgeon Va. Hosp. Ctr., Arlington, v.p. med. staff, 1980-83, dir. Hand Surgery Svc., 1975-85; chief orthop. surgery No. Va. Cmty. Hosp., 1971-82; founding dir. Nirschl Orthop. Ctr. for Sports Med. and Joint Reconstruction, 1974—, Nirschl Orthop. Sports Med. Ctr. Orthop. Sports Med. Fellowship Program Va. Hosp. Ctr., Arlington, 1987—; mem. clin. faculty Georgetown U. Med. Ctr., 1965—; orthop. cons. Pres.'s Coun. Phys. Fitness, Washington, 1981-87; mem. sports sci. com. USTA, N.Y.C., 1987-94; course dir. numerous symposia in field. Author: Arm Care, 1981, rev. edit., 1996, Isoflex Exercise System, 1983; chief med. editor Orthop. Today, 1983-93; mem. editl. bd. The Physician and Sportsmedicine, 1992—, The Med. Sentinel, 1996-02, Orthopedics Today, 2003-; creator 6 video programs; contbr. chpts. to books and over 125 articles to profl. pubs.; patentee in field. Chmn. Jeffersonian Health Policy Found., Williamsburg, Va., 1994-97; mem. Va. Bd. Medicine, 2000-04. Grantee Pfizer Inc., 1992-93, Sano Corp, 1993-94, Iomed Corp., 1999—. Mem. AMA, Am. Acad. Orthop. Surgery (health fin. com. 1994-00, bd. counselors 2000—, comm. and state soc. coms. bd. of counselors 2000-03), Am. Orthop. Sports Medicine Soc. (ethics com. 1992-97, bd. dels. 2002-), Soc. Tennis Medicine and Sci. (exec. com.), Ea. Orthop. Assn., Washington Orthop. Soc., Va. Orthop. Soc. (pres. 1998-99), Med. Soc. Va. (chmn. sports medicine com. 1973-84, trustee polit. action com. 1990-02, legis. com. 1995—), Arlington County Med. Soc. (pres. 1977, chmn. legis. com. 1987—, Welburn award 1995), Washington Golf and Country Club. Republican. Roman Catholic. Avocation: fitness activities. Office: Nirschl Orthop Sports Medicine Clinic 1715 N George Mason Dr Ste 504 Arlington VA 22205-3670 E-mail: nirschl@erols.com.

NISBET, THOMAS K. architect; b. Richland Center, Wis., Jan. 9, 1931; s. Thomas Kenneth and Eva Louise (Klein) N.; m. Lynnette Patricia MacIntyre, Aug. 27, 1954; children: Bruce W., Jay T., Christopher W. Student, Columbia Coll., 1949-51; BArch, Columbia U., 1955. Registered arch., N.Y., Wis. Apprentice arch. Albert M. Skinner AIA, Watertown, N.Y., 1946-49; asst. editl. Archtl. Record, N.Y.C., 1950-51; draftsman Weiler/Strang, Madison, Wis., 1952-55; arch. H.C. Montgomery AIA, Watertown, 1958-61; arch./assoc. Flad & Assocs., Madison, 1961-83; prin. Nisbet/Archs., Madison, 1983—. Mem. Wis. Examining Bd., 1982-83, Nat. Coun. Archs. Registration Bd., 1981-. Works include co-designer Sentry Ins. home office, 1975 (honor award 1975), Wis. Telephone/ASC/WARF, 1970-75 (merit awards 1970-75), U. Wis. Libr./Vilas Hall (merit award 1974); awarded commission for Tri State Vets. Meml. with Severson/Schultz Sculptors. Deacon Westminster Presbyn. Ch., Madison, 1964; v.p., bd. dirs. Nakoma Golf Club, Madison, 1976-82. Recipient Columbia U. traveling fellowship Europe, 1957-58. Mem. AIA, Wis. Archs. Found. (pres. 1981-85). Avocations: art, photography. Office: Nisbet/Architects 4340 Hillcrest Cir Madison WI 53705-5017 Office Phone: 608-233-2320. Personal E-mail: tknisbet@chorus.net.

NISBET, TOMA A. nursing administrator; Diploma with honors, St. Mark's Hosp. Sch. Nursing, 1967; BSN with honors, No. Ill. U., 1969, MSN with honors, 1973. Internship Winnebago County Dept. Pub. Health-Health Adminstrn. & Family Planning; night staff nurse Sycamore Municipal Hosp., Ill., 1967-68; evening relief supr., charge nurse DeKalb County Nursing Home, Ill., 1969; pub. health nurse DeKalb County Health Dept., Ill., 1969-71; divsn. dir. nursing svcs. Winnebago County Dept. Pub. Health, Rockford, Ill., 1974-84; pub. dir. nursing svcs. divsn. of health & med. svcs. State of Wyo., Cheyenne, 1985-87, policy devel. & spl. projects state program mgr. divsn. of health & med. svcs., 1987-88, state bd. nursing exec., 1988—. Spokesperson for NLX D-A-Y Pub. Rels. for Burroughs Welcome, N.Y.C., 1987; project coord. for health svcs. No. Ill. U. Sch. Nursing, DeKalb, 1973-74, instr. 1979-84. Author of numerous articles. Awarded numerous rsch. grants. Mem. ANA, Nat. Coun. State Bds. of Nursing (del. 1988-95, AEC com. mem. 1990-94, mem. nomination com. 1991-92, ednl. program task force 1994-95, alternate examination com. 1994-95), Wyo. Commn. on Nursing & Nursing Edn., Wyo. Orgn. Nurse Execs., Wyo. State Bd. of Nursing Home Adminstrs. (sec. 1988-89, vice-chmn. 1990-95), Wyo. Advanced Practitioner of Nursing Orgn. Office: Wyo State Bd Nursing 2020 Carey Ave Ste 110 Cheyenne WY 82002-0001

NISCE, LOURDES, radiologist; b. Manila, Apr. 13, 1925; m. Francisa N. and Elena (Zandueta) N. MD, U. Santo Tomas, Manila, 1946. Diplomate Am. Bd. Radiology. Intern Holy Name Hosp., Teaneck, N.J., 1952-53; resident N.Y. Hosp.-Cornell Med. Coll., N.Y.C., 1957-61; fellow Meml. Hosp. Sloan-Kettering Ctr., N.Y.C., 1961-62, attending radiation oncologist, 1965-86; prof. radiology N.Y. Hosp., 1965—, Cornell Med. Coll., 1965—. Contbr. articles to med. jours. Fellow Am Coll. Radiology; mem. Am. Coll. Radiologists, Radiol. Soc. N.Am., RADIUM, Am. Soc. Therapeutic Radiology and Oncology. Address: 525 E 68th St Box 575 New York NY 10021-4870

NISCHAN, MICHEL, food service executive; m. Lori Nischan; 4 children. Breakfast cook, 1980; with La Tour, Chgo., Le Perroquet, Chgo.; opened Fleur de Lis, Milw.; opening chef Interstate Hotels Corp.; chef, co-owner Restaurant Miche Mache, Conn.; corp. cons. chef Nieporent's Myriad Restaurant Group; exec. chef Heartbeat, N.Y.C. Active James Beard Found., Peter Kump's Cooking Sch. Restaurant Miche Mache featured BBC, London Times. Named Restaurant Miche Mache in Top Ten, Zagat Restaurant Guide, Best Chef in Conn., Conn. Mag. Office: Heartbeat 149 East 49th St New York NY 10017

NISCHKE, ANN M. state legislator; b. Jan. 19, 1951; BS, U. Wis., Eau Claire, 1977. Real estate marketer; exec. dir. C. of C.; mem. Wis. State Assembly, Madison, 2002—, vice chair econ. devel. com., mem. aging and long-term care com., mem. edn. reform com., mem. energy and utilities com., mem. fin. instns. com., mem. small bus. com. Republican. Office: State Capitol Rm 8 N PO Box 8953 Madison WI 53708-8953 Address: 246 N Racine Ave Waukesha WI 53186

NISENHOLTZ, MARTIN ABRAM, telecommunications executive, educator; b. Phila., Apr. 1, 1955; s. Louis William and Rhoda Greta (Koenig) N.; m. Anne Ermine Stockler, July 26, 1987; children: Johanna, Marjorie. BA, U. Pa., 1977, MA, 1979. Research scientist NYU, N.Y.C., 1979-83; mgr. Ogilvy & Mather, N.Y.C., 1983-84, v.p., 1984-89, sr. v.p., 1989-94; dir. content strategy Ameritech Corp., Chgo., 1994-95; pres. N.Y. Times Electronic Media Co., 1995-99; CEO N.Y. Times Digital, 1999—. Mem. oper. Ogilvy & Mather Direct, 1992—94; adj. assoc. prof. NYU, 1983—; bd. dirs. internet advtsg. bur. Ctr. for Comm., 1999. Mem. Annenberg Sch. Alumni Bd., 1996—. Recipient Merrill Panott Citizenship award, 1997, Ten award, 2003; grantee Nat. Endowment Arts, 1981. Mem.: Online Pubs. Assn. (founding chmn. 2001—), Interactive Svcs. Assn. (dir. 1985—94, chmn. 1991, Disting. Svc. award 1994). Office: NY Times Digital 500 7th Ave New York NY 10018 Business E-Mail: martin@nytimes.com.

NISENSON, JAMES HOWARD, retired government agency administrator; b. Cleve., May 12, 1944; s. Morris Abraham and Florence Lillian (Starkoff) Nisenson; m. Barbara Joy Shichtman, June 15, 1986. BS in Econs., John Carroll U., 1968. Dep. clk. Cuyahoga County Juvenile Ct., Cleve., 1969—70; pub. health inspector USPHS, Honolulu, 1971—73; safety inspector City of Cleve., 1973—78; fraud investigator Cuyahoga County Welfare, Cleve., 1979—81, State of Ohio, Cleve., 1981—2000. Author: Loyal Subject?, 2002. Mem. Beachcliff Number One Homeowners Assn., 1977—; founder, pres. Ohio (Blues) Music Soc., Cleve., 1982—86. Recipient W.C. Handy award, Blues Found., Memphis, 1985. Republican. Jewish. Avocations: lobbying public officials, writing, antiques, coin collecting/numismatics, stamp collecting/philately. Home: 19802 Battersea Blvd Rocky River OH 44116 Office Phone: 440-356-1391. E-mail: jhnisenson@msn.com.

NISH, WAYNE PAUL, chef, restaurant owner; b. N.Y.C., July 23, 1951; s. John and Dorothy (Bugelli) N.; children: Caitlin Nicola, Alexandra Jane. Student, Long Island U., 1969-70, Cornell U., 1972-73, CCNY, 1973-74; diploma, N.Y. Restaurant Sch., 1983. Assoc. chef The Quilted Giraffe, N.Y.C., 1984-87; pvt. chef Anne Bass, N.Y.C., 1987-88; exec. chef La Colombe d'Or, N.Y.C., 1988-89; chef, co-owner March Restaurant, N.Y.C., 1990—. Adv. bd. mem. N.Y. Restaurant Sch., 1991—. Fund raiser Women's Camapign Fund, 1992, 93, 94. Recipient Three Stars award N.Y. Times, 1988, 92, 95, Forbes Mag., 1989, Four Stars award Forbes Mag., 1993, 94; named Am.'s top Restaurant Zagat Survey, 1993, 94, 95. Mem. Am. Inst. Wine and Food, James Beard Found. Democrat. Roman Catholic. Avocations: cooking, photography, driving. Office: March Restaurant 405 E 58th St New York NY 10022-2302 Home: 418 Cedar Ave Nyack NY 10960-1312

NISHI, YOSHIO, electronics executive, laboratory administrator; b. Yokohama, Japan, Mar. 1, 1940; came to U.S., 1986; s. Fumio and Mineko (Koizumi) N.; m. Miwako Miyake, Sept. 15, 1969; children: Toshiya, Miho. BS, Weseda U., Tokyo, 1962; PhD, U. Tokyo, 1973. Mem. tech. staff R & D Ctr. Toshiba, Kawasaki, Japan, 1962-69, supr. semiconductor div., 1969-71, sr. supr. R & D Ctr., 1971-75, sect. mgr. R & D Ctr., 1976-79, dept. mgr. semiconductor devic lab., 1979-85; lab. dir. Hewlett-Packard Labs., Palo Alto, Calif., 1986-95; sr. v.p., dir. R & D Tex. Instruments, Dallas, 1995—. Bd. dirs. KLA Instrument Copr., Santa Clara, Calif., TMA Inc., Palo Alto; cons. prof. elec. engrng. Stanford U., 1986—; mem. Com. of Japan, NRC, Washington, 1988—. Author: Silicon Integrated Circuit, 1981; editor: LSI Handbook, 1983; patentee in field; contbr. articles to tech. jours. Disting. speaker Stanford U. Computer Forum, 1986; named one of 100 in Indsl. R D, Chgo., 1982, 84, 86. Fellow IEEE (Jack A. Morton award 1995); mem. The Electrochem. Soc., Inst. Electronics and Communication Engrs. (Best Paper award Japan), Japan Soc. Applied Physics. Office: Tex Instruments MS225 13510 N Central Expy Dallas TX 75243-1108

NISHIDA, MIEKO, educator; arrived in U.S., 1985; BA, Hiroshima (Japan) U., 1982; MA, U. Tsukuba, Japan, 1984, Johns Hopkins U., 1987, PhD, 1991. Rockefeller Found. postdoctoral fellow U. Tex., Austin, 1992—93; postodoctoral fellow Emory U., Atlanta, 1993—95; lectr. in history U. Va., Charlottesville, 1996—97; postdoctoral fellow U. Md., College Park, 1997—98; asst. prof. Hartwick Coll., Oneonta, NY, 1998—2004, assoc. prof., 2004—. Contbr. articles to profl. jours.; author: Slavery and Identity: Ethnicity, Gender and Race in Salvador, Brazil, 1808-1888, 2003. Fellow Predoctoral Rsch. fellow, Carter G. Woodson Inst., U. Va., 1989—91; Summer Vis. Scholar fellow, U. Chgo.-U. Ill. Urbana-Champaign Joint Ctr. for Latin Am. Studies, 2000, Trustee Rsch. grantee, Hartwick Coll., 1999, 2001, 2002, Libr. Scholars Summer grantee, David Rockefeller Ctr. for Latin Am. Studies, Harvard U., 2000, Albert J. Beveridge grantee, Am. Hist. Assn., 2001. Mem.: The Hist. Soc., Conf. on Latin Am. History, Oral History Assn., Brazilian Studies Assn., Latin Am. Studies Assn., Am. Hist. Assn. Office: Hartwick Coll Dept History Oneonta NY 13820 Office Phone: 607-431-4839. E-mail: nishidam@hartwick.edu.

NISHIMURA, JOSEPH YO, retired retail executive, accountant; b. Berkeley, Calif., Nov. 4, 1933; s. Masamoto and Kimiko (Ishihara) N.; m. Joyce Toshiye Mori, Sept. 1, 1956; children: Brenda Joyce, Stephen Lloyd. AB cum laude, Princeton U., 1956; MBA, Stanford U., 1961. CPA, Calif., N.Y.; cert. Employee Benefit Specialist. Audit supr. Touche Ross & Co., San Francisco, 1961-66; contr. Scott Co. of Calif., Oakland, 1966-67, Purity Stores, Inc., Burlingame, Calif., 1967-69; pres. Cubit Sys. Corp., Burlingame, 1969-72; sr. v.p. Golden West Fin. Corp., Oakland, 1972-73; exec. v.p. Victory Mkts., Inc., Norwich, N.Y., 1973-90; gen. ptnr. Mori Enterprises, 1994—. Dir. Carl's Drug Co., Rome, N.Y., 1988-90, mem. site devel. com., Wakefern Food Corp., Edison, N.J., 1996—. V.p., bd. dirs. Chenango Meml. Hosp., Norwich, 1981-87; bd. dirs. United Fund, Norwich, 1984-90, N.Y. State Food Mchts. Assn., 1988-90, Binghamton (N.Y.) Philharmonic, 1988-98, treas., 1990-93. Served to lt. (j.g.) USN, 1956-59; Japan. Mem. AICPA, Calif. Soc. CPAs, Marbella Country Club, Princeton (N.Y.C.) Club. Democrat. Presbyterian.

NISHIMURA, MASAO, diversified financial services company executive; Former CEO Indsl. Bank Japan, Tokyo; chmn., co-CEO Mizuho Holdings Inc., Japan, 2000—02. Office: Maunouchi Center Bldg 6-1 Marunouchi 1 chome Chiyoda-ku Tokyo Japan

NISHIMURA, PETE HIDEO, oral surgeon; b. Hilo, Hawaii, Aug. 7, 1922; s. Hideichi and Satsuki N.; m. Tomoe Nishimura, June, 1949; children—Dennis Dean, Grant Neil, Dawn Naomi. Student, U. Hawaii, 1940-44; D.D.S., U. Mo., 1947; MSD., Northwestern U., 1949. Practice dentistry specializing in oral surgery, Honolulu, 1952—; pres. Oral Surgery Group, 1978—. Mem. coun. Nat. Bd. Dental Examination; dir. Hawaii Dental Svc., 1962-85, pres., 1970-72, 76-78; pres. State Bd. Dental Examiners, Delta Sigma Delta, Fedn. Dentaire Internat. Served with U.S. Army, 1952-54. Named Disting. Alumni, U. Mo. Hawaii, 2004; recipient Citation for outstanding pub. svc. toward the devel. of state plan for emergency mgmt. resources, Dir. Emergency Planning, Exec. Office of Pres. of U.S., 1968. Fellow Am. Coll. Dentists, Internat. Coll. Dentists; mem. Hawaii Dental Assn. (past pres.), Delta Dental Plans Assn. (dir.), Honolulu County Dental Soc., ADA, Hawaii Soc. Oral Surgeons, Am. Assn. Oral and Maxillofacial Surgeons, Western Soc. Oral and Maxillofacial Surgeons, Am. Assn. Dental Examiners, Pierre Fauchard Acad. (citation for oustanding contbn. to arts and sci. of dentistry 1987). Democrat. Home: 494 Halemaumau St Honolulu HI 96821-2135 Office: 848 S Beretania St Honolulu HI 96813-2551 E-mail: hilopete@aol.com.

NISHIYAMA, CHIAKI, economist, educator; b. Fukuoka-ken, Japan, Aug. 9, 1924; s. Michiki and Teruko (Tsuji) N.; m. Shigeko Okabe, June 9, 1957; children: Keita, Mikiko. BA in Econs., Rikkyo U., Tokyo, 1950; MA in Polit. Sci., U. Chgo., 1952, PhD in Social Thought, 1960, postgrad. in econs., 1959-60. Lectr. U. Chgo., 1957-61; assoc. prof. Rikkyo U., 1962-64, prof. econs., 1964-90, prof. emeritus, 1990—. Sr. rsch. fellow Hoover Instn., Stanford U., 1977—; prof. econs. Grad. Sch. Internat. Mgmt., U. Japan, 1994-97; lectr. Tng. Inst., Min. Trade and Industry, Japanese Govt., 1964-66, Gakushuin U., 1970-71, Waseda U., 1972-74; exec. dir. Assembly on U.S.-Japan Econ. Policy, 1972-76; prime minister's spl. envoy to White House, 1971, 75; specialist counselor Japan Employers' Assn., 1975-85; del. European Assembly, Strasbourg, France, 1982; world travel for Japanese Min. Fgn. Affairs, Japan External Trade Orgn., 1968-82; lectr. various univs., U.S. and Europe, 1976-94; mem. Am. Citizen to Citizen Econ. and Fin. Mgmt. Del. to the USSR, 1991; spl. envoy of Japan to Germany, Czechoslovakia, Hungary, Bulgaria, Ukraine, Russia, 1991. Author numerous books including: Lecture on Modern Economics, 1964, Free Economy, Its Policies and Principles, 1974, The Price for Prosperity, 1974, A Monetary History and Analysis of the Japanese Economy, 1968-70, 74, Reflection on Japanese Economy, 1976, Monetarism, 1976, The Last Chance for Creativity, Liberty and Prosperity, 1981, Human Capitalism, 1982, The Fourth Philosophy, Vol. I, 1982, Vol. II, 1983, No Limits to Growth, 1984, The Essence of Hayek, 1984, The Japanese Economy, 1987, Paradigm Shift, 1987, Japanese Economy and Life Tomorrow, 1988, A New Economics Under a New Paradigm, 1991, The End of Recession, 1994, Depression or New Prosperity, 1998, Market Economy: New Way, 1999, Chicago Boys, 2003; editl. bd. Jour. Internat. Money and Fin., 1981—. Hon. fellow Inst. Econ. Affairs, London, 1976—; mem. adv. bd. Econ. Inst. Paris, 1984-86, Carl Menger Inst., Wien, 1984; councilor The Daiwa Securities Welfare Found., 1994—. Recipient Japan Econ. Lit. award Japan Econ. Jour., 1974; Eahart fellow, 1960-61, E.C. Nef fellow, 1958-59, Woodrow Wilson Internat. Ctr. for Scholars fellow, 1976-77; grantee Relm, 1962-64, Ford, 1965-66, Lilly, 1966-67, Bank of Japan, Bankers Assn. Japan, other fin. orgns., 1978-83. Mem. Am. Enterprise Inst. (adj. scholar), Am. Econ. Assn., Econometric Soc., Japan Econs. Assn., Econ. Assn., Statis. Soc., Mont Pelerin Soc. (pres. 1980-82, sr. v.p. 1982-85, hon. v.p. 1986-88), Japan Econ. Rsch. Ctr. (spl. mem. 1964). Episcopalian. Office: Nishiyama-Kenkyushitsu 5-15-18 Kamiuma Setagaya-ku 154-0011 Tokyo Japan

NISKANEN, WILLIAM ARTHUR, JR., economist, think-tank executive; b. Bend, Oreg., Mar. 13, 1933; s. William Arthur and Nina Elizabeth (McCord) Niskanen; m. Kathryn Washburn; children: Lia, Pamela, Jaime. BA, Harvard U., 1954; MA, U. Chgo., 1955, PhD, 1962. Staff economist RAND Corp., Santa Monica, Calif., 1957—62; staff dir. U.S. Dept. Def., Washington, 1962—64; divsn. dir. Inst. Def. Analyses, Washington, 1964—70; asst. dir. Office of Mgmt. and Budget, Washington, 1970—72; prof. U. Calif., Berkeley, 1972—75; chief economist Ford Motor Co., Dearborn, Mich., 1975—80; prof. UCLA, 1980—81; mem. Coun. Econ. Advisers, Washington, 1981—85; chmn. CATO Inst., Washington, 1985—. Author: Bureaucracy and Representative Goverment, 1971, Reaganomics, 1988, Policy Analysis and Public Choic, 1998, Going Digital, 1998, Autocratic, Democratic and Optimal Government, 2004; editor: Regulation mag., 1990—96. Founder Nat. Tax Limitation Com. Mem.: Atlantic Econ. Assn. (past pres.), Pub. Choice Soc. (past pres.), Am. Econ. Assn. Republican. Office: Cato Inst 1000 Massachusetts Ave NW Washington DC 20001-5400 Office Phone: 202-789-5236. E-mail: wniskan@cato.org.

NISSEN, DAVID R. utilities executive; B, Northwestern U., 1975; MBA, U. Chgo. Staff strategic planning and bus. devel. G.E. Captial, 1981—83; mktg. G.E. Card Svcs., 1983—87, gen. mgr., 1987—90, G.E. U.S. Consumer Fin. Svcs., 1990—93; officer G.E., 1996—2001, sr. v.p., 2001—; pres., CEO G.E. Consumer Fin., 2002—. Avocations: golf, tennis, jet skiing. Office: GE Global Consumer Fin 1600 Summer St Stamford CT 06927

NISSENBLATT, MICHAEL JEFFREY, medical oncologist; b. Bronx, N.Y., 1948; MD, Columbia P&S, 1973. Diplomate Am. Bd. Internal Medicine. Intern Johns Hopkins, Balt., 1973-74, resident, 1974-75, 75-76, fellow, 1976-78; co-dir. med. oncology RW Johnson U. Hosp., New Brunswick, 1996—; staff St. Peter's Med. Ctr., New Brunswick; clin. prof. medicine RW Johnson U. Sch. Medicine, 1996—. Fellow Am. Coll. Physicians; mem. AMA, Am. Assn. Adv. Sci., Am. Radiol. Soc., Am. Soc. Clin. Oncology, Chemotherapy Found., Johns Hopkins Med. Surgeons Soc., Maimonides Soc., Middlesex County Med. Soc., N.J. Breast Cancer Coalition, others. Office: Ctrl Jersey Oncology Ctr PA 205 Easton Ave New Brunswick NJ 08901-1722 Office Phone: 732-828-9570.

NISSENSON, ALLEN RICHARD, physician, educator; b. Chgo., Dec. 10, 1946; s. Harry and Sylvia Lillian (Chapnitsky) N.; m. Charna H. Karp, May 28, 1978; 1 child, Ariel Rose. BS in Medicine, Northwestern U., 1967, MD, 1971. Diplomate Am. Bd. Internal Medicine, bd. cert. internal medicine and nephrology. Intern in medicine Michael Reese Hosp. and Med. Ctr., Chgo., 1971-72, resident in internal medicine, 1972-74; fellowship in nephrology Northwestern U., Chgo., 1974-76; assoc. medicine Northwestern U. Med. Sch., Chgo., 1976-77; asst. prof. medicine UCLA Sch. Medicine, 1977-82, assoc. prof. medicine, 1982-88, prof. medicine, 1988—; dir. dialysis program UCLA Ctr. for the Health Scis., 1977—, med. dir. renal mgmt. strategies. Adj. attending physician Northwestern Meml. Hosp., Chgo., 1976-77; asst. attending physician UCLA Ctr. for Health Scis., 1977-82, assoc. attending physician, 1988—; attending physician nephrology Wadsworth VA Hosp., 1978—; cons. on peritoneal dialysis Baxter-Travenol Labs., 1981—; mem. nephrology adv. com. Nephrology Nursing Edn. Grant, Calif. State U., 1983-90; vice chmn. Forum of End Stage Renal Disease Networks, 1988-91; mem. sci. adv. bd. Nat. Kidney Found., 1989-91, chmn. coun. on clin. nephrology, dialysis and transplantation, 1989-91; cons. on End Stage Renal Disease reimbursement Rand Corp., 1990—, others. Editor-in-chief Advances in Renal Replacement Therapy, 1993—, Hemodialysis Internat., 2004—; mem. editl. bd. Dialysis and Transplantation, 1978—, UCLA Health Insights, 1981-89, Perspectives in Peritoneal Dialysis, 1983—, Internat. Jour. Artificial Organs, 1984—, Seminars in Dialysis, 1987—, Am. Jour. Nephrology, 1989—, Am. Jour. Kidney Diseases, 1989—, Geriat. Nephrology and Urology Jour., 1989—; mem. editl. adv. bd. Contemporary Dialysis, 1983—, Nephrology Practice Today, 1989—, Hematopoietic Therapy Index and Revs., 1993—, Primary Care Reports, 1994—; editl. cons. Am. Jour. Nephrology, 1981-88; contbr. chpts. to books, abstracts and articles to profl. publs. Recipient Nat. Kidney Found. So. Calif. Cmty. Svc. award, 1981; Robert Wood Johnson policy fellow Office of Sen. Paul Wellstone, 1994-95. Fellow ACP; mem. Am. Soc. for Artifical Internal Organs, Am. Fedn. for Clin. Rsch., Am. Soc. Nephrology, Internat. Soc. Nephrology, Internat. Soc. Artificial Organs, Western Soc. for Clin. Investigation, European Dialysis and Transplant Assn., N.Am. Soc. for Dialysis and Transplantation, Renal Physicians' Assn. (bd. dirs. 1993—, sec. bd. dirs. 1994—, pres. 1999-2001), Calif. Renal Physicians (bd. dirs. 1987—). Office: UCLA Med Ctr Dialysis Ctr Ste 565-59 200 Medical Plaza Los Angeles CA 90024-6945 E-mail: anissenson@mednet.ucla.edu.

NISSIM, SHAI, special education educator, consultant; s. Oved Aicha and Nadia Aicha-Ora. MEd(hon.), Bkyn. Coll., 1995; EdD, Columbia U., 2003. Lic. N.Y. State Edn. Dept., 1995, cert. Bilingual (Hebrew/English)tchr. N.Y. State Edn. Dept., 1996. Spl. edn. tchr. United Cerebral Palsy, N.Y.C., 1991—; ESL/CLD instr. Interagency Coun. Mental Retardation, N.Y.C., 1996—; ednl. evaluator N.Y. Devel., N.Y.C., 1999—2002. Sgt Isreali Defense Forces, 1980—83. Mem.: Tchrs. English to Spkr. of other Languages (assoc.), Am. Assn. Mental Retardation (assoc.). Democrat. Jewish. Avocations: travel, swimming, camping. Office: PO Box 7069 New York NY 10116 Personal E-mail: snissim1@aol.com.

NISSINEN, MIKKO PEKKA, dancer; b. Helsinki, Finland, Mar. 4, 1962; arrived in U.S., 1987; s. Pekka and Pirkko (Pulkkinen) Nissinen. Grad., Finnish Nat. Ballet Sch., 1977; postgrad., Leningrad Acad. Ballet Sch., 1979-80. Mem. corps de ballet Finnish Nat. Ballet, Helsinki, 1977-79, soloist, 1980-82; grand sujete Dutch Nat. Ballet, Amsterdam, The Netherlands, 1982-84; soloist Basel (Switzerland) Ballet, 1984-87, San Francisco Ballet, 1987-88, prin. dancer, 1988-96; artistic dir. Marin Ballet, 1996-97, Alberta Ballet, Calgary, Canada, 1998—2002, Boston Ballet, 2001—. Guest artist La Bayadere Nat. Ballet Can., 1989; guest artist Oberlin Dance Collective, 1993; bd. dirs. Le Don Des Etoiles; guest tchr. Royal Acad. Danciang, 1993, Kennedy Ctr. Ednl. Program, 1994, Nat. Ballet Sch., Toronto, 1994; lectr. on dance history and state of dance today Stanford U., Leathbridge U., St. Mary's Coll., Christensen Soc.; artistic com. N.Y. Choreographic Inst. Dancer Sleeping Beauty, San Francisco Ballet, Swan Lake, Bizet Pas de Deux, Handel-a Celebration, Haffner Symphony, Variations de Ballet, Rodin, Rodeo, Con Brio, Ballet d'Isoline, Giuliani: Variations on a Theme, Tchaikovsky Pas de Deux, Symphony in C, Theme and Variations, Ballo della Regina, The Nutcracker, Airs de Ballet, Maelstrom, Dark Elegies, Harvest Moon, Napoli, Job, The Wanderer Fantasy, In the middle, somewhat elevated, Calcium Light Night, Le Corsaire Pas de Deux, Dreams of Harmony, Pulcinella, The Dream, Don Quixote, Giselle, A Midsummer Night's Dream, Les Biches, Sleeping Beauty, Pyrrich Dances, Masse, Le Tombeau de Couperin, Symphony in C, The Four Temperaments, The Prodigal Son, Rodin, Pierrot Lunaire, La Fille mal gardée, Swan Lake, Henze, Five Tangos, In and Out, Bits and Pieces, Jeu de Cartes, Gala Des Etoiles, Can. Internat. Ballet Gala, 1989, 1990, 1991, 1992, 1993, 1994, 1995, Reykjavik Arts Festival, 1990, Internat. Ballet Gala, Kuodio, Finland, 1992, Vail, Colo., 1993, Night of Stars Ballet Gala, Helsinki, 1993, choreographer Full Evening Nutcracker, Marin Ballet, 1996, Alta. Ballet, 2000. Recipient 1st prize Nat. Dance Competition, Kuopio, Finland, 1978; fellowship exec. program for non-profit leaders, Stanford Univ. Office: Boston Ballet 19 Clarendon St Boston MA 02116-6100

NISSMAN, DAVID M. lawyer; b. 1953; m. Carolina Zapata Nissman; 3 children. BA magna cum laude, Emory U., 1975; JD, U. Oreg., 1978. Dep. dist. atty., Eugene, Oreg.; adj. law prof. U. Oreg.; U.S. atty. St. Croix, V.I.; pub. Office of Legal Edn., Dept. of Justice; U.S. atty. Dist. of Virgin Islands. CEO Bridge Capital, Corpus Juris Pub. Co. Author: Proving Federal Crimes, 2001. Recipient Chief Inspector's Award, USPS, 1991, NRC Award, 1994, Environmental Div. Award, U.S. Dept. Justice, 2000, Dir. Awards, Exec. Office U.S. Attys. Office: US Courthouse 5500 Veterans Dr Rm 260 St Thomas VI 00802

NISWENDER, GORDON DEAN, physiologist, educator; b. Gillette, Wyo., Apr. 21, 1940; s. Rex Lel and Inez Irene (Dillinger) N.; m. Joy Dean Thayer, June 14, 1964; children: Kevin Dean, Kory Dean. BS, U. Wyo., 1962; MS, U. Nebr., 1964; PhD, U. Ill., 1967. NIH postdoctoral fellow U. Mich., 1967-68, asst. prof. physiology, 1968-72; mem. faculty Colo. State U., Ft. Collins, 1972—, prof. physiology, 1975—; assoc. dean research Coll. Veterinary Medicine and Biomed. Scis., 1982-95, dir. animal reproduction and biotech. lab., 1986—, disting. prof., 1987—. Mem. rev. panels NIH; cons. FDA. Recipient Merit award NIH, 1988-99, grantee, 1968—. Mem.: Soc. Study Reprodn. (treas. 1972-75, pres. 1981-82, editor-in-chief Biology of Reprodn. 1995—99, Rsch. award 1988, Disting. Svc. award, 2001), Am. Assn. Animal Scientists (Outstanding Young Scientist award western sect., 1974, animal Physiology and Endocrinology award 1983). Office: Colo State U Animal Reprod & Biotech Lab College Of Veterinary Med Fort Collins CO 80523-1683

NITECKI, JOSEPH ZBIGNIEW, librarian; b. Dabrowa Górnicza, Poland, Jan. 31, 1922; came to U.S., 1951, naturalized, 1956; s. Henryk W. and Antonina S. N.; m. Sophie V. Zboinski, June 17, 1945; children: Zbigniew H., Danuta A. BA in Philosophy, Wayne State U., 1955; MA, Roosevelt U., 1959; MA in L.S., U. Chgo., 1963. Various profl. and adminstrv. positions in libraries U. Chgo., 1961-63, Chgo. City Coll., 1963-66, U. Wis., Milw., 1967-70, Temple U., Phila., 1970-78; prof., exec. dir. libraries U. Wis., Oshkosh, 1978-80; dir. libraries SUNY, Albany, 1980-88, prof. Sch. Info Sci. and Policy, 1988-90, prof. emeritus, 1990—. Cons. library issues. Author, editor compiler and reviewer in field; ref. and manuscript reader. Served with Polish Armed Forces under Brit. command, 1939-48. Recipient 1st. prize Polish Émigré Poetry Contest, 2001. Mem. ALA, Beta Phi Mu. Home: 430 Coburg Village Way Rexford NY 12148-1461 E-mail: jzniteckisr@aol.com.

NITIKMAN, FRANKLIN W. lawyer; b. Davenport, Iowa, Oct. 26, 1940; s. David A. and Janette (Gordon) N.; m. Adrienne C. Drell, Nov. 28, 1972. BA, Northwestern U., 1963; LLB, Yale U., 1966. Bar: Ill. 1966, U.S. Dist. Ct. (no. dist.) Ill. 1967, U.S. Tax Ct. 1972, Fla. 1977, D.C. 1981. Assoc. McDermott, Will & Emery, Chgo., 1966-72, ptnr., 1973—. Co-author: Drafting Wills and Trust Agreements, 1990. Bd. dirs. Owen Coon Found., Glenview, Ill., 1985—, Jewish Fedn. Met. Chgo., Jewish United Fund, 1994—2003, Spertus Inst. Jewish Studies, Chgo., 1991—, chmn. bd., 1999—2002. Fellow Am. Coll. Trust and Estate Coun., Am. Bar Found.; mem. Standard Club, Arts Club (Chgo.). Home: 365 Lakeside Pl Highland Park IL 60035-5371 Office: McDermott Will & Emery 227 W Monroe St Ste 4700 Chicago IL 60606-5096 E-mail: fnitikman@mwe.com.

NITKA, ALICE W. social services administrator, state representative; b. Little Falls, N.Y., Dec. 13, 1944; m. Martin Nitka; children: Abigail, Molly. Ba, Russell Sage Coll., 1967. Social worker; with Vt. Achievement Ctr., Inc.; rep. Vt. State Ho. Reps., 1999—. Justice of the peace; mem. Ludlow Planning Commn., Zoning Bd. Adjustment; bd. dir. Ludlow Bd. Civil Authority; chmn. bd. Rutland Regional Bd. Family Svcs. Mem.: Vt. Foster and Adoptive Families Assn., Black River Valley Rod and Gun Club. Democrat. Home: North Hill PO Box 136 Ludlow VT 05149

NITOWSKY, HAROLD MARTIN, physician, educator; b. Bklyn., Feb. 12, 1925; s. Max and Fannie (Gershowitz) N.; m. Myra Heller, Nov. 28, 1954; children— Fran Ellen, Daniel Howard. AB, N.Y. U., 1944, MD, 1947; MS, U. Colo., 1952. Intern Mt. Sinai Hosp., N.Y.C., 1947-48; resident pediats. U. Colo. Med. Center, 1948-50; USPHS postdoctoral fellow U. Colo., 1950-51; staff Sinai Hosp., Balt., 1953-67, dir. pediat. rsch., 1960-67; faculty Johns Hopkins Sch. Medicine, 1953-67, assoc. prof. ob-gyn., pediats., molecular genetics, 1962-67; prof. pediats. and genetics Albert Einstein Coll. Medicine, 1967—. Cons. Nat. Inst. Child Health and Human Devel., 1966—; Sr. surgeon USPHS, 1951-53 Contbr. articles on nutrition, metabolism, genetics to profl. jours. Mem. Am. Pediat. Soc., Soc. Pediat. Rsch., Am. Soc. Human Genetics. Home: 25 Devonshire Rd New Rochelle NY 10804-3925 Office: Albert Einstein Coll Med Dept Ob-Gyn Divsn Reproductive Genetics 1695 Eastchester Rd Bronx NY 10461-2374 Office Phone: 718-405-8150. Personal E-mail: nidoc@aol.com.

NITSCHE, JOHANNES CARL CHRISTIAN, mathematics professor; b. Olbernhau, Germany, Jan. 22, 1925; came to U.S., 1956; s. Ludwig Johannes and Irma (Raecke) N.; m. Carmen Dolores Mercado Delgado, July 1, 1959; children: Carmen Irma, Johannes Marcos and Ludwig Carlos (twins). Diplom für Mathematik, U. Göttingen, 1950; PhD, U. Leipzig, 1951; Privatdozent, Tech. U. Berlin, 1955. Asst. U. Göttingen, 1948-50; rsch. mathematician Max Planck Institut für Strömungsforschung Göttingen, 1950-52; asst. Privatdozent Tech. U., Berlin, 1952-56; vis. assoc. prof. U. Cin., 1956-57; assoc. prof. U. Minn., Mpls., 1957-60, prof. math., 1960—2000, head Sch. Math., 1971-78, prof. emeritus, 2000—. Vis. prof. U. P.R., 1960-61, U. Hamburg, 1965, Tech. Hochschule Vienna, 1968, U. Bonn, 1971, 75, 77, 80, 81, U. Heidelberg, 1979, 82, 83, U. Munich, 1983, U. Florence, 1983, Tech. Hochschule Aachen, 1997, 98, 99, 2001; keynote spkr. Festive Colloquium, U. Ulm, 1986; co-organizer workshop statis. thermodynamics and differential geometry U. Minn., 1991; keynote spkr. Meml. Colloquium Tech. U. Berlin, 1991, spkr. Internat. Workshop on Geometry and Interfaces, Aussois, France, 1990, others. Author: Vorlesungen uber Minimalflachen, Springer-Verlag, 1975, Lectures on Minimal Surfaces, 1989; mem. editorial bd. Archive of Rational Mechanics and Analysis, 1967-91; editor: Analysis, 1980—; assoc. editor: Contemporary Math., 1980-88, Zeitschrift für Analysis und ihre Anwendungen, 1993—; contbr. articles to profl. jours. Mem. Am. del. joint Soviet-Am. Symposium on Partial Differential Equations, Novosibirsk, 1963, U.S.-Japan Seminar on Differential Geometry, Tokyo, 1977; speaker 750th Berlin Anniversary Colloquium, Free U. Berlin, 1987. Recipient Lester R. Ford award for outstanding expository writing, 1975, George Taylor Disting. Svc. award U. Minn. Found., 1980, Humboldt prize for sr. U.S. scientists Alexander von Humboldt Found., 1981; Fulbright rsch. fellow Stanford, 1955-56. Fellow AAAS; mem. Am. Math. Soc., Circolo Matematico di Palermo, Deutsche Mathematiker-Vereinigung, Edinburgh Math. Soc., Gesellschaft für Angewandte Mathematik und Mechanik, Math. Assn. Am., N.Y. Acad. Scis., Österreichische Mathematische Gesellschaft, Soc. Natural Philosophy. Home: 2765 Dean Pky Minneapolis MN 55416-4382

NITTA, DOUGLAS, family practice physician; b. Seattle, Mar. 30, 1954; s. Susumu and Donna (Tokuda) N. BA in Chemistry magna cum laude, U. Wash., 1976, MD, 1980. Diplomate Am. Bd. Family Practice. Internship, resident Irvine Med. Ctr. U. Calif., 1980-83; mem. active staff St. Jude Med. Ctr., Fullerton, Calif., 1982—, chmn. dept. family practice, 1989—. Pres., bd. dirs. St. Jude Med. Group, Inc., Fullerton, Calif., 1996—; mem. adv. bd. St. Jude Heritage Health Found., 1997-99; chmn. primary care dept. St. Jude Med. Ctr., 1999. Fellow Am. Acad. Family Physicians; mem. Calif. Med. Assn., Phi Beta Kappa. Office: 301 W Bastanchury Rd Ste 155 Fullerton CA 92835-3477

NITTOLY, PAUL GERARD, lawyer; b. Bklyn., July 13, 1948; s. Edward Joseph and Philomena (Lorenzo) Nittoly; m. Maryann Racioppi, May 31, 1970; children: Melissa Beth, Matthew Edward. AB, Rutgers U., 1970; JD, NYU, 1973. Bar: N.J., U.S. Dist. Ct. NJ 1973, U.S. Supreme Ct. 1979, U.S. Ct. Appeals (3d cir.) 1990, U.S. Dist. Ct. (so. and ea. dist.) NY 1998, cert.: NJ Supreme Ct. (trial atty. civil and criminal law). Asst. prosecutor, sr. trial atty. Essex County Prosecutor's Office, Newark, 1974-79; ptnr. Shanley & Fisher, P.C., Morristown, NJ, 1979-99, Drinker Biddle & Shanley LLP, Florham Park, NJ, 1999—2003, Drinker Biddle & Reath, LLP, Florham Park, 2003—. Moot trial ct. judge Seton Hall Law Sch., Newark, 1982—; lectr. symposium perinatal malpractice ACOG and Rutgers U. Med. Sch., Morristown, NJ, 1984; mem. practitioner's adv. group U.S. Sentencing Commn., 1992—. Author: Readings in White Collar Crime, 1991; mem. editl. adv. bd. Corporate Criminal Liability Reporter; contbr. chapters to books. Past pres., master C. Willard Heckel Am. Inn. of Ct.; del. adv. Am. Bd. Trial Advs.; trustee Pub. Interest Law Ctr. N.J., 1998—2003; v.p. Legal Svcs. Found. Essex County. Capt. U.S. Army, 1972. Mem.: ABA, Assn. Fed. Bar State N.J. (trustee 2000—), Trial Attys. N.J. (v.p.), Assn. Criminal Def. Attys. N.J., Nat. Assn. Criminal Def. Lawyers, Morris County Bar Assn., Essex County Bar Assn. (pres. 1998—99), N.J. Bar Assn., Park Ave. Club (Morristown), Delta Upsilon. Roman Catholic. Home: 275 Meetinghouse Ln Mountainside NJ 07092-1305 Office: Drinker Biddle & Reath LLP 500 Campus Dr Fl 4 Florham Park NJ 07932-1047 Office Phone: 973-549-7180. E-mail: paul.nittoly@dbr.com.

NITZARIM, YOEL DAVID, language educator; b. Chgo., Aug. 29, 1949; s. Maurice and Elaine Pearl Smith; m. Esther Marsha Nitzarim; children: Rachel Sarah, Gavriella Leebah. BA, Northeastern Ill. U., Chgo., 1974; MEd, Northeastern Ill. U., 1983. English tchr. Austin Career Edn. Ctr., Chgo., 1989—92; asst. prof. of English East-West U., Chgo., 1999—2002; English instr. Benedictine U., Lisle, Ill., 2002—03, Morton Coll., Cicero, Ill., 2004—. Author: (essays, poetry, photography, short stories) Affair of the Mind; contbr. articles to profl. jours. Mem.: English Teachers Assn. of Israel. Jewish. Avocations: reading, writing music, travel, dogs. Office: Morton College 3801 South Central Ave Cicero IL 60804-4398 Office Phone: 708-656-8000. Personal E-mail: ynitzari1@aol.com. E-mail: hamakor 469@aol.com.

NITZE, WILLIAM ALBERT, government official, lawyer, not-for-profit developer, energy executive; b. NYC, Sept. 27, 1942; s. Paul Henry and Phyllis (Pratt) N.; m. Ann Kendall Richards, June 5, 1971; children: Paul Kendall, Charles Richards. BA, Harvard U., 1964, JD, 1969; BA, Oxford U., 1966. Bar: N.Y. 1970, U.S. Supreme Ct. 1987. Assoc. Sullivan and Cromwell, N.Y.C., 1970-72; v.p. London Arts, Inc., N.Y.C., 1972-73; counsel Mobil South, Inc., N.Y.C., 1974-76; gen. counsel Mobil Oil Japan, Tokyo, 1976-80; asst. gen. counsel exploration and producing divsn. Mobil Oil Corp., N.Y.C., 1980-87; dep asst. sec. for environment, health and natural resources U.S. Dept. State, Washington, 1987-90; pres. Alliance to Save Energy, Washington, 1990-94; asst. adminstr. for internat. activities U.S. EPA, Washington, 1994-2001; pres. Gemstar Group, Washington, 2001—; chmn. Equinox Energy Solutions Inc., 2003—. Mem. adv. com. Sch. Advanced Internat. Studies, Washington, 1982-95, professorial lectr., 1993-94, 2001—; vis. scholar Environ. Law Inst., Washington, 1990; bd. dirs. Charles A. Lindbergh Fund, Mpls., 1990-94, Nat. Symphony Orch. Assn., Washington, 1990-2002, Atlantic Coun. U.S., Washington, 2002—; bd. dirs. Charles Darwin Found., Inc., 2001—, Falls Church, Va., vice chmn. 2002—03, chmn. 2003-; bd. dirs. Climate Inst., Washington, 2001-, vice chmn., 2001-02, chmn., 2002—. Trustee Aspen Inst., Queenstown, Md., 1988—, Krasnow Inst., Fairfax, Va., 1996-2001. Mem.: Coun. on Fgn. Rels., Assn. Bar City NY, Links Club, Cosmos Club, Met. Club. Republican. Episcopalian. Avocations: running, piano, collecting art. Home: 1537 28th St NW Washington DC 20007-3059 Office: Gemstar Group Ste 100 1785 Mass Ave NW Washington DC 20036 Office Phone: 202-756-2800. Business E-Mail: wanitze@gemstargroup.org.

NIVARTHI, RAJU NAGA, anesthesiology educator; b. Nandyal, India, June 16, 1964; came to U.S., 1993; s. Kameswara Sarma and Suseelamma Nivarthi; m. Aparna Nagaraju Nivarthi; children: Nidhi, Aditya. BSc with Chemistry, Zoology and Botany, Sri Venkateswara U., Tirupati, India, 1984; MSc in Biochemistry, Sri Kirshnadevaraya U., Anantapur, India, 1986; PhD, U. Hyderabad, 1996. Fellow Sch. Life Scis., U. Hyderabad, India, 1987-93; rsch. asst. prof. dept. anesthesiology NYU Med. Ctr., N.Y.C., 1996, scientist, 1996-99, Wyeth-Ayerst Rsch., Pearl River, N.Y., 1999-2001; sr. scientist, mgr. analytical biochemistry Bristol-Myers Squibb, Syracuse, NY, 2001—. Contbr. articles to profl. jours. Jr. Rsch. fellow Coun. Sci. and Indsl. Rsch., India, 1987, Sr. Rsch. fellow Coun. Sci. and Indsl. Rsch., 1990, Postdoctoral fellow NIH, 1998; recipient cert. of merit Pharmacia & Biotech Prize for Young Scientists, 1997, named 2000 Outstanding Scientist of 20th Century, 1998, Internat. Biographical Ctr. Mem. AAAS, Acad. Med. Cmty., Am. Chem. Soc., Am. Soc. Anesthesiologists, Am. Soc. Biochemistry and Molecular Biology, Internat. Anesthesia Rsch. Soc., Internat. Soc. for Study of Xenobiotics, Nat. Geographic Soc., N.Y. Acad. Scis. Office: Bristol-Myer Squibb 6000 Thompson Rd East Syracuse NY 13057-5050 Home: 161 North Way Camillus NY 13031-1253 Office Phone: 315-432-9612. Personal E-mail: rnivarthi@yahoo.com.

NIVISON, DAVID SHEPHERD, Chinese and philosophy educator; b. Farmingdale, Maine, Jan. 17, 1923; s. William and Ruth (Robinson) N.; m. Cornelia Green, Sept. 11, 1944; children— Louise, Helen Thom, David Gregory, James Nicholas. AB summa cum laude, Harvard U., 1946, MA, 1948, PhD, 1953. Instr. Chinese Stanford U., 1948-52, Ford Found. faculty fellow, 1952-53, instr. Chinese and philosophy, 1953-54; Fulbright research scholar Kyoto, Japan, 1954-55; lectr. philosophy Stanford U., 1955-58, asst. prof. Chinese and philosophy, 1958-59, assoc. prof., 1959-66, prof., 1966-88, Walter Y. Evans-Wentz prof. Oriental Philosophies, Religions and Ethics, 1983-88, chmn. dept. philosophy, 1969-72, 75-76, acting chmn. dept. Asian langs., 1985-86, emeritus, 1988—. Author: The Life and Thought of Chang Hsüeh-ch'eng, 1738-1801, 1966, The Ways of Confucianism: Investigations in Chinese Philosophy, 1996; co-author: Chinese Language, Thought and Culture: Nivison and His Critics, 1996; editor, co-compiler: Stanford Chinese Concordance Series, 1979; co-editor: Confucianism in Action, 1959, Studies on the Modern Text of the Bamboo Annals (in Chinese), 2002; contbr. articles to profl. jours. and encys. Served with AUS, 1943-46. Recipient Prix Stanislas-Julien Inst. de France, 1967; Am. Council Learned Socs. fellow, 1973; John Simon Guggenheim fellow, 1973-74 Mem. Assn. Asian Studies, Am. Philos. Assn. (v.p. Pacific div. 1978-79, pres. 1979-80), Am. Oriental Soc. (Western br. v.p. 1964-65, sec. 1965-70, pres. 1971-72), AAUP (pres. No. Calif. Conf. 1964-66), Internat. Acad. Chinese Culture (Beijing, Peoples Republic of China), Phi Beta Kappa. Home: 1169 Russell Ave Los Altos CA 94024-5066 E-mail: dnivison@stanford.edu.

NIX, BARBARA LOIS, real estate broker; b. Sept. 25, 1929; d. Martin Clayton and Norma (Gunter) Westfield; m. B. H. Nix, July 12, 1968; children: William Martin Dahl, Theresa Irene Dahl stepchildren: Dennis Leon, Denise Lynn. Student, St. Elizabeths Sch. Nursing, Yakima, Wash., 1949-50; AA, Sierra Coll., 1978; student, Calif. State U., Sacramento, 1984. Bookkeeper, office mgr. Lakeport (Calif.) Tire Svc., 1966-69, Dr. K. J. Absher, Grass Valley, Calif., 1972-75; real estate sales and office mgr. Rough and Ready Land Co., Penn Valley, Calif., 1976-77, co-owner, v.p., sec., 1978—, Wildwood West Real Estate, Gateway Real Estate. Co-owner Nix's Antiques, 1996—. Youth and welfare chmn. Yakima Federated Jr. Women's Club, 1957; den mother Cub Scouts, 1959—60; leader Girls Scouts U.S., 1961—62; mem. Friends of Hospice, Sierra, Nev. Meml. Hosp. Found.; adv. bd. dirs., v.p. Roots and Wings Ednl. Found., 1991—95; mem. Nevada County Sch. Dist. Redistricting Bd. Recipient Pres.'s award, Sierra Coll., 1973, others. Mem.: Sierra Nev. Meml. Hosp. Aux., Penn Valley (founder, pres. 1978), Lake Wildwood Women's Club, Job's Daus. (life). Republican. Roman Catholic. Home: 19365 Wildflower Dr Penn Valley CA 95946-9735 Office: POBox 191 Penn Valley CA 95946

NIX, EDMUND ALFRED, lawyer; b. Eau Claire, Wis., May 24, 1929; s. Sebastian and Kathryn (Keirnan) N.; m. Mary Kathryn Nagle Daley, Apr. 27, 1968; children: Kim, Mary Kay, Norbert, Edmund Alfred, Michael. BS, Wis. State U., 1951; LL.B., U. Wis., 1954, postgrad. in speech, 1956-57. Bar: Wis. 1954. Practice in, Eau Claire, 1954-65; dist. atty. Eau Claire County, 1958-64; U.S. atty. Western Dist. Wis., Eau Claire, 1965-69, U.S. magistrate, 1969-70; dist. atty. La Crosse County, Wis., 1975-77; mcpl. judge City of La Crosse, 1992—. Co-chmn. United Fund, Eau Claire, 1958; Pres. Young Democrats Wis., 1951-53; mem. adminstrv. bd. Wis. Dem. party, 1953-54; chmn. 10th Congl. dist., 1965; sec. Kennedy for Pres. Club Wis., 1959-60. Served with AUS, 1954-56. Mem. Fed. Bar Assn., Wis. Bar Assn. (state chmn. crime prevention and control com.), La Crosse County Bar Assn. (pres.), Nat. Dist. Attys. Assn., KC. Roman Catholic. Office: 123 4th St N La Crosse WI 54601-3235 E-mail: nixe@ffax.net.

NIX, JAMES RAYFORD, nuclear physicist, consultant; b. Natchitoches, La., Feb. 18, 1938; s. Joe Ebbin and Edna (Guin) N.; m. Sally Ann Wood, Aug. 19, 1961; children: Patricia Lynne, David Allen. BS in Physics, Carnegie Inst. Tech., 1960; PhD in Physics, U. Calif., Berkeley, 1964. Summer physicist Lawrence Livermore (Calif.) Nat. Lab., 1961; rsch. asst. Lawrence Berkeley Lab., 1961-64, postdoctoral physicist, 1966-68; NATO postdoctoral fellow Niels Bohr Inst., Copenhagen, 1964-65; mem. staff Los Alamos (N.Mex.) Nat. Lab., 1968-77, 89-94, group leader, 1977-89, fellow, 1994-98, sci. cons.,

1998—. Vis. prof. Centro Brasileiro de Pesquisas Fisicas, Rio de Janeiro, 1974; cons. Calif. Inst. Tech., Pasadena, 1976, 79; chmn. Gordon Research Conf. Nuclear Chemistry, New London, NH, 1976; chmn. physics divsn. adv. com. Oak Ridge (Tenn.) Nat. Lab., 1976, 97; chmn. nuc. sci. divsn. vis. com. Lawrence Berkeley Lab., 1979—80. Contbr. articles to numerous publs. Recipient Alexander von Humboldt Sr. U.S. Scientist award, Univ. Munich and Max-Planck Inst. for Nuc. Physics, 1980—81; fellow, Phi Kappa Phi, Berkeley, 1960—61; scholar, Alfred P. Sloan Found., Pitts., 1956—60. Fellow: Am. Phys. Soc. (exec. com. 1973—75); mem.: AAAS, Phi Kappa Phi, Sigma Xi. Democrat. Home and Office: 12 Los Pueblos Los Alamos NM 87544-2659 Office Phone: 505-662-7459. E-mail: j_r_nix@hotmail.com.

NIX, JEFFREY ALAN, photographer; s. Reese Wallis and Esther Alene (Whitley) Nix. AS in Drafting, Roosevelt Warm Springs Inst.Rehab., Ga., 1981. Author: (non fiction self-help book) Hope Beyond Hell (Achieved #1 Status on website best seller list, 2002), (website) http:/www.hopebeyondhell.com, (poetry) Fighting To Find The Love Inside Of Me. Asst. scoutmaster Boy Scouts Am., Columbus, Ga., 2000—02. Named Most Likely To Succeed, Student Body Roosevelt-Warm Springs Inst. Rehab., 1980; recipient Letter of Commendation, Mayor Frank K. Martin, 1993, 1994, Third Pl. Winner, Mayor's Ethics In The Workplace, Columbus Consol. Govt., 1999. Baptist. Avocations: writing, photography, genealogy. Office: Columbus ConsolGovtt 420 10th St Columbus GA 31902 Office Phone: 706-225-3949. E-mail: jnix@columbusga.org.

NIX, JERRY W. automotive executive; Sr. v.p. fin. Genuine Parts Co., 1979—. Office: 2999 Circle 75 Pkwy SE Atlanta GA 30339-3050

NIX, KATHERINE JEAN, medical case manager; d. Samuel Watson and Dorothy Lee (Woods) Lewis; m. Robert Milton Nix, May 5, 1963 (div. Feb. 1988); children: Araina Catrice, Cynthia Lathier. AA in Safety and Health, Merritt Coll., 1976; AA in Nursing, Chabot Coll., 1974; BSN, U. San Francisco, 1979. RN Calif. Staff nurse Highland Hosp., Oakland, Calif., 1961-73; nurse cmty. health Alameda County, Oakland, Calif., 1973-75; nurse occupational health Caterpiller Tractor Co., San Leandro, Calif., 1975-77, inspector safety hygiene, 1981-84; nurse cons. occupational health Intel Corp., Livermore, Calif., 1981-84; cons. health & safety Quaker Oats Co., Oakland, 1984-86; nurse cons. occupational health Rawson Drug & Sundry Co., San Leandro, 1986-89; rehab. nurse Continental Rehab. Resources, Pleasanton, Calif., 1989-91; rehab. nurse cons. GAB, Campbell, Calif., 1991-93; med. case mgr. Conservco Travelers Ins. Co., Walnut Creek, Calif., 1993-95, Olsten Kimberly Quality Care, San Leandro, Calif., 1995—. Health advisor Black Women Organized for Polit. Action, Oakland, 1979—, Alemeda (Calif.) Coll., 1982-86. Fellow Nat. Safety Coun., Rehab. Nurses Group. Democrat. Avocations: skiing, reading, stage plays. Home: PO Box 5834 Oakland CA 94605-0834 Office: St Marys Hosp 450 Stanyan St San Francisco CA 94117-1079

NIX, LINDA ANNE BEAN, public relations executive; b. Sept. 20, 1943; d. Norman Arthur and Gladys Mae (Charlton) Bean, Jr.; m. Henry Taylor Betts, Jr., Sept. 5, 1964 (div. 1970); m. John Asa Nix, Nov. 24, 1971 (div. 1990). Student, Syracuse U., 1961-64; BA, Scarritt Coll., 1965; postgrad., Middle Tenn. State U., 9171-73. Mobile coord. Children's Mus., Nashville, 1967-69; promotion dir. Sta. WDCN-TV/8, Nashville, 1969-82; dir. pub. info. Sta. WYES-TV/12, New Orleans, 1982—; mktg. dir. Sta. KOFY-TV Radio San Francisco, 1989-91, Sta. KUSI-TV, San Diego, 1992-93; self-employed in pub. rels., 1992—. Mem. pub. info. adv. com. Pub. Broadcasting Service, Washington, 1977-80, chmn. 1979-80, mem. festival task force, 1979-80. Author, editor: (tchr. workbook) Yellow Submarine, 1968; contbr. Great Chefs, 2001—; contbr. articles to profl. jours. Bd. dirs. Nashville League for Hearing Impaired, 1973-76, Tennessee Williams/New Orleans Literacy Festival, 1995—; chmn. membership com. Coun. Cmty. Svcs., Nashville, 1978-80; mem. allocation panel United Way Greater Nashville, 1979-81, United Way Greater New Orleans, 1982-86. Mem. Pub. Rels. Soc. Am. (chmn. accreditation com. 1985, pres. New Orleans chpt. 1988), Broadcast Promotion and Mktg. Execs., Inc. (Promax) (bd. dirs. 1982-91, pres. 1989-90). Avocations: flying (multi-engine, commercial), sewing. Home and Office: PO Box 7068 Metairie LA 70010-7068 E-mail: lagator@mindspring.com.

NIX, MICHAEL CHARLES, musician, educator; b. Manchester, N.H., Sept. 24, 1953; s. Patricia Lee and John Paul Nix(Stepfather), Albert E. Devitt; m. Tracey Physioc Brockett, June 11, 1994; 1 child, Elizabeth Karyn. MusM in Composition, U. of Mass., 1987; MusB cum laude, Keene State Coll., 1980. Composer, performer NixWorks, Greenfield, Mass., 1976—; guitarist Monadnock Classical Guitar Duo, Keene, NH, 1979—83; co-founder NixWorks Performance Ensemble, Greenfield, 1988—; guitarist The Moser/Nix Duo, Greenfield, 1995—; owner NixWorks Pub. and Rec., Greenfield, Mass., 1995—; adj. faculty-music theory Greenfield C.C., Greenfield, Mass., 1990—; instr., music composition and guitar performance U. of Massachusetts-Amherst, Performing Arts Divsn., Amherst, Mass., 1987—95. Classical music critic The Recorder, Greenfield, 1984—98; curriculum cons. music Humanities, Greenfield, 1998—99; mng. dir. Valley Cmty. Music Sch., Greenfield, 1993—94; music graphics cons. Nat. Evaluation Sys., Amherst, Mass., 1990—95; music critic, feature writer The Keene Sentinel, 1980—83; reveiwer new music scores Mandolin Quar., Md., 1997; founding mem. Mythos classical music group, Greenfield, 1985—90, Multi-Media Project, Greenfield, 1999—; adj. faculty music theory Greenfield C.C., 1990—; instr. music composition and guitar performance performing arts divsn. U. Mass., Amherst, 1987—95; lectr. Keene State Coll., 1980—87; Mass. touring roster Mass. Cultural Commn., Boston, 1997—; arts touring program N.H. Commn. on Artts, Concord, 1980—85; Segovia outreach program featured performer Conn. Classical Guitar Soc., Hartford, 1988—92. Composer: (guitar quartet) Small Moon, 1993, (modern dance score) Labyrinth, 2002, (song cycle) The Very Rich Hours, 1991 (Mass. Music Teacher's Assn.Composer of the Yr., 1991), rev. edit., 2002, (CD) Preludes, Airs, and Dances, 1991; musician: East & West, 1995; librettist: Operas Liombruno, 1998; author: (book) Beginning Guitar, 1985, Intermediate Guitar Theory and Technique, 1987. Adv. bd. Mohawk Trail Concerts, Music in Deerfield, Shelburn Falls, Mass., 1999—2001; com. mem. Bus. Fund for the Arts, Greenfield, Mass., 1989; mem. formation com. Valley Cmty. Music Sch., Greenfield, 1990; organ commn. com. 1st Ch. of Deerfield, Mass., 1999—2002; bd. dirs. Greenfield Arts Lottery Commn., 1987—89. Mem.: ASCAP, Guitar Found. of Am., Soc. of Composers. Office: NixWorks PO Box 400 Greenfield MA 01302 Personal E-mail: mnix@nixworks.com. E-mail: mnix@nixworks.com.

NIX, PATRICIA, artist; d. Nobe Astin Briggs and Lela Mae (Lucas) Rockstrom; m. (dec.); children: Pandora Nix Shaw, William Riley Jr., John Houston. BA, NYU, 1982. One-woman shows include Tower Gallery, Southampton, N.Y., 1978—82, 1985, NYU, 1980, Sutton Gallery, N.Y.C., 1982—83, Baumgartner Gallery, Washington, 1984, S.I. (N.Y.) Mus., 1986, Andre Zarre Gallery, N.Y.C., 1987, S.I. (N.Y.) Mus., 1988, Nerlino Gallery, N.Y.C., 1988, Andre Zarre Gallery, 1991, U. Windsor (Ont., Can.) Mus., Griffin McGear Modern Gallery, N.Y.C., 1989, San Angelo (Tex.) Mus. of Art, 1991, Hurlbutt Gallery, Greenwich, Conn., 1990, Galerie Donguy, Paris, 1994, Dillon Gallery, N.Y.C., 1994—98, exhibited in group shows at New Mus. Contemporary Art, 1985, Bess Cutler Gallery, 1985, NAD Mus., 1978, 1988, 1990—91, 1993, 1995, 1997, 1999, Nat. Mus. Am. Art, Smithsonian Instn., Washington, 1983, Galerie Zug (Switzerland) Glas Haus, Galerie Richard Mark, Zurich, Rene Foutoui Gallery, N.Y.C., Griffin McGear Gallery, 1989, Merrill Chase Galleries, Chgo., 1999, Hilligoss Galleries, 2000—03, Tex. Tech. Mus., Lubbock, 2000; represented in numerous permanent collections, designer sets and costumes (ballets) Petrushka, Pulcinella, Jeu de Cartes, 2002.

NIXON, AGNES ECKHARDT, television writer, producer; m. Robert Nixon (dec.); 4 children. Student, Sch. Speech, Northwestern U. Writer for radio and TV; freelance writer for: TV programs Hallmark Hall of Fame, Robert Montgomery Presents, Studio One; creator, packager, head writer: daytime TV series All My Children; creator nighttime mini-series The Manions of America; creator, packager daytime TV series One Life to Live; creator, packager: daytime TV series Loving; co-creator: daytime TV series As The World Turns; formerly head writer, The Guiding Light, daytime TV series Another World; creator, story cons. The City. Recipient Trustees award Nat. Acad. TV Arts and Sci., 1981, Super Achiever award Jr. Diabetes Found., 1981, Wilmer Eye Inst. award, 1981, Communicator award Am. Women in Radio & TV, 1984, Gold Plate award Am. Acad. Achievement, 1993, Popular Culture Lifetime Achievement award Popular Culture Assn., 1995, Pub. Svc. award Johns Hopkins Hosp., 1995, Humanitarian award Nat. Osteoporosis Found., 1996; inducted into TV Hall of Fame, 1993. Mem. Internat. Radio and TV Soc. Nat. Acad. TV Arts and Scis., Harvard Found. (bd. dirs.), Mus. TV and Radio (bd. dirs.), The Friars Club. Address: All My Children 320 W 66th St New York NY 10023-6304

NIXON, ARLIE JAMES, gas and oil company executive; b. Ralston, Okla., May 22, 1914; s. James Gordon and Wella May (Platt) N.; m. Wylie Elizabeth Jones, Apr. 21, 1939 (div May 1950); children: Cole Jay, Kathleen (Mrs. S. Brent Joyce); m. Lisa Marie Grant, Dec. 7, 1981 (div. June 1989). BS, Okla. State U., 1935. Airline capt. Trans World Airlines, N.Y.C., 1939-74; pres. Crystal Gas Co., Jennings, Okla., 1960—, Blackburn Gas Co., Jennings, 1964—, Blackberry Oil Co., Jennings, 1969—. Represented U.S. in several ofcl. dels. to internat. aviation tech. meetings, also represented Internat. Fedn. Air Line Pilots Assns. at internat. confs. Lt. (j.g.) USNR, 1935-63. Mem. Internat. Fedn. Air Line Pilots Assn. (regional v.p. 1972), Internat. Platform Assn., Wings Club. Democrat. Home: RR 2 Box 8651 Jennings OK 74038-9324 Office: PO Box 68 Jennings OK 74038-0068

NIXON, CAROL HOLLADAY, retired park and recreation director; b. Salt Lake City, Dec. 25, 1937; m. William L. Nixon; children: William H., Joan, Michael, Jennifer, Jacqueline, John. From dep. chief of staff to chief of staff to gov. State of Utah, Salt Lake City, 1991-93, dir. Cmty. Devel. Divsn., 1993-96; pres., CEO This Is the Place Heritage Park, Salt Lake City, 1996—2001, ret., 2001. Fax: 801-584-8325.

NIXON, CHARLES WILLIAM, acoustician; b. Wellsburg, W.Va., Aug. 15, 1929; s. William E. and Lenora S. (Treiber) Nixon; m. Barbara Irene Hunter, May 19, 1956; children: Timothy C., Tracy Scott. BS, Ohio State U., 1952, MS, 1953, PhD, 1960. Tchr. spl. edn. Ohio and W.Va. Pub. Schs., Wheeling, 1954—56; rsch. audiologist Aeromed Lab., Wright Patterson AFB, Ohio, 1956—67; supervisory rsch. audiologist Armstrong Lab., Wright Patterson AFB, 1967—96, Veridian, Dayton, 1996—. Chair W4 Am. Nat. Stds. Inst., N.Y.C., 1968—96; U.S. rep. hearing protection Internat. Stds. Orgn., Geneva, 1968—96; USAF rep. NRC-NAS Hearing Com., Washington, 1976—94; chair robotics panel Joint Dirs. Labs., Washington, 1987—88. Author: reports and book chpts. Cpl. U.S. Army, 1953—55. Recipient Meritorious Svc. medal, U.S. Dept. Def., Dayton, Ohio, 1986, Outstanding Civilian Svc. award, 1996. Fellow: Acoustical Soc. Am.; mem.: Rsch. Soc. Am. Achievements include research in noise exposure, voice communications, hearing protection, sonic boom, active noise reduction, 3-D audio displays, others. Home: 4316 Sillman Pl Dayton OH 45440-1141 E-mail: cwnixon@woh.rr.com.

NIXON, CYNTHIA, actress; b. New York, Apr. 9, 1966; d. Walter and Anne Nixon. BA in English, Barnard Coll., 1988. Founding member The Drama Dept., 1996. Actor: (plays) The Philadelphia Story, 1980 (Theatre World Award, 1981), Indiscretions, 1996 (Tony Award nom., 1996); (films) Little Darlings, 1980, Prince of the City, 1981, Tattoo, 1981, I Am the Cheese, 1983, Amadeus, 1984, The Manhattan Project, 1986, O.C. and Stiggs, 1987, Let It Ride, 1989, Through an Open Window, 1992, The Pelican Brief, 1993, Addams Family Values, 1993, Baby's Day OUt, 1994, The Cottonwood, 1996, 'M' Word, 1996, Marvin's Room, 1996, Advice From a Caterpillar, 1999, The Out-of-Towners, 1999, Igby Goes Down, 2002, The Paper Mache Chase, 2003; (TV series) Sex and the City, 1998—2004 (Emmy nom. for Outstanding Supporting Actress in a comedy series, 2002); (TV miniseries) Tanner '88, 1988; (TV films) The Seven Wishes of a Rich Kid, 1979, The Private History of a Campaign That Failed, 1981, Rascals and Robbers: The Secret Adventures of Tom Sawyer and Huck Finn, 1982, My Body, My Child, 1982, Fifth of July, 1982, The Murder of Mary Phagan, 1988, Women & Wallace, 1990, Love She Sought, The, 1990, Face of a Stranger, 1991, Love, Lies and Murder, 1991, Kiss-Kiss, Dahlings!, 1992, Sex and the Matrix, 2000, Papa's Angels, 2000, Stage on Screen: The Women, 2002. Office: William Morris Agency One William Morris Place Beverly Hills CA 90212

NIXON, DANIEL DAVID. internist; b. L.A., Jan. 7, 1934; s. Irving I. and Sara Ruth (Cohen) N.; m. Tamara Hope Friedman, June 14, 1959; children: Asa Joel, Naomi Devorah, Victoria Eve. BA, Dartmouth Coll., 1955; MD, U. Pitts., 1959. Diplomate in internal medicine and med. oncology Am. Bd. Internal Medicine. Intern Mt. Sinai Hosp., N.Y.C., 1959-60, resident in internal medicine, 1961-62, fellow in hematology; resident in internal medicine U. Pitts., 1960-61; pvt. practice internal medicine Rockville Centre, N.Y., 1963-66; internist, chief gen. med. svc. Valley Forge Gen. Hosp., Phoenixville, Pa., 1967-68; instr. medicine Columbia U. Coll. P&S, N.Y.C., 1968-69; pvt. practice hematology and oncology Miami Beach, Fla., 1969—; clin. assoc. prof. U. Miami Sch. Medicine, 1981—; chief divsn. oncology Mt. Sinai Med. Ctr., Miami Beach, 1969—. Med. dir. Dade County Hospice Inc., Miami, 1989-93; mem. sci. adv. bd. Israel Cancer Rsch. Fund, N.Y.C., 1978—; co-dir. Mt. Sinai Comprehensive Cancer Ctr., Miami Beach, 1989—. Capt. M.C., U.S. Army, 1966-68, Vietnam. Alfred B. Stengel traveling fellow ACP, 1972. Fellow ACP; mem. Am. Soc. Hematology, Am. Soc. Oncology, Internat. Soc. Hematology, Alpha Omega Alpha. Avocations: tennis, gardening, fishing. Office: Mt Sinai Med Ctr 4306 Alton Rd Miami Beach FL 33140-2840

NIXON, DANIEL WALKER, oncologist, researcher; b. Brunswick, Ga., Sept. 8, 1943; s. Marvin Elesberry and Mildred Anita (Whitehead) N.; m. Sandra Gayle Brakefield, July 18, 1970; children: William B., Marvin A. BS, U. Ga., 1965, MD, 1969. Diplomate Am. Bd. Internal Medicine, Am. Bd. Med. Oncology; lic. physician S.C., N.Y. Asst. prof. Med. Coll. Ga., Augusta, 1973-75; from assoc. prof. to prof. Emory U., Atlanta, 1975-87; assoc. dir. divsn. cancer prevention and control, Nat. Cancer Inst. NIH, Bethesda, Md., 1987-89; v.p., prof. edn. Am. Cancer Soc., Atlanta, 1989-94; Folk prof., assoc. dir. prevention and control Hollings Cancer Ctr., Med. U. S.C., Charleston, 1994—99; pres. Inst. Cancer Prevention, N.Y.C., 1999—. Mem. sci. bd. Cancer Treatment Rsch. Found., 1996; bd. dirs. Kincaid Found., Washington. Author: Cancer Recovery Eating Plan, 1994; editor: Cancer Chemoprevention, 1994; editor-in-chief: (jour.) Preventive Medicine, 1999—; contbr. more than 100 articles to med. jours. Capt. USNR, 1987—. Recipient several found. awards; grantee NIH, 1975—. Mem. Nutrition Oncology Adjuvant Therapy Soc. (pres. 1996), Army and Navy Club, Druid Hills Country Club, Country Club of Charleston, Harvard Club N.Y. Achievements include research in cancer prevention and nutrition; chemoprevention and cancer metabolism. Office: Inst Cancer Prevention 390 5th Ave New York NY 10017

NIXON, DAVID, dancer; b. Windsor, Ont., Can. Student, The Nat. Ballet Sch. Dir. Ballet Met, Columbus, 1995-2001, dir. Northern Ballet Theatre, Eng., 2001—; prin. Deutsche Oper Ballet, Berlin, 1985-90; various guest appearance including Munich Ballet, 1990-91, Staatsoper, Berlin, 1990, Komische Oper Ballet, Berlin, 1991-93, Birmingham Royal Ballet, 1990-93. Dancer Nat. Ballet Can., 1978—84, 1st soloist, 1982—84; prodr.: David Nixon's Dance Theatre, Hebbel Theatre Berlin, 1990, 1991; choreographer Butterfly, 1983, La Follia, 1984, Dangerous Liaisons, 1990, 1996, African Fantasy, 1990, Celebrate Mozart, 1991, Sudden Impulse, 1994, A Summer's Nights Reflections, 1995, Full-Length Nutcracker, 1995, Butterfly, 1996, Beauty and the Beast, 1997, Carmen, 1997, Romeo and Juliet, 1998, Swan Lake, 1998, Dracula, 1999, A Midsummer Nights Dream, 2000, A Celebration of Dance with Music by Gershwin, 2001, Wuthering Heights, 2002. Office: Northern Ballet Theatre West Park Centre Spen Ln Leeds LS16 5BE England

NIXON, DAVID L. lawyer; b. Concord, Mass., Mar. 19, 1932; s. Louis Gerard and Patricia (Williams) N.; m. Joanne P. Nixon; children: Leslie C., Melanie D., Wendy W.N. Branch, Amy W., David Lee Jr., Louis Gerard II. BA cum laude, Wesleyan U., Middletown, Conn., 1953; LLB, U. Mich., 1958. Bar: N.H. 1958, U.S. Dist. Ct. N.H. 1959, U.S. Ct. Appeals (1st cir.) 1961, U.S. Supreme Ct. 1968. Assoc. McLane Carleton Graf Greene & Brown, Manchester, N.H., 1958-61; ptnr. King & Nixon, Manchester, 1961-69, Nixon, Christy & Tessier, Manchester, 1969-76; dir. Brown & Nixon P.A., Manchester, 1976-88; pres. Nixon, Hall & Hess P.A., Manchester, 1988-93, of counsel, 1993-94; pres., dir. Nixon, Raiche, Manning & Casinghino P.A., 1994—. Mem. N.H. Supreme Ct. Accreditation Commn., 1985—, N.H. Jud. Coun., 1980-83, 93—. Rep. N.H. Legis., Concord, 1969-74, senate pres., 1973-74; moderator Town of New Boston, N.H., 1964-92. With U.S. Army, 1953-55. Named Trial Lawyer of the Decade, N.H. Trial Lawyers Assn., 1988. Mem. ABA (ho. of dels. 1970-72), Manchester Bar Assn. (pres. 1973-74, named Manchester Lawyer of the Yr. 1995), N.H. Bar Assn. (pres. 1980-81, Disting. Svc. award 1982, award for Professionalism 1993), New Eng. Bar Assn. (pres. 1970-72), Internat. Soc. Barristers (pres. 1996-97), Inner Circle Advs., Manchester Crimeline, Inc. (dir., legal counsel), Hillsborough County law Enforcement Assn. (chmn. scholarship com.), DAV (life), Am. Legion (judge adv. Post 2). Office: Nixon Raiche Manning & Casinghino PA 77 Central St Manchester NH 03101-2423 Home: 77 Central St Manchester NH 03101-2423

NIXON, DAVID PATRICK, public relations executive; b. 1965; With N. Amer. Network, Washington, 1986—89; founder, pres. The Nixon Group, Miami, 1989—2002; exec. V.P., managing dir. Golin Harris Int., Miami, 2002—. Office: Golin Harris Int Penthouse 4500 Biscayne Blvd Miami FL 33137

NIXON, DENNIS E. financial company executive; Pres. Internat. Bancshares Corp., Laredo, Tex., 1975—. Office: Internat Bancshares Corp 1200 San Bernardo Ave Laredo TX 78040-6301

NIXON, DREW, accountant, state legislator; Student, Panola Jr. Coll.; BBA in Acctg., Stephen F. Austin State U., 1982. CPA, Tex.; lic. real estate salesman, Tex. CPA, owner acctg. firm, Carthage, Tex.; br. office operator SunAmerica Securities and McGuire/Nixon Ins. Agy., Inc.; mem. Tex. Senate Dist. 3, 1994—, vice chair state affairs com., mem. nominations com., mem. natural resources com., mem. health & human svcs. com., mem. natural resources subcom. on agr., others. Republican. Office: PO Box 12068 Austin TX 78711-2068 also: 320 North St Ste 301 Nacogdoches TX 75961-5040

NIXON, EUGENE RAY, chemist, educator; b. Mt. Pleasant, Mich., Apr. 14, 1919; s. William S. and Grace (Brookens) N.; m. Phyllis R. Jones, June 10, 1945; children— Cynthia L., Emily E. Sc.B. summa cum laude, Alma Coll., 1941; PhD, Brown U., 1947. Research chemist Manhattan Project, 1942-46; instr. chemistry Brown U., 1947-49; mem. faculty U. Pa., Phila., 1949-85, prof. chemistry, 1965-85, vice dean grad. sch., 1958-62, acting chmn. dept. chemistry, 1965-66, dir. materials research lab., 1969-72, prof. emeritus, 1985—. Vis. prof. U. London, 1963-64; vis. lectr. Bryn Mawr Coll., 1957-58 Mem. Am. Chem. Soc., Am. Phys. Soc., Soc. Applied Spectroscopy (Jour. award 1965, Spectroscopist of Yr. award Del. Valley sect. 1988), Coblentz Soc. (bd. mgrs.), Sigma Xi. Research, publs. on phys. chemistry, molecular structure and molecular spectroscopy, properties of crystals, intermolecular interactions, laser spectroscopy and laser chemistry. Home: 35 Julio Dr Apt 106 Shrewsbury MA 01545-3049

NIXON, JEREMIAH W. (JAY NIXON), state attorney general; b. DeSoto, Mo., Feb. 13, 1956; s. Jeremiah and Betty (Lea) Nixon; m. Georganne Nixon; children: Jeremiah, Will. BS in Polit. Sci., U. Mo., 1978, JD, 1981. Ptnr. Nixon, Nixon, Breeze & Roberts, Jefferson County, Mo., 1981—86; mem. Mo. State Senate from Dist 22, 1986—93; atty. gen. State of Mo., 1993—. Chmn. select com. ins. reform; creator video internat. devel. and edn. opportunity program. Named Outstanding Young Missourian, Jaycees, 1994, Outstanding Young Lawyer, Barrister's Mag., 1993; recipient Conservation Fedn. Mo award, 1992. Mem.: Mo. Assn. Trial Attys., Midwest Assn. Attys. Gen., Nat. Assn. Attys. Gen. Democrat. Methodist. Office: Atty Gen Office 207 W High St PO Box 899 Jefferson City MO 65102-0899

NIXON, JOHN TRICE, judge; b. New Orleans, La., Jan. 9, 1933; s. H. C. and Anne (Trice) N.; children: Mignon Elizabeth, Anne Trice. AB cum laude, Harvard Coll., 1955; LL.B., Vanderbilt U., 1960. Bar: Ala. bar 1960, Tenn. bar 1972. Individual practice law, Anniston, Ala., 1960-62; city atty., 1962-64; trial atty. Civil Rights Div., Dept. Justice, Washington, 1964-69; staff atty., comptroller of Treasury State of Tenn., 1971-76; pvt. practice law Nashville, 1976-77; cir. judge, 1977-78; gen. sessions judge, 1978-80; judge U.S. Dist. Ct. (mid. dist.) Tenn., Nashville, 1980—, sr. judge, 1998—. Served with U.S. Army, 1958. Mem. Fly Club (Cambridge), Harvard-Radcliffe Club (Nashville). Democrat. Methodist. Office: US Dist Ct 745 US Courthouse Nashville TN 37203

NIXON, JUDITH MAY, librarian; b. Gary, Ind., June 14, 1945; d. Louis Robert Sr. and Mable Sophia (Reiner) Vician; m. Cleon Robert Nixon III, Aug. 20, 1967; 1 child, Elizabeth Marie. BS in Edn., Valparaiso U., 1967; MA in LS, U. Iowa, 1974. Tchr. U.S. Peace Corps, Kingdom of Tonga, 1968-69; popular books libr. Lincoln Libr., Springfield, Ill., 1971-73; reference libr. Cedar Rapids (Iowa) Pub. Libr., 1974-76; reference coord. U. Wis., Platteville, 1976-82; bus. libr. U. Ariz., Tucson, 1982-84; consumer and family sci. libr. Purdue U., West Lafayette, La., 1984-93, Krannert mgmt. and econs. libr., 1993—. Editor: Industry and Company Information, 1991, Organization Charts, 1992, 2d edit., 1996, Hotel and Restaurant Industries, 1993; editor quar. serial Lodging and Restaurant Index, 1985-93. Leader Girl Scouts U.S., Lafayette, 1985—. Recipient John H. Moriarty award Purdue U. Librs., 1989. Mem. ALA (chairperson bus. reference and svcs. sect. 1995-96, GALE Rsch. award for excellence in bus. librarianship 1994). Home: 2375 N 23rd St Lafayette IN 47904-1242 Office: Purdue U Libraries KRAN Mgmt and Econs Libr 504 W State St West Lafayette IN 47907-2058 Office Phone: 765-494-2922. E-mail: jnixon@purdue.edu.

NIXON, MARNI, singer; b. Altadena, Calif., Feb. 22, 1930; d. Charles and Margaret (Wittke) McEathron; m. Ernest Gold, May 22, 1950 (div. 1969); children: Andrew Maurice, Martha Alice, Melani Christine; m. Lajos Frederick Fenster, July 23, 1971 (div. July 1975); m. Albert David Block, Apr. 11, 1983. Student, L.A. City Coll., UCLA, U. So. Calif., Tanglewood, Mass. Dir. vocal faculty Calif. Inst. Arts, Valencia, 1970-72; pvt. tchr., vocal coacn, condr. master classes, 1970—; pvt. voice tchr., coach, condr. master classes, 1970—; head apprentice divsn. Santa Barbara Music Acad. of West, 1980; formerly dir. opera workshop Cornish Inst. Arts, Seattle. Tchr. in field; judge Met. Opera Internat. Am. Music Awards, Nat. Inst. Music Theatre, 1984-87; panelist New Music, Nat. Assn. Tchrs. Singing, pres., N.Y. chpt., 1994—; dialect dir., opera recs. Actress Pasadena (Calif.) Playhouse, 1940-45, soloist Roger Wagner chorale, 1947-53, appeared with New Eng. Opera Co., L.A. Opera Co., Ford Found. TV Opera, 1948-63, San Francisco Spring Opera, 1966, Seattle Opera, 1971-73; classical recitals and appearances with symphony orchs. throughout U.S., Can., also Eng., Israel, Ireland; in motion pictures as Sister Sophia in Sound of Music, 1964, Aunt Alice in I Think I Do, 1996; appeared on (TV) Boomerang, from 1975; Broadway and off-Broadway shows: Eliza Doolittle in My Fair Lady, 1964, Edna in Taking My Turn, 1983, Sadie in Opal, 1992-94, Fraulein Schneider in Cabaret, 1998, Mrs. Willson in Ballymore, 1999, Heidi Schiller in Follies, 2001, Aunt Kate in James Joyce's The Dead, 1999-2001, Mamma in Nine, 2003; taped for Great Performances PBS-TV Role of Edna, 1994; voice dubbed for film My Fair Lady, The King and I, An Affair to Remember, West Side Story, Disney's Mulan, others; rec. artist for Columbia, Mus. Heritage Records, Capital, RCA Victor, Ednl. Records, Reference Recs., Varese-Sarabande, Nonesuch. Recipient 4 Emmy awards for best actress, 2 Action for Childrens TV awards, 1977; nominee Drama Desk award; recipient Chgo. Film Festival award, 1977, 2 Gold Records for Songs from Mary Poppins and Mulan, 2 time Grammy award nominee Nat. Acad. Rec. Arts and Scis. (1st rec. Cabaret Songs and Early Songs by Arnold Schoenberg, RCA, 1977 and 1st rec. Emily Dickinson Songs by Aaron Copland, Reference Recs., 1988). Mem. Nat. Assn. Tchrs. Singing (pres. N.Y. chpt. 1994-97). Personal E-mail: singermarnix@aol.com.

NIXON, PATRICIA SAUNDERS, music educator, performer; b. Norfolk, Va., Nov. 22, 1955; d. John Edward Saunders and Marie Ewing; m. Jimmie Larry Nixon, July 7, 1979; children: Jimmie Larry Jr.(dec.), Annette Marie. BS

in Music Edn., Norfolk State U., 1978, MusM in Vocal Performance, 1988; postgrad. in Vocal Performance, Shenandoah U. Conservatory, 2002—. Music instr. VA Sch. for Deaf, Blind and Multi-Disabled, Hampton, Va., 1978—2000; choral dir. Norview Mid. Sch. Norfolk Pub. Schs., 2000—01; choral dir. Wilson H.S. Portsmouth (Va.) Pub. Schs., 2001—02; vocal instr. Norfolk State U., 2002—, dir. jazz vocal ensemble, 2004—. Choir dir., pianist intermediate choir Ebenezer Bapt. Ch., Portsmouth, 1991—. Photography, D-Day (pub., 2002), Whose in the Drivers Seat Now?, 2003; actor: Porgy and Bess; musician: Va. Symphony Pops, I. Sherman Green Chorale, others; singer: Let My People Go. Mem. Brighton/Prentice Pk. Civic League, Portsmouth, 1998—, Va. and Nat. Minority Caucus, 1990—2002. Recipient Apple for the Tchr. award, Alpha Chi chpt. Iota Phi Lambda Sorority, Inc., 1993, Christian Svc. award, Ebenezer Bapt. Ch. Vacational Bible Sch., 2000—01, 2001 Team Ptnr. Recogition award, U. S. Olympic Com., 2001, We Teach the Children Whole Village award, Va. Edn. Assn., 2001, Outstanding Performance in A Tribute to African Am. Sacred Music award, Parkview United Meth. Ch., 2001, Black Educators' award, Delicados, Inc. Portsmouth Chpt., 1997, A Salute to Black Achievers in the Tidewater Area award, Martin Luther King, Jr. Meml. Ch. Choir, 1996; grantee VTAG, Shenandoah U., 2002. Mem.: AAUP, NEA (del. 1999—2000), NAACP, Nat. Assn. Teachers and Singing, Am. Choral Directors Assn., Intercolligiate Music Assn., Va. Choral Dirs. Assn., Hampton Edn. Assn. (pres. 1998—2000), Va. Edn. Assn., Portsmouth Edn. Assn. (assoc.), Norfolk Edn. Assn. (assoc.; del. 2000), The Am. Choral Directors Assn. (assoc.), Nat. Assn. of Negro Musicians Tidewater Area Musicians Chpt. (assoc.), Music Educators Nat. Conf. (assoc.), VA Sch. at Hampton Edn. Assn. (assoc.; pres. 1998—2000, del. 1999—2000), Chancel Choir of Ebenezer Bapt. Ch. (assoc.), Va. Opera Guild (assoc.), Alpha Kappa Alpha (co-chmn. music 49th Mid-Atlantic Regional Conf. 2002, Leadership Excel award 2000), Gamma Delta Omega Chpt. of Alpha Kappa Alpha Sorority, Inc. (assoc.; publicity chmn. 1998—99, Cert. of Appreciation 1999). Democrat. Avocations: performing, crafts, photography, computer technology, travel. Home: 1019 Centre Ave Portsmouth VA 23704-7005 Office: Norfolk State U 700 Park Ave Norfolk VA 23504 Office Phone: 757-823-8544. Personal E-mail: psnixon@aol.com. Business E-Mail: psnixon@nsu.edu.

NIXON, RALPH ANGUS, psychiatrist, educator, research neuroscientist; b. Somerville, Mass., Jan. 29, 1947; s. Ralph Angus and Eleanor Nixon; m. Katharine Sangree Faulkner, Aug. 20, 1974; children: Abigail, Rebecca. AB, Brandeis U., 1968; PhD in Cell and Devel. Biology, Harvard U., 1974; MD, U. Vt., 1976. Intern Mass. Gen. Hosp., 1976, Salem Hosp., 1977; resident in psychiatry Mass. Gen. Hosp., 1977-79, McLean Hosp., 1979-80; clin. assoc. in psychiatry Mass. Gen. Hosp., Boston, 1980-97; assoc. in neurosci. Children's Hosp Med. Ctr., Boston, 1982-88; staff physician Rehab. Ctr. for Aged, Boston, 1984-90; asst. prof. psychiatry Harvard Med. Sch., Boston, 1982-86, assoc. prof., 1986-96; assoc. neuropathologist McLean Hosp., Belmont, Mass., 1982-90, assoc. psychiatrist, 1988-93, neuropathologist, 1991; psychiatrist, 1993-97; prof. psychiatry and cell biology NYU Med. Sch., N.Y.C., 1997—, vice chmn. dept. psychiatry, 2001—; dir. rsch. Nathan Kline Inst.-NYU Med. Ctr., Orangeburg, dir. ctr. dementia rsch., 1997—. Mem. sci. rev. com. Am. Fedn. for Aging Rsch., 1990-92; mem. neurosci., behavior and sociology of aging rev. com., subcom. A, Nat. Inst. on Aging, NIH, 1991-95, chmn., 1994-95; dir. labs. for molecular neurosci. McLean Hosp., 1992; mem. adv. bd. Internat. Congress Alzheimer's Disease, 1993—. Mem. editl. bd. Jour. Neurochemistry, 1986-96, Neurochem. Rsch., 1988—, Harvard Rev. Psychiatry, 1992—, Neurobiology of Aging, 1994—, Alzheimer's Disease Rev., 1997—; contbr. over 200 biol. articles to Sci. Jour. Cell Biology, Jour. Biol. Chem., Annals N.Y. Acad. Sci., Proc. NAS, chpts. to books; Proteases and Protease Inhibitors Banner C Nixon R.A. eds. Annals Acad. Sci. vol. 67, 1992. Hon. bd. dirs. Ch. League for Civic Concerns, Boston, 1987-89. Recipient Merit award NIH, 1990, Leadership and Excellence in Alzheimer Disease award, Nat. Inst. Aging, 1992, Temple Discovery award Alzheimers Assn., 1999, N.Y. State OMH Rsch. award, 1999, Career Leadership award, Nat. Inst. on Aging, 1999, Zenith award, Alzheimer's Assn., 2003; Ethel DuPont Warren fellow, 1979-80, rsch. fellow Med. Found., 1980-82, Alfred P. Sloan Found., 1981-83, Scottish Rite Schizophrenia Rsch. Program, 1983-85. Mem. AAAS, Soc. for Neurosci., Fedn. Am. Scientists, Am. Soc. for Neurochemistry, Internat. Soc. for Neurochemistry, Am. Psychiat. Assn., Am. Soc. for Cell Biology, Am. Assn. for Geriatric Psychiatry, Gerontol. Soc. Am., Am. Assn. Neuropathologists, N.Y. Acad. Sci. Achievements include 5 patents (with others) on diagnosis and treatment of Alzheimer's disease. Office: Nathan Kline Inst NYU Med Ctr 140 Old Orangeburg Rd Orangeburg NY 10962-1157

NIXON, ROBERT OBEY, SR., business educator; b. Pitts., Feb. 14, 1922; s. Frank Obey and Margurite (Van Buren) N.; m. Marilyn Cavanagh, Oct. 25, 1944 (dec. 1990); children: Nan Nixon Friend, Robert Obey, Jr., Dwight Cavanagh. BS in bus. adminstrn., U. Pitts., 1948; MS, Ohio State U., 1964; MBA, U. Phoenix, 1984. Commd. 2d lt. USAF, 1943, advanced through grades to col., 1970, master navigator WWII, Korea, Vietnam; sales, adminstrn. U.S. Rubber Corp., Pitts., 1940-41; asst. engr. Am. Bridge Corp., Pitts., 1941-42; underwriter, sales Penn Mutual Life Ins. Corp., Pitts., 1945-50; capt., nav. instr. USAF Reserves, 1945-50; ret. USAF Col., divsn. chief Joint Chiefs of Staff, 1973; educator, cons. U. Ariz., 1973-79; bus. dept. chmn., coord., founder weekend coll. Pima C.C., Tucson, 1979-90, prof. mgmt., 1991-98, coord. weekend coll. program, 1991—. Adj. faculty Pima C.C., 1998—; founder, pres. Multiple Adv. Group ednl. cons., Tucson, 1978—. Author: Source Document: On Accelerated Courses and Programs at Accredited Two- and Four-Year Colleges and Universities, 1996; contbr. articles to profl. jours. Mem. Soc. Logistics Engrs. (sr., charter mem.), Phi Delta Theta. Presbyterian. Avocations: tennis, hiking, swimming. Home: 9241 E Holmes St Tucson AZ 85710-3151 Fax: 520-885-2378. E-mail: eb58271@goodnet.com., bnixon@pimacc.pima.edu.

NIXON, SAMUEL ANTHONY, JR., state legislator, information services executive; b. Martinsville, Va., Nov. 11, 1958; s. Samuel Anthony and Julia Catherine (Hubbard) N.; m. Carol A. Gibbs, 1988. BBA in Mktg., James Madison U., 1980. Asst. plant mgr. Prillaman Chem. Corp., Richmond, Va., 1980-84; account mgr. JBA Info. Systems, Inc., Richmond, 1984-85; sr, mktg. support analyst Unisys Corp., Richmond, 1985-91; pres. Strategic Info. Systems, 1994—; mem. from 27th dist. Va. Ho. of Dels., 1995—. Congressional action rep. Unisys Corp., Richmond, 1986—. Vice chmn. Va. Young Am. for Freedom, Richmond, 1980-82; mem. Chesterfield (Va.) Rep. Com., 1985—, chmn. fin., 1987-90. Named one of Outstanding Young Men of Am., 1983-86. Mem. Va. Jaycees (mgr. govtl. affairs program 1987-88), Chesterfield Jaycees (bd. dirs. 1986-87, treas. 1987—). Methodist. Home: 7412 Barkbridge Rd Chesterfield VA 23832-8285

NIXON, SANDRA L. retired registrar; b. Kansas City, Mo., Feb. 23, 1944; d. C. Harold and Anna Pearl Scott-Mann; m. Hiram Luttmers, Mar. 6, 1965 (div. Aug. 1973); children: Hiram Charles, Gerald Lee; m. Douglas L. Nixon, July 16, 1976; children: Karen, Katherine, Raymond, Hiram Charles, Gerald. Student, Cen. Mo. State U., 1962-63, Nat. Coll., 1991-93. Credit clk. Harzfeld's, Kansas City, Mo., 1963-65; typist/receptionist Powers Regulator Co., Overland Park, Kans., 1965-69; ins. typist Comml. Union Ins. Co., Kansas City, Mo., 1969-73; typist Social Security Admin., Kansas City, Mo., 1973-78; dir. of Mothers Day Out Birchwood Bapt. Ch., Independence, Mo., 1978-80; accompanist K.C. Mo. Sch. Dist., Kansas City, Mo., 1979-81; registrar Northeast Mid. Sch., Kansas City, Mo., 1981-2000; fashion coord. Weekenders, 2001—. Mem. ABWA (pres. 1990-91, Woman of Yr. 1992-93), VFW Aux. Post 4242 (sr. v.p. 2000-2001, pres. 2001-2004, sr. v.p. 2004—). Baptist. Avocations: piano, square dancing, precious moments. Office Phone: 816-260-4538. E-mail: sandy.nixon@fellowship.net.

NIXON, SCOTT WEST, oceanography science educator; b. Phila., Aug. 24, 1943; s. Robert Scott West and Elizabeth (Wright) West Nixon; m. Pendleton Hall, (div.); children: Carter Hall, Elizabeth Pendleton; m. Virginia Lee. BA, U. Del., 1965; PhD, U. N.C., 1970. Prof. oceanography U. R.I., Kingston, 1970—, dir. sea grant coll. program, 1983-2000. Mem. ocean studies bd. NRC, 1999—. Author: (with others) A Coastal Marine Ecosystem, 1978, The New England High Salt Marshes, 1982; editor-in-chief Estuaries, 1988—; also articles. Recipient Ketchum award Woods Hole Oceanographic Inst., 1992, Achievement award New Eng. Estuarine Rsch. Soc., 2000, Achievement award Nat. Sea Grant Assn., 2001, Lifetime appointment Nat. Assn. of Nat. Academies, 2002; grantee NSF, NOAA, EPA, Office Water Resources Rsch., State of R.I. Mem. Am. Soc. Limnology and Oceanography (governing bd. 1984-87), Estuarine Rsch. Fedn. (Odum award 2003), Am. Soc. for Environ. History. Office: Univ of RI Dept Of Oceanography Kingston RI 02881 Office Phone: 401-874-6803. E-mail: swn@gso.uri.edu.

NIZALOWSKI, JOHN ANTHONY, writer, educator; b. Endicott, N.Y., Feb. 4, 1956; s. Edward Michael and Helen Nizalowski; m. Patricia Anne Wrek, June 13, 1981 (div. Nov. 2000); children: Ursula Anne, Isadora Desiree. BA in History and English, Binghamton U., N.Y., 1978; MA in English, U. Del., 1983. Instr. U. Del., Newark, 1978—81, Va. Poly. Inst. and State U., Blacksburg, 1981—86, Coll. of Santa Fe, N.Mex., 1986—90, Mesa State Coll., Grand Junction, Colo., 1990—. Cons./seminar designer Smithsonian Vacation Seminars, Santa Fe, 1990—91; dir. writing festivals Recursos de Santa Fe, 1990; dir. writing conf. Mesa State Coll., 1995—; lit. reporter The Santa Fe New Mexican, 1988—90; book columnist The Telluride Times Jour., 1994—98. Author: (book of fiction/poetry) Hooking the Sun, 2003, (anthology) The Blueline Reader, 2003, Reading Under the Sign of Nature, 2000, The Image of Technology, 1994, The Spirit That Wants Me, 1991, Harvest From the Hills, 1984; assoc. editor Pinyon Mag., 1996—, contbg. author Inside/Outside Southwest, 2000—02; contbr. numerous articles to profl. jours. Grantee Tchg./Learning grantee, State of Va., 1982—83, OSC Joint Activities grantee, State of Colo., 2001. Mem.: Robinson Jeffers Soc., Assn. for Study of Lit. and the Environment, Phi Beta Kappa. Democrat. Zen Buddhist. Avocations: hiking, astronomy, archaeology. Home: 1619 Dolores St Grand Junction CO 81503 Office: Mesa State College 1100 North Ave Grand Junction CO 81501

NIZARD, MICHAEL, editor-in-chief; Editor-in-chief Info World Mag., San Mateo, Calif. Office: Infoworld Publishing 155 Boret Rd Ste 800 San Mateo CA 94402-3108

NIZNIK, CAROL ANN, electrical engineer, educator, consultant; b. Saratoga Springs, N.Y., Nov. 10, 1942; d. John Arthur Niznik and Rosalia Sopko; m. Donald H. Walter, Jan. 11, 1964. AAS in Engring. Sci., Alfred (N.Y.) State Coll., 1962; BSEE, U. Rochester, N.Y., 1969, MSEE, 1972; PhD in Elec. Engring., SUNY, Buffalo, 1978. Technician Taylor Instrument Corp., Rochester, 1962-64; sr. technician IBM Corp., Poughkeepsie, N.Y., 1964-68; rsch. scientist Eastman Kodak Corp., Rochester, 1969-70; sr. engr. Xerox Corp., Webster, N.Y., 1971-74; rsch. ast. prof. SUNY, buffalo, 1979-80; assoc. prof. elec. engring. U. Pitts., 1980-83; pres., cons. NW Systems, Rochester, 1975—. Adj. prof. math. Rochester Inst. Tech., 1993-94; vis. assoc. prof. Ctr. for Brain Rsch., Sch. Medicine, U. Rochester, 1983-84. Author tech. monograph on cerebellum prosthesis component; contbr. some 70 articles to profl. jours.; patentee in field. Recipient fellowships, grants and U.S. govt. contracts. Mem. IEEE (sr.), Sigma Xi, Eta Kappa Nu, Tau Beta Pi. Roman Catholic. Avocations: doll collecting, care of pets, gardening. Office: NW Sys PO Box 18133 Rochester NY 14618-0133

NJIE, VERONICA P.S. clinical nurse, educator; d. Edward G. Njie and Grace B.S. Daniels-Njie. BSN, Howard U., Washington, 1992; MSN, The Cath. U. Am., Washington, 1996. RN Washington, clin. specialist in med.-surg. nursing. Tchr. Dept. Edn., Banjul, The Gambia, 1980—82; state registered nurse (SRN) Royal Victoria Hosp., Banjul, 1985—86; rsch./field asst. Med. Rsch. Coun., Fajara, 1986—87; nurse technician Howard U. Hosp., Washington, 1988—90, clin. nurse II, 1990—96; clin. nurse N.W. Health Care Ctr. Beverly Enterprise, 1990—98; clin. instr. Montgomery Coll., Tacoma Park, Md., 1996; asst. prof. nursing Balt. City C. C., Balt., 1997. Contbr. articles to profl. jours. Recipient Intramural Rsch. Tng. award, NIH, 2000. Mem.: Md. Assn. Higher Edn., ANA, Nat. League Nursing, Sigma Theta Tau. Democrat. Roman Catholic. Avocations: reading, travel, theater, dance, movies. Office: Cath U Am Michigan Ave NE Washington DC 20064 Personal E-mail: vpnjie@aol.com.

NNADI, EUCHARIA E. academic administrator; BS in Pharmacy, Creighton U., 1977; MS in Hosp. Pharmacy, U. Minn., 1978, PhD in Social and Adminstrv. Pharmacy, 1982; JD with high honors, Fla. State U., 1993. Lic. pharmacist. Asst. prof. pharmacy adminstrn. Coll. Pharmacy and Pharm. Scis. Fla. A&M U., Tallahassee, 1981—89, prof., 1989—94, dean, 1994; former dean Coll. Pharmacy and Pharm. Scis. Howard U.; v.p. acad. affairs U. Md. Ea. Shore, Princess Anne. Reviewer health affairs divsn. Tex. Higher Edn. Coordinating Bd. Contbr. articles to profl. jours., chpts. to books. Recipient Pharmacist award, Md. Pharm. Soc., 1996. Mem.: Nat. Assn. Bds. Pharmacy (item writer), Am. Coun. on Pharm. Edn. (accreditation site visits team for colls. and schs. pharmacy), Nat. Assn. State Univs. and Land-Grant Colls. (coun. acad. affairs), Order of Coif, Rho Chi. Office: U Md Ea Shore Office VP Acad Affairs Princess Anne MD 21853

NOAH, NUER, filmmaker; b. Montreal, Quebec, Canada, July 1, 1973; s. Sam Cohen and Claire Nuer. Haute Etude Commerciale, Institut Supérieur de Gestion, 1996. Workshop facilitator Learning as Leadership, San Rafael, Calif., 1999—. Cons. & coaching Learning as Leadership, 1999—. Dir.(producer, writer, cinematographer): (films) Get a Way (R.I. Internat. Film Festival, 2002, Tiburon Internat. Film Festival, 2003, Valleyfest Independant Film Festival, 2003); contbr. articles to profl. jours. Office: Learning as Leadership Po Box 150090 San Rafael CA 94915-0090 Office Phone: 415-453-5050. E-mail: noah@learnaslead.com.

NOALL, ROGER, bank executive; b. Brigham City, Utah, Apr. 1, 1935; s. Albert Edward Noall and Mabel Clayton; m. Judith Ann Stelter, Mar. 16, 1962 (div.); children: Brennan, Tyler; m. Colleen Henrietta Mannion. BS, U. Utah, 1955; LLB, Harvard U., 1958; LLM, NYU, 1959. Legal asst. Donavan, Leisure, Newton & Irvine, N.Y.C., 1959-61; assoc. Olwine, Connelly, Chase, O'Donnell & Weyher, N.Y.C., 1961-65, ptnr., 1965-67; with Bunge Corp., N.Y.C., 1967-85, exec. v.p., 1975-83; pres., chief fin. officer Centran Corp., Cleve., 1985-85; vice chmn., chief adminstrv. officer Soc. Corp., Cleve., 1985—; sr. v.p., chief adminstrv. officer Key Corp., Cleve., 1994—. Served in USNG, 1959. Office: Society Corp 127 Public Sq Cleveland OH 44114-1306

NOAR, MARK DAVID, internist, gastroenterologist, therapeutic endoscopist, consultant, inventor; b. Boston, Sept. 10, 1953; s. Myron Theodore and Phyllis (Krinsky) N.; m. Martine Denise Motard, May 15, 1983; children: Emmanuelle, Ariane, Jean-Claude. BS in Biology, Ursinus Coll., Collegeville, Pa., 1975; MPH in Internat. Health, Tulane U., 1977; MD, U. Cen. del Este, Dominican Republic, 1980. Intern 5th Pathway program Coll. Medicine and Dentistry N.J.-Newark Beth Israel Hosp., 1980-81; resident in internal medicine U. Nebr. Med. Ctr., Omaha, 1981-84; fellow in gastroenterology SUNY Downstate Med. Ctr., Bklyn., 1984-86; fellow in therapeutic and surg. endoscopy, vis. staff Univ. Hosp. Hamburg, Germany, 1986-87; pvt. practice, Balt., 1988—; pres., CEO Md. Gastroenterology Network, Inc., 1993—. Chmn. bd. dirs. 3CPM Co., Inc.; vice chmn. bd. dirs. Americas Bank; clin. cons. in therapeutic endoscopy Bklyn. VA Med. Ctr., 1987; dir. project devel., v.p. med. devel. Ixion, Inc., Seattle, 1987—96; staff physician dept. gastroenterology St. Joseph Hosp., Balt., Franklin Square Hosp., Balt.; bd. dirs., dir. ops. Disaster Support Network, Balt., 1990—95; session co-chmn. World Congress Gastroenterology, Sydney, Australia, 1990, IX European Workshop on Therapeutic Digestive Endoscopy, Brussels, 1991; CEO, med. dir. The Endoscopy Ctr., Inc., Balt., 1990—; CEO, bd. dirs. Md. Gastroenterology Network, Inc., The Endoscopy Ctr.; course dir. internat. hands-on ERCP Conf., Balt., 1994, Balt., 95; founder, dir. Internat. ERCP Edn. Found., 1994—; founder CEO Digestive Health Edn. Found.; dir. The Hepatitis Study Ctr.; CEO, med. dir. The Endoscopy Ctr. at Bel Air, Bel Air, Calif., 2002—. Author: (with N. Soehendra and H. Grimm) A Compendium of Therapeutic Endoscopy for the General Practitioner, 1991; editor-in-chief Internat. Video Jour. Therapeutic and Diagnostic Endoscopy; assoc. editor Endoscopy Rev.; contbr. articles and abstracts to med. jours., chpts. to books; inventor robotic interactive endoscopy simulation, precurved papillotome and ERCP catheters, "Noar pump" for disinfection and cleaning of endoscopes. Pub. lectr. Am. Cancer Soc., Balt., 1988—; physician educator Doctor and Lawyer Coalition Against Drugs, Balt., 1991-92. Fellow Royal Soc. Tropical Medicine and Hygiene; mem. ACP, AMA, Am. Coll. Gastroenterology, Am. Soc. Gastrointestinal Endoscopy, Am. Gastroenterologic Assn. (instr. regional advanced endoscopy 1993—, award for achievement and edn. in diagnostic/therapeutic biliary and pancreatic endoscopy 1992), Baltimore County Med. Soc., Md. Ambulatory Surgery Assn. (legis. chmn., bd. dirs. 1995—), Sigma Xi. Avocations: guitar, banjo, sailing, orchid culture, gourmet cooking. Office: Endoscopic Microsurgery Assocs 7402 York Rd Ste 100 Baltimore MD 21204-7532

NOBACK, RICHARDSON KILBOURNE, medical educator; b. Richmond, Va., Nov. 7, 1923; s. Gustav Joseph and Hazel (Kilborn) N.; m. Nan Jean Gates, Apr. 5, 1947; children: Carl R., Robert K., Catherine E. MD, Cornell U., 1947; BA, Columbia U., 1993. Diplomate Am. Bd. Internal Medicine. Intern N.Y. Hosp., 1947-48; asst. resident Cornell Med. div. Bellevue Hosp., N.Y.C., 1958-50, chief resident, 1950-52; instr. medicine Cornell U., N.Y.C., 1950-53; asst. prof. medicine SUNY Upstate Med. Ctr., Syracuse, 1955-56; assoc. prof. medicine U. Ky. Med. Ctr., Lexington, 1956-64; exec. dir. Kansas City (Mo.) Gen. Hosp. and Med. Ctr., 1964-69; assoc. dean, prof. medicine U. Mo. Sch. Medicine, Columbia, 1964-69, founding dean Kansas City, 1969-78, prof. medicine, 1969-90, prof. and dean emeritus, 1990—. Cons. U. Tenn., U. Mich., U. Del., Northeastern Ohio Group, U. Mo., Eastern Va. Med. Sch., Tex. Tech. U. Contbr. numerous articles to profl. jours. Bd. dirs. Kansas City Gen. Hosp., Truman Med. Ctr., Wayne Miner Health Ctr., Jackson County Med. Soc., The Shepherd's Ctr., Am. Fedn. Aging Rsch., Mo. Gerontol. Inst., The Shepherd's Ctrs. of Am.; dir. Mo. Geriatric Edn. Ctr., 1985-88. Capt. USAF Med. Svcs. 1953-55. Recipient medal of honor Avila Coll., Kansas City, 1968, merit award Met. Med. Soc., 1991, recognition award Mo. Soc. Internal Medicine, 1993. Mem. AMA, Mo. Med. Assn. (former mem. ho. of dels., v.p. 1992), Am. Geriatric Soc., Alpha Omega Alpha, Phi Kappa Phi. Avocations: photography, writing, travel. Home: 2912 Abercorn Dr Las Vegas NV 89134-7440 E-mail: nanori@earthlink.net.

NOBE, KEN, chemical engineering educator; b. Berkeley, Calif., Aug. 26, 1925; s. Sidney and Kiyo (Uyeyama) N.; m. Mary Tagami, Aug. 31, 1957; children: Steven Andrew, Keven Gibbs, Brian Kelvin. BS, U. Calif., Berkeley, 1951; PhD, UCLA, 1956. Jr. chem. engr. Air Reduction Co., Murray Hill, N.J., 1951-52; asst. prof. chem. engring. UCLA, 1957-62, assoc. prof., 1962-68, prof., 1968—, chmn. dept. chem., nuclear and thermal engring., 1978-83, founding chmn. chem. engring., 1983-84. Mem. tech. staff Ramo-Wooldridge Corp., El Segundo, Calif., 1958-59. Div. editor: Jour. Electrochem. Soc, 1967-91, Electrochimica Acta, 1977-85 Served with U.S. Army, 1944-46. Mem. Electrochem. Soc. (Henry B. Linford award 1992), Am. Chem. Soc., Internat. Soc. Electrochemistry, Am. Electroplate Surfacing Fin. Soc. (Abner Brenner Gold medal 2000), Sigma Xi. Office: UCLA Dept Chemical Engring Los Angeles CA 90095-1592

NOBE, KENNETH CHARLES, international agricultural and water resource economics consultant; b. Venedy, Ill., Oct. 26, 1930; s. Elmer F. and Alvina (Froekhe) N.; m. Hazel Leona McCullough, Oct. 22, 1949; children—Sandra, Jeffrey, Michael. BS, So. Ill. U., 1953; MS, Cornell U., 1954, PhD, 1959. Mktg. agt. USDA, Ithaca, N.Y., 1954-55; instr. Cornell U., 1955-56; economist USDA, Washington, 1958-61, USPHS, Denver, 1961-63, U.S. Dept. Interior, Washington, 1963-64; econ. cons. Harza Engring. Co. Internat., Lahore, West Pakistan, 1964-65; assoc. prof. econs. Colo. State U., Ft. Collins, 1965-69, prof. econs., chmn. econs. dept., 1969-83, prof. agrl. econs., chmn. dept. agr. and resource econs., 1984-87, emeritus prof., 1987—; exec. v.p. RAD Internat. Inc., Ft. Collins, 1987—2002; sr. ptnr. Nobe Econ. Cons., 1998—; chmn. exec. coun. Environ. Resources Ctr., 1970-71; dir. Internat. Sch. Econ. Devel. Studies, 1980-83; exec. dir. Internat. Sch. Agr. and Resource Devel., 1983-85. Econ. advisor to dir. West Pakistan Water and Power Devel. Authority, 1964-65; cons. U.S. Dept. State, AID, 1966, 76-92, Ford Found., India, 1980, World Bank, 1984-88, 94-96, FAO, UN, 1988-90, Philippines Dept. Agr., 1977, U.N. Devel. Program, Viet Nam, 1993, Viet Nam Dept. Agr. and Rural Devel., 1998; Asian Devel. Bank, Pakistan, 2001; chmn. Western Agr. Econs. Coun., 1976-78. Served with USAF, 1948-50. Recipient Ill. State Farmer award Future Farmers Am., 1947, Disting. Service award Colo. State U., 1979 Mem. Omicron Delta Epsilon. Home: 3510 Terry Ridge Rd Fort Collins CO 80524-1661

NOBEL, JOEL J. biomedical researcher; b. Phila., Dec. 8, 1934; s. Bernard D. and Golda R. (Nobel) Judovich; m. Bonnie Sue Goldberg, June 19, 1960 (div.); children: Erika, Joshua; m. Loretta Schwartz, Oct. 28, 1979; 1 child, Adam. AB, Haverford Coll., 1956; MA, U. Pa., 1958; MD, Thomas Jefferson Med. Coll., Phila., 1963. Intern Presbyn. Hosp., Phila., 1963-64; resident in surgery Pa. Hosp., Phila., 1964-65; resident in neurosurgery U. Pa. Hosp., 1965-66; practice medicine specializing in biomed. engring. rsch. and health-care tech. assessment, hosp. planning and mgmt., Phila., 1968—; dir. research Emergency Care Research Inst., Plymouth Meeting, Pa., 1968-71, dir., pres., 1971—2001; pres. Plymouth Inst., 1979—2002; founder and pres. emeritus ECRI, 2001—; founder, pres. ECRI Bhd, Malaysia, 2001—; CEO The Nobel Group, 2002—. Cons. in field; bd. dirs. Consumers Union, 1976-79, 1980—, chmn. tech. policy com., exec. bd. Publisher Health Devices, 1971-2001, Health Devices Alerts, 1977-2001; contbr. articles to profl. jours. Served with USNR, 1966-68. Smith, Kline & French fgn. fellow, 1962; grantee HEW, 1968-72; grantee Am. Heart Assn., 1965-66 Mem. AMA, APHA, Assn. Advancement Med. Instrumentation, Critical Care Med. Soc., Pa. Med. Assn., Navy League, U.S. Naval Inst., Sunday Breakfast Club, Brit. Officers Club of Phila. Home: 1434 Monk Rd Gladwyne PA 19035-1315 Office: ECRI 5200 Butler Pike Plymouth Meeting PA 19462-1298 Business E-Mail: jnobel@ecri.org.

NOBIL, JAMES HOWARD, JR., real estate investor, developer, consultant, broker; b. Columbus, Ohio, Mar. 21, 1955; s. James Howard Nobil and Carol Mae (Wiesenberger) Greenbaum; m. Elizabeth Ann Corro, Apr. 16, 1983 (div. 1998); children: Jonathan James Michael, Jennifer Carrie Lee. BA in Polit. Sci., Tufts U., 1973-75; postgrad., George Washington U., 1978-80. Lic. real estate broker Md., Va., D.C., Fla.; cert. leasing specialist ICSC. Account exec. Riviere Securities Corp., Washington, 1977-78; v.p. ops. Fed. Realty Investment Trust, Bethesda, Md., 1978-83; mng. gen. ptnr. NRW Devel. Co., Vienna, Va., 1983-84; v.p. acquisitions Oxford Nat. Properties Corp., Bethesda, 1984-85; 1st v.p. Washington Real Estate Investment Trust, Bethesda, 1985-86; pres. Washington Comml. Properties, Inc., McLean, Va., 1986—, Rent Verification Svcs. (subs. of Washington Comml. Properties, Inc.), McLean, 1986—. Mem. Internat. Coun. Shopping Ctrs., Nat. Assn. Realtors, D.C. Assn. Realtors, D.C. Area Comml. Brokers Coun. Avocations: running, boating, skiing, tennis. Office: Washington Comml Properties Inc 1420 Beverly Rd #350 Mc Lean VA 22101 Office Phone: 703-847-5100.

NOBLE, ALICE L. writer, researcher; b. Rome, Ga., Apr. 20, 1934; d. Bruce Gary Landers and Lucille Mae Pyle-Landers; m. Donald Eugene Noble, May 28, 1998. Student, Anthony's Real Estate Sch., Fresno, Calif., 1967—69, Calif. Chrsitian Coll., 1970—73, Internat. Assn. Assessing Officers, Chgo., 1980—81, Writers Digest Sch., L.A., 1999—2001. Real estate agt., Fresno, Calif., 1965—73; owner White Fang Pub., Delta Junction, Ark., 2003—. Author: (novels) Elusive Autumn, 2003, On the Kenai, 2003. Mem.: Creative Writers Anchorage. Republican. Presbyterian. Avocations: hiking, stamp and coin collecting, writing. Home: 2508 Healy St Delta Junction AK 99737 Mailing: PO Box 100 Delta Junction AK 99737 Office: White Fang Pub 2508 Healy St Delta Junction AK 99737 Office Phone: 907-895-4454. Business E-Mail: dnoble@wildak.net.

NOBLE, DOUGLAS, architecture educator; BS in Architecture, Calif. State Poly. U., 1981, BArch, 1982; MArch, U. Calif., Berkeley, 1983, PhD in Architecture, 1991. Registered Calif., 1985. With Cashion-Horie-Cocke-Gonzalez Architects, 1978—84; tchg. asst. U. Calif., Berkeley, 1983—88, lectr., 1988—91, rsch. asst., 1988—89; prof. U. So. Calif., 1991—; with Kenneth S. Wing and Assocs., 1985—86. Co-editor: Software for Architects; A Guide to Software for the Architectural Profession, (conf. procs.) Mission, Method, Madness; Computer Supported Design in Architecture, 1992. Fellow:

AIA; mem.: Assn. for Computer Aided Design in Architecture (pres. 1998), Phi Kappa Phi. Office: 204 Watt Hall U So Calif Sch Architecture Los Angeles CA 90089-0291 E-mail: dnoble@usc.edu.

NOBLE, ERNEST PASCAL, pharmacologist, biochemist, educator; b. Baghdad, Iraq, Apr. 2, 1929; came to U.S., 1946; s. Noble Babik and Barkev Grace (Kasparian) Babikian; m. Inga Birgitta Kilstromer, May 19, 1956; children— Lorna, Katharine, Erik BS in Chemistry, U. Calif.-Berkeley, 1951; PhD in Biochemistry, Oreg. State U., 1955; MD, Case Western Res. U., 1962. Diplomate Nat. Bd. Med. Examiners. Sr. instr. biochemistry Western Res. U., Cleve., 1957-62; intern Stanford Med. Ctr., Calif., 1962-63, resident in psychiatry, 1963-66, research assoc., asst. prof., 1965-69; assoc. prof. psychiatry, psychobiology and pharmacology U. Calif.-Irvine, 1969-71, prof., chief neurochemistry, 1971-76, 79-81; dir. Nat. Inst. Alcohol Abuse and Alcoholism HEW, 1976-78, assoc. adminstr. sci., alcohol, drug abuse and mental health, 1978-79; Pike prof. alcohol studies, dir. Alcohol Research Ctr. UCLA Sch. of Medicine, 1981—. Mem. various med./sci. jour. editorial bds.; contbr. numerous articles to profl. jours., chpts. to books V.p. Nat. Coun. on Alcoholism 1981-84; pres. Internat. Commn. for the Prevention of Alcoholism and Drug Dependency, 1988. Fulbright scholar, 1955-56; Guggenheim fellow, 1974-75; Sr. Fulbright scholar, 1984-85; recipient Career Devel. award NIMH, HEW, 1966-69 Fellow Am. Coll. Neuropsychopharmacology; mem. Internat. Soc. Neurochemistry, Am. Soc. Pharmacology and Exptl. Therapeutics, Research Soc. on Alcoholism. Office: UCLA 760 Westwood Plz Los Angeles CA 90095-8353

NOBLE, JAMES WILKES, actor; b. Dallas, Mar. 5, 1922; s. Ralph Byrne and Lois Frances (Wilkes) N.; m. Carolyn Owen Coates, May 19, 1956; 1 child: Jessica Katherine. Student, North Tex. Coll., Arlington, 1939-41, So. Methodist U., Dallas, 1941-43, 1946-47. Lectr. acting and mime Am. Acad. Dramatic Art, 1956-59. Mem. Lydia Tarnower Modern Dance Co., 1937-39; title role in 1st TV drama, The Egoist on Dumont TV, 1943; 1st N.Y. Stage appearance Helena's Room, 1947; 1st Broadway appearance: The Big Knife, 1949; others include: The Velvet Glove, 1949; Medea, 1951; Come of Age, 1952; A Far Country, 1961; Strange Interlude, 1963; 1776, 1971; The Runner Stumbles, 1976; mem. Am. Mime Theatre, 1952-59; appeared in numerous TV dramas and soap operas; appeared in more than 200 plays in theatres throughout the world most recent: Stratford Characters in Stratford-Upon-Avon, England, T.S. Eliot in The Poet's Theatre, Cambridge, Mass., 1996, Out of Order, Calgary, Alta., Can., 1997, Moon Over Buffalo, Edmonton, Alta., 1998; TV appearances include the role of the Governor on Benson, ABC-TV, 1979-86, series First Impressions, CBS-TV, 1987, series Archies, NBC-TV, 1990, Law and Order, 1991; movies include: Dragonfly, 1965; The Sporting Club, 1967; 1776, 1972; Promises in the Dark, 1978; Ten, 1979; Being There, 1979; Airplane II, 1983; You Talkin' To Me?, 1986; Tiger's Tale, 1987, Chances Are, 1988, Absent Minded Professor, 1989, Law and Order, 1991, All My Children, 1992; numerous other appearances. Author jour. article on Am. mime. Active Lee Strasberg Theater, Theatre Artists Workshop. Served as lt. USNR, 1943-46, P.T.O. Named Hon. Gov., N.J., N.Y., 1982; appreciation award Am. Heart Assn., 1983. Mem. Actors Studio (life), Actors Equity, SAG, AFTRA. Democrat. Roman Catholic. Avocation: photography. Office: Paradigm Agy 10100 Santa Monica Blvd Los Angeles CA 90067-4003

NOBLE, JOSEPH VEACH, fine arts administrator; b. Phila., Apr. 3, 1920; s. Joseph Haderman and Helen Elizabeth (Veach) N.; m. Olive Ashley Mooney, June 21, 1941 (dec. Sept. 1978); children: Josette, Ashley, Laurence; m. Lois Cook Cartwright, Oct. 27, 1979. Student, U. Pa., 1942. Cameraman, dir. DeFrenes and Co. Studios, Phila., 1939-41; studio mgr. WPTZ, Philco TV Sta., Phila., 1941-42, DeFrenes and Co. Studios, 1946-49; gen. mgr. Murphy-Lillis Prodns., N.Y.C., 1949-50; exec. v.p. Film Counselors, Inc., N.Y.C., 1950-56, dir., 1950-82; operating adminstr. Met. Mus. Art, 1956-67, vice dir. adminstrn., 1967-70; dir. Mus. City N.Y., 1970-85; exec. dir. Soc. Medalists, 1985-95. Photog. salon exhibitor, from 1936; lectr. CCNY, 1949-51 Author: The Techniques of Painted Attic Pottery, 1965, The Historical Murals of Maplewood, 1961, Forgery of the Etruscan Terracotta Warriors, 1961; Contbr.: Ency. Brit, 1970. Trustee Corning Mus. of Glass, 1970—; mem. Morrow Meth. Ch., pres. trustees, 1972-77; chmn. N.Y. State Bd. Hist. Preservation 1972-76; co-chmn. Save Venice, Inc., 1972; trustee Brookgreen Gardens, 1971—. pres., 1976-90, chmn., 1990-95, chmn. emeritus, 1995—. With AUS, 1942-46. Recipient Venice Film Festival medal for photography in sci., 1948, Sigma Xi award 1963, Maple Leaf award Maplewood, N.J., 1966, 87, Gold medal for The Big Apple N.Y. Film Festival, 1979, Disting. Svc. award Maplewood C. of C., 1987. Fellow Soc. Antiquaries London, Am. Numismatic Soc.; mem. N.Y. State Assn. Museums (pres. 1970-72), NAD (medal 1976), Nat. Sculpture Soc. (medal 1978, 91), Artists' Fellowship (medal 1978), Archeol. Inst. Am. (treas. 1963-70), Museums Council N.Y.C. (chmn. 1965-67), Am. Assn. Museums (pres. 1975-78, Disting. Svc. Awd., 1991), Cultural Instns. Group N.Y.C. (chmn. 1984-85), Soc. Promotion Hellenic Studies; Am. Watercolor Soc. (medal 1982). Clubs: Maplewood Country; Explorers (N.Y.C.), Century Assn. (N.Y.C.). Home: 107 Durand Rd Maplewood NJ 07040-2103 Office: Brookgreen Gardens PO Box 3368 Pawleys Island SC 29585-3368 *As a classical archaeologist I always have been guided by the ancient saying, "Let the light of the past illumine a pathway to the future.".*

NOBLE, LAWRENCE ALAN, artist; b. Tampa, Fla., Nov. 11, 1948; s. Clymer Marlay and Mary Alice (Cortes) N.; m. Elizabeth Wearden, May 22, 1982; children: Casey Josephine, John Marlay. Student, Tex. Acad. Art, 1969, Houston Mus. Fine Art Sch., 1974-75. Illustrator U.S. Army, Ft. Sheridan, Ill., 1970, San Francisco, 1971; staff artist, promotion dept. The Houston Chronicle, Houston, 1972; art dir., designer, illustrator Middaugh Assocs., Houston, 1973; freelance illustrator Noble Studio, Houston, 1973-88, designer, sculptor Crestline, Calif., 1988—. Sculptor, com. mem. San Bernardino County Peace Officers Meml. Com., San Bernardino, 1995—, designer sculptor Victor Salmones galleries, 1995—, sculptor, com. mem. Jack Benny Meml. Com., 1992-93, Ft. Sheridan Centennial Com., 1989-90. Sculptor, designer various art galleries. Hon. firefighter City of Redlands Fire Dept., 1997; marshall 4th July Parade Crestline Resorts C. of C., 1996, vol. McGovern for Pres., Dem. party, 1972. With U.S. Army, 1969-71. Recipient 4th U.S. Army Leadership and Integrity medal, 1986. Mem. Nat. Sculptors Soc., Internat. Sculpture Ctr., Calif. Prof. Firefighters, Star Wars Fan Club, Star Trek Fan Club. Republican. Roman Catholic. Avocations: surfing, reading, history. Office: Noble Studio PO Box 2229 Crestline CA 92325-2229

NOBLE, LAWRENCE MARK, lawyer, association administrator; b. N.Y.C., Mar. 30, 1952; s. Hyman S. and Jeanette (Lapides) N.; m. Patricia Fay Bak, Mar. 28, 1981; children: Jonathan, David. BA, Syracuse U., 1973; JD, George Washington U., 1976; Program for Sr. Mgrs. in Govt., John F. Kennedy Sch. Govt., Boston, 1991. Bar: D.C. 1976, U.S. Dist. Ct. 1977, U.S. Ct. Appeals (D.C. cir.) 1977, U.S. Supreme Ct. 1980, U.S. Ct. Appeals (4th cir.) 1989, U.S. Ct. Appeals (5th cir.), 1992. Atty. Aviation Consumer Action Project, Washington, 1976-77; litigation atty. Fed. Election Commn., Washington, 1977-79, asst. gen. counsel for litigation, 1979-83, dep. gen. counsel, 1983-87, gen. counsel, 1987-2000; exec. dir., gen. counsel Ctr. Responsive Politics, Washington, 2001; adj. prof. law George Washington U. Law Sch., Washington, 1999—. Mem. ABA election law commn., 1988-93; mem. adminstrv. conf. U.S., Washington, 1987-96. Contbr. articles to profl. jours.; lectr., spkr. in field. Mem. Coun. on Govt. Ethics Laws (pres. 1997-98), D.C. Bar Assn. Avocations: computer graphics, photography, writing. Home: 9438 Sunnyfield Ct Potomac MD 20854-2090 Office: Ctr Responsive Politics 1101 14th ST NW Ste 1030 Washington DC 20005 E-mail: lnoble@crp.org.

NOBLE, MERRILL EMMETT, retired psychology educator, psychologist; b. Las Vegas, N.Mex., July 25, 1923; s. Merrill Emmett and Martha (Van Petten) N.; m. Joy Lind, July 18, 1953; children: Margaret Lind, Eric Severin. BA, N.Mex. Highlands U., 1947; MA, Ohio State U., 1949, PhD, 1951. Research asso. Ohio State U., 1951-54, summers 1956, 58; mem. faculty Kans. State U., 1954-67, prof. psychology, 1961-67, chmn. dept., 1962-67; prof. psychology Pa. State U., 1967-89, chmn. dept., 1967-77, ret., 1989. Vis. scientist Inst. for Perception TNO, Soesterberg, Netherlands, 1973-74, 77-78, 80, also NATO vis. lectr. several univs. Mem. editorial bd. Psychol. Bull., 1963-64, Jour. Exptl. Psychology, 1967-78, Acta Psychologica, 1978-82, Human Performance, 1987-92. Fellow APA (com. on adv. svcs. for edn. and tng. 1967-70, accreditation com. 1979-82), AAAS, Psychonomic Soc., Midwestern Psychol. Assn. (mem. coun. 1967-70), Sigma Xi. Home: 2562 Calle Delfino Santa Fe NM 87505-6488 E-mail: menoble@comcast.net.

NOBLE, MILDRED M. retired social worker; b. Ont., Can., July 13, 1925; d. Edward Paibomasai and Mary Baids; 1 child, Carol Mills. BA, Boston Coll., 1984; MS, MIT, 1988. Cert. in alcohol counseling Boston Med. Ctr. Lectr. Harvard U., Cambridge, Mass., Radcliffe Coll., U. Mass., Amherts, Boston Coll., Wheelock Coll., Wellesley (Mass.) Coll., 1997—, R.I. Mus., Providence, 1997. Author: Sweet Grass, 1998; prodr., dir. video Clan Women in the 90s, 1990 (Thanks Be to Grandmother Winifred Found. grantee). Advocate Native Am. Cmtys. in New Eng. Region, Boston Indian Coun., 1972—; cultural coord. Children's Mus., Boston, 1978; bd. dirs. Native Am. Ctr. of Boston, 1972—, Boston Writer's Room, 1997. Recipient Cert. of Recognition, Mass. Ctr. for Native Am. Awareness, Inc., 1994. Home: 255 Massachusetts Ave Boston MA 02115-3505

NOBLE, RICHARD EDWARDS, historian, educator; b. N.Y.C. s. William and Joyce Noble; m. Janice Alecia Pryor; children: Martha Alecia Clayton, Jonathan Edwards Harris. BA in History, Trinity Coll., Hartford, Conn., 1980, MA in History, 1982. Chmn. history dept. The Fay Sch., Southborough, Mass., 1982—. Chaplan coord. The Fay Sch., 1982—2003. Author: Fences of Stone, Brantwood: A History; columnist Southborough Villager; author: Bantam Baseball, 1981, The Touch of Time, 1983, Brantwood, 1985, Fences of Stone, 1990, To honor the Trust, 2004. Trustee Brantwood Camp for Boys, Peterborough, NH, 1999—; chaplain Fraternal Order of Eagles, Marlboro, Mass., 2003—04. Mem.: Southborough Hist. Soc. (life), Rotary, Delta Psi St. Anthony Hall (life; pres. 1979—80). Home: The Fay Sch Southborough MA 01772

NOBLE, ROBERT B. advertising executive; b. 1945; BFA, Southwest Mo. State U. With Batz, Hodgson & Nevwoehner Advt. Agy., St. Louis, 1965-69, Noble & Assocs., Springfield, Mo., 1969—, now pres., CEO. Address: Noble & Assoc 2155 W Chesterfield Blvd Springfield MO 65807-8650

NOBLE, ROBERT WILLIAM, JR., retired elementary school educator, minister; b. Salem, Ohio, Apr. 7, 1949; s. Robert William and Grace Eleanor Noble; m. Mary Annette Lossman, Aug. 7, 1971 (div. Aug. 1994); children: Justin Robert, Jeremy David, Joshua James; m. Mary Alice Ladigo, July 1, 1995; 1 child, Robert William Tildon III. BS in Edn., Westminster Coll., 1971. Ordained min. Am. Bapt. Ch., 1976. Choral dir. Mohawk Area Schs., Bessemer, Pa., 1971—74; choral dir., chair dept. fine arts Struthers (Ohio) City Schs., 1974—2002; pastor Locust Grove Bapt. Ch., Salem, Ohio, 1990—. Founder, pres. Lost Then Found. Ministries, Struthers, 1968—2003; pres., bd. dirs. Greater Youngstown (Ohio) Teen Challenge, 1988—93; sole propr. The Choral Workbook Series, Struthers, Ohio, 1994—. Author: Educational Choral Workbook/The Choral Workbook Series, 1994, The Unmuzzled, Dizzy-Eyed, Director's Guide to Producing a Renaissance Celebration, 2003; composer: (songs) Grave Where Is Thy Victory?, over 75 contemporary Christian songs; prodr., arranger, soloist: 14 LP/CD recordings. Active cmty. theatre. Recipient Young Artist award, Erie Philharm., 1971, Lifetime Membership, Struthers PTA, 1984, award for best new talent, Youngstown Playhouse, 2001. Mem.: NEA, Ohio Edn. Assn., Music Educators Nat. Conf. (mem. state assessment com. 1991—94). Republican. Baptist. Avocations: golf, photography, woodworking. Home: 449 Sixth St Struthers OH 44471 Office: Choral Workbook Series PO Box 161 Struthers OH 44471

NOBLES, LAURENCE HEWIT, retired geology educator; b. Spokane, Sept. 28, 1927; s. Harry and Florence (Giffin) N.; m. Barbara Joanne Smith, Aug. 28, 1948; children: Heather C., Laurence F. BS, MS, Calif. Inst. Tech., 1949; PhD, Harvard, 1952. Instr. geology Northwestern U., 1952-55, asst. prof., 1955-61, assoc. prof., 1961-67, prof., 1967-90, prof. emeritus, 1990—, also asst. dean Coll. Arts and Scis., 1966-67, asso. dean, 1968-70; acting dean Northwestern U. (Coll. Arts and Scis.), 1970-72, dean adminstrn., 1972-81, v.p. adminstrn. and fin. planning, 1981-86. Trustee Adler Planetarium, 1980-86; faculty rep. Big Ten Conf., 1976-81; trustee Chgo. Acad. Scis., 1967-87, pres., 1973-78, hon. trustee, 1987—. Mem. Am. Geophys. Union, Geol. Soc. Am. E-mail: lnobles@cablespeed.com.

NOBLES, MARIA MORGUN, soil scientist, researcher; b. Moscow, Nov. 19, 1973; arrived in US, 1995; d. Evgeny Georgievitch Morgun and Tatyana Ivanovna Smolikhina. Diploma of Higher Edn., Moscow State U., 1995; PhD, Tex. A&M U., 2001. Postdoctoral rsch. assoc. dept. soil and crop scis. Tex. A&M U., College Station, 2001—. V.p. fin. Internat. Student Assn., Tex. A&M U., College Station, 1998—99. Scholar, Moscow Govt., 1993, Soros Found., 1994. Mem.: Soil Sci. Soc. Am. Office: Texas A&M University 546 Heep Center College Station TX 77843-2474 E-mail: m-morgun@tamu.edu.

NOBLITT, HARDING COOLIDGE, political scientist, educator; b. Marion, N.C., Oct. 31, 1920; s. Walter Tate and Nellie Mae (Horton) N.; m. Louise Hope Lester, July 3, 1943; 1 son, Walter Thomas. BA, Berea Coll., 1942; MA, U. Chgo., 1947, PhD, 1955. Mem. faculty Concordia Coll., Moorhead, Minn., 1950-90, prof. polit. sci., 1956-90, Wije Disting. prof., 1979-82, chmn. dept., 1964-72, prof. emeritus, 1990. Mem. editorial bd.: Discourse: A Review of the Liberal Arts, 1957-67, acting editor, 1959-60. Democratic candidate Congress, 1962; del. Dem. Nat. Conv., 1964; chmn. Profs. for Johnson-Humphrey, Minn., 1964; chmn. platform com. Dem. State Conv., 1968; mem. Gov's Citizens Council on Aging, 1963-68; mem. City Charter Commn., Moorhead, 1985—; mem. Minn. Higher Edn. Coordinating Bd., 1971-81, sec., 1974-75, pres., 1979-80. Served with AUS, 1943-46, ETO. Recipient 1st ann. Great Tchr. award Concordia Coll., 1960; recipient Flaat Disting. Service award Concordia Coll., 1982 Mem. Am. Polit. Sci. Assn., Am. Legion, Phi Kappa Phi, Pi Gamma Mu, Tau Kappa Alpha, Pi Kappa Delta Presbyterian (elder). Home: 2014 4th St S Moorhead MN 56560-4131 Office: Concordia Coll Dept Polit Sci Moorhead MN 56560

NOBLITT, NANCY ANNE, aerospace engineer; b. Roanoke, Va., Aug. 14, 1959; d. Jerry Spencer and Mary Louise (Jerrell) N. BA, Mills Coll., Oakland, Calif., 1982; MS in Indsl. Engring., Northeastern U., 1990; JD, Coll. William and Mary, 2003. Data red specialist Universal Energy Sys., Beaver Creek, Ohio, 1981; aerospace engr. turbine engine divsn. components br. turbine group aero-propulsion lab. Wright-Patterson AFB, Ohio, 1982-84, engine assessment br. spl. engines group, 1984-87; lead analyst cycle methods computer aided engr. GE, Lynn, Mass., 1987-90, Lynn PACES project coord., 1990-91; software sys. analyst Sci. Applications Internat. Corp., with artificial intelligence, 1991-92, software engring. mgr., intelligence applications integration Hampton, Va., 1992-93, mgr. test engring. and sys. support, 1993-94, mgr. configuration mgmt., 1994, mgmt. asst. to TBMCS program mgr., 1994-95; sr. simulation engr. Chem Demil, 1995-98; supervisory engr. Analytical Mechanics Assocs., Hampton, 1998-99; sr. project engr. Newport News (Va.) Shipbuilding Inc., 1999-00. Tutor math. and sci. Centerville Sch. Bd., Ohio, 1982-86; tutor math. and physics Marblehead Sch. Bd., Mass., 1988-90; tutor math., chemistry and physics Poquoson Sch. Bd., Va., 1994—; rep. alumnae admissions Boston area Mills Coll., 1987-91, trustee, bd. govs., 1995-98; mem. Citizens for Hilton Area Revitalization, 1994—. Math. and sci. tutor Centerville Sch. Bd., Ohio, 1982-86, math. and physics tutor Marblehead (Mass.) Sch. Bd., 1988-90; tutor math., chemistry and physics Poquoson Sch. Bd., Va., 1994—; rep. alumnae admissions Mills Coll., Boston area, 1987-91, trustee/bd. govs., 1995-98; mem. Citizens for Hilton Area Revitalization, 1994—. Recipient Notable Achievement award USAF, 1984, Spl. award Fed. Lab. Consortium, 1987. Mem. Soc. Mfg. Engrs., Sports and Entertainment Law Soc., Phi Alpha Delta. Avocation: book collecting. Home: 58 Hopkins St Newport News VA 23601-4034 Office: Newport News Shipbuilding Newport News VA 23607

NOBUMOTO, KAREN S. prosecutor; BA, U. Hartford, 1973; JD Southwestern U., 1989. Dep. dist. atty. County of L.A. Named Unsung Hero, KFWB Radio, 1997, Prosecutor of Yr., Century City Bar Assn., 1998, Person of Yr., Met. News-Enterprise, 2001, Lawyer of Yr., Calif. Lawyer Mag., 2003, Alumna of Yr., Southwestern U., 2003, Super Lawyer, L.A. mag., 2004. Mem.: L.A. County Bar Assn., Calif. Assn. Black Lawyers, Assn. Dep. Dist. Attys., Black Women Lawyers L.A., Women Lawyers Assn. L.A., John M. Langston Bar Assn. (pres. 1997), State Bar Calif. (pres. 2001—02), Coalition 100 Black Women, Breakfast Club, Chancery Club. Office: LA Dist Attys Office 210 W Temple St Ste 18000 Los Angeles CA 90012-3210 Office Phone: 310-288-1246. E-mail: karennobu@aol.com.

NOCAS, ANDREW JAMES, lawyer; b. L.A., Feb. 2, 1941; s. John Richard and Muriel Phyliss (Harvey) Nocas; m. Cassandra Nocas; 1 child, Scott Andrew. BS, Stanford U., 1962, JD, 1964. Bar: Calif. 1965. Assoc. Thelen, Marrin, Johnson & Bridges, L.A., 1964-71, ptnr., 1972-91; pvt. practice L.A., 1992-2000; atty. real property divsn. Office L.A. City Atty., 2000—. Del. Calif. Bar Conv., 1972—92. Served to capt. JAGC USAR. Fellow: Am. Bar Found.; mem.: ABA (chmn. arbitration com. 1981), Los Angeles County Bar Found. (trustee 1992—99), Am. Bd. Trial Advs., Los Angeles County Bar Assn. (chmn. sect. law office mgmt. 1980—82, chair errors and omissions com. 1987—88, chair litig. sect. 1988—89). Office: Office LA City Atty 200 N Main St 7th Fl Los Angeles CA 90012 Office Phone: 213-978-8197. Business E-Mail: anocas@atty.lacity.org.

NOCE, WALTER WILLIAM, JR., hospital administrator; b. Neptune, N.J., Sept. 27, 1945; s. Walter William and Louise Marie (Jenkins) N.; m. Cinda Ann Miller, Apr. 15, 1967; children: Krista Suzanne, David Michael. BA, LaSalle Coll., Phila., 1967; M.P.H., UCLA, 1969. Regional coordinator USPHS, Rockville, Md., 1969-71; v.p. Hollywood Presbyn. Hosp., Los Angeles, 1971-75; sr. v.p. Hollywood Presbyn. Med. ctr., 1975-77; v.p. adminstrn. Huntington Meml. Hosp, Pasadena, Calif., 1977-83; pres., chief exec. officer St. Joseph Hosp., Orange, Calif., 1983-90; pres. so. Calif. region St. Joseph Health System, 1987-90, exec. v.p., 1990-94; pres., CEO Children's Hosp., L.A., 1995—. Preceptor UCLA Health Services Mgmt. Program, 1977—; chmn. bd. Health Plan of Am., 1985-91; chmn. Hosp. Coun. So. Calif., 1989. Exec. v.p. Mental Health Assn. in Los Angeles County, 1979-82; regional v.p. Calif. Mental Health Assn., 1982-83. W. Glenn Ebersole finalist Assn. Western Hosp., 1969; recipient USPHS letter commendation, 1971, leadership in health affairs award Healthcare Assn. So. Calif., 1997. Mem. Am. Coll. Hosp. Adminstrs., Am. Hosp. Assn. (ho. of dels. 1994—), Nat. Assn. Children's Hosps. (bd. dirs. 1995—), Calif. Assn. Cath. Hosps. (chmn. 1990-91), Calif. Assn. Hosps. and Health Sys. (chmn. 1992), UCLA Hosp. Adminstrn. Alumni Assn. (pres. 1979-80), Pasadena C. of C. (v.p. 1980-82). Home: 1012 Glen Oaks Blvd Pasadena CA 91105-1108 Office: Childrens Hosp Los Angeles 4650 W Sunset Blvd Los Angeles CA 90027-6062 *Ambition is necessary for success, but success achieved at the expense of others is failure.*

NOCELLA, RICHARD J. lawyer; b. Roxborough, Pa., Nov. 14, 1969; BSBA cum laude, LaSalle U., Phila., 1992; JD, Widener U., Wilmington, Del., 1997. Bar: N.J. 1997, Pa. 1997, U.S. Dist. Ct. N.J. 1997, U.S. Dist. Ct. (ea. dist.) Pa. 1997, U.S. Tax Ct. 2002. Law clk. The Hon. Irvin J. Snyder, Camden Vicinage, NJ, 1997—98; atty. Parker, McCay & Criscuolo, Marlton, NJ, 1998—2001; tax mgr. PricewaterhouseCoopers LLP, Phila., 2001—. Recipient Outstanding Svc. award, Widener U. Sch. Law, Order of the Barrister, 1997. Mem.: ABA (tax sect.), Pa. Bar Assn., N.J. Bar Assn. Office: PricewaterhouseCoopers LLP 2001 Market St Philadelphia PA 19103

NOCERA, JOSEPH, editor, writer; BS in Journalism, Boston U. Contbg. editor Newsweek; exec. editor New England Monthly, Fortune Mag., editorial dir.; editor Wash. Monthly; columnist The Profit Motive column, GQ, Esquire; sr. editor Tex. Monthly Mag.; editor-at-large Fortune Mag.; columnist Money Mag., 1998—. Anchor PBS Frontline Documentary, Betting on the Market, 1997. Contbr. articles to Wall Street Journal, Newsweek, N.Y. Times, Wash. Monthly; author: Bidness: The Booms and Busts of the Texas Economy, 1986, A Piece of the Action: How the Middle Class Joined the Money Class, 1994. Named one of 100 Business News Luminaries of the Century, The Journalist and Financial Reporting, 2000; recipient John Hancock award, 1983, 1984, 1991, Gerald Loeb award, 1993, 1996, Helen Bernstein award, N.Y. Public Libr., 1995. Office: Fortune 1271 Sixth Ave 16th Flr New York NY 10020

NOCHIMSON, DAVID, lawyer; b. Paterson, N.J., June 19, 1943; s. Samuel S. and Mildred (Singer) N.; m. Roberta Maizel, June 5, 1966 (div. 1972); m. Gail Burgess, May 26, 1978. BA, Yale U., 1965; LLB, Columbia U., 1968; LLM, Australian Nat. U., Canberra, 1969. Bar: N.Y. 1970, Calif. 1977. Assoc. Paul, Weiss, Rifkind, Wharton and Garrison, N.Y.C., 1970-72; sr. v.p. Comprop Equities Corp., N.Y.C., 1972-76; assoc. Mitchell, Silberberg and Knupp, L.A., 1977-80, ptnr., 1980-83, Ziffren, Brittenham, Branca, Fischer, Gilbert-Lurie & Stiffelman, L.A., 1983—. Adv. com. UCLA Entertainment Symposium, 1979-99, co-chmn., 1981-82. Contbr. articles to Encyclopedia of Investments, 1982, profl. jours. Pres. Friends of the L.A. Free Clinic, 1994-96; trustee Santa Monica (Calif.) Mus. of Art, 1995—. Fulbright scholar, Australia, 1968-69. Mem. ABA (forum com. on entertainment and sports industries 1982—, editor The Entertainment and Sports Lawyer 1982-89, chmn. 1989-92), Internat. Bar Assn. (Vice chmn. entertainment com. 1986-90), Am. Bar Found., Beverly Hills Bar Assn. Democrat. Jewish. Avocations: tennis, racquetball, yoga, playing piano, hiking. Office: Ziffren Brittenham Branca Fischer Gilbert-Lurie and Stiffelman 1801 Century Park W Los Angeles CA 90067-6406 Office Phone: 310-552-3388.

NOCHLIN-SOTO, DAVID, neuropathologist; s. Zelman Nochlin-Pet and Esperanza Soto-Correa; children: Abraham Nochlin-Gargari, Gabriel Nochlin-Gargari. MD, Faculty Medicine, UNAM, 1965—70. Diplomate in neuropathology Am. Bd. Pathology. Rotating internship West Jersey Hosp., Camden, NJ, 1973—74; resident in neurology Kingsbrook Jewish/Downstate Med. Ctr., Bklyn., 1974—77; anatomic pathology-neuropathology fellowship Va. Commonwealth U. - Med. Coll. Va., Richmond, 1977—80; clin. asst. prof. pathology NY Med. Coll., Valhalla, 1980—84; attending neuropathologist Mexican Inst. Social Security, 1982—83; sr. staff fellow Lab. Neuroscis., Nat. Inst. Aging, Bethesda, Md., 1984—86; sr. neuropathology fellow Alzheimer's Disease Rsch. Ctr., U. Wash., Seattle, 1986—88; rsch. asst. prof. pathology U. Wash., Seattle, 1988—91, asst. prof. pathology, 1991—96, lectr., 1996—. Interim dir. neuropathology core Alzheimer's Disease Rsch. Ctr., U. Wash., Seattle, 1996—98. Contbr. articles to med. jours. Mem.: AAAS, Am. Acad. Neurology, Wash. State Med. Assn., Am. Registry Pathology, Soc. Neuroscience, U.S.-Canadian Acad. Pathology, Am. Assn. Neuropathologists (Weil Award, Hon. Mention 1989), NY Acad. Scis. (life). Business E-Mail: dnochlin@u.washington.edu.

NOCHMAN, LOIS WOOD KIVI (MRS. MARVIN NOCHMAN), retired educator; b. Detroit, Nov. 5, 1924; d. Peter K. and Annetta Lois (Wood) Kivi; m. Harold I. Pitchford, Sept. 6, 1944 (div. May 1949); children: Jean Wood Pitchford Scott, Joyce Lynn Pitchford Undiano; m. Marvin A. Nochman, Aug. 15, 1953; 1 child, Joseph Asa. AB, U. Mich., 1946, AM, 1949. Tchr. adult edn., Honolulu, 1947, Ypsilanti (Mich.) H.S., 1951-52; spl. instr. English Wayne State U., Detroit, 1953, 54; tchr. Highland Park (Mich.) Coll., 1950-51, instr. English, 1954-83; ret., 1983. Mem. exec. bd. Highland Park Fedn. Tchrs., 1963—66, 1973, del. to nat. conv., 64, 1971—74; rep. higher edn. Mich. Fedn. Tchrs. Exec. Com., 1972—76; mem. faculty adv. com. Gov's Commn. Higher Edn., 1973—. Contbr. articles to profl. jours. Tchr. Baha'i Schs., Davison, Mich., 1954—55, 1958—59, 1963—66, Beaulac, Canada, 1960, Greenacre, Maine, 1965; sec. local spiritual assembly Baha'is, Ann Arbor, Mich., 1953, sec. Detroit, 1954, chmn., 1955; mem. nat. com. Baha'is U.S., 1955—58; sec. com. and coun. Baha'i Schs., Davison, Mich., 1956, 1958, 1963—68; Baha'i lectr. subject of local TV show Senior Focus, 1992. Recipient Women's Movement plaque, Women Lawyers Assn. Mich., 1975. Mem.: MLA, NOW, Nat. Soc. Lit. and Arts, Am. Fedn. Tchrs., Mich. Coll. English Assn., Nat. Coun. Tchrs. English, Women's Equity and Action League (sec. Mich. chpt. 1975—79), Alpha Gamma Delta, Alpha Lambda Delta. Avocation: U.S. Swimming Master Champion.

NODDINGS, NEL, education educator, writer; b. Irvington, N.J., Jan. 19, 1929; d. Edward A. Rieth and Nellie A. (Connors) Walter; m. James A. Noddings, Aug. 20, 1949; children: Chris, Howard, Laurie, James, Nancy, William, Sharon, Edward, Vicky, Timothy. BA in Math., Montclair State Coll., 1949; MA in Math., Rutgers U., 1964; PhD in Edn., Stanford U., 1973; PhD (hon.), Columbia Coll., S.C., 1995. Cert. tchr., Calif., N.J. Tchr. Woodbury (N.J.) Pub. Schs., 1949-52; tchr. math. dept. Matawan (N.J.) High Sch., 1958-62, chair, asst. prin., 1964-69; curriculum supr. Montgomery Twp. Pub. Schs., Skillman, N.J., 1970-72; dir. precollegiate edn. U. Chgo., 1975-76; asst. prof. Pa. State U., State College, 1973; from asst. prof. to assoc. prof. Stanford (Calif.) U., 1977-86, prof., 1986—, assoc. dean, 1990-92, acting dean, 1992-94, Lee L. Jacks prof. child edn., 1992-98, prof. emeritus, 1998—; prof. philosophy and edn. Columbia U., N.Y.C., 1998—. Bd. dirs. Ctr. for Human Caring Sch. Nursing, Denver, 1986-92; cons. NIE, NSF and various other sch. dists. Author: Caring: A Feminine Approach to Ethics and Moral Education, 1984, Women and Evil, 1989; author: (with W. Paul Shore) Awakening the Inner Eye: Intuition in Education, 1984; author: (with Carol Witherell) Stories Lives Tell, 1991; author: The Challenge to Care in Schools, 1992, Educating for Intelligent Belief or Unbelief, 1993, Philosophy of Education, 1995, author: (with Suzanne Gordon and Patricia Benner) Caregiving, 1996; author: (with Michael Katz and Kenneth Strike) Justice and Caring, 1999; author: Starting at Home: Caring and Social Policy, 2002, Educating Moral People, 2002, Happiness and Education, 2003. Mem. disting. women's adv. bd. Coll. St. Catherine. Recipient Anne Roe award for Contbns. to Profl. Devel. of Women, Harvard Grad. Sch. Edn., 1993, medal for disting. svc. Tchrs. Coll. Columbia, 1994, Willystine Goodsell award, 1997, Laureate chpt. Kappa Delta Pi, Pi Lambda Theta award, 1999, award for disting. leadership in edn. Rutgers U., 2004; Spencer Mentor grantee, Spencer Found., 1995-97. Fellow Philosophy of Edn. Soc. (pres. 1991-92); mem. Am. Ednl. Rsch. Assn. (Div B, 2000, Lifetime achievment award), Am. Philos. Assn., Nat. Acad. Edn. (pres. 2001—), John Dewey Soc. (pres. 1994-96), Phi Beta Kappa (vis. scholar). Avocation: gardening. Office Phone: 732-988-9695. E-mail: noddings@stanford.edu.

NODDINGS, SARAH ELLEN, lawyer; b. Matawan, N.J. d. William Clayton and Sarah Stephenson (Cox) Noddings; children: Christopher, Aaron. BA in Math., Rutgers U., New Brunswick, N.J., 1965, MSW, 1968; JD cum laude, Seton Hall U., Newark, 1975; postgrad., UCLA, 1979. Bar: Calif. 1976, Nev. 1976, N.J. 1975, U.S. Dist. Ct. (ctrl. dist.) Calif. 1976, U.S. Dist. Ct. N.J. 1975. Social worker Carteret (N.J.) Bd. Edn., 1970-75; law clk. Hon. Howard W. Babcock, 8th Jud. Dist. Ct., Las Vegas, Nev., 1975-76; assoc. O'Melveny & Myers, L.A., 1976-78; atty. Internat. Creative Mgmt., Beverly Hills, Calif., 1978-81, Russell & Glickman, Century City, Calif., 1981-83, Lorimar Prodns., Culver City and Burbank, Calif., 1983-87, v.p., 1987-93; atty. Warner Bros. TV, Burbank, Calif., 1993-2001, v.p., 1993-2001, sr. atty., 1999-2001; pvt. practice, 2001—. Dir. county youth program, rsch. analyst Sonoma County People for Econ. Opportunity, Santa Rosa, Calif., 1968-69; VISTA vol. Kings County Cmty. Action Orgn., Hanford, Calif., 1965-66; officer, PTA bd. West H.S., Casimir Mid. Sch. and Arlington Elem. Sch. Mem. Acad. TV Arts and Scis. (nat. awards com. 1994-96), L.A. Copyright Soc. (trustee 1990-91), Women in Film, L.A. County Bar Assn. (intellectual property sect.), Women Entertainment Lawyers, Media Dist. Intellectual Propr. Bar Assn. (bd. dirs. 1999-2001), South Bay Marine League Bd. (B-2 rep. 2003—). Avocations: travel, tennis, skiing, bicycling, swimming.

NODDLE, JEFFREY, retail and food distribution executive; BA, U. Iowa. Various positions, including pres. 2 food divsns. Supervalu Inc., Eden Prairie, Minn., 1976-92, exec. v.p. mktg., 1992-95, exec. v.p. mktg.; pres., COO wholesale food cos., 1995-99, pres., COO, 2000-01, pres., CEO, 2001—, Chmn., 2002—. Office: Supervalu Inc 11840 Valley View Rd Eden Prairie MN 55344-3691*

NODEEN, JANEY PRICE, company executive; b. Scotland Neck, N.C., Nov. 7, 1959; d. Wade Hampton and Joyce Ann (Councill) P.; m. Thomas Nodeen. BS in Info. Sci., Christopher Newport Coll., 1987; grad., Def. Sys. Mgmt. Coll., 1994; grad. advanced mgmt. program, Nat. Def. U., 1995. Engring. analyst Newport News (Va.) Shipbldg., 1978-86; mgr. submarine info. resources and computer ops. Dept. of the Navy, Washington, 1986-93, mem. exec. devel. program, 1993-96, sr. staff Navy Acquisition Reform Exec., 1995, dep. program exec. officer Submarines for Acquisition, 1996-97; prin. Burke Consortium, Inc., Springfield, Va., 1997—. Mil. legis. fellow for Congressman Sam Gejdenson, 1994; sr. exec. fellow John F. Kennedy Sch. Govt. Harvard U., class officer, 1994. Home: 6915 Ashbury Dr Springfield VA 22152-3221 Office: Burke Consortium Inc Ste 510 5500 Cherokee Ave Alexandria VA 22312

NODELMAN, NANCY ZIEGLER, sculptor, designer; b. Scranton, Pa., Apr. 23, 1937; d. Alvin and Gertrude (Friedman) Ziegler; m. Jared Nodelman, Aug. 31, 1958 (div. Dec. 17, 1993); children: Seth, Ilisa. BS, Ohio State U., 1957, postgrad., 1958; sculpture student, San Francisco Art Inst., 1986-87. Founder Fiber Dimensions, Kentfield, Calif., 1990; co-dir. Atrium Gallery, Greenbrae, Calif., 1992—. Exhbns. include Regional Ctr. Arts Biennials, 1991, 93, Convergence Internat. Biennial, 1992 (Hon. Mention), Calif. Contemporary Design Biennial, 1992, Md. Park Commn. and Catalog, 1994, Internat. Miniature Textiles Biennial, Catalog, 1996, Gallery Strasse Hyogo, Japan, 1997, SOFA98NYC, 1998, Calif. Design 2000, Fiberarts Design Book Six; work featured in Fiber Arts mag., 1992; represented in permanent collections Szombathely Keptár Mus., Bank of Am. Marathon Plaza, Marin Gen. Hosp. Mem. humanities coun. bd. Marin Gen. Hosp., Greenbrae, Calif., 1992—; trustee Isaac Ziegler Trust, Scranton, Pa., 1996—. Recipient Hon. Mention Handweavers Am., 1992. Mem. Internat. Wine and Food Soc., Fiber Art Internat., Soc. Encouragement of Contemporary Art. Avocations: architectural, landscape and furniture design, paper toy collecting, consulting.

NODES, DANIEL JOSEPH, humanities educator, researcher; b. Hoboken, N.J., Nov. 1, 1951; s. John K. and Mary C. Nodes; m. Patricia A. Thompson, Nov. 18, 1972; children: Jennifer E., Daniel J. BA, St. Peter's Coll., Jersey City, N.J., 1969—74; MA, U. N.H., Durham, 1974—76; PhD, U. Toronto, 1977—82. Prof., classics, dean of studies Conception Sem. Coll., Mo., 1987—96; prof., dir., grad. liberal studies Hamline U., St. Paul, 1996—2001; assoc. prof., chmn., modern and classical languages Franciscan U. of Steubenville, Ohio, 2001—04; assoc. prof. classics and early Christian lit. Ave Maria U., Naples, Fla., 2004—. Mem. com. on classical tradition Am. Philosophical Assn.; panelist NEH, Washington, 1997—2001; v.p., AAUP Hamline U., St. Paul, 1997—2000. Editor: Avitus: The Fall of Man, 1985; author: Doctrine and Exegesis in Latin Biblical Poetry, 1993. Reader St. Nicholas Greek Orthodox Cathedral, Pitts. Fellow, NEH, 1995—96; grantee, 1984, 1985, 1988, 1993, 1994, Am. Coun. of Learned Socs., 1990, Vatican Libr. Microfilm Collection, Mellon Found., 1996. Mem.: N.Am. Patristic Soc., Am. Hist. Assn., Law and Humanities Inst., Renaissance Soc. of Am., Am. Philos. Assn., Medieval Acad. of Am. Republican. Greek Orthodox. Avocations: travel, hiking, history, Byzantine music. Office: Ave Maria Univ 1025 Commons Cir Naples FL 34119

NOE, ADRIANNE, museum administrator; PhD in History, U. Del. Assoc. dir. Armed Forces Inst. Pathology; dir. Nat. Mus. Health and Medicine, Washington. Adj. prof. computational biosciences George Mason U., Fairfax County, Va.; v.p. bd. dirs. Nat. Health Sci. Consortium. Fellow, Guggenheim Found.; History fellow, USAF. Mem.: Med. Mus. Assn. (past pres.), Washington Soc. for the History of Medicine (pres.), Acad. Medicine. Office: Nat Mus Health and Medicine Bldg 54 6825 16th St NW Washington DC 20306-6000*

NOE, CINDY J. state representative; b. St. Louis, Mo., Aug. 23, 1947; m. John Noe; 2 children. BS, Ind. U., 1969. Budget analyst Atlantic-Richfield, 1970—71; dir. recruiting and placement Louisville Vocat./Tech. Sch., 1971—72; former corp. sec.-treas., v.p. IHM Facility Svcs., Inc., Hamilton County, Ind., CEO, majority owner; state rep. dist. 87 Ind. Ho. of Reps., Indpls., 2001. Precinct committeeman Washington Twp. Dist. 87, Ind., 1996—; del. Ind. Rep. State Conv., 1998, 2000, 2001; v.p. bd. Character Coun. of Ind., late 1990s. Mem.: Sales and Mktg. Execs. (sec. 1994—96), Nat. Fedn. Ind. Bus. (leadership coun. 1990—), Ind. C. of C. (mem. com. 1998—2002). Republican. Office: Ind Ho of Reps 200 W Washington St Indianapolis IN 46204-2786

NOE, ELNORA (ELLIE NOE), retired chemicals executive; b. Evansville, Ind., Aug. 23, 1928; d. Thomas Noe and Evelyn (West) Dieter. Student, Ind. U.-Purdue U., Indpls. Sec. Pitman Moore Co., Indpls., 1946—60; with Dow Chem. Co., Indpls., 1960-90, pub. rels. asst. then mgr. employee comm., 1970-87, mgr. cmty. rels., 1987-90, DowBrands, Inc., Indpls., 1986-90, vice chmn. Indpls. C. of C. corp. affairs discussion group, 1988—89, chmn., 1989-90; mem. steering com. Learn About Bus. Recipient 2d pl. award as Businesswoman of Yr., Indpls. Bus. and Profl. Women's Assn., 1980, Indpls. Profl. Woman of Yr. award Zonta, Altrusa, Soroptomist & Pilot Svc. Clubs, 1985, DowBrands Great Things Cmty. Svc. award, 1991. Mem. Am. Bus. Women Assn. (Woman of Yr. award 1965, past pres.), Ind. Assn. Bus. Communicators (hon., Communicator of Yr. 1977), Assn. Women in Comm. (Louise Eleanor Kleinhenz award 1984), Zonta (dist. pub. rels. chmn. 1978-80, area dir. 1980-82, pres. Indpls. chpt. 1977-79, bd. dirs. 1993-95, 2000-02, 04—), Dow Indpls. Retiree Group (pres. 1995—). E-mail: elenoe@aol.com.

NOE, GUY, retired social services administrator; b. Brussels, Jan. 28, 1934; came to U.S., 1955, naturalized, 1961; s. Marinus Cornelis and Johana Dorothea (Beijne) N.; 1 child, Jeanette Sue. BS, Regional Agrl. Sch., Loiret, France, 1954. Social worker State of Wyo., Casper, 1962-66, dir. Natrona County (Wyo.) Dept. Public Assistance, Casper, 1966-79, Wyo. Div. Mental Health, Cheyenne, 1979-82, asst. adminstr. Divsn. of Youth Svcs., 1992-95; former mgr. Platte County Office Pub. Assistance and Social Svcs., Wheatland, Wyo., dir. low income energy assistance programs, 1994-95. Lectr. in field. V.p. Wyo. chpt. Big Bros., 1976-77; chmn. adv. coun. social svcs. State of Wyo., 1969-79; bd. dirs. Casper United Way, 1970—, Casper Salvation Army, 1970—, Casper chpt. ARC, 1977—; mem. Gov.'s Drug Abuse Adv. Bd., 1992—; pres. State Employees Assn. Named Outstanding Adminstr. State of Wyo., 1976; recipient Youth Svcs. award Wyo. Human Resources Confederation, 1988. Mem. ASPA, Am. Public Welfare Assn. (Wyo. membership chmn.), Wyo. State Employees Assn. (pres. 1996-97), Toastmasters. Democrat. Home: 2731 Deming Blvd Cheyenne WY 82001-5709

NOE, JAMES ALVA, retired judge; b. Billings, Mont., May 25, 1932; s. James Alva Sr. and Laura Madlen (Parmenter) N.; m. Patricia Arlene Caudill, Aug. 4, 1956; children: Kendra Sue, Jeffrey James, Bradley John, Kirkwood Merle. BA in Polit. Sci., U. Wash., 1954, LLB, 1957; LittD hon., Christian Theol. Sem., 1986. Bar: Wash. 1958, U.S. Dist. Ct. (we. dist.) Wash. 1958, U.S. Ct. Appeals (9th cir.) 1959. Dep. prosecuting atty. King County, Seattle, 1958-61; trial lawyer Williams, Kastner & Gibbs, Seattle, 1961-67; judge Seattle Mcpl. Ct., 1967-71, King County Superior Ct., 1971-96; ret., 1996. Moderator Christian Ch. (Disciples of Christ) in the U.S. and Can., 1977-79. Fellow: Am. Bar Found. (life); mem.: ABA (ho. of dels. 1976—78, 1982—87, 1991—96, 2003—, bd. govs. 1991—94, chmn. jud. divsn. 1988—89, chmn. nat. conf. state trial judges 1981—82, sr. lawyers divsn. coun. 2001—), Nat. Jud. Coll. (trustee 1988—91, 1995—2001, chair 1999—2001), Wash. State Superior Ct. Judges Assn. (pres. 1984—85, Wash. State Jurist of Yr. award 1991). Home: 8250 SE 61st St Mercer Island WA 98040-4902

NOE, JAMES KIRBY, computer consultant; b. Denver, June 21, 1951; s. George F. and Fern D. (Wilterdink) N. BSBA in Mgmt. Info., U. No. Colo., 1983. Cert. data processor, systems profl. Sys. supr. USN Tactical Support Ctr., Sigonella, Italy, 1978-79; tech. mgr. Empire Dispatch of No. Colo., Greeley, 1979-80; cons. Greeley C. of C., 1983; project mgr. software devel. Micro-health Sys. Corp., Denver, 1983-84; database analyst Manville Corp., Littleton, Colo., 1984; leader project devel. Citicorp Diners Club, Englewood, Colo., 1985; cons. Mountain Bell Telephone, Denver, 1985-86; computer programmer Colo. Dept. Revenue, Denver, 1986-87; cons. DST Sys., Inc., Kansas City, Mo., 1987-91, Broadcast Data Sys., Kansas City, Mo., 1991-92, U.S. Sprint, Kansas City, 1992—2001, TEK Sys., Kansas City, 2003—. Pres. Pine Tree Players, Brunswick, Maine, 1976-77, Sigonella Theatre Co., 1978; bd. dirs. Theatre Assocs. Group, Inc., Denver, 1985-86, v.p., 1987. Recipient Eagle Scout award Boy Scouts Am., 1964, bronze palm, 1965, 5-Yr. Svc. award Am. Cancer Soc., Brunswick, 1977; named Outstanding Vol. Theatre Assocs. Group, Inc., 1987. Mem. Assn. for Computing Machinery (com. mem. 1984-98, chmn. Denver chpt. 1987), Data Processing Mgmt. Assn. (com. mem. 1984-98). Republican. Presbyterian. Avocations: gemology, theater. Home: 600 E 8th St Apt 813 Kansas City MO 64106-1621

NOE, JOYCE M. architecture educator; BArch, U. Ill., 1964; M in Design Studies with distinction, Harvard U., 1998. Lic. arch., Hawaii. Assoc. prof. Arch. Sch. U. Hawaii, Honolulu, 1982—, assoc. dean, prof., practice program dir. Mem. City and County of Honolulu Bldg. Bd. Appeals, chair, 1983; mem. preservation rev. com. hist. structures Historic Hawaii Found.; mem. Mayor's Vision 2000 Team. Mem.: AIA (Honolulu chpt. urban design and profl. devel. coms., Honolulu chpt. Design award 1980, Nat. Educator award 1997), AIA Students, Gargoyle Archs. Honor Soc. Office: Univ Hawaii Sch Arch 2410 Campus Rd Honolulu HI 96822*

NOE, KENNETH WILLIAM, historian, educator; b. Richmond, Va., Nov. 9, 1957; s. Kenneth Elmo and Betty Lou (Handelman) N.; m. Nancy Jean Wahlbrink, June 22, 1985; 1 child, Jesse B. BA in Edn., Emory & Henry Coll., 1979; MA in History, Va. Poly. Inst., 1981; MLS, U. Ky., 1983; PhD in History, U. Ill., 1990. Librarian Blue Ridge Regional Libr., Martinsville, Va., 1983-85, Berea (Ky.) Coll., 1987-88; archivist Ill. Hist. Survey, Urbana, 1988-90; prof. history State U. West Ga., Carrollton, 1990-2000, Auburn (Ala.) U., 2000—. Author: Southwest Virginia's Railroad, 1994, Perryville: This Grand Havoc of Battle, 2001 (Peter Seaborg Book award 2002, Ky. Gov.'s Book award 2003); editor: A Southern Boy in Blue, 1996 (Tenn. History Book award 1996); co-editor: The Civil War in Appalachia, 1997; contbr. articles to profl. jours. Mem. Ala. Assn. Historians, Ala. Historical Assn., Appalachian Studies Assn. (program com. 1987-88), Org. Am. Historians, So. Hist. Assn. (membership com. 1994-95), Soc. Civil War Historians, Phi Alpha Theta, Beta Phi Mu, Phi Kappa Phi. Democrat. Lutheran. Avocations: gardening, model aircraft, travel, hiking. Home: 117 Carter St Auburn AL 36830 Office: Dept History Auburn Univ 310 Thach Hall Auburn AL 36849 E-mail: noekenn@auburn.edu.

NOEHREN, ROBERT, organist, organ builder; b. Buffalo, N.Y., Dec. 16, 1910; s. Alfred H. and Juliet (Egelhoff) N.; m. Eloise Southern, Aug. 27, 1938; children: Judith, Arthur. Student, Inst. Mus. Art, N.Y.C., 1929-30, Curtis Inst. Music, Phila., 1930-31; BMus, U. Mich., 1948; DMus (hon.), Davidson Coll., 1957. Instr. Davidson Coll., 1946-49; prof., univ. organist U. Mich., 1949-77, prof. emeritus, 1977—. Vis. prof. Eastman Sch. Music, 1967, U. Kans., 1975; organ builder; important instruments include organ in St. John's Roman Cath. Cathedral, Milw., 1st Unitarian Ch., San Francisco, 1st Presbyn. Ch., Buffalo, St. Andrew's Episc. Ch., Newport News, Va., Calvary Episc. Ch., Rochester, Minn.; designer, cons., 1954—; concert tours of Europe, 1948—; soloist Phila. Orch., Philharmonia Hungarica, New Sinfonia; rec. artist Lyrichord, Urania, Orion, Delos records; spl. research old organs Europe, 17th and 18th century organs in France. Author: An Organist's Reader, 1999; contbr. articles to profl. jours.; composer pieces for organ, piano, and voice; patentee combination action for organs. Recipient Grande Prix du Disque. Home: 17605 Drayton Hall Way San Diego CA 92128-2057

NOEL, BARBARA HUGHES MCMURTRY, retired music educator; b. Mt. Vernon, Wash., Feb. 27, 1929; d. Lowell Robinson and Mary Evelyn (Hayton) Hughes; children: Sarah Kathleen, Martha Elizabeth. BM, U. Ky., 1951, MM, 1952; PhD, U. Ill., 1972; student, Oberlin Conservatory, 1947-49. Instr. music Union Coll., Barbourville, Ky., 1952-54; instr. music and fine arts Annie Wright Sem., Tacoma, 1957-63; organist, choirmaster Episc. churches, Calif., Wash., 1954-66; chmn. music dept. U. Richmond (Va.), 1971-76, Mankato (Minn.) State U., 1976-78; dean coll. humanities and fine arts Tex. Woman's U., Denton, 1978-81; dean coll. visual and performing arts U. Mass. Dartmouth, North Dartmouth, 1981-89; prof. music U. Mass., Dartmouth, 1990—96, ret., 1996. Cons. for various music orgns. and univs., 1976—, textbook pubs., 1980—; reviewer Nat. Endowment for the Humanities. Book reviewer Providence Sunday Jour., 1984—; contbr. articles to music jours.; contbr. New Grove Dictionary of Music, 1974. Bd. dirs. Community Symphony Orchs., Mankato, 1976-78, New Bedford, Mass., 1981-87. Grad. fellow Danforth Found., U. Ill., 1966-71. Mem. Coll. Music Soc. (treas. 1983-87, v.p. 1979-83, coun. mem.), Nat. Assn. Schs. Music (undergrad. commr. 1978-81). Episcopalian. Avocations: reading, travel, hiking. Home: 73 Tucker Ln North Dartmouth MA 02747-3529

NOEL, DON OBERT, JR., retired editor, columnist; b. Elizabeth, NJ, Nov. 27, 1931; s. Don O. and Catherine (Pyle) N.; m. Elizabeth Bradford Foulds, Aug. 29, 1953; 1 child, Emily Rebecca. BA in Am. Studies, Cornell U., 1954. Reporter Hartford (Conn.) Times, 1958-68, asst. mng. editor, 1968-69, editorial page editor, 1969-74, editor in chief, 1974-75; sr. corr. WFSB-TV, host Face the State Post-Newsweek Stas., 1975-84; polit. columnist op-ed page Hartford Courant, 1984-97, ret., 1997. Bd. sec. Blue Hills Civic Assn., Hartford, 1988 ; bd. dirs. Conn. Civil Liberties Union, 1998 , vice-chair, 2003—. Served alt. mil. duty Am. Friends Svc. Com., Tokyo, 1954-56. Recipient Sevellon Brown Meml. award New England AP, 1964, Nat. Journalism award AMA, 1972, Nat. Journalism award Am. Soc. Planning Officials, 1972, 74; fellow Alicia Patterson Found., 1966-67; finalist Pulitzer Prize for non-deadline reporting, 1964. Mem. Soc. Of Friends. Avocations: gardening, birdwatching, language study. Home: 141 Ridgefield St Hartford CT 06112-1837 E-mail: dononoel@cs.com.

NOEL, EDWIN LAWRENCE, lawyer; b. St. Louis, July 11, 1946; s. Thomas Currie and Christine (Jones) N.; m. Nancy Carter Simpson, Feb. 7, 1970; children: Caroline, Edwin C. BA, Brown U., 1968; JD cum laude, St. Louis U., 1974. Bar: Mo. 1974, U.S. Dist. Ct. (ea. dist.) Mo. 1974, U.S. Ct. Appeals (8th cir.) 1974, U.S. Ct. Appeals (6th cir.) 1978, U.S. Ct. Appeals (7th cir.) 1994, U.S. Supreme Ct. 1986. Ptnr. Armstrong, Teasdale, LLP, St. Louis, 1974—, mng. ptnr., 1993-97. Bd. dirs. Corley Printing Co., St. Louis, Home Fed. Savs. Bank of Mo., 1988-93. Bd. dirs. Edgewood Children's Ctr., St. Louis, 1982-92, St. Louis Assn. for Retarded Citizens, 1984-87, Churchill Sch., 1988-94, Whitfield Sch., 1991-95; chmn. Mo. Clean Water Com., Jefferson City, 1982-88. Mem. Mo. Bar Assn., Bar Assn. Met. St. Louis, Attys. Liability Assurance Soc. (bd. dirs. 1995—). Republican. Episcopalian. Home: 301 S Mcknight Rd Saint Louis MO 63124-1884 Office: Armstrong Teasdale LLP 1 Metropolitan Sq Ste 2600 Saint Louis MO 63102-2740 Business E-Mail: enoel@armstrongteasdale.com.

NOEL, FRANKLIN LINWOOD, judge; b. N.Y.C., N.Y., Dec. 7, 1951; s. Charles Alexander and Mayme (Loth) N.; m. Ellen Barbara Perl, Sept. 15, 1979; children: Kate Alexandra, Charles David. BA, SUNY, Binghamton, 1974; JD, Georgetown U., 1977. Bar: D.C. 1977, U. S. Dist. Ct. D.C. 1978, U.S. Ct. Appeals (D.C. cir.) 1978, Pa. 1979, Minn. 1983, U.S. Ct. Appeals (8th cir.) 1983, U.S. Dist. Ct. Minn. 1984. Assoc. Arnold & Porter, Washington, 1977-79; asst. dist. atty. Phila. Dist. Attys. Office, 1979-83; asst. U.S. atty. U.S. Attys. Office, Mpls., 1983-89; U.S. magistrate judge U.S. Dist. Ct., Mpls., 1989—. Legal writing instr. U. Minn., Mpls., 1989-92, adj. prof. Law Sch., 1996—. Mem. League of Am. Wheelman, Phi Beta Kappa. Episcopalian. Avocation: bicycling. Office: US Dist Ct 300 S 4th St Minneapolis MN 55415-1320

NOEL, MELVINA, literature educator; b. Norfolk, Va., July 27, 1951; d. Melvin Noel, Sr. and Mattie Edith Noel. AAS, Tidewater C.C., Virginia Beach, Va., 1981, AA, 1992; BS, Hampton U., 1973; MS, Old Dominion U., 1975; EdD, George Washington U., 2000. Instr. English/drama Campostella Jr. High, Norfolk, Va., 1973—80; programming task group leader QED Systems, Virginia Beach, 1980—81; programmer analyst Computer Dynamics, Inc., Virginia Beach, 1981—83; sys. cons. Tidewater Cons. Inc., Virginia Beach, 1983—87; instr. reading/study skills Thomas Nelson C.C., Hampton, Va., 1994—2000, dir. Va. student recruitment and retention program, 1996—98; prof. reading/writing Montgomery Coll., Rockville, Md., 2001—; owner Write Now, LLC, Sterling, Va., 2003—. Author: (poetry book) Songs to the Beloved, 2002; assoc. editor: Sufism: The Science of the Soul, 2000—. Named Va. Speech Tchr. of Yr., Va. Speech Comm. Assn., 1980, Who's Who Among America's Tchrs., 1998, 2000. Mem.: Sufi Psychology Assn. (founding mem.). Avocations: poetry, reading, research, walking, studying foreign languages.

NOEL, RANDALL DEANE, lawyer; b. Memphis, Oct. 19, 1953; s. D.A. and Patricia G. Noel; m. Lissa Johns, May 28, 1977; children: Lauren Elizabeth, Randall Walker. BBA with honors, U. Miss., 1975, JD, 1978. Bar: Miss. 1978, U.S. Dist. Ct. (no. and so. dists.) Miss. 1978, Tenn. 1979, U.S. Dist. Ct. (we., mid. and ea. dists.) Tenn. 1979, U.S. Ct. Appeals (5th and 6th cirs.) 1984, U.S. Supreme Ct. 1986. Assoc. Armstrong/Allen, PLLC, Memphis, 1978-85, ptnr., 1985—, mgr. litig. practice group, 1990-94; mgmt. com. Armstrong, Allen, Prewitt, Gentry, Johnston & Holmes, Memphis, 1994—97; chief mem. Armstrong/Allen, PLLC, Memphis, 2002—. Fin. com. Memphis in May Internat. Festival, 1980-81; pres. Carnival Memphis, 1996; bd. dirs. Christ United Meth. Ch., Memphis, 1984-87, 89-91, chmn. bd. trustees, 1995; mem. Leadership Memphis, 1994-95. Fellow Am. Bar Found., Tenn. Bar Found., Memphis Bar Found.; mem. ABA (young lawyers divsn., fellow dir. 1988-90, editor The Affiliate newsletter 1987-88, dir. Affiliate Outreach project 1988—, vice-chmn. Award of Achievement com. 1986, ALI-ABA bd. 1992-97, div. dir. litig. sect., 2002, coun. litig. sect., mem. House of Dels.), Am. Counsel Assn. (pres. 1997), Tenn. Bar Assn. (pres. young lawyers divsn. 1990, pres. litig. sect. 1988, bd. govs. 1989—, pres. 1999, Pres.'s Disting. Svc. award 1988-89), So. Conf. Bar Pres. (pres. 2000), Memphis and Shelby Bar Assn. (mem. jud, recommendations, law week nominations and membership coms.), Miss. Bar Assn., Def. Rsch. Inst., Tenn. Def. Lawyers Assn., Am. Judicature Soc. (bd. dirs. 1992-96), Tenn. Legal Cmty. Found. (pres. 1999-2001). Home: 2938 Tishomingo Ln Memphis TN 38111-2627 Office: Armstrong Allen PLLC 80 Monroe Ave Ste 700 Memphis TN 38103-2467 Business E-Mail: rnoel@armstrongallen.com.

NOELKEN, MILTON EDWARD, biochemistry educator, researcher; b. St. Louis, Dec. 5, 1935; s. William Henry Noelken and Agnes (Westbrook) Burkemper; m. Carol Ann Agne, June 9, 1962. BA in Chemistry, Washington U., St. Louis, 1957, PhD in Chemistry, 1962. Rsch. chemist Ea. Regional Rsch., Dept. Agr., Phila., 1964-67; asst. prof. dept. biochemistry U. Kans. Med. Ctr., Kansas City, 1967-71, assoc. prof., 1971-81, acting chmn., 1973-74, prof., 1981—, interim chmn., 1993-94. Vis. prof. Fed. U. Minas Gerais, Brazil, 1978. Contbr. articles to profl. jours. Recipient Scholastic Achievement award Am. Inst. Chemists, Washington U., 1957; NSF fellow, Washington U., 1959. Mem. Am. Chem. Soc., Am. Soc. for Biochemistry and Molecular Biology, Biophysical Soc., Sigma Xi. Achievements include research in properties of antibody molecules related to antigen binding, stucture of collagen of basement membranes, and stability of proteins. Office: U Kans Med Ctr Dept Biochemistry 39th And Rainbow Blvd Kansas City KS 66160-7421 E-mail: mnoelken@kumc.edu.

NOETH, CAROLYN FRANCES, speech and language pathologist; b. Cleve., July 21, 1924; d. Sam Falco and Barbara Serafina (Loparo) Armaro; m. Lawrence Andrew Noeth Sr., June 29, 1946; children: Lawrence Andrew Jr. (dec.), Barbara Marie. AB magna cum laude, Case Western Res. U., 1963; MEd, U. Ill., 1972; postgrad., Nat. Coll. Edn., 1975—. Lic. speech and lang. pathologist, Ill. Speech therapist Chgo. Pub. Schs., 1965; speech, lang. and hearing clinician J. Sterling Morton High Schs., Cicero and Berwyn, Ill., 1965-82, tchr. learning disabilities/behavior disorders, 1982, dist. ednl. diagnostician, 1982-84, Title I Project tchr., summers 1966-67, lang. disabilities cons., summers 1968-69, in-svc. tng. cons., summer 1970, dir. Title I Project, summers 1973-74; learning disabilities tchr. West Campus of Morton, 1971-75; chmn. Educable-Mentally Handicapped Opportunities Tchrs. Com., 1967-68; spl. edn. area and in-sch. tchrs. workshops, 1967—. Chmn. in compiling and publishing Student Handbook, Cleve. Coll., 1962; contbr. lyric parodies and music programs J. Sterling Morton H.S. West Retirement Teas, 1972-83. Precinct elections judge, 1953-55; block capt. Mothers March of Dimes and Heart Fund, 1949-60; St. Agatha's rep. Nat. Cath. Women's League, 1952-53;

collector various charities, 1967, 93-94, 98, 99, 2000, 2001, 2002; mem. exec. bd. Morton Scholarship League, 1981-84, corr. sec., 1981-83; vol. Am. Cancer Soc., 1985—; vol. judge Ill. Acad. Decathlon, 1988—. First recipient Virda L. Stewart award for Speech, Western Res. U., 1963, Outstanding Sr. award, 1963. Mem. Am. Speech, Lang. and Hearing Assn. (life, cert.), Ill. Speech, Lang. and Hearing Assn. (life), Coun. Exceptional Children (divsn. for learning disabilities, pioneers divsn., chpt. spl. projects chmn., exec. bd. 1976-81, chpt. pres. 1979-80), Coun. for Learning Disabilities, Profls. in Learning Disabilities, Kappa Delta Pi, Delta Kappa Gamma (chmn., co-chmn. chpt. music com. 1979—, state program com. 1981-83, chpt. music rep. to state 1982—, chmn. chpt. promotion com. 1993-94, 96—), St. Norbert's Women's Club (Northbrook, Ill.), Case-Western Res. U., U. Ill. Alumni Assns., Lions (vol. Northbrook 1966-93). Roman Catholic. Home and Office: 1849 Walnut Cir Northbrook IL 60062-1245 *Personal philosophy: "This above all: to thine own self be true; and it must follow as the night the day; Thou canst not then be false to any man." (Shakespeare's Hamlet).*

NOETHER, EMILIANA PASCA, historian, educator; b. Naples, Italy; came to U.S., 1919; d. Guglielmo and Bianca (Dramis) Pasca; m. Gottfried E. Noether, Aug. 1, 1942; 1 dau., Monica Gail. AB, Hunter Coll., N.Y.C., 1943; MA, Columbia U., 1944, PhD, 1948. From instr. to asst. prof. history Douglass Coll., Rutgers U., 1947-52; rsch. assoc. Center Internat. Studies, Mass. Inst. Tech., 1952-54; from lectr. to prof. history Regis Coll., Weston., Mass., 1959-66; prof. history Simmons Coll., Boston, 1966-68, U. Conn., Storrs, 1968-87. Editor: Italian sect. Am. Hist. Rev, 1958-75, Recently Published Articles, 1976-90, Garland Modern History Dissertation Series (Italy), 1989—; author: Seeds of Italian Nationalism, 2d edit, 1969, also articles.; co-editor, contbr.: Modern Italy: A Topical History Since 1861, 1974; contbg. editor: The American Constitution as a Symbol and Reality for Italy, 1989. AAUW fellow, 1946-47, 62-63; Bunting Inst. fellow, 1961-62; sr. Fulbright scholar Florence, Italy, 1965-66; Rome, 1982; Rsch. grantee Am. Philos. Soc., summer 1970; U. Conn. Research Found., 1969-71, 73-77, 81-86 Mem. Am. Hist. Assn. (council 1975-78, chmn. com. women historians 1976), Soc. Italian Studies (chmn. prize award and citation com. 1968-69, adv. council 1979-82, adv. council v.p. 1981-83, pres. 1983-85), Berkshire Conf. Women Historians (sec. 1962-64, pres. 1967-71), Coordinating Com. on Women in Hist. Profession, AAUW, Phi Beta Kappa, Pi Gamma Mu., Phi Kappa Phi Home: 1010 Waltham St #B-346 Lexington MA 02421 E-mail: epn@comcast.net.

NOFER, GEORGE HANCOCK, lawyer; b. Phila., June 14, 1926; BA, Haverford Coll., 1949; JD, Yale U., 1952. Bar: Pa. 1953. Pvt. practice, Phila., 1953—; ptnr. Schnader, Harrison, Segal & Lewis, Phila., 1961—91, sr. counsel, 1992—. Pres. bd. sch. dirs. Upper Moreland Twp., Pa., 1965—73; trustee Beaver Coll., Glenside, Pa., 1969—76; co-trustee Oberkotter Found., 1985—, past exec. dir.; elder, trustee, deacon Abington (Pa.) Presbyn. Ch., 1956—2000; bd. dirs. Fox Chase Cancer Ctr., Phila., 1989—94; bd. dirs., vice chmn. Phila. Presbyn. Homes, Inc., 1983—98; bd. dirs. A.G. Bell Assn. for Deaf, Washington, 1992—98. Fellow Am. Coll. Trust and Estate Counsel (regent 1975—, pres. 1983-84, chmn. Pa. 1973-78), Am. Law Inst., Am. Bar Found.; mem. ABA (standing com. on specialization 1980-86, chmn. 1983-86), Pa. Bar Assn., Phila. Bar Assn., Internat. Acad. Estate and Trust Law, Phi Beta Kappa, Phi Delta Phi. Home and Office: 108 Quail Ln Radnor PA 19087-2729 Office Phone: 610-971-1535. Business E-Mail: gnofer@aol.com.

NOFFKE, FRANK EDWARD, educational planner, writer, educator; s. Harry John and Elsie Strack Noffke; m. Ruth Ann Thompson, July 23, 1943 (dec. June 20, 1978); children: James T., Cody. BA, Ind. U., Bloomington, 1938; EdM, Wash. State, Pullman, 1957. Math. instr. U.S. Mil. Acad., West Point, NY, 1945—46; asst. dean student union and activities Case Inst. of Tech., Cleve., 1946—49; planning dir. Compton student union and activities Wash. State, Pullman, 1949—59; v.p. Coll. Planning Assoc., Kalamazoo, 1959—61; planning dir. Coll. union, student activities and values rsch. Baldwin-Wallace Coll., Berea, Ohio, 1961—64; planning dir. student union (designated father of the union) Calif. State U., Long Beach, 1964—80; pres. Frank Noffke Assoc., Pentwater, Mich., 1950—; instr. grad. sch. edn. Calif. State U. at Long Beach, 1972—75. Cons. coll. union and long range planning for universities Frank Noffke Assoc., 1950—; counselor/dir. emeritus veterans affairs dept. Calif. State U., Long Beach, 1972—80; counselor Peace Edn. on campuses World U., Ojai, Calif., 1983—83; chair inter-assn. com. Assn. of Coll. Unions; chair Coun. of Nat. Student Pers. Assns.; mem. Calif. State Post-Secondary Evaluation Team for New Universities, 1984—86, 1995. Author: (books) Planning for a Coll. Union, 1965, Planning for a Coll. Union 2 edit., 1996; co-author: (information packet) O.P.E.N. Peace Edn. Network of Western Mich., (position papers and status reports); contbr. articles to profl. jours.; critic/cons.: books. Mem. UN Non-Governmental Com. on Disarmament, 1995—2000, 2003—; chair and peace adv. OPEN Peace Edn. Network of West Mich., Pentwater, Mich., 1988—; liaison rep. to Rep. Kucinich OPEN Peace Network of West Mich., Washington, 2001—. Maj. Signal Corps U.S. Army, 1941—46. Recipient cert. of appreciation, U.S. Dept. Health, Edn. and Welfare, 1979, Hon. Citizen of Tucson, Ariz., Edn. Com. Excellence award, Nat. Assn. of Veterans Program Adminstrs. Mem.: Pentwater Svc. Club, Phi Kappa Phi (life). Independent. Congregational U.C.C. Achievements include first to organize peace enclave in W. Mich; invention of regional Peacekeeper O.P.E.N. award. Avocations: tennis, reading, writing. Home: 5631 Vaughn Street Pentwater MI 49449

NOGA, STEPHEN JOSEPH, oncologist, researcher; b. York, Pa., May 27, 1954; s. Stephen Vincent and Betty Rebecca Noga; m. Jill Lee Roman, May 14, 1993; children: Sean David, Ian Roberts, Megan Elizabeth. BS in Med. Tech., U. Fla., 1976, PhD in Exptl. Pathology, 1983; MD, Johns Hopkins U., 1987. Diplomate med. oncology Am. Bd. Internal Medicine, 1999, internal medicine Am. Bd. Internal Medicine, 1997, cert. med. technologist Am. Soc. Clin. Pathology, 1976. Intern Johns Hopkins Hosp., Balt., 1987—88, resident, 1988—90, fellow in med. oncology, 1990—91; asst. prof. oncology and pathology Johns Hopkins U., Balt., 1991—, assoc. prof. oncology and pathology, 1997—; dir. hematology/med. oncology Sinai Hosp. Balt., 2001—; dir. blood and marrow transplantation/cellular therapeutics program Alvin & Lois Lapidus Cancer Inst., Sinai Hosp. Balt., 2001—. Cons. Advanced Tissue Sciences, La Jolla, Calif., 1991—94, BIS/Impath Labs., Receda, Calif., 1992—2001, Glaxo SmithKline, Research Triangle, NC, 1994—, Biometic Imaging/BD Bioscience, San Jose, 1998—2001, Amgen, Inc, Thousand Oaks, Calif., 2000—, Gambro BCT, Lakewood, Colo., 2000—, Adventis Pharmaceuticals, Union, NJ, 2002—, Ortho Biotech, Bridgewater, NJ. Grantee, NIH/NCI, 1991—, NIH, 1994—98. Mem.: Bone Marrow Tranplant Scientists Australasia (assoc.), Am. Soc. for Blood and Marrow Transplantation (assoc.), Am. Assn. Blood Banks (assoc.), Internat. Soc. for Exptl. Hematology (assoc.), European Hematology Assn. (assoc.), Transplantation Soc. (assoc.), Am. Soc. Clin. Oncology (assoc.), Am. Soc. Hematology (assoc.), Internat. Soc. for Cellular Therapy (assoc.; pres., previous v.p. 2001—03). Avocations: orchid growing, herpetology. Office: Alvin & Lois Lapidus Cancer Institute Sinai Hosp 2401 W Belvedere Ave Baltimore MD 21215 Office Phone: 410-601-4710. Personal E-mail: nogast@comcast.net. E-mail: snoga@lifebridgehealth.org.

NOGG, DONALD IRWIN, retired paper distribution executive, population researcher; b. Omaha, Feb. 17, 1930; s. Nathan L. and Ruth (Brown) N.; m. Ozzie Katz, Aug. 22, 1954; children: Kathy, Marsha, Rachel, Anthony. Student, U. Colo., 1947-51. Pres., CEO Nogg Chem. and Paper Co., Omaha, 1980-92, chmn. bd., 1992-2000, ret., 2000. Chmn. bd. Kelso Chem., Lincoln, Nebr., 1993-2000, Western Paper & Supply, Sioux City, Iowa, 1993-2000, Network Assoc. Inc., 1984-86, Airkem Profl. Products, Des Moines, 1996-2000; chmn. Hudson Pulp Adv. Com., N.Y.C., 1975-77. Pres. Chanticleer Theatre, Council Bluffs, Iowa, 1966-68, Met. Actors Guild, Omaha, 1968-70, Beth El Synagogue, Omaha, 1979-81. Fellow Am. Geog. Soc.; Population Assn. Am., Am. Names Soc. Jewish. Avocations: population geography, bicycling. Home: 1323 Jackson St Omaha NE 68102-2886

NOGINOV, MIKHAIL A. physicist, researcher, educator; b. Dolgoprudnyi, Russia, May 28, 1962; arrived in U.S., 1991; s. Anatolii M. and Lidia V. (Platonova) N.; m. Natalia Noginova (Chernova), July 3, 1982; children: Maxim M., Julia M. MSEE, Moscow Inst. Physics and Tech., 1985; PhD in Physics and Math., USSR Acad. Scis., Moscow, 1990. Engr., from jr. staff rschr. to staff rschr. Gen. Physics Inst. of USSR Acad. Scis., 1985—91; rsch. assoc. MIT, Cambridge, 1991-93; from asst. to assoc. rsch. prof. dept. physics Ala. Agrl. Mech. U., Huntsville, 1993-97; assoc. rsch. prof. Ctr. for Materials Rsch., Norfolk (Va.) State U., 1997—99, from asst. to assoc. prof. dept. physics, 1999—. Adj. assoc. prof. Va. Poly. Inst., Va. Tech., Blacksburg, 1999-2003; grant proposal reviewer NSF, CRDF; panel reviewer NSF; jour reviewer sci. jours. including Optical Soc. Am., Am. Phys. Soc., others. Contbr. over 70 articles to profl. jours., chapters to books. Mem.: IEEE, Am. Phys. Soc., Optical Soc. Am., Sigma Xi. Achievements include research in spectroscopic characterization and study of energy transfer processes in laser and nonlinear optical materials; energy transfer upconversion in laser materials; optimization of solid-state laser materials; nonlinear optics; holographic recording; studies of photorefraction mechanisms and holographic currents in dielectric and semiconductor crystals; studies of intrinsic optical bistability in broad variety of materials with different mechanisms and nonlinearity; study of stimulated emission in ensembles of micro-size, nano-size particles with optical gain, potential miniature light sources for integrated optics; optoelectronics and nanoscale devices (random lasers). Avocations: travel, windsurfing. Office: Norfolk State U Ctr for Materials Rsch 700 Park Ave Norfolk VA 23504-3993

NOGLOWS, WILLIAM P. electronics executive; BS in Chem. Engring., Ga. Inst. Tech. From various mgmt. positions to exec. v.p. Cabot Corp., Aurora, Ill., 1984—98, exec. v.p., 1998—2003; chmn. Cabot Microelectronics Corp., Aurora, 2003—, pres., 2003—, CEO, 2003—. Office: Cabot Microelectronics Corp 870 N Commons Dr Aurora IL 60504*

NOGUCHI, HIDEO, insurance company executive; b. Kyoto, Jan. 17, 1945; s. Tasao and Ishiko (Tsujii) Noguchi; m. Eleanor Kazuko Horii, May 7, 1970; children: Mark H.Y., Mitchell H.Y. BBA, U. Hawai, 1969. Buyer RCA Purchasing Co., Tokyo, 1969—73; ins. specialist Continental Ins. Agy., Honolulu, 1973—82; CEO Noguchi & Assocs., Inc., Honolulu, 1983—. Cons. in field. Named to Coll. Bus. Adminstrn. Alumni Hall of Honor, U. Hawaii, 2004; recipient Nat. New Agt. Leadership award, CNA Corp., 1974, Key Club award, CNA Co., 1975, 1979—81, Nat. New Agt. Leader II, Continental Assurance Co., Can Co., 1975, VIP Club award, Pacific Guardian Life, 1984—86. Mem.: Honolulu Assn. Life Underwriters, Nat. Assn. Life Underwriters, Internat. Platform Assn., Million Dollar Round Table, Rotary (bd. dirs. 1980), Elks. Home: 3678 Woodlawn Terrace Pl Honolulu HI 96822-1475 Office: 1314 S King St Ste 560 Honolulu HI 96814-1978 Office Phone: 808-596-2700.

NOGUCHI, THOMAS TSUNETOMI, writer, pathologist; b. Fukuoka, Japan, Jan. 4, 1927; arrived in U.S., 1952; s. Wataru and Tomika Narahashi Noguchi. D of Medicine, Nippon Med. Sch., Tokyo, 1951; prof. honoris causa, U. Braz Cubas Fedn. Faculties Mogi Das Cruzes, Sao Paolo, Brazil, 1980; DSc (hon.), Worcester State Coll., 1985. Dep. med. examiner Los Angeles County Dept. Chief Med. Examiner, L.A., 1961-67, coroner, 1967-82; prof. forensic pathology U. So. Calif. Med. Sch., L.A., 1982-99, prof. emeritus forensic pathology, 1999—. Author: Coroner, 1983 (N.Y. Times Bestseller, 1984), Coroner at Large, 1985, Unnatural Causes, 1988, Physical Evidence, 1990. Recipient Imperial medal Order Sacred Treasure, His Majesty the Emperor of Japan, 1999. Fellow: Am. Acad. Forensic Sci. (chmn. sect. 1966); mem.: AMA, AAAS, World Assn. Med. Law (v.p.), Calif. Assn. Criminalists, Calif. State Coroners Assn., Nat. Assn. Med. Examiners (pres. 1983), Internat. Acad. Legal and Social Medicine, Am. Soc. Law, Medicine and Ethics, Am. Coll. Legal Medicine. Republican. Avocations: fine arts, gourmet oriental cooking, painting stills and abstracts. Office: U So Calif Med Ctr 1200 N State St Rm 2520 Los Angeles CA 90033-1029 Fax: 323-733-9860. Business E-Mail: noguchi@hsc.usc.edu.

NOGUERAS, JUAN JOSE, surgeon; b. Rio Piedras, P.R., Apr. 23, 1956; s. Juan Jose and Agustina (Soroeta) N.; m. Michele LeMoal, Sept. 22, 1984; children: Nicole, John, Robert. AB in Biochemistry, Princeton U., 1978; MD, Jefferson Med. Coll., 1982. Diplomate Am. Bd. Surgery, Am. Bd. Colon and Rectal Surgery, Nat. Bd. Med. Examiners. Instr. surgery Wilford Hall Air Foce Med. Ctr., San Antonio, 1987-90; staff dept. colorectal surgery Cleveland Clin. Fla., Weston, 1991—, chmn. divsn. surgery, 2000—. Presenter in field. Contbg. author: Current Controversies in Breast Cancer, 1984, Pre-test Self Assessment and Review, 1987, Textbook and Atlas of Laparaoscopic Colorectal Surgery, Intestinal Stomas, 1993; reviewer: Surgical Endoscopy, 1993—, So. Med. Jour., 1993—; contbr. articles to profl. jours. Major med. corps. U.S. Army, 1987-90. Recipient A.W. Martin Marino Sr. M.D. award N.Y. Soc. Colon and Rectal Surgeons, 1991; Fellow U. Minn., 1990-91. Fellow ACS, Am. Soc. Colon and Rectal Surgeons, Soc. Am. Gastrointestinal Endoscopic Surgeons, Crohn's and Colitis Found. Am. (chmn. med. adv. com. 1992-96), Dominican Coll. Surgeons (hon.), Midwest Soc. Colon and Rectal Surgeons (pres. 1993-94), S.E. Med. Assn., S.E. Surg. Congress. Office: Cleveland Clin Dept Colorectal Surgery 2950 Cleveland Clinic Blvd Weston FL 33331

NOH, JUN-YONG, computer scientist, researcher; b. Seoul, Republic of Korea, Feb. 14, 1971; s. Hae-Kyu Noh and Yoo-im Bang. Bachelor magna cum laude, U. So. Calif., 1994, Master, 1996, PhD, 2002. Rschr. on brain-like computer Info. Scis. Inst., Marina del Rey, Calif., 1997; rschr. facial animation U. So. Calif., L.A., 1998—. CEO Digital Clone Lab., L.A., 2002—. Pvt., 1999, Seoul. Achievements include patent for expression cloning. Avocations: scuba diving, travel. Home: 13173 Pacific Promenade #101 Playa Vista CA 90094-2147

NOHNER, ALLEN M. corporate communications specialist; s. Fabian P. and Bernice M. Nohner; m. Margaret Sue Siegmund, June 18, 1977; children: Matthew A., Michael J. BS, Bemidji State U., Minn., 1966—70, MA, 1988—90. Tchr. Apollo HS, St. Cloud, Minn., 1970—74; journalist, photographer St. Cloud Daily Times, St. Cloud, Minn., 1971—74; dir. news and publications Bemidji State U., Minn., 1974—. Recipient Nat. Gold award, Admissions Mktg. Report, 1996, 1988, Award(s) of Merit, Minn. Assn. Govt. Communicators, 1990, 1991, 1992 (5), 1993, George Love Meml. Trophy, Rotary Internat. Dist. 5580, 1992. Mem.: Coun. Advancement and Support Edn. (membership coord. 1995—2004, Cir. Excellence award 1997). Office: Bemidji State U 1500 Birchmont Dr NE Bemidji MN 56601-2699 Office Phone: 218-755-2041. Business E-Mail: anohner@bemidjistate.edu.

NOHRNBERG, JAMES CARSON, English language educator; b. Berkeley, Calif., Mar. 19, 1941; s. Carson and Geneva Gertrude (Gibbs) N.; m. Stephanie Payson Lamport, June 14, 1964; children: Gabrielle L., Peter Carson L. Student, Kenyon Coll., 1958-60; BA, Harvard Coll., 1962, postgrad., 1965-68; PhD, U. Toronto, 1970. Tchg. fellow dept. English U. Coll., U. Toronto, 1963-64; jr. fellow Soc. of Fellows Harvard U., 1965-68; acting instr. dept. English Yale U., New Haven, 1968-69, lectr., 1969-70, asst. prof., 1970-75, assoc. prof., 1975; prof. English U. Va., Charlottesville, 1975—. Adj. instr. English Harvard U., Cambridge, 1967; Gauss Seminars in Criticism lectr. Princeton U., 1987; lectr. various univs., 1974—. Author: The Analogy of The Faerie Queene, 1976, 80, Like Unto Moses: The Constituting of an Interruption, 1995; mem. editl. bd. Spenser Ency., 1977-90, Spenser Studies, 1977—; contbr. articles to profl. jours. and poems to mags.; editor vols. on allegory, Bible, Homer, Dante, Boiardo, Spenser, Milton, Thomas Pynchon, Northrop Frye, among others. Recipient Am. Acad. Poets prize Harvard U., 1962; Woodrow Wilson fellow, 1962, jr. fellow Harvard U., 1965-68, Morse fellow Yale U., 1974-75, U. Va. Ctr. for Advanced Studies fellow, 1975-78, Guggenheim fellow, 1981-82, Ind. U. Inst. for Advanced Studies fellow, 1991, U. Va. Sesquicentennial fellow, 2003-2004. Mem.: MLA, Am. Computer Lit. Assn., Milton Soc., Spenser Soc., Phi Beta Kappa. Presbyterian. Avocations: poetry, collecting books and records. Home: 1874 Wayside Pl Charlottesville VA 22903-1631 Office: U Va Dept English Bryan Hall Charlottesville VA 22903 Office Phone: 434-924-6629. E-mail: jcn@virginia.edu.

NOIA, ALAN JAMES, utility company executive; b. Selbitz, Germany, Feb. 18, 1947; came to U.S., 1949; s. Fiore and Anneliese (Gossler) N.; m. Cynthia Dee Rathman BSEE, U. Va, Charlottesville, 1969. Engr. Potomac Edison Co., Hagerstown, Md., 1969-72, database adminstr., 1972-73; data base adminstr., supr. tech. svcs. Allegheny Power Svc. Corp., Greensburg, Pa., 1973-75, staff asst. N.Y.C., 1975-79; asst. v.p., treas. Allegheny Power System, N.Y.C., 1979-80, treas., 1980-82, v.p., treas., 1983-84; v.p. bulk power supply, CFO Allegheny Power System, Inc. and Allegheny Power Svc. Corp., N.Y.C., 1984-87; pres. Potomac Edison Co., Hagerstown, Md., 1990-94; pres., COO Allegheny Power, 1994—; chmn., pres., CEO Allegheny Energy. Bd. dirs. Allegheny Power Svc. Corp., Monongahela Power Co., Potomac Edison Co., West Penn Power Co., Allegheny Generating Co.; mem. Md. Econ. Devel. Com. Trustee East Ctrl. Nuclear Group, N.Y.C., 1979—; bd. dirs. Md. Symphony Orch., Southeastern Elec. Exch., Inc. Mem. Phi Eta Sigma, Eta Kappa Nu, Tau Beta Pi. Roman Catholic. Home: 9532 Childacrest Rd Boonsboro MD 21713-1507 Office: Allegheny Energy 10435 Downsville Pike Hagerstown MD 21740-1732

NOKES, JIM W. oil industry executive; b. McCook, Nebr., 1946; BA, Fort Hayes State Univ., Kans.; MBA, Univ. Ark. With Conoco Phillips, Houston, 1970—94, v.p. N. Amer. refining and market, 1994—99, pre. N. Amer. refining and market, 1998—99, exec. v.p. worldwide refining and market, 1999—2002, exec. v.p. refining and mktg., supply, & transport., 2002—. Mem. World Bus. Coun. for Suitable Devel., bd. dirs. Adv. bd. Yellowstone Pk. Found., Jr. Achievement of Southeast Tex. Inc. Office: Conoco Phillips 600 N Dairy Ashford Rd Houston TX 77079

NOKES, JOHN RICHARD, retired newspaper editor, writer; b. Portland, Oreg., Feb. 23, 1915; s. James Abraham and Bernice Alfaretta (Bailey) N.; m. Evelyn Junkin, Sept. 13, 1936; children: Richard Gregory, William G., Gail (Mrs. William M. Hulden), Douglas J., Kathy E. BS, Linfield Coll., 1936, LHD (hon.), 1988. With The Oregonian, Portland, 1936-82, city editor, 1950-65, asst. mng. editor, 1965-71, mng. editor, 1971-75, editor, 1975-82; disting. vis. prof. journalism Linfield Coll., 1982-85. Cons. editor The Hong Kong Standard, 1994. Author: American Form of Government, 1939, Columbia's River: The Voyages of Robert Gray 1787-1793, 1991, Almost a Hero: The Voyages of John Meares to China, Hawaii and the Pacific Northwest, 1998; editor Oreg. Edn. Jour., 1944. Bd. dirs. Portland U.S.O., 1968-72, U.S. Coast Guard Acad. Found., 1972-74, Portland Opera Assn., 1976-78; trustee Linfield Coll., 1977-93; v.p. Oreg. UN Assn., 1983-85, chmn. Oreg. UN Day, 1981-83. Lt. (j.g.) USNR, 1944-46; comdr. Res. (ret.). Mem. Navy League U.S. (pres. Portland coun. 1969-71), Linfield Coll. Alumni Assn. (pres. 1940), World Affairs Coun. Oreg. (pres. 1973-74), AP Mng. Editors Assn. (dir. 1973-80), Am. Soc. Newspaper Editors, N.W. China Coun., Sigma Delta Chi (pres. Willamette Valley chpt. 1975-76) Clubs: Multnomah Athletic (Portland). Republican. Methodist. Home: 11789 SW Queen Elizabeth Portland OR 97224-2601

NOLAN, CATHAL J. political scientist, educator, historian; b. Dublin, Aug. 2, 1956; came to the U.S., 1995; m. Valerie E. Duff, Sept. 7, 1985; children: Ryan Casey, Genevieve Michelle. BA in History, U. Alta., Edmonton, Can., 1978; MA in History, U. Toronto, Can., 1982, PhD in Polit. Sci., 1989; diploma in human rights, Can. Human Rights Found., 1984. CUSO vol., English and social studies instr. Govt. Secondary Sch., Kazaure, Kano, Nigeria, 1978-80, head of arts, 1979-80; contract rschr., writer Wandel Ltd., Toronto, 1982-83; cons. policy devel. and rsch. divsn. Can. Internat. Devel. Agy., Govt. Can., Ottawa, 1985-86; editl. intern Can. Jour. Polit. Sci., 1987-88; asst. prof. polit. sci. St. Francis Xavier U., 1989-90; asst. prof. internat. rels. Miami U., Oxford, Ohio, 1990-91; asst. prof. polit. sci. U. B.C., Vancouver, 1991-95, rsch. assoc. Inst. Internat. Rels., 1993-94; rsch. assoc. prof. internat. rels. Boston U., 1995-99, asst. to pres./chancellor, 1995-99, assoc. prof. history, 1999—, exec. dir. Internat. History Inst., 1999—. Lectr. in field. Author: Principled Diplomacy: Security and Rights in U.S. Foreign Policy, 1993, The Longman Guide to World Affairs, 1995, Maailma Poliitika Leksikon, 1995, Greenwood Encyclopedia of International Relations, 4 vols., 2002; editor: Ethics and Statecraft: The Moral Dimension of International Affairs, 1995, Notable U.S. Ambassadors Since 1775, 1997; founding editor (book series) Humanistic Perspectives on International Relations, 1998—; co-editor: Shepherd of Democracy? America and Germany in the 20th Century, 1992; founding co-editor: (book series) International History, 1999—; contbr. chpts. to books and articles to profl. jours. Connaught Found. Project Devel./SSHRC Project grantee, 1986, rsch. grantee Ctr. for Internat. Studies, 1986, U. Toronto, 1986, St. Francis Xavier, 1990, Consortium for the Study of Intelligence, 1990, Alumni Assn. Miami, 1990, Humanities and Social Sci., 1992, Carnegie Coun. on Ethics and Internat. Affairs, 1992, 93, 98, Cooperative Security Program, 1995, Robert R. McCormick Tribune Found., 1999, 2001; Barton fellow in peace and security, 1993. Mem. Hist. Soc., Soc. for Historians Am. Fgn. Rels., Planetary Soc. Office: Internat History Inst Boston Univ 725 Commonwealth Ave Boston MA 02215 E-mail: cnolan@bu.edu.

NOLAN, CATHERINE T. state legislator; m. Gerard Marsicano. Grad. cum laude, NYU. Apptd. ombudsman Dept. of State; mem. N.Y. State Assembly, Albany, 1984—, chmn. real property taxation com., mem. vets. com., ins. com., corps., authorities and commns. com.; commerce, industry and econ. devel. com., chmn. mass transit subcom., women vets. subcom. Chair N.Y. State Legis. Women's Caucus; mem. Assembly's Hispanic task force Somos Uno; mem. capital planning rev. bd. MTA. Co-founder Queens Displaced Homemakers Program; bd. dirs. Ridgewood Property Owners and Civic Assn.; bd. trustees Wyckoff Heights Hosp.; active supporter United Forties Civic Assn., Dutch Kills Civic Assn., Farmer's Oval Civic Assn., Hunter's Point Cmty. Coun., Queensbridge Tenant Assn., Youth Patrol and Tenant Patrol, Ravenswood Tenant Assn., Lincoln Block Assn., 56th Street Block Assn., 68th Rd. Block Assn., Cornelia Street Block Assn., Queens Spl. Olympics, Vol. Ambulance Corps., Queens Outreach Project, Ridgewood Vol. Ambulance Corps., Irish Immigration Reform Movement; adv. bd. Borden Ave. Vets. Shelter; Conrad Weiser post Steuben Soc.; mem. Queens Coalition for Political Alternatives; del. Dem. Nat. Conv., 1988; bd. dirs. Ridgeoow Dem. Club. Recipient Pres.' medal LaGuardia C.C., 1989. Mem. NAACP, Sunnyside C. of C., Astoria Kehillah, Sunnyside Kiwanis, Irish-Am. Legis. Club, Italian-Am. Legis. Club. Home: 879 Woodward Ave Ridgewood NY 11385-4465 Office: NY State Assembly 522 Legislative Office Bldg Albany NY 12248-0001

NOLAN, CHRISTOPHER ALOYSIUS, III, real estate developer, architect; b. Boston, July 17, 1950; s. Christopher Aloysius Nolan Jr. and Gladys Edna (Kiely) McMakin; m. Deborah Ellen Barham, July 22, 1982 (dec. Feb. 1999). BA, U. Toronto, 1972; MArch, Harvard, 1979; student, Sch. of Museum of Fine Arts, Boston, 1972-75. Registered architect, N.Y., N.J., Conn. Grad. architect Hugh Adams Russell Architects, Cambridge, 1977-79; architect Eli Attia and Assocs., N.Y.C., 1979-80, Haines Lundberg Waehler, N.Y.C., 1980-81, Castro-Blanco Piscioneri Feder, N.Y.C., 1981-84; chief architect Howco Investment Corp., Livingston, N.J., 1984-88; devel. mgr. Hirschfeld Realty, N.Y.C., 1988; mng. dir. Joseph Hilton & Assocs., N.Y.C. and Parsippany, 1988-96; project exec. AJ Contracting Co., Inc., N.Y.C., 1996-2000; dir. devel. LCOR Inc., N.Y.C., 2000—. Planning bd. Clermont, NY, 1991—; trustee Madison Sq. Boys and Girls Clubs, N.Y. Mem.: AIA, Harvard Club. Avocations: yoga, swimming, sustainable agriculture. Office: LCOR Inc 1 Penn Plz Ste 3310 New York NY 10119-3310 E-mail: cnolan@world.std.com., cnolan@lcor-ny.com.

NOLAN, DAVID BRIAN, lawyer; b. Washington, Jan. 1, 1951; s. John Joseph and Mary Jane Nolan; m. Cheryl Ann Cottle, June 30, 1979; children: John Joseph II, David Brian II, Christopher Dalton. BA, Duke U., 1973; MPA, Am. U., 1975; JD, U. La Verne, 1978; postgrad., Georgetown U., 1981-89. Bar: Calif. 1978, U.S. Dist. Ct. (cen. dist.) Calif. 1979, U.S. Ct. Claims 1981, U.S. Tax Ct. 1981, U.S. Ct. Appeals (D.C. cir.) 1984, U.S. Supreme Ct. 2000. Intern Congressman Joel Broyhill, 1971; asst. dir. rsch. Younger-Curb Campaign, L.A., 1978; assoc. L. Rob Werner Law Offices, Encino, Calif., 1979-80; atty. conflicts Office of Pres. Elect, Washington, 1980-81; staff atty. Office of counsel to the Pres. White House, Washington, 1981; staff asst. office of sec.

U.S. Dept. Treasury, Washington, 1981-85; spl. asst. office gen. counsel U.S. Dept. Energy, Washington, 1985-90, atty. advisor enforcement div. Office of Nuclear Safety, 1990-91, trial atty. adminstrv. litigation div. Econ. Regulatory Adminstrn., 1991-95, trial atty. Office of Gen. Counsel, 1995-2001; pvt. law practice, 2001—. Bd. dirs., treas. Energy Fed. Credit Union. Mem. editl. bd. New Guard Mag., 1983-85. Steering com. L.A. Reps., 1979-80, Reagan for Pres., L.A., 1980; chmn. 39th Assembly, Rep. Ctrl. Com., 1979-80; alt. del. 1972 Rep. Nat. Conv.; pres. N.C. Coll. Rep. Com., 1972-73; nat. treas., bd. dirs. Young Amers. for Freedom, Sterling, Va., 1983-85; corp. dir. Am. Sovereignty Task Force, Vienna, Va., 1984—, State Dept. Watch Ltd., Vienna, 1984—. Charles Edison Youth Found. scholar, 1971; named one of Outstanding Young Men in Am., Jaycees, 1976-86; recipient Mgr. of Yr. honor Dept. Energy Women's Adv. Coun., 1988, Achievement in Equal Opportunity Deptl. award, 1988. Mem. Fed. Bar Assn., Bar Assn. of D.C. (chmn. ethics com. young lawyers div. 1985-87), D.C. Bar, Calif. Bar, U.S. Supreme Ct. Soc., Federalist Soc., U.S. Justice Found. (co-founder, of counsel 1979-80), Riverside Estates Civic Assn. (pres. 2002—), Conservative Network Club, Whistle Blowers Are Patriots (co-founder 1999). Home: 8310 Wagon Wheel Rd Alexandria VA 22309-2175 Office: David B Nolan & Assocs Box 23019 Washington DC 20026-1864 Office Phone: 703-780-1864. E-mail: dbnesq1@aol.com.

NOLAN, DAVID CHARLES, lawyer, arbitrator, mediator; b. San Mateo, Calif., Oct. 12, 1940; s. Clarence Charles and Leona Henrietta (Lindeman) N.; m. Cynthia Ann James, Feb. 20, 1971; children: Matthew, John, Scott. AB, Stanford U., 1962; JD, U. Calif., Berkeley, 1965. Bar: Calif. 1966, U.S. Ct. Appeals (9th cir.) 1971, U.S. Ct. Appeals (D.C. cir.) 1975, U.S. Dist. Ct. (no. dist.) Calif. 1969, U.S. Dist. Ct. (D.C. cir.) 1970, U.S. Tax Ct., U.S. Supreme Ct. 1972. Ptnr. Graham & James, San Francisco, 1968-93; sole practitioner Walnut Creek, Calif., 1993—. Bd. dirs., officer Family Homes for Retarded, Belmont, Calif., 1978-81; founding dir. Orinda (Calif.) Baseball Assn., 1982-86; commr. Diablo Valley Baseball League, Martinez, Calif., 1983-90. Lt. comdr. USCG, 1965-68. Mem. ABA, Calif. Bar Assn., Contra Costa County Bar Assn., No. Calif. Mediation Assn., Assn. Transp. Practitioners, Commonwealth Club, Maritime Law Assn., Order of Coif. Home: 12 E Altarinda Dr Orinda CA 94563-2406 Office: 1990 N California Blvd Walnut Creek CA 94596-3742 Fax: 925-937-5442.

NOLAN, DAVID JOSEPH, author, historian; b. Cambridge, Mass., June 27, 1946; s. Joseph Thomas and Virginia Theodate (Tappin) N.; children: Sudie Ariyoshi, Hamilton Joseph. Student, U. Va., 1963-65. Field sec. Va. Students' Civil Rights Com., Lawrenceville, 1965-66; editor New South Student mag., Nashville, 1966-69; freelance writer, lectr., 1969—. Author: Fifty Feet in Paradise, 1984 (Author's award Coun. for Fla. Librs.), The Houses of St. Augustine, 1995; contbr.: The Book Lover's Guide to Florida, 1992. Pres. Marjorie Kinnan Rawlings Soc., 1993-95; trustee Ft. Mose Hist. Soc., 1996-99, 2003—; mem. Lincolnville Festival Com. Mem. Friends of St. Augustine Architecture, 40th Accord. Avocations: reading, photography, swimming. Home: 30 Park Terrace Dr Saint Augustine FL 32080-5334

NOLAN, EDMUND FRANCIS, management consultant; b. Buffalo, June 9, 1931; s. James Paul and Isabel Jane (Curry) N.; m. Chloe Dandison Nolan, Dec. 19, 1959 (div. Aug. 1979); children: Andrew Dandison, Jeffrey Stewart; m. Ann Hopkins Chadbourne, Aug. 18, 1979; stepchildren: Gay Chadbourne Canepa, Scott Holt Chadbourne. BA, Cornell U., 1953; MBA, Columbia U., 1957. Sales and mktg. staff Armstrong World Industries, Lancaster, Pa., 1957-63; mgmt. cons. Hay Group, Phila., 1963-72; dir. compensation and benefits Nashua (N.H.) Corp., 1972-76; sr. mgmt. cons. Coopers & Lybrand, N.Y.C., 1976-83; dir. compensation and benefits Svc. Systems Corp., Buffalo, 1983-87; mgmt. cons. Nolan Consulting, Falmouth, Mass., 1987—97; substance abuse counselor Miller House men's residential program Goshold Treatment Ctr., Falmouth, 1997—. Bd. dirs. J R Hess & Co., Inc., Cranston, R.I.; mem. adv. bd. L F Giampietro, PC, Falmouth. Del. Rep. state conv., Boston, 1990, Econ. Devel. Com. Town of Falmouth, 1993—; mem. Bikeways Com., Town of Falmouth, 1990—; trustee Falmouth Pub. Libr., 1994—, vice chmn. 2002—. 1st lt. U.S. Army, 1953-55, Korea. Mem. Cape Cod Cornellians (pres. 1987-89), Falmouth Sports Ctr., Woods Hole Theatre Co. (pres. 1990-95), Delta Phi (v.p. 1950—). Congregationalist. Avocations: teaching, acting, tennis, skiing, biking, running (6 marathons). Office: Miller House 165 Woods Hole Rd Falmouth MA 02540

NOLAN, JAMES LAWRY, JR., sociologist; b. Los Angeles, CA, Sept. 26, 1962; s. James Lawry and Karen Thorson Nolan; m. Catherine Elizabeth Ballou, June 25, 1988; children: Amy, David, Laura, William. BA, U. Calif., Davis, 1984; MA, U. Va., 1992, PhD, 1995. Lectr. U. Va., Charlottesville, 1995—96; asst. prof. sociology Williams Coll., Williamstown, Mass., 1996—2002, assoc. prof. sociology dept. anthropology and sociology, 2002—, chmn. dept. anthropology and sociology, 2002—04; vis. Fulbright Sch. Loughborough U, Loughborough, England, 1999—2000; dir Williams-Exeter Programme, Oxford U., 2004—06; tutor for vis. students Exeter Coll., Oxford U., 2004—06; vis. fellow Ctr. for Criminol. Rsch. Oxford U., 2004—06. Editor: The Am. Culture Wars: Current Contests, Future Prospects, 1996; author: The Therapeutic State: Justifying Gov. at Cent. End, 1998, Reinventing Justice: The Am. Drug Ct. Movement, 2001; editor: Drug Courts: In Theory, In Practice, 2002. Fellow, NEH, 1999—2000; Fulbright scholar, Fulbright Found., 1999—2000, Sorokin postdoctoral fellow, 1995—96. Mem.: Am. Sociol. Assoc. Home: 1 Moreton Rd Oxford OX2 7AZ England Office: Williams Exeter Programme 145 Banbury Rd Oxford OX2 7AN England

NOLAN, JAMES PAUL, internist, educator, medical researcher; b. Buffalo, June 21, 1929; s. James Paul and Isabel (Curry) N.; m. Christa Paul, July 23, 1956; children— Lisa, James, Christopher, Thomas. BA, Yale U., 1951, MD cum laude, 1955. Diplomate Am. Bd. Internal Medicine. Instr. in medicine Yale U., New Haven, 1961-63; intern Grace-New Haven Hosp., 1955-56, resident, 1958-60, chief med. resident, 1961-62, asso. physician, 1962-63; asst. prof. medicine SUNY, Buffalo, 1963-67, asso. prof., 1967-69, prof., 1969—, vice-chmn. dept. medicine, 1973-77, acting chmn. dept., 1978-79, chmn. dept., 1979-95, disting. svc. prof., 1996—; chief of medicine Buffalo Gen. Hosp., 1969-80, attending, 1969—; asso. attending Edward J. Meyer Meml. Hosp., Buffalo, 1963-68, attending, 1968-71, cons., 1971—; cons. physician Millard Fillmore Hosp., 1981—, Deaconess Hosp., 1973—. Attending Buffalo VA Hosp., Children's Hosp. Buffalo; cons. Roswell Park Meml. Inst., 1970—; acting dir. dept. medicine Erie County Med. Center, 1978-80, dir. dept., 1980—; trustee Buffalo Gen. Hosp., 1974—; bd. dirs. Kaleid Health, ACP Found. Editl. adv. bd. Jour. Medicine Exptl. and Clin, 1971—; reviewer: Gastroenterology, 1973—; contbr. numerous articles to med. and sci. jours. Served to lt. comdr., M.C. USN, 1956-58. NIH grantee, 1979-86; Hartford Found. grantee, 1981 Mem. ACP (master, chair bd. regents 1994-95), Am. Fedn. Clin. Rsch., AAAS, Am. Gastroent. Assn. (procedures com.), Am. Assn. Study of Liver Disease, Reticuloendothelial Soc., N.Y. Acad. Sci., Am. Clin. and Climatol. Assn., Interurban Club, Ctrl. Soc. Clin. Rsch., Internat. Assn. Study of Liver, Assn. Am. Physicians, Assn. Profs. Medicine (pres. 1993-94), Phi Beta Kappa, Alpha Omega Alpha. Office: 462 Grider St Buffalo NY 14215-3021 Address: 213 Burbank Dr Snyder NY 14226-3938 E-mail: jpnolanmd@yahoo.com.

NOLAN, JANIECE SIMMONS, health care company executive; b. Ft. Worth; d. James Coleman and Berenice Johnson Simmons; m. Robert L. Nolan; children: Douglas, Patricia, Nancy, Margaret, Sheffield, Gemini Janiece. BA, U. Tex., 1961, MA, 1963; PhD, Tulane U., 1968; MPH, U. Calif., Berkeley, 1975. Diplomate Am. Coll. Healthcare Execs. Rsch. scientist Tex. Nuc. (Nuc. Chgo.), Austin, 1963-65; head cell biology Gulf South Rsch. Inst., New Orleans, 1968-70; postdoctoral fellow dept. physiology/anatomy U. Calif., Berkeley, 1970-72; rsch. physiologist, acting assoc. chief of staff for rsch. VA Hosp., Martinez, Calif., 1970-75; COO, v.p. adminstrn. John Muir Med. Ctr., Walnut Creek, Calif., 1977-97; pres., CEO John Muir/Mt. Diablo Health Network, Walnut Creek, 1997—. Mem. med. adv. commn. Contra Costa County, Martinez, 1996, East Bay chpt. Amigos de la Americas, Orinda, 1997; commr. State Commn. Emergency Svcs., Sacramento, 1997; Bd, dirs. Calif. Healthcare Assn. Polit. Action, Sacramento, 1996. Capt. USNR, (ret.). Woodrow Wilson fellow, 1960; named Woman of Yr., Women Health Care Execs., San Francisco, 1989; recipient Navy Commendation medals (3), Humanitarian Svc. medal, 2 Armed Forces Res. medals (2). Mem.: Ind. Physician Assn., Med. Group Mgmt. Assn., Am. Mil. Surgeons of the U.S., Assn. Integrated Health Delivery Systems, Rotary (Paul Harris fellow). Avocations: international travel, genealogy research. Office: John Muir/Mt Diablo Health Network 1400 Treat Blvd Walnut Creek CA 94597-2142 Office Phone: 925-952-2880. Business E-Mail: Janiece.Nolan@jmmdhs.com.

NOLAN, JOHN BLANCHARD, lawyer; b. Providence, Aug. 30, 1943; s. John O'Leary and Elizabeth Rita (Blanchard) Nolan; m. Marguerite Ruth Hartley, Mar. 1, 1969 (dec. Aug. 1988); children: Suzanne, Caroline, Danielle; m. Lillian B. Prestley, 1989. AB, Brown U., 1965; JD, Georgetown U., 1968. Bar: Conn. 1968, U.S. Dist. Ct. Conn. 1969, U.S. Ct. Appeals (2d cir.) 1969, U.S. Dist. Ct. (so. dist.) N.Y. 1973, N.Y. 1974, U.S. Cat. Appeals (1st cir.) 1991, U.S. Dist. Ct. Ariz. 1994, U.S. Supreme Ct. 1995. Assoc. Day, Berry & Howard, Hartford, Conn., 1969-76, ptnr., 1976—. Bd. dirs. Spiritus Wines, Inc.; chmn. local rules practice adv. com. U.S. Bankruptcy Ct., 1981—. Corporator St. Francis Hosp. Med. Ctr., Hartford, 1982—; bd. dirs. Greater Hartford Arts Coun., Inc., 1993 , v.p., mem. exec. com.; mem. parish coun. Ch. St. Timothy; trustee St. Mary Home Found., 1983—, U. Hartford Art Sch., 1988—94. Fellow: Conn. Bar Found.; mem.: ABA, Insolvency Internat., Hartford County Bar Assn., Conn. Bar Assn., Am. Bankruptcy Inst., Loomis Chaffee Sch. Alumni Assn. (bd. dirs. 1996—98), Hartford Golf Club (bd. dirs. 2000—03). Democrat. Roman Catholic. Avocations: golf, skiing, travel, wines. Home: 34 Northmoor Rd West Hartford CT 06117-1709 Office: Day Berry & Howard 185 City Place Hartford CT 06103-3499

NOLAN, JOHN EDWARD, lawyer; b. Mpls., July 11, 1927; s. John E. and Teresa (Franey) Nolan; m. Joan Dobbins, June 3, 1950; children: Carol N. Klatt, John Edward III(dec.), Kelly N. Spencer, Richard Clark, Patricia N. McNeill. BS, U.S. Naval Acad., 1950; JD, Georgetown U., 1955. Bar: DC 1955, U.S. Supreme Ct. 1959, Md. 1961. Law clk. to Justice Clark U.S. Supreme Ct., 1955-56; adminstrv. asst. to Atty. Gen. Robert F. Kennedy, 1963-64; assoc. Steptoe & Johnson, Washington, 1956-62, ptnr., 1962-63, 65—. Assoc. counsel Cuban families com. Cuban Prisoners Exch., Havana, 1962—63; spl. counsel refugee subcom. Senate Jud. Com., Vietnam, 1967—68; mem. CPR Panel Disting. neutrals, Washington; mediator U.S. Ct. Appeals DC cir.; mem. exec. com. Lawyers Com. Civil Rights Under Law; vis. fellow Wolfson Coll., Cambridge (Eng.) U., 1987, 92; bd. dirs. Hooper Holmes, Inc., Iomega, Inc. Trustee Robert F. Kennedy Meml., 1969—; moderator Aspen Inst., 1980—; gen. counsel, bd. dirs. U.S. Naval Acad. Found., 1997—; bd. dirs. Fund Dem. Majority. Served from 2d lt. to capt. USMC, 1950—54, Korea. Decorated Silver Star, Bronze Star with combat V, Purple Heart. Mem.: ABA, Am. Law Inst., DC Bar Assn., U.S. Naval Acad. Alumni Assn. (bd. counsel, trustee 1997—), Univ. Club (N.Y.C.), Congl. Club, Met. Club (Washington). Roman Catholic. Office: 1330 Connecticut Ave NW Washington DC 20036-1704 Personal E-mail: jnolan@steptoe.com.

NOLAN, JOHN MICHAEL, lawyer; b. Conway, Ark., June 21, 1948; s. Paul Thomas and Peggy (Hime) N. BA, U. Tex., 1970, JD, 1973; LLM in Taxation, George Washington U., 1976. Bar: Tex. 1973, D.C. 1975, U.S. Ct. Mil. Appeals 1973, U.S. Ct. Appeals (D.C. cir.) 1975, U.S. Tax Ct. 1975, U.S. Supreme Ct. 1975. Chief counsel to chief judge U.S. Ct. Mil. Appeals, Washington, 1976-77; assoc. Winstead, McGuire, Sechrest & Minick PC, Dallas, 1977-81; shareholder Winstead Sechrest & Minick PC, Dallas, 1981—. Editor in Chief The Advocate, 1973-76. Capt. JAGC, U.S. Army, 1973-76. Named one of Outstanding Young Men in Am., U.S. Jaycess, 1976; Keeton fellow Chancellor Coun. Mem. ABA (real property, probate and trust sect., real property com., partnerships, joint ventrues, and other investment vehicles), Tex. Bar Assn. (real property, probate and trust sect.), D.C. Bar Assn., Dallas Bar Assn. (real estate group), Tex. Coll. Real Estate Lawyers, Am. Coll. Real Estate Lawyers, Coll. State Bar Tex., Real Estate Coun., Salesmanship Club Dallas, Royal Oaks Country Club. Presbyterian. Home: 6681 Crest Way Ct Dallas TX 75230-2868 Office: Winstead Sechrest & Minick 5400 Renaissance Tower 1201 Elm St Ste 5400 Dallas TX 75270-2199 Office Phone: 214-745-5251. Business E-Mail: jnolan@winstead.com.

NOLAN, JOHN THOMAS, JR., retired oil industry administrator; b. Boston, Apr. 15, 1930; s. John T. Sr. and Margaret M. (Craig) N.; m. Mary Sharkey, May 7, 1955; children: Anne, Margaret, John T. III, Stephen, Michael. AB, Cath. U. Am., 1951; PhD, MIT, 1955. Chemist Texaco, Inc., Beacon, NY, 1955—59, group leader, 1959—69, supr., 1969—79, asst. mgr., 1979—82, dir. strategic rsch., 1987—92, assoc. dir., 1982—87; ret., 1992. Contbr. over 5 articles to profl. jours. Bd. dirs. Cmty. Coll. Found., 1987—, chmn. 1989-92, chmn. planning com. 1992—. Mem. Am. Chem. Soc., Sigma Xi, Phi Beta Kappa. Achievements include patents in field. Home: 18 Relyea Ter Wappingers Falls NY 12590-5824

NOLAN, JOSEPH THOMAS, journalism educator, communications consultant; b. Waterbury, Conn., Apr. 11, 1920; s. Thomas Francis and Mary Margaret (Gaffney) N.; m. Virginia Theodate Tappin, May 6, 1943; children—Carol Nolan Rigolot, David J. AB, Holy Cross Coll., 1942; MA in English Lit., Boston U., 1945; PhD in Econs, NYU, 1973. Washington corr. UPI, 1943-49; writer, copy editor N.Y. Times, N.Y.C., 1949-55; mgr. editorial and press services RCA Corp., N.Y.C., 1955-62; sr. v.p. corporate communications Chase Manhattan Bank, N.Y.C., 1962-74; prof. journalism and pub. affairs U. S.C., Columbia, 1974-76; v.p. pub. affairs Monsanto Co., St. Louis, 1976-85; Gannett vis. prof. communications U. Fla., 1985-86; prof. communications U. North Fla., Jacksonville, 1986-92; adj. prof. bus. and comm. Flagler Coll., St. Augustine, Fla., 1985—95. Contbr. articles to various mags. Fellow Pub. Rels. Soc. Am. Roman Catholic. Home: 30 Park Terrace Dr Saint Augustine FL 32080-5334

NOLAN, MARY, state representative; Attended, Dartmouth Coll. State rep., dist. 36 Oreg. House Rep., Salem, 2001—; pres. Avrotec, Inc., Aurora, Oreg., 1990—. Mem. Agr. and Forestry Com., Student Achievement and Sch. Accountability Com., Wayns and Means Com., Natural Resources sub com. Democrat. Office: 900 Court St NE H-375 Salem OR 97301 Address: Avrotec Inc 22781 Airport Rd NE Aurora OR 97002

NOLAN, OWEN, professional hockey player; b. Belfast, Northern Ireland, Feb. 12, 1972; With Cornwall Royals, 1988—90, Halifax Citadels, 1990—91; selected 1st round NHL entry draft Que. Nordiques, 190, right wing, 1990—95, Colo. Avalanche, 1995—96, San Jose Sharks, 1996—2003, Toronto Maple Leafs, 2003—. Named to OHL All-Star 1st team, 1989-90; played in NHL All-Star Game 1992, 96. Recipient Emms Family award, 1988-89, Jim Mahon Meml. Trophy, 1989-90, Gold Medal, 2002 Olympics. Office: Toronto Maple Leafs Air Canada Centre 40 Bay St M5J 2X2 Toronto ON Canada

NOLAN, PATRICIA ANN, public health officer; MD, McGill U., Montreal, Que., Can., 1969; MPH, Columbia U., 1973. Cert. in pub. health Am. Bd. Prevention Medicine. Local pub. health adminstr., N.Y.C., 1971-75, Tucson, Ariz., 1981-88; med. adminstr. Ariz. Health Care Cost Containment Sys., 1988-92; state pub. health adminstr. Ill., 1975-81; exec. dir. Colo. Dept. Pub. Health and Environ., 1992-95; dir. R.I. Health Dept., 1995—. Adj. prof. Brown U. Mem. APHA. Office: RI Health Dept 3 Capitol Hl Providence RI 02908-5034

NOLAN, PATRICK JOSEPH, screenwriter, playwright, educator; b. Jan. 2, 1933; children: Patrick, Christian, Mark. BA, Villanova U., 1955; MA, U. Detroit, 1961; PhD, Bryn Mawr Coll., 1973. Teaching fellow and mem. faculty dept. English U. Detroit, 1959-62; instr. English Villanova (Pa.) U., 1962-80, prof., 1980—. Playwright: Chameleons, 1980, Midnight Rainbows, 1991; TV screenwriter: The Jericho Mile, 1979 (Emmy award). Vol. dir. devel. Daemion House Cmty. Counseling Ctr. Served to lt. (j.g.) USNR, 1955-59, PTO. Recipient teaching excellence award Philadelphia mag., 1980, Alumni Medallion award Villanova U., 1986. Mem. Writers Guild Am. (West chpt.), Dramatists Guild. Roman Catholic. Avocations: swimming, biking.

NOLAN, PETER JOHN, physics educator; b. NYC, Mar. 25, 1934; s. Peter John and Nora (Gleeson) Nolan; m. Barbara Nolan, 2000; children from previous marriage: Thomas, James, John, Kevin. BS in Physics, Manhattan Coll., 1956; cert. in Meteorology, UCLA, 1958; MS in Physics, Adelphi U., 1966, PhD in Physics, 1974. Engr. various corps., NJ, NY, 1956-63; systems analysis engr. on lunar module Gruman Aircraft Engring. Corp., Bethpage, NY, 1963-66; asst. prof. physics SUNY, Farmingdale, 1966-68, assoc. prof. physics, 1968-71, prof. physics, 1971—. Chmn. physics dept. SUNY, Farmingdale, 1970—77. Author: Experiments in Physics, 1982, 2d edit., 1995, Electromagnetic Theory for Electrical Technology Students, 1995, Fundamentals of College Physics, 1993, Italian Version, Fundementi Di Fisica, 1996. Mem.: Am. Assn. Physics Tchrs. Home: 59 Parnell Dr Smithtown NY 11787-2428 Office: SUNY Dept Physics Farmingdale NY 11735 Office Phone: 631-420-2271. Personal E-mail: pjnolan@optonline.net. E-mail: nolanpj@farmingdale.edu.

NOLAN, RICHARD THOMAS, clergyman, educator; b. Waltham, Mass., May 30, 1937; s. Thomas Michael and Elizabeth Louise (Leishman) N.; life ptnr. Robert C. Pingpank, Sept. 14, 1955. BA, Trinity Coll., 1960; cert. in clin. pastoral edn., Conn. Valley Hosp., 1962; diploma, Berkeley Divinity Sch., 1962; MDiv., Hartford Sem. Found., 1963; postgrad., Union Theol. Sem., N.Y.C., 1963; MA in Religion, Yale U., 1967; PhD, NYU, 1973; postgrad., Ctr. Career Devel. and Ministry, Newton Center, Mass., 1987, Harvard U., 1991. Ordained deacon Episcopal Ch., 1963, priest, 1965; cert. in death, dying and bereavement Waterbury Hosp. Health Ctr., Conn., 1977. Instr. Latin and English Watkinson (Conn.) Sch., 1961-62; instr. math. Choir Sch. of Cathedral of St. John the Divine, N.Y.C., 1962-64; instr. math. and religion, assoc. chaplain Cheshire (Conn.) Acad., 1965-67; instr. Hartford (Conn.) Sem. Found., 1967-68, asst. acad. dean, lectr. philosophy and edn., 1968-70; instr. Mattatuck C.C., Waterbury, Conn., 1969-70, asst. prof. philosophy and history, 1970-74, assoc. prof., 1974-78, prof. philosophy and social sci., 1978-92, prof. emeritus, 1992—; vicar St. Paul's Parish, Bantam, Conn., 1974-88, pastor emeritus, 1988—; pres. Litchfield Inst., Conn. and Fla., 1984-96; adj. lectr. in philosophy Palm Beach C.C., Fla., 2000—02. Ethics com. Waterbury Hosp. Health Ctr., 1984—88; vis. and adj. prof. philosophy, theology and religious studies Trinity Coll., Conn., L.I. U., U. Miami, St. Joseph Coll., Conn., Pace U., Teikyo Post U., U. Conn., Hartford Grad. Ctr., Ctrl. Conn. State U., 1964—95, Broward C.C., Fla.; lectr. philosophy and theology Barry U., Fla., 1973, 1989—92, 1997—98; adj. assoc. in continuing edn. Berkeley Div. Sch. Yale U., 1987—89; Rabbi Harry Halpern Meml. lectr., Southbury, Conn., 1987; adj. prof. philosophy Fla. Atlantic U., 1999; adj. prof. The Union Inst., Fla., 1999; faculty of cons. examiners Charter Oak State Coll., Conn., 1990—93; assoc. for edn. Christ Ch. Cathedral, Hartford, Conn., 1988—94, hon. canon, 1991—; cons. Dept. Def. Activity Non-Traditional Ednl. Support, Ednl. Testing Svc., Princeton, NJ, 1990; vis. scholar Coll. Preachers, Washington Nat. Cathedral, 1994; supply priest Episcopal Diocese of S.E. Fla., 1994—2002; ret. priest-in-residence St. Andrew's Ch., Lake Worth, Fla., 2002—; bd. regents Cathedral Church of St. John the Divine, 2002—. Author (with H. Titus and M. Smith): Living Issues in Philosophy, 7th edit., 1979, Indonesian edit., 1984, 8th edit., 1986, 9th edit., 1995; author: (with F. Kirkpatrick) Living Issues in Ethics, 1982, 2d edit., 2000, Chinese edit., 1988 (Honored Author for Books Exceeding 100,000 Copies award Wadsworth Pub. Co., 1986); editor, contbr. Diaconate Now, 1968, host Conversations With..., 1987—89; author (with Robert C. Pingpank): Soul Mates: More Than Partners, 2004. Notary pub., Fla. Rsch. fellow Yale U., 1978, 87; recipient Founder's Day award NYU, 1973. Mem. Am. Acad. Religion, Am. Philos. Assn., Authors Guild, Hemlock Soc. Fla. (adv. bd. 1998—), Interfaith Alliance, Integrity, Boston Latin Sch. Alumni Assn., Tabor Acad. Alumni Assn., McCook Fellows Soc. Trinity Coll., Cavalier King Charles Spaniel Club, Phi Delta Kappa, Lambda Legal. Avocation: Cavalier King Charles Spaniels. Home: 2527 Egret Lake Dr West Palm Beach FL 33413-2161 E-mail: canon@rtnolan.com. *Who am I? By baptism I am a resurrected child of God born to love and be loved; my pilgrimage among others is lived within this baptismal identity, more enduring than any achievement.*

NOLAN, STANTON PEELLE, surgeon, educator; b. Washington, May 29, 1933; s. James Parker and Ellen Dubose (Peelle) N.; m. Marion Faro, June 16, 1955; children: Stanton Peelle Jr., Tiphanie Ravenel Clarke. BA, Princeton U., 1955; MD, U. Va., 1959, MS, 1962. Diplomate Am. Bd. Surgery, Am. Bd. Thoracic Surgery. Intern U. Va. Med. Ctr., Charlottesville, 1959-60, asst. resident gen. surgery, 1960-61, research fellow surgery, 1961-62, sr. asst. resident gen. surgery, 1962-64, chief resident gen surgery, 1964-65, chief resident thoracic cardiovascular surgery, 1965-66; sr. rsch. assoc. Clinic of Surgery Nat. Heart Inst., NIH, Bethesda, Md., 1966-68; asst. prof. surgery U. Va. Med. Ctr., Charlottesville, 1968-70, assoc. prof. surgery, 1970-74, surgeon in charge div. thoracic cardiovascular surgery, 1970-93, prof. surgery, 1974-81, Claude A. Jessup prof. surgery, 1981-98, clin. prof. surgery, 1998—, med. dir. Thoracic Cardiovascular post-operative unit, 1989-93. Established investigator Am. Heart Assn., 1969-74; mem. surgery A study sect. NIH, Washington, 1972-76, surgery and bioengring. study sect. 1984-87, chmn. 1985-87; cons. thoracic cardiovascular surgery VA Hosp., Salem, Va., 1968-98, Am. Bd. Surgery cons. to qualifying examination com., 1988-91; surg. cons. Bur. Crippled Children, Charlottesville, 1968-93; vis. cons. cardiothoracic surgery Aga Khan U., Karachi, Pakistan, 1995. Mem. editl. bd. Jour. Surg. Rsch., 1973-79, Annals of Thoracic Surgery, 1979-88; mem. sci. adv. bd. Jour. for Heart Valve Disease, 1993—; mem. editl. adv. bd. ECRI Operating Rm. Risk Mgmt., 1992—; co-editor: Comprehensive Thoracic Surgery Curriculum, TSDA, 1995; contbr. numerous articles to profl. jours., chpts. to books. Bd. mgrs. Ctrl. Va. Health Network, 2000—. Recipient John Horsley Meml. prize U. Va. Med. Sch., 1962; Merit award Research Forum of Am. Coll. Chest Physicians, 1968; research fellow Va. Heart Assn., 1961-62, Am. Cancer Soc., 1963-64; grantee NIH, 1968-84, Am. Heart Assn., 1970-73, Medtronic Corp., 1975-81 Fellow ACS (com. allied health pers. 1996—, exec. com. 1997-2000, vice chair, exec. com. rep. to Am. Acad. Physician Assts. 1997-2003), Am. Coll. Cardiology, Am. Surg. Assn.; mem. Am. Assn. Thoracic Surgery (rep. to Assn. Am. Med. Colls., Am. Bd. Cardiovascular Perfusion, Am. Soc. Extracorporeal Tech., others), Am. Heart Assn. (coun. on cardiovascular surgery 1969-99, anesthesiology, radiology and surgery study com. 1991-94), Andrew G. Morrow Soc., Assn. Acad. Surgery, Assn. Advancement of Med. Instrumentation (chair 1998-2000, chair-elect 1996, co-chmn. cardiac valve prostheses stds. com. 1974—, mem. internat. stds. strategy com. 1989—, bd. dirs. 1990-2000, stds. bd. 1991—, edn. com. 1992-93, nominating com. 1996-2000, chair 1998-2000, exec. com. 1996-2000, govt. rels. com. 1996-2000), Internat. Stds. Orgn. (chmn. subcom. on cardiovascular surg. implants 1982—), Assn. Clin. Cardiac Surgeons, Halsted Soc. (exec. com. 1985-89), Coord. Com. on Perfusion Affairs (chmn. 1990-2000), Internat. Assn. Cardiac Biol. Implants (sci. com. 1994), Am. Assn. for Vascular Surgery, Muller Surg. Soc. (pres. 1979), Soc. Internat. de Cirurgie, Soc. Vascular Surgery, Soc. Thoracic Surgeons (ad hoc com. on industry rels. 1992-97, stds. and ethics com. 1993-95, 98-2001, edn. and resources com. 1996-97), Soc. Univ. Surgeons, Southeastern Surg. Congress, So. Surg. Assn. (2d v.p. 1982), Thoracic Surgery Found. Rsch. and Edn (chair New Century Soc. com. 1997-2000), Va. Surg. Soc. (v.p. 1980-83, pres. 1984), Va. Vascular Soc. (exec. coun. 1985-86), Soc. Critical Care Medicine, Raven Soc., Assn. Am. Med. Colls. (rep. coun. acad. socs. 1992-01), Alpha Omega Alpha, Omicron Delta Kappa. Clubs: Chevy Chase (Md.); Farmington Country (Va.); Princeton (N.Y.C.). Home: #5204 250 Pantops Mountain Rd Charlottesville VA 22911-8702 Office: U Va TCV Surgery PO Box 800679 Charlottesville VA 22908-0679 Business E-Mail: snolan@virginia.edu.

NOLAN, VAL, JR., biologist, lawyer; b. Evansville, Ind., Apr. 28, 1920; s. Val and Jeannette (Covert) N.; m. Susanne Howe, Dec. 23, 1946 (div. Aug. 29, 1980); children: Val, Ann Clare, William Alan; m. Ellen D. Ketterson, Oct. 17, 1980. AB, Ind. U., 1941, JD, 1949. Bar: Ind. 1949. Dep. U.S. marshal, 1941; agt. White House Detail, U.S. Secret Service, 1942; asst. prof. law Ind. U., 1949-52, assoc. prof., 1952-56, prof., 1956-85, prof. emeritus, 1985—, research scholar in zoology, 1957-68, prof. zoology, 1968-77, prof. biology, 1977-85; prof. emeritus, 1985—; acting dean Sch. Law, 1976, 80. Author: (with F.E. Horack, Jr.) Land Use Controls, 1955, Ecology and Behavior of the Prairie Warbler, 1978; editor Ind. Law Jour., 1945-46, Jour. Avian Biology, 1998—; co-editor Current Ornithology, 1994—. Served with USNR, 1942-46. Guggenheim fellow, 1957; recipient Ind. U. Disting. Alumni Svc. award,

1987; named to Acad. Law Alumni Fellows, Ind. U., 1988. Fellow AAAS, Am. Ornithologists Union (v.p. 1989-90, Brewster Meml. award 1986), Animal Behavior Soc.; mem. Brit. Ornithologists Union, Cooper Ornithol. Soc., Wilson Ornithol. Soc. (co-recipient Margaret M. Nice award 1998), Assn. Field Ornithologists, Ecol. Soc. Am., Am. Soc. Naturalists, Deutsche Ornithologen-Gesellschaft, Nederlandse Ornithologische Unie, Soc. for Study of Reprodn., Phi Beta Kappa, Sigma Xi. Democrat. Home: 4675 E Heritage Woods Rd Bloomington IN 47401-9312

NOLAN, VICTORIA, theater director; b. Portland, Maine, June 15, 1952; d. Herbert Wallace and Diane Katharine (Kremm) N.; m. Clarkson Newell Crolius, Aug. 30, 1980; children: Covey Emmeline, Wilhelmina Adams. BA magna cum laude, U. Maine, 1976. Publicity asst. Loeb Drama Ctr. Harvard U., Cambridge, Mass., 1975; pub. rels. asst. to dir. Sch. for Arts Boston U., 1975-76; mgmt. asst. TAG Found., N.Y.C., 1976-77; mng. dir. Ram Island Dance Co., Portland, 1977-78; dir. devel. Ctr. Stage, Balt., 1979-81, assoc. mng. dir., 1981-87; mng. dir. Ind. Repertory Theatre, Indpls., 1988-93; dep. dean, mng. dir., prof. Yale Sch. Drama, Yale Repertory Theatre, New Haven, 1993—. Program evaluator Nat. Endowment for Arts, Washington, 1988—, panelist, 1991—; mem. Indpls. Cultural Consortium, v.p., 1991-93; bd. dirs. Greater Indpls. Progress Com., Indpls. Urban League, Arts Coun. Indpls.; mem. nat. bd. Theatre Comm. Group, N.Y.C., treas., 1995-99; bd. dirs. New Haven Arts Industry Coalition, co-chair, 1997-99, treas., 1999-2002. Mem. exec. com. League Resident Profl. Theatres. Nat. Performing Arts Mgmt. fellow Exxon, Doner Fedn. and NEA, 1978; Elizabeth L. Mahaffey arts adminstrn. fellow Conn. Commn. on the Arts, 2000. Home: 120 Rimmon Rd Woodbridge CT 06525-1915 Office: Yale Repertory Theater PO Box 208244 Yale Station 222 York St New Haven CT 06520-8244

NOLAN, WILLIAM C., JR., energy executive; b. 1939; BA, Yale U., 1961, JD, 1964. Mem. law dept. Murphy Oil Corp., El Dorado, Ark., 1964—69, chmn. bd. dirs., 2002—; founding ptnr. Nolan and Alderson, Attys., El Dorado, 1969—; pres. Noalmark Broadcasting. Office: Murphy Oil Corp PO Box 7000 200 Peach St El Dorado AR 71731-7000 also: Nolan and Alderson Attys 202 W 19th St El Dorado AR 71730

NOLAN, WILLIAM JOSEPH, III, banker; b. N.Y.C., Apr. 6, 1947; s. William J. Jr. and Alice Nettleton (Edwards) N.; m. Wendy Collison French, Mar. 21, 1981; children: William J. IV, Anina Chrysler. Student, Hackley Sch., Tarrytown, N.Y., 1958-65; E.S.U. scholar, Eastbourne Coll., U.K., 1966; BA, Colgate U., 1970; MBA, Stanford U., 1973. V.p. Bankers Trust Co., N.Y.C., 1973-83; mng. dir. Becker-Paribas, N.Y.C., 1983-84; exec. v.p., treas. PaineWebber, N.Y.C., 1984-2001. Bd. trustees Adirondack Mus. (Blue Mountain), 1996—, (treas. 2000—). Mem. Pub. Securities Assn. (money market exec. com. 1985-89, chmn. 1987, bd. dirs. 1988-91, treas. 1990), Adirondack League, Piping Rock Club, Union Club of N.Y.C. Home: 1088 Park Ave New York NY 10128-1132 E-mail: billnolan1088@aol.com

NOLAND, CHRISTINE A. magistrate judge; b. 1945; BA, JD, La. State Univ. Law clk. to Hon. John V. Parker U.S. Dist. Ct. (La. mid. dist.), 5th circuit, magistrate judge, 1987—. Mem. ABA, La. State Bar, La. trial Lawyers Assn., Baton Rouge Bar Assn., Dean Henry George McMahon Inn of Ct. (counselor 1995-97). Office: Russell B Long Fed Bldg & Courthouse 777 Florida St Rm 278 Baton Rouge LA 70801-1717

NOLAND, KENNETH CLIFTON, artist; b. Asheville, N.C., Apr. 10, 1924; s. Harry C. and Bessie (Elkins) N.; m. Cornelia Langer (div.); children: Cady, William L., Lyndon; m. Stephanie Gordon, 1967 (div.); m. Peggy Schiffer; children: Samuel Jesse (div.); m. Paige Rense, 1994. Student, Ozzip Zadkine, Paris, 1948-49; studied, Black Mountain Coll., N.C., summers, 1950, 51. Tchr. Inst. Contemporary Arts, 1950-52, Cath. U., 1951-60. One man shows include Galerie Creuze, Paris, 1949, Tibor de Nagy Gallery, N.Y.C., 1957, 58, Jefferson Pl. Gallery, 1958, French & Co., N.Y.C., 1959, Bennington Coll., 1961, Andre Emmerich Gallery, N.Y.C., 15 shows from 1960-83, Andre Emmerich Gallery, Zurich, Switzerland, 1973, 76, 79, 82, David Mirvish Gallery, Toronto, Can., 1965, 67, 74, 76, Jewish Mus., 1965, Salander O'Reilly Galleries, N.Y.C., 1989, Leo Castelli Gallery, N.Y., 1995, Gana Art Gallery, Seoul, 1995-96, also other galleries in Milan, Italy, Paris, Zurich, Dusseldorf, Hamburg and Cologne, Fed. Republic Germany, London, Montreal and Toronto, Can.; retrospective show Guggenheim Mus., N.Y.C., 1977; group shows include Kootz Gallery, N.Y.C., 1954, Norman Mackenzie Art Gallery, Regina, Sask., Can., 1963, Corcoran Gallery, Washington, 1956, 59, 63, 64, 67, 70, 75, Corcoran Gallery Biennial in Italy, 1964, Fogg Art Mus., Cambridge, Mass., 1965, 72, Mus. Modern Art, N.Y.C., 1965, 68, Nat. Gallery, Washington, 1968, U.S. Pavilion Expo 67, Montreal, Art Inst. Chgo., 1962, 70, 72, 76, Balt. Mus., 1957, 70, 77, Jewish Mus., 1963, Tate Gallery, London, 1964, 74, Guggenheim Mus., 1961, 66, 70, 73-74, 76-77, L.A. County Mus., 1964, Inst. Contemporary Art, Boston, 1964, 65, 67, Whitney Mus., N.Y.C., 1961-67, 69-73, 76, Met. Mus. N.Y.C., 1968, 70, Mus. Fine Arts, Boston, 1972, Albright-Knox Gallery, Buffalo, 1978, 80, Ameringer Howard Fine Art, NY, 99; Meredith Long Gall., Houston,Tex., 99; Andre Emmerich, CLosing Exhibition of Gall., NY, 99; CHAC-Mool Gall., CA, 99, Ameringer/Howard Gall., N.Y.C, 1999-2001, Farnsworth Mus. Art, Maine, 2002, Naples (Fla.) Mus., 2002; represented in permanent collections Salander O'Reily Galleries, N.Y.C., Mus. of Fine Arts, Houston, 1994, Ft. Lauderdale, 1994; Arte Metro Roma, Rome Colosseum Ctrl. Subway Mosaic Installed, 1995. Trustee Bennington (Vt.) Coll. Recipient 1st prize Premio Nacional Internat., Inst. Torcuato de Tella, Buenos Aires, 1964, Creative Arts award Brandeis U., 1965, 4th prize Corcoran Biennale, 1967; recipient The N.C. Award/medal of arts, 1995.

NOLAN-PITERI, DAWN C. state legislator; b. McKees Rocks, Pa. m. David Piteri; 3 children. Mem. N.H. Ho. of Reps. (dist. 34), Concord, 1996—, mem. local and regulated rev. com., 1996—. Mem. Nashua Rep. City Com., 1996—. Home: Unit 64 26 Melendy Rd Milford NH 03055-3471

NOLEN, CRYSTAL ME'KELLE, poet, educator; b. Lexinton Park, Md., July 2, 1972; d. A. Jay, Jr. and Carolyn L. Nolen; children: Stanley, Garney. BA in English, Norfolk State U., 1999. Teacher's asst., sch. cmty. trainer Norfolk (Va.) Pub. Sch. Sys., 1993—. Coord. Million Woman Mar. Bus Trip, Norfolk, 1997. Actor: (plays) Summers in Suffolk, 2000. Home: PO Box 367 Portsmouth VA 23705 Personal E-mail: Cryswrites2000@aol.com.

NOLEN, JAMES ALLEN, property manager, writer; b. Elyria, Ohio, May 8, 1960; s. Anderson and Maynida Nolen. Cert. refrigeration and HVAC, Refrigeration Svcs. Engring. Soc., class II asbestos abatement tng., Law Cos. Tng. Ctr., Colo.; pool and spa operator Nat. Swimming Pool Found. Facilities maintenence engr. Hospitality Industry, Denver, 1982—2002; dir. of leasing for property mgmt. firm Willmax Capital Mgmt., Denver, 2002—. CEO Semaj Publs. Denver, 2003—04. Author: (poetry) Semaj Poetry (Poet of Merit Award/Outstanding Achievement in Poetry award, 2003). Independent. Baptist. Achievements include patents pending for SnowWhiz; Stye remover; unique shower head. Avocations: travel, billiards, fishing, camping, writing. Home: PMB 508 13918 E Mississippi Ave Aurora CO 80012 Office: Semaj PublsDenver PMB 506 13918 E Mississippi Ave Aurora CO 80012 Personal E-mail: semajpoetry@cs.com. E-mail: semajpoetry@cs.com.

NOLEN, NORMAN W. financial executive; b. 1943; MBA, U. Tex.; degree in elec. engring., U. Houston. CPA. Corp. banker Tex. Commerce Bank, 1968-80; corp. treas. Cameron Iron Works, 1980-90; sr. v.p., treas., CFO Weatherford Internat., Inc., 1991-98; sr. v.p., CFO, treas. Kirby Corp., 1999, exec. v.p., CFO, treas., 1999—. Office: Ste 1000 55 Waugh Dr Houston TX 77007

NOLEN, ROY LEMUEL, retired lawyer; b. Montgomery, Ala., Nov. 29, 1937; s. Roy Lemuel Jr. and Elizabeth (Larkin) N.; m. Evelyn McNeill Thomas, Aug. 28, 1965; 1 child, Rives Rutledge. BArch, Rice U., 1961; LLB, Harvard U., 1967. Bar: Tex. 1968, U.S. Ct. Appeals (5th cir.) 1969. Law clk. to sr. judge U.S. Ct. Appeals (5th cir.), 1967-68; assoc. Baker Botts LLP, Houston, 1968-75, ptnr., 1976-2000; co-head Corp. Dept., 1985-90; mem. exec. com., 1988-91; adminstrv. ptnr., 1997-2000; ret., 2000. Cmty. rep. instnl. animal care and use com. M.D. Anderson Cancer Ctr., 2001—. Bd. dirs. Houston Ballet Found., 1980-92, Rice Design Alliance, 1995-96; exec. com. Contemporary Arts Mus., 1990-96, 97-2002; exec. com. Houston Symphony Soc., 1994-99, gen. counsel, 1994-98; trustee Menil Found. (Menil Collection), 1999—, sr. warden Christ Ch. Cathedral, 1991-92, chancellor, 2003—; chmn. Houston area devel. initiative Episcopal Diocese of Tex., 1997. 1st lt. USMC, 1961-64. Mem.: State Bar Tex., Briar Club, Paul Jones Dancing Club, Allegro, Coronado Club. Episcopalian. Office: Baker Botts LLP One Shell Plz 910 Louisiana St Houston TX 77002-4995

NOLEN, WILLIAM GILES, lawyer, accountant; b. Fayetteville, Ark., Aug. 4, 1931; s. William Jefferson and Marie (Giles) N.; m. Carole Turner, Aug. 25, 1957; children: Kathy, Thomas (dec.). BSBA, U. Ark., 1960; JD, U. Houston, 1980. Bar: Tex. 1980; CPA, Tex. Auditor Arthur Anderson & Co., Houston, 1960-66; sec., treas. Brown & Root (U.K.) Ltd., London, 1966-69; v.p. Highlands Ins. Co., Houston, 1969-73, sr. v.p., 1973-80, dir., 1973-88; v.p. Halliburton Co., Dallas, 1980-82; sr. v.p. Brown & Root, Inc., Houston, 1982-86; exec. v.p. Highlands Ins. Co., Houston, 1986-88; of counsel Whitmore, Sheppard & Pollicoff, Houston, 1988-92, Policoff, Smith & Myres LLP, Houston, 1992-95, Policoff, Smith, Myres & Remels LLP, Houston, 1995-2000, Pollicoff, Smith & Remels, Houston, 2000—02. Maj. USAF, 1951-56. Mem. Am. Assn. Atty. CPAs (past pres., bd. dirs.), Tex. Soc. CPAs (Tex. CPA of Yr. 1961), Mensa. Presbyterian.

NOLF, DAVID M. financial consultant; b. Hartford, Conn., Nov. 25, 1942; s. Richard A. and Erreld I. (Manstan) N.; m. Linda J. Anderson, June 20, 1964; 1 child, Cristina E. BSChemE, Lafayette Coll., 1964; MBA, U. Conn., 1968. Prodn. engr. Am. Cyanamid, Wallingford, Conn., 1664-66; adminstrn. supr. Electric Boat Div. Gen. Dynamics, Groton, Conn., 1966-71; chief fin. and adminstrv. officer, corp. sec. Analysis and Tech. Inc., North Stonington, Conn., 1971—99; cons., 2001—. Bd. dirs. Reflexite Corp. Chmn. Ch. Fin. Com., Westerly, R.I., 2002—; trustee Westerly Hosp., 1993—, chmn. 2003—; bd. dirs. The Day Newspaper, 1997—. Mem.: Beta Gamma Sigme, Tau Beta Pi. Avocations: fishing, golf. Home: 347 Lantern Hill Rd Mystic CT 06355-3623

NOLFI, EDWARD ANTHONY, lawyer; b. Warren, Ohio, Sept. 30, 1958; s. Eugene Vincent Sr. and Margaret Joyce (Futey) N.; m. Sheri Ann Loue, June 5, 1982. AB, Brown U., 1980; JD, U. Akron, 1983. Bar: Ohio 1983, N.Y. 1986, U.S. Dist. Ct. (no. dist.) Ohio 1987, U.S. Tax Ct. 1987, U.S. Ct. Appeals (6th cir. 1989), U.S. Supreme Ct. 1989. Juggler Miracle Sta., Warren, 1976; instr. Sch. One, Providence, 1980; tech. writer Doctors' Hosp., Massillon, Ohio, 1982; pvt. practice Warren, 1983-84; assoc. editor Lawyers Coop. Pub. Co., Rochester, N.Y., 1985-87; pvt. practice Akron, Ohio, 1987—2003, Portage County, 2003—. Prof. Acad. Ct. Reporting, Akron, 1988-91; prof. Kent State U., 1993, Mt. Aloysius Coll., Cresson, Pa., 1996; product developer and lead case law editor LexisNexis, Miamisburg, Ohio, 1999—. Author: The Master Juggler, 1980, Basic Legal Research, 1993, Basic Wills, Trusts, and Estates, 1995; articles editor Am. Law Reports, Fed., 1986-87. Roman Catholic. Avocation: juggling. Home and Office: 4965 State Rte 14 Ravenna OH 44266-9622 Business E-Mail: enolfi@neo.rr.com.

NOLIN, JOHN CHARLES, product specialist, engineering consultant; s. Roger J. and Claire B. Nolin; m. Audra Bretton, May 1, 1992; 1 child, Marc. BS in Mech. Engring., U. of Lowell, 1988. Mech. design engr. Diversified Optical Products, Salem, NH, 1988—92, Resonetics, Nashua, NH, 1992—93; mech. engr. Alan Dick & Co. USA, Hollis, NH, 1993—95; mech. design engr. PRI Automation, Billerica, Mass., 1995—95; CAD mgr. Tech. Rsch. & Mfg., Bedford, NH, 1995—96; mech. specialist CIMLOGIC, Inc., Nashua, 1996—2000; software reviewer www.ZDNet.com, Cambridge, Mass., 1998—2001; product specialist SolidWorks Corp., Concord, Mass., 2000—04. MCAD and computer cons. DesignSmith LLC, Hollis, 1995—. Mem.: ASME (ementor 2001—02), N.H. Soc. Mfg. Engrs. (chmn. 1998—2002), Soc. of Profl. Engrs. (assoc.; EIT 1983), KC (dep. grand knight 1997—2002). Independent. Roman Catholic. Achievements include design of Granite altar for Resurrection Parish. Avocations: skiing, hiking, computing, writing, bicycling. Home: 128 Pine Hill Rd Hollis NH 03049 Personal E-mail: tjnolin@juno.com.

NOLL, RICHARD ALLAN, strategy consultant; b. Miami, Fla., Aug. 13, 1957; s. William Frederick and Doris (Bombardier) N. BS in BA, Pa. State U., 1979; MSIA/MBA with distinction, Carnegie-Mellon U., 1985. Project mgr. Air Products & Chems., Inc., Allentown, Pa., 1979-83; intern Chase Manhattan Bank, N.Y.C., 1984; v.p. Strategic Planning Assocs., Washington, 1985—. Mem. World Affairs Coun., Washington, 1990—. Elliott Dunlap Smith awardee Carnegie-Mellon U., 1985. Republican. Roman Catholic. Home: 1614 W Abingdon Dr Alexandria VA 22314-1010 Office: Strategic Planning Assocs 2300 N St NW Ste 800 Washington DC 20037-1122

NOLL, RICHARD DEAN, JR., psychologist, educator, historian; b. Detroit, Oct. 27, 1959; s. Richard Dean and Betty Ann (Adamczak) Noll; m. Mary Beth McAndrews, Apr. 27, 1986 (div. 1993); m. Susan J. Naylor, May 13, 1994 (div. 2002); 1 child, Wolfgang; 1 child, Dylan James Patterson. BA, U. Ariz., 1979; MA, New Sch. for Social Rsch., 1982; PhD, New Sch. for Rsch., 1992. Lic. clin. psychologist, Pa. Staff clin. psychologist Ancora Psychiat. Hosp., Hammonton, N.J., 1985-88; clin. psychologist in pvt. practice Phila., 1988-92; instr. dept. psychology West Chester (Pa.) U., 1992-94; postdoctoral fellow Harvard U., Cambridge, Mass., 1994-96, Lectr. in History of Sci., 1997-98; resident fellow Dibner Inst. History of Sci. and Tech. MIT, Cambridge, Mass., 1995-96; asst. prof. psychology De Sales Univ., Center Valley, Pa., 2000—. Invited lectr. Acad. Scis., Budapest, Hungary, 1991, Warsaw U., 1991, Chinese Acad. Scis., Beijing, 1994; vis. scholar MIT, 1995-96. Author: The Encyclopedia of Schizophrenia and the Psychotic Disorders, 1992, 2d rev. edit., 2000, Vampires, Werewolves and Demons: Twentieth Century Case Reports in the Psychiatric Literature, 1992, The Jung Cult, 1994 (named best book in psychology Assn. Am. Publishers 1994), The Aryan Christ, 1997, Encyclopedia of Schizophrenia and Other Psychotic Disorders, rev. 2d edit., 2000; contbr. articles to profl. jours. Wenner-Gren Found. for Anthropol. Rsch. grantee, 1993. Mem. APA, History of Sci. Soc., Soc. for Sci. of Clin. Psychology. Office Phone: 610-282-1100 ext. 1268. E-mail: richard.noll@desales.edu.

NOLL, ROGER GORDON, economist, educator; b. Monterey Park, Calif., Mar. 13, 1940; s. Cecil Ray and Hjordis Alberta (Westover) Noll; m. Robyn Schreiber, Aug. 25, 1962 (dec. Jan. 2000); 1 child, Kimberlee Elizabeth; m. Ann Seminara, Dec. 2, 2001. BS, Calif. Inst. Tech., 1962; AM, Harvard U., 1965, PhD in Econs, 1967. Mem. social sci. faculty Calif. Inst. Tech., 1965-84, prof., 1973-82, inst. prof., 1982-84, chmn. div. humanities and social scis., 1978-82; prof. econs. Stanford U., 1984—, Morris M. Doyle centennial prof. of pub. policy, 1990—2002, dir. pub. policy program, 1986—2002, dir. Am. Studies Program, 2001—02, dir. Stanford Ctr. for Internat. Devel., 2002—; Jean Monnet prof. European U. Inst., 1991; vis. fellow Brookings Instn., 1995-96, non-resident sr. fellow, 1996—2000, vis. scholar, 2003. Sr. staff economist Coun. Econ. Advisors, Washington, 1967—69; sr. fellow Brookings Instn., Washington, 1970—73; mem. tech. adv. bd. Com. Econ. Devel., 1978—82; mem. adv. coun. NSF, 1978—89, NASA, 1978—81, SERI, 1982—90; mem. Pres.'s Commn. Nat. Agenda for Eighties, 1980; chmn. L.A. Sch. Monitoring Com., 1978—79; mem. Commn. Behavioral Social Scis. and Edn. NAS, 1984—90, mem. bd. sci., tech. and econ. policy, 2000—; mem. energy rsch. adv. bd. Dept. Energy, 1986—89; mem. Sec. Energy Adv. Bd., 1990—94, Calif. Coun. Sci. and Tech., 1995—2000; mem. bd. on sci., tech. and econ. policy NRC, 2001—. Author: (book) Reforming Regulation, 1971, The Economics and Politics of Deregulation, 1991, The Economics and Politics of the Slowdown in Regulatory Reform, 1999; co-author: Economic Aspects of Television Regulation, 1973, The Political Economy of Deregulation, 1983, The Technology Pork Barrel, 1991; editor: Government and the Sports Business, 1974, Regulatory Policy and the Social Sciences, 1985, Challenges to Research Universities, 1998; co-editor: Constitutional Reform in California, 1995, Sports, Jobs and Taxes, 1997, A Communications Cornucopia, 1998; supervisory editor: Info. Econs. and Policy Jour., 1984—92. Recipient 1st ann. book award, Nat. Assn. Ednl. Broadcasters, 1974; fellow Guggenheim, 1983—84; grantee NSF, 1973—82. Mem.: Am. Econ. Assn. Democrat. Home: 4153 Hubbartt Dr Palo Alto CA 94306-3834 Office: Stanford U Dept Econs Stanford CA 94305 Office Phone: 650-723-2297. Business E-Mail: rnoll@stanford.edu.

NOLL, WALTER, mathematics professor; b. Berlin, Jan. 7, 1925; came to U.S., 1955, naturalized, 1961; s. Franz and Martha N.; m. Helga I. Schönberg, Apr. 1, 1955 (dec. Jan. 1976); children: Virginia, Peter; m. Mary T. Strauss, Jan. 4, 1979 (dec. Nov. 1999); m. Marilyn Smith Marsh, Dec. 30, 2000. Diplom-Ingenieur, Technische U. Berlin, 1951; Lincencié ès Sciences, U. Paris, 1950; PhD, Ind. U., 1954. Sci. asst. Technische U., Berlin, 1951-55; instr. U. So. Calif., 1955-56; assoc. prof. Carnegie-Mellon U., Pitts., 1956-60, prof., 1960—. Vis. prof. Johns Hopkins, 1962-63, Oxford U. and U. of Pisa, 1984-85; vis. lectr. Soc. for Indsl. and Applied Math., 1969-71 Author: (with C. Truesdell) The Non-Linear Field Theories of Mechanics, 1965, 2d edit. 1992, 3d edit. 2004, (with B.D. Coleman, H. Markovitz) Viscometric Flows of Non-Newtonian Fluids, 1966, The Foundations of Mechanics and Thermodynamics, Selected Papers, 1974, Finite-Dimensional Spaces: Algebra, Geometry, and Analysis, vol. 1, 1987. Mem. Soc. for Natural Philosophy (founding, pres. 1973-75), Am. Math. Soc., Math. Assn. Am. Achievements include research in conceptual mathematical foundations of continuum mechanics and thermodynamics. Home: 308 Field Club Ridge Rd Pittsburgh PA 15238-2422

NOLLAU, LEE GORDON, lawyer; b. Balt., Feb. 6, 1950; s. E. Wilson and Carolyn G. (Blass) N.; m. Carol A. Haughney, Aug. 12, 1978; children: Ann G., Catherine E., Margaret C. BA, Juniata Coll., 1972; MAS, Johns Hopkins U., 1975; JD, Dickinson Sch. Law, 1976. Bar: Pa. 1976, U.S. Dist. Ct. (mid. dist.) 1982, U.S. Dist. Ct. (we. dist.) 1988, U.S. Ct. Appeals (3d cir.) 1980, U.S. Supreme Ct. 1982. Instr. Juniata Coll., Huntingdon, Pa., 1976-78; asst. dist. atty. Centre County, Bellefonte, Pa., 1978-80, dist. atty., 1981; assoc. Litke, Lee, Martin, Grine & Green, Bellefonte, 1981-83, Jubelirer & Assocs., State College, Pa., 1983-87; ptnr. Jubelirer, Nollau, Young & Blanarik, Inc., State College, 1988-89, Jubelirer, Rayback, Nollau, Walsh, Young & Blanarik, Inc., State College, 1989-94, Nollau & Young, State College, 1994—. Mental health rev. officer Centre County, Bellefonte, 1982—; instr. Pa. State U. Smeal Coll. Bus., 1995—; lectr., author Pa. Bar Inst., 1995—. Author: Trial Tactics: Direct Examination of Lay Witnesses. Mem. ABA, Pa. Bar Assn., Centre County Bar, Pa. Assn. Criminal Def. Lawyers. Presbyterian. Office: Nollau & Young 2153 E College Ave State College PA 16801-7204 Office Phone: 814-235-1110. E-mail: lnollau@nollauyounglaw.com.

NOLLY, ROBERT J. pharmacist, health facility administrator, educator; b. Amsterdam, N.Y., Jan. 8, 1947; m. Diera R. Lehtonen, June 21, 1969; children: Shelby Alexandra, Kirby Alycia, Kendall Alexis. BS in Pharmacy with honor, Albany Coll. Pharmacy, 1970; MSc in Hosp. Pharmacy, Ohio State U., 1979. Pharmacy extern Matt Pharmacy, Canajoharie, N.Y., 1967-70; pharmacy intern Park Row Drugs, Canajoharie, 1970-71, asst. mgr., 1971-72; staff pharmacist Mary Imogene Bassett Hosp., Cooperstown, N.Y., 1972-74, 75-77; med. svc. rep. Dista Products Co., Eli Lilly and Co., Indpls., 1974-75; resident hosp. pharmacy Grant Hosp., Columbus, Ohio, 1977-79; asst. dir. pharmacy svcs. City of Memphis Hosp., 1979-81, U. Tenn. Bowld Hosp., Memphis, 1982, dir. pharmacy svcs. and materials mgmt., 1982-85, asst. adminstr. pharmacy svcs. and materials mgmt., 1985—90, adminstr., 1991—92, adminstr. ops., 1992—98, exec. dir., 1999—2002. Asst. prof. Coll. Pharmacy U. Tenn., Memphis, 1979-92, assoc. prof.1992-; lectr. Columbus Tech. Inst., 1978-79; trustee Diversified Svcs., Inc., Tenn. Hosp. Assn., 1990-96, mem. pharmacy adv. com., 1990; bd. dirs. Ava Marie Nursing Home, chmn. nom. com., 1988, 89, mem. long-range planning com., 1989, 90, mem. constn. and by-laws com., 1990, mem. govtl. rels. com., 1991-93; presenter in field. Editor U. Tenn. Bowld Hosp. Pharmacy Newsletter, 1987-91; mem. editl. bd. Drug and Therapeutics Newsletter, U. Tenn. Coll. Pharmacy, 1989, 90. Usher Ch. of Holy Spirit, 1988-96; mem. Am. Cancer Soc. Recipient Order of Sword award Am. Cancer Soc., 1992. Mem. Am. Soc. hosp. Pharmacists, Tenn. Soc. Hosp. Pharmacists (mem. com. 1980, constn. and by-laws com. 1985, 88, 89, 90, chmn. nominating com. 1989, orgn. and goals com. 1991, strategic planning com. 1992), Tenn. Pharmacists Assn. (pharmacy tech. task force 1988, 89, 90, ho. dels. 1988, 89, 90, 91, 92, 94, chmn. tech. curriculum com. 1991, tech. edn. accreditation com. 1991, 92, 94), Memphis Area Soc. Hosp. Pharmacists (pres.-elect 1984, pres. 1985, past pres. 1986, chmn. nominating com. 1991), Tenn. Hosp. Assn. (liaison Tenn. Med. Assn. com. 1991), Mid-South Healthcare Materials Mgmt. Assn., Kappa Psi, Rho Chi. Home: 2927 Mikeyair Dr Germantown TN 38138-7148 E-mail: rnolly@utmem.edu.

NOLPH, GEORGIA BOWER, physician; b. Appleton, Minn., Jan. 26, 1938; d. Clarence Walter and Gladys Mae (Hanson) Bower; m. Karl David Nolph, July 26, 1961; children: Erika Lynn, Kristoper Karl. BA, St. Olaf Coll., 1960; MD, Woman's Med. Coll. Pa., 1964. Pvt. practice with G.H. Ferguson MD, Bala-Cynwyd, Pa., 1965-67; civil service Walter Reed Army Med. Ctr., Washington, 1967-69; instr. community health and med. practice U. Mo., Columbia, 1969-70; asst. prof. U. Mo. Med. Sch., Columbia, 1970-77, assoc. prof. family and community medicine, 1977—. Acting med. dir. Family Med. Care Ctr., U. Mo. Hosp. and Clinics, Columbia, 1980—87; med. dir. NBA Lenoir Retirement Cmty., 1987—99, bd. dirs., 2000—, v.p., 2001—03, pres., 2003—. Assoc. editor. (profl. jour.) Continuing Education for the Family Physician, 1972-73. V.p. Parents for Drug Free Youth, Columbia, Mo., 1985-86, 86-87, pres. 1987-88, 88-89; bd. dir. Columbia Civic Orch., 2003—. Mem.: Boone County Med. Soc., Mo. State Med. Assn., Am. Bus. Women's Assn., Am. Med. Women's Assn. (state dir. 1975—2003, region VII gov. 1996—2003), Am. Legion Aux. Republican. Methodist. Avocations: music, reading, travel, needlecrafts. Home: 908 Hickory Hill Dr Columbia MO 65203-2320 Office: U Mo Med Sch Dept Family and Cmty Medicine 1 Hospital Dr Columbia MO 65201-5276

NOLTE, HENRY R., JR., lawyer, former automobile company executive; b. N.Y.C., Mar. 3, 1924; s. Henry R. and Emily A. (Eisele) Nolte; m. Frances Messner, May 19, 1951; children: Gwynne Conn, Henry Reed III, Jennifer Stevens, Suzanne Saunders. BA, Duke U., 1947; LLB, U. Pa., 1949. Bar: N.Y. 1950, Mich. 1967. Assoc. Cravath, Swaine & Moore, N.Y.C., 1951-61; assoc. counsel Ford Motor Co., Dearborn, Mich., 1961, asst. gen. counsel, 1964-71, assoc. gen. counsel, 1971-74, v.p., gen. counsel, 1974-89, Philco-Ford Corp., Phila., 1961-64; v.p., gen. counsel, sec. Ford of Europe Inc., Warley, Essex, Eng., 1967-69; gen. counsel fin. and ins. subs. Ford Motor Co., 1974-89; sr. ptnr. Miller, Canfield, Paddock & Stone, Detroit, 1989-93, of counsel, 1993—. Formerly vice chmn. and trustee Cranbrook Ednl. Cmty.; mem. Internat. and Comparative Law Ctr. of Southwestern Legal Found.; trustee Beaumont Hosp. Lt. USNR, 1943-46, PTO. Mem. ABA (past chmn. corp. gen. counsel), Mich. Bar Assn., Assn. Bar City N.Y., Assn. Gen. Counsel, Orchard Lake Country Club, Bloomfield Hills Country Club, Everglades Club (Fla.), Gulfstream Golf Club (Fla.), Ocean Club (Fla.). Episcopalian. Office: Miller Canfield Paddock & Stone 840 W Long Lake Rd Troy MI 48098-6356

NOLTE, NICK, actor; b. Omaha, Feb. 8, 1941; m. Sheila Page, 1966 (div. 1971), Sharon Haddad, May 10, 1978 (div. 1983); Rebecca Linger, Feb. 19, 1984 (div. 1995); 1 child, Brawley King. Student, Ariz. St. Univ., Eastern Ariz. Coll., Pasadena City Coll., Phoenix City Coll.; studies with, John Paul, Allen Dutton. Actor: (play) The Last Pad, 1973, (TV movies) Winter Kill, 1974, The California Kid, 1974, Death Sentence, 1974, (TV series) Adams of Eagle Lake, 1975, (TV movies) The Treasure Chest Murder, 1975, The Runaway Barge, 1975, (mini-series) Rich Man, Poor Man, 1976; (films) Return to Macon County, 1975, The Deep, 1977, Who'll Stop the Rain, 1978, North Dallas Forty, 1979, Heart Beat, 1980, Cannery Row, 1982, 48 Hours, 1982, Under Fire, 1983, The Ultimate Solution of Grace Quigley, 1984, Teachers, 1984, Down and Out in Beverly Hills, 1986, Weeds, 1987, Extreme Prejudice, 1987, Farewell to the King, 1988, Three Fugitives, 1988, New York Stories, 1989, Everybody Wins, 1989, Q & A, 1990, Another 48 Hours, 1990, Prince of Tides, 1991, Cape Fear, 1991, Lorenzo's Oil, 1992, The Player, 1992, Blue Chips, 1994, I'll Do Anything, 1994, I Love Trouble, 1994, Jefferson in Paris, 1995, Mulholland Falls, 1996, Mother Night, 1996, Nightwatch, 1997, Afterglow, 1997, U-Turn, 1997, Affliction (also exec. prod), 1998, Thin Red

Line, 1998, The Best of Enemies, 1999, Simpatico, 1999, Breakfast of Champions, 1999, The Golden Bowl, 2000, Trixie, 2000, Investigating Sex (also prod.), 2001, The Good Thief, 2002, Northfork, 2003, The Hulk, 2003.

NONNA, JOHN MICHAEL, lawyer; b. N.Y.C., July 8, 1948; s. Angelo and Josephine (Visconti) N.; m. Jean Wanda (Cleary), June 9, 1973; children: Elizabeth, Caroline, Marianne, Timothy. BA, Princeton U., 1970; JD, NYU, 1975. Bar: N.Y. 1976, U.S. Dist. Ct. (so. dist.) N.Y., 1978, U.S. Ct. Appeals (2d cir.) 1978, U.S. Ct. Appeals (9th cir.) 1980, U.S. Ct. Appeals (5th cir.) 1997, U.S. Dist. Ct. Conn. 1988, U.S. Supreme Ct. 1998. Law asst. to Hon. D.L. Gabrielli N.Y. Ct. Appeals, Albany, 1975-77; assoc. Reid and Priest, N.Y.C., 1977-84; ptnr. Werner and Kennedy, N.Y.C., 1984-99, LeBoeuf, Lamb, Greene, and MacRae, N.Y.C., 1999—. Contbr. articles to profl. jours. Dep. mayor, trustee Pleasantville, N.Y., 1990-95; mayor, 1995-2003; acting justice, 1983-89. With USNR, 1970-75. Mem. U.S. Olympic Team, 1972, 1980; Paul Harris fellow Rotary Internat. Fellow Am. Bar Found. (life); mem. ABA (torts and ins. practice sect. com. chair 1986-87, 92-93), N.Y. State Bar Assn. (chair comml. and fed. litig. sect. 1998-99, co-editor in chief 2000, N.Y. ins. law practice), Assn. Bar City N.Y., N.Y. Fencers Club (pres. 1990-93). Avocations: fencing, running, piano. Office: LeBoeuf Lamb Greene & MacRae 125 W 55th St New York NY 10019-5369 Office Phone: 212-424-8311. Business E-Mail: jnonna@llgm.com.

NOOLAN, JULIE ANNE CARROLL, management consultant; b. Adelaide, South Australia, Australia, June 14, 1944; came to U.S., 1966; d. Archibald Henry and Norma Mae (Gillett) Noolan; m. Daniel Thuering Carroll, Aug. 20, 1977. MA, U. Chgo., 1968, PhD, 1974, Exec. MBA, 1983. With State Library of South Australia, 1962-63, Repatriation Dept. South Australia, 1962-66; asst. librarian U. Chgo. Libraries, 1966-68; dir. edn. Med. Library Assn., Chgo., 1972-77; exec. dir. Assn. Coll. and Research Libraries, Chgo., 1977-84; COO Carroll Group, Inc., Chgo., 1984-95; pres. COO Carroll Group, Inc., Chgo., 1995—. Mem. faculty U. Chgo., 1968-89, Am. U., 1995—. Author: Libraries and Accreditation in Higher Education; contbr. articles to jours. U. Chgo. fellow, 1967-68, Higher Edn. Act fellow, 1969-72; Nat. Library of Medicine grantee, 1967-69; named Outstanding Young U.S. Leader 1985 Coun. on the U.S., Mem. ALA, Am. Soc. Assn. Execs., Am. Mgmt. Assn., Spol. Librs. Assn., Am. Soc. for Info. Scis. (past pres., doctoral award, Watson Davis award), ASTD, Nat. Tng. Labs. (bd. dirs. 1990-94), Orgn. Devel. Network, Internat. Assn. Neuro-Linguistic Programming (bd.dirs. 1990-93), Internat. Plant Genetic Resources Inst. (Rome, bd. dirs. 1991-98), Internat. Ctr. Agrl. Rsch. in Dry Areas (Syris, bd. dirs. 1992-98), Beta Phi Mu.

NOONAN, FRANK RUSSELL, business executive; b. Boston, July 21, 1942; s. Russell F. and Barbara (Yutronich) N.; m. Patricia Bernadette Saulnier, Aug. 22, 1964; children: Kathleen, Kelly, Kristin. BA, U. N.H., 1964. Fin. mgmt. trainee GE, Lynn, Mass., 1966-69, corp. auditor Schenectady, N.Y., 1969-74, audit adminstr., 1974-76, fin. mgr. mechanical drive turbine dept. Fitchburg, Mass., 1976-78, fin. mgr. air conditioning divsn. Louisville, 1978-81; sr. v.p., chief fin. officer Union Mutual Ins. Co., Portland, Maine, 1981-86, UNUM Corp., Portland, 1986-89; sr. v.p., group fin. The Dun & Bradstreet Corp., N.Y.C., 1989-90; chmn., CEO R.H. Donnelley Corp., Purchase, N.Y., 1991—. Bd. trustees U. N.H. Found.; dir. China Big.com. Chmn. N.Y. United Hosp. Med. Ctr., 1995—, Maine Coll. Art; trustee Found. Blood Rsch., Scarborough, Maine, 1982-89; vice chmn. bd. govs. Buick Classic, 1996—; bd. trustees Manhattanville Coll., 1998—. Mem. Yellow Pages Pubs. Assn. (bd. dirs. 1996-2000). Republican. Avocations: tennis, skiing, music, golf, model trains. Office: R H Donnelley Corp 1 Manhattanville Rd Purchase NY 10577-2100 Home: 3 Arbor Rd Falmouth ME 04105-1117

NOONAN, JACK, application developer; With field engring. and sys. devel. IBM Corp., 1967—77; from with software devel., mktg., customer svc. to v.p. corp. product support Amdahl Corp., Santa Clara, Calif., 1977—85; v.p. Product Group Candle Corp., 1985—90; pres., CEO Microrim Corp., 1990—91; pres. SPSS Inc., Chgo., 1992—, CEO, 1992—, bd. dir. Bd. dir. Morningstar, Inc., Repository Technologies, Inc., Fortel Inc.; adv. com. Geneva Tech. Ptnrs., Inc. Office: SPSS Inc 233 S Wacker Dr 11th Fl Chicago IL 60606*

NOONAN, JACQUELINE ANNE, pediatrics educator; b. Burlington, Vt., Oct. 28, 1928; BA, Albertus Magnus Coll., 1950; MD, U. Vt., 1954, DSc (hon.), 1980. Diplomate Am. Bd. Pediatrics, Am. Bd. Pediatric Cardiology. Intern N.C. Meml. Hosp., Chapel Hill, 1954-55; resident in pediatrics Children's Hosp., Cin., 1955-57; rsch. fellow Children's Med. Ctr., Boston, 1957-59; asst. prof. pediatrics State U. Iowa Sch. Medicine, 1959-61; asst. prof. pediatrics cardiology U. Ky. Coll. Medicine, Lexington, 1961-64, assoc. prof., 1964-69, prof., 1969-99, chmn. dept. pediatrics, 1974-92, emeritus prof., 1999—. Mem. embryology and human devel. study sect. NIH, 1973-78; mem. U.S.-USSR Symposium on Congenital Heart Disease, 1975; mem. sub. bd. pediatric cardiology Am. Bd. Pediatrics, 1977-82; examiner, mem. test. com. Nat. Bd. Med. Examiners, 1984-90, exec. com., 1991-95; participant various confs. in field; vis. prof. Vanderbilt U., Nashville, 1987; spkr. in field. Contbr. articles, revs. to med. publs.; mem. editl. bd. Am. Jour. Diseases Children, 1970-80, Am. Jour. Med. Edn., 1975-78, Pediatric Cardiology, 1978-90, Am. Heart Jour., 1994-96, Clin. Pediatrics, 1990-99. Mem.: AMA, So. Soc. Pediat. Rsch. (pres. 1972), Soc. Pediat. Rsch., NIH Alumni Assn., Ky. State Med. Assn., Irish-Am. Pediat. Soc. (pres. 1999—2001), Fayette County Pediat. Soc., Am. Pediat. Soc., Assn. Med. Sch. Pediatrics (dept. chmn. exec. com. 1978—81), Am. Coll. Cardiology (gov. Ky. chpt. 1989—92), Am. Acad. Pediatrics (chmn. cardiol. sect. 1972—74). Office: U Ky Coll Medicine MN 117 Lexington KY 40536-0001 Office Phone: 859-257-4679. Business E-Mail: jnoonan@uky.edu.

NOONAN, JAMES C. lawyer, mediator, arbitrator; b. Chgo., July 16, 1928; s. T. Clifford and Ethel (Jennett) N.; m. Carol Colbert, Nov. 24, 1954 (div. June 1975); children: James, Christopher, Mary, Anne, Catherine; m. Ardis Niemann, May 24, 1986. AB, U. Notre Dame, 1953, MA in Criminology, 1954; JD, William Mitchell Coll. Law, St. Paul, 1962. Bar: Minn. 1962, U.S. Dist. Ct. Minn. 1963, U.S. Ct. Appeals (8th cir.) 1971, U.S. Supreme Ct. 1969. Probation officer Ramsey County Juvenile Ct., St. Paul, 1954-57; supt. Woodview Detention Home, St. Paul, 1957-63; assoc. Firestone, Fink, Krawetz, Miley, O'Neill, St. Paul, 1963-67; ptnr. Firestone Fink, Krawetz, Miley, Maas and Noonan, St. Paul, 1967-70, Magistad & Noonan, St. Paul, 1971-75; owner James C. Noonan and Assocs., St. Paul, 1975—. Mem. adv. bd. Home of Good Shepherd, St. Paul, 1958-74; mem. citizen adv. bd. Detention and Corrections Authority, St. Paul, 1966-80. Mem. ABA, Minn. State Bar Assn., Ramsey County Bar Assn., St. Paul Amateur Radio Club, Am. Radio Relay League. Roman Catholic. Avocation: amateur radio (w9osn). Home and Office: 2015 E Edison St Tucson AZ 85719-2176 Fax: (651) 222-3340. Office Phone: 651-222-3310. E-mail: w9osn@arrl.net.

NOONAN, JEAN, lawyer; BA with highest honors, Okla. State U.; JD, U. Tex., Austin. Staff atty. FTC, McLean, Va., 1977-80, mgr. Equal Credit Opportunity Act Enforcement Program, 1980-83, asst. dir. div. credit practices, 1983-86, assoc. dir. credit practices, 1986-91; gen. counsel Farm Credit Adminstrn., 1991—. Office: Farm Credit Adminstrn 1501 Farm Credit Dr Mc Lean VA 22102-5004

NOONAN, JOHN T., JR., federal judge, law educator; b. Boston, Oct. 24, 1926; s. John T. and Marie (Shea) Noonan; m. Mary Lee Bennett, Dec. 27, 1967; children: John Kenneth, Rebecca Lee, Susanna Bain. BA, Harvard U., 1946, LL.B., 1954; student, Cambridge U., 1946—47; MA, Cath. U. Am., 1949, PhD, 1951, LHD, 1980; LL.D., U. Santa Clara, 1974, U. Notre Dame, 1976, Loyola U. South, 1978; LHD, Holy Cross Coll., 1980; LL.D., St. Louis U., 1981, U. San Francisco, 1985; student, Cath. U. Am., 1980, Gonzaga U., 1986, U. San Francisco, 1986; LLD, Duquesne U., 1995, Valparaiso U., 1996, U. San Diego, 1999; LHD, Loyola U., Chgo., 1999. Bar: Mass. 1954, U.S. Supreme Ct. 1971. Mem. spl. staff Nat. Security Council, 1954-55; pvt. practice Herrick & Smith, Boston, 1955-60; prof. law U. Notre Dame, 1961-66, U. Calif., Berkeley, 1967-86, chmn. religious studies, 1970-73, chmn. medieval studies, 1978-79; judge U.S. Ct. Appeals (9th cir.), San Francisco, 1985-96, sr. judge, 1996—. Oliver Wendell Holmes, Jr. lectr. Harvard U. Law Sch., 1972; Pope John XXIII lectr. Cath. U. Law Sch., 1973; Cardinal Bellarmine lectr. St. Louis U. Div. Sch., 1973, Ernest Messenger lectr. Cornell U., 1982; John Dewey Meml. lectr. U. Minn., 1986; Baum lectr. U. Ill., 1988; Strassberger lectr. U. Tex., 1989; chmn. bd. Games Rsch., Inc., 1961—76; overseer Harvard U., 1991—. Author: The Scholastic Analysis of Usury, 1957, Contraception: A History of Its Treatment by the Catholic Theologians and Canonists, 1965, Power to Dissolve, 1972, Persons and Masks of the Law, 1976, The Antelope, 1977, A Private Choice, 1979, Bribes, 1984, The Responsible Judge, 1993, Professional and Personal Responsibilities of the Lawyer, 1997, The Lustre of Our Country, 1998; editor: Natural Law Forum, 1961—70, Am. Jour. Jurisprudence, 1970, The Morality of Abortion, 1970; author: Canons and Canonists in Context, 1997, Narrowing the Nation's Power, 2002. Chmn. Brookline Redevel. Authority, Mass., 1958—62; cons. Papal Commn. on Family, 1965—66, Ford Found., Indonesian Legal Program, 1968, NIH, 1973, 1974; expert Presdl. Commn. on Population and Am. Future, 1971; pres. Thomas More-Jacques Maritain Inst., 1977—; trustee Population Coun., 1969—76, Phi Kappa Found., 1970—76, U. San Francisco, 1971—75; mem. com. theol. edn. Yale U., 1972—77; cons. U.S. Cath. Conf., 1979—86; sec., treas. Inst. for Rsch. in Medieval Canon Law, 1970—88; trustee Grad. Theol. Union, 1970—73; exec. com. Cath. Commn. Intellectual and Cultural Affairs, 1972—75; bd. dirs. Ctr. for Human Values in the Health Scis., 1969—71, S.W. Intergroup Rels. Coun., 1970—72, Inst. for Study Ethical Issues, 1971—73. Recipient St. Thomas More award, U. San Francisco, 1974, Christian Culture medal, 1975, Laetare medal, U. Notre Dame, 1984, Campion medal, Cath. Book Club, 1987, Alemany medal, Western Dominican Province, 1988; fellow Guggenheim fellow, 1965—66, 1979—80, Ctr. for Advanced STudies in Behaviroal Scis. fellow, 1973—74, Wilson Ctr. fellow, 1979—80, Kluge chair in Am. law and govt.w, Libr. Congress Ctr. for Scholars, 2002—. Fellow: Am. Acad. Arts and Scis., Am. Soc. Legal Historians (hon.); mem.: Am. Law Inst., Canon Law Soc. Am. (gov. 1970—72), Am. Soc. Polit. and Legal Philosophy (v.p. 1964), Phi Beta Kappa (senator United chpts. 1970—72, pres. Alpha of Calif. chpt. 1972—73). Office: US Ct Appeals 9th Cir PO Box 193939 San Francisco CA 94119-3939

NOONAN, PATRICK FRANCIS, conservation executive; b. St. Petersburg, Fla., Dec. 2, 1942; s. Francis Patrick and Henrietta (Donovan) N.; m. Nancy Elizabeth Peck, Aug. 15, 1964; children: Karen Elizabeth, Dawn Wiley. AB, Gettysburg Coll., 1961-65; M.City and Regional Planning, Catholic U. Am., 1967; MBA, Am. U., 1971. Pres. The Nature Conservancy, 1973-80; chmn., pres., CEO The Conservation Fund, 1985—2003, chmn. emeritus, 2003—; chmn. Am. Farmland Trust, 1991-97. Trustee Nat. Geog. Soc., 1990—, Nat. Geog. Edn. Found., 1995—, Gettysburg Coll., 1978—91, Duke U. Sch. Environment, 1979—, Ind. Sector, 1984—91, Am. Conservation Assn., 1986—, Natural Resources Coun. Am., 1996—2002; dir. Ashland, 1991—, Internat. Paper, 1993—, Saul Ctrs., 1993—; mem. Pres.' Commn. on Am. Outdoors, 1985—87, Pres.' Commn. on Environ. Quality, 1991—93, Pres.' Commn. on White House Fellows, 2001—. MacArthur Found. fellow, 1985-90. Home: 11901 Glen Mill Rd Potomac MD 20854-1920

NOONAN, PATRICK SUTTON, management educator; b. Springfield, Ill., July 11, 1955; s. Patrick Arthur and Julia Ann (Sutton) N.; m. M. Jo Howarth, Apr. 27, 1985; children: Paul Howarth, William Prindiville. BS in Engring. Sci., Yale U., 1977, MBA, 1984; MS in Engring. Sci., Harvard U., 1989, PhD in Decision Scis., 1992. Dir. and gen. mgr. East River Consort, Boston, 1978-80; pres. Greenpeace New Eng., Boston, 1980-82; assoc. McKinsey & Co., Inc., N.Y.C., 1984-88; cons. MicroMentor, Inc., Cambridge, Mass., 1984-89; prin. Planning Techs. Group, Inc., Lexington, Mass., 1989—98; assoc. prof. Emory U., 1993—. Prodr. record albums, including Laurasia, 1978, Undiscovered Country, 1988, Beat Noir, 1996, Scott's Red Star, 2000; prodr. film Journey to Georges Bank, 1982.

NOONAN, PEGGY, writer; b. Brooklyn, N.Y., Sept. 7, 1950; d. Jim and Mary Jane (Byrne) N.; m. Richard Kahn, Nov. 27, 1985 (div. 1990); 1 child, Will. BA in English Literature & Journalism, Fairleigh Dickinson U., Rutherford, N.J., 1974, PhD in Humane Letters (hon.), 1990. Premium adjuster Aetna Ins. Co., Newark, 1968-70; student Antiwar Protester of Vietnam; temp. agency sec. N.Y.C., 1974; news staffer WEEI Radio (CBS station), Boston, 1974, editl. dir., 1975-77; writer, editor CBS News, N.Y.C., 1977-80, commentary for Walter Cronkite and Dan Rather, 1980-81, full time commentary writer for Dan Rather, 1981-84; White House speech writing tech. Ronald Reagan, Washington, 1984-86; White House speech writer George Bush, Washington, 1988-89; contbg. editor The Wall St. Jour., Time, Good Housekeeping. Bd. dir. The Manhattan Inst. Author: What I Saw at the Revolution: A Political Life in the Reagan Era, 1990, Life, Liberty, & the Pursuit of Happiness, 1995, Simply Speaking: How to Communicate Your Ideas With Style, Substance, and Clarity, 1998, The Case Against Hillary Clinton, 2000, When Character was King: A Story of Ronald Reagan, 2001, A Heart, a Cross and a Flag, 2003; contbr. articles to Forbes, Mirabella, Newsweek, N.Y. Times, O Mag., Time, Wash. Post. Coll. Guest Editor Mademoiselle, 1990; Mother of Yr. award, 1990; Nat. Mother's Day Com., 1990. Mem. Judson Welliver Soc. Republican. Roman Catholic. also: ICM 40 W 57th St Fl 16 New York NY 10019-4001*

NOONAN, ROBERT HARRY, art and music educator; b. Mpls., Sept. 18, 1924; s. William Earl and Nellie Morene Noonan; BS in Chemistry, Northwestern State Coll., 1948; MusB in Music Edn., Centenary Coll., 1963. Cert. tchr. music, chemistry, sci., math., visually talented and musically talented La. Sr. chemist Ark. Fuel Oil Co., Shreveport, La., 1948-53; grad. asst. U. Wyo., Laramie, 1953-54; asst. chief chemist Atlas Processing Co., Shreveport, 1955-58; Frenh horn player Shreveport Symphony Orch., 1948-72; sch. sys. employee East Baton Rouge Sch. Sys., Baton Rouge, 1972-81; pub. sch. tchr. Ascension Parish Schs., Donaldsonville, La., 1981-95; tchr. visually talented St. James Parish Schs., Lutcher, La., 1997—2001. Composer, arranger: music One Step from the Edge, 1999—2000, I Am Your Child, 2000—01, Finding My Way, 2001—02; composer: symphony for Yalley Youth Orch., 2002, two string quartets, a piano trio, a sonata for clarinet and piano, music for voices and strings, theater, 2003; one-man shows include Jones Creek Libr., Baton Rouge, 1993, Donaldsonville (La.) H.S., 1994, Galvez (La.) Libr., 1994, Westbank Libr., Harvey, La., 1995, Bruno Gallery, New Orleans, 1997, exhibited in group shows, Baton Rouge, Jackson, Plaquemine, Morgan City, numerous others, Represented in permanent collections, La., Tex., Miss., Ala., Okla., others. Chmn. La. Sch. Employees Coun.l, 1977—81. With Air Corps U.S. Army, 1943—46. Grantee Goals 2000, State of La., 1995—96, Spl. Arts, 1997—99. Mem.: Jefferson Art Guild, St. Bernard Art Guild (pres. 1999—2001), New Orleans Art Assn. (v.p. 1998—2000), Am. Chem. Soc. (sr. grade chemist 1948—58), La. Partnership for the Arts. Avocations: outdoor painting, writing article for newspapers. Home: 433 Delta Ave Paonia CO 81428-8413

NOONAN, SHEILA M. energy consulting company executive; BA in Bus. Adminstrn., U. St. Thomas; postgrad., Harvard U., Boston U. Numerous positions including dir. security & fire alarm bus. Honeywell; v.p. sales Cadence Networks, Cin. Office: Cadence Networks 105 E 4th St Ste 250 Cincinnati OH 45202-4006

NOONAN, SUSAN ABERT, public relations executive; b. Lancaster, Pa., May 10, 1960; d. James Goodear and Carole (Althouse) Abert; m. David Lindsay Noonan, July 28, 1986; children: Caroline du Pont, Elizabeth Augusta. BA, Mt. Holyoke Coll., 1982. Account exec. Merill Lynch, N.Y.C., 1982-83; sr. v.p. Cameron Assocs., N.Y.C., 1983-88; pres., founder Noonan/Russo Comm. (now Euro RSCG Life NRP), N.Y.C., 1988—. Mem. Nat. Investor Rels. Inst. Office: Noonan Russo Comm Inc 220 5th Ave New York NY 10001-7708*

NOONAN, THOMAS M. utilities executive; B in Econs., Assumption Coll.; MBA, George Washington U.; grad. leadership devel. program, U. So. Calif. CPA Calif. Fin. analyst Am. Gas Assn., Nuc. Regulatory Commn., Booz-Allen & Hamilton, Washington; regulatory cost specialist Regulatory Policy and Affairs Dept. Edison Internat., with treas. dept., with contrs. dept., asst. contr., 1993, v.p., contr., 1999—. Office: Edison Internat 2244 Walnut Grove Ave Rosemead CA 91770

NOONAN, WILLIAM DONALD, lawyer, physician; b. Kansas City, Mo., Oct. 18, 1955; s. Robert Owen and Patricia Ruth Noonan. AB, Princeton (N.J.) U., 1977; JD, U. Mo., Kansas City, 1980; postgrad., Tulane U., 1981-83; MD magna cum laude, Oreg. Health Scis. U., 1991. Bar: Mo. 1980, U.S. Ct. Appeals (5th cir.) 1982, U.S. Patent & Trademark Office 1982, U.S. Ct. Appeals (D.C. cir.) 1984, Oreg. 1985, U.S. Ct. Appeals (9th Cir.) 1985. Assoc. Shurgue, Mion, Zinn, Washington, 1983-84, Keaty & Keaty, New Orleans, 1984-85; ptnr. Klarquist, Sparkman LLP, Portland, Oreg., 1985—; intern in internal medicine Portland Providence Med. Ctr., 1993-94; resident in ophthalomology Casey Eye Inst., Portland, 1994-95. Adj. prof. patent law Tulane U., New Orleans, 1984-85, U. Oreg., 1992-93. Casenotes editor U. Mo. Law Rev., 1979. Nat. Merit scholar. Mem. ABA, AMA (Leadership award 1994), Alpha Omega Alpha (pres. Oreg. chpt. 1990-91). Independent. Avocations: raising horses, running, travel, genealogy. Office: 1600 World Trade Ctr 121 SW Salmon St Portland OR 97204-2901 Office Phone: 503-226-7391.

NOONE, PALMER, academic administrator; Doctorate in higher edn. adminstrn., Union Insit.; JD, MBA, U. Iowa; BBA, U. Dubuque. Pres. U. Phoenix, 2002—, provost, sr. v.p. acad. affairs, dir. acad affairs, faculty; atty gen. civil practice Iowa; judge City of Chandler, Ariz. Office: U Phoenix 3201 E Elwood St Phoenix AZ 85034

NOONE, R. BARRETT, plastic surgeon; b. Scranton, Pa., Oct. 30, 1939; s. Robert Patrick and Margaret Ann (Barrett) N.; m. Barbara Ellen Atkins, May 29, 1965; children: Robert B. Jr., Megan J., Genevieve C., Rebecca B., Theresa Ann. BS, U. Scranton, 1961; MD, U. Pa., 1965. Diplomate Am. Bd. Surgery, Am. Bd. Plastic Surgery. Rotating intern Hosp. of U. Pa., Phila., 1965-66, resident in surgery, 1966-71, resident in plastic surgery, 1971-73; asst. prof. surgery Sch. Medicine, U. Pa., Phila., 1974-83, clin. assoc. prof. surgery, 1983-89, clin. prof. surgery, 1989—; head sect. on plastic surgery Pa. Hosp., Phila., 1974-80; chief svc. plastic surgery Bryn Mawr (Pa.) Hosp., 1977—, Lankenau Hosp., Phila., 1980-91; chmn. dept. surgery Bryn Mawr (Pa.) Hosp., 1991—; exec. dir. Am. Bd. Plastic Surgery, 1997—. Bd. dirs. Am. Bd. Plastic Surgery, Phila., 1987-94, vice chmn. 1993-94; bd. dirs. Plastic Surgery Ednl. Found., Chgo., 1981-91, pres. 1989-90. Contbr. articles to profl. jours. Bd. dirs., trustee Rosemont (Pa.) Sch. of the Holy Child, 1983-87, U. Scranton, 1998—. Capt. USAF, 1967-69. Recipient Frank J. O'Hara Disting. Alumnus award U. Scranton, 1986. Fellow ACS (bd. govs. 1994-98); mem. AMA (del. plastic surgery 1986-88), Am. Soc. Plastic and Reconstructive Surgery (bd. dirs. 1989-90, 92-95, chmn. bd. trustees 1994-95), Am. Assn. Plastic Surgeons (sec. 1995-98, v.p. 1998-99, pres.-elect 1999-2000, pres. 2000-01), Northeastern Soc. Plastic Surgeons (pres. 1985-86), Robert H. Ivy Soc. (pres. 1982-83), Merion Cricket Club, Phila. Country Club, Eagles Mere Country Club. Republican. Roman Catholic. Avocations: golf, tennis, photography, swimming, travel, reading. Home: 234 Chesworld Hill Rd Haverford PA 19041-1814 Office: Plastic & Reconstructive Surg Assocs 888 Glenbrook Ave Bryn Mawr PA 19010-2506 Office Phone: 610-527-4833.

NOONKESTER, JAMES RALPH, retired college president; b. Flatridge, Va., June 10, 1924; s. Reggie L. and Arcie (Parks) N.; m. Naomi Hopkins, June 10, 1947; children: Myron Craig, Lila. BA, U. Richmond, 1944, LLD, 1968; ThM, So. Bapt. Theol. Sem., 1947, PhD, 1949; LHD (hon.), Blue Mountain Coll., 1982; postgrad., Harvard U., 1980. Minister edn. 1st Bapt. Ch., Charlottesville, Va., 1950-52; prof., head div. religion and philosophy William Carey Coll., Hattiesburg, Miss., 1952-53, acad. dean, 1953-56, pres., 1956-89, pres. emeritus, 1989—. Pres. Miss. Fund. Ind. Colls.; mem. Edn. commn. So. Bapt. Conv., chmn., 1983; bd. dirs. Miss. Sch. Bds. Assn. Workers Compensation Trust, 1993-95, chmn., 1994. Chmn. bd. dirs. Am. Cancer Soc., Miss. divsn., 1966; campaign chmn. United Givers Fund, 1975-76, pres. 1976-77; coun. chmn. Boy Scouts Am., dir. Planned Giving Pine Burr Area Boy Scouts Am., 1990-93; trustee Hattiesburg Pub. Schs., 1990-95, pres. bd. trustees, 1992-95. Recipient award Outstanding Grad. English U. Richmond, 1944; named Hattiesburg's Outstanding Young Man of 1956.; recipient Silver Beaver award Boy Scouts Am., 1981, HUB award, 1983; named Sales and Mktg. Execs. Man of Yr., 1983 Mem. NEA, Miss. Edn. Assn., Hattiesburg Concert Assn. (bd. dir.), So. Assn. Bapt. Colls. and Schs. (pres.), Miss. Assn. Colls. (pres.), Hattiesburg C. of C. (pres. 1966), Phi Beta Kappa, Phi Delta Kappa, Chi Beta Phi, Omicron Delta Kappa. Clubs: Kiwanian. Home: 100 Lesley Ln Hattiesburg MS 39402-2922

NOOR, RONNY, language educator, writer; MA, Tech. U., Berlin, 1986, Okla. State U., 1989, PhD, 1994. Lectr. Salisbury (Md.) State U., 1995—96; sr. lectr. U. Tex., Brownsville, 1996—98, asst. prof., 1999—2004, assoc. prof., 2004—. Contbr. essays, short stories, articles to profl. jours. Mem.: South Ctrl. MLA, Popular Culture Assn. Achievements include research in literature and linguistics. Avocations: piano, tennis. Office Phone: 956-544-8849. E-mail: noor@utb.edu.

NOORDA, RAYMOND J. computer software company executive; b. Ogden, Utah. BSEE, Utah, 1949. CEO Novell Inc., 1982-94; chmn. MTI Inc. (now MTI Tech. Corp.), Anaheim, Calif., 1994—.

NOORDERGRAAF, ABRAHAM, biophysics educator; b. Utrecht, Netherlands, Aug. 7, 1929; s. Leendert and Johanna (Kool) N.; m. Geertruida Alida Van Nee, Sept. 6, 1956 (div. Jan. 2001); children: Annemiek (Mrs. James A. Young), Gerrit Jan, Jeske Inette, Alexander Abraham. B.Sc., U. Utrecht, 1953, MS, 1955, PhD, 1956; MA (hon.), U. Pa., 1971. Teaching asst. U. Utrecht, 1949-50, asst. dept. physics, 1951-53, research asst. dept. med. physics, 1953-55, research fellow dept. med. physics, 1956-58, sr. research fellow dept. med. physics, 1959-65; tchr. math. and physics Vereniging Nijverheidsonderwijs, Utrecht, 1951; research asst. U. Amsterdam, Netherlands, 1952; vis. fellow dept. therapeutic research U. Pa., Phila., 1957-58; assoc. prof. biomed. engring. Moore Sch. Elec. Engring., U. Pa., 1964-70, acting head electromed. div., 1968-69, prof. biomed. engring., 1970-97, assoc. dir. biomed. engring. tng. program, 1971-76, asso. dir. sch., 1972-74, chmn. grad. group in biomed. electronic engring., 1973-75, chmn. dept. bioengring., 1973-76, chmn. grad. group bioengring., 1975-76, dir. systems and integrative biology tng. program, 1979-84; prof. physiology Sch. Vet. Medicine U. Pa., 1976-97, prof. Dutch culture Sch. Arts and Scis., 1983-97, prof. anesthesia Med. Sch., 1990-97, prof. emeritus, 1997—. Vis. prof. biomed. engring. U. Miami, 1970-79, Erasmus U. Med. Sch., Rotterdam, The Netherlands, 1970-71, Tech. U., Delft, 1970-71, Polish Acad. Scis., Warsaw, 1975; hon. vis. prof. physiology U. Ljubljana, 1994—; mem. cardiovasc. study sect. NIH, 1985-89, temp. mem., 1998—; cons. sci. affairs divsn. NATO, 1973—; participant numerous internat. confs. in field. Author: (with I. Starr) Ballistocardiography in Cardiovascular Research, 1967, Circulatory System Dynamics, 1978; contbg. author: Biological Engineering, 1969; Editor: (with G.N. Jager and N. Westerhof) Circulatory Analog Computers, 1963, (with G.H. Pollack) Ballistocardiography and Cardiac Performance, 1967, (with E. Kresch) The Venous System: Characteristics and Function, 1969, (with J. Baan and J. Raines) Cardiovascular System Dynamics, 1978, (with Reichenbach-Consten) Two Hundred Years of Netherlands-American Interaction; sci. editor Biophysics and Bioengring. Series, 1976-94; contbr. numerous articles to profl. jours.; Referee: Biophys. Jour., 1968—, Physics in Medicine and Biology, 1969—, Bull. Math. Biophysics, 1972-84, Circulation Research, 1973—; mem. editorial adv. bd.: Jour. Biomechanics, 1969-84; assoc. editor: Bull. Math. Biology, 1973-84. Vice pres. Haverford Friends Sch. PTA, 1968-70. Recipient S. Reid Warren Jr. award U. Pa. Sch. Engring. and Applied Sci., 1986, Christian and Mary Lindback award U. Pa., 1988, Lifetime Achievement award, 2001, Internat. Order of Merit, 2003, Arthur C. Guyton award, 2003. Fellow IEEE (life, mem. adminstrv. com. engring. in medicine and biology group 1967-70, mem. edn. com. group biomed. engring. 1968-70, sec. Phila. chpt. 1974-75, mem. regional coun. profl. group engring. in medicine and biology 1974-77), AAAS, N.Y. Acad. Scis., Explorers Club, Coll. Physicians Phila., Am. Coll. Cardiology, Royal Soc. Medicine London; mem. Nederlandse Natuurkundige Vereniging, Ballistocardiograph Research Soc. U.S.A. (sec.-treas. 1965-67, pres.

1968-70), Biophys. Soc. (charter), European Soc. for Noninvasive Cardiovascular Research (co-founder 1960, sec.-treas. 1960-61, mem. com. on nomenclature 1960-61, officer 1961-62, Herman C. Burger award 1978, Disting. Rsch. Award, 1993), Cardiovascular System Dynamics Soc. (co-founder 1976, pres. 1976-80, hon. life 1986), Franklin Inst., John Morgan Soc., Biomed. Engring. Soc. (founding mem., chmn. membership com. 1978-79, dir. 1972-75), Am. Heart Assn., Instrument Soc. Am. (sr. mem.), Soc. Math. Biology (charter mem.), Am. Physiol. Soc., Microcirculatory Soc., Am. Assn. Med. Systems and Informatics, Pa. Acad. Sci., Sigma Xi, Phi Zeta. Presbyterian. Achievements include discovery (with Maximilian Moser) of impedance-defined flow, generalizing William Harvey's 1628 theory of blood circulation. Home: 620 Haydock Ln Haverford PA 19041-1208 Office: U Pa 101 Hayden Hall Philadelphia PA 19104-6392 Office Phone: 215-898-5881. Business E-Mail: anoor@seas.upenn.edu.

NOORI, MOHAMMAD NOORI, mechanical engineering educator; b. Tehran, Iran, Dec. 24, 1952; m. Nahid Bozorgi; children: Haeman, Hooman, Naudereh. BS, U. Ill., 1977; MS, Okla. State U., 1980; PhD, U. Va., 1984. Surveyor dept. civil engring. U. Ill., Urbana, 1975-77; instr. dept. civil engring. Okla. State U., Stillwater, 1977-79; civil engr. Urban Devel., Iran, 1979-80; rsch. asst. civil engring. dept. U. Va., Charlottesville, 1980-84; asst. prof. mech. and mfg. engring. Worcester (Mass.) Poly. Inst., 1984-90, assoc. prof. mech. and mfg. engring., 1998-92, prof., head mech. and aerospace engring. dept., 1991-99, John Woodman Higgins prof., 1998—2000, dir. Ctr. Loss prevention and Structural Integrity, 1998—; prof., head mech. engring. dept. North Carolina U., 1999—; R.J. Reynolds prof. and head, mach. and aerospace dept. N.C. State U., 1999—. Mem. editl. bd.: 5 internat. jours.; contbr. over 150 articles to profl. jours., chpt. to book. Fellow: ASME (chair profl. devel. com. 1988—, invitee presdl. commn. on civil infrastructures, fellow various awards 1988—), Japan Soc. Promotion of Sci.; mem.: ASCE (mem. com. 1991—), AIAA, Soc. Engring. Sci., Am. Soc. Engring. Edn. Achievements include patent pending for vibration absorber for offshore platforms, SMA Mechanism for Seismic Isolation. Office: Mech & Aerospace Engring Dept North Carolina State U Raleigh NC 27695 Office Phone: 919-513-2368. E-mail: mnoori@eos.ncsu.edu.

NOOYI, INDRA K. food products company executive; BS, Madras (India) Christian Coll.; MBA, Indian Inst. Mgmt., Calcutta; M Pub. and Pvt. Mgmt., Yale U. Product mgr. Johnson & Johnson, India, Mettur Beardsell, Ltd., India; dir. internat. corp. strategy projects Boston Cons. Group; bus. devel. exec. Motorola, v.p., dir. corp. strategy and planning; sr. v.p. strategy, planning and strategic mktg. Asea Brown Boveri; sr. v.p. strategic planning PepsiCo, Purchase, N.Y., 1994-2000, sr. v.p., CFO, 2000-01, pres., CFO, 2001—. Bd. dirs. Phoenix Home Life Mut. Ins. Co. Bd. dirs. PepsiCo Found.; trustee Convent of Sacred Heart Sch., Greenwich, Conn. Office: Pepsico Inc 700 Anderson Hill Rd Purchase NY 10577-1444

NOPAR, ALAN SCOTT, lawyer; s. Myron E. and Evelyn M. Nopar; m. Angela P. Yancey, Aug. 26, 2000. BS, U. Ill., 1976; JD, Stanford U., 1979. Bar: Ariz. 1979, U.S. Dist. Ct. Ariz. 1980, U.S. Ct. Appeals (9th cir.) 1980, U.S. Supreme Ct. 1982, Calif. 1989; CPA, Ill. Assoc. O'Connor, Cavanagh, Anderson, Westover, Killingsworth & Beshears P.A., Phoenix, 1979-85, ptnr., 1985-87; of counsel Tower, Byrne & Beaugureau, Phoenix, 1987-88; ptnr. Minutillo & Gorman, San Jose, Calif., 1989-91, Bosco, Blau, Ward & Nopar, San Jose, 1991-96; exec. v.p., gen. counsel, dir. AmeriNet Fin. Systems, Inc., Ontario, Calif., 1996-97; sole practice law Palo Alto, Calif., 1998-99; ptnr. Bosco, Ward & Nopar, Palo Alto, 2000—. Mem. Ariz. Rep. Caucus, Phoenix, 1984-88. Mem. AICPA, ABA (bus. law and law practice mgmt. sects., mem. forum com. on franchising), Ariz. Bar Assn. (bus. law sect.), Calif. State Bar Assn. (bus. law sect.). Avocations: golf, skiing, tennis. Office: 425 Sherman Ave Ste 100 Palo Alto CA 94306-1849

NORA, AUDREY HART, physician; b. Picayune, Miss., Dec. 5, 1936; d. Allen Joshua and Vera Lee (Ballard) H.; m. James Jackson Nora, Apr. 9, 1966; children: James Jackson Jr., Elizabeth Hart. BS, U. Miss., 1958, MD, 1961; MPH, U. Calif., 1978. Diplomate Am. Bd. Pediat., Am. Bd. Hematology and Oncology. Resident in pediat. U. Wis. Hosp., Madison, 1961-64; fellow in hematology/oncology Baylor U., Tex. Childrens Hosp., Houston, 1964-66, asst. prof. pediat., 1966-70; assoc. clin. prof. pediat. U. Colo. Sch. Medicine, Denver, 1970—; dir. genetics Denver Childrens Hosp., 1970-78; commd. med. officer USPHS, 1978, advanced through grades to asst. surgeon gen., 1983, cons. maternal and child health, 1978-83, asst. surgeon gen. regional health adminstr., 1983-92, dir. maternal & child health bur., health resources and svc. adminstrn., 1992-99. Mem. adv. com. NIH, Bethesda, 1975-77; mem. adv. bd. Metronet Health, Inc., Denver, 1986-92; mem. adv. bd. Colo. Assn. Commerce and Industry, Denver, 1985-92, WIC program USDA, 1989-99; mem. adv. coun. NICHD, 1992-99; pres. bd. dirs. RMC for Health Promotion and Edn., 2004-. Author: (with J.J. Nora) Genetics and Counseling in Cardiovascular Diseases, 1978, (with others) Blakiston's Medical Dictionary, 1980, Birth Defects Encyclopedia, 1990, (with J.J. Nora and K. Berg) Cardiovascular Diseases: Genetics, Epidemiology and Prevention, 1991; contbr. articles to profl. jours. Recipient Virginia Apgar award Nat. Found., 1976. Fellow Am. Acad. Pediat.; mem. Am. Pub. Health Assn. (governing coun. 1990-92, coun. mem. maternal and child health 1990—), Commd. Officers Assn., Am. Soc. Human Genetics, Teratology Soc., Western Soc. Pediatric Rsch. Presbyterian. Avocations: quilting, cooking, hiking. Office: 1973 S Kenton Ct Aurora CO 80014-4709

NORA, GERALD ERNEST, lawyer; b. Chgo., May 25, 1951; s. Gerald Edwin and Lois (Billingham) N.; m. Patricia Cunniff, June 19, 1976; children: Gerald Joseph, Thomas More, Mary Elizabeth, John Paul. Student, U. Ill., 1970-71; BA, Georgetown U., 1973, JD, 1978. Bar: Ill. 1978, U.S. Supreme Ct. 1983, U.S. Dist. Ct. (no. dist.) Ill. 1983, U.S. Dist. Ct. Ariz. 1993, U.S. Ct. Appeals (7th cir.) 1996. Exec. asst. state's atty. for policy office Cook County State's Atty., Chgo. Bd. adv. Nat. Criminal Justice Assn.; adj. faculty Layola Univ., Chgo.; mem. capital punishment reform study com. State of Ill. Mem.: Cath. Lawyers Guild, ITLA, CBA, ISBA, ABA. Office: Office of the Cook County States Atty 69 W Washington St Ste 3200 Chicago IL 60602 Office Phone: 312-603-1839.

NORA, HOPE, healthcare consultant; b. Laredo, Tex., June 4, 1949; d. Felix C. and Esperanza (Coronado) Rocha; m. Amaury Nora, June 19, 1971; children: Amaury E., Araceli E. BS, U. Houston, 1971; MS, Tex. A&I U., 1972; PhD, U. Houston, 1986. Staff psychologist, counselor Tex. Commn. for Vocat. Rehabv., Laredo, Tex., 1973-78; dir. programs Laredo State Ctr. for Human Devel., 1978-82; dir. clin. programming Los Encinas Hosp., Pasadena, Calif., 1987-89; dir. clin./support svcs. Woodland Hosp., Hoffman Estates, Ill., 1989-92; quality mgr. Ill. Dept. Mental Health and Developmental Disabilities, 1992-96; ind. healthcare cons. Houston, 1996—. Mem. Am. Soc. for Quality. Mem. Tex. Psychol. Assn. (cert.). Democrat. Avocations: reading, music. Home: 2001 Holcombe #803 Houston TX 77030 Office: Unit 803 2001 Holcombe Blvd Houston TX 77030-4214 E-mail: hopenora@hotmail.com.

NORA, JAMES JACKSON, physician, writer, educator; b. Chgo., June 26, 1928; s. Joseph James and Mae Henrietta (Jackson) N.; m. Barbara June Fluhrer, Sept. 7, 1949 (div. 1963); children: Wendy Alison, Penelope Welbon, Marianne Leslie; m. Audrey Faye Hart, Apr. 9, 1966; children: James Jackson Jr., Elizabeth Hart Nora. AB, Harvard U., 1950; MD, Yale U., 1954; MPH, U. Calif., Berkeley, 1978. Diplomate Am. Bd. Pediat., Am. Bd. Cardiology, Am. Bd. Med. Genetics. Intern Detroit Receiving Hosp., 1954-55; resident in pediat. U. Wis. Hosps., Madison, 1959-61, fellow in cardiology, 1962-64; fellow in genetics McGill U. Children's Hosp., Montreal, Canada, 1964-65; assoc. prof. pediat. Baylor Coll. Medicine, Houston, 1965-71; prof. genetics, preventive medicine and pediat. U. Colo. Med. Sch., Denver, 1971—, prof. emeritus, 1986. Dir. genetics Rose Med. Ctr., Denver, 1980—; dir. pediatric cardiology and cardiovasc. tng. U. Colo. Sch. Medicine, 1971-78; mem. task force Nat. Heart and Lung Program, Bethesda, Md., 1973; cons. WHO, Geneva, 1983—; mem. U.S.-U.S.S.R. Exch. Program on Heart Disease, Moscow and Leningrad, 1975. Author: The Whole Heart Book, 1980, 2d rev. edit., 1989; author: (with F.C. Fraser) Medical Genetics, 4th Rev. edit., 1994; author: Genetics of Man, 2d rev. edit., 1986, Cardiovascular Diseases: Genetics, Epidemiology and Prevention, 1991; author: (novels) The Upstart Spring, 1989; author: The Psi Delegation, 1989, The Hemingway Sabbatical, 1996, Panacea, 2002, What Every Senior Needs to Know About Health Care, 2004; author: (poetry) Songs from a Brazen Bull, 2001. Mem. com. March of Dimes, Am. Heart Assn., Boy Scouts Am. 2nd lt. USAAC, 1945—47. Grantee Nat. Heart, Lung and Blood Inst., Nat. Inst. Child Health and Human Devel., Am. Heart Assn., NIH; recipient Virginia Apgar Meml. award. Democrat. Presbyterian. Avocations: writing fiction, poetry.

NORA, LOIS MARGARET, neurologist, educator, academic administrator, dean; BS in Biology with honors, U. Ill., 1976; MD, Rush Med. Coll., Chgo., 1979; JD, U. Chgo., 1987; MBA, U. Ky., 2002. Fellow Am. Bd. Neurology, Am. Bd. Electrodiagnostic Medicine; bar: Ill. 1988, D.C. 1988. Intern in family medicine Cmty. Meml. Gen. Hosp., LaGrange, Ill., 1980; resident in neurology Rush-Presbyn.-St. Luke's Med. Ctr., Chgo., 1981-84, chief resident in neurology, 1983-84, fellow electromyography and neuromuscular disease, 1984-85; asst. prof. dept. neurology, asst. dean clin. curriculum Rush Med. Coll., Chgo., 1987-94, assoc. prof. dept. neurology, 1994-95; fellow Ctr. for Clin. Med. Ethics U. Chgo., 1993-95; assoc. dean acad. affairs, assoc. prof. dept. neurology U. Ky. Coll. Medicine, 1995—2002; prof. neurology U. Ky. Coll. Law, 1996—2002; pres. Northeastern Ohio Univ. Coll. of Med., 2002—, dean, 2002—. Spkr. in field. Contbr. articles to profl. jours., chpts. to books. Vice chair Epilepsy Found. of Greater Chgo., 1988-90, chair, 1991, chair strategic planning com. 1990-91, bd. dirs., 1987-94; bd. dirs. Epilepsy Found. of Am., 1992-95, co-chair quality standards com. 1992-94; mem. needs assessment com. United Way of Chgo., 1989-90; camp physician children's summer camp program Muscular Dystrophy Assn., 1984-86; vol. tchr. Christ the King Elem. Sch., 1996—2002. Mem. AMA (mem. dean's com. on family violence curriculum 1993, mem. report and resolutions subcom. for reference com. C 1997), Am. Acad. Neurology (mem. ethics com. 1997—2002), Am. Assn. Electrodiagnostic Medicine (chair profl. practice com. 1991—97, sec., treas., 1999-2002, pres.-elect, 2002-03, pres. 2003-04), Soc. Clin. Neurologists. Office: Northeastern U Coll Med PO Box 95 4209 St Rt 44 Rootstown OH 44272

NORA, WENDY ALISON, lawyer; b. New Haven, Conn., Feb. 14, 1951; d. James Jackson Nora and Barbara June (Fluhrer) P.; m. Jay Robert Vercauteren, Aug. 21, 1973 (div. Nov. 1981); children: Lucas Jay, Eric Robert. BA, U. Wis., 1971, JD, 1975. Bar: Wis. 1975, U.S. Dist. Ct. (w. dist.) Wis. 1975, U.S. Dist. Ct. (e. dist.) Wis. 1991, U.S. Supreme Ct. 1986. Pvt. practice, Cross Plains, Wis., 1975-81, Madison, Wis., 1981-84, Mpls., 1986-90, Madison, Wis., 1991—; developer, incorporator, pres. Cmty. Investment Credit Corp., Madison, 1997—. Atty. State of Wis., 1977-81, asst. pub. defender, 1983-84. Fellow U. Minn. Mem. ABA (vice-chmn. adminstrv. law sect., criminal law and juvenile justice com. 1982—). Home: 6931 Old Sauk Rd Madison WI 53717-1122 Office: 8530 Greenway Blvd 209 Middleton WI 53562-4606

NORBACK, CRAIG THOMAS, writer; b. Pitts., Nov. 14, 1943; s. Howard George and Maybelle Veronica Montaigne (Cosse) N.; m. Judith Carol Shaul, Oct. 12, 1976. BS, Washington U., St. Louis, 1967; postgrad., Drew U., 1986—. Author, co-author, compiler, producer over 150 books, including: The Misspeller's Dictionary, 1972, Everything You Can Get from the Government for Free or Almost for Free, 1975, The Dream Machine: The Golden Age of American Automobiles 1946-65, 1976, Great Songs of Madison Avenue, 1976, Great North American Indians, 1977, The Health Care Directory, 1977, The Older American's Handbook, 1977, The Educational Marketplace, 1978, Famous American Admirals, 1978, Newsweek Travel Guide to the U.S., 1978, The Dow Jones-Irwin Guide to Franchising, 1979, The Horseman's Catalog, 1979, The Must Words, 1979, The Practical Inventor's Handbook, 1979, ABC Complete Book of Sports Facts, 1980, ABC Monday Night Football, 1980-81, 1980, The Bible Almanac, 1980, Check Yourself Out, 1980, The Signet Book of World Winners, 1980, The TV Guide Almanac, 1980, The World's Great News Photos (1840-1980), 1980, The Allergy Encyclopedia, 1981, American Expressions, 1981, The Computer Invasion, 1981, The Consumer's Energy Handbook, 1981, 500 Questions New Parents Ask, 1982, Business Week Almanac, 1982, The International Yellow Pages, 1982, The Puzzle King's Bafflers, 1982, The Associated Press Sunday Crossword Puzzle Book, 1983, Chilton's Job Textbook Series: Advertising Management, 1983, Office Management, 1983, It's a Fact, 1983, National Education Association Parent and Child Success Library: Helping Your Child Read, 1983, How Letters Make Words, 1983, How to Prepare Your Child for School, 1983, Learning the Alphabet, 1983, Learning to Add, 1983, The Ultimate Toy Catalog, 1983, U.S. Publicity Directory, various years, Advertising and Promotion Management, 1983, America Wants to Know, 1983, Certified Professional Secretary modules I through VI, 1984, East Coast Publicity Directory, 1984, Human Resources Yearbook, 1987, 88, 89, 90, Princeton Area Job Finder, 1986-87, Career Encyclopedia, 1987, Travel Publicity Directory, 1987, 88, 89, 90, Arthur Young Guide to Venture Capital, 1987, Hazardous Chemicals on File, 1988, Joint Ventures, 1992. Home: 3112 Kaitlyn Ct Princeton Junction NJ 08550-5349

NORBECK, JANE S. retired nursing educator; b. Redfield, S.D., Feb. 20, 1942; d. Sterling M. and Helen L. (Williamson) N.; m. Paul J. Gorman, June 28, 1970. BA in Psychology, BSN, U. Minn., 1965; MS, U. Calif., San Francisco, 1971, DSN, 1975. Psychiat. nurse Colo. Psychiat. Hosp., Denver, 1965-66, Langley Porter Hosp., San Francisco, 1966-67; pub. health nurse San Francisco Health Dept., 1968-69; prof. U. Calif. Sch. of Nursing, San Francisco, 1975—2003, dean, 1989-99, dept. chair, 1984-89, prof. and dean emeritus, 2003. Chair study sect. Nat. Inst. of Nursing Rsch., 1990-93, mem. editl. bd. Archives of Psychiat. Nursing, 1985-95, Rsch. in Nursing and Health, 1987-2003. Co-editor: Annual Review of Nursing Research, 1996-97; contbr. articles to profl. jours. Mem. ANA, Am. Acad. Nursing, Inst. of Medicine, Sigma Theta Tau.

NORBECK, TIMOTHY BURNS, medical association executive; b. Buffalo, N.Y., June 29, 1938; s. Carl Francis N. and Helene Smith (Comstock) Browne; children: Carl, Kim, Karin; m. Michéle R. Mathieu, Mar. 24, 1990. BA, Hamilton Coll., 1960. Sales rep. Nat. Steel Corp., Detroit, Milw., Chgo., 1960-67; regional dir. AMA, Chgo., St. Louis, Chgo., 1967-73; exec. dir. R.I. Med. Soc., Providence, 1973-77, Conn. State Med. Soc., New Haven, 1977--. Bd. dirs., treas. Conn. Med. Mgmt., Inc., Wallingford, 1984--; asst. treas. Conn. Med. Ins. Co., Wallingford, 1984--; cons. Vt. State Med. Soc., Montpelier, 1987; cons. R.I. Med. Soc., Providence, 1986; bd. dirs. MD Advantage. Contbr. articles profl. jours. Chmn. bd. dirs. Am. Cancer Soc. Conn. Div., Wallingford, 1985-87, mem. nat. com. on field svcs., 1989—, bd. dirs. Conn. div.; bd. dirs. St. Louis County Narcotics Commn., 1967-70; bd. dirs. New Haven Regional Mental Health Assn., 1980-83; pres. Conn. Physicians Guild; exec. com. Gaylord Hosp., Wallingford, Conn., 1998—. Recipient Nat. Bronze medal Am. Cancer Soc., 1987, hon. MD, Conn. State Med. Soc. Mem. Am. Soc. Assn. Execs., Am. Assn. Med. Soc. Execs. (bd. dirs., pres.), Rotary. Democrat. Presbyterian. Avocations: public speaking, reading, writing speeches and articles, tennis. Home: 7 Canterbury Way North Haven CT 06473-1018 Office: Conn State Med Soc 160 Saint Ronan St New Haven CT 06511-2312 E-mail: tnorbeck@csms.org.

NORBERG, ARTHUR LAWRENCE, JR., historian, physicist, educator; b. Providence, Apr. 13, 1938; s. Arthur Lawrence Sr. and Margaret Helen (Riley) N.; children: Catherine E. Norberg Morin, Patricia A. Norberg Fetta, Timothy E., Gregory T. BS in Physics, Providence Coll., 1959; MS in Physics, U. Vt., 1962; PhD in History of Sci., U. Wis., 1974. Asst. prof. physics St. Michael's Coll., Winooski, Vt., 1961-63, 64-68; assoc. scientist Westinghouse Electric Co., Pitts., 1963-64; instr. in physics U. Wis., Whitewater, 1968-71; rsch. historian U. Calif., Berkeley, 1973-79; program mgr. NSF, Washington, 1979-81; dir. Charles Babbage Inst. for History of Info. Processing U. Minn., Mpls., 1981-93, 99—, prof. history of sci. and tech., 1995—, assoc. prof. computer sci., 1981-95, prof. computer sci., 1995—. Del. Am. Coun. Learned Socs., N.Y.C., 1981-87; mem. adv. coun. NASA, Washington, 1988-93; endowed ERA Land Grant chair U. Minn., 1989-93, 99—. Editor: Annals of the History of Computing, 1982-93; adv. editor Tech. and Culture, 1985-92, (book) Transforming Computer Technology: Information Processing for the Pentagon, Computers and Commerce; contbr. articles to profl. jours. Founding pres. City Works-A Tech. Ctr., Mpls., 1987-90; exec. dir. Charles Babbage Found., 1984-94; trustee Charles Babbage Found., 1993-96. Fellow AAAS; mem. History of Sci. Soc. (treas. 1975-80), Brit. Soc. for History of Sci., Soc. for History of Tech., Sigma Xi. Office: U Minn Dept Computer Sci 4-192 EE/CS Bldg Minneapolis MN 55455-0290 E-mail: norberg@cs.umn.edu.

NORBERG, DEBORAH DORSEY, museum administrator; b. New Haven, Conn., Jan. 31, 1950; d. Gray Lankford and Jeanne (DeVall) Dorsey; m. Henry F. Norberg, Sept. 11, 1971; children: Sarah E., Daniel G. BA, Stanford U., 1968; M in Mus. Practice, U. Mich., 1974; JD, Stanford U., 1980. Rsch. asst. San Jose (Calif.) Mus. Art, 1975, asst. to curator, 1975-76, exhibition coord., 1987-88, asst. curator, 1988-89, assoc. registrar, assoc. permanent collection curator, 1989-90, registrar, assoc. permanent collection curator, 1990—91, registrar, permanent collection curator, 1991—92, dep. dir., 1992—; assoc. Hopkins and Carley, San Jose, 1980-82. Ford Found. fellow, 1972. Mem. Phi Beta Kappa. Office: San Jose Mus Art 110 S Market St San Jose CA 95113-2383

NORCEL, JACQUELINE JOYCE CASALE, educational administrator; b. Nov. 19, 1940; d. Frederick and Josephine Jeanette (Bestafka) Casale; m. Edward John Norcel, Feb. 24, 1962. BS, Fordham U., 1961; MS, Bklyn. Coll., 1966; 6th yr. cert., So. Conn. State U., 1980; postgrad., Bridgeport U. Elem. tchr. NYC Pub. Schs., 1961-80; prin. Coventry (Conn.) Schs., 1980-84, Trumbull (Conn.) Schs., 1984—2003, Frenchtown Elem. Sch., 2003—. Guest lectr. So. Conn. State U., 1980; cons. Monson (Mass.) Schs., 1984; mem. Conn. State Prin. Acad. Adv. Bd., 1986-88; mem. adj. faculty Sacred Heart U., Fairfield, Conn., 1985—, So. Conn. State U., summer 1991; fed. rels. coord. Nat. Assn. Elem. Sch. Prins., Conn., 1999-2002. Editor: Best of the Decade, 1980; mem. editl. adv. bd. Principal Matters; contbr. articles to profl. jours. Chmn. bldg. com. Trumbull Bd. Edn., 1978-80; chmn. Sch. Benefit Com., Trumbull, 1985-86; catechist Bridgeport Diocese, Roman Cath. Ch., Conn., 1975-85, youth min., 1979-84, coord., evaluator leadership tng. workshops for teens and adults, 1979-84; mem. St. Stephen's Parish Coun., 1993-97, trustee, 1997—, Eucharist min., 1999—, lector, 1990-; com. mem. New Sch. Bldg. Town of Trumbull, 2001-04. Recipient Town of Trumbull Svc. award, 1982, Nat. Disting. Prin. award, 1988, Joseph Formica Disting. Svc. award EM-SPAC, 1994. Mem.: ASCD, Assoc. Tchrs. Math. in Conn., New Eng. Coalition Ednl. Leaders, Ea. Conn. Coun. Internat. Reading Assn., Conn. Assn. Elem. Sch. Prins., Trumbull Adminstrs. Assn. (pres.-elect 1989—91, pres. 1991—93, 2002—), Conn. Assn. Supervision and Curriculum Devel., Nat. Assn. Elem. Sch. Prins. (del. to gen. assemblies 1984—90, zone I dir. 1987—90, del. to gen. assemblies 1999—), Hartford Area Prins. and Suprs. Assn. (local pres. 1981—82), Conn. Assn. Schs. (bd. mem. 2000—), Adminstrn. and Supervision Assn. (sec. 1980—81, pres. 1981—82, exec. bd. 1982—93), Elem. Mid. Sch. Prins. Assn. (pres. 1985—86, state elected rep. 1989—90, fed. rels. coord. 1990—94, dists. 1, 2 and 3 dir. 1995—98, commr. 1997—2000, fed. rels. coord. 1999—2002, Citizen of Yr. award 1991, Pres.'s award 1981—85), N.E. Regional Elem. Prins. Assn. (rep. 1984—86, sec. 1986—87), Delta Kappa Gamma (v.p. 1996—2000), Pi Lambda Theta, Phi Delta Kappa (v.p. rsch. and projects 1993—95, Disting. Fellow award 1992). Home: 5240 Madison Ave Trumbull CT 06611-1016 Office: Frenchtown Elem Sch 30 Frenchtown Rd Trumbull CT 06611 Office Phone: 203-452-4227. Personal E-mail: norcelJ98@yahoo.com.

NORCIA, STEPHEN WILLIAM, advertising and internet advertising executive, consultant; b. N.Y.C., Jan. 21, 1941; s. William Matthew and Amelia (Marrone) N.; m. Martha Elizabeth Whelan, Apr. 22, 1978; children: Matthew F., Daniel P., Anne E. BA, U. Conn., 1962. Media planner and buyer SSC&B, N.Y.C., 1965-66; account exec. McCann-Erickson Co., Chgo., 1966-68, v.p., dep. mgr. Milw., 1971-72, v.p., mgmt. supr. N.Y.C., 1972-74, sr. v.p., gen. mgr. Atlanta, 1974-78, exec. v.p., gen. mgr. N.Y.C., 1978-81; exec. v.p., mem. exec. policy com., mem. mgmt. com. Lintas, N.Y.C., 1981-94, exec. v.p., 1989-91, world wide client dir., dir. bus. devel., 1991-94, also bd. dirs.; mng. ptnr. Earle Palmer Brown, N.Y.C., 1994-96; dir. global account DDB, N.Y.C., 1996-99, mng. dir., 1998-2000; v.p. bus. devel. Agency.com, 2000—; owner cons. co. Norcia Group, 2002—; founder, prin. Topsail Group, 2003. Account exec. Needham, Harper & Steers, Chgo., 1968-70; dir. mktg. product devel. workshop Interpub., N.Y.C., 1970-71; bd. dirs. Communication Counselors Network; adj. prof. Fordham U., Iona Coll. Bd. dirs. U. Ga. Master of Br. Mgmt. Program, 1985, 86, 87, Advt. Edn. Found., 1999—. 1st lt. U.S. Army, 1962-65. Recipient Robert E. Healy award Interpub. Group Cos., 1975, Effie award Am. Mktg. Assn., 1985, Grand Effie award Am. Mktg. Assn., 1984. Mem. Am. Assn. Advt. Agys., Advt. Club N.Y., Am. Yacht Club. Republican. Roman Catholic. Avocations: tennis, boating, skiing, bicycling. Home: 1 Topsail Ln Rye NY 10580-3116 Office: Topsail Group 1 Topsail Ln Rye NY 10580-3116 Office Phone: 914-921-3351.

NORCOTT, FLEMMING L., JR., state supreme court justice; b. New Haven, Oct. 11, 1943; BA, Columbia U., 1965, JD, 1968. Bar: Conn. 1968. Peace corps vol. U. East Africa, Nairobi, Kenya; legal staff Bedford-Stuyvestant Restoration Corp.; asst. atty. gen. Office Atty. Gen., V.I.; judge Superior Ct., 1979-87, Appellate Ct., 1987-92; assoc. justice Conn. Supreme Ct., Hartford, 1992—. Hearing examiner Conn. Commn. Human Rights and Opportunities; co-founder, exec. dir. Ctr. Advocacy, Rsch. and Planning, Ind., New Haven; lectr. Yale U. Bd. govs. U. New Haven; bd. dirs. Dixwell Community House, Ea. Collegiate Football Ofcls. Assn., New Haven Football Ofcls. Assn., Long Wharf Theatre; assoc. fellow Calhoun Coll., Yale U.; bd. trustees Yale-New Haven Hosp. Mem. Omega Psi Phi Office: 231 Capital Ave Hartford CT 06106

NORCROSS, ALVIN WATT, retired personnel administrator, consultant; b. Buffalo, N.Y., Sept. 21, 1918; s. William Watt and Nettie Anne (Alexander) Norcross; m. Charlotte Anne Guptill, Oct. 23, 1948; children: David Lichty, Nancy Dayna. BA, Baldwin-Wallace Coll., 1940; MPA, Harvard U., 1948. Employment mgr. Nat. Screw & Mfg. Co., Cleve., 1941-43; spl. asst. to dir. civilian pers. Dept. of the Air Force, Washington, 1954-58; chief of employment Gen. Svcs. Adminstrn., Washington, 1959-61; asst. dir. pers. U.S. Treasury Dept., Washington, 1961-67; dep. dir. Bur. Pers. Mgmt. Evaluation U.S. Civil Svc. Commn., Washington, 1967-73; project mgr., pub. adminstrn. advisor UN, Kubul, Afghanistan, 1975-80, chief tech. advisor Male, Republic of Maldives, 1982-84; ret., 1984. Pers. expert, cons. Agy. for Internat. Devel., Washington, 1974-75; cons. on exec. pay Orgn. Resource Counselors, Inc., N.Y.C., 1975; prin. assoc., cons. Exec. Mgmt. Svcs., Inc., Arlington, Va., 1981. Author of pamphlets. Councilman Town of Vienna, Va., 1959-65; mem. Svc. Corps of Ret. Execs., New Bedford, Mass., 1984-87, Recycling/Solid Waste Com., Westport, Mass., 1986-94; mem. citizen advd. com. Mass. Dept. Mental Health, 1989-97. 1st lt. USAF, 1943-46; lt . col. USAFR, 1946-72, ret. Mem. ASPA, Old Dartmouth Hist. Soc., Westport Hist. Soc., Westport River Watershed Alliance (bd. dirs. 1989-98), Harvard Club Greater New Bedford (adv. bd. mem. 1997-98), YMCA Greater New Bedford. Avocations: travel, tennis, drama, walking. Home: 36 Shirley St Westport MA 02790-1333

NORCROSS, MARVIN AUGUSTUS, veterinarian, retired government agency official; b. Tansboro, N.J., Feb. 8, 1931; s. Marvin A. and Katherine V. (McGuigan) N.; m. Diane L. Tuttle, Nov. 22, 1956 (div. 1991); children: James, Janet. Student, Rutgers U., 1954-55; VMD, U. Pa., 1959, PhD, 1966. Pathologist Merck Sharp & Dohme Rsch. Labs., Rahway, N.J., 1966-69, dir. clin. research, 1969-72, sr. dir. domestic vet. research, 1972-75; dir. div. vet. med. rsch. Ctr. Vet. Medicine, FDA, Rockville, Md., 1975-78, assoc. dir. for rsch., 1978-82, assoc. dir. for human food safety, 1982-84, assoc. dir. for new animal drug evaluation, 1984-87; asst. dep. adminstr., then dep. adminstr. Sci. and Tech., Food Safety and Inspection Svc. USDA, Washington, 1987-93, exec. asst. to the adminstr., 1993-94; U.S. coord. for Codex Alimentarius USDA, Washington, 1994-96, sr. sci. advisor to adminstr., 1996; cons. vet. medicine and food safety, 1996—. Adj. prof. faculty Va.-Md. Regional Coll. Vet. Medicine, Blacksburg, Va., 1980-85. Contbr. articles to profl. jours. Trustee Scotch Plains (N.J.) Community Fund, 1969-72. Served to lt. AUS, 1952-54; col. Res., 1954-83 (ret.). Recipient FDA Merit award, 1978, Meritorious Presdl. Rank award, 1989; named to Artillery OCS Hall of Fame, 2000. Mem. AAAS, Am. Assn. Avian Pathologists, Assn. Mil. Surgeons U.S., Civil Affairs Assn., Inst. Food Technologists, Nat. Assn. Fed. Veterinarians,

N.J. Acad. Sci., N.Y. Acad. Scis., Res. Officers Assn., Soc. Toxicologic Pathology, Sigma Xi. Home and Office: 14304 Brickhowe Ct Germantown MD 20874-3431 Office Phone: 877-899-9426. Personal E-mail: mjnorcross@bww.com.

NORD, ERIC THOMAS, retired manufacturing executive; b. Amherst, Ohio, Nov. 8, 1917; s. Walter G. and Virginia C. Nord; m. Jane H. Baker; children: Virginia, Emily, Carlotte, Richard. BS in Mech. Engring., Case Inst. Tech., 1939. Pres., chief exec. officer Nordson Corp., Amherst, Ohio, 1954-73, chmn., 1973-97. Also bd. dirs. Pres. Oberlin (Ohio) Bd. Edn., 1965; chmn. Oberlin City Council, 1959; bd. trustees Oberlin Coll., 1977—.

NORD, H. JUERGEN, gastroenterologist; b. Arolsen, Germany, Oct. 25, 1936; s. Rudolf and Elisabeth Nord; m. Linda M. Nord, Dec. 30, 1967; children: Dorothy, Christoph. MD, U. Frankfurt, 1964. Intern hosps., Kassel, Germany, 1964-66; resident Ind. U., Indpls., 1966-67; fellow Washington U., St. Louis, 1967-68, Ind. U., 1968-69; resident, rsch. assoc. Gutenberg U., Mainz, Germany, 1969-73; from asst. prof. to prof. medicine U. South Fla., Tampa, 1973—. Dir. divsn. digestive diseases and nutrition U. South Fla., 1990—2000. Author: Critical Care Gastroenterology, 1982, Colonoscopy: Principles and Technique, 1995. Fulbright scholar, 1963—69. Fellow: ACP, Fla. Soc. Gastrointestinal Endoscopy, Am. Soc. Gastrointestinal Endoscopy (pres. 1998—99, 1981—82), Fla. Gastroenterol. Soc. (pres. 1996—97), Am. Coll. Gastroenterology (bd. govs. 1988—92). Office: U So Fla Coll Med 4 Columbia Dr Ste 550 Tampa FL 33606-3568

NORD, HENRY J. transportation executive; b. Berlin, May 1, 1917; came to U.S., 1937, naturalized, 1943; s. Walter and Herta (Riess) N.; children: Stephen, Philip. Student, U. Oxford, Eng., 1934, Northwestern U., 1938-40, Ill. Inst. Tech., 1942; JD, De Paul U., 1949. CPA, Ill. Apprentice in export, Hamburg, Germany, 1935- 37; with GATX Corp., Chgo., 1938-85, comptroller, 1961-67, v.p., 1967-71, exec. v.p., 1971-78, sr. v.p., 1978-80, v.p., 1980-82, cons., 1982-84, fin. cons., 1982—, dir., 1964-78. Dir. Planned Lighting, Inc. to 1988. Trustee DePaul U. Served to 1st lt. AUS, 1943—46. Mem. Internat. Law Assn. Clubs: Tavern (Chgo.). Home: 1000 N Lake Shore Pl Chicago IL 60611-1308 Office: 3 First Nat Plz 70 W Madison St Ste 2100 Chicago IL 60602-4253

NORD, ROBERT EAMOR, lawyer; b. Ogden, Utah, Apr. 11, 1945; s. Eamor Carroll and Ella Carol (Winkler) N.; m. Sherryl Anne Smith, May 15, 1969; children: Kimberly, P. Ryan, Debra, Heather, Andrew, Elizabeth. BS, Brigham Young U., 1969; JD, U. Chgo., 1972. Bar: Ill. 1972, U.S. Dist. Ct. (no. dist.) Ill. 1972, U.S. Ct. Appeals (D.C. cir.) 1974, U.S. Dist. Ct. (mid. dist.) Fla. 1976, U.S. Ct. Appeals (7th cir.) 1977, U.S. Dist. Ct. (no. dist.) Ind. 1978, U.S. Dist. Ct. (no. dist.) Fla. 1979, U.S. Supreme Ct. 1981, U.S. Dist. Ct. (ea. dist.) Mich. 1984, U.S. Ct. Appeals (11th cir.) 1985, U.S. Ct. Appeals (3d cir.) 1996, U.S. Ct. Appeals (2d cir.) 2002. Assoc. Chadwell & Kayser, Chgo., 1972-75; from assoc. to ptnr. Hinshaw & Culbertson, Chgo., 1975—2002, of counsel, 2003—. Republican. Mem. Lds Ch. Home: 481 Woodlawn Ave Glencoe IL 60022-2175 Office: Hinshaw & Culbertson 222 N La Salle St Ste 300 Chicago IL 60601-1081 E-mail: robert_nord@excite.com.

NORD, WALTER ROBERT, business administration educator, researcher, consultant; b. Mt. Kisco, N.Y., July 2, 1939; s. Arthur William and Elizabeth (Reimstedt) N.; m. Ann Feagan, June 10, 1967. BA in Econs., Williams Coll., 1961; MS in Organizational Behavior, Cornell U., 1963; PhD in Social Psychology, Washington U., St. Louis, 1967. Asst. prof. organizational psychology Washington U., 1967-70, assoc. prof., 1970-73, prof., 1973-89; prof. mgmt. U. South Fla., 1989—, Disting. Univ. prof., 2001; vis. prof. faculty commerce Northwestern U., 1981, U. B.C. (Can.), Vancouver, 1975-76. Author: (with S. Tucker) Implementing Routine and Radical Innovations, 1987; editor: Concepts and Controversy in Organizational Behavior, 1972, rev. edit, 1976; (with P. Frost and V. Mitchell) Organizational Reality, 1978, rev. edit., 1982, 86, 92; (with H. Meltzer) Making Organizations Humane and Productive, 1982; (with P. Frost and V. Mitchell) Managerial Reality, 1989, HRM Reality, 1992; (with A. Brief) Meanings of Occupational Work, 1990, (with S. Clegg and C. Hardy) Handbook of Organization Studies, 1996 (George Terry Book award 1997), (with Frost, P. and Krosting, A.) Managerial and Organization Reality, Stories of Life and Work, 2004. Fellow APA; mem. Acad. Mgmt. (named Disting. Educator 2002). Home: 6004 Pratt St Tampa FL 33647-1043 Office: U South Fla Sch Bus Tampa FL 33620-5500 Office Phone: 813-974-1787. Business E-Mail: wnord@coba.usf.edu.

NORDBERG, DONALD, communications executive; b. Chgo., Nov. 11, 1949; s. Nestor and Ruth Nordberg; m. Hilary Glassborow, Aug. 25, 1979; children: Peter Hugo, Gregory William. BA English with high honors and distinction, U. Ill., 1971, MA English, 1973; MBA with distinction, Warwick U., Coventry, Eng., 1994; student application sys. dynamics to bus. strategy, London Bus. Sch., 1998. Bur. chief Reuters Ltd., Frankfurt, West Germany, 1980-84, chief corr. Zurich, Switzerland, 1984-88, fin. editor London, 1988-91; news editor Reuters Am. Inc., N.Y.C., 1991-93, v.p., 1994-96; product planning mgr. Reuters Fin. TV, London, 1996—98; dir. strategy RAW Comm., 1999—. Dir.: (reporting) 1st Clinton-Yeltsin summit meeting and coverage 1992 presdl. election campaign. Named one of the most influential journalists in Am., TFJR's Bus. News Reporter, 1996. Mem. Investor Rels. Soc. Avocations: writing, reading modern german literature and 19th and 20th century english, theater. Office: RAW Comm 28-30 Worship St London ECA 2AH England

NORDBERG, JOHN ALBERT, federal judge; b. Evanston, Ill., June 18, 1926; s. Carl Albert and Judith Ranghild (Carlson) N.; m. Jane Spaulding, June 18, 1947; children: Carol, Mary, Janet, John. Student, Carleton Coll., 1943—44, student, 1946—47; JD, U. Mich., 1950. Bar: Ill. 1950, U.S. Dist. Ct. (no. dist.) Ill. 1957, U.S. Ct. Appeals (7th cir.) 1961. Assoc. Pope & Ballard, Chgo., 1950-57; ptnr. Pope, Ballard, Shepard & Fowle, Chgo., 1957-76; judge Cir. Ct. of Cook County, Ill., 1976-82, U.S. Dist. Ct. (no. dist.) Ill., Chgo., 1982-95, sr. judge, 1995—. Editor-in-chief, bd. editors Chgo. Bar Record, 1966-74 Magistrate of Cir. Ct. and justice of peace Ill., 1957-65. Served with USN, 1944-46; PTO Mem. ABA, Chgo. Bar Assn., Am. Judicature Soc., Law Club Chgo., Legal Club Chgo., Union League Club of Chgo., Order of Coif. Office: US Dist Ct #1886 219 S Dearborn St Chicago IL 60604-1706

NORDBY, EUGENE JORGEN, orthopedic surgeon; b. Abbotsford, Wis., Apr. 30, 1918; s. Herman Preus and Lucille Violet (Korsrud) N.; m. Olive Marie Jensen, June 21, 1941; 1 child, Jon Jorgen BA, Luther Coll., Decorah, Iowa, 1939; MD, U. Wis., 1943. Diplomate Am. Bd. Orthopaedic Surgery. Intern Madison Gen. Hosp., Wis., 1943-44, asst. in orthopedic surgery, 1944-48; practice medicine specializing in orthopedic surgery Madison, Wis., 1948—. Pres. Bone and Joint Surgery Assocs., S.C., 1969—91; chief staff Madison Gen. Hosp., 1957—63; assoc. clin. prof. U. Wis. Med. Sch., 1961—; bd. dirs. Wis. Physicians Svcs., 1958—, chmn., 1979—; dir. Wis. Regional Med. Program, Chgo. Madison and No. R.R.; bd. govs. Wis Health Care Liability Ins. Plan; chmn. trustees S.M.S. Realty Corp.; mem. bd. attys. Profl. Responsibility of Wis. Supreme Ct., 1992—. Mem. editl. bd. Clin. Orthopaedics and Related Research, 1964—, Spine, 1994-2000. Pres. Vesterheim Norwegian Am. Mus., Decorah, Iowa, 1968-97, pres. emeritus, 1997—. Served to capt. M.C., AUS, 1944-46 Decorated Knight 1st class Royal Norwegian Order St. Olav; named Notable Norwegian Dane County Norwegian-Am. Fest, 1995; recipient Disting. Svc. award Internat. Rotary,1 987, Den Hoyeste Aere award Vesterheim, 1993, Lyman Smith, M.D. and Eugene J. Nordby, M.D. award for minimally invasive spine surgery established N.Am. Spine Soc., 1998, The Nordby Bldg. designated Wis. Phys. Svc. Health Ins. Co., 1998. Fellow Wisdom Hall of Fame; mem. Acad. Orthopaedic Surgeons (bd. dirs. 1972-73), Clin. Orthopaedic Soc., Assn. Bone and Joint Surgeons (pres. 1973), Internat. Soc. Study Lumbar Spine, State Med. Soc. Wis. (chmn. 1968-76, treas. 1976-97, Coun. award 1976), Am. Orthopaedic Assn., N.Am. Spine Soc., Internat. Intradiscal Therapy Soc. (sec. 1987-99, exec. dir. 1996—, Eugene J. Nordby Rsch. award established in his honor 1993), Wis. Orthopaedic Soc., Dane County Med. Soc. (pres. 1957), Nat. Exch. Club, Madison Torske Klubben (founder, pres. 1978-98, pres. emeritus 1998—), Norwegian-Am. Orthopaedic Soc., Am. Acad. Orthopedic Surgeons, Am. Orthopedic Assn., Norwegian Am. Found., Phi Chi. Lutheran. Home: 7824 Courtyard Dr Madison WI 53719 Office: 2704 Marshall Ct Madison WI 53705-2256 Office Phone: 608-831-2356. *We must remember no matter how dedicated we are to the accumulation of knowledge, it isn't always what you know that matters but what you can think of in time.*

NORDELL, HANS RODERICK, journalist, retired editor; b. Alexandria, Minn., June 26, 1925; s. Wilbur Eric and Amelia (Jasperson) N.; m. Joan Projansky, Apr. 30, 1955; children: Eric Peter, John Roderick, Elizabeth Sabin. AB magna cum laude, Harvard U., 1948; B Litt, U. Dublin, 1951. Exec. editor World Monitor: The Christian Science Monitor Monthly; with Christian Sci. Monitor, Boston, 1948-93, arts editor, 1968-73, asst. chief editorial writer, 1973-83, home forum editor, 1983-85, feature editor, 1985-87; exec. editor World Monitor: The Christian Science Monitor Monthly, Boston, 1988-93. Bd. dirs. Cmty. Music Ctr., Boston, 1970-94, corp. chair, 1994—; bd. dirs. Young Audiences, 1970-88; mem. Com. for Harvard Theatre Collection, 1977-91; trustee Berklee Coll. Music, 1970-97, trustee emeritus, 1997—. With USMCR, 1943-46. Fellowship Rotary Found., 1950-51. Mem.: Harvard Musical Assn., St. Botolph Club, Phi Beta Kappa. Christian Scientist. Home: 25 Meadow Way Cambridge MA 02138-4635

NORDENBERG, MARK ALAN, law educator, academic administrator; b. Duluth, Minn., July 12, 1948; s. John Clemens and Shirley Mae (Tappen) N.; m. Nikki Patricia Pirillo, Dec. 26, 1970; children: Erin, Carl, Michael. BA, Thiel Coll., 1970; JD, U. Wis., 1973. Bar: Wis. 1973, Minn. 1974, U.S. Supreme Ct. 1976, Pa. 1985. Atty. Gray, Plant, Mooty & Anderson, Mpls., 1973-75; prof. law Capital U. Law Ctr., Columbus, Ohio, 1975-77, U. Pitts., 1977—, acting dean Sch. Law, 1985-87, dean Sch. Law, 1987-93, interim univ. sr. vice chancellor and provost, 1993-94, Univ. Disting. Svc. prof., 1994—, interim univ. chancellor, 1995-96, univ. chancellor, 1996—. Mem. U.S. Supreme Ct. Adv. Com. on Civil Rules, Washington, 1988-93, Pa. Supreme Ct. Civil Procedure Rules Com., Phila., 1986-92; reporter civil justice adv. group U.S. Dist. Ct., Pitts., 1991-96; bd. dirs. Mellon Fin. Corp. Author: Modern Pennsylvania Civil Practice, 1985, 2d edit., 1995. Bd. dirs. Urban League of Pitts., Allegheny Conf. on Cmty. Devel., Pitts., Pitts. Coun. on Higher Edn., Pa. Assn. Colls. and Univs., Assn. of Am. Univs.; trustee Thiel Coll., Greenville, Pa., 1987—97; bd. dirs. Inst. for Shipboard Edn. Found., Pitts. Digital Greenhouse, Pitts. Life Scis. Greenhouse, Pitts. Robotics Foundry, Coun. on Competitiveness. Named Vectors Pitts. Person of Yr. in Edn., 1996, Person of Yr., 1997, Pitts. Mag. Person of Yr., 2001. Fellow Am. Bar Found.; mem. ABA, Pa. Bar Assn., Allegheny County Bar Assn., Pitts. Athletic Assn., Law Club Pitts., Univ. Club, Duquesne Club, Wildwood Golf Club, Pitts. Golf Club. Office: U Pitts Cathedral of Learning Pittsburgh PA 15260

NORDGREN, RONALD PAUL, engineering educator, researcher; b. Munising, Mich., Apr. 3, 1936; s. Paul A. and Martha M. N.; m. Joan E. McAfee, Sept 12, 1959; children: Sonia, Paul. BS in Engring., U. Mich., 1957, MS in Engring., 1958; PhD, U. Calif., Berkeley, 1962. Rsch. asst. U. Calif., Berkeley, 1959-62; mathematician Shell Devel. Co., Houston, 1963-68, staff rsch. engr., 1968-74, sr. staff rsch. engr., 1974-80, rsch. assoc., 1980-90; Brown prof. civil and mech. engring. Rice U., Houston, 1989-2000, rsch. prof., 2001—. U.S. nat. com. on theoretical and applied mechanics NRC, 1984-86, U.S. nat. com. for rock mechanics, 1991-95. Contbr. articles to profl. jours.; assoc. editor Jour. Applied Mechanics, 1972-76, 81-85; patentee in field. Fellow: ASME; mem.: NAE, Sigma Xi. Office: Rice U PO Box 1892 Houston TX 77251-1892 Business E-Mail: nordgren@rice.edu.

NORDGREN, SHARON L. state legislator; b. Chgo., Oct. 21, 1943; m. Richard Nordgren; 2 children. Student, U. Minn. N.H. state senator; mem. appropriations com.; mem. dist. 10 N.H. Ho. of Reps., 1998—. Mem. Hanover Bd. Selectman, 1979-88, chmn., 1982-88. Trustee Montshire Mus. Sci., 1984-92, chair, 1991-92; chmn. Cmty. Substance Abuse Com., 1989—; bd. dirs. N.H. Women's Lobby, 1992—; mem. Children's Trust Fund, 1990—, State Leadership Team Abuse and Neglect, 1991—; Hanover H.S. Coun., 1983—; cmty. mem. Hanover Inn Bd. Overseers, 1985—. Named Citizen of Yr., Hanover C. of C., 1992. Mem. Ch. of Christ. Avocations: fishing, hiking, sports. Home: 23 Rope Ferry Rd Hanover NH 03755-1404 Office: NH Ho Rep House of Reps Concord NH 03301

NORDGREN, WILLIAM BENNETT, engineering executive; b. Salt Lake City, Mar. 5, 1960; s. Kent Widstoe and Eliza (Schmuhl) N.; m. Carolyn B. Erickson, June 26, 1981; children: William Tyson, Cameron Lynn, Cassy Erin. BS, Brigham Young U., 1986, MS, 1989. Engr. Boeing Airplanes Co., Seattle, 1986-88; pres. CIM Engring. Assocs., Orem, Utah, 1988-89; v.p. engring. Prodn. Modeling Corp., Orem, 1989-93; pres. F & H Simulations, Inc., Orem, 1993—. Developer, polar coordinant mill. Mem. Soc. Mfg. Engrs., Inst. Indsl. Engrs. Republican. Mem. Lds Ch. Avocations: fishing, camping, sports. Office: PO Box 658 Orem UT 84059-0658

NORDHAGEN, HALLIE HUERTH, nursing home administrator; b. Apr. 2, 1914; d. Mathias James and Ethel Elizabeth (Fann) Huerth; m. Carl E. Nordhagen, May 24, 1947; children: Bruce Carl, Brian Keith. EdD, U. Wis., Superior, 1938, MA, 1949. Prin. tchr. Wis. Pub. Schs., 1932—46; supervising tchr. Wis. C.C., 1946—48; nursing home adminstr. Trempealeau County Health Care Ctr., Whitehall, Wis., 1959—. Mem. Wis. Nursing Home Adminstrs. Examining Bd.; fellow Menninger Clinic, Topeka, 1979—81. Author: Wisconsin Indians, 1966. Chmn. BRAD Assn./Alcohol and Drug Abuse; mem. Trampealeau County Alliance Drug Free Youth; mem. com. cons. to bishop Evang. Luth. Ch. Am., 1995—96. Recipient Disting. Svc. award in edn. and hosp. adminstrn., London, 1967, award for svcs. to human svcs. programs, Wis. Assn. Human Svcs., 1972, award for outstanding svcs. to exceptional children, Assn. Retarded Children, 1978, award for accomplishments in human resources, Trempealeau County Conservation Svc., 1981, citation, Wis. State Senate, 1983, Wis. Gov., 1984, Wis. State Assembly, 1989, Women of Leadership, Delta Kappa Gamma Alpha Kappa chpt. Jackson Counties, Wis., 2000. Mem.: Internat. Platform Assn., Wis. Assn. Human Svcs. Programs, Wis. Edn. Assn., Wis. Assn. County Homes, Am. Lutheran Ch. Women, Women's Club, Whitehall Country Club. Home: 35681 Claire St Whitehall WI 54773-8430 Office Phone: 715-538-4481.

NORDHAUS, ROBERT RIGGS, lawyer; b. Albuquerque, Mar. 27, 1937; s. Robert J. and Virginia (Riggs) N.; m. Jean Friedberg, June 27, 1964; children: Ronald E., Hannah E. BA, Stanford U., 1960; LLB, Yale U., 1963. Bar: N.Mex. 1963, D.C. 1981, U.S. Supreme Ct. 1982. Asst. counsel U.S. House Reps., Washington, 1963-74, counsel interstate and fgn. commerce com., 1975-76; asst. adminstr. FEA, Washington, 1977; gen. counsel Fed. Energy Regulatory Commn., Washington, 1977-80; ptnr. Van Ness, Feldman & Curtis, Washington, 1981-93; gen. counsel Dept. of Energy, Washington, 1993-97; ptnr. Van Ness Feldman, Washington, 1997—. Professorial lectr. George Washington Law Sch., Washington, 2001—. 2d. lt. U.S. Army, 1960. Mem. Fed. Energy Bar Assn. (bd. dirs. 1989-92). Office: Van Ness Feldman Ste 700 1050 Thomas Jefferson St NW Washington DC 20007-3877

NORDIN, JOHN ALGOT, economist, educator; b. Mpls., Mar. 18, 1916; s. John A. and Beda (Nelson) N.; m. Agnes June Leith, Apr. 8, 1944 (dec. June 1969); children: Karen Frances, Margaret Lynn Nordin Ragle, Barbara Jean; m. Margaret N. Lahey, Mar. 30, 1970. BA, U. Minn., 1935, MA, 1937, PhD, 1941. Mem. faculty Iowa State U., 1941-61, successively asst. prof. econs., assoc. prof., 1941-56, prof. charge instrn., 1956-61; prof. dept. econs. Kans. State U., 1961-84, prof. emeritus, 1984—. Author: (with Virgil Salera) Elementary Economics, 1954; contbr. articles to profl. jours. Served with USNR, 1942-45. Mem. Phi Beta Kappa Episcopalian. Home: Apt E563 14515 W Granite Valley Dr Sun City West AZ 85375-6024

NORDLAND, GERALD, art museum administrator, historian, consultant; b. LA; AB, JD, U. So. Calif. Dean of faculty Chouinard Art Sch., L.A., 1960-64; dir. Washington Gallery of Modern Art, 1964-66, San Francisco Mus. Art, 1966-72, Frederick S. Wight Art Galleries, UCLA, 1973-77, Milw. Art Mus., 1977-85; ind. curator, author, editor Chgo., 1985—. Author: Paul Jenkins, 1972, Gaston Lachaise/The Man and His Work, 1974, Richard Diebenkorn, 1987, rev. edit., 2001, Frank Lloyd Wright: In the Realm of Ideas, 1988, Zhou Brothers, 1994, Ynez Johnston, 1996, Lev Syrkin, 1998, Twentieth Century American Drawings, 1998, Jon Schueler: To The North, 2002, In the Spirit of the Times, 2003, Emerson Woelffer: A Solo Flight, 2003. Gaston Lachaise Found. grantee, 1973-74; John Simon Guggenheim Found. fellow, 1985-86. Home and Office: 645 W Sheridan Rd Chicago IL 60613-3316

NORDLANDER, PETER JAN ARNE, physics educator, researcher; b. Stockholm, Nov. 21, 1955; came to U.S., 1985; s. Arne Nils Ludwig and Blenda Mimmi (Sjosell) N.; m. Nancy Jean Halas, Aug. 1, 1990. MSc in Engring. Physics, Chalmers U., Sweden, 1980, PhD, 1985. Postdoctoral fellow rsch. divsn. IBM, Yorktown Heights, N.Y., 1985-86; rsch. asst. prof. Vanderbilt U., Nashville, 1987-88, adjoint asst. prof., 1988-91; sr. postdoctoral fellow Rutgers U., Piscataway, N.J., 1988-89; asst. prof. physics Rice U., Houston, 1989-93, assoc. prof., 1993-97, prof., 1997—. Cons. AT&T Bell Labs., N.Y., 1987-89; docent Chalmers U., 1991; dir. Rice quantum Inst., 2000—. Editor: Procs. Inelastic Ion Surface Collisions-10, 1994, Inelastic Ion Surface Collisions-12, 1999. 2d lt. cav. Swedish Army, 1976-77. Recipient Charles Duncan award, 1999. Fellow Am. Phys. Soc.; mem. AAAS, Am. Chem. Soc. Office: Rice U Dept Physics 6100 Main St Houston TX 77005-1827 E-mail: nordland@rice.edu.

NORDLEY, GERALD DAVID, investor, writer; b. Mpls., May 22, 1947; s. V. Gerald and Evelyn May (Whitesel) N., (div. 1973), 1 child, Sharon, m. Gayle Ann Wiesner, May 9, 1976; children: Jeffrey Goldberg, Andrew Nordley. BA in Physics, Macalester Coll., 1969; MS in System Mgmt., U. So. Calif., L.A., 1980. Enlisted USAF, 1969, commd. 2nd lt., 1970, advanced through grades to maj., 1982; inter-range ops. officer Network Ops. Div., Sunnyvale AFB, Calif., 1973-76; chief orbital ops. br. Def. Satellite Communications Directorate, L.A. AFB, 1976-81; chief spacecraft engr. br. DSCS III Program Office, L.A. AFB, 1981-82; battle dir. Mangilsan Liason Annex, Mang Il San, South Korea, 1983; chief advanced propulsion br. A.F. Rocket Propulsion Lab., Edwards AFB, Calif., 1984-86; rsch. staff mgr. ARIES office Astronautics Lab., Edwards AFB, 1986-89; ret. USAF, 1989; writer, pvt. investor Sunnyvale, 1990—. Mem. dir. Macalester Coll. Rep. Club, St. Paul, 1967-68; pres. Park Knowles Estates Property Owners Assn., Boron, Calif., 1988; co-chair Silicon Valley Writers Workshop, Cupertino, Calif., 1992, 93; treas. CONTACT: Cultures of the Imagination, 1997—. Decorated Air Force Commendation medal with 4 oak leaf clusters, Meritorious Svc. medal with 1 oak leaf cluster; recipient Anlab award Analog Mag., 1992, 93, 2000. Fellow Brit. Interplanetary Soc.; mem. AIAA (sr.; elec. propulsion com. 1984-86), Air Force Assn., Sci. Fiction Writers Am., Whensday People Writers Group, Space Access Soc., Am. Legion. Unitarian Universalist. Avocation: amateur astronomy. E-mail: gdnordley@aol.com.

NORDLIE, ROBERT CONRAD, biochemistry educator; b. Willmar, Minn., June 11, 1930; s. Peder Conrad and Myrtle (Spindler) N.; m. Sally Ann Christianson, Aug. 23, 1959; children: Margaret, Melissa, John. BS St. Cloud State Coll., Minn., 1952; MS, U. N.D., 1957, PhD, 1960. Tchg., rsch. asst. biochemistry U. N.D. Med. Sch., Grand Forks, 1955-60, James J. Hill rsch. prof. biochemistry, 1962-74, Chester Fritz disting. prof. biochemistry, 1974—, Cornatzer prof., chmn. dept. biochemistry and molecular biology, 1983-2000, Chester Fritz disting. emeritus prof., 2000—. Hon. prof. San Marcos U., Lima, Peru, 1981, 82—; emeritus prof., 2000-; NIH fellow Inst. Enzyme Rsch., U. Wis., 1960-61; mem. biochemistry study sect. NIH; merit rev. com. VA, 1994—; cons. enzymology Oak Ridge, 1961—; vis. prof. Tokyo Biomed. Inst., 1984; mem. predoctoral fellowship rev. group Howard Hughes Inst., 1990-93. Mem. editorial bd.: Jour. Biol. Chemistry, Biochimca et Biophysica Acta. Research publs. on enzymology relating to metabolism of various carbohydrates in mammalian livers, regulation blood sugar levels. Served with AUS, 1953-55. Recipient Disting. Alumnus award St. Cloud State U., 1983; recipient Sigma Xi Rsch. award, 1969, Golden Apple award U. N.D., 1968, Edgar Dale award U. N.D., 1983, Burlington No. Faculty Scholar award, 1987, Thomas J. Clifford Faculty Achievement award for excellence in rsch. U. N.D. Found., 1993. Mem. AAAS, Am. Soc. Biol. Chemistry and Molecular Biology, Am. Chem. Soc., Internat. Union Biochemists, Soc. Exptl. Biology and Medicine, Am. Inst. Nutrition, Sigma Xi, Alpha Omega Alpha. Home: 162 Columbia Ct Grand Forks ND 58203-2947 Office Phone: 701-777-2751. E-mail: rnordlie@medicine.nodak.edu.

NORDLING, BERNARD ERICK, lawyer; b. Nekoma, Kans., June 14, 1921; s. Carl Ruben Ebben and Edith Elveda (Freeburg) N.; m. Barbara Ann Burkholder, Mar. 26, 1949. Student, George Washington U., 1941-43; AB, McPherson Coll., 1947; JD, U. Kans., 1949. Bar: Kans. 1949, U.S. Dist. Ct. Kans. 1949, U.S. Ct. Appeals (10th cir.) 1970. Pvt. practice, Hugoton, Kans., 1949—; ptnr. Kramer, Nordling & Nordling, Hugoton, Kans., 1950-99; mem. Kramer, Nordling & Nordling, LLC, Hugoton, Kans., 1999—; city atty. City of Hugoton, 1951-87; county atty. Stevens County, Kans., 1957-63. Kans. mem. legal com. Interstate Oil Compact Commn., 1969-93; mem. supply tech. adv. com. nat. gas survey FPC, 1975-77. Editor U. Kans. Law Rev., 1949. Mem. Hugoton Sch. Bds., 1954-68, pres. grade sch. bd., 1957-63; trustee McPherson Coll., 1971-81, mem. exec. com., 1975-81; mem. Kans. Energy Adv. Coun., 1975-78, mem. exec. com., 1976-78; bd. trustees Kans. 4-H Found., 1987-2003. With AUS, 1944-46. Recipient Citation of Merit, McPherson Coll., 1987, Disting. Alumnus award, Kans. U. Law Sch., 1993, Lifetime Achievement award, Hugoton Kans. Area C. of C., 1994. Fellow: Am. Bar Found. (Kans.); mem.: ABA, Am. Inn of Ct., S.W. Kans. Royalty Owners Assn. (exec. sec. 1968—94, asst. exec. sec. 1994—), Nat. Assn. Royalty Owners (bd. govs. 1980—99, James L. Stafford Founder's award 2003), City Attys. Assn. Kans. (exec. com. 1975—83, pres. 1982—83), Kans. Bar Assn., Kans. U. Alumni Assn. (bd. dirs. 1992—97, Fred Ellsworth medallion 1997, James Woods Green medallion 2001), Kans. U. Endowment Assn. (trustee 1987—), U. Kans. Law Soc. (bd. govs. 1984—87), Phi Alpha Delta, Order of Coif. Address: 4404 Nicklaus Dr Lawrence KS 66047 Office Phone: 785-842-1665. E-mail: benordling@sunflower.com.

NORDLINGER, GERSON, investor; b. Washington, Feb. 2, 1916; s. Gerson and Camille (Bensinger) N. BA, George Washington U., 1935; BCS, Benjamin Franklin U., 1939. Head Navy Dept. Bur. Aeros. Budget, 1946-50; pres. Nordlinger Investment Corp., Washington, 1955—; trustee Washington Real Estate Investment Trust, 1961-98. Chmn. D.C. Arts Commn., 1965-67; v.p. Nat. Symphony Assn., 1953—, Nat. Ballet, 1966-70, Alliance Francaise, 1980—; pres. Prevention of Blindness Soc., 1960-67; treas. Friendship House, 1951-69; vice chmn. D.C. Recreation Bd., 1960-67; trustee Washington Performing Arts Soc., Mt. Vernon Coll., Washington Opera, Cathedral Choral Soc., Phillips Collection; life trustee Nat. Symphony Orch., 1952—; state com. Republican Party, 1952-64. Lt. comdr. Supply Corps, USNR, 1941-46, PTO. Recipient Angel of Arts award, 2001. Mem. D.C. Inst. CPAs, Cosmos Club, Met. Club. Home: 2700 Calvert St NW # 515 Washington DC 20008-2621 also: 3900 Galt Ocean Dr Fort Lauderdale FL 33308-6631 E-mail: gersonn@aol.com.

NORDLOH, DAVID JOSEPH, English language educator; b. Cin., May 3, 1942; s. Joseph Westerman and Josephine (Fusz) N.; m. Barbara Jane Beddow, June 29, 1968; children: Geoffrey David, Jennifer Ellen Blum. AB in English, Coll. of Holy Cross, 1964; PhD in English, Ind. U., 1969. Asst. prof. English Ind. U., Bloomington, 1969—75, assoc. prof. English, 1975—81, prof. English, 1981—, assoc. dean faculties, 2003—. Vis. assoc. prof. U. Va., Charlottesville, 1978; dir. Am. Studies Program, Ind. U., 1987-94. Gen. editor: A Selected Edition of W.D. Howells, 1974—; editor: Twayne's United States Author's Series, 1978-90; co-editor: American Literary Scholarship, 1986—; mem. editl. bd. Walter Scott Edition, 1984—; adv. bd. The Writings of James Fenimore Cooper, 1995—. Pres. Bloomington Symphony Orch., 1986-88, 93-94. Fulbright scholar, 1982-83. Mem. Am. Lit. Assn. Home: 3123 E Diana Ct Bloomington IN 47401-4407 Office: Ind U English Dept 442 Ballantine Hall Bloomington IN 47401-5048

NORDLUND, DONALD CRAIG, lawyer; b. Chgo., May 23, 1949; s. Donald E. and Jane (Houston) N.; m. Sally Baum, Sept. 7, 1975; children: Courtney Elizabeth, Michael Andrew, Laurie Katherine. AB, Stanford U., 1971; JD, Vanderbilt U., 1974. Assoc. Ware & Freidenrich, Palo Alto, Calif., 1974-77; atty. Hewlett-Packard Co., Palo Alto, 1977-87, assoc. gen. counsel, sec., 1987-99; sr. v.p., gen. counsel, sec. Agilent Technologies, Inc., 1999—. Sec. Agilent Tech. Found. and various Agilent Tech. subsidiaries, 1999—; panelist ann. disclosure doc. seminar Practicing Law Inst., 1982—2001, co-chmn., 2002—04; bd. dirs. Addison Ave. Fed. Credit Union, 1985—. Chmn., bd. dirs. Santa Clara County chpt. Jr. Achievement, 1995-97. Mem.: Am. Corp. Counsel Assn. (bd. dirs. San Francisco chpt. 1984—2000, pres. 1989—90, nat. bd. dirs. 1995—2001), Am. Soc. Corp. Secs. Inc. (pres. San Francisco region 1986—88, bd. dirs. 1987—90, mem. exec. com. 1988—89, chmn. securities law com. 1995—98, nat. chmn. 1999—2000), Foothills Tennis and Swimming Club. Avocations: tennis, skiing, sailing, golf. Office: Agilent Technologies Inc 395 Page Mill Rd Palo Alto CA 94306-2024

NORDLUND, DONALD ELMER, manufacturing executive, lawyer; b. Stromsburg, Nebr., Mar. 1, 1922; s. E.C. and Edith O. (Peterson) N.; m. Mary Jane Houston, June 5, 1948; children: Donald Craig, William Chalmers, Sarah, James. AB, Midland Coll., 1943; JD, U. Mich., 1948. Bar: Ill. 1949. With Stevenson, Conaghan, Hackbert, Rooks and Pitts, Chgo., 1948-55, A.E. Staley Mfg. Co., Decatur, Ill., 1956-85, v.p., dir., mem. exec. com., 1958-65, pres., chief operating officer, 1965-80, dir., mem. exec. com., 1965-85, also chmn., 1975-85; chief exec. officer Staley Continental, Inc., Rolling Meadows, Ill., 1985-88, chmn. and chief exec. officer, 1985-88. Past chmn. bd. trustees Millikin U., now hon. trustee; trustee Mus. Sci. and Industry, Chgo., Rush-Presbyn. St. Lukes Med. Ctr., Chgo.; bd. dirs. Lyric Opera Chgo.; mem. grad. dirs. coun. Decatur Meml. Hosp. Mem. ABA, Chgo. Bar Assn., Corn Refiners Assn. (bd. dirs., past chmn., now hon. dir.), Legal Club, Comml. Club, Chgo. Club, Tavern Club, Barrington Hills Club, Phi Alpha Delta.

NORDMAN, CHRISTER ERIC, chemistry professor; b. Helsinki, Finland, Jan. 23, 1925; came to U.S., 1948, naturalized, 1960; s. Eric Johan and Gertrud (Nordgren) N.; m. Barbara Lorraine Neal, Nov. 28, 1952 (div. 1993); children: Christina, Aleta, Eric, Carl; m. Outi Marttila, Dec. 28, 1994. Dipl. Ing., Finnish Inst. Tech., Helsinki, 1949; PhD, U. Minn., 1953. Research asso. Inst. Cancer Research, Phila., 1953-55; mem. faculty U. Mich., Ann Arbor, 1955—, prof. chemistry, 1964-95; prof. emeritus, 1995—. Mem. U.S. Nat. Com. Crystallography, 1970-72. Served with Finnish Army, 1943-44. NIH spl. fellow, 1971-72; recipient A.L. Patterson award, 1997. Fellow AAAS; mem. Am. Chem. Soc., Am. Phys. Soc., Am. Crystallographic Assn., Finnish Soc. Scis. and Letters. Home: 27 Haverhill Ct Ann Arbor MI 48105-1406 Office: Univ Mich Dept Chemistry Ann Arbor MI 48109

NORDQVIST, ERIK ASKBO, shipping company executive; b. Copenhagen, Aug. 8, 1943; s. Joergen and Lissie (Moeller) Nordqvist; m. Kirsten Vibeke Kenholt, Sept. 17, 1970 (dec. June 28, 2002); children: Ken-Martin, Alexander. Student, Danish Comml. Coll. Commerce, London, 1963-64, U. S.C., 1964-65. Vice pres. Import Center W.S., L.A., 1964-65; mgr. Denning Freight Forwarders Ltd., Toronto, Ont., Can., 1965-66; sales dir. overseas Samson Transp. Co., Copenhagen, 1967-68; mng. dir., pres. Seair AS, Copenhagen, 1969-71, Nordbird Group, Vedbaek, Denmark, 1971—, Nordbird AS, 1971—; chmn. European Steamship Line, Vedbaek, 1995—, European Airline Sys., Vedbaek, 1995—; owner Rederiet Waterest I/S, 1998—, AidsKit, Copenhagen, 2003—; part-owner Pastamannen, Klampenborg, Denmark, 2003—. Also Nordbird Oil, Nordbird Fin., Copenhagen, Nordbird Internat. Financing Ltd., Toronto, Ont.; v.p. N. Sea Products Inc., High Point, N.C., 1980—; bd. dirs. Fino Travel, Odense, Denmark, Annex Furniture Galleries, European Broadcast Comm., Vedbaek, On Holding Ltd., Gibraltar, Olsen & Nordqvist Holding, Holbaek, Denmark, pres., 1986—, NQ-Byg Aps, Holbaek, Auto Dan-Am., Holbaek, Autotel Internat., Roskilde, On Holding APS, Vedbaek Dansk-Fransk Osters Aps, 3 Danish Open, U.S., Gt. Britain, Japan, Tins and Cans, Denmark; chmn. European Broadcast Comm., Charlottenlund, Denmark, London, European Aid Found., Vedbeak, Denmark, Lac, Albanien; cons. Frederikshavns. Skibsvaerf AS, Copenhagen Cmty. Chmn. European Broadcast Comm., Copenhagen and London, 1992—, European Aid Found., Copenhagen and N.Y.C.; del. Internat. Red Cross, Copenhagen, 1994—. Recipient Devel. honor for shipping City of Le Havre, France, 1971. Mem. Det Udenrigspolitiske Selskab, Funen Soc. (founder, past pres.). Lutheran. Office: EAS/ESL/RSD 312 Ballerumvej 7700 Thisted Denmark Office Phone: 45893994. E-mail: enq@sol.dk.

NORDSTRAND, NATHALIE ELIZABETH JOHNSON, artist; b. Woburn, Mass., Nov. 6, 1932; d. Edward N. and Ruth Peterson Johnson; m. Robert I. Nordstrand, Jan. 12, 1962. AA, Bradford Jr. Coll., 1952; BA, Barnard Coll., Columbia, 1954; studies with Jay Connaway, Don Stone, Roger Curtis. Rsch. assoc. Gerontology Age Ctr. of New Eng., Boston, 1955-64; clk. corp. dir. Johnson Bros. Greenhouses, Inc., Woburn, 1958-84; owner Nordstrand Gallery, Rockport, Mass., 1970-99. Artist oils and watercolor works exhibited at Nat. Acad. Galleries, N.Y.C., Springfield Mus. Fine Arts, Hammond Mus., North Salem, N.Y.C., Bhulabha Meml. Inst., Bombay, India, Copley Soc. at Boston Symphony Hall, Hermann Fine Arts Ctr., Marietta, Ohio, Am. C. of C., Hong Kong, 1975, 76, Silvermine Guild, Conn., 1976, Wall of Fame, Balt. Watercolor Soc., 1976, Ann. Copley Masters Exhbn. Boston, others; one woman shows include Rockport (Mass.) Art Assn., 1969, Laura Knotts Art Gallery, Bradford Coll., 1982, Reading Pub. Libr. Found., 1997; paintings in Nat. Mus. Am. Art, Smithsonian Inst., 1994, Best of Watercolors, 1995, Best of Oil Painting, 1996, Landscape Inspirations, 1997, Gallery of Marine Art, 1998. Mem. planning bd. North Suburban Art Festival, 1963—68; chair. planned giving Barnard Coll., N.Y.C., 2003—. Named Citizen of Yr., Reading chpt. Am. Cancer Soc., 1983; recipient Excellence in Watercolor award, Rockport Art Assn., 1997, Philip Isenberg Meml. award, Salmagundi Club, 1997, 179 awards in nat. and regional competition, 1960—. Fellow Am. Artist Profl. League (Gold medal 1971, 75, award 1978, 79); mem. Acad. Artists Assn. (Watercolor awards 1973, 74, 76, 77, New Eng. Heritage award 1993), Copley Soc. Boston (master artist), Hudson Valley, North Shore (bd. dirs. 1964-67, 86—), Rockport Art Assn. (Lifetime Dedication to Promotion of Art award 1999), Affiliated Art Assn. Mass. (v.p. 1980), Reading Art Assn. (charter, program chmn. 1960-86, Pres.'s awards 1973-80), Am. Watercolor Soc. (juror 125th Ann. Internat. Exhbn., 1992), Allied Artists Am. (Watercolor award 1973, 74), New Eng. Watercolor Soc. (2d v.p. 1984-90), Boston Watercolor Soc. (award 1975), Guild Boston Artists (bd. dirs. 1986-99, A. Lassall Ripley award 1993), Reading Assn. Fine and Performing Arts (charter, bd. dirs. 1993), Nat. Mus. Women in Arts (charter mem.), Salmagundi Club (40 awards including MacGowin Tuttle Meml. award 1976, 78, 79, Elliot Liskin Meml. award 1988, Steven Blackman award 1988, Joseph Hartley award 1989, 2001, 2002, Mortimer Freehof Meml. award 1991, Bruce Crane award 1994, Rita Duis Meml. award 2001, Margery Saroka Meml. award 2003, Thomas Moran award 2004). Methodist. Address: 384 Franklin St Reading MA 01867-1036 E-mail: nordstrands@aol.com.

NORDSTROM, BLAKE W. retail executive; b. 1960; With Nordstrom, Inc., Seattle, 1974—, v.p. & gen. mgr. Wash./Alaska region, 1991—95, co-pres., 1995—2000, pres., 2000—. Office: Nordstrom Inc 1617 Sixth Ave Seattle WA 98101-1742

NORDSTROM, BRUCE A. department store executive; b. 1933; married. BA, U. Wash., 1956. With Nordstrom, Inc., Seattle, 1956—, v.p., 1964-70, pres., 1970-75, chmn., 1975-77, co-chmn., 1977—, dir. Office: Nordstrom Inc 1617 6th Ave Seattle WA 98101-1742

NORDSTROM, JOHN N. department store executive; b. 1937; married. BA, U. Wash., 1958. With Nordstrom, Inc., Seattle, 1958—, v.p., 1965-70, exec. v.p., 1970-75, pres., 1975-77, co-chmn., 1977—, dir. Bd. dirs. Fed. Res. Bank San Francisco. Office: Nordstrom Inc 1617 6th Ave Seattle WA 98101-1742

NORDSTROM, KARL FREDRIK, geographer, educator; b. Boston, Aug. 9, 1941; s. Karl Benard Nordstrom and Mabel Augusta Geiger. BA, Rutgers U., New Brunswick, N.J., 1963; MS, Rutgers U., 1970, PhD, 1975. From asst. prof. to prof. Inst. Marine and Coastal Sci. Rutgers U., New Brunswick, 1975—. Vis. scholar U. Amsterdam, 1995; vis. Fulbright scholar U. Greifswald, Germany, 1999; vis. instr. Universidade de Vale do Itajai, Brazil, 2002. Author: (book) Estuarine Beaches, 1992, Beaches and Dunes of Developed Coasts, 2000; editor: Estuarine Shores, 1996; mem. editl. bd. Jour. Coastal Rsch., Jour. Coastal Conservation. Capt. U.S. Army, 1964—67. NSF grantee, Nat. Geog. Soc. grantee, NOAA grantee, Nat. Park Svc. grantee, German Acad. Exch. Svc. grantee. Mem.: Coastal Edn. and Rsch. Found., Assn. Am. Geographers, Am. Shore and Beach Preservation Assn. Avocations: travel, music. Office: Inst Marine and Coastal Scis Rutgers Univ New Brunswick NJ 08901-8521

NORDYKE, ELEANOR COLE, population researcher, public health nurse; b. Los Angeles, June 15, 1927; d. Ralph G. and Louise Noble (Carter) Cole; m. Robert Allan Nordyke, June 18, 1950; children: Mary Ellen Nordyke-Grace, Carolyn Nordyke Cozzette, Thomas J., Susan Nordyke Bell., Gretchen Nordyke Worthington. BS, Stanford U., 1950; P.H.N. accreditation, U. Calif.-Berkeley, 1952; MPH, U. Hawaii, 1969. RN. Pub. health nurse San Francisco Dept. Health, 1950-52; nurse-tchr. Punahou Sch., Honolulu, 1966-67; clinic coordinator East-West Population Inst., East-West Ctr., Honolulu, 1969-75, population rschr., 1975-82, rsch. fellow, 1982-92. Cons. Hawaii Commn. on Population, Honolulu, 1970-83; mem. Hawaii Policy Action Group for Family Planning, Honolulu, 1971-89, chmn., 1976-77; nurse-cons. vol. Straub Clinic and Hosp., 2001--. Author: The Peopling of Hawaii, 1977, 2d rev. edit., 1989, A Profile of Hawaii's Elderly Population, 1984; author: (with Robert Gardner) The Demographic Situation in Hawaii, 1974; author: Pacific Images-Views from Captain Cook's Third Voyage, 1999; editor: I'm Third-An American Boy of Depression Years - Memoirs of Robert A. Nordyke, MD, 2003; mem. editl. bd. Hawaiian Jour. History, 1980—; contbr. articles to profl. jours. Bd. dirs. YMCA, Honolulu, 1970-85, YMCA Camp Erdman Br., 1985—. vice-chmn. 1978-79, chmn. YMCA Camp Erdman, 1989-92; bd. dirs. Hawaii Planned Parenthood, 1974-78, Friends of Libr. of Hawaii, 1985-87, 2002—; trustee Hawaiian Hist. Soc., 1978-82, Arcadia Retirement Residence, Honolulu, 1978-87; mem. liberal arts coun. Hawaii Pacific U., 1988—. Mem. Population Reference Bur., Am. Statis. Assn., Hawaii Econ. Assn., Hawaiian Hist. Soc., Friends of East-West Ctr., Friends of Univ. Hawaii Sch. Medicine, Stanford Nurses Alumni Assn., Stanford Alumni Assn. (bd. dirs. Hawaii chpt.), U. Hawaii Sch. Pub. Health Alumni Assn. (life), Honolulu County Geneal. Soc., Gen. Fed. Women's History Club, Adventure Club of Honolulu, Book Reading Club, Outrigger Canoe Club, Morning Music Club, Caledonian Soc., NAIC Wiki Kala Investment Club, Phi Beta Kappa. Democrat. Congregationalist. Avocations: music, art, swimming, birds, travel. Home: 2013 Kakela Dr Honolulu HI 96822-2158 Personal E-mail: rnordyke@aol.com.

NORELL, MARK ALLEN, paleontology educator; b. St. Paul, July 26, 1957; s. Albert Donald Norell and Helen Louise Soltau; m. Vivian Pan, Nov. 1, 1991; 1 chld, Inga Pan. BS, Long Beach State U., 1980; MS, San Diego State U., 1983; PhD, Yale U., 1988. Assoc. curator Am. Mus., N.Y.C., 1989-99, chmn. dept., 1996—, divsn. chmn., curator, 1999—. Adj. assoc. prof. dept. biology Yale U., New Haven, 1991—. Author: All You Need to Know About Dinosaurs, 1991, Discovering Dinosaurs, 1995, 2d edit., 2000, Searching for Velociraptor, 1996, A Dinosaur and Its Nest, 1999. Named Disting. Alumnus, Long Beach State U., 2000. Fellow: Willi Hennig Soc.; mem.: Soc. Vertebrate Paleontology (Romer prize 1987). Office: Am Museum of Natural History 79th at Central Park W New York NY 10024-5192 Office Phone: 212-769-5804. Business E-Mail: norell@amnh.org.

NORELLI, TERIE THOMPSON, state legislator; b. Orange, N.J., July 7, 1952; d. George Russell and Iverna C. (Weber) Thompson; m. Allen M. Norelli, Dec. 31, 1973; children: Gina Marie, Daniel Thompson. BS in Math. summa cum laude, U. N.H., 1985. Tchr. math. Winnacunnet H.S., Hampton, N.H., 1985-95; mem. N.H. Ho. of Reps., Concord, 1996—, sci., tech. and energy com., 1996—2003, telecomm. oversight com., 1997—2003, ho. Dem. leadership, 1998—, asst. Dem. whip, 2002—, chair clean air subcom., 1998—2003, electric utility restructuring oversight com., 1998—2003, pub. works and hwys. com., 2003—, rules com., 2003—, co-chair reproductive rights caucus, 1996—, mem. legis. caucus for children, 1997—2002. Participant in devel. series geometry insvc. workshops U. N.H., 1986-89. Area team Nat. Abortion Rights Action League of N.H., Portsmouth, 1990-94, bd. dirs., Concord, 1996-2000; chair Naral-Prochoice N.H. Pac; bd. dirs. Sexual Assault Support Svcs., Portsmouth, 1992-96, pres. bd., 1993-95; del. to Joint U.S.-China Conf. on Women's Issues, Beijing, 1995; organizing com. Bringing Back Beijing '95, Statewide Women's Conf., Concord, 1996, Beijing +5 Tri-State Preperation Conf., 1999; adv. bd. Feminist Health Ctr. Ports, Portsmouth, 1996-97; mem. Leadership Seacoast, 1995. Recipient NH Women's Lobby Meritorious Svc. award, 2002, Naral Pro-Choice N.H. Champion for Choice award, 2003, NASW-NH Legislator of Yr. award, 2004. Mem. Phi Beta Kappa, Phi Kappa Phi, Pi Mu Epsilon. Avocations: travel, arts and culture, running. Office: Rm 201 LOB State St Concord NH 03301

NOREM, RICHARD FREDERICK, SR., musician, music educator; b. Joliet, Ill., June 28, 1931; s. Oscar Lewis and Mabel Vera (Meyer) N.; m. Sally Lou Jarvis, July 24, 1954; 1 son, Richard Frederick II. Mus.B., U. Rochester, 1953, Mus.M., 1958; postgrad., Guildhall Sch., London, 1974. Instr. Joliet Musical Coll., 1951-53; tchr. Rochester Pub. Schs., N.Y., 1956-57; mem. faculty La. State U., Baton Rouge, 1957-95, prof., asst. dean music, 1969-84, prof. emeritus, 1995. Dir., sec.-treas. Bank Commerce, 1983-97; bd. dirs., sec.-treas. NBC Fin. Corp., 1988-97; mem. adv. bd. dirs. First Am. Tenn. Bank., 1997-99, AmSouth Bank, 1999-2002. Mem. Baton Rouge Symphony Orch., 1957—, Timm Woodwind Quintet, 1957-95; founder La. State U. Faculty Brass Quintet (now named Norem Brass Quintet of La. State U.), 1999. With USMC Band, 1953-56. Mem. Am. Legion (past post comdr.), Rolls-Royce Owners Club (sec.-treas. So. Delta region 1982-98, regional chmn. 1997-99), Norwegian Club Baton Rouge, La. State U. Faculty Club, Baton Rouge Model R.R. Club, Rotary. Republican. Episcopalian. Home: 4821 Sweetbriar St Baton Rouge LA 70808-8660 Office: La State U Sch Music Baton Rouge LA 70803-0001 *I have been blessed by the divine creator with an artistic talent in music to which I have dedicated my life. Early during my performing career I knew I must share with others the knowledge I had obtained in music; consequently my goals have been to train and educate the hundreds of music students I have taught during my teaching career. I have also tried to continue to bring beauty to our world in my own way as an active performing musician in the Baton Rouge Symphony Orchestra.*

NORFOLK, WILLIAM RAY, lawyer; b. Huron, S.D., Mar. 15, 1941; s. James W. and Helen F. (Thompson) N.; m. Marilyn E. Meadors; children: Stephanie G., Allison T., Meredith H. BA, Miami U., Oxford, Ohio, 1963; student, U. London, 1963-64; LLB, Duke U., 1967. Bar: N.Y. 1968, U.S. Dist. Ct. (so. and ea. dists.) N.Y. 1969, U.S. Ct. Appeals (2d cir.) 1969, U.S. Ct. Appeals (9th cir.) 1977, U.S. Ct. Appeals (5th cir.) 1979, U.S. Ct. Appeals (3d and 11th cirs.) 1981, U.S. Dist. Ct. (ea. dist.) Mich. 1986, U.S. Ct. Appeals (6th and 8th cirs.) 1986, U.S. Ct. Appeals (Fed. cir.) 1990, U.S. Ct. Internat. Trade 1990, U.S. Dist. Ct. (we. dist.) Mich. 1992. Assoc. Sullivan & Cromwell, N.Y.C., 1967-74, ptnr., 1974—. Mem. ABA, N.Y. State Bar Assn., Assn. of the Bar of the City of N.Y. Office: Sullivan & Cromwell 125 Broad St Fl 28 New York NY 10004-2489

NORGLE, CHARLES RONALD, SR., federal judge; b. Mar. 3, 1937; BBA, Northwestern U., Evanston, Ill., 1964; JD, John Marshall Law Sch., Chgo., 1969. Asst. state's atty. DuPage County, Ill., 1969-71, dep. pub. defender, 1971-73, assoc. judge, 1973-77, 78-81, cir. judge, 1977-78, 81-84; judge U.S. Dist. Ct. (no. dist.) Ill., Chgo., 1984—. Mem. exec. com. No. Dist. Ill.; mem. 7th Cir. Jud. Coun., 7th Cir. Jud. Conf. planning com., subcom. grant requests Fed. Defender Orgn., Fed. Defender Svcs. Com.; adj. faculty Northwestern U. Sch. Law, John Marshall Law Sch., Chgo.; pres. Atticus Finch Inn Ct. Mem. ABA, Fed. Bar Assn., Fed. Circuit Bar Assn., Ill. Bar Assn., DuPage County (Ill.) Bar Assn., Nat. Attys. Assn., DuPage Assn. Women Attys., Chgo. Legal Club, Northwestern Club. Office: US Dist Ct 219 S Dearborn St Ste 2346 Chicago IL 60604-1802

NORGREN, RALPH, neuroscientist; b. Washington, Mar. 22, 1943; BA, U. Pa., 1965; PhD, U. Mich., 1969. Postdoctoral Rockefeller U., N.Y.C., 1969-71, from asst. to assoc. prof., 1971-83; prof. Pa. State U. Coll. Medicine, Hershey, 1983—. Office: Pa State U Coll Medicine Dept Neural and Behavioral Sci 500 University Dr Hershey PA 17033-0850

NORGREN, WILLIAM ANDREW, retired religious denomination administrator; b. Frostburg, Md., May 5, 1927; s. William Andrew and Martha Elizabeth Leona (Richardson) N. BA, Coll. William and Mary, 1948; STB, now STM, Gen. Theol. Sem., N.Y.C., 1953; LittB, Oxford (Eng.) U., 1959; DD (hon.), Gen. Theol. Sem., N.Y.C., 1984, Berkeley Div. Sch. at Yale, 1995. Ordained to ministry Episcopal Ch., 1953. Chaplain Christ Ch. Cathedral, Oxford, 1955-59; exec. dir. Commn. on Faith and Order Nat. Coun. Chs. of Christ in U.S.A., N.Y.C., 1959-71, mem. gen. bd., 1979-95; pastoral asst. Trinity Ch., N.Y.C., 1972-74; assoc. ecumenical officer Episcopal Ch., N.Y.C., 1975-79, ecumenical officer, 1979-94, theol. cons., 1995-2000. Observer 2d Vatican Coun., Roman Cath. Ch., Vatican City, 1963-65; mem. assemblies World Co. Chs., various cities, 1961, 68, 83, 91. Editor: Living Room Dialogues, 1965, Implications of the Gospel, 1988, Toward Full Communion and Concordat of Agreement, 1991; author: Commentary on Called to Common Mission, 1999. Fellow Gen. Theol. Sem., 1953-55. Democrat. Episcopalian. Avocations: art, music, theater, walking.

NORIEGA, CAROLOS I. astronaut; b. Lima, Peru, Oct. 8, 1959; s. Rodolfo and Nora Noriega; m. Wendy L. Thatcher; 5 children. BS in Computer Sci., U. So. Calif., 1981; MS in Computer Sci., MS in Space Systems Ops., Naval Postgrad. Sch., 1990. Commd. 2d lt. USMC, 1981, advanced through grades to lt. col.; helicopter pilot Marine Corps Air Sta., Kaneohe Bay, Hawaii; base ops. officer Marine Air Base Squadron 24; aviation safety officer, instr. pilot MCAS, Tustin, Calif.; with U.S. Space Command, Colorado Springs, Colo., comdr. Space Surveillance Ctr.; staff 1st Marine Aircraft Wing, Okinawa, Japan; astronaut NASA, Houston, 1994—, mission specialist, 1996. Decorated Air medal with Combat Disting. Device, Air medal, Navy Achievement medal. Achievements include logged 461 hours in space; 19 EVA hours in 3 space walks; mem. crew on STS-84 (1997) and STS-97 (2000). Office: Astronaut Office/CB NASA Johnson Space Ctr Houston TX 77058

NORIEGA, ROGER FRANCISCO, federal agency administrator; b. Wichita, Kans., 1959; BA, Washburn U., 1981. Press sec, leg. asst. Congressman Bob Whittaker, US House Reps., 1983—86; sr. writer, editor USAID, Bureaus for Inter-Am. Affairs and Pub. Affairs, 1986—87, program off., 1987—90; sr. policy adv., alt. US rep. US Mission Organ. Am. States, Wash., 1990—93, sr. adv. publ. info., 1993—94; sr. staff mem. for com. internat. rels. US House Reps., Wash., 1994—97; sr. staff mem. for com. fgn. rels. US Senate, Wash., 1997—2001; perm. rep. US Dept. State, Organ. Am. States, Wash., 2001—03; asst. sec., bur. western hemisphere affs. U.S. Dept. State, Washington, 2003—. Bd. dirs. Inter-Am. Found. Named Gran Master of the Order of the Sun, Govt. Peru, 2001. Office: US Dept State Harry S Truman Bldg 2201 C St NW Rm 6262 Washington DC 20520

NORINS, ARTHUR LEONARD, physician, educator; b. Chgo., Dec. 2, 1928; s. Russell Joseph and Elsie (Lindemann) N.; m. Mona Lisa Wetzer, Sept. 12, 1954; children: Catherine, Nan, Jane, Arthur. BS in Chem. Engring, Northwestern U., 1951, MS in Physiology, 1953, MD, 1955. Diplomate: Am. Bd. Dermatology; subcert. in dermatopathology. Intern U. Mich., Ann Arbor, 1955-56; resident in dermatology Northwestern U., Chgo., 1956-59; asst. prof. Stanford U., 1961-64; prof., chmn. dept. dermatology, prof. pathology Ind. U. Sch. Medicine, Indpls., 1964-93, prof. emeritus, 1993—. Mem. staff Riley Children's Hosp., Univ. Hosp., Wishard Hosp.; cons. VA Hosp. Contbr. articles to profl. jours. Capt. M.C. U.S. Army, 1959-61. Recipient Pres.' award Ind. U., 1979 Fellow ACP; mem. Am. Acad. Dermatology (bd. dirs.), Am. Dermatol. Assn., Soc. Pediatric Dermatology (founder, past pres.), Am. Soc. Dermatopathology, Am. Soc. Photobiology (founder), Soc. Investigative Dermatology. Home: 10100 Torre Ave Apt 211 Cupertino CA 95014-2168 Office: 550 University Blvd Ste 3240 Indianapolis IN 46202-5149 E-mail: norinssr@ix.netcom.com.

NORKIN, CYNTHIA CLAIR, retired physical therapist; b. Boston, May 6, 1932; d. Miles Nelson and Carolyn (Green) Clair; m. Stanislav A Norkin, Feb. 19, 1955 (dec. 1970); 1 child, Alexandra. BS in Edn., Tufts U., 1954; cert. phys. therapist, Bouve Boston Coll., 1954; MS, Boston U., 1973, EdD, 1984. Instr. Bouve Boston Coll., 1954-55; staff phys. therapist New Eng. Med. Ctr., Boston, 1954-55, Abington (Pa.) Meml. Hosp., 1965-70, Ea. Montgomery Country Vis. Nurse Assn., 1970-72; asst. prof. phys. therapy Sargent Coll./Boston U., 1973-84; assoc. prof. phys. therapy, dir., founder Ohio U. Sch. Phys. Therapy, Athens, 1984-95, ret., 1995. Consult Boston Ctr Independent Living, Cambridge Vis Nurse Asn, Mass Medicaid Cost Effectiveness Project, 1978; secy Health Planning Coun Greater Boston, 1976—78; book, manuscript reviewer F A Davis Co, 1986—; arthritis adv comt Ohio Dept Health. Author (with P Levangie and C Norkin): Joint Structure and Function: A Comprehensive Analysis, 1983, 3d edit., 2001; author: (with D J White) Joint Measurement: A Guide to Goniometry, 1985, 3d edit., 2003. Trustee Brimmer and May Sch, 1980. Mem.: APHA, AAAS, Athens County Vis Nurse Asn (secy adv coun 1984—95), Mass Asn Mental health, Mass Physical Therapy Asn (chair quality assurance comt 1980—83), Am Physical Therapy Asn (on site evaluator comn on accreditation 1986—95). Episcopalian.

NORLAND, DONALD RICHARD, retired foreign service officer; b. Laurens, Iowa, June 14, 1924; s. Norman and Aletta (Brunsvold) N.; m. Patricia Bamman, Dec. 13, 1952; children: Richard Boyce, David, Patricia D. Student, Iowa State Tchrs. Coll., 1941-43, N.W. Mo. State Tchrs. Coll., 1943-44; BA, U. Minn., 1948, MS, 1950; postgrad., U. Mich., 1951-52, Grenoble (France) U., 1948-49. Instr. history and polit. sci. U. No. Iowa, 1949-51; teaching fellow U. Mich., 1951-52; with Fgn. Svc., U.S. Dept. State, 1952-81; posts include Rabat, Morocco, 1952-56, Washington, 1956-58, Abidjan, Ivory Coast, 1958-60; mem. NATO del., Paris, 1961-63, NATO delegation, The Hague, The Netherlands, 1964-69; dep. chief mission Conakry, Guinea, 1970-72; U.S. Dept. State fellow Stanford (Calif.) U., 1969-70; dep. dir. Office Mil. Assistance and Sales, Bur. Politico-Mil. Affairs, Dept. State, Washington, 1972-73, chief polit. officers counseling br. Office Pers., 1973-75; dep. dir. Office Mgmt. Ops., 1975-76; amb. to Botswana, Lesotho and Swaziland, 1976-79; amb. to Chad, 1979-81; ret. Fgn. Svc., U.S. Dept. State, 1981; lectr. African affairs; internat. cons., specialist econ. devel. Chmn. African studies Fgn. Svc. Inst. of U.S. Dept. of State, Washington, 1987-89; program dir. Ctr. for Internat. Pvt. Enterprise affiliate U.S. C. of C., Washington, 1990-91; sr. cons. World Space, Inc., 1995, sr. policy advisor, 1996—. Bd. dirs. Calvert New Africa Fund, 1995. Lt. (j.g.) USNR, 1943-46. Mem. Am. Fgn. Svc. Assn. (v.p. for retirees 1993-95, sec. 1995-97, mem. editl. bd. Fgn. Svc. Jour. 1992-95), World Space Found. (pres. 1997-98). Home: 4000 Cathedral Ave NW Apt 636B Washington DC 20016-5286

NORLING, RAYBURN, food service executive; b. 1934; Pres. Willmar (Minn) Poultry Co., Inc.; with Norling Farms, Inc., Svea, Minn., 1979—. Office: Willmar Poultry Co Inc 3735 County Road 5 SW Willmar MN 56201-9712

NORLING, RICHARD ARTHUR, health care executive; b. Waterbury, Conn., Dec. 9, 1945; s. Arthur and Alice Norling; m. Jeanne Marie Bone, Oct. 1, 1946; children: Jennifer, Stephanie. BS in Math., Tufts U., 1967; MS in Systems Engring., U. Ariz., 1969; MHA, U. Minn., 1975. Systems analyst Univ. Hosp., Tucson, 1969-70, mgr. systems engring., 1970-72, asst. to adminstr., 1972-73; adminstrv. resident Presbyn. Hosp. Ctr., Albuquerque, 1974-75; asst. dir. Calif. Med. Ctr., Los Angeles, 1975-77, assoc. dir., 1977-79, pres., exec. dir., 1979-86; exec. v.p. LHS Corp., Los Angeles, from 1986; former pres., CEO Fairview Hosp. and Healthcare Svcs., Mpls.; now chmn., CEO Premier Inc., San Diego. Mem. Joint Commn. on Accreditation of Healthcare Orgn.'s Adv. Group, 1993; chmn., Foun. for the Malcolm Balridge Nat. Quality Award, 2001-. Bd. mem. Am. Healthcare Systems, 1989, Augsburg Coll., 1992, Benefit Panel Svcs., 1991, Express Scripts, Inc., 1992, Hosp. Edn. and Rsch. Found., 1989, Minn. Bus. Partnerships, Inc., 1991.

Kings Fund fellow, 1984-90; named Emerging Health Care Leader Assn. of Western Hosps. Mem. Am. Hosp. Assn. (chmn. various coms., coun. on fin. 1980-83), Am. Coll. Healthcare Execs., Edina Country Club, Mpls. Club. Congregationalist. Avocations: golf, gardening, raquetball. Office: Premier Inc 12225 El Camino Real San Diego CA 92130

NORMAN, ALBERT GEORGE, JR., lawyer; b. Birmingham, Ala., May 29, 1929; s. Albert G. and Ila Mae (Carroll) N.; m. Catherine Marshall DeShazo, Sept. 3, 1955; children: Catherine Marshall, Albert George III. BA, Auburn U., 1953; LLB, Emory U., 1958; MA, U. N.C., 1960. Bar: Ga. 1957. Assoc. Moise, Post & Gardner, Atlanta, 1958-60, ptnr., 1960-62, Hansell & Post, Atlanta, 1962-86, Long, Aldridge & Norman, Atlanta, 1986-2000. Dir. Atlanta Gas Light Co., 1976-2000. Served with USAF, 1946-49. Mem. ABA, Ga. Bar Assn., Atlanta Bar Assn., Lawyers Club Atlanta (pres. 1973-74), Am. Law Inst., Am. Judicature Soc. (dir. 1975-78), Old War Horse Lawyers Club, (pres. 1991-92), Cherokee Town and Country Club. Episcopalian. E-mail: almarnorman@mindspring.com.

NORMAN, ALLINE L. health facility administrator; b. Homerville, Ga., Dec. 20, 1938; d. John F. and Alline D. N. BS, Ga. Coll., 1960; cert. Sch. for Med. Records, U.S. Pub. Health Svc., 1961. U.S. pub. svc. offcr. U. Cin., 1961-65; asst. chief and chief med. records U.S. Pub. Health Svc. Hosps., New Orleans, Chgo., Norfolk, 1965-70; chief med. info. section, Med. Adminstrn. Svc. VA Med. Ctr., N.Y., 1970-72, Miami, 1972-75, asst. chief Med. Adminstrn. Svc. East Orange, N.J., 1975-80, Miami, 1980-83, chief Med. Adminstrn. Svc. Augusta, Ga., 1983-85, chief field ops. divsn., Med. Adminstrn. Svc. Atlanta, 1988-89, from dep. dir. to dir. Med. Adminstrn. Svc., 1990-93, dir. Adminstrn. Svc. Office, 1993-94, dir. Lake City, Fla., 1994-97, ret., 1997, acting dir., 1998-99. Chmn. combined fed. campaign Vets. Health Adminstrn., 1991, co-chmn. chief med. dir.'s adv. com. on diversity, 1992-96, mem. task force subcom. on recommendations of commn. on future structure of vets. health car, 1992; mem. White House Nat. Health Care Task Force on Integration Govt. Sys., 1993, Sec.'s Adv. Group on Sexual Harassment, 1993-96, Interagy. Inst., 1993-94. Bd. dirs. Suwanee United Way, 1994-95, Lake City C.C. Found., 1995-96, Am. Cancer Soc., Lake City, 1995-96. Recipient Fed. Leadership award, 1992, cert. achievement Fed. Women's Interagency Bd., 1993, Sec. Meritorious Svc. award, 1994, Under Sec. Health Honor award, 1994. Mem. VA Sr. Execs. Assn. (bd. dirs. 1994). Methodist. Office: VA Med Ctr 801 S Marion St Lake City FL 32025-5827

NORMAN, ARNOLD MCCALLUM, JR., engineer; b. Little Rock, May 1, 1940; s. Arnold McCallum and Ann Carolyn (Gibson) N.; m. Sylvia Burton, July 1, 1962 (div. 1967); m. Marisha Irene Malin, June 7, 1969; children: Frank Lee, Paul James. BS in Physics, Ga. Inst. Tech., 1962. Test engr. Rocketdyne div. Rockwell Internat., Canoga Park, Calif., 1962-64, engr. in charge of various programs, 1964-75, engr. in charge, project engr. large chem. lasers, 1975-85, project engr. space sta. propulsion system, 1985-87, project engr. nat. launch system health mgmt. systems, 1987-92, project engr. kinetic energy weapons, 1993-94; project engr. advanced propulsion systems Rockwell Internat., Canoga Park, Calif., 1994-95, sr. engring. specialist, 1995-96; health mgmt. sys. team head, x-33 Aerospike rocket engine Boeing-N.Am. Rocketdyne Divsn., Canoga Park, Calif., 1996-97; cons. rocket propulsion sys., ops. and health mgmt., 1997—. Mem. ops. com. health mgmt. ctr. U. Cin., 1988-94; mem. program com. Ann. Internat. Conf. on Engring. Applications of Artificial Intelligence, 1988-90; presenter in field. Mem. editorial bd. Jour. Applied Intelligence, 1990-94; author numerous papers in field. Bd. dirs. Sebastopol Ctr. for Arts, 2000—, treas., 2003—. Fellow AIAA (assoc., sect. chair sr. adv. com. 1991-93, San Fernando Valley sect., chmn. 1989-90, sys. effectiveness & safety com. 1995-97), Inst. Advancement Engring; mem. Tau Beta Pi. Home: 4053 Bones Rd Sebastopol CA 95472-9756

NORMAN, BEN ERIC, mathematician, educator; b. Bogota, Colombia, July 25, 1967; s. Ben Burge and Cathy Norman. BS in Math., U. Calif., Davis, 1991, MA in Math., 1993. Part-time instr. math. Sacramento City Coll., 1993—; computer resource specialist U. Calif., Davis, 1997—. Author: (anthology) Honesty Awakened, 2002 (Merit award, 2002). Mem.: Math. Assn. Am. Avocations: Bible study, poetry. Office: Sacramento City Coll 3835 Freeport Blvd Sacramento CA 95822

NORMAN, BILL, information technology executive; married; 3 children. MBA, Northeastern U. Various mgmt. positions Digital Equipment Corp., 1976—94; from mem. staff to corp. v.p. Microsoft, Redmond, Wash., 1994, corp. v.p. Avocations: golf, time with family. Office: One Microsoft Way Redmond WA 98052-6399

NORMAN, BOBBY DON, artist, writer, research scientist; b. Dallas, June 5, 1933; s. Reuben Ray Norman and Bessie Mae Norman-Gregory; m. Mae Pearl Delley (dec. July 8, 2001); 1 child, Parette Michelle. Cert. grad.(hon.), S.W. Sch. Bus. Adminstrn., 1959. Mgr. Mile High Club, Dallas, 1955—57; city distbn. clk. U.S. Post Office, Dallas, 1956—66; office mgr., co-dir. So. Christian Leadership Conf., Dallas, 1969—73; cmty. liaison dir. Planned Parenthood N.E. Tex., Dallas, 1974—76; exec. v.p., gen. mgr. Davis Norman & Zanders, Inc., Dallas, 1977—78; house mgr., supr. Fed. Bur. Prisons, Dallas, 1982—83; supr. Halfway House Tex. Dept. Corrections, Dallas, 1983—84; artist, writer, scientist, publ. speaker Dallas, 1955—. Founder, pres. Assn. Advancing Artists and Writers, Inc., Dallas, 1969—72; active Internat. Platform Assn. Pub. Spkrs., Dallas, 1977—78. Author: Artistic Theological Science, 1998, Biblical Geology, 1998. Commr. Greater Dallas Cmty. Rels. Commn., 1970—72; mem. block partnership com. Greater Dallas Coun. Chs., 1970—71; organizer, tactical negotiator Dallas-Ft. Worth Coalition for the Free Flow of Info., 1970—72. Cpl. USAF, 1951—55, Korea. Recipient Tng. award, So. Christian Leadership Conf., 1969, Svc. award, Greater Dallas Cmty. Rels. Commn., 1972, Art award, Black C. of C., 1973. Mem.: Dallas Black C. of C. Baptist. Avocations: fishing, art. Office: Art Religious PO Box 191904 Dallas TX 75219-8509 Office Phone: 214-534-2584.

NORMAN, CHRISTINA, broadcast executive; b. July 30, 1963; m. Charles Hunt; children: Zoe, Asha. BA, Boston U. Freelance prodn. coord MTV, 1986—91, prodn. mgr., 1991—93, supervising prodr., on-air promotions, 1993—94, dir., on-air promotions, 1994—95, v.p., on-air promotions, 1995—97, sr. v.p., on-air promotions, 1997—99, sr. v.p., mktg. and on-air promotion, 1999—2002; exec. v.p. and gen. mgr. VH1, 2002—04, pres., 2004—. Named one of 10 Most Powerful Blacks in TV, Ebony mag., 2002; named to 100 Most Powerful Women in Hollywood list, Hollywood Reporter, 2003, 40 under 40 list, Crain's N.Y. Bus., 2003. Office: VH1 20th Fl 1515 Broadway New York NY 10036*

NORMAN, COLIN ARTHUR, astrophysics educator; b. Melbourne, Australia, May 3, 1948; came to U.S., 1984; s. Howard Arthur Norman and Jean Olice (Macgregor) Downing; m. Wen Shen, June 2, 1988; children: Alexandra Jean, Arthur Shen, Victoria Amelia. BE with honours, U. Melbourne, 1969; DPhil, Oxford U., 1973. Rsch. fellow Magdalen Coll., Oxford U., England, 1973—77, U. Calif., Berkeley, 1975—77; asst. prof. U. Leiden, Netherlands, 1977—84; prof. physics and astronomy Johns Hopkins U., Balt., 1984—, head acad. affairs div. Space Telescope Sci. Inst., 1987-91, head Hubble Fellow program Space Telescope Sci. Inst., 1991-94. Sr. rsch. fellow Inst. Astronomy, Cambridge, Eng., 1981-84, European So. Obs., Munich, 1983-84, 2000-03; vis. prof. U. Paris, 1983; Sackler lectr. Cambridge, 1995, Astor lectr. Oxford U., 2002; Prof. fellow U. Melbourne, 2002—. Editor: Stellar Populations, 1987, Quasar Absorption Lines, 1988, Massive Stars and Star Formations, 1991; contbr. articles to astrophysics jours. Rhodes scholar, 1970-73; recipient Perelberg prize Scotch Coll., Melbourne, 2002. Fellow Royal Astron. Soc.; mem. Am. Phys. Soc., Am. Astron. Soc., Amnesty Internat., Greenpeace, Johns Hopkins Club, Hamilton St. Club. Office: Johns Hopkins U Dept Physics and Astronomy Baltimore MD 21218 Office Phone: 410-516-7329.

NORMAN, DONALD ARTHUR, cognitive scientist; b. N.Y.C., Dec. 25, 1935; s. Noah N. and Miriam F. N.; m. Martha Karpati (dec.); children: Cynthia, Michael; m. Julie Jacobsen; 1 child, Eric BSEE, MIT, 1957; MSEE, U. Pa., 1959, PhD in Psychology, 1962; degree in psychology (hon.), U. Padua, Italy, 1995. Lectr. Harvard U., 1962-66; prof. dept. psychology U. Calif.-San Diego, La Jolla, 1966-92, prof. emeritus, 1992—, prof., chair dept. cognitive sci., 1988-92, chair dept. psychology, 1974-78; Apple fellow Apple Computer Inc., Cupertino, Calif., 1993-97, v.p. advanced tech., 1995-97, exec. info. appliances Hewlett Packard, Palo Alto, Calif., 1997-98; co-founder, prin. Nielsen Norman Group, Fremont, Calif., 1998—; pres. learning sys. UNext, 1999—2001; prof. dept. computer sci. Northwestern U., 2001—. Cons. to industry on human computer interaction and user-centered design. Author: Human Information Processing, 2d edit., 1977, Learning and Memory, 1982, User Centered System Design, 1986, The Psychology of Everyday Things, 1988, The Design of Everyday Things, 1989, 2002, Turn Signals Are the Facial Expressions of Automobiles, 1992, Things That Make Us Smart, 1993, The Invisible Computer, 1998, Emotional Design, 2004. Recipient Excellence in Rsch. award, U. Calif., 1983, Lifetime Achievement award, Computer Human Interaction. Fellow: Assn. Computing Machines, Cognitive Sci. Soc. (chmn., founding mem.), Human Factors & Ergonomics Soc., Am. Acad. Arts and Scis., Am. Psychol. Soc.; mem.: Am. Psychol. Assn., Inst. Design, IIT Chicago (trustee). E-mail: norman@nngroup.com.

NORMAN, E. GLADYS, retired business computer educator, consultant; b. Oklahoma City, June 13, 1933; d. Joseph Eldon and Mildred Lou (Truitt) Biggs; m. Joseph R.R. Radeck, Mar. 1, 1953 (div. Aug. 1962); children: Jody Norman, Ray Norman, Warren Norman (dec. May 1993), Dana Norman; m. Leslie P. Norman, Aug. 26, 1963 (dec. Feb. 1994); 1 child, Elayne Pearce. Student, Fresno (Calif.) State Coll., 1951-52, UCLA, 1956-59, Linfield Coll., 1986-95. Math. aid U.S. Naval Weapons Ctr., China Lake, Calif., 1952-56, computing systems specialist, 1957-68; systems programmer Oreg. Motor Vehicles Dept., Salem, 1968-69; instr. in data processing, dir. Computer Programming Ctr., Salem, 1969-72; instr. in data processing Merritt-Davis Bus. Coll., Salem, 1972-73; sr. programmer, analyst Teledyne Wah Chang, Albany, Oreg., 1973-79; sr. systems analyst Oreg. Dept. Vets. Affairs, Albany, 1979-80; instr. in bus. computers Linn-Benton C.C., Albany, 1980-95; ret., 1995. Computer cons. for LBCC Ret. Sr. Vol. Program, 1995-2002; presenter computer software seminars State of Oreg., 1991-93, Oreg. Credit Assoc. Conf., 1991, Oreg. Regional Users Group Conf., 1992; computer tchr. Linn-Benton C.C., 1999-2001; computer cons. Oremet-Wah Chang, 1996-2002, Oreg. State Yr. 2000 Project, 1997-98; adj. prof. Chemeketa C.C., 2000-02; computer cons. in field. Mem.: Assn. Info. Tech. Profls. (region treas. 1999, region sec. 2000—04), Data Processing Mgmt. Assn. (bd. dirs. 1977—84, assoc. v.p. 1988, bd. dirs. 1989—95, region sec. 1995—96, Diamond Individual Performance award 1985). Democrat. Avocations: drawing, painting, gardening. Personal E-mail: gladys33@quik.com.

NORMAN, FORREST ALONZO, lawyer; b. Renton, Pa., Nov. 21, 1929; s. Forrest Alonzo and Nellie Corley Norman; m. Christine Dende Norman, July 5, 1954; children: Sally, Forrest III, William. BBA, Western Res. U., 1952, LLB, 1954. Bar: Ohio 1954, U.S. Dist. Ct. (no. dist.) Ohio 1956, U.S. Supreme Ct. 1980. Assoc. Hauxhurst, Inglis, Sharp and Cull, Cleve., 1956-64; ptnr. Hauxhurst, Sharp, Mollison & Gallagher, Cleve., 1964-76, Gallagher, Sharp, Fulton and Norman, Cleve., 1976—. Pres. Fed. Ins. and Corp. Counsel, Walpole, Mass., 1981-82. Contbr. articles to profl. jours. Gen. chmn. Case Western Res. U. Ann. Fund, 1990-91. With USNR, 1947-52, U.S. Army, 1954-56. Recipient Disting. Svc. award Def. Rsch. Inst., 1979, 83, Centennial medal Case Western Res. U., 1995. Fellow Am. Coll. of Trial Lawyers, Ohio State Bar Found., Nat. Assn. R.R. Trial Counsel (bd. dirs. 1986—); mem. Order of Coif, Internat. Soc. Barristers, Am. Bd. Trial Advocates. Republican. Avocations: golf, gardening, reading. Home: 2977 Courtland Blvd Shaker Heights OH 44122-2803 Office: Gallagher Sharp Fulton & Norman 1501 Euclid Ave Ste 700 Cleveland OH 44115-2108 E-mail: fan@gsfn.com.

NORMAN, GREGORY JOHN, professional golfer; b. Mt. Isa, Australia, Feb. 10, 1955; m. Laura Norman, July 1, 1981; children: Morgan-Leigh, Gregory. Profl. golfer, 1976—; chmn., CEO Gt. White Shark Enterprises Inc., Hobe Sound, Fla. Winner Brit. Open Championship, 1986, 93, 18 PGA Tour titles, 68 additional internat. titles; winner Vardon trophy, 1989, 90, 94; recipient Arnold Palmer award for leading money winner, 1995, Byron Nelson trophy for the lowest scoring average, 1995; ranked #1 by Sony; named PGA Player of Yr., 1995, PGA Tour Player of Yr., 1995; named to World Golf Hall of Fame, 2001. Achievements include being the leading Money Winner PGA Tour 1986, 90.

NORMAN, JEAN REID, journalist; b. Phoenix, Feb. 13, 1957; d. James August and V. Janice (Radford) R.; m. James E. Norman, Jr., Dec. 30, 1982; children: James R., Janiece C. BS in Journalism, Northwestern U., 1979. Reporter Fallon (Nev.) Eagle-Standard, 1979-80; reporter, spl. sections editor North Las Vegas Valley Times, 1980-81; mng. editor Good Times, Santa Cruz, Calif., 1981-83; copy editor Daily Review, Hayward, Calif., 1983-85, Journal-Bulletin, Providence, R.I., 1986-89, Contra Costa Times, Walnut Creek, Calif., 1989, The Washington Post, 1990, USA Today Money Sect., Rosslyn, Va., 1990-93; mng. editor Navy Times, Springfield, Va., 1993-98; asst. metro editor Las Vegas Sun, 1998—. Vestry mem. St. Mark's Episcopal Ch., 1996-98. Democrat. Office: Las Vegas Sun 2275 Corporate Cir Ste 300 Las Vegas NV 89074 E-mail: jeanrnorman@earthlink.net.

NORMAN, JESSYE, soprano; b. Augusta, Ga., Sept. 15, 1945; d. Silas Sr. and Janie (King) N. B.M. cum laude, Howard U., 1967; postgrad., Peabody Conservatory, 1967; M.Mus., U. Mich., 1968; MusD (hon.), U. South, 1984, Boston Conservatory, 1984, U. Mich., 1987, U. Edinburgh, 1989, Cambridge U., 1989. Debut, Deutsche Oper, Berlin, 1969, Italy, 1970; appeared: in operas Die Walküre, Idomeneo, L'Africaine, Marriage of Figaro, Aida, Don Giovanni, Tannhauser, Gotterdammerung, Ariadne auf Naxos, Les Troyens, Dido and Aeneas, Oedipus Rex, Hérodiade, Les Contes d'Hoffmann; debut in operas, La Scala, Milan, Italy, 1972, Salzburg Festival, 1977, U.S. debut, Hollywood Bowl, 1972, appeared with, Tanglewood Festival, Mass., also Edinburgh (Scotland) Festival, debut, Covent Garden, 1972; appeared in 1st Great Performers recital, Lincoln Center, N.Y.C., 1973—; other guest performances include, L.A. Philharm. Orch., Boston Symphony Orch., Am. Symphony Orch., Chgo. Symphony Orch., San Francisco Symphony Orch., Cleve. Orch., Detroit Symphony, N.Y. Philharm. Orch., London Symphony Orch., London Philharm. Orch., BBC Orch., Israel Philharm. Orch., Orchestre de Paris, Nat. Symphony Orch., English Chamber Orch., Royal Philharm., London Phila. Orch., Milw. Symphony Orch., Stockholm Philharm. Orch., Vienna Philharm. Orch., Berlin Philharm. Orch.; tours, Europe, S. Am., Australia, numerous recs., Columbia, EMI, Philips Records; PBS TV spcls. include Kathleen Battle and Jessye Norman Sing Spirituals, 1991, Concert at Avery Fisher Hall, 1994; recordings include Amazing Grace, Brava, Jessye!, Jessye Norman at Notre Dame (Cable Ace award), Lucky to Be Me, Sacred Songs, With a Song in My Heart, In The Spirit. Nat. spokesperson Partnership for the Homeless, Lupus Found.; bd. mem. Ms. Found., Nat. Music Found., City-Meals-on-Wheels, N.Y.C., N.Y. Bot. Garden, Paine Coll., Augusta, Ga. Recipient 1st prize Bavarian Radio Corp. Internat. Music Competition, 1968, Grand Prix du Disque, Acad. du Disque Francais, 1973, 76, 77, 82, 84, Deutsche Schallplatten, Preis, 1975, 81, Alumni award U. Mich., 1982, Outstanding Musician of Yr. award Musical Am., 1982, Grand Prix du Disque Academie Charles Cros, 1983, Commandeur de l'Ordre des Arts et des Lettres, France, 1984, Grammy awards, 1980, 82, 85, Legion d'Honneur, France, 1989, Radcliffe medal Radcliffe Coll. Alumnae Assn., 1997, numerous other awards; named hon. life mem. Girl Scouts U.S., 1987; inductee Am. Classical Music Hall of Fame, 2002. Mem. Royal Acad. Music (hon.), Alpha Kappa Alpha, Gamma Sigma Sigma, Sigma Alpha Iota, Pi Kappa Lambda. Clubs: Friday Morning Music (Washington). Office: L'Orchidee PO Box S Crugers NY 10521-0710*

NORMAN, JOHN BARSTOW, JR., designer, educator; b. Paola, Kans., Feb. 5, 1940; s. John B. and Ruby Maxine (Johnson) N.; m. Roberta Jeanne Martin, June 6, 1967; children: John Barstow III, Elizabeth Jeanne. BFA, U. Kans., 1962, MFA, 1966. Designer and illustrator Advt. Design, Kansas City, Mo., 1962-64; asst. instr. U. Kans., Lawrence, 1964-66; art dir. Hallmark Cards, Inc., Kansas City, 1966-69; instr. dept. art U. Denver, 1969-73, asst. prof., 1973-78, assoc. prof., 1978-93, disting. prof., 1980-93, prof. emeritus, 1993—; sr. designer Mo. Coun. Arts & Humanities, 1966-67; cons. designer Rocky Mt. Bank Note Corp., Denver, 1971—. Cons. designer Signage identity System, U. Denver; bd. dirs. comm. U. Denver; tech. cons. Denver Art Mus., 1974—, designed exhbns, 1974-75; adv. cons. Jefferson County (Colo.) Sch. System, 1976—, chmn. Design and Sculpture Exhbn., Colo. Celebration of the Arts, 1975-76. One-man shows include GalleryCortina, Aspen, Colo., 1983; commd. works include Jedda, Saudi Arabia, Synegistics Corp., Denver; represented in permanent collections Pasadena Ctr. for Arts, N.Y. Arts Dirs. Club, Calif. State U./Fiber Collection, Pasadena Ctr. Arts, N.Y. Art Dirs. Club, Midland Art Coun./Fiber Collection, Geologic Soc. Am.; represented in traveling exhbns. L.A. Art Dirs. Show and N.Y. Art Dirs. Show, U.S., Europe, Japan, 1985; featured in Denver Post, 1984, Post Electric City Mag., 1984, Rocky Mt. News, 1984, Douglas County Press, 1984, Mile High Cable Vision, 1985, Sta. KWGN-TV, 1985, Les Krantz's Am. Artists, 1988; illustrated Survey of Leading Contemporaries, 1988, U.S. Surface Design Jour., 1988; co-work represented in film collectin Mus. Modern Art, N.Y.C.; selected fashion show designs displayed Sister City dels., Denver, 1987. Recipient Silver medal award N.Y. Internat. Film and Video Competition, 1976, Design awards Coun. ADvancement and Support Edn., 1969, 71, 73, 76, Honor Mention award L.A. Art Dirs. Club, 1984, Honor Mention award N.Y. ARt Dirs. Club, 1984, Native Am. Wearable Art Competition, 1985, 5th pl. Nat. Wind Sail Am. Banners Competition, Midland, Mich., 1985, also awards for surface designs in Colo. Ctr. for Arts Wearable ARt Competition, 1984-85, Foothills Art Gallery Nat. Wearable Competition, 1984-85, Fashion Group Denver Competition, 1984-85. Mem. Art Dirs. Club Denver (Gold medals 1974-82, Best of Show Gold medal 1983, Honor Mentin award 1984, 3 gold medals 1989), Univ. Dirs. Assn. Home: PO Box 507 Lake George CO 80827-0507

NORMAN, JOHN EDWARD, petroleum landman; b. Denver, May 22, 1922; s. John Edward and Ella (Warren) Norman; m. Hope Sabin, Sept. 5, 1946; children: J. Thomas, Gerould W., Nancy E., Susan G., Douglas E. BSBA, U. Denver, 1949, MBA, 1972. Clk., bookkeeper Capitol Life Ins. Co., Denver, 1940—42, 1945—46; salesman Security Life and Accident Co., Denver, 1947; bookkeeper Ctrl. Bank and Trust Co., Denver, 1947—50; automobile salesman H.A. Hennies, Denver, 1950; petroleum landman Continental Oil Co. (name changed to Conoco Inc. 1979), Denver, 1950—85; ind. petroleum landman, 1985; ind. investor, 1985—. Lectr. pub. lands Colo. Sch. Mines, 1968—83, lectr. mineral titles and landmen's role in oil industry Casper Coll., 1969—71. Mem. Casper Mcpl. Band Commn., 1965—71, mem. band, 1961—71, mgr., 1968—71; former musician, bd. dirs. Casper Civic Symphony; former bd. dirs. Jefferson Symphony, performing mem., 1972—75; mem. choir, vestryman, past dir. acolytes Episc. Ch. Served U.S. Army, World War II. Mem.: Rocky Mountain Petroleum Pioneers, Rocky Mountain Oil and Gas Assn. (pub. lands com. 1981—85), Denver Assn. Petroleum Landmen, Wyo. Assn. Petroleum Landmen (pres.), Assn. Petroleum Landmen (dir. at large, chmn. publs. for regional dir.), Elks. Episcopalian. Home and Office: 2710 S Jay St Denver CO 80227-3856

NORMAN, KENNETH GLEN, lawyer; b. Baytown, Tex., Mar. 25, 1944; s. Kenneth Glen and Eloise Fern (Crow) N.; m. Patricia L. Clark, June 17, 1978; children— Ashley Elizabeth, Chelsea Allison. B.A., Baylor U., 1966; J.D., U. Houston, 1973. Bar: Tex. 1973, Alaska 1975, U.S. Dist. Ct. Tex. 1974, U.S. Dist. Ct. Alaska 1975, U.S. Circuit Ct. (5th cir.) 1973, U.S. Ct. Appeals (9th cir.) 1975, U.S. Circuit Ct. (D.C. cir.) 1981, U.S. Supreme Ct. 1979, U.S. Tax Ct. 1982. Asst. atty. gen. State of Tex., Houston, 1973-74; asst. borough atty. Greater Anchorage Area Borough, 1974-75; asst. mcpl. atty. Anchorage Municipality, 1975-81, Cummings & Routh, 1981-83; sole practice, Anchorage, 1981-84; ptnr. Dobbs & Norman, Corpus Christi, Tex., 1983-84; counsel Cook Inlet Air Resources Mgmt. Dist., Anchorage, 1974-79; instr. environ. law Anchorage Community Coll., 1975— . Crusade atty., bd. dirs., exec. com. Alaska Billy Graham Crusade, 1982-84; elder 1st Presbyn. Ch., Anchorage, 1983— . Recipient Am. Jurisprudence award, 1970, 71; Bobbs-Merrill award, 1972; Fulbright, Crocker and Jaworski Law Rev. award, 1972; Matthew Bender award, 1973. Mem. ABA, Alaska Bar Assn., Tex. Bar Assn., Order of Barons, Phi Delta Phi, Comment and casenote editor U. Houston Law Rev., 1972-73; author: Litigation Manual for Code Enforcement Cases, 1980; contbr. articles on environ. law to profl. jours. Office: 4507 San Jacinto St Ste 400 Houston TX 77004-4949

NORMAN, LALANDER STADIG, retired insurance company executive; b. Binford, N.D., Apr. 10, 1912; s. John and Corinne (Stadig) N.; m. Garnet Johnston, Nov. 8, 1941; children: Eric John, Martha Mary Norman Neely, Carol Jean Norman Wellborn, Shirley Ann Norman Cook. AB, U. Mich., 1935, MBA, 1937. Actuarial asst. Central Life Ins. Co. of Ill., Chgo., 1937-40, mgr. Eastern dept., 1940-41; actuary Mich. Life Ins. Co., Detroit, 1941-43; asst. actuary Guarantee Mut. Life Co., Omaha, 1946-49; asso. actuary Am. United Life Ins. Co., Indpls., 1949, actuary, 1950-77, dir., 1959-77, v.p., 1962-69, sr. v.p., 1969-77; ret., 1977. Bd. mgrs. AUL Fund B, 1969-84, chmn., 1973-84; actuary Ind. Dept. Ins., 1977-79 Bd. dirs. Cyprus Village Assn., 1981, 1983—85. Served with USNR, 1943—46. Recipient Navy Commendation award, 1946, Theta Xi Distinguished Service award, 1958. Fellow Soc. Actuaries; mem. Am. Acad. Actuaries, Indpls. Actuarial Club (past pres.), Woodland Country Club (Carmel), Sugarmill Woods Golf and Racquet Club, So. Woods Golf Club, Phi Beta Kappa, Theta Xi (regional dir. 1953-59), Phi Kappa Phi, Beta Gamma Sigma. Republican. Home: Sugarmill Woods 21 Graytwig Ct W Homosassa FL 34446-4727 Office: 1 American Sq Indianapolis IN 46282-0020

NORMAN, MARY MARSHALL, alcohol/drug abuse services professional; b. Auburn, N.Y., Jan. 10, 1937; d. Anthony John and Zita Norman. BS cum laude, LeMoyne Coll., 1958; MA, Marquette U., 1960; EdD, Pa. State U., 1971. Cert. alcoholism counselor. Tchr. St. Cecilia's Elem. Sch., Theinsville, Wis., 1959-60; vocat. counselor Marquette U., Milw., 1959-60; dir. testing and counseling U. Rochester (N.Y.), N.Y., 1960-62; dir. testing and counseling, dean women, assoc. dean coll. Corning (N.Y.) C.C., Corning (N.Y.) C.C., 1962-68, asst. dean students, dir. student activities, asst. prof. ps University Park, 1962-68; rsch. asst. Ctr. for Study Higher Edn. Pa. State U., University Park, Pa., 1969-71; dean faculty South Campus C.C. Allegheny County, West Mifflin, Pa., 1971-72, campus pres., coll. v.p., 1972-82; pres. Orange County C.C., 1982-86; alcohol counselor Sullivan County Alcohol Drug Abuse Svc., 1985-90; sr. counselor Horton Family Program, 1990-96, ednl. cons., writer, 1996—. Cons. Boricua Coll., N.Y.C., 1976-77; reader NSF, 1977-78; mem. govtl. commn. com. Am. Assn. Cmty. and Jr. Colls., 1976-79, bd. dirs., 1982—; mem. and chmn. various middle state accreditation teams. Contbr. articles to profl. jours. Mem. Econ. Devel. Seneca County, Seneca County Tourism Bd.; active St. Patrick's Ch.; bd. dirs. Orange County United Way; bd. dirs. Orange County Alcoholism and Drug Abuse Coun., 1993—96; bd. dirs. Seneca County Hist. Soc., 1997—, Guild and Altar Soc., 1999. Mem. Nat. Women's Hall of Fame. Mem.: Pa. Coun. on Higher Edn., Nat. Am. Coun. on Edn. (Pa. rep. identification women for adminstrn. 1978—82, bd. dirs., pres. 1980—96), Pitts. Coun. Women Execs. (charter), Pa. Assn. Acad. Deans, Pa. Assn. Two-Yr. Colls., Am. Assn. Women in Cmty. and Jr. Colls. (charter, Woman of the Yr. 1981), Nat. Assn. Women Deans and Counselors, Am. Assn. Higher Edn., Seneca County C. of C. (bd. dirs., mem. tourism com.), Orange County C. of C. (bd. dirs.), Amnesty Internat. (charter mem. women's coun. 2000—), Concerned Citizens for Good Govt. (charter), Kiwanis (bd. dirs. Seneca Falls), Gamma Pi Epsilon. Home: 9 S Park St Seneca Falls NY 13148-1423

NORMAN, MELORA RANNEY, library director, educator; d. Lewis Putnam and Jean Turco; m. Steve Norman, Nov. 2, 2002; children: Phoebe, Siri; 1 child, Jessima Ranney. B in English-Writing Arts and Spanish, SUNY, Oswego, 1983; MLS, Syracuse U., 1986. Head circulation, instr. SUNY Agrl. & Tech. Coll., Morrisville, 1988—90; asst. registrar Tompkins Cortland C.C., Dryden, 1990—91; dir. Salina Free Libr., Mattydale, 1991—93; computer dept. head Liverpool Pub. Libr., Liverpool, 1993—93; dir. Charles M. Bailey Pub. Libr., Winthrop, Maine, 1994—2002; outreach coord. Maine State Libr., Augusta, 2002—. Webmaster Town of Winthrop, Winthrop, Maine, 2000—04; adj. instr. Ctrl. Maine Tech. Coll., Auburn, 2001—03. Webmaster Unitarian Universalist Ch., Brunswick, Maine, 2002—04. Mem.: ALA (intellectual freedom com. 2002—03, chair 2003—04, intellectual freedom round table),

Libr. Adminstrn. and Mgmt. Assn. (contbr. to developing profl. publ. 2000—02, SASS tech. svcs. com), Maine Intellectual Freedom Com. (co-chair 1995—2001), Maine Libr. Assn. (chpt. councilor 2001—03, exec. bd. 1995—, conf. com. 1995—), Rotary (winthrop rotary club pres. 1999—2000, Pres.'s Award 2000). Home: PO Box 176 Augusta ME 04332 Office: Maine State Libr 64 State House Sta Augusta ME 04333 Personal E-mail: melora@prexar.com.

NORMAN, PARALEE FRANCES, English language educator, researcher; b. Lubbock, Tex., Jan. 2, 1932; d. Hugh Redlingshafer and Hazel Irene (Brinegar) N. AB, U. Mo., 1954; MA, Drake U., 1959; PhD, U. Iowa, 1978. Cert. permanent prof., Iowa. Instr. English Mitchell Coll., New London, Conn., 1960-62; asst. prof. English W.Va. Weslyan U., Buckhannon, 1967-69, Marycrest Coll., Davenport, Iowa, 1969-70; instr. English Muscatine (Iowa) Community Coll., 1970-71; asst. prof. English Upper Iowa U., Fayette, 1978-79; prof. English Ft. Polk campus Northwestern State U. La., Leesville, 1979—, mem. grad faculty, 1991—. Cons. La. Com. for Humanities: Readings Am. Themes, Leesville-DeRidder, La., 1984; presenter 3d Internat. Short Story Conf., U. No. Iowa. Author: Marmion Wilme Savage 1804-1872: Dublin's Victorian Satirist, 2000; editor LCTE Coun. Notes, 1998-2002; contbr. articles and revs. to scholarly jours. Recipient Invitational Conf. award NEH and Vanderbilt, Phoenix, 1984, Cert. Appreciation Dept. Army, 1985, Officers' Wives Club, Ft. Polk, 1988, 91, commendations 5th Div. Tank Unit, Ft. Polk, 1989; grantee LEH, NEH, BESE for summer Tchrs. Inst., 1993, 2000. Mem. Nat. Coun. Tchrs. English (liaison officer 2003—), Irish-Am. Cultural Inst., La. Coun. Tchrs. English (sec., exec. com. 1990-92), La. Coun. Tchrs. English (1st v.p. 1992-94, pres. 1994-96), Victorian Soc. Office: Northwestern State U 3329 University Pkwy Leesville LA 71446-9041 E-mail: normanp@nsula.edu.

NORMAN, PHILIP SIDNEY, physician; b. Pittsburg, Kans., Aug. 4, 1924; s. P. Sidney and Mildred A. (Lawyer) N.; m. Marion Birmingham, Apr. 15, 1955; children: Margaret Reynolds, Meredith Andrew, Helen Elizabeth. AB, Kans. State Coll., 1947; MD cum laude, Washington U., St. Louis, 1951. Intern Barnes Hosp., St. Louis, 1951-52; resident Vanderbilt U. Hosp., Nashville, 1952-54; fellow Rockefeller Inst., 1954-56; instr. medicine Johns Hopkins U. Sch. Medicine, Balt., 1956-59, asst. prof., 1959-64, assoc. prof., 1964-75, prof., 1975—, chief allergy and immunology div., 1971-91. Editor Jour. of Allergy and Clin. Immunology, 1993-98; contbr. chpt. to books, articles to profl. jours. Served with USAAF, 1943-46; Served with USPHS, 1954-56. Fellow Am. Acad. Allergy (pres. 1975); mem. Am. Fedn. Clin. Research, Am. Assn. Immunologists, Am. Soc. Clin. Investigation, Am. Assn. Physicians, N.Y. Acad. Scis., Soc. Exptl. Biology and Medicine, Am. Thoracic Soc., Am. Clin. and Climatol. Assn., Johns Hopkins Med. Soc., Alpha Omega Alpha. Episcopalian. Office: Johns Hopkins U Asthma and Allergy Ctr 5501 Hopkins Bayview Cir Baltimore MD 21224-6821 Office Phone: 410-550-2300. Business E-Mail: pnorman@jhmi.edu.

NORMAN, RALPH LOUIS, physicist, consultant; b. Kingston, Tenn., Mar. 25, 1933; s. Walter Hugh and Helen Irene (Smith) N.; m. Agnes Irene Pickel, Sept. 5, 1964; children: Mark Alan, Max Alvin. BS, U. Tenn., 1959; LL.B., Blackstone Sch. Law, 1967, JD, 1971; certificate, Indsl. Coll. Armed Forces, 1969; MA in Pub. Adminstrn, U. Okla., 1971; D.Sci. (hon.), Apollo Research Inst., 1976. Engr. Chrysler Corp. Missile Div., Huntsville, Ala., 1959-60; physicist Army Rocket & Guided Missile Agy., Redstone Arsenal, Ala., 1960-61; asst. project mgr. Army Missile Command, Redstone Arsenal, 1961-62, project mgr., 1962-89, ret., 1989; cons. to several def. contractors, 1989—; faculty Athens (Ala.) Coll., 1970-71, Calhoun Jr. Coll., Decatur, Ala., 1971-74, 85-90, U. Montevallo, Ala., 1973-74, U. Ala. at Huntsville, 1976-77, Columbia (Mo.) Coll., 1977-79. Cons. firm Bishop and Sexton, 1973—, Athens (Ala.) State Coll.; reviewer NSF, 1974-76; FAA examiner. Contbr. articles profl. jours. Served with USN, 1951-55. Recipient Dept. Def. commendations, 1961, 65, Dept. Army commendation, 1972 Mem. N.Y. Acad. Scis., Assn. U.S. Army. Home: 102 Nobleton Ln NW Huntsville AL 35806-4014 *I strive to make the knowledge gained through my research benefit all mankind.*

NORMAN, STEPHEN PECKHAM, financial services company executive; b. Norwich, Conn., May 20, 1942; s. Richard Leonard and Mary Ellen (Carr) N.; m. Jacqueline Mary Batten, June 29, 1968; children— Adrian Gates, Hilary Batten, Philip Douglas, Matthew Jeremy Mitchell. BA, Yale U., 1964; JD, U. Pa., 1967. Bar: Conn. 1967, N.Y. 1972. Atty. Am. Express Co., N.Y.C., 1970-78, v.p. corp. office, 1978-82, sec., 1982—2003, corp. sec., chief governance officer, 2003—. Mem. bd. editors Corp. Governance. Sgt. U.S. Army, 1968—70, Vietnam. Mem. Am. Soc. Corp. Secs. (past chmn.). Clubs: Am. Yacht (Rye). Republican. Episcopalian. Home: 6 Highland Park Pl Rye NY 10580-1736 Office: Am Express Co 200 Vesey St New York NY 10285 Office Phone: 212-640-5583. E-mail: stephen.p.norman@aexp.com.

NORMAN, WILLIAM STANLEY, travel and tourism executive; b. Roper, N.C., Apr. 27, 1938; s. James Colbitt and Josephine Cleo (Woods) N.; m. Elizabeth Patricia Patterson, May 31, 1969; children: Lisa Renée, William Stanley II. BS, West Va. Wesleyan U., 1960; MA, Am. U., 1967; exec. program, Stanford U., 1976. Math. tchr. Washington High Sch., Norfolk, 1961; commd. USN, 1962; advanced through grades to comdr., 1973; naval flight officer Airborne Early Warning Squadron Eleven, 1962-65; asst. combat info. ctr. officer U.S.S. Constellation, 1965; staff officer air weapons systems analysis Office Chief Naval Ops., Pentagon, Washington, 1965-66; history and fgn. affairs instr. U.S. Naval Acad., 1967-69; social aide The White House, 1967-69; carrier div. staff officer SE Asia, 1969-70; spl. asst. to Chief Naval Ops. for Minority Affairs, 1970-72; asst. to Chief Naval Ops. for Spl. Projects, 1972-73; dir. corp. action Cummins Engine Co. Inc., Columbus, Ind., 1973-74, exec. dir. corp. responsibility, 1974-76; exec. mktg. mgr., 1976-77; exec. dir. distbn. mktg. Cummins Engine Co. Inc., Columbus, Ind., 1977-78; v.p. eastern divsn., 1978-79; v.p. sales and mktg. Amtrak, Washington, 1979-81, group v.p., 1981-84, exec. v.p., 1984-94; pres., CEO Travel Industry Assn. of Am., Washington, 1994—. Bd. dirs. Bestfoods Inc., Englewood Cliffs, N.J., Corn Products Internat., Bedford Park, Ill., Logistics Mgmt. Inst., McLean,Va. Bd. dirs. USN Meml. Found., Washington, 1980—, Internat. Consortium on Health Effects of Radiation, 1993—, An-Bryce Found., 1993—; bd. overseers Hospitality Industry Hall of Honor and Archives, 1995—; trustee W.Va. Wesleyan Coll., Buckhannon. Capt. USNR. Mem. Travel Industry Assn. Am. (bd. dirs. 1980—, chmn. bd. 1987-89, chmn. bd. dirs. of found. 1990-92), UN Assn. U.S. (bd. dirs. 1983—, bd. govs. 1985—), Coun. on Fgn. Rels., United Nations Assn. of U.S. (mem. nat. coun.), Travel and Tourism Govt. Affairs Coun. (bd. dirs. 1988—). Democrat. Episcopalian. Avocations: golf, tennis, jogging, walking, bicycling. Home: 1308 Timberly Ln Mc Lean VA 22102-2504 Office: Travel Industry Assn of Am Ste 450 1100 New York Ave NW Washington DC 20005-3934 Office Phone: 202-408-8422. E-mail: wnorman@tia.org.

NORMAN, WYATT THOMAS, III, landman, consultant; b. Austin, Tex., Dec. 30, 1952; s. Wyatt Thomas Jr. and Frances Claire (Bliss) N. BS in Agronomy, Tex. A&M U., 1975. Cert. profl. landman, environ. site assessor. Mgr. farm and ranch Bennett Bros., Inc., Pearsall, Tex., 1975-78; landman Corpus Christi, Tex., 1978—. Mem. Flour Bluff (Tex.) Vol. Fire Dept., 1984-90. Mem. Am. Assn. Profl. Landmen, Corpus Christi Assn. Profl. Landmen (exec. com.), Assn. Former Students, Century Club, Padre Isles Property Owners Assn., Internat. Game Fish Assn., Corpus Christi Town Club, Single Action Shooting Soc., Coastal Conservation Assn., Tex. Riviera Pistoleros, Paloma de Arcabus Club (charter, treas.). Republican. Presbyterian. Avocations: hunting, fishing, skiing. Home: 13946 Man O'War Ct Corpus Christi TX 78418-6340 Office: 615 Leopard St Ste 434 Corpus Christi TX 78476-2225 Personal E-mail: WTN111@aol.com.

NORMAND, GILBERT, government official; b. Montmagny, Que., Can., Mar. 31, 1943; BA, 1963; student, U. Montreal, 1965; MD, Laval U., 1970. Pvt. practice medicine, Montmagny, 1970-89; sec. of state Agr. and Agri-food, Fisheries and Oceans, Ottawa, 1997-99, Sci. Rsch. and Devel., 1999—. Mem. coun. physicians, dentists and pharmacists Hôtel-Dieu de Montmagny Hosp., 1970-97; dir. Dept. de santé communautaire de Montmagny, 1990-93; cons. physician Pub. Health Directorate of the Chaudière-Appalaches Regional Health and Social Svcs. Bd., 1993—; condr. health activities, Jamaica, 1968; active devel. "healthy cities, towns and villages" network, Senegal, 1993. Regional pres. Red Cross, Côte-du-Sud region, 1986-88; mem. founding bd. trustees Chaudière-Appalaches Health and Social Svcs. Bd., 1988-94; pres., exec. mem. Que. Healthy Cities, Towns and Villages network, 1988-94; mem. Health and Welfare Coun. Study Com., Que., 1993-95; founder Côte-du-Sud Tourism Bur., 1986, pres., 1986-93; dep. chair, then chair Côte-du-Sud Econ. Coun., 1986-93; chair econ. summit Chaudière-Appalaches region, 1990, chair regional coord. and devel. coun., 1988-92, bd. dirs. univ. svcs. founding corp., 1990-94; mayor City of Montmagny, 1985-93; asst. warden Regional County Municipality of Montmagny, 1987-93; elected MP for fed. riding of Bellechasse-Etchemins-Montmagny-L'Islet, 1997.

NORMAND, ROBERT, retired lawyer; b. Montreal, Que., Can., Sept. 24, 1936; s. Lucien and Eva (Rochon) N.; m. Madeleine Scott, Sept. 16, 1961; children: Eric, Yves, Genevieve. BA, U. Montreal, 1956; LLL, U. Sherbrooke, Que., 1960; diploma, Inst. d'etudes politiques, Paris, 1962. Bar: Que. 1960. Legal adviser Nat. Assembly, Quebec City, 1962-67, law clk., 1967-71; asst. dep. min. justice Que. Govt., Quebec City, 1970-71, dep. min. justice, 1971-77, dep. min. intergovtl. affairs, 1977-82, dep. min. fin., 1982-87; pres., pub. Le Soleil (Hollinger), Quebec City, 1987-93; v.p. corp. affairs UniMedia Inc., 1993-94, dep. min. internat. affairs, 1994-96; pres., dir. gen. Télé-Québec, 1996-99; ret., 1999. Sec. Study Com. on Expropriation 1965-67; guest prof. legis. law faculty Laval U., Ottawa U., 1971; pres. Que. Police Inst., 1974; chmn. Com. Supervising Olympic Security, 1974-76; chmn. Uniform Law Conf. Can.; dir. Caisse de Dèpot et Placement du Quèbec, 1982-87; v.p. Can. del. Diplomatic Conf. on travel contracts, Brussels, 1970; pres. Can. del. at convs. Internat. Inst. French Lang. law, 1974, 76. V.p. Hosp. du Saint-Sacrement, Quebec City, 1988-94; vice chmn. Inst. Rsch. on Pub. Policy, Montreal, 1988-94; pres. Que. Symphony Orch., Quebec City, 1989-92; consul gen. Sweden, Quebec City, 1989-94; co-pres. United Way Campaign Greater Quebec Region, 1989, hon. chmn. Telethon for Cerebral Palsy, 1990; mem. Citizens Forum, Spicer Commn., 1990-91; chmn. Ec. Nat. de l'Humour, 1997-99. Capt. Can. Army, 1954-60. Named Queen's Counsel, 1971, Comdr., Royal Order of the Polar Star, Sweden, Chevalier de la Legion d'honneur, France; recipient Pub. Adminstrn. award of excellence Nat. Sch. Pub. Adminstrn. Alumni, Quebec City, 1986. Mem. Investment Dealers Assn. Can. (dir. 1989-94), Que. Garrison Club (dir. 1991-96), Profl. Liability Ins. of Que. Bar (dir. 1991-94), Que. Bar (supervisory com. 1988-93), La Commanderie de Bordeaux. Roman Catholic. Avocations: fishing, hunting. Home: 2750 de L'Anse Sainte-Foy QC Canada G1W 2G5 E-mail: robenorm@videotron.ca.

NORMANDEAU, ANDRE GABRIEL, criminologist, educator; b. Montreal, Que., Can., May 4, 1942; s. Gabriel E. and Laurette D. (Sauve) N.; m. Pierrette La Pointe, Aug. 14, 1965; children: Alain, Louis, Jean. MA in Criminology, U. Pa., 1965, PhD in Sociology, 1968. Asst. prof. criminology U. Montreal, 1968-71, assoc. prof., 1971-76, prof., 1976—, chmn. dept. criminology, 1970-80, dir. Internat. Ctr. Comparative Criminology, 1983-89, dir. Rsch. Inst. on Police, 1990—. Author: Public Attitudes and Crime, 1970, The Measurement of Crime, 1975, Patterns of Robbery, 1980, Crimes of Violence, 1985, A Vision of the Police, 1990, Crime Prevention, 1993, Justice and Minorities, 1995, Community Policing, 1998, Death Penalty, 2003. Woodrow Wilson fellow, 1964-68 Mem. Internat. Soc. Criminology, Am. Soc. Criminology, Am. Sociol. Assn., Can. Criminal Justice Assn. Roman Catholic. Home: 3150 Ave Kent Montreal QC Canada H3S 1N1 Office: Dept Criminology U Montreal Montreal QC Canada H3C 3J7 Office Phone: 514-343-6111 ext 3999. Business E-Mail: andre.normandeau@umontreal.ca. *Happiness is achieved by working for it, not by waiting for it to come to you.*

NORMANN, MARGARET ELLA, deacon, educator; b. Providence, Jan. 13, 1931; d. Parker Edward and Margaret Millard (McDowell) Monroe; m. Conrad Neil Normann, July 17, 1953; children: Andrea Kristin Mudge, Margaret Ingrid Wierdsma, Conrad Neil, Parker Monroe. BA in Drama, Vassar Coll., 1952; MA in English, NYU, 1966; MS in Recreation and Leisure, So. Conn. State U., 1978. Ordained deacon Protestant Episcopal Ch., 1993. Human svc. officer, dir. recreation programs Town of Bedford, NY, 1975—83; cmty. edn. coord., writer, cons. Cmty. Residences Info. Svc. Program, White Plains, NY, 1983—91; initiator, exec. dir. Apropes Housing Opportunities and Mgmt. Enterprises, Inc., Bedford/Mount Kisco, NY, 1985—93; deacon Ch. of the Holy Communion, Mahopac, NY, 1993—; chaplain Four Winds Hosp., Cross River, NY, 1993—. Writing instr., tutor, evaluator SUNY Empire State Coll., Hartsdale, NY, 1984—. Recipient Disting. Svc. Alumnae award, Lincoln Sch., Providence, 1988, Cert. of Merit, State of N.Y., Albany, 1991, Mickey Leland Home for the Homless award, 1991. Republican. Home (Summer): Margaret House Box 591 Route 107 Bridgton ME 04009 Home (Winter): #511-513 1 Hamilton Heights Dr West Hartford CT 06119-6320

NORMENT, ERIC STUART, newspaper editor; b. Butler, Pa., July 26, 1956; s. Hillyer Gavin and Reva Lucille (Shepherd) N.; m. Ann Hobin, Aug. 22, 1987; chldren: Timothy Hobin, Peter John, Laura Mary, Daniel Hillyer. BA, U. Chgo., 1979; MS, Northwestern U., Evanston, Ill., 1980. Reporter Paddock Publs., Arlington Heights, Ill., 1980-83; asst. night editor Cape Cod Times, Hyannis, Mass., 1983; copy editor The Boston Herald, 1983-85, copy desk chief/news, 1985-87, features prodn. editor, 1987-88, asst. Sunday editor, 1988-94, Sunday editor, 1994—. Instr. journalism Northeastern U., Boston, 1984. Recipient Peter Lisagor Pub. Svc. award Chgo. Headline Club, 1981, Edn. Reporting award Ill. Press Assn., 1981. Office: 1 Herald St Boston MA 02118-2200 E-mail: enorment@bostonherald.com.

NORQUIST, JOHN OLAF, former mayor; b. Princeton, N.J., Oct. 22, 1949; s. Ernest O. and Jeannette (Nelson) N.; m. Susan R. Mudd, Dec. 1986; children: Benjamin Edward, Katherine Elisabeth. Student, Augustana Coll., Rock Island, Ill., 1967-69; BS, U. Wis., 1971, MPA, 1988. Assemblyman Wis. State Assembly, Madison, 1974-82, co-chmn. state joint com. fin., 1980-81; mem. Wis. State Senate, 82-88, asst. majority leader, 1984-85, 87; mayor City of Milw., 1988—2004. Adj. assoc. prof. Sch. Arch. U. Wis., Marquette U. Author: The Wealth of Cities, 1998. Bd. dirs. Congress for the New Urbanism. Sgt. USAR, 1971-77. Mem. Wis. Alliance of Cities, Congress for New Urbanism (bd. dirs.). Democrat. Presbyterian. Avocation: map collecting.

NORRBY, KLAS CARL VILHELM, pathology educator; b. Shanghai, Jan. 8, 1937; s. Åke Vilhelm and Ingrid Maria (Wedblad) N.; m. Ulla Margareta Hjort, June 17, 1961; children: Katarina, Cecilia, Jacob. BSc, Uppsala (Sweden) U., 1957; MB, Göteborg (Sweden) U., 1959, MD, 1964, PhD, 1970. Asst. prof. pathology Göteborg U., 1967-71; sr. lectr. in pathology Linköping U., 1972-84, chmn. Inst. Med. Microbiology and Pathology, 1980-84; prof. pathology, regal chair Göteborg U., 1985—; vis. prof. in cell biology Harvard Med. Sch., Boston, 1989-90; chmn. Inst. Labor Medicine Sahlgrenska U. Hosp., Göteborg, 1997-2000. Author over 200 articles to profl. jours. Sub.-lt. Royal Swedish Navy Med. Corps, 1972-86. Office: Sahlgrenska U Hosp Dept Pathology SE-41345 Göteborg Sweden

NORRID, HENRY GAIL, osteopathic physician and surgeon, researcher, educator, healthcare facility administrator; b. Amarillo, Tex., June 4, 1940; s. Henry Horatio and Johnnie Belle (Combs, Cummins) N.; m. Andreia Maybeth Hudson, Jan. 29, 1966 (dec. 1988); children: Joshua Andrew, Noah Adam; m. Cheryll Diane Payne, Mar. 19, 1989 (div. Aug. 2000); stepchildren: Kim Sheri Payne, Matthew Dominic Payne; m. Carolyn A. Layton, June 8, 2002; stepchildren: Crissey Ann Elizabeth Bruce, David Randall Marshall Bruce. AA, Amarillo Coll., 1963; BA, U. Tex., 1966; MS, W. Tex. State U., 1967; DO, Kirksville Coll., 1973. Diplomate Bd. Osteo. Physicians and Surgeons, Nat. Bd. Examiners Osteo. Physicians and Surgeons; cert. basic sci. tchr. Iowa, Tex., Colo. Intern Interboro Gen. Hosp., Bklyn., 1973-74; attending physician dept. gen. practice Osteo. Hosp. and Clinic N.Y., N.Y.C., 1974-77; gen. practice medicine specializing in osteo. Amarillo, Tex., 1978—; emergency care physician Amarillo Emergency Receiving Ctr. Amarillo Hosp. Dist., 1978-79, Ready Care Emergency Ctr., Arlington and Bedford, Tex., 1990-92, St. Anthony Hosp., Amarillo, 1992. Emeritus mem. consulting staff physician dept. family practice Northwest Tex. Hosp., Amarillo, 1995; emergency/trauma physician Tex. EM Care, 1995—; mem. mass casualty nat. disaster response team ARC, 1995; contract staff physician Tex. Tech. Univ. Sch. Medicine and Health Scis. Ctr., med. dept. and infirmary Tex. Dept. Corrections, Tex. Dept. Criminal Justice, 1992-94; med. cons. rehab. medicine vocat rehab. divsn. Tex. Rehab. Commn., Plano, 1992-94; cattleman, ranch owner, Van Zandt County, Tex.; lectr. osteo. prins. and practice, The Osteo. Hosp. and Clinic N.Y., 1974-77, mem. credentials com., 1975-76; mem. exec. com. Southwest Osteo. Hosp., Amarillo, 1983-84, chief of staff, 1984-85; sec. dept. family practice Northwest Tex. Hosp., Amarillo, 1981-82, mem. credentials com., 1984-85, joint practice com. dept. family practice, 1986-87; mem. orgnl. com. for devel. of dept. osteo. prins. and practices, chmn. N.Y.C. group N.Y. Coll. Osteo. Med., 1977; mem. founding com. N.Y. Coll. Osteo. Medicine, N.Y. Inst. Tech., Old Westbury L.I., 1976-77; mem. North Tex. Support Group, Dallas; instr. human anatomy and physiology dept. biol. scis. Amarillo Coll., 1998-2001, fall 2003. Contbr. articles to Tex. Jour. Sci., other publs. Scout physician Llano Estecato council Boy Scouts Am., Tex., 1978-85. Served to E-4 U.S. Army, 1956-63. Recipient William M. Giltner Meml. Fund award 1972, Humanitarian award Am. Cath. Conf., 1979, Century award Boy Scouts Am., 1982, Pfizer Sr. Med. Student award, 1973; Maxwell D. Warmer Meml. scholar 1973; scholar Kirksville Coll. Osteo. Medicine, 1970; Tex. Legislature scholar, 1969-73; named to Eminent Soc. Border Legionaires, 11th Armored Cavalry Regiment, Germany, 1958. Mem. Am. Coll. Gen. Practitioners, Tex. Osteo. Med. Assn. (pres. dist. I, mem. ho. of dels. 1981-82, 95), Tex. C.C. Tchrs. Assn., SAR, The Sons of Republic of Tex., Am. Congress Rehab. Medicine, Am. Osteo. Assn., World Future Soc. (profl.), Gen. Soc. War of 1812, Tex. & Southwest Cattle Raisers Assn., N.Y. Acad. Scis., Ex-Student's Assn. of The Univ. Tex. (life), 11th Armored Cavalry Regiment Assn., 36th (Tex.) Inf. Divsn. Assn. (life), Baron of the Magna Charta (Somerset chpt. Magna Charta Barrons 1994—), Masons, Am. Legion, Beta Beta Beta, Sigma Sigma Phi (pres. 1972), Alpha Phi Omega, Psi Sigma Alpha, Theta Psi, Theta Psi Clowns (1969-73). Avocations: astronomy, short wave listening, camping, fishing, anthropology.

NORRIS, ALAN EUGENE, federal judge; b. Columbus, Ohio, Aug. 15, 1935; s. J. Russell and Dorothy A. (Shrader) N.; m. Nancy Jean Myers, Apr. 15, 1962 (dec. Jan. 1986); children: Tom Edward Jackson, Tracy Elaine; m. Carol Lynn Spohn, Nov. 10, 1990. BA, Otterbein Coll., 1957, HLD (hon.), 1991; cert., U. Paris, 1956; LLB, NYU, 1960; LLM, U. Va., 1986; HLD (hon.), Capital U. Law Sch., 2001. Bar: Ohio 1960, U.S. Dist. Ct. (so. dist) Ohio 1962, U.S. Dist. Ct. (no. dist) Ohio 1964. Law clk. to judge Ohio Supreme Ct., Columbus, 1960-61; assoc. Vorys, Sater, Seymour & Pease, Columbus, 1961-62; ptnr. Metz, Bailey, Norris & Spicer, Westerville, Ohio, 1962-80; judge Ohio Ct. Appeals (10th dist.), Columbus, 1981-86, U.S. Ct. Appeals (6th cir.), Columbus, 1986—. Contbr. articles to profl. jours. Mem. Ohio Ho. of Reps., Columbus, 1967-80. Named Outstanding Young Man, Westerville Jaycees, 1971; recipient Legislator of Yr. award Ohio Acad. Trial Lawyers, Columbus, 1972. Mem. Ohio Bar Assn., Columbus Bar Assn. Lodges: Masons (master 1966-67). Republican. Methodist. Office: US Ct Appeals 328 US Courthouse 85 Marconi Blvd Columbus OH 43215-2823

NORRIS, ALBERT STANLEY, psychiatrist, educator; b. Sudbury, Ont., Can., July 14, 1926; s. William and Mary (Zell) N.; m. Dorothy James, Sept. 2, 1950; children: Barbara Ellen, Robert Edward, Kimberly Ann. MD, U. Western Ont., 1951. Intern Ottawa (Ont.) Civic Hosp., 1951-52; resident in psychiatry U. Iowa, Psychopathic Hosp., Iowa City, 1953-55, Boston City Hosp., 1955-56; practice medicine Kingston, Ont., Can., 1956-57; instr. Queen's U., Kingston, 1956-57; asst. prof. psychiatry U. Iowa, 1957-62, asso. prof., 1962-64, 1965-66, prof., 1966-72; asso. prof. U. Oreg., 1964-65; prof. So. Ill. U. Sch. Medicine, Springfield, 1972-84, chmn. dept. psychiatry, 1972-82; prof. emeritus, 1984—; practice medicine specializing in psychiatry, 1984—. Vis. prof. U. Auckland, N.Z., U. Otago, New Zealand, U. Liverpool. Contbr. chpts. to books, articles to med. jours. Fellow Am. Psychiat. Soc. (life); mem. AMA, Am. Psychopath. Assn., Soc. Biol. Psychiatry, Can. Psychiat. Soc., Am. Soc. Psychosomatic Ob-Gyn, Royal Soc. Medicine. Republican. Presbyterian. Home: 5 Penfro Dr Iowa City IA 52246-4927 Office: PO Box 1408 Cedar Rapids IA 52406-1408 *A life is only fulfilled by a quest, a vision of the future and a commitment to a greater value than one's self. A flickering candle is poor light, unless there is no other.*

NORRIS, ANDREA, government agency administrator; Dep. chief info. officer NASA, Washington. Office: NASA Headquarters Washington DC 20546

NORRIS, BRENT LANE, orthopedist; b. Louisville, June 14, 1962; MD, Med. Coll. Ga., 1989. Diplomate Am. Bd. Orthop. Surgeons. Intern U. Md., Balt., 1989—91, resident, 1991—93; resident in orthop. surgery U. N.C., Chapel Hill, 1993—95; fellow in orthop. trauma Carolinas Med. Ctr., Charlotte, NC, 1995—96; faculty Univ. Orthop. Assocs., Chattanooga, 1996—; asst. prof. orthop. surgery U. Tenn. Coll. Medicine, Chattanooga, 1998—. Office: Univ Tenn Coll Medicine 979 E 3d St Ste C-220 Chattanooga TN 37403-2178

NORRIS, CHARLES HEAD, prosecutor, manufacturing executive; b. Boston, Sept. 14, 1940; s. Charles Head and Martha Marie N.; m. Diana D. Strawbridge, July 27, 1974 (div. 1994); children: Margaret Dorrance, Cecilia Walker; m. Ceil T. Walker, Oct. 13, 2001. BA, U. Pa., 1963; JD, 1968; MA, U. Wash., 1965. Mem. Morgan, Lewis & Bockius, Phila., 1968-77; pres., chief exec. Artemis Corp., 1978-79; chmn. bd., chief exec., 1979-91; chmn. exec. com., vice-chmn. bd. Remington Rand Corp., 1979-81; ptnr. Artemis Energy Co., 1980-92; chmn., CEO Norris Investment Co., 1992—. Chmn. Norris Mfg. Co., 1994—, Garret Precision Products, 1996—; chmn., CEO AmTech Engring. Co., 1996—; trustee maj. stockholders' voting trust Campbell Soup Co., 1987-90; bd. dirs. SBSF Funds, Inc., 1988-91, Del. Trust, 1987-91. Mem. Harvard U. Overseas Com. to Visit Libr., 1989—; mem. Pa. Commn. to Crime and Delinquency, 1980-84; mem. Thouron Award Selection Com., 1985-90; mem. Pa. Electoral Coll., 1980; mem. West Pikeland Twp. Suprs., 1969-72; mem. bd. visitors Carnegie Mellon U. Sch. Urban and Pub. Affairs, 1988-90; corp. mem. Belmont Hill Sch., 1990—. Served with USAF, 1960. Mem. ABA, Pa. Bar Assn., Am. Econ. Assn., Phila., Knickerbocker, Vicmead Hunt, Everglades (bd. dirs. 1986-91, Bath and Tennis Club (treas., bd. dirs. 1985-91), Sunningdale Golf (Eng.), The Country (Brookline), Coral Beach and Tennis Club (Bermuda), Mid Ocean Club (Bermuda). Office: PO Box 112 Boston MA 02117-0112 Mailing: PO Box 772719 Memphis TN 38177-2719 Address: Clark Tower Exec Stes 5100 Poplar Ave Ste 2700 Memphis TN 38137

NORRIS, CHARLES MORGAN, laryngologist, educator; b. New Milford, Pa., Aug. 17, 1915; s. Ben Clark and Emma (Morgan) N.; m. Sarah Wistar Harwood, Nov. 6, 1948; children— Charles Morgan, Stephen Harwood. BS, Pa. State Coll., 1935; MD, Temple U., 1939; MS, 1944. Intern Temple U. Hosp, 1939-41, resident otolaryngology and broncho-esophagology, 1941-44; mem. faculty Med. Sch., 1944—, prof., chmn. dept. laryngology and broncho-esophagology, 1961-85. Recipient Alumni award Temple U., 1954 Mem. Am. Broncho-Esophalogical Assn. (pres. 1964-65), Pan. Am. Assn. Oto-Rhino-Laryngology and Broncho-Esophagology (sec. 1961-66), Internat. Bronchoesophagological Soc. (sec. 1961-83), Am. Laryngol. Assn. (pres. 1976-77), ACS, Am. Acad. Opthalomology and Otolaryngology, Am. Soc. Head and Neck Surgery (pres. 1973-74), Am. Laryngol., Rhinol. and Otol. Soc. (v.p. 1973-74), Am. Coll. Chest Physicians, Cricket Club. Home: 602 E Cathedral Rd Apt 9 Philadelphia PA 19128 Office: Chevalier Jackson Norris Clin 3401 N Broad St Philadelphia PA 19140-5103

NORRIS, CHUCK (CARLOS RAY), actor; b. Ryan, Okla., Mar. 10, 1940; m. Dianne Norris (div.); m. Gena O. Norris; children: Mike, Eric, Dina; stepchildren: Kelley, Tim. Appeared in: (films) The Wrecking Crew, 1969, Return of the Dragon, 1972, Breaker, Breaker, 1976, Good Guys Wear Black, 1977, Force of One, 1978, The Octagon, 1979, An Eye for an Eye, 1980, Silent Rage, 1981, Forced Vengeance, 1981, Lone Wolf McQuade, 1982, Missing in Action, 1984, Missing in Action II-The Beginning, 1985, Code of Silence, 1985, (co-screenwriter) Invasion, U.S.A., 1985, Delta Force, 1986, Firewalker, 1986, (co-screenwriter) Braddock: Missing in Action III, 1987, Hero and the Terror, 1988, Delta Force 2: Operation Stranglehold, 1990, The Hitman, 1991, (co-exec. prodr.) Sidekicks, 1993, Top Dog, 1995, Forrest Warrior, 1996; TV films Logan's War: Bound by Honor, 1998, The President's

Man, 2000, The President's Man: A Line in the Sand, 2002, Dodgeball: A True Underdog Story, 2004 (TV series) Walker: Texas Ranger, 1993-2001; author: The Secret Power Within Zen Solutions to Real Problems, 1996; (with Joe Hyams) The Secret of Inner Strength: My Story, 1988; host: The Ultimate Stuntman: A Tribute to Dar Robinson. Founder, pres. United Fighting Arts Fedn.; founder, chmn. Kick Drugs Out of Am. Profl. world middleweight karate champion, 1968-74

NORRIS, DARELL FOREST, retired insurance company executive; b. Pontiac, Mich., Oct. 19, 1928; s. Forest Ellis and Mabel Marie (Smith) N.; m. Thordis Marie Johansen, Aug. 21, 1955; children: Dara Lee, Jennifer, Lisa, Nancy. BS, U. Kans., 1950. CLU; ChFC. Reporter, mem. sports staff Kansas City (Mo.) Star, 1950-51; pilot TWA, 1955-58; divsn. agy. mgr. Merced (Calif.) region Farmers Group, Inc., 1959-62, sales rep. Colorado Springs (Colo.) region, 1962-64, regional agy. mgr., 1964-66, regional sales mgr. Santa Ana, Calif., 1966-69, mem. mgmt. tng. program staff, dir. agys. L.A., 1969—71, regional mgr. Austin, Tex., 1971-73, v.p. sales L.A., 1973-76, v.p. field ops. midwestern zone, 1976-79, v.p. field ops. western zone, 1979—. Pres. Farmers New World Mgmt. Co., 1977-81, v.p. staff ops., 1981-85, sr. v.p. life co. ops. and staff support svcs., 1985-90, farmers cons., 1990-93, gen. ins. cons., 1993—, vice chmn., 2. Vice chmn. bd. dirs. Northridge Hosp. Med. Found.; chmn. bd. deacons 1st Bapt. Ch., Granada Hills, Calif., 1977-89; sustaining mem. Rep. Nat. Com. Capt. USAF, 1951-55. Mem. Am. Soc. CLUs, ChFC, Ins. Edn. Assn. (trustee 1982-84). E-mail: DNorris268@aol.com.

NORRIS, FLOYD HAMILTON, financial journalist; b. L.A., Sept. 6, 1947; s. Floyd H. and Martha Leota (Buntin) N.; m. Mary Christine Bockelmann, Oct. 5, 1984; 1 child, John Buntin. Student, U. Calif., Irvine, 1965-68; MBA, Columbia U., 1982. Reporter Coll. Press Svc., Washington, 1969-70, Manchester (N.H.) Am., 1970-72, Concord (N.H.) Monitor, 1972-74, UPI, Vt. and Ala., 1974-77; press sec. Sen. John Durkin, Washington, 1977-78; fin. writer AP, N.Y.C., 1978-81; columnist Barron's, N.Y.C., 1982-88; fin. columnist N.Y. Times, N.Y.C., 1988-98, mem. editl. bd., 1998-99, chief fin. corr., 1999—. Recipient Gerald Loeb award for fin. journalism commentary and lifetime achievement. Office: N Y Times 229 W 43rd St New York NY 10036-3959 E-mail: norris@nytimes.com.

NORRIS, FRANKLIN GRAY, thoracic and cardiovascular surgeon; b. Washington, June 30, 1923; s. Franklin Gray and Ellie Narcissus (Story) N.; m. Sara Kathryn Green, Aug. 12, 1945; children: Gloria Norris Sales, F. Gray III. BS, Duke U., 1947; MD, Harvard U., 1951. Diplomate Am. Bd. Surgery, Am. Bd. Thoracic and Cardiovasc. Surgery, Am. Bd. Gen. Vascular Surgery. Resident Peter Bent Brigham Hosp., Boston, 1951-54, Bowman Gray Sch. Medicine, 1954-57, practice medicine specializing in thoracic and cardiovascular, 1957—. Prof. anatomy and physiology, Valencia C.C., Orlando, Fla., 1995—; pres. Norris Assocs., Orlando, 1985—; mem. staff Brevard Meml. Hosp., Melbourne, Fla., Waterman Meml. Hosp., Eustis, Fla., West Orange Meml. Hosp., Winter Garden, Fla., Orlando Regional Med. Ctr., Fla. Hosp., Lucerne Hosp., Arnold Palmer Children Hosp., Princeton, Fla. Hosp. N.E. and South (all Orlando). Bd. dirs. Orange County Cancer Soc., 1958-64, Ctrl. Fla. Respiratory Disease Assn., 1958-65. Capt. USAAF, 1943-45. Decorated Air medal with 3 oak leaf clusters. Mem. ACS, Fla. Heart Assn. (dir. 1958—), Orange County Med. Soc. (exec. com. 1964-75, pres. 1971-75), Ctrl. Fla. Hosp. Assn. (bd. dirs. 1980-85), Soc. Thoracic Surgeons, So. Thoracic Surg. Assn., Am. Coll. Chest Physicians, Fla. Soc. Thoracic Surgeons (pres. 1981-82), Am. Coll. Cardiology, So. Assn. Vascular Surgeons, Fla. Vascular Soc., Citrus Club, Orlando Country Club, Phi Kappa Psi. Presbyterian. (elder). Home: 1801 Bimini Dr Orlando FL 32806-1515 Office: Norris Assocs 1801 Bimini Dr Orlando FL 32806-1515 E-mail: fnorris8@hotmail.com.

NORRIS, GEOFFREY, geology educator, consultant; b. Romford, Essex, Eng., Aug. 6, 1937; came to Can., 1964; s. Alfred Frederick Henry and Winifred Lucy (Camps) N.; m. Anne Frances Facer, Sept. 20, 1958; children—Grant, Theresa, Brett, Sonia BA, Cambridge U., Eng., 1959, MA, 1962, PhD, 1964. Sci. officer N.Z. Geol. Survey, Lower Hutt, 1961-64; postdoctoral fellow McMaster U. Hamilton, Ont., Canada, 1965; rsch. scientist Pan Am. Petroleum, Tulsa, Okla., 1965-67; prof. U. Toronto, Canada, 1967—2003, chmn. dept. geology, 1980-90, prof. emeritus, 2003—. Ptnr. Austin and Cumming Exploration, Calgary, Alta., Can., 1980-87; vis. scientist Fla. Marine Rsch. Lab., St. Petersburg, 1986, Fla. Mus. Natural History, U. Fla., Gainesville, 1994; mem. Univ. Coll., 1993—; pres. Rosalex, Inc., 1996—; rswch. assoc. Royal Ont. Mus., Toronto, 1967—; A.V. Humboldt fellow Cologne U., West Germany, 1976. Contbr. articles to profl. jours. Pres. White Light Hospice Found., Toronto, 1987-96, 2003—; dir. Metro Toronto Residents Action Com. for Rail Safety, 1980-95; bd. dirs. Can. Geol. Found., 1997-02. Recipient numerous operating, equipment and travel grants, Nat. Scis. and Engring. Research Council of Can., 1967— Fellow Am. Assn. Stratigraphic Palynologists (pres. 1972), Royal Soc. Can. (sec. divsn. earth, ocean and atmospheric scis. 1990-92, dir. 1993-96), Geol. Assn. Can. (councilor 1987-90), Geol. Soc. Am.; mem. Can. Assn. Palynologists (pres. 1982), Internat. Commn. Palynology (sec.-treas. 1975-80), Internat. Union Geol. Scis. (Can. nat. com. 1990-98). Office: U Toronto Dept Geology Toronto ON Canada M5S 3B1 E-mail: rosalex@interlog.com.

NORRIS, GLENN L. lawyer; b. Clarinda, Iowa, Sept. 25, 1946; s. Harold E. and Darlene Louise (Crane) N.; m. Dale Bailey, Jan. 28, 1967 (div. June 1990); m. Tiffinny C. Sparks, Nov. 14, 1998; children: Christopher Steven, Catherine Beth, Glenn Leonard Jr., Janet Darlene. BA, Simpson Coll., 1968; JD with honors, U. Iowa, 1971. Bar: Iowa 1971, So. Dist. Iowa 1971, U.S. Dist. Ct., no. dist., Iowa, 8th circuit, 1972, U.S. Supreme Ct., 1976. Law clerk U.S. Dist. Judge Hanson, Ft. Dodge, Iowa, 1971-73; assoc. Hawkins, Hedberg & Ward, Des Moines, Iowa, 1973-78; ptnr. Hawkins & Norris, P.C., Des Moines, Iowa, 1978—. Editor: Iowa Academy of Trial Lawyers Handbook, 3d edit., 1999. Mem. tech. com. Iowa Supreme Ct. Commn. for Planning for 21st Century, 1996-98, Iowa Supreme Ct. Budget Adv. Com., 1997—; dir. men's chorus Sacred Heart Knights of Columbus. Recipient St. George award for Disting. Svc. to Cath. Scouting, Boy Scouts Am., Eagle Scout. Fellow Iowa Acad. Trial Lawyers; master C. Edwin Moore Am. Inn of Ct. (pres. 1998-2000); mem. Am. Bd. Trial Advs. (cert. civil trial advocate 2000—), Iowa State Bar Assn. (mem. fed. practice com. 1999—), Iowa Assn. Trial Lawyers (bd. govs. 1987-98). Roman Catholic. Home: 6205 Oakwood Hills Dr Johnston IA 50131-1962 Office: Hawkins & Norris PC 2501 Grand Ave Ste C Des Moines IA 50312-5311 E-mail: gnorrislaw@hotmail.com.

NORRIS, JAMES ARNOLD, federal agency administrator, consultant; b. Fargo, N.D., May 26, 1937; s. Cedric Leon and Gladys Louise (Arnold) N.; m. Catherine Anne Wright, Mar. 2, 1963; children: Suzanne, Erica, James. SB, MIT, 1959, SM, 1965; PhD, U. Calif., 1963. Economist US AID, Tunis, Tunisia, 1966-71, Jakarta, Indonesia, 1971-76, Cairo, 1976-80, dir. Bangladesh-India office Washington, 1980-82, mission dir. Dhaka, Bangladesh, 1982-84, Islamabad, Pakistan, 1988-92, Moscow, 1992-96, counselor to agy. Washington, 1984-85, dep. adminstr. Asia and Near East, 1985-88; project dir. Ralph M. Parsons Co., St. Petersburg, Russia, 1996-98; assoc. asst. adminstr. USAID, Washington, 1999; chief of party Chemonics Internat., Cairo, Egypt, 1999—. Recipient Presdl. Meritorious Svc. award President U.S., 1984, 87, Presdl. Disting. Svc. award President U.S., 1989. Address: Abdel Kader Hamza St #9 Garden City Cairo Egypt

NORRIS, JAMES HAROLD, lawyer; b. New Kensington, Pa., Sept. 18, 1953; s. J. Harold and Eleanore Rose (Arch) N.; m. Ann Marie Annase, Nov. 25, 1988; children: Ryan, Scott, Nicholas. BA, Washington Jefferson Coll., 1975; JD, Duquesne U., 1978. Bar: Pa. 1978, U.S. Dist. Ct. (we. dist.) Pa. 1978, U.S. Ct. Appeals (3d cir.) 1994, U.S. Dist. Ct. (no. dist.) W.Va. 1996, U.S. Supreme Ct., 2003. Assoc. Ruffin Hazlett Snyder Brown & Stabile, Pitts., 1979-83; ptnr. Eckert Seamans Cherin & Mellott, Pitts., 1983—; exec. v.p., gen. counsel Academy System; adj. prof. U. Pitts. Sch. Law. Chief counsel Allegheny Regional Asset Dist.; bd. dirs. Epilepsy Found. Western Pa., Western Pa. Growth Fedn., North Hills YMCA. Mem. Allegheny County Bar Assn., Pa. Bar Assn. (chmn. adminstrv. law sect. 1992-94, spl. achievement award 1993). Home: 2545 Country Side Ln Wexford PA 15090-7941 Office: Eckert Seamans Cherin & Mellott 600 Grant St Pittsburgh PA 15219-2702 Office Phone: 412-566-6159.

NORRIS, JOHN ANTHONY, health products executive, lawyer, educator; b. Buffalo, Dec. 27, 1946; s. Joseph D. and Maria L. (Suite) Norris; m. Kathleen E. Mullen, July 13, 1969; children: Patricia Marie, John Anthony II, Joseph Mullen, Mary Kathleen, Elizabeth Mary. BA, U. Rochester, 1968; JD, MBA with honors, Cornell U., 1973; cert., Harvard U., 1986. Bar: Mass. 1973. Assoc. Peabody, Brown, Boston, 1973-75; from assoc. to ptnr., exec. com., v.p., dir. Powers Hall, Boston, 1975-80; chmn. bd., pres., CEO, founder Norris & Norris, Boston, 1980-85; dep. commr., COO FDA, Washington, 1985-88, chmn. action planning and cap coms., 1985-88, chmn. reye syndrome com., 1985-87, chmn. trade legis. com., 1987-88; corp. officer, exec. v.p. Hill & Knowlton, Inc., N.Y.C., 1988-93; worldwide dir. Health Scis. Cons. Group., 1988-93; chmn. health scis. policy coun. Health Scis. Cons. Group, 1989-93; chmn. bd., pres., CEO, founder John A. Norris, Esq., PC, Boston, 1993—; pres., CEO Nat. Pharm. Coun., Reston, Va., 1995-96. Instr. Tufts Dental Sch., 1974—79, Boston Coll. Law Sch., 1976—80, Boston U. Law Sch., 1979—83, Harvard U. Pub. Health Sch., 1988—; mem. bd. editors FDA Drug Bull., FDA Consumer Report, 1985—88; bd. dirs. Summit Tech., Inc., Cytologics, Inc., Horus Therapeutics, Inc., Nat. Applied Scis., Med. Knowledge Processing, Inc.; trustee Caritas Christi Healthcare Sys. Editor-in-chief: Cornell Internat. Law Jour., 1971—73, founder, faculty editor-in-chief: Am. Jour. Law and Medicine, 1973—81, assoc. editor: Medicolegal News, 1973—75, reviewer: New Eng. Jour. Medicine Law Medicine Notes, 1980—81. Mem. U.S. Pres. Chernobyl Task Force, 1986, vice-chmn. health affects sub-com.; mem. Fed. Pain Commn.; chmn. Mass. Stuatory Adv. Com. Regulation Clin. Labs., 1977—83; mem. Mass. Gov.'s blue ribbon task force hosp. determination of need DON, 1979—80; chmn. Mass. Clin. Lab. Regulatory Commn.; mem. U.S. Intra-Govtl. AIDS Task Force, 1987; chmn. bd. dirs. Boston Holiday Project, 1981—83; bd. dirs. Mass. 4-H Found., 1982—2002, vice-chmn. bd. dirs., 1996—2002; chmn. U.S. del. Japan, Austria, Saudi Arabia, 1987, Finland, Denmark, Italy, 1986; chmn. Boston alumni and scholarship com. U. Rochester, 1979—85, mem. trustees coun., 1979—85, chmn. reunions; mem. exec. com. Cornell Law Sch. Assn., 1982—85, class pres., chmn. reunions; trustee Jordan Hosp., 1978—80, mem. exec. com., 1979—80, chmn. CEO search com., 1980; chmn. Joseph D. Norris, Esq. Health Law and Pub. Policy Fund, 1979—; mem. IOM Drug Devel. Forum, 1986—88, co-chmn. end points sub-com., 1987—88. With U.S. Army, 1972—73. Named one of Ten Outstanding Young Leaders award, Jaycees, 1982; recipient Kansas City Hon. Key award, 1988, award Merit, FDA, 1987—88, PHS award, 1987, HHS Sec. award, 1988; Comprehensive Health Planning fellow, 1970—73. Mem.: ABA (vice-chmn. medicine and law com. 1977—80), Internat. Coun. Global Health Progress (bd. dirs. 1989—95), Soc. Computer Applications Med. Care Informatics (bd. dirs. 1984—85), Am. Soc. Law and Medicine (1st v.p. 1975—80, chmn. bd. dirs. 1981—84, life mem. award 1981), Nat. Health Lawyers, Am. Soc. Hosp. Attys., Mass. Bar Assn., Phi Kappa Phi. Home: 531 W Washington St Hanson MA 02341-1067

NORRIS, JOHN HART, lawyer, director; b. New Bedford, Mass., Aug. 4, 1942; s. Edwin Arter and Harriet Joan (Winter) N.; m. Anne Kiley Monaghan, June 10, 1967; children: Kiley Anne, Amy O'Shea. BA, Ind. U., 1964; JD, U. Mich., 1967. Bar: Mich. 1968, U.S. Ct. Claims 1975, U.S. Tax Ct. 1979, U.S. Ct. Mil. Appeals 1969, U.S. Supreme Ct. 1974. From assoc. to ptnr. Monaghan, Campbell, LoPrete, McDonald and Norris, 1970-83; of counsel Dickinson, Wright, Moon, Van Dusen & Freeman, 1983-84, ptnr., 1985—; dep. asst. atty. gen. State of Mich., 1997—. Natural gas law counsel to claims mediator Columbia Gas Transmission Corp.; chpt. 11 bankruptcy procs. in Wilmington, Del. Bankruptcy Ct., 1992—; dep. asst. atty. gen. State Mich., 1997—; bd. dirs. Prime Securities Corp., Ray M. Whyte Co., Ward-Williston Drilling Co., One Stop Cap. Shop. Contbr. articles to profl. jours. Mem. Rep. State Fin. Com.; founder, co-chmn. Rep. Majority Club; bd. trustees Boys and Girls Clubs of Southeastern Mich., 1979—, Mich. Wildlife Habitat Found., Mercy Coll., Detroit, Detroit Hist. Soc., 1984—; bd. trustees, bd. dirs. African Wildlife Found.; trustee, 1st vice chmn. Salk Inst., dir. One Stop Capital Shop, Detroit, 1999—. Recipient numerous civic and non-profit assn. awards. Fellow Mich. State Bar Found.; mem. ABA (litigation and natural resources sects.), Mich. Oil and Gas Assn. (legal and legis. com.), State Bar Mich. (chmn. environ. law sect. 1982-83, probate and trust law sect., energy conservation task force, oil and gas com.), Oakland County Bar Assn., Detroit Bar Assn. (pub. adv. com.), Am. Arbitration Assn., Fin. and Estate Planning Coun. of Detroit, Def. Orientation Conf. Assn., Detroit Zool. Soc., Blue Key Nat. Hon. Fraternity, Phi Delta Phi. Clubs: Bloomfield Hills Country, Thomas M. Cooley, Detroit Athletic, Econ. (Detroit), Hundred, Prismatic, Turtle Lake, Yondotega. Roman Catholic. Home: 1325 Buckingham Ave Birmingham MI 48009-5881 Office: Dickinson Wright 38525 Woodward Ave Ste 2000 Bloomfield Hills MI 48304-2971 Office Phone: 248-433-7227. Business E-Mail: jnorris@dickinsonwright.com.

NORRIS, JOHN STEVEN, healthcare company executive; b. Chgo., Apr. 25, 1943; s. Norris Dale and Olive (Grissinger) N.; m. Susan Jean Armstrong, May 3, 1975; children: Lindsey Jean, Whitney Ann, John Scott. BA, U. Ariz., 1967; B in Fgn. Trade, Thunderbird, The Am. Grad Sch. Internat. Mgmt., 1968; MPH, U. Ariz., 1995. Diplomate Am. Coll. Healthcare Exec.; lic. nursing home adminstr., gen. contractor, real estate broker. Inspection officer Citicorp, Brazil, Columbia, Mex., 1968—73, asst. cashier NYC, 1973—74; pres., gen. mgr. Phoenix Athletic Club, 1974-76; bus. mgr. Phoenix Pub. Inc., 1976-77; project mgr. Environ. Constn. Co., Phoenix, 1977-79; pres. AGN Devel. Corp., Phoenix, 1979—, Valley View Realty, Inc., Phoenix, 1981-87; exec. v.p., sec., pres. RGW Constrn. Co., Inc.; pres. Norris/Roberts Group, Inc., Phoenix, 1987-90; CEO Christian Care Co., Inc., Phoenix, 1990—. Chmn. Covenant Health Network, 2001–. Ex officio bd. dir. Christian Care Inc.; bd. dirs. Promise Endowment, 1st Christian Ch., Dove's Transitional Housing, Inc., Alliance Purchasing Network; bd. dirs., chmn. region 1 Area Agy. Aging. Recipient award of honor Ariz. Assn. Homes and Svc. for Aging, 1999. Fellow: Am. Assn. Home Svcs. Aging (retirement housing profl.), Am. Coll. Healthcare Adminstrs.; mem.: Rotary Internat. (treas., past pres. Phoenix club, Paul Harris fellow, Service Above Self award 2002), Phi Delta Theta. Republican. Avocations: golf, skiing, racquetball. Home: 111 W Tam O'Shanter Dr Phoenix AZ 85023-6241 Office: Christian Care Cos 2002 W Sunnyside Dr Phoenix AZ 85029-3534 Office Phone: 602-443-5411. E-mail: jnorris@christiancare.org.

NORRIS, LONNIE HAROLD, dean; b. Houston, Nov. 22, 1942; m. Donna M. Farmer, June 18, 1966; children: Marlaina M., Michael A. BA in Chemistry, Fisk U., 1964; DMD, Harvard U., 1976, MPH, 1977. Asst. prof. oral & maxillofacial surgery Tufts U. Sch. Dental Medicine, Boston, 1981-88, assoc. prof., 1988-95, prof., 1995—, interim dean, 1995-96, dean, 1996—. Mem. com. dental accreditation. Mem. Gov.'s commn. Study Oral Health Staus and Accessibility Dental Care Svcs. Residents Commonwealth Mass. Named Disting. Practitioner, Nat. Acads. Practice, Dentist of the Yr., New Eng. chpt. Pierre Fauchard Acad. Fellow: Internat. Coll. Dentists, Am. Bd. Oral/Maxillofacial Surgery, Am. Assn. Oral/Maxillofacial Surgeons, Am. Coll. Dentists, Am. Acad. Dental Sci., Phi Beta Kappa, Omicron Kappa Upsilon. Avocation: travel. Office: Tufts U Sch Dental Medicine 1 Kneeland St Boston MA 02111-1527 Office Phone: 617-636-6636. E-mail: lonnie.norris@tufts.edu.

NORRIS, MELVIN, lawyer; b. Cambridge, Massachusetts, Aug. 17, 1931; BA, Northeastern U., Boston, 1954; JD, Boston Coll., 1959. Bar: Mass., 1959, U.S. Supreme Ct., 1965. Atty. FTC, Boston, 1960—62; pvt. practice Boston, 1962—76; ptnr. Norris, Kozodoy, Krasnoo, and Fong, Boston, 1976—90, Norris, Kozodoy, and Fong, Boston, 1991—96; pvt. practice Wayland, Mass., 1997—. Ethics com. for govt. lawyers Supreme Jud. Ct., Mass., 1999-2000. Bd.of editors Mass. Lawyers Weekly, 1984-93. Vice-chmn. Newton Crime Commn., 1966-67; mem. Newton Bldg. Code Revision Com., 1972-73; chmn. bd. dirs., pres. Waterville Estates Assn., Campton, N.H., 1992-94. With USCG, 1954-56. Mem. Fed. Bar Assn. (pres. Boston chpt. 1977-78, v.p. 1st cir. 1978-99, exec. com. 1982-83, Cert. Appreciation 1996, Mass. chpt. Outstanding Leadership Award 1999), Mass. Bar Assn. Office: 260 Boston Post Rd Ste 9 Wayland MA 01778

NORRIS, PAMELA MARIE, mechanical engineer, educator; b. Portsmouth, Va., Sept. 21, 1965; d. Danny Owen Norris and Nancy Light Clark; m. Edward Eric Lamb, June 13, 1999; 1 child, Abigail Marie Lamb. BS in Mech. Engring. and Mechanics, Old Dominion U., Norfolk, VA; MS in Mech. Engring., Ga. Insitute of Tech., Atlanta; PhD in Mech. Engring., Ga. Inst. of Tech., Atlanta. Vis. postdoctoral rsch. engr. and lectr. U. Calif., Berkeley; asst. prof. U. Va., Charlottesville, assoc. prof. Dir. Aerogel rsch. lab. U. Va., Charlottesville, 1996—, dir. microscale heat transfer lab., 1994—. Recipient Disting. Spkr. award, Soc. of Automotive Engineers, 1989, Tchg. Excellence award, Ctr. for the Enhancement of Tchg. and Learning, 1992, Ga. Tech. Outstanding Young Engring. Alumni award, Ga. Inst. Tech., 1996, VEF Faculty Fellow, U. of Va., 2002; grantee, NSF, 1995. Mem.: ASME (chair k-21 com. on heat transfer edn. 2001), Am. Soc. for Engring. Edn. Achievements include patents in field; patents pending in field. Office: Univ Va 122 Engineer's Way Charlottesville VA 22904-4746

NORRIS, RICHARD PATRICK, museum director, historian, educator; b. Galveston, Tex., May 21, 1944; s. William Gerard and Iris Elsa (Allington) N.; m. Therese Louise Aalid, July 27, 1974; children: William Gerard, John Patrick. BA, Ohio State U., 1966; MA, SUNY, Binghamton, 1968; PhD, U. Minn., 1976. Instr. U. Minn., Mpls., 1970-76; lectr. U. Md., Europe/Asia, 1976-78; dir. Chippewa Valley Mus., Eau Claire, Wis., 1978-80, Kalamazoo Valley Mus., 1985—; curator of history Mus. Sci. & Hist., Fort Worth, 1980-85. Lectr. Tex. Christian U., Fort Worth, Tex., 1981—85; cons. Am. Assn. Mus., Washington, 1979—, NEH, Washington, 1989; adj. prof. We. Mich. U., Kalamazoo, 1986—. Author: History by Design, 1984; book reviewer Mus. News, History News; contbr. articles to profl. jours. Mem.: Assn. Midwest Mus., Internat. Coun. Mus., Am. Assn. State and Local History, Am. Assn. Mus., Rotary (dir. Kalamazoo club 1991—93, pres. 1999—2000). Office: Kalamazoo Valley Museum PO Box 4070 Kalamazoo MI 49003-4070 E-mail: rnorris@kvcc.edu.

NORRIS, ROBERT WHEELER, lawyer, military officer; b. Birmingham, Ala., May 22, 1932; s. Hubert Lee and Georgia Irene (Parker) N.; m. Martha Katherine Cummins, Feb. 19, 1955; children— Lisha Katherine Norris Utt, Nathan Robert BA in Bus. Adminstrn., U. Ala., 1954, LL.B., 1955; LL.M., George Washington U., 1979; postgrad., Air Command & Staff Coll., 1968, Nat. War Coll., 1975. Commd. 2d lt. USAF, advanced through grades to maj. gen., dep. judge advocate gen., 1983-85, judge advocate gen., 1985-88; gen. counsel Ala. Bar Assn., Montgomery, 1988-95; ptnr. London & Yancey, Birmingham, Ala., 1995—2002; ret. Decorated D.S.M., Legion of Merit, Meritorious Svc. medal.

NORRIS, TRACY HOPKINS, retired public relations executive; b. Ainsworth, Iowa, Nov. 1, 1927; s. Lee E. and Ruth C. (Simpson) N.; m. Emilie Lathrop, Nov. 11, 1956; 1 child, Shawn Tracy. BA, Cornell Coll., Mt. Vernon, Iowa, 1952; MA, U. Iowa, 1957. Admissions counselor Cornell Coll., Mt. Vernon, 1952—54; dir. news bur. Wittenberg U., Springfield, Ohio, 1956—70; exec. dir. univ. rels. and comm. Ball State U., Muncie, Ind., 1970—88; ret., 1988. Active United Way Springfield, Ohio, Muncie, 1965—. Served with USN, 1945-48. Recipient Silver Anvil award Pub. Rels. Soc. Am., 1967. Mem. Coun. for Advancement and Support Edn., Exch. Club. Lutheran. Avocations: golf, travel, lawn and garden activities. Home: PO Box 2329 Muncie IN 47307 Personal E-mail: tnorris629@aol.com.

NORRIS, WILLIAM ALBERT, retired judge; b. Turtle Creek, Pa., Aug. 30, 1927; s. George and Florence (Clive) Norris; m. Jane Jelenko, Feb. 17, 1991; children: Barbara, Donald, Kim, Alison, David Jelenko. Student, U. Wis., 1945; BA, Princeton U., 1951; JD, Stanford U., 1954. Bar: Calif. 1955, D.C. 1955. Assoc. Northcutt Ely, Washington, 1954—55; law clk. to Justice William O. Douglas U.S. Supreme Ct., Washington, 1955—56; sr. mem. Tuttle & Taylor, Inc., L.A., 1956—80; judge U.S. Ct. Appeals (9th cir.), L.A., 1980—94; lawyer Folger, Levin & Kahn, L.A., 1997—2000, mediator, 1997—; sr. counsel Akin Gump Strauss Hauer & Feld, LLP, 2000—. Spl. counsel Pres.' Kennedy's Com. on Airlines Controversy, 1961; mem. Calif. State Bd. Edn., 1961—67; mem. bd. dir. L.A. Eye Inst., 2001—. Trustee Calif. State Colls., 1967—72, Craft and Folk Art Mus., 1979—87; pres. L.A. Bd. Police Commrs., 1973—74; founding pres., trustee Mus. Contemporary Art, L.A., Calif., 1980—92; Dem. nominee for atty. gen. State of Calif., 1974. With USN, 1945—47. Office: Akin Gump Strauss Hauer & Feld LLP Ste 2400 2029 Century Park E Los Angeles CA 90067 Office Phone: 310-229-1047. Business E-Mail: wnorris@akingump.com.

NORRIS, WILLIAM C. retired computer systems executive; b. Inavale, Nebr., July 14, 1911; s. William H. and Mildred A. (McCall) N.; m. Jane Malley, Sept. 15, 1943; children: W. Charles, George, Daniel, Brian, Constance, Roger, Mary N., David. BS, U. Nebr., 1932. Sales engr. Westinghouse Electric Mfg. Co., Chgo., 1935-41; v.p., gen. mgr. Engring. Research Assocs., 1946-55, Univac (div. Sperry Rand Corp.), 1955-57; pres. Control Data Corp., Mpls., 1957-77, past chmn., also bd. dirs.; chmn. William C. Norris Inst., Bloomington, Minn., 1988—. Bd. dirs. N.W. Bank Corp., N.W. Growth Fund, Tronchemics, Inc. Trustee Hill Reference Library; adv. com. White House Conf. on Balanced Nat. Growth and Econ. Devel., 1978— . Served to comdr. USNR, 1941-46. Recipient Nat. Medal Tech., 1986. Office: William C Norris Inst 2001 Killebrew Dr Ste 302 Bloomington MN 55425-1886

NORRIS, WILLIAM ROBERT, engineer, researcher; b. Ft. Kent, Maine, Dec. 28, 1963; m. Julie Marie Hansen, Sept. 18, 1998; children: Josh, Jeremy, Sean. BS, U. Ill., 1996, MS, 1997, PhD, 2001. Rsch. asst. Constrn. Engring. Rsch. Lab., Champaign, Ill., 1995—2001, Nat. Ctr. Supercomputer Applications, Urbana, Ill., 1996—2001; staff engr. Deere and Co., Moline, Ill., 2001—. Contbr. articles to profl. jours. Staff sgt. U.S. Army, 1986—92. Decorated Meritorious Svc. medal US Army, Army Commendation (2 awards), Army Achievement (3 awards); named Rsch. Asst. of Yr., Corps Engrs., 2000; recipient Best Paper award, Internat. Conf. Systemics, Cybernetics and Informatics, 2001, hon. mention, Internat. ASAE Conf., 2001, William A. Chittenden award, UIUC. Mem.: VFW, ASME, IEEE, Am. Assn. for Artifical Intelligence, Am. Soc. of Agrl. Engr., Soc. of Automotive Engr., Autism Soc., Mensa, Am. Legion, Alpha Epsilon, Gamma Epsilon, Sigma Xi, Tau Beta Pi, Phi Kappa Phi. Achievements include development of a method for incorporating human operators in (virtual a reality based rapid prototyping) system design; discovery of new method for and type of fuzzy logic system for multi-objective autonomous vehicle control; method for reducing rule base sizes through for incorporating control strategies. Avocations: robotics, computers, travel, reading, weightlifting, artificial intelligence. Office: Deere and Company John Deere Tech Ctr 1 John Deere Pl Moline IL 61265-8098 Office Phone: 309-765-3743. E-mail: norriswilliamr@johndeere.com.

NORSTRAND, HANS PETER, lawyer, real estate public official, municipal official; b. Cambridge, Mass., Aug. 1, 1940; s. Hans Donald and Marion (Hardy) N.; m. Janet Hoover, Dec. 30, 1967 (div.); children: Rachel Bell, Hans Christopher; m. Katherine Tallman, Feb. 5, 1994. AB, Dartmouth Coll., 1963; JD, Boston Coll., 1966. Bar: Mass., 1966; U.S. Supreme Ct., 1994. Asst. atty. gen., Mass., 1966-69; assoc. Sullivan & Worcester, Boston, 1969-74; v.p., gen. csl Kuras & Co., Inc., Boston, 1974-76; pvt. practice Boston, 1977-80; v.p., gen. counsel Boston Co. Real Estate Counsel, Inc., 1980-81; prin. Aldrich, Eastman & Waltch, Boston, 1981-91; mng. dir. Sun Capital Adv.,Inc., Boston, 1991-93; prin. State St. Global Advs., 1994—99; v.p. ASB Capital Mgmt., Inc., 1999; pvt. practice Brookline, Mass., 2000; dir. real estate Commonwealth of Mass. Divsn. Capital Asset Mgmt., Boston, 2000; dir. real estate and dep. commr, divsn. capital asset mgmt. Commonwealth of Mass., Boston, 2001—. Office: 1 Ashburton Pl 15th Fl Boston MA 02108 Office Phone: 617-727-8090. E-mail: ksthpn@aol.com., HPeter.Norstrand@state.ma.us.

NORSWORTHY, ELIZABETH KRASSOVSKY, lawyer; b. N.Y.C., Feb. 26, 1943; d. Leonid Alexander and Wilma (Hudgens) Krassovsky; m. John Randolph Norsworthy, June 24, 1961 (div. 1962), m. Nov. 26, 1977 (div. 1984); 1 child, Alexander. AB magna cum laude, CUNY, 1965; MA, U. N.C., 1966; JD, Stanford U., 1977. Bar: D.C. 1978, Mass. 1992, Vt. 1998, U.S. Ct. Appeals (D.C. cir.) 1979. Atty. applications, disclosure rev. and investment adviser regulation, divsn. investment mgmt. SEC, Washington, 1978-79, 80-82, atty. operating brs. and disclosure policy divsn. corp. fin., 1979-80, chief, spl. counsel office of regulatory policy divsn. investment mgmt., 1983-86; assoc. Kirkpatrick & Lockhart, Washington, 1986-90; ptnr. Sullivan & Worcester, Boston, 1990-92; pvt. practice Norfolk, Mass., 1992; pvt. practice in juvenile law Concord, Vt., 1996—. Pub. arbitrator, chairperson NASD; mediator, facilitator Cmty. Justice Ctr., St. Johnsbury. Mem. North Country Chorus, Wells River; chair investment com. North Congl. Ch., St. Johnsbury; mem. adv. bd. Natural Resources, Concord. Mem.: Vt. Coverts, Vt. Grass Farmers, Am. Farmland Trust, Jacob Sheep Breed Assn., Am. Livestock Breed Conservancy, Vt. Bar Assn. (ADR com., family law com.), College Club (St. Johnsbury), Athenaeum (St. Johnsbury), Catamount Arts Club (St. Johnsbury), Phi Alpha Theta, Phi Beta Kappa. Democrat. Mem. United Church of Christ. Avocations: farming, swimming, singing, environmental protection. Office: Winterbrook Farm 1342 Woodward Rd Concord VT 05824-9620 Fax: 602-695-2516. Office Phone: 802-695-1408. E-mail: ekn@kingcon.com.

NORSWORTHY, LAMAR, petroleum company executive; b. 1946; With Holly Corp., Dallas, 1967—, pres., 1971-75, treas., from 1975, now chmn., pres.; chmn., pres. Navajo Refining Co., Artesia, N.Mex., 1982—. Office: Holly Corp 100 Crescent Ct Ste 1600 Dallas TX 75201-6927 also: Navajo Refining Co 501 E Main St Artesia NM 88210-9606

NORTELL, BRUCE, lawyer; b. Nov. 19, 1946; s. Joseph and Dorothy Nortell; children: Adam, Daniel, Anthony. AB, Boston U., 1968; JD, U. Chgo., 1971. Bar: Ill. 1971, U.S. Dist. Ct. (no. dist.) Ill. 1971, U.S. Supreme Ct. 1979. Sole practice, Chgo., 1971—74; asst. dir. legal affairs AMA, Chgo., 1974—81, counsel, sec. jud. coun., 1976—81; dir. tax and fin. planning Loyola U., Chgo., 1981—88, North Ctrl. Coll., Naperville, Ill., 1988—. Contbr. articles to profl. jours.; author two books novels. Mem.: ABA, Chgo. Bar Assn., Ill. Bar Assn. (Lincoln award 1975), Phi Beta Kappa (bd.). Home: 1124 Dickens Ln Naperville IL 60563-4301 Office: 30 N Brainard St Naperville IL 60540-4607

NORTH, A. FREDERICK, physician; b. Milw., July 3, 1931; s. Alexander F. and Florence (Reineking) N.; m. Jane Whittlesey, Dec. 18, 1954; children: Lindsay Elizabeth, Robert Whittlesey, Wendy Katherine. Student, Yale Coll., 1953; MD, Yale U., 1956. Intern Strong Meml. Hosp., Rochester, N.Y., 1956-58, resident pediatrics, 1960-62; instr. pediatrics U. Rochester, 1962-66; sr. pediatrician Project Head Start, Washington, 1966-68; assoc. prof. pediatrics George Washington U., Washington, 1968-72; assoc. med. dir. Children's Hosp. of D.C., Washington, 1968-72; vis. prof. pediatrics, pub. health U. Pitts., 1972-79; physician for retarded persons Govt. of D.C., Washington, 1978-88; pvt. practice in pediat. Rockville, Md., 1988—. Cons. various locations, 1966-88. Author: Infant Care, 1980; contbr. articles to publs. Lt. USNR, 1958-60. Fellow Acad. of Pediatrics, Am. Pub. Health Assn.; mem. Am. Pediatric Soc., Ambulatory Pediatric Assn. (pres. 1966-67), Chevy Chase Club. Republican. Episcopalian. Home: 5703 Overlea Rd Bethesda MD 20816-1918 Personal E-mail: afnorth@msn.com.

NORTH, DANNY L. music educator; b. Pocatello, Idaho, Apr. 29, 1960; s. Virgil Lewis and Bertie Lee North; m. Leslie North, May 19, 1982; children: Stewart, Camille, Alex, Carl, Tasia. M in Music Edn., VanderCook Coll. of Music, Chgo., 1994; B in Music Edn., Idaho State U., Pocatello, 1987. Band and speech tchr. Madison H.S., Rexburg, Idaho, 1987—. Mem.: Idaho Music Educators Assn. (pres. 2002—04). Office: Madison HS 134 Madison Ave Rexburg ID 83440

NORTH, DOUGLAS MCKAY, academic administrator; b. Albany, N.Y., Oct. 14, 1940; s. Henry Saxe and Elsie (Sewell) N.; m. Ellen Cole, Dec. 10, 1975; children: Jeffrey, Lisa, Anton, Gabriel. BA, Yale U., 1962; MA, Syracuse U., 1964; PhD, U. Va., 1970. Asst. prof. SUNY, New Paltz, 1964-67, Wesleyan U., Middletown, Conn., 1970-71; prof. Goddard Coll., Plainfield, Vt., 1973-81, dir. devel., 1982-89; pres. Prescott (Ariz.) Coll., 1989—94; prof., pres. Alaska Pacific U., 1995—. Contbr. articles to profl. jours. Dept. Edn. grantee, Washington, 1988-91. Mem. Nat. Consortium Single Parent Educators (bd. dirs. 1988—). Office: Office of Pres 4101 University Dr Anchorage AK 99508 E-mail: dnorth@alaskpacific.edu.

NORTH, DOUGLASS CECIL, economist, educator; b. Cambridge, Mass., Nov. 5, 1920; s. Henry Emerson and Edith (Saitta) North; m. Elisabeth Willard Case, Sept. 28, 1972; children from previous marriage: Douglass Alan, Christopher, Malcolm Peter. BA, U. Calif., Berkeley, 1942, PhD, 1952; D in Natural Scis. (hon.), U. of Cologne, Federal Republic of Germany, 1988, U. Zurich, Switzerland, 1993, Stockholm Sch. of Econs., Sweden, 1994, Prague Sch. Econs., 1995. Asst. prof. econs. U. Wash., 1950—56, assoc. prof., 1957—60, prof., 1960—83, chmn. dept., 1967—79, prof. emeritus, 1983—; dir. Inst. Econ. Research, 1960—66, Nat. Bur. Econ. Research, 1967—87; Spencer T. Olin prof. in arts and scis. Washington U., St. Louis, 1983—. Pitt prof. Am. history and instns. Cambridge U., 1981—82; fellow Ctr. for Advanced Study on Behavioral Scis., 1987—88. Author: The Economic Growth of the U.S. 1790-1860, 1961, Growth and Welfare in the American Past, 1966; author: (with L. Davis) Institutional Change and American Economic Growth, 1971; author: (with R. Miller) The Economics of Public Issues, 1971, 1974, 1976, 1978, 1980; author: (with R. Thomas) The Rise of the Western World, 1973; author: Structure and Change in Economic History, 1981, Institutions, Institutional Change and Economic Performance, 1990. Recipient Nobel Prize in Econ. Sci., Nobel Found., 1993; fellow Guggenheim Found., 1972—73; grantee, Social Sci. Rsch. Coun., 1962, Rockefeller Found., 1960—63, Ford Found., 1961, 1966, NSF, 1967—73, Bradley Found., 1986—. Fellow: Am. Acad. Arts and Scis.; mem.: Econ. History Assn., The Brit. Acad. (corr.), Am. Econ. Assn. Office: Dept Economics Rm 305 Elliot Hall Box 1208 Saint Louis MO 63130

NORTH, E(DWARD) LEE, retired writer, former aerospace company professional; b. Englewood, NJ, June 2, 1924; s. Edward Louis North and Genevieve Jean (Smith) North Francais; m. Florence Kirkland Hennen, Aug. 29, 1945; children: Patrick Lee, Diane North Goncalves. *Father (1900-60) Lt. Col. U.S. Army veteran of WWI and II. Civil Engineer, built many roads, bridges, and jetties, mainly on LI. Mother (1904-96) Belle of Wethampton Beach won many ballroom dancing competitions and will never be forgotten by her children and grandchildren. Grandfather Charles W. North (1862-1942) of Guilford Lake, NY, was a successful farmer, astronomer, and swimmer. Grandmother Elizabeth Brome North (1862-1946), a lovely lady whose ancestry traced back to royalty (Henry III) through her Canfield and Wiloughby forebears.* BA, Washington & Jefferson Coll., 1946. Sports editor Washington (Pa.) Reporter, 1947-49; publicity dir. Washington and Jefferson Coll., 1949-51; writer, editor Grumman Aerospace Corp., Bethpage, N.Y., 1951-78, proposal mgr., 1978-89. Hon. consul Free Polish Govt., London, 1980-95. Author: For This One Hour, 1970, Redcoats, Redskins, and Red-Eyed Monsters: A human-interest history of West Virginia, 1979, Battling the Indians, Panthers, and Nittany Lions, 1991, The Fifty-Five West Virginias, 1998, Mark of the White Wolf, 2000, Snowflakes on the Don, 2002; co-author (with Jane Wyman): Chris, the Rhode Island Wonder Dog, 1993. Chmn. Good Govt. Party, Suffolk County, NY, 1956—57; bd. of policy Liberty Lobby, Washington, 1975—2001; chmn. Islip Town (NY) Conservative Party, 1970s; hist. Brightwaters Village, 1990—. Recipient Gold Cross of Merit Free Poland Govt., 1985. Mem.: Phi Kappa Psi, The Authors Guild, Football Writers of Am., Am. Edn. Assn. (bd. dirs. 1992—), Rep. Nat. Com., Assn. of Pub. Historians of N.Y. State. Episcopalian. Avocations: tennis, golf, bridge, Scrabble, study of wolves. Home: 55 Woodland Dr Brightwaters NY 11718 E-mail: north444@aol.com.

NORTH, GERALD DAVID WILLIAM, lawyer; b. N.Y.C., Feb. 15, 1951; s. David North and Isabella (Leonard) Cadgene; m. Jeanne Curtis, Nov. 1970 (div. 1977); m. Carmela Benvenuto, Feb. 21, 1980; 1 child, David II. BA (hon.) with distinction, U. Iowa, 1972, JD with high distinction, 1975; postgrad., Oxford (Eng.) U., 1975-76. Bar: Iowa 1975, Ill. 1977, U.S. Dist. Ct. (no. dist.) Ill. 1977, U.S. Supreme Ct. 1982, U.S. Dist. Ct. (no. dist. trial bar) Ill. 1983, U.S. Ct. Appeals (fed. cir.) 1984, Ariz. 1985, U.S. Dist. Ct. Ariz. 1985, U.S. Ct. Appeals (9th cir.) 1985. Assoc. Sidley & Austin, Chgo., 1976-81; ptnr. Brace & North, Chgo., 1981-82; v.p., gen. counsel Trans-Global Group, Chgo., 1983-84; of counsel McCabe, Polese, Pietzsch, Phoenix, 1984-87; founder, shareholder North & Barron, Phoenix, 1987-92; sr. shareholder North & Vaira, Phila., Phoenix, 1992-93; prin. counsel IMPRA, Inc., Phoenix, 1984-93; chmn. bd. Fibrin Techs., Inc., Wilmington, Del., 1993-97; prin. counsel MinTec, Inc., Freeport, Bahamas, 1995-96; bd. dirs. Fenders Auto Leasing Inc., Vancouver, Can., 1996-97; asst. sec. Summit Spirits, Ltd., Grand Cayman, Cayman Islands, 1998—; prin. counsel Am. German Gold Bond Holders Assn., Quincey, Ill., 2003—. Contbg. author: European Investment in U.S. and Canadian Real Estate, 1990, Directory of Asian High Tech Companies in the U.S., 1991. Fellow Ariz. Bar Found.; past mem. ABA (antitrust sec. 1975-93) Am. Intellectual Property Law Assn., Assn. Trial Lawyers Am., Fed. Cir. Bar Assn., Univ. Club (Chgo.), United Oxford and Cambridge Club (London), Legal Club (Chgo.); mem. National Club (Moscow), Monte Carlo Country Club, Desert Mtn. Club, Order of Coif, Phi Beta Kappa, Omicron Delta Kappa. Avocation: weightlifting.

NORTH, HELEN FLORENCE, classicist, educator; b. Utica, NY; d. James H. and Catherine (Debbold) N. AB, Cornell U., 1942, MA, 1943, PhD, 1945; LLD (hon.), Rosary Coll., 1982; DLitt (hon.), Trinity Coll., Dublin, 1984, Fordham U., 1999; LHD (hon.), La Salle U., 1985, Yale U., 1986. Instr. classical lang. Rosary Coll., River Forest, Ill., 1946-48; faculty Swarthmore Coll., 1948—91, prof. classics, 1961-91, chmn. dept., 1959-91, emerita, 1991—, Centennial prof. classics, 1966-73, 78-91, Kenan prof., 1973-78, sr. rsch. scholar, 2003—. Vis. asst. prof. Cornell U., 1952—; vis. assoc. prof. Barnard Coll., 1954-55; vis. prof. LaSalle Coll., Phila., 1965, Am. Sch. Classical Studies, Athens, 1975, 87; Blegen disting. vis. rsch. prof. Vassar Coll., 1979. Author: Sophrosyne: Self-Knowledge and Self-Restraint in Greek Literature, 1966, From Myth to Icon: Reflections of Greek Ethical Doctrine in Literature and Art, 1979, (with Mary C. North) The West of Ireland: A Megalithic Primer, 1999, Cork and the Rest of Ireland: A Megalithic Primer II, 2003; translator: John Milton's Second Defense of the English People, 1966; editor: Interpretations of Plato: A Swarthmore Symposium, 1977; co-editor: Of Eloquence, 1970; editor Jour. History of Ideas; mem. editl. bd. Catalogus Translationum et Commentariorum, 1979. Bd. dirs. Am. Coun. Learned Socs., 1977-85; trustee LaSalle U., 1972-2003, chmn. bd. trustees, 1991-93; trustee King's Coll., Am. Acad. in Rome; chmn. com. on Classical Sch. Recipient Harbison prize Danforth Found., 1969, Centennial medal Am. Acad. Rome, 1995; named Distinguished Daughter of Pa., 1989, del. of Am. Philological Assn. to Am. Coun. Learned Socs., 1991-95; grantee Am. Coun. Learned Socs., 1943-45, 73, fellow, 1971-72, 87-88; Mary Isabel Sibley fellow Phi Beta Kappa Found., 1945-46, Ford Fund Advancement Edn. fellow, Fulbright fellow Rome, 1953-54, Guggenheim fellow, 1958-59, 75-76, AAUW, 1963-64; grantee Danforth Found., 1962, Lindbach Found., 1966; Sr. fellow NEH, 1967-68; NEH Coll. Tchrs. fellow, 1983-84; Martin classical lectr. Oberlin Coll., 1972. Mem. Am. Philol. Assn. (dir. 1968—, pres. 1976—, Charles J. Goodwin award 1969, Disting. Svc. medal 1996), Classical Assn. Atlantic States, Catholic Commn. Intellectual and Cultural Affairs (chmn. 1968-69), Am. Acad. Arts and Scis., Am. Philos. Soc., Soc. Religion Higher Edn., Phi Beta Kappa (bd. vis. scholars 1975-76, senate 1991—2003), Phi Kappa Phi. Home: 604 Ogden Ave Swarthmore PA 19081-1131 E-mail: hnorth1@swarthmore.edu.

NORTH, JAMES LITTLE, lawyer; b. Anniston, Ala., Oct. 10, 1936; s. John Pelham and Winnie (Little) N.; m. Lettie Lane Hurlbert, Sept. 5, 1959; 1 child, James Little, Jr. BS, U. Ala., 1958; JD, U. Va., 1964. Law clk. U.S. Supreme Ct., Washington, 1964-65; from assoc. to ptnr. Bradley, Arant, Rose & White, Birmingham, Ala., 1965-73; ptnr. North, Haskell, Slaughter & Young, Birmingham, 1973-85, James L. North & Assocs., Birmingham, 1985—. Bd. dirs., gen. counsel Adtran, Inc. Lt. U.S. Army, 1959-61. Recipient commendation medal U.S. Army, 1961. Fellow Am. Bar Found. (life), Internat. Soc. Barristers; mem. ABA (ho. dels. 1986-88), Ala. Law Inst. (coun.), Ala. State Bar (pres. 1985-86, award of merit), Eleventh Cir. Hist. Soc. (trustee). Trustee Dem. Nat. Com.; chmn. fin. Clinton-Gore campaign, Ala., 1992, 96; bd. trustees Presbyn. Home for Children, Talladega, Ala.; bd. dirs. Pub. Affairs Rsch. Coun., Birmingham. Home: 4008 Lenox Rd Birmingham AL 35213 Office: 300 21st St N 700 Title Bld Birmingham AL 35203

NORTH, KATHRYN E. KEESEY (MRS. EUGENE C. NORTH), retired educator; b. Columbia, Pa., Jan. 25, 1916; d. Isaac and Elizabeth (French) Keesey; B.S., Ithaca Coll., 1938; M.A., N.Y. U., 1950; m. Eugene C. North, Aug. 18, 1938. Dir. music Cairo (N.Y.) Central Sch. Dist., 1938; music edn. cons. Argyle (N.Y.) Central Sch. Dist., 1939; dir. gen. music curriculum Hartford (N.Y.) Central Sch. Dist., 1939; mem. staff Del. Dept. Pub. Instrn., Dover, 1943; dir. music edn. Herricks (N.Y.) Pub. Schs., 1944-71; ret., 1971. Vis. lectr. Ithaca Coll., summers 1959, 60, 62-65, Fairleigh-Dickinson U., Rutherford, N.J., summer 1966, Albertus Magnus Coll., New Haven, summer 1968; instr. Adelphi Coll., 1954-55, Sch. Edn., N.Y.U., 1964-65. Mem. Music Educators Nat. Conf., N.E.A., N.Y. State Sch. Music Assn., N.Y. State Tchrs. Assn., Nassau Music Educators Assn. (exec. bd. 1947-58), N.Y. State Council Adminstrs. Music Edn. (chpt. v.p. 1967-68), Herricks Tchrs. Assn. (pres. 1948), Sigma Alpha Iota. Mem. Order Eastern Star. Home: 1645 Calle Camille La Jolla CA 92037-7107

NORTH, MARJORIE MARY, columnist; b. Mt. Clemens, Mich., Oct. 21, 1945; d. Robert Haller and Hilla Beryl (Willard) Wright; m. William B. Hirons; children: Laura, Christina, Angela. Student, Wayne State U., 1963—66. Features editor Elizabeth City (N.C.) Daily Advance, 1966-69; news/mng. editor Brandon (Fla.) News, 1977-78; city editor Leesburg (Fla.) Comml., 1978-79; metro editor Sarasota (Fla.) Herald Tribune, 1979-80, Fla. West editor, 1980-85, daily columnist, 1985—. Host Weekly Interview Show, SNN-TV, 1997—. Author: Sarasota: A City For All Seasons, 1994, (plays) With the Best Intentions, 1994, Back in the Game, 1998. Recipient Layout, Creativity and Overall Publ. awards Fla. Press Assn., numerous comty. awards and citations; winner Fla. shorts competition Fla. Studio Theater New Play Festival, 1994, 98; Paul Harris fellow. Avocations: tennis, entertaining, theater. Office: Sarasota Herald-Tribune PO Box 1719 Sarasota FL 34230-1719 E-mail: mnorth10@comcast.net.

NORTH, PERCY, art historian, educator; b. Balt., June 22, 1945; d. William Randolph and Leona Elizabeth (Kappler) N. BA in English, Radford Coll., 1966; MA in Art History, Pa. State U., 1968; PhD in Art History, U. Del., 1974. Asst. prof. Mary Washington Coll., Fred, Va., 1972-74; vis. asst. prof. U. Minn., Mpls., 1975; asst. prof. George Mason U., Fairfax, Va., 1976-84; lectr., adj. prof. Art History Georgetown U., Washington, 1984—; prof. Art History, coord. Art History Montgomery Coll., Rockville, Md., 1989—. Guest curator U. Minn. gallery Mpls., 1977, The Jewish Mus., N.Y.C., 1981-82, The High Mus., Atlanta, 1989-91; vis. asst. prof. Art History James Madison U., Harrisonburg, Va., 1985-86, Emory U., Atlanta, 1986-88, Vanderbilt U., Nashville, 1988-89; Fulbright prof. U. Lyon (France), 1978-79. Author: Max Weber: The Cubist Decade (1910-1920), 1991, Bernhard Gutmann: American Impressionist, 1995; numerous monographs, catalogues with essays; lectr. in field; contbr. articles to profl. jours. Smithsonian fellow, 1970-71, Royal Oak fellow, Eng., 1981. Mem.: Artable, Am. Studies Assn., Coll. Art Assn., Washington Biography Group. Home: 1916 Greenspring Valley Rd Stevenson MD 21153-0649

NORTH, ROBERT L. computer software executvie; b. Topeka, Sept. 19, 1935; BEE, Stanford U., 1953, MEE, 1958; postgrad., UCLA Grad. Bus. Sch., 1977; post grad., Stanford Grad. Bus. Sch., 1981. Tech. staff mem. Aerospace Corp., 1962-65; various positions TRW, 1965-81, v.p., gen. mgr., 1981-86; CEO HNC Software, Inc., San Diego, 1987-2000, chmn., 2000—. Mem. San Diego C. of C., 1983-84; bd. dir. San Diego Econ. Devel. Coun., 1983-84, United Way Pres. Coun., 1984 Office: Fair Isaac Corp 3661 Valley Centre Dr San Diego CA 92130-3317

NORTH, STEVEN EDWARD, lawyer, educator; b. Oct. 16, 1941; s. Irving J. and Barbara (Grubman) N.; m. Sue J. Buznitsky, Dec. 24, 1966; children: Jennifer, Samantha. BA, CCNY, 1963; JD, Bklyn. Law Sch., 1966; LLM, NYU, 1967. Bar: NY 1967, US Dist. Ct. (so. and ea. dists.) NY 1970, US Supreme Ct. 1971. Asst. dist. atty. homicide bur. NY County Dist. Atty. Office, NYC, 1967-71; spl. asst. atty. gen., bur. chief NY State Atty. Gen.'s Office, NYC, 1972-75; pvt. practice NYC, 1975. Mem. adv. com. Ann. Civil Litigation Inst., Practicing Law Inst., 1996; chmn. Assn. Bar Subcom. on Investigation into Imposition of Legis. Limits on Awards for Non-Econ. Damages, 1995; mediator US Dist. Ct. (so. dist.) NY, 1994—, apptd. jud. screening program; mem. adv. coms. solo law practice Practicing Law Inst., 1991, adv. bd. tort litigation, 1989—; vis. faculty Sch. Law, NYU, faculty workshop Cardozo Sch. Law, judge appellate argument, alumni advisor; faculty advisor Trial of Breast Cancer Case, Law Jour. Seminars, 2000; lectr. in field, Lectr., "Trial Tech.", Am. Trial Lawyers Assnt. Roscoe Pound Inst. Fordham Law Sch., 2003; Faculty, "20the Intensive Trial Advocacy Program", Cardozo Sch. of Law, 2003; Faculty, Bklyn. Law Sch. Bridge-the-Gap; "The Substantive Law of Personal Injury and Med. Malpractice" - Practicing Law Inst., 2003; NY State Trial Lawyers, Annual "Decisions" Seminar, "Damages - 2003" - Editorial Bd., NY State Trial Lawyers. Author: Prevention and Detection of Fraud in Industry, 1973, Controlling the Deposition: Winning Your Case Before Trial, 1978, Deposition Strategy, Law and Forms, vol. 1 (Introduction and Law), vol. 5 (Medical Malpractice), vol. 8 (Personal Injury), 1981, (course handbooks) Trial Mechanics, Personal Injury Desbook, 1983, Trial Mechanics and Discovery, 1985, 86, Medical Malpractice Litigation, 1988, Managing the Multi-Million Dollar Case, 1990, Objectifying Brain Damage in Closed Head Injury, 1990, Fundamentals of Medical Malpractice Litigation, 1991, Damage Update, 1992, 93, 94, 95, 96, 97—, Proving & Defending Damages, 1993, Conducting & Defending Depositions, 1993; contbr. chpts. to books; editor: Cancer Litigation Bull., 1994—, Fear of Developing Cancer; contbg. editor: Law and Order mag.; med.-legal editor Perinatology, 1983; contbr. articles to legal jour.; commentator Eyewitness News, 1994, Court TV, 1994-98, Talk News TV, 1996. Mem. leadership coun. So. Poverty Law Ctr. Mem. ATLA, NCCJ (lawyers divsn., ann. dinner com.), NOW (benefits com.), US Holocaust Mus. (charter mem.), Am. Bd. Trial Adv., Soc. Med. Jurisprudence, NY State Bar Assn. (faculty), NY State Trial Lawyers Assn. (bd. dir. 1990—, faculty chmn. Depositions in Action 2000, North's Ninety-Nine Pointers on Advanced Deposition Practices 1999), Lotos Club, Nat. Eagle Scout Assn., State Trial Lawyers Assn. (bd. dir. 1990—, seminar faculty chmn. 1993, faculty decisions program 1991—, Law Day dinner com.), NY County Lawyers Assn. (exec. com. med. malpractice sect., exec. com. gen. tort law sect.), Assn. Bar of City of NY (civil ct. com. 1980-83, legal and continuing edn. com. 1983—, legal referral svc. com., med. malpractice mediator 1994—, chmn. subcom. on imposition of legis. limits to awards for non-econ. damages), Vol. Lawyers for the Arts, Million Dollar Adv. Forum, Vol. Lawyers for the Arts, NY County Supreme Ct. Com. Med. Malpractice Litigation, NY Soc. Anesthesiologist (speaker), NY State Bar Assn. Home: 148 E 74th St New York NY 10021 Office: 148 E 74th St New York NY 10021-3542

NORTH, TERRY CLAIRE, clinical psychologist; b. Brunswick, Ga., Apr. 8, 1959; d. Henry Carlton Jr. and Jimmie Claire (Copeland) North; m. Scott Alan Yonker, Sept. 21, 1991. BA, Auburn U., 1982; MA, U. S.D., 1986, PhD, 1989. Lic. psychologist, Nebr. Neuropsychologist Immanuel Med. Ctr., Omaha, 1989-90, St. Joseph Ctr. for Mental Health, Omaha, 1990-91; psychologist in pvt. practice Heartland Psychotherapy Assocs., Papillion, Nebr., 1991-95; dir. post-traumatic stress disorder clinic Omaha VA Med. Ctr., 1995—. Clin. asst. prof. adj. faculty dept. psychiatry U. Nebr. Med. Ctr., 2000—; adj. asst. prof. dept. psychology U. SD Vermillion, 1998—; asst. clin. prof. dept. psychiatry Creighton U., 2001—. Mem.: Internat. Soc. for Traumatic Stress Studies. Avocation: dressage. Office: Omaha VA Med Ctr 41011Woolworth Ave Omaha NE 68105

NORTH, WARREN JAMES, government official; b. Winchester, Ill., Apr. 28, 1922; s. Clyde James and Lucille Adele (Bishop) N.; m. Mary Strother; children— James Warren, Mary Kay, Susan Lee, Diane. BS in Engring, Purdue U., 1947; MS, Case Inst. Tech., 1954, Princeton, 1956. Engr. and test pilot NACA, Cleve., 1947-55, asst. chief aerodynamics br., 1955-59; chief manned satellites NASA, Washington, 1959-62; chief flight crew support div. NASA (Manned Spacecraft Center), Houston, 1962-71; asst. dir. space shuttle NASA (Flight Ops. Directorate), 1972-85; pres. Spalding Edn. Found., Glendale, Ariz., 1986—. Contbr. articles to profl. jours. Served with USAAF, 1943-45. Recipient DeFlorez tng. award, 1966; NASA award for exceptional service, 1968, 69 Mem. Am. Inst. Aero. and Astronautics (asso. fellow 1955), Tau Beta Pi, Pi Tau Sigma. Clubs: Mason. Home: 6933 W Kimberly Way Glendale AZ 85308-5757 Office: Spalding Edn Found 2814 W Bell Rd Ste 1405 Phoenix AZ 85053-7531

NORTH, WILLIAM HAVEN, foreign service officer; b. Summit, N.J., Aug. 17, 1926; s. Eric M. and Gladys (Haven) N.; m. Jeanne Foote, Sept. 2, 1950; children: Jeannette Haven, William Ashby, Charles Eric. BA in History with honors, Wesleyan U., Middletown, Conn., 1949; MA in History, Columbia, 1951. Program officer ICA, Ethiopia, 1953-57; then dep. chief program divsn. ICA (African-European Regional Office), Washington, 1958—61; asst. dir. for program USAID Mission, Nigeria, until 1965; dir. Ctrl. and Western African affairs AID, Washington, 1966-70, U.S. AID mission to Ghana, 1970-76; dep. asst. adminstr. Africa Bur. AID, 1976-82, spl. asst. Office of the Adminstr., 1982-83, assoc. asst. adminstr. Ctr. Devel. Info. and Evaluation, 1983-89, ret.; pvt. cons. Internat. Devel. for World Bank, 1989—, UN Devel. Program USAID, 1989—; coord. Evaluation of Global Environ. Facility, 1993, Evaluation Spl. Program of Asst. to Africa, 1997-98, Evaluation DAC/OECD Eval. Group, 1998; evaluator UNDP Aid Coordination, 1998—. Evaluator UNDB Global Program for HIV/AIDS, 2000, African Governance Capacity Bldg, UNDP, Danida, Denmark, 2002-03; fellow Ctr. for Internat. Affairs, Harvard U., 1965-66; chmn. experts group on evaluation Devel. Assistance Commn., OECD, 1985-88; vice-chmn. editl. bd. Fgn. Svc. Jour., 1983-86; mem. adv. panel on evaluation Inter-Am. Devel. Bank, 1993-94; prin. evaluator Internat. Fin. Corp.; program dir. U.S. Fgn. Assistance Oral History Program, 1995—; cons. UN Devel. Coop. Policy Branch, 2000-02. Mem. devel. com., Cmty. Ministry Montgomery Co., 2000-03; evaluator USAID Program in Iraq, 2003-04. Served with AUS, 1944-46. Recipient Meritorious Svc. award for exemplary achievement in pub. adminstrn., W.A. Jump Honor cert., Superior Honor award for Nigerian Relief Adminstrn., Equal Employment Opportunity award, Disting. Honor award AID, Presdl. Meritorious Svc. medal, Adminstrs. Career Svc. award. Mem. Soc. for Internat. Devel., African Studies Assn., Assn. Diplomatic Studies and Tng., Am. Evaluation Assn., Applachian Mountain Club. Methodist. Home and Office: Internat Development 6748 Brigadoon Dr Bethesda MD 20817-5436

NORTHCUTT, CLARENCE DEWEY, lawyer; b. Guin, Ala., July 7, 1916; s. Walter G. and Nancy E. (Homer) Northcutt; m. Ruth Eleanor Storms, May 25, 1941. AB, U. Okla., 1939, LL.B., 1938. Bar: Okla. 1938. Pvt. practice, Ponca City, 1938—. Mem. bd. visitors U. Okla. Served with AUS, 1941-46. Decorated Bronze Star, Air medal with oak leaf cluster, Order St. John of Jerusalem; named Outstanding Citizen of Ponca City, 1982; inducted to Okla. Hall of Fame, 2001. Fellow Am. Coll. Trial Lawyers, Am. Coll. Trust and Estate Attys., Am. Bar Found.; mem. Acad. Univ. Fellows, Internat. Soc. Barristers, Am. Bd. Advocacy, Internat. Acad. Trial Lawyers, Okla. Bar Assn. (pres. 1975, bd. govs.), Ponca City C. of C. (past pres.). Clubs: Mason, Kiwanian. Democrat. Baptist. Home: 132 Whitworth Ave Ponca City OK 74601-3438 Office: PO Box 1669 Ponca City OK 74602-1669 Office Phone: 580-762-1655. E-mail: cdnorth@northcuttlawfirm.com.

NORTHCUTT, MARIE ROSE, elementary, secondary, & special education educator; b. White Plains, N.Y., Feb. 2, 1950; d. Carlo and Marcelline Marie Rose DeMarco; m. Kenneth Walter Northcutt, Mar. 17, 1984; children: James

Lee, Thomas Joseph. BA, Lynchburg Coll., 1972; MA, Columbia U., 1977. Cert. elem. and secondary tchr., N.Y. Tchr. Petersburg (Va.) Pub. Schs., 1972-74; asst. relocation mgr. Ticor Co., White Plains, 1974-75; 3rd grade tchr. Resurrection Sch., Rye, 1975-76; 6th grade tchr. Harrison (N.Y.) Cen. Sch. Dist., 1976-78, learning disabilities specialist, 1981—; tchr. of emotionally handicapped N.Y.C. Schs., 1978-80; learning evaluator Empire State Coll., White Plains, 1981-82. Ind. evaluation cons., White Plains, 1981—; chair Mid. States Sub-com. Active Harrison H.S. PTA. Mem. Assn. for Children with Learning Disabilities, Westchester County Assn. for Children with Learning Disabilities, Spl. Edn. Parents Tchrs. Assn., Orton Soc., Phi Delta Kappa. Roman Catholic. Avocations: reading, cooking. Home: 81 Griffin Pl White Plains NY 10603-3609 Office: Harrison Cen Sch Dist Union Ave Harrison NY 10528-2108

NORTHCUTT, WAYNE, history educator; b. New Orleans, July 5, 1944; s. Bernard Duke and Clara Lenoir Northcutt. BA in History, Calif. State U., Long Beach, 1966, MA in History, 1968; PhD in European History, U. Calif., Irvine, 1974; postgrad., Ecole Partique des Hautes Etudes, Paris, 1978. Asst. prof. of history and head western European area study Monterey (Calif.) Inst. of Internat. Studies, 1975-78; lectr. in history and internat. rels. Schiller Coll., Paris, 1978; tchg. assoc. U. Calif., Irvine, 1979-80; fgn. expert Chinese People's U., Beijing, 1983; coord. internat. studies program Niagara (N.Y.) Univ., 1985—2003, prof. of history, 1980—. Author: The Regions of France, 1996, Mitterrand: A Political Biography, 1992, Historical Dictionary of the French Fourth and Fifth Republic, 1946-1991, 1992, The French Socialist and Communist Party Under the Fifth Republic, 1958-1981, 1985. Office: Dept History Niagara U Niagara University NY 14109 E-mail: northcutt@niagara.edu.

NORTHEN, CHARLES SWIFT, III, retired bank executive; b. Birmingham, Ala., Jan. 25, 1937; s. Charles Swift and Jennie Hood (Hunt) S.; m. Margaret Carson Robinson, Dec. 27, 1959 (div. 1972); children: Margaret Allen, Charles Swift IV, Bryce Robinson; m. Betty Jean Taylor, Oct. 3, 1981. BA cum laude, Vanderbilt U., 1959, MA, 1961. Chartered fin. analyst. Mem. staff trust dept. Birmingham Trust Nat. Bank, 1960-64; with First Ala. Bank Birmingham, 1964-80, sr. v.p., trust officer, 1975-80, Central Bank of South, Birmingham, 1981-85; exec. v.p. 1st Ala. Bankshares, 1985-95, corp. investment officer, 1993-95; mng. dir. Sterne, Agee & Leach, Inc., Birmingham, 1995-98, investment cons., 1998—2001; ret. Lectr. So. Trust Sch., Birmingham So. Coll.; pres. First Ala. Investments Inc.; dir. Hubbard Press, Findlay, Ohio. Bd. dirs. United Presbyn. Found., N.Y.C., 1977-86; mem. Birmingham Com. Fgn. Rels., 1970—. Mem. Ala. Security Dealers Assn. (pres.), Ala. Soc. Fin. Analysts (pres.), Inst. Chartered Fin. Analysts, Newcomen Soc., SAR, Kiwanis, Mountain Brook CLub, The Club, Soc. Col. Wars. Presbyterian. Home: 3024 N Woodridge Rd Birmingham AL 35223-2748

NORTHERN, RICHARD, lawyer; b. Louisville, Dec. 17, 1948; s. James William and Mary Helen (Barry) N.; m. Mary Lou Grundy, Aug. 28, 1971; children: James Barry, Nancy Hope, Mary Grace. BA in English, U. Louisville, 1970, JD, 1976; MPA, Harvard U., 1977. Bar: Ky. 1976, U.S. Dist. Ct. (we. and ea. dists.) Ky. 1977. Staff writer Courier-Jour., Louisville, 1970-72; dir. planning devel. Jefferson County Govt., Louisville, 1972-76; legis. dir. Office of U.S. Rep. Romano Mazzoli, Washington, 1977-78; spl. asst. U.S. Sec. of Interior, Washington, 1979-80; ptnr., mem. exec. com. Wyatt, Tarrant & Combs, Louisville, 1980—. Dir. Nugent Sand Co., 1998—. Chmn. bd. dirs. Cath. Edn. Found., Inc., Louisville, 1998—; dir. Caritas Health Svcs., 1981—. White House fellow, 1979, U.S.-Japan Leadership fellow Japan Soc., Inc., 1988. Democrat. Roman Catholic. Office: Wyatt Tarrant & Combs 2800 Citizens Plz Louisville KY 40202-2898 Office Phone: 502-562-7234. Business E-Mail: rnorthern@wyattfirm.com.

NORTHEY, WILLIAM THOMAS, microbiologist, educator; b. Duluth, Minn., Aug. 10, 1928; s. William Thomas Northey and Mary Ellen Riley; m. Margaret Esparza, July 1, 1972; m. Elizabeth L. Van Laeke, Aug. 12, 1950 (div. June 15, 1970); children: Kathleen, William Northey III, Bruce, Brian, Barry, Brett, Suzanne. BA, U. of Minn., 1950; MA, U. of Kans., 1957, PhD, 1959. Rsch. asst. Abbott Labs., Chgo., 1950—51, Naval Med Rsch. Unit #4, Gt. Lakes, Ill., 1951—55; tchg. and rsch. U. of Kans., Lawrence, Kans., 1955—59; from asst. prof. to prof. emeritus Ariz. State U., Tempe, Ariz., 1959—85, prof. emeritus, 1985—. Cons. Unidynamics Corp., Goodyear, Ariz., 1960—63, AiResearch Corp., Phoenix, 1963—65; pres., dir. Iatric Corp., Tempe, 1960—92. Contbr. articles to profl. jours. Vol. United Fund, Phoenix; grant reviewer Ariz. Heart Assn., Phoenix; bd. dir. Ariz. Br. of Allergy Found. of Ariz., Phoenix. Seaman second USNR, 1946—51. Grantee, NIH, 1960—85, USAF, 1963—68. Fellow: Am. Acad. of Microbiology; mem.: Am. Soc. of Immunology, Am. Soc. of Microbiology (pres. Ariz. chpt. 1963). Achievements include development of scorpion anti-venom; research in aeroallergens in Arizona. Avocations: skiing, swimming, reading. Home: 4818 N 72nd Way Scottsdale AZ 85251-1302

NORTHRIP, ROBERT EARL, lawyer; b. Sleeper, Mo., May 8, 1939; s. Novel and Jessie (Burch) N.; m. Linda Kay Francis, June 15, 1968; children: Robert E. Jr., William F., Darryl F., David F. BA, Southwest Mo. State, 1960; MA, U. N.C., 1965; JD, U. Mo., 1968. Bar: Mo. 1968, U.S. Dist. Ct. (we. dist.) Mo. 1968, U.S. Ct. Appeals (10th cir.) 1976, U.S. Ct. Appeals (8th cir.) 1980, U.S. Ct. Appeals (9th cir.) 1983, U.S. Ct. Appeals (3d cir.) 1987, U.S. Supreme Ct. 1978. Ptnr. Shook, Hardy & Bacon, Kansas City, Mo., 1968—. Active Nelson Art Gallery, Soc. of Fellows, Kans. City, Mo. 1st lt. US Army, 1963-65. Mem. ABA, Mo. Bar Assn., Lawyers Assn. Kansas City, Mo. Orgn. Def. Lawyers, Kansas City Met. Bar Assn., U. Mo. Alumni Assn. (past pres. Kansas City chpt.), Nat. Soc. Arts and Letters. Republican. Avocations: baseball, football. Office: Shook Hardy & Bacon 2555 Grand Blvd Kansas City MO 64108-2613 Home: 6439 Wenonga Rd Mission Hills KS 66208 E-mail: rnorthrip@shb.com.

NORTHROP, EDWARD SKOTTOWE, federal judge; b. Chevy Chase, Md., June 12, 1911; s. Claudian Bellinger and Eleanor Smythe (Grimke) N.; m. Barbara Middleton Burdette, Apr. 22, 1939; children: Edward M., St. Julien (Mrs. Kevin Butler), Peter. LLB, George Washington U., 1937. Bar: Md. 1937, D.C. 1937. Village mgr., Chevy Chase, Md., 1934-41; pvt. practice, Rockville, Md., Washington, 1937-61; mem. Md. Senate, 1954-61, chmn. fin. com., joint com. taxation fiscal affairs, majority leader, 1959-61; judge U.S. Dist. Ct. Md., Balt., 1961-70; chief judge U.S. Dist. Ct. of Md., Balt., 1970-81, sr. judge, 1981—. Mem. Met. Chief Judges Conf., 1970-81; mem. Jud. Conf. Com. on Adminstrn. of Probation System, 1973-79, Adv. Corrections Council U.S., 1977, Jud. Panel on Multidist. Litigation, 1979; judge U.S. Fgn. Intelligence Surveillance Ct. of Rev., 1985—1992. Trustee Woodberry Forest Sch.; founder Washington Met. Area Coun. Govts. & Mass Transp. Agy. Served to comdr. USNR, 1941-45. Decorated Army commendation medal, Navy commendation medal; recipient Profl. Achievement award George Washington U., 1975, Disting. Citizen award State of Md., 1981, Spl. Merit citation Am. Judicature Soc., 1982. Mem. ABA, Md. Bar Assn. (Disting. Svc. award 1982), D.C. Bar Assn., Montgomery County Bar Assn., Barristers, Washington Ctr. Met. Studies. Clubs: Chevy Chase (Md.). Lodges: Rotary. Democrat. Episcopalian. Office: 4828 Broom Dr Olney MD 20832-3124

NORTHROP, MARY RUTH, retired mental health nurse; b. Washington, June 5, 1919; d. William Arthur and Emma Aurelia (Kaech) N. Diploma in nursing, Georgetown U., 1951, BS in Nursing cum laude, 1952; MS, U. Md., 1958; MA in Anthropology, U. Va., 1970. RN, Va. Asst. dir. nursing U. Md. Hosp., Balt., 1958-60; dir. nursing Georgetown U. Hosp., Washington, 1961; nursing rep. ARC, Pa., 1962, regional dir. nursing, 1963-68; pediatric nursing cons. Va. Dept. Health, Richmond, 1971-84; clin. nursing specialist Va. Dept. Mental Health and Mental Retardation, Petersburg, Va., 1988-99. Adj. asst./assoc. prof. U. Md. Sch. Nursing, Balt., 1958-60. Author: Matthew Ryan and Mary Schmitz of North Star Township, Brown County, Minnesota, 1998; editor Lively Experiment, 2001—. Nursing fellow rsch. HEW, U. Md., Bethesda, 1957-68, nursing fellow anthropology U. Va., 1968-70; recipient Recognition Georgetown U. Alumni Assn., Richmond, 1987. Mem. ANA, Va. Nursing Assn., DAR (chpt. regent 1983-86, dist. treas. 1992-95), Nat. Soc. Women Descendants Ancient and Hon. Arty. Co. (treas. Va. chpt. 1995—), Daus. of Founders and Patriots of Am. (registrar Va. 1997—), Order of First Families of R.I. and Providence Plantation (charter), Sons and Daus. of Colonial and Antebellum Bench and Bar (charter), Soc. First Families of Minn., Mensa, Sigma Theta Tau. Republican. Roman Catholic. Avocations: genealogy, reading, travel. Home: 300 W Franklin St Apt 401E Richmond VA 23220-4967

NORTHRUP, CHRISTIANE, gynecologist-obstetrician; b. Buffalo, Oct. 4, 1949; d. George Wilbur and Edna (Zwilling) N.; children: Ann Christiane, Kate Northrup. BA, Case Western Res., 1971; MD, Dartmouth Coll., 1975. Diplomate Am. Bd. Ob-Gyn. Intern Tufts New Eng. Med. Ctr. Affiliated Hosps., Boston, 1975; intern then resident Tufts New Eng. Med. Ctr., Boston, 1976-79; assoc. clin. prof. ob-gyn Tufts U. Sch. Medicine, Boston, 1979-80; clin. instr. ob-gyn U. Vt. Coll. Med., Portland, Maine, 1980—82, asst. clin. prof. ob-gyn, 1982—2001; practice medicine specializing in ob-gyn Gynecol. Assocs., South Portland, 1979-85, Women's Health Care Orgn. Women to Women, Yarmouth, Maine, 1985—96; private practice ob-gyn, Yarmouth, Maine, 1979—. Mem. high risk perinatal group Maine Med. Ctr., Portland, 1981-83. Contbr. various articles on women's health to profl. jours. Fellow Am. Coll. Ob-Gyn; mem. Am. Holistic Med. Assn. (sec. 1986-88, pres. 1988-90), Am. Holistic Med. Found. (pres. 1986-88). Achievements include appearing in 4 PBS specials discussing womens health. Avocations: music, harpist, folk singing, cross country skiing, proprioceptive writing. Office: PO Box 199 Yarmouth ME 04096

NORTHRUP, HERBERT ROOF, economist, business executive; b. Irvington, N.J., Mar. 6, 1918; m. Eleanor Pearson, June 3, 1944; children: James Pearson, Nancy Warren, Jonathan Peter, David Oliver, Philip Wilson. AB, Duke U., 1939; A.M., Harvard U., 1941, PhD, 1942. Instr. econs. Cornell U., 1942-43; sr. hearing officer Nat. War Labor Bd., 1943-45; asst. prof. econs. Columbia U., 1945-49; labor economist Nat. Indsl. Conf. Bd., 1949-52; indsl. relations cons. Ebasco Services, 1952-55; v.p. indsl. relations Penn-Texas Corp., N.Y.C., 1955-58; employee relations mgr. Gen. Electric Co., 1958-61; prof. industry Wharton Sch., U. Pa., Phila., 1961-88, prof. emeritus, 1988—, chmn. dept. industry, 1964-69, dir. indsl. rsch. unit, 1964-88, chmn. Labor Rels. Coun., 1968-85. Cons. and expert witness on manpower, pers. and labor rels. problems for many cos.; arbitrator in labor rels. disputes. Author: Organized Labor and the Negro, 1944, Unionization of Professional Engineers and Chemists, 1946, Economics of Labor Relations, 1950, 9th edit., 1981, Government and Labor, 1963, Readings in Labor Economics, 1963, Boulwarism: Labor Policies of General Electric Company, 1964, Negro and Employment Opportunity, 1965, Hours of Labor, 1965, Compulsory Arbitration and Government Intervention in Labor Disputes, 1966, Restrictive Labor Practices in Supermarket Industry, 1967, Negro in the Automobile Industry, 1968, Negro in the Aerospace Industry, 1968, Negro in the Rubber Tire Industry, 1969, Negro in Paper Industry, 1969, Negro in the Tobacco Industry, 1970, Negro Employment in Basic Industry, 1970, Negro Employment in Southern Industry, 1970, Negro Employment in Land and Air Transport, 1971, Impact of Government Manpower Programs, 1975, Open Shop Construction, 1975, The Impact of OSHA, 1978, Objective Selection of Supervisors, 1978, Black and Other Minority Participation in the All-Volunteer Navy and Marine Corps, 1979, Manpower in the Retail Pharmacy Industry, 1979, The Impact of the ATT-EEO Consent Decree, 1979, Multinational Collective Bargaining Attempts, 1979, Multinational Union Organizations in the Manufacturing Industries, 1980, Employee Relations and Regulations in the 80s, 1982, Internat. Transport Workers' Federation and Flag of Convenience Shipping, 1983, Open Shop Construction Revisited, 1984, Personnel Policies for Engineers and Scientists, 1985, Doublebreasted Operations and Pre-Hire Agreements in Construction: The Facts and the Law, 1987, The Federal Government as Employer: The Federal Labor Relations Authority and the PATCO Challenge, 1988, The Changing Role of Women in Research and Development, 1988, Government Protection of Employees in Mergers and Acquisitions, 1989, The Railway Labor Act, 1990, Union Corporate Campaigns and Inside Games as a Strike Form, 1994, Union violence: The Record and the Response by Courts, Legislatures, and the NLRB, rev. edit., 1999, Construction Union Tactics to Regain Jobs and Public Policy, 2004, The Impact of Union-Management Relations on Urban Industrial Employment, 2000, The Great Paper Strike and Its Aftermath: International Paper vs. the United Paperworkers, 2004, also over 300 articles in field. Mem. Am. Econ. Assn., Indsl. Relations Research Assn., Am. Arbitration Assn., Phi Beta Kappa. Clubs: Harvard (N.Y.C.); Harvard-Radcliffe (Phila.); University (Washington), Faculty (U. Pa.). Home and Office: 205 Avon Rd Haverford PA 19041-1612 Office Phone: 610-642-1293.

NORTHUP, ANNE MEAGHER, congresswoman; b. Louisville, Ky., Jan. 22, 1948; d. James L. and Floy Gates (Terstegge) Meagher; m. Robert Wood Northup, Apr. 12, 1969; children: David, Katherine, Joshua, Kevin, Erin, Mark. BA in Econs. and Bus., St. Mary's Coll. Notre Dame, South Bend, Ind., 1970. Mem. Ky. Ho. of Reps., Frankfort, 1987-96, U.S. Congress from 3d Ky. Dist., 1997—; mem. house appropriations com.; founder House Reading Caucus, 1998; mem. speaker's drug free task force, 1998; chair speaker's task force on education, 1998; mem. World Trade Org. congl. advisory group, 1999, free trade working group, 2000, comm. on educational accountability, 1993—95, economic development task force, 1991—92, task force to study highway needs, 1990—91, state debt capacity task force. Mem. fin. adv. bd. EPA, 1989-93; mem. home econs. adv. bd. U. Ky. Coll. Agr., 1992— Appeared on Meet the Press, Fox News Sunday, Larry King Live, CNN & Co., Hardball with Chris Matthews. Mem. exec. com. Partnership Ky. Sch. Reform, 1990—; bd. dirs. Greater Louisville Pub. Radio, 1993—, Hospice Louisville, 1994—, Ky. Cancer Consortium, 1992—; mem. cmty. adv. bd. Jr. League Louisville, 1993—; active Holy Spirit Cath. Ch. Named Outstanding Woman of Achievement St. Matthews BPW, 1990; recipient Cath. Schs. Disting. Alumni award, 1991, U. Notre Dame award of the yr. Ky. Alumni Assn., 1991, Clearing the Air award Am. Lung Assn. of Ky., 1991, Svc. Above Self award St. Matthews Rotary Club, 1992, Pub. Svc. award Am. Heart Assn., 1992, Sacred Heart Acad. Alumna award, 1994, Nat. Fedn. of Ind. Bus./Guardian of Small Bus. award, 1996, 97, 98, Legislator of Yr. award Environ. Industry Assn., 1997, Outstanding Freshman Mem. of Congress award Nat. Industries for Blind, 1997, Spirit of Enterprise award U.S. C. of C., 1997, Bulldog award Watchdogs of Treasury, 1998, Jefferson award Citizens for Sound Economy, 1998, Outstanding Support award Am. Printing House for Blind, 1998, Legislator of Yr. award Assn. Equipment Distbrs., 1999, Cmty. Healthcare Champion award Nat. Assn. Cmty. Health Ctrs., Inc., 1999, Spirit of Enterprise award C. of C., 1999, Susan B. Anthony Congl. award, 1999, Pub. Policy Adv. of Yr. award Nat. Assn. Women Bus. Owners, 1999, Honor Roll of Legis. Achievement in Econ. Devel. award So. Econ. Devel. Coun., Inc., 1999, Legislator of Yr. award Nat. Beer Whoesalers Assn., 1999. Mem. Nat. Order Women Legislators, Nat. Conf. State Legislators, Nat. Rep. Legis. Conf., Inst. Rep. Women, So. Legis. Conf. (alternate from Ky. to fiscal affairs and govtl. com.), Nat. Fedn. Ind. Bus. Republican. Roman Catholic. Office: US Ho Reps 1004 Longworth House Office Bl Washington DC 20515-1703

NORTHWAY, WANDA I. real estate company executive; b. Columbia, Mo., July 11, 1942; d. Herman W. and Goldie M. (Wood) Proctor; m. Donald H. Northway, June 12, 1965; 1 child, Michelle D. RN, U. Mo. Lic. real estate agt. Mo., grad. Realtors Inst. Realtor, 1970—81; co-owner, pres., realtor, ptnr. House of Brokers Realty, Inc., Columbia, 1981—. Pres., organizer Realtor-Assoc. Sales Club, Columbia, 1975; pres. Columbia Bd. Realtors, 1982. Contbr. articles to realty mags. Vol. ARS, local hosp.; mem. allocation com. United Way; active vol. Am. Cancer Soc. and Heart Assn.; campaign worker for various legislators; Sunday sch. tchr., girls' aux. leader Bapt. Ch. Named Realtor Assoc. of Yr., Columbia Bd. Realtors, 1974, Realtor of Yr., 1980. Mem.: Nat. Assn. Realtors (nat. dir. 1977), Realtors Nat. Mktg. Inst. (cert. residential specialist 1978), Mo. Assn. Realtors (state dir. 1974—77, Realtor Assoc. of Yr. 1977), Epsilon Sigma Alpha (state corr. sec., local pres.). Baptist. Office: House of Brokers Realty Inc 1515 Chapel Hill Rd Columbia MO 65203-5457 Office Phone: 573-446-6507.

NORTON, ANDRE ALICE, author; b. Cleve., Feb. 17, 1912; s. Adalbert and Bertha Stemm N. Librarian Cleve. Pub. Libr., until 1951; dir. High Hallack Genre Writers' Rsch. Libr., Murfreesboro, Tenn. Author: The Sword is Drawn, 1944 (Dutch Gov. award, 1946), Sword in Sheath, 1949 (Ohioana Juvenile award Honor Book, 1950), Starhunter, 1961 (Hugo award nomination World Sci. Fiction Conv., 1962), Witch World, 1963 (Hugo award nomination World Sci. Fiction Conv., 1964), Night of Masks, 1964 (Boy's Club of Am. Cert. of Merit, 1965), To the King a Daughter, 2000, Knight or Knave, 2001, Leopard in Exile, 2001, A Crown Disowned, 2002, The Elevenborn, 2002, others, (series include) Swords Trilogy, Star Ka'at Sci. Fiction series, Witch World Fantasy series, Solar Queen series, Oak series, Elvenbane series (1st vol. Science Fiction Book Club Choice for Book of Yr., 1991). Bd. dirs. High Hallack Genre Writers Rsch. Libr., 1999. Recipient Invisible Little Man award Westercon XVI, 1963, Phoenix award 1976, Gandalf Master Fantasy award World Sci. Fiction Convention, 1977, Andre Norton award Women Writers of Sci. Fiction, 1978, Balrog Fantasy award 1979, Ohioana award, 1980, Fritz Leiber award, 1983, E.E. Smith award, 1983, Nebula Grand Master award Sci. Fiction Writers of Am., 1984, Jules Verne award, 1984, Second Stage Lensman award, 1987, Favorite Book of Yr. award Sci. Fiction Book Clubs, 1991, Lifetime Achievement award SESFA, 2002; named to Ohio Hall of Fame, 1981; named to Sci. Fiction Writers Hall of Fame, 1996. Mem. Sci. Fiction Writers Am.

NORTON, CHERYL J. academic administrator; m. Henry Norton; children: Joel, Aaron. B in Phys. Edn. and Recreation with honors, Denison U., 1971; EdM, M in Applied Physiology, Columbia U., EdD in Applied Physiology, 1980. From temp. faculty mem. to full prof. Met. State U., Denver, 1976, chair dept. human performance, sport and leisure studies, 1992—96, interim assoc. dean Sch. Profl. Studies, 1996—97, provost, v.p. for acad. affairs, 1997—2004; pres. So. Conn. State U., New Haven, 2004—. Pres. Colo. Assn. for Health, Phys. Edn., Recreation and Dance; pres. Ctrl. dist. Am. Alliance Health, Phys. Edn., Recreation and Dance. Author 2 books; contbr. articles to profl. jours. Fellow: Am. Coll. Sports Medicine (past pres. regional chpt.). Office: So Conn State Univ 501 Crescent St New Haven CT 06515*

NORTON, DELMAR LYNN, candy company executive; b. Vernal, Utah, Sept. 6, 1944; s. La Mar and Velma (Hullinger) N.; m. Connie Jean Bryan, Mar. 10, 1967; children: Bryan Lynn, Christopher Max, Wendy, Nicholas Delmar. Student, U. Utah, 1962-63, Famous Artists Sch., 1966-69. Nat. sales mgr. Maxfield Candy Co., Salt Lake City, 1965-72; sec.-treas. Ice Cream & Candy Shops, Salt Lake City, 1972-73; pres., gen. mgr. Ostlers' Candy Co., Salt Lake City, 1973—; chmn. bd. Nat. Mktg. Co., Salt Lake City, 1974—; pres., gen. mgr. Rent-A-Flick, Inc., Salt Lake City.; v.p. Redi-Therm Insulation, Inc., Salt Lake City., 1991-94; nat. sales mgr. Uphill Down U.S.A., 1994—. Mem. Ch. Jesus Christ of Latter-Day Saints (missionary). Home: 4240 S 1650 E Salt Lake City UT 84124-2556 Office: PO Box 71470 Salt Lake City UT 84171-0470

NORTON, DOROTHA OLIVER, speech educator; b. Rutherford, Tenn. d. Lacey A. and Pearl (Cunningham) Oliver; m. Robert Marion Norton, Aug. 17, 1958; children: Robbie Jean Norton Eddings, Robert Marion II. BA, Union U., Jackson, Tenn., 1959; MA, Memphis State U., 1961, Murray (Ky.) State U., 1974. Cert. speech, English and bus. tchr., guidance counselor, Tenn. Tchr. Enlgish, shorthand, guidance counselor Kenton (Tenn.) H.S., 1958-66; instr., asst. prof. English and speech U. Tenn., Martin, 1966-77, assoc. prof. speech, 1977-91, prof. speech, 1991—. Author: Kenton: Folklore and Fact, 1972; contbr. articles to profl. jours. Tchr. Sunday Sch. 1st Bapt. Ch., Kenton, 1984-94, 97-2002, also narrator Christmas cantata; spkr. Kenton XYZ Sr. Citizens Club, Dyer (Tenn.) Golden Agers Sr. Citizens. Named Woman of Yr., Kenton Jaycees, 1973, Tchr. of Yr., The Pacer, U. Tenn., 1991; nominated for Coffey Outstanding Tchg. award Coll. of Humanities and Fine Arts, U. Tenn., 2001. Mem. NEA, Nat. Comm. Assn. (panelist, Ctrl. States Comm. Assn. (panelist), So. States Comm. Assn. (panelist), Tenn. Comm. Assn. (pres. 1990-91, exec. dir. 2000—, panelist, Educator of Yr. award 1992), Tenn. Edn. Assn., Gen. Fedn. Women's Clubs, Tenn. Fedn. Women's Club (dist. pres. 1978-80), Kenton Women's Club (past pres.), Phi Kappa Phi (pres. 2000-01). Avocations: reading, travel, picnicking. Home: 528 S Poplar St Kenton TN 38233-3624 Office: U Tenn 305 Gooch Hl Martin TN 38238-5099 Office Phone: 731-587-7552.

NORTON, DOUGLAS RAY, former auditor general; b. Portales, N.Mex., Mar. 23, 1933; s. Clayton G. and Lillian W. (Powers) N.; m. Wanda Jones, May 23, 1951 (div. July 1979); children: Debbie Norton Goodman, Vicki Norton Hulet, Denise Norton Jolley; m. Robertta J. Andersen, July 31, 1998. BS, U. Ariz., 1963. CPA, Ariz. Staff acct., audit supr. Ernst & Ernst, Tucson, Ariz., 1963-67; ptnr. Baker, Price & Norton, Prescott, Ariz., 1968-75, Lester Witte & Co., Prescott, Ariz., 1975-76; auditor gen. State of Ariz., Phoenix, 1976-99; ret., 1999. Former mem. Profl. Adv. Bd. Sch. Acctg. Ariz. State U., Tempe; former mem. acctg. bd. advisors U. Ariz. Pres. Prescott Bd. Edn., 1976. Served with U.S. Army, 1953-55. Mem. AICPA, Ariz. Soc. CPAs, Nat. Assn. State Auditors, Comptrollers and Treasurers (pres. 1993-94), Nat. State Auditors Assn. (pres. 1982-83), Lions (pres. Prescott chpt. 1973-74). Home: PO Box 3120 Chino Valley AZ 86323-2707

NORTON, DUNBAR SUTTON, economic developer; b. Hoquiam, Wash., Jan. 30, 1926; s. Percy Dunbar and Anna Fedelia (Sutton) N.; m. Kathleen Margaret Mullarky, Dec. 21, 1948 (dec. Apr. 1994); children: Priscilla K., Rebecca C., Jennifer A., Douglas S.; m. Mary Ethel Wolff, May 25, 1996. Student, U. Oreg., 1946-48; diploma, U.S. Army Command & Gen. Staff, 1964. Enlisted U.S. Army, 1944, commd. 2d lt., 1948, advanced through grades to lt. col., ret., 1974; dir. econ. devel. dept. Yuma (Ariz.) County C. of C., 1974-83; exec. v.p. Lakin Enterprises, Yuma, 1983-87; owner Norton Cons., Yuma, 1987—; dir. Lower Colo. River Rsch. Ctr., Ariz. West Coll./No. Ariz. U., Yuma, 1998-2000. Corp. mem. Greater Yuma Econ. Devel. Corp., 1984-96, vice chmn., 1993-95. Mem. Yuma County Indsl. Devel. Authority, 1984-90, 92—, pres., 1992—; chmn. fundraising com. Yuma Cross Park Coun., 1984-88, sec., 1988-90, v.p., 1990-92, bd. dirs., 1982-96; bd. dirs. Yuma Leadership, 1984-93, Yuma Youth Leadership, 1993-96; chmn. devel. com. Yuma County Airport Authority, 1985-92, v.p., 1992-2002, pres., 2003-04, chmn. mktg. com., 2004; vice chmn. Yuma Main St. Bd., 1988-90, Yuma County Geog. Info. Sys. Task Force, 1991-95, Yuma Kids Voting, 1990-91, bd. dirs. Ariz. Partnership Air Transp., 1990-96, v.p. 1993-95; bd. dirs. Yuma County Civic Trusteeship, 1993-95, Ariz. Western Coll. Found. Bd., 2000-02, chmn. scholar awards commn., 2000-02; chmn. The Southwest Inst., 1995-96, What's Best for Our Kids, 1995-96, Yuma Sch. Dist. No. 1 New Elem. Sch. Planning Com., 1996-97; trustee Yuma County Libr., 1996-02; chmn. Yuma County Complete Count com. U.S. Census, 1990, 95, 2000; co-chmn. maintain the level budget override com., Yuma Sch. Dist. 1, 1999-2001; mem. Yuma County Town Hall Com., 1999—. Decorated Legion of Merit with oak leaf cluster, Bronze Star, Meritorious Svc. and Army Commendation Medal with Oak Leaf Cluster. Mem. Ariz. Assn. for Econ. Devel. (bd. dirs. 1975-82, pres. 1982-83, legis. affairs com. 1987-2002, Developer of Yr. 1978, William W. Lampkin award 2001), Yuma Execs. Assn. (sec.-treas., exec. dir. 1987—). Republican. Episcopalian. Avocations: golf, swimming, singing. Home and Office: 12267 E Del Norte Yuma AZ 85367-7356 Personal E-mail: yumexec@mindspring.com.

NORTON, EDWARD, actor; b. Boston, Aug. 18, 1969; Motion picture and stage actor. Film appearances include Everyone Says I Love You, 1996 (L.A. Film Critics Assn. award, 1996), Primal Fear, 1996 (nominee Best Supporting Actor Oscar, 1996, Chgo. Film Critics Assn. award, 1997, Golden Globe award, 1996, Nat. Bd. Rev. award, 1996), The People vs. Larry Flynt, 1996, Rounders, 1998, American History X, 1998 (nominee Best Actor Oscar, 1999, Chgo. Film Critics Assn. award, 1999, Golden Satellite award, 1999), Fight Club, 1999, The Score, 2001, Death to Smoochy, 2002, Red Dragon, 2002, Frida, 2002, 25th Hour, 2002, The Italian Job, 2003, dir., prodr. Keeping the Faith, 2000. Office: Endeavor Talent Agy 9701 Wilshire Blvd Fl 10 Beverly Hills CA 90212-2010

NORTON, ELEANOR HOLMES, congresswoman, lawyer, educator; b. Washington, June 13, 1937; d. Coleman and Vela (Lynch) Holmes; m. Edward W. Norton (div.); children: Katherine Felicia, John Holmes. BA, Antioch Coll., 1960; MA in Am. Studies, Yale U., 1963, LLB, 1964. Bar: Pa., 1965, U.S. Supreme Ct., 1968. Law clk. to Judge A. Leon Higgonbotham Fed. Dist. Ct.,

1964-65; asst. legal dir. ACLU, 1965-70; exec. asst. to mayor City of N.Y., 1971-74; chmn. N.Y.C. Commn. on Human Rights, 1970-77, EEOC, Washington, 1977-81; sr. fellow Urban Inst., Washington, 1981-82; prof. law Georgetown U., Washington, 1982—; del. (at large) U.S. Congress from D.C., 1990—; mem. coms. on govt. reform and transp./infrastructure. Democrat. Office: US Ho of Reps 2136 RayburnHo Office Bldg Washington DC 20515-0001*

NORTON, ELIZABETH WYCHGEL, lawyer; b. Cleve., Mar. 25, 1933; d. James Nicolas and Ruth Elizabeth (Cannell) Wychgel; m. Henry Wacks Norton Jr., July 16, 1954 (div. 1971); children: James, Henry, Peter, Fred; m. James Cory Ferguson, Dec. 14, 1985 (div. Apr. 1988). BA in Math., Wellesley Coll., 1954; JD cum laude, U. Minn., 1974. Bar: Minn. 1974. Summer intern Minn. Atty. Gen.'s Office, St. Paul, 1972; with U.S. Dept. Treasury, St. Paul, 1973; assoc. Gray, Plant, Mooty, Mooty & Bennett, P.A., Mpls., 1974-79, prin., 1980-94, of counsel, 1995-96. Mem. Minn. Lawyers Bd. Profl. Responsibility, 1984-89; mem. U. Minn. Law Sch. Bd. Visitors, 1987-92. Trustee YWCA, Mpls., 1979-84, 89-91, co-chmn. deferred giving com., 1980-81, chmn. by-laws com., bd. dirs., 1976-77, lectr.; treas. Minn. Women's Campaign Fund, 1985, guarantor, 1982-83, budget and fin. com. bd. dirs., 1984-87; trustee Ripley Meml. Found., 1980-84; treas. Jones-Harrison Home, 1967, bd. dirs., 1962-69, 2d v.p., chmn. fin., 1968-69; mem. Sen. David Durenberger's Women's Network, 1983-88. Durant scholar. Fellow Am. Bar Found.; mem. ABA (mediation task force family law sect. 1983-84), Minn. Bar Assn. (human rights com. family law sect., task force uniform marital property act 1984-85), Minn. Bar Found. (dir. 1991-94), Hennepin County Bar Assn. (pres. 1987-88, chmn. task force on pub. edn. 1984, chmn., mem. exec. com. family law sect. 1979-94), Minn. Inst. Legal Edn., Minn. Women's Lawyers (exec. com.), Hemlock Soc. of S.W. Fla. (co-chmn. 1999-2001), U. Minn. Law Sch. Alumni Assn. (dir. 1975-81, exec. com. 1981-83), Wellesley Club (Naples, pres. 2002-04), Phi Beta Kappa. Home: 26 Water Oaks Way Naples FL 34105-7157 E-mail: betsynorton@swfla.rr.com.

NORTON, FLOYD LIGON, IV, lawyer; b. Shreveport, La., Oct. 23, 1950; s. Floyd Ligon III and Grace Louise (Julian) N.; m. Kathleen Fair Patterson, Nov. 24, 1979; children: Caroline, Elizabeth. BA with honors, U. Va., 1972, JD, 1975. Bar: Va. 1975, D.C. 1975. Assoc. Reid & Priest, Washington, 1975-83, ptnr., 1983-95, Morgan Lewis & Bockius, 1995—. Mem. ABA, Fed. Energy Bar Assn. Episcopalian. Home: 4107 Bradley Ln Bethesda MD 20815-5236 Office: Morgan Lewis & Bockius 1111 Pennsylvania Ave NW Washington DC 20004-5802 E-mail: fnorton@morganlewis.com.

NORTON, FRAN, recreation director; b. July 5, 1950; m. Richard Spitz, Jr. BFA, Rochester Inst. Tech., 1972. Park technician Frederick Douglass NHS Nat. Parks-East, Washington, 1972-75; supr. park technician John F. Kennedy Ctr. Performing Arts, Washington, 1975-80; supr. park ranger Klingle Resource Ctr. Nat. Capital Region, Washington, 1980-81, regional vol., grants mgr., 1982-84, supr. park ranger Career Conservation Devel. Corp., 1990; self employed Annapolis, Md., 1984-90; site mgr. Arlington House, Robert E. Lee Meml. George Washington Meml. Pkwy., McLean, Va., 1993-94; unit mgr. cultural resources, site mgr. Arlington House Clara Barton NHS, Glen Echo Park, Women in Mil. Svc. Am., McLean, 1994-98; chief ranger, divsn. interpretation Ft. Sumter, Sullivan's Is., S.C., 1998—. Office: 1214 Middle St Sullivans Island SC 29482-9717 Fax: 843-883-3910.

NORTON, GALE ANN, Secretary of the Interior; b. Wichita, Mar. 11, 1954; d. Dale Bentsen and Anna Jacqueline (Lansdowne) N.; m. John Goethe Hughes, Mar. 26, 1990. BA, U. Denver, 1975, JD, 1978. Bar: Colo. 1978, U.S. Supreme Ct. 1981. Jud. clk. Colo. Ct. of Appeals, Denver, 1978-79; sr. atty. Mountain States Legal Found., Denver, 1979-83; nat. fellow Hoover Instn. Stanford (Calif.) U., 1983-84; asst. to dep. sec. USDA, Washington, 1984-85; assoc. solicitor U.S. Dept. of Interior, Washington, 1985-87; pvt. practice law Denver, 1987-90; atty. gen. State of Colo., Denver, 1991—99; sr. counsel Brownstein, Hyatt & Farber, P.C., 1999—2000; sec. U.S. Dept. Interior, Washington, 2001—. Lectr. U. Denver Law Sch., 1989; transp. law program dir. U. Denver, 1978-79. Contbr. chpts. to books, articles to profl. jours. Past chair Nat. Assn. Attys. Gen. Environ. Com.; co-chair Nat. Policy Forum Environ. Coun.; candidate for 1996 election to U.S. Senate; chair environ. commn. Rep. Nat. Lawyers Assn. Named Young Career Woman Bus. and Profl. Women, 1981, Young Lawyer of Yr., 1991, Mary Lathrop Trailblazer award Colo. Women's Bar Assn., 1999. Mem. Federalist Soc., Colo. Women's Forum, Order of St. Ives. Republican. Methodist. Avocation: skiing. Office: Dept of the Interior Office of the Sec 1849 C St NW Washington DC 20240

NORTON, GERALD PATRICK, lawyer; b. West Roxbury, Mass., Jan. 25, 1940; s. Thomas W. and Genevieve (Sweeny) N.; m. Judith C. Ralphs, Apr. 24, 1965 (dec. Oct. 1969); children: Jeremy, Elizabeth; m. Amanda B. Norton, Sept. 25, 1971; 1 child, Adam. AB magna cum laude, Princeton U., 1961; LLB magna cum laude, Columbia U., 1964. Bar: N.Y. 1964, D.C. 1966. Law clk. to judge U.S. Ct. Appeals (2d cir.), N.Y.C., 1964-65; assoc. Covington & Burling, Washington, 1965-73; asst. to solicitor gen. Dept. Justice, Washington, 1973-75; dep. gen. counsel FTC, Washington, 1975-79; ptnr. Pepper Hamilton & Scheetz, Washington, 1979-92, Harkins Cunningham, Washington, 1992—. Mem. Supreme Ct. Moot Ct. panels. Mng. and research editor Columbia U. Law Rev., 1963-64; contbr. articles to profl. jours. Bd. dirs. Washington Lawyer Com. for Civil Rights & Urban Affairs, 1984—; 1st v.p., bd. dirs. Washington Met. Planning and Housing Assn., 1969-70; vol. atty. ACLU, Washington. Recipient Arthur E. Flemming award Jaycees of Nat. Capital Area, 1979; named Grad. of Yr., Province I Phi Delta Phi, 1964. Mem.: Nat. Assn. Attys. Gen., DC Bar (spl. com. on govt. lawyers and the model rules of profl. conduct 1986—88, legal ethics com. 1989—95, com. on rev. of rules and profl. conduct 1995—2001). Democrat. Office: Harkins Cunningham 801 Penn Ave NW Washington DC 20004-2615 E-mail: gnorton@harkinscunningham.com.

NORTON, GREGORY ALAN, writer; b. Linton, Ind., Nov. 21, 1948; s. Harrison Weaver and Marceline Marsha Norton; 1 child, Michael Harrison. BA in English, Western Ill. U., 1970. Mng. editor United Steelworkers, Elgin, Ill., 1991—98. Author: (novel) There Ain't No Justice, Just Us. Organizer, editor United Steelworkers, Elgin, Ill., 1991—98.

NORTON, JANE E. lieutenant governor; b. Grand Junction, Colo. d. Bus and Elinor Bergman; m. Mike Norton; children: Lacee, Tyler. BS, Colo. State U., 1976; MS in Mgmt., Regis U. With Med. Group Mgmt. Assn., Englewood, Colo.; mem. Colo. Ho. Reps., 1986—87; regional dir. U.S. Dept. Health and Human Svcs.; exec. dir. Colo. Dept. Pub. Health Environment, 1999—2002; lt. gov. Colo., 2003—. Chair Colo. Commn. on Indian Affairs. Republican. Office: 130 State Capitol Denver CO 80203

NORTON, JERRY E. law educator; b. Salina, Kans., Oct. 6, 1937; s. Frank C. and Helen M. Norton; m. Margaret A. Williams, Jan. 6, 1962. BA, Kans. Wesleyan U., Salina, 1958; JD, Washburn U., Topeka, 1962; LLM, Northwestern U., Evanston, Ill., 1967. Bar: Ill. 1968. Atty. Norton and Norton, Salina, Kans., 1962—66; asst. prof. of law Chgo.-Kent Coll. of Law, Ill. Inst. of Tech., 1967—71; prof. of law Loyola U. Chgo. Sch. of Law, 1971—. Mem. and chair, village plan commn., Oak Park, Ill., 1986—94; trustee Kans. Wesleyan U., Salina, Kans., 2004. Office: Loyola University Chicago School of Law 1 East Pearson St Chicago IL 60611 Office Phone: 312-915-7136. E-mail: jnorto1@luc.edu.

NORTON, KAREN ANN, accountant; b. Nov. 1, 1950; d. Dale Francis and Ruby Grace (Gehlhar) N. BA, U. Minn., 1972; postgrad., U. Md., 1978; MBA, Calif. State Poly. U., Pomona, 1989. CPA, Md. Securities transactions analyst Bur. of Pub. Debt, Washington, 1972-79, internal auditor, 1979-81, IRS, Washington, 1981; sr. acct. World Vision Internat., Monrovia, Calif., 1981-83, acctg. supr., 1983-87; sr. sys. liaison coord. Home Savs. Am. (name changed to Washington Mut.), 1987-97, sys. auditor, 1997-2000, sect. mgr., 2000—02, group mgr., v.p., 2003—04; project mgr. II Indy Mac Bank, 2004—. Author: (poetry) Ode to Joyce, 1985 (Golden Poet award 1985). 2d v.p. chpt. Nat. Treasury Employees Union, Washington, 1978, editor chpt. newsletter; mem. M-2 Prisoners Sponsorship Program, Chino, Calif., 1984-86. Recipient Spl. Achievement award Dept. Treasury, 1976, Superior Performance award Dept. Treasury, 1977-78; Charles and Ellora Alliss scholar, 1968. Mem. Angel Flight, Flying Samaritans, Habitat for Humanity. Avocations: flying, chess, tennis. E-mail: skypilot@pacbell.net.

NORTON, LARRY, oncologist; b. Bronx, N.Y., 1947; MD, Columbia U., 1972. Diplomate Am. Bd. Internal Medicine, Am. Bd. Oncology. Intern Bronx Mcpl. Hosp.-Einstein, N.Y.C., 1972-73, resident, 1973-74; mem. staff Meml. Sloan-Kettering Cancer Ctr., N.Y.C.; ptnr. group practice. Mem. Alpha Omega Alpha. Office: Meml Sloan-Kettering Cancer Ctr 1275 York Ave New York NY 10021-6094

NORTON, LINDA LEE, pharmacist, educator; b. Vallejo, Calif., Aug. 12, 1953; d. Don Leroy and Pearl Etta (Cain) Hartzell; m. Lawrence Henry Norton, Aug. 19, 1972; children: Joshua David, Gabriel Aaron. PharmD, U. Pacific, 1991. Lic. pharmacist, Calif., Nev. Pharmacy resident St. Joseph's Med. Ctr., Stockton, Calif., 1991-92, U. Ariz., Tucson, 1992-93; fellow in pain rsch. and drug info. U. of Pacific and Am. Acad. Pain Mgmt., Stockton, 1993-95; asst. prof. pharmacy practice U. of Pacific, Stockton, 1995-99, assoc. coord. postgrad. profl. edn., 1995-99, assoc. prof., dir. postgrad. profl. edn., 1999—. Mng. editor Enjoying Good Health, 1997-99; contbr. articles to profl. jours. Mem. shared governance com. Liberty Union H.S., Brentwood, Calif., 1995-97, health careers acad. com., 1995-97; bd. dirs. SMART Coalition, Sacramento, 1998-2000. Recipient Award for outstanding article in pain mgmt. Am. Jour. Pain Mgmt., 1997; grantee Valley Mountain Reg. Ctr., 1998-2000, Diagnostek, 1994; Thomas J. Long Faculty fellow, 1997, 98, 2000-03. Mem. Am. Assn. Colls. Pharmacy (chmn. CPE sect. 2001-2003), Am. Soc. Health-Sys. Pharmacists, Calif. Soc. Health-Sys. Pharmacists (co-chair C.E. Focus '98), Rho Chi. Avocations: small-scale farming and ranching, horse shoe pitching, fishing. Office: Univ Pacific Sch Pharmacy 751 Brookside Rd Stockton CA 95211-0001

NORTON, MARY BETH, history educator, writer; b. Ann Arbor, Mich., Mar. 25, 1943; d. Clark Frederic and Mary Elizabeth (Lunny) N. BA, U. Mich., 1964; MA, Harvard U., 1965, PhD, 1969; DHL (hon.), Siena Coll., 1983, Marymount Manhattan Coll., 1984, De Pauw U., 1989; DLitt (hon.), Ill. Wesleyan U., 1992. Asst. prof. history U. Conn., Storrs, 1969-71; from asst. prof. to prof. Cornell U., Ithaca, NY, 1971-87, Mary Donlon Alger prof. Am. history, 1987—. Author: The British-Americans: The Loyalist Exiles in England, 1774-1789, 1972, Liberty's Daughters: The Revolutionary Experience of American Women, 1750-1800, 1980 (Berkshire prize for Best Book Woman Historian 1980), Founding Mothers and Fathers: Gendered Power and the Forming of American Society, 1996 (finalist Pulitzer prize in history 1997), In the Devil's Snare: The Salem Witchcraft Crisis of 1692, 2002 (Amb. Book award of English-Speaking Union 2003); co-author: A People and A Nation, 1982, 7th rev. edit., 2004; editor: AHA Guide to Hist. Literature, 3d rev. edit., 1995; co-editor: Women of America: A History, 1979, To Toil the Livelong Day: America's Women at Work, 1790-1980, 1987, Major Problems in American Women's History, 1989, 3d rev. edit., 2003; contbr. articles to profl. jours. Trustee Cornell U., 1973-75, 83-88; mem. Nat. Coun. Humanities, Washington, 1979-84. Woodrow Wilson Found. fellow, 1964-65, NEH fellow, 1974-75, Shelby Cullom Davis Ctr. fellow Princeton U., 1977-78, Rockefeller Found. fellow, 1986-87, Soc. for Humanities fellow Cornell U., 1989-90, John Simon Guggenheim Meml. Found. fellow, 1993-94, Starr Found. fellow Lady Margaret Hall, Oxford U., 2000, Mellon postdoctoral fellow Huntington Libr., 2001. Fellow Soc. Am. Hist. (exec. bd. 1974-87, 2003—, Allan Nevins prize 1970); mem. Am. Hist. Assn. (v.p. for rsch. 1985-87), Am. Acad. Arts and Sci., Orgn. Am. Hist. (exec. bd. 1983-86), Berkshire Conf. Women Hist. (pres. 1983-85) Democrat. Methodist. Office: Cornell U Dept History 325 Mcgraw Hall Ithaca NY 14853-4601 E-mail: mbn1@cornell.edu.

NORTON, MAX C. writer, educator; b. Rigby, Idaho, Feb. 20, 1920; s. Robert Leandor and Alice Ida Norton; m. Adrianna Mae Van Konynenburg; children: Maxwel V.K., Gale Dirk, Jenni Sahlman. AA, Modesto Jr. Coll., Calif.; studied, U. Pacific, Stockton, Calif.; BA, Stanford U.; PhD, Denver U. Emeritus prof. Calif. State U., Turlock, 1985—. Mem. editl. bd. Inst. for Gen. Semantics, San Francisco, 1964. Author: The Alice Saga, 2000. Mem.: Am. Speech Language Hearing Assn. (life). Home: 5766 Stoddard Rd Modesto CA 95356 E-mail: mnorton@calstatestan.edu.

NORTON, NORMAN JAMES, retired exploration geologist, educator; b. Du Quoin, Ill., Apr. 26, 1933; s. James Harlan Norton and Helen Jane (Riley) Norton Rosen; m. Bettie Jean Greer, July 7, 1955; children— Matthew James, Jane Alison BS, So. Ill. U., 1958; MS, U. Minn., 1960, PhD, 1963. From asst. to prof. biology Hope Coll., Holland, Mich., 1964-74; prof., chmn. dept. biology Ball State U., Munice, Ind., 1974-78, acting v.p. acad. affairs, 1978-79; acting dean Ball State U. Coll. Arts and Scis., 1979-81; provost, v.p. acad. affairs Ind. U. Pa., 1981-83; cons. geologist Gulf Oil Corp., Houston, 1970-83; sr. staff geologist Gulf Oil Exploration and Prodn. Co., Houston, 1983-85; biostratigrapher, stratigraphic services, exploration Chevron Overseas Petroleum Inc., San Ramon, Calif., 1985-91; supr. biostratigraphy sect. Chevron U.S.A., Inc., Houston, 1991-93; acting divsn. geologist Chevron U.S.A. Inc., Houston, 1993-95, divsn. geologist, 1995—, geol. cons., 1997-98, ret., 1998. Contbr. articles to profl. jours. Chmn. bd. trustees Kiawah Island Natural Habitat Conservancy, 2002—. With USAF, 1952—56. Recipient Outstanding Tchr. Educator award Sr. Class of Hope Coll., 1969, acad. citation for disting. achievement Mich. Acad. Scis., Art and Letters, 1969, Outstanding Achievement award Chevron Overseas Petroleum Inc., 1990. Mem. Am. Assn. Stratigraphic Palynologists (Disting. Svc. award 1978, chmn. bd. trustees found., archives com. 1970—, constrn. revision com.). Home: 514 Ruddy Turnstone Johns Island SC 29455 E-mail: njnorto@attglobal.net.

NORTON, PATRICK H. manufacturing executive; b. Windsor, Ont., Can., May 23, 1930; s. H. Patrick and Alfreda (Haf) N.; m. Dorothy A. McAllen, Oct. 10, 1953; children: Patrick J., Mary Anne, Susan, Margaret, Michael, Thomas, John, Kathleen. BSME, U. Detroit, 1950. Pres. Ionic Internat., Inc., Detroit, 1965-75; chmn. Korest-Peterson Co., Detroit, 1975-83; chmn. and chief exec. officer Chem. Handling Equipment Co., Toledo, 1980—, also bd. dirs. Bd. dirs. Korest-Peterson Co., ECO Communications Co., JJ Bus. Products Co. Patentee in field. Mem. Zoning Bd. Appeals, Beverly Hills, Mich., 1965-68. Served with U.S. Army, 1951-53. Recipient Edward Ignatius Rice award Christian Bros. Ireland, 1986. Mem. Am. Electroplaters Soc. (bd. dirs. 1954-86). Clubs: Plum Hollow Golf (Southfield, Mich.), Burning Tree Country (Mt. Clemens, Mich.). Republican. Roman Catholic. Avocations: golf, boating. Home: 17700 Northland Park Ct Southfield MI 48075-4302 Office: Chem Handling Equipment Co Inc 5656 Opportunity Dr Toledo OH 43612-2941

NORTON, ROBERT HOWARD, entertainer, musical arranger, author; b. NYC, July 19, 1946; s. Howard R. and Lena (Triano) N.; m. Eileen Williams, Sept. 29, 1966 (div. 1976); children: Brian, Lelania. Student, Broward C.C., Ft. Lauderdale, Fla., 1970-75; community antenna TV engr. cert., Nat. Cable TV Inst., 1976. Rec. session artist Motown and various other recording labels, 1964—; entertainer various concerts, 1964—; systems technician Selkirk Communications, Ft. Lauderdale, Fla., 1979-81; cable TV engr. Gen. Instrument Corp., Hatboro, Pa., 1981-84; entertainer (with Leilani Chandler) The Sophisticats, Ft. Pierce, Fla., 1984—; owner, author, software writer Norton Music, Ft. Pierce, Fla., 1990—. Author: The Artist's and Entertainer's Tax Bible, 1990, Entertainer's Guide to Cruising, 1991—; writer mus. software: 350 User Styles, 1991—, Band-in-a-Box Supercharger, 1993—, 22 Band-in-a-Box Fake Disks, 1994—, 13 Band-in-a-Box User Style Disks, 1993—, software 475+: Gen. MIDI Sequences, 1993—; composer: numerous songs, —; arranger of more then 400 songs, —. Mem. Internat. Wind Synthesis Assn. Home and Office: Norton Music PO Box 13149 Fort Pierce FL 34979-3149 E-mail: norton@nortonmusic.com.

NORTON, ROBERT L. consumer products company executive; BSc, Cleve. (Ohio) State U., 1973. Vice chmn., CFO JoAnn Stores, Inc., 1993—96; from gen. mgr. to CEO FTD Inc., Downers Grove, Ill., 1997—99, CEO, 2000, chmn. bd. Office: FTD Inc 3113 Woodcreek Dr Downers Grove IL 60515*

NORTON, ROBERT MICHAEL, mathematician, educator, statistician; b. Richmond Heights, Mo., July 1, 1946; s. Robert and Eunice Louise Ethel (Hoffman) N.; m. Elizabeth Ferry, Aug. 6, 1972; children: Andrew Robert, Susan Hall. BS, BS in Edn., N.E. Mo. State U., 1968; MS in Math., Okla. State U., 1971, PhD in Math., 1974. Asst. prof. math. Coll. of Charleston, S.C., 1974-79, assoc. prof., 1979-86, prof., 1986—. Bd. examiners Nat. Coun. for Accreditation of Tchr. Edn., 1990-93; dir. MS program in math. U. Charleston, 1994-98, dir. EdM in sci. and math., 1997-2002; expert witness in stats.; stats. quality control cons. Author: A Quick Course in Statistical Process Control; contbr. articles to profl. jours. Dir. region III H.S. wrestling ofcls. S.C. H.S. League, 1989-96. With U.S. Army, 1969-70, Vietnam. Named S.C. Wrestling Referee of the Yr., S.C. H.S. League, Columbia, 1997. Mem. Am. Statis. Assn. (pres. S.C. chpt. 1979-80), Math. Assn. Am., Am. Soc. for Quality (sect. chair 2000-01), VFW (life).

NORTON, ROBERT R., JR., former food products executive; b. 1946; BS, Mo. Western State Coll., 1966; MBA, N.W. Mo. State U., 1968. Sec., treas. Dugdale Packing Co., St. Joseph, Mo., 1966-86; with BeefAmerica Operating Co., Inc., Omaha, 1986-96, pres., 1988-96. Office: Beef America Ste 216 3610 Dodge St Omaha NE 68131-3218

NORTON, SALLY PAULINE, lawyer; b. Elkhart, Ind., Jan. 28, 1964; d. Ronald and Peggy Hale; m. Peter Norton, Aug. 28, 1993; children: Alexander, Aileen. BA, Ind. U., 1986, JD, 1989. Bar: Ind. 1991, U.S. Dist. Ct. (no. and so. dists.) Ind. 1991. Law clk. Kalamaros & Assocs., South Bend, Ind., 1990-91, assoc., 1991—2002, Doran-Blackmond LLP, South Bend, 2000—02, prnt., 2002—. Mem. Ind. Bar Assn., St. Joseph County Bar Assn., Def. Trial Counsel Ind., Def. Rsch. Inst., Robert A. Grant Inn of Ct. Avocation: martial arts. Home: 10628 N Pheasant Cove Dr Granger IN 46530-7576 Office: Doran Blackmond LLP 211 W Washington South Bend IN 46601

NORVILLE, DEBORAH ANNE, news correspondent; b. Aug. 8, 1958; d. Zachary S. and Merle Olson Norville; m. Karl G. Wellner Dec. 12, 1987; children: Karl Nikolai, Kyle Maximilian, Mikaela Katharina. ABJ summa cum laude, U. Ga., 1979. Reporter Sta. WAGA-TV, Atlanta, 1978-79, anchor, reporter, 1979-81, Sta. WMAQ-TV, Chgo., 1982-86; anchor NBC News, N.Y.C., 1987-89; news anchor Today Show, NBC, N.Y.C., 1989, co-anchor, 1990-92; corr. Street Stories, CBS, N.Y.C., 1992-94; co-anchor America Tonight, CBS, N.Y.C., 1994; anchor Inside Edition, King World Prodns., 1994—; contbg. editor McCall's, N.Y.C.; host Deborah Norville Tonight MSNBC, N.Y.C., 2004—. Author: Back on Track: How to Straighten Out Your Life When it Throws You a Curve, 1997, I Don't Want To Sleep Tonight, 1999, I Can Fly, 2001. Bd. dirs. Greater N.Y. coun. Girl Scouts U.S., 1989-, Broadcaster's Found.; mem. steering com. Rita Hayworth Gala Alzheimer's Assn; nat. celebrity spokesperson Mother's March of Dimes, 2001, 02. Recipient Outstanding Young Alumni award Sch. Journalism, U. Ga., Emmy award, 1985-86, 89, Gracie Award, Am. Women in Radio and TV; named Person of Yr., Chgo. Broadcast Advt. Club, 1989, 91, Anchor of Yr. 2000, Washington Journalism Rev., 1989. Mem. Soc. Profl. Journalists. Office: Inside Edition King World Prod 515 W 57th St New York NY 10019-2901*

NORWALK, KELLI CURRAN, retail executive, entrepreneur; b. Cleve., Sept. 25, 1949; d. Paul Joseph and Ella (Eylar) Curran; m. Keith Otto Norwalk, Apr. 3, 1970; children: Keith Curran, Alyssa Barr. BA, Butler U., 1978. Exec. dir. Heritage Place, Indpls., 1975-77; social worker Americana Health Care, Indpls., 1978-81; pres., prin. Down By the Ducks, Inc., Indpls., 1982-85; chief exec. officer, prin. The Tarkington Tweed, Inc., Indpls., 1985—. Chmn. Spotlight, 2001, 02. Mem. Butler Tarkington Neithborhood Assn., Indpls., 1978—, Arts, Ind. Finalist Entrepreneur of Yr. award Ernst and Young Ind. Heartland, 1998. Mem. 500 Festival Assocs., Indpls. C. of C. Democrat. Roman Catholic. Avocations: painting, theater, travel. Home: 5534 Bay Landing Ct Indianapolis IN 46254-9564 Office: The Tarkington Tweed Inc 5631 N Illinois St Indianapolis IN 46208-1554

NORWITZ, TREVOR S. lawyer; b. Cape Town, South Africa, Oct. 21, 1964; came to the U.S., 1989; s. Rubin Gabriel and Marionne Joyce Norwitz; m. Shannon Lieberman, Jan. 19, 1992; children: Raphael Shai, Herschel Sam. B in Bus. Sci., U. Cape Town, 1986; BA in Juris, Oxford (Eng.) U., 1989, MA, 1993; LLM, Columbia U., 1990. Bar: N.Y. 1991. Assoc. Cravath, Swaine & Moore, N.Y.C., 1990-94, Wachtell, Lipton, Rosen & Katz, N.Y.C., 1994-98, ptnr., 1999—. Contbr. articles to profl. jours. Rhodes scholar, 1987. Mem. ABA (bus. sect. com., com. corp. laws). Office: Wachtell Lipton Rosen & Katz 51 W 52nd St Fl 29 New York NY 10019-6150

NORWOOD, BERNARD, economist; b. Boston, Nov. 21, 1922; s. Hyman and Rose (Fink) N.; m. Janet Lippe, June 25, 1943; children: Stephen Harlan, Peter Carlton. BA, Boston U., 1947; MA, Fletcher Sch. Law and Diplomacy, 1948, PhD, 1957. Internat. economist State Dept., 1949-58; joined U.S. Fgn. Svc., 1955; 1st sec. U.S. mission to European Communities, Brussels, Belgium, 1958-62; asst. chief comml. policy and treaties divsn. Dept. State, 1962; chmn. trade staff com. Office Spl. Rep. for Trade Negotiations, Exec. Office Pres., 1963-67; assigned The Nat. War Coll., 1967-68; advisor divsn. internat. fin. bd. govs. Fed. Res. Sys., 1968-75; prin. assoc., sr. cons. Nathan Assocs., Inc., 1975-94. Mem. U.S. del. to negotiations and confs. GATT, Geneva, 1953-67. Served with AUS, 1943-46. Home and Office: 5610 Wisconsin Ave # 21D Chevy Chase MD 20815-4415

NORWOOD, B.J. SCOTT, business and management educator, Russian affairs educator; b. San Diego, June 24, 1926; s. Guy Johns and Louise Elizabeth Norwood; m. Barbara Ann Norwood, Jan. 28, 1956; children: Jonathan Scott, Beverly Norwood. AA, UCLA, 1947, BS, 1949; MBA, Harvard U., 1951. Asst. prof. San Jose (Calif.) State U., 1955-58, assoc. prof., 1958-62, prof., 1962—2003, prof. emeritus, 2004—. Chmn. bd. dirs. Radiation Detection Co., Sunnyvale, Calif., 1972—83; mgmt. cons., reschr., educator, Calif., 1960—83; mgmt. cons., rschr., educator U.S. Govt., 1973—98; econ. transition advisor various govt. entities Russia, Belarus, Mongolia, 1990—95; lectr. in field. Founding editor Vectors, 1989-98; contbr. to profl. pubs. Commr. County of Santa Clara-Moscow Region Sister County Commn., 1995—. With USNR, 1944-46, PTO. Named Outstanding Prof., San Jose State U., 1976; recipient Outstanding Svc. award, Air Force ROTC, 1982, medal for superior pub. svc., Sec. of Navy, 1988, Jefferson award, FBI, Washington, 1993. Mem.: Navy League U.S. (state pres. 1986—87, region v.p.-at-large 1995—97, nat. dir. emeritus, 11 awards 1990—98), Assn. U.S. Army (state pres. and regional exec. v.p. 1988—90, regional exec. v.p. 1995—96, 7 awards 1994—98), Air Force Assn. (state chmn. bd. 1982—84, state pres., 10 awards 1981—89), Propeller Club (nat. bd. govs., pres. San Francisco Bay Region 2002—03), Knights Hospitaller (chevalier), Sovereign Order of St. John, Sovereign Mil. Order Temple of Jerusalem (knight comdr. 1995, grand officer 1999, chevalier). Avocations: Russian language, travel in Russia.

NORWOOD, BRANDY RAYANA (BRANDY), singer, actress; b. McComb, Miss., Feb. 11, 1979; d. Willie and Sonia Norwood; m. Robert Smith, 2001 (div. 2003); 1 child, Sy'rai. Student, Pepperdine U. Singer: (albums) Brandy, 1994 (NAACP Image Award: Best New Artist, 1996), De Falda Cortita, 1995, Never S-A-Y Never, 1998, Full Moon, 2002; actor: (TV series) Thea, 1996, Moesha, 1995—2001 (NAACP Image Award: Best Youth Actor/Actress, 1997), Brandy: Special Delivery, 2002; (TV films) Cinderella, 1997; actor, exec. prodr.: (TV films) Double Platinum, 1999; actor: (films) I Still Know What You Did Last Summer, 1998; voice Osmosis Jones, 2001. Named Favorite New Artist, Am. Music Awards, 1996; recipient Grammy award (with Monica) Best R&B Performance By A Duo Or Group With Vocal for song "That Boy Is Mine", 1998. Office: 15030 Ventura Blvd 710 Sherman Oaks CA 91403*

NORWOOD, CECILIA STUBBS, communications executive; b. Kansas City, Mo. married. BBA cum laude, MBA in Mktg. summa cum laude, U. North Tex. Analyst Exxon Co. U.S., 1978, sales rep. for dealer operated stores in North Tex. region, mkt. devel. analyst; v.p. corp. comms. Southland Corp., until 1996; corp. v.p. global comms. Electronic Data Sys. Corp., Plano, Tex., 1996—. Chair Conf. Bd. Coun. Corp. Comms. Strategy; pres. Dallas chpt. Nat. Investor Rels. Inst., So. Meth. U. Coll. Comms. Adv. Bd.; active U. North Tex. Pres.'s Coun.; bd. dirs. Planned Parenthood Dallas, Planned Parenthood Northeast Tex., Dallas Women's Found. Recipient Clarion award. Office: Electronic Data Sys Corp 5400 Legacy Dr Plano TX 75024-3199 Fax: 972-605-2643.

NORWOOD, CHARLES W., JR., congressman; b. Valdosta, Ga., July 27, 1941; m. Gloria Norwood; 2 children. BS, Ga. So. U., 1964; DDS, Georgetown U., 1967. Pvt. practice, Augusta, Ga., 1969-94; owner Norwood Tree Nursery, 1984—; mem. U.S. Congress from 9th Ga. dist. (formerly 10th), 1995—, mem. commerce, edn. and the workforce coms., vchmn. health subcom., chmn. workforce protection com.; pres. Georgia Dental Assoc., 1983. Capt. U.S. Army, 1967-69, Vietnam. Decorated Combat Medic badge, Bronze Star for Meritorious Svc., Bronze Star for Meritorious Achievement. Mem. Ga. Dental Assn. Republican. Methodist. Office: US Ho of Reps 2452 Rayburn Hob Washington DC 20515-1010

NORWOOD, DEBORAH ANNE, law librarian; b. Honolulu, Nov. 12, 1950; d. Alfred Freeman and Helen G. (Papsch) N.; 1 child, Nicholas. BA, U. Wash., 1972, M in Law Librarianship, 1979; JD, Willamette U., 1974. Bar: Wash., U.S. Dist. Ct. (we. dist.) 1975, U.S. Ct. Appeals (9th cir.) 1980. Ptnr. Evans and Norwood, Seattle, 1975-79; law libr. U.S. Courts Libr., Seattle, 1980-89; state law libr. Wash. State Law Libr., Olympia, 1989—2002, reporter of decisions, 1994-2001; asst. dir. pub. svcs. Jacob Burns Law Libr. George Washington U., Washington, 2002—. Mem. Freedom to Read Found. Mem. Am. Assn. Law Librs. (chmn. state, ct. and county spl. interest sect. 1995-96, chair legal info. svcs. to pub. spl. interest sect. 2001-02). Office: Jacob Burns Law Libr George Washington U 716-20th St NW Washington DC 20052 Office Phone: 202-994-7338. E-mail: dnorwood@law.gwu.edu.

NORWOOD, JANET LIPPE, economist; b. Newark, Dec. 11, 1923; d. M. Turner and Thelma (Levinson) Lippe; m. Bernard Norwood, June 25, 1943; children: Stephen Harlan, Peter Carlton. BA, Douglass Coll., 1945; MA, Tufts U., 1946; PhD, Fletcher Sch. Law and Diplomacy, 1949; LLD (hon.), Fla. Internat. U., 1979, Carnegie Mellon U., 1984, Harvard U., 1997, Rutgers U., 2003. Instr. Wellesley Coll., 1948-49; economist William L. Clayton Ctr., Tufts U., 1953-58; with Bur. Labor Stats., U.S. Dept. Labor, Washington, 1963-91; dep. commr., then acting commr. Bur. Labor Stats. Dept. Labor, Washington, 1975-79, commr. labor stats., 1979-92; sr. fellow The Urban Inst., Washington, 1992-99; counselor, sr. fellow N.Y. Conf. Bd., 2001—. Dir. Nat. Opinion Rsch. Ctr., chair adv. coun. unemployment compensation, 1993—96; dir. Inst. Global Ethics; chair panel to rev. 2000 census NAS; mem. adv. bd. Bur. Transp. Stats.; pres. COSSA, 2001—02. Author: Organizing to Count: Change in the Federal Statistical System, 1995; contbr. Named Hall Disting. Alumni, Rutgers U., 1987; recipient Disting. Achievement award, Dept. Labor, 1972, Spl. Commendation award, 1977, Philip Arnow award, 1979, Elmer Staats award, 1982, Pub. Svc. award, 1984, Presdl. Disting. Exec. Rank, 1988, Elizabeth Scott award, Com. Pres.'s Statis. Assns., 2002. Fellow: AAAS, Nat. Assn. Bus. Economists, Royal Statis. Soc., Am. Statis. Assn. (pres. 1989, Founder's award 1997); mem.: Nat. Inst. Statis. Sci. (bd. trustees 1991—2000), Nat. Acad. Pub. Adminstrn., Am. Econ. Assn., Internat. Assn. Ofcls. Stats., Internat. Statis. Inst., Douglass Coll. Soc. Disting. Achievement, Cosmos Club (pres. 1995—96). Home: 5610 Wisconsin Ave Ph 21-d Chevy Chase MD 20815-4444 Personal E-mail: janetnor@aol.com.

NOSANOW, BARBARA SHISSLER, art association administrator; b. Roanoke, Va. d. Willis Morton and Kathryn Sabin (Bradford) Johnson; m. John Lewis Shissler Jr., July 28, 1957 (dec. May 1972); children: John Lewis Shissler III, Ada Holland Shissler; m. Lewis Harold Nosanow, Oct. 15, 1973. AB, Smith Coll., 1957; MA, Case Western Res. U., 1958. Asst. mng. editor Jour. Aesthetics and Art Criticism, Cleve. Mus. Art, 1958-63; dir. publs. and rsch. Mpls. Inst. Arts, 1963-72; dir. U. Minn. Art Mus., Mpls., 1972-76; dir. exhbns. and edn. Nat. Archives, Washington, 1976-79; curator Smithsonian Instn., Washington, 1979-82; asst. dir. Nat. Mus. Am. Art, Smithsonian Instn., 1982-88; dir. Portland (Maine) Mus. Art, 1988-93, Art Spaces, 1993—; study leader, lecturer Smithsonian Study Tours of France and Russia, 1997—. Lectr. art history, also author. Past mem. various rev. panels NEH, Washington. Bd. dirs. Md. Com. for Humanities, Balt., 1980-83. Mem. Internat. Women's Forum. Avocation: travel. Office: Art Spaces 3386 Piperfife Ct Keswick VA 22947-9142 Office Phone: 434-923-0019.

NOSCO, PETER ERLING, humanities educator, consultant; b. N.Y.C., N.Y., Mar. 13, 1950; s. John and Beatrice Nosco; m. Margaret Joan Button, June 19, 1976; children: John Alexander, Jean Nosco Wright. BA, Columbia U., 1971; MA (hon.), Cambridge U., Eng., 1973; PhD, Columbia U., 1978. Prof. U. of So. Calif., Los Angeles, Calif., 1986—2003, U. Brit. Columbia, 2003—; asst. prof. St. John's U., Queens, NY, 1979—86. Project dir. Fulbright Group Projects Abroad; dir. NEH Summer Inst. for Coll. Tchrs.; pres. faculty and acad. senate U. So. Calif., 2001—02. Author: (book-length monograph) Remembering Paradise; editor: (scholarly book) Confucianism and Tokugawa Culture; translator: Some Final Words of Advice (Saikaku oritome) (Transl. Ctr. (Nat. Endowment for the Arts Columbia U.), 1980). Recipient Fulbright Sr. Rsch. fellowship, Dept. of Edn., 1986, grant to lead a Fulbright Group Projects Abroad field study of Japan, 1998; grantee grant to direct a summer inst. for coll. tchrs., NEH, 2002. Fellow: L.A. Inst. for the Humanities; mem.: Am. Acad. of Religion, Am. Hist. Assn., Assn. for Asian Studies. Office: UBC-Asian Studies 401-1871 W Mall Vancouver BC Canada V6T 1Z2 Personal E-mail: peter.nosco@ubc.ca.

NOSHER, JOHN LOUIS, radiologist; b. East Orange, N.J., Jan. 31, 1946; s. Louis P. and Pauline Nosher; m. Marjorie Theresa Dolan, 1970; children: John Christopher, Todd Matthew, Brittany Paige. BS, St. Joseph's Coll., 1967; MD, Jefferson Med. Coll., 1971. Diplomate Am. Bd. Radiology, cert. Added Qualification, vascular/interventional radiology. Intern Jefferson Med. Coll., Phila., 1971-72; resident Columbia-Presbyn. Med. Ctr., N.Y.C., 1972-75; radiologist U. Radiology Group (formerly Radiology Group New Brunswick), East Brunswick, N.J., 1975—; program dir. diagnostic radiology residency program Robert Wood Johnson Med. Sch. U. Medicine and Dentistry of N.J., New Brunswick, N.J., 1985-87, program dir. vascular/interventional fellowship program RWJ Med. Sch., 1985—, chmn. dept. radiology Robert Wood Johnson Med. Sch., 1987—, clin. prof. radiology, 1989—. Chief radiology svcs. Robert Wood Johnson U. Hosp., New Brunswick, 1985—, divsn. vascular/interventional radiology dept. radiology RWJ U. Hosp., 1985—; attending radiologist, RWJ U. Hosp., St. Peter's U. Hosp., 1975—; exec. coun. U. Medicine and Denstistry-Robert Wood Johnson Med. Sch., Ctr. Biomed. Imaging; clin. com. chmn. Robert Wood Johnson Med. Sch., Robert Wood Johnson U. Hosp., med. bd.; mem. com. Vascular Ctr. N.J.; bd. dirs. U. Radiology Group. Author: Angiography & Interventional Radiology, 1991; co-author: Interventional Radiology-A Multimedia Approach (textbook, CD-ROMS), 2000; (with others): Atlas of Radiologic Imaging, 1989, Genitourinary Radiology: A Multimodality Approach, 1990, Invasive Diagnostic Procedures, 1994, Atlas of Diseases of the Kidney, 1998. Named one of N.J.'s finest physicians N.J. Monthly, 1998. Mem. Am. Coll. Radiology, Assn. Univ. Radiologists, Soc. Chmn. Acad. Radiology Depts., Soc. Cardiovascular and Interventional Radiology, N.J. Radiol. Soc., Middlesex County Med. Soc., Assn. Program Dirs. Radiology, Roxiticus Country Club, Seaside Park Yacht Club (fleet surgeon). Avocations: skiing, surfing, sailing, golf, gardening. Office: UMDNJ Robert Wood Johnson Med Sch PO Box 19 1 Robert Wood Johnson Pl New Brunswick NJ 08903 E-mail: nosher@umdnj.edu.

NOSKI, CHARLES H. telecommunications executive; Degree, Calif. State U., Northridge, 1973. Corp. v.p., controller Hughes Elec. Corp., 1990—92, senior v.p., CFO, 1992—99, vice chmn., 1996—99; with Haskins & Sells (known as Deloitte & Touche), 1973-83, ptnr., 1983-90; v.p., CFO At&T Corp., N.Y.C., 1999—2002; vice chmn. of bd. AT&T Corp., 2002—. Office: AT&T Corp 32 Ave of the Americas New York NY 10013-2412

NOSLER, PETER COLE, construction company executive; b. Portland, Oreg., May 7, 1940; s. Lyle and Elizabeth (Lewis) N.; m. Kay Hanson, Apr. 25, 1971; 1 child, Alexander. BS in Physics and Math., Walla Walla Coll., 1962; postgrad., U. Wash., 1962-63, U. Calif., Berkeley, 1965-70. Physicist GE, Richland, Wash., 1963-65; pvt. practice Portland, 1970-72; project mgr. Stolte Constrn., San Leandro, Calif., 1972-75; v.p. ops. Rudolph & Sletten, Foster City, Calif., 1975-90; founder, pres. DPR Constrn. Inc., Redwood City, Calif., 1990—, CEO now. Lectr. Stanford U., Palo Alto, Calif., 1988—. Recipient Young Constrn. Profl. of Yr. award Jour. Bldg. Design and Constrn., 1978. Mem. Soc. Model Exptl. Engring. Avocations: model engineering and construction, history. Office: DPR Constrn Inc 1450 Veterans Blvd Redwood City CA 94063-2612

NOSLER, ROBERT AMOS, sports company executive; b. Ashland, Oreg., Apr. 21, 1946; s. John Amos and Louise (Booz) N.; m. Joan Kathleen Hilliard, July 15, 1967; children: Christie Lynn, Jill Ann, John Robert. Student, U. Oreg., 1965. V.p., gen. mgr. Nosler Bullets, Inc., Bend, Oreg., 1974-88, pres., chief exec. officer, 1988-90; pres., CEO Nosler, Inc., Bend, 1990—. Regional bd. dirs. US Bank. Editor: Nosler Reloading Manual #1, 1976. Bd. dirs. Bend C. of C., 1984-88, treas., 1988; chmn. Central Oreg. Welcome Ctr. Steering Com., 1988. With USN, 1966-70; trustee Ctrl. Oreg. Community Coll. Found., 1992-98; trustee Nat. Rifle Assn. Found., 1997—. Recipient Pres.' award Bend C. of C., 1984, 87, 88. Mem. Nat. Reloading Mfrs. Assn. (bd. dirs. 1982-86, 90-93, pres. 1984-86), Greater Bend Rotary (dir. 1989-91). Republican. Lutheran. Avocations: hunting, outdoors, sports. Office: Nosler Inc 107 SW Columbia St Bend OR 97702-1014

NOSOFSKY, ROBERT M. psychology educator; Prof. psychology Ind. U., Bloomington. Recipient Troland Rsch. NAS, 1995. Office: Ind U Dept Psychology Bloomington IN 47405

NOSTWICH, THEODORE DANIEL, literature educator, researcher; b. Akron, Ohio, Sept. 14, 1925; s. John and Amelia Rose Nostwich; m. Ann Elizabeth Baker, Mar. 21, 1953; children: Mark, Paul, Michael, Elisabeth, Sarah. BA, Ohio State U., 1948, MA, 1950; PhD, U. Tex., 1968. Asst. prof. Ferris State U., Big Rapids, Mich., 1955—58, Purdue U., West Lafayette, Ind., 1962—63, Del Mar Coll., Corpus Christi, Tex., 1963—68; asst. prof. to full prof. Iowa State U., Ames, 1968—95, prof., 1996—98; lectr. Am. Lit. U. Glasgow, Scotland, 1996. Rschr. in Am. lit. Editor: Dreiser's Heard in Corridors, 1988, Dreiser's Journalism Volume 1, 1988, Dreiser's Newspaper Days, 1991, Dreiser's "Fulfillment and Other Tales", 1992, Dreiser's "Dawn", 1998. Grantee Travel grantee, NEH, 1987—89. Mem.: Nat. Assn. Scholars, Am. Studies Assn. Avocations: classical music, art galleries, collecting postage stamps. Home: 707 Hodge Ave Ames IA 50010 Office: Iowa State Univ Dept English Ames IA 50012

NOTARBARTOLO, ALBERT, artist; b. N.Y.C., Jan. 12, 1934; m. Valerie Cervelli, June 1, 1962. Student (scholar), Nat. Acad. Fine Arts, 1950; apprentice to mural painter, Ignacio LaRussa, 1951-53. Tchr., 1967—. Represented in permanent collections, Smithsonian Instn., Washington, Mus. Modern Art, N.Y.C.; one-man shows include Hemisphere Gallery of Time-Life Inc., 1973, U. P.R., 1966, David Gavin Gallery, Millerton, N.Y., 1993; exhibited group shows, Tate Gallery, London, 1965, Corcoran Gallery Art, Washington, 1968, Del. Art Mus., Wilmington, 1970, Mus. Modern Art, N.Y.C., 1971, 74, 76, Nat. Gallery Art, Washington, 1976, Smithsonian Instn., Washington, 1976, Santa Barbara (Calif.) Mus. Art, 1976, Taft Mus., Cin., Bell Gallery, Greenwich, Conn., 1977, Huntsville (Ala.) Mus. Art, 1978, Hokin Gallery, Palm Beach, Fla., 1982, Drawing Ctr., N.Y.C., 2001. Served with AUS, 1957-59. Recipient Nat. Community Art Competition award HUD, 1973; U.S. Bicentennial Flag Competition award, A Flag for the Moon, 1976. Mem. Nat. Soc. Lit. and the Arts. Home: 99 Battery Pl Apt 27H New York NY 10280-1329 *When I turned thirteen my Aunt Rosa Pucci gave me a gift— a small packet of reproductions of Raphael's paintings. On the overleaf she inscribed, "Art does affect the lives of men; it moves to ecstasy, thus giving colour and movement to what be otherwise a rather grey and trivial affair." The intonation of this phrase today makes me believe that an act of art echoes on, invoking a continuing music, a vitality for the future while all else turns into the dust of history.*

NOTARO, ANTHONY, application developer; b. Queens County, NY, Sept. 13, 1956; s. Ignatius and Ida Notaro. AA, Nassau C.C., Garden City, NY, 1976; BS in Computer Sci., Hofstra U., 1978. Data analyst Hofstra U., Hempstead, NY, 1978; programmer Sperry Corp., Great Neck, NY, 1978—80; sys. designer L.I. Lighting Co., Hicksville, NY, 1980—84; sr. sys. analyst Grumman Corp., Bethpage, NY, 1984—85; self-employed cons. West Hempstead, NY, 1985—90; engr. Keyspan Energy Corp., Hicksville, 1990—. Plant engr. Shoreham (NY) Nuclear Power Sta., 1990—94; elec. supervising svc. operator Hewlett (NY) Elec. Ops., 1994—97. Contbr. articles on martial arts to profl. publs. Vol. Fedn. United Martial Arts, NJ, 1986—89, Fedn. Practicing Ju Jitsus, NJ, 1982—. Recipient Ismael Quiles award, South Bronx Cmty., 1988. Mem.: IEEE, Assn. Computing Machinery, Amred Forces Comms. Electronics Assn., Am. JuJitsu Assn., U.S. Navy Seals Mus. Assn. (life). Republican. Roman Catholic. Avocation: martial arts. Home: 319 Garfield Ave Hempstead NY 11552 Office: Key Span Energy Corp 175 E Oco Country Rd Hicksville NY 11801

NOTAROS, BRANISLAV M. electrical engineer, educator; b. Zrenjanin, Serbia-Monteneg (Yugoslavia), Jan. 2, 1965; s. Milivoj D and Smilja J Notaros; m. Olivera K Micic; children: Jelena, Milica. BS in elec. engring., U. of Belgrade, 1988, MS in elec. engring., 1992, PhD in elec. engring., 1995; Postdoc. elec. Engring., U. of Colo., 1999. Tchg. and rsch. asst. U. of Belgrade, Elec. Engring. Dept., 1989—96, asst. prof., 1996—98; rsch. assoc. U. of Colo., 1998—99; asst. prof. U. of Mass. Dartmouth, 1999—. Dir. of telecom. lab. Advanced Tech. and Mfg. Ctr., U. of Mass. Dartmouth, 2001—. Author: (book) Collection of Examination Questions and Problems in Electromagnetics, 1998, Collection of Examination Problems in Fundamentals of Electrical Engineering with Solutions, 1997, Electromagnetic Theory, 2003; contbr. chapters to books, 2000, articles to profl. jours. Recipient IEE Marconi Premium, Instn. of Elec. Engineers (IEE), London, UK, 1999, URSI Young Scientist award, Internat. Union of Radio Sci. (URSI), Gen. Assembly, Toronto, Can., 1999. Mem.: IEEE. Christian Orthodox. Avocations: swimming, skiing, travel. Home: 1 Aster Ln South Dartmouth MA 02748 Office: Univ of Mass Dartmouth ECE Department 285 Old Westport Rd Dartmouth MA 02747-2300 Business E-Mail: bnotaros@umassd.edu.

NOTEBAERT, RICHARD C. telecommunications industry executive; b. 1947; m. Peggy Notebaert; 2 children. B.A., U. Wis., 1969, MBA, 1983. With Wisconsin Bell, 1969-83; v.p. marketing and operations Ameritech, Chicago, 1983-86; pres. Ameritech Mobile Comm., 1986-89, Indiana Bell Telephone Co., 1989-92, Ameritech Services, 1992-93, pres., COO, 1993-94; chmn., pres., CEO Ameritech Corp., Chicago, 1994—99; pres., CEO Tellabs, 2000—02; chmn., CEO Qwest Commn. Internat., Denver, 2002—. Bd. dirs. AON Corp., Cardinal Health, Inc., Qwest Comms. Internat., Inc.; trustee, corp. leadership bd. dirs. U. Notre Dame, mem., bus. coun.; chmn., Reliability and Interoperability Coun. FCC, 2002—; apptd. mem. Nat. Security Telecom. Adv. Com., 2003—. Co-chmn. Alexis de Toqueville Soc. United Way; bd. dirs. Denver Ct. Performing Arts; vice chmn., civic com. The Comml. Club Chgo.; bd. dirs. The Executives Club, Chgo. Recipient Dist. Alumni award, U. Wis., 1999. Office: Qwest Commn Internat 1801 California St Denver CO 80202*

NOTKIN, LEONARD SHELDON, architect; b. N.Y.C., Apr. 1, 1931; s. Murry and Evelyn (Mofshatz) N.; m. Ann Mathilda Stefanko, Nov. 24, 1956; children: Jennifer, Mead. BArch, U. Pa., 1954. Registered architect, N.Y., Mass., Ohio, Pa., Nat. Coun. Archtl. Registration Bds. Architect, Percival Goodman (Architect), N.Y.C., 1956-58; Architect Bloch and Hesse (Architects), N.Y.C., 1958-59, Resnick and Green (Architects), N.Y.C., 1959-60; architect, prin., v.p. The Architects Collaborative, Inc., Cambridge, Mass., 1960-95; chief design critic Boston Archtl. Center, 1964-69; mem. Lexington (Mass.) Design Adv. Com., 1970-73, chmn., 1972; profl. studio critic Harvard Grad. Sch. Design, 1974-76; pres. Boston Design Assocs., Inc., Waltham, Mass., 1995—. Major recent works include Intermediate Sch. 137, Bronx, N.Y., 1976, Visual Arts Instructional Facility SUNY, Purchase, 1976, Lahey Clinic Med. Ctr., Burlington, Mass., 1976—, W. Penn Hosp., Pitts., 1977, St. Francis/St. George Hosp., Cin., 1978, Blue Cross/Blue Shield of Conn. Hdqrs., North Haven, Temple U. Hosp., Phila., composite hosp. Loring AFB, Limestone, Maine, Med. Facilities, Fort Drum, N.Y., Health Care Internat. Ltd., Glasgow, Scotland, Intensive Care Hosp. and Hotel, U. Ky. Cancer Rsch. Ctr., Children's Hosp. Med. Ctr. Rsch. Lab., Cin., new main entrance, lobby and admissions facilities Hosp. of U. Pa., Phila., Childrens Hosp., Kuwait, 1996, Health Facilities, Algiers, Algeria, 1996, Nigeria, 2003, Office Building/Auburn, Mass., Greenfield Comty. Coll., Mass. Served with U.S. Army, 1954-56. Recipient Design award for IBM Hdqrs., Gaithersburg, Md. Progressive Architecture mag., 1964; 1st pl. award for Worcester (Mass.) Community Center AIA, 1966; Design award for Worcester Found. Exptl. Biology bldg. Mass. chpt. AIA, 1968; Design award NIH Research Lab., Bethesda, Md. GSA, 1972; Best Bldg. of Yr. award for Norwalk (Conn.) High Sch. Assn. for Better Community Design, 1972; Honor award Conn. Soc. Architects AIA, 1974 Mem. AIA, Mass. State Assn. Architects, Boston Soc. Architects (dir. 1976-79, spl. design citation 1993). Office: Boston Design Assocs Inc 393 Totten Pond Rd Waltham MA 02451-2003 Office Phone: 781-259-9190.

NOTT, TARA LEE, Olympic athlete; b. Stilwell, Kans., May 10, 1972. Student, Colo. Began competing in weightlifting, 1995; Am. Open Gold medallist, 1996; Sr. Nat. Championships Gold medallist, 1996; Silver Dragon Team mem. Silver Medallist, 1997; World Team Trials Gold medallist, 1997; Am. Open Silver medallist, 1997; Sr. Nat. Championships Gold medallist, 1997; Sr. World Championships Gold medallist, 1997; Sr. World Championships 10th place, 1997; NACACI Team Mem. Gold medallist, 1997; Sr. Nat. Championships Bronze medallist, 1998; World Team Trials Silver medallist, 1998; Sr. World Championships 6th place, 1998; Sr. Nat. Championships Gold medallist, 1999; NACACI Team Mem. Gold medallist, 1999; Pan Am Games Gold medallist, 1999; Sr. World Championships 9th place, 1999; Sr. Nat. Championships Gold medallist, 2000; Olympic Gold medallist, 2000; Am. Open Gold medallist, 2001; Mermet Cup Team mem. Gold medallist, 2002; Am. record holder 48 kg. Snatch-82.5 kg., 48 kg. Clean and Jerk-102.5 kg., 48 kg. Total-185 kg.; 53 kg. Snatch-85.5 kg. Mem. several USA Soccer teams. Named to Colo. Coll. Hall of Fame. Achievements include only athlete to train at the U.S. Olympic Trainng Center in 3 different sports; only American Women's Olympic Gold Medallist in Weightlifting.

NOTTERMAN, DANIEL A. pediatrician, educator, scientist; BA, Cornell U.; M in Philosophy, Tufts U.; MD, NYU. Diplomate Am. Bd. Pediatrics. Intern, resident NYU Med. Ctr., N.Y.C., chief resident in pediat.; rsch. fellow clin. pharmacology Cornell Med. Ctr., N.Y.C.; dir. divsn. pediatric critical care medicine N.Y. Hosp. Cornell Med. Ctr., N.Y.C.; postdoctoral rschr., prof. Princeton (N.J.) U.; chief pediatric svcs. Bristol-Myers Squibb Children's Hosp. Robert Wood Johnson U. Hosp.; chair dept. pediat. U. Medicine and Dentistry N.J. - Robert Wood Johnson Med. Sch. Home: 19 Foxcroft Dr Princeton NJ 08540 Office: Robert Wood Johnson Med Sch 1 Robert Wood Johnson Pl MEB 306 New Brunswick NJ 08903 Business E-Mail: d.notterman@umdnj.edu.

NOTTINGHAM, EDWARD WILLIS, JR., federal judge; b. Denver, Jan. 9, 1948; s. Edward Willis and Willie Newton (Gullett) N.; m. Cheryl Ann Card, June 6, 1970 (div. Feb. 1981); children: Amelia Charlene, Edward Willis III; m. Janis Ellen Chapman, Aug. 18, 1984 (div. Dec. 1998); 1 child, Spencer Chapman. AB, Cornell U., 1969; JD, U. Colo., 1972. Bar: Colo. 1972, U.S. Dist. Ct. Colo. 1972, U.S. Ct. Appeals (10th cir.) 1973. Law clk. to presiding judge U.S. Dist. Ct. Colo., Denver, 1972-73; assoc. Sherman & Howard, Denver, 1973-76, 78-80, ptnr., 1980-87, Beckner & Nottingham, Grand Junction, Colo., 1987-89; asst. U.S. atty. U.S. Dept. Justice, Denver, 1976-78; U.S. dist. judge Dist. of Colo., Denver, 1989—. Mem. Jud. Conf. of the U.S. Com. on Automation and Tech., 1994-2000, chmn., 1997-2000. Bd. dirs. Beaver Creek Met. Dist., Avon, Colo., 1980-88, Justice Info. Ctr., Denver, 1985-87, 21st Jud. Dist. Victim Compensation Fund, Grand Junction, Colo., 1987-89. Mem. ABA, Colo. Bar Assn. (chmn. criminal law sect. 1983-85, chmn. ethics com. 1988-89), Order of Coif, Denver Athletic Club, Delta Sigma Rho, Tau Kappa Alpha. Episcopalian. Office: US Dist Ct 901 19th St Denver CO 80294 Office Phone: 303-844-5018. E-mail: NottinghamChambers@cod.uscourts.gov.

NOTTINGHAM, ROBINSON KENDALL, insurance company executive; b. Balt., Apr. 4, 1938; s. Robinson Jr. and Juliet (Moore) N.; m. Elizabeth LeViness, Aug. 26, 1960; children: Robinson Kendall Jr., Charles Denmead. BA in Polit. Sci., Johns Hopkins U., 1959; postgrad., Johns Hopkins U., Washington, 1965. With Am. Internat. Group, Inc., Hong Kong and Bangkok, 1968-71; mng. dir. Hanover Ins. Co., Universal Ins. Co., Bangkok, 1971-73, Am. Internat. Ins. Co., Lagos, Nigeria, 1973-75; regional pres. African div. Am. Internat. Underwriters, N.Y.C., 1975-78, Middle Ea. div., 1978-83, European div., 1983-86; chief exec. officer for Japan and Korea Am. Internat. Group, Inc., Tokyo, 1986-89; chmn., bd. dirs., CEO Am. Life Ins. Co., Wilmington, Del., 1989—; exec. v.p., life ins. Am. Internat. Group, 1998—. Bd. dirs. AIG Overseas Fin. (Japan) Inc., Tokyo, Am. Home Assurance Co., N.Y.C., AIU Ins. Co., N.Y.C. Pres. USO Coun., Tokyo, 1987-89; mem. world bd. govs. USO, Washington, 1987-97; mem. adv. coun. Johns Hopkins U. Sch. Advanced Internat. Studies, Washington, 1984-96. Served to lt. comdr. USNR, 1960-68. Mem. Princeton Club (N.Y.C.), Short Hills Club (N.J.), Bay Head Yacht Club (N.J.), Baltusrol Club (Springfield, N.J.), Chevy Chase (Md.) Club, Delta Phi. Republican. Episcopalian. Avocation: sailing. Office: Am Life Ins Co 1 Alico Plz Wilmington DE 19899

NOTTINGHAM, WILLIAM JESSE, retired church mission executive, minister; b. Sharon, Pa., Nov. 22, 1927; s. Jess William and Alice May (Green) Nottingham; m. Patricia Clutts, Feb. 1, 1949; children: Theodore Jess, Deborah Joan Selke, Nancy Alice, Gregory Philip. BA, Bethany Coll., W.Va., 1949, DD (hon.), 1987; BD, Union Theol. Sem., N.Y.C., 1953; PhD, Columbia U., 1962; DD (hon.), Christian Theol. Sem., Indpls., 1984. Ordained to ministry Christian Ch. (Disciples of Christ), 1945, ministerial standing United Ch. of Christ. Machinist apprentice Westinghouse, 1943—45; pastor Ch. of Christ, Canoe Camp and Covington, Pa., 1949-50; field worker Ch. of the Master, N.Y.C., 1950-53; assoc. min. Nat. City Christian Ch., Washington, 1954-58; fraternal worker Coun. on Christian Unity, France, 1958-65; with CIMADE and Centre de Glay; with youth dept. World Coun. of Chs., Geneva, 1965-68; exec. sec. for Latin Am. and Caribbean Christian Ch. (Disciples of Christ) and United Ch. Christ, Indpls., 1968-76; exec. sec. East Asia and Pacific Divsn. Overseas Ministries, Christian Ch. (Disciples of Christ), 1976-83; pres., exec. sec. Europe divsn. Overseas Ministries Christian Ch. (Disciples of Christ), Indpls., 1984-94, pres. emeritus, 2004; ret., 1994; affiliate prof. mission Christian Theol. Sem., 1995—. Author: Christian Faith and Secular Action: An Introduction to the Life and Thought of Jacques Maritain, 1968, The Practice and Preaching of Liberation, 1986, The Social Ethics of Martin Bucer 1491-1551, 1962; translator: God's Underground, 1970, Prayer at the Heart of Life, 1975, Materialist Approaches to the Bible, 1985, Madeleine Barot, 1991; contbr. articles to theol. jours. Mem. Ind. Faith and Labor Network, Com. To Free Lori Berenson. Recipient Eagle Scout award, Boy Scouts Am., 1946, Disting. Alumnus award, Union Theol. Sem., 1999, Fulbright scholarship, Strasbourg, France, 1953—54, Martin Luther King, Jr. Drum Major for Justice award, 2003. Mem.: Disciples Justice Action Network, United Christian Missionary Soc., Assn. Disciples for Theol. Discussion, Indpls. Peace and Justice Ctr. (bd.). Democrat. E-mail: patn@mibor.net., bnottingham@cts.edu.

NOTZ, JOHN KRANZ, JR., arbitrator and mediator, retired lawyer; b. Chgo., Jan. 5, 1932; s. John Kranz and Elinor (Trostel) N.; m. Janis Wellin, Apr. 23, 1966; children: Jane Elinor Notz (Mrs. Ian H. Watson), John Wellin. BA, Williams Coll., 1953; JD, Northwestern U., 1956. Bar: Ill. 1956, Fla.

1957, Wis. 1989, U.S. Supreme Ct. 1960. Assoc. 1st Nat. Bank Chgo., 1954, 1956; from assoc. to ptnr. Gardner, Carton & Douglas, Chgo., 1960-95, of counsel, 1990-95; ret., 1996. Arbitrator, mediator Am. Arbitration Assn., Chgo. Internat. Dispute Resolution Assn., NASD Dispute Resolution Inc., Nat. Futures Assn., N.Y. Stock Exch., Am. Stock Exch. Contbr. articles to profl. jours. Sec. State Corp. Acts Adv. Com., 1982-95, chmn., 1987-89; pres. Chgo. Lit. Club, 1996-97, Ill. Inst. Continuing Legal Edn., 1980-91, chmn., 1990-91; bd. dirs., pres. Black Point Historic Preserve, Inc.; trustee Graceland Cemetery; life trustee Beloit Coll. 1st lt. USAF, 1957-60. Recipient Svc. award Northwestern U., 1978 Fellow Am. Bar Found. (life), Ill. Bar Found. (life), Chgo. Bar Found. (life); mem. Am. Law Inst., Ill. State Bar Assn., Chgo. Bar Assn., Wis. State Bar, Lawyers Club City Chgo., Racquet Club Chgo., Lake Geneva (Wis.) Country Club, Mid-Day Club (Chgo.), Literary Club (Chgo.), Caxton Club (Chgo.), Cliff Dwellers (Chgo.), Soc. Archtl. Historians (treas.), Antiquarian Soc. Office: care Gardner Carton & Douglas 191 N Wacker Dr 3700 Chicago IL 60606-1698

NOUR, BAKR M. surgeon, health facility administrator; s. Mohamed Mahmoud Nour and Fatheya A. Hussein; m. Sohair A. Kheir, Dec. 23, 1976; children: May, Mohamed. MD, U. Alexandria, 1974, M in Surgery, 1978, D in Surgery, 1986. Diplomate Bd. Gen. Surgery, Egypt. Intern U. Alexandria, Egypt, 1975-76, resident in gen. & pediatric surgery, 1976-79, instr. surgery, 1979, asst. lectr. pediatric surgery, 1979-82, sr. asst. lectr. pediatric surgery, 1984-86, asst. prof. pediatric surgery, 1987-89; clin./rsch. fellow, vis. asst. prof. surgery dept. pediatric surgery U. Pitts. Med. Ctr., Children's Hosp. Pitts., 1982-84, 90; clin. fellow U. Pitts. Med. Ctr., Transplantation Inst., 1990-92, asst. prof. surgery, 1992-94; chief pediatric liver transplantation, adult liver transplant surgeon Okla. Transplantation Inst., Bapt. Med. Ctr., Oklahoma City, 1994-97; chief abdominal transplantation Okla. Transplantation Inst., Integris Bapt. Med. Ctr., Oklahoma City, 1997-98, dir. abdominal organ transplant divsn., 1998-99, interim dir., 1999-2000, dir., chmn., 2000—. Past mem. staff Presbyn. U. Hosp. Pitts., Montefiore Hosp., Pitts.; mem. human rights com. Children's Hosp. Pitts., 1993-94; mem. libr. com. Bapt. Med. Ctr. Okla. Contbr. articles to profl. jours. Founding mem. Innocent Childhood Benevolent Charity Assn., Alexandria; mem Islamic Charity Assn. Recipient World Cmty. award Results, 1998. Mem. AMA, ACS, Arab Am. Med. Assn., Am. Coll. Physician Execs., Am. Assn. Study of Liver Disease, Am. Soc. Transplant Surgeons, Egyptian Physician's Syndicate, Egyptian Med. Assn., Egyptian Soc. Surgeons, Egyptian Assn. Pediatric Surgeons, Alexandria Med. Assn., Brit. Assn. Pediatric Surgeons, Okla. State Med. Assn., Okla. County Med. Soc., Internat. Coll. Surgeons, Internat. Gastro-Surg. Club, Internat. Liver Transplantation Soc., Tex. Transplant Soc., Soc. Surgery Alimentary Tract, Alexandria Sporting Club, Oklahoma City Golf and Country Club. Moslem. Achievements include research in cell model to study bacterial translocation in transplanted small bowel, FK506 as immunosuppressive agent, small bowel transplantation, causes of anemia in transplant patients, Alpha interferon therapy, for viral hepatitis. Home: 14409 Rosebay Pl Oklahoma City OK 73142 Office: Okla Transplantation Inst Nazih Zuhdi 3300 NW Expressway Oklahoma City OK 73112-4418 E-mail: NourBM@Integris-Health.com.

NOUR, NAWAL M. obstetrician, gynecologist, health facility administrator; arrived in U.S.A., 80; BA, Brown U, 1984; MD, Harvard U., 1994; MPH, Harvard U, 1999. Chief residency Brigham and Women's Hosp., Boston, 1998; instr. dept of Obstetrics, Gynecology and Reproductive Biology Harvard Sch. of Medicine; dir. obstetric resident practice Brigham and Women's Hosp., Boston; founder African Women's Health Practice, 1999—. Recipient Commonwealth Fund Harvard U., 1999; fellow H. Rchard Nesson Fellowship, Brigham and Women's Hosp., 1999, MacArthur Found., 2003. Office: Brigham and Women's Hosp 75 Francis St Boston MA 02115

NOVA, CRAIG, writer; b. Los Angeles, July 5, 1945; s. Karl and Elizabeth (Sinclair) N.; m. Christina Barnes, July 2, 1977; children: Abigail, Tate. BA, U. Calif.-Berkeley, 1967; M.F.A., Columbia U., 1969. Author: Turkey Hash, 1972, The Geek, 1975, Incandescence, 1978, The Good Son, 1982, The Congressman's Daughter, 1986, Tornado Alley, 1989, Trombone, 1992, The Book of Dreams, 1994, The Universal Door, 1997, Brook Trout and the Writing life, 1999, Wetware, 2001, Cruisers, 2004. Recipient Harper-Saxton prize Harper and Row, Pubs., 1972; recipient award in lit. Am. Acad. and Inst. Arts and Letters; Guggenheim Found. fellow, 1977; fellow Nat. Endowment for Arts, 1973, Nat. Endowment for Arts, 1975, Creative Artists Pub. Service, 1976; NEA fellow, 1985; story included in Best Am. Short Stories, 1987.

NOVACK, ALVIN JOHN, physician; b. Red Lodge, Mont., Mar. 11, 1925; s. John and Anna Geraldine (Maddio) N.; m. Betty P. Novack, Jan. 10, 1952; children— Vance, Deborah, Michelle, Mitchel, Craig, Brad, Mary Ellen, Garth. MD, U. Wash., 1952. Intern Harper Hosp., Detroit, 1952, resident in surgery, 1953; resident in otolaryngology Johns Hopkins U., 1954-57; resident in surgery Columbia-Presbyn. Med. Center, N.Y.C., 1957-60, fellow head and neck surgery, 1957-60; dir. head and neck surgery Swedish Hosp., Seattle, 1960-91; dir. otolaryngology Children's Orthopedic Hosp., Seattle, 1965-78; ret., 1991. Contbr. articles to med. jours. Served to lt. AUS, 1940-43. Nat. Cancer Inst. fellow, 1957-60 Fellow A.C.S.; mem. AMA, Am. Acad. Otolaryngology and Head and Neck Surgery, Soc. Head and Neck Surgeons, North Pacific Surg. Assn., Pacific Coast Surg. Assn., Seattle Surg. Soc.

NOVACK, KENNETH JOSEPH, lawyer; b. Boston, Aug. 25, 1941; s. Hyman and Dorothy Ruth N.; m. Marianne Margaret Lefebvre; children: Laura Ann, Sara Elizabeth, Emily Kate, Jeffrey Nicholas. BA (Rufus Choate scholar), Dartmouth Coll., 1963; LL.B., Harvard U., 1966. Bar: Mass. 1966, D.C. 1972. With Mintz, Levin, Cohn, Ferris, Glovsky and Popeo, P.C., Boston, 1996—98, 2004—, named ptnr., 1970, mem. exec. com., 1972—98, mng. ptnr, 1972—78, pres., CEO, 1991-94, sr. counsel, 2004—; vice chmn. AOL Inc. (AOL and Time Warner merge, 2001), 1998—2001, Time Warner Inc. (formerly AOL Time Warner), 2001—04. Bd. dirs. Time Warner Inc., 2001—, Paratek Pharms., 2002—. Vice chmn. Mus. Sci., Boston, Tufts-New England Med. Ctr., Combined Jewish Philanthropies; pres. Teen Action Campaign Inc.; trustee Facing History and Ourselves, Novack Family Found. Mem. ABA, Internat. Bar Assn., Boston Bar Assn. (co-chmn. securities law com. 1970-85), D.C. Bar Assn., Am. Law Inst. Clubs: St. Botolph, Harvard of Boston. Office: Mintz Levin Cohn Ferris Glovsky and Popeo PC 1 Financial Ctr Fl 39 Boston MA 02111

NOVACK, TEVOR D. surgeon, consultant; b. Boston, Sept. 6, 1928; MD, Harvard Med. Sch., 1954. Diplomate Am. Bd. Surgery. Intern Beth Israel Hosp., Boston, 1954-55; resident in surgery Beth Isreal Hosp., Boston, 1955-56; resident in gen. surgery Letterman Gen. Hosp., San Francisco, 1957-59; resident in thoracic surgery Walter Reed Gen. Hosp., Washington, 1966-68; staff Meth. Hosps., Gary and Merrillville, Ind., St. Anthony Med. Ctr., Crown Point, Ind.; med. dir. Gary works U.S. Steel, 1979-94; cons. in occupl. medicine, 1995—; clin. asst. prof. surgery N.W. Ctr. for Med. Edn., Ind. U. Med. Sch., 1982—. Col. U.S. Army, 1956-79. Fellow Am. Coll. Surgeons, Am. Coll. Occupl. and Environ. Medicine; mem. AMA.

NOVAK, ALAN LEE, retired pharmaceutical company executive; b. Chgo., Ill., Oct. 25, 1928; s. Samuel Adolph and Tina Lillian (Oris) N.; m. Delores Jane Tonkel, Dec. 17, 1950; children: Shaya Ray, G. Alexander, Cheryl Lynn. BS, Fla. So. Coll., 1951. Cert. purchasing mgr. Police officer Lakeland (Fla.) Police Dept., 1952-53; sales rep. Sinclair Refining Co., Tampa, Fla., 1954-58; prin. Novak's Texaco s/s and Fuel Co., Tampa, 1958-62; sales rep. Burroughs Wellcome Co., Columbus, Ohio, 1962-70, purchasing agt. Research Triangle Park, N.C., 1970-74, dir. purchasing, 1974-94. Bd. dirs. Eastern N.C. Better Bus. Bur., 1989-96. Active N.C. Coun. on the Holocaust, 1996—2002; vol. Friends Helping Friends Vet. Sch., N.C. State U., 1994—; records dept. Raleigh Polic Dept., 1994—; area contact Am. Israel Polit. Affairs Coun., Raleigh, 1984—86; fin. sec. Temple Beth Or, Raleigh, 1975—77, treas., 1996—97; pres. Raleigh Chpt. B'nai B'rith, 1999—2000. With U.S. Army, 1946—47, Japan. Mem. Am. Legion Jewish War Vets. 1st Cav. Divsn. Assn., Drug, Chem., and Allied Trades Assn. (area rep. 1975-78, bd. dirs. 1978-84, treas. 1985, v.p. 1986, pres. 1987-88), Nat. Assn. Purchasing Mgmt., Purchasing Mgmt. Assn. Carolinas-Va., Triangle Purchasing Assn., Raleigh C. of C., Burroughs Wellcome Retirees Club (pres.), Tau Kappa Epsilon, Omicron Delta Kappa. Lodges: B'nai B'rith (Double Chai award 1985-87), AMRAN Shrine Temple (charter). Republican. Jewish. Avocations: hunting, fishing. E-mail: zayden@bellsouth.net.

NOVAK, ALAN P. political organization administrator; m. Caroline Anderson Novak. BA, Ursinus Coll.; JD, Villanova Univ. Sch. Law. Atty., ptnr. Conrad, O'Brien, Gellman and Rohn, 1995—; chair Pa. State Rep. Party, Harrisburg, 1996—. Mem. Coatesville City Coun., 1981—84; chmn. Mgmt. Training for Elected Officials, 1993—95, Pa. Delegation to Rep. Nat. Convention, 2000; committeeman Coatesville City Rep. Com., 1980—84; chmn. Rep. Com. Chester County Grassroots Training, 1991—95; vice chmn. Rep. Com. Chester County, 1992—94, chmn., 1994—; mem. Rep. State Com. Pa., 1994—, RNC Northeastern State Chmn.'s Assn., 1996—, chmn., 1999—; mem. RNC Standing Com. Rules, 1997—; RNC Com. on Arrangements, 2000. Office: 112 State St Harrisburg PA 17101-1024

NOVAK, BARBARA, art history educator; b. N.Y.C. d. Joseph and Sadie (Kaufman) N.; m. Brian O'Doherty, July 5, 1960. BA, Barnard Coll., 1951; MA, Radcliffe Coll., 1953, PhD, 1957. TV instr. Mus. Fine Arts, Boston, 1957-58; mem. faculty Barnard Coll., Columbia U., N.Y.C., 1958-98, prof. art history, 1970—, Helen G. Altschul prof., 1984-98, prof. emeritus, 1998—. Adv. council Archives of Am. Art, NAD Author: American Painting of the 19th Century, 1969, Nature and Culture, 1980, rev. edit., 1995, The Thyssen-Bornemisza Collection 19th Century American Painting, 1986, Alice's Neck, 1987, The Margaret-Ghost, 2003, (novels) The Ape and the Whale, 1995, (play) The Ape and the Whale: Darwin and Melville in Their Own Words, 1987 (performed at Symphony Space 1987), Dreams and Shadows: Thomas H. Hotchkiss in 19th Century Italy, 1993; co-editor: Next to Nature, 1980; mem. editorial bd. Am. Art Jour. Commr. Nat. Portrait Gallery. Fulbright fellow Belgium, 1953-54; Guggenheim fellow, 1974; Nat. Book Critics nominee, 1980; L.A. Times Book Award nominee, 1980; Am. Book Award paperback nominee, 1981; recipient disting. tchg. award Coll. Art Assn., 1997, Lawrence Fleishman award for outstanding scholarship Archives Am. Art, 1999, medal of distinction, Barnard Coll., 2002. Fellow Soc. Am. Historians, Phila. Atheneum; mem. Soc. Am. Historians, Am. Antiquarian Soc., Coll. Art Assn. (dir. 1974-77, Disting. Tchg. of Art History award 1997), PEN.

NOVAK, CAMILLE, small business owner, consultant; d. Edward Sherrill Arnold, Sr. and Nila Ruth (Grow) Arnold; m. Robert Novak, Nov. 1, 1975. AA, St. Louis C.C., St. Louis, Mo., 1996; BA in Media Comm., Webster U., St. Louis, Mo., 1998; BA in History, Webster U., 1998; MA in Media Comm., Webster U., St. Louis, Mo., 2000; Ph.D. Candidate in Am. History, St. Louis U., St. Louis, Mo., 2000—01. Paralegal Cert.: Nat. Acad. of Paralegals 1991; Leadership Devel. Cert. Phi Theta Kappa Internat. Honor Soc., 2001. Exec. adminstrn. Christian Appalachian Project, Lancaster, Ky., 1974—77, St. William's Cath. Ch., Lancaster, 1974—77; comm. adminstr. First Bapt. Ch. of St. John, St. Louis, 1978—82; owner Novak Enterprises, St. Louis, Mo., 1982—; writer: features, film/theatre rev., oped, edn. The Montage Newspaper, St. Louis, Mo., 1993—98; adminstrn. mgmt. Lyss Fine Arts, St. Louis, 1993—; social & behavioral sciences/history & govt. tutor program adminstr. St. Louis C.C., St. Louis, 1996—2000; intern Ky. filmmakers collection U. of Ky. Spl. Collections and Archives, 1998—98; adminstrn. support St. Louis Assn. for Retarded Citizens (ARC), St. Louis, 1999—; instr. St. Louis C.C. Dist., St. Louis, 2000—02, meramec global studies programadministrative support, 2000—01. Actor: (A World of Their Own), (The Big Brass Ring), (King of the Hill), (Soul of the Game); prodr.: (graphic design) The New Millennium (The Eichling Yearbook Internat. Award, 2000); dir.(editor, cinemtographer): (film) The Star-True life acctg. about an Appalachian African Am. youth with cognitive & phys. disabilities who taught the true meaning of life to a class of misfits (Mind over TV Best of Camille show 1997, Meramec Classic Film Festival, 1997, various U.S. film and video festivals, 1997); author: (journalistic writing) Body of Work (Internat. Bus. Communicators Assn. Award, 1996, The Press Club of Met. St. Louis Milton Ferman Meml. Award, 1997), (novels) The Stewart Chronicles, (pub.) Film Hist.:The Age of Aquarius: The Dawning of The New Hollywood., (The Liguorian Mag.) The Star; prodr.(animator): (animated film emphasizing global unity) Scarlet Ribbons (Presented at Meramec Classic Film Festival and Mind Over TV Best of Camille show, 1997), (editor) (documentary) Psalm 23-an alternative reading of 20th Century hist. as filtered through post- modern media; actor: (films) Lights, Camera, Propanda Starring American Film as Propaganda Tool: 1938-1945. Founder/prodr./dir./steering com. Meramec Classic Film Festival, St. Louis, 1999—2000; founder/prodr./dir. Dollars for Scholars Scholarship programming, St. Louis, 1997—2002, Petey K. Bear Says Reading is FUN! state-wide literacy project, St. Louis, 1998—99. Nominee Presidents Merit Award for Excellence in Academics, SLCC-Meramec Campus Pres., 1996; recipient Most Disting. Chpt. Advisor, Mo. Phi Theta Kappa, 2002, ALL-USA TODAY Academic Team Scholar Campus Representative, St. Louis C.C., 1997, Mo. State All-Academic First Team, Mo. C.C. Assn., 1997, US Achievement Acad. All-American Scholar, 1997, Meramec Honors Program Honors Grad. (and Scholarship Recipient), 1993-2000; Graduate in 1996, 1997, Commencement Spkr., SLCC-Meramec Coll., 1996, Horizon Award for Advisors, Mo. Phi Theta Kappa, 2002, Paralegal Student of Mo., Nat. Acad. of Paralegal Studies, 1992, Nat. Acad. for Paralegal Studies Scholarly Distinction of Merit, NAPS, 1992, West Ednl. Pub. Paralegal Student Award, West Ednl. Pub. Co., 1992, Nat. Deans List, 1996, 1997, 1998, 1999, 2000, Campus Deans List, SLCC and Webster U., 1993-2000, Phi Theta Kappa Internat. Paragon Award for New Advisors Nominee, Phi Theta Kappa Internat., 2002, Honors Program Instr. Recognition Award, Forest Pk. C.C. Honors Program, 2002, Rotary Internat. Amb. of Goodwill Alt., Rotary Internat. of Mo., 1997, Phi Theta Kappa Internat. Disting. Regional Officer Award, 1999, Phi Theta Kappa Internat. Disting. Chpt. Pres. Award, 1997; scholar Guistwhite Scholar, Phi Theta Kappa Internat., 1997, Hites Scholar, St. Louis C.C., 1997, Am. Bus. Women's Assn. Scholar, ABA, 1996, St. Louis Journalism Found. Scholar, 1996-1997-1998-only 3 time awardee, Phi Theta Kappa Transfer Scholar, Webster U., 1996-1998, A. E. Hotchner Scholar, Scholarship Found. of St. Louis, 1996—2002, Alpha Kappa Alpha, 1997. Master: The Spirit of St. Louis Alumni Assn. (life; assn. advisor 2002—03); mem.: Am. Film Inst., The Am. Hist. Assn., Phi Theta Kappa Internat. Honor (life; chpt. & regional pres. 1996—99, chpt. advisor 2000—02, Internat. Disting. Regional Officer Award (99) & Internat. Disting. Chpt. Pres. Award (97) 1999, 1997 respectively, Mo. Region Disting. Chpt. & Regional Pres., Advisor 1996—99). Home: 9930 Carlyle Ave Saint Louis MO 63114-1305

NOVAK, DAVID, Judaic studies educator, rabbi; b. Chgo., Aug. 19, 1941; s. Syd and Sylvia (Wien) N.; m. Melva Ziman, July 3, 1963; children: Marianne, Jacob George. AB in Classics and Ancient History, U. Chgo., 1961; M in Hebrew Lit., Jewish Theol. Sem. Am., 1964; PhD, Georgetown U., 1971. Ordained rabbi, 1966. Rabbi Shaare Tikvah Congregation, 1966-69; dir. Jewish chaplaincy St. Elizabeth's Hosp., 1966-69; rabbi Emanuel Synagogue, Oklahoma City, 1969-72, Beth Tfiloh Congregation, Balt., 1972-77, Congregation Beth El, Norfolk, Va., 1977-81, Congregation Darchay Noam, Far Rockaway, N.Y., 1981-89; Edgar M. Bronfman prof. modern Judaic studies U. Va., Charlottesville, 1989-97; J. Richard and Dorothy Shiff chair of Jewish studies U. Toronto, 1997—. Lectr. philosophy Oklahoma City U., 1969-72, New Sch. for Social Rsch., 1982-84; lectr. Jewish studies Balt. Hebrew Coll., 1972-77; adj. asst. prof. philosophy Old Dominion U., 1977-81; vis. assoc. prof. Talmud Jewish Theol. Sem. Am., 1986-88; adj. assoc. prof. Baruch Coll., CUNY, 1984-88, adj. prof., 1989; founder, v.p., coord. panel Halakhic Inquiry Union Traditional Judaism/Inst. Traditional Judaism; disting. vis. prof. religion and corp. ethics Drew U., 1995; Yarnton/Lancaster lectr. Oxford U., 1996. Contbg. editor First Things. Sec.-treas. Inst. on Religion and Pub. Life. Essay winner Hyman G. Enelow prize Jewish Theol. Sem. Am., 1975; recipient Rabbi Jacob B. Augus award Jewish Theol. Sem. Am., 1984, Best Book Constructive Religious Thought award Am. Acad. of Religion, 2000; Woodrow Wilson Internat. Ctr. for Scholars fellow, 1992-93. Fellow Acad. for Jewish Philosophy, Am. Acad. for Jewish Rsch.; mem. Am. Theol. Soc., Assn. for Jewish Studies, Am. Acad. Religion. Office: Univ Coll 15 King's College Cir Toronto ON Canada M5S 3H7 Office Phone: 416-946-3229. E-mail: david.novak@utoronto.ca.

NOVAK, DAVID C. restaurant company executive; Sr. v.p., mktg. Pizza Hut, 1986—90; exec. v.p., mktg. and nat. sales Pepsi-Cola Co., 1990—92, COO, N. Am., 1992—94; pres., CEO N. Am. Kentucky Fried Chicken, 1994—97; group pres., CEO, Pizza Hut, KFC Tricon Global Restaurants, Inc., Louisville, 1996—97, vice-chmn., 1996—97, pres., 1997—, CEO, 2000—; chmn. Yum! Brands, Inc. (formerly Tricon Global Restaurants, Inc.), 2001—. Bd. dirs. Bank One Corp., Yum Brands, Inc., 1997—. Office: Yum Brands Inc 1441 Gardiner Ln Louisville KY 40213-1914*

NOVAK, DENNIS E. physician; b. East Liverpool, Ohio, Jan. 5, 1946; BA, Bklyn. Coll., 1966; Lic. in Med. Scis., U. Brussels, 1972; MD, Rutgers U., 1974. Diplomate Am. Bd. Family Practice, Nat. Bd. Med. Examiners. Resident in family practice Monmouth Med. Ctr., Long Branch, N.J., 1974-77; clin. instr. to clin. asst. prof. Robert Wood Johnson Med. Sch., 1977—; chmn. dept. family practice, mem. med. exec. com. Cmty. Med. Ctr., 1990—; pvt. practice specializing in family medicine, 1977-96; group practice, exec. com. Cmty. Health Assocs. of St. Barnabas Health Care Sys., 1996-2000; pvt. practice, 2001—. Attending physician utilization rev. com. Cmty. Meml. Hosp., 1987-88, quality assurance com., 1988, dept. family practice quality assurance com.; physician reviewer, quality assurance HealthSouth Rehab. Hosp. Mem. exec. adv. bd. Ocean County coun. Boy Scouts Am., asst. scoutmaster Ocean Coun., 1997-2002, com. chair Troop 165, 2000—; trustee United Way Ocean County., Area VII Physician Rev. Org., 1983-86; bd. dir. Interfaith Hospitality Network Ocean County Homeless Program. Named one of Top Docs in N.J., Castle-Connolly N.J. Monthly, 2001—03. Fellow Am. Acad. Family Practice; mem. Ocean County Acad. Family Practice (v.p. 1983), Ocean County Med. Soc. (bd. trustees 1983-87). Avocations: photography, scuba, guitar. Address: PO Box 780 1001 Lacey Rd Forked River NJ 08731-1042

NOVAK, GORDON S., JR., computer scientist, educator; b. Colo., 1947; m. Susan Raye Strawn, May 7, 1977; children: Genevieve, Courtney. BSEE, U. Tex., 1969, MA in Computer Sci., 1971, PhD in Computer Sci., 1976. Mgr. sys. programming Tracor Inc., Austin, Tex., 1966-76; instr. U. Tex., Austin, 1976-77, asst. prof., 1978-81, 83-84, assoc. prof., 1984-98; prof., 1998—; dir. Artificial Intelligence Lab. U. Tex., Austin, 1984-99; computer sci. SRI Internat., Menlo Park, Calif., 1977-78. Vis. asst. prof. Stanford (Calif.) U., 1981-83. Contbr. articles to profl. jours. Office: U Tex Dept Computer Sci Austin TX 78712

NOVAK, GREGORY, marketing professional; b. Johnstown, Pa., Oct. 19, 1949; s. Eugene F. and Joan (Tross) N.; m. Naomi Sosia Wall; children: Rebecca, Jeffrey, Jacqueline. BA, U. Vt., 1971. Project dir. Dun & Bradstreet, N.Y.C., 1973-74; sr. analyst Colgate Palmolive, N.Y.C., 1974-76; mgr. brand rsch. R.J. Reynolds, Winston-Salem, N.C., 1976-77, mgr. group new brand rsch., 1977-80, dir. new bus., 1980-81, dir. group mktg., 1981-84; nat. dir. mktg. Deloitte Haskins & Sells, N.Y.C., 1984-90; pres. Novak Mktg. Inc., 1990—. Office: Novak Mktg Inc 29 Brandon Dr Mount Kisco NY 10549-3720 E-mail: NovMkt@aol.com.

NOVAK, JAMES F. physician; b. Portland, May 5, 1944; s. John Martin and Mary Ruth Novak; m. Marilynn L. Grosso, July 10, 1971; children: Vincent, Mark. BS, U. San Francisco, 1966; MD, Oreg. Health Science U., Portland, 1970. Diplomate Am. Bd. Family Practice; cert. Md. Intern Hennepin County Gen. Hosp., Mpls., 1970-71; physician emergency room Merle West Med. Ctr., Klamath Falls, Oreg., 1971-72; physician and ptnr. Klamath (Oreg.) Med. Clinic, 1972—; clin. instr. Cascade East Family Practice Residency, Klamath Falls, 1994—. Chief of staff Merle West Meml. Ctr., Klamath Falls, 1978-79; pres. Oreg. Acad. Family Practice, 1997-98; past pres., bd. dirs. Klamath Youth Devel. Ctr., Klamath Falls, 1980—, Klamath Lake CARES, PHP Health Plan; Oreg. del. to Am. Acad. Family Physicians Congress of Dels., 2001—. Pres. Klamath County Rotary Club, 1995-96. Fellow Am. Acad. Family Practice; mem. AMA, Oreg. Med. Assn., Klamath County Med. Soc. (pres.). Avocations: sailing, fishing, skiing, wine making. Office: Klamath Med Clinic 1905 Main St Klamath Falls OR 97601-2649 Personal E-mail: novja@aol.com.

NOVAK, JO-ANN STOUT, chemical engineer; b. Glen Ridge, N.J., June 25, 1956; d. Herbert Austin and Anna (Messina) Stout; m. John Robert Novak Jr., Oct. 30, 1976. B in Chem. Engring., Ga. Inst. Tech., 1977; MBA, Oakland U., 1984. Cert. engr.-in-tng., Ga.; registered profl. engr., Mich. Trainee AC Spark Plug divsn. GM, Flint, Mich., 1977-78, chemist, 1978-79, exptl. chemist, 1979-81, mfg. engr., 1981-84, sr. mfg. engr., 1984-87; sr. mfg. project engr., 1987-89; mgr. bus. and engring. processes, 1989-90; program planning mgr., 1990-92; supr. engring.-info. and sys., 1992-94; staff engr. chem. and metall. processes, 1994—; advanced mfg. engr., 2001—. Mem. AIChE, NSPE, Am. Electroplaters Soc. (dir. Saginaw Valley br. 1981-83, ednl. chmn. 1984-85, sec.-treas. 1984-86, 2d v.p. 1986-87, 1st v.p. 1987-88, pres. 1988-89), Soc. Mfg. Engrs., Engring. Soc. Detroit. Office: Delphi Auto Sys 1300 N Dort Hwy Flint MI 48506-3956 Home: 661 Southshore Dr Oxford MI 48371-3558

NOVAK, JOE, artist; b. Springfield, Mass., Oct. 15, 1930; s. Benjamin D. and Mae (Lavitt) N. BA, Dartmouth Coll., 1952; JD, Harvard U., 1955. One-man shows include Vered Gallery, East Hampton, NY, 1985, 87-88, Milari Ltd., N.Y.C., 1989, Light Emanations, Tesuque, N.Mex., 1992, Bank of Santa Fe, 1996, Davidson & Daughters, Portland, Maine, 1997, McKesson Plz., San Francisco, 1998, Sirius Art Gallery, Santa Fe, 2000, Circle Elephant Art, LA, 2001, 03, Evo Gallery, Santa Fe, 2001, 02, 04, Hood Mus. Art, Dartmouth Coll., 2002, Etherton Gallery, Tucson, 2004; exhibited in group shows at Parrish Art Mus., Southampton, N.Y., Guild Hall Mus., East Hampton, NY, Mus. Fine Arts, Santa Fe, Vered Gallery, Milari, Ltd., Olaf Clasen Gallery, Cologne, Germany, Lewallen Gallery, Santa Fe, Circle Elephant Art, LA, Anderson Contemporary Art, Santa Fe, Evo Gallery, Santa Fe Art Inst., others; works in pub. collections include Boston Mus. Fine Arts, Guild Hall Mus., U. Tex.-Pan Am., Mus. Fine Arts, Santa Fe, Mus. Art, Ft. Lauderdale, Fla., Hood Mus. Art, Dartmouth Coll., U. Calif.-Berkeley Art Mus., Art Mus. Fla. Internat. U., Miami, Cin. Art Mus., Mus. Fine Arts, Springfield, Mass.; subject of articles. Lt. USN, 1955-58. Recipient awards for art. Home: PO Box 393 Tesuque NM 87574-0393 E-mail: kiva1015@comcast.net.

NOVAK, JOSEPH ANTHONY, law librarian; b. Detroit; s. Thomas Paul and Mary Cecilia N. AA, Macomb C.C., Warren, Mich., 1984; BA, Oakland U., 1986; JD, Mich. State U., 1991; M Libr. and Info. Sci., Wayne State U., 1998. Intern Wayne County Pub. Defender's Office, Detroit, 1986; intern Office of Jud. Assistance 3d Jud. Ct. Mich., Detroit, 1993, law clk. to Hon. Diane M. Hathaway, intern, 1996; law libr. St. Louis Correctional Facility, 2000—01, Mid-Mich. Correctional Facility, 2001—03; asst. libr. Mound Correctional Facility, 2003—. Vol., Vol. Income Tax Assistance Program, Detroit, 1995-2001. Recipient Outstanding Vol. Volunteer Income Tax Assistance Program, 1995, 96, 98, 99, 2000, The Spirit of Am. Is In the Heart of Its Volunteers IRS, 1995, 96, 97, 99. Mem. Am. Assn. Law Librs., Am. Corrections Assn., Spl. Librs. Assn., Acctg. Aid Soc., County and State Agy. Librs., Mich. Corrections Assn., KC. Democrat. Roman Catholic. Avocations: coin and stamp collecting, biking, walking. Home and Office: 3524 Hamlet Sterling Heights MI 48310-6905

NOVAK, JOSEPH DONALD, science educator, knowledge studies specialist; b. Mpls., Dec. 2, 1930; s. Joseph Daniel and Anna (Podany) N.; m. Joan Owen, July 18, 1953; children: Joseph Mark, Barbara Joan, William John BS, U. Minn., 1952, MA, 1954, PhD, 1958; Doctorate (hon.), U. Comanhue, Neuquen, Argentina, 1998, Pub. U. Navarra, 2002. Teaching asst. U. Minn., Mpls., 1952-56, instr., 1956-57; asst. prof. Kans. State Tchrs. Coll., 1957-59, Purdue U., West Lafayette, Ind., 1959-62, assoc. prof., 1962-67; prof. Cornell U., Ithaca, N.Y., 1967-95, prof. emeritus, 1995—; pres. Joseph D. Novak Knowledge Consultants, Inc.; sr. rsch. scientist U. West Fla. Knowledge constrn. and orgn. cons. to Procter & Gamble and other cos.; cons. to over 400 schs. and colls., 1975—; vis. fellow Harvard U., 1965-66; disting. vis. prof. U. N.C., Wilmington, 1980, U. West Fla., 1987-88; vis. prof. U. South Fla., 1995; sr. rsch. scientist U. West Fla., 1996—. Author: Learning How to Learn, 1984, in 10 langs. 1984-96, Educational Psychology: A Cognitive View, 1978, A Theory of Education, 1977, Aprendizaje Significativo: Techieas y Aplica-

ciones, 1997, Learning, Creating, and Using Knowledge: Concept Maps as Facilitative Tools for Schools and Corporations, 1998, Teaching Science for Understanding, 1998, Assessing Science Understanding, 2000, Una aportacion a la mejora de la calidad de la docentia universitaria: Los mapas Conceptuales, 2000, Errores Conceptuales: Diagnosis, Tratamientoy Reflexiones, 2001, 15 others; contbr. over 120 chpts. to books; contbr. over 100 articles to profl. jours. Fellow Tozer Found., Lydia Anderson, 1955-56; research assoc. Harvard U., 1965-66; Fulbright-Hayes Sr. Scholar, Australia, 1980 Fellow AAAS (sec. sect. Q); mem. NSTA, Nat. Assn. Rsch. in Sci. Tchr. (Outstanding Contbns. Sci. Tchg. Through Rsch. award 1990), Nat. Assn. Biology Tchrs. (hon.), Assn. for Edn. of Tchrs. of Sci., Am. Ednl. Rsch. Assn., Coun. Sci. Soc. Pres.'s (1st hon. award for rsch. in sci. edn. 1998), Sigma Xi. Avocations: hiking, swimming, dance, music. Home: 90 Highland Ave S Club 3 Unit 302 Tarpon Springs FL 34689 Office: Cornell U Dept Edn Kennedy Hall Ithaca NY 14853 Home (Summer): 77 Alcott Cir Taunton MA 02780-1056 Business E-Mail: jdn2@cornell.edu.

NOVAK, KIM (MARILYN NOVAK), actress; b. Chgo., Feb. 13, 1933; d. Joseph A. and Blanche (Kral) N.; m. Richard Johnson, April 1965 (div. 1966), m. Robert Malloy, Jan. 1977. Student, Wright Jr. College, Chgo.; AA, Los Angeles City College, 1958. Appeared in: (films) The French Line, 1953, Pushover, 1954, Phffft, 1954, Five Against the House, 1955, Son of Sinbad, 1955, Picnic, 1955, The Man with the Golden Arm, 1956, The Eddie Duchin Story, 1956, Jeanne Eagles, 1957, Pal Joey, 1958, Vertigo, 1958, Bell, Book and Candle, 1958, Middle of the Night, 1959, Strangers When We Meet, 1960, Pépé, 1960, Boys' Night Out, 1962, The Notorious Landlady, 1962, Of Human Bondage, 1964, Kiss Me Stupid, 1964, The Amorous Adventures of Moll Flanders, 1965, The Legend of Lylah Clare, 1968, The Great Bank Robbery, 1969, Tales That Witness Madness, 1973, The White Buffalo, 1977, Just a Gigolo, 1979, The Mirror Crack'd, 1980, The Children, 1990, Liebestraum, 1991; (TV movies) Third Girl from the Left, 1974, Satan's Triangle, 1975, Malibu, 1983, Obsessed with Vertigo, 1997; (TV series) Falcon Crest, 1986-87, Alfred Hitchcock Presents, 1985, Liebestraum, 1989; (TV appearances) Cleopatra: The Film that Changed Hollywood, 2001. Named one of 10 most popular movie stars by Box-Office mag. 1956, All-Am. Favorite 1961, Brussels World Fair poll as favorite all-time actress in world 1958. Office: William Morris Agency care Norman Brokaw 151 S El Camino Dr Beverly Hills CA 90212-2775*

NOVAK, LESLIE HOWARD, lawyer; b. Chgo., May 10, 1944; s. Sidney and Sadie (Jensky) N.; m. Nancy Ruth Sherman, July 2, 1967; children: Heidi Ellen, Shani Beth. BS in Bus. with high distinction, U. Minn., 1966, JD cum laude, 1969. Bar: Minn. 1970, U.S. Dist. Ct. Minn. 1970, U.S. Ct. Appeals (8th cir.) 1974, U.S. Supreme Ct. 1995. Assoc. Robins, Kaplan, Miller & Ciresi, Mpls., 1969-77, ptnr., 1977-92, Mackall, Crounse & Moore, PLC., Mpls., 1992—, mng. ptnr., 1997-99. Bd. dirs. Am. Israel C. of C. and Industry of Minn., Mpls., 1981—, founding pres., 1981-91; founding sec., founding bd. dirs. Assn. N.Am.-Israel Chambers Commerce, Inc., 1993—; bd. dirs. United Jewish Fund and Coun., St. Paul, 1986—; founding dir. Illusion Theater and Sch.; past bd. dirs., past pres. Jewish Family Svc. of St. Paul; past bd. dirs. Mt. Zion Temple. Named Leading Am. Atty., Am.'s Registry Outstanding Profls. Mem. Hillcrest Country Club, Gopher Golf Boosters Club (sec., bd. dirs.), Phi Delta Phi, Beta Gamma Sigma. Avocations: biking, golf, tennis, skiing. Office: Mackall Crounse & Moore PLC 1400 AT&T Tower 901 Marquette Ave Minneapolis MN 55402-2859 Business E-Mail: lhn@mcmlaw.com.

NOVAK, MARK, lawyer; b. Buffalo, N.Y., Jan. 28, 1952; s. Eugene Francis and Joan (Tross) N.; m. Charlene Mary Ingoglia, Sept. 2, 1972; children: Jason Charles, Jennifer Rose. BA, U. Rochester, 1974; JD, Loyola U., Chgo., 1977. Bar: Ill. 1977, U.S. Dist. Ct. (no. dist.) Ill. 1977, U.S. Ct. Appeals (7th cir.) 1978. Assoc. Anesi, Ozmon & Lewin, Ltd., Chgo., 1977-83; ptnr. Anesi, Ozmon, Rodin, Novak & Kohen, Ltd., Chgo., 1983—. Fundraiser Christmas is for Kids Charity, Chgo., 1992—. Mem. ATLA (product liability sect. 1985—), ABA, Ill. Trial Lawyers Assn., Trial Lawyers for Pub. Justice, Chgo. Bar Assn. (jud. evaluation com. 1995—). Avocations: painting, gardening, travel. Home: 1212 N Lake Shore Dr Chicago IL 60610-2371 Office: Anesi Ozmon Rodin Novak & Kohen Ltd 161 N Clark St Fl 21 Chicago IL 60601-3206

NOVAK, MAXIMILLIAN ERWIN, retired language educator; b. N.Y.C., Mar. 26, 1930; s. George and Elsie (Loewy) Novak; m. Estelle Gershgoren, Aug. 21, 1966; children: Ralph, Daniel, Rachel. PhD, UCLA, 1958; D.Phil., St. John's Coll., Oxford U., Eng., 1961. Asst. prof. English, U. Mich., Ann Arbor, 1958-62; prof. English UCLA, 1962—2001, Clark Library prof., 1973-74, prof. emeritus, 2001—. Author: Economics and the Fiction of Daniel Defoe, 1962, Defoe and the Nature of Man, 1963, Congreve, 1971, The Wild Man Within, 1972, English Literature in the Age of Disguise, 1977, Realism, Myth and History in the Fiction of Daniel Defoe, 1983, Eighteenth-Century English Literature, 1983, Passionate Encounters, 2000, Daniel Defoe Master of Fictions, 2001, Enchanted Ground, 2004; editor: Augustan Reprint Society Dryden: Works, vol. 10, 1970, vol. 13, 1984, Southerne Oroonoko, 1976, Stoke Newington Daniel Defoe, 1999—. Fulbright fellow, 1955—57, Guggenheim fellow, 1965—66, 1985—86, Am. Philos. Soc. fellow, 1979, NEH fellow, 1980—81, Beinecke Libr. fellow, 1991, Pres.' fellow, U. Calif., 1991—, Huntington Libr. fellow, 1991—. Mem.: MLA, Western Soc. Eighteenth Century Studies, Johnson Soc. So. Calif., Am. Soc. 18th Century Studies. Democrat. Jewish. Home: 451 S El Camino Dr Beverly Hills CA 90212-4221 E-mail: novak@humnet.ucla.edu.

NOVAK, MICHAEL (MICHAEL JOHN NOVAK), religion educator, author, editor; b. Johnstown, Pa., Sept. 9, 1933; s. Michael John and Irene (Sakmar) N.; m. Karen Ruth Laub, June 29, 1963; children: Richard, Tanya, Jana. AB summa cum laude, Stonehill Coll., North Easton, Mass., 1956; BT cum laude, Gregorian U., Rome, 1958; MA, Harvard U., 1966; LLD, Keuka (N.Y.) Coll., 1970, Stonehill Coll., Mass., 1977, Thomas More Coll., 1992; LHD, Davis and Elkins (W.Va.) Coll., 1971, LeMoyne (N.Y.) Coll., 1976, Sacred Heart U., 1977, Muhlenberg Coll., 1979, D'Youville Coll., 1981, Boston U., 1981, New Eng. Coll., 1983, Rivier Coll., 1984, Marquette U., 1987; D en Ciencias Sociales, U. Francisco Marroquin, Guatemala, 1993, Jacksonville U., 1994; HHD, Saint Xavier U., 1995. Tchg. fellow Harvard U., 1961-63; asst. prof. Stanford U., 1965-68; assoc. prof. philosophy and religious studies State U. N.Y., Old Westbury, 1968-71; assoc. dir. humanities Rockefeller Found., N.Y.C., 1973-75; provost Disciplines Coll., SUNY, Old Westbury, 1969-71; vis. prof. Jan. session Carleton Coll., Northfield, Minn., 1970, Immaculate Heart Coll., Hollywood, Calif., 1971, U. Calif., Santa Barbara, 1972, Riverside, 1975; Ledden-Watson disting. prof. religion Syracuse U., 1977-79; journalist nat. elections Newsday, 1972; writer in residence The Washington Star, 1976, syndicated columnist, 1976-80, 84-89; columnist Forbes Mag., 1989—; resident scholar Am. Enterprise Int., Washington, 1978—83; George Frederick Jewett chair pub. policy and religion Am. Enterprise Inst., Washington, 1983—, dir. social and polit. studies, 1987—; chmn. working seminar on family and Am. welfare policy Ind., 1986; faculty U. Notre Dame, Ind., 1986-87, vis. W. Harold and Martha Welch Prof. Am. Studies, 1987, 88. Judge Nat. Book awards, 1971, DuPont Broadcast Journalism awards, 1971-80; speechwriter nat. polit. campaigns, 1970, 72; mem. Bd. Internat. Broadcasting, 1983—; mem. Presdl. Task Force Project Econ. Justice, 1985-87, Council Scholars Library of Congress, 1986—; mem. monitoring panel UNESCO, 1984; vice chmn. Lay Commn. Cath. Social Teaching and U.S. Economy, 1984-86; U.S. Ambassador to Experts Meeting on Human Contacts of the Conf. On Security and Cooperation in Europe, Bern, Switzerland, 1986; U.S. rep. to human rights commn. UN, 1981-83; hon. prof. U. Cuyo, Argentina, 1992. Author: (novel) The Tiber was Silver, 1961, A New Generation, 1964, The Experience of Marriage, 1964, The Open Church, 1964, Belief and Unbelief, 1965, 3d edit., 1994, A Time to Build, 1967, A Theology for Radical Politics, 1969, American Philosophy and the Future, 1968, Story in Politics, 1970, (with Brown and Herschel) Vietnam: Crisis of Conscience, 1967, Naked I Leave, 1970; Politics: Realism & Imagination, 1971, Ascent of the Mountain, Flight of the Dove, 1971, A Book of Elements, 1972, All the Catholic People, 1971, The Experience of Nothingness, 1970, The Rise of the Unmeltable Ethnics, 1972, Choosing Our King, 1974, The Joy of Sports, 1976, The Guns of Lattimer, 1978, The American Vision, 1978, Rethinking Human Rights I and II, 1981, 82, The Spirit of Democratic Capitalism, 1982, Confession of a Catholic, 1983, Moral Clarity in the Nuclear Age, 1983, Freedom with Justice, 1984, Human Rights and the New Realism, 1986, Will It Liberate? Questions About Liberation Theology, 1986, Character and Crime, 1986, The New Consensus on Family and Welfare, 1987, Taking Glasnost Seriously: Toward an Open Soviet Union, 1988, Free Persons and the Common Good, 1989, This Hemisphere of Liberty, 1990, The Spirit of Democratic Capitalism, 1991 (Anthony Fisher award 1992), Choosing Presidents, 1992, The Catholic Ethic and the Spirit of Capitalism, 1993, Awakening from Nihilism, 1995, Joy of Sports, rev. 1995; Belief and Unbelief, rev, 1995; Business as a Calling, 1996, The Fire of Invention, 1997, with daughter Jana Novak, Tell Me Why: A Father Answers His Daughter's Questions About God, 1998, On Cultivating Liberty, 1999, To Empower People, anniv. ed, 1995, A Free Society Reader, 2000, Three in One, 2001 (essays on Dem. Capitalism 1976-2000), On Two Wings, 2002; numerous other articles and books transl. into all maj. langs.; assoc. editor Commonweal mag., 1966-69; contbg. editor Christian Century, 1967-80, Christianity and Crisis, 1968-76, Jour. Ecumenical Studies, 1966-77, This World, 1982-89, First Things, 1990—; religion editor Nat. Rev., 1979-86, founder, pub. Crisis, 1982—, editor-in-chief, 1993-95. Decorated K.M.G., Soverign Mil. Order of Malta, 1987, Order of the Byzantine Cross Republic of Slovakia, 1996; Kent fellow, 1961-65; fellow Hastings Inst., 1970-76; named Most Influential Prof. Sr. Class Stanford U., 1967, 68; Man of Yr. Johnstown, Pa., 1978; recipient Faith and Freedom award Religious Heritage Am., 1978, HIAS Liberty award, 1981, Friend of Freedom award, 1981; Newman Alumni award CCNY, 1984; George Washington Honor medal, 1984; award of Excellence, Religion in Media, 8th annual Angel Awards, 1985, Ellis Island Honor medal, 1986, Anthony Fisher award, 1992, Wilhelm Weber Prize, 1993, Templeton prize for progress in religion, 1994, Internat. prize Inst. World Capitalism, 1994, Award for the Arts City of Bratislava, 1998, Gold Medal Slovak Acad. Scis., 2000, Masaryk award Czech Republic, 2000, IDI Award for Econs., Fondazione Istituto Dirigenti, Rome, 2000, Cezanne medal City of Aix-en-Provence, 1998, Boyer award Am. Enterprise Inst., 1999, Internat. Prize for Cath. Culture, Italy, 1999, Gold medal Pa. Soc., 2001, Milan R. Stefanik award Slovak-Am. Cultural Ctr., 2002, Maritain medal for Scholarly Excellence, Am. Maritain Assn., 2002; diploma as vis. prof. U. Francisco Marroquin, 1985; named acad. corr. mem. from U.S., Argentina Nat. Acad. Scis., Morals & Politics, 1985, others. Mem. Soc. Religion in Higher Edn. (ctrl. com. 1970-73), Am. Acad. Religion (prog. dir. 1968-72), Coun. Fgn. Rels., Cath. Theol. Soc., Soc. Christian Ethics, Inst. Religion and Democracy (dir. 1981—), Nat. Ctr. Urban and Ethnic Affairs (dir. 1982-86). Office: Am Enterprise Inst 1150 17th St NW Washington DC 20036-4603 E-mail: mnovak@aei.org. *Many persons have found a certain emptiness at the heart of human life — an experience of nothingness. Hidden in it, implicit in it, are prior commitments to honesty, courage, freedom, community. To increase the frequency of such acts in our lives is to grow, and to feel them diminish is to wither.*

NOVAK, RANDI RUTH, engineer, computer scientist; b. Chgo., July 10, 1954; d. Bernard Richard and Shirley Ann (Fiedorczyk) Novak; children: Rona Rachel Reich, Bonnie Shaina Reich. BS in Math., BA in Econs. with honors, U. Calif., Santa Cruz, 1976; postgrad., U. Rochester, 1976-78. Rsch. asst. U. Calif., Santa Cruz, 1974-76; Russian translator U. Chgo., 1977—78; intern economist Congl. Budget Office, Washington, 1977; engr. Lockheed MSC, Sunnyvale, Calif., 1978-82; software engr. contractor Silicon Valley Systems, Belmont, Calif., 1982, 83-84, Data Encore (subs. of Verbatim), Sunnyvale, 1982-83; systems programmer CompuPro/Viasyn Corp., Hayward, Calif., 1984-87; mem. tech. staff Network Equipment Techs., Redwood City, Calif., 1987-89; v.p. engring., founder Segue Setups, Burlingame, Calif., 1989-92, ptnr., 1992—; sr. tech. staff NEC Am., San Jose, Calif., 1992—94; sr. systems engr. Hitachi Computer Products, Santa Clara, Calif., 1994-96; prin. engr. Rapid-City Comms./Bay Networks/Nortel Networks, Santa Clara, Calif., 1996—2002, Trapeze Networks, Pleasanton, Calif., 2002—04; prin. engr. tech. staff Foundry Networks, San Jose, 2004—. Fellow Dept. Treasury, 1974-76, NSF, 1977-78, U. Rochester, Rush Rhees fellow. Mem. IEEE Computer Soc., Am. Math. Assn., Computer Profls. for Social Responsibility, Soc. for Computing and Info. Processing, Internat. Platform Assn., Calif. Scholarship Fedn. (life). Avocations: piano, oboe, physics, photography, mathematics. Home: 4166 School St Pleasanton CA 94566-6218 Office Phone: 408-941-7201.

NOVAK, RAYMOND FRANCIS, environmental health/toxicology research institute director, pharmacology educator; b. St. Louis, July 26, 1946; s. Joseph Raymond and Margaret A. (Cerutti) N.; m. Frances C. Holy, Apr. 12, 1969; children: Jennifer, Jessica, Janelle, Joanna. BS in Chemistry, U. Mo., St. Louis, 1968; PhD in Phys. Chemistry, Case Western Res. U., 1973. Assoc. in pharmacology Northwestern U. Med. Sch., Chgo., 1976-77, asst. prof. pharmacology, 1977-81, assoc. prof., 1981-86, prof., 1986-88; prof. pharmacology Wayne State U. Sch. Medicine, Detroit, 1988—; dir. Inst. Environ. Health Scis. Wayne State U., Detroit, 1988—, dir. EHS Ctr. in Molecular and Cellular Toxicology with Human Application, 1994—. Mem. toxicology study sect. NIH, Bethesda, Md., 1984-88; adj. sci. Inhalation Toxicology Rsch. Inst., Lovelace Biomed. and Environ. Rsch. Inst., 1991-98; program leader Epidemiology and Environ. Carcinogenesis, Karmanos Cancer Inst. and Comprehensive Cancer Ctr., 1996-98. Assoc. editor Toxicol. Applied Pharmacology, 1992-96; editor Drug Metabolism and Disposition, 1994-2000; mem. editorial bd. Jour. Toxicology and Environ. Health, 19 87-92, In Vivo, 1986—, Toxic Substances Jour., 1993-98; mem. bd. pub. trustees Am. Soc. Pharmacology and Experimental Therapeutics, 1994-2000; contbr. articles to profl. jours. Recipient Disting. Alumni award U. Mo., St. Louis, 1988; grantee Nat. Inst. Environ. Health Sci., 1979—, Gen. Medicine sect. NIH, 1979-82, 89-94. Mem. Am. Soc. for Biochem. and Molecular Biology, Soc. Toxicology (councilor 1996-98, chmn. cont. edn. com. 1995-96), Am. Assn. for Cancer Rsch., Am. Soc. for Pharmacology and Exptl. Therapeutics (bd. publ. trustees 1994-99), Am. Soc. Hematology, Internat. Soc. for Study Xenobiotics. Office: Wayne State U Inst Environ Health Scis 2727 2nd Ave Rm 4000 Detroit MI 48201-2671 Office Phone: 313-577-0100.

NOVAK, RICHARD L. health products executive; Various positions Smith-Kline Beecham Clin. Labs., Inc.; exec. v.p. ea. ops. Lab. Corp. Am. Holdings, Burlington, N.C., 1997-98, exec. v.p., COO, 1998—. Office: Lab Corp Am Holdings 430 S Spring St Burlington NC 27215

NOVAK, ROBERT DAVID SANDERS, newspaper columnist, television commentator; b. Joliet, Ill., Feb. 26, 1931; s. Maurice Pall and Jane Anne (Sanders) N.; m. Geraldine Williams, Nov. 10, 1962; children: Zelda, Alexander. AB, U. Ill., 1952; LLD (hon.), Kenyon Coll., 1987; LittD (hon.), U. Ill., 1998. Reporter Joliet (Ill.) Herald-News, 1947-51, Champaign-Urbana (Ill.) Courier, 1951-52, AP, Omaha, Lincoln, Nebr., Indpls. and Washington, 1954-58, Wall St. Jour., Washington, 1958-63; syndicated columnist N.Y. Herald-Tribune, Washington, 1963-66; commentator Corinthian Broadcasting, Washington, 1963-65, Metromedia, Washington, 1966-76, RKO-Features, Washington, 1976-78; syndicated columnist Chgo. Sun-Times, Washington, 1966—; commentator Cable News Network, Washington, 1980—, Am. Voice, 1993—. Pub. Evans-Novak Polit. Report, Washington, 1967—, Evans-Novak Tax Report, Washington, 1985-92, Evans-Novak Japan Report, Washington, 1989-92; contbg. editor Readers Digest, 1979—. Author: Completing the Revolution, 2000; co-author: (with Rowland Evans) The Agency of the GOP, 1965, Lyndon B. Johnson: The Exercise of Power, 1967, Nixon In The White House, 1971, The Reagan Revolution, 1981. Trustee Bullis Sch., Potomac, Md., 1987-98, Phillips Found., 1991—, Children Charities Found., 1994—. 1st lt. U.S. Army, 1952-54. Recipient ACE award Cable Broadcasting Industry, 1990, Laureate Order of Lincoln, Lincoln Acad. Ill., 1999. Mem. Soc. Profl. Journalists, Washington Gridiron Club, Nat. Press Club, Army and Navy Club. Home: 801 Pennsylvania Ave NW Washington DC 20004-2615 Office: Ste 1203 1750 Pennsylvania Ave NW Washington DC 20006-4501

NOVAK, ROBERT DENNIS, contractor, real estate developer; b. Poughkeepsie, N.Y., Jan. 12, 1954; s. William Henry and Terese Edna Novak; m. Barbara Jean Owen, Aug. 21, 1999; m. Deborah Ann Cross (div.); children: Jessica Ann, Jennifer Lee, Jonathan Charles. Grad high sch., N.Y. Pres. Wilro Constrn., Inc., Hopewell Junction, 1973—; v.p. Billings Plz. Corp., 1987—2001; pres. Lamp Light Assocs., 1987—2001. Mem.: Nat. Homebuilders Assn. Avocations: bicycling, scuba diving, camping, motorcycling. Office: Wilro Constrn Inc 25 Clove Hollow Rd Hopewell Junction NY 12533 Office Phone: 845-724-4697.

NOVAK, TERRY LEE, public administration educator; b. Chamberlain, SD, Sept. 1, 1940; s. Warren F. and Elaine M. N.; m. Barbara Hosea, Aug. 29, 1981; 1 child, David. B.Sc., S.D. State U., 1962; postgrad. (Rotary fellow), U. Paris, 1962-63; M.P.A., Colo. U., 1965, PhD, 1970. Asst. city mgr. City of Anchorage, 1966-68; city mgr. City of Hopkins, Minn., 1968-74, City of Columbia, Mo., 1974-78, City of Spokane, Wash., 1978-91; v.p. bus. and fin. Ea. Wash. U., Cheney, 1991—94, prof. public adminstrn., 1992—, dir. grad. program pub. administrn., 1994-95; dir. Spokane Joint Ctr. for Higher Edn., 1995-98; bus. mgr. Riverpoint campus Wash. State U., 1998-99; prof pub. adminstrn. Eastern Wash. U., 1999—. Asst. adj. prof. U. Mo., Columbia, 1975, 77; adj. instr. Gonzaga U., Spokane, 1986-88; mem. nat. adv. coun. on environ. policy and tech. EPA. Author: Special Assessment Financing in American Cities, 1970; contbr. articles to profl. jours. Mem. ASPA, Internat. Pers. Mgmt. Assn., Internat. City Mgrs. Assn. (Acad. Profl. Devel.). Episcopalian. Office: 668 N Riverpoint Blvd Spokane WA 99202-1677 E-mail: tnovak@terrynovak.net.

NOVAK, VICKI ANN, human resources specialist; Bachelor's, U. Tenn., 1973. Various positions in human resources Dept. of Commerce, Washington, Dept. of Housing and Urban Devel., Washington, Dept. of Transp., Washington; spl. asst. to dir. of personnel NASA, Washington, chief of agy. personnel policy br.; personnel officer NASA Hqrs., Washington; dir. personnel NASA, assoc. adminstr. for human resources and edn. Mem. Internat. Personnel Mgmt. Assn., Sr. Exec. Assn., Phi Beta Kappa. Office: NASA Human Resources and Edn 300 E St SW Washington DC 20546-0005

NOVAKOV, GEORGE JOHN, JR., gifted and talented educator, consultant, administrative assistant; b. New Orleans, Apr. 1, 1945; s. George John Novakov Sr. and Gloria (Edwards) Frost; m. Ann Marie Mariano, Dec. 27, 1969; children: Jay, Jaime. BA, U. New Orleans, 1967, MEd, 1970, postgrad., 1985, Tulane U., Loyola U., 1985. Tchr. New Orleans Pub. Schs., 1967—, adminstrv. asst., dir. admission Edna Karr Secondary Sch., 1994—, student data mgr. Edna Karr Secondary Sch., 1994—. Grant writer asst. Edna Karr Secondary Sch., New Orleans Pub. Libr., 1987-99. Author: (play) The Christmas Caper, 1980. Ind. Study Humanities fellow, 1991. Mem. La. Assn. of Computer Using Educators (assoc. editor newsletter, 1992), Greater New Orleans Coun. of Tchrs. of English, Presenter at Nat. Edn. Computer Conf., 1998, 2002. Democrat. Roman Catholic. Avocations: opera, science fiction, computers. Home: 7340 Edward St New Orleans LA 70126-2012 Office: Edna Karr Secondary Sch 3332 Huntlee Dr New Orleans LA 70131-7046 E-mail: george_novakov@nops.k12.la.us.

NOVALES, RONALD RICHARDS, zoologist, educator; b. San Francisco, Apr. 24, 1928; s. William Henry and Dorothy (Richards) N.; m. Barbara Jean Martin, Dec. 19, 1953; children: Nancy Ann, Mary Elizabeth. BA, U. Calif., Berkeley, 1950, MA, 1953, PhD, 1958; postgrad., UCLA, 1951-52. Asst. prof. biol. scis. Northwestern U., Evanston, Ill., 1958-64, assoc. prof., 1964-70, prof., 1970-80, prof. neurobiology and physiology, 1981-93, emeritus prof. neurobiology and physiology, 1993—. Cons. A.J. Nystrom Co., 1969 Mem. editorial bd.: The American Zoologist, 1969-73; Contbr.: articles to profl. jours. Ency. Brit. Book of Year. Served with U.S. Army, 1953-55. NSF research grantee, 1959-73, 75-78 Fellow AAAS. Unitarian Universalist. Home: 2008 Mcdaniel Ave Evanston IL 60201-2125 *Remember not to "die on the barbed wire" of all the conflicting demands of your work. It is possible for you to cut through the individual strands and to make a successful rush for the enemy's trench.*

NOVELLO, ANTONIA COELLO, state health commissioner, former surgeon general, pediatric nephrologist, educator, retired federal agency administrator; b. Fajardo, P.R., Aug. 23, 1944; d. Antonio and Ana D. (Flores) Coello; m. Joseph R. Novello, May 30, 1970. BS, U. P.R., Rio Piedras, 1965; MD, U. P.R., San Juan, 1970; MPH, Johns Hopkins Sch. Hygiene, 1982; DrPh (hon.), Johns Hopkins U., 2000; DSc (hon.), Med. Coll. Ohio, 1990, U. Ctrl. Caribe, Cayey, P.R., 1990, Lehigh U., 1992, Hood Coll., 1992, U. Notre Dame, Ind., 1991, N.Y. Med. Coll., 1992, U. Mass., 1992, Fla. Internat. U., 1992, Cath. U., 1993, Washington Coll., 1993, St. Mary's Coll., 1993, Ea. Va. Med. Sch., 1993, Ctrl. Conn. State U., 1993, Georgetown U., 1993, U. Mich., 1994, Mt. Sinai Sch. Medicine, 1995; LHD (hon.), Alvernia Coll., 1996; HHD (hon.), Kings Coll., 1996; D in Health Sci. (hon.), Ponce Sch. of Medicine, 1996; D in Law (hon.), Gannon U., 1997; LHD (hon.), Loyola U., 1997; DSc (hon.), U. North Tex., Ft. Worth, 2002, Howard U., 2003, NYU, 2003, Pace U., 2003, others. Diplomate Am. Bd. Pediatrics. Intern in pediatrics U. Mich. Med. Ctr., Ann Arbor, 1970-71, resident in pediatrics, 1971-73, pediatric nephrology fellow, 1973-74, Georgetown U. Hosp., Washington, 1974-75; project officer Nat. Inst. Arthritis, Metabolism and Digestive Diseases NIH, Bethesda, Md., 1978-79, staff physician, 1979-80; exec. sec. gen. medicine B study sect., div. of rsch. grants NIH, Bethesda, 1981-86; dep. dir. Nat. Inst. Child Health & Human Devel., NIH, Bethesda, 1986-90; surgeon gen. USPHS-HHS, Washington, 1990-93; spl. rep. for health and nutrition UNICEF, N.Y.C., 1993—96; vis. prof. health policy and mgmt. Johns Hopkins U. Sch. of Hygiene and Pub. Health, 1996—99; commr. of health New York, 1999—. Clin. prof. pediatrics Georgetown U. Hosp., Washington, 1986, 89, Uniformed Svcs. U. of Health Scis., 1989; adj. prof. pediatrics and communicable diseases U. Mich. Med. Sch., 1993; adj. prof. internat. health Sch. Hygiene and Pub. Health, Johns Hopkins U., Balt.; prof. dept. health policy mgmt. and behavior SUNY, 1999—; clin. prof. pediats. U. Rochester, N.Y., 1999—; mem. Georgetown Med. Ctr. Interdepartmental Rsch. Group; legis. fellow U.S. Senate Com. on Labor and Human Resources, Washington, 1982-83; mem. Com. on Rsch. in Pediatric Nephrology, Washington; participant grants assoc. program seminars Nat. Inst. Arthritis, Diabetes and Digestive and Kidney Diseases, NIH, Bethesda, 1980-81; pediatric cons. Adolescent Medicine Svc., Psychiat. Inst., Washington, 1979-83; nephrology cons. Met. Washington Renal Dialysis Ctr. affiliate Georgetown U. Hosp., Washington, 1975-78; phys. diagnosis class instr. U. Mich. Med. Ctr., Ann Arbor, 1973-74; chair Sec.'s Work Group on Pediatric HIV Infection and Diseases, DHHS, 1988; cons. WHO, Geneva, 1989; mem. Johns Hopkins Soc. Scholars, 1991. Contbr. numerous articles to profl. jours. and chpts. to books in field; mem. editorial bd. Internat. Jour Artificial Organs, Jour. Mexican Nephrology. Served in USPHS, 1978-99. Recipient Intern of Yr. award U. Mich. Dept. Pediatrics, 1971, Woman of Yr. award Disting. Grads. Pub. Sch. Systems, San Juan, 1980, PHS Commendation medal HHS, 1983, PHS Citation award HHS, 1984, Cert. of Recognition, Divsn. Rsch. Grants, NIH, 1985, PHS Outstanding medal HHS, 1988, PHS Unit Commendation, 1988, PHS Surgeon Gen.'s Exemplary Svc. medal, 1989, PHS Outstanding Unit citation, 1989, DHHS Asst. Sec. for Health Cert. of Commendation, 1989, Surgeon Gen. Medallion award, 1990, Alumni award U. Mich. Med. Ctr., 1991, Elizabeth Blackwell award, 1991, Woodrow Wilson award for disting. govt. svc., 1991, Congl. Hispanic Caucus medal, 1991, Order of Mil. Med. Merit, 1992, Washington Times Freedom award, 1992, Charles C. Shepard Sci. award, 1992, Golden Plate award, 1992, Elizabeth Ann Seton award, 1992, Ellis Island Congl. Medal of Honor, 1993, Legion of Merit medal, 1993, Athena award Alumnae Coun., 1993, Nat. Citation award Mortar Bd., 1993, Disting. Pub. Svc. award, 1993, Healthy Am. Fitness Leaders award, 1994, Pub. Leadership Edn. Network Mentor award, 1994, Disting. Svc. award Nat. Coun. Cath. Women, 1995, James E. Van Zandt Citizenship award, 1995, Ronald McDonald Children's Charities Excellence award, 1995, Hispanic Heritage Leadership award, 1998, Disting. Alumnus award Am. Assn. of State Colls. and Univs., 1997, Humanitarian award Am. Cancer Soc., 2001, James Smithson Bicentenial medal Smithsonian Inst., 2002; named Health Leader of Yr., COA, 1992; inductee Nat. Women's Hall of Fame, 1994, Internat. Pediatric Hall of Fame Miami Children's Hosp., 1996, Am. Med. Women Assn. Hall of Fame, 2002. Fellow Am. Acad. Pediatrics (Excellence Pub. Svc. award 1993); mem. AMA (Nathan Davis award 1993, Meritorious Svc. award 1993, Luther L. Terry award, 2000), Inst. Medicine, Internat. Soc. Nephrology, Am. Soc. Nephrology, Latin Am. Soc. Nephrology, Soc. for Pediatric Rsch.,

Am. Pediatric Soc., Assn. Mil. Surgeons U.S., Am. Soc. Pediatric Nephrology, Pan Am. Med. and Dental Soc. (pres.-elect, sec. 1984), D.C. Med. Soc. (assoc.), Johns Hopkins U. Soc. Scholars, Alpha Omega Alpha. Avocation: collecting antique furniture. Office: NY State Health Commr Corning Tower Empire State Plz Albany NY 12237*

NOVELLY, PAUL ANTHONY, petrochemical and refining company executive; b. St. Louis, 1943; m. Mary Katherine Novelly; 4 children. B. in commerce, St. Louis U., 1965. With Shell Oil Co., St. Louis, 1962-68, Apex Oil Co., Inc., St. Louis, 1968—; pres. Apex Oil Co., Inc., St. Louis, 1980—; chmn., CEO Apex Oil Co., Inc., St. Louis. Dep. chmn. bd. dirs. Liquid Funding, Ltd., 2001—; vice chmn. bd. dirs. Clark Oil & Refining Co., St. Louis; bd. dirs. The Bear Stearns Companies, N.Y.C., 2002—. Recipient Horatio Alger award, 2000. Office: Apex Oil Corp 8235 Forsyth Blvd Ste 400 Clayton MO 63105*

NOVETZKE, SALLY JOHNSON, former ambassador; b. Stillwater, Minn, Jan. 12, 1932; married; 4 children. Student, Carleton Coll., 1950-52; PhD (hon.), Mt. Mercy Coll., 1991. Amb. to Malta, Am. Embassy, Valletta, 1989-93. Past mem., legis. rep. Nat. Coun. on Vocat. Edn.; past mem. adv. coun. for career edn., past mem. planning coun. Kirkwood C.C.; bd. dir., life trustee Cedar Rapids Cmty. Theater, Cedar Rapids; past bd. dir. James Baker III Pub. Policy Inst., Rice U.; past trustee, v.p. bd. dir. Shattuck-St. Mary's Sch., Faribault, Minn., Mt. Mercy Coll., Cedar Rapids; vice chmn., life trustee, mem. exec. com. Hoover Presdl. Libr., 1982—, v.p. Hoover trustees; mem. Coun. Am. Amb.; trustee 4-Oaks Juvenile Facility; chmn. Nat. Coun. Youth Leadership; adv. coun. Shattuck-St. Mary's Sch., Faribault, Minn.; state chmn. Iowa Rep. Ctrl. Com., 1984—86; co-chair rep. Ctrl. Com.; chmn. Linn County Rep. Com., 1980—83; mem. adv. bd. Nat. Rep. Women, 1987—89; co-chmn. V.P. Bush Inauguration, 1980; Iowa co-chmn. George Bush for Pres.; trustee Am. U. in Rome, 2001—; bd. dir. Amb. Forum. Decorated dame Order of Knights of Malta; recipient Disting. Alumnus award Stillwater High Sch., 1991; Disting. Alumni award for outstanding achievement Carleton Coll., 1994. Republican. Home: 4747 Mount Vernon Rd SE Cedar Rapids IA 52403-3941

NOVICH, BRUCE ERIC, chemicals executive; b. Phila., Mar. 15, 1957; s. Samuel David and Vivian Rose Novich; m. Susan S. Novich, Sept. 5, 1982; children: Scott, Spencer, Corey. BA, Colgate U., 1979; BSChemE, MIT, 1980, MS in Geology, MSCE, MIT, 1982, ScD in Materials Processing, 1984. V.p. R & D and engring. Ceramics Process System, Milford, Mass., 1984-95; global bus. dir. electronics-zebralink PPG Industries, Pitts., 1995-2000; global bus. dir. Arch Chem.s Microelectronics and Semicondr., 2000—. Contbr. over 50 articles to profl. jours. Recipient 2 R&D 100 awards. Achievements include over 20 patents in ceramics, composites and electronic packaging. Office: Arch Chems 80 Circuit Dr N North Kingstown RI 02852 Office Phone: 401-996-2333. Business E-Mail: bnovich@archchemicals.com.

NOVICH, NEIL S. metals distribution company executive; BA in Physics summa cum laude, Harvard U.; MS in Nuclear Engring., MS in Mgmt., MIT. Former dir. Bain & Co.; chmn., pres., CEO Ryerson Tull, Inc., Chgo., 1994—. Dir. W.W. Grainger, Inc. Trustee Field Mus. Natural History, Children's Home & Aid Soc. Ill.; mem. vis. com. Divsn. Phys. Scis., U. Chgo. Nat. Sci. Found. scholar, Ford scholar. Mem. Phi Beta Kappa. Office: Ryerson Tull Inc 2621 W 15th Pl Chicago IL 60608

NOVICK, ANDREW CARL, urologist; b. Montreal, Apr. 5, 1948; came to U.S., 1974; s. David and Rose (Ortenberg) N.; m. Thelma Silver, June 29, 1969 (div. Dec. 1983); 1 child, Lorne J.; m. Linda Friedman, May 24, 1992; children: Rachel H., Eric D. BSc, McGill U., Montreal, 1968, MD, CM, 1972. Diplomate Am. Bd. Urology. Resident in surgery Royal Victoria Hosp., Montreal, 1972-74; resident in urology Cleve. Clinic Found., 1974-77, staff dept. urology, 1977—, head sect. renal transplant, 1977—, chmn. Urol. Inst., 1985—, chmn. Organ Transplant Ctr., 1985—. Trustee Am. Bd. Urology, 1995—2001, Urology Residence Rev. Com., 1997—2002. Editor: Vascular Problems in Urology, 1982, Stewart's Operative Urology, 1989, Renal Vascular Disease, 1995, Innovations in Urologic Surgery, 1997; contbr. more than 500 articles to profl. jours. Fellow ACS, Med. Coun. Can.; mem. Am. Urol. Assn., Am. Assn. Genito-Urinary Surgeons, Clin. Soc. Genito-Urinary Surgeons. Home: 2660 George Zeiger Dr Ste 906 Beachwood OH 44122 Office: Cleve Clinic Found 9500 Euclid Ave A100 Cleveland OH 44195-0001

NOVICK, JULIUS LERNER, theater critic, educator; b. N.Y.C., Jan. 31, 1939; s. Solomon Joseph and Ethel (Lerner) N.; m. Phyllis Belle Spaeth, May 27, 1983; 1 child, Ilana BA, Harvard U., 1960; D.F.A., Yale U., 1966. Theatre critic WNDT-TV, Channel 13, N.Y.C., 1968-70; asst. prof. English NYU, N.Y.C., 1969-72; assoc. prof. lit. SUNY-Purchase, 1972-80, prof., 1980—2001, prof. emeritus, 2002—; theatre critic The Village Voice, N.Y.C., 1958-89, The N.Y. Observer, N.Y.C., 1987-91, Newsday, N.Y.C., 1992-94, Kempner Disting. prof., 1997-99. Vis. lectr. drama div. Juilliard Sch., N.Y.C., 1966-71; dramaturg The Acting Co., N.Y.C., 1971-73; vis. critic Dartmouth Summer Repertory Co., Hanover, N.H., 1976, 79, 80, 82, 83, 84; master critic Nat. Critics Inst., Waterford, Conn., 1971— Author: Beyond Broadway, 1968. Fulbright scholar, 1960-61; Woodrow Wilson fellow, 1961-62; Guggenheim fellow, 1977; recipient George Jean Nathan award for dramatic criticism, 1981-82 Mem.: Am. Theatre and Drama Soc., Assn. for Theatre in Higher Edn., Assn. for Jewish Studies, Am. Theatre Critics Assn., Am. Soc. for Theatre Rsch. Jewish. E-mail: Jluddite@aol.com.

NOVICK, MARVIN, investment company executive; b. N.Y.C., July 16, 1931; s. Joseph and Anna Novick; m. Margaret A. Blau, Apr. 9, 1960; children: Jeffrey, Stuart, Barry. BBA, CCNY, 1952; MBA, NYU, 1955, postgrad., 1955-58. CPA N.Y., Mich., La., N.C. Sr. v.p. Mich. Blue Cross/Blue Shield, Detroit, 1961-70; v.p., dir. ops. underwriting Meadowbrook Ins., Southfield, Mich., 1970-72; ptnr. Touche Ross and Co., Detroit, 1972-84; vice chmn. Dura Corp., Southfield, 1984-87, Wesnovtek Corp., Birmingham, Mich., 1987-91; pres. R&M Resources Inc., Birmingham, 1991—; advisor Meadowbrook Ins. Group, Southfield, 1995—. Trustee Mich. Assn. Emotional Children, 1965—, also past pres.; chmn. pers. com. Jewish Welfare Found., 1987—91, assoc. chmn. cultural and edn. fedn. com., 1984—97; chmn. adv. com. Marrow Found., 1996—; trustee, treas. Mariners Inn, 1996—2000, Karmanos Cancer Inst.; mental health ctr. dir. Rose Hill Ctr., 1995—; chmn. Oak Park-Huntington Woods-Pleasant Ridge (Mich.) Dem. Orgn., 1970—72, 18th Dem. Congl. Dist., 1972—74; trustee, vice chmn. Union Am. Hebrew Congregation, 1981—; chmn. fin. com., fin. sec. World Prog. Judaism-Internat., 1985—99; mem. com. Jewish Agy. in Isreal, 1987—99; trustee Temple Beth El, Birmingham, Mich., 1968—, past pres.; mem. various coms. Jewish Welfare Fedn.; trustee Providence Hosp., Southfield, 1975—83, past chmn., trustee bldg. bd., 1982—89; vice chmn. fin. com., trustee Sinai Hosp., 1988—92, mem. audit com., 1995—97; bd. dirs. B'nai B'rith Centennial Lodge, 1970—79, past pres.; trustee, mem. exec. com. Rose Hill Ctr., Inc., 1992—; mem. com. Hillel Ctr., U. Mich. Named one of Outstanding Young Men Am., Outstanding Am. Found., 1968; recipient Honor and Svc. cert., Oak Park Bd. Edn., 1972, Past Pres. award, Mich. Assn. Emotionally Disturbed Children, 1986. Mem.: AICPA, N.Y. State Assn. CPAs, Mich. Assn. CPAs. Home: 12820 Burton St Oak Park MI 48237-1679

NOVICK, NELSON LEE, dermatologist, internist, writer, consultant, dermatological surgeon; b. Bklyn., June 27, 1949; s. Benjamin and Vivian (Meltzer) N.; m. Meryl Sohnis, June 20, 1971; children: Yonatan, Yoel, Ariel, Daniel, Avraham, Shmuel, Yehudah. BA in Biology magna cum laude, Bklyn. Coll., 1971; MD, Mt. Sinai Sch. Medicine, 1975. Diplomate Am. Bd. Internal Medicine, Am. Bd. Dermatology, Am. Bd. Med. Examiners. Resident internal medicine Mt. Sinai Med. Ctr., N.Y.C., 1975—78, postgrad. preceptee, 1980—83, outpatient dept. clinic chief, dermatology svc., 1983—2003, attending, 2004—; resident Skin and Cancer Unit NYU Med. Ctr., N.Y.C., 1978—80; clin. prof. Mt. Sinai Sch. Medicine, N.Y.C., 2004—. Cons. Westwood-Squibb Skin Care Info. Ctr., Vaseline Intensive Care Rsch., Bausch & Lomb, Schering-Plough, Sandoz Internat., Procter & Gamble, Lever-2000, Novartis, Bradley Pharms., Merz Pharms., Inst. for Med. Info., Collagenesis Corp., PediFix, Biocell Tech., others. Author: Saving Face, Skin Care for Teens, Super Skin, Baby Skin, You Can Do Something About Your Allergies, You Can Look Younger at Any Age, Diseases of the Mucus Membranes, (novel) In the Path of the Wolf, (audiotape series) Keeping That Baby Skin Look, Healthier and Younger-Looking Skin, Lunchtime Beauty Fixes for a Prettier Face, Breathing Easier, Fido, Food and Fumes; co-author: The External Ear; reviewer Annals Internal Medicine, Jour. Am. Acad. Dermatology, Jour. Dermatol. Surgery, Internat. Jour. Dermatology; editl. advisor Exec. Health's Good Health Report, Snyder Comm., Your Baby Wallboard Program; former med. editor Current Podiatric Medicine, Jour. Am. Analgesia Soc.; contbr. articles to profl. jours. Regent's Coll. scholar, 1971, Max and Leah Strauss Fund scholar, 1971, Grand St. Found. scholar, 1971; recipient Dept. Dermatology award for contbg. to edn. of residents, 2000-01, Dept. Dermatology award for exceptional svc. in patient care, 2001-02. Dept. Dermatology award for two decades of outstanding svc. Fellow ACP (direct election), Am. Acad. Dermatology, Am. Soc. Dermatol. Surgery, Am. Acad. Cosmetic Surgery, Skin Cancer Found. (hon.); mem. AMA, AAAS, Soc. Investigative Dermatology, Skin Phototrauma Found., Internat. Soc. for Androgenic Disorders, Skin Cancer Found. (charter), N.Y. Acad. Scis., N.Y. County Med. Soc., Am. Soc. Dermatologic Surgery, Am. Analgesia Soc. (past bd. dirs.), Am. Soc. Cosmetic Dermatology & Aesthetic Surgery (charter), Nature Conservancy, Audubon Soc., Nat. Geog. Found., N.Y. Zool. Soc., Am. Mus. Natural History, Smithsonian Instn., Nat. Wildlife Fedn., The Wilderness Soc., Author's Guild, Author's League Am., Phi Beta Kappa. Jewish. Office: 328 E 75th St New York NY 10021-3317 Office Phone: 212-772-9300. E-mail: nnovickmd@aol.com. *The true measure of a person's success in life is not how much he accomplished, but how much of his God-given potential he has used.*

NOVICK, STEPHEN ALAN, cardiologist; b. Hackensack, NJ, July 25, 1938; m. Rita Lynn Schneider; children: David, Michael, Jonathan. BA in Chemistry magna cum laude, Bklyn. Coll., 1959; MD with honors, SUNY, 1963. Intern L.I. Coll. Hosp., Bklyn., 1963—64, resident, chief resident in internal medicine, 1965—67; fellow cardiology Mt. Sinai Med. Ctr., N.Y.C., 1967—69; dir. prenatal cardiology clinic Mt. Sinai Hosp., N.Y.C., 1969—. Dir. cardiac clinic Mt. Sinai Hosp., N.Y.C., 1970—2000; dir. cardiology, dir. ICU Yonkers (N.Y.) Profl. Hosp., 1972—79; cons. cardiologist St. John's Riverside Hosp., Yonkers, NY; cons., presenter in field. Contbr. articles to profl. jours. Founder, dir. Little TOR Homeowners Assn., New City, NY, 1973—75, Bklyn. Coll. Soc. for Free Discussion of Politics, 1955—59. Recipient cardiology fellowship, NIH, 1967—69. Fellow: N.Y. Cardiol. Soc.; mem.: Phi Beta Kappa. Avocations: history, violin, singing, writing. Office: 133 E 73rd St New York NY 10021 also: 984 N Broadway Yonkers NY 10701 Office Phone: 914-423-7267.

NOVIK, STEVE, finance company executive; BSBA, U. Mo., 1972; MBA, Washington U., 1974. Ptnr. KPMG Peat Marwick; from gen. prin. to CFO Steve Novik, St. Louis, 1983-95; CFO Edward Jones, St. Louis, 1995—. Office: Edward Jones 12555 Manchester Road Saint Louis MO 63131

NOVIKOFF, HAROLD STEPHEN, lawyer; b. N.Y.C., Apr. 5, 1951; s. Eugene Benjamin and Vivian (Hirsch) N.; m. Amy Pearl, Aug. 20, 1972; children: Sara Heather, Elyse Fana. AB, Cornell U., 1972; JD, Columbia U., 1975. Bar: N.Y. 1976, U.S. Dist. Ct. (so. dist.) N.Y. 1976. Ptnr. Wachtell, Lipton, Rosen & Katz, N.Y.C., 1975—. Mem. ABA, N.Y. State Bar Assn., Assn. Bar City N.Y. (bankruptcy and reorgn. com. 1995-99, chair 1999-2002), Nat. Bankruptcy Conf. (exec. com.). Office: Wachtell Lipton Rosen Katz 51 W 52nd St Fl 29 New York NY 10019-6150 Office Phone: 212-403-1249. Business E-Mail: hsnovikoff@wlrk.com.

NOVIKOV, SERGEI PETROVITCH, mathematician; b. Gorky, Russia, Mar. 20, 1938; s. Peter Sergeevitch and Ludmila (Keldysh) N.; m. Eleonora Vikentievna Tsoi, Oct. 2, 1962; children: Irina, Maria, Peter. B.Math., Moscow State U., 1960; Dr. Math., Steklov Math. Inst., Moscow, 1965; Hon. Dr., U. Athens, 1988. Rsch. prof. math. Steklov Math. Inst., Moscow, 1964-75; chmn. math. dept. Landau Inst. Theoretical Physics, Moscow, 1975-96; prof. of math U Maryland, Coll. Park, 1996—. Chmn. geometry and topology Steklov Math. Ins., 1983—, Moscow State U., 1983—. Contbr. articles to profl. jours. Recipient Lenin Prize, 1967, Fields medal Internat. Math. Union, 1970, Lobachevskii Internat. Prize, Acad. of Sci. of the USSR, 1981. Mem. Moscow Math. Soc. (pres. 1985-96), Internat. Assn. of Math. Physicists (v.p. 1986-90), London Math. Soc. (hon. mem.), Serbian Acad. of Sci. and Art (hon. mem.), Acad. of Sci of the USSR (corresponding mem. 1966-81, full mem. 1981—), elected foreign mem. of the Academia de Lincei, Italy, 1991, mem. Academia Europea, 1992, foreign mem. of the NAS, 1994, mem of the Pontifical Acad. of Sci. (Vatican), 1996. Office: Landau Inst Kosygin St 2 Moscow Russia also: Dept of Math Math Bldg U of Maryland College Park MD 20742-4015

NOVINS, DOUGLAS K. psychiatrist, educator; Prof. psychiatry divsn. child and adolescent psychiatry U. Colo., Denver. Recipient Presdl. Scholar award Am. Acad. Child and Adolescent Psychiatry, 1993. Office: U CO Divsn Child & Adolescent Psychiatry Health Scis Ctr PO Box C-259 42 Denver CO 80262-0001

NOVITCH, MARK, physician, retired pharmaceutical executive, educator; b. New London, Conn., Apr. 23, 1932; s. Charles Weinger and Mary (Margolick) N.; m. Katherine Louise Henderson, Oct. 9, 1971; 1 dau., Julia Drummond. AB, Yale U., 1954; MD, N.Y. Med. Coll., 1958. Intern, asst. resident in medicine Boston City Hosp., 1958-60; rsch. fellow Harvard Med. Sch., 1960-62, asst. in medicine, 1962-64, instr. medicine, 1964-67; mem. med. staff Peter Bent Brigham Hosp., Boston, 1962-67; asst. physician Univ. Health Svcs., Harvard U., 1961-67; asst. to dep. asst. sec. for health and sci. affairs HEW, Washington, 1967-71; dep. assoc. commr. for med. affairs FDA, Washington, 1971-78, assoc. commr. for health affairs, 1978-81; dep. commr. food and drugs HHS, 1981-85; corp. v.p. The Upjohn Co., Kalamazoo, 1985-86, sr. v.p. sci. adminstrn., 1986-88, exec. v.p., 1989-90, vice-chmn. bd. dirs., 1991-93; prof. health scis. George Washington U., Washington, 1994-97. Adj. prof. George Washington U., 1997—2001; bd. dirs. Guidant Corp., Neurogen Corp., Kos Pharms., Inc., Alteon, Inc., Nat. Acad. Soc. Ins.; chmn. bd. dirs. Food and Drug Law Inst., 2001—02; trustee U.S. Pharmacopeial Conv. Inc., 1999—2000, pres., 1990—95. Bd. dirs. Nat. Fund Med. Edn., Nat. Acad. Social Ins., 2003—. USPHS fellow, 1960-62; Brookings Instn. fed. exec. fellow, 1970-71 Mem. Mass. Med. Soc., Am. Soc. Clin. Pharmacology and Therapeutics. Home: 3558 Albemarle St NW Washington DC 20008-4214

NOVITZ, CHARLES RICHARD, television executive; b. Chgo., Oct. 25, 1934; m. Eve Krzyzanowski, Feb. 11, 1988; 1 child, Alexandra Maris. BS in Journalism, U. Ill., Champaign-Urbana, 1956; MS, Columbia U., 1960; MPA, NYU, 1971. Reporter, writer, editor City News Bur., Chgo., 1956-57, UPI, Chgo., 1957-59; editor, writer, field producer NBC News, N.Y.C. and Chgo., 1959-60; with ABC News, 1960-79; mgr. ABC News (TV network syndication), 1973-79; mng. dir. Ind. TV News Assn., N.Y.C., 1979-81; producer, exec. NBC News, N.Y.C., 1982-85, 87; assoc. Rowan & Blewitt, Inc./Exec. TV Workshop, N.Y.C., 1985-95; pres. NovaNews Comm. Cons., N.Y.C., 1994—. On-air talent Money Call News, 1988; freelance TV producer, cable and pub. TV series, 1985—; adj. instr. LIU, 1967-69, NYU, 1969-70; asst. adj. prof. Lehman Coll., 1970-71; adj. prof., producer interactive televised course CUNY, 1972-75 Mem. Silurians, Broadcast Pioneers, Radio TV News Dirs. Assn., Alumni Assn. Columbia Grad. Sch. Journalism (pres. 1979), Deadline Club N.Y.C. (pres. 1969), Deadline Club Found. (pres. 1999—), Soc. Profl. Journalists-Sigma Delta Chi (pres. 1981-82). Office: 160 West End Ave Apt 29D New York NY 10023-5616 also: 392 Moonstone Beach Rd Wakefield RI 02879-5102 Office Phone: 212-787-6908. Personal E-mail: evevideo@earthlink.net.

NOVOA, YANIRA, diplomat; b. San Salvador, El Salvador, Mar. 5, 1956; arrived in U.S., 1977; d. Numa Pompilio and Donna Rodriguez Novoa. BA, Mount Marty Coll., Yankton, S.D., 1977—81. Coun. gen. Min. Fgn. Affairs, El Salvador, 1990—98, min. counselor, 1998—2002, free trade agreement investment chpt. mem., 1997—2002. Recipient Mother Jerome scholarship, Mount Marty Coll. Mem.: Internat. Ct. Justice. Address: 4800 N 15th Apt 211 Lincoln NE 68521-5605 Home: PO Box 6421 Lincoln NE 68506-0421

NOVOGROD, NANCY GERSTEIN, editor; b. NYC, Jan. 30, 1949; d. Max and Hilda (Kirschbaum) Gerstein; m. John Campner Novogrod, Nov. 7, 1976; children: James Campner, Caroline Anne. AB, Mt. Holyoke Coll., 1971. Sec. fiction dept. The New Yorker, NYC, 1971-73, reader, 1973-76; asst. editor Clarkson Potter/Pubs., NYC, 1977-78, assoc. editor, 1978-80, editor, 1980-83, sr. editor, 1984-86, exec. editor, 1987; sr. editor HG (House & Garden mag.), NYC, 1987-88, editor-in-chief, 1988-93, Travel + Leisure, NYC, 1993—; editl. dir. Am. Express Pub., NYC, 2000—. Bd. dirs. NY Bot. Garden, 1991—; exec. com., bd. dirs. Mount Holyoke Coll., 1992—97; adv. bd. Breast Cancer Rsch. Found., 1993; bd. dirs. Children's Advocacy Ctr. Manhattan, 2003. Mem.: Am. Soc. Mag. Editors (bd. dir.). Office: Travel + Leisure 1120 Avenue of the Americas New York NY 10036-6700 E-mail: nnovogrod@travelandleisure.com.

NOVOTNEY, DONALD FRANCIS, superintendent of schools; b. Streator, Ill., July 10, 1947; s. Andrew Stephen and Irene Marie (Lux) Novotney; m. Jane Francis Loeffelholz, June 3, 1973; children: Nicole, Tara, Thomas, Michael, Theresa. BA, Loras Coll., 1969; MS in Tchg., U. Wis., Platteville, 1973; MS, U. Dayton, 1985. Cert. tchr., Wis.; cert. tchr. and adminstr., Ohio. Prin. Holy Ghost Sch., Dickeyville, Wis., 1969-75, St. John Sch., Green Bay, Wis., 1975-76, Beaver Dam (Wis.) Cath. Schs., 1976-83; coord. Jordan Cath. Schs., Rock Island, Wis., 1983-85; supt. schs. Diocese of Fargo, N.D., 1985-86, Diocese of La Crosse, Wis., 1987—2001, Diocese of Jefferson City, Mo., 2002—. Mem. Nat. Cath. Edn. Assn. (del. to nat. congress for cath. schs.). Republican. Roman Catholic. Avocations: athletics, travel. Home: 4000 Terra Bella Jefferson City MO 65109 Office: Diocese of Jefferson City 402 N Clark Ave Jefferson City MO 65102 Office Phone: 573-635-9127. Personal E-mail: donjanen@aol.com.

NOVOTNY, DONALD WAYNE, electrical engineering educator; b. Chgo., Dec. 15, 1934; s. Adolph and Margaret Novotny; m. Louise J. Eenigenburg, June 26, 1954; children: Donna Jo Kopp, Cynthia Mason. BEE, Ill. Inst. Tech., 1956, MS, 1957; PhD, U. Wis., 1961. Registered profl. engr., Wis. Instr. Ill. Inst. Tech., 1957-58; mem. faculty U. Wis., Madison, 1958—, prof. elec. engring., 1969-96, chmn. dept. elec. and computer engring., 1976-80, Grainger prof. power electronics, 1990—96, prof. emeritus, 1996—. Vis. prof. Mont. State U., 1966, Eindhoven (The Netherlands) Tech. U., 1974, Tech. U. Louvain, Belgium, 1986; Fulbright lectr. Tech. U. Ghent, Belgium, 1981; dir. Wis. Elec. Machines and Power Electronics Consortium, 1981-96; assoc. dir. Univ.-Industry Rsch. Program, 1982-93; chmn. elec. engring. program Nat. Technol. U., 1989—2003; cons. to industry. Author: Introductory Electromechanics, 1965, Vector Control and Dynamics of AC Drives, 1996; also rsch. papers; assoc. editor: Electric Machines and Power Systems, 1976—99. Recipient Kiekhofer tchg. award U. Wis., 1964, Benjamin Smith Reynolds tchg. award, 1984, Holdridge tchg. award, 1995, Nat. Technol. U. Outstanding Instr. award, 1996-2001, IEEE-IAS Outstanding Achievement award, 1998; Outstanding paper award Engring. Inst. Can., 1966; named IEEE-IAS Disting. Lectr., 1995; fellow GE, 1956, Ford Found., 1960; grantee numerous industries and govt. agys. Fellow IEEE (prize paper awards 1983, 84, 86, 87, 90, 91, 93, 94, 3d Millennium Medal 2000); mem. Am. Soc. Engring. Edn., Sigma Xi, Tau Beta Pi, Eta Kappa Nu. Lodges: Rotary. Congregationalist. Home: 1421 E Skyline Dr Madison WI 53705-1132 Office: U Wis Dept Elec and Computer Engring 1415 Engineering Dr Madison WI 53706-1607 Office Phone: 608-262-6926. Business E-Mail: novotny@engr.wisc.edu.

NOVOTNY, F. DOUGLAS, lawyer; b. Mineola, N.Y., Mar. 10, 1952; s. Frank Joseph and Eleanor Evans (Rose) N.; m. Norma R. Federici, Sept. 7, 1991; children: Nicholas, Christina, Alexander. BA cum laude, SUNY, Albany, 1974; postgrad., NYU, Hofstra U., C.W. Post U.; JD cum laude, Albany Law Sch., 1979. Bar: N.Y. 1980, U.S. Dist. Ct. (no. dist.) N.Y. 1980. Confidential law asst. Appellate Divsn. 3d Dept., Albany, 1979-80; ptnr. DeGraff, Foy, Conway, Holt-Harris & Mealey, Albany, 1980-91; pvt. practice Saratoga, N.Y., 1991-93; mng. atty. Law Offices of F. Douglas Novotny, 1993—; staff counsel Am. Internat. Group, Inc., 1993—. Mem. Albany County Arbitration Panel, 1984-88. Editor Albany Law Rev., 1978-79; contbr. articles to profl. jours. Mem. ATLA, Justinian Soc., Assn. Trial Lawyers Am., Capital Dist. Trial Lawyers Assn. Presbyterian. Home: 27 Mallard Lndg S Waterford NY 12188-1037

NOVOTNY, VLADIMIR, educator, consultant; b. Olomouc, Czech Rep., Aug. 30, 1938; came to U.S., 1969, naturalized, 1983; s. Vladimir and Frantiska Novotny; m. Lynn Emily Braasch, June 14, 1975; children: Paul Martin, Eric Vladimir. Diploma in Engring., Tech. U., Brno, Czech Rep., 1963, degree in Sci., 1968; PhD, Vanderbilt U., 1971. Rsch. engr. Water Mgmt. Inst., Brno, Czech Rep., 1962-69; rsch. assoc. Vanderbilt U., Nashville, 1969-71; project engr. Aware, Inc., Nashville, 1970-73; pres. Aquanova Internat., Ltd., Mequon, Wis., 1989—; prof. Marquette U., Milw., 1973—2002, prof. emeritus, 2003—; CDM chair, prof. Northeastern U., Boston, 2003—. Dir. Inst. Urban Environ. Risk Mgmt. Marquette U., Milw., 1998—2002; dir. workshop NATO, Vienna, 1994; expert pollution abatement Venezia Nuova, Venice, Italy, 1989—2001. Author: Handbook of Nonpoint Pollution, 1981, Water Quality, 1994, 2002; editor: Management of Degraded River Basins, 1995. Rsch. grantee, Water Environ. Rsch. Found., Alexandria, Va., 1992, 1995, U.S. EPA, Washington, 1993, 1997, 2003, Ill. EPA, 2000—03. Mem. Internat. Water Assn. (chm. com. 1993-98, chair internat. conf., Chgo., 1993, Edinburgh, 1998, Milw. 2001), Internat. Water Resource Assn., Am. Water Resources Assn. (dir. 1985-89), Water Environ. Fedn. Office: Harvard Univ 655 Huntington Ave Boston MA 02115 Home: 780 Centre St Apt C Newton MA 02458-2539 E-mail: novotny@coe.neu.edu.

NOWACKI, JAMES NELSON, lawyer; b. Columbus, Ohio, Sept. 12, 1947; s. Louis James and Betty Jane (Nelson) N.; m. Catherine Ann Holden, Aug. 1, 1970; children: Carrie, Anastasia, Emma. AB, Princeton U., 1969; JD, Yale U., 1973. Bar: Ill. 1973, N.Y. 1982, U.S. dist. Ct. (no. dist.) Ill. 1973, U.S. Ct. Appeals (7th cir.) 1978, U.S. Ct. Appeals (6th cir.) 1987, U.S. Supreme Ct. 1992. Assoc. Isham, Lincoln & Beale, Chgo., 1976-79; ptnr. Kirkland & Ellis, Chgo., 1980—. Mem. Winnetka Sch. Bd. Dist. 36, Ill. 1983-91, bd. pres., 1989-91; mem. New Trier Sch. Bd., 1997-99, pres., 1997-98. Harlan Fiske Stone prize Yale U., 1972. Mem. ABA (forum com. on constrn. industry, litigation sect.), Mid-Am. Club, Skokie Country Club. Home: 708 Prospect Ave Winnetka IL 60093-2320 Office: Kirkland & Ellis LLP 200 E Randolph St Fl 60 Chicago IL 60601-6636

NOWAK, GREGORY JOSEPH, lawyer, educator; b. Phila., Aug. 5, 1959; s. Joseph Michael and Mary Anne N.; m. Denise Marie Maggetti, May 25, 1985. BA, La Salle U., 1981; JD, Cornell U., 1984; LLM, NYU, 1988. Bar: Pa. 1984, N.J. 1984, U.S. Dist. Ct. (ea. dist.) Pa. 1984, U.S. Dist. Ct. N.J. 1984, U.S. Tax Ct. 1985. Assoc. Stradley, Ronon, Stevens & Young, Phila., 1984-92, ptnr., 1993-99; exec. v.p. for mergers and acquisitions and product devel. Villanova Capital, Conshohocken, Pa., 1999—. Instr. Inst. for Paralegal Edn., Phila., 1986-89; bd. dirs. Marian Juniata Fed. Credit Union, Phila., 1978-99. Contbr. articles to popular mags. Bd. dirs. Holy Redeemer Found. Christian Bros. scholar, 1978-81, Lindback scholar, 1981. Mem. ABA (chmn. regulated investment cos. com.), Phila. Bar Assn. (chmn. exempt orgn. com. 1997-99), Pa. Econ. League. Avocations: golf, running. Office: Villanova Capital 1200 River Rd Conshohocken PA 19428-2436

NOWAK, JACQUELYN LOUISE, state agency administrator, artist, realtor, consultant; b. Harrisburg, Pa., Sept. 2, 1937; d. John Henry and Irene Louise (Clark) Snyder; children: Andrew Alfred IV, Deirdre Anne. Student, Pa. State U., 1973-74; BA, Lycoming Coll., 1975. Editl. writer Patriot News Co., Harrisburg, 1957-58; dir. West Shore Sr. Citizens Ctr., New Cumberland, Pa., 1969-72; exec. dir. Cumberland County Office Aging, Carlisle, Pa., 1972-80; bur. dir. Bur. Advocacy/Pa. Dept. Aging, Harrisburg, 1980-88; exec. asst. to Senator John D. Hopper Senate Com. on Aging and Youth, Pa., 1989; assoc. Century 21 Piscioneri Realty, Inc., Camp Hill, Pa., 1989-94; adminstrv. officer

Am. Trauma Soc., 1994-2000; exec. asst. to dep. sec. pub. health programs Pa. Dept. Health, 2000—03, mgr. diabetes program, 2003—. Owner D&J Prodns./Art and Handcrafted Teddy Bears, 1986, Ted E. Bear's Emporium, Harrisburg, 1988-92; adminstr. Country Meadows West Shore II, Mechanicsburg, Pa., 1993-94; recorder Pa. Gov's Coun. Aging Cen. Region, 1972-74, chmn. pub. rels., 1973-74; state planning com. Pa. State conf. Aging, 1974, panelist, 1975-78; mem. state bd. Pa. Coun. Homemakers-Home Health Aide Svcs., 1972-80, v.p., 1975, chmn. ann. meeting, 1973-75; sr. citizens subcom. chmn. Pa. Atty. Gens. Commn. to Prevent Shoplifting, 1983. Spl. projects coord. Pa. divsn. Am. Trauma Soc., 1991-93; adv. com. Tri-County Ret. Sr. Vol. Program, 1972-74; bd. dirs. Coun. Human Svcs. Cumberland, Dauphin, and Perry Counties, 1973-74, Cumberland County Unit Am. Cancer Soc., 1964-76, state del., 1964-66, chmn. county pub. rels., 1965-66, cancer crusade chmn., 1964; svc. com. Family and Children's Svc. Harrisburg, 1970-74, policy com. 1973-74 Recipient Herman Melitzer award Pa. Conf. Aging, 1978; named Woman of Yr. Sta. WIOO Radio, Carlisle, Pa., 1979. Mem. Nat. Assn. Area Ags. on Aging (bd. dirs. 1975-80, pres. 1976-77, sec. 1978-79), Nat. Soc. Decorative Painters (bd. dirs. Penns Woods Painters chpt. 1995—, sec. 1996-97, v.p. 1998-99, pres. 2000-2001), Pa. Watercolor Soc., Harrisburg Art Assn., Mechanicsburg Art Ctr. (pres. 1987-90, bd. dirs. 1984-95), Am. Trauma Soc. (state bd. Pa. divsn. 1985-88), Older Womens League (founder chpt.), Lycoming Coll. Alumni Assn. (exec. bd. 1987-89), Pa. Fedn. Womens Club (divsn. chmn. 1972-76), Torch Club (pres. 1987-88, 2d v.p. 1985-86), Zonta Internat. (sec. 1986-89). Home: 15 Paddock Ln Camp Hill PA 17011-1268 E-mail: jlnowak@aol.com.

NOWAK, JERRY (GERALD C. NOWAK), music educator, musician, writer; b. Detroit, Mich., Apr. 16, 1936; s. John and Lucille Nowak; m. Judith C. Christian, Sept. 30, 1937; children: Amy Elizabeth DeGrgorio, Christopher Gerald. BS in Music Edn., Coll. of N.J., 1954—58, MA, 1968. Music tchr. Hunterdon Ctrl. Regional H.S., Flemington, NJ, 1958—69; prof. of music Bucks County C.C., Newtown, Pa., 1969—. Co-author: Conducting Music, Not the Musicians, 2002, The Art of Expressive Playing, 2004, musician (founding mem.) Phila. Saxophone Quartet, N.J Saxophone Quartet; musician: (composer, arranger) more than 800 pub. compositions and arrangements for instrumental and vocal ensembles (ASCAP each yr. since 1988); condr.: rec. sessions in N.Y.C., Phila., Washington and London. Pres. Raritan Twp. Athletic Assn., Flemington, NJ, 1980—82. Home: 42 Madison Ave Flemington NJ 08822 Office: Bucks County CC Swamp Rd Newtown PA 18940 Personal E-mail: jerrynowak@blast.net.

NOWAK, JOHN E. law educator; b. Chgo., Jan. 2, 1947; s. George Edward and Evelyn (Bucci) N.; m. Judith Johnson, June 1, 1968; children: John Edwin, Jeffrey Edward. AB, Marquette U., 1968; JD, U. Ill., 1971. Law clk. Supreme Ct. of Ill., Chgo., 1971-72; asst. prof. U. Ill., Urbana, 1972-75, assoc. prof., 1975-87, law prof., 1978—, grad. coll. faculty, 1982—, Baum prof. Law, 1993—. Chmn. Constl. Law Sch. Sect.; faculty rep. Big Ten Intercollegiate Conf., Schaumburg, 1981—91; vis. prof. law U. Mich., Ann Arbor, 1985; Lee disting. vis. prof. Coll. William and Mary, 1993; Williams vis. prof. law U. Richmond, 2003. Co-author: Constitutional Law, 7th edit. 2004, Treatise on Constitutional Law, 1986, 3d edit., 1999, Story's Commentaries on the Constitution, 1987. Scholar-in-Residence, U. of Ariz., Tucson, 1985, 87. Mem. Assn. of Am. Law Schs. (chmn. constl. law sect., accreditation com. 1980-88), Nat. Collegiate Athletic Assn. (mem. infractions com. 1987—), Am. Law Inst., Am. Bar Assn., Ill. Bar Assn., Order of the Coif (Triennial Book award com.). Roman Catholic. Home: 1701 Mayfair Rd Champaign IL 61821-5522 Office: U Ill Coll Law 504 E Pennsylvania Ave Champaign IL 61820-6909

NOWAK, JUDITH ANN, psychiatrist; b. Albany, N.Y., Feb. 18, 1948; d. Jacob Frank and Anne Patricia Nowak. BA, Cornell U., 1970, MD, 1974. Diplomate in psychiatry Am. Bd. Psychiatry and Neurology. Resident U. Va. Hosp., Charlottesville, 1974-77; fellow in psychiatry Westchester divsn. Cornell U. Med. Coll. Westchester Div., White Plains, N.Y., 1977-78; clin. affiliate Cornell U. Med. Coll., White Plains, N.Y., 1978-79; staff psychiatrist Chestnut Lodge Hosp., Rockville, Md., 1979-81; med. officer in psychiatry St. Elizabeths Hosp., Washington, 1981; pvt. practice Washington, 1981—. Clin. asst. prof. of psychiatry, George Washington U., Washington, 1981-89; clin. assoc. prof. psychiatry, George Washington U. 1989-94, clin. prof. psychiatry, 1994—. Mem. Am. Psychiat. Soc. (pub. affairs rep. 1995), Am. Psychoanalytic Soc., Washington Psychiat. Soc. (sec. 1989-90, 2001-2003, pres. 1991-92), D.C. Med. Soc. (speaker ho. of dels. 1996-98, chair coun. med. specialty socs. 1998-2000). Office: 908 New Hampshire Ave NW Washington DC 20037-2049 Office Phone: 202-887-5495.

NOWAK, NANCY STEIN, judge; b. Des Moines, Sept. 17, 1952; d. Russell D. and Christine (Evanoka) Stein; m. Raymond A. Nowak, May 26, 1973. BA, Drake Univ., Iowa, 1974, MA, 1976; JD, George Washington Univ., D.C., 1980. Bar: D.C. 1980, Iowa 1982, Tex. 1986. Briefing atty. Judge Jamie Boyd, 1983-84, Judge Edward Prado, 1984-87; asst. U.S. atty., 1987-88; asst. U.S. trustee, 1988-89; magistrate judge U.S. Dist. Ct. (Tex. we. dist.), 5th circuit, San Antonio, 1989—. Office: US Courthouse 655 E Durango Blvd San Antonio TX 78206-1100

NOWE, RONALD JOHN, state legislator, small business owner; b. Gloucester, Mass., Feb. 7, 1946; children: Ronald Jr., Miguel, Valierie. Student, Hesser Coll., 1976. Owner, mgr. Now Ins. Agy., Epping, N.H., agy. mgr.; propr., mgr. Kamper Kampania Kampground, 3d Street Grocery; mgr., propr. Oak Grove Golfing; mem. N.H. Ho. of Reps. Mem., chmn. wildlife and marine resources com., com. whip, legis. adminstrn. chmn., chmn. sheriff com., mem. long range planning com. Mem. Pub. Water Access Adv. Bd.; vice chair Epping Planning Bd. Mem. DAV (jr. vice. comdr. 1983-94), VFW, Am. Legion, Masons. Republican. Home: PO Box 327 Epping NH 03042 Office: Legis Office Bldg Rm 308 Concord NH 03301

NOWELL, LIONEL L. food products executive; BS in Bus. Adminstrn., Ohio State U., 1976. CPA. Various fin. analysis positions Owens-Corning Fiberglas Corp., Packard Electric Divsn., GM, Inc.; various audit and control positions Pizza Hut divsn. PepsiCo., Inc., 1983-91; v.p., controller audit activities food and internat. retail Pillsbury Co., 1991, v.p., CFO Haagen-Dazs, v.p. fin. bakeries and foodservice unit; v.p. fin. Pillsbury N.Am., 1996-98; sr. v.p. strategy and bus. devel. RJR Nabisco Holdings Corp., N.Y.C., 1998—99; controller PepsiCo, Inc, 1999—2000; cfo Pepsi Bottling Co, Inc, 2000—01; sr. v.p., treasurer PepsiCo, Inc., 2001—. Dir. Gifts in Kind Internat. Mem. AICPAs. Office: 700 Anderson Hill Rd Purchase NY 10577

NOWELL, PETER CAREY, pathologist, educator; b. Phila., Feb. 8, 1928; s. Foster and Margaret (Matlack) Nowell; m. Helen Worst, Sept. 9, 1950; children: Sharon, Timothy, Karen, Kristin, Michael. BA, Wesleyan U., Middletown, Conn., 1948; MD, U. Pa., 1952. Intern Phila. Gen. Hosp., 1952—53; resident pathology Presbyn. Hosp., Phila., 1953—54; med.-teaching, research specializing in cancer Phila., 1956—; from instr. to prof. pathology Sch. Medicine U. Pa., 1956—, chmn. dept. pathology, 1967—73; dir. (Cancer Center), 1973—75. Lt. M.C. USNR, 1954—56. Recipient Rsch. Career award, USPHS, 1964—67, Parke-Davis award, 1965, Lindback Disting. Tchg. award, 1967, Passano award, 1984, Rous-Whipple award, Am. Assn. Pathology, 1986, de Villers award, Leukemia Soc. Am., 1987, Mott prize, GM Cancer Rsch. Found., 1989, 3M award, FASEB, 1993, Lasker Found. award, 1998. Home: 345 Mount Alverno Rd Media PA 19063-5313 Office: U Pa Sch Medicine Dept Pathology & Lab Medicine Philadelphia PA 19104-6082 Office Phone: 215-898-8061. Business E-Mail: nowell@mail.med.upenn.edu.

NOWICK, ARTHUR STANLEY, metallurgy and materials science educator; b. NYC, Aug. 29, 1923; s. Hyman and Clara (Sperling) N.; m. Joan Franzblau, Oct. 30, 1949; children: Jonathan, Steven, Alan, James. AB, Bklyn. Coll., 1943; A.M., Columbia U., 1948, PhD, 1950. Physicist NACA, Cleve., 1944-46; instr. U. Chgo., 1949-51; asst. prof., then assoc. prof. metallurgy Yale U., 1951-57; mgr. metallurgy research IBM Corp Research Center, Yorktown Heights, N.Y., 1957-66; prof. metallurgy Columbia U., 1966-90, Henry Marion Howe prof. metallurgy and materials sci., 1990-95, prof. emeritus, 1996—. Adj. prof. CBEMS dept. U. Calif., Irvine, 2001; Frank Golick lectr. U. Mo., 1970; vis. prof. Technion, Haifa, Israel, 1973; co-chmn. Internat. Conf. Internal Friction, 1961, 69; cons. in field. Author: Crystal Properties Via Group Theory, 1995; co author: Anelastic Relaxation in Crystalline Solids, 1972, co-editor: Diffusion in Solids, 1975, Diffusion in Crystalline Solids, 1984; contbr. articles to profl. jours. Named David Turnbull lecturer Materials Rsch. Soc., 1994; gold medalist Internat. Conf. Internal Friction, 1989. Fellow AIME, Am. Phys. Soc.; mem. Materials Rsch. Soc. (Turnbull lectr. 1994), Sigma Xi (pres. Kappa chpt. 1983-85). Home: 24 Hillsdale Dr Newport Beach CA 92660-4234 Office: U Calif Irvine 916 Engineering Tower Irvine CA 92697-2575 Business E-Mail: anowick@uci.edu.

NOWICKI, GEORGE LUCIAN, retired chemical company executive; b. Rutherford, N.J., Dec. 4, 1926; s. Justin Nowicki; m. Mary Elisabeth Baker, Aug. 30, 1947; children: Barbara, Peter, Paul, James. BSChemE, CCNY, 1949; MSChemE, NYU, 1956. Registered profl. engr., N.Y., Pa. Chemist Ideal Toy Co., N.Y.C., 1949; chem. engr. Bklyn. Union Gas Co., 1949-50, Sonotone Corp., Elmsford, N.Y., 1950-52; dept. head Burroughs Wellcome Co., Tuckahoe, N.Y., 1952-70; v.p. mfg. Quaker Chem. Corp., Conshohocken, Pa., 1970-79, v.p. domestic ops., 1984-89, ret., 1989; pres. Selby Batersby Co., Phila., 1979-81; mng. dir. Quaker Chem. Holland BV, Uithoorn, The Netherlands, 1981-84. Chmn. bd. Overdale Corp., Alsip, Ill., 1987-89, Quaker Chem. Can. Ltd., Toronto, 1985-89. Pres. Ctrl. Sch. Dist. 7, Hartsdale, N.Y., 1960-69, Westchester County Sch. Bds. Assn., White Plains, N.Y., 1965; bd. dirs. Suburban Gen. Hosp., Norristown, Pa., 1986; mem. governing bd. Vt. Common Cause, 1993-2001; bd. dirs. Martha Canfield Libr., Arlington, Vt., 1994-2000; counselor Svc. Corps Ret. Execs., 1993-95. With USN, 1944—46, WWII. Mem. Am. Inst. Chem. Engrs., Mfrs. Assn. Del. Valley (bd. dirs. 1987-89). Avocations: swimming, skiing, video photography, stamps. Home: 1268 Berwal Rd Arlington VT 05250-8821

NOWIK, DOROTHY ADAM, medical equipment company executive; b. Chgo., July 25, 1944; d. Adam Harry and Helen (Kichkaylo) Wanaski; m. Eugene Nicholas Nowik, Aug. 9, 1978; children: George Eugene, Helen Eugene. A.A., Columbia Coll., 1980. Cert. lactation counselor, lactation educator, lactation cons. Sec., adminstrv. asst. to pres. Zenco Engring Corp., Chgo., 1970-71, sales rep. Medizenco USA Ltd., Chgo., 1971-73, pub. Pacific Med. Systems, Inc., Bellevue, Wash., 1973-76, pres., 1976—. Mem. NAFE, Pacific Mothers Support, Inc. (pres. 1991), Wash. Assn. Lactation Cons. (treas. 1994—). Mem. Orthodox Ch. Am. Home: 303 126th Ave NE Bellevue WA 98005-3217 Office: 1407 132nd Ave NE # 10 Bellevue WA 98005-2259

NOWIK, HENRY IAN, marketing executive, consultant; b. Posen, Poland, Feb. 3, 1917; came to U.S., 1979; s. Alexander Joseph and Elizabeth Augusta (von Kuhn) N.; m. Evelyn Phyllis Barnard, Sept. 17, 1949 (dec. 1992); m. Kathleen Yvonne Jones, May 12, 1995. BS in Econs., London U., 1949; PhD, U. Lyon, 1948. Student advisor U. London, 1948-52; export mktg. exec. Parke Davis Ltd., Eng., 1952-54; mgr. market rsch. Mather & Crowther, Eng., 1954-56; mgr. new products Hoover Ltd., Eng., 1956-58; mgr. market rsch. Petfoods Ltd. div. Mars, Inc., Eng., 1958-64; v.p. mktg., sales Uncle Ben's, Australia, 1964-68, gen. mgr., mng. dir., 1968-78; v.p. mktg. Mars, Inc., U.S., 1979-80, group pres., 1980-84; cons. mktg., 1984—; sr. cons. Food System Assocs., Washington, 1985—. Prof., lectr. Georgetown U., Washington, 1984—. Author: Disciplined Entrepreneur, 1976, Research in Marketing, 1964, (with others) Product and Process Development in the Food Industry, 1985; contbr. articles to profl. jours. Justice of Peace, Sydney, Australia, 1973; bd. dirs. Australian Ballet Found., Melbourne, 1975; trustee World Wildlife Fund, Australia, 1976; chmn. Decentralization Adv. Bd., Canberra, Australia, 1977-78. Served with RAF, 1939-45. Decorated Officer of Most Excellent Order Brit. Empire, Officer of Order of Australia, Comdr. with Star of Polonia Restituta, Polish Gold Cross of Merit, Knight Supreme Mil. Order Temple Jerusalem. Fellow Royal Statis. Soc., Brit. Inst. Mgmt., Australian Inst. Mgmt., Advt. Inst. Australia, Inst. Dirs. Australia; mem. Internat. Law Assn., Acad. Polit. Sci. (life), Lloyds of London (underwriting), Market Rsch. Soc., Chartered Inst. of Mktg., Am. Mgmt. Assn., N.Y. Acad. Sci., London Reform Club, Georgetown Club (Washington), Royal Yacht Squadron Club (Sydney, Australia). Roman Catholic. Avocations: collecting coins, stamps and first edition books.

NOWIK, JOHN DAVID, music educator, musician; b. Allentown, Pa., Aug. 26, 1960; s. Stanley John and Helen Mary Nowik; m. Martha Elizabeth Huddleston, Jan. 9, 1982; children: Clare Magdalena children: Elizabeth J., Anna M., Krystyna H., Sofia M., Katerina T., Lucia F., Johanna C., Alexander S., Monica R. MusB, Westminster Choir Coll., 1982; MusM, Emory U., 1996. Organist, choir dir. St. Joseph the Worker Ch., Fallsington, Pa., 1980—83; instr., organist St. Joseph's Prep. Sem., Princeton, NJ, 1981—85; cathedral organist, dir. music Cathedral St. Francis of Assisi, Metuchen, NJ, 1983—2001; univ. organist Seton Hall U., South Orange, NJ, 1996—; dir. music, organist Immaculate Conception Sem., South Orange, NJ, 1996—. Dir. concerts, arts Cathedral Concert Series, Metuchen, NJ, 1984—2001; assoc. condr. Brunswick Symphony Orch., New Brunswick, NJ, 1985—2001. Editor (contributor) hymnal. Recipient Excellence in Achievement award, Middlesex County Cultural and Heritage Commn., 1993; scholar, Emory U., 1995—96. Mem.: Conf. Roman Cath. Cathedral Musicians, Am. Guild Organists (dean 1993—95). Roman Catholic. Avocations: composing, music, bicycling, stamp collecting/philately. Office: Seton Hall U 400 South Orange Ave South Orange NJ 07079 Personal E-mail: nowikjoh@shu.edu.

NOWLAN, CHARLES F. controller; married; 3 children. B. U. Ala., 1976. CPA 1979. Mem. audit staff Coopers & Lybrand, 1977—80; with acquisition, tax and pension areas McWane, 1980—91, v.p., controller, 1991—. Mem. pres.'s coun. Fla. Coll., Tampa; elder Cahaba Hts. Ch. of Christ. Mem.: AICPA, Birmingham C. of C. Office: McWane 2900 Hwy 280 Ste 300 Birmingham AL 35223

NOWLAND, JAMES FERRELL, lawyer; b. Talladega, Ala., Dec. 7, 1942; s. James Franklin and Wilma Delene (Dean) N.; m. Faye Roberts, Aug. 28, 1964; children: Angela Roschelle, James Ferrell II. BS, Jacksonville (Ala.) State U., 1967; BS in Med. Technology, U. Ark., 1972; grad., U. Ark. Med. Ctr., 1974; JD, Oglethorpe U., 1983. Bar: Ga. 1984, U.S. Dist. Ct. (no. dist.) Ga. 1984, U.S. Ct. Appeals (11th cir.) 1984, U.S. Supreme Ct. 1988. Chemist U.S. Army C.E., Marietta, Ga., 1972-97; pvt. practice Cobb County, Ga., 1984—. Capt. USAF, 1967-72. Mem. ABA, Ga. Bar Assn., Cobb County Bar Assn. Home: 50 Mt Calvary Rd Marietta GA 30064-1918 Office: PO Box 1847 Marietta GA 30061-1847

NOWLAND-CURRY, BETSY, state official; m. David Curry. Grad., U. Ky. Dir. Tng. and Leadership Ctr. Ky. League of Cities; dir. comm. and tng. Gov. Paul E. Patton, 1998—2000; exec. dir. Ky. Women's Leadership Network, Lexington YWCA; dir. cmty. edn. Transylvania U.; exec. dir. Ky. Commn. on Women, Frankfort, 2000—. Wrote grant to establish YWCA Spouse Abuse Ctr., 1976. Named Outstanding Bus. Woman of Frankfort, 1979, Outstanding Kentuckian, Gov. Martha Layne Collins, 1982; named one of Outstanding Young Women of Am., 1978; recipient Lexington Outstanding Young Woman of Yr. award, 1981. Office: Ky Commn on Women 312 W Main St Frankfort KY 40601

NOWLIN, JAMES ROBERTSON, federal judge; b. San Antonio, Nov. 21, 1937; s. William Forney and Jeannette (Robertson) N. BA, Trinity U., 1959, MA, 1962; JD, U. Tex., Austin, 1963. Bar: Tex. 1963, Colo. 1993, U.S. Dist. Ct. D.C. 1966, U.S. Ct. Claims 1969, U.S. Supreme Ct. 1969, U.S. Dist. Ct. (we. dist.) Tex. 1971. Assoc. Kelso, Locke, & King, San Antonio, 1963-65; assoc. Kelso, Locke & Lepick, San Antonio, 1966-69; legal counsel U.S. Senate, Washington, 1965-66; propr. Law Offices James R. Nowlin, San Antonio, 1969-81; mem. Tex. Ho. of Reps., Austin, 1967-71, 73-81; judge U.S. Dist. Ct. for Western Dist. Tex., Austin, 1981-99, chief judge, 2000—03, sr. judge, 2003—. Instr. Am. govt. and history San Antonio Coll., 1964-65, 71-73. Capt. U.S. Army, 1959-60, USAR, 1960-68. Fellow State Bar Found (life); mem. San Antonio Bar Assn., Colo. Bar Assn. Republican. Presbyterian. Avocations: pilot, skiing, hiking, jogging. Office: US Courthouse 200 W 8th St Austin TX 78701-2325

NOYES, RICHARD HALL, bookseller; b. Evanston, Ill., Feb. 12, 1930; s. George Frederick and Dorothy (Hall) N.; m. Judith Claire Mitchell, Oct. 10, 1953; children— Catherine, Stephanie, Matthew. BA, Wesleyan U., 1952. Tng. program, elementary-high sch. salesman Rand McNally & Co., Colo., Utah, Idaho, Wyo., 1955-59; founder, owner, mgr. The Chinook Bookshop, Colorado Springs, Colo., 1959—. Contbr. to A Manual on Bookselling, 1974, The Business of Book Publishing, 1984; contbr. articles to newspapers and trade jours. Co-chmn. Colo. Media Coalition, 1974—; bd. dirs. Colorado Springs Fine Arts Ctr., 1977-81, Citizens Goals for Colorado Springs, 1976-88; trustee Fountain Valley Sch., 1979-81; vice chmn. Colorado Springs Charter Rev. Commn., 1991-92; mem. adv. com. U. Colo., Colorado Springs, 1997—, Downtown Partnership, 1998—. Served with AUS, 1952-54. Recipient Intellectual Freedom award Mountain Plains Librs. Assn., 1977, Disting. Svc. award U. Colo., 1980, Recognition award Pikes Peak Arts Coun., 1989, Charles S. Haslam award, 1990), Entrepreneur of Yr. award U. Colo., 1992, Gordon Saull award for outstanding bookseller Mountains and Plains Booksellers Assn., 1996. Mem. Am. Booksellers Assn. (pres., dir.) Home: 1601 Constellation Dr Colorado Springs CO 80906-1609 Office: The Chinook Bookshop Inc 210 N Tejon St Colorado Springs CO 80903-1385

NOYES, ROBERT EDWIN, publisher, writer; b. N.Y.C., June 22, 1925; s. Clarence A. and Edith (LaDomus) N.; m. Janet Brown, Mar. 24, 1952 (div. June 1963); children— Keith, Steven, Mark, Geoffrey; m. Mariel Jones, July 24, 1964; children— Rebecca, Robert. BS in Chem. Engring, Northwestern U., 1945. Chem. engr. Am. Cyanamid Co., Pearl River, N.Y., 1947; sales exec. Titanium Pigment Corp., N.Y.C., 1948-55; market research mgr. U.S. Indsl. Chem. Co., N.Y.C., 1956-58; sales mgr. atomic energy Curtiss Wright Export, N.Y.C., 1958-60; founder, pres., chmn. bd. Noyes Data Corp., Westwood, N.J., 1960-99; pub. Noyes Press, Noyes Publs., Westwood, 1961-99, Noyes Strategic Pubs., Saddle River, N.J., 1999—. Author numerous books in fields of internat. fin., devel., tech., space, military. Served to lt. (j.g.) USNR, 1945-47. Mem.: AIAA, Am. Inst. Chem. Engrs., Am. Chem. Soc., N.Y. Yacht Club. Episcopalian. Home: 224 W Saddle River Rd Saddle River NJ 07458-2620 Office Phone: 201-760-9049.

NOYES, RONALD TACIE, agricultural engineering educator; b. Leedey, Okla., Jan. 4, 1937; s. Johnnie Lyle and Anna Madeline (Allen) N.; m. Zona Gail McMillen, Apr. 16, 1960; children: Cynthia Gail, Ronald Scott, David Eric. BS in Agrl. Engring., Okla. State U., 1961, MS in Agrl. Engring., 1964; postgrad., Purdue U., 1966-68; PhD in Higher Edn., U. Okla., 1998. Profl. engr., Ind., Okla. Asst. prof. Purdue U., West Lafayette, Ind., 1964-68; chief engr. Beard Industries, Inc., Frankfort, Ind., 1968-81, v.p. engring., 1981-85; assoc. prof. Okla. State U., Stillwater, 1985-88, prof., 1988—. Cons. Ronald T. Noyes, Profl. Agrl. Engr., Stillwater, 1988—. Co-author: Designing Pesticide and Fertilizer Containment Facilities, 1991, revised edit., 1995; contbr. 5 chpts. to books; co-editor, co-author: The Mechanics and Physics of Modern Grain Aeration, 1999, International Engineering Textbook on Stored Grain Aeration, 1999. 1st lt. U.S. Army, 1961-63. Recipient Disting. Svc. award U.S. Dept. Agr., 1992, Outstanding Ext. Faculty award Okla. State U., 1991. Fellow Am. Soc. Agrl. Engrs.; mem. Aircraft Owners and Pilots Assn., Nat. Agrl. Aviation Assn. (assoc.), Exptl. Aircraft Assn. Achievements include 6 patents in field; developed new aeration management procedure for controlling insects in stored grain that reduces chemical use, manifolded phosphine fumigation process for grain tanks and silos that reduces chemical use. Home: 1116 Westwood Dr Stillwater OK 74074-1116 Office: Oklahoma St Univ Dept Biosys & Agrl Engring 111 Ag Hall Stillwater OK 74078-6016

NOYES, RUSSELL, JR., psychiatrist; b. Indpls., Dec. 25, 1934; s. Russell and Margaret (Greenleaf) N.; m. Martha H. Carl, Nov. 13, 1960; children: Marjorie Noyes-Aamot, Nancy Heifner, James R. BS, DePauw U., 1956; MD, Ind. U., 1959. Diplomate Am. Bd. Psychiatry and Neurology. Intern Phila. Gen. Hosp., 1959-60; residency U. Iowa, Iowa City, 1961-63, asst. prof. psychiatry, 1966-71, assoc. prof., 1971-78, prof., 1978—2002, prof. emeritus, 2002—. Co-author: The Anxiety Disorders, 1998; editor: Handbook of Anxiety, 1988-91; contbr. 250 articles to profl. jours. With USN, 1963-65. Fellow Am. Psychiat. Assn., Acad. Psychosomatic Medicine (pres. 1990-91); mem. Iowa Psychiat. Soc. (pres. 1986-87). Republican. Lutheran. Avocation: gardening. Home: 326 MacBride Rd Iowa City IA 52246-1716 Office: Psychiatry Rsch Med Edn Bldg Iowa City IA 52242-1009

NOZARI, MOE S. manufacturing executive; b. Iran; BS, Hope Coll., 1965; PhD in Organometallic Chemistry, U. Detroit; MS, U. Ill. Sr. rsch. chemist 3M Co., 1971, consumer products mgmt., group v.p., consumer and other markets group, 1996—99, exec. v.p., consumer and other bus. dept., 1999—. Bd. trustees Mpls. Inst. of the Arts. Recipient Acad. Award, Sci. and Engring. Award, Lab. Divsn., 1982. Office: 3M Co 3M Ctr Saint Paul MN 55144

NOZIERE, BARBARA, science educator, researcher; PhD in phys. chemistry, U. Bordeaux, France, 1991—94. Post-doctoral fellow Nat. Ctr. Atmospheric Rsch., Boulder, 1998—2001; rsch. asst. prof. U. Miami/RSMA /MAC, 2001—. Office: U Miami 4600 Rickenbacker Causeway Miami FL 33149

NOZISKA, CHARLES BRANT, lawyer; b. Oakland, Calif., Aug. 28, 1953; s. Charles Richard and Shirley Ann (Orme) N. BA, Colo. Coll., 1975; JD magna cum laude, U. San Diego, 1982. Bar: Calif. 1982, U.S. Dist. Ct. (so. dist.) Calif. 1982. Ptnr. Thorsnes, Bartolotta, McGuire & Padilla, San Diego, 1982—. Co-author: Landslide and Subsidence Liability, 1988. Mem. Assn. Trial Lawyers Am., Calif. Trial Lawyers Assn., San Diego Trial Lawyers Assn., San Diego County Bar Assn. Democrat. Avocation: ocean sports. Office: Thorsnes Bartolotta McGuire & Padilla 2550 5th Ave Ste 11 San Diego CA 92103-6612

NOZZOLILLO, ANTHONY, utilities executive; CFO, sr. v.p. Long Island Lighting Co.; exec. v.p. ops. KeySpan Energy, Bklyn. Office: KeySpan Energy One Metro TEch Ctr Brooklyn NY 11201

NRIAGU, JEROME OKON, environmental geochemist; b. Ora-eri Town, Anambra, Nigeria, Oct. 24, 1942; arrived in U.S., 1993; s. Martin and Helena (Anaekwe) N.; children: Chinedu Delbert, Uzoma Vivian, Osita Jide. BSc with honors, U. Ibadan, Nigeria, 1965, DSc, 1987; MS, U. Wis., 1967; PhD, U. Toronto, Ont., 1970. Rsch. scientist Environment Can., Burlington, Ont., 1970-93; prof. environ. chem. sch. of pub. health U. Mich., Ann Arbor, 1993—; dir. environ. health scis. program, 1996-99; rsch. scientist Ctr. for Human Growth and Devel., U. Mich., 1997—. Adj. prof. U. Waterloo, Ont., 1985—96; vis. scientist NOAA, Ann Arbor, 1992; bd. dirs. Ecology Ctr. Mich., Alliance to End Childhood Lead Poisoning, Washington, 1998—. Author: Lead and Lead Poisoning in Antiquity, 1983; editor: (book series) Advances in Environmental Science and Technology, 1982—, Trace Metals in the Environment, 1996—, 29 books on various environ. topics, 1979—, Sci. of the Total Environment, 1983—; mem. editl. bds.: 9 jours.; contbr. articles to profl. jours. Recipient Rigler medal, Can. Soc. Limnologists, 1988; Fulbright sr. fellow, 2002. Fellow Royal Soc. Can. (Romanowski medal 1999); mem. Am. Pub. Health Assn., Geochem. Soc. Roman Catholic. Avocations: photography, reading (African authors), travel. Office: Univ Michigan Environ/Indsl Health 109 Observatory St Ann Arbor MI 48109-2029

NSOFOR, LESLIE MONAGOLUM, food scientist, researcher; b. Oguta, Nigeria, July 10, 1955; arrived in U.S.A., 1997; s. Francis Chukwudifu Nsofor and Florence Chinelo Anamaleze; m. Obianuju Nwamaka Ikpeze, Apr. 29, 1983; children: Leslie, Valentine, Stephanie. BS in microbiology, U. Nigeria, 1978; MS in food sci., Utah State U., 1983, PhD in food sci., 1984. Lectr. Kaduna (Nigeria) Poly., 1978—80; grad. rsch. asst. Utah State U., 1981—84, post doctoral rsch. fellow, 1984—85; assoc. prof., assoc. dean Fed. U. Tech., Owerri, Nigeria, 1986—97; adj. assoc. prof. Mich. State U., 1999—; rsch. dir., co-owner, dep. CEO Soy Ultima LLC, East Lansing, Mich., 2000—. Acting

head of dept. Abia State U., Uturu, Nigeria, 1990—92; mem. senate Fed. U. Tech., Owerri, Nigeria, 1994—96. Co-author 27 jour. articles, Instrument for Measuring Milk Coagulation in Cheese Vat. Ch. harvest com. St. Joseph Cath. Chaplaincy, Imo State Univ., Owerri, Nigeria, 1996—97. Rsch. grant, Internat. Found. Sci., 1989. Roman Catholic. Achievements include patents for soy beverage mfg. method. Avocations: jogging, jazz, travel. Home: 4436 Wagon Wheel Ln Lansing MI 48917 E-mail: lensofor@aol.com.

NUBEL, MARIANNE KUNZ, cultural administrator, writer, composer; b. Cin., Sept. 14, 1966; d. Walter Charles and Marjorie (Larson) Kunz; m. Christopher Robert Nubel, Aug. 12, 1989. BS in Cmty. Arts Mgmt., East Carolina U., 1989. Exec. dir. Cmty. Arts Ctr., Wilmington, N.C., 1989-94; dir. film and media svcs. and cultural arts coord. City of Wilmington, 1994—. Founding mem., v.p. 5 & Dime Cultural Prodns., Wilmington, 1992-96,Big Dawg Productions, 1995; bd. dirs. Arts Coun. of the Lower Cape Fear, Wilmington, 1991-95, sec., 1994-95; pres. prodn. bd. Cape Fear Shakespeare, Wilmington, 1994—, music dir., coord., 1994—; pres. adv. bd. Journey Prodn. Performance Edn. Theatre, 2000—; mem. adv. bd. Big Dawg Theatre Co, 2001—. Composer for children's theatre. Music dir. Pied Piper Theatre, Jr. League, Wilmington, 1989-95; mem. co. Bessie's Underground Mole Players, Wilmington, 1995-99; mem. Arts Coun. Lower Cape Fear, Opera House Theatre Co. Recipient Arts and Humanities award N.C. Recreation and Parks Soc., 1993, 94, Cmty. Svc. award Thalian Assn. Cmty. Theatre, 1993, 94. Mem. Theatre N.O.W., Blues Soc. of the Lower Cape Fear (bd. dirs. 1990-92, 1st woman dir.), Big Dawg Theatre Co., Lower Cape Fear Hist. Soc., Opera House Theater Co., Wilmington Choral Soc. Avocations: writing, composing, community theatre, children's theatre, travel. Office: 5745 Tholozan Ave Wilmington NC 28402-1810 E-mail: Marianne.Nubel@ci.wilmington.nc.us., mknubel@hotmail.com.

NUCCIARONE, A. PATRICK, lawyer; b. Denville, N.J., Aug. 29, 1947; s. H. Joseph and Alice Marie (McGuirk) N. BA, U. So. Calif., 1969; JD, George Washington U., 1973. Bar: N.J. 1973, N.Y. 1981, Vt. 1984, U.S. Dist. Ct. N.J. 1973, U.S. Dist. Ct. (no. dist.) Ohio 1986, U.S. Ct. Appeals (3d cir.) 1976, U.S. Supreme Ct. 1995. Com. staff asst. U.S. House of Reps., Washington, 1971-72; staff asst. Exec. Office of Pres. of U.S., Washington, 1972-73; asst. U.S. Atty. Office of U.S. Atty., Newark, 1974-83, chief environ. sect., 1978-83; spl. asst. Atty. Gen. Office of Atty. Gen., Montpelier, Vt., 1984; ptnr. Hannoch Weisman, Roseland, N.J., 1984-91, Dechert, Price & Rhoads, Princeton, N.J., 1991-95; fed. monitor U.S. Dist. Ct., SD, 2001—. Co-chmn. N.J. Hazardous Task Force, Trenton, 1978-83; supr. Rutgers U. Environ. Law Clinic, Newark, 1978-83; mem. Environ. Expn. Adv. Bd., Trenton, 1985-90; chmn. ann. seminar on impacts of environ. law bus. trans. Practicing Law Inst., 1986-92, mem. adv. com. on environ. law, 1986—; mem. faculty NYU Summer Inst. on Environ. Law, 1991-94. Contbr. articles to profl. jours. Recipient Outstanding Service award U.S. Dept. Justice, Washington, 1980, Spl. Achievement awards U.S. Dept. Justice, 1978, 79, Presdl. Citation for Excellent Performance Exec. Office of Pres., Washington, 1973. Mem. ABA (vice chmn. sect. on natural resources, energy and environ. law 1987-93), N.J. State Bar Assn. (bd. dirs. environ. law sect. 1985-89). Office: 1540 Hwy 138 Ste 107 Wall NJ 07719-3766 Office Phone: 732-280-4800.

NUCKOLLS, JOHN HOPKINS, physicist, researcher; b. Chgo., Nov. 17, 1930; s. Asa Hopkins and Helen (Gates) N.; m. Ruth Munsterman, Apr. 21, 1952 (div. 1983); children: Helen Marie, Robert David; m. Amelia Aphrodite Liaskas, July 29, 1983. BS, Wheaton Coll., 1953; MA, Columbia U., 1955; DSc (hon.), Fla. Inst. Tech., 1977. Physicist U. Calif., Lawrence Livermore Nat. Lab., 1955—, assoc. leader thermonuclear design divsn., 1965-80, assoc. leader laser fusion program, 1975-83, divsn. leader, 1980-83, assoc. dir. physics, 1983-88, dir., 1988-94, assoc. dir. at large, 1994-97, dir. emeritus, 1997—. Mem. U.S. Strategic Command Strategic adv. group; tech. adv. bd. Network Physics, Inc.; cons. def. sci. bd. Dept. Def.; mem. adv. coms. to dir. CIA, 1989-99. Recipient E.O. Lawrence award Pres. and AEC, 1969, Fusion Leadership award, 1983, Edward Teller medal Internat. Workshop Laser Interaction and Related Plasma Phenomena, 1991, Resolution of Appreciation, U. Calif. Regents, 1994, Sec. of Def. Outstanding Pub. Svc. medal, 1996, Disting. Assoc. award U.S. Dept. Energy, 1996, Career Achievement award Fusion Power Assocs., 1996. Fellow AAAS, Am. Phys. Soc. (J.C. Maxwell prize 1981); mem. NAE. Office: Lawrence Livermore Nat Lab PO Box 808 Livermore CA 94551-0808 Office Phone: 925-422-5435. E-mail: jhnuck@aol.com.

NUDING, DORIS LEONA, law librarian, legal assistant, researcher; b. Chgo., Dec. 26, 1949; d. Donald Harold and Leona Elvira (Fremgen) Thompson; m. William E. Nuding Jr., July 13, 1949; children: Tracy, Kelly. Cert. legal asst., Roosevelt U., 1987. Lic. real estate assoc. Clk./typist Continental Ill. Nat. Bank, Chgo., 1968-70; clk./typist Personal Trust Banking Attys. W. Clement & Jesse Stone Found., 1972-74; sec., asst. to dir. pub., dir. achievment motivation Nat. Com. for Prevention of Child Abuse, Chgo., 1974-83; sales coord. Arnstein & Lehr, Chgo., 1981-91; legal asst., sec. Querry & Harrow, Chgo., 1991—; real estate assoc. Barid & Warner, 2003—. Mem. Am. Assn. Law Librs., Chgo. Assn. Law Librs., Solo Libr. Soc., Am. Legion Aux. (pres. 1995-98, sec. 1999-2004). Avocations: reading, computers, grandchildren. Office: Barid & Warner 3236 Vollmer Olympia Fields IL 60461-2827 Personal E-mail: dnuding1@juno.com. Business E-Mail: dnuding@querrey.com., doris.nuding@baridwarner.com.

NUECHTERLAIN, JAMES HOWARD, music educator; b. Frankenmuth, Mich., Sept. 14, 1953; s. Howard and Erema Nuechterlain; m. Donna Sue Nuechterlain, June 23, 2001; children: Patrick, Joshua. MM Music Edn., Mich. State U., East Lansing, Michigan, 1988; BME, Grand Valley State U., Allendale, Michigan, 1980; BS Bus. Adminstrn., Ferris State U., Big Rapids, Michigan, 1975. Band and orch. dir. Monroe Pub. Schools, Monroe, Mich., 1988—; band dir. Marcellus Cmty. Schools, Marcellus, Mich., 1984—88, Vicksburg Cmty. Schools, Vicksburg, Mich., 1980—81; dept. head JC Penny Co., Battle Creek, Mich., 1975—76. Mem.: Mich. Sch. Band and Orch. Assn., Nat. Edn. Music Conf. Office: Monroe High School 901 Herr Road Monroe MI 48161 E-mail: nuechten@monroe.k12.mi.us.

NUERNBERG, WILLIAM R(ICHARD), lawyer; b. Pitts., July 7, 1946; s. William W. and Frances (Hubler) N. BA cum laude, Denison U., 1968; JD cum laude, U. Mich., 1971. Bar: Pa. 1971, U.S. Dist.Ct. (we. dist.) Pa. 1971, Fla. 1995. Mem. Eckert Seamans Cherin & Mellott LLC, 1981-98; ptnr. Duane Morris LLP, Miami, 1999—. Bd. govs. Big Bros. Big Sisters Greater Miami. Pitt fellow U. Pitts. Sch. Bus., 1987-88. Mem. ABA, Pa. Bar Assn., Fla. Bar Assn., Miami City Club. Office: Duane Morris LLP 200 S Biscayne Blvd Ste 3400 Miami FL 33131-2318

NUESSLE, WILLIAM RAYMOND, surgeon; b. Bismarck, N.D., Sept. 17, 1951; s. Robert Frederick and Margaret Elizabeth (Bergeson) N.; m. Anna Maria Marlow, June 26, 1982; children: Aaron, Alexa, Matthew. BS, U. N.D., 1973, BS Medicine, 1975; MD, U. Ala., 1977. Diplomate Am. Bd. Surgery and Colon and Rectal Surgery. Resident gen. surgery Ochsner Found., New Orleans, 1977-1982; resident colon and rectal surgery U. La., Shreveport, 1982-83; colon and rectal surgeon Quain and Ramstat Clinic, Bismarck, N.D., 1983-90, Clinic for Colon & Rectal Surgery, Huntsville, Ala., 1990—, Huntsville (Ala.) Hosp., 1990—, Crestwood Hosp., Huntsville, 1990—. Fellow ACS, Am. Soc. Colon and Rectal Surgeons; mem. SAGES. Avocations: tennis, fishing, music. Office: Clinic for CRS 115 Manning Dr SW Ste D101 Huntsville AL 35801-4341 Office Phone: 256-533-6070. E-mail: wrn@hiwaay.net.

NUGENT, GORDON WALKER, writer; b. Peoria, Ill., July 25, 1926; s. William Walker and Vesta Maude (Collins) Nugent; m. Irene Maria Schneidmann, May 28, 1952; children: Barbara Barli Nugent Wakefield, Thomas Walker. Student in mech. engring., Purdue U., 1944—46; BS in Math., Bradley U., 1949; MS in Journalism, Columbia U., 1952. Copy boy, fgn. desk clerk N.Y. Times, 1950—52; pub. rels. staff writer GE Co., Schenectady, NY, 1953—60; cmty. rels. dir. Glass Container Manufacturers Inst., NY, 1960—64; editor, employee pubs. Union Carbide Corp., NY, 1967—78; mgr. employee comm. Stauffer Chem. Co., Westport, Conn., 1979—81. Officer candidate V-12 USNR, 1944—46. Recipient 3 awards, Internat. Assn. Indsl. Communicators, N.Y., 1981. Mem.: Ancient Free and Accepted Masons Conn. (sr. steward 2001—03, master mason), Fairfield County Computer Users Group (sec. 2002—04, dir.). Achievements include patents in field. Avocations: piano, bridge. Home and Office: Nugent Tool Co 160 Rivergate Dr Wilton CT 06897-3611

NUGENT, HELEN JEAN, history educator; b. Indpls., Oct. 14, 1934; d. John Isaac and Ruth Augusta (Mather) McClelland; m. Paul Thomas Nugent, Aug. 19, 1935; children: Paula Jean Nugent Barickman, Thomas J. II, Ruth E. B. Nugent Simard. BA, Franklin Coll., 1956; MA, U. Ill., 1965, Ind. U., 1971; PhD, Mich. State U., 1983. Lifetime cert. in secondary edn., Ind. Tchr. grades 9-12 Union City (Ind.) H.S., 1956-57, Seven Mile (Ohio) H.S., 1957-58; tchr. history St. Rose Acad., Vincennes, Ind., 1962-64; instr. history Margaret Hall Sch., Versailes, Ky., 1964-66; lectr. history Ind.U./Purdue U., Columbus, 1976-82; vis. lectr. Ind. U./Purdue U., Columbus, 2001; dir. Can. studies Franklin (Ind.) Coll., 1984-95, chair dept. history, 1996-99, prof. emerita history, dir. emerita Can. studies, 1999—. Contbr. numerous articles, papers to profl. jours., chpts. to books. Mem. Franklin Coll. Alumni Coun., 2002—. Recipient Alumni award Franklin Coll., 1997. Mem. Mid West Assn. Can. Studies (v.p. 1990-92, exec. coun. 1992-94), Assn. Can. Studies U.S. (exec. bd. 1993-97), Phi Alpha Theta, Theta Alpha Phi, Delta Kappa Gamma, Phi Kappa Phi. Roman Catholic. E-mail: hnugent@franklincollege.edu.

NUGENT, JEFFREY M. cosmetics executive; Various sr. mgmt. positions Johnson & Johnson, 1972-95; worldwide ops. Neutrogena Corp., 1995-99; pres., CEO Revlon Inc., N.Y.C., 1999—. Office: Revlon Inc 625 Madison Ave Fl 4 New York NY 10022

NUGENT, JOHN HILLIARD, communications executive; b. Paterson, NJ, Aug. 20, 1944; s. James Joseph and Jacqueline Ann (Storms) N.; m. Mary Elizabeth Maher, June 3, 1967; 1 child, Jill Frances. BA, Columbia U., 1970; MSA, Southeastern U., 1978; DBA, Bus. Sch., Lausanne, Switzerland, 1989. CPA; cert. fraud examiner Nat. Assn. Cert. Fraud Examiners, Austin. Adminstr. Chase Manhattan Bank, N.Y.C., 1970-71; analyst U.S. Dept. of Army, Washington, 1971-72; chmn. Strategic Planning & Rsch. Corp., Dallas, 1977-95; pres. AT&T Aviation Tech. and Sys., Ltd., Arlington, Va., Hong Kong, Beijing, 1993; exec. CDX, Inc., Dallas, 1995; pres., bd. dirs. SA Telecomm., Inc., Richardson, Tex., 1996-97, also bd. dirs., pres., 1996; mng. dir. Cordoba Capital, Southport, Conn., 1998-99. V.p., fin. acct. AdCon Inc./Internat. Bank, Reston, Va., 1971-79; CFO HDS, Inc., Reston, 1979-82; pres. Group L Corp., Herndon, Va., 1983-85; pres., bd. dirs. AT&T/Datotek, Dallas, 1985-92; asst. prof. telecomms. Grad. Sch. Mgmt. U. Dallas, 1999—. Author: Corporate Decline: Causes, Symptoms, and Prescriptions for a Turnaround, 1989, Plan to Win: Analytical and Operational Tools-Gaining Competitive Advantage, 2002, 2nd edit., 2003. Cpl. USMC, 1962-66. Mem. AICPAs, Greater Washington Soc. CPAs, Tex. Soc. CPAs, Nat. Assn. Accts., Dallas Com. on Fgn. Rels., Columbia Club of N.Y. Republican. Avocation: reading. Office: Grad Sch Mgmt U Dallas Irving TX 75062-4736 Address: 2469 County Road 855 Mc Kinney TX 75071 Office Phone: 214-682-8025. Business E-Mail: jnugent@gsm.udallas.edu. E-mail: jnugent@texoma.net.

NUGENT, JOHNNY WESLEY, state legislator, tractor company executive; b. Cleve., July 18, 1939; s. Carl Howard and Velma (Holland) N.; m. Nancy Carol Whiteford, Dec. 16, 1960; 1 child, Suzette. Grad. high sch., Aurora, Ind. Owner, mgr. Nugent Tractor Sales, Lawrenceburg, Ind., 1960—; mem. Ind. Senate from 43rd dist., Indpls., 1978—. Bd. dirs. 1st Nat. Bank Aurora. Commr. Dearborn County, Lawrenceburg, 1966-74. With USAR, 1957-64. Republican. Baptist. Office: Ind Senate Dist 43 200 W Washington St Indianapolis IN 46204-2728

NUGENT, NELLE, theater, film and television producer; b. Jersey City, May 24, 1939; d. John Patrick and Evelyn Adelaide (Stern) N.; m. Donald G. Baker, June 6, 1960 (div. 1962); m. Benjamin Janney, June 22, 1969 (div. Apr., 1980); m. Jolyon Fox Stern, Apr. 7, 1982; 1 child, Alexandra Fox Stern. BS, Skidmore Coll., 1960, DHL (hon.), 1981. Chmn. bd. McCann & Nugent, Prodns. Inc., N.Y.C., 1976-86; pres. Foxboro Prodns., Inc., N.Y.C., 1985-94; pres., CEO Foxboro Entertainment, 1990-94; pres. The Foxboro Co., Inc.; co-prin. Golden Fox Films, Inc. Adj. faculty NYU, N.Y.C., 2003—04. Stage mgr. various off-Broadway shows, 1960-64; prodn. asst.: Broadways plays Any Wednesday, 1963-64, Dylan, 1964, Ben Franklin in Paris, 1964-65; stage mgr. Broadway shows, 1964-68; prodn. supr., then gen. mgr., 1969-76, assoc. mng. dir. Nederlander Corp., operating theaters and producing plays in, N.Y.C. and on tour, 1970-76; prodr.: Dracula, 1977 (Tony award), The Gin Game (Tony nom,), The Elephant Man, 1978 (Tony award, Drama Critics award), Morning's at Seven, 1980 (Tony award), Home, 1980 (Tony nomination), Amadeus, 1981 (Tony award); also produced: Rose and Piaf, 1980, Otherwise Engaged, The Life and Adventures of Nicholas Nickleby, 1981 (Tony award, Drama Critics award), The Dresser (Tony award nominee), 1981, Mass Appeal, 1981; The Lady & The Clarinet, 1982; The Glass Menagerie (revival), 1983; Painting Churches (Obie award), 1983; Total Abandon, 1983; All's Well That End's Well, 1983 (Tony nominee); Pilobolus Dance Company, 1983; Pacific Overtures (revival), 1984; Much Ado about Nothing/Cyrano de Bergerac (repertory) (Tony award nominees), 1984; Leader of the Pack (Tony award nominee), 1985, The Life and Adventures of Nicholas Nickleby (revival) (Tony award nominee), 1986; prodr.: TV spls.; Morning's At Seven, Piaf; Pilobolus; prodr. A Fighting Choice, 1986-88, A Conspiracy of Love, 1987, The Final Verdict, 1990 (Cable Ace award nominee Best Picture); exec. prodr. (TV pilot) Morning Maggie, 1987, Dick Clark Prodns., 1988-90, (feature films) Student Body, 1993, Getting In, 1994, Jane Doe, 1996; (TV films) In the Presence of Mine Enemies, 1995-96 (Houston Festival Silver Star award), A Town Has Turned to Dust, 1997 (World Festival Silver medal 1998), After the Storm (Best Feature Film N.Y. Internat. Independent Film & Video Festival, 2000), Angelciti Festival (Best Feature 2001), Houston Worldfest (Platinum award, Best Film Made for TV 2001), (Broadway prodn.) The Smell of the Kill, 2002, Sly Fox, 2004. Mem.: League Am. Theaters, Prodrs. Guild Am. (exec. com.), Am. Women's Econ. Devel. Corp. (bd. dirs.). Office: Foxboro Co Inc 133 E 58th St Ste 301 New York NY 10022-1236

NUGENT, ROBERT J., JR., fast food company executive; b. 1942; BBA, U. Cin., 1964. Loan officer Citizens Savs., 1964-67; asst. v.p. Gem City Savs., 1967-69; v.p. Ponderosa System Inc., 1969-78, Ky. Fried Chicken, 1978-79, Foodmaker Inc., San Diego, from 1979, exec. v.p. ops., mktg., 1985-95, CEO, pres., 1995-99, Jack in the Box, Inc., San Diego, 1999—. Office: Jack in the Box Inc 9330 Balboa Ave San Diego CA 92123-1598

NUGENT, S. GEORGIA, academic administrator; m. Thomas J Scherer. B cum laude, Princeton U., 1973; PhD in classics, Cornell U. Instr. Swarthmore Coll.; assoc. prof. Brown U., 1985; asst. prof. Princeton U., 1979, dean, Harold McGraw Jr. Ctr. for tchg. and learning, asst. to pres., 1992—95; assoc. provost, 1995; pres. Kenyon Coll., 2003—. Author books. Recipient Wriston award for excellence in tchg. Office: President Ransom Hall Kenyon Coll Gambier OH 43022

NUGENT, SHANE VINCENT, lawyer; b. Bozeman, Mont., July 14, 1962; s. John Vincent Nugent and Marilyn Jean (Piotrowski) Cloven; m. Lori Sue Meyer, June 14, 1986; children: Justine Nicole, Cole Tyler. BA, Knox Coll., 1984; JD, Northwestern U., 1987. Bar: Ill. 1987. Assoc. Lord, Bissell & Brook, Chgo., 1987—93; pvt. practice Barrington, Ill., 1993-94; of counsel Blatt Hammestahr & Eaton, Chgo., 1994-96; pvt. practice Barrington, 1996-98; exec. v.p., COO Intelligent Learning Sys., Inc., Austin, Tex., 1998—2003; pvt. practice, 2003—. Contbr. articles to profl. jours. Recipient NASA Space Act award, 2000; named one of Outstanding Young Men Am., 1987. Mem. Chgo. Bar Assn., Beta Theta Pi (Ray M. Arnold prize Xi chpt. 1984, chpt. advisor 1987-92, asst. gen. sec. 1992-97), Xi Alumni (pres. 1992-2004). Office Phone: 847-778-9666.

NUGENT, TIMOTHY SCOTT, alcohol/drug abuse services professional; b. Iowa City, Apr. 23, 1947; s. Stephen Francis and Ina Kammeyer Nugent; m. Katherine Werner, Nov. 26, 1970 (div. Nov. 10, 1986); children: Patrick Stephen, Lisa Kathleen; m. Susan Thorne, Apr. 3, 1992. BA, U. Fla., 1969, MEd, 1972. Cert. addictions profl. 2000. Field rep. Pa. Dept. Justice, Pitts., 1972—74; program dir. S. Fla. Regional Planning Coun., Miami, 1974—76; dir. regulatory Deltona Corp., Miami, 1977—81; exec. dir. Ybor Redevel. City of Tampa, Fla., 1981—85; dir. downtown redevel. City of Tallahassee, Tallahassee, 1991—93; govtl. and devel. cons., 1985—91; exec. dir. Lee County Fla. Redevel. Agy., 1994—96; therapist S.W. Fla. Addiction Svcs., Ft. Myers, 1996—. Oral exam evaluator, bd. dirs. Fla. Cert. Bd., Tallahassee, 2000—. Mem.: Nat. Assn. Alcoholism and Drug Abuse Counselors (bd. dirs. Fla. chpt., pres.-elect), Ybor City C. of C. (pres. 1987). Home: 2373 Woodland Ter Fort Myers FL 33907-5818 Office: SW Fla Addiction Svcs Inc 2516 Grand Ave Fort Myers FL 33907

NUGENT, WALTER TERRY KING, historian; b. Watertown, N.Y., Jan. 11, 1935; s. Clarence A. and Florence (King) Nugent; m. Suellen Hoy, 1986; children from previous marriage: Katherine, Rachel, David, Douglas, Terry, Mary. AB, St. Benedict's Coll., 1954, DLitt, 1968; MA, Georgetown U., 1956; PhD, U. Chgo., 1961. Instr. history Washburn U., 1957-58; asst. prof. Kans. State U., 1961-63, Ind. U., 1963-64, assoc. prof., 1964-68, prof., 1968-84, assoc. dean Coll. Arts and Scis., 1967-71, dir. overseas study, 1967-76, chmn. history dept., 1974-77; Andrew V. Tackes prof. history U. Notre Dame, 1984-00, Andrew V. Tackes prof. emeritus, 2000—. Paley lectr., Fulbright vis. prof. Hebrew U., Jerusalem, 1978—79; summer seminar dir. NEH, 1979, 84, 86; vis. prof. U. Hamburg, U. Warsaw, 1982; Mary Bell Washington Fulbright prof. U. Coll., Dublin, 1991—92. Author: (book) The Tolerant Populists, 1963, Creative History, 1967, The Money Question During Reconstruction, 1967, Money and American Society 1865-1880, 1968, Modern America, 1973, From Centennial to World War: American Society 1876-1917, 1977, Structures of American Social History, 1981, Crossings: The Great Transactlantic Migrations 1870-1914, 1992; author: (with Martin Ridge) The American West: The Reader, 1999, Into the West: The Story of Its People, 1999 (Caughey award, 2000); author: Making Our Way: A Family History, 2003. Bd. dirs. U.S.-Israel Ednl. Found., 1985—89. Recipient medal of Merit, Warsaw U., 1992; Newberry Libr. fellow, 1962, Guggenheim fellow, 1964—65, Huntington Libr. fellow, 1979, 1985, Beinecke fellow, Yale U., 1990. Mem.: Soc. Historians the Gilded Age and Progressive Era (pres. 2000—02), Soc. Am. Historians, Western Hist. Assn. (hon. life mem.). Democrat. Catholic. Business E-Mail: wnugent@nd.edu.

NUGTEREN, CORNELIUS, air force officer; b. Colton, S.D., Feb. 7, 1928; s. Adrian Joe and Marie Johanna N.; m. Liane Albrecht, Sept. 22, 1956; children: Cecile, Aneli. BA, Central Coll., Pella, Iowa, 1951. Commd. 2d lt. USAF, 1953, advanced through grades to maj. gen., 1980; advisor Vietnam Air Force, 1970-71; served in Germany, 1971-77; vice comdr. (Air Logistics Center), Utah, 1977-79; comdr. (Aerospace Rescue and Recovery Service), Scott AFB, Ill., 1979-81; chief (Joint U.S. Mil. Aid Group), Greece, 1981-82; comdr. Air Logistics Ctr., Robins AFB, Ga, 1983-88; ret.; cons. for def. industries, 1988-94; v.p. Chem. Tech. Internat., Warner Robins, Mercer U. Engring. Rsch. Ctr., Warner Robins, 1996—. Decorated D.S.M., Legion of Merit, Bronze Star, Superior Service medal; recipient USAF EEO award, 1979; named to Ga. Aviation Hall of Fame, 2004. Mem. Air Force Assn., Order Daedalians, Internat. Order Hansen, Order of the Sword. Office: 114 Holly Dr Warner Robins GA 31088-6615 E-mail: gennewt@aol.com. *Service to one's country is not just a job...it's a calling. Integrity to and within the institution to which you belong is an absolute necessity. Loyalty to peers and subordinates is equally important as loyalty to your superiors. Attitude toward life, humankind and profession is key determinant to success. Goals should be set high enough so as to be unattainable. Standard of conduct must always include duty, honor, country.*

NÜHN, ADRIAAN, food products executive; b. 1953; BA, Eindhoven Hogere Econ. Sch., Netherlands; MBA, U. Puget Sound, Tacoma, Wash. With Xerox Corp., Rochester, NY, Richardson Vicks/Procter & Gamble; mng. dir. Procter & Gamble, Vienna; gen. mgr., household and body care divsn. Sara Lee/DE, Netherlands, 1990—91, pres., Kortman Intradal, 1991—94, regional v.p., Beneleux countries, 1994, regional v.p., continental Europe, 1994—95, corp. v.p., CEO worldwide household and body care divsn., bd. mgmt., 1995—96, chmn., bd. mgmt., 2003—; corp. sr. v.p. Sara Lee Corp., 1996—99, pres., worldwide coffee & tea divsn., 1999—2003, exec. v.p., 2003—. Office: Sara Lee Corp Three First Nat Plaza Chicago IL 60602-4260

NULAND, ANTHONY C. J. lawyer; b. N.Y.C., 1943; AB cum laude, Princeton U., 1965; JD, NYU, 1968. Bar: N.Y. 1969, D.C. 1977, Ga. 1978. Asst. dir. divsn. market regulation SEC, 1975-76, assoc. dir. divsn. market regulation, 1976-77; now ptnr. Seward & Kissel, N.Y.C., 1977—. Office: Seward & Kissel 1200 G St NW Ste 350 Washington DC 20005-3881

NULAND, SHERWIN, surgeon, writer; b. N.Y.C., Dec. 8, 1930; s. Meyer and Violet (Lutsky) N.; m. Sarah Peterson, May 29, 1977; children: Victoria Jane, Andrew Meyer, William Peterson, Amelia Rose. BA, NYU, 1951; MD, Yale U., 1955. Surgeon Yale-New Haven Hosp. (Conn.), 1962—92; clin. prof. surgery Yale Sch. Medicine, New Haven, 1962—. Author: The Origins of Anesthesia, 1983, Doctors: The Biography of Medicine, 1988, Medicine: The Art of Healing, 1991, How We Die: Reflections on Life's Final Chapter, 1994 (Nat. Book award for non-fiction, 1994, Pulitzer prize finalist, 1995), The Wisdom of the Body: How We Live, 1997, The Mysteries Within: A Surgeon Reflects on Medical Myths, 2000, Leonardo da Vinci, 2000, Lost in America, 2003, The Doctors' Plague, 2003; contbg. editor The New Republic, The American Scholar, mem. editl. bd. Perspectives in Biology and Medicine. V.p. Conn. Hospice, New Haven, 1978-80. Fellow AAAS, ACS, Yale Inst. Social & Policy Studies; mem. New Eng. Surg. Soc., Assocs. of Yale Med. Sch. Libr. (chmn. 1982-94), Yale-China Assn. (chmn. med. 1988-93), History of Medicine and Allied Scis. (chmn. bd. jour. 1979-2002). Democrat. Jewish. Avocation: tennis. Home: 29 Old Hartford Tpke Hamden CT 06517-3523 Office: PO Box 6356 Hamden CT 06517-0356 Office Phone: 203-776-5635. E-mail: snuland@comcast.net.

NULL, ELISABETH HIGGINS, librarian, writer; b. Worcester, Mass., Dec. 1, 1942; d. Carter Chapin Higgins and Katharine Huntington (Bigelow) Doman; m. Henry Harrison Null IV, July 13, 1963 (div. 1970); children: John Higgins, Jacob Van Vechten. BA, Sarah Lawrence Coll., Bronxville, N.Y., 1983; MA, Yale U., 1985, MPhil in Am. History, 1989; MA in Folklore, U. Pa., 1987; M Libr. and Info. Sci., Cath. U. Am., 1995. V.p. Abington Pub. Co., Clark's Summit, Pa., 1966-70; CEO Green Linnet Records, Danbury, Conn., 1971-81; vis. lectr. Am. Musical Life, Georgetown U., 1991-98; libr. and conversion specialist nat. digital libr. program Libr. of Congress, Washington, 1996-98, expert cons., 1995; writer on edn. issues Rural Sch. and Cmty. Trust, 1999—2004; rsch. coord. congl. campaign Janine Selendy (Dem.) N.Y. Dist. 17, 2002, 2004. Bd. dirs. Maine Folklife Ctr.; Horizon Internat., New Haven; program co-chair Washington Folk Festival, 1999-2000; program chair Folklore Soc. Greater Washington, 1993-94; humanities scholar-in-residence Conn. Coun. for Humanities and Conn. Dept. for the Arts, Waterbury, Conn., 1986-87; fieldworker in folklore Waterbury Ethnic Music Project, 1986-87. Singer 2 recordings: The Feathered Malden, 1977, American Primitive, 1981; performance career with guitarist Bill Shute included 6 appearances with Garrison Keillor's A Prairie Home Companion; major venues include Phila. Folk Festival, Bklyn. Mus., Mus. Natural History. Incorporator John Woodman Higgins Armory, Worcester, Mass., 1966—; sec. Stanton Park Neighborhood Assn., Washington, 1990; bd. dirs. John and Clara Higgins Found., 1999—; rsch. coord. Selendy for Congress, 2002. Folger Shakespeare Libr. Seminar fellow, 1989-91. Mem. ALA, Am. Folklore Soc., Soc. for History of Early Am. Rep. Democrat. Episcopalian. Avocations: folk music performer, song writer. Home and Office: 706 Bonifant St Silver Spring MD 20910-5534 Office Phone: 301-587-2286. E-mail: elisabeth.null@tcs.wap.org.

NULL, WILLIAM SETH, lawyer; b. N.Y.C., Apr. 15, 1954; s. Douglas P. Null and Barbara M. (Black) Schacker; m. Lauren E. Thaler, May 10, 1981; children: Danielle, Evan. BA, Hampshire Coll., 1977; JD, Yeshiva U., 1980.

Bar: N.Y. 1981, U.S. Dist. Ct. (ea. and so. dists.) N.Y. 1981, U.S. Supreme Ct. 1987. With Null & Null, P.C., Garden City, N.Y., 1980-83, Kraver & Martin, N.Y.C., 1983-85, Cuddy & Feder LLP, White Plains, NY, 1985—, mng. ptnr., 1999—. Dir. The Housing Partnership, Elmsford, NY, 1995—2001, White Plains Bridge of Friendship Found., 1994—; dir. Westchester chpt. Juvenile Diabetes Rsch. Found. Internat., 1998—2003, pres., 2004—; dir. Gilda's Club Westchester, 2001—, The Briarcliff Manor Edn. Found., 2001—03, White Plains Hosp. Ctr., 2002—. Office: Cuddy & Feder LLP 90 Maple Ave White Plains NY 10601-5105 Office Phone: 914-761-1300. E-mail: wnull@cuddyfeder.com.

NULTON, WILLIAM CLEMENTS, retired lawyer; b. Pittsburg, Kans., Feb. 22, 1931; s. Perley Edgar and Mary Celia (Anderson) N.; m. Vicki Smith, Aug. 20, 1956; children: Carnie, Erica. BA, Kans. U., 1953, LLB with honors, 1958; postgrad., NYU, 1953-54. Bar: Kans. 1958, Mo. 1959. Sr. atty. Great Lakes Pipe Line Co., Kansas City, Mo., 1958-66, asst. sec., 1961-66; assoc. Blackwell, Sanders, Matheny, Weary & Lombardi, Kansas City, 1966-68, ptnr., 1968-81; assoc. Shughart Thomson & Kilroy, Kansas City, 1981-83, ptnr., 1983-94. Contbr. articles to profl. jours. Bd. dirs. Corinth Hills Home Assn., Shawnee Mission, 1974-76, Faith Friends, 1999-2004, Front Porch Alliance, 1999—, Ivanhoe neighborhood coun., 2003—; pres. Beta Theta Pi Kansas City Alumni Assn., 1977; mem., elder Village United Presbyn. Ch., Prairie Village, Kans., 1976—, trustee, 1992-94, endowment bd., 1997-2001; bd. dirs. Prairie Village Mcpl. Found., 1987—, v.p., 2000—; bd. dirs. Kansas City Civil Rights Consortium, 1993—, Marillac Acad., 1994-99; Kans. adv. com. U.S. Civil Rights Commn., 1994—, acting chmn., 1998; active Shawnee Mission Unified Bd. Edn., 1969-73, v.p., 1973; pres. Corinth Elem. Bd. Edn., Johnson County, Kans., 1969; chmn. Full Employment Task Group on Employment Disabled, Kansas City, 1987. Summerfield scholar Kans. U., 1949-53, Root-Tilden scholar NYU, 1953-54. Mem. ABA (mgmt. chmn. labor and employment law sect., com. on arbitration and collective bargaining 1989-92), Am. Acad. Hosp. Attys. (co-chmn. task group on bylaws for small rural hosps. 1992-93), Mo. Bar Assn. (chmn. labor law com. 1982), Nat. Health Lawyers Assn. (co-chmn. task group on alternative dispute resolution in health care field 1990-91), Phi Beta Kappa, Order of Coif. Republican. Home: 7908 El Monte St Shawnee Mission KS 66208-5047

NUMANN, PATRICIA JOY, surgeon, educator; b. Bronx, N.Y., Apr. 6, 1941; BA, U. Rochester, 1962; MD, SUNY Health Sci. Ctr., Syracuse, 1965. Intern, resident SUNY Health Sci. Ctr., Syracuse, 1970, from asst. prof. to assoc. prof. surgery, 1970-89, assoc. dean Coll. Medicine, 1978-84, assoc. dean Coll. Medicine Clin. Affairs, prof. surgery, 1989—, Lloyd S. Rogers prof. of surgery, med. dir., 1997—. Dir. breast care program SUNY Health Sci. Ctr., Syracuse, 1986—; presenter in field. Contbr. chpts. to books, articles to profl. jours. Found. bd. dirs. Vera House, Syracuse, 1993-94; hon. bd. dirs. F.A.C.T., Syracuse, 1994. Named one of Women of Distinction, N.Y. State Gov. Mario Cuomo, 1994, Disting. Tchg. Prof. SUNY, 1994, Disting. Svc. Prof.; recipient Disting. Surgeon award Assn. Women Surgeons, 1991. Mem. AMA (coun. sci. affairs), ACS (com. on cancer grad. med. edn. com., 2nd v.p. 1999, 2d v.p. 1999-2000), Am. Bd. Surgeons (bd. dirs. 1994—, chair 2001), Am. Assn. Endocrine Surgeons (v.p. 1992), Assn. for Surg. Edn. (pres. 1985), Corinthian Club. Office: SUNY Health Sci Ctr 750 E Adams St Syracuse NY 13210-1834 Office Phone: 315-464-6365. Business E-Mail: numannp@upstate.edu.

NUMMINEN, TEPPO, professional hockey player; b. July 3, 1968; With Winnipeg Jets/Phoenix Coyotes, 1998—. Played in NHL All Star Game, 1999 & 2000. Achievements include winning a silver and bronze medal with the Finnish Olympic team. Office: America West Arena/Cellular One Ice Den 9375 E Bell Rd Scottsdale AZ 85260

NUNES, DEVIN, congressman; b. Tulare, Calif., Oct. 1, 1973; m. Elizabeth Tamariz. BS in Agrl. Bus., Calif. Poly. State U., 1995, MS in Agrl., 1996; BS, Coll. Sequoias. Calif. state dir. USDA; congressman 21st Dist. Calif. U.S. Ho. Reps., 2003—. Mem. Coll. Sequoias Bd. Trustees, 1996—2002; grad. Calif. Agr. Leadership Fellowship Program, 2000. Republican. Roman Catholic. Office: 1017 Longworth HOB Washington DC 20515-0521

NUNEZ, FABIAN, state representative; b. Logan Heights, Calif. children: Estaban, Teresa, Carlos. BA, Pitzer Coll.; student, U. Calif., San Diego. Education leg. analyst; polit. dir. LA County Fedn. Labor; dir. govt. rels. LA Unified Sch. Dist.; mem. Calif. Assembly, 2002—. Founder Latino Forum Small Bus. Devel. Ctr. Democrat. Office: PO Box 942849 Rm 2117 Sacramento CA 95841 Address: 320 W 4th St Ste 1050 Los Angeles CA 90013

NUÑEZ, JOE C. federal agency administrator; m. Lilly Nuñez; 4 children. BA, U. No. Colo.; MAE, InterAm. U. P.R.; honors grad. Japanese Lang. Inst., Yale U. Commd. officer USAF, advanced through ranks to lt. col.; regional rep. Region VIII U.S. Dept. Labor, 1986—93; mem. Colo. Ho. Reps., 1999—2001, mem. appropriations com., vice chmn. state, mil. and vets. affairs com., mem. edn. com.; regional rep. Region VIII U.S. Dept. Health and Human Svcs., Denver, 2001—. Decorated Bronze Star, two Meritorious Svc. medals, Nat. Def. Svc. medal, Air Force Commendation medal, Vietnamese Svc. medal, Republic of Vietnam Gallantry Cross, Republic of Vietnam Campaign medal. Office: US Dept HHS Rm 1076 1961 Stout St Denver CO 80294

NUNEZ-LAWTON, MIGUEL G. international finance specialist; b. Havana, Cuba, Feb. 8, 1949; came to U.S., 1964; s. Miguel Nunez-Cancio and Silvia Lawton-Alfonso. BSBA, Georgetown U., 1971, postgrad. in Econs., 1973. Asst. treas. Deltec Securities Corp., N.Y.C., 1971; debt specialist internat. econs. dept. World Bank, Washington, 1973-95; internat. cons. Miami, Fla., 1996—; World Bank del. Paris Club Debt Renegotiation for Senegal, 1982. UN Conf. in Trade and Devel. cons. Nat. Bank Angola, Luanda, 2000; chief tech. adviser UN Conf. Trade and Devel. Bur. Treasury, Manila, 1989—90. Bd. dirs., treas. Friends of Art Mus. of the Americas, OAS, Washington, 1988-90; bd. dirs. Friends of Peru, 1991-1996, Friends of the Cuban Heritage Collection, U. Miami, 2003—; panel mem. The Lawrenceville Sch., 1992; mem. Presdl. Inaugural Com., Washington, 1997. Roman Catholic. Avocations: art collecting, genealogy. Home: 8860 SW 123rd Ct Apt K106 Miami FL 33186-4152 Office Phone: 305-606-0983. Personal E-mail: mnlawton@hotmail.com.

NUNEZ-PORTUONDO, RICARDO, investment company executive; b. N.Y.C., June 9, 1933; s. Emilio and Maria (Garcia) N-P.; m. Dolores Maldonado, Sept. 7, 1963; children— Ricardo Jose, Emilio Manuel, Eduardo Javier. LL.D., U. Havana, Cuba; postdoctoral in law, U. Fla., 1975. Bar: Cuba, Fla. Editor Latin Am. div. USIA, Miami, Fla., 1961-71, editor Washington, 1961-71; nat. dir. Cuban Refugee Program, Washington, 1975-77; pres. Cultural Pub., Inc., Miami, 1994—, Central Investment Trust, Coral Gables, Fla., 1977—; chmn. bd. Interstate Bank of Commerce, Miami, 1986-88; v.p. Century 21, Coral Gables, 1989—. Author: A Critique on the Linowitz Report, 1975, Cuba: La Otra Imagen, 1994, Un Procer Cubano, 1994, Cuban Refugee Program, The Early Years, 1995. Dir. Nat. Hispanic Scholarship Fund, San Francisco, 1978—; dir. COSSMHO, Washington, 1980—; trustee emeritus Fla. Internat. U., 1984—; pres. Mercy Hosp. Found., Miami, 1985—; bd. dirs. ARC, Greater Miami. Recipient numerous awards for civic contbns. including day named in honor Ricardo Nunez Day, Miami, 1975. Mem. Cuban Lawyers Assn., Cuban Acad. History, Metro. Club, Lyford Cay Club, Ocean Reef Club, Key Biscayne Yacht Club, Big Five Club, 200 Club. Republican. Roman Catholic. Home: 4651 W Flagler St Apt 9 Miami FL 33134-1532 Office: PO Box 141720 Coral Gables FL 33114-1720

NUNN, CHARLES BURGESS, religious organization executive; b. Richmond, Va., May 1, 1931; s. Charles Burgess Sr. and Virginia Atkinson (Goode) N.; m. Helen Agnes Parker, Sept. 1, 1957; children: Patsy Virginia, Catherine Louise, Stephen Charles, Stewart Gavin. BA in Econs., Randolph Macon Coll., 1953; BD, Southwestern Bapt. Theol. Sem., 1959, MDiv, 1969; DMin, Pitts. Theol. Sem., 1979. Ordained to Gospel ministry, 1954. Pastor Warwick Rd. Bapt. Chapel, Richmond, Va., 1952-53, Garrett's Bluff Bapt. Ch., Arthur City, Tex., 1954-56, Plymouth Haven Bapt. Ch., Alexandria, Va., 1959-68, First Bapt. Ch., Bluefield, W.Va., 1968-77; exec. dir. missions Richmond (Va.) Bapt. Assn., 1977-97; adminstr., treas. So. Bapt. Conf./Assoc. Dirs. Missions, 1997—2003. Trustee Bluefield (Va.) Coll., 1972-82, U. Richmond, Va., 1989-93; first v.p. Va. Bapt. Gen. Bd., Richmond, 1974-75; dir. Home Mission Bd., So. Bapt. Conv., Atlanta, 1976-84. Author: (children's book) Following Jesus, 1968. Commr. Bluefield (W.Va.) Urban Renewal Authority, 1971-74; chmn. Bluefield (W.Va.) Beautification Commn., 1972-73; pres. North Chamberlayne Civic Assn., Richmond, 1989-91. Recipient Disting. Svc. award City of Bluefield, 1970, Disting. Alumnus award Alumni Soc. Randolph Macon, Ashland, Va., 1992, Vol. Missions award Richmond Regional Devel. Coun. of the Fgn. Mission Bd., So. Bapt. Conv., 1995. Mem. Richmond Rotary Club (bd. dirs. 1990-92), Sandston Rotary Club, Pawleys Island Rotary Club, Omicron Delta Kappa. Avocations: travel, fishing, photography, baseball. E-mail: cbnunnjr@aol.com.

NUNN, GRADY HARRISON, political science educator emeritus; b. Arlington, Tex., Apr. 12, 1918; s. William Roy and Floy Brooke (Dugan) N.; m. Ann Torrey Welsh, June 15, 1951 (dec. 1980); 1 child, Therese von Hohoff.; m. Virginia Cotton Chivington, Dec. 18, 1982. BA, U. Okla., 1939, MA, 1941; PhD (Penfield fellow), N.Y.U., 1961. Instr. N.Y.U., 1946-49; from instr. to asso. prof. U. Ala., Tuscaloosa, 1949-65, prof., chmn. dept. polit. sci. Birmingham, 1969-83, prof. emeritus, 1983—; vis. asst. prof. Ind. U., 1960-61; asst. prof., asso. prof. U. Pitts. at Ahmadu Bello U., Nigeria, 1964-68; assoc. prof. U. Pitts., 1968, Auburn U., 1968-69. Bd. dirs. Unitarian Universalist Service Com., 1978-84, v.p., 1981-82 Assoc. editor: Background on World Politics, 1957-62; Contbr. to: Readings in Government in American Society, 1949, Federalism in the Commonwealth, 1963, The Politics and Administration of Nigerian Government, 1965, editorial bd.: Jour. of Politics, 1971-74. Mem. Birmingham Regional Planning Commn., 1995-2000. Capt. F.A., AUS, 1942-46. Ford Found. Fgn. Area fellow, 1956-57 Mem. Am. Polit. Sci. Assn., So. Polit. Sci. Assn. (exec. council 1974-77), Royal African Soc., AAUP (pres. Ala. conf.), Phi Beta Kappa, Pi Sigma Alpha, Phi Eta Sigma, Alpha Tau Omega, Omicron Delta Kappa. Unitarian Universalist. Home: 805 Rockhurst Ln Birmingham AL 35209 E-mail: ghnunn@aol.com.

NUNN, MARGARET BAKER, owner boutique; b. Blue Creek, W.Va., Dec. 24, 1912; d. Arthur and Ethel (Reynolds) Baker; m. William L. Nagy, Aug. 27, 1932 (dec. July 1971); children: William L., Beverly N. Nicklaus; m. Harold Denton Nunn, Nov. 21, 1972. Student, W.Va. Sch. Bus., Fairmont, 1931, Evening Vocat. Sch., Tampa, Fla., 1967. Salesperson S. S. Klein Agy., Pitts., 1936-46; owner, broker Beverly Realty Co., Pitts., 1946-59; owner Christmas Shoppe, St. Pete Beach, Fla., 1961-64, Barefoot Browser, St. Pete Beach, 1964-80, Peg Nunn's Pla. 100, St. Petersburg, Fla., 1979—. Founder Boys Club of St. Petersburg, 1972, Abilities Rehabilitation Ctr. Guild, Clearwater, Fla., 1977; pres. Women's C. of C., Treasure Island, Fla., 1966-67, Soroptimist Internat., Treasure Island, 1972; dir. corp. bd. Boys Clubs of Pinellas County, Pinellas Park, Fla., 1972-89, Pinellas County Anti-Crime Com., St. Pete Beach, 1972; elected mem. Castle Shannon Sch. Bd., Pitts., 1959. Named Queen of Hearts, Am. Heart Assn., St. Petersburg, 1977, Woman of the Yr., Beta Sigma Phi, St. Petersburg, 1981, to Hall of Fame, Women's Svc. League, St. Petersburg, 1988; recipient Suncoast Woman & Youth award Boys & Girls Clubs, 1993, Am. Svc. to Youth award, 1997; JCPenney Gold Medallion award, 1997, Sunshine Sr. Ctr. award, St. Petersburg, Fla., 2001, Everyday Shero award Resource Ctr. for Women, St. Petersburg, 2002; given Key to the City, St. Petersburg., 2001. Mem. The Pla. Shoppes Mchts. (pres. 1987-89), Beach Mchts. Assn. (v.p. 1986-89), NAFE. Republican. Lutheran. Avocation: volunteer civic work. Home: One Beach Dr Ste 2205 St Petersburg FL 33701 Office: 111 2nd Ave NE Ste 100 Saint Petersburg FL 33701-3439

NUNN, PATARICA DIAN, poet; b. Arkadelphia, Ark., Aug. 10, 1951; m. Freddie Lee Nunn, Mar. 16, 1979; children: Katarica Lakisha, Roshonda Lanae, Ophelia Lorraine, Opal Laverne. Student, Ouachita Bapt. U., 1971—72. Dir. assistance operator Southwestern Bell Tel. Co., Hot Springs, Ark., 1978—2003; ret., 2003. Songwriter My Moment of Miles, Time, 1998, Mellow Drifting, 2002, Sassy Sassy Lady, 2003; author: (poetry) Sacred Memories, 1996, A True Mother's Love, 1997, A True Father's Love, 1998 (Hon. Mention Nat. Authors Registry), Out in Left Field, 1998, A Breathe of Fresh Air, 2002. Bd. dirs., mem. adv. com. Nat. Libr. Poetry. Named to Internat. Poetry Hall of Fame, 1997; recipient elected into the Internat. Poetry Hall of Fame, 1997, elected into the Internat. Hall of Fames's Mus. on the Internet's World Wide Web., http:/www.poets.com, Bd. of Dir. and Adv. Com. of The Nat. Libr. of Poetry, mentioned "A True Fathers Love", Iliad Press, 1998, hon. mention "Contemporary Verse From Around the World Edit.", The Nat. Authors Registry, 1997, hon. mention,"Sacred Memories", Whispers In The Garden edit., The Poetry Guild, 1997. Mem.: Poetry Guild, Nat. Author's Registry. Democrat. Home: 4 Stillman Dr Little Rock AR 72209

NUNN, SAMUEL (SAM NUNN), former senator, lawyer; b. Perry, Ga., Sept. 8, 1938; s. Samuel Augustus and Elizabeth (Cannon) N.; m. Colleen O'Brien, Sept. 25, 1965; children: Michelle, Brian. Student, Ga. Tech., 1956-59; AB, LL.B., Emory U., 1962. Bar: Ga. 1962. Legal counsel armed services com. U.S. Ho. Reps., 1963; mem. firm Nunn, Geiger & Rampey, Perry, Ga., 1964-73; mem. Ga. Ho. Reps., 1968-72; U.S. senator from Ga., 1972-96; ranking Dem. mem., chmn. armed svcs. com.; mem. govtl. affairs com., intelligence com., small bus. com.; ptnr. King & Spalding, Atlanta, 1997—2003; co-chmn. Nuc. Threat Initiative, Washington, 2003—. Former ranking Dem., former chmn. Permanent Subcom. on Investigations of Govt. Affairs; bd. dirs. Chevron Texaco Corp., Coca-Cola Co., Dell Computer Corp., GE, Internet Security Systems Inc., Scientific-Atlanta; disting. prof. Sam Nunn Sch. Internat Affairs Ga. Tech. Office: Nuc Threat Initiative 1747 Pennsulvania Ave NW Ste 700 Washington DC 20006

NUNN, STEPHEN R. state representative; b. Glasgow, Ky, Nov. 4, 1952; m. Tracey Nunn; children: Mary, Robert, Courtney. Attended, Univ. of Louisville, Sch. of Law, 1976, Univ. of Ky; BA, Transylvania Univ., 1975. State Rep. House of Rep., Dist. 23, 1990—; phys. recruiter TJ Samson Hosp., 1998—; ins. specialist Larry Glass Construction Co., 1995—98; co-owner Calvert & Nunn Ins., 1988—95; farmer Dairy/Tobacco/Beef, 1979—87. Bd. mem. Long Term Policy Rsch. Ctr. Bd., 1994—, Atty. Gen. Task Force on Older Kentuckians, 1995; adv. Forgy for Gov., 1995; mem. Atty. Gen. Task Force on Child Sex Abuse, 1994, Tobacco Task Force, 1992—93; chair Young Rep. for Nunn, 1979; mem. White House Intern Program, 1974, Appropriations & Revenue; vice chair Health & Welfare; mem. Labor & Industry. Mem.: South Ctrl. Cultural Ctr. (pres.), People for People Campaign (co-chair 1995—96), Longterm Policy Rsch. Ctr., Glasgow/Barren Chamber of Commerce, Ducks Unlimited, Comty. Farm Alliance, Mus. of the Barrens (bd. of dir.), YMCA (bd. mem.), Ky. League of Sportsmen, Boy Scouts of Am. Republican. Christian. Office: Capitol Capitol Annex Rm 316A Frankfort KY 40601 also: Campaign 136 Fairway Pl Glasgow KY 42141 also: Campaign 2 640 S 4th St Ste 201 Louisville KY 40202 also: Dist 136 Fairway Pl Glasgow KY 42141 E-mail: snunn@snunn4gov.com.

NUNNALLY, KNOX DILLON, lawyer; b. Haynesville, La., Jan. 26, 1943; s. Miles Dillon and Linnie Mat (Knox) Nunnally; m. Kay Clyde Webb; 1 child, Kevin Knox. BBA, U. Tex., 1965, LLB, 1968. Bar: Tex. 1968, U.S. Dist. Ct. (ea. dist.): Tex. 1970, U.S. Dist. Ct. (so. dist.): Tex. 1969, U.S. Dist. Ct. (we. dist.): Tex. 1976, U.S. Ct. Appeals (5th cir.): 1978, Diplomate Tex. Bd. Legal Specialization:. Ptnr. Vinson & Elkins LLP, Houston, 1976—. Mem.: ABA, Houston Bar Assn., Tex. Bar Assn., Am. Coll. Trial Lawyers. Home: 3421 Meadow Lake Ln Houston TX 77027-4106 Office: Vinson & Elkins LLP 1001 Fannin St Ste 2300 Houston TX 77002-6760

NUNNELLEY, CAROL FISHBURNE, editor newspaper; b. Montgomery, Ala., Dec. 25, 1942; m. William A. Nunnelley; 1 child, Meg. BA, Samford U., 1965; postgrad., U. Ky., 1965-66. Reporter The Birmingham (Ala.) News, 1966-78, city editor, 1978-92, mng. editor, 1992—. Recipient reporting and writing awards Ala. Soc. Porfl. Journalists, Ala. Press Assn., Ala. Associated Press, Journalist of the Yr. award Troy State U., Achievement award Birmingham Emancipation Assn. Mem. Soc. Profl. Journalists, Leadership Birmingham, The Women's Network. Office: The Birmingham News 2200 4th Ave N Birmingham AL 35203-3840

NUNZ, GREGORY JOSEPH, aerospace engineer, program manager, educator, entrepreneur; b. Batavia, N.Y., May 28, 1934; s. Sylvester Joseph and Elizabeth Marie (Loesell) N.; m. Georgia Monyea Costas, Mar. 30, 1958; children: Karen, John, Rebecca, Deirdre, Jaimie, Marta. BSChemE, Cooper Union, 1955; postgrad., U. So. Calif., Calif. State U.; MS in Applied Math., Columbia Pacific U., 1991, PhD in Mgmt. Sci., 1993. Adv. design staff, propulsion mgr. U.K. project Rocketdyne div. Rockwell, Canoga Park, Calif., 1955-65; mem. tech. staff Aerospace Corp., El Segundo, Calif., 1965-70; mem. tech. staff propulsion div. Jet Propulsion Lab., Pasadena, Calif., 1970-72; chief. monoprop. engring. Bell Aerospace Corp., Buffalo, N.Y., 1972-74; group supr. comb. devices Jet Propulsion Lab., Pasadena, 1974-76; dep. group leader, asst. div. leader, program mgr. internat. HDR geothermal energy program, program mgr. space-related projects Los Alamos (N.Mex.) Nat. Lab., 1977—. Assoc. prof. electronics L.A. Pierce Coll., Woodland Hills, Calif., 1961-72; instr. No. N.Mex. C. C., Los Alamos, 1978-80, div. head scis., 1980-92; adj. prof. math. U. N.Mex., Los Alamos, 1980—; sr. mgmt. rep. Excel Telecom., Inc., 1995-98; ptnr. JRB Rsch., 2000—. Author: Electronics Lab Manual I, 1964, Electronics in Our World, 1972; co-author: Electronics Mathematics, vol. I, II, 1967, Imotep to Khufu: How It Can Be Done, 2001; contbg. author Prentice-Hall Textbook of Cosmetology, 1975, Alternative Energy Sources VII, 1987; contbr. articles to profl. jours.; inventor smallest catalytic liquid N2H4 rocket thrustor, co-inventor first monoprop/biprop bimodal rocket engine, tech. advisor internat. multi-prize winning documentary film One With the Earth. Mem. Aerial Phenomena Research Orgn., L.A., 1975. Fellow AIAA (assoc., liquid propellants com. on stds.); mem. Arista, Math. Assn. Am. Avocations: travel, archaeology, foreign languages, golf. Office: Los Alamos Nat Lab PO Box 1663 Los Alamos NM 87545 0001 also: U NMex Los Alamos Br 4000 University Dr Los Alamos NM 87544-2233 Office Phone: 505-667-0137. E-mail: gnunz@lanl.gov.

NUOVO, BETTY A. state representative; b. Englewood, N.J., Dec. 10, 1931; m. Victor L. Nuovo, 1953; two children. BS, Bucknell U., 1953. State rep. Vt. Ho. of Reps., Middleury, 1981-90, 96—; pvt. law practice Middleury, 1974—94. Jud. com. Ho. of Reps., 1981-88, chmn. 1985-88, chmn. jud. rules com. 1985-86, adminstrv. rules com. 1985-88, vice-chmn. 1987-88, ways and means com. 1989-90, Middlebury natural resources and energy com., 1996-2000, jud. com., 2001-02, agr. com., 2003—. Chair Vt. State Dem. Platform Com., Middlebury Charter Comn., Vt., Addison County Dem. Com.; bd. dirs., exec. bd. Addison County Regional Planning Com; bd. selectmen Middlebury; bd. dirs. Vt. YMCA; mem. Middlebury LWV. Office: PO Box 347 Middlebury VT 05753-0347

NURENBERG, DAVID, retired oil company executive; b. N.Y.C., Mar. 25, 1939; s. Abraham S. and Katherine G. N.; m. Brenda G. Schwait, Sept. 1963; children— Jill Suzanne, Brian Michael. BS in Marine Engring, U.S. Mcht. Marine Acad., 1960; MS in Indsl. Mgmt, Columbia U., 1963, PhD in Mgmt. Sci, 1965. With Exxon Corp., 1963-67; employee relations mgr. Esso Pappas, Athens, Greece, 1968-72; labor relations and compensation mgr. Esso Europe, London, 1972 77; corp. sec. Esso Eastern Inc., Houston, 1977 82; mgr. exec. compensation Exxon Corp., N.Y.C., 1982-90, mgr. compensation and exec. programs Irving, Tex., 1990-98; ret. Past mem. coun. exec. compensation Conf. Bd., past chmn.; adj. prof. Union Inst. Past mem. exec. edn. adv. bd. Wharton Sch., U. Pa.; past mem. adv. bd. Ctr. for Effective Orgns., U. So. Calif. Mem. Am. Compensation Assn. (bd. dirs., chmn., exec. comp. coun., bd. steering com.), Am. Contract Bridge League (Silver life master).

NURHUSSEIN, MOHAMMED ALAMIN, internist, geriatrician, educator; b. Adwa, Ethiopia, Apr. 4, 1942; came to U.S., 1972; s. Hagos and Teberih (Yusuf) N.; m. Zahra Said, June 10, 1972; children: Nadia, Siham, Safy. BS, Haile Selasie Mil. Acad., Harar, Ethiopia, 1961; MD, Zagreb (Yugoslavia) U., 1968. Intern, resident, then fellow Bklyn.-Cumberland Med. ctr., 1972-77; emergency rm. physician Cumberland Hosp., Bklyn., 1977-79; attending physician in medicine Kings County Hosp. Ctr., Bklyn., 1979—; faculty practice medicine, geriatrics SUNY Univ. Hosp., Bklyn., 1983—. Instr., then asst. prof. SUNY Health Sci. Ctr., bklyn., 1979—; med. cons., dir. drug abuse treatment Coney Island Hosp., Bklyn., 1982-84; adv. bd. Bklyn. Alzheimer's Disease Assistance Ctr., 1992—. Fellow ACP; mem. Am. Geriatric Soc., Am. Lung Assn., N.Y. Acad. Scis., Amnesty Internat., Physicians for Human Rights. Democrat. Moslem. Office: SUNY Health Sci Ctr 450 Clarkson Ave Brooklyn NY 11203-2056

NURICK, CARL J. writer, consultant, poet; b. Harrisburg, Pa., Mar. 29, 1934; s. Gilbert and Sylvia Nurick; m. Elizabeth Parker Nurick; children: Kim, Scott, Todd, Craig. BA, Pa. State U., 1955; advanced studies, Mich. State U., Columbia U. Area v.p. AT&T, Pa., 1982—86; internat. v.p. Internat. Alliance, Phila., 1987—93; exec. v.p. Transnet, Huntington Valley, Pa., 1993; v.p. OutSource Internat., Norristown, Pa., 1995—96; pres., COO Vircom, West Chester, Pa., 1996—97; freelance author, cons. Tafton, Pa., 1998—. MBA adv. bd. Pa. State U. and Bloomsburg U., 1974—86; mktg. adv. bd. Drexel U., Phila., 1974—78. Author: The Truth About Islam, 2003, Living To Die, 2003, Green Street Boy, 2004. Youth activities chmn. Jr. C. of C., Harrisburg, Pa., 1957, 1958, 1989; bd. mem. Sjourbaay Gay'l Hosp., Morristown, Pa., 1979, 1980. Lt. USN, 1955—57. Mem.: Fairview Lake Assn., U.S. Naval Inst., Univ. Pk. County Club Residents Assn. Avocations: reading, exercise, boating, music. Home Fax: 570-226-8366.

NURNBERG, CHARLES GORDON, publishing company marketing executive; b. Newark, Nov. 16, 1947; s. Max and Eleanor (Gordon) N.; m. Barbara Ann Goldstein, Dec. 20, 1970; children: Jeremy, Peter, David. BA, Syracuse U., 1969. Proofreader Frederick Fell Pub., Inc., N.Y.C., 1969, editor, 1970-72, sales, 1972-74, sales mgr., 1974-75, v.p. sales, 1975-77, exec. v.p., 1977-78, pub., 1978; pub. paperbacks Sterling Pub. Co., Inc., N.Y.C., 1978-80, v.p., dir. mktg., 1980-82, sr. v.p., 1982-89, exec. v.p., 1990—2003, pres., CEO, 2003—. Mem. Book Industry Study Group com., 1992-95. Mem. Assn. Am. Pubs. (mem. mktg. com. 1970-73, chmn. pubs. forum com. 1973-79), Marlboro Soccer Assn. (bd. dirs., coach 1974, boys travel team). Avocations: writing, travel, exercise. Home: 25 Whitman Rd Morganville NJ 07751-1442 Office: 387 Park Ave S New York NY 10016-8810 E-mail: cnurnberg@sterlingpub.com.

NURNBERGER, JOHN I., JR., psychiatrist, educator; b. N.Y.C., July 18, 1946; married; 3 children. BS in Psychology magna cum laude, Fordham U., 1968; MD, Ind. U., 1975, PhD, 1983. Diplomate Am. Bd. Psychiatry and Neurology. Resident in psychiatry Columbia Presbyn. Med. Ctr., N.Y.C., 1975-78, med. officer sect. psychogenetics, 1977-78; sr. staff fellow, outpatient clinic adminstr. sect. psychogenetics NIH, Bethesda, Md., 1978-83, staff psychiatrist, chief NIMH Outpatients Clinic, 1983-86, acting chief sect. clin. genetics, 1986; prof. psychiatry, dir. Inst. Psychiatric Rsch., rsch. coord. dept. psychiatry Ind. U. Med. Ctr., Indpls., 1986—; prof. med. psychiatry, neurobiology and med. genetics Ind. U. Grad. Sch., Indpls., 1987—; Joyce and Iver Small prof. psychiatry, dir. Inst. Psychiat. Rsch., Ind. U., Indpls. Clin. cons. Cold Spring VA Hosp., 1986—; cons., lectr. in field. Editor-in-chief: Psychiatric Genetics; field editor: Neuropsychiatric Genetics; contbr. articles to profl. jours. NSF fellow, 1968; recipient NAMI Exemplary Psychiatrist award Nat. Alliance Mentally Ill, 1992, 94. Fellow Am. Psychiatric Assn., Am. Psychpathological Assn.; mem. AAAS, Am. Soc. Human Genetics, Internat. Soc. Psychiatric Genetics (bd. dirs.), Am. Coll. Neuropsychopharmacology, Soc. Light Treatment and Biol. Rhythms, Soc. Neursci., Assn. Rsch. in Nervous and Mental Disease, Soc. Biol. Psychiatry, Sigma Xi. Office: Ind U Sch Medicine Psychiatric Rsch Inst 791 Union Dr Indianapolis IN 46202-2873

NURSE, SIR PAUL M. academic administrator; BSc, U. Birmingham, 1970; PhD, East Anglia, 1973. Dir. rsch. Imperial Cancer Rsch Fund, 1993—96; dir. gen. Imperial Cancer Rsch. Fund, 1996—2002; chief exec. Cancer Rsch. U.K., London, 2002—03; pres. Rockefeller U., N.Y.C., 2003—. Recipient Gairdner Internat. award, Gairdner Found., 1992, Royal medal Royal Soc., 1995, H. P. Heineken prize for biochemistry and biophysics Royal Netherlands Acad. Arts and Scis., 1996, Dr. Josef Steiner prize, Cancer Found., Bern, Switzerland, 1996, Alfred P. Sloan Jr. prize and medal, GM Cancer Rsch. Found., 1997,

Albert Lasker award USA, 1998, Berkan Judd award, 1998, Nobel Prize in Physiology or Med., The Nobel Found., 2001. Fellow: Royal Soc., 1989; mem.: NAS (foreign assoc.), 1995. Office: Rockefeller U 1230 York Ave New York NY 10021-6399*

NUSBACHER, GLORIA WEINBERG, lawyer; b. NYC, July 22, 1951; d. Murray and Doris (Togman) Weinberg; m. Burton Nusbacher, Aug. 4, 1974; 1 child, Shoshana. BA magna cum laude, Barnard Coll., 1972; JD, Columbia U., 1975. Bar: N.Y. 1976. Assoc. Hughes Hubbard & Reed LLP, NYC, 1975-83, counsel, 1983-91, ptnr., 1991—. Lectr. in field. Mem. Columbia Law Rev.; contbr. articles to profl. jours. Troop leader, leader trainer Girl Scouts USA, 1991-97. Mem. ABA (employee benefits and exec. compensation com. 1987—, fed. regulation securities com., subcom. employee benefits, exec. compensation and sect. 16, 1983—, task force Sect. 16, 1991-97, vice-chair com. employee benefits and exec. compensation 2001-03, chair subcom. fed. and state securities laws of com. employee benefits and exec. compensation 1994-2001, 03-, mem. task force exec. compensation 1992-94). Office: Hughes Hubbard & Reed LLP 1 Battery Park Plz New York NY 10004-1482 Office Phone: 212-837-6719.

NUSBAUM, ALAN B. real estate executive; Chmn. bd. S.L. Nusbaum Realty Co., Norfolk, Va., 1961—. Office: SL Nusbaum Realty Co PO Box 2491 Norfolk VA 23501-2491 Fax: 757-640-2207.*

NUSBAUM, BENNETT, printing/copying company executive; CFO Kinko's Inc., Ventura, Calif. Office: 255 W Stanley Ave Ventura CA 93001-1348

NUSIM, ROBERTA, publisher; b. N.Y.C., Dec. 1, 1943; BA in English, CCNY, 1964; MA, CUNY, 1966. Tchr. N.Y.C. Bd. Edn., 1964-73; v.p. program devel. Mind, Inc., Westport, Conn., 1973-76; pres. Mind Media, 1976-78; founder, pres. Lifetime Learning Systems, Fairfield, Conn., 1978-90; founder dir. The Film Study Guild, 1979-90; founder, pres. The Work & Family Publishing Group, Inc., 1991-94; founder, pres. Youth Mktg. Internat., Ltd., 1995—. Editor: Let's Talk About Health, 1980. Mem. ASCD, NAFE, Am. Film Inst., Women in Comm., Ednl. Press Assn. Am., Ptnrs. for Global Edn. (founder). Avocations: reading, painting. Office Phone: 212-286-1000. Personal E-mail: schoolroom@aol.com.

NUSIM, STANLEY HERBERT, chemical engineer, consultant; b. N.Y.C., Oct. 2, 1935; s. Seymour and Ranna T. (Weiner) N.; m. Marcia Anne Borsig, Feb. 21, 1960; children: David Mark, Jill Wendi. BChemE, CCNY, 1957; MChemE, N.Y. U., 1960, PhD, 1967. Rsch. engr. Battelle Meml. Inst., Columbus, Ohio, 1956; researcher, chem. engring. rsch. and devel. Merck Rsch. Labs. Div., Rahway, N.J., 1957-68, sect. mgr., 1968-70; tech. svcs. mgr. Merck Chem. Mfg. Div., Rahway, 1970-73, mfg. mgr., 1973-80; dir. subsidiary projects Merck Internat. Div., Rahway, 1981-82, exec. dir. Latin Am., Far East, Near East ops., 1982-88; exec. dir. licensee, Latin Am., Far East, Asia ops. Merck Pharm. Mfg. Div., Rahway, 1989-92; exec. dir. licensee ops. worldwide Merck Mfg. Divsn. Merck & Co. Inc., Whitehouse Station, NJ, 1992-94; v.p. mfg. and ops. Therics Inc., Princeton, NJ, 1994-97; pres. S.H. Nusim Assocs., Inc., Aventura, Fla., 1994—. Mem. adv. bd. CCNY Sch. Engring., 1982—; bd. dirs. AGI Dermatics Inc., Freeport, NY. Author: Kinetic Studies on C4 Hydrocarbon Systems, 1967. V.p. men's club Temple Beth Shalom, Livingston, N.J., 1975-78; rep. to bd. edn. Livingston Home and Sch. Assn., 1982-83; bd. govs. Turnberry Isle Yacht and Racquet Club, Aventura, Fla., 1992-94. Mem. Am. Inst. Chem. Engrs. (bd. dir. N. Jersey sect. 1968-71, scholarship award 1955), Am. Chem. Soc., Tau Beta Pi, Garden State Yacht Club (bd. govs. 1987-88), Otis Woodlands Club (bd. dirs. 2002—). Achievements include U.S. and foreign patents on the continuous manufacture of halogenated acetone, development of "clean room" concepts for pharmachemical manufacturing, development of sophisticated training techniques for sterile pharmaceutical manufacturing. Home: 400 E 56TH St #31J New York NY 10022-4147

NUSS, BARBARA GOUGH, artist; b. Washington, Apr. 11, 1939; d. Gaines Homer Gough and Edwerta Barbara (Beyer) Barber; m. Frederick A. Johnson, Sept. 30, 1968 (div. 1975); 1 child, Mark Eugene; m. Fred Dean Nuss, Dec. 18, 1982. BFA, Syracuse U., 1960; postgrad., Schuler Sch. Fine Arts, Balt., 1986—87. Art dir. Chappell's Dept. Store, Syracuse, NY, 1960-62, 66; mgr., illustrator Holman Anderson & Moore, Washington, 1967-70; art dir., advt. mgr. Ad-Media & Howard Advt. Assocs., Columbia, Md., 1970-75; acct. exec. Graphic Arts Inc., Alexandria, Va., 1975-77; sales mgr. The Jour. Newspapers, Washington, 1977-82; tchr., adult edn. Montgomery Coll., Rockville, Md., 1984-85; pvt. tchr. fine arts, Woodbine, Md., 1982-96; instr. Plein air painting workshop, 1998—. Chmn. Montgomery County Juried Art Exhibit, Rockville, 1988, Mid-Atlantic Regional Watercolor Exhibit, 1998—99; pres. Nuss Fine Arts, Inc., 1992—; judge Am. Landscape Show Art League Torpedo Factory, Alexandria, Va., 2002; judge Mountain State Forest Festival Fine Art Exhibition, Elkins, W.Va., 2002, Potomac Valley Watercolorists Ann. Juried Show, 2004, Mont. County Art Assn. Ann. Show, 2004. One-woman shows include Pa. State U., 1986, NIH, Bethesda, Md., 1989—90, Md. Nat. Capital Pk. and Planning Commn., 1991, Art League Gallery, Alexandria, 1992, Bendann Art Galleries, Towson, Md., 1999—2000, Troika Gallery, Easton, Md., 2004, Strathmore Hall Art Ctr., Bethesda, Md., 2004, Washington County Arts Coun. Gallery, Hagerstown, Md., 2004, Grand Style Gallery, Balt., 2004, exhibited in group shows at Art League at the Torpedo Factory, 1987—92, 2002, Mid-Atlantic Regional Watercolor Exhbn., 1989—90 (Holbein award), Heritage Gallery Classical Realism, 1989—90, Art Barn Gallery, Washington, 1990, Carmen's Gallery, 1991—2000, Art Showcase 100 Md. Artists, 1991—92, Assn. pour la Promotion du Patrimoine Artistique Francais, Galerie Jean Lammelin, Argenteuil, France, 1991, Salmagundi Club 14th Ann. Exhbn., 1991, Atrium Gallery Georgetown U., Washington, 1991, 18th Ann. Exhbn., 1995, Mid-Atlantic Regional Watercolor Exhbn., 1996, State House, Annapolis, 1996, World Trade Ctr., Balt., 1996, Bendann's Art Gallery, Towson, 1997—2002, Principle Gallery, Alexandria, 1998—2004, Miniature Painters, Sculptors and Gravers Soc. Washington, 1999, Addison/Ripley Fine Art Gallery, Washington, 1999, Rock Creek Gallery, 1999, Main St. Gallery, Annapolis, 1999—2000, Miniature Art Soc. Fla., 2000, Oil Painters Am., 2000—01, Rock Creek Gallery, Washington, 2001, Troika Gallery, Easton, 2001—04, Washington County Arts Coun. Gallery, Hagerstown, 2001—04, Brazier Fine Art, Richmond, Va., 2002, Grand Style Gallery, Balt., 2002—04, Black Rock Ctr. for the Arts, Germantown, Md., 2003—04, Kushnir Taylor Gallery, Ellicott City, Md., 2003—04, Represented in permanent collections Am. Coun. Edn., NIH, Bell Atlantic, Kiplinger Washington Editors, Fairhaven Retirement Cmty., Md. State Treas.'s Office, NIH; work represented in: Art from the Parks, How Did You Paint That?, 2000; author: 14 Formulas for Painting Fabulous Landscapes, 2003. Finalist still life competition, Artist's mag., 1996, landscape competition, 2003; recipient 1st prize for watercolor, C&O Canal Show, 1987, 1st prize for oil painting, Rockville Art League, 1987, Montgomery County Art Assn., 1983, 1989, Gaithersburg Fine Arts Assn., 1983, 1989, grand champion award for oil painting, Howard County Fair, 1989, one of Top 100 award for oil painting, Nat. Arts for Parks, 1989, 1991, 1992, 2001, Top 200, 1990, 1993, 1996, Best in Show award, Nat. League Am. Pen Women, Md. Biennial Conv., 1999, 1st prize watercolor, 1st prize oils, Best in Show award, 2003. Mem. Nat. League Am. Pen Women (sec. Bethesda, Md. 1989, treas. 2000-03), Balt. Watercolor Soc. (bd. dirs. 1997-99), Washington Soc. Landscape Painters (sec. 1999, pres. 2000-03, Baustian award for Excellence 1999), Salmagundi Club (NYC), Oil Painters Am. Avocations: quilting, crossword puzzles. Home: 3132 Cabin Run Woodbine MD 21797-7933 Office Phone: 301-854-6447.

NUSS, JOANNE RUTH, sculptor, artist; b. Gt. Bend, Kans., May 2, 1951; d. Melvin Oliver and Ruth Helen (Brauer) N. Student, Valparaiso U., 1969-71, U. Kans., 1972-73, U. Copenhagen, 1974; BA, Ft. Hays State U., 1975; MFA, Santa Fe Inst. Fine Arts, 1991. Lectr. Noon Edition Sta. KCMO-TV, Kansas City, 1981, Menoriah Hosp., Brookridge Elem. Sch., The Jill Shurin Show Telecable 10, Kansas City, 1982, Barton County C.C., Gt. Bend, Nelson-Atkins Mus., Kansas City, Mo., 1984; artist-in-residence Helen Wurlitzer Found., Taos, N.Mex., 1984, 90. One-woman shows include Bette Moses Gallery, Great Bend, 1980, Art Expo Ctr., San Francisco, 1981, Univ. Gall., Ft. Hays State U., 1985, Am. Legation Mus., Tangiers, Morocco, 1986, Inma Gallery, Dhahran, Saudi Arabia, 1994, Bab Rouah Gallery, Rabat, Morocco, 1996, Agora Gallery, Soho, New York, 2001, Amsterdam Whitney Internat. Fine Art Gallery, N.Y.C., 2003, others, exhibited in group shows at Second Internat. Sculpture Fair, Boston, 1980, Joan Cooke Gallery, Kansas City, Mo., 1983, The Batz Lawrence Gallery, Kansas City, 1984, Galerie de Rond Point des Champs Elyssees, Paris, 1989, Tetouan & La Kabila Gallery, Tetouan, Morocco, 1991, N.Mex. Sculptors Guild, Fuller Lodge Art Gallery, Los Alamos, 1992, Hermosas Fine Arts Gallery, Durango, Colo., 1995, Tanjah Flandria Art Gallery, Tangiers, 1997—99, Shidoni Gallery, Tesuque, N.Mex., 1999—2002, Birger Sandzen Gallery, Lindsborg, Kans., 2000, Nat. Assn. Women Artists, Sarasota Visual Arts Ctr., 2000, U. No. Iowa, Cedar Falls, 2001 (1st pl., 2001), Coplan Gallery, Boca Raton, Fla., 2002, Attleboro (Mass.) Mus., 2002, Jeanette Hare Art Gallery, West Palm Beach, Fla., 2002, Twelfth Ann. Benefit Auction, Attleboro (Mass.) Mus., 2003, 114th Ann. Exhbn. Nat. Assn. Women Artists Fifth Ave. Gallery, N.Y.C., 2003, Attleboro Mus., Mass., 2003, Baker Arts Ctr. 7th Nat. Juried Art Exhbn., 2004; featured artist Artist Spectrum Mag.; exhibitions include Nat. Assn. Women Artists, 2003, Baker Arts Ctr., 2004, exhibited in group shows at The Carolina Exhibitions: McDopwell Arts amd Crafts Assn., Shelby Arts, Ashe County Arts Coun., 2004—05. Recipient 1st Kans. Artist Purchast award Ft. Hays State U., 1985, Best 3-D Works award Wichita Art Assn., 1983; 1st female fgn. artist commd. for archtl. major project, Tangiers, 1988-90, 98-2004. Mem. Nat. Assn. Women Artists, Nat. Sculpture Soc., Nat. Mus. of Women in the Arts, N.Mex. Women in Arts, Internat. Sculpture Ctr., Kans. Sculptor's Assn., Internat. Platform Assn. Avocations: travel, working with other artists, gardening.

NUSS, LAWTON R. judge; b. Salina, Kans., Dec. 30, 1952; m. Barbara Nuss; 5 children. BA in English and History, U. Kans., 1975, JD, 1982. With Clark Mize & Linville law firm, 1982; justice Kans. Supreme Ct., Topeka, 2002—. Mediator U.S. Dist. Ct. (Kans.). Combat engring. officer USMC. Mem.: Kans. Assn. Def. Counsel (pres.), Kans. Bar Assn. (chmn. bd. editors jour.). Office: Kans Jud Ctr 301 SW 10th Topeka KS 66612-1507

NUSSBAUM, ARNOLD, pediatrician; b. N.Y.C., Dec. 20, 1925; s. Jack and Clara (Gewirtz) N.; m. Helen P. Coble, June 30, 1951; children: Andrea, Jack, Paul, Robert. BS, Bklyn. Coll., 1949; MD, SUNY, Downstate Med. Ctr., Bklyn., 1954. Diplomate Am. Bd. Pediatrics. Intern USPHS, S.I., N.Y., 1954-55; resident in pediats. Jewish Hosp. Med. Ctr., Bklyn., 1955-57; pvt. practice Bklyn., 1957-77, Brook Island Pediats. Group, Bklyn., 1977—. With U.S. Navy, 1943-46, PTO. Mem. AMA, Kings County Med. Soc. Democrat. Jewish. Avocation: racing thoroughbred horses. Home: 67 Barlow Dr N Brooklyn NY 11234-6719 Office: 2462 E 65th St Brooklyn NY 11234-6718 also: 299 Guyon Ave Staten Island NY 10306-4134

NUSSBAUM, JEFFREY JOSEPH, musician; b. N.Y.C., July 7, 1952; s. Eli and Dorothy (Wolkowitz) N.; m. Alison Knopf (div. 1984); m. Joan Feigenbaum, April 5, 1990; 1 child, Samuel Leonard Baum. BA in Music, Hunter Coll., N.Y., 1977; MA in Edn., Bklyn. Coll., 1987; MFA in Early Music, Sarah Lawrence Coll., Bronxville, Tex., 1989. Cert. N.Y.S., N.Y.C. Freelance musician (trumpet, cornetto, natural trumpet), 1979—; tchr. music Park West H.S., N.Y., 1984—. Pres., founder Historic Brass Soc., N.Y., 1989—; dir. Manhattan Early Wind Ensemble, N.Y., 1992—, Pan Brass Quintet, N.Y., 1978-84; organized Internat. Hist. Brass Symposium, Amherst, Mass., 1995; organizer Early Brass Colloquium, Royal Acad. Music, London, 1997, Internat. Hist. Brass Symposium, co-sponsored by Cité de la Musique, Paris, 1999, Internat. Symposium co-sponsored with Stimu, Utrecht, Germany, 2000, HBS Cornetto Symposium, Bate Coll., Oxford U.; co-organizer Toronto 2000: Musical Intersections, 2000. Author: Brass Teaching and Learning: History, Development and Technology of Brass Instruments, 1998; contbr. articles to jours. in field. Mem. Am. Fedn. Musicians, Am. Musicological Soc., Internat. Trumpet Guild, Galpin Soc. Jewish. Home: 148 W 23rd St Apt 5F New York NY 10011-2447 Business E-Mail: president@historicbrass.org.

NUSSBAUM, LEO LESTER, retired college president, consultant; b. Berne, Ind., June 27, 1918; s. Samuel D. and Margaret (Mazelin) N.; m. Janet Nell Gladfelter, Nov. 25, 1942; children: Felicity Ann, Luther James, Margaret Sue. BS, Ball State U., 1942, MA, 1949; PhD, Northwestern U., 1952; postgrad., U. Mich., 1963. Tchr. Monmouth H.S., Decatur, Ind., 1946-48; dean men, asst. prof. bus. Huntington (Ind.) Coll., 1948-51; dean coll. liberal arts, assoc. prof. edn. and psychology U. Dubuque, Iowa, 1952-60; dean coll., prof. edn. and psychology Austin Coll., 1960-67; dean coll., prof. psychology Coe Coll., 1967-82, pres., 1970-82, pres. emeritus, 1982—; dir. Acad. Sr. Profls. Eckerd Coll., 1983-87; dir. PEL-ASPEC Project, 1988-95; coord. faculty ASPEC Colleagues, St. Petersburg, 1992-97. Cons. pvt. practice St. Petersburg, Fla., 1982—; Fulbright lectr. U. Mysore, India, 1958-59; cons., evaluator So. Assn. Colls. and Schs., Atlanta, 1963-67, North Cen. Assn. Colls. and Schs., 1959-60, 67-82, dir. I.E. Industries and Iowa Electric Light and Power Co., Cedar Rapids, 1982-91, dir. emeritus, 1991-92. Contbr. articles to profl. jours. Bd. dirs. Cedar Rapids Symphony, 1968-70; mem. cabinet Cedar Rapids United Way, 1980-82; elder Presbyn. Ch., moderator Presbytery of S.W. Fla., 1989. Sgt. U.S. Army, 1942-46. Recipient Disting. Alumnus award Ball State U., 1976, Alumni Merit award Northwestern U., 1977. Mem. Assn. Colls. Midwest (chmn. 1975-77), Iowa Assn. Ind. Colls. and Univs. (chmn. 1976-77), Danforth Assocs., Rotary (Cedar Rapids pres. 1975-76), Phi Delta Kappa, Blue Key, Pi Gamma Mu Home: 6909 9th St S Apt 336 Saint Petersburg FL 33705-6207 E-mail: cnussbau@tampabay.ar.com.

NUSSBAUM, MARTHA CRAVEN, philosophy and classics educator; b. N.Y.C., May 6, 1947; d. George and Betty (Warren) Craven; m. Alan Jeffrey Nussbaum, Aug., 1969 (div. 1987); 1 child, Rachel Emily. BA, NYU, 1969; MA, Harvard U., 1971, PhD, 1975; LHD (hon.), Kalamazoo Coll., 1988, Grinnell Coll., 1993. Asst. prof. philosophy and classics Harvard U., Cambridge, 1975-80, assoc. prof., 1980-83; vis. prof. philosophy, Greek and Latin Wellesley (Mass.) Coll., 1983-84; assoc. prof. philosophy and classics Brown U., Providence, R.I., 1984-85, prof. philosophy, classics and comparative lit., 1985-87, David Benedict prof. philosophy, classics and comparative lit., 1987-89, prof., 1989-95; prof. law and ethics U. Chgo., 1995-96, prof. philosophy dept., 1995—, prof. Divinity Sch., 1995—, Ernst Freund prof. law and ethics Law Sch./Divinity Sch., 1996-99, assoc. mem. classics dept., 1996—. Rsch. advisor World Inst. Devel. Econs. Rsch., Helsinki, Finland, 1986-93; vis. prof. law U. Chgo., 1994. Author: Aristotle's De Motu Animalium, 1978, The Fragility of Goodness, 1986, Loe's Knowledge, 1990, The Therapy of Desire, 1994, Poetic Justice: The Literary Imagination and Public Life, 1996, For Love of Country, 1996; editor: Language and Logos, 1983; (with A. Rorty) Essays on Aristotle's De Anima, 1992, (with A. Sen) The Quality of Life, 1993, (with J. Brunschwig) Passions & Perceptions, 1993, (with J. Glover) Women, Culture and Development, 1995, Poetic Justice, 1996, Cultivating Humanity, 1997, Sex and Social Justice, 1998. Soc. Fellows Harvard U. jr. fellow, 1972-75, Humanities fellow Princeton U., 1977-78, Guggenheim Found. fellow, 1983, NIH fellow, vis. fellow All Souls Coll., Oxford, Eng., 1986-87; recipient Brandeis Creative Arts award, 1990, Spielvogel-Diamondstein award, 1991; Gifford lectr. U. Edinburgh, 1993. Fellow Am. Acad. Arts and Scis. (membership com. 1991-93, coun. 1992-96), Am. Philos. Soc.; mem. Am. Philos. Assn. (exec. com. Ea. divsn. 1985-87, chair com. internat. coop., ex-officio mem. nat. bd. 1989-92, chair com. on status of women 1994-97), Am. Philol. Assn., PEN. Office: U Chicago The Law Sch 1111 E 60th St Chicago IL 60637-2776

NUSSBAUM, MICHEL ERNEST, physician; b. L.A., Nov. 7, 1947; s. Schymen and Jeannette Eleanor (Pequignot) N.; m. Joyce Wendy Laudon, Nov. 1, 1981; children: Eleanor, Anna. BA, Cornell U., 1969; MD, Free U. Brussels, 1977. Intern internal medicine N.Y. Hosp. Med. Ctr. of Queens, Flushing, 1977-78, resident, 1978-80, fellow gastroenterology, 1980-82, attending physician, 1982—; physician pvt. practice, Flushing, N.Y., 1982—; attending physician Flushing Hosp. Med. Ctr., 1987—; clin. instr. medicine Cornell U. Med. Coll., N.Y.C., 1994-98, clin. asst. prof. medicine, 1998—; med. dir. Franklin Ctr. for Nursing and Rehab., Flushing, 1995-99. Physician in charge endoscopic svcs. N.Y. Hosp. Med. Ctr. of Queens, 1990—, asst. dir. gastroenterology, 1998—, pres. med. staff soc., 1992-96, chmn. med. bd., 1997—2003, bd. trustees, 1998-2003, acting dir. gastroenterology, 2004—. Fellow ACP, Am. Coll. Gastroenterology. Office: 142-43 Booth Memorial Ave Flushing NY 11355-5343 Office Phone: 718-886-1919.

NUSSBAUM, PAUL A. retired hospitality executive; Ret. chmn., CEO Wyndham Internat.; chmn. Panco Svcs., Inc., Dallas. Office: PO Box 1425 Washington CT 06793-0425 E-mail: panussbaum@earthlink.net.

NUSSDORF, GLENN, distribution executive; CEO Quality King Distbrs., Ronkonkoma, N.Y. Office: Quality King Distbrs 2060 9th Ave Ronkonkoma NY 11779

NUSSDORF, LAWRENCE C. real estate/construction executive; Degree, U. Pa.; JD, Rutgers U., Georgetown U. Tax mgr. Arthur Andersen & Co.; v.p. fin. Clark Enterprises Inc., Bethesda, 1977-80, exec. v.p., 1980-98, pres., COO, CFO, 1998—. Office: Clark Enterprises Inc 7500 Old Georgetown Rd Bethesda MD 20814

NUSSLE, JAMES ALLEN, congressman; b. Des Moines, June 27, 1960; s. Mark S. and Lorna Kay (Fisher) N.; m. Leslie J. Harbison, Aug. 23, 1986; 2 children. BA, Luther Coll., Decorah, Iowa, 1983; JD, Drake U., 1985. Bar: Iowa 1985. Pvt. practice law, Manchester, Iowa, 1986; states atty. Delaware County Atty., Manchester, 1986-90; mem. U.S. Ho. of Reps. from 2d Iowa dist., Washington, 1991—, mem. house ways and means com., chmn. house budget com. Republican. Lutheran. Avocation: guitar. Office: US Ho of Reps 303 Cannon Hob Washington DC 20515-0001

NÜSSLEIN-VOLHARD, CHRISTIANE, medical researcher; b. Magdeburg, Germany, Oct. 20, 1942; d. Rolf Volhard and Brigitte (Haas) Volhard. Diploma in Biochemistry, U. Tübingen, 1968, PhD, 1973; ScD (hon.), Yale U. Rsch. assoc. lab. of Dr. Schaller Max-Planck Inst. for Devel. Biology, Tübingen, 1972-74; postdoctoral fellow lab. of Dr. W. Gehring, Biozentrum, Basel, Switzerland, 1975-76; postdoctoral fellow lab of Dr. K. Sander U. Freiburg, 1977; head rsch. group European Molecular Biology Lab., Heidelberg, 1978-80; rsch. group leader Friedrich-Miescher Lab. Max-Planck-Gesellschaft, Tübingen, 1981-85; sci. mem. Max-Planck Assn., dir. Max-Planck Inst. for Devel. Biology, Tübingen, 1985-90, dir. genetics dept., 1990—. Hon. prof. U. Tübingen. Contbr. numerous articles to profl. jours. Recipient Albert Lasker Basic Med. Rsch. award Albert and Mary Lasker Found., 1991, Louisa Gross Horowitz prize Columbia U., 1992, Forderpreis award Deutschen Forschungsgemeinschaft, 1986, Franz Vogt prize U. Giessen, 1986, Carus medal German Acad. Leopoldine, 1989, Rosenstiel medal Brandeis U., Nobel prize in physiology or medicine, 1995; Schering prize, Berlin, 1993. Mem. European Molecular Biology Orgn., Berlin Brandenburgische Acad., Am. Philosophical Soc. Achievements include rsch. in using embryos, created a series of genetic screens that led to the identification of most of the genes responsible for the organism's body segment development, establishing that genes encode signaling molecules that tell cells where they are in the organism's overall structure and what their function is to be. Office: Max-Planck-Institut fur Entwicklungsbiologie Abt III Genetik D-72076 Tübingen Germany*

NUSYNOWITZ, MARTIN LAWRENCE, nuclear medicine physician; b. N.Y.C., July 21, 1933; s. Morris and Esther Clara (Pober) Nusynowitz; m. Harriet Rubinstein, Aug. 28, 1955; children: Murray Mark, Russell Neil, Leah Rachel. Student, Fordham U. Coll. Pharmacy, 1951—53; BA, NYU, 1954; MD cum laude, SUNY, Syracuse, 1958. Diplomate Nat. Bd. Med. Examiners, Am. Bd. Internal Medicine with subspeciality in endocrinology and metabolism, Am. Bd. Nuclear Medicine. Intern Letterman Army Med. Ctr., San Francisco, 1958—59; resident in internal medicine Tripler Army Med. Ctr., Honolulu, 1959—62; commd. 2d lt. U.S. Army, advanced through grades to col., 1977, various med. assignments, 1962—65; chief med. R&D, nuclear medicine, endocrine svcs. William Beaumont Army Med. Ctr., El Paso, Tex., 1965—77; ret., 1977; assoc. clin. prof. radiology George Washington U., Washington, 1974; clin. prof. medicine Tex. Tech. U., Lubbock, 1974; chief nuclear medicine Bexar County Hosp., San Antonio, 1977—82; prof., head nuclear medicine U. Tex. Health Sci. Ctr., San Antonio, 1977—82, U. Tex. Med. Br., Galveston, 1982—92; clin. nuclear medicine Surgeon Gen., U.S. Army, Washington, 1972—77, Audie Murphy Meml. VA Hosp., San Antonio, 1977—82. Cons. in endocrinology and nuclear medicine Brooke Army Med. Ctr., San Antonio, 1978—. Contbr. articles to profl. jours., chpts. to textbooks. Bd. dirs. El Paso Diabetes Assn., 1970—72; bd. dirs., mem. steering com. Gulf Coast Coun. on Fgn. Affairs, Galveston, 1982—. Decorated Legion of Merit; recipient Bos of Yr. award, Am. Bus. Women's Assn., 1975. Fellow: Am. Coll. Endocrinology, Am. Coll. Nuclear Physicians (pres.-elect 1996, pres. 1997), ACP; mem.: Southwestern Clin. Ligand Assay Soc. (pres. 1984—85, 1991—93), Am. Bd. Nuclear Med. (life), Endocrine Soc., Soc. Nuclear Medicine (sec.-treas. 1996—98). Jewish. Avocations: dance, sailing. Home: 15726 Brook Forest Dr Houston TX 77059-6402 Office: U Tex Med Br Sect Nuclear Medicine Galveston TX 77555-0793 Office Phone: 409-772-8016.

NUTBROWN, EDWIN EMANUEL, safety engineer, writer; b. Canonsburg, Pa., May 4, 1949; s. Samuel Edward and Anna Catherine Nutbrown; m. Nancy Lynn Hoellerman, Apr. 15, 1972; children: Lora Lynn, Stephen Michael, Jason Peter. BS in Bus. Mgmt., Pa. State U., Univ. Pk., Pa., 1971. Gen. supr. Container Recovery Corp., Marion, Ohio, 1980—85; maintenance mgr. Grossman Industries, Columbus, Ohio, 1985—87; maintenance supr. Glen Gery Brick, Iberia, Ohio, 1988—91; project mgr. Marion Christian Ctr., Marion, Ohio, 1991—92, Christian Internat., Santa Rosa Beach, Fla., 1992—94; mgr. engring. and safety Sika Corp., Marion, Ohio, 1994—. Chairperson Marion County Emergency Planning Com., Marion, Ohio, 1997—2003. Author: Our Time To Speak, The World-Wide Taxation Elimination Handbook, (autobiography) Edwin E. Nutbrown. Conservative. Christian. Achievements include discovery of documented the global process by which tax-based public financing and interest-based economic systems will be eliminated. Home: 1260 Lawrence Rd Caledonia OH 43314 Office: Sika Corp 1682 Marion-Williamsport Rd Marion OH 43302 Personal E-mail: eenutbrown1@aol.com. Business E-Mail: nutbrown.edwin@sika-corp.com.

NUTE, LESLIE F. lawyer; BA, Bates Coll., 1963; JD, U. Chgo., 1966. Bar: Ind. 1966, Mich. 1973, Pa. 1998. Sr. v.p., gen. counsel, sec. Bayer Corp., Pitts., 1991—. Office: Bayer Corp 100 Bayer Rd Pittsburgh PA 15205-9741

NUTT, ROBERT L. lawyer, educator; b. New Castle, Pa., Mar. 30, 1945; s. James Earl and Dorothy Nutt; children: David, Jonathan. BA, Grove City Coll., 1967; JD, U. Pa., 1970. Bar: N.Y., Mass. Law clerk U.S. Ct. Appeals (2d cir.), N.Y.C., 1970-71; assoc. Ropes & Gray, Boston, 1971-79, ptnr., 1979—. Lectr. in law Boston U., 1989-98. Contbr. articles to profl. jours. Trustee Shore County Day Sch., Beverly, Mass., 1986-2001; moderator First Ch. of Christ, Marblehead, Mass., 1993-2000; trustee Grove City Coll., 1998—. Mem. ABA (bus. law sect. com. on corp. laws), Boston Bar Assn. (bus. law sect. chair 1990-93). Congregationalist. Avocations: skiing, golf, upland bird hunting. Office: Ropes & Gray LLP One International Pl Boston MA 02110-2624 Office Phone: 617-951-7384. Business E-Mail: rnutt@rupesgrog.com.

NUTT, TAMI LEE, academic administrator; d. Ronald and Charlotte Tanner; m. C. Scott Nutt. BA, Howard Payne U., 1995—99; MA, Baylor U., 1999—2001. Program coord. Bill of Rights Inst., Arlington, Va., 2001—03; asst. dir., Baylor interdisciplinary core Baylor U., 2003—. Writer (curriculum guide) Citizenship & Character; editor: (curriculum guide) Bill of Rights and You, 2nd Edit. Women's ministry mem.

NUTTALL, RICHARD NORRIS, management consultant, physician; b. Hamilton, Ont., Can., Feb. 7, 1940; s. James William and Margaret Gay (Walsh) N.; m. Ethel Jane Pickering, July 9, 1977; children: Andrew Richard, John Patrick. BSA, U. Toronto, 1961; MPA, Harvard U., 1964; MB, BS, U. London, 1974; MPH, TM, James Cook U., 2003. Cert. Coll. Family Physicians Can.; mgmt. cons. Zone dir. Health and Welfare Can., Prince Rupert, 1977-79, regional dir. Edmonton, 1980-82; pres. Rutland Consulting Group, Ltd., Vancouver, Canada, 1982-87, Richmond Assocs. Internat., Vancouver,

1988-90; med. health officer Govt. N.W. Ters., Yellowknife, Canada, 1990-93, Regina (Can.) Health Dist., 1993-97; pres. Anjohn Med. Svcs., Inc., Victoria, Canada, 1997—. Staff physician Royal Jubilee Hosp., Victoria Gen. Hosp. Fellow Am. Coll. Preventive Medicine, Am. Coll. Healthcare Execs., Can. Coll. Health Svc. Execs.; mem. Can. Pub. Health Assn. (bd. dirs. 1991-93). Office: 1494 Fairfield Rd Victoria BC Canada V8S 1E8 Office Phone: 250-598-5158.

NUTTELMAN, DORIS GRAVES, nursing administrator; b. Mass., Apr. 20, 1930; Student, Lynn (Mass.) Hosp., 1951; MS, U. Mass., 1975, MA in Teaching, 1973; EdD, Vanderbilt U., 1989. RN, Mass., N.H. Dir. nursing div. Am. Internat. Coll., Springfield, Mass., 1975-77; chair dept. nursing Colby-Sawyer Coll., New London, N.H., 1980-84; exec. dir. N.H. Bd. of Nursing, Concord, 1990—. Mem. ANA, APHA, Nat. League of Nursing, Sigma Theta Tau.

NUTTER, DAVID GEORGE, urban planner; b. Manchester, Conn., Nov. 25, 1939; s. George Huitt and Catherine Lavina (Casey) N.; m. Ellen Marie Manfredonia, Sept. 7, 1968; children: Susan Katherine, Anne Amelia. BA in English cum laude, Tufts U., 1961; MS in Urban Planning, Columbia U., 1967. City planner Balt. City Planning Commn., 1967-69; dir. planning Charles Ctr.- Inner Harbor Mgmt., Inc., 1969-72, v.p., 1972-76; pvt. cons., 1976-83; dir. downtown mall mgmt. dist. Denver Partnership, Inc., 1983-85; exec. dir. Rochester Downtown Devel. Corp., NY, 1985-87; prin. Nutter Assocs., 1987-2000; dir. Salisbury-Wicomico Planning and Zoning Commn., Md., 2000—02; prin. Nutter Assocs., 2002—. Author: Selecting a Developer, 1983, The 2003 Greater Vienna Comprehensive Plan, 2003, The 2004 Greater Laurel Comprehensive Plan, 2004. Bd. dirs. Soc. Preservation of Fed. Hill, Balt., 1969-73, Arts for Greater Rochester, 1986-90, Nabb Rsch. Ctr. Delmarva History and Culture, Salisbury (Md.) U., 1998-2003, Lower Eastern Shore Heritage Com., 2000-2002; chmn. Town of Brighton (N.Y.) Conservation Bd., 1992-95. Sgt. U.S. Army, 1962-65. William F. Kinne fellow for travel in Europe, Columbia U., 1967. Mem. Am. Inst. Cert. Planners, Am. Planning Assn., Urban Land Inst. (assoc.), Canal Soc. of N.Y. State. Avocations: historical map and atlas collecting, American and English history, computer mapping, hiking, history of settlement and urbanism. Home: 507C South Blvd Salisbury MD 21801 E-mail: dnutter@aol.com.

NUTTER, FRANKLIN WINSTON, lawyer; b. Charleston, W Va, Apr. 17, 1946; s. Frank Hamilton and Marie Agnes (Pyles) N.; m. Linda Jean Davis, Sept. 2, 1972; children: Alycia Marie, Aaron Davis. BBA in Econs., U. Cin., 1968; JD, Georgetown U., 1974. Bar: DC, Va., US Dist. Ct. (no. dist.) Va., US Ct. Appeals (9th and DC cir.), US Supreme Ct. 1993. Gen. counsel Nat. Flood Ins. Assn., Washington, 1975-78, Reins. Assn. Am., Washington, 1978-81, pres., 1981-84, 91—, Alliance Am. Insurers, Schaumburg, Ill., 1984-91, Property Loss Rsch. Bur., Schaumburg, Ill., 1984-91. Bd. overseers Inst. Civil Justice subs. Rand Corp., 1984-91; chair Natural Disaster Coalition. Bd. dir. Advs. for Hwy. and Auto Safety, 1989-91; trustee Nat. Commn. Against Drunk Driving. Lt. (j.g.) USN, 1968-72. Mem. ABA (torts and injury practice sect., past chmn. internat. ins. law, excess and surplus lines and reins. com., coun. tort and ins. practice sect.), Va. Bar Assn., Ins. Inst. Hwy. Safety (bd. dir. 1984-91), Workers' Compensation Rsch. Inst., Industry Sector Adv. Coun. on Svc., Adv. Bd. Ctr. for Health and Global Environ., Harvard Med. Sch., 2002-; Bd. Bermuda Bio Ctr. for Rsch., 2000-; Bd Internat. Hurricane Ctr., 2000-. Home: 8458 Portland Pl Mc Lean VA 22102-1708 Office: 1301 Pennsylvania Ave NW Washington DC 20004-1701

NUTTER, WALLACE LEE, paper manufacturing executive; b. 1944; BA, U. Washington, 1967; grad. advanced mgmt. program, Harvard U., 1987. Ops. asst. N.W. timber div. ITT Rayonier Inc., Stamford, Conn., 1967-69, contract logging foreman, 1969-70, contract logging supt., 1970-71, mgr. log sales and purchases, 1971-78, mgr. wood resources sales and procurement, 1978-80, regional dir. forest and wood products N.W. regional ops., 1980-82, dir. timber and wood products N.W., 1982-84, dir. forest products ops., 1984-85, v.p. forest and wood products ops., from 1985, v.p. pulp mfg.; exec. v.p. Rayonier (no longer divsn. of ITT), Stamford, Conn., 1987-96, pres., COO, 1996—. Office: Rayonier 50 N Laura St Ste 1900 Jacksonville FL 32202-3638

NUTTER, ZOE DELL LANTIS, retired public relations executive; b. Yamhill, Oreg., June 14, 1915; d. Arthur Lee Lantis and Olive Adelaide (Reed) Lantis-Hilton; m. Richard S. West, Apr. 30, 1941 (div. Nov. 1964); m. Ervin John Nutter, Dec. 30, 1965. Assoc. in Bus., Santa Ana Jr. Coll., 1944. Cert. spl. emergency secondary tchr., Calif.; FAA cert. lic. commercial, instrument, single/multi engine land airplanes pilot. Promoter World's Fair & Comml. Airlines Golden Gate Internat. Expn., San Francisco, 1937-39; pirate theme girl, official hostess Treasure Island's World Fair, San Francisco, 1939-40; prin. dancer San Francisco Ballet, 1937-41; artist, 1941-45; program dir. Glenn County H.S., Willows, Calif., 1952-58; pub. rels. Monarch Piper Aviation Co., Monterey, Calif., 1963-65; pilot, pub. rels. Elano Corp., Xenia, Ohio, 1968-85. Bd. dirs. Nat. Aviation Hall of Fame, Dayton, Ohio, pres., chmn., 1989-92, bd. trustees, 1976—, chmn. bd. nominations, 1992—; bd. trustees Ford's Theatre, Washington, Treasure Island Mus., San Francisco; charter mem. Friends of First Ladies, Smithsonian, Washington, 1990-93. Assoc. editor KYH mag. of Shikar Safari Internat., 1985-87; contbg. columnist Scripps Howard San Francisco News, 1938. Bd. dirs. Cin. May Festival, 1976-80, San Francisco Aero. Soc., 1997-; cen. com. Glenn County Rep. Party, Willows, 1960-64; state cen. com. Rep. Party, 1962-64; adv. bd. Women's Air & Space Mus., Dayton, 1987-94. Warrant officer, Civil Air Patrol, 1967-69. Recipient Civic Contbn. Honor award Big Brothers/Big Sisters, 1991, John Collier Nat. award Camp Fire Girls & Boys, 1988, Tambourine award Salvation Army, 1982, State of Ohio Gov.'s award for Volunteerism, 1992, Spirit of Innovation award Wright State U., 2001, Amb. award Wright Bros. Heritage Benefit, 2001, East Ann. Zoe Dell Nutter Dayton Air Show award, 2003, In grateful appreciation of contbn. 1909 Wright Flyer Monument award INVENTING FLIGHT, 2003; named Most Photographed Girl in World, News Burs. & Clipping Svcs., 1938-39. Mem., founder Dancers Over 40, NYC; Fellow Pres.'s Club U. Ky., Ohio State U., Wright State U.; mem. 99's Internat. Women Pilots Orgn. (life, hospitality chmn. 1968), San Francisco Aeronaut. Soc. (bd. dirs. 1997—), Monterey Bay Chapter 99's (mem. chmn. 1964-65), Walnut Grove Country Club, Rotary (Paul Harris fellow 1987), Shikar Safari Internat. (host com. 1976), Country Club of the North. Achievements include established ann. Zoe Dell Nutter Dayton Air Show award, 2003. Avocations: aviation, flying, horseback riding, hunting, shooting, fashion. Home: 986 Trebein Rd Xenia OH 45385-9534

NUTTING, MAUREEN MURPHY, historian, educator; b. N.Y.C. d. Patrick Joseph and Marie (Clarke) Murphy; m. Theodore Michael Nutting, May 3 1975; children: Teresa, Andrew, Stephen, Eileen. BA in History, Fordham U., Bronx, N.Y., 1968; MA in Am. Studies, U. Notre Dame, Ind., 1969, PhD in History, 1975. Asst. prof. history Humboldt State U., Arcata, Calif., 1972-75, Chaminade U., Honolulu, 1975-77; asst. dir. minorities & women's scholarly & profl. interests Am. Hist. Assn., Washington, 1979-81; asst. prof. history U. Miami, Coral Gables, Fla., 1987-90, Seattle U., 1990-91; instr. history Seattle Ctrl. C.C., 1992-96; prof. history, chair North Seattle C.C., 1996—. Vol. Seattle Pub. Sch. Dist., 1982—86, 1990—98; chair local draft bd. U.S. Selective Svc., Seattle, 1998—, mem. local draft bd., 1992—; vol. homeless ministry St. James Cathedral, Seattle, 1994—. Recipient rsch. travel grants Asian Studies Devel. Program, East-West Ctr., China, 1996, India, 1995, Summer Inst. grants NEH, Hawaii, 1994, Brazil, 1998, Guatemala, Honduras and Mex., 2002, trustees' lifetime learning award Seattle C.C. Dist., 1999; selected rsch. seminar Libr. of Congress, Am. Hist. Assn., C.C. Humanities Assn., Washington, 1999. Mem.: Cmty. Coll. Humanities Assn., Coordinating Coun. for Women's History, Western Assn. Women Historians, Immigration and Ethnic History Soc. (program com. 1999—2002), C.C. Humanities Assn. (chair nat. conf. program 2001), Orgn. Am. Historians, Am. Hist. Assn. (mem. coun. 2001—04, mem. task force on pub. history 2001—, bd. dirs. nat. history ctr. 2004—, chair annual meetins local arrangements com. 2005). Roman Catholic. Office: North Seattle CC 9600 College Way N Seattle WA 98103-3514 Office Phone: 206-526-7010. Business E-Mail: mnutting@sccd.ctc.edu.

NUTTING, PAUL ALBERT, medical educator, medical science administrator; b. Aug. 24, 1944; m. Kaia M. Gallagher; children: Paul James, Kaia Elise. AB in Psychology, Cornell U., 1966; MD, U. Kans., 1970; MSPH, U. Colo., 1988. Diplomate Am. Bd. Family Practice, Am. Bd. Preventive Medicine. Intern in pediat. U. Pitts., 1970—71; resident in preventive medicine U. Ariz., 1973—75; clin. dir. Santa Rosa (Ariz.) Clinic Indian Health Svc., 1971—72, maternal and child health officer Sells (Ariz.) Svc. Unit, 1972—73, med. rsch. office Office of R&D, 1973-77, assoc. dir. rsch. Office of R&D, 1977-83; sr. scholar-in-residence Inst. Medicine-NAS, Washington, 1983-84; dir. Office of Primary Care Studies Health Resources and Svc U.S. Dept. Health and Human Svcs., Rockville, Md., 1984-86; resident in family medicine Mercy Med. Ctr., Denver, 1986-88; dir. rsch. Indian Health Svc., Tucson, 1989-90; dir. divsn. primary care and dep. dir. Ctr. for Gen. Health Svcs. Rsch., DHHS, Rockville, Md., 1990—93; dir. Ambulatory Sentinel Practice Network, Denver, 1993—; prof. family medicine dept. family medicine U. Colo. Health Scis. Ctr., 1993—; dir. rsch. Ctr. for Rsch. Strategy, Denver, 1999—. Rsch. assoc. prof. dept. family and cmty. medicine U. Ariz., 1981—87, 1988—89; clin. assoc. prof. dept. cmty. and family medicine Georgetown U. Sch. Medicine, 1983—86; mem. subcom. on cardiovascular disease Sec.'s Task Force on Black and Minority Health, 1984—85; mem. interagy. com. on infant mortality USPHS, 1990—93, chair rsch. sub-com., clin. preventive svcs. steering com., 1991—93, nat. steering com. primary care-substance abuse linkage initiative, 1991—93; chairperson Workshop on Early Detection of Prostate Cancer Nat. Cancer Inst., Bethesda, 1993; cons. in field. Author (with L.A. Green): From Research to Policy to Practice: Closing the Loop in Clinical Policy Development in Primary Care, 1994; editor: Community-Oriented Primary Care: From Principle to Practice, 1987; co editor: Primary Care Research: Theory and Methods, 1991. Capt. USPHS, 1982. Recipient Cert. appreciation, Nat. Indian Health Bd., 1982, Modern Medicine award for disting. achievement, 1993. Mem.: APHA (sect. in med. care, epidemiology, internat. health), Soc. Tchrs. Family Medicine, Soc. for Epidemiologic Rsch., N.Am. Primary Care Rsch. Group (bd. dirs. 1994—, chair com. on bldg. capacity for rsch. in family practice 1994—), Am. Acad. Pediat. (mem. steering com. pediat. rsch. in office settings 1993—), Am. Acad. Family Physicians (liaison mem. com. on rsch. 1993—), Inst. Medicine-NAS. Office: Ctr Rsch Strategy 225 E 16th Ave Ste 1150 Denver CO 80203-1694

NUTTING, PAUL JOHN, city manager; b. Oswego, N.Y., July 6, 1952; s. Robert Truman and Joan Violet (Joyce) N. BA, SUNY, Oswego, 1974; MPA, SUNY, Albany, 1977. Adminstrv. asst. City of League City, Tex., 1978-79, acting city adminstr., 1979-80, 81, asst. city adminstr., 1980-81, exec. asst. to mayor, 1981-82, city adminstr., 1982-95; city mgr. City of Springfield, Tenn., 1995—. Bd. dirs. Tenn. Energy Acquisition Corp., Five Rivers Resource Conservation and Devel. Coun. Bd. dirs. League City Family Welfare Coun., 1978-89; chmn. United Way, Robertson County, 2003; mem. exec. bd. Mainland Communities United Way, Texas City, Tex., 1991-94; adv. dir. League City Mchts. and Bus. Assn., 1989-95, North Galveston County C. of C., Dickinson, Tex., 1989-95. Mem. Internat. City and County Mgmt. Assn., Tenn. City Mgmt. Assn., Texas City Mgmt. Assn., Am. Soc. for Pub. Adminstrn. (pres. Houston area chpt. 1991-93, dir. 1990-91, 93-95), Springfield-Robertson County C. of C., League City Rotary Club (pres. 1985-86, 93-94), Rotary. Roman Catholic. Avocations: golf, history. Home: 333 Walnut St Springfield TN 37172-2125 Office: City of Springfield 405 N Main St Springfield TN 37172-2408

NUTTING, WALLACE HALL, army officer; b. Newton, Mass., June 3, 1928; s. Gerry B. and Ethel M. (Hall) N.; m. Jane Anne Walker, June 17, 1950; children: Elizabeth J., John T., Katherine A., Sally W. BS, U.S. Mil. Acad., 1950; MA in Internat. Affairs, George Washington U., 1963; postgrad., Naval War Coll., 1963, Nat. War Coll., 1968; D of Mil. Arts & Scis. (hon.), Norwich U., 1984. Commd. cavalry officer/platoon ldr. U.S. Army 2nd Infantry Divsn., Republic of Korea, 1950-52; advanced through grades to gen. U.S. Army; comdr. 1st Squadron 10th Cavalry, Vietnam, 1966-67; asst. dir. plans Dept. Army, Washington, 1968-70, dep. dir. plans, 1973-74; comdr. 11th Armored Cavalry Regiment, Vietnam, 1970-71; dep. comdr. ops. 1st brigade 5th Inf. Div., Vietnam, 1971; Army mem. chmn.'s staff group Orgn. Joint Chiefs of Staff, Washington, 1971-73; comdg. gen. 1st Inf. div. forward, Fed. Republic Germany, 1974-75; dir. strategy plans and policy Dept. Army, 1975-77; comdg. gen. 3d Armored div., Fed. Republic Germany, 1977-79; comdr. in chief U.S. So. Command, Quarry Heights, Panama, 1979-83; comdr.-in chief U.S. Readiness Command, dir. Joint Deployment Agy., MacDill AFB, Fla., 1983-85; assoc. fellow Ctr. for Internat. Affairs, Harvard U., 1986; sr. fellow Inst. Higher Def. Studies, Nat. Def. U., Washington, 1986-96. Mem. exec. bd. Trans-Atlantic coun. Boy Scouts Am., 1977-79, Panama Canal coun., 1979-83; mem. Gulf Ridge coun. Boy Scouts Am., 1983-85, dist. chmn. Pine Tree coun., 2002; bd. dirs. No. York County YMCA, 1992, Maine Cancer Found., 1996-2004; chair Osher Lifelong Learning Inst., 1996-2004; mayor City of Biddeford, Maine, 2003. Decorated Defense D.S.M. with oak leaf cluster, Silver Star, Legion of Merit with 2 oak leaf clusters, Soldier's medal, Bronze Star with oak leaf cluster, Air medal (7), Purple Heart with oak leaf cluster, Army Commendation medal with oak leaf cluster, Presdl. Unit citation, Korean Svc. medal with 5 stars, Vietnam Svc. medal with 4 stars, U.N. Svc. medal, JCS Identification badge, Gen. staff Identification badge, Vietnamese Cross of Gallantry with palm and silver star, Brazilian Order Mil. Merit, Order Mil. Merit Dominican Republic, Cross of Venezuelan Armed Forces, Mil. Star Armed Forces Chile, Cross Armed Force Republic of Honduras, Order Mil. Merit in grade grand officer (Argentina), Order Mil. Merit (Panama); recipient Silver Beaver award, 1985, Living Legacy award So. Maine Agy. on Aging, 2000, Lyman L. Lemnitzer award Assn. U.S. Army, 1996. Mem. U.S. Armor Assn., Coun. on Fgn. Rels. Congregationalist. Home: PO Box 96 Biddeford Pool ME 04006-0096 Office: Dept of Army Gen Officer Mgmt Ofc Washington DC 20310-0001

NUVEMAN, STACEY, Olympic athlete; b. Apr. 26, 1978; BA in Sociology, UCLA. Commentator Women's Coll. World Series, ESPN, 2003; mem. U.S. Women's Softball Team, Sydney Olympic Games, 2000, U.S. Women's Softball Team, Athens Olympic Games, 2004. Named NFCA/ Diamond Sports Div. I Catcher of the Yr., 2001, USA Softball Collegiate Player of the Yr., 2002, USA Softball Player of the Yr., 2002, Pac-10 Newcomer of the Yr., 1997, NFCA First-team All Am., 1997, 1999, 2001, 2002; named to All WCWS Tournament Team, 1997, 2002. Achievements include mem. NCAA Champion UCLA Bruins, Women's Coll. World Series, 1999; NCAA all-time career leader in home runs (90) and slugging percentage (.945); mem. Gold medal U.S. Nat. Team, ISF World Championships, 2003; second player in history named Pac-10 player of the yr. three times; mem. Gold medal U.S. Nat. Team, U.S. Cup, 2002; mem. Gold medal U.S. Nat. Team, Pan Am. Games, 1999, 2003; mem. U.S. Women's Softball Gold medal Team, Sydney Olympics, 2000. Office: USA Softball Complex 4845 S Shields Blvd Oklahoma City OK 73129*

NUWER, HENRY JOSEPH (HANK NUWER), journalist, educator; b. Buffalo, Aug. 19, 1946; s. Henry Robert and Teresa (Lysiak) N.; m. Alice May (Cerniglia), Dec. 28, 1968 (div. Mar. 1980); 1 child, Henry Christian; m. Jenine (Howard), Apr. 9, 1982 (sep. 2003); 1 child, Adam. BS English, State Univ. Coll. of N.Y., Buffalo, 1968; MA English, Highlands U., N. Mex., 1971; PhD equivalency, Ball State U., Muncie, Ind., 2002—. Freelance author, journalist, 1969—; asst. prof. Clemson U., SC, 1982—83; assoc. prof. Ball State U., Muncie, Ind., 1985—89; sr. editor Rodale Press, Emmaus, Pa., 1990—91; editor in chief Arts Ind. Mag., Indpls., 1993—95; assoc. prof. journalism U. Richmond, Va., 1995—97. Expert lectr. Hazing, 1990—; hazing cons. NBC Movie-of-the-Week, Moment of Truth: Broken Pledges, Indpls., 1994, U.S. Dept. Edn., 2002—; adj. prof. journalism Ind. U. Sch. Journalism, Indpls., 1995—; Anderson U., 1998-2002; asst. prof. journalism, Franklin (Ind.) Coll., 2002—; nat. advisor NCAA study and survey on hazing in coll. athletic groups Alfred U., 1999. Author: Steroids, 1990; Broken Pledges: The Deadly Rite of Hazing, 1990; How to Write Like an Expert, 1995; The Legend of Jesse Owens, 1998; Wrongs of Passage, 1999, revised edit., 2002; High School Hazing, 2000, At The Crest, 2003; To the Young Writer, 2002; The Hazing Reader, 2003, At the Crest, 2004; mem. editl. staff Chic Mag., 1976-77; contbg. articles to profl. jour. Grantee: Nat. Endowment for the Arts, 1976; Idaho Humanities Coun., 1985; Gannett Found., 1988; named New Mag. Adviser of Yr., Coll. Media Advisers, 1988; Disting. Alumnus, Buffalo State Coll., 1999. Mem. Soc. Profl. Journalists (3d. pl., Best Bus. Article Ind. competition 2002), Investigative Reporters and Editors, Soc. Profl. Journalism, Phi Kappa Phi, Alpha Lambda Delta. Democrat. Roman Catholic. Office: Franklin Coll Journalism Dept 501 E Monroe St Franklin IN 46131-2598 also: Ind Univ Sch Journalism 902 W New York St ES 4104 Indianapolis IN 46202 Personal E-mail: hnuwer@hanknuwer.com.

NUXOLL, CARLA, federal official; m. Jim Braukmann. Degree in polit. sci. and history, Gonzaga U. English tchr. Mead H.S., Spokane, 1972; pres. Wash. Edn. Assn., 1989-93; apptd. sec.'s regional rep. U.S. Dept. Edn. Region X, Seattle, 1994—. Avocations: avid fly fisherwoman, bridge player, reader of detective novels. Office: US Dept Edn Region X Jackson Fed Bldg 915 2nd Ave Seattle WA 98174-1009

NUZZO, ANTHONY GERALD, services executive; b. New Haven, Aug. 9, 1951; s. Michael Anthony and Theresa Mary (Aitro) N.; m. Julie Nuzzo, Mar. 22, 1975; children: Beth, Michael, Cortney. BA, Boston Coll., 1973; MBA, Columbia U., 1975. CLU, cert. in long-term care. Brand asst. Procter & Gamble, Cin., 1975-76, sales rep., 1976, asst. brand mgr., 1976-77; asst. product dir. Johnson & Johnson, New Brunswick, NJ, 1977-78, spl. project dir., 1978-79, product dir. Milltown, NJ, 1979-82, group product dir., 1982-84; v.p. Am. Express Travel Related Svcs., NYC, 1984-87; v.p., exec. com. Am. Express Can., Inc., Markham, 1987-88; v.p. internat. mktg. Am. Express, NY, 1988; v.p. Chem. Bank, NYC, 1988-90, sr. v.p., 1990-91; pres., CEO Chem. Bank Del., Wilmington, 1991-92; pres., founder Advanced Mktg. Assocs., Inc., East Brunswick, NJ, 1992-93; pres., CEO Fidelity Trust Co., Salt Lake City, 1993-98, chmn., 1998-99; pres., CEO Fidelity TempWorks/TempSource, Boston, 1998-99; chmn., pres., CEO @Bank, Framingham, Mass., 1999-2000; pres., CEO Engage, Andover, Mass., 2000—01; pres., CEO, founder The Nuzzo Group, Inc., Wellesley, Mass., 2001—; fin. adviser The Commonwealth Fin. Group, Newton, Mass., 2002—. Mem. Visa Mktg. Advisors, 1989—92, 1993—98. Editor: Physiology, 1984. Dir., co-chair, co-founder Citizens Against UnSafe Environments, East Brunswick, 1981-93; bd. dirs. Utah Bd. Fin. Instns., 1995-98. Named to PS&D Merchandising Hall of Fame Procter & Gamble, Cin., 1977, named Scholar of the Coll., Boston Coll., 1973; recipient Bus. Sch. Svc. award Columbia U., 1975, Excellence award Package Designer Coun., NYC, 1980, Clio Creative Excellence award Clio Adv. Body, NYC, 1981, Effie award, NYC, 1989. Mem. Boston Coll. Alumni Assn., Columbia Bus. Sch. Alumni Assn. (dir. NY club 1975), Utah Bankers Assn. (bd. dirs. 1996-98), Utah Assn. Fin. Svcs. (bd. dirs. 1993-98, treas. 1995-96). Avocations: golf, skiing, reading. E-mail: agnuzzo@aol.com.

NWACHUKU, LEVI AKALAZU, social sciences and behavioral studies educator; b. Okpala, Nigeria, Aug. 23, 1940; came to U.S., 1963; s. Moses Akalazu and Evangeline (Enwere-Uzo) N.; m. Ugochi Justina Nwachuku, Dec. 19, 1981; children: Uchenna, Nneka, Chimereze, Chinomso, Enyinna. BA, Lincoln U., Pa., 1967; MA, Howard U., 1969; PhD, Mich. State U., 1973. V.p. acad. Shorter Coll., Little Rock, 1977; assoc. prof. U. Mich., Flint, 1977-81, dir. Black studies, 1973-81; reader history U. Maiduguri, Nigeria, 1981-88; coord. African Am. studies Lincoln U., 1989-94, chair dept. history, 1993—, dean faculty social scis., 1994-97. Co-author: Troubled Journey: Nigeria Since the Civil War, 1994, Exploring the African-American Experience, 1995. Named Outstanding Male Faculty Mem., NAACP, 1995. Mem. Phi Alpha Theta, Alpha Phi Alpha. Home: PO Box 153 Lincoln Univ PA 19352-0153 Office: Lincoln U Lincoln University PA 19352

NWAGBARAOCHA, JOEL ONUKWUGHA, academic administrator, educator; b. Victoria, Cameroons, Nov. 21, 1942; came to U.S., 1964; naturalized, 1974; s. John O. and Christiana (Ihejeihu) N.; m. Patsy Coleman, Aug. 27, 1977; children: Jason, Jonathan, John, Eric. BS in Math., cert. in physics, Norfolk State U., 1969; EdM, Harvard U., 1970, EdD (Univ. fellow), 1972. Tchr. math. and physics Emmanuel Coll., Owerri, Nigeria, 1960-64; asst. dir. Manpower Rsch. Inst./Norfolk (Va.) State Coll., 1969-70; rsch. assoc. Harvard U. Grad. Sch. Edn., 1969-72; assoc. dir. co-op acad. planning program Inst. for Svcs. to Edn., Washington, 1972-74, dir. instnl. planning and mgmt. program, 1974-76, dir. divsn. acad. planning and faculty devel., 1976-78; assoc. prof. edn., v.p. planning and ops. analysis Morgan State U., Balt., 1978-87; v.p. acad. affairs Voorhees Coll., Denmark, S.C., 1987-80; pres. Barber-Scotia Coll., Concord, N.C., 1990-94; prof. edn., bus. adminstrn. Strayer U., Washingtn, 1994—, dir. grad. studies, 2000—. Dean Tacoma Park Campus, Strayer Coll., Washington; cons. in higher edn. planning and evaluation system devel., 1972—. Co-author: Operational Manual for ollege Planning Development, 1977, Planning Management and Evaluation System, 1979; mem. editl. bd. Spartan Echo, 1967-69; contbr. articles to profl. jours. Mem. AAAS, Am. Coun. on Edn., Nat. Coun. on Social Studies, Am. Assn. for Higher Edn., Am. Humanist Assn., Soc. for Coll. and Univ. Planning, Am. Assn. Univ. Adminstrs., Am. Mgmt. Assn., Higher Edn. Group of Washington, Smithsonian Nat. Assoc., Alpha Kappa Mu, Phi Beta Sigma, Beta Kappa Chi, Phi Delta Kappa. Home: 10928 Battersea Ln Columbia MD 21044-2701 Office: Strayer Univ Washington DC Campus 1025 15th St NW Washington DC 20005-2601

NWANGWU, JOHN TOCHUKWU, epidemiologist, public health educator; b. Ogidi, Anambra, Nigeria, Apr. 16, 1952; came to U.S., 1973; s. Sidney N. and Phoebe Nwangwu; m. Chioma Ugonwa Nwokolo, Sept. 3, 1988; children: Nmadinobi, Tobenna, Kamsiyo. MB, U. Nebr., Omaha, 1979; MPH, Loma Linda U., 1981; PhD, Columbia U., 1988; postgrad., Erasmus U., Rotterdam, The Netherlands, 1991. Cons. WHO, 1982-87; instr. Columbia U., N.Y.C., 1983-85, St. Joseph's Coll. Hosp., Bklyn., 1986-88; asst. prof. SUNY, 1988-89; chief epidemiologist Kern County Health Dept., Bakersfield, Calif., 1989-90, dir. epidemiology and data mgmt., 1990; assoc. prof. pub. health Conn. State U., New Haven, 1991-95, prof. pub. health, 1995—. Vis. prof. Calif. State U., Bakersfield, 1990, Yale U., New Haven, 1992, adj. prof. epidemiology Sch. Medicine, 1995—; epidemiologist/rsch. affiliate faculty Yale U. Sch. Medicine, 1993—; cons. Hosp. of St. Raphael, New Haven, 1995—; cons. to fgn. countries, 1982—; presenter in field; adj. prof. cmty. medicine Sch. Medicine U. Conn., 1995—; vis. prof. Harvard Sch. Pub. Health, 1998; vis. scholar Dana-Farber Cancer Inst., Harvard U., Boston; cons. in infectious disease VA Hosp., Rocky Hill, Conn., 1998. Contbr. articles to profl. publs. Erasmus U. fellow, 1991. Fellow Royal Soc. Medicine, Am. Coll. Epidemiology; mem. APHA, Internat. Epidemiol. Assn., N.Y. Acad. Scis., Assn. Tchrs. Preventive Medicine. Avocations: badminton, squash, reading. Home: 898 Greenway Rd Woodbridge CT 06525-2413 Office: Conn State U Dept Pub Health 144 Farnham Ave Dept Pub New Haven CT 06515-1202 also: Yale U Sch Medicine Dept Epidemiology and Pub Health 60 College St New Haven CT 06510-3210 E-mail: jnwangwu@hotmail.com.

NWEEIA, MARTIN THOMAS, dentist, musician, composer, anthropologist; b. New Britain, Conn., Apr. 15, 1954; s. Alexander and Nellie (Lazar) N. BA in English and Biology, Trinity Coll., Hartford, Conn., 1977; DDS, Case Western Res. U., 1984; cert., Brånemark Clinic, Göteborg, Sweden, 1989. Pvt. practice, Honolulu, 1984—95, Sharon, Conn., 1995—; clin. faculty Harvard Sch. Dental Medicine, 2002—. Dental corr. Sta. KGMB-TV, 1988—92; dental columnist Honolulu Star-Bull., 1988—95; expert witness for dental malpractice MedQuest, 1998—; attending cons. Sharon Hosp., 1995—; leader expdn. to study adult tooth morphology of living Ticuna Indians of Colombian Amazon, 1978; leader expdn. to study childhood dental diseases of Micronesia Ulithi Atoll, Yap State, 83; prin. investigator Narwhal Tooth Expdn., Baffin Island, 2000—03. Author: (pamphlet) Baby-Bottle Tooth Decay, 1989, The Whole Tooth, Answers to Questions You Always Wanted to Ask Your Dentist, 1999; editor Hawaii Dental Jour., 19990-94 (Golden Pen award 1994); contbr. articles to profl. jours. including Am. Jour. Dental Rsch., Internat. Jour. Dental Rsch., Am. Jour. Phys. Anthropology; music dir. As One Hawaii, 1992, Do It Together, Honolulu, 1993, Cool Notes, Hawaii Dept. Edn., 1994; PBS documentaries including; Light in Art, 1988, Facets, 1989 (Kona Gold, Blue Ribbon Am. Film and Video Assn.), Dark After Daylight, Taiwan, 1990, Dialog, 1994, to debut video for Waikiki Aquarium Jellyfish (Cine Golden Eagle 1994). Rsch. grantee in anthropology Explorers Club N.Y., Colombian Amazon, 1978; Joseph Silber fellow Am. Cancer Soc., 1982-83, grad. student rsch. fellow Smithsonian Instn., 1981. Fellow Amer. Col. of Dentists, Acad.

Gen. Dentistry (Editl. award of excellence 1999), Acad. Dentistry Internat. (hon.), Internat. Coll. Dentists (hon.), Pierre Fauchard Acad. (hon.), Explorers Club (nat.); mem. Hawaii Dental Assn. (trustee 1993-95), Hawaii Acad. Gen. Dentistry (pub. info. award 1990-93, pres. 1993-95, nat. award for cmty. involvement 1990, nat. award for media rels. 1992, nat. award for editorials, 1999). Republican. Mem. United Ch. of Christ. Avocations: documentary composer and arranger, anthropologist, windsurfing, skiing, tennis and squash. Home: 16 Grandview Ln Sharon CT 06069-2040 also: 358 Kupaua Pl Honolulu HI 96821-2152 Office: 6 New St Sharon CT 06069-2077 E-mail: boo@snet.net.

NWOKOYE, PATRICK IKECHUKWU, priest, researcher; b. Amawbia, Nigeria, Mar. 25, 1970; arrived in U.S., 1997; s. Anizoba and Nwakaego Nwokoye. BA, Lateran U., Rome, 1992, MA in Philosophy, 1994, PhD, 1997; MA, MDiv, Kenrick Sch. Theology, 2002. Clergy Diocese of Springfield-Cape Girardeau, Mo., 1997—. Tchr. Notre Dame H.S., Mo., 1999—2000; co-host talk show Raidue, Rome, 1995—96. Youth dir. St. Mary Cathedral, Cape Girardeau, Mo., 1999—2000. Mem.: Internat. Lateran Assn., World Phenomenology Inst., Fellowship of Cath. Scholars. Roman Catholic. Avocations: soccer, ping pong/table tennis, basketball, ballet, hockey. E-mail: pul1997@hotmail.com.

NYBERG, STANLEY ERIC, cognitive scientist; b. Boston, Jan. 30, 1948; s. Leroy Milton and Anna Maria (Olson) N. PhD, SUNY, Stony Brook, 1975; MBA, Yale U., 1984. Postdoctoral fellow U. Calif., Berkeley, 1975-76; asst. prof. North Park Coll., Chgo., 1976-79, Barnard Coll., Columbia U., N.Y.C., 1979-82; sys. mgmt. Interactive Data Corp., Lexington, Mass., 1984-88, Dept. of Revenue, Commonwealth of Mass., Boston, 1988-2000; with Dept. of Environ. Protection, Commonwealth of Mass., 2000—01; registrar vital records and stats. Commonwealth of Mass., 2001—. Co-author: Human Memory: An Introduction to Research and Theory, 1982. Bd. dirs. Childrens Home of Cromwell, Conn., 1988-94, Decade Fund, Yale U. Sch. Mgmt., 1984-85; ch. coun. Luth. Ch. of Redeemer, Woburn, Mass., 1991-97, West Roxbury Rugby Football Club, 1984-87; v.p., sec. L Street Running Club, South Boston, 1987—; mem. divsn. ecumenism New Eng. Synod, Evang. Luth. Ch. in Am., 1997—2002; bd. dirs. Scandinavian Charitable Soc. Greater Boston, 2000—. Fellow Am. Psychol. Soc.; mem. Soc. for Applied Rsch. in Memory and Cognition, Eastern Psychol. Assn., Midwestern Psychol. Assn., Am. Psychol. Assn. E-mail: snyberg@aol.com.

NYBORG, KENNETH WAYNE, retired social sciences educator, small business owner; b. Mountain Lake, Minn., May 27, 1939; s. Lester C. and Clara E. Nyborg; m. Carol E. Nyborg; children: Glen, David, Solveig Kruse. BA, St. Olaf Coll., 1961; MSEd, Winona State U., 1970. Cert. life gen. secondary tchr. Calif. Tchr. Barstow (Calif.) Unified Sch. Dist., 1964—2002; bus. co-owner Nyborg's Music, Barstow, 1979—91. Dist. tech. lead Barstow Unified Sch. Dist., 1992—96; tech. lead Barstow H.S., 1994—98, dept. chair social studies, 1997—2001, co-chair WASC accreditation com., 1999—2001. Mem. Barstow C. of C., 1979—91. Named Small Bus. of Yr., Barstow C. of C., 1988, Tchr. of Yr., Barstow H.S., 2001. Mem.: Calif. Ret. Tchrs. Assn. (newsletter co-editor 2001—02). Lutheran. Avocations: reading, travel, golf, church choir, computers. Home: 921 Windy Pass Barstow CA 92311 Personal E-mail: knyb@hotmail.com.

NYBORG, WESLEY LEMARS, physics educator; b. Ruthven, Iowa, May 15, 1917; s. Isaac and Eva (Larson) N.; m. Beth Woolsey, Sept. 8, 1945; 1 dau., Elsa Beth. BA, Luther Coll., 1941; MS, Pa. State U., 1944, PhD, 1947. Asst. prof. physics Pa. State U., Univ. Park, 1948-50; asst. prof. Brown U., Providence, 1950-54, asso. prof., 1954-60; prof. U. Vt., Burlington, 1960-86, acting chmn. physics dept., 1978-79, prof. emeritus, 1986—. Vis. scientist Oxford (Eng.) U., 1960-61, Univ. Coll., Cardiff, Wales, 1969, U. of Rochester, 1987; Exec. council Am. Inst. Ultrasound in Medicine, 1972-74, 76-78, chmn. bioeffects com., 1976-78; adv. bd. Bur. Radiol. Health, 1972-75; cons. FDA, 1976—; chmn. sci. com. 66 Nat. Council Radiation Protection and Measurements, 1980—; mem. working group on biol. effects ultrasound, WHO, 1982, 85, 88; mem. study sect. diagnostic radiology NIH, 1982-85; adv. mem. Rochester Ctr. for Biomed. Ultrasound, 1986; Lauriston S. Taylor lectr. Nat. Coun. Radiation Protection and Measurements, Bethesda, Md., 2001. Author: Intermediate Biophysical Mechanics, 1975; co-editor: Biological Effects of Ultrasound, 1985; Editorial bd.: Ultrasound in Medicine and Biology, Clinics in Diagnostic Ultrasound; internat. adv. editor: Ultrasonics; co-editor Proc. Symposium on Safety and Standardization in Med. Ultrasound, 2d World Fedn. Ultrasound in Medicine and Biology, 1989; contbr. to profl. jours. Recipient Presdl. recognition award Am. Inst. Ultrasound in Medicine, 1977, Univ. scholar award in phys. scis. U. Vt., 1984, Disting. Svc. award Luther Coll., 1996, Vt. Acad. Sci. and Engring., 1997, Lauriston S. Taylor Lectr. award 2001; USPHS fellow MIT, 1956-57; research grantee NIH, 1955—. Fellow AAAS, Acoustical Soc. Am. (exec. coun. 1965-68, Silver medal 1990), Am. Inst. Ultrasound in Medicine (Joseph H. Holmes award 1985, W.J. Fry Lecture award 1990), Ultrasonic Soc. India (hon.); mem. Nat. Acad. Engrs., Am. Phys. Soc., Biophys. Soc., Am. Assn. Physics Tchrs., Sigma Xi, Sigma Pi Sigma. Home: 2 Stirling Pl Burlington VT 05401-2634 E-mail: wnyborg@zoo.uvm.edu.

NYCE, JOHN DANIEL, lawyer; b. York, Pa., Sept. 7, 1947; s. Harry Lincoln and Dorothy (Wagner) Nyce; m. Deborah Dvorak; children: Joshua David, Laura Kimberly. BA, SUNY, Buffalo, 1970; JD, U. Miami, 1973. Bar: Fla. 1973, U.S. District Ct. (so. dist.) Fla. 1973, U.S. Dist. Ct. (middle dist.), Fla. 1973, U.S. Ct. Appeals (5th and 11th cirs.) 1986, U.S. Supreme Ct. 1984. Assoc. Ralph P. Douglas, Pompano Beach, Fla., 1974, Coleman, Leonard & Morrison, Ft. Lauderdale, Fla., 1975-78; ptnr. Nyce and Smith, Ft. Lauderdale, 1979; sole practice Ft. Lauderdale, 1980—. Adj. prof. bus. law, inernat. bus. law and orgn. Lynn U., Boca Raton, Fla., 2001—. *Mr. Nyce, a highly rated business law adjunct college professor, represents major churches/ministries and served in state/national leadership of Operation Rescue, being instrumental in criminal defense of numerous rescuers. He specializes in Estate Planning/Probate, Real Property, Family Law/Divorce, Adoptions (exceeding 600), Corporate Law, Trial Law, and Bankruptcy. Serving on the Florida Adoption Advisory Counsel, he authored the putative father registration codified in F.S. 63.054. In 1985, he secured Florida's first Christian adoption license, serving as the main catalyst in opening the floodgate of adoption license in Florida. His appellate victory, Johnson vs. Johnson 455 So. 2nd 1332, helped define Florida's Shared Parental Responsibilities.* Author: Proof of God's Existence in the Seven C's and Christian Handbook of Lists, 2003. Mem. Social Register Ft. Lauderdale; mem. Broward County Right to Life, Operation Rescue, South Fla., Beach Street Aid to the Homeless of Ft. Lauderdale, Legis. Adv. Coun. on Adoptions, Nat. Right to Life Com., Inc.; founder, past pres., bd. dirs. Broward County Christian Lawyers Assn.; mem. Christian Legal Soc.; mem. exec. com. Broward County Rep. Party; Broward Citizens bd. U. Miami; mem. Conservative Caucus of Broward County; bd. dirs. Shepherd Care Ministries, Inc.; co-founder Christian Adoption Svcs. of Shepherd Care Ministries, Inc.; cert. trainer Evangelism Explosion III Internat., Inc.; legal counsel and evangelism trainer Coral Ridge Presbybn. Ch., Christ the Rock Cmty. Ch., First Bapt. Ch., West Hollywood, Fla., Calvary Chapel of Ft. Lauderdale Ch.; bd. dirs. Alliance for Responsible Growth, Inc. Mem.: Nat. Acad. Elder Law Attys., Attys. Title Ins. Fund, S.D. Rifle and Hunting Assn., U. Miami Alumni Assn., SUNY Buffalo Alumni Assn., Holiday Park Tennis Ctr., U.S. Tennis Assn., U. Miami Hurricane Club, Sports Fitness Clin., Palm Aire Golf and Country Club. Republican. Presbyterian. Office: PO Box 11071 Fort Lauderdale FL 33339-1071 Office Phone: 954-567-3305. E-mail: miamijd73@aol.com.

NYCKLEMOE, GLENN WINSTON, bishop; b. Fergus Falls, Minn., Dec. 8, 1936; s. Melvin and Bertha (Sumstad) N.; m. Ann Elizabeth Olson, May 28, 1960; children: Peter Glenn, John Winston, Daniel Thomas. BA, St. Olaf Coll., 1958; MDiv, Luther Theol. Sem., St. Paul, 1962; D of Ministry, Luth. Sch. Theology, Chgo., 1977. Ordained to ministry Am. Luth. Ch., 1962. Assoc. pastor Our Savior's Luth. Ch., Valley City, N.D., 1962-64, Milw., 1964-67, co-pastor, 1967-73, sr. pastor Beloit, Wis., 1973-82, St. Olaf Luth. Ch., Austin, Minn., 1982-88; bishop Southeastern Minn. Synod, Evang. Luth. Ch. in Am., Rochester, 1988—2001. Bd. dirs. Luth. Social Svcs. of Minn., Mpls., Bd. of Social Ministries, St. Paul, Minn. Coun. Chs., Mpls. Mem. bd. regents St. Olaf Coll., Northfield, Minn., 1988—. Lutheran. Avocations: skiing, trap shooting, golf.

NYCUM, SUSAN HUBBELL, lawyer; BA, Ohio Wesleyan U., 1956; JD, Duquesne U., 1960; postgrad., Stanford (Calif.) U. Bar: Pa. 1962, Calif. 1964, U.S. Supreme Ct. 1967. Sole practice law, Pitts., 1962-65; designer, adminstr. legal rsch. sys. U. Pitts., Aspen Sys. Corp., Pitts., 1965-68; mgr. ops. Computer Ctr., Carnegie Mellon U., Pitts., 1968-69; dir. computer facility Computer Ctr., Stanford U., 1969-72, Stanford Law and Computer fellow, 1972-73; cons. in computers and law, 1973-74; sr. assoc. MacLeod, Fuller, Muir & Godwin, Los Altos, LA and London, 1974-75; ptnr. Chickering & Gregory, San Francisco, 1975-80; ptnr.-in-charge high tech. group Gaston Snow & Ely Bartlett, Boston, NYC, Phoenix, San Francisco, 1980-86; mng. ptnr. Palo Alto office Kadison, Pfaelzer, Woodard, Quinn & Rossi, LA, Washington, Newport Beach, Palo Alto, Calif., 1986-87; sr. ptnr., chmn. U.S. intellectual property/info. tech. practice group Baker & McKenzie, Palo Alto, 1987—, mem. U.S. leadership team, 1987-97, mem. Asia Pacific regional coun., 1995—. Founder Tech. Disputes Resolution Svcs., Inc., 2002—; trustee EDUCOM, 1978-81; mem. adv. com. for high tech. Ariz. State U. Law Sch., Santa Clara U. Law Sch., Stanford Law Sch., U. So. Calif. Law Ctr., Harvard U. Law Sch., U. Calif.; U.S. State Dept. del. OECD Conf. on Nat. Vulnerabilities, Spain, 1981; invited spkr. Telecom., Geneva, 1983; lectr. N.Y. Law Jour., 1975—, Law & Bus., 1975—, Practicing Law Inst., 1975—; chmn. Office of Tech. Assessment Task Force on Nat. Info. Sys., 1979-80. Author-:(with Bigelow) Your Computer and the Law, 1975, (with Bosworth) Legal Protection for Software, 1985, (with Collins and Gilbert) Women Leading, 1987; contbr. monographs, articles to profl. publs. Fellow Am. Bar Found.; mem. Town of Portola Valley Open Space Acquisition Com., Calif., 1977; mem. Jr. League of Palo Alto, chmn. evening div., 1975-76 NSF and Dept. Justice grantee for studies on computer abuse, 1972-. Fellow Am. Bar Found., Assn. Computer Machinery (mem. at large of coun. 1976-80, nat. lectr. 1977—, chmn. standing com. on legal issues 1975—, mem. blue ribbon com. on rationalization of internat. propr. rights protection on info. processing devel. in the '90s 1990—), Coll. Law Practice Mgmt. (trustee 2002—); mem. ABA (chmn. sect. on sci. and tech. 1979-80), Computer Law Assn. (v.p. 1983-85, pres. 1986—, bd. dirs. 1975—), Calif. State Bar Assn. (founder first chmn. econs. of law sect., vice chmn. law and computers com.), Internat. Bar Assn. (U.S. mem. computer com. of corps. sect.), Nat. Conf. Lawyers and Scientists (rep. ABA), Strategic Forum on Intellectual Property Issues in Software of NAS, Internat. Coun. for Computer Comm. (gov. 1998). Office: 35 Granada Ct Portola Valley CA 94028-7736 Office Phone: 650-888-7786. Business E-Mail: susan@nycum.net.

NYDEGGER, RICK D. lawyer; b. Salt Lake City, Utah, Apr. 24, 1949; s. A. Don and Jean Virginia (Hansen) N.; m. Denise Winegar, Oct. 22, 1970; children: Dan L., Chad E., Kurt D., Brittney, Trent R. BSEE cum laude, Brigham Young U., 1974, JD cum laude, 1977. Bar: Utah 1977, U.S. Dist Ct. (ctrl. dist.) Utah 1977, U.S. Patent Office 1977, U.S. Ct. Appeals (5th and 10th cirs.) 1980, U.S. Supreme Ct. 1990, U.S. Ct. Appeals (fed. cir.) 1994. Assoc. Fox, Edwards, & Gardiner, 1977-81, shareholder, dir., 1981-84; founding shareholder, dir., officer Workman, Nydegger & Seeley, Salt Lake City, Utah, 1984—. Adj. prof. U. Utah Coll. Law, 1988-99, Brigham Young U. Coll. Law, 1998-2002. Contbr. articles to profl. jours. Bd. dirs. Nat. Inventors Hall of Fame, 2000— bd. dirs. NIHF Found., 1998—, pres.-elect, 2002; trustee Am. Intellectual Property Law Edn. Found., 2001—. Fellow Am. Intellectual Property Law Assn. (founding mem., chmn. electronic computer law com. 1990-93, bd. dirs. 1993-96, editl. bd. quar. jour., vice-chmn. ad hoc com. PCT practice, 1994-98, nominations com. 1997, chmn. mid-winter Inst. 2000 planning com., 2d v.p. 2000-01, 1st v.p. 2001-02, pres.-elect 2002-03); mem. ABA, Utah State Bar (chmn. patent, trademark, copyright sect. 1985-87), Fed. Cir. Bar Assn., U.S. Supreme Ct. Hist. Soc. (10th cir. rep. 1993-94, Utah rep. 1992-93), Nat. Coun. Intellectual Property Law Assn. (chmn. 2000-01), Order of Coif. Office: Workman Nydegger & Seeley 60 E South Temple Ste 1000 Salt Lake City UT 84111-1011

NYE, ERIC W. English language and literature educator; b. Omaha, July 31, 1952; s. William Frank and Mary Roberta (Lueder) N.; m. Carol Denison Frost, Dec. 21, 1980; children: Charles William, Ellen Mary. BA, St. Olaf Coll., 1974; MA, U. Chgo., 1976, PhD, 1983; postgrad., Queens' Coll., Cambridge, England, 1979-82. Tutor in coll. writing com. U. Chgo., 1976-79, tchg. intern, 1978; tutor Am. lit. Cambridge (Eng.) U., 1979-82; asst. prof. English and religious studies U. Wyo., Laramie, 1983-89, assoc. prof., 1989—, dir. English honors program, 1985—89, 1992—93, 2002—04. V.p., bd. dirs. Plainview Tel. Co., Nebr.; hon. vis. fellow U. Edinburgh (Scotland) Inst. for Advanced Studies in the Humanities, 1987; guest lectr. NEH summer Inst., Laramie, Wyo., 1985, Carlyle Soc. of Edinburgh, 1987, Wordsworth summer Conf., Grasmere, Eng., 1988, cons. NEH. Contbr. articles and reviews to profl. jours. Mem. Am. Friends of Cambridge U., Friends of Cambridge U. Libr. (life), Gen. Soc. Mayflower Descendants; elected mem. Wyo. Coun. for Humanities, 1992-96, mem. exec. com., 1993-94; mem. adv. bd. Wyo. Ctr. for the Book, 1995—; mem. Peripatetics, 1989-, leader Boy Scouts Am. Named Nat. Merit Scholar St. Olaf Coll., 1970-74; recipient Amb. Fellowship, Rotary Found., 1979-80, grant Am. Coun. of Learned Socs., 1988, Disting. Alumnus award, Lincoln (Neb.) E. High Sch., 1986. Mem.: Guild Book Workers, Bibliog. Soc. London (hon. sec.-treas. for N.Am. 2002—), Soc. History of Authorship, Reading, and Pub., Assn. Lit. and Linguistic Computing, Assn. Computers and the Humanities, Modern Lang. Assn. (del. assembly 1991—93), Assn. Literary Scholars and Critics (life), Queens' Coll. Club (Cambridge), Carlyle Soc. (life), Coleridge Soc. (life), Friends of Dove Cottage (life), Jane Austen Soc. N.Am. (life), Wyo. State Hist. Soc. (life), Penn Club (London), The Victorian Inst., Charles Lamb Soc., Tennyson Soc. (life), Royal Oak Found., Phi Beta Kappa (rep. Triennial Couns. 1988, pres., v.p., sec. Wyo. chpt. 1988—, rep. Triennial Couns. 1994, 2000, 2003). Home: 1495 Apache Dr Laramie WY 82072-6966 Office: U Wyo Dept English PO Box 3353 Laramie WY 82071-3353

NYE, ERLE ALLEN, electric power industry executive, lawyer; b. Ft. Worth, June 23, 1937; s. Ira Benjamen N.; m. Alice Ann Grove, June 5, 1959; children: Elizabeth Nye Janzen, Pamela Nye Schneider, Erle Allen Jr., Edward Kyle, Johnson Scott. BEE, Tex. A&M U., 1959; JD, So. Meth. U., 1965. With Dallas Power & Light Co., 1960-75, v.p., 1975-80, Tex. Utilities Co. (dba TXU Corp.), Dallas, 1980, exec. v.p., 1980-87, pres., 1987-95, pres., CEO, 1995-97, chmn., CEO, 1997—2004, chmn., 2004—. TU Svcs., 1982-97, chmn., CEO, 1997—, Tex. Utilities Properties Inc., 1994, Tex. Utilities Commn., Dallas, 1995-97, chmn., CEO, 1997—; pres. Tex. Utilities Fuel Co., 1982-97, chmn., CEO, 1997—; chmn. Tex. Utilities Australia Pty., Ltd., 1996—, chmn. and CEO ENSERCH Corp., Enserch Devel. Corp., Dallas, 1997—, chmn. Enserch Energy Svcs. Inc., 1997—; dir. The Energy Group PLC, London, 1998—; chmn. and CEO Tex. Energy Industries Inc., Dallas, 1997—, Southwestern Electric Svc. Co., 1997—, chmn. Lufkin-Conroe Comm. Co., 1997—, chmn. bd., CEO Tex. Utilities Integrated Solutions Inc., 1997—. Bd. dirs. Dallas Bar Found., 1980-83, Dallas Cen. Bus. Plan Com., 1980-83, Inroads/Dallas-Ft. Worth Inc., 1984-88, trustee Baylor Dental Coll., Dallas, 1985-94; mem. Dallas Together Forum, 1989—, Dallas Com. Fgn. Rels., 1991—, Bd. of Boys & Girls Clubs of Am., 1991—; The Dallas Found., 1994—; The Science Pl., Dallas, 1995-99; The Salvation Army's Dallas County Adv. Bd., 1995-99. Mem. ABA, Dallas Bar Assn., Tex. State Bar Assn., Dallas C. of C. (bd. dirs. 1991-95, vice chmn. 1992-95). Clubs: Engineers (pres. 1982-83), Northwood (Dallas). Methodist. Home: 6924 Desco Dallas TX 75225 Office: TXU Corp 1601 Bryan St Fl 41 Dallas TX 75201-3411

NYE, GENE WARREN, retired art educator; b. Sacramento, July 3, 1939; s. Charles Frederick and Dorthy Dell Nye; m. Alena Mae Nye, Sept. 20, 1974; children: Dirk, Ronni, Anthony, Timothy. AA, American River Coll., Sacramento, 1962; AB, Sacramento State U., 1964; cert. Secondary Art Tchr., U. Calif., Berkeley, 1966. Printer Roseville (Calif.) Press Tribune, 1957-60; typographer Oakland (Calif.) Tribune, 1960-65; tchr. art Long Beach (Calif.) Unified Sch. Dist., 1965-67; tchr., chair art dept. Woodland (Calif.) Unified Sch. Dist., 1967-98; retired, 1998. Freelance artist Wildcat Art, Sacramento, 1985—; cons. in field; workshop presenter, including Nat Assn. Workshop Dirs., Nat. Assn. Student Couns., Calif. Assn. Dir. of Activities, Nat. Assn. Secondary Sch. Prins., others. Author: (workbook set and video) Posters Made EZ, 1990; How to Create Successful Posters, on CD, 2001; (video and CD) Communication: the vitality of an organization, 2003. Mem. task force Constn. Revision of CADA, L.A., 1988-89. Named to Calif. Assn. Dirs. of Activities Hall of Fame, 1992. Mem. NEA (life), Calif. Tchrs. Assn., Calif. Retired Tchrs. Assn., Woodland Edn. Assn. (v.p. 1971-72), Calif. Art Edn. Assn., Nat. Art Edn. Assn., Calif. League Mid. Schs., U. Calif.-Berkeley Alumni Assn. (life). Home: 2200 Eastern Ave Sacramento CA 95864-0805

NYE, JOHN ROBERT, furniture company executive, transportation consultant; b. Phila., Apr. 18, 1947; s. William E. and Mary B. (Brick) N.; m. Judy Burris, May 31, 1969 (div. Dec. 1977); children: Keith, Lanny, John; m. Grace M. Adams, Feb. 28, 1981 (div. Aug. 1993); children: Annette, Mark. BA, N.C. State U., Raleigh, 1969. Prodn. mgr. Highland House, Hickory, N.C., 1969-79; distbn. mgr. Hickory Chair Co., 1979-97; mgr. Tydings House, Hickory, 1983—; distbn. mgr. Baker Furniture, 1998—. Owner J.R. Investments, 1989. Mem. Catawba Valley Traffic Club; vice-chmn. Catawba County Mayors Com. for Handicapped, 1987-89. Mem. Met. Planning Assn. Republican. Lutheran. Home: PO Box 3136 Hickory NC 28603-3136

NYE, JOSEPH SAMUEL, JR., dean, political science educator; b. South Orange, N.J., Jan. 19, 1937; s. Joseph S. and Else (Ashwell) N.; m. Molly Harding, June 10, 1961; children— John Bundy, Joseph Benjamin, Daniel Tupper AB in Pub. Affairs, Princeton U., 1958; BA in Philosophy, Politics and Econs., Oxford U., Eng., 1960; PhD in Polit. Sci., Harvard U., 1964. Prof., govt. Harvard U., Cambridge, Mass., 1964—95, program dir., Ctr. for Internat Affairs, 1969—72, dir., Ctr. for Science & Internat. Affairs, Kennedy Sch. Govt., 1985—90, assoc. dean internat. rels., 1989-92, dir. Ctr. for Internat. Affairs, 1989-93, Clarence Dillon prof., internat. affairs, 1989—93; dep. undersec. state, security assistance, science & tech. U.S. Dept. State, Washington, 1977-79, cons., 1979; asst. sec. def., internat. security affairs U.S. Dept. Def., Washington, 1994—95; Dean and Don K. Price prof. public policy, dean pub. policy Harvard U. JFK Sch. of Govt., 1995—. Cons. Dept. Energy, Washington, 1979; U.S. rep. UN Adv. Bd. on Disarmament; chmn. Nat. Intelligence Coun., 1993-94. Author: Pan Africanism and East African Integration, 1965, Peace in Parts: Integration and Conflict in Regional Organization, 1971 (with Robert O. Keohane) Power and Interdependence: World Politics in Transition, 1977, The Making of America's Soviet Policy, 1984, (with Graham Allison and Albert Carnesale) Hawks, Doves and Owls: An Agenda for Avoiding Nuclear War, 1985, Nuclear Ethics, 1986, Bound to Lead: The Changing Nature of American Power, 1990, (with Kurt Biedenkopf and Motoo Shiina) Global Competition After the Cold War: A Reassessment of Trilateralism, 1991, Understanding International Conflicts: An Introduction to Theory and History, 1993, The Paradox of American Power: Why the World's Only Only Superpowr Can't Go It Alone, 2002, (with Yukio Satoh and Paul Wikinson) Addressing the New International Terrorism: Prevention, Intervention, and Multilateral Cooperation, 2003; co-editor: Canada and the United States: Transnational and Transgovernmental Relations, 1974, Energy and Security, 1980, Global Dilemmas, 1985, Seeking Stability in Space: Anti-Satellite Weapons and the Evolving Space Regime, 1987, On The Defensive? The Future of SDI, 1988, Fateful Visions: avoiding Nuclear Catastrophe, 1988, democracy.com?: Governance in a Networked World, 1999, Governance in a Globalizing World, 2000. Recipient: Dept. State Disting. Honor award, 1979; Rhodes scholar Oxford U., 1958-60, Montague Burton Professorship, U. Edinburgh, 1990, Intelligence Cmty. Disting. Service medal, 1994, Dept. Def. Disting. Service medal with Oak Leaf Cluster, 1995; fellow, Woodrow Wilson Internat. Ctr., Smithsonian Inst., 1993, Hon. fellow, Exeter Coll, Oxford, 1996. Fellow Am. Acad. Arts and Scis., Aspen Inst. for Humanistic Study (sr. fellow, 1983-93); mem. Amer. Assoc. for the Advancement of Science: Com. on Science, Arms Control, and Nat. Security, 1984-90, bd. dirs., Amer. Council on Germany, 1985-93, bd. govts., Atlantic Inst. for Internat. Affairs, 1974-77, Internat. Inst. Strategic Studies (council), Coun. Fgn. Rels., Trilateral Commn., Am. Acad. Diplomacy. Office: Harvard U JFK Sch Govt Office of Dean 79 John F Kennedy St Cambridge MA 02138-5801 E-mail: josephnye@harvard.edu.*

NYE, RANDALL WAYNE, music educator; s. John Barlow and Kathryn Viola Nye; m. Donna Sheryl Fraser, Mar. 18, 1995; 1 child, Benjamin Christopher. MusB, So. Meth. U., 1977, MusM, 1980. Educator Eastfield Coll., Mesquite, Tex., 2004—. Editor: The Guitar Ensemble: A Collection. Music scholar, So. Meth. U., 1974—77. Mem.: Dallas Classic Guitar Soc. (adv. bd. 1990—2003), Phi Theta Kappa. Office: Eastfield Coll 3737 Motley Dr Mesquite TX 75150 Personal E-mail: rnye@cccd.edu. Business E-Mail: randy.nye@dcccd.edu.

NYE, W. MARCUS W. lawyer; b. N.Y.C., Aug. 3, 1945; s. Walter R. and Nora (McLaren) N.; m. Eva Johnson; children: Robbie, Stephanie, Jennifer. BA, Harvard U., 1967; JD, U. Idaho, 1974. Bar: Idaho 1974, U.S. Dist. Ct. Idaho 1974, U.S. Ct. Appeals (9th cir.) 1980; lic. pilot. Ptnr. Racine, Olson, Nye, Budge & Bailey, Pocatello, Idaho, 1974—. Vis. prof. law U. Idaho, Moscow, 1984; adj. prof. Coll. Engring. Idaho State U., 1993-96; Idaho State U. Found.(pres. 2001-2003), U. Idaho Coll. Law Found. Commr., Idaho State Centennial Found., 1985-90. Recipient Alumni Svc. award U. Idaho, 1988. Fellow ABA (bd. govs. 1997-2000), Am. Bar Found. (stat. chmn. 1992-95); mem. Am. Bd. Trial Advs. (nat. bd. dirs.), Am. Coll. Trial Lawyers, Idaho State Bar Assn. (pres. 1987-88), Idaho Def. Counsel Assn. (pres. 1982), 6th Dist. Bar Assn. (pres. 1982). Avocation: travel. Home: 173 S 15th Ave Pocatello ID 83201-4056 Office: Racine Olson Nye Budge & Bailey PO Box 1391 Pocatello ID 83204-1391 Office Phone: 208-232-6101.

NYE, WILLIAM ROGER, psychologist; b. Haverhill, Mass., Oct. 23, 1940; s. Kenneth Enoch and Virginia Pauline (Cook) N.; children: Michael Shepherd Abowitz Nye; 1 stepson, Christopher J. Wells. BA, Yale U., 1962; MDiv, Union Theol. Sem., N.Y.C., 1965; PhD, Adelphi U., Garden City, N.Y., 1981. Lic. psychologist, N.Y. Pastor Ch. of the Evangel, Bklyn., 1965-77; asst. minister Plymouth Ch. of the Pilgrims, Bklyn., 1977-82; pastor All Souls Bethlehem Ch., Bklyn., 1983—2003; exec. dir. Blanton-Peale Counseling Ctrs., 1983—. Past pres. Met. Assn. of N.Y. Conf. of United Ch. of Christ, 1969-73. Pres. Pastoral and Ednl. Svcs., Bklyn., 1983-87, The Vinmont Found., N.Y.C., 1988—. Mem. Am. Psychol. Assn. Democrat. United Ch. of Christ. Home: 888 E 19th St Brooklyn NY 11230-3108 Office Phone: 718-253-9001. E-mail: realbilnye@aol.com.

NYENHUIS, JACOB EUGENE, college official; b. Mille Lacs County, Minn., Mar. 25, 1935; s. Egbert Peter and Rosa (Walburg) N.; m. Leona Mae Van Duyn, June 6, 1956; children: Karen J. Louwsma, Kathy J. Kurtze, Lorna J. Cook, Sarah Van Duyn Nyenhuis. AB in Greek, Calvin Coll., 1956; AM in Classics, Stanford U., 1961, PhD in Classics, 1963; LittD (hon.), Hope Coll., 2001. Asst. in classical langs. Calvin Coll., Grand Rapids, Mich., 1957-59; acting instr. Stanford (Calif.) U., 1962; from asst. prof. to prof. Wayne State U., Detroit, 1962-75, dir. honors program, 1964-75, chmn. Greek and Latin dept., 1965-75; prof. classics, dean for humanities Hope Coll., Holland, Mich., 1975-78, dean for arts and humanities, 1978-84, provost, 1984—2001, prof. and provost emeritus, 2001—; sr. rsch. fellow A.C. Van Raalte Inst., 2001—02, dir., 2002—. Cons. Mich. Dept. Edn., Lansing, 1971-72, Gustavus Adolphus Coll., St. Peter, Minn., 1974, Northwestern Coll., Orange City, Iowa, 1983, Whitworth Coll., Spokane, Wash., 1987, The Daedalus Project, 1988, Albion Coll., 2002-03, Kalamazoo Coll., 2003—04; reviewer NEH, Washington, 1986-87, panelist, 1991; reviewer Lilly Endowment, Indpls., 1987-89, U.S. Dept. Edn., 1993, Mich. Humanities Coun., 1999-2001; vis. assoc. prof. U. Calif., Santa Barbara, 1967-68, Ohio State U., Columbus, 1972; vis. rsch. prof. Am. Sch. Classical Studies, Athens, Greece, 1973-74, mng. com.; vis. scholar Green Coll. Oxford U., 1989; mem. editl. adv. bd. Christianity and The Arts, 1998-2001, chmn., 1999-2001. Co-author: Latin Via Ovid, 1977, rev. edit., 1982, A Dream Fulfilled: The Van Raalte Sculpture in Centennial Park, 1997; editor: Petronius: Cena Trimalchionis, 1970, Plautus: Amphitruo, 1970; author: Centennial History of 14th Street Christian Reformed Church, Holland, Michigan, 2002, Myth and the Creative Process:

Michael Ayrton and the Myth of Daedalus, the Maze Maker, 2003; contbr. articles to profl. jours. Elder Christian Ref. Ch., Palo Alto, Calif., 1960—62, elder, clk. Grosse Pointe, Mich., 1964—67, Holland, Mich., 1976—85, v.p., 1988—91, exec. com., 1994—95, trustee Calvin Theol. Sem., 2001—, mem. exec. com., 2002—, v.p., 2003—; chmn. human rels. coun. Open Housing Com., Grosse Pointe, 1971—73. Mem. Am. Philol. Assn., Danforth Assocs. (chmn. regional com. 1975-77), Mich. Coun. for Humanities (bd. dirs., 1976-84, 88-92, 96-99, chmn. 1980-82, Disting. Svc. award 1984), Nat. Fedn. State Humanities Couns. (bd. dirs. 1979-84, pres. 1981-83), Gt. Lakes Colls. Assn. (bd. dirs. 1991-93), Coun. on Undergrad. Rsch. (councilor-at-large 1993-99), Green Coll. Soc., Mortar Board, Phi Beta Kappa, Eta Sigma Phi. Democrat. Avocations: photography, carpentry. Office: Hope Coll Van Raalte Inst PO Box 9000 Holland MI 49422-9000 Office Phone: 616-395-7678. E-mail: nyenhuis@hope.edu.

NYERGES, ALEXANDER LEE, museum director; b. Rochester, N.Y., Feb. 27, 1957; s. Sandor Elek and Lena (Angeline) N.; m. Kathryn Gray; 1 child, Robert Angeline. BA, George Washington U., 1979, MA, 1981. Intern The Octagon, Washington, 1976-79; archeol. asst. Smithsonian Instn., Washington, 1977; curatorial intern Nat. Mus. Am. History, 1978-79; adminstrv. asst. George Washington U., Washington, 1979-81; exec. dir. DeLand Mus. Art, Fla., 1981-85, Miss. Mus. Art, Jackson, 1985-92; dir. Dayton (Ohio) Art Inst., 1992—. Mem. grants panel Nat. Endowment for the Arts, 1988—; field surveyor Inst. Mus. Svcs., Washington, 1985-88, nat. review panel, 1990-92; treas., bd. dirs. Volusia County Arts Coun., Daytona Beach, Fla., 1983-85. Author: Selections from the Permanent Collection, 1999, In Praise of Nature: Ansel Adams and Photographers of the American West, The Harold W Shaw Collection: Pre Columbian Treasures, 2003, Edward Weston: A Photographer's Love of Life, 2004; contbr. articles to profl. jours. Bd. dirs. West Volusia Hist. Soc., 1984-85; pres. Miss. Inst. Arts and Letters, 1987-88; trustee Cultural Arts Ctr., DeLand, 1984-85, Miami Valley Cultural Alliance, 1993-95, Intermus. Conservation Lab., 1993-99, Montgomery County Arts and Culture Dist., 1994-2001; trustee, chmn. Dayton-Montgomery County Conv. and Visitors Bur. U.S. Dept. Edn. scholar, 1973. Mem. DeLand Area C. of C. (bd. dirs., tourist adv. com. 1984-85), Assn. Art Mus. Dirs., Am. Assn. Mus. (S.E. regional rep. to non-print media com. 1983-85, nat. legis. com. 1986-93), Miss. Mus. Assn., Southeastern Mus. Conf. (bd. dirs. 1991-92), Fla. Mus. Assn., Fla. Art Mus. Dirs. Assn., Cultural Roundtable (pres. 1993-95), Ohio Mus. Assn. (trustee 1993-98), Phi Beta Kappa. Avocations: photography, music, writing, sports, scuba diving. Home: 229 Volusia Ave Dayton OH 45409-2226 Office: Dayton Art Inst 456 Belmonte Park N Dayton OH 45405-4700 Office Phone: 937-223-5277. E-mail: anyerges@aol.com.

NYGAARD, LANCE COREY, nurse, data processing consultant; b. Casper, Wyo., June 21, 1952; s. Miles Adolph and Jenile Hansine (Mosman) N.; m. Susan Leigh Wilson, May 8, 1995; 1 child from previous marriage, Kari Melissa. AA in Nursing, U. S.D., 1980; BS in Chemistry, 1974; MLS, U. Ill., 1975. Libr. asst. Brookings Pub. Libr., S.D., 1971-75, asst. dir., 1975-77; emergency med. technician Brookings Hosp., 1976-78; sr. emergency med. technician Vermillion Ambulance, S.D., 1978-80; nurse McKennan Hosp., Sioux Falls, S.D., 1980-91, VA Hosp., 1991-96, Sioux Valley Hosp., 1996—, cardiovasc. data sys. coord., 1997—; owner operator Data Processing Svcs., Sioux Falls, 1983—; applications cons. Computer Dimensions, Sioux Falls, 1984-85. Fin. sec., mem. ch. coun. Holy Cross Luth. Ch., Sioux Falls, S.D., 1986-91, info. resources coord., 1991-92; troop leader Minn-Ia-Kota coun. Girl Scouts U.S., 1989—, region troop supr., 1991-95. Mem. Vermillion Chemistry Club (pres. 1973-74), Sioux Valley Rose Soc. (v.p. 1988-89, pres. 1989-90), Sons of Norway (guard 1976-77). Republican. Lutheran. Avocations: World War II military history, photography, amateur radio. Home: 3500 S Grace Cir Sioux Falls SD 57103-7226 Office: Sioux Valley Hosp 1100 S Euclid Ave Sioux Falls SD 57105-0496

NYGAARD, RICHARD LOWELL, federal judge; b. Thief River Falls, MN, 1940; BS cum laude, U. So. Calif., 1969; JD, U. Mich., 1971. Mem. Orton, Nygaard & Dunlevy, 1972—80; judge Ct. Common Pleas, 6th Dist. Pa., Erie, 1981—88, U.S. Ct. Appeals (3d cir.), Erie, Pa., 1988—; sr. lecturer Penn State Univ., 1999—2003. Councilman Erie County, Pa., 1977—81. With USNR, 1958—64. Mem.: ABA, Erie County Bar Assn., Pa. Bar Assn. Office: James A Byrne Courthouse 601 Market St Rm 2100 Philadelphia PA 19106 also: 17 S Park Row # B230 Erie PA 16501-1164

NYGARD, PAUL DAVID, social sciences educator; b. Brockton, Mass., Sept. 17, 1958; s. David Paul and Nancy Jean (Ohrn)) Nygard; m. Mary Lee McKinley, Dec. 27, 1986; children: Shanda Marie, Jason David, Kirsten Renee Nygard-Gage, Daniel Brandon, Casey Elizabeth. BA in History, So. Ill. U., 1990, MA in History, 1992; PhD in Am. Studies, St. Louis U., 1997. Asst. prof. St. Louis C.C., 1999—2002, assoc. prof., 2002—, chair dept. social and behavior sciences, 2002—. Contbr. encyclopedia, articles to profl. jours. With USAF, 1977—85. Recipient Excellence in Tchg. award, State of Mo., 2001—02; Am. Studies fellow, St. Louis U., 1992—97. Mem.: St. Louis Area Hist. Assn. (pres. 1998—2003). D-Liberal. Lutheran. Avocations: radio announcing, travel, peanuts collectors club, Maine literature. Home: 11 Leo St Fairview Heights IL 62208 Office: St Louis Cmty Coll 3400 Pershall Rd Saint Louis MO 63135 Office Phone: 314-513-4419. Personal E-mail: pnygard@stlcc.edu. E-mail: pnygard@stlcc.edu.

NYHART, ELDON HOWARD, employee benefits consultant, lawyer; b. Lafayette, Ind., Jan. 17, 1927; s. Howard E. and Mabel (Keller) N.; m. Frieda Ernie, Apr. 12, 1971; children: Maria, Malott, Sallie, Eldon Jr. AB cum laude, Princeton U., 1948; JD, Ind. U., 1952. Exec. v.p. The Nyhart Co., Inc., Indpls., 1953-55, pres., chief exec. officer, 1955-60, chief exec. officer, 1960-91, chmn. bd. dirs., 1991-96, chmn. emeritus, 1996—. Lectr. Purdue U., Lafayette; tchr. Ind. U. Grad. Sch. Bus., Bloomington, dir. Midwest Pension Conf. Contbr. articles to profl. jour. Life trustee Indpls. Mus. Art, bd. govs., 1990—; bd. dirs. Ind. Swiss Found., pres. 1991—, Ind. State Symphony Soc., 1990—, Eiteljorg Mus., 1990, Contemporary Art Soc., 1991—, Friends of Herron Gallery, 1990—; del. White House Conf. on Aging. Mem. ABA, Internat. Bar Assn., Ind. Bar Assn., Assn. Pvt. Pension and Welfare Plans, trustee 1987-91, Am. Judicature Soc., Am. Pension Conf., Woodstock Club, Chgo. Racquet Club, Univ. Club (Indpls.), Princeton Club (N.Y.). Episcopalian. Home: 6454 Holliday Dr W Indianapolis IN 46260-4257 Office: Nyhart Co Inc 9320 Priority Way W Dr Indianapolis IN 46240-1468

NYHUS, LLOYD MILTON, surgeon, educator; b. Mt. Vernon, Wash., June 24, 1923; s. Lewis Guttorm and Mary (Shervem) N.; m. Margaret Goldie Sheldon, Nov. 25, 1949; children: Sheila Margaret, Leif Torger. BS, Pacific Luth. Coll., 1945; MD, Med. Coll. Ala., 1947; Doctor honoris causa, Aristotelian U., Thessalonika, Greece, 1968, Uppsala U., Sweden, 1974, U. Chihuahua, Mex., 1975, Jagallonian U., Cracow, Poland, 1980, U. Gama Filho, Rio de Janeiro, 1983, U. Louis Pasteur, Strasbourg, France, 1984, U. Athens, 1989. Diplomate Am. Bd. Surgery (chmn. 1974-76). Intern King County Hosp., Seattle, 1947-48, resident in surgery, 1948-55; practice medicine specializing in surgery Seattle, 1956-67, Chgo., 1967—; instr. surgery U. Wash., Seattle, 1954-56, asst. prof., 1956-59, assoc. prof., 1959-64, prof., 1964-67; Warren H. Cole prof., head dept. surgery U. Ill. Coll. Medicine, 1967-89, emeritus head, 1989—, prof. emeritus, 1993. Emeritus surgeon-in-chief U. Ill. Hosp.; sr. cons. surgeon Cook County, West Side VA, Hines (Ill.) VA hosps.; cons. to Surgeon Gen. NIH, 1965-69. Author: Surgery of the Stomach and Duodenum, 1962, 4th edit., 1986, named changed to Surgery of the Esophagus, Stomach and Small Intestine, 5th edit., 1995, Hernia, 1964, (book name change) Nyhus and Condon's Hernia, 5th edit., 2002, Chinese (Mandarin) edit., 2003, Abdominal Pain: A Guide to Rapid Diagnosis, 1969, 95, Spanish edit., 1996, Russian edit., 2001, Manual of Surgical Therapeutics, 1969, latest rev. edit., 1996, Mastery of Surgery, 1984, 3d edit., 1997, Spanish edit., 1999, Surgery Ann., 1970-95, Treatment of Shock, 1970, 2d rev. edit., 1986, Surgery of the Small Intestine, 1987; editor-in-chief Rev. of Surgery, 1967-77, Current Surgery, 1978-90, emeritus editor, 1991—; assoc. editor Quar. Rev. Surgery, 1958-61; editl. bd. Am. Jour. Digestive Diseases, 1961-67, Scandinavian Jour. Gastroenterology, 1966-97, Am. Surgeon, 1967-89, Jour. Surg. Oncology, 1969-99, Archives of Surgery, 1977-86, World Jour. Surgery, 1977-95; contbr. articles to profl. jours. Served to lt. M.C. USNR, 1943-46, 50-52. Decorated Order of Merit (Poland); postdoctoral fellow USPHS, 1952-53; recipient M. Shipley award So. Surg. Assn., 1967, Rovsing medal Danish Surg. Soc., 1973; Disting. Faculty award U. Ill Coll. Medicine, 1983, Disting. Alumnus award Med. Coll. Ala., 1984, Disting. Alumnus award U. Wash., 1993, 99; Guggenheim fellow, 1955-56. Fellow ACS (1st v.p. 1987-88), Assn. Surgeons Gt. Brit. and Ireland (hon.), Royal Coll. Surgeons Eng. (hon.), Royal Coll. Surgeons Ireland (hon.), Royal Coll. Surgeons Edinburgh (hon.), Royal Coll. Physicians and Surgeons Glasgow (hon.), Internat. Soc. Surgery Found. (hon., sec.-treas. 1992-2001); mem . Am. Gastroent. Assn., Am. Physiol. Soc., Pacific Coast Surg. Assn., Am. Surg. Assn. (recorder 1976-81, 1st v.p. 1989-90), Western Surg. Assn., Ctrl. Soc. Clin. Rsch., Chgo. Surg. Soc. (pres. 1974), Ctrl. Surg. Assn. (pres. 1984), Seattle Surg. Soc., St. Paul Surg. Soc. (hon.), Kansas City Surg. Soc. (hon.), Inst. Medicine Chgo., Internat. Soc. Surgery (hon. fellow 2001, pres. U.S. sect. 1986-88, pres. 34th World Congress 1991, internat. pres. 1991-93), Internat. Soc. for Digestive Surgery (pres. III world congress Chgo. 1974, internat. pres. 1978-84), Soc. for Surgery Alimentary Tract (sec. 1969-73, pres. 1974), Soc. Clin. Surgery, Soc. Surg. Chmn., Soc. U. Surgeons (pres. 1967), Duetschen Gesellschaft für Chirurgie (hon.), Polish Assn. Surgeons (hon.), L'Academie de Chirurgie (France) (corr.), Nat. Acad. of Medicine (France, Argentina and Brazil, hon.), Swiss Surg. Soc. (hon.), Brazilian Coll. Surgeons (hon.), Surg. Biology Club, Warren H. Cole Soc. (pres. 1981), Japan Surg. Soc. (hon.), Assn. Gen. Surgeons of Mex. (hon.), Columbian Surg. Soc. (hon.), Costa Rican Coll. Medicine & Surgery (hon.), Assn. Surgeons Costa Rica (hon.), Internat. Fedn. Surg. Colls. (hon. treas. 1992-99), Sigma Xi, Alpha Omega Alpha, Phi Beta Pi. Home: 310 Maple Row Northfield IL 60093-1036 Office: U Ill Coll Medicine Dept Surgery MC 958 840 S Wood St Chicago IL 60612 7322 Office Phone: 312-996-1680 Personal E-mail: lmn_23@msn.com.

NYIRJESY, ISTVAN, obstetrician, gynecologist; b. Budapest, Hungary, Nov. 14, 1929; came to U.S., 1954, naturalized, 1960; s. Sandor D. and Margit (Bertalan) N.; m. Michelle Shoepp, June 16, 1956; children— Francis, Paul, Christine. MD, Catholic U. Louvain, Belgium, 1955. Diplomate: Am. Bd. Ob-Gyn. Intern Cath. U. Louvain and Little Co. Mary Hosp., Evergeen Park, Ill., 1954-55; resident in gynecology obstetrics, 1960-63; chief obstetrical research Nat. Naval Med. Center, Bethesda, Md., 1966-68; ret., 1968; practice medicine specializing in Ob-Gyn, 1968—. Clin. prof. Ob-Gyn Georgetown U., 1968—; cons. NIH, 1974—, FDA, 1977-88. Lit. editor Breast Disease: contbr. articles to med. jours.; author: Prevention and Detection of Gynecologic and Breast Cancer, 1994. Pres., Internat. Found. for Gynecol. Cancer Detection and Prevention, 1993—. Officer M.C. USN, 1956-68; advanced through grades to comdr. Recipient Sword of Hope pin Am. Cancer Soc., 1973, Vicennial medal Georgetown U., 1988. Fellow ACOG (Host award 1964), Hungarian Gynecologic Soc. (hon.), Internat. Coll. Surgeons; mem. Montgomery County (Md.) Med. Soc. (chmn. profl. edn. com. 1971-72), Am. Soc. of Breast Disease (past pres.), Assn. Profs. Ob-Gyn., Am. Soc. Reproductive Medicine, Washington Gynecol. Soc. (v.p. 1993-94, 1st v.p. 1994-95, pres. 1996-97). Office: 5301 Westbard Cir Ste 5 Bethesda MD 20816-1429 Office Phone: 301-654-0445.

NYKOLYN, IRMA M. product manager; d. Wilfredo Arroyo and Ambrosia Rosado; m. Dennis J. Nykolyn, 1988; 1 child, Miranda. BA, SUNY, Albany, 1982; cert. in corps. law, Adelphi U., 1986; MA, NYU, 1996. Product mgr. Symantec Corp., Melville, N.Y., 1998-2000; product mktg. mgr. Vigilante, Melville, 2000—01; mktg. cons. Huntington, 2001—. Regents scholar N.Y. Regents, 1978. Mem. Assn. for Ednl. Comm. and Tech., Phi Beta Kappa. Roman Catholic. Avocation: travel. Personal E-mail: irmoi@hotmail.com.

NYKROG, PER, French literature educator; b. Copenhagen, Nov. 1, 1925; came to U.S., 1979; s. Kai S. Nathanson and Karen E. (Olsen) Nykrog; m. Vibeke H. Rasmussen, 1951 (dec. 1977); children: Thomas, Jakob; m. Usha Saksena Nilsson, Jan. 2, 1981. Grad., U. Copenhagen, 1952; PhD, U. Aarhus, Denmark, 1957. Asst. prof. U. Aarhus, 1953-57, prof., 1957-79; prof. French lang. and lit. Harvard U., Cambridge, Mass., 1979-98. Author: Les Fabliaux, 1957, La Pensée de Balzac, 1965, L'Amour et la Rose, 1986, La Recherche du Don perdu, 1987, Chrétien de Troyes romancier discutable, 1995. Mem. Royal Soc. Scis. Denmark. Home: 243 Concord Ave Cambridge MA 02138-1360 Office: Harvard U Dept Romance Langs Boylston Hall Cambridge MA 02138

NYLANDER, JANE LOUISE, museum director, lecturer, writer; b. Cleve., Jan. 27, 1938; d. James Merritt and Jeannette Cayford; m. Daniel Harris Giffen, 1963 (div. 1970); children: Sarah Louise, Thomas Harris; m. Richard Conrad Nylander, 1972; 1 child, Timothy Frost. AB, Brown U., 1959; MA, U. Del., 1961; postgrad., Attingham (Eng.) Summer Sch., 1970; PhD (hon.), New Eng. Coll., 1994. Curator Hist. Soc. York (Pa.) County, 1961-62, N.H. Hist. Soc., Concord, 1962-69; instr. New Eng. Coll., Henniker, NH, 1964-65, Monadnock C.C., Peterborough, NH, 1966-69; curator of textiles and ceramics Old Sturbridge (Mass.) Village, 1969-85; adj. assoc. prof. Boston U., 1978-85; sr. curator Old Sturbridge Village, 1985-86; dir. Strawbery Banke Mus., Portsmouth, NH, 1986-92, Soc. for Preservation of New Eng. Antiquities, Boston, 1992-93, pres., 1993—2002, pres. emerita, 2002—. Adj. prof. art history and Am. studies Boston U., 1993-96; trustee Worcester (Mass.) Hist. Mus., 1978-84, trustee Hist. Deerfield (Mass.), Inc., 1981-94, 2003—, hon. trustee, 1994-2003, chmn. strategic planning com., 2003—; trustee Hist. Mass. Inc., 1991-93, Portsmouth Athenaeum, 1988-90, Japan Soc. N.H., 1988-92, Fort Ticonderoga, 2000-02; bd. govs. Decorative Arts Trust, 1991—; mem. adv. bd. Concord (Mass.) Mus., 1986-94, Wentworth-Coolidge Commn., 1991-96, John Nicholas Brown Ctr. for Am. Studies, Providence, 1995—; mem. adv. com. Wentworth-Coolidge, 1996—; mem. adv. bd. dept. Am. decorative arts Mus. Fine Arts, Boston, 1971-99, Art of the Ams., 1999-2000; mem. adv. com. Lakes Region Conservation Trust, 2002-03; mem. coun. Colonial Soc. Mass., 1993-96; advisor, house com. Moffatt Ladd House, 1973—; mem. interpretation com. N.H. Hist. Soc., 2003—; bd. dirs. Castle Preservation Soc., 2003—; cons. in field. Author: Fabrics for Historic Buildings, 4th edit., 1990, Our Own Snug Fireside: Images of the New England Home 1760-1860, 1993, paperback edit., 1994, Windows on the Past, 2000, The Art of Family, 2002; mem. editl. bd.: Hist. N.H., 1993—2000, The Dublin Seminar, 1984—; contbr. numerous articles to profl. jours. Mem. adv. bd. New Eng. Heritage Ctr., 1993-2002; active State House Adv. Com., Boston, 1984-85, Gov.'s Coun. for Wentworth Coolidge Mansion, Concord, 1964-66; mem. Com. for Preservation of N.H. State Flags, 1989-92; mem. H.F. duPont award com. Winterthur Mus., 1993—, Mt. Vernon adv. com. for 1999, 1996-99, collections com. N.J. Hist. Soc., 1994-96; designator The Henderson Found., 1992-2004. Recipient Charles F. Montgomery prize Decorative Arts Soc., 1985, (with Richard C. Nylander) The Anne and Roger Webb award Hist. Mass., Inc., 1996, John F. Ayer award Bay State Hist. League, 2002, Boston History award Bostonian Soc., 2003. Mem.: N.H. Hist. Soc. (interpretation com. 2003—), Costume Soc. Am. (bd. dirs. 1977—83), New Eng. Hist. Geneal. Soc., N.H. Humanities Coun., Soc. Preservation of N.H. Forests, Soc. Winterthur Fellows, Mass. Hist. Soc., Portsmouth Athenaeum, Royal Oak Assn., Nat. Trust for Hist. Preservation, Am. Assn. for State and Local History (Cert. of Commendation 2001), Am. Antiquarian Soc., Friends of the Moffatt Ladd Huse., Colonial Soc. Mass., Nat. Soc. Colonial Dames in N.H. (bd. dirs. 1967—73, program chair 2002—), Friends of Hist. Deerfield, Lakes Region Conservation Trust, St. Botolph Club, Brown Club N.H. (trustee 1988—93). Episcopalian. Home: 17 Franklin St Portsmouth NH 03801-4501 E-mail: jane.nylander@verizon.net.

NYMAN, CARL JOHN, JR., university dean and official; b. New Orleans, Oct. 21, 1924; s. Carl John Sr. and Dorothy (Kraft) N.; m. Betty Spiegelberg, July 15, 1950; children: Gail Katherine, John Victor, Nancy Kraft. BS, Tulane U., 1944, MS, 1945; PhD, U. Ill., 1948. Jr. technologist Shell Oil Co., Wilmington, Cal., 1944; instr. chemistry U. Ill., 1948, Wash. State U., Pullman, 1948-50, asst. prof., 1950-55, assoc. prof., 1955-61, prof., 1961-88, prof. emeritus, 1988—, vice provost for rsch., 1981-86, acting dean grad. sch., 1968-69; dean, 1969-87; dean and vice provost emeritus for rsch. grad. sch. Wash. State U., 1988—. Vis. asst. prof. Tulane U., summer, 1950, adj. prof., 1986-87; vis. fellow Cornell U., 1959-60, Imperial Coll. Sci. and Tech., 1966-67; vis. fellow Swiss Fed. Inst. Tech., Zurich, 1973; chmn. Acad. Coun. Ctr. Grad. Study, Richland, Wash., 1968-70, N.W. Assn. Colls. and Univs. for Sci., 1969; mem. Gov.'s Adv. Coun. on Nuclear Energy, 1968-70, Washington State High Tech. Coord. Bd., 1984-86; mem. exec. com., coun. on rsch. policy and grad. edn. Nat. Assn. State Univs. and Land Grant Colls., 1972-75; bd. dirs. Coun. of Grad. Schs. in U.S., 1977-80. Author: (with G. B. King and J. A. Weyh) Problems for General Chemistry and Qualitative Analysis, 4th edit., 1980, (with R. E. Hamm) Chemical Equilibrium, 1967, (with W. E. Newton) Procs. of the 1st Internat. Conf. Nitrogen Fixation; contbr. articles to profl. jours. Mem. Am. Chem. Soc. (chmn. Wash.-Idaho border sect. 1961-62), AAAS, Sigma Xi, Phi Lambda Upsilon, Alpha Chi Sigma, Omicron Delta Kappa. Home: 1419 E Cambridge Ln Spokane WA 99203-3962

NYMAN, MICHAEL S. marketing executive; BA, U. So. Calif., 1986. Prin. Bragman, Nyman, Cafarelli, Inc., Beverly Hills, Calif., 1990—. Office: Bragman Nyman Cafarelli Inc 9171 Wilshire Blvd Ste 300 Beverly Hills CA 90210-5515

NYQUIST, JOHN DAVIS, retired radio manufacturing company executive; b. Peoria, Ill., May 28, 1918; s. Eliud and Linnea (Widen) N.; m. Alice Schmidt, June 5, 1942; 1 child, Sarah Lynn. BS in Mech. Engring, U. Ill., 1941. With Collins Radio Co., Cedar Rapids, Iowa, 1941—, v.p., gen. mgr. Iowa region, 1965-69, v.p. operations, 1969-70, sr. v.p., 1970-73, also dir.; ret., 1973; cons. Rockwell-Collins. Dir. Norwest Bank Iowa N.A. (formerly Peoples Bank & Trust Co.), Cedar Rapids. Bd. dirs. Am. Cancer Soc., YMCA, St. Lukes Hosp. Recipient award for outstanding achievement Am. Inst. Indsl. Engrs., 1966, Indsl. Engring. award, 1969, Coll. Engring. Alumni Honor award, 1977; both U. Ill.). Mem. Iowa Mfrs. Assn., Am. Mgmt. Assn., Am. Inst. Indsl. Engrs., IEEE, Cedar Rapids C. of C. (dir.) Clubs: Cedar Rapids Country. Home: 3279 Jordans Grove Rd Springville IA 52336-9786

NYQUIST, MAURICE OTTO, federal agency administrator, scientist; b. Fairmont, Minn., May 30, 1944; s. Carl Arther and Wilda Yvette (Freitag) N.; m. Mary Maud Magee, Aug. 8, 1977; children: Gretchen, Beth. BS in Biology, Hamline U., 1966; MA in Biology, Mankato State U., 1968; PhD in Zoology, Wash. State U., 1973. Asst. prof. zoology Wash. State U., Pullman, 1973-74; scientist Nat. Park Svc., Lakewood, Colo., 1974-76, mgr., 1979-93; mgr., scientist Nat. Biol. Svc., Denver, 1993-96, USGS, Denver, 1996—; coord. The Aurora Partnership, 1999—. Affiliate faculty Sch. Natural Resources, Colo. State U., Ft. Collins; mem. peer rev. coms. for academia, govt. and pvt. industry; agy. rep. Fed. Geographic Data Com., chair biol. data working group, mem. standards working group and coordination group, vegetation subcom. Dir. prodn. interactive computer exhibit on remote sensing for Denver Mus. Nat. History; contbr. sci. articles to profl. jours. Bd. dirs. Nat. Park Service Equal Employment Opportunity Com., Denver, 1981, chmn., 1982. Recipient Mgrs. award Nat. Park Service, Lakewood, 1981, Performance Commendation award, 1988, Excellence of Svc. Team awrd U.S Dept. Interior, 1999; NRA rsch. grantee, 1972. Fellow Am. Soc. Potogrammetry and Remote Sensing (exec. com., bd. dirs. 1988-90, v.p. 1992, pres.-elect 1993, pres. 1994, dir. remote sensing applications divsn. 1987-89); mem. Am. Congress on Surveying and Mapping (joint satellite mapping and remote sensing com.), The Wildlife Soc., GRASS Users Group (steering com. 1986—, treas. 1987—), ELAS Users Group (co-chmn. 1985-86, chmn. 1986-87), Sigma Xi. Avocations: tennis, skiing, soccer. E-mail: maury_nyquist@usgs.gov. *Personal philosophy: We need to view the land as a community to which we all belong, instead of a commodity for individual gain. (adopted from Aldo Leopold's A Sand County Almanac, 1949).*

NYQUIST, THOMAS EUGENE, consulting business executive; b. Froid, Mont., June 20, 1931; s. Richard Theodore and Lydia (Baker) N.; m. Corinne Elaine Johnson, Dec. 22, 1956; children: Jonathan Eugene, Lynn Marie Nyquist Bergstrausser. BA, Macalester Coll., 1956; MA, U. Mont., 1958; PhD, Northwestern U., 1966. Prof. SUNY, New Paltz, 1968-76, adminstr. cen. div. Albany, 1976-90; pres. Nyquist Assocs., New Paltz, N.Y., 1991—. Mem. adv. bd. George Washington's Hdqrs., Newburgh, N.Y., 1980-92; acad. dir. N.Y. Edn. Dept., Kenya, 1982; head del. House of Peace and Friendship/Village of New Paltz delegation, St. Petersburg, Russia, 1992; chmn. Japan Com., 1997-99; co-chair Scenic Byways Com, 2002-2003; chmn. Regatta Com., 2000—03. Author: (monograph) Urban Africans in South Africa, 1977, (book) African Middle Class Elite, 1983. Mem. Ulster County Legislature, 1976-79; dep. mayor Village of New Paltz, 1983-87, mayor, 1987-2003, mem. exec. bd., N.Y. Conf. Mayors, 2000-2003; chmn. New Paltz Centennial Com., 1986-87; bd. dirs. Ulster Region Credit Union, Kingston, N.Y., 1976-87, Ulster Performing Arts Ctr., 1978-82, Friends of Cuttington Coll., Liberia, 1994-98; bd. dirs. Internat. Partnership for Svc. Learning, 1985—, treas., 2003-; mem. exec. bd., 1998—; treas. Lower Hudson Conf., 1988, 89-90, 91-92; chair Thomas & Corinne Nyquist Found., 2004—. With U.S. Army, 1952-54. Fellow SUNY, South Africa, 1975; Ford Found. grantee, 1986. Mem. African Studies Assn., N.Y. African Studies Assn. (exec. bd. dirs. 1973—, co-editor newsletter 1974—), Am. Polit. Sci. Assn. Democrat. Avocations: hiking, cross county skiing. Home: 140 Huguenot St New Paltz NY 12561-1018 Office: Nyquist Associates 140 Huguenot St New Paltz NY 12561-1918 Office Phone: 845-255-3003. Personal E-mail: nyq@hvi.net.

NYREN, NEIL SEBASTIAN, publisher, editor; b. Boston, June 13, 1948; s. Karl Edwin and Dorothy Elizabeth (Smith) N.; m. Lois Miriam Sharfman, Oct. 11, 1970; 1 child, Alexander BA, Brandeis U. V.p. G.P. Putnam's Sons Pub., N.Y.C., 1997—; editor Random House Pubs., N.Y.C., 1974-77, Arbor House Pubs., N.Y.C., 1977-78; exec. editor Atheneum Pubs., N.Y.C., 1978-84; sr. editor G.P. Putnam's Sons Pub., N.Y.C., 1984-86, editor-in-chief, 1986—, pub., 1989—, sr. v.p., 1997—. Democrat. Jewish. Office: GP Putnam's Sons 375 Hudson St New York NY 10014-3658 E-mail: nnyren@penguinputnam.com.

NYROP, DONALD WILLIAM, airline executive; b. Elgin, Nebr., Apr. 1, 1912; s. William A. and Nellie (Wylie) N.; m. Grace Cary, Apr. 19, 1941; children: Nancy, William, Karen, Kathryn. AB, Doane Coll., 1934; LL.B., George Washington U., 1939. Bar: D.C. 1938. Atty. Gen. Counsel's Office, CAA, Washington, 1939-41; exec. officer to chmn. CAB, 1942, chmn., 1952; rep. U.S. airlines; mem. ofcl. U.S. delegations Internat. Civil Aviation Orgn. Assemblies, 1946, 47; dep. adminstr. for ops. CAA, 1948-50, adminstr., 1950-51; chmn. CAB, 1951-52; pres. Northwest Airlines, Inc., 1954-78. Served with Air Transport Command USAAF, 1942-46. Decorated Legion of Merit. Mem.: Minneapolis, Minnesota. Home: 4505 Golf Ter Minneapolis MN 55424-1510

NYSTROM, LORNE, member of parliament; B in Polit. Sci., U. Saskatchewan, Can. Cert. tchr. Can. Mem. 37th parliament House of Commons, Ottawa, Canada, 1968—; owner consulting firm, 1993—97. Mem. privy coun. House of Commons, 1992, critic for fin. and Dem. reform, dep. house leader; spkr. in field. Author: Just Making Change, 2002. Mem. New Dem. Party, 1975—95, chair task force employment and parliamentary reform. Recipient l'Ordre de la Pléiade, French Rep. New Dem. Party. Office: House of Commons 710 Justice Bldg Ottawa ON K1A 0A6 Canada also: 1059 Albert St Regina SK S4R 2P9 Canada

NYÚL, LASZLO G. mathematician, educator, researcher; b. Várpalota, Hungary, Sept. 4, 1970; s. László Nyúl and Éva Milassin. BSc, József Attila U., Szeged, Hungary, 1992, MSc, 1994; PhD, U. Szeged, 2003. Programmer József Attila U., Szeged, 1994—95, asst. lectr., 1995—2000, U. Szeged, 2000—03, asst. prof., 2003—. Contbr. chapters to books Advances in Multiple Sclerosis, 3D Image Processing-Techniques and Clinical Applications, articles to profl. jours. Scholar, Ctrl. European Exch. Program for U. Studies, 2000; TEMPUS scholar, Hungarian Ministry of Edn., 1993—94, Eötvös scholar, 1998. Mem.: Hungarian Assn. Image Analysis and Pattern Recognition, John von Neumann Computer Soc. Achievements include patents for standardizing MR imaging intensity. Office: Univ Szeged Arpád tér 2 Szeged H-6720 Hungary Office Phone: +36 62 546-396. Office Fax: +36 62 546-397. E-mail: nyul@inf.u-szeged.hu.

OAK, CLAIRE MORISSET, artist, educator; b. St. Georges, Quebec, Can., May 31, 1921; came to U.S., 1945; d. Louis and Bernadette (Coulombe) Morisset; m. Alan Ben Oak, July 2, 1947. Student, Ecole des Beaux Arts, 1938-42, Parsons Sch. Design, N.Y.C., 1945, Art Students League, 1945-46. Staff artist Henry Morgan & R. Simpson, Montreal, 1942-45; artist illustrator W.B. Golovin Advt. Agy., N.Y.C., 1947-49; freelance illustrator Arnold Constable & Advt. Agy., N.Y.C., 1948-50, Le Jardin des Modes, Paris, 1950-51, May & Co., L.A., 1956, Katten & Marengo Advt., Stockton, Calif., 1962-84; pvt. practice illustrator, designer San Joaquin Valley, Calif., 1984-92; art instr. San Joaquin Delta Coll., Stockton, 1973—. Owner Fashion Illustrator's Workshop, N.Y.C., 1953-54; instr. Bauder Coll., Sacramento, 1975-76; painting workshop leader Lodi Art Ctr., 1991—; watercolor workshop leader D'Pharr Painting Adventures, Virginia City, Nev., 1992; on-going watercolor workshop Galerie Iona, Stockton, Calif., 1993—. Named S.B. Anthony Woman of Achievement in the Arts, U. Pacific, 1982. Mem. Stockton Art League, Lodi Art Ctr., Ctrl. Calif. Art League, The League of Carmichael Artists, Delta Watercolor Soc. (bd. mem. 1988—). Avocations: outdoor painting, drawing from a model. Home: 2140 Waudman Ave Stockton CA 95209-1755 *You are a success in the visual arts if you teach others how to see.*

OAK, JEFFREY CHARLES, ethicist; b. Weymouth, Mass., July 1, 1959; s. Wayne LeRoy and Myrna Eloise (Noble) O.; m. Carol Pinkham, Oct. 11, 1986; children: Nathaniel Charles, Julia Elizabeth. BA, Gettysburg (Pa.) Coll., 1981; MDiv, Yale U., 1985, STM, 1986, PhD, 1996. Ordained Methodist Church. Clergyman United Meth. Conf. Ea. Pa., Valley Forge, 1986-87, United Meth. Conf. N.Y., White Plains, 1987-91; lectr., tchg. asst. Yale U., New Haven, 1991-96; healthcare ethicist Arden Hill Health Care, Goshen, N.Y., 1996-98; v.p. corp. integrity and ethics Arden Hill Sr. Health System, Goshen, 1998-99; sr. v.p. Coun. of Ethical Orgns., Alexandria, Va., 1999-2001; chief ethics and compliance officer Vets. Health Adminstrn., Washington, 2001—. Chmn. U.S. code of ethics Health Care Compliance, Phila., 1998-99, chmn. nat. edn. com., 1998-99. Editor Pastin Report on Healthcare Compliance, 2000; assoc. editor Report on Healthcare Compliance, 1999—; contbr. articles to profl. jours. Trustee, vice chair Arden Hill Health System, Goshen, 1993-96; chmn. ethics com. Arden Hill Hosp., Goshen, 1990-99, Hospice of Orange County, Middletown, N.Y., 1996-99; mem. steering com. Hudson Valley Healthcare Ethics Network, Bronx, 1993-97; trustee Health Care Compliance Assn., 2001-, Southold Yacht club, 2001-. Recipient Keith Pappas award Gettysburg Coll., 1981, Disting. Alumni award Manheim Twp. H.S., 1998; John Wesley fellow Found. for Theol. Edn., 1992-95, Yale U. fellow, 1994. Avocations: sailing, woodworking, jogging, kayaking, nordic skiing. Office: Vets Health Adminstn Office Compliance (10B3) 810 Vermont Ave NW Washington DC 20420 E-mail: jcoak@att.net.

OAKAR, MARY ROSE, congresswoman; b. Cleve., Mar. 5, 1940; d. Joseph M. and Margaret Mary (Ellison) O. BA in English, Speech and Drama, Ursuline Coll., Cleve., 1962, LHD (hon.); MA in Fine Arts, John Carroll U., Cleve., 1966; LLD (hon.), Ashland U., 1978, Ursuine Coll., 1984, St. Mary's Notre Dame, 1989, Baldwin Wallace Coll., 1988; LHD (hon.), Trinity Coll., 1987. Instr. English and drama Lourdes Acad., Cleve., 1963-70; asst. prof. English, speech and drama Cuyahoga Community Coll., Cleve., 1968-75; mem. Cleve. City Council from 8th Ward, 1973-76, 95th-102nd Congresses from 20th Dist. Ohio, 1977-92; mem. Pepper Commn. on Long Term Health Care, chair subcom. internat. devel., fin., trade and monetary policy; chair task force on social security, elderly, women; chair subcom. on personnel and police; mem. banking, fin. and urban affairs com., select com. on aging, post office and civil service com., com. on house adminstrn., also numerous subcoms.; Ptnr. Mary Rose Oakar and Assocs. Apptd. to Sec. Conf. to Establish Nat. Action Plan on Breast Cancer, 1994, by Pres. Clinton to bd. dirs. Bldrs., For Peace, 1994, to policy to White House Conf. on Aging. Founder, vol.-dir. Near West Side Civic Arts Center, Cleve., 1970; ward leader Cuyahoga County Democratic Party, 1972-76; mem. Ohio Dem. Central Com. from 20th Dist., 1974; trustee Fedn. Community Planning, Cleve., Health and Planning Commn. Cleve., Community Info. Service Cleve., Cleve. Soc. Crippled Children, Public Services Occupational Group Adv. Com., Cuyahoga Community Coll., Cleve. Ballet, Cleve. YWCA. Recipient Outstanding Service awards OEO, 1973-78, Community Service award Am. Indian Center, Cleve., 1973, Community Service award Nationalities Service Center, 1974, Community Service award Club San Lorenzo, Cleve., 1976, Cuyahoga County Dem. Woman of Yr., 1977, Ursuline Coll. Alumna of Yr. award, 1977, awards Irish Nat. Caucus, awards West Side Community Mental Health Center, awards Am. Lebanese League, awards Cleve. Fedn. Am.-Syrian Lebanese Clubs, Breast Cancer Awareness award Nat. Women's Health Resource Ctr., 1989, 1st lay recipient Barbara Bohen-Pfeiffer award Italian-Am. Found. Cancer Rsch., 1989, Disting. Svc. award Am. Cancer Soc., 1989, Myrl H. Shoemaker award Ohio Dem. Party, 1992, Philip Hart award Consumer Fedn. Am., 1987; cert. appreciation City of Cleve.; Woman of Yr. award Cuyahoga County Women's Polit. Caucus, 1983; decorated Knight of Order of St. Ladislaus of Hungary, Women in Aerospace Outstanding Ach. award, Black Focus Woman of the Decade award. Office: 1888 W 30th St Cleveland OH 44113-3447

OAKES, CLAUDIA, museum administrator; Asst. dir. pub. programs Utah Mus. Nat. History, Salt Lake City; asst. dir. exhibits & ops. Utah Mus. Natural History & Hansen Planetarium, Salt Lake City, assoc. dir. mus. affairs; v.p. pub. programs Milw. Pub. Mus., Milw.; assoc. curator, acting aeronautics dept. chmn. Smithsonian Inst. Nat. Air & Space Mus., Washington. MAP III surveyor; reviewer IMLS-GOS. Mem.: Am. Assn. Mus. (v.chmn.), Nat Assn. Mus. Exhib. (bd. dir.), We. Mus. Assn. (bd. dir.). Office: Utah Museum Natural History 1390 E Presidents Circle Salt Lake City UT 84112-0050

OAKES, DENNIS, lawyer, insurance company executive; b. 1951; B, Hamilton Coll., 1973; JD, Cath. U. of Am., 1977. With Wolf, Block Schorr and Solis-Chohen; chief of staff Mayor of Phila., 1980—84; adminstrv. asst. Phila. Congressman William J. Green, 1973—77; with U.S. Healthcare; spl. counsel Ronald O. Perelman, 1989—93; exec. dir., acad. medicine and managed care forum Aetna Inc., 1996—2001, chief investor rels., 2001—03, v.p., 2003—. Office: Aetna Inc 151 Farmington Ave Hartford CT 06156

OAKES, DUWAYNE EARL, retired principal; b. Fillmore, ND, May 28, 1926; s. Ralph William Oakes and Ella Catherine (Anderson) Baril; m. Elva Jean Jacobsen, Nov. 6, 1948; children: Jon, Robert, Kathleen, Mary. BA in Edn., Pacific Luth. U., 1952, MA, 1972. Tchr. DuPont Ft. Lewis Sch. Dist., Wash., 1952-59, prin., 1959, Clover Pk. Sch. Dist., Lakewood, Wash., 1959-71. Author: God's Call to Communion, 1982; contbr.: National Poetry Library Anthology, 1995-96, God's Plan, 1999; inventor fishing rod socket. Inductee Internat. Poetry Hall of Fame, 1996. Mem. Norwegian Lodge, Eagles Club. Christian Socialist. Lutheran. Avocations: singing in church choir, Normanna Chorus. Home: 8515 94th St SW Lakewood WA 98498-4527

OAKES, FRED D. editor; Editor Elks mag. The Elks of the USA, Chgo. Office: The Elks of the USA 425 W Diversey Pkwy Chicago IL 60614-6107

OAKES, JAMES L. federal judge; b. Springfield, Ill., Feb. 21, 1924; m. Evelena S. Kenworthy, Dec. 29, 1973 (dec. Oct. 1997); m. Mara A. Williams, Jan. 1, 1999; m. Rosalyn Landon, Oct. 2, 1945; 3 children. AB, Harvard Coll., 1945; LLB, Harvard U. Law Sch., 1947; LLD, New Eng. Coll., 1976, Suffolk U., 1980, Vt. Law Sch., 1995. Bar: Calif. 1949, Vt. 1950. Pvt. practice, Brattleboro, Vt.; spl. counsel Vt. Pub. Svc. Commn., 1959—60; counsel Vt. Statutory Revision Commn., 1957—60; mem. Vt. Senate, 1961—65; atty. gen. Vt., 1967—69; U.S. dist. judge, 1970—71; judge U.S. Ct. Appeals 2d Cir., Brattleboro, 1971—, chief judge, 1989—92. Adj. faculty Duke U. Law Sch., 1985—96, Iowa U. Coll. Law, 1993—97. Office: US Ct Appeals PO Box 696 Brattleboro VT 05302-0696

OAKES, JUDY DIANNE, real estate broker; b. Charleston, W.Va., Aug. 14, 1950; d. William E. and Betty A. Hager; m. Gary H. Oakes, Dec. 21, 1968; children: Scott E., Christina D. McDaniel, Brian M. Real estate sales Bishop Realtors, Cleve., 1973-82, Armstrong Realty, Riverside, Calif., 1986-88; real estate broker Remax All Stars, Riverside, Calif., 1988-94, Realty Exec., Riverside, Calif., 1994—2001. Named #1 Agt. in Co., Real Estate Sales, 1994—2002. Mem. Cert. Residential Specialist, Magnolia Ave. Bapt. Ch., Inland Valley Assn. Realtors (bd. dirs. 1995). Avocations: reading, rose garden, ocean. Office: Judy Oakes Real Estate Group 3742 Tibbetts St #101 Riverside CA 92506 E-mail: judy@judyoakes.com.

OAKES, LAURA, radio personality; Grad. Comms. and History, U. Minn.; postgrad., Brown Inst. With radio, Fergus Falls, Minn.; with radio and TV Duluth; news reporter, morning news anchor Sta. KDLH-TV; co-anchor 5 pm Sta. WCCO News Hour. Mem.: Minn. AP Broadcasters Assn. (bd. dirs.). Avocations: competitive figure skater, music, theater, sports. Office: WCCO 625 2nd Ave S Minneapolis MN 55402

OAKES, LESTER CORNELIUS, retired electrical engineer, consultant; b. Knoxville, Oct. 11, 1923; s. Charles Vaughn and Maude Cornelia (Harrison) O.; m. Kathleen Clark, Dec. 27, 1947; children: Michael, Richard, Cynthia, Melissa. BS in E.E., U. Tenn., 1949, MS, 1962. Registered profl. engr., Tenn. Engr. Fairchild Engring. and Aircraft, Oak Ridge, 1949-51; engr. I&C div. Oak Ridge Nat. Lab., 1951-68, dep. head I&C div., 1968—, asst. dir. I&C div., 1971-90; cons. Oak Ridge Nat. Lab., electric Power Rsch. Inst., Nuclear Regulatory Commn., 1990—. Contbr. articles to profl. jours.; patentee in field. Served with USAF, 1943-46. Martin Marietta Corp. fellow. Fellow IEEE Presbyterian. Home: 710 Pleasant Hill Rd Maryville TN 37803-7337 E-mail: lesoakes@aol.com.

OAKES, MARIA SPACHNER, nurse; d. A. William and Roberta Mae (Linville) Stephens; m. John Cullwell Oakes, Nov. 27, 1976; children: John Cullwell II, Laura Suzann. Diploma Sch. Nursing, King's Daughters' Hosp. Cert. med./surg. nurse. Staff nurse Ohio State U. Hosp., Columbus, Lawrence County, Ironton; head nurse, neonatal intensive care King's Daughters' Med. Ctr., Ashland, Ky. Staff nurse neonatal IC, Huntington Hosp. Behavioral Medicine. Bd. dirs. Am. Cancer Soc.; deacon bd. sessions, pres. Women's Assn. First Presbyn. Ch.; v.p. West Ironton Parent-Tchr. Group; pres. Kingsbury Parents for Better Schs.; past pres. Kings Daus. Hosp. Sch. Nursing Alumni Assn.; mem. strategic planning com. Ironton City Sch. Dist., Acad. Boosers Assn., H.S. Band Boosters mem., band nurse. Mem.: ANA, Cabell Lincoln County (work camp project co-dir.), Ky. Nurses Assn. (state offices nursing practice com., legis. com., state nominating com., nurse practice commn., past pres., v.p., treas. Dist. 4, program chmn., seminar planner, continuing edn. coord, current v.p. Dist. 4, mem. ad hoc com. health care reform), Ironton Coop. Club (past pres.). Home: 2210 N 3rd Ave Ironton OH 45638-1068

OAKES, NANCY, chef, restaurant owner; Student, San Francisco Art Inst. Formerly chef Alexis, San Francisco; formerly chef, co-owner Barnacle, San Francisco, L'Avenue, San Francisco; chef, co-owner Boulevard, San Francisco, 1993—. Named Best Chef in Calif., James Beard Found., 2001. Office: Boulevard 1 Mission St San Francisco CA 94105

OAKES, ROBERT JAMES, physics educator; b. Mpls., Jan. 21, 1936; s. Sherman E. and Josephine J. (Olson) O.; children: Cindy L., Lisa A. BS, U. Minn., 1957, MS, 1959, PhD, 1962. NSF fellow Stanford U., 1962-64; asst. prof. physics, 1964-68; assoc. prof. physics Northwestern U., 1968-70, prof. physics, 1970-76, prof. physics and astronomy, 1976—. Vis. staff mem. Los Alamos Sci. Lab., 1971-92; vis. scientist Fermi Nat. Accelerator Lab., 1975—, CERN, 1966-67; mem. Inst. for Advanced Study, Princeton, 1967-68; vis. scientist DESY, 1971-72; faculty assoc. Argonne Nab. Lab., 1982—; U.S. scientist NSF-Yugoslav joint program, 1982-92; panelist Nat. Rsch. Coun., 1990-98. A.P. Sloan fellow 1965-68; Air Force Office Sci. Rsch. grantee, 1969-71, NSF grantee 1971-87, Dept. Energy grantee, 1987—; named Fulbright-Hays Disting. prof. U. Sarajevo, Yugoslavia, 1979-80; recipient Natural Sci. prize China, 1993. Fellow Am. Phys. Soc., AAAS; mem. N.Y. Acad. Sci., Ill. Acad. Sci., Physics Club (Chgo.), Sigma Xi, Tau Beta Pi. Clubs: Physics (Chgo.). Office: Northwestern U Dept Physics 2145 Sheridan Rd Evanston IL 60208-0834

OAKES, TERRY LOUIS, retail clothing store executive; b. Denver, June 12, 1953; s. Robert Walter and Stella Marie (Ray) O.; m. Cynthia Alison Bailey, Jan. 10, 1981; children: Madeleine Bailey, Robert Alan. BBA, So. Meth. U., 1975. Dept. mgr. Woolf Bros., Dallas, 1975-76; buyer I.K.O. Dry Goods, Denver, 1976-79, gen. sales mgr., 1979-81, exec. v.p., mdse. mgr., 1981-86; nat. sales mgr. Fresh Squeeze div. Bayly Corp., Denver, 1986-88; owner, pres. Bolderdash, Denver, 1988—. Tchr., mem. adv. bd. fashion mdse. divsn. Colo. Inst. Art., Denver, 1991-98. Bd. dirs. Cherry Creek North Bus. Improvement Dist., Vail Racquet Club, Vail, Colo. Mem. Vail Racquet Club (bd. dirs.). Democrat. Presbyterian. Home: 5390 S Geneva St Englewood CO 80111-6205 Office: Bolderdash 2717 E 3d Ave Denver CO 80206-4919 E-mail: bolderdash@earthlink.net.

OAKES, THOMAS WYATT, environmental engineer, computer engineer; b. Danville, Va., June 14, 1950; s. Wyatt Johnson and Relia (Sceacre) O.; m. Terry Lynn Jenkins, June 15, 1974; 1 child, Travis Wyatt. BS in Nuclear Engring., Va. Polytechnic U., 1973, MS in Nuclear Engring., 1975; MS in Environ. Engring., U. Tenn., 1981. Ordained deacon Bapt. Ch., 1989. Health physics asst. Va. Polytechnic U., Blacksburg, 1972-74; radiation engr. Babcock and Wilcox Co., Lynchburg, Va., 1974-75; dept. mgr. Oak Ridge (Tenn.) Nat. Lab., 1975-78, environ. mgr., 1978-85; corp. environ. coord. Martin Marietta, Oak Ridge, 1985-87; asst. v.p. Sci. Applications Internat. Corp., Oak Ridge, 1987-90; environ. mmgr. Westinghouse Environ. and Geotech. Svcs., Knoxville, Tenn., 1990-91; mgr. S.E. region environ. svcs. ATEC & Assocs., Inc., Marietta, Ga., 1991-93; asst. v.p. environ. svcs. Scitek, Ft. Campbell, Ky., 1993-98; ind. sr. cons., 1998—; pres. T30 Nat. Svc. Inc., 1998—. Safety dir. DSSI/MOEC, 2002—. Contbr. over 107 articles to scholarly and profl. jours. Recipient Spl. Recognition award Union Carbide Corp., 1980, Best Paper award Nat. Safety Coun., 1982, Tech. Publs. award Soc. Tech. Communications, 1987. Mem. AAAS, Am. Indsl. Hygiene Assn., N.Y. Acad. Scis., Health Physics Soc. (sec.-treas. environ. sect. 1984-85), Am. Naval Soc., Am. Soc. for Quality Control. Office: 11130 Kingston Pike Ste 1-328 Knoxville TN 37922-2800 E-mail: t30oakes@inetmail.att.net.

OAKES, WALTER JERRY, pediatric neurosurgeon; b. De Soto, Mo., July 10, 1946; s. Marvin Melton and Mildred Florene (Link) O.; m. Linda Helen Maas (div. Jan. 1985); 1 child, Kathleen Suzanne; m. Jean Evans, Dec. 1988; children: Matthew Marvin, Peter Clifford. BA in Chemistry, U. Mo., 1968; MD, Duke U., 1972. Diplomate Am. Bd. Neurol. Surgeons. Neurosurgery resident Duke U., Durham, N.C., 1972-78, asst. prof. neurosurgery, 1979-90, assoc. prof. neurosurgery, 1991—, asst. prof. pediatrics, 1981-92, assoc. prof. pediatrics, 1992; pediatric neurosurgery resident U. Toronto Hosp. for Sick Children, Ont., Can., July-Dec., 1975; registrar pediatric neurosurgery U. London Hosp. for Sick Children, Eng., Sept., 1978-Feb., 1979; prof. neurosurgery and pediat. U. Ala., Birmingham, 1992—, Dan Hendley chair pediatric neurosurgery, 2002—. Fellow: ACS. Office: Children's Hosp Ala 1600 7th Ave S Ste 400 Birmingham AL 35233-1785 Office Phone: 205-939-6914. Business E-Mail: wjomd@uab.edu.

OAKLEY, ANDREW ARTHUR, journalist, educator; b. Chgo., Oct. 22, 1958; s. Arthur George and Dolores Margarite (Hernandez) O.; m. Suzanna Pinter, Sept. 7, 1985; children: Glen Matthias, Ryan Arthur. BS in Journalism, Northwestern U., 1980, MS, 1981. Reporter Woodstock (Ill.) Daily Sentinel, 1980-81; police reporter Herald-Palladium, St. Joseph, Mich., 1981-82; city hall reporter Daily Herald, Arlington Heights, Ill., 1982-84; instr. journalism Oakton C.C., Des Plaines, Ill., 1984-85; features editor North Shore Mag., Winnetka, Ill., 1985-86; news editor City and State, Chgo., 1986-93; journalism editor P.O. Publ. Co., Port Murray, N.J., 1993-2000; newsletter editor All Aboard for Hackettstown, N.J., 1996-98. Lectr. Northwestern U., Evanston, Ill., 1990-96; columnist Daily Herald, Arlington Heights, Ill., 1995-96; copy editor Full Time Dads Mag., Clifton, N.J., 1997-2000; corr. Daily Herald, Arlington Heights, 1995—. *Having worked as a newspaper journalist and fiction writer, Andy Oakley has developed a college curriculum that emphasizes literary journalism to his writing students. Both his professional and academic work propound a synthesis between fiction and non-fiction writing. He stresses during his college courses and public speaking engagements that the best writers are masters of both fiction and non-fiction; this is especially necessary due to the upheaval in communication technology that will make some writing forms, including daily newspaper journalism, obsolete. Still, he believes that basic newspaper reporting is a solid foundation for the construction of a writing career.* Author: Eighty-Eight, 1988, Issues Confronting City and State Governments, 1992, Beginning Journalism Packet, 1994; cons. editor P.O. Pub. Co., Skokie, Ill., 1988-92. Lifetime mem. N Club, 1980—; commr. Skokie Human Rels. Commn., 1987-94; advisor Mcpl. Alliance Lit. Club, 1997-98; U.S. Soccer Fedn. coach, referee, 1999—; edn. chmn. Charleston (Ill.) Alliance Ch., 2000-04. Mem. Medill Alumni Assn., Evanston Running Club. E-mail: OAKLEYANDY@aol.com.

OAKLEY, CAROLYN LE, state legislator, city manager, director; b. Portland, Oreg., June 28, 1942; d. George Thomas and Ruth Alveta Victoria (Engberg) Penketh; children: Christine, Michelle. BS in Edn., Oreg. State U., 1965. Educator Linn County (Oreg.) Schs., 1965-76; owner Linn County Tractor, 1965-90; mem. Oreg. Legis. Assembly, Salem, 1989—, asst. majority leader, 1993—, majority whip, 1994; apptd. regional dir. region 10 Dept. Health and Human Svcs., Seattle, 2002—. Mem. exec. bd. Oreg. Retail Coun., 1987-90. Chmn. Linn County Rep. Ctrl. Com., 1982-84; chmn. bd. dirs. North Albany Svc. Dist., 1988-90; chair Salvation Army, Linn and Benton Counties, 1987—; vice chmn. bd. trustees Linn-Benton C.C. Found., 1987—; pres. Women for Agr., Linn and Benton Counties, 1984-86; mem. STRIDE Leadership Round Table, 1991—; state chair Am. Legis. Exch. Coun., 1991-96; nat. bd. dirs., 199-99, exec. com., 1995, 1st vice chair, 1998; mem. Edn. Commn. of the States, 1991—, com. policies and priorities, 1993—, steering com., 1998—, exec. com., 1998; mem. Leadership Coun. on Higher Edn., 1995—; mem. nat. policy bd. Danforth Found., 1995—; state dir., Women in Govt., 1996—; state dir., Nat. Order Women Legislators, 1993—; hon. mem. Linn-Benton Compact Bd., 1993—; active Linn County Criminal Justice Coun., 1994—. Named Woman of Yr. Albany chpt. Beta Sigma Phi, 1970. Mem. Nat Conf. State Legislators (chmn. edn. com. 1992—), Albany C. of C. (bd. dirs. 1986-93, 96—), Linn County Rep. women (legis. chmn. 1982-91). Republican. Methodist. Avocations: gardening, camping. Office: 2201 6th Ave RX-01 Seattle WA 98121-0001 Home: 3197 NW Crest Loop Albany OR 97321-9627 Office Phone: 541-928-7745. Personal E-mail: cloakley@juno.com.

OAKLEY, CHARLES, professional basketball player; b. Cleve., Dec. 18, 1963; Student, Va. Union U., 1984—85. With Chgo. Bulls, 1986—88, N.Y. Knicks, 1989—98, Toronto Raptors, 1998—2001, Chgo. Bulls, 2001—02, Wash. Wizards, 2002—. Office: MCI Center 601 F St NW Washington DC 20004

OAKLEY, FRANCIS CHRISTOPHER, history educator, former college president; b. Liverpool, Eng., Oct. 6, 1931; arrived in U.S., 1957, naturalized, 1968; s. Joseph Vincent and Siobean (NiCurean) O.; m. Claire-Ann Lamenzo, Aug. 9, 1958; children: Deirdre, Christopher, Timothy, Brian. BA, Corpus Christi Coll., Oxford U., 1953, MA, 1957; postgrad., Pontifical Inst. Medieval Studies, Toronto, 1953—55; MA, Yale U., 1958, PhD, 1960; LLD, Amherst Coll., 1986, Wesleyan U., 1989; LHD, Northwestern U., 1990, North Adams State Coll., 1993, Bowdoin Coll., 1993; LittD, Williams Coll., 1994. Mem. faculty Yale U., 1959-61, Williams Coll., Williamstown, Mass., 1961—, prof. history, 1970—2002, dean faculty, 1977-84, Edward Dorr Griffin prof. history of ideas, 1984—85, pres., 1985-94, pres. emeritus, 1994—, Edward Dorr Griffin prof. history of ideas, 1994—2002, prof. emeritus, 2002—; interim pres. Am. Coun. Learned Socs., 2002—03, pres. emeritus, 2003—; hon. fellow Corpus Christi Coll., Oxford U., 1991—; sr. fellow Oakley Ctr. Humanities, Williams Coll., 2002—. Vis. lectr. Bennington (Vt.) Coll., 1967; Sir Isaiah Berlin vis. prof. Oxford U., 1999-2000; Merle Curti lectr. U. Wis., Madison, 2001; Étienne Gilson lectr Pontifical Inst. Medieval Studies, Toronto, 2002; mem. Inst. Advanced Study Princeton, 1981-82; assoc. Nat. Humanities Ctr., 1991; guest scholar Woodrow Wilson Internat. Ctr. for Scholars, 1994; chair bd. dirs. Am. Coun. Learned Socs., 1993-97; trustee Sterling and Francine Clark Art Inst., 1985—, pres. 1998—; trustee Mass-MoCA Found., 1995—, Willamstown Art Conservation Ctr., 1995-98, Williamstown Theatre Festival, 1985-93, Nat. Humanities Ctr., 1996-02, 2003—, chmn. bd. trustees, 2004—, Lake Forest Coll., 1997-2001; trustee Inst. Advanced Cath. Studies, 1998—, vice chair, 2002—; mem. MassMoCA Cultural Devel. Commn., 1988—; mem. adv. coun. Ctr. for Study of Religion, Princeton U., 1999—. Author: The Political Thought of Pierre d'Ailly: The Voluntarist Tradition, 1964, Kingship and the Gods: The Western Apostasy, 1968, Council over Pope?, Towards a Provisional Ecclesiology, 1969, Medieval Experience: Foundations of Western Cultural Singularity, 1974, rev. England edit., The Crucial Centuries, 1979, Spanish edit., 1980, 95, Medieval Acad. edit., 1988, 93, The Western Church in the Later Middle Ages, 1979, rev. edit., 1985, 88, 91, Natural Law, Conciliarism and Consent in the Late Middle Ages, 1984, Omnipotence, Covenant and Order: An Excursion in the History of Ideas, 1984, Community of Learning: The American College and the Liberal Arts Tradition, 1992, Scholarship and Teaching: A Matter of Mutual Support, 1996, Politics and Eternity: Studies in the History of Medieval and Early Modern Political Thoughts, 1999, The Leadership Challenges of a College Presidency, 2002, The Conciliarist Tradition, 2003; editor: (with Daniel O'Connor) Creation: The Impact of an Idea, 1969, (with Bruce Russett) Governance, Accountability and the Future of the Catholic Church, 2003; contbr. articles to profl. jours. Lt. Brit. Army, 1955-57. Goldsmith's Co. London fellow, 1953-55, Social Sci. Rsch. Coun. fellow, 1963, Am. Coun. Learned Socs. fellow, 1965, 69-70, Weil Inst. fellow, 1965, Folger Shakespeare Libr. fellow, 1974, NEH fellow, 1976, 81-82; recipient Wilbur Lucius Cross medal Yale Grad. Sch., 1997. Fellow Medieval Acad. Am. (pres. fellows 1999-2002), Am. Acad. Arts and Scis.; mem. Am. Hist. Assn., Am. Cath. Hist. Assn., Am. Ch. History Soc., New Eng. Medieval Conf. (pres. 1983-84), The Century Assn., Am. Cusanus Soc. (adv. bd. 1997—). Democrat. Roman Catholic. Office: Williams Coll Oakley Ctr Humanities & Soc Sci Williamstown MA 01267 Office Phone: 413-597-2149. Business E-Mail: francis.c.oakley@williams.edu.

OAKLEY, GODFREY PORTER, JR., medical educator, former health facility administrator; b. Greenville, N.C., June 1, 1940; s. Godfrey Porter and Carrie O.; m. Mary Ann Bryant, Sept. 2, 1961; children: Martha Gray, Susan Herndon, Robert Bryant. Student, Duke U., 1958-61; MD, Bowman Gray Sch. of Medicine, 1965; MS in Preventive Medicine, U. Washington, 1972. Diplomate Am. Bd. Pediatrics, Nat. Bd. Med. Examiners, Am. Bd. Preventive Medicine, Am. Bd. Med. Genetics. Intern in straight pediatrics Cleve. Met. Gen. Hosp., 1965-66, resident in pediatrics, 1966-68; sr. fellow in teratology and human embryology U. Washington Sch. of Medicine, Ctrl. Lab. Human Embryology, Dept. of Pediatrics, Seattle, 1970-72; sr. fellow U. Washington Sch. Pub. Health and Community Medicine, Seattle, 1971-72; EIS officer leukemia sect. Ctrs. Disease Control and Prevention (CDC), Atlanta, 1968-70, chief etiology studies sect., bur. epidemiology, cancer and birth defects, 1972-81; chief birth defects br., chronic diseases divisn. Nat. Ctr. Environ. Health, Ctrs. Disease Control and Prevention, Atlanta, 1981-85, dir. divsn. birth defects and devel. disabilities, 1985-94; clin. asst. prof. pediatrics divsn. med. genetics Emory U., Atlanta, 1968-70, 72-85, clin. asst. prof. gynecology-obstetrics divsn. med. genetics, 1981-85; mem. visiting med. staff Grady Meml. Hosp., Atlanta, 1974-84; vis. prof. epedemiology Rollins Sch. Pub. Health, Emory Univ., 1998—. Med. adv. bd. Ctrs. Disease Control & Prevention (CDC); mem. task force on predictors of hereditary disease or congenital defects NIH Consensus Conf., 1979; mem. genetics coordinating com. NIH/CDC; mem. adv. com. biometric and epidemiological methodology FDA/CDC; cons. bur. med. svcs. FDA; mem. Chronic Diseases Surveillance Working Group; mem. patient registry com. Cystic Fibrosis Found., med. adv. coun., 1978—; mem. drug experience coordinating com. Dept. Health, Edn. and Welfare; mem. genetics com. Ga. Dept. Human Resources, 1980—; ex-officio mem. genetic diseases rev. and adv. com. Health Svcs. Adminstrn., 1981; mem. master community health program, interdisciplinary faculty com., curriculum com. Emory U.; mem. working group on heart disease epidemiology Nat. Heart, Lung and Blood Insts., 1978; mem. ad hoc com. on Alpha-fetoprotein Pub. Health Svc.; mem. profl. adv. coun. Spina Bifida Assn.

Am., 1981—; mem. WHO EURO-China Consultation, Beijing, China, 1983; lectr. in field. Mem. editorial bd. Pediatric & Perinatal Epidemiology, 1987-89; contbr. articles to profl. jours., chpts. to books. Nancy Lybrook Lasater scholar 1961-67; recipient Physician's Recognition award AMA, 1973-76, Outstanding Svc. medal Pub. Health Svc., 1981, Meritorious Svc. award, 1988, Spl. Recognition award, 1993, President's Excellence award Spina Bifida Assn. Am., 1988-89, Disting. Alumnus award U. Washington Sch. Pub. Health, 1990, Hebert L. Needleman award Am. Pub. Health Assn., 1996; named Person of Week, World News Tonight, 1996. Mem. Am. Acad. Pediatrics (past com. drugs/CDC liaison, com. genetics 1990, exec. com. 1990—, CDC rep. Ga. chpt. 1993), Am. Soc. Human Genetics, Am. Coll. Epidemiology, Am. Coll. Med. Genetics, Atlanta Genetics Soc., Greater Atlanta Pediatric Soc., Atlanta Obstetrical and Gynecological Soc. (assoc.), Soc. Epidemiologic Rsch., Soc. Pediatric Rsch., Teratology Soc. (pres. elect 1983-84, pres. 1984-85, editorial bd. Teratology 1978-83, edn. com. 1988), Internat. Clearinghouse Birth Defects Monitoring Systems (chmn. 1981-82, vice chmn. 1982-83, chmn. 1983-84), Pub. Health Leadership Inst., Alpha Omega Alpha, Inst. Medicine, 2004. Office: Rollins Sch Pub Health Emory U Dept Epedemiology 1510 Clifton Rd NE Atlanta GA 30322-4218

OAKLEY, JAMES LOUIS, marketing educator, researcher; b. Hinsdale, Ill., Oct. 30, 1971; s. James Clifton and Annette Marie Oakley; m. Lorraine Emily Pecknold, May 6, 1995; children: Rachel Christine, Brandon Paul, Emily Nicole. BS in Psychology, U. Ill., 1993; MS in Mgmt., Purdue U., 1995; PhD in Mktg., Northwestern U., 2002. Project mgr. First Bank Sys., Inc., St. Paul, 1995—96; bus. devel. analyst Capital One Fin. Corp., Richmond, Va., 1996—99; rsch. assoc. Media Mgmt. Ctr. Northwestern U., Evanston, Ill., 1999—2001, mktg. instr., 2001—02; asst. prof. mgmt. Purdue U., West Lafayette, Ind., 2002—. Recipient Dissertation award, State Farm Cos. Found.; grantee, Ctr. for E-Business Edn. and Rsch., 2003. Mem.: Acad. Mgmt., Inst. Ops. Rsch. and the Mgmt. Scis., Soc. Consumer Psychology, Assn. Consumer Rsch., Am. Mktg. Assn. Office: Purdue U 100 S Grant St West Lafayette IN 47907-2076 E-mail: joakley@krannert.purdue.edu.

OAKLEY, JOHN HOWARD, humanities educator; b. Elizabeth, N.J., Nov. 6, 1949; s. Howard Thurston and Marjorie Ethel (Deyo) O.; m. Evi Gertrud Hessler, May 8, 1990; children: Nicholas Todd, Jacob Travis. BA, Rutgers U., 1972, MA, 1976, PhD, 1980. Asst. prof. Coll. William and Mary, Williamsburg, Va., 1980-86, assoc. prof., 1986-93, prof. classical studies, 1993—, chancellor prof., 1993—, Forrest D. Murden, Jr. prof., 2000—, dept. chair, 2001—. Vis. prof. Canterbury U., Christchurch, N.Z., 1997; Whitehead vis. prof. Am. Sch. Classical Studies, Athens, 1997-98, dir. summer session, 1986, mng. com., 1982—; adv. coun. Am. Acad. in Rome, 1985—; vis. fellow classics dept. Princeton U., 2000-01; vis. prof. Freiburg U., Germany, 2003. Author: The Phiale Painter, 1990, Corpus Vasorum Antiquorum-Baltimore, 1992, The Achilles Painter, 1997, others; co-author: The Wedding in Classical Athens, 1993, Coming of Age in Ancient Greece: Images of Childhood from the Classical Past, 2003, PIcturing Death in Classical Athens: The Evidence of The White Lekythre, 2004; editor: Corpus Vasorum Antiquorum, 1985—, Bryn Mawr Electronics Resources Rev., 1997-2002; adv. bd. Am. Jour. Archaeology, 1992-93; contbr. articles to profl. jours. 1st lt. U.S. Army, 1972-80. Recipient Phi Beta Kappa Award for Advancement of Scholarship, 1990; Alexander von Humboldt Stiftung fellow, 1988-89, 91-92, NEH fellow, 1997-98, Andrew W. Mellon fellow Met. Mus. Art, 2000-2001. Mem. Archaeol. Inst. Am. (pres. Williamsburg soc. 1995-97, travelling lectr. 1989-91, 95—), Classical Assn. of Mid. West and South. Avocation: Black Belt. Home: 2864 Hidden Lake Dr Williamsburg VA 23185-8020 Office: College William and Mary Dept Classical Studies Williamsburg VA 23187

OAKLEY, MARY ANN BRYANT, lawyer; b. Buckhannon, W.Va., June 22, 1940; d. Hubert Herndon and Mary F. (Deeds) Bryant; m. Godfrey P. Oakley, Jr., Sept. 2, 1961; children: Martha, Susan, Robert. AB, Duke U., 1962; MA, Emory U., 1970, JD, 1974. Tchr. Winston-Salem/Forsyth County Schs., N.C., 1961-65; assoc. Margie Pitts Hames, Atlanta, 1974-80; ptnr. Stagg Hoy & Oakley, Atlanta, 1980-83, Oakley & Bonner, Atlanta, 1984-90; pvt. practice, 1990-96; ptnr. Holland & Knight LLP, Atlanta, 1996—. Adj. prof. trial practice Ga. State U., 1986-95; adj. prof. pretrial Emory U. Law Sch., 1991, 95; bd. dirs. Nat. Employment Lawyers Assn., 1989-94; founding coord. NELA, Ga.; mem. Ga. Supreme Ct. Commn. on Racial and Ethnic Bias, 1994-95; mem. Ga. Bd. Bar Examiners, 1990-94, chmn., 1994. Author: Elizabeth Cady Stanton, 1972; mem. editl. rev. bd.: The Ga. Labor Letter, 1997—2001, notes and comments editor: Emory Law Jour., 1973—74; contbr. articles to law jours. Bd. dirs. Atlanta Met. YWCA, 1975-79, 1st v.p., 1978-79; mem. Leadership Atlanta, 1979; bd. dirs. Ga. chpt. ACLU, 1981-83, Holland & Knight Charitable Found. Bd., 2002—, Ga. Legal Svcs. Program, 1991-98; trustee Unitarian Universalist Congregation Atlanta, 1977-80, pres., 1979-80, mem. Unitarian Universalist Commn. Appraisal, 1980-85; bd. dirs. Unitarian Universalist Service Com., 1984-90, v.p., 1986-88, pres., 1988-90. Nat. Merit scholar, 1958. Fellow: Ga. Bar Found., Am. Bar Found.; mem.: ABA, Gate City Bar Assn., Ga. State Bar Disciplinary Bd. (investigative panel 1985—88, chmn. 1987—88), Ga. Assn. Women Lawyers (Kathleen Kessler award 1998), Lawyers Club Atlanta, Atlanta Bar Assn., State Bar Ga. (chmn. individual rights sect. 1979—81, Disting. Svc. award 1998, H. Sol Clark Pro Bono award 1996), Am. Judicature Soc., Order of Coif, Phi Beta Kappa, Bleckley Inn of Ct. (pres. 1996—99). Home: 2224 Kodiak Dr NE Atlanta GA 30345-4152 Office: 1201 W Peachtree St One Atlantic Ctr Ste 2000 Atlanta GA 30309-3400 Office Phone: 404-817-8500. Business E-Mail: maruann.oakley@hklaw.com.

OAKLEY, PHYLLIS ELLIOTT, retired diplomat; b. Omaha, Nov. 23, 1934; d. Thomas Myron Elliott and Elsa (Kerkow) Elliott Garabedian; m. Robert Bigger Oakley, June 8, 1958; children: Mary Oakley Kress, Thomas Elliott. BA, Northwestern U., 1956; MA, Fletcher Sch. Law & Diplomacy, 1957. Commd. fgn. svc. officer Dept. State, 1957-58, 74-99, ret., 1999. Asst. cultural affairs officer, Kinshasa, Zaire, 1979-82, desk officer, Afghanistan, 1982-85, Pearson Exchange officer Senator Mathias, 1985-86; dep. spokesman, 1986-89, AID Afghan Humanitarian Assistance program, Islamabad, 1989-91, dep. asst. sec. INR Bur., 1991-93, sr. dep. PRM, 1993-94, asst. sec. PRM, 1994-97, INR Bur., 1997—. Mem. Coun. Fgn. Rels., Cosmos Club, Phi Beta Kappa. Office: Dept of State INR Bur 2201 C St NW Washington DC 20520-0001

OAKLEY, ROBERT ALAN, insurance executive; b. Columbus, Ohio, Nov. 1, 1946; s. Bernard Harmon and Mary Evelyn (Mosier) O.; m. Ann Lucille Liesenhoff, Aug. 3, 1968; children: Jeff, David. BS in Aero. Engring., Purdue U., 1968; MBA, Ohio State U., 1969, PhD in Fin., 1973. Mgr. fin. projects Nationwide Mut. Ins. Co., Columbus, 1976-79, regional controller, 1979-82, dir. ops. controls, 1982-83, v.p., corp. controller, 1983—, exec. v.p., CFO, 1993—. Author: Insurance Informations Systems, 1985. Capt. USAF, 1972-76. Mem. Fin. Mgmt. Assn., Fin. Execs. Inst., Am. Soc. CLU's. Avocations: golf, reading, teaching. Office: Nationwide One Nationwide Plz Columbus OH 43215-2220

OAKLEY, ROBERT LOUIS, law librarian, educator; b. N.Y.C., Nov. 6, 1945; s. Bert Tuttle Oakley and Allese (Duffin) Vestigo; m. Madeleine Cohen, Aug. 13, 1971 (div. 2002); children: Esther Shulamit, Daniel Isaac-Meir. BA, Cornell U., 1968; MLS, Syracuse U., 1972; JD, Cornell U., 1976. Bar: N.Y. 1977, U.S. Dist. Ct. (no. dist.) N.Y. 1977. Assoc. dir. law libr. Cornell U., Ithaca, N.Y., 1976-79; dir. law libr., assoc. prof. Boston U. Law, 1979-82, Georgetown U., Washington, 1982-87, dir. law libr., prof., 1987—. Contbr. articles to profl. jours. Mem. Libr. of Congress, mem. Network Adv. Com., 1986-92, 95—; adv. nat. commn. on Preservation and Access, 1988-94; bd. dirs. Montgomery County (Md.) Pub. Librs., 1988-92. Mem. ABA, ALA, Am. Assn. Law Librs. (Washington Affairs rep. 1989—, mem. exec. bd. 1991-94, v.p. 1999-2000, pres. 2000-01), Assn. Am. Law Schs. Avocations: photography, music, personal computers, amateur radio. Office: Georgetown U Law Ctr 111 G St NW Washington DC 20001-1417

OAKS, DALLIN HARRIS, lawyer, church official; b. Provo, Utah, Aug. 12, 1932; s. Lloyd E. and Stella (Harris) Oaks; m. June Dixon, June 24, 1952 (dec. July 1998); children: Sharmon, Cheri Lyn, Lloyd D., Dallin D., TruAnn, Jenny June; m. Kristen McMain, Aug. 25, 2000. BA with high honors, Brigham Young U., 1954, LLD (hon.), 1980; JD cum laude, U. Chgo., 1957; LLD (hon.), Pepperdine U., 1982, So. Utah U., 1991. Bar: Ill. 1957, Utah 1971. Law clk. to Chief Justice Earl Warren U.S. Supreme Ct., 1957—58; with firm Kirkland, Ellis, Hodson, Chaffetz & Masters, Chgo., 1958—61; mem. faculty U. Chgo. Law Sch., 1961—71, assoc. dean and acting dean, 1962, prof., 1964—71, mem. vis. com., 1971—74; pres. Brigham Young U., Provo, Utah, 1971—80; also prof. law J. Reuben Clark Law Sch., 1974—80; justice Utah Supreme Ct., 1981—84; mem. Coun. of Twelve Apostles Ch. Jesus Christ of Latter Day Sts., 1984—, pres. Phlippines area, 2002—04. Legal counsel Bill of Rights com. Ill. Constl. Conv., 1970. Author (with G.G. Bogert): Cases on Trusts, 1967, 1978; author: (with W. Lehman) A Criminal Justice System and The Indigent, 1968; author: The Criminal Justice Act in the Federal District Courts, 1969; author: (with M. Hill) Carthage Conspiracy, 1975; author: Trust Doctrines in Church Controversies, 1984, Pure in Heart, 1988, The Lord's Way, 1991, His Holy Name, 1998, With Full Purpose of Heart, 2002; editor: The Wall Between Church and State, 1963; contbr. Mem. adv. com. Nat. Inst. Law Enforcement and Criminal Justice, 1974—76; mem. Wilson coun. Woodrow Wilson Internat. Ctr. for Scholars, 1973—80; trustee Intermountain Health Care Inc., 1975—80; regional rep. Ch. of Jesus Christ of Latter-day Saints, 1974—80, past 1st counselor Chgo. South Stake; bd. dirs. Notre Dame Ctr. for Constl. Studies, 1977—80, Rockford Inst., 1980—2000, Pub. Broadcasting Svc., 1977—85, chmn., 1980—85; bd. dirs. Polynesian Cultural Ctr., 1987—96, chmn., 1988—96. Fellow: Am. Bar Found. (exec. dir. 1970—71); mem.: Am. Assn. Pres. Ind. Colls. and Univs. (pres. 1975—78, dir. 1971—78), Order of Coif. Mem. Ch. Of Jesus Christ Of Latter-Day Saints. Office: Quorum of Twelve 47 E South Temple Salt Lake City UT 84150 1200

OAKS, MAURICE DAVID, retired pharmaceutical company executive; b. Everett, Pa., Jan. 22, 1934; s. Jacob Garvin and Hannah Alma (Young) O.; m. Judith Ann Rayne; 1 child, Kimberly. BS in Biology, Franklin and Marshall Coll., 1956. Sales rep. Squibb Pharm, Salisbury and Balt., Md., 1959-69; div. sales mgr. Squibb Pharm., Columbus, Ohio, 1969-71, product mgr. Princeton, N.J., 1971-76, group product dir., 1976-78, dir. product planning, U.S., 1979-80, v.p. world wide mktg. devel., 1980-82, v.p. mktg. svcs., 1983-85, pres. Princeton Pharm. Products, 1985-89; exec. v.p. Squibb Pharm. Group U.S., Princeton, N.J., 1989-90; v.p. worldwide ops. planning Bristol-Myers Squibb Pharms. Ops., Princeton, 1990-92. Bd. dirs. Nat. Pharm. Coun., McLean, Va., 1985-90, mem. exec. com., 1988-90; bd. dirs., mem. audit com Penn Engring. Mfg., Danboro, Pa., chmn. compensation com., 2000-01, chmn. nominating com., 2002—. Mem. coun. Franklin and Marshall Coll. Commn. on Found. and Corp. Support, Lancaster, Pa., 1987-90, ann. fund class capt., 1991-97; mem., pres. Mid-Atlantic regional adv. coun. Franklin and Marshall Coll., also mem. phys. scis. labs. renovation com., 1996-97; bd. dirs. Surf's Edge Condo Assn., Ocean City, Md., 1995-99; active YMCA, Doylestown, Pa. With U.S. Army, 1956-58. Mem. Doylestown (Pa.) Country Club. Republican. Methodist. Avocations: tennis, golf, bicycling.

OATES, CARL EVERETTE, lawyer, director; b. Harlingen, Tex., Apr. 8, 1931; s. Joseph William and Grace (Watson) O.; m. Eileen Noble Hudnall; children: Carl William, Gregory Carl Hudnall, Patricia O. Chase, Matthew Noble Hudnall. BS, U.S. Naval Acad., 1955; LLB, So. Meth. U., 1962. Bar: Tex. 1962, D.C. 1977, Nebr. 1985. Assoc. Akin, Gump, Strauss, Hauer & Feld, Dallas, 1962-64, ptnr., 1965-91. Asst. atty. gen. State of Texas, 1992-94, spl. coun., Tex. Dept. Banking, 1994-95, prin. Carl E. Oates, P.C. Chmn. bd. trustees S.W. Mus. Sci. and Tech., Dallas; v.p. S.W. Sci. Mus. Found., Dallas; bd. dirs. Kiwanis Wesley Dental Ctr., Inc., Dallas; pres. Wesley Dental Found., Dallas. Lt. USN, 1955-59. Mem. ABA, D.C. Bar Assn., Tex. Bar Assn., Dallas Bar Assn., Barristers, Northwood Club, Delta Theta Phi. Personal E-mail: coates00@aol.com.

OATES, JOHN ALEXANDER, III, medical educator; b. Fayetteville, NC, Apr. 23, 1932; s. John Alexander and Isabelle (Crowder) O.; m. Meredith Stringfield, June 12, 1956; children: David Alexander, Christine Larkin, James Caldwell. BS magna cum laude, Wake Forest Coll., 1953; MD, Bowman Gray Sch. Medicine, 1956. Intern, asst. resident medicine N.Y. Hosp.-Cornell U. Med. Center, N.Y.C., 1956-58, 61-62; from clin. assoc. to sr. investigator Nat. Heart Inst., 1958-63; faculty Vanderbilt U. Sch. Medicine, Nashville, 1963—, prof. medicine and pharmacology, 1969—, Werthan prof. investigative medicine, 1974-84, chmn. dept. medicine, 1983-97, Thomas F. Frist Sr. prof. medicine, 1984—. Drug rsch. bd. Nat. Acad. Scis.-NRC, 1967-71; chmn. pharmacology and toxicology tng. com. Nat. Inst. Gen. Med. Scis., 1969-70; adv. coun. Nat. Heart, Lung and Blood Inst., 1985-89. Master ACP; fellow Am. Acad. Arts and Scis., Am. Assn. Advancement Sci.; mem. Am. Fedn. Clin. Rsch. (pres. 1970-71), Am. Soc. Clin. Investigation (v.p. 1976-77), Assn. Am. Physicians (pres. 1981-82), Am. Soc. Pharmacology and Exptl. Therapeutics (chmn. exec. com. divsn. clin. pharmacology 1967-69), Inst. of Medicine. Achievements include co-discovery of antihypertensive effect of methyldopa, elucidation of a number of interactions between drugs in man; research in biochemistry and pathophysiology of eicosanoids. Home: 2032 Sunset Hills Terr Nashville TN 37215 Office: Vanderbilt Med Ctr 536 RRB Nashville TN 37232-6602 Office Phone: 615-343-4845. Business E-Mail: john.oates@vanderbilt.edu.

OATES, JOHN FRANCIS, classics educator; b. Holyoke, Mass., Aug. 7, 1934; s. William Adrian and Lilian (Woods) O.; m. Rosemary Walsh, June 27, 1957; children: Elizabeth, Emily, John Francis, Sarah. BA, Yale U., 1956, MA, 1958, PhD, 1960; postgrad. (Fulbright fellow), Am. Sch. Classical Studies in Athens, Greece, 1956-57. Instr. classics Yale U., 1960-63, asst. prof., 1963-67; asso. prof. ancient history Duke U., 1967-71, prof., 1971—2002, prof. emeritus, 2002—, chmn. dept. classical studies, 1971-80, chmn. humanities coun., 1975-80, dir. database of documentary papyri, 1982—, dir. papyrus catalog project, 1992-95. Hon. rsch. asst. Univ. Coll. London, 1965-66; vis. prof. Smith Coll., Northampton, Mass., 1967, 68; mem. mng. com. Intercollegiate Ctr. Classical Studies in Rome, Italy, 1972-77, Am. Sch. Classical Studies in Athens, 1973—, mem. com. on coms., 1975-77; mem. Coun. for Internat. Exch. of Scholars, 1974-77; v.p., trustee Triangle Univs. Ctr. for Advanced Study, Inc., 1975-90; trustee Nat. Humanities Ctr., 1977-90, trustee emeritus, 1990—; adv. coun. Sch. Classical Studies, Am. Acad. in Rome, 1976—; dir. summer seminar Nat. Endowment Humanities, 1978; dir. Nat. Fedn. State Humanities Couns., 1980-83; mem. N.C. Humanities Com., 1977-83, chmn. 1980-82. Author: The Status Designation, 1963 (with A.E. Samuel and C.B. Welles) Yale Papyri in the Beinecke Library, 1967, A Checklist of Papyrological Editions, 5th edit., 2001, (with Willis) Duke Data Bank of Documentary, Papyri (CD-ROM), 1996, The Basilikos Grammateus, 1995; mem. adv. bd. Greek, Roman and Byzantine Studies, 1977—, Humanities Report, 1981-83. ACLS fellow, 1973-74 Mem. Am. Philol. Assn. (chmn. com. computer activities 1974-75, dir. 1975-78, mem. nominating com. 1980-83), Archaeol. Inst. Am., Am. Hist. Assn., Am. Soc. Papyrologists (v.p. 1971-73, pres. 1976-80, dir.), Assn. Internationale de Papyrologues, Classical Assn. Middle West and South (v.p. 1972-74, pres. So. sect. 1974-76). Home: 843 Inglenook Rd Durham NC 27707-3961 Office: Duke U Dept Classical Studies Durham NC 27708-0103 Fax: 919-681-4262. E-mail: joates@duke.edu.

OATES, JOYCE CAROL, author; b. Lockport, N.Y., June 16, 1938; d. Frederic James and Caroline (Bush) O.; m. Raymond Joseph Smith, Jan. 23, 1961. BA, Syracuse U., 1960; MA, U. Wis., 1961. Instr. English U. Detroit, 1961-65, asst. prof., 1965-67; prof. English U. Windsor, Ont., Can., 1967-87; writer-in-residence Princeton (N.J.) U., 1978-81, prof., 1987—. Author: (short story collections) By the North Gate, 1963, Upon the Sweeping Flood, 1966, The Wheel of Love, 1970, Marriages and Infidelities, 1972, The Hungry Ghosts, 1974, The Goddess and Other Women, 1974, Where Are You Going, Where Have You Been?: Stories of Young America, 1974, The Poisoned Kiss and Other Stories From the Portuguese, 1975, The Seduction and Other Stories, 1975, Crossing the Border, 1976, Night-Side, 1977, All the Good People I've Left Behind, 1978, The Lamb of Abyssalia, 1980, A Sentimental Education: Stories, 1981, Last Days: Stories, 1984, Wild Nights, 1985, Raven's Wing: Stories, 1986, The Assignation, 1988, Heat: And Other Stories, 1991, Where is Here?: Stories, 1992, Haunted: Tales of the Grotesque, 1994, Will You Always Love Me? and Other Stories, 1995, The Collector of Hearts: New Tales of the Grotesque, 1996, Faithless: Tales of Transgressions, 2001, Small Avalanches: And Other Stories, 2003, I Am No One You Know, 2004; (novels) With Shuddering Fall, 1964, A Garden of Earthly Delights, 1967 (Nat. Book award nomination 1968), Expensive People, 1967 (Nat. Book award nomination 1969), them, 1969 (Nat. Book award for fiction 1970), Wonderland, 1971, Do With Me What You Will, 1973, The Assassins, 1975, Childwold, 1976, The Triumph of the Spider Monkey, 1976, Son of the Morning, 1978, Unholy Loves, 1979, Cybele, 1979, Bellefleur, 1980 (L.A. Times Book award nomination 1980), A Sentimental Education, 1981, Angel of Light, 1981, A Bloodsmoor Romance, 1982, Mysteries of Winterthorn, 1984, Solstice, 1985, Marya, 1986, You Must Remember This, 1987, (as Rosamond Smith) The Lives of the Twins, 1987, American Appetites, 1989, (as Rosamond Smith) Soul-Mate, 1989, Because It Is Bitter, and Because It Is My Heart, 1990, (as Rosamond Smith) Nemesis, 1990, I Lock My Door Upon Myself, 1990, The Rise of Life on Earth, 1991, Black Water, 1992, (as Rosamond Smith) Snake Eyes, 1992, Foxfire: Confessions of a Girl Gang, 1993, What I Lived For, 1994 (PEN/Faulkner award nomination 1995), Zombie, 1995, First Love, 1996, We Were the Mulvaneys, 1996, Man Crazy, 1997, Devil's Half Acre, 1997, Come Meet Muffin!, 1998, My Heart Laid Bare, 1998, Broke Heart Blues, 1999, Starr Bright Will Be With You Soon, 1999, Blonde, 2000, The Barrens, 2001, Faithless: Tails of Transgression, 2001, Middle Age: A Romance, 2001, Big Mouth and Ugly Girl, 2002, I'll Take You There, 2002, Freaky Green Eyes, 2003, Rape: A Love Story, 2003, Where Is Little Reynard, 2003, The Tattooed Girl, 2004; (non-fiction) The Faith of a Writer: Life, Craft, Art, 2003; (poetry collections) Women in Love, 1968, Expensive People, 1968, Anonymous Sins, 1969, Love and Its Derangements, 1970, Angel Fire, 1973, Dreaming America, 1973, The Fabulous Beasts, 1975, Season of Peril, 1977, Women Whose Lives are Food, Men Whose Lives are Money: Poems, 1978, The Stepfather, 1978, Celestial Timepiece, 1981, Invisible Women: New and Selected Poems, 1970-1972, 1982, Luxury of Sin, 1983, The Time Traveller, 1987; (plays) The Sweet Enemy, 1965, Sunday Dinner, 1970, Ontological Proof of My Existence, 1970, Miracle Play, 1974, Three Plays, 1980, Daisy, 1980, Presque Isle, 1984, Triumph of the Spider Monkey, 1985, In Darkest America, 1990, I Stand Before You Naked, 1990, The Perfectionist and Other Plays, 1995; (essays) The Edge of Impossibility, 1972, The Hostile Sun: The Poetry of D.H. Lawrence, 1973, New Heaven, New Earth, 1974, Contraries: Essays, 1981, The Profane Art, 1984, On Boxing, 1987, (Woman) Writer: Occasions and Opportunities, 1988; editor, compiler: Scenes from American Life: Contemporary Short Fiction, 1973, (with Shannon Ravenel) Best American Short Stories of 1979, 1979, Night Walks, 1982, First Person Singular: Writer's on Their Craft, 1983, (with Boyd Litzinger) Story: Fictions Past and Present, 1985, (with Daniel Halpern) Reading and Fights, 1988, The Oxford Book of American Short Stories, 1992, The Sophisticated Cat: An Anthology, 1992; editor (with Raymond Smith) Ontario Rev.; contbr. to nat. mags. including N.Y. Times Book Rev., Mich. Quarterly Rev., Mademoiselle, Vogue, North Am. Rev., Hudson Rev., Paris Rev., Grand Street, Atlantic, Poetry, Esquire. Recipient O. Henry award, 1967, 73, Rosenthal award Nat. Inst. Arts and Letters, 1968, O. Henry Spl. award continuing achievement, 1970, 86, Award of Merit Lotos Club, 1975, St. Louis Lit. award, 1988, Rea award for the Short Story, 1990, Alan Swallow award for fiction, 1990, Nobel Prize in Lit. nomination, 1993; Guggenheim fellow, 1967-68, Nat. Endowment for the Arts grantee, 1966, 68. Mem. Am. Acad. and Inst. Arts and Letters. Office: care John Hawkins 71 W 23rd St Ste 1600 New York NY 10010-4102 also: Princeton U Dept Creative Writing 117 185 Nassau St Princeton NJ 08544-0001*

OATES, MARY JOSEPHINE, historian, educator; b. Boston, Apr. 18, 1935; d. Thomas Francis and Mary (Folan) Oates. BA (summa cum laude), Cath. U. of Am., DC, 1963; MA, Yale U., Conn., 1964, PhD, 1969. Mem. Congregation of the Sisters of St. Joseph of Boston, 1952—; asst. prof. econs. Regis Coll., Weston, Mass., 1970—74, assoc. prof. econs., 1974—80, prof. econs., 1980—2000, rsch. prof. econs., 2000—. Chair com. on internat. fellowships and awards AAUW, Washington, 1978—80, chair com. on fellowships to Am. women, 1983—85; mem. nat. adv. bd. Project on Religion and Am. Culture, Ind. U., Purdue U., Indpls., 1988—90; mem. com. on rsch. Nat. Fedn. of Congregations of Sisters of St. Joseph, U.S. and Can., St. Louis, 1988—96; cons. religion divsn. program Lilly Endowment, Indpls., 1992; mem. currriculum devel. project Ctr. for the Study of Philanthropy, CUNY, N.Y.C., 1996—99; chair com. on Cath. women U. of Notre Dame - Lilly Endowment Rsch. Initiative in Twentieth Century Studies in Am. Catholicism, Notre Dame, Ind., 1997—2000. Author: (book) The Role of the Cotton Textile Industry in the Economic Development of the American Southeast, 1900-1940; editor: Higher Education for Catholic Women: An Historical Anthology; author: The Catholic Philanthropic Tradition in America (Hon. Mention, Staley-Robeson-Ryan-St. Lawrence prize, Nat. Soc. of Fund Raising Execs., 1996), Catholic Philanthropy in America, Curriculum Guide, (book chpt.) The Textile Industry and Its Business Climate, Catholic Boston: Studies in Religion and Community, 1870-1970, A Guide to the History of Massachusetts, Faith, Moral Reasoning, and Contemporary Life, Catholic Women's Colleges in America, Charity, Philanthropy, and Civility in American History, Religion, the Independent Sector, and American Culture, Women in Spiritual and Communitarian Societies in the United States, American Catholic Women: An Historical Exploration. Mem. history adv. bd. Mus. of Women's History - The Leadership Ctr., N.Y.C., 2000—03; cons. U.S. CSC - Boston Region, 1971; mem. women's strategy group Giving New Eng., Associated Grant Makers, Boston, 2001—03; mem. ad hoc com. on stewardship Nat. Conf. of Cath. Bishops, Washington, 1990; mem. investment com. Congregation of the Sisters of St. Joseph of Boston, 1977—2003; mem. bd. dirs. Takayasu's Arteritis Assn., Bedford, NH, 1998—2002. Recipient Disting. Historian award, Conf. on the History of Women Religious, 2001; fellow Charlotte Dickson Fisher Fellowship, AAUW, 1966—67, Fellowship in Academic Adminstrn., Am. Coun. on Edn., 1969—70, Faculty Fellowship in Sci., Harvard U., NSF, 1976—77, Rsch. Fellowship, Mary I. Bunting Inst., Radcliffe Coll., 1980—81; grantee Kress Grant, Baker Libr., Harvard U. Grad. Sch. of Bus. Adminstrn., 1972, Rsch. Grant, Am. Philos. Soc., 1976, Curriculum Devel. Grant, Shelby Cullom Davis Found., 1978, Course Devel. Grant, Assn. of Am. Colls., 1986—89, Rsch. Grant, 1988, Lilly Endowment, 1988, 1990—92, Louisville Inst., 1997, Spencer Found., 2002—03. Mem.: Mass. Hist. Soc., Am. Cath. Hist. Assn. (chair, book prize com. 1997—98), Econ. History Assn. (program com. 1971—73), Social Sci. History Assn. (chair, book prize com. 1990—91, program com. 1982), Assn. for Rsch. on Nonprofit Orgns. and Voluntary Action (book prize com. 2001), Orgn. of Am. Historians, Am. Hist. Assn., Phi Beta Kappa. Roman Catholic. Office: Regis Coll 235 Wellesley St Weston MA 02493

OATES, SHERRY CHARLENE, portraitist, artist, photographer; b. Houston, Sept. 11, 1946; d. Charles Emil and Berniece Faye (Lohse) O. Student North Tex. State U., 1965-66; student under Martin Kellogg; BA in English, Health and Phys. Edn., Houston Bapt. U., 1968. Cert. art tchr., Tex. Tchr. Jackson Jr. High Sch., Houston, 1968-69, Percy Priest Sch., Nashville, 1969-70, Franklin (Tenn.) High Sch., 1970-84; freelance illustrator Bapt. Sunday Sch. Bd., Nashville, 1978-85, United Meth. Pub. House, Nashville, 1980-85; portraitist in oils, owner Portraits, Ltd., Nashville, 1984—. Portraits include corp. leaders, educators, politicians, hist. and equestrian subjects, society figures and children; participated in various exhbns. at Bapt. Sunday Sch. Bd. and All State and Ctr. South Exhibits at the Parthenon. Recipient 3d place in graphics Ctrl. South Exhbn. at The Parthenon-Tenn. Art League, 1986. Mem. Tenn. Art League. Republican. Baptist. Avocation: antiques. Studio: 816 Kirkwood Ave Nashville TN 37204-2602

OATES, STEPHEN BAERY, retired history educator; b. Pampa, Tex., Jan. 5, 1936; s. Steve Theodore and Florence (Baer) O.; divorced; children: Gregory Allen, Stephanie. BA magna cum laude, U. Tex., 1958, MA, 1960, PhD, 1968; Litt.D. (hon.), Lincoln Coll., 1981. Prof. history U. Mass., Amherst, 1971—98, Paul Murray Kendall prof. biography, 1980—98, adj. prof. English, 1981—98. Author: Confederate Cavalry West of the River, 1961, Rip Ford's Texas, 1963, Republic of Texas, 1968, Visions of Glory, 1970, To Purge This Land With Blood: A Biography of John Brown, 1970, Portrait of America, 2 vols., 1973, rev. edits., 1976, 83, 86, 90, 94, 98, 2002, The Fires of Jubilee: Nat Turner's Fierce Rebellion, 1975, With Malice Toward None: The Life of Abraham Lincoln (Christopher award for outstanding lit., Barondess/Lincoln

award N.Y. Civil War Round Table 1977), Our Fiery Trial: Abraham Lincoln, John Brown, and the Civil War Era, 1979, Let the Trumpet Sound: The Life of Martin Luther King, Jr., 1982 (Christopher award, Robert F. Kennedy Meml. Book award), Abraham Lincoln, The Man Behind the Myths, 1984, Biography as High Adventure: Life Writers Speak on Their Art, 1986, William Faulkner: The Man and the Artist, 1987, A Woman of Valor: Clara Barton and the Civil War, 1994, The Approaching Fury: Voices of the Storm, 1820-1861, 1997, The Whirlwind of War: Voices of the Storm, 1861-1865, 1998; contbr. articles and essays to periodicals; lectr. Presdl. Writers award, 1985; Master Tchr. award U. Hartford, 1985; Silver Medal award Case Council for Advance and Support of Edn., Prof. of Yr., 1986, 87, Kidger award New Eng. History Tchrs. Assn., Nevins-Freeman award Chgo. Civil War Round Table, 1993; Guggenheim fellow, 1972; sr. summer fellow NEH, 1978. Fellow Tex. State Hist. Assn.; mem. Tex. Inst. Letters, Soc. Am. Historians, Am. Antiquarian Soc., Phi Beta Kappa. Office: U Mass Dept History Amherst MA 01003

OATES, THOMAS R. university executive; married; 4 children. BA in English and Philosophy, St. Louis U., 1964, MA in English, 1970; postgrad., Am. Film Inst. Ctr., Beverly Hills, Calif., 1971; PhD in Am. Lit., St. Louis U., 1979. Coord., dir. program assts. and counselors upward bound pgm. Webster Coll., 1970-71, dir. media/journalism degree program, 1974-81, coord. MA program in media comms., 1975-81; chair, assoc. prof. dept. journalism St. Michael's Coll., 1981-85; campus dean U. Wis. Ctr., Richland Center, 1985-89; dir. U.S. ops. and acad. programs Coop. Assn. of States for Scholarships, Georgetown U., Washington, 1989-94; pres. Spalding U., Louisville, 1994—2002, Rocky Mountain Coll., Billings, Mont., 2002—. Mem. media adv. com. Mo. State Coun. of Arts, 1973-77; mem. planning commn. State Dept. of Higher Edn., Baton Rouge, 1979-80; mem., rep. Mo.'s ind. colls. and univs. Cen. Ednl. Network Mo., 1979-81; mem. adv. bd. Tri-State Bilingual Tng. Program, St. Michael's Coll., 1981-83; mem. Vt. Cath. Press Assn. Bd., 1984-85; mem., appointed chair Internat. Edn. Coun., U. Wis. Sys., 1987-88, designer, author Ctr. of Excellence project, 1988; mem. acad. staff adv. bd., U. Wis. Ctr. Sys., 1987-89, chair acad. staff grievance com., 1988; mem. 9-person state commn. to develop criteria for legal evaluations of devel. projects reviewed under Act 250 environ. law, Vt., 1984-85; presenter on internat. ednl. regional and nat. meetings of various orgns. Author, designer: (slide-tape program on history of early French and English explorers in mid-west) Old Land, New Land, 1985; author, designer: (book) Images, Values, and Development in Chittenden County, 1984; prodr.: (documentary photographic study on 5 rural Alaskan comtys.) Images of Continuity, Images of Change, 1977; prodr., dir.: (16mm documentary film) The Faces of British Honduras, 1974. Grantee Mo. Coun. on Arts, 1972, 76, NEH, 1975, U. Alaska, 1978, Mo. Coun. on Humanities, 1979, Vt. Coun. on Humanities, 1981, IBM, 1982, U. Wis. Ext., 1988, Wis. Coun. for Humanities, 1989, Orgn. for Petroleum Exporting Countries, 1992, C.C.'s for Internat. Devel., 1992. Office: Spalding U 851 S 4th St Office Pres Louisville KY 40203-2188

OATES, WILLIAM ARMSTRONG, JR., investment company executive; b. Pitts., July 27, 1942; s. William Armstrong and Margaret (Nichols) O.; m. Elizabeth Dick Macy, Sept. 7, 1968; children: Elizabeth N., Katherine M., Emily E.A. BA, Colby Coll., 1965; MBA, Harvard U., 1972. Asst. treas. Morgan Guaranty Trust, N.Y.C., 1966-70; trustee, dir. Northeast Investors Trust, Boston, 1972—; pres. Northeast Investors Growth Fund, Boston, 1980—; ptnr. Guild, Monrad & Oates, Inc., 1984—. Dir. Horn Corp., Ayer, Mass., Furman Lumber Co., Boston, Clifford Inc., Bethel, Vt. Pres. bd. trustees Groton (Mass.) Sch., 1979; trustee, treas. Roxbury Latin Sch., West Roxbury, Mass., 1975—. Served to 2d lt. Army N.G., 1966-70. Mem.: Harvard (Boston); Brookline Country (Brookline, Mass.); Somerset (Boston). Republican. Episcopalian. Home: 201 Village Ave Dedham MA 02026-4230 Office: NE Investment Mgmt Inc 150 Federal St Ste 1000 Boston MA 02110-1745

OATMAN, MICHAEL JAMES, artist, art educator; b. Burlington, Vt., Aug. 7, 1964; s. Gordon and Shirley Oatman; m. Bree Edwards, Aug. 4, 2001. BFA, RISD, 1986; MFA, SUNY, Albany, 1992. Tchg. asst. RISD, Providence, 1983—86, Harvard U., Cambridge, Mass., 1988; lectr. U. Vt., Burlington, 1992—98; adj. faculty SUNY, Albany, 1993—98; clin. asst. prof. Rensselaer Poly. Inst., Troy, NY, 1999—; rotating faculty mem. Vt. Coll. and Union Inst., Montpelier, Vt. Cons. Alice Austen Ho., S.I., NY, 2001; vis. critic RISD, 1986—. One-man shows include U. Wyo., Laramie, Williams Coll. Mus. Art, Ziehersmith Gallery, N.Y.C., two person show, Lenore Gray Gallery, Providence, exhibited in group shows at University Art Museum, SUNY, Albany, Museum of Contemporary Art, North Adams, Mass., Hermen Gooded Gallery, Bklyn., Art in General, N.Y.C., U. RI Fine Arts Ctr. Galleries, Kingston, DeCordova Museum and Sculpture Park, Lincoln, Mass., Scope Art Fair, Gershwin Hotel, N.Y.C., Samek Art Gallery, Bucknell U., Aldrich Mus. Contemporary Art, Ridgefield, Conn. Chmn. artists' com. Arts Ctr. of Capital Region, Troy, 1999—2003. Recipient Juror's award Exhbn. of Artists of Mohawk /Hudson Region, SUNY, Albany, 1999, 1994, 2003; grantee, Nancy Graves Found., NY, NY, 2003, Vt. Coun. on the Arts, 1995; Edna Lawrence Meml. scholar, RISD, 1983, Alumni scholar, 1984—86, Benevolent grantee, SUNY, Albany, 1990, tchg. fellow, Phillips Acad., Andover, Mass., 1986—87, S.O.S. grantee, NY State Coun. on the Arts, 1997, 1996. Mem.: Coll. Art Assn. Avocations: travel, industrial archaeology. Home: 623 River St Troy NY 12180 Office: Rensselaer Poly Inst 110 8th St Troy NY 12180-3590 Personal E-mail: oatman@rpi.edu.

OATWAY, FRANCIS CARLYLE, corporate executive; b. Bermuda, Nov. 29, 1936; s. Charles Y. and Josephine (McLellan) O.; m. Ann Thomason; children— Stephen F., Karen E., Andrew C., Christopher M. BSBA, Boston Coll., 1960. CPA, Mass., N.Y., others. With Deloitte Haskins & Sells, N.Y.C., 1960-80, ptnr., 1970-80; v.p. taxation Continental Group, Inc., Stamford, Conn., 1980-81, v.p. treasury and taxation, 1981-82, v.p. fin., 1982-83, v.p., chief fin. officer, 1983; exec. v.p., pres., dir. Continental Forest Industries, Inc., Stamford, Conn., 1984-85; pres. Hargro Assocs., S. Pomfret, Vt., 1985—; pres., CEO, dir. Hargro Enterprises, Inc., S. Pomfret, 1985—. Chmn., CEO, bd. dirs. NER Data Products, Glassboro, N.J., 1985—; pres., bd. dirs. Covent Ins. Co. Ltd., Hamilton, Bermuda, 1980-85; chmn. bd., mng. dir. CCC Finanz A.G., Zug, Switzerland, 1980-85; mng. dir. Continental Group Overseas Fin. N.V., Curacao, Netherlands Antilles, 1981-85; bd. dirs. Suecia Ins. Co. Am., Tarrytown, N.Y., chmn. bd. Apple Syndicate Corp., Westport, Conn., 1983-85. Contbg. editor: Federal Income Taxation of Banks and Financial Institutions, 1968, Professional Responsibility in Federal Tax Practice, 1970; contbr. articles to fin. jours. Trustee Convent of Sacred Heart, Greenwich, Conn., 1979-83; mem. acctg. adv. bd. Columbia U. Grad. Sch. Bus., N.Y.C., 1982-86; mem. exec. com. Boston Coll. Wall St. Coun., 1989-2002; trustee Conn. Pub. Expenditure Coun., Inc., Hartford, 1984-85; mem. pres.'s adv. bd. Weston Sch. Theology, Cambridge, 1993-99. Mem. Woodstock Country Club, Orchid Island Golf and Beach Club, Quail Valley Golf Club (Fla.) Roman Catholic. Also: Hargro Assocs PO Box 62 South Pomfret VT 05067-0062

OBAID, THORAYA AHMED, international organization official; b. Baghdad, Iraq, Mar. 2, 1945; married; 2 children. BA, Mills Coll., Oakland, Calif., 1966; MA, Wayne State U., Detroit, 1968, PhD, 1974; LLD (hon.), Mills Coll., 2002. Asst./assoc. social affairs officer Econ. and Social Commn. Western Asia, 1975—81, women and devel. prog. mgr., 1981—92, chief, social devel. and population divsn., 1992—93, dep. exec. sec., 1993—98; dir. divsn. arab states and Europe UN Population Fund, 1998—2000, exec. dir., 2001—; under-sec. gen. UN, 2001—. Coord. group on women Econ. and Social Commn. for Western Asia, 1989—90, v.p. staff coun., 1980—82; chair Inter-agy. Task Force on Gender, Amman, Jordan, 1996. Mem. editl. bd. Jour. Arab Women, 1984—90. Recipient award for outstanding commitment to global pub. svc., N.Y. Wagner Sch. Pub. Health, NYU, 2001, Borderless Giving award, Global Philanthropy Forum, 2002, George P. Younger award, Com. Religious Non-Govtl. Orgns., UN, 2002, medal and key to the city, Mayor of City of Santiago, Managua, Nicaragua, 2003, The Pedro Joaquin Chamorro award, Pres. Nicaragua, 2003, Second Century award for Excellence in Health Care, Columbia U. Sch. Nursing, 2003. Mem.: Assn. Working Mothers, Al Nadha Women's Assn. Office: 220 E 42nd St New York NY 10017

O'BAIRE, MARIKA, nurse, writer; b. Manila, Oct. 3, 1947; d. Gerald John and Giovanna (BelForti) Barry; children: Matthew, Alexei, Rita, D. Patrick. Student, U. Conn., 1964-65; diploma, Ellis Hosp. Sch. Nursing, 1977; BSN, Russell Sage Coll., 1980, postgrad., 1983, 94; grad. ontological design, Logonet Inc. ODC-J, 1993; postgrad. in humanities, Calif. State U., Dominguez Hills, 1995—; postgrad., Univ. Dundee, 2000—. RN N.Y.; lic. avatar master/wizard Star's Edge Internat., 1999. English tchr. Lang. Inst., Taipei, Taiwan, 1971-73; team leader, staff nurse in acute psychiatry Samaritan Hosp., Troy, N.Y., 1978-80; staff nurse, pediatric ICU Albany (N.Y.) Med. Ctr., 1980-84, 97—; rsch. nurse Commn. on Quality Care for Mentally Disabled, Albany, 1984; staff nurse Columbia-Greene Med. Ctr., Catskill, N.Y., 1984-89; night charge nurse Conifer Park, Scotia, N.Y., 1991-92; nursing educator St. Clare's Hosp., Schenectady, N.Y., 1992-96; adjunct clin. educator Albany Med. Ctr. So. Vt. Coll., Bennington, 1997—2001. Philosophy coaching Cmty. Hospice Saratoga, N.Y., 1998—; founder Future Design: Create What You Prefer, Avatar Tech. & Skills, 2000, Favorite Nurses, Colonie, N.Y., 2002—. Contbr. Echo Mag.; author: (screenplays) Dragon, 2002, About Love, (novels) Future Joyous, 2002, (screenplays) Syin. Vol. curriculum designer in gifted and talented programs. Mem. Childreach Plan Internat., Upstate Independent Filmmakers/Screenwriters. Home and Office: 90 Lincoln Ave Saratoga Springs NY 12866-4536 Personal E-mail: mobaire@nycap.rr.com.

OBAMA, BARACK H. state legislator; b. Honolulu, Hawaii, Aug. 4, 1961; m. Michelle Obama; children: Malia Ann, Natasha. B, Columbia U., 1983; JD, Harvard U., 1991. Editor-in-chief Harvard Law Review; exec. dir. PROJECT VOTE!, Ill., 1992; atty. Miner, Barnhill & Galland, P.C., 1993—; mem. Ill. Senate Dist. 13, Springfield, 1997—; mem. judiciary & local govt. com. Ill. Senate, Springfield, chmn., pub. health & human svcs. com. Sr. lecturer U. Chgo. Law Sch.; keynote speaker Dem. Nat. Convention, Boston, 2004. Author: (Memoir) Dreams From My Father, 1995. Chmn., Chgo.Annenberg Challenge; bd. dirs. Woods Fund Chgo., the Ctr. for Neighborhood Tech., the Chgo. Lawyers Com. for Civil Rights Under the Law and Pub. Allies, Joyce Found., 1994-. Recipient 40 Under 40 award, Crains Chgo. Bus., 1993, Monarch award for Outstanding Public Service, 1994, "Legal Eagle" award, IVI-IPO, 1995. Mem: Cook County Bar Assn. Democrat. Office: Sen 13th Dist M114 Capitol Bldg Springfield IL 62706 also: Obama for Ill PO Box 802799 Chicago IL 60680-2799 also: Miner Barnhill & Galland PC 14 W Erie St Chicago IL 60610-3811*

OBAMOGIE, MERCY A. physician; b. Lagos, Nigeria, Jan. 18, 1954; d. Godwin I and Janet E. (Amiolemen) O.; m. Abiodun O. Odunmbaku, June 20, 1980 (div. 1995); children: Abisola, Adenike, Abiodun. BS, Columbia U., 1980; MD, U. Medicine and Dentistry N.J., Piscataway, 1984; MPH, Johns Hopkins U., 1987; MBA, U. Calif., Irvine, 2000. Diplomate Am. Bd. Family Practice, Nat. Bd. Med. Examiners. Intern in internal medicine Muhlenberg Hosp., Plainfield, N.J., 1984-85; resident in gen. preventive medicine Johns Hopkins U., Balt., 1985-86; resident in family practice Georgetown U./Providence Hosp., Washington, 1986-89; pvt. practice Washington, Greenbelt, Md., 1989—; med. dir. Doctors Slim and Fitness Ctr., Greenbelt, 1996-98. Med. adv. bd. Metra Health Ins. Co., 1992-94; utilization com. Aetna Ins. Co., 1993-95, credentialing com., 1996; med. adv. com. United Health-Care, 1997; mem. planning com. Providence Hosp., Washington, 1996-98; with Prince George's Hosp. Ctr., Cheverly, Md., Howard U. Hosp., Washington, Doctors Cmty. Hosp., Lanham, Md., Providence Hosp., Washington; pres., med. dir. Mercy Med. Ctr., Benin City, Nigeria, 1996—; pres., CEO ASAKI Corp., Greenbelt, Md., 2000—. Contbr. articles to profl. jours. Home: 25 Atwood Ct Silver Spring MD 20906-2089 Office: 7323 Hanover Pkwy Ste A Greenbelt MD 20770-3617 E-mail: aimmercy@aol.com.

O'BANNION, MINDY MARTHA MARTIN, nurse; b. Cushing, Okla., Aug. 19, 1953; d. John William and Martha Florence (Vineyard) Martin; children: Mindi Martha Mae, William Neale Aaron. Student, Okla. State U., 1971-73, Oscar Rose Jr. Coll., 1973; grad., St. Anthony Sch. Nursing, 1975. RN, Tex. Med. clk. Martin Clinic, Cushing, Okla., 1968-72; nursing asst. Cushing Mcpl. Hosp., 1973-75, head nurse surg. fl., 1975-76, charge nurse med. unit, 1978-79, 82-83; staff nurse Met. Hosp., Dallas, 1985; staff nurse med. unit Mesquite (Tex.) Cmty. Hosp., 1985-87; nurse post partum unit, breastfeeding and discharge educator post partum unit Trinity Med. Ctr. Tenet Healthcare System, Carrollton, Tex., 1987—. Ind. beauty cons. Mary Kay Cosmetics, Dallas, Tex., 1993-99. Social com. Royal Haven Bapt. Ch. Women's Missionary Union, Dallas, 1977-78; mem. extension dept. nursery First Bapt. Ch., Cushing, 1979-82, extension dept. presch., 1982-84; mem. extension dept. presch. Royal Haven Bapt. Ch., Dallas, 1986-87; mem. Montgomery Elem. Sch. PTA, Farmers Branch, Tex., 1986-94, Vivian Field Jr. H.S. PTA, Farmers Branch, 1993-97, Valwood Park Bapt. Ch., Farmers Branch, 1994-2002, R.L. Turner H.S. PTA, R.L. Turner H.S. Orch. Booster Club, 1995-2001, Farmers Branch/Carrollton, 1995-2001, Prestonwood Bapt. Ch., Plano, Tex., 2002-; treas., nominating com. Joyce Harms group Women's Missionary Union; clk., charter mem. Brookhaven Bapt. Ch., Farmers Branch, 1989-92. Mem. Am., Tex., Okla. State Nurses Assns., St. Anthony Hosp. Sch. Nursing Alumnae, Bluebonnet Shelties (founder), Tau Beta Sigma (Alpha chpt.), Alpha Xi Delta (epsilon Omicron chpts. corr. sec. 1973). Baptist. Home: 13505 Onyx Ln Dallas TX 75234-4912

O'BARA, KENNETH J. physician; b. Detroit, Feb. 27, 1947; s. John Joseph and Catherine (Levens) O'Bara; m. Marianne Schwartz, July 29, 1972; children: Thomas, Mickel. BSE, U. Mich., Ann Arbor, 1969, MD, 1976. Diplomate Am. Bd. Emergency Medicine. Resident Truman Med. Ctr., Kansas City, Mo., 1976-79; mem. staff St. Joseph Mercy Hosp., Ann Arbor, 1979-80, Centralia (Wash.) Gen. Hosp., 1980-81, St. Helen's Hosp., Chehalis, Wash., 1980-81, Valley Med. Ctr., Renton, Wash., 1981—. ACLS affiliate faculty Am. Heart Assn., Seattle, 1982-86; co-dir. Assn. Emergency Physicians, Seattle, 1983-85. Fellow Am. Coll. Emergency Physicians, Wash. State Med. Soc., King County Med. Soc. Office: 8009 S 180th St Ste 103 Kent WA 98032-1042

OBATA, GYO, architect; b. San Francisco, Feb. 28, 1923; s. Chiura and Haruko (Kohaski) O.; m. Majel Chance, 1947 (div. 1971); children: Kiku, Nori, Gen; m. Courtney Bean, Nov. 28, 1984; 1 child, Max. BArch, Washington U., St. Louis, 1945; MArch in Urban Design, Cranbrook Acad. Art, 1946. Registered architect 39 states, D.C. Sr. designer Skidmore, Owings, & Merrill, Chgo., 1947-51; designer Hellmuth, Yamasaki & Leinweber, Detroit, 1951-55; pres., chmn. bd. dirs. Hellmuth, Obata & Kassabaum, Inc., St. Louis, 1955-93. Affiliate prof. Washington U., 1971; frequent lectr. design and urban environment; serves on competition juries on design throughout country. Projects include Nat. Air and Space Mus., King Saud U., Riyadh, Saudi Arabia, Dalls and Houston Gallerias, King Khaled Airport, Riyadh, hdqrs. Kellogg Co., hdqrs. BP America, World Bank, Washington, St. Louis Union Sta., Met. Sq., Dallas-Ft. Worth Airport, Squibb Corp. Rsch. Ctr., Lawrenceville, N.J., Burger King Corp. Hdqrs., numerous others. Fellow AIA; mem. Log Cabin Club, Noonday Club, St. Louis Club. Avocations: skiing, tennis. Office: Hellmuth Obata & Kassabaum Inc 211 N Broadway # 600 Saint Louis MO 63102-2733

OBEAR, FREDERICK WOODS, academic administrator; b. Malden, Mass., June 9, 1935; s. William Fred and Dorothea Louise (Woods) O.; m. Patricia A. Draper, Aug. 30, 1959 (dec. Dec. 1993); children: Jeffrey Allan, Deborah Anne, James Frederick; m. Ruth Crowley Sundell, Feb. 21, 1998. BS with high honors, U. Mass., Lowell, 1956, LHD, 1985; PhD, U. N.H., 1961. Mem. faculty dept. chemistry Oakland U., Rochester, Mich., 1960-81, prof., 1979-81, v.p. for acad. affairs, provost, 1970-81; chancellor U. Tenn., Chattanooga, 1981-97, univ. prof., chancellor emeritus, 1997—. Mem. nat. adv. panel Nat. Commn. on Higher Edn. Issues, 1981; mem. pres. commn. NCAA, 1991-94. Trustee Marygrove Coll., 1973-79. Am. Council Edn. fellow, 1967-68 Mem. AAAS, Am. Assn. State Colls. and Univs. (bd. dirs. 1992-96, chair 1995), Am. Chem. Soc., Am. Assn. Higher Edn., Sigma Xi. Roman Catholic. Office: 417H Fletcher Hall 615 McCallie Ave Chattanooga TN 37403-2504 E-mail: frederick-obear@utc.edu.

OBER, DORIS ANN, writer, editor, consultant; b. NY, Nov. 21, 1944; d. Emil Howard and Betty Novick Ober; m. Richard Kirschman, Sept. 13, 2001. Student, Tex. Western Coll., El Paso, Tex., 1962, Syracuse Univ., Syracuse, N.Y., 1963—64. Acct. exec. D.L. Blair Corp., N.Y., 1960—62; promotion, mkgt. asst. mgr. Arlans Dept. Stores, N.Y., 1968—69; ptnr., bus. mgr. One Age Graphics, Tucson, 1970—77; publ. rels. dir. Oakland Ballet, Oakland, Calif., 1977—79; self-employed San Fransicso/Dogtown, 1980—. Cons. in field. Contbg. editor: The World Rushed In: California Gold Rush Experience, 1981, And the Band Played On: Politics, People and the Aids Epidemic, 1987, Conduct Unbecoming: The Homosexual Subculture in the U.S. Military, 1993, The Bug in the Martini Olive, 1991, Simple is Powerful: Anecdotes for a Complex World, 1992, Tales of Two Cities, A Persian Memoir, 1996, I Love A Cop: What Police Families Need to Know, 1997, Secrets of Six-Figure Women, 2002, 45 Effective Ways for Hiring Smart: How to Predict Winners and Losers in the Incredibly Expensive People Reading Game, 1998; collaborator: The Alaska Deception, 1983, Tantra: The Art of Conscious Loving, 1989, American Daughter Gone to War: On the Front Lines with an Army Nurse in Vietnam, 1992, Covarrubias, 1994, Sometimes My Heart Goes Numb: Love and Service in a Time of AIDS, 1995, Thousands of Words You Already Know in Spanish, 1995, Finding Hope When a Child Dies, 1999, Make a Name for Yourself: The Eight Steps to Becoming an Unforgettable Brand in Your Business, 2000, Ordinary People Doing the Exraordinary: The Story of Ed and Joyce Koupal and the Initiative Process, 2002, TransFats: The Hidden Killer in Our Food, 2004.

OBER, RICHARD FRANCIS, JR., lawyer, banker; b. Balt., Dec. 12, 1943; s. Richard Francis and Caroline Fisher Ober; m. Carol Laycock Munger, Aug. 25, 1973; children: Julia Keyser, Margaret Delancey. AB cum laude, Princeton U., 1965; LLB, Yale U., 1968. Bar: Md. 1968, Pa. 1970, N.J. 1977. Law clk. to chief judge Md. Ct. Appeals, Annapolis, 1968; assoc. Ballard, Spahr, Andrews & Ingersoll, Phila., 1969-75; gen. counsel Summit Bancorp, Princeton, NJ, 1975—2001. Sec. Summit Bancorp, Princeton, 1978-2001, sr. v.p., 1982-88, exec. v.p., 1988-2001; bd. dirs. sec. Summit Credit Life Ins. Co., Summit Credit Corp.; sec. Summit Bank, Summit Leasing Co., Summit Venture Capital, Inc. Fire commr. South Brunswick (N.J.) Fire Dist. 3, 1981-85; Republican county committeeman, 1975—; v.p. Republican Assn. Princeton, 1995-96; trustee Princeton Day Sch., 1986-92, treas., 1988-92, vice-chmn., 1990-92; trustee Yale Law Sch. Assn. N.J.; first vice-chmn., dir N.J. Spl. Olympics. Mem. ABA, Bank Corp. Counsel Com. (chmn. 1979-80), N.J. Bar Assn. (gen. coun. 1982-85, 93-94, exec. com. banking law sect. 1979-94, sec. sect. 1980-81, vice-chmn. 1981-82, chmn. 1984-85), N.J. Corp. Counsel Assn. (exec. com. 1980-91, 2d v.p. 1982-85, pres. 1985-86, chmn. banking and fin. instns. com. 1984-85), Am. Bankers Assn. (exec. com. bank counsel unit 1990-95, vice-chmn. 1993-94, chmn. 1994-95), N.J. Bankers Assn. (chmn. bank lawyers coun. 1993-94, chmn. legal and tax com. 1994-95), N.J. Bus. and Industry Assn. (legis. affairs com.), Pa. Bankers Assn. (legal affairs com.), Phila. Bar Assn., Assn. Corp. Counsel Am., Princeton Bar Assn., Fin. Svcs. Roundtable, Lawyers Coun., Bedens Brook Club (Princeton). Episcopalian.

OBER, RUSSELL JOHN, JR., lawyer; b. Pitts., June 26, 1948; s. Russell J. and Marion C. (Hampson) O.; children: Lauren Elizabeth, Russell John III; m. Sandi J. Antill. BA, U. Pitts., 1970, JD, 1973. Bar: Pa. 1973, U.S. Dist. Ct. (we. dist.) Pa. 1973, U.S. Tax Ct. 1982, U.S. Ct. Appeals (4th cir.) 1976, U.S. Ct. Appeals (3d cir.) 1979, U.S. Ct. Appeals (D.C. cir.) 1985, U.S. Ct. Appeals (2d cir.), 1990, U.S. Ct. Appeals (7th cir.) 1993, U.S. Supreme Ct. 1976, U.S. Ct. Appeals (6th cir.) 2000. Asst. dist. atty. Allegheny County, Pitts., 1973-75; ptnr. Wallace Chapas & Ober, Pitts., 1975-80, Rose, Schmidt, Hasley & DiSalle, Pitts., 1980-92, Meyer, Unkovic & Scott, Pitts., 1992—. Bd. dirs. Parent and Child Guidance Ctr., Pitts., 1983-90, treas., 1985-86, pres., 1986-88; bd. mgmt. South Hills Area YMCA, 1989-91; mem. Mt. Lebanon Traffic Commn., 1976-81; bd. dirs. Whale's Tale Youth Family Counseling Ctr., 1990-95. Mem. ABA (discovery com. litigation sect. 1982-88, ho. of dels. young lawyers div. 1982-83), Pa. Bar Assn. (ho. of dels. 1983—), Allegheny County Bar Assn. (chmn. young lawyers sect. 1983, bd. govs. 1984, fin. com. 1984-88, mem. coun. civil litigation sect. 1991-93), Nat. Bd. Trial Advocacy (diplomate), Acad. Lawyers Allegheny County (fellow 1983—, bd. govs. 1988-90) U. Pitts. Law Alumni Assn. (bd. govs. 1984-89, v.p. 1985-87, pres. 1987-88), Rivers Club. Office: Meyer Unkovic & Scott 1300 Oliver Bldg Pittsburgh PA 15222 E-mail: rjo@muslaw.com.

OBER, STUART ALAN, investment consultant, book publisher; b. NYC, Oct. 2, 1946; s. Paul and Gertrude E. (Stollerman) Ober; m. Allison Craig; children: Erik Kenneth Michaels-Ober, Alexander Gabriel. BA, Wesleyan U., Middletown, Conn., 1968; postgrad., U. Sorbonne, Paris, 1972, CUNY, 1976—77. Pres., editor-in-chief Beekman Pubs. Inc., NYC, 1972—2004; pvt. practice, 1972—; expert witness, 1979—; with Moseley, Hallgarten & Estabrook, 1974—75, Loeb, Rhoades & Co., 1976—77; divsn. dir. tax investment dept. Josephthal & Co., Inc., 1977—78; mgr. tax investment dept. Bruns, Nordeman, Rea & Co., 1978—79; pres. Ober Investment Cons., 1979—80, Securities Investigations, Inc., 1981—. Arbitrator Nat. Futures Assn., 2003—, Am. Arbitration Assn.; chairperson NASD, NYSE. Author: Everybody's Guide to Tax Shelters; editor-in-chief: Ober Income Letter, 1983-88; pub.: Tax Shelter Blue Book, 1983—. Bd. dirs., v.p. Woodstock Playhouse Assn., 1985-87; trustee Maverick Concerts, 1986—; chmn. Woodstock Arts and Cultural Com., 1988. Mem.: Inst. Cert. Fin. Planners (fin. products stds. bd. 1986—90, treas. 1988—90). Office: PO Box 888 Woodstock NY 12498-0888

OBERAI, ASSAD A. engineer, researcher; m. Vidya Ramaswamy. PhD, Stanford U., 1994—98. Rsch. assoc. Stanford U., Calif., 1998—2001; asst. prof. Boston U. Contbr. articles to profl. jours. Mem.: USACM, APS. Office Phone: 607-353-7331.

OBERDORFER, LOUIS F. federal judge; b. Birmingham, Ala., Feb. 21, 1919; s. A. Leo and Stella Maud (Falk) O.; m. Elizabeth Weil, July 31, 1941; children: John Louis, Kathryn Lee, Thomas Lee, William L. AB, Dartmouth, 1939; LL.B., Yale, 1946. Bar: Ala. bar 1946, D.C. bar 1949. Law clk. to Justice Hugo L. Black, 1946-47; pvt. practice, 1947-51; mem. firm Wilmer, Cutler, & Pickering (and predecessors), 1951-61, 65-77; asst. atty. gen. tax div. Dept. of Justice, 1961-65; judge, now sr. judge U.S. Dist. Ct. (D.C. dist.), 1977—. Vis. lectr. Yale Law Sch., 1966-71; adv. com. Fed. Rules Civil Procedure, 1962-84; co-chmn. lawyers com. Civil Rights Under Law, 1967-69; adj. prof. law Georgetown U., Washington, 1993-97. Editor-in-chief Yale Law Jour., 1941. Served to capt. AUS, 1941-46. Mem. ABA, D.C. Bar Assn. (bd. govs. 1972-77, pres. 1977), Ala. Bar Assns., Am. Law Inst., Yale Law Sch. Assn. (pres. 1971-73) Office: US Dist Ct 333 Constitution Ave NW Washington DC 20001

OBERFIELD, RICHARD ALAN, oncologist; b. N.Y.C., July 29, 1932; s. George B. and Frances Oberfield; m. Valerie I. Oberfield, Feb. 14, 1954 (dec. Jan. 1980); children: Elizabeth A., Alice A.; m. Keren G. Oberfield, July 28, 1988. BA cum laude, Alfred U., 1953; MD, NYU, 1957. Lic. physician, Mass., N.Y.; diplomate Am. Bd. Internal Medicine. Intern Greenwich (Conn.) Hosp., 1957-58; USPHS sr. asst. surgeon venereal disease br. Detroit Receiving Hosp., 1958-60; tng. fellow pathology NYU Med. Ctr., N.Y.C., 1960-61; resident in medicine Dartmouth Med. Ctr. Affiliated Hosps., Hanover, N.H., 1961-63, fellow in hematology and cancer chemotherapy, 1963-65; staff physician sect. med. oncology dept. internal medicine Lahey Clinic Med. Ctr., Burlington, Mass., 1965—, head sect. med. oncology dept. internal medicine, 1969-85. Hosp. appts. include New Eng. Bapt. Hosp., Boston, 1965—80, New Eng. Deaconess Hosp., Boston, 1965—97, Mary and Arthur R. Clapham Hosp., Lahey Clinic Med. Ctr., Burlington, 1980—97; chmn. emeritus sect. med. oncology dept. internal medicine Lahey Clinic Med. Ctr., Burlington, 1997—; clin. rsch. cons. dept. rsch., 1997—; clin. instr. medicine Harvard Med. Sch., Boston, 1972—; asst. prof. dept. medicine Tufts U. Sch. Medicine, 2000—. Contbr. numerous articles to profl. publs. Fellow ACP (Meade Johnson postgrad. scholar 1962-63); mem. AMA (Cert. Merit 1966), Internat. Assn. for Study of Lung Cancer (founding mem.), Nat. Bd. Med. Examiners (diplomate), Am. Assn. for Cancer Rsch., Inc., Am. Soc. Clin. Oncology, Am. Assn. for Cancer Edn., Mass. Med. Soc., Mass. Soc. Internal Medicine, New Eng. Cancer Soc., Mass. Soc. Clin. Oncologists. Avocations: piano, writing, running, reading. Office: Lahey Clinic Med Ctr 41 Mall Rd Burlington MA 01805 Office Phone: 781-744-8383.

OBERFIELD, SHARON ELEFANT, pediatric endocrinologist; b. N.Y.C., Aug. 14, 1950; d. Nicholas and Anna (Weiss) Elefant; m. Richard A. Oberfield; 2 children. AB in Biology, Cornell U., 1970, MD, 1974. Diplomate in pediatrics and pediatric endocrinology Am. Bd. Pediatrics. Intern in pediatrics The N.Y. Hosp., 1974-75, resident in pediatrics, 1975-76, fellow in pediatric endocrinology, 1976-79, asst. attending pediatrician, 1979-84; asst. attending pediatrian endocrinology Meml. Sloan Kettering Cancer Ctr., N.Y.C., 1986—2001. Provisional pediatrician to outpatient dept. N.Y. Hosp., 1976-79; assoc. attending pediatrician St. Luke's-Roosevelt Hosp. Ctr., N.Y.C., 1984-91, Presbyn. Hosp., N.Y.C., 1991, Tisch Hosp., Bellevue Hosp., N.Y.C., 1992—, Children's Hosp. of N.Y.-Presbyn. Hosp., 1998—; asst. attending pediatrician Meml. Sloan Kettering Cancer Ctr., 1979-84; asst. prof. pediatrics Cornell U. Med. Coll., N.Y.C., 1979-84, Columbia U. Coll. Physicians & Surgeons, N.Y.C., 1984-91, assoc. prof. clin. pediatrics, 1991, prof., 1998—, dir. pediat. endocrinology; assoc. prof. clin. pediatrics NYU Med. Ctr., 1992-95. Grantee NIH, 1978-84, Hoffman-LaRoche, 1985-89, Eli Lilly, 1986-92. Children's Brain Tumor Found., 1995-98; recipient Mitchell Spivak Meml. prize in pediatrics, 1974. Mem. Am. Med. Women's Assn. (citation 1974), N.Y. Acad. Scis., N.Y. Pediatric Soc., Soc. Pediatric Rsch., Endocrine Soc., Lawson Wilkins Soc., Pediatric Endocrinology, Alpha Omega Alpha, Alpha Epsilon Delta. Office: Divsn Pediat Endocrinology 630 W 168th St PH-5E-522 New York NY 10032

O'BERG, ROBERT MYRON, minister; b. Long Beach, Calif., Apr. 21, 1961; s. Robert Ronald and Carolyn Ruth (Smith) O'B.; m. Kristen Johnson, Mar. 22, 1986; children: Erin Kristine, Robert William. BA, U. Calif., Riverside, 1983; MA, Claremont Grad. Sch., 1990; MDiv, Pacific Luth. Theol. Sem., 1991. Ordained to ministry Evang. Luth. Ch. in Am., 1991. Assoc. pastor Trinity Luth. Ch., Fresno, Calif., 1999—. Book reviewer Augsburg Fortress Pub. House; initial interviewer multi-synodical candidacy com. Evang. Luth. Ch. in Am.; relief chaplain Simi Valley Hosp. and Health Care Svcs., 1994-99; convener Simi Valley Ecumenical Coun. (Luth., Episcopal and Roman Cath.), 1993-95. Mem. steering com. Luth. Social Svcs. Cen. Coast, 1993; bd. dirs. Vols. for You, 1997-99. Recipient Disting. Svc. award Luth. Social Svcs., 1993; named Pastor of Day, Sta. KKLA-FM, 1995. Mem. Aid Assn. for Lutherans, Luth. Brotherhood, U. Calif.-Riverside Alumni Assn., Claremont Grad. Sch. Alumni Assn., Pacific Luth. Theol. Sem. Alumni Assn. Democrat. Avocations: writing, reading, hunting, music. Home: 722 N Clovis Ave Clovis CA 93611-0360 Office: Trinity Luth Ch 3973 N Cedar Ave Fresno CA 93726-5299

OBERHAUS, JAMES EDWARD, secondary school educator; b. Defiance, Ohio, Sept. 11, 1952; s. Raymond G. and Lorena S. Oberhaus; m. Linda S. Oberhaus, Sept. 11, 1950; children: Kimberly Kay, Kevin James. B of Music Edn., Bowling Green State U., 1974; M of Music Edn., Vandercook Coll. Music, 1988. Assoc. dir. Barbershop Chorus, Defiance, Ohio, 1978—. Mem.: Am. Choral Dirs. Assn., Ohio Music Educators Assn. (adjudicator 1989—, choral clinician 1992—). Home: 15828 State Rte 281 Holgate OH 43527 E-mail: jmoberhaus@aol.com.

OBERHAUSEN, JOYCE ANN WYNN, aircraft company executive, artist; b. Plain Dealing, La., Nov. 12, 1941; d. George Dewey and Jettie Cleo (Farrington) Wynn; m. James J. Oberhausen, Oct. 15, 1966; children: Georgann, Darla Renee Estein Oberhausen Christopher, Dale Henry Estein Oberhausen. Student, Ayers Bus. Sch., Shreveport, 1962-63; student, U. Ala., 1964-65. Stenographer, sec. Lincoln Nat. Life Co., Shreveport, 1965-66; co-owner Precision Splty. Co., Huntsville, 1966—; internat. art tchr. Huntsville, Ala., 1974—; sec. Baifield Industries, Shreveport, 1975-86. Co-owner Mil. Aircraft, Huntsville, 1979—; pres., owner Wynnson Galleries Pvt. Collections, Florist, Meridianville, 1987; owner North Ala. Wholesale Flowers, 1988—, Wynnson Enterprises Mil. Packaging Co., 1988—. Contbr.: Huntsville New Beginnings, 2002; contbr. articles to profl. jour. Co-founder Nat. Mus. Women in Arts; judge 20th Biennial Conv. Internat. Porcelain Arts Tchrs., 1998. Mem. NAFE, Internat. Porcelain Guild, People to People, Porcelain Portrait Soc., United Artists Assn., Am. Soc. of Profl. and Exec. Women Hist. Soc., Nat. Trust Hist. Preservation, Internat. Platform Assn., Met. Mus. Art., Smithsonian Assn., Assn. Cmty. Artists, Rep Senatorial Inner Cir., Ala. Sheriffs Assn., C. of C., Better Bus. Bur., Huntsville Art League and Mus. Assocs. Avocations: painting, antiques, handcrafts, gourmet cooking, horseback riding. Home: 156 Spencer Dr Meridianville AL 35759-2023 Office: Wynnson Enterprises Inc 12043 Highway 231 431 N Meridianville AL 35759-1201

OBERHELMAN, DOUGLAS R. tractor company executive; CFO Caterpillar Inc., Peoria, Ill., v.p., dir. engine products divsn. Office: Caterpillar Inc 100 NE Adams St Peoria IL 61629-0002

OBERHELMAN, HARRY ALVIN, JR., surgeon, educator; b. Chgo., Nov. 15, 1923; s. Harry Alvin and Beatrice (Babel) O.; m. Betty Jane Porter, June 12, 1946; children: Harry Alvin III, James I., Robert P., Thomas L., Nancy L. Student, Yale U., 1942-43; BS, U. Chgo., 1946, MD, 1947. Diplomate: Am. Bd. Surgery. Intern U. Chgo. Clinics, 1947-48, resident in surgery, 1948-51, 52-57; asst. prof., then assoc. prof. surgery U. Chgo. Sch. Medicine, 1957-60; mem. faculty Stanford (Calif.) Sch. Medicine, 1960—, prof. surgery, 1964-95, Emer prof. surgery, 1995—. Mem. div. licensing Calif. Bd. Med. Quality Assurance, 1970-82 Author papers in field. Served with USAF, 1951-53. Mem. AMA, Calif. Med. Assn., Soc. Univ. Surgeons, Am., Western, Pacific Coast surg. assns., Soc. Alimentary Tract, Halsted Soc., Fedn. State Med. Bds. U.S. (bd. dirs. 1979-82) Home: 668 Cabrillo St Stanford CA 94305-8404 Office Phone: 650-723-5672. Personal E-mail: hoberhelman@hotmail.com.

OBERLANDER, HERBERT, retired physiologist; b. Manchester, N.H., Oct. 2, 1939; BA cum laude in Zoology, U. Conn., 1961; PhD in Biology, Western Res. U., 1965. Postdoctoral fellow U. Zurich, Switzerland, 1965-66; asst. prof. Brandeis U., Waltham, Mass., 1966-71; rsch. physiologist USDA, Agrl. Rsch. Svc., Gainesville, Fla., 1971-76, rsch. leader, physiology unit, insect attractants lab, 1976-84, lab. dir. insect attractants, behavior/basic biology rsch., 1984-96; dir. Ctr. for Med. Agrl. and Vet. Entomology, Gainesville, 1996—2001; prof. entomology U. Fla., Gainesville, 1979—2001; ret., 2001. Grantee U.S.-Israel BARD, 1989-93; NSF fellow, 1961-65; NIH fellow, 1965-66; NSF rsch. grantee, 1966-71, 83. Fellow Entomol. Soc. Am. (Founders' Meml. award 1995); mem. Tissue Culture Assn., Phi Beta Kappa, Sigma Xi, Phi Kappa Phi. Office: USDA -ARS - CMAVE PO Box 14565 1700 SW 23rd Dr Gainesville FL 32608-1069

OBERLIN, EARL CLIFFORD, III, securities brokerage company executive; b. Bryan, Ohio, Dec. 10, 1956; s. Earl Clifford II and Pauline Lois (Weber) O. BS in Acctg. and Fin., Miami U., Oxford, Ohio, 1979; MS, Cin. Coll., 1980. CFP; CPA, PFS, Ohio; gen. securities prin., mcpl. bond prin., registered options prin. V.p. MFI Investments Corp., Bryan, 1977-80, treas., 1980-84, pres., chief exec. officer, vice chmn. Toledo (Ohio) and Bryan, 1984—; v.p. Merit Co., Bryan, 1979-87, pres., chief exec. officer, 1988-95; v.p. Oberlin-Ford, Inc., Bryan, 1979-87; vice-chmn. Oberlin and Ford, Inc., Bryan, 1979-95, pres., chief exec. officer, 1988-95; chmn. Sky Investments Corp., 1996-2000; chmn. bd. R&O Memorials, Inc., 2000—; CEO Oberlin Fin. Corp., 2000—, Oberlin Fin. Mortgage Group, LLC, 2000—. Pres., chief exec. officer Quality Care Med. Equipment, Bryan, 1980-85; pres., chief exec. officer, vice chmn. MFI Advisors, Inc., Bryan and Toledo, 1987-95. Author: Building a High End Financial Services Practice, 2004; bi-weekly columnist Personal Investing for Women, 1987. Bd. dirs. Jr. Achievement N.W. Ohio Inc., 1989—; pres., bd. dirs. Jr. Achievement, Bryan, 1989-91. Jr. Achievement NW Ohio scholar, 1975. Mem. AICPA, Inst. CFPs, Internat. Assn. for Fin. Planning (broker/dealer coun., chmn.-elect 1991, chmn. 1992), Young Pres.'s Orgn., Nat. Assn. Securities Dealers (dist. 8 bus. conduct com. 1994-96, chmn. dist. 8 nominating com. 1999), Toledo Club, Rotary (Paul Harris fellow), Eagles, Moose. Republican. Methodist. Avocations: sailing, skiing. Home: 127 Country Club Rd Bryan OH 43506-9139 Office: Oberlin Financial Corp PO Box 998 Bryan OH 43506-0998 Office Phone: 419-636-4001.

OBERLY, KATHRYN ANNE, lawyer, diversified financial services company executive; b. Chgo., May 22, 1950; d. James Richard and Lucille Mary (Kraus) Oberly; 1 child, Michael W. Goelzer; m. Haynes B. Johnson, June 29, 2002. Student, Vassar Coll., 1967—69; BA, U. Wis., 1971, JD, 1973. Bar: Wis. 1973, D.C. 1981, N.Y. 1995. Law clk. U.S. Ct. Appeals, Omaha, 1973-74; trial atty. U.S. Dept. Justice, Washington, 1974-77, spl. asst., 1977-81, spl. litig. counsel, 1981-82, asst. to Solicitor Gen., 1982-86; ptnr. Mayer, Brown & Platt, Washington, 1986-91; assoc. gen. counsel Ernst & Young LLP, Washington, 1991-94, vice-chair, gen. counsel N.Y.C., 1994—. Bd. dirs. Appleseed Found., 2003—. Named one of 50 Most Influential Women Lawyers in Am., Nat. Law Jour., 1998. Mem. ABA, Am. Law Inst. (coun. mem.), Am. Acad. Appellate Lawyers, Wis. Bar Assn., D.C. Bar Assn. Democrat. Office: Ernst & Young LLP 5 Times Sq New York NY 10036 Business E-Mail: kathryn.oberly@ey.com.

OBERMAN, MICHAEL STEWART, lawyer; b. Bklyn., May 21, 1947; s. Hyman Martin and Gertrude O.; m. Sharon Land, Oct. 8, 1975; 1 child, Abigail Land. AB, Columbia U., 1969; JD, Harvard U., 1972. Bar: N.Y. 1973, U.S. Dist. Ct. (so. and ea. dists.) N.Y. 1973, U.S. Ct. Appeals (2d cir.) 1973, U.S. Supreme Ct. 1976, Calif. 1981, U.S. Dist. Ct. (no. dist.) Calif. 1981, U.S. Ct. Appeals (9th cir.) 1981, U.S. Dist. Ct. (so. and cen. dists.) Calif. 1982, U.S. Ct. Appeals (5th cir.) 1989, D.C. 1992, U.S. Ct. Appeals (7th cir.) 1993. Law clk. to Hon. Milton Pollack, U.S. Dist. Ct. (so. dist.) N.Y., 1972-73; assoc. Kramer Levin Naftalis & Frankel LLP, N.Y.C., 1973-79, ptnr., 1980—. Contbr. articles to profl. jours. Recipient Nathan Burkan prize ASCAP, 1973. Mem. N.Y. State Bar Assn. (mem. ho. of dels. 1989-91, exec. com. comml. and fed. litigation sect.). Office: Kramer Levin Naftalis & Frankel LLP 919 3rd Ave New York NY 10022-3902

OBERMAN, SHELDON ARNOLD, writer, educator; b. Winnipeg, Man., Can., May 20, 1949; s. Allan and Dorothy Oberman; m. Lee Anne Block, Sept. 8, 1973 (div. Mar. 9, 1990); children: Adam, Mira; m. Lisa Ann Dveris, Sept. 2, 1990; 1 child: Jesse. BA in English, U. Winnipeg, 1972; BA in English with honors, U. Jerusalem, Israel, 1973; teaching cert., U. Man., 1974. Tchr. W. C. Millar Collegiate, Altona, Man., Can., 1975-76, Joseph Wolinsky Collegiate, Winnipeg, Man., Can., 1976-95. Author: The Folk Festival Book, 1983, Lion in the Lake: A French English Alphabet Book, 1988, Julie Gerond and the Polka Dot Pony, 1988, TV Sal and the Game Show From Outer Space, 1993, This Business With Elijah, 1993, The Always Prayer Shawl, 1994, The White Stone in the Castle Wall, 1995, By the Hannukah Light, 1997, The Shaman's Nephew: A Life in the Far North, 1999, The Wisdom Bird: A Tale of Solomon and Sheba, 2000; co-editor: A Mirror of a People: The Canadian Jewish Experience in Poetry and Prose, 1985 (Sydney Taylor honor 2000, McNalley Robinson Book award 2001), Island of the Minotaur: Greek Myths of Crete, 2003. Recipient Parents Choice Silver Honour, 1999, Norma Fleck award for children's non fiction, 1999, Parents Coun. Outstanding Book, 1999, Nat. Jewish Book award Jewish Book Coun., 1995, Sydney Taylor award, 1995, Best Book of the Yr. A Child's Mag., 1994, Pick of the List award Am. Bookseller, 1994, Can. Author Short Story award Canadian Author's Assn., 1987, Bliss Carmen Poetry prize Banff Sch. of Fine Arts, 1980; various writer and film maker grants. Avocations: public address, acting, collage sculptor, canoing. Home: 822 Dorchester Ave Winnipeg MB Canada R3M 0R7 E-mail: soberman@mts.net.

OBERMANN, RICHARD MICHAEL, governmental technology and policy analyst; b. May 21, 1949; s. Baird J. and Phyllis L. (Weber) Obermann; m. Grace Karaffa; 1 child, Pearl Louise. BS of Engring. in Aerospace and Mech. Scis. cum laude, Princeton U., 1971, PhD in Engring., Aerospace and Mech. Scis., 1977; MS of Engring. in Astronautics and Aeros., Stanford U., 1972; postgrad., Va. Poly. Inst. and State U., Am. U. With MITRE Corp., McLean, Va., 1977-88, engr. transp. systems analysis, transp. energy analysis, telecommunications, project leader, mem. tech. staff in communications and system design; sr. staff officer aeros. and space engring. bd. NRC, Washington, 1988-90, study dir. and analyst technol. and policy issues; mem. profl. staff for space subcom. US Ho. of Reps. Com. on Sci., Space and Tech., Washington, 1990-95; minority staff dir., space and aeronautics subcom. US House of Reps. Com. on Sci., Washington, 1995—. Author tech. papers and presentations. Fellow AIAA (internat. activities public policy com.), Brit. Interplanetary Soc., Am. Astronaut. Soc. (bd. dirs., exec. com., internat. policy com.); mem. IEEE, AAAS, NY Acad. Sci., Asia Soc., Nat. Space Club, Pacific Telecomms. Coun., Women in Aerospace (bd. dir.), Internat. Acad. Astronautics, World Affairs Coun., elected full mem. of Internat. Acad. of Astronautics, 2001. Avocations: Japanese, Chinese and Spanish langs., sports, trumpet.

OBERMAYER, HERMAN JOSEPH, newspaper publisher; b. Phila., Sept. 19, 1924; s. Leon J. and Julia (Sinsheimer) O.; m. Betty Nan Levy, June 28, 1955; children: Helen O. Levy-Myers, Veronica O. Atnipp, Adele O. Malpass, Elizabeth Rose. Student, U. Geneva, Switzerland, 1946; AB cum laude, Dartmouth Coll., 1948. Reporter L.I. Daily Press, Jamaica, N.Y., 1950-53; classified advt. mgr. New Orleans Item, 1953-55; asst. to pub. Standard-Times, New Bedford, Mass., 1955-57; editor, pub. Long Branch (N.J.) Daily Record, 1957-71, No. Va. Sun, Arlington, 1963-89; adj. prof. journalism U. Md., 1989-93; vis. lectr. U. West Indies, Jamaica, 1994-95; publ. com. Commentary Mag., 1989—. Pulitizer Prize juror, 1983, 84; lectr. publs. mgmt. Hungary, Poland, Lithuania, Latvia, Estonia, Ukraine, Moldova, Slovenia, Macedonia, Russia, Croatia, Serbia, 1990-2002, Internat. Ctr. Journalists, 1992—. Author: Jews in the News, 2001; contbr. articles to popular mags., local newspapers. Bd. dirs. Monmouth Med. Ctr., 1958-71; mem. exec. coun. Monmouth Boy Scouts Am., 1958-71, mem. exec. com. Nat. Capital coun., 1971-79, v.p., 1974-77; mem. Va. Legis. Alcohol Beverage Control Study Commn., 1972-74; trustee Arlington (Va.) Bicentennial Commn., Am. Jewish Com. Cmty. Svc. award, 1986, nat. bd. govs., 1989-96, nat. coun., 1996—; trustee Jewish Inst. for Nat. Security Affairs, 1996—. With AUS, 1943-46, ETO. Rhineland Campaign Star; Recipient Silver Beaver award Boy Scouts Am., 1977, Knight Internat. Press fellow, 1994-95. Mem. Am. Soc. Newspaper Editors, So. Newspaper Pubs. Assn. (dir. 1981-84), Mont. Pelerin Soc., Nat. Press Club (Washington), Cosmos Club (Washington), Washington Golf and Country Club (Arlington, Va.), Dartmouth Club (N.Y.C.), Econ. Club (Washington), Sigma Chi. Jewish. Rotarian. Home: 4114 N Ridgeview Rd Arlington VA 22207-4711

OBERMAYER, MICHAEL ERIK MAX, management consultant; b. Stockholm, May 8, 1948; s. Adolf Max and Gerd Sigrid Ulrica (Malm) O.; m. Marianne Linnander, May 2, 1991; children: Anna Catharina, Johan Georg, Marie Louise, Erik Richard. MSChemE, Royal Inst. Tech., Stockholm, 1973; DSc in Biochemistry with honors, Ludwig Maximilians U., Munich, 1976; MBA with honors, European Inst. Adminstrn. Affairs, Fontainebleau, France, 1977. Fellow Max Planck Inst. Biochemistry, Munich, 1974-76; assoc. McKinsey & Co., Copenhagen, 1977-83, prin. Stockholm, 1983-86, prin., head of office Oslo, 1986-90, dir., head of office Stockholm, 1990-93, dir., chmn. Ea. Europe St. Petersburg, Russia, 1993-94, chmn. Ea. Europe Prague, Czech Republic, 1994-96, Moscow, 1996-2000, London, 2000—. Vis. prof. bus. strategy Faculty Econs. Moscow State U., 1996—. Mem. adv. bd. State Hermitage Mus., St. Petersburg, 1994; mem. Mir Iskusstvo/World of Art Found., Moscow, 1997. Lt. C.E., German Army, 1967-68.

OBERMEIER, TOM, architectural firm executive; m. Tina Poe. BArch, MArch in Urban Design, U. Colo. Lic. Colo., Calif., Oreg., Ariz., Wyo., Wash., Tex., N.Mex., Utah, Idaho, cert. Nat. Coun. Archtl. Registration Bds. Founding prin. OZ Arch., Denver. Mem.: AIA. Achievements include invention of Cygnus Curtain Wall System. Office: OZ Architecture Inc 3012 Huron St Ste 100 Denver CO 80202*

OBERMEYER, THERESA NANGLE, sociology educator; b. St. Louis, July 25, 1945; d. James Francis and Harriet Clare (Shafer) Nangle; m. Thomas S. Obermeyer, Dec. 23, 1977; children: Thomas Jr., James, Margaret, Matthew. BA, Maryville U., St. Louis, 1967; MEd, St. Louis U., 1970, PhD, 1975. Lic. real estate broker Alaska, 1979, cert. Type A teacher Alaska, 1979. Dir. student activities Lindenwood Univ., St. Charles, Mo., 1969-70; asst. dean of students Loyola Coll., Balt., 1972-73; asst. dir. student activities St. Louis C.C., 1973-78; dir. student activities U. Alaska, Anchorage, 1978-79; instr. sociology Chapman U., Anchorage, 1981-93; secondary tchr. McLaughlin Youth Ctr. for Juvenile Delinquents, 1984-90. Mem Anchorage Munic Health Commn., 1980—81; elected alt. coun. urban bd edn. Nat Sch. Bds. Assn., 1994; maj. party nominee US Senate Gen. Election, 1996; founder, mem. Alaska Women's Polit. Caucus, 1979—; elected Anchorage Sch. Bd., 1990—94, treas., 1993. Recipient Fed Women's Equity Act, US Dept Educ Univ Alaska, 1978—79; fellow Fulbright, Project India, 1974, Project Jordan, 1977; grantee Title I, Univ Md and Loyola Col, 1972—73; scholar NDEA, 1968—70. Mem.: AAUW (bd. dirs. Anchorage br. 1980—81), DAR (regent col. John Mitchell chpt. 1992—94), Am. Soc. Pub. Adminstrn. (pres., bd. dirs. south ctrl. chpt. 1981). Avocations: athletics, swimming, horseback riding, skiing, running. Home and Office: 3000 Dartmouth Dr Anchorage AK 99508-4413 Fax: 907-278-9455. Office Phone: 907-278-9455. E-mail: tobermeyer@gci.net.

OBERNAUER, MARNE, corporate executive; b. Pitts., Mar. 6, 1919; s. Arthur H. and Anna (Somerman) O.; m. Joan Strassburger, Aug. 1, 1941; children: Marne Jr., Wendy Damon. Grad., Cornell U., 1941. Vice chmn. Beverage Distbrs. Corp. and BDH Inc., Aurora, Colo.; pres. Doric Securities Co. Bus. cons., pvt. investor. Pres., bd. dirs. The Obernauer Found., Inc. Served to lt. USNR, 1942-45. Mem. Concordia Club (Pitts.), Century Country Club (Purchase, N.Y.), Banyan Golf Club (Palm Beach, Fla.). Home: 2 North Breakers Row Palm Beach FL 33480 Office: 60 E 42d St Ste 1912 New York NY 10165 Fax: 561-659-2132.

OBERNAUER, MARNE, JR., business executive; b. Lakehurst, NJ, July 1, 1943; s. Marne and Joan Carolyn (Strassburger) O.; m. Marion Fleck Gislason, Aug. 22, 1976 (dec. Jan. 1996); children: Matthew Gene, Michael Sidney. BA, Yale U., 1965; MBA, Harvard U., 1972. With First Nat. City Bank (Citibank, N.A.), NYC, 1965-70, Donaldson, Lufkin & Jenrette, NYC, 1972-74, Devon Group, Inc., NYC and Stamford, Conn., 1974-98, pres., 1978, CEO, 1980-98, chmn. bd., 1986-98; vice chmn. Applied Graphics Techs., Inc., 1998—2003, also bd. dirs. Chmn. bd. dirs. Beverage Distbrs. Co. Trustee The Trinity Sch., The Obernauer Found., Inc.; bd. dirs. Com. for Responsible Fed. Budget. Mem.: Am. Bus. Conf. Found. for Econ. Growth (chmn.), Am. Bus. Conf. (bd. dirs.), Assn. Yale Alumni (treas. 2002—03, bd. govs. 1999—2003), Maroon Creek Club, Century Country Club, Yale Club NYC. Office: Ste 1912 60 E 42d St New York NY 10165

OBERNDORF, MEYERA E. mayor; m. Roger L. Oberndorf; children: Marcie, Heide. BS in Elem. Edn., Old Dominion U., 1964. Broadcaster Sta. WNIS, Norfolk, Va.; chair Pub. Libr. bd., Va.; mem. city coun. City of Virginia Beach, Va., 1976—, vice-mayor, 1986—88, mayor, 1988—. Mem. exec. bd. Tidewater coun. Boys Scouts Am.; bd. dirs. Va.Beach Pub. Libr., 1966-76, chmn. bd., 1967-76; past pres. Va. Muncipal League; bd. dir. Hampton Roads Partnership; Econ. Develop. Alliance; adv. com. Va. Inst. of Gov. Named 25 Most Dynamic Mayors in the US, Newsweek. Mem. AAUW, U.S. Conf. Mayors (trustee), Va. Mcpl. League (exec. bd.), Nat. League Cities (vice-chmn., mem. adv. bd., past chair Energy, Environ., and Natural Resources Steering Com.), Princess Anne Women's Club; chair Standing Com. on Internat. Affairs. Jewish. Home: 5404 Challedon Dr Virginia Beach VA 23462-4112 Office: 2401 Courthouse Drive City Hall Bldg 1 Municipal Ctr Virginia Beach VA 23456 Office Phone: 757-427-4581. Office Fax: 757-426-5669.

O'BERRY, CARL GERALD, former career officer, electrical engineer; b. Lansing, Mich., Apr. 11, 1936; s. Gerald Ray and Edith Lenore (Watson) O'B.; m. Charlene Marice Bussche, June 21, 1958; children: Brian, Eileen, Kevin, Bradley, Kathleen. BSEE, N.Mex. State U., 1972; MS in Systems Mgmt., Air Force Inst. Tech., 1977. Commd. 2d lt. USAF, 1961, advanced through grades to lt. gen., 1993; comdr. 2019 Communications Squadron, Griffiss AFB, N.Y., 1974-76; project engr. Rome Air Devel. Ctr., Griffiss AFB, 1979-81; asst. dep. chief of staff requirements Air Force Systems Command, Andrews AFB, Md., 1982-84; comdr. Rome Air Devel. Ctr., Griffiss AFB, 1984-86; joint program mgr. WWMCCS info. system Hdqrs. USAF, Washington, 1986-88; dir. command, control and communications U.S. European Command, Stuttgart, Fed. Republic Germany, 1988-90; dir. command control systems and logistics U.S. Space Command, Peterson AFB, Colo., 1990-92; command control comm. and computers DCS, HQ USAF, Washington, 1992-95; v.p., dir. strategic planning Motorola Space and Sys. Tech. Group, Scottsdale, Ariz., 1995-98; tech. cons. Def. Sci. Bd., Washington, 1998—; v.p., gen. mgr. govt. info. and comms. sys., space group The Boeing Co., Anaheim, Calif., 2000—. Mem. Air Force Assn., Armed Forces Communications-Electronics Assn., Soc. Logistics Engrs. Roman Catholic. Office: The Boeing Co PO Box 4921 3370 Miraloma Ave Anaheim CA 92803

O'BERRY, PHILLIP AARON, veterinarian; b. Tampa, Fla., Feb. 1, 1933; s. Luther Lee and Marjorie Mae (Mahlum) O'B.; m. Terri Martin, July 31, 1960; children: Kelly, Eric, Holly, Danny, Andy, Toby, Michael Asefa. BS in Agr., U. Fla., 1955; DVM, Auburn U., 1960; PhD, Iowa State U., 1967. With Agrl. Rsch. Svc. USDA, 1956—2003, asst. to dir. vet. scis. rsch. div., 1967-72; asst. dir. Nat. Animal Disease Ctr., Ames, Iowa, 1972-73, dir., 1973-88, tech. transfer coord., 1988—2003; prin. scientist Office Agr. Biotech., USDA, 1988-90; ret., 2003. Adj. prof. Coll. Vet. Medicine, Iowa State U., 1973—; mem. expert panel livestock infertility FAO; sci. adv. com. Pan Am. Zoonosis Ctr., Buenos Aires; mem. Fed. Coun. Sci. and Tech.; mem. com. animal health, world food and nutrition study NRC; cons. Govt. of Italy, Govt. of Mex., USDA, Govt. of Egypt; mem. nat needs grad. fellowship rev. panel USDA, 1989-91, cons. agr. biotech. rsch. adv. com.; mem. sci. adv. bd. Biotech. R&D Corp., 1992-2001, sci. review bd. Am. Jour. Vet. Rsch., 1990-92; mem. USDA Patent Review Com., 1988-2003. Author 27 rsch. publs.; mem. editl. adv. bd. Food Safety mag. Recipient Cert. of Merit, Agrl. Rsch. Svc., 1972, 84, Alumni Merit award Iowa State Club of Chgo., 1982, Cert. Appreciation, 1988, Tech. Transfer award 1989, USDA Disting. Alumnus award Auburn U., 1991; named Hon. Diplomate Am. Coll. of Vet. Microbiologists, 1995, Ames Citizen of the Yr., 2000, Iowa Gov.'s Vol. award, 2001. Mem. APHA, AVMA, AAAS, Nat. Assn. Fed. Vets., Iowa Vet. Med. Assn., N.Y. Acad. Scis., Conf. Rsch. Workers Animal Diseases, Am. Soc. Microbiology, Am. Assn. Lab. Animal Sci., U.S. Animal Health Assn., Am. Assn. Bovine Practitioners, Livestock Cons. Inst., Sigma Xi, Phi Zeta, Phi Kappa Phi, Gamma Sigma Delta (Alumni award Merit 1976), Alpha Zeta, Spades, Blue Key. Democrat. Home: 3319 Woodland St Ames IA 50014-3550 E-mail: tmoberry@aol.com.

OBERST, RICHARD B. military officer, hospital administrator; b. Wyo. Bs in Zoology and Physiology, U. Wyo., 1972; MS in Microbiology, U. Pitts., 1975; PhD in Parasitology and Lab. Practices, U. N.C., 1985. Commd. USN, 1975, advanced through grades to capt.; rschr. Malaria br. CDC, Atlanta; head clin. microbiology Naval Regional Med. Ctr., Portsmouth, Va., Oakland; dir. lab. svcs. Navy Environ. Unit 6, Okinawa, Japan, 1977—79; head parasitology Naval Med. Rsch. Unit 2, Manila, Philippines, 1985; naval med. rsch. dir. Naval Med. Rsch. Inst., officer in charge, dep. dir. infectious disease dept., product mgr. pharm. systems divs.; commdg. officer Naval Med. Rsch. Ctr., Silver Spring, Md., 1998—. Decorated Meritorious Svc. medal (2), Navy Commendation medal, Navy Achievement medal. Office: Naval Medical Rsch Ctr 503 Robert Grant Ave Silver Spring MD 20910

OBERSTAR, JAMES L. congressman; b. Chisholm, Minn., Sept. 10, 1934; s. Louis and Mary (Grillo) O.; m. Jo Garlick, Oct. 12, 1963 (dec. July 1991); children: Thomas Edward, Katherine Noelle, Anne-Therese, Monica Rose; m. Jean Kurth, Nov. 1993; stepchildren: Corinne Quinlan Kurth, Charles Burke Kurth, Jr. BA summa cum laude, St. Thomas Coll., 1956; postgrad. in French, Laval U., Que., Can.; MS in Govt. (scholar), Coll. Europe, Bruges, Belgium, 1957; postgrad. in govt, Georgetown U. Adminstrv. asst. Congressman John A. Blatnik, 1963-74; adminstr. Pub. Works Com. U.S. Ho. of Reps., 1971-74; mem. 94th-108th Congresses from 8th Minn. Dist., 1975—, ranking minority mem. transp. and infrastructure com. Mem. Am. Polit. Sci. Assn. Democrat. Office: US Ho of Reps 2365 Rayburn Hob Washington DC 20515-2308

OBERT, CHARLES FRANK, retired banker; b. Cleve., Apr. 28, 1937; s. Carl William and Irene Frances (Urban) O.; m. Linda Marie Thoss, June 3, 1961; children— Lisa Marie, Charles David. Student, Ohio State U., 1955-57. With Ameritrust Corp., Cleve., 1958-92, sr. v.p. affiliate bank div., 1975-80, sr. v.p. corp. service div., 1980-87, sr. v.p. br. adminstrn., 1987-92, mgmt. cons., 1993-2000; ret. Acoustical Cleaning Systems Inc., 2000, pres. Mem. Solon (Ohio) Recreation Commn., 1978-94, Solon Bd. Edn., 1986-94. Mem. Am. Inst. Banking, Am. Bankers Assn., Ohio Bankers Assn., Bank Adminstrn. Inst., Internat. Assn. Laryngectomees, Cleve. Hearing and Speech Ctr., Greater Cleve. Growth Assn., Solon C. of C. Home and Office: 8270 Pebble Creek Ct Chagrin Falls OH 44023-4866

OBERT, KEITH DAVID, lawyer; b. Talladega, Ala., Nov. 22, 1962; s. Sam R. and Alice M. Obert; m. Alaine Anderson, Aug. 3, 1991; 1 child, Baylor Anderson. BS in Acctg., U. Ala., 1984; JD, U. Miss., 1988. Bar: Miss. 1988, Tenn. 1988, Ala. 1989. Acct. Challenger Lighting Co. Inc., Olive Branch, Miss., 1984-85; atty. Wells, Moore, Simmons, Stubblefield and Neeld, Jackson, Miss., 1988-89, Copeland, Cook, Taylor & Bush, Jackson, Miss., 1989-97; shareholder Akers & Obert, P.A., Brandon, Miss., 1997—2002, Obert Law Group P.A., Madison, Miss., 2002—. Verger, lector, usher, acolyte Chapel of the Cross, Madison, Miss. Mem. ABA, Miss. Bar Assn. (dir. young lawyers divsn., chmn. nomination com., code adv. com., chmn. membership svcs. com. chmn. pub. rels. com., bus. law sect. co-editor newsletter, Outstanding Young Lawyer in Miss. 2001, inducted fellow young lawyer, 2002), Rankin County Bar Assn., Hinds County Bar Assn. (dir., co-chmn. golf tournament com., mem. bench/bar com., newsletter editl. bd.), Tenn. Bar Assn., Ala. State Bar, Bar Assn. of the Fifth Fed. Cir., Miss. Def. Lawyers Assn., Def. Rsch. and Trial Lawyers Assn., Miss. Claims Assn., Jackson Young Lawyers Assn. (pres., v.p., treas., dir., chmn. bench/bar com., chmn. social com., chmn. golf com.), U. Ala. "A" Club, Public Info. Com. (chmn. 2002-03). Avocations: golf, hunting, skiing. Office: Obert Law Group One Woodgreen Pl Ste 200 Madison MS 39110

OBERT, PAUL RICHARD, lawyer, manufacturing executive; b. Pitts. s. Edgar F. and Elizabeth T. Obert. BS, Georgetown U., 1950; JD, U. Pitts., 1953. Bar: Pa. 1954, D.C. 1956, Ohio 1972, Ill. 1974, U.S. Supreme Ct. 1970. Sole practice, Pitts., 1954-60; asst. counsel H.K. Porter Co., Inc., Pitts., 1960—62, sec., gen. counsel, 1962-71, Addressograph-Multigraph Corp., Cleve., 1972-74; v.p. law Marshall Field & Co., Chgo., 1974-82, sec., 1976-82; v.p., gen. counsel, sec. CF Industries, Inc., Long Grove, Ill., 1982—, also officer, dir. various subs. Served to lt. col. USAF. Mem. ABA (corp. gen. counsel com.), Pa. Bar Assn., Allegheny County Bar Assn., Ill. Bar Assn., Chgo. Bar Assn., Am. Soc. Corp. Secs., Am. Retail Fedn. (bd. dirs. 1977-80), Georgetown U. Alumni Assn. (bd. govs.), Pitts. Athletic Assn., Univ. Club (Chgo.), Delta Theta Phi. Office: CF Industries Inc 1 Salem Lake Dr Long Grove IL 60047-8401

OBERWETTER, JAMES C. ambassador; BA, U. Tex. Press sec. Rep. George H.W. Bush, U.S. Ho. Reps.; chmn. Tex. Commn. on Alcohol and Drug Abuse; sr. v.p. govtl. and pub. affairs Hunt Consol., Inc., 1974—2003; U.S. amb. to Saudi Arabia U.S. Dept. State, Washington, 2004—. Office: American Embassy Unit 61307 APO AE 09803-1307*

OBEY, DAVID ROSS, congressman; b. Okmulgee, Okla., Oct. 3, 1938; s. Orville John and Mary Jane (Chellis) O.; m. Joan Therese Lepinski, June 9, 1962; children: Craig David, Douglas David. BS in Polit. Sci, U. Wis., 1960, MA, 1962. Mem. Wis. Gen. Assembly, 1963-69, asst. minority leader, 1967-69; mem. U.S. Congress from 7th Wis. dist., 1969—; ranking minority mem. appropriations com. Mem. adminstrv. com. Wis. Dem. Com., 1960-62 Named Edn. Legislator of Yr., Rural div. NEA, 1968; recipient Legislative Leadership award Eagelton Inst. Politics, 1964, award of merit Nat. Council Sr. Citizens, 1976, citation for legis. statesmanship Council Exceptional Children, 1976. Democrat. Office: US Ho of Reps 2314 Rayburn HOB Washington DC 20515-4907

OBIECHINA, EMMANUEL NWANONYE, humanities educator; b. Nkpor, Anambra, Nigeria, Sept. 20, 1933; came to U.S., 1987; s. Obiechina Enyibuaku Olisakwe and Nwayioye Udenweze Obierika; m. Maria Obiageli Enekebe, Apr. 25, 1964; children: Nnonye, Nneka, Ikenna, Chioma, Nkemjika, Joy. BA in English with honors, Univ. Coll., Ibadan, Nigeria, 1961; PhD in English, Cambridge (Eng.) U., 1967. Asst. sec. Ministry Fgn. Affairs, Lagos, Nigeria, 1961-62; lectr. U. Nigeria, Nsukka, 1967-74, prof., 1974, chair dept. English, 1975-78, 80-81, dean grad. sch., 1981-85; dir. Nigerian Univs. office Embassy of Nigeria, Washington, 1987-90; vis. prof. English Hobart & William Smith Colls., Geneva, N.Y., 1990-92; vis. prof. humanities U. Pitts., Bradford, Pa., 1992-95; Gerry Carruthers chair U. N.Mex., Albuquerque, 1996; Williams/NEH disting. prof. humanities Ferrum (Va.) Coll., 1997—99; vis. prof. Eng. and African-Amer. Studies Univ. Kansas, Lawrence, KS, 2000—. Ahiajoku ann. lectr. Imo State Govt. of Nigeria, Owerri, 1994, fellow, DuBois Inst. for African Am. Rsch., Harvard U., 2001-02, vis. scholar, Harvard U., Dept. Afro-Am. Lit. and Lang., 2002-03. Author: An African Popular Literature, 1973, Culture, Tradition and Society in the West African Novel, 1975, Language and Theme, 1990, Masksong For Our Times, 2003; editor: Baldwin's Go Tell It On the Mountain, 1966. Sec. Nat. Guidance Com., Biafra, 1967-70; mem. coun. Nigerian Inst. Internat. Affairs, 1978-84; exec. mem. Assn. Nigerian Authors, 1982-87; mem. Nat. Anthem Com., Nigeria, 1977-78. Commonwealth Academic fellow, Cambridge, 1972-73, Woodrow Wilson fellow, 1979-80, NEH summer fellow, 1991, 1994-98; non-resident fellow, DuBois Inst., African Am. Rsch., Harvard U., 2003-, Nigerian Acad. of Letters, 2004. Mem. MLA, African Lit. Assn., African Studies Assn., Internat. Comparative Lit. Assn., Clare Coll. Assn., Nigerian Inst. Internat. Affairs (life), Internat. Assn. of Univ. Profs. of English, 2000. Roman Catholic. Avocations: gardening, writing, music, tennis. Home: 14125 Parker Farm Way Silver Spring MD 20906-6326 Office: WEB DuBois Inst for African and African Am Rsch Barker Ctr 12 Quincy St Cambridge MA 02138-3879 E-mail: obiechin@fas.harvard.edu., emmanuelobiechina@yahoo.com.

OBIEDAT, MOHAMMAD AHMAD, education educator, researcher; b. Yobla, Irbid, Jordan, Dec. 2, 1968; s. Ahmad Diab and Wisal Mhmood Obiedat; m. Enas Faisal Khrais, July 25, 2003. PhD in math., Mid. East Tech. U., 1998. Asst. prof. math. Gallaudet U., Washington, 1999—2003. Contbr. articles. Home: 837 Pleasant Hill Lane Bowie MD 20716 Office: Gallaudet U 800 Florida Ave NE Washington DC 20002 Office Phone: 202-651-5315.

OBIORA, CHRIS SUNNY, architect; b. Lagos, Nigeria, Sept. 2, 1954; came to U.S., 1978; s. Patrick M. and Virginia E. Obiora. Diploma in Physics, Chemistry, and Biology, Christ the King Coll., Onitsha, Anambra, 1974; A in Econs. and Current Affairs, Christ the King Coll., 1976; postgrad., Tex. A&M U., 1986, Coll. Profl. Mgmt., Lintas, Lagos, 1992. CFP; cert. tng. adminstr. Accounts clk. Lintas, Ltd., Lagos, 1976-78, media accounts clk., 1977-78; with San Jacinto Jr. Coll., Houston, Tex., 1980-81; The Wacherhit Corp., Coral Gables, Fla., 1980-84; gen. merchant Joncod Overseas Ltd., Lagos, 1974—, world trade strategist Houston, 1987—; retail trader Star Liquor Store, Hempstead, Tex., 1987—; owner, prin. Chris & Chris Assocs., 1989. Coord. Jancod/Bexpharm, Houston, 1987-88; cost acct. Jancod Overseas Ltd., Houston, 1980—; founder, pres. Joncod Internat., Inc., 1987—; founder, com. group head Star Liquor Store, Hempstead, 1987—. Active ARC, 1967-70, PTO, also numerous charitable activities, Lagos, 1970-74. Recipient Professionalism Cert. AMA, 1994, Meritorious Svc. award AIA Students, 1985, Recognition award Nat. Fire Protection Assn., 1986. Fellow The Highlanders Club (svcs. prof. 1993—), Nat. Shrine, Oxford Club, Oblates Mission Mary Immaculate; mem. ACLU, NAFE, ATLA, AIChE, N.Y. Acad. Sci., Am. Chem. Soc., Am. Fin. Assn., Nat. Audubon Soc., Internat. Assn. Fin. Planners, Soc. Applied Learning Tech., Assn. Corp. Tech. Computer Profls., Instr. of Profl. Mgmt. and Adminstrn., Internat. Assn. of Account Practitioners, Constrn. Specs. Inst., Nat. Hist. Soc., Nat. Soc. Accts., Sherrifs Assn. Tex., Soc. Human Rels. Mgmt. Avocations: table and lawn tennis, photography, swimming. Office: Joncod Overseas Ltd PO Box 87549 Houston TX 77287-7549

OBLINGER, JAMES L. academic administrator; b. Ashland, Ohio, Nov. 3, 1945; s. Richard Bruce and Pauline (Frary) O.;m. Diana G. Oblinger. BA in Bacteriology, DePauw U., Greencastle, Ind., 1967; MS in Food Tech., Iowa State U., 1970, PhD in Food Tech., 1972. Asst. prof. to prof. food sci. and human nutrition U. Fla., Gainesville, 1972-84; assoc. dean, dir. resident instrn. Coll. Agr., U. Mo., Columbia, 1984-86; assoc. dean, dir. acad. affairs Coll. Agr. and Life Sci., N.C. State U., Raleigh, 1986—97; dean, exec. dir. for agrl. programs N.C. State U., Raleigh, 1997—2003, provost and exec. vice chancellor for acad. affairs, 2003—. Mem. joint coun. of food and agrl. scis. U.S. Dept. Agr. Contbr. articles to profl. jours., chpts. to books. Recipient Award of Merit, Inst. of Food and Agrl. Scis., 1981, Tchr. of the Yr., 1977. Mem. Inst. Food Technologists (Wm. V. Cruess Nat. Award Excellence 1983), So. Assn. Agrl. Scientists (Profl. Scientist Award 1976), Coun. for Agrl. Sci. and Tech. (pres. 1990—), Am. Assn. Higher Edn., Internat. Assn. Milk, Food and Environ. Sanitarians, Nat. Assn. Colls. and Tchrs. Agr., Sigma Xi, Phi Kappa Phi, Gamma Sigma Delta, Phi Tau Sigma, Phi Epsilon Phi. Episcopalian. Office: NC State U 109 Holladay Hall PO Box 7101 Raleigh NC 27695-7101

O'BLOCK, ROBERT, entrepreneur, publishing executive; BS in Sociology, Pittsburg (Kans.) State U., 1972, MS in Sociology, 1973, EdS, 2001; PhD, Kans. State U., 1976; MA in Psychology, Newport U., 1998, PsyD in Psychology, 2000; MDiv, Trinity Coll., 2001, DMin, 2003. Ordained deacon So. Episcopal Ch., 1999; ordained priest Anglican Cath. Ch., 2002. Patrolman Frontenac (Kans.) Police Dept., 1971-73; probation officer Crawford County Juvenile Ct., 1973-74; spr. Children's Ct. Ctr., 1974; adminstrv. asst. to dean student affairs/cmty. svc. Labette Cmty. Jr. Coll., 1976; dir. night sch. Marymount Coll., 1976; asst. prof. dept. adminstrv. justice Wichita State U., 1977-79; assoc. prof. dept. criminal justice/polit. sci. Appalachian State U., Boone, N.C., 1979-89; prof., chair dept. adminstrn. of justice Coll. of Ozarks, Point Lookout, Mo., 1989-93; exec. dir. Am. Coll. Forensic Examiners, Springfield, Mo., 1994—. Founder Am. Bd. Forensic Medicine, Am. Bd. Forensic Examiners, Am. Bd. Forensic Psychol. Specializations, Am. Bd. Forensic Dentistry, Am. Bd. Forensic Engring. and Tech., Am. Bd. Forensic Nursing, Am. Bd. Law Enforcement Experts, Am. Bd. Forensic Acctg., Am. Bd. of Forensic Counselors, Am. Bd. Forensic Social Work; lectr., cons. in field. Author: Criminal Justice Research Sources, 1983, 3d edit., 1992, (with others) Security and Crime Prevention, 2d edit., 1990; founder, pub. The Forensic Examiner, Annals of the Am. Psychotherapy Assn., co-founder E Bus. Techs., contbr. articles to profl. jours., holder 14 U.S. fed. trademarks. Adv. bd. Larnard State Hosp. Named Knight Chevalier, Sovereign Military Order of Temple of Jerusalem, 2001; grantee, Gov.'s Commn. on Criminal Adminstrn., 1976—77. Fellow: Am. Ctr. for Study of Religion and Soc., Oxford Soc. Scholars; mem.: Am. Assn. Integrative Medicine (co-founder, CEO), Am. Coll. Forensic Examiners (founder), Am. Psychotherapy Assn. (founder, chmn., CEO). Office: 2750 E Sunshine St Springfield MO 65804-2047 Home: 3686 E Kingswood Dr Springfield MO 65809-4635 Office Phone: 417-881-3818 121. E-mail: rloblock@aol.com.

O'BLOCK, ROBERT PAUL, management consultant; b. Pitts., Mar. 9, 1943; s. Paul Joseph and Mary Elizabeth (Galicic) O'B.; m. Megan Marie. BSME, Purdue U., 1965; MBA, Harvard U., 1967. Rsch. and tchg. fellow in fin., econs. and urban mgmt. Harvard U., 1967-70; assoc. in real estate mgmt. and fin. McKinsey & Co., Inc., Boston, 1969-78; gen. and mng. ptnr. Freeport Ctr., Clearfield, Utah, 1971—; prin. McKinsey & Co., Inc., Boston, 1979-84, dir., 1984-98. Vis. lectr. urban econs. Yale Law Sch., Princeton U.; cons. Mass., N.J. housing fin. agys., Rockefeller Assn., HUD, 1968-76; chmn. mgmt. com. Snowbird Lodge (Utah), 1974-86. Contbr. articles to profl. jours. Mem. nat. adv. bd. Snowbird Arts Inst., 1977-83; mem. budget com. N.Y. Pub. Libr., 1977-79; mem. adv. bd. Internat. Tennis Hall of Fame, 1986-89, bd. dirs., 1989-95; mem. bd. overseers Boston Symphony Orch., 1988-2000, vice-chmn. bd. overseers, 1992-95, chmn., 1995-2000, trustee, 2000—, vice chmn. bd. trustees, 2002—; trustee U.S. Ski Ednl. Found., 1989-2001, Park Sch., 1997—2003. Mem. Devon Yacht Club, Maidstone Club, Nat. Golf Links Am., The Country Club (Brookline). Office: 60 Cramond Rd Chestnut Hill MA 02467-2803

OBLOY, LEONARD GERARD, priest; b. Cleve., Sept. 1, 1951; s. Henry Joseph and Ruth Elsie (Walter) Obloy. AB, Borromeo Coll. of Ohio, 1973; MDiv, St. Mary's Sem., 1977; SSL, Pontifical Bibl. Inst., Rome, 1983, postgrad., 1984. Ordained priest Roman Cath. Ch., 1977. Assoc. pastor St. Helen Parish, Newbury, Ohio, 1977-80, St. Rose of Lima Parish, Cleve., 1984-88; vice-rector Mt. St. Mary's Sem., Emmitsburg, Md., 1988-97, asst. prof. sacred scripture and computer sci., 1988-99, dir. aux. svcs., 1997-99; assoc. pastor St. Francis of Assisi Parish, Gates Mills, Ohio, 1999—2002; pastor St. William Parish, Euclid, Ohio, 2002—. Adj. prof. St. Mary's Sem., Cleve., 1984—88, Cleve., 1999—; dean grad. divsn. Cath. Distance U., Hamilton, Va., 1995—2003, dean emeritus, 2003—; guest lectr. Our Lady of Holy Cross Coll., New Orleans, 1998—2003; lectr. in field. Author, narrator pub. TV series And God Said, Witness; author various pamphlets, audio casettes for Cath. Distance U. Mem.: IEEE Computer Soc., Vatican Radio, Sacred Congregation for Doctrine of Faith, Nat. Cath. Edn. Assn., Corp. for Pub. Broadcasting, Cath. Bibl. Fedn., NY Acad. Scis., Assn. for Computing Machinery. Avocations: computers, audio engineering, audio recording, auto mechanics. Office: St William Parish 367 E 260th St Euclid OH 44132 Office Phone: 216-731-1515. E-mail: lgobloy@aol.com.

OBNINSKY, VICTOR PETER, lawyer; b. San Rafael, Calif., Oct. 12, 1944; s. Peter Victor and Anne Bartholdi (Donston) Obninsky; m. Clara Alice Bechtel, June 8, 1969 (div. Oct. 30, 2003). BA, Columbia U., 1966; JD, U. Calif., Hastings, 1969. Bar: Calif. 1970. Sole practice, Novato, Calif., 1970-2001, Tiburon, Calif., 2001—02, Sonoma, Calif., 2003—. Arbitrator Marin County Superior Ct., San Rafael, 1979—; superior ct. judge pro tem, 1979—; lectr. real estate and partnership law. Author: The Russians in Early California, 1966. Bd. dirs. Calif. Young Reps., 1968-69, Richardson Bay San. Dist., 1974-75, Marin County Legal Aid Soc., 1976-78; baseball coach Little League, Babe Ruth League, 1970-84; mem. nat. panel consumer arbitrators Better Bus. Bur., 1974-88; leader Boy Scouts Am., 1970-84; permanent sec. Phillips Acad. Class of 1962, 1987—; mem. Phillips Acad. Alumni Coun., 1991-95; bd. cmty. advisors Buck Ctr. for Rsch. on Aging, 1990-2001. Mem ABA, State Bar Calif., Marin County Bar Assn. (bd. dirs. 1985-91, treas. 1987-88, pres.-elect 1989, pres. 1990), Sonoma Bar Assoc. Phi Delta Phi, Phi Gamma Delta. Republican. Russian Orthodox. Home and Office: 21453 Shainsky Sonoma CA 95476-8412 Office Phone: 707-935-7427. Personal E-mail: vpobninsky@cs.com. *An all-out intellectual attempt to understand baseball thoroughly may give sufficient insight to understand oneself; the so-called "designated hitter" rule shoold be abolished immediately.*

OBOLENSKY, IVAN, investment banker, foundation consultant, writer, publisher; b. London, May 15, 1925; s. Serge and Alice (Astor) O. (parents Am. citizens); m. Claire McGinnis, 1949 (div. 1956); children: Marina Ava, Ivan Serge, David; m. Mary Elizabeth Morris, 1959; 1 child, Serge. AB, Yale U., 1947. Pres. Hotel Investments, Inc., N.Y.C., 1950-58; v.p., treas. Serge Obolensky Assocs., 1952-75; Ivan Obolensky Inc. and Astor Books, pubs. Ivan Obolensky Inc., pubs., 1956-65; dir. Silver Bear Inc., Atlanta; ptnr. A.T. Brod & Co., investment bankers, Dominick & Dominick Inc., investment bankers, 1965-70, Middendorf Colgate, investment bankers, 1970-73; v.p. C.B. Richard, Ellis/Moseley Hallgarten, investment bankers, 1974-81, Sterling Grace & Co., investment bankers, N.Y.C., 1982-87; sr. v.p. Jesup, Josephthal & Co., investment bankers, N.Y.C., 1987-90; gen. ptnr. Astor Capital Mgmt. Assocs., 1980—; v.p. Capital Mgmt. Assocs., 1990—, Shields & Co., N.Y.C., 1990—. Bd. dirs. Gold Canyon Resources, 1996—; cons. and lectr. in field. Author: Rogues' March, 1956, Who, 1962; contbr. to Nihon Keizai Shimbun, Tokyo, on precious metals, 1985—, program com. N.Y. Soc. of Security Analysts for pub., aerospace, metals and mining, oil and gas; contbr. articles to profl. publs. Bd. dirs. Police Athletic League, N.Y.C., 1975-85, exec. com., 1980-85, 96—, U.S.O., 1987—, Audubon Canyon Ranch, Calif., 1989—, Tolstoy Found., 1994—, Soldiers', Sailors', Marines' and Airmen's Club, 1976—, pres., 1987-2000, chmn.,ceo, 2000—, Russian Nobility Assn. in Am., 1990—, treas., 1991—, v.p., 1995—, Musicians Emergency Fund, 1985-93, pres.1987-92, Children's Blood Found., N.Y. Hosp., 1952—, pres., 1981-95, pres. emeritus, 1995—; pres., dir. Josephine Lawrence Hopkins Found., 1971—, pres. Whitemarsh Found., 1980-90, Masonic Brotherhood Found., 1996—. Lt. (j.g.) USNR, 1943-45, ret., 1980. Published works by James Agee: A Death in the Family and Tad Mosel; All the Way Home, which received Pulitzer prizes, 2 Caldecott awards. Mem. Am. Legion, Mil. Order Loyal Legion U.S. (sr. vice-comdr. 1955, comdr. 1967-70), St. Elmo Soc., Met. Mus. Art (life), Knickerbocker Club, N.Y. Yacht Club, New Eng. Soc. N.Y., St. Georges Soc. N.Y., The Navy League, Army and Navy Club, Explorer's Club, Masons (Holland #8 master 1981, dist. dep. grand master 1st Manhattan 1983-84, grand treas. 1994-96), DeMolay (hon. mem.). Office: Shields & Co 140 Broadway New York NY 10005-1101 Office Phone: 212-320-3000. Personal E-mail: Iobolensky@aol.com.

OBOLENSKY, MARILYN WALL (MRS. SERGE OBOLENSKY), metals company executive; b. Detroit, Aug. 13, 1929; d. Albert Fraser and Christine (Frischkorn) Wall; m. Serge Obolensky, June 3, 1971. Student, Duschesne Jr. Coll., 1947. Chmn. bd. Wall-Colmondy Corp., Detroit, 1959-61, exec. sec., 1961—. Chmn. bd. Wall-Gases Inc., Morrisville, Pa., 1959-61; pres. Serge Obolensky Assocs. Bd. dirs. Heart and Lung Assn. N.Y.C., 1963— . Mem.: Bathing Corp. (Southampton, N.Y.), Southampton. Republican. Roman Catholic. Address: 45 Preston Pl Grosse Pointe Farms MI 48236-3035

O'BOYLE, MAUREEN, television show host; News prodr., anchor Sta. KREM-TV, Spokane, Wash.; reporter, prodr., writer, co-anchor Sta. WMAZ-TV, Macon, Ga.; nightside reporter, anchor Sta. WECT-TV, Wilmington, N.C.; morning news anchor Sta. WITN-TV, Washington, N.C.; anchor A Current Affair; anchor, sr. corr. Extra, Glendale, Calif., 1995-96, co-host, 1997—; host In Person With Maureen O'Boyle, 1996-97. Office: PO Box 509 Hurley NY 12443-0509

OBRAMS, GUNTA IRIS, medical officer; b. Düsseldorf, Germany, Sept. 2, 1953; came to U.S., 1961; d. Robert and Olga (Baltins) O.; m. Malcolm DeWitt Patterson, Dec. 22, 1975; 1 child, Andrew McDougal Patterson. BS in Biology cum laude, Rensselaer Poly. Inst., 1977; MD, Union U., Albany, N.Y., 1977; MPH, Johns Hopkins U., 1982, PhD, 1988. Resident in obstetrics and gynecology Ea. Va. Grad. Sch. Medicine, Norfolk, 1977-78; community physician Southampton Meml. Hosp., Franklin, Va., 1978-81; resident in gen. preventive medicine sch. hygiene and pub. health Johns Hopkins U., Balt., 1981-84, project dir., 1983-85, med. dir., 1985-86; med. officer divsn. cancer etiology Nat. Cancer Inst., Bethesda, Md., 1986-89, dep. chief, 1989-90, chief, 1990-96, dir. extramural epidemiology & genetics program, 1996-2001; mgmt. US Coast Guard Health Svcs., 2001—. Editor: (with M. Potter): The Epidemiology and Biology of Multiple Myeloma, 1991; contbr. articles to profl. jours. With USPHS, 1987—. Recipient Nat. Cancer Inst. Nat. Rsch. Svc. award, 1981, Rsch. Career award Nat. Inst. Occupational Safety & Health; scholar Am. Med. Women's Assn., 1977. Mem. Phi Beta Kappa, Delta Omega, Alpha Omega Alpha. Office: Health Svcs Mgmt Dvsn US Coast Guard Hdqts G-WKH-3 2100 Second St SW Washington DC 20593

OBRECHT, MARGARET M. H. cultural organization administrator; b. June 12, 1938; married; 3 children. AB in Religion, Goucher Coll., 1960; MA in Theology, St. Mary's Sem. Ecumen. Inst., 1978; cert. in hosp. chaplaincy, Archdioc. Balt. Health Affairs, 1979; postgrad., St. Mary's Sem. Ecumen. Inst., 1987-88. Admissions counselor admissions office Goucher Coll., Towson, Md., 1965-70; cons. Sevynmor Farm, Inc., Kennett Square, Pa., 1986-87; dir. ch. rels. U.S. Holocaust Meml. Mus., Washington, 1989—. Lectr. in field. Chairperson residential gifts divsn. United Way, 1975, chairperson individual spl. gifts divsn., 1980-81; bd. dirs. Anne Frank Inst. of Phila., 1978-89, pres. pro tem, 1985; adj. chaplain Johns Hopkins Hosp., 1979—; chairperson adv. com. Women's Detention Ctr., 1987-93; foster parent Balt. City Dept. Social Svcs., 1987—; bd. dirs. St. Mary's Sem. and U. Alumni Assn., 1982-84, 87—, Ecumenical Inst. of St. Mary's Sem., 1982-87, Red Cross Holocaust and War Victims Tracing and Info. Ctr., 1990-97. Recipient Disting. Alumnae award Bryn Mawr Sch., 1996, Chevra Ahavas Chesed, Inc., Humanitarian award, 1994, Benemerenti Papel award 2000; Holywell Trust Grant lectr., No. Ireland, 1995; fellow Shalom Hartman Inst. for Advanced Judaic Studies, Jerusalem, 1984. Office: US Holocaust Meml Mus Dept Ch Rels 100 Raoul Wallenberg Pl SW Washington DC 20024-2126

O'BRIAN, HAROLD SAMUEL, lawyer; b. Phila, Pa, Dec. 9, 1933; s. Harold S. and Estelle A. (Wilson) O'Brian; m. Judith Bremer, May 21, 1964; children: Jonathan, Geoffrey, Andrew. BA, Amherst Coll., 1954; LLB, U. Pa, 1960; LLM, NYU, 1967; MBA, Rutgers U, 1984. Bar: Pa. 1961, NJ 1975, Calif. 1980. Assoc. Paul & Paul, Phila., 1965—67; asst. US atty. Phila., 1967—70; assoc. counsel Campbell Soup Co., Camden, NJ, 1970; gen. counsel, v.p. and corp. sec. Rsch. Cottrell Inc., Somerville, NJ, 2003—. Mem.: ABA (past chmn. small bus. tax com.). Office: Research Cottrell Inc PO Box 1500 Somerville NJ 08876-1251

O'BRIEN, ANNMARIE, education educator; b. N.Y.C., Nov. 10, 1949; d. Hugh and Margaret (Doherty) O'B.; m. William James McGinty, Dec. 30, 1976; children: Michael Hugh, Liam Patrick. BS in Elem. Edn., Boston U., 1971; MS in Early Childhood Edn., Queens Coll., 1976; EdD in Ednl. Leadership, Portland State U., 1994. Tchr. St. Gerard Majella Elem. Sch., Hollis, N.Y., 1972-76, Lower Kuskokwim Sch. Dist., Bethel, Alaska, 1977-85; child sexual abuse prevention coord. Resource Ctr. for Parents and Children, Fairbanks, Alaska, 1986; grad. asst., project evaluator Portland (Oreg.) State U., 1989-92, student tchr. supr., 1992; prof. edn., rsch. assoc. Inst. Social and Econ. Rsch. U. Alaska, Anchorage, 1993-96; prin. Old Harbor Sch., Kodiak Island Borough Sch. Dist., Kodiak, Alaska, 1996-99; dir. curriculum and instr. Northwest Arctic Borough, Kotzebue, Alaska, 1999—. Author: A Child Abuse Prevention Training Manual for Educators, 1976; co-author: The Academy for Future Educators Guidebook, 1992. Recipient scholarship Portland State U., 1991. Mem. ASCD, Kappa Delta Pi. Office: NWA BSD PO Box 51 Kotzebue AK 99752-0051 E-mail: aobrien@nwarctic.org.

O'BRIEN, BEA JAE, artist; b. Oshkosh, Wis., Dec. 4, 1940; d. Harry A. and Mammie Anna (Smith) Mac Farlane; m. John Walsh O'Brien, July 27, 1965; 1 child, John Christian. BA, U. Wis. Profl. artist B.J.'s Fine Arts, Moraga, Calif. Art included in various art publs.; exhibitions include Dennos Mus., Calif. Art & Wine Festival, 2001, Internat. Art Show, 2001, Valley Art Gallery, Calif., 2001—03, Calif. Art (3 awards), Internat. Art Show, Chgo., First Cyberspace Art Exhibit, New Zealand, Internat. Collage Constrn. Mus., Mexico City, one-woman shows include, Moraga, Calif., 1996—2001. Vol. children's art publ. Moraga Sch. Sys.; vol. local sch. projects Calif. Open Art Exhbits, 2003; vol. organizer Cmty. Art Gallery, Moraga Gallery, 2000—01; donated, vol. Outreach Art Funds and Scholarships, Calif. Recipient 1st pl. award, Calif. Art and Wine Festival, 1999, Bay Area Art Festival, 1999, 2000. Mem.: Digital Image Art Career, Intuitive Layering Art Group, Valley Arts Ctr., Collage Artists Am., Nat. Collage Soc. (award 1997—99, 2004, signature), Internat. Soc. Exptl. Artists (Nautilus award 2003, signature), Lamorinda Arts Alliance, Coll. Art Am., Women in Arts Mus. (honor roll). Avocations: reading, volunteering. Office: BJs Fine Arts 34 Sea Pines Moraga CA 94556-1029 Office Phone: 925-376-8018.

O'BRIEN, CATHERINE LOUISE, museum administrator; b. NYC, July 21, 1930; d. Edward Denmark and Cathrine Louise (Browne) O'B.; m. Philip R. James (div.); m. Sterling Noel (div.). BA, Finch Coll., 1952; postgrad, Williams Coll., 1954, Marymount Coll., 1954. Reprodn. mgr. Met. Mus. Art, N.Y.C., 1975—; dir. sales Simon Pearce Gallery, N.Y.C. Exhibited in group shows at Parrish Art Mus., Southampton, NY, 1965-70, Met. Mus. Art, NYC, 1975-85, Guild Hall Exhibit, East Hampton, NY, 1965-85. Mem. aux. Southampton Hosp., 1970-85; founder East Hampton Horse Show, Ladies Village Improvement Soc., East Hampton, 1970—; fair coms. St. James Ch., NYC, St. Luke's Ch., East Hampton, 1970-85; alumnae adv. bd. Marymount Coll., NYC, 1984-86, chmn. alumnae event, 1994; active Women's Nat. Rep. Club, NYC, John Drew Theater Co., Guild Hall, 1956-59; chmn. Landmark and Tree Planting Com. for Madison Ave. Assn., NYC, 1994—; mem. founding com. Internat. Debutante Ball, Waldorf Astoria, NYC, 1955; founding mem. Williamstown (Mass.) Theater, 1955; founder Parrish Art Mus.

Players, Southampton, NY, 1955. Mem. DAR (founding; vice regent East Hampton chpt. 1974-85), Colonial Dames Am. (archives com. 1980-85), Daus. Brit. Empire (historian 1978-85), United Daus. Confederacy (state historian 1970-85), Daus. Colonial Wars (corr. sec. 1983-85), Sons and Daus. of Pilgrims (corr. sec. 1983-85), Victorian Soc., Soc. Mayflower Descs. (life), English Speaking Union, New Eng. Soc. (mem. ball com. 1983-86), Daus. of Cin. (historian 1979-85), Squadron "A", Devon Yacht, Maidstone, Southampton Yacht, Metropolitan Club (women's com., chmn. debutante ball 1980-84), Reciprocal/India House, St. Anthony Union League. Republican. Episopalian. Avocations: show horses, dogs. Home: 605 Park Ave New York NY 10021-7016 also: Seacote PO Box 1488 East Hampton NY 11937-0711 Office: Met Mus of Art 5th Ave New York NY 10028 also: Simon Pierce Gallery 500 Park Ave New York NY 10022-1606

O'BRIEN, CHARLES H. lawyer, retired state supreme court chief justice; b. Orange, N.J., July 30, 1920; s. Herbert Rodgers and Agnes Sidman (Montanya) O'B.; m. Anna Belle Clement, Nov. 9, 1966; children: Merry Diane, Steven Shawn (dec.), Heather Lynn. LLB, Cumberland U., 1947. Rep. Tenn. Legislature, Memphis, 1963-65, senator, 1965-67; assoc. judge Tenn. Ct. Criminal Appeals, Crossville, 1970-87; assoc. justice Tenn. Supreme Ct., 1987-94, chief justice, 1994-95; ret., 1995; pvt. practice, 1995—. Bd. dirs. Lake Tansi Village Property Owners Assn., 1984-89, chmn., 1989. With U.S. Army, 1938-45, ETO, 1950, UN Command, Tokyo. Decorated Bronze Star, Purple Heart with oak leaf cluster. Fellow Tenn. Bar Found.; mem. Tenn. Bar Assn., Cumberland County Bar Assn., Am. Legion, Lake Tansi Village Chowder and Marching Soc. (pres.). Democrat. Avocation: outdoor activities.

O'BRIEN, CHARLES P. psychiatrist, educator; BA, Tulane U., 1960, MS, MD, 1964, PhD in Neurophysiology, 1966. Resident in internal medicine Mass. Gen. Hosp., 1964—65; neurologist, psychiatrist Tulane U., 1965—67, Nat. Hosp. Nervous Disorders, London, 1967—68; psychiatrist U. Pa., Phila., 1968—69, from instr. to asst. prof. to assoc. prof., 1969—78, prof. psychiatry, 1978—, vice chmn., 1986—. Tchg. asst. neurophysiology Tulane Med. Sch., 1965—66, instr., 1966—67; vis. prof. Sch. Medicine Hahnemann U., 1980—95; Pfizer vis. prof. Albert Einstein Coll. Medicine, 1990; Inst. Med. Nat. Sci. Acad., 1991. Fellow: APA, Am. Coll. Neuropsychopharmacology; mem.: Assn. Rsch. Nervous and Mental Diseases (pres. 1989—90), Soc. Neurosci., Coll. on Problems of Drug Dependence, Am. Psychosomatic Soc., Soc. Psychotherapy Rsch., Am. Acad. Neurology, Psychiat. Rsch. Soc. Office: U Pa Treatment Rsch Ctr 3900 Chestnut St Philadelphia PA 19104-3120 E-mail: obrien@mail.trc.upenn.edu.

O'BRIEN, CONAN, writer, performer, talk show host; b. Brookline, Mass., Apr. 18, 1963; m. Liza Powel, Jan. 2002; 1 child, Neve. BA Am. Hist., Lit., Harvard U., 1981-85. Staff mem. The Harvard Lampoon, 1981-85 (pres. 1983, 84); head Conaco. Stage appearances with: The Groundlings (L.A.) 1985-87; writer, performer The Happy Happy Good Show (L.A., Chgo.) 1988; writer (TV) Not Necessarily the News (HBO) 1985-87, Saturday Night Live, 1988-91 (NBC, Emmy Outstanding Writing in Comedy series 1989), Lookwell (NBC) 1991; writer, prodr. The Simpsons (Fox) 1991-93, The Wilton North Report (syndicated) 1987, Late Night with Conan O'Brien (NBC) 1993— (Best Writing in Comedy/Variety Show Writer's Guild award 1997, TV award Writers Guild Am. 2000), host, Emmy Awards 2002; TV appearances include Mr. Show, The Single Guy, Arli$$, (voice) Dr. Katz, Professional Therapist, Veronica's Closet, Spin City, LateLine, Space Ghost Coast to Coast, (voice) Futurama, Tomorrow Night, 1998, Barenaked in America, 1999, Saturday Night Live: 25th Anniversary, 1999, (video) Elmopalooza!, 1998. Named one of 25 Most Intriguing People, People Mag., 50 Funniest People Alive, Entertainment Weekly. Office: Late Night with Conan O'Brien NBC 30 Rockefeller Plz New York NY 10112-0002

O'BRIEN, DAN, writer; b. N.Y.C., Dec. 4, 1973; s. Gerald Patrick and Kathleen Welsh O'Brien. BA in English and Theatre, Middlebury Coll., 1996; MFA in Creative Writing, Brown U., 1999. Playwright-in-residence Manhattan Theatre Club, N.Y.C., 1999—2000; faculty mem. Sewanee Writers Conf., Tenn., 2003; lectr. dept. theatre Princeton U., NJ, 2003—04. Fellow, Brown U., 1997—99; Thomas J. Watson fellow, 1996—97, Tennessee Williams fellow, Sewanee U. of South, 2002—03. Mem.: Dramatic Guild Am. (solo rep. writer, dir. lab. 2001—02), Primary States New Am. Writes Group. Office: c/o Beth Blickers Abrams Artists 275 Seventh Ave 26th Fl New York NY 10011

O'BRIEN, DANIEL J. lawyer; b. Los Alamos, N.Mex., Nov. 18, 1951; BS, U. N.Mex., 1975, MBA, 1980, JD, 1983. Bar: N.Mex. 1983, Tex. 1993, U.S. Dist. Ct. N.Mex. 1984, U.S. Ct. Appeals (10th cir.) 1987. Atty. DAniel J. O'Brien & Assocs., Albuquerque. Mem.: ABA, Albuquerque Bar Assn., N.Mex. Trial Lawyers Assn., N.Mex. Def. Lawyers Assn. (pres. 1999—2000), State Bar N.Mex. (bd. commrs. 1994—2000, v.p. 2002). Office: Daniel J O'Brien and Assocs 6301 Indian Sch NE Ste 800 Albuquerque NM 87110

O'BRIEN, DAVID A. lawyer; b. Sioux City, Iowa, Aug. 30, 1958; s. John T. and Doris K. (Reisch) O'B. BA, George Washington U., 1981; JD with distinction, U. Iowa, 1984. Bar: Iowa 1985, U.S. Dist. Ct. (no. dist.) Iowa 1985, Nebr. 1990, U.S. Dist. Ct. Nebr. 1990. Legis. asst. Nat. Transp. Safety Bd., Washington, 1978-81; assoc. O'Brien, Galvin & Kuehl, Sioux City, 1985-88; ptnr. O'Brien, Galvin Moeller & Neary, Sioux City, 1989-94; chair Wage Appeals Bd. & Bd. of Svc. Contract Appeals U.S. Dept. Labor, Washington, 1994-96, acting dir. Office Adminstrv. Appeals, 1995-96, chair adminstrv. review bd., 1996-98; atty. White & Johnson, P.C., Cedar Rapids, Iowa, 1998-2000; ptnr. Willey, O'Brien, Mullin, Laverty & Hanrahan, PLC, Cedar Rapids, 2000—. Dem. candidate for Congress, 6th dist. of Iowa, Sioux City, 1988; chmn. Woodbury County Dem. Party, Sioux City, 1992-94, chair Iowa campaign Clinton for Pres., Des Moines, 1992; bd. dirs. Mid-Step Svcs. Inc., Sioux City, 1986-91, Mo. River Hist. Devel., Sioux City, 1989-94. Mem.: Iowa Trial Lawyers Assn. (bd. govs. 1991—94, bd. govs. 2002—), Nat. Assn. Trial Lawyers. Roman Catholic. Avocations: sports, politics. Office: Willey O'Brien Mullin Laverty Hanrahan 3519 Center Pointe Rd NE Cedar Rapids IA 52402 Office Phone: 319-390-5555. Home Fax: 319-378-1413.

O'BRIEN, DAVID PETER, gas industry executive, lawyer; b. Montreal, Que., Can., Sept. 9, 1941; s. John Lewis and Ethel (Cox) O'Brien; m. Gail Baxter Cornell, June 1, 1968; children: Tara, Matthew, Shaun. BA in Econs. with honors, Loyola Coll., Montreal, 1962; BCL, McGill U., Montreal, 1965. Assoc. and ptnr. Ogilvy, Renault, Montreal, 1967-77; v.p., gen. counsel Petro-Can., Calgary, 1977-81, sr. v.p., 1982-85, sr. v.p. fin. and planning, 1982-85, exec. v.p., 1985-89; pres., CEO Noverco Inc., Montreal, 1989; chmn. bd., pres., CEO PanCan. Petroleum Ltd., Calgary, 1990—95; pres., COO Can. Pacific Ltd., Montreal, 1995—96, chmn., pres., CEO Calgary, 1996—2001; chmn., CEO PanCan. Energy Corp., 2001—02; chmn. EnCana Corp., 2002—. Bd. dirs. Inco Ltd., Royal Bank Can., chmn., 2004—; bd. dirs. EnCana Corp., Fairmont Hotels and Resorts, TransCan. PipeLines Ltd., Molson Inc. Mem.: Calgary Golf and Country Club, Calgary Petroleum Club, Glencoe Club. Office: 4460 Bankers Hall West 888 3d St SW Calgary AB Canada T2P 5C5 Business E-Mail: marilynn.prentice@encana.com.

O'BRIEN, DENNIS SEAN, lawyer; b. June 19, 1953; s. Edward Patrick and Virginia (Davlin) O'B.; m. Laurie Lynne Barnes, Aug. 6, 1977; children: Sean Patrick, Kathleen Erin, Elizabeth Honora, Conor James. AA, Springfield Coll., Ill., 1973; BA, Rosary Coll., 1975; JD, Loyola U., Chgo., 1978. Bar: Ill. 1978, U.S. Dist. Ct. (no. dist.) Ill. 1978; U.S. Dist. Ct. (cen. dist.) Ill. 1980. Asst. states atty. felony div. Lake County States Atty.'s Office, Waukegan, Ill., 1978-80; ptnr. Livingstone, Mueller, O'Brien & Davlin, Springfield, 1980—, v.p., sec., 1999—. Presenter seminar Ill. State Bar Assn., Ill. Inst. for Continuing Legal Edn., Nat. Bus. Inst., Lohrman Edn. Svcs. Bd. dirs. Springfield Mcpl. Opera, 1971-75, 88-92, 94-97, 99-2004, pres., 1990-92; bd. dirs. Springfield Theatre Ctr., 1986-88; mem. Leading Lawyers Network Adv. Bd., 2003—. Named to Outstanding Young Men. Am., U.S. Jaycees, 1976. Mem.: ABA, Ill. Bar Assn. (workers compensation sect. coun. 1988—90), Sangamon County Bar Assn. (bd. dirs. 1995—97). Roman Catholic. Home: 2013 S Glenwood Ave Springfield IL 62704-4517 Office: Livingstone Mueller O'Brien and Davlin 620 E Edwards St Springfield IL 62703-1639 Office Phone: 217-525-1070. E-mail: dsob@livingstonelaw.com.

O'BRIEN, DERMOT J. human resources specialist; b. Dublin; B of Fin., Pace U. With Morgan Stanley; various positions Merrill Lynch; exec. v.p. human resources TIAA-CREF, N.Y.C., 2003—. Office: TIAA-Cref 730 3d Ave New York NY 10017

O'BRIEN, DONALD EUGENE, federal judge; b. Marcus, Iowa, Sept. 30, 1923; s. Michael John and Myrtle A. (Toomey) O'B.; m. Ruth Mahon, Apr. 15, 1950; children: Teresa, Brien, John, Shuivaun. LL.B., Creighton U., 1948. Bar: Iowa bar 1948, U.S. Supreme Ct. bar 1963. Asst. city atty., Sioux City, Iowa, 1949—54; county atty. Woodbury County, Iowa, 1955—59; mcpl. judge Sioux City, Iowa, 1959-60; U.S. atty. No. Iowa, 1961-67; pvt. practice law Sioux City, 1948—61; U.S. Dist. judge, 1978—; chief judge U.S. Dist. Ct. (no. dist.) Iowa, Sioux City, 1985-92, sr. judge, 1992—; pvt. practice law Sioux City, 1967—78. Rep. 8th cir. dist. ct. judges to Jud. Conf. U.S., 1990-97. Served with USAAF, 1942-45. Decorated D.F.C., air medals. Mem. Woodbury County Bar Assn., Iowa State Bar Assn. Roman Catholic. Office: US Dist Ct PO Box 267 Sioux City IA 51102-0267 E-mail: Don_OBrian@iand.uscourts.gov.

O'BRIEN, EDWARD IGNATIUS, private investor, corporation director; b. N.Y.C., Sept. 15, 1928; s. Edward I. and Marguerite (Malone) O'B.; m. Margaret M. Feeney, June 29, 1957; children: Edward Ignatius III, Margaret Mary, Thomas Gerard, John Joseph. AB, Fordham U., 1950; LLB, St. John's U., 1954; grad., Advanced Mgmt. Program, Cornell U., 1965. Bar: N.Y. 1954. With firm Hale, Kay & Brennan, N.Y.C., 1954-55; with Bache & Co., Inc., N.Y.C., 1955-74, gen. counsel, 1960, gen. ptnr., 1964, sec., 1968, v.p., 1965-68, sr. v.p., mem. exec. com., 1969, exec. v.p., 1969, chmn. exec. com., 1971-74; pres. Securities Industry Assn., 1974-93; retired, 1993. Bd. dirs. 8 corps.; lectr. Am. Law Inst., Practising Law Inst., Am. Mgmt. Assn.; exch. ofcl. Am. Stock Exch., 1972; mem. adv. bd., mem. exec. com. Securities Regulation Inst., U. Calif., 1975—. Mem. Cardinal's com. Laity Cath. Archdiocese N.Y., mem. Cardinal's com. for edn.; chmn. Fordham U. Coun., 1971-73; bd. dirs. 3 non-profit orgns.; chmn. corp. devel. com. Fordham U.; trustee, chmn. bd. trustees Fordham Prep. Sch., 1975-77, Capt. USAR. Mem. N.Y. State Bar Assn,. Am. Arbitration Assn., Am. Soc. Internat. Law, Guild Cath. Lawyers, Securities Industry Assn. (chmn. publicly owned firms com. 1972), Nat. Assn. Securities Dealers (dist. com. 1973-74), Shenorock Shore Club (Rye, N.Y.), Town Club (Scarsdale, N.Y.), Met. Club (Washington). Home and Office: 12 Woods Ln Scarsdale NY 10583-6408

O'BRIEN, EDWARD JOHN, musician, vocalist; b. Oxford, England, Apr. 15, 1968; Student in Econs., Manchester (Eng.) U. Barman; photographer's asst.; guitarist, vocalist Radiohead, 1992—. Musician (and vocalist): (albums) Pablo Honey, 1993, The Bends, 1995, OK Computer, 1997 (Grammy award, 1997), Kid A, 2000 (Grammy award, 2000), Amnesiac, 2001, I Might Be Wrong: Live Recordings, 2001, Hail to the Thief, 2003. Office: Capital Records 1750 North Vine St 10th Fl Hollywood CA 90028

O'BRIEN, EDWIN FREDERICK, archbishop; b. Bronx, N.Y., Apr. 8, 1939; BA, St. Joseph's Sem., Yonkers, N.Y., 1961, MDiv, 1964, MA, 1965; STD, Algelicum U., Rome, 1976. Ordained priest Roman Cath. Ch., 1965. Parish priest, chaplain U.S. Mil. Acad., West Point, NY, 1965—70; commd. 2d lt. U.S. Army, 1970, advanced through grades to capt., 1973, chaplain, 1970—73, 82nd Airborne Divsn., Ft. Bragg, NC, 1970—71, 173rd Airborne Brigade, 1st Calalry Brigade, Vietnam, 1971—72; post chaplain Ft. Gordon, Ga., 1972—73; assoc. pastor St. Patrick's Cathedral, N.Y.C., 1976—81; vice chancellor Archdiocese N.Y., 1976—81, dir. comm., 1981—83, sec. Cardinals Terence Cooke, John O'Connor, 1983—85; rector St. Joseph's Sem., Dunwoodie, NY, 1985—89, 1994—97, Pontifical N. Am. Coll., Rome, 1990—94; titular bishop Diocese of Tizica, 1996—99; auxillary bishop Diocese of N.Y., 1996—97; archbishop Archdiocese of Mil. Svcs., Washington, 1997—. Bd. dirs. Nat. Conf. Cath. Bishops, Basilica Nat. Shrine Immaculate Conception; Trustee St. Joseph's Sem., Pontifical Coll. Josephinum; chmn. bd, trustees Pontifical N. Am. Coll. Mem.: Fellowship Cath. Scholars. Roman Catholic. Office: Mil Archdiocese PO Box 4469 Washington DC 20017-0469 E-mail: archbishop@erols.com.

O'BRIEN, ELMER JOHN, librarian, educator; b. Kemmerer, Wyo., Apr. 8, 1932; s. Ernest and Emily Catherine (Reinhart) O'B.; m. Betty Alice Peterson, July 2, 1966. AB, Birmingham So. Coll., 1954; Th.M., Iliff Sch. Theology, 1957; MA, U. Denver, 1961. Ordained to ministry Methodist Ch., 1957; pastor Meth. Ch., Pagosa Springs, Colo., 1957—60; circulation-reference librarian Boston U. Sch. Theology, 1961—65; asst. librarian Garrett-Evang. Theol. Sem., Evanston, Ill., 1965—69; librarian, prof. United Theol. Sem., Dayton, Ohio, 1969—96, prof. emeritus, 1996—; abstractor Am. Bibliog. Center, 1969—73; dir. Ctr. for Evang. United Brethren Heritage, 1979—96; acting libr. Iliff Sch. Theology, 2000—01. Chmn. div. exec. com. Dayton-Miami Valley Libr. Consortium, 1983-84; rsch. assoc. Am. Antiquarian Soc., 1990. Author: Bibliography of Festschriften in Religion Published Since 1960, 1972, Religion Index Two: Festschriften, 1960-69; contbg. author: Communication and Change in American Religious History, 1993, Essays in Celebration of the First Fifty Years, 1996; pub. Meth. Revs. Index, 1818-1985, 1989-91; contbr. essay to profl. jour. Recipient theol. and scholarship award Assn. Theol. Schs. in U.S. and Can., 1990-91; Assn. Theol. Schs. in U.S. and Can. library staff devel. grantee, 1976-77, United Meth. Ch. Bd. Higher Edn. and Ministry research grantee, 1984-85 Mem. ALA, Acad. Libr. Assn. Ohio, Am. Theol. Libr. Assn. (head bur. personnel and placement 1969-73, dir. 1973-76, v.p. 1977-78, pres. 1978-79), Am. Antiquarian Soc. (rsch. assoc. 1990), Delta Sigma Phi, Omicron Delta Kappa, Eta Sigma Phi, Kappa Phi Kappa. Clubs: Torch Internat. (v.p. Dayton club 1981-82, pres. 1982-83). Home: 4840 Thunderbird Dr Apt 281 Boulder CO 80303-3829 E-mail: Ejobr@aol.com.

O'BRIEN, ERIN, auditor; b. Marlton, N.J., Sept. 25, 1976; d. Edward Patrick and Christine O'Brien. BA in Sociology and Anthropology, Coll. of N.J., 1998; MSW, Rutgers U., N.J., 2001. LSW N.J., 2002. Client support svcs. Prevention Edn. Inc., Lawrenceville, NJ, 1998—2001; social work intern Planned Parenthood, Camden, NJ, 1999—2000, Buttonwood Hosp., Pemberton, NJ, 2000—01; housing dir. Cherry Hill (N.J.) Twp., 2001—02; internal auditor N.J. Dept. Cmty. Affairs, Trenton, 2002—. Resource devel. com. Prevention Edn. Inc., Lawrenceville, NJ, 2002—; mem. Maple Shade Twp. Zoning Bd., 2004—. Recipient Vol. award, Govs. Office on Volunteerism, N.J., 2003. Mem.: Nat. Assn. Social Workers (N.J. chpt.), Alpha Delta Mu (Gammi Psi chpt.), N.J. Commn. on Nat. and Cmty. Svc., Planned Parenthood Action Network, Nat. Orgn. of Women. Democrat. Avocations: reading, writing. E-mail: eobrien76@hotmail.com.

O'BRIEN, EVA FROMM, lawyer; b. Herne, Germany, May 6, 1956; came to U.S., 1959; d. Georg and Eva (Aust) F.; m. John J. O'Brien, Feb. 12, 2000. BS in Chem. Engring., Syracuse U., 1978; JD, U. Houston, 1985. Bar: Tex. 1985, U.S. Dist. Ct. (so. dist.) Tex. 1987, U.S. Ct. Appeals (5th cir.) 1997. Engr. Chrysler Corp., Deer Park, Mich., 1978-79; process engr. Mobay Chem. Co., Baytown, Tex., 1980, ETI Engrs. Inc., Houston, 1981-82; engr. Petromas Inc., Houston, 1982-83; sr. chem. engr. NUS Corp., Houston, 1983-84; briefing clk., assoc. Hill Parker Franklin Cardwell & Jones, Houston, 1985-86; assoc. Fulbright & Jaworski LLP, Houston, 1986-93, ptnr., 1994—. Author, editor: Texas Environmental Law Handbook, 1989, 5th edit., 2000, (book chpt.) Environmental Aspects of Real Estate Transactions, 2d edit., 1999. Mem. ABA (co-chair real estate and probate sect., underground storage tank and RCRA com. 1994-95), Houston Bar Assn. (co-chair legal line com. 1988-90; sec. environ. law sect. 1991, vice-chair 1992, chair 1993). Home: 19 Serenity Woods Pl Houston TX 77383 Office: Fulbright & Jaworski LLP 1301 Mckinney St Ste 5100 Houston TX 77010-3031

O'BRIEN, GAYLE ANN, nurse; b. Warren, Ohio, July 11, 1957; d. James Allen Lipscomb and Delores Pauline (Vauple) Swindler; children: Veronica N., Steven J. BSN, Kent State U., 1980, MSN, 1985. Cert. profl. healthcare quality; clin. nurse specialist, APN. Nurse mgmt. critical care Robinson Meml. Hosp., Ravenna, Ohio, 1980—88; instr. U. Akron (Ohio), 1988-90; clin. nurse specialist in critical care, dir. quality improvement, patient safety officer Akron Gen. Med. Ctr., 1990—. Pres. Bd. of Health, City of Kent, Ohio, 2001—. Recipient award of Leadership, Sigma theta Tau, 2003. Mem.: Am. Soc. Quality, Ohio Assn. Nurse Execs., Ohio Assn. Healthcare Quality, Nat. Assn. Healthcare Quality. Office: Akron Gen Med Ctr 400 Wabash Ave Akron OH 44307-2463 E-mail: gobrien@agmc.org.

O'BRIEN, GEOFFREY PAUL, editor, writer; b. N.Y.C., May 4, 1948; s. Joseph Aloysius and Margaret Dorothy (Owens) O'B.; m. Carly Francis O'Brien, Mar. 18, 1977; 1 child, Heather. Student, Yale U., 1966—67, SUNY, Stony Brook, 1968—70. Editor Reader's Catalog, N.Y.C., 1987-91; exec. editor Libr. of Am., N.Y.C., 1992-97, editor-in-chief, 1998—. Author: Hardboiled America, 1981, Dream Time, 1988, A Book of Maps, 1989, The Phantom Empire, 1993, The Hudson Mystery, 1994, Floating City: Selected Poems, 1978-1995, 1996, The Times Square Story, 1998, Bardic Deadlines: Reviewing Poetry 1984-95, 1998, The Browser's Ecstasy, 2000, Castaways of the Image Planet, 2002, Sonata for Jukebox, 2004; contbr. poetry, essays and revs. to profl. jours.; contbg. writer The Village Voice, 1982—90; editor: Frogpond, 1980—81; co-editor: Montemora, 1974—76; author: A View of Buildings and Water, 2002. Recipient Writing award Whiting Found., 1988; fellow N.Y. Inst. Humanities, 1998—, John Simon Guggenheim Meml. Found., 1999, Rockefeller Found., 2002. Office: Libr of Am 14 E 60th St New York NY 10022-1006 E-mail: BardicG@aol.com.

O'BRIEN, GEORGE ALOYSIUS, JR., paper company executive; b. Port Arthur, Tex., Dec. 13, 1948; s. George Aloysius and Avril Colleen (Adkins) O'B.; m. Cynthia Jean McCaa, Aug. 16, 1973; children: Erin Colleen, Meghan Anne, Caitlin Jean. BS in Petroleum Engring., U. Tex., 1971, MBA, 1975. Engr. Tesoro Petroleum Corp., San Antonio, 1972-73; exec. asst. Mesa Petroleum Co., Amarillo, Tex., 1975-79; v.p., treas. Transco Energy Co., Houston, 1979-82; sr. v.p., chief fin. officer Spectrum Energy Co., Houston, 1982-83; v.p. Smith Barney Harris Upham & Co., Houston, 1984-86; 1st v.p. E.F. Hutton & Co., N.Y.C., 1986-88; v.p., dir. corp. devel. Internat. Paper Co., Purchase, N.Y., 1988-91, v.p. land and timber, sr. v.p. forest resources Savannah, Ga., 1997—2001; CFO Carter Holt Harvey Pulp, Paper & Tissue, Auckland, New Zealand, 1991-94, CEO, 1995-97; sr. v.p. forest products Internat. Paper Co., 1997—. Dir. Nat. Tree Trust, Savannah C. of C., United Way of Savannah, Arbor Gen LLC. Mem.: Savannah Harbour Golf Club. Republican. Roman Catholic. Avocations: golf, tennis, sailing. Office: Internat Paper Co PO Box 1391 Savannah GA 31402-1391 Home: 3 Marsh Harbor Dr Savannah GA 31410

O'BRIEN, GEORGE DENNIS, retired academic administrator; b. Chgo., Feb. 21, 1931; s. George Francis and Helen (Fehlandt) O'B.; m. Judith Alyce Johnson, June 21, 1958; children: Elizabeth Belle, Juliana Helen, Victoria Alyce. AB in English, Yale, 1952; PhD in Philosophy, U. Chgo., 1961. Tchr. humanities, Carnegie rsch. fellow U. Chgo., 1956-57; from instr. to asst. prof., asst. dean Princeton (N.J.) U., 1958-65; on leave in Athens, Greece, 1963-64; spl. honors seminars LaSalle Coll., spring 1963, fall 1964, spring 1965; assoc. prof. philosophy Middlebury (Vt.) Coll., 1965-71, prof., 1971-76, dean of men, 1965-67, dean of coll., 1967-74, dean faculty, 1975-76; pres. Bucknell U., 1976-84, U. Rochester, N.Y., 1984-94; ret., 1994. Dir. Salzburg Seminar in Am. Studies. Author: Hegel on Reason in History, 1975, God and the New Haven Railway, 1986, What to Expect from College, 1991, All the Essential Half-Truths About Higher Education, 1997, The Idea of a Catholic University, 2002; contbr. articles to profl. jours. Trustee LaSalle Coll., Phila., 1965—; bd. dirs. Union Theol. Sem., 1985-90, Rsch. Librs. Group, 1994-96; chair Commonweal Found., 2002—. Fellow Am. Coun. Learned Socs., London, 1971-72; Nat. Phi Beta Kappa scholar, 1996-97. Mem. Am. Philos. Assn., Phi Beta Kappa. Home: 153 Wildflower Ln Middlebury VT 05753-9172 Office Phone: 802-388-1376. Business E-Mail: gdob@middlebury.edu.

O'BRIEN, GERALD JAMES, utilities executive; b. St. Paul, May 1, 1923; s. Dewey Joseph and Henrietta Elizabeth O'B.; m. Patricia Margaret McCorison, Feb. 23, 1946; children: Kathleen, Thomas, John, Andrew. Student, St. Thomas Coll., 1940-41, 45-46; B.C.S., Drake U., 1948. Staff acct. Haskins & Sells, Mpls., 1948-50; with Donovan Cos., Inc., St. Paul, 1950-81, sec., asst. treas., 1977-81; utility rate cons., 1981-84. Dir. Alumbaugh Coal Co., Donovan Constrn. Co., So. Tier Gas Corp., Gas Distbrs. Info. Service. Served with U.S. Army, 1942-45. Decorated Purple Heart. Address: 11111 River Hills Dr Apt 235 Burnsville MN 55337

O'BRIEN, GREGORY MICHAEL ST. LAWRENCE, academic administrator; b. N.Y.C., Oct. 7, 1944; s. Henry Joseph and Mary Agnes (McGoldrick) O'B.; m. Mary K. McLaughlin, Dec. 28, 1968; children: Jennifer Jane, Meredith Kathleen. BA with honors, Lehigh U., 1966; MA, Boston U., 1968, PhD, 1969. Assoc. in psychology Lab. Community Psychology, Harvard Med. Sch., Boston; dir. Human Svcs. Design Lab., Sch. Applied Social Scis., Case Western Res. U., Cleve., 1970-74; dean, prof. Sch. Social Welfare, U. Wis., Milw., 1974-78; provost, prof. psychology U. Mich.-Flint, 1978-80; prof. social work and psychology, v.p. acad. affairs U. South Fla., Tampa, 1980-83, provost, 1983-87, prof. mgmt., 1986-87; chancellor U. New Orleans, 1987—2003; interim supr. New Orleans Paris Schs., 1999; chancellor Argosy U., Chicago, Ill., 2004—; DeBlois Endowed Chair in Private/Public Initiatives U. New Orleans, 2004—. Evaluation research cons. Cambridge Dept. Health and Hosps. and USPHS, 1968; bd. dirs. WLAE-TV (PBS), Bank One New Orleans Region, Entergy New Orleans, Nat. Coalition for Advanced Mfg., Nat. Assn. State Univs. and Land-Grant Colls. Contbr. chpts. to books, articles to profl. jours. State of La. Econ. Devel. Coun., 1997—; vice chmn. State of La. Film and Video Commn., 1993-94, mem., 1993—; chmn. Metro. Coun. Govts. MetroVision, 1992—; adv. mem. Bus. Coun. New Orleans and the River Region; bd. dirs. The Chamber/New Orleans and the River Region, 1988—; mem. Kellogg Commn. on Future of Land Grant Colls. and State Univs., 1996—. NIMH fellow, 1968-69 Fellow Am. Coll. Mental Health Adminstrs. (founding fellow, pres. 1984-86); mem. NCAA (chair pres. commn. 1992-93), Nat. Assn. Social Workers, Nat. Conf. Social Welfare, Soc. Gen. Systems Research, Am. Psychol. Assn., Am. Public Health Assn., Metrovision Partnership Found. (1992-93), Council Social Work Edn. (presdl. task force on structure of assn.), Indsl. Relations Research Assn. Roman Catholic. Home: 2468 Lark St New Orleans LA 70122-4322 Office: Argosy U 2 First National Plz 20 S Clark St 3d Fl Chicago IL 60603

O'BRIEN, HELEN MARGARET, healthcare educator, environmentalist; d. Patrick John O'Brien and Antonette Knaperek; m. Edward R. Schweser (div. 1980); adopted children: Jeffrey Richard Schweser, Gary Ronald Schweser, Laurie Darlene Schweser Svitak. Degree in nursing, Danbury, Conn.; BSN, SUNY; M Health and Environ., Goddard U., 1980. Nurse Red Cross Blood Bank, Louisville, 1943—44; US army nurse Eng. Gen. Hosp., Atlantic City, 1945; sch. nurse, tchr. Levittown (NY) Schs., 1955—70; health educator Peace Corps, Botswana, 1971—73, Project Hope, Antigua and Barbuda, 1974—76; asst. instr. Sam Houston State U., Tex., 1976—77. Cons. Kappa Sys., Arlington, Va., 1979—80, Med. Svc. Cons., Arlington, 1978, Pacific Cons., Inc., Washington, 1979, Westinghouse Corp., Columbia, Md., 1979, MetaMetrics, Inc., Washington, 1980, Concerned Women Family Planning, Washington, 1980, Nat. Coun. Internat. Health, Washington, 1980, Pragma Corp., Falls Ch., Va., 1983, World Bank, Washington, 1983—84, Office Fgn. Disaster Assistance/AID, Washington, 1985—86; project dir. women's internat. network study Concern, Inc., Washington, 1982—83; team mem. Pritech, Arlington, Va.; founder Cherish the Earth, Inc., 1992—2000. Author: A Manual for Health Education in Botswana, 1971, Manual for Community Health Education for the Caribbean, 1976; co-author: Health Education Program Teaching Modules, 1982; author: (slide course) Preventing Pesticide Poisoning in Developing, 1984. Cons. Mormon Health Missionary Corps, Salt Lake City; evaluator health programs for Native Americans Navajo Indian Reservation, Ariz. and N.Mex.; developer gardening project for srs. Raleigh, NC. Home and Office: 6620-613 Rockglen Way Raleigh NC 27615 E-mail: hobrien@bellsouth.net.

O'BRIEN, J. WILLARD, lawyer, educator; b. N.Y.C., Oct. 19, 1930; s. J. Willard and Anna C. (Carroll) O.'B.; m. Peggy J. O'Brien. BS, Fordham U., 1952, JD, 1957. Bar: N.Y. 1957. Assoc. Cahill, Gordon, Reindel & Ohl, N.Y.C., 1957-62; asst. prof. law Syracuse U. Coll. Law, 1962-65; prof. law Villanova (Pa.) U. Sch. Law, 1965-98, dean, 1972-83, dir. Connelly Inst. Law and Morality, 1983-95, dean and prof. of law emeritus, 1998—. Mem. Pa. Fed. Jud. Nominating Commn., 1977-80, vice chmn., 1978-80; mem. Pa. Law and Justice Inst., 1972-73, chmn. exec. com., 1973-75, pres., 1975-77 Editor-in-chief Fordham Law Rev, 1956-57. Bd. dirs. Nat. Inst. on Holocaust, 1984-85; bd. dirs. Phila. Coordinating Council on the Holocaust, 1983—2003. Served with USAF, 1952-54; Served with N.Y. Air N.G., 1954-58. Mem. ABA, N.Y. State Bar Assn., Pa. Bar Assn., Canon Law Soc. Am. Roman Catholic.

O'BRIEN, JACK GEORGE, artistic director; b. Saginaw, Mich., June 18, 1939; s. J. George and Evelyn (MacArthur Martens) O'B. AB, U. Mich., 1961, MA, 1962. Asst. dir. APA Repertory Theatre, N.Y.C., 1963-67, asso. dir., 1967-69; worked with San Diego Nat. Shakespeare Festival, 1969-82, A.C.T., 1970-80, Loretto Hilton, 1975, Ahmanson, Los Angeles, 1978-80, San Francisco Opera, Houston Grand Opera, Washington Opera Soc.; artistic dir. N.Y.C. Opera, 1982, Old Globe Theatre, San Diego, 1981—. Dir.: (Broadway plays) Cock-A-Doodle Dandy, 1969, The Time of Your Life, 1975, Porgy and Bess, 1976, 1983, The Most Happy Fella, 1979, Two Shakespearean Actors, 1992, Damn Yankees, 1994—95, Getting Away With Murder, 1996, The Little Foxes, 1997, More to Love, 1998, The Full Monty, 2000—02 (Tony nom. best dir. of a musical, 2001), Imaginary Friends, 2003, Hairspray, 2002 (Tony award best dir. of a musical, 2003), Henry IV, 2003—04 (Tony award best dir. of a play, 2004); art. dir. (Broadway plays) Into the Woods, 1987—89, Rumors, 1988—90, The Piano Lesson, 1990—91, Two Trains Running, 1992, Redwood Curtain, 1993, Play On!, 1997, Oldest Living Confederate Widow Tells All, 2003. Mem. Actors' Equity, Am. Soc. Composers and Performers, Soc. Stage Dirs. and Choreographers, Dirs. Guild Am. Office: Old Globe Theatre PO Box 122171 San Diego CA 92112-2171*

O'BRIEN, JAMES ALOYSIUS, foreign language educator; b. Cin., Apr. 7, 1936; s. James Aloysius and Frieda (Schirmer) O'B.; m. Rumi Matsumoto, Aug. 26,1961. BA, St. Joseph's Coll., 1958; MA, U. Cin., 1960; PhD, Ind. U., 1969. Instr. English, St. Joseph's Coll., Rensselaer, Ind., 1960-62; asst. prof. Japanese, U. Wis., Madison, 1968-74, assoc. prof., 1974-81, prof., 1981—2003, prof. emeritus, 2003—, chmn. East Asian langs and lit., 1979-80, 82-85, 1996—2000. Author: Dazai Osamu, 1975, Akutagawa and Dazai: Instances of Literary Adaptation, 1988; translator: Selected Stories and Sketches (Dazai Osamu), 1983, Three Works (Muro Saisei), 1985, Crackling Mountain and Other Stories (Dazal Osamu), 1989. Mem. MIddleton City Common Coun., 1996—. Ford Found fellow, 1965-66; Fulbright-Hays and NDEA fellow, 1966-68; Social Sci. Research Council fellow, 1973-74; Japan Found. fellow, 1977-78 Mem. Assn. Asian Studies, Assn. Tchrs. of Japanese (exec. com. 1981-84, dir. devel. 1981-83, pres. 1984-90) Home: 2533 Branch St Middleton WI 53562-2812

O'BRIEN, JAMES EDWARD, lawyer; b. Mpls., June 10, 1937; s. Thomas Edward and Virginia Ann (Balster) O'B.; m. Patricia Jo Ann Cole, Mar. 1, 1958; children: Daniel J., Martin J. BA, U. Alaska, 1962; JD, U. Minn., 1965. Bar: Minn. Assoc. Moss & Barnett, Mpls., 1965—, chmn., CEO. With USAF, 1957-62. Mem. Unilaw (chmn.), Fund for Legal Aid Soc. (bd. dirs.), Kiwanis Internat. (George Hixon fellow 1996), Kiwanis Mpls. (bd. dirs.). Avocations: fishing, boating.

O'BRIEN, JAMES J. manufacturing executive; degree in Acctg., Fin., MBA, Ohio State U. Exec. asst. to chmn. Ashland Inc., 1992—94; v.p., gen. mgr. branded mktg. Ashland Petroleum Co., 1994; v.p. Ashland Inc.; pres. Valvoline; with Ashland Inc., 1976—, sr. v.p., 1997, group oper. officer, pres., COO, 2002, chmn., CEO, 2002—. Nat. bd. dirs. Big Bros. Big Sisters Am.; adv. bd. sch. bus. Ohio State U.; chmn. bd. trustees Midway Coll. Ky. Mem.: Am. Chemistry Coun., Assn. Governing Bds. Univ. Colls. Office: 50 E River Ctr Blvd Covington KY 41012-0391

O'BRIEN, JAMES JEROME, construction management consultant; b. Phila., Oct. 20, 1929; s. Sylvester Jerome and Emma Belle Filer (Fulforth) O'B.; m. Carmen Hiester, June 10, 1952 (div. Aug. 1, 1984); children: Jessica Susan, Michael, David; m. Rita F. Gibson, Nov. 1, 1984 BCE, Cornell U., 1952; postgrad., U. Houston, 1957-58. Registered profl. engr., N.Y., N.J., Pa., Ga., Conn., Maine. Project engr. Rohm & Haas, Phila. and Tex., 1955-59, RCA Corp., Moorestown, N.J., Greenland and Alaska, 1959-62; cons. Mauchly Assocs., Fort Washington, Pa., 1962-65; founding ptnr., exec. v.p. Meridian Engrng. Co., Phila., 1965-68; pres. MDC Systems, Cherry Hill, 1968-72; ptnr. James J. O'Brien P.E., Cherry Hill, 1972-77; pres. O'Brien-Kreitzberg & Assocs., N.Y.C., Pennsauken, San Francisco, 1977-80, chief exec. officer, 1980-89, chmn. bd. dirs., 1989-93, vice chmn., 1993—2002. Author: CPM in Construction Management-Scheduling by the Critical Path Method, 1965, CPM in Construction Management-Project Management with CPM, 5th edit., 1999, Management Information Systems-Concepts, Techniques and Applications, 1970, Management with Computers, 1972, Construction Inspection Handbook, 1974, 4th edit., 1997, Value Analysis in Design and Construction, 1976, Construction Delay-Risks, Rsponsibilities and Litigation, 1976, Preconstruction Estimating: Budget to Bid, 1994, Construction Documentation, 3d edit., 1995; co-author: Construction Management: A Professional Approach, 1974; editor: Recollections (L.D. Miles), 1987; author, editor: Scheduling Handbook, 1969, Contractor's Management Handbook, 1971, 2d edit., 1990, Standard Handbook of Heavy Construction, 3d edit., 1996, Construction Change Orders, 1998; contbr. articles to profl. jours. Lt. 1952-55, USN. Recipient Profl. Mgr. award N.Y. chpt. Soc. Advancement Mgmt., 1969 Fellow ASCE (Constrn. Mgmt. award 1976, v.p. 1985, pres. South Jersey br. 1985, Disting. Engr. South Jersey br. 1986, pres. N.J. sect. 1987-89, mem. com. on quality in civil engrng. profession 1990-97), Project Mgmt. Inst. (sec. 1971, v.p. 1972, pres. 1973, chmn. bd. 1974-75, v.p. edn. 2002, charter mem. Coll. of Scheduling, award for contbn. to project mgmt. 1983, Fellow award 1989, project mgmt. profl.), Constrn. Mgmt. Assn. Am. (bd. dirs. 1990-92, Fellow award 1993, Constrn. Mgr. of Yr. award N.Y.-N.J. chpt. 1994), Cornell Soc. Engrs. (dean's adv. com. sch. civil and environ. engrng. 1986-87); mem. Soc. Am. Value Engrs. (cert. value specialist, v.p. N.E. region 1986-87, Fallon Value-in-Life award 1993), Miles Value Found. (bd. dirs. 1987-90, 99, trustee 1990-99), Port Authority NY & NJ, Regional Alliance for Small Contractors (bd. dirs. 1989-95), Tau Beta Pi, Chi Epsilon. Home: 2 Linden Ave Riverton NJ 08077-1124 Office: O'Brien Kreitzberg URS 8 Penn Ctr 21st Fl 1628 Jfk Blvd Philadelphia PA 19103-2125 E-mail: jimobriendd527@aol.com.

O'BRIEN, JAMES PHILLIP, lawyer; b. Monmouth, Ill., Jan. 6, 1949; s. John Matthew and Roberta Helen (Cavanaugh) O'B.; m. Laurene Reason, Aug. 30, 1969 (div. 1980); m. Lynn Florsheim, Sept. 5, 1987. BA, Western Ill. U., 1971; JD, U. Ill., 1974. Bar: Ill. 1974. Asst. atty. gen. State Ill., Springfield, 1974-75; jud. clerk Ill. Appellate Ct., Springfield, 1975-76; assoc. Graham & Graham, Springfield, 1976-81; corp. counsel Am. Hosp. Assn., Chgo., 1981-84; ptnr., chmn. health care dept. Katten, Muchin Zavis Rosenman, Chgo., 1984—. Task force med. malpractice reform legislation Am. Hosp. Assn., 1983-84, tax adv. com., 1987-91, tax reporting and compliance com., 1990-91; spkr. in field. Contbr. numerous articles to profl. jours. Recipient cert. recognition Ill. Dept. Children and Family Svcs., 1981; Edward Arthur Mellinger Found. scholar, Western Ill. U. 1971. Mem.: Am. Arbitration Assn. (Task Force Health Care Dispute Resolution 1982—84), Am. Health Lawyers Assn. Office: Katten Muchin Zavis Rosenman 525 W Monroe St Ste 1600 Chicago IL 60661-3693 Office Phone: 312-902-5630.

O'BRIEN, JANE MARGARET, academic administrator; b. Washington, Nov. 17, 1953; d. Thomas and Edith (Pedersen) O'B; m. James A. Grube, June 28, 1975; children: William Howard Grube-O'Brien, Harold Thomas Grube O'Brien. BS in Biochemistry, Vassar Coll., 1975; PhD in Chemistry, U. Del., 1981. Rsch. asst. U. Vt., Burlington, 1978-79; asst. prof. chemistry Middlebury (Vt.) Coll., 1980-88, assoc. provost, 1988-89, assoc. prof. chemistry, 1988-91, dean of faculty, 1989-91; pres. Hollins Coll., Roanoke, Va., 1991—. Ednl. chmn. biology task force New Eng. Consortium Undergraduate Sci., 1988-91; project mgr. H. Hughes Med. Inst. Instl. Awards, 1988-91; mem. steering com. Sloan New Liberal Arts Initiative, 1988-91. Implementation com. Vermont EPSCoR, 1989-91; bd. dirs. Coun. Ind. Colls. in Va., 1991—, Va. Found. for Ind. Colls., 1991—; ednl. adv. com. Rainforest All, 1991—. Grad. fellow U. Del., 1975-76, Kellogg fellow W.K. Kellogg Found., 1989-92, Internat. fellow Assoc. Am. Colls., 1990-91, Regional fellow finalist White House Fellowship, 1991. Home: General Delivery Annapolis MD 21405-9999 Office: Hollins Coll Office of the President Hollins College VA 24020

O'BRIEN, JIM, professional basketball coach; m. Sharon O'Brien; children: Jack, Shannon, Caitlyn. B in Mgmt., Mktg., St. Joseph, 1974; MBA, U. Md., 1981. Asst. coach N.Y. Knicks, 1987—88, U. Ky., 1994—97; head coach Wheeling Jesuit Coll., 1982—87, U. Dayton, 1989—94, Boston Celtics, 2001—04, Philadelphia 76ers, 2004—. Asst. coach 6 different colls. Named to St. Joseph's Hall of Fame, 1988, Big Five Hall of Fame, 1989. Office: c/o Philadelphia 76ers Wachovia Center 3601 S Broad St Philadelphia PA 19148*

O'BRIEN, JOAN SUSAN, lawyer, educator; b. New York, Apr. 14, 1946; d. Edward Vincent O'Brien and Joan Therese (Kramer) Quinn; m. Michael P. Wilpan, May 27, 1979; children: Edward B. Wilpan, Anabel T. Wilpan. BA, NYU, 1967; JD, Georgetown U., 1970. Bar: N.Y. 1971, Mass. 1971, U.S. Dist. Ct. (so and ea. dist.) N.Y. 1972, U.S. Ct. Appeals (2d cir.) 1971. Law clk. to Hon. Frank J. Murray U.S. Dist. Ct. Mass., Boston, 1970-71; asst. U.S. atty. Office of U.S. Atty. U.S. Dist. Ct. (ea. dist.) N.Y., Bklyn., 1972-76; pvt. practice N.Y.C., 1976-79; trial atty. Mendes & Mount, N.Y.C., 1979-84; asst. prof. St. Johns U., Jamaica, N.Y., 1984-90; adminstrv. law judge N.Y. State Workers Compensation Bd., Hempstead, N.Y., 1990-93; appellate atty. Scheine, Fusco, Brandenstein & Rada, Woodbury, N.Y., 1993-97; trial atty. Grey & Grey, L.L.P., Farmingdale, N.Y., 1997—. Editor: Georgetown Law Jour., 1968-70. Pres. Nassau County Dem. Com. Women's Caucus, Westbury, N.Y., 1988-90; leader Girl Scouts Nassau County, 1990-93. Unitarian-Universalist. Office: Grey & Grey LLP 360 Main St Farmingdale NY 11735-3592 Office Phone: 516-249-1342.

O'BRIEN, JOHN CONWAY, economist, educator, writer; b. Hamilton, Lanarkshire, Scotland; s. Patrick and Mary (Hunt) O'B.; m. Jane Estelle Judd, Sept. 16, 1966; children: Kellie Marie, Kerry Patrick, Tracy Anne, Kristen Noël. B.Com., U. London, 1952, cert. in German lang., 1954; tchr.'s cert., Scottish Edn. Dept., 1954; AM, U. Notre Dame, 1959, PhD, 1961. Tchr. Scottish High Schs., Lanarkshire, 1952-56; instr. U. B.C., Can., 1961-62; asst. prof. U. Sask., Can., 1962-63, U. Dayton, Ohio, 1963-64; assoc. prof. Wilfrid Laurier U., Ont., Can., 1964-65; from asst. to full prof. Econs. and Ethics Calif. State U., Fresno, 1965—. Vis. prof. U. Pitts., 1969-70, U. Hawaii, Manoa, 1984, U. Queensland, Brisbane, Australia, 1994; keynote speaker Wageningen Agrl. U., The Netherlands, 1987; presenter papers 5th, 6th, 10th World Congress of Economists, Tokyo, 1977, Mexico City, 1980, Moscow, 1992; presenter Schmoller Symposium, Heilbronn am Neckar, Fed. Republic Germany, 1988, paper The China Confucius Found. and "2540" Conf., Beijing, 1989, 6th Internat. Conf. on Cultural Econs., Univ. Umeä, Sweden, 1990, Internat. Soc. Intercommunication New Ideas, Sorbonne, Paris, 1990, European Assn. for Evolutionary Polit. Economy, Vienna, Austria, 1991; active rsch. U. Göttingen, Fed. Republic Germany, 1987; acad. cons. Cath. Inst. Social Ethics, Oxford; presenter in field. Author: Karl Marx: The Social Theorist, 1981, The Economist in Search of Values, 1982, Beyond Marxism, 1985, The Social Economist Hankers After Values, 1992; editor: Internat. Rev. Econs. and Ethics, Internat. Jour. Social Econs., Ethical Values and Social Econs., 1981, Selected Topics in Social Econs., 1982, Festschrift in honor of George Rohrlich, 3 vols., 1984, Social Economics: A Pot=Pourri, 1985, The Social Economist on Nuclear Arms: Crime and Prisons, Health Care, 1986, Festschrift in honor of Anghel N. Rugina, Parts I and II, 1987, Gustav von Schmoller: Social Economist, 1989, The Eternal Path to Communism, 1990, (with Z. Wenxian) Essays from the People's Republic of China, 1991, Festschrift in Honor of John E. Elliott, Parts I and II, 1992, Communism Now and Then, 1993, The Evils of Soviet Communism, 1994, Ruminations on the USSR, 1994, The Future Without Marx, 1995, Essays in Honour of Clement Allan Tisdell, 1996, Essays in Honor of Clement Allan Tisdell, Part I, 1996, Part II and III, 1997, Part IV and V, 1998, Part VI, 1999, Part VII and VIII, 2000, Social Economists at Work, 1999, Our Fragile Civilization, 2001; translator econ. articles from French and German into English; contbr. numerous articles to profl. jours. With British Royal Army Service Corps, 1939-46, ETO, NATOUSA, prisoner of war, Germany. Recipient GE Corp. award Stanford U., 1966, Ludwig Mai Svc. award Assn. for Social Econs., Washington, 1994; named Disting. Fellow of Internat. Soc. for Intercomm. of New Ideas, Paris, 1990. Fellow Internat. Inst. Social Econs. (mem. coun., program dir. 3d World Cong. Social Econs. Fresno Calif. 1983, keynote spkr. 4th conf. Toronto 1986), Internat. Soc. for Intercomm. New Ideas (disting.); mem. Assn. Social Econs. (dir. west region 1977—, pres.-elect 1988-89, program dir. conf. 1989, pres. 1990, presdl. address Washington 1990, Thomas Divine award 1997), Western Econ. Assn. (organizer, presenter 1977-95), History Econs. Soc., Soc. Reduction Human Labor (exec. com.), European Assn. Evolutionary Polit. Econs., Ga. Acad. Econ. Scis. (Republic of Ga. fgn. mem.). Roman Catholic. Avocations: jogging, collecting miniature paintings, soccer, tennis, photography. Home: 9000 E San Victor Rd 112 Scottsdale AZ 85258 Office Phone: 559-661-2121. Personal E-mail: johnconwayobrien@aol.com.

O'BRIEN, JOHN F. former insurance company executive; Grad., Harvard Coll., 1965; MBA, Harvard Business Sch., 1968. With Fidelity Mng. & Rsch. Co., 1968—89; pres., CEO First Allmerica Fin. Life Ins. Co., Worcester, Mass., 1989—95; also bd. dirs. State Mut. Life Assurance Co. Am., Worcester, Mass.; chmn., CEO Allmerica Property & Casualty Co., Inc., Worcester, Mass., 1992—95; also bd. dirs. Citizens Corp., pres., CEO, 1992—95, Allmerica Fin. Corp., Worcester, Mass., 1995—2002; chmn. The Hanover Ins. Co., Worcester. Dir., CEO Allmerica Property & Casualty Cos., Inc., First Allmerica Life Ins. Co.; pres., CEO, chmn. bd. Citizens Corp; pres., chmn. bd. Allmerica Fin. Life Ins. and Annuity Co.; chmn. bd. Hanover Ins. Co., Citizens Ins. Co. Am.; bd. dirs. Am. Coun. Life Ins., Cabot Corp.; trustee Worcester Poly. Inst.; vis. com. bd. overseers Harvard Coll., 1990—, com. on univ. resources, 1990—, com. on mng. acad. resources, 1990—. Mem. Am. Coun. Life Ins. (bd. dirs. 1992—), Life Ins. Assn. Mass. (bd. dirs. 1989—), Harvard Alumni Assn. (exec. com. 1991—, past pres.).

O'BRIEN, JOHN MATTHEW, psychologist, educator; b. Waltham, Mass., June 27, 1965; s. Paul Joseph and Carol Ann O'Brien. BA in Psychology, Boston Coll., 1987; MA in Counseling Psychology, Tufts U., 1989; PhD in Counseling Psychology, Mich. State U., 1996. Lic. psychologist Maine. Guidance counselor Wayland (Mass.) H.S., Mass., 1989—91; psychology intern Dallas VA Med. Ctr., 1995—96; outpatient therapist Spring Harbor Counseling, Portland, Maine, 1996—2000; lic. psychologist Mental Health Assocs. Maine, Portland, 1998—. Ad hoc reviewer Archives Family Medicine; v.p. West Suburban Guidance Assn., Wayland, 1990—91; adj. faculty U. Maine, Augusta, 1998—. Contbr. articles to profl. jours. Vol. pre/post HIV test counselor The AIDS Project, Portland, 1997—98; bd. mem. AIDS Lodging Ho., Portland, 1997—99. Mem.: APA (chair sect. on lesbian, gay and bisexual awareness divsn. counseling p 2000—03, divsn. ind. practice, divsn. soc. for the psychol. study of gay men and lesbians), Phi Kappa Phi. Democrat. Avocations: running, motorcycling, german, weightlifting. Office: Mental Health Assocs Maine Ste 700 465 Congress St Portland ME 04101 Office Phone: 207-773-2828 1310. Personal E-mail: obrien@mhame.com.

O'BRIEN, J(OHN) PATRICK, psychiatrist, educator; b. Washington, Aug. 25, 1941; s. John Francis and Gertrude Estelle (Offutt) O'B. BA magna cum laude, Yale U., 1963; MD, Johns Hopkins U., 1968. Diplomate Am. Bd. Psychiatry and Neurology. Intern U. Pa.-Phila. Gen. Hosp., 1970-71; resident Mass. Gen. Hosp., Boston, 1971-74, asst. in psychiatry, 1974-83, asst. psychiatrist, 1983—; clin. fellow psychiatry Harvard U., Boston, 1971-74, clin. instr. psychiatry, 1974-79, asst. clin. prof. psychiatry, 1979—. Lectr. Harvard Ext. Sch., Boston, 1985-88. Author: The Disorganized Mind, 1978, poems; translator: (jour.) Formations, 1987. Fellow Royal Soc. Medicine; Am. Psychiat. Assn., NY Acad. Scis., Mass. Psychiat. Assn., Yale Club Mass., Phi Beta Kappa. Democrat. Office: Mass Gen Hosp ACC 806C 15 Parkman St Boston MA 02114-3117

O'BRIEN, JOHN STEININGER, clinical psychologist; b. Lewisburg, Pa., June 3, 1936; s. Peck Zanders and Esther (Steininger) O'B.; children: Peck David, Timothy. AB, Pa. State U., 1967; MA, So. Ill. U., 1969; PhD, Boston U., 1980. Diplomate Internat. Acad. Profl. Psychotherapists, Internat. Acad. Behavioral Medicine/Psychotherapy. Asst. tchr. educable retarded children Selin's Grove (Pa.) State Sch., 1964-66; clin. rsch. asst. Pa. State U., State Coll., 1966-67; rsch. technician Anna (Ill.) State Hosp., 1968; intern Boston City Hosp., 1968-69, from coord. alcohol study unit to psychologist, 1969-73; clin. instr. psychiatry Sch. Medicine Tufts U., St. Elizabeth's Hosp., Brighton, Mass., 1973-81; dir. psychol. svcs. Baldpate Hosp., Georgetown, Mass., 1981-94, dir. outpatient substance abuse rehab. program, 1991-94; clin. psychologist Brockton (Mass.) Hosp., 1994—. Bio-behavioral cons. Behavioral Medicine Inst., Quincy, Mass., 1985-88; clin. dir. Social Learning Ctr., Quincy, 1971—; behavioral therapist, clin. coord. TAP Boston Childrens Svc., 1973-76; lectr. in psychology Curry Coll., Milton, Mass., 1994—. Author: Moments with Peck, 1982, Peck's Boat; A Duffy & Duffy, 1991; contbr. 45 articles to profl. jours. Mem. APA, Nat. Register Health Svcs. in Psychology, Soc. Study of Addiction, Assn. Advancement Behavioral Therapy, Am. Assn. Clin. Counselors, Biofeedback Soc. Am., Internat. Acad. Profl. Counselors and Psychotherapists. Avocations: ocean cruising, deep sea fishing, photography, gardening. Home and Office: 30 Oak St Ext Apt 110 Brockton MA 02301-1161 Office Phone: 508-584-6335.

O'BRIEN, JOHN WILFRID, economist, emeritus university president, educator; b. Toronto, Ont., Can., Aug. 4, 1931; s. Wilfred Edmond and Audrey (Swain) O'B.; m. Joyce Helen Bennett, Aug. 4, 1956; children: Margaret Anne, Catherine Audrey. BA, McGill U., 1953, MA, 1955, PhD, 1962, LLD, 1976; postgrad., Inst. Polit. Studies, Paris, 1954; DCL, Bishop's U., 1976; LLD, Concordia U., 2004. Lectr. econs. Sir George Williams U., Montreal, 1954-57, asst. prof., 1957-61, assoc. prof., 1961-63, asst. dean U., 1961-63, dean arts, 1963-68, vice-prin. acad., 1968-69, prof., 1965-96, prin., vice chancellor, pres., 1969-74; rector, vice chancellor, pres. Concordia U., Montreal, 1974-84, rector emeritus, 1984—. Provincial ednl. TV com. Dept. Edn. Que., 1962-66, dep. chmn., 1965-66, mem. tchr. tng. planning com., 1964-66; mem. Gauthier Ad Hoc Com., Univ. Operating Budgets, 1965-68, Council Univs., 1969-76; pres. Conf. Rectors and Prins. Que. Univs., 1974-77; mem. council Assn. Commonwealth Univs., 1975-78; bd. dirs. Assn. Univs. and Colls., Can., 1977-79; mem. Conseil Consultatif sur l'Immigration, Que. Gov., 1977-79, Corp. Higher Edn. Forum, 1983-84; bd. govs. YMCA, 1969-89, Vanier Coll., 1975-79, Fraser-Hickson Inst., 1975-2000, pres. 1989-92, Que. div. Can. Mental Health Assn., 1977-79, Montreal World Film Festival, 1985—; sec., treas., Cinematheque Can., 1988-96, bd. dirs.; sec., treas. World Film Fest. Found., 1989-96; exec. mem. Alliance Que., 1989-96, chmn., 1990-96, bd. dirs.; hon. mem. Corp. Higher Edn. Forum, 1984-2000; hon. v.p. Que. Provincial council Boy Scouts Can., 1974-90; hon. councillor Montreal Mus. Fine Arts, 1969—. Author: Canadian Money and Banking, 1964, (with G. Lermer) 2d edit., 1969.

O'BRIEN, JOHN WILLIAM, JR., investment management consultant, finance educator; b. Bronx, NY, Jan. 1, 1937; BS, MIT, 1958; MS, UCLA, 1964. Sr. assoc. Planning Rsch. Corp., LA, 1962—67; dir. fin. systems group Synergetic Scis., Inc., Tarzana, Calif., 1967—70; dir. analytical svcs. divsn. James H. Oliphant & Co., LA, 1970—72; chmn. bd., CEO, pres. Wilshire Assocs. (formerly O'Brien Assocs. Inc.), Santa Monica, Calif., 1972—75; v.p. A.G. Becker Inc., 1975—81; chmn., CEO Leland O'Brien Rubinstein Assocs., 1981—97; mng. dir. Credit Suisse Asset Mgmt., NYC, 1997—2000; adj. prof. fin. U. Calif. Berkeley Haas Sch. Bus., 2000—. Recipient Graham and Dodd award Fin. Analysts Fedn., 1970, Matthew McArthur award Investment Mgmt. Consultants Assn., 2004; named Businessman of Yr. Fortune Mag., 1987. Mem.: Delta Upsilon. Home: 119 Jasmine Creek Dr Corona Del Mar CA 92625-1418 Office Phone: 510-643-1396. E-mail: obrien@jwobrien.com.

O'BRIEN, KATHLEEN ANN, academic administrator; b. Springfield, Mass., June 25, 1944; D. William Edward and Helen Maude (Smith) O'B. BA, Alverno Coll., Milw., 1967; MBA, Vanderbilt U., Nashville, 1976; PhD, U. Wis., 1988. Tchr. St. Patrick Grade Sch., Fremont, Nebr., 1967-68, St. Agatha Grade Sch., Howard, S.D., 1968-69, Pope John XXIII High Sch., Elgin, Nebr., 1969-71, Ryan High Sch., Omaha, 1971-73; adminstr. Sch. Sisters of St. Francis Province, Omaha, 1972-74; prof. mgmt. Alverno Coll., Milw., 1976—, dean sch. bus., 1988-91, acad. dean, 1991—, interim pres., 2003—04. Mem. Sch. Sisters of St. Francis, Milw., 1962—; edn. cons., 1989-90; cons. Project on Future of Higher Edn., 2001—. Bd. dirs. Girl Scouts of Greater Milw., 2002—. Recipient Faculty award for disting. achievement Vanderbilt U., Nashville, 1976. Mem. Acad. Mgmt., Am. Assn. for Higher Edn., Rotary Club of Milw. Roman Catholic. Home: 3250 S 43rd St Milwaukee WI 53219-4803 Office: Alverno Coll PO Box 343922 Milwaukee WI 53234-3922 Office Phone: 414-382-6084. E-mail: kathleen.obrien@alverno.edu.

O'BRIEN, KEVIN, musician, radio producer; b. Newark, Sept. 16, 1968; s. Merle and Shirley O'Brien; m. Stacy Brier, May 7, 2002; 1 child, Harley Maxim Brier-O'Brien 1 stepchild, Sophia Grace Brier-Heimbach. AA, Union County Coll., 1989; MusB, Montclair State U., 1997, MusM, 2002. Music tchr., adminstr. Montclair State U., Upper Montclair, NJ, 1995—99; musician, drummer Sony/Island/RCA Records, 1998—2003; board operator, prodr., co-host KGEO AM 1230, Bakersfield, Calif., 2003—. Pvt. drum tchr., Bakersfield, 1987—; ind. composer radio jingles, session musician, 2003—; performer Carnegie Hall, Montreux Jazz Festival, MTV, VH1. Songwriter, prodr.: album NASH, 2003 (Album of Yr., 03), drummer: Scream 3 soundtrack, 1999 (Gold Album, 99). Scholar, Union County Coll., 1987; Found. scholar, Montclair State U., 2002. Avocations: exercise, movies, reading. E-mail: prestonnash@yahoo.com.

O'BRIEN, KEVIN D. medical educator; BS summa cum laude, U. Idaho, 1980; MD honors, U. Wash., 1984. Diplomate Am. Bd. Internal Medicine, Cardiovascular Diseases Am. Bd. Internal Medicine. Intern, resident U. Wash., Seattle, 1984—87, chief med. resident, 1987—88, assoc. prof. medicine, 1988—. Med. student rsch. fellow Fred Hutchinson Cancer rsch. Ctr., Seattle, 1981; attending physician U. Wash. Med. Ctr., Seattle, 1988—. Contbr. articles to profl. jours. Mem.: Am. Fedn. Med. Rsch. (pres. 2001—02, found. pres. 2002—03). Office: Univ Wash Med Ctr Campus Box 356422 1959 NE Pacific St Seattle WA 98195-6422 Office Phone: 206-543-7249.

O'BRIEN, KEVIN JAMES, investment banking executive; b. Tucson, July 19, 1956; s. Murray Andre and Sigrid (Kostoff) O'B. BSBA in Fin., No. Ariz. U., 1983. V.p. spl. situations Drexel Burnham Lambert, Inc., L.A., 1983-91; spl. projects mgr. Gtr. Flagstaff (Ariz.) Econ. Coun., Inc., 1992-95; pres. Sovereign Capital, Inc., Flagstaff, 1995—. Advisor World Bank, Washington, 1995—. Contbr. articles to profl. jours. Bd. dirs. No. Ariz. Econ. Devel. Dist., Flagstaff, 1992-95, No. Ariz. U. Students in Free Enterprise, Flagstaff, 1998. Mem. Nat. Tax Lien Assn. (charter). Avocations: flying, skiing, writing, travel, hiking. Office: # 309-109 8987 E Tanque Verde Rd Tucson AZ 85749-9610

O'BRIEN, MARK J. real estate/residential construction executive; With Pulte Constrn., Bloomfield Hills, Mich., 1982—, pres. Pulte Homes West Fla. divsn., pres. Pulte Fla. region, pres. Pulte Home, COO, 1997—2002, CEO, 2002—. Office: Pulte Corp Ste 200 33 Bloomfield Hills Pkwy Bloomfield Hills MI 48304

O'BRIEN, MARK STEPHEN, pediatric neurosurgeon; b. West New York, NJ, Jan. 2, 1933; s. Mark Peter and Hannah (Dempsey) O'B.; m. Mary Morris Johnson, June 3, 1961 (div.); children: David, Derek, Marcia; m. Karen-Marie Sampson, June 1, 1984; children: Blythe, Blake, Lauren-Blair, Connor. AB cum laude, Seton Hall U., 1955; MD, St. Louis U., 1959. Diplomate Am. Bd. Neurol. Surgery, Am. Bd. Pediat. Neurol. Surgery. Intern St. John's Hosp., St. Louis, 1959-60, resident in surgery, 1960; resident in neurology Charity Hosp.,

New Orleans, 1962-63; resident in neurosurgery St. Vincent's Hosp., N.Y.C., 1963-64, resident in surgery, 1965; sr. resident, chief resident Cin. Children's Hosp., U. Cin., 1965-68, research fellow in neurosurgery, 1966-67, 67-68; NIH spl. fellow in neuroradiology Albert Einstein Coll. Medicine, N.Y.C., 1968-69; mem. faculty dept. surgery Emory U. Sch. Medicine, Atlanta, 1969—, prof. surgery, assoc. prof. pediatrics, 1979—; chief neurosurgery Henrietta Egleston Hosp. for Children, Atlanta, 1971—. Trustee Elaine Clark Center for Exceptional Children; mem. med. adv. bd. Nat. Found., March of Dimes; trustee Henrietta Egleston Hosp. for Children; mem. profl. adv. panel Spina Bifida Assn. Am. Editorial bd. Pediatric Neurosurgery; contbr. chpts. to books, articles to med. jours. Served with USNR, 1960-62. Mem. Am. Assn. Neurol. Surgeons, Soc. Neurol. Surgeons, Congress Neurol. Surgeons, Internat. Soc. Pediatric Neurosurgery, Greater Atlanta Pediatric Soc., Med. Soc. Atlanta, AMA, ACS, Ga. Neurosurg. Soc., Am. Acad. Pediatrics, Am. Soc. Pediatric Neurosurgery, Pediatric Oncology Group, Am. Bd. Pediatric Neurol. Surgery (sec.), Acad. Pediatric Neurosurgeons. Home: 889 W Wesley Rd NW Atlanta GA 30327-1306 Office: 1900 Century Blvd NE Ste 4 Atlanta GA 30345-3307 Personal E-mail: mobrien33@aol.com.

O'BRIEN, MARY DEVON, communications executive, consultant; b. Buenos Aires, Feb. 13, 1944; came to U.S., 1949, naturalized, 1962; d. George Earle and Margaret Frances (Richards) Owen; m. Gordon Covert O'Brien, Feb. 16, 1962 (div. Aug. 1982); children: Christopher Covert, Devon Elizabeth; m. Christopher Gerard Smith, May 28, 1983 BA, Rutgers U., 1975, MBA, 1976. Project mgmt. cert., 1989. Contr. manpower Def. Comm. divsn. ITT, Nutley, N.J., 1977-80, adminstr. program, 1977-78, mgr. cost, schedule control, 1978-79, voice processing project, 1979-80, mgr. project Avionics divsn. ITT, Nutley, 1980 81, sr. mgr. projects, 1981-93, cons. strategic planning, 1983-95; pres. Anamex, Inc., 1995—. Bd. trustees South Mountain Counseling Ctr., 1987-98, chmn. bd. trustees, 1994—; bd. dirs. N.J. Eye Inst.; session leader Internet Conf., Florence, Italy, 1992; session moderator, panel mem. MES Conf., Cairo, Egypt, 1993, spkr., session leader Vancouver, 1994, keynote spkr. New Zealand, 1995; lectr. in field Author: Pace: System Manual, 1979, Voices, 1982; contbr. articles to profl. jours. and Maplewood Community calendar. Chmn. Citizens Budget Adv. Com., Maplewood, N.J., 1984-87, chmn. recreation, libr., pub. svcs., 1982-83, 94-96, chmn. pub. safety, emergency svcs., 1983-84, chmn. schs. and edn., 1984-85, chmn. gen. gov. and fin., 1998-2000; first v.p. Maplewood Civic Assn., 1987-89, pres., 1989-91, 2000—, sec. 1993-94, bd. dirs., officer, 1984—; chmn. Maple Leaf Svc. award Com., 1987-89, 94—, Community Svc. Coun. of Oranges and Maplewood Homelessness, Affordable Housing, Shelter Com., 1988—; chmn. speaker's bur. United Way, 1989-93; bd. trustees United Way Essex and West Hudson Cmty. Svc. Coun., 1988—; v.p. mktg. United Way Community Svc. Coun. of Oranges and Maplewood, 1990-93, v.p. 1994; mem. Maplewood Zoning Bd. of Adjustment, 1983-95; officer, mem. exec. bd. N.J. Project Mgmt. Inst., 1985—, pres., 1987-88, 95-2000, v.p. adminstrn., 1994-95; bd. dirs. Performance Mgmt. Assn.; chmn. Charter Com.; chmn. Internat. Project Mgmt. Inst. Jour. and Membership survey, 1986-87, mktg. com., 1986-89, long range planning and steering com., 1987—; bd. dirs., vice chmn. Coun. Chpt. Pres. Interaction Com., 1986-90, chmn., 1991—, pres. Internat. Project Mgmt. Inst., 1991, chmn., 1992, v.p. Region II, 1989-90; adv. bd. Project Mgmt. Jour., 1987-90, N.J. PMI Ednl., 1987—; liaison officer, PMI internat. liaison to Australian Inst. of Project Mgmt. and Western Australia Project Mgmt. Assn.; apptd. fellow Leadership N.J., 1993—, Internat. Project Mgmt. Inst. and Performance Mgmt. Assocs.; mem. MCA/N.J. Blood Bank Drive; chmn. Maplewood Community Calendar, 1990-98; trustee community svc. coun. and edn. program United Way Essex and West Hudson, 1988—, also, chmn. leadership div., chmn. speakers bur., 1991— and mem. communications com.; pres. N.J. Project Mgmt. Inst., 1995—; chmn. Maplewood Rep. County Com., 1996—; chair, sec. Essex County Rep. County Com. Recipient Spl. commendation for Community Svc. Twp. Maplewood, 1987; First Place award Anti-Shoplifting Program for Distributive Edn. Club Am., 1981, N.J. Fedn. of Women's Clubs, 1981, 82, Retail Mchts. Assn., 1981, 82; Commendation and Merit awards Air Force Inst. Tech., 1981; Pres.'s Safety award ITT, 1983; State award 1st Pl. N.J. Fedn. of Women's Clubs Garden Show, 1982, Outstanding Pres. award Internat. Project Mgmt. Inst., 1988, Outstanding Svc. and Contbrn. award 1986-87; Cert. Spl. Merit award N.J. Fedn. of Women's Clubs, 1982, Disting. Contbn. award United Way, 1990, Pursuit of Exellence Cost Savings Achievement award ITT Avionics, 1990, Meritorious Svc. Recognition award Internat. Project Mgmt. Inst., 1989-90, Maple Leaf award for outstanding community svc., 1992, Phoebe and Benjamin Shackelford award United Way, 1992, U.S. Ho. Reps. citation, 1992, N.H. Gen. Assembly Senate resolution for Community Leadership and Svc., 1992, resolution of Appreciation Township of Maplewood; N.J. Leadership fellow, 1993, awarded fellow of Internat. Project Mgmt. Inst., 1995. Mem. Internat. Platform Speakers Assn., Grand Jury Assn., Telecommunications Group and Aerospace Industries Assn., Women's Career Network Assn., Nat. Security Indsl. Assn., Assn. for Info. and Image Mgmt., Internat. Project Mgmt. Inst. (liaison officer pres. 1991—), Performance Mgmt. Assn, Indsl. Rels. Rsch. Assn., ITT Mgmt. Assn., NAFE, Rutger's Grad. Sch. Bus. Mgmt. Alumni Assn., Maplewood LWV (chair women and family issues com., voter registration bd. dirs.), Maplewood Women's Evening Membership Div. (pres. 1980-82), Lions (Maplewood dir. 1992-95, program chmn. 1991-92, treas. 1994-95, N.J. dist. 16E zone gov., chmn. 1992-93, 95-96, cabinet sec. internat. dist., region chmn. 1993-94, 96—, trustee Eye Bank N.J., internat. dist. 16-E cabinet sec. 1994-95, dist. 16-E chmn. peace poster contest 1995-99, pres. Newark 1995-97, sec. 1997—, N.J. State chmn. youth outreach and quest 1995-98, internat. dist. 16-E gov., 1999—, dist. MD16 treas., 1999—). Home: 594 Valley St Maplewood NJ 07040-2616 Office: 21 Madison Plz Ste 152 Madison NJ 07940-2354

O'BRIEN, MORGAN EDWARD, communications executive, lawyer; b. Washington, Dec. 14, 1944; AB Classical with honors, Georgetown U., 1966; JD, Northwestern U., 1969. Bar: Ill. 1969, Washington 1971. Lawyer Mobile Svcs. divsn. Common Carrier Bur. FCC, Washington, 1970-72; asst. bur. chief Spectrum Mgmt. Pvt. Radio Bur. FCC, Washington, 1976-87; co-founder, chmn. bd. Nextel Comm., Inc., Reston, Va., 1987-96, vice chmn., 1996—. Ptnr. Jones, Day, Reavis & Pogue, Washington, 1986-90; pvt. practice, Washington, 1979-90. Office: 1101 30th St NW Ste 320 Washington DC 20007

O'BRIEN, NANCY LYNN, bank executive; b. Norfolk, Nebr., Sept. 6, 1951; d. Robert Sammie and Betty Ann (Petersen) Auten; m. Leo E. O'Brien, Aug. 3, 1984. BSE, U. Nebr.-Lincoln, 1972, U. Nebr.-Omaha, 1975; PhD, U. Nebr.-Lincoln, 1979. Tchr. spl. edn. Omaha Pub. Schs., 1973—79; devel. studies specialist Metro Tech. Community Coll., Omaha, 1979—80; mgr. tng. Omaha Nat. Bank, 1981—84, mgr. employment and tng, 1984—. Area rep/travel cons. Am. Leadership Study Groups, Worcester, Mass., 1977—; grant mgr. Coun. Exceptional Children, 1978; adj. faculty Coll. St. Mary's, Omaha, 1983—. Active United Way, Omaha; pres. Child Abuse Coun., Omaha, 1982—83, Coun. for Exceptional Children, 1981. Grantee, Coun. for Exceptional Children, 1978. Mem.: ASTD (dir.). Democrat. Lutheran. Home: 22627 Wilson Ave Waterloo NE 68069-9797

O'BRIEN, NANCY PATRICIA, librarian, educator; b. Galesburg, Ill., Mar. 17, 1955; d. Leo Frederick O'Brien and Yvonne Blanche (Uhlmann) O'Brien Tabb; 1 child, Nicole Pamela. AB in English, U. Ill., 1976, MS in LS, 1977. Vis. instr. U. Ill., Urbana, 1977-78, asst. prof. libr. adminstrn., 1978-84, assoc. prof., 1984-91, prof., 1991—, serials bibliographer, 1977-78, social sci. bibliographer collection devel. div., 1979-81, project dir. Title II-C grant, 1987-88, acting libr. and info. sci. libr., 1989-90, head Edn. and Social Sci. Libr., 1994—, coord. social scis. divsn., 1996—2003, edn. subject specialist, 1981—. Discussion leader Ill. White House Conf. on Libr. and Info. svcs., 1990; mem. nat. adv. bd. Office Ednl. Rsch. and Improvement, U.S. Dept. Edn., 1989-91; grant proposal reviewer NEH, 1991; mem. adv. bd. Ctr. for Children's Books, 1992-97; cons. Ark. Coll., 1989; chmn. rev. team Instrnl. Materials Ctr., U. Wis., Madison, 1989; chair exec. com. Nat. Edn. Network Nat. Libr. Edn. U.S. Dept. Edn., 1998—2002; presenter in field. Author: Test Construction: A Bibliography of Resources, 1988, (with Emily Fabiano) Core List of Books and Journals in Education, 1991; Education: A Guide to Reference and Information Sources, 2d edit., 2000, (with John Collins III) Greenwood Dictionary of Edn., 2003; co-editor Media/Microforms column Serials Rev., 1979-82; mem. editl. bd. Bull. Bibliography, 1982-90; asst. editor Libr. Hi Tech., 1983-85; editor EBSS Newsletter, 1990-91; contbr. articles to profl. jours., chpts. to books. Mem. ALA (Whitney-Carnegie grantee 1990-91), Am. Ednl. Rsch. Assn. (spl. interest group on libr. resources and info. tech.), Assn. Coll. and Rsch. Librs. (access policy guidelines task force 1990-95, vice chmn., chmn.-elect edn. and behavioral scis. sect. 1993-94, chmn. 1994-95, acad. status com. 1996—2000, Disting. Edn. and Behavioral Scis. Libr. 1997), Libr. Adminstrn. and Mgmt. Assn. (edn. and tng. com. pub. rels. sect. 1990-95), Resources and Tech. Svcs. Divsn.(micropub. com. 1982-85, chmn. 1983-85, cons. 1985-87). Office: U Ill Edn & Social Sci Libr 100 Main Libr 1408 W Gregory Dr Urbana IL 61801-3607 Office Phone: 217-333-2408. E-mail: npobrien@uiuc.edu.

O'BRIEN, ODESSA LOUISE, protective services official; m. John Daniels O'Brien, May 30, 1964; children: James John, Jeanne Jacqueline, Kevin Raymond. B.Elective Studies, St. Cloud State U., 1975. Lic. pilot. Stewardess Northwest Airlines, St. Paul; personnel officer Minn. Wing Civil Air Patrol, St. Paul, 2001—. Area rep. Youth for Understanding, Brainerd, Minn., 1979—82; v.p. Christian Women's Club, Brainerd, 1976—80; chmn. St. Francis Ch. Women's Guild, Brainerd, Minn., 1978—79, St. Francis Parochial Sch. Bd., Brainerd, Minn., 1979—80; mem. coun. St. Francis Ch., Brainerd, Minn., 1979—80; adv. bd. Pine County Vo-Tech Sch., Pine City, Minn., 1967—71. Recipient Outstanding Woman of Collier County, Am. Bus. Women's Assn., 1983—85, Comdrs. Commendation, Naples Sr. Squadron, Civil Air Patrol, 1983, Grover Loening award, Minn. Wing Civil Air Patrol, Air Force Aux., Paul E. Garber award, Civil Air Patrol, 2003, Gill Robb Wilson award, 2004. Mem.: AAUW (life; pres. Naples br. 1983—85), USAF Aux., Civil Air Patrol, Collier Automotive Mus. (sec. of vol. docents), Naples Woman's Club (internat. chmn.), Phi Theta Kappa (life). Roman Catholic. Avocations: bridge (Bronze Life Master), flying, travel, tennis, reading. Office: Minn Wing Civil Air Patrol PO Box 11230 Saint Paul MN 55111-0230 also: 5861 Paradise Cir Naples FL 34110

O'BRIEN, ORIN YNEZ, musician, educator; b. Hollywood, Calif., June 7, 1935; d. George Joseph and Marguerite Graham (Churchill) O'Brien. Studied with Frederick Zimmermann, Milton Kestenbaum and Herman Reinshagen; diploma, The Juilliard Sch., 1957. Double bassist N.Y.C. Ballet Orch., 1956—66, Saidenberg Little Symphony, Music Aeterna, Am. Symphony (with Stokowski), N.Y. Philharm., N.Y.C., 1966—; faculty Manhattan Sch. Music, N.Y.C., 1969—, Mannes Coll. Music, N.Y.C., 1988—, The Julliard Sch., N.Y.C., 1990—, co-chair double bass dept., 1992—2002. Participant numerous chamber music festivals, including Marlboro; featured in 1st performances of Gunther Schuller Quartet for 4 double basses; artist for GM, CBS and RCA Recording cos. Mem.: Internat. Soc. Bassists, Am. Fedn. Musicians, The Bohemians. Avocations: reading, writing, cooking.

O'BRIEN, PAT, television personality; b. Sioux Falls, S.D., Feb. 14, 1948; m. Linda O'Brien, 1973; 1 child, Sean. Grad., U. S.D., 1970; postgrad., Johns Hopkins U. Prodn. asst. The Huntley-Brinkley Report; reporter WMAQ-TV, Chgo., KNXT-TV (now KCBS-TV), L.A.; host The Krypton Factor, 1981; anchor CBS Sports, 1981—97; host Overtime...with Pat O'Brien, 1990, How'd They Do That?, 1993—94; host (TV spls.) The Road to Olympic Gold, 1996, 2000; host CNBC coverage of the Sydney Olympics, 2000; corr. NBC coverage of the Utah Olympics, 2002; co-anchor Access Hollywood, 1997—2004; host NBC coverage of the Athens Olympics, 2004, The Insider, 2004—. Author: Talkin' Sports: A B.S.-er's Guide, 1998; columnist: N.Y. Daily News, Inside Sports, Live!, TV Guide, Ego, Men's Health, gadget editor: Gear Mag. Recipient newswriting award, L.A. Press Club, 1987. Office: Paramount Studios 5555 Melrose Ave Los Angeles CA 90038*

O'BRIEN, PATRICK KARL, economic history educator; b. London, Aug. 12, 1932; s. William Patrick and Elizabeth (Stockhausen) O'B.; m. Cassy Cobham, Apr. 15, 1959; children: Karen, Helen, Stephen. BSc in Econs., London Sch. Econs., 1958; DPhil, Oxford (Eng.) U., 1966, MA, 1970; D (hon.), U. Carlos III, Madrid, 1999, U. Uppsala, 2000. Rsch. fellow Sch. Oriental and African Studies, London, 1960-63, lectr., 1964-66, reader, 1966-70; reader, profl. fellow St. Anthony's Coll., Oxford, Eng., 1970-90, lectr., fellow, 1970-83; prof., dir. Inst. Hist. Rsch. London U., 1990-98; Centennial prof. London Sch. Econs., 1999—. Vis. prof. Yale U., European U., Florence, Princeton U., Columbia U., U. Calif., San Diego, Va. U., Carlos III U., Madrid. Author: The Revolution in Egypt's Economic System, 1966, The New Economic History of Railways, 1977, Economic Growth in Britain and France, 1780-1914, 1978, The Industrial Revolution and British Society, 1992. Fellow Royal Hist. Soc., Brit. Acad., Academica Europa, Royal Soc. Arts, Econ. History Soc. U.K. (pres. 1997-2000). Home: 66 St Bernards Rd Oxford OX2 6EJ England Office: Dept Economic History London Sch Econs Houghton St Aldwych London WC2A 2AE England

O'BRIEN, PATRICK MICHAEL, library administrator; b. Newport, R.I., Mar. 17, 1943; s. Joseph Xavier and Loretta (DeCotis) O'B.; m. Roberta Luther, Nov. 27, 1977; children— Megan MacRae, Brendan Watters. BA in Eng. Lit., Merrimack Coll., North Andover, Mass., 1964; M.L.S., U. R.I., Kingston, 1965; MBA, Case Western Res. U., Cleve., 1983. Reference libr. Newsweek mag., N.Y.C., 1965-72; asst. dir. rsch. FIND/SVP, N.Y.C., 1972-74; head cen. libr., cultural ctr. Chgo. Pub. Libr., 1974-79; dir. Cuyahoga County Pub. Libr., Cleve., 1979-84; dir. librs. Dallas Pub. Libr., 1984-92; dir. Alexandria (Va.) Libr., 1992—. Mem. editorial bd. Handel's Nat. Directory for Performing Arts; contbr. articles to profl. jours. Participant, alumnus Leadership Dallas Program, 1984-85, Leadership Cleve. Program, 1981; mem. nat. adv. com. to Libr. of Congress; mem. adv. coun. Tex. State Libr., Libr. Svcs. and Constrn. Act, 1986-89; co-chair, del. selection com. Tex. Conf. on Librs. and Info. Svcs.; mem. com. Goals for Dallas, 1985; mem. exec. bd. univ. librs. So. Meth. U., 1985-93; bd. dirs. Urban Community Sch., Cleve., 1982-84, Mus. African-Am. Life and Culture, 1985-86; mem. client data base com. Dallas Assn. Svcs. to Homeless, 1988-90; mem. Latchkey Children's Task Force, 1985-90. Recipient Servant as Leader award City of Dallas, 1989, Disting. Alumnus award U. R.I. Grad. Sch. Libr. and Info. Studies, 1990. Mem. ALA (coun. mem. 1987-95), Am. Libr. Trustee Assn. (bd. dirs.), Pub. Libr. Assn. (pres. 1985-86), Pub. Libr. Systems Sect (pres. 1983), Tex. Libr. Assn. (legis com. 1986-92), Tex. Women's Univ. Sch. Libr. and Info. Studies Vis. Com., Tex. Ctr. for Book Dallas Pub. Libr., Cleve. Area Met. Libr. Systems (pres. bd. 1980), Chgo. Libr. Club (pres. 1978), D.C. Libr. Assn., Va. Pub. Libr. Dirs. Assn. (bd. dirs. 1994-96), Va. Libr. Assn., Online Computer Libr. Ctr. (bd. trustees 1992-98), The White House Conf. on Librs. and Info. Svcs. (del. 1991), Pub. Lib. Adminstrs. N.Tex. (pres. 1990-91), Dallas 40, Rotary of Alexandria (bd. dirs. 1996-97, pres. 2002-03, Rotarian of Yr. 2001), Alexandria Commn. on Info. Tech., Beta Gamma Sigma. Office: Alexandria Libr 5005 Duke St Alexandria VA 22304-2903

O'BRIEN, PATRICK WILLIAM, lawyer; b. Chgo., Dec. 5, 1927; s. Maurice Edward and Ellen (Fitzgerald) O'B.; m. Deborah Bissell, July 2, 1955; children: Kathleen, Mariellen, Patrick, James, Patricia. BS in Mech. Engring., Northwestern U., 1947, JD, 1950. Bar: Ill. 1951, U.S. Dist. Ct. (no. dist.) Ill. 1954, U.S. Dist. Ct. (so. dist.)Ill. 1956, U.S. Ct. Appeals (7th cir.) 1955, U.S. Ct. Appeals (8th cir.) 1972, U.S. Supreme Ct. 1970. Assoc. Bell, Boyd, Marshall & Lloyd, Chgo., 1950—51, Mayer, Brown, Rowe & Maw, Chgo., 1953—62, ptnr., 1962—94, sr. counsel, 1995—. Served to capt. USAF, 1951-53. Fellow Am. Coll. Trial Lawyers; mem. ABA, Ill. Bar Assn., Chgo. Bar Assn. Clubs: Chgo., Mid-Day, University, Westmoreland Country, Cliff Dwellers, Dairymen's Country. Republican. Roman Catholic. Office: Mayer Brown Rowe & Maw 190 S La Salle St Ste 3140 Chicago IL 60603-3441 Home: 2606 Park Pl Evanston IL 60201-1318

O'BRIEN, RAYMOND FRANCIS, transportation executive; b. Atchison, Kans., May 31, 1922; s. James C. and Anna M. (Wagner) O'B.; m. Mary Ann Baugher, Sept. 3, 1947; children: James B., William T., Kathleen A., Christopher R. BS in Bus. Adminstrn., U. Mo., 1948; grad., Advanced Mgmt. Program, Harvard, 1966. Accountant-auditor Peat, Marwick, Mitchell & Co., Kansas City, Mo., 1948-52; contr., treas. Riss & Co., Kansas City, Mo., 1952-58; regional contr. Consol. Freightways Corp. of Del., Indpls., also, Akron, Ohio, 1958-61; contr. Consol. Freightways, Inc., San Francisco, 1961—, v.p., treas., 1962-63, bd. dirs., 1966, v.p. fin., 1967-69, exec. v.p., 1969-75, pres., 1975—, chief exec. officer, 1977-88, 90-91, chmn., 1988—; now chmn. emeritus CNF Transportation. Pres. CF Motor Freight subs. Consol. Freightways, Inc., 1973; dir. Transam. Corp., Watkins-Johnson, Inc.; past chmn. WesternHwy. Inst., Champion Road Machinery, Ltd. Former mem. bus. adv. bd. Northwestern U., U. Calif., Berkeley; bd. dirs., regent, former chmn. bd. trustees St. Mary's Coll.; bd. dirs., regent Charles Armstrong Sch., 1991—; mem. Pres.'s Adv. Herbert Hoover Boys and Girls Club; dir. Boy Scouts Am. Bay Area Coun. Served to 1st lt. USAAF, 1942-45. Recipient Disting. Svc. Citation Automotive Hall Fame, 1991; named Outstanding Chief Exec. five times Financial World Mag. Mem. Am. Trucking Assn. (bd. dirs. Found., exec. com.), Pacific Union Club, World Trade Club, Commonwealth Club (San Francisco), Menlo Country Club. Home: 26347 Esperanza Dr Los Altos CA 94022-2601 Office: 3240 Hillview Ave Palo Alto CA 94304

O'BRIEN, RAYMOND VINCENT, JR., banker; b. Bronx, N.Y., Sept. 23, 1927; s. Raymond Vincent and Blanche (Harper) O'B.; m. Theresa Sweeney, Mar. 29, 1952 (dec. June 1981); children: Susan, Raymond, Christopher, Sean, Carol, Nancy Meisenzahl; m. Ellen Boyle, July 24, 1982. BA, Fordham U., 1951, JD, 1958; postgrad., Harvard U. Advanced Mgmt. Program, 1969. With Chase Manhattan Bank, N.A., N.Y.C., 1953-74; chief exec. officer, chmn. bd. Emigrant Savs. Bank, N.Y.C., 1978—93, pres., 1974-77. Bd. dirs. Internat. Shipholding Corp. Trustee Fordham U., 1979-92; chmn. bd. trustees Regis H.S., 1988-92; past chmn. Cmty. Bankers Assn., N.Y., Nat. Assn. Cmty. Bankers. Served with AUS, 1946-47, 51-53. Mem. Guild Cath. Lawyers, Sky Club, Navesink Country Club (Middletown, N.J.), Plantation Country Club (Ponte Vedra, Fla.), K.M., Friendly Sons St. Patrick. Republican. Roman Catholic. Home: 102 Lands End Ponte Vedra Beach FL 32082-3906

O'BRIEN, RICHARD ALAN, research scientist; b. Sioux City, Iowa, June 16, 1961; s. Richard Henry O'Brien. BS, S.D. State U., 1985; MS, U. N.D., 1987; PhD, U. Nebr., 1992. Rsch. scientist Rieke Metals, Inc., Lincoln, Nebr., 1992-93, TPL, Inc., Albuquerque, 1993-97, Hexcel Corp., Decatur, Ala., 1997—. Active Decatur Concert Assn., 1997-98. Mem. Am. Chem. Soc. Office: Hexcel Corp 3300 Mallard Fox Dr NW Decatur AL 35601-7575

O'BRIEN, RICHARD FRANCIS, advertising agency association executive; b. Everett, Mass., Aug. 3, 1942; s. James Raymond and Gertrude Lucille O'B.; m. Clare Lynch, Apr. 7, 1973; children: Catherine Lynch, Miles Edward. AB magna cum laude, Boston Coll., 1964; MA, Ind. U., 1965; MBA, Columbia U., 1967. With Grey Advt. Inc., N.Y.C., 1967-83, v.p., mgmt. supr., 1973-77, sr. v.p., mgmt. rep., 1977-80, exec. v.p., mgmt. rep., 1980-83; exec. v.p., mgmt. dir. Dancer Fitzgerald Sample, Inc. (name changed to Saatchi & Saatchi Advt.), N.Y.C., 1983-88; vice chmn. Dancer Fitzgerald Sample, Inc. (became Saatchi & Saatchi Advt.), N.Y.C., 1988-97; bd. dirs. Saatchi & Saatchi Advt. Worldwide, 1989-97; exec. v.p. Spl. Olympics Internat., 1997-2000; exec. v.p., dir. govt. rels. Am. Assn. Advt. Agys., 2001—. Bd. dirs. Spl. Olympics Internat., 1983-97. Office: Am Assn Advt Agys 1203 19th St NW 4th Fl Washington DC 20036

O'BRIEN, RICHARD L(EE), medical educator, academic administrator, physician, cell biologist; b. Shenandoah, Iowa, Aug. 30, 1934; s. Thomas Lee O'B. and Grace Ellen (Sims) Parish; m. Joan Frances Gurney, June 29, 1957; children: Sheila Marie, Kathleen Therese, Michael James, Patrick Kevin. MS in Physiology, Creighton U., 1958, MD, 1960. Diplomate Nat. Bd. Med. Examiners. Intern and resident Columbia med. divsn. Bellevue Hosp., N.Y.C., 1960-62; postdoctoral fellow in biochemistry Inst. for Enzyme Rsch., U. Wis., 1962-64; asst. prof. to prof. pathology Sch. Medicine, U. So. Calif., L.A., 1966-82, dep. dir. Cancer Ctr., 1975-80, dir. rsch. and edn. Cancer Ctr., 1980-81, dir. Cancer Ctr., 1981-82; dean Sch. Medicine Creighton U., Omaha, 1982-92, acting v.p. health scis., 1984-85, v.p. health scis., 1985-99, prof. health policy and ethics, Univ. prof., 2000—, dir. office of interprofl. edn., 2002—. Vis. prof. molecular biology U. Geneva, 1973-74; cons. in field; mem. cancer control rsch. grants rev. com. NIH, Nat. Cancer Inst.; mem. Cancer Ctr. Support grant rev. com. Nat. Cancer Inst., 1984-88, chmn. 1987-88; co-chmn. United Way/CHAD Pacesetter campaign, 1988, 94. Contbr. articles to profl. jours.; editor various profl. jours. Served to capt. U.S. Army, 1964-66. Spl. fellow Nat. Cancer Inst., 1967-69; Combined Health Agys. Drive-Health Citizen of Yr., 1986. Mem. ACP, Am. Assn. Pathologists, Am. Assn. Cancer Rsch., Am. Assn. Cancer Edn., AAAS, Am. Assn. Cancer Insts. (dir. 1982-83), Assn. Am. Med. Colls. (chmn. MCAT evaluation panel 1987-88, liaison com. on med. edn., 1988-93, co-chmn, 1989-93, adv. panel Strategic Planning Health Care Reform 1992-96), Assn. Acad. Health Ctrs. (long-range planning com. 1986, 2000, nominating com. 1987, 96, Task Force Health Care Delivery 1992, mem. task force on leadership and instl. values 1993-99, bd. dirs. 1998-99), Am. Cancer Soc. (adv. com. Inst. rsch. Grants 1977-80, Outstanding Leadership award, dir. Calif. divsn. 1980-82, dir. Nebr. divsn. 1992-96), Am. Hosp. Assn. (com. on med. edn. 1986-89), Alpha Omega Alpha. Home: 9927 Essex Dr Omaha NE 68114-3873 Office: Creighton Univ California At 24th Omaha NE 68178-0001 Office Phone: 402-280-2017. Business E-Mail: rlo@creighton.edu.

O'BRIEN, ROBERT BROWNELL, JR., investment banker, consultant, yacht broker, opera company executive; b. NYC, Sept. 6, 1934; s. Robert Brownell and Eloise (Boles) O'B.; m. Sarah Lager, Nov. 28, 1958; children: Robert Brownell III, William Stuart, Jennifer. BA, Lehigh U., 1957; postgrad., NYU, Am. Inst. Banking. Asst. treas., credit officer, br. locations officer Bankers Trust Co., N.Y.C., 1957-63; v.p., dir. bus. devel. George A. Murray Co., gen. contractors, N.Y.C., 1964; also v.p. Bowery Savs. Bank, 1964-69; dir., chief exec. officer Fed. Savs. & Loan Ins. Corp., Washington, 1969-71; chmn. exec. com. Fed. Home Loan Bank Bd., 1969-71; v.p. Bowery Savs. Bank, N.Y.C., 1972; exec. v.p. First Fed. Savs. & Loan Assn., N.Y.C., 1973-75; chmn., chief exec. officer Carteret Savs. Bank, Morristown, 1975-91, also bd. dirs.; mng. dir. Printon Kane Group Inc., Short Hills, N.J., 1991-94; dir., former chief exec. officer Govs. Bank Corp., West Palm Beach, 1992-94; pres., CEO Hubert Johnson Inc., 1998—. Bd. dirs. Fed. Home Loan Bank N.Y., Govs. Bank Corp., Ocean Med. Ctr. Found., Ocean City Atty. Ethics Com.; vice chmn. 1st Mortgage Capital Corp., Vero Beach, Fla.; chmn. Neighborhood Housing Svcs. Am., 1972-91; vice chmn., bd dirs. U.S. League Savs. Instns., Washington, O'Brien Yacht Sales. Contbr. articles to trade mags. Trustee Trinity Pawling Sch., Palm Beach County Housing Partnership, Lehigh U.; chmn. Housing Opportunities Found.; trustee, pres. Toms River Seaport Soc., N.J. Mus. Boating; trustee, past chmn. Cmty. Found. of N.J., 1987—; trustee, pres. Bay Head Hist. Soc.; vice chmn., bd. dirs. Dalt Found.; chmn. adv. bd. Palm Beach Maritime Mus., Peanut Island, Fla.; active Nat. Commn. on Neighborhoods; past chmn., exec. dir. N.J. State Opera. Mem. Nat. Coun. Savs. Instns. (past chmn.), Essex County Savs. and Loan League (past chmn.), N.J. Savs. League (past chmn.), N.J. Hist. Soc. (past chmn.), Greater Newark C. of C. (bd. dirs.), N.J. C. of C. (bd. dirs.), Union League Club, Delray Beach Yacht Club (past commodore), New York Yacht Club, Morris County Golf Club, Somerset Hills Golf Club, Palm Beach Yacht Club, Bay Head Yacht Club (past commodore). Republican. Episcopalian. Home: 500 Club Dr Bay Head NJ 08742-5016 Office Phone: 732-295-2072. E-mail: bob@woodenboatsnj.com.

O'BRIEN, ROBERT EMMET, insurance company executive; b. St. Louis, Sept. 13, 1923; s. Algernon Francis Adams and Adeline (von Weisert) O'B.; m. Mary Lou Gallagher, July 20, 1946 (div. 1978); children: Robert Jr., Gardnar, Scott, Derek, Mary Berkeley; m. Marian Strong Achilles, June 30, 1983. BBA, St. Louis U., 1946, MBA, 1947. Prin., ptnr. R. Newman & R. O'Brien, St. Louis, 1946-52; mem. Lloyd's of London, 1952—; dir. Hunter Engring. Co., St. Louis, 1946-72, Atlas Mfg. Co., St. Louis, 1965-80, Narragansett Corp., St. Louis and Moberly, Mo., 1965-80, Mid-America Coffee Co., St. Louis, 1970-75, Golden-Dipt Corp. and DCA (N.Y.), N.Y.C., 1948-1970; cons. internat. ins. The Law Firm of Honorable Wilbur D. Mills and Herman E. Talmadge, Washington, London, 1976—. Pres. North Atlantic Assurance Co. Ltd., London, 1962-75; elected hon. dir. Atlantic Coun. of the U.S. Treas. St. Louis Trust Coun., 1949-65; apptd. to Bd. Life Govs. Royal Hosp. Putney, West Hill, London, 1969; councillor The Athletic Coun. of U.S., Atlantic Coun. of U.S., Carnegie Found.; mem. U.S. Olympics (Ice) Speed Skating

Team, 1939; trustee Errol Flynn Estate, Jamaica and London, 1959-64; mem. Hiberian United Svcs. Club, Dublin, Ireland. With AC U.S. Army, 1942-45, ETO, NATOUSA. Decorated DFC (Eng.). Mem. DAV (life), Royal Air Force Soc., Zurich Internat. Insurers (apptd.), Life Underwriters, Million Dollar Round Table (life), Mid-Atlantic Club, Royal Yacht Club Hobart Tasmania, Royal Yacht Club Tasmania, Army and Navy Club Washington (hon.), Devonshire Club (London), Irish Nat. (London), Liberal Club (London), Royal Jamacia Yacht Club (life), Mo. Athletic Club, Royal Yacht of Fiji, Royal Scots Mil. Club (Edinburgh), U.S. SAMOA Soc. So. Pacific, Bridlespur Hunt and Polo Club. Home: 117 Old Wharf Rd North Chatham MA 02650-1129

O'BRIEN, ROBERT JOHN, JR., public relations executive, former government official, air force officer; b. Wheeling, W. Va., Apr. 16, 1935; s. Robert John and Martha Virginia (Hunter) O'B.; m. Margaret Eugenia Schultz BS in Journalism, Northwestern U., 1957; MA in Journalism, U. Wis., 1970; grad., Indsl. Coll. Armed Forces, 1977. Comnd. officer U.S. Air Force, 1957, advanced through grades to col.; dir. pub. affairs N. Am. Air Def. Command, Colorado Springs, Colo., 1977-80, Air Force Systems Command, Camp Springs, Md., 1980-82; dir. def. info. Office Sec. Def., Washington, 1982-83, dep. asst. sec. def., 1983-86; dir. pub. rels., Washington McDonnell Douglas Corp., Arlington, Va., 1986-97; v.p. pub. rels. The Boeing Co., Arlington, Va., 1997-99. Decorated D.S.M., Legion of Merit, Bronze Star, Air medal, Medal of Honor (Republic Vietnam). Mem. Air Force Assn., Pub. Rels. Soc. Am., Aviation/Space Writers Assn., U.S. Space Found., Ret. Officers Assn., Williamsburg Nat. Golf Club (Williamsburg, Va.), Nat. Press Club. Republican. Methodist. Avocations: golf, stamp collecting/philately, model railroading.

O'BRIEN, ROBERT S. state official; b. Seattle, Sept. 14, 1918; s. Edward R. and Maude (Ransom) O'B.; m. Kathryn E. Arvan, Oct. 18, 1941 (dec. June 1984). Student public schs. With Kaiser Co., 1938-46; restaurant owner, 1946-50; treas., 1950-65, 1965-89; chmn. Wash. State Fin. Com., 1965-89, Wash. Public Deposit Protection Commn., 1969-89, Wash. Public Employees Retirement Bd., 1969-77, Law Enforcement Officers and Firefighters Retirement System, 1971-77, Wash. State Investment Bd., 1981-89; retired, 1989. Mem. Wash. Data Processing Adv. Bd., 1967-73; Gov.'s Exec. Mgmt. and Fiscal Affairs Com., 1978-80, Gov.'s Cabinet Com. on Tax Alternatives, 1978-80; trustee Wash. Tchr.'s Retirement System, 1965-89; bd. dirs. Centennial Bank, Olympia, Wash. Recipient Leadership award Joint Council County and City Employees-Fedn. State Employees, 1970, Eagles Leadership award, 1967 Mem. Nat. Assn. State Auditors, Comptrollers and Treasurers (pres. 1977), Nat. Assn. Mcpl. Fin. Officers, Nat. Assn. State Treasurers, Western State Treasurers Assn. (pres. 1970), Wash. County Treas. Assn. (pres. 1955-56), Wash. Assn. Elected County Ofcls. (pres. 1955-58), Olympia Area C. of C., Soap Lake C. of C. (pres. 1948) Clubs: Elks (hon. life); Moose, Eagles, Lions, Olympia Yacht, Olympia Country and Golf; Empire (Spokane); Wash. Athletic (Seattle). Democrat. Address: 1136 Tullis St NE Olympia WA 98506

O'BRIEN, SHANNON PATRICIA, state treasurer; b. Boston, Apr. 30, 1959; m. Emmet Hayes; 1 child, Regan Ann; 1 stepchild: Jill. BA, Yale U., 1981; JD, Boston U., 1985. State rep., 1987-93; state senator, 1993-95; health care exec., 1995-97; lectr. Boston U., 1997-98; treas. State of Mass., Boston, 1999—. Office: State House Rm 227 Office Of Treasurer Boston MA 02133

O'BRIEN, SOLEDAD, newscaster, news anchor; m. Brad Raymond; children: Sofia, Cecilia, Charlie, Jackson. Student, Harvard U. Prodr. Second Opinion, reporter Health Week in Review Sta. KISS-FM, Boston; assoc. prodr., newswriter Sta. WBZ-TV, Boston; prodr. NBC News, 1991—93; co-host The Know Zone Discovery Channel; chief East Bay bur. Sta. KRON-TV, San Francisco, reporter, 1993—96; co-host The Site, Nightly News, Weekend Today MSNBC, 1996—99; anchor, Weekend Today NBC, 1999—2003; co-anchor, American Morning CNN, 2003—. Recipient Emmy. Office: CNN 820 1st St NE Washington DC 20002-4243*

O'BRIEN, TERRENCE LEO, federal judge; b. Lincoln, Nebr., Aug. 8, 1943; s. Leo James and Luella Mildred (Benting) O'B.; m. Dorothy Marguerite Driskill, Mar. 30, 1966; children: Sean Brendan, Heather Kathleen. BS in Acctg., U. Wyo., 1965, JD with honors, 1972. Bar: Wyo. 1972, U.S. Dist. Ct. Wyo. 1972, U.S. Ct. Appeals (7th and 10th cirs.) 1972, U.S. Ct. Appeals (8th, 9th and D.C. cirs.) 1973, U.S. Ct. Appeals (2d and 4th cirs.) 1974, U.S. Supreme Ct. 1975. Staff atty. Land and Natural Resources-U.S. Dept. Justice, Washington, 1972-74; ptnr. Omohundro & O'Brien, Buffalo, Wyo., 1974-80; judge 6th Jud. Dist. Wyo., Gillette, 1980—2001; pres. Visionary Communications Inc, 2000—01; private practice Wyo., 2001—02; judge U.S. Ct. Appeals (10th Cir.), 2002—. Justice of Peace Johnson County, Buffalo, 1975-80. Mem. Wyo. Community Coll. Commn., 1978-80. Capt. U.S. Army, 1966-69. Mem.: Rotary. Republican. Office: US Courthouse 2120 Capitol Ave Ste 2212 Cheyenne WY 82001

O'BRIEN, THOMAS HENRY, former bank holding company executive; b. Pitts., Jan. 16, 1937; s. J. Vick and Georgia (Bower) O'B.; m. Maureen Sheedy; children: Thomas Henry, Lauren C., Timothy B. BS in Commerce, U. Notre Dame, 1958; MBA, Harvard U., 1962. Joined Pitts. Nat. Bank, 1962, v.p., 1967-73, sr. v.p., 1973-80, exec. v.p., 1980-83, vice chmn., 1983-84; bd. dirs., CEO PNC Fin. Corp., 1985—2000, also chmn., 1988—2001; chmn. PNC Bank Corp., Pitts., 1988—, CEO, 1988-2000, chmn., 1988—2001; ret. Bd. dirs. Hilb, Rogal & Hamilton Co., Bell Atlantic Corp., Internat. Monetary Conf., Black Rock, Inc., Verizon Comm. Bd. dirs. United Way Southwest Pa., Extra Mile Found., Carnegie Museums of Pitts., Pitts. Opera, Allegheny Conf. Cmty. Devel., U. Pitts., Res. City Bankers; mem. bd. visitors U. Pitts. Grad. Sch. Bus. Named Industrialist of Yr. Soc. Indsl. and Office Realtors, 1996. Mem. Assn. Res. City Bankers, Pa. Bankers Assn., Fox Chapel Golf Club. Clubs: Duquesne, Allegheny (bd. dirs.), Pitts. Field, Rolling Rock, Laurel Valley Golf. Roman Catholic. Avocation: golf.*

O'BRIEN, TIM, writer; b. Austin, Minn., Oct. 1, 1946; s. William Timothy and Ava Eleanor (Shultz) O'B.; m. Ann Elizabeth Weller. BA, Macalester Coll., 1968; LHD (hon.), Miami (Ohio) U., 1990. Reporter The Washington Post, 1973-74. Author: (memoir) If I Die in a Combat Zone, 1973; (novel) Northern Lights, 1975, Going After Cacciato, 1978 (Nat. Book award 1979), The Nuclear Age, 1985, The Things They Carried, 1990 (Heartland award 1990, Melcher Book award 1991, nominee Pulitzer prize and Nat. Book Critics Cir. award 1991), In the Lake of the Woods, 1994, Tomcat in Love, 1998. Sgt. U.S. Army, 1968-70, Vietnam. Nat. Ednowment for the Arts fellow, 1976, 87, Best Am. Short Stories fellow Houghton Miffin Co., 1977, 87, Guggenheim Found. fellow, 1981; recipient O. Henry prize Doubleday Pub. Co., 1976, 78, 82. Address: Bantam Books Author Svcs 1540 Broadway New York NY 10036-4039

O'BRIEN, TIMOTHY ANDREW, writer, journalist, lawyer, educator; b. N.Y.C., July 11, 1943; s. Timothy Andrew and Hildegarde J. (Schenkel) O'B.; m. Maria de Guadalupe Margarita Moreno, Jan. 15, 1971; children: Theresa Marie, Tim A. BA in Comm., Mich. State U., 1967; MA in Polit. Sci., U. Md., 1972; postgrad., Tulane U., 1974-75; JD, Loyola U., New Orleans, 1976. Bar: La. 1976, D.C. 1977, U.S. Supreme Ct 1981. News writer, reporter, anchor WKBD-TV, Detroit, 1968-69, WTOP-TV, Washington, 1969-72, WDSU-TV, New Orleans, 1972-74, WVUE-TV, New Orleans, 1974-77; law corr. ABC News, 1977-99; corr. Cable News Network (CNN), 2001—. Leo Goodwin Prof. Law Southeastern U., 1997; disting. prof. law Hofstra U., Sch. Law, 2000, St. Thomas Sch. Law, Miami, 2001, Nova U., 2002; disting. vis. prof. law, Nova Southeastern U., 1999, 2001, Loyola Sch. of Law, 2003. Contbr. articles to profl. jours. Bd. govs. Woodward Acad., College Park, Ga.; bd. visitors Loyola U. Sch. Law., 1997—. Recipient AP award for outstanding reporting of extraordinary event, 1976, New Orleans Press Club award for non-spot news reporting, 1976, Emmy award for documentary on D.C., 1969, ABA awards of merit, 1979 (2), 80, 85, Gavel award for documentary, 1980, Nat. award for human rights reporting Women in Comm., 1981, Disting. Alumnus award Mich. State U., 1996. Mem. Am. Law Inst., Radio-TV Corrs. Assn. Washington, Am. Judicature Soc. (bd. dirs. 1991-97). Office: CNN 820 First St NE Washington DC 20002 Office Phone: 301-704-1160.

O'BRIEN, TIMOTHY JAMES, lawyer; b. Detroit, Nov. 4, 1945; m. Hyon Baek, Jan. 31, 1970; children: Jean, Jane. AB, Yale U., 1967; JD, Harvard U., 1976. Bar: N.Y. 1977, Hong Kong, 1999. Assoc. Cleary, Gottlieb, Steen & Hamilton, N.Y.C., 1976-80; ptnr. Coudert Bros., N.Y.C. and Hong Kong, 1980—, mng. ptnr. Hong Kong office, 2000—. Lectr. symposium on internat. investment Southwestern Law Found., 1995. Mem.: Harvard Law Rev., 1975—76; contbr. articles to profl. jours.; co-author: Corporate Governance in Korea at the Millennium, 2002. Assoc. dir., vol. Peace Corps, Republic of Korea, 1967-73. Mem. ABA (co-chmn. conf. on Korea-U.S. trade and investment 1990-92), Assn. of Bar of City of N.Y. (internat. law com., Asian affairs com. 1989-94), The Korea Soc. (N.Y., sec., bd. dirs. 1996-99). Office: Coudert Bros Gloucester Tower 11 Pedder St Landmark 39th Fl Central Hong Kong Hong Kong Fax: 852-2218-9200. E-mail: obrient@coudert.com.

O'BRIEN, WILLIAM J., III, lawyer; BS, Holy Cross Coll., 1965; LLB, Yale U., 1969. Bar: N.Y. 1970, Mich. 1985. With Hughes Hubbard and Reed, N.Y.C. and Paris, 1969-75; asst. gen. counsel Chrysler Corp., Highland Park, 1983, assoc. gen. counsel, 1984, dep. gen. counsel, 1986, v.p., gen. counsel, sec., 1987; sr. v.p., gen. counsel DaimlerChrysler AG, 1998—2002, exec. v.p., gen. counsel, 2002—. Office: DaimlerChrysler Corp CIMS 485-14-96 1000 Chrysler Dr Auburn Hills MI 48326-2766

O'BRIEN, WILLIAM JEROME, II, lawyer; b. Darby, Pa., Oct. 22, 1954; s. Richard James O'Brien and Margaret (McGill) Hahn. BA in Econ. and Polit. Sci., Merrimack Coll., 1976; JD, Del. Law Sch., 1981. Bar: Pa. 1982, U.S. Dist. Ct. (ea. dist.) Pa. 1983, U.S. Supreme Ct. 1986. Law clk. Commonwealth Ct. of Pa., Harrisburg, 1982-83; assoc. Philips, Curtin and DiGiacomo, Phila., 1983-86, O'Brien & Assocs. PC, Phila., 1986—. Bd. dirs. New Manayunk Corp., Phila. counselor, 1987-98. Bd. dirs. North Light Inc., 1986-94, sec., 1988-90, pres., 1990-92; bd. dirs. Manayunk Cmty. Ctr. for Arts, 1988-90, chmn. Chaminouix Mansion, 1989—, chmn., 1991—; spl. asst. to U.S. Senator H. John Heinz, 1976-78; Rep. candidate for Phila. City Coun., 1991, for Phila. City Contr., 1997; mem. Rep. State Com. Pa., 1998-2000; mem. Phila. Rep. Exec. Com. Mem.: Bus. Assn. Manayunk (bd. dirs. 1987—89), Pa. Bar Assn., Phila. Bar Assn., Del. Law Sch. Alumni Assn. (sec. 1985—87), Racquet Club (mem. com. 1985—87). Roman Catholic. Avocations: squash, court tennis, scuba, golf. Office: O'Brien & Assocs PC 4322 Main St Philadelphia PA 19127-1421

O'BRIEN, WILLIAM JOHN, ecology researcher; b. Summit, N.J., Nov. 30, 1942; m. Mavion Meier, 1964; children: Connor, Shay, Lia BA, Gettysburg Coll., 1965; postgrad., Cornell U., 1965-69; PhD, Mich. State U., 1970. sch. rsch. assoc. Ctr. Northern Studies, 1977; disting. lectr. Kans. Acad. Sci., 1990. From asst. prof. to prof. aquatic ecology U. Kans., Lawrence, 1971—2000, full prof., 1982—, dir. exptl. and applied ecology program, 1994—99, chair dept. sys. and ecology, 1991—96. Rsch. scientist Ecosys. Ctr. Marine Biol. Lab., 1986—. Grantee NSF, 1975—. Mem.: Internat. Assn. Theoretical and Applied Limnology, Am. Fisheries Soc., Am. Soc. Limnology and Oceanography. Office: U NC Dept Biol 310 Eberhart Bldg Greensboro NC 27402

O'BRIEN-PALMER, MICHELLE ANN, educational writer, consultant; b. Long Beach, Calif., Apr. 8, 1954; d. Michael William O'Brien and Joanna Jacobson; m. Louis Gideon Palmer, Mar. 22, 1980; 1 child, Nicholas Gideon Palmer. BA, U. of Wash., 1979, MS, 1980; EdD, Fielding Grad. Inst., Santa Barbara, Calif., 2003. Co-pres., cons. Action Consulting, Kirkland, Wash., 1984—93; pres., ednl. writer MicNik Publs., Inc., Woodinville, Wash., 1988—2003. Educator Group Health Coop., Seattle, 1980—83; author-in-residence Lake Washington Sch. Dist., Redmond, 1991—2001. Author: (ednl.text) How the Earth Works, (children's poetry book) Through My Eyes, (ednl. text) Poetry Projects with Pizzazz, Watch Me Grow (Rated Outstanding by Parents' Coun., 2001), Healthy Me, Sense-Abilities (Childrens' Lit. Choice award, 1999); writer, graphic designer: ednl. series Let's Learn About Story Elements: Book 1-Character, Book 2-Setting, Book 3-Plot (Benjamin Franklin award finalist in Edn., 1996), ednl. text Great Graphic Organizers, Beyond Book Reports, composer, musician: ednl. rec. Book-Talk: Singable Songs for Lifelong Readers. Mem.: ASCD, Alumni Assn. U. of Wash., Am. Ednl. Rsch. Assn., Internat. Soc. for Tech. in Edn. Achievements include research in The Effect of Learning Web Site Design on Higher-Order Thinking Skill Development in Fourth Grade Students. Personal E-mail: micnik@aol.com. E-mail: micnik.com.

O'BRIENT, DAVID WARREN, sales executive, consultant; b. Toledo, Oct. 2, 1927; s. Earl James and Jessie Carlton (Edwards) O'B.; m. Enid Jo Wynne O'Brient, Feb. 21, 1962 (div. Apr. 1978); 1 child, David Warren Jr. BS in Archtl. Engring., U. Tex., 1949. Registered profl. engr., Tex. Sales engr. Smith Engring. Co., Houston, 1949-53; dist. sales mgr. Dunham-Bush, Inc., Hartford, Conn., 1953-60; sales mgr. W.L. Lashley & Assoc., Houston, 1960-67; pres., owner OJ & C. Co., Inc., Houston, 1967-78, exec. v.p., 1980-83; pres., owner O'Brient Engring. Co., Houston, 1983-89. Mem., phone solicitor Rep. Party, Houston, 1962—; mem. adminstrv. bd. First United Meth. Ch., Houston, 1969—. With USN, 1945-46, 50-52, PTO, Korea. Mem. ASHRAE, Phi Eta Sigma, Tau Sigma Delta, Tau Beta Pi. Avocations: sports, music. Home and Office: 9550 Ella Lee Ln Apt 811 Houston TX 77063-1238

OBROU, KOUADIO OLIVIER, physics professor, researcher; b. Assié-Orié, Cote d'Ivoire, Jan. 1, 1969; s. Louis Obrou and Antoinette Apo Adouby; m. Leontine Alika Kouadio, Apr. 1, 2000; 1 child, Henoc Kadjo. BS, U. Cocody, Cote d'Ivoire, 1991; MS, U. Cocody, 1993, PhD in atmospheric physics, 1997. Tchg. asst. U. Cocody, asst. prof. Rsch. fellow Internat. Centre Theoretical Physics, Trieste, Italy, 1998—98, NASA Goddard Space Fligt Ctr., Greenbelt, Md., 2001. Mem. U. Teachers Labor Union, Abidjan, Cote d'Ivoire (Ivory Coast), 1998—2003; chmn. Socioeconomic Devel. Mut. Soc., 2003—; vice chair United Meth. Ch. Youth Union, Adzope, 1990—93. Recipient Young Scientist Award, Internat. Union of Radio Sci. (URSI), 1996, 1999, 2002; grantee NSF Grant, 2001, African Sr. Rsch. Scholar Program, US Fulbright Grant, 2003. Fellow: COSPAR/URSI Working Group. Office: University of Cocody Boulevard de l'Université Cocody Abidjan 22 BP 582 Cote d'Ivoire Office Phone: +225 22 44 48 77. Office Fax: +225-22440412. Personal E-mail: okobrou@ifrance.com. E-mail: okobrou@ifrance.com.

O'BRYAN, JAMES A. communications specialist, political organization administrator; BS, Boston U., 1978. Sen. U.S. V.I., 1985-87; dir. youth prevention program Dept. Human Svcs., V.I., 1987-90; press sec. to gov. of V.I. Office of Gov., 1990-95, asst. to gov. pub. affairs, 1999—2003, dist. dir. comms. for congresswoman Christian Christensen, 1997; adminstr. St. Thomas/Water Island, 2003—. Chmn. Dem. State Party, 1998—. Mem. Assn. State Dem. Chairs. Office: PO Box 501 Saint Thomas VI 00804-0501

O'BRYANT, DANIEL R. manufacturing executive; BS in Mgmt. Sci., Calif. State Polytechnic U., Pomona, Calif.; MBA, U. So. Calif. From dir. cap. planning to sr. v.p. fin., CFO Avery Dennison, Pasadena, Calif., 1990—2001, sr. v.p. fin., 2001—, CFO, 2001—. Office: Avery Dennison Corp Ctr 150 North Orange Grove Blvd Pasadena CA 91103-3596

O'BRYANT-SEABROOK, MARLENE LORETTA LINTON, retired educator; b. Newberry, S.C., Aug. 21, 1933; d. Fletcher Arthur and Arabella Greenwood Linton; m. Evans O'Bryant Jr., Apr. 7, 1956 (div. 1968); children: Kim Denise, Evans III, Wayne Anthony, Darryl Fletcher; m. Arthur Herman Seabrook, Feb. 18, 1977. BS, S.C. State U., 1955; MA in Tchg., The Citadel, 1972; PhD, U. S.C., 1975. Cert. elem. edn., learning disabilites, mental retardation, elem. adminstrn., psychology, S.C. Tchr. Columbia (S.C.) Pub. Schs., 1955-57; social investigator Dept. Social Welfare, Bklyn., 1961-62; tchr. Charleston (S.C.) County Schs., 1962-72, dir. diagnostic/prescriptive tchg. program, 1972-75, head spl. edn. H.S., 1980-87; asst. prof. The Citadel, Charleston, 1972-75, 75-80; ret., 1987. Cons. Lake Greenwood Project, Laurens, S.C., 1972-73, Delaware County Intermediate Unit, Media, Pa., 1972-75, State Divsn. Instn., Raleigh, N.C., 1973-77, U. Mass. Spl. Edn. Dept., Amherst, 1975-77, Upward Bound Coll. Charleston, 1978-81, Follow Through program U.S. Ofice Edn., 1972-74. Pres. Avery Inst. African-Am. History and Culture, Charleston, 1990-94, v.p., 1998-99, pres., 1999-2001; bereavement counselor Hospice of Charleston, 1992—, bd. dirs., 1998—; mem. edn. bd. Gibbles Mus. Art, Charleston, 1997—. Mem. League Allied Arts (pres. 1998—), Alpha Kappa Alpha (Gamma Xi Omega chpt. v.p. 1996-98, pres. 1998-2000, Soror of Yr. 1998, 99). Episcopalian. Avocations: quilting, cross-stitching, smocking, knitting, painting. Home: 939 Rutledge Ave Charleston SC 29403-3205 E-mail: marlobs@awod.com.

O'BRYON, JAMES FREDRICK, defense executive; b. Schenectady, N.Y., Oct. 1, 1941; s. Frederick Stanley and Elizabeth Mary O'B.; m. Margaret Adina Bell, Oct 23, 1965; children: Daniel, Douglas, Cris, Kera. BS in Math., King's Coll., Briarcliff, N.Y., 1964; MSA in Ops. Rsch., George Washington U., 1973; SM in Elec. Engring., MIT, 1975. Mathematician Ballistics Rsch. Lab. Aberdeen (Md.) Proving Ground, 1966-74, asst. to dir. Ballistics Rsch. Lab., 1975-76, ops. rsch. analyst smart munitions group Ballistics Rsch. Lab., 1976-79, chmn. red-on-blue working group Joint Tech. Coord. Group, 1979-85, chief combat survivability and tech. U.S. Army Materiel Systems Analysis Activity, 1985-86; asst. dep. undersec. def. Office Sec. Def., Washington, 1986-88, dir. live-fire testing, 1988-95, dep. dir. operational test and evaluation, 1995—2001; chmn. The O'Bryon Group, 2001—, Mobius Bus. Solutions, 2002—. Dir. Live Fire Test Program, Washington, 1986-2001; mem. Conventional Sys. Com., Washington, 1987—; panel mem. NAS, 2000—; newscaster, radio personality WRBS-FM, Balt., 1965-80; chmn. Mobius Bus. Solutions, 2002—. Recorded albums Until Then, 1968, Portrait of a Man, 1972, My Favorite Song, 1977, Celebration of Praise, 1982; co-author: (manual) Red-on-Blue Weapons, Effects, 1983; contbr. over 75 articles to profl. jours. Active edn. coun. MIT, Cambridge, 1980—; trustee Dettmer Charitable Trust, Conn.; bd. dirs. Internat. Bible Soc. Found., Colo.; mem. adv. bd. N.Y. Theol. Sem. With U.S. Army, 1964-66. Named Outstanding Young Man in Am., Jaycees, 1970, Disting. Lectr., Def. Systems Mgmt. Coll., 1988. Fellow Ctr. Advanced Engring. Study MIT; mem. AIAA, Nat. Def. Indsl. Assn. (chmn. Test and Evaluation divsn.), Internat. Test and Evaluation Assn., Sigma Xi. Home: 1608 S Tollgate Rd Bel Air MD 21015-5825 Office Phone: 443-528-2711. Business E-Mail: jamesobryon@obryongroup.com.

O'BRYON, LINDA ELIZABETH, television station executive; b. Washington, Sept. 1, 1949; d. Walter Mason Ormes and Iva Genevieve (Batrus) Ranney; m. Dennis Michael O'Bryon, Sept. 8, 1973; 1 child, Jennifer Elizabeth. BA in Journalism cum laude, U. Miami. News reporter Sta. KCPX (now KTVX), Salt Lake City, 1971-73; documentary and pub. affairs prodr. Sta. WPLG-TV, Miami, Fla., 1974-76; producer, reporter, anchor, news dir. then v.p. for news and pub. affairs, exec. editor, sr. v.p. Nightly Business Report Sta. WPBT (PBS), Miami, 1976—. Recipient award Fla. Bar, Tallahasse, 1977, 2 awards Ohio State U., 1976, 79, award Corp. for Pub. Broadcasting, 1978, Econ. Understanding award Dartmouth Coll., 1980, award Fla. AP, 1981, 1st prize Nat. Assn. Realtors, 1986, Bus. News Luminary award TJFR, 1990, Am. Women in Radio and TV award, 1995, 98, Disting. Achievement award Soc. Am. Bus. Editors and Writers, 2004; named Most Influential Woman Bus. News Exec., TJFR, 2001. Mem. NATAS (past bd. dirs. So. Fla. chpt., regional Emmy award), Radio-TV News Dirs. Assn., Am. Pub. TV (trustee). Republican. Roman Catholic. Avocations: aerobics, tennis, golf. Office: Sta WPBT 14901 NE 20th Ave Miami FL 33181-1121

O'BRYON, MAUREEN, lawyer; b. Marshalltown, Iowa, Apr. 3, 1946; d. Robert Maurice and Ruth Ida (Bratzel) O'B.; m. John P. Rupp, 1968; children: Megan, Erin O'Bryon. BA magna cum laude, U. Iowa, 1968; JD, Georgetown U., 1975. Bar: D.C. 1975, U.S. Supreme Ct. Assoc. Donovan Leisure Newton & Irvine, Washington, 1975-84, ptnr., 1984-86, Hogan & Hartson, Washington, 1986—. Mem. exec. com., trustee Washington Lawyers Com. for Civil Rights and Urban Affairs, Washington, 1977—. Mem. ABA (litigation and antitrust sects.), Phi Beta Kappa, Chi Omega.

OBUCHOWSKA, WIESLAWA TERESA, mathematician, educator; d. Antoni Chrostowski and Maria Chrostowska; children: Peter Obuchowski, Agnes Krystyna. M in Math., U. Wroclaw, Poland, 1970; PhD, Wroclaw U. Econs., 1980; MSc in Applied Math., U. Windsor, Ont., 1990; PhD, U. Windsor, 1995. Asst. and assoc. prof. Wroclaw U. Econs., 1980—90; NSERC postdoctoral fellow Royal Mil. Coll. of Can., Kingston, 1995—96; asst. prof. U. Nebr., Omaha, 1996—99; vis. asst. prof. SUNY, Fredonia, 1999—2000; asst. prof. Chowan Coll., Murfreesboro, NC, 2000—. Contbr. articles to profl. jours. Fellow, Natural Scis. and Engring. Rsch. Coun., 1995—96; postgrad. scholar, 1991—93, grad. scholar, Province of Ont., 1993—94, travel grantee, NSF-AWM, 1999, 2003. Mem.: Math. Programming Soc. Office: Chowan Coll Dept Math 200 Jones Dr Murfreesboro NC 27855 Office Phone: 252-398-6476. Business E-Mail: obuchw@chowan.edu.

OBUCHOWSKI, MICHAEL J. state legislator; b. Bellows Falls, Vt., Feb. 4, 1952; Student, Harvard U. Staff Basketville Inc., Putney, Vt.; mem. Vt. Ho. of Reps., Montpelier, 1973—, spkr., 1995—2001. Former mem. joint energy com., judicial retention com., former chmn. appropriations com., edn. and energy coms., Vt. Ho. of Reps., spkr. of house 1995—; incorporator New Eng. Kurn Hattin Homes; former mem. Vt. Health Policy Corp. Former mem. New Eng. Bd. Higher Edn.; mem. Rockingham and Windham County Dem. Com.; bd. dirs. Rockingham Meml. Hosp. Bd. Mem. Bellows Falls H.S. Alumni Assn. (sec.), Elks. Democrat. Address: 72 Atkinson St Bellows Falls VT 05101-1321 E-mail: obie@leg.state.vt.us.

O'BYRNE, MICHAEL, management consultant; b. Butte, Mont., Dec. 26, 1938; s. Michael E. and Margaret F. (Turner) O'B.; m. Penny L. Graham, Nov. 14, 1964; children: Jennifer L. McLellan, Gregory M. O'Byrne, Andrew G. O'Byrne. BSME, U. Wash., 1961. Cert. engr., Wash. V.p. PACCAR, Inc., Bellevue, Wash., 1969-84; pres. Mobi-Dock, Inc., Mercer Island, Wash., 1985-86; ptnr. The Catalyst Group, Mercer Island, 1986-89; pres. Raima Corp., Bellevue, 1988-89, Pacific North Equiptment Co., Kent, Wash., 1990-95; cons. Master Performance, Inc., Bellevue, 1995-2000, Vehicle Monitor Corp., Redmond, Va., 1996—. Council mem. Hunts Point, Wash., 1980-97; mem. bd. dirs. Mcpl. League of King County, Seattle, 1994-95; dist. chmn. Boy Scouts Am., Seattle, 1994-98; pres. USO Puget Sound Area, 1997-2004. Lt. comdr. USN, 1961-69. Mem. Soc. Automotive Engrs., Assoc. Equipment Distributors (chpt. pres. 1994-95), Rotary Internat., Seattle Yacht Club. Republican. Avocations: sailing, skiing, fishing. Home and Office: 4224 Hunts Point Rd Bellevue WA 98004-1106 E-mail: michael.obyrne@comcast.net.

O'CALLAGHAN, JAMES PATRICK, neuroscientist; b. West Palm Beach, Fla., Mar. 6, 1949; s. James Patrick and Paula Ann (Reinholtz) O'C. BS in Biology, Purdue U., 1971; PhD in Pharmacology, Emory U., 1975. Postdoctoral fellow N.Y. State Office of Drug Abuse Svcs., Bklyn., 1975-78; staff fellow NIH, Bethesda, Md., 1978-81; sr. sci. adviser neurotoxicology divsn., rsch. lab. EPA, Research Triangle Park, N.C., 1981-97; head molecular neurotoxicology CDC-NIOSH, Morgantown, W.Va., 1997—. Cons. N.Y. U. Med. Ctr., N.Y.C., 1986—, Cato Rsch. Ltd., Durham, N.C., 1990—, Rockefeller U., N.Y.C., 1986—. Author more than 120 sci. papers. Mem. Soc. for Neuroscis., Am. Soc. for Pharmacology of Exptl. Therapeutics, Soc. of Toxicology, AAAS, N.Y. Acad. Sci. Office: CDC-NIOSH 1095 Willowdale Rd Morgantown WV 26505-2845 Office Phone: 304-285-6079. Business E-Mail: jdo5@cdc.gov.

O'CALLAGHAN, JERRY ALEXANDER, government official; b. Klamath Falls, Oreg., Feb. 23, 1922; s. Jeremiah Patrick and Marie Jane (Alexander) O'C.; m. Florence Marie Sheehan, Aug. 6, 1949; children— Jane Mary, Susan Margaret. BS with honors, U. Oreg., 1943, MA with honors, 1947; PhD, Stanford, 1951. Acting instr. history Stanford, 1951-52, U. Wyo., 1952-53; oil editor Tribune-Herald, Casper, Wyo., 1953-55; acting asst. prof. U. Wyo., 1955-56; legis. asst. to Senator Joseph O'Mahoney (Wyo.), 1956-60; exec. asst. to Senator Joseph Hickey(Wyo.), 1961; asst. dir. lands and minerals mgmt. Bur. Land Mgmt., Dept. Interior, 1961-62, asst. dir. plans and legislation, 1962-64, chief legislation and coop. relations, 1964-69, chief div. coop. relations, 1969-80, chief hist. studies, 1980-82, historian emeritus, 1982—. Author: Disposition of the Public Domain in Oregon, 1960, America

200— The Legacy of Our Lands, 1976. Bd. govs. St. Columba's Episc. Nursery Sch., 1959-71; vestryman Episc. Ch., 1964-68, outreach leader, 1985-90; lay ministry St. Columba's, 1990—. With AUS, 1943-46. Mem. Soc. of Forest History, Fed. Profl. Assn. (pres. 1972), Fossils, Phi Kappa Psi. Home: 5607 Chesterbrook Rd Bethesda MD 20816-1301

O'CALLAGHAN, R.J. PATRICK, lawyer; b. Mpls., Aug. 8, 1924; s. Robert Desmond and Claire Marie (Moe) O'C.; married Albina Julie Sepich, June 4, 1949; children: Michael, Edward, Catherine, Diana, Robert, Daniel. BA, Drake U., 1949; JD, U. Denver, 1951. Bar: Colo. 1951, U.S. Dist. Ct. Colo. 1956, U.S. Tax Ct. 1971, U.S. Ct. Appeals (10th cir.) 1978. Pvt. practice law, Denver, 1952-53, Rangely, Colo., 1953-63; real estate broker Grand Junction, Colo., 1963-65; ptnr. Bellinger, Faricy, Tursi & O'Callaghan, Pueblo, Colo., 1965-73; pvt. practice law Pueblo, 1973-76; ptnr. Lattimer, O'Callaghan & Ware P.C., Pueblo, 1978-81; of counsel Quiet & Dice, Denver, 1981-83; pvt. practice law Pueblo, 1983—. Atty. Town of Rangely, 1953-63; bd. atty. Pueblo Bd. Realtors, 1971-82; instr. real estate U. Colo., 1968-79; sr. cert. valuer Internat. Real Estate Inst. Pres. Homes for Sr. Citizens Inc., Pueblo, 1978-80; pres. Mt. Carmel Credit Union, 1972-74; adv. bd. dirs. Pueblo Salvation Army, 1987-91. With USNR, 1943-46. Mem. ABA, Colo. Bar Assn., Pueblo County Bar Assn., Nat. Network Estate Planning Attys., Elks (exalted ruler Rangley Lodge No. 1907). Republican. Roman Catholic. Avocation: photography. Address: 125 E 7th Ste 100 Pueblo CO 81003-3407 Office Phone: 719-543-8371. E-mail: patoc@qwest.net.

O'CALLAGHAN, WILLIAM LAWRENCE, JR., lawyer; b. Atlanta, Aug. 6, 1941; s. William Lawrence and Martha Kathryn (Fitzpatrick) O'Callaghan; m. Bonnie Faye Whitmire, Dec. 18, 1964; children: Diana Lee, John Patrick, Michael Lawrence. BBA, U. Ga., 1963, JD cum laude, 1965; LLM in Taxation, Georgetown U., 1968. Bar: Ga. 1965, U.S. Supreme Ct. 1971. Assoc. Sutherland, Asbill & Brennan, Atlanta, 1965; ptnr. Gambrell, Russell et al, Atlanta, 1968-74; chmn. O'Callaghan, Saunders & Stumm, Atlanta, 1974-90; ptnr. Branch, Pike, Ganz & O'Callaghan, Atlanta, 1990—93, O'Callaghan & Stumm LLP, 1993—2002, Alston & Bird, LLP, Atlanta, 2002—. Bd. dirs. Atlanta Jr. Golf Assn., pres., 1987—88; bd. dirs. Phoenix Soc. Atlanta, 1985—87. Served to capt. U.S. Army, 1965—68. Mem.: ABA (chmn. 1983—89, mem. com. fed. tax real property sect., mem. real property sect., mem. tax sect.), State Bar Ga., Atlanta Bar Assn., Atlanta Estate Planning Coun., Sandy Springs (Ga.) C. of C. (bd. dirs. 1982—83), Atlanta Athletic Club (bd. dirs. 1987—96, pres. 1992—94), Optimists (pres. Sandy Springs chpt. 1978), Rotary (v.p. Sandy Springs chpt. 1986, mem. Robert R. Jones, Jr. scholarship com. 1992—). Avocations: golf, travel, model building. Office: Alston & Bird LLP 1201 W Peachtree St Atlanta GA 30309-3424 Office Phone: 404-881-7818.

OCASIO, WILFRED, writer; b. Bklyn., Mar. 17, 1969; s. Wilfredo Juarbe Ocasio and Carmen Gloria (Moles) Reyes. Diploma in engring., Oberlin (Ohio) Coll., 1991. Video co-star Tom of Videocraft, Bklyn., 1987; burlesque performer Gaiety, N.Y.C., 1987; waiter Grand Prospect Hall, Bklyn., 1990; freelance author Liberty of Congress, Washington, 1990—. Decorated Gold Stars and Stripes Mil. Mem.: ISKCON. Avocations: Spanish, creative writing, exercise, dance, music. Home: 807 8th Ave Apt 2F Brooklyn NY 04215-4118 Office Phone: 417-623-5016.

OCASIO-MELENDEZ, MARCIAL ENRIQUE, history professor; b. San Juan, P.R., Aug. 22, 1942; s. Manuel C. and Amparo (Melendez) Ocasio; m. Mimi Rivera, Apr. 15, 1973 (div. 1976). BA, U. P.R., 1964, MA, 1977; PhD, Mich. State U., 1988. Tchr. sci. P.R. Dept. Edn., San Juan, 1966-67; tchr. sci., history Nyack (N.Y.) Schs., 1967-71; tchr. sci. Robinson Prep. Sch., Condado, P.R., 1971-72; instr. P.R. Jr. Coll., Rio Piedras, 1972-80; teaching asst. Mich. State U., E. Lansing, 1979-83; instr. history Caribbean U., Bayamon, P.R., 1983-85; instr. Inter Am. U., Bayamon, 1985-87, U. P.R., Rio Piedras, 1983-87; vis. asst. prof. Mich. State U., E. Lansing, 1987-88; asst. prof. history U. Mich., Flint, 1988-91; prof. history U. P.R., Rio Piedras, 1991—, dir. grad. program history, 1991-93, assoc. dean acad. affairs Coll. Humanities, 1993-95, dir. internat. rels., 1995—2001; prof. Ctr. Advanced Grad. Studies P.R. and The Caribbean; chair, dept. history U. P.R., Rio Piedras, 2004—. Vis. prof. U. Zaragoza, Spain, 2001; bd. dirs. Spanish Speaking Info. Ctr., Flint; lectr. Universidad del Valle, Cali, Universidad de Los Andes, Bogota, Universidad Pedagogica Nacional, Tunja, U. del Norte Barranquilla, Colombia; dir. Rockefeller Found. Caribbean 2000 Project, U. P.R., 1994-95, Urban Preservation Project of Rio Piedras, P.R., 1994-95; pres. P.R.'s Bd. Hist. Preservation, 1999—; mem. editl. bd. Caribbean Studies, 1994-99. Author: Rio Piedras Notas, 1985, Las Americas, Su Tierra, Su Gente, 1997, Capitalism and Development, Tampico 1876-1924, 1998. Pres. P.R. Bd. Hist. Preservation, 1999-2002. Mich. State U. scholar 1981, urban affairs grantee, 1982-83; Fulbright scholar (Colombia) 1989, 90, 2001-; Fulbright scholar specialist, 2002—; NEH fellow, 1973, 78-79, 91, 2002-. Mem. Social Sci. Studies Assn., Coun. L.Am. History, Am. Hist. Assn., L.Am. Studies Assn., Assn. P.R. Historians (pres. 1995-97), Joint Border Rsch. Inst., Assn. Caribean Historians, Caribbean Studies Assn., Hispanic Coun. on Internat. Rels., Phi Alpha Theta. Office: Univ PR History Dept PO Box 23350 San Juan PR 00931-3350 Office Phone: 787-764-0000 3777. Personal E-mail: kokoroko9@hotmail.com.

OCCHIATO, MICHAEL ANTHONY, city official; b. Pueblo, Colo. s. Joseph Michael and Joan Occhiato; m. Peggy Ann Stefonowicz, June 27, 1964 (div. Sept. 1983); children: Michael, James, Jennifer. BBA, U. Denver, 1961; MBA, U. Colo., 1984; postgrad., U. So. Colo. Grad. Real Estate Inst. Sales mgr. Tivoli Brewing co., Denver, 1965-67, acting brewmaster, prodn. control mgr., 1967-68, plant mgr., 1968-69; adminstrv. mgr. King Resources Co., Denver, 1969-70; ops. mgr. Canners Inc., Pepsi-Cola Bottling Co., Pueblo, 1970-76; pres. Pepsi-Cola Bottling Co., Pueblo, 1978-82; gen. mgr. Pepsi-Cola Bottling Group div. PepsiCo., Pueblo, 1982, area v.p., 1982-83; ind. cons. Pueblo, 1983—; broker assoc. Sound Venture Realty, Pueblo, 1996-98, Jones Healy Better Homes & Gardens, 1998—. V.p. Colo. Soft Drink Assn., 1978, pres., 1979; regional dir. Pepsi Cola Mgmt. Inst. divsn. Pepsi Co., 1979-82; pres. Ethnic Foods Internat. dba Taco Rancho, Pueblo, Exodus 20, 1996—; chmn. Weifang (China) Sister City Del., 1991—; bd. dirs. Pueblo Diversified Industries, Pueblo Crime Stoppers, Pueblo Regional Bldg; rancher, 1976—; land devel. real estate broker assoc., 1996—; real estate designator, GRI, CRS. Mem. Pueblo City Coun., 1978—93, 2001—, pres., 1986—87, 1991; mem. Pueblo Bd. Health, 1978—80, Pueblo Regional Planning Commn., 1980—81, Pueblo Action Inc., 1978—80, Pueblo Planning and Zoning Commn., 1985; chmn. Pueblo Area Coun. Govts., 1980—82; mem. Pueblo Econ. Devel. Corp., 1983—91; chmn. fundraising Pueblo chpt. Am. Heart Assn., 1983—; active Earth Wise Pueblo, 1991; pres. Pueblo City Coun., 2002; bd. dirs. Pueblo Urban Renewal Authority, 1993—; mem. Pueblo Regional Bldg. Bd., 2003—; bd. dirs. Pueblo Crime Stoppers, 2001—, El Pueblo Boys Ranch; v.p. Colo. Soft Drink Assn., 1979—80, pres., 1980—81; del. 1st World Conf. Local Elected Ofcls. to 1st UN Internat. Coun. for Local Environ. Initiative. Lt. USN, 1961—65. Mem. So. Colo. Emergency Med. Technicians Assn. (pres. 1975), Am. Saler Assn., Am. Quarter Horse Assn., Colo. Cattle Assn., Pueblo C. of C., Rotary, Pi Kappa Alpha (v.p. 1960). Home and Office: 11 Harrogate Ter Pueblo CO 81001-1723

OCHEJ, HELEN WANDA, biologist, researcher, information scientist; b. Treysa, Germany, Oct. 3, 1946; d. Frank Ochej and Luba Kopytko; m. David R. Sutkoff, Aug. 30, 1980; 1 child, Anne Q. Sutkoff. BS, Lycoming Coll., Williamsport, PA, 1968. Rsch. asst. McNeil Labs, Fort Washington, Pa., 1968—72, Max Planck Inst. Brain Rsch., Koln, Germany, 1972—74, U. Rochester Cancer Ctr., Rochester, NY, 1975—85, supr. facility, 1975—85; contract med. indexer Kessler, Herner, Caelum, Rockville, Md., 1986—95; tech. info. specialist Nat. Libr. Medicine, Bethesda, Md., 1995—. Pres. Grad. Women Sci., Rochester, NY, 1978—79; focus group NLM Exhibit, Md., 2001—01; treas. Am. Soc. Indexers, Md., 2002—. Contbr. articles to profl. jours. V.p. Neighborhood Assn., Rochester, NY, 1978—79; adv. bd. Gifted and Talented Edn., Montgomery County, Md., 1991—95; active Seneca Valley Pony Club, Md., 1996—98. Grantee Rsch. Grant, Max Planck Inst., 1972-1974. Mem.: Am. Soc. Indexers, Am. Med. Writers Assn. Avocations: gardening, tibetan meditation, yoga, travel, hiking. Office: National Library of Medicine 8600 Rockville Pike Bethesda MD 20894 E-mail: helen.ochej@nlm.nih.gov.

OCHELTREE, RICHARD LAWRENCE, lawyer, retired forest products company executive; b. Springfield, Ill., Oct. 9, 1931; s. Chalmer Myerly and Helen Margaret (Camm) O.; m. Ann Maureen Washburn, Apr. 11, 1958; children: Kirstin Ann, Lorraine Page, Tracy Lynn. AB, Harvard U., 1953, LL.B., 1958. Bar: Calif. 1959. Sec., gen. counsel Am. Forest Products Corp./Bendix Forest Products Corp., San Francisco, 1961-81; v.p. adminstrn., sec., gen. counsel Am. Forest Products Co., 1981-87. Served with USAF, 1953-55. Mem. Am., San Francisco bar assns. Home: 1446 Floribunda Ave Apt 102 Burlingame CA 94010-3810

OCHMANEK, DAVID ALAN, defense analyst; b. Oak Park, Ill., Apr. 10, 1951; s. Edwin Joseph and Phyllis Jean (Straass) O.; m. Barbara Jane Larson, June 16, 1973; children: James Edwin, Anne Skaaden. BS in Internat. Affairs, Polit. Sci., USAF Acad., 1973; MPA in Pub. Affairs and Internat. Rels., Princeton U., 1980. Fgn. svc. officer U.S. Dept. State, 1980-85; profl. staff The Rand Corp., 1985-93, 95—; dep. asst. sec. of def. for strategy Washington, 1993-95; sr. def. analyst The RAND Corp., Washington, 1995—. Author: Military Operations Against Terrorist Groups Abroad, 2003, NATO's Future: Implications for U.S. Military Capabilities and Force Posture, 2000; co-author: (with Edward L. Warner III) Next Moves: An Arms Control Agenda for the 1990's, 1989, (with Christopher Bowie et al) The New Calculus, 1993, (with Zalmay Khalilzad) Strategic Appraisal, 1997, (with Edward Harshberger el at) To Find and Not to Yield, 1998, (with Anthony Lake) The Real and the Ideal, 2001; contbr. articles to profl. jours., chpts. to books. Capt. USAF, 1973-78. Lutheran. Office: The RAND Corp 1200 S Hayes St Arlington VA 22202-5050 Office Phone: 703-413-1100.

OCHOA, ARTHUR J. lawyer, hospital administrator; b. LA, Calif., Sept. 16, 1968; s. Arthur P. and Josephine E. Ochoa; m. Daniele J. Worth, Jan. 25, 1998; children: Madeleine Worth, Eloise Worth. BA, U. of So. California, 1986—90; JD, Yale Law Sch., 1992—95. Bar: State of Calif. 1995. Policy coord. Youth Svc. Am., Washington, 1990—92; assoc. O'Melveny & Myers LLP, LA, Calif., 1995—98; atty. Irell & Manella LLP, Century City, 1998—2001; dir. of planned giving Cedars-Sinai Med. Ctr., LA, 2001—04, sr. v.p. cmty. rels., 2004—. Mem. and sec., bd. of directors Youth Svc. Am., Washington, 1997—98; adj. faculty mem., mba program U. of Judiasm, LA, 2001—; adv. bd. mem. Neopets Found., Glendale, 2001—. Vice chmn. tax exempt orgn. com. LA County Bar Assn., 1998; mem., bd. of trustees Mexican Am. Bar Found., LA, 2002. Mem.: Nat. Eagle Scout Assn., Yale Club of N.Y.C., Phi Beta Kappa. Office: Cedars-Sinai Medical Ctr 8700 Beverly Blvd TSB 190 Los Angeles CA 90048 E-mail: ochoaa@cshs.org.

OCHOA, ELLEN, astronaut; b. L.A., May 10, 1958; d. Roseanne Ochoa; m. Coe Fulmer Miles; one son. BS in Physics, San Diego State U., 1980; MSEE, Stanford U., 1981, PhD in EE, 1985. Rsch. engr. Sandia Nat. Labs., Livermore, Calif., 1985—88; chief intelligent systems tech. br. NASA/Ames Rsch. Ctr./Moffet Field Naval Air Sta., Mountain View, Calif.; Astronaut NASA, Houston, 1991—, dep. dir., flight crew ops. Recipient two Space Act Tech Brief Awards, 1992, Space Flight Medals 1993, 1994, 1999, 2002; Outstanding Leadership Medal, 1995, Exceptional Svc. Medal, 1997, Women in Aerospace Outstanding Achievement Award, the Hispanic Engr. Albert Baez Award for Outstanding Tech. Contribution to Humanity, the Hispanic Heritage Leadership Award, San Diego State U. Alumna of the Year. Mem. Optical Soc. Am., Am. Inst. Aeronautics and Astronautics, Phi Beta Kappa, Sigma Xi, Pres. Commn. on the Celebration of Women in Am. History. Achievements include being the first female Hispanic astronaut chosen for Space Shuttle program. Office: NASA Johnson Space Ctr Astronaut Office Houston TX 77058*

OCHOA, MANUEL, JR., oncologist; b. N.Y.C., Apr. 22, 1930; s. Manuel and Maria (Diaz) O.; m. Suzanne Ellen Recca, Sept. 1, 1956; children: Elizabeth, Suzanne Elise. AB, Columbia Coll., 1951; MD, Columbia U., 1955. Diplomate Am. Bd. Internal Medicine; lic. physician, N.Y., Mass. Asst. in medicine U. Rochester (N.Y.) Med. Sch., 1958-61; instr. medicine, assoc., asst. prof. Columbia U., N.Y.C., 1964-68; attending physician Meml. Sloan-Kettering Cancer Ctr., N.Y.C., 1973—. Investigator Marine Biol. Lab., Woods Hole, Mass., 1965; assoc. prof. clin. medicine Cornell U., N.Y.C., 1982-96, prof., 1996—; cons. Harlem Hosp. Ctr., N.Y.C., 1966-68, Kingston (N.Y.) Hosp., 1970-85; vis. prof. U. Hawaii, Honolulu, 1971, U. Mex., Mexico City, 1979. Contbr. articles to profl. jours. Capt. USAF, 1956-58, ETO. Fellow Lalor Found., 1965. Fellow ACP, ACS. Republican. Roman Catholic. Achievements include discovering genetic code and protein synthesis in cancer cells, cancer chemotherapy. Home: 82 E Middle Patent Rd Bedford NY 10506-2106 Office: Meml Sloan-Kettering Cancer Ctr 1271 York Ave New York NY 10021-6007

OCHOA-BRILLEMBOURG, HILDA MARGARITA, investment banker; b. July 8, 1944; BS in Econs., U. Catolica Andres Bello, Caracas, Venezuela; MPA, Harvard U.; postgrad. in fin., Harvard Bus. Sch. Chief investment officer, pension investment div. World Bank, 1976—87; mng. dir. Emerging Markets Investment Corp.; founder, pres., CEO Strategic Investment Group, 1987—. Bd. dirs. Harvard Mgmt. Co., World Bank / Internat. Monetary Fund Credit Union, Gen. Mills, Inc., McGraw-Hill Inc.; treas. C.A. Luz Electrica de Venezuela, Caracas, 1967—71; lectr. U. Catolica Andres Bello, 1970; ind. cons. in econs. and fin. Published articles in Fin. Analyst Jour. and Pensions & Investments. Bd. dirs. Nat. Symphony Orch., Washington Opera, Cath. Charities Found.; chmn. bd. dirs. Youth Orch. of the Americas; mem. investment com. Rockefeller Family Fund; vice chair, Group of 50 Carnegie Endowment for Internat. Peace; mem. adv. com. Rockefeller Ctr. for Latin Am. Studies, The Hauser Ctr. at Harvard U., Small Enterprise Asst. Funds. Named one of Top 50 Hispanic Women in Bus., Hispanic Mag., Top 50 Smartest Women in Bus., Money Mag., 2000; Fulbright-Hays fellow. Office: 1001 19th St N 16th Fl Arlington VA 22209-1722 Office Phone: 703-243-4433.

OCHS, CAROL REBECCA, theologian, philosophy and religion educator; b. N.Y.C., May 7, 1939; d. Herman and Clara Florence (Michaels) Blumenthal; m. Michael Ochs, Sept. 27, 1959; children: Elisabeth Amy, Miriam Adina. BA, CUNY, 1960, MA, 1964; PhD, Brandeis U., 1968. Philosophy lectr. CUNY, 1964-65; from asst. prof. to prof. philosophy Simmons Coll., Boston, 1967-92, prof. emerita, 1992—. Adj. faculty Grad. Sch. Union Inst., Cin., 1992—97, Hebrew Union Coll.-Jewish Inst. Religion, N.Y.C., 1994—97, dir. grad. studies, vis. prof. philosophy, 1997—2001, dir. grad. studies, adj. prof. Jewish Religious Thought, 2001—; cons. Inst. for Svc. to Higher Edn., Chestnut Hill, Mass., 1972, St. Mary's Coll., South Bend, Ind., 1980; scholar-in-residence Hollins Coll., Roanoke, Va., 1987, numerous temples and synagogues; mem. selection com. Kent Postdoctoral Fellowships Bunting Inst., Radcliffe Coll.; lectr. in field. Author: Behind the Sex of God: Toward a New Consciousness Transcending Matriarchy and Patriarchy, 1977, Women and Spirituality, 1983, 2d edit., 1997, An Ascent to Joy: Transforming Deadness of Spirit, 1989, The Noah Paradox: Time as Burden, Time as Blessing, 1991, Song of the Self: Biblical Spirituality and Human Holiness, 1994, Jewish Spiritual Guidance, 1997, Our Lives as Torah: Finding God in Our Own Stories, 2001, Reaching Godward: Voices from Jewish Spiritual Guidance, 2004; contbr. articles to profl. jours. Mem. Jewish-Cath. Dialogue, Boston, 1989-93; mem. Cath.-Jewish com. Archdiocese of Boston, 1989-93. Fellow NEH, 1976, 88, Nat. Humanities Inst., U. Chgo., 1978-79, Danforth Found., 1981-86, Coolidge Rsch., Colloquium, 1985, Resource Theologian, 1995-99. Fellow Soc. for Values in Higher Edn. (bd. dirs. 1982-88, chair ctrl. com. 1985-87, v.p. 2004-), Assn. for Religion and Intellectual Life (mem. editl. bd. 1986—). Office: Hebrew Union Coll 1 W 4th St New York NY 10012 Office Phone: 212-824-2267.

OCHS, ELINOR, linguistics educator; Prof. dept. TESL and applied linguistics UCLA. Co-editor: Developmental Pragmatics, 1979, Language Socialization Across Cultures, 1986, Interaction with Grammar, 1996; author: Culture and Language Development: Language Acquisition and Language Socialization in a Samoan Village, 1988, (with L. Capps) Constructing Panic, The Discourse of Agoraphobia, 1995; contbr. articles to profl. publs. MacArthur fellow J.D. and C.T. MacArthur Found.; grantee NSF, 1986-89, Nat. Inst. Child Health and Devel., 1986-89, Spencer Found., 1990-93, 94-97, U.S. Dept. Edn., 1993-96 Achievements include research on discourse structures, grammar in context, language and affect, spoken and written language, cross-cultural communication. Office: UCLA Dept Applied Linguistics TESL 330 Rolfe Hall Room 3326 PO Box 951531 Los Angeles CA 90095-1531

OCHS, MICHAEL, editor, librarian, music educator; b. Cologne, Germany, Feb. 1, 1937; came to U.S., 1939, naturalized, 1945; s. Isaac Julius and Claire (Baum) O.; m. Carol Rebecca Blumenthal, Sept. 27, 1959; children—Elisabeth Amy, Miriam Adina BA, CCNY, 1958; MS, Columbia U., 1963; A.M., NYU, 1964; D.A., Simmons Coll., 1975. Cataloguer CCNY, 1963-65, lectr. in music, 1964; music libr. Brandeis U., Waltham, Mass., 1965-68, creative arts libr., 1968-74; asst. prof. libr. sci. Simmons Coll., Boston, 1974-78; libr. Eda Kuhn Loeb Music Libr., Harvard U., Cambridge, Mass., 1978-88, Richard F. French libr., 1988-92; lectr. music Harvard U., Cambridge, Mass., 1978-81, sr. lectr. music, 1981-92, also libr. cons., 1977-78; music editor W. W. Norton and Co., N.Y.C., 1992-2001; pres. Ochs Editl., 2001—. Libr. cons. Biblioteca Berenson, Florence, Italy, 1983, Columbia U., 1987; project dir. U.S. Répertoire International des Sources Musicales Manuscript Inventory Ctr. at Harvard U., NEH, Cambridge, Mass., 1985-88. Editor Notes, Jour. Music Libr. Assn., 1987-92, Music Librarianship in America, 1991; contbr. articles to profl. jours., 1976—. Mem. Am. Musicol. Soc. (bd. dirs. 2000-02), Internat. Assn. Music Librs. (pres. rsch. librs. br. 1987-90), Music Libr. Assn. (chmn. New Eng. chpt. 1968-69, chmn. com. on bibliog. description 1971-73, chmn. music libr. adminstrn. com. 1975-76, chmn. fin. com. 1976-78, bd. dirs. 1976-78, chmn. publs. com. 1983-87, pres. 1993-95). Office Phone: 212-987-1089.

OCHS, RICHARD WAYNE, artist, gallery owner; b. Newburgh, NY, Dec. 26, 1938; s. Harold John Ochs and Gertrude Adelaid Goetchius; m. Cindy Ochs, Apr. 14, 1968. AB in Econs. and Math., Hamilton Coll., 1960; postgrad., SUNY, New Paltz, 1961-70. Cert. secondary tchr., N.Y. Math. tchr. Newburgh Sch. Dist., 1960-92; artist, owner Richard Ochs Gallery, Newburgh, 1993—. Represented by Art Nook Gallery, Newburgh, 1979-93, Gallery Frame Shop, New Paltz, N.Y., 1996-, Jordane Artworks, Fort Myers Beach, Fla., 1998-2003, Nadeja Gallery, Newport, R.I., 2001—, Watermark Gallery, Tuckerton, NJ, 2003-; mem. Coast Guard Artists' Program. Treas. Newburgh Tchrs.' Assn., 1965; pres. Dutchess County Art Assn., Poughkeepsie, N.Y., 1979, trustee, 1975-76. Staff sgt. N.Y. ARNG, 1963-69. Recipient Grumbacher Gold medal Mt. St. Mary Coll., 1997, 98, George Gray award USCG. Fellow Am. Artist's Profl. League; mem. Artist's Fellowship, Hudson Valley Art Assn. (bd. dirs.), Kent Art Assn. (exec. bd. 1996—, 2d v.p. 1999-2000), North East Watercolor Soc. (treas. 1984-94, 1st v.p. 1995-97, pres. 1997-2002, 1st v.p., 2003—, trustee 2001—), Mo. Watercolor Soc. (signature), Cmty. Arts Assn. (exec. bd. 1996—), Soc. Creative Artists of Newtown, Middletown, NY Artist's Group, Watercolor Soc. Ala., Soc. Marine Artists, Artist's Fellowship, Ctrl. NY Watercolor Soc., Morris County Art Assn. (tchg. faculty 2003—), Salmagundi Club. Home and Office: 62 Dalfonso Rd Newburgh NY 12550-7203 Office Phone: 914-561-8489. E-mail: ROchsWcrGallery@aol.com.

OCHS, SIDNEY, neurophysiology educator; b. Fall River, Mass., June 30, 1924; s. Nathan and Rose (Kniaz) O.; m. Bess Ratner; children: Rachel F., Raymond S. Susan B. PhD, U. Chgo., 1952. Rsch. assoc. Ill. Neuropsychiat. Inst., Chgo., 1952-54; rsch. fellow Calif. Inst. Tech., Pasadena, 1954-56; asst. prof. dept. physiology U. Tex. Med. Br., Galveston, 1956-58; assoc. prof. dept. physiology Ind. U., Indpls., 1958-61, prof., 1961-94, prof. emeritus, 1994—. Author: Elements of Neurophysiology, 1965, Axoplasmic Transport and Its Relation to Other Nerve Functions, 1982, A History of Nerve Functions: From Animal Spirits to Molecular Mechanisms, 2004; founding editor, editor-in-chief Jour. Neurobiology, 1969-76, assoc. editor, 1977-86. Served with U.S. Army, 1943-45 Mem. Internat. Brain Rsch. Orgn., Internat. Soc. Neurochemistry, Internat. Soc. Hist. Neurosciences, Am. Physiol. Soc., Soc. Neurosci., Am. Soc. Neurochemistry, Peripheral Nerve Soc., Hist. Sci. Soc. Democrat. Jewish. Office: Ind U Med Ctr Dept Cellular & Integ Physiology 635 Barnhill Dr Indianapolis IN 46202-5126 Office Phone: 317-274-7940. Business E-Mail: sochs@iupui.edu.

OCHS, WALTER J. civil engineer, consultant; b. Springfield, Minn., May 20, 1934; s. Walter Minrod and Cleo (Schultz) O.; m. Connie Mae Strate, Sept. 15, 1956; children: Julie, Brian. BS in Agrl. Engring., South Dakota U., 1957. Registered profl. civil engr., Mich. Engr. in training USDA, Soil Conservation Svc., Watertown, S.D., 1957-58, project engr. Britton, S.D., 1958-61, area engr. Sioux Falls, S.D., 1961-63, asst. state conservation engr. East Lansing, Mich., 1963-66, state conservation engr., 1966-69, asst. state conservationist Saint Paul, Minn., 1969-71, nat. drainage engr. Washington, 1971-86; drainage adviser World Bank, Washington, 1986-96; internat. ind. water mgmt. cons., 1996—. Bd. dirs. Internat. Inst. for Land Reclamation and Improvement Postgrad Land Drainage Course, The Netherlands, 1990-98; particpated in project work over 30 countries; mem. Internat. Commn. Irrigation and Drainage. Contbr. to profl. jours. Named Federal Engr. Of The Year, Nat. Soc. Profl. Engrs., 1982; recipient Outstanding Alumnus award South Dakota State Univ., 1977, Outstanding Contributions award Corrugated Plastic Tubing Assn., 1981; named to Internat. Drainage Hall of Fame, 1996. Fellow: Am. Soc. Agrl. Engrs.; mem.: ASCE (chmn. drainage com. 1975—76, Royce J. Tipton award 2001). Office: 6731 Fern Ln Annandale VA 22003-1903

OCHSNER, JOHN LOCKWOOD, thoracic-cardiovascular surgeon; b. Madison, Wis., Feb. 10, 1927; s. Edward William Alton and Isabel (Lockwood) O.; m. Mary Lou Hannon, Mar. 20, 1954; children: John L., Joby Hannon, Katherine Lockwood, Frank Hannon. MD, Tulane U., 1952. Diplomate Am. Bd. Thoracic Surgery (chmn. 1993-95), Am. Bd. Surgery, Am. Bd. Vascular Surgery. Intern Univ. Mich. Hosp., Ann Arbor, 1952-53, resident, 1953-54, Baylor U. Affiliated Hosp., Houston, 1956-58, 1958-59; chief surg. resident Tex. Children's Hosp., 1959-60; instr. Baylor U., Houston, 1960-61; mem. staff Ochsner Clinic, New Orleans, 1961—, chmn. dept. surgery, 1966-87, chmn. emeritus dept surgery, 1987—; clin. asst. prof. Tulane U., New Orleans, 1961-65, clin. assoc. prof., 1965-70, clin. prof. surgery, 1970—. Author: (with others) Coronary Artery Surgery, 1978. Pres. Tennis Patrons Assn. New Orleans, 1972; image amb. City of New Orleans, 1982; bd. dirs. Internat. Trade Mart, New Orleans, 1983. Capt. USAF, 1954-56. Recipient award Life Mag., 1961, Golden Plate Acad. Achievement award, 1962, medal of honor, Ecuador, 1981. Mem. Internat. Soc. Cardiovascular Surgery (pres. N.Am. chpt. 1983-84, internat. pres. 1989-91), Am. Assn. Thoracic Surgery (sec. 1979-83, pres. 1992-93), New Orleans Surg. Soc. (pres. 1977-78), So. Surg. Assn. (pres. 1991), So. Assn. for Vascular Surgery (pres. 1983), Boston Club, La. Club, New Orleans Country Club, City Club, Alpha Omega Alpha. Republican. Home: 84 Audubon Blvd New Orleans LA 70118-5540 Office: Ochsner Clinic Found 1514 Jefferson Hwy New Orleans LA 70121-2483

OCHSNER, OTHON HENRY, II, importer, restaurant critic; b. Chgo., May 19, 1934; s. Othon Henry and Louise Catherine (Schlichenmaier) O. AA, Chgo. City Coll., 1961. Pub. rels. staff Walgreen Co., Chgo., 1961-65; sales mgr. Porsche Car Imports, Northbrook, Ill., 1966-67; nat. sales mgr. Pirelli Tire Corp., N.Y.C., 1968-73; pres., CEO Ochsner Internat., Chgo., 1974—. Bd.dirs., pres. Swiss-U.S.A. Racing Team, Chgo., 1976—. Author: Ochsner Pocket Guide to the Finest Restaurants and Hotels in the World, 1st edit.; author Ochsner Restaurant Newsletters, 1986—. Pres., exec. dir. Louise Catherine Schlichenmaier and Othon Henry Ochsner I Charitable Family Found., 2000—. With U.S. Army, 1957-59. Mem. The Am. Inst. Wine and Food, Am.-Swiss C. of C., Swiss-Am. Hist. Soc., Swiss Gourmet Soc. (pres. U.S. chpt.), Swiss Travel Club, Swiss Club Chgo., The Bagatelle Club, Conf. de la Chaine des Rotisseurs, Ordre des Canariers. Baptist. Avocation: visiting and reviewing world class french and swiss restaurants worldwide. Home: 701 Bluff Rd Lake Bluff IL 60044-2116 Office: The Ochsner Bldg 246 E Marquardt Dr Wheeling IL 60090-6430

OCHSNER, SEYMOUR FISKE, radiologist, editor; b. Chgo., Nov. 29, 1915; s. Albert Henry Ochsner and Fleda Fiske; m. Helen Keith, Sept. 8, 1945 (dec. Jan. 1976); children: Anne, Diana, Lida; m. Bobbie Sue Mercer, Dec. 31, 1981 (dec. Jan. 1997). AB, Dartmouth Coll., 1937; MD, U. Pa., Phila., 1947. Diplomate Am. Bd. Radiology, 1953. Intern Johnston-Willis Hosp., Richmond, Va., 1949-50; staff radiologist Ochsner Clinic, New Orleans, 1953-90, also chmn. dept., 1969-77; clin. prof. radiology Tulane Med. Sch., New Orleans, 1955-75; editor Orleans Parish Med. Bulletin, New Orleans, 1985-91. Contbr. articles to profl. jours. Pres. PTA, Metairie, La., 1964. Recipient Disting. Svc. medal So. Med. Assn., 1972, Disting. Svc. award AMA, 1993, fellow, Alton Ochsner Med. Found., New Orleans, 1950-53. Mem. Radiol. Soc. La. (pres. 1965), So. Radiol. Conf. (pres. 1968), Am. Coll. Radiology (pres. 1972, Gold medal 1982), Am. Roentgen Ray Soc. (pres. 1975, Gold medal 1986), Rex Orgn., So. Yacht Club, Candlewood Club. Republican. Episcopalian. Avocations: reading, gardening, travel, sailing. Home: 107 Holly Dr Metairie LA 70005-3915

OCKERBLOOM, RICHARD C. newspaper executive; b. Medford, Mass., Dec. 19, 1929; s. Carl F. and Helen C. (Haraden) O.; m. Anne Joan Torpey, Sept. 17, 1955; children: Catherine, Carl, Gail, Mark, John, Peter. BSBA, Northeastern U., 1952; D Pub. Svc. (hon.), Westfield State Coll., 1989; LLD (hon.), Northeastern U., 1995. With Boston Globe, 1948—, salesman, 1955-63, asst. nat. advt. mgr., 1963-70, nat. advt. mgr., 1970-72, asst. advt. dir., 1972-73, advt. dir., 1973-77, v.p. mktg. and sales, 1977-81, exec. v.p., 1981—, gen. mgr., chief operating officer, 1984-86, pres., chief operating officer, 1986-93, vice chmn., 1993-94; ret.; retired; chmn. bd. Met. Sunday Newspapers. Bd. dirs. Greater Boston Conv. and Visitors Bur., Winchester Hosp., United Way Mass. Bay; vice chmn. bd. trustees Northeastern U.; mem. adv. bd. U. Mass., Boston. With U.S. Army, 1952-54. Mem. Algonquin Club (pres.), WInchester Country Club, Phi Kappa Phi. Nat. Honor Soc. Home: 80 Arlington St Winchester MA 01890-3735

OCKERMAN, HERBERT W. agricultural studies educator; b. Chaplin, Ky., Jan. 16, 1932; m. Frances Ockerman (dec.). BS with Distinction, U. Ky., 1954, MS, 1958; PhD, N.C. State U., 1962; postgrad., Air U., 1964-70, Ohio State U., 1974, postgrad., 1983, postgrad., 1987, postgrad., 2001, postgrad., 2003, postgrad., 2004. Asst. prof. Ohio State U., Columbus, 1961-66, assoc. prof., 1966-71, prof., 1971—. Former mem. Inst. Nutrition and Food Tech.; judge regional and state h.s. sci. fairs, 1965—, Ham Contest, Ky. State Fair, Sausage and Ham Contest, Ohio Meat Processing Groups; cons. Am. Meat Inst., 1977-88, USDA, 1977-2003, CRC Press., Inc., 1988—; bd. examiners U. Calcutta, 1987-88; examiner U. Mysore, India, 1990-97; expert witness, various firms, 1992—, UN expert 95; mem. expert cons. com. FAO/WHO, 2003; hon. mem. vet., med. faculty Assiut U., Egypt; mem. adv. bd. Bull. Vet. Inst. Poland, 2004; presenter, cons. in field. Contbr. more than 196 articles to profl. jours., 81 chpts. to books. Comdr. USAF, 1955-58. Fisher Packing scholar; named Highest Individual in Beef Grading, Kansas City Meat Judging Contest, 1952; recipient Cert. of Appreciation, Ohio Assn. Meat Processors, 1987-2003, Profl. Devel. award Cahill faculty, commendation for internat. work in agr. Ohio Ho. of Reps., badge of merit for svc. to agr. Polish Govt., plaque Argentina Nat. Meat Bd., animal sci. award Roussel UCALF, France, U. Assiuit, Egypt, silver platter Nat. Meat Bd., Sec. Agr., Livestock and Fishery, Argentina, Svc. award Coun. Grad. Students, Pomerance Tchg. award, Outstanding Alumni award U. Ky., also named to Hall of Disting. Alumni, 1995, award for outstanding ednl. achievements Argentine Soc. Agr., Coop. award vet. faculty U. Cordoba, Svc. award Panoma Legis. Br., Brazil; veterinary faculty U. Cordoba, Spain, 1982, 94, Nat. Chung-Hsing U., 1982, 95, Vet. Mus. Ciechanowcu, Poland, Internat. award Assn. Nat. Tech. en Alimentos de Mexico, Can. Indst. Food Sci. and Tech., 1998, Appreciation plaque Republic of Argentina, 1999, Candle Stick of Knowledge, Ludhiana U., Punjab, India, 1999, Internat. award Am. Meat Sci. Assn., 1999, 2000, Appreciation Plaque Am. Coll. Commerce, 1999, Appreciation Plaque, Taiwan, 1999, Plaque, Selcuk U., Turkey, 1999, Folklore and Cultural memento Sudanese Socs., Sudan U., 1999, Homage and Acknowledgment, Argentine Sec. Agr., 2000, Am. Most. Sci. Assoc. Internat. award, 2000, Most Honored Guest, Weifang, China, 2001, World History award Jhadong U., China, 2001, plaque Congress of Ham, Cordoba, Spain, 2001, Michal Oczapowski award Polish Acad. Sci., 2002, Sausage Maker award, Poland, 2001, Great Educator award, China, 2001, Silver Medallion award INTA Argentina, 2001, Pub. award Taiwan, 2001, Animal Sci. Plaque, China, 2002, Food award, China, 2002, Michal Oczapowski medal 2002, Publ. award, Dayeh U., Taiwan, 2003, award for cooperation with Cath. U., Argentina, 2004. Mem. NAS, NCR, ASTM, Am. Meat Sci. Assn., Am. Soc. Animal Sci. (Rsch. award 1987), Reciprocal Meat Conf., European Meeting of Meat Rsch. Workers, Polish Vet. Soc. (hon.), Inst. Food Technologists (nat. and OVS chpts.), Inst. Food Tech. (Internat. award 1998, 2000), Can. Meat Sci. Assn., Internat. Congress Meat Sci. and Tech., Rsch. in Basic Sci., Phi Beta Delta (treas. 1987, pres. 1991, Internat. scholar award 1991, Internat. Faculty award 1991, Presdl. medallion award), Gamma Sigma Delta (Rsch. award 1977, Internat. award of merit 1988), Sigma Xi (outstanding advisor in coll. award 1995), Phi Beta Kappa (Outstanding Tchg. award 1997, Extension Diversity award 1997, Pomerene Tchg. Enhancement award 1997, Outstanding Internat. Faculty award 1997), Internat. Gamma Sigma Delta (Disting. Achievement Nat. award 1998), Phi Kappa Phi. Office: Ohio State U Meat Lab Animal Sci 2029 Fyffe Rd Columbus OH 43210-1007 Office Phone: 614-292-4317. Business E-Mail: ockerman.2@osu.edu.

OCKEY, RONALD J. lawyer; b. Green River, Wyo., June 12, 1934; s. Theron G. and Ruby O. (Sackett) O.; m. Arline M. Hawkins, Nov. 27, 1957; children: Carolyn S. Ockey Baggett, Deborah K. Ockey Christiansen, David, Kathleen M. Ockey Hellewell, Valerie Ockey Sachs, Robert. BA, U. Utah, 1959, postgrad., 1959-60; JD with honors, George Washington U., 1966. Bar: Colo. 1967, Utah 1968, U.S. Dist. Ct. Colo. 1967, U.S. Dist. Ct. Utah 1968, U.S. Ct. Appeals (10th cir.) 1969, U.S. Ct. Claims 1987. Missionary to France for Mormon Ch., 1954-57; law clk. to judge U.S. Dist. Ct. Colo., 1966-67; assoc. ptnr., shareholder, v.p., treas., dir. Jones, Waldo, Holbrook & McDonough, Salt Lake City, 1967-91; pres. IntelliTrans Internat. Corp., 1992-94; mem. Utah Ho. of Reps., 1988-90, Utah State Senate, 1991-94; of counsel Mackey Price & Williams, Salt Lake City, 1995-98; asst. atty. gen. Utah, 1998—. Trustee SmartUtah, Inc., 1995-2002; trustee Utah Tech. Fin. Corp., 1995-98; lectr. in securities, pub. fin. and bankruptcy law. Mem. editl. bd. Utah Bar Jour., 1973-75; mem. staff and bd. editors George Washington Law Rev., 1964-66; contbr. articles to profl. jours. State govtl. affairs chair Utah Jaycees, 1969; del. state Rep. Convs., 1972-74, 76-78, 80-82, 84-86, 94-96, del. Salt Lake County Rep. Conv., 1978-80, 88-92; sec. Wright for Gov. campaign, 1980; legis. dist. chmn. Utah Rep. Party, 1983-87; trustee Food for Poland, 1981-85, pres., trustee Unity to Assist Humanity Alliance, 1992-95; bd. dirs. Utah Opera Co., 1991-94; trustee Utah Info. Tech. Assn., 1991-2000. Lt. U.S. Army, 1960-66, to capt. JAG, USAR, 1966-81. Mem. ABA, Utah State Bar Assn. (various coms.), Nat. Assn. Bond Lawyers (chmn. con. on state legislation 1982-85), George Washington U. Law Alumni Assn. (bd. dirs. 1981-85), Order of Coif, Phi Delta Phi. Home: 4502 Crest Oak Cir Salt Lake City UT 84124-3825 E-mail: roah@darnfast.com.

O'CONNELL, BRIAN, community organizer, public administrator, writer, educator; b. Worcester, Mass., Jan. 23, 1930; s. Thomas J. and Mary (Carroll) O'C.; m. Ann C. Brown, July 11, 1953; children: Todd, Tracey, Matthew. BA, Tufts Coll., 1953; postgrad., Maxwell Sch. Citizenship and Pub. Adminstrn., 1953-54; also numerous hon. degrees. Field rep. Am. Heart Assn., Pa., 1954-56, Md. exec. dir., 1956—61, Calif. exec. dir., 1961—66; exec. dir. Nat. Assn. Mental Health, 1966-78, dir. emeritus, 1978—; pres. Nat. Council on Philanthropy, 1978-80; exec. dir. Coalition of Nat. Vol. Orgns., 1978-80; pres. Ind. Sector, 1980-95, founding pres., pres. emeritus, 1995—; prof. pub. svc. Tufts U., Medford, Mass., 1995—. Mem. U.S. Pres.'s Com. Employment of Handicapped, 1966-68; chmn. Liaison Group Mental Health, 1969-72. Author: Effective Leadership in Voluntary Organizations, 1976, Finding Values That Work: The Search for Fulfillment, 1977, America's Voluntary Spirit, A Book of Readings, 1983, The Board Members Book, 1985, Philanthropy in Action, 1987, Our Organization, 1987, Volunteers in Action, 1989, People Power: Service Advocacy, Empowerment, 1994, Board Overboard, 1995, Powered By Coalition: The Story of Independent Sector, 1997, Voices from the Heart: In Celebration of America's Volunteers, 1999, Civil Society: The Underpinnings of American Democracy, 1999, Fifty Years in Public Causes: Stories From a Road Les Traveled, 2004. Mem. Alumni Coun. Tufts U., 1970-80, trustee, 1988-2000, trustee emeritus, 2000—, chmn. pres. search com., 1992; trustee Points of Light Found., 1989-95; bd. dirs. Hogg Found., 1990-95; chmn. organizing com., 1st chmn. Civicus: World Alliance for Citizen Participation, 1992-96; bd. dirs. E.M. Kaufman Found., 1994—2003, The BridgeSpan Group, 1999—, The Cape Cod Found., 2003—. Recipient outstanding agy. prof. award United Way Am., 1979, Lincoln Filene Citizenship award, 1985, John W. Gardner Leadership award, 1994, Gold Key award Am. Soc. Assn. Execs., 1994, Chmns. award, NSFRE, 1994, The Tiffany award, 1998. Fellow Am. Pub. Health Assn., Nat. Acad. Pub. Adminstrn. (trustee 1993-2000), Nat. Com. Patients' Rights (chmn. 1975-77). Home: 50 Chase St Chatham MA 02633-2404 Office: Univ Coll Citizenship and Pub Svc Tufts U Medford MA 02155

O'CONNELL, BRIAN MICHAEL, computer scientist, educator; b. Hartford, Conn., Nov. 2, 1960; s. Robert F. and Elizabeth S. O'Connell; m. Sarah E. Cox, Oct. 31, 2000. BA, Trinity Coll., Hartford, 1983; JD, U. Conn., 1987. Bar: Conn. 1988, U.S. Supreme Ct. 1992. Assoc. prof. ethics law, computing Ctrl. Conn. State U., New Britain, 1997—. Recipient Franklyn S. Haiman, Nat. Commn. Assn., 1999. Mem.: IEEE (pres. social implications tech. 2003). Office: Central Conn State Univ 1615 Stanley St New Britain CT 06050 E-mail: oconnellb@ccsu.edu.

O'CONNELL, BRIAN MORGAN, music educator; b. Cambridge, Mass., Sept. 11, 1947; s. Donald Paul and Mary Elizabeth (Jackson) O'Connell; m. Beth Holden Williams, Aug. 13, 1974 (div. Jan. 1984); m. Gail Andrea Leicher, May 18, 1985; children: Caley, Jamie, Alexander, Tira. B in music edn., U. Lowell, 1969; M in music choral conducting, Boston Conservatory of Music, 1987; postgrad., Boston U., 1991—93. Cert. voice therapy Boston Conservatory of Music, 1978. Chairman Berklee Coll. of Music, Voice Dept., Boston, 1972—87; lead tchr. BU/Chelsea Partnership, Chelsea, Mass., 1991—93; tchr. Boston U., 1991—93; dir. of choral activities Tufts U., Medford, Mass., 1997—99; tchr. New England Conservatory of Music, 1995—2000, U. Mass., Lowell, 2002—; guest condr. Northeastern U., Boston, 2001; dir. of choral activities Lexington HS, Mass., 1993—; condr. youth chorus Handel and Haydn Soc., Boston, 1995—97; dir. Sarteano Chamber Choral Workshop, Tuscany, Italy, 2004—. Condr. Cambridge Chorale, 1973—75, Nashua Choral Soc., 1978—79, Quincy Choral Soc., 1985—88, Neposett Choral Soc., 1999—2000, Nashoba Valley Chorale, 2001—. Pres. Mass. Am. Choral Dir. Assoc., 1997—99, tres., 1993—95; tchr. adv. com. Boston Symphony Orch., 1993. Recipient President's medal, Lithuanian soc., 1985; grantee, Lexington Edn. Found., 1995, 2003. Mem.: Mass. Music Educators Assoc., Am. Choral Dir. Assoc., Phi Delta Kappa. Avocations: hiking, birdwatching, gardening. Home: 27 Patterson Rd Lexington MA 02421 Office: Lexington HS 251 Waltham St Lexington MA 02421 E-mail: occonnell@sch.ci.lexington.ma.us.

O'CONNELL, CARMELA DIGRISTINA, appraisal executive, consultant; b. Johnstown, Pa., Nov. 8, 1925; d. Salvatore and Josephine (Riggio) Digristina; m. Maurice F. O'Connell, Sept. 21, 1974 (dec. Feb. 1984); children: Geraldine, John, Bernard. Diploma, Eastern Secretarial Sch., N.Y.C., Sch. Interior Design. From typist to sec.-treas. Philip P. Masterson Co., N.Y.C., 1942-72; exec. v.p., bd. dirs. Masterson & O'Connell Inc., N.Y.C., 1972-80, cons., 1981—; founder, pres. N.Y. Appraisal Corp., N.Y.C., 1971-80; co-founder, pres. Park Ave. Appraisal, N.Y.C., 1981—. Mem. N.Y. Rep. Com., 1974—, Met. Opera Guild, N.Y.C., 1986; chmn. Ch. of Our Saviour, N.Y.C., 1986; mem. Ladies of Charity, Cath. Charities Archdiocese of N.Y., 1990; bd. dirs. 80 Park Avenue Condominiums, 1997—. Recipient Amita award for Bus. Woman of Yr., 1977, Lena Madesin Phillips award N.Y. League/Fortune 500 Bus. and Profl. Women, 1989. Mem. Nat. Fedn. Bus. and Profl. Women's Clubs Inc. (2d v.p. 1964, 1st v.p. 1966). Roman Catholic. Home: 2421 Old Collier Rd Land O Lakes FL 34639

O'CONNELL, DANIEL CRAIG, psychology educator; b. Sand Springs, Okla., May 20, 1928; s. John Albert and Letitia Rutherford (McGinnis) O'C. BA, St. Louis U., 1951, Ph.L., 1952, MA, 1953, S.T.L., 1960; PhD, U. Ill., 1963. Joined Soc. of Jesus, 1945; asst. prof. psychology St. Louis U., 1964-66, asso. prof., 1966-72, prof., 1972-80, trustee, 1973-78, pres., 1974-78; prof. psychology Loyola U., Chgo., 1980-89, Georgetown U., Washington, 1990-98, emeritus, 1998—, chmn., 1991-96. Vis. prof. U. Melbourne, Australia, 1972, U. Kans., 1978-79, Georgetown U., 1986, Loyola U., Chgo., 1998-2003; Humboldt fellow Psychol. Inst. Free U. Berlin, 1968; sr. Fulbright lectr. Kassel U. W. Ger., 1979-80. Author: Critical Essays on Language Use and Psychology, 1988; contbr. articles to profl. jours. Recipient Nancy McNeir Ring award for outstanding teaching St. Louis U., 1969; NSF fellow, 1961, 63, 65, 68; Humboldt Found. grantee, 1973; Humboldt fellow Tech. U. of Berlin, 1987. Fellow Am., Mo. psychol. assns., Am. Psychol. Soc.; mem. Midwestern, Southwestern, Eastern psychol. assns., Psychologists Interested in Religious Issues, Psychonomic Soc., Soc. for Scientific Study of Religion, N.Y., Mo. acads. sci., AAUP, AAAS, Phi Beta Kappa. Home and Office: Hallahan House 4511 W Pine Blvd Saint Louis MO 63108-2191 Office Phone: 314-758-7143. Business E-Mail: doconnel1@jesuits-mis.org. *Were it over, it would have been more than my expected share already. The challenge of learning to serve others has moved it along at a quick pace, and I am grateful that I have always received more than I've been able to give in return—from the Lord and from many good people.*

O'CONNELL, DANIEL F. lawyer; b. Orange, NJ, May 5, 1943; BS with honors, Villanova U., 1965; JD, Rutgers U., 1968. Bar: N.J. 1968, N.Y. 1980, U.S. Supreme Ct. 1980. Ptnr. Drinker Biddle & Reath LLP, Florham Pk., NJ. Mem. Supreme Ct. N.J. Dist. VII Ethics Com., 1978-83, sec., 1980-83; chmn. N.J. Commn. Legal and Ethical Problems in the Delivery of Health Care, 1986-90. Mem. ABA (labor and employment law sect., antitrust law sect., health law sect. 1977—), N.J. State Bar Assn. (labor law sect., health and hosp. law sect.), Somerset County Bar Assn. (exec. com. 1977-81, pres. 1979), Am. Health Lawyers Assn., Am. Hosp. Assn. Office: Drinker Biddle & Reath 500 Campus Dr Florham Park NJ 07932-1047 E-mail: doconnell@dbr.com.

O'CONNELL, DAVID M. academic administrator; b. Phila., Apr. 21, 1955; BPh magna cum laude, Niagara U., 1978; ThM, Mary Immaculate Seminary, 1981, DivM, 1983; PhD in Canon Law, Cath. U., 1987; Licentiate in Canon Law, Cath. U. Am., 1990. Ordained Cath. priest 1982. Religion tchr., dir. student activities Archbishop Wood H.S. for Boys, Warminster, Pa.; registrar, asst. acad. dean, asst. prof. philosophy, homiletics and canon law Mary Immaculate Seminary, Northampton, Pa., 1987—90; prof. theology St. John's U., Jamaica, NY, 1990—98, acad. dean, dean faculty Coll. Liberal Arts and Scis., 1991—98, assoc. v.p., 1996—98; interim acad. v.p. Niagara U., 1994—95; pres. Cath. U. Am., Washington, 1998—. Canonical cons. and ecclesiastical judge on the tribunals Diocese of Harrisburg, Pa., Diocese of Birmingham, Ala., Diocese of Scranton, Pa.; co-host, commentator during papal visit to U.S. CBS-TV, 1995; trustee Consortium Univs. Washington Met. Area. Contbr. articles to profl. jours. Trustee Cath. U. Am., St. John's U., Archbishop John Carroll H.S., Washington, Basilica of the Nat. Shrine of the Immaculate Conception; active Greater Washington Bd. Trade; mem. adv. bd. U. St.Thomas, St. Paul. Mem.: Assn. Cath. Colls. and Univs., Ea. Regional Canon Lawyers Assn., Canon Law Soc. Am. Office: Office Pres Cath Univ Am Nugent Hall 620 Michigan Ave NE Washington DC 20064*

O'CONNELL, EDWARD JAMES, JR., psychology educator, computer applications and data analysis consultant; b. Sterling, Ill., Aug. 15, 1932; s. Edward James and Elizabeth E. (Clapham) O.; m. Pamelia Canon Floyd, Aug. 21, 1959; children— Edward James III, John Matthew BS in Psychology, Ill. Inst. Tech., 1958; MA in Psychology, Northwestern U., 1961, PhD in Psychology, 1962. NSF postdoctoral fellow Carnegie Inst. Tech., Pitts., 1962-63, asst. prof. psychology, 1963-65; psychology faculty Syracuse (N.Y.) U., N.Y., 1965-93, prof., 1975-93, prof. emeritus, 1993—. Cons. Rand Corp., Santa Monica, Calif., 1962-64, Abt Assocs., Boston, 1970-73, Marcy Psychiat. Hosp., N.Y., 1979-82 Served to cpl. U.S. Army, 1952-54 NSF predoctoral fellow, 1959-62: NSF postdoctoral fellow, 1962-63; Northwestern U. predoctoral fellow, 1958-59 Mem. Sigma Xi. Democrat. Avocations: billiards, computer programming. Address: PO Box 570 Cashiers NC 28717-0570 E-mail: ejoconn@dnet.net.

O'CONNELL, FRANCIS V(INCENT), textile printing company executive; b. Norwich, Conn., July 8, 1903; s. Thomas Francis and Isabelle (Gelino) O'C.; m. Marie Louise Lemoine, Nov. 7, 1940. LLB, Blackstone Coll. Law, 1932, JD, 1940, LLM, 1942. Textile screen printer U.S. Finishing Co., Norwich, 1921-30; foreman Ahern Textile Print Co., Norwich, 1930-36; pres., owner Hand Craft Textile Print Co., Plainfield, Conn., 1936—. Roman Catholic. Home: PO Box 165 Plainfield CT 06374-0165 Office: Bishop's Crossing Plainfield CT 06374

O'CONNELL, GERLAD M. communications executive; b. Stamford, Conn., 1962; BA in English and History, Middlebury (Conn.) Coll., 1983. House painter, Middlebury, 1983; mktg. exec. Productivity Inc., 1984; product mgr. Comp-U-Mall, CUC Internat., 1985-87; founder, ptnr. Modem Media Inc. (merged with Poppe Tyson, 1998), Westport, Conn., 1987—; now chmn. & CEO Modem Media Inc. Avocation: fishing. Office: Modem Media 230 East Ave Norwalk CT 06855-1935

O'CONNELL, HUGH MELLEN, JR., retired architect; b. Oak Park, Ill., Nov. 29, 1929; s. Hugh M. and Helen Mae (Evans) O'C.; m. Frances Ann Small, Apr. 13, 1957; children: Patricia Lynn, Susan Marie, Jeanette Maureen. Student mech. engring., Purdue U., 1948-50; BS in Archtl. Engring, U. Ill., 1953. Registered architect, Ariz., Calif., La., Nev., Nat. Council Archtl. Registration Bds. Designer John Mackel; structural engr. Los Angeles, 1955-57; architect Harnish & Morgan & Causey, Ontario, Calif., 1957-63; self-employed architect Ventura, Calif., 1963-69; architect Andrews/O'Connell, Ventura, 1970-78; dir. engring. div. Naval Constrn. Bn. Center, Port Hueneme, Calif., 1978-91, supervisory architect, 1991-93; ret., 1993. Mem. tech. adv. com. Ventura Coll., 1965-78; sec. Oxnard Citizens' Adv. Com., 1969-79, v.p., 1970-72, pres., 1972—; chmn. Oxnard Beautification Com., 1969, 74, Oxnard Cmty. Block Grant adv. com., 1975-76; mem. Oxnard Planning Commn., 1976-86, vice chmn., 1978-79, chmn., 1980-81. Mem. Oxnard Art-in-Pub. Places Commn., 1988-93, 2003—. Served with AUS, 1953-55. Mem. AIA (emeritus, pres. Ventura chpt. 1973), Am. Concrete Inst., Soc. Am. Registered Architects (Design award 1968, dir. 1970), Am. Legion, Soc. for Preservation and Encouragement of Barbershop Quartet Singing in Am. (chpt. pres. 1979, chpt. sec. 1980-83), Acad. Model Aeros. (#9190 1948—), Channel Islands Condors Club (treas. 1986-99), Sports Flyers Assn., Alpha Rho Chi (Anthemios chpt.). Presbyterian (elder 1963, deacon 1967). Lodges: Kiwanis (pres. 1969, div. sec. 1974-75), Elks. Home and Office: 520 Ivywood Dr Oxnard CA 93030-3527 Personal E-mail: hughoarch@msn.net.

O'CONNELL, JEANNE, financial planner, insurance broker; b. Stoneham, Mass., Dec. 9, 1951; d. Kenneth Edward and Frances Evelyn (Matulewicz) O'C.; 1 child, Ryan Sulloway. Student, U. Oreg., 1971-72; BFA cum laude, U. Mass.-Amherst, 1974, U. Calif.-Sacramento, summer 1973; postgrad., Northeastern U., 1975; MBA, Suffolk U., 1984. CPCU, CLU; chartered fin. cons.; assoc. in underwriting; enrolled agt. designation. Ins. clk. S.B. Swaim & Co., Boston, 1969-72, Hollis Perrin & Co., Boston, 1972; underwriting asst. Pub. Svc. Mut. Ins. Co., Newton, Mass., 1974-77; personal lines analyst Comml. Union Ins. Co., Boston, 1977-80, sr. personal lines analyst, 1980-83, tech. specialist, 1983-88; pvt. practice fin. cons., brokerage Boston, 1988—. Instr. ins. and fin. planning Ins. Libr. Boston, 1988—; speaker in field; ind. tax preparer; pub. arbitrator NASD, BBB, AMEX; founder, dir. Red Dragon Arts Coop., Boston, 1983; potter, artist Radcliffe Pottery Studio, Boston, 1980-85. Mem. exec. student adv. bd. Suffolk U., 1982—83, student liaison mem. between Exec. MBA Program and regular MBA Program and dean's adv. bd., coord. Exec. MBA Program Policy Seminar Weekend, 1983; v.p., trustee Friends Waltham Pub. Libr., 1998, 1999, asst. treas., 2000, 2000—. Fellow Nat. Tax Practice Inst.; mem. Internat. Assn. Fin. Planners, Nat. Soc. Enrolled Agts., Nat. Soc. Accts., Nat. Assn. Tax Preparers, Waltham Garden Club (photographer 1997—), Delta Mu Delta. Avocations: reading books on tape, photography, rubber stamps, gardening. Studio: 229 School St Waltham MA 02451-4546 Office Phone: 781-891-1721. E-mail: reddragonarts@rcn.com.

O'CONNELL, JEFFREY, law educator; b. Worcester, Mass., Sept. 28, 1928; s. Thomas Joseph and Mary (Carroll) O'C.; m. Virginia Kearns, Nov. 26, 1960 (dec. 1994); children: Mara, Devin. Grad. cum laude, Phillips Exeter Acad., 1947; AB cum laude, Dartmouth Coll., 1951; JD, Harvard U., 1954. Bar: Mass. 1954, Conn. 1954, Va. 1983, hon. admittance to Ark. and Minn. bar. Instr. speech Tufts U., 1953-54; assoc. Sherburne, Powers & Needham, 1954-57, Hale & Dorr, Boston, 1958-59; asst. prof., then assoc. prof. law U. Iowa Coll. Law, 1959-62; assoc. dir. automobile claims study Harvard Law Sch., 1963-64; assoc. prof. law U. Ill. Coll. Law, 1964-65, prof., 1965-79; prof. law U. Va. Law Sch., 1980-83, John Allan Love prof., 1983-90, Samuel H. McCoy II prof., 1990—, Class of 1948 rsch. prof., 1994-97. Summer vis. prof. Northwestern U., 1963, U. Mich., 1966, 75, So. Meth. U., 1972, U. Tex., 1977, U. Wash., 1979; John Marshall Harlan vis. prof. N.Y. Law Sch., 1991; vis. fellow Centre for Socio-Legal Studies, Wolfson Coll., Oxford (Eng.) U., 1973, 79; Thomas Jefferson vis. fellow Downing Coll. Cambridge U., Eng., 1989; mem. U. Va. Ctr. for Advanced Study, 1980-83. Author: (with R.E. Keeton) Basic Protection for the Traffic Victim, 1965, After Cars Crash: The Need for Legal and Insurance Reform, 1967, (with Arthur Myers) Safety Last: An Indictment of the Auto Industry, 1966, (with R.E. Keeton, John McCord) Crisis in Car Insurance, 1968, (with Wallace Wilson) Car Insurance and Consumer Desires, 1969, The Injury Industry, 1971, (with Rita James Simon) Payment for Pain and Suffering, 1972, Ending Insult to Injury: No-Fault Insurance for Products and Services, 1975, (with Roger Henderson) Tort Law, No-Fault and Beyond, 1975, The Lawsuit Lottery: Only the Lawyers Win, 1979, (with C. Brian Kelly) The Blame Game: Injuries, Insurance and Injustice, 1986, (with Lester Brickman and Michael Horowitz) Rethinking Contingency Fees: A Proposal to Align the Contingency Fee System with its Policy Roots and Ethical Mandates, 1994, (with Peter Bell) Accidental Justice: The Dilemmas of Tort Law, 1997 Mem. Nat. Hwy. Safety Adv. Com., 1967-70; ednl. adv. bd. John Simon Guggenheim Found., 1973-87; bd. dirs. Consumers Union, 1970-76; mem. com. on competitive safeguards and med. aspects of sports NCAA, 1985-87. Served as 1st lt. USAF, 1954-57. Recipient Robert B. McKay award for ins. scholarship Tort and Ins. Practice sect. ABA, 1992; Guggenheim fellow, 1972-73, 79-80. Mem. ABA, Va. Bar Assn., Casque and Gauntlet, Farmington Country Club, Cosmos Club (Washington), Phi Beta Kappa, Psi Upsilon. Democrat. Roman Catholic. Home: 505 Oak Cir Charlottesville VA 22901-3220 Office: U Va Sch Law 580 Massie Rd Charlottesville VA 22903-1738 Office Phone: 434-924-7809. E-mail: jo@virginia.edu.

O'CONNELL, JOHN BERNARD, JR., medical educator, chairman department of medicine; b. Chgo., July 27, 1949; s. John B. O'C; m. Mary Owens, Jan. 12, 1980; children: Jessica, Moira, Claire, Sheila, John. BS, U. Ill., Chgo., 1971; MD magna cum laude, Loyola U., Maywood, Ill., 1974. Diplomate Nat. Bd. Med. Examiners, Am. Bd. Internal Medicine, Am. Bd. Cardiovascular Disease. Intern Loyola U. Med. Ctr., Maywood, 1975-76, resident in internal medicine, 1976-78, chief resident in internal medicine, 1977-78, fellow in cardiology, 1978-80, staff physician emergency dept., 1979-81, attending cardiologist, 1980-86, med. dir. Cardiac Transplantation Program, 1984-86; clin. instr. in medicine Loyola U., Stritch Sch. Medicine, Maywood, 1977-80, asst. prof. medicine, 1980-85, assoc. prof. medicine, 1985-86; asst. chief med. svc. Hines VA Hosp., Maywood, 1981-83; attending cardiologist LDS Hosp., Salt Lake City, 1986-91, U. Utah Med. Ctr., Salt Lake City, 1986-91; assoc. prof. medicine Sch. Medicine, U. Utah, Salt Lake City, 1986-91, prof., 1991; attending physician Univ. Hosp., U. Miss. Med. Ctr., Jackson, 1991—97; prof. medicine U. Miss. Med. Sch., Jackson, 1991—97, chmn. dept. medicine, 1991—97; prof., chair dept. internal medicine Wayne State U., Detroit, 1997—. Cons. Salt Lake VA Med. Ctr., Salt Lake City, 1988-91, Primary Children's Med. Ctr., Salt Lake City, 1988-91; med. dir., chmn. exec. com. UTAH Cardiac Transplant Program, Salt Lake City, 1986-91; chmn. adv. bd. Exptl. Organ Transplantation Procedures, apptd. by Gov. of Ill., 1985-86;

mem. working group on myocarditis Nat. Heart, Lung and Blood Inst., 1985; com. mem. Internat. Symposium Inflammatory Heart Disease, Snowmass, Colo., July, 1988; mem. sci. coun. Internat. Soc. and Fedn. Cardiology, 1990—; mem. spl. study sect. NIH, 1990; mem. sci. bd. Internat. Congress of Cardiology on Cardiovascular Pharmacotherapy and Cardiomyopathies, Greece, 1990; mem. adv. com. Miss. Health Scis. Info. Network, 1992-94; med. dir. Miss. Organ Procurement Agy., 1992-93; mem. sci. com. Internat. Workshop on the Cardiomyopathies, LaCoruna, Spain, 1993. Co-editor (monographs): Myocarditis: Precursor of Cardiomyopathy, 1983, Drug Therapy of Dilated Cardiomyopathy and Myocarditis, 1988, Intrathoracic Transplantation 2000, 1993; mem. editorial bd. Jour. Heart and Lung Transplantation, 1986—, Internat. Jour. Cardiology, 1992—, Transplantation, 1993—; manuscript cons. numerous publs.; contbr. articles to profl. jours. Recipient Norris L. Brookens Outstanding Resident award Ill. Soc. Internal Medicine, 1978, Robert Kark, M.D. Rsch. award Chgo. Soc. Internal Medicine, 1981, Outstanding Young Citizen award Chgo. Jr. Assocs. Commerce and Industry, 1985, Shinshu U. medal Matsumoto City, Nagano, Japan, 1992; grantee Earl M. Bane Charitable Trust, 1979-83, Fraternal Order Eagles, 1983-86, BRSG, 1983-84, NHLBI, 1986-91, Deseret Found., 1987-91, Bristol Myers Squibb, 1988-91, Burroughs Wellcome, 1992—, Otsuka Pharm., 1993—, Smith Kline Beecham Pharm., 1993—. Fellow ACP, Am. Coll. Chest Physicians, Am. Coll. Cardiology (cardiac transplantation com. 1991—, conf. steering com. 1991-92), Am. Coll. Angiology; mem. AMA, AAAS, Assn. of Profs. of Medicine (bd. dirs. 1997—, treas. 1998-2001, pres.-elect 2001-02, pres. 2002-03), Am. Soc. Transplant Physicians (mem. tng. and manpower com. 1990—, mem. pub. policy com. 1993—, numerous others), N.Y. Acad. Scis., Internat. Soc. Heart and Lung Transplant (mem. sci. program com. 1987, 89, 90, councilor 1989-91, pres.-elect 1991-92, pres. 1993-94, past pres. 1993-94, others), Transplantation Soc., Assn. Profs. Medicine, Rsch., Miss. (bd. dirs.), Jackson Acad. Medicine, So. Soc. Clin. Investigation, Am. Fedn. Clin. Rsch. (sen. midwest sect. 1983-86), So. Soc. Clin. Rsch., Ctrl. Soc. Clin. Rsch., Miss. State Med. Assn., Ctrl. Med. Soc., Am. Heart Assn. (bd. dirs. West Cook County 1982-86, v.p. 1985-86, chmn. 1990-92, numerous others), United Network for Organ Sharing (mem. coalition on organ doning 1991-92, mem. thoracic com. 1992—, mem. sci. adv. com. 1993—), Alpha Omega Alpha. Home: 2959 Chestnut Run Dr Bloomfield Hills MI 48302-1108 Office: Wayne State Univ UHC-2E 4201 Saint Antoine Detroit MI 48201 Office Phone: 313-745-8244. Business E-Mail: joconell@med.wayne.edu.

O'CONNELL, KEVIN, lawyer; b. Boston, Sept. 4, 1933; s. Michael Frederick and Kathryn Agnes (Kelley) O'C.; m. Mary Adams, July 14, 1990; children: Tiffany W., Elizabeth H., Dana A., Liesel E. AB, Harvard, 1955, JD, 1960. Bar: Calif. 1961. Assoc. firm O'Melveny & Myers, L.A., 1960-63; asst. U.S. atty. criminal div. Cen. Dist. Calif., L.A., 1963-65; staff counsel Gov. Calif. Commn. to Investigate Watts Riot, L.A., 1965-66; ptnr. Tuttle & Taylor, L.A., 1966-70, Coleman & O'Connell, L.A., 1971-75; pvt. practice law L.A., 1975-78; of counsel firm Simon & Sheridan, L.A., 1978-89; ptnr. Manatt, Phelps & Phillips, L.A., 1989—; adj. prof. law U. So. Calif. Law Sch., 2002—. Bd. editors: Harvard Law Rev., 1958-60. Mem. Los Angeles County (Calif.) Democratic Central Com., 1973-74; bd. dirs. Calif. Supreme Ct. Hist. Soc. Lt. USMCR, 1955-57. Mem. Am. Law Inst. Home: 426 N Mccadden Pl Los Angeles CA 90004 1026 Office: Manatt Phelps & Phillips Trident Ctr E Tower 11355 W Olympic Blvd Los Angeles CA 90064-1614 Office Phone: 310-312-4222. Business E-Mail: koconnell@manatt.com.

O'CONNELL, MARUEEN C. state legislator, lawyer; m. Don O'Connell; 1 child, Don. BS in Health Care Adminstrn., St. Josephs Coll.; JD, St. John's U.; RN, Flushing Hosp. Med. Ctr. Mem. adv. bd. Nassau Cmty. Coll., Molloy Coll. Sch. of Nuring. Recipient Am. Jurisprudence award. Mem.: Oncology Nursing Soc., Nassau Co. Bar Assn., Am. Cancer Soc. Democrat. Office: 224 7th St Garden City NY 11530-5781

O'CONNELL, MARY ANN, state legislator, small business owner; b. Albuquerque, Aug. 3, 1934; d. James Aubrey and Dorothy Nell (Batsel) Gray; m. Robert Emmett O'Connell, Feb. 21, 1977; children: Jeffery Crampton, Gray Crampton. Student, U. N.Mex., Internat. Coun. Shopping Ctrs. Exec. dir. Blvd. Shopping Ctr., Las Vegas, Nev., 1968-76, Citizen Pvt. Enterprise, Las Vegas, 1976; media supr. Southwest Advt., Las Vegas, 1977—; owner, operator Meadows Inn, Las Vegas, 1985—99, 3 Christian bookstores, Las Vegas, 1985-99; mem. Nev. State Senate, 1985—, chmn. govtl. affairs com., vice chmn. commerce and labor com. Vice chmn. Legis. Commn., 1985—86, 1995—96, mem. edn. com. to rewrite standards; mem. Edn. Commn. of the States, 1997—; rep. Nat. Conf. State Legislators; past vice chair State Mental Hygiene and Mental Retardation Adv. Bd. Pres. explorer div. Boulder Dam Area coun. Boy Scouts Am., Las Vegas, 1979-80, former mem. exec. bd. mem. adv. bd. Boulder Dam chpt.; pres., bd. dirs. Citizens Pvt. Enterprise, Las Vegas, 1982-84, Secret Witness, Las Vegas, 1981-82; vice chmn. Gov.'s Mental Health-Mental Retardation, Nev., 1983-; past mem. community adv. bd. Care Unit Hosp., Las Vegas; past mem. adv. bd. Kidney Found., Milligan Coll., Charter Hosp.; tchr. Young Adult Sunday Sch.; 1st vice chmn. Clark County Rep. Party, 2001-03. Recipient Commendation award Mayor O. Grayson, Las Vegas, 1975, Outstanding Citizenship award Bd. Realtors, 1975, Silver Beaver award Boy Scouts Am., 1980, Free Enterprise award Greater Las Vegas C. of C., Federated Employers Assn., Downtown Breakfast Exch., 1988, Award of Excellence Women in Politics, 1989, Legislator Yr. award Bldg. and Trades, 1991, Legislator Yr. award Nat. ASA Trade Assn., 1991, 94, Guardian Liberty award Nev. Coalition Conservative Citizens, 1991, Internat. Maxi Awards Promotional Excellence, Guardian Small Bus. award Nat. Fedn. Ind. Bus., 1995-96, Legislator Yr. award Nev. Med. Polit. Com., 1999, Assoc. Builders and Contractors, New Mortgage Brokers, 2000, Nev. Ind. Check Cashing Assn., 2001, Nev. Phys. Therapists, 2002, Atty. Gen. award Women's Role Model, 2002, Nicholas J. Horn award Nev. State Med. Assn., 2003; named Nev. Public Health Assoc. Legislator Yr., Nev. Retail Assn., 1992, New Assn. Bldg. Contractors, 1999, Nev Polit. Med. Action Com., 1999; inducted into Nev. Vets. Citizens Hall Fame, 1999; named one of 25 Notable Las Vegas Women, 2004. Mem. Retail Mchts. Assn. (former pres., bd. dirs.), Taxpayers Assn. (bd. dirs.), Greater Las Vegas C. of C. (past pres., bd. dirs., Woman of Achievement Politics women's coun. 1988). Republican. Mem. Christian Ch. Avocations: china painting, reading. Office: Nev Legislature Senate 401 S Carson St Carson City NV 89701-4747

O'CONNELL, MAURICE DANIEL, lawyer; b. Ticonderoga, N.Y., Nov. 9, 1929; s. Maurice Daniel and Leila (Geraghty) O'C.; m. Joan MacLure Landers, Aug. 2, 1952; children: Mark M., David L., Ann M., Leila K., Ellen A. Grad., Phillips Exeter Acad., 1946; AB, Williams Coll., 1950; LLB, Cornell U., 1956. Bar: Ohio 1956. Since practiced in, Toledo; assoc. Williams, Eversman & Black, 1956-60; ptnr. Robison, Curphey & O'Connell, 1961-95, of counsel, 1996—; spl. hearing officer in conscientious objector cases U.S. Dept. Justice, 1966-68. Mem. complaint rev. bd. Bd. Commrs. on Grievance and Discipline of Supreme Ct. Ohio, 1987. Mem. Ottawa Hills Bd. Edn., 1963-66, pres., 1967-69; former trustee Toledo Soc. for Handicapped; past trustee Woodlawn Cemetery; past trustee Toledo Hearing and Speech Center, Easter Seal Soc.; mem. alumni council Phillips Exeter Acad. Served to 1st lt. USMCR, 1950-53. Fellow Ohio State Bar Found.; mem. NW Ohio Alumni Assn. of Williams Coll. (past pres.), Ohio Bar Assn., Toledo Bar Assn. (chmn. grievance com. 1971-74), Kappa Alpha, Phi Delta Phi. Clubs: Toledo. Home: 3922 W Bancroft St Toledo OH 43606-2533 Office: 9th Flr Four SeaGate Toledo OH 43604

O'CONNELL, MIKE, professional sports team executive; m. Rosemary O'Connell; children: Kristen, Matthew, Gregory. Hockey player Ontario (Can.) Hockey League, Chgo. (Ill.) Blackhawks, 1975—80, Boston (Mass.) Bruins, 1980—86, Detroit (Mich.) Red Wings, 1986—90; head coach San Diego (Calif.) Gulls, 1990—91, Providence Affiliate League, 1992—94; asst. gen. mgr. Boston (Mass.) Bruins, 1994—2000, v.p., 1998—, gen. mgr., 2000—. Named to All Star Game, 1984; recipient Seventh Player award, WSBK-TV, 1984. Office: 1 Fleetcenter Ste 250 Boston MA 02114*

O'CONNELL, PHILIP RAYMOND, retired lawyer, paper company executive; b. N.Y.C., June 2, 1928; s. Michael Joseph and Ann (Blaney) O'C.; m. Joyce McCabe, July 6, 1957; children: Michael, Kathleen, Jennifer, David. AB, Manhattan Coll., 1949; JD, Columbia U., 1956; grad., Advanced Mgmt. Program, Harvard U., 1967. Bar: N.Y. 1956, U.S. Supreme Ct. 1961, Conn. 1988. Assoc. Dewey, Ballantine, Bushby, Palmer & Wood, N.Y.C., 1956-61, 62-64; gen. counsel, sec. Laurentide Finance Corp., San Francisco, 1961-62; gen. counsel Wallace-Murray Corp., 1964-66, div. mgr., 1966-70; pres., chief exec. officer, dir. Universal Papertech Corp., Hatfield, Pa., 1970-71; sec. Champion Internat. Corp., Stamford, Conn., 1972-90, v.p., 1979-81, sr. v.p., 1981-90. Mem. legal adv. com. N.Y. Stock Exch., 1985-88, corp. governance subcom., legal adv. com., 1985-94; chmn. lawyers steering com. corp. governance task force The Bus. Roundtable, 1981-87, mem., 1981-94. Mem. Champion Internat. Found., 1979-90; mem. bd. visitors Fairfield Univ. Sch. Bus., 1981-93, chmn., 1983-93; bd. dirs. Kearney-Nat. Corp., 1975-78. With USNR, 1951-54. Mem. Am. Soc. Corp. Secs. (hon.; chmn. 1988-89).

O'CONNELL, RALPH ANTHONY, dean, psychiatrist, educator; b. N.Y.C., Jan. 26, 1938; s. Ralph E. and Agnes H. (O'Connell) O'C.; m. Jane Burke, June 15, 1963; children: Ralph E. III, Ellen C., John B. AB cum laude, Coll. of Holy Cross, Worcester, Mass., 1959; MD, Cornell U., 1963. Diplomate Am. Bd. Psychiatry and Neurology. Intern St. Vincent's Hosp. and Med. Ctr. N.Y., N.Y.C., 1963-64, resident, 1964, 67-69, rsch. psychiatrist, 1969-71, chief inpatient dept. psychiatry, 1971-76, clin. dir. and vice chmn. psychiatry, 1974-95; prof. psychiatry N.Y. Med. Coll., Valhalla, 1984—, dean and provost, 1996—. Editor-in-chief Comprehensive Psychiatry, 1983-96. Served to capt. U.S. Army, 1965-66. Fellow Am. Psychiat. Assn., N.Y. Acad. Medicine (trustee 1989—). Clubs: Univ. (N.Y.C.). Roman Catholic. Office: NY Med Coll Valhalla NY 10595

O'CONNELL, ROBERT FRANCIS, physics educator; b. Athlone, Ireland, Apr. 22, 1933, came to U.S., 1958, s. William and Catherine (O'Reilly) O'C.; m. Josephine Molly Buckley, Aug. 3, 1963; children: Adrienne Molly, Fiona Catherine, Eimear Kathleen. BSc, Nat. U. Ireland, Galway, 1953, DSc, 1975; PhD, U. Notre Dame, 1962. Telecommunications engr. Dept. Posts and Telegraphs, Dublin, Ireland, 1954-58; scholar Inst. Advanced Studies, Dublin, 1962 63; systems analyst IBM, Dublin, 1963-64; sr. rsch. assoc. Inst. Space Studies, N.Y.C., 1966-68; asst. prof. physics La. State U., Baton Rouge, 1964-66, assoc. prof., 1966-69, prof., 1969-86, Boyd prof., 1986—. Editor for theoretical physics Hadronic Jour.; former bd. mem. Phys. Rev. A; contbr. articles to profl. jours. Named Disting. Rsch. Master, La. State U., 1975; NAS NRC fellow, 1966 68, Sci. Rsch. Coun. (Eng.) sr. vis. fellow, 1976. Fellow Am. Phys. Soc.; mem. Am. Astron. Soc., Internat. Astronomy Union, Internat. Soc. Gen. Relativity and Gravitation. Republican. Roman Catholic. Avocation: tennis. Home: 522 Bancroft Way Baton Rouge LA 70808-4807 Office: La State Univ Dept Physics And Astronomy Baton Rouge LA 70803-0001

O'CONNELL, ROBERT JOHN, diversified financial services company executive; b. N.Y.C., May 16, 1943; m. Claire M. Costantini; children: Kristin, Jared. BA, Fordham U., 1965; MA, U. Pa., 1966. With N.Y. Life Ins. Co., N.Y.C., 1970-89, v.p., 1983-86, sr. v.p., 1986-89; sr. v.p. group mgmt. divsn. AIG, 1989-91; pres., CEO AIG Life Ins. Cos., 1991-98; also bd. dirs. A.I. Life; pres., CEO Mass. Mutual Life Insurance, Springfield, Mass., 1998-2000, chair., pres., & CEO, 2000—. Bd. dirs. AIG Life Ins. Co., AIG Equity Sales Corp., Delam Life Ins. Co.; mem. adv. com. to Cato Inst. project on Social Security Privatization. Mem. State Dept. Fin. Svcs. Corps Mission to Czechoslovakia. Mem. Am. Coun. Life Ins., Am. Internat. Life Assn. N.Y. (bd. dirs.). Office: Mass Mutual 1295 State St Springfield MA 01111-0001*

O'CONNELL, ROBERTA M. realtor; b. Whitinsville, Mass., Nov. 17, 1962; d. Robert F. McMorrow, Jr., James H. and Mary F. Wojdylak; m. David G. O'Connell, July 14, 1984. Lic. Cosmetologist, Kenneth's Inst. Hair Design, Framingham, Mass., 1982; Lic. Real Estate Agt., Am. Real Estate Acad., Waltham, Mass., 2001; student, Children's Inst. Lit., Ill., 2001—03. Sec. to the treas. Davna Corp., Millis, Mass., 1986—90; data entry staff Potpourri Collections, Medfield, Mass., 1990—92; stylist, nail technician Rafael Bertoldi's Hair Salon, Medfield, 1992—96; top stylist, esthetician Changes Hair Salon, Medway, Mass., 1996—2000; top stylist, esthetician, nail technician Expressions Hair Salon, Medway, 2000—01; lic. real estate salesperson Carlson GMAC Real Estate, Milford, 2001—02; realtor ERA Key Realty Svc., Milford, 2002—, ERA Key Realty Svc. Leadership Team, Whitinsville, 2003. Appeared (films) Celtic Pride, 1995, Jesus, Mary & Joey, 2003, Mohegan Sun Commerical, 2003. CCD tchr., catechist Our Lady of the Valley, Uxbridge, Mass., 1996—; mem. music ministry St. Mary's Parish, Uxbridge, 1999—. Named #1 Facialist, People's Choice Awards, Medway, 1998, #1 Pedicurist, 1998; recipient Boston Broker Coun. award multi-million dollar sales, 2003. Mem.: Milford C. of C. Roman Catholic. Avocations: painting, writing, reading, cooking, sledding. Home: 3 Jesters Way Uxbridge MA 01569 Office: ERA Key Realty Svcs 55 Church St Whitinsville MA 01588

O'CONNELL, TAAFFE CANNON, actress, publishing executive; b. Providence; d. Joseph Ceril and Edith Ethelyn (Dent) O'C. BA, MFA, U. Miss. Regional supr. Gloria Marshall Figure Salons, S.C.; v.p., co-founder Doc Sox Inc., Pacific Palisades, Calif., 1988-90; pres., founder Canoco Pub., L.A., 1991—, 1-800-266-DYNE, L.A., 1992-93. Founder Rising Star Distbn., Yes I Can Actor's Workshops, 2001—, Get Inside the Agent's Head Seminars, 2003; exec. prodr. Beanie/Twigg 1999-, Canoco Prodn. Appeared in films, including Men Without Dates, Dangerous, Hot Chili, Cheech & Chong Nice Dreams, Rocky II, Galaxy of Terror, New Years Evil, Rich Man Poor Man Book I, Caged Fury; TV appearances include Malubu Branch, General Hospital, Dangerous Women, Dallas, Knight and Daye, The New Gidget, Knight Rider, Three's Company, Dr. Joyce Brothers Show, Blansky's Beauties, Peter Lupus Show, Fix-It City, Happy Days, Laverne & Shirley, Wonder Woman, The Incredible Hulk; theater appearances include Too True to be Good, Damn Yankees, Anastasia, Star Spangled Girl, The Beaux Stratagem, The Canterbury Tales; founder, pub. Astrocaster, 1991, Power Agent, 1993; Jan. founder Rising Star Distbn. and Canoco Prodns., 1999—, Get Inside the Agents' Head Seminars, Yes I Can Actors Workshops; exec prodr.: Beanie & Twigg, Paranormal Private Eyes, Inside the Industry, 2000; founder Get Inside the Agents Head, 2003. Mem. Screen Actors' Guild, Am. Fedn. TV Radio Artists, Actor's Equity, Actor's Forum (bd. dirs. 1985-94). Avocations: singing, spinning, sailing, travel. Office: Canoco Pub 11611 Chenault St Ste 118 Los Angeles CA 90049-4574 Office Phone: 310-471-2287. E-mail: industryedge@earthlink.net.

O'CONNELL, WILLIAM EDWARD, JR., finance educator; b. N.Y.C., Sept. 16, 1937; s. William Edward and Helen Margaret (Brazel) O'Connell; m. Janet Elinor Shields, Aug. 15, 1965; children: William Edward III, Cathleen Anne. AB, Manhattan Coll., 1959; MBA, Columbia U., 1961; D in Bus. Adminstrn. with honors, Ind. U., 1967; JD, Coll. William & Mary, 1974. Fin. analyst Pfizer, Inc., N.Y.C., 1962-64; asst. prof. U. Conn., Storrs, 1967-69; Morris prof. banking U. Va., Charlottesville, 1988; Chessie prof. bus. Coll. William and Mary, Williamsburg, Va., 1969—. Mem. faculty Va. Bankers Sch., Charlottesville, 1975—99, Stonier Grad Sch. Banking, Newark, 1977—91, Bank Adminstrn. Inst., Madison, Wis., 1978—97; bd. dirs. C. & F Fin. Corp., Citizens & Farmers Bank, Citizens & Commerce Bank. Author: (book) Asset & Liability Management, 1979, Advanced Financial Planning, 1984, Financial Planning for Credit Unions, 1989, Strategic Financial Management for Commercial Banks, 1993. Mem.: Fin. Mgmt. Assn., Am. Fin. Assn., Fords Colony Country Club, Omicron Delta Epsilon, Beta Gamma Sigma. Roman Catholic. Home: 102 Overlook Dr Williamsburg VA 23185-4434 Office: Coll William & Mary Sch Bus Williamsburg VA 23187-8795 Office Phone: 757-221-2880. E-mail: william.oconnell@business.wm.edu.

O'CONNELL, WILLIAM RAYMOND, JR., educational consultant, retired academic administrator; b. Richmond, Va., Jan. 4, 1933; s. William Raymond and Mary Helen (Wenenger) O'C.; m. Peggy Annette Tucker, June 29, 1957; 1 child, William Raymond III. B of Music Edn., Richmond Profl. Inst., 1955; MA, Columbia U., 1962, EdD, 1969; HLD (hon.), New Eng. Coll., 1995. Asst. to provost Richmond (Va.) Profl. Inst., 1955-57, dean of men, 1957-59, dean of students, dean of men, 1959-61; asst. to provost, dir. student info. ctr. Tchrs. Coll. Columbia U., N.Y.C., 1962-65, rsch. asst. inst. of higher edn. Tchrs. Coll., 1965-66; rsch. assoc. So. Regional Edn. Bd., Atlanta, 1966-69, dir. spl. programs, 1969-73, project dir., undergrad. edn. reform, 1973-79; dir. curriculum and faculty devel. Assn. Am. Colls., Washington, 1979-80, v.p. for programs, 1980-82, v.p., 1982-85; pres. New Eng. Coll., Henniker, NH, 1985-95, pres. emeritus, 1995—; vis. sr. fellow Assn. Am. Colls. and Univs., 1995—97; dir. health edn. and leadership program Nat. Assn. Student Pers. Adminstrs., 1996—2002, 2003—. Cons. Coun. for Advancement Small Colls., 1975; adv. com. project on instnl. renewal through improvement of tchg. Soc. for Values in Higher Edn., 1975-78; evaluator N.H. Postsecondary Edn. Commn., 1987-95, vice chmn., 1990-92, chmn., 1992-94; evaluator Nat. Ctr. for Rsch. to Improve Postsecondary Tchg. and Learning, 1987-90, New Eng. Assn. Schs. and Colls., 1988, 91; higher edn. rev. panel awards for pioneering achievements in higher edn. Charles A. Dana Found., 1988, 89. Author, editor: articles to profl. publs. Pres. Richmond Cmty. Amb. Project, 1958-60, bd. dirs., 1960-61; bd. dirs. Alumni Assn. Acad. divsn. Va. Commonwealth U., 1970-73; chmn. fundraising com. Atlanta Boys Choir, Inc., 1976-77, trustee 1978-79; trustee Atlanta Coun. for Internat. Visitors, 1973-76, 78-79; pres. UN Assn., Atlanta, 1976-77; steering com. Nat. Coun. chpt., divsn. pres. UN Assn. U.S., 1977-79, nat. coun., 1980-90; steering com. Leadership Concord, 1992-95, chmn., 1994-95. Named Cmty. Amb. to Sweden Cmty. Amb. Project of the Experiment in Internat. Living, 1956. Fellow Royal Soc. of the Arts (U.K.); mem. N.H. Coun. on World Affairs (bd. dirs. 1993-95), Greater Concord C. of C. (bd. dirs. 1989-93), Coordinating Coun. for Internat. Univs. (bd. dirs. 2001—), Phi Delta Kappa. Methodist. Avocations: antiques, travel. E-mail: wroconn@cox.net.

O'CONNER, LORETTA RAE, lawyer; b. Denver, Dec. 23, 1958; d. Ronald Lee and Norma Jareene (Warner) Barkdoll; m. George Ellis Bentley, Dec. 31, 1976 (div. 1979); m. Donald Hugh O'Conner, Feb. 3, 1987; children: Justin Lee, Brandon Craig. AS, Denver Acad. Ct. Reporting, 1983; BA summa cum laude, Regis U., 1992; JD, U. Colo., 1996. Bar: Colo., 1996. Ct. reporter, Denver, 1983-87; dist. ct. reporter Jud. Dept., State of Colo., Pueblo, 1987-91; ct. reporter Pueblo, 1991-93; student atty. Pueblo County Legal Svcs.; pvt. practice Pueblo, 1997—. With Jud. Dept. State of Colo. Chief justice Student govt. Ct. U. So. Colo., Pueblo, 1992; trained facilitator Kettering Found., Pub. Policy Inst., Dayton, Ohio, 1992; sec. So. Colo. Registered Interpreters for the Deaf, Pueblo, 1991; bd. dirs. Concerned Parents of Pueblo, 1999—2002. President's scholar U. So. Colo., 1991-92, Alumni Assn. scholar, 1991-92; grantee Kettering Found., 1992; Colo. Legislature grantee and scholar Regis U., 1992; Colo. Legislature grantee U. Colo. Sch. Law, 1993-95, Dean's scholar, Dazzo Scholar, King scholar U. Colo. Sch. Law, 1993-96. Mem.: ATLA, Pueblo County Bar Assn., Colo. Womens Bar Assn., Colo. Bar Assn., Colo. Trial Lawyers Assn., Walking Stick Assn. (sec. 2000—), Phi Delta Phi (clk. 1994—95), Golden Key. Avocations: reading, writing, community board memberships. Home: 4310 Muirfield Rd Pueblo CO 81001-1167 Office: 9071 E Mississippi Ave Apt 13E Denver CO 80247-2019 Fax: (719) 584-2233.

O'CONNOR, ABIGAIL ELIZABETH, mathematician, educator, science educator; b. New Brunswick, N.J., Feb. 18, 1978; d. Samuel Margulies and Jennifer Alman Michaels; m. George O'Connor, Jr., Aug. 18, 2002; 1 stepchild, Nathan Edward. BA in Math., Rutgers U., 1999; MS in Applied Math., Rensselaer Poly. Inst., 2002. Adj. math. lectr. Rutgers U., New Brunswick, NJ, 1999—2000; comml. pilot, flight instr. O'Connor Aviation, Inc., Albany, NY, 2000—01; owner, flight instr. No. Flight Acad., Inc., Scotia, NY, 2002—; instr. math. and physics Schenectady (N.Y.) County CC, 2002—03; instr. math Albany Coll. Pharmacy, NY, 2003—. Presenter in field. Fellow, Claire Booth Luce Found., 2001—02. Mem.: Aircraft Owner and Pilot Assn., Am. Math. Soc. Avocations: alpaca farming, geology, home improvement, aviation. Home: 64 Stratton Ln Stillwater NY 12170 Office Phone: 518-664-2880. Business E-Mail: abby@oconnorfarm.com.

O'CONNOR, BETTY LOU, hotel executive, food service executive; b. Phoenix, Oct. 29, 1927; d. Georg Eliot and Tillie Edith Miller; m. William Speori O'Connor, Oct. 10, 1948 (dec. Feb. 1994); children: Thomas W., William K., Kelli Anne. Student, U. So. Calif., 1946-48, Calif. State U., Los Angeles, 1949-50. V.p. O'Connor Food Svcs., Inc., Jack in the Box Restaurants, Granada Hills, Calif., 1983-93; pres. O'Connor Food Svcs., Inc., Granada Hills, Calif., 1994—, Western Restaurant Mgmt. Co., Granada Hills, 1986—, C.E.O. Foods, Inc., Victorville, Calif., City Snippers, Inc., Santa Clarita, Calif. Mem. adv. bd. Bank of Granada Hills; bd. dirs. Nat. Franchise Purchasing Coop., nc. Recipient Frannie award Foodmaker, Inc., Northridge, Calif., 1984, First Rate award, 1992. Mem. Jack in the Box Franchisee Assn., Spurs Hon. (sec. U. So. Calif. 1947-48), Associated Women Students (sec. U. So. Calif. 1946-47), Gamma Alpha Chi (v.p. 1947-48), Chi Omega. Republican. Roman Catholic. Avocation: sewing. Office: O'Connor Food Svcs Inc 17545 Chatsworth St Granada Hills CA 91344-5720

O'CONNOR, BRIAN D. A. music educator, French Horn musician; b. Albuquerque, Dec. 6, 1951; s. Joseph Fredrick and Mary Adger (King) O'Connor; m. Coral Lynn Johnson, Sept. 21, 1972 (dec. July 1993); 1 child, Sean Adger; m. Wendy Anne Gunby, July 14, 1995; 1 stepchild, Nicola G. Perry. Student, New Eng. Conservatory of Music, Boston, 1970—72; BFA, Calif. Inst. of the Arts, Valencia, 1973. Recording musician French horn L.A. Recording Orch., 1974—; prof. horn UCLA, 1998—. Horn clinician Calif State Music Edn., L.A., 2001—; French horn performer Pacific Serenades, L.A., 2000—, UCLA Faculty Chamber Group, Westwood, 2001—; hornist/soloist over 1000 film scores and numerous TV scores including Crimson Tide, Contact, Backdraft, Star Trek-First Contact, others. Mem.: Recording Musicians Assn. of L.A. (pres. 1999—). Avocations: soccer, running, flying, bicycling. Office: 20335 Ventura Blvd Ste 400 Woodland Hills CA 91364

O'CONNOR, BRIAN KEVIN, pediatric cardiac electrophysiologist, researcher; b. Woodbury, N.J., Dec. 27, 1960; s. Frederick V. and Patricia Mary O'Connor. BS magna cum laude, U. Notre Dame, 1981; MD, Georgetown U., 1985. Pediat. resident, Boston, 1985-88; pediat. cardiology fellow U. Mich., Ann Arbor, 1988-91; pediat. electrophysiology fellow S.C. Children's Heart Ctr., Charleston, 1993-95; asst. prof. pediats. Sch. Medicine NYU Med. Ctr., N.Y.C., 1995—, dir. divsn. pediat. electrophysiology, 1995—. Author: (with others) Perspectives in Pediatric Cardiology, Vol. 2, 1990, Practical Pediatric Cardiac Pacing, 1995, Clinical Pediatric Cardiac Arrhythmias, 1998; contbr. articles to profl. jours. including Pacing and Clin. Electrophysiology, Pediat. Annals, Circulation, and Jour. Am. Coll. Cardiology. Fellow Am. Coll. Cardiology-Bristol-Meyers Squibb, 1994. Mem. Am. Coll. Cardiology, N.Am. Soc. Pacing and Electrophysiology, Phi Beta Kappa. Office: Children's Hosp NJ 201 Lyons Ave Newark NJ 07112-2027

O'CONNOR, BRYAN D. astronaut; b. Orange, Calif., Sept. 6, 1946; m. Susie O'Connor; children: Thomas, Kevin. BS in Engring., U.S. Naval Acad., 1968; MS in Aeronautical Systems, U. West Fla., 1970; grad., Naval Postgrad. Sch., Monterey, Calif., 1972, Naval Air Test Ctr., Patuxent River, Md., 1976. Commd. 2d lt. USMC, 1968, advanced through grades to col.; attack pilot; test piot Strike Test Directorate Naval Air Test Ctr., Patuxent River, Md., project officer, 1977—79; dept. program mgr. Naval Air Systems Command, Washington; astronaut NASA, Houston, 1980, aviation safety officer Astronaut Corps, asst. to space shuttle program mgr., chmn. Space Flight Safety Panel, 1988—89, dep. dir. flight crew ops., 1988—91; commdg. officer Marine Aviation Detachment Naval Air Test Ctr., 1991, dep. dir., chief of staff flight test and engring. group; dep. assoc. adminstr. for space flight NASA, dir. space sta. redesign, dir. Space Shuttle Program, 1994—96; aerospace cons., 1996—. Decorated DFC; named Aviation Week and Space Tech. Laureate; recipient Sys. Effectiveness and Safety award, AIAA, Barry M. Goldwater Edn. award. Achievements include logged over 5,000 hours in over 40 types of aircraft; logged over 386 hours in space; pilot STS-61B Atlantis (1985); crew comdr. STS-40 Columbia (1991). Avocations: hiking, scuba diving, music, travel. Office: Astronaut Office/CB NASA Johnson Space Ctr Houston TX 77058

O'CONNOR, CHARLES EDWARD, JR., state government official, lawyer; b. Philadelphia, PA, Feb. 21, 1960; s. Charles Edward O'Connor, Ruth Pauline Cardamone-O'Connor; m. Lori Marie Ruszkiewicz; 1 child, Charles Henry. Juris Doctor, Widener University School of Law, Wilmington, Delaware, 1985—88; Bachelor of Arts, LaSalle College, Philadelphia, Pa, 1978—82.

Election Clerk County Commissioners' Office, Philadelphia, PA, 1978—81; Parcel Post Machine Clerk United States Postal Service, Philadelphia, PA, 1982—83, Letter Carrier Abington, PA, 1983—85; Bail Interviewer Supervisor Common Pleas Court of Philadelphia, Philadelphia, PA, 1985—89; Law Clerk to The Honorable John T.J Kelly Jr. Superior Court of Pennsylvania, Philadelphia, PA, 1989—92, Chief Law Clerk to The Honorable John T.J. Kelly Jr., 1992—97, Deputy Prothonotary for the Eastern District of Pennsylvania, 1997—2001; Executive Director 2001 Legislative Reapportionment Commission, Harrisburg, PA, 2001—02. Member 2nd District Police Advisory Council, Philadelphia, PA, 1998—2002; Counsel Summerdale Boys Club, Philadelphia, PA, 1993—97; Member 24th Police District Advisory Council, Philadelphia, PA, 1989—92. Member 53rd Ward Republican Executive Committee, Philadelphia, 1978—82, 25th Ward Republican Executive Committee, Philadelphia, 1988—89; Counsel & Civic Improvement Chairman Friends of Summerdale Civic Association, Philadelphia, 1995—99, President, 1999—2004. Mem.: OSIA, Saint Martin of Tours Ch. Parish (coun. mem.), Custodes Pacis Lodge#2085, Grand Army of The Republic Museum, Ancient Order of Hiberians Division#87 (First Degree 2000), Pennsylvania Historical Society, Brehon Law Society. Roman Catholic. Avocation: Pennsylvania History, Neighborhood Clean-up/Graffiti Removal, Old Car Repair and Restoration, Urban Affairs. Home: 9040 Wesleyan Rd Philadelphia PA 19136-1113 Office: Superior Ct Pa 530 Walnut St Ste 315 Philadelphia PA 19106 Office Phone: 717-705-9901. Office Fax: 717-705-9906. Business E-Mail: fsmdcivic@aol.com.

O'CONNOR, CHARLES P. lawyer; b. Boston, Sept. 29, 1940; m. Mary Linda Hogan; children: Jennifer, Amy, Austin, Catherine. Bachelors degree, Holy Cross Coll., Worcester, Mass., 1963; LLB, Boston Coll., 1966. Bar: Mass. 1966, D.C. 1968, U.S. Supreme Ct. 1974. Atty., gen. counsel's office NLRB, Washington, 1966-67; assoc. Morgan, Lewis & Bockius, LLP, Washington, 1968-71; ptnr. Morgan, Lewis & Bockius, Washington, 1971—2003, chmn. labor and employment law sect., 1996-99, mng. ptnr. Washington office, 1995-97; v.p., gen. counsel Maersk, Inc., 2003—. Gen. counsel Major League Baseball Player Rels. Com., N.Y.C., 1989-94. Contbr. numerous articles on labor and employment law to law jours. Spl. counsel elections com. U.S. Ho. of Reps., Washington, 1968-69. Fellow Coll. Labor and Employment Lawyers; mem. ABA, D.C. Bar Assn., Met. Club Washington, Belle Haven Country Club, N.Y. Athletic Club, Cape Cod Nat. Golf Club. Home: 424 S Lee St Alexandria VA 22314

O'CONNOR, CLINT HAYNIE, electrical engineer; b. Corpus Christi, Tex., June 23, 1955; s. Robert Barnard Jr. and Edith H. (Haynie) O'C.; m. Christine Ann Schroeder, Mar. 30, 1985. BA, Wabash Coll., Crawfordsville, Ind., 1978. Pres., dir. R&D Analytical Engines, Austin, Tex., 1982-86; sr. project engr. Gould Indsl. Automation, Andover, Mass., 1986-88; mgr. elect. engring. Webtron Corp., Fort Lauderdale, Fla., 1988-93; sr. tech. strategist Dell Computer Corp., Austin, 1993—. Chmn. bd. Analytical Engines, 1982-86; cons. Marine Sci. Inst., Galveston, Tex., 1980. Vol. Dolphin Rsch. Ctr., Grassy Key, Fla., 1989-90. Mem. Sigma Xi. Achievements include development of first 68000 co-processor for Apple II, 68010 co-processor for IBM PC; author 68000 Applesoft BASIC compatible interpreter; software development of Gould C986 co-processor, printing press control systems, development of Dell battery gauge, Dell control, Dell PC-card central and utilities for Dell Latitude portables; 13 patents in field. Office: Dell Computer One Dell Way Round Rock TX 78682

O'CONNOR, DANIEL WILLIAM, retired religious studies and classical languages educator; b. Jersey City, Mar. 17, 1925; s. Daniel William and Emma Pauline (Ritz) O'C.; m. Carolyn Lockwood, June 26, 1954; children—Kathlyn Forssell Beal, Daniel William III BA, Dartmouth Coll., 1945; MA, Columbia U., 1956, PhD, 1960; M.Div., Union Theol. Sem., 1950. Ordained to ministry United Ch. of Christ, 1950. Mem. exec. com., bd. home missions Congl. Chs., 1946-51; pastor Paramus Congl. Ch., N.J., 1950-55; assoc. sec. Student Christian Movement YMCA, N.Y., 1947-48; exec. sec. Earl Hall Columbia U., N.Y.C., 1948-50; tutor asst., dept. N.T. Union Theol. Sem., N.Y.C., 1958-59; successively asst. prof., assoc. prof., prof. religious studies and classical langs. St. Lawrence U., Canton, N.Y., 1959-67, dir. summer session, 1966, assoc. dean coll., 1967-68, Charles A. Dana prof. religious studies and classical langs., 1967-89, chmn. dept. religious studies and classical langs., 1974-89, Charles A. Dana emeritus prof., 1989—. Lectr. Elderhostels and Sr. insts., N.Y. and Fla., 1990—. Author: Peter in Rome, 1969; contbr. articles to Ency. Britannica and profl. jours., also revs. Trustee Silver Bay Assn. YMCA, N.Y., 1978-86, 86-92, Lit. Vols. Am., St. Lawrence County, N.Y., 1991-94; bd. dirs. U.S. Power Squadron, St. Lawrence Squadron, N.Y., 1972-75. With USNR, 1943-45. Grantee Lilly Found., Columbia U., 1969-70, Mellon Found., Am. Schs. Oriental Research, Jerusalem, 1979 Mem. AAUP, Am. Assn. Ret. Persons, Nat. Assn. Watch and Clock Collectors, Rotary (pres. Canton Club 1972-73, Rotary Found. scholarship selection com. dist. 7040 1983-87, 96-2000, gov. dist. 7040 1987-88, dist. 7040 ext. com. 1988-89, youth exch. com. dist. 7040 1990-93, lit. com. 1991-93). Home: 3 Hillside Cir Canton NY 13617-1409 E-mail: timeout@1000islands.net.

O'CONNOR, DAVID, talent agent; Talent agt. Creative Artists Agy., Beverly Hills, Calif., ptnr., mng. dir., 1996—. Office: Creative Artists Agy 9830 Wilshire Blvd Beverly Hills CA 90212-1825

O'CONNOR, DORIS JULIA, non-profit fundraiser, consultant; b. Apr. 30, 1930; 1 dau., Kim C. BA cum laude in Econs., U. Houston, 1975. Adminstrv. asst. Shell Cos. Found. Inc., N.Y.C., 1966-71, asst. sec. Houston, 1971-73, sec., 1973-76, sr. v.p., dir., mem. exec. com., 1976-93; prin. Doris O'Connor & Co., 1993—. Corp. assoc. United Way of Am., Washington, 1976-93; corp. advisor Bus. Com. of Arts, N.Y.C., 1976-91, del., 1982-87; dir. Ind. Sector, Washington, 1981-89, vice chmn., 1983-87; mem. contbns. coun. Conf. Bd., N.Y.C., 1976-93; advisor Coun. of Better Bus. Burs., Washington, 1975-94, vice chmn., 1983-87; commr. adv. commn. on work-based learning, Dept. Labor, 1991-93; mem. Houston/Harris County Arts Task Force, 1991-93, Houston Ind. Sch. Dist. Task Force, 1991-93; trustee Houston Grand Opera, 1993-99, Houston Symphony Soc., 1993-99, Soc. Performing Arts, 1993-99, Cultural Arts Coun., 1993-96, Greater Houston Coalition Edn. Excellence, 1993-96; mem. adv. bd. Houston Zool. Soc., 1993-99; mem. New Orleans Mus. of Art, Opera Assn. Mem. Houston Com. Fgn. Rels., Houston Philos-.Soc., Plaza Club (bd. givs. 1987-89), Omicron Delta Epsilon.

O'CONNOR, EDWARD GEARING, lawyer; b. Pitts., May 5, 1940; s. Timothy R. and Irene B. (Gearing) O'C.; m. Janet M. Showalter, June 17, 1972; children: Mark G., Susan M. BA, Duquesne U., 1962, JD, 1965. Bar: Pa. 1965, U.S. Dist. Ct. (we. dist.) Pa. 1965, U.S. Ct. Appeals (3d cir.) 1968, U.S. Supreme Ct. 1976. Assoc. Eckert, Seamans, Cherin & Mellott, Pitts., 1965-72, ptnr., 1973-99, sr. counsel, 2000—. Mem. adv. com. on appellate ct. rules Supreme Ct. Pa., 1986—92, mem. procedure rules com., 1998—2004; bd. dirs., mem. audit com., compliance com. Federated Investors, Inc. Editor Duquesne U. Law Rev., 1964-65. Chmn. Hampton (Pa.) Twp. Planning Commn., 1986-87; mem. Hampton (Pa.) Twp. Zoning Hearing Bd., 1997—; bd. dirs. Duquesne U. Recipient Disting. Alumni award Duquesne U. Law Rev., 1985, Disting. Law Alumni award Duquesne U. Sch. Law, 1991, Disting. Svc. award Hampton Twp., 1991, McAnurlty Svc. award Duquesne U., 1992; named Century Club Disting. Alumni, Duquesne U., 1985. Fellow: Pa. Bar Found., Am. Bar Found.; mem.: Ally City Bar Found. (chair fellows com. 2000—01), Acad. Trial Lawyers Allegheny County (bd. govs. 1986—89, 1998—), Pa. Bar Assn. (ho. of dels. 1985—90), Pitts. Athletic Assn., Duquesne U. Alumni Assn. (pres. 1980—82, 1988—90, bd. govs. 1982—90, bd. dirs. 1988—89), Duquesne Club. Republican. Roman Catholic. Home: 4288 Green Glade Ct Allison Park PA 15101-1202 Office: Eckert Seamans Cherin & Mellott 600 Grant St Ste 44th Pittsburgh PA 15219-2702 Office Phone: 412-566-6000. E-mail: ego@escm.com., eoconnor@eckertseamans.com.

O'CONNOR, EILEEN J. federal agency administrator; Grad., Columbus State U., Cath. U. Ptnr. Office Fed. Tax Svcs. Grant Thornton, 1984—99; officer for tax svcs. Aronson, Fetridge and Weigle; asst. atty. gen. tax divsn. U.S. Dept. Justice, Washington, 2001—. Adj. prof. law George Mason Law Sch., Georgetown U. Law Sch. Office: US Dept Justice Tax Divsn 950 Pennsylvania Ave NW Washington DC 20530-0001

O'CONNOR, FRANCIS X. financial executive; b. Bklyn., May 7, 1929; s. Richard B. and Mary (McCafferty) O'C.; m. Leona A. Windorf, June 30, 1951; children: Francis X., Edward K., Brendan T., Richard B. III, A. Bruce, Marianne, Margaret, Leona. BS, St. Peter's Coll., 1951. CPA, N.Y., N.J. Audit mgr. Coopers & Lybrand, N.Y.C., 1951-65; controller Ward Foods, Inc., N.Y.C., 1965-66, v.p. fin., CFO, 1966-72, also bd. dirs., 1968-73; v.p. fin., CFO UMC Industries, Inc., N.Y.C., 1973-76; v.p. fin. and corp. devel., CFO SKF Industries, Inc., King of Prussia, Pa., 1976-87; v.p. corp. fin. Moore & Schley Securities Corp., Morristown, N.J., 1987-89; mng. dir. Sterling Manhattan Corp. Investment Bankers, N.Y.C., 1989-93. Adv. bd. Boyden Cons. Corp. Mem. AICPA, AIM, N.Y. State Soc. CPAs. Fin. Excs. Inst., Nat. Conf. on Power Transmission (trustee), Machinery and Allied Products Inst. Fin. Coun., St. Peter's Coll. Alumni Assn. (trustee, past pres. Monmouth chpt.), Navy League U.S., Spring Lake Golf Club, (past pres., trustee), Seaview Country Club (N.J.), Green Gables Croquet Club (past pres.), Legacy Golf Club (Ft. Pierce, Fla.), Yacht and Country Club (Stuart, Fla.). Home: 2355 NE Ocean Blvd Stuart FL 34996-2945 Office: 16 St Clair Ave Spring Lake NJ 07762

O'CONNOR, SISTER GEORGE AQUIN (MARGARET M. O'CONNOR), academic administrator, sociology educator; b. Astoria, N.Y., Mar. 5, 1921; d. George M. and Joana T. (Loughlin) O'C. BA, Hunter Coll., 1943; MA, Catholic U. Am., 1947; PhD (NIMH fellow), NYU, 1964; LL.D. Manhattan Coll., 1983; D of Pedagogy (hon.), Dowling Coll., 1997; DHL, St. Francis Coll., 1997, St. Joseph's Coll., 1997. Mem. faculty St. Joseph's Coll., Bklyn., 1946—, prof. sociology and anthropology, 1966—, chmn. social sci. dept., 1966-69, pres., 1969-97; pres. emeritus. Fellow African Studies Assn., Am. Anthrop. Assn.; Bklyn. C. of C. (dir. 1973-97), Alpha Kappa Delta, Delta Epsilon Sigma. Author: The Status and Role of West African Women: A Study in Cultural Change, 1964. Named one of N.Y. State Senate's Women of Distinction. Office: Saint Joseph's Coll 245 Clinton Ave Brooklyn NY 11205-3602

O'CONNOR, G(EORGE) RICHARD, ophthalmologist; b. Cin., Oct. 8, 1928; s. George Leo and Sylvia Johanna (Voss) O'C. AB, Harvard U., 1950; MD, Columbia U., 1954. Resident in ophthalmology Columbia-Presbyn. Med. Center, N.Y.C., 1957-60; research fellow Inst. Biochemistry, U. Uppsala, Sweden, 1960-61, State Serum Inst., Copenhagen, 1961-62; asst. prof. ophthalmology U. Calif., San Francisco, 1962-68, prof., 1972-84; dir. Francis I. Proctor Found. for Research in Ophthalmology, 1970-84. Mem. Nat. Adv. Eye Council NIH, 1974-78 Author: (with G. Smolin) Ocular Immunology, 1981; asso. editor: Am. Jour. Ophthalmology, 1976-81. Served with USPHS, 1955-57. Recipient Janeway prize Coll. of Physicians and Surgeons, Columbia U., 1954; Doyne medal Oxford U., 1984; NIH grantee, 1962-84 Mem. Am. Bd. Ophthalmology (examiner), Assn. for Rsch. in Vision and Ophthalmology (trustee 1979-83, pres. 1982-83, Weisenfeld award 1990), Am. Ophthal. Soc., Calif. Med. Assn., Frederic C. Cordes Eye Soc., Pan Am. Ophthal. Assn. Clubs: Faculty. Republican. Presbyterian. Home: 22 Wray Ave Sausalito CA 94965-1831 Office: U Calif Med Ctr 315 S San Francisco CA 94143-0001 Office Phone: 415-332-4994. Business E-Mail: rconnor@itsa.ucsf.edu.

O'CONNOR, JAMES E. waste management executive; m. Cathy O'Connor; children: Kerry O'Connor Stiles, James, Kevin. Staff acct. Waste Mgmt., Oakbrook, Ill., 1972-78, with, 1982-87, v.p. southeastern region, 1987-91, sr. v.p. N.Am., 1991-92, area pres., 1992-98; CEO Republic Svcs., Inc., Ft. Lauderdale, Fla., 1998—, also bd. dirs. Bd. dirs. Broward Workshop, Children's Cardiac Found.; mem. bd. advisors Broward Econ. Devel. Coun., Broward County Make-A-Wish Found.; trustee Fla. Tax Watch, Mus. Art, St. Thomas Aquinas H.S. Found. Recipient Tree of Life award Jewish Nat. Fund, 1995. Office: Republic Svcs Inc 110 SE 6th St 28th Fl Fort Lauderdale FL 33301

O'CONNOR, JAMES G. auto company executive; With Ford Motor Co., 1964—, gen. mgr., parts & svcs. div., 1989—90; pres., COO Ford Motor Co. of Can. Ltd., 1990—92, pres., CEO, 1992—94; exec. dir., N Amer. mktg. ops. & plans Ford Motor Co., 1994—96, pres., Lincoln Mercury div., 1996—99, pres., Ford div., 1999—2002, group v.p., N. Amer. mktg, sales, & svcs., 2002—. Office: Ford Motor Co One Amer Rd Dearborn MI 48126-1899

O'CONNOR, JAMES JOHN, retired utility company executive; b. Chgo., Mar. 15, 1937; s. Fred James and Helen Elizabeth O'Connor; m. Ellen Louise Lawlor, Nov. 24, 1960; children: Fred, John (dec.), James, Helen Elizabeth. BS, Holy Cross Coll., 1958; MBA, Harvard U., 1960; JD, Georgetown U., 1963. Bar: Ill. 1963. With Commonwealth Edison Co., Chgo., 1963-98, asst. to chmn. exec. com., 1964-65, comml. mgr., 1966, asst. v.p., 1967-70, v.p., 1970-73, exec. v.p., 1973-77, pres., 1977-87, chmn., 1980-98, CEO, also bd. dirs., 1998; chmn., CEO Unicom Corp., Chgo., 1994-98, ret., 1998. Bd. dirs. Corning, Inc., Trizec Properties, Inc., United Air Lines, Smurfit-Stone Container Corp. Mem. The Bus. Coun.; bd. dirs. Lyric Opera, Joffrey Ballet, Helen Brach Found.; bd. dirs., trustee Mus. Sci. and Industry, Chgo. Symphony; past chmn. Met. Savs. Bond Campaign; trustee Northwestern U.; bd. dirs., past chmn. Chgo. Urban League, Chicagoland C. of C.; past chmn. bd. trustees Field Mus. Natural History; life trustee Adler Planetarium, Mus. Sci. and Industry; mem. exec. bd. Chgo. Area coun. Boy Scouts Am.; chmn. Cardinal Bernardin's Big Shoulders Fund; exec. v.p. The Hundred Club Cook County; dir., past pres. Cath. Charities; past chmn., hon. dir. Am. Cancer Soc., Chgo. Conv. and Tourism Bur. With USAF, 1960-63.

O'CONNOR, JAMES T. civil engineering educator; b. Tulsa, Oklahoma, Feb. 28, 1956; s. Joseph Walter and Mary Lois (Walker) O'C.; m. Catherine (Morris), Jan. 7, 1995; children: Catherine Claire, James Patrick. BS, Okla. State U., 1979; MArch, U. Ill., 1980; PhD, U. Tex., 1983. Registered profl. engr. Tex. Archtl. engr. intern Murray, Jones, and Murray, 1977-80; prof. U. Tex., Austin, 1984—. Engr. and mgmt. cons. Arco Chem.; Dallas Area Rapid Transit; FSB, Inc.; City of Austin, U. Tex. Sys.; Fla. Power and Light; Cuyahoga County, Ohio. Contbg. articles to profl. jour.; author five course manuals in field. U.S. Army Corp Engr., 1975-77. Recipient Nat. Value Engring. Award, Am. Assn. of State Hwy. Transp. Ofcl., 1997; Tex. Quality Initiative Award, State of Tex., 1998; Nat. Quality Initiative Award Assn. State Hwy. Transp. Ofcl., Fed. Hwy. Adminstrn., 1999. Mem. ASCE (Rowland prize 1995, 97); Tex. Soc. Profl. Engr., Constrn. Specifications Inst. Roman Catholic. Achievements include rsch. on project constructability, planning from startup, value mgmt. process and highway constrn. productivity rates. Home: 1200 Yaupon Valley Rd Austin TX 78746-4331 Office: U Tex Dept Civil Engring ECJ 5 2 Austin TX 78712 Business E-Mail: jtoconnor@mail.utexas.edu.

O'CONNOR, JENNIFER, lawyer; b. Somerville, Mass., Feb. 12, 1966; m. Paul J. Meyer, Nov. 13, 1993. BA in Govt. magna cum laude, Harvard U., 1987; MPA, Columbia U., 1993; JD magna cum laude, Georgetown U., 1997. Dep. press sec., econ. devel. assoc. Office of Manhattan Borough Pres Ruth Messinger, N.Y.C., 1990-92; budget specialist, N.E. regional polit. dir. Presdl. Transition Office, Little Rock, 1992-93; dep. dir. Office of Mgmt. and Adminstrn. The White House, Washington, 1993, spl. asst. to Pres. for Cabinet affairs, 1993-95, spl. asst. to Pres. Office Dep. Chief of Staff, 1995-96; dep. asst. sec. policy U.S. Dept. Labor, Washington, 1997; law clk. to judge U.S. Ct. Appeals/D.C. Cir., 1997-98; assoc. Miller, Cassidy, Larroca & Lewin/Baker Botts (merged), Washington, 1998—2002; counsel Wilmer, Cutler and Pickering, 2002—. Field. dir. N.Y. primary campaign, polit. dir. N.J. primary campaign, dep. mgr. at Dem. Nat. Conv., state dir. Vt. gen. election campaign Clinton for Pres./Clinton-Gore '92, 1992. Democrat. Office: Wilmer Cutlre Pickering LLP 2445 M St NW Washington DC 20037

O'CONNOR, JOHN DENNIS, biology professor; b. Chgo., Mar. 20, 1942; married, 1964; 3 children. BS, Loyola U, Chgo., 1963; MS, DePaul U., 1966; PhD, Northwestern U., 1968. NIH fellow Mich. State U., East Lansing, 1968-70; asst. prof. biology UCLA, 1969-74, assoc. prof., 1974-77, prof. biology, 1977-81, chmn. biology, 1979-81, dean, life scis., 1981-87; vice chancellor for research, dean of grad. sch., prof. biology U. N.C., prof. biology, 1988-91; chancellor, prof. biology U. Pitts., 1991-95; provost Smithsonian Instn., Washington, 1996-99, under sec. for sci., 2000—02; v.p. rsch., dean grad. studies U. Md., College Park, 2002—04, prof. biology, 2004—. Vis. prof. U. Nijmegen, Netherlands, 1975-76, Monash U., 1977. Fellow AAAS; mem. Am. Soc. Zoology, Soc. Devel. Biology, Am. Soc. Molecular Biology and Biochemistry, Bus. Higher Edn. Forum (vice chair 1994-96, chair 1996-98), Assn. Univs. for Rsch. in Astronomy (bd. dirs.). Office: U Md 2133 Lee Bldg College Park MD 20742-5121*

O'CONNOR, JOHN JAY, III, lawyer; b. San Francisco, Jan. 10, 1930; s. John Jay and Sally (Flynn) O'C.; m. Sandra Day, Dec. 20, 1952; children: Scott, Brian, Jay. AB, Stanford U., 1951, LLB, 1953. Bar: Calif. 1953, Ariz. 1957, D.C. 1981. Mem. Fennemore, Craig, von Ammon & Udall, Phoenix, 1957-81, Miller & Chevalier, Washington, 1982-88; ptnr. Bryan Cave, Washington and Phoenix, 1988-99, of counsel, 2000—. Judge pro-tem Superior Ct. State of Ariz., 1979-81. Chmn. Ariz. Crippled Children's Svcs., 1968; Chmn. planning and zoning commn. Town of Paradise Valley, 1967; Chmn. Maricopa County Young Republicans, 1960, Ariz. Young Rep. League, 1962; bd. dirs. Ariz. Tax Rsch. Assn., 1966-81; chmn. bd. dirs. Maricopa County Gen. Hosp., 1967-70; exec. com. bd. visitors Stanford Law Sch., 1976-80; pres. Stanford Law Fund, 1980-82; mem. nat. coun. Salk Inst. Biol. Studies, San Diego, 1977-90; pres. Phoenix-Scottsdale United Way, 1977-79; bd. dirs. World Affairs Coun. of Phoenix, 1970-81, Legal Aid Soc. Phoenix, Maricopa County Mental Health Assn.; trustee Meridian House Internat., Washington, 1982-88; mem. policy devel. com. Phoenix Cmty. Svc. Fund, 1978; mem. exec. com. Valley Leadership, 1979-81; bd. dirs. Trusteeship for St. Luke's Hosp., 1979-81; mem. adv. com. Nat. Postal Mus., Washington, 1992-98. Served to 1st lt. AUS, 1954-57. Mem. ABA, Stanford Assocs., Paradise Valley Country Club, Ariz. Club (pres. 1979-81), Valley Field Riding and Polo Club, Stanford Club of Phoenix (pres.), Iron Springs Club (pres. 1974-76), Bohemian Club, Met. Club, Alfalfa Club, Alibi Club, Delta Upsilon, Phi Delta Phi. Office: Bryan Cave 700 13th St NW Fl 7 Washington DC 20005-5921

O'CONNOR, JOHN JOSEPH, operations executive; b. Smyrna, Tenn., June 1, 1959; s. John O'Connor and Dolores Jane (Bell) Brem; m. Lea Ann Bradford, Sept. 6, 1986; 1 child, Colleen Michelle. BS, Tex. A&M U., 1981. Cert. marine engr. 3rd asst. engr. Marine Engrs. Beneficial Assn., Houston, 1981-84; asst. engr. Biehl Ship Mgmt., Houston, 1984; balance technician Hickham Industries, Inc., LaPorte, Tex., 1984-86, prodn. scheduler/Sulzer, 1986-87, project engr./Sulzer, 1987-88, engring. mgr./Sulzer, 1988-89, ops. mgr./Sulzer Huntington Beach, Calif., 1989-93, sr. engr., corp. mergers and acquisitions La Porte, Tex., 1993-94; tech. and field svc. mgr. Sulzer Turbosys. Internat., Houston, 1994-98; engring. projects mgr. Hickham Industries, Inc., LaPorte, Tex., 1998—. Guest speaker Tex. A&M U., Galveston, Tex., College Station, Tex., 1981-89, U. Houston, 1986-89; moderator Power Machinery and Compressor Conf., Houston, 1989. Prin. engr. inventions in field (Achievement awards 1989); author: Steam Turbine Overhaul and Repair Specifications, 1994. Bd. dirs. Cedar Lawn Assn., pres., 1998-2001; bd. dirs. East End Presch., pres., 1998-99; bd. dirs. (pres.) Galveston Alliance of Island Neighborhoods, 1998-2003; adv. bd. Galveston Hist. Found., 1999. Recipient Outstanding Records in Engring., Gulf Oil Corp., Galveston, 1981. Mem. ASME (guest speaker convs.), Pacific Energy Assn. (guest speaker convs. 1990-92), Assn. of Former Students/Tex. A&M. Avocations: hiking, camping, travel, automotive restoration, litigation. Business E-Mail: john.oconnor@sulzerhickham.com.

O'CONNOR, JOHN MORRIS, III, retired humanities educator; b. Evanston, Ill., Sept. 21, 1937; s. John Morris and Clare Evelyn (Merrick) O'Connor; m. Mary Bittner, Dec. 30, 1960 (div.); 1 child, Emily; m. Miranda E. P. Ind, Aug. 14, 1971 (div.); 1 child, Amanda. Student, Georgetown U., 1955—56; BA, Cornell U., 1959; MA, Harvard U., 1962, PhD, 1965. Instr. Vassar Coll., 1964-66, asst. prof. philosophy, 1966-68; asst. prof. Case Western Res. U., Cleve., 1968-70, assoc. prof., 1970-77; exec. sec. Am. Philos. Assn. U. Del., Newark, 1977-84, assoc. prof., 1977-83; asst. dir. programs Nat. Humanities Ctr., Research Triangle Park, NC, 1983-87; dean Sch. Humanities William Paterson Univ., Wayne, NJ, 1987—91, dean Sch. Humanities, Mgmt. and Social Scis., 1991-92; coord. spl. projects Office of Provost William Paterson Coll., Wayne, NJ, 1992-93, prof. philosophy, 1992-2001; ret., 2001. Editor (with others): Introductory Philosophy, 1967, Modern Materialism, 1969, Moral Problems in Medicine, 1976; contbr. articles to profl. jours. Woodrow Wilson Nat. fellow, 1959—60. Home: 523 Guilford Ave Chambersburg PA 17201

O'CONNOR, JOHN THOMAS, civil engineering educator; b. N.Y.C., Feb. 11, 1933; married, 1966; 2 children. BCE, Cooper Union, 1955; MSCE, N.J. Inst. Tech., 1958; EngD, Johns Hopkins U., 1961. Sanitary engr. Elson T. Killam Sanit & Hydraulic Consulting Engrs., 1955-56; civil engr. George A. Fuller Constrn. Co., N.Y., 1956-57; sanitary engr. Parsons, Brinckerhoff, Quade & Douglas, 1957; from asst. prof. to prof. civil engring. U. Ill., Urbana-Champaign, 1961-75; prof. civil engring. U. Mo., Columbia, 1975-92, chmn. dept., 1975-89; chief Ill. State Water Survey, 1992-95; pres. H2O'C Engring., LLC, 1995—. Mem. ASCE, Am. Chem. Soc., Am. Water Works Assn., Am. Soc. Limnology and Oceanography, Water Environment Fedn. Achievements include research on drinking water treatment processes; removal of arsenic, microorganisms, organic substances, iron and manganese, radionuclides; wastewater treatment and disinfection; solid and hazardous waste site remediation. E-mial. Address: 2401 Tahoe Ct Columbia MO 65203-1444 E-mail: john@h2oc.com.

O'CONNOR, KAREN, political science educator, researcher, writer; b. Buffalo, Feb. 15, 1952; s. Robert J. and Norma (Wilton) O'C.; m. F. Allen McDonogh, June 7, 1974 (div. 1986). 1 child, Meghan; m. Richard Cupitt, July 31, 1992. B.A., SUNY-Buffalo, 1973, J.D., 1977, Ph.D., 1979. Bar: Ga. 1978. Instr. polit. sci. Emory U., 1977-78, asst. prof., 1978-83, assoc. prof., 1983-88; prof., 1988-95; prof. Am. Univ., 1995—, dir. Women & Politics Inst., 1999—. Author: Women's Organization's Use of the Courts, 1980; (with N.E. McGlen) Women's Rights, 1983, (with L. Sabato) American Government, 8th edit., 2004; Mem. editorial bd. Women & Politics, 1980—, editor, 1999-2003, Law & Policy, 1982—, Jour. of Politics, 1984-87, Am. Politics Quarterly, 1987-90, Women and Congress, 2002, Women, Politics and American Society, 2004; Contbr. articles to profl. jours. Mem. Am. Polit. Sci. Assn. (exec. council 1985-87), So. Polit. Sci. Assn. (pres. 2000-01), Nat. Capitol Area Pol. Sci. Assn. (pres. 2001-02), Cosmos Club. Home: 4383 Westover Pl NW Washington DC 20016-5555

O'CONNOR, KAREN LENDE, Olympic athlete; b. Feb. 17, 1958; m. David O'Connor, 1993. Mem. US Equestrian Olympic Team, Seoul, Korea, 1988, Atlanta, 1996, U.S. Equestrian Team, 2000. Winner CCI, Boekelo (Holland), 1984, CCI, Chesterland (Pa.), 1985, placed 1st Role/Kentucky Internat. CCI Three Day Event, 1991, 1st Tetbury (Eng.) Horse Trials, 1991, 1st Fair Hill (Md.) Horse Trials, 1991, 3rd Burghley Three Day Event CCI (Eng.), 1991, 6th World Three Day Event Rider Rankings L'Annee Hippique, 1991, 3rd CCI, Loughanmore (Ireland), 1992, 6th Blenheim Audi Internat. Horse Trials (Eng.), 1993, 1st CCI, Punchestown (Ireland), 1993, 10th CCI Internat. de Saumur, 1994; recipient Silver medal, Olympic Games, Atlanta, 1996; named U.S. Combined Trg. Assn. Lady Rider of the Year, 1989, 90, 91, 95, 96, 97, 98, Female Equestrian Athlete of the Year Olympic Com., 1993, USET spring champion, winning Kentucky CCI, USET FAll Reserve champion, 2nd Fair Hill, 1999, World Equestrian Games Bronze Medal Team, 1998, USET spring champion, winner Kentucky CCI, 1997; grantee USET, 1991. Office: care US Equestrian Team Inc PO Box 355 Gladstone NJ 07934-0355

O'CONNOR, KARL WILLIAM (GOODYEAR JOHNSON), lawyer; b. Washington, Aug. 1, 1931; s. Hector and Lucile (Johnson) O'C.; m. Sylvia Gasbarri, Mar. 23, 1951 (dec.); m. Judith Ann Byers, July 22, 1972 (div. 1983); m. Eleanor Celler, Aug. 3, 1984 (div. 1986); m. Alma Hepner, Jan. 1, 1987 (div. 1996); children: Blair, Frances, Brian, Brendan; m. Allie O'Connor, Jul.

15, 2000. BA, U. Va., 1952, JD, 1958. Bar: Va. 1958, D.C. 1959, Am. Samoa 1976, Calif. 1977, Oreg. 1993. Law clk. U.S. Dist. Ct. Va., Abingdon, 1958-59; practice law Washington, 1959-61; trial atty. U.S. Dept. Justice, Washington, 1961-65; dep. dir. Men's Job Corps OEO, Washington, 1965 67; mem. civil rights div. Dept. of Justice, chief criminal sect., prin. dep. asst. atty. gen., 1967-75, spl. counsel for intelligence coordination, 1975; v.p., counsel Assn. of Motion Picture and Television Producers, Hollywood, Calif., 1975-76; assoc. justice Am. Samoa, 1976; chief justice, 1977-78; sr. trial atty. GSA Task Force, Dept. Justice, 1978-81; insp. gen. CSA, 1981-82; spl. counsel Merit Systems Protection Bd., Washington, 1983-86; U.S. atty. for Guam and the No. Marianas, 1986-89; ret.; pvt. practice, 1989—; Am. counsel O'Reilly Vernier Ltd., Hong Kong, 1992-93; ptnr. O'Connor & Vernier, Medford, Oreg., 1993-94; pvt. practice Medford, 1994—. Served with USMC, 1952-55. Mem. Oreg. Bar Assn., D.C. Bar Assn., Va. Bar Assn., Calif. Bar Assn., Am. Samoa Bar Assn., Soc. Colonial Wars, Phi Alpha Delta, Sigma Nu. Home: Box 126 6743 Griffin Ln Jacksonville OR 97530 Office: Brehon House 915 W 10th St Medford OR 97501-3018

O'CONNOR, KATHLEEN MARY, lawyer; b. Camden, Jan. 14, 1949; d. John A. and Marie V. (Flynn) O'C. BA, U. Fla., 1971, JD, 1981. Bar: Fla. 1981, U.S. Ct. Appeals (11th cir.) 1982, U.S. Supreme Ct. 1987. Atty. Walton, Lantaff, Schroeder & Carson, Miami, Fla., 1981-84, Thornton, Davis & Murray PA, Miami, 1984-98, Thornton, Davis & Fein, P.A., Miami, 2002—. Exec. editor U. Fla. Law Rev., 1981; contbr. articles to profl. jours. Legal advocate Miami Project to Cure Paralysis, 1992-97. Mem. ABA, Dade County Bar Assn. (vice chair appellate cts. com. 1981, 2003, chair 2004—), Def. Rsch. Inst., Fla. Def. Lawyers Assn., Fla. Assn. for Women Lawyers (bd. dirs. Miami-Dade County chpt. 2002—), Fla. Bar (mem. appellate rules com. 2002—). Office: Thornton Davis & Fein PA 80 SW 8th St Ste 2900 Miami FL 33130 Home: 7445 SW 147 St Palmetto Bay FL 33158 E-mail: oconnor@tdflaw.com.

O'CONNOR, KAY F. state legislator; b. Everett, Wash., Nov. 28, 1941; d. Ernest S. and Dena (Lampers) Wells; m. Arthur J. O'Connor, Sept. 1, 1959; 6 children. Diploma, Lathrop H.S., Fairbanks, Alaska, 1959. Office mgr. Blaylock Chemicals, Bucyrus, Kans., 1981-84; store mgr. Copies Plus, Olathe, Kans., 1984-86; acct. Advance Concrete Inc., Spring Hill, Kans., 1986-92; mem. Kans. Ho. of Reps. from 14th dist., 1993-2000, Kans. Senate from 9th dist., 2001—. Exec. dir. Parents in Control, Inc.; bd. dirs. Hometel Ltd.; author sch. voucher legis. State of Kans., 1994-2002; corrections and juvenile justice oversight com., judiciary com., fed. and state affairs com., vice chair elections and local govt. com. Kans. Senate, 2001—. Republican. Roman Catholic. Avocations: choir directing, statue renovations, speaking on school vouchers. Home: 1101 N Curtis St Olathe KS 66061-2709 Office: PO Box 2232 Olathe KS 66051-2232 E-mail: kayoisok@comcast.net.

O'CONNOR, KEVIN, computer programing executive; BSEE with honors, U. Mich. Co-founder ICC Software Co., Atlanta, 1983—91; chief tech. officer, v.p. rsch. DCA, Atlanta, 1992—95; funded and built ISS Group, Atlanta, 1995, chmn. bd. dirs., 1995—; co-founder, chief exec. officer Internet Advt. Network, 1995—; co-founder, pres., chief exec. officer DoubleClick, NY, 1996—. Office: DoubleClick 111 Eighth Ave 10th Fl New York NY 10011 Office Phone: 212-683-0001., 212-271-2542. Office Fax: 212-287-1203.*

O'CONNOR, KEVIN, electronics executive; b. 1958; Degree in Mgmt., Ariz. State U. With Sperry Flight Sys.; with Frito-Lay PepsiCo; various positions Dell Computer; sr. v.p. global human resources Iomega Corp., Axcelis Technologies; sr. v.p. Worldwide Human Resources Solectron Corp., Milpitas, Calif., 2002—. Mem.: Am. Compensation Assn., Asian Human Resource Alliance, Soc. Human Resources Mgmt., Am. Lung Assn., North Shore C. of C., Boys and Girls Clubs Weber County. Office: Solectron Corp 777 Gibraltar Dr Milpitas CA 95035

O'CONNOR, KEVIN JAMES, lawyer; b. Hartford, Conn., May 3, 1967; s. Dennis Edmund and Mary Theresa (Leahy) O'Connor. BA, U. Notre Dame, 1989; JD, U. Conn., 1992. Conn. 1992, N.Y. 1993, U.S. Dist. Ct. Conn. (so. and ea. dists.) N.Y. 1994, U.S. Ct. Appeals (2d cir.) 1994. Law clerk Hon. William H. Timbers, U.S. Ct. Appeals (2d cir.), N.Y.C., 1992-93; assoc. Cahill, Gordon & Reindel, N.Y.C., 1993-95; sr. counsel Divsn. Enforcement U.S. Securities & Exchg. Commn., Washington, 1995-97; ptnr. Day Berry & Howard, Hartford, 1999—2002; US atty. U.S. Dept. Justice, Conn., 2002—. Adj. prof. George Washington U. Law Sch., Washington, 1996-97, U. Conn. Law Sch., 1998—. Republican. Roman Catholic. Office: Conn Finl Ctr PO Box 1824 New Haven CT 06508 Office Phone: 203-821-3700.

O'CONNOR, KEVIN JOHN, psychologist, educator; b. Jersey City, July 18, 1954; s. John Lanning and Marilyn (Reynolds) O'C.; m. Ryan Michael, Matthew Benham. BA, U. Mich., 1975; PhD, U. Toledo, 1981. Clin. psychologist Blythedale Children's Hosp., Valhalla, N.Y., 1980-83; dir. psychol. svcs. Walworth Barbour Am. Internat. Sch., Kfar Shmaryahu, Israel, 1983-84; adj. asst. prof. dept. psychology Iona Coll., New Rochelle, N.Y., 1984; clin. psychologist No. Westchester Guidance Clinic, Mt. Kisco, N.Y., 1985; exec. dir., newsletter editor Assn. for Play Therapy, Fresno, Calif., 1982-97; cons. psychologist Fresno (Calif.) Treatment Ctr., 1986-87, Diagnostic Sch. for Neurologically Handicapped Children, Fresno, Calif., 1986-90; adj. faculty Pacific Grad. Sch. of Psychology, Palo Alto, Calif., 1997—2001, Calif. Sch. Profl. Psychology, Berkeley, Calif., 1988-89; prof. Alliant Internat. U., Calif. Sch. Profl. Psychology, Fresno, 1985—, dir. clinical PsyD and PhD programs, 1985—. Contbr. numerous presentations in field. Named Psychologist of Yr. San Joaquin Psychol. Assn., 1994. Fellow APA; mem. Assn. for Play Therapy. Democrat. Avocations: travel, art, ceramics. Office: Calif Sch Profl Psych Alliant Internat U 5130 E Clinton Way Fresno CA 93727-2014 Office Phone: 559-456-2700 x2273.

O'CONNOR, KEVIN THOMAS, religious organization administrator; b. Dubuque, Iowa, Oct. 9, 1950; s. Francis John and Marion Helen (Rhomberg) O'C.; m. Abbie J. O'Connor, July 17, 1993; 1 child, Sean Francis. BS, Regis Coll., Denver, 1973. Spl. agt. Northwestern Mut. Life, Denver, 1973-78; account exec. Blue Cross/Blue Shield of Colo., Denver, 1978-82; pres., owner O'Connor Ins. Cons., Denver, 1982-92; dir. devel. Archdiocese of Denver, 1992-95, mgr. Cath. appeal, 1995-96; dir. devel. Archdiocese of L.A., 1996—. Chmn. Regis Coll. Telefund, Denver, 1987-88, 90-91; treas., 1st vice chmn. Serra Trust Fund for Vocations, 1988-93, chmn., 1993-96; mem. fin. coun. St. James Parish, 1988-95, chmn. autumn bazaar, 1985, 87, mem. choir, 1993-95; sec. Mother Teresa Com., 1989; mem. choir St. Bede The Venerable, La Canada, Calif., 2001—. Recipient Share Serra Comm. award Serra Internat., 1989, Spl. Project award Dist. 6, 1986, 88, Spl. Recognition award, 1989, Outstanding Serran award, 1995, Jan Berbers award, 1996, Alumni Svc. award Regis Coll., 1990, Disting. Alumnus award Wahlert H.S., 1994. Mem. Serra Club L.A., Serra Internat. (trustee 1997-2003, sec. bd. 1998-2001, chmn. internat. vocation com. 2000-01, v.p. 2001-03, co-founder Pueblo chpt., 1992, Colo. Springs chpt., 1995, Greeley chpt., 1996, pres. Denver chpt., 1991-92, dist. 6 gov., 1995-96). Roman Catholic. Avocations: golf, tennis, mountain climbing, handball, running. Home: 3510 Fallenleaf Pl Glendale CA 91206-4803 Office: Archdiocese LA 3424 Wilshire Blvd Los Angeles CA 90010-2241 Office Phone: 213-637-7617. Personal E-mail: kevinabbie@charter.net. Business E-Mail: ktoconnor@la-archdiocese.org.

O'CONNOR, MAUREEN, judge; b. Washington, Aug. 7, 1951; d. Patrick and Mary E. O'Connor; children: Alex, Ed. BA, Seton Hill Coll., 1973; postgrad., SUNY, 1975-76; JD, Cleve. State U., 1980. Pvt. practice, 1981-85; referee Probate Ct., 1985-93; judge Common Pleas, 1993-95; prosecutor Summit County, 1995-99; lt. gov., dir. Dept. Pub. Safety State of Ohio, 1999—2003; Supreme Ct. Ohio Supreme Ct. Justice, Ohio, 2003. Dir. Summit County Child Support Enforcement Agy.; spkr. in field. Parishioner St. Vincent's Ch.; vol. Comty. Drug Bd., Am. Cancer Soc., bd. dirs.; bd. dirs. Victim Assistance, St. Edward Home, Fairlawn, Furnace St. Mission. Recipient MADD Law Enforcement award, 1997, Cleve. State Disting. Alumnae award for Civic Achievement, 1997. Mem. MADD, Nat. Dist. Attys. Assn., Nat. Child Support Enforcement Assn., Nat. Coll. Dist. Attys. Assn., Ohio Prosecuting Attys. Assn. (exec. com.), Ohio Family Support Assn., Atty. Gen.'s Prosecutor Liaison Com., Summit County Police Chiefs Assn., Summit Forum, Summit County Child Mortality. Republican. Office: Ohio Supreme Ct 30 E Broad St Fl 3 Columbus OH 43215

O'CONNOR, MICHAEL E. lawyer; b. Syracuse, NY, Sept. 15, 1948; s. Leo T. and Geraldine (Hager) O'Connor; m. Margaret A. Soplop, June 3, 1972. AA, Auburn (N.Y.) C.C., 1968; BA, SUNY, Buffalo, 1970; JD, Syracuse U., 1974. Bar: N.Y. 1975, U.S. Supreme Ct. 1983. Assoc. Coulter, Fraser, Bolton, Bird & Ventre, Syracuse, 1975-80, ptnr., 1981-90, Hancock & Estabrook, 1990-94, DeLaney & O'Connor LLP, 1994—. Pres. Onondaga Title Assn., 1979, Ctrl. N.Y. Estate Planning Coun., 1981; adj. prof. law U. Syracuse; pres. Most Holy Rosary Home Sch. Assn., 1985—86, Aurora of CNY, Inc., 1988—90. Bd. dirs. Syracuse Symphony Orch. Assn., CNY Cmty. Found.; pres. Citizens Found., Inc., 1983—85. Fellow: Am. Coll. Trust and Estate Counsel (state chair); mem.: ABA, Onondaga County Bar Assn. (chmn. estate and surrogates ct. com. 1981—87, bd. dirs. 1984—86), N.Y. State Bar Assn. (ho. of dels. 1982—85, chair elder law sect. 1999—2000, chair elect trusts and estates sect.), Century Club of Syracuse, Lions (pres. 1984—85). Republican. Roman Catholic. Home: 154 Robineau Rd Syracuse NY 13207-1644 Office: DeLaney & O'Connor LLP One Lincoln Ctr Syracuse NY 13202 Office Phone: 315-476-8450. Personal E-mail: meoconnor1@twcny.rr.com. Business E-Mail: oconnor@delaneyoconnor.com.

O'CONNOR, MICHOL, judge; b. Houston, Nov. 30, 1942; d. Charles Cary O'Connor and Ida Mae (Mueller) Baird; 1 child, Baird James Craft. BA, U. Tex., Austin, 1966; JD, U. Houston, 1973. Bar: Tex. 73, cert.: Tex. Bd. Legal Specialization (appellate law). Law clk. 1st Ct. Civil Appeals, Houston, 1974—75; asst. dist. atty. Harris County Dist. Attys. Office, Houston, 1975—76; assoc. firm Kronzer, Abraham & Watkins, Houston, 1976—78; asst. US atty. so. dist. US Atty.'s Office, Houston, 1978—81; corp. counsel Century Devel. Corp., 1981—82; of counsel Haight, Gardner, Poor & Havens, 1985—86; pvt. practice Houston, 1986—88; justice Tex. Ct. Appeals 1st Cir., Houston, 1989—2000; CEO Jones Mc Clure Pub. Inc., 2001—. Lectr. in field. Author: O'Connor's Texas Civil Appeals, 1993-1998, O'Connor's Texas Rules and Civil Trials, 1997-2004; co-author: O'Connor's Causes of Action, 2001, 2004; contbr. articles to profl. jours. Recipient Jour. Article award, Tex. Bar Found., 1978. Mem.: ABA, Houston Young Lawyers (bd. dirs. 1975—76, Outstanding Contbn. award 1975), Houston Bar Assn. (bd. dirs. 1977—79), Tex. Bar Assn. (chmn. adminstrn. justice com.), Order of Barons. Office Phone: 713-335-8200. Business E-Mail: moc@jonesmcclure.com.

O'CONNOR, OTIS LESLIE, lawyer, director; b. Charleston, W.Va., July 6, 1935; s. Robert Emmett and Julia Elizabeth (Aultz) O'C.; m. Elizabeth Frances Morris, Aug. 7, 1965; children: Otis Leslie, James M. AB, Princeton U., 1957; JD, Harvard U., 1963; MBA, W.Va. Coll. Grad. Studies, 1979; MA, Trinity Theol. Sem., 2003. Bar: W.Va. 1963, U.S. Dist. (so. dist.) W.Va. 1963. Assoc. Steptoe & Johnson, Charleston, 1963-69, ptnr., 1969—. Pres. Daymark, Inc., 1981—82. Served with USN, 1957—60, served to comdr. JAGC USNR, 1960—81. Mem. ABA, W.Va. Bar Assn., Kanawha County Bar Assn., Res. Officers Assn., Rotary Internat. Club (Charleston). Presbyterian. Home: 890 Chester Rd Charleston WV 25302-2817

O'CONNOR, PAT, film director; b. Ardomore, Ireland, 1943; BA, UCLA. Motion picture dir. Dir., writer: (films) The Ballroom of Romance, 1982; dir. (films) Cal, 1984, A Month in the Country, 1987, Stars and Bars, 1988, January Man, 1989, Fools of Fortune, 1990, Circle of Friends, 1995, Inventing the Abbotts, 1997, Dancing at Lughnasa, 1998, Sweet November, 2001, (T.V. movie) Zelda, 1993, Force of Duty, 1992. Office: c/o Andrew Connava United Talent Agency 9560 Wilshire Blvd Ste 500 Beverly Hills CA 90212-2427

O'CONNOR, PAUL DANIEL, lawyer; b. Paterson, N.J., Nov. 24, 1936; s. Paul Daniel and Anne Marie Christopher O'C.; m. Melissa Monson; children: Steven Paul, Sheryl Lynn, Laura Ann. BS in Engring, U.S. Naval Acad., 1959; LLB, U. Va., 1965. Bar: N.Y. 1965, Calif. 1995. Assoc. firm Winthrop, Stimson, Putnam & Roberts, N.Y.C., 1965-72, partner, 1972-80; sr. v.p., gen. counsel Singer Co., Stamford, Conn., 1980-86; chief exec. officer Citation Builders, 1986-95; trustee Valley Trusts, Oakland, Calif., 1986—; of counsel Clement, Fitzpatrick & Kenworthy, 2003—. 1st lt. USAF, 1959-62. Mem.: Sonoma County Bar Assn., Bar Assn. San Francisco, Assn. Bar City NY, Fairfield County Hunt Club. Home: 1150 Lombard St # 2 San Francisco CA 94109-9103 Office: 3333 Mendocino Ave Ste 200 Santa Rosa CA 95403 also: Valley Trusts 1939 Harrison St Ste 555 Oakland CA 94612-3586 Office Phone: 707-523-1181.

O'CONNOR, R. D. retired health care executive; BS in Psychology and Sociology, U. So. Miss., 1960, MS Adminstrv. Pers., 1961, PhD Mgmt. and Orgnl. Comm., 1983. Asst. dean student affairs Holmes Jr. Coll., Goodman, Mo., 1961-64; spl. counselor vocat. rehab. divsn. Dept. Edn., Jackson, Mo., 1964-65; asst. adminstr. Hinds Gen. Hosp., Jackson, Mo., 1965-68; adminstr. Rankin Gen. Hosp., Brandon, Mo., 1968-76; v.p. Human Resources/ Mktg. Delta Mgmt. Systems, Metairie, La., 1976-79; asst. to pres. Bapt. Med. Ctr., Jacksonville, Fla., 1979-82; pres. RiverGroup Riverside Hosp., Rivercorp Inc., Riverside Found., Jacksonville, Fla., 1982-87; owner O'Connor & Assocs., Jacksonville, Fla., 1987-91; pres. Fla. 1st: Managed Health Care, Winter Haven, Orlando & Tampa, Fla., 1991-94; dir. orgn. devel. Mid Florida Med. Svcs. Inc., Winter Haven, Fla., 1994-97. Instr. U. So. Miss., Hattiesburg, Ms.; tchr., lectr. various univs., C.C.s, military acads.; grad. faculty coord. Webster U.; online instr. for univs. Contbr. articles to profl. jours. and books. Commr. Cleary Heights Sewer Dist., 1978-79; pres'. selective task force Induction Procedures, 1969; chmn. personnel com. San Jose Baptist Ch., 1981-86, strategic planning com., 1986-87; gov's. com. Statewide Planning Vocat. Rehab., 1968; bd. dirs. Rankin County C. of C., 1970-73, exec. com., chmn. health affairs com., 1970-72, chmn. highway com. 1970-74, fin. com. 1971-73), Family Blood Assurance Program, 1972-77, v.p. 1977, Vol. Action Coun., 1973-76, United Givers Fund, 1973-76. With Army Security Agy., Air Nat. Guard, Med. Svc. Corps., ret. Fellow Am. Coll. Healthcare Execs. (life); mem. Fla. Hosp. Assn. (com. chmn. 1984), Greater Jacksonville Area Hosp. Coun. (chmn. 1985), Jackson-Vicksburg Hosp. Coun. (chmn. 1974), Nat. Assn. Mental Health (bd. dirs. 1973-74), Miss. Assn. Mental Health (pres. 1972-74), Miss. Hosp. Assn. (bd. dirs .1973-76, exec. devel. com. 1972-75, mgmt. engring. adminstrv. bd. 1973, fin. com. 1972-74, chmn. nominating com. 1971, coord. divsn. profl. practice 1970). Home: 12837 Julington Forest Dr E Jacksonville FL 32258-2294

O'CONNOR, RALPH STURGES, investment company executive; b. Pasadena, Calif., Aug. 27, 1926; s. Thomas Ireland and Edith Masury (Sturges) O'C.; m. Alice Maconda Brown, Apr. 28, 1950; children— George Rufus, Thomas Ireland III, Nancy Isabel, John Herman. BA, Johns Hopkins U., 1951; postgrad., Harvard U., 1967. With Highland Resources, Inc., Houston, 1951-87, exec. v.p., 1961-64, pres., 1964-87; pres., chief exec. officer Ralph S. O'Connor and Assocs., 1987—. Chmn. bd. Arnaud's Restaurant, New Orleans, Texas Ice, Clear Lake, Tex. Trustee emeritus Rice U., Johns Hopkins U., Oldfields Sch., Glencoe, Md.; pres., The Marian and Speros Martel Found., Houston, 1983-2003. With USAAF, 1943-46. Mem. NAS (Pres.'s Circle), Am. Assn. Petroleum Landmen, All Am. Wildcatters, Houston Landmen's Assn. (past pres.), The Johns Hopkins Instns., Presdl. Counselors, Bayou Club (Houston), River Oaks Country Club (Houston), Petroleum Club (Houston). Home: 5627 Indian Cir Houston TX 77056-1006 Office: Ralph S O'Connor & Assocs 10000 Memorial Dr Ste 510 Houston TX 77024-3422 Office Phone: 713-682-3441. E-mail: ralphsoconnor@yahoo.com.

O'CONNOR, ROBERT EDWARD, JR., lawyer; b. Omaha, June 1, 1950; s. Robert Edward Sr. and Agnes (Flynn) O'C.; m. Jean Patricia Mergens; children: Maureen, Kathleen. undergrad. degree, JD, Creighton U., 1974. Bar: Nebr. 1974, U.S. Dist. Ct. Nebr., U.S. Ct. Appeals (8th cir.). Sole practice, Omaha, 1974—. Mem. Nebr. State Bar Assn. (del. 1982-84, pres. 2001-02), Nebr. Assn. Trial Attys. (del.), Assn. Trial Lawyers Am. (del.). Democrat. Roman Catholic. Avocation: sailing. Office: 2433 S 130th Cir Omaha NE 68144-2528

O'CONNOR, ROD, chemist, consultant, inventor; b. Cape Girardeau, Mo., July 4, 1934; s. Jay H. and Flora (Winters) O'C.; m. Shirley Ann Sander, Aug. 7, 1955; children: Mark Alan (dec.), Kara Ann, Shanna Suzanne, Timothy Patrick. BS, S.E. Mo. State Coll., 1955; PhD, U. Calif., Berkeley, 1958. Asst. prof. chemistry U. Omaha, 1958-60, Mont. State Coll., 1960-63; assoc. prof. chemistry Mont. State U., Bozeman, 1963-66; assoc. prof., coordinator gen. chemistry Kent (Ohio) State U., 1966-67; prof., dir. 1st year chemistry U. Ariz., Tucson, 1968-72; staff assoc. Adv. Council on Coll. Chemistry Stanford (Calif.) U., 1967-68; vis. prof. Wash. State U., Pullman, 1972-73; prof. chemistry Tex. A&M, College Station, 1973-86; pres. Texas ROMEC Inc., College Station, 1983-98; prof. environ. studies Baylor U., Waco, Tex., 1996-99. Cons. insect venoms Hollister-Stier Labs., Spokane, Wash., 1963-67; lab. separates editor W.H. Freeman Co., 1968-78; ednl. cons. TUCARA-4 Media Resources, Inc., 1971-74; mem. Coll. Chemistry Cons. Service; vis. scientist, tour lectr. Am. Chem. Soc., 1970-86. Author: (with T. Moeller) Ions in Aqueous Systems, 1972, Fundamentals of Chemistry, 1981, (with C. Mickey and A. Hassell) Solving Problems in Chemistry, 1981, (with L. Peck and K. Irgolic) Fundamentals of Chemistry in The Laboratory, 1981, (with T.E. Taylor and P. Glenn) Toward Success in College, 1981, (with A. Hassell and C. Mickey) Advanced Problems in Applied Chemistry, 2000; films Laboratory Safety, 1971; Contbr. articles to profl. jours.; patentee in field Recipient nat. teaching award Mfg. Chemists Assn., 1978; 4 regional teaching awards. Fellow AAAS, Am. Inst. Chemists, Sigma Xi; mem. Internat. Soc. Toxinology, Am. Chem. Soc. Office: Chem Consulting Svcs 1300 Angelina Cir College Station TX 77840-4855 Office Phone: 979-693-5804. E-mail: docroc34@hotmail.com.

O'CONNOR, RORY, pharmaceutical company executive, medical director; b. Liverpool, United Kingdom, July 21, 1955; m. Catherine Doyle, Aug. 12, 1995; children: Sinead children: Mairead, Ruairi Joe, Ciara, Niamh. MB ChB, U. Liverpool, Faculty Medicine, 1973—78. Mfpm Faculty Pharm. Medicine, Royal Coll. Physicians, UK, 1996. Sr. dir. med. affairs and clin. ops. Europe, Pfizer Pharms. Group, N.Y.C., 1996—, med. dir., Pfizer Ctrl. Rsch., Sandwich, England, 1994—96. Office: Pfizer Inc 235 E 42nd St New York NY 10520 Office Phone: +1 212 733 4202.

O'CONNOR, SANDRA DAY, United States Supreme Court Justice; b. El Paso, Tex., Mar. 26, 1930; d. Harry A. and Ada Mae (Wilkey) Day; m. John Jay O'Connor, III, Dec. 1952; children: Scott, Brian, Jay. AB in Econs. with great distinction, Stanford U., 1950, LLB, 1952. Bar: Calif., Ariz. Dep. county atty., San Mateo, Calif., 1952—53; civilian atty. Q.M. Market Ctr., Frankfurt am Main, Germany, 1954—57; pvt. practice Phoenix, 1958—65; asst. atty. gen. State of Ariz., 1965—69; state senator Ariz., 1969—75; chmn. com. on state, county and mcpl. affairs, 1972—73; majority leader, 1973—74; judge Maricopa County Superior Ct., 1975—79, Ariz. Ct. Appeals, 1979—81; assoc. justice U.S. Supreme Ct., 1981—. Referee juvenile ct. Maricopa County, 1962—64; chmn. vis. bd. Maricopa County Juvenile Detention Home, 1963—64; mem. Maricopa County Bd. Adjustments and Appeals, 1963—64, Anglo-Am. Legal Exchange, 1980, Maricopa County Superior Ct. Judges Tng. and Edn. Com., 1977—79, Maricopa Ct. Study Com.; chair com. to reorganize lower cts. Ariz. Supreme Ct., 1974—75; faculty Robert A. Taft Inst. Govt.; mem. Ariz. Criminal Code Commn., 1974—76; bd. visitors Ariz. State U. Law Sch., 1981, liaison com. on med. edn., 81. Mem. bd. editors: Stanford (Calif.) U. Law Rev. Mem. Ariz. Pers. Commn., 1968—69, Nat. Def. Adv. Com. on Women in Svcs., 1974—76; trustee Heard Mus., Phoenix, 1968—74, 1976—81, pres., 1980—81; mem. adv. bd. Phoenix Salvation Army, 1975—81; trustee Stanford U., 1976—81, Phoenix County Day Sch.; mem. citizens adv. bd. Blood Svcs., 1975—77; nat. bd. dirs. Smithsonian Assocs., 1981—, Colonial Williamsburg Found., 1988—2000; exec. bd. Ctrl. Eastern European Law Initiative, 1990—; adv. bd., v.p. NCCJ, Maricopa County, 1977—81; bd. dirs., sec. Ariz. Acad, 1969—75, Cathedral chpt. Washington Nat. Cathedral, 1991—99; past Rep. dist. chmn.; bd. dirs. Phoenix Cmty. Coun., 1969—75, Jr. Achievement Ariz., 1975—79, Blue Cross/Blue Shield Ariz., 1975—79, Channel 8, 1975—79, Phoenix Hist. Soc., 1974—78, Maricopa County YMCA, 1978—81, Golden Gate Settlement. Named Woman of Yr., Phoenix Advt. Club, 1972, National Women's Hall of Fame, 1995; recipient Ann. award, NCCJ, 1975, Disting. Achievement award, Ariz. State U., 1980, Sara Lee Frontrunner award, 1997, ABA medal, 1997. Mem.: ABA (select law enforcement revision commn. vice chair 1979—80), Maricopa County Bar Assn. (referral svc. chair 1960—62), Calif. Bar Assn., Ariz. Bar Assn. (legal edn., pub. rels. com., lower ct. reorgn. com.), Soroptimist Club (Phoenix). Office: US Supreme Ct Supreme Ct Bldg 1 First St NE Washington DC 20543

O'CONNOR, SHEILA ANNE, freelance writer; b. Paisley, Scotland, Jan. 20, 1960; came to the U.S., 1988; d. Brian Aubrey Witham and Margaret Kirk (Reid) Davies; m. Frank Donal O'Connor, Aug. 9, 1986; children: David Michael, Andrew James, Christine Charlotte. BA in French and German, Strathclyde U., 1980, postgrad. diploma in office studies, 1981, MBA, 1992. Office asst. BBC, London, 1982-83; asst. to mng. dir. Unimatic Engrs. Ltd., London, 1983-84; freelance word processing operator London, 1984-88; staff asst. Internat. Monetary Fund, Washington, 1988-94; prin. Internat. Media Assn., Washington, 1988—. Co-author: Chocolate for a Woman's Spirit, 1999; contbr. articles to profl. jours. Mem. Am. Mktg. Assn., Bay Area Travel Writers Assn., Calif. Writers Club. Avocations: animals, travel. Home and Office: 1974 46th Ave San Francisco CA 94116-1005 E-mail: sheila.oconnor@juno.com.

O'CONNOR, SYLVIA CANNON, association legislative liaison, analyst, retired; b. Chgo., Sept. 9, 1934; d. LeGrand and Helen (West) Cannon; m. William Searls Van Bergen, Aug. 25, 1956 (div. 1983); children: Louise Van Bergen Holzhauer, Carolyn Van Bergen-Rylander, Amy E. Van Bergen; m. Raymond James O'Connor, Nov. 28, 1987. BA, Sangamon State U., 1984, MA with honors, 1986. Legis. liaison Chgo. Bar Assn., Springfield, Ill., 1983-84; asst. to bur. chief Ill. Dept. Aeronautics, Springfield, 1984-86; dir. Springfield Right to Life, 1986-89; Ill. capitol city task force coord. Am. Assn. Retired Persons, Washington, 1988-92; ret., 1992. Mem. policy com. Ill. Dept. Aging, Springfield, 1989—; chmn. fundraiser Christ Episc. Ch., Springfield, 1990, vestry mem., 1987-90; mem. Symphony Guild. Mem. PEO (v.p. 1981-82, 91—), Questers (pres.), Kappa Alpha Theta (alumnae rush chmn. 1980, pres. Alumnae Club of Sarasota 1997, 98). Republican. Episcopalian. Avocations: reading, symphony, theater, classic films, art. Home (Summer): 4460 Deer Trail Blvd Sarasota FL 34238-5606

O'CONNOR, THOMAS C. gas industry executive; BS in Biology cum laude, U. Mass., Lowell, 1977, MS in Environ. Studies, 1980. Dir. mktg. svcs., dir. bus. devel. Tex. Ea. Transmission Corp.; pres. PanEnergy Devel. Co.; from supr. environ. compliance to mgr. mkt. devel. algonquin gas transmission divsn. Duke Energy Corp., Charlotte, NC, 1987—89, sr. v.p. mktg. and capacity mgmt., v.p. mktg., v.p. east coast mktg. NE pipeline group, 1994—2002, pres. gas transmission divsn., 2002—; pres. Maritimes & NE Mgmt. Co. Office: Duke Energy Corp 526 S Church St Charlotte NC 28202-1803

O'CONNOR, THOMAS EDWARD, petroleum geologist, management consultant; b. Boston, Dec. 16, 1936; s. John Stephen and Lucille (Arnold) O'C.; m. Jeannette Canuel, June 30, 1962 (dec. Mar. 1976); children: Kevin Patrick, David Andrew, Shelley Elizabeth; m. Moufida Banawi, Apr. 28, 1977; children: Tammer Thomas, Amr Adel Hammouda. BSc, Stanford U., 1958; MSc., U. Colo., 1961. Geologist Amoco Prodn. West, Denver, 1963-67, Amoco Netherlands, Utrecht, 1968-69, Amoco Europe, London, 1969-74; chief geologist Gulf of Suez Petroleum Co., Cairo, 1974-79; geol. mgr. Amoco Africa, Mid East, Houston, 1979-80; v.p. Aminoil, Houston, 1980-84; prin. petroleum engr. The World Bank, Washington, 1985-98; internat. petroleum mgmt. cons., 1998—; chmn. bd. dirs. Benchmark Oil & Gas AB, Malmo, Sweden, 2003—. Adj. prof. George Washington U. Grad. Sch. Polit. Mgmt., 2003—. Presenter numerous sci. confs., seminars, workshops in U.S. and abroad, 1976—. Lt. USNR, 1960-63. Mem. AAAS, Am. Assn. Petroleum Geologists (cert. petroleum geologist), Geol. Soc. Am., Houston Geol. Soc. Moslem. Home and Office: 937 5th St Camano Island WA 98282 Office Phone: 202-210-1305. E-mail: teoconnor@aol.com.

O'CONNOR, THOMAS PATRICK, screenwriter; s. Thomas Robertson and Barbara (Gumbel) O'Connor; m. Virginia Elizabeth Perlo, 1971 (div.); m. Barbara Piazza Cox, 1991 (div.); 1 stepchild, Thad. BFA, NYU, 1971, MA, 1981; PhD in Social Svcs., Berne U., 2004. Chaplain Mountain Chaplaincy, Park City, Utah, 1998—2002; chief, safety and security V.I. Port Authority, 1992—94; gen. mgr. Telluride (Colo.) Cmty. TV, 1989—91; v.p. Lake Tahoe (Nev.) Pub. TV, 1988; asst. dep. commr. N.Y. Police Dept., 1971—72; writer prodr. Special Report, Incline Village, Nev., 2002—. Nat. def. exec. res. Fed. Emergency Mgmt. Agy., NY, 1984—86. Screenwriter The Nemesis Factor (Telluride IndieFest Screenwriting award, 1999). Mem. Washde County Sheriff's Citizen's Homeland Security Coun., 2003. Mem.: AFTRA, SAG, Writers Guild of Am., Radio-TV News Dirs. Assn., Internat. Assn. Chiefs of Police. Home: PO Box 5592 Incline Village NV 89450

O'CONNOR, VARLEY, writer, education educator; b. Paterson, N.J., Oct. 7, 1953; d. Donald Herbert and Louise Mann Varley. BFA, Boston Univ., Mass.; MFA, Univ. Calif., Irvine, Calif., 1989. Writing instr. Univ. Calif., Irvine, Calif., 1986—91, Marymount Manhattan Coll., N.Y., 1997—2000, Bklyn. Coll., Bklyn., 2001—02, Hofstra Univ., Hempstead, NY, 2003—. Author: (novels) A Company of Three, 2003, Like China, 1991.

O'CONNOR, WILLIAM CHARLES, automobile agency finance executive; b. Poplar Bluff, Mo., July 19, 1943; s. Thomas Francis and Luella Darlene (Davis) O'C.; m. Leigh Volkening, Dec. 21, 1975 (div. May 1992); children: Kelli, Megan, Katie. BA in English, Memphis State U., 1966. High rigger Boiler Makers Union, St. Louis, 1968-70; br. mgr. Pub. Fin. Corp., St. Louis, 1970-74; fin. specialist Pat Ryan & Assocs., Chgo., 1974-77; fin. mgr. Drew Ford, La Mesa, Calif., 1978-80; fin. dir. Honda of Pasadena, Calif., 1980-89, Goudy Honda, Alhambra, Calif., 1989-94, Honda of Pasadena, Calif., 1995-99. Cons. Am. Honda Fin. Corp., Torrance, 1987—. Contbr. articles to profl. jours. Mem. Fin. and Ins. Profls., KC, Jr. C. of C., Young Dems. Orgn. (pres. 1968-69). Avocations: L.A. marathon 1987, golf, fishing. Office: 1965 E Foothill Blvd Pasadena CA 91107-3218 Home: 80 N Grand Ave Pasadena CA 91103

O'CONNOR, WILLIAM MATTHEW, lawyer; b. Pensacola, Fla., Apr. 5, 1955; s. William Francis and Rosalind (Shea) O'C.; m. Mary Patricia Keepnews, Oct. 13, 1984; children: William Lawrence, Thomas Patrick, Robert Austin. BS in Psychology, Fordham U., 1977, JD, 1980. Bar: N.Y. 1981, N.J. 1987, U.S. Dist. Ct. N.J. 1987, U.S. Dist. Conn. 1988, U.S. Dist. Ct. (so., ea., no. and we. dists.) N.Y., 1981, U.S. Ct. Appeals (2nd cir.) 1983, U.S. Ct. Appeals (3d cir.) 1996. Intern N.Y. Atty. Gen., N.Y.C., 1978-79; legis. intern Am. Lung Assn., N.Y.C., 1979; assoc. Keane & Butler, N.Y.C., 1979-81, Keane & Beane, White Plains, N.Y., 1981-83, Cooperman, Levitt & Winikoff, P.C., N.Y.C., 1983-86; sr. assoc. Sullivan, Donovan, Hanrahan & Silliere, N.Y.C., 1986-87; ptnr. O'Connor Reddy & Seeler, N.Y.C., 1987-95, Harris Beach & Wilcox LLP, N.Y.C., 1995-2000, Buchanan Ingersoll PC, N.Y.C., 2000—. Author: Lobbying Guidebook Am. Lung Assn., 1979. Contbr. articles to profl. jours. Legis. com. pub. schs., White Plains, 1981-82; councilman Town of Pelham, N.Y., 1998—. Mem. ABA, Fed. Bar Coun., N.Y. State Bar Assn. (mem. comml. and fed. litigation sect., creditor's rights com. 1989—), Westchester Bar Assn. (editor in chief Jour. 1983-89, mem. labor law com. 1981—, com. on profl. ethics 1989—), Fordham ILJ Alumni Assn. (bd. dirs. 1984—), New Rochelle Bar Assn. Republican. Roman Catholic. Home: 684 Esplanade Pelham NY 10803-2403 Office: Buchanan Ingersoll PC 140 Broadway New York NY 10005 E-mail: oconnorwn@bipc.com.

O'CONNOR, WILLIAM MICHAEL, search company executive; b. Chgo., Sept. 28, 1947; s. Maurice Francis and Margaret (Brand) O'C.; m. Karen Jean Gipson, Jan. 30, 1972; children: Sean, Mary, William, David. BA in History, Loyola U., Chgo., 1970. Interviewer Ill. State Employment Svc., Chgo., 1970-73; ins. agt. Equitable Life Assurance Soc., Chgo., 1973-76; recruiting officer U.S. Army, Chgo., 1977-78; profl. employment rep. GTE Network Systems, Northlake, Ill., 1978-81; employment mgr. Molex, Inc., Lisle, Ill., 1981-85, Rand McNally & Co., Skokie, Ill., 1986; v.p. Richards Cons., Ltd., Chgo., 1987-88; v.p., ptnr. Chestnut Hill Ptnrs., Deerfield, Ill., 1988-95; v.p. Kennedy & Co., Chgo., 1995-2001; pres. Edgewood Internat., Woodridge, Ill., 2001—. Mem. Art Inst. Chgo., Smithsonian Inst., Field Mus. Natural History, Rep. Nat. Com., 1984—. Lt. col. USAR, 1971-99. Decorated Chevalier, Sovereign Mil. Order of Temple of Jerusalem, 1998—. Mem. Res. Officers Assn., U.S. Armor Assn. (Order of St. George), Mil. Police Assn., 337th Cavalry Regiment (Order of the Spur), Bus. Mobilized for Loyola U. Roman Catholic. Home: 3018 Edgewood Pky Woodridge IL 60517 Office: Edgewood Internat 3018 Edgewood Pkwy Woodridge IL 60517 E-mail: theheadhuntingone@yahoo.com., wocatedgewood@aol.com.

O'CONNOR, WILLIAM THOMAS, retired surgeon; b. Elizabeth, N.J., Sept. 17, 1925; MB, BChir, Nat. U. Ireland, 1954. Diplomate Am. Bd. Surgery. Intern Jersey City Med. Ctr., 1954-55; resident E. Orange VA Hosp., N.J., 1956-61, Francis Delafield Hosp., N.Y.C., 1957; pvt. practice, 1961—2001; ret., 2001. Fellow ACS; mem. AMA. Address: PO Box 1329 Sykesville MD 21784 E-mail: wiltcon@att.net.

O'CONNOR TAYLOR, SHERYL ANN, medical services administrator; b. Rome, Ga., Jan. 26, 1951; d. Robert W. and Phyllis M. (Lambert) Nippler; 1 child, Ashley. BS, Ea. Mich. U., 1972; LPN, Washtenaw Community Coll., Ann Arbor, Mich., 1976; RN, Santa Ana Coll., 1980; MA Bus. Mgmt., U. Redlands, 1983. Cert. RN, cert. pub. health nurse, lic. healthcare risk mgr., cert. case mgr., cert. quality assurance/utilization mgmt., cert. med. staff coord., cert. provider credentialing specialist, cert. legal nurse cons., registered health information tech. Med.-surg./oncology nurse Western Med. Ctr., Santa Ana, Calif.; community health nurse Vis. Nurse Assn., Orange, Calif.; hosp. adminstr. USNR Med. Svcs. Corps., Jacksonville, Fla., 1985-88; ins. coord. Blue Cross/Blue Shield Fla., Pensacola, Fla., 1988-90; ctr. dir. Singleday Surgery, Jacksonville, 1990-91; dir. quality mgmt. Humana Hosp., Orange Park, Fla., 1991—93; dir. quality and med. affairs Humana Health Plans, Maitland, Fla., 1991—93; dir. health svcs. PCA/Century Med. Health Plans, Inc., Orlando, Fla., 1993-94; dir. nursing Nations Healthcare Inc., Jacksonville, Fla., 1994-95; dir. central credentials and privileging dept. USN Healthcare Support Office, Jacksonville, Fla., 1995-99; corp. risk mgr. Universal Health Svcs. Inc., King of Prussia, Pa., 1999-2001; dir. risk mgmt. Children's Nat. Med. Ctr., Washington, 2001—02; v.p. clin. effectiveness, quality improvement, patient safety Main Line Health Sys., Bryn Mawr, Pa., 2002—04; dir. quality resource mgmt. Parrish Med. Ctr., Titusville, Fla., 2004—. Mem. Am. Coll. Healthcare Execs., Am. Bd. Quality Assurance and Utilization Physicians, Naval Res. Assn., Nat. Assn. Med. Staff Svcs., Am. Soc. Healthcare Risk Mgmt., Am. Health Info. Mgmt. Assn. Personal E-mail: soconn@bellsouth.net.

O'CONNOR VOS, LYNN, healthcare group executive; b. NY; BS, Alfred U. CEO, pres. Grey Healthcare Group, Inc., NY. Mem.: Am. Skin. Assn., Healthcare Businesswomen's Assn., Multiple Myeloma Rsch. Found. Office: Grey Healthcare Group Inc 114 Fifth Ave New York NY 10011 Office Phone: 212-886-3000. Office Fax: 212-886-3097. E-mail: voc@ghgroup.com.

OCVIRK, OTTO GEORGE, artist; b. Detroit, Nov. 13, 1922; s. Joseph and Louise (Ekle) O.; m. Betty Josephine Lebie, June 11, 1949; children: Robert Joseph, Thomas Frederick, Carol Louise. B.F.A., State U. Iowa, 1949, M.F.A., 1950. Advt. artist apprentice Bass-Luckoff Advt. Agy., Detroit, 1941; engring. draftsman Curtiss-Wright Aircraft Corp., Buffalo, 1942; faculty Bowling Green (Ohio) State U., 1950—, assoc. prof., 1960-65, prof. art, 1965-85, prof. emeritus, 1985—. Exhibited in group shows at, Denver Mus. Art, 1949, 50, 53, Detroit Inst. Art, 71948, 49, 50, 53, 56, Dayton (Ohio) Art Inst., 1950, 51, 56, Ohio State U., 1953, Walker Art Center, Mpls., 1948, 49, Library of Congress, Washington, 1949, Bklyn. Mus., 1949, Joslyn Mus., Omaha, 1949, Colorado Springs Fine Arts Center, 1949; represented in permanent collections, Detroit Inst. Arts, Dayton Art Inst., Friends of Am. Art, Grand Rapids, Mich., State U. Iowa, Iowa City, Bowling Green State U.; (Recipient 24 nat., regional juried art exhbn. awards 1947-57, others.); Author: (with R. Stinson, P. Wigg, R. Bone and David Cayton) Art Fundamentals— Theory and Practice, 1960-97, 7th edit., 1994, 8th edit., 1997, 9th edit., 2001. Scoutmaster Toledo Area council Boy Scouts Am., 1960-63, asst. scoutmaster, 1963-74, dist. commr., 1978-80. Served with AUS, 1943-46. Recipient Silver Beaver award Boy Scouts Am., 1976, Magnifico award Medici Circle, Bowling Green State U., 1987. Mem. Delta Phi Delta (hon.) Methodist. Home and Office: 231 Haskins Rd Bowling Green OH 43402-2206 *"Freedom for expression" keys creative thought into a productive whole.*

ODAR, FUAT, nuclear engineer; b. Harbin, China, May 8, 1934; arrived in U.S., 1957; s. Ibrahim and Hatice Odar; m. Zehra Agi, Oct. 9, 1979; m. Penelope Marie Hays, Dec. 28, 1959 (div. May 30, 1978); children: Deniz Ardelle, Holly Rosemarie. Diploma in engring, Tech. U., Istanbul, Turkey, 1956; PhD, Northwestern U., 1962, MS, 1958. Rsch. phys. scientist U.S. Cold Regions Rsch. Lab, Hanover, NH, 1962—67; nuclear engr. Westinghouse Electric Corp, West Mifflin, Pa., 1967—74; sr. reactor engr. U.S. Nuc. Regulatory Commn., Rockville, Md., 1974—2003. Contbr. articles to profl. jours. Mem.: Am. Nuc. Soc. Personal E-mail: frankodar@earthlink.net.

O'DAY, ANITA BELLE COLTON, entertainer, musician, vocalist; b. Chgo., Dec. 18, 1919; d. James and Gladys (Gill) C. Student, Chgo. public schs. Singer and entertainer various Chgo. Music Clubs, 1939-41; singer with Gene Krupa's Orch., 1941-45, Stan Kenton Orch., 1944, Woody Herman Orch., 1945, Benny Goodman Orch., 1959; singing tours in U.S. and abroad, 1947—; rec. artist Polygram, Capitol, Emily Records, Verve, GNP Crescendo, Columbia, London, Signature, DRG, Pablo; million-seller songs include Let Me Off Uptown, 1941, And Her Tears Flowed Like Wine, 1944, Boogie Blues, 1945; appeared in films Gene Krupa Story, 1959, Jazz on a Summer's Day, 1960, Zigzag, 1970, Outfit, 1974; TV shows 60 Minutes, 1980; Tonight Show, Dick Cavett Show, Today Show, Big Band Bash, CBS Sunday Morning, CNN Showbiz Today; inductee Jazz Hall of Fame, Tampa, 1997, Nat. Endowment Fellowship. Author: High Times, Hard Times, 1981, rev. edit., 1989; performed 50 yr. anniversary concert Carnegie Hall, 1985, Avery Fisher Hall, 1989, Tanglewood, 1990, JVC Festival Town Hall, 1993, Rainbow and Stars, 1995, JVC Festival Carnegie Hall, 1996, JVC Festival Avery Fisher Hall, 1999, Hollywood Palladium, 1999, Blue Note, N.Y.C., 2000, Atlas Supper Club, Los Angeles, 2000, Fez, N.Y.C., 2001, Plush Room, San Francisco, 2002, Iridium, N.Y.C., 2003, Blue Note, N.Y.C., Jazz Alley, Seattle, 2003; currently touring worldwide; albums include Drummer Man, Kenton Era, Anita, Anita Sings The Most, Pick Yourself Up, Lady is a Tramp, An Evening with Anita O'Day, At Mr. Kelly's, Swings Cole Porter, Travelin' Light, All the Sad Young Men, Waiter Make Mine Blues, With the Three Sounds, I Told Ya I Love Ya Now Get Out, Uptown, My Ship, Live in Tokyo, Anita Sings the Winners, Incomparable, Anita 1975, Live at Mingos, Anita O'Day/The Big Band Sessions, Swings Rodgers and Hart, Time for Two, Tea for Two, In a Mellowtone (Grammy nomination 1990), At Vine St. Live, Mello'Day, Live at the City, Angel Eyes, The Night Has a Thousand Eyes, The Rules of the Road, Jazz Masters, Skylark, Swingtime in Hawaii, SS 'Wonderful (Carnegie Hall), Jazz Past Midnight, Compact Jazz, Let Me Off Uptown, The Complete Verve/Cleff Sessions, Ultimate Anita O'Day, After Midnight, Hi-Ho Trailus Bootwhip, Legends of the Swing Era, The Legacy Lives On, Finest Hour, complete Signature and London Recordings, The Young Anita. Jazz Masters fellow Nat. Endowment for the Arts, 1997. Mem. AFTRA, Screen Actors Guild, BMI. Office: Alan Eichler 6064 Selma Ave Los Angeles CA 90028-6415 *From the time I was twelve or thirteen, my life was music. I never thought about being on top. I only wanted to be a part of the scene.*

O'DAY, DENIS MICHAEL, ophthalmologist, educator; b. Melbourne, Victoria, Australia, Dec. 10, 1935; came to U.S., 1967; s. Kevin John and Bernadette John (Hay) O'D.; m. Ann Georgina Despard, May 28, 1966; children: Luke Gerard, Simon Patrick, Edward Daniel. Diploma, Xavier Coll., 1953; MBBS, Melbourne U., 1960. Diplomate Am. Bd. Ophthalmology. Intern St. Vincent's Hosp./U. Melbourne, 1961; resident in internal medicine St. Vincent's Hosp., 1962-64, chief resident dept. medicine, 1964, clin. asst. medicine, 1965-66; 3d asst., mem. asst. Royal Victoria Eye & Ear Hosp., Melbourne, 1967-70; resident in ophthalmology U. Calif., San Francisco, 1970; Wellcome rsch. fellow in corneal disease Inst. Opthalmology, London, 1970-72; asst. prof. ophthalmology Vanderbilt U. Sch. Medicine, Nashville, 1972-74, assoc. prof. ophthalmology, 1974-77, prof. ophthalmology, now chmn., 1977-92, chmn. ophthalmology dept., 1992—; exec. dir. Am. Bd. Ophthalmology, Bala Cynwyd. Cons. ophthalmologist Royal Commonwealth Soc. of Blind, Nigeria, 1972; cons. VA Hosp., 1973-74, active staff, 74; mem. active staff Nashville Gen. Hosp., 1974, Park View Hosp., 1980, Vanderbilt Hosp., 1972; mem. cons. staff St. Thomas Hosp.; bd. dirs. Am. Bd. Ophthalmology, Phila., 1988—; proctor lectr. U. Calif., San Francisco, 1993; co-med. dir. Lions Eye Bank and Sight Svc., 1973-86, med. dir. 1986—; bd. dirs. Lions Eye Bank Mid. Tenn., 1987—; ad-hoc mem. NIH Visual Sci. Study Sect., 1977. Author: Management of Functional Impairment due to Cataract, 1993; contbr. numerous articles, abstracts to profl. publs., chpts. to books. Chair ethics com. Cath. Pub. Policy Commn., Nashville, 1991—. Joyn Hayden rsch. fellow, 1965; recipient Felton Bequest and Potter Found. awards, 1967, recognition award Alcon Rsch. Inst., 1983, Sr. Sci. Investigator award Rsch. to Prevent Blindness, 1987, Health Profl. of Yr. award Tenn. chpt. Assn. for Edn. and Rehab. of Blind and Visually Impaired, 1990. Fellow ACS, Royal Australia Coll. Physicians, Royal Soc. Medicine, Am. Acad. Ophthalmology (sec. quality of care com. 1993—, Honor award for Ednl. Contbns. 1981-85, dir. clin. alert program, pub. health com. 1985-88); mem. AMA, AAUP, Am. Ophthalmol. Soc., Assn. for Rsch. in Vision and Ophthalmology, Nashville Acad. Medicine, Nashville Acad. Ophthalmology (v.p. 1980-81), Oxford Ophthalmol. Soc., Royal Australasian Coll. Physicians, Tenn. Acad. Medicine, Tenn. Acad. Ophthalmology. Roman Catholic. Avocation: sailing. Office: Vanderbilt U Med Ctr East Dept Ophthalmology Med Ctr Fl 8 Nashville TN 37232-0001

O'DAY, JOHN IGNATIUS, retired computer science educator; b. Buffalo, May 30, 1938; s. John Ignatius and Jean Irene (McCarthy) O'D.; m. Giovanna Rose Foderaro, Aug. 24, 1963 (dec. May 1994); children: Domenique, Jeanne d'Arc, John Ignatius III, Cathleen, Frank; m. Theresa Marie Marzec, July 30, 2000. BS, Canisius Coll., 1963. Programmer analyst N.Y. State Civil Svc. Dept., Albany, 1964-66, U. Buffalo, 1966-67, Computer Task Group, Buffalo, 1967-70; info. systems mgr. Erie County Medicaid, Buffalo, 1974-81; v.p. LODOC, Inc., Buffalo, 1981-83; asst. prof. info. systems mgmt. Buffalo State Coll., 1983-88; dir. data processing Erie County, 1988-99, ret., 2000. Cons. in field. Contbr. articles to profl. jours. Active Erie County Dem. Com., Buffalo, 1976-82, Hamburg Dem. Com., 2000—; zone chmn., 30th Zone City Buffalo, 1978-82. Mem. N.Y. All Campus Computer Procurement Com., Frontier Dems. Club (Buffalo) (chmn. steering com. 1982—). Roman Catholic. Avocations: Evolutionary biology, jazz piano. Home: 3682 Briarwood Ct Hamburg NY 14075-2247

O'DAY, KATHLEEN M. federal official; Assoc. gen. counsel bd. mems. office Fed. Res. Sys., Washington. Office: Fed Res Sys Bd Mems Office 20th & C Sts NW Ofc Washington DC 20551-0001

O'DAY, PAUL THOMAS, trade association executive; b. May 2, 1935; s. James Thomas and Jeannette Irene (Deschenes) O'D.; m. Nancy Frances Eitler, June 16, 1962; children: Kathleen, Maureen, Michael, Ellen. BA, Am. Internat. Coll., Springfield, Mass., 1958; JD, Georgetown U., 1963; MPA, Am. U., 1967; D of Pub. Adminstrn. honoris causa, Am. Internat. Coll., 1997. Bar: D.C. 1964, U.S. Supreme Ct. 1974. Patent examiner U.S. Patent Office, Washington, 1959-62; exec. sec. panel high-speed ground transp., auto. air poll. Dept. Commerce, Washington, 1965-66, staff asst. to sec., 1967-69, exec. asst. to sec., 1969-71, dep. dir. bur. domestic commerce, 1972-74; dep. dir. Nat. Bus. Coun. for Consumer Affairs, Washington, 1971-72; cons. to Gen. Counsel GE, Fairfield, Conn., 1974-75; asst. trade rep. Exec. Office of the Pres., Washington, 1975-77; dep. asst. sec. U.S. Dept. Commerce, Washington, 1978-84; pres. Am. Fiber Mfrs. Assn., Washington, 1984—. Chmn. Fiber Econs. Bur., 1984—; pres. Eisenhower World Affairs Inst., 1993-99, exec. com., 2000—. Corporator Am. Internat. Coll., 1974—; mem. governing coun. Shakespeare Theater Guild, 1989-2001. Recipient Constl. Law award Georgetown U. Law Ctr., 1962; Alumni award Am. Internat. Coll., 1970; Pres.'s Meritorious Exec. award., 1984; Nat. Inst. Pub. Affairs fellow Princeton U., 1964 Mem.: AAAS, Am. Chem. Soc., World Econ. Forum, Jussi Bjorling Soc. USA (charter), O'Dea Clan Assn. (Corofin, Ireland), Fed. City Club, Cosmos Club. Home: 8261 Private Ln Annandale VA 22003-4471 Office: Am Fiber Mfrs Assn 1530 Wilson Blvd Ste 690 Arlington VA 22209 Office Phone: 703-875-0432.

ODDIS, JOSEPH ANTHONY, associations executive; b. Greensburg, Pa., Nov. 5, 1928; s. Giacinto and Felicetta (D'Amico) O.; m. Jeanne Trevena, July 10, 1954; children— Joseph Michael, Marie Theresa/ BS, Duquesne U., 1950; DSc (hon.), Mass. Coll. Pharmacy, 1975, Phila. Coll. Pharmacy and Sci., 1975, Albany Coll. Pharmacy, Union U., 1976, Duquesne U., 1989, Mercer U., 1995; LHD (hon.), L.I. U., 1991. Staff pharmacist Mercy Hosp., Pitts., 1950-51, asst. chief pharmacist, 1953-54; chief pharmacist Western Pa. Hosp., Pitts., 1954-56; staff rep. hosp. pharmacy Am. Hosp. Assn., Chgo., 1956-60; dir. div. hosp. pharmacy Am. Pharm., Washington, 1960-62; exec. v.p. Am. Soc. Health-System Pharmacists, Washington, 1960-98. Pres. Am. Soc. Hosp. Pharmacists Research and Edn. Found., 1986-98. Active Boy Scouts Am., Camp Fire Girls; Sec. Am. Soc. Health-System Pharmacists Research and Edn. Found., 1970-86. Served with AUS, 1951-53. Recipient 1st cert. Honor award Duquesne U. Sch. Pharmacy, 1969, named Outstanding Alumnus, 1978; recipient Harvey A.K. Whitney award Am. Soc. Hosp. Pharmacists, 1970, Julius Sturmer Meml. Lecture award Rho Chi soc. Phila., 1971, Howard C. Newton Lecture award 1977, Samuel Melendy Lecture award, 1978, Hugo H. Schaefer award, 1983, Reed and Alice Henninger Lecture award, 1984, Donald E. Francke medal, 1986, Remington medal award, 1990. Fellow AAAS; mem. Am. Pharm. Assn., Am. Soc. Hosp. Pharmacists, Am. Inst. History Pharmacy, Internat. Pharm. Fedn. (pres. hosp. pharmacy sect. 1977-81, v.p. 1984-86, pres. 1986-90), Drug Info. Assn., Am. Soc. Assn. Execs., Can. Soc. Hosp. Pharmacists (hon.), Soc. Hosp. Pharmacists Australia (hon.), Pharm. Soc. Gt. Britain (hon.), Pharm. Soc. Nigeria (hon.), Nat. Coun. Patient Info. and Edn. (sec. 1982-85), Israel Pharm. Soc. (hon.), Rho Chi, Kappa Psi (hon.), Duquesne U. Century Club (charter). Home: 6509 Rockhurst Rd Bethesda MD 20817-1661 Office: Am Soc Health-System Pharmacists 7272 Wisconsin Ave Bethesda MD 20814-4836

ODDSSON, LARS INGIMAR EUGEN, biomedical researcher; b. Reykavik, Iceland, May 7, 1954; came to U.S., 1993; s. Ingimar and Anna-Stina (Johnsson) O.; m. Annette Xenopoulos; 1 child, Mattias, 2001. Student program for civil engring., Linköping U., 1973-76; BSc, U. Coll. Phys. Edn. and Sports, Stockholm, 1981; D Med. Sci., Karolinska Inst., Stockholm, 1990. Cert. tchr., nat. team coach instr. Tchr., lectr. Sch. Phys. Edn. Karolinska Inst., Stockholm, 1982-93, rsch. engr., 1986-88; postdoctoral fellow NeuroMuscular Rsch. Ctr. Boston U., 1993, rsch. asst. prof., 1994-96, rsch. assoc. prof., 1996—. Investigator Nat. Space Biomed. Rsch. Inst., 2000—; head coach Sollentuna VK, Stockholm, 1982-91; asst. nat. team coach, Sweden, 1982-91. Contbr. articles to profl. jours.; inventor. Recipient Leadership in Sports Honor, Swedish Sports Fedn., 1985, Coach of Yr. award Swedish Volleyball Assn., 1989, Rsch. Grant Whitaker Found., 1995. Mem. Scandinavian Physiol. Soc., Internat. Soc. Biomechanics, Internat. Soc. Electrophys. Kinesiology. Avocations: composing, photography, skiing, tennis, volleyball. Office: Boston U Neuro Muscular Rsch Ctr 19 Deerfield St Boston MA 02215-1904 Office Phone: 617-358-0717. E-mail: loddsson@bu.edu.

O'DEA, DENNIS MICHAEL, lawyer; b. Lowell, Mass, Nov. 1, 1946; s. James Lawrence and Carol France (Gibbons) O'D.; m. Mary Gail Frawley; children: Emily C., Dennis C., Daniel P., Mollie G., Sally K., Igor Ibradzic. BA in Govt., U. Notre Dame, 1968; JD magna cum laude, U. Mich., 1972. Bar: Mass. 1972, D.C. 1980, Ill. 1981, N.Y. 1994. Assoc. Goodwin, Procter & Hoar, Boston, 1972-74, Fine & Ambrogne, Boston, 1974-77; assoc. prof. Syracuse U. Coll. Law, NY, 1977-78; vis. assoc. prof. Nat. Law Ctr., George Washington U., 1978-80; ptnr. Keck Mahin & Cate, NYC, 1980-96; pvt. practice, 1996-97; ptnr. Wolf, Block, Schorr and Solis-Cohen LLP, NYC, 1997—. Co-dir. The Gilmore Inst., 1995—. Mem. Order of the Coif, Chgo. Lit. Club (pres. 1993). Presbyterian. Home: 5 Opal Ct New City NY 10956-7021 Office: Wolf Block Schorr & Solis-Cohen 250 Park Ave Ste 1000 New York NY 10177-0001

O'DEA, J. DAVID, psychologist, educator; b. Ellsworth, Kans., Feb. 17, 1924; m. Teresa Eleanor Cordova, June 21, 1980. BS in Psychology, Emporia State U., 1948, MS in Psychology, 1949; PhD in Psychology, Oreg. State U., 1952. Lic. psychologist Fla. Assoc. prof. Fla. State U., Tallahassee, 1953—56; sr. staff assoc. IBM, Dunedin, Fla., 1956—82. Cons. psychologist, Dunedin, 1982—92; vis. prof. Notre Dame U., South Bend, Ind., 1953, U. Va., Charlottesville, 1956, Oreg. State U., Corvallis, 1964, U. Miami, 1969—70; chmn. bd. Caladesi Nat. Bank, Dunedin, 1967—72, Clearwater (Fla.) Oaks Bank, Clearwater, 1973—82. Contbr., author: book Counseling Selected Readings, 1962; contbr. articles to profl. jours. and mags. Mem. adv. counsel for pres. Berea (Ky.) Coll.; bd. dirs. Dunedin Pub. Libr., 1991—. With USN, 1942—45, WWII. Named Ky. col., Hon. Order of Ky. Cols., 1982. Mem.: VFW, APA (licentiate; Fla. state pres. 1969—70), Ye Mystic Krewe of Neptune (charter mem. Tampa Bay, dir. 1979—), KC (4th degree, Family of Month 1980), Elks (life). Roman Catholic. Avocations: travel, reading, civil volunteering, genealogy. Home: 509 Baywood Dr S Dunedin FL 34698

O'DEA, WILLIAM PATRICK, research and development company executive; b. Jersey City, Feb. 20, 1959; s. William Patrick O'Dea Sr. and Blanche (Zakzrewski) O'Dea. BS in polit. sci., St. John's U., 1981; BS in criminal justice, Seton Hall Law Sch., 1982. Project mgr. Elizabeth (NJ) Devel. Co., 1993—94, UEZ dir., 1994—95, deputy exec. dir., 1995—. City coun. mem. City of Jersey City, 1985—93; freeholder County of Hudson, Jersey City, 1997—; mem. Jersey City Planning Bd., 1985—89; v. chmn. Jersey City Edn. Devel. Co., 1985—89, PR Org. for Econ. Edn. Devel., Elizabeth, 1996—. Co-author: (plays) The Pitts, 2003 (Producer award, 2003), (screenplays) A Clown in Babylon, 1994 (Producer award, 1996); author: (plays) Therapy, 1993 (Producer award, 1993). Bd. mem. Friends of the Loew's, Jersey City, 2003; elected mem. NJ Dem. Com., Trenton, 2000—; bd. mem. Big Brother/Big Sister, Hudson County, 1997—. Recipient Advocate for People award, Chirstopher Columbus Found., 2003. Mem.: Knights of Columbus 475, Moose Lodge 266, Nat. Honor Soc. Democrat. Catholic. Achievements include directed nation's #1 Enterprise Zone program as selected by the Nat. Assn. of State Devel. agencies, 1998. Avocations: chess, mentor, playwriter, script writer, catechism thr. Home: 143 Mallory Ave Jersey City NJ 07304 Office: Elizabeth Devel Co 288 N Broad St Jersey City NJ 07304 E-mail: wodea@edcnj.org.

ODEGARD, MARK ERIE, geophysicist, consultant; b. Plentywood, Mont., Nov. 1, 1940; s. Harold Theodore and Edna Marcella (Jacobsen) O.; m. Elisabeth Snow, June 17, 1967; 1 child, Liv. AA, Dawson Coll., Glendive, Mont., 1960; BA, U. Mont., 1962; MS, Oreg. State U., 1965; PhD, U. Hawaii, 1975. Asst. prof. Hawaii Inst. Geophysics, Honolulu, 1974-78; dir. geology and geophysics program Office Naval Rsch., Arlington, Va., 1978-81; assoc. prof. N.Mex. State U., Las Cruces, 1981-83; staff rsch. geophysicist Sohio Petroleum Co., Dallas, 1983-86; prin. scientist Basalt Waste Isolation Program, Richland, Wash., 1986-88; rsch. assoc. Unocol Sci. & Tech., Brea, Calif., 1988-93; mgr. Potential Fields Group, Unocal, Sugar Land, Tex., 1993-98; bd. dirs., v.p. U.S. ops. Geophys. Exploration Tech., Sugar Land, 1998—. Contbr. over 50 articles to sci. jours. Chmn. San Bernardino County (Calif.) Svc. Area 48 Adv. Com., 1989-91; vice chmn. Chino Hills Planning Commn., 1992-93; mem. Chino Hills (Calif.) Mcpl. Adv. Coun., 1990-91. Recipient Antarctica Svc. medal U.S. Congress, 1966. Mem. Soc. Exploration Geophysicists, Am. Geophys. Union, Sigma Xi, Am. Planning Assn. Avocations: skiing, golf, hunting, fishing, marathon running. Home: 3418 El Dorado Blvd Missouri City TX 77459-2414 Office: Ste 510 12503 Exchange Dr Stafford TX 77477-3607

O'DELL, ELIZABETH ANN, controller; b. Jersey City, Apr. 27, 1960; d. William P. and Madeline M. (Conheeney) O'D.; m. Dennis Polizzi, Sept. 7, 1985. BBA, MBA, Pace U., 1982. CPA, N.J. Sr. auditor Touche Ross & Co., Newark, 1982-85; supr. Coopers & Lybrand, Newark, 1985-87; controller/dir.

internal ops. Kratos Analytical Inc., Ramsey, N.J., 1987-91; controller Radiodetection Corp., Mahwah, N.J., 1991—. Mem. AICPA, N.J. State Soc. CPA's, NAFE, Am. Woman's Soc. CPA's. Office: Alteon Inc 6 Campus Dr Parsippany NJ 07054-4406

ODELL, HERBERT, lawyer; b. Phila., Oct. 20, 1937; s. Samuel and Selma (Kramer) O.; m. Valerie Odell; children: Wesley, Jonathan, James, Sarah, Samuel. BS in Econs., U. Pa., 1959; LLB magna cum laude, U. Miami, 1962; LLM, Harvard U., 1963. Bar: Fla. 1963, Pa. 1968, D.C. 2002. Trial atty. tax div. U.S. Dept. Justice, Washington, 1963-65; assoc. Walton, Lantaff, Schroeder, Carson & Wahl, Miami, Fla., 1965-67; from assoc. to ptnr. Morgan, Lewis & Bockius, Phila., 1967-89; ptnr. Zapruder & Odell, Phila., 1989-98, Odell & Ptnrs., Phila., 1998-99, Miller & Chevalier, Chartered, Phila., 2000—. Adj. prof. U. Miami, Villanova U.; lectr. various tax insts. Contbr. articles to profl. jours. Ford fellow, 1962-63. Mem.: ABA, D.C. Bar Assn., Phila. Bar Assn., Pa. Bar Assn., Fla. Bar Assn., Harvard Club, Beta Alpha Psi, Omicron Delta Kappa, Phi Kappa Phi. Avocations: sailing, running, tennis, scuba diving, fishing. Office: Miller & Chevalier 401 E City Ave Ste 815 Bala Cynwyd PA 19004-1121 Office Phone: 610-617-7510. E-mail: hodell@milchev.com.

O'DELL, JAMES E. newspaper publishing executive; V.p. ops. and techs. Chgo. Tribune, 1993-97, Chgo. Tribune Pub., 1997—. Office: Chgo Tribune Pub 435 N Michigan Ave Chicago IL 60611-4066

O'DELL, JANE, automotive company executive; Co-owner Westfall GMC Truck Inc., Kansas City, Mo. Office: Westfall GMC Truck Inc 3915 Randolph Rd Kansas City MO 64161-9383

O'DELL, JOAN ELIZABETH, lawyer, mediator, consumer products company executive, educator; b. East Dubuque, Ill., May 3, 1932; d. Peter Emerson and Olive (Bonnet) O'Dell; children: Dominique R., Nicole L. BA cum laude, U. Miami, 1956, JD, 1958. Bar: Fla. 1958, U.S. Supreme Ct. 1972, DC 1974, Ill. 1978, Va. 1987; lic. real estate broker Ill., Va., W.Va. Trial atty. SEC, Washington, 1959-60; asst. state atty. Office State Atty., Miami, Fla., 1960-64; asst. county atty. Dade County Atty.'s Office, Miami, 1964-70; county atty. Palm Beach County Atty.'s Office, West Palm Beach, Fla., 1970-71; regional gen. counsel Region IV EPA, Atlanta, 1971-73, assoc. gen. counsel Washington, 1973-77; sr. counsel Nalco Chem. Co., Oakbrook, Ill., 1977-78; v.p., gen. counsel Angel Mining, Washington and Tenn., 1979-96; pres. S.W. Land Investments, Miami, 1979-88; v.p. Events U.S.A., Washington, 1990—. Mem. Exec. Women's Coun., Tucson, 1982—85; co-chmn. sch. improvement coun. Harpers Ferry Jr. HS, 2000—04; bd. dirs. Tucson Women's Found., 1982—84, U. Ariz. Bus. and Profl. Women's Club, Tucson, 1981—85, LWV, Tucson, 1981—85, pres., 1984—85, chmn. nat. security study, bd. dirs. Palm Beach County, Fla., 1990—92, Jefferson County Visitors and Conv. Bur., Harpers Ferry, W.Va., 2001—04. Mem.: Ill. Bar Assn., Va. State Bar Assn., DC Bar Assn., Fla. Bar Assn. Avocations: camping, hiking, skiing. Office Phone: 304-724-1763. Personal E-mail: treetopsjodell@adelphia.net.

ODELL, JOHN H. construction executive; b. Toledo, Oct. 31, 1955; s. John H. and Doris Odell; m. Kathryn Lau, Oct. 1, 1988; children: Ceara, Heather, Victoria. B in Environ. Design, U. Miami, Oxford, Ohio, 1977. Staff arch. Richard Halford and Assocs., Santa Fe, 1978-79; ptnr. B.O.A. Constrn., Santa Fe, 1980-84; owner John H. Odell Constrn., Santa Fe, 1985—; v.p. Los Pintores Inc., Santa Fe, 1990-92; pres. Uncle Joey's Food Svcs. Inc., 1991—, John H. Odell Assocs. Inc., Santa Fe, 1995—. Musician: Huntington (W.Va.) Cmty. Orch., 1972—73, Santa Fe Cmty. Orch., 1982. Mem. citizen rev. com. Santa Fe Sch. Bd., chmn., 1999—, mem. bond and mil. levy com., 2000—. Recipient Hist. Preservation award, City of Santa Fe, 1997. Mem.: AIA (assoc.; treas., bd. dirs. Santa Fe chpt. 1988—, mem. liaison com. design 1987—, Cmty. Svc. award 1993), Santa Fe Remodeler Coun., Nat. Assn. Home Builders, Vine and Wine Soc. (N.Mex No. Rio Grande chpt. pres., bd. dirs., v.p.). Avocations: skiing, scuba diving, handball, racquetball. Home: PO Box 2967 Santa Fe NM 87504-2967 Office: John H Odell Assn 1523 Taos St Santa Fe NM 87505-3835 E-mail: johnoinc@aol.com.

O'DELL, KIMBERLY JANE, historian, educator; d. A. Truman O'Dell and Barbara Jane Young. BA in History, Jacksonville (Ala.) State U., 1991, MA in History, 1992, MS in Edn., 1997; EDS in Adult Edn., Auburn U., 2003. Cert. tchr. Ala., 1997. Owner, sec., treas. Goal Post BBQ, Anniston, Ala., 1994—98; instr. Cheaha Regional Adult Edn. Program, Anniston, 2000—02; curriculum developer, instr. Family Svcs. of Calhoun and Cleburne Counties, Anniston, 2002; instr. Fast Track Program Ala. Works, Anniston, 2002—03; instr. office careers Gadsden State C.C., Anniston, 2003—. Adj. instr. Gadsden State C.C., Anniston, 1997; cons. Brown & Kughn, Anniston, 1999. Author: Calhoun County, Alabama, 1998, Anniston, Alabama, 2000. Recipient Alumni Author award, The Donoho Sch., 1998. Mem.: Ala. Assn. Pub. Continuing Adult Edn., Nat. Hist. Trust, Ala. Hist. Assn., Drayton Hall Soc., Phi Alpha Theta.

O'DELL, LYNN MARIE LUEGGE (MRS. NORMAN D. O'DELL), librarian; b. Berwyn, Ill., Feb. 24, 1938; d. George Emil and Helen Marie (Pesek) Luegge; m. Norman D. O'Dell, Dec. 14, 1957; children: Jeffrey, Jerry. Student, Lyons Twp. Jr. Coll., La Grange, Ill., 1957, No. Ill., Coll. of Dupage. Sec. Martin Co., Chgo., 1957-59; dir. Carol Stream (Ill.) Pub. Libr., 1964—. Chmn. automation governing com. DuPage Library System, v.p., 1982-85, pres. exec. com. adminstrv. librarians, 1985-86, chair automation search com., 1991-92. Named Woman of Yr., Wheaton Bus. and Profl. Woman's Club, 1968. Mem. ALA, Ill. Libr. Assn., Libr. Adminstrs. Conf. No. Ill., Pub. Libr. Assn. Lutheran. Home: 182 Yuma Ln Carol Stream IL 60188-1917 Office: 616 Hiawatha Dr Carol Stream IL 60188-1634 E-mail: lodell@cslibrary.org.

ODELL, M. CAROL, music educator; b. Bunkie, La., Feb. 12, 1936; d. James William and Marguerite Viola (Harper) Durham; children: Lydia Brown, Melanie Tipton. B in music edn., So. Ark. U., 1957. Choral tchr. Forest Heights Jr. H.S., Little Rock, 1957—58, Jacksonville Jr. H.S., Ark., 1958—63; dir. of child care Marshall Rd. Bapt. Ch., Jacksonville, 1978—96; piano tchr. pvt., Jacksonville, 1958—2000, voice tchr., 1958—78; ch. pianist Marshall Rd. Bapt. Ch., Jacksonville, 1976—2000; piano tchr. Olive Bapt. Ch. Art Sch., Pensacola, Fla., 2000—03. Pianist Northside Bapt. Ch., 2002—; mem. Little Rock Coterie, 1958—59, 1997—2000. Mem.: Nat. Guild of Piano Teachers, Pensacola Music Teachers Assn., Fla. Music Teachers Assn., Music Teachers Nat. Assn. Home: 1328 N 57th Ave Pensacola FL 32506

O'DELL, NANCY, television personality; b. Myrtle Beach, SC; d. Leonard and Betty Humphries; m. Richard O'Dell. Grad, Clemson U. Reporter, anchor WPDE-TV, Myrtle Beach, SC; morning news anchor, crime reporter WCBD-TV, Charleston; co-anchor, investigative reporter WTVJ-TV, Miami; entertainment reporter A Current Affair, 1995—96; weekend co-anchor, weekday corr. Access Hollywood, 1996—99, co-anchor, 1999—; host Nashville Star, USA Network, 2003—. Contbr. reports NBC News's The Today Show and Dateline; host Emmys Pre-Show, Fox, 1999, Emmys Pre-Show, ABC, 2000; co-host Emmys Post Show, NBC, 2002, Hollywood Christmas Parade, 1999, 2000, 02, Tournament of Roses Parade coverage, NBC, 2001, 02, 03, 04, Golden Globes Arrivals Show, NBC, 2002, 03, 04, Miss USA, 2004. Actress (films) Scream 2, 1997, The Adventures of Ragtime, 1998, The Bachelor, 1999, Scream 3, 2000, Outta Time, 2002, (TV series) General Hospital, 1998, Days of Our Lives, 2002—03. Mem. Nat. Celebrity Cabinet, Am. Red Cross, 2002—; internat. bd. mem Best Buddies; Celebrity Amb. Childhelp USA; spokesperson March of Dimes. Named State SC Hall of Fame, 1998; recipient 2 AP Awards, 2 Soc. Profl. Journalists Awards, Spirit of Leadership Award, Best Buddies, 2002. Office: Access Hollywood NBC Studios 3000 W Alameda Ave Burbank CA 91523*

ODELL, PATRICK LOWRY, mathematics professor; b. Watonga, Okla., Nov. 29, 1930; s. Max Vernon and Pamela (Massey) Odell; m. Norma Lou Maddox, Aug. 16, 1958 (dec. May 1980); children: James M., David L., Michael R.L., Julie K., Patricia L., Deborah L.; m. Dovalee Dorsett, Aug. 3, 1985. BS, U. Tex., 1952; postgrad., UCLA, 1953-54; MS, Okla. State U., 1958, PhD, 1962. Mathematician White Sands (N.Mex.) Proving Grounds, 1952-53, Kaman Nuclear, Albuquerque, 1958-59, U.S. Naval Nuclear Ordnance Evaluation Unit, 1959-62, Ling-Temco Vought Aeros., 1962; asst. prof. math. U. Tex., Austin, 1962-66; prof., chmn. dept. math. Tex. Technol. U., Lubbock, 1966-71, coordinator insts., dir. rsch., Coll. Arts and Sci., 1971-72; prof math. scis. and environ. scis. U. Tex., Dallas, 1972-88, prof. emeritus, 1988—; prof. emeritus math. sci. Baylor U., Waco, Tex., 1988—2001; exec. dean grad. studies and rsch. U. Tex., Dallas, 1972-75. Assoc. dir. Tex. Ctr. for Rsch., Austin, 1964—66; rsch. scientist Def. Rsch. Lab., 1963—65; cons. math. statistician, 1962—. Capt. USAF, 1953—57. Fellow: Am. Statis. Assn., Tex. Acad. Sci. (Disting. Tex. Scientist award 1994); mem.: Soc. Indsl. and Applied Math. Home: 3200 Windsor Ave Waco TX 76708-3113

O'DELL, RICHARD, trucking executive; With Yellow Corp., 1987—95, v.p. fin. and adminstrn. WestEx subs., 1995—97; v.p. fin. and adminstrn. Saia Motor Freight Line, Inc., Duluth, Ga., 1997—99, pres., CEO, 1999—. Office: Saia Motor Freight Line Inc 11465 Johns Creek Pky Ste 400 Duluth GA 30097*

O'DELL, WALDEN WESLEY, manufacturing executive; b. St. Louis, July 19, 1945; s. Walden W. and Nettie Ann (Chaffin)O'D.; m. Patricia Marie Gormley, Aug. 19, 1967; children: Micahael Thomas, Jennifer Mary, Patrick Brian, Kathleen Elizabeth. BS, St. Louis U., 1967, MS, 1970; MBA, Stanford U., Calif., 1972. Engr. Emerson Electrics-E&S, St. Louis, 1966-70; asst. to v.p. engr. Boise Cascade, St. Louis, 1971; engr., asst. to v.p., int. mgr., int. adminstr. Emerson Electric - Corp. Int., St. Louis, 1970-75; v.p. intl. Emerson Electric - Alco Controls, St. Louis, Emerson Electric - USEM, Milford, Conn., 1979-81; pres. Emerson Electric - Louisville Ladder, 1981-85, Emerson Electric - Krautkramer Branson, Lewistown, Pa., 1985-87, Emerson Electric Co., Lewistown, 1987—; pres. & CEO Diebold, Inc., North Canton, OH, 1999—. Mem. Cin. Council on World Affairs, 1987--. Mem. Valve Mfrs. Assn., Hyde Park Country Club. Office: Diebold Inc 5995 Mayfair Rd Canton OH 44720-8077*

ODELL, WILLIAM DOUGLAS, physician, educator, research scientist; b. Oakland, Calif., June 11, 1929; s. Ernest A. and Emma L. (Mayer) O.; m. Margaret F. Reilly, Aug. 19, 1950; children: Michael, Timothy, John D., Debbie, Charles. AB, U. Calif., Berkeley, 1952; MD, MS in Physiology, U. Chgo., 1956; PhD in Biochemistry and Physiology, George Washington U., 1965. Intern, resident, chief resident in medicine U. Wash., 1956-60, postdoctoral fellow in endocrinology and metabolism, 1957-58; sr. investigator Nat. Cancer Inst., Bethesda, Md., 1960-65; chief endocrine service NICHD, 1965-66; chief endocrinology Harbor-UCLA Med. Center, Torrance, Calif., 1966-72, chmn. dept. medicine, 1972-79; vis. prof. medicine Auckland Sch. Medicine, New Zealand, 1979-80; prof. medicine and physiology U. Utah Sch. Medicine, Salt Lake City, 1980-99, chmn. dept. internal medicine, 1980-96, prof. medicine and physiology, 1996-99, emeritus prof. medicine and physiology, 1999—. Pres. med. staff U. Utah Sch. Medicine, 1995-96. Mem. editorial bds. med. jours.; author, editor 8 books in field; contbr. over 330 articles to med. jour. With USPHS, 1960-66. Recipient Disting. Svc. award U. Chgo., 1973, Pharmacia award for outstanding contbn. to clin. chemistry, 1977, Gov. award State of Utah Sci. and Tech., 1988, also rsch. awards, Mastership award ACP, 1987, Laureate award (Utah). Mem.: Soc. Exptl. Biol. Medicine (councillor), Western Soc. Clin. Rsch. (Mayo Soley award), Western Assn. Physicians (pres.), Pacific Coast Fertility Soc. (pres.), Soc. Study of Reprodn. (bd. dirs.), Endocrine Soc. (v.p., Robert Williams award 1991), Am. Soc. Andrology (pres.), Assn. Am. Physicians, Am. Physiol. Soc., Am. Soc. Clin. Investigation, Alpha Omega Alpha. E-mail: owodell@aol.com.

O'DELL, WILLIAM FRANCIS, retired business executive, writer; b. Detroit, Jan. 24, 1909; s. Frank Trevor and Garnett (Aikman) O'C.; m. Bess Baer, June 10, 1933 (dec. July 1986); m. Helen M. Porter, May 16, 1987 (dec. 1997); children: Peggy, David. BS, U. Ill., 1930. With Penton Pub. Co., 1933-37; v.p. Ross Fed. Research Corp., 1937-44; mng. dir. Statis Research Co., 1944-45; pres. Market Facts, Inc., 1946-64, chmn., 1964-74; pres. ROC Internat., 1961-64; mem. census adv. bd. Dept. Commerce, 1963-73; prof. mktg. McIntire Sch. Commerce U. Va., 1965-78. Vis. prof. Chinese U. of Hong Kong, 1969 Author: Marketing Decision, 1968, Marketing Decision Making, 1976, 4th edit., 1988, How to Make Lifetime Friends—With Peers and Parents, 1978, Twelve Families—An American Experience, 1981, Effective Business Decision Making and the Educated Guess, 1991; mem. editorial rev. bd. Jour. Mktg, 1964-73. Recipient Leader in Mktg. award, 1970, Jour. Mktg. Research editorial award, 1979; William F. O'Dell professorship in commerce named in his honor U. Va., 1983; named Pioneer in Mktg. Rsch., 1998. Mem. Am. Mktg. Assn. (pres. 1960-61), Colonnade Club (Charlottesville), Cornerstone Soc., Rotary, Delta Upsilon, Beta Gamma Sigma. Home: 15010 Shell Point Blvd Fort Myers FL 33908-1637 E-mail: biode@aol.com.

O'DELL, WILLIAM H. state legislator, manufacturing executive; b. Ware Shoals, S.C., Oct. 11, 1938; s. William B. and Sara Francis O'Dell; m. Aedra Gaily Tisdale; children William B., Patricia Michelle. BA, The Citadel, 1960, hon. degree, 1997. CEO, O'Dell Mop Co., Inc., Ware Shoals; mem. S.C. Gen. Assembly, Columbia, 1990-91, S.C. Senate, Columbia, 1989—. Mem. agr. and natural resources com., fin. com., gen. com., invitations com., labor, commerce and industry com., transp. com. Bd. visitors The Citadel, 1981-88, Piedmont Inst. Tech., 1987-88; vice chmn. Ware Shoals Sch. Dist. 51, 1974-81, Abbeville Devel. Bd., 1987; pres. Ware Shoals Cmty. Found., 1985-88; chmn. Ware Shoals United Fund, 1986. Mem. S.C. N.G., 1956-58. Recipient Palmetto award The Citadel, 1994. Democrat. Office: 510 Gressette Bldg Columbia SC 29202 also: PO Box 540 Ware Shoals SC 29692-0540

ODELL-SCOTT, DAVID WINFIELD, education educator; s. Willis W and JoAnn Scott; m. Lauren M. Odell-Scott, 1975; children: Megan, Paul. BA, Tex. Christian U., 1975; MDiv, Vanderbilt U., 1980, PhD, 1989. Asst. prof. philosophy and religion Fisk U., Nashville, 1987—90, chair dept., 1989—90; asst. prof. philosophy Kent State U., Ohio, 1990—95, assoc. prof., 1995—, coord. religion studies, 1996—2003, chair dept. philosophy, 2003—. Author: A Post-Patriarchal Christology, Paul's Critique of Theocracy: A Theocracy in Corinthians and Galatians, 2003; editor: Democracy and Religion: Free Exercise and Diverse Visions; contbr. Handbook of Postmodern Biblical Interpretation. Co-min. Eastwood Christian Ch. (Disciples of Christ), Nashville, 1983—90. Rsch. grant, The Pluralism Project At Harvard U., 1998, 1999. Mem.: Am. Philos. Assn., Soc. of Bibl. Lit. (program chair, semiotics and exegesis sect. 2002—), Am. Acad. of Religion. Office: Philosophy Dept Kent State U Kent OH 44242-0001 Office Phone: 330-672-0271.

ODEN, JEAN P(HIFER), special education educator; b. Chgo., May 2, 1936; d. Dillard James and Lena (Conner) Phifer; m. James Edward Oden, Apr. 26, 1959; 1 child, Eric James. BE, Chgo. Tchrs. Coll., 1958; MEd in Learning Disabilities, Chgo. State U., 1973; postgrad., Nat. Coll. Edn., Evanston, Ill., 1986—, cert. advance studies, 1987; EdD, Nat.-Louis U., 1995. Tchr. elem. schs. Chgo., 1958-73, tchr. learning disabilities elem. schs., 1973-81, cons. spl. edn., ind. edn. program facilitator, 1981; learning disability specialist Phillips High Sch., Chgo., 1982-87, Englewood High Sch., Chgo., 1987-94, Harold Washington Elem. Sch., Chgo., 1994-98. Mem. Ill. Guidelines for Learning Disabilities Devel. Com., Springfield, Ill., 1981-82, Com. to Devel. State Test for Learning Disabilities Tchrs., Springfield, 1986—; speaker Who's Who Congress, Cambridge, Eng., 1992; mem. del. to Vietnam, 1993, China, 1994, Oxford U., 1997, South Africa, 2001; mem. African Affairs Adv. Coun. to Chgo. Human Rels. Commn., 1999, People to People Internat. Worldwide Conf., 2002; chair edn. com. Chgo. Southside Br. NAACP, 2000. Sec. Nat. Urban League N.Y.C. conf., 1980; mem. Congl. Victory Fund, Chgo., 1985, SCLC Met. Chgo., 1979-81, Mayoral Summit Parent-Community Coun. on Ednl. Reform, 1987—, Chgo. Mayor's Edn. Summit on Sch. Reform, 1988; charter mem. Rep. Presdl. Adv. Task Force, 1989, Rep. Inner Circle, 1991, Ctr. for Study of the Presidency, 1998; mem. Coalition Black Trade Unionists, 1991—, cons. pool Nat. Juvenile Justice Resource Ctr., 1991—, NAACP; state chair African Am. Econ. Devel. Task Force, Ill. Legis. Black Caucus, 1992—; bd. dirs., African Scientific Rsch. Mus. Inst., 2003. U.S. Dept. Edn. grantee, 1986; recipient Citizenship award Chgo. mayor, 1984, Cert. merit NAACP South Side Br., 1978; named state advisor U.S. Congl. Adv. Bd., 1985; speaker edn. seminar 19th Congress on Arts and Communicatiion, Cambridge, Eng. Mem. ASCD, LWV, NAACP (chair edn. com. 2000, sec. Chgo. Southside br., 2003), Minority Mainstream, United Neighborhoods Intertwined for Total Equality (founder, exec. dir., rschr.), Assn. for Citizens with Learning Disabilities, Coun. for Exceptional Children (liaison to state bd. Ill. Divsn. for Citizens with Learning Disabilities 1980), Spl. Edn. Tchrs. Assn. (1st pres., founder), Black Parents United for Edn. and Related Svcs. (founder), Kappa Delta Pi, Lehigh (Fla.) Country Club, Thousand Trails Club (Ottawa, Ill.). Mem. Carter C.M.E. Ch. Avocations: hiking, racketball, travel, camping. Fax: 773 821-4456. *Personal philosophy: Those of us in society who are fortunate to reach levels of influence should share skills and talents with the less fortunate. A society which maintain masses of people in an undeveloped state is doomed to class conflict and cultural extinction. Those who don't study history are bound to repeat it.*

ODEN, JOHN TINSLEY, engineering educator, mathematician, consultant; b. Alexandria, La., Dec. 25, 1936; s. John James and Sara Elizabeth (Lyles) O.; m. Barbara Clare Smith, Mar. 19, 1965; children: John Walker, Elizabeth Lee. BS, La. State U., 1959; MS, Okla. State U., 1960, PhD, 1962; doctorate in sci. (hon.), Tech. U. Lisbon, Portugal, 1986; Doctorate (hon.), Polytechnique de Mons, Belgium, 2000, Tech. U. Krakow, Poland, 2001. Registered profl. engr., Tex., La. Teaching asst. La. State U., Baton Rouge, 1959; asst. prof. Okla. State U., Stillwater, 1961-63; sr. structures engr. Gen. Dynamics, Fort Worth, 1963-64; prof., head dept. engring. mechanics U. Ala., Huntsville, 1964-73; prof. U. Tex., Austin, 1973—, Carol and Henry Groppe prof. engring., Ernest and Virginia Cockrell chair in engring., 1987-93, Cockrell Family Regents prof. engring. 2, 1993—, assoc. v.p. rsch., 2003—. Prof. Coope U. Fed., Brazil, 1974; dir. Inst. Computational Engring and Sci., 2003, assoc. v.p. for rsch., 2003—; mem. Sci. Rsch. Coun. vis. scholar Brunel U., Eng., 1981; com. on computational mechanics NRC; chmn. U.S. Nat. Com. on Theoretical and Applied Mechanics, 1992-94; founder, CEO computational Mechanics Co., Inc., 1982-96. Author, editor 45 books; editor Jour. Computer Methods in Applied Mechanics and Engring., 1980—; contbr. numerous articles to profl. jours. Decorated chevalier Ordre des Palms Academique (France); recipient rsch. award Southeastern Conf. on Theoretical and Applied Mechanics, 1978, Lohmann medal Okla. State U., 1991, Computational Mechanics medal Japan Soc. Mech. Engrs., 1993; elected Nat. Acad. Engring. Brazil, 1998. Fellow ASCE (Outstanding Svc. award 1968, Walter Huber rsch. award 1973, Theodore von Karman medal 1992, Joe J. King Prof. Engring. award 1994), ASME (Worcester Reed Warner medal 1990, Timoshenko medal 1996), NAE, Soc. Engring. Sci. (pres. 1978, Eringen medal 1991, Hocutt Rsch. award, 1992), Am. Acad. Mechanics (pres. 1990-94, Disting. Svc. medal 1995); mem. Soc. Indsl. and Applied Math., Internat. Assn. Computational Mechanics (pres. 1990-94, Congress-Gauss-Newton medal 1994), U.S. Assn. Computational Mechanics (pres. 1990-92, John Von Neumann medal 1993), Soc. Natural Philosophy, Nat. Acad. Engring. Mex., Nat. Acad. Engring. Brazil. Home: 7403 W Rim Dr Austin TX 78731-2044 Office: Univ Tex Austin ICES Campus Code CO200 Austin TX 78712

ODEN, KEITH D. real estate company executive; MBA, U. Tex. Lic. realtor Tex. Mgmt. cons. Deloitte, Haskins and Sells Century Devel. Corp., dir. fin. planning, pres. Camden Property Trust, Houston, COO, trust mgr. Office: Camden Property Trust 3 Greenway Plaza Ste 1300 Houston TX 77046*

ODEN, ROBERT A., JR., academic administrator; m. Teresa Oden; children: Robert, Katherine. BA in History and Lit., Harvard Coll.; MA in Religious Studies/Oriental Langs., Cambridge U.; MA in Theology, Harvard Divinity, 1972; PhD in Near Eastern Langs. and Lit., Harvard U., 1975; MA (hon.), Dartmouth Coll., 1987. Faculty Dartmouth Coll., 1975—89, prof., 1985—89, chair dept. of religion, 1983—89; dir., founder Dartmouth's Humanities Inst.; headmaster Hotchkiss Sch., Lakeville, Conn., 1989—95; pres. Kenyon Coll., Gambier, Ohio, 1995—2002, Carleton Coll., Northfield, Minn., 2002—. Chmn. com. on orgn. and policy Dartmouth Coll., com. on admissions and fin. aid; lectr. in field. Author: The Bible Without Theology, 1987. Mem.: Conn. Assn. Ind. Schs. (bd. dirs.). Avocations: fishing, running, religious studies, archaeology. Office: Carleton Coll 1 North College St Northfield MN 55057

ODEN, ROBERT RUDOLPH, surgeon; b. Chgo., Dec. 2, 1922; s. Rudolph J. E. and Olga H. (Wahlquist) Oden; m. Nancy Clow; children: Louise, Boyd, Beach, Lisbeth. BS, U. Ill., 1943; MD, MS in Anatomy, Northwestern U., 1947. Intern Augustana Hosp., Chgo., 1947-48, resident in surgery, 1948-49; resident in orthopaedics Hines Vets. Hosp., Chgo., 1949-51; resident in children's orthopaedics Shriner's Hosp., 1953-54; pvt. practice Chgo., 1954-57, Aspen, Colo., 1957—. Clin. assoc. prof. orthopedics U. Colo.; orthop. surgeon U.S. Olympic Com., 1960, 72, 76, 80; founder, trustee Pitkin County Bank, 1983—. Assoc. editor: Clin. Orthopedics and Related Rsch. Founder Aspen Inst. Theol. Futures, 1978, Gt. Tchrs. and Preachers Series Episc. Ch., 1989; trustee U.S. Ski Ednl. Found., 1967—82, Aspen Valley Hosp., 1978—86; founder Aspen Orthop. and Sports Medicine Pub. Found., 1985; mem. organizing com. Aspen World Cup, 1976—92; founder Aspen Pitkin Employee Housing, 1975. Named to Aspen Hall of Fame, 1996, Colo. Ski Hall of Fame, 2002, U.S. Ski Hall of Fame, 2002; recipient Biegan award Most Outstanding Svc. to U.S. Skiing, 1985, Halsted award, U.S. Ski Assn., 1987. Mem.: SICOT, ACS, Internat. Knee Inst., Internat. Soc. Knee, ACL Study Group, Internat. Ski Safety Soc., Am. Orthop. Soc. Sports Medicine (Hall of Fame 2004), Can. Orthop. Assn., Rocky Mountain Traumatologic Soc., Am. Assn. Bone & Joint Surgeons, Western Orthop. Assn., Internat. Coll. Surgeons, Am. Acad. Orthop. Surgeons, Phi Beta Kappa. Home: PO Box 660 Aspen CO 81612-0660 also: PO Box 172 Captiva FL 33924-0172 Office: 100 E Main St Aspen CO 81611-1778

ODEN, WILLIAM BRYANT, bishop, educator; b. McAllen, Tex., Aug. 3, 1935; s. Charles Alva and Evea (Bryant) O.; m. Marilyn Brown, July 12, 1957; children: Danna Lee Oden Bowen, William Dirk, Valerie Lyn, Charles Bryant. BA, Okla. State U., 1958; MDiv, Harvard U., 1961, postgrad., 1964; ThD, Boston U., 1964; DD (hon.), Oklahoma City U., 1980; LHD (hon.), Centenary Coll., 1990. Ordained to ministry Meth. Ch., 1961. Pastor Aldersgate United Meth. Ch., Oklahoma City, 1963-69, St. Stephen's United Meth. Ch., Norman, Okla., 1969-76, Crown Heights United Meth. Ch., Oklahoma City, 1976-83; prof. Phillips Grad. Sem., Enid, 1976-88; pastor 1st United Meth. Ch., Enid, 1983-88; bishop United Meth. Ch., Baton Rouge, 1988-96, bishop for the Dallas area, 1996—. Ecumenical del. to Lambeth Conf., 1998. Pres., United Meth. Coun. Bishops, 2000—; pres. SCJ Coll. of Bishops, 1989-90; del. Gen. Conf., 1976, 80, 84, 88; chmn. Okla. Del. to Gen. and Jurisdictional Confs., 1984, 88; Jackson lectr. Perkins Sch. Theology, So. Meth. U., 1975, Wilson lectr. SCJ Bishop's Week, 1989; co-chair World Meth.-Anglican Dialogue, 1991—; bd. dirs. Wesley Works Project; pres. Gen. Bd. Higher Edn. & Ministry, 1996—; pres. Coun. of Bishops, 2000-01, United Meth. Comm., 2000—. Author: Oklahoma Methodism in the Twentieth Century, 1968, Liturgy as Life Journey, 1976, Wordeed: Evangelism in Biblical and Wesleyan Perspective, 1978; contbr.: Send Me: The Itenerancy in Crisis, 1991, Vision and Supervision, 2003. Trustee Oklahoma City U., 1980-88, Southwestern U., Winfield, Kans., 1983-88, Centenary Coll., 1988-96, Dillard U., 1988-96, So. Meth. U., 1996—. Named to Okla. State U. Hall of Fame, 2003; Charles E. Merrill fellow, Harvard U., 2003. Mem. Am. Acad. Homiletics. Methodist. Avocations: writing, reading biographies, mountain climbing, backpacking.

ODENATH, DAVID R., JR., diversified financial services company executive; Sr. v.p., dir. sales, Investment Consulting Group Paine Webber; pres. Prudential Investments Prudential Fin., Inc., Newark, 1999—2003, pres. annuities, 2003—. Office: Prudential Financial Inc 751 Broad St Newark NJ 07102-3777

ODENIGBO, INNOCENT CHUKWUNWIKE, linguist, consultant; arrived in U.S., 2004; s. Lazarus Okonkwo and Rosaline Ama Odenigbo; m. Monica Chinwe Akpu, Oct. 6, 1996; m. Felicia Umekwulu Egesi, Sept. 26, 1967 (div. Sept. 16, 1996); children: Uchenna Zephyrina, Ifeanyi Innocent, Chukwuemeka John-Mary, Uzoamaka Assumpta. BA in languages, U. de Grenoble, 1968—71; studied at, Universite de Besancon, 1974—75; studied advanced television production, CIRNEA, Paris, 1990—94; PhD in languages, Am. West U., 1999—2002; MBA, Dowling Coll., 2000—02. Lang. prof. Inst. of

Mgmt. and Tech., Enugu, Nigeria, 1971—73; rsch. officer Nigerian Nat. Supply Co., London Office (now defunct), London, 1973—78; sr. news presenter Nigerian TV Authority, Enugu, 1979—81; chief editor, anchorman Anambra Broadcasting Svc., Awka, Nigeria, 1983—98; pres. IMC Info. Services, Newark, 2003—. Cons. IMC Info. Services, Newark, 2003—. Author: (poetry) Thank God for America. Recipient Best Broadcaster award, Nigeria Union Journalists, 1984. Mem.: Soc. of Profl. Journalists, Internat. Soc. of Poets (Disting. Mem. 2000, 2001). Office Phone: 973-399-7220. E-mail: imcodenigbo@aol.com.

ODENWELLER, ROBERT PAUL, philatelist, association executive, retired airline pilot; b. Sept. 19, 1938; s. Charles Joseph and Robina Katharine (Watson) O.; m. Jane Blackistone Rawlings, June 24, 1965; 1 stepchild, Joy McCorriston; 1 child, Liesl Hasbrouck. BS, U.S. Air Force Acad., 1960. Commd. USAF, 1956, advanced through grades to capt., 1963, resigned, 1956-66. Mem. Collectors Club Inc., N.Y.C., 1964—, gov. 1969—, program chmn., 1970-80, 2004—, mem. editl. bd., 1975—, sec. 1979-82, v.p. 1983-86, pres. 1987-90, trustee, 1992-98; trustee, vice chmn. then chmn. expert com. Philatelic Found., N.Y.C., 1970—. Author: The FIP Guide to Exhibiting and Judging Traditional and Postal History Exhibits, 1993; author, editor: Philatelic Vocabulary in Five Languages, 1978 (Vermeil medal 1979); editor: Opinions VI, 1992 (Gold medal), The Stamps and Postal History of Nineteenth Century Samoa, 2004 (Gold medal, Nat. Grand award); contbr. articles to profl. pubs. Recipient Grand Prix d'Honneur, Zeapex Orgn., 1980; selected to sign Roll of Disting. Philatelists, Brit. Philatelic Fedn., 1991, Alfred Lichtenstein Meml. award Collectors Club, N.Y., 1993, TWA Flight Ops. Meritorious Achievement award 1995, award of Excellence, 1995, 2000. Fellow Royal Philatelic Soc. London (spl. rep. for U.S. 2003-, membership and conduct com. 2004-), Royal Philatelic Soc. N.Z.; mem. Fedn. Internat. de Philatelie (pres. commn. traditional philately 1978-96; Grand Prix d'Honneur 1980, Svc. medal 1996), Am. Philatelic Soc. (bd. dirs. 1981-84, 89-90, named Champion of Champions 1973, Luff award 1996, chmn. 2003-), Assn. Internat. Des Experts Philateliques (expert 1980-, bd. dirs. 1987-), Fedn. New Zealand Philatelic Socs., Grand Prix Club Internat. (sec., treas. 1980-89, bd. dirs. 1989-92, 94-00, v.p. 1994-96, pres. 1996-2000), Soc. Australasian Specialists (pres. 1969-72), U.S. Chess Fedn., European Acad. Philately. Republican. Episcopalian. Avocations: stamp collecting/philately, photography, languages, chess, bridge. Home: Chalon Round Top Rd Bernardsville NJ 07924 Office: Collector's Club Inc 22 E 35th St New York NY 10016-3806 E-mail: rpodenwel@cs.com.

ODER, BROECK NEWTON, school emergency management consultant; b. Ill. s. Bruce Newton and Mary Louise Oder; m. Jolene Marie Peragine, 1975 (dec. June 1979). BA in History, U. San Diego, 1974, MA in History, 1975; postgrad., U. N.Mex., 1976-79. Life C.C. tchg. credential, Calif. Rsch. asst. to pres. U. San Diego, 1975; grad. asst. U. N.Mex., Albuquerque, 1976-79; tchr. history, chmn. dept. Santa Catalina Sch., Monterey, Calif., 1979—, asst. dean students, 1981-83, dir. ind. study, 1981-95, dean students, 1983-91, dir. emergency planning, 1986—, dean campus affairs, 1991-94, dir. security, 1994—. Disaster preparedness coun. Monterey County Office Edn., 1988-99; chair Diocesan Sch. Emergency Preparedness Coun, 1991-98. Mem. bd. of tchrs. The Concord Rev.; contbr. articles to profl. publs. including American National Biography, Safety and Security Adminstrn. in Sch. Facilities, 2d edit. Participant Jail and Bail, Am. Cancer Soc., Monterey, 1988, 89; reviewer sch. emergency plans, Monterey, 1989—. Recipient award of merit San Diego Hist. Soc., 1975, Outstanding Tchr. award U. Chgo., 1985, Outstanding Young Educator award Monterey Peninsula Jaycees, 1988, resolution of commendation Calif. Senate Rules Com., 1988, cert. of commendation Calif. Gov.'s Office Emergency Svcs., 1991, nat. cert. of achievement Fed. Emergency Mgmt. Agy., 1991, Outstanding High Sch. Tchr. award Tufts U., 1998, High Sch. Tchr. of Excellence, U. Calif. at San Diego, 1998, Outstanding Tchr. of Am. History award Calif. DAR, 2001-02; nominee Disney Tchr. award, 2002, 03. Mem. ACLU, NAACP, NRA (life), Am. Hist. Assn., Orgn. Am. Historians, Nat. Coun. on History Edn., Soc. for History Edn., Second Amendment Found., Law Enforcement Alliance Am., Calif. State Sheriffs Assn., Nat. Assn. Sch. Resource Officers, Phi Alpha Theta. Avocations: reading, sports, target shooting. Office: Santa Catalina Sch 1500 Mark Thomas Dr Monterey CA 93940-5291

ODERMATT, DIANA B. development consultant; b. Hollywood, Calif., Nov. 25, 1938; d. Harold and Mary H. (Wilson) Birtwistle; m. Robert Allen Odermatt, June 9, 1960; children: Kristin Odermatt Lee, Kyle David Odermatt. BA, Mills Coll., 1960. Assoc. dir. admissions Mills Coll., Oakland, Calif., 1978-82, dean admissions and fin. aid, 1982-85; dir. devel. Head-Royce Sch., Oakland, 1985-91; major gift officer univ. rels. U. Calif., Berkeley, 1992-95, cons. Coll. Environ. Design, 1995-96; dir. devel. Bentley Sch., Oakland, 1996-99. Tchr., trainer Coun. for the Advancement and Support of Edn., Washington, 1980-93; bd. mem. European Coun. Ind. Schs., Washington, 1982-85; cons. The Coll. Bd., N.Y.C., 1985-92. Contbr. articles to profl. jours. Home: 39 Drury Ln Berkeley CA 94705-1615 Personal E-mail: dbomatt@aol.com.

ODERMATT, ROBERT ALLEN, architect; b. Oakland, Calif., Jan. 3, 1938; s. Clifford Allen and Margaret Louise (Budge) O.; m. Diana Birtwistle, June 9, 1960; children: Kristin Ann, Kyle David. BArch, U. Calif., Berkeley, 1960. Registered architect, Calif., Oreg., Nev., Colo., Hawaii; cert. Nat. Coun. Archtl. Registration Bds. Draftsman Anderson Simonds Dusel Campini, Oakland, 1960-61; architect James R. Lucas, Orinda, Calif., 1961-62, ROMA Architects, San Francisco, 1962-76, architect, pres., 1976-84; prin. ROMA Design Group, San Francisco, 1962-92; pres. The Odermatt Group, Berkeley, Calif., 1992—. Prin. spkr. Internat. Conf. on Rebuilding Cities, Pitts., 1988; mem. U.S. Design in Am. Program, Sofia, Bulgaria, Armenian Disaster Assn. Team, 1989, NA Collateral Internship Mgmt. Com.; prin. State of Calif. Bay Arera Facilities Plan, 1992, Greece Resort Privatization Program, 1993. Prin. designer U.S. Embassy, Bahrain, Grand Canyon Nat. Park, 1977, Yosemite Nat. Park, 1987; prin. planner hotel complex Westin Hotel, Vail, Colo., 1982, Kaanapali Resort, 1987, Las Montanas Resort, San Diego; master plan U. Calif., Berkeley, 1988, Kohanaiki and Mauna Lani resorts, 1989, Calif. State Strategic Real Estate Plan, 1992, Greek Resort/Marina Privatization Program, 1993, Tektronix Strategic Plan, 1994, United Labs, Manila Master Plan, 1995, State of Calif. Real Estate Orgn. Plan, 1996, Ford Island Pearl Harbor Master Plan, 1996, Pearl Harbor Visitor Ctr. Plan, 1997, Albiano Resort Study, 1998; master plans include Trefethen Vineyards, Bell Garden, Napa Valley Expo. Bd. dirs. Nat. Archtl. Accrediting Bd., 2003—, also v.p.; mem. Santa Cruz Downtown Assessment, Eisenhower E. Plan, Alexandria, Va., Upper Potomac W. Plan, Alexandria, King St. Revitalization Study, Alexandria, 2004, Oakland Mayor's Com. on High Density Housing, 1982, Oakland Gen. Plan Congress, 1994; mem. waterfront plan adv. com. City of Oakland, 1996, Westpark Town Ctr., 2003, Koa Ridge Cmty., Oahu, Hawaii, King St. Retail Plan, Alexandria. Fellow AIA (dir. East Bay chpt. 1969-71, pres. 1980-81, dir. Calif. coun. 1979-81, Disting. Svc. award Calif. chpt., 1991, nat. dir. 1983-86, nat. v.p. 1986-87, chair AIA internat. steering com. 1993-94, graphic stds. adv. com. 1991-92, U. Calif. archtl. review commn. 1992-96, exec. com. Coll. Fellows 1996-98, vice chancellor Coll. Fellows 1999, chancellor 2000, East Bay medal 1997, Edward C. Kemper medal for outstanding svc. 2004), Am. Archtl. Found. (regent, bd. dirs.).

O'DESS, MARY ABIGAIL, lawyer; b. Detroit, May 21, 1954; d. Laurence G. and Naomi V. (Michau) O'Dess.; m. William J. Hein, Nov. 19, 1983. (dec.). BS, No. Mich. U., 1975; JD, U. Mich., 1977. Bar: Wis. 1978, U.S. Dist. Ct. (ea. dist.) Wis. 1978. Assoc. Jacobson & Hupy, S.C., Milw., 1978-91; ptnr. Maculak, Robertson, & O'Dess S.C., Milw., 1991—2003, O'Dess and Assocs., S.C., Milw., 2003—. Mem. Jr. League Milw., 1983-85; sec. Wis. Coalition for Adv., Madison, 1982-83; bd. dirs. Milw. Women's Ctr., 1981-83, pres., 1983. Mem. Wis. Bar Assn., Phi Kappa Phi, Omicron Delta Nu, Phi Alpha Theta. Avocations: volunteer activities, reading. Office: O'Dess and Associates, SC 1414 Underwood Aveune, Suite 403 Wauwassa WI 53213 Office Phone: 414-727-1591. E-mail: aodess@aol.com.

ODGERS, RICHARD WILLIAM, lawyer; b. Detroit, Dec. 31, 1936; s. Richard Stanley and Elsie Maude (Trevarthen) O.; m. Gail C. Bassett, Aug. 29, 1959; children: Thomas R., Andrew B. AB, U. Mich., 1959, JD, 1961. Bar: Calif. 1962. Assoc. Pillsbury, Madison & Sutro, San Francisco, 1961—69, ptnr., 1969—87, 1998—2000; exec. v.p., gen. counsel Pacific Telesis Group, San Francisco, 1987-98; ptnr. Pillsbury Winthrop, San Francisco, 2001—. Chmn., bd. dirs. Legal Aid Soc. Employment Law Ctr.; dir. Legal Cmty. Against Violence; dir., sec.-treas. Van Loben Sels Charitable Found.; bd. dirs. Immigrant Legal Resource Ctr., Fed. Dist. Ct. Hist. Soc.; active Calif. Legal Svcs. Trust Fund Commn. With USNR. Fellow Am. Bar Found., Am. Judicature Soc., Am. Coll. Trial Lawyers; mem. ABA (spl. com. on gun violence), Am. Law Inst., Coll. Law Practice Mgmt. Office: Pillsbury Winthrop 50 Fremont St San Francisco CA 94105-2228 Office Phone: 415-983-1202. Business E-Mail: rwodgers@pillsburywinthrop.com.

ODIERNO, RAYMOND T. career military officer; b. Rockway, N.J. s. Raymond J. and Helen Odierno; m. Linda Odierno. BS, U.S. Mil. Acad., West Point, N.Y., 1976; MS in Nuc. Effects Engring., N.C. State U.; MA in Nat. Security and Strategy, U.S. Naval War Coll. Commd. lt. U.S. Army, advanced through grades to maj. gen., 2001, nuc. rsch. officer, chief acquisition support divsn. Def. Nuc. Agy., 1986—87, various positions, commdr. 2d bat., 1992—94, commdr. artillery divsn., 1995—97, dir. requirements and force mgmt. Office Dep. Chief Staff Ops. and Plans Washington, commdg. gen., 4th Infantry Divsn. (Mechanized) Ft. Hood, Tex., 2002—. Decorated The Legion of Merit with three oak leaf clusters U.S. Army, Meritorious Svc. Medal with three oak leaf clusters, Def. Meritorious Svc. Medal. Office: US Army Fourth Infantry Divsn Mechanized Fort Hood TX 76544*

ODISHOO, SARAH A. English language educator; b. Chgo., July 12, 1939; d. Saul Eshoo and Nanajan Odishoo; divorced; children: Elizabeth, Leslie. BA in English Lit., Ill. Wesleyan U., 1961; MA in Poetry and English Lit., N.E. Ill. U., 1980. Instr. English composition No. Ill. U., 1982—85; prof. English, world lit., mythology and writing Columbia Coll., Chgo., 1985—, prof. lit., 1992—. Co-dir. freshman writing program, dir. profl. writing program and seminars Columbia Coll., 1985-89, pres. faculty orgn., 1990-92, dir. myth. workshops, 1998, guest poet/collaborator CD/sound collaboration, deep sound, 1999, liaison to bd. trustees, CCFO rep., 1999-2000; faculty adv. coun. Ill. Bd. Higher Edn., 1985-89; coord. PEN Midwest Reading Series, 1988-89; archeol. dig for study of mythology of early Jewish and Christian nomadic cultures, Nitzana, 1992; artist in-residence Nitzana (Israel) Ednl. Project, dept. history Ben Gurion U. Negev, 1993, U. Wyo., 1999, Byrdcliffe Colony, Woodstock (NY) Guild, 2000; lectr. River Oaks Art Coun., Oak Pk., Ill., 2000, Chgo. Cultural Ctr., 2003; guest tchr. Hyde Sch., Bath, Maine, 2003; Mythic Path Instr., Hyde Sch., Bath, Maine, 2003. Office: Columbia Coll Chgo 600 S Michigan Ave Chicago IL 60605 E-mail: sodishoo@colum.edu.

ODLAND, STEVE, retail executive; B, U. Notre Dame; M in Mgmt., Northwestern U. Sr. v.p., gen. mgr. snacks divsn. Sara Lee, 1996—98, pres. bakery foodsvc. divsn., 1997—98; pres., CEO Tops Markets, Inc., 1998—2000; COO Ahold USA, Inc., 2000—01; chmn., pres., CEO Autozone Inc., 2001—. Office: 123 S Front St Memphis TN 38103

ODLE, ROBERT CHARLES, JR., lawyer; b. Port Huron, Mich., Feb. 15, 1944; s. Robert Charles and Elizabeth Dagmar (Lassen) O.; m. Lydia Ann Karpinol, Aug. 2, 1969. BA, Wayne State U., Detroit, 1966; JD, Detroit Coll. Law, 1969, LLD (hon.), 1992. Staff asst. to pres. of U.S., 1969-71; dir. adminstrn. Com. Re-election of President, 1971-73; dep. asst. sec. HUD, 1973-76; Washington corp. affairs rep. Internat. Paper Co., 1976-81; asst. sect. Dept. Energy, 1981-85; ptnr. Weil, Gotshal & Manges, 1985—. Mem. Mich. Bar Assn., D.C. Bar Assn., Delta Theta Phi. Clubs: University (Washington). Republican. Roman Catholic. Home: 476 S Union St Alexandria VA 22314-3826 Office: Weil Gotshal & Manges 1501 K St NW Ste 100 Washington DC 20005

O'DOHERTY, BRIAN, writer, filmmaker; b. Ballaghadereen, Ireland; came to U.S., 1957; m. Barbara Novak, 1960. MB BCh, Univ. Coll. Dublin, Nat. U. Ireland, 1952, DPH with honors, 1955; MS in Hygiene, Harvard U., 1958. TV host Invitation to Art, Mus. Fine Arts, Boston, 1958-61; art critic N.Y. Times, 1961-64; host Dialogue, WNBC, 1961-64; vis. prof. Berkeley U., 1967; dir. visual arts Nat. Endowment for Arts, 1969-76, dir. media arts, 1976-94; dir. Millennium Projects, 1994-96. Art and architecture critic Today Program, 1971-77; adj. prof. Barnard Coll., 1969-96; editor-in-chief Art in Am., 1971-74; Univ. prof. fine arts and media L.I. U.-Southampton Campus, 1997—. Author: (art book) Object and Idea: A New York Art Journal, 1961-67, 1967; editor: (museum study) Museums in Crisis, 1972, (Art Book) American Masters, The Voice and the Myth, 1973, 2d edit., 1995, Inside the White Cube, 1986, revised edit., 1999, (novels) The Strange Case of Mile P., 1992 (Saggitarius award, 1993), The Deposition of Father McGreevy, 1999 (Booker prize short list, 2000); dir.: (films) Hooper's Silence, 1981; contbr. articles to profl. jours. Recipient Mpls. Citizens award, 1961, Eire Soc. Gold medal for contbns. to culture, 1963, Grand Prix Montreal Internat. Festival of Arts Film award, 1982, Emmy nominations; Smith-Mundt fellow. Fellow Royal Coll. Physicians Ireland (hon.); mem. Irish Hist. Soc. (bd. dirs.), Whitney Mus. Am. Art (bd. dirs. 1996-2000), Coll. Art Assn. (life; Mather award 1964). Office: 15 W 67th St New York NY 10023-6226

ODOM, FLOYD CLARK, surgeon; b. Cisco, Tex., 1946; MD, U. Tex., San Antonio, 1972. Diplomate Am. Bd. Colon & Rectal Surgery, Am. Bd. Surgery. Intern Bexar County Hosp., San Antonio, 1972-73, resident in gen. surgery, 1973-77; fellow in colon & rectal surgery Baylor Med. Ctr., Dallas, 1977-78; colorectal surgeon Presbyn. Hosp., Dallas, 1997—. Fellow ACS, Am. Soc. Colon and Rectal Surgeons. Office: 8220 Walnut Hill Ln Dallas TX 75231-4406

ODOM, JEROME D. academic administrator; BS, U. N.C., 1964; PhD in Inorganic Chemistry, Ind. U., 1968. Postdoctoral fellow U. Bristol, England, 1968—69; asst. prof. U. S.C., Columbia, 1969—74, assoc. prof., 1974—77, prof., 1977—, chair dept. chemistry, 1985—91, interim project dir. S.C. Alliance for Minority Participation, 1993—94, dean Coll. Sci. and Math., 1994—97, provost, exec. v.p. for acad. affairs, 1997—, chair strategic directions and initiatives com., 2001—02. Author five general chemistry textbooks; contbr. articles to profl. jours. Achievements include patents in field. Office: Office of the Provost 102 Osborne Adminstrn Bldg Univ SC Columbia SC 29208*

ODOM, JUDY, software company executive; b. 1952; BBA in Acctg., Tex. Tech. U., 1974. CPA. With Coopers & Lybrand, Dallas, 1974-76, Grant Thornton, Dallas, 1976-85; co-founder, owner Software Spectrum, 1983—2002, CEO, 1988—2002. Bd. dirs. Storage Tek, Leggett & Platt Inc., Harte-Hanks Inc. Named to, Computer Reseller News Industry Hall of Fame, 2003.

ODOM, KENNETH JAMES, information technology executive; b. Camp LeJeune, NC, Mar. 28, 1974; s. Arnold William and Lula McCoyle Odom. AAS in microcomputer systems, Isothermal C.C., 1994—96. Sales TaskMaster Computer Ctr., Forest City, NC, 1996—98; helpdesk technician Rutherford County Internet, Forest City, NC, 1998—99; acquisitions/computer support technician Isothermal C.C., Spindale, NC, 1999—. Sys. adminstr. CMC Libr. Consortium, Spindale, NC, 1999—; mem. of talc instl. effectiveness com. Isothermal C.C., Spindale, NC, 2002—. Recipient 2nd Pl., Info. Tech., NC State Chpt., Phi Beta Lambda, 1996, 6th Pl., Info. Tech., Nat. Chpt., Phi Beta Lambda, 1996. Independent. Avocations: reading, music. Office: Isothermal Cmty Coll 286 ICC Loop Rd Spindale NC 28160 E-mail: kodom@isothermal.edu.

ODOM, LAMAR JOSEPH, professional basketball player; b. Jamaica, NY, Nov. 6, 1979; Student, UNLV; grad., U. Rhode Island, 2001. Player LA Clippers, 1999—2003, Miami Heat, 2003—04, LA Lakers, 2004—. Mem. US Olympics Basketball Team, Athens, Greece, 2004. Named to All-Rookie First Team, 2000. Office: c/o LA Lakers 555 N Nash St El Segundo CA 90245

ODOM, MARJORIE MILDRED MORGAN, retired librarian; b. Lavernia, Tex., July 22, 1924; d. Andrew Jackson and Estella Fledia (Phillips) Morgan; m. Steven Odom, Jr., June 25, 1944 (dec.). Cert. in cosmetology, C.J. Walker Beauty Coll., 1943; BA in Libr. Sci., Our Lady of Lake U., San Antonio, 1964, MA in Edn., 1979. Ordained deacon Bapt. Ch., 1985. Mgr. Mme. C.J. Walker Beauty Salon, San Antonio, 1944—52; propr. Ross Hotel Beauty Salon, San Antonio, 1952—63; asst. supr. children's dept. San Antonio Pub. Libr., 1964—65; secondary sch. librarian San Antonio Ind. Sch. Dist., 1965—90; ret., 1990. Past sponsor Libr. Reading Club, San Antonio; past mem. Tex. Senator's adv. coun. on legis. affairs; del. Bexar County Presdl. Senatorial Dist. conv., 1984, 1988; mem. Dist. 19 Tex. Dem. conv., Ft. Worth, 1990; del. Dem. State Conv., El Paso, 2002; elected Dem. Precinct chair, 2002; del. Tex. State Dem. Convention, 2004; chmn. evangelism com. Corinth Bapt. Ch., San Antonio, 1983—86, mem. evangelism and witnessing team, 1984—, Sunday sch. tchr., 1983—; trainer Evangelism Explosion, 1987—. Recipient outstanding award analysis and design, Kappa Pi Sigma, 1978, appreciation plaque, PTA, 1981, cert., Internat. Ctr. Learning, 1982—83, Nat. Sunday Sch. and Bapt. Temperance Union Congress, 1967—70. Mem.: NEA (life), San Antonio Area Ret. Tchrs. Assn. Democrat. Home: PO Box 8374 San Antonio TX 78208-0374

ODOM, RICHARD B. dermatologist, educator; b. Ahoskie, NC; MD, Bowman Gray U., 1963. Diplomate Am. Bd. Dermatology, Dermatopathology Am. Bd. Dermatology. Intern U. Fla., Gainesville, 1964; resident Walter Reed Army Med. Ctr., Washington, 1969; head dermatology dept. U. Calif. Med. Ctr., San Francisco, 1970—. Prof. U. Calif. San Francisco. Mem.: PDA, Am. Dermatology Assn., Am. Acad. Dermatology (Excellence in Edn. award 2001). Office: Univ Calif Sch Medicine Derm Dept 3d Fl 1701 Divisardero St San Francisco CA 94123

ODOM, ROD D., JR., telecommunications industry executive; b. Miami; Grad., U. Fla. Acct. exec. So. Bell, West Palm Beach, Fla., 1972—83; dir, new venture planning Bellsouth Corp., 1983—2000, exec. v.p. network ops., 2000—02; pres. network svcs. Bellsouth Corp, Atlanta, 2002—. Bd. dirs. Oglethorpe U., Sheltering Arms, Piedmont Hosp., Fla. Found.; mem. engring. adv. bd. U. Fla. Methodist. Office: Bellsouth Corp 1155 Peachtree St NE Atlanta GA 30309-3610

ODOM, SARAH BERNICE, elementary school educator; b. Orange, Tex., Dec. 17, 1965; d. William Ogden and Thelma Louise (Ball) Gilpatrick; m. Armond G. Odom, Jr., Dec. 15, 1978 (div. Oct. 1999); children: Wesley, Clinton, Cody. AS, Panola Jr. Coll., Carthage, Tex., 1989; BS in Edn. cum laude, U. Tex., Tyler, 1990; M in Elem. Edn., Lamar U., 2001. Cert. life elem. self-contained grades 1-8 tchr., life elem. reaing tchr. grades 1-8, life generic spl. edn. tchr. grades PK-12. Tchr. Mauriceville (Tex.) Middle, 1991—95, Little Cypress Jr. High, Orange, Tex., 1995—99, Little Cypress Intermediate, Orange, Tex., 1999—2001, Little Cypress Jr. High, Orange, Tex., 2001—. Nominee Disney's Am. Tchr. award. Avocations: reading, painting, writing, outdoor activities. Home: 502 Camellia Orange TX 77630 Office: Little Cypress Jr High 6765 Fm Rd 1130 Orange TX 77632

ODOM, STEVE, information technology executive; m. LeeAnn O.; children: Brittany, Kristi, Steven. Exec. v.p., founder Instrument Repair Svc., 1974; pres. PCS divsn. Executone Info. Sys., 1987-90; cons. World Access, 1990-94; chmn., CEO Restor Industries, 1994-00, Cereus Tech. Partners; CEO Verson Techs., 2000—. Named honorary ambassador State of Ga.; mem. C. of C. State of Ga. Recipient Ernst & YOung Entrepreneur Yr. award, 1997. Office: Verso Techs Inc 400 Galleria Pkwy Ste 300 Atlanta GA 30339

ODOM, WILLIAM ELDRIDGE, army officer, educator; b. Cookeville, Tenn., June 23, 1932; s. John Albert and Callie Frances (Everhart) O.; m. Anne Weld Curtis, June 9, 1962; 1 child, Mark Weld. BS, U.S. Mil. Acad., 1954; MA, Columbia U., 1962, PhD, 1970; DSc (hon.), Middlebury Coll., 1987. Commd. 2nd lt. U.S. Army, 1954, advanced through grades to lt. gen., 1984; mem. U.S. Mil. Liaison Mission to Soviet Forces, Germany, 1964-66; from asst. prof. to assoc. prof. govt. U.S. Mil. Acad., West Point, 1966-69, 74-76; asst. Army attache U.S. embassy, Moscow, 1972-74; nat. security staff mem. White House, 1977-81; asst. chief of staff for intelligence Dept. Army, Washington, 1981-85; dir. Nat. Security Agy., Fort Meade, Md., 1985-88; dir. nat. security studies Hudson Inst., 1988—. Adj. prof. polit. sci. Yale U., 1989—; chmn. bd. dirs. Am. Sci. and Engring., V-ONE (Virtual Open Network Environment). Author: The Soviet Volunteers, 1973, On Internal War, 1992, Trial After Triumph, 1992, America's Military Revolution, 1993, (with Robert Dujarric) Commonwealth or Empire? Russia, Central Asia and The Transcaucasus, 1995, The Collapse of the Soviet Military, 1998, Fixing Intelligence, 2003, (with Robert Dujarric) America's Inadvertent Empire, 2004; contbr. articles to profl. jours. Trustee Middlebury Coll., 1987-97. Decorated Def. D.S.M. with oak leaf cluster, D.S.M. with oak leaf cluster, Legion of Merit, Nat. Security medal, Nat. Intelligence D.S.M.; grand cross Order of Merit with Star (Fed. Republic Germany); Order Nat. Security Merit (Republic of Korea), officer Nat. Order of Merit (France). Mem. Coun. on Fgn. Rels., Am. Assn. for Advancement of Slavic Studies, Internat. Inst. for Strategic Studies, Am. Polit. Sci. Assn., Acad. Polit. Sci. Office: Hudson Inst 1015 18th St NW Ste 300 Washington DC 20036-5200

O'DONNELL, BERNARD JOSEPH, JR., lawyer; b. Cleve., Oct. 31, 1969; s. Bernard Joseph and Afkam O'Donnell. BA in English, Mary Washington Coll., Fredericksburg, Va., 1993; MA in English magna cum laude, Loyola U. Chgo., 1996; JD summa cum laude, Fla. State U., 2000. Bar: Fla. 2000. Adj. prof. English Palm Beach Atlantic Coll., West Palm Beach, Fla., 1997—98, Fla. State U., Tallahassee, 1998—2000, U. Fla., Gainesville, 2000—03; pvt. practice law Gainesville, 2000—03; assoc. Henderson, Franklin, P.A., Ft. Myers, Fla., 2003—. Pro-bono atty. Guardian Ad Litem, Ctrl. Fla., 2001—03. Contbr. articles to profl. jours. Recipient Excellence in Tchr. award, U. Fla., 2002, Excellence in Tchg. award, U. Fla. Anderson Scholars, 2002, 2003; Lester Crow scholar in edn., 1993, Dean's scholar in law, 1998, Katzentine-Simon scholar in law, 1999, Grinter fellow in English, 2000—03. Mem.: ABA, MLA, Fla. Bar Assn., Order of the Coif. Roman Catholic. Avocations: reading, basketball, guitar. Home: 1520 Jackson St 6 Fort Myers FL 33901-2952 Office: Henderson Franklin PA 1715 Monroe St Fort Myers FL 33902-0280

O'DONNELL, CATHERINE ROSE, lawyer; b. South Charleston, W.Va., Feb. 15, 1964; d. Philip John and Madeline Marie Ripepi; m. Neil Taney O'Donnell, May 6, 1989; children: Neil Philip, Renata Marie. BA in Bus. and Econs., U. Pitts., 1984, JD, MBA, U. Pitts., 1987. Bar: D.C. 1988, Pa. 1988, U.S. Dist. Ct. (ea. dist.) Pa. 1988, U.S. Dist. Ct. (ctrl. dist.) Pa. 1990. Assoc. Drinker Biddle & Reath, Phila., 1988—90; assoc. to shareholder Elliott Reihner Siedzikowski & Egan, Scranton, Pa., 1990—2000; dist. justice Wilkes-Barre, Pa., 2000—02; assoc. O'Donnell Law Offices, Wilkes-Barre, 2002—. Mem. parish coun. St. Therese Ch., Wilkes-Barre, 1990—93, mem. fin. coun., 2000—, cantor, 2001—; bd. dirs. Wyoming Valley Montessori Sch., Kingston, Pa., 1997—2000; pres. Wyoming Valley Montessori Sch. PTA, Kingston, Pa.; bd. dirs. Osterhout Libr., Wilkes-Barre, 1999—2000, Cath. Youth Ctr., Wilkes-Barre, 1996—99, Wyoming Valley Habitat for Humanity, Kingston, 1991—93, Luzerne County LWV, Kingston, 1999—2000, Wyo. Sem. Lower Sch. Parents Assn., 2003—. Mem.: ATLA (bd. dir.), ABA (bd. dir. Pa. chpt.), Northeast Trial Lawyers Assn., Lackawanna County Bar Assn., Wilkes-Barre Law and Libr. Assn., Pa. Trial Lawyers Assn., Pa. Bar Assn. Office: O'Donnell Law Offices 22 E Union St Wilkes Barre PA 18701 Office Phone: 570-821-5717. Business E-Mail: cro@odonnell-law.com.

O'DONNELL, CHRIS, actor; b. Winnetka, Ill., 1970; m. Caroline Fentress, Apr. 19, 1997; children Lilly Ann, Christopher Jr. Student, Boston Coll. Actor: (films) Men Don't Leave, 1990, Fried Green Tomatoes, 1991, Scent of a Woman, 1992 (Golden Globe award nomination best supporting actor 1992), School Ties, 1992, The Three Musketeers, 1993, Blue Sky, 1994, Circle of Friends, 1995, Mad Love, 1995, Batman Forever, 1995, In Love and War, 1996, The Chamber, 1996, Batman & Robin, 1997, Cookie's Fortune, 1999,

Vertical Limit, 2000, Twenty-nine Palms, 2002; actor, prodr. The Bachelor, 1999; prodr. (TV films) The Triangle, 2001, Miracle on the 17th Green, 1999. Office: Creative Artists Agy care Josh Lieberman 9830 Wilshire Blvd Beverly Hills CA 90212-1804*

O'DONNELL, DENISE ELLEN, lawyer; BS in Polit. Sci., Canisius Coll., 1968; MSW, SUNY, Buffalo, 1973, JD summa cum laude, 1982. Bar: NY 1983, U.S. Dist. Ct. (we., no., ea. and so. dists.) NY, U.S. Ct. Appeals (2d cir.), U.S. Supreme Ct. Law clk. Hon. M. Dolores Denman NY Appellate Divsn. 4th Dept., Buffalo, 1982-85; asst. U.S. atty. Western Dist. N.Y., Buffalo, 1985-90, appellate chief, 1990-93, 1st asst. U.S. atty., 1993—97, U.S. atty., 1997-2001; ptnr. Gen. Litigation Practice Group, Hodgson, Russ, LLP, Buffalo, 2001—. Part-time instr. trial technique program SUNY, 1990—; lectr. ethics, evidence and trial practice Office Legal Edn.U.S. Dept. Justice, 1988—2000; lectr. NITA seminar Western NY Trial Acad., 1994, 98; mem. Atty. Gen.'s Adv. Com., 1999—2001, vice-chair, 2000—01. Mem. Vol. Lawyers Program, 1997—2001; bd. dirs. NCCJ, 2000—; sec. Nat. Women's Hall of Fame, 2001—, bd. dirs., 2001—. Mem.: ABA, Nat. Assn. Former U.S. Attys. (bd. dirs.), Western NY Trial Lawyers Assn., Women's Bar Assn. State NY (founding mem. Western NY chpt. 1985), Bar Assn. Erie County (dep. treas. 1992—93, treas. 1993—94), West Side Rowing Club. Office: Hodgson Russ LLP One M&T Plz Ste 2000 Buffalo NY 14203-2931 Office Phone: 716-848-1314. E-mail: dodonnel@hodgsonruss.com.

O'DONNELL, EDWARD FRANCIS, JR., lawyer; b. Waterbury, Conn., May 13, 1950; s. Edward Francis and Dorothy Patricia (Breheny) O'D.; m. Jayne Ann DeSantis, Dec. 29, 1972; children: Ryan Anderson, Brooke Stires. BA, St. Anselm Coll., Manchester, N.H., 1972; JD, U. Conn., 1977. Bar: S.C. 1978, Conn. 1977, U.S. Dist. Ct. S.C. 1978, U.S. Dist. Ct. Conn. 1980, U.S. Ct. Appeals (1st and 2d cirs.) 1980. Assoc. Ogeltree, Deakins, Nash, Smoak & Stewart, Greenville, S.C., 1977-79; ptnr. Siegel, O'Connor, Zagari, O'Donnell & Beck, P.C., Hartford, Conn., 1979—. Contbr. articles to profl. jours. Mem. ABA, Conn. Bar Assn., S.C. Bar Assn., Hartford Bar Assn., Hartford Club, Phi Alpha Theta. Roman Catholic. Office: Siegel O'Connor Zangari O'Donnell & Beck PC 150 Trumbull St Fl 5 Hartford CT 06103-2400

O'DONNELL, EDWARD JOSEPH, bishop, former editor; b. St. Louis, July 4, 1931; s. Edward Joseph and Ruth Mary (Carr) O'Donnell. Student, Cardinal Glennon Coll., 1949-53; postgrad., Kenrick Sem., 1953-57. Ordained priest Roman Cath. Ch., 1957, consecrated bishop, 1984; assoc. pastor in 5 St. Louis parishes, 1957-77; pastor St. Peter's Ch., Kirkwood, Mo., 1977-81; assoc. dir. Archdiocesan Commn. on Human Rights, 1962-70; dir. Archdiocesan Radio-TV Office, 1966-68, Archdiocesan Vocation Council, 1965; editor St. Louis Rev., 1968-81; vicar-gen. Archdiocese of St. Louis, 1981-84, aux. bishop, 1984-94; bishop Diocese of Lafayette, Lafayette, LA, 1994—. Bd dirs Nat Cath Conf Interracial Justice, 1980—85; chmn Interfaith Clergy Coun Greater St Louis, 1963—67; NAACP, 1964—66; bd dirs Urban League St Louis, 1962—68. Named to Golden Dozen, Int Soc Weekly Newspaper Eds, 1970, 1977. Mem.: Nat Asn TV Arts and Scis, Cath Press Asn. Roman Catholic. Office: 7500 Cromwell Clayton MO 63105

O'DONNELL, F. SCOTT, state agency administrator; b. Brownsville, Pa., Sept. 20, 1940; s. Francis Horner and Rebecca (Warren) O'D.; m. Ann Bukmir, Dec. 30, 1976. BA, Grove City (Pa.) Coll., 1962; postgrad., U. Wis. Grad. Sch. Banking, 1970, Internat. Sch. Banking, U. Colo., 1972. Nat. bank examiner Comptroller of Currency, Cleve., 1965-71; sr. v.p. First Nat. Bank, Steubenville, Ohio, 1971-75; supt. of banks State of Ohio, Columbus, 1975-77; exec. v.p. Heritage Bancorp, Steubenville, 1977-80; from v.p. to exec. v.p. Soc. Corp., Cleve., 1980-95; dep. tax commr. State of Ohio, Columbus, 1996-99; supt. fin. instns. divsn. Ohio Dept. Commerce, 1999—. Mem. state banking bd. Div. of Banks, Columbus, 1979-85, govt. affairs com. Ohio Bankers Assn., 1982-84. Served with USCG, 1963-69. Mem. Columbus Athletic Club, Pitts. Univ. Club, Belmont Hills Country Club, Lakewood Country Club. Avocations: travel, politics, antiques. Office: Ohio Divsn Fin Instns 77 S High St Fl 21 Columbus OH 43266-0121*

O'DONNELL, JAMES FRANCIS, retired health science administrator; b. Cleve., July 22, 1928; s. John Michael and Mary Louise (Hayes) O'D.; m. Winifred Locke, Sept. 10, 1955; children— Anne Catherine, Patrick John, Mary Elizabeth BS in Biology, St. Louis U., 1949; PhD in Biochemistry, U. Chgo., 1957. Asst., then. assoc. prof. biol. chemistry and exptl. medicine Coll. Medicine, U. Cin., 1957—68; grants assoc., divsn. rsch. grants NIH, Bethesda, Md., 1968—69; program dir. population and reprodn. grants br. Ctr. for Population Research, Nat. Inst. Child Health and Human Devel., NIH, 1969—71; asst. dir. divsn. rsch. resources NIH, Bethesda, 1971—76, dep. dir. divsn. rsch. resources, 1976—90, acting dir. divsn. rsch. resources, 1981—82, dir. Office of Extramural Programs, Office of the Dir., 1990-99; ret., 1999; cons. Commonwealth Health Rsch. Bd., Richmond, Va., 1999—. Scientific cons. Commonwealth Health Rsch. Bd., Richmond, Va., 1999—. Served with U.S. Army, 1950-52 Home: 11601 Bunnell Ct S Rockville MD 20854-3603 Personal E-mail: jfwlodonnell@erols.com.

O'DONNELL, JAMES JOSEPH, classicist, educational administrator; b. Giessen, Fed. Republic Germany, Feb. 26, 1950; s. James J. and Helen T. (Murphy) O'D. BA, Princeton U., 1972; PhD, Yale U., 1975; MA (hon.), U. Pa., 1982. Lectr. in Latin Bryn Mawr (Pa.) Coll., 1975-76; asst. prof. Catholic U. Am., Washington, 1976-77, Cornell U., Ithaca, N.Y., 1977-81; assoc. prof., grad. chair U. Pa., Phila., 1981-89, prof., 1990—, vice provost info. sys. and computing, 1996—. Vis. prof. Johns Hopkins, 1993, U. Wash., 1995. Author: Cassiodorus, 1979, Boethius, Consolatio Philosophiae, 1984, Augustine, 1985, Augustine, Confessions, 3 vols., 1992; contbr. numerous article to profl. jours.; medieval editor Bryn Mawr Latin Commentaries, 1982—; mem. editorial bd. Traditio, 1985-96; founding editor Bryn Mawr Classical Review, 1990—, Bryn Mawr Medieval Review, 1993—. NEH grantee, 1982, 84, 89, 91, 92, 93, 94, Am. Coun. Learned Socs. grantee, 1983; Guggenheim fellow, 1989. Mem. Am. Philol. Assn. (bd. dirs.), Medieval Acad. Am. (councillor 1996—), North Am. Patristics Soc., Soc. for the Promotion of Eriugenian Studies. Roman Catholic.

O'DONNELL, JAMES P. food service executive; B in Econs., U. Ky.; MBA in Fin., Xavier U. CMA. With fin. dept. Borden, Inc.; with ConAgra, 1978—, sr. v.p., CFO, exec. v.p., CFO, corp. sec., 1997—. Office: Conagra Inc One ConAgra Dr Omaha NE 68102-5001

O'DONNELL, JOHN LOGAN, retired lawyer; b. Chgo., Mar. 6, 1914; s. William Joseph and Elizabeth (McLogan) O'D.; m. Mary Ellen Sipe, Sept. 2, 1939 (dec. Dec. 29, 1979); 1 son, John Logan; m. Michele G. Fischer, May 9, 1981. BA, Williams Coll., 1934; JD, Northwestern U., 1937. Bar: Ill. 1937, N.Y. 1943, D.C. 1977. Asso. firm Defrees, Buckingham, Jones and Hoffman, Chgo., 1937-38; staff atty. Office Gen. Counsel, SEC, 1938-41; instr. Cath. U. Law Sch., 1938-41; assoc. Cravath, Swaine & Moore, N.Y.C., 1941-52; ptnr. Olwine, Connelly, Chase, O'Donnell & Weyher, N.Y.C., 1952-91, of counsel, 1991, Twomey, Hoppe & Gallanty, N.Y.C., 1991—2003; ret., 2003. Bd. dirs. Near East Found., 1968-84. Fellow Am. Coll. Trial Lawyers; mem. Assn. Bar City N.Y., Am., Fed., bar assns., Beta Theta Pi, Phi Delta Phi. Clubs: Union, Univ., Williams, (N.Y.C.). Roman Catholic. Avocations: piano, sports. Home: 181 E 73rd St New York NY 10021-3549

O'DONNELL, JOSEPH MICHAEL, electronics executive; BS, U. Tenn., 1968, MBA, 1970. Sales mgr. telecomm. ITT, Chgo., 1970—75, dir. mktg. comm. Hartford, Conn., 1975-77; dir. mktg. Gen. Instrument Corp., N.Y.C., 1977-81, gen. mgr. Post Falls, Idaho, 1981-84; v.p. Conrac Corp., Stamford, Conn., 1984-87; pres. OD & S Ventures, Stamford, 1987-88; v.p. Handy & Harman, N.Y.C., 1988-89; CEO, GO/DAN Industries, New Haven, 1990-92; pres., CEO Savin Corp., Stamford, Conn., 1993-94; pres., CEO, Artesyn Techs. Inc., Boca Raton, Fla., 1994—. Office: Artesyn Techs Inc 7900 Glades Rd Boca Raton FL 33434-4167

O'DONNELL, KATHLEEN C. artist; b. Clifton, N.J., Nov. 15, 1919; d. George Francis and Alvina Rose (Munzell) Denzel; m. John Joseph O'Donnell, Feb. 17, 1942; children: John Joseph, Sharon Rose. BA cum laude, Montclair (N.J.) State Coll. Designer Denzell Mfg. Co., Passaic, NJ, 1937—38, clk., 1939—41; sec. Marschalk Ins., Clifton, NJ, 1941—42; clk. The Fair, Passaic, 1968—69; designer Arise Ministry, Lakewood, NJ, 1983—91; assoc. N.J. Bell, Clifton & Totowa, NJ, 1969—85. One-woman shows include Dwight Eisenhower Libr., Totowa, 1982, No. Lights Art Gallery, Clifton, 1985, YWHA, 1988, Fine Arts Ctr., Passaic, 1988, Denville Libr., 2003, exhibited in group shows at Fine Arts Ctr., Passaic, 1983, 1988, Willowbrook Mall, Wayne, N.J., 1984, YWHA, Clifton, 1985, Clifton Libr., 1988, The Nathan's Art Gallery, West Paterson, N.J., 1994, Montclair Country Club, 1994, Montclair State U., 1995, 1998, Westbeth Gallery, N.Y.C., 1996, Caldwell (N.J.) Women's Club, 1999, Botto House, Haledon, N.J., 1999, Clifton (NJ) Arts Ctr., 2001, Hamilton House, Clifton, 2002, Clifton Arts Ctr., 2003, 2004, represented in numerous pvt. collections, exhibited in group shows at Denville Lib., 2003. Mem.: Roxbury Assn. Art, Clifton Assn. Artists, Bell Atlantic Pioneers. Roman Catholic.

O'DONNELL, KATHLEEN MARY, social services administrator; b. Bklyn., Dec. 29, 1965; d. Maureen Grace O'D. BA in Psychology, Tchr. of Handicapped, Kean Coll. N.J., 1990; MS in Psychiat. Rehab., U. Medicine and Dentistry N.J., 2000. Cert. social worker, psychosocial rehab. practitioner. Nursing asst. Carrier Found., Belle Mead, N.J., 1988; tutor Kean Coll. N.J., Union, 1989; case mgr. Project Live, Inc., Newark, N.J., 1990-92, U. Medicine & Dentistry N.J., New Brunswick, 1992-2000. Vol. Childrens Specialized Hosp., Mountainside, NJ, 2003—, Make-a-Wish Found., NJ, 2003—. Mem. Internat. Assn. Psychiat. Rehab. Practitioners. Avocations: bowling, dance, music, travel.

O'DONNELL, KEVIN, retired metal products executive; b. Cleve., June 9, 1925; s. Charles Richard and Ella (Kilbane) O'Donnell; m. Ellen Blydenburgh, Aug. 16, 1965; children: Kevin, Susan, Michael, John, Maura, Neil, Megan, Hugh. AB, Kenyon Coll., Gambier, Ohio, 1947, PhD (hon.) in Law, 1980; MBA, Harvard U., 1947; PhD in Econs. (hon.), Pusan (Korea) Nat. U., 1970; PhD in Humanities (hon.), Ohio Wesleyan U., 1972. Gen. sales mgr. Steel Improvement & Forge Co., Cleve., 1947-60; mgmt. cons. Booz, Allen and Hamilton, Cleve., 1960-62, gen. mgr., dir. Atlas Alloys-Rio Algom Corp., Cleve., 1963-66; dir. Peace Corps, Seoul, Republic of Korea, 1966-70, dir. adminstrn. and fin., then dep. acting dir., 1970-71; assoc. dir. internat. ops. ACTION, 1971-72; exec. v.p. SIFCO Industries, Inc., Cleve., 1972-75, pres., chief oper. officer, 1976-83, pres., chief exec. officer, 1983-89, chief exec. officer, 1989-90, chmn., exec. comm., 1990-94; ret., 1994. Bd. dirs. Ctrl. Pk. Media Corp., N.Y.C., Doyle Pacific Industries, Ltd., Hong Kong, Whole Health Mgmt., Inc., Cleve.; adv. dir. Plz. Group, Houston, Capital Strategies, Inc., Cleve. Mem. Washington Inst. Fgn. Affairs, Cleve. Com. Fgn. Rels., chmn., 1979—82, CCWA, 1982—89; pres. Guest Ho., Inc., 1990—92; trustee Alcohol Svcs., Cleve., 1993—, Cleve. Coun. World Affairs, Nat. Peace Corps. Assn. Decorated Order Civil Merit Republic of Korea. Mem.: Harvard Bus. Sch. Alumni Assn. (dir. Boston 1991—94), Army-Navy Club (Washington), Westwood Country Club, Union Club, 50 Club, First Friday Club, Harvard Bus. Sch. Club Cleve., Knights of Malta (master knight). Republican. Roman Catholic. Avocations: golf, reading. E-mail: kevodoncle@aol.com.

O'DONNELL, LAURENCE GERARD, editorial consultant, former managing editor The Wall Street Journal; b. Bklyn., June 30, 1935; s. Thomas Edward and Dorothy (Clark) O'D.; m. Joan M. Coniglio, Jan. 9, 1960; children: Christopher, Carolyn, Jeffrey, Anthony. AB, Holy Cross Coll., 1957. Reporter Wall Street Jour., N.Y.C., 1958-66, chief Detroit Bur., 1966-74, asst. mng. editor, N.Y.C., 1974-77, mng. editor, 1977-83; assoc. editor Dow Jones & Co., Inc., N.Y.C., 1983-90, cons., 1991-99. Pres. Dow Jones Newspaper Fund, 1988-93; bd. dirs. Dow Jones Newspaper Fund; vis. lectr. Queens Coll./CUNY, 1992-99. Trustee Holy Cross Coll., 1982-90; mem. journalism adv. bd. Queens Coll./CUNY, 1989-2003; juror Pulitzer Prize, 1982, 83; bd. dirs. Interam. Press Assn., 1986-2001. Mem. Am. Soc. Newspaper Editors. Mem. Natl. adv. com., Robert Wood Johnson Found., 2002-. Office: Dow Jones Newspaper Fund PO Box 300 Princeton NJ 08543-0300

O'DONNELL, LAWRENCE, III, waste management executive; b. Houston, Dec. 14, 1957; s. Lawrence Jr. and Annell O'D.; m. Dare Boswell, May 22, 1981; children: Linley, Lawrence IV. BS in Archtl. Engring., U. Tex., 1980; JD cum laude, U. Houston, 1983. Bar: Tex. 1983. Assoc. Wood, Campbell, Moody & Gibbs, Houston, 1983-84; ptnr. Campbell & Riggs, Houston, 1984-91; dep. gen. counsel Baker Hughes Inc., Houston, 1991-94; v.p., gen. counsel Baker Hughes Oilfield Ops., Houston, 1993-95; corp. sec. Baker Hughes Inc., Houston, 1991-96, v.p., gen. counsel, 1995-2000; sr. v.p., gen. counsel, sec. Waste Mgmt., Inc., Houston, 2000-01, exec. v.p., gen. counsel, corp. sec., 2001—, exec. v.p. western ops., 2001—03, exec. v.p. ops. support, CAO, 2003—04, pres., COO, 2004—. Bd. dirs., mem. exec. com. Spring Br. Edn. Found.; bd. dirs. Am. Arbitration Assn., U. Tex. Med. Br.; mem. energy planning coun. State of Tex., 2004. Trustee. Houston Police Activities League.; adv. bd. Brookwood. Mem.: ASCE, ABA, Houston Bar Assn., Tex. State Bar, Order of Barons, Phi Delta Phi. Avocations: golf, sailing, skiing. Office: Waste Mgmt Inc 1001 Fannin St Ste 4000 Houston TX 77002-6711

O'DONNELL, MAUREEN STACEY, editor; b. Fresno, Calif., July 21, 1965; d. Stanley and Rosanna G. O'Donnell; m. John Purcell, June 12, 2000. BA in English, U. Wash., 1986. Mng. editor, sr. editor Workz.com, Seattle, 1999—2001; editor S&T Onsite, 2001—02, NYTEC, Inc., 2002—03. Author: (short stories) Penthouse mag., 2002, Avalon Press, 2002, Cleansheets.com, 2003.

O'DONNELL, MICHAEL JAMES, computer scientist; b. Spartanburg, S.C., Apr. 4, 1952; s. William Joseph and Linnie Lucille (Hynds) O'D.; m. Julie Ann Nerini, Feb. 6, 1982; children: Benjamin Michael, Mary Kathleen. BSc, Purdue U., 1972; PhD, Cornell U., 1976. Rsch. assoc. U. Toronto, Ont., Can., 1976-77; asst. prof. Purdue U., West Lafayette, Ind., 1976-81, assoc. prof., 1981-85, Johns Hopkins U., Balt., 1984-85; prof. U. Chgo., 1985—, assoc. chair computer sci., 1986-87, chair computer sci., 1987-90, sr. fellow Computation Inst., 2000—. Pvt. cons., 1999—; vis. prof. U. Iowa, Iowa City, 1996-97; vis. assoc. prof. Johns Hopkins U., Balt., 1983-84; adv. bd. Founds. of Computation Lab., Queensland, Australia, 1989—. Author: Computing in Systems Described by Equations, 1976, Equational Logic as a Programming Language, 1985; co-author: A Programming Logic, 1978; editl. bd. Jour. of Functional and Logic Programming, 1995—, mng. editor Chgo. Jour. of Theoretical Computer Sci., 1994—2000. Grantee NSF, 1989-94. Mem. IEEE Computer Soc., IEEE Signal Processing Soc., Assn. for Computing Machinery (chmn. SIGSound 2001—), Acoustical Soc. of Am., Midwest Soc. for Programming Langs. and Systems (pres. 1987-94), Free Software Found. Achievements include invention and first implemention of lazy evaluation for functional programs; discovery of first practical example of Gödel incompleteness. Office: U Chgo 1100 E 58th St Chicago IL 60637-1588 Office Phone: 773-702-1269. E-mail: michael_odonnell@acm.org.

O'DONNELL, PAT A. state representative; b. Holyoke, Mass., Oct. 15, 1954; m. Robert J. O'Donnell; 4 children. Degree, Holyoke (Vt.) C.C. Salesperson; rep. Vt. State Ho. Reps., 1999—. Clk. Vernon (Vt.) Selectboard; mem. Vernon (Vt.) PTC, Vernon (Vt.) ELF; chmn. Vernon (Vt.) Sch. Bd. Roman Catholic. Home: PO Box 355 Vernon VT 05354

O'DONNELL, PIERCE HENRY, lawyer; b. Troy, N.Y., Mar. 5, 1947; s. Harry J. and Mary (Kane) O'Donnell; m. Dawn Donley, Mar. 17, 1995; children: Meghan Maureen, Brendan Casey, Courtney Dawn, Pierce Dublin, Aidan Yeats. BA, Georgetown U., 1969, JD, 1972; LLM, Yale U., 1975. Bar: D.C. 1973, U.S. Supreme Ct. 1975, Calif. 1978. Law clk. to Justice Byron R. White U.S. Supreme Ct.; law clk. to Judge Shirley M. Hutstedler U.S. Ct. Appeals (9th cir.); assoc. Williams & Connolly, Washington, 1975-78; ptnr. Beardsley, Hufstedler & Kemble, L.A., 1978-81, Hufstedler, Miller, Carlson & Beardsley, L.A., 1981-82, O'Donnell & Gordon, L.A., 1982-87, Kaye, Scholer, Fierman, Hays & Handler, L.A., 1988-95, O'Donnell & Shaeffer, L.L.P., L.A., 1996—. Exec. asst. U.S. Sec. Edn., 1979; spl. counsel Commn. Jud. Performance, San Francisco, 1979; chmn. Nat. Media, Inc., 1984—92. Co-author: (book) Fatal Subtraction: The Inside Story of Buchwald v Paramount, 1992, Toward A Just and Effective Sentencing System: Agenda for Legislative Reform, 1976; author: Dawn's Early Light, 2001; contbr. articles to profl. jours. Chmn. Friends Cal Tech YMCA, 1983—84, Verdugo-San Rafael Urban Mountain Park Fund, 1980—84; bd. dirs. Foothill Family Svc., 1979—85, chmn., 1984—85; bd. dirs. Interfaith Ctr. To Reverse Arms Race, 1984—90, pres., 1987—88; mem. Econ. Round Table of L.A., 1979—, pres., 2000—01; chmn. Calif. Coast Baseball Acad., 2001—; mem. Santa Barbara Sheriff's Coun., 2003—; bd. dirs. Firends of Altadena Libr., 1979—81, Pasadena-Foothill Urban League, E. Altadena Little League, 1993—97. Fellow: Internat. Acad. Trial Lawyers; mem.: NAACP, PEN, Cal Tech Assocs., Am. Law Inst., Am. Bd. Trial Advocates, Sierra Club, Calif. Club, Gridiron Club (Georgetown U.), Bel Air Country Club. Roman Catholic. Office: O'Donnell & Shaeffer LLP 550 S Hope 20th fl Los Angeles CA 90071-2027 Home: 735 Picacho Ln Santa Barbara CA 93108-1226 Office Phone: 213-532-2000. Business E-Mail: pod@oslaw.com.

O'DONNELL, ROBERT PATRICK, priest; b. Gary, Ind., June 11, 1919; s. Liquori Alphonsus and Carolyn Emily (Senn) O'D. Student, Art Inst., Chgo.; BA, U. Chgo., 1943; MA, Cath. U., 1945; postgrad., Gregorian U., Rome, 1980-81. Ordained priest Roman Cath. Ch., 1949. Asst. Sacred Heart Ch., Russellville, Ky., 1950-52; adminstr. Our Lady of Lourdes Ch., Otway, Ohio, 1953-55; pub. rels. Glenmary Home Missioners, Glendale, Ohio, 1956-60; chaplain Glenmary Sisters, Fayetteville, Ohio, 1960-66; pastor Holy Redeemer Ch., Vancebury, Ky., 1987-94, St. Agnes Ch., Elkton, Ky., 1981-87, St. Mary & St. James Ch., Guthrie, Ky., St. Francis De Sales Ch., Idabel, Okla., 1987-94; with Glenmary Home Missioners, Cincinnati, 1994—. Editor, photographer, illustrator Glenmary's Challenge, Cin., 1952-80; designer/builder seven chs. in Ky., Ohio, N.C., 1952-64. Founder/designer: Appalachian Studios-resident artist, gen. mgr., 1966-80; composer music, producer: (musical) From Sheeba They Came, 1990; producer: (movie) Glenmary Story, 1958, other. With USN. With maritime svc. USN, 1943, ATO. Recipient Thomas Jefferson award, U.S. Office of Pres., 1979, Four Chaplains Nat. award Office of Four Chaplains Found., Phila., 1981; Art scholar U. chgo. Mem. Rotary (internat. exc. chmn. 1989-91), Phi Kappa Psi (pres. 1943), AFL CIO, KC. Home and Office: 100 Compton Rd 5C3 Cincinnati OH 45215-4141

O'DONNELL, ROSIE, television personality, actress, comedienne; b. Commack, N.Y., Mar. 21, 1962; m. Kelli Carpenter, Feb. 26, 2004; children: Parker Jaren, Chelsea Belle, Blake Christopher. Attended, Dickinson Coll., Boston Univ. Appearances include (TV series) Gimme A Break, 1986-87, Stand By Your Man, 1992, Women Aloud, 1992, Stand-up Spotlight, VH-1 (American Comedy award nomination best female performer in a TV special 1994, Cable ACE award nomination best entertainment host 1994), (TV) host The Rosie O'Donnell Show, 1995-2002 (Daytime Emmy awards 1997, 98, 99, 2000, 2001), (TV movie) The Twilight of the Golds, 1997; (films) A League of Their Own, 1992, Sleepless in Seattle, 1993 (American Comedy award nomination best supporting female in a motion picture 1994), Another Stakeout, 1993 (American Comedy award nomination best actress in a motion picture 1994), Car 54, Where Are You?, 1994, I'll Do Anything, 1994, The Flintstones, 1994, Exit to Eden, 1994, Now and Then, 1995, Beautiful Girls, 1996, Harriet the Spy, 1996, A Very Brady Sequel, 1996 (uncredited), Wide Awake, 1996, Get Bruce, 1999, Jackie's Back, 1999, Tarzan, 1999 (voice), Flintstones in Viva Rock Vegas, 2000; Broadway shows include Grease, 1994, Seussical the Musical, 2001; author: Find Me, 2002; editor: Rosie mag., 2000-2002, prodr.: Taboo (Broadway) 2003-2004. Office: ICM 8942 Wilshire Blvd Beverly Hills CA 90211*

O'DONNELL, TERRENCE, lawyer; b. N.Y.C., Mar. 3, 1944; s. Emmett and Lorraine (Muller) O'Donnell; m. Margaret Lynne Kidder; children: Stephanie T., Erin K., Victoria L. BS, U.S. Air Force Acad., 1966; JD, Georgetown Law Sch., 1971. Bar: D.C. 1971, U.S. Ct. Appeals (D.C. cir.) 1978, U.S. Ct. Appeals (4th cir.) 1987, U.S. Dist. Ct. Md. 1986, U.S. Ct. Mil. Appeals 1990, U.S. Ct. Fed. Claims, U.S. Supreme Ct., others. Commd. 2d lt. USAF, 1966, advanced through grades to capt., various positions, 1966-72, resigned, 1972; spl. asst. Pres. of U.S., The White House, Washington, 1972-77; appointments sec. Pres. Ford, Washington, 1974-77; assoc. Williams & Connolly, Washington, 1977-82, ptnr., 1982-89; gen. counsel Dept. Def., Washington, 1989-92; ptnr. Williams and Connolly, Washington, 1992—; exec. v.p., gen. counsel Textron Inc., 2000—. Presdl. appointee to bd. visitors U.S. Air Force Acad., Colorado Springs, 1982-87, chmn., 1985-86; U.S. corr. and rep. UN Program to Prevent Crime, Washington and N.Y.C., 1977-81; bd. dirs. IGI Inc., MLC Holdings. Trustee Gerald R. Ford Found., Grand Rapids, Mich., 1987—; mem. Adminstrv. Conf. U.S., 1991-92; mem. adv. com. U.S. Ct. Fed. Claims; mem. code com. U.S. Ct. of Mil. Appeals for the Armed Forces, 1993-95; bd. dirs. Falcon Found., 1988—. Decorated Bronze star; recipient Disting. Pub. Svc. medal Dept. of Def., 1992, Disting. Svc. award U.S. Atty. Gen., 1992. Mem. ABA, D.C. Bar Assn., Bar of U.S. Supreme Ct., and others. Home: 5133 Yuma St NW Washington DC 20016-4336 Office: Williams and Connolly 725 12th St NW Washington DC 20005-5901 Office Phone: 401-457-2555. Business E-Mail: todonnell@textron.com. E-mail: todonnell@wc.com.

O'DONNELL, THOMAS LAWRENCE PATRICK, lawyer; b. Taunton, Mass., Aug. 12, 1926; s. Patrick Francis and Ellen Balfe (Brady) O'D.; m. Carol Hodgdon, Feb. 16, 1952; children— Ellen, Thomas, Janet Gael, Christopher Hodgdon AB magna cum laude, Harvard U., 1947, LL.B., 1949. Bar: Mass. 1950. Assoc. Ropes & Gray, Boston, 1949-52, 54-61, ptnr., 1962-97, chmn., 1984-90, of counsel, 1998—. Dir. Rath & Strong, Inc., 1985-96. Trustee, Trustees of Reservations, 1970—, chmn. bd., 1975-76; bd. dirs. Mass. Land Conservation Trust, 1975-2002, chmn. bd., 1986-2002; bd. dirs. Mass. Taxpayers Found., 1972—, chmn. bd., 1977-79, 93-95, mem. exec. com., 1976—; bd. dirs. Boston Mcpl. Rsch. Bur., 1965—, chmn. bd., 1967-72; mem. pub. pension task force Mass. Bus. Roundtable, 1983-86; bd. dirs., sec. Jobs for Mass., Inc., 1981-83; moderator Town of Hingham, 1967—; del. Rep. Nat. Conv., 1972, all Rep. State convs., 1960-94; overseer Harvard U., 1986-92; bd. dirs. United Way Mass. Bay, 1987—, mem. exec. com. 1993—, chmn. bd. 1997-2000. Lt. USNR, 1994-45, 52-54. Recipient Cushing award Labor Guild of Archdiocese Boston, 1973, Humanitarian award The Nat. Conf. Greater Boston, 1997, The Harvard medal, 1997; mem. Knights of Malta, 1983— Fellow Am. Bar Found.; mem. ABA, Mass. Bar Assn., Boston Bar Assn., Am. Arbitration Assn., Indsl. Rels. Rsch. Assn. (pres. Boston chpt. 1980), Harvard Alumni Assn. (bd. dirs. 1978-81; 1st marshal class of 1947). Clubs: Harvard of Boston (bd. govs. 1985-91), Union of Boston; Hingham Yacht, Comml. Roman Catholic. Home: 7 South Ln Hingham MA 02043-2446 Office: Ropes & Gray LLP 1 International Pl Boston MA 02110-2624 E-mail: todonnell@ropesgray.com.

O'DONNELL, THOMAS MICHAEL, former brokerage firm executive; b. Cleve., Apr. 9, 1936; s. John Michael and Mary L. (Hayes) O'D.; m. Nancy A. Dugan, Feb. 4, 1961; children: Christopher, Colleen, Julie BBA, U. Notre Dame, 1959; MBA, U. Pa., 1960. Cert. Chartered Fin. Analyst. Fin. analyst Saunders Stiver & Co., Cleve., 1960-65; rsch. dir. McDonald & Co., Cleve., 1965-66, exec. v.p. corp. fin., 1967-83, gen. ptnr., 1968-83; pres. McDonald & Co. Investments, Inc./McDonald & Co. Securities, Cleve., 1984-88; chmn., chief exec. officer McDonald & Co. Securities, Cleve., 1988-98. Bd. dirs. Seaway Food Town; mem. regional firms adv. com. N.Y. Stock Exch., 1986-92, chmn., 1991-92; dir. C.I.D. Venture Funds. Author: The Why and How of Mergers, 1968 Bd. dirs. Greater Cleve. Growth Assn., Inroads Northeast Ohio, PlayHouse Square Found.; bd. regents St. Ignatius High Sch., Cleve.; steering com. Leadership Cleve. Mem. Cleve. Soc. Security Analysts (cert.), Securities Industry Assn. (dir. 1988-94, chmn. 1993), Union Club, Westwood Country Club, 50 Club Cleve., Pepper Pike Club, Double Eagle Club. Roman Catholic. Avocation: golf. Home: 1790 Century Oaks Dr Cleveland OH 44145-3654

O'DONNELL, THOMAS P. mechanical engineer; b. Pitts., Jan. 7, 1963; s. William J. and Joanne M. O'Donnell; m. Patricia A. Pinyot, Nov. 4, 2000. BSME, Pa. State U., 1985; M Engring., Carnegie Mellon U., 1987; PhD in Mech. Engring., U. Pitts., 1994. Registered profl. engr., Pa. Sr. engr.

Westinghouse Electric Corp., Pitts., 1987-96; sr. project engr. John J. McCullen and Assocs., Pitts., 1996-97; sr. engr. Geo-Centers, Inc., Pitts., 1998—; v.p. O'Donnell Cons. Engrs., Inc., Bethel Park, Pa., 1988—. Cons. Design Analysis Svcs., Inc., Pitts., 1996—, Decamedics, Columbus, Ohio, 1999—; biomed. engr. artificial heart program U. Pitts. Med. Ctr., Pitts., 1991-2003; intra-aortic balloon pump engr. UPMC STAT MedEvac Flight Team, Pitts., 1998-2003; instr. Pa. State U., 1990-2001. Contbr. articles to profl. jours.; author conf. procs. in field. Mem. Nat. Ski Patrol, 1982—85. Keck Bioengring. fellow Keck Found., 1991-92. Mem. ASME, Tau Beta Pi, Pi Tau Sigma. Avocations: skiing, horseback riding, tennis, travel, water sports. Home: 4717 Doverdell Dr Pittsburgh PA 15236 Office: O'Donnell Cons Engrs 2940 S Park Rd Bethel Park PA 15102

O'DONNELL, WILLIAM DAVID, retired construction firm executive; b. Brockton, Mass., Aug. 21, 1926; s. John Frank and Agnes Teresa (Flanagan) O'D.; m. Dixie Lou Anderson, Jan. 31, 1951; children— Craig Patrick, Ginger Lynn BS, U. N.Mex., 1953. Registered profl. engr., Ill., 1958. Engr. State of Ill., 1953-59; with Gregory-Anderson Co., Rockford, Ill., 1959—, gen. mgr., 1960-61, sec., 1961-81, pres., 1981-94; ret. Bd. dirs. Growth Enterprise, Davis Meml. Park, BankOne, Rockford. Dir. St. Anthony Med. Ctr., Youth Svcs. Network, Cath. Conf. of Ill.; bd. dirs. Rockford YMCA, pres., 1984. Served with USN, 1943-47 Recipient Friend of the Boy award Optimist Club, 1966, Excalibur award for cmty. svc. Rockford Register Star, 1971; named Titan of Yr., Boylan H.S., 1974, Papal Knight Order of St. Gregory the Great; fellow Wisdom Hall of Fame. Fellow: NSPE, ASCE, Soc. Am. Mil. Engrs.; mem.: VFW (life), No. Ill. Bldg. Contractors, Amateur Trapshooting Assn., World Future Soc., Aircraft Owners & Pilots Assn., Balloon Fedn. Am., Am. Polar Soc., Nat. Sporting Clays Assn., Old Antarctic Explorers Assn., Forest Hills Country (Rockford), Metropolitan Club (Chgo.); Adventurers (Chgo.), Adventurers Club, Metropolitan Club, Forest Hills Country Club, Rotary (Service Above Self award 1972; v.p. Rockford chpt. 1983, pres. 1984), Rotary (v.p. Rockford chpt. 1983, pres. 1984, Svc. Above Self award 1972), Am. Legion (life), Tau Beta Pi, Chi Epsilon, Sigma Tau. Home: 2004 Bradley Rd Rockford IL 61107-1258 Office: PO Box 900 Rockford IL 61105-0900

O'DONNELL, WILLIAM JAMES, engineering executive; b. Pitts., June 19, 1935; s. William James and Elizabeth (Rau) O'D.; m. Joanne Mary Kusen, Jan. 31, 1959; children: Suzanne, Janice, William, Thomas, Kerry, Amy. BSM.E., Carnegie Inst. Tech., 1957; MSM.E., U. Pitts., 1959, PhD, 1962. Jr. engr. Westinghouse Research Lab., 1957-58, asso. engr., 1958; with Westinghouse Bettis Atomic Power Lab., West Mifflin, Pa., 1961-70, adv. engr., 1966-70; pres., chmn. bd. O'Donnell & Assos., Inc., Pitts., 1970—. Contbr. numerous articles on engring. and mechanics to profl. jours.; holder patents on processes and devices. Served with C.E. AUS, 1963-64. Recipient Machinery's Achievement award as outstanding mech. designer, 1957, Pi Tau Sigma Gold medal for achievements in engring., 1967, Pressure Vessel and Piping award ASME, 1994, Disting. Alumni award U. Pitts. Sch. Mech. Engring., 1996. Fellow ASME (nat. award for outstanding contbn. to engring. profession 1973, internat. award for best publ. in pressure vessels and piping 1988, Engr. of Yr. award 1988, Pressure Vessel and Piping medal 1994); mem. NSPE, AAAS, ASTM, Soc. Exptl. Mechanics, Am. Nuclear Soc., Am. Soc. Metals Internat., The Minerals, Metals and Materials Soc., Sigma Xi. Home: 121 Sunrise Ln Venetia PA 15367 Office: O'Donnell Consulting Engrs 2940 S Park Rd Pittsburgh PA 15102 Office Phone: 412-835-5007. Business E-Mail: wjo@odonnellconsulting.com.

O'DONNELL, WILLIAM W. theater educator, lighting designer; b. Sharon, Pa., Dec. 1, 1954; s. William W. and Dorothy A O'Donnell; life ptnr. Craig W. Eslep, Nov. 24, 1987. BFA, Pa. State U., 1977; MFA, Wayne State U., 1979. Asst. prof. theatre Bloomsburg U. of Pa., 1983—86; lighting designer Pitts. Ballet Theatre, 1986—87; prodn. mgr. New Works Festival, Pitts., 1991—93; resident lighting designer City Theatre, Pitts., 1991—2002; freelance lighting designer Pitts. Area, 1992—; assoc. prof. theatre California U. of Pa., 1993—; prodr. CalRep Pa., California, Pa., 1994—2003. Bd. dirs. Chartiers Valley Arts Coun., Carnegie, Pa., 1990—93. Lighting designer (play) Major Barbara (Galway Arts Festival, 2003). Exec. com. Unitarian Universalist Ch. of Smithton, Pa., 2000—03; union del. Assn. of Pa. State Coll. and U. Faculties, California, 2003—04. Mem.: ACLU, Safe Zone (founding mem. 1999—2004), Theatre Comm. Group, U.S. Inst. of Theatre Tech., PADI, People for the Am. Way, Human Rights Campaign, Rainbow Alliance of Calif. (faculty advisor 1997—2004, Svc. to Gay Cmty. 2003), Alpha Psi Omega (life). Democrat. Unitarian Universalist. Achievements include founding producer of CalRep Pa. Avocations: gay rights advocate, scuba diving. Office: California Univ of Pa 250 University Dr California PA 15419 Business E-Mail: odonnell@cup.edu.

O'DONOVAN, LEO JEREMIAH, former academic administrator, priest, theologian; b. N.Y.C., Apr. 24, 1934; s. Leo J. O'Donovan Jr. AB, Georgetown U., 1956; Licentiate in Philosophy, Fordham U., 1961; STB, Woodstock Coll., 1966, Licentiate in Sacred Theology, 1967; ThD, U. Münster, Fed. Republic Germany, 1971; LittD (hon.), Sogang U., Seoul, 1993; DHL, Loyola Coll., 1991, Coll. St. Rose, 2000; MD (hon.), Georgetown U., 2001. Ordained to ministry Cath. Ch., 1966. Instr. philosophy Loyola Coll., Balt., 1961—63; asst. prof. Woodstock Coll., Woodstock, 1971—74; assoc. prof. Weston Sch. Theology, Cambridge, Mass., 1974—81, prof., 1981—89; pres. Georgetown U., Washington, 1989—2001, prof., 2001—. Provincial asst. formation Md. Province S.J., Balt., 1985—88; cons. Nat. Conf. Cath. Bishops, Washington, 1986—89; bd. dirs. The Riggs Nat. Bank, Walt Disney Co., 2001—, MedStar Health, Inc. Bd. dirs. U. Detroit Mercy, 1986—95; mem. Consortium of Univs. Washington Met. Area, 1989—2001, chair, 1994—96; mem. Fed. Cuty Coun., 1993—2001, Bus.-Higher Edn. Forum, 1989—2001, Nat. Coun. Arts, 1994—98, Consortium Fin. Higher Edn., 1990—98, chmn., 1995—97; mem. Am. Reads Stery Com., 1997—. Recipient Knight Comdr.'s Crodd, Germany; fellow, Danforth Found., 1956—71, vis. fellow, Woodstock Theol. Ctr.; grantee teaching grantee, Assn. Theol. Schs., 1978—79; scholar, Fulbright Found., U. Lyon, France, 1956—57. Fellow: Soc. Values in Higher Edn. (bd. dirs. 1989—); mem.: Boston Theol. Soc., Assn. Cath. Colls. and Univs. (bd. dirs. 1994—2000), Assn. Jesuit Colls. and Univs., Univ. Club. Office: Georgetown U 37th and O St NW Washington DC 20057-1789

ODORIZZI, MICHELE L. lawyer; b. Chgo., July 12, 1952; BA, Northwestern U., 1973; JD cum laude, U. Chgo., 1976. Bar: Ill. 1976, U.S. Ct. Appeals (7th cir.) 1976, U.S. Dist. Ct. (no. dist.) Ill. 1977, U.S. Supreme Ct. 1980, U.S. Ct. Appeals (4th, 9th, 10th cirs.). Ptnr. Mayer, Brown & Platt, Chgo. Office: Mayer Brown & Platt 190 S La Salle St Ste 3100 Chicago IL 60603-3441

O'DOWD, DONALD DAVY, retired university president; b. Manchester, N.H., Jan. 23, 1927; s. Hugh Davy and Laura (Morin) O'D.; m. Janet Louise Fithian, Aug. 23, 1953; children: Daniel D., Diane K., James E., John M. BA summa cum laude, Dartmouth Coll., 1951; postgrad. (Fulbright fellow), U. Edinburgh, Scotland, 1951-52; MA, Harvard U., 1955, PhD, 1957. Instr., asst. prof. psychology, dean freshmen Wesleyan U., Middletown, Conn., 1955-60; assoc. prof., prof. of psychology, dean Univ. Oakland Univ., Rochester, Mich., 1960-65, provost, 1965-70; pres. Oakland U., Rochester, Mich., 1970-80; exec. vice chancellor SUNY, Albany, 1980-84; pres. U. of Alaska Statewide System, 1984-90. Carnegie Corp. fellow, 1965-66 Mem. APA, AAAS, Phi Beta Kappa, Sigma Xi. Home and Office: 1550 La Vista Del Oceano Santa Barbara CA 93109-1739

O'DOWD, NIALL OLIVER, publishing executive, writer; b. Thurles, Ireland, May 18, 1953; arrived in U.S., 1979; s. Donal O'Dowd and Kathleen Devins; m. Debbie McGoldrick, Aug. 9, 1996; 1 child, Alana. BA, Univ. Coll. Dublin, 1977, diploma in Edn., 1978. Founder, editor Irishman Newspaper, San Francisco, 1979—85, Irish Am. Mag., N.Y.C., 1985—, Irish Voice Newspaper, N.Y.C., 1987—. Author: Fire in the Morning, 2002. Dir. Emerald Isle Immigration Ctr., N.Y.C., 1994—. Recipient Irish Am. Peace prize, Irish Am. Dems., 1997, Peace Process award, Flax Trust, Belfast, No. Ireland, 1998. Mem.: Irish Am. Hist. Soc. (dir. 2000—). Achievements include intermediary between IRA and the White House during Irish Peace Process, 1991-1995. E-mail: irvoice@aol.com.

ODRE, STEVEN M. lawyer; B in Chemistry, Union Coll., 1971; M in Analytical Biochemistry, Purdue U., 1973; JD, Chgo. U., 1977. Patent counsel G.D. Searle, 1983—86; dir. intellectual property Amgen, 1986—88, assoc. gen. counsel, 1988—98, v.p. intellectual property, assoc. gen. counsel, 1998—2000; sr. v.p., gen. counsel, sec. Amgen Inc., Thousand Oaks, Calif., 2000—. Office: Amgen Inc 1 Amgen Center Dr Thousand Oaks CA 91320-1799

O'DRISCOLL, SHAWN WILLIAM, surgeon, researcher; b. Toronto, Can., Apr. 28, 1955; arrived in U.S., 1989; m. Chantal O'Driscoll; children: Colin, Christopher, Jesse, Pierre. BS, Univ. Tornto, Can., 1976; MD, Univ. Toronto, Can., 1980; PhD, Int. Med. Sci. Univ. Toronto, Can., 1984. Lic. Med. Coun. Can., Coll. of physicians and Surgeons, Can., diplomate Nat. Bd. of Med. Examiners, U.S., lic. Minn. State Bd. of Med. Examiners, diplomate Am. Bd. of Orthopedic Surgery. Rotating intern Toronto East Gen. and Orthop. Hosp., 1980—81; resident U. Toronto, 1981—87; fellow St. Michael's Hosp., 1988, Toronto We. Hosp., 1988, Mayo Clin., 1989; staff surgeon Toronto We. Hosp., Canada, 1988—; asst. prof. dept orthop. surgery Mayo Clin., 1989; orthop. surgeon St. Michae'ls Hosp., 1990—92; assoc. prof. Mayo Clin., 1992—95, prof. orthop. surgery, 1995—. Dir. cartilage/connective tissue rsch. lab Mayo Clin., 1995—; vis. prof. Univ. Nagoya, Japan, 1993, Univ. Fla., 1995; guest lectr. St. Marianna Univ., Japan, 1996, Hiroshima Hand Club, Japan, 1996; vis. prof. Mt. Sinai Med. Ctr., 2001, Cleve. Orthop. Soc., Ohio, 2003, Abbott Soc. Conf., San Francisco, 2003. Contbr. scientific papers 138 pub. to profl. jour. (Zimmer award, 1982, 1983, Honourable Mention, 1983, many others), articles over 100 pub. to profl. jour., chapters to books over 46 pub. Recipient Can. Orthop. Rsch. Edn. award, 1990; grantee MRC Oper. Grant, 1990, Connaught, 1990, PSI Oper. Grant, 1990—91, Arthritis Soc. Oper. Grant, 1991, many others; scholar MRC Scholarship, 1990. Fellow: Royal Coll. of Surgeons of Can.; mem.: Am. Shoulder and ELbow Surgeons, Am. Bd. of Orthop. Surgery, Am. Shoulder and Elbow Surgeons, Orthop. Rsch. Soc., Minn. St. Bd. of Med. Examiners, Coll. of Physicians and Surgeons, Can. Med. Assn., Ontario Med. Assn., Sigma Si Rsch. Soc. Avocations: hockey, kayaking, canoeing, music, scuba diving. Office: Mayo Clin 200 1st SW MSB 3-69 Rochester MN 55905

ODUM, JEFFERY NEAL, mechanical engineer; b. Bristol, Tenn., Sept. 11, 1956; s. Herschel S. and Minnie Lee (Carrier) O.; m. Stacy Elaine Ferrell, mar. 18, 1989; 1 child, Charles Wesley Ferrell. BSME, Tenn. Technol. U., 1978; MS in Engring., U. Tenn., 1983. Sr. project engr. TVA, Knoxville, 1978-81; sr. constrn. engr. Stone & Webster Engring. Corp., Boston, 1981-84; div. engr. E.I. DuPont de Nemours & Co., Aiken, S.C., 1984-89; engring. mgr. Flour Daniel, Greenville, S.C., 1989-92; mgr. of projects, Pharmaceutical Bus. Group CRS Sirrine Engrs., Inc., Raleigh, N.C., 1992-93; sr. project mgr. Gilbane Bldg. Co., Raleigh, 1993-95; dir. engring. Gilbane Process Group, Vacaville, Calif., 1995-98; biopharm. office leader Clark, Richardson and Biskup, Cons. Engrs., Cary, NC, 1998—. Author: Sterile Product Facility Design and Project Management, 1996, Large Scale Biomanufacturing, 2004; contbr. articles to profl. jours. Vol. Spl. Olympics, Habitat for Humanity; mem. bd. govs. U. Tenn., 2002—03. Recipient DuPont Engring. Achievement award 1986, 88, 89, Nat. Svc. Alumni award Univ. Tenn. Mem. Parenteral Drug Assn., Internat. Soc. Pharm. Engrs. (bd. dirs., pres. Carolina chpt. 1996-97, chair N.Am. Chpt. Coun. 1998, chair publs. com. 2000-01, chair chpt. excellence 2000-01, chair tng. 2002, Svc. award 1999, 2001, Richard Purdy Outstanding Achievement award 2002), U. Tenn. Nat. Alumni Assn. (pres. Augusta chpt. 1987-89, bd. govs.), Order Engr., Kappa Sigma. Republican. Presbyterian. Avocations: sports, biking, cooking, physical fitness, writing. Office: Clark Richardson & Biskkup 1225 Crescent Green Dr Ste 300 Cary NC 27511-8107

ODUSHKIN, TARAS, mathematician; b. Lviv, Ukraine, Jan. 6, 1969; s. Volodymyr and Vira Odushkin. BS in Physics, Lviv State U., 1993; MS in Stats., U. Tex., Dallas, 2003; MS in Applied Math., U. Tex., 2001. Rschr. Ukrainian Nat. Acad. Sci., Lviv, 1993—97; tchg. asst. U. Tex., Dallas, 1997—. Presenter in field. Mem.: Am. Math. Soc. (licentiate), US Chess Fedn. (licentiate). Home: 700 Custer Rd Apt 266 Richardson TX 75080 Office: Univ Tex 2601 N Floyd Rd Richardson TX 75083 Personal E-mail: taras_od@yahoo.com. Business E-Mail: taras@utdallas.edu.

O'DWYER, BRIAN, lawyer, educator; b. NYC, Oct. 10, 1945; s. Paul and Kathleen (Rohan) O.; m. Marianna Page, Sept. 7, 1968; children: Brendan, Kathleen. BA, George Washington U., 1967, LLM, 1976; MA, Middlebury Coll., 1968; JD, Georgetown U., 1971. Bar: N.Y. 1972, U.S. Dist. Ct. (so., ea. and no. dists.) N.Y. 1973, U.S. Ct. Appeals (2d cir.) 1975, U.S. Supreme Ct. 1983. Atty. NLRB, Newark, 1972-73, N.Y. State Labor Bd., 1973-74; mng. ptnr. O'Dwyer & Bernstein, N.Y.C., 1974—. Commr. N.Y.C. Commn. on Human Rights, 1993-96; dir. Malcom King Coll., 1980-88; pres. Bohola Enterprises Inc.; mem. Pres. Commn. on White House Fellows, 1998-2001. Trustee Clara Miller Found., Mayo Found for the Handicapped; nat. v.p. Irish Ams. for Clinton Gore; chmn. Emerald Isle Immigrant Ctr. Mem. ABA, Brehon Law Soc., Kappa Sigma (nat. pres.). Democrat. Roman Catholic. Home: 350 Central Park W New York NY 10025-6547 Office: O'Dwyer & Bernstein 52 Duane St Fl 5 New York NY 10007-1250 Personal E-mail: bjodwyer@aol.com.

O'DWYER, MARY ANN, automotive executive; BS, DePaul U.; MS, Benedictine U. CPA. With Ernst and Young, McDonald's Corp.; various positions CC Industries (a Henry Crown Co.); sr. v.p. fin. ops., CFO Wheels, 1991—; sr. v.p. fin & ops., CFO Frank Consol. Enterprises. Office: Frank Consol Enterprises 666 Garland Pl Des Plaines IL 60016

ODZA, RANDALL M. lawyer; b. Schnectady, May 6, 1942; s. Mitchell and Grace (Mannes) O.; m. Rita Ginness, June 19, 1966; children: Kenneth, Keith. BS in Indsl. and Labor Rels., Cornell U., 1964, LLB, 1967. Bar: N.Y. 1967, U.S. Ct. Appeals (2d cir.) 1970, U.S. Dist. Ct. (so. and ea. dists.) N.Y. 1969, U.S. Dist. Ct. (we. dist.) N.Y. 1970. Assoc. Proskauer, Rose, Goetz & Mandelsohn, N.Y.C., 1967-69, Jaeckle, Fleischmann & Mugel, Buffalo, 1969-72, ptnr., 1972—. Past trustee, legal counsel, treas. Temple Beth Am; bd. trustees Buffalo Philharm. Orch. Soc. Recipient Honow award Western N.Y. Retail Mchts. Assn., 1980. Fellow Coll. Labor and Employment Lawyers; mem. ABA, Indsl. Rels. Rsch. Assn. Western N.Y., Erie County Bar Assn., N.Y. State Bar Assn. Office: Jaeckle Fleischmann & Mugel 12 Fountain Plz Rm 700 Buffalo NY 14202-2292

OECHLER, HENRY JOHN, JR., lawyer; b. Charlotte, N.C., Apr. 9, 1946; s. Henry J. and Convere Jones (McAden) O. AB, Princeton U., 1968; JD, Duke U., 1971. Bar: N.Y. 1972, U.S. Ct. Appeals (2d cir.) 1974, U.S. Ct. Appeals (D.C. cir.) 1975, U.S. Ct. Appeals (8th cir.) 1986, U.S. Ct. Appeals (9th cir.) 1995. Assoc. Chadbourne & Parke, N.Y.C., 1971-80, ptnr., 1980—. Avocation: studying airline schedules. Office: Chadbourne & Parke 30 Rockefeller Plz Fl 31 New York NY 10112-0129

OECHSLI, CHRISTOPHER GEORGE, foundation administrator; b. Costa Rica, Dec. 31, 1953; s. L. Paul and Helen (George) Oechsli; m. Julie Ann Dakin; children: Annika, Alexander. AB, Occidental Coll., 1975; MA in Fgn. Affairs, U. Va., 1978, JD, 1981. Assoc. Wickwire, Goldmark & Schorr, Seattle, 1981-85; prof. East China Law Inst., Shanghai, 1985-86; assoc. McCutchen, Doyle, Shanghai, 1987-90; gen. counsel Gen. Atlantic Group, London, 1990—; dir., pres. Gen. Atlantic Corp., 1995—; program dir. Atlantic Philanthropies (Seattle), Inc., Bainbridge Island, Wash., 2000—; ptnr. Estancia Buenaventura, Salta, Argentina, 1998—. Avocations: organic farming, guitar. Home: 14930 Sunrise Dr Bainbridge Island WA 98110-1113 Office: Atlantic Philanthropies (Seattle) Inc The Dockside Bldg, Suite 130 203 Parfitt Way SW Bainbridge Island WA 98110

OEFFNER, BARBARA DUNNING, writer, educator, scriptwriter; b. Southampton, N.Y., Aug. 25, 1944; d. Walter Arnold and Grace Dominy (Werner) Renkens; m. Michael Arthur Dunning, Oct. 1, 1966 (div. June 1984); children: Brendan, Ania, Amie, Heidi, Matt; m. F. Thomas Oeffner, Oct. 2, 1991. BS in Journalism, Northwestern U., 1966; MLS and Info. Studies, Fla. State U. Film copywriter Ency. Britannica, Chgo., 1966-69; pub. rels. dir. Eldred Auctions, East Dennis, Mass., 1982-85; editor Sandscript, Cummaquid, Mass., 1975-95; ins. agt. State Farm Ins., Delray Beach, Fla., 1992-95; biographer Cape Cod Writers, Inc., Cummaquid, 1995—. V.p. Caribbean Coatings Corp., Moore Haven, Fla., 1996—, Native Am. Prodns., Palm Beach, Fla., 1994—; lectr. Glades County Hist. Soc. Author: (screenplay) The Cuban Accident, 1996; co-author: (screenplay) Chief, 1994; author: (book) Chief: Champion of the Everglades, 1995. Tchr. Meth. Bible Sch., Moore Haven, 1997; activities dir. Campers Club Am., Moore Haven, 1996-97. Grantee Mary Roberts Rinehart Found., 1975, Commonwealth of Mass.-Dept. of Arts and Humanities, 1984, Coord. Coun. Lit. Mags., 1976. Mem. DAR. Democrat. Avocations: water aerobics, line dancing, hiking, travel, gardening. Home: Box 1236 306 Yacht Club Way Moore Haven FL 33471-2809 Office: Belle Glade Libr 530 Main St Belle Glade FL 33430 Office Phone: 561-996-3453., 561-996-2304. Business E-Mail: deffnerb@pbclibrary.org.

OEHLER, RICHARD DALE, lawyer; b. Iowa City, Dec. 9, 1925; s. Harold Lawrence Oehler and Bernito Babb; m. Rosemary Heineman, July 11, 1952, (div.); m. Maria Luisa Holguin-Zea, June 11, 1962; children: Harold D., Richard L. BA in Med. Scis., U. Calif., Berkeley, 1951; JD, Loyola U., L.A., 1961. Bar: Calif. 1962, Fla. 1968. Sales rep. Abbott Labs., Pasadena, Calif., 1951-63; with claims dept. Allstate Ins., Tampa, 1963-70; pvt. practice Tampa, 1970—. Instr. Dale Carnegie Courses West Fla. Inst., Tampa, Scott Hitchcock & Assocs., Tampa, 1969—. Pres. U. South Fla. Parents Assn., Tampa, 1986-87. Mem. Fla. Bar Assn., Hillsborough County Bar Assn., Acad. of Fla. Trial Lawyers, Assn. of Trial Lawyers of Am., Masons (32d degree), Shriners, Phi Beta Kappa. Republican. Presbyterian. Avocations: jogging, road races, target shooting, fishing. Office: 200 N Pierce St Tampa FL 33602-5020 E-mail: doehler@mindspring.com.

OEHLER, RICHARD WILLIAM, lawyer; b. N.Y.C., Nov. 24, 1950; s. John Montgomery and Florence Mae (Jahn) O.; m. Linda Tyson. BA, Dartmouth Coll., 1972; JD, Harvard U., 1976. Bar: Calif. 1976, Wash. 1987, D.C. 1988, U.S. Dist. Ct. (no. dist.) Calif. 1976, U.S. Dist. Ct. Wash. 1987, U.S. Claims Ct. 1979, U.S. Ct. Appeals (fed. cir.) 1982. Assoc. Pillsbury, Madison & Sutro, San Francisco, 1976-78; trial atty. U.S. Dept. Justice, Washington, 1978-87; of counsel Perkins Coie, Seattle, 1987-90, ptnr., 1990—. Mem. ABA, Nat. Contract Mgmt. Assn. (Spl. Achievement award 1990-92), Wash. State Bar Assn. Office: Perkins Coie 1201 3rd Ave Fl 40 Seattle WA 98101-3029 Office Phone: 206-359-8419. Business E-Mail: roehler@perkinscoie.com.

OEHLERT, WILLIAM HERBERT, JR., cardiologist, administrator, educator; b. Murphysboro, Ill., Sept. 11, 1942; s. William Herbert Sr. and Geneva Mae (Roberts) O.; m. L. Keith Brown, Mar. 14, 1976; children: Emily Jane, Amanda Elizabeth. BA, So. Ill. U., 1967; MD, Washington U., St. Louis, 1967; M in Med. Mgmt., Tulane U., 1999. Diplomate Nat. Bd. Med. Examiners, Am. Bd. Internal Medicine, Am. Bd. Cardiovascular Disease, North Am. Soc. Pacing and Electrophysiology, Am. Coll. Physician Execs. Med. intern Union Meml. Hosp., Balt., 1967-68, resident, 1968-69, U. Iowa, Iowa City, 1969-70, cardiology fellow, 1970-72; asst. prof. medicine, dir. coronary care units U. Okla. Health Sci. Ctr., Oklahoma City, 1972-74, asst. clin. prof. medicine, 1974-82, assoc. clin. prof. medicine, 1982-88, clin. prof. medicine, 1988—; chmn. dept. cardiology Bapt. Med. Ctr., 1992-95; pvt. practice Oklahoma City, 1974—. Med. dir. cardiovasc. svcs. Integris Bapt. Med. Ctr., 1993-98; pres. Cardiovasc. Clinic, Oklahoma City, 1987-91, chmn. exec. com., 1987-91; med. dir. Cardiovasc. Imaging Svcs. Corp., Oklahoma City, 1987-92; v.p. Plaza Med. Group, 1992-93; CEO W.H. Oehlert, MD, P.C., 1993—; prin. clin. coord Okla. Found. Med. Quality, 1998-2002, med. clin. coord., 2002—. Author: Arrhythmias, 1973, Cardiovascular Drugs, 1976; contbr. articles to profl. jours. Fellow ACP, Am. Heart Assn. (nat. program com. 1979-82, pres. Okla. affiliate 1985-86, bd. dirs. 1974-88, ACLS nat. affiliate faculty 1987-90, bd. dirs. Oklahoma City 1999—), Am. Coll. Cardiology; mem. AMA, ACP-Am. Soc. Internal Medicine, Nat. Assn. Residents and Interns, Am. Coll. Physician Execs. (cert.), Am. Diabetes Assn. (western coun. 2000-03, ea. coun. 2000-01), Okla. County Med. Assn. (chmn. quality of care com. 1990-91), Okla. State Med. Assn. (trustee 2001—, chmn. Physicians Campaign for Healthier Okla., 2003—04, chmn. CME accreditation rev. com. 2003—04, chmn. CME planning com. 2004—), Okla. City Clin. Soc., Okla. Cardiac Soc. (pres. 1978-79), Osler Soc., Soc. Nuc. Medicine, Okla. Found. for Med. Quality (bd. dirs. 1995-98), Wilderness Med. Soc., Stewart Wolf Soc., Sportman's Club (bd. dirs. 2003—), Phi Eta Sigma, Phi Kappa Phi. Home: 3017 Rock Ridge Pl Oklahoma City OK 73120-5713 Office: Okla Found for Med Quality 5801 Broadway Ext Ste 400 Oklahoma City OK 73118-7484 Office Phone: 405-840-2891. Office Fax: 405-840-1343. E-mail: woehlert@okqio.sdps.org.

OEHME, FREDERICK WOLFGANG, medical researcher, educator; b. Leipzig, Germany, Oct. 14, 1933; arrived in U.S., 1934; s. Friedrich Oswald and Frieda Betha (Wohlgamuth) Oehme; m. Nancy Beth McAdam, Aug. 6, 1960 (div. June 1981); children: Stephen Frederick, Susan Lynn, Deborah Ann, Heidi Beth; m. Pamela Sheryl Ford, Oct. 2, 1981; 1 child, April Virginia. BS in Biol. Sci., Cornell U., 1957, DVM, 1958; MS in Toxicology and Medicine, Kans. State U., 1962; DMV in Pathology, Justus Liebig U., Giessen, Germany, 1964; PhD in Toxicology, U. Mo., 1969. Diplomate Am. Bd. Toxicology, Am. Bd. Vet. Toxicology, Acad. Toxicol. Scis. Resident intern, Large Animal and Ambulatory Clinic Cornell U., 1957-58; gen. practice vet. medicine, 1958-59; from asst. to assoc. prof. medicine Coll. Vet. Medicine Kans. State U., 1959-66, 69-73, dir. comparative toxicology labs., 1969—, prof. toxicology, medicine and physiology Coll. Vet. Medicine, 1974-96, prof. toxicology, pathobiology, medicine and physiology, 1996—; postdoctoral research fellow in toxicology, NIH U. Mo., 1966-69. Cons. FDA, Washington, Ctr. for Vet. Medicine, Rockville, Md.; cons. animal care com. U. Kans., Lawrence, 1969—76, Syntex Corp., Palo Alto, Calif., 1976—77; mem. sci. adv. panel on PBB Gov.'s Office, State of MIch., 1976—77; mem. Coun. for Agrl. Sci. and Tech. Task Force on Toxicity, Toxicology and Environ. Hazard, 1976—83; cons., mem. adv. group on pesticides EPA, Cin., 1977—; expert state and fed. witness; advisor WHO, Geneva; presenter numerous papers to profl. meetings. Reviewer: Toxicology and Applied Pharmacology, Spectroscopy, numerous others. Mem. adv. coun. Cub Scouts Am., Eagle Scouts; mgr., coach Little League Baseball; active PTA; mem. Manhattan Civic Theatre; trustee Manhattan Marlin Swim Team; dir. meet Little Apple Invitational Swim Meet, 1984; mem. coun. Luth. Ch. Am., mem. sr. choir, numerous coms. Recipient Disting. Grad. Faculty award, Kans. State U., 1977—79, Dir.'s Letter of Commendation, FDA, 1983, Kenneth P. DuBois award, Midwest Soc. Toxicology, 1991, Kenneth F. Lampe award, Am. Acad. Toxicology, 1993, John Doull award, Ctrl. States Soc. Toxicology, 1994, medal, Azabu U., 1994, Silver award, Aristotelian U., 1995, others; fellow, Morris Animal Found., 1967—69. Fellow: Am. Acad. Vet. and Comparative Toxicology (past sec.-treas., numerous coms.), Am. Acad. Toxicology (past pres., numerous coms.); mem.: NRC (subcom. on organic contaminants in drinking water, safe drinking water com., adv. ctr. on toxicology assembly life scis. 1976—77, panel on toxicology marine bd., assembly of engring. 1976—79), AVMA (com. on environmentology 1971—73, adv. com. coun. on biol. and therapeuric agts. 1971—74, Samuel Shiedy award 1999), Nat. Ctr. Toxicol. Rsch. (vet. toxicology rep. sci. adv. bd., sci. adv. bd. 1974—77), N.Y. Acad. Scis., Soc. Toxicologic Pathologists, World Fedn. Clin. Toxicology Ctrs. and Poison Control Ctrs. (past pres.), Soc. Toxicology (past pres., numerous coms., Edn. award 2003), Cornell U. Athletic Assn., Manhattan Square Dance Club, Cornell U. Crew Club, Sigma Xi, Phi Zeta, Omega Tau Sigma. Republican. Avocations: historical readings, scientific writings, nature tours and walks, travel. Home: 148 S Dartmouth Dr Manhattan KS 66503-3079 Office: Kans State Univ Comparative Toxicology Labs 1800 Denison Ave Manhattan KS 66506-5660 E-mail: oehme@vet.ksu.edu.

OEHME, REINHARD, physicist, researcher; b. Wiesbaden, Germany, Jan. 26, 1928; arrived in U.S., 1956; s. Reinhold and Katharina (Kraus) O.; m. Mafalda Pisani, Nov. 5, 1952. Dr. rer. nat., U. Goettingen, Germany, 1951; Diplom Physiker, U. Frankfurt am Main, Germany, 1948. Asst. Max Planck Inst. Physics, Goettingen, 1949-53; research asso. Fermi Inst. Nuclear Studies, U. Chgo., 1954-56; mem. faculty dept. physics and Fermi Inst., 1958—, prof. physics, 1964—; mem. Inst. Advanced Studies, Princeton, 1956-58. Vis. prof.

Inst. de Física Teórica, São Paulo, Brazil, 1952-53, U. Md., 1957, U. Vienna, Austria, 1961, Imperial Coll., London, Eng., 1963-64, U. Karlsruhe, Fed. Republic Germany, 1974, 75, 77, U. Tokyo, 1976, 88; vis. scientist Internat. Centre Theoretical Physics, Miramare Trieste, Italy, Brookhaven Nat. Lab., Lawrence Radiation Lab., U. Calif., Berkeley, CERN, Geneva, Switzerland, Max Planck Inst., Munich, Fed. Republic Germany, Rsch. Inst. for Fundamental Physics, Kyoto (Japan) U. Author articles in field, chpts. in books. Guggenheim fellow, 1963-64; recipient Humboldt award, 1974, Japan Soc. for Promotion of Sci. Fellowship awards, 1976, 88. Fellow: Am. Phys. Soc. Achievements include discovery of chargeconjugation non-invariance. Office: U Chgo Enrico Fermi Inst 5640 S Ellis Ave Chicago IL 60637-1433 Office Phone: 773-702-7299. E-mail: oehme@theory.uchicago.edu.

OEHME, WOLFGANG WALTER, landscape architect; b. Chemnitz, Germany, May 18, 1930; came to the U.S., 1957; s. Walter Gustav and Elisabeth Elsa (Neumann) O.; 1 child, Roland. Degree in horticulture, Bitterfeld Trade Sch., 1950; degree in landscape architecture, U. Berlin, 1954. Exch. student Waterer & Sons Nurseries, Bagshot, United Kingdom, 1954-56; landscape architect Baltimore County Planning, Towson, Md., 1958-65, The Rouse Co., Columbia, Md., 1965-66; asst. prof. U. Pa., Phila., 1962-64, U. Ga., Athens, 1965; pvt. practice Balt., 1965-74; CEO Oehme, Van Sweden and Assocs., Inc., Washington, 1974—. Co-author: Bold Romantic Gardens, 1990, Gardening with Water, 1995, Process Architecture, 1996, Gardening with Nature, 1997. Recipient Spl. Resolution for Disting. and dedicated vol. svc. Baltimore County Coun., 2003; mamed to Hall of Fame, Towson Devel. Corp., 1995; named Man of Yr., German Soc. Md., 1996. Fellow Am. Soc. Landscape Architects, mem. Perennial Plant Assn. (Disting. Svc. 1988), Garden Writers Assn. (Quill and Trowel award 1991), Mass. Hort. Soc. (George Robert White medal of honor 2002). Home: 511A W Joppa Rd Baltimore MD 21204-3819 Office: 800 G St SE Washington DC 20003-2816 E-mail: oehme@ovsla.com.

OEHNINGER, SERGIO C. endocrinologist, obstetrician, gynecologist; b. Montevideo, Uruguay, Oct. 24, 1952; s. Carlos F. Oehninger and Elena Gatti; m. Maria L. Fornella, Jan. 16, 1953; children: Sergio F., Juan S., Natalia, Matthew T. MD, U. of the Republic, Montevideo, Uruguay, 1980; MS, Rutgers U., 1981; PhD, U. Stellenbosch, Capetown, South Africa, 2002. Diplomate Uruguay. Prof. dept. of ob-gyn Ea. Va. Med. Sch., Norfolk, Va., 1998—, dir. dept. ob-gyn divsn. reproductive endocrinology, The Jones Inst Reproductive Medicine, 2000—. Vis. prof. U. Stellenbosch, Capetown, South Africa, 1999—2002. Mem. editl. bd. Biology of Reproduction, 2000—02, Reproduction, U.K., 2000—02, Andrologia, Germany, Revista Latinoamerican de Fertilidad y Reproduccion Humana; contbr. articles to profl. jours. Fulbright scholar, Rutgers U., 1980—81. Fellow: Am. Gynecol. Obstet. Soc. (assoc.); mem.: European Soc. Human Reproduction and Embryology (assoc.), Soc. for the Study of Reproduction (assoc.), Soc. for Gynecol. Investigation (assoc.), Am. Soc. Andrology (assoc.), Am. Soc. for Reproductive Medicine (assoc.). Office: Eastern Virginia Medical School 601 Colley Ave Norfolk VA 23507 E-mail: oehninsc@evms.edu.

OEHRLEIN, MARY LOU, architect; b. Clinton, Iowa, Dec. 7, 1950; d. Gilbert Joseph and Virginia Marie (Thrun) O.; m. David Evans Heacock, Jan. 16, 1979. BArch, Iowa State U., 1973. Registered architect, D.C., Md., Va. Staff architect Hist. Am. Bldgs. Survey U.S. Nat. Parks Service, Washington, 1972-74; archtl. conservator Universal Restoration, Inc., Washington, 1975; v.p. Bldg. Conservation Tech., Washington, 1975-83; sr. assoc., dir. Washington office The Ehrenkrantz Group, 1978-83; prin. Oehrlein & Assocs., Washington, 1984—. Reviewer State of Va. Div. Hist. Landmarks, Richmond, 1985-96; commn. fine arts Old Georgetown Bd., 1996—; bd. dirs. Cosmos Club Hist. Preservation Found., Washington, 1987-95. Author handbooks on hist. property and maintenance. Bd. dirs. D.C. Preservation League, 1987-96. Recipient Cert. Appreciation Town of Leesburg, Va., 1987. Fellow AIA (v.p. Washington chpt. 1987, pres. 1988—, numerous awards 1983-99); mem. Assn. Preservation Tech., Constrn. Specifications Inst. (bd. dirs. Washington chpt. 1983-85), Preservation Round Table, Cosmos Club. Office: Oehrlein & Assocs 1350 Connecticut Ave NW Washington DC 20036-1722

OELBERG, DAVID GEORGE, neonatologist, educator, researcher; b. Waukon, Iowa, May 26, 1952; s. George Robert and Elizabeth Abigail (Kepler) O.; m. Debra Penuel, Aug. 4, 1979; children: Anna Elizabeth, Benjamin George. BS with highest honors, Coll. William and Mary, 1974; MD, U. Md., 1978. Diplomate in pediat. and in neonatal-perinatal medicine Am. Bd. Pediat. Intern U. Tex. Med. Br., Galveston, 1978-79, resident, 1979-81, house pediat. staff, 1978-81; postdoctoral fellow in neonatal medicine U. Tex. Med. Sch., Houston, 1981-84, asst. prof. dept. pediat., 1984-90, assoc. prof., 1990-93; assoc. prof. pediat., head perinatal rsch. Ctr. Pediat. Rsch. Ea. Va. Med. Sch., 1993-2001, prof., interim chmn. dept. pediat. Ctr. Pediat. Rsch., 2001—, dir. divsn. neonatal-perinatal medicine. Mem. hosp. staff Hermann Hosp., Houston, 1983-93; physician Crippled Children's Svcs. Program, Houston, 1985-93; mem. hosp. staff Lyndon B. Johnson County Hosp., 1990-93; vis. prof. Wyeth-Ayerst Labs., 1992; med. dir. Office Rsch., Children's Hosp. of King's Daus., 1993—, v.p. for acad. devel., 2001—; med. dirs. Office of Rsch., Sentara-Norfolk Gen. Hosp., 1993—, pres.-elect med. staff. Mem. editl. adv. bd. jour. Neonatal Intensive Care; contbr. articles to profl. jours.; ad hoc reviewer profl. jours.; patentee in field. Physician cons. Parents of Victims of Sudden Infant Death Syndrome, Houston, 1984; chmn. Instl. Animal Care and Use Com. Recipient award in analytical chemistry Am. Chem. Soc., 1974, NIH Clin. Investigator award NHLBI, 1989-94; rsch. grantee Am. Lung Assn., 1989-90, NIH, 1989-94. Fellow Am. Acad. Pediat. NY Acad. Scis.; mem. AMA, NAS, Soc. Exptl. Biology and Medicine, So. Soc. Pediatric Rsch. (councilor, pres.), Soc. Pediatric Rsch. Achievements include development of a method for optical measurement of bilirubin in tissue. Home: 1624 W Little Neck Rd Virginia Beach VA 23452-4720 Office: Ea Va Med Sch Ctr Pediatric Rsch 855 W Brambleton Ave Norfolk VA 23510-1005

OELBERG, ROBERT NATHAN, landscape architect; b. Washington, May 7, 1956; s. George Robert and Elizabeth Abigail (Kapler) Oelberg; m. Katherine Jane Shoffner, Nov. 9, 2002; stepchildren: Forrest Dungan, Katelyn Dungan. BA in Art magna cum laude, Maharishi Internat. U., Fairfield, Iowa, 1981; M.Landscape Arch., U. Va., 1985. Registered landscape architect, N.C. Landscape architect, sr. project mgr. Land Design Inc., Alexandria, Va., 1985-93; owner Robert N. Oelberg ASLA PA, Boone, N.C., 1994-97, 99—; dir. HMR Land Planning and Landscape Arch., Boone, 1997-99. Project landscape architect Heavenly Mountain Resort, Boone, 1994—, mem. archtl. rev. bd. and exec. bd., 1997—. Bd. dirs. Mcoi Devel. Corp., Washington, 1989-91; chmn. Boone Country Dancers. With USMC, 1974-76. DuPont fellow, 1984. Mem. Am. Soc. Landscape Architects. Democrat. Episcopalian. Office: 155 Briar Rose Trl Boone NC 28607-9422 E-mail: rnola@bellsouth.net.

OELGESCHLAGER, GUENTHER KARL, publisher; b. Jersey City, Apr. 19, 1934; s. Herman Wilhelm and Frieda Johanna (Onken) O.; m. Jacqueline L. Braley, July 16, 1962; children: Stacey, Lauren, Amy. BA cum laude, Princeton U., 1958; postgrad., Columbia U., 1959. Nat. sales mgr. Harper & Row Pubs., N.Y.C., 1959-67; dir. coll. div. F.A. Praeger Co., N.Y.C., 1968; v.p., gen. mgr. D.C. Heath & Co., Lexington, Mass., 1969-72; pres., dir. Ballinger Pub. Co., Cambridge, Mass., 1973-78; v.p., dir. J.B. Lippincott Co., Phila., 1973-78; pres. Oelgeschlager, Gunn & Hain, Pubs., Inc., Cambridge, 1979-87; chmn., pres. bd. dirs. Falcon Software Inc., Wellesley, Mass., 1989—. With U.S. Army, 1954-56. Mem. Software Pubs. Assn. Democrat. Episcopalian. Home: 245 Merriam St Weston MA 02493-1350 Office: PO Box 154 Weston MA 02493-0001 E-mail: karl@falconsoftware.com.

OELMAN, ROBERT SCHANTZ, retired manufacturing executive; b. Dayton, Ohio, June 9, 1909; s. William Walter and Edith (Schantz) O.; m. Mary Coolidge, Oct. 17, 1936; children: Bradford Coolidge, Robert Schantz, Jr., Kathryn Peirce, Martha Forrer. AB summa cum laude, Dartmouth Coll., 1931, MA, 1963, LL.D. (hon.), 1981; postgrad., U. Vienna, 1931-32; H.H.D. (hon.), U. Dayton, 1959; LL.D. (hon.), Miami U., Oxford, Ohio, 1960, Wright State U., 1976; L.H.D. (hon.), Wilmington Coll. (Ohio), 1965. With NCR Corp., Dayton, 1933-80, asst. to pres., 1942-45, v.p., 1946-50, exec. v.p., 1950-57, pres., 1957-62, chmn., pres., 1962-64, chmn., 1962-74, chmn. exec. com., 1974-80, dir., 1948-80; ret., 1980. Trustee Dartmouth Coll., 1961-76; Mem. Bus. Council, 1965—; chmn. bd. trustees Wright State U., 1961-76; bd. dirs. Miami Conservancy, 1967-79, pres., 1975-79; chmn. Air Force Mus. Found., Dayton, 1970-80; trustee C.F. Kettering Med. Center, 1971-80; ind. dir. tournament policy bd. PGA Tour, Ponte Vedra, Fla., 1974-83, chmn., 1978-83. Mem. Country Club of Fla., Ocean Club of Fla., Augusta Nat. Club (Ga.), Delray Beach Yacht Club.

OEMLER, AUGUSTUS, JR., astronomer, educator; b. Savannah, Ga., Aug. 15, 1945; s. Augustus and Isabelle Redding (Clarke) O.; children: W. Clarke, Bryan S. AB, Princeton U., 1969; MS, Calif. Inst. Tech., 1970, PhD, 1974. Postdoctoral assoc. Kitt Peak Nat. Obs., Tucson, 1974-75; instr. astronomy Yale U., New Haven, 1975-77, asst. prof., 1977-79, assoc. prof., 1979-83, prof., 1983-96, chmn. dept., 1988-96; dir. Carnegie Obs., Pasadena, Calif., 1996—2003, staff astronomer, dir. emeritus, 2003—. Contbr. articles to profl. jours. Alfred P. Sloan fellow, 1978-80 Mem. Am. Astronom. Soc., Internat. Astronom. Union Republican. Roman Catholic. Office: Carnegie Obs 813 Santa Barbara St Pasadena CA 91101-1232

OERDING, JAMES BRYAN, military educator; b. Roseburg, Oreg., June 21, 1935; s. William Arthur and Naomi Eileen Oerding. BS, U.S. Mil. Acad., 1960; MA, U. Fla., 1975-77; candidate in philosophy, U. Calif., Davis, 1978-80. Cert. community coll. tchr., Calif. Commd. 2nd lt. U.S. Army, 1960, advanced through grades to maj., various assignments, officer 7th Spl. Forces Group, 1973-74, research specialist 1st Psychol. Ops. Bn., 1975-78; internat. plans & tng. specialist U.S. Army Western Command Hdqrs., Ft. Shafter, 1980-85; internat. security assistance analyst U.S. Army, Washington, 1985-86, dir. Army sr. fellowship program, 1986-89; comdt. U.S. Army Mgmt. Engring. Coll., Rock Island, Ill., 1989-91, dep. for strategic plans, 1991-92, regional rep. East Coast D.M.E.C., 1992-94; ret., 1994. Cons. on travel and mgmt. Escapes Unltd., Greencastle, Pa., 1988—; cruise lectr., 1994-. Regents' fellow U. Calif. at Davis, 1978, Chancellor's fellow, 1980. Mem. Spl. Forces Assn. (life), Am. Indochina Vets. Legion (N.C. state chmn. 1975-76), VFW, Disabled Am. Vets. Republican. Avocations: stamp collecting/philately, writing. Office Phone: 717-597-2484. E-mail: escapes_unlimited@hotmail.com.

OERTEL, GOETZ KUNO HEINRICH, physicist, professional science administrator; b. Stuhm, Germany, Aug. 24, 1934; arrived in US, 1957; s. Egon F.K. and Margarete W. (Wittek) O.; m. Brigitte Beckmann, June 17, 1960; children: Ines M.H. Oertel Downing, Carsten K.R. Abitur, Robert Mayer, Heilbronn, Fed. Republic Germany, 1953; vordiplom, U. Kiel, Fed. Republic Germany, 1956; PhD, U. Md., 1963. Aerospace engr. Langley Ctr. NASA, Hampton, Va., 1963-68, chief solar physics Washington, 1968-75, policy analyst for sci. advisor to Pres. and Office Mgmt. and Budget, 1974-75; head astronomy divsn. NSF, Washington, 1975; dir. def. and civilian nuc. waste programs U.S. Dept. Energy, Washington, 1975-83; acting mgr. sav. river ops. office Aiken, S.C., 1983-84; dep. mgr. ops. office Albuquerque, 1984-85; dep. asst. sec. of energy for EH, Washington, 1985-86; pres., CEO Assn. Univs. for Rsch. in Astronomy, Inc., Washington, 1986-99; also bd. dirs. Assn. Univs. for Rsch. in Astronomy, Inc. (AURA, Inc.), Washington, disting. advisor, 2000—. Cons. Los Alamos Lab., N.Mex., 1987-92, Westinghouse Electric, 1988-99, Lampadia Found., Fundacion Andes of Santiago de Chile, Vitae Found. Sao Paulo, Brazil; bd. dirs. Inst. for Sci. and Soc., Ellensburg, Wash., IUE Corp.; mem. bd. internat. sci. orgns. NRC; chmn. bd. Sch. of Computational Sci., George Mason U., 2002-03; mem. U.S. Com. for CODATA, 1993-2003, chmn. 1997-2000; U.S. nat. del. CODATA ICSU, 1999-2003; mem. peer rev. com. ASME, 1996—; cons. conicyt, Govt. of Chile, 2000-, VITAE Found., Brazil, 2001-, Fundacion Andes, Chile, 2000-; chmn., bd. dirs. Ctr. of Excellence for Hazardous Materials Mgmt., Carlsbad, N.Mex.; nat. assoc. Nat. Acads. Wash., 2003. Contbr. articles to profl. jours. Fulbright grantee, 1957. Fellow AAAS; mem. Am. Phys. Soc., Am. Astron. Soc., Internat. Astron. Union, N.Y. Acad. Scis., Internat. U. Exch., Inc. (bd. dirs.), Cosmos Club, Sigma Xi. Lutheran. Achievements include patents in field. Avocations: exercise, chess, computing, genealogy. Home: 8833 Watts Mine Ter Potomac MD 20854-5439 Office: PO Box 388 Cabin John MD 20818-0388 E-mail: goetz@oertel.org.

OERTEL, YOLANDA CASTILLO, pathologist, educator, diagnostician; b. Lima, Peru, Dec. 14, 1938; came to U.S., 1966; d. Leonardo A. and Dalila (Ramirez) C.; m. James E. Oertel, Sept. 24, 1969. MD, Cayetano Heredia, Lima, 1964; Dr. honoris causa, U. Peruana Cayetano Heredia, 1999. Diplomate Am. Bd. Pathology (mem. test com. for cytopathology 1988-94). Internat. postdoctoral fellowship NIH, Bethesda, Md., 1966-68; asst. prof. pathology Sch. Medicine George Washington U., Washington, 1975-78, assoc. prof., 1978-84, prof., 1984-98, prof. emerita, 1998—. Adj. prof. pathology and lab. medicine MCP Hahnemann U. Sch. Medicine; cons. Registry Cytology Armed Forces Inst. Pathology, Washington, 1981—. Author: Fine Needle Aspiration of the Breast, 1987; contbr. chpts. to books, articles to profl. jours. Decorated comendador de la Orden Cayetano Heredia, 1999; recipient Francisco A. Camino prize Peruvian Med. Assn., 1965, cert. Meritorious Svc. Armed Forces Inst. Pathology, 1974; named Disting. Alumna Cayetano Heredia Med. Sch., 1989. Mem. Assn. Mil. Surgeons (hon.), Colombian Soc. Pathology (hon.), Argentinian Soc. Pathology (hon.), Peruvian Soc. Pathologists (hon.), Argentinian Soc. Cytopathology, (hon.), Am. Soc. Cytopathology, Internat. Acad. Pathology, Soc. Latinoamericana Patologia, Am. Soc. Clin. Pathologists (coun. on cytopathology 1982-88), Coll. Am. Pathologists, Arthur Purdy Stout Soc. Surg. Pathologists, Am. Thyroid Assn., L.Am. Thyroid Soc. Avocations: reading, opera. Office: Washington Hosp Ctr Pathology Dept Washington Cancer Inst 110 Irving St NW Washington DC 20010-2975 Office Phone: 202-877-2740. Office Fax: 202-877-0197. Business E-Mail: Yolanda.C.Oertel@medstar.net.

OERTER, CYNTHIA LYNN, medical technologist; b. Waupaca, Wis., Mar. 8, 1948; d. Lavern Charles and Geraldine Mae (Huffcutt) Trinrud; m. Gregory Van Oerter, June 8, 1968; children: Nathan, Justin. BS, U. Wis., Oshkosh, 1971; MS, Cardinal Stritch Coll., 1993. Cert. Am. Soc. Clin. Pathologists. Med. technologist Mercy Med. Ctr., Oshkosh, Wis., 1970-76, Iola (Wis.) Hosp., 1978-86, wellness cons., 1985-86, Riverside Med. Ctr., Waupaca, Wis., 1986-93, med. technologist, hematology supr., insvc. coord., cons., 1987-95; pres. Pro Health Consul, Inc., Waupaca, Wis., 1994—; bus. ptnr., adminstr. Garden Park House, 1994—2000, owner, adminstr., 2000—; owner Back Door Bakery, 2003—, Secret Garden Cafe, 2003—. Tchr. Fox Valley Coll., Appleton, Wis., 1986, 87; organizer Overeaters Anonymous, Iola, 1985-89; owner Green Fountain Inn, 1995—. Mem. parent's com. for gifted and talented Waupaca Sch. Sys., 1984, charter mem. edn. employment coun., 1989-92, mem. adv. com. guidance program K-12, 1992; vol. Nat. Wellness Inst., 1986-97, Am. Lung Assn., 1986-87; tchr. smokeless program Am. Inst. Preventative Medicine, 1988-93; com. mem. Main St. Design, 1999-2001. Mem. NAFE, Nat. Platform Assn., Am. Sch. Health Assn. (com. mem.), Waupace C. of C. (mem. tourism com. 2002—), Rotary (sec. 1996-98, bd. dirs. 1995—, pres. elect 1999-2000, pres. 2000-2001, Athena award 2003). Republican. Lutheran. Avocations: gardening, gourmet cooking, sailing, bible study, hobby farm. E-mail: greenfountain@gglbbs.com.

OESTERLE, CAROLYN SCHERER, pediatric ophthalmologist; b. Detroit, Apr. 12, 1949; d. Ernest Francis and Margaret (Palm) Scherer; m. Eric Adam Oesterle, Sept. 15, 1973; children: Adam Clark, Allison Margaret. BS in Chemistry with honors, U. Mich., 1971; postgrad., U. Wis., 1971-72; MD with distinction, Northwestern U., Chgo., 1977. Am. Bd. Ophthalmology. Intern Evanston (Ill.) Hosp., 1977-78; resident in ophthalmology U. Ill. Eye and Ear Infirmary, Chgo., 1978-81; fellow in pediat. ophthalmology Childrens Hosp. Nat. Med. Ctr., Washington, 1981-82; ophthalmologist Evanston Ophthalmologists, 1982-83; pediat. ophthalmologist Wheaton (Ill.) Eye Clinic, 1983—; attending physician Ctrl. DuPage Hosp., Winfield, Ill., 1983—; assoc. in ophthalmology Northwestern U. Med. Sch., Chgo., 1984—. Lectr. in organic chemistry U. Mich., 1973. Contbr. articles to profl. jours. James B. Angell scholar, 1969. Fellow Am. Acad. Ophthalmology; mem. AMA, Am. Assn. Pediat. Ophthalmology and Strabismus, Am. Assn. Ophthalmology, DuPage Med. Soc., Ill. Assn. Ophthalmology, Phi Beta Kappa, Phi Lambda Delta, Alpha Omega Alpha. Home: 645 Lake Rd Glen Ellyn IL 60137-4249 Office: Wheaton Eye Clinic 2015 N Main St Wheaton IL 60187-3190

OESTERLE, ERIC ADAM, lawyer; b. Lafayette, Ind., Dec. 2, 1948; s. Eric Clark and Germaine Dora (Seelye) O.; m. Carolyn Anne Scherer, Sept. 16, 1973; children: Adam Clark, Allison Margaret. BS, U. Mich., 1970, JD, 1973. Bar: Ill. 1973, U.S. Dist. Ct. (no. dist.) Ill. 1973, U.S. Ct. Appeals (7th cir.) 1987, U.S. Supreme Ct. 1986. Assoc. Sonnenschein, Carlin, Nath & Rosenthal, Chgo., 1973-80; ptnr. Sonnenschein Nath & Rosenthal, Chgo., 1980—. Major gifts com. U. Mich. Law Sch., 2002—. Mem. ABA, Ill. Bar Assn., Chgo. Bar Assn. Home: 645 Lake Rd Glen Ellyn IL 60137-4249 Office: Sonnenschein Nath & Rosenthal 8000 Sears Tower 233 S Wacker Dr Ste 8000 Chicago IL 60606-6491 E-mail: eoesterle@sonnenschein.com.

OESTERLING, THOMAS OVID, retired pharmaceutical executive; b. Butler, Pa., Mar. 6, 1938; s. Victor Kenneth and Marjorie Gertrude (Oswald) O.; m. Janet Westrick, Dec. 30, 1960 (div. 1983); children: Thomas, Jennifer, Daniel; m. Cynthia Adler, 1984 (div. 1987). BS, Ohio State U., 1962, MS, 1964, PhD, 1966. Rsch. assoc., rsch. head Upjohn Co., Kalamazoo, 1966-76; dir. R&D dermatol. divsn. Johnson & Johnson Corp., New Brunswick, N.J., 1976-78, dir. pharm. R&D, 1978-79; v.p. med. products R&D Mallinckrodt, Inc., St. Louis, 1979-83; sr. v.p. R&D Collaborative Rsch. Inc., Bedford, Mass., 1984-86, pres., 1986-89; chmn., pres., CEO Gliatech Inc., Cleve., 1989-2000; ret. Mem. faculty Arden House Conf. on Stability Evaluation Pharm. Dosage Forms, 1979 Contbr. numerous sci. articles to profl. jours.; patentee in field. Recipient Disting. Alumni award Ohio State U. Coll. Pharmacy, 1982; Parke Davis rsch. grantee, 1962-64; Am. Found. for Pharm. Edn. fellow, 1964-66 Mem. Am. Chem. Soc., Soc. Nuclear Medicine, Acad. Pharm. Scis., Soc. for Neurosci.

OESTERREICHER, JAMES E. former department stores executive; b. 1941; BS, Mich. State U., 1964. With J. C. Penney Co. Inc., 1964—; pres. Western Region J. C. Penney Co. Inc., 1987-88, exec. v.p., 1988-94; chmn., CEO J.C. Penney Co. Inc., 1994—2000. Dir. Brinker Internat., The Dial Corp., TXU. Office: Brinker International 6820 LBJ Freeway Dallas TX 75240-6515

OESTING, DAVID W. lawyer; b. Chgo., Aug. 6, 1944; AB, Earlham Coll., 1967; JD, Wash. U., 1970. Bar: Wash. 1970, Alaska 1981. Ptnr. in charge of Anchorage Office Davis Wright Tremaine, Anchorage, 1980—. Editor-in-chief Wash. U. Law Quarterly, 1969-70. Mem. ABA, Am. Coll. Trial Lawyers, Wash. State Bar Assn., Alaska Bar Assn., Anchorage Bar Assn., Order of Coif. Office: Davis Wright Tremaine 701 W 8th Ave Ste 800 Anchorage AK 99501-3467 Office Phone: 907-257-5300. Business E-Mail: daveoesting@dwt.com.

OESTMANN, MARY JANE, retired senior radiation specialist; b. Chgo., May 22, 1924; d. Charles Edward and Harriet Evelyn (Stoltenberg) O. BA in Math, Chemistry with honors, Denison U., 1946; MS, U. Wis., 1948, PhD, 1954; DSc., Denison U., 1975. Research chemist Inst. for Atom Energy, Oslo, 1954—55; vis. scientist AB Atom Energy, Stockholm, 1955—56; vis. prof. chem. dept. U. Iowa, Iowa City, 1957; sr. scientist Battelle Meml. Inst., Columbus, Ohio, 1957—61; assoc. chemist Argonne Nat. Lab, Ill., 1961—71; environ. project mgr. U.S. AEC, Washington, 1971—75; sr. radiation specialist U.S. Nuclear Regulatory Commn., Glen Ellyn, Ill., 1975—87; ret. Bd. dirs. U. Wis.-Madison Alumni Assn. of the So. Lakes, 1992—. Contbr. numerous articles to scientific jours. Mem. planning and zoning commn. Town of Burlington, 1992--; bd. trustees Plymouth Congl. UCC Ch. Burlington, 1993-96. Recipient Internat. Women's Yr. award Nuclear Regulatory Commn., 1975, Dist. Alumni citation Denison U., 1971. Fellow Am. Inst. Chemists, Am. Nuclear Soc. (bd. dirs. 1983-86); mem. Am. Chem. Soc., Inst. Environ. Sci. and Tech. (sr. mem.), Health Physics Soc. (sec.-treas. Midwest chpt. 1978, exec. com. 1983-86), N.Y. Acad. Scis., Wis. Acad. Scis., Arts and Letters, Wis. Fedn. Rep. Women (1st Congl. Dist.), Nat. Parks Conservation Assn., Nat. Conservancy, Burlington Woman's Club (treas., chair scholarship com. 1993—), Browns Lake Yacht Club (Burlington), Rep. Women Racine County-West Club (v.p. 1992-93, pres. 1994—, Anita Hunt award, Bovay award), Sigma Xi, Phi Beta Kappa, Sigma Delta Epsilon, Iota Sigma Pi. Home: 2520 Cedar Dr Burlington WI 53105-9174

OESTREICH, CHARLES HENRY, retired university president; b. Columbus, Ohio, June 8, 1932; s. Henry F. and Martha (Schwartz) O.; m. Rhoda J. Haseley, Aug. 26, 1957; children: Martha, Mary, David. BS, Capital U., 1954; MS, Ohio U., 1956, PhD, 1961; LLD, Capital U., 1986. Instr. chemistry Va. Mil. Inst., 1956-57, Capital U., Columbus, 1960-62, asst. prof., 1962-64, assoc. prof., 1965-69; acad. dean Tex. Luth. U., Seguin, 1969-76, interim pres., 1976-77, pres., 1977-95, pres. emeritus, 1995—. Postdoctoral rsch. fellow Vanderbilt U., 1965-66 Bd. dirs., past pres. Mid-Tex. Symphony; v.p., bd. dirs. St. Luke's Health Ministries; v.p. ECLA Luth. Men in Mission. Mem. Goud County Geneal. Soc. (v.p.), Rotary (past pres. Seguin). Home and Office: 2269 S Abbey Loop New Braunfels TX 78130-8965 Fax: 830-625-8306. E-mail: charleso@axs4u.net.

OETJEN, DAVID L. (JON DAVID DOUGLAS), writer, film producer; b. Washington, Iowa, May 23, 1938; s. Walter Theodor Oetjen and Alyce Marie Peterson. BA, U. of Iowa, 1960. Prodr. Home Shopping Network, Clearwater, Fla.; broadcast prodn. dir. Barlow/Johnson Advt., Syracuse, Albany, Buffalo, Springfield, 1969—73; dir. of promotion, advt. mgr. Sta. WTVH-TV, Meredith Corp., Syracuse, NY, 1977—91. Prodr.: (TV series, television) Dari-Lean "Magic", 1971 (Chgo. Film Festival, 1971); author: (novels) Cody, A Boy's Odyssey, 2002, Place Out of Time, 2003. Citizen's adv. Bayfront Med. Ctr., St. Petersburg, 1997—99; advisor Office of the Mayor, Syracuse, 1988—91, Syracuse (N.Y.) Symphony, 1988—90; prodr. Bring Them Home Alive-Missing Childrens' Clearing House, Tampa Bay. Recipient Silver Shaker award for Winterfest, CNY-Pub. Rels. Soc. Am., 1989, 1st Pl. TV Promotion award for Gimmie Five!, Syracuse Advt. Club, 1988, 1st Pl. TV Promotion award for Tell 'Em, 1989, Media award, CNY Parks and Recreation Soc., 1985, Award of Appreciation for svc. as dir. of broadcast promotion and publicity, AAU/USA Jr. Olympics, 1987. Mem.: Broadcast Promotion Assn., Village Writers' Group. Home: 1617 Duran Dr The Villages FL 32162 Personal E-mail: dleeo@earthlink.net.

OETTGEN, HERBERT FRIEDRICH, physician; b. Cologne, Germany, Nov. 22, 1923; came to U.S., 1958; s. Peter and Minna (Kaul) O.; m. Trudi Hesberg, Feb. 16, 1957; children: Hans Christoph, Joerg Peter, Anne Barbara. MD, U. Cologne, 1951. Diplomate Bd. Internal Medicine, Fed. Republic of Germany. Resident in pathology City Hosp., Cologne, 1952-54, resident in medicine, 1955-58; fellow Meml. Sloan-Kettering Cancer Ctr., N.Y.C., 1958-62, assoc. to assoc. mem., 1963-69, mem., 1972—, attending physician, 1971—; prof. medicine Cornell U. Med. Coll., N.Y.C., 1972—. Assoc. dir. Cancer Rsch. Inst., N.Y.C., 1985—. Author over 350 publs. in hematology, cancer rsch., immunology and clin. oncology. Recipient award for cancer rsch. Wilhelm Warner Found., Hamburg, Fed. Republic Germany, 1970, Lisec-Artz award for cancer rsch. Friedrich Wilhelm U., Bonn, Fed. Republic of Germany, 1982. Presbyterian. Avocations: violin, woodworking. Home: 48 Overlook Dr New Canaan CT 06840-6825 Office: Meml Sloan-Kettering Cancer Ctr 1275 York Ave New York NY 10021-6094 Business E-Mail: oettgenh@mskcc.org, hoettgen@licr.org.

OETTINGER, ANTHONY GERVIN, mathematician, educator; b. Nuremberg, Germany, Mar. 29, 1929; came to U.S., 1941, naturalized, 1947; s. Albert and Marguerite (Bing) O.; m. Marilyn Tanner, June 20, 1954; children: Douglas, Marjorie. AB, Harvard U., 1951, PhD, 1954; Henry fellow, U. Cambridge, Eng., 1951-52; Litt.D. (hon.), U. Pitts., 1984. Mem. faculty Harvard, 1955—, asso. prof. applied math., 1960-63, prof. linguistics, 1963-75, Gordon McKay prof. applied math., 1963—, chmn. program on info. resources policy, 1972—, mem. faculty of govt., 1973—, prof. info. resources policy, 1975—. Mem. command control comm. and intelligence bd. Dept. Navy, 1978-83; mem. sci. adv. group Def. Comm. Agy., 1979-90; chmn. bd. visitors Joint Mil. Intelligence Coll., 1986—; chmn., dir. Ctrl. Intelligence

Sci., 1994—; cons. Arthur D. Little, Inc., 1956-80, Office Sci. and Tech., Exec. Office of Pres., 1960-73, Bellcomm, Inc., 1963-68, Sys. Devel. Corp., 1965-68, Nat. Security Coun., Exec. Office of Pres., 1975-81, Pres.'s Fgn. Intelligence Adv. Bd., 1981-90; chmn. Computer Sci. and Engring. Bd., Nat. Acad. Scis., 1968-73; mem. Mass. Cmty. Antenna TV Commn., 1972-79, chmn., 1975-79; mem. rsch. adv. bd. Com. for Econ. Devel., 1975-79; trustee Babbage Inst., 1991—; panel mem. Naval Studies Bd. NAS/NRC, 1993-95; mem. banking and fin. team Pres.' Commn. on Critical Infrastructure Protection, 1998; mem. Def. Sci. Bd., 2003—. Author: A Study for the Design of an Automatic Dictionary, 1954, Automatic Language Translation: Lexical and Technical Aspects, 1960, Run Computer Run: The Mythology of Educational Innovation, 1969, High and Low Politics: Information Resources for the 80s, 1977, Behind the Telephone Debates, 1988, Mastering the Changing Information World, 1993; editor: Proc. of a Symposium on Digital Computers and Their Applications, 1962; contbr. chpts. to The Information Resources Policy Handbook: Research for the Information Age, 1999. Fellow Am. Acad. Arts and Scis., AAAS, IEEE, Assn. Computing Machinery (mem. coun. 1961-68, chmn. com. U.S. Govt. Rels. 1964-66, editor computational linguistics sect. Commn. 1964-66, pres. 1966-68); mem. Soc. Indsl. and Applied Math. (mem. coun. 1963-67), Coun. on Fgn. Rels., Phi Beta Kappa, Sigma Xi. Clubs: Cosmos (Washington); Harvard (N.Y.C.). Home: 65 Elizabeth Rd Belmont MA 02478-3819 Office: Harvard U Maxwell Dworkin 125 33 Oxford St Cambridge MA 02138-2901 E-mail: anthony@deas.harvard.edu.

OETTINGER, JULIAN ALAN, lawyer, pharmaceutical executive; BS, U. Ill., 1961; JD, Northwestern U., 1964. Bar: Ill. 1964. Atty. SEC, 1964-67, Walgreen Co., Deerfield, Ill., 1967-72, sr. atty., 1972-78, dir. law, 1978-89, v.p., gen. counsel, corp. sec., 1989-2000, sr. v.p., gen. counsel, corp. sec., 2000—. Office: Walgreen Co 200 Wilmot Rd Deerfield IL 60015-4616*

OETTINGER, REGINA MARIE, music educator; b. Greenville, Pa., Jan. 13, 1979; d. Paul Wesley and Carolyn Lee Bell; m. Philip Lee OEttinger, July 1, 2000; 1 child, Devon Tyler. BA, Alleghany Wesleyan Coll., 2001. Tchr. piano pvt. opractice, Salem, Ohio, 1997—98; dietary aide, housekeeper Essex of Salem, 1999—2001; tchr. music Liberty Bible Acad., 2001—03. Mem.: Ohio Music Tchrs. Assn. Republican. Avocations: camping, fishing, gardening.

O'FARRELL, MARK THEODORE, religious organization administrator; b. Milw., Apr. 13, 1948; s. Theodore Wolfred and Ernestine (Shelhammer) O.; m. Phillis Gilley, Sept. 18, 1948; children: Gwen, Kevin. BA, Columbia Bible Coll., 1970; DD, Toccan Falls Coll., 1996. Asst. pastor 1st Alliance Ch., Macon, Ga., 1970-71, sr. pastor Port Charlotte, Fla., 1981-86, Belle Glade (Fla.) Alliance Ch., 1971-81; asst. to dist. supt., ext. dir. Southeastern Dist. of Christian and Missionary Alliance, Orlando, Fla., 1986-93, dist. supt., 1993—. Recipient Spiritual Aims award Kiwanis. Home: Christian & Missionary Alliance Southeastern District 2450 Donaldson Dr Orlando FL 32812 Office: PO Box 720430 Orlando FL 32872-0430 E-mail: sedistrict@cmalliance.org.

O'FARRELL, TIMOTHY JAMES, psychologist, educator; b. Lancaster, Ohio, Apr. 22, 1946; s. Robert James and Helen Loretta (Tooill) O'F.; m. Jayne Sara Talmage, May 19, 1973; 1 child, Colin. BA, U. Notre Dame, 1968; PhD in Psychology, Boston U., 1975. Instr. Harvard U. Med. Sch., Boston, 1977-82, asst. prof., 1982-86, assoc. prof., 1986-2000, prof., 2000—. Chief Harvard Families and Addiction Program, 1991—; staff psychologist VA Med. Ctr., Brockton, Mass., 1975-78, dir. Alcoholism Clinic, 1978-83, dir. Counseling for Alcoholics' Marriages Project, 1978—, chief Alcohol and Family Studies Lab., 1981-91; chief, Harvard Families and Addiction Program, 1991—; assoc. chief psychology svc., 1988—; VA predoctoral grantee, 1969-72; rsch. grantee VA, 1978—, Nat. Inst. on Alcohol Abuse and Alcoholism, 1991—, Smithers Found., 1991—, Guggenheim Found., 1993-94. Author: Alcohol and Sexuality, 1983, Treating Alcohol Problems: Marital and Family Interventions, 1993, Accreditation Guide for Substance Abuse Treatment Programs, 1997; editl. bd. numerous scientific jours.; contbr. articles to profl. jours. Fellow APA, Behavior Therapy and Rsch. Soc.; mem. NIAAA (psychosocial rsch. rev. group 1989-93), Assn. Advancement Behavior Therapy, Eastern Psychol. Assn. Home: 14 Wadsworth Ln Duxbury MA 02332-5116 Office: VA Med Ctr 116B1 Brockton MA 02301 E-mail: timothy_ofarrell@hms.harvard.edu.

OFFENBERGER, ALLAN ANTHONY, electrical engineering educator; b. Wadena, Sask., Can., Aug. 11, 1938; s. Ivy Viola (Hagglund) O.; m. Margaret Elizabeth Patterson, Apr. 12, 1963; children: Brian, Gary. BS, U. B.C., 1962, MS, 1963; PhD, MIT, 1968. Asst. prof. U. Alta., Edmonton, Can., 1968-70, assoc. prof., 1970-75, prof., 1975-95, prof. emeritus, 1996—. Cons. Lawrence Livermore (Calif.) Nat. Lab., 1996-2003, numerous univs., govts. and industries; vis. prof. U.K. Atomic Energy Agy., Abingdon, Oxon, Eng., 1975-76; project dir. Laser Fusion Project, Edmonton, 1984-91; mem. strategic adv. com. Nat. Fusion Program, Atomic Energy of Can. Ltd., Chalk River, Ont., 1987-96; vis. prof. U. Oxford, U.K., 1992, U. Osaka, Japan, 2000; served on several execs., bds. and sci. adv. and rsch. grant committees; hosted internat. scholars; lect. at more than 100 internat. insts. and confs. Mem. editorial bd. Laser and Particle Beams, 1987—; contbr. over 150 sci. articles on lasers and plasma physics. Killam Rsch. fellow Can. Coun., 1980-82. SERC rsch. fellow, Eng., 1992. Mem. Can. Assn. Physicists (exec. officer, v.p. elect 1987-88, pres. 1989-90), Am. Phys. Soc., Sigma Xi. Achievements include establishing a major center for high power laser research and development (particularly krypton fluoride lasers) for fusion energy and other applications. Home: 412 Lessard Dr Edmonton AB Canada T6M 1A7 Office: U Alta Dept Elec Computer Engring Edmonton AB Canada T6G 2V4 E-mail: aao@ece.ualberta.ca.

OFFER, STUART JAY, lawyer; b. Seattle, June 2, 1943; m. Judith Spitzer, Aug. 29, 1970; children: Rebecca, Kathryn. BA, U. Wash., 1964; LLB, Columbia U., 1967. Bar: D.C. 1968, U.S. Tax Ct. 1968, Calif. 1972. Atty., advisor U.S. Tax Ct., Washington, 1967-68; assoc. Morrison & Foerster, LLP, San Francisco, 1972-76, ptnr., 1976—. Trustee Am. Tax Policy Inst. Served as capt. U.S. Army, 1968-72. Mem. ABA (chmn. taxation sect., corp. tax com. 1991-92, coun. dir. 1995-98, vice chmn. adminstrn. 1998-2000), Internat. Fiscal Assn. (regent), Am. Coll. Tax Counsel. Office: Morrison & Foerster LLP 425 Market St San Francisco CA 94105-2482 Office Phone: 415-268-7052. Business E-Mail: soffer@mofo.com.

OFFERMAN, JOSE ANTONIO DONO, professional baseball player; b. San Pedor de Macoris, Dominican Republic, Nov. 8, 1968; Student, Colegio Biblico Cristiano, Dominican Republic. Shortstop L.A. Dodgers, 1990-96, Kansas City Royals, 1996-99; infielder Boston Red Sox, 1999—. Selected to N.L All-Star Team, 1995. Office: Boston Red Sox Fenway Park 4 Yawkey Way Boston MA 02215-3496

OFFERMANN, PETER, financial executive; b. Teaneck, N.J., Dec. 6, 1944; s. Henry and Theresa O.; m. Kathleen Joanne Spray, Aug. 31, 1968; children: Thomas Peter, Christine Lynne. BA, Rutgers State U., 1966. Mng. dir. B.T. Securities (a divsn. of Bankers Trust Co.), N.Y.C., 1968-94; exec. v.p., chief fin. officer TLC Beatrice Internat. Holdings, N.Y.C., 1994-99; chmn. bd., CEO ATC Group Svcs., Woburn, Mass., 2000—. Bd. dirs. Jan Bell Mktg., Inc. Sunrise, Fla., Nat. Auto Fin., Inc. Boca Raton, Fla. Mem. Nat. Assn. Corp. Dirs., Family Firm Inst., Turnaround Mgmt. Assn. Roman Catholic. Avocations: aviation, flying. Home: 154 N Mountain Ave Montclair NJ 07042-2350 Office: ATC Group Svcs 600 W Cummings Park Ste 6000 Woburn MA 01801

OFFIT, MORRIS WOLF, investment advisory executive; b. Balt., Jan. 22, 1937; s. Michael and Rhea (Wolf) O.; m. Nancy Silverman, Nov. 26, 1959; children: Ned S., Daniel W. BA in History, Johns Hopkins U., 1957, LHD (hon.), 1996; MBA in Fin., U. Pa., 1959. V.p. investment dept. Mercantile Safe Deposit and Trust, Balt., 1960—68; gen. ptnr. Salomon Bros. Inc., N.Y.C., 1968-80; pres. Julius Baer Securities, N.Y.C., 1980-82; now CEO Offit Hall Capital Mgmt. LLC, 2002—; CEO Offit Assoc. Inc., NYC, 1983—2001. Trustee, former chmn. bd. trustees Johns Hopkins U.; chmn. adv. coun. Nitze Sch. Advanced Internat. Studies; trustee Jewish Mus., former chmn.; trustee Jewish Theol. Sem., Thirteen-WNET, United Jewish Appeal Fedn. N.Y., Am. Jewish Com. Mem. Coun. on Fgn. Rels. Office: Offit Hall Capital Mgmt LLC 65 E 55th St New York NY 10022

OFFIT, SIDNEY, writer, educator; b. Balt., Oct. 13, 1928; s. Barney and Lillian (Cohen) O.; m. Avodah Crindell Komito, Aug. 8, 1952; children: Kenneth, Michael Robert. BA, Johns Hopkins U., 1950; DHL (hon.), L.I. U., 1999. Editorial staff Mercury Publs., N.Y.C., 1952-53, Macfadden Publs., N.Y.C., 1953-54; contbg. editor Baseball mag., Washington, 1955-58; faculty NYU, 1964—2002; assoc. editor Intellectual Digest, 1970-72, sr. editor, 1972-74; adj. prof. creative writing NYU, 1977—2003. Lectr. creative writing New Sch. U., 1965—; curator George Polk Awards for Journalism, 1977—; commentator Channel 5 TV, NYC, 1975-85, Channel 11 TV, 1992. Author: He Had it Made, 1959, The Other Side of the Street, 1962, Soupbone, 1963, Topsy Turvey, 1965, The Adventure of Homer Fink, 1966, The Boy Who Made a Million, 1968; short stories Not All the Girls Have Million Dollar Smiles, 1971; Only a Girl Like You, 1972, What Kind of Guy Do You Think I Am?, 1977, Memoir of the Bookie's Son, 1995; series sports books for boys, 1961-65, also essays, revs., short stories; book editor: Politics Today, 1978-80. Selection com. Dist. Sch. Bd., NYC, 1968; exec. bd. Lexington Democratic Club, 1957-60, NY Dem. County Com., 1966-; chmn. 19th Precinct Cmty. Coun. NYC, 1964-80. Recipient Disting. Alumni award Valley Forge Mil. Acad., 1961, Otty Cmty. Svc. award, 1975, Tchg. Excellence award NYU, 1981, commendation for achievment as teacher, scholar, communicator NY State Legislature, 1983, proclamation for contbns. to city, NYC Coun., 1983, Police Athletic League citation for svc. to children of NYC, 1991, 96, 2002, Honors Convocation award Marymount Manhattan Coll., 1994, Detlev W. Bronk award Johns Hopkins Alumni Assn., 1994, Disting. Univ. Tchg. award New Sch. U., 2000. Mem. Tudor and Stuart Club, Authors Guild Found. (pres. 1993—), Authors Guild (coun. 1970-77, 79—, v.p. 1993-95), Authors League (nat. coun. 1976), Authors League Fund (v.p. 1998—, acting pres. 2004—), Am. Ctr. PEN (exec. com. 1969, 2003—, v.p. 1970-74, internat. del. 1971-72, 74), Century Assn. Club (NYC), Coffee House Club (NYC). Home: 23 E 69th St New York NY 10021-4919 *I have been guided by a strong devotion to my family and friends and moderate ambition. In both these priorities I have been influenced by my parents. With my writing I have tried to fulfill my own needs, and for the most I have been satisfied by the reception. I do not aspire to fame or great fortune, and this leaves me free to enjoy the sharing of experiences with my friends and family. I consider myself a lucky man and this keeps me grateful to whatever forces there are that contrive man's fortune.*

OFFNER, ERIC DELMONTE, lawyer; b. Vienna, June 23, 1928; came to U.S., 1941, naturalized, 1949; s. Sigmund J. and Kathe (Delmonte) O.; m. Julie Cousins, 1955 (dec. 1959); m. Barbara Ann Shotton, July 2, 1961; 1 son, Gary Douglas; m. Carol Sue Marcus, Jan. 12, 1980 (dec. 1983) BBA, CCNY, 1949; JD in Internat. Affairs, Cornell U., 1952. Bar: N.Y. 1952. Assoc. Langner, Parry, Card & Langner, N.Y.C., 1952-57; ptnr. Haseltine, Lake, Waters & Offner, N.Y.C., 1957-77; sr. ptnr. Offner & Kuhn, 1978-83; pvt. practice N.Y.C., 1965—74. Instr. George Washington U. Law Sch., Cornell U. Law Sch.; spl. prof. law Hofstra Law Sch., 1974-92; jazz disc jockey ProgressiveRadioNetwork.com. Author: International Trademark Protection, 1964, Japanese edit., 1977, International Trademark Service, Vols. I-III 1970, Vol. IV, 1972, Vol. V., 1973, Vol. VI, 1976, Vol. VII, 1981, Vols. I-VII, 2d edit., 1981, Legal Training Course on Trademarks, 1982; editor in chief: Cornell Law Forum, 1950-51; mem. editorial bd.: Trademark Reporter, 1961-64, 69-72; book reviewer Jour. Humanism and Ethical Religion; contbr. articles to profl. jours.; prodr. jazz concerts N.Y.C., 1996—, jazz video and jazz CDs. V.p. Riverdale Mental Health Clinic, N.Y.C., 1966-67; pres. Riverdale Mental Health Assn., 1967-69, Ethical Culture Soc., Riverdale-Yonkers, 1964-67, Ethical Cultural Retirement Ctr., 1975-94; trustee Am. Ethical Union, 1967-73, Internat. Alliance of Holistic Lawyers; bd. dirs. Fit Kids; pres. The Sidney Bechet Soc., Ltd., 1997—. Mem. N.Y. Patent Law Assn. (assoc. editor Bull. 1961-66, gov. 1973-76), ABA, City N.Y. Bar Assn. (sec. 1962-64), U.S. Trademark Assn., World Peace Through Law (charter), Trademark Soc. Washington (charter), Inst. Trade Mark Agts. (London), Sidney Bechet Soc. Ltd. (pres. 1997—), Australian Patent Inst., Internat. Assn. Protection Indsl. Property, Nat. Coun. Patent Law Assn., Internat. Patent, Trademark Assn., Phi Alpha Delta. Home: 20 Joy Dr New Hyde Park NY 11040-1109 E-mail: eoffner@optonline.net. *Do unto others so as to elicit the best in them and thereby the best in yourself.*

OFFUTT, REBECCA SUE, business and sales executive; b. Wheeling, W.Va., Jan. 20, 1951; d. John Howard and Mary Concetta (Lanzuisi) Warden; m. Denver C. Offutt, Apr. 13, 1970 (div. 1990); children: Kimberly Dawn, Jody Monroe. Student, W.Va. U., 1968-70, W.Va. State Coll., 1973-75. Founder, pres. Marabec Designs, Inc., Charleston, W.Va., 1980-82; realtor, sales assoc. McQuire Realty Co., Huntington, 1988-89; sales assoc. Focus Mktg. Consultants, Charleston, 1987-90; ter. mgr. Quorum Corp., Hurricane, W.Va., 1990—96; network sales specialist Danka Office Imaging, Charleston, 1996—99; founding ptnr. Komax Bus. Sys., LLC, South Charleston, W.Va., 1999—. Developer five-yr. plan Jr. League, Charleston and Huntington, 1984; docent Huntington Galleries; pres. Pea Ridge Elem. PTA, Huntington, 1986-87; del.-at-large Ohio Valley Tennis Assn., 1986-87. Recipient Local, Dist. and Regional winner Ricoh Corp., 1993. Mem.: South Charleston Area Devel. Coun. (U.S. Congl. bus. adv. chmn. 2004, Nat. Rep. Congrl. Bus. Adv. Coun. Businessman of Yr., W.Va. 2003, W. Va. Businessman of Yr. 2004), South Charleston Conv. and Visitors Bur. (sec./treas. 2000—02, bd. dirs. 2004), Putnam County Rotary (charter mem.) (Disting. W. Virginian 2004). Home: 318 Southpointe Dr Charleston WV 25314 Office Phone: 304-744-7440.

OFFUTT, SUSAN ELIZABETH, economist; b. Newport, R.I., Apr. 17, 1954; d. William Franklin and Carol Dorothy (Chieves) O. BS, Allegheny Coll., 1976; MS, Cornell U., 1980, PhD, 1982. Asst. prof. agrl. econs. U. Ill., Urbana, 1982-87; sect. leader Econ. Rsch. Svc. USDA, Washington, 1987-88; chief agr. br. U.S. Office Mgmt. and Budget, Washington, 1988-92; exec. dir., bd. agr. Nat. Rsch. Coun., Washington, 1992-96; adminstr. U.S. Dept. Agrl./Econ. Rsch. Svc., Washington, 1996—. Office: Econ Rsch Svc 1800 M St NW Rm 4145 Washington DC 20036-5802

O'FLAHERTY, JAMES DANIEL, council executive; b. Chgo., Nov. 4, 1942; s. James Carneal O'Flaherty and Lucy Maupin Ribble; m. Cynthia Lane Keyworth, May 21, 1971 (div. July 1983); m. Mayra Gazelle Lacayo, Aug. 9, 1984. BA, Williams Coll., 1965; BA, MA (Rhodes scholar), Oxford (Eng.) U., 1967; MA, Harvard U., 1971. Asst. prof. U. of the South, Sewanee, Tenn., 1971-74; profl. staff Senate Select Com. on Intelligence, Washington, 1974-75; sr. assoc. Carnegie Endowment for Internat. Peace, Washington, 1975-83; asst. dir. Group of Thirty, N.Y.C., 1983-86; v.p. Nat. Fgn. Trade Coun., Washington, 1987—; exec. dir. U.S.-South Africa Bus. Coun., Washington, 1993—. Bd. advisors Patterson Sch. of Diplomacy U. Ky., Lexington, 1987-95; U.S. adv. com. Robert F. Kennedy Ctr. for Human Rights, Durban, South Africa, 2000—. Contbr. articles to profl. jours. Chmn. Alexandria Dem. Party, 1977—80; mem. Va. Dem. Ctrl. Com., 1977—80. Mem. Coun. on Fgn. Rels. Avocations: classical history, chess. Home: 804 Janneys Ln Alexandria VA 22302 Office: Nat Fgn Trade Coun 1625 K St NW #200 Washington DC 20006 E-mail: doflaherty@nftc.org.

O'FLYNN, THOMAS M. investment company executive; m. Cheryl O'Flynn; 1 child. BA in Econ., Northwestern U., 1982; MBA, U. Chgo., 1986. Mng. dir. global power and utility group, head N.Am. region Morgan Stanley, 1986—2000; exec. v.p., CFO Pub. Svc. Enterprise Group, Newark, 2001—. Office: Pub Svc Enterprise Group Inc 80 Park Plz Newark NJ 07101

OFNER, WILLIAM BERNARD, investor; b. L.A., Aug. 24, 1929; s. Harry D. and Gertrude (Skoss) Offner; m. Florence Ila Maxwell, Apr. 13, 1953 (div. 1956). AA, L.A. City Coll., 1949; BA, Calif. State U., L.A., 1953; LLB, Loyola U., L.A., 1965; postgrad., Sorbonne, 1951; cert. de Langue Francaise, 1987; postgrad., U. So. Calif., 1966; post grad., Glendale Cmty. Coll., 1986-92. Bar: Calif. 1966, US Dist. Ct. Calif. 1966, US Supreme Ct. 1972. Assoc. Thomas Moore and Assoc., LA, 1967-69; pvt. practice LA, 1969-70, 74—; assoc. Peter Lam, LA, 1981-94, mng. atty., 1993—. Assoc. C.M. Coronel, 1986-87, Jack D. Janofsky, 1987-89, Mario P. Gonzalez, 1990-92, Genaro Legorreta, Jr., 1997-98; lectr. Van Norman U., 1975; property mgr., 1982—; investor 1984—. Electronics instr. USNR, 1949—54. Mem. Inst. Gen. Semantics, Toastmasters, Safari Athletic Club. Democrat. Avocations: photography, linguistics, tutoring, painting. Office: PO Box 163 Chino Hills CA 91709 Office Phone: 909-590-4484.

OFODILE, FERDINAND, plastic surgeon; b. Nnobi, Anambara, Nigeria, Oct. 20, 1941; came to U.S., 1962; s. Julius and Regina (Eruchalu) O.; m. Caroline N. Ofodile, July 15, 1969; children: Uchenna, Ikechukwu, Nnaemeka, Nnamdi. BS, Northwestern U., Evanston, Ill., 1964; MD, Northwestern U., Chgo., 1968. Diplomate Am. Bd. Surgery, Am. Bd. Plastic Surgery. Rotating intern Columbia U./Harlem Hosp. Program, N.Y.C., 1968-69, resident in gen. surgery, 1971-73, resident in plastic surgery, 1973-75; resident in gen. surgery Columbia Presbyn. Hosp., N.Y.C., 1969-71; fellow in plastic surgery Mayo Clinic, Rochester, Minn., 1975-76; sr. lectr., cons. in plastic surgery dept. surgery Univ. Coll. Hosp./U. Ibadan, Nigeria, 1977-82; assoc. attending in plastic surgery St. Lukes/Roosevelt Hosps., N.Y.C., 1985—; chmn. plastic surgery residency program Harlem Hosp. Ctr., N.Y.C., 1982—, chief plastic surgery svc., 1982—; clin. prof. surgery Columbia U., N.Y.C., 1997—. Vis. prof. U. Sokoto, 1993; mem. internat. symposium com. Plastic Ednl. Found., 1989-98; lectr. in field. Contbr. numerous articles to profl. jours. Fellow ACS, West African Coll. Surgeons, Am. Assn. Plastic Surgeons; mem. Am. Soc. Plastic and Reconstructive Surgeons, Assn. Acad. Chmn. Plastic Surgery, Mayo Alumni Soc., N.Y. Regional Soc. Plastic and Reconstructive Surgery (sec. 1996-97), Webster Soc., N.Y. State Med. Soc., N.Y. County Med. Soc., Manhattan Med. Soc. Achievements include design of ofodile nasal implant for rhinoplasty in blacks and Hispanics; determination of serum levels of vitamins E, C and essential elements in ulcer patients; role of thombin in hemostasis in burns; anthropometric measurements of the Black face; elucidation of the anatomy, morphology and surgery of the Black nose; cosmetic and reconstructive surgery of the breast in Blacks. Office: 2590 Frisby Ave Bronx NY 10461

OFSTAD, EVELYN LARSEN BOYL, retired primary school educator, radio personality, film producer; b. Laurel, Oreg., Sept. 11, 1918; d. Walter Winfred and Nellie Lyle (Gellatly) Larsen; m. Robert Morris Boyl (dec.); children: Kathleen Roberta Boyl, Robert Morris Boyl Jr., Shannon Gae Boyl, Brian Larsen Boyl; m. Olaf Ofstad, Nov. 15, 1988. BS, Oreg. State U., 1940; MS in Tchg., Portland State U., 1968. Cert. learning specialist. Radio announcer Sta. KOAC, Corvallis, Oreg., 1939-40; announcer, script writer Sta. KWIL, Albany, Oreg., 1940-42, operator, announcer, 1941-42; sec. Higgins Ship Bldg., New Orleans, 1943-44; elem. tchr. Portland Pub. Schs., 1968-71; learning specialist North Clackamas Schs., Milw., Ore., 1972-85, home instr. Milwaukie, Oreg., 1985-86. Prodr., actor (video travelogues) Portland Cable Access, 1987—; actor: Oreg. Sr. Theater, 1987—95, Plz. Players, 1999—. Co-leader Girl Scouts Am., Oak Grove, Oreg., 1954—55, Webelos Boy Scouts Am., 1956—57, 1970—71; videographer Ptnrs. Ams., Oreg., 1990—91; head video prodn. Channel 29 In-House TV Ret., 1999—2004; prodr. biweekly travel show, weekly activities show; mem. synchronized swim team Holladay Park Plz., 2003—04. Mem.: AAUW (pres. Albany chpt.). Avocations: painting, video production, bell playing, travel, synchronized swimming.

OFTE, DONALD, business executive; b. N.Y.C., Aug. 23, 1929; s. Sverre and Ingeborg Ofte; m. Margaret Mae McHenney, July 23, 1955; children: Marc Christian, Nancy Carolyn Appleby, Kirk Donald Jr. BA in Chemistry, Dana Coll., 1952; postgrad. study metall. engring., Ohio State U., 1958-60. Jr. chemist Inst. Atomic Research, Ames, Iowa, 1952-53; sr. research chemist Monsanto Research Corp., Miamisburg, Ohio, 1958-66; ops. engr. AEC, Miamisburg, 1966-69, br. chief, div. dir. ops. office Albuquerque, 1969-73, mgr. Pinellas area office Largo, Fla., 1973-79; mgr. Rocky Flats area office Dept. Energy, Golden, Colo., 1979-82, asst. mgr. devel. and prodn. Albuquerque, 1982-83, dep. mgr. ops. office, 1983-84; prin. dep. asst. sec. Dept. Energy Defense Programs, Washington, 1984-87; mgr. ops. office Dept. Energy, Idaho Falls, Idaho, 1987-89; mgmt. cons. Idaho Falls, 1989-92; v.p. govt. ops. United Engrs. & Constructors (Raytheon Engrs. & Constrn.), Denver, 1992-93; v.p. Adv. Scis., Inc., Albuquerque, 1993-94; pres. FERMCO (also known as Fluor Daniel, Fernald), Cin., 1994-96; chmn., bd. mgrs. Washington Group BWXT Oper. Svcs., LLC, 2004—. V.p. Fluor-Daniel, Inc., 1994-96; affiliate prof. Idaho State U., 1990-92; bd. dirs. Denver Fed. Exec. Bd., 1979-82; bd. dirs., chmn., Washington BWXT Operating Sys., LLC, 2004—. Author: (with others) Plutonium 1960, 1965, Physicochemical Methods in Metals Research; contbr. articles to profl. jours. on metallurgy and ceramics. Campaign chmn. United Way Pinellas, St. Petersburg, Fla., 1978; bd. dirs. Bonneville County United Way, Idaho Rsch. Found.; mem. adv. bd. Teton Peaks Council Boy Scouts of Am., 1987-92, Eastern Idaho Tech. Coll.; chmn. Excellence in Edn. Fund Com., 1990-92; vice chmn., bd. dirs. Rio Grande Ch. ARC, Albuquerque, 1982-84; trustee, bd. dirs. Nat. Atomic Mus., 1999—2003. Served to lt. (j.g.) USN, 1953-57. Recipient citation AEC for Apollo 12 SNAP 27 Radioisotope Generator, 1969, High Quality Performance award AEC, 1968, Group Achievement award NASA, 1972; Meritorious Svc. award Dept. Energy, 1985, Disting. Career Svc. award, 1989. Mem. Am. Chem. Soc. (emeritus), Am. Nuclear Soc., Am. Soc. Metals, Nat. Contract Mgmt. Assn., Am. Soc. Pub. Adminstrs., Suncoast Archeol. Soc., Idaho Falls C. of C. (bd. dirs., cmty. svc. award 1990), Rotary Internat. (Paul Harris fellow). Avocations: reading, bridge, gardening, golf. Home: 1129 Salamanca St NW Albuquerque NM 87107-5643 Office Phone: 505-878-1351. E-mail: dofte@wgint.com.

OGAN, RUSSELL GRIFFITH, business executive, retired air force officer; b. Reading, Pa., Nov. 20, 1923; s. Russell John and Edna Gwendlyn (Griffith) O.; m. Gloria Mae Withers, Oct. 30, 1943; children: Susan Ann (Mrs. Greg Gunn), Russell Lee. Student, Wyomissing Polytech. Inst., 1942, Air Command Staff Coll., 1948; grad., Nat. War Coll., 1963. Enlisted as pvt. U.S. Army, 1942; advanced through grades to brig. gen. USAF, 1970; fighter squadron comdr. Dover AFB, Del., 1951; dir. combat operations (11th Air Div.), Ladd AFB, Alaska, 1951-53; dir. (Combat Operations Center), Hamilton AFB, Calif., 1953-56; with (Hdqrs. Air Def. Command), Ent AFB, Colo., 1956-60; dir. (Aerospace Def. Systems Office, Air Force Ballistic Missile Div.), 1960-62; from dep. dir. plans to comdr. Sector Operation Ctr. NATO, Germany, 1963-66; dep. dir. personnel data and records (USAF Mil. Personnel Center), Randolph AFB, Tex., 1966-68; comdr. 71st Missile Warning Wing, then vice comdr. (14th Aerospace Force), Ent AFB, Colo., 1968-71; dep. dir. personnel programs Hdqrs. USAF, Washington, 1971-72; dir. Prisoner of War and Missing in Action Affairs, Office Sec. Def., Washington, 1972-74; former pres. Vacation Interval Mktg.; real estate broker Fishermen's Village, Punta Gorda, Fla. Decorated D.S.M., Legion of Merit with bronze oak leaf cluster, Air medal with 1 silver and 1 bronze oak leaf cluster. Mem. Daedalians, T.R.O.A., Kingsway Country Club. Flew 62 missions as fighter pilot over France and Germany, 1944-45. Home: 12413 SW Kingsway Cir Lake Suzy FL 34269

O'GARA, BARBARA ANN, soap company executive; b. Newark, Aug. 8, 1953; d. Frank Percy and Rose Stevens. AA, Keystone Jr. Coll., 1973; BS, U. Ariz., 1976. Media buyer Wells, Rich, Green/Townsend, Irvine, Calif., 1977-80; dist. sales mgr. Dial Corp., Phoenix, 1980-82; regional sales mgr. Guest Supply, Inc., North Brunswick, N.J., 1982-85; dir. hotel mktg. and sales Neutrogena Corp., L.A., 1985-92, v.p. hotel mktg. and sales, 1992-96; cons. Bath and Body Works; owner O'Gara & Assocs., Ltd., 1996—. Recipient Outstanding Sales Accomplishment award, Armour-Dial, 1981; scholar Keystone Jr. Coll., 1972, Morris County scholar, 1971. Mem.: Network Exec. Women in Hospitality, Am. Hotel and Motel Assn., Am. Mgmt. Assn., Am. Mktg. Assn. Republican. Roman Catholic. Avocation: tennis, reading, yoga, skiing, photography. Home and Office: PO Box 305 Mountain Lakes NJ 07046-0305 E-mail: barbara.ogara@rcn.com.

O'GARA, WILLIAM B. state legislator, real estate agent; Real estate agt.; mem. Dist. 33 Maine Ho. of Reps., Augusta, 1985-95; mem. Dist. 29 Maine Senate, Augusta, 1995—; mem. edn. com. Maine Ho. of Reps. Address: 29 Cardinal St Westbrook ME 04092-3802

OGATA, KATSUHIKO, engineering educator; b. Tokyo, Jan. 6, 1925; came to U.S., 1952; s. Fukuhei and Teruko (Yasaki) O.; m. Asako Nakamura, Sept. 6, 1961; 1 son, Takahiko. BS, U. Tokyo, 1947; MS, U. Ill., 1953; PhD, U. Calif., Berkeley, 1956. Research asst. Sci. Research Inst., Tokyo, 1948-51; fuel engr. Nippon Steel Tube Co., Tokyo, 1951-52; mem. faculty U. Minn., 1956—, prof. mech. engring., 1961—; prof. elec. engring. Yokohama Nat. U., 1960-61, 64-65, 68-69. Author: State Space Analysis of Control Systems, 1967, Modern Control Engineering, 1970, 2001, Dynamic Programming, 1973, Ingenieria de Control Moderna, 1974, 1998, Metody Przestrzeni Stanow w Teorii Sterowania, 1974, System Dynamics, 1978, 2003, Engenharia de Controle Moderno, 1982, 2003, Teknik Kontrol Automatik, 1985, Discrete-Time Control Systems, 1986, 1995, Gendai Seigyo Riron, 1986, Dinamica de Sistemas, 1987, Solving Control Engineering Problems with MATLAB, 1994, Gendai Seigyo Kogaku, 1994, Designing Linear Control Systems with MATLAB, 1994, Kejuruteraan Kawalan Moden, 1996, Sistemas de Control en Tiempo Discreto, 1996, Projeto de Sistemas Lineares de Controle com MATLAB, 1996, Solucao de Problemas de Engenharia de Controle com MATLAB, 1997. Recipient Outstanding Adv. award Inst. of Tech., U. Minn., 1981, John R. Ragazzini Edn. award Am. Automatic Control Coun., 1999 Fellow ASME; mem. Sigma Xi, Pi Tau Sigma. Office: U Minn Dept Mech Engring Minneapolis MN 55455

OGATA, SADAKO, United Nations official; b. 1927; Min. Japan's Mission to UN, N.Y.C., 1978-79; spl. emissary UN; Japanese rep. Comm. on Human Rights, UN, 1982-85; former chair. exec. bd. UNICEF; former dir. Inst. Fgn. Rels. Sophia U., Tokyo, dean faculty of fgn. studies; high commr. UN High Commn. for Refugees, Geneva, 1991—. Office: UNHCR Case postale 2500 1211 Geneva 2 depot Switzerland

OGAWA, JOICHI RAPHAEL, director, consultant; b. Tokyo, July 2, 1958; arrived in U.S., 2002; s. Isamu and Yoshiko Ogawa. BA in Econs., Keio U., Tokyo, 1982, BA in Psychology, 1986, MA in Sociology, 1989, PhD in Human Rels., 1993. Tchr. Jogakukau Girls' HS, Tokyo, 1988—90; rschr. Inst. Behavioral Sci. Uchido Yoko Co. Ltd., Tokyo, 1989—90; lectr. Fukuoka Prefecture U., Tagawa-shi, Japan, 1992—93; mgr. info. planning divsn. Nippon Kouatsu Electric Co. Ltd., Obu-shi, Japan, 1993—97; gen. mgr. cons. Shinjuku Gen. Acctg. Firm, Tokyo, 1997—98; liaison mgr. O'Hara Coll. Bus. San Jose (Calif.) State U., 1997—2002; program coord. Palo Alto (Calif.) Ctr. Devel. Studies, Inc., 2002—. Rschr. human sensory Ministry of Internat. Trade and Industry, Tokyo, 1990—92; cons. Long Term Credit Bank, Tokyo, 1991—93; family psychologist Nagoya (Japan) Nat. Hosp., 1991—92; clin. psychologist Azabu HS, Tokyo, 1997—2000. Mem.: APA, Acad. Mgmt., Internat. Soc. Psychodynamic Studies Orgn. Office: Palo Alto Ctr Devel Design 520 N 6th St, Apt # 107 San Jose CA 95112-3262 Office Phone: 408-205-7517. Office Fax: 408-920-2593. Personal E-mail: joichi.ogawa@aol.com.

OGAWA, SEIJI, research scientist, biophysicist; b. Tokyo, Jan. 19, 1934; came to U.S., 1962; s. Shimpei and Mitsu O.; m. Kazuko, Mar. 10, 1962; 1 child, Miwako. BS, U. Tokyo, 1957; PhD, Stanford U., 1967. Rsch. assoc. Mellon Inst., Pitts., 1962-64; postdoctoral Stanford U., Calif., 1967-68; disting. mem. tech. staff Bell Labs., Murray Hill, NJ, 1968—2001; dir. Ogawa Laboratories for Brain Function Rsch., Hamano Life Science Research Found., Tokyo, 2001—. Elected mem. Inst. of Medicine, 2000. Recipient Japan Internat. prize, 2003, Gairdner award, 2003. Fellow Internat. Soc. Magnetic Resonance (Gold medal 1995); mem. Biophysical Soc., Am. Physical Soc. (Biol. Physics prize 1996), Neurosci. Office: Hamano Life Sci Rsch Found 12 Daikyo-cho Shinjuku-ku Tokyo 160-0015 Japan

OGBAR, JEFFREY OGBONNA GREEN, history professor; b. June 10, 1969; BA, Morehouse Coll., 1991; MA, Ind. U., 1993, PhD, 1997. Jeffrey Campbell fellow St. Lawrence U., Canton, N.Y., 1996-97; asst. prof. U. Conn., Storrs, 1997—2003, assoc. prof., 2003—. Rsch. fellow W.E.B. DuBois Ctr. for Afro-Am. Rsch., Harvard U., 1999-2000; fellow Schomburg Ctr. for Rsch. in Black Culture, Scholars-in-Residence Program, N.Y. Pub. Libr., N.Y.C., 2001-2002.

OGBONNAYA, CHUKS ALFRED, entomologist, agronomist, environmentalist; b. Akoli-Imenyi, Abia, Nigeria, June 30, 1953; came to U.S., 1975; s. Alfred Agbaeze and Christy (Agubuche) Ogbonnaya; m. Joyce Elizabeth Belgrave, Mar. 30, 1985; children: Latoya, Oluchi, Kelechi, Chioma. BS, U. Nebr., 1979, PhD, 1985; MS, N.W. Mo. State U., 1981. Cert. profl. crop scientist, profl. agronomist. Lab. asst. U. Nebr., Lincoln, 1976-78, rsch. asst., 1978-80, 82-85, postdoctoral fellow, 1985; asst. prof., fellow Mountain Empire Coll., Big Stone Gap, Va., 1985-90, prof., 1990—, coord., prof. environ. sci. dept., 1986—, asst. dean, 1996—99. Disting. scholar-in-residence Pa. State U., summer 1990, vis. prof., 1990. Soccer coach Parks and Recreation, Big Stone Gap, 1989; mem. Va. Water Resources Statewide Adv. Bd., govt.-mined land reclamation adv. bd. Recipient Times Teaching award, 1990, Chancellor's Profs. award Va., 1990; Fulbright sr. scholar, 1993-94. Mem. Am. Soc. Agronomy, Crop Sci. Soc. Am., Entomol. Soc., Va. Acad. Sci., Va. Mining Assn. (Outstanding Contbn. to Comty. award 1993), Internat. Platform Assn., Phi Beta Kappa. Methodist. Avocations: tennis, soccer. Home: 520 Bays View Rd Kingsport TN 37660-3202

OGBUREKE, KALU UGWA EMMANUEL, oral surgeon, oral and maxillofacial pathologist, molecular biologist; b. Dorowa-Babuje, Nigeria, May 30, 1955; came to U.S., 1993; s. Kalu Ugwa and Ihudiya Grace O.; m. Ezinne Ihuoma Enyioma, Aug. 25, 1991; children: Chinasa, Kalu, Erinma. B of Dental Surgery, U. Ibadan, Nigeria, 1986; MSc in Med. Scis., U. Glasgow, Scotland, 1993; DMSc, Harvard Sch. Dental Medicine, 2001; JD, Suffolk U., 2002. Lic. Med. Dental Coun. Nigeria. Accounts clk. Nigerian TV Authority, Aba, 1978-79; house surgeon Ahmadu-Bello U. Tchg. Hosp., Kaduna, Nigeria, 1986-87; vis. registrar oral and maxillofacial surgery Ahmadu-Bello U. Tch. Hosp., Kaduna, 1991; dental surgeon Hebgreen Dental Clinic, Portharcourt, Nigeria, 1987-88, Nigerian Mil. Hosp., Portharcourt, 1988—89; resident oral and maxillofacial surgery, instr. U. Nigeria Tchg. Hosp., Enugu, 1989-91. Contbr. articles to profl. jours. Sec. African and Carribean Christian Fellowship, Glasgow, Great Britain, Ireland, 1992, pres., 1992-93. Recipient Nat. Rsch. Sci. award NIH, 1996-99; Gani Fawehinmi Undergrad. scholar, 1984, Wanda scholar Harvard Com. Gen. Scholarship, 1999; Primary fellow West African Coll. Surgeons, 1990, Postgrad. Tng. fellow U. Nigeria, 1991-93, Rsch. fellow Harvard Sch. Dental Medicine, 1996-2001, Postdoc. fellow Forsyth Inst., 1998-2001, Clin. Rsch. fellow NIDCR, NIH, 2002—. Fellow Royal Coll. Surgeons (Eng.); mem. AAAS, Internat. Assn. Oral Maxillofacial Pathologist, Am. Acad. Oral Maxillofacial Pathology, Am. Assn. Cancer Rsch. Avocations: sports, travel. Home: 7730 Goodfellow Way Derwood MD 20855 Office: NIDCR Bethesda MD 20892

OGBURN, HUGH BELL, chemical engineer, consultant; b. Lexington, Va., July 13, 1923; s. Sihon Cicero Jr. and Bettie Mae (Bell) O.; m. Anne Wotherspoon, Mar. 2, 1946 (div.); children: Margaret Mathews Berenson, Scott A.; m. Nancy Wrenn Petersen, Sept. 5, 1974. BS, Princeton U., 1944, MS, 1947, PhD, 1954. Sect. dir. research and devel. dept. Atlantic Refining Co., Phila., 1950-61; mgr. process engring. M.W. Kellogg Co., N.Y.C., London, 1961-67; dir. research and engring. Union Carbide Corp., N.Y.C., 1967-69; dir. new bus. devel. Weyerhaeuser Co., Tacoma, 1969-72; pres. H.B. Ogburn Assocs., Greenwich, Conn. and Honolulu, 1971—; v.p., dir. Incontrade Inc., Stamford, Conn., 1973-78; v.p. Pacific Resources Inc., Honolulu, 1978-83; chmn. Pacific Oasis, Los Angeles, 1983-85. Dir. Danmore Corp., Planning Research Corp.; cons. AEC; prof. chem. engring. Drexel U., Phila., 1951-61 Contbr. articles to profl. jours.; patentee in field. Pres. bd. trustees Woman's Hosp., Phila., 1954-62, Kapiolani Women's and Children's Med. Ctr., 1980-90; mem. adv. bd. Princeton U., 1960-70. Served to lt. j.g. USNR, 1942-46, PTO. Mem. AIChE, Am. Chem. Soc., Research Engrs. Soc., Pacific (Honolulu) Club, Greenwich Field (Conn.) Club, Princeton (N.Y.C.) Club, Phi Beta Kappa, Sigma Xi, Tau Beta Pi. Republican. Presbyterian. Home and Office: 4340 Pahoa Ave Apt 16 A Honolulu HI 96816-5032

OGBURN, NANCY WRENN, civic volunteer; b. Honolulu, Sept. 16, 1926; d. Heaton Luse and Carolene (Cooke) Wrenn; m. Hugh Gerhard Petersen Jr., July 1, 1948 (div. 1972); children: Hugh G. Petersen III, Suzanne Elise Petersen, Monte Cooke Petersen, Alexander Wrenn Petersen; m. Hugh Bell Ogburn, Sept. 5, 1974. BA, Wellesley Coll., 1948. With outside sales dept. Harris Travel, Greenwich, Conn., 1974-78. Guide Hawaiian Mission Children's Soc., Honolulu, 1978-81, Lyon Arboretum; treas. Rep. precinct, Honolulu, 1993. Recipient Carey E. Quinn award Am. Daffodil Soc., 1964, Roberta C. Watrous award, Medal of Merit Garden Club Am., 1966, Corning medal, 1991. Fellow Honolulu Acad. Arts; mem. Greenwich Garden Club (non-resident, Horticultural Com. award (2)), Garden Club Honolulu (chmn. various coms., Horticultural Com. award). Republican. Episcopalian. Avocations: bridge, travel, grandchildren, hiking. Home: 4340 Pahoa Ave Apt 16A Honolulu HI 96816-5032

OGDEN, ALFRED, lawyer; b. Bklyn., Oct. 14, 1909; s. Alfred Trecartin and Sophronia (Wisner) O.; m. Mary Fell Jordan, June 25, 1938; 1 child, Alfred Trecartin II. Grad., Phillips Acad., 1928; BA, Yale, 1932; LL.B., Harvard, 1935. Bar: N.Y. 1936. Since practiced, N.Y.C.; partner Alexander & Green, 1955-75; of counsel firm Morgan, Lewis & Bockius, 1979-80, c/o Reboul, MacMurray, Hewitt, Maynard & Kristol, 1980—. Pres., dir. C. Tennant, Sons & Co., N.Y.C., 1952-54 Trustee Fay Sch., Southborough, Mass., 1950-70, Population Reference Bur., 1963-68, Daniel and Florence Guggenheim Found., 1972—, Lavenberg Found., 1986—; trustee Mystic Seaport Mus., Mystic, Conn., 1959—, chmn., 1982-83, chmn. emeritus, 1983—; bd. mgrs., bd. overseers Meml. Sloan Kettering Cancer Ctr., 1959-97; trustee, exec. com. Robert Coll., Istanbul, Turkey, 1952-73, chmn., 1955-63; bd. dirs., v.p. English Speaking Union U.S., 1950-92, acting pres., 1983-84; bd. dirs., mem. exec. com. Winston Churchill Meml. Fund., 1966—; trustee Planned Parenthood N.Y.C., 1977-83; bd. dirs. Children's Mus. Manhattan, 1985-87, Nat. Trust Historic Presentation, 1998—. Served to lt. col. Gen. Staff Corps AUS, 1942-46. Decorated Legion of Merit. Mem. ABA, Internat. Law Assn., Soc. Colonial Wars, Pilgrims of U.S., Coun. on Fgn. Rels., Century Assn., Yale Club (N.Y.C.), Wadawanuck Club (Stonington, Conn.), Cosmopolitan Club, Thursday Evening Club. Home: 150 E 73rd St New York NY 10021-4362 also: PO Box 214 Stonington CT 06378-0214 Office: 45 Rockefeller Plz Fl 10 New York NY 10111-1099 *There is nothing permanent except change.*

OGDEN, ANITA BUSHEY, nursing educator; b. Malone, N.Y., May 23, 1938; d. John Richard and Eleanor Miriam (Wright) Bushey; m. William Alan Ogden, Dec. 27, 1972. Nursing diploma, N.Y. Med. Coll., 1959; BSN, Columbia U., 1962; MS in Adult Health, SUNY, Buffalo, 1968; PhD, Cornell U., 1984. Faculty Flower-Fifth Ave. Sch. Nursing, N.Y.C., 1959-62, Meth. Hosp., Bklyn. Sch. Nursing, N.Y.C., 1962-66, Hartwick Coll., Oneonta, N.Y., 1968-73; faculty, chair divsn. nursing edn. Corning (N.Y.) C.C., 1973-89; faculty Alfed U., Alfed Station, N.Y., 1984-88; prof., dir. nurse edn. Elmira (N.Y.) Coll., 1989—; clin. staff nurse various orgns., 1959—. Cons. curriculum devel., 1978—. Mem. adv. coun. Alfed U., Alfed Station, 1984-87; mem. bd. dirs. Cmty. Health Svcs. for Elderly, Elmira, 1992—; nursing cons. St. Kitts/Nevis U.S. Aid Ptnrs. Ams., 1986-87. Mem. ANA (various offices), N.Y. State and Dist. Nurses Assn. (various offices), Internat. Resources Instructional Svcs. (faculty 1990—), Nat. League for Nursing (regional bd. dirs. 1973—, ednl. cons. 1982—), LWV (regional coord.), Order Ea. Star (various offices), Delta Kappa Gamma (scholarship award 1981, 83), Delta Kappa Gamma (pres., bd. dirs. 1970), Sigma Theta Tau. Republican. Avocations: bicycling, hand crafts, cats. Home: 104 Fairview Ave Painted Post NY 14870-1215

OGDEN, BENJAMIN, language educator; b. Merced, Calif., Jan. 16, 1960; s. Dale and Joy Ogden. ABD, Vanderbilt U., 1988—92. Asst. prof. of spanish Truman State U., Kirksville, Mo., 1992—, coord. of computing support for I&l, 1993—. Computer programmer (software development for spanish, var. computer programs).

OGDEN, BRADLEY M. chef, restauranteur; m. Jody Ogden. Grad. with honors, Culinary Inst. Am., 1977. From sous chef to exec. chef Am. Restaurant, Kansas City, Mo., 1979—83; exec. chef Campton Pl. Hotel Restaurant, San Francisco, 1983—89; exec. chef, co-owner Lark Creek Inn, Larkspur, Calif., 1989—, One Market Restaurant, San Francisco, Birch Creek, Roseville, Calif., Yankee Pier, Larkspur, Lark Creek Cafe, Walnut Creek, Calif., San Mateo, Calif. Named Best Calif. Chef, James Beard Found., 1993; named one of Gt. Am. Chefs, Internat. Wine and Food Soc.; recipient Golden Plate award, Am. Acad. Achievement. Office: The Lark Creek Inn 234 Magnolia Ave Larkspur CA 94939-2099

OGDEN, BRUCE E. pediatrician, neonatologist; b. Oakland, Calif., Aug. 16, 1948; s. J. Edward Ogden and Betty Rulene Woster; m. Lynda Dell Simons, Sept. 4, 1970; children: Melanie Lyn Ogden Sorensen, Maren Elizabeth, Lauren Brooke Ogden Wilkins. BS, Brigham Young U., 1972; postgrad., U. Utah, 1973, MD, 1978. Diplomate pediat. and neonatal/perinatal medicine Am. Bd. Pediat. Intern, resident in pediatrics U. Utah Coll. Medicine, Salt Lake City, 1978-80; neonatal-perinatal fellow U. N.Mex. Sch. Medicine, Albuquerque, 1980-82; mem. hosp. staffs in Albuquerque, 1980—82, L.A., 1982—83, Colorado Springs, Colo., 1983—84, Tulsa, 1985—88, Sioux Falls, 1988—90, Las Vegas, 1990—2002, Provo, Utah, 2002—; med. dir. dept. neonatology McKennan Hosp., Sioux Falls, SD, 1988—90, Women's Hosp., Las Vegas, 1990-94; mem. staff Univ. Med. Ctr., Las Vegas, 1992—2002; staff pediatrician, neonatologist Lake Mead Hosp. Med. Ctr., North Las Vegas, Nev., 1995—2002; staff pediatrician Valley Hosp. Med. Ctr., Las Vegas, 1995—2002. Mem. pediat. staff Mountain View Hosp. Med. Ctr., Las Vegas, 1997—2002, Summerlin Hosp. Med. Ctr., Las Vegas, 1997—2002, Desert Springs Hosp., Las Vegas, 2000—02; staff dept. neonatology Utah Valley Regional Med. Ctr., Provo, 2002—. Contbr. Mem.: Am. Acad. Pediat. Office: Utah Valley Regional Med Ctr 1034 N 500 W Provo UT 84604-3380 Office Phone: 801-357-7707.

OGDEN, DANIEL MILLER, JR., government official, educator; b. Clarksburg, W.Va., Apr. 28, 1922; s. Daniel Miller and Mary (Maphis) O.; m. Valeria Juan Munson, Dec. 28, 1946; children: Janeth Lee Martin, Patricia Jo Hunter, Daniel Munson. BA in Polit. Sci., Wash. State U., 1944; MA, U. Chgo., 1947, PhD, 1949. From instr. to assoc. prof. Wash. State U., Pullman, 1949-61; staff asst. resources program U.S. Dept. Interior, 1961-64; asst. dir. U.S. Bur. Outdoor Recreation, 1964-67; dir. budget U.S. Dept. Interior, Washington, 1967-68; dean Coll. Humanities and Social Scis. Colo. State U., Ft. Collins, 1968-76; disting. vis. prof. Lewis and Clark Coll. and Portland (Oreg.) State U., 1977-78; dir. Office of Power Mktg. Coordination U.S. Dept. Energy, 1978-84; mgr. Pub. Power Coun., Portland, Oreg., 1984-88, ret., 1988. Mem. profl. staff com. interstate and fgn. commerce U.S. Senate, 1956-57; spll. asst. to chmn. Dem. Nat. Com., 1960-61; lectr. Mgmt. Devel. Ctrs., U.S. Office Pers. Mgmt., 1966—. Co-author: Electing the President, rev. edit., 1968, American National Government, 7th edit., 1970, American State and Local Government, 5th edit., 1972, Washington Politics, 1960, How National Policy is Made, 4th edit., 1999. Committeeman Wash. Dem. Ctrl. Com., 1952-56; chmn. Whitman County Dem. Ctrl. Com., 1958-60; chmn. 49th Legis. Dist. Dem. Com., 1990-94; chmn. Clark County Dem. Ctrl. com., 1994-98, 1999-2000, vice chair, 1998-99. With inf. U.S. Army, 1943-46. Mem. Phi Beta Kappa, Phi Kappa Phi, Pi Sigma Alpha, Sigma Delta Chi. Mem. Unitarian Ch. Home: 3118 NE Royal Oak Dr Vancouver WA 98662-7435 Office Phone: 360-254-8886.

OGDEN, JAMES RUSSELL, marketing educator, consultant, lecturer, writer; b. Paris, Ill., Nov. 4, 1954; s. Russell Lee and Marianne (Johnson) O.; children: David James, Anne Marie, Kari Kristine; m. Denise T. Alarid, 1989. B of Bus. Edn., Ea. Mich. U., 1978; MS, Colo. State U., 1981; PhD, U. No. Colo., 1986. With acctg. and fin. dept. Hydra-Matic Divsn. GM Motors, 1978; dir. mktg. Mich. Tech. Inst., 1979; grad. fellow Colo. State U., Ft. Collins, 1979—81, asst. mgr. family housing, 1979—81; placement counselor U. No. Colo., Greeley, 1981—83, instr. mktg., 1982—83; CEO, pres. Ogden, Ogden Latshaw & Assocs., Coopersburg, Pa., 1982—; chair advt. and mktg. dept., assoc. prof. Adams State Coll., Alamosa, Colo., 1983—89; dept. chair, prof. mktg. Coll. Bus. Kutztown U., Pa., 1989—, bd. bus. advisors Students in Free Enterprise Coll. Bus., 1996—. Interim dir. Small Bus. Devel. Ctr., Adams State Coll., 1988-89; adj. prof. Ctrl. Mich. U., Mt. Pleasant, 1987—, Cedar Crest Coll., Allentown, 1989—, Pa. State U., 1994-95, Nova Southeastern U., doctoral com. chair, Ft. Lauderdale, Fla., 1995—; spkr. in field; mktg. and advt. cons.; corp. trainer; textbook reviewer, editl. cons. Merrill Pub. Co., Allyn & Bacon, Inc., Richard Irwin, Inc., Macmillan Pub., John Wiley & Sons, Inc., Prentice-Hall, Houghton & Mifflin Co., Austen Press, Simon & Schuster; textbook reviewer Fairchild Books and Visuals, Inc.; tech. editor Rsch. and Edn. Assn.; doctoral com. mem. Nova Southeastern U., Drexel U., Phila., Pace U., N.Y.C., Temple U., Phila.; bd. dirs. Z-Coil, Inc., Albuquerque Author: Developing a Creative and Innovative Integrated Marketing Communication Plan, 1998, The Power of Point-of-Purchase Advertising: Marketing at Retail, 2004; co-author: The Best Test Preparation for the CLEP College-Level Examination Program Principles of Marketing, 1996; contbg. author, editor: Principles of Business, 1991, Essentials of Advertising, 1992, rev. edit., 1994, Marketing's Powerful Weapon: Point-of-Purchase Advertising, 2001; editor: Essentials of Marketing, 1994; contbr. over 40 articles to profl. jours. Treas. Com. to Elect Jorge Amaya County Commr., Colo., 1985, Bob Pastore for Senate Com.; senator Assoc. Student and Faculty Senate, Adams State Coll., 1984-85; bd. dirs. Am. Advt. Fedn. Acad. Com., 1991-97, Alamosa Personnel Bd., 1986-88, Alamosa County Devel. Corp., 1987-89, Alamosa Tourism Com., 1988-89, trustee bd. dirs. Creede Repertory Theatre, 1987-89; expert witness in tourism and mktg. State of Colo.; advisor team entries into Nat. Student Advt. Competition, Coll. World Series of Advt., 1989-90, 93—; trustee Dr. R.L. Ogden Meml. Scholarship, Colo. State U. Found., 1992—; faculty advisor Students in Free Enterprise Nat. Competition, 1997—, faculty advisor, bus. adv. bd. Kutztown U. chpt. Recipient award for Excellence in Econ. Edn., Freedoms Found. Valley Forge, 1986, Capital award for contbn. to edn., Nat. Leadership Coun., 1991-92; named Outstanding Educator of Sch. Bus., Adams State Coll., 1987-88; Sam Walton fellow Students in Free Enterprise, 1997, 98, Outstanding Educator award, 1998. Fellow Direct Mktg. Assn.; mem. Am. Advt. Fedn. (faculty advisor 1987—, bd. dirs. acad. com. 1991-97), Western Mktg. Educators Assn. (paper reviewer), Nat. Guild Hypnotists (cert.), Acad. Mktg. Sci., Advt. Club N.Y., Point of Purchase Advt. Inst., Am. Collegiate Retailing Assn., Assn. Nat. Advertisers, Nat. Assn. Hispanic Profs. of Bus. Adminstrn. and Econs., New Eng. Bus. Adminstrn. Assn., Ctrl. Pa. Advt. Club, Phi Kappa Phi, Alpha Sigma Alpha (fin. advisor 1992—), Alpha Kappa Psi (dist. dir.). Democrat. Avocations: scuba, music, travel. Office: Kutztown U Coll Bus Dept Mktg Kutztown PA 19530 Office Phone: 610-683-4396. E-mail: ogden@kutztown.edu.

OGDEN, JONATHAN, professional football player; b. Washington, July 31, 1974; B.A. in History, UCLA, 1996. Tackle Balt. Ravens, 1996—. Founder Jonathan Ogden Found.; bd. trustee's Urban League. Named First Team All-American, 1995, NFL First Team All-Pro, 2000; named to NFL Pro-Bowl, 1997—2003. Achievements include mem. Super Bowl XXV Champion Balt. Ravens, 2001; had his jersey number retired by UCLA, 1997. Office: c/o Baltimore Ravens 1101 Russel st Baltimore MD 21230*

OGDEN, MAUREEN BLACK, retired state legislator; b. Vancouver, B.C., Nov. 1, 1928; came to U.S., 1930; d. William Moore and Margaret Hunter (Leitch) Black; m. Robert Moore Ogden, June 23, 1956; children: Thomas, Henry, Peter. BA, Smith Coll., 1950; MA, Columbia U., 1963; M in City and Regional Planning, Rutgers U., 1977. Researcher, staff asst. Ford Found., N.Y.C., 1951-56; staff assoc. Fgn. Policy Assn., N.Y.C., 1956-58; mem. Millburn (N.J.) Twp. Com., 1976-81; mayor Twp. of Millburn, N.J., 1979-81; mem. N.J. Gen. Assembly, Trenton, 1982-96. Chmn. Assembly Environment Com., N.J. Gen. Assembly; chmn. Energy and Pub. Utilities Com., Coun. State Govts., 1991-92; mem. adv. bd. Sch. Policy and Planning, Rutgers Univ., New Brunswick, N.J., 1992-96. Author: Natural Resources Inventory, Township of Millburn, 1974. Bd. govs. N.J. Hist. Soc., Newark, 1992-2000; trustee N.J. chpt. The Nature Conservancy, 1994-99; hon. trustee Paper Mill Playhouse, Millburn, 1990—; former trustee St. Barnabas Med. Ctr., Livingston, N.J.; former pres. N.J. Drug Abuse Adv. Coun.; chair Gov.'s Coun. on N.J. Outdoors, 1996-99; mem. Palisades Interstate Park Commn., 1996-99; chair Garden State Preservation Trust, 1999—; mem. policy com. N.J. Conservation Found., 2000—. Recipient citation Nat. Assn. State Outdoors Recreation Liaison Officers, 1987, cert. appreciation John F. Kennedy Ctr. for the Performing Arts, The Alliance for Art Edn., 1987, disting. svc. award Art Educators N.J., 1987, ann. environ. quality award EPA Region II, 1988, citation Humane Soc. U.S., 1989, award N.J. Hist. Sites Coun., 1989, N.J. Sch. Conservation, 1990, pres.'s award The Nature Conservancy, 1995, pub. policy award Nat. Trust for Hist. Preservation, 1995. Republican. Episcopalian. Home: 59 Lakeview Ave Short Hills NJ 07078-2240 E-mail: mrogden@worldnet.att.net.

OGDEN, MAURICE B. retired minister, writer; b. Whizbang, Okla., Sept. 25, 1923; s. Arthur Omer Ogden and Hazel Mae Hartman; m. Ruth Lair Arnold (div.); 1 child, Michael Arnold; m. Kathryn Louise Freeman, June 3, 1990. BA in Letters and English, U. Okla., 1949. Freelance writer/editor, Oklahoma City, 1945—; tech. writer Paul Omohundro Co., Paramount, Calif., 1955—60; min. Unitarian Ch. Orange County, Anaheim, Calif. Creative writing instr. Coastline C.C., Fountain Valley, Calif., 1983—98, critical thinking instr., 1983—98. Author: Hangman, poetry, fiction, drama, short stories. With USAAF, 1942—43. Recipient O'Henry award for short stories, 1940. Green Party. Unitarian. Avocations: reading, cryptograms, crossword puzzles, sailing.

OGDEN, PEGGY A. retired personnel director; b. N.Y.C., Mar. 21, 1932; d. Stephen Arnold and Margaret (Stern) O. BA with honors, Brown U., 1953; MA, Trinity Coll., Hartford, Conn., 1955. Asst. dir. YMCA Counseling Svc., Hartford, 1953-55; employment interviewer R.H. Macy & Co., N.Y.C., 1955; asst. pers. dir. Inst. Internat. Edn., N.Y.C., 1956-59; pers. advisor Girl Scouts U.S.A., N.Y.C., 1959-61; store and pers. mgr. Ohrbachs, Inc., N.Y.C., 1961-74; dir. pers. N.Y.C. Coll. Tech., CUNY, Bkyn., 1974-2000, ret., 2000. Arbitrator, mediator Better Bus. Bur., N.Y.C., 1988—; cons. Girl Scout Coun. N.Y., N.Y.C., 1988-89. Advocate Am. Diabetes Assn., 1999—. Mem APA, AAAS, Am. Assn. U. Adminstrs., Women in Human Resources, N.Y. Pers. Mgmt. Assn. Home: 1100 Park Ave New York NY 10128-1202

OGDEN, STEVE, oil and gas company executive, state legislator; m. Beverly Ogden, Dec. 1973; children: Michael, Stephanie, Kristen. BS, U.S. Naval Acad., 1973; grad., Naval Nuc. Power Sch., 1974; MBA, Tex. A&M U., 1987. Pres. Ogden Resources Corp.; mem. Tex. Ho. of Reps., 1990-97, Tex. Senate, 1997—, mem. intergovtl. rels. com., mem. jurisprudence com., mem. natural resources com., mem. internat. rels., trade and tech. com., others. Lt. comdr. USN. Republican. Office: PO Box 12068 Austin TX 78711-2068 also: 7607 Eastmark Dr Ste 241 College Station TX 77840-4028

OGDEN, VALERIA MUNSON, management consultant, state representative; b. Okanogan, Wash., Feb. 11, 1924; d. Ivan Bodwell and Pearle (Wilson) Munson; m. Daniel Miller Ogden Jr., Dec. 28, 1946; children: Janeth Lee Ogden Martin, Patricia Jo Ogden Hunter, Daniel Munson Ogden. BA magna cum laude, Wash. State U., 1946. Exec. dir. Potomac Coun. Camp Fire, Washington, 1964-68, Ft. Collins (Colo.) United Way, 1969-73, Designing Tomorrow Today, Ft. Collins, 1973-74, Poudre Valley Community Edn. Assn., Ft. Collins, 1977-78; pres. Valeria M. Ogden, Inc., Kensington, Md., 1978-81; nat. field cons. Camp Fire, Inc., Kansas City, Mo., 1980-81; exec. dir. Nat. Capital Area YWCA, Washington, 1981-84, Clark County YWCA, Vancouver, Wash., 1985-89; pvt. practice mgmt. cons. Vancouver, 1989—; mem. Wash. Ho. of Reps., 1991—2002, spkr. pro tempore, 1999—2002. Mem. adj. faculty pub. adminstrn. program Lewis and Clark Coll., Portland (Oreg.) State U., 1979-94; mem. Pvt. Industry Coun., Vancouver, 1986-95; mem. regional Svcs. Network Bd. Mental Health, 1993-2003. Author: Camp Fire Membership, 1980. County vice-chair Larimer County Dems., Ft. Collins, 1974-75; mem. precinct com. Clark County Dems., Vancouver, 1986-88; mem. Wash. State Coun. Vol. Action, Olympia, 1986-90; treas. Mortar Bd. Nat. Found., Vancouver, 1987-96; bd. dirs. Clark County Coun. for Homeless, Vancouver, 1989-2004, chmn., 1994; bd. dirs. Wash. Wild Life and Recreation Coalition, 1995-2002, Human Svcs. Coun., 1996-02, State Legis. Leaders Found., 2001-02; mem. adv. bd. Wash. State U., Vancouver, 2002—; chair arts and tourism com. Nat. Conf. State Legis., 1996-97, exec. com., 2000-02; bd. dirs.

Wash. State Hist. Soc., 1996—, Affordable Cmty. Environments, 1998—, Clark County Skill Ctr. Found., 2003-; spkr. pro tem Wash. Ho. of Reps., 1999-2002; pres. Nat. Order of Women Legislators, 1999-2001; chair Wash. State Interagy. Com. for Outdoor Recreation, 2003, Wash. State Historic Preservation Fund; mem. Columbia Springs Edn. Ctr. Found.; co-chair S.W. Wash. Ctr. for the Arts, 2003-; bd. mem. Clark County Skill Ctr. Found., 2003, Columbia Springs Environ. Edn. Found., 2003-. Named Citizen of Yr. Ft. Collins Bd. of Realtors, 1975, State Legislator of Yr., Wash. State Labor Coun., 2000; recipient Gulick award Camp Fire Inc., 1956, Alumna Achievement award Wash. State U. Alumni Assn., 1988; named YWCA Woman of Achievement, 1991; named Citizen of Yr., Vancouver, Wash., 2002. Mem. Internat. Assn. Vol. Adminstrs. (pres. Boulder 1989-90), Nat. Assn. YWCA Exec. Dirs. (nat. bd. nominating com. 1988-90), Sci. and Soc. Assn. (bd. dirs. 1993-97), Women in Action, Philanthropic and Ednl. Orgn., Phi Beta Kappa. Democrat. Avocations: hiking, travel. Home and Office: 3118 NE Royal Oak Dr Vancouver WA 98662-7435 Office Phone: 360-254-8886. Personal E-mail: repval@comcast.net.

OGE, MARGO TSIRIGOTIS, environmentalist; b. Athens, Greece, Feb. 20, 1949; came to U.S., 1968; d. John Tsirigotis and Joana Lambrinakos; m. Cuneyt Oge, Aug. 24, 1975; children: Nicole, Marisa. Degree in Plastic Tech., Lowell U., 1972, degree in Plastic Engring., 1975. Chem. engr. EPA, Washington, 1980-83, sect. chief, 1983-85, dep. dir. toxic substances office, 1986-88, dir. radon divsn., 1988—; legis. asst. to Sen. Chafee U.S. Senate, Washington, 1985; dir. transp. air quality EPA, Washington, 1994—. Avocations: reading, tennis, skiing, travel. Office: EPA Ariel Rios Blvd N MC6401A 1200 Pennsylvania Ave NW Washington DC 20460-0001

O'GEARY, DENNIS TRAYLOR, retired contracting/engineering company executive; b. Waverly, Va., Feb. 20, 1925; s. King William and Mary Virginia (Traylor) O'G.; m. Alice Stuart Baum, Aug. 3, 1947; children: Dennis Patrick, Mary Alice O'Geary Eisenbarth, Elizabeth Christina O'Geary Bernstorf. Surveying degree, Tri-State U., 1943; BS in Civil Engring., Ill. Inst. Tech., 1947. Resident engring trainee Va. Hwy. Dept., Richmond, 1947-50; civil engring. supt. Wiley Jackson Co., Roanoke, Va., 1950-57; engr., asst. estimator, project mgr., v.p. and asst. to area mgr. S.J. Groves & Sons Co., Mpls. and Springfield, Ill., 1957-77, v.p., area mgr., 1978-82, v.p., asst. divsn. mgr., divsn. estimator Atlanta, 1982-84; pres. Peabody S.W., Inc., Houston, 1984-85; v.p. Houston ops. J.D. Abrams, Inc., Austin, Tex., 1985-99; ret., 1999. Cons. J.D. Abrams, Inc. Served with USNR, 1943-46. Mem. ASCE (life), Am. Concrete Inst. (50 yr. mem.), Soc. Am. Mil. Engrs. (50 yr. mem.), Nat. Maritime Hist. Soc. Christian (Disciples Of Christ). Home: 15402 Cresent Oaks Ct Houston TX 77068-2079 Office: 111 Congress Ave Austin TX 78701-4050 E-mail: daogeary@aol.com.

OGEDE, ODE, literature educator; b. Uchenyim Igede, Benue, Nigeria, Sept. 16, 1956; came to the U.S., 1994; s. Ogede and Margaret (Ogwuna) Ode; m. Shianyisimi Asabe, Apr. 5, 1986; children: Ochuole, Ogede, Shekwaga. BA in English Lit. with honors, Ahmadu Bello U., Zaria, Nigeria, 1979, MA in African Lit., 1982, PhD in English, 1987. Sr. lectr. in English Ahmadu Bello U., Zaria, 1988-94; Andrew Mellon faculty fellow U. Pa., Phila., 1994-95; vis. prof. Lincoln U., Pa., 1995-96; English prof. N.C. Ctrl. U., Durham, 1996—. Author: Art, Society and Performance, 1997, Ayi Kwei Armah: Radical Iconoclast, Pitting Imaginary Worlds Against the Actual, 1998, Achebe and the Politics of Representation, 2000, Teacher Commentary On Student Papers: Conventions, Beliefs, and Practices, 2002; editor SAIWA (Roots), 1989-94; mem. editl. bd. Studies of Nigerian Cultures and Society, 1990-94; contbr. articles to profl. jours. Mem. MLA, MLA of Nigeria (v.p. 1989-91), African Lit. Assn. Am. Home: 129 Celeste Cir Chapel Hill NC 27517-8916 Office: NC Central U Comms Bldg Rm 327 Durham NC 27707

OGG, JAMES ELVIS, microbiologist, educator; b. Centralia, Ill., Dec. 24, 1924; m. Betty Jane Ackerson; 2 children. BS, U. Ill., 1949; PhD, Cornell U., 1956. Bacteriologist Biol. Labs., Ft. Detrick, Md., 1950-53, cons., 1953-56, med. bacteriologist, 1956-58; prof. microbiology Colo. State U., Ft. Collins, 1958-85, prof. emeritus, 1985—; asst. dean Grad. Sch., 1965-66, head dept. microbiology, 1967-77. Dir. Advanced Sci. Edn. Program div. grad. edn. in sci. NSF, Washington, 1966-67; Fulbright-Hays sr. lectr. in microbiology, Nepal, 1976-77, 81; acad. adminstrn. advisor Inst. Agr. and Animal Sci., Tribhuvan U., Nepal, 1988-91; cons. NASA, 1968-69, NSF, 1968-73, Martin Marietta Corp., 1970-76; cons.-evaluator North Central Assn. Colls. and Secondary Schs., 1974-89; cons. Consortium for Internat. Devel., 1990-98, Winrock Internat. Inst. for Agrl. Devel., 1992—. Contbr. articles to profl. jours. Served with AUS, 1943—53. Fellow: AAAS, Am. Acad. Microbiology; mem.: Am. Soc. Microbiology (chmn. pub. svc. and adult edn. com. 1975—80), Fulbright-Hays Alumni Assn., Phi Kappa Phi. Home: 1442 Ivy St Fort Collins CO 80525-2348 E-mail: jeogg@lamar.colostate.edu.

OGG, ROBERT DANFORTH, corporate executive; b. Gardiner, Maine, June 10, 1918; s. James and Eleanor B. (Danforth) O.; m. Nancy Foote, Oct. 21, 1978; children by previous marriage: Richard Aasgaard, Robert Danforth, James Erling. Student, U. Calif., Berkeley, Stanford U. Utilities engr. State of Calif., 1946-48; gen. mgr. Danforth Anchors, Berkeley, 1948-51, prse., CEO, 1951-59; mng. dir. Danforth divsn. The Eastern Co., Berkeley, 1959-79, dir., 1972-80, Hodgdon Bros., East Boothbay, Maine, 1961-65; pres. Brewers Boatyard, West Southport, Maine, 1963-65; v.p. Henry R. Hinckley Co., Manset, Maine, 1974-79; pres. Ogg Oceans Systems, Manset, Maine, 1980—; chmn. Alpha Ocean Systems, Manset, Maine, 1983—. Author: Anchors & Anchorin (8 edits.); contbr. chpts. to books, articles to profl. jours.; patentee in field; inventor The Danforth Anchor, Inertial Altimeter, Digital Depth Sounder, others. Mem. adv. com. U. Calif. Rsch. Expeditions Program, 1979, co-chmn., 1983—; trustee U. Calif.-Berkeley Found., 1981, exec. com., 1983—, chmn. audit com., 1984-89, fellow, 1990, lifetime emeritus trustee; advisor Lawrence Hall Sci.; founder, sr. warden St. Ann's Episcopal Ch., Windham, Maine, 1976-79; life fellow U. Calif., Berkeley; contbr. to ABC and BBC documentaries on Pearl Harbor. With USN Intelligence, 1941-46, lt. comdr. USNR, ret. Recipient Wheeler Oak meritorious award U. Calif., 1987. Fellow Explorers Club (life), Calif. Acad. Scis. (life); mem. Navy League (founder Marin coun.), Soc. Naval Architects & Marine Engrs., Am. Soc. Naval Engrs., Am. Boat & Yacht Coun., Boating Writers Internat., Am. Geophys. Union, IEEE, Chancellors Cir. U. Calif., Sports Adv. Coun. U. Calif., Bodega Marine Lab., U.S. Naval Inst., R.G. Sproul Assocs., Tail Hook Assocs., Woodshole Assocs., Buncke Microsurg. Found. (bd. dirs. 1994—), Sierra Club, U. Calif.-Berkeley Alumni Assn., Engring. Alumni Assn., N.Y. Yacht Club, Pacific Union Club, Elks, Bear Backers Club, U. Calif. Berkeley Chancellor's Cir. Club, U. Calif. San Francisco Heritage Club. Address: 4225 Wayvern Dr Apt 224 Santa Rosa CA 95409-7134

OGG, WILSON REID, lawyer, retired judge, poet, publishing executive, educator; b. Alhambra, Calif., Feb. 26, 1928; s. James Brooks and Mary (Wilson) Ogg. Student, Pasadena Jr. Coll., 1946; AB, U. Calif., Berkeley, 1949; JD, U. Calif., 1952; Cultural D in Philosophy of Law, World U. Roundtable, 1983. Bar: Calif. 1955. Assoc. trust dept. Wells Fargo Bank, San Francisco, 1954-55; pvt. practice Berkeley, 1955—. Instr. Taegu English Lang. Inst., 1954, 25th Sta. Hosp., Taegu, Republic of Korea, 1954; rsch. atty., legal editor dept. of continuing edn. bar U. Calif., 1958—63; curator-in-residence, Pinebrook, 1964—2003; adminstv. law judge, 1974—93; real estate broker, cons., 1974—; trustee World U., 1976—80; dir. admissions internat. Soc. Phil. Enquiry, 1981—84; dep. dir. gen. Internat. Biog. Ctr., England, 1986—; dep. gov. Am. Biog. Inst. Rsch. Assn., 1986—; owner Pinebrook Press, Berkeley, Calif., 1988—2004; sci. faculty Cambridge U. *Judge Ogg's career combines not only outstanding achievement in the legal profession but also as in science with a major analysis of the problems of distinguishing co-existence from causality in medicine and natural science. He has formulated the unified theory or the two-way flow theory of consciousness and matter published on the internet at wilsonogg.com under which principles of quantum mechanics, black notes, light, expansion and contraction of manifestation, and physical and biological evolutions are derivative from the basic postulates of the theory.* Author: (book) The Unified Theory; contbr. articles to profl. jours., poems to mags. With AUS, 1952—54. Named to Internat. Poetry Hall of Fame, Nat. Libr. Poetry, 1997; recipient Internat. Peace prize, Auth. of United Cultural Conv., U.S., 2002, 50 Yr. Commemorative medal, Albert Schweitzer Assn., 2003. Mem.: ACLU, ASCAP, ABA, VFW, AAAS, London Diplomatic Acad., Inst. Noetic Scis., Intertel, Calif. Soc. Psychical Study (pres., chmn. bd. 1963—65), Am. Arbitration Assn. (nat. panel arbitrators), San Francisco Bar Assn., State Bar Calif., Internat. Soc. Individual Liberty, Internat. Platform Assn., Faculty Club of the U. Calif. at Berkeley (emeritus), Men's Inner Cir. Achievement, Amnesty Internat., Marines Meml. Club, Elks, Shriners, Masons, Am. Legion. Unitarian Universalist. Home: 8 Bret Harte Way Berkeley CA 94708-1607 Office Phone: 510-845-7155. Home Fax: 510-540-6052. Business E-Mail: wilsonogg@calberkeley.edu.

OGIER, WALTER THOMAS, retired physics educator; b. Pasadena, Calif., June 18, 1925; s. Walter Williams and Aileen Vera (Polhamus) O.; m. Mayrene Miriam Gorton, June 27, 1954; children: Walter Charles, Margaret Miriam, Thomas Earl, Kathryn Aileen. BS, Calif. Inst. Tech., 1947, PhD in Physics, 1953. Research fellow Calif. Inst. Tech., 1953; instr. U. Calif. at Riverside, 1954-55, asst. prof. physics, 1955-60, Pomona Coll., Claremont, Calif., 1960-62, assoc. prof., 1962-67, prof. physics, 1967-89, prof. emeritus, 1989—, chmn. dept., 1972-89. Contbr. articles on metals, liquid helium, X-rays and proton produced X-rays to profl. jours. Served with USNR, 1944-46. NSF Sci. Faculty fellow, 1966-67 Mem. Am. Phys. Soc., Am. Assn. Physics Tchrs. (pres. So. Calif. sect. 1967-69), Tau Beta Pi. Home: 8555 San Gabriel Rd Atascadero CA 93422-4928 E-mail: ogierwrt@tcsn.net.

OGILBY, BARRY RAY, lawyer; b. Dixon, Ky., Jan. 19, 1947; s. Jesse Bryan and Ann (Sutton) O; m. Carolyn Cowser, May 30, 1969 (div. 1973); m. Charlene Marie Coehlo, July 2, 1983; children: Kevin Glenn, Brandon Jesse. BS in Geology, U. Ky., 1969; JD, U. Memphis, 1972. Bar: Tenn. 1972, Tex. 1972, Ky. 1973, Calif. 1985, U.S. Dist. Ct. (cen. and no. dists.) Calif. 1987, U.S. Ct. Appeals (9th cir.) 1989. Litigation atty. Exxon U.S.A., Houston, 1972-74, mktg. atty. Memphis, 1975-76, labor, environ. atty. L.A., 1976-78, refinery atty. Benicia, Calif., 1978-81; asst. gen. counsel Exxon Pipeline Co., Houston, 1981-84; assoc. div. atty. Exxon Co. USA, Thousand Oaks, Calif., 1985-86; pvt. practice Calabasas, Calif., 1986—91; gen. counsel Marine Spill Response Corp., 1991-94; of counsel Bingham McCutchen LLP, Walnut Creek, Calif., 1995—; ptnr. Cooper, White & Cooper, LP, Walnut Creek, 2004—. Adj. prof. environ. law La Verne Coll., 1989-90; lectr. Am. Labor Inst.-ABA legal Edn. Seminar, San Francisco, 1980, 82, 2002, 2003. Contbr. articles to profl. jours. Mem. ABA (nat. resources law com., marine resources com. 1998—). Office: Cooper White & Cooper Ste 450 1333 N California Blvd Walnut Creek CA 94596 Business E-Mail: bogilby@cwclaw.com.

OGILVIE, DONALD GORDON, bankers association executive; b. N.Y.C., Apr. 7, 1943; s. John B. and Ann (Stephens) O.; m. Fan Staunton, Apr. 18, 1966; children: Jennifer B., Adam C. BA, Yale U., 1965; MBA, Stanford U., 1967. Systems analyst Dept. of Def., Washington, 1967-68; pres., dir. ICF Inc., Washington, 1969-73; dep. assoc. dir. Office of Mgmt. and Budget, Washington, 1973-74, assoc. dir., 1974-76; assoc. dean Yale U., New Haven, 1977-80; v.p. Celanese Corp., N.Y.C., 1980-85; exec. v.p. Am. Bankers Assn., Washington, 1985—2002, pres., CEO, 2002—. Dir. Colonial Bancorp, 1979-85, MacDermid Corp., 1986—, Marine Spill Response Corp., 1991-2001. Bd. dirs. N.Y.C. Ballet, 1981-88, Hospiec Edn. and Rsch., New Haven, 1978-81; mem. adv. bd. Yale Sch. Orgn. and Mgmt., 1992-94. Home: 3133 Connecticut Ave NW Apt 923 Washington DC 20008-5111 Office: Am Bankers Assn 1120 Connecticut Ave NW Washington DC 20036-3902

OGILVIE, KELVIN KENNETH, university president, chemistry educator; m. Emma Roleen; children: Kristine, Kevin. BS with honors, Acadia U., 1964, DSc (hon.), 1983; PhD, Northwestern U., 1968; DSc (hon.), U. N.B., Can., 1991, McGill U., 1998. Assoc. prof. U. Man., Winnipeg, 1968-74; prof. chemistry McGill U., Montreal, 1974-88, Can. Pacific prof. biotech., 1984-87; bd. dirs. Sci. Adv. Bd., Biologicals, Toronto, Ont., 1979-84; dir. Office of Biotech. McGill U., 1984-87; prof. chemistry Acadia U., Wolfville, 1987—, v.p. acad. affairs, 1987—93, pres., vice-chancellor, 1993—2003. Invited lectr. on biotech. Tianjin, People's Republic of China, 1985; Snider lectr. U. Toronto, 1991; Gwen Leslie Meml. lectr., 1991; Centennial Mossman lectr. McGill U., 1998; mem. Nat. Adv. Bd. Sci. and Tech., 1994-95; chair selection com. Indsl. Postgrad. Scholarship program NSERCC, 1994; mem. Coun. N.S. Univ. Pres. 1993-2003; mem. Coun. of Applied Sci. and Tech. for N.S., 1988-93; mem. Nat. Biotech. Adv. Com., 1988-99; mem. Fisher (Can.) Biotech. Adv. Ctr., 1989-92; mem. sci. adv. bd. Allelix Biopharms., 1991-93; chair adv. bd. NRC Inst. for Marine Bioscis., 1990-93; mem. steering com. on biotech. labor Can., 1990-92; mem. Atlantic regional com. Prime Min.'s Awards for Tchg. Excellence in Sci., Tech. and Math., 1993—; chair regional planning forum for a pharm. industry, Atlantic, Can., 1993; mem. Atomic Energy Control Bd., Can., 1997-99; chair sci. adv. bd. Quanta Nova Can., 1998-2001; mem. Can. Electronic Bus. Roundtable, 1999-2002, Can. Global Bus. Dialogue on Electronic Commerce, 1999, Coun. of Ministers Com. on Online Learning, 2000-01; mem. IBM Global Edn. Policy Coun., 2000—, The Can. e-Bus. Initiative, 2002—; chair Premier's Coun. on Innovation, N.S., 2003—. Mem. editl. bd. Nucleosides and Nucleotides, 1981-92; contbr. over 150 articles to profl. jours.; holder 14 patents. Bd. dirs. Plant Biotech. Inst., 1987-90. Decorated Order of Can., Knight of Malta; named Hon. Col. 14th Air Maintenance Squadron, RCAF, 1995-2000; recipient Commemorative medal for 125th Anniversary of Confedn. Can., 1992, Buck-Whitney medal, 1983, Manning Prin. award, 1992, Queen Elizabeth Golden Jubilee medal, 2002; named to McLean's Honor Roll of Canadians Who Made a Difference, 1988; E.W.R. Steacie Meml. fellow, 1982-84; inducted into Discovery Ctr. Sci. and Tech. Hall of Fame, 2002. Fellow Chem. Inst. Can.; mem. Am. Chem. Soc., Ordre des Chemists of Que., Assn. Univs. and Colls. Can. (standing com. on rsch. 1993-2000), Atlantic Univ. Athletic Assn. (pres. 1995-97). Achievements include inventing of BIOLF-62 (ganciclovir), antiviral drug used worldwide; developed general synthesis of RNA; developed original 'gene machine'; developer complete chemical synthesis of large RNA molecules. Home: PO Box 307 Canning NS Canada B0P 1HO Office: Acadia U Dept Chemistry Wolfville NS Canada B4P 2R6 E-mail: kelvin.ogilvie@acadiau.ca.

OGILVIE, RICHARD IAN, clinical pharmacologist; b. Sudbury, Ont., Can., Oct. 9, 1936; s. Patrick Ian and Gena Hilda (Olson) O.; m. Ernestine Tahedl, Oct. 9, 1965; children— Degen Elisabeth, Lars Ian. MD, U. Toronto, 1960. Intern Toronto (Ont.) Gen. Hosp., 1960-61; resident Montreal Gen. and Univ. Alta. hosps., 1962-66; fellow in clin. pharmacology McGill U., Montreal, 1966-68, asst. prof. medicine, pharmacology and therapeutics, 1968-73, assoc. prof., 1973-78, prof., 1978-83, chmn. dept. pharmacology and therapeutics, 1978-83. Prof. emeritus, U. Toronto, 2002-, clin. pharmacologist Montreal Gen. Hosp., 1968-83, dir. div. clin. pharmacology, 1976-83; prof. medicine and pharmacology U. Toronto, 1983—2002; dir. div. cardiology Toronto Western Hosp., 1983-88, div. clin. pharmacology, 1983-91; mem. pharm. grants com. Med. Research Coun. Can., 1977-82, chmn. 1980-82; mem. med. adv. com. Que. Heart Found., 1976-82, chmn. 1977-81. Editor Hypertension Canada, 1989—. Bd. dirs. PMAC Health Care Found., 1986-92; hon. sec.-treas. Banting Research Found., 1984-87, chmn. grant rev. com., 1985-86 Decorated knight comdr. Sovereign Mil. Order St. John of Jerusalem, Knights of Malta, 1987, nat. chmn., recipient prize in med. ethics, 1988-98, sci. advisor to the prior, 1987—, Knight Grand Cross, 1990; jury mem. Can. Prix Galien, 1994-99; grantee Can. Kidney Found., J.C. Edwards Found., Med. Rsch. Coun., Que. Heart Found., Can. Found. Advancement Therapeutics, Conseil de la recherche en sante du Que. Fellow ACP, Royal Coll. Physicians of Can.; mem. Can. Soc. Clin. Investigation (coun. 1977-80), Can. Hypertension Soc. (bd. dirs. 1979-81, 89-94, 96—, v.p. 1991-92, pres. 1992-93, Disting. Svc. award, 2002), Can. Found. Advancement Clin. Pharmacology (dir. 1978-86), Canadian Soc. for Clin. Pharmacology (pres. 1979-82, Sr. Investigator award 1993), Internat. Union Pharmacology (coun. mem. clin. pharmacology sect. 1981-84, chmn. 1984-87), Pharm. Soc. Can., Can. Cardiovascular Soc., Am. Soc. Pharmacology and Exptl. Therapeutics, Am. Soc. Clin. Pharm., Toronto Hypertension Soc. (pres. 1988-98). Home: 79 Collard Dr King City ON Canada L7B 1E4 Office: Toronto Western Hosp 399 Bathurst St Toronto ON Canada M5T 2S8 Office Phone: 416-603-5176. Business E-Mail: ri.ogilvie@utoronto.ca.

OGILVIE, T(HOMAS) FRANCIS, engineer, educator; b. Atlantic City, Sept. 26, 1929; s. Thomas Fleisher and Frances Augusta (Wilson) O.; m. Joan Husselton, Sept. 11, 1950; children: Nancy Louise, Mary Beth, Kenneth Stuart. BA in Physics, Cornell U., 1950; M.Sc. in Aero. Engring., U. Md., 1957; PhD in Engring. Sci., U. Calif., Berkeley, 1960; D in Naval Arch./Marine Engring. (hon.), Nat. Tech. U. Athens, 1996. Physicist, David Taylor Model Basin, Dept. Navy, Bethesda, Md., 1951-62, 64-67; liaison scientist Office of Naval Research, London, 1962-63; assoc. prof. naval architecture and marine engring. U. Mich., Ann Arbor, 1967-70, prof. fluid mechanics, 1970-81, chmn. dept. naval architecture and marine engring., 1973-81; prof. ocean engring. MIT, Cambridge, 1982-96, prof. emeritus, 1996—, head dept., 1982-94. Vis. prof. naval architecture Osaka (Japan) U., 1976; vis. prof. math. U. Manchester, Eng., 1976; founding mem. Ariz. Sr. Acad., Tucson, 1997. Contbr. articles to profl. jours. Recipient Meritorious Pub. Svc. award U.S. Dept. of Transp., 1982. Fellow Soc. of Naval Architects and Marine Engrs. (coun. 1977-82, exec. com. 1978-80, 83-84, William H. Webb medal 1989); mem. Sigma Xi, Phi Beta Kappa. Home: 7559 S Eliot Ln Tucson AZ 85747-9627

OGIRRI, DENNIS AREKPITA, educator, political/business management consultant; b. July 10, 1949; arrived in U.S., 1981; s. Ogirri Idor and Asimawu (Ekekwe) O.; m. Esther O. Ogirri, Nov. 15, 1978; children: Osi, Aghie, Pita. BS, U. Ibadan, Nigeria, 1974; MURP, U. Pitts., 1983; PhD, W.Va. U., 1991. Exec. officer, sr. adminstrv. officer Bendel State Civil Svc., Nigeria, 1975-81; stenographic/confidential sec., 1964-71; asst. prof. Johnson C. Smith U., Charlotte, NC, 1989—94, assoc. prof., 1995—, head dept., 1994—96, mem. honors coll. core faculty, 1995—. Adj. prof. U. N.C., Charlotte, 1999, Queens Coll., Charlotte, 2000, Montreat Coll., Charlotte Campus, N.C., 1998—, Shaw U., Kannapolis, 1993-97; presenter/lectr. in field. Reviewer, referee for jours. and pubs.; contbr. articles to profl. jours. Mem. scholar Urban Rsch. Group, Charlotte, 1997—; vol. Charlotte-Mecklenburg Schs., Charlotte, 1994-96; TV polit. analyst/panelist, 1991-97, 2001-02. Recipient Par Excellence Teaching award Bank of Am., 2000. Mem. Am. Polit. Sci. Assn. (Outstanding Tchr. 2000), Acad. Polit. Sci., Southeastern Regional Sem. on African Studies, African Studies Acad., Assn. Am. Colls. and Univs., Urban Affairs Assn., N.C. Polit. Sci. Assn. (panel chair, moderator, presenter). Avocations: reading, soccer, organizing/participating in african cultural presentations. Home: PO Box 563132 Charlotte NC 28256 Office: Johnson C Smith U 100 Beatties Ford Rd Charlotte NC 28216 E-mail: dogirri@carolina.rr.com., dogirri@jcsu.edu.

OGLE, D. CLARK, textiles executive; b. 1947; Buyer and numerous positions Super Valu, Eden Prairie, Minn., 1968-74; pres. W.Va. div. Fox Grocery Co., 1974-78; pres., COO, bd. dirs. Scrivner, Inc., 1978-87; pres., CEO Affiliated Food Stores, Keller, Tex., 1987-90; industry cons. Hoover, Ala.; CEO Peter J. Schmitt; pres., CEO various pvt. cos., 1987-96; mng. dir. KPMG Peat Marwick, LLP; pres., CEO Johnston Industries, Inc., 1998—. Office: Johnston Industries Inc 2401 Brookstone Centre Pkwy #200 Columbus GA 31904 Fax: 706-641-3159.

OGLE, DAVID WILLIAM, art educator, sculptor, ceramist, printmaker; b. Richmond, Calif., May 17, 1944; s. Robert Ray Sr. and Dorothy O.; m. Carol Jo Gudenkauf, July 7, 1968; 1 child: Ashley Christina. AA in Art, Contra Costa Coll., San Pablo, Calif., 1964; BA in Ceramics, San Jose State U., 1969, MA in Sculpture, 1970; postgrad., San Francisco State U., 1988. Cert. instr. art C.C., Calif. Owner David Ogle Ceramics and Sculpture, Los Gatos, Calif., 1968—; instr., art lab. technician West Valley Coll., Campbell, Calif., 1971-72, instr. art, founder ceramics dept. Saratoga, Calif., 1973—, chmn. dept. sculpture, 1973—, chmn. dept. art, 1976-78, chmn. ceramics, 1978—. Foundry apprentice San Francisco Art Foundry, 1974-75; lectr. Corcoran Sch. Art, Washington, 1976—, San Jose State U., Calif. 1986—; chmn. Olympiad of Arts Coll. Divsn., Saratoga, 1993-97; juror numerous art exhbns., Calif., Oreg. Contbg. author Ceramics Monthly Mag., 1985-97, Claytimes Mag., 2004; author: Workbook for Ceramics, 1997; one-man shows include San Jose Mus., 1979; exhibited in group shows at San Francisco Mus. Modern Art, Oakland Mus., De Young Mus., Triton Mus., Los Gatos Mus., Crocker Mus., Arts Coun. Gt. Britain-White Chapel Gallery, Musee d'Art Moderne, Paris, France, La Jolla Mus., Palo Alto Cultural Ctr., Esther Robles Gallery, L.A., William Sawyer Gallery, San Francisco, Smith-Anderson Gallery, Palo Alto, Calif., Fendrick Gallery, Washington, Gargoyle Gallery, Aspen, Colo., Jalbert Gallery, Saratoga, The Art Foundry Gallery, Sacramento, The Art Object Gallery, San Jose, Calif.; represented in permanent collections Addison Gallery Am. Art, Brit. Coun. for Arts; prin. works include Figurescapes, Chi the Vital Spirit, Fates and the Unknown Artist, Richmond Projects Series; represented in numerous pvt. collections; curator (exhibits) Art Object Gallery, San Jose, Calif., The Art Gallery, Saratoga, Calif. Mentor 2+2+2 Off to Coll. program West Valley Coll., 1993—; vol. Young Authors program VanMeter Elem. Sch., Los Gatos, 1990-92; vol. Montalvo Art Assn., Saratoga, 1992; active San Francisco Mus. Modern Art, 1975—. Recipient numerous sculpture awards, Calif., 1970-80; grantee sabbatical West Valley Coll., 1981-82, profl. growth and devel. grantee West Valley Coll., 1996. Mem. Nat. Coun. Edn. for Ceramic Arts, Faculty Assn. C.C., Los Gatos Athletic Club. Avocations: skiing, racquetball, landscaping, writing, home design and construction. Home: 16555 Topping Way Los Gatos CA 95032-5645 Office: West Valley Coll 14000 Fruitvale Ave Saratoga CA 95070-5640 E-mail: brnzpnut@aol.com.

OGLE, ROBBIN SUE, criminal justice educator; b. North Kansas City, Mo., Aug. 28, 1960; d. Robert Lee and Carol Sue (Gray) O. BS, Ctrl. Mo. State U., 1982; MS, U. Mo., 1990; PhD, Pa. State U., 1995. State probation and parole officer Mo. Dept. Corrections, Kansas City, 1982-92; collector J.C. Penney Co., Mission, Kans., 1990-92; instr. U. Mo., Kansas City, 1990-92; grad. lectr. Pa. State U., University Park, 1992-95; prof. criminal justice dept. U. Nebr., Omaha, 1995—. Author: Battered Women Who Kill: A New Framework, 2002; contbr. articles to profl. jours. Athletic scholar Ctrl. Mo. State U., Warrensburg, 1978-82. Mem. AAUW, ACLU, NOW, Am. Soc. Criminology, Acad. Criminal Justice Scis., Am. Correctional Assn., Phi Kappa Phi. Avocations: reading, watching basketball, walking dog. Office: U Nebr Dept Criminal Justice 1100 Neihardt Lincoln NE 68588-0630 Home: 2410 N 99th St Omaha NE 68134-5642 Office Phone: 402-472-3677. Personal E-mail: rsogle@webtv.net.

OGLESBY, JOSEPH WOODSON (MIKE ENGLISH), writer, publishing executive; b. Louisville, Aug. 14, 1931; s. Joseph Woodson Oglesby, Sr. and Mary Lee (Wiggington) Oglesby; m. Marianna Bachmann, Sept. 4, 1971; 1 child, Shane Woodson. BA, U. Louisville, 1953. Staff writer Louisville Times, 1954—56, asst. editor, 1954—56; city editor New Albany Tribune, Ind., 1956—59; editor Frankfort Crusader, Ky., 1960, pub., 1960; investigative reporter Tonawanda News, North Tonawanda, NY, 1961—63; exec. editor Voice Newspapers, Louisville, 1964—70; pub., CEO Lucky Pubs., Louisville, 1988—2000; freelance writer, 1970—. Founding mem. Ky. Thoroughbred Media, Lexington, Ky., 1990; pub. rels. adv. Nat. Kitchen Cabinet Assn., Louisville, 1970—72, Contact Lens Soc. of Am., Louisville, 1972. Author: (novels) The Devil's Disciple, 1977, Ghost Riders of the Staked Plains, (plays) The Dodge, 1998 (nominee Pulitzer prize, 1999), monographs on Ky. history; contbr. articles to newspapers and magazines. Vice chmn. bd. dir. YMCA, St. Matthews, Ky., 1970; mem. bd. dir. Talbot Ho., Louisville, 1962; pub. rels. adv. Recovery, Inc., Louisville, 1960—62. Nominee Eclipse award, 1998; recipient Best Feature award, Ky. Press Assn., 1967, Short Story award, Writer's Digest, 1982, 1985; grantee, P.E.N. Internat. Ctr., NYC, 1983. Mem.: Mystery Writers of Am., Authors Guild, Authors Legacy Soc., Hon. Order Ky. Cols., Omicron Delta Kappa. Democrat. Avocations: travel, history, thoroughbred handicapping, coin collecting/numismatics. Home: No 5 2312 Alta Ave Louisville KY 40205 Personal E-mail: novelistjosephoglesby@msn.com.

OGLESBY, ROGER, publishing executive; BJ, U. Mo.; JD, U. Calif. With Knight-Ridder's San Jose (Calif.) Mercury News, Omaha World Herald; CEO, pres. California Community News; editor, v.p. Allentown (Pa.) Morning Call; pres. Los Angeles Times (Orange County edit.); pub., editor Seattle-Post Intelligencer, 2000—. Office: Seattle Post-Intelligencer Hearst Newspapers PO Box 1909 Seattle WA 98111-1909 also: Seattle Post-Intelligencer 101 Elliot Ave W Seattle WA 98119

OGLIARUSO, MICHAEL ANTHONY, retired chemist, educator, actor; b. Bklyn., Aug. 10, 1938; s. Andrea and Anna (Bianco) O.; m. Basila Gallo, Apr. 2, 1961; 1 child, Michael Dana. BS, Poly. Inst. Bklyn., 1960, PhD, 1965. Postdoctoral rsch. assoc. UCLA, 1965-67; asst. prof. chemistry Va. Poly. Inst. and State U., Blacksburg, 1967-72, assoc. prof., 1972-78, prof., 1978-95, assoc. dean Coll. Arts and Scis., 1984-95; ret. Coll. Arts and Scis.; profl. actor. Contbr. articles to profl. jours. Served with C.E. U.S. Army, 1960-61. Mem. Am. Chem. Soc., Va. Acad. Sci., Sigma Xi, Phi Lambda Upsilon. *I have been fortunate to be associated with the most personally rewarding profession available today, the professional education of young men and women. This career is best suited to persons who wish to remain young in spirit, since regardless of your age you are always surrounded with students who are between 18 and 22 years old. This is the best way I know to remain spiritually young.*

OGNIBENE, ANDRE JOHN, physician, army officer, educator; b. N.Y.C., Nov. 18, 1931; s. Morris S. and Josephine C. (Macaluso) O.; m. Margaret A. Haug, Apr. 21, 1957; children: Judy, Andrea, Adrienne, Marc, Eric. BA cum laude, Columbia U., 1952; MD, NYU, 1956. Diplomate Am. Bd. Internal Medicine, Am. Bd. Geriatrics, Am. Bd. Med. Mgmt. Intern in medicine Bellevue Hosp., N.Y.C., 1956-57, resident in medicine, 1957-59; commd. capt. U.S. Army M.C., 1957, advanced through grades to brig. gen., 1978; resident in medicine Manhattan VA Hosp., N.Y.C. and chief resident in medicine, 1959-60; chief med. service U.S. Army Hosp., Nurnburg, Germany, 1961-62, chief dept. medicine, 1962-64; fellow in cardiology Walter Reed Gen. Hosp., Washington, 1964-65, asst. in cardiology, 1965-66, asst. chief dept. medicine, 1969-72; chief dept. medicine, chief profl. services U.S. Army Hosp., Ft. Meade, Md., 1966-68; cons. in medicine Hdqrs. U.S. Army, Vietnam, 1969; asst. chief dept. medicine Walter Reed Army Med. Ctr., 1970-72; from chief dept. medicine to dir. med. edn. Brooke Army Med. Center, Ft. Sam Houston, Tex., 1972-78, dir. med. edn., 1976-78, dep. comdr. and chief profl. services, 1976-78, comdr., commanding gen., 1978-81; hosp. dir. San Antonio State Chest Hosp., 1981-85; program dir. internal medicine Canton, Ohio, 1985-95; prof. medicine N.E. Ohio U., Rootstown, 1985-98, prof. emeritus, 1998—, chmn. dept. medicine, 1989-98, assoc. dean for med. edn., med. dir., 1995-98; v.p., treas. Majomed Corp., San Antonio, 1999—. Instr. medicine NYU, 1960; assoc. clin. prof. Georgetown U., 1970-72; clin. prof. U. Tex. Health Sci. Ctr., San Antonio, 1973-85, mem. postgrad. adv. com., 1977-78; mem. Instl. Rev. Bd., 1981-85; pres. Bexar Met. unit Am. Cancer Soc., 1984; dir. Eisenhower Nat. Bank; bd. dirs. Cancer Therapy and Rsch. Ctr.; chmn. South Tex. Epilepsy Found., 1985. Contbr. articles to med. publs. and chpts. to books; editor, prin. author Internal Medicine in Vietnam, Vol. II, 1982; editor-in-chief: Internal Medicine in Vietnam, vol. I, 1977. Trustee Regina Health Ctr., 1992-97; mem. med. adv. bd. Access Health Inc., 1998-2000. Decorated Disting. Service medal, Legion of Merit; named among Am. Top Physicians, Consumer Rsch. Coun., 2003. Master ACP (laureate, master tchr.); fellow Am. Coll. Physician Execs. (cert.), Am. Coll. Angiology; mem. N.Y. Acad. Scis., Am. Fedn. Clin. Rsch., Bexar County Med. Soc., Stark County Med. Soc., Assn. Profs. Medicine, Tex. Med. Found., Alpha Omega Alpha. Home and Office: 27671 Ramblewood St San Antonio TX 78261-2013 *Compassion must remain the universal prescription in medical practice. Technology can provide no solutions in the absence of humanity.*

OGNIBENE, FREDERICK PETER, internist; b. Jamestown, N.Y., Aug. 30, 1953; s. Vincent Larry and Alma Linda (Martinelli) O. BA, U. Rochester, 1975; MD, Cornell U., 1979. Diplomate Am. Bd. Internal Medicine, Am. Bd. Internal Medicine-Critical Care. From intern to resident N.Y. Hosp./Cornell Med. Ctr., 1979-82; from med. to sr. staff fellow Critical Care Medicine Dept. NIH, Bethesda, Md., 1982-87, sr. investigator, 1987—, fellowship dir., 1998—2003. Assoc. clin. prof. George Washington U., Washington, 1996—; adj. assoc. prof. U. Md., 2000—; dir. clin. rsch. tng. program NIH, 2000—, dir. office clin. rsch. tng. and med. edn., 2003—. Manuscript reviewer; contbr. articles to profl. jours., chpts. to books. Mem. adv. bd. Washington Project of the Arts/ Corcoran; bd. dirs. Cultural Devel. Corp. D.C., 2003—. Capt. USPHS, 1985—. Fellow ACP, Am. Coll. Critical Care Medicine (chair credentials com. 1992-94, bd. regents 1994-2000); mem. Cornell U. Med. Coll. Alumni Assn. (bd. dirs.), Am. Fedn. Clin. Rschs. (nat. coun. 1987-95, sec.-treas. ea. sect. 1987-91, chair-elect 1991-92, chair 1992-93), Am. Fedn. Clin. Rsch. Found. (trustee), Soc. Critical Care Medicine (co-chair symposium 1998, governing coun. 2000-04, sec. 2004—), Alpha Omega Alpha. Democrat. Roman Catholic. Avocations: travel, studying Italian language, collecting contemporary american art. Home: 1661 Crescent Pl NW Apt 308 Washington DC 20009 Office: NIH Rm BIL401 9000 Rockville Pike Bldg 10 Bethesda MD 20892 Office Phone: 301-496-9425. Business E-Mail: fognibene@nih.gov.

O'GORMAN, MAURICE R.G. medical researcher; s. Bernard Joseph and Joyce Ann Elaine O'Gorman; m. Lori Ann O'Gorman, Sept. 21, 1986; children: Nicholas Joseph, Trevor Maurice. PhD, U. of B.C., Vancouver, 1988. Diplomate Am. Bd. of Med. Lab. Immunology, 1994. Dir., diagnostic immunology and flow cytometry labs. The Children's Meml. Hosp., Chgo., 1991—, vice chmn. - pathology and lab. medicine: bus. affairs and outreach, 2003—, acting dir., pathology flow cytometry lab. Chicago, Ill., 1991—94; assoc. prof. Northwestern U., Chgo., 1999—; dir., adult hiv and spl. studies cytometry lab. Northwestern Meml. Hosp., Chgo., 1992—, cons. dir., clin. flow cytometry, dept. of pathology, 1992—94; cons. PharMingen/Becton Dickinson, Inc., San Diego, 1997—2000; cons., dept. of microbiology/immunology, microbiology reference labs Focus Technologies, Herndon, Va., 1992—94; faculty, flow cytometry preceptorship ASCP-Rush Presbyn. St. Luke's Program, Chgo., 1992—94; cons. Biometric Imaging, Inc., Mountain View, Calif., 1994—96. Insp. Am. Soc. Clin. Pathologists Lab. Accreditation Program, Chgo., 1990—; reviewer Cytometry, Jour. of Leukocyte Biology, Clin. Immunology and Immunopathology, Jour. Immunol. Methods, Archives of Pathology and Lab. Medicine; examiner Am. Soc. Clin. Pathology Bd. of Registry Cytometry Qualification, Chgo. Sect. editor (newsletter) Molecular Diagnostics, mem. editl. bd. (book) Clinical and Diagnostic Laboratory Immunology, American Society for Microbiology Publications Board. Mem.: 'Assn. of Med. Lab. Immunologists (pres. 2002—03). Office Phone: 773-880-3070. Personal E-mail: mogorman@northwestern.edu.

OGRA, PEARAY L. pediatrician, educator; b. Srinagar, Kashmir, India, Mar. 19, 1937; came to U.S., 1961, naturalized, 1969; s. Govinda Kaul and Gunvati (Daftari) O.; children: Sanjay, Monica. MB, Christian Med. Coll., Ludhiana, India, 1961. Intern Binghamton (N.Y.) Gen. Hosp., 1962-63; resident U. Chgo., 1963-64, N.Y. U.-Bellevue Med Center, 1964-66, fellow in infectious diseases, 1966-68; asst. prof. pediatrics SUNY, Buffalo, 1968-71, assoc. prof. pediatrics and microbiology, 1972-74, prof., 1974-91; John Sealy disting. chair, prof. U. Tex. Med. Br., Galveston, 1991-2000, chmn. dept. pediatrics, 1991-99; prof. pediatrics Children's Hosp., Buffalo, 2000—. Dir. divsn. virology Children's Hosp. Buffalo, 1969-81, chief dept. infectious diseases, 1970-91; dir. Clin. Labs. Children's Hosp., 1985-90; mem. study sect. NIH, 1979-85, maternal child health com., 1987-91; mem., chmn. bd. Internat. Pediat. Rsch. Found., Inc., 1984-89; mem. com. on vaccines for 21st century Inst. of Medicine NAS, 1997-2000, com. in infant formula, 2002. Recipient E. Mead Johnson award for Pediatric Research Am. Acad. Pediatrics, 1978; Kalhana award Kashmir Sci. Culture and Soc., 1984; Stockton Kimball award SUNY, 1985; Buswell fellow, 1968-71. Fellow Royal Soc. Medicine, Assn. Am. Physicians, Am. Acad. Pediatrics, Am. Acad. Microbiology; mem. Am. Soc. Clin. Investigation, Soc. Pediatric Rsch., Infectious Disease Soc. Am., Soc. Exptl. Biology and Medicine, Am. Assn. Immunologists, Am. Soc. Microbiology, AAAS, Am. Fedn. Clin. Rsch., Am. Soc. Virology. Home: 163 Troy Del Way Williamsville NY 14221-4505 Office Phone: 716-878-7290. Business E-Mail: pogra@upa.chob.edu.

O'GRADY, BEVERLY TROXLER, investment executive, counselor; d. Robert Andrew and Beverly Beam (Barrier) Troxler; m. Robert Edward O'Grady, Aug. 6, 1966. BA, St. Mary's Coll., 1963; MA, Columbia U., 1965. Exec. v.p. Wilkinson & Hottinger Inc., N.Y.C., 1973-94, Helvetia Capital Corp., N.Y.C., 1987-94; pres. Wilkinson O'Grady & Co., Inc., N.Y.C., 1994—. Mem. adv. bd. Charles Schwab Fin., San Francisco, 1991-93. Active Women's Nat. Rep. Club, N.Y.C., 1991-94; trustee St. Mary's Coll., Notre Dame, Ind., 2002—. Mem. Assn. Investment Mgrs., N.Y. Soc. Security Analysts, Women's Bond Club (pres. 1992-94), Univ. Club. Roman Catholic. Office: Wilkinson O'Grady & Co Inc 520 Madison Ave New York NY 10022-4213

O'GRADY, DENNIS JOSEPH, lawyer; b. Hoboken, N.J., Nov. 16, 1943; s. Joseph A. and Eileen O'Grady; m. Mary Anne Amoruso, Sept. 9, 1966 (div. Apr. 1984); 1 child, Kara Anne. AB, Seton Hall Coll., 1965; MA, U. So. Calif., 1969; JD, Rutgers U., 1973. Bar: N.J. 1973, U.S. Ct. Appeals (3d cir.) 1975, U.S. Dist. Ct. N.J., U.S. Supreme Ct. 2000. Ptnr. Riker, Danzig, Scherer, Hyland & Perretti, Newark, Trenton and Morristown, N.J., 1974—. Adj. asst. prof. of bus. law St. Peter's Coll., Jersey City, 1973—; adj. prof. law Rutgers U. Law Sch., 1997—. Fellow: Am. Coll. Bankruptcy Lawyers; mem.: ABA (bus./bankruptcy sect.), NJ Turnaround Assn. (bd. dirs.), Am. Bd. Cert. (faculty subcom.), Am. Bankruptcy Inst. (health career subcom., bd. profl. cert.), Fed. Bar Assn., N.J. State Bar Assn. (debtor/creditor sect.). Democrat. Roman Catholic. Office: Riker Danzig Scherer Hyland & Perretti 1 Speedwell Ave Ste 2 Morristown NJ 07960-6823 E-mail: dogrady@riker.com.

O'GRADY, JAMES S. retired elementary school educator; b. Battle Creek, Mich., Aug. 14, 1936; s. John Stanley and Bernadine Yeo O'Grady. BA in Social Scis., Calif. State Coll., 1972. Cert. tchr. Calif., 1976. Tchr. Standiford Elem. Sch., Modesto, Calif., 1973—87, The Firs Jr. Sch., Bishop Stortford, England, 1987—88, C.F. Brown Elem. Sch., Modesto, Calif., 1988—94; coord., tchr. Ave. Libr./Homework Ctr., Ventura, 1998—2002; ret. Vol. tutor Project Understanding, Ventura, 1997—98, vol. story reader Grandparents and Books, 1997—98. Author: (picture book) Good-Bye Strawberry Pie. With U.S. Army, 1959—65. Avocations: baseball, writing, travel, reading, bird-watching.

O'GRADY, MICHAEL J. federal agency administrator; Bachelor's Degree, Alfred U.; D in Polit. Sci., U. Rochester. Sr. analyst Biopartisan Commn. on the Future of Medicare; health analyst Senate Fin. Com.; sr. rsch. dir. Project Hope's Ctr. for Health Affairs; sr. health economist Joint Econ. Com., U.S. Congress; asst. sec. for planning and evaluation U.S. Dept. Health and Human Svcs., Washington, 2003—. With Medicare Payment Adv. Commn., Physician Payment Rev. Commn., Congl. Rsch. Svc., Libr. Congress, Office for Civil Rights, Dept. Health Edn. and Welfare and Dept. Edn. Office: US Dept Health and Human Svcs 200 Independence Ave SW Washington DC 20201

OGREAN, DAVID WILLIAM, sports executive; b. New Haven, Feb. 7, 1953; s. Richard Berton and Dorothy (Nystrom) O.; m. Maryellen Harvey, Aug. 10 1974; children: Matthew David, Tracy Erin, Dana Marie. BA in English cum laude, U Conn., 1974; MS in Film, Boston U., 1978. Asa S. Bushnell intern Ea. Coll. Athletic Conf., Centervill, Mass., 1977-78; pub. rels. dir. Amateur Hockey Assn. U.S., Colorado Springs, Colo., 1978-80; mng. editor Am. Hockey and Arena mag., 1979-80; comm. rep. ESPN, Inc., Bristol, Conn., 1980-83, program mgr., 1983-88; asst. exec. dir. for TV Coll. Football Assn., Boulder, Colo., 1988-90; dir. of broadcasting U.S. Olympic Com., Colorado Springs, 1990-93; exec. dir. USA Hockey, Colorado Springs, 1993-99; chmn. Colorado Springs Sports Corp., 1996-97; dep. exec. dir. mktg. U.S. Olympic Com., Colorado Springs, 1999-2000; pres., CEO Colorado Springs Sports Corp., 2000—02. Chmn. legis. com. U.S. Olympic Com., 1997-99, 2000—; exec. dir. USA Football, 2002—. Office: 8300 Boone Blvd Ste 870 Vienna VA 22182 Office Phone: 703-918-0007.

OGREN, ROBERT EDWARD, biologist, educator; b. Jamestown, N.Y., Feb. 9, 1922; s. David Paul and Mary Gladys (Ahlstrom) O.; m. Jean Blose Jackson, Aug. 28, 1948; children: Paul Robert, Philip Edward. BA, Wheaton Coll., 1947; MS, Northwestern U., 1948; PhD, U. Ill., 1953. Asst. prof. biology Ursinus Coll., Collegeville, Pa., 1953-57, Dickinson Coll., Carlisle, Pa., 1957-63; mem. faculty Wilkes Coll., Wilkes-Barre, Pa., 1963—, prof. biology, 1981-86, prof. emeritus, 1986—. Author: Meet the Pastors of First Presbytarian Church, Wilkes-Barre, 1770-1996, 1997, The First Presbytarian Church of Wilkes-Barre, Pennsylvania: History of the Sanctuary, Stained Glass Windows and Pipe Organs, 1996-1998, 1998. Bd. dirs. Northeastern Pa. chpt. Am. Heart Assn., 1971-88; chmn. bd. Northeastern Pa. chpt. Am. HeartAssn., 1973-76; bd. dirs. Wyo. Valley West Sch. Dis., 1973-79, pres., 1979. Served with AUS, 1943-46. Recipient Frank B. Shepela Meml. Vol. award Northeastern Pa. Heart Assn., 1977; NSF grantee, 1960, 63, 65 Fellow AAAS; mem. Am. Soc. Zoologists, Am. Soc. Parasitologists, Am. Micros. Soc., Soc. Protzoologists, Electron Micros. Soc. Am., Wyo. Commemorative Assn., Pa. Acad. Sci. (editor procs. 1961-62 Darbaker award 1989), N.Y. Acad. Sci., Ecol. Soc. Am., Western N.Y. Geneol. Soc., Wyo. Hist. and Geol. Soc., Sigma Xi (chpt. pres. 1981-82) Republican. Presbyterian. Home: 88 Lathrop St Kingston PA 18704-4811 Office: Wilkes Univ Dept Biology S Franklin St Wilkes Barre PA 18701-1201 Personal E-mail: ogrenrob2@hotmail.com. *To be involved as a citizen in some aspect of community life. To use academe as an opportunity to prepare scholarly works for publication advancing knowledge in your discipline. To work beyond your limitations. To recognize opportunities and use them for making progress. To be positive, honest, creative and persevering. To enjoy the fruits of your labor and the freedom of expression and movement in our great land.*

OGRETMEN, BESIM, science educator, molecular biologist, researcher; b. Ankara, Turkey, Jan. 5, 1966; s. Necati and Ayse Ogretmen; m. Sarita Ogretmen, Nov. 6, 1993; children: Ari Cem, Talia Bahar. PhD, Ill. Inst. of Tech., 1989—94. Post-doctoral fellow The U. of Chgo., 1994—96; rsch. assoc. Med. U. of SC., 1996—2000, asst. prof., 2000—. Contbr. articles to profl. jours. Rsch. grant, Nat. Cancer Inst., 2002. Mem.: Am. Soc. for Biochemistry and Molecular Biology, Am. Assn. for Cancer Rsch. Office: Med U of South Carolina 176 Ashley Ave Dept of Biochemistry Charleston SC 29425

OGUL, MORRIS SAMUEL, political science educator, consultant; b. Detroit, Apr. 15, 1931; s. Jack and Sarah (Zimmerman) O.; m. Eleanor Simon, Aug. 26, 1954. BA, Wayne State U., 1952; MA, U. Mich., 1953, PhD, 1958. Instr. polit. sci. U. Pitts., 1957-59, asst. prof., 1959-64, assoc. prof., 1964-67, prof., 1967-98, prof. emeritus, 1998—. Cons. U.S. Ho. of Reps., 1973, 83, U.S. Office Personnel Mgmt., Washington, 1975—, U.S. Senate, 1977 Author: (with William J. Keefe) American Legislative Process, 1964, 7th edit., 1989, 8th edit., 1993, 9th edit., 1997, 10th edit., 2001, Congress Oversees the Bureaucracy, 1976. Carnegie Corp. research grantee, 1965-68 Mem. Am. Polit. Sci. Assn., Midwest Polit. Sci. Assn. (council 1982-84), Pa. Polit. Sci. Assn. Democrat. Home: 1500 Cochran Rd Apt 814 Pittsburgh PA 15243-1068 Office: U Pitts Dept Polit Sci 4N24 Forbes Quadrangle Pittsburgh PA 15260-7454 Office Phone: 412-648-7281. E-mail: morrisogul@comcast.net.

OGUNLESI, ADEBAYO O. investment banker; b. Nigeria; m. Amelia Quist-Ogunlesi; children: Geoffrey, Carl. BA with honors, Oxford U.; MBA, Harvard U., 1978, JD magna cum laude, 1979. Law clerk Thurgood Marchall, Assoc. Justice, 1980—81; former atty., corp. practice group Cravath, Swaine & Moore, NY; joined as an assoc. First Boston Corp., 1983, named dir., 1989, mng. dir., head of project fin., 1993—97; mng. dir., head of project fin. and global energy Credit Suisse First Boston LLC (First Boston Corp. acquired by Credit Suisse in 1997, now Credit Suisse First Boston), 1999—2002; global head, investment banking Credit Suisse First Boston, NYC, 2002—, mem. oper. com., exec. bd. Lectr. Yale U. Scho. Orgn. and Mgmt. Trustee St. Bernard's Sch., NYC. Named one of the 50 Most Powerful Black Executives in Am., Fortune Mag., 2002; recipient Nigerian Lawyers Assn. Merit award, 2002. Mem.: D.C. Bar Assn. Office: Credit Suisse First Boston 11 Madison Ave New York NY 10010-3629

OGUNYEMI, OMOLOLA IJEOMA, medical educator; b. Ibadan, Oyo State, Nigeria, Dec. 19, 1972; d. E. Olanrewaju and Chikwenye Okonjo Ogunyemi. BA, Barnard Coll., 1993; MSE, U. of Pa., 1994, PhD, 1999. Rsch. assoc. Brigham and Women's Hosp., Boston, 1999—; instr. ITMS, Boston, 1999—2003; asst. prof. Harvard Med. Sch., Boston, 2003—. Bd. mem. Fate Found. USA, Boston, 2002—03. Recipient 2nd Pl. winner, PhD divsn., AT&T rsch. student poster competition, AT&T Rsch., ACM, 1998; RO3 Rsch. Grant, NIH, 2002—, RO1 Rsch. Grant, 2002—. Mem.: Am. Med. Informatics Assn., IEEE, Assn. for Computing Machinery. Avocation: creative writing.

OH, ANGELA E. lawyer; b. L.A., Sept. 8, 1955; BA, UCLA, 1977, MPH, 1981; JD, U. Calif., Davis, 1986. Bar: Calif. 1986. Lawyer, 1987—. Lawyer del. 9th Cir. Jud. Conf., 1995-96, lawyer rep.; mem. Senator Boxer's Jud. Noms. Com. for Ctrl. Dist. Calif., 1994-95; bd. dirs. Calif. Women's Law Ctr., Lawyers Mut. Ins. Co.; mem. cmty. adv. bd. First Interstate Bank Calif.; spkr. in field. Contbr. articles to profl. jours. and newspapers. Spl. counsel to the Assembly Spl. Com. on the L.A. Crisis. Mem. ABA, State Bar Calif., Korean-Am. Bar Assn. So. Calif. (pres.), L.A. County Bar Assn. Office: PO Box 7000 639 Redondo Beach CA 90277

OH, CHRISTOPHER J. advertising executive; Pres., CEO OH Comm., Louisville. Office: OH Comm PO Box 99529 Louisville KY 40269-0529

OH, JOHN KIE-CHIANG, political science educator, university official; b. Seoul, Korea, Nov. 1, 1930; came to U.S., 1954, naturalized, 1971; s. Sung-Jun and Duk-Cho (Kim) O.; m. Bonnie Cho, Sept. 5, 1959; children: Jane J., Marie J., James J. BS, Marquette U., 1957; postgrad., Columbia U., 1957-58; PhD, Georgetown U., 1962. Asst. prof. St. Thomas Coll., St. Paul, 1962-66; assoc. prof. polit. sci. Marquette U., Milw., 1967-71, prof., chmn., 1971-77, dean grad. sch., 1977-85; acad. v.p. Cath. U. Am., Washington, 1985-89, Banigan scholar, prof. dept. politics, 1990-2001, prof. emeritus, 2001—. Adviser Republic of Korea Embassy, 2001—03; nat. chmn. Asian Sect. Fulbright Hays Program. Author: Korea: Democracy on Trial, 1968, (with Peter Cheng et. al.) Emerging Roles of Asian Nations in the 1980's, 1979, Democratization and Economic Development in Korea, 1990, Korean Politics: The Quest for Democratization and Economic Development, 1999, The Korean Embassy in America, 2003; contbr. articles to profl. jours. Chmn. scholarship com. World Affairs Coun., 1976-78; mem. Wis. Gov.'s Commn. for UN, Madison, 1971-74; chmn. Korean Studies com., Assn. Asian Studies, 1975-76. Grantee Hill Found., 1963, Relm Found., 1968, Social Sci. Rsch Coun., 1973, Am. Coun. Learned Socs., 1973. Mem. Am. Polit. Sci. Assn., Assn. Asian Studies, Internat. Polit. Sci. Assn., Midwest Conf. Assn. Affairs (pres. 1970-71), Assn. Cath. Colls. and Univs. (bd. dirs. 1983-87), Indian Spring Country Club (bd. govs. 2000—). Roman Catholic. Home: 8807 Maxwell Dr Potomac MD 20854-3123 Personal E-mail: JNBOH@aol.com.

OH, MARK EDWARD, minister; s. Kap Soo and Boonhak Oh; m. Rosemary McGuire, Aug. 20, 1965; children: Christopher Douglas, Jonathan David. BA, Keimyung U., 1958; MA, San Francisco Theol. Sem., 1963; MRE, New Orleans Bapt. Theol. Sem., 1964; MDiv, We. Sem. Portland, 1968; PhD, Calif. Grad. Sch. Theology, 1971; D of Ministry, Fuller Theol. Sem., 1988. Ordination Crescent-Bay Bapt. Assn., CA, 1968. Pastor Internat. Bible Ch., L.A., 1972—. Pres. Christ Bible Coll., L.A., 2001—. Mem.: Am. Assn. Christian Counselors (charter). Office Phone: 213-382-7925.

OH, TAI KEUN, business educator; b. Seoul, Korea, Mar. 25, 1934; s. Chin Young and Eui Kyung (Yun) O.; came to U.S., 1958, naturalized, 1969; B.A., Seijo U., 1957; M.A., No. Ill. U., 1961; M.L.S., U. Wis., 1965, Ph.D., 1970; m. Gretchen Brenneke, Dec. 26, 1964; children: Erica, Elizabeth, Emily. Asst. prof. mgmt. Roosevelt U., Chgo., 1969-73; assoc. prof. Calif. State U., Fullerton, 1973-76, prof. mgmt., 1976—; vis. prof. U. Hawaii, 1983-84, 86; advisor Pacific Asian Mgmt. Inst., U. Hawaii; internat. referee Asia-Pacific Jour. of Mgmt., 1990—; cons. Calty Design Research, Inc. subs. Toyota Motor Corp. The Employers Group; seminar leader and speaker. Named Outstanding Prof., Sch. Bus. Adminstrn. and Econs., Calif. State U., Fullerton, 1976, 78. NSF grantee, 1968-69, recipient Exceptional Merit Service award Calif. State U., 1984, Meritorious Performance and Profl. Promise award Calif. State U., 1987. Mem. Acad. Mgmt., Indsl. Relations Research Assn., Acad. Internat. Bus. Editorial bd. Acad. Mgmt. Rev., 1978-81; contbg. author: Ency. Profl. Mgmt., 1978, Handbook of Management 1985; contbr. articles to profl. jours. Home: 2044 E Eucalyptus Ln Brea CA 92821-5911

OH, WILLIAM, physician; b. The Philippines, May 22, 1931; came to U.S., 1958, naturalized, 1970; s. Bun Kun and Chay Suat (Lim) O.; m. Mary Oh, June 4, 1960; children— Kenneth Albert, Kerstin Amy. MD, U. Santo Tomas, Phillipines, 1958; MA (hon.), Brown U., 1974; DSc (hon.), R.I. Coll., 1985. Diplomate Am. Bd. Pediatrics, Am. Bd. Neonatal Perinatal Medicine. Intern Deaconess Hosp., Milw., 1958-59; resident in pediatrics Michael Reese Hosp., Chgo., 1959-63; fellow in neonatology Kavolinska Inst., Stockholm, 1963-65; dir. neonatology Michael Reese Hosp., Chgo., 1965-69; dir. neonatology, assoc. prof. pediatrics UCLA, 1969-73, prof., 1973-74; prof. pediatrics and obstetrics Brown U., Providence, 1974-88, Sylvia Kay Hassenfeld prof. pediatrics, chmn. dept., 1989—2003; pediatrician-in-chief Women and Infants Hosp. of R.I., Providence, 1974—89, R.I. Hosp.; prof., chmn. dept. pediatrics Brown U., 1989—2003; prof. pediat. Women and Infants' Hosp., Brown U., 2003—. Mem. NIH study sect. on human embryology and devel., chmn., 1985-93; mem. pediatric test com. Bd. Med. Exam., 1985-89; mem. sub-bd. of neonatal-perinatal medicine Am. Bd. Pediatrics, 1982-88; chair com. on Fetus and Newborn, Am. Acad. Pediatrics; mem. Nat. Adv. Coun. for Child Health, 1995-99. Author book in field; contbr. chpts. to books, numerous articles to profl. jours.; editor profl. jour. Adv. com. Nat. Found. of March of Dimes. NIH grantee. Mem. Am. Pediatric Soc., Am. Acad. Pediatrics (fetus and newborn com. 1986-90), Soc. Pediatric Research, Perinatal Research Soc. (pres. 1981), Am. Inst. Nutrition, Fedn. Am. Socs. Exptl. Biology. Roman Catholic. Home: 24 Robbins Dr Barrington RI 02806-2612 Office: 593 Eddy St Providence RI 02903-4923 E-mail: woh@wihri.org.

O'HAGAN, JAMES JOSEPH, lawyer; b. Chgo., Dec. 29, 1936; s. Francis James and Florence Agnes (Dowgialo) O'H.; m. Suzanne Elizabeth Wiegand, June 28, 1958; children: Timothy, Karen, Peggy, Kevin. B in Commerce, De Paul U., 1958, JD, 1962. Sr. ptnr. O'Hagan, Smith & Amundsen, Chgo., 1997—. Mem. Cook County Pres.'s Com. on the Cts. for the 21st Century, chmn. suburban subcom., 1998—2000; lawyer Chgo. Claim Mgrs. Assn., 1992—; chmn. USLaw Network, Inc., 2001—03. Mem. ABA, Ill. Bar Assn. Chgo. Bar Assn., Internat. Assn. Def. Coun., Def. Rsch. Inst., Profl. Liability Underwriters Soc. Roman Catholic. Avocations: golf, tennis, physical conditioning, painting, reading. Office: O'Hagan Smith & Amundsen 150 N Michigan Ave Chicago IL 60601-7553 E-mail: johagan@osalaw.com.

O'HALLERAN, MICHAEL D. insurance company executive; m. Kay; children: Meghan, Connor. Degree in acctg. and fin., U. Wis., Whitewater. Sr. exec. Wausau Ins. Cos., Gen. Reins., Alexander Re; sr. operating positions Aon Corp., Chgo., 1987, pres., COO; also bd. dirs. Bd. dirs. Cardinal Health, Inc., Optimark Techs., Inc.; COO Aon Group Inc. Dir. Spl. Children's Charities, Providence-St. Mel High Sch., Angus Robinson, Jr. Meml. Found.; mem. arts and letters adv. bd. U. Notre Dame; trustee Dublin City U., Ireland, dir. Coll. Ins. Mem. Econ. Club Chgo., Young Pres.'s Orgn.

O'HALLORAN, THOMAS ALPHONSUS, JR., physicist, researcher; b. Bklyn., Apr. 13, 1931; s. Thomas Alphonsus Sr. and Nora (Sheehan) O'H.; m. Barbara Joyce Hug, June 4, 1954; children: Theresa Joyce, Maureen Ann, Kevin Thomas, Patrick Joseph. Student, San Jose State U., 1948-50; BS in Physics & Math., Oreg. State U., 1953, MS in Physics, 1954; PhD, U. Calif., Berkeley, 1963. Rsch. asst. Lawrence Berkeley Lab., U. Calif., 1963-64; rsch. fellow Harvard U., Cambridge, Mass., 1964-66; asst. prof. physics U. Ill., Urbana, 1966-68, assoc. prof., 1968-70, prof., 1970-93, prof. emeritus, 1993—; vis. scholar U. Utah, Salt Lake City, 1990-93, rsch. prof. physics, 1993-97. Mem. program adv. com. Argonne Nat. Lab., Lemont, Ill., Fermi Lab., Batavia, Ill., Brookhaven Nat. Lab., Upton, L.I.; vis. scientist Lawrence Berkeley Lab., U. Calif., 1979-80. Contbr. numerous articles on elem. particle physics to profl. jours. Lt. USNR, 1954-58. Guggenheim fellow, 1979-80. Fellow Am. Phys. Soc. Home: 4614 Ledgemont Dr Holladay UT 84124-4735 Personal E-mail: toh-boh@earthlink.net.

OHAMA, GARY LOUIS, dental ceramist; b. Abington, Pa., Dec. 9, 1948; s. Benjamin Saburo and Kuniko Hirokawa Ohama; 1 child from previous marriage, Jennifer Suzanne. BS, Pa. State U., 1971. Owner, ceramist Ohama Dental Studio, Inc., Abington, 1973—91; finisher Nakashima Woodworkers, New Hope, Pa., 2000—02; dental ceramist Ft. Washington (Pa.) Dental Lab., 2002—. Cons., lectr. on dental ceramics N.Y. Dental Lab. Congress, Dentsply INternat., Ney Co., Sterngold, Colo., others. Served with USAR, 1971—77. Recipient Outstanding Alumni award, Pa. State U., 1982. Methodist. Achievements include development of internal translucency and effects of refractive index in dental ceramics. Avocation: Aikido. Home: 207 Quigley Ave Willow Grove PA 19090 Office Phone: 212-628-4944.

O'HANDLEY, DOUGLAS ALEXANDER, retired astronomer; b. Detroit, May 7, 1937; s. Malcolm Joseph and Georgie Roberta (McPherson) O'Handley; m. Christine Jeannette Stube, July 20, 1991; 1 child, Douglas Alexander. AB, U. Mich., 1960; MS, Yale U., 1964, PhD, 1967. Astronomer U.S. Naval Obs., Washington, 1960-67; scientist Jet Propulsion Lab., Pasadena, Calif., 1967-85; dir. space sta. Ames Rsch. Ctr., Moffett Field, Calif., 1984-86, dir. astrobiology acad., 1992—99; mgr. TRW Space Tech. Group, Redondo Beach, Calif., 1986-88; dep. asst. adminstr. office exploration NASA, Washington, 1988-92; ret., 1999. Chmn. com. for protection of human subjects in med. rsch., 1982—85; lectr. grad. sch. Georgetown U., Washington, 1964—67; adj. prof. physics Santa Clara (Calif.) U., 1997—; v.p. Sci. and Tech. Corp., Hampton, Va., 2001—; spkr. in field. Contbr. articles to profl. jours. Extraordinary min. St. Catherine Cath. Ch.; bd. dirs. Big Bros. Fellow: AAS, ASMA, AIAA (assoc.), Royal Soc. Medicine; mem.: Internat. Acad. Astronautics, Internat. Astron. Union. Home: 16865 Zinfandel Cir Morgan Hill CA 95037-7076 Personal E-mail: dohphd@earthlink.net.

OHANIAN, MIHRAN JACOB, nuclear engineering educator, research dean; b. Istanbul, Turkey, Aug. 7, 1933; came to U.S., 1956, naturalized, 1967; s. Mark and Mary Catherine (Sayabalian) O.; m. Sandra Jean Blair, Apr. 22, 1962; children: Heather Jean Allen, Holly Lynn Welty. BSE.E. with high honors, Robert Coll. Engring. Sch., Istanbul, 1956; M.E.E., Rensselaer Poly. Inst., 1960, PhD in Nuclear Engring. and Sci., 1963. Lectr. nuclear engring. Rensselaer Poly. Inst., 1963, instr., 1958-62; asst. prof. nuclear engring. U. Fla., Gainesville, 1964-67, assoc. prof., 1967-70, prof., 1970-2001, prof. emeritus, 2001—, chmn. dept., 1969-79, assoc. dir. Engring. and Indsl. Expt. Sta., 1977-99, assoc. dean for rsch., 1979-90, assoc. dean for adminstrn. and planning, 1990-91, assoc. dean for rsch. and adminstrn., 1991-98, interim v.p. rsch., dean of grad. sch., 1998-99, pres. Rsch. Found., 1998-99, interim dean Coll. of Engr., assoc. v.p. Engring. and Indsl. Experiment Station, 1999-2001; sabbatical leave Inst. Energy Analysis, Oak Ridge, 1976-77, on assignment, 1977-78. Cons. Fla. Power Corp., Batelle Meml. Inst., Fla. Nuc. Assocs., Oak Ridge Nat. Lab., Inst. Energy Analysis, Argonne Nat. Lab., Savannah River Lab., U. Va., Tex. Higher Edn. Bd., NSF; U. Fla. rep. U.S. Nuc. Energy Inst., 1972-2001, mem. adv. coun., 1972-80; U. Fla. rep. to Oak Ridge Assoc. Univs., 1972-76; mem. engring. accreditation commn. Accreditation Bd. Engring. and Tech., 1984-88; mem. rev. com. reactor analysis and safety divsn. Argonne Nat. Lab, 1982-88, chmn. 1986-87, mem. rev. com. reactor engring. divsn., 1992-2001; mem. adv. com. Consol. Fuel Reprocessing Program Oak Ridge Nat. Lab., 1982-88; mem. com. on univ. rsch. reactors Energy Engring. Bd., NRC, 1986-88; mem. U.S. Dept. Energy's Adv. Com. on Nuc. Facility Safety (ACNFS), 1988-90; bd. dirs., chmn. Fla. Inst. Phosphate Rsch., 1990-2001. Contbr. articles to profl. jours. Trustee Fla. Defenders of the Environment, 1969-71, treas., 1969-70, mem., 1969—. Recipient valor medal Am. Legion, 1966, Disting. Faculty award Fla. Blue Key, 1984; Alumnus fellow Rensselaer Poly. Inst., 1994. Fellow AAAS, Am. Nuclear Soc. (v.p., pres.-elect 1989-90, pres. 1990-91, bd. dirs. 1974-77, 84-93, vice chmn., chmn. edn. divsn. 1975-76, exec. com. nuclear fuel cycle divsn. 1978-81, mem. profl. devel. and accreditation com., chmn. tech. program of internat. conf. Washington, 1980, mem. nominating com., 1980-81, 87-88, chmn., 1991-92, exec. com., 1986-92, honors and awards com. 1997—, chmn. 2004—, Exceptional Svc. award 1980, adv. editor Nuclear Sci. and Engring. Jour. 1989-2004, hon. chmn. ann. conf. 1997, hon. chmn. 10th Internat. Conf. on Robotics, 2004), Engr. Coun. Profl. Devel. (dir. 1976-78), Am. Assn. Engring. Soc. (awards com. 1985-86, bd. dir. 1990-91, exec. com. 1990-95, sec.-treas., 1992, chair-elect 1993, chair 1994, chair nominating com. 1995, chair awards com. 1996), Am. Soc. Engring. Edn. (adv. com. Ford Found. Resident Fellow Program 1971-79, sec.-treas. nuc. engring. divsn. 1981-82, vice chmn. 1982-83, chmn. 1983-84, projects bd. 1981-87, chmn. awards com. 1985-87; mem. Nat. Audubon Soc. (pres. 1965-66), Ret. Faculty U. Fla. Inc. (pres. 2004—), Rotary (Paul Harris fellow), Sigma Xi, Tau Beta Pi (eminent engr.), Alpha Nu Sigma (pres. 1981-83), Eta Kappa Nu, Phi Kappa Phi, Epsilon Lambda Chi. Presbyterian. Home: 6095 Twin Lakes Rd Keystone Heights FL 32656-9728 Business E-Mail: johanian@ufl.edu.

O'HANLON, MICHAEL A. finance company executive; BA, Phila. Coll. Textiles & Sci.; MBA, U. Conn. Sr. exec. Pitney Bowes; pres., CEO Concord Leasing, Inc.; exec. v.p. DVI Inc., Doylestown, Pa., 1993-94, pres., COO, 1994-95, pres., CEO, 1995—, also bd. dirs. Office: DVI Inc 2500 York Rd Jamison PA 18929-1042

O'HANLON, RICHARD THOMAS, counseling educator; b. Chichester, Eng., Dec. 16, 1956; came to U.S., 1957; s. Thomas Joseph and Agnes Cecilia (Mahoney) O'H. BA in Philosophy, St. Hyacinth Coll., 1974; MS in Pastoral Counseling, Loyola Coll., 1987, cert. in advanced studies, 1988. Tchr. St. Francis H.S., Athol Springs, N.Y., 1974-82, Archbishop Curley H.S., Balt., 1982-84; editor Franciscan Press, Balt., 1984-90; counselor Lighthouse, Catonsville, Md., 1986-87, County of Balt., 1987-88, Human Life Internat., Gaithersburg, Md., 1990-91; prof. Washington Theol. Union, 1990-98; eap Bank of Am., 1998—. Dir. Franciscan Bros., Balt., 1985-88; treas. Cupertino Franciscans, Ellicott City, Md., 1988-97; pres. Continuing Edn. Commn., Balt., 1991-94. Named Citizen of the Yr., Union League, 1969. Mem. ACA, APA, Am. Assn. Christian Counselors, Am. Psychol. Soc., Md. Assn. Counseling and Devel., Md. Assn. for Religious and Value Issues in Counseling, Assn. for Religious and Value Issues in Counseling. Avocation: dramatics. Office: Bank of Am 4401 Coastal Hwy Ocean City MD 21842-6800 Home: 119 133rd St Ocean City MD 21842-4503 Office Phone: 410-289-6818.

O'HARA, CATHERINE, actress, comedienne; b. Toronto, Mar. 4, 1954; m. Bo Welch, 1992. Actress, writer with Second City, Toronto, 1974; co-founder of SCTV, 1976 (Emmy award); films include After Hours, 1985, Heartburn, 1986, Beetlejuice, 1988, Dick Tracy, 1990, Betsy's Wedding, 1990, Home Alone, 1990, Little Vegas, 1990, There Goes The Neighborhood, 1992, Home Alone II: Lost In New York, 1992, (voice) The Nightmare Before Christmas, 1993, The Paper, 1994, Wyatt Earp, 1994, A Simple Twist of Fate, 1994, Tall Tale, 1995, Waiting for Guffman, 1996, The Last of the high Kings, 1996, (voice) Pippi Longstocking, 1997, Home Fries, 1998, The Life Before This, 1999, (voice) Bartok the Magnificent, 1999; TV, SCTV, Comic Relief, Dream On (dir.), Hope, 1997; co-writer SCTV, Cinemax, 1984, Really Weird Tales, HBO, 1986; dir. (TV series) Dream On, 1990; writer Really Weird Tales, 1987; TV guest appearances The Simpsons Show, The Larry Sanders Show, 1992, The Outer Limits, 1995.

O'HARA, CYNTHIA O'CONNOR, writer, columnist, food consultant; b. New Hartford, N.Y., Sept. 17, 1963; d. Miles Joseph and Janice Louise O'Connor; m. Michael Timothy O'Hara, June 17, 1989; children: Colleen Meghan, Kelly O'Connor. Grad., Utica Sch. Commerce, 1984. Culinary instr. Bd. of Coop. Ednl. Svcs., New Hartford, 1996—; newspaper columnist Observer-Dispatch (Gannett News Svc.), Utica, N.Y., 1997—; TV personality numerous TV stas., 1997—. Spkr. N.Y.C. pub. librs., orgns., bus.; food demonstrator various stores, N.Y.C. Author: The Harried Housewife's Cookbooks, 1997; contbr. articles to mags. Leader Girl Scouts Am., Utica, N.Y., 1996-97. Mem. Internat. Assn. Culinary Profls., Mohawk Valley Business-women's Network. Roman Catholic. Avocations: cooking, gardening, reading. Office: The Harried Housewife PO Box 16 Whitesboro NY 13492-0016 Fax: 315-768-2714. E-mail: harried@borg.com.

O'HARA, DELIA IGLAUER, family nurse practitioner; b. Cin., Feb. 5, 1942; d. Arnold and Virginia Iglauer; children: Robert, Matthew, William; m. Herbert G. Johnson, Sept. 23, 2000. BS, Simmons Coll., 1965; Cert. Nurse Practitioner, George Washington U., 1975; JD, Howard U., 1987. Bar: D.C.; cert. family nurse practitioner. Dir. home care program for cancer patients George Washington U. Med. Ctr., 1975-79; occupational health nurse practitioner Libr. of Congress, Washington, 1979-84; lawyer FTC, Washington, 1987-89; dir. student health svcs. Presdl. Classroom for Young Ams., 1987-98; health svcs. mgr. Time-Life Books, Inc., Alexandria, Va., 1990-92; pvt. practice law Washington, 1990-99; occupational health nurse practitioner Washington Hosp. Ctr., 1993-96, nurse practitioner Admissions Testing Ctr., 1996-98; nurse practitioner dept. pre-surgery Kaiser Permanente Med. Ctr., Oakland, Calif., 1998—; quality liason nurse practitioners East Bay Kaiser Permanente, Oakland, Calif., 2003—. Chmn. D.C. Home Care Task Force; vol. Winterhaven Shelter for Homeless Women; active Bd. Nursing, Washington; vestrywoman St. John's Episcopal Ch., Montclair, 1999—2001; mentor edn. ministry EFM Ministries, Montclair, 2001—03. Recipient Trustee's scholarship Howard U. Fellow Am. Acad. Nurse Practitioners (bd. dirs. region 3 rep. 1991-94, rec. sec. 1994-96, treas. 1996-97, pres. 2004—), Am. Acad. Nurse Practitioners Found. (bd. dirs. 1996-2004, pres. 2001), Nurse Practitioner Assn. of D.C. (pres. 1992-95), Capitol Area Network of Nurse Attys. (v.p. 1992-93), Simmons Coll. Alumnae Assn. (class sec. Class of 1964, 1989-94). Home: 2525 Alida St Oakland CA 94602-2503 Office: Kaiser Permanente Med Ctr 280 W Macarthur Blvd Oakland CA 94611-5642

O'HARA, JOHN PATRICK, lawyer, accountant; b. N.Y.C., Jan. 11, 1930; s. Thomas James and Anne (Henry) O'H.; m. Mary Ann Leavey, Oct. 15, 1955; children: Ann O'Hara Carroll, Kathleen O'Hara Geary, Maureen O'Hara-Padden. BBA, St. John's U., N.Y.C., 1952; JD, U. Balt., 1960. Bar: Md. 1960. Spl. agt. FBI, 1955-62; chief counsel, staff dir. emeritus subcom. on investigations and oversight Com. on Pub. Works and Transp., Ho. of Reps., Washington, 1962-86; dir. corp. security Flying Tiger Ln., L.A., 1986-89; ptnr. Burgess & O'Hara, Upper Marlboro, Md., 1990-91; cons. Legal Svcs. Corp., Washington, 1990-91, pres., 1991-94; cons., 1994—. 1st lt. USMC, 1952-54. Decorated Nat. Def. Svc. medal, UN medal, Korean Svc. medal. Mem. Md. Bar Assn., Bolling AFB Officers Club, Marines Meml. Assn., Am. Legion. Home: 5904 Mount Eagle Dr Apt 911 Alexandria VA 22303-2539 also: 4490 Vincitor St Las Vegas NV 89135 E-mail: johnpohara@aol.com.

O'HARA, JOHN PAUL, III, orthopedic surgeon; b. Detroit, June 10, 1946; m. Randy Baird, Mar. 11, 1987; children: Riley Anne, Nolan Baird, Evan John. BA, U. Mich., 1968, MD, 1972. Resident U. Va. Med. Ctr., Charlottesville, 1973-77; fellow Nuffield Orthopaedic Ctr., Oxford, Eng., 1977; practice medicine specializing in orthopaedic surgery Southfield, 1978—; staff Providence Hosp., Southfield, Mich., 1978—, pres. elect med. staff, 1990, pres. med. staff, 1991; sect. chief orthopedics; pres. Porretta Orthopedic Ctr., 1996—, med. dir., 2001—. Pres. Providence Hosp. Med. Staff Research Found., 1984-85, bd. dirs., 1982—; bd. dirs. Mich. Master Health Plan, Southfield, 1982. Contbr. articles to profl. jours. Pres. Birmingham (Mich.) Little League Baseball. Recipient Disting. Alumni award Brother Rice High Sch., 1986. Fellow Am. Acad. Orthopaedic Surgery, Mid Am. Orthopaedic Soc.; mem. Detroit Orthopaedic Soc., Mich. Orthopaedic Soc., Detroit Acad. Orthopaedic Surgeons (past pres.), Oakland Hills Country Club (Birmingham, Mich.), Beverly Hills (Mich.) Club. Avocations: earthwatch vol., travel, sports. Home: 627 Waddington St Bloomfield Hills MI 48301-2346 Office: Porretta Orthopedic Ctr 22250 Providence Dr Ste 401 Southfield MI 48075-6212

O'HARA, KAREN ANN, mathematician, educator; b. Long Beach, Calif., Oct. 30, 1971; d. Robert John and Penny Ann Bradford; m. Marc Edward O'Hara, July 25, 1992; children: Peyton Bryana, Auston Galen, Quinton Mathieu. BS in Math., Calif. State U., Fullerton, 1994; MS in Math., Vanderbilt U., 1996, PhD in Math., 2002. Asst. prof. math. High Point U., High Point, NC, 1999—. Mem.: Am. Women in Math., Am. Math. Assn., Math. Assn. of Am. Avocations: hiking, reading. Home: 6028 Weant Rd Archdale NC 27263 Personal E-mail: kohara@math.highpoint.edu.

O'HARA, KEVIN J. information technology executive; Grad., Drexel U., 1983. Mgmt. staff Peter Kiewit Sons', Inc.; area mgr. Kiewit Network Tech., Inc.; v.p. network svcs. MFS Telecom.; pres. MFS Devel.; pres., CEO MFS Global Network Svcs.; COO Level 3 Comm., Inc., Broomfield, Colo., 1998—, pres., 2000—. Recipient Alumni Achievement award, Drexel U. Coll. Engring., 2001. Office: Level 3 Comm 1025 Eldorado Blvd Broomfield CO 80021

O'HARA, MAUREEN (MAUREEN FITZSIMONS), actress; b. Dublin, Aug. 17, 1920; d. Charles and Marguerite (Liburn) FitzSimons; m. George Hanley Brown (annulled), Will Price, Dec. 29, 1941 (div. 1952); 1 child, Bronwyn Bridget Fitzsimons; m. Charles Blair, 1967. Pres. Antilles Air Boats, St. Croix, V.I., 1978-81, chief exec. officer, 1978-79; owner, columnist The Virgin Islander, 1975-80. Actress in numerous prodns. including: (movies) Jamaica Inn, Hunchback of Notre Dame, 1939, A Bill of Divorcement, Dance, Girls, Dance, 1940, They Met in Argentina, How Green Was My Valley, 1941, To the Shores of Tripoli, 1942, Ten Gentlemen from West Point, 1942, The Black Swan, 1942, This Land is Mine, 1943, Immortal Sergeant, 1943, The Fallen Sparrow, 1943, Buffalo Bill, 1944, The Spanish Main, 1945, Do You Love Me?, 1946, Rio Grande, At Sword's Point, 1952, Kangaroo, 1952, Flame of Araby, 1952, The Quiet Man, 1952, Against All Flags, 1952, Redhead from Wyoming, 1953, War Arrow, 1953, Sinbad the Sailor, 1947, Miracle on 34th St., 1947, Lady Godiva, 1955, Wings of Eagles, 1957, Our Man in Havana, 1960, The Parent Trap, 1961, The Deadly Companions, 1961, Mr. Hobbs Takes a Vacation, 1962, McClintock, 1963, Spencer's Mountain, 1963, The Rare Breed, 1966, The Battle of the Villa Fiorita, 1965, How Do I Love Thee, 1970, Big Jake, 1971, Only the Lonely, 1991; (TV film) The Christmas Box, 1995, Cab to Canada, 1998, The Last Dance, 2000; (play) Christine, 1960; (TV) The Red Pony, Mrs. Miniver, Scarlet Pimpernel, Spellbound, High Button Shoes, Who's Afraid of Mother Goose. Recipient Heritage award, Am. Ireland Fund, 1991. Address: care Charles FitzSimons 11445 Berwick St Los Angeles CA 90049-3415*

O'HARA, PATRICIA A. dean, law educator; BA summa cum laude, Santa Clara U., 1971; JD summa cum laude, Notre Dame, 1974. Bar: Calif. 1974. Assoc. Brobeck, Phleger & Harrison, 1974—79, 1980—81; assoc. prof. law Notre Dame Law Sch., 1981, prof., 1990, v.p. student affairs, 1990—99, dean, law educator, 2001—. Contbr. chapters to books, articles to law jours. Office: U Notre Dame 203 Law Sch PO Box R Notre Dame IN 46556 E-mail: Patricia.A.O'Hara.3@nd.edu.

O'HARA, PAUL ANTHONY, JR., retired art educator, artist; b. Indiana, Pa., Sept. 16, 1938; s. Paul Anthony and Hilda M. (Henderson) O;H.; m. Barbara Ann Zolock, May 24, 1965; children: Paul Anthony III, Polly Ann, Rebecca, Mark. BS in Art Edn., Edinboro (Pa.) U., 1961; MA in Painting/Sculpture, Pa. State U., 1965; postgrad., U. Pitts., Calif. U. Pa., 1963-64. Cert. tchr. K-12, supr., Pa. Tchr. jr. h.s. art Chartiers Valley Schs., Pitts., 1961—95. Photographer Pa. State U., University Park, 1977-78; instr. ceramics Allegheny C.C., Pitts.; instr. art Everyday Poeple, Monessen and Donora, Pa. Sculptor, printmaker, painter; one-man shows include Calif. U. Pa., 1962-64, Lutheran Assn. State Coll, Pa., 1964, Pitts. Ctr. Arts, 1964, 68, St. Francis Coll., Ft. Wayne, Ind., 1968, U. Iowa, Iowa City, 1968, U. Pitts., 1969, Pa. State U., University Park, 1972, Pitts. History and Landmarks Mus., Pitts., 1973, 74, Adam's Art, Bellefonte, Pa., 1994, Frank L. Melega Art Mus., Brownsville, Pa., 2000, Fayette Campus Pa. State U., 2001; exhibited in group shows at Erie Mus. Spring Art Show, 1959-60, 89, 93, 95-96, 2000, Everyman Art Exhbn., The Women's Club, Erie, Pa., 1960, Soc. Sculptors, Pitts., 1963-66, 68-84, Associated Artists, Pitts., 1962-63, 66-67, 68, 70, 72-73, 75-79, 81, 84, 86, Mini Print Internat., Cadaques, Spain, 1989-2003, Mini Print Internat. traveling show, 1989, Museo Nacional de la Estampa Ciutat de Mexico, 1989, Spain, 1993-98, Galeria Article, 26, Barcelona, Spain, 1995-97, Ateneu de Canet de Mar, Canet de Mar, Barcelona, Spain, 1993, Certamen d'Arq Vitectura de La Vila de Canet de Mar, Canet de Mar, Barcelona, Spain, 1988-89, Italy, 1989, Sala del Silenzio, Comune di Bologna, Italy, Colombia, 1989, Festival Internacional de Teatro, Manizales, Colombia, Cadaques, 1990-2002, Japan 1991, Japan: Gallery Fukuda I Palus, Fukuoka, Gallery Oish, Hankyu Dept. Store, Osaka, Daimaru Dept. Store, Kochi, Nipponbashi Takashi Maya Interior Gallery, Tokyo, Matsuyama Frame Shop, Muroran, Bunqadoh, Hakodate, Tomamidoh, Tomakomai, Sasati Gallery, Kushiro, Japan, Korea, 1994-95, Joensuun Taidemuseo, Joensov, Finland, 2000, Wingfield Festival Arts & Music, Wingfield England, 1992-2003, Galeria L'Etand d'Art, Bages, France, Spain, 1990-2003, Tallergaleria Fort, Cadaques, Spain, Catalona: Museu D'Art De Sabadell, Barcelona, Capella De Sant Joan, VilaFranca Del Penedes, Barcelona, Museu Del Suro, Palafrugell, Girona, Palau De L'abadia, Sant Joan De Les Abadeses, Girona, Puigcerda, Girona, Castell De La Bisbal, La Bisbal, Girona, Portal Del Pardo, El Vendrell, Tarrgona, Serveis Territorials, Tortosa, Tarragona, Pa. State U., University Park, Boston Printmakers, Boston, 1969, Pittman's 33rd Annual Art Show, Penn State U., University Park, 1963, Vendome Gallery, Pitts., Pratt Internat., 1971, Pratt Internat. traveling show, 1971-74, William Penn Mus., Harrisburg, Pa., Pa. State traveling show, 1972-74, Ball State U., Muncie, Ind., 1973-74, Delmar Coll., Corpus Christie, Tex., 1973, Three Rivers Art Festival, Pitts., 1961-67, 71, 73-74, 76-78, 80, Pitts. Connection, Dunfermline, Scotland, 1985, Butler Inst. Am. Art, Youngstown, Ohio, 1987, Seton Hill Coll., Greensburg, Pa., 1989, Greensburg Mus. Art, 1989, Pitts. Ctr. Art, 1962-68, Ann. Holiday Ornaments Exhbn. Palmer Mus. Art, Pa. State U., University Park, 1997-99, Soc. Am. Graphics Artists 67th Nat. Mems. Exhbn. Prince St. Gallery, N.Y.C., 68th Am. Graphic Artists, 1999, Stephen Gang Gallery, N.Y.C., 2000, Soc. Am. Graphic Artists 69th Nat. Juried Exhbn. Art Students League NY, 2002, Nemacolin Woodlands Resort, Farmington Pa., 2000, 11th Internat. Miniature Print Exhbn., Seoul, 2000, Sept. 11 Meml. Portfolio Exhibits, Am. Print Alliance, 2002, Thomas Hosp., Fairhope, Ala., 2002, Cape Cod C.C., 2002, DuBois (Pa.) Regional Med. Ctr., 2003. Recipient Frick award Frick Found., 1964. Mem.: Am. Print Alliance, Soc. Am. Graphic Artists, Internat. Sculpture Ctr., Internat. Assn. for the Diffusion of Graphic Arts Print Group, The Print Ctr., Erie Art Mus. Democrat. Roman Catholic. Avocations: landscaping, renovation, genealogy. Home: PO Box 132 Roscoe PA 15477-0132

O'HARA, ROBERT SYDNEY, JR., lawyer; b. Englewood, N.J., Apr. 26, 1939; s. Robert Sydney and Katharine (Drayton) O'Hara; m. Elizabeth Crocker, June 17, 1961 (div.); children: Jennifer, Isabelle; m. Bonnie Durkin, July 19, 1975. AB, Princeton U., 1960; JD, U. Pa., 1963. Bar: N.Y. 1964. Ptnr. Milbank, Tweed, Hadley & McCloy, N.Y.C., 1965—. Served to capt. AUS, 1963—65. Office: Milbank Tweed Hadley & McCloy 1 Chase Manhattan Plz Fl 47 New York NY 10005-1413

O'HARA, SABINE U. academic administrator, dean, economist, educator; b. Ludwigsburg, W. Germany, Oct. 29, 1955; d. Wolfgang E. and Margarete Maier; m. R. Philip O'Hara, Mar. 17, 1983; children: Daniel, David, Dennis. Doctorate, U. Gottingen, Germany, 1984. Dir. pub. policy N.Y. State Coun. Chs., Albany, 1990—93; asst. prof. econs. Rensselaer Poly. Inst., Troy, NY, 1994—99, dir. grad. studies in econs., 1996—99; provost and prof. econs. Green Mountain Coll., Poultney, Vt., 1999—2002; v.p. acad. affairs and dean Concordia Coll., Moorhead, Minn., 2002—04; pres. Roanoke Coll., Salem, Va., 2004—. Lectr. in field. Author: (books) Economic Theory for Environmentalists, 1996; contbr. articles to profl. jours. Steering com. Downtown Revitalization Initiative, Poultney, 2001—02; bd. dirs. Girls Inc. of the Greater Capital Dist., Albany, NY, 1998—2000, Employee Ownership Project, Albany, 1997—2000; vice chair Schenectady Econ. Devel. Initiative, NY, 1994—97. Recipient Outstanding Paper award for excellence, Internat. Jour. Social Econs., 1996, 2000, Outstanding Svc. award, N.Y. State Coun. Chs., 1997; grantee Rsch. grantee, Hewlett Found., Froehlich Found., Sloan Found. Mem.: Am. Econ. Assn., Internat. Assn. Feminist Econs., Assn. Social Econs., Internat. Soc. Ecol. Econs. E-mail: ohara@cord.edu.

O'HARA, THOMAS PATRICK, managing editor; b. Phila., July 15, 1947; s. Hugh James and Agatha Mary (Gilroy) O'H.; m. Juliet Munro, 1970 (div. 1974); m. Pamela Smith, Oct. 8, 1977; children: Rachel Kathleen, Patrick Graham. BA in English, Rutgers South Jersey, 1972; MA in Communications, U. Fla., 1974. Sports reporter Gainesville SUN, 1972-74; reporter Orlando (Fla.) Sentinel, 1974-76, Daytona Beach (Fla.) News Jour., 1976-78; various editing and reporting positions Miami (Fla.) Herald, 1978-86, city editor Palm Beach ed., 1985-86; asst. met. editor Palm Beach Post, West Palm Beach, Fla., 1986-87, met. editor, 1987-88, asst. mng. editor, 1988-89, mng. editor, 1989—2000, The Plain Dealer, Cleve., 2000—. Sgt. USAF, 1969-71. Home: 8890 Spring Valley Dr Broadview Heights OH 44147-2573 Office: The Plain Dealer 1801 Superior Ave Cleveland OH 44114 E-mail: tohara@plaind.com.

O'HARA, WILLIAM DESMOND, JR., lawyer; b. Corning, N.Y., July 18, 1938; s. William D. Sr. and Mary Margaret (Fleming-Burke) O'H.; m. LaVerne Mary Smith, Nov. 22, 1980. BA, U. Notre Dame, 1960; JD, Chgo.-Kent Coll. Law, 1968. Bar: Ill. 1968, U.S. Supreme Ct. 1971, Colo. 1971, Minn. 1976, U.S. Dist. Ct. Ill., U.S. Dist. Ct. Minn., U.S. Ct. Appeals (7th and 8th cirs.). Atty. McKenna Storer Rowe White and Haskell, Chgo., Law Office Dale Schlafer, Chgo., Ruff & Grotefeld, Chgo., Sachs Latz & Kirschbaum, Mpls., O'Hara Fossum Hill & Lothspeich, Brainerd, Minn., William D. O'Hara Jr. Ltd., Brainerd. Mem. Minn. Trial Lawyers Assn., Minn. State Bar Assn., Trial Lawyers Club Chgo., Elks Club, Sertoma. Home: 20446 Legionville Point Tr Brainerd MN 56401 Office: 417 Laurel St PO Box 624 Brainerd MN 56401-0624 Office Phone: 218-828-3398. E-mail: oharalaw@brainerd.net.

OHARAH, JACK, academic administrator; m. Elaine Oharah; 3 children. BS, MS, Kans. State Coll.; EdS in C.C. Adminstrn., PhD Higher Edn., C.C. Admin./Vocat. Ed., U. Iowa. Dean coll., acting pres. Muscatine C.C., Iowa, 1976-86; instr. Scott C.C., Davenport, Iowa; exec. v.p. instrn. and devel. Butler County C.C., El Dorado, Kans., 1986-96; pres. Edmonds C.C., Lynnwood, Wash., 1996—. Mem. ACCT Pres.' Adv. Com., Corrections Edn. Com. Operating Budget Com.; mem. exec. com. State Computer Info. Svcs. Wash. Comty. and Tech. Colls.; mem. AACC Commn. on Publs. and Pub. Rels., Edmonds Alliance for Econ. Devel. Bd., Wash. State Higher Edn. Bd.'s Project Coord. Team. Hon. bd. dirs. Cascade Symphony Orch., Big Bros./Big Sisters; vice-chmn. Puget Sound Ctr. for Tchg., Learning and Tech. Mem. South Snohomish County C. of C. (co-chair), Snohomish County Econ. Devel. Bd. Office: Edmonds C C 20000 68th Ave W Lynnwood WA 98036-5912 Fax: 425-640-1532. E-mail: joharah@edcc.edu.

O'HARE, DANIEL JOHN, electrical engineer; b. Bay City, Mich., Dec. 17, 1955; s. John William and Vida Flo (Roberts) O'H.; m. Betty Joanne Luczak, May 23, 1979; children: Jennifer Louise, Meghan Elizabeth, Amanda Jayne. BSEE, Mich. Technol. U., 1978; postgrad., U. Minn., 1979-84, SUNY, Binghamton, 1985. From jr. engr. to adv. engr. IBM, Rochester, Minn., 1978—91, adv. engr. interdivsnl. project leader, 1991—95; program mgr. storage adapter all IBM server syss., 1995-97; sr. program mgr. AS/400 Asia Pacific Mktg., 1997—2001, exec. project mgr. IBM eServer iSeries, 2001—02; tech. support mktg. leader storage software divsn. IBM, 2002—. Coach competitive cheerleading squad Minn. ICE elite, 2003—. Referee Rochester Youth Baseball Assn., 1988, 89, coach, 1992, 93; line judge Rochester Youth Soccer, 1989; vol. tchr. for gifted and talented edn. at local pub. elem. sch., 1989-94; asst. youth competitive cheerleading squad, Rochester Youth Cheerleading Assn., 1995-98, h.s. cheerleading asst. coach, 1999-2003; judge Destination Imagination, 2001. Roman Catholic. Avocations: model building, computers, photography. Home: 2607 Westview Ln NW Rochester MN 55901-2362 Office: IBM Hwy 52 at 37th St NW Rochester MN 55901 E-mail: djohare@attglobal.net.

O'HARE, DEAN RAYMOND, insurance company executive, director; b. Jersey City, June 21, 1942; s. Francis and Ann O'H.; m. Kathleen T. Walliser, Dec. 2, 1967; Dean, Jason. BS, NYU, 1963; MBA, Pace U., 1968. Trainee Chubb Corp., N.Y.C., 1963-64, tax advisor, 1964-67, asst. v.p., mgr. corp. fin. devel., 1968-72, sr. v.p., mgr. corp. fin. devel. dept., from 1979, chief fin. officer, 1979-94, pres., 1986-88, chmn., CEO, 1988—2002; ret., 2002. Chmn. Chubb Life Ins. Co. N.H., 1981—; chmn., pres. Fed. Ins. Co., 1988—, Vigilant Ins. Co., 1988—; chmn., dir. Bellemead Devel. Corp., 1973—; chmn. Colonial

Life Ins. Co. Am., 1980—, Chubb Life Ins. Co. Am., 1980—; bd. dirs. Chubb Ins. Co. Can., Fed. Ins. Co., Vigilant Ins. Co. Dir. Coalition Svc. Industries, The N.J. Partnership; trustee com. for econ. devel., WDC. Mem. Am. Ins. Assn., The Links Club (N.Y.C.).*

O'HARE, JAMES RAYMOND, energy company executive; b. Evergreen Park, Ill., July 20, 1938; s. Raymond Clarence and Helen (Nickel) O'H.; m. Nan Jane Raleigh, Sept. 18, 1965; children: Joan, Daniel, Colleen, Patrick. BS, Marquette U., 1960; MBA, U. Calif. at Los Angeles, 1961. C.P.A., Ind., Ill., Ky., Calif., Tex. Mgr. Peat, Marwick, Mitchell & Co., Chgo., 1961-68, South Bend, Ind., 1968-69; controller Essex Internat., Inc., Fort Wayne, Ind., 1969-76, Am. Air Filter Co., Inc., Louisville, 1976-80; fin. v.p. and treas. Petrolane Inc., Long Beach, Calif., 1980-85; treas. Tex. Eastern Corp., Houston, 1985-87, v.p., treas., 1987-88; sr. v.p. fin. and adminstrn. Tex. Ea. Gas Transmission Co., Houston, 1988—89; v.p., CFO Enclean Inc., Houston, 1991—93; fin. cons., 1993—97; v.p., CFO Ascendant Healthcare Group, Inc., Houston, 1997, John March Ptnrs., Inc., Houston, 1998—2004, Sensor Microsystems, Inc., San Antonio, 2004. Served with USNR, 1962-68. Mem. Evans Scholars, Fin. Execs. Inst., The Woodlands Country Club, Beta Gamma Sigma. Personal E-mail: johare@swbell.net.

O'HARE, JOSEPH ALOYSIUS, academic administrator, priest; b. NYC, Feb. 12, 1931; s. Joseph Aloysius and Marie Angela (Enright) O'H. AB, Berchmans Coll, Cebu City, Philippines, 1954, MA, 1955; STL, Woodstock Coll., Md., 1962; PhD, Fordham U., 1968; DHL (hon.), Fairfield U., 1980, Rockhurst Coll., Kansas City, Mo., 1984, Ateneo de Manila U., 1990, CUNY, 1991, Coll. of St. Rose, Albany, NY, 1995, St. Francis Coll., Bklyn., 1996, St. Peter's Coll., 1997, Albertus Magnus Coll., 2004; DLitt (hon.), Coll. New Rochelle, 1984; D.D. (hon.), Muhlenberg Coll., 1998; DLitt (hon.), Fordham U., 2003. Joined S.J., 1948, ordained priest Roman Cath. Ch., 1961. Instr. Ateneo de Manila U., 1955-58, prof. philosophy, 1968-72; assoc. editor Am. Mag., N.Y.C., 1972-75, 2003—, editor-in-chief, 1975-84; pres. Fordham U., Bronx, NY, 1984—2003, Regis HS, N.Y.C., 2004—. Author weekly column Of Many Things (Best Original Column award Cath. Press Assn. 1976, 78, 81, 84) Office Phone: 212-581-4640. Business E-Mail: johare@fordham.edu.

O'HARE, SANDRA FERNANDEZ, education educator; b. N.Y.C., Mar. 19, 1941; d. Ricardo Enrique and Rosario de Los Angeles (Arenas) Fernandez; m. S. James O'Hare, Oct. 12, 1963; children: James, Richard, Michael, Christopher. BA, Marymount Coll., 1962; MA, U. San Francisco, 1980. Cert. elem. and coll. tchr.; bilingual and lang. devel. specialist. Instr. adult edn., Guam, 1964-66, Spanish Speaking Ctr., Harrisburg, Pa., 1977-79; tchr. Colegio Salesiano, Rota, Spain, 1973-74, 84, Alisal Sch. Dist., Salinas, Calif., 1979—81, Liberty Sch., Petaluma, Calif., 1981-85, Cinnabar Sch., Petaluma, 1985—; instr. Chapman U., 1994-98; also summer migrant edn. programs, 1990-91. Instr. Santa Rosa (Calif.) Jr. Coll., 1982-83; mem. math. curriculum com. Sonoma County Office Edn., Santa Rosa, 1988; mem. Summer Sci. Connections Inst., Sonoma State U., 1994, Redwood Empire Math. Acad., summer 1995; mem. Sonoma County Math Project, 1995-96; summer '96 NEH stipend to Harvard U. Translator: Isabel la Catolica, 1961. Mem. Asian relief com. ARC, Harrisburg, 1975, Boy Scouts Am., Petaluma, 1983, Mechanicsburg, Pa., 1974, Monterey, Calif., 1971, Sonoma County Adult Literacy League, 1996—. Sarah D. Barder fellow Johns Hopkins U., 1990. Mem. NEA, AAUW (chair edn. founds. com. 1985-86), Calif. Assn. Bilingual Educators, Club Hispano-Americano Petaluma (pres. 1987-89), M3 Investment Club. Roman Catholic. Avocation: travel. Home: 1289 Glenwood Dr Petaluma CA 94954-4326

O'HARE, VIRGINIA LEWIS, human resources administrator; b. Pitts., May 2, 1951; d. Robert Edward and Ellen Marie (Saylor) Lewis; m. John Francis O'Hare, Sept. 17, 1994; 1 child, Merit Elisabeth. BS in Edn., U. Pitts., 1973; MS in Human Resources Mgmt., Laroche Coll., 1984. Legal asst. Meyer, Darragh, Buckler, Bebenek & Eck, Pitts., 1973-85; legal office mgr. Rockwell Internat., Pitts., 1985-86; pers. mgr. Rose, Schmidt, Hasley & DiSalle, Pitts., 1986-88; legal adminstr. Duquesne Light Co., Pitts., 1988-99; mgr. human resources Klett Lieber Rooney & Schorling, Pitts., 1999—. Mem. Assn. Legal Adminstrs., Pitts. Legal Adminstrn. Assn. (sec. 1989-93, membership chair 1993-97, edn. chair 1997-2000, pres.-elect 2000-2001), Pa. Bar Assn., Allegheny Bar Assn., Pitts. Human Resources Assn. Republican. Avocations: horseback riding, target shooting, walking, biking. Office: Klett Lieber Rooney Lieber & Schorling 40th Fl 1 Oxford Ct Pittsburgh PA 15219-1407

OHASHI, SHOICHI, business administration educator; b. Seto, Aichi, Japan, Mar. 7, 1932; s. Mitsuo and Yoshie Ohashi; m. Kimiko Ohashi, Nov. 20, 1957; 1 child, Reisaku MBA, Kobe (Japan) U., 1957, DBA, 1967. Acad. asst. Kansai U., Suita, Japan, 1957-60, lectr., 1960-63, assoc. prof., 1963-70, prof. bus. adminstrn., 1970-2000, vice dean students div., 1972-74, vice dean faculty commerce, 1977-78, dean faculty commerce, 1979-80, dean vocat. div., 1982-86, acad. v.p., 1986-92, dean of entrance divsn., 1993-99; prof., dean faculty tourism, acad. v.p. Osaka Meijo U., Kumatori, Japan, 2000—. Lectr. Osaka U. Fgn. Studies, 1968-74, Kobe U., 1971, Ritsumeikan U., Kyoto, Japan, 1971-73, Kwanseigakuin U., Nishinomiya, Japan, 1979-80, 94-97. Author: Theories on Works Community, 1966, Theory of Business Administration, 1992; co-author: Workers' Participation, 1979; co-editor: Information Society Business, 1988, Business Administration, 1991, Lexicon of Business Administration, 1994, An Inquiry into the Japanese Management, 1996. Researcher com. Rsch. Fund Commn. Japan Ministry Edn., 1987-89. Mem. Japan Soc. Bus. Adminstrn. (internat. com. 1980-83, exec. com. 1983-89, 92-95, v.p. 1995-98), Assn. for Comparative Study of Mgmt. (exec.com. 1980-84, pres. 1994-96), Soc. for the History of Mgmt. Theories (exec. com. 1993-96, v.p. 1996-99). Home: 5-40-602 Mukogawacho Takarazuka Hyogo 665-0844 Japan Office: Osaka Meijo U 5-3-1 Okubo-Minami Kumatori Osaka Japan *Books published as author, editor or co-editor since a first book in 1966, a dissertation book, until 1998 are 25. Being engaged these days in research into Japanese management system sponsored by Japan Ministry of Education and Japan Society for the promotion of Science. Recent accomplishments as Dean of Entrance Division include a successful increase of about 10% in applicants for Kansai University in 1997 entrance examination amid overall decrease of the applicable in Japan.*

OHAYON, MAURICE M. research center administrator, psychiatrist; b. Casablanca, Morocco, June 22, 1948; arrived in Can., 1990; MD, U. Aix Marseille II, France, 1979, Cert. d'Etudes Spéciales Psychiatry, 1980, D in Computer Scis., 1992; PhD in Human Biology, U. Calude Bernard, Lyon, France, 1997. Resident in psychiatry and neurology C.H.U. Marseille, 1975-77; hosp. psychiatrist France, 1980-90; sci. dir. Rsch. Ctr. Fernand Seguin, Montreal, Que., Can., 1990-92; dir. rsch. ctr. Inst. Philippe Pinel, Montreal, 1992—; rsch. coord. U. Montreal, 1992-96; pres. Ctr. Evaluation and Statistics, Montreal, 1998—; project dir. Ctr. for Human Sleep Rsch. Stanford (Calif.) U. Med. Ctr. Assoc. prof. U. Que. Trois-Rivières, 1993—; sci. conseiller Ctr. Hos. Vinatier, France, 1994—; vis. clin. scientist St. Mary's Hosp., London, 1995—; cons. prof. psychiatry Stanford U., 1995—; adj. prof. psychiatry NYU, 1998—. Author: Intelligence Artificielle et Psychiatrie, 1989, Apprentissage, Adaptation et Réadaptation: Etat de la Recherche, 1995; Dis-moi comment tu dors, 1997. Mem. APHA, Can. Psychol. Assn., N.Y. Acad. Scis. Office: Ctr Rsch Philippe Pinel 10905 Henri Bourassa E Montreal QC Canada H1C 1H1 also: Ctr for Human Sleep Rsch Stanford Univ Med Ctr 401 Quarry Rd Ste 3301 Stanford CA 94305

O'HEARN, JANE E. state legislator; b. Gardner, Mass., Feb. 20, 1949; m. Robert O'Hearn; children: Megan, Matthew. BA, Anna Maria Coll., 1971; student, Fitchburg State Coll., Worcester State Coll. Tchr. Lunenburg Sch. Sys., 1971-77; tutor, 1979-92; mem. N.H. No. of Reps. from 26th Dist., Concord, 1993-2000, N.H. Senate from 12th Dist., Concord, 2001—, mem. edn., enrolled bills, interstate coop. coms., 2001—, mem. pub. instns., health and human svcs. coms., 2001—. Vol. coord. Birch Hall Sch./Nashua Sch. Dist., 1986-90; vice chair N.H. House Edn., 1996-97, chair, 1997-2000; adv. bd. CHADD; vol. Am. Cancer Soc., Heart Fund, Devel. Disabilities Coun., PTO; dir. Sch. Vol. Program, After Sch. Ski Program; mem. N.H. Fedn. Rep. Women; mem. Commn. on Adequate Edn. and Adequate Fin., 1999-2000; chair Pub. Higher Edn. Study Commn., 1999-2000; mem. Spl. Edn. Adv. Commn., 1999-2000; mem. Commn. on Deaf Studies, 1996; mem. steering com. Office of Spl. Edn. Programs, 2000; mem. N.H. Edn. Improvement Assessment Program, 1997-2000; mem. nominating com. N.H. Higher Edn. Assistance Found., 2000. Home: 7 Pope Cir Nashua NH 03063-3307 Office: State House 107 N Main St Concord NH 03301 Fax: (603) 886-6728.

O'HEARN, ROBERT RAYMOND, stage designer; b. Elkhart, Ind., July 19, 1921; s. Robert Raymond, Sr. and Ella May (Stoldt) O'H. BA, Ind. U., 1939-43; student, Art Students League, 1943-45. Designer Brattle Theatre, Cambridge, Mass., 1948-52; prof. stage design, chmn. design dept. Sch. Music Ind. U., 1989—. Instr. Studio and Forum Scenic Design, 1968-88. Stage designer: Broadway shows The Relapse, 1950, Loves Labor's Lost, 1953, Othello, Festival, 1955, The Apple Cart, Child of Fortune, 1956; asst. designer: Broadway shows Kismet, 1953, Pajama Game, 1955, My Fair Lady, 1956, West Side Story, 1958; designer: for film A Clerical Error, 1955; designer prodns. Central City Opera House, 1959-63, Opera Soc. Washington, 1958-61, L'Elisir D'Amore at Met. Opera House, 1960, Die Meistersinger, 1962, Aida, 1963; stage designer: As You Like It, Stratford, Conn., 1961, Troilus and Cressida, Stratford, 1961, Kiss Me Kate, Los Angles Civic Light Opera, 1964, N.Y.C. Center, 1965, Samson and Delila, Met. Opera, 1964, La Sylphide, Am. Ballet Theatre, 1964, Italian Symphony, 1971, Adam Cochrane, Broadway, 1964, Pique Dame, Met. Opera, 1965, La Ventana, 1966, Die Frau Ohne Schatten, 1966, Porgy and Bess, Vienna Volksoper, 1965, Bregenzer Festspiele, 1971, Otello, Boston Opera, also Hamburg State Opera, 1967, Hansel and Gretel, Met. Opera, 1967, Nutcracker Ballet, San Francisco Ballet, 1967, L.A. Ballet, 1979, La Traviata, Santa Fe Opera, 1968, Rosalinda, L.A. Civic Light Opera, 1968, Der Rosenkavalier, Met. Opera, 1969, Tallis Fantasia, N.Y.C. Ballet, 1969, Boris Godunov (unproduced), Met. Opera, 1970, Parsifal, Met. Opera, 1970, Porgy and Bess, Bregenz Festspiel, Austria, 1971, Falstaff, Marriage of Figaro, Gianni Schicci, Central City Opera House, 1972, Barber of Seville, 1973, The Enchanted, Kennedy Center, 1973, The Mind with the Dirty Man, Los Angeles, 1973, Midsummer Night's Dream, Central City Opera, 1974, Coppelia, Ballet West, 1974, Carmen, Strasbourg, 1974, The Pearl Fishers, Miami Opera, 1974, N.Y.C. Opera, 1980, Don Pasquale, Miami Opera, 1976, Scipio Africanus, Central City Opera, 1975, Swan Lake, Strasbourg, 1975, Marriage of Figaro, Met. Opera, 1975, Die Meistersinger, Karlsruhe, Germany, 1975, Girl of the Golden West, Houston Opera, 1976, N.Y.C. Opera, 1977, Vienna Staatsoper, 1976, Boris Godunov, Strasbourg, 1976, Der Rosenkavelier, Karlsruhe, 1976, Don Quixote, Ballet West, 1977, Die Meistersinger, Chgo. Lyric Opera, 1977, Adriana Lecouvreur, Miami Opera, 1978, La Boheme, 1978, Coppelia, Pacific N.W. Dance, Seattle, 1978, Andrea Chenier, N.Y.C. Opera, 1978, Der Rosenkavelier, Can. Opera Co., Toronto, 1978, Taming of the Shrew, Pa. State U., 1980, Die Fledermaus, Miami Opera, 1980, Tosca, Miami Opera, 1981, West Side Story, Bregenz Festspiel, Austria, 1981, Mich. Opera Theatre, 1985; Pique Dame, San Francisco Opera, 1982, La Traviata, Miami Opera, 1982, Of Mice and Men, Miami Opera, 1982, Carousel, Annie Get Your Gun, Miami Opera, 1984, Lucia di Lammermoor, 1984, L'Italiana in Algeri, 1985, Porgy and Bess, Met. Opera, 1985, West Side Story, Mich. Opera Theatre, 1985, Aida, Don Giovanni, Opera Colo., 1986, My Fair Lady, Mich. Opera Theatre, 1986, Samson and Delilah, Manon Lescaut Opera Colo., 1987, Annie Get Your Gun, Paper Mill Playhouse, 1987, Peter Grimes, Ind. U., 1987, Madama Butterfly, N.J. State Opera, 1990. Mem. vis. com. Costume Inst., Met. Museum. Mem. United Scenic Artists. Home: 2604 E 2nd St Bloomington IN 47401-5351

O'HERN, DANIEL JOSEPH, retired state supreme court justice; b. Red Bank, N.J., May 23, 1930; s. J. Henry and Eugenia A. (Sansone) O'H.; m. Barbara Ronan, Aug. 8, 1959; children: Daniel J., Eileen, James, John, Molly. AB, Fordham Coll., 1951; LLB, Harvard U., 1957. Bar: N.J. 1958. Clk. U.S. Supreme Ct., Washington, 1957-58; assoc. Abramoff, Apy & O'Hern, Red Bank, N.J., 1966-78; commr. N.J. Dept. Environ. Protection, 1978-79; counsel to Gov. N.J. Trenton; assoc. justice N.J. Supreme Ct., Trenton, 1981—2000; counsel Gibbons, Del Deo, Dolan, Griffinger & Vecchione, Newark, 2000—. Former mem. adv. com. profl. ethics N.J. Supreme Ct.; commr. Nat. Conf. Commrs. Uniform State Laws, 2001-. Past trustee Legal Aid Soc. Monmouth County, (N.J.); mayor Borough of Red Bank, 1969-78, councilman, 1962-69. Served as lt. (j.g.) USNR, 1951-54. Fellow Am. Bar Found.; mem. ABA, N.J. Bar Assn., Monmouth County Bar Assn., Harvard Law Sch. Assn. N.J. (past pres.) Office: NJ Supreme Ct 151 Bodman Pl Red Bank NJ 07701-1070 also: NJ Supreme Ct PO Box 970 Trenton NJ 08625-0970 Office: Gibbons Del Deo Dolan et al One Riverfront Plaza Newark NJ 07102

OHGA, NORIO, retired electronics executive; b. Numazu, Shizuoka, Japan, Jan. 29, 1930; m. Midori Ohga. Grad., Tokyo Nat. U. Fine Arts and Music, 1953, Kunst U., Berlin, 1957. Cons., advisor Tokyo Tsushin Kogyo (later Sony Corp.), 1953-59; gen. mgr. tape recorder divsn., product planning divsn., indsl. design divsn. Sony Corp., Tokyo, 1959, bd. dirs., 1964-72, mng. dir., 1972-74, sr. mng. dir., 1974-76, dep. pres., 1976-82, pres., chief oper. officer, 1982-89, pres. and CEO, 1989-95, chmn. and CEO, 1995-99, chmn., rep. dir., 1999-2000, chmn. bd., 2000—03; CEO Nobuyuki Idei. Sr. mng. dir. CBS/Sony Group, Inc., 1968-70, pres., 1970-80, chmn., 1980-91; chmn. Sony Corp. Am., 1988-98; vice chmn. Keidanren, 1998. Decorated Cmdr. Cross First Class of the Order of Merit of the Rep. of Austria, 1987, Medal of Honor with Blue Ribbon by J.M. the Emperor of Japan, 1988, Officier de l'Ordre Nat. de la Legion d'Honneur France, 1996, Grande Ufficiale dell'Ordine Al Merito della Repubblica Italiana award Pres. Italian Republic, 1998. Mem. Japan Fedn. Econ. Orgn. (vice-chmn. 1998), Tokyo C. of C. and Industry (vice chmn.). Office: Sony Corp 7-35 Kitashinagawa 6-chome Shinagawa-ku Tokyo 141 Japan also: Sony Corp Am 550 Madison Ave New York NY 10022-3211

OHIRA, KAZUTO, theatre company executive, writer; b. Hiroshima, Japan, Jan. 5, 1933; s. Kitaro and Ryo (Sugimoto) O.; m. Evelyn Lanham, Sept. 3, 1964. BA, Waseda U., Tokyo, 1956. Theatre mgr. Toho's La Brea Theatre, L.A., 1961-63; gen. mgr. Toho Cinema, N.Y.C., 1963-64; publicity mgr. Towa Co., Ltd., Tokyo, 1965-69; rep., dir., mgr. Toho Internat. Inc., N.Y.C., 1969, chief exec. officer, 1988-97; pres. Internat. Cultural Prodn. Inc., N.Y.C. Producer (dance performance and drama) Yasuko Nagamine's Musume Dojoji, 1982, Mandara, 1985, (drama) Yukio Ninagawa's Media, 1987, Takarazuka Show at Radio City Music Hall, N.Y., 1989, KanashibetsU: Furano Group at La Mama, Takarazuka Dance Concert at Joyce Theater, 1992, Sotoba Komachi, Yasuko Nagamine and Co., Beauty of Tokyo, Met. Tokyo, City Ctr., N.Y., 1993, Virtue Senpo Sugihara, Danny Kay Theater, N.Y.C., 1997, Gen: Hiroshima Atom Bomb's Kid, Danny Kay Theater, N.Y.C., 1998, The Winds of God, Am. Pl. Theater, N.Y.C., 1999, Rent, Japan, 2000, Boonah, Come Down, N.Y.C., 2000, Thank You, Broadway at Lincoln Center, Alice Tally Hall, 2002; author: Broadway parts I and II, 1982, 2d edit., 1987, Broadway, Broadway, 1987, Performing Arts of New York, 1989, Haiku Collection: Though The Travel is Short, The Charms of Broadway, 1994, Broadway Criticism: Walk on Broadway, 1995, Japanese translation of Show Business Is No Business by Al Hirshfeld, 1997, Haiku Collection Flower Garden, 2002. Bd. dirs. Japan Musical Award Com. in U.S., 1994—; chair bd. dirs. Saeko Ichinohe Dance Co., 1993-2002. Recipient 2d Fumiko Yamaji Cultural award, 1985, 1st Cultural Bridge award, 1998, Fgn. Min. Commendation award Japan, 2004. Mem. N.Y. Waseda Univ. Alumni Assn. (hon. dir.). Avocation: golf. Home and Office: 235 W 48th St New York NY 10036

OHL, JOAN E. federal agency administrator; b. Harrisburg, Pa; m. Ronald E. Ohl. Grad., U. Del., 1967; EdM, SUNY, Buffalo, 1969; post grad., Pa. State U. Cons. CE "Jim" Compton of FIVE-J Energy & Grafton Coal Co., 1984—93; W.Va. cabinet sec., chief adminstr. Dept. Health and Human Resources, 1997—2001; commr. Adminstrn. on Children, Youth and Families U.S. Dept. HHS, Washington, 2002—. Asst. to v.p. Fairleigh Dickson Univ., Rutherford, NJ, 1975—82. Recipient Disting. West Virginian award, 2000, Joan E. Ohl Rural Health Leadership award, W.Va. Rural Health Assn., 2000, Leadership Award, Multi-CAP, Inc., 2000, Bateman Award, WV Hosp. Assoc., 2000, Leadership Award, WV Pub. Health Assoc., 2000. Mem.: Ind. Coll. Fund of NJ & the Assoc. of Ind. Coll. & Univ. in NJ (v.p. 1982—83), WV Health Care Cost Review Authority (bd. mem. 1993—97). Office: Dept HHS Adminstrn on Children Youth and Families 330 C St SW Rm 2134 Washington DC 20447*

OHLE, DAVID H. military career officer; b. Youngstown, Ohio, Oct. 16, 1944; m. Susan Thomas; children: Amanda, Darren. BS, U. Mil. Acad., 1968; MA in Social Sci., Ohio State U. Commd. officer US Army, 1968, advanced through grades to lt. gen., comdr. Ranger Co., comdr. inf. bn., comdr. infantry brigade Schofield Barracks, Hawaii, asst. divsn. comdr. 1st Inf. Divsn. Ft. Riley, Kans., chief of staff of the Army chairholder Nat. War Coll., chief exec. svcs. divsn. Office of the Chief of Staff, exec. officer to the dep. chief of staff for ops. and plans, exec. officer to chief of staff of the Army, dir. La. Maneuvers Task Force, dep. comdt. U.S. Army Command and Gen. Staff Coll., dir. Officer Pers. Mgmt. Sys. XXI Task Force, asst. dep. chief of staff for personnel, office of dep. chief of staff for personal, 1997—98, lt. gen., dep. chief of staff for personnel, 1998—. Decorated Silver Star, three Legions of Merit, three Bronze Stars one with V device for valor, Def. Meritorious Svc. medal, two Air medals one with V device for valor. Office: US Army 300 Army Pentagon Washington DC 20310-0300*

OHLGREN, JOEL R. lawyer; b. Mpls., July 21, 1942; BA, UCLA, 1965, JD, 1968. Bar: Calif. 1969. Ptnr. Sheppard, Mullin, Richter & Hampton LLP, L.A. Fellow Am. Coll. Bankruptcy; mem. ABA, State Bar Calif., Los Angeles County Bar Assn. (past chmn. comml. law and bankruptcy sect.), Fin. Lawyers Inst., Am. Bankruptcy Inst., Turnaround Mgmt. Assn., Internat. Insolvency Inst. Office: Sheppard Mullin Richter & Hampton LLP 333 S Hope St Fl 48 Los Angeles CA 90071-1406 Office Phone: 213-620-1780. Business E-Mail: johlgren@sheppardmullin.com.

OHLINGER, KRISTIE L, music educator; b. Reading, Pa., Nov. 7, 1975; d. Michael D. and Jacquelyn Roth; m. Matthew J. Ohlinger, Nov. 10, 2000. BS, Millersville U., 1993—97; Post Grad. Work, U. of the Arts, 2000—03; student masters in music edn., Lebanon Valley Coll., 2004—. Gen. music educator Ephrata Mid. Sch., Ephrata, Pa., 1997—, vocal instr., 1997—2004, musical choreographer, 2000—; colorguard instr. Gov. Mifflin Mid. Sch., Shillington, Pa., 2000—; pvt. woodwind instr. Don Randell's Music, Lancaster, Pa., 1997—98; woodwind instr. Gov. Mifflin H.S. Marching Band, Shillington, Pa., 1997—99; indoor color guard artistic dir. Gov. Mifflin H.S., Shillington, Pa., 1997—2000. Artistic dir. and dance instr. grades 7 through 12 Ephrata Area Sch. Dist., Pa., 2002—. Actor: (theatre) Lend Me a Tenor; singer (dancer): (theatre) Chicago, the Musical, Cabaret, the Musical; musician: Cabaret the musical; actor(lead role): (Musical) Sweet Charity, 2004. Mem.: Music Educators Nat. Conf. (assoc.; collegiate officer 1995—97), Nat. Tchr. Assn. (assoc.). Home: 41 Misty Lane Ephrata PA 17522 Office: Ephrata Middle School 957 Hammon Ave Ephrata PA 17522 Personal E-mail: k_ohlinger@easdpa.org. E-mail: k_ohlinger@easdpa.org.

OHLKE, AMANDA ANNE, museum association administrator, museum educator; b. Bethesda, Md., Aug. 8, 1964; d. Clarence Carl and Frances Nicholson O.; m. Michael Joseph Kapsa, Mar. 10, 2001; 1 child, Jeremy Clarence. M of Arts and Tchg., George Wash. U., Washington, DC, 1991. Edn. outreach specialist Md. Hist. Soc., Balt., 1991—94; adult programs coord. Nat. Bldg. Mus., Washington, 1994—96; assn. mgr. Mus. Trustee Assn., Washington, 1996—2001, exec. dir., 2001—04; mgr. adult edn. Internat. Spy Mus., Washington, 2004—. Bd. dirs. Cleve. Pk. Hist. Soc., Washington, D.C. Preservation League, Washington. Editor: (newsletter) Network. Mem. D.C. Preservation League, 1997—2003. Home: 3706 Reno Rd NW Washington DC 20008 Office: Internat Spy Mus 800 F St NW Washington DC 20004 E-mail: aohlke@spymuseum.org.

OHLMAN, DOUGLAS RONALD, commodities and securities trader, investment consultant, lawyer; b. Rockville Centre, N.Y., Mar. 25, 1949; s. Maxwell and Miriam (Frucht) O.; m. Elat Menashe, Dec. 4, 1983 (div. Nov. 1996). B.A., Columbia Coll., 1971; J.D., Hofstra U., 1974. Bar: N.Y. 1975, U.S. Dist. Ct. (so. and ea. dists.) N.Y. 1976, (no. and we. dists.) N.Y. 1978, U.S. Tax Ct. 1978, U.S. Supreme Ct. 1978, U.S. Ct. Claims 1978, U.S. Customs Ct. 1978. V.p. Info. & Research Services, Inc., Roslyn, N.Y., 1975-81; assoc. Baer & Marks, N.Y.C., 1974-75, Rains, Pogrebin & Scher, Mineola, N.Y., 1975-76, Weisman, Celler, Spett, Modlin & Wertheimer, N.Y.C., 1976-79, Hoffberg, Gordon, Rabin & Engler, N.Y.C., 1979-80, Bergner & Bergner, Blum & Ruditz, N.Y.C., 1980-81; gen. counsel Greenfield Ptnrs., N.Y.C., 1981-86, gen. ptnr., 1982-86, dep. mng. ptnr., 1984-86, chief operating officer, sr. v.p., sec., dir. V.W. Investors, Inc., J.L. Investors, Inc., N.Y.C., 1985-88; commodities and securities trader for proprietary accts. Highland Beach, Fla., 1988—; dir. Track Data Corp., N.Y.C., 1983-87; allied mem. N.Y. Stock Exchange, Inc., 1982-88, options prin., 1985, 87. Mem. radio news team WKCR-FM, N.Y.C. (Writers Guild award, Peabody nomination 1968); notes and comments editor Hofstra Law Rev., 1973-74. Communications dir., dep. radiol. officer Nassau County Civil Def., Town of Roslyn, N.Y., 1964-74; mem. com. Nassau County Liberal Party, 1982. Mem. ABA, N.Y. State Bar Assn., N.Y. County Lawyers Assn., Assn. of Bar of City of N.Y. Home: 401 NE Mizner Blvd Apt T502 Boca Raton FL 33432-4024

OHLMEYER, DONALD WINFRED, JR., film and television producer; b. New Orleans, Feb. 3, 1945; s. Donald W. and Eva Clare (Bivens) O.; m. Linda Jonsson, 2003; children by previous marriage: Justin Drew, Christopher Brett, Todd Bivens, Kemper Perry. BA in Comms., U. Notre Dame, 1967. Pres. Roadblock Prodns., 1977—; chmn. bd., CEO, Ohlmeyer Comms., L.A., 1982—92; pres. west coast NBC, Burbank, Calif. Adj. prof. Pepperdine U. Assoc. dir. ABC Sports, N.Y.C., 1967-70, dir., 1971-72, prodr., 1972-77; dir. Olympic Games, 1972; prodr., dir. Summer and Winter Olympics, 1976; prodr. ABC Monday Night Football, 1972-76; exec. prodr. NBC Sports, N.Y.C., 1977-82; exec. prodr.: 1980 Olympic Games, Crime of Innocence, 1985, Under Siege, Bluffing It, 1987, Right to Die, 1987, Special Bulletin, The Golden Moment: An Olympic Love Story (also writer) 1980, Crazy in Love, 1992, Cold Sassy Tree, The Heroes of Desert Storm (also dir.) 1991; prodr.: The Emmy Awards Show, Fast Copy, Crimes of the Century, Lifestories; creator, dir.: MTV Awards Show, 1983-86, The Skins Game. Recipient 15 Emmy awards 1975-99, Cine Golden Eagle award, 1979, Miami Film Festival award 1979, award Nat. Film Bd., 1980, award Glaad Media, 1991, Humanities prize, 1983, 96. Mem. Dirs. Guild Am., Acad. TV Arts and Scis. Clubs: Bel-Air (Calif.); The Reserve (Indian Wells). Office: DWOCO Inc 10880 Wilshire Blvd Ste 920 Los Angeles CA 90024-4101

OHLOTT, PATRICIA J. cultural organization administrator; b. Elizabeth, N.J., Apr. 30, 1961; d. Robert Paul Ohlott and Kathleen Elizabeth Ohlott (nee Milot); m. Thomas G Trocano, Apr. 16, 1988. BA in Psychology, Yale U., New Haven, Conn., 1983; ABD in Bus. Adminstrn., Duke U., Durham N.C., 1996. Social sci. asst. Yale U. Family TV Rsch. and Consultation Ctr., New Haven, 1983—84; rsch. technician Yale U. John B Pierce Found., New Haven, 1984—85; rsch. and tchg. asst. Duke Fuqua Sch. of Bus., Durham, NC, 1985—92; rsch. asst. Ctr. for Creative Leadership, Greensboro, NC, 1987—88, rsch. assoc., 1988—95, project mgr., 1996—2002, sr. assoc., 2003—. Chair, profl. standards com. Ctr. for Creative Leadership, Greensboro, NC, 2003—; mem. Ctr. for Creative Leadership Instrument Rev. Team, Greensboro, NC, 2000—; assoc. editor Career Forum, Acad. of Mgmt. Author: (book) Standing at the Crossroads: Next Steps for High-Achieving Women, Managerial Promotion: The Dynamics for Men and Women, The Realities of Management Promotion, Learning from Life: Turning Life's Lessons into Leadership Experience, Traps and Pitfalls in the Judgment of Executive Potential; contbr. book, articles to profl. jours., chapters to books. Reach to recovery area coord. Am. Cancer Soc., Alamance County, NC, 2001—04; grant com. Susan G. Komen Found., Raleigh, NC. Mem.: Soc. for Indsl./Orgnl. Psychology, APA, Acad. of Mgmt. Democrat. Home: 1807 Keogh St Burlington NC 27215-1935 Office: Center for Creative Leadership PO Box 26300 Greensboro NC 27438-6300 Office Phone: 336-286-4423. Office Fax: 336-286-4434. Personal E-mail: pohlott@aol.com. E-mail: ohlott@leaders.ccl.org.

OHLSON, DOUGLAS DEAN, artist, educator; b. Cherokee, Iowa, Nov. 18, 1936; s. Lloyd E. and Effie O. (Johnson) O. BA, U. Minn., 1961. Prof. art Hunter Coll., N.Y.C., 1964—. One man shows include Fischbach Gallery, N.Y.C., 1964, 66-70, 72, Susan Caldwell Gallery, N.Y.C., 1974, 76, 77, 79, 81, 82, 83, Portland (Oreg.) Ctr. for Visual Arts, 1977, Ruth Siegel Gallery, N.Y.C., 1985, 87, Andre Zarre Gallery, N.Y.C., 1985, 90, 92, 93, 95, 2000,

Andre Zarre Gallery, N.Y.C., 2004, Gallery 99, Miami, Fla., 1986, Nina Freudenheim Gallery, Buffalo, 1986, Jaffe Gallery, Miami, 1989, Doug Ohlson 20 Years of Painting: 1982-2002,; group shows include Mus. Modern Art, N.Y.C., 1968, Tate Gallery, London, 1969, Whitney Mus., N.Y.C., 1969, 71, Corcoran Gallery, Washington, 1972, 73, UCLA, 1975, Born in Iowa: The Homecoming, 1986-87, Hunter Coll./Times Sq. Gallery, N.Y.C.; invitational Am. Acad. Arts and Letters, 1992, 94, 97, 2002; represented in permanent collections Met. Mus. Art, N.Y.C., Nat. Gallery Art, Washington, Am. Fedn. Art, Mus. Modern Art, Frankfurt, Fed. Republic Germany, Lowe Art Mus., Miami, Fla., Karl Ernst Osthaus Mus., Hagen, Germany, Mus. Contemporary Art, Helsinki, Mpls. Inst. Art, Dallas Mus., Bklyn. Mus., Whitney Mus., N.Y.C., Harvard Art Mus., Cambridge, Mass. Served with USMC, 1955-58. Guggenheim fellow, 1968; Creative Artists Public Service grantee, 1974; Nat. Endowment for Arts grantee, 1976 Home: 35 Bond St New York NY 10012-2426

OHLSSON, ERIC PAUL, music educator; b. Hastings, Nebr., Sept. 30, 1952; s. Gordon Lewis and Mary Elizabeth (Armstrong) Ohlsson; children: Eric Loren, Jennie Kirsten. B of Music Edn., James Madison U., 1974; MusM, Ohio State U., 1976, D of Musical Arts, 1980. Co-prin. oboist Columbus (Ohio) Symphony, Ohio, 1978—80; asst. prof. music U. SC, Columbia, 1980—86; from asst. to assoc. prof. music in oboe Fla. State U., Tallahassee, 1986—93, prof. music in oboe, 1993—. Faculty Brevard (NC) Music Ctr., 1994—; artist-in-residence SC Gov's Sch. for the Arts, Greenville, 1983—93; prin. oboe Tallahassee Symphony, 1986—. Naples (Fla.) Philharmonic, 1986—96, Palm Beach Opera Orch., West Palm Beach, Fla., 2002—. Democrat. Presbyterian. Avocation: golf. Office: Fla State Univ Sch Music Tallahassee FL 32306

OHM, HERBERT WILLIS, agronomy educator; b. Albert Lea, Minn., Jan. 28, 1945; s. Wilhelm Carl and Lena Ann (Finkbeiner) O.; m. Judy Ann Chrisinger, Aug. 8, 1964; children: Cari Lynn, David William. BS in Agrl. Edn., U. Minn., St. Paul, 1967; MS in Plant Breeding, N.D. State U., 1969; PhD in Plant Genetics and Breeding, Purdue U., 1972. Cert. agronomist. Asst. prof. Purdue U., West Lafayette, Ind., 1972-77, assoc. prof. agronomy, 1977-83, prof., 1983—. Team leader Interdisciplinary Wheat and Oat Genetics and Breeding Program, West Lafayette, 1980—, Interdisciplinary Purdue/AID Devel. Program, Burkina Faso, West Africa, 1983-85; mgr. hard red winter wheat rsch. Pioneer Hi-Bred Internat., Inc., Hutchinson, Kans., 1980. Contbr. book chpts. Recipient Soils and Crops Merit award Ind. Crop Improvement Assn., 1988, Merit award Orgn. of African Unity, 1989, Meritorious Svc. award Sci., Tech. and Rsch. Commn., 1989, Agronomic Acheivement award American Soc. of Agronomy, 1994, Sch. of Agr. Team award, 2000. Fellow: AAAS, Crop Sci. Soc. Am. (chmn. divsn. 1991), Am. Soc. Agronomy; mem.: Am. Registry Cert. Profls. in Agrl. Crops and Soils (cert.), Coun. Agrl. Sci. and Tech., Nat. Oat Improvement Coun. (chmn.), Am. Oat Workers Conf. (chmn.). Avocations: woodworking, music. Office: Purdue U Dept Agronomy Lilly Hall Life Scis West Lafayette IN 47907-1150 Office Phone: 765-494-8072. E-mail: hohm@purdue.edu.

OHMAN, DIANA J. government agency administrator, former state official; b. Sheridan, Wyo., Oct. 3, 1950; d. Arden and Doris Marie (Carstens) Mahin. AA, Casper Coll., 1970; BA, U. Wyo., 1972, MEd, 1977, postgrad., 1979—. Tchr. kindergarten Natrona County Sch. Dist., Casper, Wyo., 1971-72; tchr. rural sch. K-8 Campbell County Sch. Dist., Gillette, Wyo., 1972-80, rural prin. K-8, 1980-82, prin. K-6, 1982-84, assoc. dir. instrn., 1984-87; dir. K-12 Goshen County Migrant Program, Torrington, Wyo., 1988-89; prin. K-2 Goshen County Sch. Dist., Torrington, Wyo., 1987-90; state supt. pub. instrn. State of Wyo., Cheyenne, 1991-94, secretary of state, 1995-98; dir. Dept. Def. Dep. Schs., 2002—. Chmn. Campbell County Mental Health Task Force, 1986-87; mem. Legis. Task Force on Edn. of Handicapped 3-5 Yr. Olds, 1988-89. State Committeewoman Wyo. Rep. Party, 1985-88. Recipient Wyo. Elem. Prin. of Yr. award, 1990; named Campbell County Tchr. of Yr. 1980, Campbell County Profl. Bus. Woman of Yr. 1984, Outstanding Young Woman in Am., 1983. Mem. Coun. of Chief of State Sch. Officers (Washington chpt.), Internat. Reading Assn., Wyo. Assn. of Sch. Adminstrs., N.Am. Securities Adminstrs. Assn., Kappa Delta Pi, Phi Kappa Phi, Phi Delta Kappa. Republican. Lutheran. Office: CMR 443 Box 111 APO AE 09096-9111

OHMAN, FRANKLIN ERIC, ballet educator, choreographer; b. L.A., Jan. 7, 1939; s. Eric Ohman and Irene Iris Harsen; m. Gloria Isaksen, June 24, 1978 (div. Aug. 1984); 1 child, Johan Eric. Grad. h.s., Ontario, Calif., 1957. Dancer San Francisco Ballet, 1959—62, N.Y.C. Ballet, 1962—84; dir. N.Y. Dance Theatre, 1974—. Artistic dir. N.Y. Dance Theatre, 1974—; choreographer, tchr. Ohman Sch. Ballet, L.I., NY, 1980—; choreographer Boston Ballet, Am. Movie Classics (divsn. Rainbow Cablevision), Broadhollow Players, L.I.; tchr., choreographer Long Lake Performing Arts Camp, NY. Co-author (with Emily Berkowitz): Mr. Balanchine my teacher/my friend. Pvt. U.S. Army, 1961—67. Grantee, NY State Coun. on Arts, Suffolk County Office of Cultural Affairs. Avocations: painting, choreography, writing. Office: Ohman Sch Ballet Calvert Ave Commack NY 11725

OHMAN, JOHN MICHAEL, lawyer; b. Dec. 22, 1948; s. John W. and D. Jeanne (Forster) O.; m. Desiree Ohman; children: Brittany Michelle, Andrea Michaela. BS in Bus. Adminstrn., Creighton U., 1971, JD, 1972. Bar: Nebr. 1972, Idaho 1973, U.S. Dist. Ct. Idaho 1973, U.S. Dist. Ct. Nebr. 1973, U.S. Ct. Appeals (9th cir.) 1978., U.S. Supreme Ct. 1978. Atty. Cox & Ohman, Idaho Falls, Idaho, 1978—. Lectr. various locations; chmn. Idaho Transp. Dept. Author: Federal Judges: The Complexity of Recruitment, Appointment, Tenure and Removal; contbr. articles to profl. jours. Exec. bd. Assn. Humanities in Idaho, legal advisor; active United Way, YMCA; past pres. Am. Cancer Soc.; judge advocate Intermountain dist. Civitan Internat., also past pres. Idaho Falls chpt.; legal adv. Mayor's Com. for Handicapped, Mayor's Com. for Swimming Pool, Community Concert Assn., Idaho Falls Symphony Soc., Eastern Idaho Spl. Services Agy.; dir. Group Homes, Inc.; campaign coordinator Gov. Idaho; mem. State Dem. Cen. Com.; precinct committeeman. Served to capt. U.S. Army. Recipient Outstanding Pres. award Civitian Internat., Century Club mem. YMCA, Idaho Safe Pilot award; named del. to Hong Kong, to People's Republic of China and Japan by Idaho Bus. Leaders. Mem. ABA (litig. sect., family law sect., tort and ins. practice sect., divsn. law and procedures com.), Am. Soc. Law and Medicine, Am. Judicature Soc., Idaho State Bar Assn. (adv. coun. continuing legal edn.), Nebr. State Bar. Assn., Seventh Jud. Dist. Bar Assn., Am. Trial Lawyers Assn., Idaho Trial Lawyers Assn., Idaho Assn. Def. Counsel, Def. Rsch. Inst., Idaho Law Found., Unauthorized Practice Law Com., Western Assn. State Hwy. and Transp. Officials, Assn. Humanities Idaho (past mem. exec. bd.), Am. Assn. State Hwy. and Transp. Officials, Smithsonian Inst. (assoc.), Internat. Platform Assn., Assn. Interstate Commerce Practitioners, 7th Jud. Dist. Bar Assn., Am. Mus. Natural History, Airplane Owners and Pilots Assn., Nat. Arbor's Day Found., Idaho Falls C. of C. (chmn. legis. com.), Phi Alpha Delta, Omicron Delta Epsilon, Phi Kappa Psi. Lodges: Elks (legal advisor). Democrat. Roman Catholic. Avocations: aquatic sports, coin collecting/numismatics, reading, aviation, racquetball. Office: Cox and Ohman PO Box 51600 Idaho Falls ID 83405-1600 Office Phone: 208-522-8606. Fax: 208 520-8618. E-mail: johman3419@aol.com., cobjmo@ida.net.

OHNO, APOLO ANTON, Olympic athlete; b. Seattle, May 22, 1982; Mem. U.S. Elite Short Track Speedskating Team. Named U.S. Champion, 1997, World Jr. Short Track Champion, 1999, World Cup Overall Champion, 2001, 500 meter champion, 2001, 1000 meter champion, 2001, 1500 meter champion, 2001; recipient U.S. Champion, 1999, 2001, 2002, 1500 meter Gold medal, 2002 Olympic Games, 1000 meter Silver medal. Achievements include was a national champion and record holder in indoor inline skating, earned a state championship as a swimmer in the breaststroke. Avocations: music, badminton, basketball, break dancing, friends. Address: US Speedskating PO Box 450639 Westlake OH 44145

O'HOLLAREN, SEAN B. federal agency administrator; BS in Polit. Sci. and Psychology, Willamette U.; completed intensive studies program, Georgetown U. Former dir. Washington affairs-environment subs. Union Pacific Corp., primary co. liaison to U.S. Customs Svc.; legis. asst. to U.S. Sen. Mark Hatfield; asst. sec. govt. affairs U.S. Dept. Transp., Washington, 2002—. Office: US Dept Transp Govtl Affairs 400 7th St SW Washington DC 20590

O'HORGAN, THOMAS FOSTER, composer, director; b. Chgo., May 3, 1924; BA, MA, DePaul U. Chgo. Debut performance in Fallout; off-Broadway revue, 1959; directing debut with prodn. The Maids, 1964; dir.: Hair (Tony award nominee 1968), Lenny (Drama Desk award 1971), Jesus Christ Super Star, Inner City, Six from La Mama, The Hessian Corporal, Futz (Obie award 1967, Drama Desk award 1968), Tom Paine (Drama Desk award 1968), Massachusetts Trust, Dude, The Leaf People, Sergeant Pepper's Lonely Hearts Club Band on the Road, Capitol Cakewalk, 1990, The Architect and The Emperor of Abyssinia, The Other Side of Broadway, 2002; composer: music for numerous prodns. including Open Season at Second City Senator Joe (also dir.), 1989, The Body Builder's Book of Love, 1990; music for films including Futz, 1969, Alex in Wonderland, 1970, Rhinocerous, 1974; performer in: film All Men Are Apes, 1965. Recipient Creative Arts award Brandeis U., 1968 Office: care Dirs Guild Am 840 Broadway New York NY 10003-4823 also: 346 W 46th St New York NY

OHRENSTEIN, ROMAN ABRAHAM, economics educator, economist, rabbi; b. Slomniki, Poland, June 12, 1920; arrived in U.S., 1951, naturalized, 1957; s. Joseph Barukh and Gena (Fiefkopf) O.; m. Ruth Silberstein, Aug. 30, 1953; children: Gena Ann, Ilana Rose. MA in Econs., U. Munich, 1948, PhD in Econs. cum laude, 1949, postgrad. in medicine, 1949—51; MHL, Jewish Theol. Sem. Am., 1955; postgrad., Columbia U., 1963—64. Ordained rabbi, 1955. Rabbi, Auburn, NY, 1955—57, Pittsfield, Mass., 1957—60, Atlanta, 1960—62, NYC, 1962—66; prof. econs. Nassau Coll., SUNY, Garden City, 1964-99, chmn. econs. dept., 1976-78, 82-84, prof. emeritus, 1999—, campus chaplain, 1970—; chaplain Nassau County Civic Preparedness, NY, 1965—; mem. Coll. Coun. Am. Coll. Jerusalem, 1967-73, prof. econs., 1968-73. Vis. prof. U. Newcastle, Australia, 1985, vis. rsch. prof., 1989; past chaplain Kiwanis, Police Dept. Cayuga County, NY, 1955-57, Mt. Sinai Hosp., NYC, 1963-64; mem. Coun. of Orgns., U.S.A., 1978-85; mem. spl. com. on Jewish law Rabbinical Assembly, 1971; condr. seminars U. Queensland, Sydney U., Nat. Univ., Australia, 1989, Sorbonne, Paris, 1990; lectr., guest spkr. on radio, TV, Jewish civic and profl. orgns. Author: (series) Economic Thought in Talmudic Literature, 1968, 70, 83, 86, 87, 89, 91-93, 96, 2003 (citation Am. Biog. Inst. 1985), Inventories During Business Fluctuations, 1973, Inventory Control as an Economic Shock Absorber, 1975, Economic Analysis in Talmudic Literature, 1992, ed edit., rev. and enlarged, 2003; contbr. chpt. to anthology: Ancient and Medieval Economic Ideas, 1998; mem. editl. adv. bd. Internat. Rev. Econs. and Ethics; columnist Algemeiner Jour., NYC; contbr. articles to profl. jours. Mem. nat. exec. comm. Am. Profs. for Peace in the Mid. East, 1971-73; mem. adv. bd. Am. Acad. Alliance for Israel, 1995—. Recipient 1st Faculty Disting. Achievement award Nassau Coll., SUNY, 1992, 95, Citation of Excellence, Anbar Electronic Intelligence, Eng., 1996, Poineering Rsch. in Talmudic Economics, 1968; SUNY fellow, 1968, 70. Mem. Nat. Assn. Jewish Chaplains, Rabbinical Assembly NY Bd. Rabbis, Am. Econ. Assn., History of Econs. Soc., Assn. Social Econs., Learned Soc., NY Acad. Scis., Internat. Soc. for Intercommunication New Ideas, Literati Club (Eng.). Home: 28-74 208th St Bayside NY 11360-2421 Office: Nassau Coll Dept Econ Stewart Ave Garden City NY 11530 *I kept my faith in God coupled with loyalty to tradition, sharpened my mind while maintaining discipline of the heart; tenacity in the face of adversity, turning stumbling blocks into stepping stones while never losing sight of life's supreme purpose: to leave the world a little better than I found it.*

OHRING, GEORGE, meteorologist; b. NYC, June 20, 1931; s. Aron and Anna (Wasserman) O.; m. Jean Ohring, Dec. 19, 1953; children: Marshall, Peter, Richard. BS, CCNY, 1952; MS, NYU, N.Y.C., 1954, PhD, 1957. Asst. meterologist NYU, N.Y.C., 1953-57; atmospheric physicist Air Force Cambridge Rsch. Lab., Bedford, Mass., 1957-60; mgr. meteorology lab. GCA Corp., Bedford, 1960-71; assoc. prof. Tel Aviv (Israel) U., 1971-83; chief land scis. br. NOAA, Washington, 1983-84, chief satellite rsch. lab., 1984-96, chief climate rsch. and applications divsn., 1996—2000, cons., 2001—. Chmn. Commn. A. of Com. on Space Rsch., Paris, 1986-92. Author: Weather on the Planets, 1966; contbr. articles to profl. jours. Grantee U.S. Army, NOAA, U.S.-Israel Bi-Nat. Sci. Found., Israel Acad. Scis., 1970's. Fellow AAAS, Internat. Assn. Meteorology and Atmospheric Physics (exec. com. 1988-96), Am. Meteorology Soc., Am Geophys. Union. Home: 6100 Wpd College Park MD 20740 Office: NOAA Nat Environ Satellite Data & Info Svc Washington DC 20233-0001

OHRT, WILLIAM F. manufacturing executive; B in Acctg., Wayne State U., 1975; MBA in Fin., U. Detroit, 1981. Joined AlliedSignal, Inc., 1979, v.p. fin. AlliedSignal Turbocharging Sys., 1995—97; v.p. fin. ITT Automotive Elec. Sys., 1997—98; v.p., CFO truck group Navistar Internat. Transp. Corp., 1998—99; v.p., CFO Dura Automotive Sys., Inc., 2000—01; exec. v.p., CFO Walter Industries, Inc., Tampa, Fla., 2001—. Office: Walter Industries Inc 4211 W Boy Scout Blvd Tampa FL 33607*

OHS, KARL, lieutenant governor; b. Havre, Mont., Nov. 18, 1946; m. Sherri Ohs; children: Brad, Eric, Brian, Elizabeth. Student in Agrl. Econ., Mont. State U. Founder Mont. Agrl. Producers, Inc., 1988—; rep. Mont. House Rep., 1995; prin., owner AAA Storage, Helena, 1996—; majority whip Mont. House Rep., 1997, 1999; lt. gov. State of Mont., Helena, 2000—. Prin. negotiator Freeman standoff FBI, Jordan, Mont., 1996. Bd. dir. Harrison Sch. Bd., Mont., 1974—83. Recipient Lou Peters award, FBI, 1998. Office: State Capitol Capitol Station, Rm 207 PO Box 200801 Helena MT 59620-0801

OINAS, FELIX J. retired Slavic language educator; b. Tartu, Estonia, Mar. 6, 1911; m. Lisbet Kõve, July 12, 1937; children: Helina (Mrs. Charles Piano), Valdar. Student in Finno-Ugric and Slavic langs., Budapest (Hungary) U., 1935-36; MA in Finno-Ugric Lang., Tartu U., 1938; student in Slavic and English langs., Heidelberg (Germany) U., 1946-48; PhD in Linguistics and Slavic Lang., Ind. U., 1952; Doctorate (hon.), Tartu U., 1999. Lectr. various univs., 1938-50; lectr. Russian studies Ind. U., Bloomington, 1950-52, instr. Slavic studies, 1952-55, asst. prof., 1955-61, assoc. prof. Slavic langs. and lits., 1961-65, prof., 1965-81, prof. Uralic and Altaic studies, 1965-81, fellow Folklore Inst., 1965-81, prof. emeritus, 1981—. Vis. prof. Slavic and Finnic folklore, U. Calif., Berkeley, spring 1976; lectr. and presenter in field. Author 26 books, including: Truth and Justice of Vargamäe: Essays, 1984, Studies in Finnic Folklore: Homage to the Kalevala, 1985, Essays on Russian Folkore and Mythology, 1985, Immortal Kalevipoeg, 1994, others; editor: How Writers Write Lund, 1978, European Folklore: Readings from the Journal of the Folklore Institute, 1981, others; mem. adv. bd. Russian Lang. Jour., 1976-77; cons. Ency. Am. Popular Beliefs and Superstitions, 1984; mem. editl. com. The Slavic and East European Jour., 1966—; assoc. editor Uralic and Altaic Series, 1960—; contbr. 26 books, 450 articles, 50 notes and comments, 130 book reviews. Recipient Cultural award Found. Estonian Arts and Letters, 1978, Kalevala medal Finnish Govt., 1985, Lauri prize Found. Estonian Culture in U.S., 1985, medal of Kreutzwald's Mus., Võru, 1991, awarded Presdl. Order of the Estonian State Coat of Arms, II Class, 1997; Finno-Ugric, Slavic and Folklore fellow Tartu U., 1942-44; Fulbright grantee for Finland, 1961-62, Guggenheim grantee, 1961-62, 66-67, Fulbright-Hays grantee for Yugoslavia, 1964-65, grantee Am. Philos. Soc., 1966, Ford Found., summer 1967, travel grantee ACLS, 1973, Rsch. grantee NEH, 1974-75; named hon. doctor Thrtu U., 1999. Mem. Estonian Sci. Soc. (hon.), Folklore Fellows Internat. (hon.). Fax: (812) 855-2107. E-mail: iuslavic@indiana.edu.

OJALVO, MORRIS, civil engineer, educator; b. NYC, Mar. 4, 1924; s. Nissim and (Fanny) O.; m. Anita Bedein, Dec. 26, 1948; children— Lynne, Joseph, Howard, Isobel. B.C.E., Rensselear Poly. Inst., Troy, N.Y., 1944, M.C.E., 1952; PhD, Lehigh U., Bethlehem, Pa., 1960; JD, Ohio State U., Columbus, 1978. Bar: Ohio bar 1979. Draftsman Am. Bridge Co., Elmira, N.Y., 1946-47; tutor civil engring. CCNY, 1947-49; instr. Rensselear Poly. Inst., 1949-51; asst. prof. Princeton U., 1951-58; research instr. Lehigh U., 1958-60; mem. faculty Ohio State U., 1960—, prof. civil engring., 1964-82, prof. emeritus, 1982—; vis. prof. U. Tex.-Austin, 1982-83. Author: Thin-Walled Bars With Open Profiles, 1990; contbr. papers in field; patentee warp restraining device. With USN, 1943—46. Mem. ASCE, Structural Stability Research Council. Home and Office: 1024 Fairway Ln Estes Park CO 80517-7156 Office Phone: 970-577-0237.

OJEDA, JOSEPH A. psychotherapist; b. N.Y.C., Mar. 25, 1950; s. Benigno Ojeda and Maria Luisa Ayala; children: Kenneth, Lorraine. Doctor of Naturopathy, Westbrook U., Weirton, W.Va., 2004; PhD in Hypnotherapy, LaSalle U., Mandeville, La., 2002; DD, U. of Universal Life, Modesto, Calif., 1975; Master's in Holistic Healing, Westbrook U., 1996. Diplomate Am. Coll. Forensic Examiners, 1997, Am. Psychotherapy Assn., 1998, bd. cert. Am. Acad. of Experts in Traumatic Stress. Psychotherapist/clergy Counseling Ch. of the Universal Living God, Jamaica, NY, 1972—97; psychotherapist Holistic Healing, Hypnotherapy & Psychotherapy Family, Middletown, 1998—. Marriage officiant Counseling Ch. of the Universal Living God, 1976—, pastoral counseling, 1976—; free counseling walk-in clinic, Counseling Ch. of the Universal Living God, 1972—97. Author: (book) Re-education & Reprogramming with Hypnotherapy..., 2001, Integration of Behavioral & Relaxation Approaches..., 2002, Application of Self-Hypnosis Reprogramming Procedure..., 2002. Recipient award for poem Mysterious Woman, Nat. Libr. of Poetry, 1997, Medal of Merit for cmty. involvement, Pres. Ronald Reagan, 1986, award letter for emergency control ctr. assistance, Commr. Joseph V. Terrenzio, Dept. of Hosp. Bur., 1970. Fellow: Am. Acad. of Experts in Traumatic Stresss. Home and Office: 27 Sproat Street Middletown NY 10940

OJEDA, NORMA, social sciences educator, researcher; b. Mexico, D.F., Mexico, June 12, 1954; arrived in U.S., 1989; d. Jose Heriberto Ojeda and Maria Del Rosario De La Peña; m. Marc Techner, Jan. 1, 1988; 1 child, Jose-Marc Techner. BA in sociology, Nat. Autonomous U. of Mex., 1981; MA in demography, Coll. de Mex., Mex. City, 1982; PhD in sociology, U. Tex., Austin, 1987. Part time prof. Nat. Autonomous U. of Mex., 1981—82, asst. prof., 1982—87, assoc. prof., 1987—88; prof. Coll. De La Frontera Norte, Mexico, 1988—99; asst. prof. San Diego State U., Calif., 1999—2000, assoc. prof., 2001—. Adj. rschr. Coll. De La Frontera Norte, Mexico, 2001. Author: (books) Genero, Familia Y Salud, 1999, El Cicló De Vida Familiar, 1989, Familias Transfronte Rizas, 1996. Pres. bd. dir. Fronteras Unidas Pro-Salud, Baja, Calif., 2000—02. Recipient Nat. Rschr. award, sci. and tech. coun., Ministry of Edn., 1987, leadership award in population, Coll. De La Frontera, 1994. Avocations: music, dance, swimming, movies, reading. Office: San Diego State Univ 5500 Campanile Dr San Diego CA 92182-4423

OJIMA, IWAO, chemistry educator; b. Yokohama, Japan, June 5, 1945; came to U.S., 1983; s. Masaharu and Sumiko (Takatsuki) O.; m. Yoko Ogino, Apr. 24, 1971. BS, U. Tokyo, 1968, MS, 1970, PhD in Organic Chemistry, 1973. Rsch. fellow Sagami Inst. for Chem. Rsch., Japan, 1970-76, sr. rsch. fellow, group leader, 1976-83; assoc. prof. chemistry SUNY, Stony Brook, 1983-84, prof., 1984-91, leading prof., 1991-95, disting. prof., 1995—, chmn., 1997—. Editor: Catalytic Asymmetric Synthesis, 1993, 2d edit., 2000, Taxane Anticancer Agents, 1994, Biomedical Frontiers of Fluorine Chemistry, 1996, Anticancer Agents-Frontiers in Cancer Chemotherapy, 2001; contbr. numerous articles to profl. jours.; numerous patents in field. Named fellow J.S. Guggenheim Meml. Found., 1995-97. Fellow AAAS, N.Y. Acad. Sci.; mem. Am. Chem. Soc. (editl. adv. bd. 1995-2000, exec. com. divsn. organic chemistry 1998-2000, A.C. Cope Scholar award 1994, E.B. Hershberg award 2001), Chem. Soc. Japan (Nat. Young Investigator award 1976, Disting. Achievement award 1999), N.Y. Acad. Scis., Sigma Xi. Achievements include research in homogenous catalysis of transition metal complexes; asymmetric synthesis; organic synthesis by means of organometallic reagents; peptides and peptide mimetics; beta-lactam chemistry; organoflourine chemistry, medicinal chemistry especially in regard to enzyme inhibitors and taxane anticancer agents. Home: 41 Roslyn Ct Port Jefferson NY 11777-1462 Office: State U New York Dept Chemistry Stony Brook NY 11794-3400 E-mail: iojima@notes.cc.sunysb.edu.

OJINNAKA, BECKY, publishing executive; b. Orlu, Nigeria, July 27, 1956; d. Kevin and Felicia Anasott. BSBA, Southeastern U., Washington, 1978, MBA, 1980; PhD, Fell Sem., Calif., 1996; DBA, Calif. Coast U., 1999. Youth svc. ACB-Bank, Lagos, Nigeria, 1981-82; with Fin. Merchant Bank, Lagos, 1982-86; sr. mgr. CCB Bank, Lagos, 1986-92; asst. gen. mgr. Winggold Savings, Lagos, 1992-96; pres. World Achievers, Lagos, 1994—, Jireh Shammah, Lagos, 1998—. Author: Be You Own Cosmetics, 1985, Cosmetician, 1990, Part 1 and 2. Cons. to First Lady of Nigeria, 1996-98. Mem. DBA Execs., Nigerian Assn. Female Execs. (cons. 1994). Home: 6703 Kerman Ct Lanham Seabrook MD 20706-2186

OKA, TAKASHI, journalist, consultant, educator; b. Tokyo, Oct. 21, 1924; s. William Masakazu and Fumiko Mary Oka; m. Hiroko Imai, Sept. 8, 1956; children: Megumi, Sakuya. B in Econs., Rikkyo U., 1947; BA, Principa Coll., 1950; MA, Harvard U., 1954. Asst. to fgn. editor Christian Sci. Monitor, Boston, 1954-59, fgn. corr. Hong Kong, Saigon, Moscow, 1959-68, Paris, London, Beijing, and Tokyo, 1971-92; bur. chief Tokyo office N.Y. Times, 1968-71; staff dir. internat. dept. New Frontier Party, Tokyo, 1994-98; Washington rep. Liberal Party of Japan, 1999—2002; vis. scholar Sigur Ctr. George Washington U., Washington, 1998-99, 2003—04. Rsch. assoc. Internat. Inst. of Strategic Studies, London, 1976-78; rsch. fellow Carnegie Endowment for Internat. Peace, 1992-95. Author: Prying Open the Door: Foreign Workers in Japan, 1995. Avocation: tennis. Home and Office: 2555 Pennsylvania Ave NW Washington DC 20037-1614

OKA, TAKESHI, physicist, chemist, astronomer, educator; b. Tokyo, June 10, 1932; arrived in U.S., 1981, naturalized, 2004; s. Shumpei and Chiyoko O.; m. Keiko Nukui, Oct. 24, 1960; children: Ritsuko, Noriko, Kentaro, Yujiro. B.Sc., U. Tokyo, 1955, PhD, 1960; DSc (hon.), U. Waterloo, 2001, Univ. Coll., London, 2004. Rsch. assoc. U. Tokyo, 1960-63; fellow NRC Can., Ottawa, Ont., 1963-65, asst., 1965-68, assoc., 1968-71, sr. rsch. physicist, 1971-80; prof. U. Chgo., 1981—, Robert A. Millikan disting. prof., 1989—; prof. Enrico Fermi Inst., 1993—2004, emeritus, 2004—. Mem. editorial bd. Chem. Physics, 1972-92, Jour. Molecular Spectroscopy, 1973—, Jour. Chem. Physics, 1975-77. Recipient Steacie prize, 1972; Earle K. Plyler prize, 1982, Norman McLean award U. Chog., 2004. Fellow Royal Soc. Can., Royal Soc. London (Davy medal 2004), Am. Phys. Soc., Optical Soc. Am. (William F. Meggers award 1997, Ellis R. Lippincott award 1998), Am. Acad. Scis. and Arts; mem. Am. Astron. Soc; Am. Chem. Soc. (E. Bright Wilson award, 2002). Office: U Chgo Dept Chemistry Astronomy & Astrophysics Chicago IL 60637 Office Phone: 773-702-7070. Business E-Mail: t-oka@uchicago.edu.

OKADA, RYOZO, educator, clinician and researcher; b. Kiryu, Gummaken, Japan, July 20, 1931; s. Kenji and Sachi (Ishihara) O.; m. Shigeko Shindo, May 25, 1958; children: Kyoko, Taro. MD, Tokyo U., 1956, PhD, 1961. Intern then resident; asst. Tokyo U. Sch. Medicine, 1962-63; rsch. fellow Hektoen Inst. Cook County Hosp., Chgo., 1963-66; attending physician Yoikuin Hosp., Tokyo, 1966-68; assoc. prof. Sch. Med. Juntendo U., Tokyo, 1968-83, prof., 1983-97, dir. cardiovascular lab., 1985-97, prof. emeritus, 1997—; rector Gumma Paz Gakuen Coll., Japan, 1998—; dir. Misato Rsch. Inst., Japan, 2000—. Councilor Cardiovasc. Inst. Roppongi, Tokyo, 1990—, Indsl. Medicine Found., 1995—. Contbr. chapters to books, articles to profl. jours. Bd. dirs. Shirane Kaizen Sch.; Hotaka juridical person, Gumma, Japan. Fellow: Japanese Geriat. Soc., Japanese Angiology Soc., Japanese Circulation Soc., Coun. Prevention Heart Disease, Am. Heart Assn., Internat. Electrocardiology, Am. Geriat. Soc., Internat. Cardiovasc. Pathology, Am. Diabetes Assn., Internat. Union Angiology; mem.: Sports Medicine Occupl. Medicine, Japanese Soc. Medicine. Avocation: travel. Office: Gumma Paz Gakuen Coll 6859-251 Nakayama Takayamamura Gummaken 377-0702 Japan Home: 25-9 Asahigaoka Kanagawaku Yokohama 221-0814 Japan Office Phone: 0279-63-3366.

OKADA, SHIGERU, pathology educator; b. Okayama, Japan, Feb. 15, 1940; s. Keizo and Moyoko (Nishigaki) O.; m. Naoko Kobashi, Nov. 7, 1965; children: Satoru, Rie, Mari. MD, Okayama U., Japan, 1964, PhD, 1969. Chief pathologist Kyoto (Japan) City Hosp., 1977-80; lectr. Sch. Medicine Kyoto U., 1980-90; asst. Med. Sch. Okayama U., 1969-71, lectr., 1971-77; prof.

Okayama U. Med. Sch., Japan, 1990—2001; dir. Isotope Ctr. Okayama U., Japan, 1995—2001, advisor to the pres., 1999—2001; prof., dean Okayama U. Sch. of Medicine, 2003—. Head radiation protection com. Okayama U., 1991-2001. Contbr. articles to profl. jours. Mem. Japan Pathol. Soc. Tokyo, Japan Haematological Soc. Kyoto, Internat. Soc. Hematology, Japanese Cancer Assn. Tokyo, N.Y. Acad. Sci. Office: Okayama U Grad Sch Medicine and Dentistry 2-5-1 Shikata Okayama 700-8558 Japan

OKAFOR, EMEKA, professional basketball player; b. Houston, Tex., Sept. 28, 1982; BA in Finance, U. Conn., 2004. Player Charlotte Bobcats, 2004—. Mem. US Olympics Basketball Team, Athens, Greece, 2004. Named Most Outstanding Player, NCAA Final Four, 2004, Co-Nat. Player of the year, NABC, 2004, Big East Player of the Year, 2004, Defensive Player of the Year, 2004, Academic All-American first team, 2003—04; named to All-American First Team, AP, 2004. Achievements include Mem.of NCAA Nat.Championship Team U. Conn Huskies, 2004; First ever draft pick (second overall) of expansion Charlotte Bobcats, 2004. Office: c/o Charlotte Bobcats 129 W Trade St Ste 700 Charlotte NC 28202

OKAFOR, VICTOR O. journalist, educator; s. Christopher C. and Grace I. Okafor; m. Victoria N. Morah, Aug. 26, 2000; 1 child, Emeka C. BA in Journalism, Ind. U., 1986, M in Pub. Affairs, 1988; PhD in African Am. Studies, Temple U., Phila., 1994. Cert. online course designer and instr. e-Coll., 2001. Asst. prof. N.C. State U., 1994—95; assoc. prof. Ea. Mich. U., Ypsilanti, Mich., 1995—2004, prof., 2004—. Grad. instr. Temple U., Phila., 1989—94. Author: (book) Towards An Understanding of Africology, 2002. V.p. Black Faculty & Staff Assn. of Ea. Mich. U., Ypsilanti, 2003. Mem.: So. Conf. on African Am. Studies, Phi Kappa Phi. Achievements include design of Online Univ. courses. Avocations: writing, reading, travel. Office: Ea Mich Univ 620 Pray Harrold Ypsilanti MI 48198 Office Phone: 734-487-3460. Office Fax: 734-487-6891. Personal E-mail: victor.okafor@emich.edu. E-mail: victor.okafor@emich.edu.

OKAMOTO, SEIZO, transportation executive; b. Wakayama, Japan, 1942; m. Tomoko Okamoto; 2 children. Degree in Engring., Osaka U., 1965. From engr. to pres., CEO Toyota Motor Mfg., Ind., Inc., Princeton, Ind., 1965—96, pres., 1996—, CEO, 1996—. Office: Toyota Motor Manufacturing Indiana Inc 4000 Tulip Tree Dr Princeton IN 47670 Mailing: PO Box 4000 Princeton IN 47670-4000

OKAMURA, ARTHUR SHINJI, artist, educator, writer; b. Long Beach, Calif., Feb. 24, 1932; s. Frank Akira and Yuki O.; m. Elizabeth Tuomi, Aug. 7, 1953 (div.); children: Beth, Jonathan, Jane, Ethan; m. Kitty Wong, 1991. Student, Art Inst. of Chgo., 1950-54, U. Chgo., 1951, 52, 57, art seminar Yale, 1954. Faculty Ctrl. YMCA Coll., Chgo., 1956, 57, Evanston (Ill.) Art Center, 1956-57, Art Inst. Chgo., North Shore Art League, Winnetka, Ill., Acad. Art, San Francisco, 1957, Calif. Sch. Fine Arts, 1958, Ox Bow Summer Art Sch., Saugatuck, Mich., 1963, Calif. Coll. Arts and Crafts, Oakland, 1958-59, prof. arts, 1966-97, prof. emeritus, 1997—. Instr. watercolor painting, 1987; dir. San Francisco Studio Art, 1958; tchr. watercolor workshops, Bali, Indonesia, 1989, 92; lectr. in field. Author (with Robert Creeley): 1, 2, 3, 4, 5, 6, 7, 8, 9, 0, 1971; author: (with Joel Weishaus) Ox-Herding, 1971; author: (with Robert Bly) Basho, 1972, Ten Poems by Issa, 1992; author: (with Steve Kowit) Passionate Journey, 1984; author: Magic Rabbit, 1995, The Paper Propeller, 2000; one-man shows include Charles Feingarten Galleries, Chgo., 1956, 1958, 1959, San Francisco, 1957, Santa Barbara Mus. Art, 1958, Oakland Mus. Art, 1959, Legion Honor, San Francisco, 1961, Dallas, 1962, La Jolla (Calif.) Mus., 1963, U. Utah, 1964, San Francisco Mus. Art, 1968, Hanssen Gallery, 1968, 1971, Ruth Braunstein, San Francisco, 1981, 1982, 1984, 1986—88, 1990, 1994, 1997, 2000, 2003, Commonweal Gallery, Bolinas, Calif., 2001, exhibited in group shows at Pa. Acad. Fine Art, U. Chgo., U. Wash., U. Ill., Art Inst. Chgo., L.A. County Mus., Am. Fedn. Art, Denver Mus., NAD, De Young Mus., San Francisco, Knoedler Gallery, N.Y.C., Feingarten Galleries, Whitney Mus. Art, others; retrospective at Bolinas Mus., 2002, Claudia Chapline Galleries, Stinson Beach, Calif., 1995; Represented in permanent collections Art Inst. Chgo., Borg-Warner Collections, Chgo., Whitney Mus. Art, Santa Barbara Mus. Art, San Francisco Mus. Art, Ill. State Normal, Corcoran Mus., Nat. Collection Fine Arts, Smithsonian Instn., many others. Served as pvt. AUS, 1955-56. Recipient 1st prize religious art U. Chgo., 1953; Ryerson travelling fellow, 1954; Martin Cahn award contemporary Am. paintings Art Inst. Chgo., 1957; purchase award U. Ill., 1959; purchase award Nat. Soc. Arts and Letters, N.Y.C., 1960; Neysa McMein purchase award Whitney Mus. Art, 1960; Schwabacher-Frey award 79th Ann. of San Francisco Mus. Art, 1960 Mem.: Commonweal (bd. dirs. 1993—2002). Home: 210 Kale Rd Bolinas CA 94924 E-mail: arthurokamura@earthlink.net.

O'KANE, MARGARET E. non-profit organization executive; children: Katie, Beth. BA in French, Fordham U., 1969; MHS in Health Adminstrn. and Planning, Johns Hopkins U. Sch. Hygiene and Public Health. Second grade tchr. St. Ambrose Sch., Bklyn., 1970-72; neurology rsch. asst. Children's Hosp., Boston, 1972-73; respiratory therapist St. Elizabeth's Hosp., Boston, U. Va. Med. Ctr., Charlottesville, Va., Children's Hosp., Washington, DC, 1973-78; program analyst office of planning, evaluation, legislation health svcs. adminstrn. U.S. Dept. Health and Human Svcs., Washington, 1979-81; rsch. assoc. intergovernmental health policy project (IHPP) The George Washington U., Washington, 1981-83; public health svc. fellow U.S. Dept. Health and Human Svcs. Nat. Ctr. for Health Svcs. Rsch., Washington, 1983-84, special asst. to dir., 1985-86; dir. med. dirs. divsn. Am. Assn. Health Plans (formerly Group Health Assn. of Am., Inc.), Washington, 1986-89; dir. quality mgmt. Group Health Assn., Inc., Washington, 1989-90; pres. Nat. Com. Quality Assurance, Washington, 1990—. Elected mem. Inst. of Medicine, 1999. Named Health Person of Yr. Medicine & Health Jour., 1996; recipient Founder's award Am. Coll. Med. Quality, 1997. Office: Nat Com for Quality Assurance 2000 L St NW Ste 500 Washington DC 20036-4918*

OKANTAH, MWATABU S. writer, educator; b. Orange, NJ, July 18, 1952; s. Gladys Smith and Wilbur T. Smith, Sr.; m. Aminah M. Smith, May 18, 1991; m. Lanette M. Okantah (div.); children: Jamila T., Afrikiti M., Ile-Ife A., Sowande A., Berhane S., Janeia N., Ta-Seti M. Okantah-Donald. BA, Kent State U., Ohio, 1970—76; MA creative writing, CC NY, 1978—82. Asst. dir. Cleve. State U., Cleve., 1981—89; asst. prof. Kent State U., 1996—. Dir., ctr. pan-african culture Kent State U., 1999—. Author poetry; contbr. anthology. Named Featured Writer, Poets' League Greater Cleve., 2000; recipient Vis. Minority Scholars, Artist Residence Program, U. Wis., Eau Claire, 1996; fellow Rotary Group Study Exch. Fellow, Rotary Internat., 1988. Mem.: Nat. Coun. Black Studies. Office: Dept Pan-African Studies Kent State U Kent OH 44242-0001 Personal E-mail: mkepoet1@neo.rr.com. Business E-Mail: mokantah@kent.edu.

OKAY, JOHN LOUIS, management consultant; b. Emmett, Mich., Mar. 27, 1942; s. Stanley John and Mildred Isabell (Little) O.; m. Judith Ann Gerlach, Aug. 22, 1964; children: Stephen, Christopher, Douglas. BS in Agr., Mich. State U., 1964, MS in Agrl. Econs., 1967, PhD in Resource Econs., 1974. Agrl. economist U.S. Soil Conservation Svc., East Lansing, Mich., 1967-73, program analyst Washington, Mich., 1974-83, dir. info. systems, 1983-85; assoc. dir. info. systems USDA, Washington, 1985-91, dir. info. systems, 1991-95; dep. commr. Fed. Technology Svc., GSA, Falls Church, Va., 1995-97; sr. v.p. Fed. Sources Inc., McLean, Va., 1997-99; pres. J.L. Okay Cons., Oak Hill, Va., 1999—. Recipient Meritorious Exec. award Pres. of U.S., 1989, 97. Mem. Armed Forces Comm. and Electronics Assn. (bd. dirs. 1994-98), Sr. Execs. Assn. (bd. dirs. 1989-98). Office: 2857 Fox Mill Rd Oak Hill VA 20171-1829 E-mail: john.okay@erols.com.

O'KEEFE, DONALD MARTIN, detective-lieutenant; b. San Francisco, Mar. 30, 1956; s. William J. and Jane T. (English) O'K. Grad., FBI Nat. Acad., Quantico, Va., 1993; BS in Human Svcs., Coll. of Notre Dame, Belmont, Calif., 1995; MPA, U. San Francisco, 1999. Cert. advanced Commn. on Peace Officer Stds. and Tng. (POST), Calif. Dep. sheriff San Mateo County Sheriff's Office, Redwood City, Calif., 1980-88, detective, 1988, sgt., 1988-91, detective sgt., 1991-98, detective lt., 1998—. Recipient commendation for outstanding svc. Am. Legion, Redwood City, 1993, City of East Palo Alto, Calif., 1997. Mem. Calif. Narcotics Officers Assn., Calif. Homicide Officers Assn., Calif. Sexual Assault Officers Assn., Calif. Robbery Investigators Assn., FBI Nat. Acad. Assocs. Republican. Roman Catholic. Avocations: golf, tennis, weightlifting, skiing. Office: San Mateo County Sheriff's Office 400 County Ct Ofc Redwood City CA 94063-1662

O'KEEFE, EDWARD FRANKLIN, lawyer; b. S.I., N.Y., June 9, 1937; s. Francis Franklin and Bertha (Hall) O'K.; m. Toni Lynne McGohan; children: Kira Kathleen, Douglas Franklin, Andrew Franklin, Alison Elizabeth, Theadore William, Nigel Francis. AB, U. N.C., 1959; JD, U. Denver, 1961. Bar: Colo. 1962. Law clk. Colo. Supreme Ct., Denver, 1962-63; assoc. gen. counsel Hamilton Mgmt. Corp., Denver, 1966-69, sec., 1968-76, v.p. legal, gen. counsel, 1969-76; ptnr. Moye, Giles O'Keefe, Vermeire & Gorrell, Denver, 1976—. Assoc. gen. counsel, sec. ITT Variable Annuity Ins. Co., Denver, 1969, v.p. legal, gen. counsel, 1969-70; sec. Hamilton Funds Inc., Denver, 1968-76 Served with USNR, 1963-66. Mem. Nat. Assn. Security Dealers (dist. conduct com., chmn. 1976), Colo. Assn. Corporate Counsel (pres. 1974-75) also: 2680 Mariners Way SE Southport NC 28461 Office: Moye Giles O'Keefe Vermeire 1225 17th St Fl 29 Denver CO 80202-5534 Home: 2680 Mariners Way SE Southport NC 28461-8512 E-mail: ed.okeefe@moyelaw.com.

O'KEEFE, FREDRICK REA, bishop, consultant, educator, writer; b. Washington, Mar. 26, 1944; s. Roy Fox and Kathryn Isabelle (Rea) O'Keefe; stepson of James Michael O'Keefe. Student, Fordham U., 1970-72; STD (hon.), StarReach Inst., Putnam Valley, N.Y., 1973; student, St. Augustines Sch. Theology, Fla., 1984; HHD (hon.), Trinity Hall Coll. & Sem., Santa Monica, 1987. Mgmt. trainer Sears Roebuck, Peekskill, NY, 1971-76, div. mgr., 1970-76; pres. Dreadnought Corp., Peekskill, NY, 1974-76, gen. mgr. R. Shaw Co., Laguna Beach, Calif., 1977, N.D. Burger Co., LA, 1980-84; mgmt., sales and mktg. trainer, v.p. mktg. Grand Am. Computers and Software Only, Irvine, Calif., 1984-86; tchr. Confraternity Christian Doctrine, Myrtle Beach, SC, 1967-68; deacon to priest Old Cath. Ch. in N.Am., Peekskill, NY, 1975 82; consecrated bishop Old Episcopal Ch., Scotland, 1982; vicar gen. Lomita, Calif., 1982-83; presiding bishop Redondo Beach, Calif., 1983—; archibishop-abbot Incarnation Abbey Found., Order of St. Benedict, 1987—; dir. customer svc. divsn., mgr. MIS networks Peter Lowe Internat. Inc., Tampa, Fla., 1992-94; mgmt. cons. Power Support Engring., Inc., Tampa, 1997-2000; v.p. mktg. Nat. Lightning Safety Inst., 2002; dir. Comprehensive Writing Corp., 2003—. Dir. Conlegium Spiriti Refulgentis, Redondo Beach, 1975—; exec. dir. Am. Bd. Examiners in Pastoral Counseling, Washington, 1986—, sec., treas., 1982—; exec. dir. Am. Coun. on Sch. and Coll., Washington, 1982—; chmn. Grad. Coll. Theology, LA, 1983-87; chaplain LA Sheriff's Dept., 1983-86; cons. CSR Cons., Clearwater, Fla., 1975-98, CEO, 1984-98, also dir.; dir. customer svc. IT Dir. Peter Lowe Internat., Inc., 1992-94; bd. dir. Corp. Mgmt. Trust, Advanced Indsl. Tech. Contbr. articles to mag.; author numerous poems; assoc. editor, journalist, mng. editor ANCHOR Mag., 1984—. Trustee St. Petersburg (Fla.) Theol. Sem., 1993-95; chmn. Trinity Hall Coll. and Sem., 1998—; bd. dir. Carrollwood Civic Assn., Fla., 1995-97, Camp Endeavor, 1996-2000. With USAF, 1964-70. Recipient John Philip Sousa award, 1963. Mem. ASCAP, Am. Ministerial Assn. (sec. 1982-86, bd. dir. 1985—, internat. pres. 1998—), Nat. Writers Union (grievance officer, contract adv. 2003-, at-large trustee, del. 2002-2003, nat. trustee 2004-), Fla. Writers Assn. (regional dir. 2003-), Westchase Cmty. Assn. (dir. 1999-2000, voting mem. 1999—), Anglican Soc. N.Am., The Confraternity of the Blessed Sacrament, Silicon Valley Computer Soc., Pinellas IBM-PC Users Group, Inc., Internat. Order of St. Luke the Physician (award 1975), Soc. Christian Letters, Soc. Mfg. Engr., Small Press, Writers and Artists Orgn., Soc. Profl. Journalists, Planetary Group Writers Club, Order of the Holy Redeemer, Ecumenical Ch. Fedn., Anglican Inst. Ecumenical Coun. of Cath. and Orthodox Bishops, Tampa Bay Skeptics Soc., Bay Area Profl. Writers Guild (editor, pres. 2004), Internat. Fed. Journalists, Investigative Reporters and Editors, Patrons of Husbandry, Carrollwood Sertoma Club. Avocations: composing, carpentry, screenwriting, liturgics. Office: 13014 N Dale Mabry Hwy #363 Carrollwood FL 33618-2814

O'KEEFE, GARY RAYMOND, actor; b. Riverside, Calif., Oct. 3, 1940; s. Harold Clarence and Geraldine Amelia (Richardson) O'K.; m. Annette Barbara Dimeo, June 2, 1967. Grad. high sch., Santa Monica, Calif. Actor, L.A., 1969—. Appeared in over 200 movies, TV shows and on stage. Chmn. Gower Gulch Neighbor Assn., Hollywood, Calif., 1978-79. Sgt. U.S. Army, 1960-66, Europe, Korea, Vietnam. Decorated Purple Heart with oak leaf cluster. Mem. SAG, AFTRA, VFW (life), 28th Inf. Assn. Democrat. Avocation: ironman triathlons (finished 5 times).

O'KEEFE, JAMES PAUL, epidemiologist; b. Evanston, Ill., May 19, 1946; married; 3 children. BS, Marquette U., Milw., 1964—67; MD, Loyola U., Maywood, Ill., 1967—71. Cert. Am. Bd. Internal Medicine, 1974, infectious diseases Am. Bd. Internal Medicine, 1978. Intern Phila. Gen. Hosp., 1971—72; resident, internal medicine Loyola U. Stritch Sch. Medicine, Maywood, Ill., 1972—74; fellow, infectious diseases Veterans Adminstn. Hosp., Sepulveda, Calif., 1974—75, Tufts New England Med. Ctr., Boston, 1975—77; asst. prof., medicine Loyola U. Stritch Sch. Medicine, Maywood, Ill., 1977—82, dir., divsn. infectious diseases, 1977—2001, assoc. prof., medicine, 1983—91, prof., medicine, 1991—; med. dir. Maywood Primary Care Clinic, Ill., 1987—; med. dir., med. specialties practice Loyola Outpatient Ctr. Subspecialty Medicine, Maywood, Ill., 1999—; assoc. chmn., dept. medicine Loyola U. Med. Ctr., Maywood, Ill., 2001—. Mem., dept. medicine postgraduate evaluation com. Loyola U.; bd. dirs., mem. exec. com. Loyola U. Physicians Found.; bd. dirs., ctr. for home care and hospice Loyola U. Med. Ctr., mem., infection control com., mem., quality assurance coord. coun. Mem. adv. bd. Cath. Charities Chgo.; chmn. HIV/AIDS Task Force, Cath. Charities Chgo.; mem. Cook County TB Task Force Com. Mem.: ACP, Chgo. Infectious Disease Soc., Infectious Disease Soc. Am., Alpha Omega Alpha. Office: Loyola Univ Chgo 2160 S First Ave 54/149 Maywood IL 60153 Office Phone: 708-216-8563.

O'KEEFE, JAMES WILLIAM, JR., investment manager and banker; b. Troy, N.Y., Oct. 23, 1948; s. James William and Antoinette (Shannon) O'K.; m. Ann Palmer Ghiglione, June 4, 1977; 1 child, Courtney Anne. BA, Georgetown U., 1970; MBA, Harvard U., 1972. Mng. dir. Morgan Stanley & Co. Inc., N.Y.C., 1972-87, Kidder, Peabody & Co. Inc., N.Y.C., 1987-92; CEO Aetna Realty Investors, Inc., 1993—. Bd. dirs. Fishers Island Devel. Co. Mem. bd. advisors Georgetown Univ. Coll., NYU Real Estate Inst. Mem. Urban Land Inst., Nat. Assn. Real Estate Investment Trusts, Nat. Realty Com., Pension Real Estate Assn., Nat. Assn. of Real Estate Investment Mgrs., N.Y. Athletic Club, Fishers Island Club. Avocation: golf. Office: UBS Realty Investors LLC 242 Trumbull St Hartford CT 06103-1213*

O'KEEFE, JOHN DAVID, investment specialist; b. N.Y.C., Nov. 16, 1941; s. Timothy J. and Agnes V. (Timlin) O.; m. Stefanie Carreau Keegan, Jan. 28, 1978; children: Douglas G., Hillary C., John M., Meredith B. BBA, Iona Coll., 1963; MBA, L.I. U., 1968. Analyst L.I. Lighting Co., Mineola, N.Y., 1965-69, Pershing and Co., N.Y.C., 1969-72; mng. dir. Kidder, Peabody and Co., Inc., N.Y.C., 1972-89; v.p. Smith Barney, N.Y.C., 1989—. Bd. dirs. Heisman Found. Sgt. USMC, 1963-65. Mem.: Securities Industry Assn., Touchdown Club of Am., Inc. (bd. dirs. 2001—), Union Club (N.Y.C.), Downtown Athletic Club (gov. 1986, 1988, chmn. Heisman Trophy com. 1987—88). Republican. Home: 31 Linden Tree Rd Wilton CT 06897-1613 Office: Smith Barney 200 Nyala Farms Rd Westport CT 06880-6267 Office Phone: 203-221-6082. E-mail: john.cl.o'keefe@smithbarney.com.

O'KEEFE, KATHLEEN MARY, state government official; b. Butte, Mont., Mar. 25, 1933; d. Hugh I. and Kathleen Mary (Harris) O'Keefe; m. Nick M. Baker, Sept. 18, 1954 (div. 1970); children: Patrick, Susan, Michael, Cynthia, Hugh, Mardeen. BA in Comm., St. Mary Coll., Xavier, Kans., 1954. Profl. singer, mem. Kathie Baker Quartet, 1962-72; rsch. cons. Wash. Ho. of Reps., Olympia, 1972-73; info. officer Wash. Employment Security Commn., Seattle, 1973-81, dir .pub. affairs, 1981-90, video dir., 1990-95, ret., 1995. Freelance writer, composer, producer, 1973—. Author: Job Finding In the Nineties, The Third Alternative, handbook on TV prodn., (children: So You Want to be President, 1995; composer numerous songs, also writer, dir., prodr. numerous spots. Founder, pres. bd. Eden, Inc., visual and performing arts, 1975—; pub. rels. chmn. Nat. Women's Dem. Conv., Seattle, 1979, Wash. Dem. Women, 1976-85; bd. dirs., composer, prodr., dir. N.Y. Film Festival, 1979; Dem. candidate Wash. State Senate, 1968. Recipient Silver medal Seattle Creative Awards Show for composing, directing and producing Rent A Kid, TV Pub. Svc. spot, 1979. Mem. Wash. Press Women. Roman Catholic. Home: 4426 147th Pl NE # A12 Bellevue WA 98007-7191 Office Phone: 425-881-7800. E-mail: kathie@nwrain.com.

O'KEEFE, MARTIN D. priest, philosopher, educator, classicist; b. Denver, Sept. 7, 1935; s. Thomas Aloysius and Kathleen Marguerite (Brennan) O'Keefe. BA, St. Louis U., 1959, MA, PhL, St. Louis U., 1960; B in sacred theology, Woodstock Coll., 1965, Licentiate in sacred theology, 1967; PhD, Mich. State U., 1969. Latin tchr. St. Louis U. HS, St. Louis, 1960—63; asst philos. instr. Mich. State U., East Lansing, 1967—69; dean St. Louis U. Coll. of Philos., 1970—75; asst to provincial Mo. Provincial of Soc. of Jesus, St. Louis, 1970—83; vp Gonzaga U., Spokane, Wash., 1979—83; USA regional sec. Jesuit Curia, Rome, 1983—84; assoc. prof. Gonzaga U., 1984—91; adj. prof. St. Louis U., 1991—2004; assoc. editor Inst. of Jesuit Sources, St. Louis, 1991—. Bd. of dirs. Georgetown U., Wash., 1972—78, St. Louis U., 1974—78; exec. sec. Nat. Seminar on Jesuit Higher Edn., Wash., 1972—80. Author (translator): Known From The Things That Are, 1987, Oremus, 1993, For Matters of Greater Moment, 1994, Exsultemus, 2002. Republican. Roman Catholic. Home: Jesuit Hall 3601 Lindell Blvd Saint Louis MO 63108 Office: Inst of Jesuit Sources 3700 W Pine Blvd Saint Louis MO 63108 E-mail: okeefemd@slu.edu.

O'KEEFE, MAURICE TIMOTHY, editor, writer, photographer, educator; b. NYC, Mar. 7, 1943; s. Maurice Edward and Jeanne Elizabeth (Murphy) O'K.; 1 child, Timothy Patrick. BA, Washington, Lee U., 1965; MA, U. NC, 1967, PhD, 1968. Instr., prof. U. Ctrl. Fla., Orlando, 1968—2002, head journalism divsn. Nicholson Sch. Comm., 1998—2002, prof. emeritus, 2003—; pub. Guide to Caribbean Vacations.com. Author: Internat. Divers Guide, 1972-78, AAA Photo Journey to Central Florida, 1991, Diving to Adventure, 1992, Caribbean Afoot!, A Hiking & Walking Guide to 29 Islands, 1993, 2d edit., 2001, Manatees, Florida's Vanishing Mermaids, 1993, 2d edit., 1995, Hiking Florida, 1993, 2d edit., 2000, Sea Turtles, The Watcher's Guide, 1995, Great Adventures in Florida, 1996, 2d edit., 2000, Seasonal Guide to the Natural Year: Florida and the Alabama and Georgia Coasts, 1996, Caribbean Hiking, 2001; (with Larry Larsen) Fish and Dive the Caribbean, 1991, Fish and Dive Florida & The Keys, 1992; editor: www.guide to caribbean vacations.com, 2004—.; contbr. to National Geographic Guide to Caribbean Family Vacations, 2003; contbr. photos to newspapers and mags. Past pres. Fla. Outdoor Writers Assn. Recipient of more than 50 regional and nat. awards for writing and photography, 1973-2003, including Best Book (Seasonal Guide to the Natural Year), Best Photojournalism and Best Spl. Interest Publ., Fla. Outdoor Writers Assn., 1997, Best Mag. Photo, Best Article Series (Fla. Fishing) and Best Book (Spicy Camp Cook Book), Fla. Outdoor Writers Assn., 1998, Best Mag. Feature award Fla. Outdoor Writers Assn., 1999, Best Photojournalism award Fla. Outdoor Writers Assn., 1999-2003, Best Mag. Photo award Fla. Outdoor Writers Assn., 1999-2003, Best Travel Destination award Fla. Outdoor Writers Assn., 1999, 2003; named Fla.'s Premier Outdoor Photographer and Writer, Tampa Bay Mag. Mem. Nat. Writers Union, Am. Soc. Media Photographers, Soc. Am. Travel Writers (1st v.p. Atlantic-Caribbean chpt. 2002-2004, pres. 2004-). Home: 307 Fox Squirrel Ln Longwood FL 32779-4904 Office Phone: 407-788-3062.

O'KEEFE, MICHAEL DANIEL, lawyer; b. St. Louis, Jan. 3, 1938; s. Daniel Michael and Hanoria (Moriarty) O'K.; m. Bonnie Bowdern, July 11, 1964; children: Collen Coyne, Daniel Michael. AB, LLB, St. Louis U., 1961; postgrad., George Washington U., 1963. Bar: Mo. 1961, U.S. Ct. Appeals (8th cir.) 1961, U.S. Dist. Ct. (ea. dist.) Mo. 1961, Ill. 1975, U.S. Dist. Ct. (so. dist.) Ill. 1975, U.S. Ct. Appeals (5th and 7th cirs.) 1983, (10th cir.) 1995. Asst. cir. atty. U.S. Ct. Appeals, St. Louis, 1961—62, 1964—65; pvt. practice St. Louis, 1964-67; ptnr. Lucas, Murphy & O'Keefe, St. Louis, 1967-74, Thompson & Mitchell, St. Louis, 1974-96. Adj. prof. trial practice Sch. of Law, St. Louis U., 1992—. Editor: American Maritime Cases, 1985—. Trustee St. Louis U. Capt. USAF, 1962-64. Fellow Am. Coll. Trial Lawyers; mem. Internat. Assn. Def. Counsel, Fedn. Ins. and Corp. Counsel, Maritime Law Assn., Nat. Assn. Railroad Trial Counsel, Am. Law Inst. Democrat. Roman Catholic. Avocations: reading, tennis, fencing, archaeology, microbiology. Home: 372 Walton Row Saint Louis MO 63108-1909 Office: Thompson Coburn One US Bank Plz Saint Louis MO 63101-1643 Office Phone: 314-552-6092. Business E-Mail: mokeefe@thompsoncoburn.com.

O'KEEFE, PATRICIA M. state legislator; b. Methuen, Mass., Feb. 28, 1955; BA in Psychology, U. N.H. Commr. Seabrook Beach Village Dist., 1989-91; mem. dist. 21 N.H. Ho. of Reps., Concord, mem. health, human svcs. and elderly affairs com. Bd. dirs. Seacoast Vis. Nurses, 1992—, Granite State AIDS consortium, 1995-97; mem. Seabrook Budget Com., 1989-90, 96-97; trustee Seabrook Town Libr., 1995-97. Democrat. Roman Catholic. Home: PO Box 145 Seabrook NH 03874-0145 Office: NH Ho of Reps State Capitol Concord NH 03301

O'KEEFE, PAUL, editor; b. Chgo. Heights, Ill., Mar. 23, 1956; s. Philip and Rita Rose (Nee Keniery) O'Keefe. Student, U. Pa., 1974—78. Assoc. editor Worral Cmty. Newspapers, Bloomfield, NJ, 1993—2000; mng. editor Verona and Cedar Grove (N.J.) Observers Essex Cmty. Newspapers, 2000—. Contbr. several stories to fantasy mags. Roman Catholic. Avocations: chess, fictional writing. Home: 552 Pompton Ave Cedar Grove NJ 07009 Office: Essex Cmty Newspapers 550 Pompton Ave Cedar Grove NJ 07009 Office Phone: 973-571-0246. Office Fax: 973-571-7184. E-mail: cgonews@aol.com.

O'KEEFE, RAYMOND PETER, lawyer, educator; b. N.Y.C., Jan. 16, 1928; s. William Bernard and Catherine Irene (Smith) O'Keefe; m. Stephanie Ann Fitzpatrick, June 19, 1954; children: Raymond, William, Ann, Kevin, Mary, James, John. AB cum laude, St. Michael's Coll., 1950; JD, Fordham U., 1953. Bar: N.Y. 1954, Fla. 1976, U.S. Dist. Ct. (so. dist.): N.Y. 1955, U.S. Ct. Claims: 1960, U.S. Ct. Appeals (2d cir.): 1963, U.S. Supreme Ct.: 1971. Assoc. Thayer & Gilbert, N.Y.C., 1953—55; prof. law Fordham U. Sch. Law, N.Y.C., 1955—63; sr. assoc. Carter, Ledyard & Milburn, N.Y.C., 1963—68; ptnr. Ide & Haigney, N.Y.C., 1968—74; sr. ptnr. McCarthy, Fingar, Donovan, Drazen & Smith, White Plains, NY, 1974—. Adj. prof. Pace U. Sch. Law, White Plains, 1979—, Fordham U. Sch. Law, 1983—; lectr. N.Y. Med. Coll., Valhalla, NY, 1979—; prof. St. Thomas of Villanova Miami Sch. Law, 1984—; vis. prof. Thomas M. Cooley Sch. Law, Lansing, 1991, Fordham U. Sch. Law, 1992; justice State of N.Y. Justice Ct., 1978—81. Trustee Am. Irish Hist. Soc.; chmn. bd. Westchester Halfway House, 1974—78; bd. dirs. Westchester Youth Shelter, 1980. With USN, 1945—48. Recipient Alumni award, St. Michael's Coll., 1961, Humanitarian award, Fordham Law Sch., 1999. Mem.: ABA (commn. on youth, drugs and alcoholism 1984), Assn. of Bar of City of N.Y., N.Y. State Trial Lawyers Assn., Assn. Trial Lawyers Am., Fla. Bar Assn., N.Y. State Bar Assn. (chmn. spl. com. on lawyer alcoholism and drug abuse 1979—), Surf Club, Harbor View Club, Larchmont Shore Club. Home: 802 Kure Village Way Kure Beach NC 28449-4900

O'KEEFE, ROBERT JAMES, retired bank executive; b. Boston, Dec. 30, 1926; s. James J. and Irene (Egan) O'K.; m. Mary U. Hughes, Oct. 12, 1951 (dec.); children: Mary F., Robert James; m. Simone A. Charbonneau, Apr. 3, 1976. AB, Boston Coll., 1951. Mem. staff Mass. Inst. Tech., Cambridge, 1951-55; cons. Arthur D. Little, Inc., Cambridge, 1955-58; with Chase Manhattan Bank, N.Y.C., 1958-79, v.p., 1964-69, sr. v.p., 1969-79, Am. Security Bank, Washington, 1979-89; exec. v.p. MNC Info. Svcs., Balt., 1989-90, ret. Trustee Boston Coll., 1974-82, trustee assoc., 1982-86; mem. computer sci. and engring. bd. Nat. Acad. Sci., 1971-73. Served with AUS, 1945-46. Recipient Alumni medal Boston Coll., 1970 Mem. Boston Coll. Alumni Assn. (pres. 1973-74), Am. Legion, KC. Home: 190 Pocono Rd Apt 360 Denville NJ 07834

O'KEEFE, SEAN CHARLES, federal agency administrator; b. Monterey, Calif., Jan. 27, 1956; s. Patrick Gordon and Patricia Carlin O'Keefe; m. Laura Jean McCarthy, Oct. 7, 1978; children: Lindsey, Jonathan, Kevin. BA, Loyola U., New Orleans, 1977; MPA, Syracuse U., 1978. Budget analyst U.S. Dept. Def., Washington, comtr., CFO, sec. of the Navy; profl. staff U.S. Senate Appropriations Com., Washington, staff dir.; prof. Pa. State U., University Park, Maxwell Sch., Syracuse (N.Y.) U.; adminr. NASA, Washington, 2001—; dept. dir. OFE of Mgmt. and Budget, 2001—01. Bd. dirs. J. Ray McDermott, S.A., New Orleans; trustee CNA Corp., Alexandria, Va.; bd. advisor Pa. State Applied Rsch. Lab., University Park. Editor: Defense Industry in Post Cold War Era, 1998. Staff rep. platform com. Rep. Nat. Com., New Orleans, 1988, advisor, Washington, 1994-97. Fellow Nat. Acad. Pub. Adminstrn.; mem. Bohemian Club San Francisco, Cavalry Club. Republican. Roman Catholic. Avocations: golf, fishing. Office: NASA Adminr Office 300 E St NW Washington DC 20546-0005

O'KEEFE, THOMAS MICHAEL, academic administrator; b. St. Cloud, Minn., Mar. 25, 1940; s. Thomas William and Genevieve B. (McCormick) O'K.; m. Kathleen Marie Gnifkowski, Aug. 20, 1966; children: Steven Michael, Ann Catherine. Student, Marquette U., 1961-65, BS, 1965; MS in Nuclear Physics, U. Pitts., 1968; DHL, Hamline U., 1989. Dir. edn. planning HEW, Washington, 1969-70, dep. asst. sec., 1977-80; v.p. Carnegie Found. for Advancement of Teaching, Washington, 1980-83; pres. Consortium for Advancement Pvt. Higher Edn., Washington, 1983-89; exec. v.p. McKnight Found., Mpls., 1989-99; commr. Dept. Human Svcs., State Minn., St. Paul, 1999—2002; pres. Mpls. Coll. Art and Design, 2002—. Dir. Washington internships in edn. George Washington U., 1970-73; dir. policy analysis and evaluation U. Ill., Chgo., 1973-74, assoc. v.p. acad. affairs, 1974-77; head U.S. del. to Orgn. Econ. Coop. and Devel., 1979, 80; mem. Carnegie Forum on Edn. and the Economy, 1985-88; mem. N.J. Commn. on Ind. Higher Edn., 1986-88; mem. task force on ind. higher edn. Edn. Commn. States, 1987-89; co-chair Edn. Program, The Aspen Inst., 1987—. Contbr. articles to profl. jours.; contbg. editor: Change mag., 1985—2001; bd. dirs.: Editl. Project in Edn., 1984—93. Bd. dirs. The Edn. Resources Inst., Boston, 1987-94, Minn. Coun. on Founds., 1994-99, Minn. Pub. Radio, 1999—, Alliance for Excellence in Edn., 2004—; trustee Buena Vista Coll., Storm Lake, Iowa, 1984-90; mem. Coun. on Fgn. Rels., 1995-99; bd. regents U. Minn., 1996-2002. Mem.: Mpls. Club. Democrat. Office: Mpls Coll Art and Design 2501 Stevens Ave S Minneapolis MN 55404 Office Phone: 612-874-3737. E-mail: michael_okeefe@mcad.edu.

O'KEEFE, VINCENT THOMAS, clergyman, educational administrator; b. Jersey City, Jan. 10, 1920; s. James and Sarah (Allen) O'K. AB, Georgetown U., 1943; MA, Woodstock Coll., 1945, Ph.L., 1944; Th.L., St. Albert de Louvain, Belgium, 1951; student, Muenster (Germany) U., 1951-52; S.T.D., Gregorian U., Rome, 1954. Ordained priest Roman Cath. Ch., 1950. Instr. Latin and math. Regis High Sch., N.Y.C., 1944-47; assoc. prof. fundamental theology Woodstock Coll., 1954-60; acad. v.p. Fordham U., Bronx, N.Y., 1960-62, exec. v.p., 1962-63, pres., 1963-65, rector Jesuit community, 1984-88; gen. asst. to superior gen. Soc. of Jesus, Rome, 1965-83, v.p. spl. projects Jesuit Conf., 1988-90, superior, writer provincial residence, 1990-94; superior Am. House, N.Y.C., 1994-2000. Mem. regents exams. and scholarship center N.Y. State Dept. Edn.; pres., dir., mem. exec. com. Council Higher Ednl. Instns. of N.Y.C. Author: The History and Meaning of Ex Attrito Fit Contritus, 1957; Contbr. articles to religious publs., also book reviews. Dir. N.Y. World's Fair, 1964-65; Corp. Bd. mgrs. New York Bot. Garden; dir., mem. bd. Center Intercultural Formation, Cuernavaca, Mexico; trustee Fordham U. Fellow Royal Soc. Encouragement Arts Mfrs. and Commerce (London); mem. Council Higher Edn. City N.Y., Religion Council Cath. Secondary Schs. Archdiocese of N.Y., Cath. Bibl. Assn., Cath. Theol. Assn. Am., Religion Ednl. Assn., NEA, Jesuit Ednl. Assn., Nat. Cath. Edn. Assn., Internat. Assn. Univs., Soc. Cath. Coll. Tchrs. Sacred Doctrine, Phi Beta Kappa. Roman Catholic. Office: 106 W 56th St New York NY 10019-3803 Office Phone: 212-581-4640.

OKEKE, CHRISTIAN NWACHUKWU, law educator; b. Obinofia, Enugu, Nigeria, June 8, 1941; s. Stephen Agueze and Sussana Nwaduvu Okeke; m. Justina Nwanagu Okeke. LLM Summa Cum Laude, Kiev State U., Ukraine, 1969; PhD, Free U., Holland, 1973. Lic. Nigerian Coun. Legal Edn. Sr. Lectr. U. Nigeria, Enugu, Nigeria, 1974—85; pioneer dean emeritus Nnamdi Azikiwe U., Awka, Nigeria, 1985—91; dep. vice chancellor, dean of law emeritus Enugu State U. of Sci. Tech., Enugu, Nigeria, 1991—95; fellow MaxPlanck Inst., Heidelberg, Germany, 1994—95; law prof. Golden Gate U., San Francisco, 1996—. Ptr. ILegbune, Okeke & Co., Enugu, Nigeria, 1980—94; cons. African Network for Prevention of Child Abuse and Neglect, Enugu, 1974—; trustee mem. Internat. First Aid Soc., Enugu, 1974—. Author: Expansion of New Subjects of International Law, 1973, Controversial Subject of Contemporary International Law, 1974, Theory & Practice of International Law in Nigeria, 1986. Exec. dir. Internat. First Aid Soc., Inc., Antioch, Calif., 1994—. Rsch. fellowship, Hague Acad. of Internat. Law, 1970, fellowship, Cambridge U., England, 1971. Mem.: Nigerian Bar Assn., Nigerian Soc. of Internat. Law. Home: 4320 Mink Ct Antioch CA 94531 Office: Golden Gate U Sch of Law 536 Mission St San Francisco CA 94105 Office Phone: 415-442-6695. Office Fax: 415-442-6756. E-mail: cokeke@ggu.edu.

O'KELLEY, WILLIAM CLARK, federal judge; b. Atlanta, Jan. 2, 1930; s. Ezra Clark and Theo (Johnson) O'K.; m. Ernestine Allen, Mar. 28, 1953; children: Virginia Leigh O'Kelley Wood, William Clark Jr. AB, Emory U., 1951, LLB, 1953. Bar: Ga. 1952. Pvt. practice, Atlanta, 1957-59; asst. U.S. atty. No. Dist. Ga., 1959-61; partner O'Kelley, Hopkins & Van Gerpen, Atlanta, 1961-70; U.S. dist. judge No. Dist. Ga., Atlanta, 1970—, chief judge, 1988-94. Mem. com. on adminstrn. of criminal law Jud. Conf. U.S., 1979-82, exec. com., 1983-84, subcom. on jury trials in complex criminal cases, 1981-82, dist. judge rep. 11th cir., 1981-84, mem. adv. com. of fed. rules of criminal procedure, 1984-87; bd. dirs. Fed. Jud. Ctr., 1987-91, adv. com. history program, 1989-91, com. on orientation of newly appointed dist. judges, 1985-88; mem. Com. Jud. Resources, 1989-94; mem. Jud. Coun. 11th Cir., 1990-96, exec. com., 1990-96; mem. Fgn. Intelligence Surveillance Ct., 1980-87; mem. Alien Terrorist Removal Ct., 1996—; corp. sec., dir. Gwinnett Bank & Trust Co., Norcross, Ga., 1967-70. Mem. exec. com., gen. counsel Ga. Republican Com., 1968-70; mem. fin. com. Northwest Ga. Girl Scout Coun., 1958-70; trustee Emory U., 1991-97. Served as 1st lt. USAF, 1953-57; capt. USAFR. Mem. Fed. Bar Assn., Ga. State Bar, Atlanta Bar Assn., Dist. Judges Assn. 5th Cir. (sec.-treas. 1976-77, v.p. 1977-78, pres. 1978-80), Lawyers Club Atlanta, Kiwanis (past pres.), Atlanta Athletic Club, Sigma Chi (named Significant Sig 1983), Phi Delta Phi, Omicron Delta Kappa. Baptist. Home: 550 Ridgecrest Dr Norcross GA 30071-2158 Office: US Dist Ct 1942 US Courthouse 75 Spring St SW Atlanta GA 30303-3309 Office Phone: 404-215-1530.

O'KELLEY, WINNIE, editor; m. Patrick McGeehan; 2 children. Grad., Northwestern U., 1984. Asst. copy desk chief Adv. Age, 1985; with Am. Banker, 1988; mng. editor Banking Week; dep. bus. editor NY Times, NYC, 1993—. Recipient Best in Bus. for Overall Excellence Cert. Merit, Am. Bus. Editors and Writers, 2003. Office: NY Times Bus Section 229 W 43rd St New York NY 10036 Office Phone: 646-728-9200.

O'KELLY, EUGENE D. accounting company executive; BS, Pa. State U.; MBA, Stanford U. Joined KPMG LLP, San Francisco, 1972, elected ptnr., 1982, mng. ptnr., 1988, dir. banking nat. industry, 1994—98, vice chmn. fin. svc., 1998—2002, chmn., CEO Am., 2002—. Office: KPMG LLP 345 Park Ave New York NY 10154-0102 Office Phone: 212-758-9700. Office Fax: 212-758-9819.

OKEN, MARC, bank executive; Fellow Securities and Exchange Commn., 1981—83; with Price Waterhouse, 1983—89; from mem. staff to CFO Bank Am. Corp., Charlotte, NC, 1989—98, CFO, 1998—. Office: Bank America Corp 100 North Tryon St 18th Fl Charlotte NC 28255*

OKEN, ROBERT, neuroscientist, researcher, consultant; b. NYC, Oct. 15, 1929; s. Milton and Etta (Weiner) O. BA, NYU, 1949, PhD, 1958. V.p., dir. Oken Fabrics Inc., N.Y.C., 1959-68, 71-73; rschr., cons. U.S. Army, USN, Washington, and Frederick, Md., 1955-56, Teller Environ. Systems, N.Y.C., 1969-70; businessman R.A. Siegel Galleries, N.Y.C., 1978-87; cons. to dir. N.Y. State Inst. for Basic Rsch., Staten Island, 1991-93; cons. Gerex Biotech. P.L. McGeer, Vancouver, Canada, 1994—98. Editl. advisor NIMH, 2001—, Neurosci. Rsch., 1998—. Contbr. articles to profl. jours. including Schizophrenia Bull., Am. Jour. Psychiatry, Annals of Pharmacotherapy, Jour. Dental Rsch., Alzheimer's Disease and Associated Disorders, Medical Hypotheses, Parkinson/Alzheimer Digest, Focus on Parkinson's Disease, Psychiatry Rev. Series. Scientific advisor Lifer Environ. Group, Roxbury, N.J., 1984-87; vol. Dover (N.J.) Gen. Hosp., 1989-90. With U.S. Army. 1955-56. Recipient medal of achievement Dover Gen. Hosp., 1990. Mem. AAAS, Am. Chem. Soc., Am. Philatelic Soc., N.Y. Acad. Scis., N.Y. Neuropsychology Group, Mensa Internat., Intertel, Phi Beta Kappa. Home and Office: PO Box 412 Hopatcong NJ 07843-0412 Office Phone: 973-770-0006. Personal E-mail: robertjoken@nac.net.

OKERE, CHUMA ONYEAGHALA, neuroscientist; b. Enugu, Nigeria, Mar. 20, 1964; s. Geoffrey Chukwuma and Marian Nnenna (Ike) O.; m. Maria Anayo Iwuoha, Jan. 17, 1993; children: Chukwumerije Uzoma, Tochukwu Eziihe, Enyichukwu Nneoma. BSc, U. Ibadan, Nigeria, 1987, MSc, 1990; PhD, Kochi (Japan) Med. Sch., 1997. Lectr. U. Maiduguri, Nigeria, 1990-93; rsch. assoc. Kochi Med. Sch., 1999-2000, postdoctoral rsch. fellow, 1997-99; rsch. fellow Med. Coll. Pa. Drexel U., Phila., 2000—. Fgn. Rsch. fellow Ministry Sci. Culture and Sports, Japan, 1993. Mem. AAAS, Internat. Behavioral Neurosci. Soc., Japan Neuroendocrine Soc. Avocations: reading, nature viewing. Office: Hahnemann U Med Coll Pa 2900 Queen Dr Philadelphia PA 19129 Home: Apt C27 5115 Wissahickon Ave Philadelphia PA 19144-4061 Office Phone: 215-991-8428. Personal E-mail: writetochuma@yahoo.com. Business E-Mail: chuma.okere@drexel.edu.

OKERLUND, ARLENE NAYLOR, university official; b. Emmitsburg, Md., Oct. 13, 1938; d. George Stiles and Ruth Opal (Sensenbaugh) Naylor; m. Michael Dennis Okerlund, June 6, 1959 (div. Apr. 1983); 1 dau., Linda Susan. BA, U. Md., 1960; PhD, U. Calif.-San Diego, 1969. Instr. sci. Mercy Hosp. Nursing Sch., Balt., 1959-63; prof. English San Jose (Calif.) State U., 1969-80, 94—, dean humanities and arts, 1980-86, acad. v.p., 1986-93. Cons. Ednl. Testing Svc., Berkeley, Calif., 1976-80 Editor: San Jose Studies, 1975-80; contbr. articles on the humanities to profl. jours. Bd. dirs. World Forum Silicon Valley; mem. Peninsula Banjo Band. Grantee NEH, 1979; grantee San Jose State U., 1971-72. Mem. Philol. Assn. Pacific Coast (sec.-treas. 1975-78), MLA (del. to assembly, west coast rep. 1976-77), Internat. Coun. Fine Arts Deans, Calif. Coun. Fine Arts Deans (pres. 1984-86), Am. Beethoven Soc. (vice chmn. bd. dirs.). Democrat. Office: San Jose State U Dept English Washington Sq San Jose CA 95192-0090 Business E-Mail: okerlund@email.sjsu.edu.

OKHAMAFE, IMAFEDIA, English literature and philosophy educator; b. Otuo, Nigeria; s. Obokhe and Olayemi Okhamafe. Double PhD, Purdue U., 1984. Prof. philosophy and English U. Nebr., Omaha, 1993—. Office: U Nebr Annex 26 Omaha NE 68182-0001 also: U Nebr Philosophy Dept Omaha NE 68182-0001 E-mail: imafedia@unomaha.edu.

O'KIEF, W. GERALD, lawyer; b. Portland, Oreg., Feb. 19, 1937; s. William G. and Alice M. (Zilmer) O'K.; m. Sharon M. Moran, June 26, 1966; children: Gregory, Mary, John, Paul. AB, LLB, Creighton U., 1960; LLM, Harvard U., 1961. Pvt. practice, Valentine, Nebr., 1961—. Bd. dirs. First Nat. Bank, Valentine, Nebr. Mem. Nebr. Bar Assn. Office: Box 766 111 E 3rd St Valentine NE 69201-1809

OKIGBO, FRANKLIN C. engineering company executive; b. Lagos, Nigeria, Jan. 30, 1961; arrived in US, 1985; s. Alexandria and Veronica Okigbo; married, Sept. 11, 1998; children: Adaora, Nwando, Chinelo. BS in finance, So. Ill. U., 1990; MBA, Southeastern U., 1995; PhD in info. sys., Walden U., 2003. Cert. Network Assoc. Computer Info. Sys. Co., network Profl. Computer Info. Sys. Co.; Microsoft Sys. Engr. Network engr. Social Security Office, Balt., sr. network engr., FAA, Wash.; pres., ceo Worldtech Inc., Hyattsville, Md., 1998—. Named one of 50 influential minority in bus., MBPN, 2002; recipient Outstanding Support with Golftrac Program, Us Army. Mem.: Porter Ednl. Svcs. Avocations: volleyball, basketball, golf, tennis. Home: 13003 Englisthurn Dr Silver Spring MD 20904 E-mail: franklin@worldtechinc.com.

OKIISHI, THEODORE HISAO, mechanical engineering educator; b. Honolulu, Jan. 15, 1939; s. Clifford Muneo and Dorothy Asako (Tokushima) O.; m. Rae Wiemers, May 28, 1963; children: Christopher Gene, John Clifford, Mark William, Kenneth Edward. Student, U. Hawaii, 1956-57; BS, Iowa State U., 1960, MS, 1963, PhD, 1965. Registered profl. engr., Iowa, Ohio. From asst. prof. to prof., assoc. dean coll. engring. Iowa State U., Ames, 1967—. Cons. on fluid dynamics Contbr. articles to profl. jours. Served to capt. C.E., U.S. Army, 1965-67 Decorated Joint Services Commendation award; named Outstanding Prof., Iowa State U. student sect. ASME, 1983, Mech. Engring. Dept. Prof. of Yr., Iowa State U., 1977, 86, 90; recipient award for research NASA, 1975; Ralph R. Teetor award Soc. Automotive Engrs., 1976, Engring. Coll. Superior Teaching award Iowa State U., 1987, Cardinal Key Iowa State U., 1991. Fellow ASME (Melville medal 1989, 98); mem. AIAA, Sigma Xi. Republican. Mem. Ch. of Jesus Christ of Latter-day Saints. Club: Osborn Research Home: 2940 Monroe Dr Ames IA 50010-4362 Office: Iowa State U 104 Marston Hl Ames IA 50011-0001 Office Phone: 515-294-4395. Business E-Mail: tedo@iastate.edu.

OKIMOTO, GLENN MICHIAKI, state official; b. Honolulu, Mar. 12, 1953; s. Sueo and Matsue (Kojima) O.; m. Hope Kayoko Okabe, Aug. 29, 1981; 1 child, Lauren. BS, U. Hawaii, 1976, MS, 1978, PhD, 1981, Cert. in Pub. Adminstrn., 1983. Economist Dept. of Transp., State of Hawaii, Honolulu, 1981-89, program analysis mgr., 1989-94, dep. dir., 1994—. Rsch. asst. U. Hawaii, Honolulu, 1976-81, lectr., 1987—; mgr. family bus., Honolulu, 1986—. Del. Dem. Party of Hawaii, Honolulu, 1996; speech contest judge Am. Legion, Honolulu. Mem. Govt. Fin. Officers Assn., Gamma Sigma Delta. Avocations: family, golf, tennis. Home: 94-243 Pulelo Pl Waipahu HI 96797-5051 Office: State of Hawaii Dept of Transportation 869 Punchbowl St # 54 Honolulu HI 96813-5036

OKINAGA, LAWRENCE SHOJI, lawyer; b. Honolulu, July 7, 1941; s. Shohei and Hatsu Okinaga; m. Carolyn Hisako Uesugi, Nov. 26, 1966; children: Carrie, Caryn, Laurie. BA, U. Hawaii, 1963; JD, Georgetown U., 1972. Bar: Hawaii 1972, U.S. Dist. Ct. Hawaii 1972, U.S. Ct. Appeals (9th cir.) 1976. Adminstrv. asst. to Congressman Spark Matsunaga, Honolulu, 1964, 65-69; law clk. to chief judge U.S. Dist. Ct. Hawaii, Honolulu, 1972-73; assoc. Carlsmith Ball, Honolulu, 1973-76, ptnr., 1976—. Mem. Gov.'s Citizens Adv. Com. Coastal Zone Mgmt., 1974-79; sec. Hawaii Bicentennial Corp., 1975-77, chmn., 1985-87, vice chmn., 1983-85; mem. Jud. Selection Commn., State of Hawaii, 1979-87, vice chmn., 1986; mem. consumer adv. coun. Fed. Res. Bd., 1984-86; chmn. State of Hawaii Jud. Conduct Commn., 1991-94; apptd. mem. Fed. Savs. and Loan Adv. Coun., Washington, 1988-89; mem. nat. adv. coun. U.S. SBA, 1994-2000; mem. adv. coun. Fed. Res. Bank of San Francisco, 1995-2002. Bd. dirs. Moiliili Cmty. Ctr., Honolulu, 1965-68, 73-86, trustee 1993—; bd. visitors Georgetown U. Law Ctr., 1993—; trustee Kuakini Med. Ctr., 1984-88, 89-96; bd. dirs. Pub. Sch. Hawaii Found., 2004—. Capt. USAFR, 1964-72, 74-76. Mem. ABA (ho. of dels. 1991-94, standing com. on jud. selection tenure and compensation 1993-96, standing com. on jud. independence 1999-2002), Hawaii Bar Assn. (sec., bd. dirs. 1981), Am. Judicature Soc. (bd. dirs. 1986, treas. 1995-97, pres. 1997-99), Georgetown U. Law Alumni Assn. (bd. dirs. 1986-91), Omicron Delta Kappa. Office: Carlsmith Ball PO Box 656 Honolulu HI 96809-0656

OKITA, GEORGE TORAO, pharmacologist educator; b. Seattle, Jan. 18, 1922; s. Kazuo and Fusao (Muguruma) O.; m. Fujiko Shimizu, Nov. 29, 1958; children: Ronald Hajime, Sharon Mariko, Glenn Torao. Student, U. Cin., 1943-44; BA, Ohio State U., 1948; PhD, U. Chgo., 1951. Rsch. asst., rsch. assoc., instr., then asst. prof. U. Chgo., 1949-63; assoc. prof. Northwestern U. Med. Sch., 1963-66, prof. pharmacology, 1966-90, prof. emeritus, 1990—, acting chmn. dept. molecular pharmacology and biol. chemistry, 1968-70, 76-77. Contbr. articles to profl. jours.; Asst. editor: Jour. Pharmacology and Exptl. Therapeutics, 1965-68. Served with AUS, 1944-46. NIH Postdoctoral fellow, 1952 Mem. AAAS, AAUP, Am. Soc. Pharmacology and Exptl. Therapeutics, Internat. Soc. Biochem. Pharmacology, Am. Heart Assn., Cardiac Muscle Soc., Sigma Xi. Achievements include research in med. field. Home: 95-1058 Kihene St Mililani HI 96789 E-mail: gtoki@aol.com.

OKKARMA, THOMAS B. biotechnology company executive; AB, Dartmouth Coll.; MD, PhD, Stanford U. Faculty dept. medicine Stanford U., 1980—85; sci. founder, v.p. R&D Applied Immune Scis., Inc., 1985—96, chmn., CEO; sr. v.p. Rhone-Poulenc Rorer, 1995—96; v.p. R&D Geron Corp., Menlo Park, Calif., 1998—99, pres., CEO, dir., 1999—. Dir. Geron Bio-Med Ltd. Office: Geron Corp 230 Constitution Dr Menlo Park CA 94025

OKLAK, DENNIS D. real estate company executive; BS in Acctg. magna cum laude, Ball State U., 1977. CPA. Tax mgr. Duke Realty Corp., Indpls., 1986, contr., v.p., treas., exec. v.p., chief adminstv. officer, 1997—2002, co-COO, 2002—03, pres., COO, 2003—. Mem.: AICPA, Ind. CPA Soc. Office: Duke Realty Corp Ste 100 600 E 96th St Indianapolis IN 46240*

OKOJIE, FELIX A. research administrator; b. Esan, Nigeria, Feb. 13, 1957; s. John and Mary (Elebor) O.; m. Elizabeth Oboh, Dec. 21, 1993; 1 child, Clyde. BS, Auchi Poly. U., 1980; MA, Atlanta U., 1983, EdD, 1985. V.p. Fornafric Group Cos., Nigeria, 1980-82; rsch. assoc. Atlanta U., 1985-87; asst. prof. Jackson (Miss.) State U., 1988-90; dir. ctr. cmty. svc., ednl. technologist Miss. Dept. Edn., Jackson, 1990-93; assoc. prof., to asst. v.p. rsch. & devel. Jackson State U., 1993-99, interim v.p. rsch. & devel., 1999—. Bd. dirs. Hinds Pvt. Industry Coun., Jackson, 1996—; cons. in field; bd. dirs. F&K Group, Jackson. Mem. Am. Statis. Assn., Am. Soc. on Aging, Soc. Rsch. Adminstrn., Jaycees, Alpha Kappa Delta, Phi Delta Kappa. Avocations: ping pong/table tennis, walking, reading, movies, hiking. Home: 119 Longwood Dr Brandon MS 39042-2800

OKOJIE, ROBERT SYLVESTER, electronics engineer, researcher, aerospace scientist; arrived in U.S., 1986; PhD, N.J. Inst. Tech., Newark, 1996. Sr. scientist Kulite Semiconductor Products, Inc, Leonia, NJ, 1993—97; sr. rsch. engr. Ford Microelectronics, Inc., Colo. Springs, 1998—99; engr. NASA Glenn Rsch. Ctr., Cleve., 1999—. Author: (research) Silicon Carbide for Harsh Environments (Nat. Tech. Assn. Tech. Achiever-Scientist Category, 2002). Achievements include discovery of transformation of hexagonal polytype silicon carbide crystal to cubic polytype; patents in field. Office: NASA Glenn Rsch Ctr 21000 Brookpark Rd Cleveland OH 44135 Office Phone: 216-433-6522. E-mail: robert.s.okojie@nasa.gov.

OKOLSKI, CYNTHIA ANTONIA, psychotherapist, social worker; b. N.Y.C., July 26, 1954; d. Augusto and Valerie (Toffolo) Zaccari; m. Andrzej L. Okolski, Jan. 8, 1983; children: Gabriel, Christian. BA, Hofstra U., 1976; MA, Columbia U., 1978, MSW, 1983; cert. psychoanalytic psychotherapy, Advanced Ctr. Analytic Therapy, 1986. Counselor, instr. Hofstra U., Hempstead, N.Y., 1975-76; recreational dir. Residence for Young Adults Hostel, Hempstead, 1976-78; rsch. asst. Ctr. Policy Rsch., N.Y.C., 1978-79, Ctr. Psychosocial Studies, N.Y.C., 1979-81; group leader Fidel Sch., Glen Cove, N.Y., 1981; rsch. asst. Assn. of Jr. League, N.Y.C., 1982; social worker Children's Aid Soc., N.Y.C., 1983-84, Manhattan Psychiat. Ctr., N.Y.C., 1984-85; psychotherapist Advanced Inst. Analytic Psychotherapy, Jamaica, N.Y., 1986—. Supervising psychotherapist in therapeutic foster care program St. Christopher-Ottillie, 1994—. Mem. NASW, Acad. Cert. Social Workers, Alpha Kappa Delta.

O'KON, JAMES ALEXANDER, engineering company executive; b. N.Y.C., Aug. 8, 1937; s. A.C. and Rita O'Kon; m. Carol Ann Smith, 1988; children: Sean Fitzgerald, Katherine Shannon. BCE, Ga. Inst. Tech., 1961; MCE, NYU, 1970. Registered profl. engr., Tenn., N.Y., Mo., Conn., Ill., Fla., Tex., Miss., Calif., Ga., Mass., La. N.J., S.C., Ala., Ky., Va., N.C., Kans., Colo., Mich., Wyo. Hwy. engr. Ga. Hwy. Dept., Atlanta, 1960-62; structural engr. Robert & Co., Atlanta, 1962-64; project coord. So. Design, Spartanburg, S.C., 1964-67; project engr. Crawford-Russell, Stamford, Conn., 1967-68, Farkas Barron Ptnr., N.Y.C., 1968-69; v.p. Lev Zetlin Assocs., N.Y.C., Atlanta, 1969-77; pres. O'Kon and Co. (formerly Lev Zetlin Assocs.), Atlanta, 1977-2000; v.p. O'Kon divsn. RBA Group, Atlanta, 2000—03; pres. O'Kon & Co., Atlanta, 2003—. Mem. Bd. Constrn. Rsch. Ga. Tech. Author: Guidelines for Failure Investigation, 1989, Methodology For The Life Prediction of Buildings, 1989, Floating Factory to Produce Precast Concrete Components, 1973, Methods to Reduce Errors Due to Dependency on Computers, 1994, Bridge From the Past, 1995, Maya Intersite Scabe System, 1997, Error Avoidance in Light Weight Space Frames, 1999, Computer Design of Space Frames, 2000, Seismic Analysis of Large Structures, 2001, Maya Suspension Bridge, Yaxchilan, 2003. Recipient Grand award Builder's Mag., 1983, Archtl. Excellence award Am. Inst. Steel Constructors, 1984, Engring. Excellence award Am. Consulting Engrs. Coun. Ga., 1983, 88, Grand Award for Engring. Excellence, 1988-89, 91-93, USAF Air Mobility award, 1997, Nat. Grand prize Steel Joist Inst., 1999, Grand Nat. Design award Am. Inst. of Steel Constrn., 2000, Grand award ACEC, 2001. Fellow Explorers Club (nat. fellow), ASCE (chmn. tech. com. forensic engring.); mem. Am. Inst. Archaeology, Ga. Tech. Bldg. Rsch. Ctr. (Ga. Tech. continuing edn. com.), Bldg. Futures Coun., Soc. Am. Mil. Engrs., Smithsonian Inst., Am. Arbitration Assn. (panel of arbitrators). Democrat. Roman Catholic. Office: O'Kon & Co Inc 26104 Plantation Dr Atlanta GA 30324 Office Phone: 404-885-6000. E-mail: jamesokon@okon.com.

OKOSHI-MUKAI, SUMIYE, artist; b. Seattle; One-woman shows include Gallery Internat., N.Y.C., 1970, Miami Mus. Modern Art, 1972, Galerie Saison, Tokyo, 1982, St. Peter's Ch., Living Room Gallery, N.Y.C., 1987, Viridian Gallery, 1987, 1992, 1996, 1999, Port Washington (N.Y.) Pub. Libr., 1985, NAS, Washington, 1991—92, exhibited in group shows at Bergen Mus. Art and Scis., 1983, Am. Acad. Arts and Scis., 1984, Port Washington Pub. Libr., 1985, Hudson River Mus., 1985, Sao Paulo and N.Y. Culture Exch., 1988, Hyundai Gallery, Pusan, Korea, 1988, Gary Snyder Fine Art, N.Y.C., 2002, Represented in permanent collections The Mitsui & Co., N.Y., Hotel Nikko, Atlanta, Bank of Nagoya, N.Y., Palace Hotel, Guam Island, Port Washington Pub. Libr., Lowe Gallery-U. Miami, Miami Mus. Modern Art, Nat. Women's Edn. Ctr., Saitama-ken, Japan, NAS, Hammond Mus., North Salem, N.Y., The Jane Voorhees Zimmerli Art Mus., N.J., Asian Traditions Modern Expressions; included in Collage-Techniques, 1994. Mem. Nat. Women Artists Assn. (Belle Cramer award Zluta and Joseph Fund award, Ralph Mayer Meml. award, Doris Kreindler Meml. award 2002), Nat. Mus. Women in the Arts (charter mem. 1994).

OKPALANMA, CHIKA, psychiatrist; b. Owerri, Nigeria, Mar. 30, 1949; MD, St. Georges U., Grenada, 1984. Diplomate Am. Bd. Psychiatry. Intern Bronx (N.Y.) Lebanon Hosp., 1988-89, resident, 1989-91, chief resident, 1991-92, attending psychiatrist, 1992—, unit chief, 1996—. Clin. instr. psychiatry Albert Einstein Coll. Med., N.Y.C., 1992-94, clin. asst. prof. psychiatry, 1994—. Recipient Tchr. of Yr. award, Bronx Lebanon Hosp. Ctr., 2002, Ams. Top Psychiatrists, Consumer's Rsch. Coun. of Am., 2002—03. Fellow: Am. Psychiat. Assn., Am. Coll. Forensic Examiners (Tchr. of Yr. award 2002); mem.: AMA, Black Psychiatrists of Am., Am. Soc. Addiction Medicine. Office: Bronx Lebanon Hosp Ctr 1276 Fulton Ave Bronx NY 10456-3402 also: 1452 E Gun Hill Rd Ste B Bronx NY 10469-3037 Fax: 718-652-8492. E-mail: cokpalanma@aol.com.

OKRENT, DANIEL, writer; b. Detroit, Apr. 2, 1948; s. Harry and Gizella (Adler) Okrent; m. Cynthia Jane Boyer, June 23, 1969 (div. Aug. 1977); m. Rebecca Kathryn Lazear, Aug. 28, 1977. BA, U. Mich., 1969; DHL, Mass. Coll. Liberal Arts, 1988. Editor Alfred A. Knopf, Inc., N.Y.C., 1969–73; editorial dir. Grossman Pubs., Inc., N.Y.C., 1973—76; editor-in-chief Harcourt Brace Jovanovich, N.Y.C., 1976—77; pres. Hilltown Press, Inc., Worthington, Mass., 1978—91, Tex. Monthly Press, Inc., Austin, 1978—83; editor New Eng. Monthly, Northampton, Mass., 1984—89; asst. mng. editor Life mag., N.Y.C., 1991—92, mng. editor, 1992—96; editor new media Time Inc., N.Y.C., 1996—99, editor-at-large, 1999—2001; dir. Zinio, Inc., 2001—; pub. editor N.Y. Times, 2003—; dir. TESSCO Techs., Inc., 2004—. Columnist Esquire mag., N.Y.C., 1985—89. Author: Nine Innings, 1985, The Way We Were: New England Then and Now, 1989, Great Fortune: The Epic of Rockefeller Center, 2003; co-author: Baseball Anecdotes, 1989; co-editor: The Ultimate Baseball Book, 1979; appeared in (films) Sweet and Lowdown, 1999. Chmn. Nat. Portrait Gallery, 2001—. Mem.: Century Assn. Jewish. Office: NY Times 229 West 43rd St New York NY 10036

OKRENT, DAVID, engineering educator; b. Passaic, N.J., Apr. 19, 1922; s. Abram and Gussie (Pearlman) O.; m. Rita Gilda Holtzman, Feb. 1, 1948; children: Neil, Nina, Jocelyne. ME, Stevens Inst. Tech., 1943; MA, Harvard, 1948, PhD in Physics, 1951. Mech. engr. NACA, Cleve., 1943-46; sr. physicist Argonne (Ill.) Nat. Lab., 1951-71; regents lectr. UCLA, 1968, prof. engring., 1971-91, prof. emeritus, rsch. prof., 1991—. Vis. prof. U. Wash., Seattle, 1963, U. Ariz., Tucson, 1970-71; Isaac Taylor chair Technion, 1977-78 Author: Fast Reactor Cross Sections, 1960, Computing Methods in Reactor Physics, 1968, Reactivity Coefficients in Large Fast Power Reactors, 1970, Nuclear Reactor Safety, 1981; contbr. articles to profl. jours. Mem. adv. com. on reactor safeguards AEC, 1963-87, also chmn., 1966; sci. sec. to sec. gen. of Geneva Conf., 1958; mem. U.S. del. to all Geneva Atoms for Peace Confs. Guggenheim fellow, 1961-62, 77-78; recipient Disting. Appointment award Argonne Univs. Assn., 1970, Disting. Service award U.S. Nuclear Regulatory Commn., 1985. Fellow Soc. for Risk Analysis, Am. Phys. Soc., Am. Nuclear Soc. (Tommy Thompson award 1980, Glenn Seaborg medal 1987), Nat. Acad. Engring. Home: 439 Veteran Ave Los Angeles CA 90024-1956 Business E-Mail: okrent@ucla.edu.

OKTAVEC, EILEEN M. anthropologist, artist; b. Apr. 9, 1942; d. Albert W. and Margaret (O'Reilley) O. Student, Cooper Union, N.Y.C., 1960-61; BA in Anthropology, SUNY, Stony Brook, 1973; MA in Anthropology, U. Ariz., 1975. Instr. anthropology White Pines Coll., Chester, N.H., 1975-76; art dir. Great Walks, Inc., Goffstown, N.H., 1989—. Author: Answered Prayers: Miracles and Milagros Along the Border, 1995; photographs in: Great Walks of Acadia National Park and Mount Desert, 1990, Great Walks of Southern Arizona, 1991, Great Walks of Big Bend National Park, 1991, Great Walks of the Great Smokies, 1992, Great Walks of Yosemite National Park, 1993, Great Walks of Sequoia and Kings Canyon National Parks, 1994, Great Walks of Acadia National Park and Mount Desert Island, 1994, Great Walks of the Olympic Peninsula, 1999, The Woodland Garden, 1996; exhibited in group shows at Rockport (Mass.) Art Festival, 1977, 78, Berkshire Art Assn., Pittsfield, Mass., 1979, The Ogunquit (Maine) Art Ctr., 1982, 83, N.H. Art Assn., Manchester, 1985, Concord (Mass.) Art Assn., 1988, 91, 92, 96-98, Sharon (N.H.) Art Ctr., 1998. Winner Southwest Book award for Answered Prayers, 1997. Mem. Concord Art Assn., Sharon Arts Ctr. Office: Great Walks Inc PO Box 410 Goffstown NH 03045-0410 Home: PO Box 410 Goffstown NH 03045-0410

OKUHARA, TETSU, artist, photographer; b. L.A., Mar. 3, 1940; Student, U. Chgo., 1958-61, The Cooper Union, 1970-71. Lectr., workshop leader Otis Coll., L.A., Hartwick Coll., Oneonta, N.Y., NYU, Rutgers U., New Brunswick, N.J., Sch. Visual Arts, N.Y.C., New Sch., N.Y.C., Wesleyan U., Middletown, Conn, Cornish Inst., Seattle. Exhibited in one person and group shows at Los Angeles County Mus., 2002, Small Works, NYU, 1999, Fotomassan, Goteborg, Sweden, Chgo. Cultural Ctr., 1997, Gotland Konst Mus., Sweden, 1995, San Francisco Camera Work, 1994, Art Inst. Boston, 1994, Artist Space, N.Y.C., 1992, Chgo. Art Inst., 1991-92, Art in General, N.Y.C., 1990, Cleve. Mus. Art, 1978, San Francisco Mus. Modern Art, 1979, numerous others; represented in permanent collections Mus. Modern Art, N.Y.C., Met. Mus. Art, N.Y.C., ADP, Chgo., Hasselad Collection, Goteborg, Sweden, Tokyo Met. Mus. Photography, Art Inst., Chgo., San Francisco Mus. Modern Art, Los Angeles County Mus., numerous others; contbr. mags., newspapers. Grantee Creative Artist Pub. Svc., 1973-74, 75-76, N.Y. Found. for the Arts, 1988-89, Nat. Endowment for the Arts, 1988-89, La Napoule Found./Nat. Endowment for the Arts, France, 1989, Intercambio, San Juan, P.R., 1991, James P. Phelan Art Award, San Francisco, 1993-94; Guggenheim fellow, 1975-76, N.Y. Found. for Arts fellow, 2000. Home: 202 E 42nd St New York NY 10017-5808

OKUN, DANIEL ALEXANDER, environmental engineering educator; b. N.Y.C., June 19, 1917; s. William Howard and Leah (Seligman) O.; m. Elizabeth Griffin, Jan. 14, 1946; children: Michael Griffin, Tema Jon. BS, Cooper Union, 1937; MS, Calif. Inst. Tech., 1938; ScD, Harvard U., 1948, U. N.C., 2000. Registered profl. engr., N.C., N.Y. With USPHS, 1940-42; tchg. fellow Harvard U., 1946-48; with Malcolm Pirnie, N.Y.C., 1948-52; from assoc. prof. dept. environ. scis. and engring. to prof. U. N.C., Chapel Hill, 1952-73, Kenan prof., 1973-82, Kenan prof. emeritus, 1982—, head dept. environ. scis. and engring., 1955-73. Vis. prof. Tech. U. Delft, 1960-61, Univ. Coll., London, 1966-67, 73-75, Tianjin U., 1981; editor environ. scis. series Acad. Press, 1968-75; cons. to industry, cons. engrs., govtl. agys. World Bank, WHO, UNDP, with spl. svc. in Switzerland, Israel, Jordan, Peru, Egypt, Colombia, Brazil, Venezuela, Thailand, Indonesia, Kenya, Zambia, Tunisia, Australia, Taiwan, Bangladesh, Argentina, Chile, New Zealand, Jamaica, Guatemala, Turkey, Finland, Eng., Morocco, China, The Philippines, India; environ. coun. Rohm & Haas Co., Inc., 1985-92; chmn. expert panel on N.Y.C. water supply EPA, 1992-93. Author: (with Gordon M. Fair and John C. Geyer) Water and Wastewater Engineering, 2 vols., 1966-68, Elements of Water Supply and Wastewater Disposal, 1971; (with George Ponghis) Community Wastewater Collection and Disposal, 1975; Regionalization of Water Management—A Revolution in England and Wales, 1977; editor: (with M.B. Pescod) Water Supply and Wastewater Disposal in Developing Countries, 1971; (with C.R. Schulz) Surface Water Treatment for Communities in Developing Countries, 1984; contbr. articles to profl. jours. Chmn. Chapel Hill Fellowship for Sch. Integration, 1961-63; adv. bd. Ackland Meml. Art Mus., 1973-78; bd. dirs. Warren Regional Planning Corp., 1971-77, Inter-Faith Coun. Housing Corp., 1975-83, N.C. Water Quality Coun., 1975-77; mem. adv. com. for med. rsch. Pan Am. Health Orgn., 1976-79; chmn. Washington Met. Area Water Supply Study Com., 1976-80, NAS-NRC; bd. sci. and tech. for internat. devel. NRC, 1978-81, vice chmn. environ. studies bd., 1980-83, chmn. water sci. and tech. bd., 1991-94; com. on human rights NAS, 1988-94; pres. Chapel Hill chpt. N.C. Civil Liberties Union, 1991-93. Maj. AUS, 1942-46, PTO. Decorated Philippine Liberation medal; recipient Harrison Prescott Eddy medal for rsch. Water Pollution Control Fedn., 1950, Gordon Maskew Fair award Am. Acad. Environ. Engrs., 1973, Thomas Jefferson award U. N.C. at Chapel Hill, 1973, Gordon Y. Billard award N.Y. Acad. Scis., 1975, 1st Thomas R. Camp Meml. lectr. Boston Soc. Environ. Engrs., Gordon Maskew Fair medal Water Pollution Control Fedn., 1978, First Allen Hazen lectr. New Eng. Water Works Assn., 1990, Donald R. Boyd award Assn. Met. Water Agys., 1993, Jones award Chapel Hill chpt. ACLU N.C., 1998, Gano Dunn award for profl. achievement in sci. and engring. The Cooper Union, 2002; Friendship medal Inst. Water Engrs. and Scientists (Gt. Britain), 1984; NSF fellow, 1960-61; Fed. Water Pollution Control Adminstrn. fellow, 1966-67; Fulbright-Hayes lectr., 1973-74; Daniel A. Okun Disting. Professorship in Environ. Engring. established by U. N.C., 1999. Mem. NAE, AAUP (pres. U. N.C. chpt. 1963-64), ASCE (hon., chmn. environ. engring. divsn. 1967-68, 1st Simon W. Freese award 1977), Am. Water Works Assn. (hon., N.C. Fuller award 1983, Best Paper award ednl. divsn. 1985, Abel Wolman award of Excellence 1991, Best Paper Water Resources Divsn. 1999), Inst. Medicine, Water Environ. Fedn. (hon., chmn. rsch. com. 1961-66, dir.-at-large 1969-72), Am. Acad. Environ. Engring. (pres. 1969-70, hon. diplomate, Kappe lectr. 1995), Assn. Environ. Engring. Profs. (Founders' award 1994), N.C. Pub. Health Assn. (Jarrett award 1994), U. N.C. Order of Golden Fleece), Sigma Xi (pres. U. N.C. chpt. 1968-69). Home: 750 Weaver Dairy Rd Apt 204 Chapel Hill NC 27514-1466 Office: ESE U NC CB 7431 Chapel Hill NC 27599-7431 Office Phone: 919-918-3500. Business E-Mail: dokun@unc.edu.

OKUN, DEANNA T. government agency administrator; BA in Political Science, Utah State U.; JD, Duke U. Sch. of Law. Research assoc. Competitive Enterprise Inst., Washington; assoc. attorney and mem. of Internat. Trade Group Hogan & Hartson law firm, Washington; legislative asst. to Senator Frank Murkowski; counsel for internat. affairs to Sen. Frank Murkowski, 1993—99; chmn U.S. Internat. Trade Comm., 2002—04, vice chmn., 2004—. Office: US Internat Trade Commission 500 E Street SW Washington DC 20436

OKUN, HERBERT STUART, diplomat, educator; b. NYC, Nov. 27, 1930; s. Irving and Ida Muriel (Levine) O.; m. Lorraine Joan Price, Dec. 5, 1954 (div. 1985); children: Jennifer, Elizabeth, Alexandra; m. Enid Curtis Bok, Dec. 27, 1990. AB with great distinction, Stanford U., 1951; postgrad., Syracuse U., 1951—52, Princeton U., 1952; Hochschule fuer Politische Wissenschaft, Munich, 1956—57; MPA, Harvard U., 1959. Mem. US Fgn. Svc., 1955—91, Munich vice consul, 1955—57; with Bur. Intelligence and Rsch., Dept. State Office Soviet Union Affairs, Washington, 1959-61, alt. dir., 1971-73; 2d sec. Am. Embassy, Moscow, 1961-63; consul, prin. officer Am. Consulate, Belo Horizonte, Brazil, 1964-65; 1st sec., prin. officer Am. Embassy, Brasilia, Brazil, 1965-66, counsellor embassy, prin. officer, 1967-68; assigned to Naval War Coll., 1968-69; spl. asst. to sec. of state Dept. State, Washington, 1969-71, dep. chmn. U.S. Del., U.S.-USSR Talks on Prevention Incidents at Sea, 1971-72; polit. advisor and spl. asst. for internat. affairs to comdr.-in-chief NATO So. Command, Naples, Italy, 1973-74; min.-counsellor, dep. chief mission Am. Embassy, Lisbon, Portugal, 1975-78; dep. chmn. U.S. del. Strategic Arms Limitation Talks with Soviet Union, Geneva, 1978-79; vice chmn. U.S. del. to trilateral U.S.-U.K.-USSR Talks on comprehensive test ban treaty, Geneva, 1979-80; amb. to German Dem. Rep. Berlin, 1980—83; amb.-in-residence Aspen Inst., Washington, 1983-85; amb., dep. permanent rep. of U.S. to the UN N.Y.C., 1985-89. Rep. of US to Gen. Assembly UN, to UN Security Coun., 1985-89, to Com. on Peaceful Uses of Outer Space, 1986-87, to Disarmament Commn. UN, 1985-89, to Commn. Human Rights, 1985-89, to com. on program and coordination of Econ. and Social Coun., 1987, 89; amb. in residence Carnegie Corp. NY, 1989-90; US mem. UN Sec. Gen's. Expert Group on Enhancing UN Structure for Drug Abuse Control, 1990, UN Internat. Narcotics Control Bd., Vienna, Austria, 1992-2002; founding exec. dir. Fin. Svcs. Vol. Corps, NYC, 1990-97; vis. lectr. Yale Law Sch., New Haven, 1991-2002; professorial lectr. in internat. rels., internat. law and instns. Johns Hopkins. U. Sch. Advanced Internat. Studies, Washington, 2002—; spl. adviser, dep. personal envoy of the sec. gen. UN, Yugoslavia and Nagorno-Karabakh, 1991-92; spl. adv., dep. co-chmn. Internat. Conf. on former Yugoslavia, 1992-93; UN mediator Dispute between Greece & former Yugoslav Republic of Macedonia, 1993-97; adv. bd. Chazen Inst. Internat. Bus. Grad. Sch. Bus., Columbia U.; bd. dirs. World Rehab. Fund; adv. bd. Minority Rights Group USA; spl. advisor Carnegie Commn. on Preventing Deadly Conflict. Commr. U.S.-Poland Action Commn; mem. Internat. Coun., Found. Inter-Ethnic Rels., The Hague, Netherlands, 1995—, mem. Adv. Com., Human Rights Watch, N.Y., 1995—; mem. group internat. advisors Internat. Com. Red Cross, Geneva, 1996-2000; bd. overseers Curtis Inst. Music, Phila.; adv. bd. internat. security studies Yale U., New Haven; mem. adv. bd. Portuguese-Am. Leadership Coun.; bd. dirs. Internat. Ctr. N.Y., 2004-. Served with AUS, 1952-54. Recipient Meritorious Honor award Dept. of State, 1972, Superior Honor award Dept. of State, 1980, Presdl. Meritorious Svc. award, 1983. Mem. Am. Fgn. Policy (nat. com.), Am. Acad. Diplomacy, Lawyers Alliance World Security (nat. bd. dirs.), Washington Inst. Fgn. Affairs, Phi Beta Kappa. Home: 1133 Park Ave Apt 16-E New York NY 10128-1246

OKUN, MAURY, dance company executive; Exec. dir. Eisenhower Dance Ensemble, Troy, Mich., 1996—; co-founder, exec. dir. Detroit Chamber Winds & Strings; exec. dir. Great Lakes Chamber Music Festival. Office: Eisenhower Dance Ensemble Ste 214 755 W Big Beaver Troy MI 48084 also: Detroit Chamber Winds & Strings 17348 W 12 Mile Rd, Suite 102 Southfield MI 48076

OKUN, NEIL JEFFREY, vitreoretinal surgeon; b. St. Louis, Nov. 21, 1957; s. Edward and Barbara J. (Braham) O.; m. Joan A. Sosnoff, May 19, 1984; children: David E., Sarah E. AB, Dartmouth Coll., 1980; MD, Washington U., 1984. Diplomate Am. Bd. Ophthalmology. Intern internal medicine Jewish Hosp. at Washington U., St. Louis, 1984-85; resident ophthalmology Washington U. Med. Ctr., St. Louis, 1985-88; fellow vitreoretinal Retina Cons., Ltd., Washington U., St. Louis, 1988-89; vitreoretinal surgeon Fla. Retina Inst., Jacksonville, Fla., 1990-91, Retina Assocs. Ctrl. Fla., Orlando, 1991—. Instr. dept. ophthalmology Washington U. Sch. Medicine, St. Louis, 1988-89; clin. asst. prof. dept. ophthalmology U. South Fla., Tampa, 1992—; chmn. dept. ophthalmology Fla. Hosp. Orlando, 1996—. Recipient Upjohn Achievement award for endocrinology and metabolism Washington U. Sch. Medicine, St. Louis, 1984. Fellow ACS, Am. Acad. Ophthalmology; mem. AMA (Physicians's Recognition award for continuing med. edn. 1992—), Am. Soc. Retina Specialists, Assn. for Rsch. in Vision and Ophthalmology, Fla. Med. Assn., Fla. Soc. Ophthalmology, Ctrl. Fla. Soc. Ophthalmology, Orange County Med. Soc., Vitreous Soc., Paul Cibis Club. Avocations: music, art. Office: Retina Assocs Ctrl Fla 2501 N Orange Ave Ste 401 Orlando FL 32804-4644 Office Phone: 407-896-1224.

OLAFSON, FREDERICK ARLAN, philosophy educator; b. Winnipeg, Man., Can., Sept. 1, 1924; s. Kristinn K. and Fredericka (Björnson) O.; m. Allie Lewis, June 20, 1952 (dec.); children— Peter Niel, Christopher Arlan, Thomas Andrew. AB, Harvard U., 1947, MA, 1948, PhD, 1951. Instr. philosophy and gen. edn. Harvard U., 1952-54; asst. prof. philosophy, then assoc. prof. Vassar Coll., 1954-60; assoc. prof. Johns Hopkins U., 1960-64; prof. edn. and philosophy Harvard Grad. Sch. Edn., 1964-71; prof. philosophy U. Calif., San Diego, 1971-91, chmn. dept., 1973-76, assoc. dean grad. studies and research, 1980-85. Author: Principles and Persons, 1967, Ethics and Twentieth Century Thought, 1973, The Dialectic of Action, 1979, Heidegger and the Philosophy of the Mind, 1987, What Is A Human Being?, 1995, Heidegger and the Ground of Ethics, 1998, Naturalism and the Human Condition, 2001. Served to lt. (j.g.) USNR, 1943-46. Mem. Nat. Acad. Edn. Home: 6081 Avenida Chamnez La Jolla CA 92037-7404

OLAFSSON, OLAFUR JOHANN, writer, media company executive; b. Reykjavik, Iceland, Sept. 26, 1962; s. Olafur Sigurdsson; m. Anna Olafsson; children: Arni, Olaf. Degree in physics, Brandeis U. Joined Sony Corp., San Jose, Calif., 1984; v.p., spl. projects Sony USA, N.Y.C., 1989—91; founder, pres., CEO Sony Interactive Entertainment Inc. (formerly Sony Electronic Pub. Co.), N.Y.C., 1991—96; pres. Advanta Corp., 1998—99; vice chmn. Time Warner Digital Media, N.Y.C., 1999—2003; exec. v.p. Time Warner Inc., N.Y.C., 2003—. Author: (short stories) Nine Keys, 1986, (novels) Marketplace of the Gods, 1988, Absolution, 1994, The Journey Home, 2000, Walking Into The Night, 2003, (plays) The Feast of Snails, 2002. Office: Time Warner Inc 75 Rockefeller Plz New York NY 10019-6990*

OLAGUNJU, AMOS OMOTAYO, computer science educator, consultant; b. Igosun, Kwara, Nigeria, Nov. 27, 1954; came to U.S., 1980; s. Solomon Atoyebi and Ruth Ebun (Adegoke) O.; m. Janet; 1 child, Amanda. EdD, U. N.C., Greensboro, 1987; PhD, Kensington U., 1990; cert. in cryptography and info. systems, MIT, 1996, cert. in design and analysis experiments, cert. in digital comm. networks, MIT, 1999, cert. in bioinformatic principles, 2001. Cert. bioinformatic prins. MIT, 2001. Dir. mgmt. info. sys. Barber-Scotia Coll., Concord, NC, 1981-82; lectr. NC A&T State U., Greensboro, NC, 1982-87, asst. prof., 1987-90; mem. tech. staff Bell Comm. Rsch., Piscataway, NJ, 1986-90; vis. prof. Mich. State U., East Lansing, Mich., 1990-91; coord. acad. computing, assoc. prof. Del. State U., 1991-92, prof., chair dept. math. and computer sci., 1992—2001; collegiate prof. UMUC-Asia, 2001—02; prof. computer networking and applications St. Cloud State U., Minn., 2002—. Cons. NSF, Washington, 1991-93, Edn. Testing Agy., Princeton, NJ, 1995—. Author: Lecture Notes Series in Language C, Systems Programming, Database Systems, Theoretical Aspects of Computing, File Structures, Introduction to Computer Science and Scientific and Engineering Applications of Fortran, 1991-96; mem. editl. bd. Sci. World Jour., 2003—; contbr. articles to Software Metrics, Automatic Indexing, Perfect Hashing, Number Theory, Efficient Statis. Algorithms. Del. State News. Pres. Ahmadu Bello Assn. Computer Univ. Students, Zaria, Nigeria, 1976, Orgn. United Africans, Concord, NC, 1982. Recipient Queen's Grad. award Queen's U., Kingston, Ont., 1979; Navy-Am. Soc. for Engring. Edn. fellow, 1997, sr. fellow 1998, 2000. Mem. Internat. Assn. Sci. Tech. Devel. (reviewer 2001—), Assn. for Modelling and Simulation in Enterprises (program chair 1989-90, editor), Assn. for Computing Machinery (reviewer), NC Acad. Sci. (program chair 1991—, mem. editl. bd. 1999—), NY Acad. Sci. Achievements include invention of the Bell Communication Rsch. Software Daily Software Report and Analysis Measurement System and Generic Administrative Quantitative Decision Support System. Home: 1617 Highland Trail Saint Cloud MN 56301 Office Phone: 320-308-5696. Personal E-mail: blessamos@yahoo.com.

OLAH, GEORGE ANDREW, chemist, educator; b. Budapest, Hungary, May 22, 1927; arrived in U.S., 1964, naturalized, 1970; s. Julius and Magda (Krasznai) Olah; m. Judith Agnes Lengyel, July 9, 1949; children: George John, Ronald Peter. PhD, Tech. U. Budapest, 1949, D (hon.), 1989; DSc (hon.), U. Durham, 1988, U. Munich, 1990, U. Crete, Greece, 1994, U. Szeged, Hungary, 1995, U. Veszprem, 1995, Case Western Res. U., 1995, U. So. Calif., 1995, U. Montpellier, 1996, SUNY, 1998, U. Pecs, Hungary, 2001, U. Debrecen, 2003. Mem. faculty Tech. U. Budapest, 1949—54; assoc. dir. Ctrl. Chem. Rsch. Inst., Hungarian Acad. Scis., 1954—56; rsch. scientist Dow Chem. Can. Ltd., 1957—64, Dow Chem. Co., Framingham, Mass., 1964—65; prof. chemistry Case Western Res. U., Cleve., 1965—69, C.F. Mabery prof. rsch., 1969—77; Donald P. and Katherine B. Loker disting. prof. chemistry, dir. Hydrocarbon Rsch. Inst., U. So. Calif., LA, 1977—. Vis. prof. chemistry Ohio State U., 1963, U. Heidelberg, Germany, U. Colo., 1969, Swiss Fed. Inst. Tech., 1972, U. Munich, 1973, U. London, 1973—79, Louis Pasteur U., Strasbourg, France, 1974, U. Paris, 1981; hon. vis. lectr. U. London, 1981—95; cons. to industry. Author: Friedel-Crafts Reactions, Vols. I-IV, 1963—64; author: (with P. Schleyer) Carbonium Ions, Vols. I-V, 1969—76; author: Friedel-Crafts Chemistry, 1973, Carbocations and Electrophilic Reactions, 1973, Halonium Ions, 1975; author: (with G.K.S. Prakash and J. Somer) Superacids, 1984; author: (with Prakash, R.E. Williams, L.D. Field and K. Wade) Hypercarbon Chemistry, 1987; author: (with R. Malthotra and S.C. Narang) Nitration, 1989; author: Cage Hydrocarbons, 1990; author: (with Wade and Williams) Electron Deficient Boron and Carbon Clusters, 1991; author: (with Chambers and Prakash) Synthetic Fluorine Chemistry, 1992; author: (with Molnar) Hydrocarbon Chemistry, 1995; author: (with Laali, Wang, Prakash) Onium Ions, 1998; author: A Life of Magic Chemistry, 2001; author: (with Pranash) Across Conventional Lines, 2003; contbr. chapters to books, articles to profl. jours.; patentee in field. Recipient Alexander von Humboldt Sr. U.S. Scientist award, 1979, Calif. Scientist of Yr. award, 1989, Pioneer of Chemistry award, Am. Inst. Chemists, 1993, Mendeleev medal, Russian Acad. Scis., 1992, Kapitsa medal, Russian Acad. Natural Scis., 1995, Order of the Hungarian Corvin-Chain, 2001, Albert Einstein medal, Russian Acad. Natural Scis., 2002, Bolyai prize, Hungarian Acad. Sci., 2002; Guggenheim fellow, 1972, 1988. Fellow: AAAS, Chem. Inst. Can., Brit. Chem. Soc. (hon.; hon./centenary lectr. 1978, Centenary lectr. 1978); mem.: NAS, Indian Nat. Acad. Sci. (fgn.), Can. Royal Soc., Royal Soc. Sci. Arts Barcelona, Royal Acad. Sci. and Arts, Am. Acad. Arts and Sci., Chem. Soc. Japan (hon.), Italy Chem. Soc. (hon.), Royal Chem. Soc. (hon.), Hungarian Acad. Sci. (hon.), Am. Philos. Soc., Am. Chem. Soc. (award petroleum chemistry 1964, Leo Hendrik Baekeland award N.J. sect. 1966, Morley medal Cleve. sect. 1970, award Synthetic Organic Chemistry 1979, Roger Adams award in organic chemistry 1989, Arthur C. Cope award 2001), European Acad. Arts, Sci. and Humanities, Royal Soc. London (fgn. mem.), Italian Nat. Acad. Sci. Lincei, Grand Cordon of the Order of the Rising Sun (Japan). Home: 2252 Gloaming Way Beverly Hills CA 90210-1717 Office: U So Calif Loker Hydrocarbon Rsch Inst Los Angeles CA 90007 Office Phone: 213-740-5976. Business E-Mail: olah@usc.edu. *America still is offering a new home and nearly unlimited possibilities to the newcomer who is willing to work hard for it. It is also where the "main action" in science and technology remains.*

OLAJUWON, AKINOLA, investment company executive; Prin., owner Olajuwon Holdings, Inc., Houston, Tex., 1994—. Office: Olajuwon Holdings Inc 800 W Sam Houston Pkwy S Houston TX 77042-1912 Fax: 713-723-1159.

OLAJUWON, HAKEEM ABDUL, former professional basketball player; b. Lagos, Nigeria, Jan. 21, 1963; s. Salaam and Abike Olajuwon. Student, U. Houston, 1980—84. With Houston Rockets, 1984—2001, Toronto Raptors, 2001—02. Mem. NBA Championship Team, 1994—95. Named Most Valuable Player, 1993—94, NBA Defensive Player of Yr., 1993—94, Most Valuable Player, NBA Finals, 1994—95; named to All-Am. 1st team, Sporting News, 1984, All-Rookie team, NBA, 1985, All-Star team, 1985—90, 1992—94, All-NBA 1st team, 1987—89, 1993—94, All-Defensive 1st team, NBA, 1987—88, 1990, 1993—94; recipient award, IBM, 1993.

OLANDER, RAY GUNNAR, retired lawyer; b. Buhl, Minn., May 15, 1926; s. Olof Gunnar and Margaret Esther (Meisner) O.; m. Audrey Joan Greenlaw, Aug. 1, 1959; children: Paul Robert, Mary Beth. BEE, BBA, U. Minn., 1949; JD cum laude, Harvard U., 1959. Bar: Minn. 1959, Wis. 1962, U.S. Patent Office 1968. Elec. engr. M. A. Hanna Co., Hibbing, Minn., 1950-56; assoc. Leonard, Street & Deinard, Mpls., 1959-61; comml. atty. Bucyrus Internat. Inc., South Milwaukee, Wis., 1961-70, dir. contracts, 1970-76, v.p. comml., 1976-88, gen. atty., 1978-80, corp. sec., 1978-88, gen. counsel, 1980-88, vice chmn., dir., 1988-92; ret. Bd. dirs. Ballet Found. Milw., Inc., 1978-92, Pub. Expenditure Rsch. Found., Inc., Madison, Wis., 1978-94, Pub. Expenditure Survey Wis., Madison, 1978-82. With USN, 1944-46. Mem. ABA, Wis. Bar Assn., Wis. Intellectual Property Law Assn., Am. Soc. Corp. Secs., Inc., Am. Corp. Counsel Assn., VFW, Harvard Club (N.Y.C.), Harvard of Wis. Club, Bonita Bay Club. Republican. Roman Catholic. Home: 3708 Woodlake Dr Bonita Springs FL 34134-8605 Personal E-mail: rogunnarna@aol.com. *Strive for success in whatever you endeavor in every honorable way. Respect the dignity and rights of all persons with whom you come in contact, irrespective of their station in life. Recognize your own shortcomings and allow for those of others.*

OLANSKY, SIDNEY, retired dermatologist; b. Boston, Jan. 11, 1914; s. Samuel and Anna Olansky; m. Marian Elizabeth Freehafer, June 30, 1945; children: Leann, Alan, David, Sidney. BS, NYU, 1934; MD, Glasgow (Scotland) U., 1940. Diplomate Am. Bd. Dermatology. Intern Met. Hosp., N.Y.C., 1940-42; commd. officer USPHS, 1942, advanced through grades to med. dir., 1950; med. officer in charge Rapid Treatment Ctr., Washington, 1943-46; resident dept. dermatology Duke U. Hosp., 1946-48; pvt. practice dermatology Washington, 1948-50; dir. V.D. Rsch. Lab., Chamblee, Ga., 1950-55; assoc. prof. dermatology Duke U. Med. Ctr., 1955-59; prof. medicine, chief divsn. dermatology Emory U. Sch. Medicine, Atlanta, 1959-81, emeritus prof., 1981—. Rschr. USPHS, Gallinger Meml. Hosp., 1948-50; mem. nat. serology adv. com. to Surgeon Gen. of Pub. Health Svc.; cons. 3rd Army Hdqs.; mem. med. sci. com. Dermatology Found. Contbr. articles to profl. jours. Fellow ACP; mem. AMA, Am. Acad. Dermatology and Syphilology (bd. dirs.), Am. Dermatol. Assn., Am. Venereal Disease Assn. (pres. 1971-72), Am. Fedn. Clin. Rsch., Med. Assn. Ga., Med. Assn. Atlanta, Southeastern Dermatol. Assn. (sec., pres. 1971-73), Atlanta Dermatology Assn. (pres. 1971-72). Avocations: reading, sports. Office: 2045 Peachtree St NE Ste 800 Atlanta GA 30309-1412

O'LAUGHLIN, JOANIE, broadcast executive; b. Pasadena, Calif. Student, San Diego St. Sales rep. Blair TV, 1961-63, nat. sales coord., traffic mgr., 1963-75, ops. mgr., 1975-82, sta. mgr., 1982-95; v.p., gen. mgr. Sta. XETV-TV, San Diego, 1996—. Adv. bd. Shared Vision Found.; bd. trustees San Diego Lions Club Welfare Found. Office: Sta XETV TV 8253 Ronson Rd San Diego CA 92111-2004

OLAZABAL, ANN MORALES, business law educator; b. Phoenix, Ariz., July 3, 1963; d. Gilbert G. and Audrey Jean Morales; m. F. David Olazabal, Feb. 23, 2001; 1 child, Francisco Christian. BA, Tex. Christian U., 1984; JD,

U. of Notre Dame, 1987; MBA, U. of Miami, Coral Gables, 1997. Bar: Ariz. 1987. Atty. Gallagher & Kennedy, PA, Phoenix, 1987—89, Scult French Zwillinger, PA, Phoenix, 1989—94, Morrison & Hecker, Phoenix, 1994—95; v.p., gen. counsel Exko Svcs., Inc., Miami, Fla., 1995—97; lectr. law dept. U. of Miami, Coral Gables, Fla., 1997—99, asst. prof. of bus. law Sch. Bus. Adminstrn., 2000—. Author: (monthly column) Credit & Collection Managers' Letter; contbr. articles to legal jours. Recipient Grad. and Profl. Opportunity fellowship, U. of Notre Dame Law Sch., 1984—87. Mem.: Southeastern Acad. of Legal Studies in Bus. (pres.-elect 2003—04), Acad. of Legal Studies in Bus., Notre Dame Club of Miami, Riviera Country Club, Beta Gamma Sigma, Alpha Kappa Psi (hon.). Democrat. Roman Catholic. Office: U Miami Bus Law Dept 5250 University Dr 323E Coral Gables FL 33146 E-mail: aolazabal@miami.edu.

OLAZABAL, JOSE MARIA, professional golfer; b. Fuenterrabla, Spain, Feb. 5, 1966; Profl. golfer PGA European Tour, 1985—; mem. European Ryder Cup Team, 1987, 89, 91, 93, 97, Kirin Cup Team, 1987, Four Tours World Championship Team, 1989, 90, World Cup Team, 1989, Dunhill Cup Team, 1986, 87, 88, 89, 92. Winner Italian Amateur award, 1983, Spanish Amateur award, 1983, European Masters-Swiss Open, 1986, Sanyo Open, 1986, Belgian Open, 1988, German Masters, 1988, Tenerlfe Open, 1989, Dutch Open, 1989, Benson & Hedges Internat., 1990, Irish Open, 1990, Lancome Trophy, 1990, Visa Talhoyo Club Masters, 1989, 90, Catalonia Open, 1991, Turespana Open de Tenerlfe, 1992, Open Mediterrania, 1992, British Boys Champion, 1993, British Amateur Champion, 1994, Masters, 1994, Mediterrania pen, 1994, Volvo PGA, 1994, British Youth Champion, 1995, Open Ferrier de Paris, 1995, Turespana Masters, 1997; tour victories include NEC World Series of Golf, 1990, The Internat., 1991, Dubai Desert Classic, 1998, Masters, 1999, Benson & Hedges Internat. Open, 2000. Avocations: music, cinema. Office: PGA European Tour Wentworth Dr Virginia Water Surrey GU25 4LX England

OLBERT, STANISLAW, physicist; b. Lwow, Poland, May 9, 1923; m. Norma Louise DeVivo, 1954; children: Elizabeth, Thomas. Student, U. Munich, 1946-49; PhD, MIT, 1953. Rsch. scientist divsn. sponsored rsch. MIT, Cambridge, Mass., 1953-57, from asst. prof. to prof. emeritus, 1957-88, prof. emeritus, 1988—, cons. ctr. ednl. computing initiatives, 1999—2003. Vis. prof. U. Rome, 1986, 87, U. Florence, 1986, 87, Inst. Cosmic Studies, Warsaw, Poland, 1991. Co-author: Introduction to the Physics of Space, 1970; contbr. articles to profl. jours. Office: MIT Ctr Space Rsch 77 Massachusetts Ave Cambridge MA 02139

OLBRICK, VALERIE LYN, management consultant, information technologist; b. Pitts., Feb. 9, 1959; d. Kenneth Donald and LaVerne Estelle (Aiken) O. BS, Grove City Coll., 1981. Sr. telecomm. analyst Timken Co., Canton, Ohio, 1981-85; network planning mgr. Leaseway Transp. Inc., Cleve., 1985-87; group mgr. Network Strategies, Fairfax, Va., 1987-88; sr. mgr. Ernst & Young, L.A., 1988-95, prin. N.Y.C., 1995, dir. tech. planning and deployment Internat. divsn., 1995—. Avocations: sailing, skiing, bicycling, gardening, reading. Office: Ernst & Young Internat 787 7th Ave Fl 14 New York NY 10019-6085

OLCOTT, JOHN WHITING, aviation executive; b. Orange, N.J., Oct. 20, 1936; s. Egbert Whiting and Marion Richmond (Braillard) O.; m. Hope Bennett Phillips, May 14, 1966 (div. Feb. 1987); children: David Whiting, Bradley Phllips, Carter Howell; m. Isobel Waxman Ritter, Nov. 25, 1989. BS in Aero. Engring., Princeton U., 1960, MS in Aero. Engring., 1964; MBA in Gen. Mgmt., Rutgers U., 1970. V.p. Linden (N.J.) Flight Svc., 1960-66; flight rsch. specialist Princeton (N.J.) U., 1966-68; v.p. corp. devel., sr. cons. Aero. Rsch. Assocs. Princeton, Inc., 1968-74; v.p., group pub., editorial dir. McGraw-Hill Aviation Week Group, Rye Brook, N.Y., 1973-92; pres. Nat. Bus. Aviation Assn., Inc., 1992—2003, Gen. Aero Co., Inc., 2003—. Rsch. engring. and devel. adv. com. FAA, 1990-2003; mem. bd. govs. Flight Safety Found., 1992-2000; bd. dirs. ARINC, Inc., Annapolis, Md., 1997-2003, NASA, Aerospace Tech. Adv. Com., 1998-2003; co-chair FAA Safer Skies Program, 1999—2003; chmn. Be A Pilot, 2003-; mem. Small AircraftTransp. System. Coun. NASA, 2002—; bd. dirs. Nat. Coalition for Aviation Mobility, 2004—. Crew chief, mem. New Vernon (N.J.) Vol. First Aid Squad, 1974-92; bd. dirs. Aviation Rsch. and Edn. Found., Washington, 1988-92; mem. bd. visitors Aircraft Owner and Pilots Assn. Air Safety Found., Frederick, Md., 1988-93; trustee Embry-Riddle Aero. U., Daytona Beach, Fla., 1988-93, 95-97; chmn. panel on gen. aviation and commuter tech. NASA, Washington, 1974-86; chmn. panel gen. aviation safety FAA, Washington, 1983-88. Recipient Meritorious Svc. award Flight Safety Found., 1983, 2003, Dir.'s award FAA Ctral Region, 1984, Am. Spirit award Nat. Bus. Aviation Assn., 2003, Commendation cert. FAA, 1984, Gill Robb Wilson award Embry-Riddle Aero. U., 1986, Journalism award Helicopter Assn. Internat., 1990; inducted N.J. Aviation Hall of Fame, 2001. Republican. Presbyterian. Office: Gen Aero Co Hangar One 1 Airport Rd Morristown NJ 07960 Office Phone: 973-734-9994. E-mail: jack@generalaerocompany.com.

OLCOTT, RICHARD M. architectural firm executive; b. Princeton, NJ; BA Bachelor of arch., Cornell Univ., 1979; work study, Arch. Assoc., London, Eng. Intern Polshek Ptnr., 1979—98, ptnr., 1998—. Project, Oklahoma City Civic Ctr. Mus. Hall, Iris and B. Gerald Cantor Ctr. for Visual Arts, Stanford Univ., Seamen's Ch. Inst., The New York Times Printing Plant. Preservation Comm. Mcpl. Art Soc., New York, NY, 1989. Recipient Founders Rome Prize Fellowship, Am. Acad. in Rome, 2003—04. Mem.: NY City Landmarks Preservation Commn. (commissioner 1996—). Office: Polshek Ptnr LLP 320 W 13th St New York NY 10014-1278

OLCZYK, ED, professional athletics coach; Hockey player Chgo. (Ill.) Blackhawks, 1983—87, 1998—2000, Toronto (Can.) Maple Leafs, 1987—90, Winnipeg Jets, 1990—92, 1995—96, N.Y. Rangers, 1992—95, LA (Calif.) Kings, 1996—97, Pitts. (Pa.) Penguins, 1997—98, head coach, 2003—. Mem. Team USA Olympic Hockey Team, 1984, World Championships Tournament, 1985—87, 1989, Can. Cup Tournament, 1987, 91. Mailing: 1 Chatham Ctr Ste 400 Pittsburgh PA 15219*

OLCZAK, PAUL VINCENT, psychology educator; b. Buffalo, N.Y., May 25, 1943; s. Vincent Henry and Helen (Babula) O.; m. Marie Rose Oliveri, Oct. 20, 1973; children: Paul V. II, Patrick J., Drew M. MA, No. Ill. U., 1969, PhD, 1972. Clin. psychologist Family Ct. Psychiat. Clinic, Buffalo, 1975-77, cons. supervisory psychologist, 1977—; supr. psychol. svcs. Hopevale, Inc., Hamburg, N.Y., 1977-89; clin. psychologist Amherst (N.Y.) Police Dept., 1989—; asst. prof. psychology SUNY, Geneseo, 1977-83, assoc. prof. psychology, 1983-90, prof. psychology, 1990—, chairperson, 1999—; clin. psychologist child and adolescent psychiatry Niagara Falls Meml. Hosp., 1996—. Co-editor: Community Mediation, 1991; contbg. author: The POI in Clinical Situations: A Review, 1991, Self-actualization-Polemics Surrounding Its Use, 1991; contbr. articles to profl. jours./publs. Mem. APA, Ea. Psychol. Assn., Midwestern Psychol. Assn., Psychonomic Soc., Soc. Exptl. Social Psychology, Internat. Assn. for Conflict Mgmt., Psi Chi, Sigma Xi. Home: 150 Briarhill Rd Buffalo NY 14221-1811 Office: SUNY Dept Psychology Geneseo NY 14454 E-mail: olczak@geneseo.edu.

OLD, HUGHES OLIPHANT, research theologian, clergyman; b. Redondo Beach, Calif., Apr. 13, 1933; s. Shadburne Edward and Emma Coulter (Oliphant) O.; m. Mary Chase McCaw, June 12, 1982; children: Hannah Chase, Isaac Houghton Chambers. BA, Centre Coll., 1955; BD, Princeton Theol. Sem., 1958; postgrad., U. Tubingen, 1964-66; ThD, U. Neuchatel, 1971. Ordained to ministry Presbyn. Ch., 1959. Minister Presbyn. Ch., Atglen, Pa., 1959-64, Faith Presbyn. Ch., West Lafayette, Ind., 1972-85; mem. Ctr. for Theol. Inquiry, Princeton, N.J., 1985—. Lectr. Princeton Theol. Sem., 1998—. Author: Patristic Roots of Reformed Worship, 1975, Worship, 1984, enlarged edit. 2002, Shaping of the Reformed Baptismal Rite, 1992, Leading in Prayer, 1995, Themes and Variations for A Christian Doxology, 1992, The Reading and Preaching of Scripture in the Worship of the Christian Church, Vols. I and II, 1998, Vol. III, 1999, vol. IV, 2002; contbr. numerous articles to scholarly jours. Fellow N.Am. Acad. Liturgy; mem. Union League Phila. Republican. Avocations: painting, music. Home: 818 Lower Ferry Rd Trenton NJ 08628-3501

OLD, LLOYD JOHN, cancer biologist; b. San Francisco, Sept. 23, 1933; s. John H. and Edna A. (Marks) Old. BA, U. Calif., Berkeley, 1955; MD, U. Calif., San Francisco, 1958; MD (hon.), Karolinskia Inst., 1994, U. Lausanne, Switzerland, 1995, Univ. Coll. London, 1997. Rsch. fellow Sloan-Kettering Inst. Cancer Rsch., N.Y.C., 1958—59, rsch. assoc., 1959—60, assoc., 1960—64, assoc. mem., 1964—67, mem., 1967—; rsch. assoc. biology Sloan-Kettering div. grad. sch. Med. Scis., Cornell U., N.Y.C., 1960—62, asst. prof. biology, 1962—66, assoc. prof. biology, 1966—69, prof. biology, 1969—81, prof. immunology, 1981—; acting assoc. dir. research planning Sloan-Kettering Inst. Cancer Rsch., N.Y.C., 1972, v.p., assoc. dir., 1973—76, v.p., assoc. dir. for sci. devel., 1976—83; assoc. dir. for rsch. Meml. Sloan-Kettering Cancer Ctr. and Meml. Hosp., N.Y.C., 1973—83, William E. Snee Chair cancer immunology, 1983—. Harvey Soc. lectr., 1972; G.H.A. Clowes Meml. lectr., 80; assoc. med. dir. N.Y. Cancer Rsch. Inst. Inc., 1970; med. dir. Cancer Rsch. Inst., Inc., 1971—74, dir. sci. adv. coun., 1974—; vis. prof. clin. investigation GM Cancer Rsch. Found., Dana-Farber Cancer Inst.; vis. prof. pathology Harvard U., 1986; fgn. adj. prof. med. faculty Karolinska Inst., 1994—; cons. in field. Adv. editor: Jour. Exptl. Medicine, 1971—76, 1990—95, Progress in Surface and Membrane Sci., 1972—74, assoc. editor: Virology, 1972—74, mem. editl. adv. bd.: Cancer Rsch., 1967—70, Cancer, 1968—71, Recent Results in Cancer Rsch., 1972, mem. editl. bd.: Immunobiology, 1987—. Sci. dir., mem. Emeritus Sci. Com. Ludwig Inst. Cancer Rsch., 1971—86, chmn. sci. com., 1988—, bd. dirs., 1989—, CEO, 1995, dir. N.Y. unit, 1990; mem. med. and sci. adv. bd., trustee Leukemia Soc. Am. Inc., 1970—73; mem. sci. adv. bd. Jane Coffin Childs Meml. Fund for Med. Rsch., 1970—75; mem. rsch. coun. Pub. Health Rsch. Inst. City N.Y., 1977—80, bd. dirs., 1979—89, vice chmn. exec. com., 1984—89; adv. bd. biology divsn. N.Y. Hall of Sci., 1985—. Recipient Roche award, 1957, Alfred P. Sloan award cancer rsch., 1962, Lucy Wortham James award, James Ewing Soc., 1970, Louis Gross award, 1972, Founders Tumor Immunology award, Cancer Rsch. Inst., 1975, Rabbi Shai Shacknai Meml. award, 1976, Rsch. Recognition award, Noble Found., 1978, Robert Roesler de Villiers award, 1981, N.Y. Acad. Medicine medal, 1985, Robert Koch prize, 1990. Mem.: AAAS, NAS, Inst. Medicine of NAS, Am. Assn. Immunologists, Am. Assn. Cancer Rsch. (bd. dirs. 1980—83), Am. Acad. Arts and Scis., Harvey Soc., N.Y. Acad. Scis., Alpha Omega Alpha, Sigma Xi, Phi Beta Kappa. Office: Ludwig Inst for Cancer Rsch 605 Third Ave 33rd Fl New York NY 10158

OLDAKER, BRADLEY RUSSELL, lawyer; b. Washington, Sept. 5, 1962; s. William B. and Lois L. (Westfall) O.; m. Marianne E. Kaufman. BA magna cum laude, W.Va. Wesleyan Coll., 1984; JD, W.Va. U., 1987. Bar: W.Va. 1987, Ky 2002, Sup. Ct. US 2002, U.S. Dist. Ct. (no. and so. dists.) W.Va. 1987, U.S. Ct. Appeals (4th cir.) 1989. Assoc. Wilson & Bailey, Weston, W.Va., 1987-88, ptnr., 1988—. Contbr. W.Va. Law Rev., 1986. Mem. ATLA, W.Va. Trial Lawyers Assn. Democrat. Methodist. Office: Wilson & Bailey 122 Court Ave Weston WV 26452-1966

OLDEN, KENNETH, federal agency administrator, medical researcher; b. Parrottsville, Tenn., July 22, 1938; s. Mack L. and Augusta (Christmas) Olden; m. Sandra L. White; children: Rosalind, Kenneth, Stephen, Heather. BS, Knoxville Coll., 1960; MS, U. Mich., 1964; PhD, Temple U., 1970; DSc (hon.), U. Rochester, 2003; LHD (hon.), Coll of Charleston, 2003. Rsch. fellow, physiology instr. Harvard U., Cambridge, Mass., 1970—74; sr. staff fellow NIH, Nat. Cancer Inst., Bethesda, Md., 1974—77, biochemistry expert, 1977—78, rsch. biologist, 1978—79; assoc. dir. rsch. Howard U. Med. Sch. Cancer Ctr., Washington, 1979—82, dep. dir., 1982—85, dir., 1985—91; dir. Nat. Inst. Environ. Health Scis. and Nat. Toxicology Program NIH, Rsch. Triangle Park, NC, 1991—. Author numerous books, assoc. editor Cancer Rsch., 1990—2000, Jour. Nat. Cancer Inst., 1990—, Molecular Biology of the Cell, 1991—93, Environ. Health Perspectives, 1992—; contbr. articles to profl. jours. Mem. awards bd. GM Cancer Rsch. Found., Detroit, 1992—96. Recipient Disting. Svc. award, DHHS Sec., 1995, Am. Coll. Toxicology, 1995, Presdl. Meritorious and Disting. Exec. Rank awards, Pres. Clinton, 1996, 1997, City of Medicine award, Durham, N.C., 1996; fellow Porter Devel. postdoctoral, NIH, 1970—73, Macy Faculty, Macy Found., 1973—74. Mem.: Internat. Soc. Study Comparative Oncology, Inst. Medicine NAS, Metastasis Rsch. Soc., So. Biol. Response Modifiers, Am. Soc. Biol. Chemistry, Am. Soc. Cell Biology. Baptist. Avocations: tennis, hiking, bicycling, cooking. Home: 19 Quail Ridge Rd Durham NC 27705-1871 Office: Nat Inst Environ Health Scis & Nat Toxicology Prog PO Box 12233 Research Triangle Park NC 27709 E-mail: olden@niehs.nih.gov.

OLDENBURG, CLAES THURE, artist; b. Stockholm, Jan. 28, 1929;, naturalized, 1953; s. Gosta and Sigrid (Lindforss) O.; m. Patricia Joan Muschinski, Apr. 13, 1960 (div. Apr. 1970); m. Coosje van Bruggen, July 22, 1977. BA, Yale, 1951; student, Art Inst., Chgo., 1952-54. One-man shows include Reuben Gallery, NYC, 1960, Green Gallery, 1962, Sidney Janis Gallery, 1964—70, Galerie Ileana Sonnabend, Paris, 1964, Robert Fraser Gallery, London, 1966, Moderna Museet, Stockholm, 1966, 1977, Mus. Contemporary Art, Chgo., 1966, 1977, Irving Blum Gallery, L.A., 1968, Mus. Modern Art, NYC, 1969, Stedelijk Mus., Amsterdam, 1970, 1977, Tate Gallery, London, 1970, Pasadena (Calif.) Art Mus., 1971, Nelson-Atkins Mus., Kansas City, Mo., 1972, Art Inst. Chgo., 1973, Leo Castelli Gallery, NYC, 1974, 1976, 1976, 1980, 1990, Margo Leavin Gallery, LA, 1975—76, 1978, 1988—89, Walker Art Ctr., Mpls., 1975, 1992, Art Gallery Ont., Toronto, 1976, Ctr. Georges Pompidou, Paris, 1977, Rijksmus. Kröller-Muller Otterlo, 1979, Mus. Ludwig, Cologne, 1979, Wave Hill, Bronx, N.Y., 1984, Solomon R. Guggenheim Mus., NYC, 1986, 1995, Mus. Haus Esters Krefeld, Germany, 1987, Kunstmus., Basel, 1992, Pace Gallery, 1992, 1994, Nat. Gallery Art, Washington, 1995, Mus. Contemporary Art, LA, 1995, Kunst und Ausstellungshalle der Bundersrepublik Deutschland, Bonn, 1996, Hayward Gallery, London, 1996, Whitney Mus. Am. Art, NYC, 2002, two person show with Coosje van Bruggen, No. Ctr. Contemporary Art, Sunderland, 1988, Leeds City Art Gallery, 1988, Palais des Beaux-Arts, Brussels, 1988, IVAM Ctr. Julio González, Valencia, 1988, Galleria Christian Stein, Milan, 1990, Leo Castelli Gallery, NYC, 1990, 1990, Pace Gallery, 1994, Mus. Correr, Venice, 1999, Mus. Serralves, Porto, Portugal, 2001, Met. Mus. Art, NYC, 2002, PaceWildenstein, 2002, Frederick Meijer Gardens and Scupture Park, Grand Rapids, Mich., 2002, exhibited in group shows at Martha Jackson Gallery, NYC, 1960—61, Dallas Mus. Contemporary Art, 1962, Sidney Janis Gallery, NYC, 1962, 1964, Inst. Contemporary Arts, Lndon, 1963, Art Inst. Chgo., 1962—63, Mus. Modern Art, NYC, 1963, 1988, 1990—91, Washington Gallery Modern Art, 1963, Am. Pavilion, Venice, 1964, 1968, Moderna Museet, Stockholm, 1964, Whitney Mus. Am. Art, N.Y.C., 1964—66, NYC, 1968, 1970, 1974, 1981, 1984, 1999, Solomon R. Guggenheim Mus., 1965, Inst. Contemporary Art, Boston, 1966, Mus. Fridericianum, Kassel, 1968, 1972, 1977, 1982, Richard Feigen Gallery, Chgo., 1968—69, Minami Gallery, Tokyo, 1975, Mus. Contemporary Art, Chgo., 1980, Westfalisches Landesmus. Kunst und Kulturegeschichte, Munster, 1987, 1997, Venice Biennale, 1997, Mus. Nat. Modern Art, Ctr. Georges Pompidou, 1989, La Grande Halle-La Villette, Paris, 1989, Royal Acad. Arts, London, 1991, Mus. Contemporary Art, L.A., 1992, exhibited in group shows, Guggenheim Mus., SoHo, NYC, 1993, Nat. Gallery, London, 2000, exhibited in group shows, others, Represented in permanent collections Solomon R. Guggenheim Mus., NYC, Mus. Modern Art, Albright-Knox Art Gallery, Guffalo, Ctr. Georges Pompidou, Stedelijk Mus., Tate Gallery, Mus. Ludwig, Moderna Museet, Rose Art Mus. Brandeis U., Waltham, Mass., Oberlin Coll., Nat. Gallery Art, Canberra, Art Gallery Ont., Art Inst. Chgo., Hirshorn Gallery and Sculpture Garden, Whitney Mus. Am. Art, Mus. Contemporary Art, LA, others, exhibitions include public exhibitions and sculptures with Coosje van Bruggen Rijksmus. Kröller-Muller, Otterlo, The Netherlands, 1979, Nollen Plz. Civic Ctr., Greater Des Moines, Iowa, 1984, Vitra Internat. AG, Weil am Rhein, 1988, Mpls. Sculpture Garden, Walker Art Ctr., Mpls., 1990, Parc de la Villette, Paris, 1993, Ctrl. Gardens, Middlesbrough, Eng., 1994, Nelson-Atkins Mus. Art, Kansas City, Mo., 1996, Tokyo Internat. Exhbn. Ctr., 1996, Guggenheim Found., 2000, Piazzale Cadorna, Milan, 2000, Eindhoven, The Netherlands, 2001, Neumarkt Galerie, Cologne, Germany; author: Store Days, 1967, Notes in Hand, 1971, Raw Notes, 1973, Multiples in Retrospect, 1991; author: (with Coosje van Bruggen) Claes Oldenburg: Sketches and Blottings Toward the European Large-Scale Project, 1994, Claes Oldenburg Coosje van Bruggen, 1999, Down Liquidambar Lane: Sculpture in the Park, 2001. Recipient Sculpture award, Brandeis U., 1971, Skowhegan Sculpture medal, 1972, Am. Ann., Chgo. Art Inst., 1976, medal, AIA, 1977, Wilheml-Lehmbruck prize, Germany, 1981, prize, Wolf Found., 1989, Creative Arts award, Brandeis U., Jack I. and Lillian Poses medal, 1993, Lifetime Achievement award, Internat. Sculpture Ctr., 1994, award, Rolf Schock Found., Stockholm, 1995, Nathaniel S. Saltonstall award, ICA, Boston, 1996, Nat. Medal Arts, Washington, 2000. Mem.: Am. Acad. Arts and Scis., Am. Acad. Inst. Arts & Letters.

OLDENBURG, RICHARD ERIK, auction house executive; b. Stockholm, Sept. 21, 1933; came to U.S., 1936, naturalized, 1959; s. Gösta and Sigrid Elisabeth (Lindforss) O.; m. Harriet Lisa Turnure, Dec. 17, 1960 (dec. Apr. 1998); m. Mary Ellen Meehan, June 11, 2003. AB, Harvard U., 1954. Mgr. design dept. Doubleday & Co., Inc., N.Y.C., 1958-61; mng. editor trade div. Macmillan Co., Inc., N.Y.C., 1961-69; dir. publs. Mus. Modern Art, N.Y.C., 1969-72, dir., 1972-94, dir. emeritus, hon. trustee, 1995—; chmn. Sotheby's North and South America, N.Y.C., 1995-2000, hon. chmn., 2000—. Served with AUS, 1956-58. Home: 447 E 57th St New York NY 10022-3064 Office: Sotheby's Inc 1134 York Ave New York NY 10021-8300

OLDENBURG, WARNER ANDREW, vascular surgeon; b. Cleve., Apr. 22, 1953; MD, Case Western Res. U., 1980. Diplomate Am. Bd. Surgery. Intern Mayo Clinic, Rochester, Minn., 1980-81, resident in surgery, 1981-85, fellow in vasc. surgery, 1985-86; staff St. Luke's Hosp., Jacksonville, Fla. Assoc. prof. surgery Mayo Grad. Sch. Mem. Fla. Med. Assn., Internat. Soc. Cardiovasc. Surgery, Peripheral Vascular Soc., Priestly Soc., So. Assn. Vasc. Surgery, Soc. for Vascular Surgery. Home: Mayo Clinic 4500 San Pablo Rd Jacksonville FL 32224 Office Phone: 904-953-2000. E-mail: oldenburg.warner@mayo.edu.

OLDER, JAY JUSTIN, ophthalmic plastic surgeon; b. Jersey City, N.J., Feb. 7, 1940; m. Lois Rosner; children: Benjamin, Jessica. AB, Rutgers U., 1961; MD, Stanford U., 1966. Diplomate Am. Bd. Ophthalmology. Intern, resident in internal medicine Cornell U./Bellevue Hosp. Ctr., N.Y.C., 1968; resident in ophthalmology Stanford (Calif.) U., 1973; fellow in ophthalmic plastic and reconstructive surgery Stanford U., San Francisco, 1974; pvt. practice Tampa, Fla., 1974—. Clin. prof. ophthalmology U. South Fla. Coll. Medicine, Tampa, 1975—, dir. oculoplastic svc., 1974—99. Author: Eyelid Tumors: Clinical Diagnosis and Surgical Treatment, 1987, 2d edit., 2003. Fellow Am. Acad. Ophthalmology (Sr. Honor award 1995), Am. Soc. Ophthalmic Plastic and Reconstructive Surgery (pres. 1987, sec. 1983-84), ACS; mem. Phi Beta Kappa (v.p. Greater Tampa Bay Assn. 1995-96). Office: Older & Slonim Eyelid Inst 4444 E Fletcher Ave Ste D Tampa FL 33613-4937

OLDER, SUSAN, editor; Editor, chief UPI, Washington, 1997—. Office: UPI 1510 H St NW Fl 6 Washington DC 20005-1000

OLDERMAN, GERALD, retired medical device company executive; b. N.Y.C., July 16, 1933; s. Cass and Hilda (Klein) O.; m. Myrna Ruth Schwartz, Aug. 3, 1958; children: Sharon, Neil, Lisa. BS in Chemistry, Rensselaer Poly Inst., 1958; MS Phys. Chemistry, Seton Hall U., 1971, PhD, 1972. Rsch. chemist Nat. Cash Register, Dayton, Ohio, 1958-61; tech. mgmt. positions Johnson & Johnson, New Brunswick, N.J., 1961-75, dir. R & D, bd. dirs. surg. products hosp. divsn., 1972-75, v.p. R & D, Surgikos divsn., 1975-78; v.p. R & D, bd. dirs. Am. Convertors divsn. Am. Hosp. Supply corp., Evanston, Ill., 1978-85; v.p. internat. R & D Pharmaseal divsn. Baxter Healthcare Corp., Valencia, Calif., 1985-91; v.p. R & D, bd. dirs. cardiopulmonary divsn. C.R. Bard, 1991-96; cons. R.F. Caffrey & Assoc., Inc., Brownsville, Vt., 1996—; exec. v.p. R&D tech. and commercialization, bd. dirs. Quick-Med Techs., Inc., Wilmington, Del., 1998—. With USMC, 1954-56. Recipient Robert Wood Johnson medal Johnson & Johnson, 1969. Fellow Am. Inst. Chemists; mem. Assn. Advancement Med. Instrumentation, INDA, Assn. Nonwovens Industry (bd. dirs., corp. rep. 1986, 87), Nat. Fire Protection Assn. (industry rep.), Am. Soc. Artificial Internat. Organs. Home: 17 Pickman Dr Bedford MA 01730-1009 Office: RF Caffrey & Assoc Inc PO Box 319 Brownsville VT 05037-0319 also: Quick Med Techs Inc 401 NE 25th Terr Boca Raton FL 33431 Office Phone: 781-271-9893. E-mail: jolderman@aol.com.

OLDERMAN, MURRAY, columnist, cartoonist; b. N.Y.C., Mar. 27, 1922; s. Max and Jennie (Steinberg) O.; m. Nancy J. Calhoun, Feb. 28, 1945; children: Lorraine Imlay, Marcia Lynn, Mark. BJ, U. Mo., 1943; BS in Humanities, Stanford U., 1944; MJ, Northwestern U., 1947. Sports editor Rockland Leader, Spring Valley, N.Y., 1938-40; cartoonist, writer McClatchy Newspapers, Sacramento, 1947-51, Mpls. Star-Tribune, 1951-52; cartoonist, writer, exec. editor Newspaper Enterprise Assn., N.Y.C., 1952-87; asst. prof. San Francisco State U., 1974-80, U. Redlands, Calif., 1987, U. Oreg., Eugene, 1991-97; sr. editor Palm Springs (Calif.) Life, 1995—2003, Hiway III Mag., 2003—. Project dir. Hall of Fame, Oakland (Calif.) Raiders, 1995-99. Author: (books) The Pro Quarterback, 1966, The Running Back, 1969, The Defenders, 1972, Tennis Clinic, 1979, Super: "Just Win, Baby", 1984, Starr, 1987, Mingling with Lions, 2002; (book series) My Best Year, 1969-71. Pres. Calif. Alliance for Mentally Ill, Sacramento, 1994-95. Lt. M.I., U.S. Army, 1944-45, ETO. Recipient Bert McGrane award Football Writers Assn. Am., 1991; named to Nat. Sportswriters and Sportscasters Hall of Fame, Salisbury, N.C., 1993, Internat. Jewish Sports Hall of Fame, Netanya, Israel, 1997. Mem. Nat. Cartoonists Soc. (Best Sports Cartoonist 1973, 78), Golf Writers Assn. Am. (Best Feature 1982), Pro Football Writers Assn. (Dick McCann award 1979, Best Feature 1983), Baseball Writers of Am., Basketball Writers of Am. (Best Feature 1959), Football Writers Assn. Am. (pres. 1960-61), Phi Beta Kappa. Democrat. Avocations: tennis, photography. Home: 832 Inverness Dr Rancho Mirage CA 92270-1451 E-mail: molde55574@aol.com.

OLDERSHAW, LOUIS FREDERICK, retired lawyer; b. New Britain, Conn., Aug. 30, 1917; s. Louis A. and Annie Louise (Bold) O.; m. Virginia Wakelin, Nov. 30, 1940; children: Peter W., Robert L., David L. AB, Dartmouth Coll., 1939; LLB, Yale U., 1942. Bar: Mass. 1946, Fed. 1947. Mem. legal staff Army Ordnance Dist., Springfield, Mass., 1942-43; with firm Lyon, Green, Whitmore, Doran & Brooks, Holyoke, Mass., 1947-49; ptnr. firm Davenport, Millane & Oldershaw, Holyoke, 1949-64; treas. Nat. Blank Book Co., Inc., Holyoke, 1964-65, pres., 1965-78, chmn. bd., 1978-83; group v.p., dir. Dennison Mfg. Co., Framingham, Mass., 1967-82; counsel Bulkley, Richardson & Gelinas, Springfield, Mass., 1983—2002, ret., 2002. Mem. editl. bd.: Yale Law Jour, 1941-42. Trustee Mt. Holyoke Coll., 1966-76, Greater Holyoke YMCA; bd. dirs. emeritus Holyoke C.C. Found., Sta. WGBY-TV. Lt. USNR, 1943-47. Mem.: Abanahee Club (Biddaford Pool, Maine), Orchards Golf Club, Rotary, Colony Club, Longmeadow (Mass.) Country Club. Republican. Mem. United Congl. Ch. Home: 30 Bayon Dr South Hadley MA 01075 Office: Baybank Tower 1500 Main St Ste 2700 Springfield MA 01115-0001 E-mail: loldershaw@bulkley.com.

OLDFIELD, BARNEY, entertainment executive; b. Boston, June 28, 1956; s. Wilbur Joseph and Thelma Florence (Coombs) O. AB, Harvard U., 1979, Cert. Advanced Studies, 1981; Cert. Bus. Entertainment, NYU, 1996. Editor Musicians, 1979-83; copy editor Social Register Assocs., N.Y.C., 1983-87; advt. dir. Local Listings, N.Y.C., 1987-89; mkt. rep. Societa Italiana Lavor Oro, N.Y.C., 1989-90; bus. mgr. Al-Bab Internat., N.Y.C., 1990-92, McKenzie Internat., N.Y.C., 1992-96; gen. mgr. Angelika Entertainment, N.Y.C., 1996—; CEO Angelika Releasing, 1999—, Angelika.Com, 1999—; pres. Angelika TV.com, 2000—. Bd. dirs. Anthology Film Archives, N.Y.C., 1995—, Havana Film Festival in N.Y., Howl Arts Festival; chair bd., coord. Harvard Ind. Film Group; mem. adv. com. Internat. Film and TV Exch., exec. prodr. New Filmmakers Series; exec. prodr. Metro Angelika Film Festival. Prodr.: Too Much Sleep, Zero Day, Another Deep Breath, All Ivy, Maniac Z; columnist: So. Voice newspaper, 1976—79; editor: Harvard Today, 1997—; prodr.: Maniac 2. Mem. Soc. Calif. Pioneers, San Francisco, 1981—. Mem. Friars Club of Calif., Harvard Club of N.Y., Harvard Club of Boston, Harvard Club

of So. Calif., Harvard Faculty Club, Union League Club N.Y. Republican. Anglican. Avocations: squash, tennis. Office: PO Box 4956 New York NY 10185-4956 Office Phone: 212-410-9404. Office Fax: 212-876-4635. Business E-Mail: barney@angelikafilm.com.

OLDFIELD, EDWARD HUDSON, neurosurgeon, researcher; b. Mount Sterling, Ky., Nov. 22, 1947; s. Ellis Hudson Oldfield and Amanda Caroline Miller; m. Susan Shawler Wachs Oldfield, June 8, 1974; 1 child, Caroline Talbott. BA in Physics, U. Ky., 1969, MD, 1973. Diplomate Am. Bd. Neurol. Surgery. Pvt. practice, Lexington, Ky., 1980—81; senior staff fellow NIH, Bethesda, Md., 1981—83, dep. chief clin. neurosurgery, 1983—84, chief neurosurgery, 1984—. Med. dir. VHL disease Family Alliance, 1993—; adv. bd. brain cancer McDonnell Found., 1997—. Mem. editl. bd. Jour. Neurosurgery, 1994—2002. Recipient The Grass Award, Soc. Neurol. Surg., 1995, Farber Award, Am. Assn. Neurol. Surg., 1999. Achievements include patents in field of convective-enhanced drug distribution to the Central Nervous System; and advances in the understanding and treatment of brain tumors, pituitary tumors, syningomyleia, spinal aneteniovenous malformations, and drug delivery to the brain and spinal cord. Home: PO Box 309 Philomont VA 20131 Office: Nat Inst Health NINDS/SNB 10 Center Dr Rm 5D37 Bethesda MD 20892 Office Phone: 301-496-5728.

OLDFIELD, JAMES EDMUND, nutrition educator; b. Victoria, B.C., Can., Aug. 30, 1921; came to U.S., 1949; s. Henry Clarence and Doris O. Oldfield; m. Mildred E. Atkinson, Sept. 4, 1942; children: Nancy E. Oldfield McLaren, Kathleen E. Oldfield Sansone, David L., Jane E. Oldfield Imper, Richard A. BSA, U. B.C., 1941, MSA, 1949; PhD, Oreg. State U., 1951. Faculty Oreg. State U., Corvallis, 1951-90, head dept. animal sci., 1967-83, dir. Nutrition Rsch. Inst., 1986-90. Mem. nat. tech. adv. com. on water supply U.S. Dept. Interior, Washington, 1967-68; bd. dirs. Coun. for Agrl. Sci. and Tech., Ames, Iowa, 1978-84; mem. nutrition study sect. NIH, Bethesda, Md., 1975-80, 85-87; cons. Selenium Tellurium Devel. Assn., Grimbergen, Belgium, 1990-2002. Editor: Selenium in Biomedicine, 1967, Sulphur in Nutrition, 1970, Selenium in Biology and Medicine, 1987; author: Selenium in Nutrition, 1971, Selenium World Atlas, 1999. Served to maj. Can. Army, 1942-46, ETO. Decorated Mil. Cross Can.; recipient Klaus Schwarz medal Internat. Assn. Bioinorganic Scientists, 1998; Fulbright rsch. scholar U.S. Dept. State, 1974, Massey U., New Zealand. Fellow Am. Soc. Animal Sci. (pres. 1966-67, Morrison award 1972), Am. Inst. Nutrition; mem. Am. Chem. Soc., Am. Registry Profl. Animal Scientists (pres. 1990, editor: Profl. Animal Scientist 1993-96), Fedn. Am. Socs. Exptl. Biol., Pacific Fisheries Technologists (pres. 1966), Kiwanis (pres. 1964, lt. gov. 1986). Republican. Episcopalian. Home: 1325 NW 15th St Corvallis OR 97330-2604 Office: Oreg State Univ Dept Animal Sci Corvallis OR 97331 Fax: 541-737-4174. Office Phone: 541-737-1894. Business E-Mail: james.e.oldfield@oregonstate.edu.

OLDFIELD, KAREN, transportation executive; Pres., CEO Halifax Port Authority, Canada. Office: Halifax Port Authority PO Box 336 Halifax NS Canada B3J 2P6

OLDHAM, DARIUS DUDLEY, lawyer; b. Beaumont, Tex., July 6, 1941; s. Darius Saran and Mary Francis (Carraway) O.; m. Judy J. White, Jan. 23, 1965; children: Steven, Michael BA, U. Tex., Austin, 1964; JD, U. Tex., 1966. Bar: Tex. 1966, U.S. Dist. Ct. (so., no., ea. and we. dists.) Tex. 1966, U.S. Supreme Ct. 1974, U.S. Ct. Appeals (3rd, 5th and 11th cirs.) 1968; cert. arbitrator and mediator. Assoc. Fulbright & Jaworski, Houston, 1966—74, ptnr., 1974—, mem. policy com., 1980—97, 2001—, mem. exec. com., 1997—2000, mem. litigation mgmt. com., 1998—2003, chair, 2001—02. Mem. faculty grad. litigation program U. Houston; lectr. on corp. def. ins. and product liability. Former mem. bd. editors Aviation Litigation Reporter, Personal Injury Def. Reporter, Internat. Ins. Law Rev.; contbr. articles to profl. jours. Mem. Nat. Jud. Coll. Adv. Coun.; mem. liberal arts adv. coun. U. Tex.; bd. dirs. FDCC Found.; past bd. dirs. Houston Pops Orch. Fellow Am. Coll. Trial Lawyers (chair complex litigation and jud. com.), Tex. Bar Found. (life), Am. Bar Found. (life), Houston Bar Found. (life), Am. Bd. Trial Advs. (pres. Houston chpt. 1999); mem. ABA (mem. ho. of dels. 1996-98, chair tort and ins. practice sect. 1994-95, mem. coun. tort and ins. practice sect. 1988-98, presdl. emissary 1993-95, chmn. Standing Com. on Independence of the Judiciary 2001-04, chmn. Select Commn. on Jud. Campaign Fin. 2000-01), U. Tex. Law Sch. Alumni Assn. Exec. Com., 2003—, Tex. Bar Assn. (chmn. liaison fed. jud. com. 1989-90, pattern jury charges Vol. IV com. 1988-92), Tex. Young Lawyers Assn. (bd. dirs., chmn.), Fed. Def. and Corp. Counsel (pres. 1989-90, chmn. bd. 1990-91, exec. com. 1988-91), Tex. Assn. Def. Counsel, Maritime Law Assn. U.S., Am. Counsel Assn. (bd. dirs. 1982-83, 89-94), Def. Rsch. Inst. (chmn. aerospace com. 1984-87, Presdl. Achievement award 1987, bd. dirs. 1989-92, exec. com. 1991-92), Lawyers for Civil Justice (bd. dirs. 1988-98, chmn. 1998, exec. com. 1990-98, pres. 1997), River Oaks Country Club, Houston Ctr. Club, Sigma Chi, Phi Delta Phi. Office: Fulbright & Jaworski 1301 Mckinney St 51st Fl Houston TX 77010-3031 Office Phone: 713-651-5397. E-mail: doldham@fulbright.com.

OLDHAM, GRANVILLE MURL, JR., conductor, educator; b. Dyersburg, Tenn., Apr. 22, 1961; s. Granville Murl Oldham, Sr. and Theresa Fuller; BA in Music Edn., U. Pacific Conservatory Music, 1986; MA in Choral Conducting, San Jose State U., 1994; postgrad., U. So. Calif. Thornton Sch. Music, 2000—04. Asst. prof. U. Ala. Sch. Music, Tuscaloosa, 1994—99; lectr., condr. choral dept. U. So. Calif., Thornton Sch. Music, L.A., 2000—04; cathedral choir dir. Second Bapt. Ch., 2003—; heavenbound choir dir. Hollywood Presbyn. Ch., Hollywood, 2003—04; choral coord., condr. L.A.'s Best After Sch. Arts Program, Calif., 2003—. Scholar, U. Pacific Sch. Edn., 1985—86. Mem.: Am. Choral Dirs. Assn. (assoc.; women's chorus chair 1996—98), Pi Kappa Lambda. Home: 748 S Orange Grove Ave Los Angeles CA 90036 Office: USC Thornton School of Music 840 West 34th Street Los Angeles CA 90089-0851 Office Phone: 213-748-0318. Personal E-mail: gmoldham@aol.com.

OLDHAM, J. THOMAS, lawyer, educator; b. Cleve., Jan. 20, 1948; s. Vern Lawrence and Pauline Adams (Drake) O.; m. Chaille Linn Cooper, Feb. 4, 1995. BA, Denison U., 1970; JD, UCLA, 1974. Bar: Calif. 1974, D.C. 1977, Tex. 1983. Pvt. practice, Beverly Hills, Calif., 1974-81; prof. law U. Houston, Beverly Hills, 1981—. Vis. prof. law U. Colo., 1984, George Washington U., 1988-89, Cambridge (Eng.) U., 1992, U.of Copenhagen, 1999; past chair family and juvenile law sect. Am. Assn. Law Sch. Author: Divorce Separation and the Distribution of Property, 1987, Texas Homestead Law, 1991, Texas Marital Property Rights, 1996, Family Law Cases and Materials, 1998, Child Support: The Next Frontier, 2000; mem. bd. editors Family Law Quar., Family and Children's Law Abstracts. Pres. Mus. Area Mcpl. Assn., 1986-90; bd. dirs. Main St. Theater, Houston, 1991-97. Mem. Houston Bar Assn. Office: U Houston Law Sch 4800 Calhoun St Houston TX 77204-0001 Business E-Mail: toldham@central.uh.edu.

OLDHAM, JOE, editor; b. Bklyn., Aug. 1, 1943; BS, NYU, 1965. Editor Car Model OLR Pub., North Arlington, NJ, 1966—68; assoc. editor Automobile Internat. Johnston Internat. Publs., NYC, 1968—70; spl. projects editor Magnum-Royal Publs., NYC, 1970—72; book devel editor Hearst Corp., NYC, 1972—77, editor Motor Mag., 1977—81, exec. editor Popular Mechanics, 1981—85, editor-in-chief Popular Mechanics, 1985—. Contbr. (numerous articles) to various mags. Recipient Cert. of Appreciation, Nat. Inst. for Automotive Svc. Excellence, 1976, Automotive Svc. Couns., 1979, Northwood Inst., 1981, Cert of Appreciation, Automotive Hall of Fame, 1981. Mem.: Am. Auto Racing Writers and Broadcasting Assn., Internat. Motor Press Assn. (pres. 1973—74, 1981—82), Am. Soc. Mag. Editors, Soc. Profl. Journalists, Detroit Press. Office: Popular Mechanics The Hearst Corp 224 W 57th St New York NY 10019-3299

OLDHAM, JOHN MICHAEL, physician, psychiatrist, educator; b. Muskogee, Okla., Sept. 6, 1940; s. Henry Newland and Alice Gray (Ewton) O.; m. Karen Joan Pacella, Apr. 24, 1971; children: Madeleine Marie, Michael Clark. BS in Engring., Duke U., 1962; MS in Neuroendocrinology, Baylor U., 1966, MD, 1967. Licensed physician N.Y., N.J., S.C., Tex.; diplomate in psychiat. and forensic psychiatry Am. Bd. Psychiatry and Neurology. Intern pediatrics St. Luke's Hosp., N.Y.C., 1967-68; resident psychiat. Columbia U. Dept. Psychiat., N.Y.S. Psychiatric Inst., N.Y.C., 1968-70; chief resident in psychiatry Columbia U., N.Y. State Psychiat. Inst., N.Y.C., 1970-71; grad. Columbia Psychoanalytic Ctr., N.Y.C., 1977; dir. psychiatric emergency svcs. Roosevelt Hosp., N.Y.C., 1973-74, dir. residency tng. dept. psychiat., 1974-77; dir. short term diagnostic and treatment unit N.Y. Hosp. Westchester Divsn., White Plains, N.Y., 1977-80, dir. divsn. acute treatment svcs., 1980-84; deputy dir. N.Y. State Psychiatric Inst., N.Y.C., 1984-89, acting dir., 1989-90, dir., 1990—2002; assoc. chmn. dept. psychiatry Columbia U. Coll. Physicians & Surgeons, N.Y.C., 1986-96, vice chmn., 1996-2000, acting chmn., 2000—02; chief med. officer N.Y. State Office Mental Health, Albany, 1989—2002; chmn. dept. psychiatry and behavioral sci. Med. U. SC, 2002—, exec. dir. Inst. Psychiatry, 2002—. From instr. clin. psychiatry to prof. clin. psychiatry Columbia U. Coll. P.&S., 1974-96, 1988-96, Elizabeth K. Dollard profl clin. psychiatry medicine and law, 1996-2002; prof. psychiatry Med. U. S.C., 2002—; asst. prof. psychiatry Cornell U. Med. Coll., N.Y.C., 1977-83, assoc. prof. clin. psychiatry, 1983-84; attending staff dept. psychiatry Roosevelt Hosp., N.Y.C., 1973-77; assoc. attending in psychiatry, N.Y. Hosp., 1977-84, Presbyn Hosp., N.Y.C., 1984-88, attending in psychiatry, 1988-2002; tng. and supervising psychoanalyst Columbia Psychoanalytic Ctr., N.Y.C., 1983-2002; coord. med. student edn., dept. psychiatry Cornell U. Med. Coll., Westchester Divsn., White Plains, N.Y., 1977-84; coord. clin. clerkships in psychiatry Roosevelt Hosp., Columbia U. Coll. P.&S., N.Y.C., 1974-77; spl. adv. bd. Freedom From Fear, Inc.; examiner Am. Bd. Psychiatry and Neurology; chmn. acute divsn. rsch. group, Westchester Divsn., N.Y. Hosp., 1981-84, co-project dir. borderline rsch. group, 1982-84, co-prin. investigator familial transmission DSM III personality disorders, 1982 84; prin. investigator personality disorders in bulimia, N.Y.S. Psychiat. Inst., 1985-90, structured DSM III assessment psychoanalytic patients, Columbia Psychoanalytic Ctr., 1986-91; co-prin. investigator validity DSM III R personality disorders, N.Y. State Psychiat. Inst., 1987-94; co-investigator NIMH, 1996—. Author: (with L.B. Morris) The Personality Self-Portrait, 1990; editor Jour. Psychia. Practice; contbg. editor Jour. Personality Disorders; sect. editor Psychiatry; dep. editor Am. Psychiat. Pub., Inc.; mem. exec. editl. bd. Psychiat. Quar.; reviewer Psychiat. Svcs., Jour. of Neuropsychiatry; contbr. numerous articles to profl. jours.; more than 100 presentations in field. Recipient John J. Weber prize Excellence in Psychoanalytic Rsch. Columbia Psychoanalytic Ctr., 1990. Fellow Am. Coll. Psychiatrists (treas. 2004—), Am. Psychiat. Assn. (chmn. com. psychoanalytic liaison N.Y. County dist. br. 1986-87, pres. 1989-90, com. rsch. psychiat. treatment 1987-93, coun. rsch., steering com. practice guidelines, chmn. sci. program com. 1992-95, cons. 1991-92, 95-96, chmn. com. quality indicators 1999-2003, chmn. coun. quality care 2003—), Am. Psychopath. Assn., N.Y. Acad. Medicine;mem. Am. Psychoanalytic Assn. (cert.), Assn. Psychoanalytic Medicine (pres. 1989-91), Internat. Psychoanalytical Assn., N.Y. Acad. Sci., N.Y. State Med. Soc., Assn. Rsch. Personality Disorders (bd. dirs.), Internat. Soc. for Study of Personality Disorders (pres. 2000—03). Office: Med Univ SC Dept Psychiatry and Behavioral Sci PO Box 250861 67 President St Charleston SC 29425 Business E-Mail: oldhamj@musc.edu.

OLDHAM, KEITH T. surgeon; b. St. Louis, Aug. 24, 1950; s. Richard Thomas and Gladys (Althen) O.; m. Karen Sue Guice, May 9, 1981; children: Christian, Brian. BA, U. N.C., Chapel Hill, 1971; MD, Med. Coll. Va., 1976. Diplomate Am. Bd. Surgery with subspecialty in surg. critical care and pediat. surgery. Intern U. Wash., Seattle, 1976-77, resident in gen. surgery, 1977-81; fellow in pediat. surgery U. Cin. Children's Hosp., 1981-83; asst. prof. surgery U. Tex. Med. Br., Galveston, 1983-85; asst. prof./assoc. prof. surgery U. Mich., Ann Arbor, 1985-91; prof. and chief divsn. pediat. surgery Duke U. Med. Ctr., Durham, N.C., 1991-98; prof., chief divsn. pediat. surgery Med. Coll. Wis., 1998—; surgeon-in-chief Children's Hosp. of Wis., Milw., 1998—. Author/editor: Surgery of Infants and Children, 1997, 2004, Surgery: Principles and Practice, 2001; contbr. numerous articles to profl. jours.; editl. bd. Jour. Surg. Rsch., 1995. Trustee Am. Pediat. Surgery Assn. Found., 1997-2000 Mem. ACS, Am. Acad. Pediat. Surgery, Am. Surg. Assn., Am. Pediat. Surg. Assn. (sec. 1997-2000), Soc. Univ. Surgeons. Office: Childrens Hosp of Wis PO Box 1997 Milwaukee WI 53201-1997 Office Phone: 414-266-6557. Business E-Mail: koldham@mcw.org.

OLDHAM, MAXINE JERNIGAN, real estate broker; b. Whittier, Calif., Oct. 13, 1923; d. John K. and Lela Hessie (Mears) Jernigan; m. Laurance Montgomery Oldham, Oct. 28, 1941; 1 child, John Laurence. AA, San Diego City Coll., 1973; student Western State U. Law, San Diego, 1976-77, LaSalle U., 1977-78; grad. Realtors Inst., Sacramento, 1978. Mgr. Edin Harig Realty, LaMesa, Calif., 1966-70; tchr. Bd. Edn., San Diego, 1959-66; mgr. Julia Cave Real Estate, San Diego, 1970-73; salesman Computer Realty, San Diego, 1973-74; owner Shelter Island Realty, San Diego, 1974—. Author: Jernigan History, 1982, Mears Geneology, 1985, Fustons of Colonial America, 1988, Sissoms. Mem. Civil Svc. Commn., San Diego, 1957-58. Recipient Outstanding Speaker award Dale Carnegie. Mem. Nat. Assn. Realtors, Calif. Assn. Realtors, San Diego Bd. Realtors, San Diego Apt. Assn., Internationale des Professions Immobilieres (internat. platform speaker), DAR (vice regent Linares chpt.), Colonial Dames 17th Century, Internat. Fedn. Univ. Women. Republican. Roman Catholic. Avocations: music, theater, painting, genealogy, continuing edn. Home: 3348 Lowell St San Diego CA 92106-1713 Office: Shelter Island Realty 2810 Lytton St San Diego CA 92110-4810

OLDHAM, TODD, fashion designer; b. Corpus Christi, Tex., 1960; s. Jack and Linda Oldham. Founder Times 7, Dallas; founder, designer Todd Oldham, N.Y.C., 1989; design dir. Escada, Munich, 1994; dorm room furniture designer Target Corp., 2001—03; furniture designer La-Z-Boy Inc., 2002—. Host, dir. Todd Time MTV House of Style, 1993-96; guest Tracy Takes On with Tracy Ullman, 1994, The Nanny, 1996, Roseanne, 1996; designer spl. collection for Batman Forever, 1995, MTV's Choose or Lose bus, 1996, GM Bravada to raise money for cancer rsch., 1997; music video co-dir. (with Hype Williams) Maxi Priest's That Kind of Girl, 1996; music video dir. Us3's Come on Everybody, 1997. Active Design Industries Found. for AIDS, People for the Ethical Treatment of Animals, POWARS, Pet Pals. Recipient Rising Star award Internat. Apparel Mart, Dallas, 1991, Fashion Execellence award Internat. Apparel Mart, Dallas, 1993; named Designer of Yr. Calif. Fashion Industry Friends of AIDS Project, 1996. Mem. Coun. Fashion Designers Am. (Perry Ellis award for new fashion talent 1991). Office: Todd Oldham Store NY 120 Wooster St Frnt 3 New York NY 10012-5200

OLDLAND, KEVIN BRADLEY, architect; b. Uniontown, Pa., Sept. 20, 1964; s. Paul Richard and Martha Louise (Newcomer) O.; m. Karen Evans Oldland, May 11, 1991; children: Matthew Stephen, Kelsey Lynne. BA, U. N.C., Charlotte, 1989, BArch, 1992. Registered profl. arch., N.C., Del., N.J., Md., Pa., Va. Designer, intern Edwin Bouldin Arch., P.A., Winston-Salem, N.C., 1985, 86; project designer, mgr., intern Thomas H. Hughes and Assocs., Winston-Salem, N.C., 1988-91; prin. designer Kevin B. Oldland, Residential Designer, Clemmons, N.C., 1992-95; prodn. supr. W.R. Watkins Arch., Winston-Salem, 1992-95; prin. arch. Kevin B. Oldland Arch., Lewisville, N.C., 1995-98; project arch. W.R. Watkins Arch., Winston-Salem, N.C., 1995-99; prin. arch. Oldland Archtl. Studio, Lewisville, N.C., 1999-00; assoc. Design Exchange Arch., Inc., Lewes, Del., 2000—01; sr. project mgr. Design Exchange Arch., Inc./Tetra Tech. Inc., 2001—03; sr. project architect AWB Engrs., Salisbury, Md., 2003—. Sports dir. Lewisville Civic Club, 1998—2000; dist. insp. U.S. Lighthouse Soc., 2001—; mem. Del. River and Bay Lighthouse Found., 2000—; asst. cubmaster Cub Scout Pack 95; mem. zoning com. Town of Georgetown, Del., 2002—03, hon. chmn. bus. adv. coun., 2003; newsletter editor Luth. Ch. of the Epiphany, Winston-Salem, 1995—2000, min. for congl. life, 1993—95, archtl. liaison needs assessment com. and bldg. com., 1998—2000; mem. Downtown Master Plan Com., Town of Lewisville, 1999; mem. planning bd. Town of Lewisville, 2000. Mem. Nat. Coun. Archtl. Registration Bds., Constrn. Specifications Inst. (cert. constrn. documents technologist), Nat. Fire Protection Assn., Lewes C. of C., Rehoboth Beach C. of C., Alpha Rho Chi (leadership medal 1992). Republican. Lutheran. Avocations: travel, motorboating, deep sea fishing, painting, photography. Office: AWB Engineers Inc 1942 Northwood Drive Salisbury MD 21801

OLDMAN, ALFRED MAURICE, accountant, management consultant; b. London, May 12, 1948; s. Joseph and Dorothy O.; m. Marilyn Spiro, Jan. 16, 1983. MSc in Mgmt. Studies, U. Bradford, Eng., 1972; DBA, Henley Mgmt. Coll., 1997. Chartered acct., England. Gen. mgr. Europe The Torrington Co., Paris, 1983-87; dir. AMO Cons., Bath, Eng., 1987—. European contr. Measurex Corp., Datchet, Eng., 1979-82; asst. contr. North Europe, Norton Co., Welwyn Garden City, Eng., 1977-79; sr. corp. auditor Am. Express Co., N.Y.C. Editor: Handbook of Cost Management, 1998; author: Cost Management and its Interplay with Business Strategy and Context, 1999. Fellow Inst. Chartered Accts. in Eng. and Wales. Jewish. Avocations: music, antiques, mountain climbing, jogging. Office Phone: 44 7778 450080. E-mail: dramoldman@aol.com.

OLDS, JACQUELINE, psychiatrist, educator; b. Springfield, Mass., Jan. 4, 1947; d. James and Marianne (Ejier) O.; m. Richard Stanton Schwartz, Aug. 26, 1978; children: Nathaniel Leland, Sarah Elizabeth. BA, Radcliffe Coll., 1967; MD, Tufts U., 1971. Diplomate Am. Bd. Psychiatry and Neurology. Resident in adult psychiatry Mass. Mental Health Ctr., Boston, 1974; resident in child psychiatry McLean Hosp., Belmont, Mass., 1976, assoc. attending child psychiatrist, 1979—; psychiatrist-in-charge inpatient unit McLean Hall-Mercer Children's Ctr., Belmont, 1976-79; assoc. child psychiatry Beth Israel Hosp., Boston, 1979—; cons. in child psychiatry Mass. Gen. Hosp., Boston, 1994—. Instr. psychiatry Harvard U. Med. Sch, Boston, 1976-86; asst. prof. clin. psychiatry, 1986-2000, assoc. clin. prof. psychiatry, 2000—; cons. North Shore Mental Health Ctr., Salem, 1981-82. Author: Overcoming Loneliness in Every Day Life, 1996, Marriage in Motion, 2000, editor Clin. Challenges column in Harvard Rev. of Psychiatry; contbr. articles to profl. jours.; author (translator into Spanish): Matrimonio in Moviemento. Recipient Mentoring award Mass. Gen. Hosp. Dept. Child Psychiatry, 1998. Disting. fellow, Am. Psychiat. Assn.; mem. Mass. Psychiat. Soc. (ethics com. 1988-93, mem. pub. affairs com. 1992—), Am. Acad. Child Psychiatry, Am. Psychoanalytic Assn., New England Coun. Child and Adolescent Psychiatry (bd. dirs.). Democrat. Avocations: piano, writing, cooking, watercolors. Office Phone: 617-547-5920.

OLDS, JOHN THEODORE, banker; b. N.Y.C., Dec. 24, 1943; s. Richard J. and Barbara (Moses) O.; m. Candace Rose; children: Richard W., Samantha. Grad., Hill Sch., 1961; BA, U. Pa., 1965. Mng. dir. J.P. Morgan & Co., N.Y.C., 1972-97; vice chmn., CEO Devel. Bank Singapore, 1997-2001, advisor to chmn., 2001—. Trustee Singapore Civil Svc. Coll., Calif. Hist. Soc.; bd. dirs. Internat. Monetary Conf. Mem. Bedford Golf and Tennis Club, Mid-Ocean Club, Knickerbocker Club. Episcopalian. Home: 2450 Steiner St San Francisco CA 94115-1715 Office: DBS Bank 6 Shenton Way DBS Bldg Tower 1 Singapore 068809 Singapore

OLDS, JOHN WARD, internist; b. Apr. 25, 1935; s. Thayer Stevens and Dorris (La Vanture) O.; m. Rosemary Burns, July 10, 1957; children: David, James, Miriam. BS, Iowa State U., 1956; MD, U. Tenn., 1967. Diplomate Am. Bd. Internal Medicine, Am. Bd. Infectious Diseases, cert. physician exec. Intern San Francisco Gen. Hosp., 1967—68; resident, fellow U. N.Mex., 1968—72; practice internal medicine Des Moines, 1972—2002; dir. continuing med. edn. Iowa Meth. Med. Ctr., 1983—93, cons. infectious diseases, 1972—2002, attending physician, 1972—2002; asst. clin. prof. U. Iowa, Iowa City, 1978—95; co-dir. infectious disease and epidemiology Iowa Meth. Med. Ctr., 1985—93, dir. med. affairs, 1989—93; Medicare med. dir. for Iowa, 1993—97; Part A Medicare med. dir. for Iowa and S.D., 1997—; med. dir. Medicare RHHI, 1997—. Contbr. articles to med. jour. Lt. USNR, 1956—61. Recipient Roche award, U. Tenn., 1966. Fellow: ACP, Infectious Diseases Soc. Am., Am. Coll. Physician Execs.; mem.: AMA, Iowa Found. Med. Care (dist. chmn. 1981—83, bd. dirs. 1985—), Iowa Med. Soc. (councilor 1980—84), Med. Libr. Club (pres. 1985—86). Avocation: squash. Office: 400 E Court Ave Des Moines IA 50309 Business E-Mail: jolds@cahabagba.com.

OLDS, WILLIAM BELLAMY, physician; b. Scotland Neck, N.C., July 28, 1946; s. Hiawatha and Mary Lee (Lamberson) O.; m. Gloria Sonja Grant, Feb. 22, 1975; children: Grant Kandia, Rena Barika. BS, N.C. A&T State U., 1968; MD, U. N.C., 1981. Diplomate Am. Bd. Family Physicians. Rsch. technician N.C. Meml. Hosp., Chapel Hill, 1975-77; physician Person Family Med. Ctr., Roxboro, N.C., 1984-91; pvt. practice Roxboro, 1991—. Capt. USAF, 1968-75. Mem. Old North State Med. Soc. (asst. treas., Dr. of Yr., 1994), Nat. Med. Assn., Am. Acad. Family Physicians, N.C. Acad. Family Physicians. Avocations: tennis, listening to music. Home and Office: PO Box 1738 Roxboro NC 27573-1738

OLDSHUE, JAMES Y. chemical engineering consultant; b. Chgo., Apr. 18, 1925; s. James and Louise (Young) O.; m. Betty Ann Wiersema, June 14, 1947; children: Paul, Richard, Robert. BS in Chem. Engring., Ill. Inst. Tech., 1947, MS, 1949, PhD in Chem. Engring., 1951. Registered engr., N.Y. Chem. engr. Manhattan Project, Los Alamos, N.Mex., 1945-46; With Mixing Equipment Co., Rochester, NY, 1950-92, dir. research, 1960-63, tech. dir., 1963-70, v.p. mixing tech., 1970-92; pres. Oldshue Techs. Internat., Rochester, NY, 1992—; tchr. Sarasota (Fla.) Sch. Dist., 1992—. Adj. prof. chem. engring. Beijing U. Chem. Tech., 1992—. Author: Fluid Mixing Technology, 1983; contbr. chpts. and articles to books and jours. Chmn. budget com. Internat. div. YMCA; bd. dirs. Rochester YMCA. Served with AUS, 1945-46. Recipient 1st Disting. Svc. award N.E. YMCA Internat. Com., 1979, J.E. Purkyne medal Czech Republic Acad. Sci.; named Rochester Engr. of Yr., 1980. Fellow AIChE (pres. 1979, treas. 1983-89, chmn. 75th anniversary com. 1983, chmn. internat. activities com. 1989-92, Founders award 1981, Eminent Chem. Engr. award 1983, Svc. to Soc. award 1989, F.J. and Dorothy van Antwerpen award for Svc. to the Inst. 1999, centennial com. 2001—); mem. NAE, Am. Assn. Engring. Socs. (chmn. 1985, K.A. Roe award 1987), Am. Chem. Soc., Czech Soc. Chem. Engring. (hon.), World Congress Chem. Engrs. (v.p. 1986, pres. 1992-96), N.Am. Mixing Forum (chmn. 1990-93, Mixing Achievement rsch. award 1992), Interam. Confedn. Chem. Engrs. (sec. gen. 1991-93, v.p. 1993-95, pres. 1995-96), Victor Marquez award 1983), Rochester Engring. Soc. (pres. 1992-93, Rochester Engr. of Yr. 1980), UN Assn. of Rochester (pres. 2001-2003). Mem. Reformed Ch. in Am. (gen. program coun.). Achievements include design and scale-up procedures in field of fluid mixing. Home and Office: 141 Tyringham Rd Rochester NY 14617-2522 Office Phone: 941-349-0257. E-mail: ninetofive@juno.com.

OLDSON, JO, state representative, lawyer; b. Ft. Dodge, Iowa, May 15, 1956; BA, JD, Drake U. First dep. ins. commr., 1994—99; policy advisor to Gov. Tom Vilsack, 1999—2000; state rep. dist. 61 Iowa Ho. of Reps., 2003—; mem. commerce, regulation and labor com.; mem. govt. oversight com.; mem. state govt. com.; mem. ways and means com.; mem. oversight appropriations subcom. Vol. Young Women's Resource Ctr. Democrat. Office: State Capitol East 12th and Grand Des Moines IA 50319

OLDSTONE, MICHAEL BEAUREGARD ALAN, immunologist, educator; b. N.Y.C., Feb. 9, 1934; MD, U. Md., 1961. Fellow USPHS U. Md. Sch. Med., Balt., 1958; intern Medicine U. Hosp., Balt., 1961, resident, 1962-63, resident in Neurology, 1963-64, chief resident, 1964-66, fellow Dept. Pathology, 1966-69, assoc., 1969-71; head Neurology rsch. Scripps Rsch. Inst., 1969—; prof. Dept. Immunology and Neuropharmacology U. Calif., San Diego, 1978—, prof. Neurosci. and Pathology, 1988—. Adj. prof. Pathology U. Calif. San Diego, 1971—, adj. prof. Neurosci., 1972—; sci. coun. NIH, 1991-96; cons. WHO, 1992—. Recipient NIH-AID career devel. award, 1969, Maurice Pincoffs award, 1984, Cotzias award, 1986, Abraham Flexner Lectr. award for contributions in biomed. rsch., 1988, Rouse-Whipple award, 1993, Kakolin Sci. award, 1994. Mem. Inst. Med. Nat. Acad. Sci., Am. Assn. Immunology, Am. Soc. Neurology, Am. Soc. Virology, Am. Assn. Physicians, Am. Soc. Clin. Investigation, British Soc. Microbiology, Scandinavian Soc. Immunology, Office: Dept Neuropharm Scripps Mail Drop IMM6 10550 N Torrey Pines Rd La Jolla CA 92037-1000

OLEARCHYK, ANDREW, cardiothoracic surgeon, educator; b. Peremyshl, Ukraine, Dec. 3, 1935; s. Symon and Anna (Kravéts) O.; m. Renata M. (Sharan), June 26, 1971; children: Christina N., Roman A., and Adrian S.

Grad., Med. Acad., Warsaw, Poland, 1961, U. Pa., 1970. Diplomate Am. Bd. Surgery, Am. Bd. Thoracic Surgery. Chief divsn. anesthesiology, asst. dept. surgery Provincial Hosp., Kielce, Poland, 1963-66; resident in gen. surgery Geisinger Med. Ctr., Danville, Pa., 1968-73; resident in thoracic, cardiac surgery Allegheny Gen. Hosp., Pitts., 1980-82; pvt. practice medicine splty. in cardiac, thoracic and vascular surgery Phila. and Camden, NJ, 1982—. Author: A Surgeon's Universe, 2003; contbr. articles to profl. jours. Achievements include description of mimicking of the subclavian steat syndrome (2004), recognition of a triad of the severe atherosclerosis of the aortic valve, a low incidence of coronary artery disease and rheumatic fever in patients with a congenital bicuspid aortic valve (2002); modification of a vertical reduction aortoplasty by a distal external synthetic grafting for surgical treatment of aneurysms of the ascending aorta (2002); treatment of a bullous emphysema of the lung by a conservative resection of bullae and a local application of a biological glue (2001); noted association between congenital diaphragmatic defect with peritoneopericardial communication and congenital bicuspid aortic valve (2000); applied a staged treatment of the left subclavian steal syndrome and coronary artery disease by the left carotid-subclavian and coronary artery bypasses (1999); establishing that in patients with coronary artery disease, the causes of congestive heart failure in those with a mild to moderate reduction of the left ventricular ejection fraction were hypertension, myocardial infarction or ishemic insufficiency of the mitral valve, and in those with severe reduction of the left ventricular ejection fraction were left ventricular dysfunction alone, or in combination with ischemic mitral regurgitation (1999); repair of a pseudoaneurysm of the ascending aorta on a beating heart (1997); ligation of bilateral coronary-pulmonary artery fistulas on a beating heart (1996); internal repair of the coronary sinus (Valsalva) aneurysm (1996); grafting of the internal thoracic to coronary arteries without touching the atherosclerotic ascending aorta, on cardiopulmonary bypass with a beating, warm and vented heart and bradycardia induced by beta-blockers (1994); design of Olearchyk R Triple Ringed Cannula Spring Clip to secure vein grafts over blunted cannulas in coronary artery bypass surgery (1989); combined right femoral and iliac retroperitoneal surgical approach to remove retained intraaortic balloon device (1989); technique a side graft during replacement of the ascending aorta in proximal aortic dissection (1989); intro. of endarterectomy and external prosthetic grafting of ascending and transverse aorta under hypothermic circulatory arrest (1987); first to combine insertion of the inferior vena cava filter with a protected iliofemoral venous thrombectomy (Olearchyk's operation, 1986); pioneering promotion of grafting of diffusely diseased coronary arteries with the internal thoracic artery (1980-82) and of the left anterior descending coronary artery sys. during resection of cardiac aneurysms (1979-80); recognized that alcoholism and smoking were common habits of patients with stomach cancer (1975); description of a combined treatment of advanced gastic carcinoma by resection and chemotherapy (1975); demonstration of safety of simultaneous use of fluothane and curare as gen. anesthesia (1966); description of combined treatment of advanced testicular seminoma with chemotherapy, resection and radiotherapy (1961). Address: 129 Walt Whitman Blvd Cherry Hill NJ 08003-3746 Office Phone: 856-428-0505. E-mail: asolearchyk@yahoo.com.

O'LEARY, DANIEL BRIAN, lawyer, educator; b. May 20, 1947; s. John Patrick and Cecilia Frances (May) O'Leary; m. Patricia Anne Adams, June 22, 1974. BA, U. Minn., 1972; JD, William Mitchell Coll. Law, 1976. Bar: Minn. 1976, U.S. Dist. Ct. Minn. 1977. Assoc. Mansur & Mansur, St. Paul, 1976—81; ptnr. Mansur O'Leary & Gabriel, PA, St. Paul, 1981—96, Mansur & O'Leary, P.A., St. Paul, 1996—. Adj. prof. William Mitchell Coll. Law, St. Paul, 1981—90; mem. Charter Commn. West St. Paul, Minn., 1984—90, 2001—; pres. Douglas K. Amdahl Inn of Ct., 2002—03. Mem.: ATLA, ABA, State Bar Assn. Civil Trial Cert. Coun., Minn. Trial Lawyers Assn. (bd. govs. 1976—). Roman Catholic. Home: 1660 Humboldt Ave Saint Paul MN 55118-3905 E-mail: olearytriallaw@yahoo.com.

O'LEARY, DANIEL FRANCIS, academic administrator, priest; b. Boston, Apr. 17, 1923; s. Dennis Joseph and Catherine Mary (O'Connell) O'L. BA, Oblate Coll., 1950; EdM, U. Buffalo, 1953, EdD, 1956. Tchr. gen. sci., biology Bishop Fallon High Sch., Buffalo, 1951-62, asst. prin., 1962-65; dir. edn. Oblate Fathers, Washington, 1963-68; prin. Bishop Fallon H.S., Buffalo, 1968-74; dir. spl. programs Niagara (N.Y.) U., 1974-77, dean spl. programs, 1977-81, prof. edn., 1982—, dean edn. and continuing studies, 1982-88, prof., dean Coll. Edn., 1982-98, assoc. v.p. acad. affairs, 1998—. Adj. prof. Mt. St. Joseph's Tchrs. Coll., Buffalo, 1956-64, edn. evaluator reading clinic, 1956-64. Asst. dir. family life dept. Diocese of Buffalo, 1953-64. Mem. AAUP, ASCD, Assn. Tchr. Educators, Am. Assn. Sch. Adminstrs., Nat. Coun. for Adminstrn. Tech. Edn., Nat. Coun. for Accreditation of Tchr. Edn., N.Y. State Assn. Tchr. Educators, Am. Assn. Colls. for Tchr. Edn., Phi Delta Kappa. Roman Catholic. Office: Niagara U Assoc VP Acad Affairs Alumni Hall Niagara University NY 14109 Fax: 716-286-8349. E-mail: dfo@niagara.edu.

O'LEARY, DANIEL VINCENT, JR., lawyer; b. Bklyn., May 26, 1942; s. Daniel Vincent and Mary (Maxwell) O'L.; m. Marilyn Irene Gavigan, June 1, 1968; children: Daniel, Katherine, Molly, James. AB cum laude, Georgetown U., 1963; LLB, Yale U., 1966. Bar: Ill. 1967. Assoc. Wilson & Mc Ilvaine, Chgo., 1967—75, ptnr., 1975—87, Peterson & Ross, Chgo., 1987—94, Schwartz & Freeman, Chgo., 1994—95; of counsel Mandell, Menkes & Surdyk, LLC, Chgo., 1995—. Pres., bd. dirs. Jim's Cayman Co., Ltd.; pres. TV and Radio Purchasing Group Inc.; asst. sec. L.M.C. Ins. Co. Bermuda, 1990—; pres. Wagering Ins. N.Am. Purchasing Group Inc., 1997—. Lt. comdr. USNR, ret. Roman Catholic. Avocations: fishing, scuba diving. Office: Mandel Menkes & Surdyk LLC Ste 300 333 W Wacker Dr Chicago IL 60606 Office Phone: 312-251-1000. E-mail: doleary@mms-law.net.

O'LEARY, DAVID, priest, theologian, educator; b. Lynn, Mass., Mar. 11, 1958; BA, St. John's Sem., Boston, 1981, MDiv, 1985; MEd, Boston Coll., 1986; STL, Weston Jesuit Sch. Theology, 1990; DPhil, Oxford U., Eng., 1999; Cert. in Alcohol Counseling/Substance Abuse, Boston Coll Sch. Social Work, 1982; Cert. in Spiritual Direction, St. Mary's Sem. and U., Balt., 1995; Cert. in Human Sexuality, Christian Inst. for Study of Human Sexuality, Bosotn, 1995. Ordained priest Boston Archdiocese, 1985. From spl. edn. tchr. to dir. spl. edn. program St. John's Sem., Boston, 1977—81; tchr., film editor, and writer Office Religious Edn. Arcdiocese Boston, 1981—82; co-leader group therapy, case worker Brigham & Women's Hosp., Kenmore Sq. De-Tox, Boston, 1982—83; substance abuse counselor St. John/St. Hugh, Roxbury, Mass., 1983—84; deacon intern Immaculate Conception Ch., Malden, Mass., 1984—85; parochial vicar Immaculate Conception Parish, Everett, Mass., 1986-91; parochial vicar, dir. religious edn. St. Augustine's Parish, South Boston, 1991-93, St. Theresa's Ch., North Reading, Mass., 1993-95; asst. prof. moral theology, spirituality,sexual ethics St. Mary's Sem. and U., Balt., 1995—; assoc. U. chaplain, dir. Cath. Ctr. Tufts U., Medford, Mass., 1998—2002, U. chaplain, 2002—, 2nd prof. Adj. faculty lectr. in moral theology and social ethics St. John's Sem. Pastoral Inst., 1991; vis. lectr. in social ethics USAF Acad., Denver, 1992, USAF Chaplain Sch., Squadron Oficer Sch.,Air Command and Staff Coll., Air War Coll., Maxwell AFB, Ala., summer, 1992; adj. faculty Christian Inst. for Study of Human Sexuality and St. Luke's Inst., Silver Springs, Md., 1995—98; theol. cons. Md. Cath. Conf. of Bishops and St. Luke's Inst., Silver Springs, Md., 1995—98; mem. Human Investigation Rev. Com. New Eng. Med. Ctr. and Tufts U., 1998; chmn. instn. rev. bd. Tufts U., Medford, Mass., 2001; elected to bd. ministry Harvard U., Cambridge, Mass., 2002. Author: (Book) A Vision of Catechesis for Today and Pointers on Catechetical Instruction, 1996, Roman Catholic Beliefs and Prayers: A Handbook for Those on a Spiritual Journey, 1999, The Roman Catholic Perspective on the Morality of Withdrawing or Witholding Food and Fluid Administered Artificially to an Individual in the Persistent Vegitative State, 2001, Seeking the Path of God's Justice: an Analysis of the U.S. Bishop's Letter on Economic Justice, 2001; contbr. articles to profl. jours. Resident dir. Exceptional Citizens Week for disadvantaged, Gilmanton, N.H., 1990-94; bd. dirs. Camp Giving summer camp for physically and mentally challenged, 2001. Chaplain, major USAF, 1982—94. Mem.: Nat. Assn. of Coll. and Univ. Chaplains, Cath. Theol. Soc. Am., Am. Acad. Religion, USAF Assn., Soc. Biblical Lit. Republican. Avocation: long distance running. Office: Office of Univ Chaplain Tufts U Goddard Chapel 3 The Green Medford MA 02155 Office Phone: 617-627-3427.

O'LEARY, DEANNA KAY, analyst, consultant; b. Corcoran, Calif., Feb. 14, 1967; d. Harold Devoe and Glenda Lea Hoppert; m. Michael Patrick O'Leary, Nov. 16, 1996. BA, U. Fresno, 2000. Cert. six sigma green belt 2003. Benefit analyst CIGNA HealthCare, Visalia, Calif., 1991—96, project specialist, 1996—99, sr. claims examiner, 1999—2000, process and orgn. evaluation analyst, 2000—02, sr. process and orgn. evaluation analyst, 2002—. Author: inspirational short book, poems (Featured in Sparrowgrass Poetry Forum, 1996, featured in Famous Poets Soc., 2004); composer, musician, singer (inspirational music) Beyond the Clouds; author: Don't Miss It - Reflections on the Journey of Life, 2003. Trainer of ergonomics and time/motion economy City of Visalia, Visalia, 2002—02; asst. to vols. Youth Vision, Visalia, Calif., 2002—03; v.p. Children's Mus. of the Sequoias, Visalia, 2002—02; music dir., min. Tulare (Calif.) Missionary Bapt. Ch., 1998—, ins. com., 2001—03; ladies choir dir. Visalia Missionary Bapt. Ch., 1993—96; vol. Gift of Life Found., Visalia, 2002—03, v.p., 2003—; promoter and vol. Calif. Transplant Donor Network, Central Valley, Calif., 1996—2001. Recipient U. Merit award, Fresno Pacific U., 1999. Republican. Baptist. Avocations: writing inspirational and motivational works, songwriting and performing, enrichment of others, volunteer work, motion and time study. Home: 2602 S Silvervale St Visalia CA 93277 Office: CIGNA HealthCare 5300 W Tulare Ave Visalia CA 93277 Office Phone: 559-738-2153. E-mail: kismet01@sbcglobal.net.

O'LEARY, DENIS JOSEPH, retired physician, insurance company executive; b. Ireland, Feb. 5, 1924; came to U.S., 1949, naturalized, 1954; s. Joseph and Mary Christine (Dennis) O'L.; m. Audrey Mary Ryan, Nov. 26, 1952; children: Michael, Brian, Denis, Kevin. MD, Nat. U. Ireland, Cork, 1947. Intern St. Michael's Hosp., Toronto, Ont., Can., 1947-48, resident, 1948-49, St. Vincent's Hosp., N.Y.C., 1949-50, Triboro Hosp., Jamaica, N.Y., 1950-51; with N.Y. Life Ins. Co., N.Y.C., 1952-88, med. dir. employees' health, 1961-70, v.p., 1970-82, sr. v.p., 1982-88; asst. attending physician Bellevue Hosp., N.Y.C., 1955-69, assoc. attending physician, 1969-77, attending physician, 1977-84, sr. attending physician, 1984-87. Instr. medicine, Columbia U., 1958-63, assoc. in medicine, 1963-68; asst. prof. clin. medicine NYU, 1968-86; sec. N.Y. Lung Assn., 1962-67, 69-71, v.p., 1967-69, dir., 1961-86, pres.-elect, 1983, pres., 1985-86. Bd. dirs. Nat. Council on Alcoholism, N.Y.C., 1979-86, pres., 1984-86. Served as capt. M.C. AUS, 1953-55. Fellow Am. Coll. Chest Physicians, Am. Occupational Med. Assn., Am. Pub. Health Assn.; mem. AMA, N.Y. State, New York County med. socs., Am. Thoracic Assn., Soc. Alumni Bellevue Hosp., N.Y. Occupational Med. Assn. (exec. com. 1967—, pres. 1973-74). Clubs: Scarsdale (N.Y.) Golf (gov. 1981-84), Country Club Rancho Bernardo.

O'LEARY, DENNIS SOPHIAN, medical organization executive; b. Kansas City, Mo., Jan. 28, 1938; s. Theodore Morgan and Emily (Sophian) O'L.; m. Margaret Rose Wiedman, Mar. 29, 1980; children: Margaret Rose, Theodore Morgan. BA, Harvard U., 1960; MD, Cornell U., 1964. Diplomate Am. Bd. Internal Medicine, Am. Bd. Hematology. Intern U. Minn. Hosp., Mpls., 1964-65, resident, 1965-66, Strong Meml. Hosp., Rochester, NY, 1966—67, chief resident and hematology fellow, 1967—68; asst. prof. medicine and pathology George Washington U. Med. Ctr., Washington, 1971-73, assoc. prof., 1973-80, prof. medicine, 1980-86, assoc. dean grad. med. edn., 1973-77, dean clin. affairs, 1977-86; pres. Joint Commn. on Accreditation Healthcare Orgns., Oakbrook Terrace, Ill., 1986—. Med. dir. George Washington U. Hosp., 1974-85, v.p. Univ. Health Plan, 1977-85; pres. D.C. Med. Soc., 1983. Chmn. editl. bd. Med. Staff News, 1985-86; contbr. articles to profl. jours. Founding mem. Nat. Capital Area Health Care Coalition, Washington, 1982; trustee James S. Brady Found., Washington, 1982-87; bd. dirs. D.C. Polit. Action Com., 1982-84, Nat. Quality Forum, Nat. Adv. Coun. Agy. for Healthcare Rsch. and Quality. Maj. U.S. Army, 1968-71. Recipient Community Service award D.C. Med. Soc., 1981, Key to the City, Mayor of Kansas City, Mo., 1982. Master ACP; fellow Am. Coll. Physician Execs.; mem. AMA (resolution commendation 1981), Soc. Med. Adminstrs., Am. Hosp. Assn. (del. 1984-86, resolution commendation 1981), Internat. Club (Chgo.). Avocation: tennis.

O'LEARY, JOHN, international trade consultant, former ambassador; b. Phila., Jan. 16, 1947; m. Patricia Cepeda; 2 children. BA, Yale U., 1969, JD, 1974; MA, Cambridge U., Eng., 1971. Bar: Maine 1974. With Pierce Atwood, Portland, Maine, 1974-98; amb. to Chile Santiago, 1998—2001; prin. O'Leary & Barclay internat. strategic advisers, Washington, 2001—, Santiago, 2001—, John O'Leary LLC, 2001—. Trustee Santiago Coll.; mem. adv. bd. L.Am. studies program George Washington U.; mem. adv. com. ABA L.Am. Law Initiative Coun.; assoc. Inter-Am. Dialogue; mem. Western Hemisphere Task Force U.S. C. of C. Contbr. articles to profl. jours. Mayor City Portland, 1980-81. Mem.: Ford L.Am. Group, Washington Inst. Fgn. Affairs, Coun. on Fgn. Rels., Assn. for Diplomatic Studies and Tng. (bd. mem.), Coun. Am. Ambs. (bd. dirs.), Chilean-Am. C. of C. (pres.). Office: Chilean Am C of C Ste 600 South 601 13th St NW Washington DC 20005-3807*

O'LEARY, JOHN CLARENCE, retired radiologist; b. Washington, Nov. 16, 1922; MD, U. Tex., 1946. Diplomate Am. Bd. Radiology. Intern U.S. Naval Hosp., Long Beach, 1946-47; resident in internal medicine Scott-White Meml. Hosp., Temple, Tex., 1949-52; resident in radiology U.S. Naval Hosp., Bethesda, Md., 1956-59; resident in radiol. therapy Walter Reed Army Med. Ctr., Washington, 1959-60; mem. staff Brazosport Meml. Hosp., Lake Jackson, Tex., 1960-92, ret., 1992. Mem. AMA, Am. Coll. Radiology, Am. Inst. Ultrasound Medicine.

O'LEARY, KATHLEEN ANN, writer; b. Washington, Dec. 17, 1946; d. Patrick Christopher and Hilda Elizabeth (Gobrecht) O'Leary; children: Kara Ann Topper, Scott Patrick Thompson, Ryan Arthur Thompson, Kelly Marie Shifflett. Student, Montgomery Jr. Coll., 1964-66, Colo. State U., 1973-74; BS in Bus. Adminstrn., U. Md., 1975. Acct. exec. Sta. WSBT-AM-FM-TV, South Bend, Ind., 1972-74; mgr. advt. and promotion Sta. WGHP-TV, High Point, N.C., 1978-83, Am. Women in Radio and T.V., 1978—84; acct. exec. Wheat, First Securities, Greensboro, N.C., 1983-85; investment broker Legg Mason Wood Walker, Greensboro, 1985-88; investment exec. Ferris, Baker Watts, Inc., Bethesda, Md., 1988-90. Legal sec., paralegal complex civil and criminal investigation and def. practice Washington, 1988-94; legal staffer Morgan, Lewis & Bockius LLP, Washington; lectr. in investment field, 1986-2002. Exec. prodr. TV documentary Classic Memories, 1985. Founder, 1st pres., bd. dirs. Big Brothers/Big Sisters of High Point, 1981-85; founder, sec.-treas. Furniture City Classic, Inc., High Point, 1981-88; founder, bd. dirs. Henredon Classic LPGA Golf Tourament, High Point, 1981-88; mem. Leadership High Point, 1987-89; Challenge: High Point grad. and steering com. mem. High Point C. of C., 1984-85; bd. dirs. met. bd. YMCA of High Point, 1981. 82, Adams Meml. YWCA, High Point, 1985-87, Salvation Army Boys Club, 1980-81, Vols. to Ct., Guilford County, 1980-81; Sunday sch. tchr. Immaculate Heart of Mary Ch., High Point, 1980-87; exec. bd. mem. Greater Washington Open LPGA Golf Tourament, 1980-90. Democrat. Roman Catholic. Avocations: creative writing, classical piano. Office Phone: 301-549-3114.

O'LEARY, MARION HUGH, university dean, chemist; b. Quincy, Ill., Mar. 24, 1941; s. J. Gilbert and Ruth Elizabeth (Kerr) O'L.; m. Sandra E. Eisemann, Sept. 5, 1964 (div. 1979); children— Catherine, Randall, Jessica; m. Elizabeth M. Kean, Jan. 24, 1981. BS, U. Ill., 1963; PhD, MIT, 1966. Asst. prof. chemistry U. Wis., Madison, 1967-73, assoc. prof., 1973-78, prof. chemistry and biochemistry, 1978-89; prof. and head dept. biochemistry U. Nebr., Lincoln, 1989-96; dean Coll. Natural Scis. and Math., Calif. State U., Sacramento, 1996—. Cons. Institut Pertanian Bogor, Indonesia, 1983-84; vis. prof. Universitas Andalas, Padang, Indonesia, 1984-85, Australian Nat. U., 1982-83. Author: Contemporary Organic Chemistry, 1976. Editor: Isotope Effects on Enzyme-Catalyzed Reactions, 1977. Contbr. articles to sci. publs. Grantee, NSF, U.S. Dept. Agr., Dept. Energy, NIH; Guggenheim Found. fellow, 1982-83; Sloan Found. fellow, 1972-74. Fellow AAAS; mem. Am. Chem. Soc., Am. Soc. Biochemistry and Molecular Biology. Home: 6428 Orange Hill Ln Carmichael CA 95608-4580 Office: Calif State U Coll Natural Scis Math 6000 J St Sacramento CA 95819-6123 E-mail: moleary@csus.edu.

O'LEARY, PATRICK J. manufacturing executive; BS in Acctg. and Law, U. Southampton, England. From acct. to ptnr. Boston (Mass.) Office Deloitte & Touche, 1978—88, ptnr. Boston (Mass.) Office, 1988—94; CFO, dir. Carlisle Plastics, Inc., 1994—96; v.p. fin., treasurer, CFO SPX, Charlotte, NC, 1996—. Office: SPX 13515 Ballantyne Corporate Pl Charlotte NC 28277

O'LEARY, PAUL GERARD, investment executive; b. Boston, June 22, 1935; s. Gerard Paul and Marie Agnes (Hennessey) O'Leary; m. Elizabeth Jane Pollins, Oct. 14, 1961; children: Paul Hennessey, William Gerard, Mary Elizabeth Conroy, James Daniel. AB cum laude, Harvard U., 1956; MBA, U. Pa., 1958. Alumni dir. Wharton Grad. Sch., U. Pa., Phila., 1958-60; asst. sec. Empire Trust Co., N.Y.C., 1960-65; sr. investment analyst Blyth & Co., Inc., N.Y.C., 1965-70; v.p. William D. Witter, Inc., N.Y.C., 1970-76, also bd. dirs.; investment sr. v.p. Prudential Ins. Corp. Am., Newark, 1977—2002; retired. Instr fin Univ Pa, 1957—60. V.p. Prudential Found., Newark, 1986—96. Mem.: Boston Latin Sch. Alumni Assn., N.Y. Property Ins. Underwriting Assn. (mem. investment com. 1994—2002), Ins. Inst. Hwy. Safety (mem. investment com. 1983—2002), Assn. Ins. and Fin. Analysts (pres. 1973—74), Am. Nuc. Insurers (chmn. investment com. West Hartford, Conn. 1989—96), Inst. Chartered Fin. Analysts, Hobbyists Unltd. (Ridgewood, N.J.), Harvard Club N.Y.C., Upper Ridgewood Tennis Club, Harvard Club N.J. (pres. 1983—84). Roman Cath. Avocations: tennis, philately, cartography, history. Home: 719 Belmont Rd Ridgewood NJ 07450-1300

O'LEARY, PRENTICE LEE, lawyer; b. L.A., May 6, 1942; BA, UCLA, 1965, JD, 1968. Bar: Calif. 1969. Ptnr. Sheppard, Mullin, Richter & Hampton, L.A., 1974—. Bd. dirs. Legal Aide Found. L.A., 1987—93, 2000—. Mem. ABA (bus. bankruptcy com.), State Bar Calif., Los Angles County Bar Assn. (chmn. bankruptcy com., chmn. comml. law and bankrupt sect. 1985-86), Am. Coll. Bankruptcy Profls., Order of Coif. Office: Sheppard Mullin Richter & Hampton 333 S Hope St Fl 48 Los Angeles CA 90071-1406

O'LEARY, ROBERT C. publishing and media executive; CFO Cox Enterprises Inc., Atlanta. Office: Cox Enterprises Inc PO Box 105357 Atlanta GA 30348-5357

O'LEARY, THOMAS MICHAEL, lawyer; b. N.Y.C., Aug. 16, 1948; s. James and Julia Ann (Connolly) O'L.; m. Luise Ann Williams, Jan. 13, 1978; 1 child, Richard Meridith. BA, CUNY, 1974; JD, Seattle U., 1977. Bar: Wash. 1977, U.S. Ct. Mil. Appeals 1978, U.S. Ct. Appeals (9th cir.), U.S. Supreme Ct. 1983. Dep. pros. atty. Pierce County, Tacoma, 1978; commd. 1st lt. U.S. Army, 1978, advanced through grades to capt., 1978; chief trial counsel Office of Staff Judge Adv., Ft. Polk, La., 1978-79, trial def. counsel, trial def. svc., 1979-81; chief legal advisor Office Insp. Gen., Heidelberg, Fed. Republic of Germany, 1981-82; sr. def. counsel Trial Def. Svc., Giessen, Fed. Republic of Germany, 1982-84; asst. chief adminstrv. law U.S. Army Armor Ctr., Ft. Knox, Ky., 1984-85, chief adminstrv. law, 1985, chief legal asst., 1985-86; ret. U.S. Army, 1996; sr. trial atty. Immigration and naturalization Svc., Phoenix, 1987; sector counsel, spl. asst. U.S. atty., U.S. Border Patrol, Tucson, 1987-90; enforcement counsel U.S. Immigration and Naturalization Svc., Tucson, 1990-95, asst. dist. counsel Phoenix litigation, 1995-97. Apptd. U.S. Immigration Judge, U.S. Immigration Ct., Imperial, Calif., 1997-2000, apptd. sr. U.S. Immigration Judge, Tucson, 2000—; adj. prof. Embry-Riddle Aero. U., Tucson, 2002- Decorated Purple Heart, Cross of Gallantry (Vietnam). Mem. Judge Advs Assn., Wash. State Bar Assn., Order Ky. Cols. (commd. col. 1985). Home: 9080 E 25th St Tucson AZ 85710-8675 Office: US Immigration Ct 1705 E Hanna Rd Ste 366 Eloy AZ 85231-9612 Office Phone: 520-466-3671.

OLECHNO-HUSZCZA, CZESLAW, retired translator and educator; b. Estate Zadworze Wilno, Poland, Aug. 6, 1918; came to U.S., 1952; s. Vincent and Pelagia Olechno-Huszcza; m. Ethel Gillian Taylor, Aug. 25, 1951; 1 child, William Vincent. BA in Latin, U. London, 1950; diploma in edn., U. Leeds, Eng.; MA, U. So. Calif., 1958; postgrad., UCLA, 1960-65. Tchr. langs. Morningside H.S., Inglewood, Calif., 1958-80; head lang. dept., asst. tennis coach. Grad. lang. examiner UCLA, 1964-70; lectr. Polish lang. Loyola Marymont U., L.A., 1976-77; translator books and articles in Latin, Russian, Polish. Translator: The Warsaw Ghetto, 1970, Warsaw Aflame, 1970. Officer Polish Am. Hist. Assn., 1978; chmn. scholarship com. Polish Univ. Club L.A., Inc., 1947-99. Flying officer RAF, 1940-50. Decorated War medal, Air Force medal, Order Knights of Cross of Republic of Poland. Mem. Am. Translators Assn. (founder So. Calif. chpt. 1960), Polish Univ. Club. Democrat. Roman Catholic. Avocations: bridge, tennis, stamp collecting/philately. Home: 1841 Saint John Rd Seal Beach CA 90740-4380 E-mail: jillret@mailstation.com.

OLEEN, LANA, state legislator; b. Kirksville, Mo., Apr. 26, 1949; d. Robert James and Frances (Primm) Scrimsher; m. Kent E. Oleen; children: Brooke, Bentson. BS in Edn., Ks. State Tchrs. Coll., 1972; MS in Curriculum, Emporia State U., 1977. Tchr., Council Grove, Kans., 1972-74, St. George, Kans., from 1978; communications coord. Woodward-Clyde Cons., San Francisco, 1974-75; dir. communication Kans. Dept. Human Resources; mem. Kans. State Senate, 1988—. Mem. Rep. Precinct Com., 1978—. Active Kans. Rep. Women, Riley County Rep. Women. Mem. NEA, Nat. Coun. Tchrs. of English. Lutheran. Office: Kansas Senate State Capitol Rm 136-N Topeka KS 66612 Address: 1619 Poyntz Ave Manhattan KS 66502-4148

OLEFSKY, JERROLD M. medical educator, researcher; Prof. medicine, rschr. U. Calif., San Diego; chief U. Calif. & VA San DiegoHealth Care System divsn. of endocrinology and metabolism. Sci. dir. Whittier Inst. for Diabetes, La Jolla, Calif. Grantee MERIT award, Nat. Inst. Diabetes and Digestive and Kidney Diseases, 1994—97, 2001—06. Mem.: Nat. Acad. Scis. Inst. of Medicine. Office: Univ Calif San Diego Med Ctr Mailbox 0673 200 W Arbor Dr San Diego CA 92103-0673 E-mail: jolefsky@ucsd.edu.

OLEJINICZAK, RONALD M, corporate financial executive; B in acctg., Canisius Coll. CPA. Sr. audit mgr. Price Waterhouse; v.p.,mgr. fin. reporting and acctg. policy Shawmut Nat. Corp., 1992—95; dir. of corp. acctg. policy Aetna Inc., 1995—97, v.p., fin. reporting analysis, 1997—2001, v.p., contr., 2001—. Mem.: NY State Soc. of Cert. Pub. Accountants, Am. Inst. Cert. Pub. Accountants. Office: Aetna Inc 151 Farmington Ave Hartford CT 06156

OLEJNICZAK, BERNARD CHARLES, education educator; b. Green Bay, Wis., Aug. 23, 1930; s. Bernard Clement and Helen Josephine (LeClair) Olejniczak; m. Mary Jean Barrett-Terry, Oct. 13, 1956 (div. Dec. 1979); children: Ann Marie, Mary Rose, Patrick James, Thomas Bernard; m. Margaret Jean Olson, Sept. 19, 1980. BA in Philosophy, St. Norbert Coll., 1953; MA in Counseling, U. Wis., 1966. Tchr. in Latin, French and journalism Pulaski (Wis.) H.S., 1957—71; adminstr. Pulaski Elem. Schs., 1971—92; ednl. cons., 1993—96; tech. lectr. U. Wis., Oshkosh, 1996—. Chmn. spirituality curriculum U. Wis. Learning in Retirement, 1997—, chmn. curriculum, 2004—. Editor (newsletter): Polish Heritage, 1993—, Wisconsin Counselor, 1995—. Pres. Village Bd., Pulaski, 1965—70; v.p. Bd. Edn., Pulaski, 1992—96; sec. Pulaski C. of C., 1958—64; pres. Brown County Libr. Bd., Green Bay, Wis., 1985—96, Nicolet Fed. Libr., Green Bay, Wis., 1987—92. Named Trustee of Yr., Wis. Libr. Assn., 1997; recipient Profl. Writing award, Wis. Counselors Assn., 1999. Mem.: Lions Club (newsetter editor, sec. 1993—), Phi Delta Kappa. Democrat. Roman Catholic. Avocations: reading, computers. Home: 1625 Graber St Oshkosh WI 54901 Office: Univ Wis Coll Edn 800 Algoma Blvd Oshkosh WI 54901 E-mail: olejnicz@uwosh.edu.

OLEN, MILTON WILLIAM, JR., marketing executive; b. Providence, Sept. 15, 1950; s. Milton William and Elizabeth Amanda (Goodrich) O.; m. Kathleen A. Windridge, June 15, 2001. Student, Fla. So. Coll., 1969-72; BS in Behavioral Scis. magna cum laude, Nova U., 1978. Lic. comml. pilot, USCG capt.; lic. residential contractor, Fla. Mfr.'s rep. for Fla., The Siemens Corp., Ft. Lauderdale, Fla., 1972-77; product mgr., exec. salesman, sales mgr. The Ritter Dental Co., Romulus, Mich., 1977-85; gen. mgr., exec. salesman Olen Homes Internat. Inc., Fort Lauderdale, Fla., 1981—; gen. mgr. Windridge Yacht Charters. Mem. Nat. Assn. Home Builders, C. of C. Miami Beach, Better Bus. Bur. Roman Catholic. Avocations: boating, travel. Office: PO Box 70156 Fort Lauderdale FL 33307-0156

OLENCHAK, FRANK RICHARD, music educator, musician; b. Scranton, Pa., Aug. 5, 1928; s. Francis Richard and Helen Anita Olenchak; m. Patricia Maye Ingram, June 15, 1949; children: Francis Richard III, Rebecca Lynn, Jeffrey Stuart. MusB, James Madison U., 1950; MEd, Pa. State U., University Park, Pa., 1957, CASE, postgrad., Johns Hopkins U., 1965, PhD in Music. Music Edn., U. of Mich., 1977. Cert. music tchr. Md., Va. Supr. of music, band dir. Galax (Va.) Pub. Schs., 1950—54; h.s. band dir. Harford County Schs., Bel Air, Md., 1954—58, Balt. City Schs., 1958—61; elem. instrumental music tchr. Balt. County Schs., Towson, Md., 1961—66; emeritus prof. edn. and profl. devel. Western Mich. U., Kalamazoo, 1966—84; adj. coord. of student tchg. Ea. Mich. U., Ypsilanti, 1984—85; dir., CEO Music on the Move of Mich., Ann Arbor, 1985—87; chair dept. of music Allen U., Columbia, SC, 1989—; CEO, record prodr. Myrtle Records, Columbia, SC, 1997—. Post-doctoral rschr. Columbia U., 1981; vis. scholar U. Mich., Ann Arbor, 1981—82. Author: Exploratory Music, (periodical) The Instructor, 1968; editor: (newsletter) Michigan Association of Teacher Educators, (books) SchoolMATES, 3 vols., 1981, 1982. Choir dir. Trinity Luth. Ch., Columbia, 1999—2002; dir. of music 3d Luth. Ch., Balt., 1960—62. Recipient doctoral tchg. fellowship, U. of Mich., 1969—70, acad. scholarship, Shenandoah Conservatory of Music, 1947. Mem.: Am. Fedn. of Musicians, Assn. of Tchr. Educators (pres., comms. chair 1978—83, Meritorious Svc. award 1980), Phi Delta Kappa (pres. 1978—87, 1991—94, Disting. Svc. Key 1985). Achievements include Creator of NUMCOMPO, a system for teaching musical notation to children with no prior knowledge of music. Avocations: sports, bridge, checkers, record collecting, travel. Office: Allen U 1530 Harden St Columbia SC 29204 E-mail: myrtrec@earthlink.net.

OLENDER, JACK HARVEY, lawyer; b. McKeesport, Pa., Sept. 8, 1935; m. Lovell Olender. BA, U. Pitts., 1957, JD, 1960; LLM, George Washington U., 1961. Bar: D.C. 1961, U.S. Supreme Ct. 1965, Md. 1966, Pa. 1985; diplomate Am. Bd. Trial Advocates,Inner Cir. Advocates. Pvt. practice, Washington, 1961-79; prin. Jack H. Olender & Assocs., P.C., Washington, 1979—. Contbr. articles to profl. jours. Active World Peace through Law, Washington. Named to Hall of Fame Nat. Assn. Black Women Attys., 1987, D.C. Hall of Fame, 2000, Washington Bar Assn. Hall of Fame, 2000; recipient Presdl. award Nat. Bar Assn., 1996, 2000, 02, Advocate for Justice award Nat. Bar Assn., 2000, Internat. B'nai B'rith Pursuit of Justice award, 2001, Champion Justice award Trial Lawyers Assn., D.C., 2004. Fellow Am. Coll. Trial Lawyers, Internat. Acad. Trial Lawyers and Inner Cir. Advs.; mem. ATLA, Nat. Bar Assn. (adv. for justice 2000), Am. Bd. Profl. Liability Attys. (bd. dirs.), Trial Lawyers Pub. Justice (bd. dirs.), Internat. Assn. Jewish Lawyers and Jurists (bd. dirs.), Bar Assn. of D.C. (pres. 1999-2000). Office: Jack H Olender & Assocs PC 888 17th St NW Fl 4 Washington DC 20006-3939 Office Phone: 202-879-7777.

OLENDORF, DONNA, editor; b. Chgo., Sept. 11, 1949; d. Camille Frank Vozar and Lea Bertani Vozar Newman; m. Donald Olendorf, June 29, 1969; children: Patrice LeeAnn Boettcher, Sara Elizabeth Ortolan, Donald Patrick. BA with distinction, U. Mich., 1969; MA in Edn., Ea. Mich. U., Ypsilanti, 1973; MA in English cum laude, Wayne State U., Detroit, 1982. From asst. editor to sr. editor, project mgr. Gale Group, Farmington Hills, Mich., 1982—; editor in chief St. Luke's Epistle, Utica, Mich., 1998—2001; review panel manuscript Jour. Coll. Sci. Reading Nat. Sci. Tchrs. Assn., Arlington, Va., 1998-2000; with editl. bd. The Record, Detroit, 2000—; with Gale Group, Farmington Hills, Mich.; series project mgr., editor select vols, Grzimek's Animal Life Ency., 2d edit., 2002—. Prodn. editor: Notable Twentieth Century Scientists, 1995 (RASD Outstanding Reference Books citation, 1995, Best Reference Libr. Jour., 1995); editor: Gale Encyclopedia of Medicine, 1999 (RUSA award Outstanding Ref., 2000, Editor's Choice award RRB/Booklist, 2000), Something about the Author, 1990-92, Contemporary Authors, 1992-94. Active Eisenhower Dance Ensemble, Rochester Hills, Mich., 1997—; clerk of vestry St. Luke's Episcopal Ch., Utica, Mich., 1998-2000. Recipient Blue Ribbon award for gen. excellence, Diocese of Mich., 2000, Red Ribbon award for gen. excellence, 2001. Mem.: Project Mgmt. Inst. Avocations: ballet, gardening. Office: Gale Group 27500 Drake Rd Farmington Hills MI 48331 E-mail: donna.olendorf@gale.com.

OLENDORF, WILLIAM CARR, JR., small business owner; b. Albany, N.Y., Oct. 3, 1945; s. William Carr Sr. and Mary Zilpha (Gillies) O.; m. Barbara Kay Cowan, Aug. 14, 1966; children: Mark, Julie, Jennifer. Student, Columbia Coll., 1964-65, So. Ill. U., 1965-66. Prodn. asst. Sta. WTTW-TV, Chgo., 1962-64; radio announcer Sta. WERX, Wyoming, Mich., 1967-68; sales rep. Sta. WCFL, Chgo., 1968-70, Sta. WJJD-AM & FM, Chgo., 1970-72; v.p. Promotion Network, Chgo., 1972-74; account exec. AVCO-TV, Chgo., 1974-76, Peters, Griffin & Woodward, Chgo., 1976-82, Petry TV, Chgo., 1982-83; owner, pres. Point South KOA Resort, Yemassee, S.C., 1983—. Commr. Point South Pub. Svc. Dist., 1987-88, Lowcountry & Resort Island Tourism Commn., 1994—; mem. tourism tax adv. bd. Jasper County, S.C., 1985—; chmn. Jasper County Hist. Preservation Commn., S.C., 1994-99; trustee S.C. Battleground Preservation Trust, Inc., 1994-98, 2003-2004; mem. Low Country Revolutionary War Trail Commn. Recipient S.C. Honor award for Historic Preservation, Palmetto Trust for Historic Preservation, S.C. Dept. Archives and History, 1997. Mem. Nat. Campground Owners Assn. (campground nat. adv. bd. 1989-93, Take Pride in Am. award 1992), Kampground Owners Assn. (S.C. regiona pres. 1994-97, Award of Merit 1990), S.C. Campground Assn. (pres. 1987-88), Point South Mchts. Assn. (pres. 1990—), Jasper County Hist. Soc., Jasper County C. of C. (bd. dirs. 2001-2003). Republican. Episcopalian. Avocation: amateur radio operator. Home and Office: PO Box 1760 Yemassee SC 29945-1760 E-mail: pskoa@mykoa.com.

OLER, WESLEY M., IV, portfolio manager; b. Washington, Apr. 13, 1955; s. Wesley Marion III and Virginia (Craemer) O.; m. Debra Brown, Apr. 16, 1993; children: Wesley V, Phoebe. BA, Yale U., 1978. CFA. Deputy mgr. instl. sales Brown Bros. Harriman & Co., Zurich, 1982-88, mgr. internat. bankers N.Y.C., 1988-95, sr. mgr. equity trading, 1995-99; sr. portfolio mgr., pvt. client group, 1999—. Mem. ITS/CAES subcom. Nasdag Stock Market, N.Y.C., 1996—; mem. N.Y. Stock Exch., N.Y.C., 1998. Mem. Endowment Commn. Christ Ch., Greenwich, Conn. Mem. SAR (treas. 1995-96), Soc. Colonial Wars (coun. mem. 1993-94), Soc. Mayflower Descs., Securities Industry Assn. (mem. instnl. brokerage com. 1997—), N.Y. Soc. Security Analysts (mem. High Net Worth Investors Com.). Office: Brown Bros Harriman & Co 1450 Broadway 5th Fl New York NY 10005- E-mail: wesley.oler@bbh.com.

OLERUD, JOHN GARRETT, professional baseball player; b. Seattle, Aug. 5, 1968; s. John E. Olerud. Student, Washington State U. Player Toronto Blue Jays, 1989-96, NY Mets, 1997-99, Seattle Mariners, 2000—04, New York Yankees, 2004—. Named to Am. League All-Star Team, 1993, 2001; recipient Am. League Gold Glove Award, 2000, 2002, 2003. winner A.L batting title, 1993. Office: c/o New York Yankees E 161st street and river ave Bronx NY 10452*

OLES, PAUL STEVENSON (STEVE OLES), architect, perspectivist, educator; b. San Antonio, Sept. 26, 1936; s. Paul Stevenson Sr. and Suda (Willis) O.; m. Carole Simmons, Oct. 11, 1963 (div. 1991); children: Brian Thomas, Julia Oles Carr; m. Susan Thompson, Sept. 26, 1992. BArch, Tex. Tech U., 1960; MArch, Yale U., 1963. Registered architect, Mass. Draftsman The Architects Collaborative, Cambridge, Mass., 1963-65, Cambridge Seven Assocs., Cambridge, 1965-67; architect MIT, Cambridge, 1968-70; prin. architect Interface Architects, Newton, Mass., 1971—. Vis. faculty RISD, Providence, 1974-79; lectr. architecture Harvard Grad. Sch. Design, Cambridge, 1984-88, vis. scholar, 1989-91. Author: Architectural Illustration, 1979, Drawing the Future, 1988. Mem. vestry Episcopalian Ch., 1995-98. Named Loeb fellow Harvard Grad. Sch. Design, 1982. Fellow AIA (inst. honor 1983, fellow 1989), Boston Soc. Architects, Am. Soc. Archtl. Perspectivists (founder, pres. 1986-90, bd. dirs. 1993-97, Hugh Ferriss Meml. prize 1996). Democrat. Avocations: music, painting, photography. E-mail: steve@psoles.com.

OLES, STUART GREGORY, lawyer; b. Seattle, Dec. 15, 1924; s. Floyd and Helen Louise (La Violette) O.; m. Ilse Hanewald, Feb. 12, 1954; children: Douglas, Karl, Stephen. BS magna cum laude, U. Wash., 1947, JD, 1948. Bar: Wash., 1949, U.S. Supreme Ct. 1960. Dep. pros. atty. King County, Wash., 1949, chief civil dept., 1949—50; gen. practice law Seattle, 1950—95; sr. ptnr. firm Oles, Morrison & Rinker and predecessor, 1955—90, of counsel, 1991—95. Author: A View From the Rock, 1994, On Behalf of My Clients -- A Lawyer's Life, 1998. Chmn. Seattle Cmty. Concert Assn., 1955, pres. Friends Seattle Pub. Libr., 1956; mem. Wash. pub. Disclosure Commn., 1973-075; trustee Ch. Divinity Sch. of Pacific, Berkeley, Calif., 1974-75; mem. bd. curators Wash. State Hist. Soc., 1983; former mem. Seattle Symphony Bd.; pres. King County Ct. House Rep. Club, 1950, U. Wash. Young Rep. Club, 1947; Wash. conv. floor leader Taft, 1952, Goldwater, 1964; Wash. chmn. Citizens for Goldwater, 1964; chmn. King County Rep. convs., 1966, 68, 76, 84, 88, 90, 92, 96, Wash. State Rep. Conv., 1980. Served with USMCR, 1943-45. Mem. ABA (past regional vice-chmn. pub. contract law sect.), Wash. Bar Assn., Order of Coif, Scabbard and Blade, Am. Legion, Kapoho Bay Club (pres.), Am. Highland Cattle Assn. (v.p. and dir.), Phi Beta Kappa, Phi Alpha Delta. Home: 22715 SE 43rd Ct Issaquah WA 98029-5200 also: Cape St Mary Rnch Lopez Island WA 98261 also: RR 2 Pahoa HI 96778-9802

OLESKIEWICZ, FRANCIS STANLEY, lawyer, retired insurance executive; b. Chicopee, Mass., Jan. 2, 1928; s. Francis and Agata (Gniady) O.; m. Ruth M. Ventrice, June 16, 1951; children— Francis H., Laurie BS, Am. Internat. Coll., Springfield, Mass., 1953; LL.B, Western New Eng. Coll., 1961. Bar: Mass. 1962. With Ins. Co. N.Am., 1953-67; property mgr. Employers-Comml. Union, Boston, 1967-69; pres., chmn. Lexington Ins. Co., Boston, 1969-86; v.p. Am. Internat. Group, N.Y.C., 1979-86, retired, 1986; limited sole practice law Framingham, Mass., 1986—. Chmn. bd. Risk Specialists Cos., Inc., Boston; vice chmn. Starr Assocs., N.Y.C., C.V. Starr & Co., Inc., Calif.; bd. dirs. Audubon Ins. Co., Baton Rouge, Union Atlantique d'Assurances S.A., Brussels; bd. trustees, mem. trustee com. We. New England Coll., Springfield, Mass., 1987—. Served as pfc. USMC, 1946-47, PTO Mem. Mass. Bar Assn. (vol. law speaker, 1988—), Marine Corps League, Am. Legion, Alpha Chi Home: 19 Hickory Hill Ln Framingham MA 01702-6113

OLEVSKY, EUGENE A. research scientist, educator; b. Kiev, Ukraine, Mar. 6, 1962; came to U.S., 1995. s. Alex Isaak and Levina Jacob Olevsky; m. Renata Arn Kleiner, Apr. 12, 1987; children: Marina, Anna. MSME with honors, Kiev Poly. Inst., 1985; MS in Math. with honors, Kiev State U., 1986; PhD Powder Metallurgy/Composite Material, Ukraine Nat. Acad. Scis., Kiev, 1990. Rsch. assoc. Inst. for Problems of Materials Sci. NAS of Ukraine, Kiev, 1985-92; Alexander von Humboldt fellow Max Planck Inst., Stuttgart, Germany, 1992-94; rsch. fellow Cath. U. Leuven, Belgium, 1994-95; prof. San Diego State U., 1998—. Vis. scholar NSF Inst. for Mechanics and Materials, San Diego, 1995-98; invited prof. U. Metz, France, 1999. Contbr. numerous articles to sci. publs. Recipient Young Investigator (Career) award NSF, 2000, award for excellence in tchg. TRW, 2000; Long-term rsch. grantee Soros Internat. Sci. Found., 1994; scholar Bd. Govs., NSF Inst. for Mechanics and Materials, 1995-98. Mem. ASME, Internat. Inst. for Sci. of Sintering, Am. Powder Metallurgy Inst., Am. Soc. Engring. Edn. Office: San Diego State U 5500 Campanile Dr San Diego CA 92182-0002 Fax: (619) 594-3599. E-mail: olevsky@kahuna.sdsu.edu.

OLGAARD, ANDERS, economics educator; b. Aabenraa, Denmark, Sept. 5, 1926; s. Axel O. and Anna Lebeck; m. Alice Christiansen, 1951; three children. Dr. Polit., Univ. Copenhagen, 1966. Civil servant Econ. Sec., 1953-60; prof. econs., Univ. Copenhagen, 1962-96; adviser in Malaysia, Harvard U. Devel. Adv. Service, 1968-69; mem. Econ. Council, 1966-68, chmn., 1970-76. Author: Growth, Productivity and Relative Prices, 1966; The Danish Economy, EEC Economic and Financial Series, 1980. Mem. Danish Econ. Assn. (pres. 1983-88). Home: 12 Lerbaekvej DK-2830 Virum Denmark Office: U Copenhagen Inst Econs Studiestraede 6 DK-1455 Copenhagen Denmark

OLIAN, JOANNE CONSTANCE, curator, art historian; b. N.Y.C. d. Richard Edward and Dorothy (Singer) Wahrman; m. Howard Olian; children: Jane Wendy, Patricia Ann Student, Syracuse U.; BA, Hofstra U., 1969; MA, NYU/Inst. Fine Arts, 1972. Grad. internship Met. Mus., N.Y.C., 1973; asst. curator Mus. of City of N.Y., 1974, curator costume collection, 1975-91; cons. curator Costume Collection, 1992-95, curator emeritus, 1995—. Lectr. Parsons Sch. Design; vis. lectr. Musée des Arts Decoratifs, Paris, summer 1983, 84, 85. Author: The House of Worth: The Gilded Age, 1860-1918, 1982; editor: Authentic French Fashions of the Twenties, 1990, Everyday Fashions of the Forties, 1992, Children's Fashions from Mode Illustrée 1860-1914, 1994, Wedding Fashions, 1862-1912, 1994, Everyday Fashions, 1909-1920, 1995, La Mode Illustrée, 1997, Victorian and Edwardian Fashions, 1998, 80 Godey's Full-Color Fashions Plates, 1838-1880, 1998, Full-Color Victorian Fashion, 1870-1893, 1999, Everyday Fashions of the Sixties, 1999, Parisian Fashions of the Teens, 2002, Everyday Fashions of the Fifties, 2002, Children's Fashions, 1900-1950, 2003; contbr. articles to profl. jours., chpts. to books. Mem. Internat. Council Mus. (costume com.), Costume Soc. Am. (dir. 1976-79, 83-86), Fashion Group (bd. dirs. 1985-86), Centre Internat. d'Etude des Textiles Anciens. Clubs: Cosmopolitan (N.Y.C.). Home and Office: Shepherds Ln Sands Point NY 11050 E-mail: joanneolian@aol.com.

OLIAN, JUDY D. dean; b. Australia; BS in psychology, Hebrew U., 1974; MS in indsl. rels., U. Wis., 1977, PhD in indsl. rels., 1980. Lectr. to full prof. mgmt. and orgn. Robert H. Smith Sch. Bus., U. Md., 1979—2000; fellow Am. Coun. Edn. to pres., U. Md., 1990—91, special asst. to pres., 1991—92; founder, dir. IBM-TQ Project, U. Md., 1991—92; sr. assoc. dean Robert H. Smith Sch. Bus., U. Md., 1999—2000; dean, prof. mgmt. Smeal Coll. Bus., Penn State U., 2000—. Exec. com. Personnel and Human Resources divsn. Acad. Mgmt., 1984—87, 1991—94; exec. com. bd. dirs. Assn. to Advance Collegiate Sch. Bus., 2000—01. Author: (syndicated weekly column) About Business; past mem. editl. bd.: Jour. Quality and Mgmt., Acad. Mgmt. Review. Bd. dirs. The Second Mile, Penn State Found. Recipient award for curriculum innovation, Md. Assn. for Higher Edn., 1996. Office: Dean's Office Smeal Coll Bus Adminstrn Pa State Univ 801-H Bus Adminstrn Bldg University Park PA 16802 Office Phone: 814-863-0448. Office Fax: 814-865-7064. Business E-Mail: jdo10@psu.edu.

OLIAN, ROBERT MARTIN, lawyer; b. Cleve., June 14, 1953; s. Robert Meade and Doris Isa (Hessing) Olian; m. Terri Ellen Ruther, Aug. 10, 1980; children: Andrew Zachary, Alix Michelle, Joshua Brett. AB, Harvard U., 1973, JD, 1977, M in Pub. Policy, 1977. Bar: Ill. 1977, U.S. Dist. Ct. (no. dist.) Ill., U.S. Ct. Appeals (7th cir.) 1983, U.S. Dist. Ct. (no. dist. trial bar) Ill. 1992, U.S. Dist. Ct. (we. dist.) Mich. 1994, U.S. Dist. Ct. (cen. dist.) Ill. 2004. Assoc. Sidley & Austin, Chgo., 1977-84; ptnr. Sidley Austin Brown & Wood LLP, Chgo., 1985—. Editor: (book) Illinois Environmental Law Handbook, 1988, 1997. Panel atty. Chgo. Vol. Legal Svcs., 1983—; bd. dirs. Friends IDF, 2003—; trustee North Shore Congregation Israel, 1990—, sec., 1995—96, v.p., 1996—2003, first v.p., 2004—; mem. regional strategic/mktg. com. Alexian Bros. Ill., Inc., Elk Grove, 1985—88; mem. dean's alumni leadership coun. JFK Sch. Govt., Havard U., 2003—. Mem.: ABA, Chgo. Bar Assn., Harvard Club (Chgo.), Std. Club. Jewish. Home: 85 Oakmont Rd Highland Park IL 60035-4111 Office: Sidley Austin Brown and Wood LLP Bank One Plz 10 S Dearborn St #5200 Chicago IL 60603-2003 Office Phone: 312-853-7208. Business E-Mail: rolian@sidley.com.

OLICK, PHILIP STEWART, lawyer; b. N.Y.C., Oct. 2, 1936; s. Jack and Anita (Babsky) O.; m. Alice D. Chait, Mar. 25, 1961; children: Jonathan A., Jeffrey K., Diana M. BA, Columbia U., 1957; LL.B., NYU, 1960. Bar: N.Y. 1961, Mo. 1966. Ptnr. Benjamin, Galton, Robbins & Flato, N.Y.C., 1961-65; gen. counsel, v.p., sec. Nat. Bellas Hess, Inc., Kansas City, Mo., 1965-69, dir., 1970-76; ptnr. Burke & Burke, N.Y.C., 1970-73, Townley & Updike, 1973-89, Moses & Singer, 1989—. Bd. arbitrators N.Y. Stock Exch. Bd. dirs. Univ. Glee Club N.Y.C., v.p.; bd. dirs. The Young Peoples Chorus of N.Y.C. With AUS, 1960-61. Mem. N.Y. Bar Assn., Assn. of Bar of City of N.Y., Univ. Club (N.Y.C.), Columbia Club. Home: 860 5th Ave # 19J New York NY 10021-5856 Office: 1301 Avenue Of The Americas New York NY 10019-6022 also: 4 Rosebud Ln East Quogue NY 11942-3627 Office Phone: 212-554-7891. E-mail: polick@mosessinger.com., philipolick@earthlink.net.

OLIET, SEYMOUR, endodontics educator, dean, dentist; b. Perth Amboy, NJ, July 12, 1927; s. Asher Jacob and Sarah Oliet; m. Sherry Roseff, July 2, 1949; children: Eric Jay, Amy Ellen Oliet Heller. Student, Rutgers U., 1945-46, 47-49; DDS with distinction, U. Pa., 1953. Diplomate Am. Bd. Endodontics. Instr. oral medicine Sch. Dental Medicine U. Pa., 1953 56, assoc. oral medicine, 1956-61, asst. prof. oral medicine, 1961-65, assoc. prof. oral medicine, 1965-71, prof. oral medicine, dir. undergrad. endodontics, 1971-72, founding chmn. dept. endodontics, 1972-80, prof. endodontics, interim chmn. endodontics, 1990-91, prof. emeritus, 1994—; attending dentist Albert Einstein Med. Ctr., Phila., 1953-60, sr. attending, chmn. endodontics, 1960-84; prof. endodontics Coll. Dental Medicine Nova Southeastern U., Ft. Lauderdale, Fla., 1996—, chmn. task force to estab. Dental Sch., 1995-96, dean Coll. Dental Medicine, 1996—2001, dean emeritus, 2001—. Cons. endodontics U.S. Army, Ft. Dix, N.J., and Walter Reed Army Hosp., Washington, 1955-80, VA Hosp., Phila., 1965-80; chmn. internat. to estab. I.B. Bender Endowment Fund, Israeli Endodontic Soc., Hebrew U., 1990-91; reviewer Jour. Am. Dental Assn., 1970—. Author: (with others) Endodontics Practice, 11th edit., 1988, Diagnosis and Treatment of Endodontic Emergences, 1981, Current Therapy in Dentistry, 1977, Diagnosis and Treatment Planning in Management of Diseases of the Pulp, 1963, Programmed Text Endodontics; editor Alpha Omega, 1956, (newsletter) Am. Assn. Endodontics, 1966-69; contbr. articles to profl. jours. Named Hon. Citizen of New Orleans; inducted Perth Amboy H.S. Hall of Fame, 1998; recipient Mayor's Citation, Perth Amboy, 1998. Fellow AAAS, Royal Soc. Health (Brit.), Internat. Assn. Dental Rsch., Am. Assn. Endodontists, Am. Coll. Dentists (sec.-treas. Phila. chpt. 1965-76, pres.-elect 1976-77, pres. 1976-77), Internat. Coll. Dentists, Phila. Coll. Surgeons; mem. ADA (life), Pa. Acad. Endodontics (founder, pres. 1977-79, adv. to pres. 1979), Phila. County Dental Soc. (membership com. 1954, indsl. dentistry com. 1954, chmn. sci. program com. 1963, chmn. essay and clins. com. 1964-65, chmn. mediation com. 1965-66, bd. govs. 1985-87, chmn. ad hoc com. ins. 1985-96, com. peer rev. 1985-96, com. on continuing edn. 1989-96, dir. liberty dental conf. 1987-91, gen. chmn. 1991-92, chmn. awards and banquets 1988-89, dir. sci. exhibits and programs 1989-90, del. Pa. Dental Assn. 1985-96, long-range planning com. 1993-96, historian, bd. govs. 1994-96), Brazilian Dental Soc. (hon.), N.Y. Acad. Sci., Am. Assn. Endodontists (arrangements com. 1958-60, libr. com. 1960-61, membership com. 1961-67, publ. chmn., editor newsletter, sci. 1966-69, sci. prof. chmn. 1970-71, bd. govs., exec. com. 1972-78, awards and hons. com. 1992-95), Eastern Dental Soc. (chmn. membership 1956-57, program com. 1957-59, chmn. publicity, editor 1957-59, sec. 1960-62, bd. dirs. 1958X, pres.-elect chmn. bd. govs. 1968-69, pres. 1969-70), Acad. Stomatology, Am. Assn. Dental Editors, Alpha Omega (Phila. alumni chpt., editor 1956, treas. 1956-60, adv. to alumni chpt., regent 1960-61, nat. dept. marshall 1961-62, pres.-elect 1961-63, pres. 1963-64). Avocations: tennis, golf, horseback trail riding, fishing. Office: Nova Southeastern U Coll Dental Medicine 3200 S University Dr Fort Lauderdale FL 33328-2018

OLIGARIO, MAX, retired accountant; b. Port-Au-Prince, Haiti, Sept. 17, 1920; arrived in U.S., 1958; s. Felix and Guillermina (Gonzales) Oligario; m. Gnislaine Romulus; children: Natasha, Sagine, Max Oligario Jr.; m. Fernande St. Leger (div.); 1 child, Carole. AS in Engring. Scis., Nassau C.C., 1965; BBA, Hofstra U., 1969; MS in Pub. Acctg., C.W. Post Coll., 1972. CPA N.Y.; ordained 1999. Mgr. Champs Ednl. Supplies, Mineola, NY, 1958—66; asst. supr. cost acctg. Gt. Lakes Carbon, NY, 1966—69; supr., auditor Sperry/Unisys, Nassau County, NY, 1969—88; pvt. practice Brentwood, NY, 1988—89; ret., 1990. Mem. Rep. Presdl. Task Force Presdl. Commn., Washington, 1986; mem. Presdl. Round Table, Washington, 1993—; life mem. Rep. Presdl. Task Force, Washington, 1989. Named Donor of Yr., Hospitalized Vets., 2002; recipient Order of Merit, Rep. Presdl. Legion of Merit, 1994, Cert. of Appreciation, Nat. Pk. Trust, 1995, Nat. Children's Cancer Soc., 2001, Royal honor, Principality of Hutt River Province, 1996—97. Home: 8784 Middlebrook Dr Fort Myers FL 33908

OLIKER, DAVID WILLIAM, healthcare management administrator; b. Elkins, W.Va., Mar. 29, 1948; married; 3 children. BA in Sociology and Anthropology, East Carolina U., 1970; MA in Social Anthropology, Am. U., 1973; Cert. in Healthcare Adminstrn., George Washington U., 1977. Health svcs. specialist United Mine Workers Am. Health and Retirement Funds, 1976-78; health planner Health Sys. Agy. Western Md., Cumberland, 1978-79; ops. mgr. Md.-Individual Practice Assn., Inc., Rockville, 1979-81; project dir. N.Y. Health Maintenance Plan, Inc., N.Y.C., 1981-82; pres., CEO MVP Health Plan, Schenectady, N.Y., 1982—. Mem. APHA, Am. Assn. Health Plans, N.Y. State HMO Conf. (bd. dirs.), Nat. Managed Care Inc. (chmn.). Office: MVP Health Plan PO Box 2207 Schenectady NY 12301-2207

OLIKER, VLADIMIR, mathematician, educator; b. Ulianovsk, Russia, Oct. 7, 1945; came to U.S. 1975, naturalized 1980; s. Yosef and Sonia (Bakelman) Oliker; m. Elena Matis, Mar. 20, 1969; children: Olga, Aviva, Yosef Matis. MS, Leningrad U., Russia, 1967; PhD, Leningrad U., 1971. Sr. researcher Hydrometeorological Inst., Leningrad, Russia, 1970-72; group leader Dept. Transportation, 1972-74; vis. prof. Temple U., Phila., 1975-77; assoc. prof. to prof. U. Iowa, Iowa City, 1977-80, 80-84; prof. math. Emory U., Atlanta, 1984—. Vis. mem. Math Scis. Research Inst., Berkeley, Calif., 1983; vis. prof. U. Florence, Italy, 1983, Technische U., Berlin, 1982, U. Heidelberg, Fed. Republic Germany, 1981 Contbr. articles to profl. jours. Jewish. Home: 1565 Adelia Pl NE Atlanta GA 30329-3805 Office: Emory U Dept Math And Computer Sci Atlanta GA 30322-0001 Business E-Mail: oliker@mathcs.emory.edu.

OLIM, AUGUST SOUZA, counselor; b. Honolulu, Aug. 11, 1940; s. Frank Souza and Hilda Lucy (Leong) O; m. Sharon Jean Warren, Dec. 28, 1963; children: Warren Kalani Olim, Tamera Meilani Olim. BA, U. N. Colo., 1958-63; MS, Pepperdine U., 1973-75. Cert. Exceptional Children (Life), Educable Mentally Retarded Gen. Elem. (Life), Pupil Pers. Ryan Adminstrn. Clear, Learning Handicapped. Tchr. Educable Mentally Retarded Centennial Intermediate, Norwalk-LaMirada, Calif., 1963-65, Walton Intermediate, Garden Grove, Calif., 1965-67; tchr. Learning Handicapped Ralston Intermediate, Garden Grove, Calif., 1967-70; tchr. Learning Disability Group Chapman Jr. High Sch., Garden Grove, Calif., 1970-74, 9th grade English tchr., 1974-76, 7th, 8th, 9th grade counselor, 1976-81; project facilitator Clinton Elem. Sch., Garden Grove, Calif., 1981-84; counselor, co-adminstr. Lake Continuation High Sch., Garden Grove, Calif., 1984-95; prin. Cook Elem., Jordan Spl. Edn., Garden Grove, Calif., 1988, Lincoln Adult Edn. Ctr., Garden Grove, Calif., 1992, Chapman Adult Edn., 1995—2000. Pres. Coun. for Exceptional Children, Orange County, Calif., 1976-80; regional dir. Pacific Am. Concerns HEW, Wash., 1977-81; treas. Asian/Pac/Islander Nat. Edn. Assn., Wash., 1977-81; v.p. Very Spl. Arts, So. Calif., 1989-90. Dir. Jr. Miss Pageant Fountain Valley (Calif.) Jaycees, 1970—72; treas., v.p. Fountain Valley Jaycees, 1972—74; state dir. Calif. Jaycees, 1975; dir. Jr. Miss Inc. Dist. Eight Jaycees Orange County, Calif., 1976; sch. bd. Speech Lang. Ctr., Buena Park, 1994—99; bd. Crippled Children Soc. Orange County, 1995—; bd. dirs. Ainahau o Kaleponi Hawaiian Civic Club, 1997—; co-founder Asian Pacific Islander Cultural Heritage Coun., 1999—. Recipient Life Hon. PTA Lampson, Garden Grove, Calif., 1967, Spoke award Fountain Valley (Calif.) Jaycees, 1972; named Outstanding State Dir. Calif. Jaycees, 1976, Outstanding Bd. Mem. Asian Pacific Islander Tchrs., HI, 1979. Mem. Calif. State Fedn. Coun. for Exceptional Children (mem. ethnic and multicultural concerns com.), Garden Grove Pupil Pers. Assn., Very Spl. Arts Calif., Spl. Olympics Beauty Pageant, Minority Affairs Commn. Nat. Edn. Assn., Interagy. for Legis. of Spl. Edn., Phi Delta Kappa. Roman Catholic. Avocations: music, tennis, cooking, gardening. Home: 25535 Sun City Blvd Sun City CA 92586-3846

OLIN, KENT OLIVER, banker; b. Chgo., July 27, 1930; s. Oliver Arthur and Beatrice Louise Olin; m. Marilyn Louise Wood, May 27, 1956. BS in Econs., Ripon Coll., 1955. Dist. sales rep. Speed Queen Corp., Ripon, Wis., 1955—57; v.p. United Bank, Denver, 1957—71; exec. v.p., pres. Bank One Boulder (formerly Affiliated First Nat. Bank), Boulder, 1971—74; pres., CEO Bank One Colorado Springs, 1971—86; CEO Bank One Colo. (formerly Affiliated Bankshares of Colo.), Denver, 1986—91, vice chmn. bd., 1992—94, also bd. dirs. Trustee Colo. Coll., Colorado Springs, 1983-89, Falcon Found., Colorado Springs, 1983—; trustee El Pomar Found., Colorado Springs, 1992—, chair

investment com.; trustee Colorado Springs Fine Arts Ctr., 1992-95; sec. Air Force Acad. Found., Colorado Springs, 1988; dir., chair exec. com. Garden City (Kans.) Co.; bd. dirs. Rocky Mountain Arthritis Found., Denver, 1989-94, Goodwill Industries, Colorado Springs, 1993-99. Staff sgt. USAF, 1950-54. Mem. Broadmoor Golf Club (dir. 1975-88, 93-98). Office: El Pomar Found 10 Lake Cir Colorado Springs CO 80906-4201 Home: 7499 E Mariposa Grande Dr Scottsdale AZ 85255-3459

OLIN, MARGARET, art educator; b. Chgo., Mar. 1, 1948; d. Lester Kenneth and Rosalyn Wechter Olin; m. Robert S Nelson, Sept. 27, 1947; children: R. Benjamin Nelson, I. Sheba Nelson. PhD, U. of Chgo., 1976—82. Prof. Sch. of the Art Inst. of Chgo., 1986—. Author: (academic book) Forms of Representation in Alois Riegl's Theory of Art, The Nation Without Art: Examining Modern Discourses in Jewish Art; editor: Monuments and Memory, Made and Unmade. Fellowship, Nat. Endowment for the Humanities, 1999, Residence-fellowship, J. Paul Getty Rsch. Inst., 2000, Rsch. grant, Am. Coun. of Learned Societies, 1985—86, PhD fellowship, Whiting, 1979—80, fellowship, Vienna, Austria, Fulbright-Hays, 1979—80. Mem.: Coll. Art Assn. Jewish. Avocations: photography, music. Office: School of the Art Institute of Chicago 112 S Michigan Ave Chicago IL 60603 Office Phone: 312-345-3771.

OLIN, MARILYN, secondary school educator; b. Rochester, N.Y. BA in English, Nazareth Coll. Rochester, 1965; MS in English Edn., SUNY, Brockport, 1971. Nat. bd. cert. tchr. 1999. Tchr. Rochester Diocese Cath. Schs., 1965—68, Rochester Pub. Schs., Duval County (Fla.) Pub. Schs., 1972—, Paxon Sch. for Advanced Studies, Jacksonville, Fla., 1996—. Mem.: Nat. Forensic League, Nat. Bd. for Profl. Tchg. Stds. (bd. mem.). Office: Paxon Sch for Advanced Studies 3239 Norman E Thagard Blvd Jacksonville FL 32254 Office Phone: 904-693-7583 ext 161.

OLIN, WILLIAM HAROLD, orthodontist, educator; b. Menominee, Mich., Mar. 7, 1924; s. Harold H. and Lillian (Hallgren) Olin; m. Bertha Spitters, May 6, 1950; children: William Harold, Paul Scott, Jon Edward. DDS, Marquette U., 1947; MS, U. Iowa, 1948. Asst. prof. orthodontics Univ. Hosps., U. Iowa, Iowa City, 1948, assoc. prof., 1963-70, prof., 1970-93, prof. emeritus, 1995—. Chmn. bd. dirs. Hills Bank. Author: (book) Cleft Lip and Palate Rehabilitation, 1960; contbr. articles to profl. jours. Fund raiser, participant Ops. Smile. Served to capt. U.S. Army, 1952—54. Mem.: Am. Acad. Sports Dentistry (bd. dirs., sec./treas. 1989—95), Am. Cleft Palate Assn. (pres. 1970), Iowa Orthodontic Soc. (pres. 1959), Midwest Orthodontic Soc. (pres. 1968—69), Angle Orthodontic Soc. Midwest (pres. 1982), Univ. Athletic Club (bd. dirs.), Rotary (pres. Iowa City). Republican. Methodist. Avocations: coins, antique music boxes, sports, travel, political memorabilia. Home: 426 Mahaska Dr Iowa City IA 52246-1610 Office Phone: 319-338-1054. E-mail: w.olin@mchsi.com.

OLINGER, ANGELA MARIE, adult education educator; b. Eugene, Oreg., Nov. 14, 1965; d. Theodore Michael Colombo and Jean Annette Eyman; m. Jon Dru Olinger, June 29, 2003; children: Benjamin Michael Goff, Nicholas Keith Goff, Emily Rebecca Goff. AA, Ohio State U., 1990—94. Chemical Operations Specialist US Army Chem. Sch., 1986, Light Fighter Rite of Passage US Army, 7th Inf. Divsn. (Light), 1987, Basic Military Fire Suppression Nat. Wildlife Coordinating Group, 1994, Primary Leadership Development US Army, Pacific, 1996. Chem. ops. specialist US Army, Ft. Ord, Calif., 1986—88; nuc. biol. chem. specialist Ohio Army N.G., Columbus, Ohio, 1988—94; decontamination/bn. ops. US Army, Ft. Riley, Kans., 1994—96, nuc. biol. chem. specialist Schofield Barracks, Hawaii, 1996—99, Ft. Lewis, 1998—99; instr. Madison Adult Edn., Manfield, Ohio, 2002—. Author: (instructors manual) Civilian Nuclear Biological Chemical Protection Against Weapons of Mass Destruction. Sec. Vet. Connection, Akron, Ohio, 2000—01; vice pres./founder Colombo & Assoc. Emergency Preparedness and Safety Tng., Ashland, Ohio, 2002—04. Sgt/e-5 US Army, 1986—99, United States. Decorated Army Achievement medal US Army, Army Commendation medal Ohio Army N.G., Nat. Svc. Def. medal, Humanitarian Svc. medal US Army Force Command. Mem.: Chem. Corp Rgt. (life). Achievements include US Army expert qualifications M16A2 rifle. Avocations: diamond grading, gardening, reading. Home: 1079 County Rd 2075 Ashland OH 44805 Office: Madison Adult Education 600 Esley Lane Mansfield OH 44905 Personal E-mail: angiegoff@aol.com.

OLINGER, CARLA D(RAGAN), medical advertising executive; b. Cin., Oct. 8, 1947; d. Carl Edward and Selene Ethel (Neal) Dragan; m. Chauncey Greene Olinger, Jr., May 30, 1981. BA, Douglass Coll., 1975. Mgr. info. retrieval services Frank J. Corbett, Inc., N.Y.C., 1976—77; editor, proofreader, prodn. asst. Rolf W. Rosenthal, Inc., N.Y.C., 1977—78, copywriter, 1978—80, copy supr., 1980—82, v.p. copy dept., 1982—83; v.p., group copy supr., adminstrv. copy supr. Rolf W. Rosenthal, Inc., divsn. Ogilvy & Mather, 1984—89; v.p., assoc. creative dir. RWR Advt., 1989; v.p., copy supr. Barnum & Souza, N.Y.C., 1990—92, Botto, Roessner, Horne & Messinger, Ketchum Comm., N.Y.C., 1992—95, Lyons Lavey Nickel Swift, N.Y.C., 1995—. Editor: Antimicrobial Prescribing (Harold Neu), 1979. Mem.: St. George's Soc. N.Y., Ch. Club N.Y. Office: Lyons Lavey Nickel Swift 220 E 42nd St New York NY 10017-5806

OLINGER, CHAUNCEY GREENE, JR., investment company executive, editorial consultant; b. Long Beach, Calif., Jan. 16, 1933; s. Chauncey Greene and Cora Blount (Urquhart) O.; m. Carla R. Dragan, May 30, 1981. BA in Philosophy with honors, U. Va., Charlottesville, 1955; MA, Columbia U., N.Y., 1971. CFP Bd. Stds. Coadjutant in philosophy Rutgers U., New Brunswick, NJ, 1968—72; rep. N.Y. World Federalists, USA, N.Y.C., 1970; dir. subcom. U.S. sec. of state adv. com. Dept. of State, Washington, 1972; editl. cons. Columbia U., N.Y.C., 1973—82; editor, pres. Metropolitan Rsch. Co., N.Y.C., 1982—91; investment exec. First Albany, N.Y.C., 1991—92, Janney Montgomery Scott LLC, N.Y.C., 1992—. Sec. seminar on human nature Columbia U., N.Y.C., 1968—72, mem. seminar on orgnl. mgmt., 1972—84, mem. com. to increase corp. philantrophic giving, 1980—83; founder, co-chmn. U. seminar Hist. of Columbia U., 1998—. Editor: World Enough, (Margaret Mead and Ken Heyman), 1975, A Celebration of Thanksgiving For the Life of I.I. Rabi, 1991, Columbia and the City: The University's Commitment to New York City, 1993, Courtney C. Brown: In Memory, 1995; author: New York City: An Economic Resource Profile, 1989, The I.I. Rabi Memorial Room, 1996. Pres. Fellowship of Young Churchmen, Episcopal Diocese of So. Va., 1950-52; trustee Cathedral Ch. St. John the Divine, 1988; nat. chmn. Coalition to Stop SST Environmental Damage, N.Y., 1975-78; pub. mem. human rights in rsch. com. N.Y. Hosp.-Cornell Med. Ctr., 1975-80; pres. grad. faculty alumni Columbia U., N.Y., 1977-81, pres. student coun., 1963-64; bd. dirs. Bar Harbor (Maine) Festival, 1969-74, Bloomingdale House of Music, N.Y.C., 1976-81. Lt. (j.g.) USN, 1955—58. Recipient Conspicuous Alumni Svc. medal Columbia U., 1980, Svc., Loyalty and Dedication award Grad. Faculty Alumni of Columbia U., 1988. Mem. Am. Philos. Assn., Nat. Inst. Social Science (dir. 1988-92), Fin. Planning Assn., Pilgrims of the U.S., Am. Soc. Most Venerable Order of Hosp. of St. John of Jerusalem, St. Andrew's Soc. of the State of N.Y. (sec. 1991-95), St. George's Soc. N.Y., 1977—, Century Assn., Emeritus Profs. in Columbia (assoc.), The Ch. Club of N.Y. (v.p. 1985-86, 88-89, 96-97, pres. 1997-2000, 1st v.p. 204—, trustee 1983-89, 93-2000, 2001-2004), Laymen's Club of the Cathedral of St. John the Divine (pres. 1988, gov. 1982—, v.p. 2004—). Episcopalian. Avocations: reading, writing, walking, theater, ballet. Office: Janney Montgomery Scott LLC 575 Lexington Ave New York NY 10022-6102

OLINGER, GORDON NORDELL, surgeon; b. Denver, 1942; MD, U. Rochester, 1968. Intern UCLA, 1968-69, resident, 1969-70, 72-74; resident in surgery NIH Clinic, Bethesda, Md., 1970-72; with Froedert Meml. Luth. Hosp.; prof. Med. Coll. Wis. Mem. ACS, Soc. Thoracic Surgery, Am. Assn. for Thoracic Surgery, Am. Surg. Assn. Office: Acad Faculty 9200 W Wisconsin Ave Milwaukee WI 53226-3522

OLINS, ROBERT ABBOT, communications research executive; b. Cambridge, Mass., Sept. 25, 1942; s. Harry and Janice Olins; m. Irma Westrich, June 16, 1967; 1 son, Matthew Abbot. Student, Hobart Coll., 1961-62, San Francisco Art Inst., 1962; BA, U. Mass., 1967; postgrad., U. Tampa, 1968; MA, U. Mo., 1969, PhD, 1972. With Marsteller, 1972, N.W. Ayer, 1972, Post, Keys & Gardner, Chgo., 1973, Young & Rubicam, Chgo., 1973-76, mng. dir. comm. rsch. divsn., 1976-77; pres., CEO, subs. Comm. Rsch. Inc., Chgo., 1978—, owner, chmn., 1979—. Pres., CEO Insights, Chgo., 1976—; assoc. prof. Howard Univ., 2004— Contbr. articles to profl. jours. Recipient Chgo./4 award for creative excellence, 1974; overall winner Chgo. Mackinac race, 1981; Am. Assn. Advt. Agys. grantee, 1968-71. Mem.: Mid North Assn. (bd. dirs., chmn. planning), Am. Mktg. Assn., Chgo. Yacht Club, Lake Mich. Yachting Assn., U.S. Sailing Club, Skyline Club. Avocations: skiing, sailing, power boating. Office Phone: 202-806-5119.

OLIPHANT, CHARLES FREDERICK, III, lawyer; b. Chattanooga, Sept. 25, 1949; s. Charles Frederick and Jayne (Shutting) O.; m. Nancy Ann Stewart, May 15, 1976; children: James Andrew, Alexander Stewart. BA in Econs., U. N.C., 1971; JD, U. Mich., 1975. Bar: D.C. 1975. Assoc. Miller & Chevalier, Chartered, Washington, 1975-81, mem. firm, 1982—. Bd. adv. Jour. of Pension Planning and Compliance. Fellow Am. Coll. Employee Benefits Counsel; mem. ABA, Bar Assn. D.C. Episcopalian. Avocations: music, reading. Office: Miller & Chevalier Chartered 655 15th St NW Ste 900 Washington DC 20005-5799 E-mail: foliphant@milchev.com.

OLIPHANT, CHARLES ROMIG, retired physician; b. Waukegan, Ill., Sept. 10, 1917; s. Charles L. and Mary (Goss) R.; m. Claire E. Canavan, Nov. 7, 1942; children: James R., Cathy Rose, Mary G., William D. Student, St. Louis U., 1936-40, MD, 1943; postgrad., Naval Med. Sch., 1946. Intern Nat. Naval Med. Ctr., Bethesda, Md., 1943; pvt. practice medicine and surgery San Diego, 1947-99; ret., 1999. Bd. dirs. Midway Med. Enterprises; former chief staff Balboa Hosp., Doctors Hosp., Cabrillo Med. Ctr.; chief staff emeritus Sharp Cabrillo Hosp.; mem. staff Mercy Hosp., Children's Hosp., Paradise Valley Hosp., Sharp Meml. Hosp.; sec. Sharp Sr. Health Care, S.D., 1985-98; mem. exec. bd., program chmn. San Diego Power Squadron, 1985-93, 95; charter mem. Am. Bd. Family Practice. Served with M.C., USN, 1943-47. Recipient Golden Staff award Sharp Cabrillo Hosp. Med. Staff, 1990; inducted into Wisdom Hall of Fame, 2003. Fellow Am. Geriatric Soc. (emeritus), Am. Acad. Family Practice, Am. Assn. Abdominal Surgeons; mem. AMA, Calif. Med. Assn., Am. Acad. Family Physicians (past pres. San Diego chpt., del. Calif. chpt.), San Diego Med. Soc., Pub. Health League, Navy League, San Diego Power Squadron (past comdr.), SAR, San Diego Yacht Club, Douglas County Scottish Soc. Home: Riverview Terr Unit # 109 1970 W Harvard Ave Roseburg OR 97470-2746

OLIPHANT, NAOMI JOYCE, music educator, performer; b. Toronto, Ont., Can., Jan. 24, 1953; d. James Leroy and Joyce Grace Gwendolyn (Stephens) O. BMus, U. Toronto, 1975, MMus, 1976; D of Musical Arts, U. Mich., 1982. Cert. tchr. piano. Lectr. U. Toronto, 1978; coach accompanist Banff (Ala.) Summer Sch. of Fine Arts, 1979, 80; asst. prof. music Brock U., St. Catharines, Ont., Can., 1976-83; prof., chair keyboard-vocal performance dept. U. Louisville, 1983-98, assoc. dean, 1998—, dir. Kentuckiana summer music festival piano program, 1986—2001. Clinician Frederick Harris Music Co., Ont., 1997—; com. mem. Nat. Conf. on Piano Pedagogy, 1988-95; pianist The McHugh/Oliphant violin and piano duo, 1983—; Disting. tchg. prof. U. Louisville, 1994. Piano soloist orchs. including Louisville Orch., Toronto Symphony, Hamilton Philharm., Niagara Symphony, many solo and chamber concerts, U.S., Can., Japan. Grantee Ky. Bus. and Profl. Women's Found., 1989, 96, Ky. Arts Coun., 1991, 92, 95, So. REgional Edn. Bd., 1989, 95; recipient Disting. Svc. Award Ky. Music Tchrs. Assn., 2003. Mem. Louisville Bach Soc., Music Tchrs. Nat. Assn., Greater Louisville Music Tchrs. Assn., Ky. Music Tchrs. Assn. Presbyterian. Avocations: reading, walking, puzzles, swimming, needlecrafts, gardening. Office: U Louisville Sch Of Music Louisville KY 40292

OLIPHANT, PATRICK, cartoonist; b. Adelaide, Australia, July 24, 1935; came to U.S., 1964; children: Laura, Grant, Susan. L.H.D. (hon.), Dartmouth Coll., 1981. Copyboy, press artist Adelaide Advertiser, 1953-55, editorial cartoonist, 1955-64; world tour to study cartooning techniques, 1959; editorial cartoonist Denver Post, 1964-75, Washington Star, 1975-81, L.A. Times Syndicate, 1965-80, Universal Press Syndicate, 1980—; represented by Susan Conway Gallery, Washington. Author: The Oliphant Book, 1969, Four More Years, 1973, An Informal Gathering, 1978, Oliphant! A Cartoon Collection, 1980, The Jellybean Society, 1981, Ban this Book, 1982, But Seriously Folks, 1983, The Year of Living Perilously, 1984, Make My Day, 1985, Between a Rock and a Hard Place, 1986, Up to There in Alligators, 1987, Nothing Basically Wrong, 1988, What Those People Need Is a Puppy, 1989, Fashions for the New World Order, 1991, Just Say No, 1992, Why do I Feel Uneasy?, 1993, Waiting for the Other Shoe to Drop, 1994, Off to the Revolution, 1995, Maintain The Status Quo, 1996, So That Where They Come From, 1997, Oliphant's Anthem, 1998, Are We There Yet?, 1999, Now We'll Have to Spray for Politicians, 2000, When We Can't See the Forest for the Bushes, 2001. Recipient 2d Place award as funniest cartoonist Internat. Fedn. Free Journalists in Fleet St., London, 1958, Profl. Journalism award Sigma Delta Chi, 1966, Pulitzer prize for editl. cartooning, 1967, Cartoonist of Yr. award Nat. Cartoonist Soc., 1968, 72, Best in Bus. award Washington Journalism Rev., 1985, 87, Premio Satira Politica award Forte de Marmi, 1992, Thomas Nast award, 1992. Office: Universal Press Syndicate 4520 Main St Ste 700 Kansas City MO 64111-7701

OLIPHANT, RANDALL, financial executive; B.Comm., U. Toronto, 1984. Acct. Coopers & Lybrand; with Barrick Gold Corp., Toronto, Ont., Can., 1987—, v.p. corp. devel., v.p., treas., CFO, 1994-99, exec. v.p., CFO, 1999, pres., CEO, 1999—2003, dir., 1997—. Office: Barrick Gold Corp BCE Pl Ste 3700 161 Bay St PO Box 212 Toronto ON M5J 2S1 Canada

OLIPHANT, URETZ JOHN, physician, surgeon; b. Chgo., May 9, 1953; s. John and Letha (Fryson) O.; m. Mercidita DeJesus, Jan. 11, 1985; children: Michael, Jonathan, Kathryn. AB, Boston U., 1976; MD, U. Minn., 1983. Diplomate Am. Bd. Surgery. Fellow in trauma/critical care Ill. Masonic Hosp./U. Ill., Chgo., 1991-92; attending surgeon Carle Found. Hosp., Urbana, Ill., 1992—, head divsn. trauma, 1995—; clin. assoc. prof. dept. surgery U. Ill. Coll. Medicine, Urbana, 1994—, head dept. surgery, 1996—. Chmn. bd. dirs. Frances Nelson Cmty. Health Ctr., urbana, 1994—; chmn. Region 6 Trauma Com., Urbana, 1995-97. Founding mem. Nat. Safe Kids, Champaign, Ill., 1995—. Recipient Golden Apple Tchg. award U. Ill. Coll. Medicine, 1994, 95, 97, 99. Fellow ACS, Internat. Coll. Surgeons. Avocations: chess, basketball. Office: Carle Found Hosp 602 W University Ave Urbana IL 61801-2530

OLITSKI, JULES, artist; b. Snovsk, USSR, Mar. 27, 1922; came to U.S., 1923, naturalized, 1943; s. Jevel and Anna (Zarnitsky) Demikovsky; m. Gladys Katz, 1944 (div. 1951); 1 dau., Eve; m. Andrea Hill Pearce, Jan. 21, 1956 (div. 1974); 1 dau., Lauren; m. Kristina Gorby, Feb. 29, 1980. Student, Academie de la Grande Chaumiere, Paris, 1949-50; BA, NYU, 1952, MA, 1954; postgrad., Beaux Arts Inst., N.Y.C., 1940-42, Nat. Acad. Design, 1939-42, Ednl. Alliance, 1947, Ossip Zadkine Sch. Sculpture, Paris, 1949; hon. Doctorate of the Arts, U. of Hartford, CT, 1997, U of New Hampshire, NH, 1998. Assoc. prof. art SUNY, New Paltz, N.Y., 1954-55; curator Art Edn. Gallery, NYU, 1955-56; chmn. fine arts div. C.W. Post Coll. L.I.U., Greenvale, N.Y., 1956-63; tchr. Bennington Coll., 1963-67. Exhibited in many one-man shows including Galerie Huit, Paris, 1951, Iolas Gallery, N.Y.C., 1958, French & Co., N.Y.C., 1959-61, Poindexter Gallery, N.Y.C., 1961-68, Bennington (Vt.) Coll., 1962, Kasmin, Ltd., London, 1964-75, 89, Galerie Lawrence, Paris, 1964, David Mirvish Gallery, Toronto, Ont., Can., 1964-78, Nicholas Wilder, L.A., 1966, Corcoran Gallery, Washington, 1967, 74, Am. Pavillion, Venice Biennale Art Exhbn., 1966, 88, Andre Emmerich Gallery, N.Y.C., 1966-96, Zurich, Switzerland, 1973-78, Met. Mus. Art, N.Y.C., 1969, Inst. Contemporary Art, U. Pa., 1968, 86, Lawrence Rubin Gallery, N.Y.C., 1969, 71, 72, 73, Knoedler Contemporary Art, 1973-77, 79, 81, 83, 85, 87, Dart Gallery, Chgo., 1975, FIAL, Paris, 1976, Berlinische Galerie, 1977, Downstairs Gallery, Edmonton, Can., 1980, 82, Janus Gallery, L.A., 1981, Gallery One, Toronto, 1980-90, Yares Gallery, Scottsdale, Ariz., 1986-89, Galerie Wentzel, Hamburg and Cologne, Fed. Republic Germany, 1975, 77, 81, 89, Mus. Fine Arts, Boston, 1973, 77, Whitney Mus. Am. Art, 1973, Galleria Dell'Ariete, Italy, 1974, Corcoran Gallery Art, 1974-76, Waddington Gallery, London, 1975, Galerie Templon, Paris, 1984-85, Hirshhorn Mus., Washington, 1977, Edmonton (Alta., Can.) Art Gallery, 1979, Martha White Gallery, Louisville, 1982, Harcus/Krakow Gallery, Boston, 1978, 81, 82, Harcus Gallery, Boston, 1984, 86, Meredith Long, Houston, 1981, 82, 87, 90, (retrospective) Fondation du Chateau de Jau, Perpignon, France, 1984, La Musee de Valence, France, 1985, Hokin Gallery, Palm Beach, Fla., 1988, Associated Am. Artists, N.Y.C., 1989, (retrospective) Buschlen/Mowatt Gallery, Vancouver, B.C., Can., 1990, Salander-O'Reilly Galleries, N.Y.C., 1990, 92, 94, Gallery Camino Real, Boca Raton, Fla., 1987, 88, 90, 92, 94, 95, 96, 97, Thorne-Sagendorph Art Gallery, Keene, N.H., 1993, 96, 99, Long Fine Arts, N.Y.C., 1994, 95, 97, 98, 99, U. Miami, Coral Gables, Fla., 1994, C.S. Schulte Gallery, Milburn, N.J., 1995, 97, Drabinsky Friedland Gallery, Naples, Fla., and Toronto, 1996, 97, 99, Dorthy Blau Gallery, Bay Harbor Island, Fla., 1996, 97, 2001, Hodecker Gallery, Waterville Valley, NH, 1997, Belknap Mills, Laconia, NH, 1997, Butler Institute, Youngstown, OH, 1997, 2000, Portland Museum, ME, 1998, Grimaldis Gallery, Baltimore, MD, 1998, Virginia Lynch Gallery, Tiverton, RI, 1998, 99, 2000, 2001, Gould Academy, Bethel, ME, 1998, Bernard Jacobsen Gallery, London (Paintings 1965-75), 1999, Marianne Friedland Gallery, Naples, FL, 1999, 2000, 02 Galeria Metta, Madrid, 1999, Mary McGowan Fine Art, Concord, NH, 1999, Philharmonic Center for the Arts, Naples, FL, 1999, Annandale Galleries, Sydney, Australia, 2000, 2002, Charles Nodrum Gallery, Melbourne, 2000, The Butler Institute of American Art, Youngstown, OH, 2000, Ameringer-Howard Gallery, N.Y.C., 2000, Bunnington Gallery Notthingham Trent U., UK, 2001, Ameringer-Howard Fine Art, Boca Raton, FL, 2001; exhibited in many group shows including Carnegie Internat., Pitts., 1961, 1965, Washington Gallery Modern Art, 1963, Los Angeles County Mus., 1964, Fogg Art Mus. Harvard, 1965, Pasadena Art Mus., 1965, Mus. Basel, Switzerland, 1965, 74, Whitney Mus. Am. Art, 1972, 73, Musée d'Art Contemporain, Montreal, 1973, Hirshhorn Mus., 1974, Corcoran Gallery Art, 1975, Everson Mus. Art, Syracuse, N.Y., 1976, Bass Mus., Miami, Am. Embassy, Madrid, 1984, Ft. Worth Art Mus., Mus. Art, Ft. Lauderdale, 1986, Joseloff Gallery, Hartford, Conn., 1994, Galerie Piltzer, Paris, 1994, N.Y. Studio Sch., N.Y., 1996, Andre Emmerich Gallery, N.Y.C., 1997, 1998, Suzanne Lemberg Usdan Gallery, Bennington College, VT, 1998, Yares Gallery, Scottsdale, Ariz., 1998, Mus. Fine Arts, Boston, 2000, Portland Mus., Oreg., 2001; represented in permanent collections including Mus. Modern Art, N.Y.C., Art Inst. Chgo., Whitney Mus., Corcoran Art Gallery, Nat. Gallery Can., Met. Mus. Art, N.Y.C., Bklyn. Mus., Hirshhorn Mus., Washington, Everson Mus. Art, Syracuse, N.Y., Mus. Fine Arts, Boston, Norman MacKensie Art Gallery, Regina, Can., Portland Mus., Oreg.;also pvt. collections; subject book Jules Olitski by Kenworth Moffett, 1981, Nat. Acad. Design, N.Y., 1993, illustrator of limited edition book, Small Mountains (with W.D. Wetherell), 2000. Recipient 2d prize Carnegie Internat. 1961, 1st prize Corcoran Biennial, Washington, 1967, Award for Distinction in the Arts Univ Union, U. S.C., 1975, The Milton and Sally Avery Disting. Professorship, Bard Coll., 1987; named Assoc. Nat. Academician Nat. Acad. of Design, 1993, named Distinguished Artist, Arkansas Celebration of the Arts, Hot Springs, Arkansas, 1996. Fellow AAAS, Nat. Acad. Arts and Scis. E-mail: jolitski@sover.net.

OLIVA, LAWRENCE JAY, former academic administrator, history educator; b. Walden, N.Y., Sept. 23, 1933; s. Lawrence Joseph and Catherine (Mooney) Oliva; m. Mary Ellen Nolan, June 3, 1961; children: Lawrence Jay, Edward Nolan. BA, Manhattan Coll., 1955; MA, Syracuse U., 1957, PhD, 1960; postgrad., U. Paris, 1959; DHL (hon.), Manhattan Coll., 1987; LLD (hon.), St. Thomas Aquinas Coll., 1988; DHL (hon.), Hebrew Union Coll., 1992; DLitt, Univ. Coll., Dublin, 1993; PhD, Tel Aviv U., 1994. Prof. history NYU, 1969—, assoc. dean, 1969—70, vice dean, 1970—71, dean faculty, 1971—72, dep. vice chancellor, 1970—75, v.p. acad. planning and services, 1975—77, v.p. acad. affairs, 1977—80, provost, exec. v.p. acad. affairs, 1980—83, chancellor, exec. v.p., 1983—91, pres., 1991—2002, pres. emeritus, 2002—. Author: Misalliance: A Study of French Policy in Russia during the Seven Years' War, 1964, Russia in the Era of Peter the Great, 1969; editor: Russia and the West from Peter to Kruschev, 1965, Peter the Great, 1970, Catherine the Great, 1971; contbr. articles to profl. jours. Trustee Inst. Internat. Edn.; active Onassis Found., UN Assn. of N.Y. Adv. Coun., N.Y.C. Partnership, Assn. for Better N.Y., Am. Mus. Immigration; adv. bd. U. Athletic Assn.; bd. dirs. Chatham House, Royal Inst. Internat. Affairs, Am. Bd. Dirs. Coun. for U.S. and Italy Nat. Collegiate Athletic Assn., Pres.'s Commn.; adv. bd. Pres.'s Coun.; bd. dirs. N.Y. State Commn. on Nat. and Cmty. Svc. Recipient Medal of Sorbonne, U. Paris, 1992, Man. in Edn. award, Italian Welfare League, medal of honor, Ellis Island; fellow Fribourg fellow, 1959. Mem.: Irish-Am. Cultural Inst., Assn. Colls. and Univs. of State of N.Y, Am. Coun. Edn., Soc. Fellows NYU, Phi Gamma Delta, Phi Beta Kappa. Home: 33 Washington Sq W New York NY 10011-9154 Office: 60 Wash Square S 503 New York NY 10012

OLIVA, TERENCE ANTHONY, marketing educator; b. Rochester, N.Y., Feb. 21, 1943; s. Anthony J. and Teresa Oliva; children: Mark, Andrea. BA in Math. and Art, St. Mary's Coll., Calif., 1964; MBA with distinction, Fresno State U., 1971; PhD, U. Ala., 1974. Assoc. prof. mgmt. La. State U., Baton Rouge, 1974-82; vis. assoc. mktg. Columbia U., N.Y.C., 1982-83; assoc. prof., mktg. Rutgers U., Newark, 1983-88; vis. assoc. prof. Wharton Sch., U. Pa., Phila., 1985-87, assoc. prof., 1989-90; prof., dep. dir. Ctr. for Electronic Mktg. Temple U., 1990—. Mem. editl. bd. Org. Sci., 1993—. Author, editor: Production Mgmt., 1981; assoc. editor Mgmt. Sci. Dept. Tech., 1989-91; editl. bd. mem. Org. Sci.; contbr. 32 articles to profl. jours. Capt. USAF, 1965-69, Vietnam. Decorated Bronze Star; recipient Andrisani/Frank Undergrad Tchg. award, Leadership in Rsch. award SBM, 1998, Lindback Found. Tchg. award, 2001. Mem. Am. Mktg. Assn., INFORMS, Sigma Kappa Phi (Prof. of Yr. award), Phi Delta Kappa, Omicron Delta Epsilon, Mu Kappa Tau. Home: 605 S 48th St Philadelphia PA 19143-2010 *Swimming upstream is often very productive. Just be prepared to jump obstacles and have a hard head.*

OLIVARES, JAIME RAMON, history professor, researcher; b. Houston, Nov. 7, 1967; s. Daniel Ramon and Monserrat Olivares; m. Norma Guerra, July 31, 1998; children: Martin Christopher Hernandez, Marcus Arnold Hernandez, Matheus Joshua Hernandez. PhD in History, U. Houston, 2002. Prof. history Houston C.C., 2000—. Campaign Bill White for Mayor, Houston, 2003. Fellow, Hagley Mus. and Libr., 2001—02. Mem.: Orgn. Am. Historians (assoc.), Conf. Latin Am. Historians (assoc.), Am. Hist. Assn. (assoc.). Roman Catholic. Avocations: tennis, baseball, reading, football, automobiles. Home: 11415 Carvel Ln Houston TX 77072 Office: Houston Cmty Coll 1300 Holman St Houston TX 77004 E-mail: jaime.olivares@hccs.edu.

OLIVARES-CUHAT, GABRIELA ANTONIA, literature and language professor; b. Santiago, Chile, Apr. 2, 1968; d. Manuel Antonio Olivares and Rosa Ester Menchaca; m. Daniel R. Cuhat, May 23, 1998; 1 child, Antoine Daniel Cuhat. BA in English Secondary Edn., Cath. U., 1990; MA in Liberal Arts, Purdue U., 1994, PhD in Liberal Arts, 1998. Tchr. high sch. English Colegio del Sagrado Corazon, Santiago, 1990—90; tchg. asst. Spanish Purdue U., West Lafayette, Ind., 1992—98; asst. prof. Spanish Aquinas Coll., Grand Rapids, Mich., 1998—99, Cleve. State U., 1999—2004. Co-chair elect presdl. com. on the role and status of women Cleve. State U., Cleve., 2003—, summer resident dir. study abroad program, 2002—03, grad. faculty rev. com., 2003—04, student life com. mem., 2002—03, undergraduate advisor for spanish, 2001—03; Spanish immersion specialist Our Lady Guadalupe, Dubuque, Iowa, 2003—04. Contbr. articles to profl. jours. Organizer ann. hispanic cmty. forums Cleve. State U., 2001—03; prin. investigator Cleve. Mcpl. Sch. Dist. and Cleve. State U., 2001—03. Recipient Walter J. Johnson award, Purdue U., 1997; grantee, Ctr. Tchg. and Learning, Cleve. State U., 2000, Ctr. Urban Child and Sch. Collaboration and Martha Holden Jennings, 2002, Purdue Rsch. Found., 1996—98; scholar, Am. Assn. Teachers Spanish and Portuguese, 2002. Mem.: Am. Assn. Tchrs. Spanish and Portuguese, Phi Kappa Phi, Delta Sigma Pi. Home: 11469 Robin Hood Drive Dubuque IA 52001 Office: Cleveland State University 2121 Euclid Avenue Rt1619 Cleveland OH 44114 Office Phone: 216-687-4646. Personal E-mail: gabycuhat@yahoo.com. E-mail: g.olivarescuhat@csuohio.edu.

OLIVAS, PHIL, secondary school educator; b. Colorado Springs, Colo., Jan. 27, 1971; s. Richard and Joy Olivas; m. Christine May, Sept. 14, 1996; 1 child, Brandon. B Music Edn., U. Colo., 1994. Cert. tchr. Colo. Tchr. Janitell Jr. High, Fountain, Colo., 1994—97; chmn. performing arts Mesa Ridge H.S., Colorado Springs, 1997—, dir. bands, 1997—. Recipient Dist. Arts Tchr. award, Arts Bus. Edn. Consortium, 2004. Mem.: Colo. Band Masters Assn., Colo. Music Educators, Phi Beta Mu (life). Avocations: music composition, classic car restoration, home rennovation. Office: Mesa Ridge HS 6070 Mesa Ridge Pkwy Colorado Springs CO 80911

OLIVE, DAVID MICHAEL, magazine writer, magazine editor; b. Toronto, Ont., Canada, Nov. 9, 1957; s. Harold Leslie and Alison Linton (Black) O.; m. Margaret Anne O'Reilly, Feb. 13, 1982 (div. June 1992). B of Applied Arts in Journalism, Ryerson Polytech. U., 1979. Copy editor Toronto Life Mag., 1979-81; assoc. editor Can. Bus. Mag., Toronto, 1981-84; sr. writer Report on Bus. Mag., Toronto, 1984-87, Toronto Life Mag., 1988-90; editorial writer The Globe and Mail, Toronto, 1990-91, current affairs columnist, 1991-92, bus. ethics columnist, 1996-98; editor Report on Bus. Mag., 1991-97, sr. writer, 1997-98, Fin. Post, 1998, Nat. Post, Toronto, 1998—2001; bus. columnist Toronto Star, 2001—. Dir. Can. Ctr. for Ethics and Corp. Policy, 1988-91, Jessie's Ctr. for Teenagers, 1994—; pres. Jessie's Ctr. Non-Profit Homes Corp., 1994—; pres. Nat. Mag. Awards Found., 1988-90. Author: Just Rewards: The Case for Ethical Reform in Business, 1987, White Knights and Poison Pills: A Cynic's Dictionary of Business Jargon, 1990, Political Babble: The 1,000 Dumbest Things Ever Said by Politicians, 1992, Gender Babble: The Dumbest Things Men Ever Said About Women, 1993, Canadian Political Babble: A Cynic's Dictionary of Political Jargon, 1993, More Political Babble: The Dumbest Things Ever Said by Politicians, 1996, Canada Inside Out: How We See Ourselves, How Others See Us, 1996, No Guts, No Glory: How Canada's Greatest CEOs Built Their Empires, 2000, A Devil's Dictionary of Business Jargon, 2001, The Quotable Tycoon: A Treasury of Business Quotations, 2002. Recipient Silver, Nat. Mag. awards, 1987, Gold, 1988, hon. mention, 1983, 1985, 1987, 1989, 1996, Nat. Bus. Book awards, 2001. Mem. Can. Soc. Mag. Editors, Ethics Practitioners Assn. Can.

OLIVER, ANN BREEDING, secondary school educator; b. Hollywood, Fla., Sept. 21, 1945; d. Harvey James and Ruth (Lige) Breeding; m. John Russell Kelso, July 22, 1972 (div. Feb. 1984); 1 child, Anna Liege; m. Ted J. Oliver, June 29, 1996. BA in Fgn. Lang., U. Ky., 1967; MA in History of Art, Ohio State U., 1971. Curatorial intern Lowe Art Mus., Coral Gables, Fla., 1972; adj. faculty Fla. Atlantic U., Boca Raton, Fla., 1972-73, 78; lectr. Miami (Fla.) Dade C.C., 1974, with art-music workshop, 1980-81, lectr.-cons., 1972—, adj. faculty music dept., 1991; curator of edn. Ctr. for the Fine Arts, Miami, 1987-92, High Mus. of Art, Atlanta, Ga., 1992-96; Spanish tchr. Sprayberry H.S., Cobb County Bd. Edn., Marietta, Ga., 1997—. Mem. Artists in Edn. Panel, Ga. Coun. for Arts, 1994; field reviewer Inst. Mus. Svcs., 1994; adj. faculty in art history Kennesaw State U., Marietta, Ga., 1996—; Spanish tchr. Cobb County Bd. Edn., Atlanta, Spray H.S., Marietta, Ga. Contbg. editor African Art: An Essay for Teachers, 1993; project mgr. and contbg. author: Rings: Five Passions in World Art: Multicultural Curriculum Handbook, 1996. Mem. Cobb County Com. for Fgn. Lang. Curriculum Alignment. Recipient Nat. award for graphics Mead Paper Co., 1989, Gold Medal of Honor publication design S.E. Mus. Educators Publ. Design, 1994. Mem. Am. Assn. of Mus., Inst. Mus. Svcs., Nat. Art Edn. Assn., Am. Coun. Tchrs. Fgn. Langs., Fla. Art Edn. Assn. (dir. mus. divsn.), Ga. Art Edn. Assn. (dir. mus. divsn., Mus. Educator of Yr. 1993), Fgn. Lang. Assn. of Ga. Home: 2420 Mitchell Rd NE Marietta GA 30062-5321

OLIVER, ANTHONY THOMAS, JR., lawyer; b. San Jose, Calif., July 19, 1929; s. Anthony Thomas and Josephine Gertrude (Bem) O.; m. Beverly J. Wirz, Jan. 27, 1952; children: Jeanne M. Hall, Marilyn M Guins, Cynthia M. Eschardies, Michelle M. Rogan.; m. Margaret E. Gurke, Mar. 31, 1984; 1 child, Christopher A. BS, U. Santa Clara, 1951; JD, 1953. Bar: Calif. 1954, U.S. Supreme Ct. 1979. Asst. counsel Bank Am. Legal Dept., L.A., 1953-57; assoc. Taylor & Barker, L.A., 1957-58, John F. O'Hara, L.A., 1958-63; sr. shareholder, chmn. emeritus labor dept. Parker, Milliken, Clark, O'Hara & Samuelian A Profl. Corp., L.A., 1963—. Mem. Town Hall Calif., 1981—; bd. visitors U. Santa Clara Coll. Law, 1982—. Served to lt. col. USAR. Recipient Edwin J. Owens Lawyer of Yr. award, U. Santa Clara Coll. Law, 1976. Mem. ABA, (co-chmn. com. labor arbitration 1985-88), LA County Bar Assn. (chmn. labor law sect. 1985-86), Indsl. Rels. Rsch. Assn. (nat. exec. bd. 2002—), Am. Arbitration Assn., Coll. of Labor and Employment Lawyers, NG Assn. US, NG Assn. Calif., State Bar Calif., So. Calif. Indsl. Rels. Rsch. Assn. (pres. 1972-73), Orange County Indsl. Rels. Rsch. Assn. (pres. 1999-2000), Chancery Club (LA). Roman Catholic. Office: 333 S Hope St Fl 27 Los Angeles CA 90071-1488 Office Phone: 213-683-6618. Personal E-mail: aoliver818@charter.net. Business E-Mail: ato@pmcas.com.

OLIVER, BRUCE LAWRENCE, retired information systems specialist, educator; b. Westfield, Mass., Nov. 20, 1951; s. Ernest Lawrence and Elizabeth (Welchek) O. AS, Greater Hartford C.C., 1972; BS, U. Mass., 1974; MBA, U. Hartford, 1989. Cert. tchr. sec. and vocat. edn., Mass., Conn.; cert. asset protection and fin. privacy cons. Comml. sales Gordon Realty, Enfield, Conn., 1972—75; forestry tech. rsch. Dept. Environ. Protection State of Conn., Hartford, 1973—74; res. sales Forsman Realty, Enfield, 1975—77; substitute secondary tchr. Enfield Sch. Sys., 1975—78; collections mgr. New Eng. Bank & Trust, Enfield, 1978—79; ops. CCEC/McCullahg Leasing, Inc., S. Windsor, Conn., 1979—81; pres. Ollie & Ike's, Inc., Enfield, 1985—86; MBA Adj. U. Hartford, West Hartford, Conn., 1988—89; workstation engr. Travelers, Hartford, 1982—89; ret., 1989. V.p. 1st Class Expert Sys., Inc., Wayland, Mass., 1989-90, Microsoft Corp., Boston, 1991-94; cons., pres. Profl. Office Solutions, Enfield, 1981—; pres. New Venture Inc., Enfield, 1994—; owner, nvi: Ednl. Multimedia Group, nvi: Webmaster Internet Devel.; del. leader Comparative Studies Assn.; Internat. Cultural Exch. with China, Washington; pub. spkr. Spkrs. Bur., U. Hartford; vis. mem. faculty mgmt. info. sci. U. Hartford, 1989-91; realtor Sentry Real Estae Svcs., Inc., 2004—. Author: A Novice's Guide to Personal Computer Buying, New Ventures to Egypt, New Ventures to China, Faith, Hope and Love: Coping With Life and Death. Gubernatorial appointee Conn. bd. trustees Reg. C.C.s, 1985-89; vice chmn. Student Affairs and Acad. Policies Com. Hartford, 1987; chmn., trustee Conn. Data Processing Curriculum Com., Hartford, 1989; elected com. mem. Enfield Dem. Com., 1975; chmn. regional adv. coun. Asnuntuck C.C.; notary pub. Conn., 1972—; gubernatorial appointee Conn. bd. trustees Cmty. Tech. Colls., 1990-93. Recipient CTM degree Toastmaster Internat., Hartford, 1987, State Farmer degree Conn. Future Farmers Am., DeKalb Agrl. Accomplishment award, cert. of recognition Bicentennial (USA) Commn., Enfield, 1976, Vigil Hon. BSA Order of the Arrow, Hartford, 1972, Merit award State of Conn. Cmty.-Tech. Colls. Bd. Trustees, 1994. Mem. World Affairs Coun. of Hartford, Computer Soc. of IEEE, Am. Assn. for Artificial Intelligence, Assn. C.C. Trustees, Am. Assn. Cmty. and Tech. Colls., Microsoft AlumNet Assn., Internat. Platform Assn., Oldefield Farms Homeowners' Assn. (residence com. sec. 1990-91), Hartford County Soil and Water Conservation Dist., Nat. Press Club Found., Robert Schueller's Eagles Club, Masons. Republican. Roman Catholic. Avocations: travel, refinishing antiques, tennis, hiking, real estate investment, photography. Home: 71 Oldefield Farm Enfield CT 06082-4565 Office Phone: 866-225-0772. E-mail: Bruce@Oliver.ws.

OLIVER, CHARLES MONTGOMERY, retired English educator; b. Champaign, Ill., July 8, 1932; s. William Albert and Mary Maud (Thompson) O.; m. Helen Marie Vanover, Sept. 4, 1954; children: Mark Lee, Kent Thompson, Karl Henderson. BS, Western Ky. Coll., 1954; MA, U. Mo., Columbia, 1958; PhD, Bowling Green U., 1970. Sports writer Springfield News-Leader, Mo., 1958-60, South Bend Tribune, Ind., 1960-62; English tchr. Mt. Vernon HS, Ill., 1962-65; prof. English Ohio No. U., Ada, 1965-92; ret., 1992. Author: Hemingway A to Z, 1999; editor A Moving Picture Feast: The Filmgoer's Hemingway, 1989; editor The Hemingway Rev., 1979-92, The Hemingway Newsletter, 1979—. With US Army, 1954-56. NEH grantee, 1975. Avocations: reading, writing. Home: 1417 Ricky Rd Charlottesville VA 22901-2609 Personal E-mail: cmo7798@earthlink.net.

OLIVER, DALE HUGH, lawyer; b. Lansing, Mich., June 26, 1947; s. Alvin Earl and Jean Elizabeth (Stanton) Oliver; m. Sarah Elyse Sanders, Mar. 18, 2001; children: Nathan Corey, John Franklin. BA, Mich. State U., 1969; JD cum laude, Harvard U., 1972. Bar: DC 1973, Calif. 1991, US Dist. Ct. (DC dist.) 1973, US Ct. Appeals (DC cir.) 1976, US Supreme Ct. 1980, US Ct. Appeals (fed. cir.) 1983, US Ct. Claims 1983. Assoc., ptnr. Jones, Day, Reavis & Pogue, Washington, 1975—79; ptnr. Crowell & Moring, Washington, 1979—84, Gibson, Dunn & Crutcher, Washington, 1984—87, Jones, Day, Reavis & Pogue, Washington, 1987—92, Quinn Emanuel Urquhart & Oliver, L.A., 1992—. Editor: (jour.) Pub. Contracts Law, 1980—86; contbr. articles to profl. jours. Spl. counsel 1980 Presdl. Inaugural Com., Washington, 1980; bd. dirs. L.A. coun. Boy Scouts Am., 1991—. Capt. USAF, 1973—75. Mem.: ABA (com. chmn. pub. contract sect. 1979—), Nat. Security Indsl. Assn., Nat. Contract Mgmt. Assn., Harvard Law Sch. Assn., Mich. State U. Alumni Club of Washington (pres., dir. 1984—88). Office: Quinn Emanuel Urquhart & Oliver & Hedges 865 S Figueroa St Fl 10 Los Angeles CA 90017-2543 Office Phone: 213-624-7707. E-mail: daleoliver@quinnemanuel.com.

OLIVER, DIANE FRANCES, publisher, writer; b. NYC, Feb. 7, 1935; m. Ben Martin Oliver, Sept. 3, 1960 (div. 1973). BA, Syracuse U., 1955. Reporter Millinery Rsch. mag., NYC, 1956-58; with NYC Bur., London Daily Mail and London Daily Sketch, 1964-69; editor The Celebrity Bull., Celebrity Svc. Inc., NYC, 1971-78; pub. The Celebrity Bull., pres., owner Celebrity Svc. Ltd., London, 1978—. Former publicist Lake Lucerne (NY) Playhouse, Bklyn. Acad. Music, Statler Hilton Hotel, NYC. Author: Older Woman/Younger Man, 1975; columnist Palm Beach Social Pictorial mag., 1981-85. Avocations: music, ballet, films, theater, travel. Home: 44 Lennox Gardens London SW1X 0DJ England Office: Celebrity Service Ltd 4th Fl Kingsland House 122 124 Regent St London England W1B 5SA E-mail: celebritylondon@aol.com.

OLIVER, DOMINICK MICHAEL, business educator; b. Niagara Falls, N.Y., Apr. 12, 1962; s. Dominick Jr. and Priscilla (Prenatt) O.; m. Vicki Anne Sellig, May 18, 1991. AAS, Niagara County C.C., Sanborn, N.Y., 1982; BS in Bus., Niagara U., N.Y., 1984, MS in Edn., 1986. Lic. tchr. bus. and distributive edn., N.Y.; bus. sch. lic. bus., mgmt., acctg., gen. academics, N.Y. Temporary instr. Niagara County C.C., Sanborn, 1986-87; tchr. on spl. assignment LaSalle Sr. H.S., Niagara Falls, N.Y., 1986-87; instr. St. Joseph Parochial Elem. Sch., Niagara Falls, 1987-88; instr., acad. dean Kelley Bus. Inst., Niagara Falls, 1988-91; instr. Cheryl Fell's Sch. Bus., Niagara Falls, 1991-92; instr., advisor Bryant and Stratton Bus. Inst., Buffalo, 1992—99, sr. mentor, portfolio textbook curriculum com., 1996—99; sr. instr., math coordinator The Huntington Learning Ctr., 1999—2000; adj. instr. comp. sci. SUNY Buffalo, 2000—, Niagara County Cmty. Coll., 2001—; asst. prof. office mgmt. and admin. Erie Cmty. Coll., 2002—. Bus. mgr. Dove Artworks, Buffalo, 1996—; instr. Adopt-A-H.S., Seneca Vocat. H.S., Kensington H.S., Lafayette H.S., Riverside H.S., Buffalo, 1996-1999; evaluator Empire State Coll., 2003—. Life mem. Buffalo and Erie County Naval and Servicemen's Park, Buffalo, 1991—. Republican. Roman Catholic. Avocations: sports (baseball, football, hockey), political history of united states, reading classical literature. Home: 119 Wendover Ave Buffalo NY 14223-2731 Office: Erie CC 4041 Southwestern Blvd Orchard Park NY 14127-2199

OLIVER, DONNA H. secondary school educator; AB, Elon Coll.; MEd, U. N.C.; MS, N.C. State U.; PhD, U. N.C. Tchr. biology Hugh M. Cummings High Sch., Burlington, NC; v.p. academic affairs Bennett Coll., Greensboro, NC, 1989—. Office: Bennett College 900 E Washington St Greensboro NC 27401

OLIVER, EDWARD CARL, retired state legislator, retired insurance company executive, small business owner; b. St. Paul, May 31, 1930; s. Charles Edmund and Esther Marie (Bjugstad) O.; m. Charlotte Severson, Sept. 15, 1956; children: Charles E., Andrew T., Peter A. BA, U. Minn., 1955. Sales rep. Armstrong Cork Co., N.Y.C., 1955; registered rep. Piper, Jaffray & Hopwood, Mpls., 1958; mgr. Mut. Funds Inc., subs. Dayton's, Mpls., 1964, NWNL Mgmt. Corp. subs. Northwestern Nat. Life Ins. Co., Mpls., 1968-72, v.p., 1972-81, pres., dir., 1981-90; mem. Minn. State Senate, 1992—2003, asst. minority leader, 1998—2003; owner Oliver Fin., 2003—. Arbitrator/mediator, Nat. Assn. Securities Dealers, 1988—; bd. dirs. 1st Minn. Bank, N.A. Mem. Gt. Lakes Commn., 1993—; bd. dirs. Minn. State Arts Bd., 2003—; ch. elder Calvin Presbyn. Ch. of Orono. Mem. Internat. Assn. Fin. Planners (past pres. Twin City chpt., nat. governing com.), Psi Upsilon, Mpls. Athletic Club. Home: 20230 Cottagewood Rd Excelsior MN 55331-9300 Office: 401 2d Ave S Ste 429 Minneapolis MN 55401-2349 Office Phone: 612-259-0107. E-mail: oliverfinancial@earthlink.net.

OLIVER, ELIZABETH KIMBALL, writer; b. Saginaw, Mich., May 21, 1918; d. Chester Benjamin and Margaret Eva (Allison) Kimball; m. James Arthur Oliver, May 3, 1941 (div. July 1967); children: Patricia Allison (dec.), Dexter Kimball. BA, U. Mich., 1940. Tchr. Dexter (Mich.) High Sch., 1940-41; libr. Sherman (Conn.) Libr. Assn., 1966-75; pres. Sherman (Conn.) Libr. Assn., 1983-84; writer, historian, 1976—. Reporter Sherman Sentinel, 1965-70; editor newsletter Sherman Hist. Soc., 1977-78; columnist Citizen News, Fairfield County, Conn., 1981-83. Author: History of Staff Wives-AMNH, 1961, Background and History of the Palisades Nature Association, 1964, History and Architecture of Grace United Methodist Church, 1990, Legacy to St. Augustine, 1993, Franklin W. Smith and His Casa Monica Hotel, 2000, Viewpoint of a St. Augustine Columnist, 2004; guest columnist Mandarin News, 1995-97; columnist St. Augustine Record, 1998—, Viewpoint of St. Augustine, 2004. Vol. N.Y. Hist. Soc., N.Y.C., 1961-65; treas. Coburn Cemetery Assn., Sherman, 1976-82; historian Greenbrook-Palisades Nature Assn., Tenafly, N.J., 1962-64; mem. St. Augustine Hist. Soc., Naromi Land Trust (life), Cedar Key Hist. Soc.; adv. bd. IBC (Eng.). Mem. AAUW, Friends of Libr. (life), Inst. Am. Indian Studies, Marjorie Kinnan Rawlings Soc. (charter), St. Augustine Woman's Club (archivist, cert. of appreciation 1990), Sherman Hist. Soc., Mandarin Hist. Soc., Smithsonian Nat. Mus. of the Am. Indian (charter). Republican. Congregationalist. Avocations: sacred choral music, research, reading, piano and dulcimer playing, botany. Home: 2292 Commodores Club Blvd Saint Augustine FL 32080-9161 *There are four words which I endeavor to live up to in my work, my personal contacts and every day life. They are the guideposts which I use in all I do: love, courage, integrity and steadfastness.*

OLIVER, GARY JACKSON, psychologist, educator; b. Great Falls, Mont., Sept. 20, 1947; m. Carrie Elizabeth Oliver, Dec. 27, 1980; children: Nathan, Matthew, Andrew. ThM, Fuller Sem., 1977; MA, U. Nebr., 1980, PhD, 1984. Cert. clin. psychology, Nebr., Colo., Ark. Sr. staff psychologist Lincoln (Nebr.) Family Med. Group, 1984-86; clin. dir. S.W. Counseling Assocs., Littleton, Colo., 1986-98; exec. dir., prof. The Ctr. for Marriage and Family Studies, John Brown U., Siloam Springs, Ark., 1998—. Program dir., prof. Denver Sem., 1988—; sr. fellow Coun. Christian Colls. and Univs. Author/Co-author: (with Carrie Oliver) Raising Sons...And Loving It!, 2000, (with H. Norman Wright) Raising Kids to Love Jesus, 1999, Fears, Doubts, Blues & Pouts, 1999, Good Women Get Angry, 1996, Made Perfect in Weakness: The Amazing Things God Can Do With Failure, 1998, Real Men Have Feelings Too, 1993; editor: Marriage and Family Christian Journal; contbr. over 100 articles to profl. jours. Mem. APA, ACA, Am. Assn. Christian Counselors (bd. mem.), Am. Assn. for Marriage and Family Therapy, Assn. for Psychol. Type, Nat. Coun. on Family Rels., Christian Assn. for Psychol. Studies. Office: John Brown U Ctr for Marriage and Family Studies 2000 W University St Siloam Springs AR 72761-2112 E-mail: cmfs@jbu.edu.

OLIVER, G(EORGE) BENJAMIN, educational administrator, philosophy educator; b. Mpls., Sept. 17, 1938; s. Clarence P. and Cecile (Worley) O.; m. Paula Rae Foust, Sept. 15, 1963; children: Paul Benjamin, Rebecca Lee. BA with honors, U. Tex., 1960; MDiv, Union Theol. Sem., N.Y.C., 1963; MA, Northwestern U., 1966, PhD, 1967. Lectr. Northwestern U., Evanston, Ill., 1966-67; asst. prof. Hobart & William Smith Coll., Geneva, N.Y., 1967-71, chmn. dept. philosophy, 1969-77, assoc. prof., 1971-77, prof., 1977; dean Southwestern U., Georgetown, Tex., 1977-89, provost, 1986-89; pres. Hiram (Ohio) Coll., 1989-2000, pres. emeritus, 2000—. Bd. dirs. Global Ry. Sys., Inc.; chmn. Coun. Acad. Deans and V.P.s of Tex., 1987-88. Contbr. articles to profl. jours. Trustee John Cabot U., Rome, 1989-2000, Grand River Acad., Austinburg, Ohio, 1991-2000, N.E. Ohio Coun. Higher Edn., 1991-2000, Ohio Found. Ind. Coll., 1989-2000, vice-chair, 1999-2000, exec. com., 1994-2000, co-chair strategic planning com., 1997-98; trustee Assn. Ind. Colls. and Univs. Ohio, 1993-2000, Nat. Assn. Ind. Colls. and Univs. Pol. Com. on Student Aid, 1999-2000, Am. Coun. Edn. Commn. Govtl. Rels., 1994-97, Cleve. Coun. on World Affairs, 1996-2000; chmn. bd. trustees East Ctrl. Coll. Consortium, 1993-95; bd. dirs. Global Rail Sys., Inc., 2003—. Rockefeller Found. fellow, 1960-61, Internat. fellow Columbia U., 1962-63; rsch. grantee NEH, 1973-74. Mem. AAUP, Am. Coun. Edn. (commn. on govtl. rels.), Soc. for Values in Higher Edn., Assn. Ind. Coll. and Univs. Ohio (treas. 1993-94), East Ctrl. Colls. Consortium (chair, bd. trustees 1993-95), Ohio Found. Ind. Colls. (exec. com. 1994-2000, vice chair elect 1999-2000), Am. Assn. Higher Edn., Cleve. Coun. on Fgn. Rels. Episcopalian. Office: Hiram Coll Office of Pres Hiram OH 44234 E-mail: olivergben@msn.com.

OLIVER, HARRY MAYNARD, JR., retired brokerage house executive; b. Kansas City, Mo., Jan. 21, 1921; s. Harry Maynard and Marie (Curtin) O. BA, Williams Coll., 1943. Pres. M.A. Gesner & Co., Marsh & McLennan Co., Chgo., 1947-88. Chmn. Chgo. Commn. for Sr. Citizens, 1960-69; mem. Chgo. Bd. Edn., 1966-69; pres. Vol. Agys. Chgo., 1956-86; mem. vis. com. Sch. Edn. and div. of social scis., U. Chgo.; pres., bd. dirs. Benton House Settlement, 1953-58; bd. dirs. Adult Edn. Council Greater Chgo., Nat. Fedn. Settlements and Community Centers, 1961-67; trustee Old Peoples Home Chgo., Pub. Sch. Tchrs. Pension and Retirement Fund Chgo., 1966-69, George M. Pullman Ednl. Found., Field Mus. Natural History, 1971-75. Served to lt. (j.g.) USNR, World War II. Mem. Chgo. Club, Racquet Club, Commonwealth Club, Tavern Club, Onwentsia Club (Lake Forest, Ill.), Chi Psi. Home: 1948 N Lincoln Ave Chicago IL 60614-5476 also: PO Box 1319 Big Pine Key FL 33043 also: New Richmond PO Box 100 Fennville MI 49408-0100

OLIVER, JACK ERTLE, geophysicist, educator; b. Massillon, Ohio, Sept. 26, 1923; s. Chester L. and Marie (Ertle) O.; m. Gertrude van der Hoeven, Apr. 16, 1964; children: Cornelia Oliver, Amy Oliver. AB, Columbia U., 1947, MA, 1950, PhD, 1953; DSci (hon.), Hamilton Coll., 1988. Rsch. asst., then rsch. assoc. Columbia, 1947-55, mem. faculty, 1955-73, prof. geology, 1961-71, chmn. dept., 1969-71, adj. prof., 1971-73; Irving Porter Church prof. engring. dept. geol. scis. Cornell U., 1971-93, prof. emeritus, 1993—, chmn. dept., 1971-81; chmn. exec. com. COCORP. Terrestrial physicist USAF Cambridge (Mass.) Rsch. Labs., 1951; dir. Inst. for Study of the Continents, 1981-88; cons. AEC, 1969-72, ACDA, 1962-74, USAF Tech. Applications Ctr., 1959-65; mem. Polar Rsch. Com., 1959-71, also nat. commn. uppermantle program, 1963-71; mem. panel solid earth problems NAS, 1962; mem. adv. com. U.S. Coast and Geodetic Survey, 1962-66, on seismology, 1960-72, chmn., 1966-70; mem. Geophysics Rsch. Bd., 1969-70; U.S. coord. 2d U.S.-Japan Earthquake Prediction Conf., Palisades, 1966; earth sci. panel NSF, 1962-65; mem. USAF Sci. Adv. Bd., 1960-63, 64-69; mem. geophysics adv. panel Office Sci. Rsch., USAF, 1961-74, chmn., 1966-68; U.S. del. Test Ban Conf., Geneva, Switzerland, 1958-59; intergovtl. meeting seismology and earthquake engring., mem. exec. com. IASPEI, 1968-71; mem. governing com. Internat. Seismol. Summary Commn., 1963-67, 75-76; mem. exec. com. UNESCO, Paris, France, 1964; U.S.-Japan Earthquake Prediction Conf., Tokyo, 1964; mem. UNESCO Joint Com. on Seismology and Earthquake Engring., 1965-71; chmn. exec. com. Office Earth Scis., NRC, 1976-79, Internat. Seismol. Centre, 1976-78; mem. U.S. Geodynamics Com., 1979-87, chmn., 1984-87; mem. Geol. Scis. Bd., Assembly of Math. and Phys. Scis., NRC, 1981-84; Cabot Disting. vis. scholar U. Houston, 1985-86; commn. on phys. scis., math. and resources NRC, 1987-90, commn. on geoscis., environ. and resources, 1990—. Served with USNR, 1943-46. Recipient Hedberg award Inst. for Study of Earth and Man, So. Meth. U., 1990. Fellow Am. Geophys. Union (pres. seismology sect. 1964-68, Walter H. Bucher medal 1981), Geol. Soc. Am. (coun. 1970-73, v.p. 1986, pres. 1987, Woollard medal 1990, Penrose medal 1998), Geol. Soc. London (hon.); mem. AAAS (chmn. geol. geog. sect. 1993), NAS, Seismol. Soc. Am. (pres. 1964-65, bd. dirs. 1961-70, 72-76, Eighth medal 1984), Soc. Exploration Geophysicists (Virgil Kauffman Gold medal 1983), European Union Geoscis. (hon. fgn. fellow), Sigma Xi. Home: 340 Savage Fram Dr Ithaca NY 14850 Office Phone: 607-255-2377. Business E-Mail: oliver@geology.cornell.edu.

OLIVER, JAMIE, chef, television personality; b. Essex, England, May 1, 1975; s. Trevor and Sally Oliver; m. Juliette Norton; children: Poppy, Daisy. Grad., Westminster Catering Coll., London. Head pastry chef Neal Street Restaurant, London, 1991—97; chef River Cafe, London, 1997—2002; consulting chef Monte's, London, 2000; founder, owner Fifteen Restaurant, London, 2002—. Former columnist GQ mag.; former feature writer The Times Mag., London; designer cookware & tableware line Royal Worcester. Host, chef (TV series) The Naked Chef, 1999-2001 (BAFTA award 2001), Jamie's Kitchen, 2002-04, Oliver's Twist, 2004-; author (cookbooks) The Naked Chef, 1999, The Return of The Naked Chef, 2000, Happy Days with The Naked Chef, 2001, Jamie's Kitchen, 2003, Jamie's Dinners, 2004. Founder Cheeky Chops Found., 2002. Decorated MBE; named GQ Man of the Yr., 2000; recipient GQ Best Chef award, 2000, Tatler Best Restaurant award (for Fifteen Restaurant), 2003, Excellence award, Tio Pepe Carlton London Restaurant Awards, 2003, Time Out special award for outstanding achievement, 2003, Glenfiddich Food and Drink award, 2003. Office: Fifteen Restaurant & Cheeky Chops Found Westland Place London N1 7LP England also: c/o Penguin Group 375 Hudson St New York NY 10014*

OLIVER, JERRY ALTON, former police chief; 4 children. BS in Criminal Justice, Ariz. State U., MS in Pub. Adminstrn., 1988; postgrad., Police Exec. Rsch. Forum, Washington. From patrolman to supr. Phoenix Police Dept., from supr. to asst. chief of police, 1971-90; dir. drug policy Memphis Police Dept.; chief of police Pasadena (Calif.) Police Dept., 1991—94, Richmond (Va.) Police Dept., 1995—2002, Detroit, Mich., 2002—03. Founder Spl. Friends Project, Richmond, 1988—. Inductee Ariz. State U. Coll. Pub. Programs Hall of Fame, 1989; recipient Phoenix chpt. Image award NAACP, 1990, People of the Ur. award Law Enforcement News, 1999, Richmonder of the Ur. award Richmond Style Mag., 1999, U.S. Atty. Gen.'s award for outstanding contbns. to cmty. partnership for pub. safety, 2000, othrs.

OLIVER, JOHN PERCY, II, lawyer, consultant; b. Alexander City, Ala., Dec. 3, 1942; s. Samuel William and Sarah Pugh (Coker) D.; m. Melissa Vann, June 11, 1966. AB, Birmingham (Ala.) So. Coll., 1964; JD, U. Ala., 1967. Bar: Ala. 1967, U.S. Dist. Ct. (mid. dist.) Ala. 1969, U.S. Supreme Ct. 1971, U.S. Ct. Appeals (5th cir.) 1975, U.S. Ct. Appeals (11th cir.) 1981, U.S. Dist. Ct. (mid. dist.) Ga. 1989. Assoc. Samuel W. Oliver, Atty., Dadeville, Ala., 1967; prin. John P. Oliver II, Atty., Dadeville, 1967-71; ptnr. Oliver & Sims, Attys., Dadeville, 1972-83, Oliver, Sims & Jones, Attys., Dadeville, 1984-85, Oliver & Sims, Attys., Dadeville, 1985—2002, Oliver-Treadwell Attys., Dadeville, 2002—. Dir. Bank of Dadeville. Mem. State Dem. Exec. Com., Tallapoosa County, Ala., 1986-94; judge Tallapoosa County Dist. Ct., Dadeville, 1973-76; mcpl. judge, Dadeville, 19765; spl. probate judge Tallapoosa County Probate Ct., Dadeville, 1987-88. Mem. Ala. State Bar Assn. (bd. bar commrs. 1992-98), Ala. Trial Lawyers Assn. (exec. com. 1975-77), Tallapoosa County Bar Assn. (pres. 1990). Baptist. Avocations: sailing, skiing. Office: Oliver-Treadwell 129 W Columbus St Dadeville AL 36853-1308

OLIVER, JOHN PRESTON, chemistry professor, dean; b. Klamath Falls, Oreg., Aug. 7, 1934; s. Robert Preston and Agnes May (McCornack) O.; m. Elizabeth Ann Shaw, Aug. 12, 1956; children: Karen Sue Oliver Vernon, Roy John, Gordon Preston. BA, U. Oreg., 1956; PhD, U. Wash., 1959. Asst. prof. chemistry Wayne State U., Detroit, 1959-64, assoc. prof., 1964-67, prof., 1967—, assoc. dean R&D, Coll. Liberal Arts, 1987-91, acting dean, 1991-92, interim dean Coll. Sci., 1992-93, dep. provost, 1996—2003, v.p. for rsch., 2003—. Chmn. organizing com. XIV Internat. Conf. on Organometallic Chemistry. Mem. Ferndale (Mich.) Bd. Edn., 1984-88. Mem. Am. Chem. Soc., Detroit sect. Am. Chem. Soc., Sigma Xi. Office: Wayne State Univ Rm 4043 FAB Detroit MI 48202-3489 E-mail: jpo@wayne.edu.

OLIVER, JOHN WILLIAM POSEGATE, minister; b. Vincennes, Ind., Apr. 9, 1935; s. Dwight L and Elizabeth (Posegate) Oliver; m. Cristina Shepard Hope, Oct. 19, 1968; children: John William Posegate Jr, Sloan Christian Shepard. BA, Wheaton Coll., 1956; BD, Fuller Theol. Sem., 1959; ThM, So. Bapt. Theol. Sem., 1963; DD, Western Conservative Bapt. Sem, 1996. Ordained to ministry Presby Ch, 1962. Asst. pastor Covenant Presbyn. Ch., Hammond, Ind., 1964-66, Trinity Presbyn. Ch., Montgomery, Ala., 1966-69; pastor 1st Presbyn. Ch., Augusta, Ga., 1969-97, Trinity Presbyn. Ch., Montgomery, Ala., 1997-99; prof. preaching and practical theology Reformed Theol. Sem., Charlotte, N.C., 1999—. Bd dirs Equip, Inc; moderator Cent Ga Presby, Presby Ch Am, 1976. Founder, trustee Westminster Schs, Augusta, 1972—97; bd. commrs. Augusta Housing Authority, vice chmn., 1976—93; trustee, chmn. bd. Columbia Internat. U., 1978—; dir. Bailey Manor Retirement Ctr., Clinton, SC, 1992—97; chmn. clergy Augusta United Way Campaign, 1974; exec. bd. clergy staff Univ. Hosp., Augusta, 1975—76; bd. dirs. Mission to the World, Presbyn. Ch. Am, 1984—89, bd dirs, 1992—96; ministerial adv. bd. Ref. Theol. Sem., Jackson, Miss., 1978—85, 1989—93, Charlotte, 1996—99. Mem.: Evang Theological Soc, Wynlakes Country Club, Nassau Club, Kappa Sigma. Home: 731 Stanhope Ln Matthews NC 28105-1516 Office: 2101 Carmel Rd Charlotte NC 28226-6318

OLIVER, JOSEPH MCDONALD, JR., lawyer; b. Savannah, Ga., July 26, 1946; s. Joseph McDonald and Louise (Myers) O.; m. Patricia Clark, Sept. 8, 1965 (div. Mar. 1983); children: Joseph McDonald III, Catherine McCay; m. Meredith Bennett, May 11, 1985. BA, U. Va., 1967; JD, U. Ga., 1970. Bar: Ga. 1970, D.C. 1971. Law clk. U.S. Ct. Claims, 1970-71; assoc. Jones, Day, Reavis & Pogue, Washington, 1971-77, ptnr., 1978-79, Crowell & Moring LLP, Washington, 1979—2000, sr. counsel, 2000—. Mem. ABA, Fed. Energy Bar Assn. Episcopalian. Home: PO Box 446 Washington VA 22747 Office: Crowell & Moring LLP 1001 Pennsylvania Ave NW Fl 10 Washington DC 20004-2595 Office Phone: 202-624-2625. E-mail: joliver@crowell.com.

OLIVER, JOYCE ANNE, journalist, editorial and film consultant, columnist; b. Coral Gables, Fla., Sept. 19, 1958; d. John Joseph and Rosalie Cecile (Mack) O. BA in Communications, Calif. State U., Fullerton, 1980, MBA, 1990. Corp. editor Norris Industries Inc., Huntington Beach, Calif., 1979-82; pres. J.A. Oliver Assocs., La Habra Heights, Calif., 1982—. Corp. editorial cons. Norris Industries, 1982, Better Methods Cons., Huntington Harbour, Calif., 1982-83, Summit Group, Orange, Calif., 1982-83, UDS, Encinitas, Calif., 1983-84, MacroMarketing, Costa Mesa, Calif., 1985-86, PM Software, Huntington Beach, Calif., 1985-86, CompuQuote, Canoga Park, Calif., 1985-86, Nat. Semicondr. Can. Ltd., Mississauga, Ont., Can., 1986, Maclean Hunter Ltd., Toronto, Ont., 1986-90; Frame Inc., Fullerton, Calif., 1987-88, The Johnson-Layton Co., L.A., 1988-89, Corp. Rsch. Inc., Chgo., 1988, Axon Group, Horsham, Pa., 1990-91, Am. Mktg. Assn., Chgo., 1990-92, Kenzaikai Co., Ltd., Tokyo, 1991, Penton Pub., Cleve., 1991, Bus. Computer Pub., Inc., Peterborough, N.H., 1991-92, Helmers Pub., Inc., Peterborough, 1992, Schnell Pub., Co., Inc., N.Y.C., 1992-93, Diversified Pub. Group, Carol Stream, Ill., 1993; mem. Rsch. Coun. of Scripps Clinic and Rsch. Found., 1987-92; pres. Oliver Vingtaine, 1999—. Contbg. editor Computer Merchandising/ Resell, 1982-85, Computer Reselling, 1985, Reseller Mgmt., 1987-89; contbg. editor Can. Electronics Engring., 1986-90, west coast editor, 1990, Chem. Bus. mag., 1992-93; spl. feature editor Cleve. Inst. Electronics publ. The Electron, 1986-89; bus. columnist Mktg. News, 1990-92; contbr. articles to profl. jours. and mags. Bd. dirs. Action Comms., 1993—. Mem. IEEE, AAUW, Internat. Platform Assn., Soc. Photo-optical Instrumentation Engrs., Inst. Mgmt. Scis., Nat. Writers Club (profl.), Internat. Mktg. Assn., Soc. Profl. Journalists, L.A. World Affairs Coun., Internat. Order of Merit, Nat. Trust for Hist. Preservation. Republican. Roman Catholic. Avocations: sailing, water-skiing, travel, languages. Office: PO Box 2607 La Habra CA 90631-8213

OLIVER, KAREN LEE, writer; b. Poughkeepsie, N.Y., Oct. 1, 1959; d. Robert Fuller Oliver and Leoneida Mazzara. Student, SUNY, Albany, 1982. Dancer Am. Ballet Theater, N.Y.C., 1974—76. Author: (book) Pergola, 2002. Recipient Regents scholarship, State of N.Y., 1976.

OLIVER, KATHERINE C. museum director; Exec. dir. Mid Ga. Hist. Soc. Inc., Macon. Office: Mid Ga Hist Soc Inc 935 High St Macon GA 31201-2034

OLIVER, LEANN MICHELLE, government official; b. Eureka, Calif., Nov. 15, 1955; d. George L. and Laura Maxine (Jennings) O. BS, Willamette U., 1977; MPA, SUNY, Albany, 1980; cert., Nat. Comml. Lending Sch. of Am. Bankers Assn., Norman, Okla., 1982. Mgmt. trainee U.S. GAO, Albany, 1979-80; presdl. mgmt. intern U.S. SBA, Washington, 1980-83, fin. analyst, policy and program devel., 1983-89; dep. dir. for program devel. Office Econ. Devel., 1989-92; dep. dir. Office of Rural Affairs and Econ. Devel., 1992-94; acting dir. One Stop Office, Capital Shop Project, 1994; acting dir. Office Rural Affairs and Econ. Devel. SBA, Washington, 1995, dir. divsn. Program Devel., 1995-2000, dep. assoc. adminstr. for fin. assistance, 2000—. Bd. dirs. Lafayette Fed. Credit Union, Washington, 1986—, treas., 1997-2000, asst. treas., 2000-04, treas., 2004—. Mem. Internat. Platform Assn. Roman Catholic. Office: SBA 409 3rd St SW Ste 8300 Washington DC 20416

OLIVER, MADISON E. retired engineering executive, mechanical engineer; b. Hermosa Beach, Calif., Apr. 14, 1925; s. Eldon Seymour and Gertrude Helen Oliver; m. Virginia E. Kellis. BS Applied Sci., Chico State U., 1951; BSME, Wash. State U., 1953. Registered profl. engr. N.Mex., 1956. Staff mem. Sandia Corp., Albuquerque, 1953—56, sect. supr. Livermore, Calif., 1957—60; design engr. Aerojet Gen. Corp., Sacramento, 1960—63; dep. dir. pub. works Govt. of Am. Samoa, Pago Pago, 1963—67, dir. pub. works, 1967—69; project mgr. Parsons Hawaii (unit of Ralph M. Parsons Co.), Honolulu, 1970—74, sr. project mgr., mng. engr., 1974—82, gen. mgr., 1982—91; v.p. Parsons Overseas Co., Hawaii, 1990—91. Territorial bldg. ofcl. Govt. of Am. Samoa, Pago Pago, U. S. Territory of American Samoa, 1967—69; sec. bd. of dirs. Marine Dry Dock, Pago Pago, 1968—69; project mgr. New Saipan Internat. Airport, 1970—76, Trust Ter. of the Pacific Islands Airport Sys. Plan, 1975—76, New Guam Internat. Air Terminal, 1976—82; program dir. TRUK Capital Improvements, 1975—77; prin. project mgr., engring. design and constrn. Palau Hosp., 1988—91; spkr. in field. Mem. Pacific & Asian Affairs Coun., Honolulu, 1982—90; mem., transp. com. Chamber of Commerce, Honolulu, 1982—90; bd. dirs. Marina Towers Condominium, Honolulu, 1980—83, pres. bd. dirs., 1983—86. Motor machinist's mate first class USN, 1943—46, PTO. Recipient Airport Beautification Award, Saipan Internat. Airport, FAA, Saipan, No. Mariana Islands, 1976. Mem.: Soc. Am. Mil. Engineers, ASME, Toastmasters Internat. (gov., area VI, dist. 39 1963—63), Toastmasters Internat., Raconteur Club, Folsom, Calif. (pres. 1962—63), Masonic Lodge (Golden Veterans Award 2000). Avocation: golf, writing, and fishing. Home: 1821 Jansen Way Woodburn OR 97071

OLIVER, MARGUERITE BERTONI, food service executive; b. Ann Arbor, Mich., June 5, 1929; d. Ralph Angelo and Margaret Amelia (Rovegno) Bertoni; m. William John Oliver, May 28, 1949; children: R. Scott, Catherine Oliver Allen, Susan M. Mgr. complaint dept. Sears Roebuck Co., Ann Arbor, 1949-50; dir. meals-on-wheels program U. Mich. Hosp., Ann Arbor, 1974-76; fund raiser U. Mich. Art Sch., Ann Arbor, 1976-80; founder Pastabilities (named outstanding pasta shop in U.S. by CNN TV), Ann Arbor, 1980—; prodr., dir. 500th Anniversary Program for Columbus Day, CNN, 1992. Participant, speaker Midwest Assn. State Depts. Agr., 1987; mem. adv. com. Gov.'s Conf. on Future of Mich. Agr., 1988; co-chmn. Gov.'s Conf. on Agr., 1989. Bd. dirs. Washtenaw County Commn. Aging, 1970-74, Hands-On-Mus., Ann Arbor, 1980-82; mem. market commn. Ann Arbor, 1982-2000; founded Internat. Neighbors; mem., adv. com. Mich. Future 2020 Team; bd. dirs. Found. Washtenaw C.C., 1989-96; mem. Mich. Dept. Agr. Industry Task Force, 1990; invited del. Moscow Bus. Conf., 1991; fundraiser Mott Children's Hosp. U. Mich., 1979-80; fundraiser U. Mich. Musical Soc., 1997. Recipient Washtenaw Community Service award Washtenaw Community Coll., 1985. Roman Catholic. Home: 2892 Bay Ridge Dr Ann Arbor MI 48103-1704 Office: Pastabilities 708 State Cir Ann Arbor MI 48108-1648

OLIVER, MARLYS MAE, retired editor, writer; b. St. Paul, Mar. 23, 1930; d. Earle R. and Margaret A. (Parrott) Benner; m. Alfred Leo Oliver, Apr. 28, 1951; children— Stephanie Margaret, David Earle. AA, Lakewood C.C., 1970; student Metro State U., 1976-77. Graphic artist Lakewood C.C., White Bear Lake, Minn., 1968-70; corr. Women Sports mag., N.Y.C., 1973-77; editor Press Publs., White Bear Lake, 1972-76; mng. editor Frogtown Forum, St. Paul, 1976-77; mayor City of Birchwood, Minn., 1977-83; exec. editor Press Publs., White Bear Lake, 1982-92; owner Dolls by Marlys, 1992—; host weekly cable tel. talk show Come for Coffee, 1988-90; pres., dir. Cable Access Corp., 1985-87. Mem. White Bear Lake Arts Council, dir., 1975; bd. dirs. Lakeshore Players, 1984-85, White Bear Lake Area Hist. Soc.; chmn Ramsey Washington Counties Cable TV Commn. Recipient numerous awards in journalism. Mem. Minn. Press Women (past treas.), Midwest Writers Conf (com.) Mem. Democratic Farm Labor Party. Lodge: Job's Daus. (Queen 1949). Contbr. numerous articles and poems to popular mags. Home: 2626 Ryan Dr Saint Paul MN 55119-7135

OLIVER, MARY, poet; b. Maple Heights, Ohio, Sept. 10, 1935; d. Edward William and Helen Mary (Vlasak) O. Student, Ohio State U., 1955—56, Vassar Coll., 1956—57. Chmn. writing dept. Fine Arts Work Ctr., Provincetown, Mass., 1972-73, mem. writing com., 1984; Banister poet-in-residence Sweet Briar Coll., 1991-95. William Blackburn vis. prof. creative writing Duke U., 1995; Catharine Osgood Foster prof. Bennington Coll., 1996-2001. Author: No Voyage and Other Poems, 1963, enlarged edit., 1965, The River Styx, Ohio, 1972, The Night Traveler, 1978, Twelve Moons, 1979, American Primitive, 1983, Dream Work, 1986, House of Light, 1990, New and Selected Poems, 1992, A Poetry Handbook, 1994, White Pine, 1994, Blue Pastures, 1995, West Wind, 1997, Rules for the Dance, 1998, Winter Hours, 1999, The Leaf and the Cloud, 2000, What Do We Know, 2002, Owls and Other Fantasies, 2003, Why I Wake Early, 2004, Long Life, 2004, Blue Iris, 2004; contbr. to Yale U. Rev., Kenyon Rev., Poetry, Atlantic, Harvard mag., others. Recipient Shelley Meml. award, 1970, Alice Fay di Castagnola award, 1973, Cleve. Arts prize for lits., 1979, Achievement award Am. Acad. and Inst. Arts and Letters, 1983, Pulitzer prize for poetry, 1984, Christopher award, 1991, L.L. Winship award, 1991, Nat. Book award, 1992, Lannan award, 1998; Nat. Endowment fellow, 1972-73; Guggenheim fellow, 1980-81. Mem. PEN. Home: care Molly Malone Cook Lit Agy PO Box 619 Provincetown MA 02657-0619

OLIVER, MARY MARGARET, state legislator; BA, Vanderbilt U.; degree in law, Emory U. Bar: Ga., chair individual rights sect., mem. letgis. correctional facilities, servicing coms. Staff atty., mng. atty. Ga. Legal Svcs. Program; former mem. Ho. of Reps., former mem. judiciary, transp., indsl. rels. coms.; mem. Ga. Senate, Atlanta, 1992—, chmn. judiciary com., vice chmn. edn. com., mem. appropriations, ehtics, rules coms. Mem. task force Commn. Mental Health, Retardation and Substance Abuse Delivery; adj. prof. Emory U.; asst. prof. law Boston Coll.; former hearing officer Sec. of State Joint Examining Bd., Ga. Dept. Med. Assistance; past assoc. magistrate DeKalb County Magistrate Ct. Past pres. Coun. for Children, Inc.; v.p. bd. dirs. CHARLEE Homes; bd. dirs. Ga. Legal Svc. Program. Honors received Ga. Mcpl. Assn., Parents Support Network, Ga. Psychol. Assn., Mental Health Assn. Metro Atlanta, NASW, Ga. Hosp. Assn., Ga. Coun. on Aging, Ga. Assn. Gifted Children; recipient Disting. Svc. award Ga. Bar Assn., 1996. Mem. Lawyers Club Atlanta. Democrat. Office: State Capitol Rm 421 Atlanta GA 30334 also: Ste 480 150 East Ponce Deleon Ave Decatur GA 30030

OLIVER, NANCY LEBKICHER, artist, retired elementary education educator; b. Stockton, Calif., 1939; d. John B. and Marjorie Lebkicher; m. Douglas C. Oliver, 1963; children: Charles, Elaine. BA with honors, San Jose State U., 1961. Summer playground dir. Recreation Dept., Redwood City, Calif., 1956-61; 1st grade tchr. Redwood City (Calif.) Elem. Sch. Dist., 1961-63; kindergarten tchr. Ukiah (Calif.) Unified Sch. Dist., 1963-67; assoc. tchr. kindergarten San Carlos (Calif.) Elem. Sch. Dist., 1976-81. Shopper for dept. store Macy's, San Francisco, 1975-82; asst. in hist. rsch., 2000—. Sunday sch. dir. St. Peter's Episcopal Ch., Redwood City, 1973-78; active White Oaks PTA, San Carlos, 1973-81, newsletter editor, 1978-81; leader Girl Scouts U.S.A., San Carlos, 1978-81; bd. mem. Sequoia H.S. Ednl. Found., co-chmn., 2000-2002, chmn. 2002—; bd. dirs. San Mateo County Hist. Resources Adv. Bd., 2000-. Mem. AAUW (San Carlos br. newsletter editor 1972-74, editor historic tour booklet 1981, editor historic resources booklet 1989, chmn. historic preservation sect. 1979—, pres. Willits br. 1966-67, co-pres. San Carlos br. 2002—, Named Gift honoree 1976), San Carlos Heritage Assn. (founder, dir. 1995—), Sequoia H.S. Alumni Assn. (founding sec., membership chmn. 1985—, centennial coord. 1992-95, pres. 1996-98, sec. 2oo2-, newsletter editor, 2003-, Unsung Hero award 1998), Internat. Order Rainbow Girls (grand officer Calif. 1957-58, mother advisor Redwood City 1987-89), SeriPrinters (serigrapher 1986—). Democrat. Episcopalian. Avocations: needlecrafts, historic preservation activities, walking, calligraphy, classical music. Home: 147 Belvedere Ave San Carlos CA 94070-4818

OLIVER, ROBERT BRUCE, retired investment company executive; b. Brockton, Mass., Aug. 1, 1931; s. Stanley Thomas and Helen (Sabine) O.; m. Sylvia E. Bell, Feb. 17, 1954; children: Susan Pamela, Robert Bruce. AB, Harvard U., 1953; postgrad., Bus. Sch., 1971, Boston U. Law Sch., 1955-57; MA, Mich. State U., 1958. Ret. chmn., pres., chief exec. officer John Hancock Income Securities Trust, Boston, 1989. Ret. chmn., pres. chief exec. officer John Hancock Investors Trust, John Hancock Bond Trust, John Hancock Growth Trust, John Hancock Tax Exempt Cash Mgmt. Trust, John Hancock Govt. Securities Trust, John Hancock Tax Exempt Income Trust, John Hancock Cash Mgmt. Trust, John Hancock Spl. Equities Trust, John Hancock Global Trust, John Hancock World Trust, John Hancock High Income Trust, John Hancock Tax Exempt Series Trust; chmn., dir. John Hancock Distbrs.; vice chmn., chief exec. officer John Hancock Advisers, Inc.; chmn., mng. dir. John Hancock Advisers Internat. Ltd. 1st lt. USMCR, 1953-55. Mem. Marine Corps League Home: 6619 Trident Way Naples FL 34108-8243

OLIVER, ROBERT C. financial company executive; City exec. Wachovia Bank, Gainesville, Ga., 1983-92; head N.E. Ga. ops. Ctrl. and So. Holding Co., 1990-92, pres., CEO, 1992-97; pres., COO Premier Bancshares, Atlanta, 1997—. Office: Premier Bancshares Inc 2180 Atlanta Plz 950 E Paces Ferry Rd NE Atlanta GA 30326-1180

OLIVER, RONALD, retired medical technologist; b. New Orleans, July 16, 1949; s. Wilbert and Everlina (Theard) O.; m. Ora Grant, July 12, 1995; children: Nannette Marie, Joseph Byron. Diploma in bus. adminstrn., Meadows-Draughon Coll., New Orleans, 1972; AS in Environ. Health Tech., Delgado C.C., New Orleans, 1976; BS in Biology Edn., So. U., 1980, BS in Chemistry Edn., 1983; MA in Hosp. Adminstrn., Southwest U., La., 1986; PhD in Hosp. Adminstrn., Southwest U., 1987; cert., Charity Hosp. Sch. Nuclear Med, 1986; PhD in Pub. Health, Columbia State U., La., 1992; PhD in Health Adminstrn., Kennedy-Western U., 1993; PhD in Environ. Engring., Kensington U., Glendale, Calif., 1994; PhD in Electrophysiology, Summit U., New Orleans, 1995. Med. technologist, med. technologist supr. Charity Hosp., New Orleans, 1969-95, retired, 1995; mem. faculty Pacific Western U., 1993—, Kensington U.; rsch. scientist La. State U. Med. Ctr., New Orleans, 1999. Mem. faculty Tulane U. Pub. Health and Tropical Med. Sch., 1975-81, Kensington Univ., Glendale, Calif., 1990-92; rsch. scientist Tech. La. State U. Med. Sch., New Oreleans; ex-faculty, staff mem. Delgado C.C. Author 7 books, including A Primer in Electrocardiography with Technical and Some Evaluative Values, 1991, 2d edit., 1995, Electrocardiography, Theories, Applications and Practice, 1997; also articles. V.p. Friends of Amistad Rsch., Tulane U.; mem. U.S. Trade Adv. Bd., 1996. Recipient Outstanding Svc. award Charity Hosp., 1972, acknowledgement letter Nobel Found., 1992, cert. of acknowledgement Coll. Am. Pathologists, 1981, Am. Ex-mem. Assn. Profl. Cons.; candidate Pulitzer Prize, 1995. Mem. Am. Med. Technologists, Am. Coll. Healthcare Execs. (cert. of acknowledgment), La. Environ. Health Assn. Methodist. Achievements include over 30 copyrights in the field of electrophysiology in Library of Congress; discovered the sigma wave in electrocardiography, the electrical alternan theory, the intracerebral-intracranial theories; patentee in field, 1 registered U.S. Dept. Commerce. Home: 5131 Bundy Rd PO Box 8536 New Orleans LA 70182-8536

OLIVER, ROSEANN, lawyer; b. Chgo., Oct. 7, 1947; BA, Northwestern U., 1969; JD, Loyola U., 1972. Bar: Ill. 1972, U.S. Dist. Ct. (no. dist.) Ill. 1974, U.S. Ct. Appeals (7th cir.) 1974. Legal writing instr. I.I.T. Chicago-Kent Coll. Law, 1973-74, Loyola U., 1974-75; mem. Cook County Bd. Ethics. Articles editor Loyola Law Jour., 1971-72; contbr. articles to profl. jour. Mem. Ill. State Bar Assn., Chgo. Bar Assn. (spl. counsel 1981-82, chmn. standing com. on litigation 1985-88, amicus curiae com. 1989-95), 7th Cir. Bar Assn., Inns of Ct. Office: Cahill Christian & Kunkle 224 S Michigan Ave Ste 1300 Chicago IL 60604-2583

OLIVER, SAMUEL WILLIAM, JR., lawyer; b. Birmingham, Ala., Apr. 18, 1935; s. Samuel William and Sarah C. Oliver; m. Anne Holman Marshall, Aug. 26, 1961; children: Sarah Bradley Oliver Crow, Samuel William III, Margaret Nelson Oliver Little. BS, U. Ala., 1959, JD, 1962. Bar: Ala. 1962, U.S. Dist. Ct. (no. dist.) Ala. 1963. Law clk. Supreme Ct. Ala., Montgomery, 1962-63, U.S. Dist. Ct. (no. dist.) Ala., Birmingham, 1963; assoc. Burr & Forman LLP, Birmingham, 1964-65, ptnr., 1966—, also chmn. bus./corp. law sect., 1990-93. Dir. Metalplate Galvanizing Inc., Birmingham, 1975-2004; mem. panel arbitrators comml. Am. Arbitration Assn., Atlanta, 1981-99. Chmn. bd. govs. The Relay House, Birmingham, 1985-89; mem. Leadership Birmingham, 1990; bd. dirs. Jr. Achievement Greater Birmingham, Inc., 1975-2003; mem. diocese coun. Episcopal Diocese Ala., Birmingham, 1981-85; chmn. bd. trustees Highlands Day Sch. Found., Inc., Birmingham, 1980-81; bd. dirs. Ala. Kidney Found., Birmingham, 1990-94, hon. mem., 1995—. With U.S. Army, 1956-58. Mem. ABA (bus. law sect. 1965—, negotiated acquisitions com. 1990—, task force on model stock purchase agreement 1990-95, model asset purchase agreement 1994-2001, model joint venture agreement 1994-2003, corp. counsel com.), Southeastern Corp. Law Inst. (planning com. 1996—), Birmingham Bar Assn., Ala. Bar Assn., Monday Morning Quarterback Club, Rotary Club, Venture Club, Newcomen Soc. U.S. Episcopalian.

OLIVER, SANDRA, art dealer, painter; b. Bronxville, N.Y., Apr. 2, 1941; d. Clarence Charles and Mary Bell E. (McTeique) Simoni; m. Paul Alan Williams, May 2, 1982; children: John Mortimer Wilson, Melissa Anne Wilson, PHilip Keith Wilson. BA, BFA, Marymount Coll., 1963. Art and art history tchr. N.Y.C. Sch. System, 1963-65; art tchr. Diocese Cath. Sch., Westchester, N.Y., 1963-65; comml. artist rep. Weston, Conn., 1979-84; pres. Sandi Oliver, Weston, 1984—. Author catalog: American Impressionist Paul Williams: His Garden and His Oil Paintings, 1994. Recipient 1st prize Christmas Show, Pelham (N.Y.) C. of C., 1960, Bravo award, Revlon Corp., 1980, 1st prize, Braswell Galleries, 1998, honors, Westport Art Show, 2001, award, The Westport Downtown Merchants Assn., 2002, auction record (paintings), 1988—2001. Mem. New Eng. Appraisers Assn., Allied Arts Am. Inc., Am. Fedn. Artists, Nat. Mus. Women in Arts (charter mem.). Avocations: painting, antique collecting, gardening, walking, raising dogs. Home: 11 Tubbs Spring Dr PO Box 1203 Weston CT 06883-0203 Office: Sandi Oliver PO Box 1203 Weston CT 06883-0203 Office Phone: 203-226-4469. E-mail: sandioliver@aol.com.

OLIVER, SOLOMON, JR., judge; b. Bessemer, Ala., July 20, 1947; s. Solomon Sr. and Willie Lee (Davis) O.; married; 2 children. BA, Coll. of Wooster, 1969; JD, NYU, 1972; MA, Case Western Res. U., 1974. Bar: Ohio 1973, U.S. Dist. Ct. (no. dist.) Ohio 1977, U.S. Ct. Appeals (6th cir.) 1977, U.S. Supreme Ct. 1980. Asst. prof. dept. polit. sci. Coll. of Wooster, Ohio, 1972-75; sr. law clk. to Hon. William H. Hastie U.S. Ct. Appeals (3d cir.), Phila., 1975-76; asst. U.S. atty. U.S. Atty.'s Office, Cleve., 1976-82, chief civil divsn., 1978-82; spl. asst. U.S. atty., chief appellate divsn. Dept. Justice, Cleve., 1982, spl. asst. U.S. atty., 1982-85; prof. law Cleve. State U., 1982-94, assoc. dean faculty and adminstrn., 1991-94. Lectr. in law, trial practice Case Western Res. U., Cleve., 1979-82; vis. scholar Stanford U. Coll. Law, 1987; vis. prof. Comenius U., Bratislava, Czechoslovakia, 1991, Charles U., Prague, Czechoslovakia, 1991. Chair O.K. Hoover Scholarship com. Bapt. Ch., 1987-89; trustee Coll. of Wooster, Ohio, 1991-97, 2000—. Mem. ABA, Nat. Bar Assn. Office: 801 W Superior Ave Cleveland OH 44113-1838

OLIVER, SUSAN M. air transportation executive; b. Des Moines, Iowa, July 6, 1947; married; 3 children. BS, George Washington U., 1970; JD, U. Denver, 1980. Atty. Kempell, Huffman and Ginder, 1983—84; asst. counsel Wein Airlines, 1984—85; labor rels. cons. City of Reno, 1985—86; counsel employee rels. Am. Airlines, 1986—90, mng. dir. flight svcs., 1990—96, mng. dir. strategic planning, 1996—97, v.p. employee rels., 1997—2000, sr. v.p. human resources, 2000—. Office: AMR Corp 4333 Amon Carter Blvd Fort Worth TX 76155

OLIVER, THOMAS, hotel executive; m. Jane Oliver. Econs. degree, U. Pa. Sr. mgmt. positions Fed. Express, 1978-93, COO, exec. v.p. worldwide customer ops.; pres., CEO VoiceCom, Atlanta; chmn., CEO AudioFAX, Inc., Atlanta, Bass Hotels & Resorts, Atlanta. Mem/bd. dirs. Bass PLC Exec. Com. Bd. counselors Carter Ctr. Office: Bass Hotels & Resorts 3 Ravinia Dr Ste 2900 Atlanta GA 30346-2143

OLIVER, THORNAL GOODLOE, health care executive; b. Memphis, Aug. 26, 1934; s. John Oliver and Evelyn Doris (Goodloe) Mitchell; m. Pauline Reid, Oct. 1, 1959. B.S., Tenn. State U., Nashville, 1956; M.H.A., Washington U., St. Louis, 1973. Cert. nursing home adminstr., Mo. Asst. dir., King Meml. Hosp., Kansas City, Mo., 1973-75; evening mgr. Truman Med. Ctr., Kansas City, Mo., 1975-77; asst. adminstr. Mid-Am. Radiation Ctr. U. Kans. Coll. Health Sci., Kansas City, Kans., 1977-81; dir. CHS, Inc., Leawood, Kans., 1981-82; adminstr. Poplar Bluff Hosp., Mo., 1982-83; adminstr. The Benjamin F. Lee Health Ctr., Wilberforce, Ohio, 1983-86; asst. clin. prof. Dept. Community Medicine, Wright State U., Dayton, 1986-89; asst. patent adminstr. Munson Army Hosp., Ft. Leavenworth, Kans., 1987—; cons. Urban Health Assocs., Nashville, 1986-87, others. Contbr. articles to profl. jours. Served with U.S. Army, 1957-59, USAR, 1959-63. Fellow Am. Coll. Hosp. Adminstrs.; mem. Am. Hosp. Assn., Nat. Assn. Health Services Execs., Am. Med. Record Assn., Mo. League of Nursing Home Adminstrs. Home: 10641 N Grand Ave Kansas City MO 64155-1655 Office: Munson Army Hosp Fort Leavenworth KS 66027

OLIVER, TRAVIS, advertising agency executive; COO Alcone Mktg. Group, Irvine, Calif. Office: Alcone Mktg Group 13 Whatney Irvine CA 92618-2837

OLIVER, WILLIAM ALBERT, JR., paleontologist, researcher; b. Columbus, Ohio, June 26, 1926; s. William Albert and Mary-Maud (Thompson) O.; m. Johanna L. Kramer, Sept. 1, 1948 (dec.); children: Robert A., James A. BS, U. Ill., 1948; MA, Cornell U., 1950, PhD, 1952. From instr. to asst. prof. geology Brown U., Providence, 1952-57; rsch. geologist-paleontology U.S. Geol. Survey, Washington, 1957—70, research geologist-paleontology, 1971—93, emeritus scientist, 1993—; rsch. prof. geology George Washington U., 1970—71; rsch. assoc. dept. paleobiology U.S. Nat. Mus. Natural History-Smithsonian Instn., Washington, 1967—; mem. U.S. Nat. Com. on Geology, 1975-79, chmn., 1978-79; U.S. rep. Internat. Subcommn. on Devonian Stratigraphy, 1973-92; chmn., 1984-89; rsch. prof. in geology George Washington U., 1970—71. Contbr. articles to profl. jours. Recipient Meritorious Svc. award Interior Dept., 1993. Fellow AAAS (coun. 1971-73), Geol. Soc. Am.; mem. Paleontol. Soc. (councilor 1964-69, 73-76, editor Jour. 1964-69, pres. 1974-75), Palaeontol. Assn. (London), Palaeontol. Rsch. Inst. (trustee 1976-89, pres. 1984-86, Harris award, 1994), Am. Geol. Inst. (dir. 1974-77, v.p. 1975-76, pres. 1976-77), Internat. Assn. for Study of Fossil Cnidaria (coun. 1971-88, pres. 1983-88), Internat. Palaeontological Assn. (sec. gen. 1984-89). Home: 4203 McCain Ct Kensington MD 20895-1321 Office: Smithsonian Instn MRC 137 Natural History Bldg E-305 Washington DC 20013-7012

OLIVER, WILLIAM DONALD, orthodontist; b. Montreal, Dec. 14, 1945; s. Austen William and Margaret Kay (Donald) O. BS in Physics, Mt. Allison U., 1964; DDS, McGill U., 1968; MSD in Orthodontics, U. Pa., 1970. Pres. Orthodontic Enterprises Internat., Geneva, 1973-78; orthodontist Barrington,

RI, 1979—94; pvt. practice Everett, Wash., 1993—. Instr. Frankfurt Carolinium, 1972-74; witness Senate Armed Services Com., 1975. Inventor Piezo Electric Bone Healing; contbr. articles to profl. jours. Mem. Olympic Ski Team, Squaw Valley, 1960. Served with USAF, 1970-73. Recipient Carter Meml. award, 1964, M.T. Dohan prize, 1966. Mem. ADA, Can. Assn. Orthodontists, Am. Assn. Orthodontists, European Orthodontic Soc., Can. Dental Assn., Fedn. Internat. d'Automobile (qualified and registered mem.), Royal Ocean Racing Club. Republican. Office: 10812 19th Ave SE Everett WA 98208-5153 E-mail: braces@seanet.com.

OLIVER, WILLIAM JOHN, pediatrician, educator; b. Blackshear, Ga., Mar. 30, 1925; s. John Wesley and Katherine (Schalwig) O.; m. Marguerite Bertoni, May 28, 1949; children: Ralph Scott, Catherine, Susan. Student, Ga. Southwestern Coll., 1942-43, Mercer U., 1943-44; MD cum laude, U. Mich., 1948. Diplomate Am. Bd. Pediatrics (examiner), Subsplty. Bd. Pediatric Nephrology. Intern, resident U. Mich. Med. Center, 1948-53, dir. pediatric labs., 1959-67; pvt. practice medicine specializing in pediatrics Ann Arbor, Mich., 1953—; instr. dept. pediatrics U. Mich., 1953-56, asst. prof., 1956-61, assoc. prof., 1961-65, prof., 1965, chmn. dept. pediatrics, 1967-79; chief pediatric service Wayne County Hosp., 1958-61. Co-chmn. task force on recent advances of coordinating com. on continuing edn. and recertification Am. Bd. Pediats. and Am. Acad. Pediats., 1977-80; mem. task force for pediatric rev. edn. program, 1980-88; mem. com. program for renewal certification in pediat. Am. Bd. Pediat., 1989-91, mem. exam writing com. for cert. pediatric nephrology, 1989-93, PRCP pilot test com., 1993-96; mem. rev. and question writing com. for Pediat. in Rev. Am. Acad. Pediat., 1991-97; cons. U. Riyadh, Saudi Arabia, 1980, Rsch. Rev. Com. on Pediat., 1989; ednl. cons. dept. pediat. Stanford U. Hosps., 1991-98; mem. self-assessment program for Pediat. in Rev., 1990-98; investigator adaptation primitive So. Ams. Indians, 1976—, African Pygmies, 1987—, worldwide primitive socs., 1997. Author: Primitive Peoples Without Salt, 1998; mem. editl. bd. IRCS Jour. Med. Sci., 1975-90. Pres. Mich. Kidney Disease Found., 1969, Washtenaw County br. Mich. Childrens Aid Soc., 1964; trustee Ann Arbor Hands-On Mus., 1983-88; pres. bd. trustees Perry Nursery Sch., Ann Arbor, 1989-90. With USNR, 1950-52. Fellow Am. Acad. Pediatrics (chmn. com. med. edn. 1974-80, chmn. council on pediatric edn. 1975-80, chmn. task force oversight of pediatric rev. and edn. program 1984-88, Clifford G. Grulee award 1979); mem. Soc. Pediatric Research, Midwest Soc. Pediatric Research (pres. 1968), Am. Soc. Nephrology, Assn. Med. Sch. Pediatric Dept. Chairmen (mem. council 1977-79), Soc. for Exptl. Biology and Medicine, Am. Pediatric Soc., Alpha Omega Alpha, Gamma Sigma Epsilon. Home: 2892 Bay Ridge Dr Ann Arbor MI 48103-1704 Personal E-mail: wjoandmbo@aol.com.

OLIVERI, EUGENE ALFRED, gastroenterologist; b. N.Y.C., Apr. 30, 1937; children: Gregory, Lisa, Michelle. Student, Bklyn. Coll., 1954-56, 58-60; DO summa cum laude, Kansas City Coll., 1964; LHD, U. Health Scis., 2000; MSc, Trinity So. U., 2003. Diplomate Am. Bd. Internal Medicine, Am. Bd. Gastroenterology. Intern Detroit Osteo. Hosp., 1964-65; resident in internal medicine Botsford/Ziegler Hosps., 1965-67; fellowship in gastroenterology VA Hosp., East Orange, N.J., 1967-68; asst. dean Coll. Osteo. Medicine Mich. State U. Prof. dept. internal medicine sect. of gastroenterology Botsford Gen. Hosp., assoc. program dir. gastroenterology residency emeritus, mem., courtesy staff emeritus dept. of internal medicine Huron Valley Hosp. Trustee Pikeville (Ky.) Coll., 1998—, U. New Eng., Biddeford, Maine, 2001—. With U.S. Army, 1956—58. Recipient Highest Acad. Achievement award Mead-Johnson, 1964, Outstanding Alumni Achievement award U. for Health Scis., Coll. Osteo. Medicine, 1991, Dr. J.O. Watson Disting. Lecr. Ohio Osteo. Assn., 1991, Walter Patenge medal for humanitarian svc. MSU, 1999, Phillips medal Pub Svc., Ohio U., 2002; named Physician of Yr. Mich. chpt. Ileitis and Colitis Found., 1985, Botsford Profl. Staff, 1994. Fellow Am. Coll. Gastroenterology (master); mem. Am. Osteo. Assn. (pres. 1999-2000, trustee mem. bd.), Mich. Assn. Osteo. Physician and Surgeons (pres. 1991-92), Oakland County Osteo. Assn., Am. Coll. Osteo. Internists (pres. 1982-83, Disting. Svc. award 1982, Disting. Lectr. award 1983), Am. Coll. Gastroenterology, Am. Soc. Gastrointestinal Endoscopy, Am. Soc. Addiction Medicine, Am. Osteo. Found. (bd. dirs., pres. bd. dirs., chair com. on awards), Am. Soc. Parenteral and Enteral Nutrition, Mich. Osteo. Coll. Found. (chair, trustee, bd. dirs.), Crohn's and Colitis Found. Am. (Physician of Yr. 1991), Psi Sigma Alpha, Sigma Sigma Phi. Avocations: chef, health policy wonk. Home: 844 Old Milford Farms Milford MI 48381-3363 E-mail: docoli@aol.com.

OLIVERI, PAUL FRANCIS, lawyer; b. Far Rockaway, N.Y., Feb. 27, 1954; s. Alphonse J. and Rita (Gregorace) O.; m. Debra Lynn Malkin, Aug. 7, 1977; children: Jason, Evan, Rebecca. BA, NYU, 1976; JD, St. John's U., Queens, N.Y., 1978. Bar: N.Y. 1979, U.S. Dist. Ct. (ea. and so. dists.) N.Y. 1980. Assoc. Fuchsberg & Fuchsberg, N.Y.C., 1979-83; ptnr. Oliveri & Schwartz, N.Y.C., 1983—. Mem. N.Y. State Bar Assn., Am. Trial Lawyers Assn., N.Y. State Trial Lawyers Assn. (dir. emeritus). Avocations: music, coin collecting/numismatics. Office: Oliveri & Schwartz 30 Vesey St New York NY 10007-2914

OLIVERIO, MICHAEL ANGELO, II, insurance agent, state legislator; b. Fairmont, W.Va., Aug. 6, 1963; s. Michael Angelo and Julia Rose (Barber) O.; m. Melissa Kirk. BSBA, W.Va. U., 1985, MBA, 1986. Life ins. agt. Northwestern Mut. Life, Morgantown, W.Va., 1988—; mem. W.Va. State Senate, 1994—. Mem. W.Va. Ho. of Dels., 1992-94; chmn. Gov.'s Com. on Crime, Delinquency and Corrections, 1990-92; mem. Family Protection Svcs. Bd., 1990-92. Capt. U.S. Army, 1987. Recipient Nat. Quality award Nat. Assn. Life Underwriters, 1990, 92, 93, 95. Mem. W.Va. Jaycees, Am. Heart Assn. (chmn. Monongalia County Unit 1990). Democrat. Roman Catholic. Home: 95 Hartford St Morgantown WV 26501-4361 Office: Northwestern Mut Life 121 Simpson St Morgantown WV 26501-5921

OLIVERIO, PONZIO, protective services official, educator; b. San Diego, Calif., June 14, 1958; s. Ponzio and Harriet Jean Oliverio; m. Amy Amber Edsall, Nov. 19, 1983; children: Giulia Marie, Giana. BA in Humanities, Thomas Edison Coll., Trenton, N.J., 1992; JD, U. San Diego Sch. Law, 1996. Bar: Calif. 1997; cert. in hostage negotiations FBI, 2004. Dep. sheriff San Diego County Sheriff, 1985—; prof. Nat. U., San Diego, 1999—; adj. faculty San Diego Regional Police Acad., 2000—; prof. U. Phoenix, San Diego, 2003—; guest lectr., criminal procedure U. San Diego Sch. Law; instr. USN, Master-at-Arms Sch., San Diego. Uniform com. mem. San Diego Sheriff, 1993—95, process improvement team mem., 2003—, tng. officer. Columnist The Silver Star Holding Court, San Diego County Herald Cuff Links; co-author: (training manual) Crime-Free Mobile Housing Man.; publication in True Blue, Jimmy, 2004. Moot ct. judge U. San Diego Sch. Law, 2002—04; com. mem. State Bar Domestic Violence Com., Santa Ana, Calif.; facilitator Domestic Violence Restraining Order Clinic, San Diego, 1995—96. Recipient Letter of Appreciation, Calif. Dept. Corrections, 2000, Chula Vista, Calif. Police Dept., 2000, U.S. Border Patrol, 2001, Award of Exemplary Performance, San Diego Sheriff, 2000, Medal of Valor, 2001. Mem.: Statewide Calif. Coalition for Battered Women (assoc.), Dep. Sheriff's Assn. (assoc.), Fraternal Order of Police (assoc.). Conservative. Avocations: hunting, fishing. Home: 2208 Boulders Ct Alpine CA 91901 Personal E-mail: ponzio2@cox.net.

OLIVER-WARREN, MARY ELIZABETH, retired library science educator; b. Hamlet, N.C., Feb. 23, 1924; d. Washington and Carolyn Belle (Middlebrooks) Terry; m. David Oliver, 1947 (div. 1971); children: Donald D., Carolyn L.; m. Arthur Warren, Sept. 14, 1990 (dec. Feb. 1995). BS, Bluefield State U., 1948; MS, South Conn. State U., 1958; student, U. Conn., 1977. Cert. tchr., adminstr. and supr., Conn.; cert. pub. sch. substitute tchr., K-12, N.J. Media specialist Hartford (Conn.) Pub. Schs., 1952-86; with So. Conn. State U., New Haven, 1972—, asst. prof. Sch. Libr. Sci. and Instructional Tech., 1987-95, ret., 1995; substitute tchr. K-12 Windsor, Conn., 1999—. Mem. dept. curriculum com. So. Conn. State U., 1987-95, adj. prof., 1995—; cert. substitute tchr. Somerset County Pub. Schs., 1997—; cert. substitute tchr. Windsor, Conn. Sch. Sys., 1999-. Author: My Golden Moments, 1988, The Elementary School Media Center, 1990, Text Book Elementary School Media Center, 1991, I Must Fight Alone, 1991, (textbook) I Must Fight Alone, 1994. Mem. ALA, Conn. Ednl. Media Assn., Black Librs. Network N.J. Inc., Assn. Ret. Tchrs. Conn., Black and Hispanic Consortium, So. Conn. State U. Women's Assn., Cicuso Club (v.p.), Friends Club (v.p.), Delta Kappa Gamma, Alpha Kappa Alpha. Avocations: reading, music, piano, walking. Office: So Conn State U 501 Crescent St New Haven CT 06515-1330 Home: PO Box 871 Cairo GA 39828-0871

OLIVIER, DAVID M. pharmaceutical company executive; BS, U. San Francisco, 1965; MBA, U. Calif., Berkeley, 1967; grad. advanced mgmt. program, Harvard U. Pres. Monoject divsn. Sherwood Med. Co. (subs. Am. Home Products Corp. 1982—), 1979-84; pres. domestic divsn. Sherwood Med. Co., 1984-86; exec. v.p., COO Wyeth-Ayerst Internat., Inc., 1986-88, pres., 1988-96; sr. v.p. Am. Home Products Corp., Madison, N.J., 1996—. Office: American Home Products Corp 5 Giralda Farms Madison NJ 07940-1021

OLIVIER, KATHY RICKS, college basketball coach; b. Placentia, Calif. 1 child, Alexis. Student, Calif. State U., Fullerton; grad., U. Nev., 1982. Various coaching positions U. Nev., U. Calif.-Irvine, U. So. Calif., 1981-86; asst. coach UCLA Bruins, 1986; reached NCAA Sweet 16, 1991-92; head coach UCLA Bruins, 1993—. Achievements include finished 2nd in conf. (sch. record), 1997-98. Office: c/o Athletic Dept UCLA Women's Basketball PO Box 951361 Los Angeles CA 90095-1361

OLIVIERI JR. VINCENT RONALD, sound designer; b. Virginia Beach, Va., Aug. 6, 1976; s. Vincent Ronald and Patricia Hope Olivieri; m. Sarah Hodges Olivieri, May 30, 2004. BA, U. of Richmond, 1994—98; MFA, Yale U., 1998—2001. Resident sound designer Actors Theatre of Louisville, 2001—04; freelance sound designer Self-employed, Louisville, 1997—. Avocations: music, travel, gastronomy. Home: 369 W 150 St Apt 2A New York NY 10031

OLK, FREDERICK JAMES, county official, paralegal; b. Clintonville, Wis., Apr. 30, 1952; s. James Howard and Bernice Helen (Durben) O. Student, Inst. Comp. Polit.& Econ. Sys., 1973; BS in Liberal Arts, U. Wis. River Falls, 1976; cert., Wis. Sch. Real Estate, Milw., 1980. Notary pub., Ill. Libr. asst. U. Wis., Stevens Point and Oshkosh, 1977-80; contract libr. U.S. Dept. Justice, Oxford, Wis., 1980; editl. libr. The Chgo. Cath. newspaper Archdiocese of Chgo., 1980-89; tax. examiner Cook County, Chgo., 1990—. Congl. intern U.S. Ho. of Rep., Washington, 1973; sales rep. Waupaca (Wis.) Pub. Co., 1978-79; freelance paralegal, Chgo., 1988—; security guard, account mgr. Glenbrook Security Svcs., Glenview, Ill., 1988—; asst. reference libr. Cicero (Ill.) Pub. Libr., 1989; genealogy rschr. Lineage Search Assocs., Mechanicsville, Va., 1980-99; v.p. New World Credit Union, Chgo., 1981-86. Columnist Looking back Chgo. Cath., 1985-89. Tutor Mercy Home for Boys, Chgo., 1987—88; coord. Friends of Vatican Libr., Chgo., 1995—; mem. exec. bd. customer adv. coun. U.S. Postal Svc., Cicero, 1997—; Cicero rep. for Ill. 43d dist. Anti-Crime Adv. Bd., 1999—2001; precinct capt. Wis. and Ill. Rep. coms., 1973—; Rep. judge of election Cook County, 1980—; mem. Rome tour St. John Cantius Parish Resurrection Choir, 2001, sang at St. Peter's Basilica, 2001. Named adm. Nebr. Navy, State of Nebr., 1982, col. State of Ala., 1988, Internat. Citizen of Yr., Hutt River Province, Australia, 1995; recipient Legion of Merit Rep. Nat. Com., 1997, Order of the Arrow, Boy Scouts Am., 1971. Mem. Am. Soc. Notaries (life, chmn. govt. rels. 1984-85), Nat. Assn. Investigative Specialists, Am. Legion (life), Amtrak Hist. Soc. (asst. archivist 1996—), Chgo. Geneal. Soc. (life, bd. dirs. 1988-90), 20th Century R.R. Club (sec. 1994-98, Century Club 1996, dir. 1998-2004), KC (del. archdiocesan pastoral coun. 1996—). Avocations: rail travel, genealogy, reading, music, stamp collecting/philately. Home: 845 Busse Hwy Unit 202 Park Ridge IL 60068 Office: Cook County Clk 118 N Clark St Ste 434 Chicago IL 60602-1382

OLKIN, INGRAM, statistician, educator; b. Waterbury, Conn., July 23, 1924; s. Julius and Caroline Olkin; m. Anita Mankin, May 19, 1945; children: Vivian Louise, Rhoda Joyce, Julia Ann Meza. BS, BCNY, 1947; MA, Columbia U., 1947; PhD, U. N.C., 1951; DSc (hon.), DeMontfort U., Leicester, Eng., 1997. Asst. to assoc. prof. math. Mich. State U., East Lansing, 1951—60; prof., math., chair dept. stats. U. Minn., Mpls., 1960—61; prof. stats. and edn. Stanford U., Palo Alto, Calif., 1961—, chair dept. stats., 1973—76. Bd. trustees Nat. Inst. Statis. Scis., Research Triangle Park, NC. Co-author: Statistical Methods for Meta-analysis, 1985, Inequalities, 1979, Probability Models, 1980. 1st lt. Air Corps U.S. Army, 1943—46. Recipient Wilks medal, Am. Statis. Assn., Washington, 1992; grantee Lady David fellow, 1984; Guggenheim fellow, 1995, Fulbright fellow, 1979, Alexander von Humboldt fellow, 1997. Fellow: Inst. Am. Stats. (pres.). Avocations: music, hiking, travel. Home: 950 Lathrop Pl Stanford CA 94305 Office: Stanford U Dept Stats Stanford CA 94305 E-mail: iolkin@stat.stanford.edu.

OLKINETZKY, SAM, artist, retired museum director and educator; b. N.Y.C., Nov. 22, 1919; s. Isidor and Jennie O.; m. Sammie Lee Sturdevant, Dec. 20, 1959; children: Jov Shan, Tova Shana. BA, Bklyn. Coll., 1942; postgrad., Inst. Fine Arts, N.Y. U., 1946-47. Asst. prof. art and humanities Okla. A&M U., Stillwater, 1947-57; vis. asst. prof. art U. Okla., Norman, 1957-58; assoc. prof. art Mus. of Art, 1959—; dir. Mus. Art U. Okla., Norman, 1959-83. Vis. prof. art and humanities U. Ark., Fayetteville, 1962-63, 67-68, Langston (Okla.) U., 1969-70; art cons. Kerr-McGee Industries, Inc.; advisor State of Okla. Visual Arts; mem. State Art Collection Com.; Mem. Norman Arts and Humanities Council One-man exhbns. include Arts Place II, Okla. Art Ctr., Firehouse Art Ctr., Norman, 1989; other exhbns. include Mus. Non-Objective Art, N.Y.C., Mus. Modern Art, N.Y.C.; 50-yr. Retrospective Exhbn., 1942-92, Norick Art Ctr., Oklahoma City, 1992; represented in permanent collections Philbrook Art Ctr., Tulsa, Okla. Art Ctr., Mus. Art. U. Okla., Philbrook Art Mus., Tulsa, Oklahoma City Mus. of Art. Served with USAAF, 1942-45. Recipient Gov.'s Art award, 1981. Mem. Okla. Museums Assn. (pres. 1978-79), Internat. Council Museums, Mountain-Plains Museums Assn., Am. Assn. Museums, Art Mus. Assn.

OLLAYOS, CLARE M. chiropractor; b. Elgin, Ill., Nov. 18, 1954; d. Robert W. and Margaret Irene (Knight) O.; m. Scott R. Fladland, Feb. 15, 1992. Student, Smith Coll., 1972-74; BS summa cum laude, Boston U., 1977; BS in Human Biology, Nat. Coll. Chiropractic, 1985, D of Chiropractic, 1987. Cert. acupuncturist Nat. Coll. Chiropractic; advanced cert. spine treatment of CAD injuries Rsch. Inst. San Diego; lic. chiropractic physician Ill., Mass. Instr. ballet Lisa Boehm Sch. of the Ballet, Elgin, 1975, 79-84; motor coordination remediation therapist Landmark Sch., Pride's Crossing, Mass., 1979, Summit Sch., Dundee, Ill., 1979-82; pvt. practice Elgin, 1988—. Lectr. in field. Soloist Lisa Boehm Ballet Theatre Nutcracker Ballet, 1970-76. Trustee Elgin C.C., 1995—, vice chmn., 1998—, chmn. bd. trustees, 2001—, cmty. chmn. Art a la Carte for grand opening of Visual and Performing Arts Ctr., 1993—94, mem. 50th Anniversary Task Force, chmn. opening event, 1999; mem., co-chair capital campaign Elgin C.C. Found., 1994—95; mem. Elgin Cultural Arts Commn., 1991—98, chmn., 1993—95, founder, chmn. Recognition Night, 1995—98; chmn. Smithsonian Midwest Region Sculpture Restoration and Preservation Conf., 1997; presenter Midwest Mus. Conf., Chgo., 1993; bd. dirs. Elgin Pub. Mus., 1993—. Named Outstanding Young Woman of Elgin, Elgin Jr. Woman's Club, 1986, Star Vol. of Yr., YWCA, 2001; recipient Margaret Hillis award for the arts, 1989, Elgin Image award, Elgin Image Adv. Commn., 1994, Spl. Recognition award, Elgin Cultural Arts Commn., 1998, Mayor's award for preservation, City of Elgin, 2000. Mem.: Ill. C.C. Coll. Trustees Assn. (govt. rels. com. 1996—, regional vice chmn. 1997—98, awards com. 1998—99, chmn. elect 1999—2000, state awards chmn. 2000, 2001), Assn. Cmty. Coll. Trustees (voting del. 1996—97, presenter), Fox Valley Chiropractic Coun., Ill. Chiropractic Soc., Am. Chiropractic Assn., Altrusa Internat. Avocations: ballet, reading, egyptology. Home and Office: 1161 Florimond Dr Elgin IL 60123 E-mail: claremollayos@juno.com.

OLLE, DAVID ARTHUR, writer, researcher; m. Cecilia de San Juan; children: Andrea Lee de San Juan Olle, Priscilla de San Juan Olle. BS in Agr., Ohio State U., 1962; MS in Biochemistry, Fairleigh Dickinson U., 1975. Cert. pub. schs. tchr. U. Mass., 1990. Animal nutritionist Diamond Shamrock Chem. Co., Harrison, NJ, 1968—76; owner/mgr. New Eng. Bioresearch Labs, Guilford, Vt., 1977—80; animal sci. cons. Sao Jose dos Campos, Brazil, 1980—89; med. writer Eastshire Comm., Guilford, Vt., 1991—. Adj. instr. chemistry C.C. Vt., Brattleboro, 1991—94. Mem.: New Eng. Sci. Writers, Am. Med. Writers Assn. (pres. 1999—2000). Achievements include patents for a new animal growth promotant; first to perform large scale synthesis of pheromones for use against crop pests. Avocations: travel, gardening, reading, web site design. Home: 3296 Sweet Pond Rd Guilford VT 05301-8360 Office Phone: 802-254-3899. Personal E-mail: dolle@sover.net.

OLLER, WILLIAM MAXWELL, retired energy company executive, retired naval officer; b. Lancaster, Pa., Apr. 7, 1924; s. John Secrist and Mabel Margaret (Coffman) O.; m. Doris Seitz Greenleaf, June 15, 1946; children: Arthur G., J. Richard. BS, U.S. Naval Acad., 1946; MBA, George Washington U., 1960. Commd. ensign USN, 1946, advanced through grades to rear adm., 1972; svc. in Samoa, Philippines and Italy; exec. officer Naval Supply Ctr., Newport, R.I., 1966-67, Ships Parts Control Ctr., Mechanicsburg, Pa., 1970-72; comdr. Def. Fuel Supply Ctr., Alexandria, Va., 1972-76; comdg. officer Naval Supply Ctr., Norfolk, Va., 1976-77; gen. mgr. corp. supply and distbn. Champlin Petroleum Co., Houston, 1977-79, Ft. Worth, 1979-81; sr. v.p. Petroleum Ops. and Support Svcs., Inc., New Orleans, 1981-82, pres., 1982-84; spl. asst. to pres., CEO Kaneb Svcs., Inc., Houston, 1984-85; exec. v.p. Tex. Ea. Products Pipeline Co., Houston, 1986-90. Pres. Am. Leadership Forum, Houston, 1986. Decorated Legion of Merit with gold star, Meritorious Svc. medal with gold star, Joint Svc. Commendation medal. Mem. River Creek Club. Home: 46847 Grissom St Sterling VA 20165-3592

OLLEY, ROBERT EDWARD, economist, educator; b. Vendun, Que., Can., Apr. 16, 1933; s. Edwin Henry and Elizabeth (Reed) O.; m. Shirley Ann Dahl, Jan. 19, 1957; children— Elizabeth Anne, George Steven, Susan Catherine, Maureen Carolyn BA, Carleton U., Can., 1960; MA, Queen's U., Can., 1961, PhD in Econs., 1969. Vis. asst. prof. Queen's U., Kingston, Canada, 1967-68; asst. prof. econs. U. Sask., Saskatoon, Canada, 1963-67, 68-69, assoc. prof., 1969-71, 73-75, prof., 1975-93, prof. emeritus, 1993—; pres. Gen. Econs. Ltd., 1993—. Dir. rsch. Royal Commn. on Consumer Problems and Inflation, 1967-68, econ. advisor Bell Can., Montreal, Que., 1971-73, 78-79, Can. Telecom. Carriers Assn., 1978-85, Sask. Power Corp., 1980-83; econ. advisor AT&T, 1980-90, Waste Mgmt., Inc., 1990-92, SaskTel, 1989-93; chmn. adv. com. on consumer stds. Stds. Coun. Can., 1992-93; Can. rep. to ISO/COPOLCO, Geneva, 1992-93. Author, editor: Consumer Product Testing, 1979, Consumer Product Testing II, 1981, Consumer Credit in Canada, 1966, Economics of the Public Firm: Regulation, Rates, Costs, Productivity Analysis, 1983, Total Factor Productivity of Canadian Telecommunications, 1984; Consumer Reps. Conf. Procs., 1st-4th, 1982-91. Bd. dirs. Can. Found. for Econ. Edn., 1974-82, Can. Gen. Stds. Bd., 1977-81; v.p. Niagara-on-the-Lake Hosp. Found., 2000-03, bd. dirs., 1998-. Recipient Her Magesty The Queen Silver Jubilee medal, 1977, Can.'s Jean P. Carriere Exptl. Contbr. Vol. Standardization award, 1995. Mem. Royal Econ. History Soc., Royal Econs. Assn., Econ. History Assn., Am. Econ. Assn., Can. Econ. Assn., Consumers Assn. Can. (v.p. 1967-75, chmn. 1975-77), Can. Stds. Assn. (dir., mem. exec. com. 1971-93, vice chmn. 1985-87, chmn. 1987-89, Award of Merit 1995), Consumer's Assn. Found. Can. (v.p. 1989-95), Can. Comm. Rsch. Ctr. (dir. 1992-97), Internat. Telecom. Soc. (bd. dirs. 1986-2004), Shaw Guild, Niagara Hist. Soc. (bd. dirs. 1997-99), Niagara-on-the-Lake Golf Club (bd. dirs. 2001—, v.p. 2002—). Home and Office: PO Box 1040 374 Queen St Niagara-on-the-Lake ON Canada L0S 1J0 E-mail: olley@niagara.com.

OLLIE, PEARL LYNN, artist, singer, scriptwriter; b. Highland Park, Mich., Oct. 15, 1953; d. Sam and Estelle Theresa Ollie; m. Christopher John Keyes, Nov. 29, 1975 (div. Nov. 1978); 1 child, Shane Michael Fiondella. Student, Henry Ford C.C., Dearborn, Mich., 1988-89, Soc. Arts and Crafts Coll., 1971-74, Ctr. for Creative Study, 1980-81. Tchr. ceramics Detroit Head Start, Mt. Zion, Mich., 1973; logo designer, platemaker, printer and painter Island Art Ctr., St. Simons Island, Ga., 1976-79; sec., receptionist High Performance Tube Inc., St. Simons Island, 1976-79; personal legal sec. State Senator Bill Littlefield, St. Simons Island, 1979; art coord., booking agt. Club Savoy Tivoli, San Francisco, 1979; tchr. art Redmond Hall, Skamokawa, Wash., 1980; artist Hollywood Costumes, Dearborn, 1980-90; account mgr. ins. Dr. Sheryl A. Ollie, Lynn, Mass., 1990; staff artist, acting, costumes Creative Currents, Ferndale, Mich., 1990—; art tchr. Art in Nahant, Mass., 1991-97. Make-up artist Paramount Costumes (was Hollywood Costumes), Dearborn; art tchr. music St. Lukes Montessori Sch., Detroit; artist Mich. Art and Design, Detroit, Dearborn Awnings, Lincoln Park, Mich.; instr. Aups, Provence, France, 1997. Make-up artist TV commls. and shows, movies; commd. portrait artist, illustrator; guest TV program All Star Kids. Co-pres. Nahant PTO, Johnson Sch., 1991-92; tchr. 8th grade religious edn.; vocalist area ch. chorus; choir dir. St. Anselms; vocal instr. Axis Music Musicians Inst.; instr. art, music and drama Hope of Detroit Acad. Roman Catholic. Avocations: paint, sculpting, singing, writing, piano. Home and Office: 480 Newfound Harbor Dr Merritt Island FL 32952-2627

OLLINGER, W. JAMES, lawyer; b. Kittanning, Pa., Apr. 5, 1943; s. William James and Margaret Elizabeth (Reid) Ollinger; m. Susan Louise Gerspacher, Oct. 20, 1979; children: Mary Rebecca, David James. BA, Capital U., Columbus, Ohio, 1966; JD, Case Western Res. U., 1968. Bar: Ohio 1968, US Dist Ct (no dist) Ohio 1971. Ptnr. Baker & Hostetler, Cleve., 1968—. Mem. Bentleyville Village Coun., Ohio, 1990—93; mayor Bentleyville, 1997—99. Mem.: Order of Coif, Phi Delta Phi. Office: Baker & Hostetler 3200 Nat City Ctr 1900 E 9th St Ste 3200 Cleveland OH 44114-3475 E-mail: jollinger@bakerlaw.com.

OLMAN, MARYELLEN, human resources administrator; b. Grand Rapids, Mich., Dec. 24, 1946; d. Norman Adolph and Mary Irene (McCarthy) O.; m. Richard Isaac Fine, Nov. 25, 1982; 1 child, Victoria Elizabeth. BA in Cmty. Svc., Mich. State U., 1968. Legis. rschr. to Hon. Gerald R. Ford, U.S. Ho. of Reps., 1969-71, spl. asst. to Hon. Jack F. Kemp, 1971-74; personnel analyst L.A. City Housing Authority, 1975-78; profl. placement rep. Gen. Telephone of Calif., Santa Monica, 1978-81, mgmt. staffing adminstr., 1981-84; human resource adminstr. Law Offices Richard I. Fine & Assocs., 1985—. Mem. Founders Cir., L.A. Music Ctr., L.A. World Affairs Coun., Chmn.'s Cir., L.A. Art Mus., Mus. Contemporary Art. Republican. Home: 12097 Summit Cir Beverly Hills CA 90210-1376

OLMOS, EDWARD JAMES, actor; b. L.A., Feb. 24, 1947; m. Kaija Keel, 1972 (div.); m. Lorraine Bracco, Jan. 28, 1994 (div.); 2 children. AA in Sociology, East Los Angeles City Coll.; postgrad., Calif. State U., L.A.; hon. degree, U. Colo., Whittier Coll., Calif. State U., Fresno, Occidental Coll., Film Inst., Hollywood, Calif. Exec. dir. Lives in Hazard Ednl. Project, nat. gang prevention program. Performed in exptl. theater, L.A.; actor (play) Zoot Suit (Tony nominee, Los Angeles Drama Critics Circle award, Theatre World award), Broadway and Los Angeles, 1978-80; actor, producer film The Ballad of Gregorio Cortez, 1982, Triumph of the Spirit, 1989; actor, co-producer film Stand and Deliver, 1988 (nominee best actor Acad. Awards 1988); actor films Wolfen, 1981, Zoot Suit, 1981, Blade Runner, 1982, (also assoc. prodr., composer, music adapter) The Ballad of Gregorio Cortez, 1983, Saving Grace, 1986 (also prodr.) Stand and Deliver, 1988, Triumph of the Spirit, 1989, Talent for the Game, 1991, (also dir., prodr.) American Me, 1992, A Million to Juan, 1994, My Family, 1995, Caught, 1996, Selena, 1997, Death in Granada, 1997, The Wonderful Ice Cream Suit, 1998, The Wall, 1998, Gossip, 1999, (voice) The Road to El Dorado, 2000, Gossip, 2000, Jack and Marilyn, 2002; (TV series) Miami Vice, 1984-89 (Emmy award for best supporting actor in drama series 1985, Golden Globe award 1986); (TV miniseries) The Fortunate Pilgrim, 1988, Menendez: A Killing in Beverly Hills, 1994, The Burning Season, 1995 (Golden Globe award for Best Supporting Actor in a TV Movie, Miniseries or Series 1994), Mirage, 1995, Slave of Dreams, 1995, Roosters, 1995, American Family, 2002, Battlestar Galactica, 2003, The Batman, 2004; (TV movies) The Pricess and the Barrio Boy, 2000, The Judge, 2001, In the Time of the Butterflies, 2001; star ABC miniseries Dead Man's Walk (prequel to Lonesome Dove), 1996; co-star TV movie 12 Angry Men, 1997; prodr., dir. (TV documentary) Lives in Hazard, 1994, The Limbic Region, 1995. U.S. goodwill amb. UNICEF; nat. spokesman for voter registration, Juvenile Diabetes Found., AIDS Awareness Found.; bd. dirs. Heal L.A., Recruiting New Tchrs., 20th Century Fund, UCLA Sch. Film and Theater, Miami

Children's Hosp., L.A. Children's Hosp., Nat. Coun. on Adoption, Children's Action Netowrk, Hollywood Supports, Nat. Hispanic U., Plaza del Raza, Whittier Coll.; spkr. at numerous chs., charities and juvenile instns. throughout U.S. Address: Olmos Productions 18034 Ventura Blvd Ste 288 Encino CA 91316-3516 Office: The Artists Agency Ste 301 1180 S Beverly Dr Los Angeles CA 90035-1154*

OLMSTEAD, CECIL JAY, lawyer; b. Jacksonville, Fla., Oct. 15, 1920; s. Cecil Jay Sr. and Bessie (Irby) O.; m. Frances Hughes; children: Cecil Jay III, Frank Hughes, Jane Olmstead Murphy, Amy Olmstead Vanecek. BA, U. Ga., 1950, LLB, 1951; Sterling Grad. fellow, Yale Law Sch., 1951-52; LLD (hon.), U. Hull, Eng., 1978. Bar: Ga. 1950, U.S. Supreme Ct 1964, D.C. 1978. Asst. to legal adviser Dept. State, counsel Mut. Security Agy., counsel Hoover Commn. on Orgn. Exec. Br. of Govt., 1952-55; prof. N.Y. U. Sch. Law, 1953-61; dir. Inter-Am. Law Inst., 1958-61, adj. prof. law, 1961-69; atty. Texaco, Inc., N.Y.C., 1961-62, asst. to chmn. bd., 1962-70, v.p., asst. to chmn. bd., 1970, v.p., asst. to pres., 1970-71, v.p., asst. to chief exec. officer, 1971-73, exec. dept., v.p., 1973-80; mem. firm Steptoe & Johnson, Washington, 1980—. Wang Disting. vis. prof. St. Johns U., 1987-90; mem. adv. panel on internat. law to sec. state; adv. com. law of sea State Dept.; also adv. com. transnat. enterprise; U.S. del. UN Com. on Law of Sea, 1972-73; U.S. del. UN Conf. on Law of Sea, 1974-76; Eisenhower lectr. Nat. War Coll., 1973; mem. U.S. del. UN Conf. on Code of Conduct for Transnat. Corps., ann. 1984-90; mem. World Bank's panel of conciliatiors of the Internat. Ctr. for Settlement of Investment Disputes, 1988-95; vis. fellow All Souls Coll., Oxford U., 1988; vis. scholar Yale Law Sch., 1990-91. With USAF, 1943-46, 8th and 20th Air Forces. ETO, PTO. Recipient Gold medal City of Brussels (Belgium, 1973, Gold medal City of Paris (France), 1984; named Commdr. Brit. Empire (hon.), 1990. Mem. Internat. Law Assn. (pres. Am. br. 1966-73, pres. 1972-75, vice chmn. exec. coun. 1975-86, chmn. exec. coun. 1986-88, Disting. Svc. award2004), Am. Law Inst. (assoc. reporter Restatement of the Fgn. Rels. Law of the U.S., 1st edit. 1964, advisor 3d edit.), Coun. on Fgn. Rels., Washington Inst. Fgn. Affairs, Nat. Fgn. Trade Coun. (dir. 2004), Am. Coun. on Germany (hon. dir.), Coun. on Ocean Law (dir.), Knickerbocker Club, Yale Club, Fairfield County Hunt Club (Westport), Cosmos Club (Washington), Order of Coif, Phi Beta Kappa. Home: 4 Sprucewood Ln Westport CT 06880-4021 Office: 1330 Connecticut Ave NW Washington DC 20036-1704

OLMSTEAD, LUCINDA SUE, English professor; b. Gloversville, N.Y., July 1, 1941; d. Albert Pellegrino and Lois Beverly Harding; m. Robert Lloyd Olmstead, Dec. 23, 1964; children: Kimberly Joy Woloszyn, Kelly Olmstead Masline. BA, Barrington (R.I.) Coll., 1963; MA, SUNY, Albany, N.Y., 1990. Cert. tchr. N.Y. State Tchr. Certification Assn., 1990. Instr. English Gloversville (N.Y.) Sch. Dist., 1963—64, Johnstown (N.Y.) Sch. Dist., 1967—68; instr. English and history Liverpool (N.Y.) Sch. Dist., 1964—66; substitute tchr. Capital Region Schs., NY, 1968—90; prof. English Bryant & Stratton Coll., Albany, NY, 2001—. Chmn. English dept. Bryant & Stratton Coll., 2001—, chmn. comm. com., 2001—, advisor Drama Club, 2001—. Musician: (plays) Lucinda Sings Broadway; contbr. columns in newspapers. Mem. bd. edn. Gloversville Schs.; mem. adv. coun. N.Y. State Assembly, Gloversville, 1985—86. Mem.: Nat. Coun. Tchrs. English (life). Avocations: singing, music, acting, writing. Home: 233 Shaker Park Dr Loudonville NY 12211 Office: Bryant & Stratton College 1259 Central Avenue Albany NY 12205 Office Phone: 518-437-1802. Business E-Mail: olmstead.lucinda@al.bryantstratton.edu.

OLMSTEAD, MARJORIE ANN, physics educator; b. Glen Ridge, N.J., Aug. 18, 1958; d. Blair E. and Elizabeth (Dempwolf) Olmstead. BA in Physics, Swarthmore Coll., 1979; MA in Physics, U. Calif., Berkeley, 1982, PhD, 1985. Rsch. staff Palo Alto (Calif.) Rsch. Ctr. Xerox Corp., 1985-86; asst. prof. physics U. Calif., Berkeley, 1986-90, U. Wash., Seattle, 1991-93, assoc. prof., 1993-97, prof., 1997—. Prin. investigator sci. materials divsn. Lawrence Berkeley Lab., 1988—93. Contbr. articles to profl. jours. Named Presdl. Young Investigator, NSF, 1987; recipient Devel. award, IBM, 1986, 1987, Rsch. award, A. von Humboldt Found., 2000. Fellow: Am. Phys. Soc. (chair com. on status of women in physics 1999, Maria Goeppart-Mayer award 1996), Am. Vacuum Soc. (Peter Mark Meml. award 1994); mem.: Assn. Women in Sci., Sigma Xi, Phi Beta Kappa. Office: U Washington Dept Physics PO Box 351560 Seattle WA 98195-1560 Office Phone: 206-685-3031. E-mail: olmstd@u.washington.edu.

OLMSTEAD, WILLIAM EDWARD, mathematics professor; b. San Antonio, June 2, 1936; s. William Harold and Gwendolyn (Littlefield) Olmstead; m. Adele Cross, Aug. 14, 1957 (div. 1967); children: William Harold, Randell Edward. BS, Rice U., 1959; MS, Northwestern U., 1962, PhD, 1963. Mem. rsch. staff S.W. Rsch. Inst., San Antonio, 1959—60; Sloan Found. postdoctoral fellow Johns Hopkins, 1963—64; prof. applied math. Northwestern U., Evanston, Ill., 1964—, chmn. dept. engrng. scis. and applied math., 1991—93. Vis. mem. Courant Inst. Math. Scis. NYU, 1967—68; faculty visitor U. Coll. London, 1973, Calif. Inst. Tech., 1987, 90; editor Options Prof. Newsletter, Spear Capital Mgmt., 2003—. Contbr. articles to profl. jours. Named Technol. Inst. Tchr. of Yr., 1980, Charles Deering McCormick prof., 1994—97; recipient Award for Tchg. Excellence, Northwestern Alumni Assn., 1993. Mem.: Am. Contract Bridge League (silver life master), Soc. Indsl. and Applied Math. (editl. bd. jour. 1998—), Am. Phys. Soc., Am. Math. Soc., Am. Acad. Mechanics, Soc. Engrng. Sci. (bd. dirs. 1998—2000), John Evans Club, Sigma Tau, Tau Beta Pi, Sigma Xi. Episcopalian. Home: 153 E Laurel Ave #203 Lake Forest IL 60045 Office: Northwestern U Dept Engrng Scis And Applie Evanston IL 60208-0001

OLMSTEAD-SAWYER, JEANETTE, pastor; b. Norwalk, Conn., Jan. 9, 1936; d. George Francis Olmstead and Sarah Mildred Hamilton-Olmstead; m. Eddie Lee Sawyer, Aug. 25, 1962; children: Gina Monet, Nancilee, Douglas Scott, Elizabeth LeeAnn, Michael Jason. BS, Ctrl. State Coll., 1958; MA, Bridgeport U., 1964; MDiv, Yale Divinity Sch., 1994; D of ministry, Hartford Seminary, 2001—05. Cert. Conn. Inst. Christian Religion. Sch. tchr. Norwalk Pub. Schools, Conn., 1958—83; adj. tchr. Conn. Inst. of Christian Religion, 1990—2003; founder of Outreach Living Bread of Life Evangelistic Ministries, 1990—; assoc. min. Calvary Bapt. Ch., Norwalk, Conn., 1990—94; pastor First Congregational Ch., United Ch. of Christ, 1994—. Moderator Fairfield West Assn., Conn., 1998—99; chmn. Fairfield Cty. Adv. Bd., Conn., 1996—99; pres. Norwalk Interfaith Clergy Assn., 1999—2001, Interdenominational Ministers Fellowship, 2002—. Author: (chemistry card game) Periodic Table Rummy, 1980 (celebration of excellence, 1987). Councilwoman at large Norwalk Common Coun., 2001—; org. Mothers Against Violence, 1997; chaplain Norwalk Emergency Shelter, 1990—. Recipient Black Women's award, Norwalk, Conn., 1991, Rose of Sharon, 2002. Mem.: Interdenominational Ministries Fellowship (pres. 1992—), Norwalk Interfaith Clergy Assn. (pres. 1994—). Democrat. United Ch. Of Christ. Achievements include First woman ordained at Calvary Bapt. Ch., first black pastor at First Congregational Ch., Norwalk, Conn. Avocations: golf, tennis, walking, football, jazz. Home: 5 Margaret St Norwalk CT 06851 Office: First Congregational Church Park/Lewis St Norwalk CT 06851 Office Phone: 203-847-1568.

OLMSTED, DAVID JOHN, capital management company executive; b. Kearney, N.J., Aug. 18, 1939; s. Lawrence Joseph and Jane Veronica (Carberry) O.; m. Carole Colacurcio, June 29, 1962 (div. May 1974); children: David John, Kimberly Carole; m. Carol Ann Sunderlin, Oct. 12, 1974; children: Lauren Caryl, Kristy Lynne. BS in Mgmt., Fairleigh Dickinson U., 1968, postgrad., 1968-70. V.p. Midlantic Nat. Bank/Citizens, Englewood, N.J., 1968-77; exec. v.p. Trident Investment Mgmt. Co., Paramus, N.J., 1977-82; v.p. Donaldson, Lufkin & Jenrette, N.Y.C., 1982-84; pres. Centurion Capital Mgmt. Co., Nutley, N.J., 1984—. Sec. GT USA, Nutley, 1985—; pres. CCM Comm., Nutley, 1997—, Digital Creek Publ., Inc., 1999—. Chmn. Vincent Meth. Ch. Commn., Nutley, 1982-90; v.p. Nutley Recreation Soccer League, 1980-90, Nutley Recreation Basketball League, 1986-90; head coach Nutley Twp. Girls Softball Team, 1988-90; chmn. Essex coun. Boy Scouts Am., 1989-90. With USMC, 1958-61. Fellow Fin. Analysts Fedn., N.Y.C., 1976; named to United Way Hall of Fame, Newark, 1973, benefactor Boy Scouts Am., Newark, 1990. Mem. Assn. for Investment Mgmt., Paramus C. of C., Nutley Lions Club. Republican. Methodist. Avocations: coin-stamp-baseball card collecting, softball, volleyball, basketball. Home: 1 11th St Jamesburg NJ 08831

OLMSTED, JERAULD LOCKWOOD, telephone company executive; b. Des Moines, Aug. 26, 1938; s. George Hamden and Virginia (Camp) O.; m. Mary Karen Autenrieth, June 20, 1962 (div. Dec. 1986); children: Scott H., Victoria L., Jerauld; m. Gisele A. Child, June 17, 1988. BS, Iowa State U., 1961; MBA, George Washington U., 1979; Cert. mgmt. accountant. Vice-pres. First Nat. Bank of Washington, 1969; v.p., dir. Intermediate Credit Corp., 1969-73, Internat. Gen. Industries, Inc., 1974-79, pres., dir., 1980-82, IB Credit Corp., 1982-85, N.Am. Communications, Inc., Bethesda, Md., 1985—. Sr. v.p., dir. Internat. Bank, 1978-85. Bd. govs. Iowa State U. Found., 1980—; chmn. corporate adv. bd. div. arts and humanities U. Md., 1982—; sec.-treas. George Olmsted Found., 1970— . Served with U.S. Army, 1961-63. Decorated Knight of Malta, Order of St. John Mem. Fin. Execs. Inst., Mensa, Soc. Cincinnati, Met. Club, Georgetown Club, Bethesda Country Club, Beta Alpha Psi., Beta Gamma Sigma. Republican. Episcopalian. Home and Office: 7735 Arrowood Ct Bethesda MD 20817-2821 Office Phone: 301-365-7225.

OLMSTED, THOMAS JAMES, archbishop; b. Oketo, Kans., Jan. 21, 1947; BS in Philosophy, St. Thomas Sem. Coll., 1969; MA in Theology, 1977, PhD in Canon Law, 1979. Ordained priest Roman Cath. Diocese, 1973, ordained bishop Roman Cath. Diocese, 1999. Assoc. pastor Cathedral of Risen Christ, Lincoln, Nebr., 1973—76; asst. Secretariat of State of Holy See Pontifical N.Am. Coll., Rome, 1979—88; pastor St. Vincent de Paul Parish, Seward, Nebr., 1989—93; dean personal formation Pontifical Coll. Josephinum, Columbus, Ohio, 1993—97, rector, 1997—99; coadjutor bishop Diocese of Wichita, Kans., 1999—2001, bishop, 2001—03, Roman Cath. Diocese Phoenix, 2003—. Com. mem. U.S. Conf. Cath. Bishops, 1999—; mem. adminstrv. com. U.S. Bishops, mem. com. consecrated life; bd.dir. Cath. Legal Immigration Network. Office: Diocese of Phoenix 400 East Monroe St Phoenix AZ 85004-2336*

OLNESS, KAREN NORMA, pediatrics and international health educator; b. Rushford, Minn., Aug. 28, 1936; d. Norman Theodore and Karen Agnes (Gunderson) O.; m. Hakon Daniel Torjesen, 1962. BA, U. Minn., 1958, BS, MD, 1961. Diplomate Am. Bd. Pediat., Am. Bd. Med. Hypnosis. Intern Harbor Gen. Hosp., Torrance, Calif.; resident Nat. Children's Hosp. Med. Ctr., Washington; asst. prof. George Washington U., Washington, 1970-74; assoc. prof. U. Minn., Mpls., 1974-87; prof. pediat., family medicine and internat. health Case Western Res. U., Cleve., 1987—. Named Outstanding Woman Physician, Minn. Assn. Women Physicians, 1987; recipient Christopherson award Am. Acad. Pediat., 1998, Aldrich award, Am. Acad. Pediat., 1999, Ann. award Soc. Devel. and Behavioral Pediat., 2003; named to Cleve. Med. Hall of Fame, 2000. Fellow Am. Acad. Pediat. (chair internat. health sect. 2001), Am. Acad. Family Physicians, Am. Soc. Clin. Hypnosis (pres. 1984-86), Soc. Clin. and Exptl. Hypnosis (pres. 1991-93); mem. Soc. for Devel. and Behavioral Pediat. (pres. 1991-92), Northwestern Pediat. Soc. (pres. 1977), Internat. Hypnosis Soc. (pres. 2003—). Office: Case Western Res U 11100 Euclid Ave Cleveland OH 44106-6038 Office Phone: 216-368-4368. Business E-Mail: kno@case.edu.

OLNEY, JAMES, English language educator; b. Marathon, Iowa, July 12, 1933; s. Norris G. and Doris B. (Hawk) L.; children: Nathan, Marina Gobnait. BA, U. Iowa, 1955; MA, Columbia U., 1958, PhD, 1963. Asst. prof. Drake U., Des Moines, 1963-67; Fulbright lectr. Cuttington Coll., Liberia, 1967-69; prof. English N.C. Central U., Durham, 1970-83; Voorhies prof. English La. State U., Baton Rouge, 1983—. Vis. prof. Northwestern U., 1974, Amherst Coll., 1978—79. Author: Metaphors of Self, 1972, Tell Me Africa, 1973, the Rhizome & the Flower, 1980, The Language(s) of Poetry, 1993, Memory and Narrative, 1998 (Christian Gauss award 1999); editor: Autobiography, 1988; editor So. Rev., 1983—. Fellow NEH, 1975-76, Guggenheim Found., 1980-81, Nat. Humanities Ctr., Research Triangle Park, N.C., 1980-81 Mem. MLA (exec. coun. 1983-87), Am. Acad. Arts & Scis. Office: La State U Southern Review 43 Allen Hall Baton Rouge LA 70803-0001 Home: 8 Whistler Ct Irvine CA 92612

OLNEY, JOHN WILLIAM, psychiatry educator; b. Marathon, Iowa, Oct. 23, 1931; married, 1957; 3 children. BA, U. Iowa, 1957, MD, 1963. Diplomate Am. Bd. Psychiatry, Am. Bd. Neurology. Intern Kaiser Permanente Found., San Francisco, 1963-64; resident, 1964-68; from instr. to assoc. prof. psychiatry Washington U., St. Louis, 1968-77, prof. psychiatry and neuropathology Sch. Medicine, 1977—. NIMH biol. sci. trainee Washington U., 1966-68; asst. psychiatrist Barnes Hosp., 1968—; cons. psychiatrist Malcolm Bliss Mental Health Ctr., 1968—; elected to Inst. Medicine/NAS, 1996. Recipient Wakeman award Rsch. Neurosci., 1992; co-recipient Charles A. Dana award for Pioneering Achievements in Health, 1994. Mem. APA, Am. Assn Neuropathology, Soc. Neurosci. Assn. Rsch. Nervous & Mental Disorders, Psychiatric Rsch. Soc. Achievements include research in role of excitatory neurotoxins in disorders of the nervous system. Office: Washington U Dept Psychiatry Sch Med Saint Louis MO 63110

OLNEY, ROBERT C. diversified products manufacturing executive; b. Bklyn., Aug. 19, 1926; s. Herbert Mason and Martha L. (Otten) O.; m. Wanda G. Olney, July 17, 1948 (dec. 1988); children: Robert C. Jr., Thomas J., Douglas P.; m. Ann Waters Bell, Mar. 14, 1992. BA in Econs., Cornell U., 1946. With Chem. Bank, N.Y.C., 1946-48; various mgmt. positions 3M Co., from 1948; v.p., gen. mgr. 3M-Nat. Adv. Co., Bedford Pk., Ill., 1976-80; chmn., mng. dir. 3M UK plc, Bracknell, Eng., 1980-86; dir. Yale-Valor plc, Chiswick, London, Eng., 1986-91; chmn. Nutone Inc., Cin., 1987-91. Cons. Outdoor Consulting Inc., N.Y.C.; bd. dirs. Honeytree Inc., Mich. Mem. Greenville Country Club, Worshipful Co. of Upholders (London), Royal Automobile Club (London). Avocation: skiing. Home: PO Box 223 Montchanin DE 19710-0223 also: Oatlands Park 32 Lakeside Grange Weybridge Surrey England KT139ZE also: PO Box 1764 Avon CO 81620-1764

OLOFSON, TOM WILLIAM, computer executive; b. Oak Park, Ill., Oct. 10, 1941; s. Ragnar V. and Ingrid E. Olofson; m. Jeanne Hamilton, Aug. 20, 1960; children: Christopher, Scott. Various mgmt. positions Bell Telephone Co. of Pa., Pitts., 1963-67; sales mgr. Xerox Corp., Detroit, 1967-68, nat. account mgr. Rochester, N.Y., 1968, mgr. govt. planning, 1969, mgr. Kansas City (Mo.) br., 1969-74; corp. v.p. health products group Marion Labs., Inc., Kansas City, 1974-78, sr. v.p., mem. Office Pres., 1978-80; exec. v.p., dir. Electronic Realty Assocs., Inc., 1980-83; chmn. bd., CEO Emblem Graphic Sys., Inc., 1983-88, EPIQ Sys., Inc., 1988—. Dir. DemoGraFX, Elinco Internat., Access Industries, Inc., Saztec Internat., Capital Ptnrs. Bd. visitors U. Pitts., Joseph M. Katz Grad. Sch. Bus.; past trustee Barstow Sch.; past chmn. bd. trustees Village United Presbyn. Ch. Mem. Carlton Club (Chgo.), Kansas City Club, Omicron Delta Kappa, Sigma Chi. Republican. Presbyterian. Office: EPIQ Sys Inc 501 Kansas Ave Kansas City KS 66105-1309

OLOGBENLA, ADESOJI OLAPOSI, financial advisor; b. Ile-Ife, Nigeria, Mar. 25, 1958; came to U.S., 1984; s. Adetunji Michael and Victoria (Adunni) O.; m. Olanike Adebimpe, Nov. 1, 1989; children: Adedeji Adedapo, Adedoyin. BS in Acctg., Brescia Coll., Owensboro, Ky., 1986; MBA in Fin., Delta State U., Cleveland, Miss., 1996. Acct. Walters Assocs., Miami, Fla., 1986-88; officer Devcom Mcht. Bank, Lagos, Nigeria, 1989-90; mgr. Chartered Bank, Lagos, 1990-94; pres. S&N Assocs., Durham, N.C., 1996—. Vol. Bapt. Ch., Miami, 1986-88; mentor N.C. Ctrl. U., Durham, 1996—. Named to Outstanding Young Men of Am., 1987.

OLOPADE, OLUFUNMILAYO FALUSI, oncologist, geneticist, educator; b. Nigeria; MBBS with distinction, U. Ibadan, Nigeria, 1980. Diplomate Am. Bd. Internal Medicine, Am. Bd. Med. Oncology, Am. Bd. Hematology; lic. MD Ill., Ind. Intern in medicine, surgery, pediatrics, ob-gyn. Univ. Coll. Hosp., Ibadan, 1980—81; intern in internal medicine Cook County Hosp., Chgo., 1983—84, resident in internal medicine, 1984—86, chief resident in medicine, 1986; postdoctoral fellow jt. sect. hematology/oncology U. Chgo., 1987—91; clin. instr. U. Ill. Abraham Lincoln Sch. Medicine, Chgo., 1986—87; asst. prof. hematologyo/oncology, Pritzker Sch. Medicine U. Chgo., 1991—, mem. Cancer Rsch. Ctr., 1991—, mem. Cancer Biology com., 1994—, mem. Genetics com., 1996—, assoc. prof. medicine, 2002—. Attending physician Cook County Hosp., Chgo., 1987; dir. Cancer Risk Clinic, U. Chgo., 1992—, dir. fellowship program hematology and oncology sect., 1993—. Ad hoc reviewer Jour. AMA, Genes, Chromosomes and Cancer, Genomics, Human Molecular Genetics, Cancer Rsch., Blood, Molecular Carcinogenesis, New Eng. Jour. Medicine; contbr. articles to profl. jours. Mem. AAAS, Am. Assn. Cancer Rsch. (membership credentialing com. 1994-95, program com. carcinogenesis subcom. 1993), Am. Soc. Clin. Oncology (mem. program com. subcom. tumor biology and genetics 1997), Am. Assn. Preventive Oncology, Women in Cancer Rsch., Am. Soc. Hematology, Am. Cancer Soc. (adv. com. cancer control investigations, epidemiology, diagnosis, therapy 1994-97). Office: U Chgo Med Ctr 5841 S Maryland Ave # Mc2115 Chicago IL 60637-1463

O'LOUGHLIN, JOHN KIRBY, retired insurance executive; b. Bklyn., Mar. 31, 1929; s. John Francis and Anne (Kirby) O'L.; m. Janet R. Tag, July 5, 1952; children: Robert K., Steven M., Patricia A., John A. BA in Econs., St. Lawrence U., Canton, N.Y., 1951. State agt. Royal Globe Ins. Group, 1953-58; with Allstate Ins. Co., 1958—, mktg. v.p., group v.p., then exec. v.p., 1972—; pres. Allstate Life Ins. Co., 1977—; chmn. bd. Allstate Ins. Co. and Life Co. Can., 1976—, sr. exec. v.p., chief planning officer, 1980-90; ret. Bd. dirs. all cos. in Allstate Ins. Group and Allstate Enterprises, Inc.; former pres. Allstate Enterprises, Inc.; pres., CEO Royal Link Ventures, Ltd., Pinehurst, N.C. Trustee St. Lawrence U.; bd. trustees, pres. U.S. Marine Corps U. Found., Inc.; bd. dirs. Marine Corps Assn., Am. Ireland Fund, USMC Scholarship Found. Inc., Coun. on Ind. Colls.; past chmn. No. Suburban Chgo. United Way; elder 1st United Presbyn. Ch. Capt. USMCR, 1951-53. Mem. Sales and Mktg. Execs. Internat. (bd. dirs., past chmn., pres.), Whispering Woods Golf Club, Pinehurst Country Club, Lahinch Club, Country Club of N.C., Army-Navy Club, Washington. Office: Royal Links Ventures Ltd PO Box 3579 Pinehurst NC 28374-3579

O'LOUGHLIN, SANDRA S. lawyer; b. Buffalo, Jan. 15, 1942; BA summa cum laude, Rosary Hill Coll., 1973; JD cum laude, U. Buffalo, 1978. Bar: N.Y. 1979. Atty. Hiscock & Barclay, LLP, Buffalo, 1978-79, ptnr., 1990—. Chmn. character and fitness com. appellate divsn. 4th dept. 8th jud. dist. N.Y. Supreme Ct., 1986—; adj. prof. SUNY Law Sch., Buffalo. Note editor Buffalo Law Rev., 1977-78. Mem. Erie County Legis. Task Force Mental Health, 1979-81; mem. adv. bd. Congregation of Sisters of St. Joseph, 1987—. Mem. ABA (bus. law com. on securities), Nat. Assn. Bond Lawyers, N.Y. State Bar Assn. (ethics com. 1984-94, 2000-03, vice chmn. 1987-92, unauthorized practice of law com. 1998-2002, mem. com. on securities regulation 1999—, com. standards atty. conduct 2004—), Erie County Bar Assn. (ethics com. 1984-87, chmn. 1987-89, corp. law com. 1984, grievance com. 1993—). Office: Hiscock & Barclay LLP 1100 M&T Ctr 3 Fountain Plaza Buffalo NY 14203-1486 Business E-Mail: sologhlin@hiscockbarclay.com.

OLOWOKANDI, MICHAEL, professional basketball player; b. Apr. 3, 1975; Student, U. Pacific, 1998. Guard, center L.A. Clippers, 1998—2002; player Min. Timberwolves, 2003—. Named to Schick All-Rookie Second Team, 1998—99. Achievements include recording 16 points and game-highs of 17 rebounds and 3 steals against the Vancouver Grizzlies; scored in double figures in six consecutive games; logged two double-doubles. Office: Min Timberwolves 600 First Ave N Minneapolis MN 55403

OLPADWALA, PORUS, architecture educator, dean; Bachelor's, U. Calcutta, 1962; MBA, Cornell U., 1972, MRP, 1976, PhD, 1979. Prof. dept. city and regional planning Coll. Arch., Art and Planning Cornell U., 1982—, dir. program internat. studies in planning, 1982—91, dir. grad. studies dept. city and regional planning, 1990—92, chair dept. city and regional planning, 1994—98, chair A.D. White profs.-at-large program, interim dean Coll. Arch., Art and Planning, 1998—99, dean Coll. Arch., Art and Planning, 1999—. Contbr. articles to profl. jours. Home: 319 Winthrop Dr Ithaca NY 14850 Office: Dean's Office Coll Arch Art and Planning Cornell U 129 Sibley Dr Ithaca NY 14853

OLSCHWANG, ALAN PAUL, lawyer; b. Chgo., Jan. 30, 1942; s. Morton James and Ida (Ginsberg) O.; m. Barbara Claire Miller, Aug. 22, 1965; children: Elliot, Deborah, Jeffrey. BS, U. Ill., 1963, JD, 1966. Bar: Ill. 1966, N.Y. 1984, Calif. 1992. Law clk. Ill. Supreme Ct., Bloomington, 1966-67; assoc. Sidley & Austin and predecessor firms, Chgo., 1967-73; with Montgomery Ward & Co. Inc., Chgo., 1973-81, assoc. gen. counsel, asst. sec., 1979-81; ptnr. Seki, Jarvis & Lynch, Chgo., 1981-84, dir., mem. exec. com.; dir. Mitsubishi Electric & Electronics USA, Inc. and predecessors, N.Y.C., 1983-91, Cypress, Calif., 1991—. Mem. ABA, Am. Corp. Counsel Assn., Calif. Bar Assn., Ill. Bar Assn., Chgo. Bar Assn., N.Y. State Bar Assn., Bar Assn. of City of N.Y., Am. Arbitration Assn. (panel arbitrators). Office: Mitsubishi Elec & Electronics USA Inc PO Box 6007 5665 Plaza Dr Cypress CA 90630-0007 Office Phone: 714-236-6167.

OLSEN, ALFRED JON, lawyer; b. Phoenix, Oct. 5, 1940; s. William Hans and Vera (Bearden) O.; m. Susan K. Smith, Apr. 15, 1979. BA in History, U. Ariz., 1962; MS in Acctg., Ariz. State U., 1964; JD, Northwestern U., 1966. Bar: Ariz. 1966, Ill. 1966, U.S. Tax Ct. 1970, U.S. Supreme Ct. 1970; C.P.A., Ariz., Ill. cert. tax specialist. Acct. Arthur Young & Co., C.P.A.s, Chgo., 1966-68; dir. firm Ehmann, Olsen & Lane (P.C.), Phoenix, 1969-76; dir. Streich, Lang, Weeks & Cardon (P.C.), Phoenix, 1977-78; v.p. Olsen-Smith, Ltd., Phoenix, 1978—. Chmn. tax adv. commn. Bd. Legal Specialization, 1990-92. Bd. editors: Jour. Agrl. Law and Taxation, 1978-82, Practical Real Estate Lawyer, 1983-95. Mem. Phoenix adv. bd. Salvation Army., 1973-81. Fellow: Am. Coll. Tax Counsel, Am. Coll. Trust and Estate Counsel (state chair); mem.: ABA (chmn. com. on agr., sect. taxation 1976—78, chmn. CLE com. sect. taxation 1982—84), AICPA, Internat. Acad. Estate and Trust Law (exec. coun. 1994—99), Nat. Cattlemen's Assn. (tax com. 1979—88), Am. Law Inst. (life; chmn. tax planning for agr. 1971—82), Ctrl. Ariz. Estate Planning Coun. (pres. 1972—73), State Bar Ariz., Ariz. Soc. CPAs, Phi Beta Kappa, Phi Kappa Phi, Beta Gamma Sigma, Sigma Nu Internat. (pres. 1986—88). Office: 3300 Virginia Fin Pla 301 E Virginia Ave Phoenix AZ 85004-1218 Office Phone: 602-254-1040.

OLSEN, ASHLEY FULLER, actress; b. Sherman Oaks, Calif., June 13, 1986; d. David and Jarnette Olsen, Mackenzie Olsen (Stepmother). Co-founder, prin. Dualstar Entertainment, Calif., 1993—. To Grandmother's House We Go, 1992, Double, Double, Toil and Trouble, 1993, The Little Rascals, 1994, How the West Was Fun, 1994, It Takes Two, 1995, The Challenge, 2003, Charlie's Angles: Full Throttle, 2003; (TV films) Billboard Dad, 1998; (TV series) Full House, 1987—95, Two of a Kind, 1998; actor, prodr.: So Little Time, 2001; Mary-Kate and Ashley in Action!, 2001; actor, actor, prodr.: (films) Switching Goals, 1999; Passport to Paris, 1999; Our Lips are Sealed, 2000; Winning London, 2001; Holiday in the Sun, 2001; Getting There, 2002; When In Rome, 2002; New York Minute, 2004; (video series) The Adventures of Mary-Kate and Ashley; You're Invited to Mary-Kate and Ashley; prodr.: (TV series) Tough Cookie, 2002, Fashion Forward: Spring 2001, 2001. Named one of 100 Most Powerful Women in Hollywood, Hollywood (Calif.) Reporter, 2003. Office: Dualstar Publications c/o Thorac and Co 1801 Century Park East Los Angeles CA 90067*

OLSEN, CHRISTOPHER JOHN, education educator; b. Fargo, N.D., Mar. 19, 1966; s. Richard Donald and Verna Jean Catherine Olsen; m. Jennifer Ann Ross, Mar. 18, 1995; children: Emma Catherine, Charlotte Ann. BA, N.D. State Univ., Fargo, N.D., 1988; MA, Univ. Nebraska, Lincoln, 1990; PhD, Univ. Fla., Gainsville, Fla., 1996. Asst. prof. Va. Wesleyan Coll., Norfolk, Va., 1996—99, Indiana State Univ., Terre Haute, Ind., 1999—2002, assoc. prof., chmn. dept., 2003—. Hist. cons. Friends of Ferry Farm, Va. Beach, Va., 1997—99; assoc. editor The Southern Historian, Tuscaloosa, Ala., 1994—97; faculty advisor Phi Alpha Theta, Terre Haute, Ind., 1999—. Author: Political Culture and Secession in Mississippi: Masculinity Honor, and the Antiparty

Tradition, 1830-1860, 2000; contbr. articles to profl. jour. Grantee Univ. Rsch. Grant, Indiana Stat Univ., 2001—02, Mednick Rsch. Grant, Va. Found. of Ind. Coll., 1998. Mem.: Southern Hist. Soc., Phi Beta Kappa. Democrat. Avocation: golf. Office: Indiana State Univ Dept Hist Terre Haute IN 47809 Office Phone: 812-237-2710.

OLSEN, DAVID ALEXANDER, insurance executive; b. Bklyn., Nov. 29, 1937; s. Alexander and Meile (Anderson) O.; m. Roberta Ruth Garverick, May 11, 1963; children: Bradford, Amy. BA, Bowdoin Coll., 1959. With marine dept. Gt. Am. Ins. Co., N.Y.C. and Chgo., 1959-62; acct. exec. Johnson & Higgins, San Francisco, 1966-71, v.p., mgr. marine dept. Chgo., 1971-78, exec. v.p. Ill. br., 1978-79, br. mgr., exec. v.p. Houston, 1979-80, chmn., bd. dirs. Tex. br., 1980-85, exec. v.p. N.Y.C., 1985-87, pres., COO, 1987-93, CEO, 1990-97, chmn., 1991-98; dir. Marsh & McLennan, N.Y.C., 1998—. Bd. dirs. U.S. Trust Corp. Trustee Bowdoin Coll., South St. Seaport Mus., Salisbury (Conn.) Congl. Ch., Vis. Nurse Assn., Landmark Vols. 1st lt. U.S. Army, 1960-62. Mem. India House, River Club, Sharon Country Club, Psi Upsilon. Avocations: art, photography, antiques, scuba diving, tennis, skiing. Office: J&H Marsh & McLennan 1166 Avenue Of The Americas New York NY 10036-2708

OLSEN, DONALD EMMANUEL, architect, educator; b. Mpls., July 23, 1919; s. Clarence Edward and Thea (Scharnell) O.; m. Helen Karen Ohlson, Apr. 2, 1944; 1 child, Alan Edward. B.Arch., U. Minn., 1942; M. Arch., Harvard U., 1946; postgrad. in civic design, U. Liverpool, Eng., 1953; postgrad. in philosophy of sci., London Sch. Econs., 1962-63, 68. Registered architect, Calif. Archtl. designer Saarinen, Swanson & Saarinen, Bloomfield Hills, Mich., 1946; project mgr. Skidmore, Owings & Merrill, San Francisco, 1948; designer, draughtsman Wurster, Bernardi & Emmons, San Francisco, 1949-51; pvt. practice architecture Berkeley, Calif., 1954—; prof. architecture U. Calif.-Berkeley, 1954-90, prof. emeritus, 1990—. Guest prof. various univs., lectr. in field, U.S., Eng., Germany, Denmark; lectr., tchr. Ecoles D'Art Améicaines de Fontainebleau, France; nominator Carnegie Grant Personality Assessment and Research Creativity Study Architects, 1959; profl. adviser City of San Francisco, 1961-62; juror, critic, evaluator, various programs, projects Contbr. articles, chpts. to profl. publs.; subject of numerous profl. publs. Numerous exhibits throughout U.S., Europe; prin. works include numerous design commns. Recipient awards, including nat. awards of Excellence Archtl. Record, Houses of 1966; scholar Harvard U., Cambridge, Mass., 1945-46; A. W. Wheelwright fellow Harvard U., 1953 Fellow AIA (2 nat. honor awards 1970, 8 various regional, local Honor, Excellence and Merit awards 1967-89); mem. Brit. Soc. for Philosophy of Sci., Soc. for Philosophy and Tech., Open Soc. and Its Friends Avocations: philosophy, travel, photography, opera. Office: Donald E Olsen & Assocs Architects 771 San Diego Rd Berkeley CA 94707-2025

OLSEN, EDGAR OLIVER, economics professor; b. New Orleans, Mar. 13, 1942; s. Edgar Oliver and Georgie Walker (Thompson) Olsen; m. Barbara Elliott Beasley, June 4, 1966; children: Robert Buckner, Melanie Guerry. BA, Tulane U., 1963; PhD, Rice U., 1968. Postdoctoral fellow Ind. U.-Bloomington, 1967—68; from asst. prof. to assoc. prof. U. Va., Charlottesville, 1970—83, prof., 1983—, chmn. dept. econs., 1993—96. Vis. assoc. prof. econs. U. Wis., Madison, 1975—76, vis. prof., 1982—84; economist Rand Corp., Santa Monica, Calif., 1968—70; vis. scholar HUD, Washington, 1978—79, cons., 1973—2003; bd. editors Am. Econ. Rev., Princeton, NJ, 1985—91; cons. GAO, Washington, 1999—2001; v.p. So. Econ. Assn., 2003—. Contbr. articles to profl. publs. Congl. Testimony, 2001, 2003. Recipient Cert. Spl. Achievement, HUD, 1979; NIH fellow, 1983. Mem.: Am. Real Estate and Urban Econ. Assn., Am. Econ. Assn., Assn. Pub. Policy Analysis and Mgmt., So. Econ. Assn. Home: 1606 Jamestown Dr Charlottesville VA 22901-3016 Office: Dept Econs U Va Charlottesville VA 22903 Business E-Mail: eoo@virginia.edu.

OLSEN, EDWARD JOHN, geologist, educator, curator; b. Chgo., Nov. 23, 1927; s. Edward John and Elizabeth (Bornemann) O.; children— Andrea, Ericka. AB, U. Chgo., 1951, MS, 1955, PhD, 1959. Geologist Geol. Survey Can., 1953, U.S. Geol. Survey, 1954—, Canadian Johns-Manville Co., Ltd., 1956, 57, 59; asst. prof. Case Inst. Tech., also Western Res. U., 1959-60; curator mineralogy Field Mus. Natural History, 1960-91, chmn. dept. geology, 1974-78; research assoc. prof. dept. geophys. scis. U. Chgo., 1977—. Adj. prof. U. Ill., Chgo. Circle, 1970-91. Assoc. editor Geochim. et Cosmochim. Acta., 1985-91. Fellow Mineral. Soc. Am.; mem. Mineral. Assn. Can., Geochem. Soc., Meteoritical Soc. Achievements include spl. research stability relations of minerals in earth's mantle and meteorites. Office: U Chgo Dept Geophys Sci Chicago IL 60637

OLSEN, FRANCES ELISABETH, law educator, theorist; b. Chgo., Feb. 4, 1945; d. Holger and Ruth Mathilda (Pfeifer) O.; m. Harold Irving Porter, June 8, 1984. Cert., Roskilde (Denmark) Højskole, 1967; BA, Goddard Coll., 1968; JD, U. Colo., 1971; SJD, Harvard U., 1984. Bar: Colo. 1972, U.S. Dist. Ct. Colo. 1972. Law clk. hon. Arraj U.S. Dist. Ct. Colo., Denver, 1972; lawyer Am. Indian Movement, Wounded Knee, S.D., 1973; pvt. practice Denver, 1973-74; law prof. U. Puget Sound, Tacoma, Wash., 1975-79, St. John's U., Jamaica, N.Y., 1982-83, UCLA, 1984—. Vis. fellow New Coll., Oxford (Eng.) U., 1987; vis. prof. U. Mich., Ann Arbor, 1988, Harvard U., Cambridge, Mass., 1990-91, U. Berlin, Germany, 1995, Ochanomizu U., Tokyo, 1997, U. Tokyo, 1997, Cornell U., 1997, French U. Reunion, 2000, Hebrew U. Jerusalem, 2001, Haifa U., 2001, Tel Aviv U., 2001, 2002, Addis Ababa U., 2002, Bar Ilan U., 2002, Alberto Hurtado U., Santiago, Chile, 2004; sr. Fulbright prof. U. Frankfurt, Germany, 1991-92; overseas fellow Churchill Coll., Cambridge, Eng., 1997-99; mem. faculty law Cambridge U., 1997-99; del. UN 4th World Conf. on Women, Beijing, China, 1995, NGO Forum, Huairou, China, 1995. Co-author: Cases and Materials on Family Law: Legal Concepts and Changing Human Relationships, 1994; editor: Feminist Legal Theory I: Foundations and Outlooks, 1995, Feminist Legal Theory II: Positioning Feminist Theory Within the Law, 1995; contbr. articles to law revs. Named Outstanding Alumnus U. Colo., 1989. Mem. Assn. Am. Law Schs. (chair jurisprudence sect. 1987-88, chair women in law tchg. sect. 1995-96), Conf. on Critical Legal Studies, European Conf. Critical Legal Studies, Internat. Bar Assn. Avocations: scuba diving, kayaking, long distance hiking. Office: UCLA Sch Law 405 Hilgard Ave Los Angeles CA 90095-1476 Office Phone: 310-825-6083. E-mail: olsen@law.ucla.edu.

OLSEN, GREGORY H. fiber optic manufacturing executive, researcher; b. Bklyn., 1945; 2 children. BS in physics; BSEE in physics, MS in physics magna cum laude, Fairleigh Dickinson U.; PhD in materials sci., U. Va., 1971. Tech. staff RCA Lab. (now Sarnoff Corp.), Princeton, NJ, 1972—83; founder, pres., CEO EPITAXX Inc. (acquired by Nippon Sheet Glass, 1990 and by JDS Uniphase, 1999), 1984; co-founder Sensors Unlimited, Inc. (acquired by Finisar Corp., 2000, bought back 2002), Princeton, 1991; pres., CEO Sensors Unlimited, Inc., Princeton, 1991—2000, 2002—, pres., 2000—02; chmn. bd. dirs. Sensors Unlimited Inc.; officer, dir. Finisar Corp., 2000—02. Vis. scientist physics dept. U. Port Elizabeth, South Africa; lectr. in field; bd. dir. Princeton Power Sys., Achieve 3000, Eye Response Tech. Author over 100 papers, co-author several books on crystal growth and semiconductor devices; contbr. articles for trade jour. Investor NJ Tech. Coun. Venture Fund; adv. com. Princeton U., U. So. Calif. Photonics Ctr., U. Fla. Microelectronics Ctr., U. Va., City Coll. NY. Named Inventor Yr., NJ Inst. Tech., NJ Small Bus. Person Yr., US Small Bus. Adminstrn., Entrepreneur Yr., Arthur Young/Inc. Mag.; recipient Young Authors award, Am. Assn. Crystal Growth. Mem.: NJ Crystal Growth Assn., IEEE Laser & Electro-Optics Soc. (LEOS) (bd. gov., Aron Kressel award, named disting. leader), IEEE (fellow, named disting. leader), IEEE Electro, Electrochemical Soc., Internat. Soc. Optical Engring. (SPIE). Achievements include 12 US patents; named next Pvt. Space Explored, 2003, third person in history. Office: Sensors Unlimited Inc 3490 Rt 1 Bldg 12 Princeton NJ 08540-5914 Office Phone: 609-520-0610. Office Fax: 609-520-1663. Business E-Mail: golsen@sensorinc.com.*

OLSEN, HANS H. semiconductor company executive; BSEE, Copenhagen Tech. U.; MSEE, U. Copenhagen. Engring. and mgmt. positions Christian Rovsing A/S, Copenhagen, 1973—82; co-founder, CEO Electronic Designs, Inc., 1982—83; founder, CEO IChips Corp. (acquired by Paradigm Tech., Inc.), 1993—96; v.p. mktg. Paradigm Tech., Inc., 1996—97; v.p. graphics mktg., v.p. N.Am. sales Trident Microsystems, 1997—98; v.p. ops. Pixelworks, Inc., Tualatin, Oreg., 1998—2001, exec. v.p., COO, 2001—. Office: Pixelworks Inc Ste 300 8100 SW Nyberg Rd Tualatin OR 97062*

OLSEN, HANS PETER, lawyer; b. Detroit, May 21, 1940; s. Hans Peter and Paula M. (Olsen) O.; m. Elizabeth Ann Gayton, Sept. 14, 1968; children: Hans Peter, Heidi Susanne, Stephanie Elizabeth BA, Mich. State U., 1961; JD, Georgetown U., 1965; LLM, NYU, 1966. Bar: Mich. 1967, Pa. 1969, R.I. 1974. Law clk. Monaghan, McCrone, Campbell & Crawmer, Detroit, 1964, U.S. Ct. of Claims, Fed. Appellate Ct., Washington, 1966—68; assoc. Pepper, Hamilton & Scheetz, Phila., 1968—72; ptnr. Hinckley, Allen, & Snyder, Providence, 1974—. Adv. planning com. U. R.I. Fed. Taxation Inst.; continuing legal edn. adv. bd., tax symposium adv. bd. Bryant Coll.; mem. Gov.'s State Task Force, R.I. Pub. Expenditure Coun.; cons. Bur. Nat. Affairs; liaison Bar Assn. and North Atlantic region IRS; tax adminstrs. adv. com. R.I.; lectr. tax insts. and other profl. groups N.Y., L.A., Phila., Boston, R.I.; advisor R.I. Econ. Policy com. Contbr. numerous articles on taxation to legal jours. Fellow Am. Bar Found.; mem. ABA (sect. taxation, exempt orgns. com., subcom. healthcare, corp.-shareholders rels. com., partnerships com.), R.I. Bar Assn. (sect. taxation, sec.-treas. 1977-80, liaison with CPAs, specialization com., mem. various coms.), Providence C. of C., R.I. C. of C. (chmn. com. on bus. taxes and public spending, mem., past chmn. legis. action council), Mich. State Bar, Pa. State Bar. Home: 274 Olney St Providence RI 02906-2305 Office: 1500 Fleet Ctr Providence RI 02903 also: 28 State St Boston MA 02109-1775 also: 14 South St Concord NH 03301-3744 Personal E-mail: hpeterolsen@cox.net. Business E-Mail. holsen@haslaw.com.

OLSEN, HAROLD FREMONT, lawyer; b. Davenport, Wash., Oct. 17, 1920; s. Oscar E. and Dorothy (Sprowls) O.; m. Jeanne L. Rounds, Aug. 30, 1942; children: Eric O., Ronald R., Margaret Ruth. BA, Wash. State U., 1942; LLB, Harvard U., 1948. Bar: Wash. 1948, U.S. Ct. Claims 1970, U.S. Supreme Ct. 1982; CPA, Wash. Instr. Oxford Bus. Sch., Cambridge, Mass., 1946-47; examiner Wash. State Dept. Pub. Utilities, 1948; with firm Perkins Coie (and predecessors), Seattle, 1949—, ptnr., 1954-88, of counsel, 1989—. Trustee Exec. Svcs. Corp. Wash., 1990-96. Bd. dirs. Northwest Hosp. Found., Northwest Hosp., 1980-90; trustee Wash. State U. Found., chmn. 1986-88; mem. adv. coun. Wash. State U. Sch. Bus. and Econs., 1978-90; trustee, mem. exec. com., pres. Mus. of Flight, 1991-92, chmn., 1993; trustee Horizon House, 1994-97. Maj. USAAF, 1942-45, NATOUSA, Mid. East, ETO. Decorated Silver Star. Mem. ABA, Wash. Bar Assn., Seattle Bar Assn., Aircraft Industry Assn. (chmn. legal com. 1957), Phi Beta Kappa, Phi Kappa Phi, Tau Kappa Epsilon, Rainier Club, Queenstown (New Zealand) Golf Club, Seattle Golf Club (pres. 1986-87), Sr. N.W. Golf Assn. Congregationalist. Home: 8875 Overlake Dr W Medina WA 98039-5347 Office: 1201 3rd Ave Ste 4500 Seattle WA 98101-3029 Office Phone: 206-583-8503. Business E-Mail: olseh@perkinscoie.com. E-mail: olseh@seanet.com.

OLSEN, HARRIS LELAND, diplomat, writer, real estate company executive, educator; b. Rochester, NH, Dec. 8, 1947; s. Harries Edwin and Eva Alma (Turmelle) O.; m. Mimi Kwi Sun Yi, Mar. 15, 1953; children: Garin Lee, Gavin Yi, Sook Ja. AS, SUNY, Albany, 1983, BS, 1988; MA in Polit. Sci., U. Hawaii, 1990; PhD in Internat. Bus. Adminstrn., Kennedy Western U., Idaho, 1993. Enlisted USN, 1967, advanced through grades to, served in various nuclear power capacities, 1971-76, 1976-87, ret., 1987; v.p. Waiono Land Corp., Honolulu, 1981-92, dir., 1993-95; v.p. Asian Pacific Electricity, Honolulu, 1988-89, Kapano Land Assocs., Honolulu, 1988-92, 94-95, MLY Networks, Inc., Honolulu, 1989-99, THO Consultants Corp., 1991—2002, Clarix Internat. Corp., 1994; consulate gen. Papua New Guinea, 1996—2002. Staff cons. Mariner-Icemakers, Honolulu, 1982-84, Transpacific Energy Corp., Honolulu, 1982-84; dir. Asian Pacific Devel. Bank, 1983; sr. cons. Western Rsch. Assocs., Honolulu, 1984-87, 94-95; quality assurance cons. Asian Pacific, Inc., Honolulu, 1987-88; instr., lectr. Asian history and culture U. Chaminade in Honolulu, 1991; nuclear reactor plant specialist Pearl Harbor Emergency Recall Team, 1991-95; instr. nuclear reactor theory Pearl Harbor, Hawaii, 1992-95; v.p. Schwartz, Inc., 1992-98, dir. Schwartz Jewelry Sch., 1996-98; cons. Waiono/Kapano Devel. Co., 1993; bd. dirs., sec. Pacific Internat. Engring. Corp., 1994-95; Keiretsu sec. Global Ocean Cons., Inc. and Assocs., 1994-95; joint venture Premier Fisheries Pty. Ltd., Papua New Guinea, 1995-98; cons. BFD Devel. Group, 1995-96; co-drafter Nat. Tuna Industry Devel. Plan for Papua New Guinea, 1995; quality analyst, Pearl Harbor, 1995; rep. for Min. for Fisheries, Papua New Guinea, Bi-lateral Fisheries Access Rights Japan and Papua New Guinea, 1996-97, drafter Bi-Lateral Fishing Treaty Japan and Papua New Guinea, 1996; U.S. del. to 4th World Tuna Conf., Manila, 1995, U.S. del. to 5th Aquatic Coninent Conf., Maui, Hawaii, 1995, 6th, 1996; apptd. rep. Abau Electorate, Papua New Guinea Timber Sales, 1995-98; apptd. hon. consul gen. and trade rep., dep. trade min. for Govt. of Papua New Guinea in Honolulu, 1996-2001; bd. dirs. Island Art; cons. Pew Global Devel. Corp., 1998-99, Niugini Enterprises LLC, 1999-2001, Niugini Millenium Co., Ltd., 1999-2001. Author: The Price for Gold, 2002, Candi, 2003, Sialon, 2003, Small Prices, 2004, Silent, 2004; contbr. articles to profl. jours. Head coach USN Men's Softball, Honolulu, 1978-79; pres. Pearl Harbor (Hawaii) Welfare and Recreation Com., 1983-84; mem. Rep. Senatorial Inner Cir.; commd. hon. consul gen. Ind. State Papua New Guinea, 1996; mem. Consular Corps of Hawaii, 1997-2001. Named Alumnus of Yr., Kennedy Western U., 1993; recipient Citation of Leadership, Rep. Nat. Com., 1996, Letter of Commendation for Svc. During Aitape Tidal Wave Disaster in Papua New Guinea, 1998; selected to represent Hawaii at Presdl. Inauguration, Rep. Leadership U.S. Senate, 2001. Mem.: Navy League, USCG Aux., Delta Epsilon Sigma. Republican. Roman Catholic and Buddhist. Achievements include invention of alternate power supply sys. Avocations: chess, philosophy, japanese haiku poetry, native american cultures. Home and Office: 94 1025 Anania Cir Apt 56 Mililani HI 96789-2045 Personal E-mail: HarryTho@aol.com.

OLSEN, INGER ANNA, retired psychologist; b. Copper Mountain, B.C., Can., Dec. 25, 1926; BS, Wash. State U., 1954, MS, 1956, PhD, 1962. Psychiat. nurse Provincial Mental Health Svcs. B.C., 1947-51, psychologist, 1956-58, Vancouver (B.C.) City Met. Health Svcs., 1958-60; psychologist Student Counseling Ctr., Wash. State U., Pullman, 1960-62; sr. psychologist Met. Health Svcs., Vancouver, 1962-66; instr. psychology Langara Coll., Vancouver, 1966—87. Contbr. articles to profl. jours. Docent Vancouver Aquarium Assn.; bd. dirs. Second Mile Soc., 1975—89. Mem. APA, Gerontol. Soc. Am., Can. Assn. Gerontology, Phi Beta Kappa, Sigma Xi, Alpha Kappa Delta. Home: 1255 Bidwell St Apt 1910 Vancouver BC Canada V6G 2K8

OLSEN, JOHN WILLIAM, political organization administrator; b. Greenwich, Conn., Mar. 27, 1950; s. William and Helen (Coombs) O.; m. Rose Smeriglio, Apr. 18, 1971; children: Amy, Elizabeth, Christopher. Student, Wright Tech. Sch., 1973. Apprentice Greenwich Plumbing and Heating, 1969-79; journeyman Stockenboyjer Plumbing and Heating, Greenwich, 1979-81; bus. mgr. U.A. Local 133, Greenwich, 1981-87, pres., 1978-79; sec., treas. Conn. State AFL-CIO, West Hartford, 1987-88, pres., 1988—. Trustee Fairfield-New Haven Apprenticeship Sch., Bridgeport, 1983—, Conn. Plumbers and Pipefitters Pension Fund, Wallingford, 1979—; mem., subchair Conn. Employment and Tng. Com., Wethersfield, 1989—; mem. Conn. Innovations, Inc., Rocky Hill, 1989—. Former mem. Greenwich Dem. Town Exec. Com.; mem. Dem. State Cen. Com., Hartford, 1986—, Gov.'s Bldg. and Constrn. Adv. Com., Hartford, 1987-90, Gov.'s Mgmt. Study Commn., Hartford, 1989-91, State Democratic Chmn., Conn., 1995. Mem. Greenwich Bldg. and Constrn. Trades (pres. 1983-87), Kiwanis (2d v.p. Greenwich chpt. 1987-88). Democrat. Roman Catholic. Office: Conn State AFL-CIO 56 Town Line Rocky Hill CT 06067 also: Conn Democratic Party 380 Franklin Ave Hartford CT 06114

OLSEN, JOSEPHINE K. federal agency administrator; B, U. Utah; MSW, PhD, U. Md. Vol. Peace Corps, Tunisia, 1966—68, various positions incuding chief of staff, regional dir. North Africa, Near East, Asia and the Pscific, country dir. Togo, 1979—84, 1989—92; exed. dirs. Coun. Internat. Exch. of Scholars, 1992—97; sr. v.p., dir. Peace Corps, 1997—2002, deputy dir., 2002—. Office: Peace Corps 1111 20th St NW Washington DC 20526-0001

OLSEN, KATHIE LYNN, federal agency administrator; b. Portland, Oreg., Aug. 3, 1952; d. Roland Berg and Gladys Elizabeth (Eldreth) O. BS, Chatham Coll., 1974; PhD, U. Calif., Irvine, 1979. Postdoct. fellow Harvard Med. Sch., Boston, 1979-80; rsch. scientist Long Island Rsch. Inst., Stony Brook, N.Y., 1980-83; rsch. asst. prof. SUNY, Stony Brook, 1982-85, asst. prof., 1985-89; assoc. program dir. NSF, Washington, 1984-86, program dir., 1988, leader neurosci., 1991; assoc. director, tech. Off. Science and Tech. Policy, Washington, 1999—. Adj. assoc. prof. George Washington U., Washington, 1989—; cons. editor Hormones and Behavior, 1988—. Contbr. articles to profl. jours, chapters to books. Mem. Soc. Neurosci., Endocrine Soc., Women in Neurosci., Sod. Study of Reproduction, Internat. Acad. Sex Rsch. Office: Exec Off of the Pres Off Science and Tech Policy EEOB, 17th & Pennsylvania Ave NW Washington DC 20502

OLSEN, KENNETH HAROLD, geophysicist, astrophysicist; b. Ogden, Utah, Feb. 20, 1930; s. Harold Reuben and Rose (Hill) O.; m. Barbara Ann Parson, June 15, 1955; children: Susan L., Steven K., Christopher P., Richard S. BS, Idaho State Coll., 1952; MS, Calif. Inst. Tech., 1954, PhD, 1957. Grad. rsch. asst. Calif. Inst. Tech., Mt. Wilson and Palomar Obs., Pasadena, 1952-57; staff member, group leader Los Alamos (N.Mex.) Nat. Lab., 1957-89; lab. assoc. Los Alamos Nat. Lab., 1989-95; geophys. cons. GCS Internat., Lynnwood, Wash., 1989—. Vis. rsch. fellow Applied Seismol. Group, Swedish Nat. Def. Inst., Stockholm, Sweden, 1983; sr. vis. scientist fellow Norwegian Seismic Array, Oslo, Norway, 1983; vis. scholar Geophysics Program, Univ. Wash., Seattle, 1989-91. Author, editor: Continental Rifts: Evolution, Structure, Tectonics, 1995; contbr. articles to profl. jours. Mem. Am. Geophys. Union, Geol. Soc. Am., Seismol. Soc. Am., Am. Astron. Soc., Royal Astron. Soc. Home: 1029 187th Pl SW Lynnwood WA 98036-4986

OLSEN, KENNETH HARRY, manufacturing executive; b. Bridgeport, Conn., Feb. 20, 1926; s. Oswald and Svea (Nordling) Olsen; m. Eeva-Liisa Aulikki Valve, Dec. 12, 1950. BS in Elec. Engring, MIT, 1950, MS, 1952. Elec. engr. Lincoln Lab., MIT, 1950-57; founder, pres. Digital Equipment Corp., Maynard, Mass., 1957-92, pres. emeritus, 1992—; chmn. Advanced Modular Solutions, Inc., Boxborough, Mass. Bd. dirs. Polaroid Corp., Ford Motor Co. Mem. Pres.'s Sci. Adv., 1971—73; trustee, v.p. Joslin Diabetes Found.; mem. corp. Wentworth Inst., Boston, MIT, Cambridge; trustee Gordon Coll., Wenham, Mass. With USNR, 1944—46. Named Young Elec. Engr. of Year, Eta Kappa Nu, 1960; recipient of Nat. Medal of Tech., Nat. Sci. Found., 1993. Mem.: NAE. Achievements include patents for magnetic devices. Office: EXT STE 304 150 Baker Ave Concord MA 01742-2199

OLSEN, M. KENT, lawyer, educator; b. Denver, Mar. 10, 1948; s. Marvin and F. Winona (Wilker) O.; m. Shauna L. Casement; children: Kristofor Anders, Alexander Lee, Nikolaus Alrik, Amanda Elizabeth. BS, Colo. State U., 1970; JD, U. Denver, 1975. Bar: Colo., U.S. Dist. Ct. Colo. 1982, U.S. Tax Ct. Law clk. Denver Probate Ct., 1973 75; assoc. ptnr. Johnson & McLachlan, Lamar, Colo., 1975-80; assoc. Buchanan, Thomas and Johnson, Lakewood, Colo., 1981-82, William E. Myrick, P.C., Denver, 1982-83; referee Denver Probate Ct., Denver, 1983-89; ptnr. Haines & Olsen, P.C., Denver, 1989-95; pvt. practice Denver, 1995—2001; ptnr. Olsen & Traeger, LLP, 2001—. Adv. bd. Denver Career Coll., 1993—, Elder Law Inst., 1994—. Active Gov.'s Commn. on Life and the Law, Denver, 1991-2000; bd. dirs. Adult Care Mgmt., Inc., Denver, 1985-95, Colo. Guardianship Alliance, Denver, 1990-91, Arc of Denver, Inc., 1990—, pres., 1995-97, 2004—; bd. dirs. Colo. Fund for People with Disabilities, 1994—, pres., 1994-2000. Recipient Outstanding Vol. Svc. award Adult Care Mgmt., 1990, Outstanding Svc. award The Arc of Denver, 1991, Vol. Svc. award Colo. Gerontol. Soc., 1997, Pres.'s award Arc of Denver, 1998. Mem. ABA, Colo. Bar Assn. (past chair probate sect.), First Jud. Dist. Bar Assn., Acad. Elder Law Attys., Colo. Assn. Homes and Svcs. to the Aging, Denver Bar Assn., Denver Estate Planning Coun., Denver C. of C. Avocations: running, skiing, racquetball, art, hiking. Home: 3030 S Roslyn St Denver CO 80231-4153 Office: 650 S Cherry St Ste 850 Denver CO 80246-1805 Office Phone: 303-329-4670. E-mail: mkolsen@olsentraeger.com.

OLSEN, MARTIN E. obstetrician, educator; b. Morgantown, W.Va., 1959; m. Natalie Ann Maschmann, June 25, 1985; 1 child, Karen Rebeca. MD, Med. Coll. Ohio, 1985. Diplomate Am. Bd. Ob-Gyn., Am. Bd. Family Practice. Resident in family practice Akron (Ohio) Gen. Med. Ctr., 1985-88; resident in ob-gyn. U. Tenn., Chattanooga, 1989-91; mem. faculty E. Tenn. State U., Johnson City, 1992—, chmn. dept. ob-byn., 1999—; dir. residency program Johnson City Med. Ctr., 1994—. Contbr. articles to profl. jours. Office: PO Box 70569 Johnson City TN 37614-1707 Office Phone: 423-439-8097. Business E-Mail: olsen@mail.etsu.edu.

OLSEN, MARY ANN, lawyer; b. Hoboken, NJ, Aug. 5, 1948; d. Charles Joseph and Margaret Nora (Power) O.; 1 child, Matthew Ellisen. AAS, Purdue U., 1973; BS, St. Peter's Coll., Jersey City, 1973; JD, Rutgers U., 1989. Bar: NJ, NY 91; RN. Pvt. practice, Bayonne, N.J., 1991—. Cons. atty. Hudson County Protective Svc., West New York, N.J., 1993-96. Pres. bd. trustees Jersey City Cmty. Charter Sch.; bd. dirs. St. Joseph's Home for the Blind; trustee Guardianship Assn. NJ, Inc. Mem. N.J. Bar Assn., Hudson County Bar Assn., Hudson Inn of Ct. Office: 8 E 35th St Bayonne NJ 07002-3925 Office Phone: 201-436-0401. Personal E-mail: maryannolsenlaw@aol.com.

OLSEN, MARY-KATE, actress; b. Sherman Oaks, Calif., June 13, 1986; d. David and Jarnette Olsen, Mackenzie Olsen (Stepmother). Co-founder, prin. Dualstar Entertainment, LA, 1993—. Actor: (films) To Grandmother's House We Go, 1992, Double, Double, Toil and Trouble, 1993, The Little Rascals, 1994, How the West Was Fun, 1994, It Takes Two, 1995, The Challenge, 2003; (TV films) Billboard Dad, 1998; (TV series) Full House, 1987—95, Two of a Kind, 1998; actor, prodr.: (films) Switching Goals, 1999; Passport to Paris, 1999; Our Lips are Sealed, 2000; Winning London, 2001; Holiday in the Sun, 2001; Getting There, 2002; When In Rome, 2002; actor: Charlie's Angels: Full Throttle, 2003; actor, prodr.: New York Minute, 2004; (TV series) So Little Time, 2001; Mary-Kate and Ashley in Action!, 2001; (video series) The Adventures of Mary-Kate and Ashley; You're Invited to Mary-Kate and Ashley's; prodr.: (TV series) Tough Cookie, 2002, Fashion Forward: Spring 2001, 2001. Named one of 100 Most Powerful Women in Hollywood, Hollywood (Calif.) Reporter, 2003. Office: Dualstar Publications c/o Thorne and Co 1801 Century Park East Los Angeles CA 90007*

OLSEN, REX NORMAN, trade association executive; b. Hazeltown, Idaho, Apr. 9, 1925; s. Adolph Lars and Pearl (Robbins) O. B.J., BA in English, U. Mo., 1950. Editor Clissold Pub. Co., Chgo., 1950-54; copy editor Am. Peoples Ency., Chgo., 1955; asst. editor Am. Hosp. Assn., Chgo., 1956-59, mng. editor, 1959-64, dir. jours. div., 1964-69, dir. publs. bur., 1969-75, exec. editor, asso. pub., 1975-79; v.p., treas. Am. Hosp. Pub., Inc., 1980-85; pres. Words Ltd., 1985—. Dir. publs. ETNA Comms., Chgo., 1997—. Served with USNR, 1943-46. Mem. Soc. Nat. Assn. Pubs. (sec. 1975-76, 2d v.p. 1976-77, 1st v.p. 1977-78, pres. 1978-79), Chgo. Bus. Publs. Assn. (dir. 1974-78, 4th v.p. 1978-79), Sigma Delta Chi. Home and Office: 5510 N Sheridan Rd Unit 12-A Chicago IL 60640-1630 Office Phone: 773-784-8244. E-mail: rexorudy@aol.com.

OLSEN, RICHARD GALEN, biomedical engineer, consultant; b. Colorado Springs, Colo., Aug. 10, 1945; s. Floyd Edwin and Ruth Elizabeth (Robinson) O.; m. Karen Fidler Brubaker, June 17, 1973 (dec.); children: Kathryn Elizabeth, Nickolas Robert. BSEE, U. Mo., Rolla, 1968; MS, U. Utah, 1970, PhD, 1975. Registered profl. engr., Fla. Engr. Bendix Corp., Kansas City, Mo., 1968-69; elec. engr. Naval Aerospace Med. Rsch. Lab., Pensacola, Fla., 1975-79, chief engring. systems divsn., 1979-82, head bioengring. divsn., 1982-94; head bioengring. dept. Naval Health Rsch. Ctr. Detachment, Brooks AFB, Tex., 1994-2000; cons. in bioelectromagnetics Pensacola, 2001—. Tech. cons. Naval Sea Sys. Command, Arlington, Va., 1989—91, Naval Surface

Warfare Ctr., Dahlgren, Va., 1989—95, Armstrong Lab. USAF, 1991—99, Naval Command, Control and Ocean Surveillance Command, San Diego, 1996—97, Selicor, Inc., 2001—. Contbr. articles to profl. jours. and books. With U.S. Army, 1970-72. Recipient Fred A. Hitchcock award Aerospace Physiologist Aerospace Med. Assn., 1987, Award for Excellence in Tech. Transfer, Fed. Lab. Consortium, 2004; named Engr. of the Yr., N.W. Fla. Engrs. Coun., 1991. Mem. IEEE (sr., chmn. Pensacola sect. 1982-83, SCC-28 and SCC-34 coms. 1982-2000, cert. of appreciation 1983), Bioelectromagnetics Soc. (charter, editl. bd. 1990-96), Sigma Xi, Eta Kappa Nu, Tau Beta Pi, Phi Kappa Phi. Achievements include conducting the first shipboard measurements of specific absorption rate (SAR) and of electromagnetic pulse (EMP) induced body current; patents in RF medical device to treat vascular insufficiency, elastic wire conductor, RF coil for hypothermia resuscitation, RF dosimetry system, personal microwave and RF detector, and RF warming of submerged extremities. Home and Office: 1503 N Baylen St Pensacola FL 32501-2101 E-mail: olsen116@bellsouth.net. *Live an ordinary life except in attainment.*

OLSEN, RICHARD JAMES, artist, educator; b. Milw., Nov. 15, 1935; s. Edward Marinus and Ann Frances (Keymar) Olsen; m. Nina Marsh Civilette-Olsen, July 25, 1969; children: Dayna Kim, Dawn Beth(dec.), Josh Keymar. BS, U. Wis., 1958, MFA in Painting and Printmaking, 1966. Tchg. asst. U. Wis., 1965-66; art tchr. grade 8 Winnequah Grade Sch., Monona, Wis., 1966-67; instr. printmaking Oper. Area Arts, Green Bay, Wis., 1967-69; from instr. painting and drawing to prof. emeritus U. Ga., Athens, 1969—2001, emeritus prof., 2001—; represented by Berman Gallery, Atlanta, 1986-97, Novus Inc., Atlanta, 1990—, Maurine Littleton Gallery, Washington, 1990, Miriam Perlman Gallery, Chgo., 1991, EDL & Assocs., Atlanta, 1994, Elements of Art, Columbus, Ohio, 1995, Ellen Wallace-Paushter, Art Cons., Chgo., 1999, Mercury Art Works, Athens, Ga., 2001—. Wrestling coach Monona Grove (Wis.) H.S., 1966-67; panelist Steinham Arts Festival St. Lawrence U., N.Y., 1987, Crossroads in Cultural Studies, Tampere, Finland, 1996; head praparator Reflexes and Reflections Russell Rotunda Capitol Hill, Washington, 1983, Lincoln Ctr., N.Y.C., 1984. One-man shows include Claywork Gallery, Atlanta, 1986, H. Smith Gallery U. SC, Spartanburg, 1991, Nat. Vietnam Vets. Art Mus., Chgo., 1999, Mercury Art Works, Athens, Ga., 2003, numerous group shows including most recently, exhibited in group shows at Am. Visionary Mus., Balt., 2001—, Peace Mus., Chgo., 2002—, Aurora (Ill.) Hist. Ctr., 2003, U. N.Mex., 2004, Represented in permanent collections Nat. Vietnam Vets. Art Mus., Chgo., Nat. Mus. Fine Art, Hanoi, Vietnam., Ga. World Congress Ctr., Atlanta, U. Ga. Complex Carbohydrate Rsch. Ctr.; featured (in over 150 mags.); Exhibited in group shows at U. N.Mex., 2004, Represented in permanent collections Bank South Ga., Tifton, Ga. . With U.S. Army, 1959-63, Vietnam. Decorated Purple heart, 1963; Visual Arts fellow So. Arts Fdn./NEA, 1988; Sr. Faculty grantee U. Ga. Rsch. Found., Inc., 1991-93, 96-98, Individual Artist grantee Ga. Coun. Arts, 1993-94; recipient Purchase award 8th Annual Maine/Maritime Internat. Flatworks Exhibn., 1990, Merit award Forth Ree Works 29th Juried Exbhn., Lydon House Arts Center, Athens, Ga., 2004. Mem. VFW, Mil. Order of the Purple Heart (comdr. 1999-2000), Vietnam Helicopter Pilots Assn. Home: 165 Springdale St Athens GA 30605-1237 Personal E-mail: richard.j.olsen@att.net.

OLSEN, ROBERT C., JR., academic administrator, military officer; b. Bklyn. m. Maureen Olsen; 2 children. BS, USCG Acad., 1969; MS in Adminstrn., U.S. Naval Postgrad. Sch., Monterey, Calif., 1979; MA in Nat. Security and Strategic Studies, Naval War Coll., 1990. Commd. USCG, advanced through grades to rear admiral; exec. officer USCGC Madrona; commdg. officer various cutters USCG; commandant of cadets USCG Acad., asst. supt., maritime law enforcement and intelligence br. chief for 3d Coast Guard Dist.; mgr. surface forces Coast Guard Atlantic Area; detailer for officer assignments USCG Hdqrs., mem. tng. and edn. staff, dir. pers. mgmt.; supt., pres. USCG Acad., New London, Conn. Decorated Legion of Merit (3), Meritorious Svc. medal, Coast Guard Commendation medal (4), Humanitarian Svc. medal (2). Office: US Coast Guard Academy 15 Mohegan Ave New London CT 06320-8100

OLSEN, STEVEN KENT, dentist; b. Spanish Fork, Utah, Nov. 20, 1944; s. Earl Clarence and Adela (Faux) O.; children: Christopher, Sara Kate, Vanessa. BS, Brigham Young U., 1969; DDS, U. Pacific, 1974. Ptrn. practice dentistry in surg. and endodontics Brooks & Olsen, Salt Lake City, 1974—; gen. practice dentistry Steven K. Olsen, D.D.S., San Francisco, 1974-75; pres. S.K. Olsen, P.C., San Francisco, 1975—; ptnr. Olsen, H. & P., San Francisco, 1977-83; instr. U. Pacific, San Francisco, 1978—. Chmn. bd. Am. Dentists Ins. Corp., Grand Cayman, W.I., 1978-81; instr. Stanford (Calif.) Inst., Chabot Coll. Inst., 1979-82; med. staff Latter-day Saints Hosp.; cons. Calif. Inst., San Francisco, 1981—; ptnr. J.B. Devel. Co., Russell Harris Restorations, Ryan Bott Restorations, Jason Herget Restorations, D.W. Mmgt. Co., Bob Steck Mgmt. Co., Dave Olsen & Co.; chmn. bd., pres. R.O.R., 1977-80; bd. dirs. Wilks & Topper, Inc., San Francisco, Curt Facchino Ltd., Woodside. Author: Accolade, 1963, (play) Lancer Ballade, 1963, (acad. course) World Religions, 1979; editor corr. course Calif. Inst., 1981. Recipient Good Citizenship medal SAR, 1963, Golden State award, 1988, others. Mem. Assn. Coll. of Physicians and Surgeons, ADA, Calif. Dental Assn., Utah Dental Assn., Physicians and Surgeons Club (San Francisco), Alpha Epsilon Delta. Home: 385 Old La Honda Rd Woodside CA 94062-2617 Office: 2 Embarcadero Ctr Promenade San Francisco CA 94111

OLSEN, TAVA MARYANNE LENNON, industrial and operations engineering educator; b. Aarhus, Denmark, Dec. 20, 1969; came to U.S., 1990; d. Michael James and Jennifer Anne Lennon; m. Timothy Robert Olsen, Dec. 30, 1995. BSc in Math. with honors, U. Auckland, New Zealand, 1989; MS in Stats., Stanford (Calif.) U., 1992, PhD in Ops. Rsch., 1994. Asst. prof. indsl. and ops. engring. U. Mich., Ann Arbor, 1994—2001; assoc. prof. Olin Sch. Bus., Wash. U. in St. Louis, 2001—. Mem. Inst. Ops. Rsch. and Mgmt. Sci., Sigma Xi. Office: Campus Box 1133 PO Box 1133 Saint Louis MO 63188-1133

OLSEN, THOMAS RICHARD, SR., air force officer; b. Houston, June 28, 1934; s. Oscar Leonard and Catherine (Byers) O.; children: Thomas Richard Jr., Lisa Kendrick Olsen Wesolick; m. Jacquelyn Beasley Keels, June 28, 1998. BSME, Tex. A&M U., 1956; MS in Internat. Affairs, George Washington U., 1968. Mech. engr. Tex. Gas Corp., Houston, 1956; commd. 2d lt. USAF, 1957, advanced through grades to maj. gen., 1986; pilot trainee Greenville AFB, Miss., 1957-58; fighter pilot 326 FIS/526 FIS, U.S. and Fed. Republic Germany, 1958-65, 614 TFS/615 TFS, England AFB, La., 615 TFS, Phan Rang AB, Vietnam, 1966-67; instr. U.S. Naval Amphibious Sch., Coronado, Calif., 1968-71; fighter pilot 391 TFS, Mt. Home AFB, Idaho, 1971-72, squadron ops. officer, squadron comdr., 1972-74; chief rated officer Mgmt. Hdqrs. AFMPC, Randolph AFB, Tex., 1975-78; chief of staff Hdqrs. 9th Air Force, Shaw AFB, S.C., 1978-79; dep. comdr. Hdqrs. 314th Air Div., Seoul, Republic of Korea, 1979-81; dir. ops. Hdqrs. 5th Air Force, Yokota AFB, Japan, 1981-82; wing comdr. 51 TFW, Osan AB, Republic of Korea, 1982-83; dep. dir. ops. Hdqrs. Pacific Command, Camp Smith, Hawaii, 1983-85; asst. chief of staff ops. Hdqrs. AFCENT, NATO, Brunsuum, The Netherlands, 1985-87; dep. comdr., chief of staff Hdqrs. 4 ATAF, NATO, Heidelberg, Fed. Republic Germany, 1987-89; vice comdr. Hdqrs. 9th Air Force, Shaw AFB, S.C., 1989-91; dep. comdr. U.S. Cen. Command Air Forces (Desert Shield/Desert Storm), Riyadh, Saudi Arabia, 1990-91; ret., 1991. Exec. dir. Sumter Base Defense Com., 1994—. Mem. Optimist Club, Coronado, 1969-71. Mem. Air Force Assn., Ret. Officers Assn., Daedalians, Kiwanis, Rotary. Presbyterian. Home: 1008 Sparkleberry Ct Sumter SC 29150-2337 E-mail: tolsen@usc.net.

OLSEN-DUNBAR, JESSICA IDA, sign language educator; b. Waterloo, Iowa, Dec. 7, 1977; d. Loren David and Deborah Ann Olsen; m. Stephen Leo Dunbar, Sept. 30, 1965. BA, U. No. Iowa, 2000; Master's, McDaniel Coll., 2003. Am. sign lang. instr. U. No. Iowa, Cedar Falls, 2000—. Club advisor Am. Sign Lang. Club of U. No. Iowa, Cedar Falls, Iowa, 2002—. Treas. Miss Deaf Iowa Pageant Com., 1997. Named Miss Deaf Iowa, 1995—97. Mem.: Iowa Assn. Deaf (assoc.), Miss Deaf Iowa Pageant Com. (assoc.), Cedarloo Assn. Deaf (assoc.; v.p. 1999—2001, del. 1999—2001). Home: 736 Home Park Boulevard Waterloo IA 50701-2954 Office: University of Northern Iowa 1222 West 27th Street Cedar Falls IA 50614-0001 Personal E-mail: jessicaiolsen@mchsi.com. E-mail: jessica.olsen@uni.edu.

OLSHAKER, MARK BRUCE, author, film maker; b. Washington, Feb. 28, 1951; s. Bennett and Thelma A. (Abramson) O.; m. Carolyn M. Clemente, Aug. 28, 1977. BA, George Washington U., Washington, 1972. Spl. correspondent St. Louis Post Dispatch, Washington Bur., 1974-75; writer, author, film maker Washington Area, 1972—. V.p. Unicorn Projects, Inc., Washington, 1983—, Mindhunters, Inc. Vienna, Va., 1995—; bd. dirs. Shakespeare Guild, Washington. Author: (novels) Einstein's Brain, 1981, Unnatural Causes, 1986, Blood Race, 1989, The Edge, 1994, The Mindhunters: Broken Wings, 1999; (anthology) Unusual Suspects, 1996; (non-fiction) The Instant Image, 1978; co-author (with John Douglas), Mindhunter, 1995 (Anthony award nomination, Brit. Gold Dagger nomination, Edgar nomination, Mystery Writers of Am.), Unabomber: On the Trail of America's Most-Wanted Serial Killer, 1996, Journey into Darkness, 1997, Obsession, 1998, The Anatomy of Motive, 1999, The Cases That Haunt Us, 2000; (with C.J. Peters) Virus Hunter, 1997; (screen writing) Stormchasers, 1995, (CINE Golden Eagle), The Edge, 1996 (TV Writing and Prodn.) We All Came to America, 1974, A Moment in Time, 1975, Patent Pending, 1975 (silver medal Inst. Film & TV Festival N.Y.), Lewis Mumford: Toward Human Architecture, 1979, Castle, 1983 (Am. Film Festival Red Ribbon), Cathedral, 1985 (Am. Film Festival Blue Ribbon, Cine Golden Eagle) Pyramid, 1988 (CINE Golden Eagle, Nat. Ednl. Film and Video Festival Gold Apple), What's Killing the Children?, 1990, Discovering Hamlet, 1990 (Am. Film Festival Red Ribbon, Bronze medal Inst. Film & TV Festival N.Y.), Mind of a Serial Killer, 1992 (Emmy nomination news and documentary 1993), Roman City, 1994 (Emmy award), Bridge, 1998, Mill Times, 2001, Bioterror: Dealing with a New Reality, 2001, Avoiding Armageddon, 2003; contbr. articles to newspapers, mags., wrote exhibition films for Nat. Park Svc., and Nat. Bicentennial Grand Parade, 1976. Media advisor, NEH, Corp. Pub. Broadcasting, Washington, 1984, 89, 91, 98, D.C. Comm. Arts and Humanities; hearing com. D.C. Ct. of Appeal Bd. on Profl. Responsibility, 1988-91. Mem. Writers Guild of Am. East, The Authors Guild, The Cosmos Club, Nat. Press Club. Office: PO Box 1957 Vienna VA 22183-1957

OLSHAN, REGINA, lawyer; b. Kiev, Ukraine, 1964; m. Yves Cantin; children: Maxime, Gabrielle. AB cum laude, Harvard U., 1985; cert. in European Studies, Coll. d'Europe, 1986; JD, Yale U., 1989. Bar: Conn. 1991, N.Y. 1994. Law clk. Hon. José Cabranes U.S. Dist. Ct. Conn., 1989—90; atty. Skadden, Arps, Slate, Meagher & Flom LLP, N.Y., 1990—98, ptnr., 1998—. Scholar, Fulbright Found. Office: Skadden Arps Slate Meagher & Flom LLP Four Times Square New York NY 10036

OLSON, A. CRAIG, foundation administrator, former retail executive, retail executive; m. Cathy; 1 child, Sarah. BS in Acctg., U. Idaho, 1974. CPA, Idaho. From checker to sr. v.p., CFO Albertson's, Inc., Boise, Idaho, 1967-91, sr. v.p., CFO, 1991—2001; exec. dir. J.A. and Kathryn Albertson Found., Boise, Idaho, 2002—. Adv. bd. U. Idaho Coll. Bus. & Econs., bd. dirs. Bogus Basin Recreational Assn. Mem. Am. Inst. CPAs, Idaho Soc. CPAs, Financial Exec. Inst. Avocations: family, sailing, running, skiing. Office: JA & Kathryn Albertson Found PO Box 70002 Boise ID 83707-0102

OLSON, BARBARA FORD, physician; b. Iowa City, June 15, 1935; d. Leonard A. and Anne (Swanson) Ford; m. Robert Eric Olson, 1959 (div. 1973); children: Katherine Gee, Eric Ford, Julie Marie. BA, Gustavus Adolphus Coll., 1956; MD, U. Minn., 1960. Diplomate Am. Bd. Family Practice, Am. Bd. Geriat. Medicine, added qualification geriat. medicine. Intern St. Paul-Ramsy Med. Ctr., 1960-61; resident in anesthesiology U. Hosp. Cleve., 1961-62, U. Minn. Hosp., Mpls., 1962-63; pvt. practice anesthesiology St. Johns Hosp. and Devine Redeemer Hosp., St. Paul, 1963-67, Mercy Hosp., Coon Rapids, Minn., 1967-74; staff physician Oak Terrace Nursing Home, Minnetonka, Minn., 1974-88; staff physician, med. dir. geriatric evaluation clinic VA Med. Ctr., St. Cloud, Minn., 1988—. Pres. Alpha Epsilon Iota Med. Found., Mpls., 1980—86, bd.dirs., 1980—86, 2003—. Mem. Minn. Med. Assn., Minn. Women Physicians (pres. 1981-82), Minn. Nursing Home Med. Dirs. Home: PO Box 7306 Saint Cloud MN 56302-7306 Office: VA Med Ctr 4801 8th St N Saint Cloud MN 56303-2015 Business E-Mail: Barbara.Olson@med.va.gov.

OLSON, CAROL LEA, lithographer, educator; b. Anderson, Ind., June 10, 1929; d. Daniel Ackerman and Marguerite Louise Olson. AB, Anderson Coll., 1952; MA, Ball State U., 1976. Pasteup artist Warner Press, Inc., Anderson, 1952-53, apprentice lithographer stripper, 1953-57, journeyman, 1957-63, lithographic dot etcher, color corrector, 1959-73, prepres coord. art dept., 1973-81, prepres tech. specialist, 1981-83, color film assembler, 1983-96. Part-time photography instr. Anderson Univ.; tchr. photography Anderson Fine Arts Ctr., 1976-79; instr. photography, photographics Anderson U., 1979-2003, Ind. U. East, 2003-054 mag. photographer Bd. Christian Edn. of Ch. of God, Anderson, 1973-86; freelance photographer. One person show Anderson U., 1979; exhibited in group shows Anderson U., 1980—, Purdue U., 1982. Instr. 1st aide ARC, Anderson, 1969-79; sec. volleyball Anderson Sunday Sch. Athletic Assn., 1973-2000. Recipient Hon. mention, Ann Arbor, Mich., 1977, Anderson Fine Arts Ctr., 1977, 78, 83, 1st Pl., 1983, Hon. Mention, 1983, 2d Pl., 1988, Hon. Mention, 1988, 93, Best of Show, 1983, 91, 92, Best Nature Catagory Anderson Fine Arts Ctr., 1994. Mem. AAUW, Associated Photographer Internat., Nat. Inst. Exploration, Profl. Photographers Am. Mem. Ch. of God. Avocations: camping, travel, canoeing. Home: 2604 E 6th St Anderson IN 46012-3725

OLSON, CHARLES ERIC, economist; b. Wausau, Wis., June 2, 1942; s. Roland Anthony and Lois (Erickson) O.; m. Pamela Ann Templin, July 1, 1967 (div. Oct. 1973); children: Sonja Anne, Erika Christine; m. Carole Emily Collesian, Dec. 1, 1973 (div. Oct. 1990); children: Cora Elizabeth, Sarah Emily; m. Jeanne Esther Katz, Apr. 14, 1991. Student, U. Wis., Marathon County, 1960-62; BBA with honors, U. Wis., Madison, 1964; MS, U. Wis., 1966, PhD (Villas fellow), 1968. Instr. U. Wis., Madison, 1966-68; asst. prof. U. Md., College Park, 1968-71, assoc. prof. bus. adminstrn., 1971-76; sr. economist H. Zinder & Assocs., Washington, 1976-77, v.p., 1977-79, sr. v.p., 1979—80, pres., 1986-2000, Olson & Co., Inc., 1980-86; tchg. prof. R.H. Smith Sch. Bus., U. Md., College Park, 2000—. Cons. Devel. Adv. Service, atty. gens. N.C., Minn., Ky., Mass., Va. U.S. Postal Rate Commn., Dept. Def., numerous electric and gas utilities in U.S. and Can. Testified numerous pub. utility rate cases, before Senate Subcom. on Inter-govtl. Relations; mem. advisory com. research and devel. and energy conservation Fed. Power Commn., 1973-74, vice chmn. rate design task force, 1976—. Author: Cost Considerations for Efficient Electricity Supply, 1970; contbr. chpts. to books, articles to profl. jours. Mem. Prince Georges County (Md.) Citizens Airpark Advisory Com., 1970-71. Grantee Inst. Pub. Utilities, 1967-68; U. Md. 1970, 76. Mem. Transp. and Pub. Utilities Group, Beta Gamma Sigma. Home: 10822 Alloway Dr Rockville MD 20854-1503 Office: RH Smith Sch Bus Univ Md College Park MD 20742 E-mail: colson@rhsmith.umd.edu.

OLSON, CLIFFORD LARRY, management consultant, entrepreneur; b. Karlstad, Minn., Oct. 11, 1946; s. Wallace B. and Lucille I (Pederson) O.; m. B.A. Blue Blodgett, March 18, 1967; children: Derek, Erin. BChemE, B in Physics, U. Minn., 1969; MBA, U. Chgo., 1972; Licence en Sci. Econ., U. Louvain, Brussels, 1972. CPA, Cert. mgmt. cons. Project engr. Procter & Gamble, Chgo., 1969-71; engagement mgr. McKinsey & Co., Chgo., 1972-75; ptnr., midwest regional dir. mgmt. cons. Peat, Marwick, Mitchell, St. Louis, 1976-87; chmn. Casson Group, Inc., Mpls., 1987—; CEO AbelConn, 1997—. Mem. AICPA, Union League Club Chgo., Interlachen Country Club. Avocations: skiing, carpentry. Office: 9210 Science Center Dr New Hope MN 55428-3621

OLSON, CORY M. food products executive; Product mgmt. officer Gainer Bank Corp., 1985—88; mng. dir. capital markets Bank One Corp., 1988—99; v.p., treas. Suiza Foods, 1999—2001; sr. v.p. fin., treas. Dean Foods, Dallas, 2002—. Office: Dean Foods Co 2515 McKinney Ave Dallas TX 75201-1945

OLSON, DALE C. public relations executive; b. Fargo, N.D., Feb. 20, 1934; s. Arthur Edwin and Edith (Weight) Olson Neubauer. Sr. v.p., prin., pres. motion picture divsn. Rogers and Cowan, Inc., Beverly Hills, Calif., 1967-85; prin. Dale C. Olson & Assocs., Beverly Hills, 1985—; mktg. dir. Hollywood History Mus., 2003. Cons. Filmex, L.A., 1972-83; U.S. del. Manila Film Festival, 1982-83. Editor L.A. edit. Theatre ann. Best Plays, 1963-67. V.p. Diamond Cir. City of Hope, Duarte, Calif., 1980-83; mem. adv. bd. Calif. Mus. Sci. and Industry, L.A., 1975-81; memb. bd. govs. Film Industry Workshops, Inc., 1965-80; pres. Hollywood Press Club, 1963-66; assoc. Los Angeles County Art Mus., 1981-83; bd. trustees Hollywood Arts Coun.; chair 1999 jury USA Film Festival, Dallas; cons. L.A. 2000. Recipient Golden Key, Pub. Rels. News, 1982, Les Mason and pub. svc. awards Publicists Guild, Golden Satellite award for lifetime achievement Internat. Press Acad., 1999, Prism award for pub. svc. Entertainment Industries Coun., 2000. Mem. NATAS, Acad. Motion Picture Arts and Scis. (chmn. pub. rels. coordinating com. 1982—), Actors Fund Am. (chmn. Western coun. 1991, trustee 1992, exec. com. 1998), Hollywood Arts Coun. (bd. dirs.), Pres.'s Club, Thalians. Lutheran. Office Phone: 323-876-9331. E-mail: dolson2000@earthlink.net.

OLSON, DAVID JOHN, political science educator; b. Brantford, N.D., May 18, 1941; s. Lloyd and Alice Ingrid (Black) O.; m. Sandra Jean Crabb, June 11, 1966; 1 dau., Maia Kari. BA, Concordia Coll., Moorhead, Minn., 1963; Rockefeller fellow Union Theol. Sem, N.Y.C., 1963-64; MA (Brooklings Instn. predoctoral research fellow 1968-69), U. Wis., Madison, 1966, PhD (univ. fellow 1967), 1971. Community planner Madison Redvel. Authority, 1965-66; lectr. U. Wis., 1966-67; from lectr. to asso. prof. polit. sci. Ind. U., Bloomington, 1969-76; prof. polit. sci. U. Wash., Seattle, 1976—, chmn. dept., 1983-88, Harry Bridges endowed chairlabor studies, 1992-94; bd. dirs. Harry Bridges Inst.; dir.Ctr. Labor Studies U. Wash., 1992-94; Disting. lectr. in labor studies San Francisco State U., 1994. Vis. prof. U. Bergen, 1987, Harvard U., 1988-89, U. Hawaii, 1989, U. Calif., Berkeley, 1996. Co-author: Governing the United States, 1978, Commission Politics, 1977, To Keep the Republic, 1975, Black Politics, 1971; co-editor: Theft of the City, 1974. Recipient Disting. Teaching award Ind. U., 1973, faculty fellow, 1973, Alumni Achievement award Concordia Coll., 1998. Mem. Am. Polit. Sci. Assn., Western Polit. Sci. Assn. (v.p. 1984, pres. 1985), Midwest Polit. Sci. Assn., So. Polit. Sci. Assn. Democrat. Lutheran. Home: 6512 E Green Lake Way N Seattle WA 98103-5418 Office: U Wash Dept Polit Sci Seattle WA 98195-0001 Office Phone: 206-543-7948. Business E-Mail: davidols@u.washington.edu.

OLSON, DENNIS OLIVER, lawyer; b. Seminole, Tex., Oct. 19, 1947; s. Edwin and Beulah Matilda (Strang) O.; m. Leonee Lynn Claud, Jan. 30, 1971; children: James Edwin, Stacy Rae. BA in English, U. Tex., 1969; JD, Tex. Tech U., 1974. Bar: Tex. 1974, U.S. Ct. Mil. Appeals 1974, U.S. Dist. Ct. (no. dist.) Tex. 1978, U.S. Dist. Ct. (we. dist.) Tex. 1978, U.S. Ct. Appeals (5th cir.) 1984, U.S. Supreme Ct. 1985, U.S. Dist. Ct. (ea. dist.) Tex. 2002. Commd. USMC, 1969, advanced through grades to capt., 1973, infantry officer various locations including Vietnam, 1969-74, judge advocate, 1974-78, resigned, 1978; assoc. Carr, Evans, Fouts & Hunt, and predecessor, Lubbock, Tex., 1978-81, ptnr., 1981-85; pvt. practice Dallas, 1985-88; shareholder, co-chmn. bankruptcy sect. Godwin & Carlton, P.C., Dallas, 1989-94; ptnr. Olson Nicoud & Gueck, LLP and predecessor, Dallas, 1994—. Bd. dirs. Presbyn. Ctr. Doctors Clinic, Lubbock, 1983-85, United Campus Ministry, Tex. Tech U., Lubbock, 1984-85, Discovery Sch.of Canyon Creek, Richardson, 1999-2002; elder Canyon Creek Presbyn. Ch., Richardson, Tex.; treas., bd. dirs. Lubbock chpt. ARC, 1981-83; vol. Lubbock United Way, 1978-80. Decorated Bronze Star; named Outstanding Young Man of Am., 1983. Fellow Tex. Bar Found. (sustaining life); Dallas Bar Assn., Lubbock County Bar Assn. (bd. dirs. 1983-85), Tex. Young Lawyers Assn. (bd. dirs. 1981-83), Judge Advocates Assn. (bd. dirs. 1976-78), Lubbock C. of C. (grad. Leadership Lubbock program 1981), U. Tex. NROTC Alumni Found., (bd. dirs. 2001-), Phi Delta Phi. Home: 313 Forest Grove Dr Richardson TX 75080-1937 Office Phone: 214-979-7302. E-mail: denniso@dallas-law.com.

OLSON, DONALD RICHARD, mechanical engineering educator; b. Sargent, Nebr., Dec. 26, 1917; s. Harry T. and Gyneth E. (Wittemyer) O.; m. Nancy Walker Benton, June 17, 1944; children: Walter H., Sally, Timothy W. BS, Oreg. State U., 1942; M.Engring., Yale U., 1944, D.Engring., 1951. Profl. engr., Conn. Asst. prof., asso. prof. mech. engring. Yale U., New Haven, 1951-62; prof. mech. engring. Pa. State U., University Park, 1962-83, prof. emeritus, 1983—; head underwater power plants Applied Research Lab., 1962-72, head dept. mech. engring., 1972-83; mem. engring. accreditation commn., 1979-82. Contbr. tech. papers in field to publs. Mem. ASME, Soc. Automotive Engrs. (dir. 1968-71), Sigma Xi. Home: 621 Glenn Rd State College PA 16803-3475 E-mail: dro@psu.edu.

OLSON, ERIC N. molecular biologist, educator; PhD. Prof. and chmn. molecular biology U. Tex. Southwestern Med. Ctr., Dallas. Office: Nancy B & Jake L Haman Biomed Rsch Bldg U Tex SoW Med Ctr 6000 Harry Hines Blvd Dallas TX 75390 E-mail: eric.olson@utsouthwestern.edu.

OLSON, FERRON ALLRED, metallurgist, educator; b. Tooele, Utah, July 2, 1921; s. John Ernest and Harriet Cynthia (Allred) O.; m. Donna Lee Jefferies, Feb. 1, 1944; children: Kandace, Randall, Paul, Jeffery, Richard. BS, U. Utah, 1953, PhD, 1956. Ordained bishop LDS Ch., 1962. Research chemist Shell Devel. Co., Emeryville, Calif., 1956-61; assoc. research prof. U. Utah, Salt Lake City, 1961-63, assoc. prof., 1963-68, chmn. dept mining, metall. and fuels engring., 1966-74, prof. dept. metallurgy and metall. engring., 1968-96, prof. emeritus, 1996—. Cons. U.S. Bur. Mines, Salt Lake City, 1973-77, Ctr. for Investigation Mining and Metallurgy, Santiago, Chile, 1978; dir. U. Utah Minerals Inst., 1980-91. Author: Collection of Short Stories, 1985, (hist. book) Seymour Brunson: Defender of the Faith, 1998, (novel) Harriet Cynthia Allred Olson, 1995; contbr. articles to profl. jours. Del. State Rep. Conv., Salt Lake City, 1964; bishop, 1962-68, 76-82, missionary, 1988. With U.S. Army, 1943-46, PTO. Named Fulbright-Hayes lectr., Yugoslavia, 1974-75, Disting. prof. Fulbright-Hayes, Yugoslavia, 1980, Outstanding Metallurgy Instr., U. Utah, 1979-80, 88-89, Disting. Speaker U. Belgrade-Bor, Yugoslavia, 1974. Mem. Am. Inst. Mining, Metall. and Petroleum Engrs. (chmn. Utah chpt. 1978-79), Am. Soc. Engring. Edn. (chmn. Minerals div. 1972-73), Fulbright Alumni Assn., Am. Bd. Engring. and Tech. (bd. dirs. 1975-82). Republican. Achievements include research on explosives ignition and decomposition; surface properties of thoria, silica gels, silicon monoxide in ultra high vacuum; kinetics of leaching of Chrysocolla, Malachite and Bornite; electrowinning of gold; nodulation of copper during electrodeposition. Home: 1862 Herbert Ave Salt Lake City UT 84108-1832 E-mail: donnaolson1@mailstation.com.

OLSON, FLOYD PALMER, retired service company executive; b. Glencoe, Minn., May 12, 1932; s. Oscar Peter and Hazel Anna (Wolff) O.; m. Sandra Rae Larson, Feb. 5, 1955; children: Douglas, David, Clayton, Sarah. BS, U. Minn., 1954. Mgmt. trainee Wilson Meat Packing Co., Albert Lea, Minn., 1957-60, dept. mgr. Memphis, 1960-62, area mgr. Sao Paulo, Brazil, 1962-69, plant mgr. Oklahoma City, 1969-76; pres. Gol-Pak Corp., Oneida, N.Y., 1976-78; asst. West Coast mgr. Hygrade Food Products, Tacoma, Wash., 1978-79; owner, dir. Servpro, Gig Harbor, Wash., 1979-2000; ret., 2000. Bd. mem. Peninsula Light Co., Gig Harbor, 1992-95; state dir. Servpro Industries, Wash., 1982-2000. Organizer Jr. Achievement, Albert Lea, Minn., 1959; pres. couns. ch., 1975-74. With U.S. Army, 1955-57. Mem. Rotary Internat. (pres. Gig Harbor 1990-91, presdl. citation 1996, dist. gov. 1994-95, zone chmn. 1996-97, dir. elect, Paul Harris fellow 1993). Republican. Avocations: motorhoming, golf, travel.

OLSON, FRANK ALBERT, car rental company executive; b. San Francisco, July 19, 1932; s. Alfred and Edith Mary (Hazeldine) O.; m. Sarah Jean Blakely, Oct. 19, 1957; children: Kimberly, Blake, Christopher. AA, City Coll. San Francisco, 1961. V.p. and gen. mgr. Barrett Transp. Inc., San Francisco,

1950-64; v.p., gen. mgr. Valcar Co. subs. Hertz Corp., San Francisco, 1964-68; mgr. N.Y. zone Hertz Corp., N.Y.C., 1968-69, v.p., mgr. Ea. region, v.p., gen. mgr. rent-a-car divsn., exec. v.p. rent-a-car divsn. gen. mgr., also bd. dirs., 1973-77, pres., 1977-80; CEO, 1977-99; chmn. bd. dirs. Hertz Corp., N.Y.C., 1980, also dir., CEO, 1982—; chmn., CEO Allegis Corp., 1987; pres., CEO United Airlines, 1987; chmn., CEO Hertz Corp., Park Ridge, NJ, 1987-99, chmn. bd. dirs., 1999—. Bd. dirs. Amerada Hess Corp., Becton Dickinson & Co., Fund Am. Enterprises Holdings, Inc. Bd. dirs., mem. exec. com. World Travel and Tourism Coun. Mem. Am. Assn. Sovereign Mil. Order of Malta, Pine Valley Golf Club (N.J.), Royal and Ancient St. Andrews (Scotland), Blind Brook Club, Met. Club (N.Y.C.), Seminole Golf Club (Fla.), Cypress Point Club (Calif.). Republican. Roman Catholic. Office: Hertz Corp 210 Summit Ave Montvale NJ 07645

OLSON, GARY DUANE, history educator; b. Spring Grove, Minn., July 30, 1939; s. Raymond G. and Ethel N. (Storlie) O.; m. Rosaaen Marie Skifton, Sept. 4, 1960; children: Erik Lee, Timothy Karl, Lars Christian. BA, Luther Coll., 1961; MA, U. Nebr., 1965, PhD, 1968. Tchr. social studies Kerkhoven Pub. Schs., Minn., 1961-63, asst. prof. history Augustana Coll., Sioux Falls, S.D., 1968-73, assoc. prof., 1973-79, prof., 1979—, dean acad. svcs., 1981-87, v.p. acad. affairs, dean, 1987-95. Cons.-evaluator North Ctrl Assn., 1992—. Author: (with H. Krause) Prelude to Glory, 1974, (with E.L. Olson) Sioux Falls, South Dakota: A Pictorial History, 1985, 2003; contbr. articles to profl. jours. Mem. Orgn. Am. Historians, S.D. Hist. Soc., Vesterheim Mus. Assn., Norwegian-Am. Hist. Assn. Home: 2505 S Main Ave Sioux Falls SD 57105-4820 Office: Augustana Coll Sioux Falls SD 57197-0001 E-mail: gary_olson@augie.edu.

OLSON, GARY ROBERT, banker; b. Milw., May 9, 1946; s. Ward Louis and Mary Jane (Brown) O.; m. Mia Kristina Sohn, Feb. 26, 1972; children: Kristin Anne, Brian Ward. Student, Loyola U., Rome, 1966-67; AB, Marquette U., 1968; M Internat. Mgmt., Am. Grad. Sch. Internat. Mgmt., Glendale, Ariz., 1973. Instr. Sogang Jesuit U., Seoul, 1968-70, Hankuk U. Fgn. Studies, Seoul, 1971-72; grad. asst. Am. Grad. Sch. Internat. Mgmt., 1972; credit analyst Chase Manhattan Bank, N.A., N.Y.C. and Tokyo, 1973-75, asst. treas. N.Y.C., 1975-77, 2d v.p. Madrid, 1977, Paris, 1977-80, v.p., mgr. Regional Banking Office Chgo., 1980-83; v.p., regional mgr. Case Nat. Corp. Svcs., San Francisco, 1983-87; sr. v.p. Chase Bank Ariz., Phoenix, 1987-90; v.p. Bklyn. and S.I. commercial mgr. Chase Manhattan Bank, N.A., Bklyn., 1990-93, v.p., team leader Nassau mid. mkt. mgr. Melville, L.I., 1993-97; mgr. corp. banking L.I. Dime Savs. Bank, Huntington Station, N.Y., 1997-99; sr. v.p. comml. banking Dime Savings Bank, 2000—. Advisor English program USIS, Seoul, 1969; alumni domestic counselor Am. Grad. Sch. Internat. Mgmt., 1990—, Marquette U., 1990—; vol. Spl. Olympics, Phoenix, 1988-89; fund drive capt. Phoenix Econ. Growth Corp., 1988; trustee, bd. dirs. Variety Pre-schooler's workshop, 1994—; bd. dirs. L.I. chpt. Robert Morris Assocs., 1994—, chmn., 1995—; trustee, bd. dirs., mktg. com., chmn.'s coun. Hecksher Mus., Huntington, N.Y., 1995—. Mem. Robert Morris Assocs. (assoc.), Econ. Club Phoenix, World Trade Club. Republican. Roman Catholic. Avocations: reading, skiing, swimming, golf. Office: Washington Mutual Bank 1377 Motor Pkwy Farmingville NY 11749 E-mail: garyolson281@hotmail.com.

OLSON, GEN, state legislator; b. May 20, 1938; BS in Edn. with distinction, EdD, U. Minn. Mayor, Minnetrista, Minn., 1981-82; mem. Minn. Senate from 34th dist., St. Paul, 1983—. Former mem. Park and Recreation Commn., Planning and Zoning Commn., Police Commn., City Council. Republican. Office: Minn State Senate State Capitol Building Saint Paul MN 55155-0001

OLSON, GENE L. food products executive; Sr. v.p. fin. Golden State Foods, Irvine, Calif. Office: Golden State Foods 18301 Von Karman Ave Ste 1100 Irvine CA 92612-0133

OLSON, HAROLD ROY, computer company executive; b. Escanaba, Mich., Apr. 8, 1928; s. Roy A. and Sara Calla Margarita (Carlson) O.; m. Angela Davis Hennessy, Sept. 26, 1959. BA in Journalism and Advt., Mich. State U., 1950. Mail clk. McCann Erickson Co., N.Y.C., 1950, 52-53; book promotion specialist, mgr. mag. promotion McGraw-Hill, N.Y.C., 1953-56; mgr. mag. promotion Reinhold Pub. Co., N.Y.C., 1956-58; space salesman McCall Corp., N.Y.C., 1959-60; pres. Visual Identity, Inc., N.Y.C., 1960-68; mktg. rep. Honeywell Info. Sys., Inc., N.Y.C., 1969-86; pres. Hal Olson's EDGE-BUY Express, Inc., 1986—. With U.S. Army, 1950-52. Republican. Episcopalian. Avocation: sailing. Office: 240 E 27TH St #265 New York NY 10016-9277

OLSON, HERBERT THEODORE, trade association executive; b. Bridgeport, Conn., Feb. 9, 1929; s. Herbert Theodore and Inez Evelyn (Lindahl) O.; children: Christina, Victoria; m. Kathleen A. Harrison, Dec. 27, 1988. Student, Heidelberg Coll., 1947-49; AB, Ohio U., 1951, postgrad., 1951-52. Asst. to dean of men Ohio U., Athens, 1951-52; with Union Carbide Corp., 1952-71, mgr. employee rels., coord. pub. affairs, 1969-71; exec. v.p. Am. Assn. for Aging, Washington, 1971-75; dir. spl. projects Am. Healthcare Assn., Washington, 1975-79; pres. Promotional Products Assn. Internat., Irving, Tex., 1979-96, pres. emeritus, 1996—. Event coord.-supplier Stars Showcase, 1998-2000; mem. adv. bd. Allied Bank. Mem. nat. exploring com., vice chmn. nat. events com., ann. meetings com., mem.-at-large nat. coun. Boy Scouts Am., 1980—; treas. U.S. Found. for Internat. Scouting, 1988—99, chmn. audit com., 1984—87, mem. internat. com., 1998—2003, mem. direct svc. coun. bd., 1997—2002; mem. long-term care for elderly rsch. rev. and adv. com. Dept. Health, 1972—77; mem. Longterm Care grant rev. com. HEW, 1972—77; mem. planning commn. City of Torrance, Calif., 1962—64, city councilman, 1964—67; chmn. Gov.'s Operation Leegit; mem. adv. bd. Irving Hosp.; chmn. bd. dirs. Irving Cancer Soc., 1997—; exec. bd. cir. 10 coun. Boy Scouts Am.; bd. dirs. Irving Conv. and Visitors Bur., 2001—, DFW Humane Soc., 2001—. Lord Baden Powell fellow, 1986; recipient Disting. Eagle award Boy Scouts Am., 1974, Silver Beaver award, 1968, Silver Buffalo award, 1998; named person of Yr. in Promotional Products in Counselor Mag., 1995, Hall of Fame Promotional Products Assn. Internat., 1997, Hall of Fame Can. Promo Prod. Assn., 1996. Mem. Meeting Planners Internat. (charter), Am. Soc. Assn., Execs., U.S. C. of C., Washington Soc. Assn. Execs., Nat. Assn. Exhibit Mgrs., Small Bus. Legis. Coun. (chmn. bd. 1993-95), Dallas Ft. Worth Soc. Assn. Execs. (v.p. 1985-87), Irving C. of C. (bd. dirs. 1999—), Am. Advt. Fedn., Tex. Sox. Assn. Execs., Las Colinas Country Club, Rotary (bd. dirs.), Masons, Shriners, Kiwanis (lt. gov.), DFW Humane Soc. Irving (bd. dirs. 2000-). Baptist. Home: 2910 Pacific Ct Irving TX 75062-4624 Office: 807 W Pioneer Dr Irving TX 75061

OLSON, JACK CONRAD, JR., geriatrician; b. Muskegon, Mich., 1955; BS, BA, Mich. State U., 1977; MD, U. Mich., 1984. Bd. cert. internal medicine, bd. cert. geriatric medicine. Intern U. Wis. Hosps. and Clinics, Madison, 1984—85, resident internal medicine, 1985—87, fellow geriatrics, 1987—89; assoc. med. dir. Mendota Mental Health, U. Wis., 1989—92; dir. Windermere Sr. Health Ctr., U. Chgo., 1992—99; asst. clin. prof., fellowship dir. Rush U. Med. Ctr., Chgo., 1999—. Office: Ste 319 1725 W Harrison St Chicago IL 60612 Office Phone: 312-942-7030.

OLSON, JAMES CLIFTON, historian, university president; b. Bradgate, Iowa, Jan. 23, 1917; s. Arthur Edwin and Abbie (Anderson) O.; m. Vera Blanche Farrington, June 6, 1941; children: Elizabeth, Sarah Margaret. AB, Morningside Coll., 1938, LLD, 1968; MA, U. Nebr., 1939, PhD, 1942, LittD, 1980, Chonnam Nat. U., Korea, 1978. Instr. Northwest Mo. State Tchrs. Coll., summers 1940-42; dir. Nebr. State Hist. Soc., 1946-56; lectr. U. Omaha, 1947-50, U. Nebr., 1946-54, part-time assoc. prof., 1954-56, prof., chmn. dept. history, 1956-65, Bennett S. and Dorothy Martin prof. history, 1962-65; dean Grad. Coll., univ. research administr., 1966-68, vice chancellor, 1968; chancellor U. Mo.-Kansas City, 1968-76; interim pres. U. Mo. System, 1976-77, pres., 1977-84, pres. emeritus, 1984—; OAS prof. Am. history El Colegio de Mexico, Mexico City, 1962. Vis. prof. U. Colo., summer 1965. Author: J. Sterling Morton, 1942, The Nebraska Story, 1951, History of Nebraska, 1955, 3d edit. (with Ronald C. Naugle), 1997, (with Vera Farrington Olson) Nebraska is My Home, 1956, This is Nebraska, 1960, Red Cloud and the Sioux Problem, 1965, paper edit., 1975, 79, (with Vera Farrington Olson) The University of Missouri: An Illustrated History, 1988, Serving the University of Missouri: A Memoir of Campus and System Administration, 1993, Stuart Symington A Life, 2003; contbg. author: The Army Air Forces in World War II, 1951, 53; editor: Nebraska History, 1946-56; contbr. articles to profl. jours. and encys. Bd. dirs. Mid-Am. Arts Alliance; trustee Midwest Rsch. Inst., Kansas City. Mem. Am. Assn. State and Local History, Coun. Basic Edn., Am. Hist. Assn., Orgn. Am. Historians, State Hist. Soc. Mo. (1st v.p.), Nebr. State Hist. Soc., We. Hist. Assn., Cosmos Club, Phi Beta Kappa, Omicron Delta Kappa, Phi Kappa Phi, Pi Gamma Mu. E-mail: olsonja@umkc.edu.

OLSON, JAMES R. automotive executive; married; 1 child. BA, Stanford U.; MSJ, Northwestern U. Mgr. engring. ops. Lincoln-Mercury divsn., Ford divsn. and sales ops. Ford Motor Co., 1969—85; joined Toyota, 1985—; sr. v.p. external affairs and pub. policy Toyota Motor N.Am., N.Y.C., 2000—. Past chmn. Automotive Hall Fame; past mem., exec. com. Alliance Automobile Mfrs. and Automotive Retailing Today. Office: Toyota Motor NAm Ste 4900 Nine West 57th St New York NY 10019

OLSON, JAMES RICHARD, retired transportation executive; b. Alexandria, Minn., Mar. 11, 1941; s. Orie D. and Theresa Marie (Erickson) O.; m. Ronna Lee, Feb. 1, 1969 (dec.); 1 child, Trevor James. BS, N.D. State U., 1963; LLD, U. Minn., 1966; MBA, Harvard U., 1968. Asst. to v.p. finance Cargill Inc., Mpls., 1968-69; with Graco Inc., Mpls., 1969-75, v.p. finance, 1972-75; exec. v.p. finance Ponderosa System, Inc., Dayton, Ohio, 1975-77; v.p. planning Pillsbury Co., Mpls., 1977-79, v.p. restaurant group, 1979-80; group v.p.-restaurants The Carlson Cos., Inc., Mpls., 1981-83; exec. v.p., chief fin. and adminstrv. officer Schneider Nat., Inc., 1983-87, pres. van group, 1987-92, pres. transp. sector, 1992-98. Bd. dirs., chair compensation com. Meritex Enterprises, Inc. Mem. Harvard Bus. Sch. Club Minn. (past pres.) Lutheran. Home: Winslow House # 807 100 2d St NE Minneapolis MN 55414-2131 Personal E-mail: jrolson1@att.net.

OLSON, JAMES WILLIAM PARK, architect; b. St. Louis, Oct. 6, 1940; s. James William Park; s. Louis Garfield and Gladys Helen (Schuh) O.; m. Katherine Fovargue, June 11, 1971; children: Park, Reed. BArch, U. Wash., 1963. Registered architect, Wash., Oreg., Calif., Ill., Colo., Hawaii, Ga., Fla. Ptnr. Olson Sundberg Kundig Allen Architects, Seattle, 1985—. Assoc. architect New Seattle Art Mus., 1991. Prin. works include Pike and Virginia Bldg. (AIA Honor award 1980), Seattle's Best Coffee Retail Locations (AIA Honor award 1984), Hauberg Residence (AIA Honor award 1997), Mayer Lodo residence, Denver (AIA Honor award 1998, AIA N.W. and Pacific Regional Merit award 1999, AIA We. Internat. Design award 2000), St. Mark's Cathedral Renovation (AIA Commendation award), Seattle (IFFRA award 1998, AIA citation 1998, AIA and Pacific Regional Merit award 2000), numerous residences nationwide; (subject of monologue) Monacelli Press: Architecture, Art and Craft. Bd. dirs. Ctr. Contemporary Art, Seattle, 1982-86, Artist Trust, Seattle, 1986-90, U. Wash. Henry Art Gallery, Seattle, 1986-92, Seattle Art Mus., 1996—. Recipient Best Architect award Seattle Mag., 1985. Fellow AIA; mem. NEA (juror). Avocation: art. Office: Olson Sundberg Kundig Allen Architects 159 South Jackson St 6th Fl Seattle WA 98104-2557 Office Phone: 206-624-5670. Business E-Mail: jim@olsonsundberg.com.

OLSON, JOHN KARL, lawyer; b. Springfield, Mass., Aug. 14, 1949; s. Harold Gunnar and Louise Theodora (Shukis) Olson; m. Ann Catherine Sullivan, June 16, 1973; children: Elizabeth Ann, Katherine Louise. AB, Harvard Coll., 1971; JD, Boston Coll., 1975. Bar: Fla. 1975, U.S. Dist. Ct. (mid. and so. dists.) Fla. 1976, U.S. Ct. Appeals (5th cir.) 1979, U.S. Supreme Ct. 1979, U.S. Ct. Appeals (11th cir.) 1981. From assoc. to ptnr. Carlton, Fields, Ward et al., Tampa, Fla., 1975-86; exec. v.p., gen. counsel, dir. Jet Fla., Inc., Miami, 1986-88; ptnr. Stearns Weaver Miller Weissler Alhadeff & Sitterson P.A., Tampa, 1988—. Author: (book) Creditors and Debtors Rights in Florida, 1979, 2d edit., 1989, Collier Bankruptcy Practice Guide, 1986. Trustee Tampa Mus. Art, 1992—98; mem. parent bd. U. Del., 1998—2002, co-pres., 2000—02. Fellow, U. Tampa, 1986—. Mem.: ABA (vice chmn. bankruptcy com. 1984—86), Fla. Bar Assn. (chmn. bus. law sect. 1988—89), Am. Bankruptcy Inst., Harvard Club (pres. 1982—84). Home: 2632 W Prospect Rd Tampa FL 33629-5358 Office: Sun Trust Fin Ctr 401 E Jackson St Tampa FL 33602-5233 Office Phone: 813-222-5048. E-mail: jolson@swmwas.com.

OLSON, JUDITH MARY REEDY, retired public information officer, former state senator; b. Mitchell, S.D., June 24, 1939; d. John Marvin and Camille (Murphy) Reedy; m. Robert George Olson, Aug. 5, 1961; children: Jeffrey, Jennifer, Jon, Jaime, Jason, Jeremy. EdB, U. Tucson, 1961; MEd, S.D. State U., 1984; postgrad., U. S.D., 1985—. Cert. secondary tchr., edn. adminstrn. Tchr. jr. high sch. Mpls. Pub. Schs., 1961-63; mem. State Bd. Edn., S.D., 1972-83, pres., 1975-78; dir. S.D. Edn. Policy Seminar, 1975-79; substitute tchr. Rapid City (S.D.) Schs., 1979-81, tchr. adult basic edn., 1979-81, supr. community relations, 1981-88, supr. community edn., pub. info., 1988—95; senator S.D. Legis. (dist. 33), Pierre, SD, 1989—95; edn. dir. Career Learning Center of the Black Hills. Speaker, cons. sch. bds., adminstrs., tchrs., sch. dists., pub. relations, various states, 1972—. Bd. dirs. Black Hills Symphony, 1987—; chair, S.D. State Democratic Party, 1998—. Mem. AAUW (Women of Worth award), Rotary, PEO, Delta Kappa Gamma. Democrat. Roman Catholic. Avocations: reading, spectator sports. Office: South Dakota Democratic Party 207 East Capitol Pierre SD 57501-2724 Home: 1106 Hyland Dr Rapid City SD 57701-4456

OLSON, KEITH WALDEMAR, history educator; b. Poughkeepsie, N.Y., Aug. 4, 1931; s. Ernest Waldemar and Elin Ingeborg (Rehnstrom) O.; m. Marilyn Joyce Wittschen, Sept. 10, 1955; children: Paula, Judy. BA, SUNY, Albany, 1957, MA, 1959; PhD, U. Wis., 1964; PhD (hon.), U. Tampere, Finland, 2000. Mem. history faculty Syracuse U., N.Y., 1963-66; mem. history faculty U. Md., College Park, 1966—, prof. history. Fulbright prof. U. Tampere, 1986-87, 2004, U. Oulu, Finland, 1993, U. Jyväskylä, Finland, 1994. Author: The G.I. Bill, the Veterans and the Colleges, 1974; Biography of a Progressive: Franklin K. Lane, 1979, Watergate: The Presidential Scandal That Shook America, 2003. Pres. Am. Scandinavian Found., Washington, 1977-79. Served with U.S. Army, 1952-54. U.S. Office Edn. grantee, 1965-66; U. Md. grantee, 1971, 76, 78. Mem. Am. Hist. Assn., Orgn. Am. Historians, Wis. Hist. Soc., Swedish Am. Hist. Soc., Finnish Hist. Soc. (hon.), Soc. Historians of Am. Fgn. Rels., Cen. Study of Presidency, Am. Scandinavian Assn. (pres. 1989-90). Unitarian Universalist. Home: 10746 Kinloch Rd Silver Spring MD 20903-1226 Office: U Md Dept History College Park MD 20742-0001 Office Phone: 301-405-4286. E-mail: KO6@umail.umd.edu.

OLSON, KENNETH PAUL, vocational consultant; b. Providence, June 26, 1935; s. Gustave Frederick and Beatrice Evelyn (Backstrom) O.; m. Judith Luellan Hazard, Nov. 12, 1965; children: Glenn Edward Johnson. BA in Sociology, U. Denver, 1960; MA in Sociology, U. Colo., 1973. Cert. rehab. counselor, vocat. specialist; lic. profl. counselor, Colo. Exec. dir. Goodwill Industries, Colorado Springs, Co., 1960-65, San Francisco, 1965, Ft. Worth, 1966-70; counselor II Colo. Div. Rehab., Colorado Springs, 1972-83; pres. Olson Vocat. Svcs., Colorado Springs, 1983-97; pvt. practice vocat. cons. Colorado Springs, 1997—. Vocational expert Social Security Adminstn., Denver, 1984—; rehab counselor U.S. Dept. Labor, Denver, 1984-89. V.p. Bus. Arts Ctr., Manitou Springs, 1988—89; councilman Manitou Springs, 1975—78; mem. Commn. for Rehab. Counselor Cert., 1979—85, Bd. for Rehab. Cert., 1984—86; pres. Manitou Art Project, 1994—95; mem. socio-econ. adv. com. Pikes Peak Area Coun. of Govts., 1999—2002; bd. dirs. Manitou Springs Devel. Co., 1998—2002, econ. devel. coun., 2002—03. With USN, 1954—56. Fellow Nat. Rehab. Counseling Assn.; mem. Colo. Rehab. Counseling Assn. (pres. 1979, named Counselor of Yr. 1976), Great Plains Rehab. Assn. (pres. 1982-83), Colo. Rehab. Assn., Colo. Career Devel. Assn., El Paso County Assn. Lic. Profl. Counselors (treas. 1994-96), Colorado Springs C. of C. (Small Bus. Person of Yr. award 1991), Manitou Springs C. of C. (pres. 1986). Home: PO Box 226 Manitou Springs CO 80829-0226 Office: Kenneth P Olson MA CRC LPC Ste A 620 S Cascade Colorado Springs CO 80903-1814 E-mail: ken@kenolson.org.

OLSON, KRISTINE, prosecutor; b. N.Y.C., Aug. 9, 1947; d. Harold John and Arline (Schneider) Olson; children: Karin, Tyler. B.A., Wellesley Coll., 1969, J.D., Yale U., 1972. Bar: Oreg. 1973, U.S. Dist. Ct. Oreg. 1974, U.S. Ct. Appeals (9th cir.) 1975. Asst. U.S. atty. Dept. Justice, Portland, Oreg., 1974-84; vice chair State Indigent Def. Bd., Salem, Oreg., 1985-87; assoc. dean, prof. law Lewis & Clark Coll., 1989-94; U.S. atty. Dept. Justice, Dist. Oreg., Portland, 1994—; adj. prof. Lewis and Clark Coll. Northwestern Sch. Law, 1975-89, U. Oreg. Law Ctr., 1984—; mem. 9th Cir. Task Force on Tribal Cts. Contbr. articles to profl. jours. Bd. dirs., chmn. bd. Oreg. Council on Crime and Delinquency, 1981-87; bd. dirs. State Bd. Police Standards and Tng., 1976-80; chmn. Community Corrections Adv. Bd. Multnomah County, Portland, 1978-80; chmn. women's rights project ACLU Oreg., 1977; mem. World Affairs Council Oreg.; commr., mem. exec. com. Met. Human Relations Commn., mayor's appointee, 1986—. Root Tilden fellow, 1969. Mem. Soc. Am. Archaeology Native Am. Rights Fund, Earthwatch, 1000 Friends of Oreg., Archaeol. Conservancy, Nature Conservancy. Democrat. Clubs: Early Keyboard Soc., City Club of Portland (bd. govs. 1984—, pres.-elect 1995), Multnomah Athletic (Portland). Home: 900 SW 83rd Ave Portland OR 97225-6308

OLSON, LARRY D. electronics executive; b. 1957; B, Gustavus Adolphus Coll.; MBA, U. ST. Thomas, St. Paul. With Ragon Electronics, St. Paul; exec. v.p. sales distbn. Kent Electronics Corp., Sugar Land, Tex., 1994-96, pres., CEO, 1998—; pres. Kent Components, Sugar Land, 1996-97, K*TEC Electronics, Sugar Land, 1997-98. Office: Kent Electronics Corp 1111 Gillingham Ln Sugar Land TX 77478 Fax: 281-243-4002.

OLSON, LEROY CALVIN, retired educational administration educator; b. Kane, Pa., Mar. 7, 1926; s. Vernon Reinhold and Gertrude Viola Olson; m. Miriam Marie Vogler, June 19, 1954; children— David Lee, Thomas Edward, Steven Andrew. BS, Clarion State Coll., 1949; M.Ed., Pa. State Coll., 1950; Ed.D., Pa. State U., 1962; postgrad., U. Del., 1964-65. Tchr.-counselor Boiling Springs (Pa.) High Sch., 1950-52, Gordon Jr. High Sch., Coatesville, Pa., 1952-54; guidance dir. Cen. Dauphin Sch. Dist., Harrisburg, Pa., 1954-57; coordinator pupil personnel services, asst. supt. for instrn. and personnel, acting supt. Alfred I. duPont Sch. Dist., Wilmington, Del., 1957-65; prof. edn. adminstrn. Temple U., Phila., 1965-92, prof. emeritus, 1992—. Cons. to schs. bds. and dists., also Nat., Wis., Pa. sch. bds. assns. Contbr. articles to profl. jours. Trustee Luth. Ch., 1963-66, chmn. bd., 1976-78, chmn. various coms., discussion groups. Served with USNR, 1944-46, PTO. Recipient Disting. Alumni award Clarion State Coll., 1972 Mem. Am. Personnel and Guidance Assn., AAUP, Am. Assn. Sch. Personnel Adminstrs., Assn. Supervision and Curriculum Devel., Council Profs. Instrn. Supervision, Nat. Staff Devel. Council, Am. Legion, Phi Delta Kappa, Phi Kappa Phi. Republican. Home: 231 Prospect Dr Wilmington DE 19803-5331 *God's gift of life is a marvelous thing. My attempt to make the best use of that gift is to try to live an integrated and balanced life. This means that active attention must be paid to the physical, social, spiritual, and recreational aspects as well as to the work or career dimension. It also means we must share that gift through loving and caring about others.*

OLSON, LYNDON LOWELL, JR., ambassador; b. Waco, Tex., Mar. 7, 1947; s. Lyndon Lowell and Frances (McLaughlin) O.; m. Nancy Swenson, Mar. 6, 1970 (div. Dec. 1980); m. Kathleen Woodward, Nov. 22, 1982. BA in Polit. Sci. and Religion, Baylor U., 1969, postgrad. Mem. Tex. Legislature, 1973-78; apptd. chmn. Tex. State Bd. Ins., Austin, 1979-81, 83-87, apptd. mem., 1981-83; pres. and chief exec. officer Nat. Group Ins. Cos., Waco, Tex., 1987—; chmn., CEO Travelers Ins. Holdings, N.Y.C., 1990-98; amb. to Sweden Stockholm, 1997. Bd. dirs. Central Nat. Bank; lectr. UN Conf. on Trade and Devel., Phillipines, 1985; mem. Expert Com. on Reinsurance for UN, Geneva, 1986-87; negotiator U.S.-Israeli Free Trade Agreement, 1986-87. Leader trade delegation People to People for Russia and People's Republic of China, 1985; chmn., bd. dirs. Tex. Arts Alliance, Austin, 1984, chmn. and pres. Tex. Opera Theater, Houston, 1980-82; mem. exec. com. Houston Grand Opera, 1985—; pres. Tex. Lyceum, The Woodlands, 1987; chmn. Baylor U. Honors Council, 1969; bd. dirs. Paul Quinn Coll., 1987; bd. trustees Scottish Rite Hosp. for Children, Dallas. Recipient Disting. Alumni award Baylor U., 1985, 98, Distinguished Pub. Servant award Tex. Med. Assn., 1986, Gates of Jerusalem award State of Israel, 1986; named Outstanding Pub. Ofcl. Tex. Mcpl. League, 1986, Disting. Grad. Waco Pub. Schs., 1998. Mem. Nat. Assn. Ins. Commrs. (pres. 1983),Baylor Alumni Assn. (pres. 1996), Am. Polled Hereford Assn., Scottish Rite, Masons. Lodges: Masons. Democrat. Presbyterian. Office: Am Embassy Stockholm Sweden Dept State Washington DC 20521-0001

OLSON, LYNN, sculptor, painter, writer; b. Chgo., Mar. 23, 1952; s. Ellen (Nelson) Olson. Instr. direct cement sculpture workshops Montoya Art Studios, West Palm Beach, Fla., 1988—89, Alta. Sculptors Assn., Edmonton, Canada, 1990, Mendocino (Calif.) Art Ctr., 1992—93, Sierra Nev. Coll. Lake Tahoe, Incline Village, 1993, Lighthouse Art Ctr., Crescent City, Calif., 1990—96, Elisabet Ney Sculpture Conservatory, Austin, 1995, Tarrant County Jr. Coll., Ft. Worth, 1995, Art Students League Denver, 2000, Indpls. Art Ctr., 2002. Artist-in-residence St. Joseph Coll., 2000. Prin. works include Good Shepherd, Chy. Good Shepherd, Albion, Ind., Kneeling Figure, Manta Ray. World Concrete, Addison, Ill., Rose, Carter Meml., Chesterton, Ind., Redwood Tree, Lighthouse Art Ctr., Crescent City, George Bartholomew Meml., Bellefontaine, Ohio, Color Concerto, Purdue U., Hammond, Ind., Continuity III, Tower East, Shaker Heights, Ohio, Aluma Beam, Aluma Corp., Toronto, Amobius, St. Joseph Coll., Rensselaer, Ind., Flying Fish, Lake Sara, Effingham, Ill., Kim (stone sculpture), one-man shows include U. Ill., Chgo., 2001, No. Ind. Arts Assn., 1999, Munster, CCT Gallery, Evanston Hall, Northwestern U. Settlement, Chgo., 2000—, 18 Artists Gallery, Chesterton, Ind., Marion Coll., Indpls., 2003, Ill. Ctrl. Coll., East Peoria, 2003, exhibited in group shows at Danada Sculpture Show, Cantigny Park, Wheaton, Ill., 1999—2001, Prairie Arts Coun., Rensselaer, Ind., 2000, Ind. U. N.W., 2001, Effingham's 3d Ann. Sculpture on Ave. Exhbn., Ill., 2001, McHenry CC, Crystal Lake, Ill., 2002, 4th Ann. Sculpture on Aves. Exhibit, Effingham, 2002, 5th Ann., 2003, 6th Ann., 2004, 15th Ann. Outdoor Sculpture Exhibit, Lawrence, Kans., 2002, Art Pub. Places, Cedar Rapids, Iowa, 2002, 2003, 2004, Torso, Delta State U., Cleveland, Miss., 2002, 5th Ann. Sculpture in Pk., White River State Pk., Indpls., 2003, Barrington (Ill.) Area Libr. Sculpture Garden, 2003, Tall Grass Arts Assn., Park Forest, Ill., 2004, Davlan Park, Mass. Ave. Urban Art Gallery, Indpls., 2004; author, pub.: Sculpting with Cement, 1981—2004; contbr. articles to profl. jours. Mem.: Am. Concrete Inst. (mem. com. 124 concrete aesthetics). Home and Office: Steelstone 4607 Claussen Ln Valparaiso IN 46383-1526 Office Phone: 219-464-1792.

OLSON, LYNN, editor; m. Steve Olson; 2 children. Grad., Yale U. Sr. editor Edn. Week, 1990—. Author: The School to Work Revolution: How Employers and Educators Are Joining Forces to Prepare Tomorrow's Skilled Workforce, 1997. Recipient award, Edn. Writers Assn., Nat. Assn. Secondary Sch. Prins., Internat. Reading Assn.; grantee, Alfred P. Sloan Found., N.Y., 1995. Mem.: Carnegie Found. for Advancement Tchg. (bd. mem.). Office: Editl Projects in Edn Inc Ste 100 6935 Arlington Rd Bethesda MD 20814-5233

OLSON, MARIAN KATHERINE, management executive, consultant, publisher; b. Tulsa, Oct. 15, 1933; d. Sherwood Joseph and Katherine M. (Miller) Lahman; m. Ronald Keith Olson, Oct. 27, 1956 (dec. May 1991). BA in Polit. Sci., U. Colo., 1954, MA in Elem. Edn., 1962; EdD in Ednl. Adminstrn., U. Tulsa, 1969. Tchr. pub. schs., Wyo., Colo., Mont., 1956-67; tchg. fellow, adj. instr. edn. U. Tulsa, 1968-69; asst. prof. edn. Eastern Mont. State Coll., 1970; program assoc. rsch. adminstrn. Mont. State U., 1970-75; on leave with Energy Policy Office of White House then with Fed. Energy Adminstrn., 1973-74; with Dept. Energy and predecessor, 1975—, program analyst, 1975-79, chief planning and environ. compliance br., 1979-83; regional dir. Region VIII Fed. Emergency Mgmt. Agy., 1987-93; exec. dir. Search and Rescue Dogs of the U.S., 1993—. Pres. Marian Olson Assocs., Bannack Pub. Co Contbr. articles in field. Bd. dirs. Disaster Preparedness and Emergency Response Assn. Internat. Grantee Okla. Consortium Higher Edn., 1969, NIMH, 1974. Mem. Internat. Assn. Emergency Mgrs., Am. Soc. for Info. Sci., Am. Assn. Budget and Program Analysis, Assn. of Contingency Planners, Nat.

Inst. Urban Search and Rescue (bd. dirs.), Nat. Assn. for Search and Rescue, Colo. Search and Rescue, Search and Rescue Dogs of U.S., Colo. Emergency Mgmt. Assn., Front Range Rescue Dogs, Kappa Delta Pi, Phi Alpha Theta, Kappa Alpha Theta. Republican. Home: 203 Iowa Dr Golden CO 80403-1337 Office: Marian Olson Assocs 203 Iowa Dr Ste B Golden CO 80403-1337 Personal E-mail: mlolson@ix.netcom.com.

OLSON, MARK WALTER, banker; b. Fergus Falls, Minn., Mar. 17, 1943; s. Walter Roland and Agnes Marie (Peterson) O.; m. Renee Irene Korda, July 5, 1980; children: Benjamin, Stephanie. BA, St. Olaf Coll., 1965. With First Bank, St. Paul, 1966-70; legis. dir. Congressman Bill Frenzel, Washington, 1971-72; with Andrews Allen Co., St. Paul, 1972-74; dist. dir. Congressman Bill Frenzel, 1974-76; pres. Security State Bank, Fergus Falls, Minn., 1976-88; ptnr. Ernst & Young (formerly Arthur Young & Co.), 1988-1999, staff dir. Securities Subcomm., Banking, Housing, and Urban Affairs Comm., U.S. Senate, 2000-01, gov. FRS, 2001-. Bd. dirs. Pioneer Home, Fergus Falls, 1977-86, Lake Region Hosp., Fergus Falls, 1978-88, Fergus Falls Area YMCA, 1977-83, Security State Bank, Fergus Falls, 1976-88. Mem. Am. Bankers Assn. (chmn. govt. relations council, dir. 1982-84, pres. 1986-87), C. of C. (dir. 1980-84). Republican. Lutheran. Office: Fed Reserve System Bd of Gov 20th & C Streets NW Washington DC 20551*

OLSON, NORMAN FREDRICK, food science educator; b. Edmund, Wis., Feb. 8, 1931; s. Irving M. and Elva B. (Rhinerson) O.; m. Darlene Mary Thorson, Dec. 28, 1957; children: Kristin A., Eric R. BS, U. Wis., 1953, MS, 1957, PhD, 1959. Asst. prof. U. Wis.-Madison, 1959-63, assoc. prof., 1963-69, prof., 1969-93, dir. Walter V. Price Cheese Research Inst., 1976-93; dir. Ctr. Dairy Research, 1986-93; disting. prof. U. Wis.-Madison, 1993-97, prof. emeritus, 1997—. Cons. to cheese industry, 1997—. Author: Semi-soft Cheeses; inventor enzyme microencapsulation; sr. editor Jour. Dairy Sci., 1996-2000. Lt. U.S. Army, 1953-55. Recipient Laureate award Nat. Cheese Inst., 1998, Disting. Svc. award Coll. Agrl. Life. Sci., U. Wis., 2002; named Highly Cited Rschr. ISI, 2002. Fellow Inst. Food Technologists (Macy award 1986), Am. Dairy Sci. Assn. (v.p. 1984-85, pres. 1985-86, Pfizer award 1971, Dairy Rsch. Inc. award 1978, Borden Found. award 1988, Hon. award 1997); mem. Inst. Food Technologists. Democrat. Lutheran. Avocation: cross country skiing. Home: 114 Green Lake Pass Madison WI 53705-4755 Office: U Wis Dept Food Sci Babcock Hall Madison WI 53706 Office Phone: 608-263-2001.

OLSON, PAMELA FAITH, lawyer; b. Fargo, N.D., July 6, 1954; d. Norman Clifford and Inga (Larson) O.; m. Grant Douglas Aldonas, Apr. 12, 1980; children: Nicole Helen, Kirsten Inga, Noah Grant. BA magna cum laude, U. Minn., 1976, JD, 1980, MBA, 1984. Bar: D.C. 1981. Instr. U. Minn., Coll. Bus. Adminstrn., Mpls., 1979; atty., advisor Office of Chief Counsel, IRS, Washington, 1981-84, spl. asst. to chief counsel, 1984-86; assoc. Skadden, Arps, Slate, Meagher & Flom, Washington, 1986-90, ptnr., 1990—. Precinct chair-woman Ind.-Rep. Party, 1980; coun. mem. Holy Trinity Luth. Ch., Falls Church, Va., 1988-91, pres., 1990; bd. dirs. Arlington (Va.) Forest Club, Inc., 1990-92; trustee Millenium Inst., 1993—. Mem. ABA (vice chmn. employment taxes com. 1988-90, chmn. 1990-92, com. on govt. rels. 1992—, com. on coms. 1992—, com. on women and minorities 1993—, com. on membership and mktg. 1993—, coun. dir. sect. on taxation 1993—), Equipment Leasing Assn., D.C. Bar Assn. (chmn. legis. and regulations com.), U. Minn. Law Sch. Alumi Assn. (bd. dirs. 1992—). Avocations: children, volunteering, cooking, softball, skiing. Office: Skadden Arps Slate Meagher & Flom 1440 New York Ave NW Ste 600 Washington DC 20005-6000

OLSON, PAUL RICHARD, Spanish literature educator, editor; b. Rockford, Ill., Nov. 2, 1925; s. Oscar Wilhelm and Jenny Ingeborg (Taube) O.; m. Phyllis Elizabeth Edwards, Jan. 10, 1953; children: Thomas Jeremy, John Stephen, Carl Philip, Paul Andrew. AB, U. Ill., 1948, A.M., 1950; PhD, Harvard U., 1959. Instr. Dartmouth Coll., Hanover, N.H., 1956-59, asst. prof., 1959-61; asst. prof. modern Spanish lit. Johns Hopkins U., Balt., 1961-63, assoc. prof., 1963-67, prof., 1967-91, prof. emeritus, 1991—. Author: Circle of Paradox, 1967, Unamuno: Niebla, 1984, Unamuno and the Primacy of Language, 1989, The Great Chiasmus: Word and Flesh in the Novels of Unamuno, 2003; editor: Unamuno: Como se hace una novela, 1977; gen. editor Modern Lang. Notes, 1983—86. Guggenheim Found. fellow, 1964; Fulbright grantee, 1964-65; Am. Council Learned Socs. grantee, 1969 Mem.: MLA, Assn. Internat. Hispanistas, Nat. Assn. Scholars.

OLSON, PETER, publishing executive; b. Chgo., May 1, 1950; m. Candice Carpenter, Sept. 8, 2001. Grad., Harvard Coll., 1972; JD, Harvard Law Sch.; MBA, Harvard Bus. Sch. Assoc. Baker & Botts, Wash., DC, 1976—77, Hamada & Matsumoto, Tokyo, 1977—79; officer, internat. group Dresdner Bank, Frankfurt, 1979—81, deputy mgr., corp. bus. dept. Tokyo, 1981—84, mgr., credit dept., 1984—87, v.p. planning dept., treasury div. Frankfurt, Germany, 1987—88; mgr. Bertelsmann AG, 1988, sr. v.p., Doubleday Book and Music Clubs, 1989—90, pres., Bertelsmann, Inc., 1990—92, exec. v.p., CFO, Bantam Doubleday Dell Pub. Group, 1992—94; exec. v.p., chief admin. officer, Bantam Doubleday Dell Pub. Group, 1992—94; chmn, CEO Bertelsmann book group N. Am. Bertelsmann AG, 1994—98, mem. exec. bd., Bertelsmann Book AG, 1994—98, chmn., CEO, Random House Inc., 1998—, exec. bd. mem., trade book pub. worldwide, 2001—. Office: Random House Inc 201 E 50th St New York NY 10022-7703 also: Random House Inc 1540 Broadway New York NY 10036-4039*

OLSON, PETER WESLEY, international business educator; b. Amityville, N.Y., June 13, 1950; s. Wesley Harry and Mildred Constance (Petersen) O.; m. Donna Marie Marmorale, July 13, 1974; children: Jessica Marie, Jacqueline Nicole, Stephanie Anne. BA, L.I. Univ., 1972, MBA, 1977; PhD, Columbia U., 2002. Svc/sales rep. Otis Elevator Co., L.I. City, N.Y., 1973-75, internat. sales rep. N.Y.C., 1975-79; exec. asst. to v.p. NAO United Techs., Inc., Farmington, Conn., 1979-81; internat. sales mgr. Allied Bronze Corp., L.I. City, 1981-83; pres. Internat. Techs., Inc., Windsor, Conn., 1983-88; prof., curriculum chair, internat. mgmt. Hartford Grad. Ctr., Hartford, Conn., 1988—92; exec. dir. internat. devel. Conn. World Trade Inst. (subs. Conn. World Trade Assn., Hartford, 1989—95; prof. internat. mgmt. Rensselaer Poly. Inst. Lally Sch. Mgmt. and Tech., Hartford. Bd.dirs. China Investment Group, N.Y.C.; mem. adv. bd. dirs. Conn. World Trade Assn., Hartford, 1988-95, mem. edn. com., 1988-95; chief fin. officer Women's Health Internat., New Haven, 1995--. Bd. dirs. Antiquarian Landmark Soc., Hartford, mem. exec. fin. com., pub. rels. com.; chmn. Spl. Olympics, Windsor, 1983-84; bd. dirs. Earthside Found., Ocala, Fla., 1984-86; elder, mem. edn. com. Trinity Luth. Ch.; capt. Engine # 1 Locust Valley Vol. Fire Dept., 1987—. Mem. Am. Mgmt. Assn., Entrepreneurs Assn., Fireman's Exempt Assn., Masons, Master of Roome Lodge #742, Kiwanis (v.p. Windsor club 1984), Delta Mu Delta (Nu chpt. pres. 1977-78). Republican. Lutheran. Avocations: skiing, golf, tennis, flying. Home: 6 Cedar Ave Locust Valley NY 11560-2341 Office: Rensselaer Poly Inst 275 Windsor St Hartford CT 06120-2910

OLSON, PHILLIP DAVID LEROY, agriculturist, chemist; b. Anchorage, Feb. 3, 1940; s. Marvin Willard and Bernadette (McName) O.; m. Deborah Andreé Butler, Apr. 10, 1982; children from a previous marriage: Jamie Kay, Samuel Phillip, Jill Andre. BS, U. Idaho, 1963; MS, Oreg. State U., 1972. Technician U. Calif., Riverside, 1963-65; rsch. staff Oreg. State U., Corvallis, 1965-75; mgr. R & D, Hoechst-Roussel Agri-Vet Co., Somerville, N.J., 1975-91; owner, pres. Profl. Agrl. Cons., Palm Desert, Calif., 1991—. R & D cons. and quality assurance rsch. contractor, ret., 2000. Mem. Am. Mus. Natural History. Mem. Nat. Space Soc., Soc. Quality Assurance, Pacific Regional Quality Assurance Soc., Oreg. State U. Found. (hon.), Smithsonian Instn., Archaeol. Soc. Am., Acad. Model Aeronautics, Elks, Am. Mus. of Natural History, Planetary Soc., Scale Ship Modelers Assn., Oasis Country CLub SCGA Golf Assn. Avocations: reading, fishing, rc model building, scale boat modeling, ho train modeling. Home and Office: 42908 Scirocco Rd Palm Desert CA 92211-7697 E-mail: pdolson100@cs.com.

OLSON, PHILLIP ROGER, naval officer; b. Elmhurst, Ill., June 23, 1939; s. Willard Clarence and Carol (Schulz) O.; m. Marsha Andrea Lippert, July 10, 1966; children: Christine Carole, Phillip Roger Jr. B in Naval Sci., U.S. Naval Acad., 1962; M in Physics, Naval Postgrad. Sch., 1968. Commd. ens. USN, 1962, advanced through grades to rear adm., 1987, instr. ship material readiness group, 1978-81, commdg. officer USS Pharris (FF 1094) Norfolk, Va., 1981-82, commdg. officer USS Mississippi (CGN 40), 1983-86, sr. instr. ship material readiness group Newport, R.I., 1986-87; dep. dir. ops. Joint Staff, Washington, 1987-88; dep. dir. strategy & policy Joint Staff USN, Washington, 1988-89, comdr. logistics group two Norfolk, 1989-90, comdr. cruiser-destroyer group one San Diego, 1990-92, pres. bd. inspection & survey Norfolk, 1992-96; retired, 1996. Cons. on navy logistics support and operational engring.; exec. v.p. The Sigmon Group. Decorated Disting. Svc. medal. Mem. Surface Navy Assn. Lutheran. Avocations: golf, tennis.

OLSON, RANDY, photographer; Grad, Univ. of Kans., Univ. of Mo. Photographer Pitts. Press, Pitts.; staff photographer Nat. Geo. Mag., Wash., DC, 1993—. Olson was awarded the Alicia Patterson Fellowship for suppport in a seven-yr. project documenting a family with AIDS and earned him a Robert F. Kennedy Award in 1991 for social documentary of the disadvantaged (for a story on the problems with Section 8 housing). Randy Olson has spent the last ten years working for Nat. Geo. Mag. in places as diverse as Siberian arctic, Sudan, Pakistan, India, Thailand, Newfoundland, Guyana, Am. Samoa, Turkey, Republic of Georgia and So. Pacific. Office: National Geographic Magazine Photo Dept 1145 17th St NW Washington DC 20036-4688

OLSON, RICHARD DAVID, psychology educator; b. Reading, Pa., Oct. 10, 1944; s. Milton Stuart and Sarah Ellen (Moyer) O.; m. M. Gayle Augustine, Aug. 26, 1967. BA, U. Redlands, 1966; MS, St. Louis U., 1968, PhD, 1970. Lic. psychologist, La. Asst. prof. psychology U. New Orleans, 1970-74, assoc. prof., chmn. dept. psychology, 1974-79, prof., chmn. dept., 1979-81, assoc. dean Grad. Sch., 1981-82, dean, 1982-88, vice chancellor, 1984-88, rsch. prof., 1988—2000, prof. emeritus, 2000—; chmn. dept. psychology, 1995—2000. Cons. psychologist, New Orleans, 1973—2002; pres. Statis. Cons. of New Orleans, 1977-82 Editor: Learning in the Classroom, 1971, The Comma After Love, The Selected Poems of Raeburn Miller, 1994, The Collected Poems of Raeburn Miller, 1997; contbr. articles to profl. jours. Grantee HEW, 1976-81 Fellow APA, Am. Psychol. Soc.; mem. Soc. for Neurosci., Am. Statis. Assn. Home: 40 Infinity Dr Poplarville MS 39470 Office: U New Orleans Dept Psychology Lake Front New Orleans LA 70148 Office Phone: 601-795-4838. Personal E-mail: redoak1@netdoor.com.

OLSON, RICHARD E. paper company executive; AB in Chemistry, Knox Coll.; MA in Paper Chemistry, PhD in Paper Chemistry, Inst. Paper Sci. and Tech.; postgrad., Columbia U., Dartmouth Coll. From sr. project engr. to exec. v.p. Champion Internat. Corp., Stamford, Conn., 1967—96, chmn., CEO, 1996—2000. Dir. Weldwood Can., Ltd. subs. Champion Internat. Corp. Mem.: Tech. Assn. Pulp and Paper Industry. Office: Champion Internat Corp 1 Champion Plz Stamford CT 06921-0001

OLSON, ROBERT EDWARD, coal mining executive; b. Phila., Aug. 5, 1927; s. Oscar E. and Marie B. (Kilgallon) O.; m. Jean Emilie Wadsworth, Dec. 31, 1955 (dec. Aug. 1997); children: Grace Olson, Nancy Olson Ashcraft, Karen Olson Culbertson. Student, U. Richmond, 1945, Duke U., 1945-46, U. Pa., 1946; BS in Mining Engring., Pa. State U., 1952. Registered profl. engr., Pa., W.Va. Indsl. engr. Island Creek Coal Co., Holden, W.Va., 1952-55; dir., treas., sr. assoc. Coal Standards, Inc., mgmt. cons., Charleston, W.Va., 1955-61; v.p. adminstrn. Rochester & Pitts. Coal Co., Indiana, Pa., 1961-81; pres., COO Valley Camp Coal Co., Oil City, Pa., 1981-86, vice chmn., dir., mem. exec. com., 1986-88, ret., 1988. Past pres., chmn., dir. Kanawha and Hocking Coal & Coke Co., Kelley's Creek and Northwestern R.R. Co., Valley Camp Coal Sales Co.; pres., chief exec. officer Gt. Lakes Coal & Dock Co.; chmn., dir. Donaldson Mine Co., Elm Grove Coal Co., Shewsbury Coal Co., Helen Mining Co., Valley Camp of Utah Inc.; chmn., CEO Pa. and W.Va. Supply Co. Bd. dirs. United Way of Venango County, 1983-88; pres. bd. trustees Venango County Cmty. Area Found., 1988-94, former dir.; mem. Ind. County C. of C., 1973-81, pres., 1976-77; mem. vestry Christ Episc. Ch., Oil City, 1989-92, 98; charter mem. Haverford (Pa.) State Hosp. Task Force, 1999-2002; mem. Haverford Twp. Environ. Adv. Com., 2002. With USN, 1945-47. Mem. Ind. Rotary (club pres. 1979-80), Merion Cricket Club, Theta Delta Chi, Sigma Phi Sigma. Home: The Quadrangle Ste 8259 3300 Darby Rd Haverford PA 19041-2104

OLSON, ROBERT EUGENE, physician, biochemist, educator; b. Minn., Jan. 23, 1919; s. Ralph William and Minnie (Holtin) O.; m. Catherine Silvoso, Oct. 21, 1944; children: Barbara Lynn, Robert E., Mark Alan, Mary Ellen, Carol Louise. AB, Gustavus Adolphus Coll., 1938; PhD, St. Louis U., 1944; MD, Harvard, 1951; MD (hon.), Chiang Mai U., Thailand, 1983. Diplomate: Nat. Bd. Med. Examiners, Am. Bd. Nutrition (pres. 1962-63). Postgrad. research asst. biochemistry St. Louis U. Sch. Medicine, 1938-43, asst. biochemistry, 1943-44, Alice A. Doisy prof. biochemistry, chmn. dept. biochemistry, 1965-82, assoc. prof. medicine, 1966-72, prof. medicine, 1972-82; vis. prof. (sabbatical) dept. biochemistry U. Freiburg, Breisgau, West Germany, 1970-71; also Hoffman-La Roche Co., Basel, Switzerland, 1970-71; instr. biochemistry and nutrition Harvard Sch. Pub. Health, 1946-47; research fellow Nutrition Found., 1947-49, Am. Heart Assn., 1949-51, established investigator, 1951-52; house officer Peter Bent Brigham Hosp., Boston, 1951-52; prof., head dept. biochemistry and nutrition Grad. Sch. Pub. Health U. Pitts.; lectr. medicine Sch. Medicine, 1952-65; mem. panel malnutrition Japan-U.S. Med. Scis. Program, 1965-69; dir. Nutrition Clinic, Falk Clinic, 1953-65; mem. sr. staff Presbyn. Hosp., dir. metabolic unit, 1960-65; mem. staff St. Louis U. Hosp., 1965-81; prof. biochemistry, prof. medicine, assoc. dean acad. affairs U. Pitts. Sch. Medicine, 1982-84; prof. medicine, prof. pharm. scis. SUNY-Stony Brook, 1984-90, prof. emeritus, 1990—; prof. pediatrics U. South Fla., Tampa, 1994—. Cons. Mercy Hosp., U. Pitts. Med. Center; assoc. in medicine St. Margaret's Meml. Hosp., Pitts., dir. metabolic unit, 1954-60; cons. divsn. rsch. grants USPHS, 1954-69, 72-76; dir. Anemia and Malnutrition Center, Chiang Mai, Thailand, 1967-77; vis. scholar dept. biochemistry Oxford (Eng.) U., 1961-62; vis. prof. dept. biochemistry U. Freiburg, West Germany, 1970-71; food and nutrition bd. NRC, 1977-83; adv. council Nat. Inst. Arthritis, Diabetes, Digestive and Kidney Diseases, 1981-85; William A. Noyes lectr. U. Ill., Urbana, 1980. Assoc. editor Nutrition Revs., 1954-56, editor, 1978-88; assoc. editor Am. Jour. Medicine, 1956-65, Circulation Rsch., 1956-76, Am. Heart Jour., 1958-65, Am. Jour. Clin. Nutrition, 1960-66, Methods in Med. Rsch., 1963-70, Biochem. Medicine, 1967-90, Molecular and Cellular Cardiology, 1967-78, Ann. Rev. Nutrition, 1979-84, editor, 1984-94; co-editor: Vitamins and Hormones, 1975-81. Bd. dirs. Nat. Nutrition Consortium, 1977-81, Am. Council on Sci. and Health, 1984-91. Served as lt. (j.g.) USNR, 1944-46. Recipient Fulbright award, 1961-62, Guggenheim Found. award, 1961-62, 70-71, McCollum award, 1965, Joseph Goldberger award, 1974; named Atwater Meml. lectr., 1978; Geiger Meml. lectr., 1979, William A. Noyes lectr. U. Ill., 1980, H. Brooks James lectr. N.C. State U., 1981, Virginia Beal lectr. U. Mass., 1990. Fellow ACP, Internat. Acad. Cardiovasc. Scis., Am. Pub. Health Assn. (chmn. food and nutrition sect. 1960-61), Am. Inst. Nutrition (pres. 1981-82, Conrad Elvehjem award 1998), Assn. Am. Physicians; mem. AAAS (sec. med. scis. N. sect. 1965-67), Am. Assn. Cancer Research, Am. Heart Assn., AMA (mem. council food and nutrition 1959-67, vice chmn. 1962-67), Royal Soc. Health (London), N.Y. Acad. Scis., Am. Fedn. Clin. Research, Am. Soc. Clin. Investigation, Boyleston Med. Soc., Am. Chem. Soc. (pres. biochemistry group Pitts. sect. 1960-61), Am. Soc. Biol. Chemists, Soc. Exptl. Biology and Medicine, Am. Soc. Clin. Nutrition (pres. 1961-62, McCollum award 1965, Herman award 2002), Assn. Med. Sch. Depts. Biochemistry (pres. 1979-80), Pa., St. Louis, Allegheny County med. socs., Am. Soc. Study Liver Diseases, Phi Beta Kappa, Sigma Xi, Phi Lambda Upsilon, Alpha Omega Alpha, Alpha Sigma Nu. Clubs: Cosmos (Washington), Countryside Country Club (Clearwater, Fla.). Home: 2673 Camille Dr Palm Harbor FL 34684-2217 Office: U South Fla Dept Pediatrics 17 Davis Blvd Ste 200 Tampa FL 33606-3438 E-mail: rolson@hsc.usf.edu., roberteolsonr@cs.com.

OLSON, ROBERT GRANT, lawyer; b. Ft. Dodge, Iowa, Mar. 29, 1952; s. Grant L. and R. June (Pohlmann) Olson; m. Cynthia Lynn Murray, Sept. 7, 1978; children: Brendon, Elisabeth, Jeffrey, Daniel. BS, Iowa State U., 1973; JD, U. Iowa, 1976. Bar: Mo. 1978, Ill. 1977. Ptnr. Thompson & Mitchell, St. Louis, 1976-92, Riezman & Blitz, P.C., St. Louis, 1992-2000, Stone, Leyton & Gershman, P.C., St. Louis, 2000—. Editor: Jour. Corp. Law, 1975—76. Vol. Habitat for Humanity, Gephardt for Pres. Campaign, 1988, Carnahan for Lt. Gov. Campaign, 1988, Carnahan for Gov. Campaign, 1992; arbitrator Better Bus. Bur., Taxpayer Assistance Program. Mem.: ABA, Met. St. Louis Bar Assn., Ill. Bar Assn., Mo. Bar Assn., Downtown St. Louis Lions Club (pres. 1990—91). Home: 424 E Jackson Rd Saint Louis MO 63119-4128 Office: Stone Leyton & Gershman 7733 Forsyth Blvd Ste 500 Saint Louis MO 63105-1817 Office Phone: 314-721-7011.

OLSON, ROBERT HOWARD, lawyer; b. July 6, 1944; s. Robert Howard and Jacquiline (Wells) O.; m. Diane Carol Thorsen, Aug. 13, 1966; children: Jeffrey, Christopher. BA in Govt. summa cum laude, Ind. U., 1966; JD cum laude, Harvard U., 1969. Bar: Ohio 1969, Fla. 1980, Ariz. 1985, Calif. 2001, U.S. Supreme Ct. 1973. Assoc. Squire, Sanders & Dempsey, L.L.P., Cleve., 1969, 70-71, 76-81, ptnr., 1981—, Phoenix, 1985—2002, Squire, Sanders & Dempsey, San Francisco, 2002—; sr. law clk. U.S. Dist. Ct., No. Dist., Ind., 1969-70; chief civil rights divsn. Ohio Atty. Gen.'s Office, Columbus, 1971-73, chief consumer protection, 1973-75, chief counsel, 1975, 1st asst. (chief of staff), 1975-76. Instr. Ohio State U. Law Sch., Columbus, 1974; Cen. Phoenix com. to advise city council and mayor City of Phoenix, 1987—89; bd. dirs. Orpheum Theater Found., 1989—2002, sec., 1989—90, pres., 1990—97, exec. com., 1997—99, The Ariz. Ctr. for Law in the Pub. Interest, 1989—2001, treas., 1992—93, 1997—2001, v.p., 1993—94; mem. Ariz. Ctr. for Disability Law, 1994—96, treas., 1994—95; mem. Valley Leadership Class XIV; rsch. com. Ariz. Town Hall, 1998—2002. Contbr. articles to profl. jours. Bd. dirs. 1st Unitarian Ch. Phoenix, 1987-89, 98-2001, v.p., 1987-89, 2000-2001, pres. 1998-99; bd. dirs. 1st Unitarian Ch. Found., 1987-93, pres., 1990-93. Named Arts Advocate of Yr. Bus. Vols. Arts/Phoenix, 1997. Mem. Ariz. State Bar Assn., Calif. Bar Assn., Phi Beta Kappa. Democrat. Office: Squire Sanders & Dempsey LLP One Maritime Plaza Suite 300 San Francisco CA 94111-3492

OLSON, ROBERT WALLACE, voice educator; b. Superior, Wis., Jan. 6, 1933; s. Olaf Sigurd and Martha (Mast) Olson; m. Beverly A. Davis, Mar. 17, 1955; children: Joyce S. Olson-Kapell, Robert Wilhelm; 1 child, Jennifer L. MusB cum laude, U. Ariz., Tucson, 1956; MusM, U. Ariz., 1958; student, Vienna Acad. (Opera Sch.), 1963—64; MusD, U. Ill., 1972. Profl. singer Omaha Civic Opera, Skylight Opera Co., Milw., 1964—65; adj. prof. Offenline Laererskole, Berhen, Norway, 1965—67; asst. prof. N.D. State U., Fargo, 1967—71, assoc. prof., 1971—75, prof., 1975—94. Mem. faculty senate N.D. State U., Fargo, 1969—72, 1979—82; ptnr. The Voice Inst., Fargo, 1990—97; vis. prof. Makamske Ind. U., Fairfield, Iowa, 1994—99, MSUM, Moorhead, Minn., 1996—. Performer and concerts Operas. Frequent performer of concerts, oratorio, opera, lectr. on vocal health. Capt. USAF, 1956—76. Grantee Postdoctoral grant, NEH, 1976, Opera Rsch. grant, 1986. Mem.: ACLU, AAUP (pres. N.D. 1970—75), Nat. Assn. Tchrs. of Singing (lt.gov. N.D. 1972—75). Mem. Unitarian United Ch. Home: 1329 10th St N Fargo ND 58102-2501 Office Phone: 701-293-3503. E-mail: O_Bob@msn.com.

OLSON, ROBERT WILLIAM, writer, retired counselor; b. Chgo., Feb. 5, 1930; s. Milton Olaf Olson and Leonore Stillman; m. Seiko Itoyama, Jan. 16, 1955. BA, George Williams Coll., 1952; MA, U. Chgo., 1959; 7th yr. cert. counselor-cons., Oreg. State U., 1967. 6th grade tchr. Matteson (Ill.) Elem. Sch., 1956-59; sch. counselor, cons. elem. schs., jr. and sr. h.s., various cities, Ill.,Wash., 1959-91; counseling instr. U. Wash., Seattle, 1979-81; family counselor Seattle, 1980-091. Behavioral rschr., U. Wash., 1979-81. Author: Memories with a Christmas Attitude, 1994; editor FOKUS Newsletter, 1998—; contbr. numerous articles to profl. counseling jours. Vol., Love and Forgiveness Seminar, Monroe Penitentiary, 1996—; bd. mem. Children Around the World Resource Ctr.; pres., King County (Wash.) Guidance Assn., 1978-79. With U.S. Army, 1952-56, Korea. Mem. NEA (life), Wash. Edn. Assn., Internat. Assn. Near-Death Studies, Full Gospel Businessmen Internat. (vol. King County Jail 1998—), Eastside Writers Assn. (hospitality chmn. 1999—), Northwest Christian Writers Assn. Avocations: ceramics, storytelling, swimming. Home and Office: 252 168th Ave SE Bellevue WA 98008

OLSON, ROBERTA JEANNE MARIE, art historian, author, educator, curator; b. Shawano, Wis., June 1, 1947; d. Robert Bernard Olson and Emma Pauline (Dallmann) Hoops; m. Alexander Buchanan Vance Johnson, June 15, 1980; 1 child, Allegra Alexandra Olson Johnson. BA, St. Olaf Coll., 1969; MA, U. Iowa, 1971; MFA, Princeton U., 1973, PhD, 1976. Preceptor Princeton U., 1972-74; contbg. editor Arts Mag., N.Y.C., 1973-75; art news editor The Soho Weekly News, N.Y.C., 1976-78; from asst. prof. to assoc. prof. Wheaton Coll., Norton, Mass., 1975-88, prof., 1988-2000, chmn. art dept., 1987-89, 92-93, 97-98, A. Howard Meneely chair, 1990-92. Mary L. Heuser faculty chair in the arts Wheaton Coll., 1997—2000; assoc. curator of drawings The N.Y. Hist. Soc., N.Y.C., 1999—; cons. Smithsonian Instn., Washington, 1984—86; bd. dirs. The Drawing Soc., N.Y.C., 1989—94, The Friends of Art; bd. advisers Halley's Comet Soc., 1986—; mem. collections com. drawing and print dept. Met. Mus. Art, 1993—; coll. com. drawing dept. Fogg Art Mus., Harvard U., 1997—; mem. vis. com. Paper Conv., Met. Mus. Art, 2004—; presenter in field; curator, guest-curator art exhibns. in various mus. Author: Italian Nineteenth Century Drawings and Watercolors: An Album, 1976, Italian Drawings 1780-1890, 1980 (N.Y. Times Best Art Book award, 1981, Whole Earth Book award), Fire and Ice: A History of Comets in Art, 1985, Italian Renaissance Sculpture, 1992, French edit., 1993, Ottocento: Romanticism and Revolution in 19th Century Italian Painting, 1993; editor: The Art of Drawing: Selections from the Wheaton College Collection, 1997, Fire in the Sky: Comets and Meteors, the Decisive Centuries, in British Art and Science, 1998, The Florentine Tondo, 2000, Seat of Empire, 2002; guest curator Art Mus. Princeton U., 1974, Nat. Gallery of Art, 1980, N.-Y. Hist. Soc., 1990; author: (art exhbn. catalogs) Six Centuries Sculptor's Drawings, 1981, Disegni di Tommaso Minardi, 2 vols., 1982, Galleria Nazionale d'Arte Moderna, Old Master Drawings from the Mus. Art RISD, 1983; contbr. articles various prof. publications. Fellow Samuel H. Kress Found., 1973—74, Whiting Found. for Humanities, 1974—75; grantee, NEH, 1982—83, 1987—88, Am. Philos. Soc., 1989, Am. Coun. Learned Socs., 1990—91, Getty sr. rsch. grantee, 1994—95, Samuel H. Kress Found., 1996, 1999—2000, Getty grantee, 2003—05. Fellow: The Morgan Libr.; mem.: Renaissance Soc. Am., Art Table, Coll. Art Assn., Italian Art Soc., Drawing Soc., Assn. Univ. Profs. Italian, Phi Beta Kappa (pres. Kappa chpt. 1980—82). Avocations: running, yoga, collecting, horseback riding. Home: 1220 Park Ave Apt 3-c New York NY 10128-1733 Office: N-Y Hist Soc Two West 77th St New York NY 10024 E-mail: rolson@nyhistory.org.

OLSON, RONALD LEROY, lawyer; b. Carroll, Iowa, July 9, 1941; s. Clyde L. and Delpha C. (Boyens) Olson; m. Jane Tenhulzen, June 21, 1964; children: Kristin, Steven, Amy. BS, Drake U., 1963; JD, U. Mich., 1966; Diploma Law, Oxford U., Eng., 1967. Bar: Wis. 1966, Calif. 1969, US Dist. Ct. (cen. dist.)/Calif. 1969, US Dist. Ct. (so. dist.)/Calif. 1973, US Ct. Appeals (9th cir.) 1974, US Ct. Appeals (10th cir.) 1980, US Ct. Appeals (5th cir.) 1982, US Supreme Ct. 1976, US Dist. Ct./Alaska 1983. Atty. US Dept. Justice, 1967; clk., chief judge US Ct. Appeals (DC cir.), Washington, 1967—68; ptnr. Munger, Tolles & Olson, Los Angeles, Calif., 1968—; lawyer del. Ann. 9th Cir. Conf., 1984—89; lectr. in field; mem. editorial bd. Alternatives, 1983—. Adv. trainer task force, 1986; mem. standing com. fed. judiciary. Contbr. articles legal jour. Recipient Burton scholar, U. Mich.; fellow Am. Coll Trial Lawyers. Mem.: 9th Cir. Jud. Conf. (exec. com. 1984—89), Chancery, LA County Barristers (pres. 1976), Assn. Bus. Trial Lawyers (mem. adv. com. trial ct. improvement fund for Calif. jud. coun. 1988—), State Bar Calif. (bd. dir. 1985, v.p. 1986—87), LA County Bar Assn., Am. Arbitration Assn. (bd. dir. 1983, comml. panel 1983), LA Bar Found. (bd. dir. 1977), Am. Judicature Soc., Human Rights (editorial bd., publ. sect. ind. rights and responsibilities 1986—), Soviet Exchange Program (litig. sect. com. 1983—), ABA (litig. sect. council 1976, chmn. sp. com. on dispute resolution 1976—86, chmn. 1981—82), Am. Bar Found., Skid Row Housing Trust of LA (mem. 1986—), U. Mich. Law Sch. (com. visitors 1986—), Salzburg Seminar (bd. dir.), Legal Aid Found. LA (bd. dir. 1975—86, pres. 1984—85), Claremont U. Ctr. and

Grad. Sch. (chmn. bd. fellows 1984), Sequoia Nat. Pk. Natural History Assn., Drake U. (trustee 1977), Ford Found. Oxford U., Alternatives (mem. editorial bd. 1983—88), LA Arts Festival (sec. 1985), Lawyers Alliance for Nuclear Arms Control (adv. com. Los Angeles and Orange Counties chpt.), Frat. of Friends of Music Ctr. (bd. dir., pres. 1978). Democrat. Episc. Office: Munger Tolles & Olson 355 S Grand Ave Fl 35 Los Angeles CA 90071-1560

OLSON, ROY ARTHUR, retired government official; b. Dec. 8, 1938; s. Elof Herman and Beatrice Lorraine (Dolezal) O.; m. Elisabeth Rigge Behrens, June 24, 1967; children: Heather Elisabeth, Peter Roy. BS, Northwestern U., 1960. Lic. real estate salesman, Ill. Writer, editor Chgo. Am., 1956-68; pres, Roy Olson Pub. Rels. Co., Oak Park, Ill., 1968-70; asst. regional adminstr. SBA, Chgo., 1970-95; Chgo. spokesman Ill. Dept. Transp., 1995—2004. Dir. Am. Food Industries, Chgo., Covenant Village Retirement Ctr., Northbrook, Ill., 1975-81, Brandel Care Ctr., Northbrook, 1975-81, Swedish Covenant Hosp., Chgo., 1995—. Chmn. Northbrook Covenant Ch., 1980-81, 97-2000. Mem. Soc. Profl. Journalists, Art Inst. Chgo., City Club (media com.), Execs. Club, Chgo. Press Club, Chgo. Headline Club (past dir. 1964-66), Northwestern Club. Home: 2015 Prairie St Glenview IL 60025-2824 E-mail: olsons2015@yahoo.com.

OLSON, SANDRA FORBES, neurologist; b. East Chicago, Ind., Jan. 8, 1938; MD, Northwestern U., 1963. Diplomate Am. Bd. Psychiatry and Neurology. Intern Chgo. Wesley Meml. Hosp., 1963—64, resident in internal medicine, 1964—65; resident in neurology Northwestern Med. Sch., Chgo., 1965—68, fellow in electroencephalography, 1968—69; pvt. practice neurology Chgo., 1969—; assoc. attending physician Northwestern Meml. Hosp., Chgo., 1969—75; attending physician Northwestern Meml. Hosp., Chgo., 1975—; prof. clin. neurology Northwestern U., Chgo. Bd. dirs. Accreditation Coun. for Grad. Med. Edn., 2004. Bd. dirs. Northwestern Meml. Found., 2004. Mem.: AMA, CNS, AE, Am. Acad. Neurology (pres.-elect 2002—03, pres. 2003—). Office: Northwestern U Feinberg Sch Medicine Abbott Hall 11th Fl 710 N Lake Shore Dr Chicago IL 60611-3078 Office Phone: 312-503-4658. E-mail: sfolsonnw@aol.com.

OLSON, STEPHEN M(ICHAEL), lawyer; b. Jamestown, N.Y., May 4, 1948; s. Charles R. and Marilyn (Dietzel) O.; m. Linda C. Hanson, Aug. 24, 1968; children: Kevin, Darren. AB cum laude, Princeton U., 1970; JD, U. Chgo., 1973. Bar: Pa. 1973, U.S. Dist. Ct. (we. dist.) Pa. 1973, U.S. Ct. Appeals (3d cir.) 1975, U.S. Ct. Appeals (1st and D.C. cirs.) 1986, U.S. Ct. Appeals (7th cir. and 8th cir. 1988), U.S. Supreme Ct. 1986. Assoc. Kirkpatrick & Lockhart, Pitts., 1973-81, ptnr., 1981—. Mem.: ABA (rlwy./airline labor law com.), Allegheny County Bar Assn., Pa. Bar Assn., Princeton Alumni Assn. West Pa., Duquesne Club. Avocations: photography, bicycling. Office: Kirkpatrick & Lockhart Henry W Oliver Bldg 535 Smithfield St Pittsburgh PA 15222-2312

OLSON, THEODORE BEVRY, lawyer, former federal agency administrator; b. Chgo., Sept. 11, 1940; 2 children. BA, U. Pacific, 1962; LL.B., U. Calif.-Berkeley, 1965. Bar: Calif. 1965, D.C. 1982. Assoc. Gibson, Dunn & Crutcher LLP, Los Angeles, 1965—71, ptnr., 1972—81, 1984—2001, 2004—, co-chair, appellate & constitutional law practice group, 2004—; asst. atty. gen. Dept. Justice, Washington, 1981—84, U.S. solicitor gen., 2001—04. Mem. Calif. Commn. on Uniform State Laws, 1972-74; del. Republican Nat. Conv., 1976, 80. Fellow Am. Acad. of Appellate Lawyers, Am. Coll. Trial Lawyers; mem. ABA, L.A. County Bar Assn. Republican. Office: Gibson Dunn & Crutcher LLP 1050 Connecticut Ave NW Washington DC 20036 E-mail: tolson@gibsondunn.com.

OLSON, WALTER JUSTUS, JR., management consultant; b. Paterson, N.J., July 27, 1941; s. Walter Justus and Viola Patricia (Trautvetter) O. BS, BA, Brown U., 1964; MBA, Columbia U., 1967. CPA, Va. Design engr. Rockwell Internat., Inc., Downey, Calif., 1964-65; mgmt. officer CIA, Washington, 1969-73; sr. cons. Booz, Allen and Hamilton, Inc., Washington, 1973-78; corp. planning coordinator Washington Gas Light Co., Washington, 1978-82; prin. Walter J. Olson & Assoc., McLean, Va., 1982-83; dep. asst. sec. for export adminstrn. U.S. Dept. Commerce, Washington, 1983-86; prin. Walter J. Olson & Assoc., Washington, 1986—; sr. rsch. analyst U.S. House Select Com. Technology Transfer to PRC, Washington, 1998-99. Vice-chmn. fin. com. Fairfax County (Va.) Reps., 1982-83. Served to 1st lt., USAF, 1967-69. Mem. AICPA, Greater Wash. Soc. CPAs, Strategic Leadership Forum (pres. Washington chpt. 1990-91). Republican. Episcopalian. Home: 7348 Dartford Dr Mc Lean VA 22102-7348 Office: 8180 Greensboro Dr Ste 1070 Mc Lean VA 22102-3860 Office Phone: 703-356-6919.

OLSON, WARREN KINLEY, operations research analyst, engineer, physicist; b. Minot, N.D., Aug. 11, 1943; s. Arthur Conrad and Dorothy Elenor (Kinley) O.; m. Colleen Kay Ude, Dec. 18, 1965; children: Christine Kay, Cynthia Dorine. BA in Physics and Math., St. Olaf Coll., 1965; MS in Stats., U. Del., 1974; PhD in Sci. Tech. and Pub. Policy, George Mason U., 2000. Mathematician Ballistics Rsch. Lab., Aberdeen Proving Ground, Md., 1962-69; ops. rsch. analyst Army Material Systems Analysis Agy., Aberdeen Proving Ground, 1969-76; br. chief USA TRADOC Systems Analysis Activity, White Sands Missile Range, N. Mex., 1976-85; dir. rsch. USA TRADOC Ops. Rsch. Activity, White Sands Missile Range, 1985-86; div. chief USA TRADOC Analysis Command, White Sands Missile Range, 1986, dir. rsch., 1986-87; sr. staff engr. Honeywell Defense Systems Group, Edina, Minn., 1987-90, Alliant Techsystems, Inc., Hopkins, Minn., 1990-93; rsch. mem. Inst. for Def. Analysis, Alexandria, Va., 1993—2002, cons./tchr., 2002—. Mem. sci. staff NATO Joint Field Trials, Munich, Germany, 1973-74; chmn. U.S. Army ABCA QWG/AOR Spl. Work Group, White Sands, 1979-87; mem. def. sci. bd. MOBA Study, 1994; tech. expert on computer simulation, virtual reality; vis. prof. Ga. Inst. Tech., 2002—; cons. SAIC, 2002—, Rockwell Collins, 2003—. Co-author: (with others) (text) Military Strategy and Tactics, 1975, (handbook) Military Operations Research, 1994; contbr. tech. reports to profl., military publs., 1965-97. Elder Peace Luth. Ch., El Paso, Tex., 1985-87; mem. St. Olaf choir, 1963-65. Recipient Citizenship award, DAR, 1956, Civilian Svc. Commander's award, U.S. Army, Washington, 1979. Mem. Soc. for Preservation and Encouragement of Barber Shop Quartet Singing (bd. dirs. El Paso 1977-79, Internat. medalist 1991, 92, 93, Gt. No. Union Chorus), Mil. Ops. Rsch. Soc., Am. Def. Preparedness Assn., Nat. Mil. Intelligence Assn., Sigma Pi Sigma. Avocations: music, skiing, scuba diving, photography, model railroading, chess. Home and Office: 1755 Columbine Village Dr Woodland Park CO 80863-8390

OLSON, WILLIAM CLINTON, anthologist, international affairs administrator; b. Denver, Aug. 19, 1920; s. Albert Merrill and Frances (Murray) O.; m. Mary Elizabeth Matthews, Aug. 16, 1943; children: Jon Eric, Peter Murray, Elizabeth Ann. AB, U. Denver, 1942; PhD, Yale U., 1953; DHL (hon.), U. Denver, 1992; hon. diploma, Inter-Am. Def. Coll., 2001. Chmn. com. on internat. rels. Pomona Coll., 1953-61; sr. mem. St. Antonys Coll. Oxford (Eng.) U., 1959-60; assoc. dean sch. internat. affairs Columbia U., N.Y.C., 1965-67; assoc. dir. for social scis. Rockefeller Found., N.Y.C., 1967-79; dean Am. U. Sch. Internat. Svc., Washington, 1979-86; vis. rsch. fellow Royal Inst. Internat. Affairs, London, 1986-87; dir. Bellagio Study and Conf. Ctr. of Rockefeller Found., Villa Serbelloni, Italy, 1970-79. Life fellow Clare Hall, Cambridge; cons. to vice chancellor U. Colombo, Sri Lanka, 1983. Author, editor: The Theory and Practice of International Relations, 1960, 9th edit., 1994; co-author: Internat. Relations Then and Now: Origins and Trends in Interpretation, 1991; bd. editors: Cambridge Studies in Internat. Relations, 1983-91. Mem. Brady Leadership Coun., 1999—; trustee Social Sci. Found. U. Denver, 1967, v.p., 1988—. Recipient Disting. Alumnus award Grad. Sch. Internat. Studies, Denver, 1986; received medal and named Hon. Ancien, NATO Def. Coll., 1989. Mem. Coun. Fgn. Rels., Washington Inst. Fgn. Affairs, Internat. Studies Assn. (nat. pres. 1968-69), Cosmos Club (Washington), Phi Beta Kappa (pres. Gamma of Calif. 1957-58), Sigma Iota Rho (founder). E-mail: deanolson@aol.com.

OLSON, WILLIAM HENRY, neurology educator, administrator; b. Haxtun, Colo., Sept. 2, 1936; s. William Henry and Burdene (Anderson) O.; m. Shirley Gorden, July 24, 1967; children: Erik, Marnie. BA, Wesleyan U., 1959; MD, Harvard U., 1963. Diplomate: Am. Bd. Psychiatry and Neurology. Intern Beth Israel Hosp., Boston, 1963-65; resident Children's Hosp. Med. Ctr., Boston, 1965-67; staff assoc. NIH, Bethesda, Md., 1969-70; asst. prof. neurology and anatomy Vanderbilt U., Nashville, 1970-73, assoc. prof. neurology and anatomy, 1973-75; prof., chmn. dept. adult neurology U. N.D., Fargo, 1975-80; chmn., prof. dept. neurology U. Louisville, 1980—. Co-author: Practical Neurology and the Primary Care Physician, 1981, Symptom Oriented Neurology, 1994. Fulbright scholar Tubingen, Germany, 1958-59 Fellow Am. Acad. Neurology; mem. Phi Beta Kappa Home: 331 Zorn Ave # 1 Louisville KY 40206-1542 Office: Univ Louisville Dept Neurology Louisville KY 40292-0001

OLSON, WILLIAM JEFFREY, lawyer; b. Paterson, N.J., Oct. 23, 1949; s. Walter Justus and Viola Patricia (Trautvetter) O.; m. Janet Elaine Bollen, May 22, 1976; children: Robert J., Joanne C. AB, Brown U., 1971; JD, U. Richmond, 1976. Bar: Va. 1976, D.C. 1976, U.S. Ct. Claims 1976, U.S. Ct. Appeals (4th, 6th, 10th,11th and D.C. cirs.) 1976, U.S. Supreme Ct. 1982. Assoc. Jackson & Campbell, Washington, 1976-79; ptnr. Gilman, Olson & Pangia, Washington, 1980-92; prin. William J. Olson PC, McLean, Va. and Washington, 1992—. Sec., treas. bd. dirs. Victims Assistance Legal Orgn., McLean, Va., 1979—; presdl. transition team leader Legal Svcs. Corp., Washington, 1980; chmn. and bd. dirs. nat. Legal Svcs. Corp., 1981-82; mem. Pres.'s Export Coun. Subcom. on Export Adminstrn., Washington, 1982-84; spl. counsel bd. govs. U.S. Postal Svc., Washington, 1984-86. Author: Tuition Tax Credits and Alternatives, 1978; co-author: Debating National Health Policy, 1977, Executive Orders and National Emergencies, 1999, An Evaluation of Postal Service Worksharing, 2003. Trustee Davis Meml. Goodwill Industries, Washington, 1980-86, 88-93; chmn. Fairfax County Rep. Com., Fairfax, Va., 1980-82; mem. Rep. State Ctrl. Com., Richmond, Va., 1982-86. Mem. Va. Bar Assn., Assn. Trial Lawyers Am., Va. Trial Lawyers Assn. Republican. Baptist. Avocation: gardening. Office: 8180 Greensboro Dr Ste 1070 Mc Lean VA 22102-3860 E-mail: wjo@mindspring.com.

OLSON-HELLERUD, LINDA KATHRYN, elementary school educator; b. Wisconsin Rapids, Wis., Aug. 26, 1947; d. Samuel Ellsworth and Lillian (Dvorak) Olson; m. H. A. Hellerud, 1979; 1 child, Sarah Kathryn Hellerud. BS, U. Wis., Stevens Point, 1969, tchg. cert., 1970, MST, 1972; MS, U. Wis., Whitewater, 1975; EdS, U. Wis., Stout, 1978. Cert. K-12 reading tchr. and specialist. Clk. U. Counseling Ctr. U Wis., Stevens Point, 1965—69; elem. sch. tchr. Wisconsin Rapids, Wis., 1970-76; sch. counselor, 1976-79; dist. elem. guidance dir., 1979-82; elem. and reading tchr., K-2 early intervention team, reading assessment team, 1982—. Cons. in field; instr. Summer Remedial Reading Program. Advocate Literacy Tutoring Program; adv. Moravian Ch. Sunday Sch. Mem.: NEA, Ctrl. Wis. Reading Assn. (reading and tech. com.), Internat. Reading Assn., Wood County Lit. Coun. (cons.), Wis. Reading Assn. (family literacy com.). Avocations: literacy activities, piano, Spanish, technology, aerobics. Home: 1011 16th St S Wisconsin Rapids WI 54494-5371 Office: Howe Elem Sch Wisconsin Rapids WI 54494

OLSSON, ANN-MARGRET See ANN-MARGRET

OLSSON, BJÖRN ESKIL, railroad supply company executive; b. Kristianstad, Sweden, Oct. 7, 1945; came to U.S., 1990; m. Cecilia Lindblad, July 6, 1968; children: Fredrik, Karin, Eva. M Bus. and Adminstrn., U. Lund, Sweden, 1968. Internal auditor Kockums Mek. Verkstad, Malmö, Sweden, 1969-71, mgr. acctg., 1971-74; v.p. fin. and adminstrn. Kockums Industri, Söderhamn, Sweden, 1974-76, Linden Alimak, Skellefteå, Sweden, 1976-81, Sonessons, Malmö, 1981-82; pres. Sab-Nife, Malmö, 1982-87; v.p. corp. devel. Investment AB Cardo, Malmö, 1987-90; pres., CEO Harmon Industries Inc., Blue Springs, Mo., 1990—. Bd. dirs. BJ Papperats, Malmo, Green & Co., Malmö; mem. adv. bd. Ctrl. Mo. State U. Bus. Sch., Warrensburg, 1991—. Staff sgt. Swedish Army, 1964-65. Avocations: golf, skiing. Office: Harmon Industries Inc PO Box 600 Grain Valley MO 64029-0600

OLSSON, CARL ALFRED, urologist, department chairman; b. Boston, Nov. 29, 1938; s. Charles Rudolph and Ruth Marion (Bostrom) O.; m. Mary DeVore, Nov. 4, 1962; children: Ingrid, Leif Eric. Grad., Bowdoin Coll., 1959; MD, Boston U., 1963. Diplomate Am. Bd. Urology (trustee 1988-94, pres. 1993-94). Asst. prof. urology Boston U. Sch. Medicine, 1971-72, assoc. prof., 1972-74, prof., chmn. dept., 1974-80; dir. urology dept. Boston City Hosp., 1974-77; chief urology dept. Boston VA Med. Ctr., 1971-75; urologist-in-chief Univ. Hosp., Boston, 1971-80; John K. Lattimer prof., chmn. dept. urology Coll. Phys. and Surgs., Columbia U., N.Y.C., 1980—. Dir. Squier Urol. Clinic, urology service Presbyn. Hosp., N.Y.C.; lectr. surgery Tufts U. Sch. Medicine. Boston Interhosp. Organ Bank, 1976-79; mem. working cadre Nat. Prostate Cancer Project, Nat. Cancer Inst., 1979-84; mem. adv. coun. Nat. Inst. Diabetes, Digestive Disease and Kidney; mem. integration panel for prostate cancer rsch. Dept. of Def., 1998-2002, chmn., 2000-01. Editl. bd. Jour. Prostate, World Jour. Urology, Jour. Urodynamics and Neurourology, Jour. Urology; asst. editor Jour. Urology, 1978-2004; contbr. chpts. to books, articles to med. jours. Recipient Disting. Alumnus award Boston U., 1985. Fellow ACS; mem. Am. Urol. Assn. (coord. continuing med. edn. New Eng. sect. 1977-80, del. rsch. com., bd. dirs. 2001—, exec. com. 2002—, sec. 2002—, Gold Cystoscope award 1979, Grayson-Carroll award 1971, 73, Hugh Hampton Young award 2001), Boston Surg. Soc. (exec. com. 1976-80), Am. Assn. Clin. Urologists, Am. Surg. Assn., Am. Assn. Genitourinary Surgeons, Clin. Soc. Genitourinary Surgeons, Transplantation Soc., Soc. Urologic Oncology (pres. 1993), Soc. Pelvic Surgeons, Soc. Univ. Urologists (pres. 1990), N.Y. Sect. Am. Urol. Assn. (pres. 2002), AMA, Assn. Acad. Surgery, Am. Soc. Artificial Internal Organs, Am. Soc. Transplant Surgeons, Assn. Med. Colls., Can. Urol. Assn., Societe Internationale d'Urologie, Internat. Urodynamics Soc., Mass. Med. Soc., Soc. Govt. Urologists, Australasian Urol. Soc. (hon.), New Eng. Handicapped Sportsmen's Assn. (exec. com. 1977-81), U.S. Yacht Racing Union, Yacht Racing Union L.I. Sound, N.Y. Yacht Club, Cottage Park Yacht Club, Larchmont Yacht Club, Storm Trysail Club, Alpha Omega Alpha, Am. Found. Urol. Diseases (bd. dirs. 2002—, exec. coun. 2002—). Episcopalian. Office: Columbia-Presbyn Hosp Irving Pavilion 161 Ft Washington Av New York NY 10032-3702 Office Phone: 212-305-0100. Business E-Mail: CA02@columbia.edu.

OLSSON, NILS WILLIAM, former association executive; b. Seattle, June 11, 1909; s. Nils A. and Mathilda (Lejkell) O.; m. Dagmar T. Gavert, June 15, 1940; children: Karna B., Nils G. and Pehr C. (twins). Student, North Park Coll., Chgo., Northwestern U., U. Minn., 1929-34; A.M., U. Chgo., 1938, PhD, 1949, U. Uppsala, Sweden, 1968; LHD, North Park Coll., Chgo., 1990. Admissions counselor, instr. Swedish North Park Coll., 1937-39; asst. Scandinavian U. Chgo., 1939-42, instr., 1945-50, asst. prof., 1950; mem. U.S. diplomatic service, 1950-67; 2d sec., pub. affairs officer Am. legation, Reykjavik, Iceland, 1950-52; attache, pub. affairs officer Am. embassy, Stockholm, Sweden, 1952-55, 1st. sec., consul, 1955-57; pub. affairs adviser Dept. State, 1957-59; chief Am. sponsored schs. abroad, 1959-62; 1st sec. Am. embassy, Oslo, Norway, 1962-64, counselor for polit. affairs, 1964-66; diplomat in residence Ind. U., 1966-67; dir. Am. Swedish Inst., Mpls., 1967-73; exec. dir. Swedish Council of Am., 1973-84. Author: Swedish Passenger Arrivals in New York 1820-1850, 1967, Swedish Passenger Arrivals in U.S. Ports (except New York) 1820-1850, 1979, Tracing Your Swedish Ancestry, 1974, (with Erik Wiken) Swedish Passenger Arrivals in the U.S. 1820-1850, 1995; editor: A Pioneer in Northwest America, 1841-1858, vol. I, 1950, vol. II, 1959, Veckobladet, 1934-35; editor, pub.: Swedish American Genealogist, 1981—; editor: A Swedish City Directory of Boston 1881, 1986; contbr. to hist. and ednl. jours. Mem. bd. Evang. Covenant Hist. Commn., Chgo., 1958; asst. naval attache Am. legation, Stockholm, 1943-45. Served from lt. (j.g.) to lt. comdr. USNR, 1942-45. Decorated knight Order Vasa 1st class, knight comdr. Order North Star, Sweden; recipient Swedish Pioneer Centennial medal, 1948; King Carl XVI Gustaf Bicentennial Gold medal, Carl Sandburg medal Swedish Pioneer Hist. Soc., 1982, Charlotta Medal Emigrant Inst. Växjö, Sweden; named Swedish Am. of Yr. Stockholm, 1969; recipient Hans Mattsson Plaque, Önnestad, Sweden, 1992; Victor Örnberg prize, Sweden, 1994. Fellow Geneal. Soc. (Finland), Geneal. Soc. (Sweden), Am. Soc. Genealogists; mem. Wermländska Sällskapet Stockholm (hon.), Nat. Geneal Soc., Carl Johan Soc. Sweden, Swedish-Am. Hist. Soc. (exec. sec. 1949-50, 57-68, pres. 1986-88), Royal Acad. Belles Lettres, History and Antiquities (Sweden, fgn. corr.), Pro Fide et Christianismo (Sweden, hon.), Royal Soc. Pub. Manuscripts Dealing with Scandinavian History (Sweden, fgn.). Address: 1620 Mayflower Ct Winter Park FL 32792 E-mail: nwolsson@mpinet.net.

OLSSON-HUME, IRENA, music educator; arrived in U.S., 1994; d. Dragogub D. and Gordana Bukvić; m. Jeremy Dale Hume, Sept. 5, 1999. MusB in Piano Performance summa cum laude, Oklahoma City U., 1998, MusM in Piano Performance with highest honors, 2000. Accompanist Performance Acad. Oklahoma City U., 1998—2000, piano instr., 1998—2002; owner, operator pvt. piano studio Oklahoma City, 2002—. Mem.: Ctrl. Okla. Music Tchrs. Assn., Okla. Music Tchrs. Assn., Music Tchrs. Nat. Assn., Alpha Chi, Pi Kappa Lambda.

OLSTAD, ROGER GALE, science educator; b. Mpls., Jan. 16, 1934; s. Arnold William and Myra (Stroschein) O.; m. Constance Elizabeth Jackson, Aug. 20, 1955; children: Karen Louise, Kenneth Bradley. BS, U. Minn., 1955, MA, 1959, PhD, 1963. Instr. U. Minn., Mpls., 1956-63; asst. prof. U. Ill., Urbana, 1963-64; mem. faculty U. Wash., Seattle, 1964—, asso. prof. sci. edn., 1967-71, prof., 1971-95, asso. dean grad. studies Coll. Edn., 1971-85; prof. emeritus, 1995—. Chair environ. quality commn. City of Lake Forest Park, Wash., 1997-2000, city coun., 2000—. Fellow AAAS; mem. NSTA (bd. dirs.) Wash. Sci. Tchrs. Assn. (pres. 1973-74), Nat. Assn. Rsch. Sci. Teaching (pres. 1977-78, bd. dirs.), N.W. Sci. Assn. (chmn. 1966-68), Assn. Edn. Tchrs. in Sci. (regional pres. 1966-68, pres. 1991-92), Nat. Assn. Biology Tchrs., Biol. Scis. Curriculum Study (chmn., bd. dirs. 1989-94), U. Wash. Faculty Club, Phi Delta Kappa. Home: 20143 53rd Ave NE Seattle WA 98155-1801 Office: U Wash Coll Edn Seattle WA 98195-0001

OLSTEAD, CHRISTOPHER ERIC, financial consultant, entertainment executive; b. Gainesville, Fla., Feb. 10, 1956; s. George Elias Olstead and Myra (Mahlow) Hinman; m. Rebecca Lynn Jeffries, Feb. 14, 1978; 1 child, Reneé. BS, SUNY, Albany, 1991; MBA in Internat. Bus., U. St. Thomas, 1994. Control sys. specialist Soltex Polymer, Etc., Houston, 1975-82; sr. instrument inspector Sohio Constrn. Co., Prudhoe Bay, Alaska, 1983-84; instrument engr. Arco Alaska, Kuparuk, 1984-85, Standard Alaska Prodn. Co., Prudhoe Bay, 1985-87; control sys. supr. S & B Engring., Houston, 1987-88; sr. control sys. engr. Bechtel Corp., Houston, 1988-90, microcomputer ops. mgr., 1990-92, project quality mgr., 1992-95, supply chain mgr., 1995-97; sr. exec. Arthur Andersen Bus. Cons., Houston, 1997-99; COO U.S. Space & Rocket Ctr., Huntsville, Ala., 1999-2000; sr. exec. Arthur Andersen Bus. Cons., Houston, 2000—02, Deloitte Cons., Houston, 2002—. Spkr. ASME-IEEE Internat. Conf., Boston, 1990; panelist Constrn. Industry Inst., San Antonio, Tex., 1993, Constrn. Productivity Inst., Austin, Tex., 1993. Lead author: Advances in Applied Business Strategies, 1995; contbr. articles to profl. jours. Mem. Project Mgmt. Inst., Instrument Soc. Am. (bd. dirs. 1989-92). Avocation: entertainment and management collectibles. Office: Deloitte Consulting Ste 2600 333 Clay St Houston TX 77002 E-mail: colstead@deloitte.com.

OLSZANSKI, S. MICHAEL, college program administrator; b. Hammond, Ind., Mar. 6, 1945; s. Sylvester Frank and Elizabeth Olszanski; life ptnr. Sue Ann O'Leary; m. Barbara Angela Tomazewski (div. Mar. 12, 1980); m. Caryl Jean Gavel (dec. Dec. 31, 1994); children: Robert Michael, Sallie Marie Vicino. B in Gen. Studies with highest distinction, Ind. U., Gary, 2001; cert. in labor studies, Ind. U., 2001. Steelworker Inland Steel Co., East Chicago, Ind., 1963—98; exec. bd. United Steelworkers Am., East Chicago, 1976—88, pres. Local 1010, 1987—88, founder, chair dist. 31 environ. com., founder, chair local 1010 environ. com.; asst. dir., Swingshift Coll. Ind. U., Gary, 1998—. Exec. bd. Calumet Cmty. Congress, Gary, 1972—73, Lake Mich. Fedn., Chgo., 1977—80; del. constl. conv. United Steelworkers Am., 1976—90; labor studies adv. bd. Ind. U., Gary, 1977—80; rep. Internat. Metalworkers Fedn., Berlin, 1987. Co-editor, contbr.: book Steelworkers Fight Back; contbr. book The Cold War Against Labor; contributor/editor: newspaper Voice of the Rank & File; contbr. newspaper Steelworker. Exec. bd. Save the Dunes Coun., Beverly Shores, Ind., 1978—82; cons. US EPA Region V, Chgo., 1978—79; bd. Bailly Alliance, Gary, 1978—80. Recipient Environ. Advancement award, Gary Post Tribune, 1978; scholar, J & F Morgan Swain, 1999—2000; Merit scholar, Ind. U., 1995—98. Avocation: antique radios.

OLTION, JERRY, author science fiction; b. 1951; m. Kathy Oltion. Author: Frame of Reference, 1987, German edit., 1992, Alliance, 1990, French edit., 1992, Humanity, 1990, Love Songs of a Mad Scientist, 1993, The Darkness Before the Dawn, 1995, Tales From the Yuletide, 1994, Twilights End, 1996, Buried Treasures, 1996, Mudd in Your Eye, 1997, You Only Die Twice, 1997, Hard Crase and Prophet's Power, 1998, Where Sea Meets Sky, 1998, Singing in the Rain, 1998, The Flaming Arrow (with Kathy Oltion), 2000, Abandon in Place, 2000, The Getaway Special, 2001, (e-book) The Astronaut from Wyoming, 2001; author numerous short stories, novelettes, novellas. Winner 1997 Nebula award for novella, Abandon in Place. Office: Tor Books 175 5th Ave 14th Fl New York NY 10010

OLTMAN, JOHN HAROLD, patent lawyer; b. Nov. 18, 1929; s. Peter Harold and Hazel Evelyn (Kelly) O.; m. Lita Marilyn Hagen, Aug. 16, 1952; children: David K., Laura G., John K. BS in Chem. Engring., U. Mich., 1952, JD, 1957. Bar: Ill. 1957, Ariz. 1964, Mich. 1965, Fla. 1968. Mem. firms Mueller & Aichele (Attys.), Chgo. and Phoenix, 1957—64, Barnes, Kisselle, Rasich & Choate (Attys.), Detroit, 1964—65, Settle, Batchelder & Oltman (Attys.), Detroit, 1965—67, Settle & Oltman (Attys.), Detroit and Ft. Lauderdale, 1967—72, Oltman and Flynn (Attys.), Ft. Lauderdale, 1972—90, Oltman, Flynn & Kublev, Ft. Lauderdale, 1990—. Served with USMC Res., 1952—54. Mem.: IEEE, ABA, Fla. Engring. Soc., Intellectual Property Law Assn. So. Fla., Am. Intellectual Property, Broward County Bar Assn., Fla. Bar Assn., Kiwanian (dir. Ft. Lauderdale Club 1972—74, 1977—78, pres. 1983—, chmn. Key Club com. 1970—78), Tau Beta Pi, Phi Eta Sigma. Home: 2130 NE 55th St Fort Lauderdale FL 33308-3155 Office: 915 Middle River Dr Fort Lauderdale FL 33304-3544

OLUBODUN, JOEL OLADAPO, medical researcher, physician; b. Ipoti, Ekiti, Nigeria, July 12, 1950; came to U.S., 1996; s. Samson Folayan and Alice Olawande O.; m. Margaret Olufunke, Feb. 21, 1981; children: David Oluwaseun, Israel Olaoluwa, Elizabeth Ifejesu. BS, MB, U. Ibadan, Nigeria, 1977. Houseman Adeoyo Specialist Hosp., Ibadan, Nigeria, 1977-78; resident in internal medicine U. Coll. Hosp., Ibadan, 1979-85; rsch. fellow cardiology Freeman Hosp., Newcastle Upon Tyne, U.K., 1985-86; physician, cardiologist, sr. lectr. Ogun State U. Tchg. Hosp., Shagamu, Nigeria, 1988-91; sr. rschr. fellow U. Newcastle & Freeman Hosp., Newcastle Upon Tyne, 1991-96; resident U. Pa. Health Sys., Presbyn. Med. Ctr., Phila., 1996-2000; rschr. drug devel. Tufts U. Pfizer Global Rsch. and Devel., Boston, 2000—. Chmn. cardiovas. svcs. bd. Ogun State U. Tchg. Hosp., 1989-91, disciplinary bd., 1990-91, acting head medicine dept., 1990-91, dept. rep. U. senate, 1989-91; cons. in field. Contbr. numerous articles to profl. jours.; editl. bd. Jour Ethnicity & Disease, 1999—. Active vol. African Christian Fellowship, 1996—. Med. officer 22d. armoured bridage, Ilorin, Nigeria, 1978-79. Recipient Elizabeth Wherry award, 1995, Searle Dist. Rsch. award 1996, med. degree (MRCP), Royal Coll. Physicians of Ireland, 1995, award Am. Coll. Clin. Pharmacology, 2001, 02, award Am. Soc. Clin. Pharmacology and Therapeutics, 2002, James A. Bain Young Scientist award World Congress Pharmacologists, 2002; fellow Assn. Commonwealth Univs., London, 1991, Pfizer, 1991. Fellow Postgrad. Med. Coll. Physicians Nigeria; mem. Royal Coll. Physicians Ireland, Royal Coll. Physicians Nigeria, Am. Coll. Physicians (bd. cert.), Internat. Soc. Hypertension in Blacks (editl. bd. 1990—, manuscript reviewer). Avocations: chess, travel, writing. Home: 214 Chestnut W Randolph MA 02368 Office: Tufts Univ Med Sch 136 Harrison Ave Boston MA 02111 E-mail: olubodun@yahoo.com.

OLVER, FRANK WILLIAM JOHN, research mathematician; b. Croydon, Eng., Dec. 15, 1924; came to U.S., 1961; s. John Adlbert and Susan Mary (Barnes) O.; m. Grace E. Smith, Sept. 25, 1948 (dec. 1980); children: Peter J., Linda M. (dec.), Sally E. Sondergaard; m. Claire L. Kellogg, June 22, 1990. BSc, U. London, 1945, MSc, 1948, DSc, 1961. Sr. prin. sci. officer Nat. Physical Lab., Teddington, Eng., 1945-61; mathematician Nat. Bureau of Standards, Washington, 1961-86; rsch. prof. U. Md., Coll. Park, 1969-92, prof. emeritus, 1992—. Author: Asymptotics and Special Functions, 1974, Selected Papers, 2 vols., 2002; mem. editl. bd. SIAM Jour. on Mathematical Analysis, 1969-94, Mathematics of Computation, 1984-95, Methods and Applications of Analysis, 1992-2000; math. editor NIST Digital Libr. Math. Functions, 1998—; contbr. numerous articles to profl. math. jours. and books. Recipient Silver medal U.S. Dept. of Commerce, Washington, 1969. Fellow Inst. Math. and Its Applications; mem. Am. Math. Soc., Soc. for Indsl. and Applied Maths., Math. Assn. Am., Royal Soc. Scis. Uppsala (fgn. mem.), Sigma Xi. Avocation: billiards. Office: U Md Inst Phys Sci And Tech College Park MD 20742-2431

OLVER, JOHN WALTER, congressman; b. Honesdale, Pa., Sept. 3, 1936; s. Helen Fulleborn Olver; m. Rose Alice Richardson, Sept. 12, 1959; 1 child, Martha. BS, Rensselaer Poly. Inst., 1955; MS, Tufts U., 1956; PhD, MIT, 1961. Asst. prof. chemistry U. Mass., Amherst, 1962-67; mem. Mass. Ho. of Reps., Boston, 1969-72, Mass. Senate, 1973-91, U.S. Congress from 1st Mass. dist., 1991—, mem. com. on appropriations; mem. subcoms. on transp. and mil. constrn., mil. appropriations; whip-at-large Dem. Caucus. Congressman; b. Honesdale, Pa., Sept. 3, 1936; s. Helen Fulleborn Olver; m. Rose Alice Richardson, Sept. 12, 1959; children: Martha. BS, Rensselaer Poly. Inst., 1955; MS, Tufts U., 1956; PhD, MIT, 1961. Asst. prof. chemistry, U. Mass., Amherst, 1962-68; mem. Mass. Ho. of Reps., Boston, 1969-72, Mass. Senate, 1973-91; mem. 101st-105th Congresses from 1st Mass. dist., 1991—, mem. com. on appropriations, mem. subcoms. on transp. and mil. constrn. Contbr. articles to profl. jours. Democrat. Avocations: hiking; gardening; tennis. Contbr. articles to profl. jours. Democrat. Avocations: hiking, gardening, tennis. Office: US Ho of Reps 1027 Longworth Hob Washington DC 20515-0001

OLVERA, CARLOS NELSON, mechanical engineer, executive; b. Antioch, Calif., Aug. 16, 1942; s. Manuel Olvera and Faye Ames; m. Pamela Lords, Oct. 20, 1966 (div. 1979); children: Jason, Jared, Jamie, Janel; m. Georgelean Suitter, Mar. 19, 1983. BSME, Brigham Young U., 1972. Registered profl. engr., Calif., Idaho. Mgr. Westinghouse, Idaho Falls, Idaho, 1972-83; sr. engr. So. Calif. Edison, San Clemente, Calif., 1983-97; v.p., bd. dirs. SAI Engrs., inc., Santa Clara, Calif., 1997—2001; v.p. constrn. SAI Geothermal, Inc., Santa Clara, 1997—2001. Cons. in field, 2000-. Author: Los Olvera, Journey to America. Chmn. Dana Point (Calif.) Planning Commn., 1990; pres. Dana Point Hist. Soc., 1992-94; foreman Grand Jury, Orange County, Calif., 2002-03. Served with USN, 1963-69, USNR, 1974-90, comdr. ret. Mem. ASME. Home: 24901 Danafir Dana Point CA 92629-3153

OLYAN, SAUL MITCHELL, religious studies educator; b. Toronto, Ont., Can., Feb. 2, 1959; s. Sidney David and Eve (Eisenberg) O.; life ptnr. Frederik Schockaert. BA, York U., Toronto, Ont., 1981; AM, Harvard U., 1984, PhD, 1985. Asst. prof. U. Winnipeg, 1985-87, Yale U., New Haven, Conn., 1987-92, Brown U., Providence, 1992-94, assoc. prof., 1994-2000, prof., 2000—. Author: Asherah and the Cult of Yahweh in Israel, 1988, A Thousand Thousands Served Him: Exegesis and the Naming of Angels in Ancient Judaism, 1993, Rites and Rank: Hierarchy in Biblical Representations of Cult, 2000, Biblical Mourning: Ritual and Social Dimensions, 2004; dissertation series editor Soc. Bibl. Lit., 1999-2002; mem. editl. bd. Jour. Bibl. Lit., 1993-98, Jour. History Sexuality, 1996-2000; coordinating editor (monograph) Brown Judaic Studies; contbr. articles to profl. jours. Mem. Soc. Bibl. Lit. (coun. 1999—2002), Am. Hist. Assn., European Assn. Bibl. Studies. Democrat. Jewish. Avocations: coin collecting/numismatics, music, travel, antiques. Office: Brown U 163 George St Providence RI 02906 Office Phone: 401-863-7565. E-mail: saul_olyan@brown.edu.

OLYMPIO, MICHAEL ALLEN, anesthesiologist, researcher; b. Elizabeth, N.J., Oct. 1, 1957; BS, U. Fla., 1979, MD, 1982. Diplomate Am. Bd. Anesthesiology, 1986. Instr. anesthesiology Wake Forest U. Sch. of Medicine, Winston-Salem, NC, 1986—87, asst. prof. anesthesiology, 1987—94, assoc. prof. anesthesiology, 1994—2002, prof. anesthesiology, 2002—. Staff anesthesiologist Iredell Meml. Hosp., Statesville, NC, 1985—86, Rowan Meml. Hosp., 1985—86; vice chair edn. Wake Forest U. Sch. Medicine, Winston-Salam, 2003—; lectr. in field. Contbr. articles to profl. jours., chapters to books. Recipient Am. Top Physicians, Consumers Rsch. Coun. Am., 2003, Best Doctors Am., 2003-2004. Achievements include development of Patient Simulation Laboratory of Wake Forest University School of Medicine. Office: Wake Forest U Sch Medicine Medical Center Blvd Winston Salem NC 27157-1009 Office Phone: 336-716-4498. E-mail: molympio@wfubmc.edu.

OLYPHANT, DAVID, cultural, educational association executive; b. N.Y.C., Feb. 3, 1936; s. John Kensett Olyphant and Adele (Hammond) Emery; m. Pamela Moore, Apr. 27, 1962 (div. Aug. 1988); children: Hillary, Fanny, David K., Elgin, Flora; m. Tatyana Doughty, Oct. 22, 1988 (div.); m. Eloise S. Watt, May 26, 2000. BA, Harvard U., 1958. V.p. Citibank, N.Y.C., 1959-75; ptnr. Harold Denton Assocs., Princeton, N.J., 1975-76; owner/operator Clucerna Farm, Pittstown, N.J., 1976-87; exec. dir., sec. English Speaking Union US, N.Y.C., 1987-2000; ret. Treas.-sec. Am. Trust for Brit. Libr., 1992-99; mem. adv. bd. N.Y. Marble Cemetery, 2001—. Fellow Met. Mus. Art (life), NAD (life); mem. St. Andrew's Soc. (life), Harvard Club N.Y., Porcellan Club (Cambridge, Mass.), Pilgrims of U.S. Presbyterian.

OLYPHANT, TIMOTHY, actor; b. Hawaii, May 20, 1968; m. Alexis Knief. Student, U. So. Calif. Actor: (films) The First Wives Club, 1996, A Life Less Ordinary, 1997, Scream 2, 1997, 1999, 1998, Go, 1999, No Vacancy, 1999, Advice From a Caterpillar, 1999, The Broken Hearts Club: A Romantic Comedy, 2000, Gone in Sixty Seconds, 2000, Auggie Rose, 2000, Head Over Heels, 2001, Doppelganger, 2001, The Safety of Objects, 2001, Rock Star, 2001, Coastlines, 2002, Dreamcatcher, 2003, A Man Apart, 2003, The Girl Next Door, 2004; (TV series) Deadwood, 2004—; (TV films) Ellen Foster, 1997, When Trumpets Fade, 1998, Shadow Realm, 2002. Office: c/o HBO 1100 Avenue of the Americas New York NY 10036*

OLZEROWICZ, SHARON, information technology executive; Founder Matrix, Rochelle Park, NJ, 1986—. Office: Matrix Info Consulting Inc 365 W Passaic St Rochelle Park NJ 07662

O'MALLEY, BERT WILLIAM, JR., head and neck surgeon, educator, researcher; b. Pitts., Sept. 7, 1962; s. Bert. W. and Sally A. (Johnson) O'M.; m. Cheryl Anne Moore, Jan. 17, 1987; children: Bartley, Annette, Michael. Student, U. Notre Dame, 1980-81; BA in Biochemistry, U. Tex., 1984; MD, U. Tex., Dallas, 1988. Gen. surgery resident U. Tex. Southwestern, Parkland Meml. Hosp., Dallas, 1984-88; otolaryngology and head and neck surgery resident Baylor Coll. Medicine, Houston, 1988-90; head and neck oncology and cranial base surgery fellow U. Pitts., 1994-95; clin. instr. dept. otorhinolaryngology Baylor Coll. Medicine, Houston, 1993-94; clin. instr. dept. otolaryngology and head and neck surgery U. Pitts., 1994-95; asst. prof. dept. otolaryngology—head and neck surgery Johns Hopkins U. Sch. Medicine, Balt., 1995, dir. gene therapy divsn., dept. otolaryngology-HNS, 1995—99, asst. prof. dept. oncology, 1996; chief otolaryngology U. Maryland, 1999—2003; chair designate otorhinolaryngology U. Penn. Sch. Medicine, 2003—. Cons. head and neck gene therapy project GeneMedicine, Inc. The Woodlands, Tex.; lectr. dept. otolaryngology—head and neck surgery Grand Rounds, Greater Balt. Med. Ctr., 1995, U. Pitts., 1995, Johns Hopkins U., Balt., 1996, others; presenter in field. Contbr. book chpts.: Fundamentals of Molecular Biology and Gene Therapy, 1997, Surgery of the Anterior and Middle Cranial Base, 1997; contbr. articles to Transplantation Procs., Archives of Otolaryngology—Head and Neck Surgery, Human Gene Therapy, Seminars in Surg. Oncology, Cancer Rsch., others; reviewer: Otolaryngology—Head and Neck Surgery, Head and Neck, Cancer Rsch., Archives of Otolaryngology—Head and Neck Surgery, Clin. Cancer Rsch. Mem. AAAS, Am. Assn. for Cancer Rsch., Am. Soc. Gravitational and Space Biology, Am. Acad. Otolaryngology Head and Neck Surgery, Cell Transplant Soc. (founding mem.), Md. Soc. Otolaryngology. Roman Catholic. Achievements include patents pending for gene therapy to thyroid, somatic gene therapy. Office: U Penn Sch Medicine Otorhinolaryngology Dept 3400 Spruce St 5 Ravdin Bldg Philadelphia PA 19104

O'MALLEY, CARLON MARTIN, judge; b. Phila., Sept. 7, 1929; s. Carlon Martin and Lucy (Bol) O'M.; m. Mary Catherine Lyons, Aug. 17, 1957; children: Carlon Martin III, Kathleen B. O'Malley Aikman, Harry Tighe, John Todd, Cara M. O'Malley Colombo. BA, Pa. State U., 1951; LLB, Temple U., 1954. Bar: Pa. 1955, Fla. 1973, U.S. Supreme Ct. 1973. Practiced law, 1957-61; asst. U.S. atty. for Middle Dist. Pa., Dept. Justice, 1961-69, U.S. atty., 1979-82; ptnr. O'Malley & Teets, 1970-72, O'Malley, Jordan & Mullaney (and predecessor firms), 1976-79; pvt. practice Pa. and Fla., 1972-79, 82-87; judge Ct. Common Pleas of Lackawanna County (45th Judicial Dist.), 1987-97, sr. judge, 1998—. Dir. pub. safety City of Scranton, 1983-86; lectr. Lackawanna Coll., 1982-86. Editorial bd.: Temple Law Rev, 1952-53. Pres. Lackawanna County (Pa.) unit Am. Cancer Soc., 1966-67; bd. dirs. Pa. Cancer Soc., 1967-68, Lackawanna county chpt. ARC, 1967-69; mem. solicitation team, govtl. divsn. Lackawanna United Fund, 1963-68; chmn. profl. divsn. Greater Scranton (Pa.) YMCA Membership Drives; trustee Everhart Mus., Scranton, 1987—. Pilot USAF, 1955-57, Pa. N.G., 1957-59. Mem. Am. Judges Assn., Nat. Assn. Former U.S. Attys., Pa. Bar Assn., Lackawanna County Bar Assn. (bd. dirs., fin. sec.), Fla. Bar Assn., Country Club of Scranton, Elks (pres. Pa. chpt. 1978-79, judiciary com. 1985-89, justice Grand Forum 1991, 1995-97, chief justice 1992-93, nat. pres. 1997-98), K.C., Phi Kappa (pres.), Delta Theta Phi (pres.). Democrat. Office: Judges Chambers Lackawanna County Courthouse Scranton PA 18503

O'MALLEY, EDWARD, psychiatrist, consultant; b. Hudson, N.Y., May 30, 1926; s. Thomas Patrick and Helen Mary (Cornell) O. BS, St. John's U., Bklyn., N.Y., 1949; MS, Loyola U., Chgo., 1952, PhD, 1954; MD, SUNY, Bklyn., 1958. Diplomate Am. Bd. Forensic Examiners, Am. Bd. Psychiatry and Neurology. Psychiat. cons. dept. of corrections N.Y.C., 1962-68; psychiatrist Cath. Charities, N.Y.C., 1963-68; dir. of mental health Suffolk County Govt., Hauppauge, N.Y., 1968-70; commr. of mental health Orange County, Goshen, N.Y., 1970-72; dir. drug abuse services State of N.Y., Bronx, 1972-78; lic. sch. psychiatrist N.Y.C. Bd. of Edn., 1962-82; chief psychiatry services VA, Huntington, W.Va., 1982-86; med. cons. State of Calif., San Diego, 1986—, psychiat. cons. dept. of corrections, 1987—. Asst. prof. psychiatry N.J. Med. Sch., Newark, 1975—; examiner Am. Bd. of Psychiatry and Neurology, Los Angeles, 1980; assoc. prof. psychiatry U. Calif., San Diego, 1980—; prof. psychiatry Marshall U. Sch. of Medicine, Huntington, 1982-86; dir. com. on sea cadets Navy League, San Diego, 1987—; cons. HHS, Social Security Adminstrn., Office of Hearings and Appeals, 1989—. Contbr. articles to profl. jours. Bd. dirs. Suffolk Community Council, Hauppauge, 1968-70, United Fund of Long Island, Huntington, 1968-70. Capt. ret. USNR, 1960-86. Scholar N. Y. State Coll., 1946-49, SUNY Joseph Collins Med. Sch., 1955-58; Teaching and Research fellow Loyola U., 1952-54. Fellow Am. Psychiat. Assn.(disting., life); mem. San Diego Psychiat. Soc., Soc. of Med. Cons. to the Armed Forces, Soc. of Mil. Surgeons of U.S.A., N.Y. Celtic Med. Soc., Union Am. Physicians and Dentists (steward 1990—), State Employed Physicians Assn. (bd. dirs. 1993—). Roman Catholic. Home: 3711 Alcott St San Diego CA 92106-1212 Personal E-mail: omalleyedwr@aol.com. Business E-Mail: edward.p.omalley.md@ssa.gov.

O'MALLEY, EDWARD JOSEPH, JR., financial services administrator; b. Flushing, N.Y., Jan. 4, 1942; s. Edward Joseph and Elsie Anne (Ende) O'M.; m. Iris Theresa Hill, Aug. 10, 1975. BS, Widener Coll., 1963; MBA, St. John's U., Jamaica, N.Y., 1976. Ins. agt. Liberty Mut. Ins. Co., N.Y.C., 1966-67; supr. group home Children's Village, Bayside, 1967-69; unit head N.Y. Narcotic Addiction Control Commn., N.Y.C., 1970-71; exec. dir. sch. dist. drug and alcohol abuse program Howard Beach, 1971-81; spl. asst. Kings County Dist. Atty., 1982-85, adminstrv. asst., spl. advisor, 1986-89; sr. asst. comptr. City of N.Y., 1990-91, dep. comptr., 1991-93; exec. v.p. Improved Funding Techniques, Lynbrook, 1993—; COO Accts. Proprietary Fin. ServiceNet Inc., 2000—. Past chmn., sec. N.Y.C. Coalition Sch. Based Drug Prevention Programs; past vice chmn. Comprehensive Health Planning Agy., Queens, N.Y.; mem. Queens Cmty. Planning Bd.; past v.p. Flushing Boys Club; past chmn. bd. dirs. Regular Dem. Club, Rockaway, N.Y.; mem. N.Y. State Dem. Com.; mem. Parish Coun. St. Camillus Ch.; mem. Chancellor N.Y.C. Bd. Edn. Task Force on Drug Abuse; bd. dir. Queens chpt. ARC, N.Y.C. Health Systems Agy., Rockaway Task Force on Arts, Far Rockaway chpt. NAACP; chmn. Anti-Redlining Com. of Rockaways; vice chmn. Com. for Casino Gambling in the Rockaways, Surfside Housing Assn. for Tenants; mem. N.Y. State Urban Coalition Task Force Drug Abuse. Mem. Emerald Assn. L.I., Beta Gamma Sigma, Kiwanis (past pres. Rockaway club). Home: 79-19 210 St Flushing NY 11364 Office: Improved Funding Techniques 211 Broadway Ste 300 Lynbrook NY 11563-3291 also: Accts Proprietary Fin ServiceNet 622 3d Ave New York NY 10016 Office Phone: 212-319-1489. E-mail: edo@impfti.com.

O'MALLEY, JOHN DANIEL, law educator, banker; b. Chgo., Dec. 18, 1926; s. William D. and Paula A. (Skaugh) O'M.; m. Caroline Tyler Taylor, July 12, 1958; children: John Daniel, Taylor John. Grad., St. Thomas Mil. Acad., 1945; BS, Loyola U., Chgo., 1950, MA, 1952, JD, 1953; grad., U.S. Army Intelligence Sch., 1962, Command & Gen. Staff Coll., 1965. Bar: Ill. 1953, Mich. 1954, U.S. Supreme Ct. 1962. Asst. prof. law Loyola U., 1953-59, asso. prof., 1959-65; formerly spl. counsel and bond claims mgr. Fed. Ins. Co.; prof. law Loyola U. Grad. Sch. Bus., 1965—, chmn. dept. law, 1968-86. Trust officer, v.p. First Nat. Bank Highland Park (Ill.), Marina City Bank, Chgo., Hyde Park Bank & Trust Co., 1970-75; exec. v.p. Harris Bank Winnetka, Ill., 1975-95. Author: Subrogation Against Banks on Forged Checks, 1967, Common Check Frauds and the Uniform Commercial Code, 1969; Contbr. articles to profl. jours. and law revs. Served to maj. AUS, 1945-47, 61-62. Decorated knight grand cross Papal Order of Holy Sepulchre, knight comdr. with star Constantinian Order of St. George (Italy), knight of Malta. Mem. ABA, Chgo., Ill., Mich. bar assns., Chgo. Crime Commn., French Nat. Hon. Soc., Am., Chgo. bus. law assns., Mil. Govt. Assn., Order of St. Maurice and St. Lazarus (Italy, officer). Home: 1630 Sheridan Rd 6-L Wilmette IL 60091-1830 Office: Loyola U 820 N Michigan Ave Ste 1316 Chicago IL 60611-2147

O'MALLEY, KATHLEEN M. federal judge; b. 1956; AB magna cum laude, Kenyon Coll., 1979; JD, Case Western Reserve, 1982. Law clk. to Hon. Nathaniel R. Jones U.S. Ct. of Appeals, 6th circuit, 1982-83; with Jones, Day, Reavis & Pogue, Cleve., 1983-84, Porter, Wright, Morris & Arthur, Cleve., 1985-91; chief counsel, first asst. atty. gen., chief of staff Office of Atty. Gen., Columbus, 1991-94; district judge U.S. Dist. Ct. (Ohio no. dist.), 6th circuit, Cleve., 1994—. Mem. ABA, FBA, Anthony J. Celebrezze Inn of Ct., Order of Coif, Phi Beta Kappa. Office: US District Courts 801 W Superior Ave Cleveland OH 44113-1629

O'MALLEY, KEVIN FRANCIS, lawyer, writer, educator; b. St. Louis, May 12, 1947; s. Peter Francis and Dorothy Margaret (Cradick) O'M.; m. Dena Hengen, Apr.2, 1971; children: Kevin Brendan, Ryan Michael. AB, St. Louis U., 1970, JD, 1973. Bar: Mo. 1973, U.S. Ct. Appeals D.C. 1974, U.S. Ct. Appeals (8th cir.) 1979, Ill. 1993. Trial lawyer U.S. Dept. Justice, Washington, 1973-74, Los Angeles, 1974-77, Phoenix, 1977-78, asst. U.S. atty. St. Louis, 1978-83. Adj. prof. law St. Louis U., 1979—; lectr. Ctrl. and Ea. European Law Initiative, Russian Fedn., 1996, Poland, 1999. Author: (with Devitt, Blackmar, O'Malley) Federal Jury Practice and Instruction, 1990, 92, (with O'Malley, Grenig & Lee), 1999, 2000, 01; contbr. articles to law books and jours. Community amb. Expt. in Internat. Living, Prague, Czechoslovakia, 1968; bd. dirs. St. Louis-Galway (Ireland) Sister Cities. Capt. U.S. Army, 1973. Recipient Atty. Gen.'s Disting. Service award U.S. Dept. Justice, 1977, John J. Dwyer Meml. Scholarship award, 1967-70. Fellow Am. Coll. Trial Lawyers; mem. ABA (chmn. govt. litigation counsel com. 1982-86, chmn. jud. com. 1986-87, chmn. com. on ind. and small firms, chmn. trial practice com. 1991-94, health care litigation 1994-98), Am. Law Inst., Met. Bar Assn. St. Louis (chmn. criminal law sect.), Nat. Inst. Trial Advocacy, Mo. Athletic Club. Roman Catholic. Office: Greensfelder Hemker & Gale PC 10 S Broadway Ste 2000 Saint Louis MO 63102-1747 Business E-Mail: kom@greensfelder.com.

O'MALLEY, MARTIN JOSEPH, mayor, former councilman, lawyer; b. 1963; m. Katie Curran; children: Grace, Tara, William, Jack. BA, Cath. U., 1985; postgrad, U. Md. Sch of Law, 1988. Asst. state's atty., Balt., 1988-90; staff asst. U.S. Congress; city councilman Balt., 1991—99; pvt. practice law; mayor, 1999—. Co-chmn. task force on fed.-local law enforcement U.S. Conf. Mayors. Former state field dir. Senator Barbara Mikulski Senate Campaign; former state coord. Senator Bob Kerrey Dem. Primary. chmn. Com. of Taxation and Finance, chmn. of Legislative Investment. Recipient Svc. to Humanity award Md. Jaycees, 1994. Mem.: Md. Bar Assn., Friendly Sons St. Patricks. Democrat. Office: City Hall Rm 250 100 N Holliday St Baltimore MD 21202-3417 E-mail: mayor@baltimorecity.gov.

O'MALLEY, ROBERT EDMUND, JR., mathematics professor; b. Rochester, N.H., May 23, 1939; s. Robert E. and Jeanette A. (Dubois) O'M.; m. Candace G. Hinz, Aug. 31, 1968; children: Patrick, Timothy, Daniel. BS in Elec. Engring., U. N.H., 1960, MS, 1961; PhD, Stanford U., 1966. Mathematician Bell Labs., Gen. Electric Research Co., RCA, summers 1961-63; asst. prof. U. N.C., Chapel Hill, 1965-66; vis. mem. Courant Inst., NYU, 1966-67; research mem. Math. Research Ctr., Madison, Wis., 1967-68; asst. prof., assoc. prof. NYU, N.Y.C., 1968-73; prof. math. U. Ariz., Tucson, 1973-81, chmn. applied math. program, 1976-81; prof. math. Rensselaer Poly. Inst., Troy, N.Y., 1981-90, chmn. dept. math. scis., 1981-84, Ford Found. prof., 1989-90; prof., chair applied math. U. Wash., Seattle, 1990-93, prof., 1993—. Sr. vis. fellow U. Edinburgh, (Scotland), 1971-72; guest prof. Tech. U. Vienna, 1987-88; vis. Univ. Lyon 1 and Univ. of Cambridge, 1994-95, Fields Inst., 2002-03, U. Minn., 2002-03, Dublin City U., 2002-03. Author: Introduction to Singular Perturbations, 1974; editor: Asymptotic Methods and Singular Perturbations, 1976, Singular Perturbation Methods for Ordinary Differential Equations, 1991, Thinking About Ordinary Differential Equations, 1997; editor ICIAM 91 procs.; co-editor Multiscale Phenomena, 1999; contbr. numerous articles to profl. jours. Mem. Soc. for Indsl. and Applied Math. (pres. 1991-92), Am. Math. Soc. Roman Catholic. Home: 3415 W Laurelhurst Dr NE Seattle WA 98105-5345 Office: U Wash Dept Applied Math Box 352420 Seattle WA 98195-2420 Office Phone: 206-685-1905. E-mail: omalley@amath.washington.edu.

O'MALLEY, SEAN PATRICK, archbishop; b. Lakewood, Ohio, June 29, 1944; Ed., St. Fidelis Sem., Herman, Pa., Capuchin Coll. and Cath. U., Washington. Ordained priest Roman Cath. Ch., 1970. Prof. Catholic U., Washington, 1969—73; exec. dir., Centro Catolico Hispano Washington archdiocese, Washington, 1973—78, episcopal vicar of priests serving Spanish speaking, 1978-84; coadjutor bishop Roman Cath. Ch., St. Thomas, 1984, bishop, 1985—92, Fall River, Mass., 1992—2002, Palm Beach, Fla., 2002—03; archbishop Archdiocese of Boston, Brighton, 2003—. Office: 2101 Commonwealth Ave Brighton MA 02135-3192

O'MALLEY, SUSAN, professional basketball team executive; Degree in Bus. and Finance, Mt. St. Mary's, 1983. Dir. advt. Washington Bullets, 1986-87, dir. mktg., 1987-88, exec. v.p., 1988-91, pres., 1991-96, Washington Wizards, 1996—. Achievements include becoming 1st women ever to become a president of an NBA franchise. Avocations: tennis, vacations. Office: Washington Wizards 718 7th St NW Washington DC 20001-3716*

O'MALLEY, THOMAS ANTHONY, gastroenterologist, internist; b. St. Helens, Lancashire, Eng., Jan. 21, 1932; s. Michael and Margaret (Melia) O'M.; m. Margaret Mary O'Kane, Apr. 7, 1958 (dec. Apr. 1985); m. Marianne Rapier, Jan. 23, 1988; children: Anne, Patricia, Katherine, Jane, Margaret. MBChB, U. Liverpool, Eng., 1956; Lic. Medicine, U. State N.Y., 1964. Diplomate Am. Bd. Internal Medicine, State Bd. Med. Examiners Fla. House physician Royal Infirmary, Liverpool, 1956-57; house surgeon Royal Liverpool Children's Hosp., 1957; resident in medicine C.S. Wilson Meml. Hosp., Johnson City, N.Y., 1957-58; fellow internal medicine Lahey Clinic, Boston, 1958-59; USPHS trainee in gastroenterology U. Rochester (N.Y.), Strong Meml. Hosp., 1959-60; chief resident medicine/Segal Watson fellow gastroenterology Genesee Hosp., Rochester, 1960-61; gastroenterologist Cancer Clinic, Regina, Sask., Can., 1963; asst. dir. med. edn. Genesee Hosp., U. Rochester, 1964—66; sr. lectr. medicine, pvt. practice U. Rochester, 1967—72; clin. assoc. prof. medicine U. South Fla., Tampa, 1972—. Chief medicine Sarasota (Fla.) Meml. Hosp., 1973, Doctors Hosp., Sarasota, 1985. With RAF, 1961-62. Recipient Physician of Yr. award Doctors Hosp. Sarasota, 1985; listed among Best Dr.'s of Am., 1998. Fellow: ACP, Am. Coll. Gastroenterology; mem.: Cavalieri del Vini Nobili (amb. 1989—, pres. 1997), Chevalier du Tastevin (officier comdr. 2001—, comdr. 1985—). Office: O'Malley & Hall MD PA 2650 Bahia Vista St Sarasota FL 34239-2635

O'MALLEY, THOMAS D. petroleum industry executive; b. N.Y.C., 1941; Grad., Manhattan Coll., 1963. Vice chmn., dir. Salomon, Inc. (formerly Phibro-Salomon, Inc.), N.Y.C.; former chmn., CEO, pres. Phibro Energy, Inc., Greenwich, Conn.; chmn. Argus Investments (formerly Argus Resources), Stamford, Conn., 1987; chmn., CEO Tosco Corp., Conn., 1989—2001; vice chmn., dir. Phillips Petroleum, 2001; CEO, pres., chmn. Premcor Inc., St. Louis, 2002—. Bd. dirs. PETsMART, Inc., 2002. Office: Premcor 8182 Maryland Ave Ste 600 Saint Louis MO 63105-3721

O'MALLEY, TIMOTHY PATRICK, otolaryngologist; b. Washington, Oct. 19, 1958; MD, Georgetown U., Washington, 1985. Diplomate Am. Bd. Otolaryngology. Intern Naval Hosp., San Diego, 1985-86, resident otolaryngology Oakland, Calif., 1989-93, dept. head otolaryngology Rota, Spain, 1996-99, head dept. otolaryngology Pensacola, Fla., 2000—02. Master: Am. Acad. Otolaryngology, Head and Neck Surgery; fellow: Am. Coll. Surgeons. Office: Naval Med Ctr Charette Health Care Ctr Dept Oto-Head and Neck Surg 27 Effingham St Bldg 2 Portsmouth VA 23708 E-mail: tpomalley@mar.med.navy.mil.

OMAN, HENRY, retired electrical engineer, engineering executive; b. Portland, Oreg., Aug. 29, 1918; s. Paul L. and Mary (Levonen) O.; m. Winifred Eleanor Potter, June 17, 1944 (dec. Nov. 1950); m. Earlene Mary Boot, Sept. 11, 1954; children: Mary Janet, Eleanor Eva, Eric Paul. BSEE, Oreg. State U., 1940, MSEE, 1951. Registered profl. engr., Wash. Application engr. Allis Chalmers Mfg. Co., Milw., 1940-48; rsch. engr. Boeing Co., Seattle, 1948-63, engring. mgr., 1963-91. Author: Energy Systems Engineering Handbook, 1986; contbr. numerous articles to profl. jours. Mem. team that restarted amateur radio communication to the outside world from the People's Republic of China, 1981. Recipient prize paper award Am. Inst. Elec. Engrs., 1964. Fellow IEEE (founder power electronics systems confs., 1970—, v.p. Aerospace and Electronics Systems Soc. 1984-88, Harry Mimno award 1989, Third Millenium medal 2000, editor-in-chief IEEE Aerospace and Electronic Sys. mag. 1995-99/rated in top two by Inst. for Scientific Info.), AIAA (assoc. fellow); mem. AAAS (bd. dir. Pacific divsn. 1992—). Republican. Methodist. Achievements include development of concepts for solar power satellite which generates power in geo-synchronous orbit 24 hours per day and beams it to the Earth surface with a microwave beam; research in simple battery-powered electric bicycles for low-cost, pollution-free transportation in developing nations. Home: 19221 Normandy Park Dr SW Seattle WA 98166-4129

OMAN, MARK C. bank executive; b. Cedar Falls, Iowa; B, U. No. Iowa. CPA. With Delouitte, HAskins & Sells, Des Moines, Norwest Corp., 1979; CEO Wells Fargo Home Mortgage, Inc., 1989—97, chmn., 1997—; exec. v.p. mortgage svcs. Norwest, 1997—98; group exec. v.p. home and consumer fin. Wells Fargo & Co., 2002—. Office: Wells Fargo & Co 420 Montgomery St San Francisco CA 94163

OMAN, RALPH, lawyer; b. Huntington, N.Y., July 1, 1940; s. Henry Ferdinand and Annamarie (Retelsdorf) O.; m. Anne K. Henehan, Oct. 21, 1967; children: Tabitha Russell, Caroline Adams, Charlotte Ericsson. Diploma, Sorbonne U., Paris, 1961; BA, Hamilton Coll., 1962; LLD, George-

town U., 1973. Bar: D.C. 1973, U.S. Dist. Ct. Md. 1973, U.S. Ct. Appeals (4th cir.) 1974, U.S. Supreme Ct. 1977. Law clk. to U.S. Dist. Ct. judge U.S. Dist. Ct. Md., Balt., 1973-74; trial atty U.S. Dept. Justice, Washington, 1974-75; chief minority counsel patents, trademarks and copyrights subcom. U.S. Senate, Washington, 1975-77; legis. dir. Senator Charles Mathias, Washington, 1977-78; minority counsel judiciary com. U.S. Senate, Washington, 1978-81, chief counsel, staff dir. criminal law subcom., 1981-82, chief counsel patents, copyrights and trademarks subcom., 1982-85; register of copyrights U.S. Copyright Office, Washington, 1985-94; counsel Dechert Price and Rhoads, Washington, 1996—. Adj. prof. copyright law George Washington U.; speaker in field. Contbr. numerous articles to profl. jours. Served to lt. USN, 1965-70, Vietnam. Mem. ABA (chair authors com.), Fed. Bar Assn. (past pres. Capitol Hill chpt.). Episcopalian. Home: 1110 E Capitol St NE Washington DC 20002-6225 Office: Dechert Price and Rhoads 1775 Eye St NW Ste 1100 Washington DC 20006-2424 E-mail: ralph.oman@dechert.com.

OMAN, RICHARD HEER, lawyer; b. Columbus, Ohio, Jan. 4, 1926; s. B. R. Oman and Marguerite H. (Oman) Andrews; m. Jane Ellen Wert, Oct. 5, 1963; children: Sarah M., David W. BA, Ohio State U., 1948, JD, 1951. Bar: Ohio 1951. Atty. Ohio Nat. Bank, Columbus, 1951-55; ptnr. Isaac, Postlewaite, O'Brien & Oman, Columbus, 1955-71; dir. Columbus Found., 1955-77, counsel, 1955—; ptnr. Porter, Wright, Morris and Arthur (and predecessor firm), Columbus, 1972-89; of counsel Vorys, Sater, Seymour and Pease, Columbus, 1990, ptnr., 1991-96, of counsel, 1997—. Mem. Columbus Airport Commn., 1960-64; trustee Reinberger Found., Cleve., 1980—, Columbus Acad., 1981-87, Grant Hosp., 1978-86, Harding Hosp., 1978-86; sr. warden Trinity Episc. Ch., 1985-88; counsel Columbus Jewish Found., 1985—, Wexner Ctr. Found., 1990—, Found. Cath. Diocese, Columbus, 2000—. Fellow Ohio State Bar Found.; mem. ABA, Am. Coll. Trust and Estate Counsel, Ohio State Bar Assn. (past mem. bd. govs. probate and trust law sect.), Columbus Bar Assn., Columbus Club, Rocky Fork Hunt and Country Club, Nantucket (Mass.) Yacht Club, Kit Kat Club. Republican. Episcopalian. Office: Vorys Sater Seymour & Pease PO Box 1008 52 E Gay St Columbus OH 43215-3161 Fax: 614-714-4731. Office Phone: 614-464-6453. E-mail: rhoman@vssp.com.

OMAN, VIRGINIA MILLS, psychotherapist; b. Bronxville, N.Y., Aug. 2, 1952; d. William Morse and Janet (McMaster) O. AA with high honors, Bradford Coll., 1973; BA, Wells Coll., 1975; MA, U. No. Colo., 1990; postgrad., Gallaudet U., 1994-95. Lic. profl. counselor. Mental health counselor U. No. Colo., Greeley, 1989-91; psychotherapist Weld Mental Health, Greeley, 1991-95; dir. mental health svcs. deaf Pikes Peak Mental Health, Colorado Springs, Colo., 1995—; instr. deaf program Pikes Peak C.C., Colorado Springs, 1998—. Cons., counselor deaf prep. program Pikes Peak C.C., Colorado Springs, 1998—; spkr. Colo. Registry Interpresters Deaf, Colorado Springs, 1999—. Vol. counselor Nat. Multiple Sclerosis Soc., Greeley, 1989-91, bd. dirs. 1988-93; vol. City Coun. R. Skorman, Colorado Springs, 1999. Recipient Golden Rose award Nat. Assn. Deaf, 1998. Mem. Am. Deaf Rehab. Assn., Colo. Mental Health Counselors Deaf & Hard Hearing (v.p. 1998—), Pikes Peak Ctr. Deafness (bd. dirs. 1996-97, v.p. 1997—, Oustanding Svc. 1999). Democrat. Episcopalian. Avocations: animal rescue, music. Office: Pikes Peak Mental Health 179 Parkside Dr Colorado Springs CO 80910-3146

O'MARA, HUGH, artist; b. Milton, Mass., Feb. 22, 1958; Student, Northeastern U., Boston, 1977, R.I. Sch. Design, 1978, Art Inst. of Boston, 1980, U. West LA, 1990. Artist, ind. rschr., 1974—; legal asst. Law Offices, LA, 1990—2003; care provider LA, 1995—. E-mail: hugho@earthlink.net.

O'MARA, JAMES WRIGHT, lawyer; b. McComb, Miss., Jan. 7, 1940; s. Junior and Mary Jane (Wright) O'M.; m. Jeanette Walter, June 28, 1963; children: James W. Jr., Angela J. BA, U. Miss., 1962, JD with distinction, 1967. Bar: Miss. 1967. Ptnr. Butler, Snow, O'Mara, Stevens & Cannada, Jackson, Miss., 1967-97, chmn., 1990-97; sr. ptnr. Phelps & Dunbar, Jackson, Miss., 1997—. Vis. prof. Jackson Sch. Law, 1970-72. Editor-in-chief Miss. Law Jour., 1966-67. Pres. Jackson Prep. Sch., 1984-85, Woodland Hills Bapt. Acad., Jackson, 1973-84. Capt. U.S. Army, 1962-64. Fellow Miss. Bar Found.; mem. ABA, Miss. Bar Assn., Am. Bankruptcy Inst., Miss. Bankruptcy Conf. (pres. 1980-81). Baptist. Home: 42 Eastbrooke St # I Jackson MS 39216-4714 Office: Phelps & Dunbar PO Box 23066 Jackson MS 39225-3066 E-mail: omaraj@phelps.com.

O'MARA, JOHN ALOYSIUS, retired bishop; b. Buffalo, Nov. 17, 1924; arrived in Can., 1940; s. John Aloysius and Anna Theresa (Schenck) O'Mara. Student, St. Augustine's Sem., Toronto, Ont., Can., 1944-51; JCL, St. Thomas U., Rome, 1953. Ordained priest Roman Cath. Ch., 1951. Mem. chancery Archdiocese of Toronto, Canada, 1953-69; pres., rector St. Augustine's Sem., Toronto, 1969-75; pastor St. Lawrence Parish, Scarboro, Canada, 1975-76; bishop Diocese of Thunder Bay, 1976-94, Diocese of St. Catharines, 1994—2002; ret., 2002. Pres. Ont. Conf. Cath. Bishops, 1986—92. Mem. Ont. Hosp. Svcs. Commn., 1964—69; bd. dirs. Ont. Hosp. Assn., 1961—65. Named Hon. Prelate of Papal Household with title Monsignor, 1954; Hon. fellow, U. St. Michael's Coll., Toronto, 1997. Mem.: Cath. Health Assn. Ont. (bd. dirs. 1982—86, 1988—92, 1996—), Caht. Ch. Ext. Soc. (bd. dirs. 1992—96). Home: Holy Rosary Rectory 21 Queen St S Thorold ON Canada L2V 3M7 E-mail: h-rosary@computan.on.ca.

O'MARA, THOMAS PATRICK, manufacturing executive; b. St. Catharine's, Ont., Can., Jan. 17, 1937; s. Joseph Thomas and Rosanna Patricia (Riordan) O'M.; m. Nancy Irene Rosevear, Aug. 10, 1968; children: Patricia Catharine, Tracy Irene, Sara Megan. BS, Allegheny Coll., 1958; MS, Carnegie Inst. Tech., 1960. Mktg. analyst U.S. Steel Corp., Pitts., 1960-65; dir. info. systems AMPCO Pitts. (formerly Screw & Bolt Corp.), Pitts., 1965-68; v.p., gen. mgr. Toy div. Samsonite Corp., Denver, 1968-73; regional mgr. Mountain Zone, Hertz Corp., Denver, 1973-75; asst. to chmn. Allen Group, Melville, N.Y., 1975-76; group exec. v.p. fin. and adminstrn. Bell & Howell Co., Chgo., 1976-77, corp. controller, 1977-78, corp. v.p., 1978-85, pres. visual communications, 1978-85; pres., chief operating officer, dir. Bridge Product Inc., Northbrook, Ill., 1985-87; chmn., chief exec. officer Micro Metl Corp., Indpls., 1987-91; chmn. Omara Ptnrs., 1992—; CEO Engineered Materials Corp., 2002—. Bd. dirs. Loyola U. Press; chmn. Plastics Group, Engineered Materials Corp., ABC Windows. Mem. Lake Forest H.S. Bd., 1989-96, pres. 1993-96. With USAR, 1961-66. Mem. Econs. Club Chgo., Newcomen Soc. U.S., Sigma Alpha Epsilon, Knollwood Club. Home: 1350 Inverleith Rd Lake Forest IL 60045-1540

O'MEARA, ANNA M. lawyer; b. Chgo., Aug. 11, 1947; BS cum laude, Loyola U., 1969, JD cum laude, 1984. Bar: Ill. 1984, U.S. Dist. Ct. (no. dist.) Ill. 1984. Ptnr. Mayer, Brown & Platt, Chgo., 1984—. Mem. ABA, Ill. Bar Assn. Office: Mayer Brown & Platt 190 S La Salle St Ste 3100 Chicago IL 60603-3441

O'MEARA, JOHN CORBETT, federal judge; b. Hillsdale, Mich., Nov. 4, 1933; s. John Richard and Karolyn Louise (Corbett) O'M.; m. Penelope Reingier Appel, June 9, 1962 (div. Feb. 1975); children: Meghan Appel, John Richard, Corbett Edge, Patrick Fitzpatrick, Tighe Roberts; m. Julia Donovan Darlow, Sept. 20, 1975; 1 child, Gillian Darlow. AB, U. Notre Dame, 1955; LLB, Harvard U., 1962. Bar: Mich. 1962. Assoc. Dickinson, Wright, Moon, Van Dusen & Freeman, Detroit, 1962-70; mem. faculty U. Detroit, 1965-70; ptnr. Dickinson, Wright, Moon, Van Dusen & Freeman, Detroit, 1970-94, head of labor group, 1985-94; judge U.S. Dist. Ct., Detroit, 1994—. Bd. dirs. Mich. Opera Theatre, Detroit. Contr. articles to profl. jours. Fin. chmn. Dem. Party Mich., 1968-70; chmn. U.S. Cts. Com. State Bar Mich., 1984-94. Lt. USN, 1955-59. Fellow Am. Coll. Trial Lawyers, Am. Bar Found.; mem. ABA, U.S. Supreme Court Bar, Am. Judicature Soc., Mich. State Bar Assn., 6th Cir. Court Appeals Bar (life mem., 6th Cir. Jud. Conf. 1986). Office: US Dist Ct 231 W Lafayette Blvd Detroit MI 48226-2700

O'MEARA, JOHN FRANCIS, lawyer; b. Chgo., Apr. 14, 1936; s. John J. and Mary (Joyce) O'M.; children: Marcia A. Hiehle, John A., Timothy D. BS, Loyola U., 1959; JD, Northwestern U., 1960. Bar: Ill. 1961, U.S. Dist. Ct. (no. dist.) Ill. 1964, U.S. Ct. Appeals (7th cir.) 1992. Assoc., ptnr. Lord, Bissell & Brook, Chgo., 1961-74; atty. pvt. practice, Chgo. and Park Ridge, Ill, 1975—. Instr. John Marshall Sch. Law, Chgo., 1966-71. Author: Tort Liability of Illinois Land Occupiers, 1968. Bd. dirs. St. Mary of Angels, 1987—.; founder, officer Ind. Precinct Orgn., Chgo., 1969-71. With U.S. Army Res., 1960-66. Mem. Holy Name Soc. Roman Catholic. Office: 1737 N Wolcott Ave Chicago IL 60622-1350

O'MEARA, MARK, professional golfer; b. Goldsboro, N.C., Jan. 13, 1957; m. Alicia; children: Michelle, Shaun. BS in Mktg., Long Beach State U., 1980. Profl. golfer PGA, 1980—. Mem. nat. team Ryder Cup, 1985, 89, 91, 97, Nissan Cup 1985, Dunhill Corp. 1985, 86, 87, 96, 97, Pres. Cup 1996. Named All-Am., Long Beach State U., Rookie of Yr., 1981; mem. Ryder Cup team, 1985, 89, 91; won U.S. Amateur, 1979, Greater Milw. Open, 1984, Bing Crosby Pro-Am., 1985, Hawaiian Open, 1985, Fuji Sankei Classic, 1985, Australian Masters, 1986, Lawrence Batley Internat., 1987, AT&T Pebble Beach Nat. Pro-Am., 1989, 90, 92, H-E-B Tex. Open, 1990, Walt Disney World/Oldsmobile Classic, 1991, Tokia Classic, 1992, Argentine Open, 1994, Honda Classic, 1995, Bell Can. Open, 1995, Mercedes Championships, 1996, Greater Greensboro Open, 1996; tied (with Corey Pavin) Bob Hope Chrysler Classic, 1990; AT&T Pebble Beach National Pro-Am, 1997; Buick Invitational, 1997; Masters Tournament, 1998; British Open Championship, 1998. Office: c/o PGA Box 109601 Ave of Champions Palm Beach Gardens FL 33410

O'MEARA, NOEL P. priest, religious organization administrator; b. Gort, Galway, Ireland, Dec. 22, 1937; arrived in U.S., 1983; s. Thomas Joseph O'Meara and Moyna Theresa Pathe. BA, Nat. U. Ireland, Dublin, 1960, Higher Diploma, 1966; MEd, Trinity Coll., Dublin, 1973; PhD, Fordham U., 1987. Sr. dean Templeogue H.S., Dublin, 1966—73; provincial adminstr. Irish Province, Holy Spirit Order, Dublin, 1973—77; missionary priest Congrçäo do Espirito Santo, São Paulo, Brazil, 1977—83; fund raiser Brazil missions Brazil Spiritan Missions, N.Y.C., 1983—88; dir. Mission Agy. Svcs., N.Y.C., 1985; coord. Belem sector Archdiocese São Paulo, 1988—90; gen. sec. Congregation of Holy Spirit, Rome, 1990—93, provincial bursar Irish Province, Holy Spirit Order, 1994—2000, gen. bursar-adjoint, 2001—. Contbr. articles to profl. jours. Parish priest Cath. Ch., São Paulo, 1978—90; pres. Spiritan Found., Washington, 2001—; gen. bursar adjoint Congregation of Holy Spirit, 2001—; bd. dirs. Des Places Ednl. Trust, Dublin, 1997—2000; chmn. bd. dirs. Aidlink Ngo, Dublin, 1996—2000. Mem.: Fraternity of Sant. Egidio. Roman Catholic. Avocations: music, travel to underdeveloped countries, golf. Office: Spiritan Found 11411 Amherst Ave Silver Spring MD 20902

O'MEARA, ONORATO TIMOTHY, academic administrator, mathematician; b. Cape Town, Republic of South Africa, Jan. 29, 1928; arrived in U.S., 1957; s. Daniel and Fiorina (Allorto) O'M.; m. Jean T. Fadden, Sept. 12, 1953; children: Maria, Timothy, Jean, Kathleen, Eileen. B.Sc., U. Cape Town, 1947, M.Sc., 1948; PhD, Princeton U., 1953; LLD (hon.), U. Notre Dame, 1987. Asst. lectr. U. Natal, Republic South Africa, 1949; lectr. U. Otago, New Zealand, 1954-56; mem. Inst. for Advanced Study, Princeton, N.J., 1957-58, 62; asst. prof. Princeton U., 1958-62; prof. math. U. Notre Dame, Ind., 1962-76, chmn. dept., 1965-66, 68-72, Kenna prof. math., 1976-98, provost, 1978-96, provost emeritus, 1996—, Kenna prof. emeritus, 1998—. Vis. prof. Calif. Inst. Tech., 1968; Gauss prof. Göttingen Acad. Sci., 1978; mem. adv. panel math. scis. NSF, 1974-77, cons., 1960—. Author: Introduction to Quadratic Forms, 1963, 71, 73, 2000, Lectures on Linear Groups, 1974, 2d edit., 1977, 3d edit., 1988, Russian translation, 1976, Symplectic Groups, 1978, 82, Russian translation, 1979, The Classical Groups and K-Theory (with A.J. Hahn), 1989; contbr. articles on arithmetic theory of quadratic forms and isomorphism theory of linear groups to Am. and European profl. jours. Mem. Cath. Commn. Intellectual and Cultural Affairs, 1962—, Commn. on Cath. Scholarship, 1997-99; life trustee U. of Notre Dame, 1996—. Recipient Marianist award U. Dayton, 1988; Alfred P. Sloan fellow, 1960-63. Mem. Am. Math. Soc., Am. Acad. Arts and Sci., Collegium (bd. dirs. 1992-96). Roman Catholic. Home: 1227 E Irvington Ave South Bend IN 46614-1417 Office: U Notre Dame Office of Provost Emeritus 255B Hurkey Hall Notre Dame IN 46556

O'MEARA, THOMAS FRANKLIN, priest, educator; b. Des Moines, May 15, 1935; s. Joseph Matthew and Frances Claire (Rock) O'M. MA, Aquinas Inst, Dubuque, Iowa, 1963; PhD, U. Munich, Germany, 1967. Ordained priest Roman Cath. Ch., 1962. Assoc. prof. Aquinas Inst. of Theology, Dubuque, Iowa, 1967-79; prof. U. Notre Dame, South Bend, Ind., 1981-84, William K. Warren prof. of theology, 1985—. Author 14 books, including: Romantic Idealism and Roman Catholicism, 1983, Theology of Ministry, 1985, revised edit., 1999, Church and Culture, 1991, Thomas Aquinas: Theologian, 1997, Erich Przywara, S.J., His Theology and His World, 2002, A Theologian's Journey, 2002. Mem. Catholic Theol. Soc. Am. (pres. 1980). Roman Catholic. Office: St Thomas Aquinas Priory 7200 Division St River Forest IL 60305 E-mail: tomeara@nd.edu.

O'MEARA, VICKI A. lawyer; b. Mpls., May 13, 1957; d. James Michael and Joan Kathleen (Shepers) O'M.; children: Joseph O'Meara Masterman, Nicolas James Reisinger O'Meara. BA in Polit. Sci., Cornell U., 1979; JD, Northwestern U., Chgo., 1982; MA in Environment & Natural Resource, George Washington U., Washington, 1987. Bar: Minn. 1982, D.C. 1983, Ill. 1989. Asst. to Army gen. counsel U.S. Army-Pentagon, Washington, 1982-86; spl. asst. to White House Counsel The White House Fellows Program, Washington, 1986-87; dep. exec. sec., domestic policy counsel, cabinet affairs The White House, Washington, 1987; dep. gen. counsel litigation and regional ops. U.S. EPA, Washington, 1987; ptnr. Jones, Day, Reavis & Pogue, Chgo., 1988-92, 93—; asst. atty. gen. U.S. Dept. Justice, 1992; exec. vice-pres., gen. counsel Ryder Systems Inc., Miami, FL. Hon. mem. faculty U.S. Army Logistics Mgmt. Sch., Ft. Lee, Va., 1982-85; adj. prof. The Union Inst., Cin., 1989-92. Author rev. Nat. Wetlands Newsletter, 1990; contbr. articles to profl. jours. Bd. dirs. Northwestern U. Alumni Assn., Chgo., 1988-90; mem. com. Chgo. Coun. Fgn. Rels. Mem. Chgo. Econ. Club Chgo. (com. fgn. affairs). Office: Ryder System Inc 3600 NW 82nd Ave Miami FL 33166-6623

O'MEILIA, DAVID E. lawyer; b. July 1951; Grad. Okla. State U.; grad. in Law, Tulsa Coll. Atty. Tulsa County Dist. Atty.'s Office, 1980—84; asst. U.S. atty. U.S. Atty.'s Office, Tulsa, Okla., 1986—96; atty. Nichols, Wolfe, Stamper, Nally, Fallis & Robertson, 1996—99; ptnr. Lyons, Clark, Danielson & O'Meilia, Tulsa, Okla., 1999—2002; U.S. atty. No. Dist. Okla., 2002—. Office: 333 W Fourth St Ste 3460 Tulsa OK 74103

O'MELIA, CHARLES RICHARD, environmental engineer, educator; b. N.Y.C., Nov. 1, 1934; s. Charles James and Anne Frances (Dobbin) O'Melia; m. Mary Elizabeth Curley, Oct. 27, 1956; children: Kathleen Marie, Mary Margaret, Charles James, Anne Marie, John Thomas, Michael Joseph. BSCE, Manhattan Coll., 1955; M in San. Engring., U. Mich., 1956, PhD in San. Engring., 1963. Registered profl. engr., Ga. Asst. engr. Hazen & Sawyer Engrs., NYC, 1956—57; tchg. fellow, rsch. asst. U. Mich., 1957—61; asst. prof. san. engring. Ga. Inst. Tech., Atlanta, 1961—64; postdoctoral fellow Harvard U., Cambridge, Mass., 1964—65, lectr. in water chemistry, 1965—66; assoc. prof. environ. scis. and engring. U. NC, Chapel Hill, 1966—70, prof., 1970—80, dep. chmn. dept. environ. sciences and engring, 1977—80; prof. dept. of geography and environ. engring., aquatic chemistry Johns Hopkins U., Balt., 1980—, chmn. dept. geography and environ. engring., 1990—95, Charles Richard O'Melia prof. Vis. scientist Swiss Fed. Tech., 1971; vis. scholar Woods Hole Oceanographic Inst., 1975; vis. prof. environ. engring. sci. Calif. Inst. Tech., Pasadena, 1973—74; guest prof. Eidgenössische Anstalt fur Wasserversorgung Abwasserreinigung und Gewässerschutz, Zurich, Switzerland, 1988—89, Zurich, 1996; Abel Wolman Chair in environ. engring. John Hopkins, 1998; mem. engring. and urban health scis. study sec. EPA, 1970—72, com. on rsch. needs in water supply, pollution control processes peer rev. panel, 1980—, sci. adv. bd. drinking water com., 1981—89; mem. program com. Water Pollution Control Fedn., 1980—86, chmn. rsch. symposium subcom., 1980—85; chmn. waste disposal com. Marine Scis. Coun. N.C., 1970—72; dep. chmn. Gordon Rsch. Confs., Environ. Scis.: Water, 1976, chmn., 84; mem. com. on non-phosphorus detergent builders Internat. Joint Commn., 1976—83; cons. Monsanto Chem. Co.; water sci. and tech. bd. Nat. Rsch. Coun., chair, Com. on Watershed Mgmt.; cons. Union Carbide Corp., Office Gov. Puerto Rico, EPA, others. Contbr. numerous articles to profl. jours., chapters to books. Recipient Best Lectr. award, Environ. Engring. Students, U. N.C., 1969—70, 1971, Pergammon Press Publs. award, Internat. Assn. on Water Pollution Rsch. and Control, 1988. Mem.: AAAS, ASCE (Simon W. Freese lectr. 1985, Rsch. award 1969), NAE (co-chmn. safe drinking water com., subcom. on particulate contaminants 1976, com. on water treatment chems. 1983—85, wastewater mgmt. in coastal zones com. 1989—), Assn. Environ. Engring. Profs. (bd. dirs. 1977—80, 1988—, v.p. 1978—79, pres. 1979—80, Disting. Faculty award 1972, Engring. Sci. award 1975, CH2M-Hill award 1988, 1996, Outstanding Publ. award 1984, 1991), Water Environment Fedn. (Gordon Maskew Fair medal 1993), Am. Water Works Assn. (Publs. award 1965, 1985, Best Paper award rsch. divsn. 1989, A.P. Black award 1990), Am. Soc. Limnology and Oceanography, Am. Chem. Soc. (assoc. editor Environ. Sci. and Tech. 1975—83, chmn. water program environ. chemistry divsn. 1970—72), Am. Acad. Environ. Engrs. (cert.), Tau Beta Pi, Chi Epsilon, Sigma Xi. Roman Catholic. Office: Johns Hopkins U 306 Ames Hall 3400 N Charles St Baltimore MD 21218-2686 Office Phone: 410-516-7102. Business E-Mail: omelia@jhuvms.hcf.jhu.edu.*

OMENN, GILBERT STANLEY, academic administrator, internist; b. Chester, Pa., Aug. 30, 1941; s. Leonard and Leah (Miller) O.; m. Martha Darling; children: Rachel Andrea, Jason Montgomery, David Matthew. AB, Princeton U., 1961; MD, Harvard U., 1965; PhD in Genetics, U. Wash., 1972. Intern Mass. Gen. Hosp., Boston, 1965-66, asst. resident in medicine, 1966-67; rsch. assoc. NIH, Bethesda, Md., 1967-69; fellow U. Wash., 1969-71, from asst. prof. medicine to assoc. prof., 1971-79, investigator Howard Hughes Med. Inst., 1976 77, prof. medicine, 1979 97, prof. environ. health, 1981—, chmn. dept., 1981-83; dean U. Wash. Sch. Pub. Health and Cmty. Medicine, 1982-97; CEO health sys. U. Mich. Health Sys., Ann Arbor, 1997—2002; exec. v.p. med. affairs U. Mich., 1997—2002, prof. internal medicine, human genetics and pub. health, 1997—. Bd. dirs. Amgen, Rohm & Haas Co., CNAC, Population Svcs. Internat.; sci. adv. bd. 3M, Motorola, Divergence, Pac N.W. Nat. Lab.; White House fellow/spl. asst. to chmn. AEC, 1973-74; assoc. dir. Office Sci. and Tech. Policy, The White House, 1977-80; assoc. dir. human resources Office Mgmt. and Budget, 1980-81; vis. sr. fellow Wilson Sch. Pub. and Internat. Affairs, Princeton U., 1981; sci. and pub. policy fellow Brookings Instn., Washington, 1981-82; cons. govt. agys., Lifetime Cable Network; mem. Nat. Commn. on the Environment, Rene Dubos Ctr. for Human Environments, AFL-CIO Workplace Health Fund., Electric Power Rsch. Inst., Carnegie Commn. Task Force on Sci. and Tech. in Jud. and Regulatory Decision Making, adv. com. to dir., Ctrs. Disease Control, 1992-95, adv. com. Critical Technologies Inst., RAND; mem. Pres.'s Coun., U. Calif., 1992-97; chair, Pres. Congrl. Commn. on Risk Assessment and Risk Mgmt.; mem. Nat. Enterprise for the Environment. Co-author: Clearing the Air, Reforming the Clean Air Act, 1981. Editor: (with others) Genetics, Environment and Behavior: Implications for Educational Policy, 1972; Genetic Control of Environmental Pollutants, 1984; Genetic Variability in Responses to Chemical Exposure, 1984, Environmental Biotechnology: Reducing Risks from Environmental Chemicals through Biotechnology, 1988, Biotechnology in Biodegradation, 1990, Biotechnology and Human Genetic Predisposition to Disease, 1990, Annual Review of Public Health, 1991-97, Clinics in Geriatric Medicine, 1992; mem. editl. bd. Jour. Protesme Research, Environ. Health Perspective; contbr. articles on cancer prevention, human biochem. genetics, prenatal diagnosis of inherited disorders, susceptibility to environ. agts., clin. medicine and health policy to profl. publs. Mem. Pres.'s Coun. on Spinal Cord Injury; mem. Nat. Cancer Adv. Bd., Nat. Heart, Lung and Blood Adv. Coun., Wash. State Gov.'s Commn. on Social and Health Svcs., Ctr. for Excellence in Govt.; chmn. awards panel Gen. Motors Cancer Rsch. Found., 1985-86; chmn. bd. Environ. Studies and Toxicology, Nat. Rsch. Coun., 1988-91; mem. Bd. Health Promotion and Disease Prevention, Inst. Medicine; mem. adv. com. Woodrow Wilson Sch., Princeton U., 1978-84; trustee Pacific Sci. Ctr., Fred Hutchinson Cancer Rsch. Ctr., Seattle Symphony Orch., Seattle Youth Symphony Orch., Seattle Chamber Music Festival, Santa Fe Chamber Music Festival, Univ. Mus. Soc., Ann Arbor, United Way Washtenaw County, Mich.; chmn. rules com. Dem. Conv., King County, Wash., 1972. Served with USPHS, 1967-69. Recipient Research Career Devel. award USPHS, 1972; White House fellow, 1973-74 Fellow ACP, AAAS (pres.-elect), Nat. Acad. Social Ins., Western Assn. Physicians, Hastings Ctr., Collegium Ramazzini; mem. Inst. Medicine of NAS, White House Fellows Assn., Am. Soc. Human Genetics, Western Soc. Clin. Rsch., Assn. Am. Physicians, Am. Acad. Arts and Scis. Jewish. Home: 3340 E Dobson Ann Arbor MI 48105-2583 Office: Univ Mich Med Sch A510 Med Sci Res Bldg 1 1150 W Medical Center Dr Ann Arbor MI 48109-0656 E-mail: gomenn@umich.edu.

OMER, GEORGE ELBERT, JR., orthopaedic surgeon, educator; b. Kansas City, Kans., Dec. 23, 1922; s. George Elbert and Edith May (Hines) O.; m. Wendie Vilven, Nov. 6, 1949; children: George Eric, Michael Lee. BA, Ft. Hays Kans. State U., 1944; MD, Kans. U., 1950; MSc in Orthopaedic Surgery, Baylor U., 1955. Diplomate Am. Bd. Orthopaedic Surgery, 1959, (bd. dirs. 1983-92, pres. 1987-88), re-cert. orthopaedics and hand surgery, 1983, cert. surgery of the hand, 1989. 2nd lt. U.S. Army, 1945; advanced through grades to col., 1967; ret. U.S. Army, 1970; rotating intern Bethany Hosp., Kansas City, 1950-51; resident in orthopaedic surgery Brooke Gen. Hosp., San Antonio, 1952-55, William Beaumont Gen. Hosp., El Paso, Tex., 1955-56; chief surgery Irwin Army Hosp., Ft. Riley, Kans., 1957-59; cons. in orthopaedic surgery 8th Army, chief orthop. surgery 121st Evacuation Hosp. Republic of Korea, 1959-60; asst. chief orthopaedic surgery, chief hand surgeon Fitzsimons Army Med. Center, Denver, 1960-63; dir. orthopaedic residency tng. Armed Forces Inst. Pathology and Walter Reed Army Med. Ctr., Washington, 1963-65; chief orthopaedic surgery and chief Army Hand Surg. Center, Brooke Army Med. Center, 1965-70; cons. in orthopaedic and hand surgery Surgeon Gen. Army, 1967-70; prof. orthopaedics, surgery, and anatomy, chmn. dept. orthopaedic surgery, chief div. hand surgery U. N.Mex., 1970-90, med. dir. phys. therapy, 1972-90, acting asst. dean grad. edn. Sch. Medicine, 1980-81. Mem. active staff U. N.Mex. Hosp., Albuquerque, 1970—, chief of med. staff, 1984-86; cons. staff other Albuquerque hosps.; cons. orthopaedic surgery USPHS, 1966-85, U.S. Army, 1970-92, USAF, 1970-78, VA, 1970-2000; cons. Carrie Tingley Hosp. for Crippled Children, 1970-99, interim med. dir., 1970-72, 86-87, mem. bd. advisor 1972-76, chair, 1994-96. Mem. bd. editors Clin. Orthopaedics, 1973-90, Jour. AMA, 1973-74, Jour. Hand Surgery, 1976-81; trustee Jour. Bone and Joint Surgery, 1993-99, sec., 1993-96, chmn., 1997-99; contbr. more than 300 articles to profl. jours., numerous chpts. to books. Decorated Legion of Merit, Army Commendation medal with oak leaf cluster; recipient Alumni Achievement award Ft. Hays State U., 1973, Recognition plaque Am. Soc. Surgery Hand, 1989, Recognition plaque N.Mex. Orthopaedic Assn., 1991, Recognition award for hand surgery Am. Osteo. Acad. Orthopaedics, 1982, Pioneer award Internat. Socs. for Surgery Hand, 1995, Rodey award U. N.Mex. Alumni Assn., 1997, Cornerstone award U. N.Mex. Health Scis. Ctr., 1997; recognized with Endowed Professorship U. N.Mex. Sch. Medicine, 1995; recognized with named Annual Orthop. Seminar and Alumni Day Brooke Army Med. Ctr., 1999. Fellow ACS, Am. Orthopaedic Assn. (pres. 1988-89, exec. dir. 1989-93), Am. Acad. Orthopaedic Surgeons, Assn. Orthopaedic Chmn., N.Mex. Orthopaedic Assn. (pres. 1979-81, 1999-2000), La. Orthopaedic Assn. (hon.), Korean Orthopaedic Assn. (hon.), Peru Orthopaedic Soc. (hon.), Caribbean Hand Soc., Am. Soc. Surgery Hand (pres. 1978-79), Am. Assn. Surgery of Trauma, Assn. Bone and Joint Surgeons, Assn. Mil. Surgeons U.S., Riordan Hand Soc. (pres. 1967-68), Sunderland Soc. (pres. 1981-83), Soc. Mil. Orthopaedic Surgeons, Brazilian Hand Soc. (hon.), S.Am. Hand Soc. (hon.), Groupe D'Etude de la Main, Brit. Hand Soc. (hon.), Venezuela Hand Soc. (hon.), South African Hand Soc. (hon.), Western Orthopaedic Assn. (pres. 1981-82), AAAS, Russell A. Hibbs Soc. (pres. 1977-78), 38th Parallel Med. Soc. (Korea) (sec. 1959-60); mem. AMA, Phi Kappa Phi, Phi Sigma, Alpha

Omega Alpha, Phi Beta Pi. Achievements include pioneer work in hand surgery. Home: 316 Big Horn Ridge Rd NE Sandia Heights Albuquerque NM 87122 Office: U N Mex Dept Orthopaedic Surgery 2211 Lomas Blvd NE Albuquerque NM 87106-2745

OMER, ROBERT WENDELL, hospital administrator; b. Salt Lake City, Feb. 10, 1948; s. Wayne Albert and Melva Bernice (Thunell) O.; m. Deborah Jackson, May 4, 1972;children: Melinda, Carmen, Creighton, Preston, Allison. BS in Biology, U. Utah, 1972; MHA, Washington U., St. Louis, 1975. V.p. St. Luke's Hosp., Cedar Rapids, Iowa, 1974-80; asst. adminstr. Franciscan Med. Ctr., Rock Island, Ill., 1980-82, Latter Day Saints Hosp., Salt Lake City, 1982-85, Clarkson Hosp., Omaha, 1985-93, v.p., COO, 1993-97; CEO Creighton St. Joseph's Clinics, Omaha, 1998-99; pres., CEO MCH Health Sys., Blair, Nebr., 1999—2001; CEO Cooper County Hosp., Boonville, Mo., 2002—03; rural health advisor U. Mo. Health Care, 2003—; CEO Pioneers Hosp., Meeker, Colo., 2003—. Bd. dirs. ARC, Heartland chpt. Omaha; bd. dirs. Nebr. Scanning Svcs. Lt. col. USAR, 1972. Fellow Am. Coll. Healthcare Execs. (regent); mem. Nebr. Hosp. Assn., Omaha C. of C. (Leadership Omaha award 1978), Omaha Healthcare Execs. Group (pres. 1989-90), Rotary (bd. dirs. 1990). Republican. Mem. Lds Ch. Avocations: jogging, history, bicycling, backpacking, racquetball. Home: PO Box 333 Meeker CO 81641

OMHOLT, BRUCE DONALD, product designer, mechanical engineer, consultant; b. Salem, Oreg., Mar. 27, 1943; s. Donald Carl and Violet Mae (Buck) O.; m. Mavis Aronow, Aug. 18, 1963 (div. July 1972); children: Madison, Natalie; m. Darla Kay Faber, Oct. 27, 1972; 1 child, Cassidy. BSME, Heald Coll. Engring., San Francisco, 1964. Real estate salesman R. Lea Ward and Assocs., San Francisco, 1962—64; sales engr. Repco Engring., Montebello, Calif., 1964; various mfg., engring. and mgmt. positions Ford Motor Co., Rawsonville, Saline, Owosso and Ypsilanti, Mich., 1964—75; chief engr. E.F. Hauserman Co., Cleve., 1975—77; dir. design and engring. Am. Seating Co., Grand Rapids, Mich., 1977—80; pres. Trinity Engring., Grand Rapids, Mich., 1980—81, Rohnert Park, Calif., 1981—. Cons. in mfg., carrier rack apparatus, motorcycle improvements. Achievements include patents for Patentee in vertical mitre machine, merchandise display unit; underwater breathing apparatus.

OMIDYAR, PIERRE M. Internet company executive; b. Paris, 1967; arrived in U.S., 1973; m. Pam Kerr; 2 children. BS in Computer Sci., Tufts U., 1988. With developer rels. Gen. Magic, Inc.; co-founder Ink Devel. Corp.; founder, chmn. eBay, 1995—. Trustee Tufts U., Santa Fe Inst. Co-founder Omidyar Found., 1998—; co-founder, CEO Omidyar Network. Recipient Light on the Hill award (with Pam Omidyar), Tufts U. Office: eBay Inc 2125 Hamilton Ave San Jose CA 95125-5905

OMINSKY, ALAN JAY, lawyer, medical educator; b. Phila., Apr. 7, 1938; s. Benjamin B. and Ida S. (Snydman) O.; m. Marlene Lachman, Nov. 1, 1992; 1 child, Sara. BA, U. Pa., Phila., 1958, MD, 1962, JD, 1988. Bar: Pa. 1989, U.S. Supreme Ct. 1994; cert. Am. Bd. Anesthesiology, Am. Bd. Psychiatry. Assoc. prof. anesthesiology U. Pa., Phila., 1972-88, assoc. prof. psychiatry, 1975-88; assoc. Bernstein Silver & Agins, Phila., 1089-96. Mem. ABA, Pa. Bar Assn., Phila. Bar Assn. (chiar medicolegal com. 1993-95, mem. sr. lawyers, state civil, and computer users coms.), Assn. Trial Lawyers Am., Pa. Trial Lawyers Assn., Phil. Trial Lawyers Assn., Am. Soc. Anesthesiologists, Am. Psychiat. Soc., Lawyers Club Phila., Phi Beta Kappa. Home: 233 S 6th St Apt 701 Philadelphia PA 19106-3751

OMINSKY, HARRIS, lawyer; b. Phila., Sept. 14, 1932; s. Joseph and Lillian (Herman) O.; m. Rosalyn Rita Rutenberg; children— Michelle, David BS in Econs., U. Pa., 1953, LLB cum laude, 1956. Bar: Pa. 1956. Ptnr. Ominsky & Ominsky, Phila., 1958-64; ptnr. Blank, Rome, Comisky & McCauley, Phila., 1964—, Balnk Rome LLP, 1964—; mem. mgmt. com. Blank, Rome, Comisky & McCauley, Phila., 1981-84, 88-92, co-chmn. real estate dept., 1988-93. Lectr. Law Sch., Temple U., Phila., 1969-71, lectr. Real Estate Inst., 1996—. Author: Real Estate Practice: New Perspectives, 1996, Real Estate Practice: Breaking New Ground, 2001, If I'm Still Around, I Can't Be Dead, 2002; weekly columnist Ominsky's Terrain, Phila. Legal Intelligencer, 1999—; contbr. numerous articles to profl. jours. Pres. bd. Phila. Singing City Choir, 1984-88; chmn. zoning com. Merion Civic Assn., Pa., 1984-91. Fellow Am. Bar Found.; mem. ABA (Harrison Tweed spl. merit award 1988), Pa. Bar Assn. (ho. of dels. 1984—), Pa. Bar Inst. (bd. dirs. 1981—, exec. com. 1986-93, v.p. 1988-89, pres. 1989-90, lectr., planner 1969—), Phila. Bar Assn. (chmn. real estate taxes subcom. 1984-85, real property sect. 1991-92, Leon J. Obermayer Edn. award 1989, Good Deed award real property sect. 1999), Am. Coll. Real Estate Lawyers (bd. govs. 1993-95), Order of Coif. Home: 526 Baird Rd Merion Station PA 19066-1302 Office: Blank Rome LLP One Logan Sq Philadelphia PA 19103-6998 Office Phone: 215-569-5668. E-mail: ominsky@blankrome.com.

OMMAYA, AYUB KHAN, neurosurgeon, educator; b. Pakistan, Apr. 14, 1930; came to U.S., 1961, naturalized, 1968; s. Sultan Nadir and Ida (Counil) Khan; m. Ghalazala Nangiana, 1984; children: David, Alexander, Shana, Aisha, Iman, Sinan. MD, U. Punjab, Pakistan, 1953; MA, Oxford U., Eng., 1956; DSc (hon.), Tulane U. Diplomate Am. Bd. Neurological Surgery. Intern Mayo Hosp., Lahore, Pakistan, 1953-54; resident in neurosurgery Radcliffe Infirmary, Oxford, Eng., 1954-61; vis. scientist NIH, Bethesda, Md., 1961-63, assoc. neurosurgeon, 1963-68, head sect. applied rsch., 1968-74, chief neurosurgery, 1974-79; clin. prof. George Washington U. Med. Sch., 1970—. Cons. VA, Armed Forces Radiobiology Rsch. Inst.; chmn. Inter-Agy. Com. for Protection Human Rsch. Subjects of Fed. Coordinating Coun. for Sci., Engring. and Tech., NAS; chmn. biomechanics adv. com. com. Nat. Hwy. Traffic Safety Adminstrn.; mem. adv. com. Nat. Ctr. Injury Control & Prevention, Atlanta; inaugural Lewin Meml. lectr. U. Cambridge, Eng., 1983; mem. adv. coun. CDC; Snively lectr. Am. Assn. Auto. Medicine, 1988; Ibn-Sina lectr. Islamic Med. Assn. N.Am.; clin. prof. Georgetown U. Med. Ctr. Contbr. articles to profl. jours.; inventor, patentee spinal fluid flow driven artificial organs for diabetes and degenerative diseases of the nervous system. Pres. Ctr. Integrative Neurosci., Bethesda; v.p., dir. rsch. Cyborgan, Inc., Bethesda. Recipient J. W. Kirkdaldy prize Oxford U., 1956, Lifetime Achievement award Internat. Coll. Surgeons, 1996; recipient Sitara-i-Imtiaz for Achievements in Neurosurgery Govt. Pakistan, 1981; Hunterian prof. Royal Coll. Surgeons, 1968; Rhodes scholar, 1954-60 Fellow ACS, Third World Acad. Scis. (assoc., med. scis. com.), Royal Coll. Surgeons Eng.; mem. ASME (exec. affiliate), Soc. for Neurosci., Am. Assn. Neurol. Surgeons, Rsch. Soc. Neurosurgeons, Brit. Soc. Neurol. Surgeons, Am. Assn. Pakistani Physicians (pres.), Internat. Brain Rsch. Orgn. (life), Pan-Am. Med. Assn. Home: 8901 Burning Tree Rd Bethesda MD 20817-3007 Office: 8006 Glenbrook Rd Bethesda MD 20814-2608

OMOHUNDRO, WILLIAM ADDISON, research marketing executive; b. Richmond, Va. s. Floyd Alvin and Mary Elizabeth (Gilliam) O.; m. Delight V. Dixon; children: William A., Jeffrey F., Robert L. BA, U. Va.; M Indsl. Engring., Ga. Tech. U.; MS, Columbia U. Mgr. new product devel. Gen. Electric, Bridgeport, Conn., mgr. new product engring.; mgr. product strategy Sperry Rand, Bridgeport, Conn.; dir. mktg. research Carrier Corp., Syracuse, N.Y., 1979—. Bd. dirs. Megafax, Inc., Syracuse. Patentee home hair dryer, negative ion generator, others. Pres. Stony Point Assn., Westport, Conn., 1978. Mem.: Am. Mktg. Assn. Republican. Home: 21 Camping Ridge Ct Stoney Creek Wintergreen VA 22958

OMOLE, GABRIEL GBOLABO, international venture capitalist; b. Akungba-Akoko, Nigeria, Mar. 15, 1940; came to U.S., 1975; s. Amos Akindele and Victoria Ola (Olutu) O.; children: Juliana Olufunke, Esther Oluremi, Christiana Oluseun, George Abayomi. PhD, D MSc. Chmn. Gay Omole & Co., Ltd., Lagos, Nigeria, 1968—, Akoko Indsl. Devel. Ltd., 1973—, Akoko Mktg. & Investment Ltd., 1973—, Johngay Enterprises, Ltd., Accra, Ghana, 1977—, Gayom Travel & Tours, Ltd., 1977—, Unifood Industries Nigeria Ltd., 1979—, Unity Village Complex, 1979—, 1st Akoko Internat. Corp., N.Y.C., 1978—, UCM Services Corp., N.Y.C., 1979—, The Akoko Group, Ltd., London, 1983—, Gay Omole Internat. Ltd., London, 1983—, Gay Omole Investment Ltd., Brunei Internat. Investors (West Africa) Ltd.; pres., CEO Mastercard Internat. Svcs. Ltd., 1996—; mng. dir. Galleria Tourist Devel. Property Co. Ltd., Lagos, 1993—, Galleria Transp. Systems Ltd., Lagos, 1993, Combined Billionaires Network Svcs. Ltd., 1996—, Direct Resources Internat. Ltd., 1996—, Galleria City Devel. Ltd., 1996—. Co-founder Brunei Resources (West Africa) Ltd., 1990—; pres., co-founder African Continental Corp., Miami, Fla.; dir.-gen. IBB World Leaders Gallery, Gay Omole Petroleum. Chmn. bd. dirs. Akoko Specialist Hosp., N.Y.C.; trustee, chmn., Gay Omole Found., Lagos, 1979—; founder Unity Ch. Mission, 1976, chmn. devel. fund, 1979—. Mem. Am. Mgmt. Assn., Akungba Devel. Union, Am. Mgmt. Internat., Assn. Venture Founders, Akure C. of C., N.Y.C. C. of C., Nigerian-Am. C. of C., Nigerian-ASEAN C. of C., Nigerian-South Africa C. of C., N.Y. Acad. Scis., Nat. Geo. Soc., London Inst. Dirs., U.S. C. of C. Home: PO Box 74147 Victoria Island Lagos Nigeria also: PO Box 4447 Garki Abuja Nigeria

OMOLEWU, GABRIEL ADEBAYO, business educator, researcher; b. Okeho, Oyo, Nigeria, Aug. 15, 1937; s. Samuel Aiyedogbon and Sarah Funmike Omolewu; m. Elizabeth Adejumoke Omolewu, Dec. 15, 1972; children: Daniel, Margaret, Sarah, Rachel, Deborah, Jacob, Samuel. BS Acctg., Wilberforce U., Wilberforce, OH, 1977; MBA, Wright State U, Dayton, Ohio, 1980; MS, Wright State U, 1981; D of Bus. Adminstrn., Internatl. Grad. Sch. U., 1981; PhD, The U of Akron, 2000. Instr. Wilberforce (Ohio) U, Wilberforce, Ohio, 1980—85, asst. prof. mgt., 1985—89, assoc. prof. of mgmt., 1989—2000, chair bus. and econ., 2000—02, assoc. prof. of mgmt., 2002—. Author: State and Local Govt. Employment in Dayton SMSA., Study of Relationship Between Print Promotion and Hiring of Minorities in Public Service Organizations, Presidency of Bishop Stokes Wilberforce U. Recipient Recognition for Tchg. Bus. Ethics, Gov. of Ohio, 1986, Nissan Fellowship award, Nissan Motors, 1991. Bapt. Avocations: real estate, Sunday school teacher, choir member, church deacon, reading. Office: Walker Ctr 223 Wilberforce U 1055 N Bickett Rd PO Box 1001 Wilberforce OH 45384-1001

O'MORCHOE, CHARLES CHRISTOPHER CREAGH, anatomical sciences educator, science administrator; b. Quetta, India, May 7, 1931; came to U.S., 1968; s. Nial Francis C. and Jessie Elizabeth (Joly) O'M.; m. Patricia Jean Richardson, Sept. 15, 1955; children: Charles Eric Creagh, David James Creagh. BA, Trinity Coll., Dublin (Ireland) U., 1953, MB, BCh, BAO, 1955, MA, 1959, MD, 1961, PhD, 1969, DSc, 1981. Resident Halifax Gen. Hosp., U.K., 1955-57; lectr. in anatomy Sch. Medicine Trinity Coll., Dublin (Ireland) U., 1957-61, 63-65, lectr. in physiology, 1966-67, assoc. prof. in physiology, 1967-68; instr. in anatomy Harvard Med. Sch., Boston, 1962-63; vis. prof. physiology U. Md. Sch. Medicine, Balt., 1961-62, assoc. prof. anatomy, 1968-71, prof. anatomy, 1971-74; chmn. anatomy bd. State of Md., 1971-73; prof., chmn. dept. anatomy Stritch Sch. Medicine Loyola U., Maywood, Ill., 1974-84; dean Coll. Medicine, U. Ill., Urbana-Champaign, 1984-98, prof. anat. scis. and surgery, 1984-98, emeritus dean and prof., 1998—. WHO cons., vis. prof. physiology Jaipur, India, 1967, S.M.S. Med. Coll., U. Rajasthan, vis. prof. anatomy, 1971; vis. scholar U. Wash. Sch. Medicine, 2003—. Assoc. editor: Anatomical Record, 1978-98, Am. Jour. Anatomy, 1987-91; contbr. articles to profl. jours. Elected fellow Trinity Coll., Dublin U., 1966; named faculty mem. of yr. Loyola U., Chgo., 1982. Mem. N.Am. Soc. Lymphology (v.p. 1982-84, pres. 1984-86, sec. 1993-98, Cecil K. Drinker award 1992), Am. Assn. Anatomy Chairmen (emeritus), Am. Assn. Anatomists (dir. placement svc. 1981-91), Internat. Soc. Lymphology (exec. com. 1987-97, pres. 1993-95, Presdl. award 2001), Alpha Omega Alpha. Mem. Church of Ireland. Home: 5645 NE Lincoln Rd East Poulsbo WA 98370-7756 Office: U Ill Coll Medicine 190 Med Sci Bldg 506 S Mathews Ave Urbana IL 61801-3618 Business E-Mail: cccom@uiuc.edu.

OMOSHEYIN, ROTIMI, electronics specialist, real estate company executive; b. Yaba, Labos, Nov. 4, 1960; arrived in U.S., 1982; s. Matthew and Eunice Olamita Omusheyin; m. Rochelle Smith, Oct. 27, 1990; children: Demetris, Rotimi, Dionte. BSC, Aero Space Inst., 1985; advanced cert., Harry S. Truman Coll., 1988. Lic. ins. agt. Ill.; real estate agt. Ill. Fgn. exch. specialist 1st Bank of Nigeria, Marina Lagos, 1979—82; sales cons. Century 21 Home Finder, Chgo., 1985—87; regional mgr. Al Williams and Assocs., Chgo., 1988—92; electronics specialist Marshall Field and Co., Chgo., 1986—; pres., CEO Binom Mgmt., Chgo., 1995—. Author: Monster Zunga, 1997. Amb.-in-chief Royal Amb. Bapt. Conv., Lagos, 1978. Mem.: Binom Club (pres. 1996—2000). Methodist. Achievements include invention of toddler cycle. Avocations: fishing, music, soccer, reading, travel. Home: 1455 W 115th St Chicago IL 60643 E-mail: Timiomo@yahoo.com.

OMTVEDT, CRAIG P. consumer products executive; m. Jane Omtvedt. Degree, U. Minn. Dir. of audit Fortune Brands, Inc., Lincolnshire, Ill., 1989-92, dep. contr., 1992-97, v.p., chief acctg. officer, 1997-99, sr. v.p., CFO, 1999—. Mem. Fin. Exec. Inst., Inst. of Mgmt. Accts., Tax Exec. Inst. Office: Fortune Brands Inc 300 Tower Pkwy Lincolnshire IL 60069

OMURA, GEORGE ADOLF, medical oncologist; b. N.Y.C., Apr. 30, 1938; s. Bunji K. and Martha (Pilger) O.; m. Emily Fowler, Dec. 27, 1962; children: June Ellen, Susan, Ann, George Fowler. BA magna cum laude, Columbia U., 1958; MD, Cornell U., 1962. Intern Bellevue Hosp., N.Y.C., resident, 1965-67; fellow Meml. Sloan Kettering Cancer Ctr., N.Y.C., 1967-70; asst. prof. medicine U. Ala., Birmingham, 1970-73, assoc. prof. medicine, 1973-78, prof. medicine, 1978-95, prof. emeritus, medicine, 1995—, prof. ob-gyn., 1991-95; v.p. clin. devel. BioCryst Pharms., Inc., Birmingham, 1995-99, med. dir., 1996-99; prof. emeritus, ob-gyn U. Ala., Birmingham, 1996—. Cons. Nat. Cancer Inst., 1975-97; chmn. Southeastern Cancer Study Group, 1983-87; cons. to FDA, 1994-95; cons. to pharm. industry, 2000—; prin. investigator cancer and leukemia Group B for Ala., 1986-95. Contbr. articles to profl. jours. Served with USNR, 1963-65. Am. Cancer Soc. jr. faculty clin. fellow, 1971-74. Fellow: ACP; mem.: Am. Assn. Cancer Rsch., Am. Soc. Hematology, Am. Soc. Clin. Oncology, Gynecol. Oncology Group (co-prin. investigator Ala. 1988—2003, bd. dirs. 2003—), Alpha Omega Alpha, Phi Beta Kappa. Home: 3621 Crestside Rd Birmingham AL 35223-1514 Office: University Sta Birmingham AL 35294-0001 E-mail: geoaomura@aol.com.

ONA-SARINO, MILAGROS FELIX, pathologist; b. May 8, 1940; arrived in U.S., 1965, naturalized, 1983; d. Venancio Vale Ona and Fidela Torres Felix; m. Edgardo Formantes Sarino, June 11, 1966; children: Edith Melanie Sarino, Edgar Michael Sarino, Edenn Michele Sarino. AA, U. Santo Tomas, Manila, 1959, MD meritissimus cum laude, 1964; MBA in Health Svcs. Mgmt., W.Va. U., 1999. Diplomate Am. Bd. Pathology, med. licensure N.Y., N.J., W.Va. Surgery extern Armed Forces of the Philippines, V. Luna Gen. Hosp., Manila, 1964—65; rotating intern N.Y. Infirmary, pediats., Roosevelt Hosp., N.Y.C., 1965-66; resident in anatomic and clin. pathology Lenox Hill Hosp., N.Y.C., 1966-71, asst. adj. pathologist, 1972-74; assoc. pathologist St. Francis Med. Ctr., Trenton, NJ, 1974-84, Hamilton Hosp., NJ, 1974-84; pathologist, chief pathology and lab. medicine svc. Louis A. Johnson VA Med. Ctr., Clarksburg, W.Va., 1984-98, med. dir. blood bank, 2000—, assoc. chief of staff pathology and lab. medicine, 1998—, med. dir. pathology and lab. medicine, 1999—. Clin. instr. pathology Columbia U. Coll. Physicians and Surgeons, N.Y.C., 1973—85; clin. assoc. prof. W.Va. U. Sch. Medicine. Fellow: Coll. Am. Pathologists (cert. insp.), Am. Soc. Clin. Pathologists; mem.: Am. Coll. Physician Execs., N.Y. Acad. Scis. (life), Internat. Acad. Pathology. Office: Louis A Johnson VA Med Ctr Dept Pathology Clarksburg WV 26301 E-mail: ona-sarino@clarksburg.va.gov.

ONDETTI, MIGUEL ANGEL, chemist, consultant; b. Buenos Aires, May 14, 1930; came to U.S., 1960, naturalized, 1971; s. Emilio Pablo and Sara Cecilia (Cerutti) O.; m. Josephine Elizabeth Garcia, June 6, 1958; children: Giselle Christine, Gabriel Alexander. Licensiate in Chemistry, U. Buenos Aires, 1955, D.Sc., 1957. Prof. chemistry Inst. Tchrs., Buenos Aires, 1957-60; instr. organic chemistry U. Buenos Aires, 1957-60; rsch. scientist Squibb Inst. Med. Rsch., Buenos Aires, 1957-60, rsch. investigator Princeton, N.J., 1960-66, rsch. supr., 1966-73, sect. head, 1973-76, dir. biol. chemistry, 1976-79; assoc. dir. Squibb Inst., 1980-82, v.p. rsch. cardiopulmonary disease, 1982-86, sr. v.p. cardiovascular rsch., 1987-91; pharm. cons., 1991—. Ad-hoc cons NIH; mem. adv. com. dept. chemistry Princeton U., 1982-86 Patentee in field (115); contbr. articles to sci. jours. Served with Argentine Army, 1950-51 Recipient Thomas Alva Edison Patent award R&D Coun. N.J., 1983, Ciba award for hypertension rsch. Am. Heart Assn., 1983, Perkins medal Soc. Chemistry Industry, 1991, Warren Alpert Found. award, 1991, Albert Lasker Clinical Med. Research award, 1999; scholar Brit. Coun., 1960, Squibb, 1956. Mem. AAAS, Am. Chem. Soc. (Alfred Burger award 1981, Creative Invention award 1992, Perkin medal 1992), Am. Soc. Biol. Chemists. Home: 79 Hemlock Cir Princeton NJ 08540-5405

ONDRASIK, JOHN, singer, songwriter; b. L.A. m. Carla Ondrasik; 2 children. BA in Applied Math., UCLA. Singer, pianist, guitarist, prodr. Five for Fighting, 1997—; columnist, "Hockey Rocks" Inside Hockey, 2004—. Singer, musician (albums) Message for Albert, 1997, America Town, 2000, Battle for Everything, 2004; prodr.: (soundtrack) We Were Soldiers, 2002. Nominee for Favorite Adult Contemporary. Artist, 30th Am. Music Awards. Office: Columbia Records-SONY 1020 E Lafayette St Tallahassee FL 32301*

O'NEAL, E. STANLEY (STAN O'NEAL), investment company executive; BS, Kettering U.; MBA, Harvard U. Various positions GM Corp., 1978—86; dir. investment banking Merrill Lynch, 1986, mng. dir. investment banking, head global capital mkts. group, 1997, exec. v.p., co-head corp. and instl. client group, 1998, exec. v.p., CFO, 1998—2000, pres. U.S. pvt. client group, 2000—01, COO, 2001—02, pres., 2001—, CEO, 2002—, chmn., 2003—. Bd. dirs. Merrill Lynch, GM Corp., NASDAQ; mem., capital markets divsn. N.Y. Stock Exchange. Bd. dirs. Nat. Urban League, Catalyst, Ctr. for Strategic and Internat. Studies, N.Y.C. Partnership, Lower Manhattan Devel. Corp., Ronald McDonald House, NY; trustee Buckley Sch.; mem., adv. bd. The Bronx Prep. Sch. Office: Merrill Lynch 4 World Financial Ctr 250 Vessey St New York NY 10080*

O'NEAL, EDGAR CARL, psychology educator; b. St. Louis, Apr. 30, 1939; s. Clarence Edgar O'Neal and Alyce (Mullins) Redwine; m. Ellen Rose Luther, Aug. 31, 1963; children: Colleen Ruth, Patrick Blaine BA, Duke U., 1961; M.Div., Drew U., 1964; MA, U. Mo., 1968, PhD, 1969. Ordained to ministry United Meth. Ch., 1964. Minister Community Meth. Ch., Cold Spring Harbor, NY, 1962-65; NIMH fellow U. Mo., Columbia, 1966-69; asst. prof., assoc. prof. psychology Tulane U., New Orleans, 1969-76, chmn. dept. psychology, 1978-84, prof. psychology, 1977—99, John Madison Fletcher prof. psychology, 1999—. Editor: Perspectives on Aggression, 1976; mem. editl. bd. Jour. Personality and Social Psychology, 1991-97, Jour. Non-verbal Behaviour, 1991-94, Aggressive Behavior, 1995-2004; contbr. articles to profl. jours. Fellow APA (coun. 1982-85); mem. Sigma Xi, Sigma Chi. Democrat. Methodist. Home: 7219 O'Neil Dr Harahan LA 70123-4844 Office: Tulane U Dept Psychology 2007 Stern Hall New Orleans LA 70118-5698 E-mail: edgar.oneal@cox.net., edgar.oneal@tulane.edu.

O'NEAL, HANK, entertainment producer, business owner; b. Kilgore, Tex., June 5, 1940; s. Harold Lee and Sarah (Christian) O'N.; m. Shelley M. Shier, May 14, 1985. BA, Syracuse U., 1962. With CIA, Washington and N.Y.C., 1963-76; exec. v.p. Hammond Music Enterprises, N.Y.C., 1980-83; pres., owner Chiaroscuro Records Co./Downtown Sound recording studio, N.Y.C., 1970-80, 85—; exec. v.p. HOSS, Inc., N.Y.C., 1983—, Broadway Bound, Inc., 1998—. Instr., dept. head New Sch. for Social Rsch., N.Y.C., 1970-92; bd. dirs. The Jazz Found. Am., N.Y.C., The Jazz Gallery, N.Y.C.; chair bd. govs. Jazz and Contemporary Music, New Sch. U.; pres. SOS Prodns., Wilkes Barre, Pa., 1987—. Author: Eddie Condon Scrapbook of Jazz, 1973, A Vision Shared, 1976, Berenice Abbott-American Photographer, 1982, Djuna Barnes 1978-81, 1990, Charlie Parker/The Funky Blues Date, 1995; author/photographer: The Floating Jazz Festival, 1985, The Ghosts of Harlem, 1997, Hank O'Neal, 2000; photographer: (books) Allegra Kent's Water Beauty Book, 1976, All the King's Men, 1990; producer, cover photographer/designer numerous record albums, 1967—. Capt. U.S. Army, 1963-67. Recipient various awards and prizes for books. Mem. Phi Gamma Delta. Home: Glenside PO Box 101 Thornhurst PA 18424-0101 Office: Chiaroscuro Records 830 Broadway New York NY 10003-4827 Office Phone: 212-674-0265. E-mail: chiarohank@aol.com.

O'NEAL, HARRIET ROBERTS, psychologist, psycholegal consultant; b. Covington, Ky., Dec. 28, 1952; d. Nelson E. and Georgia H. (Roberts) O'N. Student, U. Paris Sorbonne, 1972; BA in Psychology, Hollins Coll., 1974; JD, U. Nebr., 1978, MA in Psychology, 1980, PhD in Psychology, 1982. Therapist Richmond Maxi Ctr., San Francisco, 1979-81; clin. coord., therapist Pacifica (Calif.) Youth Svc. Bur., 1981-83; staff psychologist Kaiser Permanente Med. Ctr., Walnut Creek, Calif., 1983-91; pvt. practice psychotherapy Pleasant Hill, Calif., 1985-97; pvt. practice psychotherapy, psycholegal cons. San Francisco, 1995—. Cons. Employee Assistance Program, Pacific Bell, San Francisco, 1996—; psycholegal cons., Nebr., 1975-79, Calif. Bd. Behavioral Sci. Examiners, Sacramento, 1982—; psycholegal cons., presenter San Francisco State U., 1980, U. Calif., San Francisco, 1980, VA Med. Ctr., San Francisco, 1983. Cons. Nebr. Gov.'s Commn. on Status of Women, 1975, 78; vol. Make-A-Wish Found., 1992—. NIMH fellow, 1974-79. Mem. APA, Employee Assistance Profls. Assn., Phi Beta Kappa, Psi Chi. Avocations: dance, swimming, hiking, travel, bicycling.

O'NEAL, KATHLEEN LEN, communications executive, writer, management speaker, financial consultant; b. Ft. Riley, Kans., May 24, 1953; d. Leonard Arthur and Mary (Modlin) O'Neal. BS with honors, U. Mo., 1975; MBA, Calif. Coast U., Santa Ana, 1991. Cert. secondary teacher. Tchr. math. Killian Sr. H.S., Miami, Fla., 1975-78; mfg. supr. Western Electric Co., Lee's Summit, Mo., 1978-79, prodn. control supr., 1979-81; dept. mgr. Lee Wards Co., Independence, Mo., 1981-83; materials mgmt. specialist Northrup-Wilcox Electric, Kansas City, Mo., 1983-84; bus. resource planning mgr. AT&T, Lee's Summit, 1984-85, product mgr. Berkeley Heights, N.J., 1985-87, fin. mgr. Bedminster, N.J., 1987-89, info. sys. devel. mgr. Piscataway, N.J., 1989-90, sr. fin. mgr. Jacksonville, Fla., 1990-91, asst. treas., 1992-95, sr. procurement mgr., 1995-96, procurement system design dist. mgr., 1997-98, payroll dist. mgr., 1998—2001; pres Kathy O'Neal Speaks, Inc, 2001—; bd. mem., CFO and treas. Genesis Orlando Inc., 2003—; treas. Parson Pub. Inc., 2004—. Recipient Spec Recognition Award, United Way, 1980. Mem.: NOW, Am Production and Inventory Control Soc (vpres membership 1987—88, regional del 1988—89, instr inventory mgt 1987—88). Avocations: reading, antique button collecting. Office: PO Box 470863 Celebration FL 34747-0863 Personal E-mail: kathyoneal@comcast.net. E-mail: kathy@accelerated-manager.com.

O'NEAL, MICHAEL L. physician; b. St. Paul, Mar. 25, 1969; s. Lyman H. and Cynthia S. O'Neal. BS, U. S. Fla., Tampa, 1992; DO, U. Health Scis., Coll. Osteop. Medicine, Kansas City, Mo., 1998. Diplomate Bd. of Family Physicians. Resident, family medicine U. S. Fla., Tampa, 2002; physician, co-founder Ctr. Family Health and Prevention, Palm Harbor, Fla., 2002—; CEO Cooperative Med., Inc., Palm Harbor, Fla., 2003—; primary care team physician Toronto Blue Jays Major League Baseball Club. Advisor Web Directives, Clearwater, Fla., 2000—; affiliate asst. prof. U. S. Fla., Tampa, 2002—; advisor Turnef, Dunedin, Fla., 2002—; on-air health cons. Radio, Tampa, Fla., 2002—. Contbr. articles to profl. jours. Recipient Leadership Award, AMA Found., 2003. Mem.: AAFP, AMA, Med. Missions Internat. Avocations: saxophone, writing, art, basketball, jogging. Office: 2702 Tampa Rd Palm Harbor FL 34684

O'NEAL, MICHAEL RALPH, state legislator, lawyer; b. Kansas City, Mo., Jan. 16, 1951; s. Ralph D. and Margaret E. (McEuen) O'N.; children from a previous marriage: children: Haley Anne, Austin Michael; m. Cindy Wulfkuhle, Apr. 9, 1999. BA in English, U. Kans., 1973, JD, 1976. Bar: Kans. 1976, U.S. Dist. Ct. Kans. 1976, U.S. Ct. Appeals (10th cir.) 1979. Intern Legis. Counsel State of Kans., Topeka, 1975-76; assoc. Hodge, Reynolds, Smith, Peirce & Forker, Hutchinson, Kans., 1976-77; ptnr. Reynolds, Peirce, Forker, Suter, O'Neal & Myers, Hutchinson, 1980-88; shareholder Gilliland & Hayes, P.A., Hutchinson, 1988—, mng. ptnr., 1999—2000; mem. Kans. Ho. of Reps., 1984, chmn. jud. com., 1989-90, 93-94, 97—; pres. Gilliland & Hayes, P.C.,

1999-2000; minority whip Kans. Ho. of Reps., 1991-92, majority whip, 1995-96, chmn. edn. com., 1995-96, mem. fiscal oversight com., 1997—, chair redistricting com., 2001—02, mem. bus., commerce, labor com., mem. tax, commerce, transp. and jud. budget com., 2003—, chmn. reappointment com., 2001—02. Instr. Hutchinson C.C., 1977-88. Vice chmn. Rep. Ctrl. Com., Reno County, Kans., 1982-86; bd. dirs. Reno County Mental Health Assn., Hutchinson, 1984-89, YMCA, 1984-86, Crime Stoppers (ex-officio), Hutchinson; chmn. adv. bd. dirs. Wesley Towers Retirement Cmty., 1984-96; mem. Kans. Travel and Tourism Commn., 1990-94; mem. bd. govs. U. Kans. Law Sch., 1991-94; mem. Kans. Sentencing Commn., 1997-2000. Recipient Leadership award Kans. C. of C. and Industry, 1985; named one of Outstanding Young Men Am., 1986. Mem. ABA, Nat. Conf. State Legislatures (criminal justice com.), Kans. Assn. Def. Counsel, Def. Rsch. Inst., Kans. Bar Assn. (prospective legis. com., Outstanding Svc. award), Hutchinson C. of C. (ex-officio bd. dirs., Leadership award 1984), Am. Coun. Young Polit. Leaders (del. to Atlantic conf. biennial assembly), Kans. Jud. Coun., Commn. on Uniform State Laws. Avocations: basketball, tennis, golf. Home: 8 Windemere Ct Hutchinson KS 67502-2020 Office: Gilliland & Hayes PA 2d Flr Box 2977 20 W 2nd Ave Hutchinson KS 67504-2977 E-mail: mroneal@southwind.net.

O'NEAL, REAGAN See RIGNEY, JAMES JR.

O'NEAL, RODNEY, automotive executive; B, GM Inst.; M (Sloan fellow), Stanford U. Various engring. and mfg. pos. GM Inland Divsn., Dayton, Portugal, and Can., 1976—91; dir. indsl. engring. Chevrolet-Pontiac-GM of Can. Group, 1991—92, dir. mfg. GM Automotive Components Group Worldwide, Troy, Mich., 1992—94; gen. dir. warehousing and distbn. GM Svc. Parts Ops., 1994—97; v.p. GM, 1997—98; pres. Delphi Interior Systems, Troy, Mich., 1998—2000, exec. v.p. Safety, Thermal and Elec. Arch. sector, 2000—03; pres. dynamics, propulsion and thermal Delphi Corp., Troy, Mich., 2003—. Bd. dirs. Inroads, Inc., Woodward Gov. Co.; mem. Exec. Leadership Coun. Adv. bd. Focus: HOPE. Office: World Hdqrs Delphi Corp 5725 Delphi Dr Troy MI 48098-2815

O'NEAL, SHAQUILLE RASHAUN, professional basketball player; b. Newark, N.J., Mar. 6, 1972; s. Philip A. Harrison and Lucille O'Neal. Student, La. State U. Center Orlando Magic, Fla., 1992—96, L.A. Lakers, 1996—2004, Miami Heat, 2004—. Mem. Dream Team II, 1994; Owner (Clothing line and Record label) TWIsM. Actor: (films) Blue Chips, 1994, Kazaam, 1996, Steel, 1997, The Wash, 2001; performer: (albums) Shaq Diesel, 1993, Shaq Fu: Da Return, 1994, You Can't Stop the Reign, 1995, The Best of Shaquille O'Neal, 1996, Shaquille O'Neal Presents his Superfriends, Vol. 1, 2002. Named Co-MVP of NBA All-Star game, 2000, MVP of NBA All-Star game, 2004, Regular Season MVP (by media), 2000, NBA Finals MVP, 2000—02; named one of 50 Greatest Players in NBA history, 1996; named to All-Am. 1st team, Sporting News, 1990—91, NBA All-Star team, 1993—98, 2000—02, 2004, All-NBA 1st team, 1998, 2000—02, All-NBA 2nd team, 1995, 1999; recipient Rookie of Yr. award, NBA, 1993, Gold Medal, U.S. Olympic Team (Atlanta), 1996. Achievements include being first pick overall in draft, 1992, mem. of 3 consecutive championship teams, 2000-2002, NBA Scoring Champion, 1995, 2000. Office: c/o Miami Heat American Airlines Arena 601 Biscayne Blvd Miami FL 33132*

O'NEIL, J(AMES) PETER, computer software designer, educator; b. Rockville Center, N.Y., Apr. 2, 1946; s. Clement Lee and Frances Rita (Theis) O'N.; m. Carol Ann Sypniewski, June 8, 1968; children: Kelly Ann, Thomas Joseph. BA in Psychology, Loyola U., Chgo., 1968; MA in Sci. Edn., Webster Coll., St. Louis, 1972. Cert. elem. tchr. K-8, Mo., elem. tchr. K-8, Wis., dir. instruction, Wis. Tchr., student tchr. Sacred Heart Sch., Florissant, Mo., 1968-73; tchr. sci. Waunakee (Wis.) Mid. Sch., 1973-96, chmn. K-8 sci. dept., chmn. K-12 dept., 1984-92; learning coord. Deforest (Wis.) Area Sch. Dist., 1992—2000. Dir. Waunakee Summer Sci. Program, 1975-91; dir. instrn./tech. Brodhead Wis., 1996-99; designer sci. curriculum computer CD-ROM programs Sci. Curriculum Assistance Program and Elem. Sci. Curriculum Assistance Program, 1990—; dir. instrn. DeForest (Wis.) Area Sch. Dist., 2000—; adj. prof. Viterbo U., 2003—; rsch. cons. IDEAS Wis., 2002—. Feature editor: Science Scope, 1989-96; contbr. over 30 activities and articles to profl. jours. Group worker settlement houses Chgo., St. Louis; mem. Parish Coun.; dir. Waunakee Area Edn. Found. Named Master Tchr. NSF, Waunakee, 1986-96; recipient Tchr. of Yr. award Waunakee, 1984, 90, 92, Kohl Found. award, 1992, Mid. Sch. Tchr. of Yr. award Wis., 1992-93. Mem.: Wis. Soc. Curriculum Designers, Am. Soc. Curriculum Designers. Roman Catholic. Avocations: computers, sports, writing, jogging. Home: 119 Simon Crestway Waunakee WI 53597-1721 Office: Deforest Area Sch Dist 520 E Holum St De Forest WI 53532-1316 Office Phone: 608-842-6531. E-mail: jponeil@deforest.k12.wi.us.

O'NEIL, JERRY, state senator; b. Kalispell, Mont., May 10, 1943; m. Jeanne O'Neil; children: David, Wendy, Laura, Sara, Maria. AA, Flathead Valley C.C.; student, Mont. State U., U. Mont. Owner Mediator and Ind. Paralegal, 1984—; Rep. senator dist. 42 Mont. State Senate, 2000—. Pres. DREAM, Disable Ski Program, 1999-2000. Office: 985 Walsh Rd Columbia Falls MT 59912

O'NEIL, JOHN, artist; b. Kansas City, Mo., June 16, 1915; s. Michael and Emma (Harms) O'N. BFA, U. Okla., 1936, MFA, 1939; student, Taos Sch. Art, 1942, U. Florence, Italy, 1951. Dir. U. Okla. Sch. Art, 1951-65; chmn. dept. fine arts Rice U., Houston, 1965-70; dir. Sewall Art Gallery, 1972-77, Joseph and Joanna Mullen prof. art and art history, 1979-81. Vis. lectr. NYU, U. Mich., U. Mass., l'Accademia di Belle Arti, Rome, Moana Olu Coll., Hawaii. One-man show, Mus. Art, U. Okla., Sask. (Can.) Art Centers, Seattle Art Mus., M-59 Galleries, Copenhagen, Denmark, Los Robles Galleries, Calif., La. Gallery, Houston, Philbrook Art Ctr., Tulsa, Firehouse Art Ctr., Norman, Okla.; works exhibited, Carnegie Inst., Artists West of Mississippi at Colorado Springs, Denver Art Mus., San Francisco Mus., Art Inst. of Chgo., U. Ill., Dallas Mus., Cin. Mus., Sadeer Gallery, Kuwait, Kauffman Galleries, Houston, Graham Gallery, Houston, Wierzbowski Gallery, Houston, N.Y. World's Fair, Pickard Gallery, Oklahoma City, U.S. Art Expo, San Francisco, McCormick Gallery, Chgo., Am. Art, 1930-50, Mobile Ala. Art Mus.; rep. collections, Philbrook Art Center, U. Mich., Denver Art Mus., Dallas Mus., Am. Arts., Kansas City, Chgo., Rice U., others. Recipient 30 painting and graphics awards. Painting fellow Huntington Hartford Found., MacDowell Colony, Montalvo Assn. Mem. Coll. Art Assn., Southwestern, Mid-Am. art confs., Delta Phi Delta. Home: 4718 Hallmark Dr Rm 5 A-L Houston TX 77056 Office Phone: 713-850-8181.

O'NEIL, JOHN JOSEPH, lawyer; b. Detroit, July 20, 1943; s. John J. and Dora J. (Collins) O'N.; children: Meghan, Kathryn. BA, Trinity Coll., 1965; LLB, U. Va., 1968. Bar: N.Y. 1969, U.S. Ct. Appeals (2d cir.) 1969, Fla. 1979, D.C. 1982. Assoc. Jackson & Nash, N.Y.C., 1968-71, Paul, Weiss, Rifkind, Wharton & Garrison, N.Y.C., 1971-77, ptnr., 1977—. Fellow Am. Coll. Trusts and Estates Counsel; mem. ABA (com. on spl. problems of aged), N.Y. State Bar Assn. (com. on taxation, trusts and estates sect.), Assn. Bar City N.Y. (com. on trusts and estates), Pi Gamma Mu. Office: Paul Weiss Rifkind Wharton & Garrison Ste 3221 1285 Avenue Of The Americas Fl 21 New York NY 10019-6064

O'NEIL, MAUREEN, think-tank executive; BA in Sociology, LLD, Carleton U., Wilfrid Laurier U. Pres. Internat. Devel. Rsch. Ctr., Ottawa, Canada, 1997—; interim pres. Internat. Ctr. for Human Rights and Dem. Devel.; pres. North-South Inst.; dep. min. citizenship Govt. Ont. Fellow Sch. Policy Studies Queen's U.; mem. internat. bd. govs. Ctr. for Internat. Governance Innovation; bd. dirs. Internat. Inst. for Democracy and Electoral Assistance; mem. Markle Found. Global Digital Opportunity Initiative. Chair bd. govs. Carleton U.; co-chair digital divide supervisory com. World Econ. Forum; mem. adv. bd. Min. Fgn. Affairs; chair Internat. Ctr. for Human Rights and Dem. Devel., Can. Found. for the Ams.; bd. mem. Inst. for Women, Law and Devel. Office: Internat Devel Rsch Ctr 250 Albert St PO Box 8500 Ottawa ON Canada K1G 3H9*

O'NEIL, ROBERT MARCHANT, university administrator, law educator; b. Boston, Oct. 16, 1934; s. Walter George and Isabel Sophia (Marchant) O'N.; m. Karen Elizabeth Elson, June 18, 1967; children— Elizabeth, Peter, David, Benjamin AB, Harvard U., 1956, AM, 1957, LLB, 1961; LLD, Beloit Coll., 1985, Ind. U., 1987. Bar: Mass. 1962. Law clk. to Justice William J. Brennan Jr. U.S. Supreme Ct., 1962-63; acting assoc. prof. law U. Calif.-Berkeley, 1963-66, prof., 1966-67, 69-72; exec. asst. to pres., prof. law SUNY-Buffalo, 1967-69; provost, prof. law U. Cin., 1972-73, exec. v.p., prof. law, 1973-75; v.p., prof. law Ind. U., Bloomington, 1975-80; pres. U. Wis. System, 1980-85; prof. law U. Wis.-Madison, 1980-85, U. Va., Charlottesville, 1985—, pres., 1985-90; gen. counsel AAUP, 1970-72, 91-92. Author: Civil Liberties: Case Studies and the Law, 1965, Free Speech: Responsible Communication Under Law, 2d edit., 1972, The Price of Dependency: Civil Liberties in the Welfare State, 1970, No Heroes, No Villians, 1972, The Courts, Government and Higher Education, 1972, Discriminating Against Discrimination, 1976, Handbook of the Law of Public Employment, 1978, 2d rev. edit., 1993, Classrooms in the Crossfire, 1981, Free Speech in the College Community, 1997, The First Amendment and Civil Liability, 2001; co-author: A Guide to Debate, 1964, The Judiciary and Vietnam, 1972, Civil Liberties Today, 1974. Trustee Tchrs. Ins. and Annuity Assn.; bd. dirs. Commonwealth Fund, Nat. Coalition Against Censorship, Am. Law Inst. Home: 1839 Westview Rd Charlottesville VA 22903-1632 Office: Thomas Jefferson Ctr Protection Free Expression 400 Peter Jefferson Pl Charlottesville VA 22911-8691

O'NEIL, ROBERT S. engineering executive; Pres., CEO DeLeuw Cather & Co., Washington. Recipient James Laurie prize ASCE, 1995. Office: DeLeuw Cather & Co 1133 15th St NW Ste 800 Washington DC 20005-2710

O'NEIL, THOMAS FRANCIS, III, lawyer, business executive; b. Fairfield, Conn., Apr. 8, 1957; s. Thomas F. Jr. and Carmen A. (Therrien) O'N.; m. Nancy D., Aug. 14, 1982; children: Caley Elizabeth, Patrick McGee. AB magna cum laude, Dartmouth Coll., 1975-79; JD, Georgetown U., 1979-82. Bar: Md. 1982, U.S. Dist. Ct. Md. 1983, U.S. Ct. Appeals (4th cir.) 1983, D.C. 1992. Legis. asst. Congressman Stewart B. McKinney, Washington, 1980-82; law clk. Hon. Alexander Harvey II U.S. Dist. Ct. Md.; assoc. Venable, Baetjer & Howard, Balt., 1984-86; asst. U.S. atty. U.S. Dept. Justice, Balt., 1986-89; assoc. Hogan & Hartson, Balt., 1990-91, ptnr., 1992-95; chief litigation counsel MCI Comms. Corp., Washington, 1995-98; chief legal counsel, sr. v.p. MCI Worldcom, Inc., 1998—; sr. v.p., gen. counsel MCI Group, 2001—02; sr. ptnr. Piper Rudnick LLP, 2002—; chmn. Govt. Affairs Practice Group, 2003—. Bd. govs. Fed. Bar Assn., Balt., 1992; ex officio trustee Walters Art Mus., 1995—96, trustee, 1997—2002; chair William T. Walters Assocs., Georgetown U. Law Ctr., mem., bd. visitors, 1999—; mem. adv. bd. Marbury Inst., 2000—02; trustee The Contemporary Mus., 2001—. Recipient Chief Postal Insps. Spl. award U.S. Postal Svc., Washington, 1988, Letter of Commendation award Bur. of Investigation, Washington, 1989, Spl. Achievement award U.S. Dept. Justice, 1989. Mem. Serjeants Inn Law Club. Republican. Roman Catholic. Office: Piper Rudnick 1200 19th St Washington DC 20036 also: 1251 Ave of Americas New York NY 10020-1104 Office Phone: 202-861-6685.

O'NEIL, THOMAS J. mining company executive; BS in Mining Engring., Lehigh U.; MS, Pa. State U.; PhD, U. Ariz. Numerous sr. positions in minerals industry; head dept. mining and geol. engring. U. Ariz.; pres., COO Cleveland-Cliffs Inc., Cleve., 2000—. Mem. NAE, Am. Iron Ore Assn. (chmn.), Soc. Mining, Metallurgy and Exploration (dir., pres.-elect). Office: Cleveland-Cliffs Inc 1100 Superior Ave Cleveland OH 44114-2589

O'NEIL, THOMAS MICHAEL, physicist, researcher; b. Hibbing, Minn., Sept. 2, 1940; married; 1 child. BS, Calif. State U., Long Beach, 1962; MS, U. Calif., San Diego, 1964, PhD in Physics, 1965. Rsch. physicist Gen. Atomic, 1965-67; prof. physics U. Calif., San Diego, 1967—. Mem. adv. bd. Inst. Fusion Studies, 1980-83, Inst. Theoretical Physics, 1983-86; mem. plasma sci. com. NRC, 1998—, chmn., 2001—, mem. bd. on physics and astronomy, 2001—. Assoc. editor Physics Review Letters, 1979-83; correspondent Comments Plasma Physics & Controlled Fusion, 1980-84. Alfred P. Sloan fellow, 1971; recipient Disting. Alumnus award Sch. Natural Sci. CSULB, 1985, Alumni Disting. Tchg. award UCSD, 1996. Fellow Am. Phys. Soc. (award for excellence in plasma physics 1991, James Clerk Maxwell prize 1996). Achievements include research in theoretical plasma physics with emphasis on nonlinear effects in plasmas and on non-neutral plasmas. Office: Dept Physics 9500 Gilman Dr La Jolla CA 92093-5003 E-mail: toneil@ucsd.edu.

O'NEIL, WAYNE, linguist, educator; b. Kenosha, Wis., Dec. 22, 1931; s. L.J. and Kathryn (Obermeyer) O'N.; married; children: Scott Leslie, Patrick Sean, Elizabeth Erla. AB, U. Wis., 1955, AM, 1956, PhD, 1960; AM (hon.), Harvard U., 1965. Asst. prof. linguistics and lit. U. Oreg., 1961-65; prof. linguistics and edn. Harvard U., 1965-68, lectr. edn., 1968-72, vis. prof. edn., 1978-86; prof. linguistics MIT, 1968—, chmn. lit. faculty, 1969-75, chmn. linguistics program, 1986-97, head dept. linguistics and philosophy, 1989-97. Lectr. human devel. Wheelock Coll., Boston, 1991—; lectr. Beijing Normal U., 1980, Beijing and Shanghai Fgn. Lang. Insts., 1981; lectr. linguistics Shandong (China) U., 1982-83, prof., 1984—; prof. Summer Inst. on Lang. Change, NEH, 1978; vis. prof. Tsuda Coll., Tokyo, 1983, Kanda U. Internat. Studies, Makuhari, Japan, 1997, Am. Indian Lang. Devel. Inst., 2000—, Kanazawa Inst. of Tech., Japan, 2001—; co-dir. MIT-Japan Sci. and Tech. mind articulation project, 1996—. Author: (in Chinese) English Transformational Grammar, 1981, Linguistics and Applied Linguistics, 1983, (with S.J. Keyser) Rule Generalization and Optionality in Language Change, 1985, (with S. Flynn) Linguistic Theory in Second Language Acquisition, 1988, (with S. Flynn and G. Martohardjono) The Generative Study of Second Language Acquisition, 1998, (with A. Marantz and Y. Miyashita) Image, Language, Brain, 2000, (with M. Honda) Understanding First and Second Language Acquisition, 2004; mem. editl. group Radical Tchr., 1975—. Mem. steering com. Resist, 1967—, Peoples Coalition for Peace and Justice, 1970-72; co-founder, mem. Linguistics for Nicaragua, 1985—. With U.S. Army, 1952-54. Fulbright fellow in Iceland, 1961; Am. Council, Australia, 1998. Mem. AAAS, Linguistic Soc. Am., Nat. Coun. Tchrs. English, Am. Assn. Applied Linguistics, Assembly for the Tchg. English Grammar. Office: MIT Dept Linguistics and Philosophy Cambridge MA 02139-4307 Business E-Mail: waoneil@mit.edu.

O'NEIL, WILLIAM FRANCIS, academic administrator; b. Worcester, Mass., Mar. 26, 1936; s. John J. and Mary A. (Trahant) O'N.; m. Mary Elizabeth Dillon, Aug. 22, 1959; children: Kathleen, Mary Elizabeth. BS, Boston U., 1960; MEd, Worcester State Coll., 1963; diploma, U. Conn., 1970; EdD, Wayne State U., 1972; PhD in Pub. Edn. (hon.), Bridgewater State Coll., 2002; BFA (hon.), Montserrat Coll. Art, 1994. Tchr. Worcester Pub. Schs., 1960—68, cmty. sch. dir., 1968—73; assoc. prof., dir. community edn. devel. ctr. Worcester State Coll., 1973-75, dir. community svc., 1975—77, dean grad. and continuing edn., 1977—83, exec. v.p., 1983—85, Mass. Coll. Art, Boston, 1985—86, acting pres., 1986—87, pres., 1987—96; exec. officer Mass. State Coll. Coun. Pres., 1996—2002. Contbr. articles to profl. jours. Mem. Worcester Dem. City Com., Ward I Dem. Com., 1980—; pres., trustee Worcester Pub. Libr., 1977-82; mem. Mass. Bd. Libr. Commrs., 1984-89; bd. dirs. Worcester State Coll. Found., 2001—. Recipient Outstanding Alumni award field of edn. Worcester State Coll., 1996, citation Mass. Ho. of Reps., 1977, key City of Worcester, 1982; Mott fellow Charles Stewart Mott Found., 1971; Godine Cmty. Svc. medal, Mass. Coll. Art, 2002. Mem. Mass. Pub. Colls. and Univs. Pres. and Chancellors Assn. (chair 1991-92), Assn. Ind. Colls. Art and Design (bd. dirs. 1988-96), Mass. Cmty. Edn. Assn. (life; bd. dirs. 1972-77), Mass. State Colls. Pres. Assn. (chair 1992-93), Profl. Arts Consortium (v.p. Boston 1986-96, pres. 1993-94). Roman Catholic. Home: 47 Harvest Cir Holden MA 01520-3401 E-mail: woneil@worcester.edu.

O'NEIL, WILLIAM J. newspaper executive; b. Mar. 25, 1933; married; 4 children. Grad., So. Meth. U. Founder, chmn. William O'Neil + Co., Inc., 1960—, Investors Bus. Daily, 1984—. Chmn. Daily Graphs, Inc., O'Neil Data Sys., Inc., Data Analysis, Inc.; conducts investing seminars. Author: The Investor's Business Daily Almanac, 1992: The Fact, the Figures, the Trends, 24 Essential Lessons for Investment Success, 1999 (BusinessWeek bestseller, USA Today bestseller, Wall St. Jour. bestseller), How to Make Money in Stocks, 2002, The Successful Investor: What 80 Million People Need to Know to Invest Profitably and Avoid Big Losses, 2003. Named Entrepreneur Yr. Nat. Judge Chair, Ernst & Young Entrepreneur Yr. Program; recipient Classic Award Recognition, AeA high-tech group, Excellence in Sch. Choice Reporting award, John Fund. Achievements include creator of first daily computer database of US stock market, 1964. Office: Investors Bus Daily 12655 Beatrice St Los Angeles CA 90066-7303

O'NEIL, WILLIAM SCOTT, publishing executive; V.p., portfolio mgr. William O'Neil Inc., L.A., 1992—. Office: Investors Bus Daily 12655 Beatrice St Los Angeles CA 90066-7303

O'NEIL BIDWELL, KATHARINE THOMAS, fine arts association executive, performing arts executive; b. Dayton, Ohio, Mar. 23, 1937; d. Charles Allen and Margaret Stoddard (Talbott) Thomas; children: Margaret, Stephen, Thomas; m. J. Truman Bidwell. BA, Sarah Lawrence Coll., Bronxville, N.Y., 1959. Mng. dir. Met. Opera Assn., 1977-86, v.p., 1979-86; first v.p. Met. Opera Guild, N.Y.C., 1978-79, pres., chief exec. officer, 1979-86; dir. spl. projects Lincoln Ctr., N.Y.C., 1986-96. Bd. dirs. Norlin Corp.; exec. cons. N.Y.C. Opera, 1997—. Bd. dirs. Lincoln Ctr. for Performing Arts, N.Y.C., Assn. of Mentally Ill Children, 1975-76, Valerie Bettis Sch. of Theater/Dance, 1976-79, Salisbury Sch., Conn., 1982-84; trustee Sarah Lawrence Coll., 1977-86; Westminster Choir Coll., 1986-91, Greenwall Found., 1986, Vol. Cons. Group, 1986; chmn. hon. mems. of chmn. coun. N.Y.C. Opera-Lincoln Ctr. Mem. Assn. Sarah Lawrence Coll. (pres. 1975-77), Chamber Music Soc. Lincoln Ctr. (bd. dirs. 1996—). Republican. Episcopalian. Home: 435 E 57th St New York NY 10022-3065

O'NEILL, BEVERLY LEWIS, mayor, former college president; b. Long Beach, Calif., Sept. 8, 1930; d. Clarence John and Flossie Rachel (Nicholson) Lewis; m. William F. O'Neill, Dec. 21, 1952 AA, Long Beach City Coll., 1950; BA, Calif. State U., Long Beach, 1952, MA, 1956; EdD, U. So. Calif., 1977. Elem. tchr. Long Beach Unified Sch. Dist., 1952-57; instr., counsellor Compton (Calif.) Coll., 1957-60; curriculum supr. Little Lake Sch. Dist., Santa Fe Springs, Calif., 1960-62; women's advisor, campus dean Long Beach City Coll., 1962-71, dir. Continuing Edn. Ctr. for Women, 1969-75, dean student affairs, 1971-77, v.p. student svcs., 1977-88, supt.-pres., 1988—93, exec. dir. LBCC, 1983—; mayor City of Long Beach, Calif., 1994—. Advisor Jr. League, Long Beach, 1976—, Nat. Coun. on Alcoholism, Long Beach, 1979—, Assistance League, Long Beach, 1982—; bd. dirs. NCCJ, Long Beach, 1976—, Meml. Hosp. Found., Long Beach, 1984-92, Met. YMCA, Long Beach, 1986-92, United Way, Long Beach, 1986-92. Named Woman of Yr., Long Beach Human Rels. Commn., 1976, to Hall of Fame, Long Beach City Coll., 1977, Disting. Alumni of Yr., Calif. State U., Long Beach, 1985, Long Beach Woman of Yr. Rick Rackers, 1987, Assistance League Aux., 1987, Woman of Yr., Calif. Legislature 54th Dist., 1995; recipient Hannah Solomon award Nat. Coun. Jewish Women, 1984, Outstanding Colleague award Long Beach City Coll., 1985, NCCJ Humanitarian award, 1991, Woman of Excellence award YWCA, 1990, Community Svc. award Community Svcs. Devel. Corp., 1991, Citizen of Yr. award Exch. Club, 1992, Pacific Regional CEO award Assn. Community Coll. Trustees, 1992, EDDY award, 1999, Long Beach Excellence in Leadership, 1999. Mem. Assn. Calif. Community Coll. Adminstrs. (pres. 1988-90, Harry Buttimer award 1991), Calif. Community Colls. Chief Exec. Officers Assn., Rotary, Soroptomists (Women Helping Women award 1981, Hall of Fame award 1984), U.S. Conf. Mayors (trustee, 2001-), League Calif. Cities (pres. 2002-). Democrat. Office: Office Mayor Civic Ctr Plz 333 W Ocean Blvd Fl 14 Long Beach CA 90802-4604*

O'NEILL, BRIAN, research organization administrator; b. Bristol, Eng., Sept. 20, 1940; s. Raymond and Phyllis Mary (Marshall) O'N.; m. Alayne O'Neill, Aug. 31, 1969 (div. Sept. 1987); children: Allison Sarah, Stuart Douglas, Lesley Alexandra; m. Karen O'Neill, Feb. 20, 1988. BSc in Math. and Stats., Bath. U. Tech., 1965. Cons. in stats. and ops. research Unilever Ltd., London, 1965-66; research assoc. Tech. Ops. Inc., Ft. Belvoir, Va., 1966-67; mgr. applied math. dept. Wolf Research & Devel. Corp., Riverdale, Md., 1967-69; v.p., sr. v.p., exec. v.p. Ins. Inst. for Hwy. Safety, Washington, 1969-85, pres., 1985—; v.p., sr. v.p., exec. v.p. Hwy. Loss Data Inst., Washington, 1969-85, pres., 1985—. Witness at numerous fed. and state hearings on hwy. safety and transp. Contbr. numerous articles to profl. jours.; also presentations at profl. confs. Mem. Am. Pub. Health Internat. Com. on Alcohol Drugs and Traffic Safety, Royal Statis. Soc., Soc. Automotive Engrs. Office: Ins Inst for Hwy Safety 1005 N Glebe Rd Ste 800 Arlington VA 22201-5759

O'NEILL, BRIAN, national recreation area administrator; b. Washington, 1942; s. John and Virgina O'Neill; m. Marti Hendricks; 2 children. Student, U. Md., 1964. Joined Bur. Outdoor Recreation, Dept. Interior, 1965, mgr. Heritage Conservation and Recreation Svc., 1973—81, San Francisco, 1973—81; asst. supt. Golden Gate Nat. Recreation Area, San Francisco, 1981—86, supt., 1986—; acting assoc. dir. Nat. Pk. Svc. Bd. mem. San Francisco Planning and Urban Rsch. Assn.; instr. Dale Carnegie & Assocs., 1975—77. Recipient Exec. Leadership award, Dept. of the Interior, 2004. Avocations: gardening, glasswork, sailboarding, body surfing, hiking. Office: Golden Gate Nat Rec Area Fort Mason Bldg 201 San Francisco CA 94123*

O'NEILL, BRIAN BORU, lawyer; b. Hancock, Mich., June 7, 1947; s. Brian Boru and Jean Anette (Rimpela) O'N.; m. Ruth Bohan, Sept. 18, 1991; children: Dru Groves, Brian Boru, Maggie Byrne, Phelan Boru, Ariel Margaret. BS, U.S. Mil. Acad., 1969; JD magna cum laude, U. Mich., 1974; D in Pub. Svc. (hon.), Northland Coll., 1999. Bar: Mich. 1974, U.S. Dist. Ct. Minn. 1977, U.S. Ct. Mil. Appeals 1975, U.S. Ct. Appeals (6th cir.) 1975, U.S. Ct. Appeals (8th cir.) 1977, U.S. Ct. Appeals (Fed. cir.) 1983, U.S. Ct. Appeals (7th cir.) 1985, U.S. Ct. Appeals (10th cir.) 1986, U.S. Ct. Appeals (9th cir.) 1990, U. S. Ct. Claims 1981, U.S. Supreme Ct. 1981. Asst. to gen. counsel Dept. Army, Washington, 1974-77; assoc., ptnr. Faegre & Benson, Mpls., 1977—. Mem. com. vis. Mich. Law Sch., 1994—; counsel Defenders of Wildlife, Washington, 1977—, also bd. dirs; counsel Sierra Club, Audubon Soc. Mng. editor: Mich. Law Rev., 1973—74. Served to capt. U.S. Army, 1969-77. Named Environmentalist of Yr. Sierra Club North Star, 1982, 96, 97, 98; recipient William Douglas award Sierra Club, 1985, Trial Lawyer of Yr. award Trial Lawyers for Pub. Justice, 1995. Fellow Am. Coll. Trial Lawyers (regent 2003—), Internat. Acad. Trial Lawyers, Order of the Coif; mem. Mpls. Golf Club, Mpls. Athletic Club. Office: Faegre & Benson 2200 Wells Fargo Tower 90 S 7th St Ste 2200 Minneapolis MN 55402-3901 E-mail: boneill@faegre.com.

O'NEILL, BRIAN DENNIS, lawyer; b. Phila., Feb. 21, 1946; s. Harry William and Margaret Elizabeth (Miller) O'N.; m. Bonnie Anne Ryan, Aug. 17, 1968; children: Aimee Kathleen, Catherine Margaret. BA, Fla. State U., 1968, JD, 1971. Bar: Fla. 1971, D.C. 1975, U.S. Ct. Appeals (D.C. cir.) 1978, U.S. Ct. Appeals (5th and 11th cirs.) 1981, U.S. Ct. Appeals (10th cir.) 1985, U.S. Supreme Ct. 2003. Trial atty. Fed. Power Commn., Washington, 1972-75; assoc. Farmer, Shibley, McGuinn & Flood, Washington, 1975-80; ptnr. LeBoeuf, Lamb, Greene & MacRae, Washington, 1980—. Lectr. in field. Editorial bd. Energy Law Jour., Washington, 1983-84; contbr. articles to profl. jours. Bd. dirs. Immaculata Coll., Rockville, Md., 1989-91; bd. trustees Acad. of Holy Cross, Kensington, Md., 1994—; bd. visitors Fla. State U. Coll. of Law, 1994—. 2d lt. USAF, 1971-72. Mem.: ABA (chmn. coun., pub. utilities, comm. and transp. law sect.), Energy Bar Assn. (chmn. coms. 1983—84), Fla. Bar, Congl. Country Club (Bethesda, Md. bd. govs. 2002—), Phi Alpha Delta. Democrat. Roman Catholic. Office: LeBoeuf Lamb Greene & MacRae 1875 Connecticut Ave NW Washington DC 20009-5728 Office Phone: 202-986-8012. E-mail: boneill@llgm.com.

O'NEILL, BRIDGET R. lawyer; b. 1963; BSBA, Georgetown U., 1985; JD, U. Wis., 1988. Bar: Wis. 1988, Ill. 1988, N.Y. 1992. With Sidley Austin Brown & Wood, Chgo., prin., 1996—. Office: Sidley Austin Brown & Wood Bank One Plz 10 S Dearborn St Chicago IL 60603

O'NEILL, CATHERINE, cultural organization administrator; m. Richard Reeves; children: Colin, Conor, Fiona O'Neill Reeves. BA in History, St. Joseph's Coll., Bklyn.; MS in Social Welfare, Howard U.; MS in Internat. Rels., Columbia U., N.Y.C. Editl. writer KFWB Radio, L.A.; pub. affairs officer Internat. Monetary Fund, Internat. Herald Tribune, Atlantic Inst. for Internat. Affairs, Fgn. Policy Assn. of the U.S.; pub. affairs dir. RCA; dir. UN Info. Ctr., Washington, 1999—. Co-founder Women's Commn. for Refugee Women and Children, chair emeritae. Office: UN Info Ctr 1775 K St NW Ste 400 Washington DC 20006

O'NEILL, CHARLES KELLY, marketing executive, former advertising agency executive; b. Springfield, Mo., Apr. 2, 1933; s. Charles Chester and Frances (Kelly) O'N.; m. Kyoko Hirano, June 2, 1981. B.J., U. Mo., 1955. With Galvin-Farris-Alvine, Kansas City, Mo., 1957-58, copy chief, 1958; with Potts-Woodbury, Inc., Kansas City, 1958-61, chief time buyer, 1960-61; with Gardner Advt. Co., St. Louis, 1962-88, assoc. media dir., 1964-65, media dir., 1965-69, v.p., 1966-76, corp. media dir., dir. co., 1969-88, sr. v.p., 1976-78, pres., 1978-88; gen. mgr. Advanswers div., 1971-72; pres. Advanswers Media/Programming, Inc., 1973-78, chmn., 1978-88; v.p. Wells, Rich, Greene, N.Y.C., 1974-88, exec. v.p., 1979-88, dir., 1978-88; vice chmn. WRG-USA, 1981-88; chmn. O'Neill Mktg., Honolulu, 1988—; exec. v.p. Kyoko O'Neill, Inc., 1993—; dir. Colony Surf Ltd., Honolulu, 1990-94, chmn., bd. dirs., 1994. Bd. dirs. Waialae Iki Ridge Cmty. Assn., Honolulu, 1991—, 1st v.p., 1993-94. Lt. (j.g.) USN, 1955-57. Mem. St. Louis Advt. Club (gov. 1981-83), Outrigger Canoe Club (Honolulu), N.Y. Athletic Club, St. Louis Club, St. Louis Racquet Club, The Bridge (Navy League of the U.S.-Honolulu), Labrador Retriever Club of Hawaii, Sigma Chi, Alpha Delta Sigma. Episcopalian. Home: 1594 Hoaaina St Honolulu HI 96821-1345

O'NEILL, DAVID A, music educator, musician; b. Norristown, Pa., June 17, 1973; s. Robert M. and Margret M. O'Neill. BS Music Edn., West Chester U., 1994—96. Music tchr. Colonial Mid. Sch., Plymouth Meeting, Pa., 1998—, Conshohocken Elem. Sch., Pa., 1996—98. Musician: (performances) piano & trumpet concerts. Mem.: MENC. Office: Colonial Middle School 716 Belvoir Rd Plymouth Meeting PA 19462

O'NEILL, DONALD EDMUND, health science executive; b. Port Angeles, Wash., Feb. 10, 1926; s. Edward I. and Christine (Williamson) O'N.; m. Violet Elizabeth Oman, June 12, 1948; children: Shelly O'Neill Lane, Erin O'Neill Kennedy, Shawn O'Neill Hoffman. BS, U. Wash., 1949. With G.D. Searle & Co., 1950-71, regional sales dir., 1962-64, dir. med. service, 1964-68, dir. mktg., 1968-71; with Warner-Lambert Co., 1971—, v.p., 1974-77, exec. v.p. pharm. group, 1977, exec. v.p.; chmn. Internat. profl. group, 1974-76; pres. Parke-Davis & Co., 1976-78; pres., exec. dir. Warner-Lambert/Parke Davis Research Div., 1978, pres. Health Care Group, 1978-81; pres. Parke-Davis Group, 1981, Health Techs. Group, 1982-86, Internat. Ops., 1986-89; exec. v.p., chmn. internat. ops. Warner-Lambert Co, 1989-91; ret., 1991. Bd. dirs. Fujisawa U.S.A., Alliance Pharm. Immunogen Co., Fuisz Techs., Cytogen, Targeted Genetics. With USAAF, 1944-46. Mem. John's Island and Bent Pine Golf Clubs, Morris County Golf Club, Elk River Country Club.

O'NEILL, ELIZABETH STERLING, trade association administrator; b. NYC, May 30, 1938; d. Theodore and Pauline (Green) Sterling: m. W.B. Smith, June 18, 1968 (div. Aug., 1978); 1 child, Elizabeth S. Kroese; m. Francis James O'Neill, May 19, 1984. BA, Cornell U., 1958; postgrad. studies, Northwestern U., 1959-60. Social sec. Perle Mesta Ambassador Luxembourg, N.Y.C.; spl. asst. Vivian Beaumont Allen, philanthropist, N.Y.C.; rep. Prentice-Hall Pub. Co., Eastern Europe; exec. dir. New Caanan (Conn.) C. of C., 1985-97. Apptd. Commn. Small Bus. State of Conn., 1996; spkr. in field. Pres. Newcomers, New Caanan, Conn.; pub. rels. rep. Girl Scouts of U.S., Fairfield County; bd. dirs. Young Women's Rep. Club; mem. Gov. Weicker's Com. for Curriculum Reform; mem. community bd. Waveny Care Ctr., New Caanan; apptd. mem. Gov. John Roland's Commn. on Small Bus., Conn., 1996—; bd. dirs., trustee Clinton (N.J.) Mus. Art; bd. trustees, Hunterdon Mus. Art, 2000, Tewksbury Women's Club (program chair). Recipient Service awards New Caanan YMCA, N.Y. ASPCA, certs. of appreciation New Caanan Lions Club, President Bush. Mem. AAUW (bd. dirs. New Caanan chpt.), Kiwanis, Woman's Club of Tweksbury Twp. (pres. 2002-03, 2003-04). Christian Scientist. Avocations: tennis, horses, travel. Home: 17 Lance Rd Lebanon NJ 08833-5007

O'NEILL, EUGENE MILTON, retired investor; b. Richmond, Calif., Nov. 4, 1925; s. John Milton and Vivian Elda (Vogel) O'N.; m. Jane Prigmore; children: Karen, Kay, Mary. BS in Bus. and Pub. Adminstrn., Washington U., St. Louis, 1949. CPA, Mo. Acct., Jeff K. Stone & Co., St. Louis, 1948-52; controller Campbell Holton & Co. (div. Gen. Grocer Co.), Bloomington, Ill., 1953-54, pres., 1955-57; v.p. Gen. Grocer Co., St. Louis, 1957-60, pres., 1960-74, chmn. bd., pres., 1974-83. Founding trustee Food Industry Crusade Against Hunger. With USAAC, 1943-45. Mem. Food Distbrs. Internat. (past chmn.) Home: 8 Deacon Dr Saint Louis MO 63131-4803

O'NEILL, HARRIET, state supreme court justice; Undergrad. degree with honors, Converse Coll.; JD, U. S.C., 1982. Practice law, Houston; with Porter & Clements, Morris & Campbell; pvt. practice, 1982-92; judge 152d Dist. Ct., Houston, 1992; justice 14th Ct. Appeals, Houston, 1995, Tex. Supreme Ct., 1998—. Lectr. continuing edn. courses; adv. bd. CLE Inst., 1996; panelist Tex. Ctr. Advanced Jud. Studies., Austin, 1993. Contbr. articles to profl. publs. Mem. U. S.C. academic honors soc.; law sch. rep. ABA. Office: Supreme Ct PO Box 12248 Austin TX 78711-2248

O'NEILL, HARRY WILLIAM, survey research company executive; b. Atlantic City, Jan. 30, 1929; s. Harry William and Marian Elizabeth (Kuhl) O'N.; m. Carmel Gullo, Sept. 21, 1952; children: Sharon Ruth, Randal Bruce. BA, Colgate U., 1950; MS, Pa. State U., 1951. Lic. practicing psychologist, N.J. Research analyst Prudential Ins. Co., Newark, 1957-62; with Opinion Research Corp., Princeton, N.J., 1962-87, sr. v.p., 1970-73, exec. v.p., 1973-80, pres., 1980-85, vice chmn., 1985-87, NOP World, Princeton, NJ, 1988—. Mem. co-adj. faculty Rutgers U., 1959-64; vis. lectr. Woodrow Wilson Sch., Princeton U., 1980-82; mem. part-time faculty Rutgers U., 1999—. Editor Marketing Research: A Magazine of Management & Applications, 1988-93. Pres. Nat. Coun. Pub. Polls, 1984-94, trustee, 1994—; bd. dirs. Roper Ctr. for Pub. Opinion Rsch., 1984-94, chmn., 1994—; bd. dirs. Coun. Am. Survey Rsch. Orgns., 1981-83, chmn., 1982-83; vice chmn. Rsch. Industry Coalition, 1993-94, chmn., 1994-95; bd. dirs. Market Rsch. Inst. Internat., 1999—; mem. Highland Park (N.J.) Human Rights Commn., 1973-77; bd. dirs. Del-Raritan Lung Assn., 1974-88, v.p., 1977-82, chmn., 1982-84; fin. chmn. Highland Park Rep. Orgn., 1977-89. With USAF, 1951-54. Recipient Maroon citation, Colgate U., 1975, induction into Market Rsch. Coun. Hall of Fame, 1997, Lifetime Achievement award, Coun. Am. Survey Rsch. Orgns., 2001. Mem. Am. Psychol. Assn., Ea. Psychol. Assn., Am. Assn. Pub. Opinion Rsch. (Outstanding Achievement award N.Y. chpt. 1997), Assn. Consumer Rsch., Am. Mktg. Assn., Market Rsch. Coun., Highland Park Rep. Club, Masons, Elks. Presbyterian. Office: NOP World 1060 State Rd Princeton NJ 08540-1423 Office Phone: 609-683-6128. E-mail: honeill536@aol.com.

O'NEILL, JAMES F. retired health facility administrator; b. Corona, N.Y., July 3, 1923; s. James Francis O'Neill and Anita Theresa Queroli; m. Wilma Bernice Gallagher, July 17, 1948; children: Sharon, Kevin, Patricia. Med. Technologist, Bethesda Naval Med. Sch., Md., 1943; BSc, L.I. U., Bklyn., 1951, MSc, 1965; postgrad., L.I. U., 1966, Columbia U., 1970. Cert. med. lab. dir. N.Y. State. Owner Shiel Med. Lab., Inc., Queens Village, NY, 1950—56; owner, dir. State of N.Y. Med. Lab., Inc., Queens Village, NY, 1956—89, co-dir. Bklyn., 1990—95; ret., 1998. Cons. in field. With USN, 1942—46. Emeritus fellow, Am. Inst. Chemists, 2003. Fellow: Am. Inst. Chemists; mem.: KC, Rotary. Roman Catholic. Avocations: fishing, gardening, travel, computers.

O'NEILL, JAMES MARTIN, venture capitalist; b. N.Y.C., Sept. 29, 1962; s. James and Bernice N. (Grogan) O'N.; m. Kimberly A. Mika, Nov. 19, 1998; children: Matthew M., Michael C., Liam J. BA in Govt. and Econs., Dartmouth Coll., 1984; MBA, Harvard Bus. Sch., 1990. V.p. Nat. Westminster Bank USA, N.Y.C., 1984-88; assoc. corp. fin. Merrill Lynch Internat. Ltd., London, 1990-91; gen. mgr. The Coca-Cola Co., Coca-Cola Poland Ltd., Warsaw, 1991—94; mng. dir. Czech Am. Enterprise Fund, Washington, 1994-95; CEO, mng. dir. DBG Devel. Capital Ea. Europe Ltd., Jersey, Channel Islands, 1995—2002, also bd. dirs.; mng. dir. corp. devel. Metavante Corp. (W.O.S. Marshall & Isley Corp.), 2000—. Bd. dirs. DBG Osteuropa-Holding GmbH, Frankfurt. Em. European Venture Capital Assn. Avocation: travel. Home: 253 Pebble Creek Dr Barrington IL 60010-1367 Office: Metavante Corporate Development 4900 W Brown Deer Rd PO Box 240077 Milwaukee WI 53224-9004

O'NEILL, JAMES PAUL, psychiatrist; b. Elizabeth, NJ, Sept. 3, 1958; s. Paul James and Dorothy (Semansky) O'Neill; m. Patricia Ann Scott, Aug. 1989. BS in Biology, Niagara U., 1980; MD, U. N.E., Mex., 1984, U. Medicine & Dentistry NJ, 1985. Diplomate Am. Bd. Psychiatry and Neurology (added qualifications in addiction). Intern Jersey Shore Med. Ctr., Neptune, NJ, 1985-86; resident in psychiatry U. Medicine & Dentistry, Robert Wood Johnson Med. Sch., Piscataway, NJ, 1986-89, chief resident in psychiatry, 1988-89; pvt. practice Avon By The Sea, NJ, 1989—2003, Wall, NJ, 2003—. Attending psychiatrist Monmouth Med. Ctr., Long Branch, NJ; clin. asst. prof. psychiatry U. Medicine & Dentistry N.J., Robert Wood Johnson Med. Sch., Med. Coll. Pa., Drexel U. Coll. Medicine. Contbr. articles to profl. jours. Mem. com. Gov.'s coun. Addictions Managed Care Round Table, 1992—93; mem. adv. bd. Cath. Charities, Monmouth County, NJ. Named one of Am. Top Psychiatrists, Consumers Rsch. Coun. Am., 2003; NIMH fellow, 1988. Fellow: Am. Psychiatrist Assn. (disting. fellow); mem.: AMA (N.J. del. to resident physician sect. 1987—89, Physician Recognition award 1991, 1994, 1997, 2000, 2003), Med. Soc. NJ (del. Monmouth County 1990—), U.S. Life Saving Assn., Am. Soc. Addiction Medicine (officer N.J. chpt., cert.), Am. Acad. Addiction Psychiatry (N.J. chmn.), Monmouth Ocean County Psychiat. Assn. (pres.-elect 1998—99, pres. 1999—2000), NJ Psychiat. Assn. (founding pres. resident physician sect. 1987—88, treas. 2000—01, sr. v.p. 2001—02, pres.-elect 2002, pres. 2003—04, chmn. addictive disorders treatment com., counselor, officer governing coun.). Republican. Avocations: sports, travel. Office: 1540 Rt 138 Suite 307 Wall NJ 07719 Office Phone: 732-280-7555.

O'NEILL, JAMES R. aerospace transportation executive; BA, St. Anselm Coll.; exec. mgmt. courses, MIT. With Digital Equipment Corp., 1986—97; corp. officer, pres. govt. solutions Lucent Tech., 1997—2000; sr. v.p., gen. mgr. Oracle Svcs. Industries, 2000—02; pres. TASC bus. unit Northrop Grumman, 2002—04, corp. v.p., pres. info. tech. sector, 2004—. Office: 2411 Dulles Corner Park Ste 500 Herndon VA 20171-4644

O'NEILL, JEFF, professional hockey player; b. Richmond Hill, Ont., Can., Feb. 23, 1976; Ctr. Carolina Hurricanes, Morrisville, N.C., 1997—. Office: Carolina Hurricanes 1400 Edward Mills Rd Raleigh NC 27607-3624

O'NEILL, JOHN JOSEPH, JR., business consultant, former chemical company executive; b. N.Y.C., Sept. 13, 1919; s. John Joseph and Margaret (Patterson) O'N.; m. Irene Ray, Apr. 18, 1940; children— Anne, Mary (Mrs. George Schuler). BS in Chem. Engring, Mo. Sch. Mines, 1940, Chem. Engr., 1951. Research engr. Western Cartridge Co., 1940-49; with Olin Industries, Inc., 1949-60, dir. prodn. explosives operations, energy div., 1959-60; with Olin Mathieson Chem. Corp., 1960-71, asst. to pres., 1963-64, staff v.p. planning, 1964-65, v.p. comml. devel., chems. group, 1965-67, corporate v.p. plastics, 1967-70, corporate v.p. product diversification, 1970-71; cons., 1971-72; exec. v.p., chief operating officer Kleer-Vu Inc., N.Y.C., 1972-76; v.p. planning and devel. Vertac Consol., 1976-77; pres., chief exec. officer Vertac, Inc., 1977-78, cons., 1979-80, vice chmn. bd., chief oper. officer, 1980-81; cons., 1981—; pres. Jonco, Inc., 1986-89. Mem. bd. advisors Am. Express Sr. Card, 2001-2003. Contbr. articles to profl. jours.; patentee explosives, chemicals, ordnance items. Emeritus trustee St. Mary-of-Woods Coll., Terre Haute, Ind. Fellow Am. Inst. Chemists; mem. Am. Inst. Chem. Engring., Chemists Club (N.Y.C.). Clubs: Chemists (N.Y.C.). Home and Office: 7 Castlewood Ln PO Box 429 Pinehurst NC 28370-0429

O'NEILL, JOHN T. retired toy company executive; b. N.Y.C., Oct. 25, 1944; s. John and Rhoda (Dillon) O'N; m. Lois E. McGarry, Oct. 8, 1966; children: John, Margaret, Gregory, Brian. BS in Acctg., Providence Coll., 1962-66. Acct. Arthur Andersen & Co., Providence, 1966-67; ptnr. Peat Marwick, KPMG, Providence, 1970-84; mng. ptnr. Peat Marwick KPMG, 1984-87; sr. v.p. fin. Hasbro, Inc., Pawtucket, R.I., 1987-88, sr. v.p., CFO, 1988-89, exec. v.p., CFO, 1990—99; ret., 1999. Mem. pres. coun. Providence Coll.; bd. dirs., past pres. Jr. Achievement R.I.; pres., bd. dirs. Galaxy Funds. Trustee Women and Infants Hosp. R.I., Providence; treas., bd. dirs. R.I. Philharmonic Orch., Providence, C. of C.; chmn. Catholic Charity Fund, Providence. Capt. Med. Svc. Corps, U.S. Army, 1967-70. Decorated Bronze Star. Mem. AICPA, R.I. CPA Soc., Inst. Mgmt. Accts., Fin. Execs. Inst., Warwick Country Club, Hope Club, Dunes Club, Bonita Bay Club, Univ. Club. Avocations: golf, outdoors, art.

O'NEILL, JOSEPH DEAN, lawyer; b. Bayonne, N.J. s. Austin Joseph and Ann (Lynch) O'N. AB, Allegheny Coll.; JD, N.Y. Law Sch. Bar: N.J. 1968; cert. civil and criminal trial atty. Nat. Bd. Trial Advocacy. Pvt. practice, Vineland, N.J. Pres. Cumberland County Legal Aid Soc., Vineland, 1974-87. Contbr. articles to profl. publs. Assoc. counsel N.J. Jaycees. Recipient Outstanding Contbn. and Leadership award Nat. Assn. Criminal Def. Lawyers, 1978-79. Mem. Assn. Trial Lawyers Am. (pres. N.J. chpt. 1988-89, N.J. Legal PAC chmn. 1991-95), Cert. Trial Attys. (bd. dirs. 1988-90), Am. Bd. Trial Advocates (diplomate). Office: PO Box 847 30 W Chestnut Ave Vineland NJ 08360-5401 Office Phone: 856-692-2400.

O'NEILL, JOSEPH F. health science association administrator; Grad., U. Calif., San Francisco, U. Calif., Berkeley. Diplomate Am. Bd. Internal Medicine. Former med. staff Chase Brexton Clin., Baltimore; former assoc. adminstr. for AIDS Health Resources and Svcs. Adminstrn., 1997—2001; with faculty Johns Hopkins U. Sch. Medicine; dir. Office of Nat. AIDS Policy, Wash., DC, 2002—. Vol. physician Hopkins AIDS Clin. Office: Office of Nat AIDS Policy 736 Jackson Pl NW Washington DC 20503

O'NEILL, JUNE ELLENOFF, economist; b. N.Y.C., June 14, 1934; d. Louis and Matilda (Liebstein) Ellenoff; m. Sam Cohn, 1955 (div. 1961); 1 child, Peter; m. David Michael O'Neill, Dec. 24, 1964; 1 child, Amy. BA, Sarah Lawrence Coll., Bronxville, N.Y., 1955; PhD, Columbia U., 1970. Econs. instr. Temple U., Phila., 1965-68; rsch. assoc. Brookings Instn., Washington, 1968-71; sr. economist Pres.'s Coun. Econ. Advisors, Washington, 1971-76; chief human resources budget Congl. Budget Office, Washington, 1976-79; sr. rsch. assoc. The Urban Inst., Washington, 1979-86; dir. Office Policy and Rsch. U.S. Commn. Civil Rights, Washington, 1986-87; prof. econs. and fin., dir. Ctr. for Study Bus. and Govt. Baruch Coll., CUNY, 1987—; Morton Wollman Prof. Econs. Zicklin Sch. Bus. Baruch Coll., 1999—; dir. Congl. Budget Office U.S. Congress, Washington, 1995-99. Adj. scholar Am. Enterprise Inst., 1994-95, 99—; mem. Nat. Adv. Com., The Poverty Inst., U. Wis., 1988-95. Contbr. articles to profl. jours. Mem. Am. Econs. Assn. (v.p. 1998-99), Nat. Acad. Social Ins. Republican. Jewish. Home: 420 Riverside Dr New York NY 10025-7773 Office: CUNY Baruch Coll Ctr Study of Bus and Govt 17 Lexington Ave New York NY 10010-5518 E-mail: june_oneill@baruch.cuny.edu.

O'NEILL, KEVIN, professional athletics coach; b. Jan. 24, 1957; m. Chelsea Hoffman; 1 child. BA in Edn., McGill U., 1979; EdM, Marycrest Coll., 1983. Head coach North County C.C., Saranac, NY, 1980—82, Marycrest Coll., 1982; asst. coach U. Del., 1983—85, U. Tulsa, Okla., 1985, U. Ariz., 1986—89; head coach Marquette U., 1989—94, U. Tenn., 1994—97, Northwestern U., Ill., 1997—2000; asst. coach N.Y. Knicks, 2000—01, Detroit (Mich.) Pistons, 2001—03; head coach Toronto (Can.) Raptors, 2003—04.*

O'NEILL, MALCOLM R. aerospace executive; b. Chgo. m. Judy O'Neill. BS in Physics, DePaul U., 1962; MA in Physics, Rice U., 1970, PhD in Physics, 1975. Commd. U.S. Army, advanced through grades 2nd lt. to lt. gen., 1993, ret., 1996, dir. Ballistic Missile Def. Orgn., dep. dir. Strategic Def. Initiative Orgn., dir. Army Acquisition Corps, comdr. Army Lab. Command; dep. for program assessment and internat. coop. Office of the Asst. Sec. of the Army; project mgr. multiple launched rocket system U.S. Army, dep. project mgr. NATO patriot systems; program mgr. strategic fire control systems Def. Advanced Rsch. Projects Agy.; v.p. mission success, ops. and best practices in space systems Lockheed Martin, Bethesda, Md., 1996—99, v.p., chief tech. officer, 1999—. Mem. Aero. and Space Engring. Bd., NAS, Bd. Army Sci. and Tech., Air Force Sci. Adv. Bd., Space Dept. Adv. Bd. Named US Army Ordinance Hall of Fame. Fellow: AIAA; mem.: NAE, BOD Sandia Corp. Office: Lockheed Martin Corp 6801 Rockledge Dr Bethesda MD 20817

O'NEILL, MARY JANE, not-for-profit administrator, consultant; b. Detroit, Feb. 24, 1923; d. Frank Roger and Kathryn (Rice) Kilcoyne; m. Michael James O'Neill, May 31, 1948; children: Michael, Maureen, Kevin, John(dec.), Kathryn. PhB summa cum laude, U. Detroit, 1944; postgrad., U. Wis., 1949—50. Editor East Side Shopper, Detroit, 1939—45; club editor Detroit Free Press, 1945—48; reporter UP, Milw. and Madison, Wis., 1949; dir. pub. rels. Fairfax-Falls Church (Va.) Cmty. Chest, 1955—60; copy editor Falls Church Sun-Echo, 1958—60; freelance writer Washington, 1960—63; assoc. editor Med. World News, Washington, 1963—66; dir. publ. rels. Westchester Lighthouse, NY Assn. for Blind, 1967—71; dir. pub. edn. The Lighthouse, NYC, 1971—73, dir. pub. rels., 1973—80; exec. dir., CEO Eye-Bank for Sight Restoration, Inc., 1980—2000; ret., 2000. Mem. NY State Transplant Coun., 1991—2002; mem. instl. rsch. rev. bd. Manhattan Eye, Ear and Throat Hosp., 1981—; bd. dirs. NY Organ Donor Network, 1997—2003, Pro Mujer, 1997—2003, Found. of Women Execs. in Pub. Rels., 2000—. Named to Top 100 Irish Ams., Irish Am. Mag., 1999. Mem.: Pan Am. Eye Bank Assn. (bd. dirs. 1997—), Women Execs. in Pub. Rels. (dir. 1982—88, pres. 1986—87), Eye Bank Assn. Am. (lay adv. bd. 1981—83, dir. 1983—86, pres. N.E. Region 1993—96, exec. com. 1994—96, EBAA Heise award 1997), NY Acad. Scis., Women in Comm. (pres. N.Y. chpt. 1980—81), Cosmopolitan Club. E-mail: maryjaneoneill@aol.com.

O'NEILL, MICHAEL E. former bank executive; b. Oct. 31, 1946; BA in European Civilization, Princeton U., 1969; MBA, U. Va., 1974. With Continental Bank Corp (now BankAm. Corp.), 1974—2000, with internat. banking svcs., 1975-78, 2d v.p. multinat. banking svcs., 1978-79, v.p., 1979-80, mgr. multinat. banking svcs. Hong Kong, 1980-83, mgr. spl. industries svcs. in Europe London, 1983-84, U.K. country mgr., 1984-85, mng. dir., head mergers and acquisitions, 1989-90, chief of staff continental capital markets investments, 1990-92, CFO capital markets investments and trading sector, 1992-94, mgr. global equity investments U.S. corp. group, 1994-95, CFO, 1995-00; chmn., CEO Bank of Hawaii Corp. (formerly Pacific Century Financial Corp.), Honolulu, 2000—04; pvt. practice cons. to banks and corps., 1985-88. Lt. USMC, 1969-71.

O'NEILL, MICHAEL JAMES, editor, author; b. Detroit, Nov. 19, 1922; s. Michael J. and Ellen Mary (Dacey) O'Neill; m. Mary Jane Kilcoyne, May 31, 1948; children: Michael, Maureen, Kevin, Kathryn. BS, U. Detroit, 1946, LHD (hon.), 1977; postgrad., Fordham U., 1946—47. Writer Standard News Assn., N.Y.C., 1946—47; with UPI, 1947—56; Washington corr. N.Y. Daily News, 1956—66, asst. mng. editor, 1966—68, mng. editor, 1968—74, v.p., 1971—79, exec. editor, 1974—75, editor, 1975—82, exec. v.p., 1979—82, dir. Freelance writer; lectr., 1983—. Author (with L. Tanzer): The Kennedy Circle, 1961; author: (with K.M. Cahill) Preventive Diplomacy, 1996; author: China Today, 1976, Terrorist Spectaculars: Should TV Coverage Be Curbed, 1986, The Roar of the Crowd, How TV and People Power are Changing the World, 1993. Mem. Nat. Adv. Coun. Health Professions Edn., 1967—71; chmn. Fund of City of N.Y., 2003—. With U.S. Army, 1943—45, ETO. Decorated Bronze Star; recipient Nat. Affairs Reporting award, Nat. Headliner's, 1956. Mem.: Coun. Fgn. Rels., Am. Soc. Newspaper Editors (pres. 1981—82), Overseas Writers (pres. 1965), Century Club (N.Y.C. chpt.). Address: 23 Cayuga Rd Scarsdale NY 10583-6941

O'NEILL, PAUL HENRY, former government official; b. St. Louis, Dec. 4, 1935; s. John Paul and Gaynald Elsie (Irvin) O'N.; m. Nancy Jo Wolfe, Sept. 4, 1955; children: Patricia, Margaret, Julie, Paul Henry. BA, Fresno State Coll., 1960; Haynes Found. fellow, Claremont Grad. Sch., 1960-61; postgrad., George Washington U., 1962-65; MPA, Ind. U., 1966; hon. degree, Clarkson U., 1993, Edinboro U., 1997, California U. Pa., 1998, Duquesne U., 1999, Calif. State U., Fresno, 1999. Site engr. Morrison-Knudsen, Inc., Anchorage, 1955-57; systems analyst VA, Washington, 1961-66; budget examiner Bur. of Budget, Washington, 1967-69; chief human resources program div. U.S. Govt. Office of Mgmt. and Budget, Washington, 1969-70, asst. dir., 1971-72, assoc. dir., 1973-74, dep. dir., 1974-77; v.p. Internat. Paper Co., N.Y.C., 1977-81, sr. v.p., 1981-85, pres., dir., 1985-87; CEO Alcoa Inc., Pitts., 1987-99, chmn., 1987-2000; founding co-chair Pittsburgh Regional Healthcare Initiative, 1997—; sec. U.S. Dept. Treasury, Washington, 2001—02; spl. advisor The Blackstone Group, L.P., New York, 2003—. Chmn. Pres.'s Edn. Policy Adv. Com., 1989—92. Bd. dirs. Gerald R. Ford Found., 1981—. Recipient Nat. Inst. Pub. Affairs Career Edn. award, 1965, William A. Jump Meritorious award, 1971; Fellow Nat. Inst. Pub. Affairs, 1966. Mem. Nat. Acad. Social Ins. (founding mem.), Inst. Internat. Econs., Mgmt. Republican. Methodist. Office: Ste 100 One North Shore Ctr Pittsburgh PA 15212

O'NEILL, PAUL JOHN, retired psychology educator; b. Taunton, Mass., Apr. 12, 1936; s. Clarence Bernard and Edna Mary (Burke) O'N.; 1 child, Maureen Kelly O'Neill. BA, St. Bonaventure (N.Y.) U., 1960; MA, Boston U., 1961; EdD, U. Ga., 1973. Lic. psychologist. Prof. psychology Jackson (Miss.) State U., 1972-93, dir. critical thinking and outcome measures program, 1987-93. Contbr. articles to profl. jours. With U.S. Army, 1954-56, Germany. Home: 7005 Copper Cv Ridgeland MS 39157-1044 E-mail: pj31957@yahoo.com.

O'NEILL, PHILIP DANIEL, JR., lawyer, educator; b. Boston, Sept. 19, 1951; s. Philip Daniel Sr. and Alice Maureen (Driscoll) O'N.; m. Lisa G. Arrowood, June 25, 1983; children: Alexander Edwin, Sean Matthew, Madeleine Clarice. BA, Hamilton Coll., 1973; JD cum laude, Boston Coll., 1977. Bar: Mass. 1977, N.Y. 1985, R.I. 1988. Assoc. Hale and Dorr, Boston, 1977-83, ptnr., 1983-87, Edwards & Angell, Boston, 1987—. Adj. rsch. fellow John F. Kennedy Sch. Govt., Ctr. for Sci. and Internat. Affairs Harvard U., 1983—86; adj. prof. law Boston U., 1992, 2001—, Boston Coll., 1988—; Nomura lectr. in law Harvard Law Sch., 2004—; cons. Arms Control and Disarmament Agy. U.S. Dept. Def., 1983—84; panelist in internat. and domestic legal programs; arbitrator in field; lectr. in field. Contbr. chpts. to books and articles to profl. jours. Fellow Chartered Inst. Arbitrators (Eng.); mem. ABA (vice chmn. nat. security and arms control com. 2002—), Internat. Law Assn. (chmn. Am. br. arbitration com. 1985-89, rep. internat. arbitration com. 1989—), Boston Bar Assn. (chmn. internat. law sect. 1994-96, past chmn. internat. litig. and arbitration com.), Am. Soc. Internat. Law. Home: 11 Blackburnian Rd Lincoln MA 01773-4317 Office: Edwards & Angell 101 Federal St Fl 23 Boston MA 02110-1800

O'NEILL, ROBERT CHARLES, inventor, consultant; b. Buffalo, Dec. 3, 1923; s. Albert T. and Helen (Lynch) O'N.; m. Agnes Balischak; 1 dau., Eileen Anne. BS in Chemistry, Rensselaer Poly. Inst., 1945; PhD in Organic Chemistry, MIT, 1950. Sr. chemist Merck & Co., Inc., Rahway, N.J., 1950-56, marketing devel. specialist, 1956-58; v.p. Stauffer Pharms. div. Stauffer Chem. Co., N.Y.C., 1958-61; v.p., dir R & D Cooper Labs., Inc., 1961-70, exec. v.p., 1970-76, gen. mgr., 1975-76, pres., 1976-77, also dir. Cons., inventor, 1977—. Contbr. articles to profl. jours.; patentee in field. Served with USNR, 1943-46. Mem. Am. Chem. Soc., Chemists Club N.Y. Home: 10 Whitlaw Close Chappaqua NY 10514-1008

O'NEILL, ROBERT EDWARD, business journal editor; b. N.Y.C., Aug. 30, 1925; s. Joseph Michael and Ethel Agnes (Seymour) O'N.; m. Phyllis Ann Schreck, Apr. 19, 1952; children: Keith, Kathy, Kim, Karen. BA in Journalism, Syracuse (N.Y.) U., 1950. Reporter Southeasterner, Long Island, N.Y., 1950-51; rep. Bklyn. Daily, 1952; asso. editor Progressive Grocer, N.Y.C., 1952-62, sr. editor, 1962-69, exec. editor, 1970-86; editor in chief Monitor mag., Stamford, Conn., 1986-92; editorial dir. Progressive Grocer. Dir. Sopro Foods, Inc. Contbg. author/editor: Foodtown Study, 1954, Super Valu Study, 1957, Dillon Study, 1959, Colonial Study, 1961, Outstanding New Super Markets, 1961, Consumer Dynamics, 1963, A & P Study, 1970, Merchandising in Action, 1972, Consumer Behavior Study, 1976, Brand Power Study, 1977. Served with USN, 1944-47. Mem. Am. Bus. Press (editorial com. 1974-75, co-winner, Jesse H. Neal award 1961, 66, 74, 89, 90, Points of Light award 1991), Glacier Hills Assn. (pres. 1964-66), Sigma Delta Chi. Clubs: Overseas Press. Home: 67 Moraine Rd Morris Plains NJ 07950-2752 Office: O'Neill Assocs 67 Moraine Rd Morris Plains NJ 07950-2752 E-mail: lefcadio@optonline.net.

O'NEILL, ROBERT WILLIAM, marketing executive; b. Syosset, N.Y., Dec. 28, 1964; s. Robert John and Lorraine Ann (Lutter) O'N.; m. Marianne Beaman, June 19, 1993. BS in Fin., Providence Coll., 1987; MBA, Babson Coll., 1998. Dir. Bishop Svcs., Boston, 1991-93; v.p. Fidelity Investments, Boston, 1994—. Pres., cons. Robert O'Neill & Assocs., N.Y.C., 1991—. Regional coord. Reagan-Bush campaign, Providence, R.I., 1984-85, student coord. gubernatorial campaign, Providence, 1984-85; vol. VA Homeless Shelter, Boston, 1992-93; mem. InnerCity Scholarship Fund. Served to capt. U.S. Army, 1987-91, Saudi Arabia, Germany. Decorated Bronze Star, commendation medals (3), achievement medals (3); recipient Cmty. Svc. medal Westchester County, N.Y., 1991. Mem. Assn. for Investment Mgmt. and Rsch. (assoc.), Securities Industry Assn., Am. Legion, Boston C. of C. (new bus. com.), Tau Pi. Republican.

O'NEILL, RUSSELL RICHARD, engineering educator; b. Chgo., June 6, 1916; s. Dennis Alysious and Florence Agnes (Mathurin) O'N.; m. Margaret Bock, Dec. 15, 1939; children: Richard A., John R.; m. Sallie Boyd, June 30, 1967. BSME, U. Calif., Berkeley, MSME, 1940; PhD, UCLA, 1956. Registered profl. engr., Calif. Design engr. Dowell, Inc., Midland, Mich., 1940-41; design engr. Dow Chem. Co., Midland, 1941-44, Airesearch Mfg. Co., Los Angeles, 1944-46; lectr. engring. UCLA, 1946-56, prof. engring., 1956, asst. dean engring., 1956-61, assoc. dean, 1961-73, acting dean, 1965-66, dean, 1974-83, dean emeritus, 1983—; staff engr. NAS-NRC, 1954; dir. Data Design Labs., 1977-86, dir. emeritus, 1986—. Mem. engring. task force Space Era Edn. Study Fla. Bd. Control, 1963; mem. regional Export Expansion Coun. Dept. Commerce, 1960-66, Los Angeles Mayor's Space Adv. Com., 1964-69; mem. Maritime Transp. Rsch. Bd., 1974-81; bd. advisers Naval Postgrad. Sch., 1976-84; mem. Nat. Nuclear Accreditation Bd., 1983-88; mem. accrediting bd. Dept. Energy, 1992—. Trustee West Coast U., 1981-90; bd. dirs. Western region United Way, 1982-90. Mem. NAE, Am. Soc. Engring. Edn., Sigma Xi, Tau Beta Pi. Home: 15430 Longbow Dr Sherman Oaks CA 91403-4910 Office: UCLA HSSEAS Box 951600 Los Angeles CA 90095-1600 Office Phone: 310-825-2977. E-mail: russ@ea.ucla.edu.

O'NEILL, SALLIE BOYD, educational consultant, business owner, sculptor; b. Ft. Lauderdale, Fla., Feb. 17, 1926; d. Howard Prindle and Sarah Frances (Clark) Boyd; AA, Stephens Coll., 1945; m. Roger H. Noden, July 8, 1945; children: Stephanie Ann Ballard, Ross Hopkins Noden; m. Russell R. O'Neill, June 30, 1967. Course coord. UCLA Extension, 1960-72, specialist continuing edn. dept. human devel., acad. appointment, 1972-83; pres. Learning Adventures, Inc., 1985-86; v.p., CFO The Learning Network, Inc., 1985-86; ednl. cons., 1986—; sculptor, 1987—. Bd. dirs. Everywoman's Village, Sherman Oaks, Calif., 1988-98, v.p. 1993-95. Mem. Women in Bus. (founding mem., v.p., bd. dirs. 1976-77, 86-87), UCLA Assn. Acad. Women, Calif. Art Club (sculpting patron). Democrat. Home: 15430 Longbow Dr Sherman Oaks CA 91403-4910

O'NEILL, SHEILA, principal; Prin. Cor Jesu Acad., St. Louis. Recipient Blue Ribbon award U.S. Dept. Edn., 1990-91. Office: Cor Jesu Acad 10230 Gravois Rd Saint Louis MO 63123-4099

O'NEILL, THOMAS J. (TOM O' NEILL), engineering company executive; b. Buffalo, July 22, 1952; AB, Dartmouth Coll., 1973, BE, 1974. With Parsons Brinckerhoff/Tudor, Atlanta, 1974-77, Tudor Engring. Co., Atlanta, 1978-92; pres., COO, CEO Parsons, Brinckerhoff, Quade, NYC, 1992—. Mem. Chief Executive Group, L.P., Montvale, NJ. Office: Parsons Brinckerhoff 1 Penn Plz Fl 2 New York NY 10119-0021 Office Phone: 212-465-5000. Office Fax: 212-465-5096.*

O'NEILL, THOMAS NEWMAN, JR., federal judge; b. Hanover, Pa., July 6, 1928; s. Thomas Newman and Emma (Cornpropst) O'N.; m. Jeanne M. Corr., Feb. 4, 1961; children: Caroline Jeanne, Thomas Newman, III, Ellen Gitt. AB magna cum laude, Catholic U. Am., 1950; LL.B. magna cum laude, U. Pa., 1953; postgrad. (Fulbright grantee), London Sch. Econs., 1955-56. Bar: Pa. 1954, U.S. Supreme Ct. 1959. Law clk. to Judge Herbert F. Goodrich U.S. Ct. Appeals (3d cir.), 1953-54; to Justice Harold H. Burton U.S. Supreme Ct., 1954-55; assoc. Montgomery, McCracken, Walker & Rhoads, Phila., 1956-63, ptnr., 1963-83; judge U.S. Dist. Ct. (ea. dist.) Pa., 1983—; counsel 1st and 2d Pa. Legis. Reapportionment Commns., 1971, 81. Lectr. U. Pa. Law Sch., 1973 Articles editor: U. Pa. Law Rev, 1952-53. Former trustee Lawyers Com. for Civil Rights Under Law; former mem. Gov.'s Trial Ct. Nominating Commn. for Phila. County; former mem. bd. overseers U. Pa. Mus. Fellow Am. Coll. Trial Lawyers; mem. Am. Law Inst. (life), Phila. Bar Assn. (chancellor 1976), Pa. Bar Assn. (gov. 1978-81), U. Pa. Law Alumni Soc. (pres. 1976-77), Pa. Conf. County Bar Officers (pres. 1981-82), Am. Inn of Ct. (founding chmn. U. Pa.), Order of Coif (pres. U. Pa. chpt. 1971-73), Merion Cricket Club, Edgemere Club, Broadacres Trouting Assn., Phi Beta Kappa, Phi Eta Sigma. Office: US Dist Ct 4007 US Courthouse 601 Market St Philadelphia PA 19106-1713

O'NEILL, WILLIAM LAWRENCE, history professor; b. Big Rapids, Mich., Apr. 18, 1935; s. John Patrick and Helen Elizabeth (Marsh) O'N.; m. Elizabeth Carol Knollmueller, Aug. 20, 1960; children: Cassandra Leigh, Catherine Lorraine. AB, U. Mich., 1957; MA, U. Calif., Berkeley, 1958, PhD, 1963. Asst. prof. history U. Colo., 1964-66; asst. prof. U. Wis., 1966-69, asso. prof., 1969-71; prof. Rutgers U., New Brunswick, N.J., 1971—. Vis. asst. prof. U. Pitts., 1963-64; vis. asso. prof. U. Pa., 1969-70 Author: Divorce in the Progressive Era, 1967, Everyone Was Brave: The Rise and Fall of Feminism in America, 1969, rev. and repub. as: Feminism in America: A History, 1989, Coming Apart: An Informal History of America in the 1960's, 1971, The Last Romantic: A Life of Max Eastman, 1978, 2d edit., 1991, A Better World: The Great Schism: Stalinism and the American Intellectuals, 1982, repub. as: A Better World: Stalinism and the American Intellectuals, 1989, American High: The Years of Confidence, 1945-60, 1986, A Democracy at War: America's Fight at Home and Abroad in World War II, 1993. Nat. Endowment Humanities fellow, 1979-80 Mem. Am. Hist. Assn., Hist. Soc. Office: Rutgers U Dept History New Brunswick NJ 08903 Personal E-mail: wlohp@aol.com.

O'NEILL, WILLIAM WALTER, physician, educator; b. Nov. 24, 1951; m. Carol; children: Brian, Katie, Julie, Molly. BS, U. Mich., 1972; MD, Wayne State U., 1977. Diplomate Am. Bd. Internal Medicine, Am. Bd. Cardiology. Intern in internal medicine U. Wis., Madison, 1977-78; resident in internal medicine Wayne State U., Detroit, 1978-80; fellow U. Mich., Ann Arbor, 1980-82, instr. internal medicine, 1982-83, asst. prof., 1983-86, assoc. prof., 1986-87; dir. cardiac catheterization lab. U. Mich. Hosp., Ann Arbor, 1984-87; dir. divsn. cardiology William Beaumont Hosp., Royal Oak, Mich., 1987—. Attending cardiologist VA Hosp., Ann Arbor, 1982-90; chmn. govt. rels. subcom. Nat. Cardiovasc. Network; rsch. peer rev. com. Am. Heart Assn. Mich., 1988-89; chmn. publs. com. Mansfield Scientific Balloon Valvuloplasty Registry; bd. govs. William Beaumont Hosp. Rsch. Inst.; presenter in field. Author: Myocardial Revascularization by Coronary Angioplasty or Bypass Surgery During MI in Acute Myocardial Infarction: New Approaches to Evaluation and Therapy, 1986, (chpt.) Acute Coronary Intervention, 1987, Current Perspective in Coronary Care, 1987, Interventional Cardiovascular Medicine, 1994, Acute Coronary Care, 2d edit., 1995; co-author: (chpts.) Cardiovascular Review, 6th edit., 1985, 8th edit., 1987, Tissue Plasminogen Activator in Thrombolytic Therapy, 1987, Techniques and Applications in Interventional Cardiology, 1991, Atherectomy, 1992, Emergency Medicine: A Comprehensive Study Guide, 3d edit., 1992, Adjunctive Therapy for Acute Myocardial Infarction, 1992, Manual of Interventional CArdiology, 1992, Cura Intensiva Cardiologica, Primary Coronary Angioplasty in Acute Myocardial Infarction; author, co-author: (chpt.) Interventional Cardiovascular Medicine, 1994; editl. cons. Jour. Intervention Cardiology; mem. editl. bd. Catheterization Cardiovasc. Diagnosis; contbr. over 400 articles to profl. publs. Grantee Smith/Kline Beecham, 1989-90, 90—, Advanced Cardiovasc. Sys., Inc., 1988-90, 90—, Midwest Heart Rsch. Found., Abbott Labs., 1990—, Duke U., 1990—, William Beaumont Hosp. Rsch. Inst., 1990—. Fellow Am. Coll. Cardiology (chpt. sec.-treas. 1993-94, reimbursement com.), Am. Coll. Chest Physicians, Coun. Clin. Cardiology; mem. AMA, ACP, Internat. Andreas Gruentzig Soc. Office: William Beaumont Hosp 3601 W 13 Mile Rd Royal Oak MI 48073-6712

O'NEILL MCGIVERN, DIANE, nursing educator, educator; PhD, NYU, 1972. RN. Head divsn. nursing NYU, N.Y.C., Erline Perkins McGriff prof. nursing, head divsn. nursing, vice chancellor Bd. Regents, 1999—. Fellow AAN. Office: NYU Sch Edn Divsn Nursing 50 W 4th St Rm 429 New York NY 10012-1156

ONESTI, SILVIO JOSEPH, psychiatrist; b. San Francisco, Jan. 3, 1926; s. Silvio Joseph and Johanna (Kristoffy) O.; m. Jean Thomas, May 12, 1956; children: Sally Joanna, Stephen Thomas. BS, Stanford U., 1947; MD, McGill U., 1951. Diplomate Am. Bd. Psychiatry and Neurology. Instr. pediatrics Yale Med. Sch., New Haven, 1956-58; career tchr. psychiatry NIMH, Harvard Med. Sch., Beth Israel Hosp., Boston, 1963-65; head child psychiatry unit Beth Israel Hosp., Boston, 1965-73; dir. child and adolescent psychiatry McLean Hosp., Belmont, Mass., 1973-91, dir. Hall-Mercer Ctr. for children and adolescents, 1973-91; dir. child and adolescent psychiat. tng., 1973-92; dir. clin. svcs. McLean Hosp., Belmont, 1981-83; asst. prof. psychiatry Harvard Med. Sch., Boston, 1969—. Faculty Boston Psychoanalytic Soc. and Inst. Inc., Boston, 1971-81. Contbr. articles to profl. jours. With USN, 1944-46. Fellow Am. Psychiat. Assn., Am. Acad. Child and Adolescent Psychiatry, Am. Coll. Psychiatrists; mem. Group for Advancement of Psychiatry (fellow 1959-61, bd. dirs. 1987-89), Boston Psychoanalytic Soc. and Inst. Inc., Mass. Med. Soc., Alpha Omega Alpha. Home: 4 Gray Gdns W Cambridge MA 02138-2312 Office: McLean Hosp 115 Mill St Belmont MA 02478-1048 Office Phone: 617-855-2801.

ONETTO, MARC, manufacturing executive; BA in Econs., U. Lyon, France; MS in Engring., Ecole Centrale de Lyon; MS in Indsl. Adminstrn., Carnegie Mellon U. With Exxon Corp., 1976—88; with European Ops. GE, 1988—2003; exec. v.p. Worldwide Ops. Solectron Corp., Milpitas, Calif., 2003—. Office: Solectron Corp 777 Gibraltar Dr Milpitas CA 95035

ONG, CHEE-MUN, engineering educator; b. Ipoh, Perak, Malaysia, Nov. 23, 1944; came to U.S., 1978; s. Chin-Kok Ong and Say-Choo Yeoh; m. Penelope Li-Lok, July 17, 1971; children: Yi-Ping, Yi-Ching, Chiew-Jen. BE with honors, U. Malaya, 1967; MS, Purdue U., 1968, PhD, 1974. Registered profl. engr. Ind., Eng. Plant engr. Guinness Brewery, Malaysia, 1967; asst. lectr. U. Malaysia, 1968-73, lectr., 1976-78; rsch. asst. Purdue U., West Lafayette, Ind., 1973-74, vis. asst. prof., 1975-76, asst. prof., 1978-81, assoc. prof., 1981-85, prof., 1985—. Cons. SIMTECH, West Lafayette, 1978-85, L.A. Water and Power Co., 1986-88, Caterpillar, 1993-94, Franklin Electric, 1997-98, P Plus Corp., 1999-, PPlus, 1999-, Unibus, 2002. Author: Dynamic Simulation of Electric Machinery, 1998; contbr. articles to jours. in field. Fulbright-Hayes scholar, 1967-68; UNESCO fellow, 1969-70. Fellow Inst. Elec. Engrs. (U.K.); mem. IEEE (sr.). Avocations: gardening, fishing, reading. Office: Purdue U Dept Elec/Computer Engring West Lafayette IN 47907-1285 Business E-Mail: ong@ecn.purdue.edu.

ONG, GEORGE E. lawyer; b. Oakland, Calif., Jan. 6, 1936; s. Chester T.H. Ong and Lee Foon Young; m. Jennie Yep, Aug. 29, 1965; children: Gail, Lori, Ryan. BA, Stanford U., 1958; JD, Golden Gate U., 1969. Bar: Calif. Sr. trial dep. Alameda County Dist. Atty.'s Office, Oakland, 1971-79; pvt. practice, Oakland, 1979—. Adv. dir. Golden Coin Savs. Bank, Oakland, 1985-88. Scoutmaster Boy Scouts Am., Piedmont, Calif., 1990—, bd. dirs. Piedmont coun. 1993—; lectr. youth leadership tng. Chinese Am. Citizens Alliance, Oakland, 1994—. Recipient svc. award Lions Club, Oaklandt, 1989; Disting. Scouter award Piedmont coun. Boy Scouts Am., 1991, award of merit for scoutmasters Nat. coun., 1996. Mem. Asian Am. Bar Assn., Oakland County Bar Assn. (appreciation award 1981), Oakland Chinatown C. of C. (pres. 1988, svc. award 1990). Avocations: scouting, skiing, boating, youth. Office: 701 Franklin St Oakland CA 94607-3931 Office Phone: 510-465-1234.

ONG, JOHN DOYLE, ambassador, retired manufacturing executive; b. Uhrichsville, Ohio, Sept. 29, 1933; s. Louis Brosee and Mary Ellen (Liggett) O.; m. Mary Lee Schupp, July 20, 1957; children: John Francis Harlan, Richard Penn Blackburn, Mary Katherine Caine. BA, MA, Ohio State U., 1954; LLB, Harvard, 1957; LHD, Kent State U., 1982; HHD (hon.), Ohio State U., 1996; LHD (hon.), U. Akron, 1996; D in pub. svc. (hon.), SD State U., 2002. Bar: Ohio 1958. Asst. counsel B.F. Goodrich Co., Akron, 1961-66, group v.p., 1972-73, exec. v.p., 1973-74, vice chmn., 1974-75, pres., dir., 1975-77, pres., chief operating officer, dir., 1978-79, chmn. bd., pres., chief exec. officer, 1979-84, chmn. bd., chief exec. officer, 1984-96, chmn. bd., 1996-97, chmn. emeritus, 1997—; U.S. amb. to The Kingdom of Norway, 2002—. V.p. exploring Great Trail coun. Boy Scouts Am., 1974-77; bd. dirs. Nat. Alliance of Bus., 1981-84; trustee Mus. Arts Assn., Cleve., Bexley Hall Sem., 1974-81, Case Western Res. U., 1980-92, Ft. Ligonier Assn., 1997-, Kenyon Coll., 1983-85, Hudson (Ohio) Libr. and Hist. Soc., pres., 1971-72, Western Res. Acad., Hudson, 1975-95, pres. bd. trustees, 1977-95; nat. trustee Nat. Symphony Orch., 1975-83, John S. and James L. Knight Found., 1995-2002; mem. bus. adv. com. Transp. Ctr. Northwestern U., 1975-78, Carnegie-Mellon U. Grad. Sch. Indsl. Adminstrn., 1978-83; life trustee U. Chgo., 1991—; chmn. Ohio Bus. Roundtable, 1994-97; trustee Ohio Hist. Soc., 1998-2002; dir. New Amn. Schs., 1991, chmn., 1998-2002. Mem. Ohio Bar Assn. (bd. govs. corp. counsel sect. 1962-74, chmn. 1970), Rubber Mfrs. Assn. (bd. dirs. 1974-84), Chem. Mfrs. Assn. (bd. dirs. 1988-91, 94-97), Conf. Bd., Bus. Roundtable (chmn. 1992-94), Bus. Coun., Portage Country Club, Union Club, Links, Union League, Ottawa Shooting Club, Met. Club, Rolling Rock Club, Castalia Trout Club, Phi Beta Kappa, Phi Alpha Theta. Episcopalian. Home: 230 Aurora St Hudson OH 44236-2941 Office: United States Embassy Norway Drammensveien 18 0244 Oslo Norway Home: Indian Creek Farm Stahlstown PA 15687

ONG, LAUREEN E. broadcast executive; b. NYC, Sept. 24, 1952; d. Douglas and Marion (Chin) Ong; m. Richard Ong. BA in math. and speech theater arts, Montclair State Coll., N.J., 1974; MA in comm. in comm., Columbia U., N.Y.C., 1977. Mgr. sales MTM TV Distbn. Group; acct. exec. WPVI-TV, Phila.; sales mgr. KRON-TV, San Francisco; sr. exec. Rainbow Programming, 1994—96; v.p. and gen. mgr. KSAZ-TV, Phoenix, 1997—98, WTTG-TV, Washington, 1998—2000; pres. and CEO Nat. Geog. Channel, Washington, 2000—. Mem.: Cable TV Adminstrv. and Mktg. Execs., Women in Comm., Women in Cable, Nat. Cable TV Assn. Lutheran. Office: Nat Geog Channel 1145 17th St NW Washington DC 20036

ONG, MICHAEL KING, mathematician, educator, bank executive; b. Manila, Philippines, Dec. 16, 1955; s. Sanchez and Remedios (King) Ong. BS in Physics cum laude, U. Philippines, 1978; MA in Physics, SUNY, Stony Brook, 1979, MS in Applied Math., 1981, PhD in Applied Math., 1984. Asst. prof. Bowdoin Coll., Brunswick, Maine, 1984-91; sr. mathematician, fin. analyst Chgo. Rsch. & Trading Group Ltd., 1990-92; v.p., sr. rsch. analyst First Chgo. NBD, 1993-94; head market risk analysis unit First Chgo. Corp., 1994—, 1st v.p., head corp. rsch. unit, 1996-97; sr. v.p., head treasury bus. rsch. ABN-AMRO Bank, Chgo., 1997—, head of enterprise risk mgmt., 1999-2000; exec. v.p., chief risk officer Credit Agricole Indosuez, 2000—03; prof. fin. Stuart Grad. Sch. Bus. Ill. Inst. Tech., 2003—, dir. fin. program, exec. dir. Ctr. for Fin. Markets, Stuart Grad. Sch. Bus., 2003—. Adj. prof. fin. markets and trading program Stuart Sch. Bus. Ill. Inst. Tech., 1990—, bd. dirs. Carr Global Advs., 2000—. Author: Internal Credit Risk Models--Performance Measurement and Capital Allocation, 1999, Credit Ratings - Methodologies, Rationale and Default Risk, 2002, The Basel Handbook--A Guide for Financial Practitioners, 2004; editor-in-chief Jour. Credit Risk; mem. editl. bd. Jour. Fin. Regulation & Compliance, Jour. of RISK; editor Jour. of Global Financial Markets; contbr. articles to profl. jours. Mem. Am. Fin. Assn., Am. Math. Soc., Math. Assn. Am., Soc. Indsl. and Applied Math., Consortium for Math. and Its Applications, Am. Phys. Soc., Phi Kappa Phi. Avocations: writing, singing, travel, painting. Home: 2650 N Lakeview Ave Apt 4106 Chicago IL 60614-1833 Office: Ill Inst Tech Stuart Grad Sch Bus 565 W Adams St Chicago IL 60661-3691 Office Phone: 312-906-6568. Personal E-mail: michaelong123@aol.com. Business E-Mail: ong@stuart.iit.edu.

ONGAN, NILGÜN ERDAL, decorator, architect, artist; b. Istanbul, Turkey, July 5, 1935; d. Galip and Fatma Zehra (Aliye) Erdal; m. Onay Ongan, July 18, 1981. Degree in interior arch., Fine Arts Acad., Istanbul, Turkey, 1957; Master degree (hon.), Rome Fine Arts Acad., 1963. Decorator TRT Ankara, 1968-80; asst. dir. TRT Istanbul, 1980-92; head decor and fgn. svcs. Interstar, Istanbul, 1992-95; dir. Kanal D, Istanbul, 1995-96; lectr. faculty comm., radio and TV dept. Istanbul U.; dir. HBB TV, Istanbul, 1996. Dir. decor, graphics chief Istanbul Turkish Radio TV, 1974. Decorator for theatrical and operatic prodns., including Hamlet, Rome, 1963, Falstaff, Rome, 1963, Gehrden Castle, Dortmund, Germany, 1963, (film) Bible, Rome, 1966; one-woman shows at Ankara Am. Culture Ctr., 1974, Istanbul Marmara Etap Hotel, 1979, Istanbul Italian Culture Ctr., 1990, Mandir Della Pace Congress, Assisi, Italy, 2000; group exhbns. include Club Internat. de Feminin, Paris, Vichy, Frankfurt, 1966, anniversary Fine Arts Acad. Soc., 2002, Galery Temore, 2002, Internat. Film Festival Antalya, 2002; represented in permanent collections in N.Am., Peru, Italy, Switzerland; designer oldstyle Turkish coffeehouse. Recipient Hon. Plaquette of High Merit, Turkish Radio TV, 1986. Mem. Fine Arts Soc., Fine Arts Acad. (mem. grads. assembly), Interior Architects Soc. Avocations: ceramics, drawing and sketching, decorating. Home: Kucuk Bebek Cad Nurhan Apt No 51/7 Kucuk Bebek Istanbul 80810 Turkey

ONISHI, KOSUKE, trading company executive; b. Ashiya, Japan, July 28, 1963; s. Hideo and Setsuko (Takano) O.; m. Masami Wake, Sept. 17, 1993. BA, MA, U. Chgo., 1987. Assistance mgr. Mitsubishi Corp., Tokyo, 1987-98; dir. Azabu Sogo Jimsho, 1998—. Author: Preppy Life, 1991. Avocation: driving. Mailing: 115 E 57th St Fl 11 New York NY 10022-2120

ONISHI, YASUO, environmental researcher; b. Osaka, Japan, Jan. 25, 1943; came to U.S., 1969; s. Osamu and Tokiko (Domukai) O.; m. Esther Anna Stronczek, Jan 27, 1972; children: Anna Tokiko and Lisa Michiyo. BS, U. Osaka Prefecture, 1967, MS, 1969; PhD, U. Iowa, 1972. Rsch. engr. U. Iowa, Iowa City, 1972-74; sr. rsch. engr. Battelle Meml. Inst., Richland, Wash., 1974-77, staff engr., 1977-2001, mgr. rsch. program office, 1984-92, chief scientist, 2001—. Adj. grad. faculty Wash. State U., Tri-Cities, 1993—. Co-author: Principles of Health Risk Assessment, 1985, others; contbr. articles to profl. jours.; featured on TV program NOVA. Recipient Best Platform Presentation award ASTM, 1979. Mem.: IAEA (advisor on environ. issues), NAS (com. mem. "Understanding Oil Spill Dispersants: Efficacy and Effects" 2004—), ASCE (chmn. task com. 1986—96), Nat. Coun. Radiation Protection and Measurements (adj., task com. 1983—96); U.S. coord. water and soil assessment bilateral joint work on Chernobyl nuclear accident, Sigma Xi. Lutheran. Achievements include rsch. in bilateral USA/former USSR joint soil and environmental assessment of Chernobyl accident. Home: 144 Spengler Rd Richland WA 99352-1971 Office: Pacific NW Nat Labs Batelle Blvd Richland WA 99352

ONKEN, GEORGE MARCELLUS, retired lawyer; b. Bklyn., Aug. 15, 1913; s. William Henry and Lillian Charlotte (Dawe) O.; m. Mildred Ann Tausch, Dec. 13, 1958; children: Jane Elizabeth, Nancy Catherine. AB, Princeton U., 1936; LLB, Columbia U., 1948; LLM, NYU, 1952. Bar: N.Y. 1949. Asst. to pres. Welsbach Engring. and Mgmt. Corp., Phila., 1939-43; mem. legal staff L.I. R.R., 1949-78, gen. counsel, 1963-78, v.p., 1966-78, sec., 1968-78. Bd. dirs. Orphan Asylum Soc., Bklyn., 1958-2004, YMCA Greater N.Y., 1963-80, Pop Warner Little League, 1976-78; bd. mgrs. Pa. R.R. br. YMCA, N.Y.C., 1957-80, chmn., 1967-80; trustee Bklyn. YWCA, 1976-92. Lt. (j.g.) USNR, 1943-46. Recipient Man of Year award YMCA, 1977; Outstanding Svc. award Bklyn. Chpt. ARC Greater N.Y., 1994, Lifetime Commitment award Brookwood Child Care, 1998. Republican. Episcopalian (vestry 1958-64, 76-85). Clubs: Union League (N.Y.C.), Univ. (N.Y.C.), Church (N.Y.C.); Ihpetonga (Bklyn.). Home: 215 Adams St Brooklyn NY 11201-2856

ONLEY, SISTER FRANCESCA, academic administrator; Prin. Nazareth Acad. H.S.; asst. to pres. Holy Family U., Phila., 1980—81, pres., 1981—. Chair Internat. Assn. of U. Pres., UN Commn. on Disarmament Edn., Conflict Resolution and Peace. Office: Holy Family U Grant and Franklin Aves Philadelphia PA 19114

ONO, HIROMI, sociologist, researcher; d. Hirohisa and Mieko Ono. BA, Reed Coll., 1984; PhD, UCLA, 1996. Asst. rsch. scientist Inst. Social Rsch., Ann Arbor, Mich., 1998—. Abe fellow, Ctr. Global Partnership, Coun. Learned Soc., 2002—03. Achievements include research in studies of women's economic status and marriage. Office: Inst Social Rsch 426 Thompson St Ann Arbor MI 48106

ONO, KEN, mathematician, educator; b. Phila., Mar. 20, 1968; s. Sachiko Ono; m. Erika Dawn Anderson; children: Aspen, Sage. PhD, UCLA, 1993. Mem. Sch. Math., Inst. for Advanced Study, Princeton, NJ; prof. math. Pa. State U., University Park; prof. dept. math. U. Wis., Madison, 1997—. Recipient Young Investigator award, Nat. Security Agy., 1997, Career award, NSF, 1998, Presdl. Early Career award, Pre Clinton, 2000; fellow David and Lucile Packard fellow, David and Lucile Packard Found., 1999, Alfred P. Sloan Rsch. fellow, Alfred P. Sloan Found., 1999, H. I. Romnes fellow, U. Wis., 2002. Office: U Wis Dept Math 480 Lincoln Madison WI 53706

ONO, YOKO, conceptual artist, singer, recording artist; b. Tokyo, Feb. 18, 1933; U.S. citizen; m. Toshi Ichiyanagi, 1957 (div.); m. Tony Cox, 1964 (div.), children: Kyoko Chan; m. John Ono Lennon, Mar. 20, 1969 (dec. Dec. 8, 1980); children: Sean Taro. Student, Peers' Sch., Gakushuin U., Tokyo, Sarah Lawrence Coll., Harvard U.; PhD (hon.), Art Inst. Of Chicago, 1997, Liverpool U., 2001, Bard College, 2002. One-woman shows include Alchemical Wedding, Albert Hall, London, 1967, Evening with Yoko Ono, Birmingham, 1968, Event, U. Wales, 1969, Everson Mus., Syracuse, N.Y., 1971, Yoko Ono: Objects, Films, Whitney Museum of Amer. Art, 1989, Yoko Ono: A Piece of Sky, Galleria Stefania Miscetti, Rome, 1993, Endangered Species, Wacoal Art Center/Spiral Garden, Tokyo, 1993, Yoko Ono and Fluxus, Royal Festival Hall, South Bank Centre, London, 1997, Have You Seen The Horizon Lately?, Museum Of Modern Art, Oxford, 1997, Open Window, Umm El-Fahem, Israel, 2000, YES Yoko Ono, Japan Society, 2001, My Mommy Was Beautiful, Shoshana Wayne Gallery, Santa Monica, 2002, Yoko Ono Women's Room, Musée d'Art moderne de la Ville de Paris, 2003, Yoko Ono: Odyssey of a Cockroach, Institute of Contemporary Arts, London, 2004; recorded albums: (with John Ono Lennon) Two Virgins, 1968, Life With Lions, 1969, Wedding Album, 1970, Live Peace in Toronto (1969), 1970, Some Time in New York City, 1972, Double Fantasy, 1980 (Grammy award Album of Yr., 1982), Milk and Honey, 1984; solo albums include Yoko Ono Plastic Ono Band, 1970, Fly, 1971, Approximately Infinite Universe, 1973, Feeling the Space, 1973, Welcome: The Many Sides Of Yoko Ono, 1973, Season of Glass, 1981, It's Alright (I See Rainbows), 1982, Every Man Has A Woman, 1984, Starpeace, 1985, Walking On Thin Ice, 1992, Rising, 1995, New York Rock, 1995, Rising Mixes, 1996, Blueprint For A Sunrise, 2001; co-prodr. Gimme Some Truth -

The Making Of John Lennon's Imagine Album, 2001 (Grammy award best long form music video, 2001); exec. prodr. Come Together: A Night for John Lennon's Words & Music, 2001; composer numerous songs including Don't Worry Kyoko, Mummy's Only Looking for her Hand in the Snow, Walking on Thin Ice (Grammy award nomination Best Female Rock Performance on Single 1981), Don't Be Sad; author: Grapefruit, 1964, A Hole to See the Sky Through, 1971, Just Me! (Tada No Atashi), 1986, Sometime In New York City, 1995, Acorns, 1996,; author 6 film scripts, Tokyo, 1964, 13 film scores, London, 1967, John & Yoko Calendar, 1970. Recipient Helen Caldicott leadership award, 1987, Skowhegan award, 2002, Lifespire award, 2002, MOCA award, 2003. Office: c/o John Hendricks 488 Greenwich St New York NY 10013-1313*

ONOKPISE, OGHENEKOME UKRAKPO, agronomist, educator, forest geneticist, agroforester; b. Lagos, Nigeria, May 10, 1951; came to U.S., 1981; s. Jerome Esagwu and Margaret E. (Agbanobi) O.; m. Lucy Omotaka Edemo, Jan. 31, 1977; children: Oghenemaro, Omurhu, Oghogho, Onoriode. BS, U. Ife, Ile-Ife, Nigeria, 1974; MS, U. Guelph, Ont., Can., 1980; PhD, Iowa State U., 1984. Tutor Sch. Agrl., Yandev, Nigeria, 1974—75; rsch. officer Rubber Rsch. Inst. Nigeria, Benin City, 1975—81; rsch. asst. Iowa State U., Ames, 1981—85; rschr. Ohio State U., Wooster, 1985—86; asst. prof. Fla. A&M U., Tallahassee, 1986—91, assoc. prof., 1991—94, prof., 1994—. Mem. Germplasm Collection Team Internat. Rubber R&D Bd. London, Eng. in Brazil, 1981; team leader Cocoyam Breeding Team USAID, Cameroon, Republic of West Africa, 1988-90, coord. weed control project, Ghana, 1996—; sabbatical leave Inst. Forest Genetics and Tree Breeding U. Gottingen, Germany, 2002. Author: Growing Up: Tony Joins the System, 2004; contbr. articles to Commonwealth Forestry Rev. Jour., Annals Applied Biology, Plant Breeding, Acta Agronomca, Seed Sci. and Tech., African Jour. Genetics, Am. Jour. Enology and Viticulture, Indian Jour. Plant Breeding and Genetics, Silvae Genetica, Agronomie, Jour. Plantation Crops, African Tech. Forum, Women in Natural Resources Jour., Natural Resources, Salem Press, Restoration Ecology, Internat. Jour. Tropical Agr. Editor Pack 104 Club Scouts Newsletter, Boy Scouts Am., Tallahassee, 1986-88; mem. Parish Coun. St. Louis Parish, Tallahassee, 1987-88; tutor Bapt. H.S., Buea, Cameroon, 1988-89; mem. choir St. Louis Cath. Ch., 1991—. Recipient Sci. Paper award Assn. Rsch. Dirs., Washington, 1987; named Best Agrl. Instr., Agrl. Sci. Club FAMU Students, Tallahassee, 1988, 93; grantee USAID-FAMU, Cameroon, 1988-90, NASA-Fla. A&M U., 1988-91, Internat. Paper Co., 1994, USAID-Fla. A&M U.-U. Fla., Ghana, 1996-98, USDA-Fgn. Agrl. Svcs.-Fla. A&M U., Ghana, 1998—, USDA-Rsch. and Sci. Exch. Divsn.-Fla. A&M U., Ghana, 1999—; German Acad. Faculty Exch. fellow, 2002. Fellow Indian Soc. Genetics and Plant Breeding; mem. Am. Soc. Agronomy, Commonwealth Forestry Assn., Soc. of Am. Foresters (campus faculty rep., diversity com.). Achievements include development of concepts of moving forest for the tropical rain forest; growth of carrots in hydroponic system within growth chambers, inbreeding depression in polyploids with emphasis on forages; biological control of invasive species using native species. Home: 2810 Kennesaw Pl Tallahassee FL 32303-1202 Office: Fla A&M U Martin Luther King Blvd Tallahassee FL 32307 Office Phone: 850-561-2217. E-mail: o.onokpise@worldnet.att.net.

ONORATO, NICHOLAS LOUIS, retired program director, economist; b. South Barre, Mass., Feb. 24, 1925; s. Charles and Amalia (Tartaglia) O.; m. Elizabeth Louise Settergren, July 19, 1947; children: Gary, Deborah, Nicholas, Jeffrey, Glenn, Charles (dec.), Lisa. BS in Pub. Relations, Boston U., 1951; MA in Econs, Clark U., 1952, PhD, 1959. Mem. faculty Becker Jr. Coll., Worcester, Mass., 1952-54; prof. econs. Worcester Poly. Inst., 1955-68, chmn. dept. econs., govt., bus., 1968-74, dir. Sch. Indsl. Mgmt., 1972-99; prof. emeritus Worcester (Mass.) Poly Inst., 1994. Vis. prof. Clark U., Worcester, 1964-66; fin. cons. Coz Chem. Co., Northbridge, Mass., 1959-95. Contbr. to newspapers and mags. Trustee Bay State Savs. Bank, Worcester. Served with USNR, 1943-46. Mem. Torch Club (pres. Worcester 1967, 87, 95). Home: 39 Knollwood Dr Shrewsbury MA 01545-3329

ONOVWEROSUOKE, FRED, music educator, musicologist; s. Fredrick Oberuvwu Onovwerosuoke Okonedo and Agnes Orukpesheke Onovwerosuoke; m. Wendy Kristin Hymes, Feb. 24, 1994; 1 child, Omena Benjamin Oberuvwu. MBA, Lindenwood U., St. Charles, 1993. Founder & artistic dir. St. Louis African Chorus, St. Louis, Mo., 1994—; dir. Internat. Consortium for the Music of Africa & its Diaspora, New Orleans, La., 1999—. Editor The Voice of African Music, St. Louis, 1993—; music dir. Christ the King Luth. Ch., Kenner, La., 2003—. Author (choral jour.): (scholarly article) Contemplating African Choral Music: Insights for Foreign Conductors (Mo. Arts Award, 2001); composer: (music) African Choral Music; dir.: (choral workshops/clinics) African Choral Music Workshops; prodr.: (cd/album) Live! At the Sheldon, AENaO: The Sacred Music of Harcourt-Whyte. Mem. NY African Chorus, N.Y.C., 2002—03, St. Louis African Chorus, St. Louis, 1994—2003, Musical Arts Soc. of New Orleans, 2003, African Chorus, Inc., New Orleans, 2003. Grantee Grant, Regional Arts Commn., 1996-2003, Mo. Arts Coun., 1996-2003, NEA, 1999-2003. Mem.: Internat. Consortium for Music of Africa & its Diaspora (dir. 1999—2003), Internat. Soc.African-to-Am. Music (UK), Am. Choral Directors Assn., Am. Guild of Organists, The Am. Musicol. Soc. Universalist. Achievements include first to New mode of artistic expression through African choral music. Avocations: travel, tennis, world music enthusiast, multiculturalist. Office: St Louis African Chorus 634 N Grand Blvd Ste 1143 Saint Louis MO 63103 E-mail: fredo@africanchorus.org.

ONSAGER, DAVID RALPH, cardiothoracic surgeon, educator; b. Phoenix, Feb. 15, 1962; s. Ralph William and Margaret Carol (Engel) O. BA in Biochem., History & Sociology Sci., U. Pa., 1984; MD, Rush Med. Coll., 1988. Diplomate Nat. Bd. Med. Examiners, Am. Bd. Surgery, Am. Bd. Thoracic Surgery. Resident in gen. surgery Med. Coll. Wis. affiliated hosps., Milw., 1988-94; fellow in cardiopulmonary transplantation U. Wis. Hosp. and Clinics, Madison, 1994-95, fellow in cardiothoracic surgery, 1995-97, lectr. in cardiothoracic surgery, 1997-2000; attending surgeon Meth. Hosp., Omaha, 2000—01, Rush-Copley Hosp., Aurora, Ill., 2001—. Contbr. articles to profl. jours. Recipient House Staff Excellence in Tchg. award Med. Coll. Wis., 1991, Cmty. Health Svc. award Rush Med. Coll., Chgo., 1988; Cancer Ctr. grantee Med. Coll. Wis., 1991. Fellow ACS (assoc.); mem. State Med. Soc. Nebr., Internat. Soc. Heart and Lung Transplantation, Soc. Thoracic Surgeons (candidate), Coun. Healthcare and Biomed. Advisors. Dem. Avocations: tennis, basketball, skiing, sailing, flying. Home: Apt 204 511 Aurora Ave Naperville IL 60540-6289 Office: Univ Cardiovasc Surgeons 1725 W Harrison St Ste 1156 Chicago IL 60612 E-mail: donsager@earthlink.net.

ONSANIT, TAWACHAI, physician; b. Trang, Thailand, Jan. 14, 1940; arrived in U.S., 1965; s. Toon and Tanomchit (Kongsong) O.; m. Bubpha Janturagit, May 8, 1966; children: Krittika, Addie. MD, Chulalongkorn Med., Bangkok, 1964. Rotating intern Queens Gen. Hosp., N.Y.C., 1965-66; resident in gen. surgery Med. Coll. of Ohio, Toledo, 1966-70; resident in colon and rectal surgery Allentown (Pa.) Gen. Hosp., 1970-72; mem. staff Coaldale (Pa.) Hosp., 1973-77, Sentara Hosp., Virginia Beach, Va., 1977—; pvt. practice, 1973—; asst. prof. clin. surgery Ea. Va. Med. Sch., Norfolk, Va., 1993. Fellow ACS, Am. Soc. Colon and Rectal Surgery; mem. Soc. Am. Gastrointestinal Endoscopic Surgeons. Avocations: photography, ballroom dancing, reading. Office: 1020 Independence Blvd Ste 204 Virginia Beach VA 23455-5542

ONSTEAD, R. RANDALL, JR., food products executive; m. Pam Onstead; 2 children. BA in mktg., Tex. Tech. U., 1978; attended mgmt. devel. program, Harvard U., 1986. Mng. dir. Chapman Ptnrs., LLC; CEO Garden Ridge Co., 2002—03; pres., CEO Randall's Food Markets, Inc., Houston. Bd. mem. Metro YMCA, York Christian Coll., York, Nebr., Randall's Food Markets, Topco Assoc., Inc., Mem. Care Sys. Office: Dominicks Finer Foods Inc 711 Jorie Blvd Oak Brook IL 60523

ONTAI, GUY PO'OLANUI, state representative; b. Honolulu, Sept. 27, 1956; m. Pennylynn Ontai; children: Gavin, Krystalynn, Garyk. BS, U.S. Mil. Acad., West Point, 1978; MS in Physics, Mass. Inst. Tech., 1985. Tchr. advanced placement and honors Physics classes Kamehameha Schs., 1994—. Co-founder, pres. Mililani Chess Club, 1997—; scholastic dir. Hawaii Chess Fedn., 1997—. Mem.: Am. Assn. Physics Tchrs. Republican. Office: State Capitol Rm 326 415 S Beretania St Honolulu HI 96813 E-mail: repontai@Capitol.hawaii.gov.

ONTON, ANN LOUISE REUTHER, chemist; b. Bridgeport, Conn., Sept. 29, 1943; m. Aare Onton, 1965; children: Alan David, Daryl John, Julie Ann. BS in Chemistry, Purdue U., 1965. Lab. chemist Great Lakes Chem. Corp., 1965-67; rsch. asst. Geigy Chem. Corp., 1967-70; abstractor Chem. Abstracts Svc., 1970-72; rschr. Cancer Prevention II Study, 1980-90; chemist Prototek Enzyme Sys. Products, 1992-93; rsch. assoc. Applied Biotech Concepts, Inc., 1995-98, Genaissance Pharms., 1999-2000; mgr. rsch. devel. and prodn. AllExcel, Inc., 2000—. NIH grantee, 1996, 97. Mem. NAFE, AAUW, Am. Chem. Soc., Assn. for Women in Sci. Achievements include development of novel materials and methods for improved electrophoresis and DNA sequencing technologies, development of methodologies for purification and testing of enzymes, U.S.A. Nat. and world medalist in Masters and Senior Olympic Swimming. Office: AllExcel Inc 135 Wood St West Haven CT 06516-3700 E-mail: ontonalr69@yahoo.com.

ONUFROCK, RICHARD SHADE, pharmacist, researcher; b. Colorado Springs, Colo., July 5, 1934; s. Frank and Mildred Joy (Overstreet) O.; m. Karen Faye Larson, June 15, 1958 (div. 1980); children: Richard Alan (dec.), Amy Mildred. BS in Pharmacy, U. Colo., 1961; diploma, Famous Artists Schs., 1963. Registered pharmacist, Colo., Ariz., South Africa. Pharmacist Aley Drug Co., Colorado Springs, 1961-75, St. Joseph Hosp., Denver, 1976-77, Navajo Nation Health Found., Ganado, Ariz., 1977-81, Kearny (Ariz.) Kennecott-Samaritan Hosp., 1984-85, NIH, Warren G. Magnuson Clin. Ctr., Bethesda, Md., 1988—; dir. pharmacy, chief pharmacist Tintswalo Hosp., South Africa, 1981-84; pharmacist, chief pharmacist Miami (Ariz.)-Inspiration Hosp., 1985-88. Instr. Coll. of Ganado, 1979-80; asst. in textbook revision and illustration U. Colo., 1961; cons. Heritage Health Care Ctr., Globe, Ariz., 1988. Illustrator Pharmacy for Nurses, 1961, Colo. Jour. of Pharmacy, 1962-64; illustrations exhibited Colo. Springs Fine Art Ctr., 1964-66, Gilpin County Art Assn., Central City, Colo., 1968-74, 1st Nat. Space Art Show, Denver, 1969. Dem. precinct committeeman, 1974-76; den leader Boy Scouts Am., com. mem., 1975-76; fireman, lt. Ganado Vol. Fire Dept., 1977-81; compassionate med. missionary Nazarene Ch., Tintswalo Hosp. Gazankulu, South Africa, 1981-84;bd. dirs. Friends of Libr., Kearny, 1985-87; active Grace Episcopal Ch. Mem.: Pharm. Soc. of S. Africa, Washington Met. Soc. Hosp. Pharmacists, Am. Soc. Health Sys. Pharmacists, Am. Pharm. Assn., Delta Sigma Phi, Phi Delta Chi. Avocations: travel, bicycling, hiking, skiing, computers. Home: 12930 Dunbarton Dr Bristow VA 20136 E-mail: pasquache@aol.com.

ONUIGBO, MACAULAY AMECHI, physician, nephrologist, transplant physician; b. Enugu, Nigeria, Mar. 17, 1958; came to U.S., 1994; m. Nnonyelum Onuigbo, Sept. 3, 1988; children: Mark, Victor, Chimdi. MB BS, U. Nigeria, 1981, MSc, 1988. Diplomate Am. Bd. Internal Medicine, Internal Medicine and Nephrologist, cert. nephrologist and transplant physician Luther Midelfort Mayo Health Sys., Eau Claire, Wis. Renal registrar Queen Elizabeth Hosp., Birmingham, Eng., 1988; asst. prof. medicine/nephrology U. Nigeria, Enugu, 1990-94; ISN nephrology rsch. fellow U. Tex. Health Sci. Ctr., Houston, 1994-96; resident Greater Balt. Med. Ctr., 1997-99; fellow in nephrology U. Md., Balt., 2000—02; nephrologist and transplant physician Luther Midelfort Mayo Health System, Eau Claire, Wis., 2002—. Diplomate Am. Bd. of Internal Medicine, 2000. Co-author: Handbook of Physiology, 1999; contbr. over 50 articles to profl. publs. Co-founder Cream Circle League, Enugu, 1990. E-mail: onuigbo.macaulay@mayo.edu., monuigbo27@hotmail.com.

ONUKWULI, FRANCIS OSITA, computer scientist, secondary education educator, mathematician; b. Warri, Nigeria, Aug. 5, 1955; arrived in U.S., 1977; s. Chief Mathias Nwafor and Mercy (Okonkwo) O.; m. Sandra Anthonia Mgbemena, Oct. 12, 1986; children: Francis Osita, Victor Chinedu, Anthony Tochukwu, Precious Chinenye. BS in Math. and Physics, Philander Smith Coll., Little Rock, 1981; MS in Computer Sci., Atlanta U., 1983; EdD in Ednl. Leadership Higher Edn., Clark Atlanta U., 1990. Billing and credit supr. Standard Bank Nigeria Ltd., Benin, 1975-77; tutor, counselor Philander Smith Coll., 1978-81; math. rsch. asst. Atlanta U., 1982-83; instr. computer sci. Spelman Coll., Atlanta, 1983-86; asst. prof. computer sci., mgr. computer and info. sci. lab. Morris Brown Coll., Atlanta, 1986-96, assoc. prof, chmn. computer sci. dept., 1991-92; tchr. math. Lovejoy (Ga.) H.S., 1998—. Cons. PBT Engring. Co., Atlanta, 1985-86; judge Ga. Sci. Fair, 1989, 90, 93, 94, 95, 99, 2001. Co-author: Computer Applications for the Twenty-First Century; author microcomputer materials for calculus students. Mem. NSF (co-chair proposal review panelist 1989-90), Math. Assn. Am., Assn. Computing Machinery, Am. Math. Soc., Internat. Devel. Edn. Coun. (sec. 1987), Igbo Union (pres. Atlanta chpt. 1986-91), Umuoji Improvement Union (nat. v.p. U.S. and Can. 2000—, pres. Atlanta chpt.), Anambra State Assn. (nat. edn. com. chmn.). Democrat. Roman Catholic. Home: 7544 Sedona Dr Jonesboro GA 30236-2740 Office: Lovejoy HS 1587 McDonough Rd Lovejoy GA 30250 Office Phone: 770-473-2920. Personal E-mail: Dronukwuli@aol.com.

ONUSTOCK, MICHAEL R. manufacturing executive; BA in Bus. Adminstrn., U. Wash.; grad. exec. mgmt. program, Stanford U., 1987. Formerly with Boise Cascade; sales mgr. Willamette Industries, 1973—75, gen. mgr. paper, 1975—78, gen. mgr. pulp, paper and bd., 1978—79, v.p. Paper Group, 1980—88, exec. v.p. pulp and fine paper mktg., 1989—2002; sr. v.p. pulp and white paper Weyerhaeuser Co., Federal Way, Wash., 2002—. Mem. industry sector adv. com. Dept. of Commerce; mem. exec. com. AF&PA Printing and Writing Paper Bd., AF&PA Pulp Prodrs. Bd.; mem. internat. trade subcom. AF&PA. Bd. dirs. Wash. Pulp & Paper Found. Office: Weyerhaeuser Co 33663 Weyerhaeuser Way S Federal Way WA 98063-9777

ONWUCHEKWA, MICHAEL O. accountant, educator; b. Ahaba, Nigeria; s. Joseph Oji and Ego Onwuchekwa; m. Miriam C. Onwuchekwa; 1 child, Sarah C. MBA, U. Ctrl. Ark., 1990. Auditor Divsn. Taxation, Newark, 1997—2000; prof. acctg. Gibbs Coll., Montclair, NJ, 2001—. Mem.: Nat. Assn. Accts., AICPA. Democrat. Avocations: jazz, travel, jogging, reading, electronics. Mailing: PO Box 10266 New Brunswick NJ 08906-0266 E-mail: mchekwas@optonline.net.

ONYEUKU, ALFRED EME, small business owner, consultant; b. Aba, Nigeria, Apr. 30, 1948; arrived in U.S.A., 1974; s. Jeremiah and Violet Onyeuku; m. Felicia Nkpola Onyeuku, Dec. 12, 1987; children: Nasarachi, Chisom, Ngwanna, Udobi. BS, BA, U. Nebr., 1976; MBA, Sam Houston State U., 1978. Mgr. finance U.S. West Comms., Denver, 1980—95; self employed Buffalo Grove, Ill., 1995—97; sr. cons. Internat. Profit Assoc., Chgo., 1997—98; acct. adv. Parks Coll. South, Aurora, Colo., 1998—; mng. ptnr. Interglobe Svcs. Internat., Denver, 2001—. Chmn. fin. com. 100 Black Men of Denver, Denver, 1996—97; chmn. fin. Headstart, Omaha, 1987—91. Mem.: Acad. Mgmt. Avocations: tennis, reading business journals, public speaking. Office: Parks College 14280 E Jewell Ave Aurora CO 80012 Home: 225 Woodbyne Dr Fayetteville GA 30214-1295 E-mail: onyeuku@aol.com.

OOLIE, SAM, manufacturing and investment company executive; b. NYC, Aug. 11, 1936; s. Bernadt S. and Rose (Moyel) O.; m. Marjorie R. Oolie, Dec. 3, 1961; children: Janis Feldman, Caroline Gross, Tara. BS in Metallurgy, MIT, 1958; MBA, Harvard U., 1961. Chmn. Food Concepts, Inc., Rutherford, N.J., 1962-85; pres. CFC Venture Capital Corp., Fairfield, N.J., 1984-90; chmn. Oolie Enterprises, Upper Saddle River, N.J., 1985—; vice chmn. Am. Mobile, Inc., Secaucus, N.J., 1986-89; chmn. The Nostalgia Network, N.Y.C., 1987-90, New Thermal Corp., Keasbey, N.J., 1991-95, NoFire Tech., Inc., Upper Saddle River, N.J., 1995—. Bd. dirs. Comverse Tech., N.Y.C., NCT Group (formerly Noise Cancellation Tech.), Stamford, Conn. Mem. exec. com. State of N.J.-Israel Commn., 1989-93; commr. Essex County Improvement Authority, 1987-88; trustee Coun. Jewish Fedns., 1986—; bd. govs. Haifa U., 1986-90, 93-95; trustee Garden State Cancer Ctr., 1989-96, Beth Israel Med. Ctr., 1990-96, Assn. Reform Zionists Am., 1990-97, Am. Joint Distbn. Com., 1990-98; pres. United Jewish Fedn. Met. West N.J., 1988-90; vice chmn. United Jewish Appeal, 1986-96; chmn. Beth Israel Health Care Found., 1993-96. Recipient Gates of Jerusalem award Boys Town of Jerusalem, 1990, Israel 40th Ann. medal State of Israel Bonds, 1988. Mem. Harvard Club. Avocations: golf, coin collecting/numismatics. Office: 21 Industrial Ave Upper Saddle River NJ 07458 Office Phone: 201-818-1291. E-mail: samoolie@cs.com.

OOMS, VAN DOORN, economist; b. Chgo., Oct. 29, 1934; s. Casper William and Ruth P. (Miller) O.; m. Theodora J. Parfit, June 17, 1961; children: Katrina, Alex, Tamara. BA summa cum laude, Amherst Coll., 1956, LHD (hon.), 1981; BA with 1st class honors, Oxford (Eng.) U., 1958, MA, 1962, Yale U., 1960, PhD, 1965. Lectr. Yale U., 1962, asst. prof. econs., to 1968; assoc. prof. Swarthmore Coll., 1968, prof., to, 1978; chief economist U.S. Senate Budget Com., Washington, 1977-78; asst. dir. for econ. policy U.S. Office Mgmt. and Budget, Washington, 1978-81; chief economist U.S. House Budget Com., Washington, 1981-91, exec. dir. for policy, 1989-91; sr. v.p., dir. rsch. Com. for Econ. Devel., Washington, 1991—2002, sr. fellow, 2002—. Rhodes scholar, Oxford U., 1958; Ford Found. Dissertation fellow Yale U., 1965. Office: 2000 L St NW Ste 700 Washington DC 20036-4915

OORT, ABRAHAM HANS, meteorologist, researcher, educator; b. Leiden, The Netherlands, Sept. 2, 1934; came to U.S., 1961; s. Jan Hendrik and Johanna Maria (Graadt Van Roggen) O.; m. Bineke Pel, May 20, 1961; children: Pieter Jan, Michiel, Sonya. MS, MIT, 1963; PhD in Meteorology, U. Utrecht, The Netherlands, 1964. Rsch. meteorologist Koninklyk Nederlands Meteorologisch Instituut, De Bilt, The Netherlands, 1964-66, Geophys. Fluid Dynamics Lab/NOAA, Washington, 1966-68, Princeton, N.J., 1968-77, sr. rsch. meteorologist, 1977-96, ret., 1996. Prof. dept. geol. and geophys. scis. Princeton U., 1971-96; Shiatsu tchr. Kushi Inst. for Macrobiotic Studies, Becket, Mass., 1999--. Author: Physics of Climate, 1992; contbr. monographs in field. 2nd lt. Netherlands Air Force, 1959-61. NATO sci. fellow MIT, Cambridge, 1961-63; 10th Victor P. Starr Meml. lectr. MIT, 1988; recipient Gold medal U.S. Dept. Commerce, Washington, 1979. Fellow N.Y. Acad. Scis., Am. Meteorol. Soc. (Jule G. Charney award 1993), Royal Meteorol. Soc.; mem. Am. Geophys. Union. Democrat. Avocations: sculpture, shiatsu, meditation, Cranio-Sacral Therapy.

OOSTWOUDER, PETER HENRY, family physician; b. Sioux City, Iowa, June 27, 1956; s. Cornelius and Alice Theresa (Roghair) O.; m. Joanna Ruth Field, June 7, 1997; children: Christina Elaine, Cornelius Wayne, Emily Theresa. BA cum laude, Washington U., St. Louis, 1978; MD, St. Louis U., 1982. Diplomate in family practice and geriatrics Am. Bd. Family Practice. Resident in family practice United Hosp., Clarksburg, W.Va., 1982-85; family physician Jasper Med. Svcs., Heidelberg, Miss., 1985-88, Ormond Family Physicians, Ormond Beach, Fla., 1989, Ctrl. Fla. Cmty. Clinic, Sanford, Fla., 1990—. Clin. assoc. prof. Nova Southeastern Sch. Osteo. Medicine, Ft. Lauderdale, Fla., 1997—. Contbr. articles to profl. jours. Mem. Am. Acad. Family Physicians, Sigma Xi. Republican. Mem. Christian Reformed Ch. Avocations: photography, travel, scuba diving, stamp collection. Home: 198 Poinciana Ln Enterprise FL 32738-9371 Office: Ctrl Fla Family Health Ctr 2400 State Rd 415 Sanford FL 32771-6012 Office Phone: 407-322-8645. E-mail: oostwouder@pol.net.

OPACICH, MILAN, protective services official, musician; b. Gary, Ind., Apr. 12, 1928; s. Mile and Roza (Perpic) O.; m. Rosalyn Helen Nicolich, Oct. 20, 1951; 1 child, Karin Joann. Grad. h.s., Gary, Ind. Tool and die maker Gary Screw and Bolt Co., 1947-58; lt. Gary Fire Dept., 1958-78; instr. Purdue U. NW, Hammond, Ind., 1978-80; luthier Schererville, Ind., 1950—. Rev. panelist Ind. Arts Commn. Music, 2003; lectr. in field; guest on numerous radio and TV shows. Writer Serb World, USA, 1984—; exhbns. include Mall, Washington, 1976, Remwick Gallery, Washington, 1978, 79-80, Smithsonian Inst., Washington, 1981, Bailey Ctr., 1982, Balzekas Lithuanian Culture Mus., Chgo., 1988, Arie Crown Theater, Chgo., 1990, Old Town Sch. Music, 1998; represented in permanent collection Roy Acuff Mus., Nashville; recordings include Bleda Djeva, Kreni Kreni, Jamin with Julius, Drina and Mel Dokich, Vintage 59 and Patriotic Songs of the Serbs; featured in books, magazines and newspaper articles. Founder, co-dir. Tamburitza Orch. St. Sava Orthodox Ch., 1964-70; founder First Tamburitza Extravanganza, 1971—. Recipient Pres.'s award for 50 yrs. of beautiful Tamburitza music, 1999; Am. Slavic Assn. honoree, 2000; Ind. Arts Commn. grant, 2000, Master Artist grant Traditional Arts Ind., 2003; inductee Tamburitza Assn. Am. Hall of Fame. Mem.: Assn. Stringed Instrument Artisans. Ea. Orthodox. Avocations: collecting 78-rpm records, rare vintage instruments, documenting historical data, photographs, memorabilia tamburitza orchs. Home and Office: 2255 Robinhood Blvd Schererville IN 46375-1847

OPALA, MARIAN P(ETER), state supreme court justice; b. Lódz, Poland, Jan. 20, 1921; JD, Oklahoma City U., 1953, BSB in Econs., 1957, LLD (hon.), 1981; LLM, NYU, 1968; HHD, Okla. Christian U. Sci. & Arts, 1981. Bar: Okla. 1953, U.S. Supreme Ct. 1970. Asst. county atty., Oklahoma County, 1953—56; practiced law Oklahoma City, 1956—60, 1965—67; referee Okla. Supreme Ct., Oklahoma City, 1960—65; prof. law Oklahoma City U. Sch. Law, 1965—69; asst. to presiding justice Supreme Ct. Okla., 1967—68; administrv. dir. Cts. Okla., 1968—77; presiding judge Okla. State Indsl. Ct., 1977—78; judge Workers Compensation Ct., 1978; justice Okla. Supreme Ct., 1978—, chief justice, 1991—92. Adj. prof. law Okla. City U., 1962—, U. Okla. Coll. Law, 1969—; prof. law U. Tulsa Law Sch., 1982—; mem. permanent faculty Am. Acad. Jud. Edn., 1970—; mem. NYU Inst. Jud. Adminstrn.; mem. faculty Nat. Jud. Coll., U. Nev., 1975—; chmn. Nat. Conf. State Ct. Adminstrs., 1976-77; mem. Nat. Conf. Commrs. on Uniform State Laws, 1982—. Co-author: Oklahoma Court Rules for Perfecting a Civil Appeal, 1969 Mem. Adminstrn. Conf. U.S., 1993-95. Recipient Herbert Harley award Am. Judicature Soc., 1977, Disting. Alumni award Oklahoma City U., 1979, Americanism medal Nat. Soc. DAR, 1984, ABA/Am. Law Inst. Harrison Tweed Spl. Merit award, 1987, Humanitarian award NCCJ, 1991, Jour. Record award, 1995, Constn. award Rogers State U., 1996, Jud. Excellence award Okla. Bar Assn., 1997, Leo H. Whinery Disting. Svc. award, 1999, Lifetime Achievement award Oklahoma City Univ. Sch. Law, 2000, First Amendment award FOI Okla., Inc., 2002; inductee Okla. Hall of Fame, 2000. Mem. AbA (edn. com. appellate judges conf. 1984-93), Okla. Bar Assn. (Earl Sneed Continuing Legal Edn. award 1988, Jud. Excellence award 1997), Okla. County Bar Assn., Am. Soc. Legal History, Oklahoma City Title Lawyers Assn., Am. Judicature Soc. (bd. dirs. 1988-92), Am. Law Inst. (elected), Order of Coif, Phi Delta Phi (Oklahoma City Alumni award). Office: Okla Supreme Ct State Capitol Rm 238 Oklahoma City OK 73105

OPARIL, SUZANNE, cardiologist, researcher, educator; b. Elmira, N.Y., Apr. 10, 1941; d. Stanley and Anna (Penkova) Oparil. AB, Cornell U., 1961; MD, Columbia U., 1965. Diplomate Am. Bd. Internal Medicine. Intern in medicine Presbyn. Hosp., N.Y.C., 1965—66; sr. asst. resident in medicine Mass. Gen. Hosp., Boston, 1967—68, clin. and rsch. fellow in medicine, cardiac unit, 1968—71; asst. prof. medicine Med. Sch., U. Chgo., 1971—75, assoc. prof., 1975—77; assoc. prof. dept. medicine U. Ala., Birmingham, 1977—81, asst. prof. physiology and biophysics, 1980—81, assoc. prof., 1981—, prof. medicine, 1981—, dir. vascular biology and hypertension program, 1985—, prof. med. physiology and biophysics, 1993—. Mem. vis. faculty Nat. High Blood Pressure Edn. Program, 1974—, Joint Nat. Com. on Detection, Evaluation and Treatment High Blood Pressure, 1991; mem. bd. sci. advisors Sterling Drug, Inc., 1988—91; lectr. in field; Selkurt lectr. Ind. U. Sch. Medicine, 1994; hon. prof. Peking Union Med. Coll., 1994; Louis Gross-Harold Segall lectr. Jewish Gen. Hosp., Montreal, Que., 1995; Joy Goodwin Disting. lectr. Auburn U., 1996; A Ross McIntyre award U. Nebr., 1996. Author books on hypertension; editor: Am. Jour. Med. Scis., 1984—94; assoc. editor: Hpertension, 1979—83, mem. editl. bd.:, 1984—, assoc. editor: Am. Jour. Physiology-Renal, 1989—91, mem. editl. bd.: Jour. Hypertension, 1989—98; contbr. over 450 articles to profl. jours., chapters to books. Recipient Young Investigator award, Internat. Soc. Hypertension, 1979, ann. award, Med. Coll. Pa., 1984; fellow, Am. Coll. Cardiology, 1992. Fellow: Am. Coll. Cardiology; mem.: AAAS, Am. Fedn. for Clin. Rsch. (midwest councillor 1974—75, nat. councillor 1975—78, sec.-treas. 1978—80, pres.

1981—82), Assn. Am. Physicians, So. Soc. for Clin. Investigation (Founder's award 1995), Soc. Exptl. Biology and Medicine (councillor 1993—), Am. Soc. for Clin. Investigation (sec.-treas. 1983—86), Am. Physiol. Soc. (clin. physiology advd. com. 1992—, Carl Ludwig disting. lectr. 2002), Am. Heart Assn. (coun. for high blood pressure rsch. 1973—, coun. on basic scis. 1978—, mem.-at-large, exec. com. 1979—81, chmn. Louis B. Katz Prize com. 1984—86, exec. com. 1985—90, vice chmn. 1986, v.p. Ala. affiliate 1986—87, pres.-elect Ala. affiliate 1987—88, pres. Ala. affiliate 1988—89, chmn. 1988—90, chmn. budget com. 1990—91, mem.-at-large bd. dirs. 1992, Lewis K. Dahl Meml. lectr. 1993, pres.-elect Ala. affiliate 1993—94, nat. pres.-elect 1993—94, nat. pres. 1994—, Arthur C. Corcoran Meml. lectr. 1998, Irving Page-Alva Bradley Lifetime Achievement award 2002), Assn. for Women in Sci., Am. Soc. Hypertension (sci. program com. 1990—92, pub. policy com. 1990—), Inter-Am. Soc. Hypertension, Endocrine Soc., Inst. Medicine of NAS (corr. com. on human rights 1992, chmn. com. adviser Dept. Def. 1993 Breast Cancer Rsch. Program), Phi Kappa Phi, Alpha Omega Alpha (mem. nat. bd. dirs., dir.-at-large 1991, treas. 1993), Sigma Xi, Phi Beta Kappa. Avocations: horseback riding, tennis, hiking, travel. Office: U Ala 703 S 19th St ZRB 1034 Birmingham AL 35294-0007 E-mail: soparil@uab.edu.

OPAT, MATTHEW JOHN, lawyer; b. Riceville, Iowa, Nov. 5, 1952; s. Wesley John and Dolores Genevieve (Ludwig) O.; m. Therese Ann Dusheck, Aug. 13, 1977; children: Michael, Kristin, Steven. BA in History, U. Iowa, 1974; JD, Hamline U., 1977. Bar: Iowa 1977, Minn. 1977. Prin. Opat Law Office, Chatfield, Minn., 1977—. Atty. Fillmore County, 1997-2003. Mem. Fillmore County Bar Assn. (pres. 1984-85), Minn. State Bar Assn. (bd. dirs. 1985-87), Tenth Dist. Bar Assn. (chmn. ethics com. 1989-96, pres. 2001-02, 04—). Office: 22 2nd St SE Chatfield MN 55923-1203 Office Phone: 507-867-4080.

OPDAHL, VIOLA ELIZABETH, secondary school educator; b. Watervliet, NY, Jan. 6, 1925; d. Leslie Rouse and Violetta Frances (O'Bryon) Woodruff; m. Robert Clarence Opdahl, Aug. 4, 1956. BA, Skidmore Coll., 1945; MS in Edn., Cornell U., 1951; postgrad., SUNY, Albany, 1959-61. Cert. tchr. social studies, guidance. Tchr. social studies New Lebanon Ctrl. Sch., Lebanon Springs, N.Y., 1945-50, Patchogue H.S., 1951-55, Selkirk (N.Y.) Sch. Dist., 1955-56, Kingston (N.Y.) City Schs., 1956-58, secondary guidance, 1958-62, tchr. social studies, 1962-86; ret., 1986; coll. student tech. supr. SUNY, New Paltz, 1989-94; ret., 1994. Ad hoc syllabi and testing coms. N.Y. State Edn. Dept., Albany, 1967-82; adj. instr. psychology Marist Coll., 1972-86. Co-author (with Robert Opdahl): A Shaker Musical Legacy, 2004. Spl. activities organizer Town of Hurley Spl. Events Com., 1988—. Recipient Pres. award Marist Coll., 1986, Dean's award SUNY at New Paltz, 1989; named Outstanding Social Studies Tchr. Mid Hudson Soc. State Coun. of N.Y. State Coun., 1986. Mem. AAUW, LWV, Friends of the Senate House, Hurley Heritage soc. Avocations: reading, writing. Home: PO Box 218 431 Wynkoop Rd Hurley NY 12443-5108 Personal E-mail: velizabeth@msn.com.

OPDYCKE, LEONARD EMERSON, retired elementary, secondary and college-level educator, publisher; b. Boston, May 22, 1929; s. Leonard and Frances (Prescott) O.; m. Susan Wolcott, 1951 (div.); children: Susan, Deborah, Margot; m. Jeanne Bernhard, 1963 (div.); children: Sarah, Frances; m. Sandra S. Auchincloss, 1976. BA, Harvard U., 1951; MA, U. Rochester, 1965. Tchr. Southfield Sch., Shreveport, La., 1952-53, Dedham (Mass.) Country Day, Harley Sch., Rochester, NY, 1956-64; dir. Poughkeepsie (NY) Day Sch., 1965-72; chair English dept. Rhinebeck (NY) HS, 1974-77; adj. prof. Marist Coll., Poughkeepsie, 1977-84, 93-95. Co-chair citizen's adv. com. Poughkeepsie Sch. Dist., 1994—2002. Author: French Aeroplanes before the Great War, 1999; editor, pub. WWI Aero, 1961—; pub. Skyways, 1987—. Bd. dirs. Cmty. Family Devel. Day Care Ctr., 1984—, Hudson River Housing, 2003—. Mem. Phi Beta Kappa. Avocations: aviation history, linguistics, education. Home and Office: 15 Crescent Rd Poughkeepsie NY 12601-4405 Office Phone: 845-473-3679.

OPDYKE, NEIL DONALD, geology educator; b. Frenchtown, N.J., Feb. 7, 1933; BA, Columbia U., 1955; PhD, Durham (Eng.) U., 1958; DSc, U. Newcastle-upon-Tyne, 1982. Postdoctoral fellow Rice U., Houston, 1958-59, Australian Nat. U., 1959-60, U. Coll. Rhodesia and Nyasaland, Salisbury, Southern Rhodesia, 1960-63; rsch. assoc. Lamont-Doherty Geol. Observatory, 1964-66, sr. rsch. assoc., 1966-81; geology lectr. Columbia U., N.Y.C., 1967-69, adj. prof. geology, 1974-81; prof., chmn. geology U. Fla., 1981-88, prof. geology, 1994—. Vis. prof. U. Paris, 1989. Mem. editl. bd. Quaternary Rsch., 1982. Fulbright grantee, 1959, 77-78, 89. Fellow AAAS, Am. Geophys. Union (John Adam Fleming medal 1996, com. on pub. affairs 1990-91, geomagnetism and paleomagnetism sect. 1984-86, pres.); mem. NAS (geodynamics com. 1984-86), Am. Acad. Arts and Scis., Geol. Soc. Am. (George P. Woollard award 1987, assoc. editor bull. 1983, day medal com. 1982), Geol. Soc. Australia (Stillwell award 1982). Office: U Fla Dept Geology PO Box B137 1112 Turlington Hall Gainesville FL 32611-7340

OPEL, WILLIAM, medical research administrator; BA, Pepperdine U., 1968; MBA, U. So. Calif., 1993; PhD, Claremont Grad. U., 1998. Mem. staff Pasadena (Calif.) Found. Med. Rsch., Pasadena, Calif., 1961-63, rsch. assoc., 1964-70, asst. to dir., 1970-72, adminstr., 1972-76, exec. dir., 1976-82; acting exec. dir. Huntington Inst. Applied Med. Rsch., 1978-82; exec. dir. Huntington Med. Rsch. Inst., Pasadena, Calif., 1982—. Lectr. in technology, mgmt., Pepperdine U.; adj. prof. tech. mgmt. Claremont Grad. U. Mem. Beta Gamma Sigma, Phi Kappa Phi. Office: Huntington Med Rsch Insts 734 Fairmount Ave Pasadena CA 91105-3104

OPENDAK, IRENE, academic administrator; d. Leonid and Rimma Fert; m. Michael Opendak; children: Roman, Maya. MS in Engring., Kalinin Poly. Inst. Mgr. of the dept. of data processing Info. Computing Ctr., Regional Trade Ministry, Leningrad, Russia, 1976—85; dir., coll. ops. and bus. services Bryn Mawr Coll., Bryn Mawr, Pa., 1997—; info. systems mgr. U. of Pa., Phila., 1990—97. Recipient Hon. award, Am. Astron. Soc., 1991, Leadership Recognition, IBM Corp., 2001, Achievement Recognition, Bryn Mawr Coll., 2000, 2001, 2002. Mem.: Nat. Assn. of Coll. and U. Bus. Officers. D-Conservative. Achievements include lead college team in implementation of core administrative system within unprecedented 18 months accelerated schedule; first in the United States converted 20+ years of historical advancement data. Avocations: travel, skiing, interior design. Office: Bryn Mawr Coll 101 North Merion Ave Bryn Mawr PA 19010

OPENSHAW, JENNIFER, finance company executive; BA in comm. studies, MBA in comm. studies, UCLA. Press sec. Calif. State Treas.; dir. media rels. ICN Pharm., 1995; sr. v.p. Bank One; v.p. investment mgmt. svcs. group Bank Am.; dir. investment svcs. Wilshire Assoc., 1999; founder, chmn., CEO, pres. Women's Fin. Network, 1999—2000; vice chmn. Women's Fin. Network at Siebert, 2000—. Fin. commentator Wise Women, Lifetime TV; corr. Money Expert, CBS-TV, LA; columnist Women & Money, CBS MarketWatch; featured on CNBC; featured in Bus. Week publ., Wash. Times publ.; adv. bd. Wyndham Hotels, MuchoInfo. Author: What's Your Net Worth? Click Your Way to Wealth, 2001. Commr. Little Hoover Commn., Calif. Recipient Tribute to Women and Industry award, YWCA, 2001. Mem.: Young Entrepreneurs Orgn. Office: WFN at Seibert 885 Third Ave Ste 1720 New York NY 10022

OPFER, NEIL DAVID, construction educator, consultant; b. Spokane, Wash., June 1, 1954; s. Gus Chris and Alice Anna (Nibbe) Opfer. BS in Bldg. Theory cum laude, Wash. State U., 1976, BA in Econs. cum laude, BA in Bus. cum laude, Wash. State U., 1977; MS in Mgmt., Purdue U., 1982; PD in Engring., U. Wis., 2003. Cert. cost engr., project mgr., profl. constructor; lic. gen. contractor. Estimator Standard Oil (Chevron), Richmond, Calif., 1975; gen. carpenter forman Opfer Constrn. Corp., Spokane, 1976; assoc. engr. Inland Steel Corp., East Chgo., Ind., 1977-78, millwright supr., 1978-79, field engr., 1979-82, project engr., 1982-84, sr. engr., 1984-87; asst. prof. construction and construction mgmt. Western Mich. U., Kalamazoo, 1987-89, U. Nev., Las Vegas, 1989-95, assoc. prof. construction and construction mgmt., 1995—. Contbr. articles to profl. jours. Bd. dirs. Christmas in April, 1993—98, Habitat for Humanity, 1991—. Mem. Am. Welding Soc. (bd. dirs. 1982-87), Am. Inst. Constructors, Am. Assn. Cost Engrs. (nat. bd. dirs. 1995-97, Order of Engr. award 1989), Project Mgmt. Inst., Constrn. Mgmt. Assn., Tau Beta Pi (life), Phi Kappa Phi (life). Methodist. Avocations: biking, running, marathons, triathlons. Home: 1920 Placid Ravine St Las Vegas NV 89117-5961 Office: Univ Nev Civil Engring 4505 S Maryland Pkwy Las Vegas NV 89154-4015 Personal E-mail: opfern@yahoo.com.

OPFER, STEVEN EARL, education educator, researcher; s. Patricia Ann and Charles Hardy Franklin; m. Cathy Jo Vernor, Aug. 18, 1979; children: Joshua Steven, Jessica Mae. BA in Religion, Summit Sch. of Theology, 1982—85; BA, MS, Lindenwood Coll., 1988—93; PhD, Regent U. Sch. of Comm., 2003—. Instr. Norfolk State U., Va., 1993—. Exec. prodr. (TV interview program) Faces, (TV news mag.) Spartan News. Mem. Norfolk State U. Tech. Devel. Com., 2003—03. Fellow Minority Educators Fellowship, Am. Press Inst., 1994, New Journalism Educators, The Assn. for Edn. in Journalism and Mass Communication and The Freedom Forum, 1995, C-SPAN in the Classroom, C-SPAN, 1995; grantee API Minority Educators Grant, John S. and James L. Knight Found., 1994; scholar Beazley Endowed Scholarship, Regent U., 2000-2001, Azusa Endowed Scholarship, 2001-2002, 2002-2003. Office: Norfolk State U 700 Park Ave Norfolk VA 23504 Office Phone: 757-823-2444. Business E-Mail: seopfer@nsu.edu.

OPIE, CATHERINE, photographer; b. Sandusky, Ohio, 1961; BFA, San Francisco Art Inst., 1985; MFA, CalArts, Valencia, 1988. One-woman shows include Mills Coll., Oakland, Calif., 1989, 494 Gallery, N.Y.C., 1991, Kiki Gallery, San Francisco, 1994, Jack Hanley Gallery, San Francisco, 1994, Galeria Massimo de Carlo, Milan, 1995, Parco, Tokyo, 1995, Richard Fonke Galerie, Ghent, Belgium, 1995, Richard Feigen Gallery, Chgo., 1996, Ginza Art Space, Tokyo, 1997, Suzanne Hilberry Gallery, Birmingham, Mich., 1997, Mus. Contemporary Art, L.A., 1997, Jay Gorney Modern Art, N.Y.C., 1998, Wood St. Gallery, Pittsburgh, 1999, Thread Waxing Space, NY, 2000; exhibited in numerous group shows, 1985—, latest being Santa Monica (Calif.) Mus. Art, 1992, 94, 95, Inst. Contemporary Art, Boston, 1993, Long Beach (Calif.) Mus. Art, 1994, Mus. Modern Art at Heide, Melbourne, Australia, 1994, Nat. Mus. Modern Art, Paris, 1995, Los Angeles County Mus. Art, 1995, Whitney Mus. Am. Art, N.Y.C., 1995, UCLA Armand Hammer Mus. Art and Cultural Ctr., 1996, Mus. Contemporary Art, Miami, Fla., 1996, Gröoninger Mus., Gröningen, The Netherlands, 1996,, Galerie Rodolphe Janssen, Brussels, 1996, Nat. Gallery, Athens, 1996, Guggenheim Mus., N.Y.C., 1997, St. Louis Art Mus., 1997, Milw. Art Mus., 1997, Mus. Contemporary Art, L.A., 1998, Stedelijk Mus., Amsterdam, The Netherlands, 1998; represented in permanent collections Whitney Mus. Am. Art, Mus. Modern Art, San Francisco, Mus. Fine Arts, Boston, Mus. Contemporary Art, L.A., Los Angeles County Mus. Art, Long Beach Mus. Art, Gröninger Mus., Centro Cultural Arte Contemporaneo, Mexico City, Ctr. for Creative Photography, U. Ariz., Tucson; work represented in numerous publs. Address: c/o Gorney Bravin & Lee 534 W 26th St New York NY 10001-5515*

OPIE, JOHN D. retired electric power industry executive; BSMetE, Mic. Coll. Mining & Tech., 1961. With magnetic materials bus. GE, 1961-64, various carboloy sys., 1964-73, nat. sales mgr. carboloy sys., 1973-74, gen. mgr. mining bus., 1974-75, gen. mgr. battery bus., 1975-77; gen. mgr. Lexan products divsn. GE Plastics, 1977-80, v.p. Lexan products divsn., 1980-82, pres. specialty plastics divsn., 1982-83; v.p. distbn. equipment bus. GE, 1983-86, sr. v.p., 1986; pres., CEO GE Lighting, 1986-95; vice chmn., exec. officer GE, 1995—2000; interim non-exec. chmn. The Stanley Works, New Britain, Conn., 2004. Mem.: bd. dirs., The Stanley Works, 2000-. Office: The Stanley Works 1000 Stanley Dr New Britain CT 06053

OPITZ, DONALD L, science educator; b. Chgo., June 25, 1969; s. Donald O. Opitz and Angeline L. Rispoli, Antoinette I. Opitz (Stepmother); life ptnr. Gregg J. Albrecht. BS, DePaul U., 1991; MA, U. Minn., 1998, PhD, 2003. Dir. Women's Ctr. U. Minn., Mpls., 2001—02, dir. Gen. Coll. Math. Ctr., 2002—, instr. Compleat Scholar program, 2002—, instr. math., 2002—. Bd. dir. Carol E. Macpherson Scholarship, Mpls., 2001—; advisor Reentry Students' Orgn. U. Minn., Mpls., 2000—. Author: (pamphlet) Three Generations in the Life of the Minnesota Women's Center: A History, 1960-2000; contbr. biographical dictionaries American National Biography, chapters to books. Mem. OutFront Minn., Mpls., 1994—, Calhoun-Isles Cmty. Band, Mpls., 2002—. Recipient vis. studentship, U. Cambridge, 2001; fellow, U. of Minn., 1991—92; grantee, NSF, 2001; scholar, DePaul U., 1987—91. Mem.: Brit. Soc. for History of Sci., Am. Hist. Assn., History of Sci. Soc., Nat. Women's Studies Assn., Coll. Reading and Learning Assn. Dfl. Roman Catholic. Avocations: bicycling, French horn performance. Home: 5119 Red Oak Dr Mounds View MN 55112 Office: U Minn Gen Coll 128 Pleasant St SE Minneapolis MN 55455 E-mail: opitz@umn.edu.

OPLINGER, CARL SPADT, biology professor; b. Walnutport, Pa., Oct. 6, 1936; s. Barton James and Erma Agnes (Spadt) O.; m. Marilee Ann Heckman, June 17, 1961; children: Anne Arlington, Amy Allison. BS, Mulhenberg Coll., 1958; MS, Lehigh U., 1960; PhD, Cornell U., 1963. Asst. prof. to prof. Muhlenberg Coll., Allentown, Pa., 1963—. Author: Natural History of the Poconos, 1988, The Lehigh Valley: A Natural and Environmental History, 2001. Recipient Pa. Conservation Communicator of Yr., Pa. Wildlife Fedn., Harrisburg, 1989. Mem. Am. Inst. Biol. Sci., Ecol. Soc. Am., Soc. Conservation Biology, Herpetologists League. Lutheran. Home: 5071 Gary Dr Emmaus PA 18049-5051 Office: Muhlenberg Coll 2400 W Chew St Allentown PA 18104-5564 E-mail: oplinger@muhlenberg.edu.

OPP, SUSAN, science educator, researcher; PhD in Entomology, U. Mass., Amherst, 1983—88. Asst. prof. Boston U., 1988—89; prof. biol. sci. Calif. State U., Hayward, 1989—. Dir. environ. sci. Calif. State U. Named to Women's Hall Fame, Sci., Alameda County Women's Hall Fame, 2001. Office: Calif State U Hayward 25800 Carlos Bee Blvd Hayward CA 94542

OPPEDAHL, JOHN FREDERICK, newspaper publisher, publishing executive; b. Duluth, Minn., Nov. 9, 1944; s. Walter H. and Lucille (Hole) Oppedahl; m. Alison Owen, 1975 (div. 1983); m. Gillian Coyro, Feb. 14, 1987 (div. 2002); 1 child, Max. BA, U. Calif., Berkeley, 1967; MS, Columbia U., 1968. Reporter San Francisco Examiner, 1967; reporter, asst. city editor Detroit Free Press, 1968-75, city editor, 1975-80, exec. city editor, 1981, exec. news editor, 1981-82, asst. mng. editor, 1983; nat. and fgn. editor Dallas Times Herald, 1983-85, asst. mng. editor, 1985-87; mng. editor/news L.A. Herald Examiner, 1987-89; mng. editor Ariz. Republic, Phoenix, 1989-93; exec. editor Phoenix Newspapers, Inc., 1993-95; pub., CEO The Republic, 1996—2000; chmn., pub., CEO San Francisco Chronicle, 2000—03. Chmn. bd. The Daily Californian. Mem.: Am. Soc. Newspaper Editors.

OPPEDAHL, PHILLIP EDWARD, computer company executive; b. Renwick, Iowa, Sept. 17, 1935; s. Edward and Isadore Hannah (Gangstead) O.; m. Sharon Elaine Ree, Aug. 3, 1957 (dec. Aug. 1989), m. Karen Suzanne Ungar, July, 4, 2004; children: Gary Lynn, Tamra Sue, Sue Ann, Lisa Kay. BS in Naval Sci., Navy Postgrad. Sch., 1963, MS in Nuclear Physics, 1971; MS in Sys. Mgmt., U. S.C., 1978. Commd. ensign U.S. Navy, 1956, advanced through grades to capt., 1977; with Airborne Early Warning Squadron, 1957-59, Anti-Submarine Squadron, 1959-65; asst. navigator USS Coral Sea, 1965-67; basig jet flight instr., 1967-69; test group dir. Def. Nuclear Agy., 1972-74; weapons officer USS Oriskany, 1974-76; program mgt. for armament Naval Air Sys. Command, Washington, 1977-79; test dir. Def. Nuclear Agy., Kirtland AFB, N.Mex., 1979-82, dep. comdr., 1982-83; pres., CEO Am. Systems, Albuquerque, 1983—. Bd. dirs. BASIS Internat., 1991—; command pilot Angel Flight, N.Mex. Author: Energy Loss of High Energy Electrons in Beryllium, 1971, Understanding Contractor Motivation and Incentive Contracts. Decorated DSM. Mem. Nava. Inst., Am. Nuclear Soc., Aircraft Owners and Pilots Assn., Assn. Naval Aviation, Navy League (command pilot, Angel Fligt, N.Mex.). Lutheran. Home and Office: 13504 Desert Zinnia Ct Albuquerque NM 87111-7156

OPPEGAARD, GRANT E. water transportation executive; b. 1943; MBA, U. of N.H., 1968. With Dayton Hudson Corp., Mpls., 1969-71, Minstar Inc., Mpls., 1971-82, Cuyuna Engine Co., Mpls., 1982-83, Allstate Lawn Products Inc., Mpls., 1983-84, C.V.N. Cos. Inc., Mpls., 1984-89, Fingerhut Cos. Inc., Hopkins, Minn., 1989-96; CEO Genmar Holdings Inc., Mpls., 1997—. Office: Genmar Holdings Inc Ste 2900 80 S 8th St Minneapolis MN 55402-2250

OPPEL, RICHARD ALFRED, newspaper executive; b. Newark, Jan. 30, 1943; s. Alfred William and Jane Genevieve (Owen) O.; m. Carol Freeman Van Aken, Apr. 1, 1967; children: Richard Alfred, Shelby Reid BA in Polit. Sci., U. South Fla. Reporter Tampa Tribune, Fla., 1963-65; newsman, corr., chief bur. AP, Tallahassee, Tampa, Miami and Detroit, 1965-76; assoc. editor Detroit Free Press, 1976-77; exec. editor, v.p. Tallahassee Democrat, 1977-78; v.p. Charlotte (N.C.) Observer, 1978-93; editor Charlotte News, 1985-87; chief Washington bur. Knight-Ridder Newspapers, Washington, 1993-95; editor Austin (Tex.) American Statesman, Austin, Tex., 1995—. Mem. Pulitzer Bd., 2000—. Pres. N.C. First Amendment Found. Served with USMCR, 1960-65 Recipient Disting. Alumni award U. South Fla.; named Editor of Yr. Nat. Press Found., 1987, Ralph McGill Lectr. U. Ga., 1992. Mem. N.C. Press Assn. (pres. 1992-93), Am. Soc. Newspaper Editors (pres. 2000-2001). Episcopalian. Avocations: long distance running, hunting, fishing. Office: Austin Am Statesman PO Box 670 Austin TX 78767-0670

OPPENHEIM, ANTONI KAZIMIERZ, mechanical engineer; b. Warsaw, Aug. 11, 1915; came to U.S., 1948, naturalized, 1954; s. Tadeusz and Zuzanna (Zuckerwar) O.; m. Lavinia Stephens, July 18, 1945; 1 dau., Terry Ann. Diploma in Engring., Warsaw Inst. Tech., London, 1943; PhD in Engring., U. London, 1945; Diploma of Imperial Coll., 1945; DSc, U. London, 1976; Dr. Honoris Causa, U. Poitiers, France, 1981, Tech. U., Warsaw, 1989, Imperial Coll., 1995. Registered profl. engr., Calif. Research asst. City and Guilds Coll., 1942-48, lectr., 1946-48; asst. prof. mech. engring. Stanford U., 1948-50; faculty U. Calif. at Berkeley, 1950—, prof. mech. engring., 1958-86, Miller prof., 1961-62, prof. emeritus, 1986—. Prof. assoc. Sorbonne, Paris, 1960-61, U. Poitiers, France, 1973, 80; staff cons. Shell Devel. Co., 1952-60. Editor-in-chief: Acta Astronautica, 1974-79; contbr. articles to profl. jours., also monographs. Chmn. Heat Transfer and Fluid Mechanics Inst., 1958; IAA Com. on Gasdynamics of Explosions, 1968—; organizer Internat. Colloquia on Gas Dynamics of Explosions and Reactive Systems, 1967, 69, 71, 73, 75, 77, 79, 81, 83; mem. NASA, adv. com. fluid mechanics, 1963-69. Recipient Water Arbitration prize Inst. Mech. Engrs., 1948, Numa Manson medal Inst. for Dynamics of Explosions and Reactive Sys., 1981, Dionizy Smolenski medal Polish Acad. Scis., 1987, Alfred C. Egerton medal The Combustion Inst., 1988, Berkeley citation U. Calif., Berkeley, 1988. Fellow Imperial Coll.; mem. U.S. Nat. Acad. Engring, Polish Acad. Scis. Achievements include contributions to compressible fluid flow, gas turbines and internal combustion engines, heat transfer, combustion, detonation and blast waves. Home: 54 Norwood Ave Kensington CA 94707-1119 Office Phone: 510-642-0211. Business E-Mail: akd@me.berkeley.edu.

OPPENHEIM, DAVID JEROME, musician, retired university dean; b. Detroit, Apr. 13, 1922; s. Louis and Julia (Nurko) O.; m. Judy Holliday, 1948; 1 child, Jonathan; m. Ellen Adler, Apr. 14, 1957; children: Sara, Thomas; m. Pat Jaffe, June 13, 1987. Student, Julliard Sch. Music, 1939-40; MusB, U. Rochester, 1943. Dir. Masterworkd div. Columbia Records, N.Y.C., 1950-59; producer, dir., writer network news CBS-TV, N.Y.C., 1962-68; exec. producer Pub. Broadcasting Lab., N.Y.C., 1968-69; dean Tisch Sch. of Arts, NYU, N.Y.C., 1969-92, dean emeritus, 1992—. Adv. com. Sta. WNCN; mem. Tony awards com., 1983-88. Clarinet soloist Casals Festival, Prades, France, 1955, San Juan, P.R., 1959, recs. include Budapest Quartet, Brahms Clarinet Quintet, Opus 115 and Mozart Clarinet Quintet in A Maj., (Stravinsky conducting) L'Histoire du Soldat, Octet, Septet, Bernstein Sonata, Leonard Bernstein, piano (dedicated to David Oppenheim), (with Julliard Quartet) Copland Sextet, (with New Music Quartet) Douglas Moore Quintet; co-producer (play) Saul Bellow's Last Analysis on Broadway, 1962; producer documentary films on Stravinsky and Casals, CBS News. Bd. dirs. emeritus Film Soc. Lincoln Center, Inc., Town Hall Found.; bd. dirs. Am. Stefan Wolpe Soc.; bd. advisors New Sch. Concerts. With AUS, World War II, ETO. Recipient Prix Italia Radiotelevisione Italiana, 1964. Mem. Nat. Soc. Lit. and Arts, Internat. Council Fine Arts Deans, N.Y. State Arts Deans, Town Hall Found., NYU Soc. of Fellows (charter), Am. Fedn. Arts (film program) Avocations: camping, reading, gardening, hiking.

OPPENHEIM, IRWIN, chemical physicist, educator; b. Boston, June 30, 1929; s. James L. and Rose (Rosenberg) O.; m. Bernice Buresh, May 18, 1974; 1 child, Joshua Buresh. AB summa cum laude, Harvard U., 1949; postgrad., Calif. Inst. Tech., 1949-51; PhD, Yale, 1956. Physicist Nat. Bur. Standards, Washington, 1953-60; chief theoretical physics Gen. Dynamics/Convair, San Diego, 1960-61; assoc. prof. chemistry MIT, Cambridge, 1961-65, prof., 1965—. Lectr. physics U. Md., 1953-60; vis. assoc. prof. physics U. Leiden, 1955-56, Lorentz prof., 1983; vis. prof. Weizmann Inst. Sci., 1958-59, U. Calif., San Diego, 1966-67; Van der Waals prof. U. Amsterdam, 1966-67. Author: (with J.G. Kirkwood) Chemical Thermodynamics, 1961; editor: Phys. Rev. E, 1992-2001. Recipient Hildebrand award, 1998. Fellow Am. Phys. Soc., Am. Acad. Arts and Scis., Washington Acad. Sci.; mem. Phi Beta Kappa, Sigma Xi. Achievements include research in quantum statis. mechanics, statis. mechanics of transport processes, thermodynamics. Home: 140 Upland Rd Cambridge MA 02140-3623 Office: MIT 77 Massachusetts Ave #6-223 Cambridge MA 02139-4307 Business E-Mail: irwin@mit.edu.

OPPENHEIM, JEFFREY SABLE, neurosurgeon, educator; b. Queens, N.Y., Jan. 31, 1962; m. Ann Oppenheim; children: Samuel, Gabrielle, Julius. AB summa cum laude, Princeton U., 1984; MD, Cornell U., 1988. Diplomate Am. Bd. Neurol. Surgery. Resident in neurosurgery Mt. Sinai Hosp., N.Y.C., 1989-93, chief resident in neurosurgery, 1993-94; instr. Coll. Physicians and Surgeons Columbia U., N.Y.C., 1994—; attending physician Nyack (N.Y.) Hosp., 1994—, Good Samaritan Hosp., Suffern, NY, 1994—, Arden Hill Hosp., Goshen, NY, 1996—, Horton Hosp., Middletown, NY, 1997—, Mercy Cmty. Hosp., Port Jervis, NY, 1997—. Mem. bd. health Rockland County, 2001—; trustee Village of Montbello, NY, 2003—. Mem.: Med. Soc. State N.Y. (councillor 1999—), Rockland County Med. Soc. (pres. 1998—99), Am. Jewish Hist. Soc. (trustee 1995—). Office: 222 Route 59 Ste 205 Suffern NY 10901-5206 also: 30 Mathews St Ste 302 Goshen NY 10924-1963

OPPENHEIM, MARTHA KUNKEL, pianist, educator; b. Port Arthur, Tex., June 25, 1935; d. Samuel Adam and Grace (Moncure) Kunkel; m. Russell Edward Oppenheim, June 18, 1960; children: Lauren Susan, Kristin Lee Oppenheim Mortenson. MusB with honors, U. Tex., 1957, MusM, 1959; diploma in piano, Juilliard Sch. Music, 1960; student, Am. Conservatory, Fontainebleau, France, 1956, student, 1958. Soloist Amarillo (Tex.) Symphony, Austin (Tex.) Symphony, U. Tex. Orch., San Antonio Symphony, Dallas Symphony, Heilbronner Kammer Orch., Heilbron, Germany. Solo and chamber music recitals in Tex., N.Y., France; mem. Halcyon Trio, 1974—77; tchg. asst. U. Tex., 1957—59, 1968—69; pvt. piano tchr., San Antonio, 1962—; pianist in duo with cellist Dan Zollars, 1991—. Recipient 1st place award, Internat. Piano Rec. Festival, Nat. Guild Piano Tchrs., 1956, 1956, Tuesday Mus. Club Young Artist Competition, 1956, 1st place award Young Artist Competition, Amarillo Symphony, 1959, 1st place award G.B. Dealey competition, Dallas Symphony and Dallas Morning News, 1959; scholar, U. Tex., Juilliard Sch. Music. Mem.: San Antonio Music Tchrs. Assn., Tex. Music Tchrs. Assn., Music Tchrs. Nat. Assn., Tuesday Musical Club (San Antonio, bd. dirs.), Pi Kappa Lambda, Sigma Alpha Iota. Presbyterian. Home and Office: 9118 E Valley View Ln San Antonio TX 78217-5160 E-mail: moppenheim@satx.rr.com.

OPPENHEIM, ROBERT, beauty industry executive; b. N.Y.C., May 21, 1925; s. Hyman and Hannah (Lieberman) O.; m. Ruth Wigler, Feb. 7, 1954; children: Nancy Ellen, David Paul, Howard P. BS cum laude, Syracuse U., 1950. Product sales specialist McKesson & Robbins, Yonkers, N.Y., 1950-55; asst. sales mgr. Clairol, Inc., N.Y.C., 1955-60, pres. Salon div., 1976-83, chmn. Profl. Products div., 1983-87; dir. mktg. Haircolor div. Revlon, Inc., N.Y.C., 1960-68, dir. mktg. and sales Salon div., 1968-70; exec. v.p. Milton R. Barrie

Co., Inc., 1970-71; pres. Oppenheim Communications, N.Y.C., 1987—. Pub. Beauty Salon Newsletter, N.Y.C., 1971-83, Salon Update, 1988-95, The Oppenheim Letter, 1988-95; mgmt. cons., 1988—; contbg. commentator Beauty Store Bus., 1998—, Profl. Beauty Mfr., 1998-99; bd. dirs. Cosmetology Advancement Found., 1995-98, Internat. Haircolor Exch., 1995-96. Author: 101 Salon Promotions, 1999. With AUS, 1942-44, ETO. Decorated Purple Heart; recipient Spirit of Life award City of Hope, 1989, Showman Wall of Fame award Internat. Beauty Show, 1994; inducted into Nat. Cosmetology Assn. Hall of Fame, 1994, Barber & Beauty Supply Inst. Hall of Leaders, 1998. Mem. Nat. Beauty and Barber Mfrs. Assn. (pres. 1984-85), Am. Beauty Assn. (pres. 1985-86), Masons. Home: 241 Sickletown Rd West Nyack NY 10994-2905 Office: Oppenheim Communications PO Box 700 West Nyack NY 10994-0700

OPPENHEIMER, BEN R. research scientist; BA in Physics, Columbia U., 1994; PhD in Astronomy, Calif. Inst. Tech., 1999. Rsch. asst. NASA Goddard Inst. for Space Studies, 1988—91, Columbia Astrophysics Lab., 1991—94; Hubble rsch. fellow Am. Mus. Natural History, N.Y.C., 1994—2002, Kalbfleisch rsch. fellow, 2002—. Instr. Columbia U., 1993—95; instr. physics dept. Barnard Coll., 1993—94. Fellow Grad. Rsch. fellow, NSF, 1994—97, Miller Inst. for Basic Rsch. in Sci., 1999, Harvard-Smithsonian Ctr. for Astrophysics, 1999; scholar I.I. Rabi Sci. scholar, Columbia U., 1990—94, Douglass scholar, U. Ariz. Steward Obs., 2000. Mem.: AAAS, Astron. Soc. Pacific, Internat. Soc. Optical Engring., Am. Astron. Soc. Office: Am Mus Natural History Dept Astrophysics Central Park West at 79th St New York NY 10024

OPPENHEIMER, DEANNA WATSON, bank executive; Degree cum laude in Polit. Sci. and Urban Affairs, U. Puget Sound. Mktg. and govt. rels. officer Washington Mutual Inc., Seattle, 1985—89, mgr. corp. relations div., 1989—93, exec. v.p., 1993—95, exec. v.p. Consumer Banking and Corporate Relations, 1995—2000, pres. Banking and Fin. Svcs. Group, 2000—03, overseer corp. R&D and corp. rels., 1999—, pres., consumer group, 2003—. Bd. dir. Catellus Devel. Corp., U. Puget Sound. Pres. Seattle (Wash.) Children's Theatre Bd.; bd. dir. Corp. Coun. Arts, Greater Seattle (Wash.) YMCA. Named Person of Yr., Media Inc.; recipient Double Halo award, Seattle (Wash.) Advt. Fedn. Mem.: Mktg. Comm. Execs. Internat. (pres.). Office: Washington Mutual Business Banking 1201 3rd Ave Seattle WA 98101

OPPENHEIMER, FRANZ MARTIN, lawyer; b. Mainz, Germany, Sept. 7, 1919; s. Arnold and Johanna (Mayer) O.; m. Margaret Spencer Foote, June 17, 1944; children: Martin Foote, Roxana Foote, Edward Arnold. BS, U. Chgo., 1942; student, U. Grenoble, France, 1938-39; LL.B. cum laude (note editor Law Jour. 1945), Yale U., 1945. Bar: N.Y. 1946, D.C. 1955. Rsch. asst. com. human devel. U. Chgo., 1942-43; law clk. to Judge Swan, U.S. Circuit Ct. of Appeals, N.Y., 1945-46; assoc. atty. Chadbourne, Wallace, Parke & Whiteside, N.Y.C., 1946-47; atty. IBRD, Washington, 1947-57; individual practice law, 1958-59; ptnr. firm Leva, Hawes, Symington, Martin & Oppenheimer, 1959-83, Fort & Schlefer, Washington, 1984-94; pvt. practice Washington, 1995—2001; sr. of counsel Swidler Berlin Shereff Friedman (formerly Swidler & Berlin), Washington, 1996—2001; individual consulting and law practice, 2001—; atty. Internat. legal Inst., 2004—. Contbr. articles to profl. and other jours, chpts. to books. Bd. dirs. Internat. Student House; founding mem. Company of Christian Jews. Decorated officer's cross Order of Merit (Fed. Republic Germany), chevalier Nat. Order of Merit (France). Mem. ABA, Am. Soc. Internat. Law (hon. v.p., treas. 1964-76), Coun. Fgn. Rels., Yale Club, Century Assn. (N.Y.), City Tavern, Met. Club (Washington). Anglican. Home: 3248 O St NW Washington DC 20007-2847 E-mail: franzmfmo@aol.com.

OPPENHEIMER, MARTIN J. lawyer; b. Apr. 11, 1933; s. Julius and Sylvia (Haas) O.; m. Suzanne Rosenhirsch, July 3, 1958; children: Marcy, Evan, Joshua, Alexandra. BS with honors, U. Pa., 1953; LLB, Yale U., 1956. Assoc. Hays, Sklar & Hertzberg, Mendes & Mount; ptnr. Proskauer Rose Goetz & Mendelsohn, N.Y.C., 1958—. Contbr. articles to profl. jours. Chmn. City Ctr. of Music and Drama, Lincoln Ctr., N.Y., 1984—; vice chmn. N.Y.C. Opera, 1985—; bd. dir. 92nd St. YWCA, N.Y., 1985—, Lincoln Ctr. for Performing Arts, 1987—; bd. advs. Mailman Sch. of Pub. Health, Columbia U., 1991; chmn. Lincoln Ctr. Constituent Devel. Corp., 2001-02. Fulbright scholar Goethe U., Frankfurt, Fed. Republic Germany, 1956-57. Home: 400 Claflin Ave Mamaroneck NY 10543-3906 Office: Proskauer Rose et al 1585 Broadway Fl 21-76 New York NY 10036-8299

OPPENHEIMER, MAX, JR., foreign language educator, consultant; b. N.Y.C., July 27, 1917; s. Max and Louise (Pourfuerst) O.; m. Christine Backus, Oct. 14, 1942; children: Edmund Max, Carolyn Christine Oppenheimer Burns. Bachelier ès Lettres, U. Paris, 1935; BA cum laude, NYU, 1941; MA, UCLA, 1942; PhD, U. So. Calif., 1947. Instr. fgn. langs. San Diego State Coll., 1947-49; asst. prof. Romance langs. Washington U., St. Louis, 1949-51; assoc. prof. modern langs. Fla. State U., Tallahassee, 1958-61; prof., chmn. dept. Russian U. Iowa, Iowa City, 1961-67; prof. SUNY, Fredonia, 1967-76, prof. emeritus, 1976—, chmn. dept. fgn. langs., 1967-74; prof. English Yunnan Normal U., Kunming, Peoples Republic of China, 1985-86. Intelligence officer CIA, 1956-58. Author: Outline of Russian Grammar, 1962; translator: Theory of Molecular Excitons (Davydov), 1962, Theory of Ship Waves and Wave Resistance (Kostyukov), 1968, The Fake Astrologer (Calderón de la Barca), 1976, 94, The Lady Simpleton (Lope de Vega), 1976, Don Juan (Tirso de Molina), 1976, Swim First and Last, 1981, An Innocent Yank at Home Abroad, 2000, Is That What It Means?, 2004; contbr. articles to scholarly and profl. jours. Active YMCA, 1936—. Served to lt. col. M.I., AUS, 1942-46, 51-56, lt. col. Res. ret. Decorated Bronze Star; Fla. State U. grantee, 1961, Office Naval Rsch. grantee, 1965, SUNY grantee, 1973. Mem.: MLA, Am. Soc. Geolinguistics (pres. 1975—76), Mil. Officers Assn. Am., Am. Soc. Dowsers, Dobro Slovo, Am. Mensa Ltd., Elks, Phi Beta Kappa, Alpha Mu Gamma, Pi Delta Phi (nat. pres. 1946—51), Sigma Delta Pi. Avocation: swimming. Home: 10963 W Coggins Dr Sun City AZ 85351-3346 E-mail: maxojr@earthlink.net. *When you speak, always say what you think, not what you think you should say for the sake of expediency. Steadfastly, stubbornly, cling to your ideals, principles and beliefs, but be flexible enough to change whenever changing them reflects wisdom, not weakness or compromise. Avoid ego trips or being awed by your own alleged accomplishments.*

OPPENHEIMER, MICHAEL, physicist; b. Bklyn., Feb. 28, 1946; s. Harry and Shirley Oppenheimer; m. Leonie Haimson, Dec. 31, 1986; children: Chloe, Nathaniel. S.B., MIT, 1966; PhD, U. Chgo., 1970. Research fellow Harvard Coll., 1971-73; lectr. astronomy Harvard U., 1971-73; physicist Harvard-Smithsonian Center for Astrophysics, Harvard U., 1973-81, Environ. Def., N.Y.C., 1981—2001, chief scientist, 1996-2001; Albert G. Milbank prof. geoscis. and internat. affairs Princeton U., 2002—, dir. program on sci. tech. and environ. Mem. panel on atmospheric effects of aviation NRC, 1995—99; lead author Intergovernmental panel on climate change. Author: Dead Heat: The Race Against the Greenhouse Effect, 1990; contbr. articles to profl. jours. Fellow, Union Carbide, 1969—70, A.F. Morrison, 1979, Guggenheim, 1978—79. Mem.: AAAS, Am. Meteorol. Soc., Am. Geophys. Union, Am. Phys. Soc. Office: Princeton U Robertson Hall 448 Princeton NJ 08544 E-mail: michael@princeton.edu.

OPPENHEIMER, PAUL, English comparative literature educator, poet, author; b. N.Y.C., May 1, 1939; s. Fred R. Oppenheimer and Gertrude Samuels; children: Julie Sarah, Ben. BA, Princeton U., 1961; MA, Columbia U., 1963, PhD, 1970. Lectr. Hunter Coll. CUNY, N.Y.C., 1964-67, lectr., poet-in-residence City Coll., 1967-70, from asst. prof. to assoc. prof. City Coll., 1970-84, prof. City Coll., 1984—; prof. comparative lit. The Grad. Ctr./CUNY, 2001—. Exch. prof., dir. CUNY student exch. program Sorbonne nouvelle, Paris, 1984-85; exch. prof. U. North London, Eng., 1989-90, Univ. Coll. London German Dept., 1993, 95, 97, 99; Fulbright prof. U. Osnabrück, Germany, 1993-94. Author: Before a Battle and Other Poems, 1967, Beyond the Furies, 1985, The Birth of the Modern Mind: Self, Consciousness, and the Invention of the Sonnet, 1989, Evil and the Demonic: A New Theory of Monstrous Behavior, 1996, An Intelligent Person's Guide to Modern Guilt, 1997, Rubens: A Portrait, 1999, 2002, Blood Memoir, or the First Three Days of Creation, 1999, Infinite Desire: A Guide to Modern Guilt, 2000, The Flame Charts, new poems, 2002; translator: Till Eulenspiegel: His Adventures, 1972, 4th edit., 2001. Woodrow Wilson fellow, 1961-62, Alfred Hodder fellow, 1969-70, Fulbright sr. fellow, Germany, 1993-94; recipient Eisner Scholars award Rifkind Ctr. for the Humanities, 1998. Mem. Dante Soc. Am. Home: 50 W 67th St New York NY 10023-6227 Office: CCNY Dept English and Comparative Lit NAC 138 St and Convent Ave New York NY 10031 Also: The Graduate Ctr CUNY Dept Comparative Lit 365 Fifth Ave New York NY 10016 E-mail: pauloppenheimer@hotmail.com.

OPPENHEIMER, SUZI, state legislator; b. N.Y.C., Dec. 13, 1934; d. Alfred Elihu Rosenhirsch and Blanche (Schoen) O.; m. Martin J. Oppenheimer, July 3, 1960; children: Marcy, Evan, Josh, Alexandra. BA in Econs., Conn. Coll. for Women, 1956; MBA, Columbia U., 1958. Security analyst McDonnell & Co., N.Y.C., 1958-60, L.F. Rothschild Co., N.Y.C., 1960-63; mayor Village of Mamaroneck, N.Y., 1977-85; mem. N.Y. State Senate, Albany, 1985—. Ranking mem. edn., mem. fin., transp., water resources, health, ethics, environ. conservation and banking com., chmn. N.Y. State Women Legislators' Lobby, chmn. Senate Dem. Task Force on Women's Issues, treas. Legis. Women's Caucus, pres. Senate Club. Former pres. Mamaroneck LWV, Westchester County Mcpl. Ofcls. Assn., Westchester Mcpl. Planning Fedn. Recipient Humanitarian Svc. award Am. Jewish Com., 1988, Legis. Leadership award Young Adult Inst., 1988, Legis. award Westchester Irish Com., 1988, Hon. Svc. award Vis. Nurses Svcs., 1989, Humanitarian Svc. award Project Family, 1990, Meritorious Svc. award N.Y. State Assn. Counties, 1990, Friend of Edn. award N.Y. State United Tchrs., 1991, Assn. Health Care Providers award, 1993, Govtl. award Cmty. Opportunity Program, 1994, Spl. Recognition award Open Door Family Med. Group, 1995, Appreciation award, Careers for People with Disabilities, 1996, Dominican Sisters Family Health Svcs., 1996, Vets. Svc. award JWV, 1997; honoree Windward Sch. Ann. Dinner, 1992, Leadership award Westchester Dem. Com., 2003, Citizen of Yr. award NASW, 2003, others; named Legislator of Yr., N.Y. State Women's Press Club, Woman of Yr., Westchester ORT, 1990, Woman of Yr., Woman of the Yr. bus. and profl. women's club, 2001, Pub. Svc. award cmty. housing, 2002, honoree, Wash. housing alliance dinner, 2002, Hope Cmty. Svcs. Club, 2002, Westchester Fedn. Women's Clubs, 2002. Democrat. Jewish. Office: 222 Grace Church St Port Chester NY 10573-5168

OPPENLANDER, ROBERT, retired airline executive; b. N.Y.C., May 20, 1923; s. Robert and Lillian (Ahrens) O.; m. Jessie I. Major, Sept. 30, 1950; children: Kris Oppenlander Austin, Robert Kirk, Tenley. BS, MIT, 1944; MBA, Harvard U., 1948. With Metals & Controls Corp., Attleboro, Mass., 1948-53; prin. Cresap, McCormick & Paget, N.Y.C., 1953-58; comptroller, treas. Delta Air Lines, Inc., Atlanta, 1958-88, v.p. fin., 1964-67, sr. v.p. fin., treas., 1967-78, sr. v.p. fin., 1978-83, vice chmn. bd., chief fin. officer, 1983-88, ret., 1988, also adv. dir. Served to lt. USNR, 1944-46. Mem.: Capital City. Home: 3944 Powers Ferry Rd NW Atlanta GA 30342-4026

OPPER, BARBARA NEGRI, financial economist; b. Torrington, Conn., Sept. 8, 1939; d. Albert Frederick and Anna (LaRocco) Negri; m. Franz Frederick Opper, Dec. 2, 1967 (dec. Mar. 1991); children: Gretchen Elizabeth, Stephen Frederick. BA, Conn. Coll., 1961; MA in Econs., U. Mich., 1965. Analyst Conn. Gen. Ins., Hartford, 1961-63; econ. rsch. assoc. Life Ins. Assn. Am., N.Y.C., 1965-66; corp. sec., dir. Krambo Corp., N.Y.C., 1966-67; economist Fed. Res. Bd., Washington, 1967-72, sr. economist, 1976-83; fin. economist Travelers Ins. Cos., Hartford, 1972-76; lectr. Mt. Holyoke Coll., South Hadley, Mass., 1975-76; chief officer The World Bank, Wash., DC, sr. mgr., sr. advisor, Washington, 1983-98; pres. ConFirm, Chevy Chase, Md., 1998—. Sec., bd. dirs. Bank Fund Staff Fed. Credit Union, Washington, 1997—; advisor sovereign debt mgmt. U.S. Treasury, Office of Tech. Assistance, Washington, 2000—. Contbr. articles to Fed. Res. Bull. Bd. dirs. Washington Bach Consort, 1998—. Mem.: Cosmos Club, Phi Beta Kappa. Home: 7004 Meadow Ln Chevy Chase MD 20815

OPPERWALL, STEPHEN GABRIEL, lawyer; b. Racine, Wis., Aug. 14, 1953; s. Raymond and Helen Bertha Opperwall; m. Kathleen O'Neill, Oct. 27, 1990; children: Christopher Stephen, Scott O'Neill. BA, Calvin Coll., 1975; JD, U. Santa Clara, 1981. Bar: Calif. 1981, U.S. Dist. Ct. (no., ea., ctrl. and so. dists.) Calif. 1981, U.S. Tax Ct. 1994, U.S. Ct. Appeals (9th cir.) 1984; cert. specialist in creditor's rights. Tchg. asst. U. Santa Clara (Calif.) Sch. Law, 1979; judge's law clk. U.S. Ct. Appeals, 9th Cir., San Francisco, 1980; assoc. Pitto & Ubhaus, San Jose, Calif., 1980-82, Germino, Layne & Brodie, Palo Alto, Calif., 1982-87, Tarkington, O'Connor & O'Neill, San Jose, 1988-90, Smith & Smith, San Jose, 1990-92; pvt. practice Law Offices of Stephen G. Opperwall, Pleasanton, Calif., 1992—. Judge pro tem Santa Clara County Cts., 1986—, Alameda County (Calif.) Cts., 1992—; mem. adv. bd. Fremont (Calif.) Bank, 1996. Editor Santa Clara Law Review, 1980. Mem. bd. dirs. Fremont Symphony, 1994. Mem. Coml. Law League Am., Pleasanton C. of C. Avocations: golf, tennis, computers. Office: 4900 Hopyard Rd Ste 100 Pleasanton CA 94588-3149 E-mail: lawofcsgo@aol.com.

OPPEWALL, JEANNINE CLAUDIA, motion picture production designer; b. Whitinsville, Mass., Nov. 28, 1946; d. Garret Oppewall and Eva Edith Boutilier; m. Paul Schrader (div.). BA, Calvin Coll.; MA, Bryn Mawr Coll. Lectr. Harvard U., Am. Film. Inst., Otis Inst. of Art, Am. Inst. of Graphic Arts, others. Film prodn. designer L.A. Confidential, 1997 (Oscar nomination), Pleasantville, 1998 (Oscar nomination, L.A. Film Critics Assn. award for best prodn. design, 1998), Wonder Boys, 1999, The Sum of All Fears, 2001, Catch Me if You Can, 2002, Seabiscuit, 2003 (Oscar nomination), Maria's Lovers, Ironweed, The Music Box, White Palace, Love Letters, The Big Easy, Rooftops, Sibling Rivalry, The Bridges of Madison County, Snow Falling on Cedars, Tender Mercies. Recipient Best Contemporary Designed Film, Art Dir.'s Guild award. Mem.: Art Dirs. Guild, United Scenic Artists.

OPPLER, RALPH LEO, retired publishing executive, advertising executive; b. N.Y.C., June 22, 1935; s. Charles Kurt and Jetta (Samuel) O.; m. Ruth Theresa Schoen, Sept. 22, 1957; children: Charles, Robin, Stephen. Student, Bryant Coll., 1951-52. Various sales positions, 1959-71; mem. sales staff Jour. Commerce Newspaper, N.Y.C., 1972-77; regional dir. B'nai B'rith Internat., Washington, 1978-88; fundraising mgr. Juvenile Diabetes Found., Essex County, N.J., 1990-91; founder, pres. Bus. Builders Pub. Co., Inc., Fair Lawn, N.J., 1991-99; counselor Svc. Corps of Retired Execs., U.S. Sml. Bus. Adminstrn., 2000—. Fundraising cons. Williams Ctr. Performing Arts, Rutherford, N.J., 1986, March of Dimes, Bergen County, N.J., 1980, Nat. Assn. Disabled Athletes, Ft. Lee, N.J., 1985; exec. analyst George B. May Co., Chgo., 1988. Pres., mem. Ridgefield (N.J.) H.S. Booster Club, 1970-80; v.p., coach, mgr. Ridgefield Boys Athletic Orgn., 1964-80; sponsor, coach basketball team Nat. Amateur Athletic Union, N.J., 1975-76; commr. Ridgefield Pks. and Recreation Commn., 1976-80; coach, Ridgefield 7/8 Grade Basketball, 1968-80; bd. dirs. Coun. Compulsive Gambling of N.J., 1997-99. With USN, 1954-59. Mem. Commerce and Industry Assn. N.J., Fair Lawn C. of C., B'nai B'rith (Young Leadership award 1978; v.p. Paterson, N.J. lodge 1977; pres. Englewood lodge 1977-78), Jaycees (pres. Jacksonville, N.C. chpt. 1961). Democrat. Jewish. Avocations: basketball, jazz, ballroom dancing. Home: 10933 Royal Caribbean Cir Boynton Beach FL 33437-4222

OPPMAN, JOHN CHRISTOPHER, small business owner; b. Gary, Ind., Feb. 16, 1954; s. Ernest and Mary Oppman; divorced; children: Jennifer Kolosci, Elizabeth, Christine. BS in Criminal Justice, Ind. U., Gary, 1992; MPA, Western Mich. U., 1995. Asst. pers. dir. Sts. and Sanitation City of Gary, Ind., 1973; coke plant laborer U.S. Steel Corp., Gary, 1976-84; computer cons. Gary, 1985-88; drill instr. Camp Summit Juvenile Boot Camp State of Ind. Dept. Corrections, La Porte, 1995-97; owner, operator Specialty Logistics, Sawyer, Mich., 1998—. Asst. to pres. U.S.W.A. Local 1014, Gary, 1982-84. Polit. organizer Mayor Richard G. Hatcher campaign, Gary, 1970-73; campaign advisor, organizer Local 1014 presdl. campaign, Gary, 1978-84. Truman scholar, 1990. Mem. Gold Key, Sons of Italy. Episcopalian. Avocations: historical animation, interpretation.

OPPMANN, ANDREW JAMES, newspaper editor; b. Hopkinsville, Ky., Apr. 3, 1963; s. Patrick George Oppmann and Elizabeth Anne (Freeman) Peace; m. Emily Elise Wey, Oct. 8, 1988; children: Emily Katherine, Sarah Elizabeth. BA in Journalism, U. Ky., 1985. Staff writer The Orange County Register, Santa Ana, Calif., 1985-86; copy editor, staff writer Lexington (Ky.) Herald-Leader, 1986-87, bur. chief, asst. metro editor, 1988-91; urban affairs writer The Knoxville (Tenn.) News-Sentinel, 1987-88; asst. city editor The Houston Post, 1991-92, dep. met. editor, 1992, asst. to mng. editor, 1992, met. editor, 1992-94; Ky. editor The Cin. (Ohio) Enquirer, 1994-97; supervising editor The Ky. Enquirer, Ft. Mitchell, 1994-97; mng. editor Montgomery (Ala.) Advertiser, 1998-2001; exec. editor The Post-Crescent, Appleton, Wis., 2001—. Bd. vis. U. Ky. Sch. Journalism, 1994-97. Fellow U. Ky., 1984; recipient Gannett Newsroom Supr. Recognition award, 1995, 2000. Mem. U. Ky. Journalism Alumni Assn. (v.p. 1997-2000, pres. 2001-03), Soc. Profl. Journalists (bd. dirs. Queen City chpt. 1995-97), Ala. AP Mng. Editors (bd. dirs. 1998—), U. Ky. Nat. Alumni Assn. (bd. dirs. 1998-2001). Office: The Post-Crescent PO Box 59 Appleton WI 54912 E-mail: oppedit@aol.com.

OPRE, THOMAS EDWARD, retired editor, retired film company executive; b. Evansville, Ind., Nov. 6, 1943; s. William Jennings and Ruth (Strouss) O.; children: Thomas Andrew, William Hartley. AB in Journalism, Ind. U., 1965. Writer sports and outdoors Decatur (Ill.) Herald and Rev., 1965-66; outdoor editor Detroit Free Press, 1966—91; field editor Midwest div. Field and Stream mag., 1971-81; editorial dir. Gt. Lakes Sportsman mag., 1972-75; editor-at-large and sports vehicles editor Outdoor Life mag., 1981-93; pres. Tom Opre Prodns., 1967—2004. Pres. TOP Safaris, Inc., 1986—2004. Author numerous articles in outdoor and travel fields. Recipient James Henshall award Am. Fish Tackle Mfrs. Assn., 1969, Teddy award Internat. Outdoor Travel Film Festival, 1973, Environ. award EPA, 1977, Nat. Writer's award Safari Club Internat., 1977, Deep Woods Writing award OWAA, 1977, Conservation Service award Ducks Unltd., 1977; World Wildlife Found. award, 1981; named to Internat. Fishing Hall of Fame, 1968, Conservation Communicator of Yr., 1985. Mem. Outdoor Writers Assn. Am. (past dir., pres., v.p., chmn. bd.), Assn. Gt. Lakes Outdoor Writers (past dir., chmn. bd., pres., v.p.), Mich. Outdoor Writers Assn. (v.p., pres., chmn. bd. dirs.), Alpha Tau Omega. Home and Office: 255 Powers Cv NE Marietta GA 30067-1503 Personal E-mail: topsafaris@aol.com.

OPTICAN, LANCE MICHAEL, research scientist; b. Denver, Colo., May 16, 1950; s. Albert W. Optican and Arlene M. Bruno; m. Donna C. Optican, Aug. 23, 1980. BSc, Calif. Inst. Tech., 1972; PhD, Johns Hopkins Sch. Medicine, 1978. Rsch. biomedical engr. Nat. Eye Inst., Bethesda, Md., 1979—. Mem.: IEEE, Soc. for Neuroscience, Internat. Neural Network Soc. Achievements include patents for US Pat. 5, 037, 376: Apparatus and Method for Transmitting Prosthetic Information to the Brain. Office: National Eye Inst Bldg 49 Room 2A50 Bethesda MD 20892-4435 E-mail: lanceoptican@nih.gov.

O'QUINN, APRIL GALE, obstetrician, gynecologist, educator; b. Columbia, Miss., Apr. 21, 1936; d. R.V. and Anna Pauline (Cook) O'Q. Diploma, Scott and White Sch. Nursing, 1965; AA, Temple Jr. Coll., 1965; BS with honors, Baylor U., 1968; MD, U. Tex. Med. Br., 1971. Diplomate Am. Bd. Ob-Gyn. Intern U. Tex. Med. Br., Galveston, 1971-72, resident ob-gyn., 1972-75; fellow in oncology M.D. Anderson Hosp., Houston, 1976-78; practice medicine specializing in ob-gyn. Galveston, 1978-81, New Orleans, 1981—. Asst. prof. dept. ob-gyn. U. Tex. Med. Br., Galveston, 1975—81; mem. staff John Sealy Hosp., St. Mary's Hosp., Galveston, Tulane Med. Ctr., New Orleans Charity Hosp., Touro Infirmary, New Orleans; assoc. prof., dir. div. gynecol. oncology dept. ob-gyn. Tulane U. Sch. Medicine, New Orleans, 1981—85, prof., 1985—89, prof., chair dept. ob-gyn., 1989—. Fellow: ACOG, Willard R. Cooke Obstet. and Gynecol. Soc.; mem.: AMA, La. Med. Assn., Assn. Profs. in Ob-Gyn., Coun. Univ. Chmn. in Ob-Gyn., Soc. Gynecologic Oncologists, Felix Rutledge Soc. Orleans Parish. Republican. Baptist. Home: 5100 Bancroft Dr New Orleans LA 70122-1218 Office: Tulane U Sch Medicine Dept Ob Gyn New Orleans LA 70112 E-mail: aoquinn@tulane.edu.

O'QUINN, NANCY DIANE, nurse, educator, consultant; b. Walton County, Ga., Nov. 22, 1944; d. L.C. Jr. and Eula (Hegwood) Kennedy; m. Charles Frank O'Quinn; children: Robert, Spencer, Alan. Diploma, Ga. Bapt. Hosp., 1965; BSN, Valdosta State Coll., 1979, MEd, 1983; MSN, Valdosta State U., 1986; PhD in Social Work Adminstrn. & Policy, Fla. State U., 1999. Sr. nurse Tift County Health Dept., Tifton, Ga., 1979-80; instr. Abraham Baldwin Coll., Tifton, 1980-85, assoc. prof., 1992-94; asst. prof. Valdosta (Ga.) State Coll., 1985-94; asst. prof. nursing Albany (Ga.) State U., 1990-92, 94-97; rsch. assoc. Fla. State U., 1998-99, Health Occupations Cook County, Ga., 1999; asst. dir. regional econ. devel. U. Ga., 2000—02; cons. O'Quinn Cons. Svcs., 2002—; dir. Paul Coverdell INst. Ga. Coll. State U., 2004—. Lt. USNR, 1989—2002. Mem.: Alpha Chi, Sigma Theta Tau.

OR, KA LUN, research assistant; BEng in Engring.(hon.), Hong Kong U., 2001; MS (hon.), Miss. State U., 2004; PhD, U. Wis.-Madison, 2004. Ergonomics cons. Hong Kong U. Sci. and Tech., Kowloon, Hong Kong, 2001, rsch. asst., 2001, Miss. State U., Starkville, 2002—. Scholar, Enthone - OMI Co. Ltd., 1997, Polywell, 1998, Intertek Testing Svcs., 1998; Honda fellow, 2002, Barrier Grad. Engring. fellow, 2003. Mem.: Hong Kong Instn. Engrs. Office: PO Box 2636 Mississippi State MS 39762

ORAEFO, JOHNNY NDUBUISI, geologist, corporation executive, consultant; b. Jos, Plateau, Nigeria, June 26, 1945; s. George Madubike and Comfort O. (Onwuamaegbu) O.; m. Comfort Chinwe Onyekaba, July 9, 1976; children: Adaora, Ebeleann, Oge, Obi, Amy. AB, U. N.C., 1982; Diploma, Computer Electronics, 1993. Cert. profl. geologist, N.C. Dir. Flamingo Imports Exports, Inc., Raleigh, N.C., 1984—; pres., co-owner African Supermarkets and Gift Shop, Raleigh, 1987—; pres. B.J. Internat., 1994—; dir. African Safari Stores, 1995—; cons. Internat. Trades, Raleigh, 1984—. Pres. Nigerian Student Assn. of U.S.A., Raleigh, 1981; dir. World Missions Living Faith Apostolic Ministries, U.S.A., 1995—. Recipient cert. Merit Internat. Traders Assn., 1982. Mem. Am. Assn. Petroleum Geologists, Soc. Econ. Paleontologists Mineralogists, Dip. Computer Electronics Tech., Travel Internat. Club. Mem. Christian Ch. Avocations: tennis, travel, singing, ping-pong, reading. Home: 1716 River Knoll Dr Raleigh NC 27610-4582

ORAM, ROBERT W. library administrator; b. Warsaw, Ind., June 11, 1922; s. George Harry and Lottie Mae (Gresso) O.; m. Virginia White, June 16, 1949; 1 child, Richard W. BA, U. Toledo, 1949; MS in Library Adminstrn., U. Ill., 1950. Asst. to librarian U. Mo.-Columbia, 1950-56; circulation librarian U. Ill.-Urbana, 1956-67, dir. pub. service, 1968-71, assoc. univ. librarian, 1971-79, acting univ. librarian, 1975-76; dir. Central Univ. Libraries So. Meth. U., Dallas, 1979-89, dir. emeritus, 1989. Mem. adv. com. Ill. State Library, Springfield, 1975-79 Contbr. articles to profl. jours. Exec. sec. Friends of So. Meth. U. Librs., 1980-89; former mem. bd. dirs. Urbana Free Libr., Lincoln Trails Libr. Sys., Champaign, Ill.; trustee Friends Austin (Tex.) Pub. Libr., 1994-99. Mem. ALA (life, pub. com. 1975-79), Friends of Libraries U.S.A. (exec. bd. 1980-86), Ill. Library Assn. (treas. 1972-73), Democrat. Avocations: reading, music. Home: The Heritage 4409 Gaines Ranch Loop # 252 Austin TX 78735 E-mail: Roram@austin.rr.com.

ORANGE, CAROLYN, education educator; b. St. Louis, July 11, 1948; d. William, Sr. and Alma M.; m. John H. Orange, Nov. 22, 1970; children: Traci, Timothy, Tisha. BA, Harris-Stowe Coll., 1970; MS, Washington U., St. Louis, 1977, PhD, 1991. Cert. tchr., Mo. Tchr. St. Louis Pub. Schs., 1970-77; asst. staff mgr. Southwestern Bell, St. Louis, 1977-80; program dir. Maritz Motivation, St. Louis, 1983-85; instr. Maryville U., St. Louis, 1986-88; tchg. asst. Washington U., St. Louis, 1990, motivation cons., 1987-91; asst. prof. St. Louis U., 1991-93, U. Tex., San Antonio, 1993—98, assoc. prof., 1998—2004, prof., 2004—. Cons. St. Louis Pub. Schs., 1992, San Antonio Ind. Sch. Dist., Tex., 1995-97, Region 13, San Antonio, 1995, 97-98; book reviewer Merrill Edn. Prentice Hall, 1997; presenter confs. in field. Author: 25 Biggest Mistakes Teachers Make and How to Avoid Them, 2000, The Quick Reference

Guide to Educational Innovations, 2002, 44 Smart Strategies For Avoiding Classroom Mistakes, 2004; author/prodr.: (video) Using Peer Models to Teach Self-Regulation, 1996; contbr. articles to profl. jours. Publicity chair Ebony Fashion Fair, Chgo., 1996, 97, 99; mem. human rels. com. City of University City, St. Louis, 1992; bd. dirs. Greater San Antonio coun. Girl Scout U.S., 2003. Recipient four-year scholarship Harris Stowe State, St. Louis Pub. Schs., 1966-70, univ. fellow Washington U., St. Louis, 1975-77, 88-89, Spencer fellowship Woodrow Wilson Found., Chgo., 1990-91; named to San Antonio Women's Hall of Fame, 2004, others; grantee in field. Mem. Am. Ednl. Rsch. Assn., Am. Psychol. Soc., Serious About Money Investment Club (pres. 1995--), Phi Theta Kappa. Avocations: collecting costume jewelry, writing, painting, mentoring. Office: Univ Tex 6900 N Loop 1604 W San Antonio TX 78249-1130 Office Phone: 210-458-5417. E-mail: jhorange@swbell.net., corange@utsa.edu.

ORANOVE, DAVID, business educator, consultant, economist; b. N.Y.C., July 25, 1956; s. Alfred and Dorothy Dranove; m. Deborah Salgo, Aug. 21, 1983; children: Daniel, Michael. BA, Cornell U., 1977, MBA, 1979; PhD, Stanford U., 1983. Asst. prof. U. Chgo., 1983—91; Richard Paget disting. prof. strategy Northwestern U., Evanston, Ill., 1995—99, chmn. dept. mgmt. and strategy, 1996—2000, Walter McNerney disting. prof. of health industry mgmt., 2000—, founder, dir. Ctr. Health Industry Mkt. Econ., 2001—. Bd. dirs. Pediat. Faculty Found., Chgo. Author: How Hospitals Survived, 1999, Economic Evolution of American Health Care, 2001, Economics of Strategy, 2003, What's Your Life Worth?, 2003, Strategic Analysis, 2004; contbr. articles to profl. jours. Recipient John Thompson prize, Assn. Univ. Programs Health Adminstrn., 1993, Rsch. prize, NIHCM, 1998, 2003, AHSR, 1999, numerous rsch. prizes. Mem.: Am. Econ. Assn. Avocations: audiophile, sports enthusiast, fine dining enthusiast. Office: Kellogg Sch of Mgmt 2001 Sheridan Rd Evanston IL 60208 Office Phone: 847-491-8682. Business E-Mail: d-dranove@northwestern.edu.

ORANSKY, IVAN, writer, web editor; b. Nyack, N.Y., Aug. 20, 1972; s. Stanley Howard and Lesley Marsha Oransky. BA, Harvard U., 1994; MD, NYU, 1998. Editor in chief Praxis Post, N.Y.C., 2000—02; web editl. dir. The Scientist, Phila., 2002—. Adj. prof. NYU, N.Y.C., 2002—. Author: Insider's Guide to Medical Schools, 1999, Appleton & Lange's Review of Psychiatry, 6th edit., 2000. Mem.: Assn. for Health Care Journalists (bd. dirs. 2002—), Am. Soc. Bioethics and Humanities, Am. Med. Writers Assn., Nat. Assn. Sci. Writers. Personal E-mail: ivan-oransky@erols.com.

ORATOFSKY, PAUL, photographer, application developer; b. Bklyn., Jan. 21, 1943; s. Helen (Gotterer) and Solomon Oratofsky; 1 child, Daniel Marq Kohl. BA in Math. and Physics, Bklyn Coll. Computer programmer N.Y.C. Transit Authority, 1964—66, Honeywell Controls, Ltd., London, 1966—68; computer programmer analyst Bunker-Ramo Corp., Trumbull, Conn., 1968—70; writer Chauen, Morocco, 1970—71; computer sys. programmer analyst Rockefeller U., N.Y.C., 1971—75; comml. photographer Camden, Maine, 1975—78; computer applications sys. designer developer Columbia U., N.Y.C., 1978—82; computer programmer analyst Pandick Press, N.Y.C., 1982—83; sr. software specialist Digital Equip. Corp., N.Y.C., 1983—85; sr. programmer/analyst Bowne & Co., N.Y.C., NY, 1985—86; sr. programmer/analyst cons. Stochastic Models Inc., N.Y.C., NY, 1985—86; v.p. tech. Drexel Burnham Lambert, N.Y.C., NY, 1986—90; photographer N.Y.C., NY, 1992—. Tech. writer Banque Indosuez, N.Y.C., 1992—94. Scholar Sci. scholarship, N.Y. State, 1959 - 1963. Achievements include language designer, developer. Avocations: fencing, guitar. Home and Office: B&W Photography 82 W 12th St #4A New York NY 10011-8649 Business E-Mail: paul@oratofsky.com.

ORAZEM, PETER FRANCIS, economics professor; b. Ames, Iowa, Nov. 26, 1955; s. Frank and Slava (Furlan) O.; m. Patricia Mary Cotter; children: Matthew, Katherine. BA, Kans. U., 1977; M. Phil., Yale U., 1980, PhD, 1983. Asst. prof. dept. econ. Iowa State U., Ames, 1982-88, assoc. prof., 1988-94, prof., 1994—2003, univ. prof., 2003—; interim assoc. dean Coll. Liberal Arts & Scis., Ames, 1998-2000, dir. Indsl. Rels. Ctr., 2000—; co-dir. Inst. Sci. and Soc., 2002—04. Vis. scholar World Bank, 1993-94. Contbr. articles to profl. jours. Grantee Inst. Rsch. on Poverty, U. Wis., 1985, Nat. Rsch. Coun., 1986-87, NSF, 1990, Carlson Sch. Mgmt., U. Minn., 1990, USDA, 1992, 93, World Bank, 1994—, Inter-Am. Devel. Bank, 2002, Internat. Labour Orgn., 2003. Mem. Am. Econs. Assn., Am. Agrl. Econs. Assn., Midwest Econs. Assn., Soc. Labor Economists, Phi Beta Kappa. Roman Catholic. Avocations: fishing, camping, stand-up comedy. Home: 4941 Utah Dr Ames IA 50014-3004 Office: Iowa State U Dept Econs Ames IA 50011-0001 Office Phone: 515-294-8656. Business E-Mail: pfo@iastate.edu.

ORBACH, JERRY, actor, singer; b. N.Y.C., Oct. 20, 1935; s. Leon and Emily (Olexy) O.; m. Marta Curro, June 21, 1958 (div. 1975); children: Anthony Nicholas, Christopher Ben; m. Elaine Cancilla, Oct. 7, 1979. Student, U. Ill., 1952-53, Northwestern U., 1953-55; studied acting with, Herbert Berghof, Mira Rostova, Lee Strasberg, N.Y.C.; studied singing with, Hazel Schweppe, N.Y.C. Actor various films, on and off-Broadway prodns., 1956—. Profl. stage debut: Room Service, 1952; resident actor: Show Case Theatre, Evanston, Ill., summers 1953-54; N.Y.C. stage debut: Three Penny Opera, 1955; actor: (stage) Chicago, 3 Penny Opera, The Fantasticks, Carnival, Scuba Duba, Promises Promises, The Rose Tattoo, 6 Rums Riv Vu, The King and I, Guys and Dolls, The Student Prince, Annie Get Your Gun, The Trouble With People ... And Other Things, 42d Street, 1980; (films) Cop Hater, 1958, Mad Dog Coll, 1961, John Goldfarb Please Come Home, 1965, The Gang That Couldn't Shoot Straight, 1971, A Fan's Notes, 1974, Sentinel, 1977, The Prince of the City, 1982, Brewster's Millions, 1985, F/X, 1986, The Image Maker, 1986, Dirty Dancin', 1987, Someone to Watch Over Me, 1988, Crimes and Misdemeanors, 1989, Last Exit to Brooklyn, 1990, Out for Justice, 1991, Toy Soldiers, 1991, Delusion, 1991, Delirious, 1991, Beauty and the Beast, 1991 (voice only), Straight Talk, 1992, Universal Soldier, 1992, Mr. Saturday Night, 1992, The Cemetary Club, 1993, A Gnome Named Gnorm, 1994, Chinese Coffee, 2000, The Prince of Central Park, 2000, Manna From Heaven, 2001; (TV episodes) including Love American Style, Murder She Wrote; (TV series) The Law and Harry McGraw, 1987-88, Law and Order, 1992—; (TV movies) An Invasion of Privacy, 1983, Out on a Limb, 1987, Love Among Thieves, 1987, In Defense of a Married Man, 1990, Broadway Bound, 1992, Quiet Killer, 1992, The Hunt, 2001, (voice) House of Mouse, 2001; (TV miniseries) Dream West, 1986; (video) Aladdin and the King of Thieves, 1996; (voice) Beauty and the Beast: The Enchanted Christmas, 1997. Recipient New March of Dimes Horizon award, 1961, award of merit Actors Fund, 1961, Tony award Antoinette Perry Com., 1968. Mem. AFTRA, Screen Actors Guild, Actors Equity Assn., Long Star Boat Club, Friar's Club. Clubs: Lone Star Boat. Avocations: poker, pool, golf, tennis. Office: Artists Group 10100 Santa Monica Blvd Los Angeles CA 90067-4003

ORBACH, RAYMOND LEE, physicist, researcher; b. Los Angeles, July 12, 1934; s. Morris Albert and Mary Ruth (Miller) O.; m. Eva Hannah Spiegler, Aug. 26, 1956; children: David Miller, Deborah Hedwig, Thomas Randolph. BS, Calif. Inst. Tech., 1956; PhD, U. Calif., Berkeley, 1960; PhD in Policy Analysis (hon.), The Rand Grad. Sch., Santa Monica, Calif., 2002. NSF postdoctoral fellow Oxford U., 1960-61; asst. prof. applied physics Harvard U., 1961-63; prof. physics UCLA, 1963-92, asst. vice chancellor acad. change and curriculum devel., 1970-72, chmn. acad. senate L.A. divsn., 1976-77, provost Coll. Letters and Sci., 1982-92; chancellor U. Calif., Riverside, 1992—2002, chancellor emeritus, Disting. Prof. Physics emeritus, 2002—; dir. office sci. U.S. Dept. Energy, Washington, 2002—. Mem. physics adv. panel NSF, 1970-73; mem. vis. com. Brookhaven Nat. Lab., 1970-74; mem. materials rsch. lab. adv. panel NSF, 1974-77; mem. Nat. Commn. on Rsch., 1978-80; chmn. 16th Internat. Conf. on Low Temperature Physics, 1981; Joliot Curie prof. Ecole Superieure de la Physique et Chimie Industrielle de la Ville de Paris, 1982, chmn. Gordon Rsch. Conf. on Fractals, 1986; Lorentz prof. U. Leiden, Netherlands, 1987; Raymond and Beverly Sackler lectr. Tel Aviv U., 1989; faculty rsch. lectr. UCLA, 1990; Andrew Lawson lectr. U. Calif., Riverside, 1992; mem. external rev. com. Nat. High Magnetic Fields Lab., 1994—. Author: (with A.A. Manenkov) SpinLattice Relaxation in Ionic Solids, 1966; divsn. assoc. editor Phys. Rev. Letters, 1980-83, Jour. Low Temperature Physics, 1980-90, Phys. Rev., 1983—; contbr. articles to profl. jours. Recipient Whitney M. Young Humanitarian award Urban League of Riverside and San Bernardino, 1998, El Sol Azteca award La Prensa Hispana, 2000; Alfred P. Sloan Found. fellow, 1963-67; NSF sr. postdoctoral fellow Imperial Coll., 1967-68; Guggenheim fellow Tel Aviv U., 1973-74. Fellow Am. Phys. Soc. (chmn. nominations com. 1981-82, counselor-at-large 1987-91, chmn. divsn. condensed matter 1990-91); mem. AAAS (chairperson steering group physics sect.), NSF (mem. rsch. adv. com. divsn. materials 1992-93), Phys. Soc. (London), Univ. Rsch. Assn. (chair coun. pres. 1993), Sigma Xi, Phi Beta Kappa, Tau Beta Pi. Home: 2950 Van Ness St NW Apt 212 Washington DC 20008 Office: Office of Sci Dept Energy 1000 Independence Ave SW Washington DC 20585

ORBAN, KURT, foreign trade company executive; b. S.I., N.Y., Aug. 6, 1916; s. Kurt and Gertrude (Astfalck) Orbanowski; children: Robert Arnold, Robyn Ann, Kurt-Matthew, Jonathan; m. Catherine Cheng, 2002. Grad. steel fgn. trade course, Stahlunion-Export GmbH, Duesseldorf, Germany, 1938. Fgn. trade corr. Stahlunion, Dusseldorf, 1938, rep., 1939—40, Sofia, Bulgaria, 1940—41; steel export trader Steel Union Sheet Piling Co., N.Y.C., 1941; v.p. North River Steel Co., N.Y.C., 1941; chmn., pres. Kurt Orban Co., Inc., Wayne, N.J., from 1946; now sr. ptnr., chmn./CEO Kurt Orban Ptnrs. LLC. Mem. field hockey games com. U.S. Olympic Com., 1948-61; playing mgr., team capt. U.S. Field Hockey Team., London, Eng., 1948, playing coach, Melbourne, Australia, 1956; U.S. rep. Bur. Internat. Hockey Fedn., Brussels, 1954-62. Served to 1st lt., pilot USAAF, 1943-45. Field Hockey Assn. Am. named its cup for each yrs. men's team competition for him; named one of the Ten Best All-Time (1920-2003) U.S. Field Hockey Players. Mem. Am. Inst. for Internat. Steel (charter; pres. 1966-68, 78-80, bd. dirs. N.Y.C.), Am. Exporters and Importers Assn. (pres. 1972-73, bd. dirs.), Wire Assn. Internat., Am. Wire Prodrs. Assn. (charter). Avocations: tennis, skiing. Home Fax: 775-783-8881. Personal E-mail: korban@kurtorbanpartners.com.

ORBEN, JACK RICHARD, investment company executive, director; b. Bklyn., June 16, 1938; s. Stanley Souza and Helena Emily (Hall) O.; m. Patricia Wells, Dec. 17, 1960; children: Stacey Souza, Stephanie Anne, Bradford Richard. AA, Valley Forge, 1956; BA, Tufts U., 1960. Sales mgr. nat. accts. N.Y. Tel. Co., 1960-66; founder, exec. v.p. Facts, Inc., 1966-69, chmn., CEO Fiduciary Alliance, Inc., N.Y.C., 1970—2004; chmn. Oaktree Asset Mgmt., L.L.C., N.Y.C., NY, 2004—. Chmn., CEO & pres. Fiduciary Counsel, Inc., 1979-04, White Plains Charter Revision Commn.; mem. Fin. Com. City of White Plains; past pres. White Plains Child Day Care Assn., Thomas Slater Ctr.; past chmn., bd. dirs. YMCA Ctrl. and No. Westchester. With USNG, 1960-66. Mem. Larchmont Yacht Club, N.Y. Yacht Club, Union League Club, Windemere Island Club, Univ. Club, Down Town Assn., The Econ. Club of N.Y., The Pilgrims. Home: 177 Soundview Ave White Plains NY 10606-3825 Office: Oaktree Asset Mgmt LLC 30 Wall St New York NY 10005 E-mail: jrorben@aol.com.

ORBEN, ROBERT, editor, writer; b. NYC, Mar. 4, 1927; s. Walter August and Marie O.; m. Jean Louise Connelly, July 25, 1945. Humor and speech writer for entertainment personalities, bus. execs., politicians, 1946—; writer Jack Paar Show, N.Y.C., 1962-63, Red Skelton Hour, Hollywood, Calif., 1964-70; editor Orben's Current Comedy, Wilmington, Del., 1971-89; cons. to Vice Pres. Gerald R. Ford, Washington, 1974; speechwriter Pres. Gerald R. Ford, Washington, 1974-75; spl. asst. to pres., dir. White House speechwriting dept., Washington, 1976-77; speaker on uses of humor in communication, 1977—. Author: 2500 Jokes to Start 'Em Laughing, 1979, 2100 Laughs for All Occasions, 1983, 2400 Jokes to Brighten Your Speeches, 1984, 2000 Sure-Fire Jokes for Speakers, 1986, Speaker's Handbook of Humor, 2000, others. Recipient World Humor award Workshop Libr. on World Humor, 1992; Literary fellow Acad. Magical Arts, 1996. Mem. Writers Guild Am. Clubs: Nat. Press (Washington). Unitarian Universalist. Avocations: travel, theater. Home: 3709 S George Mason Dr Apt 205E Falls Church VA 22041-3700 *I have spent most of my lifetime creating laughter and consider it a lifetime well spent. Laughter is one of the glories of the human experience. It warms, amuses, instructs, and opens emotional doors. For me, laughter has been a living and a loving as well.*

ORBISON, JAMES GRAHAM, civil engineer, educator; b. Cleve., Oct. 27, 1953; s. James Lowell and Olga Andrea (Dianich) O.; m. Nancy Anne Miller, June 11, 1977; children: Ryan Brantly, Eric James. BSCE, Bucknell U., 1975; MEC, Cornell U., 1976, PhD, 1982. Project engr. English Engring. Corp., Williamsport, Pa., 1976-77; lectr. Bucknell U., Lewisburg, Pa., 1977-78, asst. prof. civil engring., 1982-87, assoc. prof., 1987-93, prof., 1993-96, Presdl. prof., 1996-99, interim dean Coll. Engring., 2000—02, dean of engring., 2002—. Reviewer ASME, ASTM, Am. Inst. Steel Constrn., Prestressed Concrete Inst, Pa. Dept. Commerce, Harper & Row Pubs. Contbr. articles to profl. jours. Mem. ASCE (Lindback award for disting. tchg. 1988), Am. Acad. Mechanics, Am. Inst. Steel Constrn., Am. Soc. for Engring. Edn. (Excellence in Instrn. Engring. Students award AT&T Found. 1990), Pa. Soc. Profl. Engrs. (Engr. of Yr. award 1985). Office: Bucknell U Coll Engring Lewisburg PA 17837 E-mail: jorbison@bucknell.edu.

ORBIT, WILLIAM (WILLIAM WAINWRIGHT), record producer; b. Eng., 1959; Hit records include Torch Song "Wish Thing", 1984, "Ecstasy", 1985, "Exhibit A", 1987, "Toward the Unknown Region", 1995, William Orbit "Orbit", 1987, "Strange Cargo", 1984-87, "Strange Cargo 2", 1990, "Strange Cargo 3", 1993, Strange Cargo "Hinterland", 1995, William Orbit "The Best of Strange Cargos", 1996, The Electric Chamber "Places in a Modern Style", 1995, Beth Orton "Superpinkymandy", 1993, Caroline Lavelle "Spirit", 1995, Bassomatic "Set the Controls for the Heart of the Bass", 1990, and "Science and Melody", 1997, Belinda Carlisle "Belinda", 1986, Madonna "Ray of Light" (album, 1999 Grammy winner for best prodn.), 1998, Wishbone Ash "Nouveau Calls", 1998, various "Guerrilla Grooves Volume 1", 1991. TV and movie appearances include "Rebellious Jukebox", 1983-84, "Bachelor Party", 1984, "Youngblood", 1986, "Texas Chainsaw Massacre 2", 1986, "Hot Shot", 1987, "Heat", 1996, and "Harald", 1997, "Pieces in a Modern Style," 2000.*

ORCHARD, ROBERT JOHN, theater producer, educator; b. Maplewood, N.J., Dec. 3, 1946; s. Robert Orchard and Beatrice (Gould) Todd; m. Pamela Marcy Pritchard, Sept. 6, 1969; children: Christopher, Katherine. Student, The Lawrence Acad., 1965; BA, Middlebury Coll., 1969; MFA, Yale U., 1972. Gen. mgr. Peterborough (N.H.) Players, 1967-70; asst. mng. dir. Yale Repertory Theatre, 1971-72, artistic admistr., 1972-73; instr. Yale Sch. Drama, 1972-73; mng. dir. Yale Repertory Theatre and Sch. Drama, 1973-79, Am. Repertory Theatre, Cambridge, Mass., 1979—2002, exec. dir., 2002—. Assoc. prof., co-chmn. theatre adminstrn. tng. program Yale Sch. Drama, 1975-79; mng. dir. Loeb Drama Ctr., Harvard U., 1979-2000, dir., 2000—, mng. dir. Inst. for Advanced Theatre Tng., 1979-2002, exec. dir., 2002—; orgn. ptnr. Inst. Arts and Civic Dialogue at Harvard U. Former mem. bd. dirs. Theatre Comms. Group; pres. bd. Mass. Cultural Edn. Collaborative, Am. Arts Alliance, Peterborough Players, Cambridge Multi-Cultural Arts Ctrs.; former exec. com. League of Residents Theatres; chmn. NEA, Profl. Theatre Cos., Opera/Mus. Theatre Panels. Office: Am Repertory Theatre 64 Brattle St Cambridge MA 02138-3443

ORCUTT, BEN AVIS, retired social work educator; b. Falco, Ala., Oct. 17, 1914; d. Benjamin A. and Emily Olive Adams; m. Harry P. Orcutt, 1946 (dec.). AB, U. Ala., 1936; MA, Tulane U., 1939, MSW, 1942; DSW, Columbia U., 1962. Social worker ARC, Lagarde Gen. Hosp., New Orleans; social worker, acting field dir. Fort Benning (Ga.) Regional Hosp., 1942-46; chief social work svc. VA Regional Office, Phoenix, 1946—51; chief social work svc. unit outpatient office VA, Birmingham, Ala., 1954-57, 58; rsch. asst. Rsch. Ctr. Sch. Social Work, Columbia U., N.Y.C., 1960-62, field advisor social work, 1962, assoc. prof. social work, 1965-76, La. State U., Baton Rouge, 1962-65; prof. social work, dir. doctoral program U. Ala., University, 1976-84; ret. Rsch. cons. Tavistock Centre, London, 1972; cons. sch. social work U. Houston, 1990, Troy State System, 1992. Author: Science and Inquiry in Social Work Practice, 1990, (with Harry P. Orcutt) America's Riding Horses, 1958, (with Elizabeth R. Prichard, Jean Collard, Austin H. Kutscher, Irene Seeland, Nathan Lefkowitz) Social Work with the Dying Patient and the Family, 1977, (with others) Social Work and Thanatology, 1980; editor: Poverty and Social Casework Services, 1974; mem. editl. bd. Jour. Social Work, 1982-84; contbr. articles to profl. books and jours. Mem. alumni bd. Sch. Social Work Columbia U., 1985—88, 1991—94. Recipient Centennial award for edn. Columbia U. Sch. Social Work, 1998; named to Ala. Social Work Hall of Fame, 1999; NIMH fellow, 1957-60; Ben Avis Adams Orcutt doctoral scholar in social work named in her honor, U. Ala. Mem. NASW, Ala. Conf. Social Welfare, Group for Advancement Doctoral Edn. (steering com., editor newsletter 1980-83), Zonta, others. Episcopalian. Home: 222 Fox Run Tuscaloosa AL 35406 Office: PO Box 870314 Tuscaloosa AL 35487-0314

ORCUTT, CHRISTOPHER C. language educator; BS summa cum laude in Philosophy, Northeastern U., 1992; cert. in secondary edn., U. Maine, 1996. Reporter Millbrook (N.Y.) Round Table, 1992—93, Poughkeepsie (N.Y.) Jour., 1993—94; Am. studies tchr. Freeport (Maine) H.S., 1996—98; dir. product devel. Actis, Inc., Portland, Maine, 1998—2000; v.p. client comm. Merrill Lynch, N.Y.C., 2000—02; adj. lectr. Baruch Coll., CUNY, N.Y.C., NY, 2002—. Web cons. QED Nat., N.Y.C., 2000. Contbr. short story,, (2nd Pl., MOTA Emerging Writers Contest, 2003), (55 Fiction World's Shortest Stories Contest Winner, 2002); author: (novel) Nick Chase's Great Escape. Mem.: Nat. Writers Union (assoc.), WWII Meml. Found., D-Day Mus., Theodore Roosevelt Assn., Phi Kappa Phi, Order of the Arrow (life). E-mail: cof11445@newton.baruch.cuny.edu.

ORCUTT, JAMES CRAIG, ophthalmologist; b. Holyoke, Colo., July 22, 1946; s. John Potter and Irene M. (Falk) O.; m. Barbara McCallum, Feb. 9, 1974; children: John, Gale. BPh in Pharmacy, U. Colo., Boulder, 1969; PhD in Pharmacology, U. Colo., Denver, 1976, MD, 1977. Diplomate Am. Bd. Ophthalmology. Intern U. Wash., Seattle, 1977-78, resident, 1978-81; fellow in orbital disease Moorfields Eye Hosp., London, 1981-82; fellow in neuro-ophthalmology Hosp. for Nervous Diseases and Great Ormond St. Hosp., London, 1982; asst. prof. ophthalmology U. Wash., Seattle, 1983-88, adj. prof. otolaryngology, 1987-88, assoc. prof. ophthalmology/adj. assoc. prof. otolargyngology, 1988-95, prof. ophthalmology, adj. prof. otolaryngology, 1995—. Chief ophthalmology Seattle Vets. Affairs Ctr., 1983—95; chief ophthalmology and eye care VA Puget Sound Health Care System, 1995—, exec. dir. surg. and perioperative care, 2000—; ophthalmology cons. Vets. Affairs Hdqrs, Washington, 1993—. Pres. bd. trustees Northwest Sch., Seattle, 1996-99. Avocations: northwest history, postal history, antique restoration. Office: U Wash Dept Ophthalmology PO Box 356485 Seattle WA 98195-6485 Business E-Mail: jorcutt@u.washington.edu.

ORD, LINDA BANKS, artist; b. Provo, Utah, May 24, 1947; d. Willis Merrill and Phyllis (Clark) Banks; m. Kenneth Stephen Ord, Sept. 3, 1971; children: Jason, Justin, Kristin. BS, Brigham Young U., 1970; BFA, U. Mich., 1987; MA, Wayne State U., 1990. Asst. prof. Sch. Art U. Mich., Ann Arbor, 1994—. Juror Southeastern Mich. Scholastic Art Award Competition, Pontiac, 1992, Scarab Club Watercolor Exhbn., Detroit, 1991, Women in Art Nat. Exhbn., Farmington Hills, Mich., 1991, U. Mich. Alumni Exhbn., 1989-90; mem. dean's adv. coun. U. Mich. Sch. Art and Design, 2001—. One-woman shows Atrium Gallery, Mich., 1990, 91; group shows include Am. Coll., Bryn Mawr, Pa., Riverside (Calif.) Art Mus., Kirkpatrick Mus., Oklahoma City, Montgomery (Ala.) Mus. Fine Arts, Columbus (Ga.) Mus., Brigham Young U., Provo, Utah, Kresge Art Mus., Lansing, Mich., U. Mich., Ann Arbor, Detroit Inst. Arts, Kirkpatrick Ctr. Mus. Complex, Oklahoma City, 1994, Riverside (Calif.) Art Mus., 1995, San Bernadino County Mus., Redlands, Calif., 1996, Neville Mus., Green Bya, Wis., 1996, Downey Mus. Art, Calif., 1996, Detroit Inst. Arts, 1996, Gallery Contemporary Art, U. Colo., Colorado Springs, 1996, Saginaw (Mich.) Art Mus., 1998, Springfield (Mo.) Art Mus., 1998, Art Inst. So. Calif., Laguna Beach, 1998, San Diego Art Inst., 1998, U. Mich., Dearborn, 1998. Hillsdale (Mich.) Coll., 1998, Ferris State U., Big Rapids, Mich., 1998, Sangre de Cristo Arts Ctr., Pueblo, Colo., 1999; works in many pvt. and pub. collections including Kelly Svcs., Troy, Mich., FHP Internat., Fountain Valley, Calif., Swords Into Plowshares Gallery, Detroit; work included in: (books) The Artistic Touch, 1995, Artistic Touch 2, 1996, Best of Watercolor-Painting Color, 1997, Best of Watercolor-Painting Light; Shadow, 1997, Artistic Touch 3, 1999; (mag.) Watercolor, An Am. Artist, 1996; subject of articles. Chairperson nat. giving fund Sch. Art U. Mich., 1993, Sch. art rep. Coun. Alumni Svcs., 1992—, mem. dean's adv. coun. Sch. Art and Design, 2001—. Recipient 1st Pl. award Swords Into Plowshares Internat. Exhbn., Detroit, 1989, Silver award Ga. Watercolor Soc. Internat. Exhbn., 1991, Pres.'s award Watercolor Okla. Nat. Exhbn., Oklahoma City, 1992, Flint Jour. award Buckham Gallery Nat. Exhbn., 1993, Ochs Meml. award N.E. Watercolor Soc. Nat. Exhbn., Goshen, N.Y., 1993, Color Q award Ga. Watercolor Soc., 1994, St. Cuthberts award Tex. Watercolor Soc., 1996, Daler-Rowney award San Diego Watercolor Soc. Internat. Exhbn., 1998, Hon. Mention award Nat. Watercolor Okla. Exhbn., 1998, Winsor:Newton award N.e. Watercolor Soc., 22d Annual Nat. Exhbn., 1998; many state and nat. painting awards. Mem. U. Mich. Alumni Assn. (bd. dirs. 1992—, Sch. Art rep.), U. Mich. Sch. Art Alumni Soc. (bd. dirs. 1989-91, pres.), Mich. Watercolor Soc. (chairperson 1992-93, bd. dirs. adv. 1993-94). Avocations: music, theater, tennis, golf, reading. E-mail: lbanksord@cox.net.

ORDAL, CASPAR REUBEN, business executive; b. Martell, Wis., May 5, 1922; s. Zakarias John and Sina Carlovna (Wulfsberg) O.; m. Ann Elizabeth Brady, June 7, 1947; Christopher Rolf, Peter Stuart. BS, Harvard Coll., 1946; M.P.A., Harvard U., 1947. Supr. central indsl. relations staff Ford Motor Co., Dearborn, Mich., 1947-53; dir. orgn. planning and mgmt. devel. Colgate-Palmolive Co., N.Y.C., 1953-65; v.p., gen. mgr. New Holland div. Sperry Rand Corp., (Pa.), 1965-76; corp. v.p. personnel Norton Simon Inc., N.Y.C., 1976-78; sr. v.p. adminstrn. Max Factor & Co., Hollywood, Calif., 1978-85. Served to 1st lt. USAAF, 1943-46. Mem. Personnel Round Table (chmn. 1983-84), Am. Mgmt. Assn. (Adv. council 1977-82), Phi Beta Kappa Clubs: Lancaster (Pa.) Country. Republican. Lutheran.

ORDEN, ALEX, management science educator emeritus; b. Rochester, N.Y., Aug. 9, 1916; s. Abraham and Esther (Katz) O.; m. Susan Rabinowitz, Dec. 8, 1946; children: Ruth Diane, David Robert, Jeanne Hannah. BS in Optics, U. Rochester, 1937; MS in Physics, U. Mich., 1939; PhD in Math, Mass. Inst. Tech., 1950. Physicist Nat. Bur. Standards, 1942-47; instr. MIT, 1947-50; mathematician Hdqrs. USAF, 1950-52; mgr. applied math. sect. Burroughs Corp., 1952-58; dir. operations analysis lab. U. Chgo., 1958-62, prof. mgmt. sci., 1958-86, prof. emeritus, 1987—. Adj. prof. U. Ill., Chgo.; vis. prof. London (Eng.) Sch. Econs., 1964, 86; vis. Vasser Woolley prof. Ga. Inst. Tech., 1966, 67, 70; program chmn. Nat. Computer Conf., 1981 Contbr. articles to profl. jours. Mem. Ill. Sci. Adv. Council, 1965-67. Mem. Inst. Mgmt. Scis. (sec. 1953, chmn. nat. meeting 1969), Assn. Computing Machinery (nat. lectr. 1965, chmn. spl. interest group in math. programming 1969-71), Math Programming Soc. (chmn. organizing com. 1970-72, vice chmn. council 1982-83, chmn. council 1983-86), Phi Beta Kappa, Sigma Xi. Home: 5715 S Kenwood Ave Chicago IL 60637-1742

ORDEN, STEWART L. lawyer; b. N.Y.C., Jan. 13, 1953; s. Charles Quigley and Esther (Ash) O.; m. Bonnie Lynn Raymond, Nov. 12, 1988; children: Molly, Justin, Tyler. BA, Clark U., 1975; JD, Bklyn. Law Sch. Biology, 1979. Bar: N.Y. 1979. Sr. trial atty. Kings Dist. Atty., Bklyn., 1979-87; ptnr. Orden & Cohen, N.Y.C., 1987-91; pvt. practice, N.Y.C., 1991—. Expert witness on trial techniques, complex personal injury, med. malpractice, comml. and white collar cases; won largest pub. settlement against NYC in discrimination case; profiled on 60 Minutes. Mem. N.Y. Coun. Def. Lawyers, Assn. Bar City N.Y., N.Y. Criminal Bar Assn., Nat. Assn. Def. Lawyers. Avocations: skiing, windsurfing, swimming, rollerblading, biking.

ORDIN, ANDREA SHERIDAN, lawyer; m. Robert Ordin; 1 child, M. Victoria; stepchildren: Allison, Richard. AB, UCLA, 1962, LLB, 1965. Bar: Calif. 1966. Dep. atty. gen. Calif., 1965-72; So. Calif. legal counsel Fair Employment Practices Commn., 1972-73; asst. dist. atty. L.A. County, 1975-77; U.S. atty. Central Dist. Calif., 1977-81; adj. prof. UCLA Law Sch., 1982; chief asst. atty. gen. Calif. L.A., 1983-90; ptnr. Morgan, Lewis &

Bockius, L.A., 1993—. Mem. L.A. County Bar Assn. (past pres., past exec. dir.). Office: Morgan Lewis & Bockius 300 S Grand Ave Ste 2200 Los Angeles CA 90071-3109 Office Phone: 213-612-1090. E-mail: aordin@morganlewis.com.

ORDONEZ, FRANCISCO A. (FRANK), automotive executive; b. Havana, Cuba; BBA, MBA, U. Detroit. Fin. mgr. GM Espana, 1981—84; fin. dir. worldwide purchasing function GM, 1984—88; various fin. and bus. planning pos., including dir. fin. Delphi Safety & Interior Systems Delphi Corp., 1988—99, gen. mgr. Product & Svc. Solutions, 1999—. Past bd. mem. U. Detroit Jesuit HS. Mem.: Motor Equipment Mfrs. Assn. (bd. mem.). Office: World Hdqrs Delphi 5725 Delphi Dr Troy MI 48098-2815 also: Delphi Product & Svc Solutions 408 Dana St PO Box 431 Warren OH 44486

ORDOVER, ABRAHAM PHILIP, lawyer, mediator; b. Far Rockaway, N.Y., Jan. 18, 1937; s. Joseph and Bertha (Fromberg) O.; m. Carol M. Ordover, Mar. 23, 1961 (dec. 1999); children: Andrew Charles, Thomas Edward; m. Eleanor Musick, Feb. 24, 2001. BA magna cum laude, Syracuse U., 1958; JD, Yale U., 1961. Bar: N.Y. 1961, U.S. Dist. Ct. (so. and ea. dists.) N.Y., U.S. Ct. Appeals (2d cir.), U.S. Supreme Ct. Assoc. Cahill, Gordon & Reindel, N.Y.C., 1961-71; prof. law Hofstra U., Hempstead, N.Y., 1971-81; L.Q.C. Lamar prof. law Emory U., Atlanta, 1981-91; CEO Resolution Resources Corp., Atlanta, 1991—; mediator and arbitrator. Vis. prof. Cornell U., Ithaca, N.Y., 1977; vis. lectr. Tel Aviv U., 1989, Am. Law Inst.; team leader nat. program Nat. Inst. Trial Advocacy, Boulder, Colo., 1980, 82, 84, 86, 89, tchr. program Cambridge, Mass., 1979-84, 88, adv. program Gainesville, Fla., 1978-79, northeast regional dir., 1977-81; team leader SE regional program, 1983; team leader Atlanta Bar Trial Tech. Program, 1981-91; lectr. in field; sr. v.p. Resolute Sys. Inc., bd. dirs. Author: Argument to the Jury, 1982, Problems and Cases in Trial Advocacy, 1983, Advanced Materials in Trial Advocacy, 1988, Alternatives to Litigation, 1993, Cases and Materials in Evidence, 1993, Art of Negotiation, 1994; prodr. ednl. films; contbr. articles to profl. jours. Bd. dirs. Atlanta Legal Aid Soc., 1984-91, 7 Stages Theatre, 1991-96. Recipient Gumpert award Am. Coll. Trial Lawyers, 1984, 85, Jacobsen award Roscoe Pound Am. Trial Lawyer Found., 1986. Fellow Am. Coll. Civil Trial Mediators; mem. ABA, N.Y. State Bar Assn., Assn. Am. Law Schs. (chair litigation sect.), Atlanta Lawyers Club, Am. Law Inst., Am. Acad. of Civil Trial Mediators. Avocation: photography. Office: Resolution Resources Corp 303 Peachtree St Atlanta GA 30308-3201 E-mail: ordover@rrcatlanta.com.

ORDWAY, ELLEN, biologist, educator, entomologist, researcher; b. N.Y.C., Nov. 8, 1927; d. Samuel Hanson and Anna (Wheatland) Ordway. BA, Wheaton Coll., Mass., 1950; MS, Cornell U., 1955; PhD, U. Kans., 1965. Field asst. N.Y. Zool. Soc., N.Y.C., 1950-52; rsch. asst. Am. Mus. Natural History, N.Y.C., 1955-57; tchg. asst. U. Kans., Lawrence, 1957-61, rsch. asst., 1959-65; asst. prof. U. Minn., Morris, 1965-70, assoc. prof. biology, 1970-85, prof., 1986-97, prof. emeritus, 1997, acad. advisor, 1997—. Cooperator, cons. USDA Bee Rsch. Lab., Tucson, 1971, Tucson, 83. Contbr. articles to profl. jours. Lectr. Morris area svc. clubs, 1972—; mgr. preserves Nature Conservancy, Mpls., 1975—; bd. dirs. county chpt. ARC, 1998—; bd. dirs. U. Minn. Morris Retirees Assn., 1997—2003, sec., treas., 1998—2003. Mem.: AAAS, Ecol. Soc. Am., Internat. Bee Rsch. Assn., Kans. Entomol. Soc., Sigma Xi. Episcopalian. Avocations: travel, photography, exploring natural environments, wilderness, areas. Office: U Minn Div Sci And Math Morris MN 56267 Business E-Mail: ordwaye@mrs.umn.edu.

ORDWAY, FREDERICK IRA, III, science educator, consultant, researcher, writer; b. N.Y.C., Apr. 4, 1927; s. Frederick Ira and Frances Antoinette (Wright) O.; m. Maria Victoria Arenas, Apr. 13, 1950; children: Frederick Ira IV, Albert James, Aliette Marisol. SB, Harvard, 1949; postgrad., U. Alger, 1950, U. Paris, France, 1950-51, 53-54, U. Barcelona, Spain, 1953, U. Innsbruck, Austria, 1954, Air U., 1952-63, Alexander Hamilton Bus. Inst., 1952-58, Indsl. Coll. Armed Forces, 1953, 63; DSc (hon.), U. Ala., 1992. Various geol., engring. positions Mene Grande Oil Co., San Tome, Venezuela, 1949-50, Orinoco Mining Co., Cerro Bolivar, Venezuela, 1950, Reaction Motors, Inc., Lake Denmark, NJ, 1951-53; with guided missiles divsn. Republic Aviation Corp., 1954-55; pres. Gen. Astronautics Rsch. Corp., Huntsville, Ala., 1955-59, 65-66; v.p. Nat. R & D Corp., Atlanta, 1957-59; asst. to dir. Saturn Systems Office, Army Ballistic Missile Agy., Huntsville, 1959-60; chief space info. systems br. George C. Marshall Space Flight Ctr. NASA, 1960-64; prof. sci. and tech. applications Sch. Grad. Studies and Rsch., U. Ala. Rsch. Inst., 1967-73; cons. Sci. and Tech. Policy Office, NSF, 1974-75; cons. ops. analysis divsn. Gen. Rsch. Corp., 1974-75; asst. to adminstr. ERDA, 1975-77, Dept. Energy, 1977-94, policy/internat. affairs dir. spl. projects office, cons., 1994—; also participant internat. energy devel. program Office of Asst. Sec. Internat. Affairs, Dept. Energy, 1978-79. Cons. to industry, Ency. Britannica, Am. Coll. Dictionary of English Lang., M.G.M. film 2001: A Space Odyssey, 1965-66, Paramount Picture Corp., The Adventurers, 1968-69; internat. lectr. space flight and energy programs. Author: (with C.C. Adams) Space Flight, 1958, (with Ronald C. Wakeford) International Missile and Spacecraft Guide, 1960, Annotated Bibliography of Space Science and Technology, 1962, (with J.P. Gardner, M.R. Sharpe, Jr.) Basic Astronautics: An Introduction to Space Science, Engineering and Medicine, 1962, (with Adams, Wernher von Braun) Careers in Astronautics and Rocketry, 1962, (with Gardner, Sharpe, R.C. Wakeford) Applied Astronautics: An Introduction to Space Flight, 1963, (with Wakeford) Conquering the Sun's Empire, 1963, Life in Other Solar Systems, 1965, (with Roger A. MacGowan) Intelligence in the Universe, 1966, (with W. von Braun) History of Rocketry and Space Travel, 1966, 1969, 75, L'Histoire Mondiale de l'Astronautique, 1968, 70, (with W. von Braun) Rockets Red Glare, 1976, (with C.C. Adams, M.R. Sharpe) Dividends from Space, 1972, Pictorial Guide to Planet Earth, 1975, (with W. von Braun) New Worlds, 1979, (with M.R. Sharpe) The Rocket Team, 1979, 2d edit., 2003, (with F.C. Durant and R.C. Seamans) Between Sputnik and the Shuttle, 1981, (with E.M. Emme) Science Fiction and Space Futures, 1982, (with von Braun, Dave Dooling) Space Travel: A History, 1985, (with Ernst Stuhlinger) Wernher von Braun: Aufbrach in den Weltraum, 1992, Wernher von Braun: Crusader for Space (2 vols.), 1994, revised 1996, also single vol. edition, 1996, (with Randy Liebermann) Blueprint for Space, 1992, Visions of Spaceflight, 2001; editor: Advances in Space Science and Technology, vols. I-XII, 2 supplements, 1959-72, (with R.M.L. Baker, N.W. Makemson) Introduction to Astrodynamics, 1960, (with others) From Peenemünde to Outer Space, 1962, Astronautical Engineering and Science, 1963; mem. editorial bd.: (with others) IX Internat. Astronautical Congress procs., 2 vols, 1959, Xth Congress procs., 2 vols, 1960; guest editor: Acta Astronautica, 1985, 94, History of Rocketry and Astronautics, Vol. IX, 1989, Digital book Mars: Target for Tomorrow Microsoft Network & Internet, 1996; Co-creation of biographical film ″ He Conquered Space″, Discovery channel, 1996, History of Astronautics Video, 1996, inter-active CD Rom, 1997, revised, 2001, interactive CD ROM and video versions) Mars: Past, Present, Future, 1998; contbr. (with others) numerous articles to profl. jours., U.S. and fgn. encys., chpts. to books, sects. to others; organizer Blueprint for Space exhbn., 1991-95, U.S. Space and Rocket Ctr., IBM Gallery of Sci. and Art, NASA Vis. Ctr., Houston, Spaceport USA, Cape Canaveral, Fla., Nat. Air and Space Mus., Washington, Va. Air and Space Ctr., exhibit Shaping The Vision contributions Art Inst. Chgo., 2001, Bruce Mus. Art and Scis., 2001, Mus. Flight, Seattle, Wash., 2002, Hampton and numerous others. Served with USNR, 1945. Recipient (with W. von Braun) diplôme d'honneur French Commn. d'Histoire, Arts et Letters, Paris, 1969; commended for contbns. to U.S. Space and Rocket Ctr., Ala. Space Sci. Exhibit. Fellow: AIAA (history com. 1975—, internat. activities com. 1980—89, sel. com. hons. and awards 1996—, 2003 Centennial of Flight Ctr. 1998—, Hermann Oberth award 1977, K.E. Tsiolkowski award 1988), AAAS, Brit. Interplanetary Soc. (guest editor Jour. Brit. Interplanetary Soc. 1992—96); mem.: Eurasian Acad. Scis., Nat. Space Soc. (bd. dirs. 1986—95, mem. publs. com. 1987—88, nominating com. 1990—92, bd. govs. 1997—, Ctr. for Lunar Rsch. com. 1998—), Am. Astron. Soc. (Emme award 1994, Nat. Space Club award 1997), Internat. Acad. Astronautics (history of astronautics com. 1983—, space activities and soc. com. 1986—, peer rev. com. 1995—, Luigi Napolitano Lit. award 1992), Arthur C. Clarke Found. (bd. dirs. 2000—), Washington Golf and Country Club, Harvard Club N.Y., Cosmos Club (bd. mgmt. 1986—91, v.p. 1988—90, award 2001). Home and Office: 2401 N Taylor St Arlington VA 22207-4021 also: 3423 Lookout Dr SE Huntsville AL 35801 Fax: 703-524-5856. E-mail: ordmars@aol.com.

ORDWAY, JOHN, ambassador; b. Calif., June 1950; m. Maryjo Ordway; children: Christopher, Julia. Grad., Stanford U., 1972; JD, U. Calif., 1975. Dep. dir. Office Soviet Affairs Dept. of State, dep. dir. Office So. African Affairs, with U.S. Mission to NATO, 1993—96, polit. officer, 1996—99, dep. chief mission, 1999—2001, U.S. amb. to Armenia, 2001—. Office: DOS Amb 7020 Yerevan Pl Washington DC 20521

ORDWAY, JOHN DANTON, retired pension administrator, lawyer, accountant; b. Mpls., Mar. 19, 1928; s. John Dunreath Ordway and Inez Adelaide (Stahl) Larson; m. Mary E. Bateman, June 16, 1951 (div. 1978); 1 child, David; m. Patricia A. Nagle, Dec. 27, 1996. BBA, Am. U., 1963, JD, 1965. Bar: U.S. Dist. Ct. D.C. 1966; CPA, Minn. Dir. ins. Nat. Automobile Dealers Assn., Washington, 1957-69; v.p. Edward H. Friend and Co., Washington, 1969-74; exec. v.p. and CEO Pension Bds. United Ch. of Christ, N.Y.C., 1974-96. Alt. mem. Planning Bd., Stamford, Conn., 1982-86. With U.S. Army, 1946-47. Mem. AICPAs. Republican. Mem. United Ch. of Christ. Club: Westwood Country (Vienna, Va.); Quail Run Golf Club (Naples, Fla.). Lodge: Kena Temple. Home: 7520 Citrus Hill Ln Naples FL 34109

O'REAR, EDGAR ALLEN, III, chemical engineering educator; b. Jasper, Ala., Feb. 24, 1953; s. Edgar Allen O'Rear Jr. and Edith Idzorek. BSChemE, Rice U., 1975; SM in Organic Chemistry, MIT, 1977; PhD, Rice U., 1981. Rsch. engr. Exxon Rsch. and Engring., Baytown, Tex., summer 1975; asst. prof. to assoc. prof. U. Okla., Norman, 1981-91, Conoco disting. lectr., 1987-92, prof., 1991—, dir. Bioengring. Ctr., 1999—, assoc. dean rsch. Coll. Engring., 1995-99. Vis. sr. rschr. Hitachi Cen. Rsch. Lab., Kokubunji, Japan, summer 1988; vis. scientist RIKEN-Inst. for Phys. and Chem. Rsch., Wako-Shi, Japan, summer 1992; vis. prof. Chulalongkorn U., Bangkok, Thailand; cons. Boehringer-Mannheim, Indpls., Baxter-Travenol, Deerfield, Ill., Associated Metallurgists, Norman; co-founder Inst. for Applied Surfactant Rsch.; organizer symposia; reviewer for funding agys. and profl. jours. Co-author: Fluid Mechanics Exam File, 1985; contbr. tech. articles to profl. jours. Usher, mem. parish coun. St. Thomas More U. Parish, Norman, GlenMary Home Missioners; People to People Phys. Scientist Del. to China; mentor Big Bros.,Big Sisters, Norman, 1984-86. Recipient Faculty Rsch. award Sigma Xi, 1986, 2003; rsch. grantee NSF, NIH, Whitaker Found., NASA, AHA, OCAST, Dept. of Def. Fellow Am. Inst. for Med. and Biol. Engring.; mem. AIChE, AAAS, Internat. Soc. Biorheology (sec. gen. 1992-99, v.p. 1999-2002, pres. 2002—), Am. Chem. Soc., Tau Beta Pi. Roman Catholic. Achievements include patent for production of polymeric films from a surfactant template; method and composition for treatment of thrombosis in a mammal. Office: U Okla Dept Chem Engring SEC T335 100 E Boyd St Norman OK 73019-1000

OREFICE, GARY JAMES, state legislator; b. Hartford, Conn. BA, U. Conn., 1964; MBA, U. Hartford, 1978. Mem. East Lyme (Conn.) Bd. Selectmen, 1981-85, East Lyme Bd. Fin., 1985-92, Conn. Ho. of Reps., Hartford, 1993—. Democrat. Address: 49 Columbus Ave Niantic CT 06357-3138 Office: Conn Ho of Reps State Capitol Hartford CT 06106

O'REGAN, DEBORAH, association executive, lawyer; b. New Prague, Minn., Aug. 30, 1953; d. Timothy A. and Ermalinda (Brinkman) O'R.; m. Ron Kahlenbeck, Sept. 29, 1984; children: Katherine, Ryan. BA, Coll. of St. Catherine, 1975; JD, William Mitchell Coll. of Law, 1980. Bar: Ala. 1982, Minn. 1980. Asst. city atty. City of Bloomington, Minn., 1978-81, asst. city mgr., 1981-82; CLE dir. Alaska Bar Assn., Anchorage, 1982-84, exec. dir., 1985—. Mem. task force on gender equality State Fed. Joint Commn., Anchorage, 1991—; mem. selection com. U.S. Magistrate Judge, U.S. Dist of Ala., 1992; mem. adv. bd. Anchorage Daily News, 1991-93. Mem. Nat. Assn. Bar Execs. (exec. com. 1993-97). Avocations: travel, outdoors, rollerblading. Office: Alaska Bar Assn 510 L St Ste 602 Anchorage AK 99501-1959

O'REILLY, ANTHONY JOHN FRANCIS, food company executive; b. Dublin, May 7, 1936; s. John Patrick and Aileen (O'Connor) O'Reilly; m. Susan Cameron, May 5, 1962 (div.); children: Susan, Cameron, Justine, Gavin, Caroline, Tony; m. Chryss Goulandris, Sept. 14, 1991. Student, Belvedere Coll., Dublin, Univ. Coll., Dublin, Wharton Bus. Sch. Overseas, 1965; BCL DCL (hon.), Ind. State U.; PhD in Agrl. Mktg, U. Bradford, Eng.; LLD (hon.), Wheeling Coll., 1974, Trinity Coll., Dublin, 1978; LL.D. (hon.), Allegheny Coll., 1983, De Paul U., Chgo., 1988; D in Bus. Studies (hon.), Rollins Coll., 1978; DHC in Civil Law (hon.), Ind. State U., 1980; DBA (hon.), Boston Coll., 1985; D in Econ. Sci. (hon.), Nat. U. Ireland, 1989. Indsl. cons. Weston Evans, 1958—62; personal asst. to chmn. Suttons Ltd., Cork, Ireland, 1960—62; lectr. dept. applied psychology Univ. Coll., Cork, 1960—62; dir. Robert McCowen & Sons Ltd., Tralee, Ireland, 1961—62; mng. dir. An Bord Bainne/Irish Dairy Bd., 1962—66; dir. Agrl. Credit Corp. Ltd., 1965—66, Nitrigin Eireann Teoranta, 1965—66; mng. dir., CEO Comhlucht Siuicre Eireann Teo. (Irish Sugar Co.) and Erin Foods Ltd., Dublin, 1966—69; joint mng. dir. Heinz-Erin Ltd., 1967—70; mng. dir. H.J. Heinz Co. Ltd., England, 1969—72; sr. v.p. N.Am. and Pacific H.J. Heinz Co., 1971—72, exec. v.p., COO, 1972—73, pres., COO, 1973—79, pres., CEO, 1979—90, also chmn., 1978—, also bd. dirs., CEO, 1978—98, non exec. chmn. bd. dirs., 1998. Chmn. Fitzwilton Plc, Ind. Newspapers Plc, Atlantic Resources, Dublin, Am. Ireland Fund; ptnr. Cawley Sheerin Wynne and Co., solicitors, Dublin; bd. dirs. Bankers Trust N.Y. Corp., Washington Post Co., London Tablet Found., Inc., Starkist Foods Inc., Ore-Ida Foods, Inc. Author: Prospect, 1962, Developing Creative Management, 1970, The Conservative Consumer, 1971, Food for Thought, 1972. Mem. Nat. Com. Whitney Mus. Art; bd. govs. Hugh O'Brian Found., L.A.; mem. coun. Rockefeller U., N.Y.C.; trustee U. Pitts., Com. for Econ. Devel.; bd. dirs. Assocs. Grad. Sch. Bus. Adminstrn. of Harvard U., Cambridge, Mass.; sr. bd. dirs. The Conf. Bd. Named Hon. Officer, Order of Australia, 1988. Fellow: Royal Soc. Arts, Brit. Inst. Mgmt.; mem.: Marks Club London, Exec. Coun. Fgn. Diplomats (bd. dirs.), Irish Mgmt. Inst. (coun.), Internat. Life Scis. Inst. Nutrition Found. (chmn., CEO coun.), Am. Irish Found., Grocery Mfrs. Am. (sec., bd. dirs.), Law Soc. Ireland (treas.), Inst. Dirs., Inc., Lyford Cay Club (Bahamas), Rolling Rock Club (Ligonier), Pitts. Golf Club, Allegheny Club, Duquesne Club, The Bd. Rm. (N.Y.C.), The Links, Union League, Les Ambassadeurs, Annabels, Univ. Club Dublin, Kildare St. Club, St. Stephens Green Club. also: Mobil Corp 150 E 42nd St New York NY 10017-5612

O'REILLY, CHARLES TERRANCE, university dean; b. Chgo., May 30, 1921; s. William Patrick and Ann Elizabeth (Madden) O'R.; m. Rosella Catherine Neilland, June 4, 1955; children: Terrance, Gregory, Kevin, Joan Bridget, Kathleen Ann. BA, Loyola U., Chgo., 1942, MSW., 1948; postgrad., U. Cattolica, Milan, Italy, 1949-50; PhD, U. Notre Dame, 1954. Instr. DePaul U., Chgo., 1948-49; asst. in psychology U. Cattolica, 1949-50; caseworker Cath. Charities, N.Y.C., 1953-54; exec. dir. Family Service, Long Branch, N.J., 1954-55; asst. prof. Loyola U., 1955-59; vis. lectr. Ensiss Sch. Social Work, Milan, 1959-60; asso. prof. U. Wis.-Milw., 1961-64; prof., asso. dir. U. Wis. Sch. Social Work, Madison, 1965-68; dean social welfare, v.p. acad. affairs SUNY-Albany, 1969-76; dean social work Loyola U., Chgo., 1976-92, dean emeritus, sr. prof., 1994—; vis. prof. sch. social work SS Maria Asunta, Rome, 1992-93. Author: OAA Profile, 1961, People of Inner Core North, 1965, Men in Jail, 1968, Italian Social Work Education 1946-1997, 1998, Italy's War of Liberation, 1998, The Enola Gay Controversy and the Smithsonian, 2004; contbr. articles to profl. jours. Pres. Community Action Commn. Dane County, Wis., 1967-68; bd. dirs. Council Community Services, Albany, Family and Children's Service, Albany; mem. adv. bd. Safer Found.; vice chmn. Ill. Pub. Aid Citizens Council. Served with AUS, 1942-46, 51-52. Fulbright scholar, 1949-50; fellow, 1959-60 Mem. AAUP, Nat. Assn. Social Workers. Roman Catholic. Home: 4073 Bunker Ln Wilmette IL 60091-1001 Office: Sch Social Work Loyola Univ Chicago IL 60611

O'REILLY, DAVID J. oil company executive; b. Dublin, Jan. 1947; BS ChemE, University Coll., Dublin, 1968, D of Sci. (hon.), 2002. Process engineer Chevron Corp., 1968—71, process engineer, operating assist., 1971—75, adviser, foreign operations, 1976—78, planning mgr., chemical div., 1979, mgr. agricultural chem., 1980—82, mgr. Salt Lake Refinery, 1983—85; mgr. manufacturing Chevron Chemical Co., 1985; gen. mgr. El Segundo Refinery, 1986—88; sr. v.p. Chevron Chemical Corp., 1989—90; v.p. Chevron Corp., 1991—94; pres. Chevron Products Co., San Francisco, 1994—98; dir., vice-chmn. Chevron Corp., San Francisco, 1998—2000, chmn. bd. dirs., CEO, 2000—01; CEO, chmn. ChevronTexaco Corp., San Francisco, 2001—. Bd. govs. San Francisco Symphony, Bay Area Coun. Mem.: Am. Soc. Corp. Execs., Bus. Coun., Nat. Petroleum Coun., Am. Petroleum Inst. (treas., bd. dirs.). Office: Chevron Corp 6001 Bollinger Canyon Rd San Ramon CA 94583-2324*

O'REILLY, HEATHER ANN, Olympic athlete; b. East Brunswick, NJ, Jan. 2, 1985; Student, U.N.C. Mem. U.S. Women's Nat. Soccer Team, 2002—, U.S. Women's Olympic Soccer Team, Athens, 2004. Named National High School Player of the Yr., 2002; named to NCAA All-Tournament Team, 2003. Achievements include mem. NCAA Champion Univ. North Carolina Tar Heels Women's Soccer Team, 2003; mem. Gold Medal U.S. Women's Soccer Team, Athens Olympic Games, 2004. Office: c/o US Soccer Federation 1801 S Prairie Ave Chicago IL 60616*

O'REILLY, JACKSON See RIGNEY, JAMES JR.

O'REILLY, JAMES THOMAS, lawyer, educator, author; b. N.Y.C., Nov. 15, 1947; s. Matthew Richard and Regina (Casey) O'R.; children: Jean, Ann. BA cum laude, Boston Coll., 1969; JD, U. Va., 1974. Bar: Va. 1974, Ohio 1974, U.S. Supreme Ct. 1979, U.S. Ct. Appeals (6th cir.) 1980. Atty. Procter & Gamble Co., Cin., 1974-76, counsel, 1976-79, sr. counsel for food, drug and product safety, 1979-85, corp. counsel, 1985-93, assoc. gen. counsel, 1993-98; adj. prof. in adminstrv. law U. Cin., 1980-97, vis. prof. law, 1998—. Cons. Adminstrv. Conf. U.S., 1981-82, 89-90, Congl. Office of Compliance, 1995-96; arbitrator State Employee Rels. Bd.; mem. Ohio Bishops Adv. Coun., Mayor's Infrastructure Commn., Cin. Environ. Adv. Coun.; city coun. Wyo., Ohio. Author: Federal Information Disclosure, 1977, Food and Drug Administration Regulatory Manual, 1979, Unions' Rights to Company Information, 1980, Federal Regulation of the Chemical Industry, 1980, Administrative Rulemaking, 1983, Ohio Public Employee Collective Bargaining, 1984, Protecting Workplace Secrets, 1985, Emergency Response to Chemical Accidents, 1986, Product Defects and Hazards, 1987, Protecting Trade Secrets Under SARA, 1988, Toxic Torts Strategy Deskbook, 1989, Complying With Canada's New Labeling Law, 1989, Solid Waste Management, 1991, Ohio Products Liability Handbook, 1991, Toxic Torts Guide, 1991, ABA Product Liability Resource Manual, 1993, RCRA and Superfund Practice Guide, 1993, Clean Air Permits Manual, 1994, United States Environmental Liabilities, 1994, Elder Safety, 1995, Environmental and Workplace Safety for University and Hospital Managers, 1996, Indoor Environmental Health, 1997, Product Warnings, Defects & Hazards, 1999, Accident Prevention Manual, 2000, Food Crisis Management Manual, 2002, Police Racial Profiling, 2002; mem. editl. bd. Food and Drug Cosmetic Law Jour.; contbr. articles to profl. jours. Mem. Hamilton County Dem. Ctrl. Com. Served with U.S. Army, 1970-72. Mem. ABA (chmn. AD law sect.), FBA, Food and Drug Law Inst. (chair program com.), Leadership Cin. Democrat. Roman Catholic. Office: 24 Jewett Dr Cincinnati OH 45215-2648

O'REILLY, MICHAEL, corporate financial executive; BS, NYU; MBA, Pace U. Securities analyst investment dept. The Chubb Corp., 1969, chief investment officer, 1986, interim CFO, 2002—03, vice chmn., 2002—03, vice chmn. and CFO, 2003—. Exec. v.p. and mng. dir. Chubb & Son. With U.S. Army, 1966—67, capt. USAR, 1968—71. Office: The Chubb Corp PO Box 1615 15 Mountain View Rd Plainfield NJ 07061-1615

O'REILLY, PATRICK JAMES, public relations executive; b. Riverside, Calif., Oct. 4, 1965; s. Patrick Gerard and Anne Mary (Caslin) O'R. BA in Internat. Rels., U. So. Calif., 1989. Account exec. Geogeson & Co., N.Y.C., L.A., 1987-89; rsch. analyst Rep. Nat. Com., Washington, 1989; campaign mgr. Riverside (Calif.) County Supr. Norton Younglove Election, 1989-90; sr. account exec. Stoorza, Ziegaus & Metzger, Riverside, 1990—2001; pres. O'Reilly Pub. Rels., 2001—. Guest speaker in field. Republican. Roman Catholic. Office: O'Reilly Pub Rels 3403 10th St 110 Riverside CA 92501

O'REILLY, RICHARD BROOKS, journalist; b. Kansas City, Mo., Feb. 19, 1941; s. Charles Alfred and Wilma Faye (Brooks) O'R.; m. Anne Pustmeuller, June 27, 1964 (div. 1978); children— Kathleen Marie, Randall Charles; m. Joan Marlene Sweeney, Jan. 1, 1981 (div. 1996); m. Julia Franco, Mar. 7, 2003. BA, U. Denver, 1966. Reporter Washington Park Times, Denver, 1963-64; mng. editor Aurora Advocate, Colo., 1964; police reporter Rocky Mountain News, Denver, 1964-66, night rewrite reporter, 1966, city hall reporter, 1966-67, statehouse reporter, 1967-68, investigative reporter, 1971-74; minority affairs reporter Denver Post, 1968-70; freelance writer St. Georges, Grenada, 1970; investigative reporter Orange County edition Los Angeles Times, 1974-78, chief county bur., 1978, asst. met. editor, 1978-80, environ. reporter, 1980-84, computer columnist, syndicated columnist, 1983-96, coord. tech. resources, 1984-89, dir. editorial computer analysis, 1989—. Adj. prof. journalism U. So. Calif., 1990-92; mem. electronic filing adv. com. Calif. Sec. of State, 1995. Named Colo. Journalist of Yr., Sigma Delta Chi, 1972; recipient Pub. Svc. award U.S. Justice Dept., 1973, McWilliams award Denver Press Club, 1974, Investigative Reporting award Orange Country Press Club, 1977, 95, Los Angeles Times, 1977, 97, Nat. Journalism award Soc. Profl. Engrs., 1983, Clean Air award Am. Lung Assn., 1985, award for non-deadline reporting Sigma Delta Chi, 1996, medal for investigative reporting Investigative Reporters and Editors, 1996. Democrat. Avocations: flying; sailing; camping. Office: Los Angeles Times 202 W 1st St Los Angeles CA 90012

O'REILLY, RICHARD JOHN, pediatrician; b. Bklyn., Apr. 29, 1943; s. John Russell and Margaret (Cronin) O'R.; m. E. Jean Capitano, Nov. 1984; children from previous marriage: John, Steven. BS, Coll. Holy Cross, 1964; MD, U. Rochester, 1968. Diplomate Am. Bd. Pediatrics. Intern U. Minn. Hosp., Mpls., 1968-69; resident in pediatrics Children's Hosp. Med. Ctr. and Beth Israel Hosp., Boston, 1971-72; with dept. pediatrics Meml. Sloan Kettering Cancer Ctr., N.Y.C., 1973—; attending pediatrician, chmn. dept. pediatrics Meml. Hosp., N.Y.C., 1986—; mem. dept. immunology Sloan-Kettering Inst. Cancer Research; prof. pediatrics Cornell U. Med. Coll., 1980, Lila Acheson Wallace prof. pediatric research, 1980, Vincent Astor prof. clin. research, 1984; chief marrow transplantation svc. Meml. Sloan-Kettering Cancer Ctr., 1981—; vice pres. elect Am. Soc. of Blood and Marrow Transplantation. Councillor Internat. Bone Marrow Transplant Registry; pres. Damon Runyon-Walter Winchell Cancer Fund, 1991-96. Editor-in-chief BBMT; assoc. editor Cancer Rsch., Clin. Cancer Rsch., Bone marrow Transplantation, NCI Study Sect. D. Served with USPHS, 1969-71. Recipient Louise and Allston Boyer-Young Investigator award for clin. research, 1980 Mem. AAAS, Am. Pediatric Soc., Am. Assn. Immunologists, Am. Acad. Pediatrics, Am. Assn. Pathologists, Soc. Pediatric Rsch., N.Y. Transplantation Soc., N.Y. Acad. Scis., Am. Assn. Clin. Radiology, Am. Soc. Hematology, Am. Soc. Blood and Marrow Transplantation (sec. 1993-95, v.p.-elect 1999). Democrat. Roman Catholic. Achievements include performing first application of marrow transplantation from unrelated donors and from genetically mismatched donors, 1973. Office: Meml Sloan-Kettering Cancer Ctr 1275 York Ave New York NY 10021-6094

O'REILLY, SALLY, musician, educator; b. Dallas, Oct. 23, 1940; Student, Curtis Inst. Music; MusB, Tex. Women's U., 1963; MusM, Ind. U., 1965. Ind. concert violinist, pianist, 1965—; faculty Manhattan Sch. Music, N.Y.C., 1972-81, La. State U., Baton Rouge, 1981-93, U. Minn., Mpls., 1993—. Sr. Fulbright lectr., Uruguay, 1982-83. Debut Dallas Symphony Orch., 1957; concert tours thru U.S., Can., S.Am., China, Mex., Europe; composer String Power Series, String Rhythms, Fiddle Magic, Quartet Sampler; rec. artist with

Caecilian Trio. Recipient Hendl award, 1957, Van Katwijk Conducting prize, 1958, Dealey award, 1958; grantee Paul Found., 1979; Fulbright scholar, Belgium, 1970-72. Office Phone: 612-624-0846. Business E-Mail: oreil004@umn.edu.

O'REILLY, TERENCE JOHN, lawyer; b. Farnborough, Eng., Apr. 12, 1945; came to U.S., 1960, naturalized, 1965; s. Arthur Francis and Doris Eileen (Burden) O'R.; m. Katharine Van Dyke Wallace, Sept. 26, 1970; children: Tobin Cooper, Matthew Wallace. BA, Loyola U., 1966; JD, U. Calif., Berkeley, 1969. Bar: Calif. 1970. Assoc. Voegelin, Barton, L.A., 1969-70, Walkup, Downing & Sterns, San Francisco, 1970-75; mem. Walkup, Shelby, Bastian, Melodia, Kelly & O'Reilly, San Francisco, 1975-87; prin. O'Reilly, Collins & Danko, San Mateo, Calif., 1987—. Lectr. Kennedy Law Sch., Moraga, Calif., 1975-76, Inner Cir. of Advocates, 1998—; bd. govs. Consumer Attys. of Calif., 1995— bd. govs., diplomate Am. Bd. Profl. Liability Lawyers, 1989—. V.p. No. Calif. Rugby Football, San Francisco, 1975-80, bd. dirs., 1975—; trustee U.S. Rugby Football Found., 1987—; trustee The Philip Brooks Sch., 1986-89, Coun. of Bancroft Libr., U. Calif. Mem. Boalt Hall Alumni (bd. dirs. 1982-85), Assn. San Francisco Trial Lawyers (bd. dirs. 1985—), Assn. San Mateo Trial Lawyers (dir. 1992—, pres. 2003), Bohemian Club, Burlingame Country Club, Menlo Circus Club, Pacific Union Club. Roman Catholic. Office: 1900 O'Farrell St Ste 360 San Mateo CA 94403 E-mail: toreilly@oreillylaw.com.

O'REILLY, THOMAS EUGENE, retired human resources consultant; b. Wichita, Kans., Sept. 7, 1932; s. Eugene William and Florence Irene (Gustner) O'R.; m. Lorraine Bryant, Feb. 9, 1957; children: Thomas Jr., Patricia, Susan, Gregory, Pamela. BA, Iona Coll., 1954; MBA, NYU, 1958. Mem. human resources staff Chase Manhattan Bank, N.Y.C., 1957-69, dir. employee rels., 1969-71, mgr. internat. personnel, 1971-75, dir. internal staffing, 1976-77, dir. mgmt. resources, 1978-80, dir. exec. resources, 1980-87; v.p., sr. cons. Lee Hecht Harrison, Inc., N.Y.C., 1988-93; ret. Spl. agt. counter-intelligence corps, U.S. Army, 1954-57. Mem. Nat. Fgn. Trade Coun., Exec. Issues Forum, Ariz. State Horseman's Assn. (1st v.p.). Republican. Roman Catholic. Home: 6200 E Cielo Run N Cave Creek AZ 85331-7645

O'REILLY, TIM, company executive; Founder, pres. O'Reilly & Assoc., Sebastopol, Calif. Office: O Reilly & Assoc 1005 Gravenstein Hwy N Sebastopol CA 95472-2811

O'REILLY, TIMOTHY PATRICK, lawyer; b. San Lorenzo, Calif., Sept. 12, 1945; s. Thomas Marvin and Florence Ann (Ohlman) O'R.; m. Susan Ann Marshall, July 18, 1969; children: T. Patrick Jr., Sean M., Colleen K. BS, Ohio State U., 1967; JD, NYU, 1971. Bar: Pa. 1971, U.S. Dist. Ct. (ea. dist.) Pa. 1971, U.S. Dist. Ct. (mid. dist.) Pa. 1972, U.S. Ct. Appeals (3d cir.) 1977, U.S. Supreme Ct. 1988. Ptnr. Morgan, Lewis & Bockius, Phila., 1978—. Editor: Developing Labor Law, 1989; contbr. articles to profl. jours. Bd. dirs. Notre Dame Acad. and Devon Preparatory Sch.; bd. govs. Aronimink Golf Club, J. Wood Platt Caddie Scholarship Trust. Elected to Coll. of Labor and Employment Lawyers. Mem. ABA (chmn. com. on devel. of the law under the Nat. Labor Rels. Act., editor-in-chief The Developing Labor Law jour., elected mem. coun. labor and employment sect.), Pa. Bar Assn., Phila. Bar Assn., Ohio State U. Alumni Assn., Aronimink Golf Club (bd. govs.). Avocation: golf. Home: 1127 Cymry Dr Berwyn PA 19312-2056 Office: Morgan Lewis & Bockius 1701 Market St Philadelphia PA 19103-2903 Office Phone: 215-963-5470. Business E-Mail: toreilly@morganlewis.com.

O'REILLY, WENDA BREWSTER, writer, researcher, management consultant; b. Frankfurt, Fed. Republic of Germany, Mar. 29, 1948; d. William Russell Brewster and Harriet Stimson Bullitt; m. James Patrick Brewster O'Reilly, July 18, 1981; children: Andrea Mariele, Noelle Christine, Mariele Angelica. BA in Psychology, U. Wash., 1975; MEd, Harvard U., 1977; MA, Stanford U., 1977, PhD in Edn., 1983. Gen. asst. King Broadcasting Co., Seattle, 1965-66; media buyer Benton & Bowles Advt. Agy., N.Y.C, 1967-68; acct. exec. Young & Rubicam Advt. Agy., Milan, 1969-70; advt. producer McCann-Erickson Advt. Agy., Milan, 1971-73; rschr., scholar Inst. for Rsch. on Women and Gender Stanford (Calif.) U., 1983-91, statis. analyst, rsch. asst., 1978-81; exec. dir. The Birth Place, Menlo Park, Calif., 1985-87. Guest lectr., seminar leader in women in mgmt., comm. and childbirth issues, 1979-93; speaker homeopathic medicine, healthcare issues, 1995—; CFO Travelers' Tales, Inc., 1998-2001; v.p. Birdcage Books, 1998-2000; pres. Birdcage Press LLC, 2001—. Author: The Beautiful Body Book, 1984; editor: Organon of the Medical Art, 1998; creator (ednl.games) The Renaissance Art Game, 2000, The Impressionst Art Game, 2001, Van Gogh and Friends Art Game, 2002, Old Mummy, 2004; contbr. articles to profl.jours. Adv. coun. Pacific Design Forum, 1991-93; v.p., bd. dirs. Calif. Assn. Free-standing Birth Ctrs., 1986-88; bd. dirs. Leavenworth Summer Theater, 1995-98, Icicle Creek Music Ctr., 1996-2000. Grantee, William H. Donner Found. Mem. Mid-peninsula Access Corp. (founding bd. dirs. Calif. chpt., v.p., founding bd. dirs. 1986-87). Democrat. Episcopalian.

O'REILLY, WILLIAM, JR., (BILL O'REILLY), commentator; s. William and Angela O'Reilly; married; 2 children. BA in history, Marist Coll., Poughkeepsie, N.Y.; MA in broadcast journalism, Boston Univ.; MA in pub. policy, Harvard Univ. Tchr. H.S., Miami, Fla.; reporter WNEP-TV, Scranton, Pa., WFAA-TV, Dallas, KMGH-TV, Denver, WFSB-TV, Hartford, WCBS-TV, N.Y.C., 1980; fgn. correspondent CBS News; anchor CBS, Boston, ABC, Boston, KATU-TV, Portland; correspondent, The World News Tonight ABC, 1986—88; sr. correspondent Inside Edition, 1988, anchor, 1989—95; host, exec. prodr. FOX News The O'Reilly Factor, 1996—; host Radio Factor, 2002—. Author: (book) The O'Reilly Factor, The No Spin Zone, Who's Looking Out for You, (novels) Those Who Trespass. Office: FOX News 1200 Ave Am New York NY 10036

OREMLAND, MELVYN J. education educator, director; b. Bklyn., May 25, 1939; m. Lenore Thier, Apr. 11, 1964; children: Patricia, Gordon. BS Mech. Engring., RPI, Troy, N.Y., 1961; MEE, N.Y.U., N.Y., 1963, MS in Physics, 1975, PhD in Physics, 1977. Engr. Bell Tel. Labs., Morristown, NJ, 1961—63; tchr. Rhodes Sch., N.Y., 1965—66; prof. physics Pace Univ., N.Y., 1966—. Chair chem. dept. Pace Univ., N.Y., 2000—02, dir. forensic sci. program, 2002—, chair faculty coun., 2004—. Mem.: Am. Acad. of Forensic Sci. Achievements include mem. all Am. winter polo team 1959-61. Office: Pace Univ Pace Plaza New York NY 10038

OREMUS, STEPHEN, composer; Grad., Berklee Coll. Music. Music dir.: Andrew Lippa's The Wild Party, Rent, regionally Into the Woods (Ordway), Dorian (World Premiere, Goodspeed), A Little Night Music, Jesus Christ Superstar (with Billy Porter and Emily Skinner), Nite Club Confidential (with Barbara Eden), The Radio City Music Hall Christmas Spectacular, vocal arranger, music supr.: Signed, Sealed, Delivered - The Music of Stevie Wonder, dir., arranger, orchestrator: Broadway plays Avenue Q, 2003, tick-.tick.BOOM!, musical dir.: Broadway plays Wicked, 2003. Office: Gershwin Theatre 222 W 51st St New York NY 10019*

OREN, BRUCE CLIFFORD, newspaper editor, artist; b. Mineola, N.Y., Aug. 31, 1952; s. Ralph and Bernice (Lands) O.; 1 child, Adam Nathaniel; m. Angela Malone Williams, Mar. 4, 1990. Student, U. Md., College Park, 1970-74. Archtl. sculptor Universal Restoration Inc., Washington, 1974-76; tech. illustrator Tex. Instruments, Stafford, Tex., 1976-77; graphic artist Houston Chronicle, 1977-79, photo editor, 1979-86, artist, 1986—, L.A. Times Syndicate, 1987-91. Named Best Art/Graphic, Hearst Newspapers, 1998, 2000; recipient Bronze medal, Soc. Newspaper Design, 1992, 1st Pl. Graphics award, Tex. Associated Press Mng. Editors, 2002. Jewish. Office: 801 Texas Ave Houston TX 77002-2904 E-mail: bruce.oren@chron.com.

OREN, JOHN BIRDSELL, retired coast guard officer; b. Madison, Wis., Dec. 27, 1909; s. Arthur Baker and Lucile Grace (Comfort) O.; m. Harriet Virginia Prentis, Feb. 9, 1934; children— Virginia Joan (Mrs. Luther Warren Strickler II), John Edward. BS, USCG Acad., 1933; MS in Marine Engring, MIT, 1942. Commd. ensign USCG, 1933, advanced through grades to rear adm., 1964; chief engring. div. (11th Coast Guard Dist.), 1957-59, (12th Coast Guard Dist.), 1960-61; dep. chief (Office Engring.), Washington, 1962-63, chief Office of Engring., 1964-68; now ret. Mem. Mcht. Marine Council, 1964—; chmn. ship structures com. Transp. Dept., 1964—; exec. dir. Maritime Transp. Research Bd., Nat. Acad. Scis., 1968—; mem. nat. adv. bd. Am. Security Council Recipient Legion of Merit. Mem. Soc. Am. Mil. Engrs. (pres. 1966, Acad. of Fellows), Am. Soc. Naval Engrs. (pres. 1965), Internat. Inst. Welding (vice chmn. Am. coun. 1964), Ret. Officers Assn. (bd. dirs. 1978), Pan Am. Inst. Naval Engring., Vinson Hall Residents Assn. (v.p. 1998), Masons. Republican. Episcopalian. Home: Apt 221 6251 Old Dominion Dr Mc Lean VA 22101-4806

ORENSTEIN, FRAN M. director, writer; b. Bklyn., N.Y., Oct. 31, 1939; s. Nathan Gitterman and Gertrude Celia Chall-Gitterman; m. Walter Orenstein, Dec. 21, 1958 (div. Jan. 1977); children: James, Susannah, Peter. BA, Bklyn. Coll., 1960; MEd, Coll. N.J., 1976; EdD, Nova Southeastern U., 1993. Lic. tchr. N.Y., N.J., guidance N.J., Calif., cert. pub. mgr. N.J. Tchr. Pub. Sch. 256-N.Y.C. Bd. Edn., Bklyn., 1960—63, Hilltop Acad., Morganville, NJ, 1973—74; editor, writer Univ. Comms., Rahway, NJ, 1975—79; tchr., content specialist East Windsor (N.J.) Regional Schs., 1979—80; sr. rehab. counselor N.J. Divsn. Vocat. Rehab., Trenton, NJ, 1980—88; disability officer Americorps N.J. Dept. Edn., Trenton, NJ, 1998—2002; program devel. specialist N.J. Dept. Cmty. Affairs, Trenton, NJ, 1998—98, 2002—. Presenter local, nat., and internat. confs. on gender equity in schs., violence prevention in schs., sexual harassment in schs and the workplace, and; cons., presenter Ednl. Visions Group, East Windsor, NJ, 1990—98. Author, editor: Bus. World for Women / Men mag., 1975—78 (Navy citation, 1977), SACC Talk, 1991—92. Campaign worker N.J. Dem. Party, NJ, 1992; founding bd. dirs. Cen. N.J. Breast Cancer Coalition, 2000—02, Am. Cancer Soc. Chpt. N.J. Breast Cancer Coalition, Manalapan, 1973—77, Freehold, 2000—; bd. dirs., newsletter editor Women's Agenda/N.J. Law, NJ, 1993—96; vol. bd. dirs. Susan B. Komen Race for the Cure, Princeton, NJ, 1995—99. Mem.: Soc. Children's Book Writers and Illustrators, Mensa, Phi Delta Kappa, Kappa Delta Pi. Avocations: reading, gardening, writing children's books. Home: 19101 Mohave DSage Way Surprise AZ 85387-7506 E-mail: franorenstein@juno.com.

ORENSTEIN, MICHAEL (IAN ORENSTEIN), philatelic dealer, columnist; b. Bklyn., Jan. 6, 1939; s. Harry and Myra (Klein) Orenstein; m. Linda Turner, June 28, 1964; 1 child, Paul David. BS, Clemson U., 1960; postgrad., U. Calif., Berkeley, 1960-61. Career regional mgr. Minkus Stamp & Pub. Co., Calif., 1964-70; mgr. stamp div. Superior Stamp & Coin Co., Inc., Beverly Hills, Calif., 1970-90; dir. stamp divsn. Superior Galleries, Beverly Hills, Calif., 1991-94; dir. space memorabelia Superior Stamp and Coin. Co., Inc., Beverly Hills, Calif., 1992-94; dir. stamp and space divsn. Superior Stamp & Coin an A-Mark Co., Beverly Hills, Calif., 1994-97; sr. buyer, appraiser Superior Stamp & Coin, Beverly Hills, Calif., 1997-2000; v.p., COO Superior Galleries, 2001; co-founder, ptnr., prin., pres. AuroraGalleries Internat., 2002—. Cons. Office Insp. Gen. NASA, Nassau County Dist. Atty., NY. Columnist: L.A. Times, 1965—93; philatelic advisor/creator The Video Guide to Stamp Collecting, 1988; author: Stamp Collecting is Fun, 1990; contbr. articles to publs. With U.S. Army, 1962—64. Recipient medal of Yuri Gagarin, Fedn. Supporting Russian Cosmonauts, 2002. Mem.: AIAA, Internat. Soc. Appraisers: Stamps, Space Memorabilia, Internat. Fedn. Stamp Dealers, Am. Philatelic Soc. (writers unit 1975—80, 1989—93), Confederate Stamp Alliance, German Philatelic Soc., C. Z. Study Group, Am. Stamp Dealers Assn. Republican. Avocation: fishing. Address: 19546 Minnehaha Northridge CA 91326 Office Phone: 818-368-6888. Personal E-mail: rightstuf@verizon.net.

ORENSTEIN, WALTER ALBERT, director; b. N.Y.C., Mar. 5, 1948; m. Diane Rauzin; children: Eleza Tema, Evan William. BS, CCNY, 1968; MD, Albert Einstein Coll. Medicine, 1972. Intern U. Calif., San Francisco, 1972—73, resident in pediat., 1973—74; EIS officer divsn. immunization CDC, Atlanta, 1974—76; med. epidemiologist divsn. immunization Ctr. for Disease Control, Atlanta, 1976—77; resident pediat. Childrens Hosp. L.A., 1977—78; fellow infectious diseases U. So. Calif. Med. Sch., 1978—80; resident preventive medicine Ctrs. for Disease Control and Prevention, Atlanta, 1980—82, chief surveillance and investigations sect., 1982—88, dir. divsn. immunization, 1988—93, dir. nat. immunization program, 1993—2004; Assoc. Dir. Emory Vaccine Ctr. Emory Univ., 2004—. Cons. smallpox eradication program WHO, Uttar Pradesh, India, 1974—75; med. adv. bd. CDC, Atlanta, 1981—84, nat. vaccine adv. com., 1988—; clin. assoc. prof. dept. cmty. health Emory U. Sch. Medicine, 1985; adj. prof. The Rollins Sch. Pub. Health, 1992—2002; cons. and presenter in field. Mem. editl. bd. Pediat. Infectious Disease Jour., 1987—2000; co-editor: Vaccines, 1999; contbr. articles to profl. jours. Asst. surgeon gen. USPHS, 1995. Fellow: Pediat. Infectious Diseases Soc. (past chmn. publs. com., past mem. coun.), Infectious Diseases Soc. Am., Am. Acad. Pediats. (com. on infectious diseases 1989—, liaison mem., nat. vaccine adv. com.); mem.: APHA, Soc. for Epidemiologic Rsch., Am. Epidemiol. Soc. Office: Emory Sch of Medicine 1440 Clifton Rd Atlanta GA 30322*

ORENTREICH, NORMAN, physician, researcher; b. N.Y.C., Dec. 26, 1922; m. Roslyn Orentreich, June 22, 1946; children: Catherine Orentreich, David S. Orentreich, Sari Mass. BS, CUNY, 1943; MD, NYU Coll. Medicine, 1948. Diplomate Am. Bd. Dermatology. Asst. chief med. examiner USN, 1950-54; med. dir. Orentreich Med. Group, N.Y.C., 1953—; dir. Orentreich Found. for the Advancement of Science, N.Y., 1961—. Head of hair clinic, skin & cancer unit NYU Med. Ctr., 1953-68; mem. bd. dirs. Animal Med. Ctr., N.Y.C., 1994, clin. prof. dermatology NYU Sch. Medicine, 1996. Fellow ACP; mem. Am. Soc. for Dermatologic Surgery (pres. 1970-72), Am. Fedn. for Aging Rsch., Am. Acad. Cosmetic Surgery, Am. Contact Dermatology Soc., Endocrine Soc., Skin Pharmacology Soc., Skin Pharmacology Soc. Avocation: research. Office: Orentreich Med Group 909 Fifth Ave New York NY 10021

ORESKES, IRWIN, biochemistry educator; b. Chgo., June 30, 1926; s. Herman and Clara (Rubenstein) O.; m. Susan E. Nagin, June 18, 1949; children: Michael, Daniel, Naomi, Rebecca. BS in Chemistry, CCNY, 1949; PhD in Biochemistry, CUNY, 1969; MA in Phys. Chemistry, Bklyn. Coll., 1956. Cert. clin. lab. dir. NYC, NY State. Chemist Tech. Tape Co., Bronx, NY, 1949; technician NYU Sch. Medicine, 1950-51; phys. chemist Kingsbrook Jewish Med. Ctr., 1951-56; rsch. fellow Poly. Inst., NY, 1957-58; rsch. assoc. Mt. Sinai Hosp., NYC, 1959-68, dir. arthritis lab., 1961-90; rsch. asst. prof. Mt. Sinai Sch. Medicine, NYC, 1969-74, rsch. assoc. prof., 1974-91; assoc. prof. Hunter Coll. Sch. Health Scis., CUNY, 1969—74, prof., 1974—2002, prof. emeritus, 2002—, dean, 1977-80; mem. doctoral faculty in biochemistry Grad. Ctr., CUNY, 1970—2002, emeritus, 2002—. Vis. prof. Johns Hopkins U. Sch. Health Svcs., 1976-77; cons. to diagnostic reagent and instrument mfrs., 1953-; mem. Internat. Sci. Coun., Albert Einstein Rsch. Inst., Buenos Aires, 1969-79; mem. bd. examiners for clin. labs. NYC Dept. Health, 1973-75; sr. cons. Biotech. Rev. Assocs., 1983-92. Co-editor: Rheumatology for the Health Care Professional, 1991; contbr. numerous articles to profl. jours. Served with U.S. Army, 1944-46. Nat. Inst. Arthritis and Metabolic Diseases grantee, 1961-69; Arthritis Found. grantee, 1961-65, 69, 72; Lupus Found. grantee, 1975-76; CUNY Found. grantee, 1982-83. Mem. Am. Chem. Soc., Am. Coll. Rheumatology, AAAS, NY Acad. Scis., Am. Assn. Immunologists, Am. Assn. Clin. Chemistry, Harvey Soc., Nat. Acad. Clin. Biochemistry, Acad. Clin. Lab. Physicians and Scientists, Clin. Immunology Soc., Sigma Xi, Phi Lambda Upsilon. Home: 670 W End Ave New York NY 10025-7313 Office: Hunter Coll Sch Health Sci 425 E 25th St New York NY 10010-2547 Office Phone: 212-481-5115. *I have always tried to live and work by the idea that strength is not harshness, caring is not sentimentality, and honesty is not vulnerability.*

ORESKES, NAOMI, science historian; b. N.Y.C., Nov. 25, 1958; d. Irwin Oreskes and Susan Eileen Nagin Oreskes; m. Kenneth Belitz, Sept. 28, 1986; children: Hannah Oreskes Belitz, Clara Oreskes Belitz. BSc with honors, Imperial Coll., London, 1981; PhD, Stanford (Calif.) U., 1990. Geologist Western Mining Corp., Adelaide, Australia, 1981-84; rsch. and tng. asst. Stanford U., 1984-89; vis. asst. prof. Dartmouth Coll., Hanover, NH, 1990-91, asst. prof., 1991-96; assoc. prof. Gallatin Sch. NYU, 1996-98, U. Calif., San Diego, 1998—. Consulting geologist Western Mining Corp., 1984-90; consulting historian Am. Inst. Physics, N.Y.C., 1990-96. Author: The Rejection of Continental Drift, 1999, Theory and Method in American Earth Science, 1999; editor: Plate Tectonics: An Insider's History of the Modern Theory of the Earth, 2001; contbr. articles to profl. jours. Recipient Lindgren prize Soc. Econ. Geologists, 1993, Young Investigator award NSF, 1994-99, George Sarton Lectr. award AAAS, 2004; fellow NEH, 1993. Mem. Geol. Soc. Am., History Sci. Soc. Jewish. Home: 14174 Bahama Cv Del Mar CA 92014-2901 Office: U Calif San Diego 9500 Gilman Dr La Jolla CA 92093-0104 Office Phone: 858-534-4695. Business E-Mail: noreskes@ucsd.edu.

ORFORD, ROBERT RAYMOND, consulting physician; b. Winnipeg, Manitoba, Can., Apr. 18, 1948; came to U.S., 1988; s. Robert Raymond and Sarah Gloria L. (Gullden) O.; m. Dale Laura Stuart, June 2, 1972; children: Carolyn Tiffany, Andrew Craig, Loren Brent. BS, McGill U., 1969, MD, 1971; MS, U. Minn., 1975; MPH, U. Wash., 1976. Assoc. prof. cmty. medicine U. Alberta, Edmonton, Can., 1978-88; dir. med. svcs. Govt. of Alberta, Edmonton, Can., 1979-81, exec. dir. occupational health svcs., 1981-85, deputy min. cmty. occupational health, 1985-88; med. dir. employee health U. Alberta Hosp., Edmonton, Can., 1988; sr. assoc. cons. Mayo Clinic, Rochester, Minn., 1988-91, cons. preventive medicine, 1991-96, Scottsdale, Ariz., 1996—. Asst. prof. Mayo Med. Sch., Rochester, 1988—; mem. Alberta Energy Resource Conservation Bd., 1988-89; chmn. divsn. preventive and occupl. medicine, dir. exec. health program, Mayo Clinic, Scottsdale, 1999—. Contbr. articles to profl. jours. Mem. Olmsted County Environ. Commn., Rochester, 1991-96, chair, 1994. Govt. of Can. Nat. Health fellow, 1975-76. Fellow Royal Coll. Physicians & Surgeons Can., Am. Coll. Occupational and Environ. Medicine, Am. Coll. Preventive Medicine, Aerospace Med. Assn.; mem. Internat. Commn. Occupational Health Medicine (nat. sec. 2001—). Presbyterian. Avocations: Spanish, skiing, travel. Home: 15516 E Acacia Way Fountain Hills AZ 85268-3158 Office: Mayo Clinic Scottsdale Divsn Preventive Medicine 13400 E Shea Blvd Scottsdale AZ 85259-5499 Office Phone: 480-301-7379. Business E-Mail: rorford@mayo.edu.

ORGEBIN-CRIST, MARIE-CLAIRE, biology professor, department chairman; b. Vannes, France, Mar. 20, 1936; License Natural Scis., License Biology, Sorbonne, U. Paris, 1957; D. Scis., Lyons U., France, 1961. Stagiaire dept. biochemistry faculty medicine, Paris, France, 1957-58; stagiaire Centre Nat. de la Recherche Scientifique, Paris, 1958-60, attachee de recherche, 1960-62; research assoc. Population Council (Med. Div.), N.Y.C., 1962-63; research assoc. dept. ob/gyn Vanderbilt Sch. Medicine, 1963-64, research instr., 1964-66, asst. prof., 1966-70, assoc. prof., 1970-73, Lucius E. Burch prof. reproductive biology, 1973—, prof. dept. anatomy, 1975—; dir. Vanderbilt Sch. Medicine (Center Reproductive Biology Research.), 1973—. Editor-in-Chief Jour. Andrology, 1983-89. Recipient Career Devel. award NIH, 1968-73, NIH Merit award, 1986,; Fogarty Internat. sr. fellow, 1977; Disting. Scientist award Am. Soc. Reproductive Medicine, 1996. Mem. Am. Assn. Anatomists, Am. Soc. Cell Biology, Am. Soc. Andrology (v.p. 1994-95, pres. 1995-96, Disting. Svc. award 1997, Disting. Andrologist award 1990), Internat. Com. on Andrology, Endoccrine Soc., Soc. for Study Fertility (Eng.), Soc. for Study Reprodn., N.Y. Acad . Scis. Office: Vanderbilt U Sch Med Ctr Reproductive Biology Rsch Rm C-3306 MCN Nashville TN 37232-0001 E-mail: m-c.orgebin-crist@mcmail.vanderbilt.edu.

ORIANI, RICHARD ANTHONY, metallurgical engineer, educator; b. El Salvador, July 19, 1920; arrived in U.S., 1929, naturalized, 1943; s. Americo and Berta (Siguenza) Oriani; m. Constance Amelia Gordon, June 26, 1949; children: Margaret, Steven, Julia, Amelia. B in Chem. Engring, CCNY, 1943; MS, Stevens Inst. Tech., 1946; MA, Princeton U., 1948, PhD, 1949. Lab. asst. CCNY, 1943; chemist Bakelite Corp., Bloomfield, NJ, 1943-46; instr. physics Miss Fine's Finishing Sch., Princeton, NJ, 1946-47; rsch. assoc. GE Rsch. Lab., Schenectady, 1949-59; asst. dir. U.S. Steel Corp. Rsch. Lab., Monroeville, Pa., 1959-80; prof. U. Minn., Mpls., 1980-89, dir. Corrosion Rsch. Ctr., 1980-87, prof. emeritus, dir. emeritus, 1989—. Cons. in field. Contbr. articles to profl. jours., chapters to books. Founder, mem. Foxwood Civic Assn., Monroeville, 1959—80; founder, v.p. Monroeville Pub. Libr., 1960—80. Recipient Alexander von Humboldt Sr. Scientist award, 1984, W. R. Whitney award, 1987. Fellow: Electrochemical Soc., Nat. Assn. Corrosion Engrs., N.Y. Acad. Scis., Am. Inst. Chemists, Am. Soc. Metals; mem.: AAAS, Am. Inst. Metall. Engrs., Am. Phys. Soc. Republican. Home: 4623 Humboldt Ave S Minneapolis MN 55409-2264 Office: U Minn 112 Amundson Hall 221 Church St SE Minneapolis MN 55455-0113 Office Phone: 612-625-5862. E-mail: orian001@umn.edu.

ORIHEL, THOMAS CHARLES, parasitology educator, research scientist; b. Akron, Ohio, Feb. 10, 1929; s. Joseph Andrew and Mary Susannah (Barno) O.; m. Dorothy Lila Williams, Dec. 27, 1952; children— Timothy Stewart, Charles Theodore, Susan Ethra, Adrianne Louise BS, U. Akron, 1950; MS, U. Wash., 1952; PhD, Tulane U., 1959. Sr. scientist Tulane Delta Primate Ctr., Covington, La., 1963-85; prof. parasitology Tulane Med. Ctr., New Orleans, 1972—99, William Vincent prof. tropical diseases, 1982—99, prof. emeritus, 1999—; dir. Tulane U. Internat. Collaboration Infectious Diseases Rsch. Program, New Orleans, 1976-89. Cons. NIH, Bethesda, Md., 1973-77; mem. expert panel WHO, Geneva, 1973-83; mem. U.S.-Japan Cooperative Med. Sci. Program, Bethesda, 1974-78; external examiner U. Queensland, Australia, U. Guelph, Ont., Can., U. Claude Bernard, Lyon, France, U. Malaya, Kuala Lumpur, Malaysia; external assessor U. Malaya, Kuala Lumpur, U. Pertanian Malaysia, Selangor. Author books on subject of medical parasitology, 1976, 81, 84, 90, 94, 95, 97; contbr. articles to Am. and internat. jours. Served to 1st lt. Med. Service Corps, U.S. Army, 1953-56, Korea Mem. Am. Soc. Tropical Medicine and Hygiene (councilor 1975-78), Royal Soc. Tropical Medicine and Hygiene, Am. Soc. Microbiology, Southwestern Assn. Parasitologists (v.p. 1972-73), Am. Soc. Parasitologists, Sigma Xi Avocations: gardening, woodworking. Home: 115 Bertel Dr Covington LA 70433-4815 Office: Tulane U Health Scis Ctr Dept Tropical Medicine 1501 Canal St New Orleans LA 70112 Office Phone: 504-988-2547. Business E-Mail: orihel@tulane.edu.

ORIN, STUART I. lawyer; Exec. v.p. corp. affairs, gen. counsel UAL Corp., Elk Grove Village, Ill., 1996—. Office: UAL Corp PO Box 66100 Chicago IL 60666-0100

ORING, STUART AUGUST, visual information specialist, writer, photographer, researcher; b. Bronx, N.Y., Aug. 28, 1932; s. Irving and Helen Flora (Greenhut) O.; m. Mary Carolyn Barth, Aug. 22, 1957; children: Carlene Marie Oring, Sheri Alyce Oring. AAS, Rochester Inst. Tech., 1957; BFA, R.I. Tech., 1959; MA, Am. U., 1970. Photo lab asst. Nat. Geographic, Washington, summer 1957; photography asst. IJBecker, Nepo-Nuss Advt Photo, Studio Assocs. & Art Green Inc., N.Y.C., 1959-61; freelance photographer pvt. practice, Washington, 1961; indsl. photographer Vitro Corp., Rockville, Md., 1962-64; health photographer Nat. Ctr. Radiol. Health, Rockville, Md., 1964-67; visual info. specialist ARS Info. div. USDA, Washington, 1967-69; audio visual specialist Nat. AV Ctr., Washington, 1969-71; photojournalist Office of Econ. Opportunity, Washington, 1971-74; visual info. specialist ASCS, U.S. Dept. Agr., Washington, 1974-94; ret., 1994. Mgr., owner ISIS Visual Comms.; photography tchr. Prince George's C.C., Largo, Md., 1975-96; guest lectr. U. Md. Balt. County, Catonsville, Corcoran Gallery of Art, Washington; spkr. in field. Author, editor and pub.: (textbook/gallery text) Understanding Pictures-A Teacher's Planning Guide, 1994, Understanding Pictures-Theories, Exercises and Procedures, 1990, rev. 1992, rev. 1995, A Beginner's Guide to Looking at Pictures, 1997; contbr. numerous articles to profl. jours.; photos published in books, mags., brochures, pamphlets. Photographer with U.S. Army, 1952-55. Recipient Cert. Recognition award Eastman Kodak Co., 1973, Nat. Ctr. Radiol. Health, Rockville, Md., 1965. Mem.: APA (divsn. 10 psychology and the arts, program spkr. 105th ann. conf., 108th ann. conf.), Inst. for Psychol. Study of Arts (program spkr.), Am. Soc. Psychopathology of Expression (bd. dirs.). Achievements include research and development of new approaches for analyzing and interpreting art and photographs. Home and Office: 2570 Redbud Ln Owings MD 20736-4308 Office Phone: 410-257-5709. E-mail: stuartoring@comcast.net., stuartoring@hotmail.com.

ORINGER, KENNETH, chef, restaurant owner; Degree, Bryant Coll.; grad., Culinary Inst. Am. Cook River Cafe, N.Y.C.; pastry chef Al Forno, Providence; chef de partie, sous chef Le Marquis de Lafayette, Boston; owner, chef Terra; chef de cuisine Silks, San Francisco; chef, ptnr. Tosca, Hingham, Mass.; exec. chef, owner Clio, Boston, 2000—. Named Best New Chef, San Francisco Chronicle, Rising Star Chef, Restaurant Hospitality, Best Chef in Boston, Boston Mag., 2000, Best Chef in N.E., James Beard Found., 2001. Office: Restaurant Clio 370 Commonwealth Ave Boston MA 02215

ORISEK, IVAN, financial executive; b. Prague, Czechoslovakia, May 29, 1945; came to U.S., 1976, naturalized, 1981; s. Frantisek and Bozena O.; m. Olga Dedina, Sept. 28, 1977; children: Philip, Vena. MSc, Czech Tech. U., Prague, 1967. Sr. rsch. analyst Rsch. Inst. Fuel and Energy Econs., Prague, 1970-75; head ops. rsch. sect. Am. Electric Power Svc. Corp., N.Y.C., 1976-81; prin. engr. Ebasco Svcs., Inc., N.Y.C., 1981-86; pres. I&O Assocs. Mortgage Corp., Forestburgh, NY, 1986—. Mem. Inst. Ops. Rsch. and Mgmt. Scis., Sports Car Club Am. Avocation: race car driving. Home: Evergreens 2488 Rte 42 Forestburgh NY 12777 Office Phone: 845-791-5500. E-mail: iomortgage@aol.com., eurorally@aol.com.

ORKAND, DONALD SAUL, management consultant; b. N.Y.C., Mar. 2, 1936; s. Harold and Sylvia (Wagner) O.; children: Dara Sue, Katarina Day; m. Kim Lim Sang, July 22, 2001; 1 child, Aaron J. BS summa cum laude, NYU, 1956, MBA, 1957, PhD, 1963. Statistician Western Electric Co., N.Y.C., 1956-58; group v.p. Ops. Rsch., Inc., Silver Spring, Md., 1960-69; pres. Ops. Rsch. Industries, Ltd., Ottawa, Ont., Can., 1968-69; pres., CEO The Orkand Corp., Tysons Corner, Va., 1970—. Bd. dirs. U. Md. Found., Inc., College Park, 1993-2002. Contbr. articles to profl. jours. Bd. visitors Coll. Bus. and Mgmt., U. Md., College Park, 1985—, Univ. Coll., 2002—; trustee Suburban Hosp., 1994-2000. 1st lt. Ordnance Corps, USAR, 1958-60. Mem. Am. Econs. Assn., Am. Statis. Assn., Ops. Rsch. Soc. Am. Republican. Jewish. Avocations: reading, theater, travel, exercise. Office: The Orkand Corp 7799 Leesburg Pike Ste 700N Falls Church VA 22043-2499

ORKIN, JENNA, writer; b. New York, NY; d. Harvey Orkin; 1 child, One. BA, Hunter Coll., NY; JD, NY Law Sch., NY; BA/MA, Oxford U., England. Press chairperson 911 Environ. Action, New York, NY, 2002—03; interviewer Exploring Post One, New York, NY, 1984—86; educator Juilliard, New York, NY, 1978—83.

ORKIN, LOUIS RICHARD, physician, educator; b. NYC, Dec. 23, 1915; s. Samuel David and Rebecca (Rish) O.; m. Florence Fine, Mar. 5, 1938; 1 dau., Rita. BA, U. Wis., 1937; MD, NYU, 1941; AAS in Marine Tech., Kingsborough Coll., 1992. Intern Bellevue Hosp., NYC, 1942, resident anesthesiology, 1946-48; practice medicine specializing in anesthesiology Bronx, NY, 1946—48; dir. anesthesiology Backus Hosp., Norwich, Conn., 1948-50; asst. prof. anesthesiology NYU Coll. Medicine, 1950-55; prof., chmn. dept. anesthesiology Albert Einstein Coll. Medicine, 1955-82, Disting. univ. prof., 1982-86, dist. univ. prof. emeritus, 1986—. Vis. prof. depts. bioengring., anesthesiology U. Calif., San Diego, 1971; Cons. VA, USPHS, USN; mem. com. anesthesiology Nat. Acad. Scis., 1964-69; mem. com. anesthetic drugs FDA, Dept. Health, Edn. and Welfare, 1970— Author: Patient in Shock, 1965, Physiology of Obstetrical Anesthesia, 1969; Contbr. articles to profl. jours. Vice pres., trustee Wood Library Mus. Served to capt. M.C. AUS, 1942-45. Decorated Bronze Star. Fellow Am. Coll. Chest Physicians, NY Acad. Sci., NY Acad. Medicine, Am. Coll. Anesthesiology (past chmn. bd. govs.); mem. NY State Soc. Anesthesiologists (past pres.; Disting. Svc. award 2000). Home: 11 Stuyvesant Oval Apt 11F New York NY 10009-2001

ORKIS, LAMBERT, musician, music educator; m. Janice Barbara Kretschmann, Feb. 19, 1972. Diploma, MusB, Curtis Inst. Music, 1965; MusM, Temple U., 1968. Prin. keyboard Nat. Symphony Orch., Washington, 1982—; prof. piano Temple U. Esther Boyer Coll. Music, Phila., 1968—. Contbr. articles to profl. jours. Nominee Grammy award, NARAS, 1996, 1997, 1999; recipient, 1999, Critic's Choice award, Nat. Pub. Radio, 1999, Cert. of Honor, Temple U. Alumni Assn., 2002. Office: PO Box 6023 Arlington VA 22206-0023 E-mail: orkispiano@lambertorkis.com.

ORLEANS, JEFFREY P. construction executive; Chmn., CEO Orleans Home Builders, 1986—, pres., 1986—92; gen. ptnr. Orleans Builders & Developers; CEO Orleans Construction Corp., 1986—93. Trustee Penn. Real Estate Investment Trust. Office: One Greenwood Sq Ste 101 3333 Street Rd Bensalem PA 19020

ORLEBEKE, WILLIAM RONALD, retired lawyer, writer; b. El Paso, Tex., Jan. 5, 1934; s. William Ronald and Frances Claire (Cook) O.; m. Barbara Raye Pike, 1955 (div. 1981); children: Michelle, Julene, David; m. Susan K. Nash, 2000. BA, Willamette U., 1956; MA, Kans. U., 1957; JD, Willamette U., 1966. Bar: Calif. 1966, US Dist. Ct. (no. dist.) Calif. 1967, US Ct. Appeals (9th cir.) 1967, US Ct. Appeals (7th cir.) 1989, US Dist. Ct. (no. dist.) Ill. 1989, US Dist. Ct. (cen. dist.) Calif. 1989. Mem. staff Travelers Ins. Co., Sacramento, 1957-61; br. claim mgr. NY Life Ins. Co., 1961-62; branch claim mgr. Transamerica Ins. Co., San Francisco, 1962-63; assoc. Eliassen & Postel, San Francisco, 1966-69; ptnr. Coll, Levy & Orlebeke, Concord, Calif., 1969-77, Orlebeke & Hutchings, Concord, Calif., 1977-89; prin. Law Offices W. Ronald Orlebeke, 1989-98; hearing officer Contra Costa County, Calif., 1981-98; arbitrator Contra Costa County Superior Ct., 1977-98, US Dist. Ct. No. Calif., 1978-98, Mt. Diablo Mcpl. Ct., 1987-89; ret., 1998. Judge pro tem Mt. Diablo Mcpl. Ct., 1973-75; criminology prof. Pioneer-Pacific Coll., 2002-03. Author: Orlebeke Family in Europe and America, 1570-1990, 1988, Don't Tell Me I Can't, 2003, (novels) Code Jeremiah, 2004, Lightning, 2004. Alumni bd. dir. Willamette U., 1978-81, trustee, 1980-81 scholar chmn. Concord Elks, 1977-79; del. Joint US/China Internat. Trade Law Conf., Beijing, 1987. With USMCR, 1952-59. Sr. scholar Willamette U., 1955-56; Woodrow Wilson fellow Kans. U., 1956-57, US Bur. Nat. Affairs fellow, 1966, others. Mem. SAR, Sons of Confederate Vets. (Merit award 1989), Sons of Union Vets. Civil War, First Marine Divsn. Assn., Order Ea. Star (worthy patron 1980), Masons (sec. Capitol Masonic Ctr., 2001-2004), Elks, Rotary (charter pres. Clayton Valley/Concord Sunrise club 1987-88, chmn. dist. 5160 Calif. membership devel. 1989-90, dist. gov. liaison dist. 5160 1990-92, dist. Rotarian of Yr. 1989-90, Paul Harris fellow 1988, 1992 dist. conf. chmn. benefactor 1990, Merit award 1990). Republican.

ORLIK, CHRISTINA BEAR, music educator; b. Detroit, Nov. 10, 1945; d. Robert William and Olive Marie (Evans) Bear; m. Peter Blythe Orlik, Aug. 18, 1967; children: Darcy Anne, Blaine Truen. BS in Edn., Wayne State U., 1967, MS in Edn., 1969. Tchr. clarinet pvt. practice, Detroit, 1961-69; elem. band dir. City Recreation Dept., Troy, Mich, 1964-67; dir. bands Crary Jr. High Sch., Waterford, Mich, 1967-69; instr. woodwind pvt. practice, Mt. Pleasant, Mich, 1970-84; dir. bands Montabella Jr. High Sch., Blanchard, Mich, 1974-76; substitute tchr. Mt. Pleasant Schs., 1976-84, libr. media profl., 1984-85, tchr. gen. music, 1985—, orch. dir., 1987—. Part-time instr. Ctrl. Mich. U. Tchr. Edn., 1989—91; organizing mem., mgr. Ctrl. Mich. Cmty. Band, Mt. Pleasant, 1973—75; clarinetist, bassoonist Alma (Mich.) Symphony Orch., 1973—86, Eddy Concert Band, Saginaw, Mich., 1973—2000; founder, mgr. Four for Strings orch. festival, 1991—. Tchr. Sunday sch. St. Andrew's Episcopal Ch., Clawson, Mich., 1966-67; treas., mem. chair LWV, Mt. Pleasant, 1972-73; chair Child Care Adv. Com., Mt. Pleasant, 1973-74. Mem. Am. String Tchrs. Assn. (program review grantee 1990), Mich. Edn. Assn., ch. Sch. Band and Orch. Assn. (Dist. 5 Orch. Tchr. of Yr. 2000), Music Educators Nat. Conf. Avocation: dance. Home: 613 Kane St Mount Pleasant MI 48858-1949 Office: West Intermediate Sch 440 S Bradley St Mount Pleasant MI 48858-3052

ORLIN, JAMES BERGER, mathematician, management scientist, educator; b. Buffalo, Apr. 19, 1953; s. Albert Norman and Roslyn Louise (Berger) Orlin; m. Donna Lynn Hogan, Jan. 3, 1982 (dec. Oct. 2000); children: Jennifer Robin, Benjamin Aaron, Caroline Anne. BA, U. Pa., 1974; MS, Caltech, 1976; MMath, U. Waterloo, Ont., Can., 1976; PhD, Stanford U., 1981. Asst. prof. MIT, Cambridge, Mass., 1979-83, assoc. prof., 1983-87, prof., 1987—, co-dir. ops. rsch. ctr., 1998—. Vis. prof. Erasmus U., Rotterdam, Netherlands, 1984—85; vis. scientist Collaborative Rsch. Inc., Waltham, Mass., 1992—93, Frictionless Commerce, 2000—01, Whitehead Inst., 1993—96. Co-author: Network Flows: Theory, Algorithms and Applications, 1993; assoc. editor: Networks, 1992—; contbr. over 75 articles to profl. jours. Recipient Young Presdl. Young Investigator award, NSF, 1985—90; Fulbright Rsch. grant, 1984—85, UPS fellow, 1991—94, 1995—96. Mem.: INFORMS (co-recipient Lanchester prize 1993), Soc. Indsl. and Applied Math., Math. Programming Soc., Assn. Computing Machinery. Home: 10 Taft Dr Winchester MA 01890-3748 Office: MIT #E40-147 77 Massachusetts Ave Cambridge MA 02139-4307

ORLIN, LOUIS LAWRENCE, literature and history educator; b. Bayonne, N.J., Nov. 7, 1925; s. Bernard and Ruth; m. Jenny Lee Gray, June 24, 1988; children: Lesley, David, Hugh, Celia. BA, U. Mich., 1949, MA, 1950, PhD, 1960. Lectr. English lang. and lit. U. Mich., Ann Arbor, 1955-58, lectr. ancient near eastern lit. and history, 1956-61, asst. prof., 1961-65, assoc. prof., 1965, prof., 1970-89, dir. residential coll., 1973, prof. emeritus, 1989—. Vis. scholar Cambridge (Eng.) U., 1967-68; vis. prof. U. Queensland, Brisbane, Australia, 1982; regional cons. Nat. Humanities series NEH, 1973-75. Author: Ancient Near Eastern Literature, 1969, Assyrian Colonies in Cappadoua, 1970; editor: Janus: Essays in Ancient and Modern Studies, 1974, Michigan Oriental Studies in Honor of George G. Cameron, 1974; TV series City of Time. Violist Ann Arbor Symphony orch., 1960-85, VA Med. Musical Group, 1990s. With U.S. Army, 1943-45, ETO. Decorated Bronze Star, Purple Heart; recipient E. Harris Harbison award for disting. tchg. Danforth Found., 1967; Danforth Found. assoc., 1967—. Mem. Am. Oriental Soc., Am. Hist. Assn., Assn. Ancient Historians, Archaeol. Inst. Am., Phi Kappa Phi. Avocations: viola, lecturing, tennis, sailing, creative writing. Home: 4734 Northgate Dr Ann Arbor MI 48103 Office: U Mich Dept Near Eastern Studies Frieze Bldg Ann Arbor MI 48109

ORLOFF, BARBARA-LEE MARGUERITE HEWITT, social worker; b. N.Y.C., Feb. 18, 1944; d. Richard Elliott Hewitt and Elise Harriet (Hofer) DeMeritt; m. Jonathan Harris Orloff, Apr. 22, 1967 (div. May 1985); children: Aleksandr Monford, Piotr Richard. BA, Chatham Coll., Pitts., 1966; postgrad., Portland State U., 1988—90. Info. and referral specialist Info. and Vol. Svcs., Pitts., 1967—70; vol. coord. Friends of Tryon Creek State Park, Portland, Oreg., 1975—81, Oreg. State Parks, Salem, 1978, Portland Dept. Parks and Recreation, 1979; exec. dir. Friend of Tryon Creek State Park, Portland, 1985—88; social svc. coord. Lake Oswego Adult Ctr., Oreg., 1985—90; program dir. N.W. Housing Alternatives, Milwaukie, Oreg., 1990—. Mem. transitional housing continnum of care bd. Clackamas County Social Svc.s, Oreg. City, Oreg., 1992—; vol. coord. book Guide to Urban Wilderness, 1978. Watercolor artist, photographer Monday Studio. Docent Portland Art Mus., 1970—74; opera evening vol. host Lake Oswego Adult Ctr., 1985—2001. Named Merit Mother of Oreg., Am. Assn. Mothers, Portland, 1991. Democrat. Episcopalian. Avocations: sailing, hiking, needlepoint, opera, literature. Home: 1400 SE Lava Dr # 14 Milwaukie OR 97222 Office: Northwest Housing Alternatives 2316 SE Willard St Milwaukie OR 97222 Office Phone: 503-654-1007 103. Business E-Mail: orloff@nwhousing.org.

ORLOVSKY, DONALD ALBERT, lawyer; b. Essex County, N.J., 1951; AB, Cornell U., 1973; JD, Rutgers U., 1976. Bar: Fla. 1976, U.S. Ct. Appeals (5th cir.) 1976, N.J. 1977, U.S. Dist. Ct. (so. dist.) Fla. 1977, U.S. Dist. Ct. N.J. 1977, U.S. Supreme Ct. 1980, U.S. Ct. Appeals (11th cir.) 1981, U.S. Ct. Appeals (8th cir.) 2003. Assoc. Smathers & Thompson, Miami, 1976-77; ptnr. McCune, Hiaasen, Crum, Ferris & Gardner, P.A., Ft. Lauderdale, Fla., 1978-86, Kamen & Orlovsky PA, West Palm Beach, 1988—. Pres. bd. dirs. Comprehensive Alcoholism Treatment Program, Inc.; sec., bd. dirs. Fla. Lawyers Assistance, Inc., supervising monitor and counselor, 1991—. Author: Nova U. Law Review, 1977, U. Miami Law Review, 1978. Recipient All-Am. recognition in springboard diving, 1966-69; inducted Hall of Fame Newark Acad., Livingston, N.J., 1997. Mem. ABA, Fla. Bar (civil procedure rules com. 1981), Acad. Fla. Trial Lawyers, Assn. Trial Lawyers Am. Episcopalian. Office: 1601 Belvedere Rd Ste 402 West Palm Beach FL 33406-1541 Office Phone: 561-687-8500. Personal E-mail: dao4law@aol.com.

ORLOWSKA-WARREN, LENORE ALEXANDRIA, art educator, fiber artist; b. Detroit, May 22, 1951; d. William Leonard and Aloisa Clara (Hrapkiewicz) Orlowski; m. Donald Edward Warren, May 11, 1990. AA, Henry Ford C.C., 1972; BS in Art Edn., Wayne State U., 1974, M in Spl. Edn., 1978; BFA, Ctr. for Creative Studies, 2000. Tchr. arts and crafts Detroit Pub. Schs., 1974—2002; fiber artist Detroit Inst. Arts. Cons. Arts Detroit Cmty. Plan, TRIACO Arts & Crafts, 1996—; instr., demonstrator weaving Detroit Inst. Arts; represented by Gallery Five, Tequesta, Fla., Ann Arbor Art Ctr. One-woman show at Dearborn C. of C., Ctr. for Creative Studies, 2000; exhibited in group shows, including alumni exhibit Henry Ford C.C., 1989, Detroit Artist Market, 1995-2000, Scarab Club, 1996, Lansing Art Gallery, 1997, Ctr. for Creative Studies, 1997, Yr. of the Woman Exhibit, 1998, Tom Thompson Meml. Art Gallery Juried Ontario Artists Exhibit, 1998, 2001, One Focus, Two Worlds Exhibit, 1999, Fashion Exhibit and Felt the Feeling of Fiber, U.245 Gallery, 1999, Ctr. Creative Studies, 2000, Ann Arbor Art Ctr., 2001, Downriver Coun. for the Arts, 2001, Alumni Fiber Artist exhibit Coll. Creative Studies, 2002, Ann Arbor Art Ctr. All Media Exhbn., 2002 (Barbara Dorr Meml. award), Outside The Lines Gallery, 2001, 02, Padziewski Gallery, 2003, Scarab Club, 2003; contbr. to Sch. Arts Mag.; represented in permanent collections Gallery Five, Tequesta, Fla., Ann Arbor Art Ctr. Mem. exec. bd. Springwells Pk. Assn., 1989-99, pres., 1994-96, chairperson youth act workshops; com. mem. Dearborn cmty. art coun. Art on the Ave., 1993-99, Gallery Crawl chairperson, 1998; chair Nat. Woman's History Month workshop, 1995. Mem.: Cranbrook Acad. Art, Am. Tapestry Alliance, Art Inst. of Chgo., Downriver Coun. for Arts, Surface Design Assn., The Textile Mus., The Nat. Mus. Women in Art Williamsburg Burgesses, Met. Mus. Art, Norton Mus. Art (Williamsburg assoc.), Mich. Surface Design, Friends of Fiber Art Internat. Assn., Coll. Art Assn., Birmingham Bloomfield Art Assn., Detroit Inst. Arts-Founders Soc., Am. Craft Coun., Mich. Art Edn. Assn. (presenter art advocacy workshop), Nat. Art Edn. Assn. (electronic gallery coord. 1992—99). Avocations: fiber art, travel, colonial gardening, reading colonial history and biographies. Home: 10 Berwick Ln Dearborn MI 48120-1102

ORLOWSKI, KAREL ANN, elementary school educator; b. Fremont, Ohio, Dec. 22, 1949; d. Karl and Angeline Marie (Oudersluys) Kooistra; m. Paul Joseph Orlowski, Apr. 28, 1973; 1 child, Jennifer Frann. BA in Music Edn., U. Mich., 1971; MS in Elem. Edn., Dowling Coll., Oakdale, N.Y., 1978. Cert. tchr., N.Y. Tchr. vocal music Patchogue-Medford Schs., NY, 1971—, lead tchr. music dept., 1986—88, 1991—94; dir. of musicals Eagle Elem. Sch., 1990—94. Dir. drama dept. River Elem. Sch., Patchogue, 1974-90, Chosen Few show choir South Ocean Mid. Sch., Patchogue, 1984-90, Notation! show choir Eagle Elem. Sch., 1990-94, 95—, A Chords show choir Barton Elem. Sch., 1994-95. Mem. N.Y. State Sch. Music Assn., Suffolk County Music Educators Assn. (co-chmn. so. divsn. I chorus 1993-95, divsn. II S.W. chorus 1996-97, asst. v.p. divsn. I festivals 1997-98, exec. v.p. for festivals 1998-2000, standing coms. 1999-2000, co-chmn. membership 2003—). Republican. Episcopalian. Avocations: reading, renaissance music, vocal jazz, nascar sk class and figure-eight racing. Home: 37 Detmer Rd East Setauket NY 11733-1912 Office: Patchogue-Medford Schs 241 S Ocean Ave Patchogue NY 11772-3787

ORLOWSKY, MARTIN L. executive manager; b. N.Y.C., Dec. 7, 1941; s. Solomon and Sylvia (Levine) O.; m. Carolyn Louise Brady, Mar. 25, 1973; children— Daniel, Keith, Matthew. BA, Long Island U., N.Y.C., 1963. Media planner Compton Advertising, N.Y.C., 1968-69; media planner Young & Rubicam Inc., N.Y.C., 1969-71; v.p. media Grey Advertising, N.Y.C., 1971-76; sr. v.p., media and mktg. services Needham, Harper & Steers, N.Y.C., 1976-77; media dir. R.J. Reynolds Tobacco Co., Winston-Salem, N.C., 1977-80, dir. mktg. services, 1980-82, v.p. brand mktg., 1982-84, sr. v.p. mktg., 1984-85, exec. v.p., 1986; pres. Grocery div. Nabisco Brands, U.S.A., Parsippany, N.J., 1986—, Planters and Life Savers div. Nabisco Brands, U.S.A., Parsippany, N.J., 1987—, DKM Holdings, 1988-90; sr. v.p. mktg. Lorillard Tobacco Co., N.Y.C., 1990-92, exec. v.p. mktg. and sales, 1992-95, pres., 1995—, pres., CEO, 1999—. Vol., Peace Corps, Bolivia, 1963-65. Served to sgt. U.S. Army, 1966-68 Avocations: fishing; tennis. Home: 21 Loch Ridge Dr Greensboro NC 27408-3869

ORM, SALLY S. music educator, consultant; d. Harvey Jacob and Lucille Mae Seyler; children: Jennifer E. Orm-Seager, Andrea Orm-Summer. Student, Eastman Sch. Music. Co-owner, ptnr. All Things Music, LLC. Founder keyboard donations Orm Music Studios, Neenah, Wis., 2001—. Treas. Regional Domestic Abuse, Oshkosh, Wis., 1984—86, pres., 1986—88; treas. Audobon Soc., Appleton, 1985—86; Gold award coord. Fox Valley Area Girl Scouts, Appleton, Wis., 1995—99. Named Mem. of the Yr. award, Fox Valley Area Girl Scouts, 1999. Mem.: Music Tchrs. Nat. Assn., Fox Valley Keyboard Tchrs. (v.p., program dir. 1999—2003, Mem. of the Yr. award 2002), World Piano Pedagogy Conf., Keyboard Music Educators Assn. (adjudicator keyboard competition 2002—). Presbyterian. Avocations: gardening, travel. Office: Orm Music Studios 749 S Commercial St Neenah WI 54956

ORMAI-BUZA, ILDIKO, soprano, composer, organist, music educator; b. Budapest, Hungary, Dec. 21, 1927; came to U.S., 1949, naturalized, 1955; d. Janos and Margit Ormai; m. George Buza, Oct. 28, 1950; children: George F., Paul L. Student in piano and theory, Hannig Conservatory, Budapest, 1938-44; student, Ecole D'Arts Coll., Freiburg, Germany, 1947-49; studied voice with Carmela Cafarelli; studied composition and orchestration, Janos Kiss. Cert. pvt. voice, piano and organ tchr., Ohio. Organist, soloist St. Raphael Cath. Ch., Bay Village, Ohio, 1957-72; concert soprano Cafarelli Opera Co., Cleve., 1957-67; organist, soloist Holy Spirit Ch., Avon Lake, Ohio, 1972-97, Our Lady of Angels Ch., Cleve., 1998-99; frequent guest, organist, soloist St. Emeric Ch., Cleve. Choir dir. Midnszenty Chamber Choir, Cleve., 1981-84; guest soloist Fatima World Congress, Germany, 1985, Portugal, 1992; guest concert soloist, U.S. and Can., 1960—. Composer: (organ and chorus) Mass of Adoration (Silver medal 1975), (choir and organ) Berzsenyi Poem: Supplication (Gold medal 1986), Piano Solos, 1996; performed solo concert Perpetual Adoration Ch., Budapest, 1989; soprano guest soloist West Suburban Philharm. Orch., Ann. Opera Concert, Cleve., 1980, 82, in concert record, 1981; commd. composer Hymn of Worldwide St. Ladislaus Order, 1989; prodr., announcer NBN weekly classical Hungarian Concert Hall Radio Hour, 1977-85; performer voice and piano Hungarian Assn., 1955—. Recipient Papal Blessing for composition Ave Maria, Pope John Paul II, 1987. Mem. Music Tchrs. Nat. Assn., Am. Guild Organists, Ohio Music Tchrs. Assn. (winner composition contest 1989, publicity com. 1981-97), St. Ladislaus Order (knighted Dame 1983, Cross of Honor 1987), Arpad Acad., Cleve. Piano Tchrs. Club. Avocations: painting, portrait drawing, sewing, dance, poetry.

ORMAN, LEONARD ARNOLD, lawyer; b. Balt., June 15, 1930; s. Samuel and Bertie (Adler) O.; m. Barbara Gold, June 9, 1978; children: Richard Harold, Robert Barton. AB summa cum laude, U. Md., 1952, JD, 1955. Bar: Md. 1955, U.S. Ct. Appeals (4th cir.) 1956, U.S. Dist. Ct. Md. 1955, Ct. Appeals Md. 1955, U.S. Supreme Ct. 1977, U.S. Ct. Claims 1990, D.C. Ct. Appeals 1987. Law clk. Hon. Frederick W. Brune, Chief Judge Md. Ct. of Appeals, 1955-56; mem. dept. legis. reference Md. Legislature, 1957-58; mem. Gov.'s Commn. to Revise Criminal Code, 1958-59; pvt. practice law Balt., 1956—. Lectr. in trial tactics. Mem. editl. bd. Md. Law Rev., 1953-55; contbr. articles to profl. jours. Pres. Young Dems. 2d Dist., Balt., 1960-63. With AUS, 1948-49; lt. col. USAF Res. ret. Rosco Pound Inst. fellow, trustee. Mem. Am. Bd. Trial Advocates (cert. civil trial adv.), Md. State Bar Assn. (com.), Balt. City Bar Assn. (com.), Nat. Coll. Trial Advocacy (trustee), Assn. Trial Lawyers Am. (com., nat. committeeman 1976-80, bd. govs. 1985—, exec. com. 1988-90, chmn. orgn. rev. com., home office and budget com., orgn. and home office com., election com., key man com., past steering com., past publ. com., past ednl. adv. group 1989-90, chmn. Stalwarts Hall of Fame com., past vice-chair ABA-ATLA liaison com., M Club, co-chair conv. site planning com., co-chair polit. insight com., long-range planning com., auth-hwy. adv. com., toy safety conf., med. malpractice adv. com., product liability adv. com., co-chair home office capital improvements adv. com., co-chmn. conv. planning com. Washington, Wiedmann/Wysocki award 1989-90, 1996, 2002), Md. Trial Lawyers Assn. (bd. govs., pres. 1984-85, Lifetime Achievement award, 2002), Order of Coif, Masons. Home: 2 Celadon Rd Owings Mills MD 21117-3010 Office: 26 South St Baltimore MD 21202-3215 Office Phone: 410-962-0400. E-mail: lorman@triallaw.com.

ORMAN, NANETTE HECTOR, psychiatrist; b. Highland Park, Ill., Feb. 1, 1943; d. William Joseph and Agnes (Daly) Hector; m. John Christopher Orman, July 2, 1964; children: Laurel Anne, Nathaniel William. BA in Journalism, U. Calif., Berkeley, 1964; postgrad., Stanford U., 1978-81; MPH in Epidemiology, U. Calif., Berkeley, 1984, MS in Health and Med. Scis., 1985; MD, U. Calif., San Francisco, 1987. Diplomate Am. Bd. Psychiatry and Neurology; lic. physician, Calif. Psychiatrist San Jose (Calif.) State U., 1989-93; pvt. practice Los Altos, Calif., 1991—; staff El Camino Hosp., 1991-94, assoc. staff, 1994—; staff Stanford (Calif.) U. Hosp. and Med. Ctr., 1998—. Asst. clin. prof. Stanford (Calif.) U. Sch. Medicine, 1995—; oral bd. examiner Am. Bd. Psychiatry & Neurology, Deerfield, Ill., 1995—, chief resident in psychiatry, 1991; spkr. and cons. in field. Editor San Mateo County Planned Parenthood Assn. Newsletter, 1968-69. Bd. dirs. Mid-Peninsula Task Force for Integrated Edn., 1972-82; consumer mem. San Mateo County Mental Health Adv. Bd., 1987. Mem. Am. Psychiat. Assn. (pub. info. com. 1989—), No. Calif. Psychiat. Soc. (chair membership com. 1996-2002, pub. info. com., media spokesperson, moderator ann. meetings 1993-94), Nat. Alliance for the Mentally Ill, San Francisco Depressive and Manic Depressive Assn. Office: 851 Fremont Ave Ste 98 Los Altos CA 94024-5602

ORMAN, SUZE, news correspondent, writer; Cert. fin. planner. Account exec. Merrill Lynch, 1980—83; v.p. investments Prudential Bache Securities, 1983—87; dir. Suze Orman Fin. Group, 1987—97. Former fin. contbr. NBC News' Today; host QVC Fin. Freedom hour. Contbr. to Self mag.; author: (PBS spl.) The Road to Wealth; co-prodr.: (PBS spl.) The Road to Wealth; host (PBS spl.) The Road to Wealth; author: (PBS spl.) The Courage to Be Rich; co-prodr.: (PBS spl.) The Courage to Be Rich; host (PBS spl.) The Courage to Be Rich; author: (PBS spl.) The 9 Steps to Financial Freedom; co-prodr.: (PBS spl.) The 9 Steps to Financial Freedom; host (PBS spl.) The 9 Steps to Financial Freedom; contbg. editor: O: The Oprah Mag.; host (nat. syndicated radio talk show) The Suze Orman Show; author: The 9 Steps to Financial Freedom, 1997 (NY Times bestsellers), The Courage to Be Rich, 1999 (NY Times bestsellers, Motivational book award Books for a Better Life, 1999), The Road to Wealth, 2001 (NY Times bestsellers), You've Earned It, Don't Lose It, 1995. Named Top 30 Power Brokers Who Most Influenced Mutual Fund Industry and Affected Money, Smart Money mag., 1999; named to 100th issue as those "who have revolutionized the way Am. thinks about money", Worth mag., 2001. Office: CNBC 2200 Fletcher Ave Ste 5 Fort Lee NJ 07024 Office Phone: 201-585-2183.

ORMASA, JOHN, retired utilities executive; b. Richmond, Calif., May 30, 1925; s. Juan Hormaza and Maria Inocencia Olondo; m. Dorothy Helen Trmble, Feb. 17, 1952; children: Newton Lee, John Trumble, Nancy Jean Davies. BA, U. Calif. Berkeley, 1948; JD, Harvard U., 1951. Bar: Calif. 1952, U.S. Supreme Ct. 1959. Assoc. Clifford C. Anglim, 1951—52, Richmond, Carlson, Collins, Gordon & Bold, 1952—56, ptnr., 1956—59; v.p. sys. gen. counsel Pacific Lighting Svc. Co., L.A., 1966—72; gen. atty., v.p., gen. counsel So. Calif. Gas Co., L.A., 1959—66; v.p. gen. counsel Pacific Lighting Corp., L.A., 1973—75, v.p., sec., gen. counsel, 1975; ret., 1975. Acting city atty. El Cerrito, Calif., 1952. With USN, 1943—46. Mem.: ABA, Richmond Bar Assn. (pres. 1959), Calif. State Bar Assn., Kiwanis (v.p. 1959). Republican. Roman Catholic.

ORME, ANTONY RONALD, geography educator; b. Weston-Super-Mare, Somerset, Eng., May 28, 1936; came to U.S., 1968; s. Ronald Albert and Anne (Parry) O.; m. Amalie Jo Brown, Nov. 18, 1984; children: Mark Antony, Kevin Ronald, Devon Anne. BA with 1st class honors, U. Birmingham, 1957, PhD, 1961. Lectr. Univ. Coll., Dublin, Ireland, 1960-68; mem. faculty UCLA, 1968—, prof. geography, 1973—, dean social scis., 1977-83. Cons. geomorphology various orgns., throughout U.S., 1968— Editor-in-chief Phys. Geog-

raphy. Recipient Award of Merit Am. Inst. Planners, 1975; recipient Outstanding Service award USAF, 1977-80, Founders' medal Brit. Geom. Rsch. Group. Mem. Geol. Soc. Am., Assn. Am. Geographers (Disting. Career award), Assn. Geography Tchrs. Ireland (pres. 1964-68), Inst. Brit. Geographers, Internat. Geog. Union. Home: 5128 Del Moreno Dr Woodland Hills CA 91364-2426 Office: UCLA Dept Geography Los Angeles CA 90095-1524 Business E-Mail: orme@geog.ucla.edu.

ORME, MELISSA EMILY, mechanical engineering educator; b. Glendale, Calif, Mar. 12, 1961; d. Myrl Eugene and Geraldine Irene (Schmuck) O.; m. Vasilis Zissis Marmarelis, Mar. 12, 1989; children: Zissis Eugene and Myrl Galinos (twins). BS, U. So. Calif., L.A., 1984, MS, 1985, PhD, 1989. Rsch. asst. prof. U. So. Calif., 1990-93; asst. prof. U. Calif., Irvine, 1993-96, assoc. prof., 1996—2002, prof. engring., 2002—. Panel reviewer NSF, Arlington, Va., 1993—; cons. MPM Corp., Boston, 1993-97; pres. RAD, Inc., 1994-1996. Contbr. articles to profl. jour. Recipient Young Investigator award NSF, 1994, Arch T. Colwell Merit award SAE, 1994. Mem. AAUW, AIAA, ASME, Am. Phys. Soc., Minerals, Metals and Materials Soc. Achievements include 14 US patents. Office: U Calif Dept Mech Engring Irvine CA 92697-0001 Office Phone: 949-824-8148. E-mail: melissao@uci.edu.

ORMES, JONATHAN FAIRFIELD, astrophysicist, science administrator, researcher; b. Colorado Springs, Colo., July 18, 1939; s. Robert Manly and Suzanne (Viertel) O.; m. Karen Lee Minnick, Dec. 26, 1960 (div.); 1 child, Laurie Kylee; m. Janet Carolyn Dahl, Sept. 12, 1964; children: Marina, Nicholas. BS, Stanford U., 1961; PhD, U. Minn., 1967. NRC assoc. Goddard Space Flight Ctr., NASA, Greenbelt, Md., 1967-69, astrophysicist, 1969, head cosmic radiations br., 1981-82, head nuclear astrophysics br. 1983-87, assoc. chief lab. for high energy astrophysics, 1987-90, chief lab. for high energy astrophysics, 1990-2000, project scientist for gamma ray astronomy obs., 1998—, dir. space scis., 2000—. Acting head high energy astrophysics NASA hdqrs., Washington, 1982-83, mem. high energy astrophysics mgmt. ops. working group, 1975-83, mem. cosmic ray program working group, 1984-91; mem. com. on space and solar physics, com. on cosmic ray physics Nat. Acad. Sci., Washington, 1991-94; adj. prof. U. Md. Balt., 2000-; adj. prof. U. Utah, 2001—. Editor: Essays in Space Science, 1987; assoc. editor astrophysics Phys. Rev. Letters, 1991-93; contbr. Astrophysics Jour., Phys. Rev. Letters, Astronomy and Astrophysics. Trustee Paint Br. Unitarian Universalist Ch., Adelphi, Md., 1987-88, chair bd. trustees, 1989, numerous positions, 1972—. Recipient Meritorious Exec. Award (presdl. rank), 2001. Fellow: Am. Phys. Soc. (various divsn. offices); mem.: Am. Geophys. Union, Am. Astron. Soc. (sec.-treas. High Energy Astrophysics divsn. 1985—87), Internat. Astron. Union. Achievements include discovery of unusual isotopic abundance of Ne in galactic cosmic rays; research on composition and energy spectra of cosmic rays, antiprotons and gamma rays from the Milky Way galaxy. Office: NASA Code 600 Goddard Space Flight Ctr Greenbelt MD 20771-0001 E-mail: Jonathan.F.Ormes@nasa.gov.

ORMOND, JULIA, actress; b. Surrey, Eng., 1965; m. Rory Edwards (div. 1993); m. Jon Rubin, 1999. Grad., Webber Douglas Acad. Drama Art, 1988. Appeared in films The Baby of Macon, 1992, Legends of the Fall, 1994, Nostradamus, 1994, Captives, 1994, First Knight, 1995, Sabrina, 1995, The Prime Gig, 2000, Resistance, 2003; TV appearances include Traffik, 1990, Young Catherine, 1991, Stalin, 1992, The 67th Annual Academy Awards, 1995, Smilla's Sense of Snow, 1997, Sibirsky Tsiryulnik, 1998, (voice) Animal Farm, 1999, Varian's War, 2001, Iron Jawed Angels, 2004; stage appearances include Faith, Hope and Charity, 1989 (London Critics best newcomer award); producer: Calling the Ghosts, 1996. Recipient Female Star of Tomorrow award Sho West Awards, 1995. Office: c/o Patrick Whitesell Endeavor 9701 Wilshire Blvd 10th Fl Beverly Hills CA 90212*

ORMOND, PAUL A. healthcare company executive; b. Aurora, Ill. B in economics with honors, Stanford U., 1971, MBA, 1973. Mem. corp. staff, positions with glass container divsn. Owens-Ill., Inc., 1973-77, nat. mktg. mgr. soft drinks, glass container divsn., 1977-78; mgr. Atlanta sales dist., glass container divsn. Owens-Ill. Inc., 1978-80, asst. gen. mgr. Gerresheimer Glas (internat. affiliate Owens-Ill. Inc.), 1980-82, v.p. glass container group, 1982-84, v.p. packaging ops., dir. market strategy and devel., 1984-91, corp. v.p., 1986-91; pres., CEO Health Care and Retirement Corp. (HCR) (subs. Owens-Ill. Inc.), Toledo, 1986-91; chmn., pres., CEO Health Care and Retirement Corp. (HCR) (now ind. co.), Toledo, 1991—98; pres., CEO HCR Manor Care Inc., Toledo, 1998—99, Manor Care, Inc., Toledo, 1999—, chmn., 2001—. Office: Manor Care 333 N Summit St Toledo OH 43604-2617*

ORMSBY, ERIC LINN, educator, researcher, writer; b. Atlanta, Oct. 16, 1941; s. Robert and Virginia (Haire) O.; m. Dorothy Louise Hoffmann, July 22, 1967; children: Daniel Paul, Charles Martin. BA summa cum laude, U. Pa., 1971; MA, Princeton U., 1973, PhD, 1981; MLS, Rutgers U., 1978. Near East bibliographer libr. Princeton (NJ) U., 1975-77, Near East curator libr., 1977-83; libr. dir. Cath. U. Am., Washington, 1983-86, McGill U., Montreal, Canada, 1986-96, assoc. prof. Inst. Islamic Studies, 1986-96, prof., 1996—. Cons. NYU, 1981-82; mem. libr. com. Mid. East Inst., Washington, 1985-87, Al Akhawayn U., Morocco, 1994-95, Saudi Arabian Monetary Agy., Riyadh, 1995-96; chmn. continuing edn. com. Washington Consortium, 1983-86; mem. bd. Ctr. Rsch. Librs., 1989-95. Author: Theodicy in Islamic Thought, 1984 (Choice Mag. award 1984), Bavarian Shrine and Other Poems, 1990 (QSPELL award for poetry 1991), (poems) Coastlines, 1992, (with others) Handlist of Arabic Manuscripts, 1986, For a Modest God: New and Selected Poems, 1997, (poems) Araby, 2001, (poems) Daybreak at the Straits, 2004, (essays) Facsimiles of Time, 2001; editor: Moses Maimonides and His Time, 1989; contbr. articles and book revs. to profl. jours., poetry and essays to various mags., including New Republic, New Yorker, Grand St., Shenandoah, The New Criterion, The Yale Rev., Studia Islamica, So. Rev. and Chelsea; weekly columnist N.Y. Sun, 2004-. Instr. Princeton Adult Sch., 1978-80. DAAD fellow German Acad. Exch., 1973-74; recipient Ingram Merrill award, 1993. Mem. Mid. East Librs. Assn. (v.p. 1981-82, pres. 1982-83), Hoelderlin Gesellschaft, Societe des Amis de Jean de la Fontaine, Can. Assn. Rsch. Librs. (v.p. 1988-89), Can. Libr. Assn., Assn. pour l'Avancement des Scis. et des Techniques de la Documentation, Conseil des recteurs et des principaux des univs. du Québec, Sous-Comité des Bibliotheques (pres. 1989-91). Roman Catholic. Office: McGill U Inst Islamic Studies 3458 McTavish St Montreal QC Canada H3A 1Y1 Office Phone: 514-398-6077.

ORNATOWSKI, CEZAR MARIA, rhetoric and communication educator, consultant; b. Gdynia, Poland, Aug. 15, 1952; arrived in U.S., 1977; s. Jerzy Ornatowski and Anna Ornatowska; life ptnr. Merrie Myoshi Sasaki. Undergraduate studies in English and Linguistics, Adam Mickiewicz U., Poland, 1975; PhD, U. Calif. San Diego, 1991. Assoc. prof. San Diego State U., 1992—. Editor: Foundations for Teaching Technical Communication; contbr. articles to profl. jours. Named English Tchg. Specialist, USIA, 1996; recipient Chairman's Excellence award, The Irvine Co., 1990, Fulbright Sr. Scholar award, William J. Fulbright Found., 1999. Mem.: MLA, Assn. for Rhetoric and Comm. in So. Africa, Assn. Tchrs. Tech. Writing, Conf. on Coll. Composition and Comm., Nat. Comm. Assn., Internat. Soc. for the History Rhetoric, Nat. Coun. Tchrs. English, Rhetoric Soc. Am., Fulbright Assn., Polish Rhetoric Assn., Soc. for Tech. Comm., Phi Beta Delta.

ORNE, EMILY CAROTA, psychologist, researcher; b. Boston, Sept. 7, 1938; d. Emil and Ruth (Farrell) Carota; m. Martin T. Orne, Feb. 3, 1962; children: Franklin Theodore, Tracy Meredith. BA, Bennington Coll., 1959. Rsch. assoc. Mass. Mental Health Ctr., Boston, 1963-64; rsch. psychologist Unit for Exptl. Psychiatry, Phila., 1964-79, sr. rsch. psychologist, 1979-83, co-dir., 1982—; rsch. assoc. psychology U. Pa. Sch. Medicine, Phila., 1983—. Trustee Inst. Exptl. Psychiatry Rsch. Found., Mass., 1964—, assoc. co-dir., 1987-97, exec. dir., 1998—; bd. dirs. False Memory Syndrome Found., 1995—. Contbr. articles to profl. jours.; assoc. editor Internat. Jour. Clin. and Exptl. Hypnosis, 1977—. Recipient Benjamin Franklin Gold medal Internat. Soc. Hypnosis, 1982, Roy M. Dorcus award Soc. Clin. and Exptl. Hypnosis, 1985, Bernard B. Raginsky award, 1993, Morton Prince award Soc. Clin. and Exptl. Hypnosis and APA, 1994. Avocations: fishing, swimming, reading. Office: U Pa Sch Medicine 1013 Blockley Hall 423 Guardian Dr Philadelphia PA 19104-6021

ORNER, LINDA PRICE, family therapist, counselor; b. Gettysburg, Pa., June 27, 1943; d. John Robert and Ruby Pearl (Vines) Price; m. Ted Arnold Orner, Mar. 29, 1963; children: Penni Ann, Jennifer Arianna. AA, North Harris Coll., 1991; BA summa cum laude, U. St. Thomas, 1994; MEd in Counseling Psychology, U. Houston, 1997, postgrad.; MA in Family Therapy, U. Houston, Clear Lake, 1999. Lic. profl. counselor. Therapist Houston VA Hosp./Trauma Recovery Program, 1996, U. Houston Counseling and Testing Svcs., 1997, U. Houston-Clear Lake Psychol. Svcs., 1998—99; intern/assoc., family therapist Houston Galveston Inst., 1998—2000; pvt. practice counselor Family Life Svcs., Colorado Springs, 2001—. Vol. Women's Ctr.; vol. seminar instr., counselor Tex. Prison; keynote spkr. Christian Women's Clubs Internat. Mem.: APA, ACA, Am. Assn. of Christian Counselors, Am. Psychotherapy Assn., Tex. Counseling Assn., Tex. Assn. for Marriage and Family Therapy, Am. Assn. for Marriage and Family Therapy. Presbyterian. Avocations: travel, scuba diving, hiking, antiques, art. Home: 4684 Stone Manor Hts Colorado Springs CO 80906-8605 Address: 2210 W Dallas # 942 Houston TX 77019 Office Phone: 719-632-4661.

ORNISH, DEAN, medical educator, administrator; MD, Baylor Coll. Medicine. Resident in internal medicine Mass. Gen. Hosp., Boston, 1981-84; clin fellow in medicine Harvard Med. Sch., 1981-84; clin. prof. medicine U. Calif., San Francisco, 1984—; founder, pres. Preventive Medicine Rsch. Inst., Sausalito, Calif., 1984—; also bd. dirs. Physician cons. to Pres. Bill Clinton, U.S. Congress, others, U.S. bd. dirs. UN High Commn. on Refugees. Author: 5 books including Dr. Dean Ornish's Program for Reversing Heart Disease, 1990, Eat More, Weigh Less, 1993, Love & Survival: The Scientific Basis for the Healing Power of Intimacy, 1998; contbr. numerous articles to profl. jours. Bd. dirs. Quincy Jones Listen Up Found. Recipient Outstanding Young Alumnus award U. Tex., 1994, U.S. Army Surgeon Gen. medal, Beckmann medal German Soc. Prevention and Rehab. Cardiovascular Diseases, 1996. Mem. Calif. Acad. Medicine. Office: Preventive Med Rsch Inst 900 Bridgeway Sausalito CA 94965-2100 Fax: 415-332-5730. E-mail: deanornish@aol.com.

ORNITZ, RICHARD MARTIN, lawyer, business executive; b. Annapolis, Md., July 4, 1945; s. Martin Nathaniel and Beatrice Cynthia (Swick) O.; m. Margareth Adams, June 15, 1971 (div. Apr. 1977); m. Janet Alma Steen, Dec. 5, 1981; children: Alexandra, Zachary, Darren, Erik, Nicholas. B.S. in Metall. Engring., Cornell U., 1967; J.D., NYU, 1970; grad. sr. exec. program, MIT, 1985. Bar: N.Y. 1971, U.S. Dist. Ct. (ea. dist.) 1972, U.S. Supreme Ct. 1984. Assoc. Cravath, Swaine & Moore, N.Y.C., 1972-77; v.p., gen. counsel, sec. Degussa Corp., Teterboro, N.J. 1977-90, mem. mgmt. com., 1987-90; of counsel, Hughes, Hubbard & Reed, N.Y.C., 1985-92; dir. Degussa Corp. subs., 1980-92; ptnr. Stroock, Stroock & Lavan, 1991-95; ptnr., chmn., fin. Coudert Bros., 1996—; speaker Risk Ins. Mgmt. Soc., 1984, 85, 86, IBA, 1986, ACCA, 1986, European Co. Lawyers Assn., 1986; Swiss Co. Lawyers Assn., 1987; Norwegian Co. Lawyers Assn., 1988; mem. pvt. law adv. com. Office of Legal Adv. U.S. Dept. State, adv. bd. Nat. Inst. Preventive Maintenance, adv. bd. corp. counsel Am. Arbitration Assn.; co-chmn. concession experts group UN, 1999—. Assoc. editor Ann. Survey of Law, NYU, 1970. Fin. com. Conn. Spl. Olympics; bd. dirs. Old Greenwich Civic Assn. Served to 1st lt. U.S. Army, 1970-72. Mem. ABA (chmn. European law sect., human relations and labor law, 1987-90), N.Y. State Bar Assn., Internat. Bar Assn., Am. Corp. Counsel Assn. (chmn. of internat. sect. com., 1986-90) European Am. Gen. Counsels Group (chmn. 1986-87), N.J. Gen. Counsels Group, Cornell Soc. Engrs. Republican. Jewish. Clubs: Old Greenwich Republican (Conn.), Innis Arden, Rocky Point, Appalachean Mountain Club, Woodchucks Hiking Club (vice comdr.), Alpine Francaise Club. Avocations: Mahoussnick dog sled excursions. Home: 18 Meadowbank Rd Old Greenwich CT 06870-2312 Office: Coudert Bros 1411 Avenue Of The Americas New York NY 10019-2512

ORNSTEIN, PETER ARNOLD, psychologist, educator; b. Bklyn., July 6, 1942; s. Jacob Arthur and Augusta Ornstein; m. Marilyn Lea Reichwald, Aug. 23, 1964; children: Miriam Leila, Naomi Anna. BA, SUNY, Binghamton, 1963; MA, CUNY, 1965; PhD, U. Wis., 1968. Asst. prof. psychology Princeton (N.J.) U., 1968—73; assoc. prof. psychology U. N.C., Chapel Hill, 1973—79, prof. psychology, 1979—2002, F. Stuart Chapin disting. prof., 2002—. Vis. prof. U. Haifa, Israel, 1979—80; dir. program in devel. psychology U. N.C., Chapel Hill, 1980—87, 1989—98, chair dept. psychology, 1999—2004. Editor: Memory Development in Children, 1978; co-editor: A Century of Developmental Psychology, 1994, Memory for Everyday and Emotional Events, 1997; contbr. articles to profl. jours., chapters to books; assoc. editor Devel. Psychology, 1988—92; co-editor: (spl. issue) Memory and Suggestibility in Child Witnesses. Bd. dirs., v.p. North Carolinians Against Racial and Religious Violence, Durham, 1985—90; pres. Beth El Synagogue, Durham, 1983—84; bd. dirs. Durham-Chapel Hill Jewish Fedn., 1995—99. Recipient Fulbright-Hayes Travel award, 1979—80; predoctoral fellow, NIMH, 1964—68, rsch. grantee, 1969—70, 1972—73, 1988—91, Nat. Inst. Child Health and Human Devel., 1973—81, 1993—98, 2000—, NSF, 2002—, postdoctoral fellow, NATO, 1971, Einstein Vis. fellow, Israel Acad. Scis. and Humanities, 1979—80. Fellow: APA (coun. reps. 2002—), Am. Psychol. Soc. (program com. 2000—03); mem.: Internat. Soc. Study of Behavioural Devel., Soc. Applied Rsch. in Memory and Cognition, Psychonomic Soc., Soc. Rsch. in Child Devel., Coun. Grad. Depts. Psychology (bd. dirs. 2002—04), Cognitive Devel. Soc. (bd. dirs. 1999—), Sigma Xi. Achievements include research in cognitive development in children, focusing especially on the factors that are responsible for developmental changes in remembering. Home: 502 Tinkerbell Rd Chapel Hill NC 27517 Office: U NC Dept Psychology Davie Hall Chapel Hill NC 27599-3270 E-mail: pao@unc.edu.

ORNT, DANIEL B. physician; b. Jan. 21, 1951; m. Jeanine Arden-Ornt. BA, Colgate U., 1973; MD, U. Rochester, 1976. Diplomate in internal medicine and nephrology Am. Bd. Internal Medicine, lic. physician N.Y., Ohio. Intern then resident U. Vt., 1976—79; fellow in nephrology U. Mich., 1979—81; from sr. instr. medicine to assoc. prof. U. Rochester (N.Y.) Sch. Medicine and Dentistry, 1981—97, prof. medicine and pediat., 1997—; assoc. dean for clin. affairs Sch. Medicine, Case Western Res. U., Cleve., 2030—. Assoc. chmn. clin. svcs. dept. medicine U. Rochester, 1998—2000, vice-chmn. dept. medicine, 2000—03, acting chief divsn. gastroenterology, 2000, assoc. program dir. gen. clin. rsch., 2002—03. Contbr. articles to profl. jours. Recipient Disting. Svc. award, Nat. Kidney Found., Inc., 1998. Fellow: ACP; mem.: Soc. for Clin. Trials, Am. Physiol. Soc., Am. Soc. Nephrology. Office: Case Western Res U Sch Medicine Rm T-101 10900 Euclid St Cleveland OH 44106 E-mail: dbo@case.edu.

ORNT, JEANINE ARDEN, lawyer; b. Apr. 29, 1955; BA, SUNY, 1977; JD, Union U., 1980. Ptnr. Greisberger, Zicari, Rochester, N.Y., 1985-89; gen. counsel med. ctr. U. Rochester, 1989—. Office: U Rochester Med Ctr 601 Elmwood Ave Rochester NY 14642-0001

ORO, ROBERT JOHN, dentist, consultant, writer; b. Bklyn., Apr. 22, 1952; s. Philip Edward and Marie Catherine (Bruno) O.; m. Debra Ann Haas, June 17, 1979; children: Philip, Anna. BS in Econs. with honors, SUNY, Queens, 1974; DMD, U. Pa., 1979; Fellow, Acad. Gen. Dentistry, 1985, Master, 1988. Lic. dentist, N.Y., Ariz. Founder, dentist Free Dental Clinic, Guadalajara, Mex., 1976; jr. resident Brookdale Hosp. and Med. Ctr., Bklyn., 1979-80, sr. resident, 1980-81; pres., CEO Hudson Valley Dental Medicine, Cortlandt Manor, N.Y., 1981-96, Penn Dental Consultants, Cortlandt Manor, N.Y., 1996; v.p. Oro-Dontics, Inc., Oro Valley, Ariz., 1996—; CEO Oro Dental Medicine, oRO vALLEY, Ariz., 1998—. Clin. instr. Brookdale Hosp. Med. Ctr., 1981-84; attending Hudson Valley Hosp. Ctr., 1981-96; officer Peekskill (N.Y.)-Yorktown Dental Soc., 1984-87, pres., 1988; co-founder, v.p. Dentistry as Children's Advocates; lectr. on patient advocacy and dental health. Author: How to Choose Your Dentist: Confessions of an Adrenaline Addict, 1997. Active health fairs/fundraisers Hudson Valley Hosp., 1981—96; fundraiser Casa del los Ninos, Tucson, 1996, 1997, St. Elizabeth's of Hungary, Tucson, 1996, 1997, Las Familias, 2000, spokesperson; active health fairs Tucson Pks. and Recreation, 1997—. Named Mr. Congeniality, Mrs. Ariz./USA Pagent, 1997; cited as one of four top clinicians Acad. Gen. Dentistry Ann. Meeting, 1997. Mem. ADA, Ariz. Dental Assn., N.Y. State Dental Soc., Pima County Dental Study Club, Peekskill Yorktown Dental Soc. (pres. 1981-96), Delta Omicron. Avocations: writing, sports, hiking. Office: Oro-Dontics Inc 991 W Wheatgrass Pl Tucson AZ 85737-8654 Home: 10260 N Camino Valdeflores Oro Valley AZ 85737-3653 Office Phone: 520-297-2227.

ORONA, ERNEST JOSEPH, real estate and construction company executive; b. Belen, N.Mex., Oct. 5, 1942; s. Joseph B. and Melinda (Sanchez) O.; m. Margaret M. Guinan, Aug. 22, 1964; children: Mary Melinda, Marie-Jeanne. BA in Latin Am. Affairs and Spanish, U. N.Mex., 1968. Vol. cmty. devel. Peace Corps, Colombia, S.Am., 1962-64; instr. Peace Corps tng. U. Mo., Kansas City, summer 1964, Baylor U., Waco, Tex., summer 1965, also U. Ariz., N.Mex. State U., Las Cruces, 1966, U. N.Mex., Albuquerque, 1966; exec. dir. Mid-Rio Grande Cmty. Action Project, Los Lunas, N.Mex., 1965-66; cmty. devel. cons. Ctr. for Cmty. Action Svcs., Albuquerque, 1967-68; project dir. Peace Corps Tng. Ctr., San Diego State U., Escondido, Calif., 1968-70; propr., developer GO Realty and Constrn. Co., Albuquerque, 1970—. Pres. La Zarzuela de Albuquerque;, Benchmark Real Estate Investment Inc. Mem. Albuquerque Sister Cities; trustee N.Mex. Performing Arts Ctr. Mem. Nat. Bd. Realtors, Albuquerque Bd. Realtors, Albuquerque C. of C., Albuquerque Com. on Fgn. Rels. Roman Catholic. Home: 733 Valverde Dr SE Albuquerque NM 87108-3467 Office: GO Realty & Constrn Co 2034 2nd St NW Albuquerque NM 87102-1043 also: Benchmark Real Estate Inv Albuquerque Profl Bldg 909 Virginia St NE Ste 103 Albuquerque NM 87108-2578

OROPEZA, JENNY, state official; b. Long Beach, Calif., Sept. 27, 1957; m. Tom Mullins. BSBA, Calif. State U. Mem. Long Beach Unified Sch. Dist. Bd. Edn., 1988—94; coun. mem. Long Beach City Coun., 1994—2000; state assembly mem. Dist. 55 Calif. State Assembly, 2000—. Mem. Latino Caucus. Democrat. Mailing: Rm 6026 PO Box 942849 Sacramento CA 94249 Office: Ste 320 One Civic Plaza Dr Carson CA 90745

O'RORKE, JAMES FRANCIS, JR., lawyer; b. N.Y.C., Dec. 4, 1936; s. James Francis and Helen (Weber) O'R.; m. Carla Phelps, Aug. 6, 1964. AB, Princeton U., 1958; JD, Yale U., 1961. Bar: N.Y. 1962. Assoc. Davies, Hardy & Schenck, 1962-69; ptnr. Davies, Hardy, Ives & Lawther, 1969-72, Skadden, Arps, Slate, Meagher & Flom, N.Y.C., 1972—. Dir. Clinipad Corp.; mem. adv. bd. Chgo. Title Ins. Co. N.Y. Trustee Mus. Am. Indian-Heye Found., 1977-80; dir. James Lenox House Assn., Inc., 1998-02. Mem. ABA, N.Y. State Bar Assn., Assn. Bar City N.Y., Am. Coll. Real Estate Lawyers, Princeton Club N.Y.C. Office: Skadden Arps Slate Meagher & Flom 4 Times Sq Fl 24 New York NY 10036-6595 Address: C/O Skadden Arps 4 Times Sq Rm 44200 New York NY 10036-6522

OROSZ, JOEL J. philanthropist, educator; b. Kalamazoo, Mich., Mar. 15, 1957; s. Joseph Frank and Caroline Mae Orosz; m. Florence Elizabeth Upjohn, Aug. 4, 1979; children: Caroline Elizabeth, Anita Jane, Marianna Margaret, Andrew Joel. BA in Am. History cum laude, Kalamazoo Coll., 1979; MA in History and Mus. Studies magna cum laude, Case We. Res. U., 1981, PhD of Am. Social History, 1986. Curator of Interpretation Kalamazoo Valley Mus., 1983—86; exec. asst., program dir. W.K. Kellogg Found., Battle Creek, Mich., 1986—2001; Disting. Prof. Philanthropic Studies Dorothy A. Johnson Ctr. for Philanthropy and Nonprofit Leadership Grand Valley State U., Grand Rapids, Mich., 2001—. Prin. Inside Philanthropy Consulting, Kalamazoo, 2001—; commr. Mich. Cmty. Svc. Commn., Lansing, 1991—2000. Author: The Insider's Guide to Grantmaking, 2000, Curators and Culture: A History of the Museum Movement, 1990; editor: For the Benefit of All: A History of Philanthropy in Michigan, 1996. Steering com., nat. adv. coun. Learning to Give, Muskegon, Mich., 1996—. Mem.: Orgn. Am. Historians, Numismatic Bibliomania Soc. (bd. dirs., historian, archivist), Am. Numismatic Soc. (assoc.). Democrat. Avocations: coin collecting/numismatics, book collecting, biographical writing, conservation of historical objects.

O'ROURKE, DENNIS, advertising executive; Former CFO, sr. v.p. Goldberg, Moser & O'Neill, San Francisco, Calif.; exec. v.p., CFO, Goldberg, Moser & O'Neill/Hill Holliday. Office: GMO Hill Holliday 600 Battery St San Francisco CA 94111

O'ROURKE, JAMES LOUIS, lawyer; b. Bridgeport, Conn., July 5, 1958; s. James G. and Margaret Elizabeth (Fesco) O'Rourke; m. Margaret C. DiCicco, Sept. 18, 1994. BS, U. Bridgeport, 1984, JD, 1987. Bar: Conn. 1988, U.S. Dist. Ct. Conn. 1989, Mashantucket Pequot Tribal Bar 1995, U.S. Supreme Ct. 1998. Pvt. practice, Stratford, Conn., 1987—. With USN, 1976—79. Mem.: ATLA, ABA, Greater Bridgeport Bar Assn., Conn. Bar Assn., Conn. Trial Lawyers Assn. Roman Catholic. Avocations: boating, gardening, fishing, bicycling, swimming. Office: The Barnum Profl Bldg 1825 Barnum Ave Ste 201 Stratford CT 06614-5333 Office Phone: 203-381-9800. Personal E-mail: js.orourke@snet.net.

O'ROURKE, JOAN B. DOTY WERTHMAN, retired school system administrator; b. N.Y.C., June 7, 1933; d. George E. Doty and Lillian G. Bergen; 10 children. BA summa cum laude, Marymount Manhattan Coll., 1953; MA, Columbia U., 1958; PhD, St. John's U., 1971. Tchr. history Marymount HS, N.Y.C., 1953-55; instr. history Marymount Manhattan Coll., 1957-59; acting chmn. history dept. Nassau C.C., Mineola, 1959-60; dir. and writer Sta. WFAS, White Plains, 1963—64; prof. history Westchester C.C., Valhalla, 1963-74; prin. Pius X Sch., Scarsdale, 1974-77; assoc. dir. alumni rels. Fordham U., N.Y.C., 1980-84; co-founder and dir. Assn. for Profl. Psychol. and Ednl. Counseling, Wilmette, Ill., 1987-91; ptnr. and pres. O'Rourke and Assoc., Wilmette, Ill., 1993-97; ret., 1997. Tchg. fellow St. John's U., Jamaica, 1968; adj. prof. social sci. Fordham U., N.Y.C., 1974—76. Mem. resident bd. Del Webb, Sun City, Calif., 2001—03; mem. fin. com. St. Francis of Assisi Ch., LaQuinta, Calif., 2001—03; bd. dir. Sun City, 2001—03, Cath. Charities Diocese of San Bernardino, 2001—04, Cath. Charities of San Bernardino, 1999—. Recipient Alumni award, Marymount Coll., 2003, Mother Raymunde McKay Cmty. Svc. award, Marymount Manhattan Coll., 2003; Dr. Joan Doty Werthman O'Rourke Scholarship established in name, 2004. Mem.: Mich. Shores Club, Order of Holy Sepulchre (lady), Soc. Mayflowers Descendats Ill. Democrat. Roman Catholic. E-mail: doctorjoan@web.tv.net.

O'ROURKE, JOHN A. insurance company executive; BS, Saint Francis Coll.; MS, CUNY. Dep. dir. Office of Health Maintenance Orgns., U.S. Dept. Health & Human Svcs.; founding pres., CEO HealthLink, Inc., 1985—97; chmn. CEO RightCHOICE, 1997—2002; pres., central region WellPoint Health Networks, Inc., 2002—. Dir., dept. econ. rsch. Am. Med. Assn. Office: WellPoint Health Networks Inc One Wellpoint Way Thousand Oaks CA 91362

O'ROURKE, MARYLYN KAY, counseling administrator, consultant; b. Perry, Okla., Aug. 28, 1942; d. George Howard and Mary Ellen Bocox; m. Roger Lloyd O'Rourke, Dec. 5, 1983 (dec. Jan. 1994); children: Roger Paul Hula, Rachel Adrienne Tiggelouen. BA, Okla. State U., 1971, MS, 1974, PhD, 1986. Lic. specialist sch. psychology Tex. Tchr. jr. high spl. edn. Ponca City Ind. Sch. Dist., Okla., 1971—73; psychometrist Regional Edn. Svc. Ctr., Cushing, Okla., 1974—77; sch. psychologist Tulsa Vocat. Tech. Sch., 1977—86; mgmt. cons. Birkman Internat., Houston, 1986—90; coord. fed. grants Kans. State Dept. Spl. Edn., 1990—92; lic. specialist sch. psychology Katy Ind. Sch. Dist., Okla., 1993—. Cons. and reviewer Tex. State Bd. Examiners of Psychologists, Austin, Tex., 2003; mgmt. cons., Houston, 1990—. Mem. Mayor's Commn. on Concerns of the Disabled, Tulsa, 1984—86; mem. adminstrn. bd. First Meth. Ch., Houston, 2003. Mem.: Coun. Exceptional Children, Tex. Assn. Sch. Psychologists (charter mem., chmn. 1993). Democrat. Avocations: yoga, ballroom dancing. Home: 12926 Kingsbridge Ln Houston TX 77077

O'ROURKE, ROBERT A. cardiologist, educator; b. San Francisco, Calif., June 12, 1936; m. Suzann Reiter, June 8, 1963; children: Michael, Kevin, Sean, Kathleen, Ryan. Student, Santa Clara U., 1954-55; BS, Creighton U., 1957, MD, 1961. Diplomate Am. Bd. Internal Medicine, Am. Bd. Cardiology. Straight med. internship Georgetown U. Hosp., Washington, 1961-62, jr. asst. resident internal medicine, 1962-63, sr. asst. resident internal medicine, 1963-64, med. houseofficer internal medicine, 1961-65, fellow cardiology dept., 1964-65, instr. in medicine cardiology, 1968-69; fellow U. Calif Cardiovasc. Rsch. Inst., Washington, 1965-66; staff cardiologist Madagan Army Hosp., Washington, 1966-68; asst. prof. medicine cardiology coll. medicine U. Ariz., Tucson, 1969-70; asst. prof. medicine cardiology, dir. clin. cardiology section, dir. heart station U. Calif., San Diego, 1970-73, assoc. prof. medicine cardiology, dir. clin. cardiology section, dir. coronary care unit, assoc. dir. myocardial infarction rsch. unit, 1973-76; acting chief medicine Audie L. Murphy Vets. Adminstrn. Hosp., 1977-78; Charles Conrad Brown disting. prof. cardiovasc. disease, dir. cardiovasc. divsn. U. Tex. Health Sci. Ctr., San Antonio, 1976—. Cons. in field for various hosps.; vis. professorships to various med. ctrs./univs. Mem. editl. bd.: Jour. Am. Coll. Cardiology, 1983-87, Am. Jour. Cardiology, 1976-81, 83—, Am. Heart Jour., 1980—, Clin. Cardiology, 1985—, Jour. Intensive Care Medicine, 1985—, Internat. Jour. Cardiology, 1981—, Annals of Internal Medicine, 1979-82, Med. Month, 1983—, Weekly Update: Cardiology, 1978-80, Cardiovasc. Medicine, 1976-80, Cardiologic Consultation, 1980—, Cardiovasc. Drugs and Therapy, 1989-90, Coronary Artery Disease, 1990—, Cardiology, 1990—, Jour. Heart Valve Disease, 1992, Current Problems in Cardiology, 1975—, assoc. editor, 1980-83, editor-in-chief, 1984—, Circulation, 1977-80, 81-83, 83-86, 86—, consulting editor, 1993, Yr. Book Cardiology, 1986-92, assoc. editor, 1986-92; assoc. editor: Jour. Applied Cardiology, 1985-90, Am. Jour. Cardiovasc. Pathology, 1985—. Recipient Sinsheimer award for Cardiovasc. Rsch., 1969-70; grantee from various sponsors. Fellow Am. Coll. Physicians, Am. Coll. Cardiology; mem. Am. Soc. Clin. Investigation, Am. Fedn. Clin. Rsch., Am. Heart Assn., Am. Physiological Soc., Assn. Army Cardiologists, Southern Soc. Clin. Rsch., Am. Soc. Echocardiography, Assn. U. Cardiologists, Alpha Omega Alpha, others. Office: The Univ Tex Health Sci Ctr VAH Rm C644 7703 Floyd Curl Drive San Antonio TX 78229-3900

O'ROURKE, THOMAS DENIS, civil engineer, educator; b. Pitts., July 31, 1948; s. Lawrence Robert and Adele Mildred (Moloski) O'R.; m. Patricia Ann Lane, Aug. 12, 1978; 1 child, Adele Christina. BSCE, Cornell U., 1970; MSCE, U. Ill., 1973, PhD, 1975. Geotech. engr. Dames & Moore, N.Y.C., 1970; rsch. asst. U. Ill., Urbana, 1970-75, asst. prof., 1975-78, Cornell U., Ithaca, N.Y., 1978-80, assoc. prof., 1981-87, prof., 1987-98, Thomas R. Briggs prof. engring., 1999—. Recipient Trevithick prize, Brit. Instn. Civil Engrs., 2002, Outstanding Paper award, Japan Gas Assn., 2003. Fellow: AAAS; mem.: ASTM (C.A. Hogentogler award 1976), ASME, NAE, ASCE (pres. Ithaca sect. 1981—82, chair exec. com. tech. coun. lifeline earthquake engr. 1998—99, Collingwood prize 1983, Huber prize 1988, C. Martin Duke award 1995, Stephen D. Bechtel pipeline engring. award 1997), U.S. Com. on Tunnelling Tech. (chmn. 1987—88), Internat. Soc. Rock Mechanics, Internat. Soc. Engring. Geology, Earthquake Engring. Rsch. Inst. (bd. dirs. 1998—2000, v.p. 2000, pres. 2002—, Outstanding Paper award 1996). Home: 10 Twin Glens Rd Ithaca NY 14850-1041 Office: Cornell U Sch Civil Environ Engring 273 Hollister Hall Ithaca NY 14853-3501 Office Phone: 607-255-6470. E-mail: tdo1@cornell.edu.

OROZCO, GABRIEL, artist; b. Jalapa, Veracruz, Mex., 1962; Student, Escuela Nat. Arte Plasticas, 1981—84, Circulo de Bellas Artes, Madrid, 1986—87. Artist-in-residence DAAD, 1995. One-woman shows include Kanaal Art Found., Kortrijk, 1993, Galerie Crousel Robelin BAMA, Paris, 1993, Mus. Modern Art, N.Y.C., 1993, Mus. Contemporary Art, Chgo., 1994, Marian Goodman Gallery, N.Y.C., 1994, 1996, 1998, Musée d'Art Moderne de la Ville de Paris, 1995, 1998, De Cardenas, Milan, 1995, Galerie Micheline Szwajcer, Antwerp, 1995, DAAD Gallery, Berlin, 1995, Art Gallery Ont., Toronto, 1996, Staalichen Mus. am Kulturforum, Berlin, 1997, Stedelijk Mus., Amsterdam, 1997, Anthony d'Offay Gallery, London, 1997, Centro Fotográfico Alvarez Bravo, Oaxaca, Mex., 1998, St. Louis Mus. Art, 1998, exhibited in group shows at Ill. Encuentro Nacional de Arte joven, Inst. Nacional de Bellas Artes, Aguascalientes, 1983 (hon. mention), Museo U. del Chopo, Mexico City, 1984, Museo Carrillo Gil, 1985, Museo de Art Moderno, 1987, Am. de Arte y Cultura, Brasilia, 1989, Bronx Mus. Art, 1990, Pasadena Art Ctr., 1991, New Mus. Contemporary Art, N.Y.C., 1993, Marian Goodman Gallery, 1993, 1994, 1998, Margo Leavin Gallery, L.A., 1994, Zacheta Nat. Gallery Contemporary Art, Warsaw, 1996, Whitney Biennial, N.Y., 1997, Berlin Biennial, 1998, numerous others. Office: care Marian Goodman Gallery 24 W 57th St New York NY 10019-3918 Fax: 212-581-5187.

ORPHANIDES, GUS GEORGE, licensing executive; b. NYC, Jan. 27, 1947; s. Gus G. and Savesta (Agapetus) O.; m. Jeanne Wood, Feb. 3, 1968; children: Alyson, Paul, Lindsay. BS with honors, Hobart Coll., 1967; PhD, Ohio State U., 1972. Chemist E.I. Du Pont de Nemours & Co., Wilmington, Del., 1974-79, Beaumont, Tex., 1979-81, Air Products, Allentown, Pa., 1981-84, applications mgr., 1984-85, comml. mgr., 1985-88, rsch. mgr., 1988-91, sr. comml. devel. mgr., 1991-95, comml. devel. mgr., 1995-96, R&D mgr., 1996-98, global tech. svc. mgr., 1998—2000, dir. applications devel., tech. svc., chem. tech., 2000—02, dir. intellectual asset mgmt. and licensing, 2002—. Contbr. articles to profl. publs.; patentee in field; developed new polymers for adhesives, non-wovens, paper coatings, polyurethane elastomers, rubber cross-linking. Phys. rehab. hosp. vol. in occupl. therapy. 1st lt. U.S. Army, 1972-74. Decorated Army Commendation medal; recipient Army Cert. of Achievment, Raker Meml. award Good Shepherd Hosp.; N.Y. State Regents scholar, 1963-67. Mem. Am. Chem. Soc., Licensing Exec. Soc. Presbyterian. Achievements include development of novel emulsion polymers and polymer intermediates, international technology transfer, technology licensing, lab-to-plant technology transfer, plant start-up, commercialized new products. Home: 4046 Providence Ct Schnecksville PA 18078-3524 Office: Air Products 7201 Hamilton Blvd Allentown PA 18195-1526 E-mail: g.orphanides@att.net.

ORPHANIDES, NORA CHARLOTTE, ballet educator; b. N.Y.C., June 4, 1951; d. M.T. and Mary Elsie (Tilly) Feffer; m. James Mark Orphanides, July 1, 1972; children: Mark, Elaine Orphanides Mastrosimone, Jennine. BA, CUNY, 1973; student, Joffrey Ballet Sch., N.Y.C., 1970-75; postgrad., Princeton Ballet Sch., 1976-86. Cert. speech and hearing handicapped tchr. With membership dept. M.M.A., N.Y.C., 1987—2002; mem. faculty Princeton (N.J.) Ballet Sch., 1983—, trustee emeritus, 1992—. Mem. cast Princeton Ballet ann. Nutcracker, 1985-90, now Am. Repertory Ballet Co., 1993—; appeared in Romeo & Juliet, 1995-96, 2000. Fundraising gala chmn. Princeton Ballet, 1985, 86, 91-92, chmn. spl. events, 1987—, trustee, 1986—, chmn. Nutcracker benefit, 1990—, Dracula benefit, 1991, honoree, 1999; dept. chmn. June Fete to benefit Princeton Hosp., 1988, 90-91, 92, 96, 2000, trustee, 1995-99; vol. Nat. Hdqrs. Recording for the Blind, 1991-93; dinner chmn. Nassau Ch. Music Festival, 1992, Handel Festival, Nassau Ch., 1993, Princeton Chamber Symphony, 1993; hon. chmn. Princeton Ballet Gala, 1993; chmn. Christmas Boutique, Princeton Med. Ctr., 1993; trustee, Princeton Med. Ctr. Aux. Bd., 1992-2002, trustee 1995—, pres., 1997-99, past pres., 2000-2002; found. bd. dirs. U. Med. Ctr. Princeton, 2004—; choreographer Stuart Country Day Sch., Princeton, 1996-99, 2001; chmn. benefit dinner Eden Inst., 2000. Named honoree Princeton Ballet, 1999, recipient Edward R. and Irene D. Farley Cmty. Stewardship award, Eden Inst. Found., 2003. Democrat. Avocations: piano, skiing, tennis. Office: 301 N Harrison St Princeton NJ 08540-3512

ORR, BOBETTE KAY, diplomat; b. Oak Park, Ill., Oct. 28, 1941; d. Robert Jay and Neta (Hoobler) Pottle; m. William Rucker Orr, Oct. 11, 1974; step children: Bridgette, Brietta, Alyson, William Jr. BA in Econs., Conn. Coll. for Women, 1963; student auditor Internat. Econs., London Sch. of Econs., 1964; postgrad. studies in Internat. Econs., George Washington U., 1964-65. Rsch. asst. C. of C. USA, Washington, 1965-66; country desk officer for Scandanavia U.S. Dept. Commerce, Washington, 1966-69, country desk officer for France, 1970-72, 79-81, country desk officer for Belgium, Netherlands, Luxembourg, 1974-77, country desk officer for Japan, 1981-82; mkt. rsch. officer United States Trade Ctr., Stockholm, 1973, trade promotion officer London, 1977-78; asst. comml. attache Am. Embassy, Paris, 1982-87; comml. attache Am. Consulate Gen., Auckland, New Zealand, 1988-92, consul gen. Edinburgh, Scotland, 1992-95; comml. counselor Am. Embassy, London, 1995-99, Cairo, 1999—2002; regional dir. Africa, Near East and South Asia U.S. Dept. Commerce, Washington, 2002—04. Mem. bd. dirs. U.S. Dept. Commerce Fed. Credit Union, Washington, D.C., 1972-77, pres., 1976-77, mem. supervisory com., 1979-81; equal employment opportunity counselor for Greater Washington Met. Area, 1972-75; mission dir. for USDOC's Concrete Constrn. Techniques Seminar Mission to Hong Kong, Singapore, Malaysia, 1980; detailed to Office of Dir. Fgn. Comml. Svc. as evaluator of candidates for Fgn. Comml. Svc., 1981. Author: (with others) 10 pamphlet series, on free enterprise, The Power of Choice, 1966; contbr. to Bus. Am., 1966-81, Overseas Bus. Reports 1966-76 (Dept. Commerce publs.). Mem. Am. Women's Club of Edinburgh, (hon. pres.), The English Speaking Union. Avocations: skiing, bicycle riding. Home: PO Box 63 Great Falls VA 22066-0063 Office: ANESA/USFCS/ITA Dept Commerce 14th and Constitution Ave NW Rm 1223 Washington DC 20230 Office Phone: 202-482-4836.

ORR, CAROLE, artist; b. Alexandria, Ind., June 10, 1933; d. Carl Victor and Marian Martha (Long) Coonse; m. Larry D. Ribble (dec. July 1953); m. Thomas LeRoy Orr, Nov. 10, 1950 (div. Oct. 1979); children: Karen Sue, Terri Ribble, David Thomas; m. Lev C. Hamblet Jr., Feb. 5, 1982 (div. Oct. 1998); stepchildren: James, Jean, Laura, Anne. Cert., Famous Artist Sch., Westport, Conn., 1956, Art Instrn. Schs., Mpls., 1962. Asst. art dir. La Gallerie du Mall, Houston, 1975—78; freelance fine artist Lantern Ln. Gallery, Houston, 1968—81, asst. mgr., design cons., 1979—81; artist Artist Showroom, Houston, 1982—. Participating artist Assistance Guild, Houston, 1968, Beaux Arts, Houston, 1968-70, Houston Gamma Phi Gallery, 1971-72, Houston Delta Gamma Found., 1978-81, Glassell Sch. of Art Houston, 1983; art instr. children's art Houston Park and Recreational Programs, 1964-68. One-woman shows include Nobler Gallery, Houston, 1967, Art Gallery, Pasadena, Tex., 1968, Gallarie La Rue, Austin, Tex., 1971, Gallery 12, Houston, 1972, Main St., Houston, 1974, La Galerie de Mall, Houston, 1976-78, Triumvirate Gallery, Santa Fe, N.Mex., 1980, Houshang's Gallery, Dallas, 1980-82, Battle Horn Galleries Ltd., Santa Fe, 1984, New Trends Inc., Santa Fe, 1985-88, Horizons Galleries, Houston, 1990-93, Houston C.C., 1992, Heinen Theatre, 1992, Windsor Gallery, Ft. Lauderdale, Fla., 1994; exhibited in group shows at Motorola Invitational, Houston, 1964, Assistance Guild Houston, 1968, Am. Gen. Bldg., Houston, 1968, Beaux Arts, Houston, 1968-70, Gamma Phi Gallery, Houston, 1971-72, Lantern Ln. Gallery, Houston, 1971-72, Delta Gamma Found., Houston, 1978-81, Glassell Sch. Art, Houston, 1983, New Trends Gallery Inc., Santa Fe, 1985-88, Pasadena (Tex.) Art Invitational, 1988, Double Tree Hotel, Houston, 1990, Horizons Gallery, Houston, 1990-93, Windsors Gallery, Dania, Fla., 1993, 2003, Magnolias Art Gallery, Town and Country Ctr., Houston, 2003-04. Art instr. adults Ch. of the Advent, Houston, 1968-70; adult edn. instr. arts Ch. Sch. Conf., Dept. Christian Edn., Trinity Ch., Diocese of Tex., Houston, 1969. Recipient Profl. Best Ann. Competition Art Instrn. Schs., Mpls., 1965; named Best-Selling Artist of Yr., 2001, Paintings DIRECT, N.Y.C., 2001, 03. Avocations: self-study in psychology, music, dance. Home and Office: Artist Showroom DBA 880 Tully Rd Apt 29 Houston TX 77079-5418

ORR, FRANK HOWARD, III, architect; b. Jasper, Ala., Sept. 4, 1932; s. Frank Howard Jr. and Lola Ruth (Lynch) O.; m. Nancy Gayle Gentry, Apr. 13, 1957; children: Mark Daniel, Steven Gentry, Karen Diann, Amy Ruth. B in Applied Art, Auburn U., 1961. Registered Ala., Ga., Ky., N.C., Tenn., Va., Miss. Assoc. architect Edwin A. Keeble Assocs., Nashville, 1962-70, Bianculli & Tyler, Inc., Chattanooga, 1970; prin. Frank Orr Architects, Nashville, 1970-76; pres., prin. Orr/Houk & Assocs. Architects, Inc., Nashville, 1976-2001; v.p. Hart Freeland Roberts, Inc. (merged with Orr/Houk), Brentwood, Tenn., 2001—04. V.p. Hart Freeland Roberts, Inc., Brentwood, Tenn.; adj. faculty O'More Sch. Design, Franklin, Tenn., 1972—77, Nashville State Tech. Inst., 1978—79; guest lectr. Sch. Arch., Victoria U., Wellington, New Zealand, 1987; exam grader Nat. Coun. Archtl. Registration Bds., Ft. Lauderdale, Fla., 1985; guest lectr. Coll. Arch., Auburn U., 2001. Author: Professional Practice in Architecture, 1982, Scale in Architecture, 1985; author (column) Urban Life, Nashville Bus. Jour., 1995; editor: Notable Nashville Architecture 1930-1980; contbr. articles to profl. jours.; prin. works include Woodmont Bapt. Ch. (design commendation 1979, Design award of Merit 1990), Appalachian Ctr. for Crafts, Two Rivers Bapt. Ch. (design commendation 1979), 1st Bapt. Ch., Hendersonville, Tenn. (design award of merit 1992), First Bapt. Ch., Athens, Ala., First Bapt. Ch., Pasadena, Tex., Tenn. Bapt. Conf. Ctrs., Carson and Linden, First Baptist Ch., Joelton, Tenn., Lake Providence Missionary Baptist Ch., Nashville. Active Citizens com. Met. Nashville Gen. Plan, 1994; mem. Play of Nashville Project, 2002—03; missionary trips, Guatemala, 1977, 1982, Mexico, 1980, Sierra Leone, 1985, 88, Poland, 1998, Brazil, 2000, Portugal, 2004. Mem.: AIA (dir. Mid. Tenn. chpt. 1971—78, chmn. Gulf States design awards com. 1985, com. environ. edn. 1972—76), Tenn. Soc. Architects (sec.-treas. 1977), Nashville C. of C. (regional transp. com. 1993—94), Scarab Archtl. Honor Soc., Auburn U. Baptist. Avocations: sketching, writing.

ORR, FRANKLIN MATTES, JR., petroleum engineering educator; b. Baytown, Tex., Dec. 27, 1946; s. Franklin Mattes and Selwyn Sage (Huddleston) O.; m. Susan Packard, Aug. 30, 1970; children: David, Katherine. BSChemE, Stanford U., 1969; PhDChemE, U. Minn., 1976. Asst. to dir. Office Fed. Activities EPA, Washington, 1970-72; research engr. Shell Devel. Co., Houston, 1976-78; sr. engr. N.Mex. Petroleum Recovery Research Ctr., Socorro, 1978-84; assoc. prof. petroleum engring. Stanford (Calif.) U., 1985-87, prof., 1987—, interim dean Sch. Earth Scis., 1994-95, dean Sch. Earth Scis., 1995—2002. Contbr. articles to profl. jours. Bd. dirs. Wolf Trap Found. for the Performing Arts, 1988-94, Monterey Bay Aquarium Rsch. Inst., 1987—, Am. Geol. Inst. Found., 1997—, David and Lucile Packard Found., 1999—; chair sci. adv. com. David and Lucile Packard Found. Fellowships for Sci. and Engring. With USPHS, 1970-72. Recipient AIME Robert Earll McConnell award, 2001. Mem. NAE, AIChE, AAAS, Soc. Petroleum Engrs. (Disting. Lectr. award 1988-89, Disting. Achievement award for petroleum engring. faculty 1993), Soc. Indsl. and Applied Math. Office: Stanford U Sch Earth Scis Mitchell Bldg Rm 101 Stanford CA 94305-2210

ORR, H. ALLEN, biologist, critic; b. Hampton, Va., July 11, 1960; s. Harold Allen and Jacqueline Shaw Orr; m. Lynne A. Hamilton, Aug. 12, 1982. BS with high honors, Coll. William and Mary, 1982, MS, 1985; PhD, U. Chgo., 1990. Postdoctoral fellow U. Calif., Davis, 1990—93; asst. prof. U. Rochester, NY, 1993—96, assoc. prof., 1996—2000, prof., 2000—. Book critic: New Yorker, New York Rev. of Books, Boston Rev., others; co-author (with Jerry A. Coyne): Speciation, 2004. Recipient Young Investigator prize, Am. Soc. Naturalists, 1992; grantee, NIH, 1995—; postdoctoral fellow in molecular evolution, Alfred P. Sloan Found., 1990—92, Packard fellow in sci. and engring., David and Lucile Packard Found., 1995—2000, Guggenheim Meml. fellow, John Simon Guggenheim Meml. Found., 2000—01, scholar in residence Bellagio Study Ctr., The Rockefeller Found., 2002. Mem.: Genetical Rsch. (mem. editl. bd.), Soc. Study of Evolution (assoc. editor 1998—2000, Dobzhansky prize 1993).

ORR, JAMES FRANCIS, marketing and information services executive; b. Phila., Oct. 10, 1945; s. James F. Jr. and Dorothy (Gallagher) O.; m. Catherine Marie Reinholt; children: Kristin Leah, Lauren Beth, James Desmond. Student, Pa. State U., 1963-64, Rutgers U., Camden and New Brunswick, N.J., 1964-67. Various sales mgmt. positions Procter & Gamble, 1967-73, dist. mgr., 1973-76, nat. accounts mgr. Cin., 1976-78, sales div. mgr., 1978-81, sales merchandising mgr., 1981-82; sales dir. Procter & Gamble Ltd., Newcastle upon Tyne, Eng., 1982-85; v.p. sales Crush Internat. Inc., Cin., 1985-88; v.p. market devel. Matrixx Mktg. Inc. subs. Cin. Bell Inc., Cin., 1989-92, pres. and CEO, 1993—; COO Cincinnati Bell Inc.; pres. & CEO Convergys Corp, Cincinnati, 2000—. Mem. parents adv. coun. Hamilton Coll., Clinton, N.Y., 1989-91, vice chmn. Parents Fund, 1989-90, chmn., 1990-91; active Grad. Leadership Cin., class XVI, 1992-93. Mem. Direct Mktg. Assn., Soc. Consumer Affairs Profls., Greater Cin. C. of C., Coldstream Country Club (trustee), Melrose Club (Daufuskie Island, S.C.). Avocations: golf, theater, antique collecting, travel. Office: Convergys Corp PO Box 1638 Cincinnati OH 45201-1638

ORR, JIM (JAMES D. ORR), editor, writer; b. Buffalo, Feb. 7, 1960; s. David James and Doris Kathleen (Wolos) O.; m. JoEllen Black, June 4, 1994. B in Journalism, Ind. U. of Pa., 1982, M in Comm., 1987. Station mgr. Sta. WIUP-TV, Ind., Pa., 1983-84; sports writer, news writer Ind. (Pa.) Gazette, 1984-88; reporter Stuart (Fla.) News, 1988-89; staff writer, columnist Gannett Rochester (N.Y.) Newspapers, 1989-96; staff writer The Bus. Jour., Fresno, Calif., 1997; sr. writer The Fresno Bee, 1998-99; features, spl. projects and weekend editor, page designer The Westerly (R.I.) Sun, 2000—. Columnist Orrdinary People, 1994-95; freelance writer, publicist, 1996—. Moderator polit. debate Edu-Cable Corp., Greece, N.Y., 1993; panelist conf. New England Soc. Newspaper Editors, 2002. Recipient Agrl. Writing 1st Place award Penn-Ag Industries, 1985, 2d place Keystone State Press award Pa. Newspaper Pub. Assn., 1987, 2 Scripps Howard writing awards, 1989, Award Gannett Enterprise Project, 1994, Cmty. Svc. award N.Y. Newspaper Pubs. Assn., 1994-95, Spl. Series 2d pl. award R.I. Press Assn., 2000, others. Home: 42 Rosewood Dr Vernon Rockville CT 06066-6229

ORR, JOSEPH ALEXANDER, educational administrator; b. West Palm Beach, Fla., Nov. 20, 1929; s. Joseph Alexander and Eula (Terry) O.; m. Ardis W. Orr (div.); children: Eric, Pamela, Tracey; m. Linda F. Orr. BS, Fla. A&M U., 1951; MS, Mich. State U., 1953; MEd, Fla. Atlantic U., 1965; PhD, Fla. State U., 1972. Sci. tchr. Roosevelt Sr. H.S., West Palm Beach, Fla., 1953-68; counselor, coord. Adult Edn. Dept. Sch. Sys., Palm Beach County, Fla., 1960-72; dean of students Palm Beach H.S., West Palm Beach, 1968-70; asst. dean Fla. A&M U., Tallahassee, 1970-72; adj. prof. Ind. U., Bloomington, 1972-73; prin. Ctrl. Sr. H.S., Louisville, 1972-74, Jupiter (Fla.) H.S., 1974-78; adj. prof. Fla. Atlantic U., Boca Raton, 1978—; asst. supt. Palm Beach County (Fla.) Sch. Bd., 1978-84, assoc. supt., 1984-92, dep. supt., chief acad. officer, 2001—; exec. dir. Palm Beach County Sch. Adminstrs. Assn., 1992-2001. Chair State Adv. Bd. for Severely Emotionally Disturbed. Contbr. articles to profl. jours. Bd. dirs. Children's Home Soc. Fla., Palm Beach County Coun. Arts; past chair Health and Human Svcs. Bd., Palm Beach County, Inst. New Dimensions, Palm Beach C.C., Assn. Retarded Citizens, Inc., West Palm Beach; past pres. Scholastic Achievement Found. Palm Beach County, Edn. Found. Palm Beach County. Recipient Disting. Svc. award NEA, Pioneer award for excellence in pub. svc. Nat. Forum of Pub. Adminstrn., Outstanding Achievement award Fla. Assn. Cmty. Educators, Four Seasons award Nat. Assn. for Year Round Edn. Mem. ASCD, Fla. Assn. Sch. Adminstrs., Am. Assn. Sch. Adminstrs., Nat. Assn. Secondary Sch. Prins., Nat. Cmty. Edn. Assn. (Sch. Leadership award), Kiwanis Internat. Democrat. Episcopalian. Avocation: boating. Office: Palm Beach County Sch Adminstrs Assn PO Box 31511 Palm Beach Gardens FL 33420 Office Phone: 561-625-6918.

ORR, KENNETH BRADLEY, academic administrator; b. Charlotte, N.C., Mar. 15, 1933; s. Frank Wylie and Kate Harriett O.; m. Ruth Douglas Currie; children: Kevin, Jeffrey, Jonathan. BA, Duke U., 1954; MDiv, Union Theol. Sem., 1960, ThM, 1961; PhD, U. Mich., 1978; LittD, Carroll Coll., 1990; DD, Presbyn. Coll., 1997. Ordained to ministry, Presbyn. Ch., 1961. Minister West End Presbyn. Ch., Roanoke, Va., 1961-64; asst. to pres. Union Theol. Sem., Richmond, Va., 1964-68, v.p., 1968-74; pres. Presbyn. Sch. Christian Edn., Richmond, 1974-79, Presbyn. Coll., Clinton, S.C., 1979-97, pres. emeritus, 1997—; sr. v.p. John McRae & Assocs., Atlanta, 1997—. Past mem. coun. presidents Nat. Assn. Intercollegiate Athletics, Kansas City, Mo., chmn. S. Atlantic Conf., 1989—91; mem. nat. adv. com. on instnl. quality and integrity U.S. Dept. Edn., 1995—2001. Contbr. to religious and ednl. publs. Mem. Assn. Presbyn. Colls. and Univs. (pres. 1994, exec. com.), Coun. Ind. Colls. (bd. dirs. 1993-96), Laurens County C. of C. (past pres.), Kiwanis. Democrat. Avocations: reading, travel, tennis, classical music.

ORR, MARCIA, child development researcher, child care consultant; b. Anamosa, Iowa, Mar. 2, 1949; d. Harold Edward Eiben and Clara Elizabeth (Hubbard) E.; m. Robert J. Orr, Sept. 6, 1969; 1 child, Jennifer. Student, U. Iowa, 1977; BS, St. Xavier U., Chgo., 1981; MEd in Early Childhood Leadership, Nat. Louis U., 1996. Bookkeeper Monticello State Bank, 1967-69; exec. sec. Davenport Bank and Trust, 1969-73; asst. educator Elisabeth Ludeman Devel. Ctr., Park Forest, Ill., 1979; tchr. Flossmoor Hills (Ill.) Elem. Sch., 1980-1984; exec. dir. Co-Care, Inc., Park Forest, 1984-89; child devel. rschr., Flossmoor, Ill., 1989—; tchr. Nazarene Nursery Sch. and Kindergarten, Chicago Heights, Ill., 1991; child care ctr. cons. Matteson Sch. Dist. 162, Park Forest, 1991—; founder, exec. dir. Before and After Sch. Enrichment, Park Forest, 1991—; adv. mem. project early start Matteson Sch. Dist. 162, Park Forest, 1991—, home-sch. coord., 1992—. Grant writer Matteson Sch. Dist. 162 and Before and After Sch. Enrichment, Inc.; officer Boleo Childcare Ctr., Iowa City, 1975-77; mentor to dirs. child care programs early childhood edn. dept. Nat.-Louis U., Ill, 1994—; co-founder Reaching New Horizons, Inc., 1996—. Tchr. religion Infant Jesus of Prague Ch., Flossmoor, Ill., 1982—; mem. Flossmoor PTO, 1987-89; music chmn. Dist. 161 PTO, 1980-90; exec. dir. Before and After Sch. Enrichment, Inc.; parent resource coord. Matteson Sch. Dist. 162. McCormick fellow, 1995—; recipient Golden Achievement award Nat. Sch. Pub. Rels. Assn., 2001; named Best Practices and Rsch. honoree Louis U., Evanston, Ill., 2001. Mem. NAFE, Nat. Assn. for Edn. Young Children (validator), Women Employed Orgn., Internat. Platform Assn., Parent Inst., South Suburban Small Bus. Assn. (charter). Democrat. Roman Catholic. Avocations: piano, classical music, travel. Home: 9411 Fox Run Ct Frankfort IL 60423-1380 Office: Before and After Sch Enrichment 210 Illinois St Park Forest IL 60466-1100

ORR, MARGARET, newscaster; b. New Orleans; married; 3 children. Grad. in English, La. State U.; grad. in Broadcast Meteorology, Miss. State U. Photographer, editor, prodr., reporter, anchor, weathercaster WCIV-TV, Charleston, SC; weathercaster WBRZ-TV, Baton Rouge; from assignment reporter to meteorologist WDSU News Channel 6, New Orleans, 1979—. Mem.: Am. Meteorol. Soc. Avocations: gardening, painting. Office: WDSU News Channel 6 846 Howard Ave New Orleans LA 70113

ORR, NANCY A. educational psychologist; b. Cin., 1952; d. Lowell and Betty Orr. BA, Ind. U., 1974, MS in Edn., 1977; PhD, U. Pa., 1988. Asst. dean of students The Coll. of Wooster, Ohio, 1977—79; asst. dean Swarthmore (Pa.) Coll., 1979—84, assoc. dean, 1984—85; rsch. assoc. Nat. Bd. Med. Examiners, Phila., 1985—97, evaluation officer, 1998—2000, sr. assessment officer, 2001—. Mem. Media (Pa.) Youth Aid Panel, 1999—. Avocations: travel, sports, gardening, quilts, cultural events. Office: Nat Bd Med Examiners 3750 Market St Philadelphia PA 19104 Office Phone: 215-590-9500.

ORR, RICHARD CLAYTON, financial modeler, futures trader; b. Oakland, Calif., Mar. 28, 1941; s. James Clayton Orr, Helen Kittle Orr; children: Robert Clayton, Debra Orr Kostoff. AB in Math., Humboldt State Coll., Arcata, Calif., 1964; MA in Math., Syracuse U., 1966, PhD in Math., 1969. From asst. prof. to assoc. prof. SUNY, Oswego, 1969—81, chmn. dept. math.; pres. Contratrend, Inc., Lexington, Mass., 1981—84; v.p. rsch. John Gutman Investments Corp., New Britain, Conn., 1984—90; pres. Chronos Corp., Lexington, Mass., 1990—95; gen. ptnr. ROME Ptnrs., Marblehead, Mass., 1995—2003; mng. dir. Calibar, LLC, Glastonbury, Conn., 2000—. Referee Market Technicians Assn., N.Y.C., 1989—2002, assoc. editor, 1985—89. Contbr. articles to profl. jours. Avocation: Meteorology, Sailing, Hiking. Office: Calibar LLC 573 Chimney Sweep Hill Rd Glastonbury CT 06033 Business E-Mail: vista@calibarllc.necoxmail.com.

ORR, ROBERT F. judge; b. Norfolk, Va., Oct. 11, 1946; married; 4 children. AB, U. N.C., 1971, JD, 1975. Bar: N.C. 1975. Pvt. practice, Asheville, NC, 1975—86; assoc. judge N.C. Ct. Appeals, 1986—94; assoc. justice N.C. Supreme Ct., Raleigh, 1994—. Mem. N.C. Beverage Control Commn., 1985—86; adj. prof. appellate advocacy N.C. Ctrl. U. Sch. Law, 1989—, adj. prof. N.C. State coll. law, 1998. Mem. Asheville-Revitalization Commn., 1977—81, Asheville-Buncombe Hist. Resources Commn., 1980—81; bd.

trustees Hist. Preservation Found. NC, 1982—85; mem. Nat. Park Sys. Adv. Bd., 1990—95, chmn., 1992—93; bd. visitors U. NC-Chapel Hill, 1993—; mem. NCBAs Appellate Rules Study com., 1999—, Gov.'s Crime Commn. With U.S. Army, 1968—71. Mem.: N.C. Bar Assn., 28th Jud. Dist., N.C. State Bar. Republican. Office: PO Box 1841 Raleigh NC 27602-1841 also: 302 Justice Bldg 2 E Morgan St Raleigh NC 27601-1428

ORR, SAN WATTERSON, JR., lawyer; b. Madison, Wis., Sept. 22, 1941; s. San Watterson and Eleanor Augusta (Schalk) Orr; m. Joanne Marie Ruby, June 26, 1965; children: San Watterson III, Nancy Chapman. BBA, U. Wis., 1963, JD, 1966. CPA Wis.; bar: Wis. 1966. Sec., tres., bd. dirs. Yawkey Lumber Co., Wausau, Wis., 1971—; pres. Forewood, Inc., Wausau, 1979—, also bd. dirs.; dir. Marshall & Ilsley Bank, Wausau, 1988—, vice chmn., 1997—; dir. Marshall & Ilsley Corp., 1994—; chmn. bd. Wausau-Mosinee Paper Corp., 1997—. Editor: U. Wis. Law Rev., 1962—63. Bd. dirs. Aytchmonde Woodson Found., Inc., Wausau, 1966—, Leigh Yawkey Woodson Art Mus., Inc., Wausau, 1981—, Wis. Taxpayers Alliance, Madison, 1983—, Competitive Wis., Inc., Milw., 1989—, Wis. Mfrs. and Commerce, 2001—, Wausau YMCA Found., 1979—, pres., 2002; bd. dirs. Nancy Woodson Spire Found., Inc., 1980—, pres., 2002; bd. dirs. Wausau Health Found., Inc., 1981—, pres., 1998—; bd. dirs. U. Wis. Found., Madison, 1991—, chmn., 2003; bd. dirs. Wis. Policy Rsch. Inst., Milw., 1995—; mem. bd. regents U. Wis. Sys., Madison, 1993—2000, pres., 1998—2000. Mem.: Am. Law Inst., Wis. Bar Assn., Ocean Club Fla., Country Club Fla., Minocqua Country Club, Wausau Club. Office: Yawkey Lumber Co 500 3rd St Ste 602 Wausau WI 54403-4857

ORR, STEVEN R. health facility administrator; b. 1947; Undergrad. degree, Macalester Coll.; M in Hosp. Adminstrn., U. Minn., 1973. Tchr., coord. master's degree program in hosp. adminstrn. U. Minn., 1974-76; v.p. corp. planning, v.p. managed and affiliated hosp. divsn. Fairfield Community Hosps., Mpls., 1976-81; COO Mid-Atlantic Health Group, 1981-83, adminstr. Monmouth Med. Ctr., 1981-83; ptnr., cons. Peat, Marwick, Main & Co., Mpls., 1984-88; chmn., pres., CEO Lutheran Health Systems, Fargo, N.D., 1988—. Office: Banner Health Systems PO Box 2989 Phoenix AZ 85062-2989

ORR, SUSAN PACKARD, business owner; BA in Econs., Stanford U., 1968, MBA, 1970; MS in Computer Sci., N.Mex. Inst. Mining and Tech., 1984. Chmn. David and Lucile Packard Found., Los Altos, Calif.; CEO Tech. Resource Assistance Ctr., Palo Alto, Calif., 1986—. Bd. dirs. Hewlett-Packard Co. Trustee Stanford U., 1998—. Office: The Packard Found 300 2nd St Ste 200 Los Altos CA 94022-3643

ORR, TERRENCE S, dancer, ballet master, artistic director; b. Berkeley, Calif., Mar. 12, 1943; m. Cynthia Gregory (div.); m. Marianna Tcherkassky. Student, San Francisco Ballet Sch. With San Francisco Ballet, 1959-65; with Am. Ballet Theatre, N.Y.C., 1965-97, soloist, 1967-72, rehearsal asst., 1970-73, prin. dancer, 1972-78, assoc. ballet master, 1973-78, ballet master, 1978-97; artistic dir. Pitts. Ballet, 1997—. Prodr. Royal Winnipeg Ballet, Nat. Ballet of Mexico, Teatro alla Scala in Millan, Nat. Ballet de Nancy in France, Teatro Colon in Buenos Aires, Pitts. Ballet Theatre, Boston Ballet, Ballet West, Dance Theatre of Harlem, N.Y.C. Ballet, Cleve./San Jose Ballet, San Francisco Ballet, Ballet Ariz., Sadler's Wells Royal Ballet, Paris Opera Ballet, Australian Ballet. Dancer (ballets) The Nutcracker, San Francisco Ballet, Fantasma, Divertissement d'Auber, Jeu des Cartes, Con Amore, Billy the Kid, Am. Ballet Theatre, Coppelia, La Fille Mal Gardee, Petrouchka, The River, Rodeo, Don Quixote, At Midnight, Dark Elegies, Fancy Free, Graduation Ball, Harbinger, Variations for Four, Pulcinella Variations, Brahms Quintet, Schubertiade, Mendelssohn Symphony, Polyandrion, Giselle, Swan Lake, La Sylphide, Gartenfest, Ontogeny; prodr.: La Sylphide, Rodeo; performer: Fancy Free; prodr.: Graduation Ball, Etudes, Billy the Kid, Fall River Legend, Giselle, Coppelia, Don Quixote, Swan Lake. Office: Pitts Ballet Theatre 2900 Liberty Ave Pittsburgh PA 15201-1511

ORR, T(HOMAS) J(EROME) (JERRY ORR), airport terminal executive; b. Charlotte, N.C., Feb. 25, 1941; m. Marcia Mincey; 3 children. BS in Civil Engring., N.C. State U., 1962. Registered profl. engr., N.C. Pvt. practice land surveyor, Charlotte, 1962-75; with Charlotte/Douglas Internat. Airport, 1975—, asst. mgr. airport ops., until 1989, aviation dir., 1989—. Chmn. employes campaign United Way of Ctrl. Carolinas, 1990; active Neighborhood Task Force, Charlotte's Cities in Schs. Program. Recipient Outstanding Support award N.C. Air Nat. Guard, 1989, Spirit award Charlotte-MJecklenburg Spirit Sq. Ctr. for Arts, 1990. Mem. N.C. Airports Assn. (past pres.), Airport Operators Coun. Internat. Office: Charlotte/Douglas Internat Airport PO Box 19066 Charlotte NC 28219-9066

ORR, ZELLIE, entrepreneur, educator, writer, researcher; b. Holly Ridge, Miss., May 12, 1951; d. Leonard and Lucille Rainey; m. Foster G. Orr Jr., Feb. 28, 1976 (div. July 14, 1998); children: Kai A., Nia Haley. Student, L.A. City Coll., 1970—71, U. Calif., Northridge, 1971—73; cert., Airline Schs. Pacific, 1974, CMLS Inst., 1979; MA in Human Letters, U. Metaphysics, 1983. Cert. real estate salesperson, Ga., 1979, pub. notary, Ga, 1985. Personal lines underwriter Kemper Ins. Co., L.A., 1976—78, Comml. Union Ins. Co., Atlanta, 1980—82, Moore Group ins. Co., Atlanta, 1982—85; lic. real estate agent Wofford Realty, Riverdale, Ga., 1979—81; owner Traffic Jam Lounge and Restaurant, Sunflower, 1986—89; documentation specialist Windsor Group, Atlanta, 1989—2001, mem. BCMS, 1991; pres., founder Comm. Unltd., Austell, Ga., 1995—. Mem. rsch. bd. advisors Am. Biog. Inst., Raleigh, NC, 1992—93. Co-author: Treasured Poems of America, 1989 (Editor's Choice award, 1989), The Best Poems & Poets of the 20th Century, 2000 (Editor's Choice award, 2000), Theatre of The Mind, 2003; contbr. poetry to mags. Organizer Sunflower Co. Civil Rights and Cmty. Reunion, Indianola, 1999; founder Charles E. Scattergood Meml. Found., Marietta, Ga., 2000; mem. So. Poverty Law Ctr., Habitat for Humanity, Feed the Children. Recipient Cert. Appreciation, Superior Ct., Calif., 1976, Cert. Recognition, CME Ch., Indianola, 1999, spl. advisor Tuskegee Airman Tribute, Columbus AFB, 2004. Mem.: NAACP, Am. Metaphysical Dr.'s Assn., Nat. Assn. Female Execs., Nat. Trust Hist. Preservation, Nat. Mus. Women in Arts, Internat. Soc. Poets, Nat. Black MBA Assn. Achievements include naming of Cox Park after 1st black Postmistress of U.S.A. (Minnie Cox); obtaining 5 posthumous medals from the military and recognition as inductee in Alcorn U. Hall of Fame for Tuskeege Airman Lt. Quitman C. Walker. Avocations: stamp collecting/philately, reading, coin collecting/numismatics, antiques, chess. Home: 3285 Doyle Ln Marietta GA 30060 Office: Comm Unltd 3999 Austell Rd Ste 303 #158 Austell GA 30106 Office Phone: 678-662-1368. E-mail: zellie@artsonwheels.com.

ORR-CAHALL, CHRISTINA, art museum director, art historian; b. Wilkes-Barre, Pa., June 12, 1947; d. William R.A. and Anona (Snyder) Boben; m. Richard Cahall. BA magna cum laude, Mt. Holyoke Coll., 1969; MA, Yale U., 1974, MPhil, 1975, PhD, 1979. Curator of collections Norton Gallery Art, West Palm Beach, Fla., 1975-77; asst. prof. Calif. Poly. State U., San Luis Obispo, 1978-81, Disting. prof., 1981; dir. art div., chief curator Oakland (Calif.) Mus., 1981-88; chief exec. officer Corcoran Gallery Art, Washington, 1988-90; dir. Norton Mus. Art, West Palm Beach, 1990—. Author: Addison Mizner: Architect of Dreams and Realities, 1974, 2d printing, 1993, Gordon Cook, 1987, Claude Monet: Am Impression, 1993; editor: The Art of California, 1984, The American Collection at the Norton Museum of Art, 1995. Office: Norton Museum of Art 1451 S Olive Ave West Palm Beach FL 33401-7162 Fax: 561-832-6529.

ORRILL, ROBERT THOMAS, foundation executive, former history educator; b. Madison, Ind., Jan. 20, 1939; s. Edward Morris and Katherine (Erny) O.; m. Linda Berg, June 22, 1963 (div. Jan. 1994); children: Andrea, Jeannie; m. Dorothy Schneirla Downie, Sept. 8, 1999. BS in English, Purdue U., 1961; BA, MA in Modern History, Oxford (Eng.) U., 1864; MA in Am. Social-Intellectual History, U. Wis., 1968. Tchg. fellow dept. history U. Wis., Madison, 1967-68; prof. dept. Am. studies Skidmore Coll., Saratoga Springs, N.Y., 1969-75; coord. for humanities, sr. acad. assoc. SUNY Empire State Coll., Saratoga Springs, 1976-78, asst. v.p. for acad. devel., 1978-82, chmn. grad. coun., chief adminstr. grad. program, 1982-85; exec. dir. Office ACad. Affairs, Coll. Bd., N.Y.C., 1985-99; prof. edn. reform Princeton U. Woodrow Wilson Sch. Pub. and Internat Affairs, NJ, 2001—02; exec. dir. Nat. Coun. on Edn. and the Disciplines, Princeton, 1999—; sr. advisor Found. Woodrow Wilson Nat. Fellowship Found., Princeton, 1999—. Advisor Alliance for Curriculum Reform, Am. Assn. Colls. and Univs., Am. Coun. on Tchg. Fgn. Langs., Am. Coun. Learned Socs., Assn. New Am. Colls., CUNY, Coun. on Basic Edn., U.S. Mil. Acad., to SUNY Faculty Task Force on Core Curriculum; co-chmn. policy task force Arts Edn. Partnership; organizer, facilitator summer insts. Coalition Essential Schs.; mem. adv. bd. Coun. Chief State Sch. Officers, EXTEND, Learning Productivity Network, NEH, Nat. Fgn. Lang. Ctr.; dir. funded project Nat. Assessment Governing Bd.; external reviewer Fund for Improvement Postsecondary Edn.; cons. to English chairs dept. Nat. Coun. Tchrs. English; evaluator Nat. Coun. Tchrs. Math., New Press, NSF. Exec. editor: Reading Reconsidered, 1988, Languages of Thought, 1989, Thinking Historically, 1990, Thinking Through Mathematics, 1990, Taking Full Measure, 1991, The Future of Educaton, 1994, The Condition of American Liberal Education, 1995, Inquiry and Learning, 1996, Literacy Redefined, 1996, Quantitatite Literacy, 1996, Education and Democracy, 1997, Why Numbers Count, 1997, Mathematics and Democracy, 2001. Rhodes scholar, 1963-64; fellow U. Wis., Yale U.; granted Fund for Improvement Postsecondary Edn., MacArthur Found., Mellon Found., Getty Ctr. for Edn. in Arts, Pew Charitable Trusts, 1999, 2000, Carnegie Corp. N.Y., 2000. Writer Neighbors for Bucks County Preservation, Inc., Solebury, Pa. Avocation: writing. Home: PO Box 442 2733 Creamery Rd Solebury PA 18963 Office: 5 Vaughn Dr Princeton NJ 08540-6313

ORRINGER, MARK BURTON, surgeon, educator; b. Pitts., Apr. 19, 1943; s. Harry B. and Alta (Moses) O.; m. Susan Michaels, June 20, 1964; children: Jeffrey Scott, Lisa Jill. BA, U. Pitts., 1963, MD, 1967. Diplomate Am. Bd. Surgery, Am. Bd. Thoracic Surgery. Resident Johns Hopkins Hosp., Balt., 1967-73; from asst. prof. to prof. surgery U. Mich. Med. Sch., Ann Arbor, 1973-80, prof. surgery, 1980—, John Alexander disting. prof. thoracic surgery, 1996. Head sect. thoracic surgery U. Mich. Med. Sch., Ann Arbor, 1985-98, head sect. gen. thoracic surgery, 1998—; dir. Am. Bd. Thoracic Surgery, 1988-95. Co-editor: (with Waldhausen) Complications in Cardiothoracic Surgery, Mosby Year Book, 1991, (with Zuidema) Shackelford's Surgery of the Alimentary Tract, vol. 1 - The Esophagus, 3d edit., 1991, 5th edit. 2002; contbr. over 200 articles to profl. jours., over 100 chpts. to books. Capt. USAR, 1974-76. Named among the Best Med. Specialists in the U.S., Town and Country mag., 1984, 89, among the 400 Best Drs. in Am., Good Housekeeping mag., 1991, One of Best Drs. in Am., 1993-2004, The 318 Top Cancer Specialists, Good Housekeeping mag., 1999, Am. Top Dr., 2001-2004; recipient Bicentennial Medal of Distinction, U. Pitts., 1987. Fellow ACS (bd. govs. 2002—); mem. Thoracic Surgery Dirs. Assn. (sec., treas. 1991-95, pres. elect 1995-97, pres. 1997-99), Soc. Thoracic Surgeons (pres. elect 2000, pres. 2001), Am. Coll. Chest Physicians, Am. Assn. Thoracic Surgery, Soc. Univ. Surgeons, Internat. Soc. Surgery, Am. Surg. Assn., Internat. Soc. Diseases Esophagus, Halsted Soc., Phi Beta Kappa, Alpha Omega Alpha. Avocations: swimming, scuba diving, hiking. Office: U Mich Med Ctr 1500 E Med Ctr Dr Ann Arbor MI 48109 Business E-Mail: morrin@umich.edu.

ORRIS-MODUGNO, MICHELE MARIE, public relations, marketing and advertising consultant; b. Norwalk, Conn., Feb. 23, 1958; d. Stephen Joseph and Arcenia (Rodriguez) O. Student, U. N.Mex., 1976-78; BA with honors, U. Bridgeport, 1980, postgrad., 1981-83. Tchr. Norwalk Pub. Schs., 1981-83; head tchr. presch. Norwalk YMCA, 1983-84; exec. dir. Norwalk Seaport Assn., 1984-86; cons., 1986-87, Barnum Festival, Bridgeport, Conn., 1987-88, P.T. Barnum Found., Bridgeport, 1987; mgr. communications Human Resources Inc., Stamford, Conn., 1987; owner, mgr. Michele Orris, Norwalk, Conn., 1988—. Dir. pub. rels. YWCA of Stamford (Conn.), 1989-90. Past sec., pres. Marvin Beach Assn., East Norwalk; asst. dir. pub. rels. Conn. Women's Celebration, 1986; chmn. subcom. auditorium com. New City Hall, Norwalk; active numerous other civic orgns.; bd. dirs. Southwestern Conn. coun. Girl Scouts U.S., 1987-88, Cmtys. In Schs. of Norwalk, Inc., 2000-01; gdn. dirs. Levitt Pavilion Performing Arts, Westport, Conn., 1991-93; mgr. Orch. New Eng., 1993-95; mem. Unquowa Parents Assn., 2000-05; pres. Unquowa Parents' Assn., 2002-04. Recipient award City of Norwalk, 1987. Mem. Greens Farms Acad. Alumni Assn. (pres., class sec.), Phi Sigma Iota (life). Democrat. Roman Catholic. Avocations: reading, tennis, bicycling, golf, art museums. Home and Office: 455 Primrose Ln Fairfield CT 06825-2343 Office Phone: 203-259-8232. Personal E-mail: ENTMOM@aol.com.

ORRMONT, ARTHUR, writer, editor; b. Albany, N.Y., July 3, 1922; m. Lora Orenstein, Oct. 6, 1956 (div. 1965); m. Leonie Rosenstiel, Aug. 22, 1995. Student, U. Ala., 1941, U. Mich., 1942-45, Cornell U., 1945; BA, U. Mich., 1945. Editl. dept. head Farrar, Straus & Co., N.Y.C., 1945-51; sr. editor Popular Libr., N.Y.C., 1951-55; exec. editor Fawcett Books, N.Y.C., 1955-57; pres., editl. dir. Author Aid Assocs., N.Y.C., 1967-97; v.p. Rsch. Assocs. Internat., N.Y.C., 1980-97; pres. Literary Cons., Albuquerque, 1997—. Lectr. creative writing CCNY, 1966, Columbia U., 1967; judge Hopwood Awards, U. Mich., 1999. Author: Love Cults and Faith-Healers, 1961, (with Capt. Marion Aten RAF) Last Train Over Rostov Bridge, 1962, Brit. edit., 1962, Indestructible Commodore Matthew Perry, 1962, Japanese edit., 1963, Amazing Alexander Hamilton, 1964, Portuguese edit., 1965, Master Detective: Allan Pinkerton, 1965 (Jr. Literary Guild selection), Chinese Gordon: Hero of Khartoum, 1966, Fighter Against Slavery: Jehudi Ashmun, 1966, Mr. Lincoln's Master Spy: Lafayette Baker, 1966, Diplomat in Warpaint: Chief Alexander McGillivray of the Creeks, 1967, Richard Burton, 1969, Brit. edit., 1969, James Buchanan Eads: The Man Who Mastered the Mississippi, 1970, (with Fr. Joseph Lauro) Action Priest, 1970, French edit., 1970, Requiem for War: The Life of Wilfred Owen, 1972; editor: (with Leonie Rosenstiel) Literary Agents of North America, 1984, 5th edit., 1995; editor Nat. Hall of Fame Biography series, 1970-72. With U.S. Army, 1942. Recipient Avery Hopwood award for short story U. Mich., 1943, 44, 45. Mem. Assn. Lit. Critics Scholars. Office Phone: 505-797-9397. Personal E-mail: rosensti@concentric.net.

ORROCK, NAN, state legislator; children: Jesse, Daniel. BA, U. Va. Mem. Ga. State Ho. of Reps., Atlanta, 1986—. Mem. Indsl. Rels. Com., Appropriations Com.; vice chmn. Health and Ecology Com. Exec. dir. Fund for So. Cmties. Mem. Unitarian Ch. Home: 1070 Delaware Ave SE Atlanta GA 30316-2470 Office: State Capitol 401 Rm 109 Capitol Square Atlanta GA 30334

ORSATTI, ALFRED KENDALL, organization executive; b. Los Angeles, Jan. 31, 1932; s. Alfredo and Margaret (Hayes) O.; m. Patricia Decker, Sept. 11, 1960; children: Scott, Christopher, Sean. BS, U. So. Calif., 1956. Assoc. prodr., v.p. Sabre Prodns., L.A., 1957-58; assoc. prodr. Ror Vic Prodns., L.A., 1958-59; bus. rep. AFTRA, L.A., 1960-61; Hollywood exec., sec. SAG, L.A., 1961-81, nat. exec. dir., 1981—, trustee Pension Welfare Plan, 1971—. Del. Los Angeles County Fedn. Labor, Los Angeles, Hollywood Film Council, Los Angeles; v.p., mem. exec. Calif. Fedn. Labor; pres. Calif. Theatrical Fedn.; chmn. arts, entertainment and media com. dept. profl. employees AFL-CIO Mem. Mayor's Film Devel. Com., Los Angeles. Mem. Actors and Artists Am. Assn. (1st v.p.) Office: SAG 5757 Wilshire Blvd Los Angeles CA 90036-3635

ORSATTI, ERNEST BENJAMIN, lawyer; b. Pitts., Nov. 14, 1949; s. Ernest Ubaldo and Dorothy Minerva (Pfeiffer) O.; m. Ingrid Zalman, May 3, 1975; 1 child, Benjamin E. BA, Marquette U., 1971; JD, Duquesne U., 1974; postgrad., Army Command and Gen. Staff Coll., 1984. Bar: Pa. 1974, U.S. Dist. Ct. (we. dist.) Pa. 1974, U.S. Ct. Appeals (3d cir.) 1977, U.S. Supreme Ct. 1978, U.S. Ct. Appeals (6th cir.) 1992. Assoc. Jubelirer, Pass & Intrieri, Pitts., 1974-81, ptnr., 1981—. Contbg. editor: The Developing Labor Law, 4th edit., 1992—2002; chpt. editor The Developing Labor Law, 4th edit., 2002—. Bd. dirs. Am. Italian Cultural Inst., Pitts. Served to capt. U.S. Army, 1975, lt. col., USAR, ret. Mem. ABA, ACLU (legal com. 1996—), Am. Arbitration Assn., Am. Trial Lawyers Assn., Pa. Bar Assn., Allegheny County Bar Assn. (profl. ethics com. 2000—), Am. Legion. Democrat. Roman Catholic. Home: 9343 N Florence Rd Pittsburgh PA 15237-4815 Office: Jubelirer Pass & Intrieri 219 Fort Pitt Blvd Pittsburgh PA 15222-1576 Office Phone: 412-281-3850. Personal E-mail: eborsatti@aol.com. Business E-Mail: ebo@jpilaw.com.

ORSBON, RICHARD ANTHONY, lawyer; b. Sept. 23, 1947; s. Richard Chapman and Ruby Estelle (Wyatt) Orsbon; m. Susan Cowan Shivers, June 13, 1970; children: Sarah Hollingsworth, Wyatt Benjamin, David Allison. BA Distng. mil. grad. ROTC, Davidson Coll., 1969; JD, Vanderbilt U., 1972; hon. grad., U.S. Army, 1972. Bar: N.C. 1972, U.S. Dist. Ct. (we. dist.) N.C. 1972, cert.: (specialist in probate and fiduciary law). Assoc. Kennedy, Covington, Lobdell & Hickman, Charlotte, NC, 1972—75, Parker, Poe et al, Charlotte, 1975—77, ptnr., 1978—. Lectr. on estate planning, probate; pres. ECO, Inc., Charlotte, 1982—. Editor (assoc., contbr.): (law rev.) Vanderbilt Law Rev., 1971—72. Mem. planning bd. Queens Coll. Estate Planning Day, 1978—, chmn., 1991; trustee Davidson Coll., 1990—91, Camp Tekoa, Hendersonville, NC; mem. YMCA basketball com.; bd. vis. Johnson C. Smith U., 1986—89; mem. Dem. state exec. com., 1980; chmn. adminstrv. bd. Myers Park United Meth. Ch., 1994—96; bd. dir. Charlotte United Way, 1983—; bd. dir. law explorer program Boy Scouts Am., Charlotte, NC, 1976—78. 1st lt. U.S. Army, 1972—73. Named Outstanding Vol., Charlotte Observer/United Way, 1984; scholar Patrick Wilson Merit, Vanderbilt U. Law Sch., 1969—72. Mem.: ABA (real property probate sect.), Charlotte Estate Planning Coun. (exec. com. 1992—, sec. 1994—, pres. 1996—97), Deans Assn. of Vanderbilt U. Law Sch. (bd. dir.), Mecklenburg County Bar Assn. (law day com., vol. lawyers program, bd. dir., chmn. 1988—89, grievance com. 1987—88), N.C. Bar Assn. Coll. of Advocacy, N.C. Bar Assn. (probate and fiduciary law sect., author, spkr. 1987—92), N.C. State Bar (cert. specialist estate planning and probate 1987), Foxcroft Swim and Racquet Club (pres. 1986—87, bd. dir. 1985—88), Davidson Coll. Alumni Assn. (bd. dir. 1983, class alumni sec. 1986—, pres.-elect 1989—90, pres. 1990—91, bd. dir. Wildcat Club 1989—, pres. 1993—98), Omicron Delta Kappa. Home: 2819 Rothwood Dr Charlotte NC 28211-2623 Office: Orsbon & FenningerLLP 4201 Congress St Ste 110 Charlotte NC 28209

ORSILLO, JAMES EDWARD, computer systems engineer, company executive; b. Elmira, N.Y., Oct. 30, 1939; s. Giacomo and Irene (Heppy) O.; 1 child, June Lynne. BEE, RCA Insts., 1962; BS in Elec. Engring. and Math., Ind. Inst. Tech., 1964; MS, Rensselear Poly., 1968; BS in Nuclear Engring., Capital Radio Electronic Inst., 1974. Communications engr. Bell Telephone Labs., Holmdel, N.J., 1962-63; video engr. Westinghouse, Elmira, N.Y., 1965-66; computer engr. GE, Pittsfield, Mass., 1966-67; systems specialist Control Data Corp., Mpls., 1968-70; software specialist Computer Sci. Corp., Morristown, N.Y., 1970-72; prin. cons. Computer Cons. Assocs., Elmira, 1972-78; CEO ORTHSTAR, Inc., Elmira, 1974—; acquired Hughes Tng., Inc. Rail Simulation Bus., 1996—. Owner, pres. Shadowstand Properties, Inc. (FKA O-K Properties), Elmira, 1984—, Thundering Hooves Stables, Elmira, 1985—. Mem. IEEE, Am. Nuclear Soc., Soc. Indsl. and Applied Math., Am. Helicopter Soc., Army Aviation Assn. Am., Internat. Flying Engrs., USAF Assn., U.S. Naval League, U.S. Polo Assn. Republican. Achievements include invention of Integrated Data Acquisition System (IDAS), of Thread Algebra used in simulation development, of Extended Sentient Non-linear Ensemble (ESNE). Office: ORTHSTAR Inc Airport Corp Park PO Box 459 Big Flats NY 14814-0459 Office Phone: 607-562-2100. Business E-Mail: orsillo@orthstar.com.

ORSINI, ERIC ANDREW, army official; b. Lodi, N.J., Jan. 7, 1918; s. Serafino and Valentina Lena (Dinino) O.; m. Mildred Jean Andre, Feb. 8, 1947; children: Donna Jean, Debra Jane. BS, Gen Edn. Devel., Fort Knox, Ky., 1948; student, Def. Sys. Mgmt. Coll., Ft. Belvoir, Va., 1978, Harvard U., 1982, George Washington U., 1986. Registered mech. engr. Commd. capt. armor U.S. Army, 1943, advanced through grades to col., 1965, transfer to Ordinance Corps., 1958, ret., 1971, appt. dep. asst. sec. for logistics, 1975—. Developer policy guidance mil. identification symbology technologies LOGMARS, 1982; policy developer mil. ordnance/maintenance policies and procedures. Decorated Purple Heart, Silver Star, Bronze Star, Legion of Merit; named to Ordnance Hall of Fame, 1991; recipient Presdl. Meritorious Exec. award, 1991, 94, Logistics Emeritus award Nat. Security Indsl. Assn., 1999. Avocations: golf, fishing. Home: 11204 Gray Fox Pt Spotsylvania VA 22553-4660 Office Phone: 703-695-3073.

ORSINI, TOM, retired telecommunications company executive; Exec. v.p. Alltel Corp., Little Rock; ret., 1999. Office: Alltel Corp One Allied Dr Little Rock AR 72202 Address: 10 Town Plz Durango CO 81301-5104

ORSKI, C. KENNETH, consulting company executive, lawyer, publisher; b. Warsaw, Mar. 7, 1932; came to U.S., 1946, naturalized, 1953; s. Thaddeus and Irene Orski; m. Jocelyne Schule, Aug. 27, 1968; children: Karine N., Monica J.; m. Barbara K. Klema, Apr. 28, 1978; 1 child, Christopher P. AB, Harvard U., 1953, LLB, JD, 1956. Atty. AEC, 1956-61; asst. to pres. Gen. Dynamics Corp., Washington, 1961-66; dir. OECD Paris; fgn. svc. officer U.S. Dept. State, 1966-73; assoc. adminstr. U.S. Dept. Transp., Washington, 1974-78; pres. Urban Mobility Corp., Washington, 1982—. Contbg. author books in field, 1982, 85; editor, pub. Innovation Briefs, 1991—; Washington corr. Traffic Tech. Internat.; contbr. articles to profl. jours. Recipient Outstanding Pub. Svc. award U.S. Dept. Transp., 1985, Disting. Svc. award, 1977, Meritorious Svc. award, 1975. Republican. Home: 10200 Riverwood Dr Potomac MD 20854-1536 Office Phone: 301-299-1996. E-mail: korski@erols.com.

ORSON, BARBARA TUSCHNER, actress; b. N.Y.C., May 19, 1929; d. Jonah Tuschner and Rebecca Traceman; m. Jay M. Orson, June 24, 1956; children: Beth-Diane, Theodore. Student, Dramatic Workshop, N.Y.C., 1948-50. Leading soubrette Am. Savoyards, N.Y.C., 1950-51, 53-55; actress Trinity Repertory, Providence, 1964—2001. Founding mem. Trinity Sq. Repertory Co., Providence, 1964—2001. Actress Edinburgh Festival, Scotland, 1968, Am. Repertory Theatre, Cambridge, Mass., 1981-85, Williamstown (Mass.) Theatre, 1985-89, Dallas Theatre Ctr., 1985, Yale Repertory Co., New Haven, Conn., 1991; appeared in: (films) Mission Hill, Code of Ethics, My One and Only, Swimming Upstream, Mr. North, Strangers in Transit (TV) Theatre in America, Feasting with Panthers, Life Among the Lowly, House of Mirth, Camera Three, RI Demon Murder, Miller's Court, Conflict of Interest (Am. premiere) The Suicide, 1980, (world premiere) Grown Ups, 1981, God's Heart, 1995; founding mem., appeared in over 100 prodns. Trinity Sq. Repertory Co., Providence, 1964—; (radio) House of Mirth, Masterpiece Radio Theatre with Jane Alexander; guest artist (Lady Macbeth), Brown U. Recipient Adrian Hall award, Trinity Repertory Co., RI, 2002. Mem. Am. Fedn. Radio and TV Artists, Screen Actors Guild, Actor's Equity Assn., Trinity Rep. Co. (founder). Home: 281 Hillside Ave Pawtucket RI 02860-6119

ORSZAG, JONATHAN MARC, economist, consultant; b. Boston, Apr. 15, 1973; s. Steven Alan and Reba Karp O.; m. Rica Rodman, June 17, 2000. AB, Princeton U., 1995; MSc, Oxford (Eng.) U., 1997. Econ. policy advisor The White House Nat. Econ. Coun., Washington, 1996-99; dir. policy and strategic planning U.S. Dept. Commerce, Washington, 1999—2000; mng. dir. Sebago Associates, Washington, 2000—, Competition Policy Assocs., Inc., Washington, 2003—. Mem. Calif. Workforce Investment Bd., Sacramento, 2000-03; mem. Calif. Tech. Adv. Group, Sacramento, 2000-03; adj. lectr. U. So. Calif., 2002-03. Recipient Leadership award, Corp. Enterprise Devel., 1999;, Marshall scholar, 1996. Mem. Pacific Coun. on Internat. Policy, L.A. World Affairs Coun., Asia Soc., Am. Econ. Assn., Am. Polit. Sci. Assn. Avocation: golf. Home: 5028 Warren St NW Washington DC 20016 Office: 1919 Pennsylvania Ave NW Washington DC 20006 Office Phone: 202-293-2626. E-mail: jorszag@competitionpolicy.com.

ORSZAG, PETER RICHARD, economist; b. Boston, Dec. 16, 1968; s. Steven Alan and Reba (Karp) O.; m. Cameron Rachel Hamill; children: Leila Madeleine, Joshua Nathaniel. AB summa cum laude, Princeton U., 1991; MS, London Sch. Econs., 1992, PhD, 1997. Econ. advisor Ministry of Fin., Moscow, 1992-93; staff economist Coun. Econ. Advisers, Washington, 1993-

94; prof. rsch. staff London Sch. Econs., 1994-95; sr. economist Coun. Econ. Advisers, Washington, 1995-96, sr. adviser, 1996; sr. econ. advisor Nat. Econ. Coun., 1997, spl. asst. to pres for econ. policy, 1998; pres. Sebago Assocs., 1998—. Lectr. in econs. U. Calif., Berkeley, 1999—2000; rsch. assoc. Ctr. Retirement Rsch., Boston Coll., 2000—; Joseph A. Pechman sr. fellow in tax and fiscal policy The Brookings Instn., 2001—; co-dir. Tax Policy Ctr., 2003—. Marshall scholar, 1991-92. Mem. Nat. Acad. Social Ins., Phi Beta Kappa. Office: The Brookings Instn 1775 Massachusetts Ave NW Washington DC 20036-2188 Business E-Mail: porszag@brookings.edu.

ORSZAG, STEVEN ALAN, applied mathematician, educator; b. N.Y.C., Feb. 27, 1943; s. Joseph and Rose (Siegel) O.; m. Reba Karp, June 21, 1964; children— J. Michael, Peter Richard, Jonathan Marc. BS, M.I.T., 1962; postgrad. (Henry fellow), St. John's Coll., Cambridge (Eng.) U., 1962-63; PhD, Princeton U., 1966. Mem. Inst. Advanced Study, Princeton, NJ, 1966—67; prof. applied math. MIT, 1967—84; prof. applied and computational math. Princeton U., 1984—, dir., 1990—92, Hamrick prof. engring., 1989—98; Smith prof. math. Yale U., New Haven, 1998—, chmn. applied math., 1999—. Cons. in field. Author: Studies in Applied Mathematics, 1976, Numerical Analysis of Spectral Methods, 1977, Advanced Mathematical Methods for Scientists and Engineers, 1978; contbr. numerous rsch. publs. in field. A.P. Sloan Found. fellow, 1970-74, Guggenheim fellow, 1989-90. Fellow Am. Inst. Physics (Otto Laporte award 1991), AIAA (Fluid and Plasmadynamics award, 1986), Soc. Indsl. and Applied Math., Soc. Engring. Sci. (G.I. Taylor medal, 1995). Office: Yale U 101 Watson Hall New Haven CT 06520-8283 E-mail: orszag@math.yale.edu.

ORTBALS, GERALD RAY, lawyer; b. St. Louis, Jan. 20, 1941; s. Ray W. and Ruth M. (Krost) O.; m. Mary L. Colligan, Aug. 13, 1966; children: Stephanie, Andrea, Joanna. BS, St. Louis U., 1963, JD, 1966; postgrad. in pub. comm., Boston U., 1968-69. Ptnr. Stinson Morrison Hecker LLP, St. Louis. Chair ctr. justice campaigen Legal Svcs. Eastern Mo., St. Louis, 1995—. Contbr. articles to newspapers. Pres. St. Patrick Ctr. Cath. Charities, St. Louis, 1996—. White House Retreat, Inc., St. Louis, 1986-87; bd. dirs. Mid-Am. Transplant Assn., Mo. and Ill., 1991—, exec. com.; dem. candidate U.S. Senate, Mo., 1994; chief staff Office Gov., Mo., 1977-78; pres. Young Dem., 1962. Capt. USAF, 1966-72. Recipient Pro Bono Publico award Mo. Bar, 1989, Alumni Leadership award St. Louis Univ. Law Sch., 1990, Vol. award United Way, 1991, Found. award St. Louis Bar Found., 1995. Mem.: Lawyers Assn. St. Louis (pres. 1986—87), Bar Assn. Met. St. Louis (pres. 1990—91), Mo. Lawyers Trust Found. (bd. dirs. 1992—97), Mo. Athletic Club (pres. 2002—03). Roman Catholic. Avocations: exercise, golf, reading, jazz. Address: 100 S 4th St Ste 700 Saint Louis MO 63102

ORTEGA, BEATRICE, construction executive; m. James Ortega. Med. technician Mount Sinai; pres. Dot Constrn. N.Y., Inc., N.Y.C., 1998—. Named to, Crain's N.Y. Bus. "40 under 40", 2004; recipient Woman of the Future award, Galaxy Awards, N.Y. Women's Agenda, 2003, Rising Star award, Latino Job Svc. Employer Com., N.Y. State Dept. Labor, 2003. Office: Dot Constrn 2855 Frederick Douglas Blvd New York NY 10039*

ORTEGA, MARIA A. security firm executive, educator; b. N.Y.C., Apr. 28, 1967; d. Humberto and Delia Margarita Ortega. BS, U. Chgo., 1992. Cert. Homeland Sec. Am. Coll. Forensic Examiners, 2003. Police officer N.Y.C. Police Dept., 1985—88; human resources mgr. Burns Internat. Security, N.Y.C., 1988—93; human resources mgr., dir. tng. Initial Security, N.Y.C., 1994—96; dir. human resources and tng. Command Security Svcs., N.Y.C., 1996—98; sr. program mgr. Opportunity Am., N.Y.C., 1998; pres., CEO Security Works Inc., N.Y.C., 1999—. Bd. dirs. N.Y. State Divsn. Criminal Justice Svc.; chmn. N.Y. State Divsn. Labor Latino JSEC, N.Y.C., 2001—. Named to Winner Circle, Burns Internat., 1989; recipient Rising Star award, N.Y. State Dept. Labor, 2000. Mem.: Nat. Assn. Chiefs of Police, ASIS Internat., Bklyn. C. of C. Avocations: basketball, music, reading, cooking. Office: Security Works Inc 4th Fl 248 Duffield St Brooklyn NY 11201 Office Phone: 718-780-4496.

ORTEGA, RAFAEL ENRIQUE, county official, educator; b. N.Y.C., Jan. 8, 1952; s. Enrique Ortega and Josefina Nieves; m. Guadalupe Cervantes, June 19, 1987 (div. May 2002); children: Gabriela, Emilio. BA, Fordham U., 1974; MSW, U. Minn., 1981, edn. policy fellow, 1987. Dir. Minn. Coun. Chs., Mpls., 1981—85; CEO Chicanos-Latinos Unidos En Servicio, Inc., St. Paul, 1985—95; county commr. Ramsey County, St. Paul, 1995—; faculty Metro State U., St. Paul, 1996—. Treas. West Side Citizens Orgn., St. Paul, 1988—92; chair Ramsey County Bd., St. Paul, 2000—02, Regional Rail Authority, St. Paul, 2002—; bd. mem. St. Paul River Front Corp., St. Paul, 1995—, YMCA, St. Paul, 2001—, Nat. Coun. LaRoza, Washington, 2002—. Democrat. Roman Catholic. Home: 66 E 9th St Saint Paul MN 55101 Office: Ramsey County Bd Commrs 220 Court House 15 W Kellogg Blvd Saint Paul MN 55102

ORTENBERG, ELISABETH CLAIBORNE See CLAIBORNE, LIZ

ORTH, DAVID NELSON, physician, educator, sculptor; b. East Orange, N.J., Mar. 5, 1933; s. John Joseph and Marjorie Adelaide (Wauters) O.; m. Linda Diana D'Errico, June 9, 1979; children by previous marriage: John Randall (dec.), Jennifer Stewart, Julie Thomas. ScB in Chemistry, Brown U., 1954; MD, Vanderbilt U., 1962. Intern, Osler med. service Johns Hopkins Hosp., Balt., 1962-63, fellow in medicine, 1962-65; asst. resident John Hopkins Hosp., Balt., 1963-65; mem. faculty dept. medicine Vanderbilt U. Sch. Medicine, Nashville, 1965—, prof., 1975-98, prof. emeritus, 1998—, joint dir. endocrinology div. dept. medicine, 1968-81, dir. cancer research and treatment ctr., 1972-77, dir. div. endocrinology, 1984-96. Scholar-in-residence Rockefeller Found. Bellagio (Italy) Study and Conf. Ctr., 1989; vis. scientist Vollum Inst. for Advanced Biomed. Rsch., Oreg. Health Scis. U., Portland, 1993-94. Contbr. numerous articles in field of endocrinology to med. jours. Served with U.S. Navy, 1954-57. John and Mary R. Markle scholar, 1968-73; Howard Hughes Med. Inst. investigator, 1969-75 Mem. AAUP, AAAS, ACP, Assn. Am. Physicians, Am. Soc. Clin. Investigation, Endocrine Soc. (sec.-treas. 1989-94, pres. 1997-98), N.Y. Acad. Scis., Am. Fedn. Clin. Rsch., So. Soc. Clin. Investigation. Office: Vanderbilt U Med Ctr 715A Mrb Ii Nashville TN 37232-0001

ORTH, PAUL WILLIAM, retired lawyer; b. Balt., May 7, 1930; s. Paul W. and Naomi (Howard Bevard) O.; m. Isle Haertle, June 15, 1956; children: Ingrid, Ilse Christine. AB, Dartmouth Coll., 1951; JD, Harvard U., 1954. Bar: Mass. 1954, Conn. 1957, U.S. Dist. Ct. Conn. 1958, U.S. Ct. Appeals (2d cir.) 1960, U.S. Ct. Appeals (1st cir.) 1983, U.S. Supreme Ct. 1960. Assoc. Hoppin, Carey & Powell, Hartford, Conn., 1957-62, ptnr., 1962-86, Shipman & Goodwin, Hartford, 1987-2000, MacDermid, Reynolds & Glissman P.C., Hartford, 2000—. Instr. Sch. Law U. Conn., 1959-81. Editor: Every Employee's Guide to the Law, 1993, 96. Chmn. Farmington Conservation Commn., 1982-83; mem. town com. Town of Farmington, 1973-81; dir. Conn. Opera Assn., 2000-02. With AUS, 1954-56. Fellow Am. Bar Found., Conn. Bar Found.; mem. ABA, Hartford County Bar Assn. (pres. 1983-84), Conn. Bar Assn. (chmn. coms.). Democrat. Office: MacDermid Reynolds & Glissman PC 86 Farmington Ave Hartford CT 06105 E-mail: porth@mrglaw.com.

ORTHWEIN, WILLIAM COE, mechanical engineer; b. Toledo, Jan. 27, 1924; s. William Edward and Millie Minerva (Coe) O.; m. Helen Virginia Poindexter, Feb. 1, 1948; children— Karla Frances, Adele Diana, Maria Theresa. BS, M.I.T., 1946; MS, U. Mich., 1951, PhD, 1959. Registered profl. engr., Ill., Ind., Ky. Aerophysicist Gen. Dynamics Co., Ft. Worth, 1951-52; research asso. U. Mich., 1952-59; adv. engr. IBM Corp., Owego, N.Y., 1959-61; dir. computer centers U. Okla., Norman, 1961-63; research scientist Ames Lab., NASA, Moffett Field, Calif., 1963-65; mem. faculty So. Ill. U., Carbondale, 1965—, prof. engring., 1967—. Cons. in field. Author: Clutches and Brakes, 1986, Machine Component Design, 1990; papers, revs., books in field. Pres. Jackson County (Ill.) Taxpayers Assn., 1976. Served with AUS, 1943-46. Mem. ASME (Outstanding Svc. award 1972), Am. Gear Mfrs. Assn., Am. Acad. Mechanis, Soc. Automotive Engrs., Ill. Acad. Sci., Ill. Soc. Profl. Engrs. (chmn. salary and employment com. 1974, chmn. ad hoc com. continuing edn. 1975), NRA, Aircraft Owners and Pilots Assn., Sigma Xi. Mem. Lds Ch. Home: 22 Meffert Ct Highland IL 62249-2699 *Success in engineering is, I believe, contingent upon one's ability to see the world as it really is, to quickly gain insight enough to detect fundamental parameters that determine behavior of the system in question, to conduct a straightforward check of one's analysis, and to simply synthesize a means of modifying and/or controlling the parameters to obtain the desired results. These ingredients apply to both physical mechanisms and to human organizations— only the means of implementation differ.*

ORTINAU, DAVID JOSEPH, marketing specialist, educator; b. Harvey, Ill., Dec. 14, 1948; s. Harold Raymond and Lois Agnice (Reich) O.; m. Shirley Keating, Aug. 15, 1975 (div. Nov. 1979); m. Renee Susan Hess, Apr. 30, 1983 (div. Aug. 1993). BS in Mgmt., So. Ill. U., 1970; MS in Bus. Adminstrn., Ill. State U., 1971; PhD in Mktg., La. State U., 1979. Sr. rsch. analyst, dir. projects Rabin Rsch. Co., Chgo., 1971-73; adminstrv. asst., instr. mktg. Coll. Bus., Ill. State U., Normal, Ill., 1973-76; grad. teaching assoc., instr. mktg. Coll. Bus., La. State U., Baton Rouge, Fla., 1976-79; from asst. prof. mktg. to assoc. prof. Coll. Bus., U. South Fla., Tampa, Fla., 1979-84; dir. mktg. and rsch. Market Rsch. Group, Tampa, Fla., 1980-83; assoc. prof. U. South Fla., Tampa, Fla., 1984-95, coord. PhD program dept. mktg., 1989-91, prof., 1995—. V.p. mktg. Neaves, Neaves and Ortinau, Normal, 1974-77. Co-author: Marketing Research: A Practical Approach in the New Millennium, 2000, Marketing Research: Within a Changing Information Environment, 2003; mem. editl. rev. bd. Jour. Acad. Mktg. Sci., 1989— (Disting. Merit award for Outstanding Reviewer 1992-93, Outstanding JAMS Rev. 1997-2000), Jour. Bus. Rsch., 2000— (Outstanding Editl. Rev. 2002); contbr. articles to Jour. Health Care Mktg., Jour. Mktg. Edn., Jour. Bus. Rsch., Jour. Svcs. Mktg., Jour. Acctg. Horizons, Jour. Retailing, others. Recipient Disting. Merit award Advt. Fedn. SW Fla., 1983, Coba Outstanding Rsch. award U. South Fla., 1987, Outstanding Tchg. award, 1980, 81, 82, 86, 90, 95, 2001. Fellow Soc. for Mktg. Advances, 2001, (bd. dirs. 1998—, co-chair doctoral consortium 1998-99); mem. Am. Mktg. Assn. (doctoral consortium fellow 1978, reviewer 1982—), Assn. Consumer Rsch., So. Mktg. Assn. (reviewer 1975—, chmn. 1976—, sec. 1990-91, treas. 1992-95, pres. elect 1995-96, pres. 1996-97, chmn. Svcs. Mktg. Customer Satisfaction Track Program 1990-92, co-chair doctoral consortium 1998, 99, Outstanding Articles award 1981, 86, 87, 90, 92), Soc. for Mktg. Advances Found. (bd. dirs., co-founder 2002—, pres. 2003—)Acad. Mktg. Sci. (reviewer 1988—, chmn. 1989, 92, Reviewer of Yr. 1992, session chair new tech. and retail store images at 1999, 2003 confs.), retailing svcs. mktg. track program chair, 2003, AMS conf. program co-chair 2004), Acad. Bus. Adminstrn. (track program chmn. 1993), Beta Gamma Sigma (pres. Fla. chpt. 1990-91). Avocations: all sports, reading, gardening, the arts. Research and consulting specializations focus on attitudinal, motivational, multivariate measurement and data analysis methods in areas of services marketing and quality, customer satisfaction and evaluation models, advertising, marketing education topics/issues, diffusion and diagnostic performance processes of product innovations, consumer services and interactive marketing technologies. Home: 2305 Windsor Oaks Ave Lutz FL 33549-5880 Office: U South Fla Mktg Dept Tampa FL 33620 E-mail: dortinau@coba.usf.edu.

ORTIQUE, REVIUS OLIVER, JR., city official, retired state supreme court justice; b. New Orleans, June 14, 1924; s. Revius Oliver and Lillie Edith (Long) O.; m. Miriam Marie Victorianne, Dec. 29, 1947; 1 child: Rhesa Marie (Mrs. Alden J. McDonald). AB, Dillard U., 1947; MA, Ind. U., 1949; JD, So. U., 1956; LLD (hon.), Campbell Coll., 1960; LHD (hon.), Ithaca Coll., 1971; LLD (hon.), Ind. U., 1983, Morris Brown Coll., 1992, Loyola U. South, 1993, Dillard U., 1996. Bar: La. 1956, U.S. Dist. Ct 1956, Eastern Dist. La 1956, U.S. Fifth Circuit Ct. of Appeals 1956, U.S. Supreme Ct 1964. Practiced in, New Orleans, 1956-78; judge Civil Dist. Ct. for Orleans Parish, 1978-92; assoc. justice La. Supreme Ct., 1993—94; chmn. New Orleans Aviation Bd., 1994—2002. Lectr. labor law Dillard U., 1950-52, U. West Indies, 1986; formerly assoc. gen. counsel Cmty. Improvement Agy.; former gen. counsel 8th Dist. A.M.E. Ch.; former mem. Fed. Hosp. Coun., 1966, Pres.'s Commn. on Campus Unrest, 1970, Bd. Legal Svcs. Corp., 1975-83; chief judge civil cts. Orleans Parish, 1986-87; spkr. in field; U.S. alt. rep. to 54th Gen. Assembly UN, 1999-2000. Contbr. articles to profl. jours. Former pres. Met. Area Com.; former mem. Bd. City Trusts, New Orleans, New Orleans Legal Assistance Corp. Bd., Ad Hoc Com. for Devel. of Ctrl. Bus. Dist. City of New Orleans; bd. dirs. Cmty. Rels. Coun., Am. Lung Assn.; trustee Antioch Coll. Law, New Orleans chpt. Operation PUSH, 1981-84; pres. Louis A. Martinet Soc., 1959; active World's Fair, New Orleans, 1984, Civil Rights Movement, 1960-79; bd. dirs., mem. exec. com. Nat. Sr. Citizens Law Ctr., L.A., 1970-76, Criminal Justice Coordinating Com., UN Assn. New Orleans, 1980—; former mem. exec. bd. Nat. Bar Found.; mem. exec. com. Econ. Devel. Coun. Greater New Orleans; past chmn. Health Edn. Authority of La.; trustee, mem. exec. com. Dillard U.; former mem. bd. mgmt. Flint Goodridge Hosp.; former mem. adv. bd. League Women Voters Greater New Orleans; former mem. men's adv. bd. YWCA; trustee AME Ch., former connectional trustee; former chancellor New Orleans Fedn. Chs.; bd. trustees Crimestoppers of New Orleans; mem. Com. for a Better New Orleans; bd. dirs. Nat. Legal Aid and Defender Assn.; trustee Civil Justice Found.; served on over 50 bds., commns. 1st lt. AUS, 1943-47, PTO. Recipient Arthur von Briesen medal Disting. Svcs. Disadvantaged Ams. NLADA, 1971, Weiss award NCCJ, 1975, Brotherhood award NCCJ, 1976, Nat. Black Achievement award, 1979, Poor People's Banner award, 1979, William H. Hastie award, 1983, Outstanding Citizen award Kiwanis of Pontchartrain, 1986, Civil Justice award, 1989, Daniel E. Byrd award NAACP, 1991, A.P. Tureaud Meml. medal La. State NAACP, 1993; Revius O. Ortique Jr. Law Libr. named in his honor, Lafayette, La., 1988; named Outstanding Young Man Nat. Urban League, 1958, Outstanding Person in La. Inst. Human Understanding, 1976, Citizen of Yr. Shreveport, 1993. Mem. ABA (del., Legal Svcs. program, Nat. adv. coun., 1964-71, jud. divsn., Thurgood Marshal award 2000), Nat. Bar Assn. (pres. 1965-66, exec. bd., Raymond Pace Alexander award, jud. coun. 1987, William Hastie award 1982, Gertrude E. Rush award 1991, Thurgood Marshall award 2000), La. State Bar Assn. (former mem. ho. of dels., Lifetime Achievement award 1986, WTC award for Exceptional Internat. Distinction, 2001), Nat. Legal Aid and Defender Assn. (past pres., mem. exec. bd.), La. District Judges Assn., Am. Judicature Soc. (bd. dirs. 1975-79), Civil Justice Found. (trustee 1989-93), Louis A. Martinet Legal Soc., World Peace Through Law (charter mem.), Blue Key Honor Soc., Phi Delta Kappa, Alpha Kappa Delta. Home: 10 Park Island Dr New Orleans LA 70122-1229 *In 1989 the National Black Law Journal in cooperation with the UCLA Law Center published: Struggle: A Power Reserved to the People, which was distributed nationwide in commemoration of Black History month, the State of Louisiana thru the office of the Secretary of State has installed a life size portrait of Justice Ortique in the gallery of the State Archives, 1986-1994, 99. Appointed U.S. Alternate Representative to the 54th General Assembly of the United Nations, 2000. Delivered U.S. position on Taliban and terrorism before General Assembly. "With little or no effort on our part, life unfolds with opportunities and rewards, except that we permit our frailties to enslave our ambitions. I am grateful that there are only horizons.".*

ORTIZ, ALBERT, police chief; Joined San Antonio Police Dept., 1972, dep. chief police, 1994—99, chief of staff, 1999—2002, chief police, 2002—. Office: San Antonio Police Dept PO Box 839966 San Antonio TX 78283-3966

ORTIZ, ANGEL VICENTE, church administrator; b. L.A., Nov. 9, 1956; s. Benjamin and Petra (Santiago) O.; m. Michele Annette Gaunt, May 5, 1979; children: Angela Nicole, Michael David. BS in Bibl. Studies, Ft. Wayne (Ind.) Bible Coll., 1982. Ordained to ministry Christian and Missionary Alliance, 1987. Pastor, ch. planter Christian and Missionary Alliance, Chula Vista, Calif., 1983-90, supt. Spanish western dist. Escondido, Calif., 1991-96, also nat. conf. spkr., evangelist; asst. to the pres. for program devel. Nyack (N.Y.) Coll., 1996-97, v.p. student devel., dean students, 1997—2002; sr. pastor First Ch. Christian and Missionary Alliance, N.Y.C., 2002—. Republican. Mem. Christian And Missionary Alliance Ch. Avocations: camping, woodworking, refinishing, travel, teaching. E-mail: angelortiz@firstchurchnyc.org.

ORTIZ, ANTHONY, hotel executive; b. Bronx, Feb. 19, 1969; s. Tony Ortiz and Elizabeth Mercado; m. Iris Elizabeth Alvarado, July 24, 1994; children: Tristan, Tyler. Student, Rockland C.C., Camden County Coll. Mgr. ops. Park Ridge Marriott, NJ, 1994—96, Newport Marriott, RI, 1996—98; event mgr. Walt Disney World, Orlando, 1998—2000; mgr. ops. Marriott Hotels, Phila., 2000—01, Sodexho, Vourhees, NJ, 2001—; pres., founder Deep Blue Films, Blackwood, NJ, 2003—. Avocations: reading, writing, movies. Office: 524 Neptune Bay #5248 Saint Cloud FL 34769 Office Phone: 407-929-2164.

ORTIZ, DAVID (DAVID AMERICO ORTIZ ARIAS), professional baseball player; b. Santo Domingo, Dominican Republic, Nov. 18, 1975; Player Minn. Twins, 1997—2002, Boston Red Sox, 2003—. Named to Am. League All-Star Team, 2004. Office: Boston Red Sox 4 Yawkey Way Boston MA 02215-3496*

ORTIZ, FELIX W. state legislator; b. La Playa de Salinas, P.R. m. Elba Ortiz; children: Felix, Daniel, Alberto. Student, U. P.R.; BS in Bus. Adminstrn., Boricua Coll., 1983; M in Pub. Adminstrn., NYU, 1986. Sr. budget analyst Office of Mgmt. and Budget, Adminstrn. of Criminal Justice, N.Y.C., 1988-90; adminstrv. mgr. Office of Mgmt. and Budget, Office of Bronx Borough Pres., 1990-95; assemblyman dist. 51 N.Y. State Assembly, Albany, 1995—. Mem. Cmty. Bd. 7, Bklyn., chair pub. safety com.; pres. 33d St. Block Assn.; mem. 72d Precinct Cmty. Coun.; mem. parish coun. Our Lady of Perpetual Help; mem. parent edn. task force Diocese of Bklyn.; mem. Sunset Park Health coun. Luth. Med. Ctr. Served with U.S. Army, 1986-88.

ORTIZ, FERNANDO, JR., commissioner; b. Havana, Cuba, Dec. 2, 1951; came to the U.S., 1961; m. Frances K. Ortiz; children: William, Fernando III. Attended, Miami-Dade C.C., 1972—74, U. Miami, Coral Gables, Fla., 1974—75, Fla. Internat. U., Miami, 1975—76; MD, U. Centro Estudios Technicos, Santo Domingo, Dominican Republic, 1981; postgrad, Syracuse U., postgrad., 1998—. Mgr. Ortiz Transp., Miami, 1981-84; ptnr. Astrum, Syracuse, N.Y., 1984-91; bus. developer Rebuild Syracuse, Inc., 1991-92; coord. Urban Bus. Opportunity Ctr. City of Syracuse, 1992-96, sr. econ. devel. officer, 1996-2000, budget dir., 2000-01, commr. cmty. devel., 2001—. Mem. adv. bd. Greater Syracuse Small Bus. Loan Program, 1993-99; bd. dirs. Consol. Industries, Inc., Child Care coun. of Onondago County; mem. educare com. Success By Six, 2000. Sec. bd. dirs. Onondaga Spanish Action League, Syracuse, 1994-95, 2003, pres., 1996-2000; Cultural Resources Coun., 1997-2000; active Onondaga Citizens League, Syracuse, 1995; bd. dirs. Syracuse Neighborhood Housing Svcs., 1997-2000, Met. Water Bd., 1998—, Leadership Greater Syracuse, 2000—, Jubilee Homes, 2001—; corp. mem. United Way Ctrl. N.Y.; mem. bus. and industry adv. bd. Onondaga C.C.; mem. Leadership Greater Syracuse Class of '93, alumni bd. dirs., bd. mem., 2001—; active F.O.C.U.S. Greater Syracuse, 1997—; sec. Syracuse Urban Renewal Agy.; bd. dirs. Syracuse Econ. Devel. Corp. Named Min. Small Bus. Adv. of Yr., U.S. SBA, Syracuse, 1995. Mem. Thursday Morning Roundtable. Avocations: reading, gardening, music. Home: 1412 Lemoyne Ave Syracuse NY 13208-1339 Office: City of Syracuse Dept Cmty Devel 201 E Washington St Rm 612 Syracuse NY 13202 Office Phone: 315-448-8620. E-mail: fortiz@ci.syracuse.ny.us., fortiz@twcny.yr.com.

ORTIZ, FRANCIS VINCENT, JR., retired ambassador; b. Santa Fe, Mar. 14, 1926; s. Francis Vincent and Margaret Mary (Delgado) O.; m. Dolores Duke, May 2, 1953; children: Christina, Francis, Stephen, James. BS, Georgetown U., 1950, postgrad., 1951-53, U. Madrid, Spain, 1950, Am. U. Beirut, Lebanon, 1952; MS, George Washington U., 1967; LLD (hon.), U. N.Mex., 1986. Joined U.S. Fgn. Service, 1951; asst. officer charge Egyptian affairs State Dept., 1951-53; 3d sec. embassy Addis Ababa, Ethiopia, 1953—55; 2d sec. Am. embassy, Mexico City, 1955—57; spl. asst. to ops. coordinator Office Undersec. State, 1957-60, staff asst. to asst. sec. interam. affairs, 1960-61; spl. asst. Am. ambassador to Mexico, 1961-63; officer charge Spanish affairs State Dept., 1963-66; assigned Nat. War Coll., 1966; chief polit. sect. Am. embassy, Lima, Peru, 1967-70, dep. chief of mission Montevideo, Uruguay, 1970-72, charge' d'affairs, 1973; country dir. for Argentina, Uruguay and Paraguay, 1973-75; dep. exec. sec. Dept. State, 1975-77; amb. to Barbados and Grenada, spl. rep. to St. Lucia, Antigua, St. Vincent, St. Kitts, Domenica, 1977—79; U.S. amb. to Guatemala, 1979—80; spl. advisor for polit. affairs U.S. So. Command, Panama, 1980-81; U.S. amb. to Peru, 1981—83; to Argentina, 1983-86; diplomat-in-residence U. N.Mex., Santa Fe, 1986-88; spl. asst. to under sec. of state for mgmt., 1988-90; ret., 1990. Regent Mus. of N. Mex., 1999. With USAAF, 1944-46. Decorated Air medal; Knight of Malta; recipient Honor award Dept. State, 1952, Superior Service award, 1964, Unit Superior Service award, 1973, Meritorious Civilian Svc. award U.S. Sec. of Def. 1981; Orden del Quetzal (Guatemala), 1980; Gran Cruz Merito Civil award (Spain), 1980; Gran Cruz Orden de Mayo (Argentina), 1991; U.S., Mexican Presdl. Chamizal Commemorative medals, 1964. Mem. Am. Fgn. Service Assn., Sigma Chi. Roman Catholic. E-mail: fvo14@aol.com.

ORTIZ, GUILLERMO, banker; BA, Universidad Nacional Autonoma de Mexico; PhD Economics, Stanford U. Economist Ministry of the Presidency of Mex., 1971—72; mgr. & deputy mgr. Econ. Rsch. Bureau of Bank of Mex., 1977—84; exec. dir. IMF, 1984—88; undersecretary of finance and public credit, 1988—94; sec. telecommunications and transportation Zedillo Adminstrn.; sec. finance and public credit Mexican Fed. Govt., 1994—97; gov. Bank of Mex., 1998—. Instr. Univ. in Mex. and U.S. Author: books and papers on econ. and finance in specialized jour. and mag. Mem.: G-30. Office: Governor Banco de Mexico Avda 5 de Mayo 2 Centro 06059 Mexico City Mexico Office Phone: 5-237-2030. E-mail: gortiz@banxico.org.mx.

ORTIZ, JAIME, business educator; b. Santiago, Chile, Jan. 20, 1958; s. Sergio Ortiz and Pilar Arizabalo; m. Pamela Caballero, June 20, 1987; children: Maria Pamela, Maria Alejandra. BSc, U. Chile, Santiago, 1980, Diploma, 1981; MA, Inst. Social Studies, The Hague, The Netherlands, 1988; PhD, Va. Poly. Inst. and State U., 1993. Freelance bus. and econ. cons., Santiago, 1980—82; econ. analyst Inter-Am. Inst. Cooperation on Agriculture, Ecuador, 1983—85; mgmt. advisor Ecumenical Ch. Loan Fund, Quito, 1985—87; rsch. asst. dept. applied econ. Va. Tech. U., 1989—93; team leader Euroconsult B.V., Quito, Ecuador, 1994—95; sr. advisor COASER, Quito, 1995—96; internat. coord. Pre-investment Orgn. OPALC, Quito, 1996—97; gen. coord. Intern Am. Devel. Bank, Quito, 1997; faculty, dir. internat. programs Fla. Atlantic U. Coll. Bus., Boca Raton, 1998—. Sr. mgmt. cons. Abastefrut S.A., Santiago, 1994, World Bank, Quito, 1995, GTZ gmbH, Quito, 1995, Inter Am. Devel. Bank, Caracas, Venezuela, 1996 Author: Small-scale Agriculture: Its Evolution in Ecuador, 1988, Small and Medium Enterprises as an Alternative to Macroeconomic Adjustments, 1997; contbr. articles to profl. jours., including Jour. Internat. Devel., Econ. Devel., Microfin., Am. Acad. Bus., Food Policy. Roman Catholic. Office: Fla Atlantic U Coll Bus 777 Glades Rd Boca Raton FL 33431-0991

ORTIZ, JAY RICHARD GENTRY, lawyer; b. Washington, Mar. 21, 1945; s. Charles and Catherine Gentry (Candlin) Ortiz; m. Lois Wright Hatcher Greer, June 12, 1982. BA, Yale U., 1967; postgrad., Stanford U., 1967—68; JD, U. N.Mex., 1972. Bar: N.Mex. 1973, Mo. 1978, Tenn. 1982, Ga. 1991, U.S. Dist. Ct. N.Mex. 1973, U.S. Ct. Appeals (10th cir.) 1973, U.S. Supreme Ct. 1977, U.S. Dist. t. (we. dist.) Mo. 1978, U.S. Dist. t. (no. dist.) Ga. 1991, U.S. Ct. Appeals (8th cir.) 1978, U.S. Ct. Appeals (11th cir.) 1991. Assoc. Rodey, Dickason, Sloan, Akin & Robb, Albuquerque, 1972—75; ptnr. Knight, Sullivan, Villella, Skarsgard & Michael, Albuquerque, 1975—77; litigation atty. Monsanto Co., St. Louis, 1977—81; environ. atty. Eastman Kodak Co., Kingsport, Tenn., 1981—84; sr. atty. AT&T, Atlanta, 1984—91; gen. counsel AMS Group, Inc., 1991—96, 1998—2002, ConsultaAmerica Internat., 1994—97, Vision Net, Inc., 1994—, Cross Constrn. Internat., Inc., 1996—97, Ophthalmic Solutions LLC, 1996—97, Univest Ltd., 1996—97; pres. VMS, Inc., 1994—2002; asst. coun. Nextel Communications, 2001—. Precinct vice chmn. Dem. Party, Albuquerque, 1971—77. Lt. (j.g.) USN, 1969—70. Mem.: ABA, English Speaking Union, Tenn. Bar Assn., Mo. Bar Assn., N.Mex. Bar Assn., Ga. Bar Assn., Yale Club of Ga., Order of the Coif, Delta Theta Phi (tribune 1972—77). Episcopalian. Home: 1000 Buckingham Cir NW Atlanta GA 30327-2704

ORTIZ, LORI J. painter, writer; d. Alan Stanley and Phyllis Audrey Galowitz. BFA, Alfred U., N.Y., 1977. Exhibited in group shows at Pierogi 2000 Gallery, Bklyn., 1997—, Sideshow Gallery, 2003; writer, critic N.Y. Arts Mag., WWW.offoffoff.com Performance Rsch. Jour., 1997; contbr. articles to profl. jours. Recipient Pollock-Krasner Award, Pollock-Krasner Found., 1989; grantee NEA/NY Times fellowship, Nat. Inst. Arts Journalism, 2004. Democrat. Home: 14 N Henry St #3R Brooklyn NY 11222 E-mail: loriortiz@earthlink.net.

ORTIZ, RAPHAEL MONTAÑEZ, performance artist, educator; b. Bklyn., Jan. 30, 1934; s. Joseph H. and Eusabia (Velazquez) O. BS, MFA, Pratt Inst., 1964; MEd, Columbia U., 1974, EdD, 1982. Instr. grad. art faculty Tchr. Coll. Columbia U., N.Y.C., 1967; instr. art NYU, N.Y.C., 1968; adj. prof. art Fordham U., N.Y.C., 1971, C. W. Post Coll., L.I., N.Y., 1971; adj. prof. art Livingston Coll. Rutgers U., New Brunswick, N.J., 1971, assoc. prof. art Livingston Coll., 1972, assoc. prof. grad. and undergrad. faculty Mason Gross Sch. Arts, 1972, prof. I Mason Gross Sch. Arts, 1991—. Panelist Sch. Visual Arts Nat. Conf. on Edn. of Artist, 1990, Artist as Activist, Mus. Modern Art, 1993, Performance is Dead Long Live Performance, Cleve. Ctr. for Contemporary Art, 1994, Internat. Exposition Art Miami Art and Tech., 1995, Conversation on Art, Destructivism in the 1960's, Whitney Mus. Am. Art, NYC, 1997, others; panelist, moderator The Artist in Multiculturalism and Art History, Alternative Mus., Soho, N.Y.C., 1992, others; The Robert Flaherty seminar spkr. Its All Digital, Wells Coll., Aurora, N.Y., 1993; lectr., presenter in field. Performed at Piano Destruction concert, BBC, London, 1966, Mother Father, Mercury Theater, London, 1966, Fordham U., NYC, 1967, Ecce Homo Gallery, NYC, 1967, Bitter End Cafe, NYC, 1967, Johnny Carson Show, 1968, Riverside Ch., NYC, 1968, Theater Ritual, Middle Atlantic States Am. Theater Assn., Temple U., Phila., 1970, Crossing, Mime Theater, NYC, 1976, San Francisco Art Inst., 1982, UCLA, 1985, Twin Palms Gallery, San Francisco, 1985, Mus. Barrio, NYC, 1988, Conz Archival Gallery, Verona, Italy, 1986, Atelier Sommering, Ko, 1990, Antiteatro U. P.R., Cleve. Ctr. Contemporary Art, 1994, Snug Harbor Cultural Ctr., S.I., NY, 1995, Whitney Mus. Am. Art, NYC, 1996, Mus. Contemporary Art, LA, 1998; co-exec. dir., participant Art and the Invisible Reality Internat. Symposium, Munich, 1988; organizer, participant Internat. Symposium Art and the Invisible-Reality, USA, Franklin-Furnace Mus., NYC, Rutgers U., New Brunswick, NJ, 1989, Vision Quest Gallery Rem, Vienna, Austria, 1988, Vision Quest II Bloomfield Coll., NJ, 1989, Alternative Mus., NYC, 1989, Exhbn. Kölnischer Kunstverein, Köln, Germany, Kunst Müller Köln, 1989, Atelier Eva Ohlaw Bildskulpturenaktionmusik, Köln, 1990, Decade Show Dance Theater, NYC, New Mus., NYC, Mus. Contemporary Hispanic Art, NYC, Harlem Mus. Contemporary Art, NYC, 1990, Alternative Mus., Soho, NYC, 1992, Mus. Modernerkunst, Stiftung Ludwig, Vienna, 1992, I.S.D.N. Video Conf. Kôlin and Kassel Germany, Electronic Cafe Gallery, Kassel, 1993, Cleve. Ctr. Contemporary Art, 1994, Mus. Barrio, NYC, 1994; (video) Whitney Mus. Am. Art, NYC, 1995-97, Mus. Contemporary Art, Tokyo, Stadt Nurenburg Kunsthalle Nurenberg, Germany, 1999—; one-man shows include Fordham U., NYC, 1967, Rene Gallery, Amsterdam, Holland, 1988, Mus. Barrio, NYC, 1988, Galerie David, Bielefeld, Germany, 1992, works Children of Treblinka in Memorium, Archaeological Find No. 3, Kunsthalle, Kôlin, 1993, Mus. Modern Art, NYC, 1993, Media Johnson Mus. Cornell U., Ithaca, NY, 1993, Whitney Mus. Am. Art, NYC, 1993, 96-97, Mitchell Algus Gallery, NYC, 1996, 2000, DaVinci Kabbala Vision, 2000, Mariboe Gallery, 2001; exhibited in group shows at Whitney Mus. Am. Art, NYC, 1965, 95, Mus. Modern Art, NYC, 1966, Franklin Furnace Mus., NYC; participated in Internat. Destruction in Art Symposium, London, 1966, Finch Coll. Mus. Art, 1968, Everson Mus. Art, Syracuse, NY, 1973, Chgo. Mus. Contemporary Art, 1979, Ancient Roots New Visions, Palacio de Mineria Mus., Mexico City, 1980, Walters Gallery Rutgers U., 1982, Mariboe Gallery, 2001, Mason Gross Sch. Arts Gallery, 2001-02, Rutgers U., New Brunswick, 2002, Ken Keleba Gallery, NYC, 2002; (computer art) Paul Robeson Gallery, Rutgers U., 1983, Salem Syndrome, Tamasulo Gallery, NJ, 1985, Francesco Conz Archival Gallery, Verona, Italy, 1986, Bonnefanten Mus., Maastricht, Holland, 1986, De-Haag, Germany, 1986, Mülheim Mus., Germany, 1986, Berlin Internat. Video and Film Festival, Coll. Art, Gwent, Wales, Eng., 1986-87, DiMaggio Mus., Milan, 1989, Ateliér Sommering, Kô, 1990, Estacion Plaza de Armas, Seville, Spain, 1992, The Kitchen, NYC, El Mus. Barrio, 1995; Infermental 9, Internat., Video Mag., Dance No. 6, 1989, Barcelona Biennale, Spain, 1989, Beograd, Yugoslavia, 1989, Kriens Videodrom, Switzerland, 1989, Vienna, Austria, 1990, Internat. Berlin Video and Film Festival, 1990, 94, Leningrad, Riga-Cine Fantom, USSR, 1990, Median Werk Statt, Vienna, 1991, Stadtisches Kunstmus., Bonn, 1990, Median Operative, Internat. Video Festival, Berlin, 1992, Bonn, 1993, Madrid, 1993, Internat. Video and TV Festival Montbeliard, France, 1992, Mus. Modern Art, Video Works Latin Am. Artists, Filmreferet Forum Stadpark, Graz, Austria, 1994, Assn. Italiana Cinema d'Essai, Milan, 1995, MTV Art Breaks, Rotterdam Fest. Behind it All, Holland, Mostra de Video Ind., Barcelona, Mediopolis, Berlin, Pandimonium, London, Cidade de Vigo, Spain, Viper, Luzern, Switzerland, Fest. Internat. Nouveau Cinema, Montreal, Internat. Audio Visual Exptl. Fest., Arnheim, Germany, Fest. Internat. Video and Art Electronicas Buenos Aires (1st prize Exptl. Vido Conversation 1996), New Visions Internat. Fest. Film, Glasgow, Glasgow Mus. Modern Art, Royal Mus. Fine Arts, Copenhagen, Cinema Video Bienniale, De Lyon, France, 1996, Video Installation Performance, Trinity Video/Inter Access/V-Tape, Toronto, Canada, 1996, Guggenheim Mus., NYC, 1997, Impakt Festival, Utrecht, Netherlands, 1998, 3rd Werkleitz Biennial, Germany, 1998, London Electronic Arts, 1998, Berkeley (Calif.) Art Mus./Pacific Film Archive, 1998, InVideo Exptl. & Art Video, Milan, 1999, OVNI Video Festival, Barcelona, 1999, Transmediale, Internat. Media Arts Festival, Berlin, 1999; represented in collections: Mus. Modern Art, Whitney Mus. Am. Art, NY, Menil Mus., Houston, Chrysler Mus., Va., Everson Mus., Syracuse, NY, Mus. Barrio, NYC, Everson Mus., Syracuse, Friedricheshof Mus., Zurndorf, Austria, Mus. Modern Art, Brussels, Ludwig Mus., Cologne, Germany, Centre Georges Pompidou, Paris, Stadishces Kunst Mus., Bonn, Neuer Belriner Kunstverein, Berlin, 1994, AIACE Assn. Italiana Cinema d'Essai, Milan, Toyo Media Links, Tokyo, Ctr. for Electronics and Media, Karlsruhe, Germany, Mus. Contemporary Art, LA. Recipient Cert. of Outstanding Achievement in Multicultural Edn., NJ Dept. Higher Edn., 1993, Grand prize Regime Lomabdia, prize Lago Maggiore XIV Festival Internat., Locarno, Switzerland, 1993 Mem. Mus. Computer Art (founder, pres. 1984), Hispanic Assn. Higher Edn. (N.J.), Art Educators N.J., Coll. Art Assn., Assn. Rsch. and Enlightenment. Office: Mason Gross Sch Vis Arts New St & Livingston Ave New Brunswick NJ 08904 Fax: 732-932-2217.

ORTIZ, SOLOMON P. congressman; b. Robstown, Tex., June 3, 1937; children: Yvette, Solomon P. Student, Del Mar Coll., Corpus Christi, Tex., 1965—67; cert., Inst. Applied Sci., Chgo., 1962; student, Nat. Sheriff's Tng. Inst., Los Angeles, 1977. Constable Nueces County, Tex., 1965—68, commr., 1969-76, sheriff, 1977—83; mem. 98th-108th Congresses from 27th Tex. dist., Washington, 1983—, ranking mem. ho. armed svcs. readiness. Mem. subcoms. for resources com.: fisheries, wildlife & oceans, energy & mineral resources; mem. Congrl. Hispanic Caucus; co-chair Congrl. Border Caucus. Served with U.S. Army, 1960-62. Named Man of Yr., Internat. Order Foresters, 1981, one of Hispanic Bus. 100 Most Influential Hispanics in U.S., Hispanic Bus. Mag., 1999. Mem. Nat. Sheriff's Assn., Sheriff's Assn. Tex. Democrat. Office: US Ho Reps 2470 Rayburn Bldg Washington DC 20515-4327

ORTIZ, WILLIAM, composer, music educator; b. Salinas, P.R., Mar. 30, 1947; s. William and Guillermina (Alvarado) O.; m. Candida, Mar. 26, 1988; children: Aleyda Enid, Nicole Samara, Amaya E. MusB, P.R. Conservatory of Music, 1976; MA in Composition, SUNY, Stony Brook, 1978; PhD in Composition, SUNY, Buffalo, 1983. Cons./auditor N.Y. State Arts Coun., N.Y.C., 1976-86; asst. dir. Black Mountain Coll. II, Buffalo, 1982-86; music advisor P.R. Symphony Orch., San Juan, 1988-90; prof. music U. P.R., Bayamon, 1986—; dir. humanities dept. U. P.R., Bayamon, 1997—. Dir./conductor, U. P.R. Band, Bayamon, 1986—, Grammy award nomination, 2001; music critic San Juan Star, 1993-94; composer-in-residence for Music-in-Motion program Atlantic Ctr. for the arts, 1996-97; artist-in-residence René Marquez Mid. Sch., 1999-2000. Composer: (music) 124 E. 107th St., 1979 (Felipe Gutierrez Internat. Composition prize 1980), Llego la Banda, 1984 (Composers Guild Internat. Composition prize 1985), Dos Gritos y una Cancion, 1986 (Composition award Ateneo Puertorriqueno 1989), Tropicalizacion, 1999 (Grammy nomination 2001); composer more than 100 works for orchestra, chamber groups, opera, others. Assoc. mem. Hispanic Womens League, Buffalo, 1982-86. Recipient commns. P.R. Symphony, San Juan, 1990, Camerata Caribe, San Juan, 1990, grants Inst. of Puerto Rican Culture, San Juan, 1990, P.R. Community Found., San Juan, 1990, Casals Festival, 1995, Orquesta Baja California, Mex., 1999, 2001; guest composer Festival Musica Nova, Sao Paulo, Brazil, 1988, Festival Latinoamericano de Musica, Caracas, Venezuela, 1991, 92, 94, 98, Am. Composers Orch. "Sonidos de las Americas," 1997, VIII Tribuna Musical para América Latina, Mex., 1997. Mem. Am. Composers Alliance, Am. Music Ctr., Coll. Music Soc., Composers Alliance of Buffalo (pres. 1984), Assn. de Compositores Puertorriquenos. Home: Plaza de La Fuente 1275 Calle España Toa Alta PR 00953 Office: U PR Bayamon Gardens Sta Bayamon PR 00959 Office Phone: 787-786-2885.

ORTIZ-BUTTON, OLGA, social worker; b. Chgo., July 12, 1953; d. Luis Antonio and Pura (Acevedo) Ortiz; m. Dennis Vesley, Aug. 11, 1973 (div. 1976); m. Randall Russell Button, Nov. 3, 1984 (div. Oct. 1993); children: Josh, Jordan, Eli. BA, U. Ill., 1975; MSW, Western Mich. U., 1981. Cert. social worker, sch. social worker. Social svcs. dir. Champaign County Nursing Home, Urbana, Ill., 1976; social svcs. and activity dir. Lawton (Mich.) Nursing Home, 1977; job developer Southwestern Mich. Indian Ctr., Watervliet, 1977-78; staff asst. New Directions Alcohol Treatment Ctr., Kalamazoo, 1978; counselor, instr. Alcohol Hwy. Safety, Kalamazoo, 1978-79; clin. social worker Mecosta County Community Mental Health, Big Rapids, Mich., 1981-84; program dir. substance abuse Sr. Svcs., Inc., Kalamazoo, 1984-85; sch. social worker Martin (Mich.) Pub. Schs., 1985-96, J.C. Huizenga Charter Schs., Grand Rapids, Mich., 1996—; owner, therapist Plainwell (Mich.) Counseling Ctr., 1989-98; co-dir. Everlasting Covenant Ministry, Kalamazoo, 1997—2004; owner Christian Counseling Ctr., 2003. S.W. cons. Med. Pers. Pool, 1993-94; founder, owner Christian Coun. Ctr., 2003—. Vol. social worker Hospice-Wings of Hope, Plainwell, 1984-85; mem. Hospice Quality Rev. Bd., 1993-96, supporter Students Against Aparteid South Africa, Kalamazoo, 1979-81; mem. World Vision and Countertop Ptnr., 1984-90; mem., vol. Christian Life Ctr., Kalamazoo, 1996; sponsor, vol. People for Ethical Treatment of Animals, 1986-91; vol. helper Sparkies for Awana Club Ch., 1989-95; consortium mem. Mich. Post Adoption Svc. System 1994-97; co-founder Everlasting Covenant Ministry, Kalamazoo, 1997; sch. social worker Nat. Heritage Acads., 1997—. Named Rural Mental Health grant, NIMH, 1979—81. Mem.: NASW, Nat. Assn. Christian Social Workers, Am. Assn. Christian Counselors, Mich. Assn. Sch. Social Workers. Avocations: jogging, plants, cross country skiing. Home: 1339 Cadet Ln Kalamazoo MI 49009-1838 Office Phone: 269-343-2117. E-mail: obutton@ureach.com.

ORTIZ MENA, ANTONIO, banker; b. Parral, Chihuahua, Mexico, 1912; Grad., Sch. Law, Nat. Autonomous U. Mexico; postgrad., Sch. Fine Arts and Philosophy, Sch. Econs.; Dr. h.c, U. Guadalajara, Mex. Chief legal counsel, then departmental rep. Mixed Agrarian Commn., Dept. Fed. Dist., Govt. Mexico, 1932-38; dir. Property Nationalization Svc.; then chief legal counsel Office of Atty. Gen., 1940-45; 1st dir. gen. professions Ministry Pub. Edn., 1945-46, dep. dir. gen., trust rep., then chmn. Banco Nacional de Obras y Servicios Públicos, 1947-52; chmn., chief exec. officer Mexican Social Security Inst., 1952-58; chmn. Permanent Inter-Am. Social Security Com., 1955-59; sec. fin. and pub. credit Govt. Mexico, 1958-70; pres. Inter-Am. Devel. Bank, Washington, 1971-88; dir. gen. Banco Nacional de Mex., 1988-91. Mem. Polit. Def. Com. of Am. Continent, World War II; cons. Mexican del. Inter-Am. Conf. to Consider Problems of War and Peace, Chapultepec, Mex., 1945; gov. for Mex. IMF, World Bank, Internat. Devel. Assn., Internat. Finance Corp., 1959-70; founding Mexican gov. Inter-Am. Devel. Bank, 1960-70, chmn. bd. govs., 1966-67; Mexico rep. Inter-Am. Econ. and Social Coun. at Ministerial Level, 1961-70, pres., 1962-63; chmn. bd. dirs. Nacional Financiera, Altos Hornos de Mex., Compañía Mexicana de Luz y Fuerza Motriz, Compañía Nacional de Subsistencias Populares, Industria Petroquimica Nacional, Guanos y Fertilizantes de Mex.; vice chmn. bd. dirs. Petroleos Mexicanos, Ferrocarriles Nacionales de Mex. Author: El Desarrollo Estabilizador, 1969, Finanzas Publicas de Mexico, 1969, Development in Latin-America, 1971-75, 76-80, El Desarrollo Estabilizador: reflexiones sobra una epoca, 1998. Decorated grand cross Order of Crown of Belgium; grand officer Legion of Honor; grand cross Nat. Order of Merit France; grand cross Order of Merit Fed. Republic Germany; Order of Flag with Banner Yugoslavia; grand cross Nat. Order of So. Cross Brazil; grand cross Order Orange-Nassau Netherlands; grand cross Order of Merit Bernardo O'Higgins Chile; others. Mem. Mexican Hwy. Assn. (life), AIM (coun. of presidents).

ORTLIP, PAUL DANIEL, artist; b. Englewood, NJ, May 21, 1926; s. Henry Willard and Aimee (Eschner) O.; m. Mary Louise Krueger, June 1981 (dec. May 2001); children from previous marriage: Carol, Kathleen, Sharon (dec.), Danielle (dec.), Michelle. Diploma, Houghton Acad., 1944; student, Art Students League, 1947—49; diploma, Acad. la Grande Chaumiere, Paris, 1950; DFA (hon.), Houghton Coll., 1988. Tchr. Fairleigh Dickinson U., Teaneck, NJ, 1956-68, artist in residence, curator Rutherford, NJ, 1968-72. Official USN artist on assignment, Cuban missile crisis, Fla., 1963, Gemini 5 Recovery, Atlantic Ocean, 1965, Vietnam, 1967, Apollo 12 recovery, Pacific Ocean, 1969, Apollo 17 recovery, Pacific Ocean, 1972, Internat. Naval Rev., NY harbor, 1976, USCG Sta., Key West, Fla., 1985; mem. USN Art Coop. and Liason Com. Exhbns. include Salonde L'Art Libre, Paris, 1950, Nat. Acad. Design, 1952, Allied Artists of Am., NYC, Acad. Sci., Rundell Gallery, Rochester, NY, Montclair Art Mus., Hist. Mus, Lima, Ohio, Butler Art Inst., Youngstown, Ohio, Fine Arts Gallery, San Diego, State Capitol Bldg., Sacramento, Capitol Mus., Olympia, Wash., Mus. Gt. Plains, Lawton, Okla., Witte Meml. Mus., San Antonio, Nimitz Meml. Mus., Fredericksberg, Tex., Pentagon Collection of Fine Arts, James Hunt Barker Galleries, Palm Beach, Fla., Nantucket, Mass., NYC, Smithsonian Inst., Gallerie Vollem Breuse, Biarritz, France, Galerie Mouffe, Paris, Guggenheim Gallery, London, Wickersham Gallery, NYC, Soc. Illustrators, NYC; retrospective exhbn. Bergen Cmty. Mus., Paramus, NJ 1970, The Curzon Gallery, 1987, 88, 89, 93, 2003, Ardennes et de l'Eifel, Charleville Mézières, France, June-Sept. 1990; represented permanent collections including Salmagundi Club NYC, Houghton (NY) Coll., Portrait Meml. J.F. Kennedy Libr., Fairleigh-Dickinson U., Nat. Air and Space Mus., Smithsonian Inst., Intrepid Sea-Air Space Mus., NYC, Hist. Mural Visitors Ctr., Palisades Interstate Pk., Ft. Lee, NJ, Vets. Med. Ctr., East Orange, NJ, USN Exhbn. Ctr., Washington Navy Yard, Am. Coll. Clin. Pharmacology, NYC, NJ U. Dentistry & Medicine, Newark, Bergen County Ct. House, Hackensack, NJ, Dickinson Coll., Carlisle, Pa., George Washingtogn Meml. Pk., Paramus, Marietta (Ohio) Coll., Mcpl. Bldg., Ft. Lee, Navy League U.S., Arlington, Va., Nat. Archives and Records Adminstrn., Washington, (mural) Pub. Libr., Fort Lee, Bush Presdl. Libr., College Station, Tex., Underwater Demolition Team Seal Mus., Fort Pierce, Fla. Served to sgt. U.S. Army, 1944-47, ETO, PTO, 1946-47. Recipient 1st prize Am. Artists Profl. League State Exhibit NJ chpt., Paramus, 1960, 1st prize U.S. Armed Forces Exhibit Far East, Seoul, Korea, Tokyo, 1946, Franklin Williams award, Salmagundi Club, NY, 1967, Outstanding Achievement award for oil painting, USN, 1968, Artist of Yr. award, Hudson Artists, Jersey City Mus., 1970, Statue of Victory World Culture prize, Academia Italia, Parma, 1982, Men of Achievement medal Cambridge, Eng., 1990, Connaissance de Notre Europe Gold medal Charleville-Mézières, France, 1990. Mem. Allied Artists Am. (art coop. and liaison com. with USN), Nat. Soc. Mural Painters, Nat. Soc. Arts and Letters, Bergen County Artists Guild (pres. 1960-62), Portrait Soc. Am., Inc., Artists Fellowship, Inc., USCG Art Program, Art Students League NY (life), Navy League U.S., VFW (life), Am. Legion, Salmagundi Club (NYC, art chmn. 1979-81), Gov.'s of the Palm Beaches Club (Fla.). Home: 2917 S Ocean Blvd Apt 703 Highland Beach FL 33487-1836 Office: c/o The Curzon Gallery 501 E Camino Real Boca Raton FL 33432-6127

ORTMAN, ELDON E. entomologist, educator; b. Marion, S.D., Aug. 11, 1934; s. Emil and Kathryn (Tieszen) O.; m. Margene Adrian, June 27, 1957; children— Karen, Connie, Nancy. AB, Tabor Coll., 1956; MS, Kansas State U., 1957, PhD, 1963. Rsch. entomologist USDA, No. Grain Insects Rsch. Lab., Brookings, S.D., 1961-68, dir., leader investigations, 1968-72; asst. prof. entomology S.D. State U., Brookings, 1961-63, assoc. prof., 1963-68, prof., 1968-72; asst. Entomology Rsch. Divsn. Office, Beltsville, Md., 1971; prof. entomology Purdue U., West Lafayette, Ind., 1972-89, head dept. entomology, 1972-89; assoc. dir. Ind. Agrl. Rsch. Programs, 1989—2001. Fellow AAAS; mem. Entomol. Soc. Am., Phi Kappa Phi, Gamma Sigma Delta, Sigma Xi. Achievements include research in plant resistance to insects and pest mgmt. Home: 3805 W Capilano Dr West Lafayette IN 47906-8881 E-mail: eeo@aes.purdue.edu.

ORTMAN, GEORGE EARL, artist; b. Oakland, Calif., Oct. 17, 1926; s. William Thomas and Anna Katherine (Noll) O.; m. Conni Whidden, Aug. 5, 1960 (dec.); 1 stepson, Roger Graham Whidden. Student, Calif. Coll. Arts and Crafts, 1947-49, Atelier Stanley William Hayter, 1949, Acad. Andre L'Hote, Paris, 1949-50, Hans Hoffman Sch. Art, 1949-50. Co-founder Tempo Playhouse, N.Y.C., 1954; Instr. painting and drawing NYU, 1962-65; co-chmn. fine arts Sch. Visual Arts N.Y.C., 1963-65; artist-in-residence Princeton U., 1966-69, Honolulu Acad. Art, 1969; head painting dept. Cranbrook Acad. Art, Bloomfield Hills, Mich., 1970-92. One-man exhbns. include Tanager Gallery, 1954, Wittenborn Gallery, 1955, Stable Gallery, 1957, 60, Howard Wise Gallery, 1962, 63, 64, 66, 69, Gimpel-Weitzenhoffer Gallery, 1972 (all N.Y.C.), Swetzoff Gallery, Boston, 1961-62, Fairleigh Dickinson U., 1962, Mirvish Gallery, Toronto, Can., 1964, Walker Art Center, Mpls., 1965, Milw. Art Center, 1966, Dallas Mus. Art, 1966, Portland Mus. Art, 1966, Akron Inst. Art, 1966, U. Chgo., 1967, Princeton U. Art Mus., 1967, Honolulu Acad. Art, 1969, Reed Coll., 1970, Cranbrook Acad. Art, 1970, 92, Indpls. Mus. Art, 1971, J.L. Hudson Gallery, Detroit, 1971, Gimpel-Weitzenhoffer, N.Y.C., 1972, 73, Gertrude Kasle Gallery, Detroit, 1976, Lee Hoffman Gallery, Detroit, 1977, Flint (Mich.) Mus. Art, 1977; other one-man exhbns. include Cranbrook Mus. Art, 1982; exhibited numerous group shows including Whitney Mus. Am. Art Annual, 1962, 63, 64, 65, 67, 73, Carnegie Internat., Pitts., 1964, 67, 70, Jewish Mus., N.Y.C., 1964, Corcoran Mus., Washington, 1964, others; represented permanent collections, Walker Art Center, Mpls., Mus. Modern Art, Whitney Mus. Am. Art, (both N.Y.C.), Guggenheim Mus., N.Y.C., Albright-Knox Mus., Buffalo, NYU, Christian Theol. Sem., Indpls., Indpls. Mus. Art, Cleve. Mus. Art, Mus. Am. Art, Washington, Honolulu Acad. Art, Newark Mus. Art, Container Corp. Am., Chgo. Ind. U. Music Bldg., Wausau (Wis.) Hosp. Center, Unitarian Ch., Princeton, Mfr. Hanover Trust Bldg., Albert Kahn & Assos., Detroit, Renaissance Center, Detroit, Mich. State Univ. Performing Arts Ctr., East Lansing, Detroit Inst. Arts. Guggenheim fellow, 1965-66; Ford Found. grantee, 1966; One of five Am. artists selected for 1965 Japanese Bi-ann.; recipient Gov. N.J.'s Purchase award 2d ann. exhbn. art, 1967; Best of Show Religion in Art Exhbn., Birmingham, Ala., 1966 Mem. Nat. Acad. of Design. also: Tim Hill Gallery 1527E 72d St Apt 12H New York NY 10021

ORTMEYER, CARL EDWARD, retired demographer; b. Charles City, Iowa, Mar. 12, 1915; s. Arthur Herman and Sarah Emilie (Stoeber) O.; m. Anne Babuska O'Brien, Aug. 3, 1947 (dec. Dec. 15, 1995); 1 child, Kerry Michael; m. Ruth Forberg, Oct. 5, 1996. BA, U. Iowa, 1939, MS, Iowa State U., 1948, PhD in Rural Sociology, Demography, 1954. Rsch. assoc. bur. pub. health econs. Sch. Pub. Health U. Mich., Ann Arbor, 1954—56; sociologist Legis. Reference Svc., Libr. Congress, Washington, 1956—57; rsch. assoc. Social Security Adminstrn. U.S. Dept. HEW, 1957—58; rsch. assoc. Sch. Medicine Howard U., 1958—59; demographer Nat. Ctr. Health, Statistics Pub. Health Svc. U.S. Dept. HEW, 1959—68, demographer Nat. Inst. Occpl. Safety and Health CDC, 1968—80. Vol. caregiver Benedictine Nursing Ctr., Mt. Angel, Oreg., 1990-96, Wesley Homes Health Ctr., Des Moines, Wash., 1996—; mem. Wesley Found., Ams. for Democratic Action. Sgt. U.S. Army, 1941-45. Travel grantee London Sch. Econs. Rockefeller Found., 1969. Fellow APHA AAAS; mem. N.Y. Acad. Sci. Democrat. Mem. United Meth. Ch. Avocation: dance. Home: 816 S 216th St Apt 211 Des Moines WA 98198-6332 E-mail: rortmeyer@aol.com.

ORTNER, DONALD J. biological anthropologist, educator; b. Stoneham, Mass., Aug. 23, 1938; s. A.W. and Marie B. (Schweizer) O.; m. Joyce E. Walker, Sept. 4, 1960; children: Donald J. Ortner Jr., Allison A. May, Karen L. Ortner. BA, Columbia Union Coll., 1960; MA, Syracuse U., 1967; PhD, U. Kans., 1970; DSc (hon.), U. Bradford, England, 1995. Asst. curator Smithsonian Instn., Washington, 1969-71, assoc. curator, 1971-76, curator, 1976—, chmn. anthropology, 1988-92; acting dir. Nat. Mus. Natural History, Washington, 1994-96. Vis. prof. U. Bradford, 1988—; pres. Paleopathology Assn., 1999—2001. Author: (book) Identification of Pathological Conditions in Human Skeletal Remains, 1981, 2d edit., 2003; editor: How Humans Adapt, 1983; co-editor: Human Paleopathology, 1991. Mem. Am. Assn. Phys. Anthropology (mem. exec. com. 1987-90), Internat. Skeletal Soc., Paleopathology Assn. Office: Smithsonian Inst Nat Mus Natural History 10th & Constitution Ave NW Washington DC 20560-0001 Business E-Mail: ortner.don@nmnh.si.edu.

ORTNER, EVERETT HOWARD, magazine editor, writer; b. Lowell, Mass., Aug. 25, 1919; s. Herman and Anne (Ehrenhaus) O.; m. Evelyn Frances Gelbman, Jan. 1, 1953. BA, U. Ark., 1939. Editor Popular Publs., N.Y.C., 1946-52; assoc. editor Popular Sci., N.Y.C., 1953-56, copy chief, 1956-70, group editor, 1970-76, mng. editor, 1976-80, editor, 1980-85. Pres. Brownstone Revival Coalition N.Y., 1968-76, chmn., 1986—; founder, pres. Back to the City, Inc., N.Y.C., 1974-83, chmn. bd., 1983—; v.p. L.I. Hist. Soc., Bklyn., 1979-83; chmn. bd Preservation Vols. Inc., 2000—. Lt. U.S. Army, 1942-46, ETO. Recipient Cinderella award Bklyn. Union Gas Co., 1978, Honor citation Borough Pres. Bklyn., 1983, Disting. Citizen award City Louisville, 1979, Quality of Life award Kings County Hosp. Ctr., Bklyn., 1976, Spirit of Life award N.Y. Congl. Home, 1994, Excellence in Hist. Preservation award Preservation League NY State, 2002, Grassroots Preservation award Hist. Dists. Coun., 2002. Mem. Overseas Press Club, Montauk Club, Ft. Hamilton Officers Club. Home: 272 Berkeley Pl Brooklyn NY 11217-3904

ORTOLANO, RALPH J. engineering consultant; b. Phila., Apr. 12, 1931; BS in Marine Engring., U.S. Mcht. Marine Acad., 1954; MBA, Santa Clara U., 1969. Registered profl. engr., Calif. Engring. watch officer USN, 1954-56; sr. design engr. marine divsn. Westinghouse, Lester, Pa., 1956-64, Sunnyvale, Calif., 1964-69; mgr. project engring. corp. cost recovery dept. Litton Ship Systems, Inc., L.A., 1969-72; consulting engr., scientist So. Calif. Edison Co., Rosemead, Calif., 1972-92, chief cons., 1993—. Formed Turbine RESCUE, 1984; cons. more than 100 power cos., numerous others, U.S. and abroad; presenter seminars in the field. Contbr. more than 100 articles to profl. jours.; holder 22 U.S. patents in field. Recipient William R. Gould award SCE, 1992, Meritorious Alumni Svc. award USMMAAA, 1989, Outstanding Profl. Achievement award USMMAAA, 1994; USMMA rifle range named Ortolano Rifle and Pistol Range in honor of being selected to 1952 and 1953 All-Am. Rifle Teams, and 1952-54 All-Am. Pistol Teams, 1999; named to USMMA Athletic Hall of Fame, 1990. Fellow ASME (past dir. ASME-SCAC power chpt., past chmn. steam turbine com., past chmn. power divsn., mem. exec. com., co-chmn. steam turbine course 1984—, George Westinghouse Gold medal 1991, past chmn. EEI steam turbine crack prevention task force). Fax: 310-377-8233. E-mail: turbinerescue@hotmail.com.

ORTON, GEORGE FREDERICK, aerospace engineer; b. Flushing, NY, Aug. 8, 1941; s. Harry and Evelyn (Brostrom) O.; m. Susan K., Dec. 21, 1962; children: Karen, Kevin, Kristen. BS in Aero. Engring., U. Md., 1964; MS in Engring. Mechanics, St. Louis U., 1971. Engr. propulsion McDonnell Douglas Co. (now The Boeing Co.), St. Louis, 1964-73, sr. engr. propulsion, 1973-77, unit chief propulsion, 1977-81, sect. chief propulsion, 1981-86, br. chief nat. aerospace plane, 1986-90, staff dir. nat. aerospace plane, 1990-92, dir. space programs, 1992-93, program mgr. Hypersonics Ctr. Excellence, 1993—, mem. air force sci. adv. bd., 2000—02. Mem. adv. bd. Ga. Inst. Tech., 1998—. Contbr. articles to profl. jours. Advisor Explorer Post 9005, St. Louis, 1980-87; sci. advisor University City (Mo.) Schs. Named to Acad. Disting. Alumni, U. Md., 2003. Fellow AIAA (assoc., mem. liquid propulsion tech. com. 1980-84, 91-96, mem. hypersonics program com. 1994—, Best Paper award 1986), St. Louis Head Injury Assn. Methodist. Achievements include patent for propellant acquisition device for zero-g engine starts, patent for propellant resupply

system, NASA technology cash award for work on shuttle auxiliary propulsion. Office: The Boeing Co PO Box 516 Mailcode S 2454055 Saint Louis MO 63166-0516 Office Phone: 314-232-7548. E-mail: george.f.orton@boeing.com.

ORTTUNG, WILLIAM HERBERT, chemistry professor; b. Phila., June 16, 1934; s. Elmer Herbert and Rosalind Orttung; married; children: Robert W., Mark. H. SB, MIT, 1956; PhD, U. Calif., Berkeley, 1961. Asst. prof. chemistry Stanford (Calif.) U., 1960-63, U. Calif., Riverside, 1963-69, assoc. prof., 1969-79, prof., 1979-94; emeritus prof., 1994—. Mem. AAAS, Am. Chem. Soc., Am. Phys. Soc. E-mail: worttung@att.net.

ORULLIAN, B. LARAE, bank executive; b. Salt Lake City, May 15, 1933; d. Alma and Bessie (Bacon) O. Cert., Am. Inst. Banking, 1961, 63, 67; grad. Nat. Mortgage Sch., Ohio State U., 1969-71; DHL (hon.), Whittier Coll., 2004. With Tracy Collins Trust Co., Salt Lake City, 1951-54, Union Nat. Bank, Denver, 1954-57; exec. sec. Guaranty Bank, Denver, 1957-64, asst. cashier, 1964-67, asst. v.p., 1967-70, v.p., 1970-75, exec. v.p., 1975-77, also bd. dirs.; chair, CEO, pres. The Women's Bank N.A., Denver, 1977-97, Colo. Bus. Bankshares, Inc., 1980-97; vice chmn. Guaranty Bank and Trust Co., Denver, 1998—. Pres., bd. dirs. Guaranty Corp., Lange Golf Co., Holladay (Utah) Bank; vice-chmn. bd. dirs. Frontier Airlines. Treas. Girl Scouts U.S., 1981-87, 1st nat. v.p., chair exec. com., 1987-90, nat. pres., 1990-96; 1st vice chair world bd. World Assn. Girl Guides Girl Scouts, London. Recipient Woman Who Made a Difference award Internat. Women's Forum, 1994; named to Colo. Women Hall of Fame, 1988; named Colo. Entrepreneur of Yr., Inc. Mag. and Arthyr Young and Co., 1989, Woman of Yr., YWCA, 1989, Citizen of Yr., EMC Lions Club, 1995, laureate Colo. Bus. Hall of Fame, 1999. Mem. Bus. and Profl. Women Colo. (3d Century award 1977), Internat. Women's Forum, Am. Bankers Assn. (adv. bd. edn. found.), Com. of 200. Independent. Mem. L.D.S. Ch. Home: 6650 W 10th Pl Denver CO 80214 Office Phone: 303-296-9600 x 1303.

ORVICK, GEORGE MYRON, church denomination executive, minister; b. Hanlontown, Iowa, Jan. 9, 1929; s. George and Mabel Olina (Mandsager) O.; m. Ruth Elaine Hoel, Aug. 25, 1951; children: Daniel, Emily, Mark, Kirsten. AA, Bethany Luth. Coll., Mankato, Minn., 1948, candidate of theology, 1953; BA, Northwestern Coll., Watertown, Wis., 1950; postgrad., U. Wis. Ordained to ministry Evang. Luth. Synod, 1953. Pastor Our Saviour Luth. Ch., Amherst Junction, Wis., 1953-54, Holy Cross Luth. Ch., Madison, Wis., 1954-86; cir. visitor Evang. Luth. Synod, Mankato, 1964-69, v.p., 1969—70, pres., 1970—76, 1980—2002, dir. dept. archives and history, 2002—; bd. regents Bethany Luth. Coll., 1957—69. Author: Our Great Heritage, 1966; columnist: The Luth. Sentinel, 1982-2002. Lutheran. Home: 224 Terrace Dr Mankato MN 56001-4728 Office: Evang Luth Synod 6 Browns Ct Mankato MN 56001-6121 Office Phone: 507-344-7308. E-mail: gorvick@blc.edu, gorvick@blc.edu.

ORWIG, MATTHEW DANE, lawyer; b. Ardmore, Okla., Jan. 2, 1959; s. Richard R. and Mary E. (Pyle) O.; m. Melissa L. Vaughan, July 11, 1981; children: Joshua Matthew, Rachel Elizabeth, Jacob Andrew. BS, Tex. Tech. U., 1981, JD, 1984. Bar: Tex. 1985, U.S. Dist. Ct. (no. dist.) Tex. 1985, U.S. Ct. Appeals (5th cir.) 1985. Legal intern for n. dist. Tex. U.S. Dept. Justice, Dallas, 1983; briefing atty. for judge U.S. Dist. Ct., Lubbock, Tex., 1984-86; ptnr. Jones, Flygare, Galey, Moody and Brown, Lubbock, 1986-89; asst. U.S. atty. U.S. Dept. Justice, Dallas, 1989—2001, U.S. atty. ea. dist., 2001—. Adj. prof. So. Meth. U. Law Sch, 1990—, Tex. Wesleyan U. Sch. Law, 1990—; legal advisor Exec. Office of U.S. Atty., Office of Legal Counsel, 1997—. Mem. ABA, State Bar Tex., Lubbock County Bar Assn., Lubbock County Young Lawyers Assn. (bd. dirs. 1987-89), Tex. Trial Lawyers Assn. Methodist. Office: 350 Magnolia Ave Ste 150 Beaumont TX 77701-2237

ORWOLL, GREGG S.K. lawyer; b. Austin, Minn., Mar. 23, 1926; s. Gilbert M. and Kleonora (Kleven) O.; m. Laverne M. Flentie, Sept. 15, 1951; children: Kimball G., Kent A., Vikki A., Tristen A., Erik G. BS, Northwestern U., 1950; JD, U. Minn., 1953. Bar: Minn. 1953, U.S. Supreme Ct. 1973. Assoc. Dorsey & Whitney, Mpls., 1953-59, ptnr., 1959-60; assoc. counsel Mayo Clinic, Rochester, Minn., 1960-63, gen. counsel, 1963-87, sr. legal counsel, 1987-91, sr. counsel, 1991-92. Gen. counsel, dir. Rochester Airport Co., 1962-84, v.p., 1981-84; gen. counsel Mayo Med. Svcs., Ltd., 1972-90; bd. dirs., sec. and gen. counsel Mayo Found. for Med. Edn. and Rsch., 1984-90; gen. counsel Mid-Am. Orthop. Assn., 1984—, Minn. Orthop. Soc., 1985-95; counsel Norwegian Am. Orthopaedic Soc., 1999—, Intl. Soc. of Amyloidosis 2002—; asst. sec./sec. Mayo Found., Rochester, 1972-91; sec. Mayo Emeritus Staff, 1998-99, vice chair, 1999-2000, chair, 2000-2001; bd. dirs. Charter House, 1986-90; dir., officer Travelure Motel Corp., 1968-86; dir., v.p. Echo Too Ent., Inc.; dir., v.p. Oberhamer Inc., 1989-99; bd. dirs. Am. Decal and Mfg. Co., 1989-93, sec., 1992-93; adj. prof. William Mitchell Coll. Law, 1978-84. Contbr. articles to profl. jours., chpts. to books; mem. editl. bd. Minn. Law Rev., 1952-53, HealthSpan, 1984-93 Trustee Minn. Coun. on Founds., 1977-82, Mayo Found., 1982-86; trustee William Mitchell Coll. Law, 1982-88, 89-98, mem. exec. com. 1990-98; bd. visitors U. Minn. Law Sch., 1974-76, 85-91; mem. U. Minn. Regent Candidate Adv. Coun., 1988-99, Minn. State Compensation Coun., 1991-97. With USAF, 1944-45. Recipient Outstanding Svc. medal U.S. Govt., 1991. Mem. ABA, AMA (affiliate), Am. Corp. Counsel Assn., Minn. Soc. Hosp. Attys. (bd. dirs. 1981-86), Minn. State Bar Assn. (chmn. legal/med. com. 1977-81), Olmsted County Bar Assn. (v.p., pres. 1977-79), Rochester C. of C., U. Minn. Law Alumni Assn. (bd. dirs. 1973-76, 85-91), Rochester U. Club (pres. 1977), The Doctors Mayo Soc., Mid Am. Orthop. Assn. (hon.), Mayo Alumni Assn. (hon.), Phi Delta Phi, Phi Delta Theta. Republican. Home: 2233 5th Ave NE Rochester MN 55906-4017 Office: Mayo Clinic 200 1st St SW Rochester MN 55905-0002 Office Phone: 507-284-2691.

ORY, STEVEN JAY, physician, educator; b. Houston, Aug. 4, 1950; s. Edwin Marvin and Norma Gertrude O.; m. Kathleen Higgins, Jan. 10, 1981; children: Eleanor Claire, Edward Michael. BA, Washington and Lee U., 1972; MD, Baylor Coll., 1976. Diplomate Am. Bd. Obstetrics and Gynecology, subsplty. cert. in Reproductive Endocrinolgy and Infertility. Asst. prof. Duke U., Durham, N.C., 1981-82, Northwestern U., Chgo., 1982-85; assoc. prof., cons. Mayo Clinic, Rochester, Minn., 1985-95, chmn. sect. reproductive endocrinology and infertility, 1985-95; pvt. practice reproductive endocrinology and infertility; mem. ob-gyn. staff Internat. U., Margate, Fla., 1995—; assoc. clin. prof. obstets. and gyn. U. Miami, Fla., 1999—. Assoc. dir. Am. Fertility Soc., Birmingham, Ala., 1986-87; bd. trustees Northwest Med. Ctr., Margate, Fla., 2003—. Asst. editor: Fertility and Sterility, 1988-96; contbr. articles to profl. jours. Mem. Internat. Soc. for Advancement of Humanistic Studies in Medicine (bd. dirs. 1999-2002), Am. Soc. Reproductive Medicine (chmn. practice com. 1998-2000, bd. dirs. 1999-2002), Soc. Reproductive Endocrinologists (sec.-treas., pres. 2001-2002), Ft. Lauderdale Ob-Gyn. Soc. (pres. 1998-2000). Address: 2825 N State Road 7 Ste 302 Margate FL 33063-5737 Office Phone: 954-247-6200.

ORYSHKEVICH, ROMAN SVIATOSLAV, retired physician, physiatrist, dentist, educator; b. Olesko, Ukraine, Aug. 5, 1928; came to U.S., 1955, naturalized, 1960; s. Simeon and Caroline (Deneszczuk) O.; m. Oksana Lishchynsky, June 16, 1962; children: Marta, Mark, Alexandra. DDS, Ruperto-Carola U., Heidelberg, Ger., 1952, MD, 1953, PhD cum laude, 1955. Cert. Am. Assn. Electromyography and Electrodiagnosis, 1964; diplomate Am. Bd. Phys. Medicine and Rehab., 1966, Am. Bd. Electrodiagnostic Medicine, 1989. Research fellow in cancer Esptl. Cancer Inst., Rupert-Charles U., 1953-55; rotating intern Coney Island Hosp., Bklyn., 1955-56; resident in diagnostic radiology NYU Bellevue Med. Ctr.-Univ. Hosp., 1956-57; resident, fellow in phys. medicine and rehab. Western Res. U. Highland View Hosp., Cleve., 1958-60; orthopedic surgery Met. Gen. Hosp., Cleve., 1959; asst. chief rehab. medicine service VA West Side Med. Ctr., Chgo., 1961-74, acting chief, 1974-75, chief, 1975-99; dir., coord. edn. U. Ill. Integrated Residency Program, Phys. Medicine & Rehab, 1974-89; clin. instr. U. Ill., 1962-65, asst. clin. prof., 1965-70, asst. prof., 1970-75, assoc. clin. prof., 1975-94, clin. prof., 1994-99; ret., 1999. Author, editor: Who and What in U.W.M.M., 1978; contbr. articles to profl. jours; splty. cons. in phys. medicine and rehab. to editl. bd. Chgo. Med. Jours., 1978-89. Founder, pres. Ukrainian World Med. Mus., Chgo., 1977; founder, 1st pres. Am. Mus. Phys. Medicine and Rehab., 1980-91. Fellow AAUP, Am. Acad. Phys. Medicine and Rehab.; mem. AAAS, Assn. Acad. Physiatrists, Am. Assn. Electromyography and Electrodiagnosis, Ill. Soc. Phys. Medicine and Rehab. (pres., dir. 1979-80), Ukrainian Med. Assn. N.Am. (dir., pres. chpt. 1977-79, fin. mgr. 17th med. conv. and congress Chgo. 1977, adminstr. and conv. chmn. 1979), World Fedn. Ukrainian Med. Assns. (co-founder and 1st exec. sec. research and sci. 1977-79), Internat. Rehab. Medicine Assn., Rehab. Internat. U.S.A., Nat. Assn. VA Physicians, Assn. Med. Rehab. Dirs. and Coordinators, Nat. Rehab. Assn., Nat. Assn. Disability Examiners, Am. Med. Writers Assn., Biofeedback Rsch. Soc. Am., Chgo. Soc. Phys. Medicine and Rehab. (pres., founder 1978-79), Ill. Rehab. Assn., Ukrainian Acad. Med. Scis. (founder, pres. 1979-80), Gerontol. Soc., Internat. Soc. Electrophysiol. Kinesiology, Internat. Soc. Prosthetics and Orthotics, Fedn. Am. Scientists. Ukrainian Catholic. Avocations: research in prosthetics, amputations, normal and pathological gaits, bracing orthotics. Home: 1819 N 78th Ct Elmwood Park IL 60707-3502

OSAKI, MARK STEPHEN, writer, development administrator; b. Sacramento, Oct. 7, 1952; s. Tadashi Melvin and Haruye (Murata) O. BA, U. Calif., Berkeley, 1974; PhD, Georgetown U., 1984. Assoc. dir. RAND Corp., Santa Monica, Calif., 1992-97, cons., 1997-2001; dir. devel. Disabled Sports USA Far West, Citrus Heights, Calif., 2000—. Comm. dir. U. Calif., 1984-90; dir. devel. Coro Found., San Francisco, 1996-97, Second Harvest Food Bank, San Jose, Calif., 1997-2000, Toigo Found., Sacramento, 1997-98. Author: Poetry of the Vietnam War, 1989, Men of Our Time: An Anthology of Male Poetry in Contemporary America, 1992. Nat. Endowment for Arts fellow, 1981. Home: 6615 Fordham Way Sacramento CA 95831 Office: c/o Disabled Sports USA Ste 2540 6060 Sunrise Vista Dr Citrus Heights CA 95610 E-mail: markosaki@msn.com., mark@dsusafw.org.

OSAKWE, CHRISTOPHER, lawyer, educator; b. Lagos, Nigeria, May 8, 1942; arrived in U.S., 1970, naturalized, 1979; s. Simon and Hannah (Morgan) Osakwe; m. Maria Elena Amador, Aug. 19, 1982; 1 child, Rebecca E. LLB, Moscow State U., 1967, PhD, 1970; JSD, U. Ill., 1974. Bar: Moscow 1967, Kazakhstan 1997. Prof. sch. law Tulane U., New Orleans, 1972-81, 86-88, Eason-Weinmann prof. comparative law, dir. Eason-Weinmann Ctr. Comparative Law, 1981-86; ptnr. Riddle and Brown, New Orleans, 1989—. Vis. prof. U. Pa., 1978, U. Mich., 1981, Washington and Lee U., 1986; vis. fellow St. Anthony's Coll. Oxford (Eng.) U., 1980, vis. fellow Christ Ch. Coll., 1988—89; vis. fellow Lomonosov Moscow State U., 1999—2004; cons. U.S. Dept. Commerce, 1980—85. Author: The Participation of the Soviet Union in Universal International Organizations, 1972, The Foundations of Soviet Law, 1981, Joint Ventures with the Soviet Union: Law and Practice, 1990, Soviet Business Law, 2 vols., 1991; author: (with others) Comparative Legal Traditions in a Nutshell, 1982, Comparative Legal Traditions - Text, Materials and Cases, 1985, 2d edit., 1994, The Russian Civil Code Annotated: Translation and Commentary, 2000, Comparative Law in Diagrams: General and Special Parts, 2000, 2d edit., 2002; editor: Am. Jour. Comparative Law, 1978—85. Carnegie fellow, Hague Acad. Internat. Law, 1969, Russian Rsch. fellow, Harvard U., 1972, USSR Sr. Rsch. Exch. fellow, 1982, Rsch. fellow, Kennan Inst. Advanced Russian Studies, 1988. Mem.: ABA, Soc. de Legis. Comparée, Supreme Ct. Hist. Soc., Am. Soc. Internat. Law, Am. Law Inst., Order of Coif. Republican. Roman Catholic. Home: 339 Audubon Blvd New Orleans LA 70125-4124 Office: 201 S Charles Ave Ste 3100 New Orleans LA 70170 Office Phone: 504-861-1272. Personal E-mail: osakwec@aol.com.

OSANDER, JOHN, secondary school educator; AB in English cum laude, Princeton U.; postgrad., U. Minn., Rider U., St. Thomas U., Macalester Coll., Yale U.; MEd in English Tchg. and Adminstrn., Harvard U. Cert. secondary sch. English and social studies tchr., cert. elem. and presch. tchr., prin. and sch. adminstr. Tchr. Blake Sch., Mpls., 1957—59, Lincoln-Sudbury Regional H.S., Mass., 1961—63; dir. admissions Princeton U., 1963—71; rschr. Exptl. Work on Writing with Children, NJ, 1972—77; sr. dep. to the pres. Carnegie Found., 1990—97; writing vol. Mpls. schs., 2000—. Cons. in field; founding dir. tchr. recruitment and placement office N.J. State Dept. Edn., 1980—88; grant writer, NY, 1975—78. Author: (novels) Country Matters, 2000, Call Me Kick, 2002; contbr. lyrics for 3 pub. and recorded musicals. Founder Cmty. Theater, Lincoln-Sudbury. Mem.: Loft Literary Ctr., Playwrights' Ctr., Authors League Am., Dramatists Guild. Home: 4831 Portland Ave S Minneapolis MN 55417 E-mail: os5555@aol.com.

OSBALDESTON, GORDON FRANCIS, business educator, former government official; b. Hamilton, Ont., Can., Apr. 29, 1930; s. John Edward and Margaret (Hanley) O.; m. Geraldine Keller, Oct. 3, 1953; children— Stephen, David, Robert, Catherine B.Commerce, U. Toronto, Ont., Can., 1952; MBA, U. Western Ont., London, 1953, LL.D., 1984, York U., Toronto, 1984, Dalhousie U., Halifax, N.S., 1985, Carleton U., Ottawa, Ont., Can., 1987. Fgn. service officer Dept. Trade and Commerce, Ottawa, 1953-54, vice consul, asst. trade commr. Sao Paula, Brazil, 1954-57, Chgo., 1957-60, consul, trade commr. Los Angeles, 1960-64, asst. dir., personnel trade commr. service Ottawa, 1964-66, asst. dir. ops. trade commr. service, 1966-67, exec. dir. trade commr. service, 1967-68; asst. dep. minister Dept. Consumer and Corp. Affairs, Ottawa, 1968-70, dep. minister, 1972-73; dep. sec. Treasury Bd. Secretariat, Ottawa, 1970-72, sec., 1973-76; dep. minister Dept. Industry, Trade and Commerce, Ottawa, 1976-78; sec. Ministry of State for Econ. Devel., Ottawa, 1978-82; undersec. of state Dept. External Affairs, Ottawa, 1982; clk. privy council, sec. to cabinet Privy Council Office, Ottawa, 1982-86; mem. Queen's Privy Coun. for Can., 1986; prof. emeritus Western Bus. Sch. U. Western Ont., 1986—. Bd. dirs. Can. Life Assurance Co., Can. Life Fin. Co., Great West Lifeco Inc., Great West Life Assurance Co., London Group Ins. Inc., London Life Co. Author: Keeping Deputy Ministers Accountable, 1989, Organizing to Govern, 1990. Decorated officer Order of Can., companion, 1997; recipient Outstanding Achievment award Can. Govt., 1981, Vanier medal Inst. Pub. Adminstrn., 1990. Mem. London Hunt and Country Club, Psi Upsilon Roman Catholic. Avocations: stamp collecting/philately, golf. Home: 1353 Corley Dr N London ON Canada N6G 4L4 E-mail: gordon5304@aol.com.

OSBERG, GREGORY JOHN, publishing company executive; b. Jamestown, N.Y., June 12, 1957; s. John Raymond and Nancy (Jones) O.; m. Linda Burton, Aug. 22, 1981; children: Eric Burton, Alexander Gregory. BS in Mktg., Colo. State U., 1979. Regional mgr. Chilton Pub., Radnor, Pa., 1979-81; account mgr. U.S. News & World Report, N.Y.C., 1981-84, Fortune, N.Y.C., 1984-85; v.p. advt. sales U.S. News & World Report, N.Y.C., 1985-90; from advt. sales dir. to v.p. Newsweek, 1992—94, v.p., 1994—97; pres. sales and mktg. CNET, Inc., 1997—99; pres. Brass Ring, Inc., 1999—2000; exec. v.p. Newsweek, 2000—, worldwide pub., 2000—. Chmn. Careers in Communications, Pitts., 1980-81. Mem. Advt. Club N.Y., Lincoln Ctr. Ctr. Circle (exec. com.), Bedens Brook Club. Avocations: golf, tennis, squash, jogging, skiing.

OSBERG, TIMOTHY MICHAEL, psychologist, educator, researcher; b. Buffalo, Aug. 11, 1955; s. John Carlton and Adeline Rose (Weichsel) O.; m. Debra A. Morreale, July 14, 1990; children: John Peter, Erika Evelyn. BA, SUNY, Buffalo, 1977, MA, 1980, PhD, 1982. Lic. psychologist NY. Intern VA Med. Ctr., Buffalo, 1981-82; asst. prof. Niagara U., N.Y., 1982-86; assoc. prof., 1986-90; prof., 1990—; pvt. practice Niagara U., Niagara Falls, NY, 1985—. Psychologist Optifast Weight Loss Program, Niagara Falls, 1989-92; editorial bd. Jour. Personality and Social Psychology, 1988-92, Teaching of Psychology, 1991-99, Jour. Correctional Edn., 1993-97, Jour. Clin. Psychology, 1999-2001; instr. Attica Correctional Facility, 1980-93; presenter in field. Contbr. articles to profl. jours. Vol. group leader pre-release program Attica (N.Y.) Correctional Facility, 1984-90, exec. com. Psychol. Assn. Western N.Y., Buffalo, 1982-87. Recipient Feldman-Cohen Meml. award SUNY, Buffalo, 1977, Disting. Faculty award Consortium of Niagara Frontier, 1993, Cmty. Svc. award Niagara County Mental Health Assn., 2000, Professionalism in Health award Niagara County Mental Health Assn., 2004. Fellow APA; mem. Am. Psychol. Soc., Eastern Psychol. Assn., Soc. for Personality Assessment, Assn. Advancement Behavior Therapy, Phi Beta Kappa. Democrat. Roman Catholic. Avocations: spectator sports, running, golf, bicycling, hockey. Home: 109 Hidden Oaks Ct Grand Island NY 14072-2575 Office: Niagara U Dept Psychology Niagara University NY 14109 Office Phone: 716-286-8524. Business E-Mail: tosberg@niagara.edu.

OSBORN, DEVERLE ROSS, insurance company executive; b. Leesburg, Ind., Sept. 29, 1925; s. Leland John and Beth (Bunnell) O.; m. Edith Helaine Germann, June 27, 1948 (dec. Mar. 1990); children: Bradford, Pamela, Andrea, Randall; m. Lillian C. Fellwock, Aug. 1990. Student, U. Notre Dame, 1944; BS in Air Transp. Engring., Purdue U., 1947. CLU. Spl. agt. FBI, Louisville, 1948, N.Y.C., 1948-53; life ins. agt. Conn. Mut. Life, N.Y.C., 1953-56; life ins. exec. Conn. Mutual Life, Hartford, 1956-65, Allentown, Penn., 1965-70, Aid Assn. Luths., Appleton, Wis., 1970-78, Evansville, Ind., 1978-91; ret. Chmn. adv. coun. Law Enforcement of Bergen County, N.J., 1955-56. Liaison State Legislators Justice Fellowship, Washington, 1982-85, chmn., 1989-92; fin. dir. Prescott, Ariz. Spl. Olympics, 1996-98; bd. dirs. Atlantic dist. Luth. Ch.-Missouri Synod, 1961-65, Habitat for Humanity, Evansville, Ind., 1991-92, Meals on Wheels, Prescott, 1997-2000, Prayer Family Internat., 1999-2002. Naval Aviation cadet, 1943-45, lt. (j.g.) res., 1950-60. Named Nat. Vol. Yr. Justice Fellowship, 1989. Mem. Soc. CLUs (v.p., pres. local chpts. 1968,70), Gen. Agt. Mgr. Assn. (treas., v.p., pres. local chpts. 1966-68), Nat. Assn. Life Underwriters. Republican. Lutheran. Avocation: flying.

OSBORN, DONALD ROBERT, lawyer; b. NYC, Oct. 9, 1929; s. Robert W. and Ruth C. (Compton) O.; m. Marcia (Lontz), June 4, 1955; (div.) children: David, Judith, Robert; m. Marie A. (Johnson), Sept. 11, 1986. BA, Cornell U., 1951; LLB, Columbia U., 1957. Bar: N.Y. 1957, U.S. Tax Ct. 1958, U.S. Ct. Claims 1961, U.S. Ct. Appeals (2d cir.) 1974, U.S. Ct. Appeals (8th cir.) 1974, U.S. Dist. Ct. (so. and ea. dist.) N.Y. 1975, U.S. Supreme Ct. 1975. Assoc. Sullivan and Cromwell, N.Y.C., NY, 1957—64, ptnr., 1964—96, sr. counsel, 1997—. Trustee Hamilton Coll., 1978-88, Mus. of Broadcasting, 1975-80; trustee, treas. Kirkland Coll., 1969-78; mem. coun. White Burkett Miller Ctr. Pub. Affairs, 1976-82; bd. dir., pres. Stevens Kingsley Found., 1967—; sec., treas. Dunlevy Milbank Found., 1974—; bd. dir. Spanel Found., 1978-88, CBS, Inc., 1975-80. Served in USN, 1951-54. Mem. ABA, N.Y. State Bar Assn., Assn. of Bar of City of N.Y., Am. Bar Found., Scarsdale Golf Club, India House, Regency Whist Club, Country Club of the Rockies. Presbyterian. Home: 1049 Park Ave New York NY 10028-1061 Office: Sullivan and Cromwell 125 Broad St Fl 32 New York NY 10004-2498 Office Phone: 212-558-3724. Personal E-mail: dromao@aol.com.

OSBORN, FREDERICK HENRY, III, foundation executive; b. Phila., Dec. 31, 1946; s. Frederick Henry Osborn Jr. and Anne de Witt (Pell) O.; m. Anne Hampton de Peyster Todd, July 10, 1971; children: Frederick Henry IV, Elisabeth Van Cortlandt, Graham Livingston. Student in Econs., Princeton U., 1964-66; BA in Bus. Adminstrn., Colby Coll., 1971; postgrad., Nat. Planned Giving Inst., 1987, Philanthropy Tax Inst., 1988. Registered investment advisor. Pres. Call-Us, Inc., Edgartown, Mass., 1969-72; exec. v.p. Hall Labs., Boston, 1972-74; fin. officer Episcopal Diocese Mass., Boston, 1972-76; diocesan adminstr. Episcopal Diocese Maine, Portland, 1976-80; dir. adminstrn. Episcopal Diocese Conn., Hartford, 1980-86; dir. of devel. and planned giving Nat. Episcopal Ch., N.Y.C., 1987-94; dir. of devel. programs Episcopal Ch. Found., N.Y.C., 1995-97; dir. devel. The Nature Conservancy of N.Y., N.Y.C., 1997-99; dir. philanthropic svcs. Episcopal Ch. Found., 1999—. Bd. dirs. Living Music, Inc., Ulysses Co., William O. Benson Co., FAN Trusts, Oslands, Inc., Boscobel Restoration, Inc., Garrison Sta. Plz., Inc., Garrison Landing Assn., Covenant Svcs., Inc.; prin. Cat Rock Counsel, Garrison, N.Y., 1990—. Co-author: Planned Giving for the Episcopal Parish, 1989, Funding Future Ministry, 2000. Bd. dirs. The Giraffe Project, chmn. 1989-93, Alice Desmond & Hamilton Fish Libr.; chmn. bd. dirs. Hudson Highlands Land Trust; v.-chair., bd. dirs. Scenic Hudson, Berkeley Divinity Sch. Yale U., Nature Conservancy (lower Hudson chpt. chair 1994-97); trustee Tabor Acad., 1993-99, Cathedral Ch. St. John the Divine, chair Hudson Highlands Music Festival, 1994-96, 99-2001, The Constn. Island Assn., Soc. for Increase of the Ministry; trustee St. Francis Found., chair, 1999-2000. With U.S. Army, 1966-68, Vietnam. Mem. Nat. Soc. Fund Raising Execs., Nat. Planned Giving Assn., Nat. Environ. Le adership Coun., Planned Giving Group Greater NY, Social Investment Forum, Coun. Econ. Priorities, Social Venture Network, Century Assn., Constitution Is. Assn., St. Andrews Soc. NY, Highlands Country Club, NY Yacht Club, Portland Yacht Club, Dauntless Club, Garrison Yacht Club, Princeton Club (NY), Internat. Platform Assn., Yale Club (NY). Avocations: sailing, music, photography. Home: PO Box 347 Garrison NY 10524-0347 Office: The Episcopal Ch Found 815 2nd Ave New York NY 10017-4563

OSBORN, GERALD GUY, psychiatrist, educator, consultant; b. Cin., Nov. 6, 1947; s. Guy Henry and Doris Irene (Taylor) O.; m. Sue Ellen Granger, July 9, 1983; children— Erica Tyrell, Eric Gerald, Ellen Stephanie. B.A., Wilmington Coll., 1969; student Schiller U., Klein-Ingersheim, Germany, 1968-69; D.O., Kirksville Coll. Osteo. Medicine, 1973; postgrad. in psychiatry U. Sheffield (Eng.), 1973; M in Philosphy Cambridge U., 1986. Diplomate Am. Osteo. Bd. Neurology and Psychiatry (bd. examiners 1982), Am. Bd. Psychiatry and Neurology. Rotating intern Lansing (Mich.) Gen. Hosp., 1973-74; resident, postdoctoral fellow dept. psychiatry Mich. State U., East Lansing, 1974-77, chief resident in psychiatry, 1976-77, instr. in psychiatry, 1974-77, asst. prof., 1977-82, assoc. prof., 1982—, dir. residency tng. osteo. div., 1979-81, assoc. dean for acad. affairs Coll. Osteo. Medicine, 1981-83; chmn. dept. psychiatry St. Lawrence Hosp., Lansing, 1986—; assoc. adj. prof. dept. history Mich. State U., 1986—; cons. in field; psychiat. reviewer Mich. Dept. Social Services; chmn. Lansing Area Psychiatry Council, 1983. Med. dir. Catholic Social Services and Family and Child Services of Lansing; active Physicians for Social Responsibility, East Lansing. Recipient Med. Writing award Mich. Osteo. Coll. Found., 1976; teaching awards Mich. State U., 1979, 80, 82, Prof. of Yr. award, 1981; Kettering scholar, 1968. Mem. Am. Osteo. Assn. Mich. Assn. Osteo. Physicians and Surgeons, Ingham County Osteo. Soc., Am. Psychiat. Assn., Mich. Psychiat. Soc., Am. Coll. Neuropsychiatrists (sr.; bd. govs. 1982—, pres.-elect 1986—), Mich. Osteo. Neuropsychiat. Soc., Osteo. Physicians and Surgeons Calif. (assoc.), Am. Assn. Dirs. Psychiat. Residency Tng., Aircraft Owners and Pilots Assn., U.S. Internat. Sailing Assn., Sigma Sigma Phi. Democrat. Quaker. Contbr. articles to profl. publs. Office: Kirksville Coll Osteopathic Med Office Dean 800 W Jefferson St Kirksville MO 63501

OSBORN, JOHN ROBERT, retired mechanical engineer; b. Kansas City, Mo., Aug. 11, 1924; married, 1945; 3 children. BS, Purdue U., 1950, MS, 1953, PhD in Mech. Engring., 1957. Jr. engr. Thiokol Chem. Corp., 1950-51; asst. Purdue U., West Lafayette, Ind., 1951-57, from asst. prof. to assoc. prof. mechanical engring., 1957-61, prof., 1961-70, 71-79, prof. aeronautical and astronautical, 1980-89, ret., 1990; br. chief Ballistics Rsch. Lab. Aberdeen Proving Ground, 1970-71. Mem.: AIAA (assoc. fellow, Wyld Propulsion award 1995), Soc. Automotive Engrs. Achievements include research in combustion instability in rockets; high frequency response instrumentation; combustion in solid rockets and interior ballistics. Address: 40 Stayman Ct Lafayette IN 47905-4446 Personal E-mail: josborn@purdue.edu.

OSBORN, JOHN SIMCOE, JR., lawyer; b. Louisville, Jan. 14, 1926; s. John S. and Ruby (Pinnell) O.; m. Mary Jo Fishback, Sept. 6, 1947; children— Robert, John, Donna LLB, U. Louisville, 1949. Bar: Ky. 1949, U.S. Dist. Ut. (ea. and we. dists.) Ky. 1952. Exec. v.p., gen. counsel Louisville Title Ins. Co., 1954-72; ptnr. Tarrant Combs & Bullitt (name changed to Wyatt Tarrant & Combs 1980), Louisville, 1972—. Chmn. bd. Beargrass Corp. Capt. JAGC, U.S. Army, 1952-54. Fellow Am. Bar Found.; mem. Ky. Bar Assn., Louisville Bar Assn., ABA, Am. Land Title Assn., Am. Coll. Real Estate Lawyers, Rotary. Democrat. Lutheran. Office: Wyatt Tarrant & Combs 2800 Citizens Plz Louisville KY 40202 Office Phone: 502-589-5235.

OSBORN, JUNE ELAINE, pediatrician, microbiologist, educator, foundation administrator; b. Endicott, N.Y., May 28, 1937; d. Leslie A. and Dora W. (Wright) Osborn; children: Philip I. Levy, Ellen D. Levy, Laura A. Jana. BA, Oberlin (Ohio) Coll., 1957; MD, Western Res. U., 1961; DSc (hon.), U. Med. Dental Sch. N.J., 1990, Emory U., 1993, Oberlin Coll., 1993, Rutgers U.,

1994, Case Western Res. U., 1997, SUNY, Stony Brook, 1999, U. Wis., 2004; DMS (hon.), Yale U., 1992; LHD (hon.), Med. Coll. Pa., 1994. Intern, resident in pediatrics Harvard U. Hosp., 1961—64; fellow Johns Hopkins, 1964—65, U. Pitts., 1965—66; prof. med. microbiology and pediat. U. Wis. Med. Sch., Madison, Wis., 1966—84, prof. pediat. and microbiology, 1974—84, assoc. dean Grad. Sch., 1975—84; dean Sch. Pub. Health U. Mich. Sch. Pub. Health, 1984—93; prof. epidemiology, pediat. and communicable diseases U. Mich. Sch. Pub. Health and Med. Sch., 1984—96, prof. emeritus, 1997—. Pres. Josiah Macy, Jr. Found., 1997—; mem. rev. panel viral vaccine efficacy FDA, 1973—79, mem. vaccines and related biol. products adv. com., 1981—85; mem. exptl. virology study sect. Divsn. Rsch. Grants, NIH, 1975—79; mem. med. affairs com. Yale U. Coun., 1981—86; chmn. life scis. associateships rev. panel NRC, 1981—84; mem. U.S. Army Med. R&D Adv. Com., 1983—85; chmn. working group on AIDS and the Nation's Blood Supply NHLBI, 1984—89; chmn. WHO Planning Group on AIDS and the Internat. Blood Supply, 1985—86. Contbr. articles to profl. jours.; mem. editl. bd.: Jour. AMA, 2002—. Active task force in AIDS, Inst. of Medicine, 1986; mem. adv. com. Robert Wood Johnson Found. AIDS Health Svcs. Program, 1986—91; mem. nat. adv. com. on health of pub. program Pew and Rockefeller Founds.; mem. health promotion and disease prevention bd. Inst. Medicine, 1987—90; mem. Global Commn. on AIDS, WHO, 1988—92; chmn. Nat. Commn. on AIDS, 1989—93; trustee Kaiser Found., 1990—98, Case Western Reserve U., Cleve., 1993—97; mem. coun. Inst. Medicine, 1995—2000; mem. Nat. Vaccine Adv. Cte., HHS, 1995—98; mem. adv. coun. Nat. Inst. on Drug Abuse, 1995—98; mem. internat adv. bd. Nat. Acads., 2002—; bd. dirs. Legal Action Ctr., 1994—2001, Ctr. for Health Care Strategies, 1998—2003, The Mind Inst., 2003—. Recipient NIH Pub. Svc. award, 2000, Scientific Freedom and Responsibility award, AAAS, 1994; grantee NIH, 1969, 1972, 1974—75, Nat. Multiple Sclerosis Soc., 1971. Fellow: Infectious Diseases Soc. Am., Am. Acad. Microbiology, Am. Acad. Arts and Scis., Am. Acad. Pediat.; mem.: Inst. Medicine, Soc. Pediat. Rsch., Am. Assn. Immunologists. Office: Josiah Macy Jr Found 44 E 64th St New York NY 10021-7306

OSBORN, KENNETH LOUIS, financial executive; b. Belleville, Ill., Jan. 9, 1946; s. William Arthur and Louise Mary (Brueggemann) Osborn; m. Roberta Marie Vodicka, Oct. 23, 1971; 1 child, David Anthony. BBA, U. N. Mex., 1968. Auditor Ernst & Ernst, Albuquerque, 1968; budget mgr. Rockwell Internat., Chgo, 1970—74; mgr. internat. acctg. Allied Van Lines, 1974—76; fin. mgr. Sealy, Inc., 1976—79; sr. fin. analyst Newark Electronics, 1979—80, internat. dir. credit, 1980—82; bus. mgr. Prime Computer, Ill., 1982—90; acctg. mgr. and CFO Flexonics, Inc., 1990—96; contr. and CFO Jackson Industries, Ill., 1996—. Fin. cons. Am. European Express. Rep. Nat. Com.; presdl. task force. With U.S. Army, 1968—70. Decorated Air medal. Mem.: Inst. Mgmt. Accts., Soc. Am. Baseball Rsch., Mensa Soc.

OSBORN, LA DONNA CAROL, clergywoman; b. Portland, Oreg., Mar. 13, 1947; d. T.L. and Daisy (Washburn) O.; m. Cory A. Nickerson, Dec. 11, 1981; children: Tommy O'Dell, LaVona Thomas, Daneesa Dolan, Donald O'Dell. Student, Assemblies of God Coll., 1963; BA, Okla. City U., 1994; DD, Bethel Coll., 1995; Doctor of Humane Letters (hon.), Wesley Synod, 1998; MA, Oral Roberts U., 2000; D in Ministry, Am. Christian Coll. and Sem., 2001; DD, Zoe Univ., 2001. Fgn. mission corr., purchaser, personnel agt. Osborn Found., Tulsa, 1969-75, exec. asst., 1975-76, internat. gen. mgr., 1976-81, internat. editor-in-chief, 1981-86, corp. pres., 1986-93; assoc. pastor Internat. Gospel Ctr., Tulsa, 1986-89, sr. pastor, 1989-94, sr. pastor, overseer, 1994-97; founder, presiding bishop Internat. Gospel Ctr. (IGC) Chs. and Mins., Tulsa, Okla., 1997—; mem. Coll. of Bishops Internat. Communion of Charismatic Chs., 1998—; v.p., CEO OSFO Internat., 1998—. Internat. minister, religious tchr., and motivational spkr. Nigeria, Kenya, Uganda, Colombia, Papua New Guinea, France, Russia, Belarus, Kazakhstan, Kyrgyzstan, Ukraine, Russia, Sweden, Eng., Holland, Can., India, Zambia, Guatemala, Ecuador, China, U.S.; internat. spiritual advisor Christian Women's Fellowship Internat. Nigeria; founder Believers' Network Internat., Women's Internat. Network. Author: Jesus & Women, 2000, God's Big Picture, 2001, New Miracle Life New, 2004, Bible tng. courses, editor. Republican. Avocations: jewish biblical history, interracial issues, biblical equality, women's issues. Home: 3111 E 89th St Tulsa OK 74137-3362 Office Phone: 918-743-0872. Personal E-mail: revldo@aol.com.

OSBORN, MALCOLM EVERETT, lawyer; b. Bangor, Maine, Apr. 29, 1928; s. Lester Everett and Helen (Clark) O.; m. Claire Anne Franks, Aug. 30, 1953; children: Beverly, Lester, Malcolm, Ernest. BA, U. Maine, 1952; postgrad., Harvard U., 1952-54; JD, Boston U., 1956, LLM, 1961. Bar: Maine 1956, Mass. 1956, U.S. Dist. Ct. Mass. 1961, U.S. Tax Ct. 1961, U.S. Claims Ct. 1961, N.C. 1965, U.S. Supreme Ct. 1979, U.S. Ct. Appeals (4th cir.) 1980, Va. 1991. Tax counsel State Mut. Life Assurance Co., Worcester, Mass., 1956-64; v.p., gen. tax counsel Integon Corp. and other group cos., Winston-Salem, N.C., 1964-81; ptnr. House, Blanco & Osborn, P.A., Winston-Salem, N.C., 1981-88; v.p., gen. counsel, dir. Settlers Life Ins. Co., Bristol, Va., 1984-89; prin. Malcolm E. Osborn, P.A., Winston-Salem, 1988—. Lectr. The Booke Seminars, Life Ins. Co., 1985-87; adj. prof. Wake Forest U. Sch. Law, Winston-Salem, 1974-82; Disting. guest lectr. Ga. State U., 1965; guest lectr. NYU Ann. Inst. Fed. Taxation, 1966, 68, 75, 80. Com. editor The Tax Lawyer, ABA, 1974-76; author numerous articles in field. Trustee N.C. Coun. Econ. Edn., 1968-76; bd. dirs. Christian Fellowship Home, 1972-80; co-founder Bereaved Parents Group Winston-Salem, 1978—. Mem. ABA (chmn. com. ins. cos. of taxation sect. 1980-82, chmn. subcom. on continuing legal edn. and publs. 1982-88), Am. Bus. Law Assn. (mem. com. fed. taxation 1968—, chmn. 1972-75), Assn. Life Ins. Counsel (com. on co. tax, tax sect. 1965—), N.C. Bar Assn. (com. taxation 1973—), Fed. Bar Assn. (taxation com. 1973—), Maine State Bar Assn., Va. State Bar Assn., Internat. Bar Assn. (com. on taxes of bus. law sect. 1973—), AAUP, Southeastern Acad. Legal Studies in Bus., Masons (Lincoln, Maine). Office: PO Box 5192 Winston Salem NC 27113-5192 Office Phone: 336-659-0613.

OSBORN, MARK ELIOT, dentist; b. Buffalo, Apr. 22, 1950; s. Thomas Earl and Ruth Frances (Martin) O. BA, U. Mo., Columbia, 1972; DDS, U. Mo., Kansas City, 1977. Dir. Westport Free Health Clinic, Kansas City, Mo., 1974-76; clinician St. Louis Dept. Health, 1977-82; gen. practice dentistry Troy, Mo., 1978-92; pvt. practice St. Louis, 1993-94; mem. gen. practice staff Gravois-Gustine Dental Group, St. Louis, 1994-96; pvt. practice gen. dentistry St. Louis, 1996-97; pvt. practice Chestnut Park Dental, St. Louis, 1997—. Mem. ADA, Greater St. Louis Dental Soc. (bd. dirs. 1999—), Am. Soc. Dentistry for Children, St. Louis Dental Rsch. Group, Delta Sigma Delta, Troy C. of C., Rotary (Troy chpt., dir. dental program 1985—, sec. 1988, pres. 1989, bd. dirs. 1989-91). Home: 360 W Point Ct Saint Louis MO 63130-4028 Office: Chestnut Park Dental 4583 Chestnut Park Plz Ste 201 Saint Louis MO 63129-3163 E-mail: meosborn@swbell.net.

OSBORN, MARVIN GRIFFING, JR., educational consultant; b. Baton Rouge, Sept. 7, 1922; s. Marvin Griffing and Mamie (Hester) O.; m. Sarah Fleming, Aug. 3, 1945; children: Jane Fleming, Charles Porter. BA, La. State U., 1942, MA, 1946; LLD, St. Xavier U., 1971; DHum, Phillips U., 1977. Pub. relations counsel La. State U., 1945-47, acting dir. bur. pub. service, 1947; assoc. prof., chmn. dept. journalism and dir. pub. relations Howard Coll. (now Frank Samford U.), 1947-49; dir. pub. relations, lectr. journalism Miss. State Coll. (now Miss. State U.), 1949-53; dir. information Washington U., 1953-58, pub. relations adviser, 1955-58, dir. Devel. Funds, 1958-61; cons. coll. and univ. adminstrn., 1961—, including Drake, Duke, Phillips, Tampa, Tex. Christian univs., Atlantic Christian Coll. (now Barton Coll.), Bethany (W.Va.), Eckerd, Loretto Heights, St. Xavier U., Tenn. Wesleyan, Webster U., Hendrix, Mercy (Detroit), Bethel (Tenn.), McMurry U., St. Scholastica, Coker Coll., Christian Ch. Found., Nat. Meth. Found. Christian Higher Edn., Lexington Theol. Sem., Memphis Theol. Sem., Nat. Benevolent Assn. Christian Ch., Sisters of Loretto. Interim pres. St. Xavier Coll., now St. Xavier U., 1968-69; mem. planning com. Conf. for Advancement Understanding and Support Higher Edn., White Sulphur Springs, W.Va., 1958; mem. exec. com. program and arrangements com. Gen. Assembly Christian Ch., 1977, 87-89. Bd. dirs. St. Louis Heart Assn., 1969-75, Fla. Christian Ctr., 1986-88; trustee Nat. City Christian Ch. Corp., 1981-85; mem. Christian Ch., bd. dirs., exec. com., sec. divsn. of higher edn., 1973-77, mem. panel to study fin. procedures of Christian Ch. (Disciples of Christ), 1987-89, Cypress Village Devel. Coun., Jacksonville, Fla., 1992-98, co-chair, 1992-98; mem. nat. fundraising com. Disciples World, 2002-04. Served from lt. to capt. 28th Inf. Divsn. AUS, 1942-45, ETO. Recipient Harry T. Ice disting. svc. award Christian Ch. Found., 1991. Mem. Am. Coll. Pub. Rels. Assn. (v.p. dists. 1951-52, v.p. membership 1952-53, sec.-treas. 1953-55, pres. 1959-60), Nat. Benevolent Assn. (amb. 1992—1998), Soc. Profl. Journalists, Omicron Delta Kappa, Sigma Chi. Home: 13655 Myrica Ct Jacksonville FL 32224-6626

OSBORN, MARY JANE MERTEN, biochemist, educator; b. Colorado Springs, Colo., Sept. 24, 1927; d. Arthur John and Vivien Naomi (Morgan) Merten; m. Ralph Kenneth Osborn, Oct. 26, 1950. BA, U. Calif., Berkeley, 1948; PhD, U. Wash., 1958. Postdoctoral fellow, dept. microbiology NYU Sch. Medicine, N.Y.C., 1959-61, instr., 1961-62, asst. prof., 1962-63; asst. prof. dept. molecular biology Albert Einstein Coll. Medicine, Bronx, N.Y., 1963-66, asso. prof., 1966-68; prof. dept. microbiology U. Conn. Health Ctr., Farmington, 1968—, dept. head, 1980—2002. Mem. bd. sci. counselors Nat. Heart, Lung and Blood Inst., 1975-79; mem. Nat. Sci. Bd., 1980-86; adv. coun. Nat. Inst. Gen. Med. Sci., 1983-86, divsn. rsch. grants NIH, 1989-94, chair, 1992-94; trustee Biosci. Info. Systems, 1986-91, chair, 1990-91; mem. German Am. Acad. Coun., 1994-97; mem. space scis. bd. NRC, 1994-2000, chair com. space biology and medicine, 1994-2000; cochair com. on indications for waterborne pathogens, 2002-03. Assoc. editor Jour. Biol. Chemistry, 1978-80; contbr. articles in field of biochemistry and molecular biology to profl. jours. Mem. rsch. com. Am. Heart Assn., 1972-77, chair, 1976-77. NIH fellow, 1959-61; NIH grantee, 1962-95; NSF grantee, 1965-68; Am. Heart Assn. grantee, 1968-71 Fellow Am. Acad. Arts and Scis. (coun. 1988-91), NAS (coun. 1990-93, com. sci. engring. and pub. policy 1993-96); mem. Am. Acad. Microbiology (bd. govs. 1994-2000), Am. Fedn. Soc. Exptl. Biology (pres. 1982-83), Am. Soc. Biol. Chemists (pres. 1981-82), Am. Soc. Microbiology. Democrat. Office: U Conn Health Ctr Dept Microbiology Ctr Farmington CT 06030-0001 Office Phone: 860-679-4206.

OSBORN, SUSAN CHANEY, writer, educator; b. Ft. Campbell, Ky., Jan. 7, 1953; d. Lawrence Elvie and Wilma Barbara (Powell) Howard; m. Nicholas Lourick, Aug. 1, 1976 (div. Oct. 1981); m. Steve Osborn, Mar. 20, 1993; 1 child. BS, Ga. State U., 1989; MS, U. Colo., 1997. Lic. tchr., Colo, pvt. occupational tchr., Colo. Owner, photographer Creative Assistance, Atlanta, 1979-89; educator St. Mary's Acad., Cherry Hills Village, Colo., 1989-90, Denver Pub. Schs., 1990-92; internet resource coord. Nat. Renewable Energy Lab., Golden, Colo., 1993-95; writer Diners Club Internat., Englewood, Colo., 1995-96; owner, writer, coord. Publs. Resolution, Denver, 1996—. Website advisor Colo. Dept. Pub. Health and Environment, Denver, 1998-99; advisor Houghton-Mifflin Co., Boston, 1992; mem. math. text seclection com. Denver Pub. Schs., 1991; cons. Hauser Chem. Co., Boulder, Colo., 1994. Author: Public Service Company Classroom Connection, 1992, photography manual. Art/photography dir. Boy's Club, Marietta, GA., 1987; art show sect. organizer Girl's Club, Atlanta, 1988; implementor Bear Creek Blvd. Civic Assn., Lakewood, Colo., 1995; pub. rels. coord. Resolve Rocky Mountain Assn., Denver, 1996. Fellow Colo. Writing Project; mem. NEA, Golden Key. Avocations: creative writing, creative photography, theater, hiking, mountain biking. Office: Publs Resolution PO Box 37263 Denver CO 80237

OSBORN, WILLIAM A. investment company executive; Chmn., CEO No. Trust Corp., Chgo. Office: No Trust Co 50 S Lasalle St Chicago IL 60675-0001

OSBORN, WILLIAM GEORGE, savings and loan executive; b. Alton, Ill., Dec. 9, 1925; s. Ralph A. and Pauline J. (Horn) O.; m. Hilda M. Alexander, Aug. 12, 1950; children: Barbara K., David A., Robert W., James A. BS in Math., Shurtleff Coll., 1947; certificate, Grad. Sch. Savs. and Loan, Ind. U., 1946-48; A.M. in Econs., St. Louis U., 1962. With Germania Fed. Savs. and Loan Assn., Alton, 1946-90, exec. officer, 1955-86, pres., 1964-86, chmn., 1981-86, chmn. trust com., 1982-86; pres. Fin. Service Assocs., Ft. Lauderdale, Fla., 1986—. Pres. Germania Fin. Corp., 1970-86; owner Fin. Guidance, Alton, 1951—; mem. Opportunities Unltd., 1954-58; instr. Am. Savs. and Loan Inst.; bd. dirs. Nat. Coun. Savs. Instns., Washington, 1984-86. Author: Savings and Loan Operating Policies Manual, 1960, Economic Factors Influencing Savings and Loan Interest Rates, 1962. Pres. Alton Wood River Community Chest, 1959; bd. dirs. Piasa Bird coun. Boy Scouts Am., 1961-88, Mississippi Valley Jr. Achievement, Alton Area United Fund, 1961-63; founder, bd. dirs., treas. New Piasa Chautauqua Ch. Assembly, 1982-86; treas. Lewis and Clark Community Coll. Found., 1976-86; bd. dirs., sec. Riverbend Civic Progress, 1984-86. Served to lt. (j.g.) USNR, 1943-46, 50-52. Mem. Nat. Assn. Bus. Economists, Nat. Economists Club, St. Louis Economists Club, Am. Inst. Mgmt. Presbyterian (elder). Clubs: Masons (Alton); Shriners; Lockhaven Country (Alton); Chautauqua (Ill.) Yacht. Office Phone: 954-776-7325.

OSBORN, WILLIAM PALMER, writer, English language educator; b. Hastings, Mich., Oct. 6, 1946; s. Palmer Osborn and Elizabeth Grose Dubuque; m. Sylvia Ayano Watanabe, Mar. 26, 1991. BA, U. Calif., San Diego, 1981; MFA, Bowling Green State U., 1983; PhD, SUNY, Binghamton, 1986. Prof. English Grand Valley State U., Allendale, Mich., 1988—. Contbr. short fiction to jours. including Carolina Quar., So. Humanities Rev., Miss. Rev., nonfiction to publs. including Chgo. Rev., Manoa, San Francisco Rev. Books. Home: 145 Crestwood NW Grand Rapids MI 49504 Office: Grand Valley State U Allendale MI 49401

OSBORNE, BARRIE M. motion picture producer; b. N.Y.C., Feb. 7, 1944; s. William Osborne and Hertha Schwarz; m. Micha Yun, July 30, 1969; 1 child, Danielle Kim. BA, Carleton Coll., 1966. Prodn. exec. New Regency Films, 1980-82; v.p. motion picture, producer Walt Disney Pictures, Burbank, Calif., 1985-87; ind. producer Los Angeles, 1987—. Prodr.(assoc. prodr.): (films) Cutter's Way, 1981, The Big Chill, 1983, Fandango, 1985; exec. prodr.: Peggy Sue Got Married, 1986, Child's Play, 1988, Dick Tracy, 1990, Wilder Napalm, 1993, China Moon, 1994, Rapa Nui, 1994, The Fan, 1996, The Matrix, 1999; prodr.: Face/Off, 1997, The Lord of the Rings: The Fellowship of the Ring, 2001 (AFI Movie of the Year, 2002, BAFTA Award for best film, 2002), The Lord of the Rings: The Two Towers, 2002, The Last Place on Earth, 2002, The Lord of the Rings: The Return of the King, 2003 (Academy Award for Best Picture, 2004). Served to 1st lt. U.S. Army, 1966-69, Korea. Mem. Dirs. Guild Am. Avocation: sailing.*

OSBORNE, BARTLEY PORTER, JR., aeronautical engineer; b. Akron, Ohio, Sept. 1, 1934; s. Bartley P. and Cordelia Inez (Sims) O.; m. Carol Ann Eubanks, Jan. 15, 1966; children: Roxane Elizabeth, Ashley Hamilton. BSME, Carnegie Mellon U., Pitts., 1956; MS in Aerospace Engring., U. So. Calif., 1962. Sr. stress analyst N. Am. Aviation, Columbus, Ohio, 1956-66; sr. design engr. Lockheed Aircraft, Burbank, Calif., 1966-70, project engr., 1970-74; staff specialist aeronautics and ocean vehicles Office Sec. of Def., Washington, 1974-78; engring. prog. mgr. Lockheed Aircraft, 1978-82, chief adv. design engr., 1982-85, chief engr. ATF, 1985-87, dep. chief adv. design engr., 1987-89; prog. mgr. Lockheed Aero. Sys. Co., Burbank, 1989-90; v.p., engr. Lockheed Aero. Systems Co., Marietta, Ga., 1990-96, v.p. advanced concepts, 1996-97; retired; cons. Aerotec Solutions, 1998—. Chmn. NASA Aeronautics Adv. Com., 1994-97; chmn. Aerospace Coun. SAE, 1997-2002; chmn. program planning com. Quiet Supersonic, 2001-02; bd. dirs. Aerofon Corp., San Diego; guest lectr. Carnegie Mellon U., 2001, Calif. Inst. Tech., 2003. Pres. Chesterfield Mews Homeowners Assn., Fairfax, Va., 1977-78. 1st lt. U.S. Army, 1956-58. Pa. State scholar, 1952; recipient Disting. Pub. Svc. medal U.S. Govt., 1997. Fellow Royal Aero. Soc., AIAA (assoc.); mem. L.A. Violin Cello Soc. Democrat. Avocation: cellist. Home: 405 White Tree Trl Palm Desert CA 92211-8947 Fax: 760-772-6842. Office Phone: 760-772-0582. E-mail: aero21st@aol.com.

OSBORNE, BURL, newspaper publisher, editor; b. Jenkins, Ky., June 25, 1937; s. Oliver and Juanita (Smallwood) O.; m. Betty S. Wilder, Feb. 14, 1974; 1 son, Burl Jonathan. Student, U. Ky., 1955-57; BA in Journalism, Marshall U., 1960; MBA, L.I. U. Sch. Bus., 1984; A.M.P., Harvard Bus. Sch., 1984. Reporter Ashland (Ky.) Daily Ind., 1957-58; reporter, editor Sta. WHTN-TV, Huntington, W.Va., 1958-60; corr. AP, Bluefield, W.Va., 1960-62, statehouse corr. Charleston, W.Va., 1963-64, corr. Spokane, Wash., 1964-67, news editor Denver, 1967-70, chief of bur. AP, Ky., 1970-72, AP, Ohio, 1972-74; asst. chief of bur. AP, Washington, 1974-76; mng. editor world hdqs. AP, N.Y.C., 1977-80; exec. editor Dallas Morning News, 1980-83, v.p., 1981, sr. v.p., editor, 1983-84, pres., editor, 1985-90, pub., editor, 1991—2001, pub. emeritus, 2001—. Bd. dirs. AP, chmn., 2002—; bd. dirs. J.C. Penney Co.; pres. publ. divsn. Belo Corp., 1995—2002; mem. journalism adv. com. Knight Found., 1991—97; bd. dirs. Nat. Kidney Found., S.W. Transplant Alliance. Bd. dirs. Pulitzer Prize, 1986—95, co-chmn. bd. dir., 1994—95. Named Newspaper Exec. of Yr., Nat. Press Found., 1992; inducted to Ky. Journalism Hall of Fame, 1994; recipient Disting. Alumnus award Marshall U., 1997, Freedoms Found. Next Millinium award, 1999. Mem.: Newspaper Assn. Am. (bd. dirs. 1996—), World Assn. Newspapers (mem. exec. com. 1998—2001, bd. dirs.), So. Newspaper Pub. Assn. (bd. dirs. 1995—2003, pres. 2000—01), Tex. Daily Newspaper Assn. (bd. dirs. 1982—92, pres. 1993), Am. Press Inst. (chmn. 1988—93), Am. Soc. Newspaper Editors (bd. dirs. 1982—91, pres. 1990—91), Orgn. Profl. Journalists. Home: 3901 Turtle Creek Blvd Dallas TX 75219 Office: Dallas Morning News PO Box 655237 Dallas TX 75265-5237 E-mail: bosborne@belo.com.

OSBORNE, CLAUDINA ROSETTA, financial analyst; b. Montserrat, Mar. 19, 1965; d. Joseph William and Mary Edith Osborne; 1 child, Bryan A. M. BS in health svcs. adminstrn., Herbert H. Lehman Coll., 1994; M in Pub. Adminstrn. and Fin., L.I. U., 2000. Fin. analyst AIG, N.Y.C., 1998—2001; sr. fin. analyst Primerica Fin. Svcs., N.Y.C., 1999 2000; ops. analyst Morgan Stanley Dean Witter, 2002—. Mem. MPA task force L.I. U., 1998-2000. Mem. Caribbean Women Orgn., Bronx, 1995-97; leader Boy Scouts of Am., 1995-97. Recipient Hiroshima Japanese scholarhip award Herbert Lehman Coll., 1993. Mem. NAFE, Am. Soc. for Pub. Adminstrn., N.Y. Women Agenda, Sigma Beta Delta. Episcopalian. Avocations: travel, reading, meeting people, tennis. Home: 2435 Boston Rd Bronx NY 10467 E-mail: dinaosborne@aol.com.

OSBORNE, DUNCAN ELLIOTT, lawyer; b. Orange, N.J., May 24, 1944; s. Walter Dodd Osborne and Anne (Boaz) Treanor; m. Elizabeth May Bachman, Dec. 29, 1965; children: Ellen Osborne Ray, Mark Elliott, Michael Cleveland. BA, Stanford U., 1966; MA, U. Tex., 1968, JD with honors, 1971. Bar: Tex. (cert. estate planning and probate law) 1971, U.S. Supreme Ct. 1975, U.S. Tax Ct. 1975, U.S. Fed. Ct. Claims 1997. Atty. Graves Dougherty, Austin, Tex., 1971-93, Osborne, Lowe, Helman & Smith L.L.P., Austin, 1993-2000, Osborne & Helman L.L.P., Austin, 2001—. Bd. dirs. Boatmen's Nat. Bank Austin, 1995-97, Hill Country Bank, Austin, 1998. Co-author, co-editor: Asset Protection: Domestic and International Law and Tactics; contbr. articles to profl. jours. Trustee Susan Vaughan Found., Houston, Still Water Found., Austin; chair bd. trustees St. Stephens Episcopal Sch., Austin, 1985-91, St. Andrews Episcopal Sch., Austin, 1978; dir. Touchstones Discussion Project, Annapolis, Md.; mem. Tex. Law Rev. Fellow Am. Coll. Trust and Estate Counsel, Coll. of State Bar of Tex.; mem. ABA, Internat. Tax Planning Assn., Internat. Bar Assn., Offshore Inst., Internat. Acad. Estate and Trust Law (exec. com.), Tex. Bar Found., Asset Protection Planning Commn. (chair 1996-98)), Order of Coif. Avocation: scuba diving. Office: Osborne & Helman LLP 301 Congress Ave Ste 1910 Austin TX 78701-2959 E-mail: deosborne@osbornehelman.com.

OSBORNE, HARRY ALAN, orthodontist; b. Youngstown, Ohio, Mar. 9, 1934; s. Kenneth L. and Marguerite (Filmer) O.; m. Carol June Williams, June 30, 1956 (dec. 1989); children: Elizabeth Ann, J. Scott, Linda J., Robert K.; m. Linda Sue Leister Simmons, May 9, 1993; stepchildren: William A. Simmons, John S. Simmons, Susan Jane Simmons. Student, Westminster Coll., New Wilmington, Pa., 1952-55; DDS, U. Pitts., 1959; MS, Northwestern U., 1962. Diplomate Am. Bd. Orthodontics. Intern Youngstown Hosp. Assn., 1959; practice dentistry specializing in orthodontics Canton, Ohio, 1964—. Supt. adv. com. North Canton Sch. Dist., 1960-87; mem. adv. com. Soc. Bank, Canton, 1962-89; chmn. bldg. com. Faith United Meth. Ch., 1975-80; chmn. cmty bd. YMCA, North Canton, 1986-96, charter mem. Heritage Club (Canton YMCA); v.p. Hills and Dales Homeowners Assn., 1993-96; trustee Christ Presbyn. Ch., Canton, Ohio, elder. Recipient Disting. Service award, Jaycees, 1968. Mem. ADA, Pierre Fauchard Acad., Am. Assn. Orthodontists, Coll. of Diplomates of Am. Bd. Orthodontists (charter), Gt. Lakes Orthodontic Assn., Ohio Dental Assn., Cleve. Orthodontic Soc. (pres. 1983), Stark County Dental Soc. (pres. 1975-76, inductee Disting. Dental Svc. Acad. 2001), World Fedn. Orthodontists, Internat. Coll. Dentists, Shady Hollow Country Club (Massillon, Ohio) (bd. dirs. 1984-85, 87—), Brookside Country Club. Republican. Avocation: golf. Home: 2410 Strathmore Dr NW Canton OH 44708-1364 Office: 1021 Schneider St SE Canton OH 44720-3857

OSBORNE, JAMES ALFRED, religious organization administrator; b. Toledo, July 3, 1927; s. Alfred James and Gladys Irene (Gaugh) O.; m. Ruth Glenrose Campbell, Nov. 26, 1945; 1 child, Constance Jean (Mrs. Donald William Canning). Grad., Salvation Army Coll., 1947; student, U. Chattanooga, 1954-55; D of Pub. Svc. (hon.), Gordon Coll., 1991. Corps officer Salvation Army, Magness, Nashville, 1947, Southside, Memphis, 1948, Owensboro, Ky., 1949-54, comdg. officer Chattanooga, 1954-61, city comdr. Miami, Fla., 1961-65, divisional sec. Ky.-Tenn. Div., 1965-68, gen. sec. N.C. and S.C. Div., 1968-70, pub. rels. sec. 15 so. states, D.C. and Mex., 1970-71, divisional comdr. Md. and No. W.Va. Div., 1971-73, divisional comdr. Nat. Capital and Virginias Div., 1973-78, divisional comdr. Fla. Div., 1978-80, chief sec. Western Ter., 1980-84, nat. chief sec., 1984-86, territorial comdr. so. states Atlanta, 1986-89; nat. comdr., Republic of Marshall Islands, Guam, P.R., Virgin Islands Salvation Army USA, 1989-93. Chmn. Salvation Army Nat. Planning and Devel. Commn., 1974-76, 84-86; exec. bd. Vision Interfaith Satellite Network, Nat. Assn. Evangelicals, Christian Children's Fund Inc.; chmn. bd. Christian Mgmt. Assn., 1993-94; exec. com. religious alliance Against Pornography; rep. Salvation Army to numerous orgns. Bd. dirs. Nat. Law Ctr. for Children and Families; sec. Tenn. Conf. on Social Welfare, 1959, v.p., 1960; pres. Fla. Conf. on Social Welfare, 1965; pres. Ky. Welfare Assn., 1970. Mem. Chattanooga Pastors Assn. (pres. 1958), Va. and W. Va. Welfare Confs., Rotary. Personal E-mail: jim@jarudsborne.com.

OSBORNE, JOAN (ELIZABETH), singer, songwriter; b. Anchorage, Ky., July 8, 1962; d. Jerry and Ruth (Yunker) O. Student, NYU. Singer various blues clubs, N.Y.C. Albums include Soul Show, 1991, Blue Million Miles, 1993, Relish (includes One of Us), 1995 (7 Grammy nominations 1996, named No. 1 album Entertainment Weekly), Early Recordings, 1996. Office: care Mercury Records Worldwide Plz 825 8th Ave New York NY 10019-7416

OSBORNE, JOHN EDWARDS, lawyer; b. Tucson, Feb. 10, 1953; s. Earle Dean and Helen Edwards Osborne; m. Diana Kuhel, Apr. 10, 1976; children: Monica, Valerie. AB with honors, Stanford U., 1975; JD, U. Tex., 1981. Bar: Ariz. Supreme Ct. 1981, U.S. Dist. Ct. Ariz. 1981, U.S. Ct. Appeals (9th cir.) 1990, U.S. Supreme Ct. 1994, White Mountain Apache Tribal Ct. Assoc. Chandler, Tullar, Udall & Redhair, Tucson, 1981-85; mng. atty. Tucson br. personal injury dept. Jacoby & Meyers Law Offices, Tucson, 1985-89; mng. ptnr. Goldberg & Osborne, Tucson, 1989—. Referee adminstr. Am. Youth Soccer Orgn., Tucson, 1997—. Fellow Ariz. Bar Found.; mem. ATLA, ABA, Am. Bd. Trial Advs. (assoc. mem., Tucson chpt.), Ariz. Trial Lawyers Assn. (sustaining mem., bd. govs.), State Bar Ariz. (cert. specialist in personal injury and wrongful death, pub. rels. com. 1985-89, trial practice sect. 1988—), Pima County Bar Assn. (pro bono com. 1982-95, v.p. young lawyers divsn. 1987-88). Avocations: private pilot, scuba diving, skiing, hunting, soccer referee. Office: Goldberg & Osborne 33 N Stone Ave Ste 1850 Tucson AZ 85701-1426

OSBORNE, JOHN L. academic administrator, educator; b. St. Catherines, Ont., Can., Aug. 28, 1967; s. John Barclay and Sharon Christine Osborne; m. Kelly Ilene Brewster, Aug. 6, 1988; children: Samuel, Riley, Seth. AA & AS, York Coll., Nebr., 1988; BS, Okla. Christian U., 1991. Tchg. cons. Mito Bd. of Ed., Japan, 1991—93; assoc. dir. Let's Start Talking, Ft. Worth,

1994—2000; dir. internat. prog. Okla. Christian U., 2000—. Cons. Let's Start Talking, 2000—, Internat. Edn. Network, Worland, Wyo., 2000—. Contbg. editor: (book) Global Perspectives, 2001, Culture Contact, 2002. Mem.: NAFSA.

OSBORNE, JOHN WALTER, historian, educator, author; b. Bklyn., Aug. 19, 1927; s. Douglas Walter and Gertrude Ann (Purcell) O.; m. Frances Patricia Hannon, Aug. 2, 1958; 1 son, David. BA, Rutgers U., 1957, MA (Louis Bevier fellow), 1959, PhD, 1961. Asst. prof. history Kean Coll. of N.J., 1961-63, N.J. Inst. Tech., 1963-64; asst. prof. Rutgers U., New Brunswick, N.J., 1964-66, assoc. prof., 1966-69, prof., 1969-93, prof. emeritus, 1993—. Author: William Cobbett-His Thought and His Times, 1966, The Silent Revolution: The Industrial Revolution in England as a Source of Cultural Change, 1970, John Cartwright, 1972; co-author: Cobbett in His Times, 1990; editor: Jour. of Rutgers U. Libraries, 1975-80; co-editor: A Grammar of the English Language, 1983; contbr. articles to profl. jours. Recipient Henry Browne award for disting. teaching Rutgers U., 1988; Am. Philos. Soc. grantee, 1966, 75 Home: PO Box 426 Ivoryton CT 06442-0426

OSBORNE, JUDITH BARBOUR, artist; b. Winnipeg, Man., Can., Oct. 14, 1950; came to U.S., 1952; d. John Anderson and Laura May (Jones) Barbour; m. Frederick Spring Osborne Jr., Feb. 15, 1986; 1 child, Sheila. BFA, Univ. of Arts, Phila., 1974; student, Vt. Studio Ctr., 1984-89; MFA, Pa. Acad. Fine Arts, Phila., 1997. Prin. Barbour CalliGraphics, Phila., 1976—2002; dir. publs. and publicity Phila. Conf. on Calligraphic Arts, Phila., 1982; mem. faculty Phila. Coll. Art (now Univ. of Arts), 1982-85, 92, 00, Drexel U., Phila., 1991—2002; faculty Innovations Internat. Calligraphy Conf., N.Y., 1987; exhbns. coord. Calleidoscope Internat. Calligraphy Conf., Trenton, NJ, 1993; guest lectr., workshop instr. Nantucket Island Sch. of Design and Arts, 2004. Guest curator Kamin Gallery, U. Pa., Phila., 1993, 95; exhbn. juror Phila. Calligraphers' Soc., 1989, 91, 94-95, 98, Phila. Sketch Club, 2002; spkr. 19th Internat. Calligraphy Conf., Guilford, Conn., 1999. One-woman shows include Rourke Art Gallery, Moorhead, Minn., 1999, Phila. Art Alliance, 1999, Artists' House, 1998, 2000, 02, Living Arts, Tulsa, Okla., 2000, Shipley Sch., Bryn Mawr, Pa., 2000, Delaware Ctr. for Contemporary Arts, 2004; exhibited in group shows at Nat. Arts Club, N.Y.C., 1990, Pa. State Mus., Harrisburg, 1994, 2000-01, Am. Coll., Bryn Mawr, Pa., 1996, Nexus Found. for Today's Art, Phila., 1997, Del. Ctr. for Contemporary Art, 2002, Parallels Gallery, Phila., 2002, Tenri Cultural Inst., N.Y.C., 2002; Shanxi Art Mus., Xian, China, 2003, Ice House Gallery, Berkeley Springs, W.Va., 2004; represented in permanent collections at Fed. Res. Bank Phila., Blue Cross, Rourke Art Gallery Mus., Moorhead, Barbour/Ladouceur Archs., Mpls.; also pvt. collections; collaborator Sophia Osborne Dance Assocs., 1999-2001; contbr. articles to mags. and newspapers including Art Matters, 1997-2001, Letter Arts Rev., 2003. Recipient Best of Show Abington (Pa.) Art Ctr., 1990; Pa. Acad. Fine Arts fellow, Phila., 1997, Independence Found. fellow, 2001. Mem. Coll. Art Assn., Phila. Calligraphers' Soc. (bd. mem., publs. editor 1980-85), Inst. Noetic Scis. Avocation: metaphysics. Home: 11 Mitchel Terr Ivoryton CT 06442-1042

OSBORNE, LOUISE, publishing executive; Pres. Osborne/Jenks Prodns., Inc., Wethersfield, Conn., 1979—. Office: care Osborne/Jenks Prodns Inc 936 Silas Deane Hwy Wethersfield CT 06109-4273

OSBORNE, MARY POPE, writer; b. Ft. Sill, Okla., May 20, 1949; d. William Perkins and Barnette (Dickens) Pope; m. William R. Osborne, May 16, 1976. BA in Religion, U. N.C., 1971. Author: Run, Run, As Fast As You Can, 1982, Love Always, Blue, 1983, Best Wishes, Joe Brady, 1984, Mo to the Rescue, 1985, Last One Home, 1986, Beauty and the Beast, 1987, Favorite Greek Myths, 1988, American Tall Tales, 1990, The Many Lives of Benjamin Franklin, 1990, Moon Horse, 1991, George Washington, Leader of a New Nation, 1991, Spider Kane Mystery Series, 1992, 1993, Magic Tree House Series, 1992—2002, Haunted Waters, 1994, Molly and the Prince, 1994, Favorite Norse Myths, 1996, One World, Many Religions, 1996, Rocking Horse Christmas, 1997, Favorite Medieval Tales, 1998, Standing in the Light, 1998, The Life of Jesus, 1998, Adaline Falling Star, 2000, My Brothers Keeper, 2000, My Secret War, 2000, Kate and the Beanstalk, 2000, The Brave Little Seamstress, 2002, After the Rain, 2002, The One-Eyed Giant, 2002, The Land of the Dead, 2002, New York's Bravest, 2002, Tales from the Odyssey, 2002, Happy Birthday, America, 2003. Recipient Disting. Alumna award, U. N.C., Chapel Hill, 1994, Distinctive Contbn. to Arts award, N.Y. Carolina Club. Mem.: PEN, Authors League Fund (bd. dirs.), Authors Guild (pres. 1993—97). Office: Brandt & Brandt Lit Agy 1501 Broadway Ste 2310 New York NY 10036-5689

OSBORNE, RICHARD DE JONGH, mining and metals company executive; b. Bronxville, NY, Mar. 19, 1934; s. Stanley de Jongh and M. Elizabeth (Ide) O.; m. Cheryl Anne Archibald, Dec. 14, 1957; children: Leslie Coleman, Lindsay Vogel, Nicholas de J., Stanley de J. AB in Econs., Princeton U., 1956. With Cuno Engring. Corp., Meriden, Conn., 1956-60; fin., planning and mktg. exec. IBM Corp., Armonk, NY, 1960-69; investment adviser Sherman M. Fairchild, N.Y.C., 1969-70; exec. v.p. fin. and bus. devel., dir. Fairchild Camera & Instrument Corp., Mountain View, Calif., 1970-74; v.p. fin. ASARCO Inc. (formerly Am. Smelting & Refining Co.), N.Y.C., 1975-77, exec. v.p., 1977-82, pres., 1982-85, chmn., pres., CEO, 1985-99. Bd. dirs. NACCO Industries, Inc., Tinker Found.; bd. dirs. (formerly non-exec. chmn.) Schering-Plough Corp.; non-exec. chmn., bd. dirs. Datawatch Corp.; treas. Ams. Soc. Mem. Nat. Mining Assn. (hon. dir.), Coun. Fgn. Rels., Econs. Club NY, River Club, Brook Club, Sakonnet Golf Club. Home and Office: 40 E 94th St Apt 32B New York NY 10128-0759 Personal E-mail: rdejo@att.net.

OSBORNE, RICHARD HAZELET, anthropology and medical genetics educator; b. Kennecott, Alaska, June 18, 1920; s. Clarence Edward and Margaret Jerenne (Hazelet) O.; m. Barbara White, Oct. 14, 1944; children: Susan, Richard, David; m. Barbara Teachman, Sept. 1, 1970. Student, U. Alaska, 1939-41; BS, BA, U. Wash., 1949; postgrad., Harvard U., 1949-50; PhD (Viking Fund Pre-doctoral fellow, Spl. fellow Inst. for Study Human Variation), Columbia, 1956; hon. doctor odontology, U. Oulu, Finland, 1994; DSc (hon.), U. Alaska, Fairbanks, 2001. Research asso. Columbia U., 1953-58; asst. Sloan-Kettering Inst., N.Y.C., 1958-60, asso., 1960-62, asso. mem., head sect. human genetics, 1962-64; prof. anthropology and med. genetics U. Wis., Madison, 1964-86, prof. emeritus, 1986—; rsch. assoc. Quatenary Ctr. U. Alaska, Fairbanks, 1993—. Asso. prof. preventive medicine Cornell Med. Coll., 1962-64; clin. geneticist Meml. Hosp. for Cancer, N.Y.C., 1963-65; vis. scientist Forsyth Dental Center, Boston, 1969-71; cons. human genetics Newington (Conn.) Childrens Hosp., 1971-73; Mem. com. on epidemiology and vets. follow-up studies NRC, 1969-73; mem. perinatal research com. Nat. Inst. Neurol. Diseases and Stroke, NIH, 1970-72; mem. cultural anthropology fellowship and rev. NIMH, 1969-73 Author: Genetic Basis of Morphological Variation, 1959, Biological and Social Meaning of Race, 1971; Editor: Social Biology, 1961-77, 81—99; contbr. articles to profl. jours. Served to maj. USAAF, 1942-46. Decorated D.F.C., Air medal with 3 oak leaf clusters.; Named Health Research Council Career Scientist City N.Y., 1962-64 Fellow Explorers Club; Mem. Am. Assn. Phys. Anthropology (exec. com. 1965-67, v.p. 1968-70), Am. Soc. for Human Genetics (dir. 1960-61, 67-69), Behavior Genetics Assn. (pres. pro-tem 1970-71), Soc. for Study Social Biology (editor Social Biology 1961-99, dir. 1981-83, 86-99), Pioneers of Alaska (life), Sigma Xi. Office: 1129 E 8th St Port Angeles WA 98362-6628 E-mail: rho6@columbia.edu.

OSBORNE, RICHARD JAY, electric utility company executive; b. N.Y.C., Feb. 16, 1951; s. Victor and Evelyn Celia (Sweetbaum) O. BA, Tufts U., 1973; MBA, U. N.C., 1975. Fin. analyst Duke Power Co., Charlotte, NC, 1975-78, sr. fin. analyst, 1978-80, mgr. fin. rels., 1980-81, mgr. treasury activities, 1981, treas., 1981-88, v.p. fin., CFO, 1988-94, sr. v.p., CFO, 1994-97; exec. v.p., CFO Duke Energy Corp., Charlotte, NC, 1997-2000, pub. rels. officer, 2000—, exec. v.p., chief risk officer, 2001—, group v.p. pub. and regulatory policy, 2004—. Chair United Way of Ctrl. Carolinas Alexis De Toqueville Soc., 2004—; bd. dirs. Charlotte Jewish Fedn., Mus. New South, Charlotte Symphony Orch., Johnson Smith U., Nuc. Elec. Ins. Ltd. Mem. Fin. Execs. Inst. Democrat. Jewish. Office: Duke Energy Corp 526 S Church St Charlotte NC 28202-1802

OSBORNE, SEWARD RUSSELL, writer; b. Catskill, NY, June 28, 1946; s. Seward Russell and Doris Virginia (Tompkins) O.; m. Jean Marie Shaver, June 22, 1968; children: Dean, Sarah. Historic site technician Senate House State Historic Site, Kingston, N.Y., 1976-77; contbg. editor Mil. Images, 1980—; contbg. author Mil. Collector & Historian, 1984—; historian Ulster County Civil War Round Table, 1994—; photographic cons. Arts and Entertainment Network, 1996. Cons. in field. Author: Holding the Left, The 20th New York State Militia at Gettysburg, July 1, 1863, 1990, The Saga of the Mountain Legion (156th N.Y. Vols.) in the Civil War and the Modest Hero Who Saved Our Flag, 1994, The Ninety Days Service of the 20th New York State Militia, 1998; editor: The Civil War Diaries of Col. Theodore B. Gates, 20th New York State Militia, 1991; contbr. articles to North South Trader's Civil War, 1970s, 1980s, Ulster County Gazette, 1970s, 1980s; photographic cons. Legacy TV Prodn. Three Days at Gettysburg, 1994. Active Friends of the Ulysses S. Grant Cottage; founder, dir. 120th Monument Restoration Fund, 1996-97; charter mem. Nat. WWII Meml., 2002—. Cited for erection 20th NY State Militia monument on the Gettysburg Battlefield, 1981, on the Battlefield of 2d Bull Run, Manassas, 1986, Rondout, NY, 2003. Fellow The Co. of Mil. Historians; mem. DAV (life), NRA, Ulster County Com. to Save the Grant Cottage (founder, chmn. 1990), N.Y. State Mil. Heritage Inst., 1997, Ulster County Geneal. Soc. (Civil War history cons.); Zadock Pratt Mus (hon. life), Kingston Area Libr. (Civil War history cons.), Friends of Nat. Parks at Gettysburg, Inc., Surratt Soc. (life), Gettysburg Battlefield Preservation Assn., Lexington Hist. Soc. (hon. life), Friends of Albany Rural Cemetery, Am. Legion. Born Again Christian. Avocations: historical sites, collecting civil war artifacts. Home: 1329 County Road 2 Olivebridge NY 12461-5417

OSBORNE, STEPHEN J. philatelist; b. Hove, Sussex, Eng., Mar. 22, 1953; s. Stephen J. and Pauline (Compton) O.; m. Vanessa Mack, 1973 (div. 1976); 1 child, Stephen; m. Nicola Edwards, Aug. 19, 1978 (div. 1990); children: Francesca, James; m. Lorraine Gaetan, Dec. 31, 1994; children: Sean, Callum. Attended, Lancing Coll., Eng. Legal analyst anti-trust law pvt. practice, 1974—. Contbr. articles to profl. jours. Parliamentary candidate for Brighton, Eng., 1974, 79; trustee Cardinal Spellman Mus., Weston, Mass., 1994-98; mem. Smithsonian Mus., Washington, 1995. Mem. Odd Fellows (hon.). Democrat. Avocation: philosophy of ludwig wittgenstein. Address: PO Box 2105 Storrington West Sussex RH20 30JH England

OSBORNE, THOMAS EUGENE, oral and maxillofacial surgeon; b. Santa Barbara, Calif., Nov. 25, 1954; s. Thomas and Inez (Terres) O.; m. Joan Boubek; children: Elisabeth, Tommy. BA, U. Calif., Santa Barbara; DDS, Loyola U., Chgo., 1982; cert. in oral and maxillofacial surgery, Johns Hopkins U., 1983-87. Diplomate Am. Bd. Oral and Maxillofacial Surgery. Asst. chief of svcs. Johns Hopkins Hosp., Balt., 1986-87; asst. prof. Sch. Dentistry Emory U., Atlanta, 1987-91; asst. chief oral and maxillofacial surgery Grady Meml. Hosp., Atlanta, 1987-91; pvt. practice oral surgery Tucker, Ga., 1991—; pres. exec. coun., COO, bd. dirs. Benchmarq Healthcare Sys., Atlanta, 1995-97, CEO, 1999—. Chmn. continuing edn. com. No. Dist. Dental Soc., Atlanta, 1993-94. Author: Hospital Dentistry, 1992; contbr. articles to profl. jours., chpt. to book. Cub scout leader Boy Scouts Am., Tucker, 1994—; vol. World Relief. Fellow Am. Bd. Oral and Maxillofacial Surgery, Hinman Dental Soc.; mem. ADA, Am. Assn. Oral and Maxillofacial Surgery, Ga. Soc. Oral and Maxillofacial Surgery, Ga. Dental Assn., Johns Hopkins Med. and Surg. Soc., Xi Psi Phi. Avocations: skiing, writing, running, rollerblading, weightlifting. Office: 2163 Northlake Pkwy Tucker GA 30084-4102 E-mail: yanker2@aol.com.

OSBORNE, TOM, congressman, former college football coach; b. Feb. 23, 1937; m. Nancy Tederman; children: Mike, Ann, Susie. BA, Hastings Coll., 1959; MA, U. Nebr., 1963, PhD in Ednl. Psychology, 1965. Flankerback Washington Redskins, NFL, 1959-61, San Francisco 49ers, NFL, 1961-62; asst. football coach U. Nebr., 1962-73, head football coach, 1973-97; coach team U. Nebr. (Cotton Bowl), 1974, U. Nebr. (Sugar Bowl), 1971, U. Nebr. (Astro-Bluebonnet Bowl), 1976, U. Nebr. (Liberty Bowl), 1977, U. Nebr. (Sun Bowl), 1980, U. Nebr. (Orange Bowl), 1979, 83, 84, 89, 92-95; prof. emeritus U. Nebr., 1998-2000; mem. U.S. Congress from Nebr. 3rd Dist., 2001—; mem. agr. com., edn. and the workforce com., resources com. Served in U.S. Army. Named Big Eight Coach of Yr., 1975, 78, 80; named Bobby Dodds Nat. Coach of Yr., 1978 Coached team to NCAA Divsn. IA Nat. Championship, 1994, 1995, 1997. Republican. Office: US Ho of Reps 507 Cannon HOB Washington DC 20515-2703

OSBOURN, JOSEPH A. information technology executive; B in Physics, U. Louisville; MBA, Memphis State U. V.p. info. svcs. Walt Disney World Co., 1989—99; sr. v.p., chief info. officer Kmart Corp., 1999—2000; exec. v.p., worldwide chief info. officer Tech Data Corp., Clearwater, Fla., 2000—. Office: Tech Data Corp 5350 Tech Data Dr Clearwater FL 33760-3122

OSBOURNE, OZZY (JOHN OSBOURNE), vocalist; b. Birmingham, Eng., Dec. 3, 1948; m. Thelma Mayfair, 1971 (div. 1981); children: Jessica Starshine, Louis Jon; m. Sharon Arden, 1982; children: Aimee Rachel, Kelly, Jack. Vocalist Black Sabbath band, 1969—79, solo career, 1980—. Albums Blizzard of Ozz, 1980, Diary of a Madman, 1981, Speak of the Devil, 1982, Bark at the Moon, 1983, The Ultimate Sin, 1986, Tribute, 1987, No Rest for the Wicked, 1988, Just Say Ozzy, 1990, No More Tears, 1981, Live & Loud, 1993, Ozzmosis, 1995, Ozzman Cometh, 1997, Down to Earth, 2001, Live at Budokhan, 2002, Essential Ozzy Osbourne, 2003, Interview Disc 97.7 Htz-Fm, 1999, albums (with Black Sabbath) Black Sabbath, 1969, Paranoid, 1970, Master of Reality, 1971, Volume 4, 1972, Sabbath, Bloody Sabbath, 1975, Sabotage, 1975, Technical Ecstasy, 1976, We Sold Our Soul For Rock and Roll, 1976, Never Say Die, 1978, Reunion, 1998, Past Lives, 2002, singles So Tired, 1984, (with Black Sabbath) Paranoid, 1970, appeared (films) Black Sabbath: Live, 1978, The Ultimate Ozzy, Ozzy Osbourne: Bark at the Moon, Trick or Treat, 1986, Decline of Western Civilization Part II: The Metal Years, Ozzy Osbourne: The Wicked Videos, 1988, Ozzy Osbourne: Don't Blame Me, 1992, The History of Rock 'N' Roll, Vol. 8, The Jerky Boys, 1995, Private Parts, 1997, Little Nicky, 2000, (TV films) Billy's Shout, 1991, (TV series) The Frank Skinner Show, 1996, South Park, 1997, The Osbournes, 2002—, (video) Ozzy Osbourne: Live and Loud, 1993, Black Sabbath: The Last Supper, 1999. Recipient Grammy award, Best Heavy Metal Performance for "I Don't Want to Change the World", 1994. Address: Epic Records 550 Madison Ave New York NY 10022-3211

OSBOURNE, SHARON ARDEN, music manager, actress, television personality; b. London, Oct. 9, 1952; d. Don and Hope Arden; m. Ozzy Osbourne; children: Aimee, Kelly, Jack; 2 stepchildren. Mgr. Ozzy Osbourne, 1980—; founder & organizer OzzFest, 1995—; co-star The Osbournes, MTV, 2002—; host The Sharon Osbourne Show, 2003—04. Named One of People Magazine's 50 most beautiful people, 2002. Office: The Osbournes MTV Networks 2600 Colorado Ave Santa Monica CA 90404

OSBURN, BENNIE I. dean; BS, DVM, Kans. State U.; PhD in Comparative Pathology, U. Calif., Davis, 1965. Diplomate Am. Coll. Vet. Pathologists. Mem. faculty Coll. Vet. Medicine, Okla. State U., 1964—68; postdoctoral fellow Johns Hopkins U. Med. Sch., 1968—70; faculty mem. U. Calif.-Davis Sch. Vet. Medicine, 1970; head Infectious Disease and Immunology Unit Calif. Regional Primate and Rsch. Ctr., 1975—83; assoc. dean for rsch. and grad. programs U. Calif.-Davis Sch. Vet. Medicine, 1975—96, dean, 1996—. Published (270 peer-reviewed publs.). Fellow: AAAS, Am. Assn. Vet. Immunologists (past pres.); mem.: Am. Coll. Vet. Pathologists (past pres.), Johns Hopkins Soc. Scholars. Office: U Calif Sch Vet Medicine Office of the Dean 1 Shields Ave Davis CA 95616*

OSBY, IRIS, education educator; d. Frank and Minnie Stone; 1 child. BE, Chgo. State U., 1970, M in Reading, 1972, diploma in lane placement reading and human rels., 1975. Tchr. Bd. of Edn., Chgo. Home: 8407 S Donchester Ave Chicago IL 60619

OSBY, ROBERT EDWARD, protective services official; b. San Diego, Oct. 29, 1937; s. Jesse William and Susie Lillian (Campbell) O.; m. Clydette Deloris Mullen, Apr. 11, 1961; children: Daryl Lawrence, Gayle Lorraine. AA in Fire Sci., San Diego Jr. Coll., 1970; BA in Mgmt., Redlands U., 1985. Recreation leader San Diego Parks and Recreation Dept., 1955-58; postal carrier U.S. Postal Service, San Diego, 1958-59; fire fighter San Diego Fire Dept., 1959-67, fire engr., 1967-71, fire capt., 1971-76, fire bn. chief, 1976-79; fire chief Inglewood (Calif.) Fire Dept., 1979-84, San Jose (Calif.) Fire Dept., 1985—. Served to 2d lt. Calif. NG, 1960-65. Mem. Calif. Met. Fire Chiefs (chmn. 1987—), Internat. Assn. Black Firefighters (regional dir. 1974-77), Brothers United (pres. 1972-75). Democrat. Avocations: fishing, jogging, landscaping. Home: 28203 Engelmann Oak Trl Escondido CA 92026-6960 Office: San Diego Fire Dept 1010 2nd Ave Ste 400 San Diego CA 92101-4970

O'SCANNLAIN, DIARMUID FIONNTAIN, federal judge; b. N.Y.C., Mar. 28, 1937; s. Sean Leo and Moira (Hegarty); m. Maura Nolan, Sept. 7, 1963; children: Sean, Jane, Brendan, Kevin, Megan, Christopher, Anne, Kate. BA, St. John's U., 1957; JD, Harvard U., 1963; LLM, U. Va., 1992; LLD (hon.), U. Notre Dame, 2002. Bar: Oreg. 1965, N.Y. 1964. Tax atty. Standard Oil Co. (N.J.), N.Y.C., 1963—65; oassoc. Davies, Biggs, Strayer, Sotel & Boley, Portland, Oreg., 1965—69; dep. atty. gen. State of Oreg., 1969—71, pub. utility commr., 1971—73; dir. Oreg. Dept. Environ. Quality, 1973—74; sr. ptnr. Ragen, Roberts, O'Scannlain, Robertson & Neill, Portland, 1978—86; judge U.S. Ct. Appeals (9th cir.), San Francisco, 1986—, mem. exec. com., 1988—89, 1993—94; mem. Jud. Coun. 9th Cir., 1991—93. Mem. U.S. Jud. Conf. Com. on Automation and Tech., 1990—; cons. Office of Pres.-elect and mem. Dept. Energy Transition Team (Reagan Transition), Washington, 1980—81; chmn. com. adminstrv. law Oreg. State Bar, 1980—81. Mem. coun. of legal advisors Rep. Nat. Com., 1981—83, mem., 1983—86; chmn. Oreg. Rep. Party, 1983—86; del. Rep. Nat. convs., 1976, 1980, chmn. Oreg. del., 1984; nominee U.S. Ho. of Reps., 1st Congl. Dist., 1974; team leader energy task force Pres.'s Pvt. Sector Survey on Cost Control, 1982—83; trustee Jesuit H.S.; bd. visitors U. Oreg. Law Sch., 1988—; mem. citizens adv. bd. Providence Hosp., 1986—92. Maj. USAR, 1955—78. Mem.: ABA (sec. Appellate Judges Conf. 1989—90, exec. com. 1990—, chmn. 1994—95, chmn. jud. divsn. 2001—02), Fed. Judges Assn., Fed. Bar Assn., Multnomah Club. Roman Catholic. Office: US Ct Appeals 313 Pioneer Courthouse 555 SW Yamhill St Portland OR 97204-1396 E-mail: JudgeO'Scannlain@ca9.uscourts.gov.

OSCARSON, KATHLEEN DALE, retired writing assessment coordinator, educator; b. Hollywood, Calif., Sept. 16, 1928; d. Chauncey Dale and Hermine Marie Rulison; m. David Knowles Leslie, June 16, 1957 (div. Aug. 1970); m. William Randolph Oscarson, Apr. 27, 1974. AB, UCLA, 1950, MA, 1952; Cert. Advanced Study, Harvard U., 1965; Diplomé Elementaire, Le Cordon Bleu U. Paris, 1972. Gen. secondary life credential, Calif. Tchr. English, counselor Palo Alto (Calif.) Unified Sch. Dist., 1954-90, H.S. writing assessment coord., 1987-2000. Cons. advanced placement English Calif. Dept. Edn., Sacramento, 1968—70; reader Calif. Assessment Program, Sacramento, 1989—2000; instr. individual study U. Calif. Ext., Berkeley, 1979—92; reader, leader Ednl. Testing Svc., Princeton, NJ, 1967—, Oakland, Calif., 1967—; reader San Jose (Calif.) State U., 1991—2000, Nat. Evaluation Systems, Sacramento, 2001—; adj. lectr. English Santa Clara (Calif.) U., 1990—91; commr. Curriculum Study Commn., San Francisco Bay araea, 1978—; chair tchrs. English Spring Asiliomar Conf., Pacific Grove, Calif., 1992, Asilomar 44, Pacific Grove, 1994; advanced placement faculty cons. in English College Bd., NJ, 1967—73, 1991—2000. Mem. lang. arts assessment adv. com. Calif. State Dept. Edn., Sacramento, 1975-90; mem.-at-large exec. bd. Ctrl. Calif. Coun. Tchrs. English, Bay Area, 1969-71; mem. Medallion Soc. San Francisco Opera, 1984—; mem. ann. summer event com., membership com. Internat. Diplomacy Coun. Mem. MLA, Nat. Coun. Tchrs. English (group leader, presenter conf. San Francisco), Calif. Assn. Tchrs. English (presenter), Internat. Diplomacy Coun. San Francisco (membership and events coms. 1996), Harvard Club San Francisco, Christopher Marlowe Soc. Avocations: cuisine, voice, writing.

OSE, DOUGLAS, congressman; b. Sacramento, 1955; m. Lynnda ose; children: Erika, Emily. BS, U. Calif., Berkeley, 1977. Project mgr. Ose Properties, Sacramento, 1977-85; owner real estate devel. and investment co., 1986—; mem. U.S. Congress from 3d Calif. dist., 1999—; mem. agr., fin. svcs., and govt. reform coms. Former bd. dirs. Citrus Heights C. of C., Sacramento Housing and Redevel. Commn.; mem. Citrus Heights Incorporation Project. Republican. Office: 236 Cannon Ho Office Bldg Washington DC 20515-0001

OSEGUERA, PALMA MARIE, retired career officer; b. Kansas City, Mo., Dec. 29, 1946; d. Joseph Edmund and Palma Louise (Utke) O'Donnell; m. Alfonso Oseguera, Jan. 1, 1977; stepchildren: Kristie M. Daniels, Michelle L. Nielson, Lori A. Kelley. BA in Phys. Edn., Marycrest Coll., 1969. Commd. 2d lt. USMC, 1969, advanced through grades to col., 1991; asst. Marine Corps exch. officer Hdqs. and Hdqs. Squadron, Marine Corps Air Sta., Beaufort, S.C., 1969-71; classified material control officer Hdqs. and Svcs. Battalion, Camp S.D. Butler, Okinawa, 1971-73; adminstrv. officer, asst. Marine Corps exch. officer Marine Corps Air Sta., El, Toro, Santa Ana, Calif., 1973-76, Marine Corps exch. officer Yuma, Ariz., 1976-77; asst. Marine Corps exch. officer Hdqrs. and Support Bn., Marine Corps Devel. and Edn. Command, Quantico, Va., 1977-79; Marine Corps exch. officer Hqrs. Marine Corps, Washington, 1979-80; adminstrv. officer Marine Air Base Squadon 46, Marine Air Group 46, Marine Corps Air Sta., El Toro, Santa Ana, 1981-83, Hdqs. and Maintanence Squadron 46, Marine Air Group 46, Marine Corps Air Sta., El Toro, Santa Ana, 1983-85, Mobilization Tng. Unit Calif. 53, Landing Force Tng. Command, Pacific, San Diego, 1985-89, 3d Civil Affairs Group, L.A., 1989; dep. asst. chief of staff G-1 I Marine Expeditionary Force, Individual Mobilization Augumentee Detachment, Camp Pendleton, Calif., 1990-91; assoc. mem. Mobilization Tng. Unit Del. 01, Del., 1992-94; adminstrn. officer Mobilization Tng. Unit, CA-53, EWTG Pac, NAB, Coronado, San Diego, 1994-96; exch. officer MWRSPT ACT IMA Det MCB, Camp Pendleton, Calif., 1996-99; ret. from 30 yrs. commissioned svc. USMCR, 1999. Choir St. Elizabeth Seaton, Woodbridge, Va., 1978-80, St. Patricks, Arroyo Grande, Calif., 1990-94; vol. Hospice, San Luis Obispo, 1995—; mem. Los Osos (Calif.) veteran's events com., 1994-2000. Mem. AAUW (past libr.), Marine Corps Assn., Marine Corps Res. Officer Assn., Marine Corps Aviation Assn. (12 dist. dir. 1987), Women in Mil. Svc. for Am., Woman Marine Assn., Marine Corps League. Republican. Roman Catholic. Avocations: skiing, gardening, reading, pet care/sitting, horseback riding. Home: 728 Scenic Cir Arroyo Grande CA 93420-1617

OSEI, JOSEPH, education educator, minister; b. Kokofu, Ghana, Dec. 10, 1951; s. Paul Kwame Osei-Assibey and Kate Afiriyie Mensah; m. Victoria Adutwumwah; children: Lucy Osei-Asare, Georgina, Sussana, Miriam Jo, Emmanuel. BA in Philosophy and Religion, U. Of Ghana, 1981; MA in Philosophy, Ohio U., 1985; PHD, Ohio State U., 1991. Cert. Theology Meth. Ch., Ghana, 1978. Vis. prof. philosophy U. of South Fla., Tampa, 2000—01, Auburn U., Ala., 2001—. Acting chair, philosophy dept. U. of Ghana, Accra, 1995—99. Sec. Ecumenical Assn. of Third World Theologians, Accra, Ghana, 1994—99. Recipient First prize In Theology, Trinity Theol. Sem., Ghana, 1978; grantee Rsch. Grant, Ohio State U., 1990; tchg. award, Young Scholar's Program, 1990. Mem.: Am. Philos. Assn. Methodist. Achievements include first to Founder, African Christian Ch., Columbus, Ohio. Avocations: soccer, volleyball. Home: 560 N Gay St Apt 212 Auburn AL Office: Auburn U 6080 Haley Ctr Auburn AL 36830 Office Fax: 334-844-2196. Personal E-mail: josephoseij@aol.com. E-mail: oseijos@auburn.edu.

OSEN, GREGORY ALAN, water conditioning company executive; b. Beloit, Wis., Mar. 14, 1951; s. Vincent Darryl and Mavis Lucille (Lasher) O.; m. Deborah Ann Churchill Bladorn, Jan. 29, 1972 (div. Jan. 1987); m.

Christine Adel Dauenbaugh Pulliam, Oct. 8, 1987; children: Leah Michelle, Felicia Ann. BA in Music Edn. with honors, Milton (Wis.) Coll., 1973; postgrad., Cardinal Stritch Coll., 1985. Machinist, assembler Nat. Detroit, Rockford, Ill., 1973-78; sales tech. Ill. Water Treatment, Rockford, 1978-79, sales engr., 1979-80, dist. sales engr., 1980-85; sales mgr. Glegg Water Technologies, Guelph, Ont., Can., 1985-2000; v.p. mktg. & sales Process Equipment Unltd., Londonderry, N.H., 2000—. Pres. Seekers, Strawbridge Meth. Ch., 1995-96, mem. adminstrv. bd., 1996, mem. choir, 1995-96; trumpeter Harris County Big Band, 1993-95. Mem. Am. Water Works Assn., AIChe Avocations: video prodn., sports cars, auto racing. Home: 6012 Canyon Rd Sanger TX 76266-7451 Office: Process Equipment Unltd 46 Nashua Rd Bldg B Ste 9A Londonderry NH 03053 also: Glegg Water Conditioning 29 Royal Rd Guelph ON Canada N1H 1G2 E-mail: peunh@aol.com.

OSENTON, THOMAS GEORGE, publisher; b. Boston, Apr. 9, 1953; s. George Thomas and Helen (Curran) O.; m. Mary Ellen Dalzell, Aug. 16, 1975; children: Curran Lynn, Matthew. BA, U. New Hampshire, 1976. Pub. relations dir. USA Hockey, Colorado Springs, Colo., 1976-78; exec. dir. Blue Line Club Wis., Madison, 1978-81; writer WCVB-TV Ch.5 ABC Affil., Boston, 1981-82; dir. olympic pub. ABC TV Network, N.Y.; dir. mktg. ABC Pub., N.Y., 1983-86; pub. Sports Mktg. News, Conn., 1986-88; pub. Am. Artist Billboard Pubs. Inc., N.Y.C., 1988-89; pres., chief exec. officer Sporting News Pub. Co., St. Louis, 1989-93; chief exec. officer thehomeschool.com, North Chelmsford, Mass., 1997-2000; pres. Courier New Media, North Chelmsford, Mass., 1993-2000; CEO Traffique.com, North Hampton, 2000—. Avocation: golf. Home: 8 Rockrimmon Rd North Hampton NH 03862-2338 Office: 8 Rockrimmon Rd North Hampton NH 03862-2338

OSER, JUDI, lawyer, artist; b. Phila., Sept. 18, 1933; d. James Isadore and Mildred (Greenspan) O.; m. Richard Hunter Hollinger, Nov. 4, 1965 (div. Nov. 1975). BA in English with honors, U. Pa., 1956; JD, New Coll. Calif., 1980; student, Sarah Lawrence Coll., Pa. Acad. Fine Arts. Bar: Calif. 1980, U.S. Dist. Ct. (no. dist.) Calif. 1980, U.S. Ct. Appeals (9th crct.) 1982. Law clk. immigration law unit North Beach-Chinatown br. San Francisco Neighborhood Legal Assistance Found., 1979; immigration atty. Law Offices of Fred C. Hite, San Francisco, 1979-81, Wong, Main and Wu, Palo Alto, Calif., 1981; assoc. Law Offices of C. H. Blagburn, San Francisco, 1981-82; staff atty. Am. Ind. Hist. Soc., San Francisco, 1982; sole practice Piedmont, Calif., 1982—. One-woman shows include Lotus Gallery, Berkeley, Calif., Mus. Coastal Arts League, Spanishtown Galleries, Half Moon Bay, Calif., Clark's Corner, San Francisco, Heart's Content, Lyndell, Pa.; exhibited in group shows and pvt. collections; contbr. articles to profl. jours. Mem. Calif. Lawyers for the Arts (atty.'s ref. panel), Eastbay Watercolor Soc. (2d place award 1992), San Francisco Women Artists (bus. sec., bd. dirs., Merit award 1988, 94), Oakland Art Assn. (corp. counsel, bd. dirs., 1st place award 1991, Merit award 1988, 90, 1st prize 30th ann. exhbn. 1987), Phila. Watercolor Club (signature membership), Pa. Acad. Fine Arts (fellowship mem. alumni assn.), Calif. Bar Assn. Office: PO Box 21342 Piedmont CA 94620-1342

OSGOOD, CHARLES, news broadcaster, journalist; b. N.Y.C., Jan. 8, 1933; s. Charles Osgood and Mary F. (Wilson) Wood; m. Jean Crafton, Dec. 5, 1973; children: Kathleen, Winston, Anne Elizabeth, Emily Jean, James Edward. BS, Fordham U., 1954; L.H.D. (hon.), St. Bonaventure U., 1977; PhD (hon.), Fordham U.; LLD, St. John's U. Program dir. Sta. WGMS, Washington, 1955—63; gen. mgr. Sta. WHCT, Hartford, Conn., 1963—64; reporter ABC Radio News, 1964—67; anchorman Sta. WCBS, 1967—71; corr. television and radio CBS, N.Y.C., 1971—; anchor CBS News Sunday Morning, 1994—. Author: Nothing Could be Finer Than A Crisis That Is Minor in the Morning, 1979, There's Nothing That I Wouldn't Do If You Would Be My POSSLQ, 1981, Osgood on Speaking, 1988, The Osgood Files, 1991, See You on the Radio, 1999. Mem.: AFTRA. Office: CBS Radio Network 524 W 57th St New York NY 10019-2924

OSGOOD, CHRIS, professional hockey player; b. Peace River, Alta., Canada, Nov. 26, 1972; Goalie Detroit Red Wings, 1991—2001, N.Y. Islanders, 2001—. Player NHLl All-Star Game, 1996. Named to WHL East All-Star 2d Team, 1990—91, Sporting News All-Star Team, 1996; recipient Bill Jennings Trophy, NHL, 1996. Office: New York Islanders Nassau Veterans Memorial Coliseum Uniondale NY 11553

OSGOOD, FRANK WILLIAM, urban and economic planner, writer; b. Williamston, Mich., Sept. 3, 1931; s. Earle Victor and Blanche Mae (Eberley) O.; children: Ann Marie, Frank William Jr. BS, Mich. State U., 1953; M in City Planning, Ga. Inst. Tech., 1960. Prin. planner Tulsa Met. Area Plnning Commn., 1958-60; sr. assoc. Hammer & Co. Assocs., Washington, 1960-64; econ. cons. Marvin Springer & Assocs., Dallas, 1964-65; sr. assoc. Gladstone Assocs., Washington, 1965-67; prof. urban planning Iowa State U., Ames, 1967-73; pres. Frank Osgood Assoc./Osgood Urban Rsch., Dallas, 1973-84; dir. mktg. studies MPSI Americas Inc., Tulsa, 1984-85, Comarc Systems/Roulac & Co., San Francisco, 1985-86; pres. Osgood Urban Rsch., Millbrae, Calif., 1986-95; freelance writer Millbrae and L.A., Calif., 1994—; VISTA vol. coord. Chrysalis, Santa Monica, Calif., 1995-96; pres. Osgood Urban Rsch., L.A., 1996—. Adj. prof. U. Tulsa, 1974-76; lectr. U. Tex., Dallas, 1979, U. Tex., Arlington, 1983. Author: Control Land Uses Near Airports, 1960, Planning Small Business, 1967, Continuous Renewal Cities, 1970, (docudrama) Region Aroused, 2003; contbr. articles to profl. jours. Chmn. awards Cub Scouts Am., Ames, 1971-73; deacon Calvary Presbyn. Ch., San Francisco, 1987-90. 1st lt. USAF, 1954-56. Recipient Community Leaders and Noteworthy Americans award 1976. Mem. Am. Inst. Cert. Planners (peninsula liaison 1987-89, dir. pro-tem 1990 No. Calif. sect., edn. coord. 1991-92, Calif., dir. N. Cen. Tex. sect., Tex. chpt. 1983), Am. Planning Assn., Am. Inst. Planners (v.p. Okla. chpt. 1975-77), Okla. Soc. Planning Cons. (sec., treas. 1976-79), Urban Land Inst., Nat. Assn. Regional Couns., So. Calif. Assn. Govts. (regional adv. coun. 1998—, vice-chmn. 1999-2000, chair 2000-01), Writer's Bloc & Novel Group, Cypress. Home: # 35H 1542 Merion Way Seal Beach CA 90740 E-mail: fwosgood@att.net.

OSGOOD, NANCY JEAN, medical educator, writer; b. July 6, 1951; d. Jack Kent and Lois Emma (Stober) Luttrell; m. Raymond Clifford Jordan, Jr., Oct. 13, 1984. BA in Sociology and Spanish, Yankton Coll., 1972; MA in Sociology, Drake U., 1974; cert. in gerontology, Syracuse U., 1979; PhD in Sociology, 1979. Rsch. assoc. Syracuse Rsch. Corp., NY, 1975—78; asst. prof. SUNY, Cortland, NY, 1979—80, Med. Coll. Va., Richmond, 1980—92, prof., 1992—. Mem. Nat. Com. on Vital and Health Stats., Washington, 1982—84. Author: Senior Settlers: Social Integration in Retirement Communities, 1982, Suicide in the Elderly: A Practitioner's Guide to Diagnosis and Mental Health Intervention, 1985, Suicide Among the Elderly in Long-Term Care Facilities, 1991; editor: Life after Work: Retirement, Leisure, Recreation and the Elderly, 1982; co-author: Seniors on Stage: The Impact of Applied Theatre on the Elderly, 1985, Suicide and the Elderly: An Annotated Bibliography and Review, 1986; co-editor: Dynamic Leisure Programming with Older Adults, 1987, The Science and Practice of Gerontology: A Multi-disciplinary Guide, 1989, Alcoholism and Aging: An Annotated Bibliography and Review, 1995, Treating Alcohol and Drug Abuse in the Elderly, 2002. Mem. selection com. King William H.S., Va., 1985; active Va. State Rehab. Bd., Am. Cancer Soc. Recipient acad. scholarship, Yankton Coll., 1969—72, N.Y. State Dept. Mental Hygiene Rsch. fellowship, 1974—75, Nat. Inst. Edn. award, 1975—78, NIMH award, 1977—79, Presdl. Invitation to White House, 1984, 1991; grantee Va. Commonwealth U., 1981—82. Fellow: Gerontol. Soc. Am.; mem.: Internat. Platform Assn., So. Gerontol. Soc., Am. Sociol. Assn., Am. Assn. Suicidology. Avocations: playing piano and clarinet, gourmet cooking, parrots. Home: PO Box 245 Manquin VA 23106-0245 Office: Med Coll Va Gerontology Dept PO Box 23298 MCV Sta Richmond VA 23298 Office Phone: 804-828-6077.

OSGOOD, RICHARD MAGEE, JR., electrical engineering educator, research administrator; b. Kansas City, Mo., Dec. 28, 1943; s. Richard Magee and Mary Neff (Russell) O.; m. Alice Rose Dyson, June 25, 1966; children—Richard Magee, III, Nathaniel David, Jennifer Anne BS in Engring., U.S. Mil. Acad., 1965; MS in Physics, Ohio State U., 1968; PhD, MIT, 1973. Rsch. assoc. dept. physics MIT, Cambridge, 1969-72, rsch. staff Lincoln Lab., 1973-80, project leader Lincoln Lab., 1980-81; assoc. prof. applied physics and elec. engring. Columbia U., N.Y.C., 1981-82, prof., 1982-91, Higgins prof., 1989—. Assoc. dir. Brookhaven Nat. Lab., Upton, NY, 2000—03; dir. Microelectronics Sci. Labs., 1984—90; mem. Army Sci. and Tech. Basic Energy Scis. Adv. Com., Def. Scis.-Advanced Rsch. Projects Agy.; cons. Los Alamos Nat. Lab.; mem. ad hoc com. Air Force Sci. Adv. Bd. Editor: Laser Diagnostics and Photochemical Processing of Semiconductor Devices, 1983; contbr. articles to profl. jours.; patentee in field Served to capt. USAF, 1965-69 Recipient Samuel Burka award USAF Avionics Lab., 1968, Leos Travelling Lectr. award, 1986-87, Disting. Travelling Lectr. APS, R.W. Wood Prize, 1991, Optical Soc. Am.; John Simon Guggenheim fellowship, 1989. Fellow IEEE, Am. Phys. Soc., Optical Soc. Am. (R.W. Wood award, 1991); mem. Am. Chem. Soc., Materials Rsch. Soc. (councillor 1983-86), Optical Device Assn. (Japanese hon. lectr. 1990), Am. Phys. Soc. (travelling lectureship 1992). Home: 345 Quaker Rd Chappaqua NY 10514-2615 Office: Columbia U Radiation Laboratory New York NY 10027

OSGOOD, ROBERT T., JR., architect, strategic planner; b. St. Louis, Sept. 25, 1958; s. Robert T. and Gale Farris (Brandau) Osgood; m. Cheryl Lenor Denler, June 26, 1982; children: Robbie, Chelsea. B cum laude in environ. design, SUNY, Buffalo, 1981; M in Architecture, Ga. Instit. Tech., 1984. Planner Stevens & Wilkinson, Atlanta, 1983—84; sr. rsch. assoc. BOSTI, Buffalo, 1984—86; sr. v.p. HOK, St. Louis, 1986—94; v.p. FLAD, Madison, Wis., 1994—98; sr. v.p. VOA, Columbus, 1999—. Lectr. Washington U., St. Louis, 1989—90, St. Louis, 1992; dir. HOK, 1986—94, FLAD, 1994—98, NBBJ, 1998—99, VOA, 1999—. Contbr. numerous articles to profl. jours. Mem. Downtown St. Louis, Mo., 1993, coach Waunakee Youth Soccer, Madison, 1995—98, BWSA Crew, Columbus, 2000—; vol. Columbus Crew, Columbus, 2000—. Recipient Planning & Design award Famous Footwear HQ, Madison Mag., 1997, Environ. Sustainability award, SC Johnson, 1997, Planning & Design award, SC Johnson HQ Bldg., AIA, 1998, Rsch. and Design awards, Progressive Architecture Jour. Mem.: Internat. Facility Mgmt. Assn., CoreNet Global, Alpha Lambda Delta, Tau Sigma Delta. Avocations: soccer, skiing, running, art, music. Office: VOA Assoc 4449 Easton Way 2nd Fl Columbus OH 43219 Office Phone: 614-934-1117. E-mail: bosgood@voa.com.

OSGOOD, RUSSELL KING, academic administrator; b. Fairborn, Ohio, Oct. 25, 1947; s. Richard M. and Mary Russell Osgood; m. Paula Haley, June 6, 1970; children: Mary, Josiah, Micah, Iain. BA, Yale U., 1969, JD, 1974. Bar: Mass. 1974, U.S. Dist. Ct. Mass. (admitted to) 1976. Assoc. Hill & Barlow, Boston, 1974—78; assoc. prof. Boston U., 1978—80; prof. Cornell U., Ithaca, NY, 1980—88, dean law sch., 1988—98; pres. Grinnell (Iowa) Coll., 1998—. Lt. USNR, 1969—71. Mem.: Selden Soc., Stair Soc., Mass. Hist. Soc. Office: Grinnell Coll 1121 Park St Grinnell IA 50112-1640 E-mail: osgood@grinnell.edu.

OSGUTHORPE, JOHN DAVID, otolaryngologist, educator; b. Fairbanks, Alaska, 1948; MD, U. Utah, 1973; grad., Med. Ed. in Otolaryngology. Intern UCLA, 1973-74, resident surgery, 1974-75, resident otolaryngology, 1975-78; prof. Med. U. SC, Charleston, SC, 1979—; otolaryngologist Med. U. Hosp., Charleston, SC. Accreditation coun. Skull Base fellowship U. Zurich. Mem.: HNS, AMA (del. 1998—), Residence Rev. Comm., Sinus Allergy Health Partnership (bd. dir. 1998—), Am. Rhinologic Soc. (bd. dir. 1998—2001, editor 1998—2001), Am. Laryngological Assn., Am. Acad. Otolaryngologic Allergy (pres. 1995), Am. Acad. Otolaryngology, Head and Neck Surgery (bd. dirs. 1997—, coord. continuing edn. 2000—, Disting. Svc. award 1995). Office: Med Univ SC Dept Otolaryngology 150 Ashley Ave Charleston SC 29401-5803 E-mail: osguthjd@att.net.

O'SHANICK, GREGORY JOHN, physician, medical association administrator; b. Akron, Ohio, Nov. 22, 1953; s. Peter and Mary (Popadics) O'S; m. Alison Moon, Oct. 8, 1991; children: Beth, Peter, Van, Alexis, Drew. Student, Ohio State U., 1971-73; MD, U. Tex., 1977. Diplomate Am. Bd. Disability Analysts, Am. Bd. Psychiatry and Neurology-Gen. Psychiatry; cert. Am. Soc. Neurorehabilitation, 1993. Intern to chief resident, fellow Duke U. Med. Ctr., Durham, N.C., 1977-81; asst. staff psychiatrist Meml. S.W. Hosp., Houston, 1981-84; assoc. The Hauser Clinic and Assoc., P.A., Houston, 1981-82; clin. asst. prof. psychiatry, clin. instr. family practice U. Tex. Health Sci. Ctr., Houston, 1981-82, asst. prof. psychiatry, assoc. dir. cons.-liason svc., 1982-84; asst. prof. psychiatry, dir. med./psychiatry svc. Med. Coll. Va., Richmond, 1984-89, asst. prof. rehab. medicine, 1985-89, dir. inpatient psychiatry svcs., 1987-90, co-dir. rehab. rsch. and tng. ctr. in brain injury, 1989-90, chmn. divsn. inpatient psychiatry, 1989-90, assoc. prof. psychiatry and rehab. medicine, 1989-91; attending physician VA Med. Ctr., Richmond, 1987-91; dir. Ctr. Neuro Rehab. Svc., Richmond, 1991—; assoc. med. dir. neurorehab. program Health South Med. Ctr., Richmond, 1993-96. Cons. neuropsychiatric PATE Rehab. Endeavors, Inc., Dallas, 1990-91; assoc. prof. dept. neurological surgery U. Va., 1998, rsch. Va. Inst. Neurological Inst., 1998; attending neuropsyhicatrist U. Va. Med. Ctr., 1999; spl. cons. traumatic brain injury initiative Nat. Inst. Handicapped Rsch., 1986-87; assoc. prof. neurosurgery U. Va. Health Sci. Ctr.; mem. neuromed. adv. bd. N.E. Ctr. for Spl. Care, 1998-2000. Author: Head Trauma Psychiatric Medicine, 1989; (with others) MMPI 168 Codebook, 1984, Psychiatric Aspects of Trauma, 1986; contbg. author: (with others) Neuropsychological Treatment of Head Injury, 1989, Principles of Medical Psychiatry, 1987, Community Reentry for Person with Traumatic Brain Injury, 1989, Psychiatric Aspects of Traumatic Brain Injury, 1994; editl. bd. Neurorehabilitation: An Interdisciplinary Jour.; numerous nat. presentations; contbr. articles, papers, letters and editls. to numerous profl. jours. Mgr., coach Huguenot Little League, Chesterfield, Va., 1991—; mem. selection com. Keep our Streets Safe and Sober, 1996; bd. dirs. Nat. Head Injury Found., 1989, chair psychiatry adv. com., 1988-90, mem. legis. com. profl. divsn., 1986-87, com. revise DSM-IV listings TBI, 1985, spl. cons., 1984; mem. task force dually diagnosed Southern Regional Edn Bd., 1986; mem. Va. Brain Injury Coun., 1987-2000, vice-chair, 1997-2000, chair, 1998-99; mem. adv. bd. Va. Head Injury Found., Inc., 1988-91; mem. task force cognitive retraining Gen. Assembly Commonwealth Va., 1992; mem. task force evaluate and modify traumatic brain injury program Woodrow Wilson Rehab. Ctr., Va., 1993; bd. dirs. Transitional Learning Cmty., Galveston, Tex., 1983-85, adv. bd. 1985-91; mem. com. psychol. edn. Am. Diabetes Assn., Houston chpt., 1983-84; mem.expert working group mild traumatic brain surgery-CDC, 2001; chmn. Blue Ribbon Panel brain injury and amusement park rider, 2002-03; cons. dopamine agonist therapy low response children following acquired brain injury, 2002-, impact littermate psychol. stress in rats, 2003-. Named Bus. Assoc. Yr. award Am. Bus. Women's Assn., Shockoe Valley chpt., 1989; Hamilton Ford award for Excellence, 1977; grantee Roering Pharm., 1983-85, UTHSCH, 1983; Va. Commonwealth Univ. Grants-In-Aid Program, 1985-86, DMHMR, 1988, 1988-89, 1989-90, 1990-91, NIDRR, 1988-89, 1986-89, 1989-93, 1989-90, 1992-93, Dept. Edn., 1991-92, N.Y. State Dept. Edn., 1993, US DOE RSA, 1995-96. Fellow Am. Psychiat. Assn. (com. mem. life, accident and health ins. 1981-89, subcom. ins. code system 1983-84, task force traumatic brain injury 1990, assoc. editor Brian Injury: Jour. Internat. Brain Injury Assn. 1985-91, disting.); mem. AMA, Am. Neuropsychiat. Assn., Am. Soc. Neurorehab., Brain Injury Assn. (med. dir. 1996—, bd. dirs. Rubin Rsch. Fund 1997), Assn. Medicine and Psychiatry, Am. Acad. for Cert. of Brain Injury Specialists (bd. dirs.), Psychiat. Soc. Va., Am. Acad. Neurology, Sigma Xi. Republican. Avocations: golf, skiing, travel, reading. Office: Ctr Neurorehab Svc 11315 Polo Pl Midlothian VA 23113-1434 E-mail: gjocns@aol.com.

O'SHAUGHNESSY, ANDREW JACKSON, historic site research director, education educator; b. Altrincham, Cheshire, Eng., Aug. 6, 1959; arrived in U.S., 1989; s. John and Marjorie O'Shaughnessy. BA, Oxford Univ., Oriel Coll., Eng., 1982, MA, 1987, PhD, 1988. Master Eton Coll., Windsor, England, 1988—89; vis. asst. prof. So. Meth. Univ., Dallas, 1989—90; prof. Univ. Wis., Oshkosh, Wis., 1990—2003; Saunders dir. Robert H. Smith Internat. Ctr. for Jefferson Studies Thomas Jefferson Found., Monticello, Va., 2003—. Adv. bd. Ctr. for the Study of the Am. Constn., 2003—. Author: An Empire Divided The American Revolution and the British Caribbean, 2000. Fellow: Royal Hist. Soc.; mem.: Am. Hist. Assn. Anglican. Avocations: swimming, classical music, theater. Home: 408 E Market St #305 Charlottesville VA 22902 Office: Thomas Jefferson Found Monticello PO Box 316 Charlottesville VA 22902 Office Phone: 434-984-7501.

O'SHAUGHNESSY, CHRISTOPHER T. lawyer; b. Princeton, N.J., Jan. 19, 1971; s. Thomas G. and Geraldine M. O'Shaughnessy; m. Renée M. Pilliod, Aug. 13, 1994; children: Michael J., Katherine Grace. BA, Ohio State U., 1993; JD, Capital U., Columbus, Ohio, 1997. Bar: Ohio 1998, U.S. Dist. Ct. (no. and so. dists.) Ohio 1999. Law clk. State of Ohio's Atty. Gen., Columbus, 1995, Ray, Alton, Todaro and Kirstein, LPA, Columbus, 1995—97, Lane, Alton & Horst, LLC, Columbus, 1997—98, atty. at law, 1998—, mem. profl. recruiting com. Atty., cons. Action Children Counsel Franklin County, Columbus, 1999—. Co-editor: (book) The ePolicy Handbook, 2001. Vol. Rep. John Kasich's Re-election, Columbus, 1990, Sen. Michael Dewine's Campaign, Columbus, 1992. Mem.: Franklin Am. Inn of Ct., Ohio Acad. of Trial Lawyers, Def. Rsch. Inst. Republican. Roman Catholic. Avocations: basketball, golf, music. Office: Lane Alton and Horst LLC 175 S Third St Columbus OH 43215 Business E-Mail: cto@lah4law.com.

O'SHAUGHNESSY, JAMES PATRICK, lawyer; b. Rochester, N.Y., Mar. 3, 1947; s. John Andrew and Margaret May (Yaxley) O'S.; m. Terry Lee Wood. BS cum laude, Rensselaer Poly. Inst., 1972; JD, Georgetown U., 1977. Bar: Va. 1977, Ohio 1979, Wis. 1987. Assoc. Squire, Sanders & Dempsey, Cleve., 1978-81; ptnr. Hughes & Cassidy, Sumas, Wash., 1981-84; patent counsel Kimberly-Clark Corp., Neenah, Wis., 1984-85; ptnr. Foley & Lardner, Milw., 1986-96; v.p., chief intellectual property counsel Rockwell Automation, Inc., Milw., 1996—, corp. officer. Founder Innovatech Co., 1996—; mem. tech. adv. coun. Ideation Internat., Inc., 1999-2004; mem. adv. bd. Licensing Econs. Rev., Intellectual Property Bus. Internat., 2002-04; mem. bd. visitors Georgetown U. Sch. Nursing, 1996-2000; mem., bd. dir. Intellectual Property Owners, 1996-2000; frequent lectr., chmn. seminars to legal and bus. groups. Contbg. author: Technology Licensing: Corporate Strategies for Maximizing Value, 1996, Profiting From Intellectual Capital: Extracting Value From Innovation, 1998; contbr. articles to profl. jours. Bd. dirs. Skylight Opera Theatre, 1991-92, Milw. Florentine Opera Co., 1999—, pres., 2002. With USN, 1964-68. Mem. CPR Inst. for Dispute Resolution (mediation/arbitration panel), Lic. Execs. Soc., Am. Intellectual Property Law Assn., Assn. Chief Patent Coun.; Disabled Am. Vets., Tau Beta Pi, Alpha Sigma Mu. Home: 3207 W Donges Bay Rd Mequon WI 53092-5119 Office: Rockwell Automation Inc 777 E Wisconsin Ave Ste 1400 Milwaukee WI 53202-5302

O'SHEA, CATHERINE LARGE, marketing and public relations consultant; b. Asheville, N.C., Feb. 27, 1944; d. Edwin Kirk Jr. and Mary Mitchell (Westall) Large; m. Roger Dean Lower, Dec. 19, 1970 (dec. Sept. 1977); children: Thaddeus Kirk Lower and David Alexander Lower (twins, dec.); m. Michael Joseph O'Shea, Dec. 29, 1980 (div. 2001). BA in History magna cum laude, Emory U., 1966. Mktg. staff mem. Time Inc., N.Y.C., 1966-69; mktg. adminstr. Collier-Macmillan Internat., N.Y.C., 1970-71; circulation mgr. Coll. Entrance Exam. Bd., N.Y.C., 1971-73; spl. asst. to pres. Wayne Dressel Assocs. Exec. Search, N.Y.C., 1973-75; freelance writer, editor, pub. rels. Princeton, N.J., 1975-78; dir. constituency rels. Emory U., Atlanta, 1978-80; devel. assoc. U. Del., Newark, 1981-83; asst. to pres. Elizabethtown (Pa.) Coll., 1983-85; assoc. v.p. Beaver Coll., Glenside, Pa., 1985; cons. mktg. and pub. rels. Phila., S.C., Ga., 1985—. Co-author: 50 Secrets of Highly Successful Cats, 1994 (trans. German edit. Schnurrende Tyrannen by Manfred Sommer, 1996); editor Elizabethtown mag., 1983-85; contbr. articles to nat. mags. and profl. jours. Founder Helping Hands Internat.; trustee Large Found.; founding trustee Newberry Opera House Found.; mem. founding com. Rachel Longstreet Found., Jessye Norman Sch. of Arts. Mem. Pub. Rels. Soc. Am. (accredited), Augusta Choral Soc. (bd. dirs.), Mortar Bd., Phi Beta Kappa, Phi Mu.

O'SHEA, ERIN K. biomedical researcher; m. Doug Jeffery O'Shea. Grad., Smith Coll.; PhD in Structural Biology, MIT. Prof., vice chair biochemistry U. Calif., San Francisco; investigator Howard Hughes Med. Inst., 2000—. Pub. Libr. Sci. Recipient award in molecular biology, NAS, 2001. Office: Univ Calif San Francisco Rm GH:S472D 600 16th St San Francisco CA 94143-2240

O'SHEA, HELENE CLAIRE, bookkeeper; b. Springfield, Ill., Dec. 22, 1935; d. David James and Catherine Agnes (Wilson) Eddington; m. David Lawrence O'Shea, July 6, 1957; children: David L. II, Maureen, Linda, Michael. Bookkeeper Harold O'Shea Builders, Springfield, Ill., 1960—. Author: A Handfull of Prisms, 2003. Roman Catholic. Avocation: grandchildren. Home: 2004 Barberry Dr Springfield IL 62704 Office: Harold O'Shea Builders 1941 S 10 1/2 St Springfield IL 62703 Office Fax: 217-522-6586. E-mail: hoshea@osheabuilders.com.

O'SHEA, JAMES, managing editor; Reporter US Army; reporter, fin. editor, Washington corr. The Des Moines Register; reporter The Chicago Tribune, 1979—90, assoc. mng. editor for foreign and nat. news, 1990—95, dep. mng. editor for news, 1995—2001, mng. editor, 2001—. Bd. gov. Oversea Press Club Am. Office: Chicago Tribune 435 N Michigan Ave Chicago IL 60611 Business E-Mail: jo'shea@tribune.com.*

O'SHEA, KAREN, public relations executive; V.p. comm., pub. rels. Lennox Internat., Richardson, Tex. Office: Lennox Internat PO Box 799900 Dallas TX 75379-9900

O'SHEA, LYNNE EDEEN, management consultant, educator; b. Chgo., Oct. 18, 1950; d. Edward Fisk and Mildred (Lessner) O'S. BA, BJ in Polit. Sci. and Journalism, U. Mo., MA in Info. Theory, 1971; PhD in Consumer Cultures, Northwestern U., 1978; postgrad., Sch. Mgmt. and Strategic Studies, U. Calif., 1988. Congl. asst., Washington, 1969-70; brand mgr. Procter & Gamble Co., Cin., 1971-73; v.p. Foote, Cone & Belding, Inc., Chgo., 1973-79; v.p. corp. comms. Internat. Harvester Co., Chgo., 1979-82; dir. mktg. and comms. Arthur Andersen & Co., Chgo., 1983-86; v.p. bus. devel. Gannett Co., Inc., Chgo., 1987-94; pres., chief oper. officer Shalit Place L.L.C., 1995—98; exec. v.p. Mus. Broadcast Comm., Chgo., 1996-97; cons. A.T. Kearney, Chgo., 1998—; pres. Ill. Women's Forum, 2003—. Prof. mktg. U. Chgo. Grad. Sch. Bus., 1979—80, Kellogg Grad. Sch. Mgmt., 1983—84, 1994—95; exec.-in-residence, prof. Kellstadt Grad. Sch. Bus., DePaul U., 2000—03; bd. dirs. AskRex.com, Clark/Bardes Inc., Motown Snacks, Robison Securities/Fleet Bank, Advocate Healthcare, Internat. Leadership Forum. Bd. dirs. Off-the-Street Club, Chgo., 1977-86; mem. adv. bd. U. Ill. Coll. Commerce, 1980-2000, Chgo. Crime Commn., 1987-90, DePaul U., 1989-95, Roosevelt U., 1994-2000, St. Mary's U., 1995-98. Recipient numerous Eagle Fin. Advt. awards, Silver medalist Am. Advt. Fedn., 1989; named Advt. Woman of Yr. Chgo. Advt. Club, 1989; named Fed. Glass Ceiling Commn., 1991-95, Com. 21st Century, 1992—; named One of Top 100 in Tech., 2003. Mem. Internat. Women's Forum (v.p. devel., v.p. comms., exec. com., bd. dirs.), Chgo. Network, Women's Forum Chgo., Women's Forum Mich., Women's Forum Ill. (pres.), Tarrytown Group, Social Venture Network, Execs. Club Chgo., Mid-Am. Club (bd. govs. 1990-92), Women's Athletic Club Chgo. Cleve. Yachting Club. Office: AT Kearney Inc 222 W Adams St Fl 25 Chicago IL 60606-5227 E-mail: lynne.o'shea@atkearney.com.

O'SHEA, WILLIAM (BILL) T. telecommunications industry executive; b. Peabody, Mass. BEE, Lowell Technol. Inst., 1969; MEE, Northeastern U., 1970; grad., MIT. Joined Bell Labs., 1972; exec. dir. Info. Tech. divsn. AT&T, 1985—88, v.p. sys. mktg. and devel. computer sys., 1988—91; sr. v.p. network products group AT&T Global Info. Solutions (formerly NCR), 1991—93, sr. v.p. worldwide mktg. for computer bus., 1993—95; v.p. worldwide mktg. AT&T Global Info. Solutions, 1993—95; acting CEO NCR Corp., 1993; joined Lucent Techs., 1995, pres. network sys. internat. regions and profl. svcs., 1995—97, pres. bus. comm. sys., 1997—99, pres. data networking sys. group, 1998—99, exec. v.p., CEO enterprise networks group, 1999—2000, exec. v.p. corp. strategy and bus. devel., 2000—, chief tech. officer, 2001—; pres. Bell Labs., Murray Hill, NJ, 2001—. Office: Bell Labs 600 Mountain Ave New Providence NJ 07974*

OSHEROFF, DOUGLAS DEAN, educator, physicist, researcher; b. Aberdeen, Wash., Aug. 1, 1945; s. William and Bessie Anne (Ondov) Osheroff; m. Phyllis S.K. Liu, Aug. 14, 1970. BS in Physics, Calif. Inst. Tech., 1967; MS, Cornell U., 1969, PhD in Physics, 1973. Mem. tech. staff Bell Labs., Murray Hill, NJ, 1972—82, head solid state and low temperature physics research dept., 1982—87; prof. Stanford (Calif.) U., 1987—, J.G. Jackson and C.J. Wood prof. physics, 1992—, chair physics, 1993—96, 2001—. Mem. Columbia Accident Investigation Bd., 2003. Rschr. on properties of matter near absolute zero of temperature, co-discoverer of superfluidity in liquid 3He, 1971, nuclear antiferromagnetic resonance in solid 3He, 1980. Co-recipient Simon Meml. prize, Brit. Inst. Physics, 1976; recipient Oliver E. Buckley Solid State Physics prize, 1981, Nobel prize in Physics, 1996; fellow John D. and Catherine T. MacArthur prize, 1981. Fellow: Am. Acad. Arts and Scis., Am. Phys. Soc.; mem.: NAS. Office: Stanford U Rm 150 Varian Physics Bldg 382 Via Pueblo Mall Stanford CA 94305-4060

OSHEROW, JACQUELINE SUE, poet, English language educator; b. Phila., Aug. 15, 1956; d. Aaron and Evelyn (Victor) Osherow; m. Saul Korewa, June 16, 1965 (div. 2003); children: Magda, Dora, Mollie. AB Magna cum laude, Radcliffe Coll., Harvard U., 1978; postgrad., Trinity Coll., Cambridge U., 1978-79; PhD in English and Am. Lit., Princeton U., 1990. Prof. English C. Utah, Salt Lake City, 1989—. Author: (poetry) Looking for Angels in New York, 1988, Conversations with Survivors, 1994, With a Moon in Transit, 1996, Dead Men's Praise, 1999. Recipient Witter Bynner prize Am. Acad. and Inst. Arts and Letters, 1990; Ingram Merrill Found. grantee, 1990; Guggenheim fellow, 1997-98, Nat. Endowment for the Arts fellow, 1999—. Mem. Poetry Soc. Am. (John Masefield Meml. award 1993, Lucille Medwick Meml. award 1995, Cecil Hemley Meml. award 1997). Jewish. Office: U Utah Dept English 255 S Central Campus Dr Rm 3500 Salt Lake City UT 84112-0494 Office Phone: 801-581-7947. E-mail: j.osherow@english.utah.edu.

O'SHIELDS, CHARLIE, marketing professional; s. John and Marlene O'Shields. BA in Studio Art(hon.), U. Mo., Kansas City, 1993. Creative dir. Lookandfeel new media, Kansas City, Mo., 1999—. Author: (children's book) The Curious Case of Miser Snoot and the Bibliomaniacs. Mem.: Am. Advt. Fedn. Office: Lookandfeel new media 106 W 14th St Suite 1400 Kansas City MO 64105 E-mail: coshields@lookandfeel.com.

O'SHIELDS, RICHARD LEE, retired natural gas company executive; b. Ozark, Ark., Aug. 12, 1926; s. Fay and Anna (Johnson) O'S.; m. Shirley Isabelle Washington, Nov. 8, 1947; children: Sharon Isabelle O'Shields Boles, Carolyn Jean, Richard Lee Jr. BS in Mech. Engring, U. Okla., 1949; MS in Petroleum Engring, La. State U., 1951. Registered profl. engr., Kans., Tex. Instr. petroleum engring. La. State U., 1949-51; prodn. engr. Pure Oil Co., 1951-53; sales engr., chief engr., v.p. Salt Water Control, Inc., Ft. Worth, 1953-59; cons. engr. Ralph H. Cummins Co., Ft. Worth, 1959-60; with Anadarko Prodn. Co. and parent co. Panhandle Eastern Pipe Line Co., 1960-88; pres. Anadarko Prodn. Co., 1966-68; exec. v.p. Panhandle Eastern Pipe Line Co., 1968-70, pres., chief exec. officer, 1970-79, chmn., chief exec. officer, 1979-83, chmn., 1983-88, also bd. dirs., 1969-93. Pres., CEO Trunkline Gas Co., 1970-79, chmn., CEO, 1979-83, chmn., 1983-88. With USAAF, 1945. Mem. Am. Petroleum Inst., Soc. Petroleum Engrs., Ind. Natural Gas Assn. Am., Gas Research Inst., Ind. Petroleum Assn. Am., So. Gas Assn., Tau Beta Pi. Republican. Methodist. Home: 511 Oakland Hills Ln Kerrville TX 78028-6427 E-mail: dick_dshields@yahoo.com.

OSHIMA, MICHAEL W. lawyer; b. Big Rapids, Mich., Apr. 4, 1957; s. Walter W. and Mitsue Oshima; m. Chiaki Tanaka, July 19, 2003. AB, Brown U., 1979; MA, Harvard U., 1984; JD, NYU, 1987. Bar: NY 1988, DC 1989. Sr. rsch. asst. Harvard U. John F. Kennedy Sch. Govt., Cambridge, Mass., 1981-84; assoc. Davis Polk & Wardwell, NYC, 1987-90, Arnold & Porter LLP, NYC, 1990-96, ptnr., 1997—. Contbr. articles, reports to profl. publs. Mem. Am. Sociol. Assn., Law and Soc. Assn., NY State Bar Assn., Assn. Bar City of NY. Office: Arnold & Porter LLP 399 Park Ave Fl 35 New York NY 10022-4690 E-mail: michael_oshima@aporter.com.

OSHIN, DIANE, publisher; married; two children. BA in Polit. Sci. and French, Tufts U.; MBA in Mktg. and Fin., Columbia U. Formerly with Woman's Day, Conde Nast Traveler, Ogilvy & Mather, others; former advt. dir. Vogue; v.p., group pub. The Parenting Group AOL Time Warner, N.Y.C., 1994—. Office: Time Inc The Parenting Grp 530 Fifth Ave New York NY 10036

OSHITA, JOHN TAKAO, musician; Diploma, Edsbergs Musikinst., Sollentuna, Sweden, 1990; BA, Yale U., 1995; MusM, U. S.C. Sch. Music, 2003. Studio tchr. Am. String Tchrs. and Suzuki Assn., 2003—; string faculty Inst. of Art Music and Sci., Bellflower, 2004—; relief cellist L.A. Philharmonic Assn., 2001—03. Adjudicator, regional evaluations Am. String Tchrs. Assn., 2003, Music Tchrs. Assn. Calif. West Valley, 2003—04. Musician (relief cellist): L.A. Philharm. European Tour; musician: (soloist) (solo debut & televised documentary) Young Soloists Concert with Helsinborg Symphony Orch., 1989; musician: 432d Young People's Concert of the N.Y. Philharm., 1984. Named Presdl. Scholar in the Arts, Nat. Found. for Advancement in the Arts / Sec. of Edn., 1987; recipient Excellence in Musical Performance award, Com. on Asian/Pacific Am. Heritage / Hon. Mayor Tom Bradley, L.A., 1983, Dr. Shinya award, Japanese-Am. Assn. of N.Y., Inc., 1991; Juliette Esselborn Geier Meml. fellow, Tanglewood Music Ctr. Fellowship Program, 1988. Mem.: L.A. Violoncello Soc., Inc. (bd. dirs. 2000—04, treas. 2001—04).

OSHMAN, MARILYN, retail executive; Chmn. bd. dirs. Oshman's Sporting Goods, Inc., Houston. Office: Oshman's Sporting Goods Inc 1050 W Hampden Ave Englewood CO 80110-2118

OSHUNRINADE, ADEYEMI OLUSEGUN, public information officer, writer; b. Ibadah, Oyo, Nigeria, June 14, 1964; arrived in US, 1995, naturalized; s. Jonathan Idowu and Elizabeth Abosede Oshunrinade. Diploma in Russian, Pushkin Inst., Moscow, Russia, 1995; BA in Russian, Bklyn. Coll., N.Y., 2000; MS in U.N. studies and Social Sci., LI U., N.Y.C., 2002. Pub. info. asst. U.N., N.Y.C., 2001—. Author: Murder of Diplomacy, 2004, (poetry) Born Beautiful, 2002. Recipient Sept. 11 cert. of Appreciation, ARC. Avocations: reading, writing, travel, soccer. Home: 2324 Beverly Rd Brooklyn NY 11226 Office: UN Rm GA 70 UN Plz 1st Ave New York NY 10017 Office Phone: 212-963-7723. E-mail: oshunrinade@hotmail.com.

OSIAS, RICHARD ALLEN, international financier, investor, real estate investment executive, corporate investor; b. N.Y.C., Nov. 13, 1941; s. Harry L. and Leah (Schank) O.; children: A. Kimberly, Alexandra Elizabeth. Student, Columbia U., 1963; postgrad., David Lipscomb U., 1988—94; PhD of Bus. Adminstrn., Shaftesbury U., 2000, PhD, DD, 1984. Owner Osias Enterprises, Inc., numerous locations, 1953—98. Mem. bus. cabinet David Lipscomb U.; bd. dirs. Am. 21; columist New York Herald Tribune, New York Daily Mirror, 1974-1983. Prin. works include city devel., residential and apt. units, developer City of Deer Park, LI, NY, founder, developer City North Lauderdale, Fla., founder, developer City of Lauderhill, Fla., complete residential housing communities, shopping centers, country clubs, golf courses, hotel chains, comprehensive housing communities; contributed Greystone Raquet and Tennis Club to Nolensville, Tenn.; owner, operator Coolsprings Exec. Plz., landmark office bldg., Internat. Common Market Shopping Complex and other office bldgs., shopping ctrs. in mid-southern region; co-author: South Florida Uniform Building Code; author: Prenuptial Bliss, 2003. Mem. North Lauderdale City Coun., 1967—, mayor, 1968, police and fire commr., 1967—; hon. police chief NYC, Ft. Lauderdale, and Nashville Met. Police, 1994—; mem. Gold Cir., Atlanta Ballet; benefactor Atlanta Symphony Soc.; founder Boys Clubs Broward County, Tower coun. Pine Crest Prep. Sch.; v.p., bd. dirs. LaCiel Park Tower Condominium Assn.; bd. dirs. Tenn. Children's Home, MADD, Tenn. chpt., Tenn. Children's Home, Agape Children's Care Ctr., Nashville, 1993—; founding bd. dirs. AGAPE, BRoward County chpt. Boys Club Am. Recipient Best Am. House award Am. Home mag., 1962, Westinghouse award, 1968, Cert. of Merit for outstanding achievement and contbn. to City of Atlanta by Mayor Andrew Young, 1982; named Builder of Yr., Sunshine State Info. Bur., Fla. and Sunshine State Sr. Citizen, Fla., 1967-73, Builder of Month, Builder/Arch. Mag., 1992, Hon. Police Chief, Nashville, Tenn., 1995, N.Y.C., 1980; profiles on nat. and internat. media, including Dateline/CBS TV, NBC TV, CBS TV and Fuji Network (Japan). Mem. Fla. Sheriff's Assn., Ft. Lauderdale BBB, N.Y. BBB, Nashville BBB, Offshore Power Boat Racing Assn., Fraternal Order Police Assn. (pres.), U.S. C. of C., Fla. C. of C., Margate C. of C., Ft. Lauderdale C. of C., Smithsonian Instn., Soc. Founders U. Miami, Tower Coun., Columns Soc., Pinecrest Prep. Sch. (founder), Nat. Assn. Home Builders, Bankers Club (Miami, Fla.), Bankers Top of First Club, Quarter Deck Club (Galveston, Tex.), Boca Raton (Fla.) Yacht and Country Club, Maunalua Bay Club (Honolulu), Tryall Golf and Country Club (Jamaica), Top of the Home Club, Svc. Plus Club (France), Ensworth Red Gables Soc., Hawaii Loa Ridge Assn., Cannes Island Yacht Club, Canary Islands Yacht Club, Collier's Reserve Country Club (Naples, Fla.), Grey Oaks Country Club (Naples), Le Ciel Club (Naples; v.p. bd. dirs.), Hawaii Loa Ridge Assn. Home: 304 Paiko Dr Honolulu HI 96821 E-mail: osias1@aol.com.

OSINSKI, MARTIN HENRY, healthcare consultant; b. N.Y.C., Apr. 23, 1954; s. Stanley and Shirley (Bobick) Osinski; m. Margie Osinski; children: Ashley, Brett. BBA in Acctg., U. Miami, 1975, MBA, 1977. Grad. asst. U. Miami, Fla., 1975-77; staff acct. Ernst & Ernst, CPA, Miami, 1977-78; asst. buyer, dept. mgr. Burdines Dept. Stores, Miami, 1978-80; buyer menswear Jefferson Ward Dept. Stores, Miami, 1980-82, Richway Dept. Stores, Atlanta, 1982-84; pres. Nat. Health Search, Inc., Miami, 1984-95; chief oper. officer MD Resources, Inc., Miami, 1989-95; prin. Am. Med. Consultants, Inc., Miami, 1996—. Bd. dirs. Congregation Bet Breira, 1994-98, 2002-. Mem.: Am. Soc. Nephrology, Nat. Assn. Physician Recruiters (bd. dirs. 1989—96, v.p. 1990—91, pres. 1991—, ethics com. 2001—, bd. dirs. 2004—, Presdl. award 1991), Iron Arrow Soc. U. Miami, Mens Club (pres. 1992—94). Office: Am Med Consultants Inc 11625 SW 110th Rd Miami FL 33176-3152 Office Phone: 305-271-9225.

OSIPOW, SAMUEL HERMAN, psychology educator; b. Allentown, Pa., Apr. 18, 1934; s. Louis Morris and Tillie Osipow; m. Sondra Beverly Feinstein, Aug. 26, 1956; children: Randall A., Jay I., Reva S., David S. BA, Lafayette Coll., Easton, Pa., 1954; MA, Columbia U., 1955; PhD, Syracuse U., 1959. Lectr. U. Wis., Madison, 1961; psychologist, asst. prof. Pa. State U., 1961-67; mem. faculty Ohio State U., Columbus, 1967-98, prof. psychology, 1969-98, chmn. dept., 1973-86, prof. emeritus, 1998—. Vis. prof. Tel Aviv U., 1972, U. Md., 1980—81; vis. rsch. assoc. Harvard U., 1965; cons. to govt. Author: Strategies in Counseling for Behavior Change, 1970, Theories of Career Development, 1968, 4th edit. 1996, Handbook of Vocational Psychology, 2 vols., 1983, 2d edit. 1995, A Survey of Counseling Methods, 1984; editor: Jour. Vocat. Behavior, 1970-75, Jour. Counseling Psychology, 1975-81, Applied and Preventive Psychology, 1993-99. Served to 1st lt. U.S. Army, 1959-61. Erskine fellow U. Canterbury, New Zealand, 1997. Mem. APA (bd. dirs. 1985-88), Nat. Register Health Svc. Providers in Psychology (bd. dirs. 1982-89, chmn. 1986-89). Home: 330 Eastmoor Blvd Columbus OH 43209-2022 E-mail: sosipow@aol.com.

OSKIN, JOELLEN ROSS, special education educator, school librarian; b. McKeesport, Pa., Apr. 26, 1943; d. Clarence Melvin Ross and Ada Mae Oliver; m. David William Oskin, Sept. 5, 1964; children: David William, Steven Ross. BS in Spl. Edn. magna cum laude, 1980, MLS So. Conn. U., 1987. Spl. edn. tchr. Greenwich (Conn.) Bd. Edn., 1980—89, Darien (Conn.) Bd. Edn., 1989—91; libr. Automated Kings Coll. Libr., Kings Coll., Auckland, New Zealand, 1992—94. Bd. dirs. Vis. Nurse/VNC Network, Wilton, Conn.; mem. adv. bd. Kids In Crisis, Greenwich, 2001—02. Mem.: AAUW. Avocations: golf, reading, travel.

OSLAND, JOYCE MARIE, finance educator, consultant; PhD, Case Western Res. U., Cleve., 1989. Prof. INCAE, Alajuela, Costa Rica, 1989—92; assoc. prof. U. Portland, Oreg., 1992—2002; prof. mgmt. San Jose (Calif.) State U., 2002—. Author: The Adventure of Working Abroad, Organizational Behavior: An Experiential Approach, The Organizational Behavior Reader. Sch. bd. pres. Costa Rica Acad., San Jose, 1990—92. Mem.: Western Acad. Mgmt. (pres. 2001—02, Ascendant scholar 1997, Joan G. Dahl President's award 2001). Office: San Jose State U COB One Washington Sq San Jose CA 95192-0070 Office Phone: 408-924-3583. Office Fax: 408-924-3555. Business E-Mail: osland_j@cob.sjsu.edu.

OSLER, GORDON PETER, retired utility company executive; b. Winnipeg, Man., Can., June 19, 1922; s. Hugh Farquarson and Kathleen (Harty) O.; m. Nancy A. Riley, Aug. 20, 1948; children: Sanford L., Susan Osler Matthews, Gillian Osler Fortier. Student, Queen's U., Kingston, Ont., Can., 1940-41. Pres. Osler, Hammond & Nanton Ltd., Winnipeg, 1952-64, UNAS Investments Ltd., Toronto, Ont., Can., 1964-72; chmn. Slater Steel Industries, Hamilton, Ont., Can., 1972-86, N.Am. Life Assurance Co., Toronto, 1986-95, TransCan. Pipelines, Toronto, 1983-89, ret., 1993. Lt. Can. Army, 1942-45, ETO. Mem. Toronto Club, York Club (Toronto), Everglades Club (Palm Beach, Fla.). Avocation: golf. Home: 17 Lamport Ave Toronto ON Canada M4W 1S7 E-mail: GOsler8660@aol.com.

OSLER, HOWARD LLOYD, retired controller; b. Camden, N.J., Nov. 24, 1927; s. Howard B. and Miriam Osler; m. Barbara C. Skufca, 1987; children by previous marriage: Carol, Peter, Andrew, Bruce. BA, Antioch Coll., 1951. CPA, D.C. Pub. acct. Peat, Marwick Mitchell & Co., Boston, 1949-55; staff asst. to corp. contr. Gillette Co., Boston, 1957-59, gen. mgr. Panamanian subs., 1959-61; asst. to pres. Gillette Co. Argentine subs., 1961-63; asst. to corp. contr. Gillette Co., Boston, 1963-65, contr. mil. Far East div., 1965-67; contr. U.S. div. Foxboro Co., Mass., 1967-68, corp. contr., 1968-87, sec., clk., 1976-86, v.p., contr., 1981-87, ret., 1987. Trustee Gilmanton Cemeteries, 1988—2002, Trust Funds, 1990—91, 1994—2001; commr. Gilmanton Corner Precinct, 1989—2002; mem. Gilmanton Budget Com., 1990—2000, Sch. Bldg. Com., 1988, 1990, Zoning Bd. Adjustment, 1990—91, 1998—2001, Gilmanton Bd. Selectmen, 1991—94. Home: PO Box 190 Gilmanton NH 03237-0190 E-mail: posler@worldpath.net.

OSMENT, LAMAR SUTTON, retired dermatologist, educator; b. Pascagoula, Miss., Apr. 9, 1924; s. Eugene Algernon and Julia Ann Maria (Lowry) O.; m. Nelda Dutton; 1 child, Rachael Osment Pippen. BS, Birmingham-So. Coll., 1945; MD, U. Ala., 1951. Instr. dermatology Sch. Medicine U. Ala., Birmingham, 1955-57, asst. prof., 1957-60, assoc. prof., 1960-70, prof., 1970-89, prof. emeritus, 1989—. Author: The Yellow Fever Epidemic of 1878, 1990, History of the University of Alabama Birmingham Department of Dermatology, 1996; contbr. chpts. to books. Bd. dirs. Arlington Antebellum Home, Birmingham, 1990—. Mem. Ala. Dermatol. Soc. (Lifetime Achievement award 1997), So. Med. Assn. (pres. 1980). Republican. Avocations: genealogy, history of medicine, tennis. Office Phone: 205-871-0639.

OSMER-MCQUADE, MARGARET, business executive, broadcast journalist; b. N.Y.C. d. Herbert Bernard and Margaret Normann (Brunjes) O.; m. Lawrence Carroll McQuade, Mar. 15, 1980; 1 son, Andrew. BA, Cornell U., 1960. Assoc. producer UN Bur., CBS News, N.Y.C., 1962-69; producer 60 Minutes, N.Y.C., 1969-72; reporter, producer Bill Moyer's Jour., Pub. Broadcasting Service, N.Y.C., 1972-73, Reasoner Report, ABC News, N.Y.C., 1973-75; corr., anchor person Good Morning Am., ABC Morning News, Washington, 1975-77; corr. ABC TV News, Washington, 1977-79; v.p., dir. programs Council on Fgn. Relations, 1979-93; pres., CEO Qualitas Internat., N.Y.C., 1994—. Dir. Dime Savs. Bank, 1980—; cons. pub. broadcasting; mem. program com. Ditchley Found. Producer, reporter: TV news shows Come Fly A Kite (Nat. Press Photographer's award 1974), Kissinger, 1970, No Tears for Rachel, 1972, Calder: Master of Mobiles, 1975; moderator, producer World in Focus, publ. TV series for Coun. Fgn. Relations/Sta. WNYC, PBS, Worldnet, 1988-93. Mem. U.S. delegation World Conf. on Cambodian Refugees, Geneva, 1980; mem. Def. Adv. Com. on Women in the Service, 1978-82; trustee Cornell U.; mem. bd. overseers Cornell U. Med. Coll., pres.'s coun. Cornell Women; mem. program com. The Ritchley Found., 1994—, task force N.Y. Sch. Vols., 1994—; vol. Nat. Svc. Learning, 1994—. Recipient Peabody award Staff of 60 Minutes, 1970 Mem. NATAS, Coun. Fgn. Relations, program comm. The Mitching Found., Task Force N.Y. Sch. Vol., Nat. Press Club, Mid. Atlantic Club., vol. Nat. Svc. Learning. Clubs: Cosmopolitan, Century.

OSMOND, DENNIS GORDON, medical educator, researcher; b. N.Y.C., Jan. 31, 1930; s. Ernest Gordon and Marjorie Bertha (Milton) O.; m. Anne Welsh, July 30, 1955; children: Roger Gordon, Martin Henry, David Richard. BSc with first class honors, U. Bristol, Eng., 1951, MB, ChB, 1954, DSc, 1975. House surgeon Royal Gwent Hosp., Newport, Eng., 1954-55; house physician Bristol Royal Infirmary, 1955; demonstrator, lectr. anatomy U. Bristol, 1957-60, 61-64; instr. anatomy U. Wash., Seattle, 1960-61; assoc. prof. anatomy McGill U., Montreal, Que., Can., 1965-67, prof., 1967-74, Robert Reford prof. anatomy, 1974-00, chmn. dept. anatomy and cell biology, 1985-95, Robert Reford emeritus prof. anatomy, 2000—. Vis. scientist Walter and Eliza Hall Inst. Med. Research, Melbourne, Australia, 1972-73; hon. sr. research fellow U. Birmingham, Eng., 1979; vis. scientist Basel Inst. Immunology, Switzerland, 1980, 96; Gaylord scholar Okla. Med. Rsch. Found., 1995. Contbr. numerous articles to profl. jours. Served with Royal Army Med. Corps, 1955-57. Fellow Royal Soc. Can.; mem. Am. Assn. Anatomists, Can. Assn. Anatomists, Anat. Soc. Gt. Britain and Ireland, Am., Can. assns. for immunology, Am. Assn. Immunology, Internat. Soc. for Exptl. Hematology. Home: 1380 Revell Dr Manotick ON Canada K4M 1K8 E-mail: dennisosmond@rogers.com.

OSMOND, MARIE, singer; b. Ogden, Utah, Oct. 13, 1959; d. George and Olive O.; m. Stephen Craig, 1982 (div.) m. Brian Blosil, 1986; children: Stephen James, Jessica Marie, Rachel. Ed. pub. schs., pvt. tutors. Appeared with The Osmond family singing group from age 7, solo act, 1973—;(TV co-star): Donny & Marie TV show, 1976-79, Donny & Marie Christmas Spl, 1979, Osmond Family Show, 1979, Osmond Family Christmas Show, 1980, Donny & Marie, 1998; (star TV spl.) Marie, 1981; appeared in TV series Maybe This Time, 1995, video Buster & Chauncey's Silent Night, 1998; (record albums) include (with Donny Osmond): Make the World Go Away, I'm Leaving It All Up To You; songs from their TV Show Goin Coconuts; (solo albums) include: Paper Roses, In My Little Corner of the World, Who's Sorry Now?, This Is The Way That I Feel, There's No Stopping Your Heart, 1985, I Only Wanted You, 1987, All In Love, 1988, Steppin' Stone, 1989, Twenty Five Hits-Special Collection, 1995; (#1 singles) include Meet Me in Montana (Best Country Duo of Yr. award with Dan Seals), 1986, You're Still New to Me, 1986, There's No Stoppin' Your Heart, 1986, I Only Wanted You, 1987, The Best Of, 1990; toured with Bob Hope, Persian Gulf, 1991; (co-author): Fun, Fame, and Family, 1973; Marie Osmond's Guide to Beauty, Health, and Style, 1980. Recipient (with Donny Osmond) Georgie award for best vocal team Am. Guild Variety Artists, 1978. Mem. Lds Ch.

OSMONT, GHYSLAIN LOUIS, accountant; b. Paris, Mar. 17, 1961; came to U.S., 1983; s. Lucien Henri and Marie-Therese Osmont; m. Macaire Henderson, Aug. 12, 1989; children: Leslie, Clara, Simon. BBA in Internat. Bus. and Acctg., U. Tex., 1987. CPA, N.Y. Acct. Mazars LLP, N.Y.C. Mem. AICPA, N.Y. Soc. CPA, N.J. State Soc. CPA, French-am. C. of C., Conseillers du Commerce Exterior, Paris-Am. Club. Home: 22 Maple Dr Colts Neck NJ 07722 Office: Mazars LLP 135 W 50th St New York NY 10020 E-mail: losmont@mrweiser.com.

OSNES, LARRY G. academic administrator; b. Scottsbluff, Nebr., Oct. 30, 1941; s. Earl E. and Rose (DeRock) O.; m. Susan C.; 1 child, Justin. BA in History, Anderson Coll., 1963; MA in History, Wayne State Coll., 1965; PhD in History, U. Cin., 1970. Asst. prof. history and govt. U. Cin., 1967-69; dir. Am. studies Anderson (Ind.) Coll., 1970-75, chmn. dept. history, 1975-76, dean acadmeic devel., 1975-78, asst. corp. sec., dean academic devel. and pub. affairs, 1978-83; pres. Minn. Pvt. Coll. Coun., St. Paul, 1983-88, Hamline U., St. Paul, 1988—. Mem. Assoc. Colls. Twin Cities (chmn. 1988-90), Mpls. Club, St. Paul Athletic Club. Office: Hamline Univ 1536 Hewitt Ave Saint Paul MN 55104-1284

OSNOS, DAVID MARVIN, lawyer, director; b. Detroit, Jan. 10, 1932; s. Max and Florence (Pollock) O.; m. Glenna DeWitt, Aug. 10, 1956; children: Matthew, Alison AB summa cum laude, Harvard U., 1953, JD cum laude, 1956. Bar: D.C. 1956. Assoc. Arent, Fox, Kintner, Plotkin & Kahn, Washington, 1956-61, ptnr., 1962—2002, chmn. exec. com., 1978-97, of counsel, 2003—. Bd. dirs. EastGroup Properties, Jackson, Miss., VSE Corp., Alexandria, Va., Washington Real Estate Investment Trust, Rockville, Md., Washington Wizards Basketball Club, Washington. Trustee Mt. St. Mary's Coll., Emmitsburg, Md., 1981-90; bd. dirs. Greater Washington Jewish Cmty. Found., Rockville, Md., Jewish Cmty. Ctr. Greater Washington, 1964-75. Avocations: tennis, music, enology. Office: Arent Fox 1050 Connecticut Ave NW Ste 600 Washington DC 20036-5339 Business E-Mail: osnosd@arentfox.com.

OSNOS, GILBERT CHARLES, management consultant; b. Detroit, Nov. 23, 1929; s. Herman Sol and Helen (Yudkoff) O.; m. Margaret N. Paysner, Aug. 18, 1957; children: Steven, Elisabeth. BA, U. Mich., 1951; MBA, Harvard U., 1953. Dept. mgr. Sams, Inc., Detroit, 1956-57, asst. buyer, 1957-58, dir. store ops., 1958, buyer, 1958-59, mdse. buyer, 1959-62; buyer Topps Divsn. Interstate Dept. Stores, N.Y.C., 1962-65; mdse. mgr. Arlans Dept. Stores, N.Y.C., 1965-68; pres. Nazareth Mills divsn. Kayser Roth, N.Y.C., 1968-73, Rosenau Bros., Phila., 1973-75, Warnaco Men's Sportswear, 1975-78; with Grisanti and Galef, 1979-81, ptnr., 1981—; pres. Grisanti, Galef & Osnos, N.Y.C., 1983—. Chmn. RKG Osnos Ptnrs., LLC, 1986—; bd. dirs. Mrs. Fields Famous Brands, Turnaround Mgmt. Assn., chmn., 1990-91. Lt. j.g. USNR, 1953-56. Mem. Am. Apparel Assn. (consumer affairs com.), Am. Bankruptcy Inst., Bus. Execs. for Nat. Security, Harvard Club, Halloween Yacht Club, Harvard Bus. Sch. Club of N.Y.C., Corinthians. Avocations: sailing, opera, classical music, photography, reading. Office: RKG Osnos Ptnrs LLP Ste 1200 20 W 22d St New York NY 10010-5804 E-mail: gosnos@rkgosnos.com.

OSNOS, PETER LIONEL WINSTON, publishing executive; b. Bombay, Oct. 13, 1943; s. Joseph Lionel and Marta (Bychowski) O.; m. Susan R. Sherer, Aug. 18, 1973; children: Katherine Mason, Evan L.R. BA, Brandeis U., Waltham, Mass., 1964; MS in Journalism with honors, Columbia U., 1965. Editorial asst. I.F. Stone's Weekly, Washington, 1964-65; corr., editor Washington Post, 1966-84; v.p, assoc. pub. Random House Trade Books and pub. Times Books, Random House, Inc., N.Y.C., 1984-96; cons. 20th Century Fund, 1996-97; pub., chief exec. Public Affairs, 1997—. Contbr. articles to profl. publs. Bd. dirs. Human Rights Watch, chmn. Europe and Ctrl. Asia divns.; bd. dirs. Baltic-Am. Partnership, U. Mich. Fellowship Journalists, 2000. Fellow NEH, 1973-74. Mem. Assn. Am. Pubs. (vice chmn. gen. pub. divsn. 1993-96), Coun. on Fgn. Rels., Century Club. Office: Pub Affairs 250 W 57th St New York NY 10107 E-mail: peter.osnos@perseusbooks.com.

OSOFF, JEFFREY ARLIN, media executive; b. Everett, Mass., June 5, 1936; s. Meyer and Minerva (Cogan) O. (dec.); m. Arlene Shuman, Sept. 23, 1962 (div. Jan. 1988); children: Judith Robin (dec.), David Eric. BA, Bowling Green State U., 1958; MS, Columbia U., 1959. Reporter Boston Post, 1954-55, Boston Globe, 1955-64, rewriteman, 1962-63, acting asst. city editor, 1963-64; dir. News Bur. Brandeis U., Waltham, Mass., 1964-67, asst. dir. pub. affairs, 1967-69, dir. pub. affairs, 1969-76; chmn. bd. Jansson, Inc., Waltham, 1976-87; pres., chief exec. officer JAO Enterprises, Ltd., Lexington, Mass., 1987—; chmn. Dorian Enterprises, Ltd., 1992—, D & J Enterprises, Ltd., Lexington, Mass., 1995—; chmn. bd. Concannon's Inc., Marlborough and Wellesley, Mass., 1990—98. Lectr. in journalism and pub. rels. cons. First v.p. Dysuatonomia Found., NY, 1965-66, bd. dirs., 1965-76, pres., 1973-74; bd. dirs. New Eng. region Anti-Defamation League. Served with USAF, 1961-62. Recipient citation for outstanding journalistic reporting Mass. N.G., 1961; several awards for high achievement in graphics. Mem. New Eng. Press Assn., Internat. Thermographic Assn., Printing Industries Am., Printing Industries

New Eng., Am. Coll. Pub. Rels. Assn., Jewish Pub. Relations Soc. Am., Pub. Rels. Soc. Am., Publicity Club Boston, Sigma Delta Chi, Zeta Beta Tau. Jewish. Home and Office: 3E Autumn Dr Hudson MA 01749-2855

OSORIO, CLAUDIO E. computer company executive; Chmn., pres., ceo CHS Electronics, Miami. Office: Price Waterhouse Coopers 10 10th St NE #1400 Atlanta GA 30309-3906

OSORIO, PEPON, artist; b. Santurce, Puerto Rico, 1955; Student, U. Inter-Am., Rio Piedras, Puerto Rico, 1974; BS, Herbert H. Lehman Coll., 1978; MA, Columbia U., 1985. Artist-in-residence El Museo del Barrio, N.Y.C., 1989—91, The Fabric Workshop and Mus., Phila., Park Ave. Shelter Homeless Women, Artist/Homless Shelter, N.Y.C., 1993, Mus. Contemporary Art, L.A., 1993, Walker Art Ctr., Mpls., 1994, Ctr. Arts at Yerba Buena Gardens, San Francisco, 1996, Manchester Craftsmen's Guild, Pitts.; artist in residence dept. visual arts Rutgers U., Ctr. Innovative Print and Paper, New Brunswick, NJ, 1998; vis. artist dept. visual arts Skidmore Coll., Saratoga Springs, NY, 1995, Temple U., Tyler Sch. Arts, Phila., 1996; vis. artist Skowhegan (Maine) Sch. Painting and Sculpture, 1998, U. Hawaii, Honolulu, 1998; vis. artist dept. fine and pub. art Calif. State U. at Monterey, 1996; vis. faculty R.I. Sch. Design, Providence, 1993, Cleve. Art Inst., 1993; mem. adv. bd. Performance Space 122, N.Y.C., 1989—93, The New Mus., N.Y.C., 1996—98, Centro de Estudios Puertoriqueños at Hunter Coll., N.Y.C., 1996—98; lectr. in field. One-man shows include Hostos Ctr. Arts and Culture, Hostos C.C., Bronx, 1985, CU Art Galleries, U. Colo., Boulder, 1991, El Museo del Barrio, N.Y.C., 1991, U. Arts, Samuel S. Fleisher Art Meml., Phila 1992, Mus. Am. Art, Acad. Fine Arts, 1992, Cleve. Inst. Art, 1993, Real Art Ways, Hartford, 1994, Storefront, 33 Broadway, Newark, 1995, Museo de Pedro Albizu, Campos, Chgo., 1996, Galerie OZ, Paris, 1996, Ronald Feldman Fine Art, N.Y.C., 1996, Otis Gallery, Otis Coll. Art and Design, Westchester, Calif., 1997, Ctr. Arts at Yerba Buena Gardens, San Francisco, 1997, South Bronx and Manhattan, N.Y., 1997, Museo Nacional Centro de Arte Reina Sofia, Madrid, 1998, Museo Alejandro Otero, Caracas, Venezuela, 1998, Hostos Art Gallery, Bronx, 1998, exhibited in group shows at Mus. Am. Art, Smithsoniann Instn., Washington, 1996, Whitney Mus. Am. Art at Champion, Stamford, Conn., 1997, Setagaya Art Mus., Tokyo, 1997, Africus Inst. Contemporary Art, Johannesburg, South Africa, 1997, The Bertha and Karl Leubsdorf Art Gallery, Hunter Coll., N.Y.C., 1998, Internat. Ctr. Photography Midtown, 1999, others, performances include, No Regrets, 1989, Broken Hearts, 1991, Historias, 1992, Familias, 1995, others, commns. include, Cafe Am., N.Y.C., 1990, Bklyn. Acad. Music, 1991, Represented in permanent collections El Museo del Barrio, N.Y.C., Nat. Mus. Am. Art, Phila., Newark Mus., Walker Ctr. Arts, Mpls., Wadsworth Atheneum, Hartford, Whitney Mus. Am. Art, N.Y.C. Recipient N.Y. Dance and Performance award, 1985, Louis Tiffany Comfort award, 1993, Mid-Atlantic Arts Found. Residency award, The Fabric Workshop, 1996, Internat. Assn. of Art Critics award, 1996; fellow Sculpture fellow, Nat. Endowment Arts, 1988, Artist fellow in sculpture, N.Y. Found. Arts, 1988, 1995, Intercultural Film/Video fellow, Rockefeller Found., 1993, Artist's fellow, Joan Mitchell Found., 1996—97, MacArthur fellow, John D. and Catherine T. MacArthur Found., 1999; Krasner Pollack Found. fellow, Theater Comm. Group and Nat. Endowment Arts fellow, 1990. Office: care Ronald Feldman Fine Arts 31 Mercer St New York NY 10013-2541

OSOWIEC, DARLENE ANN, clinical psychologist, educator, consultant; b. Chgo., Feb. 16, 1951; d. Stephen Raymond and Estelle Marie Osowiec; m. Barry A. Leska. BS, Loyola U., Chgo., 1973; MA with honors, Roosevelt U., 1980; postgrad. in psychology, Saybrook Inst., San Francisco, 1985—88; PhD in Clin. Psychology, Calif. Inst. Integral Studies, 1992. Lic. clin. psychologist, Mo., Ill., Calif. Mental health therapist Ridgeway Hosp., Chgo., 1978; mem. faculty psychology dept. Coll. Lake County, Grayslake, Ill., 1981; counselor, supr. MA-level interns, chmn. pub. rels. com. Integral Counseling Ctr., San Francisco, 1983—84; clin. psychology intern Chgo.-Read Mental Health Ctr. Ill. Dept. Mental Health, 1985—86; mem. faculty dept. psychology Moraine Valley C.C., Palos Hills, Ill., 1988—89; lectr. psychology Daley Coll., Chgo., 1988-90; cons. Gordon & Assocs., Oak Lawn, Ill., 1989; adolescent, child and family therapist Orland Twp. Youth Svcs., Orland Park, Ill., 1993; psychology fellow Sch. Medicine, St. Louis U., 1994-95; pvt. practice Chgo., Geneva and St. Charles, Ill., 1996—; founder Maximum Potential, Chgo., 1996—. Contbr., author: Transpersonal Hypnosis, 1999. Ill. State scholar, 1969-73; Calif. Inst. Integral Studies scholar, 1983. Mem. APA (chair edn. and tng. com. divsn. 30 1998-2000, chair mem. svcs. 2001—), Am. Psychol. Soc., Am. Women in Psychology, Ill. Psychol. Assn., Calif. Psychol. Assn., Mo. Psychol. Assn., Fla. Psychol. Assn., Am. Soc. Clin. Hypnosis, Chgo. Soc. Clin. Hypnosis, NOW (chair legal adv. corps, Chgo. 1974-76), Lincoln Park Bus. Devel. Inst. (chair program com. 2003—). Avocations: playing piano, gardening, reading, back-packing, writing. Office: 2210 Dean St Ste E-1 Saint Charles IL 60175 Office Phone: 630-377-8421.

OSSI, JAMES MATTHEW, artist; b. Wyckoff, N.J., Jan. 7, 1947; s. Peter and (Hildegarde) O.; m. Diana Louise Wege (divorced); children: Sara, Peter; m. Marie Decarie, Aug. 18, 1997. Grad. in Indsl. Rsch., Parsons Sch. of Design, 1970. Sculptures located in The Mus. of Modern Art, N.Y.C., 1969, MIT Mus. Cambridge, Mass., 1983, Saibu Gas Mus., Fukuoka, 1989, math. dept. Princeton U., 1998, physics lobby MIT, 2000. Recipient numerous screenwriting awards, 2002—03. Home: 21 Baywater Dr Darien CT 06820 E-mail: james.ossi@earthlink.net.

OSSOFF, ROBERT HENRY, otolaryngological surgeon; b. Beverly, Mass., Mar. 25, 1947; s. Michael Max and Eve Joan (Kladky) G.; m. Lynn Spilman, 1984; 1 child, Leslin; 1 child by previous marriage, Jacob. BA, Bowdoin Coll., 1969; DMD, Tufts U., 1973, MD, 1975; MS in Otolaryngology, Northwestern U., 1981. Intern Northwestern Meml. Hosp., Chgo., 1975-76; resident in otolaryngology Northwestern Med. Sch., Chgo., 1976-80, NIH rsch. fellow dept. otolaryngology, 1977-78, Am. Cancer Soc. clin. fellow, 1980-81, jr. faculty clin. fellow, 1981-84; pvt. practice surgery, laryngology and care of profl. voice, Chgo., 1975-86, Nashville, 1986—; chmn. dept. otolaryngology Vanderbilt U. Hosp., Nashville, 1986—; exec. med. dir. Vanderbilt Voice Ctr., 1991—. Staff Children's Meml. Hosp., Chgo., 1980—81, Nashville VA Hosp., 1986—; chief divsn. otolaryngology Evanston (Ill.) Hosp., 1983—86; chief otolaryngology VA Lakeside Hosp., Chgo., 1982—86; mem. staff Northwestern Meml. Hosp., 1981—86, Children's Meml. Hosp., 1981—84; asst. prof. Northwestern U. Dental Sch., 1980—86; assoc. prof. Northwestern U. Med. Sch., 1985—86; Guy M. Maness prof., chmn. dept. otolaryngology Vanderbilt U. Sch. Medicine, 1986—; assoc. dir. Vanderbilt Free-Electron Laser Ctr. Med. and Materials Rsch., 1992—95; assoc. vice chancellor for health affairs and chief of staff Vanderbilt U. Hosp., 1995—97, assoc. vice chancellor for health affairs, 1995—. Mem. editl. bd. Otolaryngology-Head and Neck Surgery, 1988—, sr. editor Lasers in Surgery and Medicine, 1987—94, editor-in-chief, 1995—; co-editor: Complications in Head and Neck Surgery W.B. Saunders Co., 1993—, The Larynx Lippincott Williams and Wilkins, 2002; mem. editl. bd. Clin. Laser Monthly, 1984—, Jour. of Voice, 1987—, The Laryngoscope, 1988—2003, Operative Techniques in Otolaryngology-Head and Neck Surgery, 1989—, Head and Neck Surgery, 1989—, Jour. of Laser Applications, 1989—, with editl. adv. bd. Gen. Surgery News, 1990—99, assoc. editor Diagnostic and Therapeutic Endoscopy, 1992—; contbr. articles to profl. jours., chpts. to books. Bd. dirs. Laser Inst. Am., 1984—90; dir. Am. Bd. Otolaryngology, 1995—; trustee Midwest Biolaser Inst., Chgo., 1981—86. Recipient Lederer-Pierce award Chgo. Laryngol. and Otol. Soc., 1978. Fellow: ACS (bd. govs. 1996—2002,); mem.: AMA, Cartesian Soc., Am. Laryngol. Assn. (coun. 1996—, sec. 1998—2003, pres.-elect 2003, pres. 2004, Baker lectr. 2001, Guest of Honor 2003, Presdl. citation 2003, DeRoaldes medal 2004), The Triological Soc. (coun. 1996—99, v.p. so. sect. 2002—03), Am. Broncho-Esophagological Assn. (treas. 1980—84, pres.-elect 1994—95, pres. 1995—96), Am. Soc. Head and Neck Surgery (coun. 1991—94), Soc. Head and Neck Surgeons, Am. Soc. Laser Medicine and Surgery (bd. dirs. 1985—88, pres.-elect 1988—89, pres. 1989—90, Presdl. citation 2003, William B. Mark award 1992, Presdl. citation 2003), Am. Acad. Otolaryngology-Head and Neck Surgery (chmn. laser surgery com. 1983—89, chmn. self instl. package com. 1990—96, bd. dirs. 1992—95, coord. for devel. 2001—, Cert. of Honor 1984, Disting. Svc. award 1995, Presdl. citation 1999), Am. Acad. Oral Pathology, Am. Acad. Oral Medicine. Office: Vanderbilt U Med Ctr Dept Otolaryngology S-2100 Med Ctr N Nashville TN 37232-0001 Office Phone: 615-322-6336. Business E-Mail: robert.ossoff@vanderbilt.edu.

OSSTYN, RANDOLPH BEIER, lawyer; b. Royal Oak, Mich., Apr. 24, 1943; s. Alouis and Doris Helen (Finnie) O.; children: Alicia Anne, Neal Randolph; m. Carrie Ann Wood, May 3, 1997. BA, MA, U. Mich.; JD magna cum laude, U. Detroit. Bar: U.S. Supreme Ct. 1980; bd. cert. creditors rights specialist. Tchr., dept. head Detroit Bd. Edn., 1969-76; founding ptnr. Osstyn, Bays, Ferns & Spray, Marquette, Mich., 1979—. Lectr. collection law in Mich., 2002. Treas. Prince of Peach Luth. Ch., Marquette, 1978-81; founding mem. Save the Janzen Com., Marquette, 1983-85; mem ch. council Messiah Luth. Ch., Marquette, 1984-85; bd. dirs. Marquette Mountain Racing Team, 1982-90, pres., 1986-89. Mem. ABA, Wis. Bar Assn., Mich. Bar Assn., Comml. Law League Am. Democrat. Avocations: skiing, running, bridge. Home: 43 White Oak Dr Marquette MI 49855-9450 Office: Osstyn Bays Ferns & Quinnell 419 W Washington St Ste 500 Marquette MI 49855-4322 Office Phone: 906-228-3650. E-mail: rosstyn@chartermi.net.

OSTAPENKO, ALEXIS, civil engineer, educator; b. Ukraine, Oct. 1, 1923; came to U.S. 1951; s. Peter and Natalia O.; married; 3 children. Dipl.Ing., Tech. U. Munich, Germany, 1951; ScD, MIT, 1957. Structural engr. Fay, Spofford & Thorndike, Boston, 1952, Thomas Worcester, Boston, 1952-54, various firms, 1955-57; from asst. prof. to prof. civil engring. Lehigh U., Bethlehem, Pa., 1957—94, prof. emeritus, 1994—. Rsch. grantee USN, PennDOT, USCG, U.S. Dept. of Transp., U.S. Dept Interior, U.K. Dept. Energy, Exxon, Mobil, many others, 1958—. Mem. ASCE, Sigma Xi. Office: Lehigh Univ Fritz Engring Lab 13 E Packer Ave Bethlehem PA 18015-3176

OSTAR, ALLAN WILLIAM, academic administrator, higher education consultant; b. East Orange, N.J., Sept. 4, 1924; s. William and Rose O.; m. Roberta Hutchison, Sept. 10, 1949; children. Cert. engring., U. Denver, 1943; BA, Pa. State U., 1948; postgrad., U. Wis., 1949-55; LL.D., U. No. Colo., 1968, Eastern Ky. U., 1972, Whittier Coll., 1973; L.H.D., U. Maine, 1975; D.Letters, Central Mich. U., 1975; D.P.S., Bowling Green State U., 1975, R.I. Coll., 1983; D.Higher Edn., Morehead State U., 1977; L.H.D., Appalachian State U., 1977, No. Mich. U., 1978, Dickinson State Coll., N.D., 1979, Towson State U., 1980, Salem State Coll., 1980, Mont. Coll. Mineral Sci. and Tech., 1983, Ball State U., 1984; LL.D., U. Alaska, 1978, Ill. State U., 1983, Western Mich. U., 1984; D. Polit. Sci., Kyung Hee U., Korea, 1984; L.H.D., Fitchburg State Coll., 1986, Bridgwater State Coll., 1988, No. State Coll., 1988, Harris-Stowe State Coll., 1986; LLD, Edinboro U. Pa., 1987, Loch Haven U., Pa., 1989; LHD, No. Ariz. U., 1990, Shepherd (W.Va.) Coll., 1992, SUNY, 1993, Lincoln U., Mo., 1995. Dir. nat. pub. relations U.S. Nat. Student Assn., 1948-49; exec. asst. Commonwealth Fund, N.Y.C., 1952-53; asst. to dean extension div. U. Wis., 1949-52, dir. office communications services, 1954-58; dir. Joint Office Instnl. Research, Nat. Assn. State Univs. and Land Grant Colls., Washington, 1958-65; pres. Am. Assn. State Colls. and Univs., Washington, 1965-91, pres. emeritus, 1991—, sr. cons. Acad. Search Consultation Svc., 1991—. Adj. prof. edn. Pa. State U., 1990—. Co-author: Colleges and Universities for Change, 1987; contbr. chpts. in books. Mem. 42d (Rainbow) div. U.S. Army, 1943-46. Decorated 2 Bronze Stars; recipient Centennial award for disting. svcs. to edn. U. Akron, 1970, Fogelsanger award Shippensburg (Pa.) State Coll., 1974, World Peace Through Edn. medal Internat. Assn. U. Pres., 1975, Disting. Achievement award, U. So. Colo., 1979, Chancellor's award U. Wis., 1985, Chancellor's medal CUNY, 1986, Disting. Alumnus award Pa. State U., 1989, svc. award Coun. on Internat. Ednl. Exch., 1990, Chancellor's medal Internat. Svc. U. Ark., Little Rock, 1990, Disting. Pub. Svc. medal Dept. of Def., 1991; Alumni fellow Pa. State U., 1975. Unitarian-Universalist. Home: 5500 Friendship Blvd Chevy Chase MD 20815-7219

OSTARO, See GOELE, DHRUV

OSTASZEWSKI, ALYCE VITELLA, religion educator; b. Chgo., Apr. 24, 1936; d. Peter Anthony and Cleta Earline (Chastain) Indelli; m. Gerald Earl Nelson (div. 1967); children: Peter J., Maryalice C., William P., Paula A.; m. Stanley Joseph Ostaszewski; children: Vinson Shaw, Stacean V. Grad. high sch. Immaculata, Chgo., 1954. Tchr. religious edn. St. John the Evangelist Ch., Streamwood, Ill., 1962-68; tchr. religious edn., facilitator Rite of Christian Initiation of Adults, St. Thomas More Ch., Elgin, Ill., 1980-86; tchr. religious edn., young adult min. St. Julie Billiart Ch., Newbury Park, Calif., 1987-89, confirmation coord., 1990-91; confirmation asst. coord. St. Paschal Baylon Ch., Thousand Oaks, Calif., 1991-92; master chatechist basic faith formation program L.A. Diocese, Santa Barbara Region, 1990-93. Com. mem. Santa Barbara Regional Conf., 1988-93; workshop spkr. Santa Barbara Regional Conf., 1992; confirmation tchr. Holy Cross Parish, Batavia, Ill., 1993-94; 3rd grade religion edn. tchr., 1994-96, Saturday ch. staff asst. 1997—, U. Dayton catechist formation program, 1997-98, 99, 00. Sec. Village of Streamwood Homeowners Assn., 1957-58; bd. dirs. Oak Ridge Estates Homeowners Assn., Newbury Park, Calif., 1986-88; lifetime mem. Streamwood Hist. Soc., 1993—; woman's team 7 C.R.H.P. Witness'er, 1994; mem. choir St. Thomas More, St. Julie Billiart, Holy Cross; vol. picture person program for McWayne Sch., Batavia, Ill., 1998-99. Recipient Bishop O'Neill award, 1999.

OSTBERG, A. PETER, food products/retail groceries executive; CFO Holberg Industries Inc., Greenwich, Conn. Office: Holberg Industries Inc 545 Steamboat Rd Greenwich CT 06830

OSTBERG, HENRY DEAN, corporate executive; b. Bocholt, Germany, July 21, 1928; came to U.S., 1939, naturalized, 1945. s. Fred and Lotte (Hertz) O.; m. Sydelle Burns, Dec. 13, 1987; 1 child, Neal; stepchildren: Elysa Bari, Brent Adam, Ross Jay. LLB, N.Y. Law Sch., 1950; MBA, Ohio State U., 1953, PhD, 1957. Pres. H.D. Ostberg Assocs., N.Y.C., 1950—; assoc. prof. mktg. NYU, 1954—63. Chmn. bd. Admar Group,Inc., 1960; dir. Self-Instructional Devel. Corp., Amherst Group, Porter Industries, Inc.; pres. Eastman Enterprises, Inc. Contbr. articles to profl. jours. Trustee Ostberg Found.; chmn. Givat Haviva Edn. Found. Capt. USAF, 1950—53. Jewish. E-mail: hdousa@earthlink.net.

OSTBY, FREDERICK PAUL, JR., meteorologist, retired government official, science administrator; b. New Haven, Jan. 20, 1930; s. Frederick Paul and Edna Maria (Kruckenberg) O.; m. Joanne Bernice Sorvig, Jan. 1, 1955 (div. 1989); children: Paul, Neil, Karen, Lynn; m. Barbara Richards, Mar. 17, 1989. BS in Meteorology, NYU, 1951, MS, 1960. Cert. Consulting Meteorlogist. Meteorologist TWA, N.Y.C., 1953-54, Kansas City, Mo., 1955-56, N.E. Weather Service, Lexington, Mass., 1955, Travelers Weather Service, Hartford, Conn., 1956-60; research scientist Travelers Research Center, Hartford, 1960-70; meteorologist Nat. Weather Service, Silver Spring, Md., 1970-72; dep. dir. Nat. Severe Storms Forecast Center, Dept. Commerce, Kansas City, Mo., 1972-80; dir. Nat. Severe Storms Forecast Center, 1980-96; assoc. Climatological Cons. Corp., 1997—. Severe weather cons. The Weather Channel, 1997—. Contbr. papers to profl. lit. Served with USAF, 1951-53. Fellow Am. Meteorol. Soc. (council 1977-80, 84-87). Home: 12537 Broadmoor St Overland Park KS 66209-3234 Office Phone: 913-338-4222. Personal E-mail: fostby@attglobal.net.

OSTBY, RONALD, retired dairy and food products company executive; b. 1937; BS, U. S.D., 1959. With Pillsbury Co., 1961-84, v.p. fin. planning; v.p., chief fin. officer AG Processing, 1984-86; group v.p., chief fin. officer Land O'Lakes, 1986-2000, ret.

OSTEEN, LOUIS, chef; b. Anderson, S.C. m. Marlene Osteen. Chef, owner Pawleys Island Inn, SC, 1980; chef Charleston Grill, 1989—. Former mem. food bd. New Eng. Culinary Inst. Appearances Gourmet, Bon Appetit, Southern Living, GQ, Esquire, Saveur, Food & Wine, Town & Country, Great Chefs of the South. Bd. dirs. DiRoNa; founding co-organizer Charleston's Share Our Strength State of the Nation event. Nominee James Beard Found., 1996; named to Fine Dining Hall of Fame, Nation's Restaurant News A, 1994; recipient Great Am. Express Chef S.E. award, Ivy award, Restaurants & Institutions mag., Golden Dish award, Alan Richman, GQ's Mag.'s food and wine writer, 1994. Office: Louis's Restaurant 1228 E Morehead St Ste 100 Charlotte NC 28204-2889

O'STEEN, WENDALL KEITH, neurobiology and anatomy educator; b. Meigs, Ga., July 3, 1928; s. Wellna Hubert and Lillian (Powell) O'S.; m. Sandra Lynn Kraeer, July 30, 1983; children: Lisa Diane, Kerry Keith, Buckley Powell. BA, Emory U., 1948, MS, 1950; PhD, Duke U., 1958. Asst. prof. Emory U. Jr. Coll., Valdosta, Ga., 1948-49; instr. Emory U., Atlanta, 1950-51; prof. Emory U. Sch. Medicine, Atlanta, 1968-77; from asst. prof. to prof. med. br. U. Tex., 1958-67; asst. prof. Wofford Coll., Spartanburg, S.C., 1951-53; prof., chmn. dept. neurobiology and anatomy, Bowman Gray Sch. Med. Wake Forest U., Winston-Salem, N.C., 1977-93, prof. emeritus, 1993—. Mem. anatomy com. Nat. Bd. Med. Examiners, Phila., 1982-87. Contbr. over 150 articles to books, nat. and internat. jours. Served to lt. col. USAR. Recipient Golden Apple teaching award Med. Br. U. Tex., Galveston, 1967, Outstanding Tchr. award Emory U., 1973, Williams Disting. Teaching award Emory U., 1974, award for teaching excellence Bowman Gray Sch. Medicine, Wake Forest U. Mem. Am. Assn. Anatomists (exec. com. 1980-84, v.p. 1990-92), Assn. Anatomy Chairmen (exec. com. 1982-84, pres. 1990-91), So. Soc. Anatomists (pres. 1975-76), Soc. for Neurosci., N.C. Soc. Neurosci. (pres. 1980-81), Western N.C. Soc. Neurosci. (pres. 1987-88), Assn. Rsch. in Vision and Ophthalmology, Alpha Omega Alpha. Republican. Methodist. Avocations: gardening, music. Office: Wake Forest U Bowman Gray Sch Medicine Dept Of Neurobiology & Anatomy Winston Salem NC 27157-0001

OSTEEN, WILLIAM L. federal judge; b. 1930; BA, Guilford Coll., 1953; LLB, U. N.C., 1956. With Law Office of W.H. McElwee, Jr., North Wilkesboro, N.C., 1956-58; pvt. practive Greensboro, N.C., 1958-59; with Booth & Osteen, Greensboro, 1959-69; U.S. atty. U.S. Attys. Office, Greensboro, 1969-74; ptnr. Osteen, Adams & Osteen, Greensboro, 1974-91; fed. judge U.S. Dist. Ct. (mid. dist.) N.C., Greensboro, 1991—. With USAR, 1958-51. Fellow Am. Coll. Trial Lawyers; mem. ABA, N.C. State Bar, N.C. Bar Assn. (mem. and chair subcom. N.C. sentencing commn.), U. N.C. Law Alumni Assn. Office: US Dist Ct PO Box 3485 Greensboro NC 27402-3485

OSTENDORF, LANCE STEPHEN, lawyer, educator, financial consultant; b. New Orleans, Aug. 16, 1958; 1 child, Christine Marie Ostendorf. BBA in Acctg. and Fin. summa cum laude, Loyola U., 1976, JD, 1980. Bar: La. 1980, U.S. Dist. Ct. (ea. dist.) La. 1981, U.S. Dist. Ct. La., U.S. Supreme Ct. 1980, U.S. Dist. Ct. (we. and mid. dists.) La. 1983. Founder GO Entertainment, Inc. L.A., New Orleans,Balt./Washington, L.A./Orange County, San Diego/Riverside, Ostendorf, Tate, Barnett & Wells, PLC, L.A./Orange County, San Diego/Riverside, Houston, Balt., New Orleans. Treas., CFO La. State U. Med. Ctr. Found., New Orleans, 1992—; lectr. Lorman Ednl. Seminars; bd. dirs. La. State U. Med. Ctr. Found., New Orleans, tech. transfer com.; speaker and tchr. Lorman Ednl. Svcs., Inc. Author: Insurance Law; contbr. articles to profl. jours. Mem. ABA, Fed. Bar Assn., Internat. Bar Assn., La. Bar Assn., Metairie Bar Assn., Maritime Law Assn., Comite Maritime Internat., Assn. for Transp. Law, Trucking Industry Def. Assn., Logistics and Policy, Assn. Average Adjusters of U.S., Jefferson Bar Assn., New Orleans Bar Assn., La. Restaurant Assn., Am. Trial Lawyers Assn., La. Bar Assn., Jefferson Bar Assn., Fifth Cir. Bar Assn., Def. Rsch. Inst., La. Trial Lawyers Assn., Law Def. Lawyers Assn., Houston Mariners Club, Southeastern Adm. Law Inst., St. Thomas Moore Club, La. Notary Soc., New Orleans South African Connection, Blue Key Honor Soc. Office: The Poydras Ctr Ste 1460 650 Poydras St New Orleans LA 70130 E-mail: lanceostendorf@yahoo.com.

OSTER, LEWIS HENRY, manufacturing executive, engineering consultant; b. Mitchell, S.D., Jan. 18, 1923; s. Peter W. and Lucy (Goetsch) O.; m. Mary Mills, Aug. 17, 1948; children— David, Lewis, Nancy, Susan. B.S. in Engring., Iowa State U., 1948; M.B.A., Syracuse U., 1968. Registered profl. engr., Iowa. Mgr., Maytag Co., Newton, Iowa, 1953-59; sr. staff engr., mgr. Philco-Ford Corp., Phila., 1959-62; mgr. mech. and indsl. engring. Carrier Corp., Syracuse, N.Y., 1962-75; v.p. Superior Industries Internat., Van Nuys, Calif., 1981—; v.p., gen. mgr. Superior/Ideal, Inc., Oskaloosa, Iowa, 1975—; engring. cons., Louisville, 1951-53. Author: MTM Application Manual, 1957. Leader, Boy Scouts Am., Syracuse, 1965-73; fund chmn. United Fund, Syracuse, 1965-73. Served to lt. col. USAFR, 1942—; ETO. Decorated Purple Heart, DFC, Air medal with four oak leaf clusters. Mem. Am. Inst. Indsl. Engrs. (pres. 1951-53), Oskaloosa Country Club, Ret. Officers Assn., Elks, Am. Legion.

OSTER, MARTIN WILLIAM, oncologist, educator; b. Apr. 9, 1947; s. Joseph A. and Bella Oster; m. Karen A. Strauss, May 18, 1975; children: Bonnie Felice, Michelle Rae, Nancy Meredith. BA summa cum laude, Columbia U., 1967, MD, 1971. Diplomate Am. Bd. Internal Medicine and subsplty. med. oncology. Intern, resident in medicine Mass. Gen. Hosp., Boston, 1971-73; clin. assoc. divsn. of cancer treatment Nat. Cancer Inst., Bethesda, Md., 1973-76; asst. prof. medicine Columbia Coll. Physicians and Surgeons, 1976-86, assoc. prof. clin. medicine, 1986—. Asst. attending physician Columbia-Presbyn. Med. Center, N.Y.C., 1976-86, assoc. attending physician, 1986—; vice chair protocol com. Columbia U. Cancer Ctr., 1998, chmn., 1999. With USPHS, 1973-76. Am. Cancer Soc. jr. faculty clin. fellow, 1976-79. Fellow ACP; mem. AMA (Physician Recognition awards 1976-78, 79-81, 82-84), Am. Assn. Cancer Rsch., N.Y. Cancer Soc., Am. Soc. Clin. Oncology, N.Y. Met. Breast Cancer Group, Phi Beta Kappa, Alpha Omega Alpha. Home: 6 Arrowhead Ln Armonk NY 10504-1301 Office: 161 Fort Washington Ave New York NY 10032-3713 Office Phone: 212-305-8231.

OSTER, ROSE MARIE GUNHILD, foreign language professional, educator; b. Stockholm, Feb. 26, 1934; came to U.S., 1958; d. Herbert Jonas and Emma Wilhelmina (Johnson) Hagetorn; m. Ludwig F. Oster, May 17, 1956; children: Ulrika, Mattias. Fil. mag., U. Stockholm, 1956; PhD, Kiel (Germany) U., 1958. Postdoctoral rsch. fellow linguistics Yale U., 1958-60, rsch. fellow Germanic langs., 1960-64, lectr. Swedish, 1964-66; mem. faculty U. Colo., Boulder, 1966-80, assoc. prof. Germanic langs. and lits., 1970-77, prof., 1977-80, chmn. dept., 1972-75, assoc. dean Grad. Sch., 1975-79, assoc. vice chancellor for grad. affairs Grad. Sch., 1979-80; dean for grad. studies and rsch. U. Md., College Park, 1980-83, prof. Germanic langs. and lits., 1980—, acting chair dept., 1997—2001. Mem. Fulbright Nat. Screening Com., Scandinavia, 1973, 83-87, chair, 1986-87; mem. selection com. Scandinavia Internat. Exch. of Scholars, 1982-86; cons. panelist Nat. Endowment for Humanities, 1975—, mem. bd. cons., 1980—; state coord. Am. Coun. on Edn., Colo., 1978-80, Md., 1981-83, dir. dept. leadership program, 1986-91; mem. exec. com. Assn. Grad. Schs., 1980-83; mem. dean's exec. com. African-Am. Inst., 1981-85; interim dir. Washington Sch. Psychiatry, 1994-95; cons. in field. Contbr. articles and revs. to profl. publs. Bd. dirs. Washington Sch. Psychiatry, Am.-Swedish Hist. Mus., Phila., Open Theatre, Washington; mem. nat. fellowship com. Am.-Scandinavian Found., 1997—, bd. trustees, 2001—. Carnegie fellow, 1974; grantee Swedish Govt., 1977, Am. Scandinavian Found., 1997, German Acad. Exch. Svc., 1983; recipient Translation prize Am.-Scandinavian Found., 1997. Mem. NOW, MLA (mem. Del. Assembly 1995—), AAUP, Soc. Advancement Scandinavian Studies (pres. 1979-80), Am. Scandinavian Assn. of Nat. Capital Area (pres. 1983-86, 96—), Am.-Scandinavian Found., Am. Assn. Higher Edn. Home: 4977 Battery Ln Bethesda MD 20814-4931 Office: U Md Dept Germanic Studies College Park MD 20742-0001 Office Phone: 301-405-4096. E-mail: ro8@umail.umd.edu.

OSTERBERG, EDWARD CHARLES, JR., lawyer; b. Honolulu, Jan. 1, 1942; s. Edward Charles and Emily Julia (Preston) O.; m. Susan Rhea Snider, Aug. 26, 1967; 1 child, Edward Charles III. BA, Northwestern U., 1963, JD cum laude, 1966; LLM in Taxation, So. Meth. U., 1972. Bar: Tex. 1966, Ill. 1966. Assoc. Vinson & Elkins, Houston, 1967-73, ptnr., 1974—. Reporter Internat. Fiscal Assn., Sydney, Australia, 1978, Barcelona, Spain, 1991. Contbr. articles to profl. publs. Mem. ABA (chmn. taxation com.), Houston Bar Assn. (chmn. taxation sect. 1987), Petroleum Club, Metro. Racquet Club. Methodist. Home: 11222 Wilding Ln Houston TX 77024-5308 Office: Vinson & Elkins LLP 1001 Fannin St Ste 3300 Houston TX 77002-6760 Office Phone: 713-758-2192. Business E-Mail: eosterberg@velaw.com.

OSTERBERG, JAMES NEWELL See POP, IGGY

OSTERBERG, JORJ O. retired civil engineer; Prof. Northwestern U., Chgo., prof. emeritus Evanston, Ill. Recipient Nova award for constrn. innovations, 1994. Mem. ASCE (Karl Terzaghi award 1993), Nat. Acad. Engring. Achievements include patents for Holder 11 patents. Home: 16416 E Powers Pl Aurora CO 80015-4059

OSTERBROCK, DONALD E(DWARD), astronomy educator; s. William Carl and Elsie (Wettlin) O.; m. Irene L. Hansen, Sept. 19. 1952; children: Carol Ann, William Carl, Laura Jane. PhB, SB, U. Chgo., 1948, SM, 1949, PhD, 1952, DSc (hon.), 1992, Ohio State U., 1986, U. Wis., 1997, Ohio U., 2003, U. Cin., 2004. Postdoctoral fellow, mem. faculty Princeton, 1952-53; mem. faculty Calif. Inst. Tech., 1953-58; faculty U. Wis.-Madison, 1958-73, prof. astronomy, 1961-73, chmn. dept. astronomy, 1966-67, 69-72; prof. astronomy and astrophysics U. Calif., Santa Cruz, 1972-92, prof. emeritus, 1993—. Dir. Lick Obs., 1972-81; mem. staff Mt. Wilson Obs., Palomar Obs., 1953-58; vis. prof. U. Chgo., 1963-64, Ohio State U., 1980, 86; Hill Family vis. prof. U. Minn., 1977-78. Author: Astrophysics of Gaseous Nebulae, 1974, James E. Keeler, Pioneer American Astrophysicist and the Early Development of American Astrophysics, 1984, Astrophysics of Gaseous Nebulae and Active Galactic Nuclei, 1989, Pauper and Prince: Ritchey, Hale and Big American Telescopes, 1993, Yerkes Observatory, 1892-1950: The Birth, Near Death and Resurrection of a Scientific Research Institution, 1997, Walter Baade: A Life in Astrophysics, 2001; co-author: (with John R. Gustafson and W.J. Shiloh Unruh) Eye on the Sky: Lick Observatory's First Century, 1988; editor: (with C.R. O'Dell) Planetary Nebulae, 1968, (with Peter H. Raven) Origins and Extinctions, 1988, (with J.S. Miller) Active Galactic Nuclei, 1989; Stars and Galaxies: Citizens of the Universe, 1990; letters editor Astrophys. Jour., 1971-73. With USAAF, 1943-46. Recipient Profl. Achievement award U. Chgo. Alumni Assn., 1982, Antoinette de Vaucouleurs Meml. lecture and medal U. Tex., Austin, 1994, Hans Lippershey medal Antique Telescope Soc., 1999, Alumni medal U. Chgo. Alumni Assn., 2000, LeRoy Doggett prize and lecture AAS Hist. Astronomy Divsn., 2002; Guggenheim fellow Inst. Advanced Studies, Princeton, N.J., 1960-61, 82-83, Ambrose Monnell Found. fellow, 1989-90, NSF sr. postdoctoral rsch. fellow U. Coll., London, 1968-69. Mem. NAS (chmn. astronomy sect. 1971-74, sec. class math. and phys. sci. 1980-83, chmn. class math and phys. sci. 1983-85, councilor 1985-88), Am. Acad. Arts and Scis., Internat. Astron. Union (pres. commn. 34 1967-70), Royal Astron. Soc. (assoc., Gold medal 1997), Am. Astron. Soc. (councilor 1970-73, v.p. 1975-77, pres. 1988-90, vice chmn. hist. astronomy divsn. 1985-87, chmn. 1987-89, Henry Norris Russell lectr. 1991, LeRoy Doggett prize 2002), Astron. Soc. Pacific (chmn. history com. 1982-86, Catherine Wolfe Bruce medal 1991, bd. dirs. 1992-95), Wis. Acad. Scis. Arts and Letters, Am. Philos. Soc., State Hist. Soc. Wis. Congregationalist. Home: 120 Woodside Ave Santa Cruz CA 95060-3422 Office Phone: 831-459-2605. E-mail: don@ucolick.org.

OSTERGAARD, JONI HAMMERSLA, lawyer; b. Seattle, May 26, 1950; d. William Dudley and Carol Mae (Gillett) Hammersla; m. Gregory Lance Ostergaard, May 22, 1976 (div. 1985); 1 child, Bennett Gillett; m. William Howard Patton, Jan. 1, 1988; 1 child, Morgan Hollis; stepchildren: Colin W., Benjamin C. BS, U. Wash., 1972; MS, Purdue U., 1974; JD, U. Wash., 1980. Bar: Wash. 1980, U.S. Dist. Ct. (we. dist.) Wash. 1980, U.S. Ct. Appeals (9th cir.) 1981, U. S. Ct. Claims 1983. Clin. psychol. intern Yale Med. Sch., 1976-77; law clk. U.S. Ct. Appeals (9th cir.), Seattle, 1980-81; assoc. Roberts & Shefelman, Seattle, 1982-86, ptnr., 1987, Foster Pepper & Shefelman, Seattle, 1988-92; sole practitioner Seattle, 1996—2003; dep. pros. atty. Snohomish County, Everett, Wash., 2004—. Contbr. articles to profl. jours.; notes and comments editor Wash. Law Rev., 1979-80. Recipient Sophia and Wilbur Albright scholarship U. Wash. Law Sch., 1979-80, law sch. alumni scholarship U. Wash. Law Sch., 1978-79; fellow NIMH. Avocations: gardening, reading. Office: Snohomish County Prosecuting Attys Office Civil Divsn 2918 Colby Ave Ste 203 Everett WA 98201 Office Phone: 425-388-6370. Office Fax: 425-388-6333. Business E-Mail: jostergaard@co.snohomish.wa.us.

OSTERGARD, PAUL MICHAEL, not-for-profit executive; b. Akron, Ohio, Apr. 1, 1939; s. Paul and Janette Beryl (Laube) O.; m. Elizabeth K. McCombs, Jan. 1965 (div. Nov. 1971). AB magna cum laude, Case-Western Res. U., 1961; JD, U. Mich., 1964; MPA, Harvard U., 1969; diploma in hispanic studies, U. Madrid, Spain, 1960. Bar: Ohio 1964. Atty. U.S. Steel Corp., Pitts., 1967-69; gen. atty. TWA Inc., N.Y.C., 1969-71; v.p. adminstrn., sec., counsel Pa. Co. (now Penn Ctrl. Corp.), 1971-74, and subs. Buckeye Pipe Line Co., N.Y.C., 1972-74; pub. affairs exec. GE, Fairfield, Conn., 1974-84; pres. GE Found., Fairfield, 1984-90; chmn., CEO, bd. dirs. Citigroup Found., N.Y.C., 1990-99; pres. Com. to Encourate Corp. Philanthropy, N.Y.C., 1999-2001; pres., CEO Jr. Achievement Internat., 2001—04. Bd. dirs. Bond Market Found., Found. for Tchg. Econs. Decorated Bronze Star, Legion of Merit (Vietnam); Univ. scholar, 1957-61; Littauer fellow, 1968-69 Mem. Harvard Club, Wexford Plantation Club, Phi Beta Kappa, Omicron Delta Kappa. Episcopalian. Home: 29 Oxford Dr Hilton Head Island SC 29928 E-mail: paulmo39@aol.com.

OSTERHAUS, GREG S. artist, graphic designer; b. Hinsdale, Ill., Apr. 28, 1963; s. Gordon Frederick and Leona Osterhaus; m. Janie D. Osterhaus, May 9, 1987; children: Taylor W., Madeline Q., Kyle J. BFA, Va. Poly. Inst. and State U., 1985. Artist oil paintings, also acrylics, watercolors, pastels. One-mans shows include Roanoke County Pub. Libr., 1987, Studios on the Square, Roanoke, 1994, 96, 99, YMCA Rotating Gallery, Roanoke, 1996, The Little Gallery, Smith Mt. Lake, Va., 1996, 99, Shenandoah Club, Roanoke, 1997, Frame Scapes, Roanoke, 1998, Allehany Highlands Ctr., Clifton Forge, Va., 1998, Artworks Gallery, Norfolk, Va., 1999; exhibited in group shows Depot Gallery, Roanoke, Studios on the Square, 1994, Gallery at Shanaz!, Lynchburg, Va., 1995, The Little Gallery, 1996, 97, Gallery at Szent Györgyi, Falmouth, Mass., 1998. Avocations: music, reading, guitar. Home and Office: 2351 Denniston Ave SW Roanoke VA 24015-1904

OSTERHAUS, WILLIAM ERIC, broadcast executive; b. N.Y.C., July 31, 1935; s. Eric Hugo and Helen (McAuliff) O.; m. Nancy Jean Heinemann, June 19, 1960 (dec.); children: Eric Frank, Marc Andrew; m. Annemarie Clark, Dec. 28, 1985 Student, Fordham U., 1953-54, Harvard U. Bus. Sch., summer 1970. Staff producer news and spl. events dept. Sta. WNBC-AM-TV, N.Y.C., 1956-61; exec. producer Sta. KYW-TV, Cleve., 1961-64, Sta. KPIX, San Francisco, 1964-67, gen. mgr., 1969-73; program mgr. Sta. KYW-TV, Phila., 1967-69; pres., gen. mgr. Sta. KQED Inc., San Francisco, 1973-78; pres. SiteLine Comms., Inc., San Francisco, 1979—; chmn. bd. VariCom Inc., San Francisco, 1982-86. Chmn. TV adv. com. Calif. Pub. Broadcasting Commn., 1977-78; mem. joint com. on film and broadcasting Indo-U.S. Subcommn. on Edn. and Culture., 1975-85; chmn. TV com. San Rafael Redevel. Agy., Calif., 1977-78; mem. citizens adv. com. CATV, San Rafael, 1976-77, Dominican Coll., San Rafael, 1972-80; v.p., bd. dirs. Downtown Parking Corp. Bd. dirs. The Ctr. for the Arts, San Francisco, 1985-2003; bd. dirs. Zeum, 1995—. 1st lt. U.S. Army, 1958-60. Recipient Peabody award and Hillman award for One Nation Indivisible documentary, 1968.

OSTERHELD, R(OBERT) KEITH, chemistry professor; b. Bklyn., Apr. 19, 1925; s. Albert Henry and Hilda Pearl (Heatlie) O.; m. Jean Drake Evans, June 28, 1952; children: Robert Keith, Albert Laighton, James Evans, Thomas Heatlie. BS in Chemistry, Poly. Inst. Bklyn., 1945; PhD in Inorganic Chemistry, U. Ill., 1950. Instr. Cornell U., Ithaca, N.Y., 1950-54; asst. prof. chemistry U. Mont., Missoula, 1954-58, assoc. prof., 1958-65, prof., 1965-90, prof. emeritus, 1990—, chmn. dept., 1973-90. Contbr. articles to profl. jours. Mem. Florence (Mont.) Sch. Bd., 1969-75, chmn., 1972-73, 74-75; bd. dirs. Mont. Sch. Bd. Assn., Helena, 1973-75; council mem. Florence-Carlton Community Ch., 1965-90, treas., 1965-90. Served to sgt. USAAF, 1945-47. Mem. Am. Chem. Soc., N.Am. Thermal Analysis Soc., Sigma Xi. Home: 524 Larry Creek Loop Florence MT 59833-6705 Office: U Montana Dept Chemistry Missoula MT 59812-0001

OSTERHOFF, JAMES MARVIN, retired telecommunications company executive; b. Lafayette, Ind., May 18, 1936; s. Abel Lyman and Mildred Paulene (Post) O.; m. Marilyn Ann Morrison, Aug. 24, 1958; children: Anne Michelle Bitsie, Amy Louise Olmsted, Susan Marie BSME, Purdue U., 1958; MBA, Stanford U., 1963. Staff asst. FMC Corp., San Jose, Calif., 1963-64; with Ford Motor Co., Dearborn, Mich., 1964-84; v.p. fin., CFO Ford Motor Credit Co., Dearborn, 1973-75; controller car ops. N. Am. Automotive Ops., Ford Motor Co., Dearborn, 1975-76, asst. controller, 1976-79; controller tractor ops. Ford Motor Co., Troy, Mich., 1979-84; v.p. fin., CFO Digital Equipment Corp., Maynard, Mass., 1985-91; exec. v.p., CFO U.S.West Inc., Englewood, Colo., 1991-95. Bd. dirs. Arkwright Mutual Ins. Co., FSA Ltd., GenCorp, Inc., Pvt. Sector Coun., Colo. Neurol. Inst., Goodwill Industries of Denver. Served to lt. (j.g.) USN, 1958-61. Recipient Disting. Engring. Alumnus award Purdue U.; named Outstanding Mech. Engring. Alumnus, Purdue U.

OSTERHOLZ, JOHN LOUIS, information administrator; b. N.Y.C., May 8, 1947; m. Phyllis Annette Osterholz. BA in Physics, Rutgers U.; MS in Info. Systems, George Washington U., 1994. Electronics engr. U.S. Army Electronics Command, Ft. Monmouth, N.J., 1972-74; chief satellite comm. systems divsn. Def. Comm. Agy., Arlington, Va., 1974-84; lectr. in systems engring. George Washington U., Washington, 1976-84; asst. dir. engring. Def. Mobilization Support Activity, Office of Sec. of Def., Arlington, 1984-89; asst. dir. tech., integration and systesm White House Mil. Office, Washington, 1989-92; dir. Mil. Satellite Office, Def. Info. Systems Agy., Arlington, 1992-94, dep. dir. modeling, simulation and assessment, 1994-96; dep. dir. Command, Control, Comm. and Intelligence Info., Dept. Def., Washington, from 1996; now dir. info. integration & interoperability Office Asst. Sec. Def., Washington. With U.S. Army, 1969-72, USAR, 1972-78. Avocations: hiking, golf, sketching. Home: 22 Bentley Dr Sterling VA 20165-6004 Office: Office Asst Sec Def Command Control Comm 1931 Jeff Davis Hwy Fl 7 Arlington VA 22202-3517

OSTERHOUT, RICHARD CADWALLADER, lawyer; b. Abington, Pa., Nov. 16, 1945; s. Robert Edward and Charlotte Leedom (Cadwallader) O.; m. Diane Renee Higgins, Sept. 15, 1982; children: Steven M., Schuyler C., Cody R. BA in History magna cum laude, Pa. State U., 1967; JD, Temple U., 1974. Bar: Pa. 1974, U.S. Dist. Ct. (ea. dist.) Pa. 1974, U.S. Ct. Appeals (3d cir.) 1984. Assoc. Wood & Floge, Bensalem, Pa., 1974-77; pvt. practice Trevose, Pa., 1978-85, Feasterville, Pa., 1985—. Solicitor Zoning Hearing Bd., Hulmeville, Pa., 1983—. Contbr. articles to publs. of various hist. socs. Mem. Langhorne Borough Planning Commn. (Pa.), 1974; candidate Rep. Nat. Conv., 1984. With U.S. Army, 1968-70. Mem. Pa. Bar Assn., Bucks County Bar Assn., Feasterville Business Assn. (treas. 1985, 86, v.p. 1987), Phi Beta Kappa. Home: 309 Hemlock Ave Bensalem PA 19020-7331 Office: 1744 Bridgetown Pike Feasterville Trevose PA 19053-2362 Office Phone: 215-355-2440.

OSTERHOUT, SUYDAM, internist, educator; b. Bklyn., Nov. 25, 1925; s. Howard and Edna Cornell (Davison) O.; m. Shirley Elizabeth Kirkman, Sept. 17, 1960; children— Mark, Martin, Ann. BA, Princeton, 1945; MD (Hanes fellow), Duke, 1949; PhD, Rockefeller U., 1959. Diplomate: Am. Bd. Internal Medicine. Intern pathology Cleve. City Hosp., 1950; intern internal medicine Mass. Meml. Hosp., Boston, 1950-51; resident Duke Hosp., 1953-56; faculty Duke Med. Sch., Durham, N.C., 1959—, now prof. medicine, prof. microbiology, asso. dean. Contbr. articles to profl. jours. Served with M.C. USAF, 1951-53. Recipient NIH Career Devel. award, 1960-65; Markle scholar in medicine, 1959-64 Fellow A.C.P.; mem. Am. Soc. Micro-Biology, Am. Fedn. Clin. Research, Sigma Xi, Alpha Omega Alpha. Home: 5133 N Willowhaven Dr Durham NC 27712-1956 Office: PO Box 3007 Durham NC 27715-3007

OSTERMAN, CATHERINE, Olympic athlete; b. Apr. 16, 1983; Student, U. Texas. Mem. U.S. Women's Softball Team, Athens Olympic Games, 2004. Named USA Softball Player of the Yr., 2003, Big 12 Pitcher of the Yr., 2003; named to First Team NFCA All-Am., 2003, All WCWS World Series Team, 2003. Achievements include mem. U.S. Elite Nat. Team, 2002; mem. Gold medal U.S. Nat. Team, U.S Cup, 2001; mem. Gold medal U.S. Nat. Team, Pan Am. Games, 2003; led U. Texas to Women's Coll. World Series, 2003. Home: USA Softball Complex 4845 S Shields Blvd Oklahoma City OK 73129*

OSTERMEYER, MARYANN, secondary school educator, writer; b. Indpls., Dec. 9, 1950; d. Kenneth Dale and Mary Ida Ostermeyer. AB in English, San Diego State U., 1972, M of History, 1981. Cert. secondary tchg.credential/Clad credential. Tchr. Cajon Valley Union Sch. Dist., El Cajon, Calif., 1975—; freelance writer San Diego County Office of Edn., 1983; curriculum writer Heritage Pub. Co., El Cajon, 1985—86; writer I Love a Clean San Diego, 1995—96; tchr. refugee students/ESL Internat. Rescue Com., San Diego, 1996—. Bd. dirs. Friends of Classics, San Diego; AVID dist. coord. Cajon Valley Union Sch. Dist., El Cajon, 1997—98; developer of dist. AVID programs Hillsdale Mid. Sch. and Cajon Valley Mid. Sch.; adv. comm., collaborator with Survivors of Torture Internat. Cajon Valley Mid. Sch., San Diego, 2001—02; project tchr. rep. AJA; tchr. rep., collaborator San Diego Mus. of Photographic Art. Author: El Cajon: A Pictorial History, 1986, In My Heart and On My Mind, 2003; contbr. Hope True Stories of Answered Prayers Red Rock Press, 2003, ednl. curriculum Eranos, 1983, curriculum text San Diego World in Harmony - An Environmental Awareness Curriculum for Grades 7-12, 1994. Mem. El Cajon Hist. Soc.; tchr. rep. Cmtys. Against Substance Abuse, El Cajon, 1990—92; active Mercy Outreach; Bd. dirs. City of El Cajon Fire Dept., 2001—03; Community Panel Representative - Vision 2000 City of EL Cajon Mayor's Recommendation Committee, El Cajon, CA, 1990—92. Recipient World of Difference Inst. OutstandingTchr. Recognition award, Anti-Defamation League, 1998, NEH Tchr. Summer Inst. Program, 1993, Outstanding Tchr. Yr. Emerald Mid. Sch./Cajon Valley Mid. Sch., PTA, 1985, 1991, Outstanding Tchr., Friends of Classics, 2003. Mem.: DAR, Cajon Valley Ednl. Assn. Avocations: gardening, needlepoint, writing, dog walking, community philanthropic services. Home: 1114 Evilo St El Cajon CA 92021 Office: Cajon Valley Union Sch Dist 189 Roanoke Rd El Cajon CA 92021 Personal E-mail: magistrao@aol.com.

OSTERN, WILHELM CURT, retired holding company executive; b. Geisenheim am Rhein, Germany, Sept. 29, 1923; came to U.S., 1956, naturalized, 1970; s. Wilhelm A. and Margarete R. (Seul) Ostern; m. Olga Atterbury, Nov. 24, 2001; children from previous marriage: Karen, Ellen, Wilhelm. Grad., Staatliches Realgymnasium, Geisenheim, 1941. With Bayer AG, and predecessor, 1941-88, officer and/or dir. subsidiaries and affiliates, 1956-89; vice chmn., chief fin. officer Mobay Corp., Pitts., 1974-86. Vice chmn. Bayer USA, Inc., Pitts., 1986—88, chmn., 1988—91; bd. dirs., chmn. fin. com. ACE Ltd., 1987—91; bd. dirs. Schott Corp., Inc., Carl Zeiss, Inc. Mem. Carnegie Mus. Sustaining Fund. With German Army, 1942-45. Hon. Consul Fed. Republic of Germany. Mem. Am. Coun. Germany, Soc. Contemporary Crafts Pitts. (bd. dirs.). Clubs: Brook (N.Y.C.); Duquesne (Pitts.). Home: Rhinebrook Farms Hartle Rd Sewickley PA 15143

OSTERTAG, ROBERT LOUIS, lawyer; b. N.Y.C., June 21, 1931; s. Frederick C. and Lillian (Bishop) O.; children: Thomas J., Daniel V., Debra A. BA, Fordham U., 1953; LL.B., St. John's U., Bklyn., 1956; LL.M., Georgetown U., 1960. Bar: N.Y. 1957, U.S. Dist. Ct. (so. dist.) N.Y. 1969, U.S. Tax Ct. 1965, U.S. Ct. Mil. Appeals 1959, U.S. Supreme Ct. 1960. Atty. office chief counsel IRS, Washington, 1958-60; ptnr. Guernsey, Butts & Walsh, Poughkeepsie, N.Y., 1963-90, Guernsey, Butts, Ostertag & O'Leary, Poughkeepsie, N.Y., 1991-95, Ostertag, O'Leary & Barrett, Poughkeepsie, 1995—; adj. prof. paralegal studies Marist Coll., Poughkeepsie, 1975-91; adj. prof. Fordham U. Sch. of Law, N.Y.C., 1993—. Counsel Agr. Com., N.Y. State Assembly, 1967-68; mem. Gov.'s Jud. Screening Com., 1987-93; counsel to cons. and draftsman of proposed county charters and adminstrv. codes for Dutchess, Sullivan, Fulton, Orange and Onondaga Counties, N.Y., City of Poughkeepsie, N.Y., City of Beacon, N.Y.; mem. 9th Jud. Dist. Grievance Com., 1975-79, 9th Jud. Dist. Med. Malpractice Panel, 1975-91, mem. 9th Jud. Dist. Arbitration Panel, 1980—; mem. Chief Judges Com. on Pro Bono Legal Svc., 1992-93. Trustee Joseph F. Barnard Meml. Law Libr., Poughkeepsie, 1979—; dir. Hudson Valley Philharm. Soc., 1973—76; v.p., dir. High Tor Opera Co., 1967—70; dir. United Fund of Dutchess County, 1973—78; dir. Dutchess County chpt. Am. Heart Assn., 1975—81, 1984—89; trustee Sports Mus. Dutchess County, 1989—93, chmn., 1989—90; dir. Hudson Valley Stadium Corp., 1995—, chair, 1998—; cons. Charter Revision Commn., Beacon, 2002—03; mem. Dutchess County (N.Y.) Charter Commn., 1966—67, Dutchess County Bd. Health, 1966—70, pres., 1966—70; chmn. Dutchess County Charter Revision Task Force, 1979—88; dep. supr. Town of Poughkeepsie, 1976; bd. dirs. Com. for Modern Cts., 1975—99; dir. Std. Gage Co., 1972—88; mem. adv. coun. Pace U. Sch. Law, 1975—84; paralegal adv. coun. Marist Coll., 1975—. Served to capt. JAGC USAF, 1956—58. Recipient Recognition award Cen. Poughkeepsie Exch. Club, 1967, Marist Coll. Pres.'s award, 1991. Mem.: ABA (chmn. conf. of state bar gen. practice leaders of gen. practice sect. 1980—87, mem. coun. 1982—86, ho. of dels. 1985—98, Gavel awards com. 1989—, standing com. on solo and small firm practitioners 1992—95, standing com. on profl. discipline 2002—), Dutchess County Bar Assn. (sec. 1969—79, pres. 1984—85), N.Y. State Bar Assn. (ho. of dels. 1973—79, chmn. unlawful practice of law com. 1977—81, chmn. sect. on gen. practice of law 1980—82, ho. of dels. 1980—, chmn. com. on law office econs. and mgmt. 1982, exec. com. 1983—85, com. profl. ethics 1986—90, exec. com. 1986—93, pres. 1991—92, com. profl. ethics 1996—99, chmn. comm. on future of profession 1998, spl. com. on law governing firm structure and operation 1999—, com. profl. ethics 2000—), N.Y. Bar Found., Am. Bar Found., Hudson Valley Estate Planning Coun. (pres. 1965—66, dir. 1969—74), Delta Theta Phi. Home: 8 High View Rd Poughkeepsie NY 12603 Office: 17 Collegeview Ave Poughkeepsie NY 12603-2406 Office Phone: 845-486-4300. E-mail: r.ostertag@verizon.net.

OSTERTAG, RONALD A. manufacturing company executive; b. 1941; Pres. Power Semiconductor divsn. Gen. Semiconductor, Inc., 1997—, chmn., CEO, 1997—, dir., 2000—. Office: Gen Semiconductor Inc 10 Melville Park Rd Melville NY 11747-3113

OSTERWEIL, ADAM MATTHEW, elementary school educator, writer; b. Plainview, NY, Apr. 26, 1972; s. Rheba Gerber and Michael Osterweil. BA, Cornell U., 1990—94; MA in liberal studies, Stony Brook U., 1995—96. Cert. Eng. Tchr. Secondary NY, 1998. UNIX sys. adminstr. Info. Tech., 1991—94; mid. sch. English tchr. The Springs, N.Y., 1996—. Author: (children's novel) The Comic Book Kid: Spring, 2001 (Walt Disney Adventures Best Book of the Yr. (Adventure category), Bank St. Coll. Best Children's Book of the Yr. (humor category), 2002), The Amulet of Komondor: Fall, 2003, (screenplays) The Comic Book Kid (adapted from own novel) (Scriptapalooza nat. screenwriting competition semi-finalist, 2003). Tchr. contract action com. mem. New York State Union of Teachers, East Hampton, NY, 1997—98. Recipient Nominated for the Walt Disney best tchr. of the yr. award, Walt Disney, 2001—02. Master: Springs Sch. Drama Club (play dir. 1996—99), Springs Sch. Video Game Club (club founder 1996—2004). Democrat. Avocations: treasure hunting, video games, collecting comic books, biking, cartooning. Office: Springs School 48 School St East Hampton NY 11937 Personal E-mail: adamost@optonline.net.

OSTERWEIL, LEON JOEL, dean, computer science educator; b. Newark, N.J., Mar. 27, 1944; s. Sidney Morris and Esther Server Osterweil; m. Lori Ann Rainish, July 28, 2002; children: Eric Michael, Emily Kathryn. AB, Princeton U., 1965; MS, PhD, U. Md., 1971. Prof. U. Colo., Boulder, 1971—88, U. Calif., Irvine, 1988—93, U. Mass., Amherst, 1993—2003, dean, 2001—. Contbr. articles to profl. jours. Recipient rsch. grants, NSF, several. Fellow: Assn. for Computing Machinery; mem.: IEEE Computer Soc. Business E-Mail: ljo@cs.umass.edu.

OSTERYOUNG, JANET GRETCHEN, chemistry professor; b. Pitts., Mar. 1, 1939; d. Arthur Roberts and Elizabeth Jane (Peebles) Jones; m. Bruce Ulrich, Aug. 16, 1967 (div. 1968); m. Robert Allen Osteryoung, Aug. 17, 1969; children: Anne Elizabeth, Adam Armstrong. BA, Swarthmore Coll., 1961; PhD, Calif. Inst. Tech., 1967. Asst. prof. chemistry Mont. State U., Bozeman, 1967-68; fellow Colo. State U., Ft. Collins, 1968-73, asst. prof. civil engring., 1969-73, asst. prof. civil engring., microbiology, 1972-73, assoc. prof., 1973-78, assoc. prof. civil engring., rsch. chemist, 1978-79; assoc. prof. chemistry SUNY, Buffalo, 1979-82, prof., 1982-92, faculty exch. scholar, 1987-92; head dept. chemistry N.C. State U., 1992-94; prof. NSF, 1992—, dir. chemistry divsn., 1994—. Vis. prof. Colo. Coll., 1972, Calif. Inst. Tech., 1985; Guggenheim fellow, vis. prof. U. Southampton (Eng.), 1985-86; cons. Colo. State U., Ft. Collins, 1970-72, EG&G Princeton (N.J.) Applied, 1983—; dir. program chem. analysis NSF, Washington, 1977-78, mem. ad hoc rev. panel 1988. Co-author: Models in Chemical Science, 1971; assoc. editor Electrochemica Acta, 1986—; contbr. over 180 articles to profl. jours.; patentee controlled-growth mercury drop electrode. Hon. Fulbright fellow, 1986; recipient Anachem award Soc. Analytical Chemists of Detroit, 1990, Schoellkopf medalist WNY-Am. Chem. Soc., 1992, ACS award in Electrochemistry-Electrochem. Soc., 1996. Fellow AAAS; mem., Internat. Soc. Electrochemistry (mem. divsn. 3 1985-88), Soc. Electroanalytical Chemistry (founding mem., pres. 1986-87, chmn. 1987-88), Am. Chem. Soc. (Garvan medal 1987, western N.Y. chpt., chmn. exec. com. 1981-89, Disting. Svc. award 1988), Soc. Applied Spectroscopy (Disting. Svc. award Niagara Frontier chpt. 1988), N.Y. Acad. Scis., Electrochem. Soc. (pres. Rocky Mountain sect. 1976-77), Fedn. Am. Scientists, Phi Beta Kappa, Sigma Xi, Iota Sigma Pi (Triennial Hon. mem.). Democrat. Episcopalian. Home: 4201 Wilson Blvd Ste 110 Arlington VA 22203-1859 Office: NC State U Dept of Chemistry PO Box 8204 Raleigh NC 27695-0001

OSTLER, CLYDE W. banker; b. 1947; BA, U. Calif. San Diego, 1968; MBA, U. Chgo., 1976. With Touche Ross & Co., San Diego, 1970-71; with Wells Fargo Bank NA, San Francisco, 1971, v.p., 1977-81, sr. v.p., 1981-83, gen. auditor, 1983-85, exec. v.p. 1985-86, CFO, from 1986; with Wells Fargo & Co., San Francisco, 1971—, exec. v.p., CFO, from 1986, vice chmn., now group exec. v.p. internet svcs. Office: Wells Fargo & Co 420 Montgomery St San Francisco CA 94104-1205

OSTLIND, DAN A. retired parasitologist; b. McPherson, Kans., June 19, 1936; s. Harry Dewey and Laura (Bartles) O.; m. Eleanor Ruth Ahlstedt, Oct. 5, 1958; 1 child, Dyanne Dee. MS, Kans. State U., 1962, PhD, 1966. Parasitologist Moorman Mfg. Co., Quincy, Ill., 1966-67; sr. rsch. parasitologist Merck & Co., Rahway, N.J., 1967-69, rsch. fellow, 1969-77, sr. rsch. fellow, 1977-86, sr. investigator, 1986-96. Office Phone: 908-236-9238.

OSTLING, RICHARD NEIL, journalist; b. Endicott, NY, July 14, 1940; s. Acton Eric Sr. and Christine Cathryn (Cumins) O.; m. Joan Elaine Kerns, July 8, 1967; children: Margaret Anne, Elizabeth Anne. BA, U. Mich., 1962; MS in Journalism, Northwestern U., 1963; MA in Religion, George Washington U., 1970; LittD (hon.), Gordon (Mass.) Coll., 1989. Reporter, copyreader Morning News and Evening Jour., Wilmington, Del., 1963-64; asst. news editor Christianity Today mag., Washington, 1965-67, news editor, 1967-69; staff corr. Time mag., N.Y.C., 1969-74, religion writer, 1975-94, sr. corr., 1994-98; broadcaster Report on Religion, CBS Radio, 1979-98; religion corr. Newshour with Jim Lehrer formerly MacNeil/Lehrer Newshour, 1991-98; religion writer AP, N.Y.C., 1998—. Author: Secrecy in the Church, 1974; co-author: Aborting America, 1979, Mormon America, 1999. Served with USNG, 1964-70. McCormick Found. fellow, 1962-63; recipient Supple, Templeton, Am. Acad. Religion and Wilbur awards for religion writing. Mem. Religion Newswriters Assn. (pres. 1974-76), Northwestern U. Alumni Hall of Achievement (charter), Phi Beta Kappa. Mem. Christian Reformed Ch. Home: 280 Hillcrest Rd Ridgewood NJ 07450-2400 Office: AP 450 W 33d St New York NY 10001

OSTLUND, H. GOTE, atmospheric and marine scientist, educator; b. Stockholm, June 26, 1923; came to U.S., 1963; s. Sven and Ruth (Lundin) O.; m. Doris Beck, Sept. 30, 1950; children: Stellan, Goran. Fil Kand., U. Stockholm, 1949, Fil Lic., 1958; hon. doctorate, U. Gothenburg, 1984. Research asst. U. Stockholm, 1944-46; tchr. Technol. Night Coll., Stockholm, 1946-51; research asst. Royal Inst. Tech., Stockholm, 1947, asst. instr., 1948-52; head of lab. Swedish Nitrogen Fertilizer Works, Ltd., 1952-54,

Radioactive Dating Lab., Stockholm, 1954-63; asst. instr. Royal Inst. Tech., Stockholm, 1956-57; vis. research asso. prof. Inst. Marine Scis., U. Miami (Fla.), 1960-61, asso. prof. geochemistry, 1963-67, prof. marine and atmospheric chemistry Rosenstiel Sch. Marine and Atmospheric Sci., 1967-97, chmn. div. chem. oceanography, 1970-72, coordinator Geochem. Oceans Sects., 1976-86, mem. exec. com. Geochem. Oceans Sects., 1973-86, coordinator Transient Tracers in Ocean, 1977-85, prof. emeritus, 1997—. Assoc. editor: Revs. of Geophysics and Space Physics, 1974-76; mem. editorial bd.: Marine Chemistry, 1974-93; mem. adv. bd.: Tellus B; contbr. articles to profl. jours. Served in Royal Swedish Air Force, 1943-44, 46. Mem. Am. Geophys. Union, Am. Meteorol. Soc., AAAS, Swedish Chem. Soc., Swedish Geophys. Soc., Fla. Acad. Scis. Office: U Miami 4600 Rickenbacker Cswy Miami FL 33149-1031 E-mail: gostlund@rsmas.miami.edu.

OSTMANN, CINDY, state legislator; BS, Lindenwood Coll. Tchr. Ft. Zumwalt Sch. Dist., 1958-62, 64-67, Fayetteville Sch. Sys., 1963-64; owner, mgr. residential property; mem. Mo. State Ho. of Reps. Dist. 14, 1992—, mem. children, youth and families com., mem. energy and environ. com., mem. local govt. and related matters com. Recipient Outstanding Contbr. to Edn. award Phi Delta Kappa, 1988. Mem. Coun. of Chambers Charter Govt. Com., St. Charles County Arts Coun., Grand Order of Pachyderm, Friends of St. Louis Symphony, Mo. Fedn. Rep. Women, First Capitol Rep. Club. Home: 445 Knaust Rd Saint Peters MO 63376-1713 Office: Mo Ho of Reps State Capitol Building Jefferson City MO 65101-1556

OSTRAGER, BARRY ROBERT, lawyer; b. N.Y.C., July 14, 1947; m. Pamela Goodman, Apr. 8, 1972; children: Anne Elizabeth, Katie, Jane. BA, CCNY, 1968, MA, 1973; JD, NYU, 1972. Bar: N.Y. 1973, Calif. 1996. Sr. ptnr., trial lawyer Simpson Thacher & Bartlett, N.Y.C., 1973—, co-head, litig. dept. Co-author: Modern Reinsurance Law and Practice, 2d edit., 2000, Handbook on Insurance Coverage Disputes, 12th edit., 2004. Mem. Am. Law Inst., Assn. of Bar of City of N.Y. Office: Simpson Thacher & Bartlett 26th Fl 425 Lexington Ave Fl 26 New York NY 10017-3903 Office Phone: 212-455-2655. E-mail: bostrager@stblaw.com.

OSTRANDER, ROBERT EDWIN, retired United Nations interregional advisor, petroleum company executive; b. Pitts., June 30, 1931; s. Robert Jesse and Elizabeth Raymond (Comstock) O.; m. Margaret Valentina Servello, Dec. 21, 1958; children: Robert Glen, Roseanne. BA, Cornell U., 1953. Cert. petroleum geologist; registered geol. scientist. Area reservoir engr. Mene Grande Oil Co., San Tome, Venezuela, 1956-61; dist. engr. Oasis Oil Co. of Libya, Tripoli, 1962-67; reservoir/petroleum chief engr. Occidental Oil of Libya, Tripoli, 1967-71; divsn. head Iranian Oil Consortium, Ahwaz, Iran, 1972-75; mgr. ops. Ultramar Co. Ltd., Mt. Kisco, N.Y., 1975-81; v.p. engring. Weeks Petroleum Ltd., Westport, Conn., 1982-85; mng. dir. Reomag Inc., South Salem, N.Y., 1980—. Cons. World Bank, Washington, 1981—; cons. UN Secretariat, 1994—; advisor to govts. of China, India, others in Asia, Africa, Middle East; guest lectr. Asian univs., internat. seminars. Contbr. articles to profl. jours. Sec. Rep. Com., Town of Lewisboro; chair conservation adv. coun. Town of Lewisboro; pres. Ostrander Family Assn.; mem. Rep. Com. Westchester County; past. bd. dirs. Oakridge Condominium Assn., Vista, N.Y.; fellow Herbert F. Johnson Mus. Art, Cornell U., 1999—. Served to 1st lt. U.S. Army, 1953-55. Mem. Am. Assn. Petroleum Geologists, Soc. Petroleum Engrs. Home: 5715 State Route 89 Romulus NY 14541-9546 Address: 5715 State Route 89 Romulus NY 14541-9546 E-mail: reomag@flitg.net.

OSTRANDER, THOMAS WILLIAM, investment banker; b. Detroit, July 20, 1950; s. Roland J. and Sybil (Swartout) O.; children: John Charles, Elizabeth Ann, Brian Thomas. BA, U. Mich., 1972; MBA, Harvard Bus. Sch., 1976. CPA., Mich. Staff acct. Ernst & and Whinney, Detroit, 1972-74; sr. acct. Ernst and Whinney, Detroit, 1974, Cleve., 1975; assoc. Kidder, Peabody and Co., N.Y.C., 1976-78, asst. v.p., 1978-80; v.p. Kidder, Peabody and Co., N.Y.C., 1980-86; mng. dir. Kidder, Peabody and Co., N.Y.C., 1986-89, Salomon Bros., Inc., N.Y.C., 1989-97, Salomon Smith Barney, N.Y.C., 1997—2003, Citigroup Global Markets, Inc., N.Y.C., 2003. Bd. dirs., Westmoreland Coal Co.; mem. adv. bd. Paton Sch. Accountancy U. Mich., 1984-87,; mem. vis. com. Lit., Sci., and Arts Sch., 1988-90, 95—. Pres. Ballet Hispanico, 1996—. Mem. AICPA, Met. Club, Harvard Club, Hasty Pudding Club, The Creek, Bond Club, Beaver Dam Winter Sports Club, and Theta Delta Chi. Home: 18 Pheasant Run Old Westbury NY 11568 Office: Citigrp Global Markets Inc 388 Greenwich St New York NY 10013-2339

OSTRANDER, WILLIS FREDERICK, real estate appraiser; b. Berkeley, Calif., Apr. 23, 1926; s. Willis Frederick and Grace Jackson Ostrander; m. Nancy Majors Ostrander, Jan. 2, 1950; children: Margaret Jaffee, Frederick Adam, Daphne Grace Miller, John Ellery. BA, U Calif., 1948. Cert. MAI, SRA Appraisal Inst., 1994, State Certification Real Estate Appraisal State of Calif., 1996. U.S. Merchant Marine Coast Guard, 1944—45; sales rep. Signal Oil Co. (Chevron), Alemeda, Calif., 1951—62; exec. v.p. Twin Pines Fed., Berkeley, 1962—84; pres. W.F. Ostrander & Assoc., Inc., Berkeley, 1984—. Dir. East Bay Chpt. of Soc. of Real Estate Appraisers, Calif., 1975—76. Contbr. articles to poetry mag.; author: The Hunchback and the Swan, 1978; editor: Blue Unicorn Mag., 1990—. Sec. Fair Housing and Fair Employment, Berkeley, 1965—. Mem.: Berkeley Breakfast Club, Appraisel Inst. Democrat. Roman Catholic. Home and Office: WF Osrander & Assoc Inc 5561 Country Club Dr Oakland CA 94618 Office Phone: 510-652-0546.

OSTREM, WALTER MARTIN, librarian, educator, consultant; b. Mpls., May 27, 1930; s. Oscar Martin and Helen Therese (Marcio) O.; m. Gertrud Franciska Tunkel, Aug. 6, 1956; children: Thomas, Paul, Francine. BA, U. Minn., 1953, MA, 1958; BS, Mankato State U., 1962, MS, 1964; postgrad., U. Mich., U. Iowa. Serials libr. Agr. Libr. U. Minn., 1958-59; acquisitions libr. Mankato State U., Minn., 1959-66, Eastern Mich. U., 1966-67; dir. media Iowa City Sch., 1967-69; libr. John F. Kennedy Sch., Berlin, 1969-73; disting. profl. libr. St. Paul Schs., 1973-90; libr. Open Sch. St. Pauls Schs., 1990-93; cons. in field. Librarian, educator, consultant; b. Mpls., May 27, 1930; s. Oscar Martin and Helen Therese (Marcio) O.; m. Gertrud Franciska Tunkel, Aug. 6, 1956; children— Thomas, Paul, Francine. B.A., U. Minn., 1953, M.A., 1958; B.S., Mankato State U., 1962, M.S., 1964; postgrad. U. Mich., U. Iowa. Serials librarian Agr. Library U. Minn., 1958-59; acquisitions librarian Mankato State U., Minn., 1959-66, Eastern Mich. U., 1966-67; dir. media Iowa City Sch., 1967-69; librarian John F. Kennedy Sch., Berlin, W.Ger., 1969-73; dist. profl. librarian St. Paul Schs., 1973-90; librarian Open Sch. St. Pauls Schs., 1990-93; cons. in field. Served to 1st lt. U.S. Army, 1954-55. Recipient Ency. Brit. 1st place Sch. Library Media System award, 1969. Mem. Minn. Ednl. Media Orgn., Am. Fedn. Tchrs., M Club, Phi Delta Kappa. Contbr. articles in field. Contbr. articles to profl. jours. Served to 1st lt. U.S. Army, 1954-55. Recipient Ency. Brit. 1st place Sch. Libr. Media System award, 1969. Mem. Minn. Ednl. Media Orgn., Am. Fedn. Tchrs., M Club, Phi Delta Kappa. Home: 5536 Harriet Ave Minneapolis MN 55419-1830 *Personal philosophy: I believe school libraries and school librarians are essential for increasing children's understanding of themselves and their society.*

OSTRIKER, ALICIA SUSKIN, poet; b. N.Y.C., Nov. 11, 1937; d. David and Beatrice (Linnick) Suskin; m. Jeremiah P. Ostriker, 1958; children: Rebecca, Eve, Gabriel. BA, Brandeis U., 1959; MA, U. Wis., 1961, PhD, 1964. Asst. prof. Rutgers U., New Brunswick, N.J., 1965-68, assoc. prof., 1968-72, prof. English, 1972—. Author: Vision and Verse in William Blake, 1965, Songs, 1969, Once More Out of Darkness, and Other Poems, 1974, A Dream of Springtime, 1979, The Mother/Child Papers, 1980, A Woman Under the Surface: Poems and Prose Poems, 1982, Writing Like a Woman, 1983, The Imaginary Lover, 1986 (William Carlos Williams prize Poetry Soc. Am. 1986), Stealing the Language: The Emergence of Women's Poetry in America, 1986, Green Age, 1989, Feminist Revision and the Bible, 1993, The Nakedness of the Fathers: Biblical Vision and Revisions, 1994, The Crack in Everything, 1996 (Nat. Book award finalist 1996, Paterson Poetry prize 1996, San Francisco State Poetry Ctr. award 1997), The Little Space: Selected and New Poems, 1998 (Nat. Book award finalist 1998), Dancing at the Devil's Party: Essays on Poetry, Politics, and the Erotic, 2000, The Volcano Sequence, 2002; editor: William Blake: Complete Poems, 1977. Nat. Coun. on Humanities grantee, 1968; NEA fellow, 1976-77, N.J. Arts Coun. fellow, 1982, Guggenheim Found. fellow, 1984-85, faculty fellow Rutgers Ctr. for Hist. Analysis, 1995-96, Rockefeller Found. fellow, 1982; recipient Strousse Poetry prize Prairie Schooner, 1986, Edward Stanley award Prairie Schooner, 1994, Anna David Rosenberg Poetry award, 1994, Best American Poetry award, 1996, Paterson prize, 1997, San Francisco State Poetry Ctr. award, 1997, Pushcart prize, 1999, Larry Levis prize 2001. Office: Rutgers Univ Dept of English New Brunswick NJ 08903 E-mail: ostriker@rci.rutgers.edu.

OSTRIKER, JEREMIAH PAUL, astrophysicist, educator; b. N.Y.C., Apr. 13, 1937; s. Martin and Jeanne (Sumpf) Ostriker; m. Alicia Suskin, Dec. 1, 1958; children: Rebecca, Eve; 1 child, Gabriel. AB, Harvard U., 1959; PhD, U. Chgo., 1964, degree (hon.), 1992; postgrad., U. Cambridge, Eng., 1964—65. Rsch. assoc., lectr. astrophysics Princeton (N.J.) U., 1965—66, asst. prof., 1966—68, assoc. prof., 1968—71, prof., 1971—, chmn. dept. astronomy, dir. obs., 1979—95, Charles A. Young prof. astronomy, 1982—2002, provost, 1995—2001; Plumian prof. astronomy and exptl. philosophy U. Cambridge, England, 2001—04. Author: Development of Large-Scale Structure in the Universe, 1991; editl. bd., trustee Princeton U. Press; contbr. articles to profl. jours. Recipient Vainu Bappu Meml. award, Indian Nat. Sci. Acad., 1993, Karl Schwarzschild medal, Astronomische Gesellschaft, 1999, U.S. Nat. medal of Sci., 2000; fellow Alfred P. Sloan, 1970—72; NSF fellow, U. Chgo., 1960—64. Fellow: AAAS; mem.: NAS (counselor 1992—95, bd. govs. 1993—95), Royal Netherlands Acad. Arts and Scis. (fgn.), Am. Acad. Arts and Scis., Am. Philos. Soc., Internat. Astron. Union, Am. Astron. Soc. (councilor 1978—80, Warner prize 1972, Russel prize 1980), Royal Astron. Soc. (assoc. Gold medal 2004), Am. Mus. Natural History (trustee 1997—). Home: 33 Philip Dr Princeton NJ 08540-5409 Office Phone: 609 258 4267. E-mail: jpo@astro.princeton.edu.

OSTROFF, NAT S. communications executive; Chmn. Acrodyne Comm. Inc., Blue Bell, Pa. Office: Acrodyne Comm Inc 516 Township Line Rd Blue Bell PA 19422-2197

OSTROM, DON, political science educator; b. Chgo., Mar. 9, 1939; s. Irving and Margaret (Hedberg) O.; m. Florence Horan, Jan. 13, 1972; children: Erik, Rebecca, Katherine. BA, St. Olaf Coll., Northfield, Minn., 1960; MA, Washington U., 1970, PhD, 1972. Prof. polit. sci. Gustavus Adolphus Coll., St. Peter, Minn., 1972—; state rep. Minn. Ho. of Reps., St. Paul, 1988-96. Co-editor: Perspectives on Minnesota Government and Politics, 1998. Democrat. Home: 2737 Ewing Ave S Minneapolis MN 55416 E-mail: dostrom@gac.edu.

OSTROM, ELINOR, political science educator, researcher; b. Los Angeles, Aug. 7, 1933; d. Adrian and Leah (Hopkins) Awan; m. Charles Scott, Aug. 8, 1954 (div. 1961); m. Vincent Ostrom, Nov. 23, 1963. AB with honors, UCLA, 1954, MA, 1962, PhD, 1965; D in Economics (hon.), U. Zurich, 1999. Vis. asst. prof. dept. gov. Ind. U., Bloomington, 1965-66, asst. prof., grad. adv., dept. gov., 1966-69, assoc. prof., dept. polit. sci., 1969-74, prof., polit. sci., 1974-91, Arthur F. Bentley prof. polit. sci., 1991—, prof., chmn. dept. polit. sci., 1980—84, acting chair, dept. polit. sci., 1989—90, co-dir. Workshop in Polit. Theory and Policy Analysis, 1973—, co-dir. Center for the Study Instns., Population, and Environ. Change, prof. part-time, Sch. Pub. and Environ. Affairs. Employment interviewer, asst. employee relations mgr., Godfrey L. Cabot, Inc., Boston, 1955-57; personnel analyst III, U. Calif., LA, 1957-61; bd. cons., Internat. Assn. Chiefs Police: Police Discipline Project, 1974-75; adv. bd. Nat. Evaluation Program Law Enforcement Assistance (Adminstrn.), Washington, 1975-76; mem. Nat. Adv. Panel, Nat. Acad. Pub. Adminstrn.; Neighborhood-Oriented Metropolitan Gov., 1975-76, task force on criminal justice rsch. and devel. Nat. Adv. Com. on Criminal Justice Standards and Goals, 1975-76, Nat. Sheriffs Assn.: Study of Contract Law Enforcement, 1975-76; adv. panel Div. Policy Rsch. and Analysis, NSF, Washington, 1977-78, panel on Instl. Develop., 1985; rev. panel Polit. Sci. div. NSF, 1983-84; Interuniversity Consortium for Polit. and Social Rsch. Coun., 1983-85; adv. com. nat. urban policy NAS/NRC, 1985-88, panel on Common Property Resources Mgmt., 1985-86, Scientific Com. on Problems of the Environ., 1995-98; rsch. adv. com. U.S. AID, 1989-91; local gov. rsch. adv. bd., US Adv. Commn. on Intergovernmental Rels., 1985-88; adv. bd., Inst. for Policy Reform, 1993-96; bd. dirs., Beijer Internat. Inst. Ecol. Econs., Royal Swedish Acad. Scis., 1997-; academic adv. bd., Max-Planck-Inst. für Gesellschaftsforschung, 2000-; cons. in field. Co-author: Policing Metropolitan America, 1978, Local Government in the United States, 1988, Institutional Incentives and Sustainable Development: Infrastructure Policies in Perspective, 1993, Rules, Games, and Common-Pool Resources, 1994; author: Governing the Commons, 1990, Crafting Institutions for Self-Governing Irrigation Systems, 1992; editor: Strategies of Political Injury, 1982; co-editor Jour. Theoretical Politics, 1987-95; editl. bd. mem. Am. Jour. Polit. Sci., Am. Polit. Sci. Review, Criminal Justice Review, Pub. Productivity Review, Publius, Quarterly Jour. Adminstrn., Sage Urban Affairs Ann. Review, Social Sci. Quarterly, Urban Affaris Quarterly, Ecol. Economics; contbr. articles to profl. jours. Grantee NSF, 1974-85, 87—, NIMH, 1977-81, U.S. Dept. Justice, 1978-82, AID, 1984-94, U.S. Geol. Survey, 1987-89, Ford Found., 1991—, FAO, 1992—; recipient Frank E. Seidman Disting. award in Polit. Economy, 1997, Johan Skytte prize in Polit. Sci., Upsala University, 1999, Aaron Wildavsky Enduring Contbn. award for Governing the Commons, APSA, Pub. Policy Sect., 2000, John J. Carty award for the Advancement Sci., NAS, 2004 Fellow Am. Acad. Arts and Scis., AAAS; mem. Pub. Choice Soc. (pres. 1982-84, co-chair, Duncan Black award Com., 1986-87, chair, Duncan Black award Com., 1990, exec. coun., 1982-), Am. Polit. Sci. Assn. (v.p. 1975-76, pres.-elect 1995-96, pres. 1996-97, chmn., several coms., 1978-88, mem., several coms., 1970-2002), Midwest Polit. Sci. Assn. (pres. 1984-85), Internat. Polit. Sci. Assn., Am. Econ. Assn., Internat. Assn. for Study Common Property (pres. 1990-91, program co-chair, 2000), Policy Studies Orgn., (nominating com., 1986-87, Miriam Mills award, 1996, Thomas R. Dye Svc. award, 1997), NAS. Democrat. Home: 5883 E Lampkins Ridge Rd Bloomington IN 47401-9726 Office: Ind Univ Workshop in Polit Theory & Policy Analys 513 N Park Ave Bloomington IN 47408-3895 Office Phone: 812-855-0441. Office Fax: 891-855-3150. Business E-Mail: ostrom@indiana.edu.*

OSTROM, VINCENT A(LFRED), political science educator; b. Nooksack, Wash., Sept. 25, 1919; s. Alfred and Alma (Knudson) O.; m. Isabell Bender, May 20, 1942 (div. 1963); m. Elinor Awan, Nov. 23, 1963. BA in Polit. Sci., UCLA, 1942, MA in Polit. Sci., 1945, PhD in Polit. Sci., 1950. Tchr. Chaffey Union H.S., Ontario, Calif., 1943-45; asst. prof. polit. sci. U. Wyo., Laramie, 1945-48, U. Oreg., Eugene, 1949-54, assoc. prof. polit. sci., 1954-58, UCLA, 1958-64; prof. polit. sci. Ind. U., Bloomington, 1964-90, Arthur F. Bentley prof emeritus polit. sci., 1990—. Hooker disting. vis. scholar McMaster U., 1984-85; rsch. assoc. Bur. Mcpl. Rsch., 1950, Resources for Future, Inc., 1962-64; assoc. dir. Pacific NW Coop. Program in Ednl. Adminstrn., 1951-58; founding dir. Workshop in Polit. Theory and Policy Analysis, Ind. U., Bloomington, 1973—; cons. and lectr. in field. Author: Water and Politics, 1953, The Political Theory of a Compound Republic, 1971, 2nd rev. edit., 1987, The Intellectual Crisis in American Public Administration, 1974, 2nd edit., 1989, The Meaning of American Federalism, 1991, The Meaning of Democracy and the Vulnerability of Democracies, 1997; co-author: Understanding Urban Government, 1973, Local Government in the United States, 1988; co-editor: Comparing Urban Service Delivery Systems, 1977, Guidance, Control and Evaluation in the Public Sector, 1986, Rethinking Institutional Analysis and Development, 1988, 2d. edit. 1993; mem. bd. editors Publius, 1972—; mem. editl. bd. Constnl. Polit. Economy, 1989—, Nigerian Jour. Fin. and Human Resources Mgmt., 1996—, Internat. Jour. Orgn. Theory and Behavior, 1997—; contbr. articles to profl. jours. Program coord. Wyo. Assessors' Sch., 1946-48, Budget Officer's Sch., 1947-48; exec. sec. Wyo. League of Municipalities, 1947-48; cons. Wyo. Legis. Interim Com., 1947-48, Nat. Resources, Alaska Constitutional Convention, 1955-56, Tenn. Water Policy Commn., 1956; mem. founding bd. Com. on Polit. Economy of the Good Soc., 1990—. Grantee and fellowships Social Sci. Rsch. Coun., 1954-55, Ctr. Advanced Study in Behavioral Scis., 1955-56, Ctr. Interdisciplinary Rsch., 1981-82; recipient Robert O. Anderson Sustainable Arctic award, 2003; co-recipient (with Elinor Ostrom) Lifetime Achievement award Atlas Economic Rsch. Foundation's Fund for the Study of Spontaneous Order, 2003. Mem. AAAS, Am. Polit. Sci. Assn. (Spl. Achievement award for Significant Contbns. to Study of Federalism, 1991, Best Book on Federalism and Intergovtl. Rels. award 1999), Am. Econ. Assn., Am. Soc. Pub. Adminstrn., Pub. Choice Soc., Internat. Polit. Sci. Assn. (Robert O. Anderson Sustainable Arctic award 2003, award Atlas Econ. Rsch. Found. Fund, 2003). Home: 5883 E Lampkins Ridge Rd Bloomington IN 47401-9726 Office: Ind U Workshop in Polit Theory 513 N Park Ave Bloomington IN 47408-3895 Office Phone: 812-855-0441. E-mail: workshop@indiana.edu., ghiggins@indiana.edu.

OSTROMENCKI, NANCY LEE, music educator; b. Chgo., May 2, 1954; d. George Edward and Jeanette Ann Ostromencki; m. Joshua R. Weikersheimer, Feb. 12, 1987 (div. Feb. 1989). MusB, DePaul U., 1977. Tchr., pianist North Park Coll., Chgo., 1975—88, pvt. instrn., 1975—88, Rio Rancho High Sch, N.Mex., 1989—2001, pvt. instrn., Tucson, 2001—. Co-founder The Piano Education Page. Mem.: West Mesa Music Tchrs. Assn., Music Tchrs. Nat. Assn. Home: 6760 N Calle Lomita Tucson AZ 85704

OSTROVERKHOVA, OKSANA, physicist; arrived in U.S., 1996; d. Grigoriy and Liliya Franchuk; m. Victor Ostroverkhov, June 17, 1994. Diploma in Optical Engring. and Physics with honors, Kiev Shevchenko U., 1996; PhD in Physics, Case Western Res. U., 2001—01. Rschr. Rsch. Inst. UkrAnalyt, Kiev, 1994—96; tchg. asst. Case Western Res. U., Cleve., 1996—97, rsch. asst., 1997—2001; postdoctoral fellow Stanford (Calif.) U., 2001—03; Killam meml. fellow U. Alta., Edmonton, Canada, 2003—04. Referee various sci. jours. in field, 2001—. Grantee Internat. Soros Found. grant for student excellence, 1995, Killam Meml. fellow, Killam Trust, 2002—04, Loshkarev scholarship for student excellence, Kiev Shevchenko U., 1991—96. Achievements include research in nonlinear optics of organic materials; patents pending for ultrafast spectroscopy of organic semiconductors. Home: 10145-121 St #712 Alberta Edmonton Canada T5N 1K5 Office: U Alberta 114 - 89 Avenue Alberta Edmonton Canada T6G 2J1 Office Fax: 780-492-0714. Personal E-mail: oksanao@ualberta.ca.

OSTROVSKY, LAWRENCE ZELIG, lawyer; b. Cleve., June 1, 1956; s. Peter and Yetta Ostrovsky. BA, St. John's Coll., Annapolis, Md., 1978; JD, Lewis and Clark Coll., 1982. Bar: Ohio 1982, Alaska 1983. Assoc. Berger & Kirschenbaum, Cleve., 1982, Birch, Horton, Dittner, Pestinger & Anderson, Anchorage, 1983—87; spl. asst. to the commr. of natural resources Alaska Dept. Natural Resources, Anchorage, 1987—91; assoc. dir. for energy and public lands Alaska Gov. Office, Washington, 1991—94; asst. atty. gen. oil, gas, and mining sect., Alaska Dept. Law, Anchorage, 1994—. Mem. Commonwealth North, Anchorage, 1986, Alaska Bar Assn.(bd. of governors, 1998—, pres. elect, 2003, pres. 2004). Office: Alaska Dept Law 1031 W 4th Ave Ste 200 Anchorage AK 99501-1994

OSTROW, JOSEPH W. advertising executive; b. N.Y.C., Feb. 22, 1933; s. Meyer H. and Helen (Small) O.; m. Francine Lee Goldberg, Sept. 4, 1955; children: Elizabeth Sara, Peter Mathew, William Nathan. BS in Mktg., NYU, 1955. Researcher W.R. Simmons, N.Y.C., 1954-55; with Young & Rubicam, N.Y.C., 1955-87, sr. v.p., dir. communication planning, 1972-73, exec. v.p., dir., dir. communications services, 1973-87, mem. N.Y. exec. com., U.S.A. bd. dirs.; pres., chief operating officer worldwide Direct Mktg. Group of Cos., 1983-84; exec. v.p., dir. media worldwide Foote, Cone & Belding Co., N.Y.C., 1987-94; pres., CEO Cabletelevision Advt. Bur., N.Y.C., 1994—2003; pres. Ostrow Cons., N.Y.C., 2003. Multichannel Advt. Bur. Internat.; hon. chair bd. dir. Cable Positive; past chmn. Traffic Audit Bur.; dir. Audit Bur. Circulations; bd. dir., past mem. exec. com. Advt. Info. Svc., Advt. Rsch. Found.; lectr. in field. Mem. nat. coun. Boy Scouts Am. Mem. Media Dirs. Coun. (past pres.), Am. Assn. Advt. Agys. (past vice chmn. media policy com.), Internat. Radio and TV Found. (bd. dirs.), Advt. Coun. (bd. dirs.), John Reisenbach Found. (bd. dirs.). E-mail: joe.ostrowconsulting@yahoo.com. *It is important that one continue to set goals that seem unachievable and at the same time live by standards that remain consistently high. The maintenance of integrity and adherence to principles which support it, are especially critical when dealing with consumer commercial persuasion. Anything less would be detrimental to the proper pursuit of both personal and business achievements.*

OSTROW, MICHAEL JAY, lawyer; b. Baldwin, N.Y., Apr. 25, 1934; s. Oscar I. and Ethel M. (Morganstern) O.; m. Judith L. Loewenthal, Aug. 25, 1957; children: Thomas L., Kenneth A., Nancy M. BA, Alfred U., 1955; JD, Cornell U., 1958. Bar: N.Y. 1958, U.S. Supreme Ct. 1964, U.S. Dist. Ct. (so. and ea. dists.) N.Y. 1970; diplomate Am. Coll. Family Trial Lawyers. Ptnr. Taylor & Ostrow, Mineola, N.Y., 1961-69, Taylor Atkins & Ostrow, Garden City, N.Y., 1969-96, Ostrow and Taub, Garden City, 1996-2000. Bd. dirs., lectr Advanced Practice Inst. Hofstra Law Sch., Hempstead; lectr. Practicing Law Inst., N.Y.C. Mem. ABA, Acad. Matrimonial Lawyers (pres. N.Y. chpt. 1980-81, sec. nat. acad. 1988-90, nat. v.p. 1990-94, pres.-elect 1995-96, pres. 1996-97), Internat. Acad. Matrimonial Lawyers (bd. govs. 1990-92), Am. Coll. Family Trial Lawyers (diplomate), N.Y. State Bar Assn. (chmn. family law sect. 1976-78, mem. exec. com.), Nassau County Bar Assn. (pres. 1984-85, chmn. judiciary com. 1992-93), Order of Coif, Zeta Beta Tau, Phi Delta Phi. Home: 712 Balfour Pl Melville NY 11747 Office: Schlissel Ostrow Karabatos Poepplein & Fisher PLLC 200 Garden City Plz Suite 301 Garden City NY 11530 Office Phone: 516-877-1800. E-mail: MJODIX@aol.com.

OSTROW, ROBERT, publishing executive; married; 2 children. Degree, SUNY. From account mgr. to pub. PC World, Framingham, Mass., 1986—2000, pub., 2000—. Office: PC World 492 Old Connecticut Path Framingham MA 01701

OSTROW, STUART, theatrical producer, educator, writer; b. N.Y.C. m. Ann Elizabeth Gilbert; children: Julie Elizabeth, Katherine Ann, John Stuart. Disting. univ. prof. theater U. Houston. Pres. Stuart Ostrow Found., Inc., Mus. Theater Lab.; founding mem. opera-mus. theatre panel NEA; mem. bd. overseers com. to visit Loeb Drama Ctr. Harvard U. Prodr.: We Take the Town, 1961, The Apple Tree, 1966, 1776, 1969, Scratch, 1971, Pippin, 1972, The Moony Shapiro Songbook, 1981, American Passion, 1983, M. Butterfly, 1988, La Bête, 1991, Face Value, 1993, Doll, 1995, Coyote Goes Salmon Fishing, 1996; prodr., dir.: Here's Love, 1963, Swing, 1980; author, producer: Stages, 1978; assoc. dir.; Chicago, 1975; author: A Producer's Broadway Journey, 1999, Thank You Very Much, 2002. Mem. Pulitzer Prize Drama Jury; chmn. bd. trustees Inst. for Advanced Study in Musical Theatre, 2002. Served with USAF, 1952—55.

OSTRY, SYLVIA, academic administrator, economist; b. Winnipeg, Man., Can. d. Morris J. and B. (Stoller) Knelman; m. Bernard Ostry; children: Adam, Jonathan. BA in Econs., McGill U., 1948, MA, 1950; PhD in Econs., Cambridge U. and McGill U., 1954; also 19 hon. degrees. Lectr., asst. prof. econs. McGill U.; rsch. officer Inst. Stats., U. Oxford, Eng.; assoc. prof. U. Montreal, Can.; with dept. stats. Econ. Coun. Can., Ottawa, 1964-72, chmn., 1978-79; chief statistician Stats. Can., Ottawa, 1972-75; dep. minister consumer and corp. affairs Govt. Can., Ottawa, 1975-78, dep. minister internat. trade, coordinator internat. econ. relations, 1984-85, ambassador for multilateral trade negotiations, personal rep. of Prime Minister for Econ. Summit, 1985-88; chancellor U. Waterloo, 1991-96; head dept. econs. and stats. OECD, Paris, 1979-83; chmn. Ctr. for Internat. Studies U. Toronto, Ont., Can., 1990-97, disting. rsch. fellow Munk Ctr. for Internat. Studies, 1997—. Lectr. Per Jacobssen Found., 1987; chmn. nat. coun. Can. Inst. Internat. Affairs, 1990-95; western co-chmn. Blue Ribbon Commn. for Hungary's Econ. Recovery, 1990-94; mem. adv. bd. Inst. Internat. Econs., Washington; founding mem. Pacific Coun. on Internat. Policy; Volvo Disting. vis. fellow Coun. on Fgn. Rels., N.Y.C., 1989. Author: Governments and Corporations in a Shrinking World: The Search for Stability, 1990, The Threat of Managed Trade to Transforming Economies, 1993; co-author: (with Richard Nelson) Techno-nationalism and Technoglobalism: Conflict and Cooperation, 1995; co-editor: (with Karen Knop, Richard Simeon, Katherine Swinton) Rethinking Federalism: Citizens, Markets and Governments in a Changing World, 1995; New Dimensions of Market Access, 1995, (with Gilbert R. Winham) The Halifax G-7 Summit: Issues on the Table, 1995, Who's on First: The Post-Cold War Trading System, 1997, APEC and Regime Creation in the Asia-Pacific:

The OECD Model?, 1998, Technology, Productivity and Multinational Enterprise, 1998, Intellectual Property Protection in the World Trade Organization: Major Issues in the Millennium Round, 1999, Globalization Implications for Industrial Relations, 1999, The Future of the World Trading System, 1999, Convergence and Sovereignty: Policy Scope for Compromise?, 2000, Regional Versus Multilateral Trade Strategies, 2000, Making Sense of it All: A Post Mortem on the Meaning of Seattle, 2000; The Uruguay Round North-South Grand Bargain: Implications for Future Negotiations, 2000, Regional Dominos and the WTO: Building Blocks or Boomerang?, 2000, Business, Trade and the Environment, 2000, The Changing Scenario in International Governance, 2000, Looking Back to Look Forward: The Multilateral Trading System after 50 Years, 2000, The WTO: Post Seattle and Chinese Accession, 2001, The WTO and International Governance, 2001, Dominos and the WTO: Building Blocks or Boomerang?, 2000, Business, Trade and the Environment, 2000, The Changing Scenario in International Governance, 2000, Looking Back to Look Forward: The Multilateral Trading System after 50 Years, 2000, The WTO: Post Seattle and Chinese Accession, 2001, The WTO and International Governance, 2001, Global Integration: Currents and Counter Current, 2003, What are the Necessary Ingredients for the World Trading Order?, 2003, External Transparency in Trade Policy, 2004, The World Trading System: In The Fog of Uncertainty, 2004, Summitry and Trade: What Could Sea Island Do for Doha?, 2004, External Transparency: The Policy Process at the National Levelof the Two-level game, 2004; contbg. author: China and the Long March to Global Trade, 2003; contbr. articles on empirical and policy-analytic subjects to more than 90 profl. publs. Decorated companion Order of Can., 1990; recipient Outstanding Achievement award Govt. of Can., 1987, Hon. Assoc. award Conf. Bd. of Can., 1992; Disting. vis. fellow Volvo, 1989-90. Fellow Royal Soc. Can., mem. Group of Thirty, Inst. for Internat. Econs. (adv. bd.). Avocations: films, theater, contemporary reading. Office: Munk Ctr Internat Studies U Toronto 1 Devonshire Pl Toronto ON Canada M5S 3K7 Office Phone: 416-946-8927. E-mail: sylvia.ostry@utoronto.ca.

OSTWALD, MARTIN, retired classicist; b. Dortmund, Germany, Jan. 15, 1922; arrived in U.S., 1946, naturalized, 1956; s. Max and Hedwig (Strauss) Ostwald; m. Lore Ursula Weinberg, Dec. 27, 1948; children: Mark F., David H. BA, U. Toronto, 1946; AM, U. Chgo., 1948; PhD, Columbia U., 1952; D (hon.), Fribourg (Switzerland) U., 1995, Dortmund (Germany) U., 2001. Instr. classics and humanities Wesleyan U., Middletown, Conn., 1950-51; from lectr. to asst. prof. Greek and Latin Columbia U., 1951-58; mem. faculty Swarthmore Coll., 1958—, prof. classics, 1966-92, prof. emeritus, 1992—; prof. classical studies U. Pa., 1968-92, prof. emeritus, 1992—. Vis. assoc. prof. Princeton (N.J.) U., 1964, mem. Inst. Advanced Study, 1974—75, 1981—82, 1990—91; vis. prof. U. Calif., Berkeley, 1969, Tel-Aviv U., 1996—; vis. fellow Balliol Coll. Oxford (Eng.) U., 1970—71, vis. fellow Wolfson Coll., 1987, 91; dir. fellowships-in-residence classics NEH, 1976—77; dir. d'etudes EHESS, Paris, 1991; mem. Inst. Advanced Studies, Tel Aviv, 1994, 2003. Translator: Nicomachean Ethics (Aristotle), 1962; author: (book) Nomos and the Beginings of the Athenian Democracy, 1969, Autonomia, Its Genesis and Early History, 1982, From Popular Sovereignty to the Sovereignty of Law, 1987, Anake in Thucydides, 1988, Oligarchia, 2000; author: (with T. G. Rosenmeyer and J. W. Halporn) The Meters of Greek and Latin Poetry, 2d edit., 1980; mem. editl. bd. Cambridge Ancient History, 1976—94; contbr. articles to profl. jours. Fellow, Am. Coun. Learned Socs., 1965—66, NEH, 1970—71, 1990—91; Fulbright Rsch. fellow, Greece, 1961—62, Guggenheim fellow, 1977—78, Lang. fellow, Swarthmore Coll., 1986—87. Fellow: AAAS; mem.: Soc. Ancient Philosophy, Classical Assn. Atlantic States, Classical Assn. Can., Am. Philol. Assn. (pres. 1986—87), Am. Philos. Soc., Soc. Promotion Hellenic Studies (hon.). Home: 408 Walnut Ln Swarthmore PA 19081-1137 E-mail: mostwal1@swarthmore.edu.

O'SULLIVAN, CHRISTINE, retired executive director social service agency, consultant; b. Washington, July 5, 1947; d. George Albert and Mary Ruth (Stalcup) Markward; m. Donald Phillip O'Sullivan, June 27, 1985. Sec. Gas Distributors Info. Svc., Washington, 1966-70; adminstr. asst. Nat. Airlines, Washington, 1970-71; office mgr. Tire Industry Safety Coun., Washington, 1971-75; pres. Type-Right Exec. Sec. Svc., Washington, Pitts., 1976-91; exec. dir. Eastside Cmty. Ministry, Zanesville, Ohio, 1991—2001. Chair FEMA Emergency Bd., Muskingum, Morgan and Perry Counties, Ohio, 1994-97, 99-2000; chair United Way Exec. Dirs. Coun., 1994-97, United Way agy. relations com. 2000-03, allocations com. 2002-03; v.p. Muskingum County Hunger Network, Zanesville, 1993-99. Author: Write a Good Resume, 1976. Mem. task force Literacy Coun., 1993—2000; mem. steering com. Muskingum County Operation Feed, 1992—99; trustee Disability Network of Ohio-Solidarity, 2001—; mem Zanesville City Sch. Bldg. Adv. Coun., Ohio, 2001—04; v.p. Muskingum County Women's Rep. Club, 1994, sec., 1995; mem. Downtown Clergy Assn., 1992—, pres., 1995—96; bd. dirs. Human Care Ministry, Ohio dist. Luth. Ch., Mo. Synod, PRO-Muskingum, 1995—2000; commr. Mo. Synod Luths. to Commn. on Religion in Appalachia, 1996—98; chair human care bd. Trinity Evang. Luth. Ch., 2003—; bd. dirs. Muskingum County Women's Coalition, 1994—97, Families and Children First Coun., 1995—2000, Interfaith Response to Ohio Disaster, 1988—91, Luth. Social Svcs. Emergency Assistance Com., 1998—99, Muskingum County Family Adv. Team, 2000—01. Recipient Cert. of Achievement for Mil. Family Support, U.S. Army, 1991, Excellence in Cmty. Svc. award Aid Assn. Luths., 1993, Excellence in Cmty. Svc. award Muskingum County DAR, 1994, Positive Action award, NOW, 1997, YWCA Woman of Achievement award, 1997, Americanism award VFW, 1992, Cmty. Involvement award Richvale Grange, 1997, Cmty. Citizen award State of Ohio Grange, 2000; named Outstanding Cmty. Vol. Zanesville Daybreak Rotary Club, 1997. Mem.: Nat. Multiple Sclerosis Soc. (program com. Buckeye chpt. 2001—04), Muskingum County Respiratory Assn. (bd. dirs. 2001—, sec., bd. dirs. 2003—), Disability Network Ohio Solidarity (trustee 2001—), Richvale Grange, Kiwanis (Zanesville chpt. bd. dirs. 1997—99, spiritual aims com. chair Dist. 18 of Ohio 1998—99). Avocations: creative writing, music. Office: Eastside Cmty Ministry 221 Stillwell St PO Box 965 Zanesville OH 43702-0965 Home: 62 N 3rd St Apt 201 Zanesville OH 43701 E-mail: chrissyduck@hotmail.com.

O'SULLIVAN, EUGENE HENRY, retired advertising executive, management consultant; b. Plainfield, N.J., June 8, 1942; s. Patrick J. and Helen (Callahan) O'S.; m. Tracy Ota; 1 child, Meredith. BBA, U. Notre Dame, 1964. Media buyer Foote Cone Belding, N.Y.C., 1967-68; account exec., mgmt. supr. Group Dtr, N.Y.C.; exec. v.p., dir. client svcs. Young & Rubicam, N.Y.C., 1968-84; sr. v.p., group dir. Ogilvy & Mather, N.Y.C., 1984-86, 87; exec. v.p. Hill, Holliday, Boston, 1986-87; exec. v.p., gen. mgr. McCann Erickson, N.Y.C., 1988-90; ret., 1990. Served to lt. (j.g.) USN, 1964-66. Mem. Lotos Club. Democrat. Home: 21 E 10th St New York NY 10003-5923 E-mail: eugeneo@earthlink.net.

O'SULLIVAN, JUDITH ROBERTA, lawyer, author, artist; b. Pitts., Jan. 6, 1942; d. Robert Howard and Mary Olive (O'Donnell) Gallick; m. James Paul O'Sullivan, Feb. 1, 1964; children: Kathryn, James. BA, Carlow Coll., 1963; MA, U. Md., 1969, PhD, 1976; JD, Georgetown U., 1996. Editor Am. Film Inst., Washington, 1974—77; assoc. program coord. Smithsonian Resident Assocs., Washington, 1977—78; dir. instl. devel. Nat. Archives, Washington, 1978—79; exec. dir. Md. State Humanities Coun., Balt., 1979—81, 1982—84, Ctr. for the Book, Libr. of Congress, Washington, 1981—82; dep. asst. dir. Nat. Mus. Am. Art, Washington, 1984—87, acting asst. dir., 1987—89; pres., CEO The Mus. at Stony Brook, NY, 1989—92; exec. dir. Nat. Assn. Women Judges, Washington, 1993; clk. Office Legal Adviser U.S. Dept. State, Washington, 1994—96; trial atty. Atty. Gen.'s honors program U.S. Dept. Justice, 1996—, trial atty. Criminal divsn., Domestic Security sect., 2002—; spl. asst. U.S. atty. U.S. Dist. (ea. dist.) Va., 1998—2002; asst. U.S. atty. U.S. Dist. Ariz., Tucson, 1999—2000. Summer assoc. Piper & Marbury, Balt., 1995; chair Smithsonian Women's Coun., Washington, 1988-89. Author: The Art of the Comic Strip, 1971 (Gen. Excellence award Printing Industry Am.); Workers and Allies, 1975; (with Alan Fern) The Complete Prints of Leonard Baskin, 1984, The Great American Comic Strip, 1991; editor Am. Film Inst. Catalogue: Feature Films, 1961-70, 1974-77; mem. editl. bd. Am. Film Inst. Catalog, 1979-1990. Trustee Child Life Ctr., U. Md., College Pk., 1971-74; chair Smithsonian Women's Coun., 1988-89. Univ. fellow U. Md., 1967-70, Mus. fellow, 1970-71, Smithsonian fellow Nat. Collection Fine Arts, Washington, 1972-73. Mem.: Mystery Writers of Am., D.C. Bar Assn., Md. Bar Assn. Avocations: landscape painting, mystery writing. Home: The Edgemoor 4821 Montgomery Ln # 803 Bethesda MD 20814 Office: US Dept Justice Domestic Security Sect Criminal Divsn Washington DC 20530 Business E-Mail: Judith.O'Sullivan@usdoj.gov.

O'SULLIVAN, LAWRENCE JOSEPH, retired investment counselor; b. Curragh, Ireland, Jan. 12, 1924; s. Florence Elizabeth (Heffernan) O'S.; m. Grace Ewart Logan, Dec. 24, 1947; children: Sharon, Lawrence, Maureen, James. BBA, St. John's U., Bklyn., 1953; postgrad., Coll. St. Rose, Elmira U. Sr. investment analyst Lionel D. Edie, Inc., N.Y.C., 1953-57; asst. v.p., editor Forbes IAI, Inc., N.Y.C., 1957-62; asst. v.p., registered rep. N.Y. G.C. Haas, N.Y.C., 1962-63; rsch. dir. Fin. Investment Adv. Svc., N.Y.C., 1963-70; pres. Financialite Corp., N.Y.C., 1963-80; ret. Instr. world history N.Y. State Edn. Sys., Bethpage, Hernando County Schs., Fla.; founder Star Stat Pubs., 1969. Author: W.S. Schley, Rogue Admiral?, 1985, G.E. Graham, U.S. First Black International Spy, 1969; founder Star Stat Pubs., 1992. Econ. cons. Hernando County Health Authority, Fla., 1979-82, chmn., 1983-84; dir. Watervliet (N.Y.) Hist. Club, 1995—, exec. dir., 1995; prodr., dir., performer Stage West Theater Group, Spring Hill, Fla., 1972; com. chmn. Cub pack Boy Scouts Am., Bethpage, 1960. With USNR, 1942-46. Decorated Liberation medal Philippines. Fellow Am. Fedn. Fin. Analysts (ret.); mem. N.Y. Soc. Security Analysts, DAV (life), VFW Roman Catholic.

O'SULLIVAN, LYNDA TROUTMAN, lawyer; b. Oil City, Pa., Aug. 30, 1952; d. Perry John and Vivian Dorothy (Schreffler) Troutman; m. P. Kevin O'Sullivan, Dec. 15, 1979; children: John Perry, Michael Patrick. BA, Am. U., 1974; JD, Georgetown U., 1978, postgrad., 1982-83. Bar: D.C. 1978. Ptnr. Perkins Coie, Washington, 1985-92, Fried, Frank, Harris, Shriver & Jacobson, Washington, 1993-97, Miller & Chevalier, Washington, 1997—. Mem. adv. bd. Fed. Contracts Report, 1991-97, Govt. Contract Costs, Pricing & Acctg. Report, 1997-99; mem. faculty govt. contracts program George Washington U., 1993-99; lectr. in field. Contbr. articles to profl. jours. Fellow Am. Bar Found.; mem. ABA (chair truth in negotiations com. 1991-94, chair acctg., cost and pricing com. 1996-2000, coun. sect. pub. contract law 1993-95). Office: Miller & Chevalier 655 15th St NW Ste 900 Washington DC 20005-5799 E-mail: losullivan@milchev.com.

O'SULLIVAN, MARY J. physician, maternal fetal medicine educator; b. Bklyn., Mar. 22, 1938; d. Michael and Annie (O'Donnell) Sullivan. BS, St. John's U., Bklyn., 1959; MD, Women's Med. Coll., Phila., 1963. Intern St. Vincent's Hosp., N.Y.C., 1963-64; resident in ob-gyn. Hosp. Women's Med. Ctr., Phila., 1964-68; instr. ob-gyn. N.Y. Med. Coll., 1968-73, asst. prof., 1973-77, chief obstetrics and maternal fetal medicine, 1973-77, assoc. dean, 1975-77; assoc. prof. ob-gyn. U. Miami, Fla., 1977-80, prof., 1980—, chief obstetric svcs. and perinatology, dept. ob-gyn., 1982—, chief maternal fetal medicine, 1987—. Mem. exec. bd. Am. Bd. Ob-Gyn., 1990-96. Col. USAF, 1981-93. Fellow Am. Coll. Ob-Gyn. (sec. 1989-91); mem. Soc. Perinatal Obstetricians, So. Atlantic Ob-Gyn. Soc. (membership com. 1988-90), Miami Ob-Gyn. Soc. (sec. 1988-90). Roman Catholic. Avocations: cooking, sewing, gardening, skiing. Office: U Miami Dept Ob-Gyn PO Box 16960 R-136 Miami FL 33101-6960

O'SULLIVAN, PAUL KEVIN, business executive, management and instructional systems consultant; b. Syracuse, N.Y., May 10, 1938; s. John Hugh and Helen Troy (Smith) O'S.; m. Lynda Troutman; children: Mary Kathleen and Karin Jennifer (twins), John Perry, Michael Patrick. A.B., Dartmouth Coll., 1960. Communications specialist Gen. Electric Co., Schenectady, N.Y., 1963-66; nat. inst. dir. Gen. Learning Corp., Washington, 1966-67; sr. con. ednl. systems. Aries Corp., McLean, Va., 1967-69; dir. profl. devel. Nat. Audio-Visual Assn., Fairfax, Va., 1969-74; exec. dir. Am. Soc. Tng. and Devel., Madison, Wis., 1974-80; sr. v.p. Sterling Inst., Washington, 1980-87, nat. account mgr. Orgnl. Dynamics, Inc., 1987-94; account exec. Zenger Miller, 1995-96, pres. The O'Sullivan Group, Inc., 1996—; staff dir. Nat. Audio-Visual Inst. for Effective Communications Ind. U., 1969-74; chief adminstr. Internat. Fedn. Tng. and Devel. Orgns., 1974-80; dir. Internat. Symposia for Tng. Communications in Switzerland, Australia and Middle East. Producer and dir. films and multi-media presentations; author communications and tng. courses, textbooks; contbr. articles to profl. jours. Served to lt. (j.g.), USNR, 1956-63. Recipient Honor medal for Literature Freedoms Found., 1963; Writers Gold Cup award Gen. Electric, 1966; Resolution for Outstanding Achievement Nat. Audio-Visual Assn., 1974, Pres.'s award for bus. achievement, 1989, 90, 91, 92, 93. Mem. Nat. Soc. for Performance and Instrn. (Presdl. citation 1977), Am. Soc. Assn. Execs. (Grand award for mgmt. achievement 1978), Am. Soc. Tng. and Devel. (hon. life).

O'SULLIVAN, TERENCE M. labor union administrator; Mem. local 1353 Laborers Internat. Union of No. Am., Charleston, W.Va., 1974—, asst. to gen. pres., mid-atlantic regional mgr., v.p., gen. pres., 2000—; chmn., CEO Union Labor Life Insurance Co., 2003—. V.p. exec. coun. AFL-CIO, v.p. metal trades dept., v.p. bldg. and constrn. trades; chair pension fund of ctrl. and eastern Can. Laborers Internat. Union of No. Am., chair nat. (indsl.) pension fund, chair local union-dist. coun. pension fund, chair staff pension fund, chair death benefit fund, chair polit. league. Office: The Laborers' Union 905 16th St NW Washington DC 20006 Office Phone: 202-737-8320.*

O'SULLIVAN, THOMAS J. lawyer; b. New Haven, Apr. 7, 1940; s. Thomas J. and Marjorie (Hession) O'S.; m. Anita Brady, Aug. 10, 1968; children: Kathleen, Margaret, Mary Tess, Anne Elizabeth. BA in History, Yale U., 1961; LLB, Harvard U., 1966. Bar: Conn. 1966, U.S. Dist. Ct. Conn. 1967, N.Y. 1967, U.S. Dist. Ct. (so. and ea. dists.) N.Y. 1967, U.S. Ct. Appeals (2d cir.) 1971, U.S. Supreme Ct. 1971, U.S. Dist. Ct. (no. dist.) N.Y. 1976. Assoc. White & Case, N.Y.C., 1966-74, ptnr., 1974—. 1st lt. U.S. Army, 1961-63. Mem. ABA, N.Y. State Bar Assn., Assn. of Bar of City of N.Y., Internat. Bar Assn. Clubs: Milbrook (Greenwich, Conn.); Yale (N.Y.C.). Home: 56 Hillside Rd Greenwich CT 06830-4835 Office: White & Case Bldg Ll 1155 Avenue of The Americas New York NY 10036-2787

OSVATH, LUDOVIC LAJOS, minister; b. Lupoaia, Romania, July 22, 1938; arrived in US, 1980; s. Lajos and Anna (Feher) O.; m. Jolan Pacso, May 4, 1963; 1 child, Judith. Grad., Inst. Tech., Romania, 1954, Inst. Bus., 1957, Ady Endre Coll., 1978; student, Heritage Bapt. Inst., Cleve., 1986. Ordained to ministry Bapt.Ch., 1955. Preacher Bapt. Ch., Romania, 1955—, mem. coms., 1955-65, treas., mem. com. Zalau, Romania, 1965-73; pres. Hungarian Missionary Soc. Inc., Cleve., 1989—. Del. Romanian Bapt. Congress, Bucharest, Romania, 1978; maintenance exec. Sponge, Inc., Cleve., 1985—. Underground rep. Amnesty Internat., Romania, 1977-80; founding mem. Defenders of Religious Freedom and Ideas, Romania, 1978, persecuted and excluded from the country; mem. Internat. Christian Solidarity, Zurich, Switzerland. Mem. Christian Mgmt. Assn., Bocskai Cultural Soc. (sec. 1988—).

OSVER, ARTHUR, artist; b. Chgo., July 26, 1912; s. Harry and Yetta (Woodrov) O.; m. Ernestine Betsberg, Aug. 12, 1940. Student, Northwestern U., 1930-31, Art Inst. Chgo., 1931-36, Dartmouth U., 1997. Instr. art Washington U., St. Louis, 1960-83. Works exhbtd., Art Inst. Chgo., Pa. Acad. Art, Carnegie Inst., Whitney Mus., St. Louis Art Mus., Nelson Gallery, Atkins Mus., Corcoran Art Gallery, U. Ill. Ann., Mus. Modern Art, Met. Mus., others, works in permanent collections, Whitney Mus., Toledo Mus., Isaac Delgado Mus., Peabody Mus., Rio de Janeiro Mus.; artist in residence, U. Fla., 1954-55; trustee emeritus Am. Acad Rome, 1993, artist in residence, 1957-58, one man shows, Wilson Gallery, Chgo., 1940, Grand Central Moderns, N.Y.C., 1947, 49, 51, 56, U. Tenn., 1948, Syracuse U., 1949, Hamline U., 1950, U. Fla., 1951, 55, Fairweather-Hardin Gallery, Chgo., 1953, 55, 69, Dartmouth U., Hanover, N.H., 1997, St. Louis Art Mus., 2000, others. Recipient John Barton Paine medal Va. Mus., 1944, purchase prize U. Ill., 1949, Temple gold medal and purchase prize Pa. Acad., Prix de Rome, 1952, 53, J. Henry Schiedt prize Pa. Acad. Fine Arts, award Am. Acad. and Inst. Arts and Letters, 1991, Arts & Edn. Excellence in Painting award, Arts and Edn. Coun. Greater St. Louis, 1994, Andrew Carnegie Painting award, Nat. Acad. Design, 2003; James Nelson Raymond traveling fellow, 1936-38; Guggenheim fellow, 1950-51; sabbatical leave grantee Nat. Endowment Arts. Mem. Audubon Artists, Artists Equity. Address: 465 Foote Ave Webster Groves MO 63119-1502

OSWALD, JAMES MARLIN, education educator; b. Plainview, Tex., Aug. 17, 1935; s. James Buchanan and Eula Bea (Marlin) O.; m. Dorothy Anne Veigel, Dec. 27, 1956; children: Richard, Ramona, Roberta. BS, West Tex. State Coll., 1957, MA, 1958; EdD, Stanford U., 1970. Tchr., supr. Salt Lake City Pub. Schs., 1958-66; curriculum specialist Am. Insts. Rsch., 1966-68; staff assoc. Nat. Coun. Social Studies, 1968-69; asst. prof. social studies and social sci. edn. Syracuse (N.Y.) U., 1969-72; rschr.-writer, dir. global cultural studies edn. projects Am. Univs. Field Staff, 1972-75; asst. supt. instrn. East Penn Sch. Dist., Emmaus, Pa., 1975-78; field coord. Pa., Del. and N.J. citizen edn. Rsch. for Better Schs., Phila., 1978-80; instrnl. devel. specialist C.C. Phila., 1980-96; energy conservation cons., 1959—; edn. cons., 1963—. Propr. Energy Cons. and Main Line Stoves, 1972—; pres. N.Y. State Coun. Social Studies, 1971-72; co-founder, pres. Inst. Plant Based Nutrition, 1996—; cons. in field. Author: The Monroe Doctrine: Does It Survive?, 1969; Research in Social Studies and Social Science Education, 1972; co-author: Earthship, 1974, Planet Earth, 1976, Our Home, the Earth, 1980, Marco Polo Vegan Cuisine, 1998, Christopher Columbus Vegan Cuisine, 1999, Criteria for Nutritional Guidelines for Century 21, 1999, Ferdinand Magellan Vegan Cuisine, 2000, Commemoration of Heroic Produce Grower Sacrifices, Death and Survival on September 11, 2001, 2001, Garden of Eden Vegan Cuisine, 2003, Astronaut Vegan Cuisine, 2003, New York City Vegan Cuisine, 2003, Philadelphia Vegan Cuisine, 2003; introduced concepts of global cultural studies, 1972, humanself, 1972, zero runoff landscaping, 1979, veganomics, 1998, veganocracy, 1998, veganagro, 1998, miniagro, 2001, microagro, 2003; editor quar. newsletter Plant Based Nutrition; contbr. articles to profl. jours. With U.S. Army, 1957-58, USAR, 1958-68. Recipient Sertoma Svc. to Mankind award, Salt Lake City, 1966; grantee Stanford U., NSF, U.S. Office Edn., Inst. Internat. Studies; Henry Newell fellow Stanford U., 1966-68; Fulbright-Hays SEAsia U. Singapore Study Program fellow, 1967. Mem. Am. Vegan Soc. (life), Vegan Soc. (U.K.), Vegan Organic Network Horticulture-Agr. (U.K.), Hastings-Halliburton Vegetarian Assn. (Can.), Inst. Nutrition Edn. and Rsch. (bd. advisor), Inst. Plant Based Nutrition, N.Am. Vegetarian Soc. (life), Physicians Com. for Responsible Medicine, Vegetarians of Phila., Vegetarian Resource Group, Toronto Vegetarian Assn., Main Line Vegan Soc. (founding pres.), Ctr. for Cancer Edn., Hindu Temple Soc. Am., Internat. Soc. Kirsna Consciousness, Food for Life Internat., Internat. Oak Soc., Social Sci. Edn. Consortium (life), Tex. Panhandle-Plains Hist. Soc., Utah Hist. Soc. (life), Desc. Founders of Ancient Windsor, Windsor Hist. Soc., Pa. Assn. for Sustainable Agr., Farm Animal Reform Mvmt., Pa. Hort. Soc., Pa. Forestry Assn., Pa. State Hort. Assn., Pa. Fruit Grower Assn., Pa. Vegetable Growers Assn., Pa. Nut Growers Assn., Vegetable Growers Assn. N.J., Lower Merion Hist. Soc., Va. Nut Growers Assn., Stanford Club Phila., Keystone Trails Assn., Phi Delta Kappa (emeritus). Home and Office: 333 Bryn Mawr Ave Bala Cynwyd PA 19004-2606 Office Phone: 610-667-6876. E-mail: jmoswald@bellatlantic.net.

OSWALD, ROBERT BERNARD, retired science administrator, nuclear engineer; b. Detroit, May 25, 1932; s. Robert Bernard and Leona Virginia (LeFave) O.; m. Judith Ann Dick, Feb. 3, 1964; children: Robert Vernon, Susan Marie. BS in Math., BSME, U. Mich., 1957, MSME, 1958, PhD in Nuc. Engring., 1964. Rsch. physicist Harry Diamond Labs., U.S. Army, Washington, 1964-69, chief radiation, phys. br., 1970-72, chief rsch. lab., 1972-76, assoc. tech. dir. Adelphi, Md., 1976-79; asst. to dep. dir. sci. and tech. Def. Nuc. Agy., Alexandria, Va., 1979-81; tech. dir. Electronic R&D Command, U.S. Army, Adelphi, 1981-85; corp. v.p. Sci. Application Internat. Corp., McLean, Va., 1985-87; dir. R & D C.E. Washington, 1987-96; exec. dir. strategic environ. R & D program, 1992-94; ret., 1996. Vis. prof. dept. nuc. engring. U. Mich., Ann Arbor, 1969-70. Contbr. articles to profl. jours. With USAF, 1950-53. Recipient Louis J. Hamilton award U. Mich., 1973, Disting. Exec. award Pres. of U.S., 1983, Meritorious Exec. Pres. award, 1991, 96; Boeing fellow, 1957-58, Atomic Energy Spl. fellow, 1961-63. Fellow IEEE; mem. Am. Phys. Soc., Soc. Mil. Engrs., Cath. Acad. Scis., Cosmos Club. Republican. Roman Catholic. Avocations: sailing, woodworking, gardening, golf.

OSWALD, RUDOLPH A. economist; b. Milw., Aug. 4, 1932; s. Carl J. and Anne O.; m. Mary Louise Hurney BA, Holy Cross Coll., 1954; postgrad. (Fulbright scholar), U. Munich, W. Ger., 1954-55; MS, U. Wis., Madison, 1958; PhD in Econs., Georgetown U., 1965. Research and edn. dir. Internat. Assn. Fire Fighters, Washington, 1959-63; economist research dept. AFL-CIO, Washington, 1963-72, asst. dir. edn. dept., 1975-76, dir. research dept., 1976-96, economist-in-residence George Meany Ctr for Labor Studies, 1996—. Vis. prof. Cornell U., 1997, 99, 2000; rsch. dir. Svc. Employees Internat. Union, Washington, 1972-75, instr. GM-UAW Paid Ednl. Leave program, 2001-02; adj. prof. econs. George Washington U., 1966-75; mem. Fed. Employees Pay Coun., 1970-72, Sec. Navy's Adv. Bd. Edn. and Tng., 1975-78, Nat. Commn. Employment and Unemployment Stats., Fgn. Investment Adv. Com.; mem. adv. coun. Indsl. Labor Rels. Sch., Cornell U., 1981-85, 95-99, Sch. Bus. U. S.C. 1992-98; mem. consumer adv. com. SEC, 1994-98mem. labor adv. coun. Bur. Labor Stats.; mem. Pres.'s Adv. Com. on Trade, 1984-98; mem adv. com. Ex-Im Bank, 1989-92. Bd. dirs. Nat. Industries for the Blind, 1965-71. Served with U.S. Army, 1956-57. Mem. Indsl. Rels. Rsch. Assn. (past pres.), Nat. Bur. Econ. Rsch. (dir.), Nat. Policy Assn. (dir. 1988-2003), Nat. Coun. on Econ. Edn. (dir. 1976-96). Home: 11804 Devilwood Dr Rockville MD 20854-3407 Office: George Meany Labor Studies Ctr 10000 New Hampshire Ave Silver Spring MD 20903-1706

OSWALD, STANTON S. lawyer; b. Phila., Oct. 15, 1927; s. Sylvan J. and Myra O.; m. Bernice Boorstein, June 17, 1951; children: Jane Easley, Eve Robbins, David Oswald, Beth Oswald. BA, U. Pa., 1949; LLB magna cum laude, Harvard U., 1952. Bar: Pa., 1953. Law clk. to Judge William L. Hastie U.S. Ct. Appeals Third Circuit, Phila., 1952-53; assoc. Wolf, Block, Schorr & Solis-Cohen, Phila., 1953-63, ptnr., 1963-95, of counsel, 1995—. Trustee, hon. dir. Congregation Adath Jeshurun, Melrose Park; past chmn. bd. dirs. Pa. affiliate Am. Diabetes Assn., past chmn. bd. dirs. Phila. chpt. With USAAF, 1946-47. Mem. ABA, Pa. Bar Assn., Phila. Bar Assn. Democrat. Jewish. Office: Wolf Block Schorr & Solis-Cohen LLP 1650 Arch St 22d Fl Philadelphia PA 19103-2029 Office Phone: 215-977-2192. E-mail: soswald@wolfblock.com.

OSWALT, ROY E. professional baseball player; b. Kosciusko, Miss., Aug. 29, 1977; m. Nichol Oswalt. Baseball player Houston Astros, 2001—. Named Rookie of Yr., Baseball Writers Assn. Am. (BBWAA) Houston chpt.; named to TOPPS All-Rookie team; recipient Sporting News NL Rookie Pitcher of Yr. honors. Office: Houston Astros Po Box 288 Houston TX 77001-0288

OSWELL, AUDREY S. casino executive; b. Phila. m. Marc Oswell. BA, Temple U.; MBA, Drexel U. With fin. dept. Caesars Atlantic City, from 1979; various fin., mktg. and hotel ops. positions Caesars Atlantic City and Caesars World Corp.; sr. v.p. mktg. Caesars Atlantic City Hotel/Casino; gen. mgr., exec. v.p. Caesars Atlantic City, 1996-99, pres., COO, 1999—. Also involved with Sheraton Atlantic City and Dower Downs slot machines. Bd. dirs. Miss America Orgn., N.J. State Aquarium, Atlantic County Spl. Svcs. Edn. Found.; chmn. governance bd. Success By 6; chmn. ann. F.D.R. cmty. svc. award March of Dimes. Inducted into Class of 1997, Acad. Women Achievers, YWCA, 1997; recipient honor Exec. Women N.J., Woman of Achievement award Englewood and Cliffs chpt. Women's Am. ORT; named Businesswoman of Yr., Greater Atlantic City C. of C., 1998. Mem. South Jersey C. of C. (bd. dirs.). Office: Caesars Atlantic City Atlantic City NJ 08401

OSYCZKA, BOHDAN DANNY, painter; b. Herkimer, N.Y., May 18, 1921; s. Anton and Julia Osyczka; m. Miriam Mimi Reibach, Sept. 22, 1943; children: Michael Edward, Kris Stefan, Jory Peter. Student, Syracuse (N.Y.) U., 1943. Painter, Peekskill, NY, 1943—; staff illustrator Comart Assocs.,

N.Y., 1947—69; freelance illustrator N.Y., 1970—98. Instr. Parson Sch. Design, N.Y., 1970—94; illustrator Fine Arts Exhbn. Nat. Assn. Art Svcs., 1964; illustrator Fine Arts Divsn. O. Swaroski and Co., 1967. Author: N.Y. Times, Sci., 1990. Lt. ETO USN, 1943—46. Recipient Watercolor award, Nat. Acad. Design, 1950, Purchase award, Hudson River Mus., 1976, Honor award, Osaka Mus., 1994, NY Times Sci. award, Dswaroski and Co., 1990, Jewelry Design award, 1967. Mem.: Aaron Copland Heritage Assn. (founding mem. 1993—98), NY Artist Equity Assn. (bd. dir. 1977—99), Katonah Mus. Artist Assn. (mem. adv. bd. 1992—2004). Avocations: golf, walking. Home: 1450 Summit Ave Peekskill NY 10566

OTA, KATSUHIRO JUSTIN, language educator; MA, U. Hawaii, 1986; MBA, Chaminade U., 1989; PhD, U. Hawaii, 1999. Instr. Chinese, Japanese and Taiwanese U. Hawaii at Manoa, Honolulu, 1993—. Office: U Hawaii at Manoa 1890 East-West Rd Moore Hall 382 Honolulu HI 96822 E-mail: ota@hawaii.edu.

OTAKA, HIDEAKI (HARRY OTAKA), automotive executive; Various positions in sales, mktg., and mfg. for US, Europe, Africa, the Middle East, Southwest Asia, Oceania Toyota Motor Corp., 1965—; pres., CEO Delphys Inc. subs. of Toyota (formerly Nambokusha, Inc.), 1999—2004; CEO Toyota N. Am., 2004—. Office: Toyota Motor N Am Inc 9 W 57th St Ste 4900 New York NY 10019-2701 Office Phone: 212-223-0303. Office Fax: 212-759-7670.

OTANI, MIKE, optical company executive; b. Atsumi, Aichi, Japan, July 25, 1945; s. Yuichi and Miyako (Suzuki) O.; m. Jane Ashley Campbell, Aug. 25, 1976; 1 child, Michael Taro. Degree in Internat. Fin. and Econs., Shiga U., Japan, 1967. Office mgr. Kumagai Gumi Ltd, Osaka, Japan, 1968—73; dude rancher Tumbling River Ranch, Grant, Colo., 1974—77; merchandiser Nobel, Inc., Denver, 1978—82; v.p. Charmant Eyewear, Inc., Morris Plains, NJ, 1983—88, pres., CEO, 1988—; chmn., CEO, bd. dirs. Aristar, Inc., Morris Plains, 1994—. Bd. dirs. Charmant Optical Co., Ltd., Fukui, Japan, Charmant Optical GmbH Europe, Munich, Charmant Eyewear, Inc., Charmant Eyewear, Inc., London and Paris; pres. Charmant Internat. de Mexico, 1997—. Donor Project Literacy U.S., Pitts., 1990, Pa. Coll. Optometry, Phila., 1990; organizer N.J.-Fukui Sister State Activity, 1990; active Big Bros. and Big Sisters of Morris County, 1993—. Recipient Vendor of Yr. award Walmart, Inc., 1991, Cole Nat. & Pearl Vision, 1997. Mem. Optical Mfrs. Assn. (bd. dirs. 1988-92, Star of Vision award 2002), Fukui-N.Y. Club (chmn. 1996-). Avocations: golf, horseback riding, reading, travel, fishing. Office: Charmant Eyewear Inc 400 American Rd Morris Plains NJ 07950-2461

OTELLINI, PAUL S. electronics company executive; b. San Francisco, Oct. 12, 1950; BA in Econs., U. San Francisco, 1972; MBA, U. Calif., Berkeley, 1974. Various positions to sr. v.p. Intel Architecture Bus. Group, Santa Clara, Calif., 1974—93; sr. v.p., 1993—96; exec. v.p., gen. mgr., 1996—2002; pres., COO, 2002—. Office: 2200 Mission College Blvd Santa Clara CA 95052

OTERO-SMART, INGRID AMARILLYS, advertising executive; b. Santurce, P.R., Jan. 9, 1959; d. Angel Miguel and Carmen (Prann) Otero; m. Dean Edward Smart, May 4, 1991; 1 child, Jordan. BA in Comm., U. P.R., 1981. Traffic mgr. McCann-Erickson Corp., San Juan, P.R., 1981-82, media analyst, 1982, asst. account exec., 1982-83, account exec., 1983-84, sr. account exec., 1984-85, account dir., 1985-87; account supr. Mendoza-Dillon & Assocs., Newport Beach, Calif., 1987-89, sr. v.p. client svcs., 1989-96, exec. v.p., dir. client svcs., 1996—99; Pres. & COO Mendoza-Dillon & Assoc., Aliso Viejo, Calif., 1999—. Mem. Youth Motivation Task Force, Santa Ana, Calif., 1989—; bd. dirs. Orange County Hispanic C. of C., Santa Ana, 1989-90, U.S. Hispanic Family of Yr.; mem. Santa Ana Project P.R.I.D.E., 1993. Mem. Assn. Hispanic Advt. Agys. (bd. dirs. 1998—, pres. 2002-03). Avocations: reading, writing, antiques, music, theater. Office: Mendoza-Dillon 65 Enterprise, Ste 420 Aliso Viejo CA 92656

OTHERSEN, HENRY BIEMANN, JR., surgeon, physician, educator; b. Charleston, S.C., Aug. 26, 1930; s. Henry and Lydia Albertine (Smith) O.; m. Janelle Lester, Apr. 4, 1959; children: Megan, Mandy, Margaret, Henry Biemann III. BS, Coll. Charleston, 1950; MD, Med. Coll. S.C., 1953. Diplomate: Am. Bd. Surgery, Am. Bd. Thoracic Surgery, Am. Bd. Pediatric Surgery. Intern Phila. Gen. Hosp., 1953-54; postgrad. U. Pa., 1956-57; resident in gen. surgery Med. Coll. S.C., Charleston, 1957-62; resident in pediatric surgery Ohio State U. and Columbus Children's Hosp., 1962-64; research fellow Harvard U., Mass. Gen. Hosp., Boston, 1964-65; asst. prof. pediatric surgery Med. U. S.C., Charleston, 1965-68, assoc. prof., 1968-72, prof., 1972—, chief pediatric surgery, 1972-98; med. dir. Med. U. S.C. Hosp., 1981-85, Children's Hosp., 1985—2001, med. dir. profl. staff, 1996—2001, physician liaison for documentation, 2002—; acting chief surgery VA Hosp., 2002—. Editor The Pediatric Airway; mem. editorial bd. Jour. Pediatric Surgery, Jour. Parenteral and Enteral Nutrition; contbr. articles on pediatric oncology, esophageal, tracheal strictures to profl. jours. Bd. dirs., pres. S.C. divsn. Am. Cancer Soc., 1977-79. Served with USN, 1954-56, Korea. Fellow ACS, Am. Acad. Pediatrics; mem. Am. Pediatric Surg. Assn. (bd. govs. 1986-89, pres.-elect 1996, pres. 1997), Brit. Assn. Pediatric Surgeons (overseas coun.), Am. Surg. Assn., So. Surg. Assn., Am. Trauma Soc., Charleston County Med. Soc. (pres. 1980), Alpha Omega Alpha (councilor 1978-94). Office: Pediatric Surgery PO Box 250613 96 Jonathan Lucas St Ste 418 CSB Charleston SC 29425 Office Phone: 843-792-3851. Business E-Mail: othershb@musc.edu. *A man ought to do what he thinks is right.*

OTHMAN, TALAT MOHAMAD, financial consultant, investment banker; b. Betunia, Palestine, Apr. 27, 1936; arrived in U.S., 1947, naturalized, 1954; s. Mohamad Racheed and Damelize Ahmed Othman; m. Haleema Othman; children: Joseph, Suad, Jamil, Rashid. Student, Northwestern U. With Harris Bank, Chgo., 1956—78, v.p., div. head, 1974—78; gen. mgr., CEO Saudi Arab Fin. Corp., S.A., Paris, 1978—83; pres. Dearborn Fin., Inc., Arlington Hts., Ill., 1983—95; chmn. Grove Fin. Inc., 1995—. Mem. adv. bd. Ovation Pharm., Inc.; bd. dirs. Bank One Wis. Corp., Milw., Harken Oil and Gas Co., Dallas, Pathogenesis Corp., Seattle; chmn. Dansk Internat. Designs, Inc., Mt. Kisko, NY, 1985—91, Goodson Polymer, Inc., Troy, Ohio, 1987—88. Contbr. chpts. to, articles and booklets. Bd. dirs. Inst. World Affairs, Milw., 1986—89, Khail Gibran Meml. com., Washington, 1987—89; pres. Islamic Cultural Ctr.; mem. adv. bd. Kennedy Sch. Govt. Harvard U.; mem. hon. bd. Mid East Studies Ctr. U. Chgo.; bd. dirs. St. Jude Children's Rsch. Hosp., 1991—, Ch. Alsac-Am. Lebanese Syrian Associated Charities. Recipient Outstanding Pres. award proclaiming Talat M. Othman Day in Ill., Nov. 1, 1997. Mem.: Forex Assn. of N.Am. (chmn., founding pres. Chgo. chpt. 1976, recipient plaque of Appreciation), Arab Bankers Assn. (pres. 1985—87, bd. dirs. 1984—89, recipient plaque of Appreciation), Mid. Am. Arab C. of C. (bd. dirs. 1974—78, founding pres. 1977, bd. dirs. 1984—91, recipient plaque of Appreciation), Chgo. Club. Muslim. Avocations: tennis, racquetball, reading. E-mail: grovefinancial@worldnet.att.net.

OTHS, RICHARD PHILIP, health systems administrator; b. N.Y.C., July 3, 1935; s. Philip John and Florence Violet (Kraus) O.; m. Eleanor Fuerst, May 11, 1957; children— Philip, Lisa, Eleanor, Richard. BS in Pharmacy, Fordham U., 1956; MBA in Health Care Adminstrn., CUNY, 1976. Field sales rep. E.R. Squibb & Sons, N.Y.C., 1960-63, hosp. rep., 1963-65, div. mgr., 1965-68; adminstr. operating room Mt. Sinai Hosp., N.Y.C., 1968-69, dir. admitting, 1969-71, asst. dir. hosp., 1971-76; v.p., mgr. Bethesda Hosp. Oak, Cin., 1976-84; pres. Am. Health Capital HIBI Mgmt., Inc., N.Y.C., 1984-88; pres., CEO Morristown (N.J.) Meml. Hosp., 1988-96. Atlantic Health System, Florham Park, N.J., 1996—. Goldwater fellow in hosp. adminstr. Mt. Sinai Hosp., N.Y.C., 1973; cons. Physicians Protective Trust Fund-Fla. Served with USAF, 1957-60. Recipient award E.R. Squibb-AMA, 1964. Mem. APHA, ACHA, Am. Hosp. Assn. Republican. Roman Catholic. Home: 26 Glen Gary Dr Mendham NJ 07945-3030 Office: 325 Columbia Tpke Florham Park NJ 07932-1212

OTIENO, TABITHA NYABOKE, social sciences educator, researcher; d. Alfayo Momanyi and Milka Nyambeki Otieno. PhD in Social Sci., Ohio U., 1994. Tchr. Kenya Teachers Commn., Kisii, 1981—85; lectr. Kisii Coll., 1986—89; assoc. prof. Jackson State U., Jackson, Miss., 1995—. Cons. Winona Separate Pub. Schs., Winona, Miss., 2003—04. Exhibitions include African Cultural Exhibits; contbr. articles to profl. jours. Mem.: Nat. Coun. Social Studies. Office: Jackson State University 1400 R Lynch Box 17175 MS 39217 Jackson MS E-mail: totieno@ccaix.jsums.edu.

OTIS, JACK, social work educator; b. N.Y.C., Feb. 13, 1923; s. Abraham and Esther (Goldberg) O.; children: Elisabeth H., Erich R., Greta M., Marcus H., Alicia. AB, Bklyn. Coll., 1946; MS in Social Work, U. Ill., 1948, M.Ed., 1955, PhD, 1957. Social worker Jewish Social Svc. Bur. Dade County, 1948-49; Psychiat. social worker Free Synagogue Social Service, N.Y. U., 1949-50; asso. prof. U. Ill., 1950-61; dep. dir. Office Juvenile Delinquency and Youth Devel., Dept. Health, Edn. and Welfare, 1961-65; dean Grad. Sch. Social Work U. Tex., 1965-77, prof. emeritus, 1993—. Cons. to govt., 1961—; presenter Internat. Coun. on Social Welfare, Inter-Univ. Consortium for Internat. Social Devel., Internat. Assn. Schs. Social Work, 1994; dep. dir. Pres.'s Com. Juvenile Delinquency and Youth Crime, 1961-65; spl. cons. for Am. social work edn. and rsch. European Ctr. for Social Welfare Tng. and Rsch., Vienna, Austria, 1976—; Dean Dan Sanders Meml. lectr. U. Ill., 1999. Author: (with George Barnett) Corporate Society and Education, 1961; contbr. article on child labor to Ency. Social Work, 1995. Bd. overseers Ctr. for Study Violence, Brandeis U., 1966-70; commencement spkr. U. Tex. Sch. Social Work, 2001. With AUS, 1943-46, PTO. Fulbright-Hays rsch.fellow Austria, 1977-78; established Dean Jack Otis Ann. Social Policy awards U. Tex., 2002. Mem. AAUP, Coun. on Social Work Edn. (commn. on accreditation), Philosophy of Edn. Soc., Nat. Assn. Social Workers (chair Calif. Task Force on Child Labor 2001-03), Am. Acad. Polit. and Social Sci., N.Y. Acad. Sci., Johannesburg Child Welfare Soc. (rsch. cons. South Africa chpt. 1990-91), Phi Kappa Phi (pres.). *The meaning of my life is whether I have added to the meaning of another's.*

OTIS, JOHN JAMES, civil engineer; b. Syracuse, N.Y., Aug. 5, 1922; s. John Joseph and Anna (Dey) O.; m. Dorothy Fuller Otis, June 21, 1958; children: Mary Eileen Dawn, John Leon. B in Chem. Engring., Syracuse U., 1943, MBA, 1950, postgrad., 1951-55. Registered profl. engr., Ala., Tex. Jr. process engr. GM, Syracuse, 1951-53, prodn. engr., 1954-58, process control engr., 1958-59, process engr., 1960-61; engr., writer GE, Syracuse, 1961-63, configuration control engr. Phila., 1969; assoc. rsch. engr. Boeing Co., Huntsville, Ala., 1963-65; assoc. Planning Rsch. Corp., Huntsville, 1965-67; prin. engr. Brown Engring. Co. subs. Teledyne Co., Huntsville, 1967-69; mech. designer Drever Co., Beth Ayres, Pa., 1970-71; civil engr. U.S. Army Corps Engrs., Mobile, Ala., 1971-74, Galveston, Tex., 1974—. Lector, lay minister Roman Cath. Ch. Served with USNR, 1944-50. Mem. Am. Inst. Indsl. Engrs. (past v.p. Syracuse and Huntsville chpts.), Tex. Soc. Profl. Engrs. (dir. Galveston County chpt. 1976-79, sec.-treas. 1979-80, v.p. 1980-81, pres. 1982-83), Am. Legion, Tau Beta Pi, Phi Kappa Tau, Alpha Chi Sigma, Chi Eta Sigma. Home: 2114 Yorktown Ct N League City TX 77573-5056 Office: US Army Corps Engrs Jadwin Bldg 2000 Fort Point Rd Galveston TX 77550-3038 Office Phone: 409-766-3157. E-mail: john.j.otis@swg02.usace.army.mil., jotis1@evl.net.

OTIS, LEE LIBERMAN, lawyer, educator; b. N.Y.C., Aug. 19, 1956; d. James Benjamin and Deen (Freed) L.; m. William Graham Otis, Oct. 24, 1993. BA, Yale U., 1979; JD, U. Chgo., 1983. Bar: N.Y. 1985, D.C. 1994. Law clk. U.S. Ct. Appeals (D.C. cir.), Washington, 1983-84; spl. asst. to asst. atty. gen., civil div. U.S. Dept. Justice, Washington, 1984-86, dep. assoc. atty. gen., 1986, assoc. dep. atty. gen., 1986; law clk. to Justice Antonin Scalia U.S. Supreme Ct., Washington, 1986-87; asst. prof. law George Mason U., Arlington, Va., 1987-89; assoc. counsel to the Pres. Exec. Office of the Pres., Washington, 1989-92; assoc. Jones, Day, Reavis & Pogue, Washington, 1993-94; chief judiciary coun. U.S. Sen. Spence Abraham, 1995-96; chief counsel subcom. on immigration Com. on the Judiciary, U.S. Senate, 1997-2000; gen. counsel U.S. Dept. Energy, 2001—. Adj. prof. law Georgetown Law Sch., 1995, 96. Mem. Federalist Soc. for Law and Pub. Policy (founder). Republican. Jewish. Avocations: sailing, computers.

O'TOOLE, AUSTIN MARTIN, lawyer; b. New Bedford, Mass., Oct. 5, 1935; s. John Brian, Jr. and Helen Veronica O'T.; m. Valerie Sherlock O'Toole; children: Erin Ann, Austin Martin Jr. BBA, Coll. Holy Cross, 1957; JD, Georgetown U., 1963. Bar: N.Y. 1965, D.C. 1963, Tex. 1975. Law clk. to judge U.S. Ct. Appeals, Washington, 1962-63; assoc. White & Case, N.Y.C., 1963-74; sr. v.p., sr. counsel, sec. Coastal Corp., Houston, 1974—2001. Bd. editors Georgetown Law Jour., 1962-63. Bd. dirs. Nat. Coun. on Alcoholism and Drug Dependency, Inc., 2001—; charter mem., certificated mediator Inst. for Responsible Dispute Resolution, Houston, 2000—; bd. dirs. Houston Marathon Com., 1973—2002. Officer USMC, 1957—60. Mem. ABA, Am. Soc. Corp. Secs. (bd. dirs. 1982-85), State Bar of Tex., Houston Bar Assn. (past chmn. corp. counsel sect. 1979-80), Am. Arbitration Assn. (comml. com.). Home: 2200 Willowick (10-H) Houston TX 77027 Office: 509 Nineteenth St Galveston TX 77550 E-mail: austinotoole@msn.com.

O'TOOLE, FRANCIS J. lawyer; b. Dublin, Feb. 10, 1944; came to U.S., 1960; s. Francis Herbert and Josephine (McCarthy) O'T.; m. Carole Ann Leland, Apr. 11, 1977; children: Kathleen, Kirra. AB, Harvard U., 1967; JD, U. Maine, 1970. Bar: Maine 1970, U.S. Supreme Ct. 1977, U.S. Dist. Ct. D.C., U.S. Dist. Ct. (ea. dist.) Va., U.S. Ct. Appeals (1st, 2d, 4th, 5th, 7th, 8th, 9th and 10th cirs.). Assoc. Fried, Frank, Harris, Shriver & Jacobsen, Washington, 1971-78, ptnr., 1978-92, Sidley & Austin, Washington, 1992—. Editor-in-chief U. Maine Law Rev., 1969-70; contbr. articles to profl. jours. Reginald Heber Smith fellow Calif. Indian Legal Services, 1970-71. Mem. ABA. Avocation: horse breeding and racing. Home: 7700 Burford Dr Mc Lean VA 22102-2105 Office: Sidley Austin Brown & Wood 1501 K St NW #LL Washington DC 20005-1401

O'TOOLE, JAMES JOSEPH, business educator; b. San Francisco, Apr. 15, 1945; s. James Joseph and Irene (Nagy) O'T.; m. Marilyn Louise Burrill, June 17, 1967; children: Erin Kathleen, Kerry Louise. BA, U. So. Calif., L.A., 1966; DPhil, Oxford (Eng.) U., (Eng.), 1970. Corr. Time-Life News Service, L.A., 1967-68, Nairobi, Kenya, 1967-68; mgmt. cons. McKinsey & Co., San Francisco, 1969-70; coordinator field investigations Pres.'s Comm. on Campus Unrest, Washington, 1970; spl. asst. to sec. HEW, Washington, 1970-73; prof. mgmt. U. So. Calif., L.A., 1973-93, Univ. Assocs. Chair of Bus., 1982-93; v.p. Aspen Inst., 1994-97; mng. dir. Booz-Allen & Hamilton Leadership Ctr., San Francisco, 1997—; rsch. prof. Ctr. for Effective Orgn., U. So. Calif., 1999—. Chmn. sec.'s com. work in Am. HEW, Washington, 1971-72; exec. dir. The Leadership Inst., 1990-93; bd. dirs. Radica Games. Prin. author: Work in America, 1973, Energy and Social Change, 1976; author: Work, Learning and the American Future, 1977, Making America Work, 1982 (Phi Kappa Phi prize 1982), Vanguard Management, 1985, The Executive's Compass, 1993, Leading Change, 1995, Leadership A to Z, 1999; bd. editors: Ency. Britannica, 1981-87; editor: New Management, 1983-89, The American Oxonian, 1996-98. Active Project Paideia, Chgo., 1981-83. Rhodes scholar, 1966; recipient Mitchell prize Woodlands Conf., 1979. Mem. Phi Beta Kappa. Home: 23852 Pacific Coast Hwy Ste 364 Malibu CA 90265-4879 Office: U So Calif Ctr Effective Orgns Los Angeles CA 90089-0806 E-mail: otoole_jim@bah.com.

O'TOOLE, KATHLEEN M. police commissioner; m. Dan O'Toole; 1 child. BA, Boston Coll.; JD, New Eng. Sch. Law. Bar: Mass. 1982. Officer Boston Police Dept., 1979-86; officer, supt. Met. Police Dept., 1986-90; security mgmt. Digital Equipment Corp., 1990-92; lt. col. Mass. State Police, 1992-94; sec. Office Pub. Safety, Boston, 1994—98; commr. Boston Police Dept., 2004—. Office: Boston Police Hdqs One Schroeder Plz Boston MA 02120-2014*

O'TOOLE, LAURENCE JOSEPH, public administration and policy educator, researcher; b. Syracuse, N.Y., Dec. 7, 1948; s. Laurence Joseph and Marjorie Rose (Weinheimer) O.; m. Mary Irene Gilroy, June 26, 1971; children: Conor Gilroy O'Toole, Kathleen Easton O'Toole. BS with high honors, Clarkson U., 1970; MPA, Syracuse U., 1972, PhD, 1975. Asst. prof. polit. sci. U. Va., Charlottesville, 1975-79; assoc. prof. polit. sci. Auburn U., Ala., 1979-85, prof. polit. sci., 1985-92, U. Ga., Athens, 1992—, M. Hughes and Robert T. Golembiewski prof. pub. adminstrn., 2000—, head dept. pub. admisntrn. and policy, 2002—. Vis. rsch. Internat. Inst. Mgmt. Sci. Ctr., Berlin, 1978; prof. comparative sustainability policy studies Ctr. for Clean Tech. and Environ. Policy, Twente U., The Netherlands, 1994—; sr. rsch. assoc. Carl Vinson Inst. of Govt., U. Ga., Athens, 1994-2002; mem., bd. editors Administrn. and Society, Blacksburg, Va., 1995—, Administrv. Theory and Praxis, San Francisco, 1995-2002, Beleidswetenschap Groningen, The Netherlands, 1997—, Evaluation and Program Planning, 2000—, Jour. Pub. Affairs Edn., 2001—. Co-author: American Government: Origins, Institutions and Public Policy, 1984, Regulatory Decision Making: The Virginia State Corporation Commission, 1984, Implementation Theory and Practice, 1990; editor: American Intergovernmental Relations, 1985, American Intergovernmental Relations, 2d rev. edit., 1993, American Intergovernmental Relations, 3d edit., 2000; co-editor: International Comparative Policy Research, 1992, Networks for Water Policy, 1995, Participation and the Quality of Environmental Decision Making, 1998, Advancing Public Management, 2000, Johns Hopkins Studies in Governance and Public Management, 2001—; author: Institutions, Processes and Outputs for Acidification, 1998; contbr. articles to profl. jours. Recipient outstanding prof. award Ga. Students for Pub. Adminstrn., Athens, 1994, 95; vis. scholar Erasmus U., Rotterdam, The Netherlands, 1989, 94. Mem. ASPA (Burchfield award 1979, Mosher award 1987, Stone award 1999, Levine award 2002, Wholey award 2004), Am. Polit. Sci. Assn. (chair pub. admin. sect. 1985), So. Polit. Sci. Assn., Pub. Mgmt. Rsch. Assn. (bd. dirs. 2001—, pres.-elect 2003—). Home; 190 Avalon Dr Athens GA 30606-3235 Office: Univ Ga Sch Pub and Internat Affairs Dept Pub/Adminstrn Policy/Baldwin Hall Athens GA 30602 E-mail: cmsotool@uga.edu.

O'TOOLE, ROBERT JOHN, II, telemarketing consultant; b. Binghamton, N.Y., Mar. 24, 1951; s. Robert John and Joan Ceclia (Martin) O'T.; m. Donna Sue Stevenson, Jan. 28, 1978 (div. 1984); 1 child, Irene Grace; m. Karen Irene Cady, Dec. 21, 1994. Student, Corning (N.Y.) C.C., 1969-71, SUNY, Brockport, 1970-71; BA, Wake Forest U., 1973; MBA, Southwestern Coll., 1986. Asst. dir. devel. Duvall Home for Children, DeLand, Fla., 1978-81; gen. mgr. Royale Art Advt., Odessa, Tex., 1981-82; v.p. Barnes Assocs. Advt., Odessa, 1982-84, Tex. Assn. for Blind Athletes, Austin, 1985-86; sales mgr. Los Amables Pub., Albuquerque, 1987-88; dir. devel. Albuquerque (N.Mex.) Help for the Homeless, 1988-91; chmn., CEO Advantage Ventures, Inc. (formerly Advantage Mktg., Inc.), Albuquerque, 1991—; CEO LaCourt, Medina & Sterling, Albuquerque, 1993-96. Cons. Nat. Child Safety Coun., Austin, 1985, Assn. Profl. Fire Fighters, Austin, 1985, Reynolds Aluminum, Austin, 1986, N.Mex. State Legis., 1990, Children's Charity Fund, 1996, N.Am. Found. for AIDS Rsch., 1992-93, N.Am. Pediatric AIDS Found., 1995. Author: Telemarketing Tickets, 1988, Fishing Secrets of the Florida Poachers, 1993; founder, editor: (newspaper) Albuquerque Street News, 1990; publisher: (newspaper) The New Mexican, 1991; contbr. articles to jours. Founder Permian Basin Rehab. Ctr., Odessa, 1983, Albuquerque (N.Mex.) Help for the Homeless, Inc., 1988. Recipient Cert. of Merit, Small Bus. Adminstrn., Odessa, 1984. Mem. Direct Mktg. Assn., Amnesty Internat. Avocations: restoration of historic bldgs., archeo-geomantics, travel. Office: Advantage Ventures Inc 1019 2nd St SW # B Albuquerque NM 87102-4124

O'TOOLE, WILLIAM GEORGE, lawyer; b. Chgo., Oct. 25, 1934; s. George P. and Margaret (Battenhouse) O'T.; m. Gail M. McGregor, Aug. 13, 1960; children: Joyce M. Masterton, Paul G., Katherine A. Gorski. BS, U. Detroit, 1956; JD, DePaul U., 1961. Bar: Ill. 1961, U.S. Dist. Ct. (no. dist.) Ill. 1962. Assoc. Jaros, Tittle & O'Toole (and predecessor firm), Chgo., 1961-74, ptnr., 1974-90, pres., 1990—. Mem. ABA, Ill. Bar Assn., Ill. Mortgage Bankers Assn. (bd. dirs.), Chgo. Bar Assn., Southwest Bar Assn. (past pres.), Chgo. Athletic Assn., Abbey Springs Country Club, Ridge Country Club, Elks, K.C., Beta Alpha Psi. Roman Catholic. Home: 10736 S Kolmar Ave Oak Lawn IL 60453-5349 Office: Jaros Tittle & O'Toole 20 N Clark St Ste 510 Chicago IL 60602-4188

OTOSHI, TOM YASUO, electrical engineer, consultant; b. Seattle, Sept. 4, 1931; s. Jitsuo and Shina O.; m. Haruko Shirley Yumiba, Oct. 13, 1963; children: John, Kathryn. BSEE, U. Wash., 1954; MSEE, 1957. Tech. staff Hughes Aircraft Co., Culver City, Calif., 1956-61; tech. sr. staff Jet Propulsion Lab. Calif. Inst. Tech., Pasadena, Calif., 1961—2004; ret. Cons. in field. Contbr. articles to profl. jours.; patentee in field. Treas. West L.A. United Meth. Ch., 1958-60; active Towne Singers, La Canada, Calif. Recipient New Tech. NASA award, Exceptional Svc. medal, 1994. Fellow IEEE (life); mem. Sigma Xi, Tau Beta Pi. Home: 3551 Henrietta Ave La Crescenta CA 91214-1136

OTREMBA, GERALDINE MARIE, congressional and international relations executive; b. N.Y.C., Apr. 13, 1946; d. Frank Stanley and Beatrice Gloria (O'Malley) O.; m. Stanley F. Turesky, Oct. 26, 1975; children: Sarah, Catherine. BA, St. John's U., 1967; MA, U. N.C., 1969, PhD, 1979. Dep. dir. ops. John F. Kennedy Ctr. for the Performing Arts, Washington, 1984-87, dir. planning, 1987-90, dir. ops., 1990-91, dir. govt. liaison, 1991-92, assoc. mng. dir., 1991-94; dir. of congrl. rels. Libr. Congress, Washington, 1994—99; exec. dir. Open World Leadership Ctr., 1999—. Chmn. Nat. Conf. Performing Arts Ctrs., 1990-93. Roman Catholic. Office: Open World Leadership Ctr Library of Congress 101 Independence Ave SE Washington DC 20540-9980

OTSTOTT, CHARLES PADDOCK, retired military officer, information technology executive, consultant; b. Ft. Worth, June 2, 1937; s. Daniel Dushane and Sarah May (Paddock) O.; m. Candice Lee Curley, Nov. 6, 1982; 1 child, Kelley Ann; 1 child from previous marriage, James Boyd. BS, U.S. Mil. Acad., West Point, N.Y., 1960; MS, Purdue U., 1967. Commd. 2d lt. U.S. Army, 1960, advanced through grades to lt. gen., 1990; bn. advisor Republic of Vietnam, 1964-65; co. comdr., S-3, 2d bn. 502 Inf. (Airborne) 101st Airborne Div., 1967-68; comdr. 1st bn. 46 Inf., 1st Armored Div., Erlangen, Fed. Republic Germany, 1976-78; student Nat. War Coll., Ft. McNair, D.C., 1978-79; comdr. 2d brigade 9th High Tech. Light Div., Ft. Lewis, Wash., 1979-82, chief of staff, 1982-83; exec. to SACEUR Supreme Hdqrs. Allied Powers Europe, Belgium, 1983-85; asst. div. comdr. 1st Armored Div., Bamberg, Fed. Republic Germany, 1985-86; comdg. gen. Combined Arms Combat Devel. Activity, Ft. Leavenworth, Kans., 1986-88, 25th Inf. Div. (Light), Schofield Barracks, Hawaii, 1988-90; dep. chmn. NATO Mil. Com., Brussels, 1990-92; ret., 1992; pvt. cons. strategic planning, 1992-94; with Innovative Logistics Techniques (Innolog, Inc.), 1994-96; v.p. advanced program devel. Bolt, Beranek, and Newman (BBN), 1996-99; v.p. command and control sys. Global InfoTek, 1999—2001; pvt. cons., 2001—. Instr then asst. prof. dept. physics U.S. Mil. Acad., West Point, 1968—71. Chmn. adv. com. Brussels Am. Sch., 1990-92. Decorated Def. D.S.M., Army D.S.M., Def. Superior Svc. medal, Silver Star, Legion of Merit. Avocations: golf, jogging, picture framing, woodworking. E-mail: cotstott@aol.com.

OTT, C(LARENCE) H(ENRY), ambassador, accountant; b. Richmond, Mich., Jan. 20, 1918; s. Ferdinand and Wilhelmina (Radkte) Ott; m. Helen Louise McKay, Oct. 29, 1942 (dec. Apr. 1994); children: James Richard, Dennis McKay, Richard Darrel, Delene Michelle. BA, Valparaiso U., 1940; MBA, Northwestern U., 1970; PhD, Southeastern U., 1980. CPA N.Y., cert. mgmt. acct., N.Y. Chief acct. G.E. X-Ray Corp., Chgo., 1940-41; pub. auditor Arthur Andersen & Co., Chgo., 1941-43; renegotiator contracts U.S. Army Air Corps, Chgo., 1943-45; internal auditor David Bradley Mfg. (Sears), Bradley, Ill., 1945-48; contr., treas. Manco Mfg. Co., Bradley, 1948-59; owner, operator Yellow-Checker Cab Co., Kankakee, Ill., 1959-70; chmn. acctg., prof. Rochester (N.Y.) Inst. Tech., 1970-73, Southwestern Mich. Coll., Dowagiac, Mich., 1973—; citizen amb. People to People Internat., Kansas City, Mo., 1992—. Curriculum advisor Southwestern Mich. Coll., Dowagiac, 1992—. Citizen amb. Tahiti, Bora Bora, Moorea, Cuba, Galapagos Island, Israel; del. to Russia to facilitate their transition to Dem. form of govt.; del. leader Wahrton Sch. Fin. U. Pa., Phila., 1992. Mem.: Planning Execs. Inst. (spkr., chmn.), Inst. Cert. Mgmt. Accts., Nat. Assn. Accts., Pi Gamma Mu, Pi Kappa Alpha, Alpha Kappa Psi. Republican. Avocations: travel, golf, bowling, reading, exercise. Home: 30992 Middle Crossing Rd Dowagiac MI 49047-9268

OTT, DAVID MICHAEL, engineering company executive; b. Glendale, Calif., Feb. 24, 1952; s. Frank Michael and Roberta (Michie) O.; m. Cynthia Dianne Bunce. BSEE, U. Calif., Berkeley, 1974. Electronic engr. Teknekron Inc., Berkeley, 1974-79; chief engr. TCI, Berkeley, 1979-83; div. mgr. Integrated Automation Inc., Alameda, Calif., 1983-87, Litton Indsl. Automation, Alameda, 1987-92; founder, chmn. Picture Elements Inc., Berkeley, 1992—. Inventor method for verifying denomination of currency, method for processing digited images, automatic document image revision. Mem. IEEE, AAAS, Assn. Computing Machinery, Union of Concerned Scientists. Office: Picture Elements Inc 777 Panoramic Way Berkeley CA 94704-2538

OTT, DAVID T. insurance company executive; BS in Mktg. and Bus. Mgmt., U. Mo., St. Louis, 1977. Dir., mktg. HealthLink, Inc., 1986, v.p., sales & mktg., exec. v.p., 1991—99, pres., 1999—. Office: HealthLink Hqrs 12443 Olive Blvd Saint Louis MO 63141

OTT, DORIS ANN, librarian; b. Elgin, N.D., Sept. 24, 1942; d. Oscar Edward Hirning and Lorraine Wilhelmina Gruebele; m. Richard Donald Ott, Nov. 21, 1998; m. Bernnett Gordon Reinke, Sept. 1961 (div.); 1 child, Scott Bernnett Reinke; m. James Lee Daugherty, June 1974 (div.). BS, Dickinson State U., 1964; MLS, George Peabody Coll., 1965. Lic. Ind. life tchr. Elem. tchr. Mott (N.D.) Pub. Schs., 1963-64; asst. prof. Dickinson (N.D.) State U., 1965-73; media specialist Minot (N.D.) Pub. Schs., 1973-74; head tech. svcs. Bartholomew County Libr., Columbus, Ind., 1974-75; media specialist Rushville (Ind.) Pub. Schs., 1975-86; head interlibr. loan N.D. State Libr., Bismarck, 1986-87, asst. state libr., 1987—2001, state libr., 2001—. Image cons. Beauty For All Seasons, 1984—. Mem. Humane Soc. Mem. ALA, N.D. Libr. Assn., Mountain Plains Libr. Assn. Avocation: image consulting. Office: ND State Libr 604 E Boulevard Ave Dept 250 Bismarck ND 58505-0800 Office Phone: 701-328-2492. Business E-Mail: dott@state.nd.us.

OTT, GILBERT RUSSELL, JR., lawyer; b. Bklyn., Apr. 15, 1943; s. Gilbert Russell Sr. and Bettina Rose (Ferrel) O.; m. Lisa S. Weatherford, Apr. 12, 1986; children: Gilbert R. III, Laura Elisabeth. BA, Yale U., 1965; JD, MBA, Columbia U., 1969. Bar: N.Y. 1970. Assoc. Chadbourne, Parke, Whiteside & Wolff, N.Y.C., 1969-72, LeBoeuf, Lamb, Leiby & MacRae, N.Y.C., 1972-78; assoc. gen. counsel Kidder, Peabody & Co., Inc., N.Y.C., 1978-96, asst. sec., 1978-91, asst. v.p., 1978-79, v.p., 1979-86, mng. dir., 1986-91, sr. v.p., sec., 1992-96; v.p. Kidder, Peabody Group Inc., N.Y.C., 1989-96, asst. sec., 1986-96; exec. v.p., gen. counsel, sec. Rodman & Renshaw Capital Group, Inc., Chgo. and N.Y.C., 1996-98; counsel Cadwalader, Wickersham & Taft, N.Y.C., 1998-99; dep. gen. counsel Datek Online Holdings Corp., Jersey City, 1999—2002; chief legal officer instl. divsn. Ameritrade Holding Corp., Parsippany, NJ, 2002—. Mem. Assn. of Bar of City of N.Y., Cold Spring Harbor Lab. Assn. (dir.), Piping Rock Club, Univ. Club. Home: 260 Highwood Cir Oyster Bay NY 11771-3205 Office Phone: 201-558-4061. Business E-Mail: gott@ameritrade.com.

OTT, JAMES DANIEL, journalist, educator; b. Dayton, Ky., Mar. 24, 1938; s. Arthur Daniel and Grace Mary (Bennett) O.; m. Charlotte Elizabeth Freihofer, Aug. 1, 1964; children: Alec, Stephen, Anthony, James, Michael. AB in English Lit., Thomas More Coll., 1961; MEd in Comms. Arts, Xavier U., 1973. Reporter Cin. Enquirer, 1959-65, Ky. editor, 1965-69; pub. rels. dir. Thomas More Coll., Crestview Hills, Ky., 1969-74, Cath. U. Am., Washington, 1974-78; transport editor Aviation Week and Space Tech., Washington, 1978-84, sr. transport editor, 1984-94, contbg. editor Ft. Mitchell, Ky., 1994—. Freelance writer, McGraw-Hill, Inc., Ft. Mitchell; online editor Aviation Week Group, Ft. Mitchell. Author: Jets, Airliners of the Golden Age, 1993, Airline Odyssey, 1995. Mem. adv. bd. The Messenger, 1999—. With USAR, 1956-63. Mem. Soc. Aerospace Communicators, Cathedral Found. (bd. dirs. 1997—). Republican. Roman Catholic. Avocations: swimming, hiking, reading. Office: Aviation Week and Space Tech 825 Rosewood Dr Crescent Springs KY 41017 E-mail: ott@aviationnow.com.

OTT, JOHN HARLOW, museum administrator; b. Ottawa, Ont., Can., Jan. 29, 1944; s. Thomas Gordon and Lois Elizabeth (Wright) O.; m. Lili Reineck, May 20, 1972; children— Jennie Elizabeth, Michael James Hutchins BA, Eastern Bapt. Coll., St. David's, Pa., 1966; MA, SUNY-Oneonta, 1975; postgrad. Mus. Mgmt. Inst., U. Calif., Berkeley, 1987. Curator Hancock Shaker Village, Inc., Pittsfield, Mass., 1970-72, dir., 1972-83; exec. dir. Atlanta Hist. Soc., 1983-91, B&O R.R. Mus., Inc., Balt., 1991-99, The Nat. Heritage Mus., Lexington, Mass., 1999—. Curator Ga. Hist. Soc., Savannah, 1983-87; mem. adv. bd. Concord (Mass.) Mus. Author: Hancock Shaker Village, 1976 Mem. Lexington Tourism Com., 2002—; bd. dirs. Devens Hist. Mus., 2001—03, bd. govs., 2003—. Decorated Bronze Star; named mus. profl. of yr. in Ga., 1991, profl. of yr. Acad. for Travel, Hospitality and Tourism, 1996. Mem. Am. Assn. Mus. (accrediting officer 1982—), Am. Assn. for State and Local History, Mid-Atlantic Mus. Assn., Ga. Soc. Assn. Execs., Nat. Hist. Communal Socs. Assn. (pres. 1983-84), Nat. Soc. Fund Raising Execs. (bd. dirs. Ga. chpt. 1985-91, bd. dirs. Md. chpt. 1993), Balt. City C. of C. (bd. dirs., past chmn.), Md.Assn. History Mus. (bd. dirs. 1996), Freedom's Way Heritage Assn. (bd. dirs. 2000—), Lexington C. of C. (chmn. 2002-); bd. dirs. Merrimack Valley Convention & Vis. Bureau. Republican. Episcopalian. Office: The Nat Heritage Mus 33 Marrett Rd Lexington MA 02421-5703 E-mail: jott@monh.org.

OTT, KARL OTTO, nuclear engineer, consultant; b. Hanau, Germany, Dec. 24, 1925; arrived in U.S., 1967, naturalized, 1987; s. Johann Josef and Eva (Bergmann) Ott; m. Gunhild G. Göring, Sept. 18, 1958 (div. 1986); children: Martina, Monika; m. Birgit Fehse, May 1, 1995. BS, J. W. von Goethe U., Frankfurt, Germany, 1948; MS, G. August U., Göttingen, Fed. Republic Germany, 1953, PhD, 1958. Physicist Nuc. Rsch. Ctr., Karlsruhe, Germany, 1958-67, sect. head, 1962-67; prof. Sch. Nuc. Engring. Purdue U., West Lafayette, Ind., 1967-2001, prof. emeritus, 2000—. Cons. Argonne (Ill.) Nat. Lab., 1967—. Author: (book) Nuclear Reactor Statics, 1983, 2d edit., 1989, Nuclear Reactor Dynamics, 1985, Chinese edit., 1991. Fellow: Am. Nuc. Soc. (Arthur Holly Compton award 1993). Office: Purdue U Sch Nuc Engring Lafayette IN 47907-1290 E-mail: ott@purdue.edu.

OTT, SHARON, artistic director; Theatre dir.: The Wash, Yankee Dawy You Die; artistic dir.:Berkeley Repertory Theatre; now artistic dir. Seattle Repertory Theatre. Former bd. dirs. Theatre Comms. Group, v.p. Recipient Obie award, numerous others awards. Office: Seattle Repertory Theatre 199 Mercer St Seattle WA 98109-4639

OTT, WALTER RICHARD, academic administrator; b. Bklyn., Jan. 20, 1943; s. Harold Vincent and Mary Elizabeth (Butler) Ott; m. Carla M. Narrett, May 27, 2002; children: Regina Winter Burrell, Christina W. Chiappetta, Walter R. Jr. BS in Ceramic Engring., Va. Poly. Inst. and State U., 1965; MS in Ceramic Engring., U. Ill., 1967; PhD in Ceramic Engring., Rutgers U., 1969; DSc (hon.), Alfred U., 2001. Registered profl. engr., Pa. Process engr. Corning Inc., Buckhannon, W.Va., 1965-66; staff research engr. Champion Spark Plug Co., Detroit, 1969-70; prof. engring. Rutgers U., New Brunswick, N.J., 1970-80; dean, assoc. provost N.Y. State Coll. Ceramics, Alfred, 1980-88; provost, chief acad. officer Alfred U., Alfred, 1988-2000; pres. Predictive Edge, Inc., West Orange, NJ, 2000—; v.p. enrollment mgmt. Caldwell (N.J.) Coll., 2002—. Rsch. assoc. Atomic Energy Commn.-E.I. duPont de Nemours, Aiken, S.C., 1971; cons. Haight & Hofeldt Inc., Chgo., 1984-88, Pillsbury, Mpls., 1977-79, Ctr. for Profl. Advancement, New Brunswick, 1971-79, Hammond (Ind.) Lead Products, 1970-80; bd. dirs. Victor (N.Y.) Insulator Inc., UNIPEG, 1987-88; treas. Alfred Tech. Resources N.Y.; bd. dirs. Grads Found., N.Y.C. Contbr. articles to profl. jours.; patentee in field. Recipient Ralph Teetor award Soc. Automotive Engrs., 1973, PACE award Nat. Inst. Ceramic Engrs., 1975, Ann. award Ceramic Assn. N.J., 1980; named to Greaves Walker Roll, Keramos, 1991. Fellow Am. Ceramic Soc. (trustee 1980-83, v.p. 1988-89); mem. Ceramic Edn1. Coun. (pres. 1976-77), Ceramic Assn. N.Y. (treas. 1980-88, bd. dirs.), Ceramic Assn. N.J. (bd. dirs. 1974-80), Keramos (pres. 1982-84, Greaves-Walker Roll of Honor 1991), Tau Beta Pi. Avocations: tennis, reading. Home: 165 Clarken Dr West Orange NJ 07052-3429 Office: Caldwell College Caldwell NJ 07006

OTT, WAYNE ROBERT, environmental engineer; b. San Mateo, Calif., Feb. 2, 1940; s. Florian Funstan and Evelyn Virginia (Smith) Ott; m. Patricia Faustina Bertuzzi, June 28, 1967 (div. 1983). BA in Econs., Claremont McKenna Coll., 1962; BSEE, Stanford U., 1963, MS in Engring., 1965, MA in Comm., 1966, PhD in Environ. Engring., 1971. Commd. lt. USPHS, 1966, advanced through grades to capt., 1986; chief lab. ops. br. U.S. EPA, Washington, 1971—73, sr. systems analyst, 1973—79, sr. rsch. engr., 1981—84, chief air toxics and radiation monitoring rsch. staff, 1984—90; vis. scientist dept. stats. Stanford U., 1979—81, 1990—. Vis. scholar Ctr. for Risk Analysis and dept. stats., civil engring., Stanford U., 1990—93; sr. environ. engr. EPA Atmospheric Rsch. and Exposure Assessment Lab., 1993—95; cons. prof. civil engring. Stanford U., 1995—; dir. field studies Calif. Environ. Tobacco Smoke Study, 1993—95. Author: Environmental Indices: Theory and Practice, 1976, Environmental Statistics and Data Analysis, 1995; contbr. articles on indoor air pollution, total human exposure to chems., stochastic models of indoor exposure to chems., stochastic models of indoor exposure, motor vehicle exposures, personal monitoring instruments and environmental tobacco smoke to profl. jours. Decorated Commendation medal USPHS; recipient Nat. Statistician award for outstanding contbn. to environ. stats., EPA, 1995. Mem.: Internat. Soc. Indoor Air Quality and Climate, Air and Waste Mgmt. Assn., Am. Soc. for Quality Control, Am. Statis. Assn., Internat. Soc. Exposure Analysis (v.p. 1989—90, Jerome J. Weselowski Internat. award for career achievement in exposure assessment 1995), Sierra Club, Theater Club, Jazz Club, Kappa Mu Epsilon, Tau Beta Pi, Sigma Xi, Phi Beta Kappa. Democrat. Achievements include development of nationally uniform air pollution index, first total human exposure activity pattern models. Avocations: hiking, photography, model trains, jazz recording. Home: 1008 Cardiff Ln Redwood City CA 94061-3678 Office: Stanford U Dept Stats Sequoia Hall Stanford CA 94305 Office Phone: 650-906-8442. Business E-Mail: wott1@stanford.edu.

OTTAVIANO, DORIS BAGINSKI, librarian; b. Middletown, Conn., June 14, 1938; d. Edward Francis and Genevieve M. (Recko) Baginski; m. Thomas J., April 16, 1983. BA, U. Conn., Storrs, 1960; MSLS, Syracuse (N.Y.) U., 1963. Gen. asst. Hartford Pub. Library, Conn., 1960-61; grad. asst. Syracuse U., N.Y., 1961-63; reference libr. Enoch Pratt Free Libr., Balt., 1963-64, sr. reference libr., 1964-65, subject specialist, 1965-69; suject cataloger Yale U. Libr., New Haven, 1969-70; head reference libr. U.S. Naval War Coll., Newport, R.I., 1970—. Contbr. articles to profl. jours. Mem. Spl. Libr. Assn.(pres. 1988-89, R.I. chpt.), Am. Libr. Assn., New Eng. Libr. Assn., R.I. Libr. Assn., Coalition of Libr. Advs., Beta Phi Mu (Libr. Sci. Honor Soc.), Bus. & Profl. Women's Assn. Home: 11 Admiralty Dr Apt 3 Middletown RI 02842-6254

OTTAWAY, DAVID BLACKBURNE, journalist; b. Endicott, N.Y., Oct. 27, 1939; s. James Haller Sr. and Ruth Blackburne (Hart) O.; m. Marina Seassaro, July 18, 1963; children: Eric, Robin. BA, Harvard U., 1962; MA, Columbia U., 1964, PhD, 1972. Dep. fgn. editor Washington Post, 1971-73, Africa corr., 1974-79, Mid. East corr., 1981-85, nat. security corr., 1985-90, South Africa corr., 1990-92, Ea., So. and Ctrl. South Europe corr., 1992-94, investigative reporter, 1994—. Chmn., pres. Buck Hill Falls Co., Buck Hills, Pa., 1995-98, bd. dirs., 1999—. Co-author: (with Marina Ottaway) Algeria - The Politics of a Socialist Revolution, 1965, Ethiopia - Empire in Revolution, 1978, Afro-communism, 1983; author: Chained Together - Mandela, De Klerk and the Struggle to Remake South Africa, 1993. Pres. NBO Found., 1995-98, 2001—; trustee Lawrenceville Sch., 1998—. Mem. Harvard Club of Washington. Avocations: skiing, hiking, jogging, tennis. Office: Washington Post 1150 15th St NW Washington DC 20071-0002

OTTAWAY, JAMES HALLER, JR., newspaper publisher; b. Binghamton, N.Y., Mar. 24, 1938; s. James Haller and Ruth Blackburne (Hart) O.; m. Mary Warren Hyde, June 16, 1959; children— Alexandra, Christopher, Jay. Grad., Phillips Exeter Acad., 1955; BA, Yale U., 1960; DJournalism (hon.), Suffolk U., Boston, 1970; DBA (hon.), Southeastern Mass. U., 1984. 1962reporter, mgmt. trainee New-Times, Danbury, Conn., 1960; reporter, mgmt. trainee Times Herald-Record, Middletown, NY, 1962—63; editor Pocono Record, Stroudsburg, Pa., 1963—65; publisher New Bedford (Mass.) Standard-Times, 1965—70; pres. Ottaway Newspapers, Inc., Campbell Hall, NY, 1970—85, CEO, 1976—88, chmn. bd., 1979—2003, CEO, 1998—2003. V.p. Dow Jones & Co., 1980-86, sr. v.p., 1986-2003, also bd. dirs.; dir., vice-chmn. AP, 1982-91. Past. v.p. bd. trustees Phillips Exeter Acad.; trustee Am. Sch. Classical Studies at Athens, chmn., 1996-99; trustee, vice-chmn. Storm King Art Ctr., Mountainville, N.Y., World Wildlife Fund USA, 1993-96; trustee Bard Coll., 1996—; chmn. World Press Freedom Com., 1996—; dir. Internat Ctr. Journalists, Internat. Commn. Transitional Justice, 2002—; past pres., bd. dirs. Arden Hill Hosp. Found., Goshen, N.Y. Mem. Am. Newspaper Pubs. Assn., Am. Soc. Newspaper Editors. Episcopalian. Office: PO Box 401 Campbell Hall NY 10916-0401 E-mail: jottaway@ottaway.com.

OTTE, PAUL JOHN, academic administrator, consultant, trainer; b. Detroit, July 10, 1943; s. Melvin John Otte and Anne Marie (Meyers) Hirsch; children: Deanna Kropf, John. BS, Wayne State U., 1968, MBA, 1969; EdD, Western Mich. U., 1983. With Detroit Bank and Trust Co., 1965-68; teaching fellow Wayne State U., Detroit, 1968-69; auditor, mgr. Arthur Young & Co., Detroit, 1969-75; contr., dir. Macomb Community Coll., Warren, Mich., 1975-79, v.p. bus., 1979-86; pres. Franklin U., Columbus, Ohio, 1986—, prof. undergrad. and grad. programs, 1986—. Author various tng. manuals, 1982. Cpl. USMC, 1961-65. Teaching fellow Wayne State U., 1968-69. Mem. AICPA, Mich. Assn. CPAs (chmn. continuing profl. edn. com. 1980-82, leadership com. 1981-83), Nat. Assn. Coll. and Univ. Bus. Officers (acctg. prins. com. 1986), Assn. Ind. Colls. and Univs. Ohio (bd. dirs.), Greater Detroit C. of C. (leadership award 1983), Columbus C. of C. (info. svc. com.). Roman Catholic. Avocations: travel, speaking engagements. Office: Franklin U 201 S Grant Ave Columbus OH 43215-5399

OTTEN, JEFFREY, former hospital administrator; Pres. and CEO Brigham and Women's Hosp., Boston, 1994—2002; pres. JRO Ventures, 2002—. Chmn. Ardais Corp.; bd. mem. Fossa. Recipient Outstanding Leadership in Healthcare, Linkage, Inc., 2002. Office: Ardais Corp 128 Spring St Lexington MA 02421

OTTEN, ROBIN DOZIER, state agency administrator; Supt. regulation and licensing dept. State of N. Mex., Santa Fe. Office: Off Supt Reg Licensing Dept 725 Saint Michaels Dr Santa Fe NM 87505-7605

OTTENSMEYER, DAVID JOSEPH, retired neurosurgeon, retired healthcare executive; b. Nashville, Tenn., Jan. 29, 1930; s. Raymond Stanley and Glenda Jessie Ottensmeyer; m. Mary Jean Langley, June 30, 1954; children: Kathryn Joan, Martha Langley BA, Wis. State U., Superior, 1951; MD, U. Wis., Madison, 1959; MS in Health Svcs. Adminstrn., Coll. St. Francis, 1985. Diplomate Am. Bd. Neurological Surgery. Intern then resident in gen. surgery Univ. Hosps., Madison, Wis., 1959-61, resident in neurol. surgery, 1962—65; staff neurosurgeon Marshfield Clinic, Wis., 1965-76; from instr. of neurol. surgery to clin. asst. prof. U. Wis. Med. Sch., Madison, 1964-77; CEO Lovelace Med. Ctr., Albuquerque, 1976-86, chmn., 1986-91; clin. prof. community medicine U. N.Mex., Albuquerque, 1977-79, clin. prof. neurol. surgery, 1979-92; exec. v.p., chief med. officer Equicor, 1986-90; part-time cons. pvt. practice, 1996. Bd. dirs. AABC; v.p. Marshfield Clinic, 1970-71, pres., CEO, 1972-75; pres., CEO The Lovelace Insts., 1991-96; sr. v.p., chief med. officer Travelers Ins. Co., 1990-91; served on numerous adv. and com. posts. Contbr. articles to profl. jours. Col. USAR, 1960-90. Fellow ACS, Am. Coll. Physician Execs. (pres. 1985-86); mem. Am. Group Practice Assn. (pres. 1983-84), Am. Bd. Med. Mgmt. (bd. dirs. 1989-95, chmn. 1995). Republican. Episcopalian. Avocations: flying, golf, travel. Address: 102 Crofton Ct Fairhope AL 36532-6306 E-mail: ottensmeyer@msn.com.

OTTER, CLEMENT LEROY (BUTCH OTTER), congressman; b. Caldwell, Idaho, May 3, 1942; s. Joseph Bernard and Regina Mary (Buser) O.; children: John Simplot, Carolyn Lee, Kimberly Dawn, Corinne Marie. BA in Polit. Sci., Coll. Idaho, 1967; PhD, Mindanao State U., 1980. Mgr. J.R. Simplot Co., Caldwell, Idaho, 1971-76, asst. to v.p. adminstrn., 1976-78, v.p. adminstrn., 1978-82, internat. pres., 1982—93; lt. gov. State of Idaho, Boise, 1987—2001; mem. U.S. Congress from Idaho 1st Dist., 2000—; mem. transp. and infrastructure, resources and govt. reform, energy and commerce coms. Mem. Presdl. Task Force-AID, Washington, 1982—84, U.S. C. of C., Washington, 1983—84; com. mem. invest tech. devel. State Adv. Council, Washington, 1983—84; mem. exec. council Bretton Woods Com., 1984—. With Nat. Guard, 1968—73. Mem. Young Pres.' Orgn., Sales and Mktg. Execs., Idaho Assn. Commerce and Industry, Idaho Agrl. Leadership Council, Idaho Ctr. for Arts, Idaho Internat. Trade Council, Pacific N.W. Waterways Assn., N.W. Food Producers, Ducks Unltd, Safari Club Internat. (life). Clubs: Arid, Hillcrest Country. Lodges: Moose, Elks. Republican. Roman Catholic. Avocations: jogging, music, art collecting, horse training, fishing. Office: US Ho of Reps 1711 Longworth HOB Washington DC 20515-1201

OTTER, JOHN MARTIN, III, retired television advertising consultant; b. Pottsville, Pa., Nov. 26, 1930; s. John Martin and Ruth A. (Knipe) O.; m. Susan Morgan Eaves, May 21, 1960; children— John Martin, IV, Robert Marshal. BA, Cornell U., 1953. Comml. producer Arlene Frances Home Show, 1953-55; producer Dave Garroway Today Show, 1956-59; dir. spl. programs sales NBC-TV, 1959-61, v.p. nat. sales, 1962-64, v.p. charge sales, 1965-73; cons. sta. WNET-TV, Practising Law Inst., also Dragonwk Prodns., 1973-75; v.p., dir. network programming SSC&B Inc., 1975-78; sr. v.p., dir. network programming SSC&B Lintas Worldwide, N.Y.C., 1978-84; sr. v.p. dir. nat. broadcast McCann-Erickson U.S.A., N.Y.C., 1984-88; sr. v.p. spl. projects McCann-Erickson Worldwide, N.Y.C., 1988; pres. RETTO Internat. Inc., N.Y.C., 1989-94; retired, 1994. Mem.: The Chatham Club, The Landings Yacht Club, The Landings Club. Republican. Episcopalian. Home: Four Seafarer's Cir Savannah GA 31411

OTTERBOURG, ROBERT KENNETH, public relations consultant, writer; b. N.Y.C., Jan. 26, 1930; s. Albert Marcus and Frances (Roset) O.; m. Susan Delman, Apr. 14, 1957; children— Laura Ann, Kenneth Douglas. BA, Colgate U., 1951; MS, Columbia U., 1954. Reporter, editor Fairchild Publs., N.Y.C., 1953-57; editor McGraw-Hill Pub. Co., 1957-59; v.p. pub. rels. Charles Mathieu & Co., 1959-61; pres. pub. rels. Otterbourg & Co., N.Y.C., 1962-69, 71—. Sr. v.p. Daniel J. Edelman, 1970. Author: It's Never Too Late, 1993, Retire and Thrive, 1995, 3d edit., 2003, Switching Careers, 2001; contbr. articles to profl. and consumer jours. Legis. asst. N.Y. State Senate, 1962-64; mem. exec. com. Columbia U. Sch. Journalism, N.Y.C., 1980-93, pres. exec. com., 1985-87; trustee Flat Rock Nature Ctr., pres., 1991-92; trustee Planned Parenthood Bergen County, 1985-88, v.p., 1986-88; trustee Urban League for Bergen County, 1988-93; chmn. Durham County Libr., 1997-99, Exec. Svc. Corps of the Greater Triangle; bd. dirs. Colgate U. Alumni Corp., 1969-73; bd. dirs., pres. Threshold, 2003; pres. Triangle Reading Svc., 2004. 1st lt. USAF, 1951-53. Mem. Columbia U. Grad. Sch. Journalism Alumni Assn. (pres. 1985-87). Democrat. Jewish. Home and Office: 68 Beverly Dr Durham NC 27707-2224

OTTERNESS, TOM, artist; b. Wichita, Kans., June 21, 1952; s. Garnet Otterness; m. Coleen Fitzgibbon; 1 child, Kelly. Student, Art Students League, 1970, Whitney Mus of Am. Art, 1973. One-man shows include Skoto Gallery, 2003, Marlborough Gallery, Chelsea, NY, 2002, James Corcoran Gallery, Santa Monica, Brooke Alexander, N.Y., 1990, IVAM Centre Julio Gonzalez, Valencia, Spain, Portikus/Senckenbergmuseum, Frankfurt, Germany, Haags Gemeentemuseum, The Hague, The Netherlands, 1991, The Mus. Modern Art, 1987, Nancy Drysdale Gallery, Washington, 1991, Brooke Alexander, N.Y., 1992, Galerie Weber, Muenster, Westfalen, Germany, 1993, John Berggruen Gallery, San Francisco, 1993, 99, Carnegie Mus. Art, Pitts., 1993, Gallery Contemporary Art, Krannert Art Mus., Champaign, Ill., 1994, MetroTech Ctr., Bklyn., 1995, Wichita Art Mus., 1995, Doris Freedman Plaza, 1995, Marlborough Gallery, N.Y., 1997, 2002, Marlborough Gallery, Madrid, Spain, 1999; exhibited in group exhibitions including Whitney Mus. Am. Art, N.Y.C., 1985, Marlborough Gallery, N.Y., 1995-96, Ubu Gallery, N.Y., 1995-96, Mus. Modern Art, NY, 1996, The White House, Washington, 1996, Detroit Inst. Arts, Mus. Fine Arts, Boston, Mpls. Inst. Arts, San Diego Mus. Art, Ctr. for the Fine Arts, Miami, 1996-97, John Berggruen Gallery, 1997, San Jose Mus. Art, Calif., 1997-98; pub. commns. include Edward R. Roybal Fed. Bldg., LA, 1991, Gov. Nelson A. Rockefeller Park, N.Y.C., 1992, State Libr., Munster, Germany, 1993, Roosevelt Island, N.Y., 1996, Mark O. Hatfield U.S. Courthouse, Portland, 1997, Cleve. Pub. Libr., 1998, Fed. Courthouse, Sacramento, 1999, Western Wash. U., Bellingham, 1999, Fed. Courthouse, Mpls., 1999, Hilton Times Sq., N.Y.C., 2000, MTA Arts for Transit, N.Y.C., 2000, Carl Sagan Discovery Ctr. 2000, Children's Hosp. Montefiore Med. Ctr., Bronx; represented in pvt. and permanent collections including Bklyn. Mus., Carnegie Mus. Art, Guggenheim Mus., N.Y.C., Israel Mus., Jerusalem, IVAM Ctr. Julio Gonzalez, Valencia, Spain, Mus. Modern Art, N.Y.C., Whitney Mus. Am. Art, Miyagi Mus. Art, Sendai, Japan, Mus. Tamayo, Mexico City. Active Collaborative Project, Inc., NY, 1977-82. Fellow Nat. Endowment for the Arts, 1994. Studio: 202 Plymouth St Brooklyn NY 11201-1124 E-mail: t.o.studio@rcn.com.

OTTINGER, MAURICE ARMAND, software engineer, educator; b. Knoxville, Tenn., July 10, 1962; s. Charles Love and Nana Marie (Matthews) O.; m. Lorie Lee Spin, July 20, 1985; children: Emily Marie, Maurice Allan. BMus magna cum laude, Carson-Newman Coll., 1984; MS in Adminstrn., Ctrl. Mich. U., Mt. Pleasant, 1986; postgrad., U. Tenn., 1993—. Course mgr. Jolly Frog Golf Course, Powell, Tenn., 1981-84; chief enlisted mgmt. U.S. Army Missile Sch., Redstone Arsenal, Ala., 1984-85; exec. officer/assoc. bandmaster 214th Army Band, Ft. McPherson, Ga., 1985-86; chief pers. svc. Hdqs. U.S. Army Garrison, Ft. McPherson, 1986-87; chief adminstrn. and logistics U.S. Army Recruiting, Marietta, Ga., 1988-89; chief planning and ops. Hdqs. 8th Pers. Command, Seoul, Korea, 1990-91, hdqs. co. comdr., 1991-92; adminstrv. officer 3292d USAR Forces Sch., Knoxville, 1993-96; software engr. U.S. Army Info. Support Activity, St. Louis, 1996—. Lectr. bus. and fin. St. Leo Coll., Ft. McPherson, 1987-88; instr. data processing Ga. Mil. Coll., Ft. McPherson, 1987-89. Treas. HSW Orphanage Coun., Seoul, 1991-92; active Boy Scouts Am., 1986-92; choir dir. Post Chapel, Ft. McPherson, 1987-88; acting music dir., deacon Cumberland Bapt. Ch., Knoxville, 1993-96; deacon, asst. music dir. Geyer Rd. Bapt. Ch., Kirkwood, Mo., 1997—. Maj. U.S. Army, 1984—. Recipient Meritorious Svc. medal U.S. Army, 1992, 96, Commendation medal, 1988, 89, Achievement medal, 1985. Mem. Assn. of U.S. Army, Adjutant Gen.'s Corps Regimental Assn., Officers' Christian Fellowship of the U.S.A., Nat. Eagle Scout Assn., Rev. Officers Assn. of U.S., Interallied Confedn. of Res. Officers and Med. Res. Officers Assn. Baptist. Avocation: study of comparative religion and biblical prophecy. Office: US Army Info Support Activity 9700 Page Ave Saint Louis MO 63132-1547 Home: Apt Y204 450 S Peachtree Pkwy Peachtree City GA 30269-6839

OTTINGER, RICHARD LAWRENCE, dean emeritus; b. N.Y.C., Jan. 27, 1929; s. Lawrence and Louise (Lowenstein) O.; children from previous marriage: Ronald, Randall, Lawrence, Jenny Louise; m. June Godfrey. BA, Cornell U., 1950; LLB, Harvard U., 1953. Assoc. Cleary, Gottlieb, Friendly & Hamilton, N.Y.C., 1955-56; ptnr. William J. Kridel, Law Firm, N.Y.C., 1956-60; second staff mem., dir. programs Peace Corps, L.Am., 1961-64; mem. 89th-91st Congresses, 1965-71, 94th-98th Congresses, 1975-85; prof. Pace U. Sch. Law, White Plains, N.Y., 1985—, dean, 1994—99, dean emeritus, 1999—. Bd. dirs. Environ. and Energy Study Inst., Washington. Author: Environmental Costs of Electricity, 1990. Contract mgr. Internat. Coop. Adminstrn., 1960-61; organizer Grassroots to Action, 1971-73. Office: Pace U Sch Law 78 N Broadway White Plains NY 10603-3710 E-mail: rottinger@law.pace.edu.

OTTINO, JULIO MARIO, engineering educator; b. La Plata, Buenos Aires, Argentina, May 22, 1951; came to U.S., 1976; naturalized, 1990; s. Julio Francisco and Nydia Judit (Zufriategui) O.; m. Alicia I. Löffler, Aug. 20, 1976; children: Jules Alessandro, Bertrand Julien. Diploma in Chem. Engring., U. La Plata, 1974; PhD in Chem. Engring., U. Minn., 1979; exec. program Kellogg Sch. Mgmt., Northwestern U., 1995. Instr. in chem. engring. U. Minn., Mpls., 1978-79; asst. prof. U. Mass., Amherst, 1979-83, adj. prof. polymer sci., 1979-91, assoc. prof. chem. engring., 1983-86, prof., 1986-91; Chevron vis.

prof. chem. engring. Calif. Inst. Tech., Pasadena, 1985-86; sr. rsch. fellow Ctr. for Turbulence Rsch. Stanford (Calif.) U., 1989-90; Walter P. Murphy prof. chem. engring. Northwestern U., Evanston, Ill., 1991-2000, chmn. dept. chem. engring., 1992-2000; McCormick Inst. prof., 2000—; George T. Piercy Disting. prof. U. Minn., 1998, adj. prof. mech. engring., 2001—; dir. Northwestern Inst. Complex Sys., 2004—. Cons. to U.S. and European corps.; mem. tech. adv. bd. Dow Chem.; mem. bd. dirs. Coun. Chem. Rsch.; prof. U. Minn.; lectr. in field. Author: The Kinematics of Mixing: Stretching, Chaos and Transport, 1989; contbr. articles to profl. jours.; assoc. editor Physics Fluids A, 1991—; mem. editl. bd. Internat. Jour. Bifurc. Chaos, 1991—; assoc. editor Am. Inst. Chem. Engring. Jour., 1991-95, assoc. editor., 1995—; one man art exhibit, La Plata, 1974. Recipient Presdl. Young Investigator award NSF, 1984, Alpha Chi Sigma award AIChE, 1994, W.H. Walker award AIChE, 2001, E.W. Thiele award AIChE, Chgo., 2002; Univ. fellow U. Mass., 1988, J.S. Guggenheim fellow, 2001; Lacey lectureship, Calif. Inst. Tech., 1994, Danckwerts lectureship Royal Instn., 1999, Robb lectr. Pa. State U. Fellow Am. Phys. Soc.; mem. AAAS, NAE, Am. Acad. Arts and Scis., Am. Chem. Soc., Am. Phys. Soc., Am. Soc. Engring. Edn., Sigma Xi (disting. lectr. 1997-99), Coun. for Chem. Rsch.(gov. bd. coun. 1999 2001). Achievements include research in granular dynamics, chaos, complex systems and mixing. Avocations: visual arts, painting. Home: 1092 Crescent Ln Winnetka IL 60093-1501 Office: Northwestern U Dept Chem Engring 2145 Sheridan Rd Evanston IL 60208-0834 Office Phone: 847-491-3558. Business E-Mail: jm-ottino@northwestern.edu.

OTTIS, SHERRI DANIELLE GREENE, secondary school educator, historian; b. Fort Worth, Tex., June 25, 1964; d. Derrell Lyndon Greene and Claudette Mathiot Greene-Naggs; m. Steve Ray Ottis, May 5, 1984; children: Brian Thomas, Catherine Elyse. BSc in History, Miss. Coll., 1997, MSS in History and Polit. Sci., 1999. Tchr. history Clinton (Miss.) Pub. Schs., 1999—. Adj. prof. Miss. Coll., Clinton, 1999—, Belhaven Coll., Jackson, 2002; supt.'s adv. com. Clinton (Miss.) Pub. Sch. Dist., 2002—03. Author: Silent Heroes: Downed Airmen and the French Underground, 2001. Mem.: WWII Escape Lines Meml. Soc. (U.S. rep. 2003—), Air Force Escape and Evasion Soc. Roman Cath. Avocations: reading, writing, art. Home: 717 Winding Hills Clinton MS 39056 Office: Clinton High School 401 Arrow Drive Clinton MS 39056

OTTLEY, JOHN K., JR., entrepreneur; b. Atlanta, Oct. 8, 1931; s. John King and Mary Hinton (Harvey) O.; widowed; four children. AB, Davidson Coll., 1953; MS, Columbia U., 1954; grad., U.S. Army Command/Staff Coll., Ft. Leavenworth, Kans., 1975, Army War Coll., Carlisle Barracks, Pa., 1977. Infantry unit comdr., aviator U.S. Army, 1953-58; from editl. trainee to staff reporter Charlotte (N.C.) Observer, 1958-63; from staff reporter to mng. editor Marietta (Ga.) Daily Jour., 1960-63; pub. rels. mgr. So. Svcs., Inc., Atlanta, 1963-68; v.p. Manning, Selvage & Lee, Atlanta, 1968-78; exec. dir. So. Assn. Orthodontists, Atlanta, 1978-96, Coll. Diplomates Am. Bd. Orthodontics, Atlanta, 1996-98; owner J.O. Svcs., Atlanta, 1998—. Pubs., editor Midwest Poetry Rev., 1995-2000; assoc. editor The Village Writer, 1991-93. Past dir. Families First, Atlanta; dir. Howell Pl. Condominium, 1997-98. Recipient Army Legion of Merit award, Master Army Aviator badge, Expert Infantryman badge, Three times 1st place winner Byron Herbert Reece Internat. Poetry award, Disting. Svc. award So. Assn. Orthodontists. Mem. So. Assn. Orthodontists, S.C. Assn. Orthodontists, Am. Assn. Execs., Ga. Soc. Assn. Execs., Ga. State Poetry Soc. (dir., pres. 2001—), Atlanta Writers Club, Village Writers Group, Inquiry Club (pres. 2000—), Capital City Club. Office: JO Svcs PO Box 20236 Atlanta GA 30325-0236

OTTLEY, WILLIAM HENRY, professional association director, consultant; b. N.Y.C., Mar. 7, 1929; s. James Henry and Margaret (Deeble) O. BA, Yale U., 1950; spl. cert., Georgetown U., 1953; D of Aero. Sci. (hon.), Embry Riddle Aero. U., 1979. Dir. pub. rels. Thomas A. Edison Co., West Orange, N.J., 1953-56; exec. v.p. Career Publs., Inc., N.Y.C., 1956-60; dir. spl. exhibits N.Y. World's Fair, 1960-65; exec. dir. Nat. Pilots Assn., Washington, 1965-77, U.S. Parachute Assn., Washington, 1978-92, Nat. Aero. Assn., Washington, 1992-93; pres. Internat. Gen. Aviation Commn., Paris, 1994-99. V.p. Fedn. Aero. Internat., Paris, 1994-99. Pres. Nat. Skydiving Mus. 1st lt. USAF, 1951—53. Recipient Skydiving Lifetime Achievement award, 1994. Mem. Met. Club Washington, Soc. of Cin. Republican. Episcopalian. Avocations: skydiving (world record holder 1982), flying (world record holder 1985), scuba diving, waterskiing, skiing. Home and Office: 2627 Woodley Pl NW Washington DC 20008-1525 E-mail: whottley@erols.com.

OTTO, BYRON LEONARD, lawyer, state administrator; b. Battle Creek, Mich., Oct. 4, 1940; s. Henry John and Mildred Alice (Wagner) O. BBA, St. Edward's U., 1964, MBA, 1979; JD, U. Tex., 1968. Bar: U.S. Dist. Ct. (we. dist.) 1976. Staff atty. State Welfare Dept., Austin, Tex., 1968-75; sole practice Austin, Tex., 1975-77; assoc. James R. Sloan, Austin, Tex., 1978-79; adminstr. State Comptroller, Austin, Tex., 1980—; ret., 2000. Author articles and monographs. St. Edward's U. scholar, Austin, 1978. Mem. ABA, Tex. Bar. Democrat. Roman Catholic. Home: 4604 S Lamar Blvd, Apt C-109 Austin TX 78745-1356 E-mail: byron@austin.rr.com.

OTTO, CHARLOTTE R. consumer products company executive; b. Duluth, Minn., Aug. 15, 1953; BS, Purdue U., 1974, MS in Mgmt., 1976. With Procter & Gamble, 1976—, from asst. brand mgr. to brand mgr. various products, 1977-83, assoc. advt. mgr. paper products divsn., 1984-87, assoc. advt. mgr. toilet tissue/towels, paper products div., 1987-89, dir. issues mgmt., pub. affairs divsn., 1989-90, dir. pub. rels., pub. affairs divsn., 1990-91; v.p. pub. rels. Procter & Gamble USA, 1991-93; v.p. corp. comms. Procter & Gamble Worldwide, 1993-95, v.p. pub. affairs, 1995-96; sr. v.p. pub. affairs The Procter & Gamble Co., 1996-99, global pub. affairs officer, 1999—2000, global external rels. officer, 2000—. Dir. Royal Bank Fin. Grou, Canada; adv. bd. Jour. Corp. Pub. Rels., The Medill Sch. Journalism, Northwestern Univ. Mem. nat. bd. Boys & Girls Club Am.; mem. YWCA Acad. Career Women of Acheivement; chair (past pres.) Cin. Playhouse in the Park; chair exec. com. Downtown Cin., Inc.; mem. Riverfront Advisors Commn.; v.p. exec. com. Joy Outdoor Edn. Ctr.; trustee Arts & Cultural Coun. Greater Loveland; bd. mem. Am. Red Cross, Cin. Chpt.; bd. selectors, The Jefferson Awards Am. Inst. Pub. Svc.; vice-chmn. exec. com. Greater Cin. C. of C.; bd. mem. The Port of Greater Cin. Devel. Authority, Good Samaritan Hosp., Cin. Fire Mus.; mem. Leadership Cin. - Class XIV. Recipient YWCA Career Woman of Achievement award, 1993, Woman of Distinction award Gt. Rivers Girl Scouts Coun., Inc., 1998, Purdue "Old Master", 1996; recipient Disting. Alumni, Purdue U., Krannert Sch. Mgmt. Mem. Ctr. Quality Leadership Founders, Vice Pres.'s Forum, Commonwealth Club, Women's Capital Club, Queen City Club (bd. govs.), Club at Harper's Point, Arthur Page Soc., PR Seminar Com., Kenwood Country Club. Office: Procter & Gamble Co 1 Procter And Gamble Plz Cincinnati OH 45202-3393

OTTO, FRED DOUGLAS, chemical engineering educator; b. Hardisty, Alta., Can., Jan. 12, 1935; BSc, U. Alta., 1957, MSc, 1959; PhD in Chem. Engring., U. Mich., Ann Arbor, 1963. From asst. prof. to assoc. prof. U. Alta., Edmonton, 1962-70, chmn., 1975-84, prof. chem. engring., 1970-96, dean engring., 1985-94, prof. emeritus, 1996—; pres., CEO DB Robinson & Assocs. Ltd., 1998—2002. Mem. governing coun. NRC, 1991-94. Recipient Donald L. Katz award, Gas Processors Assn., 1998. Fellow: Can. Acad. Engring.; mem.: AIChE, Can. Coun. Profl. Engrs. (bd. dirs. 1997—2003), Assn. Profl. Engrs., Geologists and Geophysicists of Alta. (1st v.p. 1995—96, pres. 1996—97, Centennial award 1993), Can. Soc. Chem. Engrs. (pres. 1986—87). Office: 12319 52d Ave Edmonton AB Canada T6H 0P5

OTTO, INGOLF HELGI ELFRIED, banking institute fellow; b. Duesseldorf, Germany, May 7, 1920; s. Frederick C. and Josephine (Zisenis) O.; m. Carlyle Miller, 1943 (div. 1960); children: George Vincent Edward, Richard Arthur Frederick. A.B., U. Cin., 1941; M.A., George Washington U., 1950, Ph.D., 1959. CPCU. Assoc. prof. fin. NYU, N.Y.C., 1960-62; prof. fin. U. Nuevo Leon, Monterrey, Mexico, 1962-65, U. So. Miss., Hattiesburg, 1965-67, U. So. Ala., Mobile, 1967-81; sr. fellow Inst. Banking and Fin., Mexico City, 1981—. Contbr. articles on fin. to profl. jours. Served to col. U.S. Army, 1941-46. Decorated Legion of Merit, Meritorious Service medal, Purple Heart. Mem. Am. Econ. Assn., N.Am. Econ. and Fin. Assn.

OTTO, JEAN HAMMOND, journalist; b. Kenosha, Wis., Aug. 27, 1925; d. Laurence Cyril and Beatrice Jane (Slater) Hammond; m. John A. Otto, Aug. 22, 1946; children: Jane L. Rahman, Mary Ellen Takayama, Peter J. Otto; m. Lee W. Baker, Nov. 23, 1973. Student, Ripon Coll., 1944-46. Women's editor Appleton (Wis.) Post-Crescent, 1960-68; reporter Milw. Jour., 1968-72, editorial writer, 1972-77, editor Op Ed page, 1977-83; editorial page editor Rocky Mountain News, Denver, 1983-89, assoc. editor, 1989-92, reader rep., 1992-99; endowed chair U. Denver, 1992-97. Founder, chmn. bd. trustees First Amendment Congress, 1979-85, chmn. exec. com., 1985-88, 89-91, pres. 1991-96, mem. bd. trustees, 1979-96; founding mem. Wis. Freedom of Info. Council. Recipient Headliner award Wis. Women in Communications, 1974; Outstanding Woman in Journalism award YWCA, Milw., 1977; Knight of Golden Quill Milw. Press Club, 1979; spl. citation in Journalism Ball State U., 1980; James Madison award Nat. Broadcast Editorial Assn., 1981; spl. citation for contbn. to journalism Nat. Press Photographers Assn., 1981, Ralph D. Casey award U. Minn., 1984; U. Colo. Regents award, 1985; John Peter Zenger award U. Ariz., 1988; Paul Miller Medallion award Okla. State U., 1990; Colo. SPJ Lowell Thomas award, 1990, Disting. Alumna award Ripon Coll., 1992, Hugh M. Hefner First Amendment Lifetime Achievement award Playboy Found., 1994; named to Milw. Press Club Hall of Fame, 1993, Freedom of Info. Hall of Fame, 1996. Mem. Colo. Press Assn. (chmn. freedom of info. com. 1983-89), Assn. Edn. in Journalism and Mass Communications (Disting. Svc. award 1984), Am. Soc. Newspaper Editors (bd. dirs. 1987 92), Soc. Profl. Journalists (nat. treas. 1975, nat. sec. 1977, pres.-elect 1978, pres. 1979-80, First Amendment award 1981, Wells Key 1984, pres. Sigma Delta Chi Found. 1989-92, chair Found. 1992-94), Milw. Press Club (mem. Hall of Fame 1993). E-mail: jottofirst@aol.com.

OTTO, LUDWIG, publisher, educator, consultant, evangelist; b. NYC, Mar. 15, 1934; s. Ludwig and Anna V. (Messina) O.; m. Sara S. Sheffield, Apr. 18, 1966 (div. 1987); children: Molly, Ryan, Matthew, Katherine; m. Maxine Z. Knight, Sept. 1, 1991; children: David, Jeffrey. LLB, Blackstone Sch., Chgo., 1958; BA, CUNY, 1975; MDiv, Southwestern Bapt. Sem., Ft. Worth, 1978, D of Ministry, 1980, PhD, Am. U., 1996, M in English, U. Dallas, 2001; MLA, So. Meth. U. Ordained min., Baptist Ch., 1975. Mgr. computer divsn. NCR, various locations, 1957-64, Honeywell, Houston, 1964-66; pres. U. Computer Scis., Houston, 1966-74; evangelist, 1971—; pastor, evangelist So. Bapt. Ch., Tex., 1974—; publ. Franklin Publ. Co., Arlington, Tex., 1987—; dir. Fed. and Found. Grants Adminstrn. Paul Quinn Coll.; pres. Prometheus Internat. Inc.; assoc. prof. English Tarrant County Coll., Tex. Exec. dir. Nat. Ethics Inst., 1992—, pres.; mem. adj. faculty El Centro Coll., Collin County C.C., Northlake Coll., Irvine, Tex., U. Tex., Arlington, Mountain View Coll., Dallas; assoc. prof., chair divsn. arts and scis. Paul Quinn Coll., Dallas, 1994—, dir. fedn. and found. rels. and grant adminstrn; v.p. Paul Quinn Cmty. Devel. Corp.; pres., CEO Franklin Devel. Corp., 1966—; prof. lit. DeVry Inst. Tech., Tarrant County Coll, Columbia Coll., Concordia U.; CEO Franklin Global Svcs., 2001; sr. ptnr. Franklin Ednl. Travel. Author: Introduction to Computer Math, 1967, 69, Training Church Members, 1980, How to Protect Your Children, 1982, Critical Thinking Strategies, 1993, Reading for Speed and Comprehension, 1993, Plato in New York, Born Poor in the USA; pub. monthly newspaper Your Opinion Counts, 1997; host radio program Your Opinion Counts, 1997. 2d lt. U.S. Army, 1950-53. Mem. North Tex. Alumni Assn. of CCNY (pres. 1993—), Prometheus Internat. (pres.), Sigma Tau Delta. Home and Office: Franklin Global Svcs 2723 Steamboat Cir Arlington TX 76006-3705 Office Phone: 817-548-1124. Personal E-mail: luotto@comcast.net.

OTTO, MARGARET AMELIA, librarian; b. Boston, Oct. 22, 1937; d. Henry Earlen and Mary (McLennan) O.; children— Christopher, Peter. AB, Boston U., 1960; MS, Simmons Coll., 1963, MA, 1970; MA (hon.), Dartmouth Coll., 1981. Asst. sci. librarian M.I.T., Cambridge, 1963, Lindgren librarian, 1964-67, acting sci. librarian, 1967-69, asst. dir., 1969-75, asso. dir., 1976-79; librarian of coll. Dartmouth Coll., Hanover, N.H., 1979—. Pres., chmn. bd. Universal Serials and Book Exch., Inc., 1980-81; bd. dirs. Rsch. Libr. Group; trustee Howe Libr., Hanover, 1988—, chmn., 1992—; mem. Brown Libr. Com., rsch. lbirs. adv. com. OCLC, 1991—, ARL; editl. com. Univ. Press New Eng., 1993—. Council on Library Resources fellow, 1974; elected to Collegium of Disting. Alumnus Boston U., 1980 Mem. ALA (task force on assn. membership issues 1993—, ad hoc working group on copyright issues), Assn. Rsch. Librs. (chair preservation com. 1983-85, bd. dirs. 1985-88, mem. stats. com., chair membership com. 1992—), Coun. on Libr. Resources (proposal rev. com. 1992—), Dartmouth Club (N.Y.C.), St. Botolph Club (Boston), Sloane Club (London). Home: 2 Berrill Farms Ln Hanover NH 03755-3205 Office: Dartmouth Coll 115 Baker Meml Libr Hanover NH 03755

OTTO, MARIE (BERTHA OTTO), educational administrator, educational consulting company executive; b. Houston, July 11, 1930; d. Robert Lillard and Bertha Irene (Allen) Davis; m. Robert Lee Otto, Jan. 7, 1950; children: Lois Ann Otto Buschmann, Barbara Jeane Otto Hunt, Robert Lee Jr. Student, Tex. Christian U., 1947-49, Hardin-Simmons U., summers 1947, 49, 54; BA in Speech, Drama and Edn., Sul-Ross State U., 1954; postgrad., U. Wyo., 1961, U. Calif., Santa Barbara, 1962, Calif. State U., Northridge, 1964; MA, Calif. State U., Long Beach, 1969, postgrad., 1980-82. Lic. tchr., Tex., secondary tchr., Wyo., Calif.; lic. psychologist; lic. marriage and family counselor. Tchr. high schs., Tex., Wyo. and Calif., 1956-64; tchr., counselor Excelsior High Sch., Norwalk, Calif., 1964-66; counselor Neff High Sch., La Mirada, Calif., 1966-69; psychologist Huntington Beach (Calif.) Union High Sch. Dist., 1969-74, project mgr., dir. pupil pers., 1974-80, asst. supt., 1980-84, supt., 1984-88, supt. emeritus, 1988—. V.p. Poole-Young-Koehler Assocs., Inc., Long Beach, 1964-79; pvt. practice marriage and family counselor, Fountain Valley, Calif., 1970—; pres. Marie Otto Assocs., Fountain Valley, 1979—; supr. student tchrs. Chapman Univ. Orange, Calif., 1988—; sec.-treas., Ctr. for Teaching Thinking, Huntington Beach, 1991—. Mem. Fountain Valley Human Svcs. Com., Huntington Beach Human Resources Commn., state planning com. Girl Scouts U.S., Worland, Wyo., 1959-61; pres. Spl. Edn. Local Plan Orgn., 1983-84; bd. dirs. Humana Hosp. Huntington Beach, Golden West Coll. Found., Huntington Beach, Huntington Beach Community Clinic, Orange County chpt. ARC, Santa Ana, Calif, No on Drugs, 1988—; sec., treas. Ctr. for Teaching of Thinking, Huntington Beach, 1992—. Recipient numerous plaques, 1985—, including Fountain Valley Human Svcs. Com., 1979, City of Fountain Valley, 1975, 79, 88, City of Huntington Beach, 1988, Fountain Valley C. of C., 1988, City of Westminster, 1988, Orange Coast Coll., 1988, Golden West Coll., 1988, Ocean View Sch. Dist., 1988, Spl. Edn. Local Plan Orgn., 1984; named Woman of Yr., Soroptimist Club, Westminster, 1984, Disting. Alumnus, Grad. Sch. Edn. Calif. State U.-Long Beach, 1988. Home and Office: 16689 Mount Hoffman Cir Fountain Valley CA 92708-2435

OTTOO, RICHARD EBIL, business educator; b. Paimol, Uganda, Dec. 28, 1958; came to U.S., 1990; s. Jevenino and Sabina (Lamoji) O.; 1 child, Emily Alimo. B of Stats., Makerere U., Kampala, Uganda, 1985; MBF, Finafrica Found., Milan, 1989; MBA, Baruch Coll., 1997; PhD, Baruch, CUNY, 1998. Spl. asst. to min. Ministry of Health, Govt. of Uganda, Entebbe, 1985-86; project mgr. Action Internationale, Kampala and Kotido, Uganda, 1986-88; lectr. Baruch Coll., N.Y.C., 1992-97; asst. prof. Pace U., N.Y.C., 1998—. Accounts trainee Nat. Water Corp., Entebbe, 1981-83; bd. dirs. Global Edn. Assocs., N.Y.C. Contbr. articles to profl. jours. Italian Ministry Fgn. Affairs scholar, 1988; Rockefeller Bros. Fund fellow, 1990; John C. Whitehead Found. fellow, 1991. Mem. Am. Fin. Assn., Fin. Mgmt. Assn., Eastern Fin. Assn., N.Y. Soc. Security Analysts. Home: 1425 Amsterdam Ave New York NY 10027-7454 Office: Pace U Lubin Sch Bus One Pace Plz New York NY 10038

OTTOSON, HOWARD WARREN, economist, retired academic administrator; b. Detroit Lakes, Minn., Sept. 18, 1920; s. John Henry and Hilma Marie (Johnson) O.; m. Margaret Jane Featherstone, Oct. 22, 1944; children— Keith Richard, John Howard, David Thomas BS, U. Minn., 1942, MS, 1950; PhD, Iowa State U., 1952. Chmn. dept. agrl. econs. U. Nebr., Lincoln, 1956-66, Bert Rodgers prof., 1965, dir., dean, 1966-79, asst. vice chancellor, 1979-81, vice chancellor, 1981-82, exec. v.p., provost, 1982-85, prof. agrl. econs. emeritus, 1985—. Cons. USDA, Washington, 1961, 64, AID, Buenos Aires, Argentina, 1962, Colombian Inst. Agr., Bogota, 1970; mem. USDA Policy Adv. Com. on Feed Grains, Washington, 1966-68; chmn. Gt. Plains Agrl. Council, Lincoln, Nebr., 1971, 79; bd. dirs. Farm Found. Bd., Chgo., 1977-85. Sr. author: Land and People in the Northern Plains Tranition Area, 1966; sr. author Agrl. Land Tenure Research bull., 1962; editor: Land Use Problems and Policies in the U.S., 1963; co-editor: Transportation Problems and Policies in the Trans Missouri West, 1967, Pelican Lakes - The History of a Minnesota Community, 2001. Pres. Lincoln Coun. Chs., Nebr., 1958-59, Nebr. divsn. UN Assn.-U.S.A., Lincoln, 1977-78; chmn. Mayor's Adv. Com. on Taxation, Lincoln, 1991; mem. Nebr. Commn. on Local Govt. Innovation and Restructuring, 1996-2000; pres. Pelican Lakes Property Owners Assn., 2000—. Served to lt. USNR, 1944-46, PTO. Mem.: LWV (bd. dir. Nebr. 1993—99), Internat. Assn. Agrl. Economists (travel fellow 1958, 1964), Am. Agrl. Econs. Assn., Open Forum (pres. 1991—92), Norden Club (pres. 1985—87), Pelican Lake Property Assn. (pres. 2000—01), Farm House, Fifty-Fifty Club, Phi Delta Kappa, Gamma Sigma Delta, Phi Kappa Phi, Sigma Xi, Alpha Zeta. Democrat. Presbyterian. Avocations: golf, skiing, woodworking, Civil War history, gardening. Home: 3001 S 51 # 2205 Lincoln NE 68506

OTTWEIN, MERRILL WILLIAM GEORGE, real estate company executive, veterinarian; b. Troy, Ill., Apr. 24, 1929; s. Oscar J. and Hilda (Bardelmeier) O.; m. Grace Marie Schmidt, Jan. 22, 1932; children: Ann Marie, Amy Sue, Paul John, Emily Carol. BS with highest honors, U. Ill., 1951, MS in Agrl. Econs., 1952, BS in Vet. Medicine, 1954, DVM with honors, 1956. Lic. veterinarian, Ill., real estate broker, Ill. Pvt. practice, Edwardsville, Ill., 1956-66; dir. Diakonia, Ch. World Svc., Honduras, 1967; mem. Ill. Senate, Springfield, 1968-70; real estate developer Cottonwood Sta. Corp., 1970-81; real estate broker Coldwell Banker, Edwardsville, 1981-91; exclusive buyer broker relocation svcs. Edwardsville, 1991—, O'Fallon, Ill., 1992—. Mem. vet. med. adv. com. U. Ill., Urbana, 1960-64. Pres. Cahokia Mounds coun. Boy Scouts Am., 1969-71; mem. bd. for world ministries United Ch. of Christ, N.Y.C., 1970-74; active local Rep. politics. Mem. Nat. Assn. Exclusive Buyer Agts. (treas. 1995, 96, pres. 1998), Ill. Assn. Realtors, Edwardsville-Glen Carbon C. of C., Edwardsville-Collinsville Bd. Realtors, Land of Goshen C. of C. (pres. 1974 75), U. Ill. Vet. Medicine Alumni Assn. (pres. 1960-61), Rotary (pres. Edwardsville 1976), Phi Kappa Phi, Alpha Zeta. Avocations: vocal and instrumental music, photography. Address: 34 Lilac Glen Carbon IL 62034 E-mail: Buyerside@aol.com.

OTUS, SIMONE, public relations executive; b. Walnut Creek, Calif., Jan. 10, 1960; d. Mahmut and Alexa (Artemenko) O. BA, U. Calif., Berkeley, 1981. Account exec. Marx-David Advt., San Francisco, 1981-82; freelance writer Mpls. and San Francisco, 1982-83; account exec. D'Arcy, MacManus & Masius, San Francisco, 1983; account supr. Ralph Silver Assocs., San Francisco, 1984-85; ptnr., co-founder Blanc & Otus Pub. Relations, San Francisco, 1985—. Address: Blanc & Otus Pub Rels 444 Castro St Fl 6 Mountain View CA 94041-2017

OTWELL, RALPH MAURICE, retired newspaper editor; b. Hot Springs, Ark., June 17, 1926; s. Walter Clement and Pearl Oda (Tisdale) O.; m. Janet Barbara Smith, July 18, 1953; children— Brian Thornton, Douglas Keith, David Smith. Student, U. Ark., 1947-48; BS, Northwestern U., 1951; postgrad. (Nieman fellow), Harvard, 1959-60. Reporter, telegraph editor So. Newspapers, Inc., Hot Springs, 1943-44, 47; asst. city editor Chgo. Sun-Times, 1953-59, news editor, 1959-63, asst. mng. editor, 1963-65, asst. to editor, 1965-68, mng. editor, 1968-76, editor, 1976-80, exec. v.p., editor, 1980-84. Mgmt. bd. newspaper div. Field Enterprises, Inc., 1967-84; lectr. Medill Sch. Journalism, Northwestern U., 1955—; charter mem. Nat. News Council, 1973-80 Trustee Garrett-Evang. Theol. Sem., 1965-79; Mem. nat. bd. Christian Social Concerns, United Meth. Ch., 1968-72; mem. bd. Community Renewal Soc., 1987-90, Chgo. Reporter, 1987-90, student publs. Northwestern U., 1968-72. Served to 1st lt. AUS, 1944-47, 51-53. Recipient Page One award Chgo. Newspaper Guild, 1964; named Ill. Journalist of Year No. Ill. U., 1974 Mem. Am. Soc. Newspaper Editors (chmn. ethics com. 1976-77), AP Mng. Editors Assn., Soc. Profl. Journalists (dir. 1966-71, sec. 1971-72, v.p. 1972-73, pres. 1973-74), Northwestern U. Alumni Assn. (dir. 1965-68, 91-93, sec. 1993-94, Merit award 1969, Svc. award 1995, chair seminar day com. 2001-2002), Sigma Delta Chi (pres. 1987-89), Kappa Tau Alpha, Econ. Club, Headline Club (pres. Chgo. chpt. 1965-66), Harvard Club Chgo., Chgo. Press Club (dir. 1968-77), Northwestern Club. Home: 2750 Hurd Ave Evanston IL 60201-1268 E-mail: ralph@otwell.com., r-otwell@northwestern.edu.

OU, LO-CHANG, physiology educator; b. Shanghai, Oct. 16, 1930; came to U.S., 1964; m. Cynthia Chin Ou, June 10, 1960; children; Winnie, Edward, Emily, Joseph. BS, Peking U., Beijing, 1954; PhD, Dartmouth Coll., 1971. Tchg. asst., dept. biochemistry Peking U., Beijing, 1954-60, lectr., dept. biochemistry, 1960-62; demonstrator, dept. physiology Hong Kong U., 1962-64; asst. prof. dept. physiology Dartmouth Med. Sch., Hanover, N.H., 1977-80, assoc. prof., 1980-85, rsch. prof., 1985—, prof. emeritus (active), 1998—. NIH rsch. grantee, 1977-94. Mem. Am. Physiol. Soc. Achievements include research on pathophysiology of high altitude. Office: Dartmouth Med Sch Dept Physiology Lebanon NH 03756 Office Phone: 603-650-7729. Business E-Mail: Lo.Chang.Ou@Dartmouth.edu.

OU, YEN-CHUAN, urologist; b. Taichung, Taiwan, Jan. 31, 1961; s. Wen-Guey and Haw (Jeng) Ou; m. Hui-Min Chen, Nov. 23, 1987; children: Hsien-Kuei, Hsien-Che, Hsien-Chi. B, Nat. Def. Med. Coll., Taipei, Taiwan, 1986. Resident Taichung Vets. Gen. Hosp., 1986—90, chief resident, 1990—91, urology specialist, 1991-92, 94—; chief urology Puli Vets. Hosp., Nan-Tou, Taiwan, 1993-94; rsch. assoc. U. Va., 1997—99, Inst. Medicine, Chung Shan Med. U., 2001—. Contbr. articles to profl. jours. Capt. Chinese Air Force, 1992-93. Nat. Sci. Coun. grantee, 1992. Mem. Urol. Assn. China, Assn. Andrology China, Surg. Assn. China. Mem. Nationalist Party. Avocations: ping pong/table tennis, basketball, travel, mountain climbing, music. Office: Taichung Vets Gen Hosp 160 SEc 3 Taichung-Kong Rd Taichung 407 Taiwan

OUBRERIE, JOSÉ R. architecture educator; Student, Supérieure des Beaux-Arts, Paris, 1955—59, Atelier Le Corbusier, 1958—65. With Le Corbusier, Arch., Paris, 1958—65; pvt. practice Paris, 1970—86; asst. prof. Unité Pédagogique d'Arch. #8, Paris, 1978—86, Columbia U., 1986—88; prof., dean U. Ky. Coll. Arch., 1988—92; prof. Ohio State U. Knowlton Sch. Arch., Columbus, 1992—, chair, head, 1992—97; co-owner Atelier Wylde-Oubrerie, Columbus, 1986—. Office: Ohio State Univ Knowlton Sch Arch 189 Brown Hall 190 W 17th Ave Columbus OH 43210*

OUDENS, GERALD FRANCIS, architect, architectural firm executive; b. Manchester, N.H., May 18, 1934; s. John and Louise Esther (Wagner) Oudens; m. Monica Elizabeth Wohlfert, June 16, 1962; children: Elizabeth Marian, Matthew Thomas, Katherine Frances. BA in Architecture cum laude, Yale U., 1956, MArch, 1958. Registered arch., D.C., Va., Md., Ind., Nat. Coun. Archtl. Registration Bds. Intern arch. Koehler & Isaak, Manchester, 1955-58; staff architect Office Surgeon Gen. USAF, Washington, 1958-61; assoc. Metcalf & Assocs., Washington, 1961-69; prin. Oudens & Knoop Architects, PC, Chevy Chase, Md., 1970—. Vis. critic, thesis advisor dept. architecture Cath. U. Am., 1968—88; mem. adv. com. Acad. Med. Ctr. Study Sch. Architecture Rice U., 1975; mem. ambulatory care adv. panel U.S. VA, 1974—75; mem. adv. panel No. Ind. Health Sys. Agy., 1977—81, AIA Rsch. Corp., 1978, Nat. Inst. Bldg. Scis., 1982—88; mem. design award juries Modern Healthcare Ann. Design Awards, 1992, 2002, Soc. Critical Care Medicine/AACN/AIA ICU Design Awards, 1992—97, 1999—2003, AIA Health Facilities Rev. Jury, 1995; presenter in field. Prin. works include NIH Master Plan, Bethesda, Md., Nat. Cancer Inst. Master Plan, Frederick, Md., Sibley Meml. Hosp., Washington, Washington Hosp. Ctr. Master Plan, Washington Adventist Hosp., Takoma Park, Md., Martha Jefferson Hosp., Charlottesville, Va., Marion (Ind.) Gen. Hosp., Humana Lucerne Hosp., Orlando, Fla., Hosp. de Pedregal, Mexico City, Fairfax Hosp., Falls Church, Va., Humana Audubon Hosp. and Heart Inst., Louisville, Humana Greensboro (N.C.) Hosp., Centre Universitaire des

Scis. de la Sante, Yaounde, Cameroon, Washington Home and Hospice, Cuttington U. Coll., Suakoko, Liberia, Escuela Agricola Panamericana, El Zamorano, FM, Honduras, others; contbr. articles to profl. jours. Recipient Nat. Capital Architecture award, D.C. Coun. Engring. and Archtl. Socs./Washington Acad. Scis., 1961, ICU Design citation, Soc. Critical Care Medicine, 1998. Fellow: AIA (acad. architecture for health 1971—, nat. healthcare policy task force 1993—, mem. adv. com. Am. Collegiate Schs. Architecture coun. archtl. rsch. 1994—, Am. Hosp. Assn. Grad. Fellowship Rev. Panel, Henry Adams award 1958, Honor award Ky. chpt. 1980, Outstanding Leadership and Commitment to Healthcare Design award 1987, Merit award Washington Met. chpt. 1989, Citations for Design Excellence 1988, 1990), Am. Coll. Healthcare Archs. (bd. regents, chmn. membership com.); mem.: Internat. Hosp. Fedn., Am. Hosp. Assn. (mem. faculty continuing edn. insts. 1972—76, adv. panel 1978), Lambda Alpha Internat. Office: Oudens & Knoop Architects PC 2 Wisconsin Cir Chevy Chase MD 20815-7003 E-mail: goudens@okarch.com.

OUELLET, ANDRÉ, business executive; b. St. Pascal, Can., Apr. 6, 1939; s. Albert and Rita (Turgeon) O.; m. Edith Pagé, July 17, 1965; children: Sonia, Jean, Olga, Pierre. BA, U. Ottawa, Ont., Can., 1960, D (hon.), 1995; LLL, U. Sherbrooke, Can., 1963. Mem. Can. Parliament, Ottawa, 1967-93, min. consumer and corp. affairs, 1974-76, 80-83, min. state urban affairs, 1976-78, min. public works, 1978-79, min. labor, 1983-84; postmaster gen. Can., Ottawa, 1972-74, 80-81; min. fgn. affairs Can. Parliament, Ottawa, 1993-96; chmn. bd. Can. Post Corp., Ottawa, 1996-99, pres., CEO, 1999—. Office: Canada Post Corp 2701 Riverside Dr Ste N1250 Ottawa ON Canada K1A 0B1 E-mail: andre.ouellet@canadapost.ca.

OUIMETTE, PAIGE, psychologist, researcher; b. Mt. Kisco, NY, Nov. 17, 1966; m. Anthony Garza, June 24, 2000; 1 child, Elizabeth Ouimette-Garza. PhD, SUNY, Stony Brook, 1989—94. Sr. rsch. assoc. VA Palo Alto Health Care Sys., Menlo Pk., Calif., 1995—2000; assoc. prof. Wash. State U., Pullman, 2000—03; rsch. assoc. Wash. Inst. Mental Illness Rsch. and Tng., Spokane, 2003—. Cons.; med. writer. Editor: (volume) Trauma and Substance Abuse: Causes, Consequences, (book) Gender and PTSD. Business E-Mail: ouimette@wsu.edu.

OUNDJIAN, PETER, conductor; b. Toronto, Canada; m. Nadine Oundjian; children: Lara, Peter. Grad, Royal Coll. Music. First violinist Tokyo String Quartet, 1981—95; artistic dir. Caramoor Internat. Music Festival, Katonah, NY, 2002; music dir. Nieuw Sinfonietta Amsterdam; prin. guest condr. Colo. Symphony, 2003; music dir. Toronto Symphony, 2004—. Adj. Yale Sch. of Music. Recipient First prize, Internat. Violin Competition in Vina Del Mar, Chile, 1980. Office: Toronto Symphony Orch 212 King St W, Ste 550 Toronto ON M5H 1K5 Canada

OUPREE, ANDERSON HUNTER, historian, educator; b. Hillsboro, Tex., Jan. 29, 1921; s. George W. and Sarah (Hunter) D.; m. Marguerite Louise Arnold, July 18, 1946; children: Marguerite Wright, Anderson Hunter. AB summa cum laude, Oberlin Coll., 1942; AM, Harvard U., 1947, PhD, 1952. Asst. prof. Tex. Tech U., 1950-52; rsch. fellow Gray Herbarium, Harvard U., 1952-54, 55-56, 81—; vis. asst. prof. U. Calif.-Berkeley, 1956-58, from assoc. prof. to prof., 1958-68, asst. to chancellor, 1960-62, dir. Bancroft Library, 1965-66; George L. Littlefield prof. Am. history Brown U., Providence, 1968-81, emeritus, 1981—; sr. vis. historian Nat. Mus. Am. History, 1975; scholar-in-residence So. Oreg. State Coll., 1983; vis. prof. history of sci. U. Minn., 1984. Cons. com. sci. and public policy Nat. Acad. Scis., 1963-64; mem. history adv. com. NASA, 1963-73, AEC, 1967-74; mem. panel on sci. and tech. U.S. Ho. of Reps. Com. on Sci. and Astronautics, 1969-73; project dir. on grants NSF, 1953-55, 61-68; mem. Smithsonian Council, 1975-84; trustee Mus. Am. Textile History, 1975-89; cons. in field. Author: Science in the Federal Government, 1957, 2d edit., 1986, Asa Gray, 1959, 2d edit., 1988; editor: Darwiniana, 1963, Science and the Emergence of Modern America, 1963, A Knowledge Policy for Peace: A Release from the Closed Universe of Friend and Foe, Technology in Society, 1994. Served to lt. USNR, 1942-46. Recipient Presdl. award N.Y. Acad. Scis., 1976; fellow Ctr. Advanced Study Behavioral Scis., 1967-68, Nat. Humanities Ctr., 1978-79 Fellow AAAS, Linnean Soc. London, Am. Acad. Arts and Scis. (sec. 1973-76); mem. Am. Hist. Assn., History of Sci. Soc. (Sarton medal 1990), Soc. History of Tech., Orgn. Am. Historians, Cosmos Club, Phi Beta Kappa. Home: 975 Memorial Dr Apt 201 Cambridge MA 02138-5755

OURISMAN, MANDELL J. automotives executive; b. Nov. 10, 1926; Student, U.S. Naval Acad., 1944, Georgetown U., 1947. Chmn., CEO Ourisman Automotive Enterprises, Marlow Heights, Md. Office: Ourisman Automotive Enterprises 4400 Branch Ave Marlow Heights MD 20748-1899 Office Phone: 301-423-4028. Personal E-mail: ourismanchev@erols.com.

OURSLER, FULTON, JR., editor, writer; b. West Falmouth, Mass., June 27, 1932; s. Fulton and Grace (Perkins) O.; m. Anne Noel Nevill, Nov. 29, 1954; children: Theresa Noel, Fulton III, Mark Nevill, James Randall, Carroll Grace. BA, Georgetown U., 1954. With Reader's Digest, Pleasantville, N.Y., 1956-87, book editor, 1968-70, sr. staff editor, 1970-72, asst. mng. editor, 1973, mng. editor, 1974-82, exec. editor, 1982-85, dep. editor-in-chief, 1986-87; editor-in-chief Guideposts mag., 1992—99; editor-in-chief, founding editor Angels on Earth mag., 1995-98, editl. dir., 1998-99; roving editor Guideposts mag., 2001—. Established: Fulton Oursler Meml. Collection, Georgetown U. Library.; editor: (commentary) Behold This Dreamer, 1964. Bd. dirs. Georgetown U. Library Assocs. Mem.: Friends of the Nyacks, Univ. Club. Home: 2 Laveta Pl Nyack NY 10960-1604 *Man makes two journeys in life: one in matter, the other in spirit. The first journey is outward and manifest; it leads to family, society, and career. The second journey is inward and invisible; it leads to the kingdom of God. The first journey is limited by logic, flesh, and time. The second is infinite, and its pathway is paradox. Self-preservation is the strongest instinct on the first journey; freedom, maturity, self-knowledge, power, and abundance seem to be important goals. But on the second journey, one learns that to find our truest selves, we must lose the sense of self; that to grow we must become as a child; that freedom is won by surrender, that the one counts for more than the many, that the meek are powerful, and the poor are rich. On both journeys, to gain life one must lose it, and be reborn.*

OUSELEY, WILLIAM NORMAN, security services consultant; b. N.Y.C., May 26, 1935; s. Norman J. Ouseley and Helen (Accurso) Loffredo; m. Josephine B. Ouseley, Mar. 3, 1962; children: John W., Elizabeth A. BA, Coll. of William & Mary, 1957; LLB, Fordham U., 1960. Spl. agt., supervisory spl. agt. organized crime FBI, nationwide, 1960-85; security rep. NFL, Kansas City, Mo., 1985-2000. Adv. bd. YMCA, Kansas City, 1987-88. Mem. Soc. Former FBI Spl. Agents (chmn. Kansas City chpt. 1992-93). Avocations: sports, outdoor activities.

OUSSANI, JAMES JOHN, stapling company executive; b. Bklyn., Jan. 3, 1920; s. John Thomas and Clara (Tager) O.; m. Lorraine G. Tutundgy, Apr. 25, 1954; children: James J., Gregory P., Rita C. B in Mech. Engring., Pratt Inst., 1942; JD (hon.), Coll. Boca Raton, Lynn U.; LLD. Dir. rsch., mfg. Supertronic Co., NYC, 1943-46; sr. ptnr. Perl-Oussani Machine Mfg. Co., NYC, 1946-49; founder The Staplex Co., Bklyn., 1949, pres., 1949—; exec. dir. Lourdes Realty Corp.; dir. Junios Corp.; prodr. air sampling equipment for radioactive fallout AEC, 1951—. Mem. Bur. Rsch. Air Pollution Control, Pres.'s Coun. on Youth Opportunity, Cardinal's Com. for Edn.; trustee Ch. of Virgin Mary; bd. dirs. St. Joan Arc Found., Boca Raton; founding mem. Lumen Christi-Palm Beach Diocese; founder, bd. dirs. Oussani Found.; founder James J. & Lorraine G. Oussani Scholarship Fund, Coll. Boca Raton; mem. cardinal's com. of laity, bishop's com. of laity; mem. Lumen Christi Found.; bd. overseers Lynn U., Boca Raton. Recipient Blue Ribbon Mining award, Sch. Mgmt. award, Aerospace Pride Achievement award; installed Knight of Jerusalem. Mem. Adminstrv. Mgmt. Soc., Office Adminstrn. Assn., Nat. Stationery and Office Equipment Assn. Office Equipment Assn., Office Execs. Assn., Nat. Office Machine Mfg. Assn., Nat. Office Machine Dealers Assn., Nat. Office Products Assn., Bus. Equipment Mfrs. Assn., Our Lady Perpetual Help Holy Name Soc., Knights of Holy Sepulchre, Knights of St. Gregory, Knights of Malta, Rotary, Salaam Club, Mahopac Golf Club (Lake Mahopac, NY), Internat. Club of Boca Raton, Boca Raton Hotel and Resort Club. Inventor automatic electric stapling machine. Patentee in field. Office: 777 5th Ave Brooklyn NY 11232-1626

OUTCALT, DAVID LEWIS, academic administrator, mathematician, educator, consultant, musician; b. Los Angeles, Jan. 30, 1935; s. Earl Kinyon and Alberta Estes Ferguson O.; m. Marcia Lee Beach, July 1, 1956; children—Jeffrey David, Kevin Douglas, Gregory Mark, Eric Matthew. BA in Math., Pomona Coll., 1956; MA in Math., Claremont Grad. Sch., 1958; PhD in Math., Ohio State U., 1963; D.Pub. Adminstrn. (hon.), Kyung Hee U., Korea, 1984. Asst. prof. math. Clarement McKenna Coll., 1962-64; asst. prof. to prof. math. U. Calif.-Santa Barbara, 1964-80, chmn. dept. math., 1969-72, dean instrnl. devel., 1977-80; vice chancellor acad. affairs U. Alaska, Anchorage, 1980-81, prof. math., 1980-86, chancellor, 1981-86; prof. natural and applied sci. U. Wis., Green Bay, 1986-93, chancellor, 1986—93, chancellor emeritus, 1998—, Hendrickson prof. econ. devel., 1994-98. Pres. Mid-Continent athletic conf., 1990-91. Author math. textbooks; contbr. articles on math. and higher edn. to profl. jours. Moderator bd. trustees Humana Hosp. Anchorage, 1982-83; mem. exec. bd. Western Alaska coun. Boy Scouts Am., 1982-86, Bay-Lakes coun., 1987-97, v.p. exploring, 1988-92, v.p. ops., 1992-93, pres., 1993-94; mem. Anchorage Symphony bd., 1986, Green Bay Symphony Bd., 1988-97, mem. Weidner Ctr. Presents Bd., 1994-98; peer reviewer NCAA, 1994-99; trustee, v.p., treas. Kauai Internat. Theatre, 1998-2000; trustee Kauai C.C. Fund, 2000—. Grantee USAF Office Sci. Research, 1964-71, U. Calif., 1975-78, NSF, 1976-79. Mem. Math. Assn. Am., Internat. Assn. Univ. Pres.'s (exec. com. 1988-96, internat. com. on tech. in higher edn. 1996-2002, N.Am. coun. exec. com. 1988-2002, vice chair, 1988-94, newsletter editor 1994-95), Greater Green Bay C. of C. (advance bd. 1987-97, bd. dirs. 1991-94, 95-97), Brown County Indsl. Devel. (pres. bd. dirs. 1994-97), Rotary (bd. dirs. Kapaa club 1999—, pres. 2002-03), Rotary Club of Kapaa Found. (bd. dirs. 2003—, chair 2003—), Sigma Xi. Mem. Congregational Ch. Home: 6414A Puupilo Rd Kapaa HI 96746-9463 E-mail: outcalt@aloha.net.

OUTIN, MARY LOUISE, business, multi-cultural history and geneology educator; b. Peak, S.C., July 18, 1948; d. Ralph T. Williams and Mary Frances Wicker-Outin, Theopolis Outin (Stepfather). BA in Bus. Adminstrn., Columbia Coll., Columbia, South Carolina, 1987; MEd, Lesley U., 1999; grad., S.C. Sch. Real Estate, 1986. Owner MO Businesses, Inc., Columbia, 2000—. N/A. Mem.: S.C. Afro-Am. Hist. and Geneal. Soc., Inc. (co-pub. rels. dir. 1998—2000), Am. Legion Aux. (Unit 219 2000). Avocations: family history research, genealogy, cooking, reading. Office: MO Businesses Inc P O Box 3393 Columbia SC 29230

OUTLAW, LANNY F. gas company executive; B in Engring., S.D. Sch. Mines and Tech. Various positions Shell Oil Co., 1958-87, Western Gas Resources, Inc., Denver, 1987-96, exec. v.p. ops., bus. devel. and engring., pres., COO, 1996-99, CEO, pres., 1999—. Office: 1099 18TH St STE 1200 Denver CO 80202-1964

OUTTEN, KRISTINA MARIE, secondary school educator; b. Ogden, Utah, Dec. 6, 1973; d. Burrett William and June J. Clay; m. Todd Edgar Outten, Nov. 16, 1996; 1 child, Nastassia Jade. BA in English Edn., U. Ariz., 1996, MA in Ednl. Psychology, 2000. Bar mgr. Bushwacker, Tucson, 1995-96; student tchr. Tucson H.S. Tucson Unified Sch. Dist., 1996, tchr. Alice Vail Mid. Sch., 1996—; bartender Applebee's Thomas & King, Tucson, 1996—2003. Com. mem. 504 rev. team, awards and site-based decision making team Vail Mid. Sch., 1998—. Author: And So It Begins..., 1999, Snakebite, 2003; contbr. poetry to Nat. Libr. of Poetry-Libr. of Congress, A View from Afar, The Peace We Knew, A Muse to Follow, Blossom in the Dawning, The Colors of Thought, Serenity at Daybreak; author poems (Editor's Choice awards 1996, 97, 98). Regents scholar U. Ariz., 1991; Vocal Talent scholar Am. Legend, 1991. Mem. Tucson Edn. Assn., Internat. Soc. Poets. Avocations: writing, singing, reading, travel.

OUTWATER, JOHN OGDEN, mechanical engineering educator; b. London, Eng., Jan. 2, 1923; came to U.S., 1924; s. John Ogden and Nenny (Boe) O.; m. Alice Hooker Davidson, Dec. 13, 1952; children— Anne Hooker, Catherine Boe (Mrs. Carl B. Colby), Alice Brookfield (Mrs. Robert B. Lang), John Ogden III. BA, Cambridge (Eng.) U., 1943, MA, 1948, PhD, 1976; Sc.D. (Timken fellow), Mass. Inst. Tech., 1950. Registered profl. engr. Research engr. DuPont Co., 1950-52; project engr. Universal Moulded Products, 1952-53; indsl. liaison officer Mass. Inst. Tech., 1954-55; prof. mech. engring. U. Vt., Burlington, 1955—71, chmn., 1955-93, prof. emeritus, 1993—. Leader archaeol. expdns. Wenner-Gren Found., Central Mexico, 1954, Yucatan, 1955, Peru-Bolivia, 1957, Haiti, 1959; cons. non-metallic materials Naval Ordnance Lab., Nat. Acad. Scis., Monsanto Research Corp., Smithsonian Instn., pres. Vt. Inst. Co., Inc. Author: (with others) Engineering Materials, 1959, Esplendor del Mexico Antigua; papers on metal cutting, plastics, archaeology, bones, ski safety, botany. Chmn. Vt. Instrument Co., Inc.; Mem. Vt. Conf. Econ. Growth; vestryman St. Paul's Cathedral, Burlington. Served as officer Brit. Army, 1943-47. Named Vt. Engr. of Year, 1970 Fellow ASME; mem. Am. Soc. Testing Materials, Holland Soc., Vt. Soc. Engrs., Delta Psi, Tau Beta Pi. Achievements include patents for. Home: 62 Overlake Park Burlington VT 05401-4012 Office: 321 S Union St Burlington VT 05401-4595 Office Phone: 802-658-3612.

OUYANG, ANN, physician, researcher, educator; b. Kaoshiung, Taiwan, Feb. 20, 1950; came to U.S., 1970; d. Mid and Ching Chao Liu O.; m. Michael Rusli; children: Andrew Ouyang Rusli, Robert Ouyang Rusli. BSc, U. London, 1971, MB BS, 1974. Diplomate Am. Bd. Medicine and sub-bd. Gastroenterology. House surgeon Guy's Hosp., London, 1974; house physician St. Olave's Hosp., London, 1974-75; intern and resident in medicine Pa. Hosp., Phila., 1975-78; fellow in gastroenterology U. Pa., Phila., 1978-80, rsch. assoc. in medicine, 1980-81, asst. prof. in medicine, 1981-90, assoc. prof. medicine, 1990-92; prof. medicine Pa. State U., Hershey, 1992—, chief divsn. gastroenterology and hepatology, 1992—. Mem. study sect. NIDDKD/NIH, Bethesda, Md., 1991-95, ad hoc mem. 1989, 90; mem. Am. Found. Aging Rsch. Nat. Screening Adv. Coun., 1995, NIH Health Reviewers Res., 1995—; mem. subsplty. bd. on gastroenterology Am. Bd. Internal Medicine, 1993—, med. sec., 1984-89. Mem. editl. bd. Annals Internal Medicine, 2000; contbr. articles to profl. jours. and chpts. to books. Recipient Career Devel. award NIH, 1986, Rsch. award, 1989. Fellow ACP (mem. publ. com. 2000, 01), Am. Coll. Gastroenterology; mem. AAAS, Am. Gastroenterological Assn. (rsch. com. 1986-89, admissions com. 1993-96, nominating com. 1993-95, chmn. 1995, abstract rev. com. Hormones and Receptors sect. 1994, tng. and edn. com. 1997-98, manpower and tng. com. chair 2000-02, chair insvc. exam devel. com. 2003—, Elsevier rsch. initiative award 1993), Am. Motility Soc. (steering com. 1991-94, sec. 2003), Am. Physiol. Soc., Am. Fedn. for Clin. Rsch., Soc. for Neurosci., Am. Soc. Gastrointestinal Endoscopists, Phila. Gastrointestinal Rsch. Group (pres. 1986-87), Sigma Delta Epsilon. Avocations: violin, art. Office: The Milton S Hershey Med Ctr Rm C5800 PO Box 850 Hershey PA 17033-0850

OUZTS, EUGENE THOMAS, minister, secondary education educator; b. Thomasville, Ga., June 7, 1930; s. John Travis and Livie Mae (Strickland) O.; m. Mary Olive Vineyard, May 31, 1956. BA, Harding U., Searcy, AR, 1956, MA, 1957; postgrad., Murray State U., KY, U. Ark., U. Ariz., Ariz. State U., No. Ariz. U. Cert. secondary tchr., Ark., Mo., Ariz.; cert. c.c. tchr., Ariz.; ordained minister Church of Christ, 1956. Min. various chs., Ark., Tex., Mo., 1957—65; tchr. various pub. schs., 1959—92; min. Ch. of Christ, Ariz., 1965—; 1st lt. CAP/USAF, 1980, advanced through grades to lt. col., 1989, chaplain, 1982—, asst. wing chaplain, 1985—. Adviser student activities Clifton (Ariz.) Pub. Schs., 1965-92; bd. dirs. Ariz. Ch. of Christ Bible Camp, Tucson, 1966—. Mem. airport adv. bd. Greenlee County, Clifton, Ariz., 1992—. Recipient Meritorious Svc. award, 1994, Exceptional Svc. award, 1997, Civil Air Patrol; named Ariz. Wing Chaplain of Yr., 1984, Thomas C. Casaday Unit Chaplain of Yr., 1985, Ariz. Wing Safety Officer of Yr., 1989, Ariz. Wing Sr. Mem. of Yr., 1994, Southwest Region Sr. Mem. of Yr., 1995, Civil Air Patrol. Mem. Mil. Chaplains Assn., Air Force Assn., Disabled Am. Vets., Am. Legion, Elks. Democrat. Avocations: flying, building and flying model aircraft, reading. Home and Office: 739 E Cottonwood Rd Duncan AZ 85534-8108

OVADIAH, JANICE, non-profit organization consultant, cultural institute executive; m. Isaac Ovadiah; children: Meir Benjamin, Simha Victoria Miriam. BA, Washington U., St. Louis, 1965; MA, Columbia U., 1967, PhD, 1978. Dir. profl. study tours Am. Odysseys, Inc., 1973-84; escort, interpreter in French U.S. Dept. State, 1978-84; asst. to exec. dir. Meml. Found. for Jewish Culture, 1984-87; exec. dir. Congregation Shearith Israel/The Spanish & Portuguese Syn., N.Y.C., 1987—, Sephardic House, N.Y.C., 1987—2003; freelance cons., 2003—. Instr. French Rutgers U., New Brunswick, N.J., 1978-79; asst. to dir. of The Maison Franclase, Columbia U., 1970-72; instr. French Columbia U., 1968-70; lectr. in field. Author: (books) Toward a Concept of Cinematic Literature: An Analysis of Hiroshima, Mon Amour, 1983, The Far Away Island of the Grey Lady, 1979, others; contbr. articles to profl. jours. E-mail: jovadiah@aol.com.

OVAERT, TIMOTHY CHRISTOPHER, mechanical engineering educator; b. Chgo., Apr. 30, 1959; s. Walter Allen and Joyce Ann (Collins) O.; m. Valerie Mora, July 16, 1988; children: Teresa Noel, Christina Lynn. BSME, U. Ill., 1981; MEM, Northwestern U., 1985, PhD, 1989. Plant engr. Wells Mfg. Co.-Dura Bar Div., Woodstock, Ill., 1981-85; mech. engr. Nat. Inst. of Standards and Tech., Gaithersburg, Md., 1986; asst. prof. Penn State U., 1989-95; assoc. prof. Pa. State U., 1995-2000, prof., 2000, U. Notre Dame, Ind., 2000—. Assoc. editor ASME Trans., Jour. Tribology, 1998—2003. Traffic safety com. Borough of State College, Pa., 1992. Named Nat. Young Investigator, NSF, 1992. Office: U Notre Dame 374 Fitzpatrick Hall Notre Dame IN 46556

OVERBECK, CARLA WERDEN, soccer player, coach; b. Pasadena, Calif., May 9, 1969; m. Greg Overbeck, Dec. 5, 1992; 1 child, Jackson. BS in Psychology, U. N.C., 1990. Asst. women's soccer coach Duke U., Durham, NC. Mem. U.S. Nat. Women's Soccer Team, 1988—, including world championship FIFA Women's World Cup team, 1991, FIFA Women's World Cup team, 95, gold medal U.S. Olympic Team, 96. Named 3-time NSCAA All Am.; named to Soccer Am. All-Freshman team. Achievements include played 63 consecutive international games, a record for any U.S. national team player. Office: US Soccer Fedn 1801 S Prairie Ave Chicago IL 60616-1319

OVERBY, OSMUND RUDOLF, art historian, educator; b. Mpls., Nov. 8, 1931; s. Oscar Rudolph and Gertrude Christine (Boe) O.; m. Barbara Ruth Spande, Mar. 20, 1954; children: Paul, Katherine, Charlotte. BA, St. Olaf Coll., 1953; B.Arch., U. Wash., 1958; MA, Yale U., 1960, PhD, 1963. Asst. in instruction dept. of history of art Yale U., 1959-60, 61-62; architect Hist. Am. Bldgs. Survey, U.S. Nat. Park Service, 1960-61, summers 1959, 62, 63, 65, 68, 69, 70, 73, 85; lectr. dept. fine arts U. Toronto, Ont., Can., 1963-64; faculty dept. art history and archaeology U. Mo., Columbia, 1964—, dept. chmn., 1967-70, 75-77, prof. art history, 1979-98, prof. emeritus, 1998—, dir. Mus. of Art and Archaeology, 1977-83. Vis. prof. dept. architecture U. Calif., Berkeley, 1980; Morgan prof. U. Louisville, 1989; vis. prof. dept. art history and archaeology Washington U., St. Louis, 1996; bd. advisors Nat. Trust for Hist. Preservation, 1974-83; cons., panelist Nat. Endowment for Humanities, 1974—; bd. Mo. Mansion Preservation Commn., 1974-87; advisor Heritage/St. Louis Survey, 1974-76; counsellor to St. Louis Landmarks Assn., 1977—; chmn. Task Force on Hist. Preservation City of Columbia, 1977-78; cons. on hist. preservation; active Mo. Adv. Council on Hist. Preservation, 1967-82; lectr., exhibitor profl. confs. in field Author: Historic American Buildings Survey, Rhode Island Catalog, 1972, William Adair Bernoudy, Architect, Bringing the Legacy of Frank Lloyd Wright to St. Louis, 1999; co-author: Laclede's Landing, a History and Architectural Guide, 1977, The Saint Louis Old Post Office, A History and Architectural Guide to the Building and Its Neighborhood, 1979; co-author, editor: Illustrated Museum Handbook, A Guide to the Collections in the Museum of Art and Archaeology, University of Missouri-Columbia, 1982; editor in chief Buildings of the United States series, 1990-96; contbr. sects. to books, articles to profl. publs. in field. Served with U.S. Army, 1953-55. Recipient various fellowships and grants in field. Mem. Soc. Archtl. Historians (bd. dirs. 1968-73, 78-81, Jour. editor 1968-73, dir. Mo. Valley chpt., session chmn. ann. meeting 1976, v.p. 1982-86, pres. 1986-88, chmn. coms.), Mid-Continent Am. Studies Assn. (editorial bd. American Studies 1965-70), Midwest Art History Soc. (bd. 1975-78, gen. chmn. annual meeting 1977), Mid-Am. Coll. Art Assn. (session chmn. annual meeting 1975), Mo. Heritage Trust (pres. 1976-79, 81-83, bd. dirs. 1979—), Coll. Art Assn., Landmarks Assn. St. Louis. Lutheran. Home: 1118 W Rollins Rd Columbia MO 65203-2221 Office: U Mo Dept Art History & Archaeolo Columbia MO 65211-0001 E-mail: overbyo@missouri.edu.

OVERBY, PETER M. journalist; b. Washington, Oct. 30, 1949; s. Kermit O. and Ethel Schlasinger Overby; m. Alexandra A. Roth; children: Graham C.R., Honora W.R. BS, Boston U., 1972. Editor Dem. Study Group, Washington, 1975—78, Plus Pubs., Washington, 1978—79; reporter Potomac News, Woodbridge, Va., 1980—83, The (Bergen) Record, Hackensack, NJ, 1983—90; staff writer, editor, sr. editor Common Cause Mag., Washington, 1991—94; Washington columnist NJ Reporter, Princeton, 1991—94; power, money and influence corr. NPR News, Washington, 1994—. Adv. com., polit. coverage project Radio and TV News Dirs. Found., Washington, 1997—2000. Co-recipient Top 10 Censored Stories award, Project Censored, 1991, 1993, 11 Best Investigative Journalism in a Mag. award, Investigative Reporters & Editors, 1993; recipient duPont-Columbia Silver Baton for Excellence in Broadcast Journalism, Grad. Sch. of Journalism, Columbia U., 2001. Unitarian. Office: National Public Radio 635 Massachusetts Ave NW Washington DC 20001 Business E-Mail: poverby@npr.org.

OVEREND, MARK G. diversified financial services company executive; CFO USA Education, Inc (formerly SLM Holding Corp.), Washington. Office: SLM Holding Corp 1050 Thomas Jefferson St NW Washington DC 20007-3837

OVERGAARD, CORDELL JERSILD, lawyer, business executive, director; b. Chgo., June 1, 1934; s. Kristin and Rose Marie (Jersild) Overgaard; m. Gail A. Gill, Sept. 5, 1959; children: Diane, Karen, Susan. BS with honors, U. Ill., 1957; LLB magna cum laude, Harvard U., 1960. CPA Ill.; bar: Ill. 1960. Assoc. Hopkins & Sutter, Chgo., 1960—67, ptnr., 1967—96, chmn. bus. fin. sect. Dir. mem. exec. com. UPI, Inc., 1982—83; pres. Cmty. Cablevision, Inc., 1980—86, Gore-Overgaard Broadcasting, Inc., 1986—; pres. bd. trustees NorthCare, 1979—81; sec. Family Weekly, Inc., 1976—80; dir. Prudential Health Care Plan, Inc., 1980—89, Cahners Pub. Co., 1970—74; dir., v.p. Small Newspaper Group, Inc., 1981—; prin. mem. Rancho Paso Grande LLC (RanchoPasoGrande.com). Editor: Harvard Law Rev., 1960. Mem. Ill. Bd. Ethics, 1973—76, chmn., 1976—80. Mem.: Chgo. Bar Assn. (chmn. corp. law com. 1972—73), February Group, Alpha Delta Phi, Beta Alpha Psi, Beta Gamma Sigma. Home: 11310 E Arabian Park Dr Scottsdale AZ 85259-4913

OVERGAARD, MITCHELL JERSILD, lawyer; b. Chgo., Jan. 9, 1931; s. Kristen Mikkelsen and Rose Eunice (Jersild) O.; m. Joan Marquardt, Aug. 2, 1958; children: Wade, Kristin Bond, Neil. BA, U. Chgo., 1950, JD, 1953. Bar: Ill. 1957, U.S. Supreme Ct. 1975. Assoc. Dale, Haffner & Grow, Chgo., 1957-63; ptnr. Overgaard & Davis, Chgo., 1963-2000, of counsel, 2001—. Dir. Cmty. Bank of Homewood-Flossmoor, Homewood, Ill., 1973—83. Trustee Village of Homewood, 1965-69, 85-95; commr. Homewood-Flossmoor Park Dist., 1969-77; past pres., bd. dirs. Family Svcs. and Mental Health Ctr. of South Cook County, Homewood Youth Coun.; bd. dirs. Ill. Philharm. Orch., 1992-95, South Star Svcs., 1998—; pres. Illiana Classis, Reformed Ch. in Am., 2004—. With U.S. Army, 1953-56. Mem.: Rotary. Mem. Reformed Ch. in America (elder) Home: 19137 Loomis Ave Homewood IL 60430-4431 Office: Overgaard & Davis 134 N La Salle St Chicago IL 60602-1086

OVERGAARD, ROBERT MILTON, retired religious organization administrator; b. Ashby, Minn., Nov. 6, 1929; s. Gust and Ella (Johnson) O.; m. Sally Lee Stephenson, Dec. 29, 1949; children: Catherine Jean Overgaard Thuleen, Robert Milton, Elizabeth Dianne Overgaard Almendinger, Barbara, Craig, David (dec.), Lori Overgaard Noack. Cert., Luth. Brethren Sem., 1954; BS, Mayville (N.D.) State U., 1959; MS, U. Oreg., 1970. Ordained to ministry Ch. Luth. Brethren Am., 1954. Pastor Elim Luth. Ch., Frontier, Sask., Can., 1954-57, Ebenezer Luth. Ch., Mayville, 1957-60, Immanuel Luth. Ch., Eugene, Oreg., 1960-63, 59th Street Luth. Ch., Bklyn., 1963-68, Immanuel Luth. Ch., Pasadena, Calif., 1969-73; exec. dir. world missions Ch. Luth. Brethren Am., Fergus Falls, Minn., 1973-86, pres., 1986—2001, ret., 2001. Editor Faith and Fellowship, 1967-75. Lutheran. Home: 806 W Channing Ave Fergus Falls MN 56537-3221 Office: Ch Luth Brethren Am PO Box 655 Fergus Falls MN 56538-0655 E-mail: rmo@clba.org.

OVERGAARD, WILLARD MICHELE, retired political scientist, jurisprudent; b. Montpelier, Idaho, Oct. 16, 1925; s. Elias Nielsen and Myrtle LaVerne (Humphrey) O.; m. Lucia Clare Cochrane, June 14, 1946; children: Eric Willard, Mark Fredrik, Alisa Claire. BA, U. Oreg., 1949; MA, U. Wis., 1955; PhD in Polit. Sci., U. Minn., 1969. Instr., Soviet and internat. affairs Intelligence Sch., U.S. Army, Europe, 1956-62, dir. intelligence rsch. tng. program, 1958-61; asst. prof. internat. affairs George Washington U., 1964-67; sr. staff polit. scientist Ops. Rsch. Inst., U.S. Army Inst. Advanced Studies, Carlisle, Pa., 1967-70; assoc. prof. polit. sci., chmn. dept., dir. Internat. Studies Inst., Westminster Coll., New Wilmington, Pa., 1970-72; prof. polit. sci. and pub. law Boise (Idaho) State U., 1972-94, chmn. dept., 1972-87, acad. dir. M.P.A. degree program, pers. adminstr. mem. humanities coun. interdisciplinary studies in humanities, 1976-87, prof. of pub. law emeritus, 1994—, dir. Taft Inst. Seminars for Pub. Sch. Tchrs., 1985-87, coord. Legal Asst. Program, 1990-95. Mem. comml. panel Am. Arbitration Assn., 1974—; mem. Consortium for Idaho's Future, 1974-75; adv. com. Idaho Statewide Tng. Program Local Govt. Ofcls., 1974-78; adv. group Gov. Idaho Task Force Local Govt., 1977; co-dir. Idaho State Exec. Inst., Office of Gov., 1979-83; grievance hearing officer City of Boise, 1981-85; arbitrator U.S. Postal Svc., 1988-90; cons. in field. Author: The Schematic System of Soviet Totalitarianism, 3 vols, 1961, Legal Norms and Normative Bases for the Progressive Development of International Law as Defined in Soviet Treaty Relations, 1945-64, 1969; co-author: The Communist Bloc in Europe, 1959; editor: Continuity and Change in International Politics, 1972; chief editor: Idaho Jour. Politics, 1974-76. Served with USAAF, 1943-45; with AUS, 1951-54; ret. maj. USAR. Named Disting. Citizen of Idaho, Idaho Statesman, 1979; Fulbright scholar, U. Oslo, 1949—50, Non-resident scholar, U. Wis., 1954—55, Adminstrv. fellow, U. Minn., 1955—56, Rsch. fellow, 1962—64. Mem. ABA (assoc.), Res. Officers Assn. (life), Am. Legion. Home: 2023 S Five Mile Rd Boise ID 83709-2316 E-mail: wgaard@velocitus.net.

OVERHAUSER, ALBERT WARNER, physicist; b. San Diego, Aug. 17, 1925; s. Clarence Albert and Gertrude Irene (Pehrson) Overhauser; m. Margaret Mary Casey, Aug. 25, 1951; children: Teresa, Catherine, Joan, Paul, John, David, Susan, Steven. AB, U. Calif., Berkeley, 1948, PhD, 1951; DSc (hon.), U. Chgo., 1979; LLD (hon.), Simon Fraser U., 1998. Research assoc. U. Ill., 1951—53; asst. prof. physics Cornell U., 1953—56, assoc. prof., 1956—58; supr. solid state physics Ford Motor Co., Dearborn, Mich., 1958—62, mgr. theoret. scis., 1962—69, asst. dir. phys. scis., 1969—72, dir. phys. scis., 1972—73; prof. physics Purdue U., West Lafayette, Ind., 1973—74, Stuart disting. prof. physics, 1974—. With USNR, 1944—46. Recipient Alexander von Humboldt sr. U.S. scientist award, 1979, Nat. medal of Sci., Pres. of U.S., 1994. Fellow: Am. Acad. Arts and Scis., Am. Phys. Soc. (Oliver E. Buckley Solid State Physics prize 1975); mem.: NAS. Home: 236 Pawnee Dr West Lafayette IN 47906-2115 Office: Purdue U Dept Of Physics West Lafayette IN 47907 Office Phone: 765-494-3037. E-mail: awo@physics.purdue.edu.

OVERHOLT, HUGH ROBERT, lawyer, retired army officer; b. Beebe, Ark., Oct. 29, 1933; s. Harold R. and Cuma E. (Hall) O.; m. Laura Annell Arnold, May 5, 1961; children: Sharon, Scott. Student, Coll. of Ozarks, 1951-53; BA, U. Ark., 1955, LL.B., 1957. Bar: Ark. 1957. Commd. 1st lt. U.S. Army, 1957, advanced through grades to maj. gen., 1981; chief Criminal Law Div., JAG Sch., Charlottesville, Va., 1971-73; chief personnel, plans and tng. Office of JAG, U.S. Army, Washington, 1973-75; staff judge adv. XVIII Airborne Corps, Ft. Bragg, N.C., 1976-78; spl. asst. for legal and selected policy matters Office of Dep. Asst., 1978-79; asst. judge adv. gen. for mil. law Office of JAG, Washington, 1979-81, asst. judge adv. gen., 1981-85, judge adv. gen, 1985-89; atty. Ward & Smith, New Bern, N.C., 1989—. Notes and comment editor Ark. Law Rev, 1956-57. Decorated Army Meritorious Service medal with oak leaf cluster, Army Commendation medal with 2 oak leaf clusters., Legion of Merit, Def. Meritorious Service medal, D.S.M. Mem. ABA, N.C. Bar Assn., Ark. Bar Assn., Assn. U.S. Army, Delta Theta Phi, Omicron Delta Kappa, Sigma Pi. Presbyterian. Office: Ward and Smith 1001 College Ct New Bern NC 28562-4972 Office Phone: 252-672-5462. E-mail: hro@wardandsmith.com.

OVERHOLT, MILES HARVARD, cable television consultant; b. Glendale, Calif., Sept. 30, 1921; s. Miles Harvard and Alma Overholt; A.B., Harvard Coll., 1943; m. Jessie Foster, Sept. 18, 1947; children: Miles Harvard, Keith Foster. Mktg. analyst Dun & Bradstreet, Phila., 1947-48; collection mgr. Standard Oil of Calif., L.A., 1948-53; br. mgr. RCA Svc. Co., Phila., 1953-63, ops. mgr. Classified Aerospace project RCA, Riverton, N.J., 1963; pres. CPS, Inc., Paoli, Pa., 1964-67; v.p. Gen. Time Corp.; mem. pres.'s exec. com. Gen. Time Corp., Mesa, Ariz., 1970-78; gen. mgr., dir. svc. Talley Industries, Mesa, 1967-78; v.p., gen. mgr. Northwest Entertainment Network, Inc., Seattle, 1979-81; v.p., dir. Cable Communication Cons., 1982—; mcpl. cable cons., 1981—; pub. The Mcpl. Cable Regulator. Served with USMCR, 1943-46. Decorated Bronze Star, Purple Heart (two). Mem. Nat. Assn. TV Officers and Advisors. Home: 8320 Frederick Pl Edmonds WA 98026-5033 Office: Cable Communication Cons 502 E Main St Auburn WA 98002-5502

OVERMAN, DEAN LEE, lawyer, investor, writer; b. Cook County, Ill., Oct. 9, 1943; s. Harold Levon and Violet Elsa (True) O.; m. Linda Jane Olsen, Sept. 6, 1969; children: Elisabeth True, Christiana Hart. BA, Hope Coll., 1965; student, Princeton Sem. and U., 1965-66; JD, U. Calif., Berkeley, 1969; postgrad. in bus., U. Chgo., 1974, U. Calif. Bar: Ill. 1969, D.C. 1977. Assoc. to ptnr. D'Ancona, Pflaum et al., Chgo., 1970-75; White House fellow, asst. to v.p. Nelson Rockefeller, Washington, 1975-76; assoc. dir. Domestic Council The White House, Washington, 1976-77; sr. ptnr. Winston & Strawn, Washington, 1977—. Cons. White House; spl. counsel to Gov. James Thompson, Springfield, Ill.; adj. faculty in secured financing U. Va. Law Sch., Charlottesville; vice chmn. J.F. Forstmann Co.; chmn. Holland Investment Co.; adj. fellow Ctr. for Strategic and Internat. Studies, 1993-95; vis. scholar, officer Harvard U., 1994-95; Templeton scholar Oxford U., 1999—. Author: Toward a National Policy on State and Local Government Finance, 1976, Effective Writing Techniques, 1980, (with others) Financing Equipment, 1973, Sales and Financing Under the Revised UCC, 1975, A Case Against Accident and Self Organization, 1997; monthly newspaper column Chgo. Daily Law Bull.; contbr. articles to profl. jours. Commencement spkr. Hope Coll., Holland, Mich., 1978; bd. dirs. Internat. Bus. Inst., White House Fellows Assn., Cmtys. in Schs., Inc.; adv. bd. The Beacon Group; former bd. dirs. U.S. Decathlon Assn. Reginald Heber Smith fellow U. Pa., 1969-70. Mme. Mensa, Intertel, ABA, Ill. Bar Assn., D.C. Bar Assn., Chgo. Bar Assn., Met. Club (D.C.), Internat. Philos. Enquiry, Triple Nine Soc., Burning Tree Club (Bethesda, Md.), Congl. Country Club (Bethesda), Harvard Club of N.Y.C., Macatawa (Mich.) Bay Yacht Club. Office: Winston & Strawn 1400 L St NW Washington DC 20005-3508

OVERMAN, LARRY EUGENE, chemistry educator; b. Chgo., Mar. 9, 1943; s. Lemoine Emerson and Dorothy Jane Overman; m. Joanne Louise Dewey, June 5, 1966; children: Michael, Jackie. BA in Chemistry, Earlham Coll., 1965; PhD in Organic Chemistry, U. Wis., 1969. Asst. prof. chemistry U. Calif., Irvine, 1971-76, assoc. prof. chemistry, 1976-79, prof. chemistry, 1979-94, chair dept. chemistry, 1990-93, disting. prof. chemistry, 1994—. Mem. sci. adv. bd. Pharmacopeia, Inc., 1993—; co-chair bd. chem. scis. and tech. NRC, 1997-2000. Editor-in-chief Organic Reactions, 1999—; bd. editors Organic Reactions, 1984-97, Organic Syntheses, 1986-94; hon. mem. editl. adv. bd. Ann. Reports in Hetero Chem., 1989-95, Synlett, 1989—, Jour. Am. Chem. Soc., 1996-, Chem. Revs., 1996-2000, Accounts Chem. Rsch., 1996-99; mem. cons. editors Tetrahedron Publs., 1995—; mem. editl. bd. Procs. NAS, 1998-2000. Recipient Sr. Scientist award Alexander von Humboldt Found., 1985-87, Jacob Javits award Nat. Inst. Neurol. Sci., 1985-92, 92-99, Disting. Faculty award Earlham Coll., 1999, S.T. Li prize for achievements in sci. and tech., 1999, Yamada prize, 2002; fellowship Japan Soc. for Promotion of Sci., 2000; predoctoral fellow NIH, 1966-69, postdoctoral fellow, 1969-71; fellow A.P. Sloan Found., 1975-77, Guggenheim fellow, 1993-94, Japan Soc. Promotion Sci. fellow, 2000; Arthur C. Cope scholar, 1989. Fellow NAS, AAAS, Am. Acad. Arts and Scis.; mem. Am. Chem. Soc. (exec. com. organic divsn., Cope Scholar award 1989, Creative Work in Synthetic Organic Chemistry award 1995), Royal Soc. Chemistry (Centenary medal 1997). Achievements include research in new methods for organic synthesis, natural products synthesis, medicinal chemistry. Office: U Calif Irvine Dept Chemistry 516 Rowland Hl Irvine CA 92697-2025 E-mail: leoverma@uci.edu.

OVERMYER, DANIEL LEE, Asian studies educator; b. Columbus, Ohio, Aug. 20, 1935; s. Elmer Earl and Bernice Alma (Hesselbart) O.; m. Estella Velazquez, June 19, 1965; children: Rebecca Lynn, Mark Edward. BA, Westmar Coll., LeMars, Iowa, 1957; BD, Evang. Theol. Sem., Naperville, Ill., 1960; MA, U. Chgo., 1966, PhD, 1971. Pastor Evangel. United Brethren Ch., Chgo., 1960-64; asst. prof. dept. religion Oberlin (Ohio) Coll., 1970-73; prof. Asian studies U. B.C., Vancouver, Canada, 1973—2000, acting head religious studies, 1984-85, head Asian studies, 1986-91, prof. emeritus, 2000—. Vis. prof. Princeton (N.J.) U., 1983, U. Heidelberg, Heidelberg, Germany, 1993, Nat. Chengchi U., Taiwan, 2002; prof. Chinese U., Hong Kong, 1996—98, hon. prof. Shanghai Normal U., China, 1997—. Author: Folk Buddhist Religion, 1976, Religions of China, 1986; (with David Jordan) The Flying Phoenix, 1986, Precious Volumes: An Introduction to Chinese Sectarian Scriptures From the Sixteenth and Seventeenth Centuries, 1999; editor Ethnography in China Today:A Critical Assessment of Methods and Results, 2002, Religion in China Today, 2003; editor spl. issue The China Quar., June 2003; contbr. articles to encys. and profl. jours. Chmn. Sch. Consultative Com., Vancouver, 1976-77; coord. Vancouver Boys Soccer League, 1979-81; adult edn. coord. United Ch. Can., Vancouver, 1981-84; co-chmn. Endowment Lands Regional Park Com., 1987-90; co-chair China and Inner Asia Coun., Assn. Asian Studies, 1992—. With USNR, 1953-61. Recipient Killam faculty rsch. prize U. B.C., 1986, Killiam faculty tchg. prize, 2000; named Alumnus of Yr., U. Chgo. Divinity Sch., 2001; NEH fellow, 1978, 79, China Rsch. fellow, 1981, sr. fellow coun. humanities Princeton U., 1983, Wang Inst. Grad. Studies fellow, 1985-86. Fellow Royal Soc. Can.; mem. Am. Soc. Study Religion, Soc. Study Chinese Religions (pres. 1985-88), Assn. Asian Studies. Democrat. Methodist. Avocations: photography, swimming, hiking, gardening. Home: 3393 W 26th Ave Vancouver BC Canada V6S 1N4 Office: UBC Ctr Chinese Rsch Vancouver BC Canada V6T 1Z2 E-mail: dano@interchange.ubc.ca.

OVERSTREET, JAMES WILKINS, obstetrics and gynecology educator, administrator; BA in Biology magna cum laude, U. South, 1967; BA in Natural Scis., U. Cambridge, Eng., 1970, PhD in Reproductive Physiology, 1973, MA in Natural Scis., 1974; MD, Columbia U., 1974. Diplomate Nat. Bd. Med. Examiners; lic. physician, Calif. NIH Med. Scientist Tng. fellow dept. anatomy coll. physicians ans surgeons Columbia U., 1970-72, NIH Med. Scientist Tng. fellow Internat. Inst. for Study Human Reproduction, 1972-74; asst. resident in ob-gyn. Presbyn. Hosp., N.Y.C., 1974; Ford Found. Postdoctoral Rsch. fellow dept. ob-gyn. Cornell U. Med. Coll., 1975-76; asst. prof. human anatomy and ob-gyn. sch. medicine U. Calif., Davis, 1976-80, assoc. prof. human anatomy, 1980-84, assoc. prof. ob-gyn. sch. medicine, 1980-85, prof. ob-gyn. sch. medicine, 1985—, chief divsn. reproductive biology and medicine dept. ob-gyn. sch. medicine, 1983-86, dir. lab. for energy-related health rsch., 1985-88, dir. Inst. Toxicology and Environ. Health, unit leader devel. and reproductive biology Primate Rsch. Ctr., 1988—. Mem. sci. rev. panel for health rsch., reviewer test rules dept. and reproductive abd devel. toxicology brs. U.S. EPA; mem. ad hoc study sect., cons. Nat. Inst. for Occupational Safety and Health; chair AIDS and related rsch. rev. group NIH; chmn. spl. study sect., mem. site visit team, mem. ad hoc reproductuve endocrinology study sect. Nat. Inst. Child Health and Human Devel.; reviewer, mem. site visit team Nat. Inst. Environ. Health Scis./NIH, Med. Rsch. Coun. Can.; mem. tech. adv. com. and site visit team contraceptive rsch. and devel. project Agy. for Internat. Devel./Ea. Va. Med. Sch.; temp. advisor spl. program rsch. devel. and rsch. tng. in human reproduction WHO; mem. reproductive and devel. toxicology program rev. panel Chem. Industry Inst. Toxicology; mem. exec. com. systemwide toxic substances rsch. and tng. program U. Calif.; reviewer NSF, Office Health and Environ. Rsch., U.S. Dept. Energy, March of Dimes Reproductive Hazards in the Workplace Rsch. Grants Program, Mt. Sinai Hosp., Alta. Heritage Cancer Grants, U.S.-Israel Binational Agrl. Rsch. and Devel. Fund; clin. cons. lab. surveys program Coll. Am. Pathologists; cons. Ctr. for Drugs and Biologics, U.S. FDA, Inst. for Internat. Studies in Natural Family Planning, Georgetown U., Internat. Devel. Rsch. Ctr. Assoc. editor Molecular Reproduction and Devel.; mem. editorial bd. Biology of Reproduction, 1983-86, Jour. In Vitro Fertilization and Embryo Transfer, 1984-89, Reproductive Toxicology, Fertilty and Sterility, 1984-92, Jour. Andrology, 1990-92; referee Jour. Reproduction and Fertilty, Jour. Exptl. Zoology, Am. Jour. Physiology, Am. Jour. Ob-Gyn., Jour. Urology, Science, Jour. Clin. Endocrinology and Metabolism, Archives Internal Medicine, Internat. Jour. Andrology, Reproduction, Nutrition, Devel., Western Jour. Medicine, Contraception, Human Reproduction, Proceedings Royal Soc. Series B.; invited lectr. in field. Georgia Fulbright scholar, 1967-68; recipient Rsch. Career Devel. award NIH, 1978-83, Disting. Career in Clin. Investigation award Columbia Presbyn. Med Ctr., 1992; grantee Syntex Rsch. Divsn., 1978-81, NIH, 1978-81, 78-83, 79-90, 81-90, 85-88, 86—, 87—, 88—, 89—, 90— (two grants), 91—, 92—, 93—, U. Calif., 1981-82, U.S. EPA, 1981-84, 82-84, Nat. Inst. for Occupational Safety and Health, 1982-84, U.S. Dept. Energy, 1985-88, Georgetown U., 1987-89, 92—, Merck Rsch. Labs., 1988-90, 92, 92—, March of Dimes, 1988-90, Semiconductor Industry Assn., 1989-92, Tobacco Related Disease Rsch. Program, 1990-93, Andrew W. Mellon Found., 1993—, Mem. Am. Fertility Soc., Am. Soc. Andrology (exec. coun. 1986-89), Soc. for Study Fertility, Soc. for Study Reproduction, Phi Beta Kappa. Achievements include research in physiology of mammalian spermatozoa, sperm transport in the female reproductive tract, in vivo and in vitro mammalian fertilization, diagnosis and therapy of human male infertility, reproductive toxicology, environmental and occupational hazards to male and female fertility, contraceptive development, reproductive endocrinology. Office: U Calif Davis Inst Toxicology & Enviro Health Rsch Office Davis CA 95616

OVERSTREET, JIM, former public relations executive; b. Savannah, Ga., Dec. 11, 1947; Reporter Atlanta Constitution, 1967-69; asst. sports editor Marietta Daily Jour., 1969-73; mktg. dir. Lake Lanier Islands Resorts, 1973-77; gen. mgr. Harlequin Theatre, 1977-78; acct. exec. Cohn & Wolfe, 1978-80, acct. supr., 1980-83, dir. acct. svc., 1983-84, exec. v.p., gen. mgr., 1984-92, gen. mgr., 1993-97, vice chair., 1997-99; bd. dirs. 360 Media Inc. Office: Cohn & Wolfe 303 Peachtree St NE Ste 2600 Atlanta GA 30308-3267

OVERSTREET, KAREN A. federal bankruptcy judge; BA cum laude, Univ. of Wash., 1977; JD, Univ. of Oregon, 1982. Assoc. Duane, Morris & Heckscher, Phila., 1983-86; ptnr. Davis Wright Tremaine, Seattle, 1986-93; bankruptcy judge U.S. Bankruptcy Ct. (we. dist.) Wash., Seattle, 1994—. Assoc. editor Oregon Law Review; dir. People's Law Sch.; mem. advisory com. U.S. Bankruptcy Ct. (we. dist.) Wash. Mem. Nat. Conf. of Bankruptcy Judges, Wash. State Bar Assn. (creditor-debtor sec.), Seattle-King County Bar Assn. (bankruptcy sec.), Am. Bar Assn., Wash. Women Lawyers Assn. Office: US Bankruptcy Ct Park Place Bldg 1200 6th Ave Ste 315 Seattle WA 98101-3130

OVERTON, EDWIN DEAN, campus minister, educator; b. Dec. 2, 1939; s. William Edward and Georgia Beryl (Fronk) O. BTh, Midwest Christian Coll., 1963; MA in Religion, Ea. N.Mex. U., 1969, EdS, 1978; postgrad., Fuller Theol. Sem., 1980. Ordained to ministry Christian Ch., 1978. Min. Christian Ch., Englewood, Kans., 1962-63; youth min. 1st Christian Ch., Beaver, Okla., 1963-67; campus min. Cen. Christian Ch., Portales, N.Mex., 1967-68, Christian Campus House, Portales, 1968—; tchr. religion, philosophy, counseling Ea. N.Mex. U., Portales, 1970—, acting chmn. religion dept., 2000. Dir. Campus Christian House, 1980—; farm and ranch partner, Beaver, Okla., 1963—. State dir. Beaver Jr. C. of C., 1964-65; pres. Beaver H.S. Alumni Assn., 1964-65; elder Cen. Christian Ch., Portales, 1985-88, 90-93; chmn. Beaver County March of Dimes, 1966; neighborhood chmn. Portales March of Dimes, 1997; pres. Portales Tennis Assn., 1977-78. Mem. U.S. Tennis Assn., Am. Assn. Christian Counselors, Ea. N.Mex. U. Faith in Life Com., Lions Club. Republican. Home: 1129 Libra Dr Portales NM 88130-6123 Office: Christian Campus House 223 S Avenue K Portales NM 88130-6643 Office Phone: 505-356-6292. Personal E-mail: campusmin@juno.com.

OVERTON, MARCUS LEE, performing arts administrator, actor, writer; b. Calhoun, Ga., Aug. 13, 1943; s. Marcus Burl Jr. and Eva Mae (Greene) O. BS in Speech and Theatre, Northwestern U., 1965. Actor, tchr. Southeastern Shakespeare Festival, Atlanta, summer 1965; actor, co. mgr. Eagles Mere Assocs. Repertory Co., Chgo., 1966; prodn. stage mgr. Lyric Opera of Chgo., 1966-72; mgr. Ravinia Festival, Highland Park, Ill., 1973-77; performing arts program mgr. Smithsonian Instn., Washington, 1983-92; exec. dir., prod. dir. Spoleto Festival U.S.A., Charleston, S.C., 1992-94; program prodr., host Who Do You Know S.C. Pub. Radio, Charleston, 1994-97; instr. in theatre and arts mgmt. Coll. Charleston, 1995-97. Narrator talking books Libr. Congress, Washington, 1982-83; adv. panelist Nat. Endowment for Arts, 1977-79, D.C. Commn. on Arts and Humanities, 1989, 90, 92; bd. dirs. Nat. Cultural Resources, 1989-90, Performing Arts Assistance Corp., 1992-97; cons. in field. Prodr. Falstaff (L.A. Philharm.), 1981-82; prodr., host Spoleto Today, S.C. Pub. Radio, 1996—, prodr. Inside Spoleto, 2001—; prodr., host Supertitles, San Diego Opera, 1999-2003. Northwestern U. scholar, 1961-65. Mem.: Actors Alliance of San Diego (bd. pres. 2001—02, chmn. 2003—). Avocations: travel, prehistoric cave art, motorcycle touring, linguistics, French culture. Address: 5581-A Adobe Falls Rd San Diego CA 92120 E-mail: marcoverton@k-online.com.

OVERTON, ROSILYN GAY HOFFMAN, financial services executive; b. Corsicana, Tex., July 10, 1942; d. Billy Clarence and Ima Elise (Gay) Hoffman; m. Aaron Lewis Overton, Jr., July 2, 1960 (div. Mar. 1975); children: Aaron Lewis III, Adam Jerome; m. Mardiros Hatsakorzian, 1991. BS in Math., Wright State U., Dayton, Ohio, 1972, MS in Applied Econs. (fellow), 1973; postgrad. N.Y. U. Grad. Sch. Bus., 1974-76; Cert. Coll. Fin. Planning, 1987. CFP. Research analyst Nat. Security Agy., Dept. Def., 1962-67; bus. reporter Dayton Jour.-Herald, 1973-74; economist First Nat. City Bank, N.Y.C., 1974, A.T. & T. Co., 1974-75; broker Merrill Lynch, N.Y.C., 1975-80; asst. v.p. E.F. Hutton & Co., N.Y.C., 1980-84; v.p., nat. mktg. dir. investment products Manhattan Nat. Corp., 1984-86; pres. R.H. Overton Co., N.Y.C., 1986—; ptnr. Brown & Overton Fin. Svcs., 1987—. Named Businesswoman of Yr., N.Y.C., 1976. Mem. Inst. Cert. Planners, Internat. Assn. Fin. Planning (pres. N.Y. chpt.), Gotham Bus. and Profl. Womens Club, Rotary Internat., Wright State U. Alumni Assn., Mensa, Zonta. Methodist. Office: 25418 Northern Blvd Ste 5 Little Neck NY 11362-1451

OVERWEG, NORBERT IDO ALBERT, physician; b. Enschede, The Netherlands; s. Ido and Bella Theresa (Lievenboom) Overweg; m. Angelique de Gorter; children: Eleanore, Elizabeth, Harold. MD, U. Amsterdam, 1957. Specialist in clin. hypertension ASH Specialists Program Inc. in affiliation with Am. Soc. Hypertension (ASH), 2003. Intern Univ. Amsterdam Hosp., 1958-60; resident Rochester (N.Y.) Gen. Hosp., 1961-62; postdoctoral fellow dept. pharmacology Columbia U. Coll. Physicians and Surgeons, 1962-65; instr. dept. public health Columbia U., 1965-66; rsch. assoc. dept. surgery Columbia U., Coll. Physicians and Surgeons, 1967-71; rsch. collaborator, asst. attending physician Brookhaven Nat. Lab., 1966-67; asst. prof. dept. physiology and pharmacology N.Y. U., 1971-78; cons. Lung Rsch. Ctr. Yale U. Sch. Medicine, New Haven, 1972-73; pvt. practice medicine specializing in internal medicine N.Y.C., 1967—. Attending staff St. Vincent's Midtown Hosp., Cabrini Med. Ctr.; clin. investigator antihypertension, anti-depressant, anti-anxiety, Alzheimer's Disease, migraine headache, panick attack, and gastro-intestinal drugs. Contbr. articles to profl. jours. NIH fellow, 1964—65. Mem. AAAS, AAUP, Am. Soc. Pharmacology and Exptl. Therapeutics, Am. Physiol. Soc., Am. Soc. Hypertension (cert. specialist in clin. hypertension), Am. Coll. Clin. Pharmacology, N.Y. Acad. Scis., Royal Dutch Soc. Advancement of Medicine, Harvey Soc., N.Y. County Med. Soc., N.Y. State Med. Soc., Netherlands Club of N.Y., Sigma Xi. Office: 133 E 73rd St New York NY 10021-3556 Office Phone: 212-861-9000. Personal E-mail: norbertoverweg@msn.com.

OVISSI, NASSER, artist; b. Tehran, Iran, Aug. 13, 1934; s. Shaban and Batool O.; m. Ruby; 1 child, maryam. LLB, Tehran U., 1959; BA, U. Rome, 1965. Diplomat fgn. ministry, 1960-79; art cons., 1979-85. Artworks exhibited in Italy, France, Eng., Greece, Germany, Switzerland, Sweden, Spain, India, Can., U.S., Turkey, Brazil, Yugoslavia, Monaco, China, and Iran; permanent collections in mus. in Athens, Barcelona, Belgrade, Brussels, Campione, Italy, N.C., Kerman, Iran, Madrid, N.Y., Ottawa, Paris, Pasadena, Calif., Rome, Tehran, Washington, in palaces in His Royal Majesty Juan Carlos of Spain and Her Imperial Majesty Farah Pahlevi of Iran. Recipient numerous awards including gold medal Internat. Salon of Campione (Italy), 1968, grand prize Internat. Art Exhbn. in Monaco, 1974, gold medal, Madrid, 1979. Home: 1381 Park Lake Dr Reston VA 20190-3936

OVITSKY, STEVEN ALAN, musician, symphony orchestra executive; b. Chgo., Oct. 12, 1947; s. Martin N. and Ruth (Katz) O.; m. Camille Levy; 1 child, David Isaac. MusB, U. Mich., 1968; MusM, No. Ill. U., 1975. Fine arts dir. Sta. WNIU-FM Pub. Radio, Dekalb, Ill., 1972-76; program mgr. Sta. WMHT-FM Pub. Radio, Schenectady, N.Y., 1976-79; gen. mgr., artistic dir. Grant Park Concerts, Chgo., 1979-90; v.p., gen. mgr. Minn. Orch., Mpls., 1990-95; v.p., exec. dir. Milw. Symphony Orch., 1995-99, pres., exec. dir., 1999—. Panelist Ill. Arts Coun., 1986, 87, 88, Chgo. Artists Abroad, 1987-91, Nat. Endowment for the Arts, 1987-89, 98-99; bd. dirs. Ill. Arts Alliance, Chamber Music Chgo.; hon. dir. Chgo. Sinfonietta. With U.S. Army, 1968-71, Korea. Mem. NARAS, Am. Symphony Orch. League. Jewish. Avocations: audio, record collecting, softball. Office: Milw Symphony Orch 700 N Water St Ste 700 Milwaukee WI 53202-4278 Business E-Mail: ovitskys@milwaukeesymphonyorchestra.org.

OVITT, GARY C. mayor; b. May 3, 1947; BA, U. Redlands, 1969. Tchr. Chaffey H.S., Ontario, Calif.; mayor City of Ontario, Calif., 1998—. Chmn. dept. edn. Chaffey Joint Unified Sch. Dist., 1970—. Mem. Ontario (Calif.) City Coun., 1992-99. Office: City Hall 303 E B St Ontario CA 91764-4105

OVITZ, MICHAEL S. communications executive; b. 1946; m. Judy Reich, 1969; 3 children. Grad., UCLA, 1968. With William Morris Agy., 1968-75; co-founder, chmn. Creative Artists Agy., L.A., 1975-95; pres. Walt Disney Co., Burbank, Calif., 1995-97; owner CKE Cos., Beverly Hills, Calif., 1998—. Chmn. exec. bd. dirs. UCLA Hosp. and Med. Ctr.; bd. advisors Sch. Theater, Film and TV UCLA; bd. dirs. Livent, Inc., Gulfstream Aero. Corp., J. Crew Group, Inc. Trustee Mus. Modern Art, N.Y.C.; bd. govs. Cedars-Sinai Hosp., L.A.; mem. exec. adv. bd. Pediatric AIDS Found. Mem. Coun. Fgn. Rels., Zeta Beta Tau. Avocations: contemporary art, african antiques, chinese furniture. Office: 2601 Colorado Ave Santa Monica CA 90404-3518

OVREBO, JUDITH, retired physical education educator; b. Wausau, Wis., Mar. 28, 1950; d. Donald Irving and Rozella Eileen (Boggs) O.; m. Harold Marvin Oberg, July 5, 1975 (div.); children: Jessica Kristine, Deborah Elisabeth. BS, U. Conn., 1972; MS in Phys. Edn., U. R.I., 1978; grad., So. Conn. State U., 1986, postgrad., 1992. Tchr. phys. edn. Fitch Jr. High Sch., Groton, Conn., 1972-79, Fitch Sr. High Sch., Groton, Conn., 1979-97. Mentor co-op. tchr. State of Conn., Groton, 1988—; evaluator New Eng. Assn. Schs. and Colls., 1993. Chairperson phys. edn. sub-com. New Eng. Assn. of Schs. and Colls., Groton, Conn., 1988-90; bd. dirs. Ledyard (Conn.) Girls Softball League, 1989—, mgr., coach, 1989—; coach Ledyard Youth Basketball

League, 1991—; mentor Take Stock in Children, Ocala, Fla.; organizer Connections, 2000—; vol. Hospice Marion County, Gerla, Fla., 2002-. Mem. AAHPERD, NEA, Am. Softball Assn., Conn. Assn. Health, Phys. Edn., Recreation and Dance, Conn. Edn. Assn., Groton Edn. Assn., Nat. Assn. Sports and Phys. Edn., Nat. Assn. Girls and Women Sports, Phi Kappa Phi. Avocations: swimming, organ. church involvement, reading. Home: 7598 SW 81st Pl Ocala FL 34476-6924 E-mail: jovrebo@cs.com.

OVSHINSKY, STANFORD ROBERT, physicist, inventor, energy executive, information company executive; b. Akron, Ohio, Nov. 24, 1922; s. Benjamin and Bertha T. (Munitz) O.; m. Iris L. Miroy, Nov. 24, 1959; children— Benjamin, Harvey, Dale, Robin Dibner, Steven Dibner. Student public schs., Akron; DSc (hon.), Lawrence Inst. Tech., 1980; DEng (hon.), Bowling Green State U., 1981; DSc (hon.), Jordan Coll., Cedar Springs, Mich., 1989. Pres. Stanford Roberts Mfg. Co., Akron, 1946-50; mgr. centre drive dept. New Britain Machine Co., Conn., 1950-52; dir. research Hupp Corp., Detroit, 1952-55; pres. Gen. Automation, Inc., Detroit, 1955-58, Ovitron Corp., Detroit, 1958—2004; pres., CTO, chief scientist Energy Conversion Devices, Inc., Rochester Hills, Mich., 2004—. Adj. prof. engring. scis. Coll. Engring., Wayne State U.; hon. advisor for sci. and tech. Beijing (China) Inst. Aeronautics and Astronautics (name changed to Beijing U. Aeros. and Astronautics); chmn. Inst. for Amorphous Studies. Contbr. articles on physics of amorphous materials, neurophysiology and neuropsychiatry to profl. jours. Recipient Diesel Gold medal German Inventors Assn., 1968, Coors Am. Ingenuity award, 1988, Karl W. Böer solar energy medal of merit U. Del. and Interna. Solar Energy Soc., 1999; named to Mich. Chem. Engring. Hall of Fame, 1983, Mich. Scientist of Yr., Impression 5 Sci. Mus., 1987, Hero for the Planet, Time mag., 1999, Hero of Chemistry, Am. Chem. Soc., 2000, Sir William Grove award IAHE, 2000. Fellow AAAS, Am. Phys. Soc.; mem. IEEE (sr.), Soc. Automotive Engrs., N.Y. Acad. Scis., Electrochem. Soc., Engring. Soc. Detroit, Cranbrook Inst. Sci. (bd. govs. 1981). Office: Energy Conversion Devices Inc 2956 Waterview Dr Rochester MI 48309

OWADA, HISASHI, judge; b. Shibata, Nigata, Japan, Sept. 18, 1932; s. Takeo and Shizuka (Tamura) O.; m. Yumiko Egashira, Oct. 7, 1962; children: Masako, Reiko, Setsuko. BA, U. Tokyo, 1955; LLB, Cambridge U., Eng., 1956. Pvt. sec. to Min. of Japan, Ministry Fgn. Affairs, Tokyo, 1971, dir. UN polit. affairs div., 1972-74, dir. treaties div., 1974-76; pvt. sec. to Prime Min. of Japan, Tokyo, 1976-78; min. Japanese Embassy, Washington, 1979-81, Moscow, 1981-84; dir.-gen. treaties bur. and for law of sea Ministry Fgn. Affairs, 1984-87, dep. vice minister, 1987-88; amb., permanent rep. of Jaoan to OECD, Paris, 1988-89; dep. min. Ministry Fgn. Affairs, Tokyo, 1989-91, vice min., 1991-93, advisor to Mins. Fgn. Affairs, 1993-94; amb., permanent rep. of Japan to UN, 1994-98; Inge Rennert disting. vis. prof. NYU Global Law Sch., 1994—; pres. Japan Inst. of Internat. Affairs, 1999—2003; advisor to Min. Fgn. Affairs, Tokyo, 1999—2003; sr. advisor to pres. of World Bank, 1999—2003; prof. Waseda U., 2000—; judge Internat. Court of Justice, Hague, Netherlands, 2003—. Adj. lectr. U. Tokyo, 1963-88; vis. prof. Harvard U., Cambridge, Mass., 1979-81, 87, 89, 99-2002; adj. prof. internat. law Columbia U., 1994-2000; vis. prof. internat law. NYU; judge Permanent Ct. of Arbitration, 2001-. Author: Japanese Practice in the Field of International Law, 1984, From Involvement to Engagement, 1994, Diplomacy, 1996, A Treatise in International Relations, 2002. Bd. hon. trust Aspen Inst., Ditchley Found. Mem. Japanese Assn. Internat. Law (exec. coun.). Avocations: skiing, mountain walking, music. Office: Internat Court of Justice Peace Place 2517 KJ Hague Netherlands Fax: 31 70 302 2409. E-mail: h.owada@icjcij.org.

OWADES, RUTH MARKOWITZ, marketing company executive; b. Los Angeles, Sept. 2, 1944; d. David and Yonina (Graf) Markowitz; m. Joseph L. Owades, Sept. 7, 1969. BA with honors, Scripps Coll., Claremont, Calif., 1966; MBA, Harvard U., 1975; postgrad. U. Strasbourg (France), 1966-67. Exec. asst. Los Angeles Econ. Devel. Bd., N.Y.C., 1968-69; copywriter D'Arcy Advt. Co., St. Louis, 1970-71; asst. program dir. KMOX-AM Radio, St. Louis, 1971-72; assoc. producer WCVB-TV, Boston, 1972-73; mktg. project mgr. United Brands Co., Boston, 1975; mktg. dir. CML Group Inc., Concord, Mass., 1975-78; founder, pres. Gardener's Eden Inc., Boston, 1978-82; pres. Gardener's Eden, div. Williams-Sonoma Inc., Emeryville, Calif., 1982-87; founder, pres. Calyx & Carolla, Inc., 1988—; bd. dirs. Hellenic Breweries S.A., Athens, Greece. Bd. of advisors An Income of Her Own; trustee Scripps Coll. Recipient Bausch & Lomb award, 1962, Disting. Alumna award Scripps Coll., 1989, Woman of Achievement award Woman's City Club Cleve., 1991, Woman Who Has Made a Difference award Internat. Women's Forum, 1991, Woman of the Yr. award Woman's Direct Response Group N.Y., 1992, Cataloger of Yr. award Target Marketing Mag., 1992, Direct Marketer of Yr. award, No. Calif. Direct Mktg. Club, 1993; Fulbright scholar, 1966; named student Goodwill Ambassador to Nagoya, Japan, 1960. Mem. Direct Mktg. Assn., Phi Beta Kappa. Club: Harvard (N.Y.C.), Women's Forum West (v.p. and treas.), Com. of 200. Home: 2164 Hyde St San Francisco CA 94109-1788 Office: 185 Berry St Ste 6200 San Francisco CA 94107-1750

OWEISS, IBRAHIM MOHAMED, economist, educator; b. Egypt, Sept. 25, 1931; came to U.S., 1960; s. Mohamed Zaki and Warda (Zeiden) O.; m. Celine M. J. Lesuisse, July 19, 1975; children: Yasmeen, Kareem. B.Com., Alexandria U., Egypt, 1952; MA, U. Minn., 1961, PhD, 1969. Tchr., 1953-55; econ. dir. indsl. projects, 1958-60; mem. faculty U. Minn., Mpls., 1961-67, Georgetown U., Washington, 1967—2002, prof. econs., 1973-75; mem. faculty Johns Hopkins U., 1971-74; first undersec. state econ. affairs Govt. Egypt, Cairo, 1977; ambassador, 1977-79; chief Egyptian Econ. Mission to U.S., 1977-79; prof. econs. Harvard U., 1997-98. Cons. econs., 1971—; mem. Pres. Coun. on Egyptian-Am. Rels., 1999—; mem. bd. regents Georgetown U., 2003—. Author: Pricing of Oil in World Trade, 1974, The Israeli Economy, 1974; editor: The Dynamics of U.S.-Arab Economic Relations, 1980, Economic Development of Egypt, 1982, Arab Civilization, Challenges and Responses, 1988, Political Economy of Contemporary Egypt, 1990, The Arab Gulf Economies: Challenges and Prospects, 2000, Economics: New Horizons, Shifting the Paradigm, 2001, A View on Islamic Economic Thought, 2003. Pres. Assn. Egyptian-Am. Scholars, 1984-88; chmn. bd. dirs. Arab-Am. Bus. and Profl. Assn., Howard and Georgeanna Jones Inst. for Reproductive Medicine, 1984-90, Egyptian Am. Cultural Assn., 1975-77, Faith and Hope Project, 1975-77. Officer Egyptian Army, 1955-58. Decorated Egyptian Merit decoration 1st Order, Order of St. John, knight Order of Queen of Sheba, grand cordon Order Mohammed Ali Pasha; Ford Found. fellow, 1979-80. Mem.: Am. Econ. Assn., Univ. Club (N.Y.C.), Cosmos Club (Washington). Muslim. Home: 4017 Glenridge St Kensington MD 20895-3708 Office: 1002 23d St NW Washington DC 20037 Business E-Mail: oweissi@georgetown.edu.

OWEN, ALLAN JACOBS, lawyer; b. Ft. Hood, Tex., Aug. 20, 1952; s. William J. and Pauline (Jacobs) O.; m. Linda Kay Whitney, Oct. 15, 1988. BS with high honors, U. Calif.-Davis, 1974; JD with distinction, U. of Pacific, 1979. Bar: Calif. 1979, U.S. Dist. Ct. (ea. dist.) Calif. 1979, U.S. Ct. Appeals (9th cir.) 1981. Assoc. Friedman, Collard Poswall & Thompson, Sacramento, 1979-84; ptnr. Friedman, Collard & Poswall, 1984-94, Owen & Owen, 1994-96; mng. ptnr. Ordas, Timmons, Owen & Owen, 1996-99, Timmons, Owen & Owen, 2000—. Mem. ABA, Consumer Attys. of Calif., Sacramento Consumer Attys., Sacramento County Bar Assn. Democrat. Jewish. Avocations: golf, reading. Office: Timmons Owen & Owen 906 G St Ste 610 Sacramento CA 95814-1812 Office Phone: 916-444-0321. E-mail: ajowen@saclaw.net.

OWEN, AMY, library director; b. Brigham City, Utah, June 26, 1944; d. John Wallace and Bertha (Jensen) Owen. BA, Brigham Young U., 1966, MLS, 1968. Sys. libr. Utah State Libr., Salt Lake City, 1968—72, dir. reference svcs., 1972—74, dir. tech. svcs., 1974—81, dep. dir., 1981—87, dir., 1987—2003. Serials com. chmn. Utah Coll. Libr. Coun., Salt Lake City, 1975—77, exec. sec., 1978—84, mem. coun., 1987—2003; mem. staff Gov.'s Utah Sys. Planning Task Force, Salt Lake City, 1982; staff liaison Utah Gov.'s Conf. on Libr. and Info. Svcs., 1977—79, chmn. exec. planning com., 1990—91; mem. pres.'s adv. panel Baker & Taylor Co., Somerville, NJ, 1977—78; panelist U.S. Dept. Edn., 1992; mem. rsch. project adv. com. U. Wis. Sch. Libr. and Info., Madison, 1992—94; mem. adv. panel Nat. Commn. Libr. and INfo. Svcs., 1985; Alumni Honor lectr. Coll. Humanities Brigham Young U., 1990; cons., trainer in field. Contbr. chpts. to books; contbg. author: various manuals. Mem. coun. Utah Endowment for Humanities, 1986—91, vice chmn., 1987—88, chmn., 1988—90; trustee Bibliographic Ctr. for Rsch., 1987—2003, mem. pers. com., 1988—89, chmn. person com., 1989—90, mem. nominating com., 1984, v.p. bd. trustees, 1989—91, pres., 1991—93; active Chief Officers of State Libr. Agys., 1987—2003, mem. stats. com., 1988—93, mem. network com., 1993—97, mem. state info. policy workshop com., 1988, bd. dirs., 1992—96; mem. conf. program com. Fedn. of State Humanities Couns., 1988; mem. coop. pub. libr. data sys. task force Nat. Commn. on Libr. and Info. Svcs., 1988—90; grant rev. panelist NEH, 1988, 1992, panel mem. reading and discussion groups, 1988; regional project mgmt. bd. mem. Intermountain Cmty. Learning and INfo. Ctr. Project, 1987—90; mem. midcontinental regional adv. com. Nat. Libr. Medicine, 1991—94; mem. adv. com. Brigham Young U. Sch. Libr. and Info. Svcs. Named Libr. of Yr., Libr. Jour., 1990. Mem.: ALA (planning, orgn. and bylaws com. 1981—85, LITA divsn. Satellite Conf. Task Force mem. 1982, bd. dirs. ASCLA divsn. 1984—86, clene roundtable mem. com. 1984—86, fin. com. 1984—86, SLAS program com. 1984—86, ALA Office for Rsch. coop. pub. libr. data sys. adv. com. 1985—89, pres. program com. 1986, nominations com. 1986—87, PLA divsn. editor column 1987—89, PLA divsn. goals, guidelines and stds. com. 1987—90, nat. adv. bd. office comms. svcs., voices and visions project 1988—89, exec. bd. mem. 1988—90, PLA pub. libr. data svc. adv. com. 1988—91, fin. com. 1989—92, chair 1990—91, PLA non MLS involvement com. 1990—91, PLA Kellogg Phase III EIC project adv. com. chmn. 1990—92, PLA strategic issues and directions com. 1991—92, exec. bd. mem. 1993—94, bd. dirs. ASCLA divsn. 1993—96, fin. com. 1993—96, pres. ASCLA divsn. 1994—95), Utah Partnership Edn. and Econ. Devel. (rsch. com. 1995—95), Utah Edn. Network (steering com. 1996—2003), Dynix Snowbird Leadership Inst. (nat. adv. bd. 1990—2002), Mountain Plains Libr. Assn. (rec. sec. 1979—80, fin. com. 1982—84, Disting. Svc. award 1989), Utah Libr. Assn. (exec. bd. 1976—80, pres. 1978—79, Spl. Svc. award 1989), Alpha Lambda Alpha, Phi Kappa Phi. Home: 4786 Naniloa Dr Salt Lake City UT 84117-5547 Office: Utah State Libr 250 N 1950 W Ste A Salt Lake City UT 84116-7901

OWEN, BRADLEY SCOTT, lieutenant governor; b. Tacoma, Washington, May 23, 1950; s. Laural Willis; m. Linda Knoll, Jan. 20, 1983; children: Shanie, Dana, Mark, Sherrie, Adam, Royce. Student pub. sch., Germany. State rep. Wash. Ho. Rep., Olympia, 1976-82; state senator Wash. State Senate, Olympia, 1983-96; lt. gov. State of Wash., Olympia, 1997—. Chmn. Legis. Com. on Economic Devel.; founder, pres. Strategies for Youth. Mem. Wash. State substance abuse coun., 1997—. Mem. Elks. Democrat. Office: Wash State Lt Gov PO Box 40400 Olympia WA 98504-0400

OWEN, CAROL THOMPSON, artist, educator, writer; b. Pasadena, Calif., May 10, 1944; d. Sumner Comer and Cordelia (Whittemore) Thompson; m. James Eugene Owen, July 19, 1975; children: Kevin Christopher, Christine Celese. Student, Pasadena City Coll., 1963; BA with distinction, U. Redlands, 1966; MA, Calif. State U., L.A., 1967; MFA, Claremont Grad. Sch., 1969. Cert. cmty. coll. instr., Calif. Head resident Pitzer Coll., Claremont, Calif., 1967-70; instr. art Mt. San Antonio Coll., Walnut, Calif., 1968-96, prof. art, 1996—, 1996-97, prof. emeritus, 1997, dir. coll. art gallery, 1972-73. Group shows include Covina Pub. Libr., 1971, U. Redlands, 1964, 65, 66, 70, 78, 88, 92, Am. Ceramic Soc., 1969, 97, 99, 2000, Mt. San Antonio Coll., 1991, The Aesthetic Process, 1993, Separate Realities, 1995, Sequence 1, 2001, San Bernardino County Mus., 1996, 97, 98, 99, Tampa Fla. Black, White & Gray, Artists Unltd., 1998, Current Clay VII, La Jolla, Calif., 1998, Westmoreland Art Nat., 1998, 99, Riverside Art Mus., 1998, Fine Art Inst. Juried Show, San Bernardino, 1998, 99, 2000, Parham Gallery, L.A., 1998, 99, Angels Gate Cultural Ctr., San Pedro, Calif., 1998, Los Angeles County Fair, Pomona, Calif., 1998, Monrovia, Arts Festival, 1998, Art for Heavens Sake Festival, 1998, 99, Riverside Art Mus., 1998, 99, 2000, Birger Sandzen Meml.Gallery McPherson, Kans., 1998, 2000, Earthen Art Works Gallery, LA, 1999, State Polytechnic U., Pomona, 1999, 2001, Mo. State U., Warrensburg, 1999, City, of Brea Gallery, 1999, 2000, All Media Exhibit, Chico, Calif. 1999, Period Gallery, Omaha, 1999, 2000, 01, 02, Mixed Media, Period Gallery, 2002, Franklin Square Gallery, Southpoet, NC, 1999, 2000, Judson Gallery, LA, 1999, San Angelo (Tex.) Mus. Fine Arts, 2000, So. Calif. Juried Art Exhbn., San Bernardino, Calif., 2000, Gallery 212, Ann Arbor, Mich., 2000, Judson Gallery, LA, 2000, Artists Unltd., Inc., Tampa, Fla., 2000, Urban Inst. Contemporary Arts, Grand Rapids, Mich., 2000, Tri-Lakes Ctr. for Arts, Palmer Lake, Colo., 2000, Santa Cruz Art League, Calif., 2000. Fine Arts Inst., San Bernardino County Mus., Redlands Calif. 2000, Vermont Artisan Designs, Brattleboro, 2000, USA Craft, 1999, New Caanan, Cons., 1999, Keith Gallery, Dexter, Mich., 1999, Claremont Forum Gallery, 1999, Parham Gallery, Santa Monica, Calif., 1999 (Grand prize 1999), City of Brea Galleries, Calif., 2000, 01, Chiarosouro Galleries, Chgo., 2000, TLD Design Ctr. and Gallery, Westmont, Ill., 2000, 2001, North Tahoe Art Ctr., Calif., 2000, Palos Verdes Art Ctr., Rancho Palos Verdes, Calif., 2000, Peck Gallery, Providence, 2000, Alder Gallery, Oreg., 2001, Rocky Mt. Arts Ctr., NC, 2001, Esmay Fine Art Gallery, Rochester NY, 2001, Hillcrest Festival, 2001, Dysfunctional, Business of Art Ctr., Manitou Springs, Colo., 2001, Nat. Juried Exhbn., Gallery 214, Montclair, NJ, 2002, Mt. San Antonio Coll., Walnut, Calif., 2001, Gallery Mia Tyson, Wilmington, NC, 2002, Millard Sheets Gallery, Pomona, Calif., 2002 (Honorable mention), Period Gallery, "Abstraction", Omaha, 2002, Rocky Mount Art Ctrs., Rocky Mount, NC, 2003, Ink & Clay 29 Exhbn., Kellogg U. Art Gallery, Calif. State Poly. U., Pomona, 2003, Period Gallery, Omaha, 2003, Feats of Clay XVI Lincoln (Calif.) Arts, 2003, Sanchez Art Ctr., Pacifica, Calif., 2003, "Containment", SKH, Great Barrington, Mass., 2003, Multi-Media Mini Show, San Bernardino County Mus., 2004, Fine Arts Acad., 2004, City of Brea Gallery, 2004; numerous others; ceramic mural commd. U. Redlands, 1991; represented in permanent collections Redlands Art Assn Gallery, Redlands; artwork in (book) Collectible Teapots, 2000; Group Internat. Exhbn. Internationale Wertbewerb Salzbrand Keramic, 2002, der Handwerks Kammer Koblenz, Galerie Handwerk, Germany, 2002. Recipient San Bernardino County Mus., 1996, Hon. Mention, 1998, 1999,; Past Pres. Monetary award, 1997, Jack L. Conte Design Cons. Purchase award Westmoreland Art Nat., 1998, 3rd Pl. Monetary award All Calif. City of Brea Galleries, 2000, Honorarium for teapots Urban Inst. Contemporary Arts, Grand Rapids, Mich., 2000. Mem. Am. Ceramic Soc. (design divsn., Design chpt. monetary award 1999), Calif. Scholarship Fedn., Coll. Art Assn. Am., Friends of Huntington Library, L.A. County Mus. Art, Redlands Art Assn., Fine Arts Inst., Sigma Tau Delta. Republican. Presbyterian.

OWEN, CHARLES THEODORE, journalist, publisher; b. Beech Grove, Ind., June 14, 1941; s. James Robert and Helen Maurine (Sayre) O.; m. Kathleen Rose Dellaria, Apr. 29, 1967. AS in Journalism, Vincennes U., 1972; BA in Social Sci., Chapman U., 1976; MBA, Nat. U. San Diego, 1984. Enlisted U.S. Marine Corps, 1959-72, commd. 2d lt., 1973, advanced through grades to capt., 1979; combat journalist, photographer, Vietnam, 1967-68; dep. dir. Joint Pub. Affairs Office, Camp Pendleton, 1976-79; dir. Pub. Affairs Office, Marine Corps Recruit Depot, San Diego, 1980-81; dir. comm. and mil. affairs divsn. Greater San Diego C. of C., 1981-82, v.p. 1987—, bd. dirs., 1982-87; pres., pub. San Diego Bus. Jour., 1987-2004, pres., CEO Carlsbad (Calif.) C. of C., 2004—; host TV program Focus on San Diego Bus. Bd. dirs. San Diego Conv. and Visitors Bur., San Diego Econ. Devel. Corp.; econ. devel. advisor to Mayor of San Diego; presenter in field. Decorated Cross of Gallantry, Joint Svc. Commendation medal with Combat V (3 awards), medal of Honor 2d class (Vietnam); recipient Thomas Jefferson award, 1981. Republican. Pub. Newswriting Program Instruction, 1972. Office: 5934 Priestly Dr Carlsbad CA 92008

OWEN, CLARENCE B. construction materials manufacturing executive; BS in mech. engring., La. Tech. U., 1972. Joined US Gypsum Co., Chgo., 1972, plant mgr., dir. tech. svcs.; v.p. oper. US Gypsum Co. Interiors; v.p. tech. svcs US Gypsum Co.; pres. mng. dir. US Gypsum Co. Europe; sr. v.p. US Gypsum Internat.; v.p., internat. tech. US Gypsum Co., v.p., chief tech. officer, 2003—. Office: US Gypsum Co 125 S Franklin St Chicago IL 60680-6721

OWEN, CLAUDE BERNARD, JR., tobacco company executive; b. Danville, Va., June 12, 1945; s. Claude Bernard and Mildred Carter (Fulton) O.; m. Mary Lamar Lewis, Aug. 14, 1965; children: Christopher E., Jennifer L. BA in Econs., Davidson Coll., 1967; MBA in Fin., U. Md., 1969. Fin. analyst Dibrell Bros., Inc., Danville, 1971-73, asst. v.p., 1973-76, v.p., 1976-81, sr. v.p., 1981-84, exec. v.p., 1984-86, pres., 1986-89, chmn., CEO, 1990-95, Dimon Inc., 1995-99. Bd. dirs. Am. Nat. Bankshares, Danville; chmn. bd. Richfood Holdings Inc., Richmond. Trustee Averett Coll., Danville, 1985, chmn. bd. trustees, 1991; pres. Danville-Pittsylvania County United Way, 1989. Served to 1st lt. U.S. Army, 1969-71. Mem. Va. C. of C. (bd. dirs. 1992—), Va. Mfg. Assn. (vice chmn. 1992, chmn. 1995—), Danville Golf Club (v.p. 1984-86), Commonwealth Club (Richmond), Country Club of Va. (Richmond), Rotary. Methodist. Avocations: golf, raquetball, skiing. Office: Dimon Inc 512 Bridge St Danville VA 24541-1406

OWEN, DANIEL BRUCE, financial consultant; b. Waterloo, Iowa, Apr. 5, 1950; s. Emlyn and Gladys Alyda (Wangen) O.; m. Suzy (Williams), Aug. 5, 1972; children: Carolyn Ann and Thomas Alexander. BS, Ea. Ill. U., 1972; MBA, Ctrl. Mich. U., 1975. Internal auditor Standard Oil Co., Ind., 1975—77; sr. internal auditor Amoco Corp., Chgo., 1977—78; operational auditor Abbott Lab., North Chgo., 1978—80, sr. mfg. cost analyst, 1980—81; controller Bulldog Jordan Co. div. Newell Co., Ft. Lauderdale, Fla., 1981—84, v.p., controller, 1984—85; corp. controller Miller Industries, Inc., Miami, Fla., 1985, dir., sec., treas., corp. controller, 1985—86, dir., pres., chief exec. officer, 1986—92; v.p., treas. Air Conditioning Equipment of Fla., Inc., Ft. Lauderdale, Fla., 1992—94; pvt. practice fin. cons., CPA Ft. Lauderdale, Fla., 1994—98; CFO Estate South East Banking Corp., Boca Raton, Fla., 1998—. Recipient Dade County (Fla.) Up and Comers Award, Price, Waterhouse, and the South Fla. Bus. Jour., 1990. Mem.: Fla. Inst. CPA, Am. Inst. CPA, Sigma Iota Epsilon. Republican. Presbyterian. Avocations: personal computing, golf, tennis, water sports, life sci. Home: 721 NW 67th Ave Fort Lauderdale FL 33317-1735 Office: South East Banking Corp 225 NE Mizner Blvd Ste 780 Boca Raton FL 33432 Office Phone: 561-447-8776 204.

OWEN, DANIEL HUGH, writer; b. Vincennes, Ind., May 26, 1922; s. William Allen and Zenith Euclid (Wilkes) O.; divorced; children: Susan, Patrick William. BS in Photography and Pub. Rels., Art Ctr. Sch., L.A., 1947; M in Edn., Ind. U., 1958; D in Comms., Syracuse U., 1963. Photographer in motion picture industry, 1947; reporter, photographer Indpls. Star, AP; instr. Ind. U. Sch. Fine Arts and Sch. Edn., Syracuse U. Sch. Fine Arts, Syracuse U. Sch. Journalism, Syracuse U. Sch. Edn.; owner photography bus.; v.p. Conklin, Labs & Bebee; founder Pizza-Porter, Inc., Dan-Lee Aviation Corp., Imagination Unlimited; v.p. Manlius Mil. Acad.; v.p. pub. rels., fundraising, advt. and student recruitment Alaska Methodist U.; pres., chmn. bd. dirs. Action Resources, Inc., Wilmington, N.C., Pitts., L.A., Detroit. Instr. Purdue U. Extension, Indpls.; spkr. in field; mem. UN coms.; bd. dirs., co-chmn. Russian Firm. Author: Circumvention of Article VI 1786, 1936, 1001 Lovers, 1968; editor The Local Paper; contbr. articles to profl. jours.; columnist La Prensa Libre. Dir. Nixon Campaign, N.Y., co-chmn.; chmn. County Republicans, Syracuse, N.Y., 1963-68; bd. dirs. Rescue Mission Syracuse, 1961-73; chmn. bus. betterment Republican Better Bus., Syracuse, 1964-67; mem. Russian Humanitarian Coms. Capt. USAF, 1941-45. Decorated Air Medal, Silver Star, Purple Heart, Presdl. Citation, French Croix de Guerre. Mem. Internat. Under Water Explorers Soc., Navy League (life), Lions, Rotary, Masonic Order, Kiwanis. Avocations: scuba diving, hot air balloon, bungee jumping, flying, archeology. Home and Office: Action Resources Inc 993C S Santa Fe Ave Ste 215 Vista CA 92083-6910 also: 5A Ave A 13-16 Zona 9 Guatemala City Guatemala

OWEN, DANIEL THOMAS, entrepreneur, venture capitalist; b. Dec. 6, 1947; s. Jesse Taylor and Loretta (Kirchner) O.; m. Margaret Wynne Chilton, Jan. 12, 1980; stepchildren: Margaret Anne Worsham Oden, Joseph Irion Worsham II. BA, U. Dayton, 1969. Dir. fundraising KERA-TV, Dallas, 1972-75; founder KERA-FM, Dallas, 1973; v.p. mktg. and programming Spectradyne, Inc., Dallas, 1975-87, exec. v.p., COO, 1987-89, internat. pres., 1989-90; founder, chmn. Focus Networks, Dallas, 1991-95; co-found. and gen. ptnr. HO2 Ptnr., Dallas, 1997—. Bd. dirs. CABC, Inc., Inner Wireless, Inc. Bd. dirs. North Tex. Pub. Broadcasting, Inc., 1994—. Mem. World Pres.'s Orgn. Episcopalian. Home: 3925 Potomac Ave Dallas TX 75205-2116 Office: HO2 Ptnrs Galleria Tower Two 13455 Noel Rd Ste 1670 Dallas TX 75240 E-mail: dan@ho2.com.

OWEN, DAVE A. finance executive; B in Acctg., Ind. U. CPA. Sr. acct., auditor Price Waterhouse; with Essex Group, Inc., 1976, contr. magnet wire and insulation divsn., 1983-85, contr. wire and cable divsn., 1985-88, dir. treasury and fin. svcs., 1988-93, treas., 1992-94, v.p. fin., CFO, 1993-94, exec. v.p., CFO, 1994—99; exec. v.p. Superior Essex (formerly Essex Group, Inc.), 1999—. Bd. dirs. Cmty. Harvest Food Bank. Office: Essex Express 1601 Wall St Fort Wayne IN 46802-4352

OWEN, DAVID TURNER, state legislator, owner, operator; b. N.Y.C., June 9, 1931; s. William Myrou Owen and Cynthia Foster Wolf; m. Marilyn Laura Clarks BA, Colo. Coll., 1955; postgrad, Northern Va. Coll., 1978. With U.S. Army, Wash., 1955-79; owner, operator Greeley (Colo.) Tonis Sales, 1979—; mem. Colo. Ho. of Reps., 1988-98, Colo. Senate, Dist. 16, Denver, 1998—. Mem. Am. Legis. Exchange Council, Nat. Assn. Antique Collecters, Western Legis., Nat. Fed. Bus. Republican. Home: 2722 W Buena Vista Dr Greeley CO 80634-7717 Office: State Capitol 200 E Colfax Ave Denver CO 80203-1776

OWEN, DIAN GRAVE, investment corporation executive; b. 1940; Pres. Owen Healthcare, Houston, 1970-96; chmn. Mansefeldt Investment Corp., Abilene, Tex., 1997—. Office: Mansefeldt Investment Corp 400 Pine St Ste 1000 Abilene TX 79601-5142

OWEN, DUNCAN SHAW, JR., internist, educator; b. Fayetteville, N.C., Oct. 24, 1935; s. Duncan S. and Mary Gwyn (Hickerson) O.; m. Irene Lacy Rose, Oct. 22, 1966; children: Duncan Shaw III, Robert Burwell, Frances Gwyn. BS, U. N.C., 1957, MD, 1960. Diplomate Am. Bd. Internal Medicine (proctor 1977-97). Intern Med. Coll. Va., Richmond, 1960-61; jr. asst. resident in medicine N.C. Meml. Hosp., Chapel Hill, 1961-62; asst. resident in medicine Med. Coll. Va., Richmond, 1964-65, fellow in rheumatic diseases, 1965-66; internal medicine and rheumatology physician Richmond, Va., 1966—; from instr. in medicine to assoc. prof. Med. Coll. Va., Richmond, 1966-78, prof. dept. internal medicine, 1978—; Taliaferro/Scott Disting. prof. internal medicine Med. Coll. Va., Va. Commonwealth U., 1989-2000, emeritus prof., 2000—; dir. residency tng. Med. Coll. Va. Hosp.; dir. rheumatology clinics. Dir. clin. tng. divsn. rheumatology, allergy, immunology, 1975-98, chmn. clin. activities comm., dept. internal medicine, 1970-90; chmn. med. adv. com. Richmond br. Arthritis Found., 1966-75, nat. patient edn. com., 1979-80; med. advisor Social Security Adminstrn., HHS, 1967-2004; co-chmn. arthritis project Va. Regional Med. Program, 1975-76; prodr. Your Health TV series Va. Ednl. TV, 1978-79; prodr. Update in Medicine, Good Morning Virginia TV show, 1980; cons. McGuire VA. Contbr. articles to profl. jours.; assoc. editor: Va. Med., 1978-98; editl. reviewer Jour. AMA, 1979—, Arthritis Rheumatism, 1981-2004, Jour. Rheumatology, 1984—. Mem. usher's guild First Presbyn. Ch., Richmond, Va., 1966-70, deacon, 1974-77, chmn. of diaconate, 1976-77, elder, 1978—, chmn. witness com., 1978-80; co-chmn. physicians statewide capital funds campaign Va. Commn. U., 1986-87; bd. dirs. Mooreland Farms Assn., 1971-73, 77-81, Va. chpt. Arthritis Found., 1970-85; mem. Va. Mus., Richmond Symphony; bd. dirs. Richmond Area Health Care Coalition, 1980-84. Capt. MC, 1962-64. Decorated Army Commendation medal; recipient Gerard B. Lambert award, 1974-75, Disting. Svc. award Arthritis Found., 1971, U. N.C., Chapel Hill, 1999; Nat. Inst. Arthritis and Metabolic Diseases fellow, 1965-66 Fellow ACP (Laureate award 1997), Am. Coll. Rheumatology; mem. AMA (expert on diagnostic and therapeutic tech. assessment program 1990-99), Am. Rheumatism Assn. (exec. com. 1979-80), Richmond Acad. Medicine (pres. 1982, chmn. bd. 1983, parliamentarian 1988-99), Med. Soc. Va. (com. on aging 1980-89, v.p. 1973, 75, del. 1972-99, scholarship com. 1980-89), Richmond Soc. Internal Medicine (bd. dirs. 1971-73), Met. Richmond C. of C. (bd. dirs. 1981-84), Jr. Clin.

Club (emeritus), Country Club Va., Custis Hunting and Fishing Club, Alpha Omega Alpha Honor Med. Soc. Avocations: hunting, fishing, photography, amateur radio. Home: 8910 Brieryle Rd Richmond VA 23229-7704 E-mail: dowen75089@aol.com.

OWEN, H. MARTYN, retired lawyer; b. Decatur, Ill., Oct. 23, 1929; s. Honore Martyn and Virginia (Hunt) O.; m. Candace Catlin Benjamin, June 21, 1952; children: Leslie W., Peter H., Douglas P. AB, Princeton (NJ) U., 1951; LLB, Harvard U., 1954. Bar: Conn. 1954, U.S. Ct. Appeals (2d cir.) 1961, U.S. Dist. Ct. Conn. 1962, U.S. Supreme Ct. 1963, U.S. Dist. Ct. Vt. 1965. Assoc. Shipman & Goodwin, Hartford, Conn., 1958-61, ptnr., 1961-94, of counsel, 1995-96; ret. Mem. Simsbury (Conn.) Zoning Bd. Appeals, 1961-67, Simsbury Zoning Commn., 1967-79; sec. Capitol Region Planning Agy., 1965-66; bd. dirs. Symphony Soc. Greater Hartford, 1967-73; trustee Renbrook Sch., West Hartford, Conn., 1963-72, treas. 1964-68, pres., 1968-72, hon. life trustee, 1972—; trustee Simsbury Free Libr., 1970-84; pres. Hartford Grammar Sch., 1987-98, trustee; corporator Hartford Hosp., 1984-96; vestry St. Alban's Ch., Simsbury, 1988-94; warden, vestry St. Paul's Ch., Brunswick, Maine, 1999-2001. Lt. USNR, 1954-57. Mem. ABA, Conn. Bar Assn., Hartford County Bar Assn., Am. Law Inst., Princeton (NYC) Club, Ivy Club (Princeton, NJ). Democrat. Episcopalian. Home: 80 Matthew Dr Brunswick ME 04011-3275

OWEN, HARRISON HOLLINGSWORTH, management consultant; b. Evanston, Ill., Dec. 2, 1935; s. Raymond Smith and Mary Crawford (Siter) Owen; m. Ethelyn Abbot, July 9, 1967; children: Cameron, Amy, Barry, Mary, Harrison Jr. BA, Williams, 1957; BD, Va. Sem., 1960; MA, Vanderbilt U., 1965. Pres. H.H. Owen & Co., Potomac, Md., 1979—. Author: Riding the Tiger, 1992, Millennium Orgn., 1994, Tales from Open Space, 1995, (users guide) Open Space Technology, 2d edit., 1997, Expanding Our Now, 1997, Growing Our Now, 1997, The Spirit of Leadership, 1999, The Power of Spirit: How Organizations Transform, 2000, The Practice of Peace, 2003. Home and Office: 7808 River Falls Dr Potomac MD 20854-3878 Office Phone: 301-365-2093. E-mail: hhowen@comcast.net.

OWEN, HENRY, former ambassador, consultant; b. N.Y.C., Aug. 26, 1920; AB, Harvard U., 1941. Economist Dept. State, Washington, 1946-55, mem. policy planning staff, 1955-62, dep. counselor, vice chmn. policy planning coun., 1962-66, chmn. coun., 1966-69; dir. fgn. policy studies Brookings Instn., 1969-77; personal rep. of Pres. U.S. with rank of ambassador to participate in preparations for summit meetings, 1977-81; sr. adviser Salomon Bros., 1981—2002; chmn. Capitol Ptnrs. for Edn., Washington, 2002—. Editor: Next Phase of U.S. Foreign Policy, 1971, (with Charles Schultze) Setting National Priorities, 1976. Served to lt. USN, 1942-46. Office: 2946 University Ter Washington DC 20016

OWEN, JOE DAVID, editor; b. Abilene, Tex., Oct. 27, 1950; s. B. Pat and Emilie (Long) O.; m. Joni Leigh Collier, Aug. 6, 1977; children: Connor Clausell, Caitlin Collier, Austin Sciever. BFA, So. Meth. U., 1976. Assoc. editor Stephenville (Tex.) Empire-Tribune, 1977; editor DeSoto (Tex.) News-Advertiser, 1978; assoc. dir. editl. svc. Boy Scouts Am., 1982-89, from mng. editor to dir., 1989-95, dir., 1995; mng. editor Boys' Life Mag., Irving, Tex., 1995-99, editor-in-chief, 1999—. Editor: Boy Scout Handbook, 10th edit., 1988. Home: 9653 Crestedge Dr Dallas TX 75238-2526 Office: Boys Life Mag PO Box 152079 Irving TX 75015-2079

OWEN, JOE SAM, lawyer; b. Gulfport, Miss., Dec. 31, 1948; s. Tofie and Amelia (Numnum) O., Sr.; m. Sandra Donohue, July 26, 1969; children— Ashley, Sam; m. 2d, Sherry Lynn Welch, Jan. 31, 1982; 1 child, Mitch. BA in History, U. Miss., 1970, JD, 1972. Bar: Miss. 1972, U.S. Dist. Ct. (no. and so. dists.) Miss. 1972, U.S. Ct. Appeals (5th cir.) 1974, U.S. Ct. Claims 1978, U.S. Tax Ct. 1978, U.S. Supreme Ct. 1978. Pvt. practice, Gulfport, Miss., 1972-82; ptnr. Blackwell, Owen & Galloway, Gulfport, Miss., 1982-83, Owen, Galloway and Dickinson, Gulfport, 1983-84, Owen and Galloway, Gulfport, 1984—; asst. dist. atty. Harrison, Hancock and Stone Counties, Miss., 1974-77; referee Harrison County Family Ct., Miss., 1971— . Mem. ABA, Miss. Bar Assn., Harrison County Bar Assn., Assn. Trial Lawyers Am., Miss. Trial Lawyers Assn., Am. Judicature Soc., Comml. Law League Am., Southeastern Bankruptcy Law Inst. Office: Owen & Galloway 1414 25th Ave Gulfport MS 39501-0673 Office Phone: 228-868-2821.

OWEN, JOHN, retired newspaper editor; b. Helena, Mont., June 10, 1929; s. John Earl and Ella Jean (McMillian) O.; m. Alice Winnifred Kesler, June 9, 1951; children— David Scott, Kathy Lynn. BA in Journalism, U. Mont., 1951. Sports editor Bismarck (N.D.) Tribune, 1953-55; wire editor Yakima (Wash.) Herald, 1956; with Seattle Post-Intelligencer, 1956-94, sports editor, 1968-80, assoc. editor, 1980-94, columnist, 1968-94. Author: Intermediate Eater Cookbook, 1974, Gourmand Gutbusters Cookbook, 1980, Seattle Cookbook, 1983, Great Grub Hunt Cookbook, 1989, Press Pass, 1994, Gluttony Without Guilt, 1997, Seattle Walks, 2000; also short stories. Served with AUS, 1951-52. Named Top Sports Writer in Wash. Nat. Sportswriters Orgn., 1966, 68, 69, 71, 74, 85, 88. Home: 611 Bell St Apt 4 Edmonds WA 98020-3065

OWEN, JOHN ATKINSON, JR., internist, educator; b. South Boston, Va., Sept. 24, 1924; s. John Atkinson and Mary Helen (Carrington) O.; m. Wanda Earle Reamy, Nov. 29, 1952; children— John Atkinson III, Ryland R. BS, Hampden-Sydney Coll., 1944; MD, U. Va., 1948. Intern Cin. Gen. Hosp., 1948-49; resident, fellow U. Va. Hosp., 1950-52; rsch. fellow Duke Med. Center, 1954-56; asst. prof. medicine Med. Coll. Ga., 1956-58, George Washington U. Med. Sch., 1958-60; mem. faculty U. Va. Sch. Medicine, 1960-96, prof., 1970-96, vice chmn. dept. internal medicine, 1972-74, James M. Moss prof. diabetes, sr. assoc. dean, 1995-96, prof. emeritus, 1997—. Mem. Va. Vol. Formulary Bd.; mem. exec. com. U.S. Pharmacopeia, 1970-75, pres., 1975-80, trustee, 1975-85 Mem. editorial bd.: Jour. Clin. Pharmacology, 1971-84; editor-in-chief: Hosp. Formulary, 1974-83. Served with USNR, 1942-45, 48-50, 52-53; capt. M.C. Res. Recipient Raven award U. Va., 1948; co-recipient Horsley Research prize, 1962, Walter Reed Disting. Achievement award, 1998; laureate ACP, 1998. Mem. AMA, ACP, Am. Fedn. Clin. Rsch., So. Soc. Clin. Investigation, Med. Soc. Va. (pres. 1990-91), Am. Diabetes Assn., Endocrine Soc. Presbyterian. (elder 1965—). Home: 106 Tally Ho Dr Charlottesville VA 22901-2034

OWEN, KAREN ANN, historian, educator; b. Brockport, N.Y., Jan. 9, 1966; d. Leland Martin Owen, Jr. and Barbara (Staffen) Owen. BS, SUNY, Brockport, 1987, MA, 1991. Math. tutor, sch. dir. Gates-Chili, Spencerport, NY, 1996—. Vol. Rochester/Monroe County Libr. Bookstore, George Eastman House. Mem.: SUNY Brockport Alumni Assn. (bd. dirs. 1998—). Avocation: Civil war and film history. Home: 204 Clark St Brockport NY 14420

OWEN, KENNETH DALE, orthodontist, real estate broker; b. Charlotte, NC, May 9, 1938; s. Olin Watson and Ruth (Watlington) O.; m. Lura Aven Carnes, Feb. 14, 1958; children: Kenneth Dale, Aven Anna. BS, Davidson Coll., 1959; DDS, U. N.C., 1963, MSc in Orthodontics, 1967. Diplomate Am. Bd. Orthodontics. Pvt. practice dentistry specializing in orthodontia, Charlotte, 1966—. Asst. clin. prof. U. N.C. Shc. Dentistry, 1969-72; bd. dirs. N.C. Dental Found., 1973-81, 89-90, exec. com., 1974-80, v.p., 1976-77, pres., 1978-79; bd. dirs. Holiday Dental Conf. Found., 1989—, v.p., 1990—, exec. dir., 1995—. Adminstrv. bd. Myers Park United Meth. Ch., 1976-79, 93-95, 99-2001. Served with Dental Corps., AUS, 1963-65. Fellow Internat. Coll. Dentists (dep. regent N.C. 1986, 87), Am. Coll. Dentists; mem. ADA (ho. of dels. 1981-92, 95, 16 trustee dist. caucus vice chmn. 1986-89, chmn. 1989-92, ADPAC bd. 1994-99, exec. com. 1997-99), Am. Assn. Orthodontists (ho. of dels. 1980-88, 90-93), So. Assn. Orthodontists (trustee 1983-85, dir. 1987-93, pres. 1991-92, Oren A. Oliver Disting. Svc. award 2001), N.C. Assn. Orthodontists (bd. dirs. 1976-80, sec. treas. 1976-78, pres. elect 1978-79, pres. 1979-80), N.C. Dental Soc. (ho. of dels. 1969-77, 81-94, parlimentarian 1994—, trustee 1980-91, sec. treas. 1987-88, pres. elect 1988-89, pres. 1989-90, N.C. Dental Polit. Action Com. chmn. 1996—, Disting. Svc. Scroll 2000), 2d Dist. Dental Soc. (editor 1967-69, sec.-treas. 1971-74, pres. 1975-76, exec. coun. 1971-77, 80-87), Charlotte Dental Soc. (chmn. various coms., dir. 1978-79, v.p. 1980-81), Stanly County Dental Soc. (program chair 1997—), Coll. Diplomates Am. Bd. Orthodontics, U. N.C. Orthodontic Alumni Assn. (sec.-treas. 1971, v.p. 1972-73, pres. 1974-75, exec. com. 1971-76), U. N.C. Gen. Alumni Assn. (life), U. N.C. Dental Alumni Assn., Orthovista Orthodontic Study Group, Delta Sigma Delta (life; pres. N.C. grad. chpt. 1970-71), Omicron Kappa Upsilon, Kappa Sigma, Alpha Epsilon Delta. Home: 3724 Pomfret Ln Charlotte NC 28211-3726 Office: 497 N Wendover Rd Charlotte NC 28211-1064 also: 325 N 2d St Albemarle NC 28001 Office Phone: 704-366-8006. Personal E-mail: holidaydental@mindspring.com.

OWEN, LANGDON TALBOT, JR., lawyer; b. Pitts., Oct. 6, 1951; s. Langdon Talbot Owen and Kathryn Agnes (Kropp) Pymm; m. Ann Nebeker, June 16, 1981; children: Brooke, Lisa, Clark, Kate. AB, U. Calif.-Berkeley, 1973; JD, U. Utah, 1977. Bar: Utah 1977, U.S. Dist. Ct. Utah 1977, U.S. Ct. Appeals (10th cir.) 1978, U.S. Tax Ct. 1978. Pvt. practice, Salt Lake City, 1977; assoc. Reynolds and Arnold, Salt Lake City, 1978-80, Watkiss & Saperstein, Salt Lake City, 1980-92; ptnr. Parsons, Kinghorn, Harris, Salt Lake City, 1992—. Comment editor, Contbr. Utah Law Rev., 1976-77. Mem.: ABA, Ctr. for Interant. Legal Studies, Am. Arbitration Assn., Salt Lake County Bar Assn., Utah Bar Assn., Am. Health Lawyers Assn. Democrat. Office: Parsons Kinghorn Harris 111 E Broadway Fl 11 Salt Lake City UT 84111 Office Phone: 801-363-4300. E-mail: lto@pkhlawyers.com.

OWEN, LARRY GENE, academic administrator, educator, electronic and computer integrated manufacturing consultant; b. Pine Bluff, Ark., Oct. 2, 1932, s. Cecil Earl and Helen Marie (Jacks) O.; m. Ruth Myra Newton, Sept. 3, 1953; children: Deborah, Patricia, Larry Gene, Shea. BS in Physics and Math., U. So. Miss., 1967; postgrad., Inst. Tech., 1974-75; MS in Ops. Mgmt., U. Ark., 1987; DPM, Masters Divinity Sch., 2004. Enlisted USAF, 1951, advanced through ranks to master sgt., 1968, electronic technician, 1951-61, comms. supt., 1961-71, ret., 1971; tchr. math. and Physics Southwestern Tech. Inst., Camden, Ark., 1971-72, tchr. electronics, 1972-75; dean tech. engring.omputer Integrated Mfg. Ctr. So. Ark. U. Tech., Camden, 1988-89, dean, dir. divsn. Computer Integrated Mfg. Ctr., 1989-91, dean, prof., 1991-97, assoc. vice chancellor, 1996-98, dean emeritus, 1996—. Adj. asst. prof. So. Ark. U.; project dir. Ark. Consortium for Mfg. Competitiveness So. Growth Policies Bd., 1988-98; vice chair South Ark. Fiber Optics Coun., 1997. Contbr. articles to profl. jours. Mem. Rep. Task Force; chair Atea Coll. Cons., 1991—. Mem. Instrumentation Soc. Am. (sr.), Am. Assn. Physics Tchrs. Am. Tech. Edn. Assn. (rep. Ark. 1989-91, 95-96, pres. so. region 1992-93, chair Coll. of Cons.), Soc. Mfg. Engrs. (sr., chmn. South Ark. chpt. 1991-92, mem. govs. mfg. network adv. com.), Am. Legion (fin. dir. post 45). Baptist. Home: 306 Lakeside Ave Camden AR 71701-3237

OWEN, MARC, health products executive; b. Wales; Grad., Oxford U.; MBA, Stanford U. Sr. ptnr. McKinsey and Co., 1988—2000; pres., CEO MindCrossing, 2000—01; sr. v.p. corp. strategy and bus. devel. McKesson Corp., 2001—. Office: McKesson Corp One Post St San Francisco CA 94104

OWEN, MICHAEL LEE, lawyer; b. L.A., Aug. 17, 1942; s. Richard M. Owen and Betty Hamilton; m. Espy Bolivar-Owen. AB in Econ. with distinction, Stanford U., 1964; LLB, Harvard U., 1967. Bar: Calif., 1968, N.Y. 1968. Assoc. Reid & Priest, N.Y.C., 1967-69; mem. legal dept. Bank of Am. NT&SA, San Francisco, 1969-81; corp. sec. BRE Properties, San Francisco, 1970-75; v.p., assoc. gen. counsel Bank of Am. NT&SA, L.A., 1979-81; ptnr. and co-chair L.Am. practice group Paul, Hastings, Janofsky & Walker, LLP, L.A., 1981—. Vice chair adv. bd. Inst. for Internat. and Comparative Law Ctr. for Am. and Internat. Law (formerly Southwestern Legal Found.). Contbr. articles to profl. jours. regarding legal issues affecting financing and investment in Latin Amer. Bd. dirs. Constnl. Rights Found. Mem. Am. Arbitration Assn. (internat. panel of arbitrators), U.S.-Mex. Law Inst. (bd. dirs.), U.S.-Mex. C. of C. (bd. dirs. Pacific chpt.). Office: Paul Hastings Janofsky & Walker LLP 515 S Flower St 25th Fl Los Angeles CA 90071-2228 Office Phone: 213-683-6214. E-mail: michaelowen@paulhastings.com.

OWEN, PRISCILLA RICHMAN, state supreme court justice; BA, Baylor U., JD, 1977. Bar: Tex. 1978, U.S. Ct. Appeals (4th, 5th, 8th and 11th cirs.). Former ptnr. Andrews & Kurth, L.L.P., Houston; justice Supreme Ct. Tex., Austin, 1995—. Liaison to Tex. Legal Svcs. for Poor Spl. Supreme Ct. Tex., Supreme Ct. Adv. Com. on Ct.-Annexed Mediations. Named Young Lawyer of Yr., Baylor U., Outstanding Young Alumna. Office: Supreme Ct Tex PO Box 12248 Austin TX 78711-2248

OWEN, RICHARD, federal judge; b. N.Y.C., Dec. 11, 1922; s. Carl Maynard and Shirley (Barnes) O.; m. Lynn Rasmussen, June 6, 1960; children: Carl R., David R., Richard. AB, Dartmouth Coll., 1947; LLB, Harvard U., 1950; MusD (hon.), Manhattan Sch. Music, 1989. Bar: N.Y. 1950. Practiced in, N.Y.C., 1950-74; assoc. Willkie Owen Farr Gallagher & Walton, 1950-53, Willkie Farr Gallagher Walton & Fitzgibbon, 1958-60; pvt. practice, 1960-65; ptnr. Owen & Aarons, 1965-66, Owen & Turchin, 1966-74; asst. U.S. atty. So. Dist. N.Y., 1953-55; trial atty. antitrust divsn. U.S. Dept. Justice, 1955-58; U.S. dist. judge So. Dist. N.Y., 1974-89, sr. judge, 1989—. Asst. prof. N.Y. Law Sch., 1951-53; adj. prof. law Fordham U. Sch. Law, 1996—. Composer, librettist operas Dismissed with Prejudice, 1956, A Moment of War, 1958, A Fisherman Called Peter, 1965, Mary Dyer, 1976, The Death of the Virgin, 1980, Abigail Adams, 1987, Tom Sawyer, 1989, Sadie Thompson, 1997. Trustee Manhattan Sch. Music, N.Y.C.; founder, bd. dirs. Maine Opera Assn., 1975-85; pres., bd. dirs. N.Y. Lyric Opera Co. 1st lt. USAAC, 1942-45. Decorated D.F.C. with oak leaf cluster, Air medal with 3 oak leaf clusters. Mem. ASCAP, Century Assn., Chelsea Yacht Club. Republican. Mem. Soc. Of Friends. Office: US Dist Ct US Courthouse Foley Sq New York NY 10007-1501 Office Phone: 212-805-6155. E-mail: operaowen@aol.com.

OWEN, ROBERT DEWIT, lawyer; b. St. Louis, Nov. 15, 1948; s. Kenneth Campbell Owen and Mary Elenor (Fish) Luebbers; m. Rebecca Roberts Baxter, June 4, 1977; children: Abigail Mary, James Roy, Charlotte Grace. BA, Northwestern U., 1970; JD cum laude, U. Pa., 1973. Assoc. Sullivan & Cromwell, N.Y.C., 1973-81; ptnr. Towne, Dolgin, Furlaud, Sawyier & Owen, N.Y.C., 1981-83, Owen & Fennell, N.Y.C., 1983-87, Owen & Davis, N.Y.C., 1987—2002, Fulbright & Jaworski, LLP, N.Y.C., 2002—. Instr. Nat. Inst. Trial Advocacy, Boulder, Colo., 1988—; faculty mem. ABA Nat. Inst. 1992, 93. Bd. dirs. St. Christopher's-Jennie Clarkson Child Care Svcs., Dobbs Ferry, N.Y., 1991-97. Mem. Assn. Bar City N.Y., Fed. Bar Coun., Nat. Assn. Securities Dealers (bd. arbitrators 1985—), Nat. Futures Assn. (bd. arbitrators 1999—), Colonial Springs Club (pres. 1986-94), India House. Episcopalian. Avocations: boating, running. Office: Fulbright & Jaworski LLP 666 5th Ave New York NY 10103-3198

OWEN, ROBERT FREDERICK, internist, rheumatologist; b. Poplar Bluff, Mo., Oct. 19, 1927; s. John Clarence and Lydia Anna (Laverty) O.; m. Edith Suzanna Trugly, June 11, 1960; 1 child, Suzanne Marie. AB summa cum laude, Princeton U., 1948; MD, Yale U., 1952. Diplomate Am. Bd. Internal Medicine, Nat. Bd. Med. Examiners. Med. intern Barnes Hosp. (Washington U.), St. Louis, 1952-53; asst. resident in internal medicine St. Louis City Hosp. (Washington U. Med. Svc.), 1953-54, 56-57, med. resident, 1957-58; pvt. practice in internal medicine and rheumatology St. Louis, 1958—98. Instr. clin. medicine Washington U. Sch. Medicine, St. Louis, 1958-98, emeritus, 1998—; cons. Arthritis Clinic Washington U. Clinics, St. Louis, 1958-78; attending physician inpatient and outpatient tchg. svcs. at Washington U. and Mo. Baptist, St. Luke's, and Deaconess Hosps., St. Louis, 1958-79. Chmn. Instnl. Rev. Bd. Mo. Baptist Hosp. (monitoring biomed. and behavioral rsch.), 1977-96; mem. St. Louis Cmty. Clin. Oncology Program Human Subjects Rsch. Instnl. Rev. Bd., 1983-96. Capt. U.S. Army Med. Corps, 1954-56, Korea. Commendation by surgeon, Eighth U.S. Army, Far East, 1955. Fellow ACP; mem. AMA (Physician's Recognition award annually 1977—), Sigma Xi, Phi Beta Kappa. Avocations: piano, organ, photography. Office: St Francois Med Ctr 1224 Graham Rd Ste 3008 Florissant MO 63031-8028

OWEN, ROBERT HUBERT, lawyer, former real estate broker; b. Birmingham, Ala., Aug. 3, 1928; s. Robert Clay and Mattie Lou (Hubert) O.; m. Mary Dane Hicks, Mar. 14, 1954; children: Mary Kathryn, Robert Hubert. BS, U. Ala., 1950; JD, Birmingham Sch. Law, 1956. Bar: Ala. 1957, Ga. 1965. Methods and procedures analyst, supr. Ala. Power Co., Birmingham, 1952-58; assoc. Martin, Vogtle, Balch & Bingham, Birmingham, 1958-63; asst. sec. So. Services, Atlanta, 1963-69; sec. Southern Co., Atlanta, 1969-71, sec., asst. treas., 1971-77; exec. v.p., sec., gen. counsel, dir. Proverbs 31 Corp., Atlanta, 1978-81, 90-97; broker Bob Owen Realty, Atlanta, 1990-97; pvt. practice law Marietta, 1978-85; v.p., gen. counsel Hubert Properties, 1985-86. Atlanta area rep. Inst. Basic Life Principles, 1970-80; elder Calvary Bapt. Ch., 1997--. Served to maj. USAF, 1951-52, 61-62. Mem.: Meteoritical Soc., Jasons, Phi Eta Sigma, Beta Gamma Sigma, Omicron Delta Kappa, Delta Chi, Delta Sigma Pi. Home and Office: 6590 Bridgewood Valley Rd NW Atlanta GA 30328-2906 Office Fax: 404-255-9479. Personal E-mail: rowen2000@comcast.net.

OWEN, ROBERTS BISHOP, lawyer, arbitrator; b. Boston, Feb. 11, 1926; s. Roberts Bishop and Monica Benedict (Burrell) O.; m. Kathleen Comstock von Schrader, Aug. 27, 1966; children— David Roberts, Lucy Leffingwell, William Atreus. Student, Dartmouth Coll., 1943-44; AB cum laude, Harvard U., 1948, LL.B. cum laude, 1951; Dip.C.L.S., Cambridge U., Eng., 1952. Bar: D.C. 1952, U.S. Ct. Appeals (D.C. cir.) 1953, U.S. Supreme Ct. 1958. Assoc. Covington & Burling, Washington, 1952-60, ptnr., 1960-79, 81—; the legal advisor U.S. Dept. State, Washington, 1979-81. Sr. advisor Sec. of State former Yugoslavia, 1995; arbitrator Fedn. Bosnia and Herzegovina, 1995; mem. Permanent Ct. Arbitration, The Hague, The Netherlands, 1980—86, 1993—98; mem. arbitration panel Internat. Ctr. for Settlement of Investment Disputes, 1995—; chair bd. dirs. Internat. Human Rights Law Group, 1996—99; mem. Claims Resolution Tribunal for Dormant Accounts in Switzerland, 1998—2000; sr. U.S. negotiator U.S.-Can. Pacific Salmon Treaty dispute, 1998; vice chair, sr. claims judge Claims Resolution Tribunal, 2001—02. Served to ensign USN, 1943-46. Fulbright scholar, 1951-52; recipient Disting Honor award Dept. of State, 1981, Sec. of State Disting. Svc. award, 1996, Sec. of Defense's medal for outstanding pub. svc., 1996. Fellow Am. Coll. Trial Lawyers; mem. ABA, Council Fgn. Relations, Am. Soc. Internat. Law (exec. council 1981-85). Clubs: Royal Ocean Racing (London); Metropolitan (Washington). Office: Covington & Burling PO Box 7566 1201 Pennsylvania Ave NW Washington DC 20004 Office Phone: 202-662-5254. E-mail: rowen@cov.com.

OWEN, SARAH-KATHARINE, language educator; b. Charlottesville, Va. d. William Davis and Carole Anne (Bradshaw) Owen. AA, Piedmont Va. C.C., Charlottesville, 1992; BS, James Madison U., 1995; MEd, U. Va., 2001, postgrad., Va. Polytech. Inst. Tchr. Spanish and French We. Albemarle H.S., Charlottesville, 1995—96; tchr. Spanish and French, activities dir. Miller Sch. of Albemarle, Charlottesville, 1996—97; tchr. Spanish and French We. Albemarle H.S., Charlottesville, 1997—98, Monticello H.S., Charlottesville, 1998—. Tchr. Spanish Crozet Elem. Sch., Charlottesville, 1997—98; instr. Spanish Piedmont Va. C.C., Charlottesville, 2002—; Fulbright tchr. exchange, Toledo, 2004 . Author: Spanish Advanced Placement Examination Reader, 2003, 2004. Avocations: reading, singing, travel, exercising. Home: 5757 Tabor St Crozet VA 22932

OWEN, STEPHEN, Canadian government official; LLB, U. B.C., 1972; LLM, U. London, 1974; MBA, U. Geneva, 1986. Bar: Can. Pvt. law practice, Vancouver, Canada, 1972—75; tchr. Can. U. Svc. Overseas, Nigeria, 1975—77; pub. law practice Vancouver, 1977—82; exec. dir. Legal Svc. Soc. B.C., 1982—86; ombudsman B.C., 1986—92; commr. Resources & Environ. B.C., 1992—95; dep. atty. gen. B.C., 1995—97; commr., v.p. Law Commn. Can., 1997—2000; mem. Parliament of Can., 2000—; parliamentary sec. to min. justice & atty. gen. of Can., 2001—02; sec. state (western econ. diversification), 2002—03; min. pub. works & govt. services, 2003—. Prof. law & pub. policy U. Victoria, Canada, 1997—2000, dir. inst. dispute resolution, 1997—2000; project leader conflict resolution in Sri Lanka Can. Internat. Devel. Agy., 2001; sr. expert IGAD Secretariat for Sudan peace negotiations, Nairobi, 2000; adv. in field; cons. in field; adj. prof. U. B.C., 1993—95; spkr. in field. Contbr. articles to profl. jours. Mem.: Can. Bar Assn. (John Tait award 2001). Office: Parliament Hill House of Commons Ste 810 Justice Bldg Ottawa 0N K1A 0A6 Canada also: Pub Works & Govt Services Can Place du Portage Phase III 11 Laurier St K1A 0S5 Hull QC Canada

OWEN, STEVEN KEITH, utilities executive; b. Enterprise, Ala., Aug. 16, 1959; s. Charlie Glenn Owen and O. Beatrice Gibson; m. Kim Cruce, July 15, 1984 (div. July 1995). BSCE, Auburn U., 1981. Asst. engr. So. Co. Svcs., Birmingham, Ala., 1981—83, AP600 project mgr., 1990—92, field engr. Augusta, Ga., 1983—84, startup test supr., 1984—87, project staff engr., 1987—89, project engring. mgr., 1989—90, So. Energy/So. Co., Atlanta, 1993—96, project dir., 1996—98, bus. unit mgr. Chgo., 1998—2000, dir. Midwest bus. units, 2000—01; v.p. Mirant Corp., Atlanta, 2001—. Coach basketball and baseball youth teams, Birmingham, 1991-93; membership chmn. So. Co. Svcs. PAC, Birmingham, 1991-93; bd. dirs. United Way, Lake County, Ind., 1998—. Mem. ASME (com. mem.), Ind. State C. of C. (environ. bd., congrl. affairs bd. 2000—), Beta Theta Pi Alumni Assn. (Auburn chpt. pres., treas. 1981-85). Avocations: golf, running, reading. Office: Mirant Corp 1155 Perimeter Center W Atlanta GA 30338

OWEN, SUE ANN, poet; b. Clarinda, Iowa, Sept. 5, 1942; d. Theodore Reynold and Elizabeth (Roderick) Matthews; m. Thomas Charles Owen, Aug. 29, 1964. BA in English, U. Wis., 1964; MFA in Writing, Goddard Coll., 1978. Poet in schs. Arts and Humanities Coun., Baton Rouge, 1980—92; artist fellowship La. Divsn. of Arts, 1993, 2001; instr. La. State U., 1992—98, poet-in-residence, 1998—. Author: Nursery Rhymes for the Dead, 1980, The Book of Winter, 1988 (Ohio State Univ. Press/The Jour. award, 1988), My Doomsday Sampler, 1999; contbr.: poems to mags., anthologies, including Harvard Mag., Iowa Rev., The Nation, Poetry, Ploughshares, So. Rev., The Best of Intro, The Poetry Anthology: 1912-2002, USA Poetry (Sweden), readings in: Boston, N.Y.C., Washington, San Francisco, New Orleans, Moscow, London. Named Profl. Artist of Yr., La. State Arts Coun., 1998. Mem.: Poets and Writers, Arts and Humanities Coun., Associated Writing Programs, Poetry Soc. Am. Home: 7825 Rue Cache Baton Rouge LA 70808

OWEN, SUZANNE, retired savings and loan association executive; b. Lincoln, Nebr., Oct. 6, 1926; d. Arthur C. and Hazel E. (Edwards) O. BSBA, U. Nebr., Lincoln, 1948. With G. F. Lessenhop & Sons, Inc., Lincoln, 1948-57, First Fed., Lincoln, 1963-91, v.p., dir. pers., 1975-81, 1st v.p., 1981-87, sr. v.p., 1987-91; ret., 1991. Mem. pers. bd. City of Lincoln, 1989-96. Mem. Lincoln Human Resources Mgmt. Assn., Wooden Spoon Club, Exec. Women's Breakfast Group, Thursday Morning Lecture Cir., Cmty. Women's Club, Lincoln Symphony Guild, Pi Beta Phi Alumnae, Order of Ea. Star, Phi Chi Theta. Republican. Christian Scientist.

OWEN, THOMAS BARRON, retired naval officer, space company executive; b. Seattle, Mar. 19, 1920; s. Thomas Barron and Ruth (Deane) O.; m. Rosemary Stolz, Dec. 24, 1944; children— Catherine Adams, Thomas Barron, James Rowell, Nancy Deane. BS cum laude, U. Wash., 1940; postgrad., U.S. Naval Postgrad. Sch., 1946-47; PhD in Chemistry, Cornell U., 1950; postgrad., U. Amsterdam, 1950-51, Indsl. Coll. Armed Forces, 1961-62, Harvard Grad. Sch. Bus. Adminstrn., 1964. Commd. ensign U.S. Navy, 1940, advanced through grades to rear adm., 1967, combat duty with Pacific Fleet, 1940-45; officer distbn. div. Bur. Naval Personnel, 1945-46; with armaments br. and mil. operations br. Office Naval Research, 1951-53; asst. repair supt. (hull) and prodn. analysis supt. Long Beach (Calif.) Naval Shipyard, 1953-57; dir. applied scis. div., dir. research and devel. planning div. Navy Bur. Ships, 1957-61; mil. asst. to dep. dir. def. research and engring. engring. and chemistry, 1962-63; assigned Office Asst. Sec. Navy Research and Devel., 1963; dir. support services Naval Research Lab., 1963-65, dir., 1965-67; chief naval research, 1967-70; ret., 1970; asst. dir. nat. and internat. programs NSF, 1970-74; assoc. dean grad. affairs and rsch. Am. U., Washington, 1974-76, asst. provost, 1976-79; asst. adminstr. NOAA, Dept. Commerce, Rockville, Md., 1979-81; mgr. program planning Fairchild Space & Electronics Co.,

Germantown, Md., 1981-83; sr. dir. systems effectiveness Fairchild Space Co., Germantown, 1983-84, v.p. procurement, 1984-86. Author profl. papers. Decorated D.S.M., Silver Star, Bronze Star. Fellow AAAS; mem. Am. Chem. Soc., U.S. Naval Inst., Philos. Soc. Washington, Sigma Xi, Phi Kappa Phi, Phi Lambda Upsilon, Tau Beta Pi, Chi Psi. Clubs: Cosmos (Washington). Home: 8409 Magruder Mill Ct Bethesda MD 20817-2746 E-mail: wonkpop@aol.com. *Demand high standards of excellence for self and others. Achieve respect of others through own performance. Be direct; avoid circumspection. Develop empathy; listen; consider feelings and rights of others. Maintain philosophy of "Onward and Upward!".*

OWEN, THOMAS JAMES, artist, educator; b. Coca-Rockledge, Fla., Aug. 20, 1945; s. Irwin Arthor and Esther Ethel (Sensinig) O.; m. Judith Lea Pasternak, June 21, 1969 (div. Feb. 1983); m. Koreen Clay, June 26, 1986; 1 child, Gillian Clay. BS in Edn., N.W. Mo. State U., 1968. Cert. tchr., Mo., Nebr. Secondary educator Avon-Grove Sch. Dist., West Grove, Pa., 1968-69, Dist. # 60 Schs., Pueblo, Colo., 1969-72, Wymore (Nebr.) Unified Dist., 1972-73; art educator Sangre De Cristo F.A.C., Pueblo, 1981-86, Colorado Springs (Colo.) F.A.C. Bemis Art Sch., 1982-96, Cottonwood Art Acad., Colo. Springs, 1997—; pvt. practice Black Forest, Colo., 1996—. Art dir. Columbine Cellers, Denver and Palisade, Colo., 1989-96; guest instr. Adams State Coll., Alamosa, Colo., 1990-95. Exhibited Kans. Watercolor Soc. (Purchase selection), Wichita Ctr. for Arts. Recipient Juror's Choice award San Diego Nat. Watermedia, 1981, Adirondack's Wilderness award, The Rouse Gold medallion, Adirondack's Nat. Exhbn. Am. Watercolors, 1995, Florene and H. Samuel Slater meml. award, 1999, Gold Medal New World Internat. Wine Label Competition, 1994, Dr. Martin's award Soc. Watercolor Artists, 1997, Silver Brush award 1999, New West award Watermedia IX, 1998, Meyer award Rocky Mt. Nat. Water Media Exhbn. Signature, 1998, 2000, Best Transparent Watercolor Watermedia X, 1999, Omni Trax award, 1999, Mid Continent Engring. award Kans. 7 state exhbn., 1999, 2000, Atlantic Papers award Western Colo. Nat. Watercolor Exhbn., 1999, Best of Show award Soc. Watercolor Artists, 2000, Carillion Gallery award, Best of Show award, 2000, Honorarium award Kans. Watercolor Soc., 2000, Connoisseur Art award, 2000, 4th Pl. medallion Pa. Watercolor Soc., 2000, Mario Cooper and Dale Myers medallion, 2003. Mem. Nat. Watercolor Soc. (signature mem., Rocky Mtn. br. bd. dirs., Hariett Wexler Bartsch Meml. award 1994), Am. Watercolor Soc. (signature mem., Mario Cooper and Dale Meyers medal 2003), Colo. Artists Assn. (v.p. 1982-86), Nickerbocker Artists (assoc.), Pikes Peak Watercolor Soc. (v.p. 1990—, Internat. Water media XIII, Silver medallion), Watercolor West (juried mem. 1999), Acad. Sertoma Club. Avocations: trout fishing, skiing, model railroading. Home and Office: 11935 Vollmer Rd Colorado Springs CO 80908-4086 E-mail: tomowen@hotbot.com.

OWEN, THOMAS LLEWELLYN, investment executive; b. Patchogue, N.Y., June 24, 1928; s. Griffith Robert and Jeanette Roberts (Hatfield) O. AB in Econs., Coll. William and Mary, 1951; postgrad., Columbia U., 1952, N.Y. Inst. Fin., 1960—62; MBA, NYU, 1966. Exec. trainee Shell Oil Co., N.Y.C. and Indpls., 1951-59, supr., 1958-59; petroleum and chem. investment analyst Paine, Webber, Jackson & Curtis, N.Y.C., 1959-62; sr. oil investment analyst DuPont Investment Interests, Wilmington, Del., N.Y.C., 1962-66, dir. rsch., 1964-66; v.p., sr. investment officer, mem. policy, investment coms. Nat. Securities and Rsch. Corp., N.Y.C., 1966-75, mutual fund portfolio mgr., 1972—75; sr. investment exec., v.p., portfolio mgr. F. Eberstadt & Co. and Eberstadt Asset Mgmt., Inc., N.Y.C., 1975-85, mem. policy com., 1979-85, also dir. portfolio rev. com.; sr. investment exec., portfolio mgr. Brown Brothers Harriman, N.Y.C., 1985-89; pres., CEO Owen Capital Mgmt., N.Y.C., 1989—. Contbr. chpt. "Oil and Gas Industries" to Financial Analysts Handbook, 1975. Former chmn. bd. trustees Congl. Ch. Patchogue, N.Y. Mem.: Investment Assn. NY, Assn. Investment Mgmt. and Rsch., Internat. Assn. Energy Economists, Nat. Assn. Petroleum Investment Analysts, Am. Petroleum Inst., Am. Econ. Assn., Oil Analysts Group N.Y., N.Y. Soc. Security Analysts, Phi Kappa Tau. Home and Office: 109Namkee Rd Blue Point NY 11715 Office Phone: 631-363-6211.

OWEN, THOMAS WALKER, banker, broker; b. Everett, Wash., June 7, 1925; s. Thomas Walker and Frances (Yantis) O.; m. Barbara May Neils, Oct. 20, 1951; children: Thomas W., Gerhard, Caroline, Jeffrey; m. Ingrid Lundgren, June 7, 1975. BA, U. Wash., 1949, MA in Finance, 1953; postgrad., Pacific Coast Banking Sch., 1956. Adminstrv. trainee Seattle Trust & Savs. Bank, 1949-54, asst. br. mgr., 1954-56, trust investment officer, 1956-57, mgr. investment dept., chmn. investment com., 1957-59; v.p., mgr. investment dept. Nat. Bank Wash., Tacoma, 1959-66, vice chmn., 1967-71; exec. v.p. bank adminstrn. Pacific Nat. Bank Wash., 1971-73; v.p. Reeder, Owen & Co., Inc., 1975-92; pres., chmn. Owen, Reeder, Inc., Merrill Lynch, 1991-92; bd. dirs. West One Bank Wash., Tacoma, 1981-93. Served with AUS, 1943-45. Decorated Bronze Star, Purple Heart. Mem. N.W. Forum, Wash. Athletic Club, Tacoma Club (past pres.), Tacoma Country and Golf Club, Phi Gamma Delta. Home: 11204 Tower Rd SW Lakewood WA 98498

OWEN, WALTER SHEPHERD, materials science and engineering educator; b. Liverpool, Eng., Mar. 13, 1920; s. Walter L. and Dorothea (Lunt) O. B.Engring., U. Liverpool, 1940, M.Engring., 1942, PhD, 1950, D.Eng., 1972. Metallurgist English Electric Co., 1940-46; mem. research staff MIT, 1951-57; prof. metallurgy U. Liverpool, 1957-66; prof., dir. materials sci. and engring. Cornell U., 1966-70; dean Tech. Inst., 1970-71; v.p. sci. and research Northwestern U., Evanston, Ill., 1971-73; prof. and head materials sci. and engring. MIT, 1973-82, prof. phys. metallurgy, 1982-85, prof. emeritus materials sci. and engring., 1985—. Cons. to industry. Author research papers. Commonwealth Fund fellow, 1951 Fellow ASM; mem. NAE, AIME, Instn. Metallurgists, N.Y. Acad. Scis., Inst. Metals, Materials Rsch. Soc., Japan Inst. Metals (hon.). Home: 1 Marine Ter Porthmadog LL49 9BL Wales E-mail: wsowen@aol.com.

OWENS, ARNE WESLEY, systems analyst; b. Burbank, Calif., Feb. 15, 1954; s. Ralph Hayes and Margaret Caroline O.; m. Arlene Austra, Sept. 11, 1982; 1 child, Wesley Paul. BS, U.S. Mil. Acad., 1977; MS, U. So. Calif., 1983. Commd. 2d lt. U.S. Army, 1977, advanced through grades to lt. col., 1994, retired, 1997; exec. asst. to asst. sec. def., pub. affairs Dept. Def., Washington, 1992-93; pub. affairs plans exec. U.S. Dept. Def., Washington, 1993-95, press spokesperson, 1995-97; dir. comm. Christian Coalition, Chesapeake, Va., 1997-98; pub. rels. cons. Virginia Beach, Va., 1998-99; dep. commr. Va. Dept. Mental Health, Mental Retardation and Substance Abuse, 2000—02; sr. analysts L3 Commn. Corp., 2002—. Mem. World Affairs Coun., Hampton Rds., Va., 1998-99. Mem. Pub. Rels. Soc. Am., Assn. U.S. Army, Army & Navy Club, Assn. Grads. U.S. Mil. Acad., The Econs. Club Hampton Rds. Republican. Baptist. Avocations: music, mountain climbing, bicycling, running, reading. Home: 12820 Pennmardel Ln Richmond VA 23233-7684

OWENS, B. MITCHELL, lab administrator; With GTE Tech. Products Divsn., Kayser-Roth Corp.; from dir. opers. to gen. mgr. Medtox Scientific Inc., 1988—2000, v.p., COO, 2000—. Office: Medtox Scientific Inc 402 County Rd D Saint Paul MN 55112*

OWENS, BILL, governor; b. Ft. Worth, Oct. 22, 1950; s. Arthur and June Owens; m. Frances Owens; children: Monica, Mark, Brett. BA, Stephen F. Austin State U., 1973; MPA, U. Tex., 1975. With Touche Ross & Co., Gates Corp.; state repr. Colo. Ho. Reps., 1983-89; state sen. Colo. State Sen., 1989-94; state treas. State of Colo., 1994-98, gov., 1999—. Guest host Mike Rosen, Ken Hamblin and Chuck Baker talk shows; lectr. Russia. Contbr. more than 50 articles to profl. jours. Named One of Country's Ten Up-and-Coming leaders Robert Novak. Republican. Office: Office Gov 136 State Capitol Bldg Denver CO 80203-1792 E-mail: governorowens@state.co.us.

OWENS, CAROL, state legislator; b. Aug. 8, 1931; Town clk, Nekimi, 1977—93; bd supvr Winnebago Cty, 1980—92; State assemblywoman, Dist 53 Wis., 1992—. Recipient Friend of Agri, 1994 & 1996. Republican. Lutheran. Office: Wis Assembly PO Box 8952 Madison WI 53708-8952

OWENS, CHARLES A. cardiovascular and interventional radiologist; b. Champaign, Ill., Nov. 8, 1956; s. Albert and Sue Ella (Baumgartner) O.; m. Susan Louise Ballin, Sept. 7, 1988; children: David Christian, Michael Charles, Katherine Louise. BS in Psychology, U. Ill., 1980, BS in Biology, 1981; MD, U. Ill., Chgo., 1985. Diplomate in radiology, diagnostic radiology, vascular and interventional radiology Am. Bd. Radiology; diplomate Nat. Bd. Med. Examiners. Resident in diagnostic radiology U. Ill. Med. Ctr., Chgo., 1987-91; fellow in interventional radiology Mass. Gen. Hosp., Boston, 1991-92; asst. prof. U. Ill. Med. Ctr., Chgo., 1992-98, assoc. prof., 1998—, physician and surgeon, 1992—. Co-dir. sect. cardiovascular and interventional radiology, dir. peripheral vascular animal lab, dir. continuing med. edn. dept. radiology U. Ill. Med. Ctr., Chgo. Contbr. articles to profl. jours. Grantee Johnson & Johnson, 1994, Dow Corning Wright, 1994, Abbott Labs., 1995, 97, Nycomed, 1995. Mem. Am. Soc. Cardiovascular and Interventional Radiology, Am. Roentgen Ray Soc., Radiol. Soc. N.Am., Cardiovascular and Interventional Soc. Europe, Assn. Univ. Radiologists, Am. Gastroenterol. Assn. Avocations: skiing, swimming, golf, basketball. Home: 331 Fuller Rd Hinsdale IL 60521-3626 Office: U Ill Med Ctr 1740 W Taylor St Chicago IL 60612-7232

OWENS, CHARLES VINCENT, JR., pharmaceutical executive, consultant; b. Kansas City, Mo., May 15, 1927; s. Charles Vincent and Helen (Barrett) O.; m. Cheryl Kreighbaum, Feb. 12, 1955; children: Melody, Kevin, Michael, John, Barbara. BS, U. Notre Dame, 1948; MS (Univ. fellow), U. N.C., 1949. Public health educator Richmond County (N.C.) Health Dept., 1949-51; with Miles Labs., Inc., Elkhart, Ind., 1951-82, pres. Ames Co. div., 1967-71, group v.p. profl. products group, 1971-77, exec. v.p. internat. ops., 1977-82; chmn., CEO Kyoto Diagnostics, Inc., 1982—85. Bd. dirs. Chronimed Inc.; CEO Genesis Inc., 1982—91. Bd. dirs. Elkhart YWCA, 1972-76, St. Jude Med. Inc., 1982-94; vice-chmn. Elkhart County Bd. Health, 1973-77; chmn. Child Abuse Task Force, Elkhart County, Ind., 1977-78; pres. Blue Crab Key Condo Assn., 1995-99, dir., 2003-04. With M.C., USAAF, 1945-47. Mem. Am. Public Health Assn., Health Industry Mfg. Assn. (dir.), Pharm. Mfrs. Assn., Nat. Pharm. Council (pres. 1970-71, dir. 1965-73), Am. Mgmt. Assn., Am. Diabetes Assn., Am. Assn. Diabetes Educators, Internat. Diabetes Fedn., Am. Soc. Med. Tech., Elcona Country Club (bd. dirs.), Nat. Notre Dame Monogram Club (bd. dirs.). Republican. Roman Catholic. Office Phone: 574-264-9720.

OWENS, DANA See QUEEN LATIFAH

OWENS, DAVID M. architect; Joined Tsoi/Kobus & Assoc. Inc., Cambridge, Mass., 1983, assoc. prin., 1998—2002, prin., 2002—. Office: Tsoi/Kobus & Assoc Inc One Brattle Sq PO Box 9114 Cambridge MA 02238-9114*

OWENS, DENNIS JAMES CAMPBELL, lawyer; b. Kansas City, Mo., Dec. 4, 1944; s. James Charles and Josephine Augusta (Wright) O.; m. Cathy Diane Campbell, Dec. 28, 1968; children: James Campbell, Mollie Kathleeen, Mary Theda, Sean Padraic Washington. BA, Rockhurst Coll., 1967; JD, U. Notre Dame, 1975. Bar: Mo. 1975, U.S. Dist. Ct. (we. dist.) Mo. 1975, U.S. Tax Ct. 1976, U.S. Ct. Claims 1976, U.S. Ct. Appeals (8th and D.C. cirs.) 1976, U.S. Supreme Ct. 1978, U.S. Ct. Internat. Trade 1983, U.S. Air Force Ct. Mil. Rev. 1983, U.S. Ct. Mil. Appeals 1983, U.S. Ct. Appeals (D.C. cir.) 1983, U.S. Ct. Appeals (6th and 11th cirs.) 1985, U.S. Ct. Appeals (9th cir.) 1986, U.S. Ct. Appeals (5th cir.) 1987, U.S. Ct. Appeals (3d cir.) 1988, U.S. Ct. Appeals (7th cir.) 1989, U.S. Ct. Appeals (4th cir.) 1991, U.S. Ct. Appeals (2d cir.) 1992, U.S. Dist. Ct. (ea. dist.) Mo. 1997, U.S. Dist. Ct. Kans. 1998, U.S. Ct. Appeals (1st cir.) 2002. Law clk. to chief justice Supreme Ct. of Mo., Jefferson City, 1975-76; sole practice Kansas City, 1976—. Editor-in-chief Notre Dame Jour. of Legis., 1974-75; author: Missouri Appellate Courts Research Manual, 1976; editor: Missouri Appellate Practice & Extraordinary Remedies, 4th edit., 1989; contbg. author, Eighth Circuit Appellate Practice Manual, 2003; contbr. articles to law revs. Bd. govs. Citizens Assn. Kansas City, 1976-94, Mo. Bar, 1997-99; trustee mid-Am. chpt. Nat. Multiple Sclerosis Soc., Kansas City, 1977-86; bd. dirs. NCCJ, Kansas City, 1978-86; vice chmn. Human Rels. Commn. Kansas City, 1979-82; bd. dirs. Rockhurst Coll. Alumni Assn., 1977-79, 1984-87; amb. Mo. Colls. Fund, Kansas City, 1982-83, chmn. bd. dirs. Coop. Social Svcs., Kansas City, 1983-87; asst. scoutmaster Boy Scouts Am., Kansas City, 1983-2002; pres. Friends of Kansas City Pub. Libr., 1984-88, gen. chmn. Alliance for Better Librs., Kansas City, 1986-88; hon. consul Republic of Austria for Western Mo. and Kans., 1987-93, consul gen., 1993—; bd. visitors Ave Maria Law Sch., Ann Arbor, Mich, 1996—; presdl. elector, Mo., 2000. 1st lt. USMC, 1968-71, Vietnam. Recipient Meritorious Achievement award Mo. Libr. Assn., 1985, Disting. Svc. award Greater Kansas City Jaycees, 1980, Jefferson award for Outstanding Cmty. Svc., Am. Inst. for Pub. Service, 1988, Steve Harvey Human Rights Hero award Justice Campaign Am., 2001, Outstanding Citizenship award SAR Del. Crossing chpt., 2002; named Outstanding Young Missourian, Mo. Jaycees, 1980, Tchr. of Yr., U. Mo.-Kansas City Dental Sch., 1980. Fellow: Am. Acad. Appellate Lawyers; mem.: ABA (8th cir. editor Cir. Ct. Newsletter 1983—87, editor-in-chief Appellate Practice Jour. 1988—, Mo. chmn. appellate practice com., Outstanding Editor award 2000—01), Assn. Bar of U.S. Ct. Appeals for 8th Cir. (bd. dirs. 2002—04), Am. Soc. Writers on Legal Subjects (SCRIBES), Nat. Lawyers Assn. (chmn. appellate practice sect. 1997—), Assn. Bar of U.S. Ct. Appeals for 10th Cir. (pres. 2002—), Lawyers Assn. Kansas City (Judge James A. Moore award 2002), Kansas City Met. Bar Assn. (chmn. appellate com. 1984—85), Notre Dame Law Assn., Mo. Bar, Federalist Soc. Law and Policy Studies, U.S. Supreme Ct. Hist. Soc., Native Sons Kansas City, Notre Dame Club (pres.), K.C. Republican. Roman Catholic. Home: 1115 Valentine Rd Kansas City MO 64111-3821 Office: Harzfeld's Building, 7th Floor 1111 Main Street Kansas City MO 64105 Office Phone: 816-474-3000. E-mail: owensappeal@aol.com.

OWENS, GARY MITCHELL, physician, educator, health facility administrator; b. Salisbury, Md., July 31, 1949; s. Avery Donovan and Elizabeth (Mitchell) O.; m. Loretta Andrews; children: Aaron David, Scott Christopher, Stefanie Erin, Avery Tyler, Thomas Edward, Danielle Caroline. BA, U. Pa., 1971; MD, Thomas Jefferson U., 1975. Diplomate Am. Bd. Family Practice, 78. Resident in family medicine Wilmington (Del.) Med. Ctr., 1975-78, chief resident, 1978, tchg. assoc. dept. family medicine, 1978-91; practice medicine specializing in family practice, Wilmington, 1978-91; tchg. assoc. dept. family medicine St. Francis Hosp., Wilmington, 1978-91; med. dir. Phoenix Steel Co., 1980-87, Delaware Valley HMO, Delaware Plan, 1985-91; assoc. med. dir. quality assurance, chmn. credentials com. Delaware Valley HMO, 1987-91; vice chmn. dept. family practice Med. Ctr. of Del., Wilmington, 1990—91; med. dir. Keystone Health Plan East, Phila., 1991-94, sr. med. dir., 1994-95; chmn. pharmacy and therapeutic com. Independence Blue Cross, 1994—, sr. med. dir., 1995—96, v.p. patient care mgmt., 1996—2003, v.p. med. mgmt. and policy, 2003—. Bd. dirs. Phila. Health Mgmt. Corp., Arthritis Found.; mem. interdisciplinary coun. on lifestyle and obesity mgmt., 1997; staff, coun. mem., chmn. reappointment com. Med. Ctr. Del., vice chmn. dept. family practice, 1990-91; cons. NorAm. Chem. Co., 1984-91; mem. Ladership Phila. Core Class, 2001-02. Fellow: Am. Acad. Family Physicians; mem.: Biotech. Med. Mgmt. Assn. (bd. dirs. 1997—2003), Am. Coll. Physician Execs., Alpha Epsilon Delta, Alpha Omega Alpha. Roman Catholic. Home: S Palmer Dr Glen Mills PA 19342 Office: PO Box 7516 1901 Market St Philadelphia PA 19101-7516 Office Phone: 215-241-2129. Business E-Mail: gary.owens@ibx.com.

OWENS, GUY, retired neurosurgeon; b. Amarillo, Tex., Jan. 25, 1926; s. Guy Fitzhugh Owens and Mary Helen Virgin; m. Lillian Janet Parkinson, June 20, 1949; children: Victoria Ann, Guy Parkinson. BS, Tufts U., 1946; MD, Harvard U., 1950. Diplomate Am. Bd. Neurol. Surgery. Intern Vanderbilt U. Hosp., Nashville, 1950—51, resident in gen. surgery, 1954—57; asst. prof. Vanderbilt U., Nashville, 1958—62; assoc. prof. SUNY, Buffalo, 1963—68; prof. surgery, head dept. U. Conn. Med. Sch., Farmington, Conn., 1968—75; pvt. practice New Britain, Conn., 1975—2003; ret., 2003. Author: Neurologic and Neurosurgical Nursing, 1975; contbr. over 130 articles to profl. jours. Home: 41 Main St Farmington CT 06032-2229

OWENS, HAROLD B. former state agency consultant; b. Knapp, Wis., Oct. 1, 1926; s. John Donald and Mabel Evelyn (Dunn) O.; m. Hazel Marie Allison, Feb. 18, 1956; children: Robert Bruce, Patrick Brian (dec.), Michael Shawn. Student, U. Mont., 1944, Rollins Coll., Winter Park, Fla., 1961-62, U. Hawaii, 1964-65. Airline transport pilot rating, FAA. Field rep. Puget Sound Power & Light, Kirkland, Wash., 1946-48; machinist Boeing Co., Seattle, 1948; commd. officer and pilot USAF, 1949, advanced through grades to col., ret. 1979; exec. dir. Tex. Soc. Energy Auditors, College Station, 1979-80; v.p. ops. Entek Assocs., Inc., College Station, 1979-88; aviation cons. Tex. Aeronautics Commn., Austin, 1983-89; research assoc. Ctr. for Strategic Tech., Tex. A&M U. System, College Station, 1979-92; ret., 1992. Aviation instr. Bryan, Tex., 1979—; ind. energy cons., 1988—. Contbr. articles to profl. jours. Commr. Bryan Hist. Landmark Commn., 1993-96; mem. SCV, 2000—. With U.S. Army, 1944-46, ETO, with USAF, 1947-79, Korea, S.E. Asia. Decorated Legion of Merit, Bronze Star, Air Medal (7). Mem. Nat. Soc. Historic Preservation, Tex. Hist. Found., Nat. R.R. Hist. Soc. (nat. dir. 1988—), Air Force Assn. (charter; chpt. pres. 1980-82, v.p. S.E. region Tex. chpt. 1998-2000), Nat. Assn. Flight Instrs., Order of Daedalians, Tex. A&M Assn. Former Students, Century Club, Faculty Club, Coll. Station Noon Lion's Club, The Ret. Officers Assn., Aircraft Owner's and Pilots Assn., Quiet Birdmen, Sons of Confederate Vets. Republican. Avocations: flying, music, sports, travel. Home: 3207 Wilderness Rd Bryan TX 77807-3222 Office Phone: 979-823-2926.

OWENS, JAMES W. manufacturing executive; Ph.D, North Carolina State U. With Caterpillar Inc., Peoria, Ill., 1972—, mng. dir., P.T. Natra Raya, 1987—90, pres., Solar Turbines Inc., 1990—93, v.p. group svcs. divsn., 1993-94, group pres., 1995—2003, vice chmn., 2003—04, chmn., CEO, 2004—. Dir. Inst. Internat. Econ., Washington; Mem. Coun. Foreign Relations, NY. Office: Caterpillar Inc 100 NE Adams St Peoria IL 61629*

OWENS, JANA JAE, entertainer; b. Great Falls, Mont., Aug. 30, 1943; d. Jacob G. Meyer and Bette P. (Sprague) Hopper; m. Sidney Greif (div.); children: Matthew N., Sydni C.; m. Buck Owens. Student, Interlochen Music Camp, 1959, Internat. String Congress, 1960, Vienna (Austria) Acad. Music, 1963—64; BA magna cum laude, MusB magna cum laude, Colo. Womens Coll., 1965. Tchr. music Ontario (Oreg.) Pub. Schs., 1965-67, Redding (Calif.) Pub. Schs., 1969-74; entertainer Buck Owens Enterprises, Bakersfield, Calif., 1974-78, Tulsa, 1979—. Concertmistress Boise (Idaho) Philharm., 1965—67, Shasta Symphony, Redding, Calif., 1969—74; founder Grand Lake Festivals, Inc., Redding, 1996—. Rec. artist (violinist, vocalist) Lark Records, 1978—. Avocations: skiing, tennis, swimming. Office: Jana Jae Enterprises Lark Record Prodns Inc PO Box 35726 Tulsa OK 74153-0726

OWENS, JEFFREY J. electronics executive; BS in Engring., Kettering U., 1978; MBA, Ball State U., 1983; grad. Global Exec. Program, Duke U., 1997. Assoc. mfg. engr. Delco Electronics Divsn., GM, Kokomo, Ind., 1978—82, 1984—90; mng. dir. HE Microwave, Tucson, 1990—94; dir. advanced engring. and systems integration Delco Electronics, 1994—95, exec. dir. emerging products and systems, 1995—97, dir. systems and software engring., 1997—98, product line exec. for Integrated Body, 1998—2000, gen. dir. engring., 2000—01, gen. dir. Bus. Line Mgmt., 2000—01; pres. Delphi Delco Electronics Systems, 2001—; v.p. Delphi Corp., 2001—. Office: World Hdqrs Delphi Delco 5725 Delphi Dr Troy MI 48098-2815 also: Delphi Delco Electronic Sys One Corporate Ctr PO Box 9005 Kokomo IN 46904-9005

OWENS, KATHLEEN C. academic administrator; married; 2 children. BS in Biology, Loyola U., Chgo.; MS in Edn. Biol. Scis., DePaul U., Chgo.; EdD in Curriculum and Instr., Loyola U., Chgo. Dean Lewis U., Romeoville, Ill., 1986—92; v.p. academic affairs St. Francis U., Loretta, Pa., 1992—2002; pres. Gwynedd-Mercy Coll., Gwynedd Valley, Pa., 2002—. Office: Gwynedd-Mercy Coll PO Box 901 1325 Sumneytown Pike Gwynedd Valley PA 19437-0901

OWENS, LUVIE MOORE, association consultant; b. Cleve., July 26, 1933; d. Dan Tyler and Elizabeth (Oakes) Moore; m. Lloyd Owens, Jan. 1, 1955 (dec. July 18, 2002); children: Luvie Owens Myers, Elizabeth, Lloyd H. Student, Smith Coll., Northampton, Mass., 1956. Tchr. Howard Jr. H.S., Wilmette, Ill., 1971-75; U.S. ops. mgr. Frank T. Ross & Co., Evanston, Ill., 1976-86; CEO Internat. Platform Assn., Winnetka, Ill., 1986—99, dir., 1972—99; ret., 1999. Mem. jr. league Cleve. Mus. Art, 1954—98, mem., 1954—2003, women's coun., Jr. League, 2004, treas., 1960—61, treas., mem. jr. coun., 1964—65; mem. alumnae bd. Madeira Sch., Greenway, Va., 1984—88; commr. Police and Fire Commn., Winnetka, 1986—87; chmn. bd. Lake Shore Unitarian Ch., Winnetka, 1986—87. Mem.: Univ. Club of Chgo., Winnetka Women's Club, Rotary.

OWENS, MAJOR ROBERT ODELL, congressman; b. Memphis, June 28, 1936; m. Marie Cuprill; children: Christopher, Geoffrey, Millard, Carlos, Cecilia. Grad. with high honors, Morehouse Coll., 1956; MS, Atlanta U., 1957. Mem. Internat. Commn. on Ways of Implementing Social Policy to Ensure Maximum Pub. Participation and Social Justice for Minorities, The Hague, Netherlands, 1972, U.S. Congress from 11th N.Y. dist., 1983—; chmn. select edn. & civil rights subcom., edn. and workforce com.; ranking minority mem. subcom. on workforce protections; mem. govt. reform and oversight com. Featured speaker White House Conf. on Librs., 1979. Pub. author and lectr. on library sci. Chmn. Bklyn. Congress Racial Equality; v.p. Met. Coun. on Housing, 1964; community coord. Bklyn. Pub. Library, 1964-66; exec. dir. Brownsville Community Coun., 1966-68; commr. N.Y.C. Community Devel. Agy., 1968-73; bd. dirs. community media program Columbia U., N.Y.C., 1973-75; mem. N.Y. State Senate, 1975-82, chmn. Dem. Ops. Com. Major R. Owens Day, named in his honor, City Bklyn., 1971. Democrat. Office: US Ho of Reps 2309 Rayburn Ho Office Bldg Washington DC 20515: 289 Utica Avenue Brooklyn NY 11213

OWENS, MARILYN MAE, elementary school educator, secondary school educator; b. Poland, Ohio, Nov. 17, 1932; d. S. Reed and Vernice Mae (Flickinger) Johnson; m. J. Edward Owens, July 23, 1953; children: Charlene, Preston, Lorraine. BS in Art Edn., Millersville State U., 1970, elem. cert., 1983; MEd in Art, Towson U., 1975; elem. prin. cert., Western Md. U., 1984. Cert. elem. and secondary tchr. art, elem. tchr., Pa.: art supr. elem. and secondry, prin. elem., Md. Tchr art. k-12 Northeastern Sch. Dist., Manchester, Pa., 1970-99; ret., 1999. Adj. instr. humanities, art appreciation York Coll. of Pa., 1977-81; mem. long range planning com., Northeastern Sch. Dist., Manchester, 1988-90, supt.'s adv. bd., 1990-91, elem. adv. bd. Orendorf Sch., 1990-92, 97-98, dist. budget com., 1991-92, elem. budget com. Conewago Elem. Sch., 1993-98, computer tech. elem. com., 1993-95, instrnl. and profl. devel. com., 1994-98, calligraphy tchr. Northeastern Adult Cmty. Edn., 1988-90. Leader Girl Scouts of U.S., Penn Laurel, York, Pa., 1963-67; mem. Northeastern Art Out-Reach program, Northeastern Edn. Assn. Comty. Rels. Com., Northeastern Sch. Dist.'s Portfolio Com.; vol. Susan B. Byrnes Health Ctr., Conewago Elem. Sch., Northeastern Sch. Dist., Spl. Olympics, York, York Co. Heritage Trust (life mem., bd. dirs. 2003—). Recipient scholarship Ind. (Pa.) State Coll., 1950; grantee Northeastern Sch. Dist., Manchester, 1989-90. Mem. AAUW, Nat. Art Edn. Assn., Northeastern Edn. Assn. (v.p. 1987-88, pres. 1988-89, cmty. rels. program 1998-99), Pa. Art Edn. Assn. (ret., Ret. Art Educator of Yr. 1999), Pa. Guild of Craftsmen (Yorktowne chpt., mailing com. 2001—), Pa. Inst. CPA (Women's Aux. S. Ctrl. chpt.), York Quilters Guild, Clearfield Hist. Soc. (life), York Art Assn., Kiwanis Club York, Phi Delta Kappa (scholarship com. 1990-94, scholarship chair 1998-99, 2000-02, Disting. Svc. award 1999). Avocations: painting, crafts, hiking, camping, sewing. Home: 2505 Schoolhouse Ln York PA 17402-3918

OWENS, MARSHA, library director; b. Birmingham, Ala., Apr. 5, 1956; d. Clarence Austin and Virginia (Hamilton) O.; m. James Alfred Smith, May 19, 1984 (div. Dec. 1990); m. William Kelly Key, Jan. 7, 1995. BS in Journalism, U. Ala., 1982, MLS, 1992. Staff photographer, reporter Daily Mountain Eagle, Jasper, Ala., 1983—84; paraprofl. librarian Birmingham Pub. Libr., 1988—90; dir. Orange Beach Pub. Libr., 1992—2002. Bd. dirs. South Baldwin Literacy Coun., Foley, Ala., 1993-97; mem. Ala. Electronic Access Com., 1997-98.

Mem. ALA, Ala. Libr. Assn. (convention com. 1994-97, 98), Beta Phi Mu. Avocations: camping, reading, sports cars, gardening, cats. Home: PO Box 814 Orange Beach AL 36561-4915 Office: Orange Beach Pub Libr 26267 Canal Rd PO Box 1649 Orange Beach AL 36561-1649 E-mail: owensm@earthlink.net.

OWENS, MARVIN FRANKLIN, JR., oil company executive; b. Oklahoma City, Feb. 20, 1916; s. Marvin Franklin and Levis (Coley) O.; m. Jessie Ruth Hay, June 15, 1941; children: Marvin Franklin III, William Earl, Jack Hay. BS, U. Okla., 1937; postgrad., Stonier Grad. Sch. Banking Rutgers U., 1960-62. Petroleum engr. Brit. Am. Oil Producing Co., Oklahoma City, 1937-41; chief petroleum engr. Bay Petroleum Corp., Denver, 1946-54; sr. v.p. Cen. Bank of Denver, 1954-81. Elder Presbyn. Ch., Denver. With U.S. Army, 1941-46; col. Res. ret. Mem. Cherry Hills Country Club. Home: 3899 S Glencoe St Denver CO 80237-1024

OWENS, MERLE WAYNE, executive search consultant; b. Barnsdall, Okla., Mar. 30, 1933; s. Jesse Raymond and Beulah Juanita (Thompson) O.; m. Nettie Natalie Norris, June 6, 1953; children: Jesse Wayne, Jennifer Lee. BBA, U. Okla., 1955. Sales engr. Nat. Supply Co., Tulsa, 1956-60; underwriter Allstate Ins., Dallas, 1960-63; regional mgr. Blue Cross Blue Shield, Dallas, 1963-78; sr. v.p. Paul R. Ray & Co., Ft. Worth, 1978-93; owner Merle Owens & Assocs., Ft. Worth, 1993—. 1st lt. U.S. Army, 1955-56. Republican. Baptist. Avocations: hunting, fishing, woodworking. Home: 420 Blue Jay Ct Bedford TX 76021-3201 Office: Merle W Owens & Assocs 401 Harwood Rd Ste B Bedford TX 76021-4151

OWENS, ROBERT GEORGE, psychologist, researcher; b. Devils Lake, N.D., Oct. 10, 1932; s. Clarence George and Anne Marie (Ebner) O.; m. Ruth Ann Johnson, Aug. 21, 1955 (dec. Sept. 1993); children: Scott George, Bruce Robert, Laura Marie. PhB, U. N.D., 1954, MA, 1955. Lic. psychologist, Wis. Lectr. U. Wis., Madison, 1964-66; cons. psychologist various mental health facilities and cts., Wis., 1966-86; profl. spkr. in field of psychology Wis., N.Y., 1962—. Founder, pub., editor The Internat. Jour. of Clin. Neuropsychology, 1979-84; contbr. articles to profl. pubs. Mem. APA, Am. Psychol. Soc., Nat. Register Health Svc. Providers in Psychology, Nat. Acad. Neuropsychologists (life). Republican. Episcopalian. Avocation: book collecting. Home and Office: 6666 Odana Rd Madison WI 53719-1012

OWENS, ROBERT W. gas industry executive; Bus. Degree, Calif. Poly. State U., 1976; MBA, Northwestern U. From mktg. trainee to dist. mgr. Mobil Oil Corp., 1976—88; corp. planner Amerada Hess, 1988—89, mgr. East Coast Branded mktg. ops., 1989—94; v.p. mktg. and svcs. Ultramar Diamond Shamrock, 1994—97; joined Sunoco, Inc., Phila., 1997, v.p. East Coast mktg., 1997—2000, sr. v.p., 2000—, v.p. Midwest mktg., 2001—. Office: Sunoco Inc Ten Penn Ctr 1801 Market St Philadelphia PA 19103-1699

OWENS, ROCHELLE, poet, playwright; b. Bklyn., Apr. 2, 1936; d. Max and Molly (Adler) Bass; m. George Economou, June 17, 1962. Writer-in-residence, Brown U., 1989; tchr. U. Calif. 1982, U. Okla., 1985, 87, 88, U. Southwestern La., 1998, Tex. A&M Univ. Author: (plays) The String Game, 1965, Istanboul, 1965 (Obie award 1966), Futz, 1967, Homo, 1966, Beclch, 1966, Futz and What Came After, 1968, He Wants Shih, 1969, Farmers Almanac, 1969, The Queen of Greece, 1969, Kontraption, 1970, The Karl Marx Play, 1971, O.K. Certaldo, 1975, Emma Instigated Me, 1976, The Widow and the Colonel, 1977, Mountain Rites, 1977, Who Do You Want, Peire Vidal, 1978, Chucky's Hunch, 1981 (Obie award 1982), Who Do You Want, Peire Vidal, 1982, Plays by Rochelle Owens, 2000, (poetry) Not be Essence That Cannot Be, 1961, Salt and Core, 1968, I am the Babe of Joseph Stalin's Daughter, Poems from Joe's Garage, The Joe 82 Creation Poems, The Karl Marx Play & Others, The Joe Chronicles, Part 2, Four Young Lady Poets, 1962, Shemuel, 1979, French Light, 1984, Constructs, 1985, Anthropologists at a Dinner Party, 1985, Who Do You Want Peire Vidal, 1986, W.C. Fields in French Light, 1986, How Much Paint Does the Painting Need, 1988, Black Chalk, 1995, New and Selected Poems: 1961-1996, Rubbed Stones: Poems from 1960-1992, 1994, The Passersby, 1993, Wild River, Poems, 1999, Luca: Discourse on Life and Death, 2001, (radio play) Sweet Potatoes, 1979 (Obie award 1982); The Passerby by Liliane Atlan (translation); (feature film) Futz, 1969 (Obie award); North American Women's Drama From Colonial Times to Present, 2004; editor: (plays) Spontaneous Combustion (Obie award 1967); recs. include: From a Shaman's Notebook, 1968, The Karl Marx Play, 1974, Totally Corrupt, 1976, Black Box 17, 1979, (play) Three Front, 1990, (radio play) Guerre a'Trois, 1991; reading performances at St. Mark's Poetry Project, Mus. Modern Art, Guggenheim, Whitney Mus., Oxford U., Am. Coll., Paris, Kelly Writer's House, Pa.; host of The Writer's Mind; prodr. radio show, U. Okla.; (video) Oklahoma Too, 1987, How Much Paint Does the Painting Need, Black Chalk, 1995; prodr.: (CD ROM) N.Am. Women's Drama, 2004; reading performance: Am. Coll. Athens, Greece. Founding mem. N.Y. Theatre Strategy, Women's Theatre Coun. Ford Found. grantee, 1965, Creative Arts Pub. Svc. grantee, 1973, Nat. Endowment for Arts grantee, 1974, Rockefeller Found. grantee, 1974; Yale Sch. Drama fellow, 1968, Guggenheim fellow, 1971; honors N.Y. Drama Critics Cir.; Rockefeller Found. Bellagio resident, 1993; recipient Nomination in poetry Okla. Ctr. for the Book, 1995. Mem. Dramatists Guild, ASCAP. Achievements include being in anthologies. Address: 226 W Rittenhouse Sq Apt 1001 Philadelphia PA 19103 *Creativity and idealism have enabled me to pursue the world of ideas, transforming itself always into art.*

OWENS, SUSAN, state supreme court justice; b. Kinston, N.C., Aug. 19, 1949; BA, Duke U., 1971; JD, U. N.C., Chapel Hill, 1975. Bar: Oreg. 1975, Wash. 1976. Judge Dist. Ct., Western Clallam County, 1981—2001; justice Wash. State Supreme Ct., 2001—. Mem.: Dist. and Mcpl. Ct. Judges' Assn. (bd. dirs., sec.-treas., v.p., pres.-elect). Office: PO Box 40929 Olympia WA 98504-0929

OWENS, TERRELL, professional football player; b. Dec. 7, 1973; Postgrad in merchandising, Univ. Tenn., Chattanooga. Wide receiver San Francisco 49ers, 1996—2003, Philadelphia Eagles, 2004—. Named to Pro-Bowl, 2000, 2001, 2002, 2003. Achievements include making NFL history for most receptions in one game in 2000. Office: c/o Philadelphia Eages 1 NovaCare Way Philadelphia PA 19145*

OWENS, THOMAS C. state representative; m. Donna Owens. Grad., Kans. State U., Washburn Sch. Law. Bar: (Kans.). Pvt. practice, Overland Park, Kans.; gen. counsel Kans. Dept. Social Rehab. Svcs.; judge pro-tem City and Dist Ct., Johnson City; chief justice Kans. Supreme Ct.; mem. Kans. Ho. of Reps. Spl. task force children and edn. Nat. League Cities, human devel. steering com., 1988, chair human devel. steering com., chair mcpl. consortium; mem. City Coun., 1981, pres., 1986, 1994, 1996, 1997. Mem.: Johnson County Bar Assn. Republican. Office: 446-N State Capitol 300 SW 10th Ave Topeka KS 66612 also: 11011 Antioch Ste 100 Overland Park KS 66212

OWENS, WILBUR DAWSON, JR., federal judge; b. Albany, Ga., Feb. 1, 1930; s. Wilbur Dawson and Estelle (McKenzie) O.; m. Mary Elizabeth Glenn, June 21, 1958; children: Lindsey, Wilbur Dawson III, Estelle, John. Student, Emory U., 1947-48; JD, U. Ga., 1952. Bar: Ga. 1952. Mem. firm Smith, Gardner & Owens, Albany, 1954-55; v.p., trust officer Bank of Albany, 1955-59; sec.-treas. Southeastern Mortgage Co., Albany, 1959-65; asst. U.S. atty. Middle Dist. Ga., Macon, 1962-65; assoc., then ptnr. Bloch, Hall, Hawkins & Owens, Macon, 1965-72; judge U.S. Dist. Ct. for Mid. Dist. Ga., Macon, 1972—, now sr. U.S. dist. judge. Served to 1st lt., JAG USAF, 1952-54. Mem. State Bar Ga., Macon Bar Assn., Am. Judicature Soc., Phi Delta Theta, Phi Delta Phi. Clubs: Rotarian, Idle Hour Golf and Country. Republican. Presbyterian. Office: US Dist Ct PO Box 65 Macon GA 31202-0065

OWENS, WILLIAM DEAN, lawyer; b. Topeka, Kans., July 3, 1931; s. Claude and Melvina Owens; m. Doris McConnell, June 10, 1953; children: Steven D., Susan Bloom, Sarah Steele. BS in Bus., U. Kans., Lawrence, 1953, JD, 1968. Bar: Kans. 1968. Mgr. McConnell Lumber Co., Lawrence, 1955-65; ptnr. Hampton & Royce, L.C., Salina, Kans., 1968—. Trustee, chmn. Kansas Wesleyan U., Salina, 1990-99, Salina Regional Health Found., 1986—; trustee Eisenhower Found., 1999—. Capt. USMC, 1953-55, Japan. Fellow Kans. Bar Found.; mem. ABA, Kans. Bar Assn. Republican. Presbyterian. Avocations: golf, travel, woodworking. Home: 2126 Melrose Ln Salina KS 67401-3543 Office: Hampton & Royce LC 119 W Iron Ave 9th Flr Salina KS 67401-2600 E-mail: wdowens@hamptonlaw.com.

OWENS, WILLIAM DON, anesthesiology educator; b. St. Louis, Dec. 12, 1939; s. Don and Caroline Wilhemena (Raaf) Owens; m. Patricia Gail Brown, Dec. 12, 1964; children: Pamela, David, Susan. AB, Westminster Coll., 1961; MD, U. Mich., 1965. Diplomate Am. Bd. Anesthesiology. Resident and fellow Mass. Gen. Hosp. and Harvard Med. Sch., Boston, 1969—72; instr. Harvard Med. Sch., Boston, 1972—73; asst. prof. anesthesiology Washington U. Sch. Medicine, St. Louis, 1973—76, assoc. prof., 1976—82, prof., 1982—, chmn. dept., 1982—92. Trustee Barnes Hosp., St. Louis, 1987—89; bd. dirs. Anesthesia Found., 1994—, pres., 1999—; sec.-treas. Am. Bd. Anesthesiology, 1991—94, pres., 1995—96, bd. dirs., 1984—96, Found. Anesthesia Edn. and Rsch., 1990—95, pres., 1994—95; mem. Mo. State Bd. Healing Arts, 2003—04. Contbr. numerous articles to profl. jours. and chpts. to books. Served to lt. comdr. USN, 1966—69. Fellow: Am. Coll. Anesthesiology; mem.: Assn. Univ. Anesthesiologists, Acad. Anesthesiology, Internat. Anesthesia Rsch. Soc., Am. Soc. Anesthesiologists (bd. dirs. 1989—99, 1st v.p. 1995—96, pres. 1997—98). Office: Washington U Sch Med Dept Anesthesiology 660 S Euclid Ave Saint Louis MO 63110-1010

OWENS-DWYER, DINA, utilities executive; b. 1963; With Dwyer Real Estate and Devel., Inc., Waco, Tex., 1981—, sec., 1989-98, dir., 1989—, co-chair bd. dirs., 1994-95, v.p. ops., 1995—, pres., CEO, 1999—; dir. Rainbow, Mr. Rooter; dir., pres. Nat. Accts. Office: The Dwyer Group Inc 1010 N University Parks Dr Waco TX 76707

OWENS-HICKS, SHIRLEY, state legislator; 2 children. Grad., Boston U., Harvard U. Adminstrv. asst. Mass. State Sen. Bill Owens; mem. Mass. Ho. of Reps., 1987—, chair fed. fin. asst. com. Pres., CEO Urban League Eastern Mass. Mem. Phi Delta Kappa, Delta Sigma Theta. Office: State Ho Rm 156 Boston MA 02133

OWEN-TOWLE, CAROLYN SHEETS, clergywoman; b. Upland, Calif., July 27, 1935; d. Millard Owen and Mary (Baskerville) Sheets; m. Charles Russell Chapman, June 29, 1957 (div. 1973); children: Christopher Charles, Jennifer Anne, Russell Owen; m. Thomas Allan Owen-Towle, Nov. 16, 1973. BS in Art and Art History, Scripps Coll., 1957; postgrad. in religion, U. Iowa, 1977; DD, Meadville/Lombard Theol. Sch., Chgo., 1994. Ordained to ministry Unitarian-Universalist Ch., 1978. Minister lst Unitarian Universalist Ch., San Diego, 1978—. Pres. Ministerial Sisterhood, Unitarian Universalist Ch., 1980-82; mem. Unitarian Universalist Svc. Com., 1979-85, pres., 1983-85. Bd. dirs. Planned Parenthood, San Diego, 1980-86; mem. clergy adv. com. to Hospice, San Diego, 1980-83; mem. U.S. Rep. Jim Bates Hunger Adv. Com., San Diego, 1983-87; chaplain Interfaith AIDS Task Force, San Diego, 1988—. Mem. Unitarian Universalist Ministers Assn. (exec. com. 1988, pres. 1989-91, African Am. minister's action com. 1995-98). Avocations: reading, walking, combating racism, promoting human rights, designing environments. Office: lst Unitarian Universalist Ch 4190 Front St San Diego CA 92103-2030

OWINGS, DONALD HENRY, psychology educator; b. Atlanta, Dec. 7, 1943; s. Markley James and Loyce Erin (White) O.; m. Sharon Elizabeth Calhoun, Jan. 29, 1966; children: Ragon Matthew, Anna Rebekah. BA in Psychology, U. Tex., 1965; PhD, U. Wash., 1972. Asst. prof. psychology U. Calif., Davis, 1971-78, assoc. prof., 1978-83, prof., 1983—, chair dept., 1989-93. Editor: (with M.D. Beecher & N.S. Thompson) Perspectives in Ethology, Vol. 12: Communication, 1997, (with R.G. Coss & K.R. Henry) Introduction to Psychobiol., 1998, 99 (2nd edit.), 2003 (3rd edit.); author: (with E.P. Morton) Animal Vocal Communication: A New Approach, 1998; contbr. articles to profl. jours., book chpts. NSF rsch. grantee, 1978-80, 82-84. Fellow Animal Behavior Soc.; mem. Internat. Soc. for Ecol. Psychology, Internat. Soc. for Behavioral Ecology, Internat. Soc. for Comparative Psychology. Democrat. Avocations: hiking, wildlife, travel, reading. Home: 815 Oeste Dr Davis CA 95616-1856 Office: U Calif Dept Psychology 1 Shields Ave Davis CA 95616-8686 Office Phone: 530-752-1673. Business E-Mail: dhowings@ucdavis.edu.

OWINGS, JOHN R, corporate financial executive; b. Chgo., 1949; BSc in acctg., No. Ill. U., 1971, MBA in fin., 1976. Sr. v.p., dir. fin., global telecom solutions segment Motorola Inc., 1998—2000, sr. v.p. fin., personal commn. segment, 2000—02; v.p., CFO Air Products, 2002—. Mem. exec. adv. coun. Coll. of Bus. at No. Ill. U., mem. bd. of exec. adv. Office: Air Products 7201 Hamilton Rd Allentown PA 18195-1501

OWINGS, MALCOLM WILLIAM, retired management consultant; b. Cin., Feb. 5, 1925; s. William Malcolm and Margaret (Benvie) O.; m. Margie M. Gehiker, Sept. 4, 1948 (dec. June 2000); children: Lynn A., Sandra S., Wendy K., Cheryl M; m. Doris Marie Gorman, Aug. 23, 2002. BS in Bus. Adminstrn., Miami U., Oxford, Ohio, 1950, LL.D., 1976; A.M.P., Harvard U., 1975. With Continental Can Co., 1950-83, corp. v.p., from 1971; v.p., gen. mgr. pub. affairs Continental Packaging Co (Continental Group, Inc.), 1982-83; owner, pres. Owings Assocs., Inc., Pinehurst, N.C., 1983-92. Dir. First Bank, Pinehurst, N.C.; adviser to Am. del. Internat. Tin Council, 1978-82 Columnist The Pilot, Southern Pines, N.C., 1997—. Dean's assoc. exec. in residence Sch. Bus., Miami U., 1973, mem. alumni coun., 1958-65, mem. pres.'s devel. coun., 1965-69, meem. resource devel. bd., 1982; trustee Village of Thiensville, Wis., 1956-59; mem. N.C. Clean, 1985-94, chmn., 1986-93; bd. dirs. Barrington Area Devel. Coun., 1974-79, Sales Mgmt. Execs. Grad. Sch., Am. Soc. Environment, 1976, Keep Am. Beautiful, 1980-81, also chmn., 1990; chmn. Keep N.C. Beautiful Coun., Raleigh, 1988-92, Moore Meml. Hosp. Found., Pinehurse, N.C., 1986-89; mem. Moore Regional Hosp. Scroll Soc., 1991—, chmn., 1992-93; chmn. Moore County (N.C.) Rep. Party, 1986-88; co-founder Rep. Presdl. Task Force; mem. U.S. Senate Bus. Adv. Bd., 1981-91; commr. Moore County, 1988-96, Youth Svcs., 1993-95; apptd. to N.C. Watershed Protection Adv. Com. by N.C. Environ. Mgmt. Commn., 1990-92; bd. dirs. Pub. Edn. Found., 1994-99, Ptnrs. for Children and Family, 1994-97, Drug-Free Moore County Inc., 1995-98, Dispute Settlement Ctr. of Moore County, 1995-97, Keep Moore County Beautiful, 1997—; mem. Moore County Bd. of Health, 1994-97; pres. Belle Meade Residents Assn., 2000. Recipient Cert. of Meritorious Svc. Miami U., 1967, Meritorious Svc. award Keep Moore County Beautiful, Inc., 1993-94; named Alumnus of Yr. Miami U., 1970; 1st Am. recipient Order of Apteryx Earth Awareness Found., 1971, Order of Long Leaf Pine. Mem. Ill. C. of C. (bd. dirs. 1976-78), Miami U. Alumni Assn. (nat. pres. 1964-65), Omicron Delta Kappa, Sigma Chi, Delta Sigma Pi Clubs: Pinehurst Country, Country of N.C. (Pinehurst). Home and Office: Belle Mead Retirement Resort 107 Caritas Ct Southern Pines NC 28387-2242 Personal E-mail: mwlmowings@earthlink.net. *The Golden Rule - "treating others as thyself" is not only a cornerstone for success, it is the foundation of personal happiness. However, it is well to remember that none of this is possible without political freedom and the contingent responsibilities that freedom requires.*

OWINGS, THALIA KELLEY, elementary school educator; b. Franklin, N.H., Apr. 11, 1948; d. James Warren and Elizabeth Louise (Chadwick) Kelley; m. Alan Morritt, June 25, 1966 (div. June 25, 1990); children: Manderlee, Tiffany, Brooke; m. Frederick Richard Owings, Dec. 31, 1994; children: Jennifer, Lisa. AA, Harvard U. Ext., 1982, BA, 1989; postgrad., Calif. State U., San Bernardino, 1996—. Cert. tchr., Calif., emergency tchr. Instr. CEA Internat., Providence, 1971-77; adminstrv. asst. Gulf Oil/Cumberland Farms, Norwood, Mass., 1989-91, So. Calif. Edison Co., Rosemead, Calif., 1991-96; substitute tchr. Palm Springs (Calif.) Unified Sch. Dist., 1996—2000. Tutor Calif. for Literacy!, Pasadena, Chino, and Palm Springs, Calif., 1991—; applicant interviewer Harvard U.; mem. edn. com. Shelter From the Storm, 2000-03, tutor com. chair, 2000—, vol. coord., 2002-03. Mem. So. Calif. Harvard/Radcliff Club, Toastmasters Internat. (v.p. pub. rels. 1995-96), Edison's Roundtable. Avocations: screenplay writing, photography, bicycling, dance, golf. Home: 407 E Laurel Cir Palm Springs CA 92262 2236

OWINO, MESHACK, history professor; b. Bondo, Nyanza Province, Kenya, Sept. 27, 1965; s. Edward and Anjeline Adhiambo Owiti; children: Anne Akinyi, Michelle Ogalo. BEd, Kenyatta U., Nairobi, Kenya, 1989, MA, 1993; PhD, Rice U., 2004, MA, 2004—04. Grad. tchr. Coast Girls' H.S., Mombasa, Kenya, 1989—89; lectr. Narok Teachers' Coll., Narok, Kenya, 1992—94; lectr. dept. history, Egerton U., Nakuru, Kenya, 1994—97; asst. prof. history (Africa) dept. history Bloomsburg U., Pa., 2004—; adj. prof. African history Tex. So. U., Houston, 2004; lectr. Rice U., Houston, 2001, lectr./tchg. asst. dept. history, 2002, lectr. dept. history, 2003; vis. lectr. Stanford U., Palo Alto, Calif. Tchr., writer African history Bloomsburg U., 2004—. Commentator Kenyan and African politics; web mgr. www.AfricaforAfricans.com. Recipient Charles Garside, Jnr. prize in history, dept. history Rice U., 2000; fellow, Rice U., 1997-2003. Mem.: Houston Area African Studies Group, Acad. Polit. Sci., African Studies Assn. Avocations: reading, travel, soccer, golf. Home: 7600 Creekbend #293 Houston TX 77071 Office: History Dept Rice U 6100 South Main St Houston TX 77251-1892 Personal E-mail: meshack@rice.edu.

OWNBEY, VANCE SCOTT, corporate financial executive; m. Elizabeth Dillon, Dec. 21, 1991. AA, Antelope Valley C.C., Lancaster, 1989; BS in Econs., Calif. Poly. State U., 1991; MBA, U. Phoenix, 1999. Fin. statement supr. Enterprise Rent A Car, Salt Lake City, 1995—2001, CFO Knight Mgmt. Ins. Svcs. LLC, LA, 2001—. Cons. in field. Co. chmn. United Way, Salt Lake City, 1998—99. 1st lt. infantry USAR, 1991—99. Mem.: AICPA, Internat. Who's Who of Bus., Inst. Mgmt. Accts., Nat. Soc. Accts. Republican. Avocations: travel, reading, music. Office: Knight Management Insurance Services LLC 4751 Wilshire Blvd Suite 111 Los Angeles CA 90010 Personal E-mail: vanceo-91@alumni.calpoly.edu.

OWNBY, DENNIS RANDALL, pediatrician, educator, allergist, researcher; b. Athens, Ohio, July 14, 1948; s. Dillard Ralph and Miriam (Lee) Ownby; m. Helen Louise Engelbrecht, May 24, 1970; children: David Randall, Kathryn Louise. BS, Ohio U., 1969; MD, Med. Coll. Ohio, 1972. Diplomate Am. Bd. Allergy and Immunology (bd. dirs. 1993-98, chair 1998, residency rev. com. 1995-2000), Am. Bd. Pediat., Nat. Bd. Med. Examiners. Intern and resident Duke U. Sch. Medicine, Durham, NC, 1972—74, asst. prof., 1977—80; staff physician Henry Ford Hosp., Detroit, 1980—97, dir. Allergy Rsch. Lab., 1986—97; prof. pediat. Case Western Res. U., Cleve., 1997; prof. pediat. and medicine Med. Coll. Ga., Augusta, 1998—. Clin. asst. prof. pediat. U. Mich., Ann Arbor, 1980—86, clin. assoc. prof. pediat., 1986—95. Contbr. articles to med. jours., chpts. to books. Fellow: Am. Acad. Allergy, Am. Acad. Pediat. Office: Med Coll Ga Sect Allergy & Immunology BG-1019 Augusta GA 30912-3790 Office Phone: 706-721-3531. E-mail: downby@mcg.edu.

OWNBY, JERE FRANKLIN, III, lawyer; b. Chicago Heights, Ill., Oct. 1, 1956; s. Jere Franklin Jr. and Emogene (Stephens) O.; m. Melissa Cooley, Mar. 17, 1990. BA, U. Tenn., 1986, JD, 1991. Bar: Tenn. 1991. Assoc. Law Offices of Peter G. Angelos, Knoxville, Tenn., 1991-2000, The Neal Law Firm, Knoxville, Tenn., 2000—02; pvt. practice, 2002—. Mem. Order of Barristers, William B. Spong Invitational Moot Ct. Team. Mem. ABA, Assn. Trial Lawyers Am., Am. Inn of Ct., Tenn. Bar Assn., Knoxville Bar Assn., Tenn. Trial Lawyers Assn., Omicron Delta Epsilon, Pi Sigma Alpha. Democrat. Avocations: gardening, raising dogs, the Life Training program. Home: 3902 Glenfield Dr Knoxville TN 37919-6635 Office: PO Box 51930 Knoxville TN 37950-1930

OWNBY, JERRY STEVE, landscape architect, educator; b. Shawnee, Okla., Jan. 25, 1939; s. Hugh H. and N. Lorraine (Hopkins) O.; children by previous marriage: Gregory Steve, Mitchell Hugh; m. Arnola Colson, Dec. 19, 1971; 1 child, Steven Cory BS, Okla. State U., 1961; MS in Landscape Architecture, Kans. State U., 1964, M in Landscape Architecture, 1970. Coun. Landscape Archtl. Registration Bds. cert. and registered landscape architect, Ariz., Kans., Okla., Mo., Tex. Extension landscape architect Kans. State U., Manhattan, 1963-64, instr., 1969-70; landscape architect Beardsley & Talley, Seattle, 1964-65; extension specialist Okla. State U., Stillwater, 1965-69, from asst. prof. to prof. landscape architecture and coordinator landscape architecture, 1970-85; pvt. practice, 1985—. Chmn. Okla. Landscape Architect Registration Bd., 1980-85; mem. 1985 Expert Panel for Uniform Nat. Exam., 1984-85; gov.'s appointee Mo. Coun. Landscape Architects, 1991-97 Designs include Las Laderas residence, 1978 (Merit award 1981), Student Union courtyard Okla. State U., 1981 (Honor award 1983). Chmn. Oklahomans for Landscape Architecture, 1979-80; chmn., vice chmn. Stillwater Park and Recreation Adv. Bd., Okla., 1971-79. Recipient Outstanding Prof. award Okla. State U. chpt. Alpha Zeta, 1975, svc. award Stillwater City Commn., 1980, design awards Springfield Planning and Zoning Commn., 1988, 89, 90, 99, design award Springfield Environ. Adv. Bd., 1990, Gov.'s landscape design award for Andy Williams' Moon River Theatre, Branson, Mo., 1992, for Charley Pride Theater, Branson, 1995, design award Watershed Com., 1993; alumni fellow Kans. State U., 1995. Fellow Am. Soc. Landscape Architects (v.p. 1983-85, Okla. chpt. svc. award 1980); mem. Nat. Coun. State Garden Clubs (accredited instr. 1964—), Nat. Coun. of Educators in Landscape Architecture, Mo. Assn. of Landscape Architects, Coun. Landscape Archtl. Registration Bds. (cert.), Phi Kappa Phi, Sigma Lambda Alpha. Republican. Baptist. Avocations: travel, photography, fishing. Home: 234 Sunset Cove # 108 Branson MO 65616-3604 E-mail: jsownby@aol.com.

OWNBY, TERRY SCOTT, music educator, director; s. John Jackie and Shirley Mae Ownby; m. Laura Reyer Reyer, May 19, 1990; children: Emily Lee, ELizabeth Lauren. MusB in Edn., U. North Ala., 1991, MA in Edn., 2004. Cert. tchr. Ala. Bd. Edn., 1991. Band dir. Muscle Shoals Mid. Sch. Band, Muscle Shoals, Ala., 1991—; asst. dir. bands Muscle Shoals H.S. Band, 1991—2004. Min. music Valley Grove Bapt. Ch., Tuscumbia, Ala., 2000, York Ter. Bapt. Ch., Sheffield, 1990—2000. Recipient citation Excellence Outstanding Contbns. to Band and Band Lit., Nat. Band Assn., 2001. Mem.: Ala. Bandmasters Assn., Ala. Music Educators Assn., Music Eudcators Nat. Conf. Conservative. Southern Baptist. Avocation: golf. Office: Muscle Shoals Board of Education 100 Trojan Drive Muscle Shoals AL 35661 Office Phone: 256-389-2642.

OWSLEY, JOHN QUINCY, III, plastic surgeon, educator; b. Manila, Luzon, Philipines, Oct. 2, 1928; came to U.S., 1930; s. John Quincy Owsley Jr. and Sara Christine Maxwell; m. Mary Leslie Marriott, Apr. 27, 1957 (div. 1969); children: John Quincy IV, Sara Elizabeth; m. Sharon Theresa Anton, Jan. 2, 1971. BA, Vanderbilt U., 1950, MD, 1953. Intern U. Calif. Med. Ctr., San Francisco, asst. resident in surgery, asst. resident, chief resident plastic surgery, 1956-60, clin. instr. to asst. prof. to assoc. prof., clin. prof. surgery, 1960-80; pvt. practice San Francisco, 1960—. Dir. Aesthetic Surgery Fellowship, 1989—; vis. prof. Columbia U. Coll. of Physicians and Surgeons, 1989, Divsn. of Plastic Surgery U. Pa., 1993; Donald P. Hause Meml. lectr. U. Calif., Davis Med. Ctr., 1993; guest reviewer Jour. of Plastic and Reconstructive Surgery; dir. ann. aesthetic surgery symposium U. Calif., San Francisco, 1989-2002. Author: Aesthetic Facial Surgery, 1994; contbr. chpts. to books and articles to profl. publs. Fellow ACS; mem. Am. Soc. of Plastic Surgeons (chmn. ethics com. 1973-76, Special Recognition award Ednl. Found. 2003), Am. Soc. for Aesthetic Plastic Surgery (sec. 1975-77), Am. Assn. of Plastic Surgeons, Am. Cleft Palate Assn. (pres. 1977-78), Bohemian Club. Avocations: sailing, bird hunting, travel. Office: 45 Castro St Ste 111 San Francisco CA 94114 E-mail: Owsley@DrjohnOwsley.com.

OWSLEY, THOMAS L. oil industry executive; b. L.A., Oct. 27, 1940; AB, Harvard U., 1962; JD, U. N.C., 1969. Bar: Conn. 1969, D.C. 1973, U.S. Supreme Ct. 1973, Md. 1983. Assoc. Davis, Cheney & Chipman, 1969—70; atty. SEC, 1970—72; legis. asst. U.S. Sen. Robert P. Griffin, 1972—73; assoc. Purcell & Nelson, 1973—75; sr. v.p., gen. counsel, corp. sec. Martin Marietta

Corp., 1976—82; pres. Crown Ctrl. Petroleum, Balt., 2003—. Lt. USN, 1962—66. Mem.: ABA, Am. Corp. Counsel Assn., Am. Soc. Corp. Secs., Md. State Bar Assn. Office: Crown Central Petroleum PO Box 1168 Baltimore MD 21201

OWYANG, CHUNG, gastroenterologist, researcher; b. Chung King, China, Nov. 20, 1945; arrived in Can., 1965; s. Chi and Ching-Ying (Fung) O.; m. Jeannette Lim; children: Stephanie, Christopher. BS with honors, McGill U., Montreal, Can., 1968, MD, 1972. Diplomate Am. Bd. Internal Medicine, Gastroenterology; lic. Gen. Med. Coun., U.K., Que., Can., Min. Med. lic., Mich. med. lic. Intern in internal medicine Montreal Gen. Hosp./McGill U., 1972-73, resident in internal medicine, 1973-75; clin. teaching fellow in internal medicine McGill U., 1974-75; fellow in gastroenterology Mayo Clinic and Found., Rochester, Minn., 1975-78; instr. internal medicine Mayo Med. Sch., Rochester, 1977-78; asst. prof. U. Mich., 1978-84, assoc. prof., 1984-88, assoc. chief divsn. gastroenterology, 1984-90, prof., 1988—, chief divsn. gastroenterology, 1991—, dir. med. procedures unit, 1992—. Assoc. dir. Gastrointestinal Peptide Rsch. Ctr., U. Mich., 1984-95, dir. 1996—; cons. Rsch. Coun. Janssen Pharmaceutica Inc., 1985—, Ann Arbor VA Med. Ctr., 1978—, NIH, Bethesda, Md., 1989-94, FDA, Bethesda, 1995—; H. Marvin Pollard chair in gastroenterology, U. Mich., 1996—; speaker, presenter in field. Co-author: Textbook of Gastroenterology, 1991, 2d edit. 1995, Atlas of Gastroenterology, 1992; mem. edit. bd. Pancreas, 1986—, Am. Jour. Physiology, 1988—, Regulatory Peptide Letter, 1988—, Gastroenterology, 1990—, guest editor, 1991—, Digestive Diseases, 1993—; contbr. numerous chpts. to books, articles to profl. jours., jours. refereed. Grantee in field. Fellow ACP; mem. Am. Assn. Physicians, Am. Soc. Clin. Investigation, Am. Gastroenterological Assn., Am. Pancreatic Assn., Am. Diabetes Assn., Am. Fedn. Clin. Rsch., Am. Motility Soc., Ctrl. Soc. Clin. Rsch., Internat. Assn. Pancreatology, Midwest Gut Club. Office: U Mich Med Ctr Divsn Gastroenterology PO Box 362 Ann Arbor MI 48106-0362

OXENHANDLER, NEAL, language educator, writer; b. St. Louis, Feb. 3, 1926; s. Joseph and Billie (Lutsky) O.; m. Jean Romano (div. May 1976); children: Noelle, Daniel, Alicia; m. Judith I. Josel, Dec. 12, 1979; stepchildren: Rebecca, Marjorie Menza. AB, U. Chgo., 1948; MA, Columbia U., 1951; PhD, Yale U., 1955; MA (hon.), Dartmouth Coll., 1973. Lectr. French St. Louis U., 1951-52; asst. instr. Yale U., New Haven, 1952-54, instr., 1954-57; asst. prof. UCLA, 1957-60, assoc. prof., 1960-65, U. Calif., Santa Cruz, 1965-66, prof., 1966-69, Dartmouth Coll., Hanover, NH, 1969—, Edward Tuck prof., 1987—, chmn. dept. comparative lit., 1980—85, chmn. dept. French and Italian, 1987-91. Dir. NEH Summer Seminar in Comparative Lit., 1981. Author: Scandal and Parade: Theater of Jean Cocteau, 1957, Aspects of French Literature, 1961, French Literary Criticism: The Basis of Judgment, 1966, Max Jacob and Les Feux de Paris, 1964, (novel) A Change of Gods, 1962, Looking for Heroes in Post-War France, 1995; adv. editor Film Quar., Berkeley, 1958-91; mem. editl. com. U. Calif. Press, Berkeley, 1966-69; asst. editor French Rev., 1969-73; contbr. articles, revs., poetry and translations to profl. jours. With U.S. Army, 1941-43, ETO, PTO. Decorated Combat Inf. badge; Fulbright scholar, Italy, 1953; Cross-Disciplinary fellow Soc. for Values in Higher Edn., France, 1966, Guggenheim fellow, France, 1962, Inst. for Shipboard Edn., 1995. Mem. MLA (adv. editor proc. 1977-80), Internat. Assn. Philosophy and Lit., Internat. Comparative Lit. Assn. Democrat. Roman Catholic. Avocation: poetry. Home: # 502 97 Sunset Dr Sarasota FL 34236 Office: Dartmouth Coll Dept French Hanover NH 03755 Office Phone: 941-330-2086. Personal E-mail: nealoxen@aol.com.

OXFORD, WILLIAM TODD, music educator; b. Dallas, July 1, 1967; s. William Franklin and Jeanette Parks Oxford; m. Thelissa Lynn Watkins, Apr. 13, 1991 (div. June 1998); m. Cara Yvonne Alden, July 12, 2003. BMus, U. Tex., Austin, 1990, MMus, 1995, DMus, 2001. Lectr., saxophone U. Mary Hardin-Baylor, Belton, Tex., 2001—03, Tex. State U., San Marcos, 2003—. Musician: (albums) It Might As Well Be Spring, 1994, Live in Chicago, 1996, Finesse, 1998, Live Through the Years, 2003, UT Wind Ensemble, 1994, TEX-SAX, 1998, USAF Band of the West, 1998, UT Wind Ensemble, 1999. Mem.: Coll. Music Soc., Tex. Music Educators Assn., Phi Mu Alpha. Avocations: movies, theater, reading, skiing, travel. Home: 817 Eventide Dr San Antonio TX 78209 Office: Music Dept Tex State Univ 601 University Dr San Marcos TX 78666 Office Phone: 512-589-5629. E-mail: wtoddoxford@aol.com.

OXLER, CORA JEAN, voice educator; d. Margaret J. Paradee; m. Matthew T. Oxler; 1 child. MusB in Edn., Hardin-Simmons U., 1996; MusM, Ind. U., 2000. Instr. voice and ear tng./sight singing Tyler Jr. Coll., Tex., 2000—. Entertainer Mayan Ranch, Bandera, Tex., 1990—2000. Singer: (soloist) Bach Magnificat, Canticle of Joy by Joseph M. Martin, What Child is This by John Leavitt. Fund raiser Komen Breast Cancer, Tyler, 2000—03, Cystic Fibrosis Found., Tyler, 2003; religious educator Cathedral of Immaculate Conception, Tyler, 2000—03. Mem.: Tyler Chamber Chorale (singer, soloist), TMEA, TCCTA, Nat. Assn.Tchrs. of Singing, Sigma Alpha Iota (sgt.of arms 1994—95). Roman Catholic. Office: Tyler Jr Coll 1400 E Fifth St Tyler TX 75701 Office Phone: 903-510-2202. E-mail: coxl@tjc.edu.

OXLEY, ANN, television executive; b. Canton, Ohio, Aug. 3, 1924; d. Edward and Dorothy (Duffy) Adang; m. Jack Raymond Oxley, Aug. 10, 1946 (dec.); children: Kathleen Oxley Wiggins, Maureen Oxley Gaff, Joseph, Jeffrey, Christeen Oxley Rhodes, Daniel (dec.), Sister Julie Marie Oxley, Jamie, Kevin, Valerie Oxley Fouch, Amy. BA with distinction, Ind. U., 1974, MPA, 1982. Advt. account salesperson Ft. Wayne (Ind.) Jour. Gazette, 1945-47; office mgr. Ind. Equestrian Assn., Ft. Wayne, 1971-73; exec. dir. Taxpayers Rsch. Assn., Ft. Wayne, 1974-76; exec. dir. Ft. Wayne Pub. TV Inc., 1976-86. Active Bicentennial Com., 1976; adviser Media Arts Panel Ind. Arts Commn.; pres. Allen County Coun. on Aging. Found., 1995-98. Mem. AAUW, Svc. Corps Ret. Execs. (publicity chair 1986, nat. mktg. dir. 1989-90), Mensa Internat. (nat. coord. Project Inkslinger Mensa Ednl. Rsch. Found. 1998-2000), C. of C. (cultural com.), Phi Alpha Alpha. Roman Catholic. Home: 4305 Arlington Ave Fort Wayne IN 46807-2635 Office: SCORE 1300 S Harrison Federal Bldg Fort Wayne IN 46807

OXLEY, DWIGHT K(AHALA), pathologist; b. Wichita, Kans., Dec. 2, 1936; s. Dwight K. Jr. and Ruth Erdene (Warner) O.; m. Patricia Warren, June 18, 1961; children: Alice DeBloois, Thomas Oxley. AB, Harvard U., 1958; MD, U. Kans., 1962. Diplomate Am. Bd. Pathology (trustee 1992—, pres. 1999), Am. Bd. Nuclear Medici ne. Pathologist Wesley Med. Ctr., Wichita, 1969-74, Eisenhower Med. Ctr., Rancho Mirage, Calif., 1974-78, St. Joseph Health Ctr., Kansas City, Mo., 1978-88; chmn. dept. pathology Wesley Med. Ctr., 1988—. Bd. editors Archives of Pathology and Lab. MEdicine, Chgo., 1984-95, Clinica Chimica Acta, Amsterdam, 1980-86, Am. Jour. Clin. Pathology, Chgo., 1974-80. Sr. warden St. Stephens Episcopal Ch., Wichita, 1994. Lt. commdr. USN, 1964-69. Fellow: Coll. Am. Pathologists (various offices), Am. Soc. Clin. Pathologists (various offices); mem.: Kans. Soc. Pathologists (pres. 1993—94), Am. Pathology Found. (bd. dirs. 1979—89). Republican. Avocations: music, athletics. Office: Wesley Med Ctr 550 N Hillside St Wichita KS 67214-4910

OXLEY, JAMES GRIEVE, mathematics professor; b. Sale, Victoria, Australia, Feb. 4, 1953; s. William A. and Dilys C. (Grieve) O.; m. Judith Danute Surkevicius; children: Margaret Catherine, David Grieve (dec.). BSc, U. Tasmania, 1974; MSc, Australian Nat. U., 1975; PhD, U. Oxford, 1978. Lectr., rsch. fellow Australian Nat. U., 1978-82; asst. prof. La. State U., Baton Rouge, 1982-85, assoc. prof., 1985-90, prof., 1990-99, alumni prof., 1999—. Vis. instr. U. N.C., Chapel Hill, 1978. Author: Matroid Theory, 1992.; mem. editl. bd. Combinatorics, Probability and Computing, SIAM Jour. on Discrete Math., Jour. Combinatorial Theory Series B; reviewer Mathematical Reviews, Zentralblatt für Mathematik; contbr. chpts. to books, articles to profl. jours. Grantee NSF, 1985-87, 89-91, La. Edn. Quality Support Fund, 1987-94, Nat. Security Agy., 1994—, others; Fulbright fellow U. N.C., 1980; named Disting. Rsch. Master of Engring, Sci. and Tech., La. State U., 1999. Mem. Am. Math. Soc., London Math. Soc. Office: La State U Math Dept Baton Rouge LA 70803-4918 Business E-Mail: oxley@math.lsu.edu.

OXLEY, MICHAEL GARVER, congressman; b. Findlay, Ohio, Feb. 11, 1944; s. George Garver and Marilyn Maxine (Wolfe) O.; m. Patricia Ann Pluguez, Nov. 27, 1971; 1 child, Michael Chadd. BA, Miami U., Oxford, Ohio, 1966; JD, Ohio State U., 1969. Bar: Ohio 1969, U.S. Supreme Ct. 1985. Agt. FBI, 1969-71; atty. Oxley, Mallone, Fitzgerald & Hollister, 1971—81; mem. Ohio Ho. of Reps., 1973-81, U.S. Congress from 4th Ohio dist., Washington, 1981—. Mem. ABA, Ohio Bar Assn., Findlay Bar Assn., Soc. Former Spl. Agts. FBI, Ohio Farm Bur., Sigma Chi. Lodges: Rotary, Elks. Republican. Office: US Ho Reps 2308 Rayburn Ho Office Bldg Washington DC 20515-3504*

OXMAN, DAVID CRAIG, lawyer; b. Summit, N.J., Mar. 10, 1941; s. Jacob H. and Kathryn (Grear) O.; m. Phyllis Statter; children— Elena, Lee AB, Princeton U., 1962; LL.B., Yale U., 1969. Bar: N.Y. 1970, N.J. 1974, U.S. Dist. Ct. (so. and ea. dists.) N.Y. 1974, U.S. Ct. Appeals (2d cir.) 1974, U.S. Tax Ct. 1977, U.S. Supreme Ct. 1974. Assoc. Davis Polk & Wardwell, N.Y.C., 1970-76, ptnr., 1977-95, sr. counsel, 1995—. Served with USN, 1962-66 Fellow Am. Coll. Trust and Estate Counsel; mem. ABA, N.Y. State Bar Assn., Assn. of Bar of City of N.Y. Office: Davis Polk & Wardwell 450 Lexington Ave New York NY 10017-3982

OXNAM, PHILIP LINTON, small business owner; b. Pomona, Calif., Nov. 5, 1945; s. Robert Fisher Oxnam and Dalys Oxnam Jaecker; m. JoAnne Buck, Sept. 30, 1989. BA, Norwich U., 1967; grad. Am. Acad. Dramatic Arts, 1972; student various acting schs., N.Y., L.A., 1972—82; grad., NYU, 1979. Lic. theatre arts tchr. Vt. Actor various orgns., N.Y., L.A., 1972—86; ind. casting dir. NY, 1985—88; owner Acting Lab., NY, 1987—89; tchr. theatre arts Lamoille Union HS, Morrisville, Vt., 1990—2000; co-owner TRIXonSTIX skis, Warren, Vt., 2002—03; owner On the Edge Skis, Monument, Colo., 2002—04. Author (various) and screenplays plays; co-creator (ski sports) TRIXonSTIX, 2002, creator (snow skis, snowboards) On the Edge Skis, 2003. Figure skating performance coach, 1998—2003. 1st. lt. U.S. Army, 1968—70, U.S., Thailand. Named Ath. Hall of Fame soccer and swimming, Norwich U., Northfield, Vt., 2002; named to All New Eng. Soccer Team, Vt. All State Swimming Team. Mem.: Norwich U. Ath. Assn., Nat. Rifle Assn., Norwich U. Golden Goal Club, Norwich U. Blue Line Club, Perry Park Country Club, Tucson Nat. Country Club. Avocations: skiing, golf, figure skating, tennis.

OXNARD, CHARLES ERNEST, anatomist, anthropologist, human biologist, educator; b. Durham, Eng., Sept. 9, 1933; arrived in Australia, 1987; s. Charles and Frances Ann (Golightly) O.; m. Eleanor Mary Arthur, Feb. 2, 1959; children: Hugh, David. BSc. with 1st class honors, U. Birmingham, Eng., 1955, MB, BChir in Medicine, 1958, PhD, 1962, D.Sc., 1975. Med. intern Queen Elizabeth Hosp., Birmingham, 1958-59; rsch. fellow U. Birmingham, 1959-62, lectr., 1962-65, sr. lectr., 1965-66, court govs., 1958-66; assoc. prof. anatomy, anthropology and evolutionary biology U. Chgo., 1966-70, prof., 1970-78, gov. biology collegiate div., 1970-78, dean coll., 1973-77; dean grad. sch. U. So. Calif., Los Angeles, 1978-83, univ. rsch. prof. biology and anatomy, 1978-83, univ. prof., prof. anatomy and cell biology, prof. biol. scis., 1983-87; prof. anatomy and human biology U. Western Australia, 1987-98, dir. ctr. for human biology, 1989-99, head div. agr. and sci., 1990-92, prof. emeritus, 1998—, sr. rsch. fellow, 1998—; Leverhulme prof. U. Liverpool (U.K.), Univ. Coll., London, 2000—03. Rsch. assoc. Field Mus. Natural History, Chgo., 1967; overseas assoc. U. Birmingham, 1968—; Lo Yuk Tong lectr. U. Hong Kong, 1973, 94, 97, 2003, hon. prof., 1978, Chan Shu Tzu lectr., 80, vis. scholar, 95, 96; Octagon lectr. U. Western Australia, 1987; Latta lectr. U. Nebr., Omaha, 1987; Stanley Wilkinson orator, 91; rsch. assoc. L.A. County Natural History Mus., 1984—, George C. Page Mus., L.A., 1986; vis. scholar Shaw Coll. Chinese U. of Hong Kong, 1995; bd. dirs. U. Western Australia Press, 1993—95; advisor on human biology World Sci. Pub. Co., 1993—; vis. prof. Northwestern U., Xian, China, 1999, U. York, England, 2003—. Author: Form and Pattern in Human Evolution, 1973, Uniqueness and Diversity in Human Evolution, 1973, Human Fossils: The New Revolution, 1977, The Order of Man, 1983, Humans, Apes, and Chinese Fossils, 1985, Fossils, Teeth and Sex, 1987, Anatomies and Lifestyles, 1990; series editor Recent Advances in Human Biology Series World Sci. Pub., Vol. I, The Origin and Past of Modern Humans, 1995, Vol. 2, Bone Structure and Remodeling, 1995, Vol. 3 The Origins and Past of Modern Humans: Towards Reconciliation, 1998, Vol. 4 The Natural History of the Doucs and Snub-nosed Langurs, 1998, Vol. 7 Morphometrics for the Life Sciences, 2000, Perspectives in Human Biology, Vol. 1 Genes, Ethnicity and Aging, 1995, Vol. 2 Humans in the Australasian Region, 1996, Vol. 3 Human Adaptability: Future Trends and Lessons from Past, 1998, Vol. 4, Is Human Evolution a Closed Chaptr, 1999, Vol. 4, Child Growth, Secular Trends and Continuing Human Evolution, Vol. 4, Dento-Facial Variation in Perspective, 1999, Vol. 5 Towards Consilience, 2000; mem. edit. bd. Annals of Human Biology; cons. editor: Am. Jour. Primatology, Jour. Human Biology, Jour. Human Evolution: Australia com. mem. Ency. Britannica, 1991-99; bibliographic referee Britannica On-Line, 1994, 99; contbr articles to anat. and anthrop. jours. Mem. Pasteur Found., 1988; bd. dirs. West Australian Inst. for Child Health, 1991-98; mem. electoral bd. Freemantle Hosp., 1991-94. Recipient Book award, Hong Kong Coun., 1984, S.T. Chan Silver medal, U. Hong Kong, 1980, Charles Darwin Lifetime Achievement award, Am. Assn. Phys. Anthropology, 2001; grantee, USPHS, 1960—71, NIH, 1974—87, NSF, 1971—87, Raine Found., 1988—91, Viertel Found., 1993—94, Australian Acad. Sci., 1995, Leverhulme Trust, Eng., 2003—06. Fellow N.Y. Acad. Sci., AAAS, So. Calif. Acad. Sci. (bd. dirs. 1985); mem. Chgo. Acad. Soc. (hon. life), Australasian Soc. for Human Biology (pres. 1987-90), Australia and New Zealand Anat. Soc. (pres. 1989-90), Anat. Soc. Gt. Britain and Ireland (councillor 1992-94), Nat. Health and Med. Rsch. Coun. (grantee 1994-97), Australian Rsch. Coun. (grantee 1988-2004), Med. and Health Infrastructure Fund, Western Australia (grantee 2001-03, Leverhulme Trust Rsch. Grant, 2003-), Soc. for Study Human Biology (treas. 1962-66), Sigma Xi (pres., nat. lectr. 1990), Phi Beta Kappa (pres. chpt.), Phi Kappa Phi (pres., Book award 1984). Office: U Western Australia Nedlands WA 6009 Australia E-mail: coxnard@cyllene.uwa.edu.au.

OXNER, GLENN RUCKMAN, financial executive; b. Greenville, S.C., July 10, 1938; s. G. Dewey and Frances O.; m. Kathleen Gallagher, 1992. Student, Duke U., 1956-57; BS, U.S.C., 1961. Trainee stock bd. broker Alester G. Furman Co., Greenville, S.C., 1961, v.p., 1964-67, exec. v.p., 1967-75; pres. S.C. Securities Co., 1975-77; sr. v.p. Interstate Securities, Charlotte, N.C., 1977-82, exec. v.p., 1982-85; chmn. First Tryon Securities, Charlotte, 1986-89; mng. dir. Nations Bank Investment Banking Co., Charlotte, 1989-92; chmn. Edgar M. Norris & Co., Charlotte, 1992-2001; exec. v.p. Scott & Stringfellow, Greenville, SC, 2001—. Served with U.S. Army, 1957. Mem. Nat. Assn. Security Dealers (com. chmn. dist. 7 1974, gov. 1981-84), Security Industry Assn. (gov. 1974), Security Dealers Carolinas (pres. 1977). Home: 18 Woodland Way Cir Greenville SC 29601-3824 Office: Scott & Stringfellow PO Box 247 Greenville SC 29602-0247

OXTOBY, DAVID WILLIAM, college president, chemistry educator; b. Bryn Mawr, Pa., Oct. 17, 1951; s. John Corning and Jean (Shaffer) O.; m. Claire Bennett, Dec. 17, 1977; children: Mary-Christina, John, Laura. BA, Harvard, 1972; PhD, U. Calif., Berkeley, 1975. Asst. prof. U. Chgo., 1977-82, assoc. prof., 1982-86, prof., 1986—2003, Mellon prof., 1987-92, dir. James Franck Inst., 1992-95, dean phys. scis. divsn., 1995—2003, William Rainey Harper prof., 1996—2003; pres., prof. chemistry Pomona Coll., Claremont, Calif., 2003—. Co-author: Principles of Modern Chemistry, 1986, Chemistry: Science of Change, 1990. Trustee Bryn Mawr Coll., 1989—, Tchrs. Acad. Math. and Sci., 1999-2003, Toyota Technol. Inst., Chgo., 2002—; mem. bd. govs. Argonne Nat. Lab., 1996-2002, Astrophys. Rsch. Consortium, 1998-2003; mem. bd. overseers Claremont Univ. Consortium, 2003—. Recipient Quantrell award U. Chgo., 1986, Alumni award of merit William Penn Charter Sch., 2003; Alfred P. Sloan Found. fellow, 1979, John Simon Guggenheim Found. fellow, 1987; Camille and Henry Dreyfus Found. tchr.-scholar, 1980. Fellow Am. Phys. Soc.; mem. Am. Chem. Soc., Royal Soc. Chemistry (Marlow medal 1983), Phi Beta Kappa. Office: Office of the Pres Pomona Coll 550 N College Ave Claremont CA 91711 Office Phone: 909-621-8131.

OYESIKU, NELSON MOBOLANLE, neurosurgeon, neuroscientist; arrived in US, 1982; s. Nelson M. and Margaret M. Oyesiku; m. Lola M. Afolabi, Nov. 20, 1982; children: Angela, Linda, Nelson III. MD, U. Ibadan, Nigeria, 1979; MSc, U. London, 1982; PhD, Emory U., 1996. Diplomate Am. Bd. Neruol. Surgery. Intern Gen. Hosp., Laos, 1980; fellow in neurosurgery Lankenau Hosp, 1984, Harford Hosp., U. Conn., 1985—86, resident in gen. surgery, 1986—87; resident in neurosurgery Emory U., Atlanta, 1987—93, asst. prof. neurol. surgery, 1993—2000, assoc. prof. neurol. surgery, 2000—. Author: (book) Patient Care in Neurosurgery, 1990; contbr. chapters to books, articles to profl. jours. Bd. dirs. Brain Injury Assn. Ga., Atlanta, 1997—99, Med. Assn. Atlanta, 1997; trustee Emory U. Alumni Exec. Bd., Atlanta, 1997—2000; bd. dirs. Druid Hills Civic Assn., Atlanta, 1994—96. Recipient Augustus McCravey award, So. Neurosurg. Soc., 1992, Young Investigator award. Brain Trauma Found./AANS/CNS, 1994, Minority Med. Faculty Devel. award, Robert Wood Johnson Found., 1994, Clinician Investigator Devel. award, NIH, 1994; fellow Young Investigator Travel fellow, Internat. Stroke Congress, 1989; scholar Commonwealth scholar, Brit. Govt., 1981. Fellow: ACS; mem.: AMA, Ga. State Med. Assn., Pituitary Soc., Nat. Med. Assn., So. Neurosurg. Soc., Med. Assn. Atlanta (bd. dirs. 1997), Ga. Neurosurg. Soc. (sec.-treas. 2001—), Am. Assn. Neurol. Surgeons, Congress Neurol. Surgeons (exec. com. 1998, v.p., pres.-elect), Atlanta Soc. Episcopalian. Avocation: golf. Home: 1917 Durand Mill Dr NE Atlanta GA 30307 Office: Emory Univ 1365B Clifton Rd NE Atlanta GA 30322

OYLER, GREGORY KENNETH, lawyer; b. Moses Lake, Wash., Sept. 16, 1953; s. Eugene Milton and Annetta Diane (Williams) O.; m. Evelyn Hartwell Wright, Oct. 18, 1986; 1 child, Elizabeth Atwood. AB, Princeton U., 1975; JD, Georgetown U., 1978; LLM, NYU, 1981. Bar: Pa. 1978, U.S. Tax Ct. 1978, U.S. Ct. Appeals (D.C. cir.) 1979, D.C. 1981, U.S. Supreme Ct. 1982, U.S. Ct. Fed. Claims 1983, U.S. Ct. Appeals (fed. cir.) 1987. Law clk. to judges U.S. Tax Ct., Washington, 1978-80; assoc. Hamel & Park, Washington, Washington, 1981-85; ptnr. Hopkins & Sutter, Washington, 1985-95, Scribner, Hall & Thompson LLP, Washington, 1995—. Mem. adv. com. IRS Info. Reporting Program, 1993—94. Mem. ABA (tax sect., ins. com.), D.C. Bar Assn. (tax sect.), Fed. Bar Assn., Soc. Preservation Md. Antiquities (bd. dirs. 1991-97), Clark-Winchcole Found. (trustee 1999—). Office: Scribner Hall & Thompson LLP 1875 Eye St NW Ste 1050 Washington DC 20006-5441

OZ, FRANK (FRANK RICHARD OZNOWICZ), puppeteer, film director; b. Hereford, Eng., May 25, 1944; s. Isidore and Frances Oznowicz. m. Robin Garsen, 1979; 2 children. Student, Oakland City Coll., 1962. Puppeteer with the Muppets, N.Y.C., 1963—; characters performed include The Mighty Favag (Saturday Night Live 1975-76), Miss Piggy, Fozzie Bear, Animal, Sam the Eagle for TV series The Muppet Show, Muppets Tonight!, 1996, films Muppet Treasure Island, 1996, Muppets From Space, 1999; voice of Bert, Grover, Cookie Monster for video Elmo Saves Christmas, 1996, film Adventures of Elmo in Grouchland, 1999, TV film Cinderelmo, 1999; voice for CDROM: The Muppets Inside, 1996; now v.p. Jim Henson Prodns., N.Y.C.; creative cons. feature film The Great Muppet Caper; appeared in films The Blues Brothers, 1980, Trading Places, 1983, Labyrinth, 1986, Innocent Blood, 1992, Blues Brothers, 2000; voice of Yoda in films The Empire Strikes Back, 1980, Return of the Jedi, 1983, Star Wars: Episode I-The Phantom Menace, 1999; dir. films The Dark Crystal (with Jim Henson), 1982, The Muppets Take Manhattan, 1984, Little Shop of Horrors, 1986, Dirty Rotten Scoundrels, 1988, What About Bob?, 1991, Housesitter, 1992, The Indian in the Cupboard, 1995, In & Out, 1997, Bowfinger, 1999, The Score, 2001, The Stepford Wives, 2004. Co-recipient Emmy award for outstanding comedy-variety or music program for The Muppet Show, 1978. Mem. AFTRA, Dirs. Guild Am., Writers Guild Am., Screen Actors Guild, Acad. TV Arts and Scis. Office: Jim Henson Prodns 117 E 69th St New York NY 10021-5004

OZ, MEHMET CENGIZ, cardiologist, writer; b. Cleve., June 11, 1960; s. Mustafa and Suna (Atabay) O. BA, Harvard U., 1982; MD, U. Pa., 1986; MBA, Wharton Bus. Sch., Phila., 1986. Resident Columbia-Presbyn. Med. Ctr., N.Y.C., 1986—93, physician, prof., vice chmn. surgery, 1993—, dir. Cardiovasc. Inst. Bd. dirs. Siga Corp.; host Second Opinion Show on Discovery Channel. Author: Healing from the Heart, 1998 (Best Book award Books Better Am.), Minimally Invasive Surgery (Doody award, 2000), Cardiac Assist Devices. Mem.: Found. Advancement of Cardiac Therapies (bd. dirs.), Am. Turkish Soc. (bd. dirs.), Global Leader Tomorrow, World Econ. Forums, Am. Soc. Artificial Internal Organs, Am. Coll. Cardiology, Am. Heart Assn., Turkish-Am. Physicians Assn., Assn. Acad. Surgery, Internat. Soc. for Heart and Lung Transplantation, Am. Bd. Surgery, Am. Bd. Thoracic Surgery, Am. Assn. Thoracic Surgeons. Office: Columbia Presbyterian Med Ctr 177 Fort Washington Ave New York NY 10032-3713 Office Phone: 212-305-4434. E-mail: mco2@columbia.edu.

OZAB, DAVID, composer, music educator; b. Virginia Beach, Va., Nov. 25, 1965; s. Lloyd J. and Dorothy L. Ozab; m. Julia Harris, June 26, 2004. PhD, U. of Oreg., 2003. Grad. tchg. fellow Sch. Music U. of Oreg., Eugene, 2002—; dir. of musical arts Cadenza Prodns., L.A., 2002—. Web designer Sansanguim LLC, Eugene, 2003—. Composer: (cd) Tempo Ficta (The Computer Music of David Ozab), 2003. Lector St. Mary's Episc. Ch., Eugene, 2002. Mem.: Internat. Computer Music Assn., Broadcast Music Inc., The Soc. for Electroacoustic Music in the U.S., Phi Kappa Lambda. Democrat. Anglo-Catholic. Home: 6236 Main St Apt 8 Springfield OR 97478-6925

OZAKI, JOSEPH, finance company executive; Contr., treas. and sec. A-Mark Fin., Santa Monica, Calif. Office: A-Mark Financial 100 Wilshire Blvd 3d Fl Santa Monica CA 90401 Office Fax: (310) 319-0346.

OZAKI, NANCY JUNKO, performance artist, performing arts educator; b. Denver, Feb. 14, 1951; d. Joe Motoichi and Tamiye (Saki) O.; m. Gary Steven Tsujimoto, Nov. 12, 1989. BS in Edn., U. Colo., 1973; postgrad., U. Colo., Denver, 1977, Metro State Coll., 1982, Red Rocks C.C., 1982-83, U. No. Colo., 1982, U. N.Mex., 1985, U. No. Colo., 1988. Elem. tchr. Bur. Indian Affairs, Bloomfield, N.Mex., 1973—75, Aurora Pub. Schs., Colo., 1977—83, Albuquerque Pub. Schs., 1983—84, Denver Pub. Schs., 1984—87, Oak Grove Sch. Dist., San Jose, Calif., 1988—89, San Mateo City Elem. Dist., Calif., 1990—92; performing artist Japanese drums Young Audiences, San Francisco, 1992—93, Denver, 1994—97; performing artist Japanese drums Epcot Ctr. Walt Disney World, Orlando, Fla., 1993—97; co-dir., mgr., performer One World Taiko Japanese Drum Troupe, Denver, 1997—2001, Seattle, 2001—; artist-in-residence Washington States Arts Commn., 2003—. Mem. Touring Arts Roster, King County. Vol. worker with young Navajo children; co-sponsor girl's sewing and camping groups. Mem. Kappa Delta Pi (Theta chpt.). Avocations: reading, sewing, skiing, hiking, snorkeling. Office: PO Box 80158 Seattle WA 98108 E-mail: oneworldtaiko@earthlink.net.

OZAKI, SATOSHI, physicist; b. Osaka, Japan, July 4, 1929; married, 1960; 2 children. BS, Osaka U., 1953, MS, 1955; PhD in Physics, MIT, 1959. Rsch. asst. physics MIT, 1956-59; rsch. assoc. Brookhaven Nat. Lab., 1959-61, asst. physicist, 1961-63, assoc. physicist, 1963-66, physicist, 1966-72, group co-leader physics, 1970-80, sr. physicist, 1972—; head Relativistic Heavy Ion Collider project Brookhaven Nat. Lab, Upton, N.Y., 1989-99, assoc. lab. dir. Relativistic Heavy Ion Collider project, 1999—. Vis. prof. Osaka U., 1975-76; dir. physics dept. Tristan Project Accelerator Dept. Nat. Lab. Higher Energy Physics, Japan, 1981-89. Fellow Am. Phys. Soc. Achievements include rsch. in high energy particle interactions, particle spectroscopy, high energy physics instrumentation, mgmt. of major accelerator constrn. projects. Office: Brookhaven Nat Lab Relativistic Heavy Ion Collider Upton NY 11973

OZANICH, CHARLES GEORGE, real estate broker; b. Aug. 11, 1933; s. Paul Anthony and Alma Bertha (Sablotna) O.; m. Betty Sue Carman, Feb. 20, 1955; children: Viki Lynn, Terri Sue, Charles Anthony, Nicole Lee. Student, Am. River Coll., Sierra Coll. Owner, broker Terrace Realty, Basic Realty, Grass Valley, Calif., 1971—, Compliance inspector Dept. Vets. Affairs. Mem. Grass Valley Vol. Fire Dept., 1965-93. Served with USAF, 1951-55, Korea. Decorated Bronze Star with three oak leaf clusters, Korean Presdl. citation, UN citation. Mem. Nevada County Bd. Realtors (dir. 1973-74). Lodges: Am.

Legion, Masons, Shriners, Moose (charter mem.). Achievements include receiving the Nat. Champion award Truck Drivers Rodeo class 5 semi-trailer 18 wheeler divsn., 1954. Home and Office: 15053 Chinook Ln Grass Valley CA 95945-8846 E-mail: cozanich@theunion.net.

OZAWA, MARTHA NAOKO, social work educator; b. Ashikaga, Tochigi, Japan, Sept. 30, 1933; came to U.S., 1963; d. Tokuichi and Fumi (Kawashima) O.; m. May 1959 (div. May 1966). BA in Econs., Aoyama Gakuin U., 1956; MS in Social Work, U. Wis., 1966, PhD in Social Welfare, 1969. Asst. prof. social work Portland (Oreg.) State U., 1969-70, assoc. prof. social work, 1970-72; assoc. rsch. prof. social work NYU, 1972-75; assoc. prof. social work Portland State U., 1975-76; prof. social work Washington U., St. Louis, 1976-85, Bettie Bofinger Brown prof. social policy, 1985—2003, Bettie Bofinger Brown Disting. prof. social policy, 2003—. Author: Income Maintenance and Work Incentives, 1982; editor: Women's Life Cycle: Japan-U.S. Comparison in Income Maintenance, 1989, Women's Life Cycle and Economic Insecurity: Problems and Proposals, 1989; editl. bd. Social Work, Silver Spring, Md., 1972-75, 85-88, New Eng. Jour. Human Svcs., Boston, 1987-95, Ency. of Social Work, Silver Spring, 1974-77, 91-95, 99-2003, Jour. Social Svc. Rsch., 1977-97, Children and Youth Svcs. Rev., 1991—, Social Work Rsch., 1994-97, 2004—, Jour. Poverty, 1997-2004. Grantee Adminstrn. on Aging, Washington, 1979, 84, NIMH, 1990-93. Mem. Nat. Assn. Social Workers (presdl. award 1999), Nat. Acad. Social Ins., Nat. Conf. on Social Welfare (bd. dirs. 1981-87), The Gerontol. Soc. Am., Soc. for Social Work and Rsch., Washington U. Faculty Club (bd. dirs. 1986-91). Avocations: photography, tennis, swimming, gardening. Home: 13018 Tiger Lily Ct Saint Louis MO 63146 4330 Office: PO Box 1196 Saint Louis MO 63188 1196 Office Phone: 314-935-6615. Business E-Mail: ozawa@wustl.edu.

OZAWA, SEIJI, conductor, music director; b. Shenyang, China, Sept. 1, 1935; s. Kaisaku and Sakura Ozawa; m. Vera Motoki-Ilyin Ozawa; children: Seira, Yukiyoshi. Student, Toho Sch. Music, Tokyo, Japan, 1953-59; studies with, Hideo Saito, Eugene Bigot, Herbert Von Karajan, Leonard Bernstein; student at the invitation of Charles Munch, Tanglewood, 1959; DMus (hon.), U. Mass., New England Conserv. Music, Wheaton Coll. Music dir. Boston Symphony Orch., 1973—2002, Vienna State Opera, 2002—. One of three asst. condrs. N.Y. Philharm., 1961—62; music dir., season Ravinia Festival, 1964—68; music dir. Toronto Symphony Orch., 1965—69, San Francisco Symphony Orch., 1970—76; apptd. artistic advisor Tanglewood Festival, 1970; condr. Evening at Symphony Boston Symphony Orch., music advisor, 1972—73, Vienna State Opera, 1988, Saito Kinen Festival, Matsumoto, Japan, 1992; mem. internat. tour Dvorak Gala, Prague, 1993, Vienna Philharm. Asia, 1993, 96, 2000, Vienna Philharm. Europe, 1997, 98, 2000; mem. concert tour Berlin Philharm. Salzburg Festival. Named Laureate, Found. du Japan, 1988, Seiji Ozawa Hall for him, Tanglewood Music Ctr., 1994, Music Dir. Laureate, Boston Symphony Orch., 2002; recipient 1st prize, Internat. Competition Orch. Condrs., 1959, Koussevitzky prize, Tanglewood Music Ctr., 1960, Inouye award for Lifetime Achievement, 1964; conducting fellow, Tanglewood Music Ctr., 1959. Office: Veroza Japan Co Ltd 2F 6-13-21 Seijo Setagaya-ku Tokyo 157-0066 Japan Office Phone: +81-(0)3-5490-6805. Office Fax: +81-(0)3-5490-6985.

OZAWA, TERUTOMO, economics educator, consultant; b. Yokohama, Japan, Jan. 17, 1935; came to U.S., 1959, naturalized, 1973; s. Hanjiro and Tsuru (Teramura) O.; m. Hiroko Aoyama, Nov. 4, 1967; children: Edwin, Clare. BA, Tokyo U. of Fgn. Studies, 1958; MBA, Columbia U., 1962, PhD, 1966. Prof. econs. Colo. State U., Ft. Collins, 1974—; vis. rsch. assoc. Ctr. for Policy Alternatives, MIT, Cambridge, Mass., 1975-76; vis. scholar Cambridge (Eng.) U., 1982-83; vis. prof. U. Paris, Sorbonne, 1993, 96, U. Tokyo, 1996; rsch. assoc. Ctr. Japanese economy and bus., Columbia Bus. Sch., 2001--; cons. to UN agys. and OECD. Author: Multinationalism, Japanese Style, 1979, Japan's General Trading Companies: Merchants of Economic Development, 1984, Recycling Japan's Surpluses for Developing Countries, 1989, Business Restructuring in Asia, 2001; also other books and articles. Mem. Am. Econ. Assn. Home: 648 Heather Ct Fort Collins CO 80525-2209 Office: Colo State U Dept Econs Fort Collins CO 80523-0001

OZER, MARTHA ROSS, psychologist, counselor; b. Richmond, Ky., Sept. 4, 1932; d. Robert Lee and Virginia Eudelle (Hurst) Ross; m. John Dudley Redden, Dec. 27, 1953 (dec. June 1969); children: Mary, Patricia, Robert, Mark; m. Mark N. Ozer, Aug. 12, 1979. BA in Elem. Edn., Georgetown Coll., 1954; MA in Counseling, Murray State U., 1966, MS in Psychology, 1968; EdD in Edn. Adminstrn., U. Ky., 1976; LLD (hon.), Georgetown Coll., 1995; postdoctoral cert. in infant and young child mental health program, Wash. Sch. Psychiatry, 1995-96. Cert. sch. psychologist with autonomous functioning Ky. Bd. Psychology, lic. sch. psychologist Va. Dept. Edn., D.C. Pub. Schs., profl. counselor D.C., nat. cert. sch. psychologist Nat. Assn. Sch. Psychologists, lic. psychologist Bd. of Psychology, D.C. Elem. tchr. Jefferson County Pub. Schs., Louisville, 1954-58, Hickman County Pub. Schs., Campbellsburg, Ky., 1960-62; tchr. emotional disturbed, dir. psychol. svcs. Paducah (Ky.) Pub. Schs., 1965-70; psychologist, program dir. Louisville Pub. Schs., 1970-74; doctoral intern Bur. Edn. for Handicapped U.S. Dept. Edn., Washington, 1974-75; program dir. project sci. tech. and disability AAAS, Washington, 1986—87; postdoctoral fellowship NYU Brain Trauma Program NYU Med. Ctr., N.Y.C., 1986-87; program dir., adminstr., asst. prof. dept. rehab. medicine Med. Coll. Va., Richmond, 1987-89; psychologist MCV Pediatric Devel. Ctr., Richmond, 1989; sch. psychologist Fairfax (Va.) County Pub. Schs., 1989-98; pvt. practice, 1998—; dir. Project Link, William Wendt Ctr. for Loss and Healing, Washington, 2000—03; psychologist Ednl. Diagnostics Inst., Inc., 1998—. Cons. Am. Coun. on Edn., Washington, 1976-97; project coord. Higher Edn. and the Handicapped Am. Coun. on Edn., 1976-86; cons. rehab. and spl. edn., Brazil, Saudi Arabia, Qatar, Turkey; numerous other profl. and disability orgns. Authored more than 20 books and contbr. articles to profl. jours. on access for persons with disabilities to sci. edn. and careers, contbn. of sci./tech. to persons with disabilities. Advisor Disability Rights, 1975—86; vol. William & Wendy Ctr. for Loss and Healing, Washington Hebrew Congreagation. Recipient U.S. Presdl. Pvt. Sector award, award Am. Coalition Citizens with Disabilities, 1980, Alumni award Geotgetown Coll., 1985, Disting. Alumni award Murray St. U., 1996; grantee U.S. Dept. Edn., 1975-86, U.S. Dept. Civil Rights, 1975-82, Grant Found., 1975-77, Exxon Found., 1976, IBM, 1976, NSF, 1977-86, Nat. Inst. for Rehab. Rsch., 1978-84. Mem.: APA (bd. dirs. rehab. sect.), NSTA (award), Am. Mental Health Assn., Am. Assn. of Mental Health Counsellors, Am. Counseling Assn., Va. Psychol. Assn., Nat. Assn. of Sch. Psychologists (nat. cert.). Avocations: photography, pottery, travel. Home: 3420 38th St NW Apt A-415 Washington DC 20016-3032

OZICK, CYNTHIA, writer; b. N.Y.C., Apr. 17, 1928; d. William and Celia (Regelson) O.; m. Bernard Hallote, Sept. 7, 1952; 1 dau., Rachel Sarah. BA cum laude with honors in English, NYU, 1949; MA, Ohio State U., 1950; LHD (hon.), Yeshiva U., 1984, Hebrew Union Coll., 1984, Williams Coll., 1986, Hunter Coll., 1987, Jewish Theol. Sem. Am., 1988, Adelphi U., 1988, SUNY, 1989, Brandeis U., 1990, Bard Coll., 1991, Spertus Coll., 1991, Skidmore Coll., 1992, Seton Hall U., 1999, Rutgers U., 1999, U. N.C., Asheville, 2000, NYU, 2001, Bar-Ilan U., Israel, 2002, Balt Hebrew U., 2004. Author: Trust, 1966, reissued, 2004, The Pagan Rabbi and Other Stories, 1971, Bloodshed and Three Novellas, 1976, Levitation: Five Fictions, 1982, Art and Ardor: Essays, 1983, The Cannibal Galaxy, 1983, The Messiah of Stockholm, 1987, Metaphor & Memory: Essays, 1989, The Shawl, 1989, Epodes: First Poems, 1992, What Henry James Knew, and Other Essays on Writers, 1994, Portrait of the Artist as a Bad Character, 1996, The Cynthia Ozick Reader, 1996, Fame & Folly, 1996, The Puttermesser Papers, 1997, (novel) Heir to the Glimmering World, 2004; (plays) Blue Light, 1994, The Shawl, 1996; guest editor Best Am. Essays, 1998, Quarrel & Quandary: Essays, 2000, Heir to the Glimmering World, 2004; also poetry, criticism, revs., translations, essays and fictions in numerous periodicals and anthologies. Phi Beta Kappa orator, Harvard U., 1985. Recipient Mildred and Harold Strauss Living award Am. Acad. Arts and Letters, 1983, Rea award for short story, 1986, PEN/Spiegel-Diamonstein award for the Art of the Essay, 1997, Harold Washington Literary award City of Chgo., 1997, John Cheever award, 1999, Lannan Found. award for fiction, 2000, Koret Found. award for lit. studies, 2001, Nat. Book Critics Circle award for nonfiction, 2001; Lucy Martin Donnelly fellow, Bryn Mawr Coll., 1992, Guggenheim fellow, 1982. Mem. PEN, Authors League, Am. Acad. of Arts and Scis., Am. Acad. of Arts and Letters, Dramatists Guild, Académie Universelle des Cultures (Paris), Phi Beta Kappa.

OZKAN, UMIT SIVRIOGLU, chemical engineering educator; b. Manisa, Turkey, Apr. 11, 1954; came to U.S., 1980; d. Alim and Emine (Ilgaz) Sivrioglu; m. H. Erdal Ozkan, Aug. 13, 1983. BS, Mid. East Tech. U., Ankara, Turkey, 1978, MS, 1980; PhD, Iowa State U., 1984. Registered profl. engr., Ohio. Grad. rsch. assoc. Ames Lab. U.S. Dept. Energy, 1980-84; asst. prof. Ohio State U., Columbus, 1985-90, assoc. prof. chem. engring., 1990-94, prof., 1994—, assoc. dean for rsch. Coll. Engring., 2000—. Contbr. articles to profl. jours. French Ctr. NAt. Rsch. Sci. fellow, 1994-95; recipient Women of Achievement award YWCA, Columbus, 1991, Outstanding Engring. Educator Ohio award Soc. Profl. Engrs., 1991, Union Carbide Innovation Recognition award, 1991-92, NSF Woman Faculty award in sci. and engring., 1991, Engring. Tchg. Excellence award Keck Found., 1994, Ctrl. Ohio Outstanding Woman in Sci. & Tech., 1996, Pitts.-Cleve. Catalysis Soc. Outstanding Rsch. award, 1998, Achievement award Soc. Women Engring., 2002, Columbus Outstanding Rsch. award ACS, 2002. Fellow Am. Inst. Chemists; mem. NSPE, N.Am. Catalysis Soc., Am. Inst. Chem. Engring., Am. Soc. Engring. Edn., Am. Chem. Soc., Combustion Inst., Sigma Xi. Achievements include research in selective oxidation, hydrogenation, NO reduction, hydrodesulfurization, hydrodeoxygenation, hydrodenitrogenation, fuel reformulation, in-situ spectroscopy. Office: Ohio State U Chem Engring 140 W 19th Ave Columbus OH 43210-1110

OZMON, KENNETH LAWRENCE, retired university president, educator; b. Portsmouth, Va., Sept. 4, 1931; emigrated to Can., 1968; s. Howard Augustine and Anna Josephine (Lynch) O.; m. Elizabeth Ann Morrison, July 6, 1968; children: Angela Francene, Kendi Elizabeth. BA in Philosophy and History magna cum laude, St. Bernard Coll., Ala., 1955; MA in Psychology, Cath. U., 1963; PhD in Psychology, U. Maine, 1968; DLitt (hon.), St. Thomas U., 2001. Instr. U. Maine, Orono, 1966-68; vis. lectr. St. Dunstan's U., P.E.I., Can., 1967; asst. prof. Calif. State U., Chico, 1968-69; chmn. dept. psychology U. P.E.I., Charlottetown, 1969-72, dean of arts, 1972-79; pres. St. Mary's U., Halifax, N.S., 1979-2000, pres. emeritus, 2000—; chmn. Optipress Inc., 2002—04, Lester B. Pearson Peacekeeping Ctr., 2002—04; dir. Ctr. for Fin. Mgmt. Ombudsman Svc., 2002—. Chmn. pres.' coun. N.S. U., 1982—85; chmn. Met. Halifax U. Pres.' Com., 1982—84, 1986—87, 1992—; co-chmn. coordinating com. Nat. Univ. Week, 1983, 1986—87; hon. prof. U. Internat. Bus. and Econs., Beijing, 1986. Contbr. numerous articles to psychol. jours. Bd. dirs. United Way Halifax-Dartmouth, 1980-82, Friends N.S. Mus. Industry Soc., 1993-95, Greater Halifax Partnership, 1995-2000, Frank H. Sobey Found., 2001—, Discovery Ctr., 2000-03; bd. dirs. Interuniv. Svcs., Inc., 1987-94, chmn., 1992-94; provincial bd. dirs. Can. Assn. Mentally Retarded, 1980-82; co-chmn. Found. for Irish and Can. Studies, 1993; mem. nat. coun. Can. Human Rights Found., 1976; mem. selection com. J.H. Moore Awards for Excellence, Toronto, 1983-92; hon. chmn. ann. campaign N.S. div. Can. Paraplegic Assn., 1985-86; mem. fundraising com. Phoenix House, 1986-88, Charitable Irish Soc. Halifax; chmn. Human Rights Commn., 1990-96; mem. adv. coun. Order of Can., 1991-95; area chair for N.S. Internat. Coun. Psychologists, 1992-93. Decorated Order of Can.; named one of 100 Nova Scotians of Century, Daily News, 2000, Can.'s Top 50 CEO's, Atlantic Bus. Mag., 2000; recipient Gov. Gen. of Can. medal for 125th Anniversary of Can. Confedn., 1993, Jerusalem award, Atlantic Jewish Congress, 1994, Disting. Cmty. Svc. award, St. Mary's U., 2000, Can.'s Top 50 CEO's, Atlantic Bus. Mag., 2001. Mem. Assn. Atlantic Univs. (vice chmn. 1983-85, chmn. 1985-87), Assn. Commonwealth Univs (governing coun. 1988-91), Assn. Univs. and Colls. Can. (exec. coun. 1985-89, vice chmn. 1990-91, chmn., 1991-93, mem. audit com. 1991—, chmn. exec. com. 1991—, vice-chmn. nominating com. 1990-91), Can. Psychol. Assn. (Nat. Univ. Week coordinating com. 1983, co-chmn. 1986-87, audit com. 1985—, co-chmn. steering com. Halifax Met. Econ. Summit II 1994), Halifax Bd. Trade (internat. trade com. 1985-91, bd. dirs. 1989-91), Halifax Club, Ashburn Golf Club. Roman Catholic. Avocations: fishing, golf, running. Home: 139 Kingswood Dr Hammonds Plains NS Canada B4B 1K4 Office: St Mary's U President Emeritus Halifax NS Canada B3H 3C3 E-mail: kenneth.ozmon@stmarys.ca.

OZNOWICZ, FRANK RICHARD See OZ, FRANK

OZOG, DIANE L. allergist; b. Chgo., July 28, 1955; MD, U. Health Scis., Chgo. Med. Sch., 1982. Cert. allergy and immunology 1987, pediat. 1987. Resident Cook County Hosp., Ill., 1982—85; fellowship Children's Meml. Hosp., Ill., 1985—87; allergist Good Samaritan Hosp. Mem.: Children's Comm. Physicians Assn. Office: 3825 Highland Ave Tower 2 Ste 204 Downers Grove IL 60515 Address: 636 Raymond Naperville IL 60563

OZOLINSH, SANDIS, professional hockey player; b. Aug. 13, 1972; Defense Fla. Panthers, 2001—, Carolina Hurricanes, 2000—01, Colo. Avalanche, 1995—2000, San Jose Sharks, 1992—96. Office: Nat Car Rental Ctr 2555 Panther Pky Sunrise FL 33323

OZZIE, RAY, Internet company executive; b. Nov. 20, 1955; B in Computer Sci., U. Ill., 1979. Sys. programmer Protection Mut. Ins. Co., 1972—73; technician dept. nuc. engring. U. Ill., 1974, sys. programmer PLATO project, 1974—79; co-founder Urbana Software Enterprises, 1978—79; with Data Gen. Corp., 1979—81; co-founder Microcosm Corp., 1981; with Software Arts, 1981—82, Lotus Devel., 1983—84; founder, pres. Iris Assocs., 1984—87; founder, chmn., CEO Groove Networks, Inc., Beverly, Mass., 1997—. Named Person of Yr., PC Mag., 1995; named one of Seven "Windows Pioneers", Microsoft, Top Five Developers of the Century, Computer Reseller News; named to Computer Mus. Industry Hall of Fame, InfoWorld Hall of Fame; recipient W. Wallace McDowell award, IEEE Computer Soc., 2000. Mem.: NRC (mem. computer sci. and telecom. bd.), World Econ. Forum (gov. IT and telecom., honored as pioneer 2001), Nat. Acad. Engring. Achievements include first to field of collaboration technology; creator, developer Lotus Notes, 1984; instrumental in development of Lotus Symphony, TK!Solver and VisiCalc. Office: Groove Networks Inc Ste 535Q 100 Cummings Ctr Beverly MA 01915

O'BRIEN-AMICO, LEAH, Olympic athlete; b. Sept. 9, 1974; m. Tommy Amico; 1 child. Mem. U.S. Women's Nat. Team, 1996—, U.S. Women's Softball Team, Atlanta Olympic Games, 1996, U.S. Women's Softball Team, Sydney Olympic Games, 2000, U.S. Women's Softball Team, Athens Olympic Games, 2004. Named Arizona State Woman of the Yr., 1997; named to First Team All-Am., 1994, 1995, 1997, All-College World Series Team, 1994, 1995, 1997. Achievements include mem. U.S. Women's Softball Gold medal Team, Atlanta Olympics, 1996, Sydney Olympics, 2000; mem. NCAA Champion Arizona Wild Cats, Women's Coll. World series, 1993, 1994, 1997; mem. Gold medal U.S. Nat. Team, ISF World Championships, 1998, 2002; mem. Gold medal U.S. Nat. Team, Pan-American Games, 1999, 2003. Office: USA Softball Complex 4845 S Shields Blvd Oklahoma City OK 73129*

O'NEILL, DANIEL J. brewery company executive; b. Canada; BA, Carleton U., 1974; MBA, Queens U., 1976. With Colgate Palmolive, Toronto, 1976—79; sr. products mgr. insect control S.C. Johnson Wax, Racine, Wis., 1981—82, category mgr., 1982—84, mktg. mgr., 1984—86, pres., gen. mgr., 1986—90, v.p. US consumer products, 1990—92, v.p. group business mgr. N.Am., 1992—93, v.p., group mng. dir. Europe, 1993—94; pres. Campbell Canada Campbell Soup Co. Ltd., Toronto, 1994—95; pres. Campbell Sales Co., Camden, NJ, 1995—97, Campbell US Soup Division, 1996—97; pres., CEO Star-Kist Foods, Inc., 1997—99; exec. v.p. N.Am. sales & pres. Heinz S.Am. H.J. Heinz Co., Pittsburgh, Pa., 1997—99; exec. v.p., COO N.Am. brewing Molson Inc., 1999—2000, pres., CEO, 2000—. Bd. dirs. H.J. Heinz Co., 1988—99, Campbell Soup Co., 1994—97, Molson Inc., 1999—. Office: Molson Inc 1555 Notre Dame St E Montreal PQ H2L 2R5 Canada*

PAANANEN, VICTOR NILES, English educator; b. Ashtabula, Ohio, Jan. 31, 1938; s. Niles Henry and Anni Margaret (Iloranta) P.; m. Donna Mae Jones, Aug. 15, 1964; children: Karl, Neil. AB magna cum laude, Harvard U., 1960; MA, U. Wis., 1964, PhD, 1967. Instr. English Wofford Coll., Spartanburg, S.C., 1962-63; asst. prof. Williams Coll., Williamstown, Mass., 1966-68, Mich. State U., East Lansing, 1968-73, assoc. prof., 1973—82, prof., 1982—2002, asst. dean Grad. Sch., 1977-82, chmn. dept. English, 1986-94, prof. emeritus, 2002—. Vis. prof. Roehampton Inst., London, 1982, 96, hon. fellow, 1992. Author: William Blake, 1977, 2d edit., 1996, British Marxist Criticism, 2000; contbr. articles to profl. and scholarly jours. Univ. fellow U. Wis., 1962, 63-64, Roehampton Inst. hon. fellow, London, 1992—; Harvard Nat. scholar, 1956-60. Home: 350 Revere Beach Blvd 5-5W Revere MA 02151-4851 E-mail: paananen@msu.edu.

PAASWELL, ROBERT EMIL, civil engineer, educator; b. Red Wing, Minn., Jan. 15, 1937; s. George and Evelyn (Cohen) P.; m. Rosalind Snyder, May 31, 1958; children: Judith Marjorie, George Harold. BA (Ford Found. fellow), Columbia U., 1956, BS, 1957, MS, 1961; PhD, Rutgers U., 1965. Field engring. asst. Spencer White & Prentis, Washington, 1954 56, engr. N.Y.C., 1957-59; rsch. scientist Davidson Lab., N.J., 1964; rsch. fellow Greater London Council, 1971-72; rsch. and teaching asst. Columbia U., 1959-62; asst. prof. civil engring. SUNY, Buffalo, 1964-68; chmn. bd. govs. Urban Studies Coll., 1973-76, assoc. prof., 1968-76, prof. civil engring., 1976-82; dir. Center for Transp. Studies and Research, 1979-82, chmn. dept. environ. design and planning, 1980-82; prof. transp. engring. U. Ill., Chgo., 1982-86, 89-90, dir. Urban Transp. Ctr., 1982-86; exec. dir. Chgo. Transit Authority, 1986-89; dir. transp. rsch. consortium, prof. civil engring. CUNY, 1990—, disting. prof., 1991—; dir. CUNY Inst. Urban Systems, 2000—. Faculty-on-leave Dept. Transp., 1976-77, cons., 1981—; v.p. Faculty Tech. Cons., Inc., Midwest Sys. Scis., Inc., 1982-86; dir. Urban Mass Transp. Adminstrn. Summer Faculty Workshop, 1980, 81; cons. transp. planning, energy and soil mechanics; spl. cons. to Congressman T. Dulski, 1973; vis. expert lectr. Jilin U. Tech., Changchun, Peoples Republic of China, 1985, hon. prof. transp., 1986—; bd. dirs. E'Escuto Archs. and Engrs., Chig, Hickling Co., Ottawa, Can., Transic Devel. Corp.; chmn. transp. steering adv. bd. Office of Tech. Assessment for Infrastructure and the Urban Core Project, 1994—; faculty Lincoln Inst. of Land Policy, 1994-95; vis. scholar Tel Aviv U., Israel, 1995—; arbitrator in productivity Met. Transp. Authority, N.Y.C., 1996 ; mem. exec. com. Coun. on Transp., 1996—, NSF Ctr. for Infrastructure Sys.; cons. Coun. of North East Govs., 1997—; faculty "Conflict Resolution," NYU, 1998—; mem. exec. com. Inst. for Civil Infrastructure Sys. (NSF), 1998—; chair panel new paradigms in transit Transp. Rsch. Bd.; bd. dirs. Transit Stds. Consortium, chmn., 2000—. Author: Problems of the Carless, 1977; contbg. author: Transport and Urban Development, 1995, Panels for Transportation Planning, 1997, Studies in Israel Planning, 1996, Dynamic Networks and Spatial Change, 1999, After the World Trade Center, 2002; editor: Site Traffic Impact Assessment, 1992; contbg. author: Decisions for the Great Lakes, 1982, World Book Encyclopedia, 1992, 93, 94, Transport and Urban Development, 1995, Israel Planning Studies, 1996, 97, Panels for Transportation Planning, 1997, New Contributions to Transportation Analysis in Europe, 1999; mem. bd. editors Jour. Environ. Systems, 1974—, Transp., 1978—, Jour. Urban Tech., 1992—; contbr. articles to profl. jours. Mem. Buffalo Environ. Mgmt. Commn., 1972-74; mem. Area Com. for Transit, Mayor's Energy Adv. Bd., 1974, Block Grant Rev. Com., City of Buffalo; chmn. com. on transp., mem. rev. adv. bd. Rsch. and Planning Coun. Western N.Y.; mem. transp. com. Chgo. 1992 Worlds Fair; mem. citizens' adv. bd. Chgo. Transit Authority, 1985—; mem. strategic planning com. Regional Transp. Authority, 1985; mem. steering com. Nat. Transit Coop. Rsch. Program, 1991—, Borough pres. (Manhattan) Trans. Adv. Bd., Bronx Ctr. Devel. Project; bd. dirs. Transit Devel. Corp., 1992—; exec. bd. Transp. Coun., 1996—; mem. exec. com. Colin Powell Ctr.; bd. dirs. York Aviation Inst., 2003—; chmn. adv. bd. Cmty. Transp. Devel. Ctr., 2003—. Recipient Dept. Transp. award, 1977, Outstanding Alumnus award, 2003; SUNY faculty fellow, 1965-66 Fellow ASCE (past pres. Buffalo sect., chmn. steering com. 1992 splty. conf. traffic impact analysis, mem. peer rev. pub. adys. com.); mem. AAAS, Transp. Rsch. Bd. (chmn. com. on transp. disadvantaged, mem. exec. com., peer rev. com. nat. transp. ctrs. 1988—), Inst. Transp. Engrs. (transit coun., exec. com., chmn. legis. policy com., rsch. com. surface transp. policy project 1995—), Coun. on Transp. (bd. dirs. 1996—), N.Y. Acad. Scis., Sigma Xi. Office: CCNY Inst Transp Systems Rm 220-Y 135th St and Convent Ave New York NY 10031

PAAVO, JARVI, conductor; b. Tallinn, Estonia; Studied under Leonard Bernstein; student in percussion and conducting, Tallinn Sch. Music; student under Otto-Werner, Max Rudolf, Curtis Inst. Music; student under Leonard Bernstein, L.A. Philharmonic Inst. Music dir. Cin. Symphony Orch., 2001—. Prin. guest conductor Royal Stockholm Philharmonic, City of Birmingham (Eng.) Symphony Orch., guest conductor N.Y. Philharmonic, Berlin Philharmonic, Munich Philharmonic, London Philharmonic, San Francisco Symphony, Phila. Orch. (Carnegie Hall debut), NHK Symphony, Tokyo Symphony, Israel Philharmonic, St. Petersburg Philharmonic, Orch. Filarmonica della Scala, L.A. Philharmonic, Philharmonic orch. and many others, (works by Bernstein) City of Birmingham Symphony Orch., Royal Stockholm Philharmonic Orch., (recordings with Estonian composers Part, Tuur, and Tubin) Searching for Roots, Sibelius' Kullervo, Lemminkainen Suite, (concerts with cellist Turls Mork); condr.: recs. with Cin. Symphony Orch. Office: Cin Symphony Orch 1241 Elm St Cincinnati OH 45210

PABST, ALFRED MARK, lawyer; b. Albia, Iowa, Mar. 8, 1908; s. Mark Dell and Myrtle Dora (Hilliard) P.; m. Mary Aileen Jenkins, June 28, 1932; children— Janis Aileen Pabst Boenker, Mark Dell, John Alfred. LL.B., U. Iowa, 1930. Bar: Iowa 1930. Sole practice, Albia, 1930-72; ptnr. Pabst & Pabst, Albia, 1972— . Fellow Am. Bar Found.; mem. ABA, Iowa Bar Assn. (gov. 1964-68, pres. 1971, advisor to bd. govs. 1972—, award of merit 1981), 8th Jud. Dist. Iowa Bar Assn. (pres. 1942). Home: 204 B Ave W Albia IA 52531-1507 Office: 212 Benton Ave W Albia IA 52531-1928

PACALA, LEON, retired association executive; b. Indpls., May 3, 1926; s. John and Anna (Ferician) P.; m. Janet Lefforge, Dec. 28, 1947 (dec. July 1987); children: Mark, Stephen, James; m. Virginia Strasenburgh, Mar. 10, 1990. AB, Franklin (Ind.) Coll., 1949; BD, Colgate Rochester Div. Sch., 1952; PhD, Yale U., 1960; LLD (hon.), Nazareth Coll., 1980; LHD (hon.), Franklin Coll., 1987. Ordained to ministry Baptist Ch., 1952. Asst. prof. philosophy and religion DePauw U., 1956-61; participant study religion undergrad. coll. Lilly Found., 1957-59; assoc. prof. religion Bucknell U., 1961-68, prof., 1968-73, chmn. dept., 1961-64, dean, 1962-73; pres. Colgate Rochester (N.Y.) Div. Sch.; also Bexley Hall, Crozer Theol. Sem., 1973-80; exec. dir. Assn. Theol. Schs. in U.S. and Can., 1980-91. Cons. acad. adminstrn. Beirut Coll. Women, 1972. Author: The Role of ATS in Theological Education, 1980-90, 1998; contbr. articles to profl. jours. Exec. com. Christian Faith in Higher Edn. Projects, 1965-68; trustee Franklin Coll., 1967-73, 98-2002; bd. dirs. Rohesters Jobs, Inc., 1973-80, Union Theol. Sem., N.Y.C., 1999—; trustee Rochester Area Colls., 1973-80; dir. Nat. Housing Ministries, Am. Bapt. Chs., 1976-80; mem. adv. bd. Colgate Rochester Div. Sch., 1997—. With USAAF, 1944-45. Internat. Rotary scholar, Louvain U., Belgium, 1952-53. Mem. Am. Conf. Acad. Deans (exec. com., treas., chmn., presiding officer 1973-74), Am. Assn. Higher Edn., Assn. Am. Colls. (commn. religion higher edn.), Assn. Theol. Schs. (com. accreditation), World Conf. Assns. Theol. Instns. (v.p. 1988-93), Am. Bapt. Assn. Sem. Adminstrs. (chmn 1975-80). Home: 56 Woodbury Pl Rochester NY 14618

PACE, CAROLINA JOLLIFF, communications executive; b. Dallas, Apr. 12, 1938; d. Lindsay Gafford and Carolina (Juden) Jolliff; m. John McIver Pace, Oct. 7, 1961. Student, Holton-Arms Jr. Coll., 1956—57; BA in Comparative Lit., So. Meth. U., 1960. Promotional advisor, dir. season ticket sales Dallas Theatre Ctr., 1960—61; exec. sec. Dallas Book and Author Luncheon, 1959—63; promotional and instl. cons. Henry Regnery-Reilly & Lee Pub. Co., Chgo., 1962—65; pub. trade rep. various cos.; instl. rep. Don R. Phillips Co., Southea. area, 1965—67; Southwestern rep. Ednl Reading Svc., Inc.-Troll Assocs., Mahwah, NJ, 1967—72; v.p., dir. multimedia divsn. Melton Book Co., Dallas, 1972—79; v.p. mktg. Webster's Internat., Inc., Nashville, 1980—82; pres. Carolina Pace, Inc., 1982—. Mem. adv. bd. Nat.

Info. Ctr. of Spl. Edn. Materials; mem. materials rev. panel Nat. Media Ctr. for Materials of Severely-Profoundly Handicapped, 1981; mem. mktg. product rev. bd. LINC Resources, 1982, 83, 84, mktg. task force, 83, adv. bd., 87; reviewer spl. edn. U.S. Dept. Edn., 1975—79, 1985; rev. cons. HHS, 1982, 83, 84, 86; product rev. task force CEC, 1984, 85, 86; cons. Ednl. Cable Consortium, Summit, NJ, 1982—87. Prodr. ednl. videos; contbr. articles to profl. jours. Mem. adv. coun. Grad. Sys. Sch. Libr. and Info. Sci. Found., U. Tex., 1987—; co-vice chair Friends Highland Park Libr., 1989; mem. focus group City Dallas Growth Policy Plan; mem. art and design com. Downtown Ctrs.; active Dallas City Wide Parking Task Force, Ctrl. Transp. Forum Ctrl. Bus. Dist., Union Sta. Art & Design Com., Downtown Transfer Ctrs., Art and Design Com., West End Task Force, Ctrl. Bus. Dist. Task Force, Tex. Parking Assn.; co-founder Operation TexRec, 1990—91; bd. dirs. Transp. Mgmt. Assn., 1995—; chair Vanpool Use Study, 1995; budget chmn. Dallas County Sesquicentennial com., 1996; mem. adv. bd. Friends of Old Red Courthouse, 1997—, Trinity River Econ. Devel. Bd., 1998—; active Downtown Dallas: Vision 2020, 2001—02; mem. com. Trinity Commons Found., 2002—; active Downtown Dallas Task Force. Mem.: DAR (Jane Douglas chpt.), Coun. Exceptional Children (conf. spkr. 1981, dir. exhibitors com., chmn. publ. com. 1979 conf.), Pub. Rels. Soc. Am., Women in Comm., Assn. Spl. Edn. Tech. (nat. dir., v.p. publicity 1980—82), Assn. Ednl. and Comm. Tech., Internat. Comm. Industries Assn., Nat. Audio Visual Assn. (conf. panelist 1979), Kimball Art Mus., Ctrl. Dallas Assn. (transp. com. 1996—, planning and greenspace com. 1998—), Dallas Plan (focus com.), Women's Nat. Book Assn., Dallas Founders, Friends of the West End (pres. 1988—), Dallas Mus. Art, Dallas West End Hist. Dist. Assn., Dallas Zool. Soc., West End Assn. Dallas (chmn. subcom. on traffic and parking 1986—87, com. demographic study 1987—88), Downtown Transp. Mgmt. Assn. (adv. bd., chmn. vanpools subcom. 1995—, citizens adv. com. 2003—, econ. devel. com. trinity project 2000—), Dallas So. Meml. Tex. Parking Assn., Alpha Delta Pi. Presbyterian. Home: 4524 Lorraine Ave Dallas TX 75205-3613

PACE, CHARLES ROBERT, psychologist, educator; b. St. Paul, Sept. 7, 1912; s. Charles N. and Lenore (Lee) P.; m. Rosella Gaarder, Dec. 18, 1937; children: Rosalind, Jenifer. BA, De Pauw U., 1933; MA, U. Minn., 1935, PhD, 1937. Instr. in gen. coll. U. Minn., 1937-40; research asso. Am. Council Edn., 1941-42; research psychologist Bur. Naval Personnel, Navy Dept., 1943-47; mem. faculty Syracuse U., 1947-61, asso. dir., then dir. evaluation service center, 1947-52, asst. to chancellor, 1948-52, prof. psychology, chmn. dept., dir. psychol. research center, 1952-61; prof. higher edn. UCLA, 1961-82, prof. emeritus, 1982—. Mem. adv. coms. Am. Council Edn., Coll. Entrance Exam. Bd., Social Sci. Research Council. Author: They Went to College, 1941, (with M. E. Troyer) Evaluation in Teacher Education, 1944, The Junior Year in France, 1959, (with F.H. Bowles and J.C. Stone) How to Get Into College, 1968, College and University Environment Scales, 2d edit, 1969, Education and Evangelism, 1972, The Demise of Diversity?, 1974, Measuring Outcomes of College, 1979, Measuring the Quality of College Student Experiences, 1984, CSEQ: Test Manual and Norms, 1987, The Undergraduates, 1990. Post-doctoral fellow Rockefeller Found., 1940-41; fellow Center Advanced Study Behavioral Scis., 1959-60; recipient citation for meritorious civilian service Navy Dept., 1946, E.F. Lindquist award Am. Ednl. Research Assn. and Am. Coll. Testing Program, 1984, Suslow award for outstanding svc. Assn. for Instl. Rsch., 1989. Mem. APA, Am. Ednl. Rsch. Assn. (Disting. Rsch. award divsn. postsecondary edn. 1992), Assn. for Study Higher Edn. (Disting. Career award 1989), Am. Assn. Pub. Opinion Rsch. Office Phone: 707-822-1204. E-mail: crp7001@axe.humboldt.edu.

PACE, ERIC DWIGHT, journalist, writer; b. N.Y.C., Oct. 13, 1936; s. Eric and Eleanor Robertson (Jones) Paepcke; m. Suzanne Monique Wiedel, June 12, 1976 (div. Jan. 1987); children: Christine, Lydia. Grad., Phillips Exeter Acad., 1953; student, U. Heidelberg, Germany, 1955-56; BA magna cum laude, Yale, 1957; MA, Johns Hopkins, 1959. Reporter San Angelo (Tex.) Standard Times and Evening Standard, 1957-58; mem. staff Life mag., N.Y.C., 1959-61, assigned to Bonn, 1961, Paris, 1961-62; corr. Time mag., Bonn., 1962-63, Hong Kong, 1963-65; mem. staff New York Times, N.Y.C., 1965-66, assigned to Saigon, 1966, Cairo, 1966-69, Paris, 1969-70, Beirut, 1970-71, N.Y.C., 1971-74, Teheran, 1974-77, N.Y.C., 1977—2004. Author: novels Saberlegs, 1970, Any War Will Do, 1973, Nightingale, 1979; contbr. articles to Fgn. Affairs, also others. Served with AUS, 1957. Recipient George Polk Meml. award Overseas Press Club, 1968, Page One award N.Y.C. Newspaper Guild, 1968 Mem. Mystery Writers Am., Crime Writers Assn. (Gt. Britain), Am. P.E.N. Clubs: Century (N.Y.C.), Squadron A (N.Y.C.). Unitarian Universalist. Mailing: 697 West End Ave New York NY 10025

PACE, ESTON A. systems administrator; b. Richmond, Va., Feb. 7, 1960; s. James Eston and Thelma Marie Winston P.; m. Wendy Jane Unison, Sept. 4, 1999. Diploma, Huguenot Acad., 1978; cert. in career studies Microsoft Network Adminstrn., J. Sargent Reynolds Coll., 2002. Microsoft Cert. network essentials, NT4.0 workstation, windows 2000, Windows 2000 destop adminstrn. Sr. officer, field tng. officer Va. Dept. of Corrections, Starkfarm, Va., 1995-2000; owner We Try Harder Computer Co., Richmond, 1998—; network adminstr. Philip Morris, Richmond, Va., 1999-2000; customer svc. analyst, network adminstr. Chaparral Steel/TXI, Petersburg, Va., 2000—02. Lt. Fine Creek Vol. Fire Dept., Powhatan, Va., 1983-85, 86-90, capt. 1985-86, chief, 1982-83, in-charge emergency med. tech. Powhatan Vol. Rescue Squad, 1974-84. Recipient Svc. award Fine Creek Vol. Fire Dept., 1986, Cert. of Appreciation, 1991; Svc. award Va. Dept. Corrections, 2000. Mem. Comp TIA-IT Profl., Internat. Internet Assn., Internat. Footprints Assn. Avocations: literature, creative cooking, amature chef, genealogy. Home: 1 Springfield St #408 Chicopee MA 01013 E-mail: EAPace02@aol.com.

PACE, GEORGE W. food products company executive; BA, MBA magna cum laude, U. N.C. Various sr. level. fin., sales and mktg. positions RJR Nabisco, 1986-88; sr. v.p. mktg. Del Monte Foods, San Francisco; v.p. sales, mktg. and distbrn. Rocco Inc., Harrisonburg, Va., 1992-96, CEO, 1996—, also bd. dirs.

PACE, JOEL FREDERIC, language educator, researcher; b. Providence, R.I., June 27, 1972; s. Joseph Frank Pace and Sharon Leigh Graves; m. Caldwell Austin Camero, July 17, 1999. BA, Providence (R.I.) Coll., 1994; MA, U. Oxford, 1996, PhD, 1999. Asst. prof. U. Wis., Eau Claire, Wis., 1999—. Rsch. fellow Brown U., Providence, 2000—03; adj. faculty Black Friar Oxford U., England. Author: Transatlantic Transcendentalist: Wordsworth in America, 2002; contbr. In Our Own Words: A Generation Defining Itself, 2001; editor: Wordsworth's American Century: 1802-1902, 2002, The Allen Rev., 1998. Fellow, Brown U., 2000; grantee, Blackfriars Oxford U., 1996, U. Wis., 2000. Mem.: Wordsworth Coleridge Assn. Am., Oxford (Eng.) Union Soc., Thoreau Soc., Modern Lang. Assn., Oxford (Eng.) U. Soc., Oxford and Cambridge Club. Avocations: musician, trumpet, singing. Home: 211 Chippewa St Eau Claire WI 54702 Office: University of Wisconsin English Dept Eau Claire WI 54702

PACE, LEONARD, retired management consultant; b. Torrington, Conn., Oct. 24, 1924; s. Anthony and Maria G. P.; m. Maureen Therese Murphy, Sept. 15, 1956; children: Leonard Anthony, Susan Maria, Daniel Graham, Thomas William, Mary Macaire, Cathleen Anne. Student, Syracuse U., 1943; BSM.E., U. Conn., 1949; postgrad., N.Y. U., 1951-52, Wayne U., 1955. Cert. mgmt. cons. With GAF, 1949-57, asst. to div. controller, 1954-57; with Deloitte Haskins and Sells, N.Y.C., 1957—, head N.Y. mgmt. adv. services, 1965-67, head Eastern region, 1967-76, nat. dir. mgmt. adv. services, 1976-85, chmn. internat. mgmt. adv. svcs. com. Served as officer, pilot USAAF, 1943-45. Mem. Am. Mgmt. Assn., Inst. Mgmt. Cons. (dir., chmn. profl. standards com.) Clubs: Baltusrol Golf, Union League, Circumnavigators. Home: 35 Little Wolf Rd Summit NJ 07901-3112

PACE, NORMAN R. science educator, microbiologist; b. Washington, Ind., Sept. 20, 1942; BA, Ind. U., 1964; PhD, U. Ill., 1967. From asst. prof. to prof. biophysics and genetics U. Colo. Med. Ctr., 1974-84; prof. biology, then disting. prof. biology and chemistry Ind. U., Bloomington, 1975-97; prof. plant and microbial biology UCLA, Berkeley, 1996—99; prof., dept. molecular, cellular and dev. biology U. Colorado, Boulder, Colo., 1999—. Fellow AAAS, Am. Acad. Arts & Scis., Nat. Speleol. Soc., Am. Acad. Microbiology (award 1996), Am. Acad. Microbiology; mem. Am. Soc. Biol. Chemists. Office: U Colorado Dept of Molecular, Cellular & Dev Bio Boulder CO 80309-0347

PACE, ORLANDO LAMAR, professional football player; b. Sandusky, Ohio, Nov. 4, 1975; Attended, Ohio State Univ. Lineman St. Louis Rams, 1997—. Donater Disadvantaged Kids; participant Spearheads Annual Offensive Line Thanksgiving Project, Chesterfield, Mo. Named to NFL Pro-Bowl, 1999—2003. Achievements include first to first player in college history to win two consecutive Lombardi awards, 1995, 1996; 1st overall pick, NFL Draft, 1997; mem. Super Bowl XXXIV Champion St. Louis Rams, 2000. Office: 1 Rams Way Saint Louis MO 63045*

PACE, PETER, military officer; b. Bklyn., Nov. 5, 1945; m. Lynne Ann Holden; children: Peter Jr., Tiffany Marie. BS, U.S. Naval Acad., 1967; MBA, George Washington U., 1972; student, USMC Command and Staff Coll., 1979-80; grad., Nat. War Coll., 1986; postgrad. in Nat. and Internat. Security, Harvard U. Commd. lt. USMC, 1967, advanced through grades to lt. gen., 1996; served in 2d Bn., 5th Marines, 1st Marine Divsn., Vietnam, 1968-69; various assignments Marine Barracks, Washington, 1969-71, 88-96; ops. officer, Security Element Marine Aircraft Group 15, 1st Marine Aircraft Wing, Nam Phong, Thailand, 1972, exec. officer, 1972; asst. majors' monitor Hdqs. Marine Corps, Washington, 1973-76; various assignments 1st Marine Divsn., Pendleton, Calif., 1976-79, 83-85; commdg. officer Marine Corps Recruiting Sta., Buffalo, 1980-83; various assignments Combined/Joint Staff, Seoul, Korea, 1986-87; dir. ops. Joint Staff, Washington, 1996; commd. US Marine Corps, Washington, 1997—2000; gen., commd. in chief US Southern Command, 2000—01; vice chmn., Joint Chiefs of Staff US Dept of Def, Washington, 2001—. Decorated Def. D.S.M., Def. Legion of Merit, Bronze Star with Combat V., Def. Superior Service medal, Def. Meritorious Service medal, Navy Commendation medal, Navy Achievement medal, Combat Action medal Office: Vice Chmn of Joint Chiefs Dept of Def Pentagon Washington DC 20301

PACE, STANLEY CARTER, retired aeronautical engineer; b. Waterview, Ky., Sept. 14, 1921; s. Stanley Dan and Pearl Eagle (Carter) P.; m. Elaine Marilyn Cutchall, Aug. 21, 1945; children: Stanley Dan, Lawrence Timothy, Richard Yost. Student, U. Ky., 1939-40; BS, U.S. Mil. Acad., 1943; MS in Aero. Engring., Calif. Inst. Tech., 1949; LLD (hon.), Maryville Coll., 1987; LHD (hon.), U. Mo., 1990. Commd. 2d lt. USAAF, 1943, advanced through grades to col., 1953; pilot, flight leader B-24 Group, 15th Air Force, 1943-44; chief power plant br., procurement div. Hdqrs. Air Materiel Command, 1945-48; assignments, procurement div. Hdqrs. Air Materiel Command, 1949-53; dep. chief prodn. Hdqrs. Air Materiel Command, 1952-53; resigned, 1954; with TRW, Inc., Cleve., 1954-85, successively sales mgr., asst. mgr., mgr. West Coast plant; mgr. jet div. Tapco plant, Cleve.; asst. mgr. Tapco group, 1954-58, v.p., gen. mgr., 1958-65, exec. v.p. co., 1965-77, pres., 1977-85, vice chmn., 1985, dir., 1965-85; vice chmn., dir. Gen. Dynamics Corp., St. Louis, 1985, chmn., chief exec. officer, 1985-90, also bd. dirs. Head United Way drive, Cleve., 1984; former council commr., pres. Great Cleve. Council Boy Scouts Am.; former trustee Nat. Jr. Achievement, Denison U., Washington U., Judson Park; former chmn. Greater Cleve. Roundtable, Cleve. Found., Nat. Assn. Mfrs., Aerospace Ind. Assn. Decorated Air medal with oak leaf clusters, Purple Heart; recipient James Forrestal award Nat. Security Indsl. Assn.; named d'Officier de lóorder de Leopold Belgium Govt. Mem. AIAA, Soc. Automotive Engrs., Union Club, Country Club, Chagrin Valley Hunt Club, Pepper Pike Club, Eldorado Country Club, Rolling Rock Club, St. Louis Country Club, Delta Tau Delta. Home: 1709 Berkshire Rd Gates Mills OH 44040-9747

PACE, STANLEY DAN, lawyer; b. Dayton, Ohio, Dec. 10, 1947; s. Stanley Carter and Elaine (Cutchall) Pace; m. Judy Roehm, Sept. 8, 1973; children: Stanley Carter, Barbara Roehm. BA, Denison U., Granville, Ohio, 1970; JD, U. Toledo (Ohio), 1975. Bar: U.S. Dist. Ct. (so. dist.) Ohio 1975, U.S. Dist. Ct. (no. dist.) Ohio 1977, U.S. Ct. Appeals (6th cir.) 1975. Atty. ARMCO Steel Corp., Middletown, Ohio, 1975-77; assoc. Spieth, Bell, McCurdy & Newell, Cleve., 1977-82, dir., 1982—, co-mng. dir., 1987—. Bd. dirs. Indsl. Rels. Resh. Assn., Cleve., 1985. Bd. dirs. pres. Judson Retirement Cmty., Cleve., 1985; bd. dirs. Arthritis Found. N.E. Ohio, Cleve., 1984, Western Res. Hist. Soc., 1998. Mem.: ABA, Greater Cleve. Bar Assn., Ohio Bar Assn., Chagrin Valley Hunt Club, Rolling Rock Club, Tavern Club, Pepper Pike Club, The Country Club. Office: Spieth Bell McCurdy & Newell 2000 Huntington Bldg Cleveland OH 44115

PACE, STEPHEN SHELL, artist, educator; b. Charleston, Mo., Dec. 12, 1918; s. John C. and Ora K. (Reeves) P.; m. Palmina Natalini, Feb. 26, 1949. Student, Inst. Fine Arts, San Miguel, 1945-46, Art Students League, N.Y.C., 1948-49, Grande Chaumiere, Paris, 1950, Inst. D'Arte Statale, Florence, Italy, 1951, Hans Hofmann Sch., N.Y.C., 1951-52; ArtsD (hon.), U. So. Ind., 2002, Maine Coll. Art, Portland, 2003. Artist in residence Washington U., 1959; instr. painting Pratt Inst., N.Y.C., 1961-69; artist in residence Des Moines Art Ctr., 1970; vis. artist U. Calif., 1968; asso. prof. Bard Coll., 1969-71, Am. U., 1975-83. One-man shows include Hendler Gallery, 1953, Artists Gallery, 1954, Poindexter Gallery, 1956, 57, Washington U., St. Louis, 1959, Holland-Goldowsky Gallery, Chgo., 1960, Howard Wise Gallery, Cleve., 1960, N.Y., 1960, 61, 63, 64, Dilexi Gallery, San Francisco, 1960, HCE Gallery, 1956-59, 61-63, 66, Dwan Gallery, L.A., 1961, Hayden Gallery, Cambridge, Mass., 1961, Ridley Gallery, Evansville, Ind., 1966, U. Calif., Berkeley, 1968, Graham Gallery, N.Y.C., 1969, Des Moines Art Ctr., 1970, U. Tex., Austin, 1970, Kansas City Art Inst., 1973, A.M. Sachs Gallery, N.Y.C., 1974, 76, 77, 78, 79, 81, 83, 85, Drew U., 1975, Bard Coll., 1975, Am. U., 1976, Roberto Polo Gallery, Washington, 1976, New Harmony (Ind.) Gallery, 1977, Farm Gallery, Far Hill, N.J., 1978, Barbara Fiedler Gallery, Washington, 1980, Chastenet Gallery, Washington, 1981, Katharina Rich Perlow Gallery, N.Y.C., 1987, 89, 91, 94, 97, 98, 2000, 02, 04, Vanderwoude-Tananbaum Gallery, N.Y.C., 1991, U. N.C., Greensboro, 1991, Evansville Mus., 1992, Maine Coast Artists, Rockport, 1994, Bates Coll. Mus., Lewiston, Maine, 1994, Union Coll., Schenectady, NY, 1999, A.J. Buecke Gallery, Northeast Harbor, Maine, 2001, Portland (Maine) Mus. Art, 2004, Farnsworth Mus., 2004; exhibited in group shows in U.S., Europe, Japan, Mid. East, India, Burma, Australia, New Zealand, Hawaii, Ctrl. and S.Am.; represented in permanent collections, Whitney Mus., Chrysler Mus., Norfolk, Va., Provincetown (Mass.) Mus., Evansville Mus., U. So. Ill., Carbondale, Michener Found., Walker Art Ctr., U. Calif., CIBA-Geigy Collection, Hallmark Collection, Bundy Art Gallery, U. N.C., Greensboro, Chase Manhattan Bank, Munson-Williams-Procter Inst., Utica, N.Y., Des Moines Art Ctr., Boston Mus. Fine Arts, Met. Mus., N.Y.C., Phillips Collection, Washington, Am. U., Washington, Corcoran Gallery, Washington, Curie Inst., Paris, Hirshhorn Mus., Washington, Bristol Myers Collection, Indpls. Mus., Portland (Maine) Mus., Bowdoin Coll. Mus., Brown U., Providence, Oberlin (Ohio) Coll. Mus, Farnsworth Art Mus., Rockland, Maine, Bates Coll. Mus., Lewiston, Maine, Nat. Mus. Am. Art, Washington, Columbus Mus. Art, Yale U., New Haven, U. of S. Indiana, Evansville, Union Coll., Schenectady, Newark Art Mus., N.J., U. No. Iowa, Cedar Falls, Colby Coll. Mus., Waterville, Maine, Rutgers U. Mus., NB, NJ, New Orleans Mus. Art, NAD, Baruch Coll., N.Y., U. Maine, Orono, U. Denver. Served with AUS, 1941-45, ETO. Recipient Dolian Lorian award for promising Am. painters, 1954, Hallmark award, 1961, Am. Acad. Arts and Letters prize, 2004; Guggenheim fellow, 1980; Creative Artists Pub. Svc. Program grantee, 1973. Mem.: NAD (Benjamin Altman prize 1993, Edwin Palmer Marine prize 2001). Address: 345 W 29th St New York NY 10001-4780

PACE, THOMAS M. lawyer; b. Mesa, Ariz., Feb. 5, 1952; s. Lemuel Max and Ann (Green) P.; m. Vi Garrett Pace, Jan. 24, 1981; children: Melanie, Brittany. BA, Stanford U., 1973; JD, U. Ariz., 1976. Bar: Ariz.; cert. real estate specialist. Assoc. Martin, Feldhacker & Freidl, Phoenix, 1976-77, Trew & Woodford, Phoenix, 1977-78; ptnr. Hecker, Phillips & Hooker, Tucson, 1978-88; sr. ptnr. O'Connor Cavanagh, Tucson, 1988-95; pvt. practice Law Office of Thomas M. Pace, Tucson, 1995—. Mem. Mayor's Housing Task Force, Tucson, 1993; bd. dirs. Tucson Urban League, 1986-96; chmn. So. Ariz. Homebuilders Polit. Action Com., 1995, 96. Mem. So. Ariz. Homebuilders (tech. com), Stanford Club So. Ariz. Democrat. Office: 2525 E Broadway Blvd Ste 102 Tucson AZ 85716-5398 Office Phone: 520-322-5511. E-mail: tpace2@mindspring.com.

PACE, WAYNE H. communications executive; Joined Price Waterhouse, 1970; exec. v.p., fin., & adminstrv. officer Turner Broadcasting Sys., Atlanta, 1993—2001; vice chmn., CFO Turner Broadcasting Sys. (now Time Warner), Atlanta, 2001; exec. v.p., CFO Time Warner Inc, N.Y.C., 2001—. Office: Time Warner Inc 75 Rockefeller Plaza New York NY 10019

PACELLA, BERNARD LEONARDO, psychiatrist; b. Toronto, Ont., Can., July 25, 1912; m. Theresa Rita Domalakes; children: Karen Pacella Oldham, Richard B., Madelyn Joyce Nichols, Bernard Leonard Jr. BS, U. Colo., 1931, MD, 1935; postgrad., N.Y. Psychoanalytic Inst., 1946-51. Cert. child, adolescent, and adult psychoanalyst; Diplomate Am. Bd. Psychiatry and Neurology. Intern Kings County Hosp., Bklyn., 1935-37, resident in pediat., 1937-38; resident in psychiatry Columbia U. and N.Y. State Psychiat. Inst., N.Y.C., 1938-40; rsch. fellow in psychiatry Columbia Presbyn. Med. Ctr., N.Y.C., 1940-41, instr. mil. psychiatry, 1943-46; lectr. clin. psychiatry Columbia U. Coll. Physicians and Surgeons, 1942-44; from assoc. clin. psychiatry to clin. prof. emeritus Columbia U., 1944-84; lectr., faculty Columbia U. Ctr. Pshychoanalytic Tng. and Rsch., 1984—; clin. prof. emeritus Columbia U., 1990—. Faculty Ctr. for Psychoanalytic Tng. and Rsch., Columbia U. Contbr. articles to profl. jours.; reviewer Psychoanalytic Quar. Pres. Margaret S. Mahler Psychiat. Rsch. Found., 1970-88, bd. dirs.; sec.-treas., bd. dirs. Sigmund Freud Archives; pres. Psychoanalytic Assistance Fund, 1974-89, bd. dirs.; bd. dirs. Freud London Mus.; co-trustee Mary S. Sigourney award, 1990. With Colo. N.G., 1930-35, M.C. USAR, 1935-40. Decorated Cavaliere Officiale dell Ordine al Merito (Italy), 1958. Fellow Am. Coll. Psychoanalysis, Am. Acad. Child and Adolescent Psychiatry, N.Y. Acad. Medicine, Am. Psychiat. Assn.; mem. AMA, Am. Soc. Adolescent Psychiatr, Am. Psychoanalytic Assn. (reviewer jour., pres.-elect 1990, pres. 1992—, treas. 1983—), Assn. Child Psychoanalysis, Group Advancement Psychiatry, Assn. Psychoanalytic Medicine, N.Y. Psychoanalytic Soc. and Inst. (bd. dirs.), Internat. Psychoanalytic Assn., N.Y. Psychiat. Soc., N.Y. Coun. Child and Adolescent Psychiatry, Alpha Omega Alpha. Home and Office: 115 E 61st St New York NY 10021-8183

PACERNICK, GARY B. literature educator, poet; b. Detroit, May 9, 1941; s. Edward and Sally Pacernick; m. Dorothea Jeanne Anton, June 4, 1968 (dec. 2002); children: Jennifer, Eden. BA with highest honors, U. Mich., 1963; MA, U. Minn., 1966; PhD, Ariz. State U., 1969. Asst. prof. English Wright State U., Dayton, Ohio, 1969—74, assoc. prof., 1974—81, full prof., 1981—. Mem. lit. panel Ohio Arts Coun., Columbus, 1970; resident artist MacDowell Colony, Petersborough, NH, 1973. Author: Memory and Fire: Ten American Jewish Poets, 1989, Sing a New Song: American Jewish Poetry Since the Holocaust, 1991, Meaning and Memory: Interviews with 14 Jewish Poets, 2002; editor: Images Mag., 1974—90; author: (poetry) Credence, 1974, Wanderers and Other Poems, 1985, The Jewish Poems, 1985, Something Is Happening, 1991, Summer Psalms, 1999; contbr. poetry to anthologies. Individual Artist's grant, Ohio Arts Coun., Columbus, 1979—80, Rapaport fellow, Am. Jewish Archives, Cin., 1989. Mem.: Phi Kappa Phi, Phi Beta Kappa. Avocations: travel, swimming, reading. Home: 419 Volusia Ave Dayton OH 45409 Office: Wright State Univ Dayton OH 45435

PACH, PETER BARNARD, columnist, editor; b. Bklyn., Aug. 3, 1951; s. Stewart Warner and Constance (Barnard) P.; m. Kathleen Ann Megan, Sept. 7, 1985; children: Nell, Samuel. BA in English, Union Coll., 1973. Reporter Record Jour., Meriden, Conn., 1974-78, Wallingford bur. chief, 1978-83; Middletown bur. chief Hartford Courant, Conn., 1983-84, columnist, 1984-95; mem. editorial bd. Hartford (Conn.) Courant, 1992—, town editls. editor, 2001—. Vis. instr. Wesleyan U., Middletown, Conn., 1985—2003. Recipient First Bus. and Econ. Reporting award New England Press Ass., 1977. Mem. Dedham County and Polo Club. Avocations: running, skiing, golf, squash, gardening. Home: PO Box 46 Middle Haddam CT 06456-0046 Office: Hartford Courant 285 Broad St Hartford CT 06115-2510

PACHECO, MANUEL TRINIDAD, retired academic administrator; b. Rocky Ford, Colo., May 30, 1941; s. Manuel J. and Elizabeth (Lopez) Pacheco; m. Karen M. King, Aug. 27, 1966; children: Daniel Mark, Andrew Charles, Sylvia Lois Elizabeth. BA, N.Mex. Highlands U., 1962; MA, Ohio State U., 1966, PhD, 1969. Mem. faculty Fla. State U., 1968—71, U. Colo., 1971; prof. edn., univ. dean Tex. A&I U., Laredo, 1972—77; prof. multicultural edn., chmn. dept. San Diego State U., 1977—78; prof. Spanish and edn. Laredo State U., 1978—80; exec. dir. Bilingual Edn. Ctr., Kingsville Tex. A&I U., 1980—82; assoc. dean Coll. Edn. U. Tex., El Paso, 1982—86, exec. dir. for planning, 1984; pres. Laredo State U., 1984—88, U. Houston-Downtown, 1986—97, U. Ariz., Tucson, 1991—97, U. Mo. Sys., Columbia, 1997—2002; ret., 2002. Cons. lang. divsn. Ency. Britannica, 1965—72; bd. dirs. Valley Nat. Bank Corp., Nat. Security Edn. Program, ASARCO; mem. exec. com. Bus.-Higher Edn. Forum. Co-editor: Handbook for Planning and Managing Instruction in Basic Skills for Limited English Proficient Students, 1983; prodr.: (videotapes) Teacher Training, 1976. Named, Most Prominent Am.-Hispanics Spanish Tchr. Mag., 1984, one of 100 Outstanding Hispanics Hispanis Bus., 1988, Man of Yr., Hispanic Profl. Action Com., 1991; recipient Disting. Alumnus award, Ohio State U., Columbus, 1984, Disting. Leadership in Higher Edn. award, Sec. of Edn. Richard Riley, 1997; Fulbright fellow, U. de Montepellier, France, 1962. Mem.: Tex. Assn. Chicanos in Higher Edn., Hispanic Assn. Colls. and Univs., Nat. Acad. Pub. Adminstrn., Am. Assn. State Colls. and Univs., Rotary, Phi Delta Kappa. Home: 11001 N 50th St Scottsdale AZ 85254-5377

PACHECO, ROBERT, state official; b. Mesilla Park, N.Mex., June 10, 1934; m. Gayle Pacheco; 5 children. AA in Bus. Adminstrn., Mgmt., East L.A. C.C.; BS in Bus. Adminstrn. and Mgmt., Calif. State U., L.A.; JD, Western U. Owner, oper. importing/mfg. corp.; former asst. v.p. corp. banking United Calif. Bank; adviser, atty. local comty.; mem. Calif. Rep. Cen. Com.; coun. mem. Walnut City Coun., 1995—98; state assembly mem. Dist. 60 Calif. State Assembly, 1998—. Chair Latino Rep. Caucus. Mem. League Calif. Cities; mem., founder Gabriel Found.; founder, mem. Walnut Edn. Found.; mem. Walnut Med. and Humanitarian Mission; mem. Founders Cir. Applause Found. Performing Arts; amb. advocate Calif. Poly. Pomona; mem. Calif. Contract Cities; del. Foothill Transit Authority. Republican. Roman Catholic. Mailing: Rm 5164 PO Box 942849 Sacramento CA 94249 Office: Ste 205 117870 Castleton St City Of Industry CA 91748

PACHECO, SUSAN, automotive executive; d. Jorge Pacheco; married; children: Alex, Adam. MBA, U. Detroit, 1989. Ford grad. tng. program Ford Motor Co., 1984—86, product design engr., 1986—89, supr. steering column and shiftsystem design and devel., 1989—92, program mgr. Ford Explorer special studies, 1992, chief program engr., pres. Ford Unlimited, dir. Mercury programs. Named one of 50 Most Important Hispanics in Bus. and Tech., Hispanic Engr. & Info. Tech. mag., 2003. Office: Ford Motor Co 1 American Rd Dearborn MI 48126-2798 Office Phone: 313-322-3000. Office Fax: 313-845-5259.

PACHECO-RANSANZ, ARSENIO, Hispanic and Italian studies educator; b. Barcelona, Feb. 8, 1932; s. Arsenio Pacheco and Jacoba Ransanz-Alvarez; m. Mercedes Olivella-Sole, Sept. 1, 1956; children: Arsenio-Andrew, David-George. MA, U. Barcelona, 1954, PhD, 1958. Tutor Colegio Mayor Hispanoamericano Fray Junipero Serra, Barcelona, 1954-56; lectr. Hochschüle für Wirtschaft und Sozialwissenschaften, Nurnberg, Germany, 1956; asst. lectr. U. Glasgow, Scotland, 1957-59; lectr. U. St. Andrews, Scotland, 1960-70; vis. prof. U. Pitts., 1966; prof. Hispanic and Italian studies U. B.C., Vancouver, Canada, 1970-97, prof. emeritus, 1997—. Editor: Historia de Xacob Xalabin, 1964, Testament de Bernat Serradell, 1971, Varia fortuna del soldado Pindaro, 1975, Obres de Francesc de la Via, 1997; contbr. articles to profl. jours. Bd. dirs. Can. Fedn. Humanities, 1981-84. Fellow Royal Soc. Can.; mem. Can. Assn. Hispanists (pres. 1978-81), Asociacion Internacional de Hispanistas,

MLA, Assn. Hispanists Gt. Britain and Ireland, N.Am. Catalan Soc. (v.p. 1984-87, pres. 1987-90), Anglo Catalan Soc., Associacio Internacional de Llengua i Literatura Catalana. Roman Catholic. Office: U BC Dept Frnch Hispanic Ital Vancouver BC Canada V6T 1Z1 E-mail: arp@interchange.ubc.ca.

PACHER, NANCY A. real estate company executive; Grad. cum laude, Georgetown U.; JD, Northwestern U. Atty. Katten, Muchin, Gitles, Zavis, Pearl & Galler (now Katten Muchin Zavis Rosenman), Chgo., 1975; sr. v.p., prin. Howard Ecker & Co.; pres., COO US Equities Realty, Chgo., 1993—. Bd. mem. Access Living Met. Chgo.; commr. City of Chgo. Plan Commn.; mem. aux. bd. Sch. Art Inst. Chgo. Mem. editl. adv. bd.: Ill. Real Estate Jour. Named Broker of the Yr., Chgo. Sun-Times; named one of 100 Most Influential Women in Chgo., Crain's Chgo. Bus., 1996; named to Who's Who in Chgo. Bus., 2002, 20th Ann. Hall of Fame, Today's Chgo. Women. Mem.: ABA, Comml. Real Estate Orgn., Comml. Real Estate Exec. Women, Chgo. Network (bd. mem.), Chgo. Bar Assn., Econ. Club Chgo., Phi Beta Kappa. Office: US Equities Realty Ste 400 20 N Michigan Ave Chicago IL 60602*

PACHNER, JAROSLAV (FRANTISEK), nuclear engineer, consultant; b. Prague, Czech Republic, Sept. 17, 1940; s. Jaroslav Pachner and Vera Zaloudkova; m. Vera Skodova, Sept. 27, 1968; children: Martin Lukas, Klara Lucia Steele. MSc, Charles U., Prague, 1963; PhD, U. BC, Vancouver, 1971. Post-doctorate fellow Chalk River (Can.) Nuc. Labs. of Atomic Energy of Can. Ltd., 1971—73; nuc. power plant tech. supr. Ont. Hydro, Rolphton, Canada, 1973—81; sr. officer Atomic Energy Control Bd., Ottawa, Canada, 1981—90; sr. engring. safety officer Internat. Atomic Energy Agy., Vienna, 1990—2002; prin. advisor Pachner Assocs., Ottawa, Canada, 2003—. Mem. expert group on npp life mgmt. Orgn. Econ. Coop. Devel. Nuc. Energy Agy., Paris, 1991—95, mem. working group on integrity and ageing, 1996—2002; mem. sub-com. on reactor instrumentation Internat. Electrotechnical Commn., Geneva, 1996—2000; chmn. adv. group on safety aspects of npp aging and life ext. Internat. Atomic Energy Agy., Vienna, 1988—89; sr. nuc. advisor dept. fgn. affairs and internat. trade Govt. Can., 2003; mem. G8 Nuc. Safety and Security Group, 2003. Tech. editor, co-author Safety Guide on Software for Computer Based Systems Important to Safety in NPPs, 2000, Safety Guide on Instrumentation and Control Systems Important to Safety in NPPs, 2002; editor: (cd-rom) IAEA Guidance on Aging Mgmt. for NPPs, 2002; editor: (co-author) Safety Guide on Periodic Safety Rev. of NPPs, 2003. Recipient Appreciation award for implementation of PSR in Korea, Nuc. Safety Symposium Org. Com., Republic of Korea, 2002. Mem.: Can. Olympic Assn., Can. Ski Assn. (v.p. 1987—90, Appreciation award 1990). Achievements include development of internationally recognized guidance on aging management of systems, structures and components, incl. universally applicable systematic aging management process; IAEA safety guide on periodic safety review of NPPs - a basis for long term safety of nuclear installations. Avocations: skiing, running, bicycling, hiking, sailing. Home: 451 Tillbury Av Ottawa ON Canada K2A 0Y6 Personal E-mail: j.pachner@rogers.com.

PACHOLCZYK, ANDRZEJ GRZEGORZ, astrophysicist; b. Warsaw, Sept. 23, 1935; arrived in USA, 1962; s. Tadeusz and Natalia (Ugniewska) Pacholczyk; m. Mary Jane Driggs, Apr. 27, 1963; children: Tadeusz J., Helen L. Arnold, Hanna G. Zoucha, Elena M. Orosco, Michelle A. Weldy. MS astronomy, Warsaw U, Warsaw, Poland, 1956, MS physics, 1957, PhD astrophysics, 1961. Rsch. fellow Polish Acad. Sci., Warsaw, 1958—62; lectr. U. Warsaw, 1958—62; Italian Fgn. ministry fellow U. Turin, Italy, 1959—60; rsch. fellow Harvard U., Cambridge, Mass., 1963—64; from asst. prof. to prof., astronomer U. Ariz., Tucson, 1965—2001, prof. emeritus, 2001—. Vis. fellow Joint Inst. for Lab. Astrophysics, Boulder, Colo., 1964—65; dir. Pachart Pub. House, Tuscon, 1970—; sr. vis. fellow U of Sussex, Falmer, England, 1973; CNR vis. fellow Inst. of Radio Astronomy, Bologna, Italy, 1973; vis. scientist Shmidt Inst. of Earth Physics, Moscow, 1962, Arecibo Ionospheric Obs., Arecibo, PR, 1968, Nat. Radio Astronomy Obs., Charlottesville, Va., 1976, Vatican Obs., Castelgandolfo, 1982, 84, 86, 88, Huazhong Normal U, Wuhan, PR, China, 1992, Swedish Inst. for Space Physics, Umea, Sweden, 1998; CEO Pachart Found., Tuscon, Ariz., 1982—; vis. prof. U of Florence, Florence, Italy, 1982—83; bd. mem. Vatican Obs. Found., Tucson, 1986—89. Author: Radio Astrophysics, 1970, Radio Galaxies, 1977, A Handbook of Radio Sources, 1978, The Catastrophic Universe, 1984; pub. (jour.) Phil. in Sci., 1983—2003; contbr. articles in prof. jour. Bd. dirs. Forum on Theology and Sci. Newman Ctr., Tucson, 1991—2003. Fellow: Royal Astron. Soc.; mem.: Polish Astron. Soc., Internat. Astron. Union, Am. Astron. Soc. Roman Catholic. Avocations: classical organ, piano, poetry. Home: 1130 San Lucas Cir PO box 35542 Tucson AZ 85740 Office: Steward Observatory Univ of AZ Tucson AZ 85721

PACHOLSKI, RICHARD FRANCIS, retired securities company executive, financial advisor, consultant; b. Seattle, June 18, 1947; s. Theodore Francis and Nellie (Tarabochia) P.; m. Dorothy Irene Nelson, May 25, 1974; children: Nicolas, Tara. BA cum laude, U. Wash., 1969, MBA summa cum laude, 1970. CPA, Wash. Mgr. Arthur Andersen & Co., Seattle, 1970-76; v.p., contr. SNW Enterprises, Seattle, 1976-82; sr. v.p., treas., sec., dir. Seattle N.W. Securities, 1982-93; cons. Carl & Co., Portland, Oreg., 1984-88, Ellis & Carl Inc., Portland, Oreg., 1979-83; pres. R. Pacholski, P.C., Redmond, Wash., 1979—. Adj. prof. U. Wash., Seattle, 1976-80. Mem. AICPA, Nat. Assn. Securities Dealers (past bd. dirs. local dist.), Wash. Athletic Club, PacWest Club (Redmond, Wash.). Roman Catholic. Home and Office: 5060 164th Ct NE Redmond WA 98052-5294 E-mail: pacholski@prodigy.net.

PACHT, ERIC REED, pulmonary and critical care physician; b. Madison, Wis., Mar. 24, 1954; s. Asher Roger and Perle (Landau) P.; m. Karen Sue Dalpiaz, Aug. 7, 1982; children: Ben, Lora. BA summa cum laude, Lawrence U., 1976; MD cum laude, U. Wis., Madison, 1980. Diplomate Nat. Bd. Med. Examiners, Am. Bd. Internal Medicine. Intern, resident Ohio State U. Hosps., 1980-83, fellow in pulmonary and critical care medicine, 1983-86; asst. prof. Ohio State U., 1986-91, assoc. prof., 1991-99; staff phys. Mt. Carmel Med. Ctr. and St. Annis Hosp., Columbus, Ohio, 1999-01, Licking Meml. Heatlh Profls., Columbus, Ohio, 2001—. Asst. dir. pulmonary and critical care Ohio State U., 1988-96, dir. pulmonary and critical care fellowship tng. program, 1988-99, med. sch. rep. to Am. Fedn. for Clin. Rsch., 1990-94, med. dir. lung transplantation program, 1992-95, dir. clin. rsch., 1993-99. Contbr. articles to profl. jours. Vol. Am. Lung Assn., Columbus, Ohio, Columbus Cancer Clinic. Recipient numerous rsch. awards. Fellow Am. Coll. Chest Physicians; mem. Am. Thoracic Soc., Ohio Thoracic Soc., Am. Fedn. Clin. Rsch., Phi Beta Kappa. Achievements include description of new form of respiratory failure and emphysema in patients with HIV. Home: 1224 Leicester Pl Columbus OH 43235-2181 Office: Bldg 2 1272 W Main St Newark OH 43055 Office Phone: 740-348-1805. Personal E-mail: EPacht@aol.com.

PACHTER, IRWIN JACOB, pharmaceutical consultant; b. N.Y.C., July 15, 1925; s. Nathan and Ethel Lillian (Thomases) P.; m. Elaine Anna White, Aug. 23, 1953; children: Wendy, Jonathan. BS, UCLA, 1947; MS, U. N.Mex., 1949; PhD, U. So. Calif., 1951; postgrad., U. Ill., 1951-52, Harvard U., 1952-53. Research chemist Ethyl Corp., 1953-55; asso. research chemist Smith Kline & French, 1955-62, asst. sec. head, 1962; dir. medicinal chemistry Endo Labs., 1962-66; dir. research Endo div. du Pont Co., 1967-70; v.p. research and devel. Bristol Labs. div. Bristol-Myers Co., 1970-82; lectr. Adelphi U., 1963-69. Contbr. articles to profl. jours.; patentee in field Trustee Gordon Research Conf., 1972-75; chmn. medicinal chemistry study group Walter Reed Inst. Research, 1975-77. Served with USN, 1944-46. Mem. Am. Chem. Soc. (chmn. div. medicinal chemistry 1974-76), Pharm. Mfrs. Assn. (chmn. research and devel. sect. 1975-76) Home: 101 Woodberry Ln Fayetteville NY 13066-1745

PACHTER, LEE M. pediatrician; b. Bklyn., Mar. 12, 1957; s. Harvey Leonard and Rosalind Blau Pachter. BA, Franklin and Marshal Coll., 1979; DO, Phila. Coll. Osteo. Medicine, 1983. Diplomate Am. Bd. Osteo. Physicians. Intern Metro. Hosp., Springfield, Pa., 1983-84; resident in pediatrics St. Christopher's Hosp. Children, Phila., 1984-87; fellow in pediatrics Children's Hosp. Phila., 1987-89; from asst. prof. to prof. pediats. and anthropology U. Conn. Sch. Medicine, Farmington, 1989—, head divsn. gen. pediat., 1998—. Trustee The Artists Collective, Hartford, Conn., 1989—. Fellow Am. Acad. Pediatrics, Soc. Applied Anthropology; mem. Am. Anthropol. Assn., Ambulatory Pediat. Assn., Soc. Rsch. & Child Devel., Soc. Applied Anthropology. Office: St Francis Hosp & Med Ctr 114 Woodland St Hartford CT 06105-1208 E-mail: lpachter@stfranciscare.org.

PACI, PIERELLA, economist; b. Rome, Aug. 18, 1957; d. Orazio and Rosa (Galassetti) P.; m. Adam Wagstaff, July 15, 1989; children: Benedict, Lilli Ruth. Grad., U. Rome, 1980; diploma, U. York, Eng., 1981; PhD, U. Manchester, Eng., 1986. Lectr. U. Sussex, Brighton, Eng., 1985-89; from lectr. to sr. lectr. City U., London, 1989-99; hon. rsch. fellow Inst. Edn., London, 1994—; sr. economist World Bank, Washington, 1998—; regional gender coord. Europe and Ctrl. Asia. Author: Wage Differentials between Men and Women: Evidence from Cohort Studies, 1996, Unequal Pay for Women and Men, 1998 (Noteworthy Books in Indsl. Rels. and Labor Econs. award 1999); contbr. articles to profl. jours. including Jour. Health Econs., Social Sci. and Medicine, Jour. Human Resources, Cambridge Jour. Econs., others. Office: The World Bank 1818 H St NW Washington DC 20433-0002 Home: 5607 Chevy Chase Pwky Nw Washington DC 20015-2519

PACIESAS, WILLIAM SIMON, astrophysicist, educator; b. Pottsville, Pa., Aug. 27, 1947; s. Simon J. and Alice A. (Bellis) P.; m. Dianne Strange, Apr. 28, 1986; children: Jack D. Darby, Rebecca M. Darby, Sylvia R., Roxanne H. BS magna cum laude, Seton Hall U., 1969; MS, U. Calif., San Diego, 1971, C.Phil., 1976, PhD, 1978. NAS/NRC resident rsch. assoc. NASA Goddard Space Flight Ctr., Greenbelt, Md., 1978-80; rsch. assoc. U. Md., College Park, 1980-82; asst. rsch. prof. U. Ala., Huntsville, 1982-88, assoc. rsch. prof., 1988-94, rsch. prof. astrophysics, 1994—. Editor: Gamma Ray Bursts, 1992; contbr. articles to profl. jours. Mem. AAAS, Am. Astron. Soc., Am. Phys. Soc., Internat. Astron. Union. Home: 1207 Bob Wallace Ave Huntsville AL 35801 Office: U Ala Dept Physics Huntsville AL 35899-0001 E-mail: william.paciesas@msfc.nasa.gov.

PACIFICO, ALBERT DOMINICK, cardiovascular surgeon; b. Bklyn., Sept. 24, 1940; s. Dominick Vincent and Amelia Catherine (Jannelli) P.; m. Vicki Lynne Overton, May 16, 1980; children: Albert D., Nicole M., Paul V. BS, St. Johns U., 1960; MD, N.J. Coll. Medicine, 1964. Diplomate Am. Bd. Surgery, Am. Bd. Thoracic Surgery. Med. intern Jersey City Med. Ctr., Seton Gall Coll. Medicine, 1964-65; asst. resident in surgery Mayo Clinic, Rochester, Minn., 1965-67; research fellow in surgery U. Ala., Birmingham, 1967-69, sr. resident, then chief resident surgery, resident in thoracic and cardiovascular surgery, 1968-72, mem. faculty dept. surgery, 1970—, prof. surgery, 1978-83, John W. Kirklin prof. cardiovascular surgery, 1983—, vice chmn. dept. surgery, 1990, dir. div. cardiothoracic surgery, 1984—, dir. Congenital Heart Disease Diagnosis and Treatment Ctr., 1985—. Mem. staff gen., thoracic and cardiovascular surgery Univ. Hosp., Birmingham, 1972—, VA Hosp., Birmingham, 1972—; mem. staff Children's Hosp., Birmingham, 1971—, chief gen., thoracic and cardiovascular surgery, 1984—. Author: (with others) Pediatric Cardiac Surgery, 1985, Cardiology, 1985, Textbook of Surgery, 13th edit., 1986, The Treatment of Congenital Cardiac Anomalies, 1986, Perspectives in Pediatric Cardiology, 1988, Current Therapy in Cardiothoracic Surgery, 1989, Decision Making in Surgery of the Chest, 1989, Cardiac Surgery: Cyanotic Congential Heart Disease, 1989, Reoperation in Cardiac Surgery, 1989, others; mem. editorial bd. Am. Jour. Cardiology, 1983—, Heart and Vessel, 1985—, Jour. Cardiac Surgery, 1985—; cons. editorial referee Ala. Jour. Med. Scis., 1974-75; contbr. articles to med. jours. Fellow ACS, Am. Coll. Cardiology, Am. Surg. Assn.; mem. AMA, Ala. State Med. Soc., Jefferson County Med. Soc., Am. Heart Assn. (Paul Dudley White Internat. Svc. Citation 1977), Am. Assn. Thoracic Surgery, Soc. Thoracic Surgeons, Am. Surg. Soc., Internat. Coll. Pediatrics, John Kirklin Soc., Congenital Heart Surgeons Soc., Assn. Acad. Surgery, Ala. chpt. Mayo Clinic Alumni Assn., Panamanian Soc. Cardiology (hon.), Peruvian Soc. Thoracic and Cardiovascular Surgery (hon.), Soc. Nat. Inst. Cardiology Mex. (hon.), Cardiac Soc. Australia and New Zealand (corr.), Peruvian Soc. Cardiology (corr.), Alpha Omega Alpha. Republican. Roman Catholic. Office: Univ Ala UAB Sta Dept Surgery Birmingham AL 35294-0001

PACIFICO, JOSEPH CARL, counselor; b. Grosse Ile, Mich., June 10, 1950; s. Carl Richard Pacifico and Mary Milano Campbell; m. Claire Lee Schlauch, Aug. 12, 1972; children: Mark Joseph, David Joseph. MBA in Mktg., U. Md., 1975; MS in Counseling Psychology, Loyola Coll., Balt., 1998. Lic. clin. profl. counselor Md., 2002. Acct. rep. Wallace Computer Svcs., Inc., Rockville, Md., 1975—99; master's level therapist Family and Marriage Therapy Ctr., Burtonsville, Md., 1998—2002, Christian Counseling Assocs., Inc., Columbia, Md., 1999—2002, clin. profl. counselor, 2002—. Leader, anger mgmt. group Christian Counseling Assocs., Inc., 2001—. Worship asst. Our Shepherd Luth. Ch., Columbia, Md., 1998—. Mem.: Christian Assocs. for Psychol. Studies. Avocations: photography, racquetball, tennis, ping pong/table tennis. Office: Christian Counseling Assocs Inc 9650 Santiago Rd # 101 Columbia MD 21045

PACIFICO, KERRY T. corporate executive; CEO Pacifico Group, Phila. Office: Pacifico Group 6701 Essington Ave Philadelphia PA 19153-3407

PACINO, AL (ALFREDO JAMES PACINO), actor, film director, film producer; b. N.Y.C., Apr. 25, 1940; s. Salvatore and Rose P.; 3 children. Student, High Sch. of Performing Arts, N.Y.C., Actors Studio, from 1966. Formerly mail deliverer editorial offices Commentary Mag.; formerly messenger, movie theatre usher, bldg. supt.; co-artistic dir. The Actors Studio, Inc., N.Y.C., 1982-84. Served apprenticeship as actor, dir. and comedy writer in Off-Off Broadway theatres, Elaine Stewart's Cafe La Mama, Julian Beck & Judith Malina's Living Theatre; appeared in New Theatre Workshop prodn. of The Peace Creeps, Dec., 1966; joined Charles Playhouse, Boston, fall, 1967, and performed in New Theatre Workshop prodn. of America Hurrah and Awake and Sing; appeared in a one-act play Off Broadway The Indian Wants the Bronx, opened Astor Pl. Theater on Jan. 17, 1968 (Obie as best actor in Off-Broadway prodn. 1967-68); made Broadway debut in Does A Tiger Wear A Necktie?, 1969 (Tony award as best dramatic actor in a supporting role, named most promising new Broadway actor in a Variety poll of metropolitan drama critics); appeared in The Local Stigmatic at Actors Playhouse, N.Y.C., opening 1969; joined Repertory Theater of Lincoln Center, N.Y.C.; other plays include The Basic Training of Pavlo Hummel, Boston Repertory Theater, 1972, Camino Real, Richard III, 1973, 79, Jungle of Cities, 1979, The Connection, Hello Out There, Tiger at the Gates, American Buffalo, Julius Caesar, 1988, Salome, Chinese Coffee (also dir.) 2000, Circle in the Square, 1992, Dir. and Performer, Hughie, 1996; (films) debut in Me, Natalie, 1969, Panic in Needle Park, 1971, The Godfather, 1972 (Best Actor award Nat. Soc. Film Critics, Acad. award nominee), Scarecrow, 1973, Serpico, 1973 (Golden Globe for best actor, Acad. award nominee), The Godfather, Part II, 1974 (BAFTA award for best actor, Acad. award nominee), Dog Day Afternoon (BAFTA award for best actor, Acad. award nominee), 1975, Bobby Deerfield, 1977, And Justice for All, 1979 (Acad. Award nomination), Cruising, 1980, Author! Author!, 1982, Scarface, 1983, Revolution, 1985, Sea of Love, 1989, Dick Tracy, 1990 (American Comedy award, Acad. award nominee), The Godfather Part III, 1990, Frankie and Johnny, 1991, Glengarry Glen Ross, 1992 (Acad. award nominee), Scent of a Woman, 1992 (Acad. award for best actor, Golden Globe for best actor), Carlito's Way, 1993, Two Bits, 1995, Heat, 1995, City Hall, 1996, Donny Brasco, 1997, Devil's Advocate, 1997, Chinese Coffee, 1999, The Insider, 1999, Any Given Sunday, 1999, People I Know, 2002, Simone, 2002, Insomnia, 2002, The Recruit, 2003, Gigli, 2003, (TV miniseries) Angels in America, 2003 (Golden Globe for best actor, Screen Actors Guild Award for best actor, 2004); actor, prodr., dir., writer Looking for Richard, 1996 (Dir. Guild of Amer. award for best dir. documentary). Recipient Cecil B. DeMille Award, 2001. Office: Creative Artists Agy care Rick Nicita 9830 Wilshire Blvd Beverly Hills CA 90212-1804*

PACINO, FRANK GEORGE, physician, educator; MD, U. Calif, Irvine, Coll. of Medicine, 1962; M.P.H., Loma Linda U., 1970. Intern Glendale Community Hosp., Calif., 1961-62; control physician, STD div. Los Angeles County Dept. Health, 1963-64, asst. chief, STD div., 1964-66; dist. health officer San Antonio Health District, 1966—92, Harbor Health Dist., 1972—92; practice medicine specializing in public health San Pedro, Calif., 1972—; med. dir. South Coast Alcohol Program, 1972—. Served with AUS, 1954-56. Recipient cert. of appreciation Los Angeles County Health Dept., 1966; commendation Los Angeles County Bd. Suprs., 1975, Patient Svcs. Improvement award Dept. Health Svcs. Los Angeles County, 1987, 88, 89. Mem. Physicians Assn. Los Angeles County (pres. 1972-73, 81-82, Physician Recognition award 1972), Am. Assn. Public Health Physicians (pres. 1975-76, pres. Calif. chpt. 1977-78, 81-82), So. Calif. Public Health Assn. (chmn. fins.), Public Health Physicians Assn. (pres. 1970-71), Am. Med. Assn. Office: 16662 Intrepid Ln Huntington Beach CA 92649-2826

PACK, ALLAN I. medical educator; MB, BChir, U. Glasgow, 1967, PhD, 1976. Dir. Ctr. for Sleep and Respiratory Neurobiology Hosp. U. Pa., Phila., prof. medicine, neurology, psychiatry. Contbr. articles to profl. jours. Achievements include research in the study of the pathogenesis of obstructive sleep apnea. Office: Hosp Univ Pa 3600 Spruce St Philadelphia PA 19104-4211 Fax: 215-662-7749. E-mail: pack@mail.med.upenn.edu.

PACK, ALLEN S. retired coal company executive; b. Bramwell, W.Va., Dec. 11, 1930; s. Paul Meador and Mable Blanche (Hale) P.; m. Glenna Rae Christian, June 21, 1952; children: Allen Scott Jr., David Christian, Mark Frederick, Andrew Ray. BS, W.Va. U., 1952. Gen. mgr. Island Coal Co., Holden, W.Va., 1969-70, pres., 1970-73, v.p. adminstrn. Lexington, Ky., 1973-75; exec. v.p. Cannelton Holding Co., Charleston, W.Va., 1975-77, pres., chief ops. officer, 1977-80, pres., chief exec. officer, 1980-91; chmn., 1991-93; ret., 1993. Bd. dirs. Bucksin coun. Boy Scouts Am., Charleston, 1976—, pres., 1980, chmn., 1994, 95, 96; bd. dirs. W.Va. Univ. Found., Morgantown, 1978-96; trustee Davis and Elkins Coll., 1981. Capt. USMC, 1952-54. Recipient Silver Beaver award Boy Scouts Am., 1981; inductee W.Va. Coal Hall of Fame, 1998. Presbyterian.

PACK, STUART HARRIS, lawyer; b. N.Y.C., Nov. 2, 1950; s. Irving and Ruth (Blum) P.; m. Robin Carol Levine, Nov. 28, 1976; children: Jennifer, Allison. BA, U. Rochester, 1972; JD, Georgetown U., 1975. Bar: Colo. 1975, U.S. Dist. Ct. Colo. 1975, U.S. Ct. Appeals (10th cir.) 1977. Ptnr. Sherman & Howard, Denver, 1975-91, Cox, Buchanan & Pack, P.C., Denver, 1991; pvt. practice Denver, 1992-96; ptnr., litigation dept. Gorsuch Kirgis LLC, Denver, 1997—. Mem. ATLA, Def. Rsch. Inst., Phi Beta Kappa. Office: Gorsuch Kirgis LLC 1515 Arapahoe St Ste 1000 Denver CO 80202-2120 Office Phone: 303-376-5000. E-mail: spackl@gorsuch.com.

PACK, SUSAN JOAN, art consultant; b. N.Y.C., June 15, 1951; d. Howard Meade and Nancy (Buckley) P. BA summa cum laude, Princeton U., 1973. Copywriter Laurence Charles & Free, N.Y.C., 1978-83, Warwick Advt., N.Y.C., 1983-85; sr. copywriter Saatchi & Saatchi Compton, N.Y.C., 1985-88; pres. The Pack Collection, 1989—. Author: Film Posters of the Russian Avant-Garde, 1995. Mem. Princeton (N.J.) U. Libr. Coun., 1985-93; trustee Pack Found. for Med. Rsch., N.Y., 1983—; bd. dirs. The Poster Soc., N.Y., 1985-87. Recipient 4 Clio awards, 1981, 1 Clio award, 1982; named one of top art collectors under 40 Art and Antiques Mag., 1985, one of top 100 collectors in U.S., 1996. Mem. Phi Beta Kappa. E-mail: spdesign@pacbell.net.

PACKARD, BONNIE BENNETT, former state legislator; b. Concord, N.H., Nov. 9, 1946; d. James Oliver and Caro Lucia (Arsenault) Bennett; m. David Bartlett Packard, Oct. 1, 1983. Mem. N.H. Ho. of Reps., Concord, 1981-82, 85-96, vice chair ho. econ. devel. com., 1992, chair ho. commerce com., 1993-96; v.p., treas. Dodd Ins. Agy., Contoocook, N.H., 1984-85; dir. govt. rels. Roussos & Hage, P.A., Attys. at Law, 1996-97, Orr & Reno, P.A., Concord, N.H., 1998—. Bd. dirs. Bus. Fin. Authority, 1994-96. State pres. N.H. Fedn. Rep. Women, 1982-83; chmn. Merrimack County (N.H.) Rep. Com., 1979-80; mem. Hillsborough County Rep. Com., 1995, chair Hillsborough County Del., 1995-96; mem. Bd. Selectmen, New Ipswich, N.H., 1989-90; nat. del. trustee Nat. Kidney Found., 1990-91, 1st v.p. N.H. chpt., 1990-91; mem. Gov.'s Task Force for Limitless Learning, 2004. Recipient Spirit of Independence award N.H. Health Underwriters Assn., 1996, Chmn.'s award Bus. Fin. Authority of State of N.H., 1996. Mem. New Ipswich Hist. Soc. Episcopalian. Avocations: sketching, antiques, political campaigns. Office: One Eagle Sq Concord NH 03301-4903 Home: 322 Alton Woods Dr Concord NH 03301-7846 Office Phone: 603-223-9136. E-mail: 66p@orr-reno.com.

PACKARD, GEORGE RANDOLPH, journalist, educator; b. Phila., May 27, 1932; s. George Randolph and Anita Porter (Clothier) Packard; m. Mary Biddle Lloyd, June 26, 1954 (div. Aug. 1978); children: Frank Randolph, Mary Wingate, William Clothier, Andrew Lloyd, Benjamin Wood, Alexander Barnes, Kent Elizabeth Davis-Packard; m. Lavinia Fletcher Plumley, July 1990. AB, Princeton U., 1954; PhD, Fletcher Sch. Law and Diplomacy, 1963; postgrad. rsch. scholar, Tokyo U., 1961—62. Spl. asst. to U.S. ambassador to, Japan, 1963—65; chief diplomatic corr. Newsweek mag., Washington, 1965—67; mng. editor Phila. Bull., 1969—73, exec. editor, 1973—75; dep. dir. Woodrow Wilson Internat. Center for Scholars, Smithsonian Instn., Washington, 1976—79; prof. Sch. Advanced Internat. Studies Johns Hopkins U., 1967—68, 1994—, dean Sch. Advanced Internat. Studies, 1979—93; vis. pres. Internat. U. Japan, 1994—98; pres. U.S.-Japan Found., 1998—. Author: (book) Protest in Tokyo: The Security Treaty Crisis of 1960, 1966, Japan, Korea and China, 1979; contbr. articles to profl. jours. Candidate U.S. Senate from Pa., 1975—76; bd. dirs. Asia Found., San Francisco, Atlantic Coun. U.S. 1st lt. U.S. Army, 1956. Ford Found. fellow, 1960—62. Mem.: Coun. Fgn. Rels. N.Y., Japan Soc. N.Y., Assn. Asian Studies, Metropolitan Club (Washington), Phi Beta Kappa. Home: 4425 Garfield St NW Washington DC 20007-1143 Office: 132 E 45th St New York NY 10017-3137

PACKARD, JOHN MALLORY, physician; b. Saranac Lake, N.Y., Sept. 25, 1920; s. Edward Newman and Mary Bissell (Betts) P.; m. Ann Maurine Schoonover, June 15, 1944; children: Michael David, John Mallory, Ann Maurine, Mary Betts, Charles Edward, Kris Asvananda, Frank Schoonover, Charlotte Mellen. BA, Yale U., 1942; MD, Harvard U., 1945. Diplomate Am. Bd. Internal Medicine. Intern Presbyn. Hosp., N.Y.C., 1945-46; resident in internal medicine Peter Bent Brigham Hosp., Boston, 1948-49; practice medicine specializing in internal medicine and cardiology Pensacola, Fla., 1954-68; prof. medicine, assoc. dean Med. Sch. U. Ala., Birmingham, 1968-76; exec. dir. Ala. Regional Med. Program, Birmingham, 1968-73; corp. v.p. med. edn. Bapt. Med. Centers, Birmingham, 1976-92; ret. Contbr. articles to med. jours. Served with USN, 1946-54. Fellow ACP, Am. Coll. Cardiology, AHA; mem. Jefferson County Med. Soc., Med. Assn. Ala., AMA, Am. Soc. Internal Medicine, Ala. Soc. Internal Medicine (pres. 1981-82), Alpha Omega Alpha. Republican. Episcopalian.

PACKARD, JULIE, aquarium administrator; d. David and Lucile P. Co-founder & exec. dir. Monterey Bay Aquarium, Monterey, Calif., 1984—, vice chair, bd of trustees, 1984—. Recipient Edward H. Bean Awd., Am. Assn. Zoological Parks and Aquariums, 1993, Audubon Medal for Conservation, 1998. Mem.: bd. David and Lucile Packard Found., Monterey Bay Aquarium Research Inst., Calif. Nature Conservancy. Office: Monterey Bay Aquarium 886 Cannery Row Monterey CA 93940-1023

PACKARD, PETER, medical educator, retired internist; b. Evanston, Ill., Mar. 14, 1927; s. George and Marianna (Dickinson) P.; m. Jenifer Carr, Aug. 28, 1951 (div. 1969); m. Mary Jane P., Nov. 8, 1969; children: Patricia Ann Langlais, Charles Barklay Langlais, Georgia Packard, Caroline L. Gregger, Louise Moskowitz-Packard, Victoria P. Aase, Adam L. Packard. BA, U. Calif., Berkeley, 1945; MD, U. Calif., San Francisco, 1948. Diplomate Am. Bd. Internal Medicine. Intern San Francisco Gen. Hosp., 1948-49; vol. arzt fellow infectious diseases Children's Hosp., Zurich, 1949-50; asst. res. in medicine Franklin Hosp., U. Calif., San Francisco, 1950-51; capt., med. corps USAF, Riverside, Calif., 1951-53; asst. res. medicine Ft. Miley VA Hosp., San Francisco, 1953-54, U. Calif. Hosp., San Francisco, 1954-55; pvt. practice Mills Hosp., Peninsula Med. Lab., San Mateo, Burlingame, Calif., 1955-91. Med. dir., vice chmn. bd. dirs., Peninsula Med. Lab., Menlo Park, Calif., 1980-94; chief of medicine, chief of staff Mills Hosp., San Mateo, 1967-74;

assoc. clin. prof. medicine, U. Calif. San Francisco, 1955—. Founding trustee, v.p. Mills-Peninsula Found., 1974-90, trustee emeritus, 1990—; pres., mem. bd. San Mateo County Heart Assn., 1964-74. Capt. M.C., USAFR, 1951-53, Korea. Mem. AMA, Calif. Med. Assn., San Mateo County Med. Assn. (various coms., bd. dirs., 1959-91), Am. Soc. Internal Medicine, Calif. Soc. Internal Medicine (del. off and on 1960-93), Calif. Soc. Medicine, U. Calif. San Francisco Assn. Clin. Faculty. Avocations: tennis, golf, teaching, history, politics. Home and Office: 720 Seabury Rd Hillsborough CA 94010-6532

PACKARD, ROBERT GOODALE, III, urban planner; b. Denver, Apr. 12, 1951; s. Robert and Mary Ann (Woodward) P.; m. Jane Ann Collins, Aug. 25, 1973; children: Jessica Nelson, Robert Gregg. BA, Willamette U., 1973; M in Urban and Regional Planning/Community Devel., U. Colo., 1976. Project mgr. Environ. Disiciplines, Inc., Portland, Oreg., 1973-75; asst. dir. planning Portland Pub. Schs., 1976-78; dir. planning Bur. of Parks, Portland, 1978-79; dir. planning and urban design Zimmer Gunsul Frasca, Portland, 1979-81, dir. project devel., 1981-84, mng. ptnr., 1984—. Co-author: The Baker Neighborhood/Denver, 1976. Contbr. articles to profl. jours. Trustee Willamette U., 1994; mem. City of Portland Waterfront Commn., 1982-83; mem. Mayor's Task Force for Joint Use of Schs., Portland, 1979-80; mem. Washington Park Master Plan Steering com., Portland, 1980-81; bd. dirs. Washington Park Zoo, 1983-86, pres. Arts Celebration Inc./Artquake, 1986—, New Rose Theatre, 1981-83; dir., pres. Grant Park Neighborhood Assn., Portland, 1981-83; pres. Pioneer Square Bd., 1997-98; bd. mem. Regional Arts and Cultural Coun.; mem. Archtl. Found. Oreg., 1992; mem. crafts bd. Oreg. Sch. Arts. Recipient Spl. Citation, Nat. Sch. Bds. Assn., 1978; Meritorious Planning Project award Am. Planning Assn., 1980, Nat. Am. Planning Assn., 1981; Meritorious Design award Am. Soc. Landscape Architects, 1981; Honor award Progressive Arch., 1983. Mem. AIA (Architecture Firm award 1991, assoc.), Am. Planning Assn., Young Pres. Assn., Racquet Club, Arlington Club, City Club, Racquet Club. Home: 3313 SW Fairmount Blvd Portland OR 97201-1478 Office: Zimmer Gunsul Frasca Partnership 320 SW Oak St Ste 500 Portland OR 97204-2737

PACKARD, RONALD C. former congressman; b. Meridian, Idaho, Jan. 19, 1931; m. Jean Sorenson, 1952; children: Chris, Debbie, Jeff, Vicki, Scott, Lisa, Theresa. Student, Brigham Young U., 1948-50, Portland State U., 1952-53; D.MD, U. Oreg., Portland, 1953-57. Gen. practice dentistry, Carlsbad, Calif., 1959-82; mem. 98th-106th Congresses from 48th (formerly 43d) Calif. dist., 1983-2001; chmn. appropriations legis. com.; former mem. pub. works and transp. com., sci., space, tech.; also chmn. appropriations fgn. ops. and transp. subcoms.; prin. Dawson & Assoc., Washington, 2001—. Mem. Carlsbad Sch. Dist. Bd., 1962-74; bd. dirs. Carlsbad C. of C., 1972-76; mem. Carlsbad Planning Commn., 1974-76, Carlsbad City Coun., 1976-78; Carlsbad chmn. Boy Scouts Am., 1977-79; mayor City of Carlsbad, 1978-82; mem. North County Armed Svcs. YMCA, North County Transit Dist., San Diego Assn. Govts., Coastal Policy Com., Transp. Policy Com.; pres. San Diego div. Calif. League of Cities. Served with Dental Corps USN, 1957-59. Republican. Mem. Ch. Lds.

PACKARD, SANDRA PODOLIN, education educator, consultant; b. Buffalo, Sept. 13, 1942; d. Mathew and Ethel (Zolte) P.; m. Martin Packard, Aug. 2, 1964; children: Dawn Esther, Shana Fanny BFA, Syracuse U., 1964; MSEd, Ind. U., 1966, EdD, 1973. Cert. tchr. art K-12, N.Y. Asst. prof. art SUNY-Buffalo, 1972-74; assoc. prof. art Miami U., Oxford, Ohio, 1974-81, spl. asst. to provost, 1979-80, assoc. provost, spl. programs, 1980-81; dean Coll. Edn. Bowling Green State U., Ohio, 1981-85; provost and vice chancellor for acad. affairs U. Tenn., Chattanooga, 1985-92; pres. Oakland U., Rochester, Mich., 1992-95, prof. edn., 1995—, dir. higher edn. doc. cognate, coord. PhD in ednl. leadership; sr. fellow, dir. tech. in edn. Am. Assn. State Colls. and Univs., 1995; coord. Nat. Coun. for Accreditation of Tchr. Edn., Washington, 1995—2001; acting dir. PhD program in end. leadership Oakland U., 2003—04. Cons. Butler County Health Ctr., Hamilton, Ohio, 1976-78, Univ. of the North, South Africa Project of the Am. Coun. on Edn., 1995; vis. prof. art therapy Simmons Coll., 1979, Mary Mount Coll., Milw., 1981; mem. corp. adv. com. Corp. Detroit Mag., 1994-95; trustee Nat. Art Edn. Found., 2004—. Sr. editor Studies in Art Edn. jour., 1979-81; mem. editl. adv. bd. Jour. Aesthetic Edn., 1984-90; editor: The Leading Edge, 1986; contbr. articles to profl. jours., chpts. to conf. papers Chmn. com. Commn. on Edn. Excellence, Ohio, 1982-83, Tenn. State Peformance Funding Task Force, 1988, Tenn. State Task Force on Minority Tchrs., 1988; reviewer art curriculum N.Y. Bd. Edn., 1985; mem. supt. search com. Chattanooga Pub. Schs., 1987-88; mem. Chattanooga Met. Coun., 1987-88, Chattanooga Ballet Bd., 1986-88, Fund for Excellence in Pub. Edn., 1986-90, Tenn. Aquarium Bd. Advisors, 1989-92, Team Evaluation Ctr. Bd., 1988-90; mem. Strategic Planning Action Team, Chattanooga City Schs., 1987-88, Siskin Hosp. Bd., 1989-92, Blue Ribbon Task Force Pontiac 2010: A New Reality, City of Pontiac Planning Divsn., 1992—; steering com., cultural action bd. Chattanooga, planning com United Way, 1987; Jewish Fedn. Bd., 1986-91; mem. coun. for policy studies Art Edn. Adv. Bd., 1982-91; ex-officio mem. Meadow Brook Theatre Guild, 1992-95; bd. chair Meadow Brook Performing Arts Co., 1992-95; chair World Cup Soccer Edn. Com./Mich. Host Com. 1993-95; bd. dirs. Ptnrs. for Preferred Future, Rochester Cmty. Schs., 1992-95, Traffic Improvement Assn. Oakland County, 1992-95, Oakland County Bus. Roundtable, 1993-95; Rochester C. of C. host com. chair on edn. World Cup, 1992-95; mem. fin. adv. com. Jewish Fedn. Detroit, 1995-97; bd. dirs. United Way Southeastern Mich., 1992-95: bd. dirs. United Way Oakland County, 1992-95, Pontiac 2010: A New Reality, mayor's transition team city/sch. rels. task force: team evaluation leader Dept. of State Am. Univ. Bulgaria, 1995; bd. trustees Cohn's & Colitis Found., 1996-97; trustee Nat. Art Edn. Found., 2004—; mem. steering com. Nat. Forum Access to Democracy Project, 2004. Am. Coun. on Edn. and Mellon fellow Miami U., 1978-79; recipient Cracking the Glass Ceiling award Pontiac Area Urban League, 1992. Fellow Nat. Art Edn. Assn. (disting.); mem. Nat. Coun. Profs. of Ednl. Adminstrn. (technology com., 2000-03), Am. Assn. Colls. for Tchr. Edn. (com. chair 1982-85), Am. Art Therapy Assn. (registered), Nat. Art Edn. Assn. Women's Caucus (founder, pres. 1976-78, McFee award 1986), Am. Assn. State Colls. and Univs. (com. profl. devel. 1993-95, state rep. 1994-95), Econ. Club Detroit (bd. dirs. 1992-95), Rotary Club, Great Lakes Yacht Club (social chmn. 1996-97, ground chmn., bd. dirs. 1997-98), Phi Delta Kappa (Leadership award 1985), Nat. Assn. Profs. of Edn. Adminstrn. (com. chair 1998-), Great Lakes Yacht Club, 1995 (bd. dir. 1996-1998). Avocation: sailing. Home: 10471 Scout Trail White Lake MI 48386 Office: Oakland U 475 Education Bldg Rochester MI 48309-4423 Office Phone: 248-370-3059. Business E-Mail: packard@oakland.edu.

PACKENHAM, RICHARD DANIEL, lawyer; b. Newton, Pa., June 23, 1953; s. John Richard and Mary Margaret (Maroney) P.; m. Susan Patricia Smillie, Aug. 20, 1983. BA, Harvard U., 1975; JD, Boston Coll., 1978; LLM in Taxation, Boston U., 1985. Bar: Mass. 1978, Conn. 1979, U.S. Dist. Ct. Mass. 1979, U.S. Dist. Ct. Conn. 1979, U.S. Ct. Appeals (1st cir.) 1981, U.S. Supreme Ct. 1985. Staff atty. Conn. Superior Ct., 1978-79; ptnr. McGrath & Kane, Boston, 1979-94, Packenham, Schmidt & Federico, Boston, 1994—. Mem. ABA, Mass. Bar Assn., Conn. Bar Assn., Boston Bar Assn., Mass CLE (faculty). Clubs: Harvard (Boston). Democrat. Roman Catholic. Home: 1062 North St Walpole MA 02081-2307 Office: Packenham Schmidt & Federico 10 St James Ave Boston MA 02116 Office Phone: 617-692-0021.

PACKER, BOYD K. church official; s. Ira Wright and Emma Jensen Packer. BA, MA, U State; PhD, Brigham Young U. Asst. to Twelve Ch. of Jesus Christ of Latter-Day Saints, 1961—70, Apostle, Quorum of the Twelve, 1970—, former pres. New England Mission, former supr. of Seminaries, acting pres. Quorum of the Twelve, 1994, 1995. Pilot, PTO, WWII. Office: LDS Church 50 E South Temple Salt Lake City UT 84150-0001

PACKER, KAREN GILLILAND, cancer patient educator, researcher; b. Washington, Apr. 27, 1940; d. Theodore Redmond and Evelyn Alice (Johnson) Gilliland; m. Allan Richard Packer, Sept. 27, 1962; 1 child, Charles Allan. Student, Duke U., 1957-59, U. Ky., 1959-60, 61-62, U. P.R. Sch. Medicine, 1960-61. Genetics researcher U. Ky., Lexington, 1959-60, 61-62; biologist Melpar Inc., Nat. Cancer Inst., Springfield, Va., 1964-66; rsch. assoc., epidemiology rsch. ctr. U. Iowa Coll. Medicine, Iowa City, 1981-85; founder, dir. Marshalltown (Iowa) Cancer Support Group, 1987—. Mem. County Health Planning Commn., Marshalltown, 1989-96; mem. adv. bd. Cmty. Svcs. Marshalltown, 1990—; v.p. Cmty. Svcs. Coun., Marshalltown, 1992-96, pres. 1996-97; mem. Marshall County Bd. of Health, 1996—. Editor The Group Gazette, 1988—. Bd. dirs. 1st United Ch. Christ, Hampton, Va., 1973-75; corr. sec. DAR, Marshalltown, 1988-92; chmn. cancer and rsch. aux. VFW, Marshalltown, 1990—; chmn. Marshall County Commn. Aging, 1999—, sec., 2000—. Recipient Leadership award Marshalltown Area C. of C., 1988, Spl. recognition Nat. Coalition for Cancer Survivorship, 1990, Iowa Senate 1995, 1st place in state award Cmty. Cancer Edn. VFW Aux., 1990-98, Nat. Vol. Hero of Yr. award Coping Mag., 1995; Genetics Rsch. grantee NSF, 1959-60, NIH, 1961-62. Mem. AAAS, Nat. Guard Bur. Officers Wives Club (publ. editor 1965-68), Nat. Alliance Breast Cancer Orgns., Nat. Cancer Registrars Assn., Iowa Cancer Registrars Assn., N.Y. Acad. Scis. Mem. Congregational Ch. Achievements include establishment of regional orgn. for cancer info. and edn. Home and Office: 1401 Fairway Dr Marshalltown IA 50158-3825

PACKER, KATHERINE HELEN, retired library educator; b. Toronto, Ont., Can., Mar. 20, 1918; d. Cleve Alexander and Rosa Ruel (Dibblee) Smith; m. William A. Packer, Sept. 27, 1941; 1 dau., Marianne Katherine. BA, U. Toronto, 1941; A.M.L.S., U. Mich., 1953; PhD, U. Md., 1975. Cataloguer William L Clements Library, U. Mich., 1953-55, U. Man. (Can.) Library, Winnipeg, 1956-59; cataloguer U. Toronto Library, 1959-63; asst. prof. Faculty Library Sci., 1967-75, asso. prof., 1975-78, prof., dean, 1979-84, prof. emeritus, 1984—. Head cataloguer York U. Library, Toronto, 1963-64; chief librarian Ont. Coll. Edn., Toronto, 1964-67. Author: Early American School Books, 1954. Mem. property tax working group Ont. Fair Tax Commn., 1991-92; mem. assessment reform working group City of Toronto, 1992-97. Recipient Disting. Alumnus award U. Mich., 1981. Mem.: Ret. Academics and Librarians at U. of Toronto, U. of Toronto Faculty Assn., Ex Libris Assn., Phi Kappa Phi. Home: 53 Gormley Ave Toronto ON Canada M4V 1Y9 Office: U Toronto Fac Info Studies 140 Saint George St Toronto ON Canada M5S 3G6 E-mail: packer@interlog.com.

PACKER, MARK BARRY, lawyer, financial consultant, foundation official; b. Phila., Sept. 18, 1944; s. Samuel and Eve (Devine) P.; m. Donna Elizabeth Ferguson (div. 1994); children: Daniel Joshua, Benjamin Dov, David Johannes; m. Helen Margaret (Jones) Klinedinst, July, 1995. AB magna cum laude, Harvard U., 1965, LLB, 1968. Bar: Wash. 1969, Mass. 1971. Assoc. Ziontz, Pirtle & Fulle, Seattle, 1968-70; pvt. practice Bellingham, Wash., 1972—. Bd. dirs., corp. sec. BMJ Holdings (formerly No. Sales Co., Inc.), 1977—; trustee No. Sales Profit Sharing Plan, 1977—; bd. dirs. Whatcom State Bank, 1995-98. Mem. Bellingham Planning and Devel. Commn., 1975-84, chmn., 1977-81, mem. shoreline subcom., 1976-82, capital improvements adv. com., 1999-01; mem. Bellingham Mcpl. Arts Commn., 1986-91, landmark rev. bd., 1987-91; chmn. Bellingham campaign United Jewish Appeal, 1979-90; bd. dirs. Whatcom Cmty. Coll. Found., 1989-92; trustee, chmn. program com. Bellingham Pub. Sch. Found., 1991-98, Heavy Culture classic lit. group, 1991—, Jewish studies group, 1993—; trustee Kenneth L. Kellar Found., 1995—; mng. trustee Bernard M. & Audrey Jaffe Found.; Torah reader; pres. Congregation Eytz Chaim, Bellingham, 1998-2000. Recipient Blood Donor award ARC, 1979, 8-Gallon Pin, 1988, Mayor's Arts award City of Bellingham, 1993. Mem. Wash. State Bar Assn. (sec. dispute resolution, real property, probate and trust, com. law examiners 1992-94). Office: PO Box 1151 Bellingham WA 98227-1151 Office Phone: 360-671-1500. Business E-Mail: Packer@nas.com.

PACKER, REKHA DESAI, lawyer; b. N.Y.C., Apr. 20, 1955; d. Rajanikant C. and Santosh (Nagpaul) Desai; m. Michael Benjamin Packer, Aug. 11, 1979. AB magna cum laude, Harvard U., 1976, JD, 1979. Bar: Mass. 1979, U.S. Dist. Ct. Mass. 1979, U.S. Tax. Ct. 1980. Assoc. Gaston & Snow, Boston, 1979-87, ptnr., 1987-91; sr. ptnr. Hale and Dorr, Boston, 1991-96; tax dir. Pricewaterhouse Coopers LLP, 1997-99; ptnr. Stradley, Ronon, Stevens & Young, LLP, Phila., 1999—. Speaker Fed. Tax Inst., 1987—, World Trade Inst., 1986—. Mem. Internat. Bar Assn. (mem. com. on investment cos., funds and trusts 1989—), ABA (mem. com. on regulated investment cos., labor law sect. 1986—, com. on U.S. activities of foreigners 1988—), Boston Bar Assn. (labor law sect. 1987—, co-chmn. internat. tax. com. 1987-89), Phi Beta Kappa. Office: Stradley Ronon Stevens & Young LLP 2600 1 Commerce Sq Philadelphia PA 19103-7098

PACKER, ROGER JOSEPH, neurologist, neuro-oncologist; b. Chgo., May 14, 1951; s. Harry and Mania (Kelmanowski) P.; m. Bernice Ruth Cizek, Mar. 28, 1976; children: Michael Joseph, Zehava Sarah. MB, Northwestern U., 1973, MD, 1976. Resident pediatrics Cin. (Ohio) Childrens Hosp., 1976-78; fellow child neurology Children's Hosp. Phila., Pa., 1978-81, attending neurologist, 1981-89; prof. neurology and pediatrics U. Pa., Phila., 1981-89; chmn. neurology Childrens Nat. Med. Ctr., Washington, 1989—, exec. dir. Ctr. for Neurosci. and Behavioral Medicine, 1999—, prin. investigator Pediat. Brain Tumor Consoritum, 1999; prof. neurology and pediatrics George Washington U., Washington, 1989—; clin. prof. neurology Georgetown U., Washington, 1992—; clin. prof. neurosurgery U. Va., Charlottesville, Va., 1993—. Chmn. brain tumor strategy group Childrens Cancer Group, Arcadia, Calif., 1989—, chmn. neurosci. com.; mem. adv. com. Neurofibromatosis, Inc. Author: New Trends in Neuro-Oncology, 1991; contbr. chpts. to books and articles to profl. jours. Grantee NIH, Am. Cancer Inst., others. Fellow Am. Acad. Pediatrics, Am. Acad. Neurology (chair sci. selection 1992—, chair neuro-oncology 1981), Child Neurology Soc. (chief liaison health plan reform 1991—); mem. N.Am. Brain Tumor Coalition Bd., Nat. Neurofibromatosis Found. (sci. bd., clin. care adv. bd.), Soc. for Neuro-Oncology (bd. dirs.), Childhood Brain Tumor Found. (sci. adv. bd.). Avocation: sports. Office: Childrens Nat Med Ctr 111 Michigan Ave NW Washington DC 20010-2916

PACKER, SAMUEL, ophthalmologist; b. N.Y.C., Jan. 26, 1941; s. Frank and Thelma (Miller) P.; m. Donna Ann Samborsky, May 24, 1957; children: Heidi, Adam, Marisa, Andrew. BA, NYU, 1962; MD, SUNY, Bklyn., 1966. Diplomate Am. Bd. Ophthalmology. Intern Kings County Hosp., Bklyn., 1966-67; resident in internal medicine Yale-New Haven Hosp., 1967-71; instnl. rev. bd. North Shore U. Cornell U. Med. Coll., Manhasset, N.Y., 1975—, med. ethics com., 1986—, chmn., 1986-92; chmn. dept. ophthalmology North Shore U. Hosp./NYU Sch. Medicine, Manhasset, 1989—. Dir. North Shore U. Hosp. Eye Surgery Ctr., Syosset, N.Y., 1996—. Contbr. numerous articles to profl. jours. Lt. comdr. USN, 1971-73. Fellow N.Y. Acad. Medicine; mem. Am. Acad. Ophthalmology (ethics com. 1990—, vice chair 1996-2000, chair 2001—), N.Y. State Ophthal. Soc. (pres. 1998—), L.I. Ophthal. Soc. (pres. 1991), Nassau Acad. Medicine (chmn. sect. ophthalmology 1987-88, bd. dirs. 1994—, pres. 1996-97), Nassau County Med. Soc. (comm. and media com., bylaws com. 1991—, sec. 1992-93), Med. Soc. State N.Y. (sci. adv. 1985-92, bioethics. com. 1993—, rules com. 1994, chmn. rules com. 1995), N.Y. State Ophthal. Soc. (bd. dirs. 1988—, pres.-elect 1996-97, pres. 1998-99), The Lions Eye Bank for L.I. (exec. dir. 1986—). Office: 600 Northern Blvd Great Neck NY 11021-5200

PACKER, ZZ (ZUWENA), writer, literature educator; b. Chgo., Jan. 12, 1973; d. Rose; m. Michael Boros, 2001. BA, Yale U., 1994; MA in Creative Writing, Johns Hopkins U., 1995; MFA, U. Iowa, 1999. Tchr. various pub. schs., Balt.; Jones lectr. Stanford U.; vis. asst. prof. Writers' Workshop U. Iowa, 2003—04. Author: (short stories) Drinking Coffee Elsewhere, 2003. Recipient Ms. Giles Whiting award, 1999, Bellingham Rev. award, 1999; grantee, Rona Jaffe Writers Found., 1997; Wallace Stegner and Truman Capote fellow, Stanford U. Office: Univ Iowa Writers Workshop 102 Dey House 507 N Clinton St Iowa City IA 52242-1000*

PACKERT, G(AYLA) BETH, retired lawyer; b. Corpus Christi, Tex., Sept. 25, 1953; d. Gilbert Norris and Virginia Elizabeth (Pearce) P.; m. James Michael Hall, Jan. 1, 1974 (div. 1985); m. Richard Christopher Burke, July 18, 1987; children: Christopher Geoffrey Makepeace Burke Packert, Jeremy Eliot Marvell Packert Burke. BA, La. Tech. U., 1973; postgrad., U. Ill., 1975—81, JD, 1985; MA, U. Ark., 1976. Bar: Ill. 1985, U.S. Dist. Ct. (no. dist.) Ill. 1985, U.S. Ct. Appeals (7th cir.) 1987, Va. 1988, U.S. Dist. Ct. (we. dist.) Va. 1989. Assoc. Jenner & Block, Chgo., 1985—88; law clk. U.S. Dist. Ct. Va. (we. dist.), Danville, 1988—89; asst. commonwealth atty. Commonwealth of Va., Lynchburg, 1989—95; pvt. practice Lynchburg, 1995—2002; ret., 2002. Notes and comments editor U. Ill. Law Rev., 1984-85. Mem. Phi Beta Kappa. Home: 3900 Faculty Dr Lynchburg VA 24501-3110

PACKHAM, MARIAN AITCHISON, biochemistry educator; b. Toronto, Ont., Can., Dec. 13, 1927; d. James and Clara Louise (Campbell) A.; m. James Lennox Packham, June 25, 1949; children: Neil Lennox, Janet Melissa. BA, U. Toronto, 1949, PhD, 1954; DSc honoris causa, Ryerson Poly. U., 1997. Sr. fellow dept. biochemistry U. Toronto, 1954-58, lectr. dept. biochemistry, 1958-63, 66-67; rsch. assoc. dept. physiol. scis. Ont. Vet. Coll., U. Guelph, 1963-65; rsch. assoc. blood and cardiovascular disease rsch. unit U. Toronto, 1965-66, asst. prof. dept. biochemistry, 1967-72, assoc. prof., 1972-75, prof., 1975—, acting chmn. dept. biochemistry, 1983. Contbr. articles to profl. jours. Royal Soc. Can. fellow, 1991; recipient Lt. Govs. Silver medal Victoria Coll., 1949; co-recipient J. Allyn Taylor Internat. prize in Medicine, 1988. Mem.: Can. Soc. Biochemistry and Molecular and Cellular Biology, Can. Atherosclerosis Soc., Internat. Soc. Thrombosis and Haemostasis, Can. Soc. Clin. Investigation, Can. Soc. Hematology, Am. Soc. Hematology. Office: U Toronto Dept Biochemistry Toronto ON Canada M5S 1A8

PACKMAN, AARON IAN, environmental engineer, educator; b. St. Louis, Mo., Sept. 19, 1969; s. Jerrold Barry and Bella Ruth Packman; m. Jennifer Suzanne Grimmer; 1 child, Ariel Rose. BSME, Wash. U., St. Louis, 1991; MS, Calif. Inst. of Tech., Pasadena, 1992, PhD, 1997. Asst. prof. Drexel U., Phila., 1997—2000, Northwestern U., Evanston, Ill., 2000—. Recipient Career award, NSF, 1999—2004; NDSEG Grad. Fellow, Office of Naval Rsch., 1991—94, Myers Fellow, Wash. U., 1987—91. Achievements include research in stream-subsurface exchange; fine sediment dynamics in streams; multi-phase contaminant transport. Office: Northwestern U 2145 Sheridan Rd Evanston IL 60208

PACOR, VICTOR J. diversified financial services company executive; MBA, Cornell U. Sr. v.p. Audio Divsns. JVC Co. Am.; with Sony Electronics, 1994—2004; pres. D&M Holdings, Suffern, NY, 2004—, COO, 2004—.*

PACTER, PAUL ALLAN, accounting standards researcher; b. N.Y.C., Jan. 26, 1943; s. Bernard David and Hilda Libby (Margolies) P. BS, Syracuse U., 1964; PhD, Mich. State U., 1967. C.P.A., N.Y. Asst. prof. N.Y.U., 1967-69; rsch. mgr. KPMG, N.Y.C., 1969-73; exec. dir. Fin. Acctg. Standards Bd., Stamford, Conn., 1973-84; commr. fin. City of Stamford, 1984-90; prof. acctg., MBA program U. Conn., Stamford, 1990-96, adj. prof., 1982-84. Adj. prof. NYU, 1982-84; project cons. Fin. Acctg. Standards Bd., 1990-96, fellow Internat. Acctg. Standards Com., London, 1993-2000, dir. Deloitte Touche Tohmatsu, Hong Kong, 2000—. Consulting editor The Jour. of Accountancy, 1968-73 Chmn. Stamford Commn. on Human Rights, 1977-84, Stamford Film Commn., 1984-90; mem. Charter Revision Commn., Stamford, 1979-80, Gov.'s Tourism Coun., Conn., 1984-90, acctg. adv. coun. U. Conn., 1984-90; pres. N. Stamford Dem. Club, 1983-84, treas., 1987-95; dir. Stamford Coliseum Authority, 1984-90; vice chmn. govtl. acctg. stds. adv. coun., 1984-91; vice chmn. China Beijing Ctr. for Asia-Pacific Fin. and Acctg. Rsch., 2000—; treas. Conn. Tourism Assn., 1987-90, North Stamford Assn., 1993-94; bd. dirs. Stamford Ctr. for the Arts, United Way Stamford, Stamford Theatre Works, Stamford Cmty. Fund, Housing Devel. Fund of Fairfield County. Earhart Found. fellow Mich. State U., 1966-67; U.S. Office of Edn. grantee, 1967 Mem. AICPA, Am. Acctg. Assn. (coun.), N.Y. State Soc. CPA's, Beta Gamma Sigma, Beta Alpha Psi. Jewish. Office: Deloitte Touche Tohmatsu 111 Connaught Rd Central Hong Kong Hong Kong E-mail: paupacter@deloitte.com.hk.

PACUSKA, ALISON BRANDI, Russian studies professional; b. Falmouth, Mass., May 23, 1974; d. Stephen C. and Margaret Anne (Nightingale) P. BA Internat. Studies, Am. U., 1996; MA in Russian Studies, George Washington U., 1999. Relocation asst. United Jewish Appeal Found., White Flint, Md., 1993—94; journalist First of Sept., Moscow, 1994; translator faculty of journalism Moscow State U., 1994; rsch. asst. Kennan Inst. for Advanced Russian Studies, Washington, 1995—96; logistics specialist Metrica, Inc., Arlington, Va., 1997—2000; litigation paralegal Armstrong, Westerman & Hattori, LLP, Washington, 2000—. Presenter U. Va. Grad. Symposium in Russian Studies, 1999. Contbr. articles to newspapers. Vol. Dem. Nat. Conv., Washington, 1993-94; participant CAAPS Peace Studies Student Conf., 1996. Presdl. scholar Am. U., 1992-94. Mem. Acad. Polit. Sci. Avocations: martial arts, music, marathons. Home: Apt 202 14134 Castle Blvd Silver Spring MD 20904-4662

PADBERG, DANIEL IVAN, agricultural economics educator, researcher; b. Summersville, Mo., Nov. 9, 1931; s. Christopher Edward and Ruth (Badgley) P.; m. Mildred Frances True, Aug. 5, 1956 (dec. Dec. 15, 1997); children: Susan Elizabeth, Jean Ellen, Carol Natalie; m. Sarah O'Brien, Dec. 30, 1998. BS, U. Mo., 1953, MS, 1955; PhD, U. Calif.-Berkeley, 1961. Asst. prof. Ohio State U., Columbus, 1961-65; project leader Nat. Commn. on Food Mktg., Washington, 1965-66; prof. Cornell U., Ithaca, N.Y., 1966-75; head dept. agrl. econs. U. Ill., Urbana, 1975-81; dean U. Mass., Amherst, 1981-83, prof. agrl. econs., 1983; cons. Farm Credit System, 1983-84; head dept. agrl. econs. Tex. A&M U., College Station, 1984-90, prof., 1990-95, ret., 1995; Fulbright chair internat. econs. U. Tuscia, Viterbo, Italy, 1997. Mem. White House Task Force on Farmer Bargaining, Washington, 1968; mem. food and nutrition bd. Nat. Acad. Sci., Washington, 1974-77; cons. Office Tech. Assessment, Washington, 1975-82; pres. Am. Agrl. Econs. Assn., 1987-88; exec. dir. Food and Agrl. Mktg. Consortium, 1993-98; chmn. Nat. Adv. Com. on Concentration in Agr l., 1996. Author: Economics of Food Retailing, 1968, Todays Food Broker, 1971; editorial council: Am. Jour. Agrl. Econs., 1970-73, Jour. Consumer Affairs, 1974-76. Pres. council First Congregational Ch., Ithaca, 1971-72. Served to lt. (j.g.) USN, 1955-58, PTO. Consumer Research Inst. grantee, 1970; FDA grantee, 1971; USDA/NRI grantee, 1992; Simon research fellow U. Manchester, Eng., 1972-73 Mem. Am. Agrl. Econs. Assn. (Quality of Discovery award 1975, Quality of Communication in Research award 1977, chmn. awards 1979-80) Home: 1405 Westlake Blvd Palm Harbor FL 34683 Personal E-mail: danpad7@hotmail.com. *Not always right, but never in doubt.*

PADBERG, HELEN SWAN, violinist; b. Shawnee, Okla. d. Frank P. and Birdie B. (Rudell) Swan; m. Frank Padberg, Feb. 6, 1943; children: Frank, Kristen. AA, Stephens Coll., 1938; MusB, U. Okla., 1940; MusM, Northwestern U., 1941; student, Jacques Gordon. Solo performances and concerts, 1932—; mem. faculty string quartet and symphony soloist Stephens Coll., 1937-38; violinist Oklahoma City Symphony Summer Concerts, 1940; soloist Northwestern U. Symphony, 1941; violinist USO Tours World War II, 1941-43; mem. Nat. Orchestral Assn. and Am. Youth Orch., N.Y.C., 1944-46; tchr. strings Maywood (Ill.), 1946-47; asst. concertmaster West Suburban Symphony, Chgo., 1947-48; mem. Chgo. Women's Symphony, Chgo. Civic Orch. and chamber music groups, 1947-51; violinist Ark. Piano Trio, 1952-58; concertmaster Ark. Symphony and Little Rock Philharm., 1953-57, Marjorie Lawrence TV Series, 1953-54; pvt. tchr. violin Little Rock, 1953-66; accompanist and performer on piano, harp. Pres. Ark. Med. Soc. Alliance, 1962-63, historian, 1963-94. Co-founder Little Rock Chamber Music Soc., 1954; pres. bd. dirs. Vis. Nurse Assn. of Pulaski County, Ark., 1967-69; bd. dirs. Internat. Visitors Ctr., Chgo., 1988—, Stephens Coll. Alumna Assn. Bd.; elder, trustee Presbyn. ch. Mem.: Mu Phi Epsilon, Internat. Women Assocs. (pres. 1988—91), Am. Opera Soc. Chgo. (v.p. and program chmn. 1981—82, pres. 1984—87), Am. Opera Soc. (historian 1987—), Am. Fedn. Musicians, Chgo. Harp Soc. (sec. 1979—84), Am. Harp Soc., English Spkg. Union (Chgo. br., bd. govs. 1997—), Musicians' Club of Women (Chgo., bd. dirs.), Women's Athletic Club of Chgo., Aesthetic Club (pres. Little Rock), Pi Beta Phi (pres. Little Rock Alumnae Club), Pi Kappa Lambda. Home: 175 E Delaware Pl Chicago IL 60611-1756

PADDEN, ANTHONY ALOYSIUS, JR., federal government official; b. Kearny, N.J., Apr. 3, 1949; s. Anthony Aloysius and Harriet Margaret (Dolan) Padden. PBA, Fairleigh Dickinson U., 1970, MA in Pub. Adminstrn., 1980;

postgrad., U. Tenn. Sch. Law, 1970. Employment interviewer N.J. Dept. Labor, Trenton, 1970—76, prin. procedure analyst, 1976—79; nat. procedure coord. Interstate Compendium Employment Svc. Activities Project, Trenton, 1979—80; mgmt. analyst Dept. Justice, Washington, 1980—83; chief clk. ct. U.S. Immigration Ct., Falls Church, Va., 1983—. Adj. faculty Nat. Judicial Coll., Reno, 1998—2003; cons., Dumfries, Va., 1978—. Author: Dept. Labor tech. report, 1980; contbr. and editor: other profl. studies. Presdl. mgmt. intern, 1980, Logan Chambers grantee, Internat. Assn. Pers. in Employment Security, 1979. Mem.: Pi Alpha Alpha (Adminstr. of Yr. 1991). Roman Catholic. Office: US Dept Justice Exec Office for Immigration Rev 5107 Leesburg Pike Ste 2545 Falls Church VA 22041-3234

PADDEN, PRESTON, broadcast executive; b. Washington, D.C., Nov. 26, 1948; m. Barbara Padden; 3 children. Grad., U. Md.; JD, George Washington U. Asst. gen. counsel Metromedia Inc.; pres. Assn. of Ind. TV Sta. Inc.; with News Corp.; chmn., CEO Am. Sky Broadcasting, 1996; pres. ABC TV Network, N.Y.C., 1997-98; exec. v.p. govt. rels. The Walt Disney Co., Washington, 1998—. Bd. dirs. The Advt. Coun., Inc. Mem. Fedr. Comm. Bar Assn., Internat. Radio TV Soc. (bd. dirs.). Office: The Walt Disney Co 1150 17th St NW Ste 400 Washington DC 20036-4622

PADDOCK, ANTHONY CONAWAY, financial consultant; b. Paris, July 9, 1935; came to U.S., 1940; s. H. Watson and Mildred V. (Decker) P.; m. Wendy E. Brewer, Apr. 24, 1971. AB, Harvard U., 1957, JD, 1960; MBA, Columbia U., 1961. Bar: N.Y. 1961. Assoc. investment bank Merrill Lynch & Co., N.Y.C., 1961-69; v.p. Chase Manhattan Bank, N.Y.C., 1970-78, Standard Rsch. Cons., N.Y.C., 1978-84; mng. dir. Benchmark Valuation Cons., N.Y.C., 1978-84; prin. KPMG Peat Marwick, N.Y.C., 1984-96; mng. dir. Empire Valuation Cons., N.Y.C., 1997—. Adj. prof. NYU, 1979-90. Trustee Sun Capital Advisors Trust, 1998—. Mem. Assoc. for Corp. Growth, Inst. Mgmt. Cons. (cert.). Episcopalian. Home: 14 N Chatsworth Ave Larchmont NY 10538-2142 Office: Empire Valuation Cons 350 5th Ave Ste 5513 New York NY 10118-5513 Office Phone: 212-714-0122. Business E-Mail: acpaddock@empireval.com.

PADEN, HARRY, municipal official; children: Shahara, Angela. Student, Am. U., 1971-73, Essex County (N.J.) Coll., 1981-83. Dir. social svcs. Unity Freedom Bapt. Ch., Newark, 1989-92; aide to freeholder pres. Essex County, 1992-96; code enforcement officer Township of Irvington, N.J., 1992-94, chief field rep. Office Neighborhood Preservation, 1994-98. Host, prodr. (cable T.V. program) Parent to Parent; contbg. writer Jersey Girl mag.; columnist Irvington Herald. Chmn. Irvington juvenile conf. com. Superior Ct.; v.p., former pres. PTA Irvington H.S.; program coord. Neighborhood Preservation, 1998—; parent coord. Essex County PTA; ednl. liaison mayor of Irvington; aide Irvington West Ward Council; celebrity reader Essex and Hudson County chpts. United Way; deacon, adminstrv. asst. to pastor Unity Freedom Bapt. Ch., Newark; mem. Irving Bd. Edn. Named Irvington African Am. Male of Yr., 1994, One of 100 Most Influential in State, City News, 1997; recipient Pinnacle award Being Single mag., 1995, Spl. Civil award Irvington C. of C. Home: 31 Civic Sq W Apt 14 Irvington NJ 07111-2425

PADEN, JOHN BRUCE, community resource executive; b. St. Louis, Aug. 19, 1944; s. John Milton Paden and Erma Maye Wheeler; m. Kristin Alexander, Nov. 17, 1983; 1 child, Rebecca Margaret. BSBA, U. Mo., 1971, MBA, 1973; cert. networks and telecom., Johnson County C.C., Overland Pk., Kans., 1994. Sr. sales exec. Xerox Corp., St. Louis, 1973-78; v.p. investments Drexel Burnham Lambert Merrill Lynch, Overland Pk., 1978-87; regional sales dir. Mark Twain Bankshares, Kansas City, Mo., 1987-88; pres., owner 1st Capital Source, Overland Pk., 1988-93; instr. Johnson County C.C., Overland Pk., 1993-96; dir. info. mgmt. St. Mary Coll., Leavenworth, Kans., 1996-2001; CEO Cmty. Resource Network, Kansas City, 2001—. Mem. adv. bd. info. tech. Johnson County C.C., Overland Pk., 1998—. Avocations: flying, skiing. Home: 12437 S Ellsworth St Olathe KS 66062-4970 Office: Cmty Resource Network 106 W Eleventh St Ste 110 Kansas City MO 64105 E-mail: bigcat39@excite.com.

PADEN, LARRY J. consulting electronics engineer, lawyer; b. Tulsa, Mar. 21, 1957; s. Jackson Taylor Jr. and Mary Lois (Dilday) P.; m. Carol Denise McAlister, July 28, 1979 (div. 2000); children: John Lawrence, Zachary Taylor, Katherine Elizabeth, Robert Nathaniel. BSEE, Okla. State U., 1979, MEE, 1980, PhD in Elec. Engring., 1991; JD, Oklahoma City U., 1995. Cert. electromagnetic compliance engr.; registered profl. engr., Okla.; bar: Okla. 1996. NSF rsch. asst. dept. physics U. Tex., Arlington, 1977; engring. intern Amoco Prodn. Rsch. Ctr., Tulsa, 1978-79; tchg. asst. Sch. Elec. and computer Engring. Okla. State U., Stillwater, 1979, grad. rsch. asst., 1979-80, rsch. asst. Consortium for Enhancement Well Log Data, 1983-85; devel. engr. AT&T Western Elec., Oklahoma City, 1980-83, 85-90; patent law clk. McCarthy & Assocs., Oklahoma City, 1993-95; electronics, computer engring.-software cons. profl. engr. Aaden Engring., LLC, Broken Arrow, Okla., 1996—2000; electronics engr. Flight Safety Internat., 2000—02. Vis. instr. computer arch. U. Okla. Sch. Elec. Engring. and Computer Sci., Norman, 1989, 91; cons. profl. engr. in electronics U.S. Post Office Maintenance Tech. Support Ctr., Norman, 1996-2000, Uptown Thrift Store, 1997-2002; ILS electronics engr. FlightSafety Internat. Simulation Sys. Divsn., Broken Arrow, Okla.; adj. prof. calculus Rogers State U., 2002—; elec. engr. Grand River Dam Authority, Pryor, Okla., 2003—. Contbr. articles to profl. jours.; newsletter editor Royal Oaks Neighborhood assn., 1988-92. Quality control sec., pres. Jr. Achievement, Tulsa, 1972-75; pres. Vocat. Indsl. Clubs of Am., Sand Springs, Okla., 1973-75; mem. Cherokee Nation, Tahlequah, Okla., 1986—; bd. dirs. Royal Oaks Neighborhood Assn., Oklahoma City, 1988-92; mem. Civic Music Assn., Oklahoma City, 1995-2001, bd. dirs., 1998-2001. Okla. State U. Regents Disting. scholar, 1975, Sigma Xi scholar, 1976, Albrecht Naeter scholar, 1977. Mem. ABA, IEEE (Oklahoma City sect. vice chmn. 1994-95, chmn. 1995-98, newsletter editor 1994-97), Okla. Soc. Profl. Engrs. (pres. Okla. City chpt. 1999-2000), Am. Assn. Individual Investors (life), Internat. Soc. for Philos. Enquiry, Citizens Police Acad. Alumni Assn., Intertel, Masons (master of ceremonies in 19th deg.), Civic Music Assn. (bd. dirs. 1998-2001), Eta Kappa Nu. Democrat. Baptist. Avocations: swimming, hiking, amateur radio, tennis, aikedo. Office: Aaden Engineering LLC 2612 S Dogwood Ave Broken Arrow OK 74012-7347 Home: 2612 S Dogwood Ave Broken Arrow OK 74012-7347 Office Phone: 918-825-0280 7709. E-mail: Aaden@aol.com.

PADEN, WILLIAM D. French literature educator; b. Lawrence, Kans., June 20, 1941; s. William D. and Dagmar Parr Paden; m. Frances Freeman, June 27, 1973; children: Catherine Miriam, William Freeman. PhD, Yale U., 1971. Prof. French Northwestern U., Evanston, Ill., 1968—. Author: Introduction to Old Occitan, 1998; editor: Poems of the Troubadour Bertran de Born, 1986, Medieval Pastourelle, 1987; editor: (contbr.) Voice of the Trobairitz, 1989, Future of the Middle Ages, 1994, Medieval Lyric: Genres in Historical Context, 2000. Fellow NEH, 1976—77, 1987—88; grantee Dir., NEH Inst., 1995. Mem.: MLA, Am. Assn. Tchrs. of French (prix du chapitre 1996—97), Medieval Acad. of Am., Société Guillaume IX (pres. 1985—92). Office: Dept French and Italian Northwestern U Evanston IL 60208-2204 E-mail: wpaden@northwestern.edu.

PADEREWSKI, SIR CLARENCE JOSEPH, architect; b. Cleve., July 23, 1908; BArch, U. Calif., 1932. Chief draftsman Sam W. Hamill, 1939-44; with Heitschmidt-Matcham-Blanchard-Gill & Hamill, 1943; prin. C.J. Paderewski, 1944-48; pres. Paderewski, Mitchell, Dean & Assoc., Inc. (and predecessor), San Diego, 1948-78. Instr. adult edn. San Diego city schs., 1939-44, U. Calif. extension div., 1945, 56; lectr. in field. Prin. works include Charactron Labs, Gen. Dynamics Corp., Convair, S.D., 1954, South Bay Elem. Schs., S.D., 1948-74; additions to El Cortez Hotel; including first exterior passenger glass elevator in the world and New Travolator Motor Hotel, S.D., 1959, Palomar Coll., San Marcos, 1951-80, San Diego County U. Gen. Hosp., San Diego Internat. Airport Terminal Bldgs., Fallbrook Elem. Schs., 1948-74, Silver Strand Elem. Sch., Coronado, Tourmaline Terrace Apt. Bldg., San Diego Salvation Army Office Bldg. Mem. adv. bd. Bayside Social Service Center, 1953-75, San Diego Polonia Newspaper, 1994—; mem. San Diego Urban Design Com.; adv. bd. Camp Oliver, 1963—, pres., 1975-76; bd. dirs. San Diego Symphony Orch. Assn., 1954-62, San Diego chpt. ARC, 1971-74; bd. dirs., chmn. coms., pres. San Diego Downtown Assn., 1963—; bd. dirs. Nat. Council Archtl. Registration Bds., 1958-66, bd. dirs. other offices, 1961-64, pres., 1965-66, chmn. internat. relations com., 1967-68, Salvation Army, vice-chmn., 1989, life mem. adv. bd., 1993—. Copernicus Found., 1994—; mem. Calif. Bd. Archtl. Examiners, 1949-61, past pres., commr., 1961—; mem. Nat. Panel Arbitrators, 1953—, Nat. Council on Schoolhouse Constrn.; hon. chmn. Ignacy Jan Paderewski Meml. Com., 1991; adv. bd. S.D. Balboa Park Cmty. Endowment Fund, 1995—. Decorated Knight Order Polonia Restituta, Polish govt. in exile, 1982, recipient Commodore cross, 2002; recipient Award of Merit for San Diego County Gen. Hosp., San Diego chpt., AIA, 1961, Honor award for San Diego Internat. Airport Terminal, Honor award Portland Cement Co., Golden Trowel award Plastering Inst., 1958-60, 4 awards Masonry Inst., 1961, award Prestressed Concrete Inst., 1976, Outstanding Community Leadership award San Diego Downtown Assn., 1963-65, 80, Polish Engring. award for outstanding arch. and achievement, 2000, Gold award Engring. Soc., 2000, Outstanding INdividual Polish Am. award Polish Ctr. of L.A., 2001. Fellow AIA (pres. San Diego chpt. 1948, 49, bd. dirs. 1947-53, chmn. several coms., spl. award 1977, Calif. Coun. Spl. award 1979, Calif. Coun. Disting. Svc. award 1982, Lifetime Achievement award 2000); mem. San Diego C. of C. (bd. dirs. 1959-62, 64-67), Am. Arbitration Assn. (San Diego adv. coun. 1969—), Sister City Soc. (bd. dirs.), Lions (past pres. Hillcrest Club, Lion of Yr. 1990, fellow internat. found. 1991), Father Serra Club (charter, past pres.), Outboard Boating Club San Diego, Chi Alpha Kappa, Delta Sigma Chi. Home: 2837 Kalmia Pl San Diego CA 92104-5418

PADGET, JOHN E. management professional; b. L.A., Aug. 26, 1948; s. LeRoy and Gladys (Black) P. BA, U. Kans., 1969, postgrad., 1970. Instr. bridge Am. Contract Bridge League, 1971-77; owner Hectors, Kirkland, Wash., 1978-84; producer TV show Sta. 2, Oakland, 1985-88; regional mgr. Keithwood Agy.-Am. Health Care Adv., Pleasanton, Calif., 1991-92; exec. v.p. J. & J. Warren Co., Walnut Creek, Calif., 1991-97; pres. BBH Ltd., 1997—. Pres. BBH Ltd. Author: Winning Style, 1977. Mem. AAAS, Mensa, Internat. Platform Soc. Jewish. Avocations: hiking, reading, travel, internet publishing.

PADGETT, GAIL BLANCHARD, lawyer; b. Douglasville, Ga., Aug. 20, 1949; d. William David and Dorothy Rose (Bennett) P. BA, Ga. State U., 1971, MEd, 1974; JD, Georgetown U., 1981. Bar: Va., Ga., D.C., U.S. Supreme Ct. Tchr. Clayton Co. Bd. Edn., Jonesboro, Ga., 1971-77; spl. asst. to dir. Community Rels Svc., Chevy Chase, Md., 1977-81, gen. counsel, 1981-89, assoc. dir., 1989-96; asst. chief immigration judge U.S. Dept. Justice, Falls Church, Va., 1996—2004, U.S. Immigration Ct., Bradentun, Fla., 2004—. Recipient Disting. Svc. award Atty. Gen. of the U.S., 1992. Home: 9448 Discovery Terrace 102 Bradenton FL 34212 Office: US Immigration Ct 515 11th St West Ste 300 Bradenton FL 34205

PADGETT, GREGORY LEE, lawyer; b. Greenfield, Ind., May 9, 1959; s. William Joseph and Anna Katherine (Hyre) Padgett; m. Ruth Anne Dorworth, June 5, 1982; children: Joshua David, William Joel, Emily Xiao Lei. BA summa cum laude, DePauw U., 1981; JD, Northwestern U., 1984. Bar: Ill., U.S. Dist. Ct. (no. dist.) Ill. 1984, U.S. Ct. Appeals (7th cir.) 1986, Ind. 1988, U.S. Dist. Ct. (no. & so. dists.) Ind. 1988. Assoc. Kirkland & Ellis, Chgo., 1984-88, Baker & Daniels, Indpls., 1988-92; ptnr. Johnson, Lawhead, Buth & Pope, P.C., Indpls., 1992-2000; of counsel Barnes & Thornburg, Indpls., 2000—04; prin. Padgett Law, Indpls., 2004—. Adj. prof. Butler U., 1989-90. Mem. Marion County Prosecutor's Rev. Task Force, Indpls., 1991; pres., bd. dirs. Theatre on the Square, Indpls., 1994-95; mem. coun. Hope Evang. Covenant Ch., 1992-96; bd. dirs. Meridian St. Found., 1994-96; bd. dirs. Ind. Arts Chorale, 2003-. Mem. Ind. State Bar Assn., Indpls. Bar Assn. (exec. com. alternative dispute resolution sect.), Christian Legal Soc., Phi Beta Kappa. Avocations: theatre arts, vocal music, hiking, writing. Office: Padgett Law Ste 230 9000 Keystone Crossing Indianapolis IN 46240 Office Phone: 317-218-0316. Business E-Mail: gp@indianaestatelaw.com.

PADGETT, NANCY WEEKS, law librarian, consultant, lawyer; b. Newberry, S.C., June 3, 1932; d. Price John and Caroline (Weeks) P.; m. David Lazar, Aug. 6, 1953 (dec. May 19, 2002). BS, Northwestern U., 1953; MLS, U. Md., 1972; JD, Georgetown U., 1977. Bar: D.C. 1977. Asst. law libr. U.S. Ct. Appeals for D.C., Washington, 1972—74, supervisory law libr., 1974—84, circuit libr., 1984—. Mem. ALA, D.C. Bar Assn., Am. Assn. Law Librs. Home: 5301 Duvall Dr Bethesda MD 20816-1873 Office: US Ct Appeals for DC Cir Judges' Libr 5518 US Court House Washington DC 20001-5618 Office Phone: 202-216-7396.

PADGETT, RON, writer; b. Tulsa, Okla., June 17, 1942; s. Wayne Merriott Padgett and Lucille Agnes Huey; m. Patricia Ann Mitchell; 1 child, Wayne. BA, Columbia U., 1964. Writer, 1964—; dir. Poetry Project, N.Y.C., 1978—80; tchr. Tchrs. and Writers Collaborative, N.Y.C., 1969—78, publs. dir., 1980—2000, also bd. dirs. Author: (book) Great Balls of Fire, 1969, You Never Know, 2002, Oklahoma Tough, 2003. Named Officier dans l'Ordre des Arts et des Lettres, 2001; recipient poetry fellowship, Guggenheim, 1986, Poetry award, Am. Acad. Arts and Letters, 1999. E-mail: ronpadgettpoet@aol.com.

PADGETT, THOMAS EUGENE, language educator; b. Mountainview, Mo., Oct. 16, 1929; s. Thomas Emory and Alta O'Tiller Padgett; m. Shirley Margaret Morris, June 1, 1952; children: Julie Beth, Becky Sue, Tammy Lynn. BA, Okla. Bapt. U., 1951; MA, U. Tex., 1962; PhD, U. Mo., 1972; LLD (hon.), Southwest Bapt. U., 1988. Tchr. high sch. Mountain View Pub. Schs., Mo., 1960—63; prof. Southwest Bapt. U., Bolivar, 1963—93. Author of poems. Bd. dirs. Friends Libr., Bolivar, 2001, libr. discussion leader, 1995—; lectr. Lucidity Poetry Jour., Eureka Springs, 1996—. Mem.: Mo. State Poetry Soc. (editor, pres., sec. 1998—), Nat. Fedn. State Poetry Socs. (chancellor 2001—03, vice chancellor 1999—2001), 37 Cents (editor 2003—), Second Tuesday (sec. 1995—2003). Republican. Baptist. Avocations: tennis, reading, movies, walking, travel. Home: 523 N Park Pl Bolivar MO 65613-1576 E-mail: tpadgett@microcore.net.

PADILLA, ALFREDO, commissioner; Commr. Bur. Fin. Insts., San Juan, PR, 2002—. Office: Fernandez Juncos Sta San Juan PR 00910

PADILLA, AMADO M. psychologist, adult education educator; s. Manuel S. and Esperanza Padilla; m. Deborah Farrington; children: Diego, Daphne, Rocky. BA, N. Mex.Highlands U., Las Vegas, NM., 1964; MS, Okla.State U., 1966; PhD, U. N. Mex., 1969. Asst. prof. State U. of N.Y., Potsdam, NY, 1969—71, U. Calif., Santa Barbara, Calif., 1971—74; assoc. prof. to full prof. UCLA, 1974—88; prof. Stanford U., Stanford, Calif., 1988—. Dir. Ctr. for Lang. Edn. and Rsch. UCLA, 1985—88; chair com. Lang., Lit., and Culture, Stanford U., 1991—98; cons. Fed. Pub. Defenders on Immigration and Assimilation, 2000—. Author various journ. publications. Mem. various co. organizations, Palo Alto, Calif., 1990—; bd. of trustees Palo Alto Unified Sch. Dist., Palo Alto, Calif., 1993—97. Recipient Disting. Rsch. Award, Am. Edn. Rsch. Assn., 1987, Paul Pimsleur Award, Am. Coun. of Tchr. of Fgn. Lang., 1989, Life Time Achievement Award, Am. Psychol. Assn. Divsn. 45, 1996. Fellow: Am. Psychol. Assn., Am. Assn. Adv. of Sci.; mem.: Am. Edn. Rsch. Assn. Democrat. Roman Catholic. Achievements include founding editor of the Hispanic Journ. of Behavorial Sci. Avocations: jogging, bicycling, hiking, gardening, writing. Home: 830 Tolman Dr Stanford CA 94305-1026

PADILLA, JAMES EARL, lawyer; b. Miami, Fla., Dec. 28, 1953; s. Earl George and Patricia (Bauer) P. BA, Northwestern U., 1975; JD, Duke U., 1978. Bar: Ill. 1978, U.S. Ct. Appeals (5th and 7th cir.) 1978, U.S. Supreme Ct. 1981, Colo. 1982, U.S. Ct. Appeals (10th cir.) 1982, D.C. 1985, N.Y. 1989. Assoc. Mayer, Brown & Platt, Chgo. and Denver, 1978-84, ptnr. Denver, 1985-87, N.Y.C., 1988-96; private investor, 1996—. Contbg. author: Mineral Financing, 1982, Illinois Continuing Legal Education, 1993. Mem. ABA, Ill. Bar Assn., D.C. Bar Assn., Colo. Bar Assn., N.Y. State Bar Assn., Univ. Club of Chgo. Avocation: golf. Office Phone: 847-259-0207. Personal E-mail: james.padilla@comcast.net.

PADILLA, JAMES JEROME, automobile executive; b. Detroit, June 13, 1946; s. David J. and Irene C. (Clos) P.; m. Alice M., Dec. 27, 1968; children: James Jr., Kathryn, Daniel. BSChemE, MS in Engring., U. Detroit, 1969, MA in Econ., 1970. Fuel econ. planning mgr. Ford Motor Co., Dearborn, Mich., 1977-78, engine planning engring. mgr. Detroit, 1979-80, engine controls dept. mgr., 1980-83, exec. engr., powertrain-electronics, 1983-85, chief engr., trim-chassis-elect-emissions, 1985, programs operations mgr., 1990, dir., small cars unit, 1991, exec. dir., engring. and mfg., Jaguar Cars, Ltd., 1992—94, dir., performance luxury vehicle lines, 1994—96, pres., Argentina and Brazil operations, 1996—98, pres. S. Am. operations, group v.p., mfg. and quality, 1999—2001, group v.p., N. Am., 2001—02, exec. v.p., 2002, pres. of the Americas, 2002—04, COO, 2004—, chmn. automotive operations, 2004—; spl. asst. to sec. commerce U.S. Govt., Washington, 1978-79. Bd. dirs. Am. Supplier Inst., Dearborn. Pres. Civic Assn., Canton, Mich., 1972-74, Plymouth (Mich.) Sch. Bd., 1981-84; mem. Plymouth Parish Council, 1980-84, Plymouth Edn. Commn., 1980-85. Served to 2d Lt. USNG, 1970-76. White House fellow U.S. Govt., Washington, 1978-79, fellow, Nat. Acad. Engring., 2001; research grantee Dow Chem. Co., Detroit, 1968-69; recipient Engr. of the Year, Hispanic Engr. Nat. Achievement Awards Conf., 2000. Mem. Soc. Automotive Engrs., Engring. Soc. Detroit. (selection com. U.S. Senate fellows 1982-84, named Outstanding Young Engr. 1980). Roman Catholic.*

PADILLA, MARIO RENÉ, literature educator, writer, actor; b. Detroit, Oct. 4, 1949; s. Marcelino Ramos and Nina Consolata (Macioce) P.; children: Francesca, Miguel, Marcello, Gabriella; m. Christine Jasiorkowski; stepchildren: Trevor, Laura. BS, Ohio State U., 1971, MA, Loyola Marymount U., 1987; PhD, U. So. Calif., 1993. Prodn. supr. CBS TV, L.A., 1972 78; actor L.A., 1980—; prof. English lit. and creative writing, Latin Am. lit. Santa Monica (Calif.) Coll., 1994—. Author: Reaching Back for the Neverendings, 1993, Borges, Faulkner, Hemingway: Young Poets of Prose, 1993 (Fulbright award 1993); composer (ballet) The Harbinger of Evolution, 1980 (ASCAP award 1981), (song) I Found Love, and numerous other songs and ballets; actor including Mario on Falcon Crest, 1981-83, Jimmy Rivera on Hunter, 1991-92, officer Lopez in General Hosp., 2000, Dragnet, 2003 (films) Losin' It, 1983, Star Trek III, 1984. Capt. U.S. Army, 1971-72. Mem. ASCAP, MLA, Screen Actors Guild, Am. Fedn. TV Radio Artists, Actor's Equity. Avocations: Karate, soccer, basketball, coaching children's sports, yoga. Home: 1211 Vienna Way Venice CA 90291-4026 E-mail: Padilla_mario@smc.edu.

PADIN, JEFFRY, aerospace engineer; s. Melquiades Padin and Norma Bonilla. BS in Aerospace Engring., Iowa State U., 1993, MS in Mech. Engring., 1994; PhD in Mech. Engring., U. Miami, 1995. Lic. Profl. Engineer, Calif., 2000. Systems engr. Aerospace Corp., El Segundo, Calif., 1997—2004; CEO JP CyberTech, Inc, El Segundo, 2002—. Author: (novel) ADAPUS, 1998. Mem.: NSPE, Rotary Club. Achievements include invention of automobile cyber entertainment system.

PADOS, FRANK JOHN, JR., investment company executive; b. Easton, Pa., Feb. 9, 1944; s. Frank John and Mary Helen (Pokrifscak) P.; m. Barbara Janselwitz, July 6, 1968; children— Frank John (dec.), Kelly Ann, Kristin, Matthew John, Kaitlyn. BA cum laude in Econs, Boston Coll., 1966; MBA, U. Pa., 1968. Securities analyst Tchrs. Ins. and Annuity Assn., N.Y.C., 1971-74, investment officer, 1975-77, v.p., 1977-78, sr. v.p., mgr. securities div., 1978-83; mng. dir. Trust Co. of the West, 1983-95; exec. v.p. Desai Capital Mgmt., N.Y.C., 1995—2003; mng. ptnr. Dublin Clark and Co., Greenwich, Conn., 2003—. Bd. dirs. Backyard Bldgs., Inc. Served with U.S. Army, 1969-70. Decorated Bronze Star. Mem. Wharton Club, Sky Club. Roman Catholic. Home: 57 Thornley Dr Chatham NJ 07928-1360 Office: 410 Park Ave Ste 830 New York NY 10022 E-mail: pados@dubinclark.com.

PADOVANI, ROBERTO, communications executive; Degree, U. Padova, Italy; MS in Elec. and Computer Engring., PhD in Elec. and Computer Engring., U. Mass. With M/A-COM Linkabit, 1984—86; from mem. staff to exec. v.p., chief tech. officer QUALCOMM Inc., San Diego, 1986—2002, exec. v.p., 2002—, chief tech. officer, 2002—. Contbr. articles to profl. jours. Mem.: IEEE (Best Paper award 1991). Achievements include patents in field. Office: QUALCOMM Inc 5775 Morehouse Dr San Diego CA 92121

PADOVANO, ANTHONY THOMAS, theologian, educator, literature educator; b. Harrison, N.J., Sept. 18, 1934; s. Thomas Henry and Mary Rose (Cierzo) P.; m. Theresa Lackamp, 1974; children— Mark, Andrew, Paul, Rosemarie BA magna cum laude, Seton Hall U., 1956; S.T.B. magna cum laude, Pontifical Gregorian U., Rome, Italy, 1958, S.T.L. magna cum laude, 1960, S.T.D. magna cum laude, 1962; Ph.L. magna cum laude, St. Thomas Pontifical Internat. U., Rome, 1962; MA, NYU, 1971; PhD, Fordham U., 1980. Ordained priest Roman Cath. Ch., 1959. Asst. chaplain Med. Center, Jersey City, 1960; asst. St. Paul of the Cross Ch., Jersey City, 1962, St. Catharine Ch., Glen Rock, N.J., 1963; prof. systematic theology Darlington Sem., Mahwah, N.J., 1962-74; disting. prof. Am. lit. and philosophy Ramapo Coll., NJ, 1971—; founding faculty mem., disting. prof. theology/religious studies Fordham U., 1973-93. Mem. Archdiocesan Commn. Ecumenical and Interreligious Affairs, 1965, Commn. Instrn. Clergy in Documents Vatican II, 1966; del. dialogue group Luth.-Roman Cath. Theol. Conversations, 1969; del.-at-large senate of priests Archdiocese of Newark; Danforth assoc., 1975—; Cath. pastor Inclusive Cmty. World Coun. Chs., 1986—; lectr. in field, also appearances on radio and TV; parish min. St. Margaret of Scotland, Morristown, N.J. Author: The Cross of Christ, the Measure of the World, 1962, The Estranged God, 1966, Who is Christ, 1967, Belief in Human Life, 1969, American Culture and the Quest for Christ, 1970, Dawn Without Darkness, 1971, Free to be Faithful, 1972, Eden and Easter, 1974, A Case for Worship, 1975, America: Its People, Its Promise, 1975, Presence and Structure, 1975, The Human Journey, 1982, Trilogy, 1982, Contemplation and Compassion, 1984, Winter Rain: A Play, 1985, His Name is John: A Play, 1986, Christmas to Calvary, 1987, Love and Destiny, 1987, Summer Lightening: A Play, 1988, Conscience and Conflict, 1989, Reform and Renewal, 1990, A Celebration of Life, 1990, The Church Today: Belonging and Believing, 1990, Scripture in the Streets, 1992, A Retreat with Thomas Merton, 1996, Hope is a Dialogue, 1998, Resistance and Renewal, 2002; editor: Centenary Issue Roman Echoes, 1959; editl. bd. The Advocate, 1966-73; contbr. articles to mags., Padovano Papers, personal and profl. papers, Archives, U. Notre Dame. With Diocese Paterson Ecumenical Commn.; founding pres. Justice and Peace Commn., Diocese of Paterson, active Resigned Priests Com. Mem. Cath. Theol. Soc. Am., Mariological Soc. Am., Nat. Fedn. Priests Couns. (ofcl. rep. to Constl. Conv., Chgo. 1968), Corpus (pres.), Fedn. Christian Ministries, Internat. Fedn. of Married Cath. Priests (v.p. for N.Am.), North Atlantic Fedn. for Renewal Cath. Priesthood (bd. dirs.). Home: 9 Millstone Dr Morris Plains NJ 07950-1536 Office: Sch of Am Internat Studies Ramapo Coll NJ Mahwah NJ 07430 Personal E-mail: tpadovan@optonline.net. *People rather than ideas have been most formative in my life. More accurately, people, as they embodied certain ideas have proved most decisive. There is nothing more persuasive than an idea which becomes so vital that it transforms the person who proclaims it.*

PADULA, FRED DAVID, filmmaker; b. Santa Barbara, Calif., Oct. 25, 1937; s. Fred and Mary (Adams) P.; married; 1 child. BA in Music, San Francisco State U., MA in Art, 1965. Adj. faculty U. Calif., San Francisco Art Inst., San Francisco State U.; artist-in-residence U. Minn., Mpls. Filmmaker: Ephesus, 1965 (1st pl. award San Francisco Internat. Film Festival, awards N.Y. Film Festival, Chgo. Internat. Film Festival, others), The Artist Speaks, Two Photographers: Wynn Bullock and Imogen Cunningham, Little Jesus (Hippy Hill), Anthology of Boats, David and My Porch, Salmon River Run, El Capitan (awards: Grand Prize Festival Internat. de Film D'Aventure Uecue, La Plagne, France, Grand Prize Film Festival Internat. Montagna Esplorazione, Trento, Italy, Grand Prize Banff Festival of Mountain Films, Can., Grand Prize Mountain Film, Telluride, Colo., Gold medal Festival Internat. du Film Alpine, Les Diablerets, Switzerland; electronic music compositions include: Barking Dogs, Charnet Loops, others; one-man shows (photography) include aerial photographic survey of Mayan Indian Ruins, Yucatan, Mex., 1989, San Francisco Internat. Airport, San Francisco Mus. Modern Art, Kalamazoo Inst. Arts, DeYoung Mus., San Francisco, San Fernando Valley State Coll.,

Bakersfield Coll., Wash. State U., West Chester Coll., Valhalla,N.Y., George Eastman House, represented in permanent collections, Kalamazoo Inst. Arts, State of Calif., George Eastman House, San Francisco Internat. Airport, Crocker Art Mus., Oakland Mus. Art, 1004 Gallery, Port Townsend, Wash., New Horizons Nat. Bank Hdqs., San Rafael, Calif., SUNY/Westchester C.C., Valhalla, N.Y., Grace Mus., Abilene, Tex. Address: PO Box 254 Mill Valley CA 94941-1551

PADULO, LOUIS, university administrator; b. Athens, Ala., Dec. 14, 1936; s. Louis and Helen (Yarbrough) P.; m. Katharine Seamans, Jan. 28, 1963; children: Robert, Joseph. BSEE, Fairleigh Dickinson U., 1959; MSEE, Stanford U., 1962; PhD, Ga. Inst. Tech., 1966. Engr. design and devel. Radio Corp. Am., 1959-60; asst. prof. elec. engring. San Jose State Coll., 1962-63; asst. prof. math. Ga. State U., 1966-67; assoc. prof. Columbia U., summer 1969, Harvard U., summer 1970; asst. prof. Morehouse Coll., 1967-68, assoc. prof., chmn. dept. math., 1968-71; dir. exchange student program Stanford U., 1969-71, assoc. prof. elec. engring., 1971-75, assoc. prof. math., summers 1971-75, dir. MITE program, 1975; prof. elec. engring. and math., dean Coll. Engring. Boston U., 1975-88, assoc. v.p., 1986-87; pres. U. Ala., Huntsville, 1988-90; pres., chief exec. officer Univ. City Sci. Ctr., Phila., 1991-96, pres. emeritus, 1997—; chmn. Invictus, Phila., 1997—. Vis. assoc. prof. Stanford U., 1969-71; vis. prof. U. Tokyo, 1986-88, MIT, 1987-88, 90-91; vis. prof. mgmt. ENPC, France, 2002-, Reims Mgmt. Sch., 2001-, Fairleigh Dickinson U., 2002—; program dir. Inst. on Computers, Logic and Automata Theory, NSF, 1969; founder, dir. dual degree program Atlanta U. Ctr. and Ga. Inst. Tech., 1968-70; numerical analyst Airesearch Corp., L.A., 1969; vis. scientist MIT, 1990-91; bd. dirs. Nemawashi, Inc., Carver Fund, Tapelicator, Inc., Ovation Products, Inc., Knite, Inc., Atlantis Components, Inc., Light Media, Inc., Nucycle, Inc., Genpathways, Inc., Workwell, Inc. Author: System Theory, 1973, Minorities in Engineering, 1974; mem. editl. adv. bd. the Scientist, DiSyCom-Digital Sys. and Comm.; contbr. chpts. to books. Pres. Valley Found., Huntsville, Ala., 1988-89, Ala. Engring. Found., Huntsville, 1989, Consortium Advancement Affordable Distance Edn., 1997—; mem. task force Vision 2000, Huntsville, 1989; bd. dirs. North Ala. Intenat. Trade Assn., 1989, Ala. Supercomputer Network, 1989, Vision 2000, Am. Poetry ctr., 1992, Benjamin Franklin Tech. Ctr., 1991-97; pres. Higher Edn. Congress, 1992-2000; bd. dirs. U.S. Japan Soc., 1990—; adv. com. United Negro Coll. Fund; trustee Fairleigh Dickinson U., 1989—, Presbyn. Found. Phila., 1993-2002, Phila. Fund for Edn., 1995-2001, Internat. House; vis. com. sch. engring. Tuskegee U., Coll. Engring. Drexel U., 1993-2004; mem. Huntsville Army Cmty. Rels. Com.; bd. vis. sch. bus. Temple U., 1993-. Recipient Excellence in Sci. and Engring. Edn. award Nat. Consortium for Black Profl. Devel., 1977, Reginald H. Jones Disting. Svc. award GE Found. and Nat. Action Coun. Minorities in Engring., 1983. Fellow IEEE, Am. Soc. Engring. Edn. (Western Electric Fund Excellence in Tchg. award 1973, Vincent Bendix award 1984, U.S. Interactive fellow 1997); mem. AAAS, ACM, Mass. Engrs. Coun., Math. Assn. Am., Union League of Phila. (life), NAACP (life), Penn Club (life). Office: Invictus 2020 Walnut St Apt 32A Philadelphia PA 19103-5645 Fax: 215-564-3988. E-mail: padulo@verizon.net.

PAETZOLD, MARY E. agricultural products supplier; b. 1950; BA in Math., Montclair State U. CPA. Audit ptnr. KPMG Peat Marwick LLP, 1973; v.p., CFO Ecogen Inc., Langhorne, Pa., 1994—, bd. dirs., 1996—. Mem. bus. adv. coun. Montclair State U. Mem. AICPA, N.J. Soc. CPA's. Office: Ecogen Inc PO Box K Belmar NJ 07719-0400

PAEZ, RICHARD A. federal judge; b. 1947; BA, Brigham Young U., 1969; JD, U. Calif., Berkeley, 1972. Staff atty. Calif. Rural Legal Assistance, Delano, Calif., 1972—74, Western Ctr. on Law and Poverty, 1974—76; sr. counsel Legal Aid Found. of LA, 1976—78, dir. litigation, 1978—79, act. exec. dir., 1980—81; judge LA Mcpl. Ct., 1981—94, superior ct. Los Angeles, 1993—94, U.S. Dist. Ct. (ctrl. dist.) Calif., LA, 1994—2000, U.S. Dist. Ct. (9th cir.), Pasadena, Calif., 2000—. Active Hollywood-Los Feliz Jewish Cmty. Ctr. Mem.: Calif. Jud. Coun., Mex.-Am. Bar Assn. LA County, LA County Bar Assn., Calif. State Bar Assn. Office: US Ct Appeals Edward R Roybal Ctr & Fed Bldg 125 S Grand AveRm 204 Pasadena CA 91105-1652

PAGAN, GILBERTO, JR., clinical psychologist; b. San Juan, P.R., Dec. 30, 1950; s. Gilberto Sr. and Juanita (Quiñones) P.; m. Grissele Camacho, Aug. 6, 1972; children: Mariel, Lauren. Exch. student, SUNY, Albany, 1969-70; BA in Psychology magna cum laude, U. P.R., 1972; MS in Devel. Psychology, Rutgers U., 1974, PhD in Clin. Psychology, 1984. Lic. psychologist, N.J.; cert. sch. psychology. Psychometrician Well Baby Clinic of New Brunswick, N.J., 1972-73; staff psychologist Community Orgn. for Mental Health and Retardation, Inc., Phila., 1976-77; intern in clin. psychology Multimodal Therapy Inst., Kingston, N.J., 1979-80; sch. psychologist New Brunswick Pub. Sch. System, 1980-83; mental health clinician Community Mental Health Ctr. U. Medicine and Dentistry N.J., Piscataway, 1983-93; sch. psychologist Perth Amboy Pub. Sch. Sys., 1993-95; pvt. practice clin. psychology Newark, 1988—; sch. psychologist Jersey City Pub. Sch. Sys., 1995-98, Elizabeth (N.J.) Pub. Sch. Sys., 1998—. Assoc. in psychiatry Univ. of Medicine and Dentistry of N.J., Piscataway, 1988-98; field supr. Rutgers U., New Brunswick, N.J., 1988—; cons. in field to clients including Bloomfield Pub. Sch. System, Div. of Youth and Family Svcs. of State of N.J., Project Head Start, Plainfield, N.J. Columnist San Juan Star, 1990-93, 97-98, El Hispano, Phila., 1977-78; contbr. profl. publs.; presenter in field. Pres. N.J. chpt. Nat. Com. for Puerto Rican Statehood, 1990-95. NIMH fellow, 1978-79; predoctoral rsch. fellow Inst. for Rsch. in Human Devel., Divsn. Psychol. Studies of Ednl. Testing Svc., Princeton, N.J., 1974-75; recipient P.R. Psychol. Assn. award, 1972, Puerto Rican Action Bds. Parents Assn. award 1985; inducted into Nat. Honor Soc. in Psychology, 1973. Mem. APA, NEA, N.J. Edn. Assn., N.J. Psychol. Assn., Elizabeth Edn. Assn. Democrat. Roman Catholic. Home: 422 Johnstone St Perth Amboy NJ 08861-3330 Office: 467 Mount Prospect Ave Newark NJ 07104-2907

PAGAN, KEITH AREATUS, music educator, academic administrator; b. Beggs, Okla., June 7, 1931; s. Areatus and Opal Gail (Facker) P.; m. Betty Lois Wallace; children: Melva Joy, Lisa Lynne, Beryl Kay. B in Music Edn., Bethany Nazarene Coll., 1952; M in Music Edn., Okla. U., 1953; D in Music Edn. with honors, Ind. U., 1970. Asst. prof. music Bethany (Okla.) Nazarene Coll., 1952-53, 55-58; prof. music Pasadena (Calif.) Coll., 1961-76; acad. dean, v.p. acad. affairs Point Loma Nazarene Coll., San Diego, 1976-88, prof. music, chair dept. music., 1989—98. Dir. S.W. Music Symposium, San Diego, 1991—; cons. Sch. for Creative and Performing Arts, San Diego, 1990—, Chula Vista, Calif., 1992—; mem. vis. team Western Coll. Assn., Calif., 1977-82. Arranger (choral) To God be the Glory, (brass) Keith A. Pagan Brass Quintet Series, The King Shall Come; mem. editorial bd. Christian Scholars Rev., 1986—, EverGreen Morning Music Press. Trustee Christian Scholars Rev., 1994—; dir. music Village Ch., Rancho Santa Fe, Calif. With U.S. Army, 1953-55. Recipient WHO award Calif. Higher Edn. Assn., 1971, Lawrence Vredevoe Disting. Leadership award 1986, Spl. Svc. to Music award Calif. Music Educators Assn., 1991; winner 4th ann. anthem contest Choral Condrs. Guild; grantee Danforth Found., 1960. Mem. Calif. Coll. and Univ. Faculty Assn. (pres. 1969-70), Music Tchrs. Assn. Calif. (parliamentarian 1971-73), Western Assn. Schs. and Coll. (accreditation liaison 1976-88). Avocations: travel, photography. Home: 5875 Friars Rd #4316 San Diego CA 92110

PAGANELLI, CHARLES VICTOR, physiologist, educator; b. NYC, Feb. 13, 1929; s. Charles Victor and Mary Paganelli; m. Barbara Harriet Slauson, Sept. 18, 1954; children: William, Kathryn, Peter, Robert, John. AB, Hamilton Coll., Clinton, N.Y., 1950; MA, Harvard U., 1952, PhD, 1957. Instr. physiology U. Buffalo, 1958-60, asst. prof., 1960-63; assoc. prof. SUNY, Buffalo, 1963-71, prof. physiology, 1971-97, disting. svc. prof., 1997—. Interim chair SUNY, Buffalo, 1991-98, emeritus, 1998. Editor: Physiological Function in Special Environments, 1990; contbr. articles to profl. jours. Recipient Elliott Coues award Am. Ornithologists Union, 1981, Newman award 1998. Mem.: Am. Physiol. Soc., Phi Beta Kappa, Sigma Xi, Alpha Omega Alpha. Office Phone: 716-829-2918. Business E-Mail: cvp@buffalo.edu.

PAGANI, ALBERT LOUIS, aerospace system engineer; b. Jersey City, Feb. 19, 1936; s. Alexander C. and Anne (Salvati) P.; m. Beverly Cameron, Feb. 23, 1971; children: Penelope, Deborah, Michael. BSEE, U.S. Naval Acad., 1957; MBA, So. Ill. U., 1971. Commd. 2d lt. USAF, 1957, advanced through grades to col., 1978, navigator, 1957-63, pilot McGuire AFB, NJ, 1963-65, command pilot Anchorage, 1965-68, mgr. airlift Saigon, Vietnam, 1968-69, chief spl. missions Scott AFB, Ill., 1969-74; commd. tactical airlift group USAF Europe, Mildenhall, England, 1974-76, dep. comdr. Rhein Main Air Base Frankfurt, Germany, 1976-78; chief airlift mgmt. USAF Mil. Airlift Command, Scott AFB, Ill., 1978-81, dir. tech. plans and concepts, 1981, dir. command and control, 1982-85; ret., 1985; program mgr. Lockheed Missile and Space Co., Sunnyvale, Calif., 1985-94; dir. data applications, dir. adv. programs PAR Govt. Sys. Corp., New Hartford, NY, 1994-97; pres. Computer Solutions Group, NY, 1997—; prin. Beval Assocs., Inc., 1997—; CEO CSG, Canada, 1999—; dir. B-Net, NY, 1999—; prin., dir. Asset Trax, Inc., 2000—. V.p. Cath. Ch. Coun., Mildenhall, 1974, pres., 1975. Decorated Legion of Merit, Bronze Star, Air medal, Vietnam Cross of Gallantry. Mem. Nat. Def. Transp. Assn. (sr.), Soc. Logistics Engrs., Air Force Assn., Armed Forces Comm. and Electronics Assn., Air Lift Assn., Inst. Noetic Scis., Daedalions, Mensa. Avocations: woodworking, neurolinguistics, volunteer senior executive consulting. Home: 8592 Red Hill Rd Clinton NY 13323-4210 Office Phone: 315-737-6875. E-mail: csq@bevalinc.com.

PAGANO, JOSEPH STEPHEN, physician, researcher, educator; b. Rochester, N.Y., Dec. 29, 1931; s. Angelo Pagano and Marian (Vinci) Signorino; children: Stephen Reynolds, Christopher Joseph. AB with honors, U. Rochester, 1953; MD, Yale U., 1957. Resident Peter Bent Brigham Hosp. Harvard U., Boston, 1960-61; fellow Karolinska Inst., Stockholm, 1961-62; mem. Wistar Inst., Phila., 1962-65; from asst. to assoc. prof. medicine & microbiology U. N.C., Chapel Hill, 1965-73, prof., 1974—, dir. divsn. infectious diseases, 1972-75; founder, dir. U. N.C. Lineberger Comprehensive Cancer Ctr., Chapel Hill, 1974-97, dir. emeritus, 1997—. Attending physician U. Hosps., Chapel Hill; vis. prof. Swiss Inst. Cancer Rsch., Lausanne, 1970-71, Lineberger prof. cancer rsch., 1986—; mem. virology study sect. NIH, Bethesda, Md., 1973-79; recombinant DNA adv. com. USPHS, 1986-90; bd. dirs. Burroughs Wellcome Fund, 1993-2001, Wachovia Bank, Chapel Hill/Durham/Cary; chmn., adv. com. N.C. Cancer Coord. and Control, 1993—2004; Mclaughlin vis. prof. U. Tex. Med. Br., 1996; Norma Berryhill Disting. lectr. U. N.C., 1997; Harry Eagle lectr. Albert Einstein Coll. Medicine, 1997; Harry F. Dowling lectr. U. Ill. Sch. Med., 1991; Gertrude & Werner Henle lectr. in viral oncology, 1990, Joseph and Ruth McCartney Hauck lectr. Mayo Clinic, 2002; Japan Soc. for Head and Neck Cancer lectr. Kanazawa U., 2003; cons. Franklin St. Ptnrs., Chapel Hill, 1998. Mem. editorial bd. Jour. Virology, Jour. Immunology, Cancer Rsch., Jour. Gen. Virology, Antimicrobial Agts. and Chemotherapy, 1974-93; contbr. articles to profl. jours., chpts. to books. Mem. awards assembly GM Cancer Rsch. Found., 1997-2001. Recipient USPHS Rsch. Career award NIH, 1968-73, N.C. award in sci., 1996. Mem. Inst. of Medicine, Am. Assn. Cancer Rsch., Am. Assn. Cancer Insts. (bd. dirs. 1992-99, pres., chmn.), Internat. Assn. for Rsch. in Epstein-Barr Virus (pres. 1990-94), Chapel Hill Tennis Club (pres. 1980-82), Carolina Club (bd. dirs. 2002—), Baldhead Island and Shoals Club. Episcopalian. Avocations: tennis, squash. Home: 114 Laurel Hill Rd Chapel Hill NC 27514-4323 Office: U NC CB7295 Lineberger Comp Cancer Ctr Chapel Hill NC 27599-0001

PAGANO, MICHAEL PRO, advertising executive; b. Tulsa, Dec. 25, 1946; s. Michael Anthony and Irene Lucille (Burns) Pagano; m. Laura Iris Silverman, Oct. 12, 1969 (div. May 1981); children: Brian Paul, Anthony Michael; m. Canera L. Jackson, June 1, 1999. BA, Okla. U., 1974, BS Physician Assoc., 1977, MA in English, 1984, PhD in Health Comm., 1990. Cert. physician asst. Lectr. U. Okla., Norman, 1984—86; physician asst. Atoka Meml. Hosp., Okla., 1986—88, Vinita Med. Assocs., Okla., 1988—92, St. Mary's Hosp., Racine, Wis., 1992—94; prof., chmn. dept. physician asst. U. Health Scis./Chgo. Med. Sch., 1992—94; physician asst. Stamford Hosp., Conn., 1995—; sr. v.p. Lyons Lavey Nickel Swift, N.Y.C., 1994—2002, assoc. creative dir., dir. internet devel.; pres., CCO DrCreative, Inc., 2002—, Pagano/Britting Comm., LLC, 2003—. Adj. faculty Sch. Labor Rels. Cornell U., N.Y.C., 1995—2000; adj. faculty U. Conn., Stamford, 2002—, Fairfield U., Conn., 2003—04, vis. asst. prof., 2004—. Author: Communicating Effectively in Medical Records, 1992, Communication Skills for Professional Nurses, 1992; contbr. articles to profl. jours. With U.S. Army, 1965—68. Recipient award of Excellence, Rx Club, 1997, 1998, 2000, AD/RX award, New Eng. Jour. Medicine, 1998, Readex award, Med Ad News, 1998; Western Speech Comm. Assn. scholar, 1987. Fellow: Conn. Acad. Physician Assts., Am. Med. Writers Assn., Am. Acad. Physician Assts.; mem.: Healthcare Mktg. and Comm. Coun. Avocations: golf, writing, reading. Home: 3 Shorefront Park Norwalk CT 06854-3752 Office: DrCreative Inc 3 Shorefront Park Norwalk CT 06854-3752 Office Phone: 203-853-6182. Business E-Mail: drmpp@drcreative.biz.

PAGANO, RICHARD DONALD, physical education educator, researcher; b. Phila., Jan. 17, 1951; s. Joe Thomas and Mary Irene Pagano; m. Ann Theresa Pagano, June 17, 1977; children: Lauren Ann, Ryan Richard. BS, East Stroudsburg U., 1973; MEd, West Chester U., 1981. Cert. tchr., Pa. Health and phys. edn. tchr. Upper Darby (Pa.) Sch. Dist., 1974—. Columnist Town Talk Newspaper, 1987— (Sportsman of Yr. 1999); author: Life of Fred Luehring, 1981, History of Delco Hall of Fame, 1988. Trustee Stuzebecker Found., 1998—; bd. dirs. Crozer-Keystone Healthplex Sports Mus., 1998—, Pa. Sports Hall of Fame, 1995—, Delaware County Athletes Hall of Fam Com., 1988—, sport historian, 1988—. Named to Delaware County Athletes Hall of Fame, 1991, Pa. Sports Hall of Fame, 1997, Ridley Twp. Old Timers Hall of Fame, 1991. Mem. Internat. Soc. Olympic Historians, AAPHERD. Avocations: sports research, writing, collecting sports books. Home: 1311 Donna Ave Woodlyn PA 19094-1126 Office: Westbrook Park Sch Westbrook Dr Clifton Heights PA 19018

PAGANO, ROSANNE V. journalism professor, media consultant; d. Benjamin and Lillian G. Pagano; m. Kenneth D. Smith, July 20, 1985; 1 child, Daniel Carter Smith. Master's of journalism, U. of Calif., Berkeley, 1981—83. Asst. prof. of journalism U. of AK Anchorage, 1999—; writer The AP, Anchorage, 1990—98. Contbr. nonfiction anthology. Bd. mem. Spirit of Youth, Anchorage, 2003, Alaska String Camps, Chugiak, 2003; rsch. chair, internships and careers interest group Assn. for Edn. in Journalism and Mass Comm., Columbia, SC. Fellow tchg., Freedom Forum, 2000, Journalism Educators, Am. Press Inst., Va., 2004. Mem.: Assn. for Edn. in Journalism and Mass Communication (rsch. chair, internships and careers interest group 2003—04). Achievements include research in The Value Of Pre-Professional Experience For Undergraduates In Journalism And Mass Communication. Office: University of Alaska Anchorage 3211 Providence Drive Anchorage AK 99508 Office Phone: 907-786-4184. E-mail: afrp@uaa.alaska.edu.

PAGAN ORTIZ, ALEX OMAR, computer systems analyst, educator; b. Ponce, P.R., Dec. 8, 1967; s. Javier E. Pagan and Brunilda Ortiz Collazo. BS in Computer Sci., Sacred Heart U., 1993; MS in Computer Sci., Temple U., 1997. Computer scientist U.S. Dept. Def., Fort Meade, Md., 1998-99; sr. cons. Oracle Corp., Columbia, Md., 1999-2000; internal sys. engr. Digital Courier Techs., Clearwater, Fla., 2000-2001; data analyst Eli Lilly Export S.A., Hato Rey, PR, 2001—02; asst. prof. Daytona Beach C.C., 2002—. Faculty assoc. Johns Hopkins U., Washington, 1998-2000. Avocations: tennis, swimming. Home: 1628 W Holden Ave # 172 Orlando FL 32839 Office: Daytona Beach CC 1200 International Speedway Daytona Beach FL 32114 E-mail: aopagan@yahoo.com.

PAGE, ALAN C. state supreme court justice; b. Canton, Ohio, Aug. 7, 1945; s. Howard F. and Georgianna (Umbles) P.; m. Diane Sims, June 5, 1973; children: Nina, Georgianna, Justin, Khamsin. BA, U. Notre Dame, 1967; JD, U. Minn., 1978; LLD, U. Notre Dame, 1993; LLD (hon.), St. John's U., 1994, Westfield State Coll., 1994, Luther Coll., 1995, U. New Haven, 1999. Bar: Minn. 1979, U.S. Dist. Ct. Minn. 1979, U.S. Supreme Ct. 1988. Profl. athlete Minn. Vikings, Mpls., 1967-78, Chgo. Bears, 1978-81; assoc. Lindquist & Vennum, Mpls., 1979-85; former atty. Minn. Atty. Gen.'s Office, St. Paul, 1985-92; assoc. justice Minn. Supreme Ct., St. Paul, 1993—. Cons. NFL Players Assn., Washington, 1979-84. Commentator Nat. Pub. Radio, 1982-83. Founder Page Edn. Found., 1988. Named NFL's Most Valuable Player, 1971, one of 10 Outstanding Young Men Am., U.S. Jaycees, 1981; named to NFL Hall of Fame, 1988, Coll. Football Hall of Fame, 1993; NCAA Theodore Roosevelt Award, 2004. Mem. ABA, Minn. Bar Assn., Hennepin County Bar Assn., Minn. Assn. Black Lawyers. Avocations: running, biking. Office: 423 Minnesota Judicial Ctr 25 Rev Dr Martin Luther King Jr Blvd Saint Paul MN 55155-1500

PAGE, ALBERT LEE, soil science educator, researcher; b. New Lenox, Ill., Mar. 19, 1927; s. Thomas E. and Hattie O. (Pease) Pugh; m. Shirley L. Jessmore, Sept. 14, 1952; children— Nancy, Thomas BA in Chemistry, U. Calif.-Riverside, 1956; PhD in Soil Sci., U. Calif.-Davis, 1960. Prof. soil sci. U. Calif.-Riverside, 1960—. Dir. Kearney Found., Univ. Calif.-Riverside, program of excellence in energy research Editor: Methods of Soil Analysis, 1983, Utilization of Municipal Wastewater and Sludge on Land, 1983, Heavy Metals in the Environment, 1977 Served as QMQ1 USN, 1945-52 Recipient Environ. Quality Research award Am. Soc. Agronomy, 1984, Disting. Teaching award U. Calif., Riverside, 1976, Disting. Svc. award USDA, 1991; Fullbright scholar, 1966-67; Guggenheim Meml. Found. fellow, 1966-67 Fellow AAAS, Am. Soc. Agronomy, Soil Sci. Soc. Am.; mem. Internat. Soil Sci. Soc., Western Soil Sci. Soc., Soc. Environ. Geochemistry and Health, Sigma Xi. Home: 5555 Canyon Crest Dr Apt 1F Riverside CA 92507-6443 Office: U Calif Dept Soil & Environ Sci Riverside CA 92521-0001 E-mail: albert.page@ucr.edu.

PAGE, ANNE RUTH, gifted education educator, education specialist; b. Norfolk, Va., Apr. 13, 1949; d. Amos Purnell and Ruth Martin (Hill) Bailey; m. Peter Smith Page, Apr. 24, 1971; children: Edgar Bailey, Emmett McBrannon. BA, N.C. Wesleyan Coll.; student, Fgn. Lang. League; postgrad., N.C. State U.; student, Overseas Linguistic Studies, France, Spain, Eng., 1978, 85, 86. Cert. tchr., N.C. Tchr. Cary (N.C.) Sr. High Sch., 1971-72; tchr., head dept. Daniels Mid. Sch., Raleigh, N.C., 1978-83; chmn. fgn. lang. dept. Martin Mid. Gifted and Talented, Raleigh, N.C., 1983—. Leadership team Senate Bill 2 Core co-chair; dir. student group Overseas Studies, Am. Coun. for Internat. Studies, France, Spain, Eng., 1982, 84, 86, 88; bd. dirs. N.T.H., Inc., Washington; cert. mentor tchr. Wake County Pub. Schs., 1989; dir. student exchs. between Martin Mid. Sch. and Sevigné Inst. of Compiegne, France. Sunday sch. tchr. Fairmont United Meth. Ch., Raleigh, 1983-85. Mem. Alpha Delta Kappa. Democrat. Home: 349 Wilmot Dr Raleigh NC 27606-1232 Office: Martin Mid Sch GT 1701 Ridge Rd Raleigh NC 27607-6737

PAGE, BERNADETTE RYAN, emergency physician; b. Chgo., Feb. 10, 1946; d. Frank James and Bernadette Rosamund (Halm) Ryan; m. Jack R. Page, Dec. 23, 1967; children: Jeremy, Sara, Alex, Rachel. MD, Loyola U., 1970. Diplomate Am. Bd. Emergency Medicine. Rotating O intern San Bernardino (Calif.) Hosp., 1970-71; resident in pediat. Orange County Med. Ctr., Anaheim, Calif., 1971-72; staff physician emergency rm. Kaiser Permanente, Bellflower, Calif., 1972-73, St. Mary's Hosp./Long Beach (Calif.) Cmty., 1973-76, Appalachian Regional Hosp., Beckley, W.Va., 1976-78, Charleston (W.Va.) Area Med. Ctr., 1978-82; staff physician, owner Doctors Urgent Care, Charleston, 1982-88; staff physician Orange Chatham Comp. Health, Carrboro, N.C., 1988-91; attending physician emergency dept. Duke U. Med. Ctr., Durham, N.C., 1991—. Chair violence prevention com. Am. Assn. Women Emergency Physicians, Durham, 1994-98; mem. adv. coun. family violence AMA, 1994-98; mem. nat. faculty ACLS Am. Heart Assn., 1976-82. Active Durham City-County Violence Prevention Com., 1993-98; co-chair Religious Coalition for a Nonviolent Durham, 1997—. Fellow Am. Coll. Emergency Physicians (mem. violence prevention com. 1997-99). Democrat. Roman Catholic. Office: Duke U Med Ctr PO Box 3096 Durham NC 27715-3096

PAGE, CHERYL MILLER, elementary school educator; BS in Social Sciences, Calif. Polytechnic State Univ., San Luis Obispo, Calif., 1975. Cert. health edn. specialist Nat. Commn. for Health Edn. Credentialing, Edn. Certification Program Calif. Polytechnic State Univ., San Luis Obispo, Calif., 1976. Elem. educator Dalles Pub. Schs., Dalles, Oreg., 1980—86, Salem-Keizer Pub. Schs., Salem, Oreg., 1986—95, middle sch. health educator, 1995—2002, health educator; prevention curriculum resource specialist Salem-Keizer Pub. Schs. Mid Valley. Named Oreg. Outstanding Elementary Health Educator, 1991, Nat. Health Edn. Profl. Yr., Oreg. Outstanding Secondary Health Educator of Yr., Vol. of Yr., Am. Cancer Soc.; recipient Tambrands award, Am. Assn. Health Edn., 1996, Health and Safety Educator of Year, NW Div. AAHPERD, 1996; Partnership Safe Sch. Healthy Students Grant, Salem, Oreg., 2002—. Mem.: Oreg. Alliance Health, Phys. Edn., Recreation and Dance (treas. 1992—96, pres. 2001—02), Oreg. Assn. for the Advancement of Health Edn. (sec./treas. 1990—92), Nat. Bd. for Profl. Tchg. Stds. (bd. mem.). Avocations: running, reading. Office: Salem-Keizer Sch Dist PO Box 12024 Salem OR 97309

PAGE, CLARENCE E. newspaper columnist; b. Dayton, Ohio, June 2, 1947; m. Lisa Johnson Cole, May 3, 1987. BS in Journalism, Ohio U., 1969. Reporter, asst. city editor Chgo. Tribune, 1969—80; dir. cmty. affairs dept. Sta. WBBM-TV, 1980—82, reporter, planning editor, 1982—84; columnist, mem. editl.l bd. Chgo. Tribune, 1984—; columnist, mem. editl. bd. Tribune Media Svcs., Washington, 1987—. Frequent guest Sta. WTTW-TV, Chgo. Tonight, Chgo. in Rev. Contbr. articles to profl. jours. Participant 1972 Chgo. Tribune Task Force Series on Vote Fraud. Recipient Cmty. Svc. award, Ill. UPI, 1980, James P. McGuire award, CLU, 1987, Pulitzer Prize for commentary, 1989. Office: Tribune Media Svcs 1325 G St NW Washington DC 20005-3104

PAGE, CURTIS MATTHEWSON, minister; b. Columbus, Ohio, Oct. 24, 1946; s. Charles N. and Alice Matthewson P.; m. Martha Poitevin, Feb. 12, 1977; children: Allison, Charles, Abigail. BS, Ariz. State U., 1968; MDiv, San Francisco Theol. Sem., 1971, D Ministry, 1985. Ordained Presbyn. Ch., 1971. Pastor Ketchum (Idaho) Presbyn. Ch., 1972-80, Kirk O'The Valley Presbyn. Ch., Reseda, Calif., 1980-90; campaign dir. Kids 1st Edn. Reform Partnership, L.A., 1990-91; sr. pastor Orangewood Presbyn. Ch., Phoenix, 1991-93, First Meridian Heights Presbyn. Ch., Indpls., 1993—. Mem. com. Ch. Devel., Ind., 1995—; bd. dirs. Express Pub., Ketchum. Chmn. com. on preparation for the ministry, San Fernando, Calif., 1988-90; chmn. Ketchum City Zoning Commn., 1979-80; L.A. Mayor's Citizen's Adv. Task Force on Ethics, 1990; co-chmn. Voice Cmty. Orgn. L.A., 1988-90; chair Family CARES, Indpls., 1995—; founding pastor AliveTime, 1995; leading innovator in mainline Protestant worship and urban ministry. Avocations: tennis, skiing, coaching softball. Office: First Meridian Heights Pres 4701 Central Ave Indianapolis IN 46205-1828 E-mail: FMHPC@aol.com.

PAGE, DAVID RANDALL, hospital administrator; b. Plainfield, N.J., Oct. 30, 1940; married BA, Davidson Coll., 1962; MA, Duke U., 1964. Administrv. resident Durham County Gen. Hosp., Durham, N.C., 1964, Duke U. Hosp., Durham, N.C., 1963-64, administrv. asst., 1964-65; asst. dir. Children's Mercy Hosp., Kansas City, 1968-69, Meml. Mission Hosp., Asheville, N.C., 1969-71, assoc. dir., 1971-81; exec. v.p., dir. Ochsner Fedn. Hosp., New Orleans, 1981-93; pres., ceo Hermann Hosp., Houston, 1993—; chief exec ofr Fairview Hosp., Minneapolis. Fellow ACHE; mem. AHA. Office: Hermann Hosp 6411 Fannin St Houston TX 77030-1599 Address: Fairview Hosp 2450 Riverside Ave Minneapolis MN 55454-1450

PAGE, ELLIS BATTEN, psychologist, educator; b. San Diego; s. Frank Homer and Dorothy (Batten) P.; m. Elizabeth Latimer Thaxton, June 21, 1952 (dec. 2000); children: Ellis Batten (Tim), Elizabeth Page Sigman, Richard Leighton. AB, Pomona Coll.; MA, San Diego State U.; EdD, UCLA, 1958. Tchr. secondary schs., Calif.; dean Coll. Edn., prof. edn. and psychology Tex. Woman's U., 1960-62; prof. ednl. psychology U. Conn., 1962-79; prof. ednl. psychology and research Duke U., 1979—. Vis. prof. U. Wis., 1960, 62, Stanford U., 1965, Harvard U., 1968-69, U. Javeriana, Bogotá, 1975; leader Ford Found. rsch. adv. team Venezuelan Ministry Edn., Caracas, 1969-70; vis. prof. Spanish Ministry Edn., 1972, 80, 82-85; rsch. cons. U.S. Office Edn.,

USN, Nat. Inst. Edn., Bur. Edn. Handicapped; chmn. nat. planning com. Nat. Ctr. Edn. Stats.; adviser Brazilian Ministry Edn., 1973, 80; chief Ministerial Commn. Edn., Bermuda, 1983-85; mem. Adv. Coun. for Edn. Stats., U.S. Dept. Edn., 1987-90; pres. TruJudge, Inc., 1993—. Author, editor in field. Capt. USMCR. Recipient Disting. Alumnus award San Diego State U., 1980; NSF fellow, 1959, IBM fellow, 1966-67. Fellow AAAS (life), APA (pres. ednl. psychology 1976-77), Am. Psychol. Soc., John Dewey Soc., Am. Assn. Applied and Preventive Psychology, Nat. Conf. Rsch. English, Philosophy Edn. Soc.; mem. Am. Coun. Assn., Am. Ednl. Rsch. Assn. (pres. 1979-80), Am. Statis. Assn. (officer N.C. chpt.), Assn. Computational Linguistics, Nat. Assn. Scholars, N.C. Assn. Rsch. Edn. (Disting. Rsch. award 1981, 91, pres. 1984-85), Rhetoric Soc. Am. (dir.), Psychometric Soc., Sociedad Española de Pedagogia (hon.), Sigma Xi, Phi Kappa Phi, Phi Gamma Delta, Psi Chi, Kappa Delta Pi, Phi Delta Kappa (life, svc. key). Episcopalian. Home: 7214 94th Ave SE Mercer Island WA 98040-5826 E-mail: EBPage@Duke.edu.

PAGE, ERNEST, medical educator; b. Cologne, Germany, May 30, 1927; came to U.S., 1936, naturalized, 1942; s. Max Ernest and Eleanor (Kohn) P.; m. Eva Veronica Gross, June 5, 1967; 1 son, Thomas J. AB, Calif., Berkeley, 1949; MD, Calif., San Francisco, 1952. Intern Peter Bent Brigham Hosp., Boston, 1952-53, resident, 1953-54, 57-58; research assoc. Harvard Med. Sch., 1957-65; assoc. prof. medicine and physiology U. Chgo. Med. Sch., 1965-69, prof. physiology, 1969-98, prof. emeritus, 1998—. Editor: (jour.) Am, Jour. Physiology: Heart and Circulatory Physiology, 1981—86; editor: (sects.) Handbook of Physiology Vol. I The Heart, 2002. Served with AUS, 1945-46. Established investigator Am. Heart Assn., 1959-65 Mem. Am. Physiol. Soc., Biophys. Soc., Am. Soc. Cell Biology, Soc. Gen. Physiologists, Assn. Am. Physicians. Home: 5606 S Harper Ave Chicago IL 60637-1832

PAGE, GEORGE ALFRED, JR., lawyer; b. Evanston, Ill., June 30, 1932; AB, Princeton U., 1954; JD, Harvard U., 1959; LLM in Taxation, Boston U., 1964. Bar: Mass 1959. From assoc. to ptnr. Peabody & Arnold, Boston, 1959—79; sr. ptnr. Csaplar & Bok, Boston, 1979—90; pvt. practice Boston, 1990—. Lectr grad tax program Boston Univ Sch Law, 1974—77; gen counsel to bd dirs and sr mgmt Woodside Mgmt Sys Inc, Boston, 1978—87. 1st lt USAR, 1954—56. Mem.: ABA (mem. real property, probate and trust law sect.), Essex County Estate Planning Coun., Boston Bar Assn. (chmn. state tax com. 1971—74, sect. taxation 1974—75, fed. tax com. 1980—82, sr. sect. 1994—96, mem. trusts and estates law sect., mem. estate planning com.). Home and Office: 1 Risley Rd Marblehead MA 01945-3720 Office Phone: 617-227-2002.

PAGE, GREGORY R. food products executive; Joined Cargill, Mpls., 1974, pres. red meat group, 1995—98, corp. v.p., sect. pres., 1998—2000, exec. v.p., 1999—2000, pres., COO, 2000—, also bd. dirs. Bd. dirs. Eaton Corp. Mem.: Am. Meat Inst. (chmn. 2000). Office: Cargill PO Box 9300 Minneapolis MN 55440

PAGE, HARRY ROBERT, business administration educator; b. Milw., Mar. 22, 1915; s. Harry Allen and Lydia (Rosendahl) P.; m. Jeanne Tompkins, Apr. 1, 1945; children: Patricia Jeanne, Margaret Berenice. AB, Mich. State U., 1941; postgrad., U.S. Army Command and Staff Coll., 1945-46, Indsl. Coll. Armed Forces, 1958-59; MBA, Harvard, 1950; PhD, Am. U., 1966. Served from 2d lt. to lt. col. U.S. Army, 1941-46; from lt. col. to col. USAF, 1947-61; exec. officer logistics directorate U.S. Joint Chiefs of Staff, Washington, 1959-61; asst. prof. bus. adminstrn. George Washington U., Washington, 1961-65, assoc. prof., chmn. dept., 1965-69, prof., chmn. dept. bus. adminstrn., 1970-74, assoc. dean, 1975-80, prof. emeritus, 1981—. Cons. Advanced Study program Brookings Instn., Washington, 1966-70, Ednl. Svcs. Inst., U.S. Postal Svc., 1985-92. Author: Church Budget Development, 1964, An Analysis of the Defense Procurement Program Decision-Making Process, 1966, Public Purchasing and Materials Management, 1980, rev. edit., 1989; co-author: Federal Contributions to Management, 1972. Chmn. task force edn. and tng. Commn. Govt. Procurement, 1972-73; bd. dirs., treas. Coun. Chs., Greater Washington, 1963-68; bd. dirs. Hunter Assocs. Lab., Inc.; deacon Rock Spring Congregational Ch., 1994-97. Decorated Air medal, Purple Heart, Legion of Merit. Fellow Nat. Contract Mgmt. Assn.; mem. Acad. mgmt., Nat. Assn. Purchasing Mgmt., Internat. Fedn. Purchasing and Materials Mgmt., Harvard Bus. Sch. Assn., Air Force Assn., Nat. Parks and Conservation Assn. (trustee), Air Force Sgts. Assn. (trustee, chmn. scholarship bd. 1971—), Harvard Bus. Club, Sch. of Wash. Club (dir., pres. 1980-81), Alpha Phi Omega, Lambda Chi Alpha Kappa Psi, Pi Sigma Alpha, Beta Gamma Sigma. Home: 3612 N Glebe Rd Arlington VA 22207-4317

PAGE, JOHN GARDNER, toxicologist, research scientist, director; b. Milw., Sept. 14, 1940; s. Raymond G. and Leone B. (Churchill) P.; m. Joyce Ann Krueger, July 7, 1962; children: Teresa Ann, Kimberly Christine. BS, U. Wis.-Madison, 1963, MS, 1966, PhD, 1967. Diplomate Am. Bd. Toxicology. Sr. scientist NIH, Bethesda, Md., 1967-69, Eli Lilly Co., Indpls., 1969-77; dir. toxicology and pathology Rhone Poulenc, Inc., Ashland, Ohio, 1977-79; dir. toxicology Toxigenics, Inc., Decatur, Ill., 1979-83; sr. rsch. advisor Battelle Meml. Inst., Columbus, Ohio, 1983-87; disting. scientist So. Rsch. Inst., Birmingham, Ala., 1987—2004; dir. NGVL-Nat. Toxicology Ctr., 2001—; disting. scientist So. Rsch. Inst., Birmingham, Ala., 2004—. Adj. prof. U. Ill., 1981-83, ctr. for AIDS rsch., U. Ala., Birmingham, 1987—, sch. pub. health, 1988—, sch. medicine, 1997—. Contbr. articles to profl. jours. Bd. dirs. Am. Cancer Soc., Greenfield, Ind., 1973-77. Recipient Rennebohm Outstanding Tchr.'s award U. Wis., 1964. Mem. AAAS, Fedn. Am. Socs. Exptl. Biology, Am. Soc. Pharm. Exptl. Therapeutics, Soc. Toxicology, Am. Coll. Toxicology, Internat. Soc. for Study Xenobiotics, Sigma Xi, Rho Chi. Avocations: photography, hiking, fishing. Home: 3700 Rockhill Rd Birmingham AL 35223-1562 Office: So Rsch Inst 2000 9th Ave S Birmingham AL 35205-5305 Office Phone: 205-581-2689. Personal E-mail: toxman1@bellsouth.net. Business E-Mail: page@sri.org.

PAGE, JOHN HENRY, JR., artist, educator; b. Ann Arbor, Mich., Jan. 18, 1923; s. John Henry and Lucille (Bennett) P.; m. Mary Lou Franks, July 22, 1945; children: Jonathan, Marilyn, Jeremy. Student, Mpls. Sch. Art, 1940-42; B.Design, U. Mich., 1948; M.F.A., U. Iowa, 1950. Instr. Mankato (Minn.) State Coll., 1950-54; asst. prof. art U. No. Iowa, Cedar Falls, 1954-55, asst. prof., 1955-59, assoc. prof., 1959-64, prof., 1964-87, acting head dept. art, 1984-85. Head art dept. U. Omaha, 1959-60 One-man shows include Luther Coll., Decorah, Iowa, 1981, Laura Musser Mus., Muscatine, Iowa, 1978, Coe Coll., Cedar Rapids, Iowa, 1975, Sheldon Gallery, Lincoln, Nebr., 1974, Creighton U., Omaha, 1969, Augustana Coll., Rock Island, Ill., 1964, Muskegon (Mich.) Mus. Art, 1983, retrospective (in three parts) Gallery of Art U. No. Iowa, Hearst Ctr. for the Arts, Cedar Falls, Iowa, Waterloo (Iowa) Mus. of Art, 1992, exhibited in group shows at 10th Nat. Print Show Bklyn. Mus., 1956, 9 Iowa Artists Gov. Exhbn., 1971—72, Walker Art Ctr., Mpls., 1973, Regional Invitational Exhbn., U. Omaha, 1978, Fragile Giants, Brunner Gallery, 1994—96, commissions include, Hearst Ctr., Cedar Falls, 2003, Represented in permanent collections Libr. Congress, Walker Art Ctr., Des Moines Art Ctr., Joslyn Art Mus., Omaha, Carnegie Inst., Pitts. Served with U.S. Army, 1943-45. Nat. Endowment Arts grantee, 1975 Unitarian Universalist. Home: 114 E Los Arcos Green Valley AZ 85614-2429 E-mail: jmlpage@earthlink.net.

PAGE, JONATHAN ROY, investment analyst; b. Harrisburg, Pa., Sept. 10, 1946; s. John and Ellen (Smith) P.; m. Patrice Marie Margerm, May 17, 1975; children: Elizabeth, Gregory, Richard, Brian. BA, Dartmouth Coll., 1968; MBA, Tuck Sch. Dartmouth, 1969. Chartered fin. analyst. Investment officer Irving Trust Co., N.Y.C., 1970-75; portfolio mgr. to mng. dir. Morgan Stanley Investment Mgmt., N.Y.C., 1975—. Vestry person St. John's Ch., Ramsey, N.J., 1984-88. Mem. N.Y. Soc. Security Analysts, Fin. Analysts Fedn. Republican. Episcopalian. Avocations: tennis, golf, skiing, landscaping. E-mail: jonathan.page@morganstanley.com.

PAGE, L. KRISTEN, biologist, educator; b. Athens, Ga., Sept. 8, 1968; d. Oscar C. and Anna Laura Page; m. Richard T. Ritchey, May 1, 1999. BS, Furman U., 1990; MS, Auburn U., 1993; PhD, Purdue U., 1998. Post-doctoral rsch. asst. biology dept. Purdue U., West Lafayette, Ind., 1998—2000; asst. prof., biology Wheaton Coll., Ill., 2000—. Mem.: Am. Sci. Affiliation, Am. Soc. Parasitologists, Am. Soc. of Mammalogists, Ecol. Soc. Am., Sigma Xi, Phi Kappa Phi. Office: Wheaton Coll Biology Dept 501 College Ave Wheaton IL 60187 E-mail: kristen.page@wheaton.edu.

PAGE, LARRY, information technology executive; BS in Engring., U. Mich.; postgrad., Stanford U. Co-founder, founding CEO Google, Inc., Mountain View, Calif., 1998—2001, pres. products, 2001—, also bd. dirs. Spkr. in field. Mem. nat. adv. com. U. Mich. Coll. Engring., Ann Arbor, Mich. Mem.: Eta Kappa Nu. Office: 1600 Amphitheatre PKWY #41 Mountain View CA 94043-1351*

PAGE, LARRY KEITH, neurosurgeon, educator; b. Rayville, La., July 7, 1933; s. Ardie Lee and Edris Estelle (Chaney) P.; m. Joan Marie Doherty, Aug. 27, 1960; children: Matthew, Elizabeth, Jennifer. BS, La. State U., 1955, MD, 1958. Diplomate: Am. Bd. Neurol. Surgery. Intern Grad. Hosp., U. Pa., Phila., 1958-59; resident Children's Hosp. and Peter Bent Brigham Hosp., Boston, 1962-66; assoc. neurosurgeon Children's Hosp., assoc. surgeon Peter Bent Brigham Hosp., 1966-71; cons. Beverly Hosp., Mass., Robert Breck Brigham Hosp., Boston, Pondville Hosp., Boston, West Roxbury VA Hosp., Boston VA Hosp.; clin. instr. neurosurgery Harvard U., Boston, 1966-71; prof., vice chmn. dept. neurosurgery U. Miami, Fla., 1971-95, prof. emeritus, 1995—, chief div. pediatric neurosurgery, 1971-95; neurosurgeon VA Hosp., Miami, 1971-88, Jackson Meml. Hosp., Miami, 1971-95, dir. neurosurgery, 1994-95; chief neurosurgery Mt. Sinai Hosp., Miami, 1990-94. Neurosurg. cons. FDA; neurosurg. cons. NASA Mem. editorial bds., contbr. articles to profl. jours. Served to lt. USN, 1959-62. Mem. ACS, Am. Acad. Pediatrics, Am. Assn. Neurol. Surgeons, Internat. Soc. Pediatric Neurosurgery, Am. Soc. Pediatric Neurosurgery, Congress Neurol. Surgeons, Fellowship of Acad. Neurosurgeons, Internat. Neurosurg. Forum, Royal Soc. Medicine, Soc. for Rsch. in Hydrocephalus and Spina Bifida, New Eng. Neurosurg. Soc., Fla. Neurosurg. Soc. (pres. 1989-90), Mass. Med. Soc., Dade County Med. Assn., Internat. Palm Soc., Alpha Omega Alpha. Roman Catholic. Home and Office: 13845 SW 73rd Ct Miami FL 33158-1213

PAGE, LESLIE ANDREW, consumer products company executive; b. Mpls., June 5, 1924; s. Henry R. and Amelia Kathryn (Steinmetz) Page; m. DeEtte Abernethy Griswold, July 6, 1952 (div. Sept. 1975); children: Randolph, Michael, Kathryn, Caroline; m. Mary Ellen Decker, Nov. 26, 1976. BA, U. Minn., 1949; MA, U. Calif., Berkeley, 1953, PhD, 1956. Asst. microbiologist, lectr. U. Calif., Davis, 1956-61; cons. San Diego Zoological Soc. Zoo Hosp., 1957-60; microbiologist, research leader Nat. Animal Disease Ctr., USDA, Ames, Iowa, 1961-79; ret., 1979; specialist in Chlamydial nomenclature and disease; med. text cons., 1979-85; founder, pres., chmn. bd. Steri-Derm Corp., San Marcos, Calif., 1987—. Cons. McCormick Distilling Co., Weston, Mo., 1994—95. Editor: Jour. Wildlife Diseases, 1965—68, Wild Diseases, 1976; contbr. chapters to books, articles to profl. jours. Pres. Garden Island Cmty. Assn., Bay St. Louis, Miss., 1980—81; chief commr. East Hancock Fire Protection Dist., Bay St. Louis, 1982—83; treas. Woodridge Escondido Property Owners Assn., 1986—88; pres. Westminster Men's Group, Westminster Presbyn. Ch., Escondido, Calif., 2002. Fellow: Am. Acad. Microbiology (emeritus); mem.: Zool. Soc. San Diego, Am. Soc. Microbiology, Wildlife Disease Assn. (pres. 1972—73, Disting. Svc. award 1980, Emeritus award 1984), Les Families Pagé d'Amérique, Sigma Xi, Phi Zeta (hon.). Achievements include patents for liquid antiseptic composition. Home and Office: 1784 Deavers Dr San Marcos CA 92069-3359 Personal E-mail: lapage1234@hotmail.com.

PAGE, LINDA KAY, bank executive; b. Wadsworth, Ohio, Oct. 4, 1943; d. Frederick Meredith and Martha Irene (Vance) P. Student, Ohio U., 1976-77; grad. banking program, U. Wis., 1982-84; BA, Capital U. cert. in pers. Am. Bankers Assn. Asst. v.p., gen. mgr. Bancohio Corp., Columbus, 1975-78, v.p., dist. mgr., 1979-80, v.p., mgr. employee rels., 1980-81, v.p., divsn. mgr., 1982-83; commr. of banks State of Ohio, Columbus, 1983-87, dir. Dept. Commerce, 1988-90; pres., CEO Star Bank Ctrl. Ohio, Columbus, 1990-92; state dir. Rural Devel/USDA, 1993-2000; pub. svc. dir. City of Columbus, 2000—04. Bd. dirs. Clark County Mental Health Bd., Springfield, Ohio, 1982-83, Springfield Met. Housing, 1982-83, Pvt. Industry Coun. Franklin County, 1990-2000—, Ohio Highe Edn. Facilities Commn., 1990-93, Ohio Devel. Corp., 1995—; bd. advisers Orgn. Indsl. Standards, Springfield, 1982-83; trustee League Against Child Abuse, 1986-90; treas. Ohio Housing Fin. Agy., 1980-90; vice chair Fed. Res. Bd. Consumer Adv. Coun., 1989-91; trustee, treas. Columbus State C.C. Found., 1990-2000, pres., 1997-99; bd. dirs. Columbus Urban league, 1992-98; mem. CompDrug Bd., 1998-2000; mem. Mid Ohio Regional Planning Commn., 2000-04. Recipient Leadership Columbus award Sta. WTVN and Columbus Leadership Program, 1975, 82, Outstanding Svc. award Clark County Mental Health Bd., 1983, Giles Mitchell Housing award, 1996. Mem.: LWV (treas. edn. fund 1992—2000), Women in Transp., Risk Mgmt. Assn., Women in Transp. (bd. trustees Ohio chpt. 2000, bd. dirs. 2002), Internat. Womens Forum, Am. Pub. Works Assn. (treas. Ohio chpt. 2000—03, treas. 2002, govt. affairs com. 2002—03), Ohio Mortgage Bankers Assn. (legis. commn. 1998), Ohio Devel. Assn., Ohio Bankers Assn. (bd. dirs. 1982—83, 1991—92), Conf. State Bank Suprs. (dist. chmn. 1984—85, sec.-treas. 1985—90, bd. dirs.), Women Execs. in State Govt., Am. Bankers Assn. (govt. rels. coun. 1990—92), Nat. Assn. Bank Women (pres. 1980—81), Rotary. Democrat. Avocations: animal protection, reading, cultural arts, travel. Home: 1477 Sedgefield Dr New Albany OH 43054-9431 Personal E-mail: lpage@insight.rr.com.

PAGE, LORNE ALBERT, physicist, researcher; b. Buffalo, July 28, 1921; s. John Otway and Laura (Stewart) P.; m. Muriel Emily Jamieson, Sept. 7, 1946; children: J. Douglas (dec.), Kenneth L., James F. (dec.), Donald S., David K. BSc, Queen's U., Can., 1944; PhD, Cornell U., 1950. Mem. faculty U. Pitts., 1950—, prof. physics, 1958-86, prof. emeritus, 1987—. Vis. physicist Stanford U., Palo Alto, Calif., 1962, Lawrence Livermore Lab., Calif., 1970. Contbr. articles to Phys. Rev., Rev. Modern Physics, Ann. Rev. Nuc. and Particle Sci. Lt. Royal Can. Navy, 1944-45. Guggenheim fellow Upsala U., Sweden, 1957-58; Alfred P. Sloan Rsch. fellow, 1961-63 Fellow Am. Phys. Soc.; mem. Sigma Xi. Episcopalian. Achievements include rsch. in definitive measurement of electron-electron (Møller) scattering, measurement of the positron's mass, identification of positronium in condensed matter; development of method for analyzing circular polarization of high energy x-rays, first measurement of inherent polarization of positive beta particles. Home: 157 Lloyd Ave Pittsburgh PA 15218-1645

PAGE, MICHEL, biochemist, researcher; b. Quebec, Que., Can., Feb. 18, 1940; s. Hector and Alma (Dussault) P.; m. Marthe Boudreau, Dec. 17, 1966; children: Brigitte, Marie, Charles, Madeleine. BA, Laval U., 1960; B.Sc., Ottawa U., 1965, PhD, 1969. Nat. Cancer Inst. postdoctoral fellow U. Colo., Boulder, 1968-70; research fellow Mt. Sinai Sch. Medicine, N.Y.C., 1970-71; clin. biochemist Hotel Dieu Hosp., Quebec, 1971-81; research scholar Nat. Cancer Inst. Can., 1975-81; prof. biochemistry U. Laval, Quebec City, 1982—; pres., founder BCM Biotech Inc., 1988, BCM Développement Inc., 1993; founder BCM Oncologia Inc., 1995. Mem. grant panels Med. Rsch. Coun., Nat. Cancer Inst.; pres. BCM Biotech Inc., BCM Devel. Inc.; sci. advisor Bioxel Pharma Inc. Author: La cuisine sans cholesterol, 1975, Cancer, 1983, Cancérologie expérimentale, 1993; contbr. over 140 articles to sci. publs; patentee in field. Mem. Ordre des Chimistes du Que., AAAS, Canadian Biochem. Soc., Canadian Immunol. Soc., Am. Soc. Cell Biology., Am. Assn. Clin. Rsch. Roman Catholic. Home: 125 Dalhousie #217 Quebec City PQ Canada G1K 4C5 Office: Faculty of Medicine U Laval Quebec City PQ Canada G1K 7P4 E-mail: bcm2@videotron.ca.

PAGE, OSCAR C. academic administrator; b. Bowling Green, Ky., Dec. 22, 1939; s. Elizabeth Page; m. Anna Laura Hood, June 12, 1965; children: Kristen, Matt. BA in Social Sci., Western Ky. U., 1962; MA in History, U. Ky., 1963, PhD in Early Modern European History, 1967. Instr. history Western Ky. U., Bowling Green, 1964; asst. prof., asst. chair history dept. U. Ga., Athens, 1967-71; dean Wesleyan Coll., Macon, Ga., 1971-78; v.p. acad. affairs Lander Coll., Greenwood, S.C., 1978-86, acting pres., 1985, provost, v.p. acad. affairs, 1986-88; pres. Austin Peay State U., Clarksville, Tenn., 1988-94, Austin Coll., Sherman, Tex., 1994—. Bd. dirs.Clarksville Nations Bank. Bd. dirs. United Way, Sherman, 1994—98; mem. pres.'s commn. NCAA, 1990—94, mem. mgmt. coun., 1998—2002; bd. dirs. Meml. Hosp., Clarksville; pres. Assn. Tex. Colls. and Univs., 1998—99. Mem.: Sherman C. of C., Rotary Club. Office: Austin Coll 900 N Grand Ave Sherman TX 75090-4440

PAGE, PATTI (CLARA ANN FOWLER), vocalist; b. Claremore, Okla., Nov. 8, 1927; m. Jerry Filiciotto, 1990. Country singer Sta. KTUL-AM, Tulsa; with Art Klauser and his Oklahomans Tulsa; with Meet Patti Page Show Sta. KTUL-AM, Tulsa; vocalist Breakfast Club, Chgo., 1948, Benny Goodman Septet, 1948; recording artist, 1950—. Appeared extensively on TV during the '50s on shows such as the Scott Music Hall, the Big Record variety show and her own shows for NBC and CBS; made several movies including "Elmer Gantry", 1960, "Dondi", 1961, and "Boys Night Out", 1962; prodr. Patti Page Pure Maple Syrup and Pancake Mix. First hit record "Confess", 1949; first million-seller "With My Eyes Wide Open I'm Dreaming"; hits throughout the '50s included "I Don't Care If the Sun Don't Shine", "All My Love" (U.S. #1), "The Tennessee Waltz", "Mockin' Bird Hill", "I Went to Your Wedding", "Once in a While", "You Belong to Me", "Why Don't You Believe Me", (How Much Is) "That Doggie in the Window", "Let Me Go, Lover", "Allegheny Moon", "Old Cape Cod." Records continued to sell well into the 1960s; last U.S. Top 10 entry 1965 title song from Bette Davis-Olivia De Havilland movie "Hush, Hush, Sweet Charlotte." In 1970s recorded mainly country material; in the '80s signed with Nashville-based Plantation Records. In 1988 gained excellent reviews when she played the Ballroom in N.Y.C., her first appearance in that city in nearly 20 years; albums: Patti Page Live at Carnegie Hall, 1999, Cocktail Hour, 2000, Brand New Tennessee Waltz, 2001, Sweet Sounds of Christmas, 2002, Child of Mine, 2002; host (radio show) Patti Page Show. Winner Grammy award for Best Traditional Popular Vocal Performance, 1999; Living Legend award Okla. Jazz Hall of Fame, 2002. Office: Filiciottos Hilltop Farm Inc 484 Lang Rd Bath NH 03740

PAGE, POLLY E. state agency administrator; b. Fairmont, W. Va. children: Larry, Paul. Student, Fairmont State Coll. Mem. Aurora City Coun., Aurora, Colo., 1987—95; commr. Arapahoe County, Colo., 1995—2000, Pub. Utilities Commn., Denver, 2000—. Chmn. Arapahoe County Pub. Airport Authority, Arapahoe Water & Wastewater Authority; bd. dir. Aurora Econ. Devel. Coun.; chmn. Denver Regional Coun. of Gov.; bd. dir. E-470 Pub. Hwy. Authority, Metro Wastewater Reclamation Dist.; chmn. S.E. Trans. Advocacy Group; bd. trustees S.W. Bus. Partnership. Auxilliary mem. Salvation Army; den mother Cub Scouts; home rm. mother; bd. dir. YMCA, Comitis Crisis Ctr. Recipient Vol. of Yr. award, Arapahoe Rep. Party. Office: Colorado Dept Regulatory Agencies PUC 158 Logan St 022 Denver CO 80203

PAGE, RANDALL, state official; b. Mt. Vernon, Ohio, Feb. 18, 1967; s. James and Nancy Page; m. Melissa Rohrman, Feb. 16, 1991; children: Julie Anne, Jason Ryan. BS, Bob Jones U., Greenville, 1990. Dir. of pub. events Office of the Gov., Columbia, SC, 1995—99; exec. v.p. Jordan and McCallum Co., Greenville, SC, 1999—2001; legislative affairs dir. Office of the Lt. Gov., Columbia, SC, 2001—03, chief of staff, 2003—04; campaign mgr. Beasley for Senate, Columbia, SC, 2004—. Bd. mem. INSIGHTS, Greenville, SC, 1994—2001; adv. bd. LifeEd, Greenville, SC, 2000—; exec. bd. SC Citizens for Life, Columbia, 2001—. Cons. George W. Bush for Pres., Columbia, SC, 2000; fourth dist. chmn. SC Rep. Party, Columbia, 2001—03; bd. mem. Kennerly Rd. Bapt. Ch., Irmo, SC, 2003—; exec. bd. mem. Greenville County Libr. Sys., SC, 1999—2001. Recipient Order of the Palmetto, Gov. David M. Beasley, SC., 1998, Hon. Order of Ky. Colonels, Gov. Paul Patton, Ky., 2003. R-Conservative. Baptist. Avocation: swimming. Office: Beasley for Senate PO Box 12321 Columbia SC 29211 Office Phone: 803-400-1606. Office Fax: 803-799-8638. Personal E-mail: govpage@sc.rr.com. E-mail: randy@beasleyforsenate.com.

PAGE, ROBERT HENRY, engineering educator, researcher; b. Phila., Nov. 5, 1927; s. Ernest Fraser and Marguerite (MacFarl) P.; m. Lola Marie Griffin, Nov. 12, 1948; children: Lola Linda, Patricia Jean, William Ernest, Nancy Lee, Martin Fraser. BS in Mech. Engring, Ohio U., 1949; MS, U. Ill., 1951, PhD, 1955. Instr., research assoc. U. Ill., 1949-55; research engr. fluid dynamics Esso Research & Engring. Co., 1955-57; vis. lectr. Stevens Inst. Tech., 1956-57, dir. fluid dynamics lab., prof. mech. engring., 1957-61; prof. mech. engring., chmn. dept. mech., indsl. and aerospace engring. Rutgers-The State U., 1961-76, prof., research cons., 1976-79; dean engring. Tex. A&M U., 1979-83, Forsyth prof., 1983-93, prof. emeritus mech. engring., 1994—. Spl. research base pressure and heat transfer, wake flow and flow separation. Contbr. over 200 articles to profl. publs.; inventor impingement nozzles. Served with AUS, 1945-47, Pacific Theatre of Operations. Recipient Western Electric Fund award Am. Soc. Engring Edn., 1968, Lindback Found. award, 1969, Disting. Alumnus award U. Ill., 1971; Disting. Svc. award, 1973, Life Quality Engring. award, 1974, James Harry Potter Gold medal, 1983, Ohio U. medal, 1983; named hon. prof. Ruhr U., Buchum, Fed. Republic Germany, 1984; named to Acad. Disting. Grads., Ohio U., 2001, Hall of Fame, Ctrl. H.S., Phila., 2002. Fellow AAAS, AIAA, ABET, Am. Astron. Soc. (chmn. nat. space engring. com. 1969-70, 72-76), Am. Soc. Engring. Edn. (Centennial medal 1993); mem. ASME (hon. mem. award 1988), Am. Phys. Soc., Pan Am. Acad. Engring. (charter). Home: 1905 Comal Cir College Station TX 77840-4818 Business E-Mail: rpage@mengr.tamu.edu.

PAGE, ROBERT WESLEY, engineering and construction company executive, federal official; b. Dallas, Jan. 22, 1927; s. Arch Cleo and Zelma (Tyler) P.; m. Nancy Ann Eaton, Sept. 17, 1952; children: Robert W. Jr., David, Mark, Margaret. BS in Archtl. Engring., Tex. A&M U., 1950. Asst. prof. Am. Univ., Beirut, 1952-54; project mgr. Aramco, The Hague and Saudi Arabia, 1954-56; dir. constrn. and devel. Internat. Coll., Beirut, N.Y.C., 1956-58; internat. mgr. Bechtel Co., N.Y.C., 1958-64; v.p. Rockresorts Co., N.Y.C., 1964-71; pres., chief exec. officer George A. Fuller Co., N.Y.C., from 1971; corp. v.p. Northrop Corp., N.Y.C., from 1971; pres., chief exec. officer Rust Engring. Co., Birmingham, Ala., 1976-81, Kellogg Rust Inc., Houston, 1981-85, chmn., chief exec. officer, dir., 1985-86; pres., chief exec. officer PM Co., Houston, 1986; asst. sec. U.S. Dept. of Army, Washington, 1987-90; chmn. Panama Canal Commn., 1989-90; exec. v.p. McDermott Internat., Washington, 1990—; sr. lectr. MIT, 1993; chmn. Pegasus Cons., Inc., Cambridge, Mass., 1996—; vice-chmn. Indevo Group, 2001—. Adj. prof. Georgetown U., Am. U.; bd. dirs. I.C.F./Kaiser Internat.; bd. dirs. Thormatrix, Inc., San Jose, Calif. Trustee Internat. Coll. Beirut; mem. Pres.'s Coun., U. Ala.; bd. dirs. Coll. Football Hall of Fame. With USNR, 1944-46, PTO. Trustee Am. U. in Cairo; trustee Wortham Theatre Ctr., Houston, Internat. Coll. Beirut; mem. Pres.'s Council, U. Ala.; mem. adv. bd. John E. Gray Inst., Lamar U.; bd. dirs. Coll. Football Hall of Fame. Served with USNR, 1944-46, PTO. Recipient Distinguished Scholar, MIT. Mem. ASME, ASCE, Rolling Rock Club (Ligoner, Pa.), Internat. Club (Washington), Army-Navy Club (Washington), Georgetown Club (Washington), Sakonnet Country Club (Little Compton, R.I.), Cosmos Club, Tau Beta Pi. Home: 3025 P St NW Washington DC 20007-3054 Office: 1850 K St NW Ste 950 Washington DC 20006-2213

PAGE, RUFFNER, bank executive; married; 3 children. BA in Philosophy and Psychology, Vanderbilt U., 1981; MBA, U. Va., 1986. With Remington Fund, 1986—89, Nat. Bank Commerce, 1989—93; from mem. staff to pres. McWane, Birmingham, Ala., 1993—. Bd. dir. Nat. Bank Commerce, Ala. Nat. Bancorporation, Protective Investment Co., O'Neal Steel, Inc., McWane, Inc. Bd. dir. Ala. Symphony, Birmingham (Ala.) Mus. Art, Emmet O'Neil Lib. Found., Vulcan Pk. Found., Altamont Sch. Mem.: Rotary. Office: McWane 2900 Highway 280 Ste 300 Birmingham AL 35223

PAGE, SALLY JACQUELYN, university official, management educator; b. Saginaw, Mich., 1943; d. William Henry and Doris Effie (Knippel) P. BA, U. Iowa, 1965; MBA, So. Ill. U., 1973. Copy editor C.V. Mosby Co., St. Louis, 1965-69; editl. cons. Editl. Assocs., Edwardsville, Ill., 1969-70; rsch. adminstr. So. Ill. U., 1970-74, asst. to pres., affirmative action officer, 1974-77; officer of instn. U. N.D., Grand Forks, 1977—, lectr. mgmt., 1978—. Polit. comentator Sta. KFJM, Nat. Public Radio affiliate, 1981-90; mem. mayor's com. Employment of People With Disabilities, 1980-97. Contbr. articles to profl. jours.

Chmn. N.D. Equal Opportunity Affirmative Action Officers, 1987-2003; chmn. NDUS Diversity Coun.; pres. Pine to Prairie coun. Girl Scouts U.S., 1980-85; mem. employment com. Ill. Commn. on Status of Women, 1976-77; mem. Bicentennial Com., Edwardsville, 1976, Bikeway Task Force, Edwardsville, 1975-77, Greater Grand Forks (N.D.) Bus. Leadership Network; bd. dirs. Grand Forks Homes, 1985—2003, pres., 1996-2001; mem. Civil Svc. Rev. Task Force, Grand Forks, 1982, civil svc. commr., 1983-98, chmn., 1984, 86, 88, 92, 96; ruling elder 1st Presbyn.; mem. Grand Forks Mayor's Adv. Cabinet, 1998-2000. Mem. AAUW (dir. Ill. 1975-77), PEO, Coll. and Univ. Pers. Assn. (rsch. and publs. bd. 1982-84), Soc. Human Resource Mgmt., Am. Assn. Affirmative Action, ADA Coords. Democrat. Presbyterian. Home: 3121 Cherry St Grand Forks ND 58201-7461 Office: U ND Grand Forks ND 58202 Business E-Mail: Sally-Page@mail.und.nodak.edu.

PAGE, STEPHEN FRANKLIN, aerospace transportation executive; b. L.A., Jan. 21, 1940; s. Steve and Milla Theresa (Raditich) Page; m. Judith Kelly; children: Stephen D., Mark C., Kathryn K. BBA, Loyola U., L.A., 1962, JD, 1968. Bar: Calif. 1969; CPA, Calif. Prin. Deloitte, Haskins & Sells, L.A., 1962-72; v.p. sec., gen. counsel McCulloch Corp., L.A., 1972-76; pres. McCulloch Mite-E-Lite, L.A., 1976-79; v.p., contr., treas. Pacific Internat. Group (div. Black & Decker), L.A., 1979-81; v.p., treas. Ams. Internat. Group (div. Black & Decker), L.A., 1981-82, Black & Decker Mfg. Co., Towson, Md., 1982-85; v.p. fin., treas. Black & Decker Corp., Towson, 1985-90, exec. v.p., CFO, 1990-92; exec. v.p. United Techs. Corp., Hartford, Conn., 1993—97, CFO, 1993—97, 2002—, dir., vice chmn., 2002—; pres., CEO Otis Elevator Co., Farmington, Conn., 1997—2002. Bd. dirs. Augat, Inc., Mansfield, Mass, Lowe's Corp.; trustee, Loyola Marymount U. Pres. Associated Cath. Charities, Balt., 1987—, The Kennedy Inst., Balt., 1988—, chmn., INROADS for Greater Hartford and Springfield Inc. Mem. ABA, AICPA, Fin. Execs. Inst. (chmn. com. on internat. bus. 1987-89, vice chair 1990). Office: United Techs Corp United Techs Bldg Hartford CT 06101*

PAGE, TIM, music critic, writer, producer; b. San Diego, Oct. 11, 1954; s. Ellis Batten and Elizabeth Latimer (Thaxton) Page; m. Vanessa Weeks, Mar. 3, 1984 (div.); children: William Dean, Robert Leonard, John Sherman; m. Julieta Stack, Oct. 12, 2002. Student, Tanglewood Music Ctr., 1970, 74, 75, Mannes Coll. Music, 1975-77; BA, Columbia U., 1979. Music critic Soho News, N.Y.C., 1979-82; music writer N.Y. Times, N.Y.C., 1982-87; music critic Newsday, N.Y.C., 1987-95; writer Washington Post, 1995—. Artistic advisor St. Louis Symphony, 1999—2000; lectr. in field. Author: Music From the Road, 1992, William Kapell, 1992, Dawn Powell: A Biography, 1998, Tim Page on Music, 2001; editor: The Glenn Gould Reader, 1984; editor: (with Vanessa Weeks Page) Selected Letters of Virgil Thomson, 1988; editor: Dawn Powell at Her Best, 1994, The Diaries of Dawn Powell, 1995, Selected Letters of Dawn Powell, 1999, The Unknown Sigrid Undset, 2001. Recipient Pulitzer prize for criticism, N.Y., 1997. Mem.: The Century Assn. Office: Washington Post 1150 15th St NW Washington DC 20071-0002

PAGE, WILLIAM MARION, lawyer; b. Columbus, Ga., July 31, 1917; s. Roger McKeene and Louise Olivia (Seals) P.; m. Lucy Quillian Page, Feb. 8, 1941 (dec. 1982); children: John Roger, Jane Quillian Page McCamy, William Franklin (dec.); m. Barbara Brown Waddell, May 10, 1985. LLB, U. Ga., 1939, JD. Bar: Ga. 1938, U.S. Supreme Ct. 1955. Ptnr. Page Scrantom Sprouse Tucker & Ford P.C., Columbus, Ga., 1939—. Bd. visitors U. Ga. Law Sch., 1969-74. With U.S. Army, 1941-46. Fellow: Am. Coll. Trial Lawyers; mem.: ABA, Columbus Bar Assn. (pres. 1946—47), Chattahoochee Circuit Bar Assn. (pres. 1948—49), State Bar Ga. (bd. govs. 1964—71), Chattahoochee River Club, Big Eddy Club, Kiwanis. Home: 916 Overlook Dr Columbus GA 31906-3029 Office: PO Box 1199 Columbus GA 31902-1199

PAGE, WILLIS, conductor; b. Rochester, N.Y., Sept. 18, 1918; Grad. with distinction, Eastman Sch. Music, Rochester., 1939. Mem. Rochester Philharm., 1937-40, Rochester Civic, 1939-40; prof. conducting Eastman Sch. Music, 1967-69; prof. conducting, dir. orchestral activities Drake U., Des Moines, 1969-71. Guest condr. Sony concerts, Chiba, Japan, 1992. Mem. Boston Symphony Orch., 1940-55; prin. bass Boston Pops, 1947-55; condr. Cecilia Soc. Boston, 1952-54, New Orchestral Soc. Boston; assoc. condr. Buffalo Philharm., 1955-59; music dir./condr. Nashville Symphony Orch., 1959-67; music dir. Linwood Music Sch., 1955-59; 1st condr. Yomiuri Nippon Symphony, Tokyo, 1962-63; condr. Des Moines Symphony, 1969-71, Jacksonville (Fla.) Symphony Orch., 1971-83; founder, condr. St. John's River City Band, 1985-86; guest condr. Boston Pops, Toronto, Rochester Civic, Eastman-Rochester, Denver, Muncie, Jerusalem, St. Louis, Colorado Springs, Memphis, Hartford orchs., Yomiuri Nippon Symphony, 1988, 92; founding condr., exec. dir. First Coast Pops Orch., 1989; condr. all-state orchs. of N.Y., Iowa, Ky., Tenn., Fla., also regional festivals; condr. 13 L.P. recordings including Symphony of the Air (Roger Williams soloist), Boston Festival Orch., Cook Labs., Nashville Symphony. Sgt. 95th inf. divsn. U.S. Army, 1943-45. Decorated Bronze Star; recipient Ford Found. European travel award, 1967. E-mail: wpage11@bellsouth.net.

PAGEL, INGA ANN, accountant; b. Silver City, N.Mex., Sept. 30, 1949; d. Lester Richard and Claudia Marcella (Huckaby) Lee; m. Russell Joseph Cortright, June 25, 1986 (dec. Jan. 2000), m. Jürgen Pagel, Sept. 6, 2003. BS in Acctg., Ariz. State U., 1976, MBA, 1978; postgrad., Walden U., 1995. CPA, Ariz., Tex. Sole practice cert. pub. acctg., Ariz., 1981—. Cons. in field. Mem. AICPA. Republican. Episcopalian. Avocation: travel. E-mail: icortright@aol.com.

PAGEL, PAUL STANLEY, anesthesiologist; b. Madison, Wis., Dec. 6, 1957; s. Gerald Gordon and Mary Ellen (Young) P.; m. Judith A. May, Sept. 13, 1996. BS, Carroll Coll., 1979; MD, Med. Coll. Wis., 1986, MS, 1991, PhD, 1994. Intern St. Josephs Hosp., Milw., 1986-87; resident Med. Coll. Wis., Milw., 1987-90, instr. anesthesiology, 1990—93, asst. prof., 1994—96, assoc. prof., 1996—99, prof. and dir. cardiac anesthesia, 1999—. Assoc. examiner Am. Bd. Anesthesiology. Contbr. articles to profl. jours.; editl. bd. Anesthesiology, Jour. of Cardiothoracic and Vascular Anesthesia. Cardiology Rsch. Anesthesiology fellow Med. Coll. Wis., 1992-93, Rsch. fellow NIH, 1990-92. Fellow Am. Coll. Cardiology, Am. Heart Assn., Am. Coll. Chest Physicians; mem. Am. Soc. Anesthesiology, Am. Soc. Pharmacology & Exptl. Therapeutics, Assn. Univ. Anesthesiologists, Internat. Anesthesia Rsch. Soc. Office: Medical College Wisconsin MEB-M4280 8701 Watertown Plank Rd Milwaukee WI 53226 Business E-Mail: pspagel@mcw.edu.

PAGEL, SCOTT B. dean, law librarian, law educator; b. Mich. State U.; MA in Libr. Sci., U. Mich.; JD, U. Calif., Berkeley. Pub. svcs. libr. Golden Gate U.; assoc. law libr. Columbia Law Sch.; dir. law libr., assoc. prof. U. Okla.; assoc. dean info. svcs., dir. law libr., prof. law Jacob Burns Law Libr. George Washington U., Washington, 1993—. Contbr. articles to profl. jours. Mem.: Am. Assn. Law Librs. Office: George Washington Univ 2000 H St NW Washington DC 20052

PAGELS, JÜRGEN HEINRICH, balletmaster, dance educator, dancer, choreographer, writer; b. Lübeck, Germany, Apr. 16, 1925; came to U.S., 1955; s. Heinrich and Margret (Haas) P. Artists diploma, Hamburg (Fed. Republic Germany) State Exam Bd., 1947; advanced soloist exam. with honors, Assn. Russian Ballet, London, 1952, advanced tchrs. exam. with honors, 1961, sr. tchrs. exam. with honors, 1969; DFA, Pacific Western U., 1988. Ballet soloist Atlantic Theater, Lübeck, 1945-46, Stadt-Theater, Lübeck, 1946-47; prin. dancer Dortmund, Fed. Republic Germany, 1947-48, Operette and Stattl. Schauspielhaus Theater, Hamburg, 1949-50; ballet soloist Ballet Theater Co., Hamburg, 1950-51; prin. dancer Ballet Legat, London, 1951-52, Ballet Legat and Yugoslav Nat. Ballet, touring throughout Europe, 1952-53; guest ballet soloist Ballet Etoile, Paris Opera, Paris, 1954; dir., owner Pagels Legat Sch. Ballet, Dallas, 1955-62; guest tchr. ballet numerous dance acads. and ballet cos., worldwide, 1962-70; prof. dance Ind. Univ., Bloomington, 1970-90; prof. emeritus Ind. U., Bloomington, 1990—. Guest tchr. ballet numerous orgns. including Vaganova Choreography Inst., Leningrad, USSR, Ballet do Rio de Janeiro, Egypt Nat. Ballet of Cairo, Ballet Intezet, Hungary, Nat. Ballet, Istanbul, Turkey, Royal Danish Ballet, Tex. Christian Univ., Ft. Worth, Legat Sch., Eng., Nat. Ballet, Nicaragua; condr. master classes for Ballet Guatemala, Escuala Nacional de Danza, San Salvador, Academia de Danza Classica, Costa Rica, Nat. Ballet Venezuela, T.W. Univ., Dallas Ballet Co., Columbia Nat. Ballet, Nat. U. Costa Rica, Bellas Artes, Honduras, Ballet Nacional Nicaragua; co-founder, dir. Dallas Civic Ballet; art dir. Ballet Guatemala, 1978-79, Nat. Ballet Salvador; guest tchr. Ulm Theatre, Germany, Ballet Co., 1995, Ballet Nat.-Mcpl., Lima, 1999, Artemis, Amsterdam, Holland, State Ballet Ecuador, Quito; Internat. Ballet competition Managua, Nicaragua, 1995; examiner Russian Ballet Soc., Eng., 1969—; guest tchr., lectr. Cuba State Ballet Co. Author of character dance books and ballet dance books in English, German and Spanish, 1991; collaborator and coach to Dame Margot Fonteyn. U.S. judge Internat. Ballet Competition, Trujillo, Peru, 1989-91, 99, Internat. Competition, Camaguey, Cuba, 1999. Served as sgt. German Army, 1942-45. Rsch. grantee, Ind. U., 1977. Avocations: exhibited sculptor, tennis, deep-sea fishing. Home: Curtius Str 6 23568 Luebeck Germany

PAGET, JOHN ARTHUR, mechanical engineer; b. Ft, Frances, Ont., Can., Sept. 15, 1922; s. John and Ethel (Bishop) Paget; m. Vicenta Herrera Nunez, Dec. 16, 1963; children: Cynthia Ellen, Kevin Arthur, Keith William. B in Applied Sci., Toronto, 1946. Chief draftsman Gutta Percha & Rubber, Ltd., Toronto, 1946—49, Viceroy Mfg. Co., Toronto, 1949—52; supr., design engr. C.D. Howe Co. Ltd., Montreal, Canada, 1952—58; sr. staff engr. Gen. Atomic, Inc., La Jolla, Calif., 1959—81. Mem.: Brit. Nuc. Energy Soc., Inst. Mech. Engrs., Soc. History Tech., ASME. Achievements include patents in field. Home: 3183 Magellan St San Diego CA 92154-1515

PAGET, RUTH PENNINGTON, academic administrator, educator, writer; b. Detroit, Dec. 12, 1963; d. Clarence and Beatrice May Pennington; m. Laurent Albert Paget, July 16, 1988; 1 child, Florence Isabelle Winifred. BA in East Asian Studies, U. Chgo., 1986. Mktg. mgr. T.L.I. Internat., Chgo., 1985—87; Japanese svcs. sec. Ernst & Young, Chgo., 1987—88; Japanese svc. coord. Deloitte & Touche, Paris, 1989—91; bilingual mkt. rschr. Chamberlain Rsch., Madison, Wis., 1996—97; focus group recruiter Martin Focus Groups, Va. Beach, Va., 1997—99; freelance reviewer Calif., 2000—; adminstrv. asst. Calif. State U., Monterey, Calif., 2002—. Contbr. reviews Monterey County Weekly, 2000—, reviews Metro Santa Cruz, 2001, articles Commerce in France, 1992; author: The Edible Tao: Munching My Way Toward Enlightenment, Eating Soup with Chopsticks: Sweet Sixteen in Japan, Edible Alchemy: Making Life Magic. V.p. young execs. Am. C. of C., Paris, 1989—91; family group sec. USS Austin USN, Norfolk, Va., 1997—99; cross-cultural trainer Youth for Understanding, Paris, 1986—94, Chgo., 1986—94; v.p. Friends of Seaside Pub. Libr. Grantee, U.S.-China Peoples' Friendship Assn., 1979; scholar, U. Chgo., 1982—86; Chrysler scholar, Youth for Understanding, 1980. Mem.: Alliance Francaise (bd. dirs.). Avocations: math, foreign languages, comparative religion, archaeology, cooking. Office: Calif State Univ Monterey 100 Campus Cr 82D Seaside CA 93955 Business E-Mail: ruth_paget@csumb.edu.

PAGET, STEPHEN A. rheumatologist, internist; b. Brooklyn, NY, Dec. 13, 1944; MD, SUNY Downstate Med. Ctr., Brooklyn, NY, 1971. Cert. Internal Medicine 1974, Rheumatology NY, 1976. Intern John Hopkins Hosp., Balt., 1971—72, resident, 1972—73; fellow rheumatology Hosp. for Spl. Surgery, NY, 1975, attending physician, physician-in-chief, dept. medicine, divsn. rheumatology, 1995—; Joseph P. Routh prof. medicine NY Hosp., Weill Med. Coll., Cornell U.; program dir. Cornell Arthritis and Multipurpose Arthritis and Musculoskeletal Diseases, Hosp. Spl. Surgery. Named Best Doctors in NY, NY Mag., 2001. Fellow: Arthritis Found. (Clin. Rsch. award 1992). Avocation: financial investment. Office: Hosp for Spl Surgery 535 E 70th St New York NY 10021 Address: 535 E 70th St Ste 721W between York Ave and East River 10021 Office Phone: 212-606-1845. Office Fax: 212-606-1170. Business E-Mail: pagets@hss.edu.

PAGILLA, PRABHAKAR REDDY, science educator, consultant; s. Bhupath Reddy and Saraswathi Pagilla; m. Padmavathy Gottam, July 2, 1999; 1 child, Riya. PhD, U. Calif., Berkeley, 1991—96. Asst. prof. Okla. State U., Stillwater, 1996—2001, assoc. prof., 2001—. Faculty rsch. fellow ALCOA, Knoxville, Tenn., 1998. Grantee, NSF, 2000—04. Mem.: ASME. Office: Okla State Univ 218 Engineering N Stillwater OK 74078

PAGLIA, CAMILLE, writer, humanities educator; b. Endicott, N.Y., 1947; d. Pasquale John and Lydia (Colapietro) P. BA in English summa cum laude with highest honors, SUNY, Binghamton, 1968; MPhil, Yale U., 1971, PhD in English, 1974. Mem. faculty Bennington (Vt.) Coll., 1972-80; vis. lectr. Wesleyan U., 1980, Yale U., New Haven, 1980-84; prof. humanities U. Arts, Phila., 1984-2000, univ. prof. and prof. humanities and media studies, 2000—. Author: Sexual Personae: Art and Decadence from Nefertiti to Emily Dickinson, 1990, Sex, Art, and American Culture, 1992, Vamps and Tramps: New Essays, 1994, Alfred Hitchcock's "The Birds", 1998; columnist: Salon.com, 1995—2001; contbg. editor: Interview Magazine, 2001—. Office: Univ Arts 320 S Broad St Philadelphia PA 19102-4994

PAGLIARO, JAMES DOMENIC, lawyer; b. Phila., Aug. 18, 1951; s. Domenic A. and Nancy I. (D'Amore) P.; m. Susan B. Boag, Aug. 25, 1973; children: Jamie C., Justin A. BA cum laude, LaSalle U., 1973; JD, Dickinson Law Sch., 1976. Bar: Pa. 1976, U.S. Dist. Ct. (ea. dist.) Pa. 1977, U.S. Ct. Appeals (3d, 4th, 8th, 9th and 10th cirs.) 1989, U.S. Supreme Ct. 1989. Regional atty. Gov. of Pa., Phila., 1976-79; sr. trial atty. office regional solicitor U.S. Dept. Labor, Phila., 1979-85; assoc. Morgan, Lewis & Bockius, LLP, Phila., 1985-88, ptnr. litigation, 1988—, mng. ptnr. litigation sect., 1999—. Chmn. Home & Sch. Bd. Norwood Acad., Chestnut Hill, Pa., 1983-87; vestry Hist. St. Paul's Ch., Elkins Park, Pa., 1993-94. Fellow Am. Coll. Trial Lawyers; mem. ABA, Pa. Bar Assn. (speaker continuing legal edn. 1987—), Phila. Bar Assn., Woolsach Honors Soc. Home: 1120 Timbergate Dr Rydal PA 19046-2509 Office: Morgan Lewis & Bockius LLP 1701 Market St Philadelphia PA 19103-2903 Office Phone: 215-963-5668. E-mail: jpagliaro@morganlewis.com.

PAGNI, ALBERT FRANK, lawyer; b. Reno, Nev., Jan. 28, 1935; s. Bruno and Daisy Rose (Recami) Pagni; m. Nancy Lynne Thomas, Aug. 12, 1961; children: Elisa, Michelle, Melissa, Michael. AB, U. Nev., 1961; JD, U. Calif., 1964. Bar: Nev. 1964. Assoc. Vargas, Dillon, Bartlett & Dixon, Reno, 1965—70; ptnr. Vargas & Bartlett and Jones Vargas, Reno, 1970—. Adv. bd. 9th Cir. Ct. Mem. Nev. Dist. Appeal Bd.; mem. hospice coun. St. Mary's Hosp.; mem. adminstrv. coun. U. Nev., 1974—81; treas. U. Nev. Legis. Commn., 1973—74, pres., 1975; bd. dirs. Better Bus. Bur. With U.S. Army, 1955—57. Recipient Outstanding Alumni award, U. Nev., 1978. Master: Am. Inns Ct.; fellow: Am. Bd. Trial Advocates (nat. bd.), Nev. Law Found. (trustee, vice chair), Am. Coll. Barristers, Am. Coll. Trial Lawyers (state chair); mem.: ATLA, ABA, State Bar Nev. (bd. govs. 1976—87, v.p. 1984—85, pres.-elect 1985—86, pres. 1986—87, mediator, arbitrator 1990—), Am. Judicature Assn., Assn. Def. Counsel Calif. and Nev. (state chmn. 1983—85), Def. Rsch. Inst., Nev. Trial Lawyers Assn., Washoe County Bar Assn., Am. Softball Found. (bd. dirs.), Wolf Club, Elks, Order of the Coif. Office: 12th Fl 100 W Liberty St Fl 12 Reno NV 89501-1962

PAGNI, PATRICK JOHN, mechanical and fire safety engineering science educator; b. Chgo., Nov. 28, 1942; s. Frank and Helen P.; m. Carol DeSantis, Dec. 26, 1970 (div. Jan. 2000); children: Christina Marie, Catherine Ann, Patrick John Jr; m. Feriel Palmer, Mar. 21, 2003. B in Aeronautical Engring. magna cum laude, U. Detroit, 1965; SM, MIT, 1967, ME, 1969, PhD, 1970. Registered profl. mechanical engr., Calif., fire protection engr., Calif. Rsch. asst. MIT, Cambridge, 1965-70; asst. prof. dept. mech. engring. U. Calif., Berkeley, 1970-76, assoc. prof., 1976-81, prof., 1981—2003, prof. emeritus, 2003—, vice chmn. grad. study, 1986-89; acting assoc. dean Coll. Engring. U. Calif., 1990; assoc. faculty scientist Lawrence Berkeley Lab., 1976—. Vis. scientist Factory Mut. Research Corp., Norwood, Mass., 1980; cons. on fire safety sci. various orgns., 1972—; affiliate prof. fire protection engring. dept. Worcester Poly. Inst., 2000—; vis. rsch. scholar U. Ulster, No. Ireland, 2000—. Editor: Fire Science for Fire Safety, 1984, Fire Safety Science--Procs. of the First Internat. Symposium, 1986, Procs. of the Second Internat. Symposium, 1989; contbr. articles to profl. jours. Grantee NSF, NASA, Nat. Bur. Standards, Nat. Inst. Standards and Tech., U.S. Forest Svc., 1971—; Applied Mechanics fellow Harvard U., 1974, 77; Pullman Found. scholar, 1960. Mem. ASME, Am. Phys. Soc. (life), Combustion Inst., Soc. Fire Protection Engrs. (Bono award for best paper 1999), Internat. Assn. Fire Safety Sci. (life mem., vice chmn., exec. com.), Tau Beta Pi, Pi Tau Sigma, Alpha Sigma Nu. Democrat. Roman Catholic. Home: 1001 Ascot Dr Moraga CA 94556-1412 Office: U Calif Coll Engring Mech Engring Dept Berkeley CA 94720-1740 E-mail: pjpagni@me.berkeley.edu.

PAGON, ROBERTA ANDERSON, pediatrics educator; b. Boston, Oct. 4, 1945; d. Donald Grigg and Erna Louise (Goettsch) Anderson; m. Garrett Dunn Pagon Jr., July 1, 1967; children: Katharine Blye, Garrett Dunn III, Alyssa Grigg, Alexander Goettsch. BA, Stanford U., 1967; MD, Harvard U., 1972. Diplomate Am. Bd. Pediat., Am. Bd. Med. Genetics. Pediatric intern U. Wash. Affiliated Hosp., Seattle, 1972-73, resident in pediat., 1973-75; fellow in med. genetics U. Wash. Sch. Medicine, Seattle, 1976-79, asst. prof. pediat., 1979-84, assoc. prof., 1984-92, prof., 1992—. Prin. investigator, editor in chief GeneTests (www.genetests.org), Seattle, 1992—; pres. Am. Bd. Med. Genetics, 2002, 03; bd. sci. counselors Nat. Human Genome Rsch. Inst., NIH, 2000—04. Sponsor N.W. region U.S. Pony Club, 1985-94. Mem. Am. Soc. Human Genetics, Am. Coll. Med. Genetics, Western Soc. Pediat. Rsch., Phi Beta Kappa. Avocations: hiking, backpacking, horseback riding. Office: Children's Hosp & Reg Med Ctr Divsn Genetics & Devel M2-9 4800 Sand Point Way NE Seattle WA 98105-0371 Office Phone: 206-987-2056.

PAGONIS, WILLIAM GUS, retired army general; b. Charleroi, Pa., Apr. 30, 1941; s. Constantinos V. and Jennie (Kontos) P.; m. Cheryl Elaine Miller, June 14, 1964; children: Gust, Robert. BS, Pa. State U., 1964, MBA in Bus. Logistics, 1970; D in Pub. Svc. (hon.), Washington Jefferson Coll., 1997. Commd. 2d lt. U.S. Army, 1964, advanced through grades to lt. gen., 1991; comdr. 1097th Transp. Co., Vietnam, 1968; div. transp. officer, then exec. officer 2d bn., 501st inf., 101st Airborne Div., Vietnam, 1970-71; pers. staff officer U.S. Army Mil. Pers. Ctr., Alexandria, Va., 1973-75; staff officer Office Chief of Legis. Liaison, Washington, 1975-76; comdr. 10th transp. bn. 7th Transp. Group, Ft. Eustis, Va., 1977-78; chief of staff 193d Inf. Brigade, Panama, 1980-81, comdr. Logistics Support Command, 1981-82; comdr. Div. Support Command, 4th Inf. Div., Ft. Carson, Colo., 1982-85; dir. transp., energy and troop support Office Dep. Chief of Staff for Logistics, Washington, 1989-90; comdg. gen. 22d Support Command, Dhahran, Saudi Arabia, 1990-91, 1990-92, 21st Support Command Europe, Germany, 1992-93; lt. gen., ret. U.S. Army, 1993; exec. v.p. logistics Sears & Roebuck Co., Hoffman Estates, Ill., 1993—. Author: Moving Mountains (Logistics Leadership and Management of the Gulf War), (one of top 30 best bus. books of 1992, top leadership book 1992 Soundview Exec. Book Summaries, 1992), 1992. Decorated D.S.M., Silver Star, Legion of Merit with oak leaf cluster, Bronze Star with 3 oak leaf clusters, Air medal with 2 oak leaf clusters, Meritorious Svc. medal with 4 oak leaf clusters, King Abdul Aziz 2d Class award Chief of Staff, Saudi Arabian Army, 1991, Kuwait Liberation medal Chief of Staff, Kuwait Army, 1992; recipient Merit and Honor award Govt. of Greece, 1991, Joseph C. Scheleen award Am. Soc. Transp. and Logistics, 1991, Man of Yr. award Modern Materials Handling, 1991, Grad. Man of Yr. award Alpha Chi Rho, 1991, AHEPA Man of Yr., 1992, Disting. Alumni award Pa. State U., 1994; named Hellenic Man of Yr., 1992; Pa. State U. fellow, 1992. Home: 25190 N Pawnee Rd Barrington IL 60010-1354 Office: Sears Roebuck & Co 3333 Beverly Rd Hoffman Estates IL 60192-3322

PAGTAKHAN, REY D. Canadian government official; b. Manila, Philippines, Jan. 7, 1935; arrived in Can., 1968, Can. citizen, 1974. m. Gloria Visarra; children: Reis, Advin, Sherwin, C.J. MD, U. Philippines, 1961, LLD (hon.), 2002; MS in Perinatal Physiology, U. Manitoba, 1969. Diplomate Am. Bd. Pediatrics. Resident in pediatrics St. Louis Children's Hosp./Washington U. Med. Ctr., 1963-65, fellow in pediat. cardiology, 1965-67; fellow in pediat. respirology Children's Hosp. of Winnipeg/U. Manitoba, 1968-71; lectr., asst. prof. to assoc. prof. U. Manitoba Faculty of Medicine, 1972-84, prof. pediatrics and child health, 1985—88; elected to House of Commons, Winnipeg North/St. Paul, 1988—, sec. of state (Asia Pacific), 2001—, min. of veterans affairs, 2002—03, sec. of state (science, research and develop.), 2002—03; min. of western econ. diversification, 2003—. Past assignments include parliamentary sec. to Prime Minister; mem. standing com. on pub. accounts, Spl. Joint House of Commons and Sen. Com. on Code of Conduct, standing com. on procedure and house affairs, sub-com. on the bus. of supply, chmn. standing com. on citizenship and immigration, mem. standing com. on human rights and status of persons with disabilities; spkr. in field; vis. prof. pediatrics U. Ariz. Coll. of Medicine, 1982-83; dir. Manitoba Cystic Fibrosis Ctr., 1974-88. Reviewer Pediatric Pulmonary Jour., Chest jour., 1984-87; contbr. numerous articles to profl. jours. and publs. Advisor Marymound Bd. dirs., 1990-96; sch. trustee, chmn. fin. and personnel coms., Winnipeg Sch. Divsn. No. 6, 1986-88; mem. Manitoba Edn. Home-Sch. Liaison Program Evaluation Com., 1987-88, Can. Internat. Devel. Agy., 1986; citizen-at-large mem. Winnipeg Police Commn., 1983-86; nat. pres. United Coun. of Fillpino Can. Assns. in Can., 1982-86; chmn. bd. pres. Can. Ethno-Cultural Coun., 1984-85, others. Recipient numerous fellowships and awards in field including Queen Elizabeth II Silver Jubilee medal, 1977 and Gold Jubilee medal, 2000. Mem. Am. Coll. Chest Physicians, Am. Thoracic Soc., Can. Assn. for Med. Edn., Can. Med. Assn., Can. Pediatric Soc., Can. Physiol. Soc., Can. Soc. for Clin. Investigation, Can. Thoracic Soc., Internat. Union Against Tuberculosis, Manitoba Med. Assn., Manitoba Pediat. Soc., Midwest Soc. for Pediat. Rsch., N.Y. Acad. of Scis., Soc. for Crit. Care Medicine. Office: House of Commons Rm 307 Confederation Bldg Ottawa ON Canada K1A OA6 also: Western Econ Diversification Can Can Place 9700 Jasper Ave T5J 4H7 Edmonton AB Canada

PAGTER, CARL RICHARD, lawyer; b. Balt., Feb. 13, 1934; s. Charles Ralph and Mina (Amelung) P.; m. Judith Elaine Cox, May 6, 1978; 1 child by previous marriage: Corbin Christopher. AA, Diablo Valley Coll., 1953; BA, San Jose State U., 1955; LLB, U. Calif., Berkeley, 1964. Bar: Calif. 1965, D.C. 1977, U.S. Supreme Ct. 1976. Law clk. Kaiser Industries Corp., Oakland, Calif., 1963-64, counsel, 1964-70, assoc. counsel Washington, 1970-73, counsel Oakland, Calif., 1973-75, dir. govt. affairs Washington, 1975-76; v.p., sec., gen. counsel Kaiser Cement Corp., Oakland, Calif., 1976-88, cons., gen. counsel San Ramon, 1988-98, cons., 1998—. Author: (with A. Dundes) Urban Folklore from the Paperwork Empire, 1975, More Urban Folklore from the Paperwork Empire, 1987, Never Try to Teach a Pig to Sing, 1991, Sometimes the Dragon Wins, 1996, Why Don't Sheep Shrink When It Rains, 2000. With USNR, 1957-61, to comdr., 1978. Mem. Calif. Bar, Am. Folklore Soc., Calif. Folklore Soc., Calif. Bluegrass Assn. (founder), Mariners Square Athletic Club. Republican. Home and Office: 17 Julianne Ct Walnut Creek CA 94595-2610

PAGULAYAN, RANDY JAY, psychologist; b. Apr. 9, 1973; PhD, U. Cin., 2000. User-testing engr. Microsoft Game Studios, Redmond, Wash., 2000—03, lead user-testing engr., 2003—. Author: (with Pagulayan, R. J., Keeker, K., Wixon, D., Romero, R., & Fuller, T.) Handbook for Human-Computer Interaction in Interactive System, 2003, (with Pagulayan, R. J., Steury, K. R., Fulton, B., & Romero, R. L.) Funology: From Usability, 2003. Achievements include patents pending for Squad Command Interface for Console-Based Video Game. Office: Microsoft Game Studios One Microsoft Way Redmond WA 98052 Business E-Mail: randypag@microsoft.com.

PAHEL, TIM ALLEN, music educator; b. Dallas, Tex., Oct. 25, 1966; s. Kenneth Ronald and Gerry Pahel(Stepmother); life ptnr. Mark Mathew Graham. MM, U. of Ill., Urbana, 1993—97. Music coord./instr. Carl Sandburg Coll., Galesburg, Ill., 1999—; dir. Galesburg Cmty. Chorus, Ill., 2000—. Dir. Carl Sandburg Coll. Choir, 1999—. Bd. mem. Nova Singers, Galesburg, 2001—03, Carl Sandburg Coll. Children's Chorus, 1999—2003. Mem.: Chorus Am., Nat. Assn. of Teachers of Singing (assoc.), Am. Choral Directors Assn. (assoc.). Office: Carl Sandburg College 2400 Tom L Wilson Blvd Galesburg IL 61401 Office Fax: 309-341-5441. E-mail: tpahel@sandburg.edu.

PAHNKE, GREG RANDOLPH, surgeon; b. Wilmington, Del., Sept. 30, 1951; MD, U. Pa., 1977. Diplomate Am. Bd. Surgery. Intern U. Tex. Health Scis. Ctr., Houston, 1977-78, resident, 1978-82; fellow in surg. oncology MD Anderson Hosp., Houston, 1982-83; staff Med. Ctr. Del., Wilmington; pvt. practice Wilmington, 1983—; med. dir. Christiana Care Breast Ctr., 1999—. Fellow ACS; mem. AMA, Stanley J. Dudrick MD Soc. Office: Lombardy Med Ctr 410 Foulk Rd Ste 200A Wilmington DE 19803-3802 Office Phone: 302-764-2380. Office Fax: 302-764-3501. E-mail: gpahnke@christianacare.org., gpahnke@dla.net.

PAICOPOLOS, ERNEST MICHAEL, public opinion research company executive; b. Boston, July 11, 1951; s. Michael Frank and Irene Anne (Bosia) P.; m. Gail Miriam Bloom, Feb. 15, 1976; 1 child, Adam Nathaniel. BS, Northeastern U., 1974, postgrad., 1974-75, U. Mass., 1976-77. Field researcher Nat. Opinion Rsch. Ctr., Chgo., 1976-77; rsch. asst. Mass. Dept. Mental Health, Boston, 1977-78; v.p. Cambridge (Mass.) Reports, Inc., 1978-88; prin. Opinion Dynamics Corp., Cambridge, 1988—; pres. Am. Insight, 1989—. Author, editor Dextra, polit. newsletter, 1971. Researcher Carter-Mondale Reelection Com., Dem. Nat. Conv., 1980; mem. fin. com. Paleologos for Lt. Gov., Boston, 1990. Mem. Am. Assn. for Pub. Opinion Rsch., Am. Assn. Polit. Cons., Cable TV Pub. Affairs Assn. Avocations: reading, photography. Home: 27 Somerset Dr Andover MA 01810-1249 Office: Opinion Dynamics Corp 1030 Massachusetts Ave Ste 3 Cambridge MA 02138-5335 E-mail: epaicopolos@opiniondynamics.com.

PAIDOUSSIS, MICHAEL PANDELI, mechanical engineering educator; b. Nicosia, Cyprus, Aug. 20, 1935; emigrated to Can., 1955, naturalized, 1976; s. Pandelis Aristeidis and Parthenope (Leptou) P. B in Engring., McGill U., 1958; PhD in Engring., U. Cambridge, 1963. Overseas fellow Gen. Electric Co., Erith, Kent, Eng., 1958-60; rsch. officer Atomic Energy of Can., Chalk River, Ont., 1963-67; with McGill U., Montreal, 1967—, prof., dept. mech. engring., 1976—, chmn., 1977-86, Thomas Workman prof., 1986—2000, 2000— Cons. and rschr. in field. Editor Jour. Fluids and Structures; contbr. articles in field. Pres. Hellenic-Can. Solidarity Com. for Cyprus, 1974-80, Com. Pan-Can. de Solidarite pour Chypre, 1978-83; hon. consul gen. Republic of Cyprus, Montreal, 1983—. Recipient Brit. Assn. medal for high distinction in mech. engring., 1958, George Stephenson prize Inst. Mech. Engrs., 1976, commemorative medal for 125th ann. of Confederation of Can., 1993, medal Can. Congress Applied Mechs., 1995. Fellow Instn. of Mech. Engrs., ASME (Fluids Engring. award 1999), Can. Soc. Mech. Engring., Royal Soc. Can., Am. Acad. Mechanics, Can. Acad. Engring.; mem. Internat. Assn. Hydraulic Rsch., Internat. Assn. Structural Mechanics in Reactor Tech., Order Engrs. Que. Home: 2930 Edouard Montpetit #PH2 Montreal QC Canada H3T 1J7 Office: 817 Ouest Rue Sherbrooke Montreal QC Canada H3A 2K6 Office Phone: 514-398-7365. E-mail: mary.fiorilli@mcgill.ca.

PAIER, ADOLF ARTHUR, computer software and services company executive; b. Branford, Conn., Oct. 27, 1938; s. Adolf Arthur and Margaret Mary (Almond) P.; m. Geraldine Shnakis, Sept. 17, 1966; children: Nathaniel Jason, Andrew Joseph, Alena Catherine. AA, Quinnipiac Coll., 1958; BS in Econs., U. Pa., 1960. Audit mgr. Touche Ross & Co., Phila., 1960-67; pres., dir. Safeguard Scientifics, Inc., Wayne, Pa., 1967-92; chmn., CEO Healthworks Alliance, Inc., King of Prussia, Pa., 1992—; pres., CEO Novus Corp., Radnor, Pa., 1992—. Bd. dirs. Deltapaper, Levittown, Pa., Analytical Graphics, Malvern, Pa. Bd. dirs. Univ. of Arts, Phila., Lincoln Ctr. Family and Youth, Bridgeport, Pa.; bd. overseers U. Pa. Mus. Archaeology and Anthropology. Mem. Chief Execs. Orgn., Phila. Pres. Orgn., Phila. Country Club (bd. govs., treas.). Office: Novus Corp 5 Radnor Corp Ctr 100 Matsonford Rd Ste 520 Radnor PA 19087-4526

PAIGE, GLENN DURLAND, political scientist, educator; b. Brockton, Mass., June 28, 1929; s. Lester Norman and Rita Irene (Marshall) P.; m. Betty Gail Grenier, Jan. 2, 1949 (div.); children: Gail, Jan, Donn, Sean, Sharon, Van; m. Glenda Hatsuko Naito, Sept. 1, 1973. Grad., Phillips Exeter Acad., 1947; AB, Princeton U., 1955; MA, Harvard U., 1957; Ph. D., Northwestern U., 1959; PhD (hon.), Soka U., 1992. Asst. prof. pub. adminstrn. Seoul Nat. U., 1959-61; asst. to assoc. prof. politics Princeton U., 1961-67; prof. polit. sci. U. Hawaii, Honolulu, 1967-92, prof. emeritus, 1992—. Cons. Fla. Martin Luther King, Jr., Inst. for Nonviolence, 1997. Author: The Korean Decision, 1968, The Scientific Study of Political Leadership, 1977, To Nonviolent Political Science, 1993, Nonkilling Global Political Science, 2002; editor: Political Leadership, 1972, (with George Chaplin) Hawaii 2000, 1973, (with Sarah Gilliatt) Nonviolence in Hawaii's Spiritual Traditions, 1991, Buddhism and Nonviolent Global Problem-Solving, 1991, (of Petra K. Kelly) Nonviolence Speaks to Power, 1993, (with Chaiwat Satha-Anand) Islam and Nonviolence, 1993; social sci. editor: Biography, 1977-2000. Program chmn. Hawaii Gov.'s Conf. on Yr. 2000, 1970; faculty UN Univ. Internat. Leadership Acad., 1997; pres. Non-profit Ctr. for Global Nonviolence, 1994—. With U.S. Army, 1948-52. Decorated Commendation medal; recipient Seikyo Culture prize, 1982, Dr. G. Ramachandran award for internat. understanding, 1986, Anuvrat award for internat. peace, 1987, Jai Tulsi Anuvrat award, 1995; named Woodrow Wilson nat. fellow, 1955-56, Princeton U. Class of 1955 award, 1987, 3rd Gandhi Meml. lectr., New Delhi, 1990. Mem. Internat. Peace Rsch. Assn., Internat. Polit. Sci. Assn., World Future Studies Fedn., Am. Polit. Sci. Assn, Phi Beta Kappa. Home: 3653 Tantalus Dr Honolulu HI 96822-5033 E-mail: cgnv@hawaii.rr.com. *Political science is a science that can help liberate humankind from violence. To do so, it must first liberate itself. This will require five related transformations: normative, empirical, theoretical, institutional, and educational. Political scientists in the 21st century must carry these transformations forward, consolidate them, and extend their influence throughout global society. A nonkilling world is possible.*

PAIGE, HILLIARD WEGNER, corporate director, consultant; b. Hartford, Conn., Oct. 2, 1919; s. Joseph Wegner and Ruth (Hill) P.; m. Dorothea Magner, Dec. 8, 1945; children: Elizabeth, Deborah, Hilliard, Jr. BSME, Worcester Poly. Inst., 1941, D of Engring. (hon), 1971. Sr. v.p. for aerospace and computer ops. Gen. Electric, N.Y.C., 1941-71; pres. Gen. Dynamics, St. Louis, 1971-73; chmn., CEO Satellite Bus. Systems, Inc., Washington, 1973-76; vice-chmn. bd. Internat. Energy Assocs., Ltd., Washington, 1976-85; chmn. bd. H.A. Knott, Ltd., Silver Spring, Md., 1984-89. Vice-chmn. The Atlantic Coun. of U.S., 1987—, Gallager Marine Systems, Inc., 1993—. Patentee in field; contbr. articles to profl. jours. Mem. Def. Sci. Bd. U.S. Dept. Def., Washington, 1973-78; trustee Worcester Poly. Inst., Mass., 1974—. Recipient Pub. Service award NASA, 1969, Order of Merit Italy, 1970, Engr. of Year award Greater Phila. Engring Council, 1960 Fellow AIAA (founding dir.), Explorers Club (nat.); mem. NAE. Clubs: Metropolitan, Chevy Chase (Washington); Conquistadores del Cielo. Republican. Congregationalist. Avocations: skiing, tennis, scuba diving, golf. Home: 905 E Boca Raton Rd Boca Raton FL 33432-4119 Office: 5163 Tilden St NW Washington DC 20016-1961 Office Phone: 202-966-6051.

PAIGE, JEFFERY MAYLAND, sociologist, educator; b. Providence, June 15, 1942; s. Charles Warren and Dorothy Frances (Rice) P.; m. Karen Ericksen, Apr. 30, 1966 (div. 1980). AB summa cum laude, Harvard U., 1964; PhD, U. Mich., 1968. Asst. prof. U. Calif., Berkeley, 1968-76; assoc. prof. U. Mich., Ann Arbor, 1976-82, prof., 1982—, dir. ctr. for rsch. on social orgn., 1992-97; vis. scholar MIT, Cambridge, Mass., 1998. Vis. lectr. U. Ctrl. Am., San Salvador, El Salvador, 1990, Fla. Internat. U., Miami, 1992; internat. observer Nicaraguan Nat. Adv. Commn. on Atlantic Coast, Managua, 1986. Author: Agrarian Revolution, 1975 (Sorokin award 1976), Coffee and Power, 1997; co-author: The Politics of Reproductive Ritual, 1981. Fulbright fellow, 1990, Kellog fellow, 1991; rsch. grantee NSF, 1990-92. Mem. Am. Sociol. Assn. (coun. chair polit. econ. of world sys. sect. 1987-89), Latin Am. Studies Assn., Sociol. Rsch. Assn. Democrat. Avocations: hiking, nordic and alpine skiing, sailing. Office: U Mich Dept Sociology Ann Arbor MI 48109

PAIGE, KATHLEEN K. naval officer; b. Schenectady, N.Y., Aug. 31, 1948; m. David Tuma. BS, U. N.H., 1970; MS, Naval Postgrad. Sch., 1976; grad., Def. Sys. Mgmt. Coll.; grad. program for execs., Cornell U. Commd. USN, advanced through grades to rear admiral; acquisition mgr. Navy's Std. Embedded Computer Resource Office; AEGIS C3 warfare officer USN; baseline mgr. combat sys. divsn. AEGIS Shipbuilding Program; chief engr. Naval Surface Warfare Ctr., Port Hueneme; tech. dir. AEGIS Program Office; comdr. Naval Surface Warefare Ctr., Arlington, Va., 1996-98, admiral, 1998—. Decorated Legion of Merit. Office: Naval Sea Systems Command SE#1100 1333 Isaac Hull Ave Washington DC 20376-1100

PAIGE, RODERICK R. secretary of education; b. Monticello, Miss., June 17, 1933; BS, Jackson State U., 1955; MS, Ind. U., 1964, Ph.D, 1969. Head football coach Jackson St. Univ., 1962—69; dean Coll. Edn. Tex. So. U., developer Ctr. Excellence in Urban Edn.; supt. Houston Ind. Sch. Dist., 1994—2000; sec. U.S. Dept. Edn., Washington, 2001—. Est. Ctr. for Excellence in Urban Edn., Tex. Southern U.; created Peer Exam., Evaluation, Redesign (PEER) program. Co-author: A Declaration of Beliefs and Visions. Mem. NAACP; mem. adv. bd. Tex. Commerce Bank, Am. Leadership Forum. Recipient Harold W. McGraw, Jr. Prize in Edn., 2000; named Supt. Yr. award, Nat. Assn. Black Sch. Educators', 2000, Nat. Supt. Yr., Am. Assn. Sch. Adminstr., 2001. Mem. review coms. Tex. Edn. Agy., State Bd. Edn. Task Force H.S. Edn.; chair, Youth Employment Issues Nat. Com. Employment Policy U.S. Dept. Labor subcom.; mem. Nat. Assn. Advancement Colored People, Edn. Com. States, Coun. Great City Schs.(recipient Richard R. Green award for Outstanding Urban Educator, 1999). Office: Dept Edn Office of Sec 400 Maryland Ave SW Washington DC 20202-0100

PAIGE, SUSANNE LYNN, financial consultant; b. Bklyn., Feb. 25, 1950; d. Abraham and Florence Roslyn (Rosenfeld) P.; divorced. BA cum laude, C.W. Post Coll., 1972, postgrad., 1975. Lic. mortgage broker, N.Y. Buyer B. Gertz and Sons, Inc., Jamaica, N.Y., 1973 76; nat. field sales mgr. LeVison Care Products, Inc., New City, N.Y., 1976-82, Am. Vitamin Products, Inc., Lakewood, N.J., 1984-85; prin. Paige & Assocs., Scarsdale, 1982-87; loan officer and fin. cons. Bayside Fed. Savs. and Loan, Jericho, N.Y., 1987-88; prin. Paige Capital Enterprises, Inc., Rye, N.Y., 1988—. Mem. Comml. Investment Divsn./Westchester Bd. Realtors, White Plains, N.Y.; pub. spkr. and lectr. in field. Author: Closing the Deal in Today's Volatile Market, 1994; satarist/polit. cartoonist C.W. Post Coll. News and Editorial, Brookville, N.Y., 1968-72; contbr. articles to profl. jours. Recipient award for Best Original Essay, Newsday Harry F. Guggenheim award, Garden City, N.Y., 1967, Hon. Mention award C.W. Post Coll. Gallery, 1982, Hon. Mention (sculpture) Fresh Meadows (N.Y.) Merchant's Assn., 1971, meritorious notation Real Estate Weekly, 1991-93; selected as Comml. Deal-Maker of Yr., N.Y. Real Estate Jour., 1992, Real Estate Personality, 1993, Northeast Fin. Work-Out Specialist N.Y. and New Eng. Real Estate Jours., 1990-93, also meritorious notation, 1990-93. Mem. Alumni Assn. C.W. Post Coll., 60's East Realty Club, Westchester Bd. Realtors, White Plains, N.Y., Assn. Commercial Real Estate. Avocations: speaker for fin. seminars, writer, traveling. Office: Paige Capital Enterprises Inc PO Box 1234 Scarsdale NY 10583-9234

PAIGEN, KENNETH, geneticist, science administrator; b. N.Y.C., Nov. 14, 1927; s. Alexander and Ida (Kantor) P.; m. Beverly Vandermolen, June 14, 1970; children: Susan, Gina, Mark, David, Jennifer AB, Johns Hopkins U., Balt., 1946; PhD, Calif. Inst. Tech., Pasadena, 1950. Staff mem. Roswell Park Meml. Inst., Buffalo, 1955-72, dept. head, 1972-82; prof. dept. genetics U. Calif., Berkeley, 1982-89; dir. Jackson Lab., Bar Harbor, Maine, 1989—2002, sr. staff scientist, 2002—. Mem. AAAS, Am. Assn. for Cancer Rsch., Internat. Mammalian Genome Soc., Human Genome Orgn., Genetics Soc. Am., Am. Soc. for Biochemistry and Molecular Biology, Sigma Xi, Phi Beta Kappa. Democrat. Jewish. Avocation: sailing. Home: Old Farm Rd Bar Harbor ME 04609 Office: Jackson Lab 600 Main St Bar Harbor ME 04609-1500 E-mail: ndb@jax.org.

PAIK, JOHN KEE, structural engineer; b. Seoul; came to U.S., 1955; s. Nam Suk and Kyong Ock (Yun) P.; m. Aine Fenoula Ievers, Feb. 20, 1970; 1 child, Brian Ievers Paik. BSCE, So. Meth. U., 1961; PhD, NYU, 1975. Lic. profl. engr. N.Y., N.J., Conn., Pa., Md., Mass., Vt., Ga., Fla., N.C. Chief engr. T.Y. Lin and Assocs., N.Y.C., 1960-67; chief structural engr. Soros Assocs., N.Y.C., 1967-68; sr. project engr. Stauffer Chem. Co., Dobbs Ferry, N.Y., 1975-77; prin., founder Paik and Assocs., Westchester County, N.Y., 1977—; chmn., founder The Future Home Tech. Inc., Port Jervis, N.Y., 1986—; chmn., pres. J.K.P. Constrn. Co. Inc., Mohegan Lake, N.Y., 1989—. Adj. assoc. prof. Grad. Sch. Engring. Manhattan Coll., Bronx, 1985; lectr. Grad. Sch. Engring. Polytech. U., Bklyn., 1973-85, Cooper Union, N.Y.C., 1972. Mem. ASCE, NSPE, Am. Inst. Steel Constrn., Prestressed Concrete Inst., N.Y. Acad. Scis., Am. Concrete Inst., Post Tensioning Inst., Constrn. Specifications Inst., Am. Arbitration Assn. (dispute arbitrator, constrn.), So. Meth. U. Alumni Club (pres. 1964), Chi Epsilon. Republican. Methodist. Achievements include the design of over 100 million sq. feet of comml., residential, indsl. and instnl. structures including several highrise bldgs. over 40 stories in N.Y.C. and White Plains, N.Y. Home: Dyckman Dr Mohegan Lake NY 10547 Office: 16 Dyckman Dr Mohegan Lake NY 10547 E-mail: jkpaik@direcway.com.

PAIK, MYUNGHEE CHO, statistician, educator; b. Seoul, Republic of Korea, Nov. 2, 1958; d. Seong-Yun Cho and Yong-Hee You; m. Yi Hyon Paik, Dec. 12, 1981; 1 child, Jane. PhD, U. Pitts., 1987. Prof. Columbia U., N.Y.C., 1988—. Author: (textbook) Statistical Methods for Rates and Proportions (Calderone Prize, 1989). Grantee, NIH. Mem.: Am. Statis. Assn. (regional adv. com. mem.). Achievements include research in biostatistics. Home: 6 Farmington Ct Princeton Junction NJ 08550 Office: Columbia U 600 W 168th St New York NY 10032

PAIK, SUN HYE, cell biologist, research scientist; b. Seoul, Republic of Korea, Oct. 28, 1963; arrived in U.S.A., 1992; d. Bong Ha and Young Ji (Hwang) Paik; m. Earl Wilson Ferguson, May 1, 1998. PharmD, U. Sao Paulo, Brazil, 1987, PharmM, 1991; PhD in Cell and Molecular Biology, U. Md., 1997. Guest worker program Ctr. for Biol. Evaluation and Rsch., Bethesda, Md., 1992—94; grad. tchg. asst. FDA, NIH, Bethesda, Md., 1992—94, U. Md., College Park, Md., 1994—97; sr. rsch. splty. Howard Hughes Med. Inst., L.A., 1997—97; post doctoral fellow UCLA, 1998—2000, vis. asst. prof., 2000—02; COO Sun Biomed. Tech., Inc., Ridgecrest, Calif., 2000—, pres. and chmn. of dirs., 2004—. Contbr. articles to profl. jours. Fed. Agy. for Grad. Edn. scholar, 1989—91, Ministry of Edn. fellow, 1991—92, Small Bus. Innovative Rsch. awardee, Dept. of Army, 2002—. Avocations: reading, travel. Office: Sun Biomedical Tech, Inc 1539 N China Lake Blvd PMB 231 Ridgecrest CA 93555-2606

PAIKEDAY, THOMAS M. lexicographer and linguistic consultant; arrived in U.S., 1962,arrived in Can., 1964; m. Mary Kurien Kizhakethottam, Jan. 4, 1967; children: Anthony, Anne-Marie. LPh, Coll. of the Jesuits, Shembaganur, India, 1955; BA with 1st class honors, Madras Christian Coll., Tambaram, India, 1958; MA, U. Madras, India, 1960; postgrad, Boston Coll., 1962—63, U. Mich., 1963—64. Lectr. English St. Joseph's Coll., Tiruchy, Madras, 1958-59, Ramjas Coll., Delhi, India, 1960-61; copy editor The Statesman, New Delhi, 1961-62; asst. lexicographer W.J. Gage Ltd., Toronto, Canada, 1964-66; editor Ont. Min. Edn., Toronto, 1966-67; head lexicography divsn. Holt, Rinehart & Winston, Toronto, 1967-73; chief lexicographer Lexicography, Inc., Brampton, Canada, 1973—. Cons. Collier-Macmillan Can., Toronto, 1980-81, Can. advisor Collins Publs., Glasgow, Scotland, 1981-82. Chief editor Winston Interm. Dictionary, 1969, Compact Dictionary of Canadian English, 1970, Winston Canadian Dictionary, elem. edit., 1975, New York Times Everyday Dictionary, 1982, The Penguin Canadian Dictionary, 1990, The User's Webster, 2000; author: The Native Speaker is Dead!, 1985; contbr. articles to profl. jours. Mem. Dictionary Soc. N.Am., MLA, Am. Dialect Soc., Am. Name Soc. Roman Catholic. Avocations: computer applications in lexicography, tennis, swimming. Office: Lexicography Inc 83 Sunny Meadow Blvd Brampton ON Canada L6R 1Z3 Office Phone: 905-790-7076. E-mail: thomaspaikeday@sprint.ca.

PAILES, WILLIAM, astronaut; b. Hackensack, N.J., June 26, 1952; married. BS in Computer Sci., USAF Acad., 1974; MS in Computer Sci., Tex. A&M U., 1981. Commd. 2d lt. USAF, 1974, advanced through grades to maj.; pilot McClellan AFB, Calif., 1975—80, Royal AFB, Woodbridge, England, 1975—80; mgr. mini-computer operating systems software devel. Hqrs. Mil. Airlift Command, Scott AFB, Ill., 1982; manned spaceflight engr. Manned Spaceflight Engring. Program, L.A. Air Force Sta., 1983—; astronaut NASA, Houston. Achievements include logged over 97 hours in space; payload specialist STS-51J Atlantis (1985). Office: Astronaut Office/CB NASA Johnson Space Ctr Houston TX 77058

PAIN, BETSY M. lawyer; b. Albertville, Ala., Aug. 29, 1950; d. Charles Riley and Jean Faye (Rains) Stone; m. William F. Pain, Nov. 18, 1977; children: Taylor Holland, Emily Anne Pain. AA, Northeastern Okla. A&M, Miami, 1970; BA, U. Okla., 1974, JD, 1976. Bar: Okla. 1977; U.S. Dist. Ct. (we. dist.) 1979. Staff atty. Okla. Dept. Corrections, Oklahoma City, 1978-79; gen. counsel Okla. Pardon and Parole Bd., Oklahoma City, 1979-84, exec. dir., 1983—88; corp. counsel Roberts, Schornick & Assocs., Inc., Norman, Okla., 1990-2000, Atkins Benham, Inc., 2002; chief legal officer The Benham Cos., Inc., Oklahoma City, 2002—. Editor: (newsletter) RSA Environ. Report, 1991—. With extended family program Juvenile Svcs., Inc. Cleveland County, Okla., 1983-91. Mem. NAFE, Okla. Bar Assn. Democrat. Methodist. Avocations: reading, needlecrafts, church activities. Office: The Benham Cos Inc 9400 N Broadway Oklahoma City OK 73114 Office Phone: 405-478-5353. E-mail: betsy.pain@benham.com.

PAINCHAUD, PHILLIP ANDRE, metrologist; b. Somerville, Mass., Apr. 24, 1919; s. Phillip Andre Painchaud and Gertrude Marie Shanley; m. Josephine Daisy Wandschneider, Dec. 18, 1943 (dec. Feb. 1988); children: Phillip A. III, Denise Michele, Valerie Yvonne; m. Arlene Roberts Painchaud, July 12, 1992 (dec. Dec. 1999). Student, MIT and U. Ill., 1943, R.I. State Coll., 1938-41; BS in Engring., Pacific States U., 1947. Lic. profl. engr., Calif. Gen. supr. metrology Northrop Corp., Anaheim, Calif., 1948-65; dir. corp. stds. E-H Rsch. Labs., Oakland, Calif., 1965-70; sr. scientist Alcon Labs., Ft. Worth, 1970-71; dir. mktg. Metron Corp., Upland, Calif., 1971-72, 78-79; cons. Painchaud Cons., Brea, Calif., 1970—. Vice-chair Calif. Profl. Metrology Com., Sacramento, 1965—74; chair Gov.'s Commn. Metrology, Sacramento, 1967—68; mem. metrology adv. bd. Calif. State Poly. U., San Luis Obispo, 1970—76. Columnist The Std., 1993— Mem. curriculum bd. Calif. State U.-Dominguez Hills, Carson, 1998—. With U.S. Signal Corps, 1942-45. Laureate Woodington award Meas. Sci. Conf. Inc., 1996; disting. vis. scholar Butler County C.C., 1996. Fellow Precision Measurements Assn. (co-founder 1958, exec. dir. 1980-89, life, pres. 1963-64), IEEE (life, sr. mem.); mem. Internat. Soc. Weighing and Measurements (life, sr. mem., gov. precision measurement divsn. 1997-99), Instrument Soc. Am. (life, sr. mem., dir. met. divsn. 1966-70), Am. Soc. for Quality (sr. mem.), ENG Club San Francisco. Avocations: computer operations, photography. Home and Office: 1110 W Dorothy Dr Brea CA 92821-2017 E-mail: painchaud4@cs.com.

PAINE (WILLIAMS), ALAN (AL) K. recording industry executive; b. Panama City, Fla., Nov. 30, 1956; s. Charles Russell and Edna Pearl (Pierce) Williams. Student, U. Nev., Las Vegas, 1978—80, Taft Coll., 1975—77. Office mgr. Visionary Integrated Sys., Las Vegas, 1990—93; adj. prof. S. Nev. CC, Las Vegas, 1996—99; pres. Diogenes Prodns., Las Vegas, 2000—. Prodr., dir., actor: (plays) What Happens to a Dream Deferred; author: (screenplays) Clear Skies on Tuesday, Shadow Chasers, The Love Child, What Kind of Fool, Twinkle, Twinkle, Little Star How I Wonder, Ode to Madonna and Other Poems, 1991, numerous poems; actor: (plays) Raisin in the Sun, Don't Bother Me, I can't Cope, No Place to be Somebody; (films) No Not One. Counselor S. Nev. Suicide Prevention Ctr., Las Vegas, 1992. Recipient Golden Poet award, World Poetry, Inc., 1991, 1992, cert. of spl. recognition, Watermark Press, award of merit, Verses, cert. of honor, Hidden Springs Rev., Critics Choice award, Nat. Libr. Poetry, 1996. Home and Office: PO Box 304 325 S Third St #1 Las Vegas NV 89101 E-mail: alanpaine@excite.com.

PAINE, DAVID M. public relations executive; b. N.Y.C., Sept. 25, 1956; BA in Polit. Sci., Union Coll., 1979. Press advanceman The White House, Washington, 1980; with N.Y. State Assembly Judiciary Com.; acct. exec. Burson-Marsteller, N.Y.C.; founder, pres. Paine & Assocs., Costa Mesa, Calif., 1986—. Mem. Pub. Rels. Soc. Am. Office: Paine PR 1900 MacArthur Blvd Irvine CA 92612

PAINE, KATHARINE DELAHAYE, communications research company executive; Journalist Washington Post.; later for Boston Herald, San Jose Mercury News-San Francisco Chronicle; dir. corp. comm. Lotus Devel. Corp.; owner, The Delahaye Group, pub. rels. and mktg. comm. rsch., until 1999; pres. Delahaye Medialink Comm. Rsch., Medialink Inc., N.Y.C., 1999—. Co-chmn. U.S. Pub. Rels. Task Force; U.S. liaison to European Stds. Task Force; spkr. in field. Contbr. numerous articles to profl. publs. Office: Delahaye Medialink Comm Rsch Medialink Inc 708 3rd Ave Fl Dave9 New York NY 10017-4201

PAINE, LYNN, academic administrator; m. Tom Paine; 3 children. Grad Summa Cum Laude, Smith Coll.; PhD in moral philosophy, Oxford U.; law degree, Harvard Law Sch. Lawyer Hill & Barlow, Boston; asst. prof. Georgetown U. Bus. Sch; prof. U. Va., Darden Sch., Nat. Cheng Chi U., Taiwan; John G. McLean prof. Harvard Bus. Sch., course head, MBA ethics module Leadership, Values, and Decision Making, 1996—2002, co-leader, MBA course: Leadership and Corporate Accountability, 2004—. Permanent mem. Luce Scholar Selection Panel, 1987—. Author: Leadership, Ethics, and Organizational Integrity, 1997, Value Shift: Why Companies Must Merge Social and Financial Imperatives to Achieve Superior Performance, 2002 (Best Bus. Books, 2002, Library Journal, 2002). Mem. adv. bd. Leadership Forum Internat.; mem. Conference Bd. Blue-Ribbon Commn. on Public Trust and Private Enterprise. Named Luce Scholar, 1976—77. Mem.: Mass. Bar Assn, Phi Beta Kappa. Office: Harvard Bus Sch Soldiers Field Boston MA 02163

PAINE, WALTER CABOT, journalist, consultant; b. Brookline, Mass., May 9, 1923; s. Richard Cushing and Ellen Eliot Paine; m. Ethel Landon Penzel, Dec. 1948 (div. Aug. 14, 1958); children: Michael, Christopher, Piera; m. Eleanor Cole Meyer, Aug. 27, 1959 (div. June 16, 1970); children: Alita, Benjamin; m. Barbara Ann Moyer, June 10, 1995. Student, St. John's Coll., Annapolis, Md., 1942—43; AB cum laude, Harvard U., 1949; postgrad., Columbia U., 1951. Cert. scuba diver, lic. capt. USCG, 1985. Assoc. editor Balt. Sunpapers, 1951—53; editor-in-chief, pub. Valley News, West Lebanon, NH, 1956—80. Pres. Keene (N.H.) Pub. Co., 1955—80; dir. Chelsea Green Pub., White River Junction, Vt., 1995—; cons. Montshire Mus. Sci., Norwich, Vt., 1990—, founder, chmn., 1974—90. Dir. Vital Comms., White River Junction; trustee U. Vt., Burlington, 1963—71. Sgt. USAF, 1943—46. Recipient Granite State award for outstanding pub. svc., N.H. State Univ. Sys., 1991. Avocations: ocean racing, marine research, music, poetry. Home: 213 Palmer Rd Enfield Center NH 03749 Office: Montshire Mus Sci 1 Montshire Rd Norwich VT 05055 E-mail: verve@valley.net.

PAINO, JAVIER E. physician; b. Lima, Peru, Mar. 5, 1965; arrived in U.S., 1989; s. Aldo L. Paino and Maria M. Scarpati. MD, Fed. Parana U., Brazil, 1990; PhD, George Washington U., 1996; postgrad., U. Miami, 1990—92; MSSM in /Neurosurgery, NYU, 1996—. Cert. Peruvian Coll. Physicians and Surgeons. Rescue diver Marine Corps, Lima, Peru, 1982—83; asst. prof. Stanley Kaplan, Washington, 1992—96, Balt., 1992—96. Cons. new product devel. Peikard Labs., Lima, PR, Peru, 1989—95. Recipient Physician of Yr. award, Mt. Sinai Sch. Medicine,NYU, 2001; scholar, Brazilian Govt., 1983—89. Mem.: N.Y. Acad. Sci., Soc. for Neurosci., Am. Assn. Neurol. Surgery, N.Am. Skull Base Soc.

PAINTER, BORDEN W. former academic administrator; BA in History, Trinity Coll., MA in History, 1959; PhD in History, Yale U., 1965; MDiv cum laude, Gen. Theol. Sem. Ordained Episc. priest. Asst. prof. history to prof. history Trinity Coll., Hartford, Conn., 1964—2004, chmn. history dept., 1974—79, 1989—93, sec. faculty, 1984—87, dean faculty, 1984—87, acting pres., 1994—95, 2003—04, pres. emeritus, 2004—. Chmn. bd. trustees, Cesari Barbieri Endowment for Italian Studies Trinity Coll., dir. Italian Programs, including Rome program and Elderhostel in Italy. Author: numerous publs. and papers. Recipient Mead History prize, 1955.

PAINTER, JACK TIMBERLAKE, civil engineer; b. Kincaid, W.Va., July 23, 1930; s. Troy Earl and Nannie Bell (Proffit) P. BSCE, W.Va. U., 1950, MSCE, 1955. Instr. civil engring. W.Va. U., 1950-51, 53-55; mem. faculty La. Tech U., Ruston, 1955—; prof. civil engring. La. Tech. U., 1962-92; Alumni Found. prof. La. Tech U., 1977-78; prof. emeritus La. Tech. U., 1992—. Vis. lectr. Manhattan Coll., Coll. Forestry, SUNY, Syracuse, Cornell U., U. Wis., summers 1954-60 Nat. pres. Circus Fans Assn. Am., 1967; lic. layreader Episcopal Ch. Served with USNR, 1951-52, comdr. res., 1966-77. Named Man of Year Omicron Delta Kappa, 1972, The Jack T. Painter Professorhhip in Engring. in his honor, 2003; Faculty fellow NSF, 1958—59. Fellow ASCE (life, 11 Outstanding Prof. award 1969-90); mem. Am. Congress Surveying and Mapping, La. Engring. Soc. (Charles M. Kerr Pub. Rels. award 1990), Am. Soc. Engring. Edn., Tau Beta Pi (Outstanding Prof. award 1963, 68, 74, 78), Chi Epsilon (Nat. Excellent Tchg. award 1985). Address: 101 Biel Lane New Bern NC 28562

PAINTER, JOHN HOYT, electrical engineer; b. Winfield, Kans., Mar. 27, 1934; s. John Paul and Marjorie Marietta (Slack) P.; m. Joy Lou Vaughan, June 7, 1955; children: John Mark, Paul Burton, William Vaughan, Joy Lynn. BS, U. Ill., 1961, MS, 1962; postgrad., Coll. William and Mary, 1967—69; PhD, So. Meth. U., 1972. Apollo comm. engr., tchr. astronauts NASA Manned Spacecraft Ctr., Houston, 1962-65; sr. engr. Motorola Govt. Electronics divsn., Scottsdale, Ariz., 1965-67; rsch. engr. NASA Langley Rsch. Ctr., Hampton, Va., 1967-74; assoc. prof. elec. engring. Tex. A&M U., College Station, 1974-79, prof. elec. engring., 1979—, prof. computer sci., 1989—, prof. aerospace engring., 1999—. Pres. ALTAIR Corp. cons., College Station, 1980—; tchr. Christian eschatology seminars. Author: The Church Visited, 2002; patentee digital signal processing and fuzzy logic. Served with USAF, 1953-58. Recipient Recognition cert. NASA, 1975; GE Found. fellow, 1962. Mem. IEEE (sr.), AIAA. Office: Tex A&M U Dept Aero Engring College Station TX 77843-3141 Business E-Mail: painter@aero.tamu.edu.

PAINTER, MARK PHILIP, judge; b. Cin., Apr. 6, 1947; s. John Philip and Marjorie (West) P.; m. Sue Ann Painter. BA, U. Cin., 1970, JD, 1973. Bar: Ohio 1973, U.S. Dist. Ct. (so. dist.) Ohio 1973, U.S. Supreme Ct. 1980. Assoc. Smith & Schnacke (now part of Thompson Hine), 1973-78; pvt. practice Cin., 1978-82; judge Hamilton County Mcpl. Ct., Cin., 1982-95, Ohio 1st Dist. Ct. Appeals, Cin., 1995—. Adj. prof. law U. Cin., 1990—; lectr. in field. Author: The Legal Writer: 30 Rules for the Art of Legal Writing, 2002, 2d edit., 2003; co-author: Ohio DUI Law, 1988, 13th edit., 2004, Ohio Appellate Practice, 2003, William Howard Taft, 2004; mem. editl. bd.: Criminal Law Jour. Ohio, 1989—92; contbr. articles to profl. jours. Mem. bd. commrs. on grievances and discipline Ohio Supreme Ct., 1993—95; mem. Rep. Ctrl. Com., Cin., 1972—82; bd. dirs. Citizens Sch. Com., Cin., 1974—76; trustee Freestore Foodbank, Cin., 1984—90, Friends of William Howard Taft Birthplace, 2002—, Mary Jo Brueggeman Meml. Found., Cin., 1981—92. Recipient Superior Jud. Svc. award Ohio Supreme Ct., 1982, 84, 85. Mem. ABA, Ohio State Bar Assn., Cin. Bar Assn. (trustee 1988-90), Am. Judges Assn., Am. Judicature Soc., Am. Soc. Writers on Legal Subjects, Potter Stewart Inn of Ct. (master of bench emeritus), Bankers Club. Home: 2449 Fairview Ave Cincinnati OH 45219-1170 Office: Ct of Appeals William Howard Taft Law Ctr 230 E 9th St Cincinnati OH 45202-2174 E-mail: JuqPainter@aol.com.

PAINTER, NELL IRVIN, historian, educator, writer; b. Houston, Aug. 2, 1942; BA, U. Calif., Berkeley, 1964; student, U. Bordeaux, France, 1962-63, U. Ghana, 1965-66; MA, UCLA, 1967; PhD, Harvard U., 1974. Teaching fellow Harvard U., Cambridge, Mass., 1969-70, 72-74; asst. prof. history U. Pa., Phila., 1974-77, assoc. prof., 1977-80; prof. history U. N.C., Chapel Hill, 1980-88, Princeton (N.J.) U., 1988-91, acting dir. Afro-Am. Studies Program, 1990-91, Edwards Prof. Am. History, 1991—. Russell Sage vis. prof. history Hunter Coll., CUNY, N.Y.C., 1985-86. Author: Exodusters: Black Migration to Kansas After Reconstruction, 1976, The Narrative of Hosea Hudson: His Life as a Negro Communist in the South, 1979, Standing at Armageddon: The United States 1877-1919, 1987, Sojourner Truth: A Life, A Symbol, 1996, Southern History Across the Color Line, 2002; editor: Gender and Am. Culture Series; mem. editl. bd. Jour. Women's History, Ency. Americana; contbr. articles to profl. jours. Ford Found. fellow, 1971-72, Am. Coun. Learned Soc. fellow, 1976-77, Charles Warren Ctr. Studies in Am. History fellow, 1976-77, Radcliffe/Bunting Inst. fellow, 1976-77, Nat. Humanities Ctr. fellow, 1978-79, Guggenheim fellow, 1982-83, Ctr. Advanced Study in Behavioral Scis. fellow, 1988-89, Kate B. and Hall J. Peterson fellow Am. Antiquarian Soc., 1991, NEH fellow, 1992-93; recipient Ccoretta Scott King award AAUW, 1969-70, Grad. Soc. medal Radcliffe Coll. Alumnae, 1984, Candace award Nat. Coalition One Hundred Black Women, 1986; named U. Calif. at Berkeley Alumnae of Yr., 1989. Mem. Am. Coun. Learned Soc., Am. Antiquarian Soc., Am. Hist. Assn. (mem. program com. 1976-78, J. Franklin Jameson fellowship com. 1978-79, Beveridge and Dunning prizes com. 1985-87, mem. coun. 1990-93), Am. Studies Assn. (mem. internat. com. 1983-88, mem. nat. coun. 1989-92, mem. adv. coun. 1991-92), Assn. Study Afro-Am. Life and History (mem. program com. 1976), Assn. Black Women Historians (mem. rsch. com. 1980—, nat. dir. 1982-84, chair Brown pub. prize com. 1983-86, 88-91), Berkshire Conf. Women Historians (mem. program com. 1976), Inst. So. Studies (mem. exec. com. 1987-88), Orgn. Am. Historians (mem. com. status women 1975-77, mem. program com. 1977-79, 83-85, Frederick Jackson Turner award com. 1983, mem. exec. bd. 1984-87, chair ad hoc com. on minority historians 1985-87, chair Avery O. Craven award 1994-95), Nat. Book Found. (chair non-fiction jury, Nat. Book awards 1994), Social Sci. Rsch. Coun. (mem. com. social sci. pers. 1977-78), So. Hist. Assn. (chair Syndor prize com. 1991-92), So. Regional Coun. (mem. Lillian Smith Book prize com. 1986, mem. exec. com. 1987), Soc. Am. Historians (chair Parkman prize com. 1993—). Office: Princeton U History Dept Princeton NJ 08544-0001

PAINTER, RICHARD WILLIAM, law educator; b. Phila., Oct. 3, 1961; s. William Hall and Marion (Homer) Painter; m. Karen Lindsley; 1 child, Elizabeth Homer. BA, Harvard Coll., 1984; JD, Yale U., 1987. Bar: N.Y. 1989, U.S. Dist. Ct. (so. dist.) N.Y., Conn., U.S. Dist. Ct. Conn., U.S. Supreme Ct. Clk. Judge John T. Noonan, Jr. U.S. Ct. Appeals, San Francisco, 1987-88; assoc. Sullivan & Cromwell, N.Y.C., 1988-91, Finn Dixon & Herling, Stamford, Conn., 1991-93; asst. prof. U. Oreg. Sch Law, Eugene, 1993-97, dir. law and enterpreneurship ctr., 1994-97; prof. law U. Ill., Champaign, 1998—, Guy Raymond and MIldred Van Voorhis Jones prof., 2003—. Vis. prof. law Boston U., 1997, Cornell U., Ithaca, NY, 1997—98, Warren Knowles; vis. prof. legal ethics U. Wis, 2001; vis. prof. U. Bielefeld, Germany, 1999, 2000, 01; vis. prof. law U. Mich., Ann Arbor, 2002; vis. scholar Humboldt U., Berlin, 2000, Harvard U. Ctr. European Studies, 2003—04. Co-author: Professional and Personal Responsibilities of the Lawyer, 1997, 2nd edit, 2001, Securities Litigation and Enforcement, 2003; contbr. articles to profl. jours. Mem.: ABA, Am. Law Inst., Havard Club Boston, Union League Club Chgo., Cosmos Club (Washington). Republican. Episcopalian. Avocation: classical music. Office: U Ill Coll Law 504 E Pennsylvania Ave Champaign IL 61820-3720 Business E-Mail: rpainter@law.uiuc.edu.

PAINTER, ROBERT LOWELL, surgeon, educator; b. Winchester, Ind., Jan. 13, 1934; s. Lowell Walter and Lillian Genevieve (Pierson) P.; m. Esther Lillian Reece, Sept. 21, 1957 (div. Sept. 1977); children: Elizabeth Haines, Bradley, Robert R., Andrew, Jane Macy-Painter; m. Nancy Sue Macy, Feb. 10, 1980. BA, Earham Coll., Richmond, Ind., 1955; MD, Ind. U., 1959. Intern and resident Hartford (Conn.) Hosp., 1959-65; resident Baylor U. Sch. Medicine, Houston, 1967-68; attending surgeon Day Kimball Hosp., Putnam, Conn., 1962-91; chmn., dir. surgery St. Francis Hosp., Hartford, 1991-98; med. practice, cons., 1999—2001. Cons. Hartford Hosp., 1969-99; assoc. prof. surgery U. Conn., 1991-99, anatomy instr., 2000—. Councilman Ct. Common Coun., Hartford, Conn., 2001—. Capt. USAF, 1965—67. Fellow ACS, Am. Coll. Physician Execs.; mem. New Eng. Surg. Soc., New Eng. Vasc. Soc., Soc. Thoracic Surgery. Republican. Avocations: hiking, gardening, bicycling, birdwatching.

PAINTER, THEOPHILUS SHICKEL, JR., internist, allergist; b. Austin, Tex., Apr. 29, 1924; s. Theophilus Shickel and Anna Mary (Thomas) P.; m. Dorothy Bulkley, July 11, 1957; children: Dana Parkey, Amy Hur, Theophilus III. BA, U. Tex., 1944, MD, 1947. Diplomate Am. Bd. Internal Medicine, Am. Bd. Allergy and Immunology. Rotating intern Univ. Hosp., U. Mich., Ann Arbor, 1947-48, resident in internal medicine, 1948-51, fellow, jr. clin. instr., 1956-58; pvt. practice, Austin, Tex., 1958—. Capt. USAF, 1951-53. Fellow ACP, Am. Coll. Allergy and Immunology, Am. Acad. Allergy and Immunology. Avocations: fishing, carving, hunting, painting. Home: 3222 Tarryhollow Dr Austin TX 78703-1639 Office: 800 W 34th St Ste 201 Austin TX 78705-1146 Office Phone: 512-454-5821. Personal E-mail: tspainterjr@cs.com.

PAINTON, RUSSELL ELLIOTT, lawyer, mechanical engineer; b. Port Arthur, Tex., Dec. 5, 1940; s. Clifford Elliott and Edith Virginia (McCutcheon) P.; m. Elizabeth Ann Mullins, July 2, 1965 (div. Dec. 1977); 1 child, Todd Elliott; m. Mary Lynn Weber, May 9, 1981. BS in Mech. Engring., U. Tex.-Austin, 1963, JD, 1972. Bar: Tex. 1972; registered profl. engr., Tex. Engr. Gulf States Utilities, Beaumont, Tex., 1963-66, Tracor, Inc., Austin, Tex., 1966-70, corp. counsel, 1973-83, v.p., gen. counsel, 1983-98, v.p., gen. counsel, corp. sec., 1991-98; atty. Brown, Maroney, Rose, Baker & Barber, Austin, 1972-73, Childs, Fortenbach, Beck & Guyton, Houston, 1973; corp. sec. Westmark Systems, Inc., Austin, 1990-91; sole practitioner, 1998—. Gen. counsel Paramount Theatre for Performing Arts, 1977-83, 2d vice chmn., 1978-80, 1st vice chmn., 1980-82, chmn. bd., 1982-84, retiring chmn., 1984-85; mem. Centex chpt. ARC; mem. adv. bd. Austin Sci. Acad., 1985-88, 93-95; mem. adv. coun. Austin Transp., 1985-88; bd. dirs. Tex. Industries for the Blind and Handicapped, 1988-95, vice chmn., 1990-91; bd. dirs. Aransas County Ind. Sch. Dist. Found., 2002—, Key Allegro Homeowners Assn., 2002-, pres. 2004. Named Boss of Yr. Austin Legal Secs. Assn., 1981. Mem.: Rockport Yacht Club (rear commodore 2002, vice commodore 2003), Am. Electronics Assn. (chmn. Austin coun. 1985—86), Better Bus. Bur. (arbitrator 1983—), Nat. Chamber Litigation Ctr., Tex. Bar Assn. (treas. corp. counsel sect. 1982—83), ABA, Houston Yacht Club, Order Blue Gavel, Austin Yacht Club (race comdr. 1968—69, treas. 1970—71, sec. 1972, 1975, vice commodore 1980, commodore 1981, fleet comdr. 1986), Delta Theta Phi. Republican. Episcopalian. Office Phone: 361-729-7010. Personal E-mail: sailor44@swbell.net.

PAIRO, PRESTON ABERCROMBIE, JR., lawyer; b. June 5, 1927; s. Preston Abercrombie and Blossom Winona (Pritchett) P.; 1 child, Preston Abercrombie III. AA, U. Balt., 1948; JD, 1951. Bar: Md. 1951. Legal investigator Office of City Solicitor, Balt., 1947-50; mem. Md. Ho. Dels., 1950-54; asst. states atty. State of Md., Balt., 1954-58; atty. Liquor Bd. City of Balt., 1958-60; savs. and loan atty., 1960—90. Mem. Md. Criminal Def. Bar (bd. dirs., past pres.), Assn. Trial Lawyers Am., Md. Bar Assn., Howard County Bar Assn. Democrat. Episcopalian. Club: Ellicott City Optimists (pres. 1968). Lodges: Ben Franklin, Masons, Shriners, Jesters. Home: 9032 Overhill Dr Ellicott City MD 21042-5221 Office: Pairo & Pairo 9050 Frederick Dr # A Ellicott City MD 21042-4014 Office Phone: 410-461-1800. Personal E-mail: pairojr@aol.com. Business E-Mail: pairo@pairo.com.

PAIROLERO, PETER CHARLES, surgeon, educator; b. Bessemer, Mich., 1938; MD, U. Mich., 1963. Diplomate Am. Bd. Surgeons, Am. Bd. Thoracic Surgeons, Am. Bd. Gen. Vascular Surgeons. Intern St. Mary's Hosp., Duluth, Minn., 1963-64; resident gen. surgery Mayo Grad. Sch. Medicine, Rochester, Minn., 1966-71, fellow cerebral vascular resch., 1968-69, resident thoracic-cardio surgery, 1971-73; fellow cerebral vascular surgery Baylor U., Houston, 1973; chmn. American Board of Thorasic Surgery, 2001—; staff surgeon Mayo Clinic, Rochester, Minn., 1974—, chair vascular surgery, 1987—90, chair gen. thoracic surgery, 1989—93, chair cardiothoracic surgery, 1992—93, chair dept. of surgery, 1993—. Served in U.S. Army, 1964—66. Mem. AMA, Am. Bd. Thorasic Surgery (chmn., 2001-). Office: 200 1st St SW Rochester MN 55905-0001*

PAISLEY, CHRISTOPHER B. business educator; B in Econ., U. Calif., Santa Barbara; MBA, UCLA. Various acctg. and fin. positions Hewlett Packard Co.; v.p. fin. Ridge Computers, 1982-85; v.p. fin., CFO, 3Com Corp., Santa Clara, Calif., 1985-2000; prof. Santa Clara (Calif.) U. Leavey Sch. Bus., 2000—. Bd. dirs. Applied Digital Access, Inc., DisCopy, ShareData. Mem. Fin. Execs. Inst. Office: Santa Clara U Leavey Sch Bus 500 El Camino Real Santa Clara CA 95053

PAIVA, CLIFFORD ANTHONY, physicist, consultant; b. Honolulu, Jan. 9, 1947; s. John Albert and Dorothy (Martin) P.; m. Jerrine Dunn, Oct. 15, 1972; children: Antonette, Alexander, Allison, Martin. BS in Geophysics, Christian Heritage Coll., El Cajon, Calif., 1978; MS in Astrogeophysics, Inst. Creation Rsch., El Cajon, Calif., 1988. Physicist Naval Warfare Assessment Ctr. Naval Weapons Sys., Seal Beach, Corona, Calif., 1979-83; physicist USAF Rsch. Lab. Rocket Propulsion Directorate Edwards AFB, Calif., 1986-91; physicist Naval Surface Warfare Ctr. Dahlgren (Va.) Divsn., 1991-2000; founder, pres. Battle Sci. Mgmt., California City, 2001—; engring. physicist, sr. infared scientist SPIRAL Techs., Inc, Lancaster, Calif., 2002—. Mem. East Asia Working Group, Ctr. for Strategic and Internat. Studies, Washington, automatic target recognition working group Def. Advanced Rsch. Agy., Theater Missile Def. Asia Pacific sector, Washington; sr. councilor Atlantic Coun. U.S., Washington, mem. physicist for Global Underwater Search Team, Global Ridge, 2000. Contbr. articles to profl. jours. Tenor Masterworks Chorus, King George, Va., 1996-98, Fredericksburg (Va.) Master Chorale, 1996-98, Antelope Valley Master Chorale, 2000—. With USAF, 1965-69. Mem.: Internat. Soc. Optical Engring./Penetrating Radiation Working Group, Am. Inst. Aeronautics and Astronautics, BSM Assn. (pres., founder), Am. Optical Soc., U.S. Naval Inst. Engrs., Creation Rsch. Soc., Optical Soc. Am., Internat. Soc. Optical Engrs., Am. Geophys. Union, APS, U.S. Naval Intelligence Profl. (life). Republican. Assemblies Of God Ch. Achievements include implementation of advanced morphological target segmentation and extraction techniques, leading to accurate predictive computer simulations of threat target sets for ballistic missile defense; research in US Dept Defense high energy laser program. Avocations: piano, guitar. Home and Office: Edwards AFB 159 Camp Fire Drive California City CA 93505 E-mail: aanthony@as.net.

PAIVA-WEED, M. TERESA, state legislator; b. Newport, R.I., Nov. 5, 1959; m. Mark Weed. BA, magna cum laude, Providence Coll., 1981; JD, Catholic Univ. of America, 1984. Bar: R.I., 1984. Asst. city solicitor city of Newport; mem. R.I. Senate, Dist. 49, Providence, 1992—; chairwoman senate com. on judiciary R.I. State Senate, 1997-98. Mem. Newport County Bar Assn., Rhode Island Bar Assn., ABA. Office: RI State Senate State House Rm 312 Providence RI 02903

PAJAK, DAVID JOSEPH, lawyer, consultant; b. Buffalo, N.Y., June 19, 1956; s. William H. and Theresa A. (Granato) P.; m. Peggy J. Fisher, Aug. 1, 1981; children: Andrew J., Karl W. BA, State Coll. Buffalo, 1978; JD, U. Buffalo, 1982. Bar: N.Y. 1983, U.S. Dist. Ct. (we. dist.) N.Y., 1991. Social svcs. counsel Genesee County Dept. Social Svcs., Batavia, N.Y., 1984-93; pvt. practice Corfu, N.Y., 1983—, Buffalo, N.Y., 1993—; town justice Town of Pembroke, N.Y., 1994—; with Genesee County Attys. Office, 2001—. Mem. legis. com. N.Y. Fed. on Child Abuse and Neglect, Albany, 1986—99, bd. dirs., 1987—89; cons. N.Y. Pub. Welfare Assn., Inc., Albany, 1987—92; pres. Social Svcs. Attys. Assn. N.Y. State, 1990—91; instr. Bill Adam's Martial Arts & Fitness Ctr., Buffalo, 1999—2002, Klassic Karate Studies, 1990—98, Filipino Karate Acad., 1989—90. Contbr. articles to profl. jours. Mem.: Western Genesee County Bus. Assn., Corfu Area Bus. Assn., Genesee County Magistrate's Assn., Genesee County Bar Assn., Erie County Bar Assn., N.Y. State Magistrate's Assn., N.Y. State Bar Assn. Republican. Avocations: Karate, martial arts. Home: 17 E Main St Corfu NY 14036-9665 Office: 7170 Transit Rd Amherst NY 14221 Office Phone: 716-630-0400. E-mail: dave@djpajak.com.

PAK, HYUNG WOONG, community advocate; b. Ham-Hoong, Korea, Nov. 6, 1932; came to U.S., 1955, naturalized, 1968; s. Kyung-Koo and Myung-Sook (Lee) P.; m. Diana Lee Stenen Woodruff, 1975; children: Jonathan Tong-Hee, Michelle Hyun-Mi Lee. AB, U. Chgo., 1958. Editor and publisher Chgo. Rev., 1958-63, cons., 1963-65; assoc. editor Ency. Britannica Press, Chgo., 1963-64, sr. editor social scis. and humanities, 1964-66; ednl. dir. Bantam Books, Inc., N.Y.C., 1966-69; gen. mgr. sch. dept. Appleton-Century-Crofts/New Century, N.Y.C., 1970-72; v.p., editorial dir. D. Van Nostrand Co., N.Y.C., 1972-74, pres., 1974-76, Chatham Sq. Press, N.Y.C., 1976-83; pub. Urizen Books, Inc., N.Y.C., 1978-81; exec. v.p. Bus. Software Mag., Palo Alto, Calif., 1983-84; pub., editor Asian High-Tech. Report, 1984-90; exec. dir. The Philip Jaisohn Meml. Found., Inc., Phila., 1990-99; pres. Asian Cmty. Devel. Corp., 2000—. Fellow Hoover Instn., Stanford, Calif., 1984-85. Author: The Pacific Rim, 1990; columnist The Phila. Bus. Rev., 1993-99. Mem. Bd. Sch. Dist. Cheltenham Twp., Pa., 1987-94; mem. Asian task force Phila. Sch. Dist., 1988-95; co-chmn. bus. adv. com. Montgomery County, Pa., 1991-93; del. Citizens' Assembly for a Greater Phila., 1991-95; chmn. Pan Asian Assn. Greater Phila., 1992-96, mem. bd. fellowship commn., 1992-95; bd. dirs. Brandywine Art Ctr., 1995-99, vice chair, 1998-99; Pa. del. The White Ho. Conf. on Aging, 1995; trustee Abington Meml. Hosp. Found., 1995-2000; mem. cmty. adv. com. Keystone Mercy Health Plan, 1998-2002; bd. dirs. Nat. Conf. Cmty. and Justice, 2000-02. Mem. ACLU (life), AHA (mem. comms. com. 1998-2000, mem. Phila. All-Am. city host com. 1998-99), Phila. Mus. Art. Home: 1015 Sharpless Rd Elkins Park PA 19027-3040 Office: PO Box 7167 Elkins Park PA 19027-0167

PAK, IGOR, mathematician, educator; b. Moscow, Sept. 5, 1971; s. Mark Aronovich and Sofia L'vovna Pak. PhD, Harvard U., 1997. J.w. gibbs instr. of math. Yale U., New Haven, Conn., 1997—2000; asst. prof. MIT, Cambridge, Mass., 2000. Home: 115 Mt Auburn St Apt 1 Cambridge MA 02138 Office: MIT Dept Math 77 Mass Ave Cambridge MA 02139

PAK, SE RI, professional golfer; b. Daejeon, Korea, Sept. 28, 1977; Professional golfer LPGA Tour, 1997—. Mem. KLPGA, 1996, 97. Recipient Rolex Rookie of Yr. award, Vare Trophy 2003, South Korea Order of Merit 1998. Winner of 22 LPGA events including four Grand Slam titles. Won the LPGA championship 1998, 2002; won the U.S. Open 1998; won the du Maurier Classic 2001. Address: LPGA 100 International Golf Dr Daytona Beach FL 32124-1082

PAK, SUCHIN, newscaster; b. Korea; Degree in polit. sci., U. Calif., Berkeley. Corres. MTV News, N.Y.C., 2001—. Office: MTV Networks 1515 Broadway New York NY 10036

PAKALUK, DEBRA LORRAINE BEHM, science educator, community service coordinator; b. North Chicago, Ill., Dec. 25, 1959; d. Thomas Gerald and Bonnie Lorraine Behm. BS, Cornell U., 1982; MA, Kans. U., 1984; tchg. cert., Washburn U., 1990. Cert. tchr. secondary biology, secondary sci., Kans. Sci. camp dir., instr. Topeka Collegiate Sch., 1984-90, sci. tchr., dept. head, 1984-91, Yeshiva Greater Washington, Silver Spring, Md., 1991-92, Norwood Sch., Bethesda, Md., 1992—. Sci. camp dir., instr. Kans. State Dept. Edn., Kansas City, 1989; workshop presenter. Contbr. articles to profl. mags. Sci-Math. fellow Coun. for Basic Edn., 1992; Fulbright Tchr. Exch. fellow, 1997; Fulbright Meml. Fund scholar, 2000. Mem. Nat. Sci. Tchrs. Assn. Avocations: travel, reading, piano, photography. Office: Norwood Sch 8821 River Rd Bethesda MD 20817-2600 E-mail: dpakaluk@norwoodschool.org.

PAKENHAM, ROSALIE MULLER WRIGHT, magazine and newspaper editor; b. Newark, June 20, 1942; d. Charles and Angela (Fortunata) Muller; m. Lynn Wright, Jan. 13, 1962; children: James Anthony Meador, Geoffrey Shepard; m. E. Michael Pakenham, Sept. 29, 2001. BA in English, Temple U., 1965. Mng. editor Suburban Life mag., Orange, N.J., 1960-62; assoc. editor Phila. mag., 1962-64, mng. editor, 1969-73; founding editor Womensports mag., San Mateo, Calif., 1973-75; editor scene sect. San Francisco Examiner, 1975-77; exec. editor New West mag., San Francisco and Beverly Hills, Calif., 1977-81; features and Sunday editor San Francisco Chronicle, 1981-87, asst. mng. editor features, 1987-96; v.p. and editor-in-chief Sunset Mag, Menlo Park, Calif., 1996—2001. Editl. cons., 2002—; tchr. mag. writing U. Calif., Berkeley, 1975—76; participant pub. procs. course Stanford U., 1977—79; chmn. mag. judges at conf. Coun. Advancement and Support of Edn., 1980, judge, 84. Contbr. numerous mag. articles, critiques, revs., Compton's Ency. Mem.: Internat. Assn. Culinary Profls., Am. Soc. Mag. Editors, Am. Newspaper Pubs. Assn. (pub. task force on minorities in newspaper bus. 1988—89, Chronicle minority recruiter 1987—94), Am. Assn. Sunday and Feature Editors (treas. 1984, sec. 1985, 1st v.p. 1986, pres. 1987, Hall of Fame 1999), Washington D.C. Women's Forum, Women's Forum West (bd. dirs. 1993—, sec. 1994), Internat. Women's Forum. Office Phone: 717-292-6969. Personal E-mail: RosalieMPakenham@aol.com. *Keep a sharp eye out for talent, recognize it and reward it, and everyone profits.*

PAKES, STEVEN P. medical school administrator; b. St. Louis, Jan. 19, 1934; married; 4 children. BSc, Ohio State U., 1956, DVM, 1960, MSc, 1964, PhD in Vet. Pathology, 1972. Vet. pathologist U.S. Army, Ft. Detrick, Md., 1960-62; chief animal colonies Pine Bluff Arsenal, Ark., 1964-66; chief comparative pathology Naval Aerospace Med. Inst., 1966-69; dir. lab. animal medicine Coll. Vet. Medicine Ohio State U., 1969-72; assoc. prof. Southwestern Med. Sch. U. Tex. Southwestern Med. Ctr., Dallas, 1972-80, Drof. comparative medicine, chmn. dept. Southwestern Med. Sch., 1980—, prof., dir. comparative medicine. Mem. exec. com. Inst. Lab. Animal Resources NAS-NRC; chmn. coun. accreditation Am. Assn. Accreditation Animal Care, 1974-76, treas., bd. trustees, 1983-90; adv. bd. Vet. Specialties, 1981-82, chmn., 1985; chmn. lab. guide rev. com. Inst. Lab. Animal Resources NAS, 1983-85; mem. Inst. Lab. Animal Resources Coun., 1985-93, chmn., 1987-93. Mem. AAAS, Internat. Coun. for Lab. Animal Scis. (sec.-gen. 1995—), Am. Assn. Lab. Animal Sci. (bd. trustees 1985-88), Am. Coll. Lab. Animal Medicine (pres. 1973, exam. com. 1968-69), Am. Vet. Medicine Assn., Am. Soc. Microbiology, Sigma Xi. Achievements include research in infectious diseases of laboratory animals, effect of spontaneous diseases of laboratory animals on biomedical research. Office: U Tex Southwestern Med Sch Dept Pathology 5323 Harry Hines Blvd Dallas TX 75390-7208

PAKTER, JEAN, maternal and child health consultant; b. N.Y.C., Jan. 1, 1911; d. David and Lillian (Kunitz) P.; m. Arnold L. Bachman, MD, Sept. 17, 1939 (dec. Dec. 1992); children: Ellen Bachman Mendelson, MD, Donald M. Bachman, MD. BS, NYU, 1931, MD, 1934; MPH, Columbia U., 1955. Diplomate Am. Bd. Pediat. Intern Mt. Sinai Hosp., N.Y.C., 1934-36, resident in pediat., 1937-39; pvt. practice, N.Y.C., 1939-43; dir. Bur. Dept. Health, Maternity, Newborn and Family Planning, N.Y.C., 1950-82; cons., lectr. maternity, child health Columbia U. Sch. Pub. Health, N.Y.C., 1984—, dep. dir. maternal and child health program, 1984-94, lectr. maternity, child health, 1970—. Contbr. numerous articles to profl. med. jours. Advisor March of Dimes, N.Y.C., 1975—. Recipient Fund for City of N.Y. Pub. Svc. award, 1974, Jacobi medal Mt. Sinai Hosp., 1975. Fellow APHA (Martha May Eliot award 1990), Am. Acad. Pediatrics, N.Y. Acad. Medicine (trustee 1979-83), N.Y. Obstet. Soc. (assoc.); mem. Pub. Health Assn. N.Y.C. (bd. dirs. 1992-96), Women's City Club, Alpha Omega Alpha. Avocations: concerts, opera, theater, reading. Home: 1175 Park Ave New York NY 10128-1211

PAL, PRABIR KUMAR (SUNNY PAL), law firm counselor; b. Chittagong, Bengal, India, Feb. 17, 1936; arrived in Can., 1969; s. Niranjan and Renuka (Mitter) P.; m. Nandinee Majumdar, Dec. 13, 1960; 1 child, Nobina Pal Robinson. BA in Law with honors, Cambridge U., 1958, MA, 1972; diploma in Indsl. Mgmt., Geneva U., 1964. Fin. and legal mgmt. positions Alcan Inc., in Can., Europe and Asia, 1959—99, v.p., chief legal officer, corp. sec., 1988—99; governance and ethics counselor Flavell Kubrick LLP, Barristers and Solicitors, Ottawa, Canada, 1999—. Bd. dir. Transparency Internat. Can. Inc., Lester B. Pearson Coll. of the Pacific. Bd. dirs. Opera Lyra Ottawa. Fellow Inst. Chartered Secs. and Adminstrs.; mem. Internat. Bar Assn., Rideau Club Ottawa. Avocations: photography, rowing. Office Phone: 613-230-6030. Business E-Mail: sunny@flavellkubrick.com.

PAL, PRATAPADITYA, curator; b. Bangladesh, Sept. 1, 1935; came to U.S., 1967; s. Gopesh Chandra and Bidyut Kana (Dam) P.; m. Chitralekha Bose, Apr. 20, 1968; children: Shalmali, Lopamudra. MA, U. Calcutta, 1958, D.Phil., 1962; PhD (U. K. Commonwealth Scholar), U. Cambridge, Eng.,

1965. Research assoc. Am. Acad. of Benares, India, 1966-67; keeper Indian collections Mus. Fine Arts, Boston, 1967-69; sr. curator Indian and Southeast Asian art Los Angeles County Mus. Art, L.A., 1970-95, acting dir., 1979; vis. curator Indian and S.E. Asian art Art Inst. Chgo., 1995—2003; rsch. fellow Norton Simon Mus., Pasadena, Calif., 1995—. Gen. editor, Marg Publs., Mumbai, 1993-; adj. prof. fine arts U. So. Calif., 1971-89; vis. prof. U. Calif., Santa Barbara, 1980, Irvine, 1994-95; William Cohn lectr. Oxford U., 1983; Catherine Mead meml. lectr. Pierpont Morgan Libr., N.Y.C., 1986; Ananda K. Coomaraswamy meml. lectr. Prince of Wales Mus., Bombay, 1987; D.J. Sibley prehistoric art lectr. U. Tex., Austin, 1989; Anthony Gardner meml. lectr. Victoria and Albert Mus., London, 1993, keynote spkr. 1st Internat. Conf. on Tibetan Art, 1994; mem. commr.'s art adv. panel IRS, Washington, 1986-96. Author: Vaisnava Iconology in Nepal, 1970, The Arts of Nepal, vol. 1, 1974, vol. 2, 1979, The Sensuous Immortals, 1977, The Ideal Image: Gupta Sculptures and its Influence, 1978, The Classical Tradition in Rajput Painting, 1978, Elephants and Ivories, 1981, A Buddhist Paradise: Murals of Alchi, 1982, Art of Tibet, 1983, Tibetan Painting, 1984, Art of Nepal, 1985, From Merchants to Emperors, 1986, Indian Sculpture, vol. 1, 1986, Icons of Piety, Images of Whimsey, 1987, Indian Sculpture, vol. 2, 1988, Buddhist Book Illuminations, 1988, Romance of the Taj Mahal, 1989, Art of the Himalayas, 1991, Pleasure Gardens of the Mind, 1993; Indian Painting, vol. 1, 1993, The Peaceful Liberators: Jain Art from India, 1994, A Collecting Odyssey, 1997, Divine Images, Human Visions, 1997, Tibet Change and Tradition, 1997, Desire and Devotion, 2001, Himalayas: An Aesthetic Adventure, 2003, Asian Art in the Norton Simon Museum, vols. 1 and 2, 2003, vol. 3, 2004; Painted Poems, 2004. Bd. dirs. Kathmandu Valley Preservation Trust, Baltimore, Am. Coun. for Cultural Policy, N.Y., John D. Rockefeller III Fund fellow, 1964, 69, fellow NEA, 1974; Getty scholar, 1995-96. Fellow Asia Soc. (Bombay, hon.); mem. Asiatic Soc. (Calcutta, B.C. Law gold medal 1993, R.P. Chanda Centenary medal, 2003).

PALACIO, JUNE ROSE PAYNE, nutritional science educator; b. Hove, Sussex, Eng., June 14, 1940; came to U.S., 1949; d. Alfred and Doris Winifred (Payne) P.; m. Moki Moses Palacio, Nov. 30, 1968 (wid. June 1999); m. Cliff Duboff, Dec. 22, 2003. AA, Orange Coast Coll., Costa Mesa, Calif., 1960; BS, U. Calif., Berkeley, 1963; PhD, Kans. State U., 1984. Registered dietitian. Asst. dir. food svc. and res. halls Mills Coll., Oakland, Calif., 1964-66; staff dietitian Servomation Bay Cities, Oakland, 1966-67; commissary mgr. Host Internat., Inc., Honolulu, 1967-73; dir. dietetics Straub Clinic and Hosp., Honolulu, 1973-80; instr. Kans. State U., Manhattan, 1980-84; prof. and program dir. Calif. State U., L.A., 1984-85; prof., asst. dean Pepperdine U., Malibu, Calif., 1985—. Instr. Kapiolani C.C., Honolulu, 1973-79, U. Hawaii, Honolulu, 1975-80, Ctr. for Dietetic Edn., Woodland Hills, Calif., 1986—; cons. Clevenger Nutritional Svcs., Calabasas, Calif., 1985—, Calif. Mus. Sci. and Industry, L.A., 1989—, Calif. State Dept. Edn., Sacramento, 1985—. Author: Foodservice in Institutions, 1988, Introduction to Foodservice, 1992, 97, 2001, The Profession of Dietetics, 1996, 2000. Mem. Am. Dietetic Assn. (del. 1977-80, 86-89, commr. Commn. for Accreditation of Dietic Edn. 1997—), Calif. Dietetic Assn. (pres. 1992-93), L.A. Dist. Dietetic Assn., Foodsvc. Systems Mgmt. Edn. Coun., Dietetic Educators of Practitioners, Gamma Sigma Delta, Omicron Nu, Phi Upsilon Omicron. Republican. Episcopalian. Avocations: tennis, running, reading, travel. Office: Pepperdine U 24255 Pacific Coast Hwy Malibu CA 90263-0002 Home: 1500 E Ocean Blvd Unit 612 Long Beach CA 90802-6931 Office Phone: 310-506-4339. Business E-Mail: june.palacio@pepperdine.edu.

PALACIOS, CHRISTINA, academic administrator; With S.W. Gas, 1984—, former mgr. human resources, adminstrn., customer rels., ops. and support, v.p. So. Nev. divsn., 1995—97, v.p. in charge of So. Ariz. divsn., 1997—; mem., asst. sec. Ariz. Bd. Regents, Phoenix. Mem. Sch. Facilities Bd., Ariz. Office: Ariz Bd Regents Ste 230 2020 N Central Ave Phoenix AZ 85004

PALACIOS, GONZALO T. education educator; b. Maracay, Venezuela, Mar. 7, 1938; s. Ricardo and Josefina (Galindo) Palacios; m. Anne E. Sullivan, June 18, 1966; children: Robert, Stephen, Michael. Architecture, The Cath. U., 1955—59; PhL in Philosophy, Gregorian U., Rome, 1963; PhD in Philosophy, The Cath. U., 1970. T.a., ethics instr. The Catholic U., Wash., DC, 1964—65; archtl. draughtman Edwin Ball, A.I.A., Riverdale, Md., 1966—68; dir./prof. philosophy St. Mary-of-the-Woods Coll., Terre Haute, Ind., 1968—69; philosophy prof. Cath. U. (U.C.A.B.), Caracas, 1970—73; min., counselor Embassy of Venezuela, Wash., DC, 1974—99; philosophy prof. (adj.) Georgetown U., 1989—2003, Prince George's Cmty. Coll., Largo, Md., 1999—2003. Cons., bd. dir. Mus. Services Internat., Wash., DC, 1980—2000; co-founder, bd. mem. Internat. Conservatory of Music, Chevy Chase, Md., 1980—2000; founder the Assn. of Latin Am. Cultural Attaches, Chevy Chase, Md.; lectr. var. U.S. universities, 1980—2000. Author: (articles) Gaceta IberoAmericana, 1981—2003, NASA Bull. 1980's. Mem.: Am. Assn. of U. Professors. Roman Catholic. Avocations: writing, drawing, translating (eng./spanish).

PALACIOS, OLGA, director; b. Bogotá, Colombia, July 6, 1964; d. Alvaro H. and Blanca L. (Gomez) Palacios; m. Heriberto Molinares, Feb. 2, 1985; children: Daniel, Francisco. BS in Ednl. Adminstrn., Fla. Nat. Coll., 1993. Asst. mgr. Comercial de Oriente, 1982—95; WIA project dir. Fla. Nat. Coll., 1997—2003, clin. rotation mgr., 1997—2003. Home: 6081 W 24th Ave #110 Hialeah FL 33016 Office: Fla Nat Coll 4425 W 20th Ave Hialeah FL 33012

PALADE, GEORGE EMIL, research scientist, educator; b. Jassy, Romania, Nov. 19, 1912; arrived in U.S., 1946, naturalized, 1952; s. Emil and Constanta Cantemir Palade; m. Irina Malaxa, June 12, 1941 (dec. 1969); children: Georgia Teodora, Philip Theodor; m. Marilyn G. Farquhar, 1970. Bachelor, Hasdeu Lyceum, Buzau, Romania; MD, U. Bucharest, Romania. Instr., asst. prof., then assoc. prof. anatomy Sch. Medicine, U. Bucharest, 1935—45; vis. investigator, asst. assoc., prof. cell biology Rockefeller U., 1946—73; prof. cell biology Yale U., New Haven, 1973—83, sr. research scientist, 1983—89; prof.-in-residence Med. Sch., U. Calif., San Diego, 1990—2001, dean sci. affairs, 1990—2001, prof. emeritus cellular and molecular medicine, 2001—. Contbr. articles to sci. jours. Recipient Albert Lasker Basic Rsch. award, 1966, Gairdner Spl. award, 1967, Horwitz prize, 1970, Nobel prize in physiology or medicine, 1974, Nat. Medal Sci., 1986. Fellow: Am. Acad. Arts Scis.; mem.: NAS, Royal Belgian Acad. Medicine, Romanian Acad., Leopoldina Acad. (Halle), Royal Soc. (London), Pontifical Acad. Sci. Achievements include correlated morphological and biochemical studies by electronmicroscopy and cell fractionation of subcellular components; discovery of ribosomes; discovery and elucidation of the secretory, exocytic pathway and studies on membrane biogenesis; discovery of and regulation of proteins and membrane traffic in animal eukaryotic cells.*

PALAHNIUK, RICHARD JOHN, anesthesiology educator, researcher; b. Winnipeg, Man., Can., Dec. 5, 1944; s. George and Teenie (Lukinchuk) P.; m. Patricia June Smando, July 15, 1967; children: Christopher, Daniel, Andrew. BS in Medicine, MD, U. Man., 1968. Head obstetric anaesthesia Health Scis. Ctr., Winnipeg, 1973-79; prof. and chmn. of anaesthesia U. Man., Winnipeg, 1979-89; prof. anesthesiology, head dept., dir. dept. anesthesiology U. Minn., Mpls., 1989—. Contbr. papers and book chpts. to profl. publs.; mem. editorial bd. Can. Jour. Anaesthesia, Toronto, 1985-89. Fellow Med. Rsch. Coun. Can., 1972, rsch. grantee, 1974-79. Fellow Royal Coll. Physicians of Can.; mem. Can. Anaesthetists' Soc., Am. Soc. Anesthesiology, Internat. Anesthesia Rsch. Soc. (editorial bd. Cleve. chpt. 1987—). Roman Catholic. Avocations: running, fishing, carpentry. Office: U Minn Med Sch Box 294 420 Delaware St SE Minneapolis MN 55455-0374

PALANCA, TERILYN, software industry analyst; b. Chicago Heights, Ill., Aug. 15, 1957; d. Raymond Anthony and Barbara Jean (Schweizer) P. BA, Coll. William and Mary, 1979; MBA, Rutgers U., 1983. Chief auditor, mgr. Williamsburg (Va.) Hilton, 1979-81; corp. auditor RCA, Princeton, N.J., 1982-83; EDP cons. Price Waterhouse & Co., N.Y.C., 1983-84; data base adminstr. Chubb & Son, Inc., Warren, N.J., 1984-85; cons., tech. mgr. Applied Data Rsch., Inc., Princeton, 1985-88; mgr. bus. devel. and product Oracle Corp., Belmont, Calif., 1988-91; mgr. market analysis Sybase, Inc., Emeryville, 1991-92, dir. product mgmt., 1993-95, sr. dir. corp. mtkg., 1996-99; rsch. dir. Giga Info. Group, Cambridge, Mass., 1999—2002; pvt. practice, 2002—. Mem. NAFE, Assn. of Inst. for Cert. Computer Profls. (cert. in data processing), Savannah Symphony Chorus. Avocations: music, literature, outdoor activities, animal and environmental aid, conservation. Office: 42 Diana Dr Savannah GA 31406 E-mail: tpalanca@bellsouth.net.

PALANCE, JACK, actor; b. Lattimer, Pa., Feb. 18, 1918; s. John and Anna (Gramiak) Palahnuik; m. Virginia Baker, Apr. 21, 1949 (div. 1969); children: Holly Kathleen, Brook Gabrielle, Cody John; m. Elaine Rochelle Rogers, May 6, 1987 (div.). Student, U. N.C., Stanford U. Appeared in stage plays The Big Two, 1947, Temporary Island, 1948, The Vigil, A Street Car Named Desire, 1948, The Silver Tassle, 1949, Darkness at Noon, 1950, Julius Caesar, The Tempest, 1955; motion pictures include Panic in the Streets, 1950, Halls of Montezuma, Sudden Fear (Acad. award nominee best supporting actor 1952), Shane (Acad. award nominee best supporting actor 1953), Arrowhead, Flight to Tangier, The Silver Chalice, Kiss of Fire, Attack!, Ten Seconds to Hell, The Big Knife, Man in the Attic, Warriors Five, Barabbas, I Died A 1000 Times, The Lonely Man, House of Numbers, Contempt, Torture Garden, Kill a Dragon, They Came to Rob Las Vegas, The Desperadoes, The Mercenary, Justine, Legion of the Damned, A Bullet for Rommel, The McMasters, The Professionals, Chato's Land, Companeros, Che, Oklahoma Crude, Craze, The Four Deuces, The Diamond, Hawk the Slayer, Gor, Bagdad Cafe, Young Guns, The Getaway, The Horsemen, The Shape of Things to Come, Hawk the Slayer, Without Warning, Tango & Cash, Batman 1989, Solar Crisis, 1990, City Slickers, 1991 (Acad. award for Best Supporting Actor 1991, Golden Globe award Best Supporting Actor 1991), Cops and Robbersons, 1994, City Slickers II: The Legend of Curley's Gold, 1994, Natural Born Killers, 1994, (voice) The Swan Princess, 1994, Marco Polo, 1998, Treasure Island, 1999, Prancer Returns, 2001, others; appeared on TV: Requiem for a Heavyweight (Sylvania award), Dr. Jekyll and Mr. Hyde, Dracula, (series) Bronk, 1975-76, (series host) Ripley's Believe It Or Not, (miniseries) Buffalo Girls, 1995, (TV) Buffalo Girls, 1995, Ebenezer, 1997, I'll Be Home for Christmas, 1997, Sarah, Plain and Tall: Winter's End, 1999, Living with the Dead (TV series), 2002. With USAF, 1942—44. Named Most Prominent Newcomer Theatre World, Best Screen Newcomer Look mag.; recipient Emmy, Best Single Performance by an Actor, Requiem for a Heavyweight, 1956. Address: William Morris Agy 151 El Camino Dr Beverly Hills CA 90212*

PALANS, LLOYD ALEX, lawyer; b. St. Louis, Aug. 6, 1946; s. Hyman Robert and Mae (Sherman) P.; m. Deborah Regn, Aug. 5, 1972; children: Emily Rebecca, Samantha Jane. BS, Tulane U., 1968; JD, U. Mo., 1972. Bar: Mo. 1972, U.S. Dist. Ct. (ea. and we. dists.) Mo. 1972, U.S. Ct. Appeals (8th cir.) 1972, U.S. Ct. Appeals (5th cir.) 1974, U.S. Supreme Ct. 1975, U.S. Ct. Appeals (9th cir.) 1992. Ptnr. Kramer, Chused, Kramer, Shostak & Kohn, St. Louis, 1972-77, Blumenfeld, Marx & Tureen, P.C., St. Louis, 1978-81, Gallop, Johnson & Neuman, St. Louis, 1981-90, Bryan Cave, LLP, St. Louis, 1990—. Adj. prof. Washington U. Sch. Law, St. Louis, 1989—. Bd. dirs. St. Louis Chpt. ARC, 1987—, St. Louis Chpt. Leukemia Soc., 1988—, Combined Health Appeal Greater St. Louis, 1988—, Combined Health Appeal of Am., 1990. Fellow Am. Coll. Bankruptcy; mem. ABA, Mo. Bar, St. Louis Met. Bar Assn. Office: Bryan Cave LLP 1 Metro Sq 211 N Broadway Saint Louis MO 63102-2733 Office Phone: 314-259-2301.

PALAST, GERI DEBORAH, federal agency administrator, Lawyer; b. L.A., Dec. 27, 1950; BA in Polit. Sci., Stanford U., 1972; JD, NYU, 1976. Bar: Calif. 1977, D.C. 1980. Atty., legis. program analyst Am. Fedn. State County and Mcpl. Employees, Washington, 1976-77; legal counsel, field rep. Nat. Treasury Employers Union, Washington, 1977-79; dir., supervising atty. Nat. Employment Law Project, Washington, 1979-81; dir. politics and legislation Svc. Employees Internat. Union, AFL-CIO, Washington, 1981-93; asst. sec. congrl. and intergovtl. affairs Dept. Labor, Washington, 1993-2000; exec. dir. justice at stake campaign Georgetown U., Washington, 2000. Home: 2737 Devonshire Pl NW Apt 402 Washington DC 20008-3475 Office: 50 F St NW #1050 Washington DC 20001

PALATNICK, FRANK SIDNEY, educational consultant; b. Bklyn., Oct. 13, 1951; s. Abraham and Miriam Palatnick; m. Klara Alexandra Gliem, June 13, 1998. Assoc. Paralegal Sci., Ashworth Coll., 2003; postgrad., So. Calif. U. Profl. Studies, 2004—; cert., Nassau Acad. Law, 2003; cert. in spl. edn. law, Nat. Bus. Inst., 2004. Cert. real estate sales agt. NY. Paralegal Albert Grant Esq., Woodbridge, NJ, 1994—96; chief paralegal Oyster Bay Paralegal Assocs., Muttontown, NY, 1996—99; sr. assoc. Foresight Inst., Palo Alto, Calif., 2000—01; chief paralegal Glen Cove (NY) Paralegal Svcs., 2001—02; accreditation examiner Distance Edn. and Tng. Coun., Washington, 2002—. Mem. Presdl. Adv. Com. on Fed. Pay, Washington, 1981—82, Nassau County Task Force, Office Mgmt. and Budget, Mineola, NY, 2002. Assoc. editor: Nassau Lawyer, 2001—, asst. editor: The Flying Lady, 2000—02, contbg. editor: jour. Cardinal Points, 2000—02. Mem. U.S. Power Squadron, USCG Auxiliary; poll taker Nassau County Dem. Com., Mineola, 2000. Recipient Letter of Appreciation, Mayor of Glen Cove, 2001, Letter of Accomplishment, Supt. of Schs., Mineola, 2003. Mem.: ABA, Coun. Adult & Experiential Learning (alumnus), Nat. Inst. Assessment Experiential Learning (alumnus), Am. Soc. Notaries, L.I. Paralegal Assn., Am. Mgmt. Assn., Suffolk County Bar Assn., Nassau County Bar Assn., Foresight Inst. (sr.), Mensa, Amnesty Internat. Avocations: stamp collecting/philately, coin collecting/numismatics. Home: 233-3838 Dr Douglaston NY 11363

PALAZZO, ROBERT PAUL, lawyer, accountant; b. LA, Apr. 14, 1952; s. Joseph Francis and Mickey Palazzo; m. Vivianne Palazzo. BA in Econs., UCLA, 1973; MBA, JD, U. So. Calif., 1976; postgrad., U. Oxford, Eng., 1979. CPA Calif., Nev., Colo.; bar: Calif. 1976, U.S. Dist. Ct. (so. dist.) Calif. 1977, U.S. Tax Ct. 1977, U.S. Ct. Appeals (9th cir.) 1978, U.S. Supreme Ct. 1980. Assoc. Graham & James, L.A., 1976-78; ptnr. Rader, Cornwall, Kessler & Palazzo CPAs, L.A., 1978-81, Palazzo & Kessler, L.A., 1978-81; pvt. practice L.A., Darwin, Calif., 1981—. Judge pro tem LA Mcpl. Ct., 1982—2000; alumni advisor UCLA, 1977—81, adv. and scholarship com., 1978—81; lectr. U. Oxford, 1979, U. So. Calif., L.A., 1986, Calif. Poly. Inst., Pomona, 1997; profl. adv. com. West L.A. Coll., 1993—96; session chair Medieval and Renaissance Conf. Ariz. State U., 2000—01, 2003; bd. dirs. Cons. Am. Oil. Co., Fin. Sys. Internat. Inc.; spkr. in field. Hist. cons. A&E Civil War Jour., (films) Death Valley Memories, hist. and archival cons. Echoes Through Death Valley, Chasing the Rainbow, hist. cons. (TV series) A&E Biography, Guns of Infamy, archival cons., hist. cons., prodr. Haunted History; editor: Gun Report; prodr.: (films) L.A. Bounty, the 20 Mule Team of Death Valley; (TV series) Magnificent Failures, 20th Century Infamous Guns; featured (TV series) Tales of the Gun, 1998—2000; contbr. articles to profl. jours. Treas. Italian Am. Civic Coalition; chmn. dist. bd. dirs. Darwin Cmty. Svcs., 1990—92; mem. ethics bd. Universal Autograph Collectors Club; founder Ohio History Flight Mus.; bd. dirs. Calif. Cancer Found., L.A., 1978—85, pres., 1979—80; bd. dirs. Friends William S. Hart Pk. and Mus., 1990—93, v.p. mus. rels. Mem.: NARAS, Ariz. Ctr. Medieval Renaissance Studies Conf. (chair 2000—01, 2003), So. Calif. Autograph Soc. (v.p.), S.E. Ohio Oil and Gas Assn., Medieval Acad. Am. (conf. session chair 2001—02), Am. Numismatic Assn. (dist. rep. Carson City 1981—82, L.A. 1982—83), Nat. Italian Am. Bar Assn., English Westerners Soc., Century City Bar Assn. (vice-chmn. estate planning, trust and probate com. 1979—80), Western Writers Assn., Italian Am. Lawyers Assn. (bd. govs. 1980—, 1st v.p. 1984—88), L.A. County Bar Assn. (arbitration com., fee dispute resolution program), Death Valley History Assn. (life), Universal Autograph Collectors Club (mem. ethics bd.), Mensa, Wig and Pen Club (London), Zeta Phi Eta, Phi Alpha Delta, Pi Gamma Mu, Beta Alpha Psi (pres. 1972), Omicron Delta Epsilon. also: 230 S Main St Darwin CA 93522

PALCHICK, BERNARD S. academic administrator, art educator; m. Lisa Palchick; children: Linnea, Benjamin. BA in Painting, Purdue U., 1967; MFA in Sculpture, RISD, 1971. Instr. art Kalamazoo Coll., 1972—74, asst. prof. art, 1974—79, assoc. prof. art, 1979—87, prof. art, 1987—, chair art dept., 1977—85, chair divsn. fine arts, 1982—95, dir. endowed artist-in-residence program, 1984—, assoc. provost, 1987—89, spl. asst. to pres. for comm., 1990, acting chair theatre dept., 1994—95, acting provost, 1996—97, v.p. for coll. advancement, 1997—, interim pres., 2004—. Mem. exhbns. selection com. Kalamazoo Inst. of the Arts, 1987—99, bd. mem., 1994—99, Plaza Arts Cir., Western Mich. U., 1999—. Mem.: Mich. Watercolor Soc., Watercolor USA Honor Soc., Coun. for Advancement and Support of Edn. Office: Kalamazoo Coll 1200 Academy St Kalamazoo MI 49006*

PALDUS, JOSEF, mathematics professor; b. Bzi, Czech Republic, Nov. 25, 1935; arrived in Can., 1968; s. Josef and Ludmila (Danicek) P.; m. Eva Zdena Bajer, Jan. 26, 1961; 1 dau., Barbara Alice. MSc, Charles U., Prague, 1958, DrSc, 1995; PhD, Czechoslovak Acad. Sci., Prague, 1961. Research scientist Czechoslovak Acad. Scis., Prague, 1961-62, 64-68; postdoctoral fellow NRC, Ottawa, Can., 1962-64; assoc. prof. applied math. U. Waterloo, Ont., Can., 1968-75, prof., 1975-2001, disting. prof. emeritus, 2001—; assoc. dir. Fields Inst., 1992-95. Vis. prof. U. Rheims, 1973, U. Louis Pasteur, Strasbourg, France, 1975-76, 82-83, Cath. U., Nijmegen, Holland, 1981, Technion, Haifa, Israel, 1983, Max Planck Inst. for Astrophysics, Munich, Germany, 1997, 98, 99; vis. scientist NRC, Ottawa, 1966-68, Free U. Berlin, 1981; adj. prof. chemistry U. Fla., Gainesville, 1984—; fellow Inst. for Advanced Study, Berlin, 1986-87. Mem. editl. bd. Comtex Sci., 1981-83, Advances in Quantum Chemistry, 1986, Jour. Chem. Physics, 1987-89, Can. Jour. Chemistry, 1994-96, Internat. Jour. Quantum Chemistry, 1996; mem. adv. editl. bd. Internat. Jour. Quantum Chemistry, 1977-88, Theoretica Chimica Acta, 1988-94, Jour. Math. Chemistry, 1989; contbr. numerous articles to profl. jours., chpts. to books. Recipient prize Chemistry divsn. Czechoslovak Acad. Scis., 1962, 67, J. Heyrovsky Gold medal Czechoslovak Acad. Sci., 1992, Gold medal Faculty of Math and Physics, Comenius U., Slovakia, 1994, Alexander von Humboldt Sr. Scientist award, 1996; Killam Rsch. fellow, 1987-89; Fields Inst. for Rsch. in Math. Scis. fellow, 2002. Fellow Royal Soc. Can.; mem. Internat. Acad. Quantum Molecular Sci., Internat. Soc. Theoretical Chem. Physics (bd. dirs.), European Acad. Scis., Arts and Letters (corr.), Czech Learned Soc. (hon.), Am. Inst. Physics, NY Acad. Scis., Applied Math. Soc. Can. Roman Catholic. Office: U Waterloo Dept Applied Math University Ave Waterloo ON Canada N2L 3G1 Office Phone: 519-888-4567 ext 6267. Business E-Mail: paldus@theochem.uwaterloo.ca.

PALEN, J(OSEPH) JOHN, sociology educator; b. Dubuque, Iowa, Feb. 24, 1939; s. Joseph John Palen and Mary (Rowan) Toner; m. Karen Ann Doody, June 9, 1962; children: Joseph John, Elizabeth Ann, Ellen Marye. BA, U. Notre Dame, 1961; MS, U. Wis., Madison, 1963, PhD, 1967. Demographer UN, Addis Ababa, Ethiopia, 1971—72; assoc. prof. U. Wis., Milw., 1972—77, prof., 1977—80; vis. prof. Nat. U. Singapore, 1983—84; prof. sociology, chmn. dept. Va. Commonwealth U., Richmond, 1980—. Author: Gentrification, Displacement and Revitalization, 1984; Urban World, 6th edit., 2002; City Scenes, 2nd edit., 1981, The Suburbs, 1995; Social Problems for the Twenty-first Century, 2001. Leader Boy Scouts Am., Wis., 1973-80, Torch Club 1980-. Grantee, Rockefeller Found., 1985, NIH, 1980—82, Ford Found., 1979, NIMH, 1976, NSF, 1985; Sr. Fulbright scholar, Taiwan, 1992, Fulbright Disting. Lectr. and Chair in N.Am. Studies, U. Calgary, 1997, Fulbright scholar, Germany, 2002, Disting. scholar, Va. Commonwealth U., 1995. Mem. Fellow Am. Sociol. Assn., So. Sociol. Soc.; mem. Urban Affairs Assn. Avocations: hiking, canoeing, civil war. Home: 500 Gardiner Rd Richmond VA 23229-6919 Office: Va Commonwealth U Dept Sociology Richmond VA 23284 Office Phone: 804-828-6826. E-mail: jjpalen@vcu.edu.

PALEN, JOSEPH WILLIAM, chemical process research company executive; b. Springfield, Mo., June 4, 1935; s. John Carlyle and Jean Allen (Gravely) P.; m. Louise Kibler, Sept. 13, 1956 (div. 1977); children: Patti, Joni, James; m. Kasdina Kasdan, June 4, 1977; children: Indradini, Indrasto, Indrastati. BS in Chem. Engring., U. Mo., 1957; MS in Chem. Engring., U. Ill., 1965; PhD in Chem. Engring., Lehigh U., 1988. Process design engr. Phillips Petroleum Co., Bartlesville, Okla., 1957-63; rsch. engr. Heat Transfer Rsch., Inc., Alhambra, Calif., 1965-68, asst., then assoc. tech. dir., 1968-86, prin. staff cons., 1988-90; prin. rsch. engr. Heat Transfer Rsch. Inc., College Station, Tex., 1992—2000, dir. rsch., 2000—; adj. prof. Bandung Inst. Tech., Indonesia, 1990-92. Patentee in field; editor: Heat Exchanger Sourcebook, 1986; contbr. to tech. publs. Lectr., UNESCO, Yugoslavia, 1981. Fellow AIChE (lectr. internat. heat transfer conf. 1986, D.Q. Kern award 1995); mem. Tau Beta Pi. Democrat. Baptist. Avocations: reading, exercise, music, personal computers. Home: 1514 Wayfarer Ln College Station TX 77845-9378 Office: Heat Transfer Rsch Inc 150 Venture Dr College Station TX 77845

PALENQUE, STEPHANIE MAHER, small business owner, writer, book indexer; b. Orange, N.J., Aug. 5, 1970; d. Peter B. and Carole Ann (Mogul) Maher; m. Jaime Antonio Palenque, Oct. 31, 1992; children: Sophia, Alexandra, Charlotte. BA in Polit. Sci., Seton Hall U., N.J., 1992, MA in English Lit., 2004. Editor Reed Ref. Publ., New Providence, NJ, 1992—96; rep., internat. liaison Little, Brown & Co., Boston, 1996—99; project editor The Coriolis Group, Scottsdale, Ariz., 1999—2001; owner The Word Nerd, Anthem, Ariz., 2001—. Author: (book) Busted! Cocaine/Crack, 2004, Busted! Marijuana, 2004, numerous articles in nat. and regional mags. Elected committeewoman Rep. Twp. Com., Chatham Twp., 1988—92; dist. rep. N.J. Legis. Assembly, 1990—92. Recipient Media award, Am. Cancer Soc., 1997, Leadership award, United Way, 1997. Mem.: Modern Lang. Assn., Am. Soc. Indexers (vice chmn. 2002—03, pres. 2004—, Honoree Order of Kohlrabi 2004). Democrat. Roman Catholic. Avocations: writing, reading, music, art. Home and Office: 3339 W Morse Dr Anthem AZ 85086 Office Phone: 866-MY-INDEX. E-mail: thewordnerd@thewordnerd.com.

PALENSKY, FREDERICK J. manufacturing executive; Joined 3M Co., 1968, v.p., dental products divsn., 1997—2001, v.p., gen. mgr., 3M ESPE, 2001, exec. v.p., specialty material mkts. & corp. svcs., 2001—02, exec. v.p., safety, security & protection svcs. bus., 2002—. Office: 3M Co 3M Ctr Saint Paul MN 55144

PALERMO, ANTHONY ROBERT, lawyer; b. Rochester, N.Y., Sept. 30, 1929; s. Anthony C. and Mary (Palvino) P.; m. Mary Ann Coyne, Jan. 2, 1960; children: Mark Henry, Christopher Coyne, Peter Stuart, Elisabeth Megan McCarthy, Julie Coyne Lawther, Gregg Anthony. BA, U. Mich., 1951; JD, Georgetown U., 1956. Bar: DC 1956, NY 1957, U.S. Supreme Ct. 1961. Trial atty. U.S. Dept. Justice, Washington, 1956-58, asst. U.S. atty. N.Y.C., 1958-60, asst. U.S. atty. in charge Rochester, NY, 1960-61; ptnr. Brennan, Centner, Palermo & Blauvelt, Rochester, 1962-81, Harter, Secrest & Emery, Rochester, 1981-94, Hodgson, Russ, Andrews, Woods & Goodyear, LLP, Rochester, 1994-97, of counsel, 1998, Woods Oviatt Gilman LLP, Rochester, 1999—. Note editor Georgetown Law Jour., 1956. Bd. dirs. McQuaid Jesuit H.S., Rochester, 1978-84, St. Ann's Home for Aged, Rochester, 1974-2001; bd. dirs., sec. St. Ann's Found., Rochester, 1989-2001; trustee, charter chmn. Clients' Security Fund N.Y. (now Lawyer's Fund for Client Protection), 1981-90; chmn. Govs. Jud. Screening Com. 4th Jud. Dept., mem. statewide com., 1987-89; chair magistrate selection com. U.S. Dist. Ct. (we. dist.) N.Y., 1995, 98; mem. N.Y. Chief Judge's Comm. on Jud. Salaries, 1997—; mem. N.Y. Office Ct. Adminstrn. Comm. on Fiduciary Appointments, 2000—. Fellow Am. Bar Found., N.Y. State Bar Found. (bd. dirs. 1978-91), Am. Coll. Trial Lawyers; mem. ABA (ho. dels. 1980-98, state del. 1982-85, bd. govs. 1985-88, 1989-93, sec. 1990-93), N.Y. State Bar Assn. (pres. 1979-80, ho. dels. 1973-75, 77—), Monroe County Bar Assn. (pres. 1973), Oak Hill Country Club. Roman Catholic. Avocation: golf. Home: 38 Huntington Meadow Rochester NY 14625-1813 Office Phone: 585-987-2800.

PALERMO, JAMES W. artistic director; b. Cleve. BMus, MMus, Ind. U. Gen. mgr. Evansville (Ind.) Philharmonic Orch., 1989-92; orch. mgr. Louisville Orch., 1992-95; artistic and gen. dir. Grant Park Orch., Chgo., 1995—. Musician Spoleo Festival Orch., Orquesta Sinfonica Del Valle, Cali, Columbia; intern Chgo. Office Fine Arts. Active Grant Park Cultural and Ednl. Cmty., program planning com. Sherwood Conservatory, search com. Chgo. Youth Symphony Orch., 25th anniversary com. Chgo. Opera Theater. Orch. Mgmt. fellow Am. Symphony Orch. League. Office: Grant Park Orch 425 E Mcfetridge Dr Chicago IL 60605-2791

PALERMO, ROBERT JAMES, architect, consultant, inventor; b. N.Y.C., Mar. 25, 1949; s. Vitorio and Simone (DiFlorio) P.; m. Lore Bernadette Bilbao, July 22, 1972 (dec. Feb. 1977); m. Patricia Dolores Ward, June 14, 1981;

children: Jaime, Justin, Kristen Leigh. BS, CCNY, 1971, BArch, 1972; MBA, Baruch Grad. Ctr., 1974; postgrad., Nat. Asbestos Tng. Inst., 1987. Lic. asbestos investigator; registered architect, N.Y., N.J. Architect Rongved, Wilcox, Erickson, N.Y.C., 1972-73, Welton Becket Assocs., N.Y.C., 1973-75; architect, prin. Jaime Lore Design, Bklyn., 1976—. Bd. dir. Nat. Meddlex Med. Constrn. Corp., Hicksville, N.Y., 1981-85; pres. Corp. Design of Am., P.C., 1989—. Mem. Am. Inst. Archs., Soc. Am. Registered Archs., Cert. Interior Decorators Assn., Phi Sigma Kappa. Republican. Roman Catholic. Avocations: rare coin collecting, philatelics, beaux art prints. Home: 160 Pelican Rd Middletown NJ 07748-3042 Office: Corp Design of Am PC 1816 Voorhies Ave Brooklyn NY 11235 Office Phone: 718-332-4119. Personal E-mail: pat32jazz@aol.com.

PALESKY, CAROL EAST, tax accountant; b. Orange, N.J., May 13, 1940; d. Neil Norell and Marie R. Reiss; m. Jacob Palesky; children: Donna, Lewis. AB, Am. Inst., Pleasantville, N.J., 1973; postgrad., Am. Inst., Portland, Maine, 1980; student, Atlantic C.C., Mays Landing, N.J., 1971-73. With mgmt. First Nat. Bank of South Jersey (now First Fidelity), Pleasantville, N.J., 1967-74; loan officer Maine Savs. Bank, Portland, 1980-81; acct., owner East Acctg. Assocs., Topsham, Maine, 1985—. Pres. Sensible Tax Limits Coalition, 1995—. Treas., bd. dirs. Congl. Term Limits Coalition, Topsham, 1993—; bd. dirs. Maine Citizens Rev. Bd., Portland, 1993—. Scholar Nat. Taxpayer Union, 1992, 94; recipient United to Serve Am. award, 1992. Mem. Nat. Assn. Small Business Owners, Maine Taxpayers Action Network (pres. 1990—), Topsham Taxpayer Assn. (pres. 1991—). Roman Catholic. Home and Office: 24 Sokokis Cir Topsham ME 04086-1615 E-mail: cep@mtan.org.

PALESTRO, CHRISTOPHER J. physician; m. Lynnette V. Stevens, May 24, 1985; children: Christopher J., Sarah Alice, Alexander Steven, Lissette Halle, Vincent Giancarlo. MD, Universidad Autonoma de Guadalajara, Mex., 1975. Diplomate Am. Bd. Nuc. Medicine, 1982. Chief nuc. medicine Norwalk (Conn.) Hosp., 1982—85; nuc. medicine physician Mt. Sinai Med. Ctr., NYC, 1985—92; chief nuc. medicine L.I. Jewish Med. Ctr., New Hyde Park, NY, 1992—. Prof. nuc. medicine and radiology Albert Einstein Coll. Medicine, Bronx, NY, 1996—. Contbr. articles to profl. jours. including Jour. Nuc. Medicine, Radiology, RadioGraphics. Fellow: Am. Coll. Nuc. Physicians; mem.: Am. Bd. Nuc. Medicine, Radiol. Soc. N.Am., Soc. Nuc. Medicine. Office: Long Island Jewish Med Ctr 270-05 76th Ave New Hyde Park NY 11040 Office Phone: 718-470-7080.

PALEVSKY, MAX, industrialist; b. Chgo., July 24, 1924; s. Isadore and Sarah (Greenblatt) P.; children: Nicholas, Madeleine, Alexander, Jonathan, Matthew. Ph.B., BS, U. Chgo., 1948; postgrad., U. Chgo., UCLA, 1951-52. Mathematician Computer div. Bendix Corp., Los Angeles, 1952-56; v.p., gen. mgr., dir. Packard Bell Electronics, Los Angeles, 1957-61; pres., chmn. bd. Sci. Data Systems; chmn. bd. Xerox Data Systems, Inc., El Segundo, Calif., 1961-72; dir. Xerox Corp., 1969-72, chmn. exec. com. of bd., 1969-72. Bd. dirs. Intel Corp., Santa Clara, Calif., Komag, Inc., Milpitas, Calif. Organized George McGovern's campaign for Pres. of U.S., 1972; organized and ran Tom Bradley's campaign for Mayor of L.A., 1973; mem. Folger com. Folger Shakespeare Libr., Washington, 1977—; mem. Dem. Adv. Com., 1968—; bd. dirs. ACLU, Constl. Rights Found.; trustee The Inst. for Advanced Study, Princeton U., 1988—. With USAAF, 1943-46. Office: 924 Westwood Blvd Ste 700 Los Angeles CA 90024-2928

PALEY, GERALD LARRY, lawyer; b. Albany, N.Y., Sept. 11, 1939; s. Arthur and Mary (Peckner) P.; m. Joyce R., June 25, 1961 (div. June 1985); children: Jonathan, Eric, Suzanne; m. Sheryl Gae, Aug. 14, 1985. BA, Union Coll., 1961; JD with distinction, Cornell U., 1964. Bar: N.Y. 1964. Assoc. Nixon, Hargrave, Devans & Doyle, Rochester, N.Y., 1964-69; assoc. solicitor Dept. Labor, Washington, 1969-71; ptnr. Nixon, Hargrave, Devans & Doyle, Rochester, 1971-87, Phillips, Lytle, Hitchcock, Blaine & Huber, Rochester, 1987—. Author: Handbook of Federal Labor Relations Laws, 1981, Understand Employee Regulations, 1984. Mem. ABA. Republican. Jewish. Office: Phillips Lytle Hitchcock et al 1400 First Federal Plz Rochester NY 14614-1981

PALEY, GRACE, author, educator; b. N.Y.C., Dec. 11, 1922; d. Isaac and Mary (Ridnyik) Goodside; m. Jess Paley, June 20, 1942; children: Nora, Dan.; m. Robert Nichols, 1972. Ed., Hunter Coll., NYU. Formerly tchr. Columbia, Syracuse U.; ret. mem. lit. faculty Sarah Lawrence Coll., Stanford, Johns Hopkins, Dartmouth, CUNY. Author: The Little Disturbances of Man, 1959, Enormous Changes at the Last Minute, 1974, Learning Forward, 1985, Later the Same Day, 1985, Long Walks and Intimate Talks, 1991, New and Collected Poems, 1992, The Collected Stories, 1994 (Nat. Book award nomination, 1994), Just As I Thought, 1998, Begin Again Collected Poems, 2000; contbr. stories to Atlantic, New Yorker, Ikon, Genesis West, others. Sec. N.Y. Greenwich Village Peace Center. Recipient Literary award for short story writing Nat. Inst. Arts and Letters, 1970, Edith Wharton award N.Y. State, 1988, 89, Rea award for short story, 1993, Vt. Gov.'s award for Excellence in the Arts, 1993, award for contbn. to Jewish culture Nat. Found. Jewish Culture; Guggenheim fellow; apptd. Vt. Poet Laureate, 2003—. Mem. Am. Acad. and Inst. Arts and Letters, Am. Acad. Arts and Scis. Office: PO Box 620 Thetford VT 05074-0620

PALEY, RUSSELL ELIOT, writer, small business owner; b. Annapolis, Md., May 23, 1969; s. Louis R and Rae Paley; m. Ronni L Krasin, July 3, 2001; 1 child, Max Andrew. BA with hons., Bryant Coll., Smithfield, R.I., 1991. Pres. Wealth Bldg. Publs., Woodbury, NY, 1995—, Wealth and Health Internat., Fla., 1991—. Author: (Book) Network Your Way to Millions, 1998. Personal E-mail: russnrole@aol.com.

PALFFY, ZIGMUND (ZIGGY PALFFY), professional hockey player; b. Skalica, Skovakia, May 5, 1972; Hockey player N.Y. Islanders, 1993—99, L.A. Kings, 1999—. Mem. Czechoslovakia Nat. Jr. Team, World Jr. Championships, Saskatoon, 1991, Czechoslavian team Can. Cup, 1991, Slovakia team Lillehammer Olympics, 1994, World Championships, 1996 Office: LA Kings Staples Ctr 1111 S Figueroa St Los Angeles CA 90015

PALIA, ASPY PHIROZE, marketing educator, researcher, consultant; b. Bombay, Nov. 27, 1944; came to U.S., 1973; s. Phiroze E. and Homai P. (Irani) P. BE in Mech. Engring., U. Bangalore, 1966; MBA, U. Hawaii at Manoa, 1976; DBA, Kent State U., 1985. Sales engr. Larsen & Toubro Ltd., 1966-72, export sales engr., 1972-73; teaching fellow Coll. Bus. Adminstrn. Kent State U., 1977-80, instr. Coll. Bus. Adminstrn., 1982-84; asst. prof. Coll. Bus. Adminstrn. U. Hawaii, Manoa, 1984-89, assoc. prof., 1990-95, prof., 1996—, pres. faculty coun., 1995-96; senator U. Hawaii Manoa Faculty Congress, 1996-98; sr. fellow dept. mktg. Nat. U. Singapore, 1998-99, vis. sr. fellow dept. mktg., 2000—02. Vis. prof. Coll. Mgmt. Nat. Sun Yat-sen U., Kaohsiung, Taiwan, 1992, Chilalongkorn U., Bangkok, 1992, 93, 97, 2003, U. Otago, New Zealand, 1995, Adminstrv. Staff Coll. India, Hyderabad, 1992, Indian Inst. Mgmt., Ahmedabad, 2000, Asian Inst. Tech., Bangkok, 2001; mem. U. Hawaii Manoa Ctr. for Teaching Excellence Faculty Adv. Group, 1991; mem. mktg. plan adv. com. U. Hawaii, Manoa, 1994, mem. honors and awards com., 1990—91, pres. faculty coun., 1995—96, mem. faculty adv. com. on acad. freedom, 1997; vis. scholar faculty bus. adminstrn. Nat. U. Singapore, 1991, Mktg. Inst. Singapore Exec. Devel. Seminars, 1991, 1994—95, 1997, Hong Kong Inst. Mktg. Exec. Devel. Seminar, 1996, Kathmandu Coll. Mgmt. Exec. Devel. Workshop, 2000; sr. fellow dept. mktg. faculty of bus. adminstrn. Nat. U. Singapore, 1998—99; affiliate faculty Japan Am. Inst. Mgmt. Sci., Honolulu, 1989—; vis. prof. Grad. Sch. Internat. Mgmt., Internat. U. Japan, Uhrasa, Yamato-machi, 1991, U. Internat. Bus. and Econs., Beijing, 1991, U. Kebangsaan Malaysia, Bangi-Selangor, Kuala Lumpur, Malaysia, 1991, 92, Mt. Carmel Inst. Mgmt., Bangalore, India, 1997; lectr., cons., presenter in field; vis. prof. Vietnam Nat. U., Hanoi Sch Bus., 2002, Singapore Mgmt. U., 2003—04, 2004; vis. scholar faculty bus. adminstrn. Boston Network Exec. Develop. Workshop, Bangkok, 2003. Editor: (with Dennis A. Rondinelli) Project Planning and Implementation in Developing Countries, 1976; assoc. editor e-Services Quar., 1999—; contbr. conf. procs. and articles to profl. jours. and books, including Indsl. Mktg. Mgmt., Internat. Bus. Jour., Asia-Pacific Jour. Mgmt., Internat. Mktg. Rev., European Jour. Mktg., Fgn. Trade Rev., Internat. Rev. Econs. & Bus., others; contbr. to numerous confs. and symposia in field; developer various mktg. decision support systems and decision-making tools for use in strategic market planning and in marketing simulations. Mem. various program rev. coms. Pacific and Asian Mgmt. Inst., Acad. Internat. Bus., Assn. Bus. Simulation and Exptl. Learning, others; bd. examiners Nat. U. Singapore Sch. Postgrad. Mgmt. Studies, 1991; external examiner Bd. Grad. Studies, Nat. U. Singapore, 2001-2002; mem. adv. bd. Soc. Coll. of Bus. Adminstrn. Alumni and Friends Exec. Com., 1991-93; adv. bd. Salvation Army Residential Treatment Facilities for Children and Youth Adv. Coun., 1989-96, vice chair, 1987-89; chair Salvation Army Family Treatment Svcs. Adv. Coun., 1997-98; mem. Salvation Army Honolulu Adv. Bd., 1997-98; treas., bd. dirs. Kings Gate Homeowners Assn., 1994-96; bd. advisors Ctr. for Nat. Competitiveness Inst. Indsl. Policy Studies, Korea, 1998—. Univ. fellow Kent State U., 1983; East-West Ctr. scholar East-West Ctr., 1973-75; Ednl. Improvement Fund grantee, 1989, Instrl. Travel and Devel. Fund grantee Office Faculty Devel. and Acad. Support, 1991, 95, joint rsch. grants U. Kebangsaan Malaysia, Nat. U. Singapore, U. So. Queensland, Australia, U. Otago, New Zealand, Lingnan Coll., Hong Kong; recipient Internat. Agreements Fund award Office Internat. Programs and Svcs., 1990-91, 91-92, ORA travel award U. Rsch. Coun., 1986, 88, 89, 91, 92, 94-98. Mem. Am. Mktg. Assn. (academia editor Honolulu chpt. 1986-87), Acad. Internat. Bus. (chair Pacific Basin Region 1995, chair Pacific Basin chpt. 1996-2002, co-chair Asia Pacific Conf. 1997), Pacific Asian Consortium for Internat. Bus. Edn. and Rsch., Assn. for Bus. Simulation and Exptl. Learning, Pan-Pacific Bus. Assn. (charter), Mortar Bd. (Outstanding Educator award 1993, Mentor award 1995), East-West Ctr. Alumni Assn. U.S. (v.p. Hawaii chpt. 1987-89, ad campaign com. 1987-88), Beta Gamma Sigma (faculty advisor, sec.-treas. Alpha of Hawaii chpt. 1990—, Outstanding Svc. award 1992-93, Bd. Govs. Commitment to Excellence award 1997, Prof. of Yr. award 2003), Mu Kappa Tau, Pi Sigma Epsilon. Avocations: music, photography, swimming, reading, hiking. Home: 2724 Kahoaloha Ln # 1605 Honolulu HI 96826-3337 Office: U Hawaii Manoa Dept Mktg 2404 Maile Way Honolulu HI 96822-2223

PALIHNICH, NICHOLAS JOSEPH, JR., retail executive; b. Montclair, N.J., Nov. 9, 1939; s. Nicholas Joseph and Lucille (Pflugh) P.; m. Diane Lorraine Parise, Nov. 12, 1966; children: Nicholas, Kristin, Danielle. BBA, U. Notre Dame, 1961. Retail buyer R.H. Macy, N.Y.C., 1961-66, Korvettes, Inc., N.Y.C., 1966-69; retail v.p., gen. mdse. mgr. Mangurians Inc., Ft. Lauderdale, Fla., 1970-72; sr. v.p. retail mgmt. Korvettes Inc., N.Y.C., 1973-79, pres., 1979-81; sr. v.p. retail mgmt. Lane Bryant, 1981-83; pres. retail mgmt. Dan Inc., 1984-86; exec. v.p. retail Bally U.S.A, 1987-93; gen. mgr. retail, dir. The Rockport Co., Canton, Mass., 1994—. Served with U.S. Army, 1962. Republican. Roman Catholic. Office: 1895 JW Foster Blvd Canton MA 02021

PALILEO, HAZEL VALENCIA, videographer; b. Pila, Laguna, Philippines, May 22, 1951; came to U.S., 1971, naturalized citizen, 1979; d. Lauro Gomez and Edna (Valencia) P. BFA in Photography and Media, Wright State U., 1976; student, DeVry Inst. Tech., 1995-97; diploma, Applied Multimedia Tng. Ctrs., 1998; cert. web designer, U. Calgary, 2002. Lab. tech. Valdhere Films, Inc., Dayton, Ohio, 1973-76; news photographer Sta. WDTN-TV, Dayton, 1977-79; videographer Sta. WKEF-TV News, Dayton, 1979-86, chief videographer, 1983-86; videographer, still photographer Wycliffe Bible Translators, Calgary, Alta., Can., 1986-92, co-mgr. media prodns. dept., 1990-92; video mgr., media coord. Cornerstone Comms., Calgary, 1992-94; photographer, videographer and multi media specialist freelance, Calgary, 1994—; media technician U. Calgary, 1998—. Videographer (TV news) Haviland Ave. Fire, 1984 (Emmy 1984). Recipient Best Video award Nat. Cath. Stewardship Conf., 1993. Mem. Anglican Ch. of Canada. Avocations: reading, photography, travel, walking. E-mail: palileo@ucalgary.ca.

PALIN, MICHAEL EDWARD, actor, screenwriter, writer; b. May 5, 1943; s. Edward and Mary P.; m. Helen M. Gibbins, 1966; 3 children. BA, U. Oxford, Eng., 1965. Writer, performer BBC Corp., 1965-69. Presenter in field. Actor, writer: (TV shows) Monty Python's Flying Circus, 1969-74, Ripping Yarns, 1976-80; (films) And Now for Something Completely Different, 1970, Monty Python and the Holy Grail, 1974, Monty Python's Life of Brian, 1978, Time Bandits, 1980, Monty Python's The Meaning of Life, 1982, American Friends, 1991; TV presenter, writer Great Railway Journeys of the World, 1980, Around the World in 80 Days, 1989, Pole to Pole, 1993, Palin's Column, 1994, Great Railway Journeys of the World, 1994, Full Circle, 1997, Michael Palin's Hemingway Adventure, 1999, Sahara with Michael Palin, 2002, Himalaya with Michael Palin, 2004; television presenter: Palin on Redpath, 1997, The Bright Side of Life, 2000, The Ladies Who Loved Matisse, 2003; actor: (TV shows) Three Men in a Boat, 1975, GBH, 1991; (films) Jabberwocky, 1976, A Private Function, 1984, Brazil, 1985, A Fish Called Wanda (Best Supporting Actor Brit. Acad. Film and TV Arts, 1989), Fierce Creatures, 1998; actor, writer and co-prodr.: The Missionary, 1982; writer (stage play) The Weekend, 1994; author: Monty Python's Big Red Book, 1970, Monty Python's Brand New Book, 1973, Dr. Fegg's Encyclopeadia of All World Knowledge, 1984, Limericks, 1985, Around the World in 80 Days, 1989, Pole to Pole, 1993, Pole to Pole: The Photographs, 1994, Hemingway's Chair 1995, Full Circle, 1997, Full Circle: The Photographs, 1997, Hemingway Adventure, 1999, Sahara, 2002, Himalaya, 2004;(children's books) Small Harry and the Toothache Pills, 1981, The Mirrorstone, 1986, The Cyril Stories, 1986. Co-recipient (with Monty Python) Michael Balcon award for outstanding contbn. to cinema, Brit. Acad. Film and TV Arts, 1987; named to CBE New Yr.'s Honours List for Svc. to TV, Drama & Travel, 2000; recipient Lifetime Achievement award, Brit. Comedy Awards, 2002. Avocations: reading, running, railways. Office: 34 Tavistock St London WC2E 7PB England

PALITZ, ANKA A. KRISER, manufacturing and distributing company executive; b. Sofia, Bulgaria, Aug. 19, 1931; came to US, 1951; d. Angel Georgieff, Rayna Tomoff Georgiewa; m. David B. Kriser (div. 1978); m. Clarence Y. Palitz Jr., 1989 (dec. Nov. 2000). BA, Art Acad., Munich, 1950. Cert. interior designer. V.p. Revlon, NYC, 1955-61; pres. Decart Design, Lancaster, Pa., 1978-83, chair, 1983-89; pres. The Baroness Collection, NYC, 1983—; art dealer NYC, 1989—; pres. Decart Design, NYC, 1978—83, chair. Contbr. articles to profl. jours. Bd. dir. NYC Opera Guild, 1965—78, Beth Israel Hosp. Guild, NYC, NY Hosp. Nursing Com., 1975—78, 910 Fifth Ave. Bldg., NYC, 1984—, Am. Ballet Theater, Career Transition for Dancers, Met. Opera, Golden Horseshoe; contbg. mem. Met. Mus., NY Philharm. Recipient Lucia Chase Award, ABT, 2003. Mem. Benefactor Coun. Soc. of the Four Arts (Palm Beach, Fla.). Avocations: the arts, travel, skiing. Home and Office: 880 Fifth Ave New York NY 10021-4951

PALIWAL, DINESH KUMAR, diplomat, educational administrator; b. Muzaffar Nagar, India, June 5, 1957; s. Rajendra Prasad and Kaushal P.; m. Neeta Paliwal, Dec. 8, 1982; children: Abhishek, Ankit. BS, Meerut U., India, 1976; MS, Agra U., India, 1979; PhD, Indian Inst. Tech., Delhi, India, 1996. Lectr. Kishan Lal Pub. Coll., Rewari, India, 1981-88; tchr. fellow Indian Inst. Tech., New Delhi, India, 1988-92; asst. ednl. adv. dept. edn. Govt. of India, New Delhi, 1992-97; consul edn. Consulate Gen. India, New York, 1997—. Contbr. articles to profl. jours. Mem. Indian Soc. Tech. Edn. Fax: 212-879-7914. E-mail: dinesh_paliwal@hotmail.com.

PALIZZI, ANTHONY N. retired lawyer, retail corporation executive; b. Wyandotte, Mich., Oct. 27, 1942; s. Vincenzo and Nunziata (Dagostini) P.; children: A. Michael, Nicholas A. PhB, Wayne State U., 1964, JD, 1966; LLM, Yale U., 1967. Bar: Mich. 1967. Prof. law Fla. State U., Tallahassee, 1967-69; prof. law Tex. Tech U., Lubbock, 1969-71; atty. Kmart Corp., Troy, Mich., 1971-74, asst. sec., 1974-77, asst. gen. counsel, 1977-85, v.p., assoc. gen. counsel, 1985-91, sr. v.p., gen. counsel, 1991-92, exec. v.p., gen. counsel, 1992—2000. Editor law rev. Wayne State U., 1964-66 Chmn. Brandon Police and Fire Bd., Mich., 1982-87. Mem. ABA, Am. Corp. Counsel Assn., Mich. State Bar Assn. Roman Catholic.

PALKO, LORRI M. automotive company executive; BS in Acctg., Indiana U. Pa. With Ernst & Whinney; pres., CEO Morgan Corp. subs. J.B. Poindexter & Co., Inc., Morgantown, Pa.; various fin. and materials mgmt. positions Dorsey Trailers, Inc., Atlanta, 1994—, pres., COO, 1997—. Office: Dorsey Trailers Inc 3850 W Main St Ste 806 Dothan AL 36305-1006

PALL, DAVID B. manufacturing company executive, chemist; b. Ft. William, Ont., Can., Apr. 2, 1914; came to U.S., 1939, naturalized, 1942; s. Adolph and Mary (Donner) P.; m. Josephine H. Blatt, Feb. 4, 1940 (dec. 1959); children: Stephanie (Mrs. Wendel Kincaid, Jr.), William, Ellen, Abigail; m. Helen R. Stream, July 10, 1960; 1 stepchild, Jane Block. B.Sc. in Chemistry, McGill U., 1936, PhD in Phys. Chemistry, 1939, D.S. (hon.), 1987; postgrad., Brown U., 1936-37; DSc (hon.), L.I. U., 1985. Group leader research labs. Interchem. Corp., 1939-44; founder Pall Corp. (successor to Micrometallic Corp.), Glen Cove, N.Y., 1944, past pres., and chmn. bd., now dir. Inventor bio-medical filters. Trustee North Shore Hosp., Manhasset, N.Y., cold Spring Harbor Lab., 1987. Recipient Nat. medal Tech. U.S. Dept. Commerce Tech., 1990. Mem. Am. Chem. Soc., Am. Soc. Metals, AAAS. Home: 25 Harbor Park Dr Port Washington NY 11050-4630 Office: Pall Corp 2200 Northern Blvd Greenvale NY 11548-1289

PALL, ELLEN JANE, writer; b. NYC, Mar. 28, 1952; d. David B. and Josephine H. (Blatt) P.; m. Richard Holmes Dicker, July 12, 1986; 1 child, Benjamin. BA, U. Calif., Santa Barbara, 1973. Freelance writer for several jours., 1987—. Staff assoc. Bread Loaf Writers Conf., Middlebury, Vt., 1986; instr. UCLA-Ext., 1980-83; adj. asst. prof. Fordham U./Coll. at Lincoln Ctr., N.Y.C., 1990-93. Author (under pen name Fiona Hill): The Trellised Lane, The Wedding Portrait, The Practical Heart, Love in a Major Key, Sweet's Folly, The Autumn Rose, The Love Child, The Stanbroke Girls, 1981, The Country Gentleman, 1987; author: (as Ellen Pall) Back East, 1983, Among the Ginzburgs, 1996, Corpse de Ballet, 2001, Slightly Abridged, 2003; contbr. articles to N.Y.Times Mag., N.Y. Times Arts & Leisure, New Yorker mag., Chgo. Tribune, Washington Post; book reviewer. Shane Stevens fellow, Bread Loaf Writer's Conf., Vt., 1983. Mem. Am. PEN (freedom to write com.). Office: care Mary Evans Inc 242 E 5th St New York NY 10003-8501

PALLADINO-CRAIG, ALLYS, museum director; b. Pontiac, Mich., Mar. 23, 1947; d. Stephan Vincent and Mary (Anderson) Palladino; m. Malcolm Arnold Craig, Aug. 20, 1967; children— Ansel, Reed, Nicholas. BA in English, Fla. State U., 1967; grad., U. Toronto, Ont., Can., 1969; MFA, Fla. State U., 1978, PhD in Humanities, 1996. Editorial asst. project U. Va. Press, Charlottesville, 1970-76; instr. English Inst. Franco Americain, Rennes, France, 1974; adj. instr. Fla. State U., Tallahassee, 1978-79, dir. Four Arts Ctr., 1979-82, dir. U. Mus. of Fine Arts, 1982—, prof. mus. studies. Mem. grad faculty Mus. Studies Cert. Program Fla. State U. Curator, contbg. editor: Nocturnes and Nightmares, Monochrome/Polychrome, Chroma; contbg. editor: Body Language; guest curator, author: Mark Messersmith: New Mythologies; curator, editor Albert Paley--Sculpture, Drawings, Graphics and Decorative Arts, Trevor Bell: A British Painter in America, and Trial by Fire: Contemporary Glass; curator, author: The Abridged Walmsley--Selections from the Career of William Aubrey Walmsley, co-curator, contbg. author: Terrestrial Forces; author: Jack Nicholson: Micro-Theatres, Alexa Kleinbard: Talking Leaves, Jake Fernandez--Ethereal Journeyman, Jim Roche-Sense of Place; editor: Athanor I-XXIII, 1980—; Represented in permanent collections Fla. Ho. of Reps., Barnett Bank, IBM. Individual artist fellow Fla. Arts Coun., 1979 Mem. Am. Assn. Mus., Fla. Art Mus. Dirs. Assn. (sec. 1989-91), Phi Beta Kappa. Democrat. Avocation: antique american fountain pen collecting. Home: 1410 Grape St Tallahassee FL 32303-5636 Office: Fla State U Mus of Fine Arts 250 Fine Arts Bldg Tallahassee FL 32306-1140 E-mail: apcraig@mailer.fsu.edu.

PALLASCH, B. MICHAEL, lawyer, director; b. Chgo., Mar. 30, 1933; s. Bernhard Michael and Magdalena Helena (Fixari) P.; m. Josephine Catherine O'Leary, Aug. 15, 1981; children: Bernhard Michael III and Madeleine Josephine (twins). BSS, Georgetown U., 1954; JD, Harvard U., 1957; postgrad., John Marshall Law Sch., 1974. Bar: Ill. 1957, U.S. Dist. Ct. (no. dist.) Ill. 1958, U.S. Tax Ct. 1961, U.S. Ct. Claims 1961, U.S. Ct. Appeals (7th cir.) 1962. Assoc. Winston & Strawn, Chgo., 1958-66, resident mgr. br. office Paris, 1963-65, ptnr. Chgo., 1966-70, sr. capital ptnr., 1971-91; sr. ptnr. B. Michael Pallasch & Assocs., 1991—. Corp. sec. Tanis, Inc., Calumet, Mich., 1972-2000, Greenbank Engring. Corp., Dover, Del., 1976-91, C.B.P. Engring. Corp., Chgo., 1976-91, Arthur Andersen Assocs., Inc., Chgo., 1976-98, Chgo. Cutting Svcs. Corp., 1977-88, L'hotel de France of Ill., Inc., Chgo., 1980-85, Water & Effluent Screening Co., Chgo., 1988-91. Bd. dirs. Martin D'Arcy Mus. Medieval and Renaissance Art, Chgo., 1975—; bd. dirs. Katherine M. Bosch Found., 1978—; asst. sec. Hundred Club of Cook County, Chgo., 1966-73, bd. dirs., sec., 1974— . Served with USAFR, 1957-63. Decorated Knight of Merit Sacred Mil. Constantinian Order of St. George of Royal House of Bourbon of Two Sicilies, Grand Officer with star Sovereign Mil. Order of Temple of Jerusalem; named youth mayor, City of Chgo., 1950; recipient Outstanding Woodland Mgmt. Forestry award, Monroe County (Wis.) Soil and Water Conservation Dist., 1975. Mem. Ill. Bar Assn. (tax lectr. 1961), Advs. Soc., Field Mus. Natural History (life), Max McGraw Wildlife Found., English Speaking Union. Clubs: Travellers (Paris); Saddle and Cycle (Chgo.). Roman Catholic. Home: 737 W Hutchinson St Chicago IL 60613-1519 Office: 35 W Wacker Dr Ste 4700 Chicago IL 60601-1614 *Personal philosophy: We define and measure success in various ways: achievement, position, wealth: and attribute it to the application of various attributes but is there any degree of success that we can achieve that is worthier than the knowledge that we have faithfully served those who depend upon and trust in us?.*

PALLEY, HOWARD A. social work educator; b. N.Y.C., Mar. 22, 1936; s. Abraham and Henrietta (Sher) Palley; m. Marian Judith Lief, Apr. 21, 1961; children: Stephen D., Elizabeth S. BA cum laude, Bklyn. Coll., 1957; MS, Yeshiva U., 1959; PhD, Syracuse U., 1963. Asst. prof. William Paterson Coll., Wayne, NJ, 1962—65, U. Wis., Milw., 1965—66; assoc. prof. Adelphi U., Garden City, NY, 1966—70, U. Md., Balt., 1970—77, prof. Sch. Social Work, 1977—, prof. dept. epidemiology and preventive medicine, 1991—. Vis. prof. Chung-Ang U., Seoul, Republic of Korea, 1990, Hebrew U., Israel, 1978, Israel, 85, Brookdale Inst. Gerontology, 1985, Otago U., New Zealand, 2000; conf. presenter in field. Co-author: (book) The Chronically Limited Elderly, 1983; author: Implementing the Canadian National Health Insurance Program, 1985; mem. editl. bd. Soc. Devel. Issues, 1983—2002; contbg. editor: Soc. Devel. Issues, 2002—; mem. editl. bd. Jour. Health and Soc. Policy, 1992—; contbr. articles to profl. jours. Recipient Fulbright Sr. Specialist award, Ukraine, Coun. Internat. Exch. Scholars, Washington, 2001, Fulbright Rsch. award, Republic of Korea, Coun. Internat. Exch. of Scholars, Washington, 1990; Disting. fellow, Inst. Human Svcs. Policy, 2002—. Mem.: NASW (co-dir. policy rsch. project 1980—82), Inter Univ. Consortium Internat. Social Devel. (instnl. rep. to bd. dirs.), Coun. Soc. Work Edn., Am. Assn. Univ. Profs., Am. Polit. Sci. Assn. Democrat. Jewish. Avocations: hiking, travel, chess. Home: 11 N Townview Ln Newark DE 19711-7416 Office: U Md Sch of Social Work 525 W Redwood St Baltimore MD 21201-1705 Office Phone: 410-706-3604. E-mail: hpalley@ssw.umaryland.edu.

PALLMEYER, REBECCA RUTH, judge; b. Tokyo, Sept. 13, 1954; arrived in U.S., 1957; d. Paul Henry and Ruth (Schrieber) Pallmeyer; m. Dan P. McAdams, Aug. 20, 1977; 2 children. BA, Valparaiso U., Ind., 1976; JD, U. Ill., Chgo., 1979. Bar: Ill. 1980, U.S. Ct. Appeals (7th cir.) 1980, U.S. Ct. Appeals (11th and 5th cir.) 1982. Judge clk. Minn. Supreme Ct., St. Paul, 1979-80; assoc. Hopkins and Sutter, Chgo., 1980-85; judge, administrv. law Ill. Human Rights Commn., Chgo., 1985-91; magistrate judge U.S. Dist. Ct. (No. Dist.), Chgo., 1991-98, dist. judge, 1998—. Mem. jud. resources com. Jud. Conf. U.S., 1994—2000. Nat. adv. coun. Christ Coll., Valparaiso U., 2001—; bd. dirs. Augustana Ctr., 1990—91. Recipient Profl. Achievement award, Chgo.-Kent Coll. of Law, 2002, President's Award for Disting. Svc., N.W. Suburban Bar Assn., 2003. Mem.: FBA (bd. mgrs. Chgo. chpt. 1995—99), Chgo. Bar Assn. (chair devel. law com. 1992—93, bd. mgrs. 2004—, David C. Hilliard award 1990—91), Fed. Magistrate Judges Assn. (bd. dirs. 1994—97), Womens Bar Assn. Ill. (bd. mgrs. 1995—98), Valparaiso

U. Alumni Assn. (bd. dirs. 1992—94). Lutheran. Avocations: choral music, sewing, running. Office: US Dist Ct 219 S Dearborn St Ste 2178 Chicago IL 60604-1877 Office Phone: 312-435-5636.

PALLONE, ADRIAN JOSEPH, research scientist; b. Lille, France, Apr. 8, 1928; came to US., 1946; s. Giovanni and Laurina (Caccia) P.; m. Teresa Maria Violino, June 12, 1954; children— John M., Anne Marie, Janet M., Joan L. BS in Aero. Engring., Poly Inst. Bklyn., 1952, MS in Aero. Engring., 1953, PhD in Applied Mechanics, 1959; cert., Sloan Sch. Mgmt., MIT, 1984. Research assoc. Poly. Inst. Bklyn., 1955-59; mgr. Avco Systems Div., Wilmington, Mass., 1959-63; mem. faculty NYU, N.Y.C., 1963-67; dir. Avco Systems Div., Wilmington, 1967-78, chief scientist, 1978-87; aerospace cons. Textron Def. Systems, Wilmington, 1987-91; pres. Aerophysics Systems & Tech., Inc., Silver Lake, N.H., 1992—. Patentee in field. Contbr. articles to sci. jours. Fellow AIAA; mem. N.Y. Acad. Scis., Sigma Xi, Sigma Gamma Tau. Roman Catholic. Avocations: skiing; sailing; hiking. Office: Aerophysics Systems & Tech Inc PO Box 189 Silver Lake NH 03875-0189

PALLONE, FRANK, JR., congressman; b. Long Branch, N.J., Oct. 30, 1951; Grad. cum. laude, Middlebury Coll., 1973; MA, Tufts U., 1974; JD, Rutgers U., 1978. Councilman City of Long Branch, 1982-88; mem. N.J. Senate, 1984-88, U.S. Congress from 6th N.J. dist., 1988—; mem. commerce com., resource com. Democrat. Roman Catholic. Office: US Ho of Reps 420 Cannon Hob Washington DC 20515-0001 Address: 504 Broadway Ste 118 Long Branch NJ 07740-5951

PALLONE, NATHANIEL JOHN, psychologist, educator; b. Chgo., Oct. 30, 1935; s. Louis T. and Adeline (Tenkach) P.; m. Letitia Clarke, Sept. 19, 1983; children: Andrea, Angela. AB, Cath. U. Am., 1957, MA, 1960; PhD, NYU, 1963. Lic. psychologist, N.J. Psychologist St. Francis Coll., Bklyn., 1960-63; asst. prof. U. Notre Dame, South Bend, Ind., 1963-66; dept. chair NYU, N.Y.C., 1966-72; assoc. dean U. Hartford, Conn., 1972-73; dean Rutgers U., New Brunswick, N.J., 1973-79, acad. v.p., 1979-87, univ. disting. prof. psychology, 1987—. Vis. prof. Harvard U., Cambridge, Mass., 1987-88; case cons. Office of Pub. Defender, New Brunswic, 1987-91; cons. social svc. agys., criminal justice agys., 1963—; chair classification rev. bd. for sex offenders N.J. Dept. Corrections, 1975— . Editor: Jour. Offender Rehab., 1989—; exec. editor Current Psychology, 1989—; sr. editor Society, 1992-98; author 35 books; contbr. numerous articles to profl. publs. Fellow Am. Psychol. Assn., Am. Coll. Forensic Psychology, Am. Psychol. Soc.; mem. Am. Bd. Profl. Psychology (diplomate), Phi Beta Kappa. Office: Rutgers Univ 215 Smithers Hall New Brunswick NJ 08903 Office Phone: 732-445-0794.

PALLOTTA, JOHANNA ANTONIA (JOHANNA STEPHEN), physician, educator, researcher; b. Boston, May 7, 1937; d. John and Antonia (Lanni) P.; m. Michael John Stephen, Aug. 13, 1966; children: Jacqueline, Antonia, Michael, Andrew. BS in Chemistry magna cum laude, Boston Coll., 1958; MD, N.Y. Med. Coll., 1962. Diplomate Am. Bds. Internal Medicine, Endocrinolgoy and Metabolism; lic. N.Y., Mass., Calif. Intern St. Elizabeth's Hosp., Boston, 1962-63; resident in medicine N.Y. Med. Coll. Metro. Hosp., N.Y.C., 1963-64; resident in medicine, fellow radioisotope svc. VA Hosp., Bronx, 1964—66; fellow metabolism and endocrinology Yale U. Sch. Medicine, New Haven, 1966-67; instr. medicine Harvard Med. Sch., Boston, 1967-69, Beth Israel Deaconess Hosp. Harvard Med. Sch., 1969-70; asst. prof. medicine Harvard Med. Sch., 1970—2003, assoc. prof. medicine, 2004—. Tutor med. scis. Harvard Med. Sch., 1972-73; dir. endocrinology clinic Beth Israel Deaconess Hosp., Boston, 1967—, dir. radioimmunoassay lab., 1972-83, clin. cons., 1984—, asst. in medicine, 1967-69, assoc. in medicine, 1969-70, asst. physician, 1970-79, assoc. physician, 1979-87, sr. physician, 1987—, dir. clin. rsch. ctr. core radioimmunoassay lab., 1984-93; cons. staff Mount Auburn Hosp., Cambridge, 1974-90; mem. numerous other coms., 1969—. Rschr. in field; contbr. articles to profl. jours. Named Carl Shapiro scholar, BIDMC-Harvard Med. Sch., 2000—; recipient S. Robert Stone Harvard Med. Sch.-BIDMC tchg. award, 1998. Fellow: ACP, Am. Assn. Clin. Endocrinologists; mem.: Am. Fedn. Clin. Rsch., Am. Thyroid Assn., Endocrine Soc., Harvard Aesculapian Club, Alpha Omega Alpha. Roman Catholic. Home: 16 Fresh Pond Ln Cambridge MA 02138-4616 Office: Beth Israel Hosp Harvard Med Sch 330 Brookline Ave Boston MA 02215-5491 Office Phone: 617-667-4016. E-mail: jpallott@BIDMC.harvard.edu.

PALLOTTI, MARIANNE MARGUERITE, foundation administrator; b. Hartford, Conn., Apr. 23, 1937; d. Rocco D. and Marguerite (Long) P. BA, NYU, 1968, MA, 1972. Asst. to pres. Wilson, Haight & Welch, Hartford, 1964-65; exec. asst. Ford Found., N.Y.C., 1965-77; corp. sec. Hewlett Found., Menlo Park, Calif., 1977-84, v.p., 1985—. Bd. dirs. N.Y. Theatre Ballet, N.Y.C., 1986-98, Austin Montessori Sch., 1993, Djerassi Resident Artists Program, 1998—, Mexican Mus., 1999—; mem. women's adv. com., nat. coun.World Wildlife Fund, 1997—; mem. program com. Ind. Sector, Washington, 1998—. Mem. Women in Founds., No. Calif. Grantmakers. Office: William and Flora Hewlett Foundation 2121 Sand Hill Rd Menlo Park CA 94025-6903

PALLOZOLA, CHRISTINE, non-profit administrator; b. St. Louis, Mar. 28, 1952; BS, U. Mo., 1974. Purchasing and sales mgmt. computer industry, Mo., 1984-92; exec. dir. Cahokia Mounds Mus. Soc., Collinsville, Ill., 1993—2001, dir. spl. events, mktg. Arts and Edn. Coun., 2001—04; exec. dir. Am. Acad. Physician and Patient, St. Louis, 2004—. Mem. Assn. Fundraising Profls. Home: 150 Burtonwood Ballwin MO 63011

PALL-PALLANT, TERI, paleontologist, inventor, behavioral scientist, design engineer, advertising agency executive; b. Somerville, NJ, Jan. 6, 1921; d. Stanley and Milicent Pall-Pallant. BA, Imperial Coll., London, 1948, MS, 1949; postgrad., Warren Sch. Aero., LA, 1950, Calif. Inst. Tech., 1951; PhD, London U., 1954, PhD, 1966; student, UCLA, 1955; PhD, Columbia U., 1963; ScD, London Inst. Applied Rsch., 1973; cert. rehab. counselor, U. So. Calif., 1975. Design engr. Simmonds Aerocessories Ltd., London, 1949, dir. vocat. rehab., 1950; founder, owner Teri Pall Advt. Agy., LA, 1951—, Pall Indsl. Surveys, Pasadena, Calif., 1952—, Pall Tech. Industries, Tarzana, Calif., 1979—. Chmn. bd. Pall Industries, Ltd., Taipei, Taiwan and Tarzana, Calif., 1980—; vertebrate paleontologist Am. Mus. Natural History, NYC, 1965-69; leader Teri Pall Trio, LA, 1951-69; exec. dir. Hoffman House, Long Beach, Calif., 1970-72; sr. adminstrv. analyst Econ. and Youth Opportunities, LA County, 1973-74; dep. dir. Head Start Program LA County, 1974-75; assoc. dir. Casa del las Amigas, Pasadena, dir. rsch. and evaluation projects Nat. Inst. Alcohol Abuse and Alcoholism, Washington, 1977; pvt. practice vocat. rehab. counseling, Beverly Hills, Calif., 1977; exec. dir. Little House LA County, 1978; robotics cons. Jet Propulsion Lab., Pasadena, 1974-95, NASA, Am. Assn. U. Women, 1990—. Author: (play) El Rancho Verde, 1951, (novel) With Banners Flying, 1953, Chinese and Western Worlds from 1800 B.C. to Modern Times, 1950, 4000 Years of Egyptian History, 1950, The Integrating Power Meter, 1956, About the Mammoth, 1962, Look, a Travelogue in Time, 1967, The History of Our Calendar, 1977; designer robotics exhibit Calif. Mus. of Sci. and Industry, LA, 1990; inventor proximity warning device for aircraft. Fossil exhibit contbr. LA County Mus., 1968-77; chmn. Mayor's Commn. on Barrier-Free Arch., 1978—; vice chmn. rsch. and coordinating com. Gov.'s Commn. on Safe Energy Alternatives, 1979—; mem. Cancer Rsch. Coordinating Com., 1979—; lectr. Long Beach Hosp., 1978; office bd. Inventor's Workshop Internat. Edn. Found., 1980—, Am. Guild of Inventors, 1990—; bd. dirs. Commn. Conserve Chinese Culture. Recipient Spl. Contbns. award Engring. and Grading Constructors Assn., 1968, Interkamera Gold award Cannes Art Festival, 1969, Spkr. of Yr. award Toastmasters Calif., 1971, Woman of Yr. for Civil Leadership award Long Beach, 1971, Outstanding Achievement award Am. Cancer Soc., 1979, others. Mem. AAUW, Statis. Quality Control Engrs. (sec. 1951—), Assn. Bus. Publs., Nat. Rehab. Counseling Assn., Archs. and Engrs. Inst., Nat. Soc. Vertebrate Paleontologists, Phi Beta Kappa. Republican. Episcopalian. Achievements include developer 2-mile cordless telephone, 1978, wrist chronograph calculator, 1979, Etch-A-Sketch, 1962, AC-DC multimeters, 1954, Miniaturized transcutaneous nerve stimulator, 1969, Electronic remote control system, 1972, proximity warning device for aircraft 1986, 4 wheel walk-a-bout 19', 2000.

PALM, CHARLES GILMAN, university official; b. Havre, Mont., Apr. 25, 1944; s. Victor F. and Laura (McKinnie) P.; m. Miriam Willits, Sept. 15, 1968. AB, Stanford U., 1966; MA, U. Wyo., 1967; MLS, U. Oreg., 1970. Asst. archivist Stanford (Calif.) U., 1971—74, dep. archivist, 1974-84, archivist, 1984-87, head libr., 1986-87, assoc. dir., 1987-90; dep. dir. Stanford U., Palo Alto, Calif., 1990—2001, dep. dir. emeritus, 2002—. Co-author: Guide to Hoover Institution Archives, 1980, Herbert Hoover, Register of His Papers in the Hoover Institution Archives, 1983. Mem. Calif. Heritage Preservation Commn., Sacramento, 1988—, vice chmn., 1993-97, chmn., 1997-2004; mem. Nat. Hist. Records and Publs. Commn., Washington, 1990-96; mem. history and edn. ctr. adv. bd. ARC, 1994—; trustee Golden State Mus. Corp., 1997-2004. Fellow: Soc. Am. Archivists; mem.: Soc. Calif. Archivists (pres. 1983—84), Bohemian Club. Republican. Office: Hoover Instn Stanford CA 94305

PALM, GREGORY K. lawyer, investment company executive; b. Binghamton, N.Y., Sept. 25, 1948; SB, MIT, 1970; MBA, JD, Harvard U., 1974. Bar: N.Y. 1977, DC 1978. Assoc. Sullivan & Cromwell, 1976—82, ptnr., 1982—92; exec. v.p., gen. counsel Goldman, Sachs & Co., N.Y.C., 1992—. Mem. Harvard Law Rev. Mem.: Am. Law Inst., DC Bar. Office: Goldman Sachs and Co Legal Dept 1 New York Plz 37th Fl New York NY 10004

PALM, MARY EGDAHL, mycologist; b. Mpls., Jan. 27, 1954; d. Lauren and Mary E.; children: Natalie Elizabeth, Christopher Steven. BA in Biology, St. Olaf Coll., 1976; MSc in Plant Pathology (mycology), U. Minn., 1979, PhD in Plant Pathology (mycology), 1983. Lab. asst. St. Olaf Coll. Biology Dept., Northfield, Minn., 1974, tchg. asst., 1975-76; rsch. asst. U. Minn. plant pathology dept., Mpls., 1976-83, post doctoral rsch. assoc., 1983-84; mycologist (botanist GS12) USDA/APHIS biol. assessment and support staff, Beltsville, Md., 1984-91; mycologist scientific svcs. USDA/Animal and Plant Health Inspection Svc., Beltsville, 1991—. Instr., coord. seminars and tng. sessions for USDA and ednl. sci. group, 1982—; adj. assoc. prof. plant pathology Pa. State U., State College, 1995. Co-author: Deuteromycetes and Selected Ascomycetes That Occur On or In Wood: An Indexed Bibliography, 1979, An Indexed Bibliography and Guide to Taxonomic Literature, 1988, A Literature Guide for the Identification of Plant Pathogenic Fungi, 1987, Fungi on Rhododendron. A World Reference, 1996, Mycology in Sustainable Development: Expanding concepts, Vanishing Borders, 1997; contbr. articles to profl. jours. including Mycologia, Plant Disease, Can. Jour. Botany, Mycotaxon. Recipient St. Olaf Coll. Hon. Biology scholarship, 1976, Disting. Alumnus Dept. Plant Pathology U. Minn., 1999; grantee U. Minn. Computer Ctr. 1979, 80, 81, 82. Mem. Am. Phytopathol. Soc. (chairperson mycology com. 1988, 89, vice chairperson 1987, mem. 1985, 86, regulatory plant pathology com. 1993—, organizer, moderator colloquim on systematics of plant pathogenic fungi 1987), Mycol. Soc. Am. (sec. 1991-94, Am. Inst. Biol. Scis. rep. 1994—, v.p. 1995-96, pres.-elect 1996-97, pres. 1997-98, other coms.), L.Am. Mycol. Assn. (U.S. liaison), Internat. Assn. Plant Taxonomy (subcom. C of com. on fungi and lichens 1986, 87, 88). Office: USDA Rm 329 B-011A 10300 Baltimore Ave Beltsville MD 20705-2350

PALMA, JACK D. lawyer; b. N.Y.C., Sept. 15, 1946; BA, Allegheny Coll., 1968; JD with honors, U. Denver, 1974. Bar: Colo. 1975, Wyo. 1976. Ptnr. Holland & Hart, Cheyenne, Wyo., 1984—. Mem. ABA, Colo. Bar Assn., Wyo. State Bar, Order St. Ives. Office: Holland & Hart PO Box 1347 Cheyenne WY 82003-1347 Office Phone: 307-778-4226.

PALMA, NICHOLAS JAMES, lawyer; b. Newark, N.J., Oct. 28, 1953; s. James Thomas and VeniceMaria (DiBenedetto) Palma; m. Mary Jo Cugliari, Sept. 1, 1973; children: Nicholas J., Valerie Michele, James Michael. BS cum laude, William Paterson U., 1975; JD, Seton Hall U., 1979. Bar: N.J. 1979, U.S. Dist. Ct. N.J. 1979, U.S. Ct. Appeals (3d cir.) 1985, N.Y. 1986, U.S. Dist. Ct. (ea. and so. dists.) N.Y. 2002; cert. firearms expert Hudson County, N.J. Investigator N.J. Pub. Defender's Office, Essex Region, Newark, 1974—75, Hudson County Prosecutor's Office, Jersey City, 1975—79, asst. prosecutor, 1979—81; ptnr. A.J. Fusco, Jr., P.A., Passaic, NJ, 1981—90; sole practitioner Clifton, NJ, 1990—. Recipient commendation, Dade County Sheriff, Fla., 1976. Mem.: N.J. State Bar Assn., Passaic County Bar Assn. Roman Catholic. Home: 221 Cedar St Cedar Grove NJ 07009-1615 Office: 1425 Broad St Clifton NJ 07013-4201 Office Phone: 973-471-1121.

PALMATIER, MALCOLM ARTHUR, editor, consultant; b. Kalamazoo, Nov. 11, 1922; s. Karl Ernest and Cecile Caroline (Chase) P.; m. Mary Elizabeth Summerfield, June 16, 1948 (dec. Oct. 1982); children: Barnabus, Timothy K., Duncan M.; m. Marie-Anne Suzanne van Werveke, Jan. 12, 1985. BS in Math., Western Mich. U., 1945; MA in English, UCLA, 1947; MA in Econs., U. So. Calif., 1971. Instr. English Pomona Coll., Claremont, Calif., 1949-51; editor Naval Ordnance Test Sta., Pasadena, Calif., 1951-54; head editl. unit Rocketdyne, L.A., 1954-55; editor The RAND Corp., Santa Monica, Calif., 1955-87, cons. editor, 1987—. Instr. English UCLA, L.A., summer 1950. Mng. editor, cons. editor Jour.: Studies in Comparative Communism, L.A., 1968-80; co-editor Perspectives in Economics, 1971; contbr. chpts. to book, book revs. and articles to profl. jours. Chmn. bd. New Start, West L.A., 1982-84. With USNR, 1943-45. Mem. Jonathan Club. Avocations: music, travel. Home: 516 Avondale Ave Los Angeles CA 90049-4804 Office: 1700 Main St Santa Monica CA 90407-2138 E-mail: Malcolm_Palmatier@rand.org.

PALMEDO, PHILIP FRANKLIN, management consulting company executive; b. N.Y.C., Mar. 11, 1934; s. Roland and Elizabeth (Franklin) P.; m. Elisabeth Sheerin, May 27, 1961; children: P. Christopher, Lawrence. BA, Williams Coll., Williamstown, Mass., 1956; MS, MIT, 1958, PhD, 1961. Physicist Brookhaven Nat. Lab., Upton, N.Y., 1964-79; pres. Internat. Resources Group, Washington, 1979-80, chmn., 1980—; pres. Kepler Fin. Mgmt., Setauket, N.Y., 1988-91, L.I. Rsch. Inst., Setauket, 1992-97, Palmedo Assocs., Setauket, 1998—. Dir. EHR Investments, Ponte Vedra Beach, Fla., Gyrodyne Corp. Am., St. James, N.Y. Co-author: Wines of Long Island, 1994, Voices in Bronze, 1999, Bill Barrett, 2003. Mem. bd. L.I. Mus. Sci. and Tech., Melville, N.Y., 1996—; trustee Gallery North, Setauket, 1987—; dir. Stony Brook (N.Y.) Found., 1987—. Avocations: writing, sports, art. Home: 4 Piper Ln Saint James NY 11780-1122 Office: Palmedo Assocs 100 N Country Rd Setauket NY 11733-1300 E-mail: ppalmedo@cs.com.

PALMEIRO, RAFAEL CORRALES, professional baseball player; b. Havana, Cuba, Sept. 24, 1964; Degree in Comml. Art, Miss. State U. With Chgo. Cubs, 1986-88, Tex. Rangers, 1988—93, Balt. Orioles, 1994-98, Tex. Rangers, 1999—2003, Balt. Orioles, 2004—. Named Nat. League All-Star Team, 1988, Am. League All-Star Team, 1991, 1998, 1999; recipient Gold Glove award, 1997-1999; led Am. League in runs (124), 1993; hit 500th career home run, May 10, 2003. Office: c/o Baltimore Orioles Camden Yards 333 W Camden St Baltimore MD 21201*

PALMER, ADA MARGARET, systems analyst, consultant; b. Feb. 8, 1940; d. Mark Lloyd Palmer and Eunice Elizabeth (Thompson) Palmer Schnitzer. AA, Colo. Woman's Coll., 1960; BA, George Washington U., 1962. Programmer, analyst U.S. Navy Dept., Washington, 1962-66, Schroder Trust, N.Y.C., 1967-68; v.p. EDP Learning Systems, N.Y.C., 1968-69; cons. JWI Assoc. Tech. Group, N.Y.C., 1969; adv. sr. programmer Merrill Lynch, N.Y.C., 1969-72; sys. analyst Tchrs. Ins. & Annuity, N.Y.C., 1972-77; sys. specialist N.Y. Times, N.Y.C., 1977-81; computer cons. Applied Sys. Resources, Inc., N.Y.C., 1981-82; asst. sec. Chase Bank, N.Y.C., 1982-94; computer cons. A.Z. Software Shop Inc., Garden City, N.Y., 1994-95; sys. acct. UN, N.Y.C., 1995-99; computer cons. AMP Consulting, Inc., 1999—. Mem. Women's Assn. of the Wichita Symphony, Allegro Movement Soc. of the Wichita Symphony. Recipient George Washington U. Alumni Svc. award, 1992. Mem. AAUW, Archeol. Inst. Am., Colo. Woman's Coll. Alumni Club, George Washington U. Alumni Club of N.Y.C. (past pres.), Am. Overseas Schs. Hist. Soc. (bd. dirs. 2002—). Republican. Presbyterian. Home and Office: Apt 1707 550 W Central Wichita KS 67203-4238

PALMER, ANN THERESE DARIN, lawyer; b. Detroit, Apr. 25, 1951; d. Americo and Theresa (Del Favero) Darin; m. Robert Towne Palmer, Nov. 9, 1974; children: Justin Darin, Christian Darin. BA, U. Notre Dame, 1973, MBA, 1975, JD, Loyola U., Chgo., 1978. Bar: Ill. 1978, U.S. Supreme Ct. 1981. Intern Wall Street Jour., Detroit, 1974; freelancer Time Inc. Fin. Publs., Chgo., 1975—77; extern, Midwest regional solicitor U.S. Dept. Labor, 1976—78; tax atty. Esmark Inc., 1978; counsel Chgo. United, 1978—81; ind. contractor Legal Tax Rsch., 1981—89; fin. and legal news contbr. The Chgo. Tribune, 1991—, Bus. Week, 1991—, Automotive News, 1993—97, Crain's Chgo. Bus., 1994—2000; contbg. editor Registered Rep, 2002—. Mem.: Woman's Athletic Club Chgo. Home: 1570 Christina Ln Lake Forest IL 60045

PALMER, ANTHONY JOHN, music educator, composer, writer; b. Youngstown, Ohio, Oct. 9, 1931; s. Frank William and Mary Ann Palmer; m. Linda Kathleen Kobylenski, July 26, 1986; m. Norma Elizabeth Johnson, Nov. 23, 1957 (div. Dec. 18, 1980); children: Carolyn Elizabeth Barnes, David William. BA (hons.), Calif. State U., LA, 1958, MA, 1960; PhD (distinction), UCLA, 1975. Tchr. Alhambra (Calif.) HS, 1963—75; assoc. prof. LA Valley Coll., Van Nuys, Calif., 1975—80, U. Tenn., Knoxville, 1980—87, UCLA, 1987—90; prof. U. Hawaii at Manoa, Honolulu, 1990—98; adj. prof. Boston U., 2000—. Freelance composer, 1957—. Staff sgt. USAF, 1950—54. Recipient Outstanding Grad., UCLA Alumni Assn., 1976; Creative Artist Fellowship, Japan-U.S. Friendship Commn., 1984—85. Mem.: Coll. Music Soc., Soc. for Ethnomusicology, Music Eductors Nat. Conf., Am. Choral Dirs. Assn., Internat. Soc. for the Philosophy of Music Edn. (bylaws chair 2003). Liberal. Office: Sch of Music Boston Univ 855 Commonwealth Ave Boston MA 02215 Office Phone: 617-353-4244. Personal E-mail: palms2@comcast.net. E-mail: ajpalmer@bu.edu.

PALMER, ARNOLD DANIEL, retired professional golfer; b. Youngstown, Pa., Sept. 10, 1929; s. Milfred Jerome and Doris M. Palmer; m. Winnie Walzer, Dec. 20, 1954 (dec. Nov. 1999); children: Peggy Palmer Wears, Amy Palmer Saunders. Student, Wake Forest Coll., LLD, 1970. Profl. golfer, 1954—; businessman, entrepreneur, 1960—. Nat. spokesman Pennzoil Petroleum Products (Shell), Sears Can., Rolex, Verizon, Golf mag., Rayovac, Textron, Lexington Furniture, Office Depot, Callaway Golf, PNC Bank Corp., Capital Mercury, KRB Seed, Encore Bank, Invacare, GlaxoSmithKline, Timing Inc., Cessna, Eisenhart Wallcoverings, Tehama, Ketel One, Administaff; designer numerous golf courses. Author: Arnold Palmer's Golf Book, 1961, Portrait of a Professional Golfer, 1964, My Game and Yours, 1965, rev. edit., 1983, Situation Golf, 1970, Go for Broke, 1973, Arnold Palmer's Best 54 Holes of Golf, 1977, Arnold Palmer's Complete Book of Putting, 1986, Play Great Golf, 1987, (with Thomas Hauser) A Personal Journey, 1994, (with James Dodson) Arnold Palmer, A Golfer's Life, 1999, Playing by the Rules, 2002. Served USCG, 1951—54. Recipient numerous golf awards including Bob Jones award U.S. Golf Assn., William D. Richardson award Golf Writers Assn. Am., Herb Graffis award Nat. Golf Found., Presdl. medal of Freedom, 2004; named Sportsman of Yr. Sports Illustrated mag., 1960, Player of Yr. Profl. Golfers Assn., 1960, 62, AP Athlete of Decade, 1969; Profl. Golfers Assn. Tour Money Leader, 1958, 60, 62, 63; elected to World Golf Hall of Fame, Profl. Golfers Assn. Hall of Fame. Mem. Latrobe (Pa.) Country Club, Laurel Valley Golf Club, Rolling Rock Club (Ligonier, Pa.), Bay Hill Club, Duquesne Club (Pitts.). Winner of over 90 major golf tournaments since 1955, including Masters Championship, 1958, 60, 62, 64, U.S. Open, 1960, U.S. Amateur, 1954, Brit. Open, 1961, 62. Home and Office: PO Box 52 Youngstown PA 15696-0052 Office Phone: 724-537-7751.

PALMER, BEN M. gas industry executive; With Arthur Andersen, Atlanta; sr. v.p., CFO, treas. EQ Svcs. Inc., Atlanta; CFO RPC Inc., Atlanta, 1996—. Office: RPC Inc 2170 Piedmont Rd NE Atlanta GA 30324-4135

PALMER, BEVERLY BLAZEY, psychologist, educator; b. Cleve., Nov. 22, 1945; d. Lawrence E. and Mildred M. Blazey; m. Richard C. Palmer, June 24, 1967; 1 child, Ryan Richard. PhD in Counseling Psychology, Ohio State U., 1972. Lic. clin. psychologist, Calif. Adminstrv. assoc. Ohio State U., Columbus, 1969-70; rsch. psychologist Health Svcs. Rsch. Ctr. UCLA, 1971-77; commr. pub. health L.A. County, 1978-81; pvt. practice clin. psychology Torrance, Calif., 1985—; prof. psychology Calif. State U., Dominguez Hills, 1973—. Reviewer manuscripts for numerous textbook pubs; contbr. numerous articles to profl. jours. Recipient Proclamation, County of Los Angeles, 1972, 1981, Fulbright scholar, Malaysia, 2001, 2004. Mem. APA. Office: Calif State U Dominguez Hills Dept Psychology Carson CA 90747-0001

PALMER, BRIAN EUGENE, lawyer; b. Mpls., May 16, 1948; s. Eugene Philip and Virginia Breeze (Rolfshus) P.; m. Julia Washburn Morrison, Dec. 29, 1972; 1 child, Julia Hunter. AB, Brown U., 1970; JD, William Mitchell Coll. of Law, 1974. Bar: Minn. 1974, U.S. Dist. Ct. Minn. 1975, U.S. Dist. Ct. (ea. dist.) Wis. 2001, U.S. Ct. Appeals (8th cir.) 1980, U.S. Ct. Fed. Claims 1984, U.S. Supreme Ct. 1980. Asst. pub. defender Hennepin County Pub. Defender, Mpls., 1974-78; assoc. Dorsey & Whitney LLP, Mpls., 1978-82, ptnr., 1983—. Home: 1190 Lyman Ave Wayzata MN 55391-9671 Office: Dorsey & Whitney LLP 50 South Sixth St Ste 1500 Minneapolis MN 55402-1498 Office Phone: 612-340-2797. E-mail: palmer.brian@dorsey.com.

PALMER, CHARLES A. lawyer, educator; b. Jackson, Mich., Jan. 25, 1945; s. Robert E. and Gertrude (Caldwell) P.; m. Barbara Ann DiTiberio, May 10, 1975; children: Robert, Joseph, Christopher. BBA, U. Mich., 1967, JD, 1970. Bar: Mich. 1970, U.S. Dist. Ct. (we. and ea. dists.) Mich. 1970, U.S. Tax Ct., U.S. Ct. Appeals (6th cir.). Jud. clk. Ingham County Cir. Ct., Lansing, Mich., 1971; assoc. Cummins, Butter & Thorburn, Lansing, 1971-72; prin. Charles A. Palmer, P.C., Lansing, 1973-88; prof. law Thomas M. Cooley Law Sch., Lansing, 1988—. Mayor, JAG, Mich. N.G., Jackson, 1978—; chmn. bd. dirs. Ind. Bank of South Mich., Leslie, 1989—. Pres. Legal Aid of Cen. Mich., Lansing. Mem. ABA, Mich. Bar Assn., Ingham County Bar Assn. Office: Independent Bank Corp 230 W Main St PO Box 491 Ionia MI 48846

PALMER, CHARLOTTE MARIE, writer; d. Floyd Bell Morgan and Louise Lillian May; m. George Saxon Palmer, Feb. 26, 1988; m. Robert John Probst, Nov. 25, 1978 (dec. Mar. 24, 1987); children: Rose Michele Watson, Tina Louise Witt, Frederick Ray Berretta Jr. Cert., Chgo. Nat. Assn. Dance Masters, 1955, Dance Masters Am., Miami, Fla., 1963, So. Dance Masters Assn., Memphis, 1961. Dir., choreographer Charlotte Morgan Sch. Dance, Memphis, 1954—67; writer, corr. Memphis Press Scimitar, Greenville, Miss., 1967—69; v.p. Probst Media Comm., Jupiter, Fla., 1981—88; freelance writer Tallahassee, 1987—. Chmn., founder Dance Promotions, Memphis, 1962—67; mktg. v.p. Fla. TV PBS Network, Jupiter, 1981—82. Prodr.: (films) The Apprentice. Docent Fla. Governor's Mansion, Tallahassee, 1995—2003; sec. Myers Pk. Neighborhood Assn., Tallahassee, 1988—2002; regent, vice regent DAR, Ft. San Luis, Tallahassee, 1987—2002. Recipient Curtains Up award, Ft. Lauderdale Civic Ballet, 1974, Disting. award, Dollars Against Diabetes, Blueprint for Cure, 1987, President's award, Fla. Heritage Found., 1991, 1992. Mem.: Capital Med. Alliance, St. Mary's Cir., St. John's Episcopal Ch., Fla. State Sch. Theater (patrons bd. mem. 1995—2003). Republican. Episcopalian. Avocations: gardening, directing productions, stage, film, and dance, poetry.

PALMER, CHRIS, professional football coach; b. Brewster, N.Y., Sept. 23, 1949; m. Donna Palmer; children: Mark, Kristin. BS, MS, So. Conn. State U. Asst. coach U. Conn., 1972-75; wide receivers coach Lehigh U., 1975-76; offensive coord. Colgate U., 1976-82; offensive line coach Montreal Concords, 1983-84; coach receivers, quarterback coach, offensive coord. N.J. Generals, 1984-86; head coach U. New Haven, 1986-87, Boston U., 1988-89; coach wide receivers Houston Oilers, 1990-92; with New Eng. Patriots, 1994-97, quarterback coach, 1996-97; offensive coord. Jacksonville Jaguars, 1997-99; head coach Cleveland Browns, 1999—2001; offensive coord. Houston Texans, 2002—. Office: The Houston Texans Two Reliant Park Houston TX 77054

PALMER, CHRISTINE (CLELIA ROSE VENDITTI), operatic singer, pianist, vocal educator; b. Hartford, Conn., Apr. 02; d. John Marion and Immacolata (Morcaldo) Venditti; m. Raymond Smith, Oct. 5, 1949 (div. June

1950); m. Arthur James Whitlock, Feb. 25, 1953. Student, Mt. Holyoke Coll., 1937-38, New Eng. Conservatory of Music, 1941-42; pvt. studies, Boston, Hartford, N.Y.C., Florence and Naples, Italy; RN with honors, Hartford Hosp. Sch. Nursing, 1941. Artist-in-residence El Centro Coll., Dallas, 1966-71. Pvt. vocal instr.-coach, specializing in vocal technique for opera, mus. comedy, supper club acts, auditions, Dallas, 1962-94; voice adjudicator San Francisco Opera Co., 1969-72, Tex. Music Tchrs. Assn., 1964-75, others; lectr. in field; appearances with S.M. Chartocks' Gilbert and Sullivan Co.; now performing lecture/entertainment circuit. Leading operatic soprano N.Y.C. Opera, Chgo., San Francisco, San Carlo, other cities, 1944-62; presented concert N.Y. Town Hall, 1951; soloist with symphony orchs. maj. U.S. Cities, 1948-62; soloist Marble Collegiate Ch., Holy Trinity Ch.; coast-to-coast concert tour, 1948; numerous appearances including St. Louis MUNY Opera, Indpls. Starlight Theatre, Lambertville Music Circus; soloist Holiday on Ice, 1949-50; TV performer, including Home Show on NBC, Telephone Hour on NBC, Holiday Hotel; performer various supper clubs, N.Y.C., Atlanta, Bermuda, Catskills, others, including Number One Fifth Avenue, The Embers, The Carriage Club, Viennese Lantern. Hon. mem. women's bd. Dallas Opera Assn.; mem. adv. bd. Tex. Opera News; mem. Tex. Music Tchrs. Cert. Bd., Collegiate Chorale, Don Craig Singers, The Vikings; mem. women's bd., Dallas Bapt. Univ. Oliver Ditson scholar, 1942; recipient Phi Xi Delta prize in Italian, 1937; named Victor Herbert Girl, ASCAP; Spl. Recognition Gold book of Dallas Soc. Mem. Nat. Assn. Tchrs. of Singing (pres. Dallas chpt. 1972-74), Nat. Fedn. Music Clubs, Tex. Fedn. Music Clubs, Dallas Fedn. Music Clubs (pres. 1972-74), Dallas Symphony League, Dallas Music Tchrs. Assn. (pres. 1971-72, Tchr. of Yr. 1974), Thesaurus Book Club (pres. 1990-91, 97-98), Friday Forum (Dallas, bd. dirs.), Dallas Women's C. of C., Eagle Forum, Pub. Affairs Luncheon Club, Dallas Fedn. Music Club, Pro Am., Wednesday Morning Choral Club, Dallas Knife and Fork Club, Prestoncrest Rep. Club. Presbyterian. Home: 6232 Pemberton Dr Dallas TX 75230-4036

PALMER, CRUISE, newspaper editor; b. Kansas City, Kans., Apr. 9, 1917; s. Thomas Potter and Margaret Scroggs (McFadden) P.; m. Dorraine Humphreys, Sept. 7, 1946; children: Thomas Cruise, Martha D. Sprague. BS in Journalism, Kans. State U., 1938. With Kansas City (Mo.) Star, 1938—, news editor, 1963-64, mng. editor, 1965-66; exec. editor and bd. Star and Times, 1967—78, cons., 1978—2002. Dir. Purtec Systems, Inc. Author: Bosses of the News Room, 1927-2006, 2003. Mem. bd. govs. Am. Royal Live Stock and Horse Show Assn., 1967-91; bd. dirs. ARC, 1978-91, Kansas City Mayor's Corps Progress, 1978-91; found. trustee Kans. State U.; trustee Kansas City Sister Cities Commn., 1978-91. Served to lt. (j.g.) USNR, 1943-46. Recipient Distinguished Service award Kans. State U., 1967; First Place award Pro-Am. Southgate Open Golf Tournament, 1973; Second Place award Pro-Am. Hawaiian Open, 1973, 85; Third Place, 1981; First Place award Jim Colbert Celebrity Tournament, 1981, First Place Team award Kansas City area Am. Cancer Soc. Golf Tournament, 1986. Mem. Am. Soc. Newspaper Editors, Soc. Profl. Journalists, Kansas City Sr. Golf Assn., Kansas City Press Club (pres. 1953-54, 64-65, permanent trustee, pres. scholarship found. 1989), Kansas City Club, Chiefs Red Coat Club, Milburn Golf and Country Club, Beta Theta Pi (Greater Kansas City Beta of Yr. 1980). Episcopalian (former vestryman and lay reader). Home: Lakeview Retirement Village 14100 W 90th Ter Apt 504 Lenexa KS 66215-5430 Office: 1729 Grand Ave Kansas City MO 64108-1413

PALMER, CURTIS DWAYNE, cardiopulmonary practitioner, microbiologist, researcher, builder; b. Leesville, La., Aug. 5, 1947; s. Curtis and Freda Elaine (Franklin) P.; children: Derrick Mitchell, Elizabeth Merritt. BSc, Northwestern U., Natchitoches, La., 1971; MSC, Northwestern U., 1972; cardiopulmonary diploma, U. Chgo., 1975. Registered respiratory therapist. From dir. pulmonary rsch. to rsch. assoc. La. State U., Shreveport, 1972-75, 79-81; pres., chmn. Pulmonary Care Assocs., Shreveport, 1975-79; med. student St. Lucia U., El Paso, Tex., 1981-83; supr. pulmonary svcs. Glenwood Reg. Med. Ctr., West Monroe, La., 1987-93; v.p. DeBlieux-Palmer Ltd., Natchitoches, La., 1994—. Contract adminstr. Therapeutic Svcs., Shreveport, 1986-90; regional mgr. TriTek Industries, Inc., 1987-93; pres., chmn. Dwayne Palmer Realty Inc., Shreveport, 1974-80; faculty Inst. Microbiology and Pulmonary Rsch., La. Sch. Medicine, Shreveport, Northwestern U. Contbr. articles to profl. jours. Bd. dirs. March of Dimes, Shreveport, 1977; realtor Bd. Realtors, Shreveport, 1975-82, Natchitoches, 1995—; contractor La. Bd. Licensing Contractors, 1976—, Palmer Constrn. Co., Inc., 1993—. Mem. Nat. Bd. Respiratory Care, Am. Assn. Respiratory Care, Nat. Assn. Home Builders, La. Soc. Respiratory Care (chmn. judiciary bd. 1976), Soc. Critical Care Medicine, Nat. Bd. Realtors, Shreveport-Bossier Bd. Realtors, Kappa Sigma (Epsilon chpt.). Republican. Methodist. Avocations: scuba diving, tennis, pilot. Home: 14150 Azalea Park Ave Ste B Baton Rouge LA 70816-1106

PALMER, DAN M. finance company executive; b. Memphis, 1943; BBA, U. Memphis, 1966; cert. in Exec. Program, Dartmouth U., 1979. Founder Electronic Fleet Sys., 1982—90; CEO Concord Computing Corp. (formerly Electronic Fleet Sys.), 1990—2003; co-CEO Concord EFS, Inc. (formerly Concord Computing Corp.), Memphis, 2003—, bd. dirs. Named Debit Exec. of Yr., Credit Card Mgmt. Mag., 2000; named one of Top 10 Leaders & success CEOs, Investors Bus. Daily, 2001. Mem.: Memphis Soc. Entrepreneurs. Office: Concord EFS Inc 2525 Horizon Lake Dr Ste 120 Memphis TN 38133*

PALMER, DAVE RICHARD, retired military officer, academic administrator; b. Ada, Okla., May 31, 1934; s. David Furman and Lorena Marie (Clardy) P.; m. LuDelia Clemmer, Apr. 13, 1957; children: Allison, J. Kersten. BS, U.S. Military Acad., 1956; MA in History, Duke U., 1966; postgrad., Army War Coll., 1972-73; PhD (hon.), Duke U., 1990. Commd. U.S. Army, 1956, advanced through grades to lt. gen.; mem. faculty dept. history U.S. Mil. Acad., 1966-69; mem. staff (Pentagon), 1973-76, Joint Chiefs of Staff, 1979-81; comdr. Baumholder Mil. Community, W. Ger., 1981-83; dep. comdt. Command and Gen. Staff Coll., Ft. Leavenworth, Kans., 1983-85; comdg. gen. 1st Armored Div., W.Ger., 1985-86; supt. U.S. Mil. Acad., 1986-91, ret., 1991; pres. Walden U., 1995-99; CEO Walden Corp., 1999-2000. Author: The River and the Rock, 1969, The Way of the Fox, 1975, Summons of the Trumpet, 1978, 1794-America, Its Army, and The Birth of the Nation, 1994, First in War, 2000, Provide for the Common Defense, 2001. Bd. dirs. Walden U., 1992-2001. Decorated Legion of Merit (3); Bronze Star (2), D.S.M.(2). Mem. Assn. U.S. Army, Armor Assn., Mil. History, Soc. Cin. Personal E-mail: lucpalmer4@cs.com.

PALMER, DAVID GILBERT, lawyer; b. Lakewood, N.J., Jan. 10, 1945; s. Robert Dayton and Lois (Gilbert) P.; m. Susan Edmundson Walsh, Aug. 17, 1968; children: Jonathan, Megan. AB, Johns Hopkins U., 1967; JD, U. Colo., 1970. Bar: Colo. 1970, U.S. Dist. Ct. Colo. 1970, U.S. Ct. Appeals (9th and 10th cirs.) 1970, U.S. Supreme Ct. 1970. Ptnr., mng. ptnr., chmn. litig. dept. Holland & Hart, Denver, 1970-87; ptnr., mng. ptnr. Gibson, Dunn & Crutcher, Denver, 1987-97; mng. ptnr. Zevnik, Horton, Palmer, Denver, 1997-2001; mng. shareholder Greenberg Traurig LLP, Denver, 2001—. Chmn. N.W. region Am. Heart Assn., Dallas, 1986—, bd. dirs., 1986—, sec., 1990—, nat. chmn., 1992-93; pres., bd. dirs. Colo. Heart Assn., Denver, 1974; bd. dirs. C.H. Kempe Nat. Ctr. for Prevention of Child Abuse, Denver, 1984-90, pres., 1989-90; bd. dirs. Goodwill Industries, Denver, 1981-84. Mem. ABA, Colo. Bar Assn., Denver Law Club, Univ. Club, Mile High Club. Home: 3120 Ramshorn Dr Castle Rock CO 80108-9073 Office: Greenberg Traurig 1200 17th St Ste 2400 Denver CO 80202 Office Phone: 303-572-6539. Business E-Mail: palmerdg@gtlaw.com.

PALMER, DAVID SCOTT, political scientist, educator; b. Boston, July 16, 1937; s. Walter S. and Jean (Stuart) P.; m. Sarah Crawford, 1966 (dec. Nov. 1985); children: Walter Scott, Henry Crawford, Asa MacAdam; m. Diane Nagel, 1998. BA in Internat. Rels. cum laude, Dartmouth Coll., 1959; MA in Hispanic Am. Studies, Stanford U., 1962; PhD in Comparative Govt., Cornell U., 1973. Vol. leader Peace Corps, Peru, 1962-64; asst. dean freshmen, asst. to dir. admissions Dartmouth Coll., Hanover, N.H., 1964-68; from instr. to asst. prof. dept. govt. Bowdoin Coll., 1972-76; professorial lectr. Sch. Advanced Internat. Studies Johns Hopkins U., Washington, 1977-88; assoc. dean for programs Fgn. Svc. Inst., Dept. State, 1984-88, chair Latin Am. and Caribbean studies, 1976-88; prof. polit. sci. Boston U., 1988—, prof. internat. rels., 1990—, assoc. chair undergrad. studies internat. rels. dept., 1997-99, chair dept. polit. sci., 1998-2001, dir. Latin Am. studies program, 1991—94, 2004—. Vis. lectr. Princeton U., 1978—79, Georgetown U., 1985; vis. scholar Inter-Am. Dialogue, 2001—02. Author: Peru: The Authoritarian Tradition, 1980, (with Kevin Middlebrook) Military Government and Political Development: Lessons from Peru, 1975 (with Robert Wesson and others) The Latin American Military Institution, 1985; editor, contbr.: Shining Path of Peru, 1992, 2d edit., 1994; contbr. chpts. to books, articles and revs. to profl. jours. Recipient Meritorious Honor award U.S. Dept. of State, 1981; Daniel Webster nat. scholar, 1955-59; Edward John Noble Found. leadership grantee 1959-62; Fulbright fellow, 1998. Mem. Latin Am. Studies Assn. (exec. com. 1983-86), New Eng. Coun. Latin Am. Studies (exec. com. 1989-98, 2000—, pres. 1993-94), Interam. Coun. of Washington (pres. 1978-79), Phi Beta Delta, Phi Kappa Phi, Sigma Delta Pi. Home: 69 Waverley St Belmont MA 02478-1958 Office: Boston U 152 Bay State Rd Boston MA 02215-1501 Office Phone: 617-353-9388. Business E-Mail: dspalmer@bu.edu.

PALMER, DEBORAH JEAN, lawyer; b. Williston, N.D., Oct. 25, 1947; d. Everett Edwin and Doris Irene (Harberg) P.; m. Kenneth L. Rich, Mar. 29, 1980; children: Andrew, Stephanie. BA, Carleton Coll., 1969; JD cum laude, Northwestern U., 1973. Bar: Minn. 1973, U.S. Dist. Ct. Minn. 1973, U.S. Ct. Appeals (8th cir.) 1975, U.S. Supreme Ct. 1978, U.S. Ct. Appeals (11th cir.) 1999. Econ. analyst Harris Trust & Savs. Bank, Chgo., 1969-70; assoc. Robins, Kaplan, Miller & Ciresi LLP, Mpls., 1973-79, ptnr., 1979—. Trustee Carleton Coll., 1984-88; mem. bd. religious edn. Plymouth Congl. Ch., 1992-95; bd. dirs. Mpls. YWCA, 1996-99; mem. Dist. Minn. Civil Justice Reform Act Adv. Group, 1990-93; bd. dirs. RKM&C Found. Edn., Pub. Health & Social Justice, 1999—. Mem. ABA, Minn. Bar Assn., Minn. Women Lawyers Assn. (sec. 1976-78), Minn. Fed. Bar Assn. (chpt. bd. dirs. 1996-98), Hennepin County Bar Assn., Hennepin County Bar Found. (bd. dirs. 1978-81), Carleton Coll. Alumni Assn. (bd. dirs. 1978-82, sec. 1980-82), Women's Assn. of Minn. Orch. (bd. dirs. 1980-85, treas. 1981-83). Home: 1787 Colfax Ave S Minneapolis MN 55403-3008 Office: Robins Kaplan Miller & Ciresi LLP 800 Lasalle Ave Ste 2800 Minneapolis MN 55402-2015 E-mail: djpalmer@rkmc.com.

PALMER, DENISE, publishing executive; m. Gregory G. Palmer. BA, U. Dayton, 1977; MS in Mgmt., N.W. U. Sr. auditor Coopers & Lybrand, Dayton, Ohio, 1977—80; corp. auditor Tribune, 1980—86, planning analyst, 1983—86, mgr. planning, 1986—88; dir. fin. WGN Radio, Chgo., 1988—93, sta. mgr., 1993; dir. fin. Chgo. Tribune, 1994—2000, v.p. devel., strategy, fin., 1998—2000; pres., CEO CLTV, Oakbrook, Ill., 2000—02; pres., pub., CEO Balt. Sun, 2002—. Office: Baltimore Sun 501 N Calvert St Baltimore MD 21278*

PALMER, DOUGLAS HAROLD, mayor; b. Trenton, N.J., Oct. 19, 1951; s. George H. and Dorothy (Vaughn) P. BS in Bus. Mgmt., Hampton U., 1973. With C.V. Hill Co., Trenton; civil svc. worker N.J. Dept. Motor Vehicles, Trenton; dir. Community Schs. Trenton; asst. dir. Trenton Bd. Edn., dir. purchasing; small bus. owner Trenton; mayor City of Trenton, 1990—. Bd. dirs. ARC, Urban League Met. Trenton, Forum Project, Rider Coll. Ednl. Opportunity Fund Program, We, Inc., Carver Ctr., NAACP, treas.; freeholder Dem. Party Mercer County, 1981-91; mgr. West End Little League, Trenton, 1965-75, treas., 1975—. Named Outstanding Young Man Am., Del. Valley United Way Bd.; recipient Fai Ho Cha award Omega Psi Phi; recipient City Livability award, US Conf. of Mayors, Twenty Year Alumnus award, Hampton U., Spirit of St. Francis award, St. Francis Hosp., Equal Justice medal, Legal Svcs. NJ, State of Israel Peace medal award, 1993, Tending the Garden State, Cmty. Develop. Leadership award, Worldworks Found. NJ, 1993. Baptist. Office: 319 E State St Trenton NJ 08608-1809*

PALMER, DOUGLAS S., JR., lawyer; b. Peoria, Ill., Mar. 15, 1945; AB cum laude, Yale U., 1966; JD cum laude, Harvard U., 1969. Bar: Wash. 1969. Mem. Foster Pepper & Shefelman PLLC, Seattle, 1975—2002, Hillis Clark Martin & Peterson, P.S., Seattle, 2002—. Office: Hillis Clark Martin & Peterson PS 500 Galland Bldg 1221 Second Ave Seattle WA 98101-2925

PALMER, EDWARD LEWIS, banker, director; b. N.Y.C., Aug. 12, 1917; s. William and Cecelia (Tierney) P.; m. Margaret Preston, Jan. 5, 1940; children: Edward Preston, Jane Lewis. AB, Brown U., 1938. With N.Y. Trust Co., 1941-59, v.p., 1952-59; with Citibank, N.A., N.Y.C., 1959-82, sr. v.p., 1962-65, exec. v.p., 1965-70, dir., chmn. exec. com., 1970-82; pres. Mill Neck Group, Inc., 1982. Bd. dirs.SunResorts Ltd., FondElec Group Inc.; dir. emeritus Corning Inc.; trustee emeritus Mut. N.Y. Trustee emeritus Met. Mus. Art, Brown U. Served to lt. comdr. USNR, 1942-46. Mem. Phi Gamma Delta. Office: 425 Park Ave New York NY 10022-3506

PALMER, GEORGE THOMAS, artist; b. Buffalo, Mar. 23, 1925; s. George Joseph and Margaret Alice P.; m. Gloria Theresa Palmer, Oct. 17, 1953; children: Lisa Haug, Maria Buscemi, Beth Palmer, Mark Palmer, Eric Palmer. Cert. art, Albright Art Sch., 1949; studied with Robert Brachman, Art Students League, 1949-52; BFA, SUNY, Buffalo, 1969. Portrait painter Little Studio, N.Y.C., 1953-56; operator George Palmer Gallery, Buffalo, 1958-65; instr. art D'Youville Coll., Buffalo, 1962-72, Genesee C.C., Batavia, N.Y., 1965-70; operator George Palmer Studio, Buffalo, 1965—. Mem. faculty Erie County C.C., D'Youville Coll., Genesee C.C.; lectr. in field; hon. exhibiting mem. Buffalo Soc. Artists. One-man shows include Art Ctr. Williamsville, N.Y., 1977, Kenan Ctr., Lockport, N.Y., 1980, Patterson Gallery, Westfield, N.Y., 1981, Washington Arts Club, 1995; exhibited in groups shows at Art Dialogue Gallery, 1996, 97, others; featured in article Artists Mag., We. N.Y. C. of C. Mag. Active Williamsville Art Soc. and Fine Arts League; founder Kenmore Art Soc.; mem. Carnegie Cultural Ctr., We. N.Y. Artists Group; mem. arts com. City Hall, Buffalo. With USN, 1943-46. Recipient Best of Show award Art 1961 Exhbn., The Promising Young Realist award Art 1961 Exhbn., Gold medal Annual Fine Arts League Show, Jr. League Buffalo Soc. Artists Annual, The Promising Young Artists award Jr. League Buffalo Soc. Artists Annual.

PALMER, HARVEY JOHN, dean; b. NYC, Apr. 3, 1946; s. Harvey Anthony and Pearl Edna (Weber) P.; m. Donna Mary Partigan, July 11, 1966; children: Harvey D., Angeline, Thomas BSC.E., U. Rochester, 1967; PhD in Chem. Engring., U. Wash., 1971. Lic. profl. engr., NY. Asst. prof. chem. engring. U. Rochester, NY, 1971-77, assoc. prof., 1977-84, prof., 1984-00, assoc. dean for grad. studies, 1983-89, chair dept. chem. engring., 1990-00; dean Kate Gleason Coll. Engring. Rochester Inst. Tech., NY, 2000—. Cons. Pfaudler Co., Rochester, 1978-79, Eastman Kodak Co., Rochester, 1982-92, Helios Corp., Mumford, NY, 1983-91, Boehringer Mannheim Corp., Indpls., 1993; bd. dirs. Transcat Inc., Rochester. Contbr. articles to profl. jour. Mem. sch. bd. Honeoye Falls-Lima Central Schs., NY, 1983-92, pres., 1988-90. Recipient Undergrad. Teaching award Coll. Engring., U. Rochester, 1979, 82 Mem. AIChE (sec. Rochester sect. 1976-77, chair 1998-00), Am. Chem. Soc., Rochester Engring. Soc. (bd. dir. 2002-03, 3d v.p. 2003—), Tau Beta Pi, Sigma Xi. Office: Rochester Inst Tech Coll Engring Rochester NY 14623-5603 E-mail: hjpeen@rit.edu.

PALMER, HUBERT BERNARD, dentist, retired military officer; b. San Antonio, Sept. 6, 1912; s. Hubert Victor and Rosemary (Garvey) P.; student St. Mary's U., 1931-34; D.D.S., Baylor U., 1938; postgrad. George Washington U., 1946-47, U. Md., 1950-53; m. Elizabeth Harriet McAlary, Aug. 16, 1945; children— Hubert Bernard II, Robert Leldon. Commd. 1st lt. USAAF, 1938, advanced through grades to col. USAF, 1971; chief dept. dental research U.S. Army, 1946-50; chief dept. exptl. dentistry, USAF, 1953-54, chief research dentistry div. 1954-56; command dental surgeon, 1958-59, 63-65, 65-68; dental staff officer, 1959-62, dir. dental services, 1968-71; dir. Eastside Dental Clinic San Antonio Met. Health Dist., 1972-81; dir. Mirasol Dental Clinic, 1982-83; clin. asst. prof. U. Tex. Dental Sch., San Antonio, 1973-76. Decorated Legion of Merit, Commendation medal First Oak Leaf Cluster, Meritorious Service medal. Fellow AAAS; mem. Am. Dental Assn., Internat. Assn. Dental Research, Soc. Gen. Microbiology, Am. Soc. Microbiology, Omicron Kappa Upsilon. Contbr. articles to profl. jours. Research reduction decalcification tooth enamel. Home: 6115 Forest Timber St San Antonio TX 78240-3357

PALMER, IRENE SABELBERG, university dean and educator emeritus, nurse, researcher, historian, genealogist; b. Franklin, N.J., May 28, 1923; d. John Joseph and May (Heiser) Sabelberg. BS, N.J. State Tchrs. Coll., 1945; diploma, Jersey City Med. Center Sch. Nursing, 1945; MA, NYU, 1951, PhD, 1963. Edn. dir. Diploma Schs. Nursing, N.J., Mass., 1948-52; ednl. dir. Glenn Dale (Md.) Hosp., D.C. Dept. Pub. Health, 1956, dir. nursing svc. and edn., 1956-61; assoc. clin. prof. nursing Georgetown U., 1960-61; USPHS trainee, 1961-62; assoc. chief nursing svc. for rsch. VA Hosp., San Francisco, 1963-64; rsch. nurse cons. HEW, USPHS, Div. Nursing, Nursing Rsch. Field Center, San Francisco, 1964-66; asst. dean, assoc. prof. nursing U. Colo. Sch. Nursing, Denver, 1966-68; dean, prof. nursing Boston U. Sch. Nursing, 1968-74; prof. Hahn Sch. Nursing, U. San Diego, 1974-91, prof. emeritus, 1991—, dean, 1974-87, dean emeritus, 1988—. Lectr. Classical Alliance of the western States, Uskudar, Turkey, 1994, Italy, 1995. Editor: Nursing Clinics of North America, 1970; Contbr. articles to profl. jours. Served to capt. Nurse Corps U.S. Army, 1953-56. Internat. Nightingale scholar; Nat. Health Svc. fellow; recipient Excellence in Nursing Scholarship award Orgn. Nurse Execs., 1993. Fellow Nat. League Nursing (bd. visitors 1977-87), Am Acad. Nursing; mem. ANA, Am. Assn. History Nursing, Am. Assn. Colls. Nursing (hon.), Boston U. Nursing Archives, German Rsch. Assn. (pres. 1995), Sigma Theta Tau (Leadership award Zeta Mu chpt. 1986, Excellence in Nursing award 1991).

PALMER, JAMES ALVIN, baseball commentator; b. N.Y.C., Oct. 15, 1945; children: Jamie, Kelly. Student, Ariz. State U., Towson State Coll., Md. Pitcher Balt. Orioles, 1966—84; commentator ABC Sports, 1984—, Home Team Sports, Bethesda, Md. Performer: TV and print advertisements; author (with Jack Clary): Jim Palmer's Way to Fitness, 1985; author: (with Jim Dale) Together We Were Eleven Foot Nine: The Twenty-Four Year Friendship of Hall of Fame Pitcher Jim Palmer and Orioles Manager Earl Weaver, 1996. Named Am. League Pitcher of Yr., The Sporting News, 1973, 1975, 1976; named to Baseball Hall of Fame, 1990, All Star Game, 1970, 1971, 1972, 1977, 1978; recipient Cy Young Meml. award, Am. League, 1973, 1975, 1976. Office: care Home Team Sports 7700 Wisconsin Ave Bethesda MD 20814-3578

PALMER, JAMES DANIEL, information technology educator; b. Washington, Mar. 8, 1930; s. Martin Lyle and Sarah Elizabeth (Hall) P.; m. Margret Kupka, June 21, 1952; children: Stephen Robert, Daniel Lee, John Keith. AA, Fullerton Jr. Coll., 1953; BS (Alumni scholar), U. Calif., Berkeley, 1955, MS, 1957; PhD, U. Okla., 1963; DPS (hon.), Regis Coll., Denver, 1977. Chief engr. Motor vehicle and Illumination Lab. U. Calif., Berkeley, 1955-57; assoc. prof. U. Okla., Norman, 1957-63, prof., 1963-66, asst. to dir. Rsch. Inst., 1960-63, cons. Rsch. Inst., 1966-69, dir. Sch. Elec. Engring., 1963-66, dir. Systems Rsch. Center, 1964-66; dean sci. and engring., prof. elec. engring. Union Coll., Schenectady, 1966-71; pres. Met. State Coll., Denver, 1971-78; rsch. and spl. programs adminstr. Dept. Transp., Washington, 1978-79; v.p., gen. mgr. rsch. and devel. div. Mech. Tech., Inc., Latham, N.Y., 1979-82; exec. v.p. J.J. Henry Co., Inc., Moorestown, N.J., 1982-85; BDM internat. prof. info. tech. George Mason U., Fairfax, Va., 1985-95, prof. emeritus, 1995—; software cons., 1995—. Bd. dirs. J.J. Henry Co., Inc.; cons. Sym Mgmt. Co., Boston, Higher Edn. Exec. Assocs., Denver, PERI, Princeton; adj. prof. U. Colo. Co-author: (with A.P. Sage) Software Systems Engineering, (with Aseltine, Beam and Sage) Introduction to Computer Systems, Analysis, Design and Application. Bd. dirs., exec. v.p. adv. com. U.S.A. Vols. for Internat. Tech. Assistance, 1967-83, exec. v.p., 1970-71, chmn. exec. com.; trustee, vice chmn. Nat. Commn. on Coop. Edn.; mem. exec. policy bd. Alaska Natural Gas Pipeline, 1978-79; trustee Auraria Higher Edn. Program, Denver; mem. Fulbright fellow Selection Com., Colo.; bd. mgrs., mem. exec. com. Hudson-Mohawk Assn. Colls. and Univs., trustee, chmn. bd., 1970-71; adv. com. USCG Acad., 1972-82, chmn. adv. com., 1979-82; mem. Colo. Gov.'s Sci. and Tech. Adv. Council; pres. Denver Cath. Community Services Bd.; mem. Archdiocesan Catholic Charities and Community Services; mem. bd. U. Okla. Rsch. Inst.; mem. adv. com. Mile-Hi Red Cross. With USMC, 1950-51. Named James D. Palmer scholarship in his honor, George Mason U., 2002; recipient U.S. Coast Guard medal, 1983; Centennial scholar, Case-Western Res., 1981. Fellow IEEE (exec. and adminstrv. coms., v.p. long-range planning and finance, chmn. com. on large scale systems, Joseph E. Wahl Outstanding Career Achievement award 1993, Millennium medal 2000); mem. Systems, Man and Cybernetics Soc. (pres., Outstanding Contbns. award 1981), alumni assns. U. Calif. and U. Okla., Inst. Internat. Edn. (bd. dir. Rocky Mt. sect.), Soc. Naval Architects and Marine Engrs., Am. Soc. Engring. Edn., Am. Mil. Engrs., N.Y. Acad. Sci., Navy League, Sigma Xi, Eta Kappa Nu, Pi Mu Epsilon, Alpha Gamma Sigma. Home: 860 Cashew Way Fremont CA 94536-2646 Office: George Mason U Sch of Info Tech & Engring Fairfax VA 22030 E-mail: jdpalmer@ix.netcom.com.

PALMER, JAMES I. government agency administrator; BS in Civil Engring., Miss. State U., 1970; JD (with hons.), U. Miss., 1977. Asst. engr. Miss. Pub. Svc. Commn.; dir. resource planning Miss. Bd. Water Commrs.; spl. asst. atty. gen. State of Miss.; adminstrv. asst., staff counsel Gov. Bill Allain, 1984; exec. dir. Office Gen. Svcs., Miss. Dept. Natural Resources, 1987—99; atty. Butler, Snow, O'Mara, STevens and Cannada, PLLC, 1999—2002; regional adminstr. US EPA, Atlanta, 2002—. Office: US EPA Region 4 Sam Nunn Atlanta Fed Ctr 61 Forsyth St SW Atlanta GA 30303

PALMER, JEFFERY DEAN, systems engineering manager, consultant; b. Monroe, La., Apr. 11, 1960; s. Kenneth Dean and Martha Jean Palmer; m. Sharman Ann Taylor. BSEE, La. State U., Baton Rouge, 1983. Registered profl. engr., Tex., 1989, EIT La., 1983, cert. reliability engr., Am. Soc. for Quality, 1998. Engr. General Dynamics, Fort Worth, Tex., 1983—90, 1991—92; sys. engr. sr. staff Lockheed Martin, Fort Worth, 1993—. Mem.: Am. Soc. for Quality. Avocation: guitar playing. Home: 228 Valley Ranch Rd Weatherford TX 76087 Office: Lockheed Martin 1000 Lockheed Blvd Fort Worth TX 76108 Personal E-mail: plmrjd@aol.com. Business E-Mail: jeff.d.palmer@lmco.com.

PALMER, JEFFRESS GARY, hematologist, educator; b. Bklyn., Oct. 7, 1921; s. William Ware and Margaret Lee (Boswell) P.; m. Jane Ann Cartwright, Feb. 2, 1951; children: Kristin Cartwright, Julie Mitchell. BS, Emory U., 1942, MD, 1944. Intern N.C. Bapt. Hosp., 1944-45; resident in medicine Emory U., Atlanta, 1947-49; fellow hematology U. Utah, Salt Lake City, 1949-52; from asst. prof. to prof. medicine U. N.C., Chapel Hill, 1952—; ret. Capt. M.C. AUS, 1945-47. Mem. AAAS, AAUP, AMA, Am. Fedn. for Clin. Rsch., So. Soc. for Clin. Investigation, N.Y. Acad. Scis., Am. Soc. Hematology. Home: Morgan Creek Rd Chapel Hill NC 27517 Personal E-mail: jgpal@med.unc.edu.

PALMER, JERRY PHILIP, medical educator, researcher, internist; b. N.Y.C., Apr. 5, 1944; BA in Biology, SUNY, 1966; MD cum laude, Upstate Med. Ctr., Syracuse, N.Y., 1970. Diplomate Am. Bd. Internal Medicine, Am. Bd. Endocrinology and Metabolism. Intern Dartmouth Affiliated Hosps., Hanover, N.H., 1970-71, resident, 1971-72; sr. rsch. fellow divsn. endocrinology dept. medicine U. Wash., Seattle, 1972-74, acting instr. dept. medicine, 1974-75, dir. adminstrn. core diabetes endocrinology ctr., 1975—; dir. clin. rsch. core Diabetes Endocrinology Rsch. Ctr. U. Wash., Seattle, 1975-88, 91—, dep. dir., 1977-96, dir., 1996—; acting asst. prof. dept. medicine U. Wash., Seattle, 1975-77, asst. prof. dept. medicine, 1977-80, assoc. prof. dept. medicine, 1980-86, prof. dept. medicine, 1986—; assoc. med. staff Univ. Hosp., Seattle, 1975—; attending physician Seattle Pub. Health Hosp., 1975-82, Pacific Med. Ctr., Seattle, 1982-89; mem. med. staff Providence Med. Ctr., Seattle, 1988-89, VA Med. Ctr., Seattle, 1989—; chief divsn. endocrinology, metabolism and nutrition Seattle VA Med. Ctr., 1989—; dir. diabetes care ctr. U. Wash. Med. Ctr., 1991—. Pfizer vis. prof. U. Tex., Houston, 1996. Assoc. editor: Diabetes, 1984, 85, 86. Mem. Am. Diabetes Assn. (Wash. affiliate bd. dirs. 1975-83, Wash. affiliate v.p. 1976, 77, Wash. affiliate chmn. peer rev. com. 1984, 85, 86, mem. rsch. com. 1985, 86, 87, 88,

ad hoc expert com. on immunotherapy of IDDM 1990, chmn. task force on profl. membership 1991-92, mem. publs. policy com. 1993-95, bd. dirs. 1994-96, mem. scientific and med. meetings oversight com. 1995—, clin. rsch. grant 1996), Am. Fedn. for Clin. Rsch., Am. Soc. for Clin. Investigation, Endocrine Soc., King County Med., Assn. Am. Physicians, We. Assn. Physicians, We. Soc. for Clin. Rsch., Immunology Diabetes Soc. (pres. 1994-95), Alpha Omega Alpha. Office: VA Puget Sound Healthcare Sys 1660 S Columbian Way Seattle WA 98108-1532

PALMER, JOCELYN BETH, volunteer; b. Salina, Kans., Dec. 19, 1927; d. Paul Franklin and Josie Murtle (Schultz) Swartz; m. Gerald Keith Palmer, Dec. 28, 1952; children: David, Paula, Brian, April. AA, Christian Coll., Columbia, Mo., 1947; BS with honors, Kans. State U., 1949; MA, U. Iowa, 1951. Grad. asst. presch. U. Iowa, Iowa City, 1949-51; instr. U. Ill., Urbana, 1951-52; co-dir. child devel. ctr. Long Beach (Calif.) City Coll., 1954-56. Mem. task force Early Childhood Edu., 2000-01. Tchr. trainer, presch. tchr., cons., chmn. nursery com., elder, deacon Presbyn. Ch.; mem. Com. to Develop Stds. for Presch. Handicapped, Salina, 1981-83; pres., bd. dirs. # 305 Salina Sch. Dist., 1975-87; com. chair, bd. dirs. St. Francis Boyd Home, Salina, Ellsworth, 1984-87; bd. dirs. YWCA, 1993-97; bd. dirs. Asburg Hosp. Aux., 1993-96, sec. 1994-96; mem. com. planning early childhood edn. USD 305. Mem. Clippership Mariners (chaplain 1991-93, logkeeper 1994-95, 2000-01, skipper 1997, chaplain, 2002-03), Saline County Med. Alliance (bd. dirs. 1992-96, 98-2000), Twentieth Century Forum (courtesy chmn. 1989-93, 2000—), PEO (pres. 1989-91, 94-95, treas. 1993-95), Salina Downtown Lioness (bd. dirs. 1988-89, 91-93, program chair 1997, pres. 2000 03), Phi Kappa Phi, Omicron Nu. Republican. Avocations: sewing, reading, music, swimming.

PALMER, JOHN ANTHONY, III, secondary school educator, music educator; b. Worcester, Mass., May 18, 1955; s. John Jr. and Barbara (Dufresne) P. BA in Spanish, Worcester State Coll., 1977, MEd in Ednl. Adminstrn., 1988. Cert. Spanish, French, German and music tchr., Mass. Tchr., head dept. fgn. langs. Mahar Regional Sch., Orange, Mass., 1979-88; tchr. French, Spanish and German, Doherty Meml. H.S., Worcester, 1993-99, Burncoat Sr. High, 1999—. Adj. prof. Spanish, Worcester State Coll., 1988-90, Fla. Atlantic U., 1991-93, Quinsigamond Cmty. Coll., 1997—; instr. voice Worcester Poly Inst., 1979-81; cantor Ch. of St. Peter, 1977-81, Worcester Eglise Notre Dame des Canadiens, Worcester, 1981-83; adjudicator vocal auditions All-State Music Educators Conf., 1988. Tenor soloist Regis Coll., Boston, Worcester Poly. Inst., Worcester Chorus, Salisbury Singers, Simmons Coll., Boston, Ft. Lauderdale Opera Co., Opera Worcester, Smith Coll., North Hampton, Wells Coll., Aurove, N.Y. Mem. ASCD, Am. Coun. Tchrs. Fgn. Langs., Nat. Assn. Secondary Sch. Prins., Mass. Assn. Sch. Supts., Mass. Fgn. Lang. Assn., Sigma Delta Pi. Democrat. Roman Catholic. Home: 14 Waterford Dr Botany Bay Worcester MA 01602 E-mail: jpalmerIII@aol.com.

PALMER, JOHN BERNARD, III, lawyer; b. Ft. Wayne, Ind., May 18, 1952; s. John Bernard and Dorothy Alma (Lauer) P. BA, Mich. State U., 1974; JD, U. Mich., 1977. Bar: Ill. 1977, U.S. Dist. Ct. (no. dist.) Ill. 1977, U.S. Ct. Appeals (fed. cir.) 2002, U.S. Tax Ct. 1979, U.S. Ct. Claims 2001. Assoc. Mayer Brown & Platt, Chgo., 1977-80, Hopkins & Sutter, Chgo., 1980-83, ptnr., 1983-2001, Foley & Lardner, Chgo., 2001—. Adj. prof. Ill. Inst. Tech.-Kent Coll. of Law, Chgo., 1984—. Mem. ABA. Office: Foley & Lardner 321 N Clark St Chicago IL 60610 Office Phone: 312-832-4575.

PALMER, JOHN DERRY, physiology educator; b. Chgo., May 26, 1932; s. John and Florence (Eley) P.; m. Carla Bianchi, Sept. 15, 1960; 1 child, John Charles. BA, Lake Forest Coll., 1957; MS, Northwestern U., 1959, PhD, 1962. Asst. prof. U. Ill., Chgo., 1961-63; fellow NSF, U. Bristol, Eng., 1963-64; prof., dept. chmn. NYU, 1964-74; prof. U. Mass., Amherst, 1974—, dept. chmn., 1974-80. Edit. bd. Marine Behavior and Physiology, 1988—, Chronobiology Internat., 1986—; author: Textbook of Modern Biology, 1968, The Biological Clock: Two Views, 1970, Biological Clocks in Marine Organisms: The Control of Physiological and Behavioral Tidal Rhythms, 1974, An Introduction to Biological Rhythms, 1976, (with others) Biological Rhythms and Living Clocks, 1977, Human Biological Rhythms, 1983, The Biological Rhythms and Clocks of Intertidal Animals, 1995, The Living Clock, 2000, The Biological Clock, 2003; contbr. articles to profl. jours. With U.S. Army, 1953-55. Fellow AAAS, Explorers Club; mem. Internat. Soc. of Chronobiology, Nat. Assn. of Scholars, Marine Biol. Lab., Phi Beta Kappa, Sigma Xi (pres., v.p., treas. N.Y. chpt., Disting. Rschr. award 1968). Avocation: trout and saltwater fishing. Office: U Mass Dept Biology 611 North Pleasant St Amherst MA 01003 E-mail: ftodd@bio.umass.edu.

PALMER, JOHN N. communications executive; BA, MBA, U. Miss. Founder, pres. Mobile Comm. Corp. Am., Jackson, Miss., 1973-89; chmn. Mobile Telecomm. Techs. Corp., Jackson, 1989—, Gulf South Capital, Jackson. Bd. dirs. Entergy Corp., Deposit Guaranty Nat. Bank, Inst. Tech. Devel. and Found. for Mid-South, U. Miss. Found.; bd. trustees Nat. Symphony Orch., EastGroup Properties, Millsaps Coll. Office: U S Embassy Lisbon Av das Forcas Armadas 1600-081 Lisbon Portugal also: 2616 Lakeward Dr #120 Jackson MS 39216-4811

PALMER, JUDITH GRACE, university administrator; b. Washington, Ind., Apr. 2, 1948; d. William Thomas and Laura Margaret (Routt) P. BA, Ind. U., 1970; JD cum laude, Ind. U., Indpls., 1973. Bar: Ind. 1974, U.S. Dist. Ct. (so. dist.) Ind. 1974. State budget analyst State of Ind., Indpls., 1969-76, exec. asst. to gov., 1976-81, state budget dir., 1981-85; spl. asst. to pres. Ind. U., 1985-86, v.p. for planning, 1986-91, v.p. for planning and fin. mgmt., 1991-94, v.p., CFO, 1994—. Bd. dirs. Ind. Fiscal Policy Inst., Kelley Exec. Ptnrs.; bd. dirs., treas. Rsch. and Tech. Corp.; bd. dirs. Ind. Farmers Mutual Ins. Bd. dirs., sec.-treas. Columbian Found., 1990-94, 2000—; bd. dirs. Columbia Club, 1989-98, pres. 1995; bd. dirs. Commn. for Downtown, 1984, mem. exec. bd., 1989-92, chmn. cmty. rels. com., 1989-93; mem. State Budget Commn., 1981-85. Named one of Outstanding Young Women in Am., 1978; recipient Sagamore of the Wabash award, 1977, 85, Citation of Merit, Ind. Bar Assn. of Young Lawyers, 1978, Appreciation award, 1980. Mem. ABA, Ind. Bar Assn., Indpls. Bar Assn. Roman Catholic. Office: Ind Univ Bryan Hall Rm 204 Bloomington IN 47405 E-mail: jgpalmer@indiana.edu.

PALMER, KIMBERLY ANNE, director; b. Lansing, Mich., June 5, 1959; d. Stan A Clapp and Ann Jedrzejek; m. Neil Raymond Palmer, June 26, 1982; children: Amanda, Ethan, Sean. BS, Mich. State U., 1982. Cert. tchr. State Dept. Of Edn., 1982. Corp. and institutional trust officer Manufactures Bank Of Detroit, 1986—90; secondary sci. tchr. Lansing Pub. Schs., Mich., 1994—2000; Curriculum, Instrn., and Assessment Coord. K-12 Math and Sci. South Lyon Cmty. Schs., South Lyon, Mich., 2000—. Cons. State Of Mich. MEAP Office - Sci. Content Adv. Com., Lansing, Mich., 1999—; contbg author - MICLiMB State Of Mich. Dept. Of Educaiton, Lansing, 2000—01. Mem. Howell Band Boosters, Mich., 2003—04. Recipient NEWMAST, NASA, 1998. Mem.: ASD, Mich. Sci. Tchrs. Assn., Oakland Rsch., Evaluation, And Assessment Com., Nat. Coun. For Tchrs. Of Math., NSTA. Office: South Lyon Community Schools 345 S Warren St South Lyon MI 48178 Office Phone: 248-573-8114. E-mail: palmerk@slcs.us.

PALMER, LARRY ISAAC, lawyer, educator; b. 1944; AB, Harvard U., 1966; LLB, Yale U., 1969. Bar: Calif. 1970. Asst. prof. Rutgers U., Camden, N.J., 1970-73, assoc. prof., 1973-75, Cornell U., Ithaca, N.Y., 1975-79, prof. law, 1979—2002, vice provost, 1979-84, v.p. acad. programs, 1987-91, v.p. acad. program and campus affairs, 1991-94; endowed chair Dept. Urban Health Policy U. Louisville, 2003—. Vis. fellow Cambridge U., 1984-85. Author: Law, Medicine, and Social Justice, 1989, Endings and Beginnings: Law, Medicine and Society in Assisted Life and Death, 2000. Mem. Am. Law Inst. Office: Inst Bioethics Health Law and Policy Sch Medicine 501 E Broadway Ste 310 Univ Louisville Louisville KY 40292 E-mail: lip1@cornell.edu.

PALMER, LOUIS THOMAS, pathologist; b. Omaha, Dec. 12, 1937; s. Harry Calvin and Helen Irene (Hansen) P.; m. Rosario Garcia, Dec. 28, 1977; children: Ria Charrise, Ryan Christopher. BS, Wash. State U., 1960; MS, Kans. State U., 1965; PhD, U. Minn., 1968. Cert. profl. plant pathologist. Plant pathologist Rockefeller Found., Mex. and India, 1968-71; extension plant pathologist U. Nebr., Lincoln, 1971-75; plant pathologist Internat. Rice Rsch. Inst., Sukamandi, Indonesia, 1975-79; dir. United Fruit Co., La Lima, Honduras, 1979-81; field devel. biologist E.I. duPont de Nemours, Campinas, Brazil, 1982-85, mgr. Madera, Calif., 1985-88; cons. Checchi & Co., Dhaka, Bangladesh, 1988-91; field rsch. mgr. Calif. Agriculture Rsch., Kerman, Calif., 1992; plant pathologist Harris Moran Seed Co., Ruskin, Fla., 1992—94, Pioneer Vegetable Genetics, Ruskin, Fla., 1995—96; pres., owner Tropical Foliage Inc., Wimauma, Fla., 1997—. Part-time asst. prof. U. Fla., 2003—; adj. prof. Fla. So. Coll., Plant City, Fla., 2004—, Lakeland, Fla., 2004. Contbr. articles to profl. jours. Advisor Boy Scouts Am., Campinas, 1983-85, councilor, Madera, 1985-88, leader Tiger Club, Dhaka, 1988-90, cubmaster, 1990-91, den. leader, Madera, 1991-92, asst. den leader Brandon, 1993, asst. scoutmaster Brandon, Fla., 1994—. Recipient Eagle Scout award Boy Scouts Am., 1955; Carl Raymond Grey scholar Union Pacific R.R., 1955, Carl J. Erickson scholar Benton County, Washington, 1956. Mem.: Am. Legion (1st vice comdr. Brandon post 2002—). Roman Catholic. Avocations: photography, swimming, tennis. Home: 1343 Monte Lake Dr Valrico FL 33594-8109 Office: Tropical Foliage Inc 5202 Bonita Dr Wimauma FL 33598

PALMER, LYNNE, writer, astrologer; b. El Centro, Calif., Dec. 14, 1932; d. Clarence Lee and Paquita Mae (Hartley) Hafer; m. Bruno Cazzaniga, Mar. 13, 1964 (div. 1965); m. Sidney Latter, Nov. 29, 1997. Student, Ch. of Light, 1957-62, Calif. Sch. Escrows, L.A., 1960; theatre mgmt. degree, Mus. Arenas Theatres Assn., N.Y.C., 1963. Asst. teller Western Mortgage, L.A., 1957-58; head teller Sutro Mortgage Svc., L.A., 1958-61; freelance astrologer N.Y.C., 1961-92, Las Vegas, Nev., 1962—; owner, operator, tchr. astrology sch. N.Y.C., 1970-72; owner Star Bright Pubs., Las Vegas, 1996—. Spkr. in field; interviewed in N.Y. Post and other major newspapers and mags. including Life and Oggi (Italy), Veja (Brazil), Wall St. Jour., People Mag., Globe, Die Welt am Sonntag (West Germany), New Woman Mag., Forbes. Author: Prosperity, Nixon's Horoscope, Astrological Almanac, Astrological Compatibility (Profl. Astrologers award 1976), Horoscope of Billy Rose, ABC Basic Chart Reading, ABC Major Progressions, ABC Chart Erection, Pluto Ephemeris (1900-2000), Daily Positions, Is Your Name Lucky For You?, Do-It-Yourself Publicity Directory, Your Lucky Days and Numbers, Money Magic, Astro-Guide to Nutrition and Vitamins, Gambling to Win, The Astrological Treasure Map, Dear Sun Signs, Are You Compatible With Your Boss, Partner, Coworkers, Employee, Client?, Bet to Win, Special Report: USA Under Attack; columnist: Self, House Beautiful, Gold; record album: Cast and Read Your Horoscope; TV appearances include The Johnny Carson Tonight Show, What's My Line, 60 Minutes, CBS News Night Watch, Cosmos (BBC), Sci. Series (Italian TV), Fantastico (Brazilian TV), Japan TV, News (Nippon), Do We Really Need It? (ASAHI), The World is Calling (Uranai); contbr. articles to mags. and newspapers. Mem. AFTRA, Am. Fedn. Astrologers (cert.). Avocation: travel. Home: 850 E Desert Inn Rd Apt 912 Las Vegas NV 89109-2100 Office: Lynne Palmer 1155 E Twain Ave Ste 108-248 Las Vegas NV 89109 Office Phone: 800-615-3352. Business E-Mail: lynnepalmer@lynnepalmer.com.

PALMER, MARCELLA, reporter; b. Edison, N.J. B, Rutgers U. News anchor Sta. WBGE-FM, Peoria; reporter Sta. WEEK, Peoria, 1993—97, Sta. WKEF-TV, Dayton, Ohio, Sta. WCBS-TV, N.Y.C., 1997—. Office: CBS 524 W 57th St New York NY 10019

PALMER, MARILYN JOAN, English composition educator; b. Mahoning County, Ohio, Mar. 3, 1933; d. Rudolph George and Marian Eleanor Wynn; m. Richard Palmer, Nov. 10, 1956 (dec. 1987); children: Ricky, Larry, Kevin. Phys. therapy cert., UCLA, 1954, BS, 1955; MA in Philosophy, Ohio State U., 1969; PhD, U. Okla., 1996. Phys. therapist Neil Ave. Sch. for Handicapped, Columbus, Ohio, 1968-69; instr. philosophy Ohio State U., Columbus, 1969; instr. English Youngstown (Ohio) State U., 1970-71; writer, editor The Economy Co., ednl. publs., Oklahoma City, 1977-81; grad. asst. in English U. Okla., Norman, 1981-87, lectr. in English, 1988-90, tech. writing instr. ind. studies, 1988-97. Free-lance editing and cons.; cons. for on-line CD-ROM to accompany a textbook, 2002. Author: Technical Writing for Science, Business and Industry, 1988, An Enthymeme as a Platform for Understanding Audience Values, 1997; editor: Kindergarten Keys Teacher's Guidebook, 1982, author parochial supplement, 1982. Fund-raiser Easter Seal Soc., 1965-68; den mother coord. Boy Scouts Am., 1966, 67. Dept. Energy grantee, 1976. Mem. AAUP, Am. Phys. Therapy Assn., Soc. for Women in Philosophy, Alpha Xi Delta (nat. editor Quill 1984-86). E-mail: doclynn@cox.net.

PALMER, MARY S. education educator, writer; d. Vivian Lawrence and Janie Cashin Schluter; m. Buddy F. Palmer, Oct. 2, 1948; children: Harry Francis, Denis John, Thomas Roderick, Michael Gerald, Marcia Ann, Stephen Lawrence. Master's in English with a Concentration in Creative Writing, U. of South Ala., Mobile, 1982—84. Author: (novel) The Callings, 2002, (essay collection) MemoraMOBILEia: Alabama Gulf Coast Potpourri, 1993, (essay) Maggie O'Hara in Mobile Bay Tales edited by Tom Franklin, poetry-published in several books. Eucharistic min. St. Dominic's Cath. Ch., Mobile, 1982—2004. R-Consevative. Roman Catholic. Avocations: travel, reading, research, cooking. Home: 4209 Aldebaran Way Mobile AL 36693-4605 Office: Faulkner State Community College Hammond Circle Bay Minette AL 36562 Personal E-mail: mlsp1@bellsouth.net.

PALMER, PAMELA S. lawyer; BA, U. Calif., Irvine, 1978; JD, U. So. Calif., 1982. Bar: Calif. 1982. Jud. clk. to Hon. Walter Ely, U.S. Ct. Appeals (9th cir.); with Heller, Ehrman, White & McAuliffe, L.A., ptnr., 1992—96, Latham & Watkins, L.A., 1996—. Office: Latham and Watkins LLP 633 W Fifth St Ste 4000 Los Angeles CA 90071

PALMER, PATRICK ASA, former banker, lecturer; b. Amherst, N.S., Can., Mar. 29, 1943; s. James Asa and Evelyn Elizabeth (Hatt) P.; m. Margaret Ann Teixeira, Feb. 8, 1964; children: Mark, Ingrid, Petrina, Kara-Lynn. B in Commerce with honors, U. Windsor, Ont., Can., 1970; FICB, U. Toronto, 1972. Mgr. mktg. program Royal Bank of Can., Toronto, Ont., 1976-78, mgr. nat. bus. met., 1978-79, mgr. comml. markets, 1979-81, v.p. comml. mktg. and svcs. Ont., 1981-82, v.p. comml. mktg., 1982-83, v.p. planning, comml. banking and nat. accounts, 1983-86, v.p. sales and svcs., 1986-88, v.p. corp. mktg. and sales, 1988-89, v.p. retail banking, 1989-94; sr. v.p. channel mgmt. RBFG, 1994-97; pres. Where Eagles Soar, Inc., 1997—. Lectr. Sheridan Coll., Oakville, Ont., 1979-81, George Brown Coll., Toronto, 1979; bd. dirs. Janes Family Foods Ltd., Kinfolk Mgmt. Inc., Penetangore Ridge, Inc; mem. adv. bd. Mphasis. founder Cappy Ride, Motorcycle Charity Ride; past bd. dirs. Ont. Export, Inc., C. of C., Ont., C. of C., CDN C. of C., Gov. Gen.'s Can. study conf., U. Windsor, CDN Tourism Assn. Econ. Devel. Assn. Can., CDN Tourism Mgmt. Ctr., other non-profit orgns.; mem. devel. bd. Windsor/Essex Hosp. Found. Contbr. articles to profl. jours. Recipient Can. 125 medal, U. Windsor Clark award, Alumni award Merit, Double Gold medalist, U. Windsor, 1970. Mem. Alliance for Ont. Univs. (hon.). Home: 8078 8th Line RR # 4 Kenilworth ON Canada NOG 2E0 Office: Where Eagles Soar Inc 5720 Timberlea Blvd Ste 201 Mississauga ON Canada L4W 4W2 E-mail: pat@whereeaglessoar.com.

PALMER, PATRICK EDWARD, radio astronomer, educator; b. St. Johns, Mich., Dec. 6, 1940; s. Don Edward and Nina Louise (Kyes) P.; m. Joan Claire Merlin, June 9, 1963; children: Laura Katherine, Aidan Edward, David Elijah. SB, U. Chgo., 1963; MA, Harvard U., 1965, PhD, 1968. Radio astronomer Harvard U., Cambridge, Mass., 1968; asst. prof. astronomy and astrophysics U. Chgo., 1968-70, assoc. prof., 1970-75, prof., 1975—. Vis. assoc. prof. astronomy Calif. Inst. Tech., Pasadena, 1972; vis. radio astronomer Cambridge (Eng.) U., 1973; vis. rsch. astronomer U. Calif., Berkeley, 1977, 86; vis. scientist Nat. Radio Astronomer Obs., 1980-2004. Contbr. articles on radio astron. investigations of comets and interstellar medium to tech. jours. Recipient Bart J. Bok prize for contbns. to galactic astronomy, 1969, Alfred P. Sloan Found. fellow, 1970-72, Helen B. Warner prize, 1975. Fellow AAAS (chmn. sect. D astronomy 1984); mem. AAUP, Am. Astron. Soc. (chmn. nominating com. 1981, mem. publs. bd. 1985-86, mem. Warner Prize selection com. 1977-78), Royal Astron. Soc., Internat. Astron. Union, U. Chgo. Track Club. Home: 5549 S Dorchester Ave Chicago IL 60637-1720 Office: Univ Chgo Astronomy & Astrophysics Ctr 5640 S Ellis Ave Chicago IL 60637-1433 Office Phone: 773-702-7972. E-mail: ppalmer@oskar.uchicago.edu.

PALMER, PAUL RICHARD, school librarian, archivist, curator; b. Cin., Jan. 21, 1917; s. Gardiner O. and Sarah Ellen (Christy) Palmer. BA, U. Cin., 1949; MS, Columbia U., 1950, MA, 1955. Asst. br. libr. Bklyn. Pub. Libr., 1950-51; libr. Columbia U., N.Y.C., 1951-67, libr. sch. libr. svc., 1968, libr., curator Brander Matthews Dramatic Mus., 1969-73, bibliographer Avery Archtl. Libr., 1974, curator Columbiana Collection, 1974—. Cons. Am. Libr. Assn., Chgo., N.Y.C., 1954—59. Contbr. articles to profl. jours. Founder fund for collection and preservation of film stills and formats Mus. Modern Art. Fellow: Pierpont Morgan Libr.; mem.: VFW, Manuscript Soc., Licoln Ctr. Film Soc., Soc. Hist. Preservation, French Inst., Am. Film Inst., Theatre Libr. Assn. (exec. coun. 1970—74), St. George Soc. N.Y., Mus. Modern Art, Am. Mus. Britain, Met. Mus. Art, Ch. Club N.Y., Grolier Club, Order St. John of Jerusalem, Phi Beta Kappa. Episcopalian. Home: 3560 Shaw Ave Cincinnati OH 45298-1455

PALMER, PHILIP EDWARD STEPHEN, radiologist; b. London, Apr. 26, 1921; Ed., Kelly Coll., Tavistock, Eng., 1938; MB BS, U. London, 1944, DMR, 1946, DMRT, 1947. Intern, then resident Westminster Hosp.; cons. radiologist West Cornwall (Eng.) Hosp. Group, 1947-54; sr. govt. radiologist Matabeleland, Rhodesia-Zimbabwe, 1954-64; prof. radiology U. Cape Town, South Africa, 1964-68; prof. U. Pa., 1968-70; prof. diagnostic radiology and vet. radiology U. Calif., Davis, 1970—. WHO cons. in field. Author: The Imaging of Tropical Diseases, 1980 and 2nd edit.: 2000; contbr. 200plus articles to profl. publs. Recipient German Röentgen award, 1993, 1st Béclère medal Internat. Soc. Radiology, 1996, 1st Antoine Béclère lectr. Internat. Soc. Radiology, 1996, Presdl. award Radiol. Soc. N.Am., 2000. Fellow Calif. Radiol. Assn., Royal Coll. Physicians (Edinburgh), Royal Coll. Radiologists (Eng.), Romanian Soc. Radiol. and Nuclear Med.; mem. Brit. Inst. Radiology, Brit. Med. Assn., Calif. Med. Assn., Internat. Skeletal Soc., Assn. Univ. Radiologists, Radiol. Soc. N.Am. (Spl. Pres.'s award 2000), Kenya Radiol. Soc., South African Coll. Medicine, Egyptian Soc. Radiology and Nuclear Medicine, Yugoslav Assn. for Ultrasound, West African Assn. Radiologists. Address: 821 Miller Dr Davis CA 95616-3622

PALMER, RICHARD CRIST, lawyer; b. New London, Conn., June 8, 1964; s. Richard Crist and Alice Frances (Linzen) P. AA, Mitchell Coll., New London, 1985; BA, Ea. Conn. State U., 1987; JD, Western New Eng. Law, Springfield, Mass., 1990. Bar: Conn. 1991, U.S. Dist. Ct. 1991. Law clk. Faulkner & Boyce P.C., New London, 1988-92; indexing editor Conn. Trial Lawyers Assn., Hartford, 1992; atty. Law Offices Theodore Ladwig, Mystic, Conn., 1993-95; indexing cons. publ. divsn. Mass. Continuing Legal Edn., Inc., Boston, 1995; sole practice Stonington, Conn., 1993—. Campaign field coord. Friends of Chris Dodd, Hartford, 1992, Clinton-Gore, 1992; registrar of voters Town of Stonington, 1997-2000, Justice of the Peace, 1995—, econ. devel. commr., 1993-98, constable, 1993-94; mem. Dem. Town Com., 1991-2000, vice chmn., 1994-95. Mem. Knights of Columbus (advocate 1992-93), Phi Alpha Delta. Democrat. Roman Catholic. Office: PO Box 126 Mystic CT 06355-0126 Business E-Mail: crisp@snet.net.

PALMER, RICHARD DOUGLAS, lawyer; b. Ann Arbor, Mich., Jan. 18, 1950; s. Donnally Woodruff and Louise (Greiner) P.; m. Jemery Mae Van Sickle, Jan. 20, 1973; children: Justin Donnally, Vanessa Louise. BA, Alma (Mich.) Coll., 1972; JD, U. Ill., 1976. Bar: Mich. 1976. Pvt. practice, Greenville, Mich., 1976—. Ajd. instr. Cornerstone U., Ctrl. Mich. U.; twp. atty. Eureka, Cato, Winfield, Crystal, Belvidere, Sidney twps.; atty. coach Greenville H.S. Mock Trial Team. Dir. Greenville Danish Festival; baseball coach Pony League, Greenville; debate instr. Greenville Pub. Sch. Saturday Scholars; lay leader First United Meth. Ch.; pres. Greenville H.S. Band Boosters; mem. dramatic prodns. Cmty. Players. Mem. Mich. Bar Assn., Montcalm-Ionia Bar Assn. (pres.). Avocations: antiques and old cars, water-skiing, song writing, tennis. Office: 111 S Lafayette St Greenville MI 48838-1933

PALMER, RICHARD N. state supreme court justice; b. Hartford, Conn., May 27, 1950; BA, Trinity Coll., 1972; JD with high honors, U. Conn., 1977. Bar: Conn. 1977, U.S. Dist. Ct. Conn. 1978, D.C. 1980, U.S. Ct. Appeals (2d cir.) 1981. Law clk. to Hon. Jon O. Newman U.S. Ct. Appeals (2d cir.), 1977—78; assoc. Shipman & Goodwin, 1978—80; asst. U.S. atty. Office U.S. Atty. Conn., 1980—83, 1987—90, U.S. atty. dist., 1991, chief state's atty., 1991—93; ptnr. Chatigny and Palmer, 1984—86; assoc. justice Conn. Supreme Ct., Hartford, 1993—. Mem. Phi Beta Kappa. Office: Connecticut Supreme Ct 231 Capitol Ave Hartford CT 06106-1548

PALMER, RICHARD WARE, lawyer; b. Boston, Oct. 20, 1919; s. George Ware and Ruth French (Judkins) P.; m. Nancy Fernald Shaw, July 8, 1950; children: Richard Ware Jr., John Wentworth, Anne Fernald. AB, Harvard U., 1942, JD, 1948. Bar: N.Y. 1950, Pa. 1959. Sec., dir. N.Am. Mfg. Co., Natick, Mass., 1946-48; assoc. Burlingham, Veeder, Clark & Hupper, Burlingham, Hupper & Kennedy, N.Y.C., 1949-57; ptnr. Rawle & Henderson, Phila., 1958-79; co-founder, ptnr. Palmer, Biezup & Henderson, Phila., 1979—97, of counsel, 1998—. Sec., bd. dirs. Underwater Technics, Inc., Camden, N.J., 1967-85; adv. on admiralty law to U.S. del. Inter-Govtl. Maritime Consultative Orgn., London, 1967, U.S. del. 30th-34th internat. confs.; mem. U.S. Shipping Coordinating Com., Washington legal sub com., 1967—; titular mem. Comité Maritime Internat.; v.p., sec., bd. dirs. Phila. Belt Line R.R.; bd. dirs. Mather (Bermuda) Ltd. Editor: Maritime Law Reporter. Mem., permanent adv. bd. Tulane Admiralty Law Inst., Tulane U. Law Sch., New Orleans, 1975—; trustee Seamen's Ch. Inst., Phila., 1967—2001, pres., 1972—84; mem. exec. com. Harvard Law Sch. Assn., Phila., 1986—; bd. dirs. Havrford (Pa.) Civic Assn., 1972—85, pres., 1976—79; consul for Denmark State of Pa., 1980—91, consul emeritus, 1992—; bd. dirs. Woodlands Cemetary Co. of Phila., Woodlands Trust for Historic Preservation. Lt. comdr. USNR, 1942—46. Fellow World Acad. Art and Sci. (treas. 1988-2002); mem. ABA (former chmn. stdg. com. on admiralty and maritime law 1978-79), N.Y.C. Bar Assn., Phila. Bar Assn., Am. Judicature Soc., Maritime Law Assn. (chmn. limitation liability com. 1977-83, 2d v.p. 1984-86, 1st v.p. 1986-88, pres. 1988-90, immediate past pres. 1990-92), Assn. Average Adjusters USA and Gt. Britain, Port of Phila. Maritime Soc., Consul Assn. of Phila., The Colonial Soc. Pa. (treas.), Danish Order of Dannebrog, Merion Cricket Club, Phila. Club, Rittenhouse Club, Geneal. Soc. Pa. (bd. dirs. 1997-2002, v.p. 2003-), Harvard Club of N.Y.C. and Phila. (exec. com. 1983-86, 94-97). Republican. Episcopalian. Home: 432 Montgomery Ave Haverford PA 19041-1527 Office: Palmer Biezup & Henderson Pub Ledger Bldg 620 Chestnut St Philadelphia PA 19106-3409 Office Phone: 610-649-3130. Office Fax: 610-649-7824.

PALMER, ROBERT BAYLIS, librarian; b. Rockville Centre, NY, Apr. 5, 1938; s. John Frederick and Marion (Baylis) P.; divorced; 1 child, Michele Palmer Fracasso. AB, Kenyon Coll., Gambier, Ohio, 1960; MS in L.S, Simmons Coll., Boston, 1965; MA in English, Middlebury (Vt.) Coll., 1965. Tchr. Brooks Sch., North Andover, Mass., 1960-65, libr., 1961-65; acting libr. Columbia Coll., 1965-66; asst. to dir. libraries Columbia U., 1965-67; dir. Barnard Coll. Libr., 1967-81. Fulbright lectr. Tribhuvan U. Library, Kathmandu, Nepal, 1972-73, Kathmandu, 1980; vol. lectr. USIS, library cons., Asia, 1976; Fulbright lectr. Wuhan, Peoples Republic China, 1984-85; library cons., advisor, Peoples Republic China, 1986-87, Zanzibar, Tanzania, 1988; lectr., cons. Kenya, Ethiopia, Zimbabwe, 1988; English lang. escort officer US Dept. State, 1989—. Mem. ALA. Address: 190 Riverside Dr New York NY 10024-1008 *Life rocks by developing an informed skepticism towards life in general and politics in particular, by thanking your teechers before it is too late, and by always having a plan B.*

PALMER, ROBERT BLUNDEN, newspaper, printing executive; b. Port Huron, Mich., Nov. 25, 1917; s. Joseph Frank and Hazel Quinn (Blunden) P.; m. Mary Bellatti (dec.), Feb. 11, 1946; children: Robert L. Palmer, Frances Lobpries, Barbara Caldwell. Office mgr. Palmer Circulation Co., Midwest, 1937-41; reporter, bus. mgr. Titus County Tribune, Mt. Pleasant, Tex., 1941-42, editor, 1946-57; pub., editor Daily Tribune, Mt. Pleasant, Tex., 1957-88; pres. Palmer Media, Inc., Mt. Pleasant, Tex., 1972—, NorTex Press, Inc., Mt. Pleasant, Tex., 1973—. Owner Palmer Real Estate, 1968—. Capt. U.S. Army, 1942-46, ETO. Presbyterian. Avocations: reading, golf, travel, music. Office: Palmer Media Inc 1705 Industrial Rd Mount Pleasant TX 75455-2235

PALMER, ROBERT ERWIN, association executive; b. Texarkana, Ark., Feb. 6, 1934; s. Burgess Prince and Ruth (Erwin) P. BJ, U. Tex., 1961. Reporter Texarkana Gazette, 1961; editor Southwestern Bell Telephone, Houston, 1961, info. specialist St. Louis, 1961-63; editor Shell Oil Co., Houston and Chgo., head office pub. relations N.Y.C.; dir. pub. relations Nat. PTA, Chgo., 1969-74; program dir. Nat. Assn. Realtors, Chgo., 1974-76; corp. communications mgr. The Milw. Rd., Chgo., 1976-78; staff v.p. Soc. Real Estate Appraisers, Chgo., 1978-83, exec. v.p., 1983-90; sr. v.p. communications, 1991—; co. exec., v.p. Appraisal Inst., Chgo., 1992-93, v.p. mem. svcs., 1993-98. Bd. dirs. Tower Advt., Chgo., Costumes Unltd. ltd., Chgo. Founding mem. Chgo. Crime Commn., 1967. Served to staff sgt. USAF, 1953-57. Recipient Award of Merit, Chgo. Internat. Film Festival, 1970, 71, Spl. Corrs. Pring Feature award, 1971, 72, Golden Trumpet award Realtor Week promotion, 1975, Golden Trumpet award Pvt. Property Week promotion, 1977, Golden Trumpet award Realtor bicentennial program, 1977, Gold Circle award Chpt.-by-Chpt. program, 1982. Mem. Pub. Relations Soc. Am., Am. Soc. Assn. Execs., Sigma Delta Chi. Clubs: Chgo. Headline. Methodist.

PALMER, ROBERT J. corporate financial executive; m. Trish Palmer; 2 children. BS in computer info. sys., Tulane U. Assoc. dir., student sys. Tulane U., New Orleans; sr. cons. Lawyers Title Ins. Corp., a LandAmerica subsidiary, 1990—93, v.p., dir. sys. devel. support, 1993—94, sr. v.p., 1994—2000; pres. Elliptus Tech., Inc., 2000; Exec. v.p., chief info. officer LandAmerica Fin. Group, Inc., 2002—. Avocations: boating, golf, fishing. Office: LandAmerica Fin Group Inc 101 Gateway Ctr Pkwy Richmond VA 23235-5153

PALMER, ROBERT LESLIE, lawyer; b. Porterville, Calif., Apr. 10, 1957; s. Harrison Rowe and Margaret Elizabeth (Witty) P.; m. Huisuk Kim, Feb. 1, 1986; 1 child, Aaron Rowe. BA, Tulane U., 1979; JD, Georgetown U., 1982. Bar: D.C. 1982, U.S. Ct. Mil. Appeals 1985, Tex. 1987, Ala. 1987, U.S. Dist. Ct. (no. dist.) Ala. 1987, U.S. Ct. Appeals (11th cir.) 1987. Assoc. Lewis Martin Burnett & Dunkle, P.C., Birmingham, Ala., 1987-89, Lewis and Martin, Birmingham, Ala., 1989-90, Martin, Drummond and Woosley, Birmingham, 1990-91, bd. dirs., 1991-92, Martin, Drummond, Woosley and Palmer, Birmingham, 1992-95; atty. Environ. Litig. Group, P.C., Birmingham, Ala., 1995—. Ala. del. 6th Joint Conf. between Korea and S.E. U.S., Kyongju, Republic of Korea, 1991, 7th Joint Conf., Atlanta, 1992. Capt. JAGC, U.S. Army, 1983-87, USAR, 1987-91. Recipient commendation Republic of Korea Ministry of Justice, 1984. Mem. ATLA, Christian Legal Soc., Phi Beta Kappa, Omicron Delta Kappa. Independent. Baptist. Home: 1408 E Whirlaway Helena AL 35080-4102 Office: Environ Litig Group PC 3529 7th Ave S Birmingham AL 35222-3210

PALMER, ROBERT P. professional association executive; b. Indpls., Dec. 29, 1967; s. Frederick Grant and Phyllis Anne Palmer; m. Kimberly Ann Palmer, July 20, 1996. BA in Polit. Sci., The Citadel, 1990; MPA, Ind. U., 1998. Exec. dir. Sheet Metal Contractors Assn. Ctrl. Ind., Indpls., 1991-93; spl. asst. Office of U.S. Rep. Steve Buyer, Kokomo, Ind., 1994; assoc. mgr. Ctrl. Ind. chpt. Nat. Elec. Contractors Assn., Indpls., 1995-97; exec. v.p. Associated Gen. Contractors Ind., Indpls., 1997—. Dean's industry adv. com. Sch. Engring. and Tech. Ind. U.-Purdue U., Indpls., 1999—; bd. dirs. Jameson Inc., Indpls. Columnist Indiana Constructor, 1997—. Bd. dirs. Christamore House, Indpls., 1999—. Mem. Am. Soc. Assn. Execs. Republican. Avocations: military history, international affairs, golf, canoeing. Office: AGC Ind 1050 Market Tower 10 W Market St Indianapolis IN 46204-2954

PALMER, ROBERT TOWNE, lawyer, bank executive; b. Chgo., May 25, 1947; s. Adrian Bernhardt and Gladys (Towne) P.; m. Ann Therese Darin, Nov. 9, 1974; children: Justin Darin, Christian Darin. BA, Colgate U., 1969; JD, U. Notre Dame, 1974. Bar: Ill. 1974, D.C. 1978, U.S. Supreme Ct. 1978. Law clk. to Hon. Walter V. Schaefer Ill. Supreme Ct., 1974-75; assoc. McDermott, Will & Emery, Chgo., 1975-81, ptnr., 1982-86, Chadwell & Kayser, Ltd., Chgo., 1987-88, Connelly, Mustes, Palmer & Schroeder, Chgo., 1988-89; of counsel Garfield & Merel Ltd., Chgo., 1990-2000. Adj. faculty Chgo. Kent Law Sch., 1975—77, Loyola U., 1976—78; adv. com. Fed. Home Loan Mortgage Corp., 1988—89; bd. dirs. Ctrl. Fed. Savs. & Loan Assn. of Chgo., chmn., 2000—; dir. Chgo. Assn. Fin. Insts., 2001—03, sec., 2002—03; mem. Chgo. Ctr. Adv. Bd. Voyageur Outward Bound Sch., 1988—91; chmn. Lake Forest Cemetery Commn., 2001—; mem. Chgo. Crime Commn., 2001—, dir., 2002—. Contbr. articles to legal jours. and textbooks. Mem. ABA, Ill. State Bar Assn. (Lincoln award 1983), Chgo. Bar Assn., Chgo. Club, Dairymen's Country Club, Lambda Alpha. Office: Central Fed Savs 1601 W Belmont Ave Chicago IL 60657-3044

PALMER, R(OBIE) MARK (ROBIE MARCUS HOOKER PALMER), banker; b. Ann Arbor, Mich., July 14, 1941; s. Robie Ellis and Katherine (Hooker) P.; m. Sushma Palmer. BA, Yale U., 1963. Copy asst. N.Y. Times, N.Y.C., 1963; asst. to producer WNDT-TV, N.Y.C., 1963-64; entered U.S. Fgn. Service, 1964; third sec. U.S. Embassy, New Delhi, India, 1964-66; internat. relations officer NATO affairs, Dept State, Washington, 1966-68; second sec. U.S. Embassy, Moscow, 1968-71; prin. speechwriter Sec. of State Rogers, Kissinger, Washington, 1971-75; counselor for polit. affairs U.S. Embassy, Belgrade, Yugoslavia, 1975-78; dir. office disarmament and control of arms Bur. of Polit.-Mil. Affairs Dept. State, Washington, 1978-81, dep. to undersec. for polit. affairs, 1981-82, dep. asst. sec. state for European affairs, 1982-86; amb. U.S. Embassy, Budapest, Hungary, 1986-90; pres., CEO Cen. European Devel. Corp., Washington, 1990-97; CEO Capital Devel., Washington, 1997—. Pres., CEO Television Devel. Ptnrs., Inc., 1996-97. Author: speeches for five Secs. of State and three Presidents Recipient Superior Honor award Dept. State, 1980, Presdl. Meritorious Service award, 1984. Mem. Council Fgn. Relations, Am. Fgn. Service Assn., Phi Beta Kappa. Episcopalian. Avocation: tennis. Home and Office: 4437 Reservoir Rd NW Washington DC 20007-2021

PALMER, ROGER CAIN, information scientist; b. Corning, N.Y., Oct. 14, 1943; s. Wilbur Clarence and Eleanor Louise (Cain) P. AA, Corning (N.Y.) C.C., 1964; BA, Hartwick Coll., 1966; MLS, SUNY, Albany, 1972; PhD, U. Mich., 1978. Tchr. Penn Yan (N.Y.) Acad., 1966-68, 70-71; dep. head, grad. libr. SUNY, Buffalo, 1972-75; asst. prof. UCLA, 1978-83; sr. tech. writer Quotron Sys., Culver City, 1984; sr. sys. analyst Getty Art History Info., Santa Monica, Calif., 1984-90, mgr. tech. devel., 1990-93; mgr. internal cons. group The J. Paul Getty Trust, Santa Monica, 1993-96, mgr. ITS Infrastructure Ops. L.A., 1996-97; v.p. China and N.Am. Bus. Assocs., Inc., 1997-2000; CIO, v.p. ops. Webchoir, Inc., 2001—. Gen. ptnr. Liu-Palmer, L.A., 1989—2000. Author: Online Reference and Information Retrieval, 1987, dBase II and dBase III: An Introduction, 1984, Introduction to Computer Programming, 1983. With U.S. Army, 1968-70. Mem. IEEE Computer Soc., ALA, Am. Soc. for Info. Scis., Spl. Librs. Assn., Art Librs. Soc. of N.Am., Assn. for Computing Machinery, Pi Delta Epsilon, Beta Phi Mu. Home: 8205 Santa Monica Blvd # 1-295 Los Angeles CA 90046-5967 Office: Webchoir Inc Los Angeles CA 90046

PALMER, ROGER FARLEY, pharmacology educator; b. Albany, N.Y., Sept. 23, 1931; m. Nelida Santiago, Apr. 1994. BS in Chemistry, St. Louis U., 1953; postgrad., Fla. State U., 1955-56, Woods Hole Marine Biology Lab., 1956; MD, U. Fla., 1960. Intern Johns Hopkins Hosp., 1960-61, resident in medicine, 1961-62; asst. dept. biochemistry U. Fla., Gainesville, 1957; asst. medicine Osler Med. Service, 1960-62; instr. pharmacology and therapeutics U. Fla., 1962, asst. prof. pharmacology, therapeutics and medicine, 1964-67, assoc. prof. pharmacology and medicine, 1967-69, prof. medicine, chief div. clin. pharmacology, 1969-70, 71-82; prof., chmn. dept. pharmacology, prof. medicine U. Miami, Fla., 1970-81, clin. prof. medicine, 1982—. Chmn. pharmacology sect. Nat. Bd. Med. Examiners, 1977—81; cons. Nat. Acad. Scis. Editorial bd. Pharmacol. Revs.; assoc. editor Advances in Molecular Pharmacology; ad hoc editor Am. Heart Jour.; editor Horizons in Clinical Pharmacology, 1976; author abstracts; contbr. over 100 articles to profl. jours. Served with USAR. Mosby scholar, 1957-60; Markle scholar in acad. medicine, 1965-70; recipient Basic Sci. Teaching award U. Miami, 1975-76; Meritorious Service medal Am. Heart Assn., 1972; citation for meritorious Service So. Region Am. Heart Assn., 1979; Visitante Distinguido award, Costa Rica, 1979; Outstanding Tchr. award U. Miami, 1982. Mem. Am. Coll. Clin. Pharmacology, Am. Fedn. Clin. Rsch., Am. Therapeutic Soc. (prize essay award 1970), Am. Soc. Pharmacology and Exptl. Therapeutics (emeritus), N.Y. Acad. Scis., So. Soc. Clin. Investigation, U.S. Pharmacopeia Revision Com., Internat. Study Group Rsch. Cardiac Metabolism, Am. Soc. Internal Medicine, Royal Soc. Health, Key Biscayne Yacht Club (bd. govs. 1994-97, fleet surgeon 1999-2000), Sigma Xi. Office: 240 Crandon Blvd Ste 215 Key Biscayne FL 33149-2009 Office Phone: 305-361-8655. E-mail: palmerpebbles@aol.com.

PALMER, ROGER RAYMOND, accounting educator; b. N.Y.C., Dec. 31, 1926; s. Archibald and Sophie (Jarnow) P.; m. Martha West Hopkins, June 7, 1986; children by previous marriage: Kathryn Sue, Daniel Stephen, Susan Jo. BS, U. Wis., 1949; MBA, Cornell U., 1951; postgrad., NYU, 1951-54. Auditor, Ernst and Ernst, CPA's, N.Y.C., 1953-54; auditor Gen. Dynamics Corp., 1956-60; mgr. corp. audits Tex. Instruments, 1960-64; auditor 1st Nat. Bank, St. Paul, 1964-68, v.p. planning, 1968-69, v.p., comptr., 1969-75, sr. v.p., contr., 1975-82; chmn. dept. fin. Coll. of St. Thomas (now U. St. Thomas), St. Paul, 1996—. Dir. First Met. Travel, Inc.; guest lectr. U. Minn., 1966; conf. leader, speaker, 1959— Contbr. articles to pubs. Bd. dirs. Waterford (Conn.) Civic Assn., 1959-60, Friends of St. Paul Pub. Library, 1967, Mpls. Citizens League; chmn. bd. dirs. Film in the Cities, 1983-85; mem. acctg. adv. council U. Minn.; trustee, chmn. fin. com. Hazelton Found. With U.S. Maritime Svc., 1945-47; with U.S. Army, 1954-56. Mem. Inst. Internal Auditors (pres. So. New Eng chpt. 1957-60, edn. chmn. Dallas 1961, Twin City chpt. 1965-66), Nat. Assn. Accts. (dir. Norwich, Conn. chpt. 1958-60), Nat. Assn. Accountants (St. Paul chpt. 1967), Assn. Bank Audit, Control and Operation, Am. Inst. Banking, Fin. Execs. Inst., Planning Forum (pres. Twin Cities chpt. 1984-85), Univ. Club (St. Paul). Clubs: St. Paul Athletic. Home: 415 Oak Ridge Dr San Marcos TX 78666 Business E-Mail: rrpalmer@stthomas.edu.

PALMER, RUSSELL EUGENE, investment executive; b. Jackson, Mich., Aug. 13, 1934; s. Russell E. and Margarite M. (Briles) P.; children: Bradley Carl, Stephen Russell, Russell Eugene, III, Karen Jean. BA with honors, Mich. State U., 1956; D in Comml. Sci. (hon.), Drexel U., 1980; MA (hon.), U. Pa., 1984; PhD (hon.), Chulalongkorn U., 1988, Free U. Brussels, 1989, York Coll., 1989. With Touche Ross & Co., N.Y.C., 1956-83, mng. ptnr., CEO, 1972-82, also bd. dirs., exec. coms.; mng. dir., CEO Touche Ross Internat., 1974-83; dean, Reliance prof. mgmt. and pvt. enterprise Wharton Sch. U. Pa., 1983-90, CEO. Bd. dirs. The May Dept. Stores Co., Honeywell Internat., Inc. Mem. Pres.'s Mgmt. Improvement Coun., 1979—80; mem. adv. bd. Salvation Army, past mem. nat. adv. bd.; former mem. adv. coun. Women's Way; bd. dirs. UN Assn. U.S.A.; former mem. adv. panel Comptr. Gen. U.S.; former chmn. bd trustees U. Pa. Health Care Sys.; trustee Acctg. Hall of Fame U. Pa.; bd. dirs. Joint Coun. Econ. Edn., 1978—83, United Fund Greater N.Y., 1980—83; mem. Bus.Com. Arts, 1977—83; bd. dirs. SEI Ctr. for Advanced Studies in Mgmt.; former mem. adv. coun. Sch. Internat. and Pub. Affairs Columbia U., Grad. Sch. Bus. Stanford U.; mem. assocs. coun. Bus. Sch. Oxford U.; mem. U.S. Sec. Labor's Commn. on Workforce Quality and Labor Market Efficiency; pres. Fin. Acctg. Found., 1979—82; pub. mem. Hudson Inst. Recipient Gavin Meml. award Beta Theta Pi, 1956, Disting. Community Svc. award Brandeis U., 1974, Outstanding Alumnus award Mich. State U., 1978, Humanitarian award Fedn. Jewish Philanthropies, 1979, Disting. Aux. Svc. award Salvation Army, 1979, LEAD Bus. award, 1984, Good Scout award Phila. coun. Boy Scouts Am., 1987. Mem. Merion Cricket Club, Conf. Bd. (bd. dirs.), Beta Gamma Sigma (mem. bd. govs.). Presbyterian. Office: The Palmer Group 3600 Market St Ste 530 Philadelphia PA 19104-2649

PALMER, SAMUEL COPELAND, III, lawyer; b. Phila., June 9, 1934; s. Samuel Copeland Jr. and Vivian Gertrude (Plumb) P.; divorced; children: Samuel C. IV, Sarah Anne, Bryan Douglas. Grad., Harvard Sch., Los Angeles, 1952; student, Yale U., 1953; AB, Stanford U., 1955; JD, Loyola-Marymount U., Marymount, 1958. Bar: Calif. 1959, U.S. Dist. Ct. (cen., ea. and so. dists. Calif.) 1959, U.S. Ct. Appeals (9th cir.) 1970, U.S. Supreme Ct. 1971. Dep. city atty., Los Angeles, 1959-60; assoc. firm Pollock & Deutz, Los Angeles, 1960-63; ptnr. firm Pollock & Palmer, Los Angeles, 1963-70, Palmer & Bartenetti, Los Angeles, 1970-81, Samuel C. Palmer III, P.C., 1981-85; ptnr. Thomas, & Snell, 1985—. Adj. prof. Calif. State U., Fresno, 1993. Trustee Western Ctr. Law and Poverty; bd. dirs. Big Bros./Big Sisters, Fresno, Arte Ams., Lively Arts Found., Nat. Sleep Found., Vols. in Parole; pres., bd. dirs. Poverello House; founder, pres. Fresno Crime Stoppers. Mem. ABA, State Bar Calif. (disciplinary subcom., bar examiners subcom.), Fresno County Bar Assn. (pres., bd. dirs. 1988-93), Pickwick Soc., Am. Bd. Trial Advocates, Chancery Club, Downtown Club, Calif. Club, Fig Garden Tennis Club, Rotary, Delta Upsilon, Phi Delta Phi. also: 820 Suffolk St Cambria CA 93428-2508 Office: Gilmore Wood Vinnard 7108 N Fresno St Ste 410 Fresno CA 93720-2953 E-mail: spalmer@thomasnell.com.

PALMER, STACY ELLA, periodical editor; b. Middletown, Conn., Oct. 25, 1960; d. Marvin Jerome Palmer and Eileen Sondra (Cohen) Palmer Burke. B in Liberal Arts and Internat. Rels., Brown U., 1982. Asst. editor Chronicle of Higher Edn., Washington, 1982-86, sr. editor, 1986-88; news editor Chronicle of Philanthropy, Washington, 1988-93, mng. editor, 1993-98, editor, 1998—. Bd. dirs. Brown Alumni Monthly, Providence, 1988-91, vice chmn., 1991-93, mem. 1996—. Mem. Comm. Network in Philanthropy, Investigative Reporters and Editors, Brown Club Washington (bd. dirs. 1993—, pres. 1994-99), Brown U. Alumni Assn. (bd. govs. 1997—). Avocations: swimming, bicycling, travel. Home: 2301 Connecticut Ave NW Apt 7C Washington DC 20008-1730 Office: Chronicle of Philanthropy 1255 23rd St NW Washington DC 20037-1125

PALMER, STUART HUNTER, sociology educator; b. NYC, Apr. 29, 1924; s. Herman G. and Beatrice (Hunter) P.; m. Anne Barbara Scarborough, June 22, 1946; 1 dau., Catherine. BA, Yale U., 1949, MA, 1951, PhD, 1955; LHD (hon.), Daniel Webster Coll., 1997. Asst. to dean Yale Coll., New Haven, 1949-51; instr. sociology New Haven Coll., 1949-51, 53-55; faculty U. NH, Durham, 1955—, prof., 1964—, chmn. dept. sociology and anthropology, 1964-69, 79-82, dean Coll. Liberal Arts, 1982-95, dir. London program, 1995-96. Disting. vis. prof. SUNY, Albany, 1970-71; vis. behavioral scientist NH Divsn. Mental Health; vis. prof. U. Sussex, Eng., 1976, U. Ga., 1977; cons. U.S. Office Edn., USPHS, U.S. Office Delinquency and Youth Devel., Dept. Justice; mem. adv. com. for sociology Com. on Internat. Exch. of Persons; mem. exec. com. NH Gov.'s Commn. on Crime and Delinquency; co-chmn. Internat. Symposium on Univs. in Twenty-First Century; co-chmn. Internat. Confs. on Stress Rsch., Nat. Commn. Arts and Scis. Author: Understanding Other People, 1955, A Study of Murder, 1960, (with Brian R. Kay) The Challenge of Supervision, 1961, Deviance and Conformity, 1970, (with Arnold S. Linsky) Rebellion and Retreat, 1972, The Violent Society, 1972, The Prevention of Crime, 1973, (with John A. Humphrey) Deviant Behavior, 1980, Role Stress, 1981, Deviant Behavior: Patterns, Sources, and Controls, 1990, The Universities Today, 1998; contbr. articles to profl. jours. Chmn. bd. trustees Daniel Webster Coll., New Eng. Aero. Inst. Served to lt. AC AUS, 1942-45; Served to lt. AC USAF, 1951-53. Decorated Air medal with 3 oak leaf clusters; fellow Henry Page. Mem. Am. Sociol. Assn., Ea. Sociol. Soc., Internat. Sociol. Soc., Internat. Soc. Criminology, Internat. Soc. Forecasters, Am. Assn. Colls., Coun. for Liberal Learning, Am. Assn. Higher Edn., Coun. Colls. Arts and Scis., Nat. Assn. State Univs. and Land-Grant Colls., AAAS, Am. Acad. Polit. and Social Scis., NY Acad. Scis., Am. Assn. Suicidology, Soc. Cross-Cultural Rsch., Am. Soc. Criminology, Assn. Gov. Bds. Univs. and Colls., Phi Beta Kappa (hon.), Sigma Xi, Alpha Kappa Delta. Home: 38A Emerson Rd Durham NH 03824-2110 *Be honest with yourself.*

PALMER, VENRICE ROMITO, lawyer, educator; b. Springfield, Mass., Jan. 11, 1952; s. Venrice Wellesley and Mildred Adlay (Foster) P. Higher diploma, U. Besançon, France, 1973; AB maxima cum laude, King's Coll., Wilkes-Barre, Pa., 1974; JD, Harvard U., 1977. Bar: N.Y. 1978, U.S. Dist. Ct. (so. and ea. dists.) N.Y. 1979, Ill. 1986, Calif. 1997. Spl. asst. atty. gen. Office N.Y. Atty. Gen., N.Y.C., 1977-79; staff atty. SEC, N.Y.C., 1979-82, br. chief, 1982-83, spl. trial counsel, 1983-85, acting asst. regional adminstr., 1984-85; sr. counsel Sears, Roebuck and Co., Hoffman Estates, Ill., 1985-97, Bank of Am., San Francisco, 1997-99; counsel McCutchen, Doyle, Brown & Enersen, LLP, San Francisco, 1999—2002, Bingham McCutchen LLP, San Francisco, 2002—. Guest lectr. St. John's U. Bus. Sch., N.Y.C., 1984; lectr. Practicing Law Inst., N.Y.C., 1995—, Glasser LegalWorks, Little Falls, N.J., 1997—, Am. Soc. Corp. Secs., 1997-99, Nat. Bus. Inst., Eau Claire, Wis., 2000—. Contbr. articles to various law publs. Recipient cert. of appreciation N.Y. State Bar Assn., 1978, Benaglia award King's Coll., 1974. Mem.: ABA, Calif. State Bar Assn. (mem. fin. instns. com. 2000—03), Alpha Mu Gamma, Delta Epsilon Sigma. Avocations: opera, ballet, reading. Home: 1200 Gough St Apt 7A San Francisco CA 94109-6616 Office: Bingham McCutchen LLP Three Embarcadero Ctr San Francisco CA 94111 E-mail: venricepalmer@bingham.com.

PALMER, VERNON VALENTINE, law educator; b. New Orleans, Sept. 9, 1940; s. George Joseph and Juliette Marie (Wehrmann) P. BA, Tulane U., 1962, LL.B., 1965; LL.M., Yale U., 1966; PhD, Pembroke Coll., Oxford U., 1985. Bar: La. 1965, U.S. Supreme Ct. 1981. Asst. prof. law Ind. Sch. Law, Indpls., 1966-70; lectr. law U. Botswana, Lesotho & Swaziland, Roma, Lesotho, 1967-69; prof. Tulane Law Sch., New Orleans, 1970—, Clarence Morrow research prof. law, 1980—, Thomas Pickles prof. law, 1989—; external examiner Nat. U. Lesotho, Roma, 1978-81. Dir. Tulane Paris Inst. European Legal Studies, European Legal Studies; reporter for revision of civil code La. Law Inst. 1979; vis. prof. Faculty Law, U. Strasbourg, 1988, The Sorbonne, U. Paris, 1986, 92, Universite des Antilles, Martinique, 1998, Universidad Ramon Llull, Barcelona, 1998, U. Trento, 1999—, U. Laussanne, 2000, U. Geneva, 2000. Author: The Roman-Dutch and Lesotho Law of Delict, 1970, The Legal System of Lesotho, 1971, The Paths to Privity, 1992, The Civil Law of Lease in Louisiana, 1997, Louisiana: Microcosm of a Mixed Jurisdiction, 1999, Mixed Jurisdictions Worldwide: The Third Legal Family, 2001; author: (with Bussani) Pure Economic Loss Europe, 2003, The Louisiana Civilian Experience, 2004, The Boundaries of Strict Liability in Europe, 2004; contbr. numerous articles to profl. jours. Pres. French Quarter Residents Assn., 1973-75, Alliance for Good Govt., 1974-75; del. Nat. Democratic Conv., N.Y.C., 1976; chmn. World Congress on Mixed Jurisdictions, 2002; pres. World Soc. Mixed Jursdiction Jurists, Titulary Mem. Internat. Acad. of Comparative Law, 2003. Decorated chevalier L'ordre des Palmes Académiques. Mem. La. Law Inst., World Soc. Mixed Jurisdiction Jurists (pres.), Titulaire Internat. Acad. Comparative Law (The Hague). Democrat. Roman Catholic. Home: 3311 Coliseum St New Orleans LA 70115-2401 Office: 6329 Freret St New Orleans LA 70118-6231 Office Phone: 504-865-5978. Business E-Mail: vpalmer@law.tulane.edu.

PALMER, VICKI R. food products executive; b. Memphis; m. John E. Palmer; 1 child, Alexandria. B in Econs. and Bus. Adminstrn., Rhodes Coll., 1975; MBA in Fin., U. Memphis, 1980. Corp. loan officer First Tenn. Bank.; head pension investment FedEx, mgr. corp. fin.; mgr. pension investments Coca-Cola Co., 1983—86; asst. treas. Coca-Cola Enterprises Inc., 1986—93, v.p., 1993—99, treas., 1993—, sr. v.p., spl. asst. to CEO, 1999—, bd. dirs., 2001—. Bd. dirs. Spelman Coll., Rhodes Coll., Woodward Acad., First Tenn. Nat. Corp. Named one of 20 Women of Power and Influence in Corp. Am., Black Enterprise Mag., 100 Black Women of Influence, Atlanta Bus. League, 1998; recipient Disting. Alumni award, U. Memphis Alumni Assn. Office: Coca-Cola Enterprises 2500 Windy Ridge Pkwy Atlanta GA 30339

PALMER, WENDY, professional basketball player; b. Aug. 12, 1974; BA in History, U. Va., 1996. Forward Oviedo, Spain, 1996—97, WMBA - Utah Starzz, Salt Lake City, 1997—99, Detroit Shock, 1999—. Named to, All-Am., 1995, 1996. Avocations: horseback riding, music. Office: 2 Championship Auburn Hills MI 48326

PALMER, WILLARD ALDRICH, III, magician, writer, actor; b. Houston, July 25, 1942; s. Willard Aldrich and Ruby Lenoir (Touchstone) P.; m. Carol Ann Houston. BA in Germanics, Rice U., 1964; MA in Letters, Music, Profl. Studies, World U. Advanced Studies of Hawaii, 1995, Phd in Germanics, 2000. Instr. Charlie Cash Music Studios, Houston, 1962-70; performer various venues, Houston, Montreal, Can., 1965—; writer Alfred Music Co., Los Angeles, 1968-86; official magician Todd Mission, Tex., 1984—; owner, operator Bill Palmer Magic Shows, Bellaire, Tex., 1984—. Dir. Tex. Renaissance Festival, Todd Mission, 1978-79; writer, dir. Ren Fair Prodns., Inc., Houston, 1979-81; writer, cons. Exclusive Magical Pubs., Houston, Mexico City, 1986— (mem. editoral bd. 1986). Author: (books) How To Play Folk and Bluegrass Banjo, 1965, A Guide For The Texas Renaissance Festival Performer, 1978, Early History of the Paddle Trick in Print, 1995, How to be a Professional Entertainer, 1996; translator: Magical Adventures and Fairy Tales (Punx) 1987, Punx's Fourth Dimensional Mysteries, 1990, Farewell Performance (Punx), 1990, Paramiracles, 1996, Shenerazade (Borodin), 2001. Dir., pres. Houston Soc. for Psychic Research, 1972—. Mem. Soc. Am. Magicians (pres. Houston chpt. 1985-86), Internat. Brotherhood Magicians (pres. Houston chpt. 1984-85), Tex. Assn. Magicians, Houston Assn. Magicians (pres. 1978-79), Magic Cir. Longon (MIMC with Gold Star), Phi Mu Alpha (warden 1966-67), Delta Phi Alpha. Lutheran. Avocation: psychic research. Home and Office: Adesso Verlag 7902 Roos Rd Houston TX 77036-6440 E-mail: bill@billpalmer.com.

PALMER, WILLIAM BERRY, II, lawyer; b. Phoenix, Jan. 15, 1954; s. William Berry Palmer I and Barbara Jean Palmer; m. Roselle Jackson Palmer, Jan. 2, 1979; children: William III, Briana, Shelby, Shanee, Blair, Tori. BS, Brigham Young U., 1978; JD, U. San Diego Sch. Law, 1981. Lic.: Nevada and Calif. 1983, cert.: fed. dist. ct. 1983. Assoc. to ptnr. Beckley, Singleton Delaney, Jenison and List, Las Vegas, 1983—89; ptnr. Harferd, Mayor and Palmer, Las Vegas, 1983—94; pvt. law practice Las Vegas, 1994—2001; ptnr. Albright, Stoddard, Warnick and Palmer, Las Vegas, 2001—, personal injury mng. ptnr., 2001—. Diplomat Trial Lawyer's Million Dollar Forum, 2000—. Scout master/chairperson Boy Scouts Am., Las Vegas, 2000; ward leadership Ch. Jesus Christ Ladder Day Saints, Las Vegas, 1983—. Recipient Duty to God award, Ch. Jesus Christ Ladder Day Saints, 1969. Mem.: Nevada Bar Assn., ABA, Assn. Trial Lawyers Am., Nevada Trial Lawyers Assn., Clark County Nevada Bar Assn. Avocations: coin collecting/numismatics, hiking, fishing, camping, gun collecting. Office: Albright Stoddard Warnick and Palmer 801 S Ranch Dr Las Vegas NV 89144

PALMER, WILLIAM D. judge; b. Adrian, Mich., 1952; BS in Mgmt. cum laude, Rensselaer Poly. Inst., 1973; JD cum laude, Boston Coll., 1976. Bar: Fla. 1976; cert. civil mediator, family mediator, arbitrator, Fla. Assoc. Carlton, Fields, Ward, Emmanuel, Smith & Cutler, Orlando, Fla., 1976-82, ptnr., 1982-97, Palmer & Palmer, PA, Orlando, 1997-2000; dist. judge 5th dist. Fla. Ct. Appeal, Daytona Beach, 2000—. Lectr. in field. Editor-in-chief Boston Coll. Environ. Affairs Law Rev., 1975-76. Past bd. dirs. Fla. Hosp. Found., Life for Kids Adoption Agy.; past chmn. bd. dirs. Ctrl. Fla. Helpline; bd. dirs. Boys and Girls Club of Ctrl. Fla. Mem.: Orange County Bar Assn. (chmn. various coms.), Fla. Bar (chair jud. nominating procedures com. 1992—94, chair Fla. Bar jour. com. 1993—95, vice chair family section amicus com. 1993—95, mem. jud. adminstrn. selection and tenure com. 1995—98, mem. litigation, appellate law and family law sects.). Office: 5th Dist Ct Appeal 300 S Beach St Daytona Beach FL 32114-5097 E-mail: palmerw@flcourts.org.

PALMER, WILLIAM JOSEPH, accountant; b. Lansing, Mich., Sept. 3, 1934; s. Joseph Flammin Lacchia and Henrietta (Yagerman) P.; m. Judith Pollock, Aug. 20, 1960 (div. Nov. 1980); children: William W., Kathryn E., Leslie A., Emily J.; m. Kathleen Francis Booth, June 30, 1990; stepchildren: Blair T. Manwell, Lindsay H. Manwell. BS, U. Calif., Berkeley, 1963. CPA. With Coopers & Lybrand, 1963—80, mng. ptnr., 1976—80; ptnr. Arthur Young & Co., San Francisco, 1980—89, Ernst & Young, San Francisco, 1989—94; prof. U. Calif., Berkeley, 1994—. Bd. dirs. Dutra Group; chair constrn. industry group Coopers & Lybrand, 1973-80, Arthur Young, 1980-89, Ernst & Young, 1989-94; guest lectr. Engring. Sch. Stanford U., 1976; lectr. Golden Gate Coll., 1975. Author: (books) Businessman's Guide to Constuction, 1981, Construction Management Book, 1984, Construction Accounting and Financial Management, 5th edit., 1994, Construction Litigation-Representing The Contractor, 1992, Construction Insurance, Bonding and Risk Management, 1996. Bd. dirs. Sacramento Met. YMCA, 1976-82, KXPR, Sacramento 1976-85, V.p., 1979-82; bd. dirs. Sacramento Symphony Found., 1977-80; asst. state fin. chmn. Calif. Reagan for Pres., 1980. Lt. USN, 1953-59. Mem. AICPA (vice chmn. com. constrn. industry 1975-81), Nat. Assn. Accts. (pres. Oakland/East Bay chpt. 1972, Man of Yr. 1968), Calif. Soc. CPA's, Assn. Gen. Contractors Calif. (bd. dirs. 1971-74), World Trade Club, Commonwealth Club (San Francisco), Del Paso Country Club, Sutter Club, Lambda Chi Alpha. Roman Catholic. Avocations: antique boats, sailing, golf, book collecting, pipe collecting. Home: PO Box 60405 Sacramento CA 95860-0405 Office: Ernst & Young 1331 N California Blvd Walnut Creek CA 94596-4537 Office Phone: 925-930-2704. E-mail: kathypalm@hotmail.com.

PALMERI, MICHAEL THOMAS, financial analyst, equity trader; b. NYC, Mar. 3, 1962; s. Michael Albert and Ruth Irene Palmeri; m. Kathryn Ann Iannizzotto, Aug. 23, 1986; children: Danielle, Michael. Student, Colo. State U., 1980—81. V.p. ops. Emergency Fin. Svcs., LA, 1995—99; equity analyst/head trader Bentley Hicks Holdings, Lake Balboa, Calif., 1999—. Pvt. first class U.S. Army, 1981—87, Ft Sill, Okla. Personal E-mail: mtp1962@netzero.net. Business E-Mail: mtp1962@netzero.net.

PALMERI, SEBASTIAN T. cardiologist, educator; MD, Georgetown U., 1975. Diplomate Cardiovascular Disease Am. Bd, Internal Medicince, 1983, Internal Medicine Am. Bd, Internal Medicince, 1979. Intern medicine Duke U. Hosp., Durham, NC, 1975—76, resident in Internal Medicine, 1976—78, fellow in Cardiovvascular Disease, 1978—80; physician dept. medicine Robert Wood Johnson U. Med. Group, New Brunswick, NJ, 1985—. Assoc. prof. medicine Robert Wood Johnson U. Hosp., New Brunswick, NJ, 1987—, dir. Inpatient and Outpatient Cardiology Consultation and Patient Care, Non-Invasiv Cardiovascular Svcs., 1987—. Office: Clin Acad Bldg Ste 5200 125 Paterson St New Brunswick NJ 08901-1977

PALMERI, SHARON ELIZABETH, freelance writer, community educator; b. Gary, Ind., July 23, 1948; d. Theodore and Alberta (Bias) Wozniak; m. John James Palmeri, Apr. 9, 1969; 1 child, Renee Suzanne. BS in Edn. English/Journalism with honors, Ind. U. Northwest, 1991. Health columnist Lake County Star, Crown Point, Ind., 1989-92; corr. Post Tribune, Gary, 1992-93, feature corr. The Munster (Ind.) Times, 1993—95; tchr. creative and news writing Merrillville (Ind.) Adult Edn., 1989—95; tchr. writers workshop continuing edn. dept. Purdue U. Calumet, Hammond, Ind., 1990—95; tchr. creative writing Purdue U. North Ctrl., Westville, Ind., 1995—; tchr. composition Purdue U., Calumet, 2001—02; corr. Post Tribune, 2002—. Dir. Write-On Hoosiers, Inc., Crown Point, 1989—; tchr. news and creative writing Bethlehem Steel Career Devel. Ctr., 1996—98; tchr. Forest Ridge Acad., 1996—; book doctor, publicity agt., local book and mag. promoter The Creative Connection. Exec. editor: Hoosier Horizon, 1991-96; co-editor: Hoosier Horizon Children's Mag., 1993—; contbr. short stories and essays to Spirits Mag., 1990, 91. Bd. dirs. N.W. Ind. Arts and Humanities Consortium, Gary, 1994—2000. Recipient Best of Show award Southlake Camera Club, Crown Point, 1975, Focal Point Camera Club, Portage, 1982. Mem. Nat. Coun. Tchrs. English, Soc. Profl. Journalists, N.W. Ind. Arts Assn. (educator 1997—), Communicators N.W. Ind., Ind. U. Alumni Assn., Kappa Delta Pi (newsletter editor 1991-94). Avocations: sailing, photography. Home and Office: 3605 Kingsway Dr Crown Point IN 46307-8934

PALMERIO, ELVIRA CASTANO, art gallery director, art historian; b. Cin., July 23, 1929; d. John and Josephine Castano; m. Carlo Palmerio, June 1, 1958 (dec.); 1 child, Marina. B Lit. Interpretation, Emerson Coll., 1950; postgrad., Pius XII Inst., Florence, Italy, 1954-55; student opera with Cesare Sturani. Curator Castano Art Gallery, Boston, 1965-78, dir. Needham, Mass., 1978-98; rschr. for Archivies of Am. Art Smithsonian Instn., Boston, 1988-89; performed voiceover in Italian for Nova PBS TV Series, Nova, Italy, 1997; gov. adv. com., 1997. Vatican translator; interpreter Italian art specializing in Macchiaioli art; Italian interpreter Ritz Carlton Internat. Festival, (Italian) Mayor's Office Sister Cities Internat. Conv.; appointed sec. World Affairs Coun., Boston; tchr. Emmanuel Coll. Boston, 1953. Mem. Rep. Presdl. Task Force, Nat. Rep. Senatorial Com., Presdl. Inner Circle; active Boston chpt. UN; bd. dirs. Needham Hist. Soc., Boston U. Women's Coun.; vol. Sail Boston, 1992; del. Presdl. Trust, 1992; apptd. Gov.'s Com. on Women's Issues; del. to Nat. Fedn. of Rep. Womens Conv., 1999, 2002; vol. WGBH. Cardinal Spellman scholar; recipient Pirandello Lyceum award, I Migliori, 1997, Vol. award Nat. Fedn. Commns. Women, 1999, Nat. Assn. Commissions for Women, 1999. Mem. UN, Boston U. Women's Coun., Boston Browning Soc., Fogg Art Mus. of Harvard U., Friends of Needham Libr., Archives Am. Art Boston, World Boston, World Affairs Coun. Boston (sec.), Nat. Mus. Women in Arts, Needham Hist. Soc. (bd. dirs.), Wellesley Hist. Soc., Nat. Italian Am. Found., French Libr., World Boston. Avocations: current events, internat. affairs, writing, travel, music. Home: PO Box 57015 Babson Park MA 02457-0015 Office Phone: 781-235-2435. E-mail: epalmerio@msn.com.

PALMERLEE, APRIL WAHLESTEDT, management consultant; b. Cheverly, Md., Apr. 9, 1968; d. James Anthony Pazienza and Beth Lewisa Catherwood; m. Claes R. Wahlestedt, June 15, 1991 (div. July 1996); m. David Luke Palmerlee, May 28, 2000. BS in Fgn. Svc., Georgetown U., 1989; M Internat. Affairs, Columbia U., 1999. Program asst. Spanish Inst., N.Y.C., 1990-92; spl. asst. Oscar de la Renta, Ltd., N.Y.C., 1992-94, 95-96; rschr. Bank Credit Analyst, Montreal, Que., Can., 1994-95; dir. comms. Coun. on Fgn. Rels., N.Y.C., 1996—2002; sr. coord. internat. women's issues U.S. Dept. State, Washington, 2002—03; dir. Potomac Ptnrs. Party, Ltd., Woolahra, Australia, 2004—. Republican. Episcopalian. Home: 27 Jersey Rd Woollahra 20016-4627 2025 Australia Business E-Mail: apalmerlee@yahoo.com.

PALMETER, N. DAVID, lawyer; b. Elmira, N.Y., Jan. 29, 1938; s. Neal Henry and Elizabeth Jane (McHale) P.; m. Mary Lee Morken, 1964 (div. 1979); m. Mary Faith Tanney, Jan. 15, 1983; children: Stephen Michael, John David, Elizabeth Jane, James Martin. AB, Syracuse U., 1960; JD, U. Chgo., 1963. Bar: N.Y. 1963, D.C. 1969. Trial atty. U.S. Dept. Justice, Washington, 1966-68; assoc. Daniels & Houlihan, Washington, 1969-73, ptnr., 1973-75, Daniels, Houlihan & Palmeter, Washington, 1975-84, Mudge, Rose, Guthrie, Alexander & Ferdon, Washington, 1984-95, Graham & James, Washington, 1995-98, Powell, Goldstein, Frazer and Murphy, 1998—2002, Sidley Austin Brown and Wood, 2002—. Author: The World Trade Organization as a Legal System, 2003; co-author: Dispute Settlement in the World Trade Organization, 1999, 2d edit., 2004; contbr. articles to profl. publs. Mem. ABA, Internat. Bar Assn. (chmn. internat. trade and customs law com. 1989-93, liaison to World Trade Orgn. 1994-96), N.Y. State Bar Assn., D.C. Bar Assn., Washington Fgn. Law Soc. (pres. 1992-93), Am. Soc. Internat. Law, Can. Coun. on Internat. Law, Brit. Inst. Internat. and Comparative Law. Home: 2804 29th St NW Washington DC 20008-4112 E-mail: dpalmeter@sidley.com.

PALMIER, DARICE, music educator; b. Terre Haute, Ind., May 19, 1953; d. Charles Eward and Bobbie Claire Goodman; m. Richard Leslie Palmier, Aug. 14, 1976; children: Lauren Elise, Justin Richard. MusB, Ea. Ill. U., 1975, MA, 1976. Instr. St. Louis C.C., 1977—79; asst. prof. Southwestern Ill. Coll., Belleville, 1979—. Accompanist Columbua Unit 4, Ill., 1990—. Mem.: Ill. State Music Tchrs. Assn. (pres. 1996—98), Nat. guild Piano Tchrs. (audition chair 1986—). Avocations: travel, reading.

PALMIERI, VICTOR HENRY, lawyer, business executive; b. Chgo., Feb. 16, 1930; s. Mario and Maria (Losacco) P.; children: Matthew B., John W.; m. Cathryn Connors, July 6, 1990. AB in History, Stanford U., 1951, JD, 1954. Bar: Calif. 1954. Assoc. O'Melveny & Myers, L.A., 1955-59; exec. v.p. Janss Investment Corp., L.A., 1959-63, pres., 1963-68; chmn. Pa. Co. and its subs. Great S.W. Corp., 1969-77; chmn. bd. Palmieri Co., N.Y.C., 1969—. Chmn. PHL Corp., Inc. (formerly Baldwin-Unitaed Inc.), Phila., 1983—87; trustee, CEO Colo.Ute Electric Assn., Inc., 1990—92; spl. dep. rehabilitator Confedn. Life Ins. Co., 1994—98; dep. rehabilitator, CEO Mut. Benefit Life Ins. Co., 1991—94; pres., CEO MBL Life Assurance Corp., 1994—95; chmn. Alix-Palmieri Assocs., 1997—99; dir. William Carter Corp., 1992—95, Outlet Comms., Inc., 1993—95, Broadcasting Ptnrs., Inc., 1994—95; bd. dirs. Mullin Cons., Inc., vice chmn., 2002—; bd. dirs. M Fin. Holdings Inc., M Benefit Solutions, M Fin. Investment Advisors. Ambassador-at-large, U.S. coord. refugee affairs Dept. State, 1979—81; chmn. Am. Learning Corp., 1970—85; dep. exec. dir. Nat. Adv. Commn. on Civil Disorders, 1967—68; mem. Coun. on Fgn. Rels.; trustee Rockefeller Found., 1979—89; pres., bd. dirs. Lincoln Ctr. Theater, 1985—89; chmn. Overseas Devel. Coun., 1985—91; bd. trustees The Police Found., 1996—2002. Office: Mullin Cons Inc 644 S Figueroa St Los Angeles CA 90017 Office Phone: 213-488-8526. Business E-Mail: Victor.Palmieri@mullinconsulting.com.

PALMISANO, DONALD J. surgeon, medical educator; b. New Orleans, 1939; m. Robin Palmisano; 3 children. MD, Tulane U., 1963; JD, Loyola U., 1982. Diplomate Am. Bd. Surgery; bar: La. Intern Charity Hosp., New Orleans, 1963-64, resident in surgery, 1964-68, Lallie Kemp Charity Hosp., Independence, 1967-68; pvt. practice; clin. prof. surgery, clin. prof. med. jurisprudence Tulane U., pres. Intrepid Resources. Mem. Gov.'s Commn. on organ donations; chair La. Med. Disclosure Panel; founding mem. La. Med. Mutual Ins. Co.; lectr. in field; commr. Joint Com. on Accreditation of Healthcare Organizations, 1999-. Contbr. articles to profl. publs. With USAF. Named one of top doctors in New Orleans, 2001; recipient Air Force Commendation medal. Fellow ACS, AMSUS, SAFCS, mem. AMA (bd. trustees 1996—, chair devel. com., Physician Outreach awards, exec com. mem. 1999-, sec-treas. 2001, pres-elect 2002, pres. bd trustees 2003-), La. State Med. Soc. (pres. 1984-85); bd. dirs. Nat. Patient Safety Found., Nat. Advisory Council, Annenberg Ctr. Health Sci. Avocation: photography. Office: AMA 515 N State St Chicago IL 60610-4325 also: Intrepid Resources 4417 Lorino St Ste 200 Metairie LA 70006

PALMISANO, SAMUEL J. information technology executive; b. July 29, 1951; m. Gaier Notman; 4 children. BA in History, Johns Hopkins U., 1973. Joined IBM, Balt., 1973, various sales, mktg. and prod. devel. positions, 1973—89, exec. asst. to IBM CEO John F. Akers, 1989; sr. mng. dir. ops. IBM Japan, 1991; pres., CEO Integrated Systems Solutions Corp., IBM subs., 1993—96; sr. v.p., group exec. IBM Personal Systems Group, 1997, IBM Global Svcs., 1998, IBM Enterprise Systems Group, 1999; pres., COO IBM, White Plains, NY, 2000—02, also bd. dirs., 2000—, pres., CEO, 2002—, chmn., 2003—. Trustee Johns Hopkins U. Avocations: golf, history, jogging, skiing. Office: IBM 1133 Westchester Ave White Plains NY 10604*

PALMITESSA, JAMES R. historian, educator; b. Teanack, NJ, Apr. 26, 1958; s. Hugo and Eleanor Palmitessa; m. Gabriela Ulovcova, July 30, 1993. BA, NYU, 1983; MA, Boston Coll., 1989; PhD, NYU, 1995. Asst. prof. history Western Mich. U., Kalamazoo, 1997—2003, assoc. prof. history, 2003—. Author: Material Culture and Daily Life in the New City of Prague in the Age of Rudolf II, 1997; contbr. articles to profl. jours. Postdoctoral fellow, Am. Coun. Learned Socs./Social Scis. Rsch. Coun., 1997—98. Mem.: Lollard Soc., Internat. Soc. Study of the Material Culture of the Mid. Ages, German Studies Assn., Sixteenth Century Studies Assn., World History Assn., Am. Hist. Assn. Avocations: travel, cooking, music, theater, exhibitions. Home: 2504 Ramblewood Dr Kalamazoo MI 49009 Office: Western Mich U Dept History 1903 W Michigan Ave Kalamazoo MI 49008-5344

PALMORE, CAROL M. state official; b. Owensboro, Ky., Jan. 13, 1949; d. P.J. and Carrie Alice (Leonard) Pate; m. John Stanley Palmore Jr., Jan. 1, 1982. BS in History and Polit. Sci., Murray State U., 1971; JD, U. Ky., 1977. Social worker Dept. Human Resources, Frankfort, Ky., 1971-74; assoc. Rummage, Kamuf, Yewell & Pace, Owensboro, 1977-81; hearing officer Ky. Bd. Claims, Frankfort, 1980-81; gen. counsel Ky. Labor Cabinet, Frankfort, 1982-83, dep. sec. labor, 1984, 1986-87, sec. labor, 1987-90, 91-94; ptnr. Palmore & Sheffer Attys., Henderson, Ky., 1984-86; dep. sec. Ky. Pers. Cabinet, Frankfort, 1996-98, acting sec., 1998, sec., 1998—. Bd. dirs. Ky. Employer's Mutual Ins., Ky. Retirement Sys., Ky. Pub. Employees Deferred Comp. Authority, Govtl. Svcs. Ctr. Authority, Gov.'s Collective Bargaining Task Force, Gov.'s Minority Mgmt. Trainee Program Task Force, State Parks Commn., Ky. Group Health Ins. Bd.; chmn. Ky. Safety & Health Stds. Bd., Frankfort, 1987-90, 91-94; co-chmn. Ky. Labor Mgmt. Adv. Coun., Frankfort, 1987-90, 91-94; bd. dirs. Ky. Workers' Comp Funding Commn., Frankfort, 1987-90, 91-94, Community Svc. Commn., Frankfort, 1993-94, Ky. Info. Resources Mgmt. Commn., Frankfort, 1994, Sch.-to-Work Partnership Coun., Frankfort, 1994; ex-officio bd. dirs. Pub. Employees Collective Bargaining Task Force, Frankfort, 1994, Ky. Workforce Partnership Coun., Frankfort, 1994. Labor liaison Jones for Gov., Lexington, 1990-91; del. Dem. Nat. Conv., N.Y.C., 1992; mem. inaugural class Ky. Women's Leadership Network, Frankfort, 1993; bd. dirs. Alliant Health Systems Adult Oper. Bd., Louisville, 1992-96, Ky. Commn. Homeless, Frankfort, 1993-94; candidate for Sec. State Commonwealth Ky., 1995; chair Dem. Women's Think Tank, 1995. Mem. Ky. Bar Assn. (del. ho. dels. 1985-86, chair law day/spkr. bur. 1985-86, mem. 1986-90), Ky. Bar Found. (bd. dirs. 1985-92, sec. 1986-89, pres. elect 1989-90, pres. 1990-91), Rotary (program chair Frankfort chpt. 1993-94). Democrat. Episcopalian. Avocations: antiques, reading, vintage jewelry, walking. Home: 2310 Peaks Mill Rd Frankfort KY 40601-9437 Office: Personnel Cabinet 200 Fair Oaks Ln Frankfort KY 40601-1134

PALMORE, JOHN STANLEY, JR., retired lawyer; b. Ancon, C.Z., Aug. 6, 1917; s. John Stanley and Antoinette Louise (Gonzalez) P.; m. Eleanor Anderson, July 31, 1938 (dec. 1980); 1 child, John Worsham (dec.); m. Carol Pate, Jan. 1, 1982. Student, Western Ky. State Coll., 1934-36; LL.B. cum laude, U. Louisville, 1939. Bar: Ky. 1938. Practice law, Henderson, 1939-42, 47-59; judge Ct. Appeals Ky. (name changed to Supreme Ct. Ky. 1975), 1959-82, chief justice, 1966, 73, 77-82; practice law Frankfort, Ky., 1983-84; ptnr. Palmore & Sheffer, Henderson, 1984-86; sr. counsel Jackson & Kelly, Lexington, Ky., 1986-92; ret., 1992. City pros. atty., Henderson, 1949-53, city atty., 1953-55; commonwealth's atty. 5th Circuit Ct. Dist. Ky., 1955-59 Served to lt. USNR, 1942-46, 51-52. Mem. VFW, Ky. Bar Assn., Am. Legion, Ky. Hist. Soc., Frankfort Country Club, Lexington Club, Frankfort Rotary Club (pres. 1993-94), Masons, Shriners, Elks, Phi Alpha Delta. Episcopalian (past vestryman, sr. warden). Home: 2310 Peaks Mill Rd Frankfort KY 40601-9437

PALMORE, RODERICK ALAN, lawyer; b. Pitts., Feb. 14, 1952; s. Jefferson and Sophie (Spencer) Palmore; m. Lynne Avril Janifer, June 3, 1978; children: Jordan, Adam. BA, Yale U, 1974; JD, U. Chgo., 1977. Bar: Pa. 1977, Ill. 1982. Assoc. atty. Berkman Ruslander Pohl Lieber & Engel, Pitts., 1977-79; asst. U.S. atty. U.S. Atty's Office, Chgo., 1979-82; assoc. atty. Wildman Harrold Allen & Dixon, Chgo., 1982-86, ptnr., 1986-93, Sonnenschein Nath & Rosenthal, Chgo., 1993-96; v.p., dep. gen. counsel Sara Lee Corp., Chgo., 1996-99, sr. v.p., gen. counsel, sec., 1999—2004, exec. v.p., gen. counsel, sec., 2004—. Commr. Oak Park Plan Commn., 1988—, chair, 1994—; lectr. Youth Motivation Program Chgo. Coun. Commerce & Industry, 1989—; bd. govs. Am. Heart Assn. Met. Chgo., 1993-94; bd. dirs. Pub. Interest Law Initiative, Legal Assistance Found. Chgo. Named one of Outstanding African-Am. Businessmen, Dollars & Sense mag., Chgo., 1991. Mem. ABA (monority ptnrs. conf. 1991—), Nat. Bar Assn., Cook County Bar Assn., Chgo. Bar Assn. (bd. dirs. 1992-94, co-chmn. minority clerkship program 1991-92), Chgo. Com. on Minorities in Law Firms (bd. dirs. 1990-92), Chgo. Bar Found. (bd. dirs. 1993-94). Baptist. Avocations: running, biking, tennis, reading. Home: 507 N Euclid Ave Oak Park IL 60302-1617 Office: Sara Lee Corp Three First National Plaza Chicago IL 60602

PALMS, JOHN MICHAEL, academic administrator, physicist; b. Rijswijk, The Netherlands, June 6, 1935; naturalized, 1956; s. Peter Joannes and Mimi Adele (DeYong) P.; m. Norma Lee Cannon, June 2, 1958; children: John Michael, Danielle Maria, Lee Cannon. BS in Physics, The Citadel, 1958, DSc (hon.), 1980; MS in Physics, Emory U., 1959; PhD, U. N.Mex., 1966. Commd. 2d lt. USAF, 1958, retired capt. Res., 1970; lectr. physics dept. U. N.Mex., 1959-60; instr. physics dept. USAF Acad., 1961-62; staff mem. Western Electric Sandia Lab., 1961-62, U. Calif. Los Alamos Sci. Lab., 1962-66, Oak Ridge Nat. Lab., 1966; asst. prof. Emory U., Atlanta, 1966-69, assoc. prof., 1969-73, chmn., assoc. prof. dept. physics, asso. prof. radiology dept. Med. Sch., 1973-74, prof., chmn. dept. physics, 1969-74, dean Coll. Arts. and Scis., 1974-80, acting chmn. dept. math. and computer sci., 1976-77, v.p. arts and scis., acting chmn. dept. anthropology, 1979-80, acting dean Emory Coll., 1979-80, acting dir. Emory U. Computing Ctr., 1980-82, v.p. acad. affairs, 1982-88, interim dean Grad. Sch., 1985-86, Charles Howard Candler prof. nuclear, radiation and environ. physics, 1988-90; pres., prof. physics Ga. State U., Atlanta, 1989-91, U. S.C., Columbia, 1991—. Bd. dirs. Fortis, Inc., N.Y.C., Exelon Corp., Chgo., NCAA, Simcom Internat. Holdings, Inc., Atlanta; adv. com. Oak Ridge Nat. Lab., 1985-89; mem. nat. nuclear accrediting bd. Inst. Nuclear Power Ops., 1985-91, mem. nat. adv. coun., 1997-2001; mem. panel for semicondr. detectors NAS/NRC, 1963-74; cons. Acad. Natural Scis., Phila., Hughes, Inc., Santa Barbara, Calif., Tennelec, Inc., Three Mile Island Environ. Study, TRW Space Sys. Divsn., L.A., Ga. Dept. Human Resources, Nat. Cancer Inst.; mem. high tech. task force Atlanta C. of C. Contbr. articles on nuclear, atomic, med. and environ. physics to profl. jours. Mem. adv. bd. The Citadel, Oak Ridge Nat. Lab.; mem. exec. bd. Atlanta Area Coun. Boy Scouts of Am., 1989-90; mem. cmty. rels. bd. U.S. Penitentiary, Atlanta; trustee, chmn. Inst. Def. Analyses, Wesleyan Coll., 1984-89, Pace Acad., 1984-89, St. Joseph's Hosp., Atlanta, 1987-89, Ga. Rsch. Alliance, 1988-89; mem. S.C. Univs. Edn. Found., Devel. Found. and Rsch. Found., S.C. Rsch. Inst. Bds.; bd. dirs. Civic-Atlanta Partnership Bus. and Edn., Inc., 1988-90, United Way; chair Rhodes scholar selection com., 1987, S.C., 1995-99; bd. dirs. Nat. Merit Scholarship Corp. Mem. AAAS, Am. Phys. Soc., Am. Assn. Physics Tchrs., IEEE (Nuclear Sci. Group), Am. Nuclear Soc., Am. Coun. Edn., Coun. Provosts and Acad. V.P.s, Am. Conf. Acad. Deans, Soc. Nuclear Medicine, Health Physics Soc., Greater Columbia C. of C. (bd. dirs.), Rotary, Columbia C. of C., Phi Beta Kappa, Sigma Xi, Phi Kappa Phi, Omicron Delta Kappa, Sigma Pi Sigma. Home and Office: Pres U SCO Osborne Bldg Columbia SC 29208-0001

PALMS, ROGER CURTIS, educator, editor, clergyman; b. Detroit, Sept. 13, 1936; s. Nelson Curtis and Winifred Jessie (Bennett) P.; m. Andrea Sisson, Aug. 22, 1959; children— Grant Curtis, Andrea Jane BA, Wayne State U., 1958; B.D., Eastern Baptist Sem., Phila, 1961, M.Div., 1971, D.D., 1977; MA, Mich. State U., 1971. Ordained to ministry Am. Bapt. Chs., 1961. Pastor Ronceverte Bapt. Ch., W.Va., 1961-64; pastor 1st Bapt. Ch., Highland Park, N.J., 1964-67; chaplain Am. Bapt. Student Found., Mich. State U., East Lansing, 1967-73; assoc. editor Decision mag. Billy Graham Evang. Assn., Mpls., 1973-76, editor, 1976-98. Guest lectr. at schs of evangelism, writers' confs., colls. and seminaries. Author 15 books including Enjoying the Closeness of God, 1989, Let God Help You Choose, 1989, An Unexpected Hope, 1998, Effective Magazine Writing, 2000, Your Best Years, 2003; newspaper columnist. Trustee No. Bapt. Theol. Sem., 1973— Mem. Evang. Press Assn. (pres. 1991-93). Baptist. *Investing in people's spiritual lives, giving time and counsel, will bring multiplied results for generations. It is one of the most far-reaching ways I can put faith to work.*

PALOMBO, LISA, artist; b. Providence, Mar. 1, 1965; d. Joseph Christopher Palombo and Catherine Ann Walsh. BFA, R.I. Sch. Design, 1987. Featured artist: (books) The Best of Oil Painting, 1996, Exploring Color, 1998. Recipient honors recognition Artist's Mag., 2003, 2004. Mem.: Oil Painters of Am., N.J. Am. Artists Profl. League. Office: Palombo Studios 55 Mountain Ave Caldwell NJ 07006 E-mail: art@lisapalombo.com.

PALSER, BARBARA F. botany researcher, retired educator; b. Worcester, Mass., June 2, 1916; d. G. Norman and Cora A. (Munson) P. AB, Mt. Holyoke Coll., 1938, A.M., 1940, D.Sc. (hon.), 1978; PhD, U. Chgo., 1942. From instr. to prof. botany U. Chgo., 1942-65; from assoc. prof. to prof. botany Rutgers U., New Brunswick, N.J., 1965-83, dir. grad. program in botany, 1973-80; adj. prof. botany U. Mass., Amherst, 1991—. Erskine fellow U. Canterbury, Christchurch, N.Z. 1969; vis. prof. Duke U., Durham, N.C., fall 1962; vis. research fellow U. Melbourne, Parkville, Victoria, Australia, fall 1984-85 Author lab. manual Principles of Botany, 1973, also numerous research papers in bot. jours.; bot. adviser Ency. Brit., Chgo., 1958-59; editor Bot. Gazette, Chgo., 1960-65 Named Outstanding Tchr., Rutgers Coll., 1977 Mem. Bot. Soc. Am. (sec. 1970-74, v.p. 1975, pres. 1976, Merit award 1985), Torrey Bot. Club (pres. 1968), Internat. Soc. Plant Morphologists, N.J. Acad. Scis. (pres. elect 1987-88, pres. 1988-89, Outstanding Svc. award 1985, 90). Avocations: hiking, stamp collecting/philately, photography. Home: 330 Spencer Dr Amherst MA 01002-3367

PALSER, BETH ANNE, painter; b. Chester, Pa., Nov. 26, 1964; d. John Frank Palser Jr. and Barbara Mower Urban; adopted d. John Frank and Anita (Dietrich) P.; m. William Joseph Quindlen III, Aug. 26, 1963. AD in Specialized Tech., Art Inst. Phila., 1984. Mech./paste-up artist, draftsman Southco, Inc., Concordville, Pa., 1985; artist, asst. David E. Gordon Studios, Phila., 1985-87; freelance artist Franklin Mint, Wawa, Pa., 1988; artist, owner Beth Palser Studios, Oxford, Pa., 1988—; represented by San Pebbles Gallery Ocean City, N.J. Bd. dirs. Rittenhouse Sq. Fine Arts Assn., Phila., 1991-94, 98—, treas., 1992-94; exhbn. chair Artist Guild of Delaware County, Springfield, Pa., 1996-98; bd. dirs. Rittenhouse Sq. Fine Arts Annual, 1998—. Exhibited in one-woman show at Darlington Fine Arts Ctr., Wawa, 1994, 95, 97; exhibited in group shows including Pavilion Galleries Nat. Art Exhbn., Mt. Holly, N.J., 1992, Camden County Cultural Heritage Regional Watercolor Exhbn., Camden, N.J., 1994 (2d place award 1994), Pearl S. Buck Found. Regional Show, Lehigh Valley, Pa., 1995, Lansdale (Pa.) Fine Art Show, 1994, 96 (Best of Show award 1994, Excellence in Watercolor award 1996), Cape May (N.J.) Promenade Art Show, 1996, Phila. Sketch Club Watercolor Exhbn., 1997, Bianco Gallery Ann. Regional Exhbn., Buckingham, Pa., 1997, Cape May (N.J.) Promenade Fine Art Show, 1997 (2d place award 1996, 1st pl. award 1997), Chestnut Hill Art Show, Pa., 1998 (hon. mention 1998, 1st pl. award 2000), Spirit of Art, Wilmington, Del., 1998 (hon. mention 1998), Roxborough Fine Art Festival, Phila., 1999 (Award of Merit, watercolor 1999), Rittenhouse Sq. Fine Arts Festival (2d place award 2000), Cape May (N.J) Promenade Art Show (2d place award 2000), Chestnut Hill Art Show (1st place award 2000); exhibited in charity art shows at Children's Hosp. Phila., 1994-95, South Jersey Arthritis Found., 1995-98, Brandywine Sch. Nursing, 1998-99, United Cerebral Palsy Del., 1998-2001, Ronald McDonald House Art Fest, Del., 1999-2001; represented in Newman Galleries, Phila, Chadds Ford Art Gallery, Pa., Tyme Gallery, Haverton, Pa., Deck the Walls, Exton, Pa.; represented by The Total Picture Gallery, Hockessin, Del., Artworks Gallery, Kennett Square, Pa., Sand Pebbles Gallery; exhibited in two-person show Artworks Gallery, Kennett Square, Pa., 1999. Recipient numerous awards for art. Mem. Balt. Watercolor Soc. (signature mem.), Chester County Art Assn., Phila. Watercolor Club, Pa. Watercolor Soc. (signature mem.). Republican. Avocations: photography, travel, cooking, aerobics. Home: 107 Midland Dr Oxford PA 19363-1125 E-mail: billnbeth@brandywine.net.

PALSHO, DOROTHEA COCCOLI, information services executive; b. Philadelphia, Pennsylvania, June 9, 1947; d. John Charles and Dorothy Lucille (Decker) Coccoli; m. Edward Robert Palsho; children: Christopher, Ryan, and Erica (stepchild). BS, Villanova Univ., 1976; MBA, Temple Univ., 1977. V.p. info. svc. Dow Jones and Co., Princeton, NJ, 1977-97, pres. bus. info. svc., 1995-97, v.p. interactive pub. N.Y.C., 1997—2002, v.p. electronic pub., 2000—02, v.p. stragetic mktg., 2002—. Named to Class of Women Achievers, YWCA Acad. of Women Achievers, 1985. Avocation: sports with the boys. Office: Dow Jones and Co Inc 200 Liberty St New York NY 10281

PALTER, ROBERT MONROE, humanities educator; b. N.Y.C., June 19, 1924; s. Meyer and Mildred (Gilder) Palter; m. Ruth Rappeport, July 15, 1945 (div. 1953); 1 child, Alixe Daphne Cielo; m. Toni Ann Inman, Apr. 5, 1955 (div. 1977); children: Geoffrey Meyer, Jennifer Thorn Allan, Nicholas Trask, Adam Finch; m. Annette B. Weiner, May 21, 1979 (div. 1982). AB, Columbia U., 1943; PhD, U. Chgo., 1952. From instr. to assoc. prof. phys. scis. and philosophy U. Chgo., 1949-64; prof. philosophy and history U. Tex., Austin, 1964-82; Dana prof. history of sci. Trinity Coll., Hartford, Conn., 1983-91, prof. emeritus, 1991—. Author: (book) Whitehead's Philosophy of Science, 1960, The Duchess of Malfi's Apricots and Other Literary Fruits, 2002; editor: Toward Modern Science, 1961, The Annus Mirabilis of Sir Isaac Newton, 1971. With U.S. Army, 1944—46. Mem.: Phi Beta Kappa.

PALTROW, GWYNETH, actress; b. L.A., Sept. 28, 1972; d. prodr. Bruce Paltrow and actress Blythe Danner; m. Chris Martin, Dec. 2003; 1 child, Apple Blythe Alison Martin. Grad. Spence Sch., N.Y.C., 1990. Appeared in films: Shout, 1991, Hook, 1991, Malice, 1993, Flesh and Bone, 1993, Mrs. Parker and the Vicious Circle, 1994, Jefferson in Paris, 1995, Moonlight and Valentino, 1995, Seven, 1995, The Pallbearer, 1996, Emma, 1996, Hard Eight, 1996, Sliding Doors, 1998, Out of the Past, 1998 (voice), Great Expectations, 1998, Hush, 1998, A Perfect Murder, 1998, Shakespeare in Love, 1998, The Talented Mr. Ripley, 1999, Duets, 1999, The Intern, 2000, Bounce, 2000, The Anniversary Party, 2001, The Royal Tenenbaums, 2001, Shallow Hal, 2001, Possession, 2002, View From the Top, 2003, Sylvia, 2003; TV films: Cruel Doubt, 1992, Deadly Relations, 1993; Theatre: Picnic, The Adventures of Huck Finn, Sweet Bye and Bye, The Seagull, Proof. Won Golden Satellite Best Actress in a Motion Picture Emma, 1997, Best Actress Oscar, American Academy Awards, Shakespeare in Love, 1999; Golden Globe Awards, Best Actress, Shakespeare in Love, 1999, Best Actress FFCC, 1999. Mem. Screen Actors Guild (Outstanding Performance with others). Office: Creative Artists Agy c/o Rick Kurtzman 9830 Wilshire Blvd Beverly Hills CA 90212-1804 also: Screen Actors Guild 5757 Wilshire Blvd Los Angeles CA 90036-3635*

PALUMBO, ANTHONY, education educator; b. N.Y.C., Dec. 4, 1938; s. John and Lucy Palumbo; m. Ellen Eskridge Palumbo, Aug. 27, 1960; children: Anna Baltrusaitis, Frank, Gordon. BA, St. John's U., 1960, MS, 1963; PD, Hofstra U., 1976, EdD, 1980. Tchr. reading, English Plainedge Pub. Schs., Massapequa, NY, 1960—98. Adj. prof. edn. St. Francis, Bklyn., 1990—92, N.Y. Inst. Tech., Greensue, 1996—99, CW Post, Brentwood, 2001—; cons. in field. Author novels, short stories; contbr. articles to profl. jours. Mem.: Internat. Reading Assn., Mystery Writers Am. Achievements include patents for underwater cutting rod. Home: 95 Le Baum Ave Amityville NY 11701

PALUMBO, BENJAMIN LEWIS, public affairs consulting company executive; b. Boston, Mar. 4, 1937; s. Guido Americo and Stella Marie (Lombardo) P.; m. Magdalene Julia Palinczar, Nov. l8, l96l; children: Matthew, Jason, Guy. BA, Rutgers U., l959, MA, l96l. Adminstrv. asst. to Gov. Richard J. Hughes, N.J., 1963-65; dir. rsch. N.J. Dem. Com., Trenton, 1965-66; asst. to commr. N.J. Dept. Transp., Trenton, 1966-70; asst. dean Woodrow Wilson Sch., Princeton (N.J.) U., 1970-71; adminstrv. asst. to Senator Harrison Williams, U.S. Senate, Washington, 1971-73, staff dir. U.S. Ho. Dem. caucus, 1975-77, Ho. subcom. on govt. activities and transp., 1977-78; nat. campaign dir. Bentsen for Pres., Washington, 1973-75; dir. fed. govt. rels. Phillip Morris, Inc., Washington, 1978-83; chmn., CEO Palumbo & Cerrell, Inc., Washington, 1983—. Bd. dirs. Nyumbani Child of God Hospice and Orphanage, pres.; bd. dirs. John Mott Found. Mem.: N.J. State Soc., Am. League Lobbyists, Nat. Dem. Club, Rutgers Club Washington, Nat. Press Club. Democrat. Roman Catholic. Office: 1717 K St NW Ste 500 Washington DC 20036-5346 Fax: 202-466-9009. Office Phone: 202-466-9000. E-mail: bpalumbo@covad.net.

PALUMBO, DANIEL P. former food products executive; B in Commerce and Fin., U. Toronto; MBA, Pa. State U. Formerly with Procter & Gamble; former chief mktg. officer Consumer Imaging Divsn. Eastman Kodak; former pres. Consumer Imaging Divsn., sr. v.p. Eastman Kodak Co.; sr. v.p., chief mktg. officer The Coca-Cola Co., Atlanta, 2003—04.

PALUMBO, JAMES FREDRICK, financial services company executive; b. Everett, Mass., Nov. 30, 1950; s. Bruno James and Lillian Elizabeth (Picardi) P.; m. Nancy Laurie Richards, July 24, 1976; children: Elizabeth Richards, Andrew Reid, Alexander Thomas. BA, Lake Forest Coll., 1973; MBA, Washington U., 1975. Market surveillance analyst Nat. Assn. of Securities Dealers, Washington, 1975-76, asst. treas., 1976-78; regional rep. Student Loan Mktg. Assn., Washington, 1978-79, mgr., 1979-81, dir., 1981-82, asst. v.p., 1982-83, v.p., 1983-87; sr. v.p. Connie Lee Mgmt. Svcs. Corp., Coll. Constrn. Loan Ins. Assn., Washington, 1987-95; with N.Y. Life Ins. Co., N.Y.C., 1995-2001, N.Y. Life Securities Inc., N.Y.C., 1995-2001; prin. Treasury Investment Svcs., Reston, Va., 1999—2003; mng. dir. TransCapital Group, Reston, 1999—2003, sr. mng. dir., 2003—04; v.p. RyanLabs Fund Mgmt. LLC, 2003—; registered broker Bedminster Fin. Group, 2003—; mng. prin. TransGlobal Capital LLC, 2004—. Participant Govt.-Univ.-Industry Rsch. Roundtable, Washington, 1986; chmn. Palumbo Properties L.L.C.; chmn. Capital Holdings Ltd., Great Falls, Va. Actor popular and children's theater, 1973-76. Chmn. sports announcers com. D.C. Spl. Olympics, Washington, 1986, 87, D.C. Regional Counsel, Lake Forest Coll., Washington, 1976-80; mem. Elliott Soc. membership com. Washington U., 1986—, Great Falls (Va.) Hist. Soc., Great Falls Citizens Assn., 1996—; bd. govs. Lake Forest Coll., 1978-82, trustee, 1992-99; trustee Abruzzo and Molise Heritage Soc., 2002-03. Mem.: Washington Soc. Investment Analysts, Nat. Assn. Ins. and Fin. Advisors, Assn. for Investment Mgmt. and Rsch., Great Falls Swim and Tennis Club (bd. dirs. 1988—91), Alpha Psi Omega. Avocations: polo, horseback riding, decoy painting. Office: TransGlobal Capital LLC 5950 Symphony Woods Rd Ste 310 Columbia MD 21044 Business E-Mail: jpalumbo@transglobalcap.com.

PALUMBO, MATTHEW ALOYSIUS, marketing executive; b. Queens, NY, Sept. 17, 1961; s. John Christopher and Seiko (Murakami) P. BS, Cornell U., 1986; MBA in Mktg. Mgmt., St. John's U., 1990. Mortgage clk. Salomon Bros., Inc., N.Y.C., 1986; mut. fund adminstr. Bank of N.Y. Co., Inc., N.Y.C., 1986-88; copywriter Pierce Assocs., N.Y.C., 1988-90; dir. mktg. cons. Palumbo Assocs., S.I., 1989-90; adj. prof. St. John's U., S.I., 1990; mktg. dir., copy dir. Flaghouse Inc., Mt. Vernon, N.Y., 1990-93; spl. projects mgr., group product mgr. Global Computer Supplies, Port Washington, N.Y., 1993-97; dir. product mktg. Cyberian Outpost, Kent, Conn., 1997—2000; pres. Palumbo Consultants, Kent, 2000—. Guest lectr. Am. direct mktg. techniques Sheffield Halleron U. (Eng.), 1993; guest lectr. designed and acquired funding Cornell U., Ithaca, 1992—. NY State Regents scholar, 1979, Annette Brodsky scholar, 1988. Mem. Am. Assn. MBA Execs., Cornell Asian Alumni Assn. (v.p. alumni affairs 1993-95), Cornell ILR Alumni, Direct Mktg. Club N.Y., Cornell Club N.Y., Cornell Club Fairfield County, Cornell U. Quadrangle Club, Beta Gamma Sigma. Avocations: reading, sports, music.

PALUMBO, MICHAEL J. air transportation executive; b. N.Y.C. BA in history, Marquette U., 1968; MBA, Fairleigh Dickinson U., 1977. Dir., banking & fin. analysis Pan Amer. World Airways, 1977—80, dir., corp. fin., 1980—81, asst. treas., 1981—83; v.p., treas. Western Airlines, 1983—84, sr. v.p., fin. & treas., 1984; v.p., treas. TransWorld Airlines, Inc., St. Louis, 1994—96, sr. v.p., CFO, 1996—99, exec. v.p., CFO, 1999—2001, Delta Air Lines, Inc., Atlanta, 2004—. Office: Delta Air Lines Inc Hartsfield Atlanta Internat Airport 1030 Delta Blvd Atlanta GA 30320-6001*

PALUMBO, RUTH ANN, state legislator; b. Lexington, Ky., July 7, 1949; d. James Keith and Dorothy Calvin (Carrier) Baker; m. John Anthony Palumbo II, June 29, 1974; children: John A. III (dec.), Joseph Edward, James Thomas, Stephen Baker. BA in Secondary Edn., U. Ky., 1972. Sales Chez Lissette Boutique, Leysin, Switzerland, 1966; sales, shoes Purcell's Dept. Store, Lexington, Ky., 1966-70; organist Ctrl. Bapt. Ch., Lexington, Ky., 1968; clk. Good Samaritan Hosp., Lexington, Ky., 1968-73; sec. Dr. Joseph Keith, Lexington, Ky., 1971-73; senate clk. aide Ky. Gen. Assembly, Frankfort, Ky., 1974; pub. rels. Palumbo Properties, Lexington, 1974-92; state rep. Ky. Gen. Assembly, 1991—. Mem. LWV, Lexington, 1990-92, Ky. Women's Polit. Caucus, Louisville, 1991-92, NAt. Order Women Legislators, Washington, 1992; sec. Ctrl. Ky. Caucus, Lexington, 1991-92. Mem. Greater Lexington Dem. Women, fin. v.p., 1982; mem. Nat. Order of Women Legislators, Washington, 1992; legis.liaison ACS Breast Cancer Detection Task Force, Ky., 1992; adv. coun. Bryan Sta. Youth Svcs. Ctr., Lexington, 1992; ball chmn. Lexington Philharmonic Women's Guild, 1990; govt. affairs Am. Symphony Orch. League Vol. Coun., Washington, 1992; bd. dirs. Philharmonic Women's Guild, pres., 1986-88; bd. dirs. Am. Cancer Soc., pres., 1988-89; bd. dirs. Lexington Phulharmonic Soc. Recipient Dorothy Moomaw Miles Svc. award Sayre Sch., 1986, Govs. Vol. Activist award Gov. Wallace G. Wilkinson, 1989, named Lexington's Outstanding Young Woman Bluegrass Jr. Woman's Club, 1982, Leadership Lexington, C. of C., 1988, Leadership Am. Found. for Women's Resources, Washington, 1989. Fellow U. Ky. Devel. Coun.; mem. Jr. League LExington (sec. 1989-90), Prof. Women's Forum, Gamma Phi Veta (pres. 1980-82). Baptist. Avocations: playing piano, singing, collecting stamps, music boxes, family. Home: 10 Deepwood Dr Lexington KY 40505-2106 Office: House of Reps State Capitol Frankfort KY 40601

PALUSKY, ALICE, missionary, educator; b. Duluth, Minn., May 3, 1928; d. Henry Albert Palusky and Catherine Wasylina. Grad., Watch Tower Bible Sch. of Gilead, 1950; student, U. Hawaii, 1979. Missionary assigned to Venezuela Watch Tower Bible and Tract Soc., Bklyn, NY, 1950, missionary, Bible instr. Valencia/Carupano, Venezuela; cert. ct. interpreter for Spanish Lang. Hawii dist. ct., 2000. Tchr. Spanish literacy, social hygiene, Bible study and family counseling Ednl. Soc. Jehovah's Witnesses, Mexico, 1967—72; tchr. ESL Internat. Lang. Svcs., Osaka, Japan, 1972; tchr. tech. English Jefri Bolkiah Sch. Engring., Brunei, 1981—83; family counseling Jefri Bolkiah Sch. Engring; tchr. ESL, Bible study classes Internat. English Ctr., Kota Kinabalu, Malaysia, 1983—89; tchr. primary sch. grades spl. edn. Hawaii Dept. Edn., Maui, 1993—. Literacy tchr., social hygiene Watch Tower Ednl. Soc., Tepic, Mexico, 1967—72; missionary to mil. and local families Watch Tower Bible and Tract Soc., Kadena, Okinawa, 1972—76, traveling missionary, Thailand, Indonesia, Malaysia, Brunei, 1976—92; instr. Internat. Lang. Sch., Osaka and Nagoya, Japan, 1972—73; engring. sch. tchr., English for spl. purposes Jefry Bolkiah Sch. of Engring., Kuala Belait, Brunei, 1982—84; lang. tchr. Internat. English Ctr., Kota Kina Balu, Malaysia, 1984—91. Mem. Kihei Congregation of Jehovah's Witnesses, 1991—. Home: 12 Uilani St Kihei HI 96753-8021 Personal E-mail: earlofmaui@juno.com.

PAMERLEAU, SUSAN L. career officer; BA in Sociology, U. Wyo., 1968; grad., Squadron Officer Sch., 1975, Air Command and Staff Coll., 1977, Indsl. Coll. Armed Forces, 1985. Commd. 2d lt. USAF, 1968, advanced through grades to maj. gen., 1997; exec. support officer 3d Civil Engring. Squadron, Kunsan Air Base, South Korea, 1973-74; chief cen. base adminstrn. 435th Tactical Airlift Wing, Rhein-Main Air Base, West Germany, 1978-79; chief force programs divsn. Dir. Plans, Programs & Analysis Air Force Mil. Pers. Ctr., Randolph AFB, Tex., 1985-87; comdr. 3700th Pers. Resources Group Air Force Mil. Tng. Ctr., Lackland AFB, Tex., 1988-89; exec. officer plans and policy divsn. Internat. Mil. Staff, NATO Hdqs., Brussels, 1989-92; chief resource allocation divsn. and pers. and support team Hdqs. USAF, Washington, 1992-93; vice comdr. Air Force Mil. Pers. Ctr., Randolph AFB, Tex., 1993-94; commandant Hdqs. Air Force Res. Officer Tng. Corps, Maxwell AFB, Ala., 1994-96; comdr. Air Force Pers. Ctr., Randolph AFB, Tex., 1996-98; dir. pers. force mgmt., dep. chief of staff pers. Hdqs. USAF, Washington, 1998—. Decorated Def. Superior Svc. medal, Legion of Merit, Meritorious Svc. medal with 2 oak leaf clusters. Office: HQ USAF/DPF 1040 Air Force Pentagon Washington DC 20330-1040

PAMIN, DIANA DOLHANCYK (DIANA DOLHANCYK), poet; b. Cleve., Dec. 13; d. Peter and Diana (Dribes) Dolhancyk; m. Leonard Pamin, Aug. 28; children: Diana Anne, Louis Peter. Grad., Titus Coll. Cosmetology. Author: The Parting in Journey of the Mind, 1994 (Editor's Choice award), The Parting in East of the Sunrise, 1995 (Editor's Choice award), Stormy in Songs on the Wind, 1994 (Editor's Choice award), Stormy in Beyond the Stars, 1995 (Editor's Choice award), Shadow Side in At Water's Edge, 1995 (Editor's Choice award), Eclipse in A Delicate Balance, 1995 (Editor's Choice award), Burnt By Love in Windows of the Soul, 1995 (Editor's Choice award), Web of Guilt in Where Dawn Lingers, 1996 (Editor's Choice award), The View in A Muse to Follow, 1996 (Editor's Choice award), The View in Portraits of Life, 1996 (Editor's Choice award), Photographer in Fields of Gold, 1997 (Editor's Choice award), Photographer in Dappled Sunlight, 1997 (Editor's Choice award), Shadow Side II in Of Moonlight and Wishes, 1997 (Editor's Choice award), Love No More in Best Poems of 1996 (Editor's Choice award), The Happening in Best Poems of the '90s, 1997 (Editor's Choice award), Rain in Journey to Our Dreams, 1996 (Accomplishment of Merit award for Literary Achievement), CAT in Promises to Keep, 1996 (Editor's Preference award of Excellence for Lit. Achievement), CAT in Starburst Jour., Winter Wedding, in Of Sunlight and Shadows, 1997 (Editor's Preference award of Excellence for Lit. Achievement), Unrequited Love, Web of Guilt, Sighs of Love, Autumn Symphony, A Dream, Happiness, Swan Song, Lost Song, in Of Sunlight and Shadows, 1997, Red Satin Box, in The Golden Wings of Time, 1997 (Editor's Preference award of Excellence for Lit. Achievement), Snowscape, Rain, Letters, Love No More, Happiness, in Best New Poems, 1996, 10 Elite award winning poems for Lit. Excellence in The Fourth Dimension, 1998, The Swing, Seasons of Love, The Goodbye, Betrothal, Not Our Own, Association, Gypsy, Heady Lilacs, Our Enchantment, Love No More, Sea of Dreams, A Furtive Tear, The Treasure, When Lips Cared, others; Association (poem), artwork cover Starburst Jour., 1999, Sea of Dreams, Starburst Jour., 1999 (elite award lit. excellence), Winter Wedding, Winds of the Universe, You, Loves Deception, The Soothing, Caress, He in Starburst Jour., 1997, His Name is Peter, "But, Isn't The Flower Lovely?," PaPa, in the Sparrowgrass Family Poetry Album, 2000, others. Inducted Internat. Poetry Hall of Fame Mus. Mem. Internat. Soc. Poets (life), Poet's Guild, Internat. Soc. Authors and Artists, Nat. Authors Registry. Home: 6282 Akins Rd North Royalton OH 44133

PAMPLIN, ROBERT BOISSEAU, SR., retired textile manufacturing executive; b. Sutherland, Va., Nov. 25, 1911; s. John R. and Pauline P. (Beville); m. Mary K. Reese, June 15, 1940; 1 child, Robert Boisseau Jr. BBA, Va. Poly. Inst. & State U., 1933; postgrad., Northwestern U., 1933-34; LLD (hon.), U. Portland (Oreg.), 1972; LHD (hon.), Warner Pacific Coll., 1976. With Ga.-Pacific Corp., Portland, 1934-76, sec., from 1936, adminstrv. v.p., 1952-55, exec. v.p., 1955-57, pres., 1957-67, chmn. bd., chief exec. officer, from 1967; ret., 1976; with R.B. Pamplin Corp., 1957—, chmn. bd., CEO, to 1996, Mt. Vernon Mills Inc. (subs. R.B. Pamplin Corp.), Greenville, S.C., retired, 1996. Office: R B Pamplin Corp Ste 2400 805 SW Broadway Portland OR 97205-3341

PAMPLIN, ROBERT BOISSEAU, JR., manufacturing company executive, minister, writer; b. Augusta, Ga., Aug. 3, 1941; s. Robert Boisseau and Mary Katherine (Reese) P.; m. Marilyn Joan Hooper; children: Amy Louise, Anne Boisseau. Student, Va. Poly. Inst., 1960-62, BSBA, 1964, BS in Acctg., 1965, BS in Econs., 1966; BS (hon.), Va. Tech., 2001; LHD (hon.), Va. Poly. Inst., 1995, Pacific U., 2001; DHL (hon.), Va. Poly. Inst., 1995; MBA, U. Portland, 1968, LLD (hon.), 1972, MEd, 1975; MA, Western Conservative Bapt. Sem. (name now Western Sem.), 1978, DMin, 1982, D of Sacred Letter (hon.), 1991, MA, 2000; PhD, Calif. Coast U.; DHL (hon.), Warner Pacific Coll., 1988; LLD (hon.), Western Baptist Coll., 1989; cert. in wholesale mgmt., Ohio State U., 1970; cert. labor mgmt., U. Portland, 1982; cert. in advanced mgmt., U. Hawaii, 1975; DD (hon.), Judson Baptist Coll., 1984; DBA (hon.), Marquis Giuseppe Scicluna Internat. U. Found., 1986; LittD (hon.), Va. Tech. Inst. and State U., 1987, LHD (hon.), Western Seminary, 1991; DD, Western Evang. Sem., 1994; DBA (hon.), U. S.C., 1996; D Pub. Svc. (hon.), DHL, U. Puget Sound, Pacific U., 1999, 2001; BS in Bus. Adminstrn. (hon.), Va. Inst. Tech., 2001. Pres., CEO R.B. pamplin Corp., Portland, Oreg., 1964—. Chmn. bd., CEO Columbia Empire Farms Inc., Lake Oswego, Oreg., 1976—, Pamplin Comms.; chmn. bd., CEO Mt. Vernon Mills Inc.,; pres., CEO Ross Island Sand & Gravel; lectr. bus. adminstrn. Lewis and Clark Coll., 1968-69; adj. asst. prof. bus. adminstrn., U. Portland, 1973-76; pastor Christ Cmty. Ch., Lake Oswego; lectr. in bus. adminstrn. and econs. U. Costa Rica, 1968, Va. Tech. Found., 1986; chmn. bd. dirs. Christian Supplly Ctrs. Inc.; prof. with tenure U. Portland, 1999. Author: Everything is Just great, 1985, The Gift, 1986, Another Virginian: A Study of the Life and Beliefs of Robert Boisseau Pamplin, 1986; author: (with others) A Portrait of Colorado, 1976, Three in One, 1974, The Storybook Primer on Managing, 1974, One Who Believed, Vol. I, 1988, vol. II, 1991, Climbing the Centuries, 1993, Heritage the Making of an American Family, 1994, American Heroes, 1995, Prelude to Surrender, 1995, Alaska Gold, 1998, Robert Reese, 1998; editor: Oreg. Mus. Sci. and Industry Press, 1973; trustee Oreg. Mus. Sci. and Industry Press, 1971, 1974—; editor: Portrait of Oregon, 1973; editor: (with others) Oregon Underfoot, 1975. Trustee Lewis and Clark Coll., 1989—, chmn. bd. trustees, 1991; hon. life pres. Western Conservative Bapt. Sem.; chmn. regents Western Sem., 1994; mem. nat. adv. coun. on vocat. Edn., 1975—; mem. Western Interstate Com. on Higher Edn., 1981-84; co-chmn. Va. Tech. $50 Million Campaign for Excellence, 1984-87, Va. Tech. Found., 1986—, Va.-Oreg. State Scholarship Commn., 1974—, chmn. 1976-78; mem. Portland dist. adv. coun. SBA, 1973-77; mem. rewards rev. com., City of Portland, 1973-78, chmn., 1973-78; bd. regents U. Portland, 1971-79, chmn. bd., 1975-79, regent emeritus, 1979—; trustee Oreg. Episc. Schs., 1979, Linfield Coll., U. Puget Sound, 1989—; dr. pub. svc., U. Puget Sound, 1999. Named Outstanding Philanthropist of Yr. award, Nat. Soc. Fund Raising Execs., 1997, Western Conservative Bapt. Sem. Lay Inst. for Leadership, Edn. Devel. and Rsch. named for R.B. Pamplin Jr., 1988, Textile World's Top 10, 1999, Portland First Citizen, Portland Met. Assn. Realtors, 1999, Parents of Yr., Juvenile Diabetes Found., 2001, Entrepreneur of Yr., Oreg. Entrepreneur Forum, 2001, Va. Tech. Coll. Bus. Adminstrn. renamed R.B. Pamplin Coll. Bus. Adminstrn. in his honor, U. Portland Sch. Bus. renamed Dr. Robert B. Pamplin, Jr. in his honor, Civil War Preservationalist of Yr., Civil War Preservation Trust, 2003; named one of 20 Most Influential Execs. Past 20 Yrs., Bus. Jour.; recipient Disting. Alumnus award, Lewis and Clark Coll., 1974, ROTC Disting. Svc. award, USAF, 1974, bronze medal, Albert Einstein Acad., 1986, Disting. Leadership medal, Freedoms Found., Disting. Bus. Alumnus award, U. Portland, 1990, Nat. Caring award, Caring Inst., 1991, Pride of Portland award, Portland Lions Club, Hero Athlete award, 1994, Herman Lay Entrepreneurship award, 1995, Thomas Jefferson award, Oreg. Hist. Soc., 1998, Aubrey R. Watzek award, Lewis and Clark Coll., 1998, Leadership award, Portland Living Mag., 1998, Unique Contbns. to Comms. award, Portland Advt. Fedn., 2001, Oliver Wendell Holmes, Jr. award for Civil War Preservationalist of Yr., 2001, Govs. Arts award, 2001, Legacy award, Civil War Preservation Trust, 2003, Gov.'s Gold award as Oregonian of Achievement, 2003. Mem. Acad. Mgmt., Delta Epsilon Sigma, Beta Gamma Sigma, Sigma Phi Epsilon, Waverley Country Club, Arlington, Multnomah Athletic Clulb, Capitol Hill Club, Greenville Country Club, Poinsett Club, Eldorado Country Club, Thunderbird Country Club, Rotary. Republican. Episcopalian. Office: RB Pamplin Corp Inc Ste 2400 805 SW Broadway Portland OR 97205-3341

PAMPUSCH, ANITA MARIE, foundation administrator; b. St. Paul, Aug. 28, 1938; d. Robert William and Lucille Elizabeth (Whaley) P. BA, Coll. of St. Catherine, St. Paul, 1962; MA, U. Notre Dame, 1970, PhD, 1972. Tchr. St. Joseph's Acad., St. Paul, 1962-66; instr. philosophy Coll. of St. Catherine, St. Paul, 1970-76, assoc. acad. dean, 1979, acad. dean, 1979-84, pres., 1984-97; Am. Council Edn. fellow Goucher Coll., Balt., 1976-77; pres. Bush Found., St. Paul, 1997—. Bd. dirs. St. Paul Cos.; head Women's Coll. Coalition, 1988-91. Author: (book rev.) Philological Quarterly, 1976; contbr. articles to profl. jours. Mem. adv. com. Instl. Leadership project, Columbia U., 1986—; dist. chmn. Rhodes Scholarship Selection com., Mo., Neb., Minn., Kans., N.D., S.D., 1987—; exec. com. Women's Coll. Coalition, Washington, 1985—. Mem. Coun. for Ind. Colls. (bd. dirs. 1987—, chair 1991—), Am. Philos. Assn., St. Paul C. of C. (bd. dirs. 1986—), St. Paul's Athletic Club, Mpls. Club, Phi Beta Kappa. Roman Catholic. Avocations: swimming, camping, reading, music. Home: 161 Stonebridge Rd Saint Paul MN 55118

PAMULA, VAMSEE K. electrical engineer, researcher; PhD, Duke U., 2000. Rsch. asst. Duke U., 1996—2000, rsch. assoc., 2000—. Pres. OmnipreSense, Durham, 1999—2000. Contbr. articles to profl. jours. Recipient Best Talk award, Duke U. Postdoctoral Assn., 2002. Mem.: IEEE, Sigma Xi, Tau Beta Pi. Achievements include patents pending for electrowetting actuation of liquid droplets on a single-sided electrode array; methods for manipulating droplets by electrowetting-based techniques; design of an accelerometer-based mouse. Office: Duke U Box 90291 Durham NC 27708

PAN, CHAI-FU, engineering educator; b. Loshon, Szechwan, China, Sept. 8, 1936; arrived in U.S., 1960; s. I-Chen Pan, Shih-Liang Shih; m. Maria Chia-Yao Shih, Aug. 18, 1962; children: Lawrence, Mariette. BS in Chem. Engring., Nat. Taiwan U., 1956; PhD in Phys. Chemistry, U. Kans., 1966. Assoc. prof. Ala. State U., Montgomery, 1966—71, prof., 1971—91, prof. emeritus, 1991—. Contbr. numerous articles to profl. jours. Recipient Rsch. award, Ala. State U., 1985; grantee Misip grantee, NSF, 1985. Fellow: Am. Inst. Chemists; mem.: Am. Chem. Soc. (referee), Phi Lambda Upsilon. Achievements include derived Pan equations; proposed methods to study hydrophilic and hydrophobic phenomena in electrolyte solutions. Avocations: reading, writing, gardening, photography. Home: 2420 Wentworth Dr Montgomery AL 36106

PAN, CYNTHIA X. geriatrician, educator, researcher; b. Taipei, Taiwan, Aug. 17, 1965; d. James T.M. pan and Hsiang Yu; m. Darrell C. Sandel. BA, Harvard/Radcliffe U., 1987; MD, SUNY, Stony Brook, 1992. Diplomate Am. Bd. Internal Medicine. Asst. prof. in geriatrics, dir. edn. palliative care program Mt. Sinai Sch. Medicine, N.Y.C., 1997—. Mem. AMA, ACP, Am. Geriatrics Soc. (com. mem.), Am. Acad. Hospice and Palliative Medicine. Avocations: swing dancing, movies, travel. Office: Mount Sinai Sch Medicine PO Box 1070 New York NY 10029-0310 E-mail: cynthia.pan@mssm.edu.

PAN, ELIZABETH LIM, information systems company executive; b. Manila, Dec. 6, 1941; came to U.S., 1961, naturalized, 1967; d. Lim Hu and Maria (Ramos) Lim; m. Jeff T. S. Pan, Jan. 17, 1962 (dec. 1978); children: Jeffrey, James. Student, U. Philippines, Quezon City, 1959-61; BA, U. Ill., 1963, MS, 1966; PhD, Rutgers U., 1974. Pres. Trulim, Inc., Inst. Info. Studies, Inc.; CEO, chmn. bd. dirs. PSI Internat. Editor: (with others) Collection Mgmt., 1977-80; editor: Annual Rev. Rehab., 1980-83; contbr. articles to profl. publs. Pres. Nat. Fedn. 8(a) Cos. (pres.) Home: 3220 Lake Edge Way Oakton VA 22124-2028 Office: 10306 Eaton Pl Ste 400 Fairfax VA 22030-2201

PAN, HENRY YUE-MING, clinical pharmacologist; b. Shanghai, Dec. 27, 1946; came to U.S. 1969; s. Chia-Liu and Siu-Ging (Sung) P.; m. Mary Agnes Tse; children: Lincoln Jonathan, Gregory Kingsley. BSc (hon.), McGill U., Montreal, 1969; MS in Toxicology, U. Hawaii, 1973, PhD in Pharmacology, 1974; MD, U. Hong Kong, 1979. Rsch. asst. U. Hawaii, Honolulu, 1969-74, tchg. asst., 1970-74; med. officer Queen Mary Hosp., Hong Kong, 1979-81; asst. prof. medicine U. Hong Kong, 1981-85; vis. asst. prof. Stanford (Calif.) U., 1983-85; from asst. clin. pharmacology dir. to exec. dir. clin. rsch. Squibb Inst. Med. Rsch., Princeton, N.J., 1985-91; v.p. clin. rsch. Bristol-Myers Squibb Pharm. Rsch. Inst., Princeton, 1991-92; v.p. clin. R & D DuPont Merck Pharm. Co., Wilmington, Del., 1992-93, sr. v.p. drug devel., 1993-96, exec. v.p. R & D, 1996-97; pres. MDS Pharm. Svcs., 1997-99; pres., CEO, mng. ptnr. Integrated Drug Devel. Svcs. and Pharmacologics, LLC, Morristown, NJ, 1998-2000; mng. dir. VennWorks LLC, N.Y.C., 2000—01; CEO VennWorks RTP, NC, 2000—01; exec. v.p., chief med. officer Neurocrine Bioscis., Inc., San Diego, 2001—. Bd. dirs. Predict, Inc., Proband, Inc.; chmn. EastWest Pharm. Internat. LLC. Contbr. articles to profl. jours. Stanford Asian Med. Fund grant, 1983-85. Fellow: Inst. Biol. and Clin. Investigation, Acad. Medicine N.J., Am. Heart Assn. Coun., Am. Coll. Cardiology, Am. Coll. Clin. Pharmacology; mem.: APSS, Am. Coll. Clin. Pharmacology, Drug Info. Assn., Am. Fedn. Med. Rsch., Am. Soc. Pharmacology and Exptl. Therapeutics, Am. Soc. Clin. Pharmacology and Therapeutics, Am. Assn. Pharm. Scientists, AMA, AAAS. Roman Catholic. Avocations: tennis, golf, bicycling, music, reading. Office: Neurocrine Bioscis 12790 El Camino Real San Diego CA 92130 Home: PO Box 675552 Rancho Santa Fe CA 92067 E-mail: henrypan@att.net., hpan@neurocrine.com.

PAN, NING, engineering educator; s. Bao Pan and Xiangyu Wu; m. Hualin Huang, July 13, 1983; 1 child, Kathleen Lin. PhD, Donghua U., 1982—85. Fellowship, Textile Inst., 1994. Mem.: The Fiber Soc. (licentiate; pres. 2001—02, Disting. Lectr. 1998). Achievements include pioneer work in several areas of fibrous materials science. Office: U of Calif at Davis One Shields Ave Davis CA 95616 E-mail: npan@ucdavis.edu.

PAN, ZHONGQI, education educator, researcher; s. Desheng Pan and Dongxian Sun; m. Shuang Zhu; 1 child, Kevin Zhu. BS, Tsinghua Univ., China, 1990, MS, 1995; PhD, U. So. Calif., L.A., 2003. Sys. engr. 301 Hosp., Beijing, 1990—92; asst. prof. Tsinghua U., Bejing, China, 1995—98, U. La. at Lafayette, La., 2003—. Contbr. articles. Recipient Nat. Invention Award, Nat. Edn. Ministry Sci. & Tech., 1998, Nat. Edn. Ministry Sci. & Tech. Advancement Award, Nat. Edn. Ministry Sci. & Technologies, 1997. Mem.: IEEE, OSA. Achievements include patents for fiber comm. Office Phone: 337-482-5899. Office Fax: 337-482-6687. Personal E-mail: zpan@louisiana.edu.

PANAGIDES, JOHN, pharmacologist; b. N.Y.C., Aug. 15, 1944; s. Chris and Sophie (Marmar) P.; m. Kathleen Ann Heimann, July 9, 1967; children: Christopher, Melissa, Adrienne. BS, CCNY, 1966; MS, U. N.C., 1968; PhD, SUNY, Buffalo, 1972. Rsch. assoc. Rockefeller U., N.Y.C., 1972-73; sr. scientist Lederle Labs., Pearl River, NY, 1973-83; sr. clin. monitor Ayerst Labs., N.Y.C., 1983-87; dir. clin. projects, CNS Organon Pharms. USA Inc., West Orange, NJ, 1987-99, sr. dir. clin. projects, CNS, 1999—. Contbr. articles to profl. jours. NDEA Title IV fellow, Chapel Hill, 1966-68. Mem. AAAS, Am. Soc. Pharmacology and Exptl. Therapeutics, Am. Coll. Neuropsychopharmacology, N.Y. Acad. Scis. Achievements include development of haemophilus influenza vaccine, 23-valent pneumococcal vaccine, fenbufen, lodine, cotazym, cotazym-S, zymase, remeron. Home: 7 Catawba Dr West Nyack NY 10994-2304 Office: Organon Pharms USA Inc 56 Livingston Ave Roseland NJ 07068 E-mail: j.panagides@organonusa.com.

PANAGIS, PETE, writer; b. N.Y.C., Aug. 23, 1952; s. Lycourgos and Elizabeth Panagis; m. Evanthia Mentonis, Sept. 2, 1973; children: Penelope, Lee. BA, Bklyn. Coll., 1974; postgrad., Bklyn Coll., N.Y.C, 1974. Lic. rea estate broker Poh's Inst., 1974. Tchr. Soterios Ellenas Parochial Sch., Bklyn., 1973—75; real estate broker Ionian Realty, Bklyn., 1975—83; gen. ptnr. Sheridan Sq. Restaurant, N.Y.C., 1983—89; gen. mgr. Del's Inc., Old Bridge, NJ, 1989—91, Charlie Brown's Steak House, Mountain Side, NJ, 1991—97; writer Freelance, South Amboy, NJ, 2001—. Contbr. articles to profl. jours. Basketball coach Old Bridge Basketball, Old Bridge, NJ, 1995—96; baseball coach Cheesequake Baseball, Old Bridge, NJ, 1988—95; basketball coach Soterios Ellenas Parochial Sch., Bklyn., 1973—75. Mem.: Ahepa (assoc.). R-Liberal. Greek Orthodox. Avocations: swimming, travel, reading, excercise. Home: 107B John St South Amboy NJ 08879 Personal E-mail: ntana@aol.com.

PANAGOTIS, DAVID TIMOTHY, editor; b. Wash., Pa., Aug. 11, 1951; s. Timothy George Panagotis and Betty Louise King-Panagotis; m. Marie Nancy Granato (dec.). BA, Marist Coll., 1991. Ct. aide NY State Supreme Ct., Queens, NY, 1982—84; data mgmt. specialist Hill & Knowlton Inc., N.Y.C., 1986—87; asst. keyboard specialist Hudson River State Hosp., Poughkeepsie, NY, 1988—89; libr. Marist Coll. Lib., Poughkeepsie, 1989—91; feature editor Awakening, Newsletter, Poughkeepsie, 1995—. Author various poet verse titles;: songs. Vol. No. Dutchess Hosp., Rhinebeck, NY, 1992—94; pres. Distributive Edn. Clubs of Am., Ocala, Fla., 1968. Mem.: Nat. Geog. Soc., Am. MENSA Ltd., Alpha Sigma Lambda. Democrat. Avocations: music appreciation, word processing, theology, philosophy, poetry.

PANARESE, WILLIAM C. civil engineer; b. Framingham, Mass., Mar. 6, 1929; s. Angelo and Stephanie (Di Profio) P. BSCE, Purdue U., 1952. Structural research engr. Assn. Am. Railroads, Chgo., 1952-55; with Portland Cement Assn., Chgo. and Skokie, Ill., 1957-76, 80-94, mgr. concrete tech. sect., 1973-76, assoc. mgr. bldg. constrn. sect., 1980-83, mgr. bldg. tech. dept., 1983-86, mgr. constrn. info. services dept., 1987-94. Author, editor: Concrete Floors on Ground, 1983, Transporting and Handling Concrete, 1987, The Homeowner's Guide to Building with Concrete, Brick and Stone, 1988, Cement Mason's Guide, 1990, Concrete Masonry Handbook for Architects, Engineers, Builders, 1991, Fiber Reinforced Concrete, 1991, High Strength Concrete, 1994, Design and Control of Concrete Mixtures, 2002, Performance of Architectural Concrete Panels in the PCA Outdoor Display, 2004, Environmental Performance of Concrete, 2004, author, editor: other bldg. guides and handbooks; editor: Concrete Constrn. mag., 1976—80, Concrete Tech. Today newsletter, 1980—94. Served with C.E. U.S. Army, 1955-57. Fellow Am. Concrete Inst. (coms. 302 on constrn. of concrete floors and slabs, 332 on residential concrete work, chmn. 332 1984-88). Roman Catholic. Home: 1625 Glenview Rd Unit 304 Glenview IL 60025-2973 Office Phone: 847-729-5885. E-mail: wmpanarese@aol.com.

PANAYOTOV, CHRISTO ANGELOV, research scientist, consultant; arrived in U.S., 1996; s. Angel Panayotov Angelov and Elena Christova Panayotova; m. Iliana Nicolova Gospodinova-Panayotova, Sept. 6, 1988. Degree in Chem. Engring., Tech. U., Sofia, Bulgaria, 1953; PhD (hon.), Tech. U., Budapest, Hungary, 1959; DSc (hon.), Humboldt U., Berlin, 1972. Prodn. mgr. Pharmachim, Sofia, 1953—67; dep. trade commr. Bulgarian Trade Commn., N.Y.C., 1967—70; chmn. biotech. com. Bulgarian Govt., Sofia, 1970—75; dept. chair, full prof. Nat. U., Sofia, 1975—89; chief trade officer Bulgarian Trade Commn., Toronto, Canada, 1989—92; engring. cons. BILES LLC Co., Toronto, 1992—96; dir. R&D B&S Machine Co., Clinton, Conn., 1996—. Rep. of Bulgaria European Union Biotechnology, Frankfurt, Germany, 1980—85; chmn. sci. policy com. World Union Scientists, Paris, 1980—85; sr. adviser World Food Program-UASA, Vienna, 1982—84; mem. adv. bd. Nobel Prize Com. on Chemistry, Stockholm, 1982—85; mem. biotech. com. State of Conn., 1998—. Author: 12 sci. books in bio-organic chemistry; editor: Acta Biotechnologica, 1982—86; contbr. articles to profl. sci. jours. Mem.: AAAS (cert. of recognition 2001). Achievements include patents in field. Avocations: ecology, reading, sports. Home: 18 Davis Farm Rd Clinton CT 06413 Office: B&S Machine Co 115 Nod Rd Clinton CT 06412 E-mail: c_angelov@yahoo.com.

PANCAKE, JOHN, newspaper editor; State news editor, environ. editor Miami Herald; arts editor Washington Post, 1996—. Office: Washington Post 1150 15th St NW Washington DC 20071-0002

PANCHALAVARAPU, POORNACHANDRA RAO, industrial engineer, consultant; s. Purushotham and AdiLakshmi Panchalavarapu; m. SriPadmaja S Ogirala; children: Manoj, Niraj. PhD, Case Western Res. U., 2000. Logistics engr. Schneider Logistics Inc., Green Bay, Wis., 1998—2001, lead logistics engr., 2001—. Contbr. articles to profl. jours.; mem. editl. bd.: Internat. Jour. Indsl. Engring., 2000—. Mem.: Inst. Ops. Rsch. and Mgmt. Sci. Hindu. Avocation: travel. Home: 2980 Conesta Dr Green Bay WI 54311 Office: Schneider Logistics Inc 3101 South Packerland Drive Green Bay WI 54313 Personal E-mail: ppc_rao@hotmail.com. E-mail: panchalavarapur@schneider.com.

PANCIERA, RICHARD CONNER, lawyer; b. Westerly, R.I., Mar. 11, 1947; s. Louis and Grace (Conner) P. BA, U. Tex., 1969; JD, U. Ariz., 1973. Bar: Ariz. 1974, U.S. Dist. Ct. Ariz. 1974, R.I. 1975, U.S. Dist. Ct. R.I., 1975, U.S. Ct. Appeals (1st cir.) 1978, U.S. Supreme Ct. 1984, U.S. Ct. Mil. Appeals 1988, U.S. Tax Ct. 1991, U.S. Claims Ct. 1991, U.S. Ct. Customs 1991, U.S. Ct. Appeals (fed. cir.) 1991, U.S. Dist. Ct. Conn. 1999. Pvt. practice, Westerly, 1975—. Legal counsel Hope Valley-Wyoming Fire Dist., R.I., 1979—. Lt. col. JAGC, USAR, 1969-2000. Mem.: ATLA, Nat. Assn. of Consumer Bankruptcy Attorneys, Washington County Bar Assn., Ariz. Bar Assn., R.I. Bar Assn. Office: PO Box 504 Westerly RI 02891-0504 Office Phone: 401-596-0311.

PANDEY, RAMESH CHANDRA, chemist, chemicals executive; b. Naugaon, Uttranchal, India, Nov. 5, 1938; arrived in US, 1967; s. Gauri Dutt and Jivanti Pandey. BSc, U. Allahabad, India, 1958; MSc, U. Gorakhpur, India, 1960; PhD, U. Poona, India, 1965. Jr. rsch. fellow CSIR Nat. Chem. Lab., Poona, 1960-64, rsch. officer, 1965-67, scientist organic divsn., 1970-72; rsch. assoc. dept. chemistry U. Ill., Urbana, 1967-70, vis. scientist, 1972-77; sr. scientist fermentation program Nat. Cancer Inst. Frederick (Md.) Cancer Rsch. Facility, 1977-82, head chem. sect., 1982-83; sr. scientist Abbott Labs., North Chicago, Ill., 1983-84; pres. Xechem, Inc., Melrose Pk., Ill., 1984-90, pres., CEO, dir. tech. devel. New Brunswick, NJ, 1990—2003; chmn., CEO, pres. Xechem Internat. Inc., 1994—2004, chmn., CEO, 2004—; chmn., CEO, pres. Xetapharm Inc., 1996—. Cons. Washington U. Sch. Medicine, St. Louis, 1976-85, LyphoMed, Inc., Melrose Park, 1984-85; vis. prof. Waksman Inst. Rutgers U., Piscataway, NJ, 1984-86; mem. life sci. adv. bd. NJTC, 1999—; mem. statewide adv. com. bd. mgrs. NJ Agrl. Exptl. Sta., Rutgers State U. NJ in Biotechnology, 2002—; founder G.D. Padney Ayurved U., New Brunswick, NJ. Mem. editl. bd. Internat. Jour. Antibiotics, 1986—; patentee graft thin layer chromatography; several US and internat. patents for the isolation and purification of antiobiotics and anticancer agents. Mem. Middlesex County (NJ) Work Force Investment Bd., 1999—; mem. adv. com. for sci. transfer and sci. tech. program Middlesex County Coll., Edison, NJ, 1999-2001. Fellow Am. Inst. Chemists; mem. Am. Chem. Soc., Am. Soc. Microbiology, Am. Soc. Mass Spectrometry, Am. Assn. Cancer Rsch., Am. Soc. Hosp. Pharmacists, Am. Soc. Pharmacognosy, Soc. Indsl. Microbiology, NY Acad. Scis., Indian Sci. Congress Assn., Am. Acad. Ayurvedic Medicine (founder, exec. trustee), Rotary Club (Paul Harris fellow 1996—, pres. New Brunswick club 1999-2000). Office: Xechem Internat Inc New Brunswick Tech Ctr 100 Jersey Ave Ste B-310 New Brunswick NJ 08901-3200 Office Phone: 732-247-3300. Business E-Mail: xechem@erols.com.

PANDEY, VIVEK K. finance educator, researcher; b. Chapra, Bihar, India, Feb. 4, 1965; came to U.S., 1987; s. Gopal K. and Shobha (Tiwary) P. BCom, Andhra U., India, 1986; MBA, Western Carolina U., Cullowhee, N.C., 1988; DBA, Miss. State U., 1994. Grad. rsch. asst. Western Carolina U., 1987-88, Miss. State U., 1988-93; instr. Miss. U. for Women, Columbus, 1993, asst. prof., 1994-98, Murray (Ky.) State U., 1998—, U. Tex., Tyler, 1999—2001, assoc. prof., 2001—. Contbr. articles to profl. jours. Recipient Outstanding Paper award Southwestern Fin. Assn., 1991, Anbar Highest Quality rsch. award, 1998, Distig. Rsch. award Allied Acads., 1999, 2000, 01; named Faculty Mem. of Yr., Divsn. of Bus., Miss. U. for Women, 1995. Mem. Am. Fin. Assn., Fin. Mgmt. Assn., Eastern Fin. Assn., So. Fin. Assn. Avocations: stamp collecting/philately, camping, biking, reading. Office: U Tex at Tyler 3900 University Blvd Tyler TX 75701-6622

PANDIT, VIKRAM S, investment company executive; MBA, Columbia Bus. Sch., 1980, PhD, 1986. Head of instl. equity divsn. Morgan Stanley, 1997—2000, co. pres., COO instl. securities divsn., 2000—03; pres. COO, instl. securities divsn. Morgan Stanley, 2003—. Office: Morgan Stanley 1585 Broadway New York NY 10036

PANDITI, SURYA, electronics executive; b. New Delhi; V.p. and gen. mgr. Telco Systems; various positions Ungermann-Bass; Intel Corp.; v.p., gen. mgr. US Robotics (acquired by 3Com); pres., CEO Avici Systems, Inc., North Billerica, Mass. Office: Avici Systems Inc 101 Billerica Ave North Billerica MA 01862-1256

PANDOLFE, JOHN THOMAS, JR., lawyer; b. Neptune, N.J., Dec. 15, 1941; s. John T. and Jeannette R. (Pullen) P.; m. Linda Lee Fritzsche, July 12, 1969; children: Leslie, Matthew. AB, U. Miami, 1965; MS, Monmouth Coll., 1973; JD, U. Miami, 1975. Bar: Fla. 1976, N.J. 1976, U.S. Dist. Ct. N.J. 1976. Ptnr. Pandolfe, Shaw & Rubino, Spring Lake, N.J. Mem. ABA, Fla. Bar Assn., N.J. Bar Assn., Monmouth Bar Assn., Spring Lake Golf Club. Office: Pandolfe Shaw and Rubino 215 Morris Ave Spring Lake NJ 07762-1360

PANDRES, DAVE, JR., science educator, researcher; b. Duncan, Okla., Jan. 10, 1928; s. Dave and Goldye (Hart) P.; m. Irene Shirley Pandres, July 21, 1953; children: Ronald Mark, Leo Philip, Keith Alan, Lisa Ann. BSEE, U. Tex., Austin, 1949, MA in Applied Math., 1956; PhD in Physics, U. Tex., 1958. Sr. engr. Chance-Vaught Aircraft Co., Dallas, 1951-52; advanced rsch. scientist Marathon Oil Co. Rsch. Ctr., Littleton, 1958-60; assoc. rsch. scientist Martin-Marietta Corp., Denver, 1960-62; sr. rsch. & devel. scientist Lockheed-California Co., Burbank, 1962-64; dir. Math. Scis. Divsn. Douglas Adv. Rsch. Labs., Huntington Beach, Calif., 1964-70; asst. prof. Dept. Math. N. Ga. Coll., Dahlonega, 1971-74, assoc. prof. Dept. Math., 1974-78, prof. Dept. Math., 1978—2002; ret., 2002. Vis. lectr. U. Calif., 1965-66; vis. prof. Inst. Math. Scis., Madras, India, 1970. Contbr. articles to profl. jours. LTJG U.S. Navy, 1952-55. Grantee NSF, 1974, 76. Mem. APS. Democrat. Jewish. Avocations: boating, photography. Home: 1244 Arbor Rd #522 Winston Salem NC 27104-3110

PANEC, WILLIAM JOSEPH, lawyer; b. Pawnee City, Nebr., June 22, 1937; s. Albert and Thelma I. (Sebring) P. BS, U. Nebr., 1962, JD, 1965. Bar: Nebr. 1965, Colo. 1999, U.S. Dist. Ct. Nebr. 1965, U.S. Supreme Ct. 1991, U.S. Ct. Appeals (8th cir.) 1991. Sole practice, Fairbury, Nebr., 1965—; county judge Jefferson County, Nebr., 1965-70. Mem. Nebr. Jud. Qualifications Commn., 1968-70; chmn. Region XIV Crime Commn., 1968-71; cons., 1971-79; cons. for regions VIII, IX, XIV Regional Jail Study, 1972; profl. instr. Nebr. Law Enforcement Adv. Council, 1972; county atty. Jefferson County, 1973-75; village atty. Diller, Nebr., 1975-95; atty. Fairbury Airport Authority, 1981—, Greeley Airport Authority, 1990-2000; organizer Nebr. Jud. Reform, 1969. Author: Probate Procedures and the Uniform Probate Code, 1969. Bd. dirs. Housing Authority, Fairbury, 1979—90, chmn., 1983—90; bd. dirs. Legal Svcs. S.E. Nebr., 1984—2000, v.p., 1992—94, pres., 1994—98; chmn. Law Day, Jefferson County, 1972, 1973, Jefferson County Mental Health Bd., 2001—. U.S. Army, 1955—56, honorably discharged Sgt. U.S. Army. Mem. Nebr. Assn. Trial Attys., Assn. Trial Lawyers Am., Am. Judicature Soc., Nebr. County Judges Assn. (v.p., pres.), Jefferson County Bar Asssn., Internat. Footprinters Assn., U. Nebr. Alumni Assn., Masons, Delta Theta Phi. Address: 1140 Main Ave Crete NE 68333-2258

PANEK, WILLIAM DOMINICK, systems engineer executive; b. Pert Amboy, NJ, Jan. 14, 1970; s. Richard William Panek and Marjaree Marie Mayne; m. Crystal Marie Pelletin, Feb. 11, 1995; 1 child, Alexandria. Assoc. degree, Computer Learning Ctr., 1994. MCSE Microsoft, 1997, Microsoft, 2001, cert. trainer Microsoft, 1997, database adminstr. Microsoft, 2000, network assoc. Cisco Corp., 2000. Microsoft cert. instr. The Associates, Shrewsbury, Mass., 1997—98; pres. Stellacon Corp, Farmington, NH, 1998—. Cons. MicroScript, Danvers, Mass., 1994—2000. Spl. advisor to the chmn. Bus. Adv. Coun., Washington, 2002—03. E4 USAF, 1988—92, Spain. Recipient NH Businessman Yr., Bus. Adv. Coun., 2003. Mem.: AOPA (corr.), NRA (assoc.). R-Consevative. Roman Catholic. Avocations: pilot, hunter, scuba. Office: Stellacon Corp 8 Polliwog Lane Farmington NH 03835

PANERO, HUGH EDWARD, broadcast executive; b. N.Y.C., Feb. 26, 1956; s. Julius and Renee (Rubin) P.; m. Mary Beth Durkin, June 21, 1987; 1 child, Sofia. BA in Govt. & Sociology, Clark U., Worcester, Mass., 1978; MBA, Baruch Coll., N.Y.C., 1989. Dep. bur. chief CableVision Mag., N.Y.C., 1980-82; v.p. mktg. Time Warner Cable of N.Y.C., 1982-93; pres., CEO Request Television, Denver, 1993—98; pres., CEO, dir. XM Satellite Radio Holdings Inc., 1998—. Mem. Cable Television Adminstrv. and Mktg. Soc., Inc. Office: XM Satellite Radio Holdings Inc 1500 Eckington Pl NE Washington DC 20002-2194*

PANES, JACK SAMUEL, publishing company executive; b. N.Y.C., Apr. 6, 1925; s. Max S. and Sophie (Levine) P.; m. Pearl Shaine, Dec. 25, 1949; children— Stephanie Jill, Michael Jonathan. BA, Bklyn. Coll., 1947; MS in Journalism, Northwestern U., 1949. Editor, pub. The Howe Service, Inc., N.Y.C., 1949-54; founder, pub. Publs. for Industry, N.Y.C., 1955—, Panes Publs., Inc., N.Y.C., 1959—; owner Drug Products Display Service Advt. Co., N.Y.C., 1955—, Supplies for Industry Co., N.Y.C., 1956—; pres. Senap Devel. Corp., Great Neck, N.Y., 1972—. Pres. Russell Woods Civic Assn., Great Neck. Served with inf. AUS, 1942-45, ETO. Decorated Silver Star medal, Bronze Star medal. Mem. Deadline Club, Sigma Delta Chi. Home: 21 Russell Woods Rd Great Neck NY 11021-4644 Office: Panes Publications Inc Great Neck NY 11021 Office Phone: 516-487-0990.

PANETH, DONALD JOSEPH, editor, writer; b. NYC, Feb. 28, 1927; s. Irving and Maud (Kramer) P.; m. Elma Olans, Apr. 10, 1949 (dec. 1987); children: Thea, Ira. BBA, CCNY, 1948; postgrad., Columbia U., 1949-50. Reporter NY Times, 1947-49; freelance journalist NYC, 1950-56, 73-75, 77-83, 94—; rewriteman Daily Mirror, NYC, 1956-63; copy editor Morning Telegraph, NYC, 1964-65, L.I. Press, Queens, NY, 1975-77; staff writer Med. Tribune, NYC, 1966-72; editor-in-chief News Dictionary: People, Places, Events, 1977-80; editor, writer Yearbook UN, NYC, 1986-93; documents editor UN Office Conf. Svcs., NYC, 1993-94; recruiting asst., crew leader US Bur. Census, 2000. Adj. lectr. English York Coll., CUNY, 1983-86; cons. study lit. far right extremist groups US Anti-Defamation League, NY, 1995-96. Author: William Baziotes: A Lit. Portrait, 1961, Current Affairs Atlas, 1979, The Ency. of Am. Journalism, 1983; contbr. articles to Commentary mag., The Nation, Village Voice, Current Biography, Peacework, WorldPaper, NY Independent, others; work included anthologies Commentary on the American Scene, 1953, New York City Folklore, 1956. Mem. Am.-Scandinavian Found., NY Soc. Libr. Avocation: reading. Home and Office: 240 Cabrini Blvd Apt 1E New York NY 10033-1113

PANETTA, JOSEPH DANIEL, biotechnology executive; b. Syracuse, N.Y., Mar. 1, 1954; s. Salvatore and Josephine Mary (Sbardella) P.; m. Karin Ann Hoffman, Oct. 21, 1978; children: Lauren Marie, Christopher Daniel. BS, LeMoyne Coll., 1976; MPH, U. Pitts., 1979. Environ. protection specialist EPA, Washington, 1979-82, sr. policy analyst, 1982-84; project leader Schering Corp./NorAm Chem Co., Wilmington, Del., 1984-85; mgr. regulatory affairs agrchems. divsn. Pennwalt Corp., Phila., 1985-88; mgr. corp. regulatory affairs Mycogen Corp., San Diego, 1988-90, dir. corp. regulatory affairs and quality assurance, 1990-92, dir. corp. regulatory, environ. affairs, 1992-97, v.p. govt. and pub. affair, 1998-99; pres., CEO BIOCOM, San Diego, 1999—. Bd. dirs. Gene Therapy Sys., San Diego (Calif.) Econ. Devel. Corp.; chmn. agr. and environment subcom. Internat. Bioindustry Forum; guest lectr. biotech. U. Calif., San Diego, and Calif. Western Law Sch.; advisor bd. on agr. NAS; mem. San Diego Pub. Utilities Adv. Commn., 2002—; adv. Com. Calif. Food Biotech., 2002-2004, U. Calif. Sch. Pharm. Sci., San Diego, Calif., 2003—, mem. adv. coun. Keck Grad. Inst., 2003—; vice chmn. Coun. State Biotech Assocs., 2002—, chmn. Coun. State Biotechnology Assn., 2004-. Columnist San Diego Daily Transcript, 1999—; contbr. articles to profl. jours. Mem. Rep. State Com. Del., 1987; bd. dirs. San Diego Work Force Partnership; mem. exec. com. Calif. Cmty. Colls. Econ. Devel. Network; mem. adv. bd. UCSD-Connect; bd. dirs. San Diego C. of C.; commissioner San Diego City Pub. Utilities commn., 2002—. Mem. Am. Crop Protection Assn. (chmn. com. biotech.), Nat. Agrl. Chems. Assn. (mem. registrations com. 1986-89), Biotech. Industy Orgn. (mem. food and agr. steering com., chmn. bipesticides com., internat. affairs com.), Calif. Indsl. Biotech. Assn. (mem. agrl. affairs com.), Am. Chem. Soc. (mem. agrl. div.), Am. Seed Trade Assn. (chmn. steering com. biotech.), Gov.'s Biotech. Coun. (Calif.), San Diego C. of C. (mem. pub. policy com.), San Diego Workforce Partnership (mem. youth coun.). Roman Catholic. Avocations: yachting, skiing, classical piano. Home: 5459 Shannon Ridge Ln San Diego CA 92130-4808 Office: BIOCOM San Diego 4501 Executive Dr San Diego CA 92121-3025

PANETTA, LEON EDWARD, federal official, former congressman; b. Monterey, Calif., June 28, 1938; s. Carmelo and Carmelina Panetta; m. Sylvia Marie Varni, July 14, 1962; children: Christopher, Carmelo, James. BA magna cum laude, U. Santa Clara, Calif., 1960, LL.B., JD, 1963. Bar: Calif. bar 1965, U.S. Supreme Ct. 1965, U.S. Dist. Ct. (no. dist.) Calif. 1965, U.S. Ct. Appeals 1965. Legis. asst. to U.S. Sen. Thomas Kuchel, Washington, 1966-69; dir. U.S. Office Civil Rights, HEW, Washington, 1969-70; exec. asst. to Mayor of N.Y.C., 1970-71; ptnr. Panetta, Thompson & Panetta, Monterey, 1971-76; mem. 95th-103d Congresses from 17th Calif. dist., 1977-93, chmn. budget com., mem. agr. com., adminstrn. com., also com. dep. majority whip for budget issues, mem. select com. on hunger; dir. U.S. Office Mgmt. and Budget, Washington, 1993-94; chief of staff The White House, Washington, 1994-97; founder Panetta Inst., CA State U., Monterey, Monterey Bay, CA, 1998—. Author: Bring Us Together, 1971. Counsel Monterey Regional Park Dists.; counsel NAACP, 1971-76; bd. trustees U. Santa Clara Law Sch.; founder Monterey Coll. Law; mem. Monterey County Dem. Cen. Com., 1972-74; v.p. Carmel Valley Little League, 1974-75. Served with AUS, 1964-66. Recipient Lincoln award NEA, 1970, Disting. Svc. award NAACP, 1972, Bread for World award, 1978, Nat. Hospice Orgn. award, 1984, Golden Plow award Am. Farm Bur. Fedn., Pres.'s award Am. Coun. on Tchr. of Fgn. Langs., 1991, Coastal and Ocean Mgmt. award Coastal Zone Found., 1991, Food Rsch. and Action Ctr. award, 1991; named Lawyer of Yr., Law Sch. U. Santa Clara, 1970. Mem.: Calif. Bar Assn. Roman Catholic. Office: The Panetta Inst Calif State U Monterey 100 Campus Ctr Bldg 86E Seaside CA 93955-8000

PANETTA, MICHAEL JON, retired state agency administrator, educator, writer, researcher; b. Lansing, Mich., Sept. 9, 1949; s. Frank Anthony P. and Elizabeth Virginia Rocchetti; m. Susan Marie Cottrill, May 1, 1971; children: Mary Elizabeth Panetta-Lowe, Michelina Anne Panetta-Cantu, Joseph Andrew. AA, Lansing (Mich.) C.C., 1970; BA, Mich. State U., East Lansing, 1971, MS, 1972, MA equivalency, 1988, DPhil, 2000. Cert. paramedic Mich., lic. emergency med. technician Mich.; pvt. detective Mich. Fed. Manpower adminstr. Manpower Area Planning Coun., Lansing, Mich., 1970—73; spl. agent med. fraud auditor State of Mich., Lansing, 1973—78, supr. fed. food stamp program, 1977—78, emergency med. svcs. program specialist, 1978—89, program specialist Gov.'s Coun. Environ. Quality, 1989—90, departmental policy and procedure specialist, 1990—91, fin. specialist, contract adminstr. child and family health programs, 1991—2002; prof. Spring Arbor U., Lansing, 2001—02; pvt. practice, cons., 2003—. Dir. youth and vet. program Nat. Alliance of Businessmen, Lansing, 1970—73; suggestion award program adminstr. Mich. Dept. Pub. Health, Lansing, 1990—91. Author: Leader Behavior & Member Response in an Institutional Setting, 1972, Citizens Perceptions of Police & Community Policing, 2000, pamphlets, booklets, guides. Co-founder, pres., v.p. Citizen's to Save Lansing Mich., Lansing, 1992—99; founder Citizens to Save Vets. Civic Ctr., Lansing, 1992—99; co-founder, v.p. Citizens Against the Rain Tax of Lansing, Lansing, 1994—2000. Recipient award, Soc. Study Social Problems Columbia U., 1986; scholar grad. rsch. scholarship, Mich. State U. Bd. Trustees, 1971. Fellow: Am. Lit. Assn.; mem.: Nat. Assn. Welfare Adminstrs., NRA, Mich. State U. Alumni Assn. (life), KC (assoc.; grand knight Richard coun. 1988—90, assoc. mem. Msgr. John A. Gabriels coun., charter grand knight Msgr. John A. Gabriels coun. 1993—95, Knight of Yr. Richard Coun. 1989, Top Proposer of Yr. Richard Coun. 1990, Knight of Yr. Msgr. John A. Gabriels Coun. 1993—95, Papal medallion 1992, Star Coun. award, Columbian award, Founders award 1993—95), Alpha Kappa Delta (life). Republican. Roman Catholic. Avocations: teaching, writing, travel, bicycling, camping.

PANG, JOSHUA KEUN-UK, trade company executive; b. Chinnampo, Korea, Sept. 17, 1924; came to U.S. 1951, naturalized, 1968; s. Ne-Too and Soon-Hei (Kim) P.; m. He-Young Yoon, May 30, 1963; children: Ruth, Pauline, Grace. BS, Roosevelt U., 1959. Chemist Realemon Co., Chgo., 1957—61; chief-chemist chem. divsn. Bell & Gossett Co., Chgo., 1961—63, Fatty Acid Inc., divsn. Ziegler Chem. & Mineral Corp., Chgo., 1963—64; sr. chemist-supr. Gen. Mills Chems. Inc., Kankakee, Ill., 1964—70; pres., owner UJU Industries Inc., Broadview, Ill., 1971—, also dir. Bd. dirs. Dist. 92, Lindop Sch., Broadview, 1976-87; chmn. Proviso Area Sch. Bd. Assn., Proviso Twp., Cook County, Ill. 1976-77; bd. dirs. Korean Am. Cmty. Svcs., Chgo., 1979-80; mem. governing bd. Proviso Area Exceptional Children, Spl. Edn. Joint Agreement, 1981-84, 85-87; alumni bd. govs Roosevelt U., 1983-89; pres. Korean Am. Sr. Ctr., 1991-92; pres. Korean Am. Srs. Assn., Chicagoland, 1992—. Mem. Am. Chem. Soc., Am. Assn. Arts and Sci., Am. Inst. Parliamentarians (region 2 treas. 1979-81, region 2 gov. 1981-82), Internat. Platform Assn., Ill. Sch. Bd. Assn., Nat. Assn. Sch. Bds., Chgo. Area Parliamentarians, Parliamentary Leaders in Action (pres. 1980-81), Nat. Spkrs. Assn. (dir. Ill. chpt. 1981-82, nat. parliamentarian 1982-84, 2d v.p. chpt.

1983-84), Toastmasters (dist. gov. 1969-70), DADS Assn. U. Ill. (chmn. Cook County 1985-98, bd. dirs. 1987-95, treas. 1990-91, v.p. 1991-92), Korean Am. Assn. Chgo. (exec. dir. 1990), World Future Soc. (Chgo. area chpt. coord. 1988-99, pres. Greater Chicagoland Futurists 1991-95, 97-98, chmn. 1998 ann. conf. World Future Soc. Chgo.), Chicagoland C. of C. (ednl., environ. and Pacific-Rim coms., internat. divsn.), Creator's Chosen Ch. of Elects (pres. 2002—). Home: 2532 S 9th Ave Broadview IL 60155-4804 Office: UJU Industries Inc PO Box 6351 Broadview IL 60155-6351 Personal E-mail: j.pang@att.com.

PANG, KATHERINE LANDEY SQUIRES, lawyer; b. N.Y.C., Mar. 28, 1959; BA, Clark U., 1980; JD, U. Dayton, 1982; LLM in Tax, Georgetown U., 1983; MDiv, Biola U., 1994, ThM, 1996, MEd, 2001. Bar: D.C. 1983, Calif. 1986, N.Y. 1999. Assoc. Kutak, Rock & Campbell, Washington, 1983—85; pres., CEO Plan Care, Inc., Irvine, Calif., 1985—88; ptnr. Finley, Kumble, Wagner et.al., Newport Beach, Calif., 1986—88, Sheppard, Mullin, Richter & Hampton, Newport Beach, 1988—89; prin. Law Office of Katherine L. Squires, Irvine, Calif., 1989—97; pres. LawPrep, Inc., LawPrep Press, Inc., 1989—97; atty., mgr. firm-wide tech. devel. tng. and forms Akin Gump Strauss Mauer & Feld, Dallas, 1997—2000; pres., COO Legal EdNet.com., Atkin EdNet.com. and TrainEd.com, Dallas, 1999—2000; chief learning officer, pres. CLE divsn. WebCE.com., LLC, 2000—; pres., chief learning officer Edway Online, 2001—03; CEO Fabricon, Inc., Dallas; COO Tech. Tng. Svs. Corp., Irvine; mng. ptnr., gen. counsel Stone Advisors LLP, Dallas, 2003—. Vis. prof. Stern Sch. Bus. NYU. Contbr. articles on taxation and comml. law to profl. jours. Rep. candidate for U.S. Senate, 1993-94; commr. Workers' Compensation Appeals Bd., 1994-96; mktg. mgr. Bowne Imaging Network, 1996. Mem. ABA (chmn. internat. law com. of gen. practice sect., 1986—), Orange County Bar Assn., Nat. Assn. Women Lawyers (chmn. bankruptcy com., 1983—), Nat. Assn. Women Execs., Newport Beach (Calif.) C. of C. Republican. Avocations: aviation, gourmet cooking, languages, architecture.

PANG, MAYBELINE MIUSZE (MAYBELINE CHAN), software testing and systems engineer, analyst; b. Shanghai, Sept. 9, 1945; came to U.S. from Hong Kong, 1964; d. Yee Sun and Margaret H. (Kong) Chan; m. Patrick Yewwah Pang, Aug. 4, 1968 (div. 1987); children: Elaine Weikay, Irene Weisum, George Siu-On. BS in Physics/Math, Lincoln U., 1967; postgrad, U. Mo., 1967-68, U. Ariz., 1984-86. Application programmer Ariz. Health Sci. Ctr., Physiology Lab., Tucson, 1984-85; software engr. System and Software Engrng. Dalmo Victor, Singer, Tucson, 1985-88, McDonnell Douglas Helicopter Co., Mesa, Ariz., 1988-90, Sperry Marine, Charlottesville, Va., 1990—. Cons., worked with Air Force (F111 Weather Simulation), Army (Advanced Apache Helicopter), Navy (Seawolf weapons, ship control, CNO-Automatic Depth Finder LPD17) projects; comml. (Integrated Software Analysis Sys.; Sperry's docking sys., Guardian Star, SRD-500 SpeedLog, Voyage Mgmt. Sys.) projects; familiar with sys. analysis and design; software devel. and testing; algorithms, pulse processing, sys. engr. and analyst for Marine Sensors; active in Sperry's New Tech. Group. Recipient Nat. Sci. Honor Soc. award, 1967, Teaching assistantship U. Mo., 1968. Avocations: chinese healing and martial arts, spirit/mind/body medicine, religion, life philosophy metaphysics, reading and research. Home: 1517 Westfield Ct Charlottesville VA 22901-1602 Office: Litton Marine Sys Seminole Trail Charlottesville VA 22901

PANIC, MILAN, pharmaceutical and health products company executive; b. Belgrade, Yugoslavia, Dec. 20, 1929; came to U.S., 1956, naturalized, 1963; s. Spasoje and Zorka (Krunich) P.; children: Dawn, Milan (dec.), Vivian; stepchildren: Jane, Mark, Patricia. BS, HU Belgrade, 1955; postgrad., U. Heidelberg, Germany, 1955-56, U. So. Calif., 1957-59. Metallurgist Kaiser Steel Corp., 1956-57; chemist Cyclo-Chem. Corp., Los Angeles, 1957-58; research asst. dept. chemistry U. So. Calif., 1958-59; research chemist Biochem. Research, Los Angeles, 1959-61; chmn. bd., chief exec. officer ICN Pharms., Inc., Costa Mesa, Calif., pres., chmn. bd., chief exec. officer, 1961—; prime min. Govt. of Yugoslavia, Belgrade, 1992-93; chmn. Ribapharm Inc. Assoc. Calif. Inst. Tech. Trustee Intra-Sci. Research Found.; sponsoring com. program health scis. and tech. Harvard-Mass. Inst. Tech.; bd. dirs. Freedom's Found., Valley Forge, Pa. Served with Yugoslavian Army in Partisan Resistance, WWII. Recipient Ellis Island Medal of Honor, 1986. Mem. Serbian Orthodox Ch. Office: ICN Pharms Inc ICN Plaza 3300 Hyland Ave Costa Mesa CA 92626-1503

PANICCIA, MARIO DOMENIC, architect; b. Torrice, Italy, May 13, 1948; s. Sebastiano and Clara (Mancini) P.; m. Tatiana Petropavlovskaya, 1995. BArch, Cooper Union, 1972. Nat. Coun. Archtl. Registration Bds.; registered arch. Conn., N.Y., Tex., Minn., N.J., R.I., Idaho, S.C., Ala., W.Va., Ga., Ill., Tenn., Ind., Mich., Mo., Fla., La., Md., Ma., N.C., Ohio, Pa., Iowa, Va., Calif., Del., D.C., Tex. (interior), Conn. (interior). With William F. Griffin & Assocs., Milford, Conn., summers 1968-72; designer Raffone, Elovitz & Fischer, Archs. & Engrs., Bridgeport, Conn., 1972-75; prin. Paniccia Assocs., Archs. & Planners, Bridgeport, 1975-86, Paniccia Archs. and Engr. Inc., Monroe, Conn., 1987—. Commr. Monroe Conservation & Water Resources and Inland Wetland Comm., 1986-90, reapptd., 1990—. Mem. AIA (nat. housing com. 1988-89, commr. conservation com. 1980—), Conn. Soc. Archs. (dir. 1979-80, commr. chpt. affairs 1979, commr. cmty. affairs 1980, commr. profl. practice 1985-86), Bridgeport Assn. Archs. (dir. 1979, v.p. 1980, 83, pres. 1981), Nat. Trust Hist. Preservation, Nat. Pks. Conservation Assn., Inst. Urban Design, Bridgeport C. of C., Elks (Fairfield, Conn.), KC (3d degree), Exch. Club (Monroe, Conn.), Pyramid Temple Shriners (Milford). Roman Catholic. Office: Paniccia Archs & Engrs Inc 25 Easton Rd Monroe CT 06468

PANICCIA, PATRICIA LYNN, journalist, writer, lawyer, educator; b. Glendale, Calif., Sept. 19, 1952; d. Valentino and Mary (Napoleon) P.; m. Jeffrey McDowell Mailes, Oct. 5, 1985; children: Alana Christine, Malia Noel. BA in Comm., U. Hawaii, 1977; JD, Pepperdine U., 1981. Bar: Hawaii 1981, Calif. 1982, U.S. Dist. Ct. Hawaii 1981. Extern law clk. hon. Samuel P. King U.S. Dist. Ct., Honolulu, 1980; reporter, anchor woman Sta. KEYT-TV, Santa Barbara, Calif., 1983-84; reporter Sta. KCOP-TV, L.A., 1984-88; reporter CNN, L.A., 1989-93. Adj. prof. comm. law Pepperdine Sch. Law, 1987, gender & the law, 1994—, adj. prof.; profl. surfer, 1977-81. Author: Worksmarts for Women: The Essential Sex Discrimination Survival Guide, 2000. Recipient Clarion award Women in Comm., Inc., 1988. Mem. ABA (chair of law and media com. young lawyers divsn. 1987-88, nat. conf. com. lawyers and reps. of media 1987-91), Calif. State Bar (mem. com. on fair trial and free press 1983-84, pub. affairs com. 1985-87), Hawaii Bar Assn., Phi Delta Phi (historian 1980-81). Office: PO Box 881 La Canada CA 91012-0881

PANICEK, DAVID, radiologist; b. Johnson City, NY, Oct. 7, 1954; MD, Cornell U., 1980. Cert. diagnostic radiology 1984. Intern Lenox Hill Hosp., N.Y.C., 1980—81; resident NY Hosp. Cornell Med. Ctr., N.Y.C., 1981—84; radiologist U. Hosp., Syracuse, NY, 1984—88; asst. prof. radiology SUNY Health Sci. Ctr., Syracuse, 1984—88, Cornell U. Med. Coll., 1988—93; radiologist Meml. Sloan-Kettering, N.Y.C., 1988—; assoc. prof. radiology Cornell U. Med. Coll., 1993—98, prof. radiology, 1999—. Office: Meml Sloan-Kettering Cancer Ctr 1275 York Ave New York NY 10021-6007

PANICH, DANUTA BEMBENISTA, lawyer; b. East Chicago, Ind., Apr. 9, 1954; d. Fred and Ann Stephanie (Grabowski) B.; m. Nikola Panich, July 30, 1977; children: Jennifer Anne, Michael Alexei. AB, Ind. U., 1975, JD, 1978. Bar: Ill. 1978, U.S. Dist. Ct. (no. dist.) Ill. 1978, U.S. Dist. Ct. (ctrl. dist.) Ill. 1987, U.S. Ct. Appeals (7th cir.) 1987, U.S. Dist. Ct. (no. dist.) Ind. 2001, U.S. Dist. Ct. (ea. dist.) Mich. 2003, U.S. Ct. Appeals (6th cir.) 2003, U.S. Dist. Ct. (so. dist.) Ill., 2004. Assoc. Mayer Brown & Platt, Chgo., 1978-86, ptnr., 1986—2001, Mayer Brown Rowe & Maw, LLP, Chgo., 2002—. Bd. dirs. Munster (Ind.) Med. Rsch. Found., 1990—, Pub. Interest Law Initiative, 2003—. Mem. ABA, Fed. Bar Assn., Ill. Bar Assn. Republican. Roman Catholic. Office: Mayer Brown Rowe & Maw LLP 190 S La Salle St Ste 3900 Chicago IL 60603-3441 Office Phone: 312-701-7198. Business E-Mail: dpanich@mayerbrownrowe.com.

PANICKER, GIRISH KUMAR, agricultural scientist, consultant; b. Paravur, Kerala, India, Jan. 11, 1949; s. Sukumar and Pankajam Panicker; m. Rani Girish Kumar, Apr. 27, 1988; 1 child, Aja Girish. BS in Agr., U. Kerala, 1972; MS in Agronomy, Alcorn State U., 1992; PhD in Hort., Miss. State U., 1999. Cert. profl. agronomist. Rsch. asst., tech. officer Dept. Agr., Kerala, 1972-78, asst. dir., 1978-80; prin. inspector agr. Dept. Sci. and Tech., Sokoto, Nigeria, 1980-89; grad. rsch. asst. agr. Alcorn State U., Lorman, Miss., 1990-92, rsch. assoc. soil conservation rsch. project USDA, 1992-96; grad. rsch. asst. Miss. State U., Starkville, 1996-99; project coord. soil conservation rsch. project USDA Alcorn State U., Lorman, 1999—2002, dir. USDA conservation rsch. project, 2002—. Recruitment bd. cons. agr. Pub. Svc. Commn., Sokoto, Nigeria, 1986-89; cons. in agronomy for gen. pub., Miss., 1997—. Contbr. more than 25 articles to profl. jours. Coord. India Assn., Sokoto, 1986-89. Mem.: Fruit and Vegetable Growers Assn., Miss. Acad. Scis. (bd. dirs. 2001—03, electred chmn. divsn. agr. and plant scis. 2002—03), Internat. Union Soil Scis., Internat. Soc. Hort. Sci., Am. Soc. Hort. Sci., World Assn. Soil and Water Conservation, Soil and Water Conservation Soc. Am., Am. Soc. Agronomy. Avocations: ornamental and vegetable gardening, reading, writing scientific articles, watching the discovery channel and national geography channel. Office: Alcorn State U 1000 Asu Dr # 1434 Lorman MS 39096-7510

PANIOTO, RONALD ANGELO, judge; b. Dec. 18, 1935; s. Judith K. Panioto; 1 child, Ronald A. Jr. BBA, U. Cin., 1963; JD, No. Ky. U., 1967. Bar: Ohio 1967. Constable Ct. Common Pleas, Cin., 1958-63, 1963-67; adminstrv. asst. U.S. Congressman Donald Clancy, Cin. and Washington, 1967-68; asst. pros. atty. Hamilton County Prosecutor's Office, Cin., 1968-75; judge Hamilton County Mcpl. Ct., Cin., 1975-82, Hamilton County Ct. Common Pleas, Cin., 1982-83, adminstrv. judge, 1983—, judge domestic rels. divsn., 1982—. Mem. Ohio State Bar Assn., Order Sons of Italy, Lawyers' Club Cin., Queen City Club, United Italian Soc. Greater Cin. (pres.), DaVinci U. Club, So. OHio Dog and Game Protective Assn., Cin. Athletic Club, Met. Club, Order Sons of Italy (pres.). Republican. Roman Catholic. Avocation: golf. Office: Hamilton County Ct Domestic Rels 800 Broadway Rm 225 Cincinnati OH 45202

PANISH, MORTON B. retired physical chemist; b. N.Y.C., Apr. 8, 1929; s. Isidore and Fanny (Glasser) P.; m. Evelyn Wally Chaim, Aug. 20, 1951; children: Steven, Paul, Deborah. Student, Bklyn. Coll., 1946-48; BS in Chemistry, Denver U., 1950; MS in Chemistry, Mich. State U., 1951, PhD in Phys. Chemistry, 1954. Chemist Oak Ridge (Tenn.) Nat. Lab., 1954-57; mem. tech. staff RAD div. AVCO Corp., Wilmington, Mass., 1957-61, sect. chief, 1961-64; mem. tech. staff Bell Telephone Labs. (now Bell Labs.), Murray Hill, N.J., 1964-69, dept. head, 1969-86, disting. mem. tech. staff, 1986-92; cons., 1992—2003. Mem. com. on microgravity rsch. NRC, 1991-96, mem. com. on future of space sci. rsch. priorities, 1994-95, space studies bd., 1996-98; mem. com. on human rights NAS, 1996-02. Co-author: Heterostructure Lasers, 1978, Gas Source Molecular Beam Epitaxy, 1993; contbr. numerous articles to profl. jours.; patentee in field. Mem. dean's adv. bd. Coll. Natural Sci., Mich. State U., 1990-95. Recipient Electrochem Soc. Electronics Divsn. award, 1972, Solid state medal, 1979, C&C Found. prize, Japan, 1986, Internat. Crystal Growth award Am. Assn. Crystal Growth, 1990, John Bardeen award The Minerals, Metals and Materials Soc., 1994, The Kyoto prize, 2001. Fellow IEEE (Morris N. Liebmann Meml. award 1991), Am. Phys. Soc.; mem. Nat. Acad. Engrng., Nat. Acad. Scis. Avocation: photography. Home and Office: 9 Persimmon Way Springfield NJ 07081-3605 E-mail: mort@att.net.

PANITZ, LAWRENCE, physician; b. Apr. 30, 1928; s. Max and Gussie (Gorenstein) Panitz; m. Adrienne Ruth Luke, June 20, 1965; children: Jennifer, Michael. BA, NYU, 1962; MD, Upstate Med. U., Syracuse, 1966. Diplomate Am. Bd. Family Practice. Intern St. Joseph's Hosp., Syracuse, NY, 1966-67; pvt. practice gen. medicine Elmsford, NY, 1967-90, Hawthorne, NY, 1968—. Affiliated with Docs Physicians Beth Israel Med. Ctr., N.Y.C., Shrub Oak, NY, Hartsdale, NY, Larchmont, NY, Yonkers, NY, Thornwood, NY, Crestwood, NY, New City, West Haverstraw, NY, others, 1992—97; mem. staff New Rochelle (N.Y.) Hosp., St. Agnes Hosp., White Plains, NY, Westchester County Med. Ctr., Valhalla, NY, N.Y. Dobbs Ferry Hosp., Beth Israel Hosp. Med. Ctr., N.Y.C., Sound Shore Med. Ctr., Phelps Meml. Hosp., North Tarrytown, NY, dep. dir. dept. family practice; dir. Elmsford Med. Ctr.; police surgeon, Tarrytown, North Tarrytown, Sleepy Hollow, Elmsford, Town of Greenburgh; med. dir. Margaret Chapman Sch. Exceptional Child, Hawthorne; med. dir., prin. rschr. Clin. Tech. Assocs., Elmsford, CNS Bioservices, Pleasantville, NY; physician Westchester County Correctional Health Dept., Valhalla; sch. physician, Elmsford; cons., expert witness Vogel & Rosenberg, N.Y.C., Britcher, Leone & Roth, LLC, Glen Rock, NJ; cons. on malpractice litigation for law firms. With U.S. Army, 1946—48, with U.S. Army, 1982—88, lt. col. M.C. USAR. Fellow: AMA, Am. Acad. Family Physicians; mem.: Westchester Acad. Medicine, Westchester County Med. Soc., Med. Soc. State of N.Y., Masons, Shriners. Jewish. Home and Office: Riveredge 3 David Ln Yonkers NY 10701-1122 Office: 5 Bradhurst Ave Hawthorne NY 10532-2154 Office Phone: 914-968-6033. E-mail: lp711md@aol.com.

PANKAU, CAROLE, state legislator; b. Aug. 13, 1947; m. Anthony John Pankau Jr.; 4 children. BS, U. Ill., 1981. Mem. Ill. Ho. of Reps. from 45th dist., 1993—. Mem. DuPage County (Ill.) Bd., 1984-92; committeeman Bloomingdale Twp. Rep. Precinct 70; mem. Keeneyville (Ill.) Sch. Dist. 20; vice chair Bloomingdale Twp. Rep. Orgn. Home: 215 Heritage Dr Roselle IL 60172-2994 Office: Ill Ho of Reps Capitol Office 234 N Stratton Office Bldg Ofc Springfield IL 62706-0001 also: One Tiffany Pointe Bloomingdale IL 60108 E-mail: carole@pankau.org.

PANKEN, PETER MICHAEL, lawyer; b. N.Y.C., Dec. 30, 1936; s. Harold Ira and Sylvia Rita (Haimes) P.; m. Beverly Muriel Goldner, June 19, 1960; children: Aaron, Melinda. BA cum laude, Haverford Coll., 1957; LLB magna cum laude, Harvard U., 1962. Bar: N.Y. 1962, U.S. Dist. Ct. N.Y. 1962, U.S. Ct. Appeals (2d cir.) 1969, (3d cir.) 1988, (10th cir.) 1989, (7th cir.) 2003, U.S. Supreme Ct. 1989. Assoc. Paul Weiss Rifkind Wharton Garrison, N.Y.C., 1962-66, Poletti Freiden Prashker Feldman & Gartner, N.Y.C., 1966-67, Parker Chapin Flattau & Klimpl, N.Y.C., 1967-72, ptnr., 1973-99, chair employment and labor law dept., 1986-99; mem. Epstein Becker & Green PC, N.Y.C., 1999—. Editor: Harvard Law Rev., 1961-62; author: A State-by-State Survey of the Law of Religion in the Workplace, 2001; contbg.: Employment Law Desk Book for Human Resources Professionals; editor-in-chief ALIABA Resource Materials: Employment and Labor Law; contbr. articles to profl. jours. Pres., bd. dirs. Fedn. of Handicapped, N.Y.C., 1984-92; bd. dirs. Fedcap Rehab. Svcs., 1993—; pres. metro N.Y. chpt. Soc. for Human Resource Mgmt., 1990-92, gen. counsel, 1993-2003. Mem. ABA (labor and employment sect., com. on NLRB law, contbg. editor The Developing Labor Law), NY State Bar Assn. (labor and employment law sect., continuing legal edn. com.), Am. Law Inst.-ABA (chmn. employment and labor law programs), Am. Law Inst. (com. on restatement of agy. and restatement of employment law), Soc. for Human Resource Mgmt. (com. on employment practices 1990-99). Office: Epstein Becker & Green PC 250 Park Ave Ste 1200 New York NY 10177-1211 Office Phone: 212-351-4840. E-mail: ppanken@ebglaw.com.

PANKEY, GEORGE ATKINSON, internist, educator, researcher; b. Shreveport, La., Aug. 11, 1933; s. George Edward and Annabel (Atkinson) P.; m. Patricia Ann Carreras, Sept. 22, 1972; children: Susan Margaret, Stephen Charles, Laura Atkinson, Edward Atkinson. Student, La. Poly. Inst., 1950-51; BS, Tulane U., 1954, MD, 1957; MS, U. Minn., 1961. Diplomate Am. Bd. Internal Medicine, Am. Bd. Infectious Disease. Intern U. Minn. Hosps., 1957-58, resident in internal medicine, 1958-60, Mpls. VA Hosp., Mpls. Gen. Hosp., 1960-61; practice medicine New Orleans, 1961—; partner Ochsner Clinic, New Orleans, 1968-99; asst. vis. physician Charity Hosp. La., New Orleans, 1961-62, vis. physician, 1962-75, sr. vis. physician, 1975-95; cons. infectious diseases Ochsner Clinic Found., 1963—, head sect. infectious diseases, 1972-94, dir. infectious disease training program, 1972—94, dir. infectious disease rsch., 1999—; instr. dept. medicine, div. infectious diseases Tulane U. Sch. Medicine, New Orleans, 1961-63, clin. instr., 1963-65, clin. asst. prof. medicine, 1965-68, clin. assoc. prof., 1968-73, clin. prof., 1973—; clin. prof. dept. medicine La. State U. Sch. Medicine, 1979—; clin. prof. oral diagnosis, medicine and radiology La. State U. Sch. Dentistry, 1983—. Cons. World Health Info. Services Inc., 1974; dir., founder Century Nat. Bank, New Orleans; mem. medicine test com. Nat. Bd. Med. Examiners, 1979-83; mem. infectious diseases adv. bd. Hoffman-LaRoche, 1982-; cons. Federal Air Surgeon, 1997—. Author: A Manual of Antimicrobial Therapy, 1969, (with Charles W. Gross and Michael G. Mendelsohn) Contemporary Diagnosis and Management of Sinusitis, 1997, 4th edit., 2004; editor: (with Geoffrey A. Kalish) Outpatient Antimicrobial Therapy - Recent Advances, 1989, Infectious Diseases Digest, 1983-95, So. Med. Assn. Program for Infectious Diseases Dial-Access, 1983-92, Ochsner Clinic Reports on Serious Hosp. Infections, 1985—, Ochsner Clinic Reports on Geriatric Infectious Diseases, 1990-93, Ochsner Clinic Reports on the Management of Sepsis, 1991-93, Infectious Disease Clinics of North America, 1994; bd. editors: Patient Care, 1969-75, Today in Medicine, 1990; mem. editl. bd. Nat. Infectious Disease Info. Network, 1983; mem. editl. adv. bd. Compendium Continuing Edn. in Dentistry, 1984—, Quinolones Bull., 1985-93, Ochsner Jour., 1999—, Infectious Disease News, 2001—; contbr. numerous articles to profl. jours. Dir. Camp Fire Inc.; Pres. New Orleans Young Republican Club, 1969-71; adv. bd. Angie Nall Sch. Hosp., Beaumont, Tex.; trustee Nall Found. for Children, Beaumont. Recipient cert. merit Am. Acad. Gen. Practice, 1969, 70 Master ACP-ASIM (laureate award La. chpt. 1997); fellow Am. Coll. Preventive Medicine, Infectious Disease Soc. Am. (Clinician award 1996), Am. Coll. Chest Physicians, Royal Soc. Medicine; mem. Am. Soc. of Transplantation, Assn. Contamination Control (chpt. pres. 1968-70), Am. Fedn. Med. Rsch., So. Med. Assn. (certificate of award 1970), Am. Soc. Internal Medicine (del. ann. meeting 1971-72), Am. Soc. Microbiology, Am. Thoracic Soc., New Orleans Acad. Internal Medicine (pres. 1977-78, 96-97), AMA, Aerospace Med. Assn., Am. Soc. Tropical Medicine and Hygiene, Am. Venereal Disease Assn., Am. Soc. Parasitologists, Internat. Travel Medicine Soc., La. Soc. Internal Medicine (pres. 1972-73), La. Med. Soc., La. Thoracic Soc. (chmn. program com. 1968, governing council 1976-80), Surg. Infection Soc., Immunocompromised Host Soc., Musser Burch Soc., Orleans Parish Med. Soc., N.Y. Acad. Scis., Pan Am. Med. Assn. (diplomate mem. sect. internal medicine 1971, sect. pres. infectious diseases and virology 1978-85), SAR, Huguenot Soc. Founders Manakin in Colony of Va., Aviation Med. Examiner, Masons (32 deg), Shriners. Home: 5910 Prytania St New Orleans LA 70115-4348 Office: Ochsner Clinic Found 1514 Jefferson Hwy New Orleans LA 70121-2483 Office Phone: 504-842-4006. Personal E-mail: gpankey@ochsner.org.

PANKIW, JIM, member of parliament; Mem. 37th Parliament, House of Commons, Ottawa, Canada. Office: House of Commons Ottawa ON K1A 0A6 Canada also: Box 2061 8th St E Saskatoon SK 57H 5N9 Canada

PANKOV, GRADIMIR KRUNISLAV, ballet artistic director; b. Skopje, Macedonia, Yugoslavia, Oct. 25, 1938; s. Krunislav Ivan Pankov and Dragica Isak (Mihajlovska); m. Margret Maria Kaufmann, Dec. 30, 1980. Baccalaureat, Josip Broz Tito Gymnasium, Skopje, 1956; diploma, State Conservatory of Dance & Music, Skopje, 1957. Dancer Nat. Theatre Macedonia, Skopje, 1956-63; guest artist Nat. Theatres, Belgrade, Zagreb, Sarajevo, 1963-67; soloist City Theatres, Nuremberg, Karlsruhe, Wuppertal, Fed. Republic Germany, Theater Am Gärtnerplatz, Munich, 1967-74, Nat. Theatre, Mannheim, Fed. Republic Germany, 1974-76; ballet master City Theatre, Dortmund, 1976-80; artistic dir., tchr. Netherlands Dance Theatre Jr. Co., The Hague, 1980-81; artistic dir. Nat. Ballet of Finland, Helsinki, 1981-84; artistic dir., tchr. Cullberg Ballet, Stockholm, 1984-88; artistic dir. Ballet du Grand Theatre, Geneva, 1988-96, Les Grands Ballets Canadiens de Montreal, 2000—. Dancer (ballets) Mercutio in Romeo and Juliet, 1963, title role in Petrushka, 1965, title role in Pulcinella, 1971, The Faun in Afternoon of a Faun, 1975, choreographer (Operas) Eugene Onegin, 1977, Carmen, 1978, Don Giovanni, 1978. Office: Les Grands Ballets Canadiens de Montreal 4816 Rivard Montreal QC Canada

PANKOVE, JACQUES ISAAC, physicist, researcher; b. Chernigov, Russia, Nov. 23, 1922; came to U.S., 1942, naturalized, 1944; s. Evsey Leib and Miriam (Simkine) Pantchechnikoff; m. Ethel Wasserman, Nov. 24, 1950; children: Martin, Simon. BSEE, U. Calif., Berkeley, 1944, MSEE, 1948; PhD in Physics, U. Paris, 1960; DSc (hon.), Nat. Poly. Inst., Grenoble, France, 2000. Mem. tech. staff RCA Labs., Princeton, N.J., 1948-70, physicist, fellow, 1970-85; prof. U. Colo., Boulder, 1985-93, prof. emeritus, 1993—, Hudson Moore Jr. Univ. prof., 1989-93, program mgr. materials and devices Ctr. for Optoelectronic Computing Systems, 1986-89; Disting. Rsch. fellow Nat. Renewal Energy Lab. (formerly Solar Energy Rsch. Inst.), 1985-93; v.p. for rsch. and tech. Astralux, Inc., 1992—. Vis. McKay lectr. U. Calif., Berkeley, 1968-69; vis. prof. U. Campinas, Brazil, 1975; Disting. vis. prof. U. Mo., Rolla, 1984; participant NAS sci. exch. program with Romania, 1970, Hungary, 1972, Yugoslavia, 1976. Mem. hon. editl. bd. Solid State Electronics, 1970-94, Solar Energy Materials, 1984—, Optoelectronics, 1986-95; regional editor Crystal Lattice Defects and Amorphous Materials, 1984-90; author: Optical Processes in Semiconductors, 1971, 75, (ednl. film) Energy Gap and Recombination Radiation, 1962; editor: Electroluminescence, 1977, Display Devices, 1980, Hydrogenated Amorphous Silicon, 1984; co-editor: Hydrogen in Semiconductors, 1991, Wide Bandgap Semiconductors, 1992, III-Nitrides, 1997, Gallium Nitride Vol. I, 1998, Vol. II, 1999; designer: laser sculpture, Bklyn. Mus., 1968; contbr. articles to profl. jours.; patentee in field. Trustee Princeton Art Assn., 1970-82; mem. Experiment-in-Arts-and-Tech., Berkeley, 1968-69. Served with U.S. Army, 1944-46. Recipient RCA achievement awards, 1952, 53, 63, Faculty Rsch. award U. Colo. Coll. Engrng. and Applied Sci., 1997, Rank Prize award Optoelectronics, 1998; David Sarnoff scholar, 1956, Disting. Alumnus award U. Calif., Berkeley, 2000. Fellow IEEE (J. J. Ebers award 1975, assoc. editor Jour. Quantum Electronics 1968-77, mem-at-large IEEE awards bd. 1992-95), Am. Phys. Soc.; mem. AAAS, NAE (hon.), Materials Rsch. Soc., Internat. Soc. for Optical Engrng., Sigma Xi. Home: 809 10th St Boulder CO 80302-7551 also: Astralux Inc 2500 Central Ave Boulder CO 80301-2864 E-mail: pankove@astraluxinc.com.

PANKRATZ, TODD ALAN, obstetrician, gynecologist; b. Henderson, NC, Dec. 10, 1965; MD, U. Nebr. Coll. Medicine, 1992. Diplomate Am. Bd. Obstetrics and Gynecology. Intern Truman Med. Ctr., Kansas City, Mo., 1992—96; staff Mercy Hosp., Iowa City, 1996—98, Mary Lanning Hosp., Hastings, Nebr., 1998; pvt. practice in ob-gyn. Obstetrics and Gynecologists, PC, Hastings, Nebr. Recipient Excellence in Medicine Leadership award, AMA Found., 2004. Mem.: AMA (state del. Young Physicians Section), Nebr. Med. Soc. Office: Obstetrics and Gynecology PC 2115 N Kansas Ave Ste 204 Hastings NE 68901 Office Phone: 402-463-6793. Office Fax: 402-463-6894.

PANNELL, CLIFTON WYNDHAM, geography educator, writer; b. Tuscaloosa, Ala., Mar. 24, 1939; s. Henry Clifton and Anne Thomas (Gary) P.; m. Laurie Preston deBuys, Feb. 14, 1964 (dec. Aug. 1992); children: Alexander, Richard, Charles, Thomas; m. Sylvia Hillyard, Dec. 9, 1994. AB, U. N.C., 1961; MA, U. Va., 1962; postgrad. Inter-Univ. Ctr., for Chinese Lang. Studies, Taipei, 1968—69; PhD, U. Chgo., 1971. Lectr. U. Md. Far East Divsn., Taiwan, 1970-71; asst. prof. geography U. Ga., Athens, 1971-75, assoc. prof., 1975-80, prof., 1980—, dir. Ctr. for Asian Studies, 1987-92, assoc. dean Franklin Coll. Arts and Scis., 1994—. Vis. prof. U.S. Mil. Acad., 1984, U. Hong Kong, 1992, 2001; mem. adv. bd. Ga. Rev., 1982-86. Author: China: The Geography of Development and Modernizatin, 1983, East Asia: Geographical and Historical Approaches to Foreign Area Studies, 1983; contbr. articles and revs. to profl. jours. and mags., chpts. to textbooks. Served to lt. USNR, 1962-66. NSF rsch. grantee 1979-82; recipient medal for creative research U. Ga. Research Found., 1981. Mem. Nat. Coun. Geog. Edn., Assn. Am. Geographers, Am. Geog. Soc. (coun. 2001—), Assn. Asian Studies, Can. Assn. Geographers. Office Phone: 706-542-3400. E-mail: cpannell@franklin.uga.edu.

PANNELL, RICHARD ANTHONY, religious organization administrator; b. NYC, Jan. 11, 1973; s. Richard Wingate and Ethel Miriam Pannell; m. Tracey Lee Brown, Sept. 7, 1978; 1 child, Richard Victor. BS in bus. adminstrn., Concordia Coll., 2000. Asst. pastor Immanuel Mennonite Ch., Harrisonburg, Va., 2001—03; social worker Rockingham County, Harrisonburg, 2001—03; dir. gospel choir Ea. Mennonite U., 2002—; dir. of LEAP Ea. Mennonite Sem., 2003—. Avocations: music, travel. Office: LEAP Easter Mennonite Sem 1200 Park Rd Harrisonburg VA 22802 Business E-Mail: richard.panne@emu.edu.

PANNER, BERNARD J. pathologist, educator; b. Youngstown, Ohio, Oct. 9, 1928; s. Morris W. and Matilda (Giber) P.; m. Molly R. Seidenberg, Feb. 11, 1962; children— Morris J., Aaron M., Daniel Z. AB, Western Res. U., 1949, MD, 1953. Diplomate Am. Bd. Pathology. Intern in internal medicine Kings County Hosp., Bklyn., 1953-54; resident in pathology Boston City Hosp., 1954-55, Strong Meml. Hosp., Rochester, N.Y., 1958-60; asst. prof. pathology Sch. Medicine, U. Rochester, 1960-67, assoc. prof., 1967-72, prof., 1972-96, emeritus prof., 1996—; pathologist Strong Meml. Hosp., Rochester, 1972-96. Cons. Genesee Hosp., Rochester, 1974-96. Contbr. articles to profl. jours. Served with USNR, 1955-57 Recipient Mapstone Teaching prize Sch. Medicine, U. Rochester, 1981 Mem. Internat. Acad. Pathology, Am. Assn. Pathologists, Internat. Soc. Nephrology, Am. Soc. Nephrology, Sigma Xi Democrat. Jewish. Home: 330 Wilmot Rd Rochester NY 14618-2947 Office: U Rochester Sch Medicine Dept Pathology 601 Elmwood Ave Rochester NY 14642-0001 Office Phone: 716-275-3188. Business E-Mail: Bernard_Panner@urmc.rochester.edu.

PANNER, OWEN M. federal judge; b. 1924; Student, U. Okla., 1941-43, LL.B., 1949. Atty. Panner, Johnson, Marceau, Karnopp, Kennedy & Nash, 1950-80; judge, now sr. judge U.S. Dist. Ct. Oreg., Portland, 1980—, sr. judge, 1992—. Recipient Am. Bd. Trial Advocates Trial Lawyer of Yr., 1973. Mem. Am. Coll. Trial Lawyers, Am. Bd. Trial Advs., Order of Coif. Office: US Dist Ct 1000 SW 3rd Ave Ste 1207 Portland OR 97204-2942

PANNKE-SMITH, PEGGY, long term care insurance and annuity agency executive; b. Chgo., Oct. 26; d. Victor E. and Leona (O'Leary) Stich; m. Craig D. Smith, July 10, 1990; children from previous marriage: Thomas Scott, David Savonne, Heidi Mireille, Peter. V.p. long term care ins. Sales & Seminars, Des Plaines, 1986-90; pres., founder Nat. Consumer Oriented Agy., Des Plaines, 1990—. Cons. on long-term care ins. The Travelers, Tchrs. Inc. & Annuity Assocs., others; spkr. Exec. Enterprises, N.Y.C., 1988—93. Columnist Sr. News, Vital Times, Daily Herald, Sr. Connection, Sr. Marketplace News, Pioneer Press, Boulder Daily Camera, Longmont Times Call, Aurora Sun, Mature Times Lifestyles. Sponsor Ill. Alliance for Aging, Chgo., 1990—, Ill. Assn. Homes for Aging, 1990-91; bd. govs. St. Matthew Luth. Home, Park Ridge, Ill., 1993-95. Recipient Spkrs. awards Health Ins. Assn. Am., Washington, 1990, Ret. Officers Assn., Glenview, Ill., 1991, 93, Nat. Assn. Sr. Living Industries, Denver, 1992, Exec. Enterprises, NYC, 1993, Gov.'s Conf. on Aging, Chgo., 1996, Golden Harvest Long Term Care award Ret. Officers Assn., 2001, Nat. awards UNUM, 2001, AIG 2002, Conseco, 2000, Allianz, 2002, Mut. of Omaha, 2003, Presidents Club, Lincoln Benefit. Mem.: Internat. Soc. for Retirement Planning, Am. Soc. on Aging, Mature Am., Nat. Coun. on Aging (ad hoc com.), Ctr. for Applied Gerontology, Nat. Assn. Long Term Care Profl., Nat. Assn. Sr. Living Industries, Friends of the Colo. Trail, Colo. Mountain Club, Boulder C. of C., Park Ridge C. of C., Kiwanis (bd. dir. Park Ridge 1992—98, pres. 1996—97), Am. Mensa (program dir. in Ill. 1983—85, Colo. chpt. 1999—, pres. Boulder chpt. 2003—). Avocations: showshoeing, travel, sketching wildflowers, hiking, trekking the Colorado Trail. Office: Nat Consumer Oriented Agy 2200 E Devon Ave Ste 359 Des Plaines IL 60018-4505 also: Cherry Creek 300 S Jackson St Denver CO 80209-3176 also: 4450 Arapahoe Ave Boulder CO 80303-9123 Office Phone: 800-554-1996.

PANOFF, STEPHEN EDWARD, music educator; b. Washington, May 24, 1961; s. Robert and Kathleen Dorothy Panoff. BS in Math. and Music, Coll. of William and Mary, Williamsburg, Virginia, 1984; MusM Edn., Shenandoah U., Winchester, Va., 1997. Cert. postgrad. profl. tchr, Va., 2001. Asst. dir. of bands Tabb (Va.) H.S., 1984—96; dir. of bands Tallwood H.S., Virginia Beach, 1996—. Adjudicator Fiesta-Val Music Festivals, Richmond, Va., 1985—86; dir. Brass Menagerie, Tabb, Va., 1990—96; asst. dir. Shenandoah U. Fine Arts Camp, Winchester, Va., 1997—2001. Contbr. world premiere musical composition Ascensions, 1992; dir.(conductor): (musical performance) Heroes, Lost and Fallen, 2000, To Those Who Serve, 2001, (music performance to honor 9/11 victims) Band-aide, 2001, (conductor) (musical performance) Danzas Brillantes, 2002. Basketball rules interpreter Peninsula Bd. #125, Newport News, Va., 2000—02, basketball ofcl., 1985—2002. Nominee for Disney Am. Tchg. Award, 1998—2002. Mem.: Internat. Jazz Educators Assn., Va. Band and Orch. Dirs' Assn., Va. Music Educator Assn. Roman Catholic. Avocation: golf. Office: Tallwood HS 1668 Kempsville Rd Virginia Beach VA 23464 Personal E-mail: spanoff@cox.net. E-mail: sepanoff@vbcps.k12.va.us.

PANOFSKY, WOLFGANG KURT HERMANN, physicist, researcher; b. Berlin, Apr. 24, 1919; arrived in U.S., 1934, naturalized, 1942; s. Erwin and Dorothea (Mosse) Panofsky; m. Adele DuMond, July 21, 1942; children: Richard, Margaret, Edward, Carol, Steven. AB, Princeton U., 1938; PhD, Calif. Inst. Tech., 1942; DSc (hon.), Case Inst. Tech., 1963, U. Sask., 1964, Columbia U., 1977, U. Hamburg, Germany, 1984, Princeton U., 1983, Yale U., 1985, U. Beijing, 1987, U. Rome, 1988; degree (hon.), Uppsala U., Sweden, 1991. Mem. staff mem. radiation lab. U. Calif., 1945-51, asst. prof., 1946-48, asso. prof., 1948-51; prof. physics Stanford U., 1951-62, prof. Stanford Linear Accelerator Ctr., 1962-89, prof. emeritus, 1989—; dir. Stanford (High Energy Physics Lab., Stanford Linear Accelerator Center), 1962-84, dir. emeritus, 1984—. Am. del. Conf. Cessation Nuclear Tests, Geneva, 1959; mem. Pres.'s Sci. Adv. Com., 1960—64; cons. Office Sci. and Tech., Exec. Office Pres., 1965—73, U.S. ACDA, 1968—81; mem. gen. adv. com. to White House, 1977—81; mem. panel Office Sci. and Techl. Policy, 1977; with nat. def. rsch. Calif. Inst. Tech. and Los Alamos, 1942—45; mem. JASON, 1965—; chmn. bd. overseers Superconducting Supercollider Univs. Rsch. Assn., 1984—93; mem. com. to provide interim oversight Dept. Energy nuclear weapons complex NAS, 1988—89; mem. panel on nuclear warhead dismantlement and special materials control Dept. Energy, 1991—92; mem. Commn. on Particles and Fields Internat. Union Pure and Applied Physics, 1985—93. Decorated officier Legion of Honor; named Calif. Scientist of Yr., 1966; recipient Lawrence prize, AEC, 1961, Nat. med. of Sci., 1969, Franklin medal, 1970, Am. Pub. Svc. award, Fedn. Am. Scientists, 1973, Enrico Fermi award, U.S. Dept. Energy, 1979, Shoong Found. award for sci., 1983, Hilliard Roderick prize Sci., AAAS, 1991, Matteucei medal, 1997. Fellow: Am. Phys. Soc. (pres. 1974); mem.: AAAS, NAS (mem. com. on internat. security and arms control 1985—, chmn. com. 1985—93, mem. scis. com. on scholarly comm. with China 1987—92), Chinese Acad. Scis. (fgn.), Nat. Acad. Lincei (Italy), Russian Acad. Scis., French Acad. Scis. (fgn.), Am. Philos. Soc. (pres. 1974—75), Sigma Xi, Phi Beta Kappa.

PANSINI, MICHAEL SAMUEL, tax and financial consultant; b. Molfetta, Italy, July 12, 1928; came to U.S., 1935; s. Ralph and Isabel (Cirilli) P.; m. Anna D'Angelo, June 5, 1949 (div. 1970); children: Elizabeth, Valerie, Michael; m. Elizabeth Bischoff, Oct. 3, 1970 (div. Feb. 1992); 1 child, Elissa Michelle. BS, NYU, 1950, MBA, 1952, LL.M., 1960; LL.D., Fordham U., 1956. Bar: N.Y. 1956, U.S. Tax Ct. Tax mgr. Pfizer Corp., N.Y.C., 1951-64; asst. treas. Hooker Chem. Corp., N.Y.C., 1964-69; treas., dir. United Indsl. Corp., N.Y.C., 1969-72; sr. v.p., gen. counsel Beker Industries Corp., Greenwich, Conn., 1972-87; pres., dir. Panmer, Inc., 1987—; tax, fin. cons., 1988—; v.p., corp. counsel Champion Energy Corp. and affiliates, 1991-93, Champion Holdings Co. and affiliates, 1993-96. V.p., chmn. various coms. Tax Exec. Inst., N.Y.C., 1963-72; pres., dir. Fed. Tax Forum, Inc., N.Y.C., 1961-72; dir. Intelligent Bus. Communications Corp. Mem. Rep. Town Com. 19th Dist., Stamford, Conn., 1993—2004; commr., vice chmn. Econ. Devel. Commn., Stamford, 1994—; bd. dirs. Stamford Sr. Ctr., 2000—; bd. dirs., treas. Women's Bus. Devel. Ctr., Inc., 2003—, Food Bank of Lower Fairfield County, 2004—. Mem. North Stamford Assn. (bd. dirs. 1999—, v.p. 2000, pres. 2001). Republican. Home and Office: 76 Lawrence Hill Rd Stamford CT 06903-2120 Office Phone: 203-329-8073.

PANTANO, DICK, advertising executive; BA in Math. and Phys. Scis. Edn., Providence Coll., 1961; BFA, RISD, 1965. Math. tchr. Warren (R.I.) schs., 1961-63; with BBDO, 1965-70; head art dir. Hill Holliday, Boston, 1970's, creative dir., 1980's. Office: Hill Holliday Cosmopoulos Inc John Hancock Tower 200 Clarendon St Boston MA 02116-5021

PANTAZAKOS, MICHAEL, law educator; b. Glen Cove, N.Y., Nov. 25, 1968; s. Achilles and Andromache Pantazakos. BA, N.Y. U., N.Y.C., 1990; JD, Benjamin N. Cardozo Sch. of Law, N.Y.C., 1994; MA, Columbia U., N.Y.C., 2003. Sr. editor Cardozo Studies in Law & Lit., N.Y.C., 1994—2001; adj. prof. of law Benjamin N. Cardozo Sch. of Law, 1996—; lectr. in law N.Y. U., 1999—2001. Sec.-treas. Law & Humanities Inst., N.Y.C., 1998—2002; bd. of editors Law & Lit., 2001—. Contbr. articles to legal jours. Office: Benjamin N Cardozo Sch of Law 55 Fifth Ave New York NY 10003 E-mail: pantazak@yu.edu.

PANTELAKOS, LAURA C. state legislator; b. Bath, Maine, Aug. 12, 1935; m. Charles Pantelakos (dec.); 7 children. Attended h.s., Bath. N.H. state rep. Rockingham County Dist. 86; mem. criminal justice and safety com. N.H. Ho. of Reps.; mem. Portsmouth City Coun., 1998—. Chmn. Portsmouth City Del., 1991-92, 1997-98; mem. Portsmouth Fire Commn., 1990-94; mem. exec. bd. Rockingham County Del. Mem. Women of Moose. Office: 528 Dennett St Portsmouth NH 03801-3621 E-mail: lpantelakos@comcast.net.

PANTENBURG, MICHEL, hospital administrator, health educator, holistic health coordinator; b. Denver, Oct. 6, 1926; d. Arthur Robert and Alice (McKenna) P. Diploma, Providence Nursing Sch., Kansas City, Kans., 1951; BS in Nursing Edn., St. Mary Coll., Leavenworth, Kans., 1958; M. in Nursing, Cath. U. Am., 1960. Joined Sisters of Charity, Roman Catholic Ch., 1945; lic. amateur radio operator. Dir. nursing Providence Hosp., Kansas City, Kans., 1958-62; nursing coordinator Sisters of Charity, Leavenworth, 1962-67; hosp. adminstr. St. Mary Hosp., Grand Junction, Colo., 1967-73, St. Vincent Hosp., Billings, Mont., 1973-81; dir. focus on leadership program Gonzaga U., Spokane, Wash., 1985-92; chaplain pastoral care dept. St. Marys Hosp. and Med. Ctr., Grand Junction, Colo., 1994-99, integrative medicine, 1999—. Dir. Norwest Bank, Billings Co-author, editor: Management of Nursing (CHA award 1969), 1967 Bd. dirs. De Paul Hosp., Cheyenne, Wyo., 1980-85, Ronald McDonald House, Billings, 1982-85, St. Joseph Hosp., Denver, 1994-97. Named Woman of Yr., Bus. and Profl. Women, Billings, 1979 Mem. Cath. Hosp. Assn. (bd. dirs., sec.), Am. Hosp. Assn. (regional del. 1975-80), Am. Coll. Hosp. Adminstrn., Mont. Hosp. Assn. (pres.), Billings C. of C. (v.p. 1977-78). Avocations: hiking; skiing. Office: Pastoral Care Dept St Marys Hosp & Med Ctr Grand Junction CO 81502

PANTOJA, SUSAN LEE, secondary school educator, literature educator; b. Jersey City, Nj, July 12, 1956; d. Allen Delk and Violet Grant McMinn; m. Gilbert Raymond Pantoja, Dec. 18, 1991; children: Zachary William Roberts, Stephen Gabriel. MA Liberal Studies, Ind. U., 1999, BA English, 1983. Professional Secondary Teaching License Ind., 1998. Tchr. English South Bend Cmty. Sch. Corp., South Bend, Ind., 1998—. D-Liberal. Non-Denominational. Avocations: writing, travel, hiking, ethnic cooking, supporter of the arts. Personal E-mail: sgpantoja@sbcglobal.net.

PANTOJAS-CONCEPCION, CARLOS A. rheumatologist; b. Santurce, P.R., Aug. 27, 1958; s. Hipolito and Carmen D. (Concepcion) Pantojas; m. Margarita S. Barbosa, Sept. 5, 1987; 1 child, Karla. MD, U. Ctrl. del Caribe, P.R., 1984. Cons. rheumatology Caguas (P.R.) Regional Hosp., 1990—, Ashford-Presbyn. Hosp., Santurce, 1992—, Pavia Hosp., Santurce, 1995—; asst. prof. San Juan Baptista Sch. Medicine, Caguas, 1995—. Pres. ethics com. Caguas Regional Hosp., 1991—. Recipient Dr.'s Choice award in Rheumatology, PR, 2000, 2001. Mem.: ACP, AMA (Physician Recognition award 1993, 1996, 1999), Women's Health Adv. Bd., Am. Acad. Pain Mgmt., PR Soc. for Pain Mgmt., Sociedad Reumatologos PR (chmn. sci. com. 2001—02, pres. 1999—2000), Am. Coll. Rheumatology.

PANTOLIANO, JOE, actor; b. Hoboken, N.J., Sept. 12, 1951; Grad. high sch., Cliffside Park, N.J. Actor: (stage prodns.) Brothers, 1982, Orphans, 1983, One Flew Over the Cuckoo's Nest, Italian American Reconciliation, The Death Star, Visions of Kerouac, (feature films) The Godfather Part II, 1974, The Idol Maker, 1980, Monsignor, 1982, Risky Business, 1983, Eddie and the Cruisers, 1983, The Mean Season, 1985, Goonies, 1985, Running Scared, 1986, The In Crowd, 1987, The Squeeze, 1987, Scenes from the Goldmine, 1987, Amazon Women on the Moon, 1987, La Bamba, 1987, Empire of the Sun, 1987, Midnight Run, 1988, Downtown, 1990, The Last of the Finest, 1990, Short Time, 1990, Zandalee, 1991, Used People, 1992, Three of Hearts, 1993, The Fugitive, 1993, Baby's Day Out, 1994, Calendar Girl, 1994, Steal Big, Steal Little, 1995, Bad Boys, 1995, Bound, 1996, Top of the World, 1997, Self Storage, 1997, Tinseltown, 1998, The Tax Man, 1998, U.S. Marshals, 1998, The Life Before This, 1999, Black and White, 1999, Tinseltown, 1999, The Matrix, 1999, Ready to Rumble, 2000, Memento, 2000, Silver Man, 2000, Cats & Dogs (voice), 2001, The Adventures of Pluto Nash, 2002, A Piece of My Heart, 2002, Daredevil, 2003, Bad Boys II, 2003, 5-25-77, 2003; (TV movies) More Than Friends, 1978, Alcatraz: The Whole Shocking Story, 1980, Destination: America, 1987, El Diablo, 1990, One Special Victory, 1991, Through the Eyes of a Killer, 1992, (voice) Olive, the Other Reindeer, 1999, (series) Sugar Hill, 1999, (TV mini-series) From Here to Eternity, 1979, Robert Kennedy and His Times, 1985, (TV spl.) Mr. Roberts, 1984 (TV Series) Free Country, 1978, The Fanelli Boys, 1990-91, The Sopranos (Emmy award best sup. actor drama, 2003), 2001-2002, (guest) Tales From the Crypt, Amazing Stories, L.A. Law, The Hitchhiker, NYPD Blue, Arlis$, Hill Street Blues, The Hitchhiker, Highlander, The Marshal. Avocations: skiing, jogging, shopping. Office: UTA care Lisa Hellerman 9560 Wilshire Blvd Fl 5 Beverly Hills CA 90212-2401

PANTOS, WILLIAM PANTAZES, mechanical engineer, consultant; b. Ann Arbor, Mich., May 15, 1957; s. William Van and Lillian William (Skinner) P. BS in Mech. Engring., Northwestern U., 1979; MS in Mech. Engring., San Diego State U., 1991. Registered profl. engr., Calif. Owner Signs & Symbols, Niles, Ill., 1975-80; engr. Hughes Aircraft, El Segundo, Calif., 1980-83, Gen. Dynamics, San Diego, 1983-85; staff engr. TRW, San Diego, 1985-90; pres. Tekton Industries, Carlsbad, Calif., 1990—. Patentee animal lift and transport apparatus. NROTC scholar USN, 1975. Mem. ASME, NSPE, Alpha Delta Phi. (pres. 1978). Greek Orthodox. Office: 300 Enterprise St Ste F Escondido CA 92029 Office Phone: 800-835-8664. E-mail: wpantos@sbcglobal.net.

PANTUSO, MICHAEL VINCENT, graphic design company executive; b. Morgantown, W.Va., Aug. 21, 1963; s. John Anthony and Bonnie Ruth (Fisher) P.; m. Shari Ann Urso, Oct. 6, 1990; children: Elliott Anthony, Biola Bella. BA, Flagler Coll., 1986. Art dir. Mktg. Comms. Firm, Chgo., 1986-90; prin., creative dir., designer Michael Pantuso Design, Chgo., 1990—. Works exhibited at AIDS Benefit, 1994, 95, Hotel d'Angleterre, 1995. Mem. Am. Inst. Graphic Arts. Avocations: painting, art collecting, travel, interactive multimedia, writing. Home: 820 S Thurlow St Hinsdale IL 60521-4328

PANTUSO, VINCENT JOSEPH, food service consultant; b. Charleston, W.Va., Aug. 13, 1940; s. Fortunato F. Pantuso and Josephine Malcom (Ginestra) Pantuso Messer; m. Carol Barber, Dec. 10, 1964 (div. 1976); children: Lisa, Barbara, Tina; m. Nancy Josephine Chellman, Sept. 30, 1978 (div. 1995). Student, Drexel U.; BSBA, St. Joseph's U., 1968; postgrad., Rollins Coll., 1984-85. Asst. mgr. Marriott Hotels, Inc., Bethesda, Md., 1962-64; v.p. sales mktg. ARA Services, Inc., Phila., 1964-72; sr. v.p. Interstate United Corp., Chgo., 1972-84; pres. V.J. Pantuso Services, Inc., Orlando, Fla., 1984—, New Vista Services, Inc., 1988-97. Mem. Nat. Assn. Concessionaires (bd. dirs. 1982—, pres. 1989-91, chmn. 1991-94, Master Concessionaire, Chgo. 1985), Nat. Assn. Food Equipment Mfrs. (doctorate 1989). Republican. Episcopalian. Avocation: fishing. Home: Apt 5 120 Monarch Cir Casselberry FL 32730-2718

PANUSKA, JOSEPH ALLAN, retired academic administrator; b. Balt., Md., July 3, 1927; s. Joseph William and Barbara Agnes (Preller) P. BS, Loyola Coll., Balt., 1948; PhD, St. Louis U., 1958; STL, Woodstock Coll., 1961; LLD (hon.), U. Scranton, 1974; LHD (hon.), Marywood Coll., 1992; D of Health (hon.), Trnava (Slovakia) U., 1997. Joined S.J., 1948; ordained priest Roman Cath. Ch., 1960. Instr. dept. physiology Emory U. Sch. Medicine, 1962-63; asst. prof. biology Georgetown U., 1963-66, assoc. prof., 1966-72, prof., 1973; provincial, bd. dirs. Jesuit Conf. Md. Province (S.J.), 1973-79; acad. v.p., dean faculties, prof. biology Boston Coll., 1979-82; pres. U. Scranton, Pa., 1982-98, pres. emeritus, 1998—2004; rector Jesuit Ctr., 1988—2003; pres. emeritus, 2004. Mem. Pa. Commn. Ind. Colls. and Univs., 1982-98, mem. exec. com., treas., 1987-91, vice chmn., 1988-89, chmn., 1990-91; mem. Pres.'s Commn., NCAA, 1989-90. Mem. editl. bd. Cryobiology, 1968-88, editor-in-chief, 1971-74; contbr. chpts. to books, articles to sci. rsch. jours. Mem. corp. Am. Found. Biol. Rsch., 1967-85, pres. bd. dirs., 1974-79, v.p., 1979-83; trustee Loyola Coll., 1979-85, St. Joseph's U., 1979-84, U. Scranton, 1970-73, 1982-98, St. Peter's Coll., 1971-72, Woodstock Coll., 1973-76, Fordham U., 1982-88, Cambridge Ctr. for Social Studies, 1973-79 (pres. 1973-79), Corp. Roman Cath. Clergymen, 1973-79 (pres. 1973-79); rector Jesuit Cmty. at Georgetown U., 1970-73; bd. dirs. United Way Pa., 1985-87, Scranton Prep. Sch., 1984-90, Scranton Area Found., 1997-98; chmn. Pa. Commn. for Ind. Colls. and Univs., 1990-91; bd. dirs. John Carroll U., 1992-98, Nat. Inst. Environ. Renewal, 1992-98, Woodstock Theol. Ctr., Washington, 1998-2001, St. Joseph's Prep. Sch., Phila., 1998-2001, Alvernia Coll., 2001—; bd. visitors Panuska Coll. Profl. Studies, U. Scranton, 1998-. NIH postdoctoral fellow, 1962-63; recipient Danforth Found. Harbison prize for disting. tchg., 1969, B'nai B'rith Americanism award, 1997, recipient from 2001, Michelini award Outstanding Svc. to Higher Edn. AICUP (Assoc. Ind. Coll. and U. Pa.), 2001; vis. fellow St. Edmunds Coll., Cambridge U., 1969; college named J.A. Panuska Coll. of Profl. Studies, Univ. at Scranton. Mem. Am. Physiol. Soc., Soc. for Cryobiology, Soc. Exptl. Biology and Medicine, Assn. Jesuit Colls. and Univs. (bd. dirs. 1982-98, treas. 1993-96), Pa. Assn. Colls. and Univs. (exec. com., adv. com. to State Bd. Edn. 1990-91), Scranton C. of C. Home and Office: Jesuit Cmty U Scranton Scranton PA 18510-4623 E-mail: panuskaji@scranton.edu. *In order to be happy in a leadership role and to succeed in it, I have to possess a sense of coherence with my life values. I also need to recognize that my own activity makes a real difference in the empowerment of others so that there is a multiplier effect which extends me beyond my own person and activity.*

PANY, KURT JOSEPH, accounting educator, consultant; b. St. Louis, Mar. 31, 1946; s. Joseph Francis and Ruth Elizabeth (Westerman) P.; m. Darlene Dee Zabish, June 3, 1971; children: Jeffrey, Michael. BSBA, U. Ariz., 1968; MBA in Mgmt., U. Minn., 1971; PhD in Accountancy, U. Ill., 1977. CPA, Ariz., cert. fraud examiner. Staff auditor Arthur Andersen & Co., Mpls., 1968-69, Touche Ross & Co., Phoenix, 1971-73; teaching asst. U. Minn., Mpls., 1969-71; teaching asst. auditing and acctg. U. Ill., Urbana, 1972-76; asst. prof. acctg. Ariz. State U., Tempe, 1977-81, assoc. prof., 1981-85, Arthur Andersen/Don Dupont prof. acctg., 1985-91. Mem. acctg. and auditing standards com. State of Ariz., Phoenix, 1989—; reviewer Jour. Acctg. and Pub. Policy, 1983—. Contbg. author: CPA Exam. Rev., 1983—; co-author: Principles of Auditing, 1988—, Auditing, 1993—; co-editor Auditing: A Jour. Practice and Theory, 1984-88; mem. editl. bd. Advances in Acctg., 1982—, Jour. Acctg. Edn., 1983—; reviewer Acctg. Rev., 1984—, ad hoc editor, 1989—; contbr. numerous articles to profl. jours. Active various child-related orgns. Peat, Marwick, Mitchell & Co. Found. grantee, 1985. Fellow AICPA (auditing stds. divsn. 1989-90, acctg. lit. selection com. 1989-90, acctg. lit. awards com. 1979-83, mem. auditing stds. bd. 1995—); mem. Am. Acctg. Assn. (tech. program com. 1980-81, chairperson Western region auditing sect. 1981-83, acctg. lit. nominating com. 1982-84, 88-89, acctg. lit. selection com. 1989-90, dir. auditing stds., chmn. auditing stds. com. 1989-90), Ariz. Soc. CPA's (auditing stds. com. 1978-81, ethics com. 1981-84). Avocation: baseball. Address: 7411 S Rita Ln Unit 116 Tempe AZ 85283-4792 Office: Ariz State U Sch Accountancy Tempe AZ 85287

PANZER, MARK, retail executive; B, Northeastern Ill. U.; MBA in fin., Loyola U. Various positions with Osco Drug, Inc., 1972—; corp. v.p., mktg., sales and gen. merchandise Albertson's Inc., 1998—2001; exec. v.p., store ops. Rite Aid Corp., 2001—02, sr. exec. v.p., store ops., 2002—. Office: Rite Aid Corp 30 Hunter Lane Camp Hill PA 17011

PANZER, MARY CAROLINE, historian, museum curator; b. Flint, Mich., May 29, 1955; d. Milton and Caroline Alice (Weis) P. BA, Yale U.; MA, Columbia U., 1980; PhD, Boston U., 1990. Asst. prof. U. Kans., Lawrence, 1989-91; curator photographs Spencer Mus. Art, Lawrence, 1989-91; asst. dir. SMART Mus. Art U. Chgo., 1991; curator photographs Nat. Portrait Gallery Smithsonian Instn., Washington, 1992-2000; ind. historian N.Y.C., 2000—; adj. faculty Hunter Coll. (CUNY), 2003—. Author: Philadelphia Naturalistic Photography, 1982, Rudolf Eickemeyer, Jr. and the Art of the Camera, 1986, Mathew Brady and the Image of History, 1997, Halsman: A Retrospective, 1998, Brady 55, 2001, Hine 55, 2002 Separate, But Equal, 2002, Nickolas Muray and Miguel Corarrubias, 2004; contbg. editor Am. Photo, 2002. Mem. Am. Studies Assn., Coll. Art Assn., Oracle, Mid-Atlantic Radical Historians Orgn., Orgn. Am. Historians.

PANZER, MARY E. state legislator; b. Waupun, Wis., Sept. 19, 1951; d. Frank E. and Verna L. P.; 1 adopted child, Melissa. BA, U. Wis., 1974; mem., Wis. State Ho. Reps. from 53rd dist. Rep. State of Wis., Madison, 1980-93; mem. Wis. Senate from 20th dist., Madison, 1993—. Home: 635 W Tamarack Dr West Bend WI 53095-3653 Office: Wis State Senate State Capital Madison WI 53702-0001

PANZER, MITCHELL EMANUEL, lawyer; b. Phila., Aug. 2, 1917; s. Max and Cecelia P.; m. Edith Budin, Apr. 13, 1943; children: Marcy C. Pokotilow, Leslie S. Katz. AB with distinction and 1st honors, Temple U., 1937; JD magna cum laude, U. Pa., 1940; LLD honoris causa, Gratz Coll., 1972. Bar: Pa. 1942, U.S. Dist. Ct. (ea. dist.) Pa. 1948, U.S. Ct. Appeals (3d cir.) 1949, U.S. Supreme Ct. 1961. Gowen Meml. fellow U. Pa. Law Sch., 1940-41; law clk. Phila. Ct. Common Pleas, No. 7, 1941-42; assoc. Wolf, Block, Schorr and Solis-Cohen, Phila., 1946-54, ptnr., 1954-88, of counsel, 1988—; spl. adv. counsel Fed. Home Loan Mortgage Corp., Fed. Nat. Mortgage Assn., 1972-82; dir. emeritus, former counsel St. Edmond's Fed. Savs. Bank; former dir. State Chartered Group, Pa. Bldg. and Loan Assn. Treas., Jewish Fedn. Greater Phila., 1981-82, v.p., 1982-86, trustee, 1963—, mem. exec. com., 1981-86, hon. life trustee, 1992—; trustee emeritus Pa. Land Title Inst., 1992—; bd. regents Gratz Coll., 1958—, pres., 1962-68. Served to capt. USAF, 1942-46. Decorated Bronze Star medal; recipient Man of Year award Gratz Coll. Alumni Assn., 1964. Mem. Am. Coll. Real Estate Lawyers, ABA (chmn. spl. com. on residential real estate transactions 1972-73), Pa. Bar Assn. (mem. spl. com. on land titles), Phila. Bar Assn. (chmn. com. censors 1966, chmn. bd. govs. 1971, parliamentarian 1965-67, 71, chmn. charter and by-laws com. 1972), Jewish Publ. Soc. (trustee 1966-81, 85-88, v.p. 1972-75, sec. 1975-78), Order of Coif (pres. 1961-63, exec. com.). Jewish. Clubs: 21 Jewel Square (Phila.); Masons. Patentee in field. Home: 505 Oak Ter Merion Station PA 19066-1340 Office: Wolf Block Schorr & Solis-Cohen 22nd Fl Arch St Philadelphia PA 19103-2097 Personal E-mail: mepanzer@erols.com. Business E-Mail: mpanzer@wolfblock.com.

PAO, CHIA-VEN, mathematics professor; b. Ho-hsien, China, Aug. 10, 1933; s. Chuan-S. and Shyu-Xi Pao; m. Mei-Shan K. Pao; children: Gene S., Bing S., Phillip S. BS, Nat. Taiwan U., 1959; M, Kans. State U., 1962; PhD, U. Pitts., 1968. Engr. Westinghouse Ele. Co., Pitts., 1962—67; teaching asst. U. Pitts., 1967—68, rsch. assoc., 1968—69, asst., assoc. prof., 1969—79; prof. N.C. State U., Raliegh, 1979—2002, prof. emeritus, 2002—. Pres. Con-Condo Corp., Raleigh, 1984—89; chmn. Cen Korlay Ptnrship., 1986—93. Contbr. articles to profl. jours. Mem.: Fedn. Nonlinear Analysis. Avocations: music, ballroom dancing, travel, reading. Office: NC State U Dept Math Box 8205 Raleigh NC 27695

PAOLANTONIO, EDMUND JOSEPH, musician, music educator; b. Bklyn., Nov. 1, 1948; s. Edward Joseph and Rose Helen Paolantonio; m. Laura Lee Lohman, Nov. 17, 1974; children: Edward Joseph, Andrew Stephen, Matthew James, Rita Helen. BS in Music Edn., SUNY, Potsdam, 1970; studied piano with, Lenny Tristano, 1971—74, Marty Holmes, 1979; MusM in Performance, U. NC, 1985. Artist in residence Piedmont Tech. Coll., Roxboro, NC, 1980—81, Wake Tech. Coll., Raleigh, NC, 1981—83; adj. instr. jazz program U. NC, Chapel Hill, 1985—89, instr. keyboard lab., 1986, instr. jazz history evening coll., 1986, vis. lectr. jazz history, 1989; leader, arranger String of Pearls, Durham, NC, 1985—90, Ed Paolantonio Trio, Durham, 1985—; instr. jazz piano Duke U., Durham, NC, 2002—. Adj. instr. jazz program Elon

Coll., Burlington, NC, 1988—90; vis. lectr. NC State U., Raleigh, 1993—94, Raleigh, 1995—96, U. NC, 1995—97, 2001, 2002—; adj. instr. NC Ctrl. U., Durham, 2002—; pianist NC Jazz Repertory Orch.; accompanist for numerous jazz artists, including Carol Sloan, Sonny Dallas Quartet, 1972—. Author: My Years with Lennie Tristano, 2001; musician: (CD) A New Level, 1990, I Believe in Little Things, 1992, In t5he Stream, 1992, Dedications, 1994, All Benny Goodman, 1998, All Duke Ellington, 1998, Dad's Blues, 1998, Defining Moments, 2001, Airmail Special, 2001, ednl. CD for Jazz Piano mag. Recipient NC Touring Program award, NC Arts Coun., 1988—89; Emerging Artist grantee, Durham Arts Coun., 1991, Jazz Composer fellow, NC Arts Coun., 1993, 1997. Mem.: Durham Music Tchrs. Assn., Music Tchrs. Nat. Assn., Internat. Assn. Jazz Educators. Republican. Roman Catholic. Avocations: reading, bicycling, hiking, camping, model trains. Home and Office: 808 Whitby Ct Durham NC 27703

PAOLILLO, REGINA M. information technology consulting executive; b. 1959; Dir. ops. GartnerGroup, 1993; sr. v.p., contr. GartnerMeasurement, 1995-97, pres., CEO, 1997-99; CEO, exec. v.p. fin., adminstrn. Gartner Inc. (previously Gartner Group Inc.), Stamford, Conn., 1999—. Office: PO Box 10212 55 Top Gallant Rd Stamford CT 06904-2212 Fax: 203-316-1100. E-mail: help@garnter.com.

PAOLINI, CLAIRE JACQUELINE, dean, educator; b. Newton, Mass., May 19, 1934; d. Frank and Angelina Landro; m. Gilberto Paolini, June 18, 1960; children: Angela J., John F. BA, Boston U., 1956; MA, Middlebury (Vt.) Coll., 1958; PhD, Tulane U., 1982. Instr. Spanish U. Mass., Amherst, 1956-60, U. New Orleans, 1970-75; from dir. internat. student affairs to assoc. dean Loyola U., New Orleans, 1975-83, assoc. dean arts and scis., 1983-97; dean coll. arts and scis., prof. spanish Sacred Heart U., Fairfield, Conn., 1997—. Author: The Narrative Art of Domingos Monteiro, 1979, Valle-Inclán's Modernism: Use and Abuse of Religious and Mystical Symbolism, 1986; editor: LA CHISPA '95: Selected Proceedings, 1995, LA CHISPA '97: Selected Proceedings, 1997; co-editor: La CHISPA '99: Selected Proceedings, 1999; assoc. editor: LA CHISPA '93: Selected Proceedings, 1993; mem. editl. bd. LA CHISPA, 1983, 85, 87, 89, NACADA Jour., 1995-97. V.p. Soc. Espanola, New Orleans, 1977-81, bd. mem. 1976-97. Mem. Nat. Assn. Academic Affairs Administrators (Administrator of Yr. award 1996-97), Modern Lang. Assn., Council Colls. Arts Scis., Am. Assn. Tchrs. Spanish and Portuguese, Coll. Consortium Internat. Studies (bd. mem. 1997—), Am. Assn. Higher Edn. Home: 3 Gregory Farm Rd Easton CT 06612-2049 Office: Sacred Heart Univ 5151 Park Ave Fairfield CT 06825-1000

PAOLINI, GILBERTO, literature and science educator; b. L'Aquila, Italy; naturalized citizen, 1954; s. John and Assunta Angela (Turavani) P.; m. Claire Jacqueline Landro; children: Angela Janet, John Frank. BA, U. Buffalo, 1957, MA, 1959; postgrad., Middlebury Coll., summer 1960, 61; PhD, U. Minn., 1965. Lectr. Spanish Rosary Hill Coll., Buffalo, 1957-58; instr. Italian and Latin lit. U. Mass., Amherst, 1958-60; instr. Spanish and Italian Syracuse U., 1962-65, asst. prof., 1965-67; assoc. prof. Spanish lit. Tulane U., New Orleans, 1967-76, prof., 1976—, dir. Tulane scholars and honors program, 1981-83, chmn. colloquia dept., 1981-83. Originator Spanish Culture Week, New Orleans, 1977, 79; chmn. adv. com. Jambalaya program Nat. Endowment Humanities, New Orleans, 1975-80; Spanish essay reader Ednl. Testing Svc., Princeton, 1979-85; founder, gen. chmn. La. Conf. on Hispanic Langs. and Lits., 1981, 83, 85, 87, 89, 93, 95, 97, 99. Author: Bartolome Soler: novelista: Procedimientos estilísticos, 1963; An Aspect of Spiritualistic Naturalism in the Novel of B.P. Galdos: Charity, 1969, La Vita Transecolare nel Contado Aquilano, 2003; mem. editl. bd.: Forum Italicum, 1967-71, Critica Hispanica, 1979—, Discurso Literario, 1985—, Letras Peninsulares, 1987—, Ojáncano, 1994—; assoc. editor: South Central MLA Bull, 1978-80; editor: La Chispa: Selected Procs., 1981-99, Papers on Romance Literary Relations, 1983; cons. editor South Central Rec., 1988-99; contbr. articles to profl. jours. With AUS, 1952-54, USAFRES, 1954-57. Recipient Disting. Service award Sociedad Espanola, 1979, Knight Cross of Order of Isabel the Catholic, 1984; subject of Festscrift Studies, Honor of Gilberto Paolini, 1996. Mem. MLA, AAUP, Am. Assn. Tchrs. Spanish and Portuguese (chmn. pub. rels. com. 1981-86, pres. La. chpt. 1979-81, 88-89), Am. Assn. Tchrs. Italian, Am. Assn. Advancement Humanities, Soc. for Lit. and Sci., Asociacion Internacional de Hispanistas, Southeastern Am. Soc. 18th Century Studies (exec. v.p.), Assn. Internat. Galdosistas, Soc. Literatura Española del Siglo XIX, Phi Sigma Iota, Sigma Delta Pi (v.p. for S.W. 1989-92). Office: Tulane Univ 304 Newcomb Hall New Orleans LA 70118 E-mail: gpaolini@tulane.edu.

PAOLINO, RONALD MARIO, clinical psychologist, consultant, psychopharmacologist, pharmacist; b. Providence, Mar. 15, 1938; s. Lawrence and Mary Corinne (Guglielmi) P.; m. Eileen Frances Quimby, June 18, 1960; children: Lisa Katherine, David Lawrence. Student, Providence Coll., 1955-56; BS in Pharmacy, U. R.I., 1959, MS, 1961; PhD in Pharmacology/Toxicology, Purdue U., 1963; postdoctoral studies Exptl. Psychology, Yale U., 1963-65; doctoral studies in clin. psychology, Purdue U., 1972-74; postdoctoral studies in existential analytic psychotherapy, Okla. Inst. Existential Analysis and Psychotherapy, 1974-75; Hostage Negotiation, FBI, 1991, Advanced Hostage Negotiation, 1995; Crisis Negotiation, FBI Acad., 1994; MA (hon.), Brown U., 1977. Lic. psychologist, R.I., pharmacist R.I.; nat. registered health svc. provider in psychology; cert. arbitrator; cert. nat. registered group psycho-therapists; cert. edn. provider N.Y.; diplomate Am. Bd. Forensic Examiners, Am. Bd. Forensic Medicine. Intern dept. psychiatry and behavioral scis. U. Okla. Health Scis. Ctr., 1974-75; David Ross predoctoral fellow dept. pharmacology/toxicology Purdue U., 1961-63; NIMH postdoctoral fellow in psychology dept. psychology Yale U., 1963-65; asst. prof. pharmacology U. Conn. Sch. Pharmacy, 1965-67; assoc. prof. psychopharmacology Purdue U., 1967-74; NIMH fellow in clin. psychology U. Okla. Health Scis. Ctr., 1974-75; coord. group psychotherapy tng. program Brown U. Program in Medicine, 1983-85, assoc. prof. psychiatry and human behavior, 1976-90; pvt. practice; chief drug dependency treatment program VA Med. Ctr., Providence, 1975-87, dir. biofeedback clinic, 1977-87, primary hostage negotiator, 1991—. Psychiatric cons. VA Police, alternative Dispute Resolution Mediator, New Eng. Veterans Integrated Svc. Network, 1996—, pain mgmt. bd., 1999—; mem. Pharmacology and Therapeutic Agts. Com., 1979-87, VA Med. Ctr., coord. VA Contracted Half-Way Project for Substance Dependent Vets., 1981-85, chmn. Pain Mgmt. Task Force, 1981-85, mem. Supervisory Level Pharmacy Profl. Standards Bd., 1990—, mem. Mgmt. Suicidal and Violent Patient Task Force, 1990-91, chmn. Com. Prevention & Mgmt. of Disturbed Behaviors, 1991—, chief crisis mgmt. program, 1993-96, advisor FBI Hostage Negotiations, 1991—, Instr. R.I. State Police Acad., 1994, Instr., Drug Recognition Experts Recert PRGM, R.I. Dept Health, 1995, Faculty, Law Enforcement Mgmt. Command Sch. U.R.I., 1991—, Va. Nat. Law Enforcement Tng. Ctr., 1997; chmn. Outpatient Psychiatry Svcs. Reorganization Task Force, 1991, mem. VA DOD Desert Storm Emergency Plan Com., 1991; advisor OSHA Dept. Labor for Violence in the Work Place, 1994-95; mem. E. Prov. Clergy & Mental Health Providers Alliance, 1995—; mem. substance abuse and prevention grant application rev. com. R.I. Adv. Coun. on Substance Abuse, 1982-92, prevention, edn. and tng. com. on substance abuse, 1981—, chmn. 1981-82; adj. assoc. prof. psychology, U. R.I., 1982—, clin. assoc. prof. pharmacy U. R.I., 1998—; mem. planning com. State Conf. on Substance Abuse in the Hispanic Community, 1986; mem. alcohol awareness commn. Episc. Diocese of R.I., 1983-85; gubernatorial appointee Gov.'s Permanent Coun. on Drug Abuse Control, 1978-82; mem. rev. com. for funding of state drug abuse programs R.I. Single State Agy. on Drug Abuse, R.I. Dept. Mental Health Retardation and Hosps., 1978-82; cons. Nurses Renewal Com., 1980-81, substance abuse prevention edn. for elem. sch. children R.I. chpt. ARC, 1977, mem. suicide prevention steering com., 1977; mem.Interagy. Drug Abuse Steering Com., Lafayette, Ind. 1969-72; bd. dirs. Providence VA Med. Ctr. Credit Union; mem. bd. cert. for alcoholism counselors R.I. Assn. Alcohol Counselors, 1979-81; mem. Gov.'s Task Force on Substance Abuse at Adult Correctional Instn., 1977-78, Gov.'s Task Force on Mental Health Svcs. at Adult Correctional Instn., 1977-78, chmn. reclassification of inmates com., 1977-78; chmn. com. on edn. and cert. biofeedback practioners Conn. Biofeedback Soc., 1977-78; summer faculty fellow U. Conn., 1967; vis. scientist lectr. Assn. Am. Colls. Pharmacy, 1972-73; cons. to bus., unions, law enforcement. Author: (2 chpts.) Drug Testing: Issues and Options, 1991; contbr. 37 articles to profl. jours. Bd. dirs. R.I. chpt. Samaritans Internat. Suicide Prevention Orgn., 1978-84; v.p. Experience Jesus Inc.; mem. com. adv. bd. Cpina Bifida Assn. R.I., 1980-83; mem. R.I. East Bay Interfaith Mental Health Alliance; congressman appointee (Patrick J. Kennedy); mem. veterans adv. commn., 1995—. Recipient Citation award for svc. and contbns. to formulation of state policy for treatment and prevention of drug abuse Gov. R.I., 1983, Letter of Commendation, Gov.'s R.I. Adv. Coun. on Substance Abuse, 1986, vc. Recognition award DAV, 1990, Spl. Contbn. award Providence VA Med Ctr., 1990, 98, 99, 2000, Outstanding Performance award, 1991, 92, 93, 94, 97, cert. appreciation for continued excellence in patient care, 1999; named to Cranston Hall of Fame, 2001. Fellow Am. Coll. Forensic Examiners; mem. AMA, Am. Psychotherapy Assn., Am. Soc. Pharmacology Exptl. Therapeutics, Internat. Brain Rsch. Orgn., Internat. Narcotic Enforcement Officers Assn., R.I. Group Psychotherapy Soc. (pres. 1991-93, continuing edn. dir. psychologists 1990-95, exec. bd. 1986—, tng. faculty 1985—, co-dir. tng. 1986-87, tng. adv. bd. 1985-86), R.I. Psychol. Assn. (chmn. substance abuse ins. subcom. 1986-87, rep. Gov.'s Coun. on Mental Health State Plan Com. 1982-84), Hostage Negotiators Am. Office: PO Box 159 Barrington RI 02806-0159 E-mail: rmpne50@aol.com.

PAOLUCCI, ANNE ATTURA, playwright, poet, English and comparative literature educator, educational consultant; b. Rome; d. Joseph and Lucy (Guidoni) Attura; m. Henry Paolucci(dec.). BA, Barnard Coll; MA, Columbia U., PhD, 1963; hon. degree, Lehman Coll., CUNY, 1995. Mem. faculty English dept. Brearley Sch., NYC, 1957-59; asst. prof. English and comparative lit. CCNY, 1959-69; univ. rsch. prof. St. John's U., Jamaica, NY, 1969-75, prof. English, 1975-77, acting head dept. English, 1973-74, chmn. dept. English, 1982-91, dir. doctor of arts degree program in English, 1982-97; ednl. cons.; editl. cons. Bagehot Coun. Fulbright lectr. in Am. drama U. Naples, Italy, 1965-67; spl. lectr. U. Urbino, summers 1966-67, U. Bari, 1967, univs. Bologna, Catania, Messina, Palermo, Milan, Pisa, 1965-67; disting. adj. vis. prof. Queens Coll., CUNY; bd. dir. World Centre for Shakespeare Studies, 1972—; spl. guest Yugoslavia Ministry of Culture, 1972; rep. US at Internat. Poetry Festival, Yugoslavia, 1981; founder, exec. dir. Council on Nat. Lits., 1974—; mem. exec. com. Conf. Editors Learned Jour.-MLA, 1975—85; del. to Fgn. Lang. Jours., 1977—85; mem. adv. bd. Commn. on Tech. and Cultural Transformation, UNESCO, 1978—80; vis. fellow Humanities Rsch. Centre, Australian Nat. U., 1979; rep. US woman playwright Inter-Am. Women Writers Congress, Ottawa, Ont., Can., 1978; organizer, chmn. profl. symposia, meetings; TV appearances; hostess Mag. in Focus, Channel 31, NYC, 1971-72; mem. N.Am. Adv. Council Shakespeare Globe Theatre Ctr., 1981—; mem. Nat. Grad. Fellows Program Fellowship Bd., 1985—87; mem. Nat. Garibaldi Centennial Com., 1981; trustee Edn. Scholarship, Grants Com. of NIAF, 1990-94; guest speaker with E. Albee Ohio No. State U., 1990; Appointed by Pres. Reagan to Nat. Council on the Humanities, 1986-1993; One of the 10 top Women in Bus. in Queens, 2003. Author (with H. Paolucci) books, including: Hegel On Tragedy, 1962, new edition, 2001, From Tension to Tonic: The Plays of Edward Albee, 1972, new edit., 2000, Pirandello's Theater: The Recovery of the Modern Stage for Dramatic Art, 1974, 2d edit. 2002, Henry Paolucci: Selected Writings on Literature and the Arts; Sci. and Astronomy; Law, Govt., and Pol. Sci., 1999, Dante's Gallery of Rogues, 2001, Do Me a Favor (and other short stories), 2001 (nominated for the Pulitzer Prize), Poems Written for Sbek's Mummies, Marie Menken, and Other Important Persons, Places, and Things, 1977, Eight Short Stories, 1977, Sepia Tones, 1985, 2nd edit., 1986, In Wolf's Clothing, 2004; plays include: Minions of the Race (Medieval and Renaissance Conf. of Western Mich. U. Drama award 1972), video version, 2002, Cipango!, 1985, pub. as book, 1985, 86, videotape excerpts, 1986, revision, 1990; performed NYC and Washington, 1987-88, Winterthur Mus., U. Del., 1990; The Actor in Search of His Mask, 1987, Italian translation and prodn., Genoa, 1987, The Short Season, Naples, 1967, Cubiculo, NY, 1973, German translation, Vienna, 1996, mini-prodn. of Minions of the Race, The Players, 1999, video prodn. 2002, In the Green Room (play), 1999, Three Short Plays, 1995; poems Riding the Mast Where It Swings, 1980, In the Green Room (orig. play), 1999; Gorbachev in Concert, 1991, Queensboro Bridge (and other Poems), 1995 (Pulitzer prize nominee 1995-96), Terminal Degrees, 1997; contbr. numerous articles, rev. to profl. jour.; editor, author intro. to: Dante's Influence on Am. Writers, 1977; gen. editor tape-cassette series China, 1977, 78; founder Coun. on Nat. Lit.; gen. editor series Rev. Nat. Lit., 1970-2000, CNL/Quar. World Report, 1974-76, semi-ann., 1977-84, ann., 1985-2000; full-length TV tape of play Cipango! for pub. TV and ednl. TV with original music by Henry Paolucci, 1990; featured in PBS psl. Italian-Americans II: A Beautiful Song, 1998; translations of Selected Poems by Giacomo Leopardi (with Thomas Bergin), 2004. Pres. Reagan appointee Nat. Grad. Fellows Program Fellowship Bd., 1985—86, Nat. Coun. Humanities, 1986—, Ann. award FIERI, 1990; bd. dirs. Am. Soc. Italian Legions of Merit, chmn. cultural com., 1990—; bd. dirs. Italian Heritage and Culture City-wide com., 1986—; pres. Columbus: Countdown 1992 Fedn.; mem. Gov. Cuomo's Heritage Legacy Project for Schs., 1989—; trustee CUNY, 1996—, chairwoman bd. trustees, 1997—99; mem. adv. com. on edn. N.Y. State Senate, 1996—. Decorated cavaliere Italian Republic, commendatore Order of Merit (Italy); named one of 10 Outstanding Italian Ams. in Washington, awarded medal by Amb. Rinaldo Petrignani, 1986; recipient Notable Rating for Mags. in Focus series N.Y. Times, 1972, Woman of Yr. award Dr. Herman Henry Scholarship Found., 1973, Amita award, 1970, award Women's Press Club N.Y., 1974, Gold medal for Quincentenary Can. trustee NIAF, 1990, ann. awards Consortium of Italian-Am. Assns., 1991, Am.-Italian Hist. Assn., 1991, 1st Columbus award Cath. Charities, 1991, Leone di San Marco award Italian Heritage Coun. of Bronx and Westchester Counties, 1992, Children of Columbus award Order of Sons of Italy in Am., 1993, 1st Nat. Elena Cornaro award Order of Sons of Italy, 1993, Golden Lion award, 1997, Can.'s Gold medal Christopher Columbus Can. Commn., 1992, Ann. award Am. Italian Cultural Roundtable, 1997, Am. Italian Tchrs. Lifetime Achievement award, 1997, Italian-Am. Legislator's award, Albany, 1997, N.Y. State Italian-Am. Legis. Lifetime Achievement award, 1997, Columbus Citizens Fedn. Ann. award, 1997, Italian Welfare League award, 1998, Queens Coun. on Arts award, 1998, N.Y. State Conservative Party Bronx com. award, 1998, Woman of Distinction award Kingsborough C.C./CUNY, 1999; named one of "Ten Top Queens Women in Bus., 2003; Columbia U. Woodbridge hon. fellow, 1961-62; Am. Coun. Learned Socs. grantee Internat. Pirandello Congress, Agrigento, Italy, 1978; recipient Woman of Distinction award N.Y. State Senate, 2000. Mem. Internat. Shakespeare Assn., Shakespeare Assn. Am., Renaissance Soc. Am., Internat. Comparative Lit. Assn., Am. Comparative Lit. Assn., MLA, Am. PEN, Hegel Soc. Am., Dante Soc. Am. (v.p. 1976-77), Am. Found. Italian Arts and Letters (founder, pres.), Pirandello Soc. (pres. 1978-85), Am. Soc. Italian Legions of Merit (bd. dir. 1990-93). Achievements include pioneering work in multi-comparative literary studies. *My own first practical premise has been to organize every task (even routine chores) so that there is always time and energy for whatever important projects come up. There is enough room in the day for doing a number of things— and for creating "space" every so often to do one's own special work (writing fiction or poetry or plays, in my case). Organization is all-important; but perhaps the basic premise in intellectual things is organic growth, letting "in" those things that are meaningful because they already suggest an intrinsic pattern. In my case, I discovered long after the projects and books themselves had taken shape and had been published, that I had been tending for a number of years more and more exclusively toward drama and dramatic criticism and theory. Well, that, obviously, was my own potential "law" organizing from within my various interests. One must continue to allow for new interests to revitalize those already familiar.*

PAOLUCCI, MASSIMO, application developer, researcher; b. Milan, Italy, Mar. 18, 1963; s. Nello Paolucci and Liliana Pinelli; m. Ulrike Habel, Oct. 4, 1997; 1 child, Anja Habel. Laurea, U.Milan, Italy; MS in Computational Linguistics, Carnegie Mellon U., Pitts., 1993; MS in Intelligent Systems, U. Pitts., 1999. Rsch. programmer U. Milan, 1990—91, U. Pitts., 1993—95; sr. rsch. programmer Carnegie Mellon U., 1999—2003, prin. rsch. programmer, 2003—.

PAONE, PETER, artist; b. Phila., Oct. 2, 1936; s. George and Angelina (Vitrella) P.; m. Alma Alabilikian, 1976. BA, Phila. Mus. Coll. Art, 1958. Head graphics dept. Fleisher Art Meml., 1959—62; instr. Positano Art Sch., Italy, 1961; tchr. Pa. Acad. Fine Arts, 1978—, chmn. graphics dept., 1978; instr. Phila. Mus. Coll. Art, Pratt Inst. One-man shows include Grippi Gallery, 1959—61, Phila. Print Club, 1961—64, Ft. Worth Mus., 1963, Clydie Jessop Gallery, London, 1968, David Gallery, Houston, 1970—72, Kennedy Gallery, NYC, 1970—72, Robinson Gallery, Houston, 1978—79, Hooks Epstein Gallery, 1978, 1980—83, Pa. Acad. Fine Arts, 1983, Phila. Print Club, 1983, Hooks Epstein Gallery, 1985, 1987—88, 1990, Rider Coll., NJ, 1991, one-woman shows include Ryder Coll., Pa., 1991, one-man shows include Merlin Verlag, Hamburg, Germany, 1996, Dresden, Germany, 1996, Pascal Robinson Gallery, Houston, 2000, exhibited in group shows at Poets, Phila. Mus. Art, 1960—61, Contemporary Am., 1961, Lehigh U., Pa., 1962, Bklyn. Mus., 1962, Poets, Phila. Mus. Art, 1963, Paris Biennial, 1963, Dallas Mus., 1964, Otis Art Inst., LA, 1964, Syracuse U., NY, 1964, La Escuela Nacional, Mexico City, 1967, Vanderbilt U., 1967, NY World's Fair Exhbn., Pakistan, 1967, 176 Anniv. Nat. Acad. Design, NYC, 2001, Poets, Nat. Acad. of Design Mus., 2003, Jersey City Mus., 2004, James A. Michener Mus., Doylestown, Pa., 2004, Represented in permanent collections Libr. Congress, Washington, DC, Phila. Mus. Art, NY Mus. Modern Art, Princeton Libr., Phila. Libr., Gen. Mills, Phila. Print Club, Rosenwald Collection, Carl Sandburg Meml. Libr., Syracuse U., Ft. Worth Mus., Victoria and Albert Mus., Brit. Mus., Art Inst. Chgo., Yale U. Recipient award of merit Phila. Print Club, 1983, Painting prize Nat. Acad., 1997; Tiffany Found. grantee, 1962, 64; John Simon Guggenheim fellow, 1965-66; grantee Penn Council for the Arts, 1985. Mem. NAD (assoc.) Home: 1027 W Westview St Philadelphia PA 19119-3718 Personal E-mail: ppaone@aol.com. *Somewhere between the world of realism and surrealism, there is a world that deals with the reality of relationships, favoring the substance of the imagination rather than the substance of everyday vision. Objects that seemingly have no real relationship to each other in their existence are juxtaposed in the life of the artist. They have touched each other and have become part of the vision, and in turn have become his iconography. There is no urgency in this vision. The private reality has always been there and always will be. The viewer is allowed to question his knowledge of it, and in doing so, he often is uneasy and bewildered before the assemblage. This, at first, implies fantasy; this is not true. Instead, this is a reconstruction of reality, not an escape from it.*

PAPA, MICHAEL JOSEPH, real estate broker; b. Bklyn., Sept. 29, 1948; s. Joseph and Lena Helen (Bellofatto) P.; m. Lana Susan Turner, Oct. 30, 1967 (div. Dec. 1969); 1 child, Dawn Michelle; m. Barbara Moehringer-Papa, May 17, 1992 (div. Dec. 1997). Lic. Real Estate Broker, Fla. Real Estate Careers, Orlando, 1992; Lic. Mortgage Broker, Kambuck Inst., Inc., Orlando, 1994, Series 6, 63 securities lic. Calif., 2001, lic. life ins. broker Calif., 2001; notary Calif. Pres. Universal Trading Co., Huntington, N.Y., 1969-70; v.p. Interspec Trading, Inc., Lake Grove, N.Y., 1970-72; pres. Quality World Ctrs., Inc., Deer Park, N.Y., 1973-83, Jewels By Shalet, Inc., Deer Park, 1983-87; v.p. Quality Treasures, Inc., Patchogue, N.Y., 1980-81; pres. Select Acquisitions, Inc., Denver, 1987-91, Watches "R" Us, Inc., Smithtown, N.Y., 1988-91, Time for You, Inc., Smithtown, 1989-91, Progressive Realty Am., Inc., Cocoa, Fla., 1993—; owner Success Foundation.com., 1998—, Realty Executives Specialists, Sacramento, 2000—; pres., chmn. Nat. Holdings, Inc., 2001—. Pres. Investors Home Realty, Inc., Cocoa, All Svc. Mortgage of Am., Universal Satellite, Success Found., 1998—; real estate and mortgage broker, owner realty-execs. specialists, Sacramento, 2000. Author: "Good Communication" A Lost Art, 1998; website founder realtyforclosure.com, 2003, info-website.com, 2003, (poetry) Words of Love, The Colors of Life publ., 2003, The Colours of the Heart internat. publ., 2004, (CD) The Sound of Poetry, 2004. Cert. Housing and Urban Devel., Brevard County, Fla., 1994-95. Mem. Rosicrusian Order (guard 1980-89). Avocations: holography, lighting effects, weapons, coins and stamps, 1st degree black belt/moo do kwan tang soo do-tai kwan do. Home and Office: 5740 Audrey Way Fair Oaks CA 95628-3004 Office Phone: 916-966-1230. E-mail: michaelpapa@realtyexecutives.com., michaelpapa@hotmail.com.

PAPA, VINCENT T. insurance company executive; b. N.Y.C., Dec. 11, 1946; s. Frank R. and Carmela (Farruggia) P.; m. Karen Ann Conroy, July 4, 1969; children: Kimberly, Jennifer, Kristen. AA, Nassau C.C., 1967; BBA, Hofstra U., 1969. CPA, N.Y. Staff acct. Arthur Andersen & Co., N.Y.C., 1969-72; comptr. Finserv Corp., N.Y.C., 1972-80; sr. v.p. Orion Capital Corp., N.Y.C., 1980-99; chmn. bd. dirs. Wm. H. McGee & Co. Inc., N.Y.C., 1995-99; CEO NYMAGIC Inc., 1999. Mem. AICPAs, Am. Mgmt. Assn. (mem. ins. and risk mgmt. coun.), N.Y. State Soc. CPAs.

PAPACHRISTOU, PATRICIA TOWNE, economics professor; b. Hartford, Conn., Oct. 16, 1946; d. George Robert and Lois Katherine (Stretch) Towne; m. Gerald Christopher Papachristou, Aug. 23, 1969; children: Mark Andrew, Angela Marie. BA in Polit. Sci. cum laude, Trinity Coll., Washington, 1968; MA in Polit. Sci., Duke U., 1970; MA in Economics, Memphis State, 1975, MBA, 1979; post grad., U. Miss., 1979—. Chair social studies dept. Immaculate Conception H.S., Memphis, 1971—78; instr. Christian Bros. U., 1980—84, asst. prof. economics, 1984—87, assoc. prof. economics, 1988—95, prof. economics, 1995—. Intern Kaiser-Permanente Health Svcs. Rsch. Ctr., Portland, Oreg., 1984. Contbr. articles to profl. jours. Non-svc. fellow, U. Miss., 1978—80, Jane Cassels Record scholar, Kaiser Health Rsch. Ctr., 1983. Mem.: Mo. Valley Econ. Assn., MidSouth Economists, Atlantic Econ. Soc., Am. Econ. Assn., Pi Gamma Mu, Omicron Delta Epsilon, Delta Sigma Pi. Roman Catholic. Avocations: bridge, camping. Home: 2858 Shelley Cv Memphis TN 38115-1814 Office Phone: 901-321-3301. E-mail: ppapachr@cbu.edu.

PAPADAKIS, CONSTANTINE N. university executive; b. Athens, Greece, Feb. 2, 1946; came to U.S., 1969; s. Nicholas and Rita (Masciotti) P.; m. Eliana Apostolides, Aug. 28, 1971; 1 child, Maria. Diploma in Civil Engring., Nat. Tech. U. Athens, 1969; MS in Civil Engring., U. Cin., 1970; PhD in Civil Engring., U. Mich., 1973. Registered profl. engr., Ohio, Greece. Engring. specialist, geotechnical group Bechtel, Inc., Gaithersburg, Md., 1974-76, supr. and asst. chief engr. geotechnical group Ann Arbor, Mich., 1976-81; v.p., bd. dirs. water resources div. STS Cons. Ltd., Ann Arbor, 1981-84; v.p. water and environ. resources dept. Tetra Tech-Honeywell, Pasadena, Calif., 1984; head dept. civil engring. Colo. State U., Ft. Collins, 1984-86; dean Coll. Engring. U. Cin., 1986-95, dir. Groundwater Rsch. Ctr., 1986-95; dir. Ctr. Hill Solid and Hazardous Waste Rsch. Ctr. EPA, Cin., 1986-93; pres. Drexel U., Phila., 1995—. Adj. prof. civil engring. U. Mich., 1976-83; cons. Gaines & Stern Co., Cleve., 1983-84, Honeywell Europe, Maintal, Fed. Republic of Germany, 1984-85, Arthur D. Little, Boston, 1984-85, Camargo Assocs., Ltd., Cin., 1986, King Fahd U. Rsch. Inst., Dhahran, Saudi Arabia, 1987, King Abdulaziz City for Sci. and Tech., Riyadh, Saudi Arabia, 1991, Henderson & Bodwell Cons. Engrs. Inc., 1991, Cin. Met. Sewer Dist., 1992, Ohio River Valley Water Sanitation Commn., 1994; acting pres. Ohio Aerospace Inst., 1988-90; interim pres. Inst. Advanced Mfg. Scis. Ohio Edison Tech. Ctr., 1989-90; bd. govs. Edison Materials Tech. Ctr., 1988-95; adv. bd., founding mem. Hamilton County Bus. Incubator, 1988-95; bd. dirs. Nat. Commn. for Coop. Edn., U. City Sci. Ctr., Ben Franklin Tech. Ctr., WHYY Inc., Fidelity Fed. Bank, Opera Co. of Phila., Corcell, Inc., Greater Phila. First, Hellenic Coll./Holy Cross Acad. Author: Problems on Strength of Materials, 1968, Sewer Systems Design, 1969; editor: Fluid Transients and Acoustics, 1978, Pump-Turbine Schemes, 1979, Small Hydro Power Fluid Machinery, 1982; Megatrends in Hydraulics, 1987; contbr. more than 65 articles to profl. jours. Mem. Greater Cin. C. of C. Blue Chip Campaign for Econ. Devel. Task Force, 1988-93, bd. dirs. Bus. Assistance Ctr., 1989-95; mem. Ohio Coun. on Rsch. and Econ. Devel., 1988, Ohio Sci. and Tech. Commn. Adv. Group, 1989-90, 92-95; coun. mem. St. Nicholas Ch. Parish, Ann Arbor, 1981-84; mem. City of Ft. Collins Drainage Bd., 1984-86; bd. dirs. Dan Beard coun. Boy Scouts Am., 1995, Intelligent Vehicle Hwy. Soc. Ohio, 1994-95; bd. dirs. Liberty Bell Coun. of the Boy Scouts of Am., 1996—. Recipient Horace W. King scholarship civil engring. dept. U. Mich., 1971-73, 6 Bechtel Merit awards, 1974-79, Young Engr. of Yr. award Mich. Soc. Profl. Engrs., Ann Arbor, Mich., 1982, Disting. Engr. award Engrs. and Scientists Cin. Tech. Socs. Coun., 1989, Acad. of Achievement in Edn. award Am. Hellenic Ednl. Progressive Assn., 1995, Hellenic Univ. Club of Phila. Achievement award, 1996, Krikos Disting. Hellene Leader award, 1996. Fellow ASCE (pres. Ann Arbor br. 1980-81, pres.-elect Mich. sect. 1983-84, hydraulics divsn. publ. com. 1980-83), ASME (chmn. fluid transients com. 1978-80, mem. fluids engring. divsn. awards com.

1981-84), Am. Soc. Engring. Edn.; mem. NSPE (legis. and govt. affairs com. 1994-95, chair profl. engrs. in edn. divsn. 1995), Order of the Engr., Internat. Assn. for Hydraulic Rsch., Ohio Engring. Dean's Coun. (chmn.-elect 1989-91), Rotary, Sigma Xi, Chi Epsilon, Tau Beta Pi. Greek Orthodox. Avocations: photography, classical music, travel, swimming, racquetball. Home: 75 Crestline Rd Wayne PA 19087-2611 Office: Drexel Univ Main Building 310 3141 Chestnut St Philadelphia PA 19104-2875

PAPADAKIS, PANAGIOTIS AGAMEMNON, financier, international business executive; b. Athens, Greece, Mar. 29, 1935; s. Agamemnon Ioannou and Anna Karyatis (Kyriakopoulou) P.; m. Alexandra Argyropoulou, July 12, 1959. Student, U. Athens, 1953-57. Registered rep., Del., Athens, Greece, Zurich, Switzerland, Chgo., NY, DC, 50 other countries. Pub., owner newspaper Peristeri, Athens, 1953-64; owner, gen. dir. printing house, advt. office, ins. agy., Athens, 1953-64; leader Nat. Radical Party Youth, Athens, 1958-59; founder, gen. dir. Servis Advt., Athens, 1963-78, Book-Servis, Athens, 1974-78; pres. Investments Promotions and Assocs. of Chgo., Athens, 1979-85; chmn. Internat. Investments World Co. Inc., Athens and Zurich, 1985—, Internat. Bus. Co. Inc., Internat. Comml. Co. Inc., Athens and Zurich, 1985—, Papadakis Internat. Fin. Co. Inc., Guarantor Co. Inc., Athens and Zurich, 1992—, Internat. Banker Fin. Co. Inc., Athens and Zurich, 1992—. Chmn. Internat. Pap Financing and Investment Group, Vaduz Liechtenstein and US, Konekt Financing Investment Group AG, Griscaviation AG; chmn., pres. 30 companies in several countries. Author, editor: Historical Biography of President Karamanlis, 1974-77; author: Why the Revolution of 21 April 1967 Happened, 1968; author numerous articles in Recently Humanity '93, Human Rights. Mem. Democracy Party, Christian Orthodox Ch. Mem. Internat. C. of C., Assn. Bus. Leaders Inc., London Diplomatic Acad., Comml. and Indsl. Chamber Athens, Greece. Mem. New Democracy Party. Christian Orthodox. Office: Internat Invest World Co Inc PO Box 140 88 115 10 Athens Greece also: Bahnhofstrasse 52 8001 Zurich Switzerland also: 24 Pontou St Ilisia 115 28 Athens Greece Office Phone: (30210) 77 95 444. E-mail: papadaki@hol.gr.

PAPADAKOS, NICHOLAS PETER, retired state supreme court justice; b. Hoboken, N.J., Jan. 24, 1925; s. Petros and Olga (Christopoulou) P.; m. Roula Sakellariou, 1950; children: Peter, James, Thomas BA, Dickinson Coll., 1949; LLB, Columbus Law Sch., Washington, 1952. Bar: D.C. 1952, Pa. 1957, U.S. Supreme Ct. 1975. Atty. Dept. Labor, Washington, 1950-55; office mgr. Pa. Dept. Labor, McKeesport, 1955-57; pvt. practice McKeesport, Pa., 1957-75; judge Ct. of Common Pleas, Pitts., 1976-84; justice Pa. Supreme Ct., 1984-95. Solicitor Versailles Sch. Dist., McKeesport, Pa., 1964-65, Port Vue Borough, Pa., 1969-75, City of McKeesport, 1974-75; instr. in bus. law Pa. State U.-McKeesport, 1960-75; mem. nat. panel arbitrators Am. Arbitration Assn., 1986. Trustee Hellenic Coll./Holy Cross Greek Orthodox Sch. of Theology; mem. charter rev. com. Greek Orthodox Archdiocese Am.; del. World Coun. Hellenes Abroad; Laic chmn. Greek Orthodox Diocese of Pitts.; past mem., past chmn. U.S. Selective Service Bd., McKeesport, Pa., early 1970s; bd. dirs. Mendelssohn Choir, Pitts. Sgt. A.C., U.S. Army, 1943-46; PTO Recipient Ellis Island Medal of Honor. Mem. Pa. State Trial Judges Conf., Greek-Am. Progressive Assn., Am. Hellenic Ednl. Progressive Assn., Tall Cedars Club, Optimists Club, Lions, Elks, Masons. Democrat.

PAPADIAS, CONSTANTINOS BASIL, electrical engineer; b. Athens, Jan. 16, 1969; s. Basil C. and Vassiliki B. Papadias. Diploma of elec. engring., Nat. Tech. U. Athens, 1991; PhD with highest honors, Ecole Nat. Supérieure des Télécomms., Paris, 1995. Cert. engr., Tech. Chamber of Greece. Mem. tech. staff Bell Labs. Wireless Rsch. Lab., Holmdel, NJ, 1997—2002, tech. mgr., 2002—. Mem. steering bd. Wireless World Rsch. Forum. Author: (book chpt.) Multiple Antenna Transceivers for Wireless Communications, 2002, (stds. contbns.) Downlink improvement through Space-Time Spreading, 1999 (Inclusion in cdma-2000 std. for 3G wireless comms., 1999); contbr. articles to profl. jours. Mem. Hellenic Assn. at Stanford (HELL.A.S), Stanford, 1995—97. Recipient FITNESS project on smart antennas rsch., European Commn., 2001—03, award for grad. studies abroad, Eugenides Found., Greece, 1991, award for top class undergrad. records, Nat. Bursaries Found. Greece, 1990, Bell Labs. Pres.'s Gold award, 2003, Young Author Best Paper award, IEEE Signal Processing Soc., 2003. Mem.: IEEE (sr.), Tech. Chamber of Greece. Achievements include patents for detectors for CDMA systems. Avocations: guitar, swimming, tennis, reading. Office: Bell Labs Lucent Techs Rm R-202B 791 Holmdel-Keyport Rd Holmdel NJ 07733-0400 Business E-Mail: papadias@lucent.com.

PAPADIMITRIOU, DIMITRI BASIL, economist, educator, academic administrator; b. Thessaloniki, Greece, June 9, 1946; came to U.S., 1965, naturalized, 1974; s. Basil John and Ellen (Takas) P.; m. Rania Antonopoulos. BA, Columbia U., 1970; PhD, New Sch. U., 1986. V.p., asst. sec. ITT Life Ins. Co. N.Y., N.Y.C., 1970-73; exec. v.p., sec., treas. William Penn Life Ins. Co. N.Y., N.Y.C., 1973-78, also dir.; exec. v.p., provost Bard Coll., 1978—, Jerome Levy prof. econs., 1978—; exec. dir. Bard Ctr., 1980—; pres. Levy Econs. Inst., 1988—; disting. scholar Shanghai Acad. Social Scis., 2002. Adj. lectr. econs. New Sch. U., 1975-76; fellow Ctr. for Advanced Econ. Studies, 1983; Wye fellow Aspen Inst.; bd. dirs. William Penn Life Ins. Co. N.Y.; bd. govs. Levy Econs. Inst., 1986—; mem. subcoun. capital allocation Competitiveness Policy Coun., 1998-2000; mem., vice-chmn. Congrl. Commn. to Rev. the Trade Deficit, 2000-02; mem. adv. com. Women's World Banking; radio econs. commentator Sta. WAMC, NPR, PRI, Money Radio, Marketplace. Author: Employment Policy Community Development and the Underclass, 1997, Employment Policy: Theory and Practice, 1998; co-author: Community Development Banking, 1993, A Path to Community Development, 1993, An Alternative in Small Business Finance, 1994, Monetary Policy Uncovered: The Federal Reserve's Experiment with Unobservables, 1994, Targeting Inflation: The Effects of Monetary Policy on the CPI and Its Housing Component, 1996, The Fed Should Lower Interest Rates More, 1998, What to Do With the Surplus, 1998, How Can We Provide for the Baby Boomers in their Old Age?, 1999, Can Social Security Be Saved, 1999, Fiscal Policy for the Coming Recession, 2001, Is Personal Debt Sustainable?, 2002, Understanding Deflation: Treating the Disease not the Symptom, 2003, Is Deficit-Financed Growth Limited? Policies and Prospects in An Election Year, 2004; editor, contbr. Profits, Deficits and Instability, 1992, Aspects of Distribution of Wealth and Income, 1994, Stability in the Financial System, 1996, Modernizing Financial Systems, 2000, Employment Policies: Theories and Evidence, 2001, Induced Investment and Business Cycles, 2004; co-editor, contbr.: Poverty and Prosperity in the USA in the Late Twentieth Century, 1993, Financial Conditions and Macroeconomic Performance, 1992; bd. editors Challenge, Rev. of Income and Wealth; book reviewer Econ. Jour., Ea. Econ. Jour. Trustee, treas. Am. Symphony Orch. Mem. Am. Econ. Assn., Royal Econ. Soc., Am. Fin. Assn., Econ. Club N.Y., The Bretton Woods Com., European Econ. Assn., Eastern Econ. Assn., Econ. Sci. Chamber of Greece, Assn. for Evolutionary Econs. Home and Office: Bard Coll Annandale On Hudson NY 12504 Office Phone: 845-758-7426.

PAPADOPOULOS, GREGORY MICHAEL, computer scientist, educator; b. Oakland, Calif., Apr. 30, 1958; s. Michael Nicholas and Imogen (Sherman) P.; m. Elizabeth Ann Woellner, Nov. 26, 1982; children: Michael Gregory, Kathryn Elizabeth. BA in Systems Sci., U. Calif.-San Diego, 1979; MS in Computer Sci., MIT, 1983, PhD in elec. engring., 1988. Programmer Scripps Inst. Oceanography, La Jolla, Calif., 1977-79; devel. engr. Hewlett-Packard, Inc., San Diego, 1979-81; sr. research scientist Honeywell, Inc., Mpls., 1981-84; co-founder, chief syss. architect PictureTel Corp., Danvers, Mass., 1984-86; co-founder, chief tech. officer A.I. Architects, Inc., Cambridge, 1985-88; project mgr. MIT lab. for computer sci., 1988-90, asst. prof. elect. engring. and computer sci., 1990-93, assoc. prof., 1993-95; sr. architect Thinking Machines Corp., Cambridge, 1993-94; chief scientist server syss. engring. Sun Microsystems, Santa Clara, Calif., 1994-95, exec. v.p., chief tech. officer, 1998—, chief scientist, 2003—; dir. Ergo, Inc., 1989-90; rsch. fellow Charles Stark Draper Labs., Cambridge, 1981-83; chief. Contbr. articles to profl. jours. Pres. Meml. chpt. Am. Field Service, Houston, 1975-76. Recipient Spl. distinction award Nat. Forensic League, 1976, Presdl. Young Investigators award, Nat. Sci. Found.; U. Calif. Regents scholar, 1978. Mem. AAAS, Phi Beta Kappa, Sigma Xi. Republican. Avocations: bicycle touring; soccer, diving. Office: Sun Microsystems 4150 Network Cir Santa Clara CA 95054

PAPAGEORGIOU, PANAGIOTIS, medical educator; b. Thessaloniki, Greece, Dec. 23, 1959; MD, Aristotelian U., Thessaloniki, 1984; PhD in Physiology, Harvard U., 1990. Cert. Ednl. Com. for Fgn. Med. Grads., FLEX; diplomate Am. Bd. Internal Medicine, subspecialty in cardiovasc. disease, cert. in clin. cardiac electrophysiology; lic. physician, Mass. Rsch. fellow Am. Heart Assn., Mass. affiliate, 1989-90; intern in medicine Beth Israel Hosp., Harvard Med. Sch., Boston, 1990-91, jr. asst. resident internal medicine, 1991-92, clin. cardiology fellow cardiovascular divsn., 1992-94, clin. electrophysiology fellow cardiovascular divsn., 1994-96, staff electrophysiologist, 1996—; dir. Pacemaker and ICD clin. Beth Isreal Hosp., Harvard Med. Sch., 1998—; tchg. fellow dept. cellular and molecular physiology Harvard U., 1985-90, clin. fellow medicine, 1990-95, instr., 1995—. Contbr. articles to profl. jours., chpts. to books. Greek Nat. scholar, 1977-84, Albert J. Ryan scholar Harvard Med. Sch., 1987-90; recipient clinician-investigator devel. award NIH, 1995, Clinician Scientist awrd AHA, Nat. Ctr., 1995. Fellow Am. Coll. Cariology; mem. ACP, AMA, Tessaloniki Med. Soc., Am. Heart Assn., Mass. Med. Soc., Biophys. Soc., Am. Heart Assn. Basic Rsch. Coun. Office: Beth Israel Hosp Med Div of Cardiology SH-446 330 Brookline Ave Boston MA 02215-5491

PAPAGEORGIS, JACK, small business owner; b. Gaitani, Zakynthos, Greece, Feb. 19, 1933; came to U.S., 1951; s. Anastasios and Effihia P.; m. Maria Papageorgis, Oct. 1, 1959 (div. Sept. 1993); 1 child, Marie D. BS, Seton Hall U., 1974, Cert. in Internat. Bus., 1983; MBA, Fairleigh Dickinson U., 1978, Seton Hall U., 1987. Gen. helper Libby's Lunch, Paterson, N.J., 1951-54, cook, 1954-56, counterman, 1956-58, mgr., 1958-63; co-owner, sec., treas. Libby's A Corp., Paterson, N.J., 1963-83, co-owner, pres., 1983-85; officer Passaic County Sheriff's Dept., Paterson, N.J., 1985-88; family svc. specialist III Divsn. Youth Family Svc., Newton-Pompton Lakes, N.J., 1990-92; food svc. assoc. Sodexho-Marriott William Paterson U., 1993—. Active St. Nicholas Greek Orthodox Ch., 1970—. Mem. Am Hellenic Progressive Assn. (25th anniversary award 1992), Panzakynthian Brotherhood (sec., v.p.). Home: 441 Preakness Ave Paterson NJ 07502-1100

PAPAI, BEVERLY DAFFERN, library director; b. Amarillo, Tex., Aug. 31, 1949; d. Clarence Wilbur and Dora Mae (Henderson) Daffern; m. Joseph Andrew Papai, Apr. 3, 1976. BS in Polit. Sci., West Tex. State U., Canyon, 1972; MSLS, Wayne State U., 1973. Head extension dept. and Oakland County Subregional Libr. The Farmington Cmty. Libr., Farmington Hills, Mich., 1973-79, coord. adult svcs., br. head, 1980-83, asst. dir., 1983-85, dir., 1985—. Cons. U.S. Office of Edn., 1978, Battelle Meml. Inst., Columbis, Ohio, 1980; presenter in field. Contbr. articles to profl. jours. Bd. dirs. Mich. Consortium, 1987-91; bd. dirs. Oakland Literacy Coun., 1998—, vice chair, 2000-01, chair, 2001—; trustee Libr. of Mich., 1989-92, vice chair, 1991, 97-98, chair, 1992; del. White House Conf. on Librs. and Info. Svcs., 1991; founder, treas., fiscal agt. METRO NET Libr. Consortium, 1993—; mem. edn. com. Child Abuse and Neglect Coun. of Oakland County, 1998-2000; mem. Commn. on Children, Youth and Families, 1996—, Multiracial Cmty. Coun., 1995—; chair Edn. and Tng. Com., 2000—04. Recipient Athena award Farmington/Farmington Hills C. of C. and Gen. Motors, 1994, Chairperson's Rainbow award, 2001, Spl. Recognition award Oakland County, 2004; Amarillo Pub. Libr. Friends Group fellow, 1972, Wayne State U. Inst. Gerontology fellow, 1972. Mem. ALA (officer), Mich. Libr. Assn. (chair specialized libr. svcs. roundtable 1975, chair conf. program 1982, chair pub. policy com. 1988-89, chair devel. com. 1994-95, chair ann. conf. and program coms. 1995-96, pres. 1996-97, Loleta D. Fyan award 1975, Libr. of Yr. award 2004), LWV of Mich., Farmington Exch. Club, Coun. on Resource Devel. Democrat. Roman Catholic. Home: 6805 Wing Lake Rd Bloomfield Hills MI 48301-2959 Office: The Farmington Cmty Libr 32737 W 12 Mile Rd Farmington Hills MI 48334-3302 E-mail: papaibev@farmlib.org.

PAPAKOSTAS, ACHILLEAS, telecommunications engineer, researcher; b. Larissa, Greece, Sept. 23, 1967; came to U.S., 1990; s. Ioannis and Dimitra Papakostas; m. Sheila Ann Papakostas, Apr. 27, 1996; children: Maria Margarita, Demitra Eleni, Erini Gianna. MS, U. Mass., 1993; PhD, U. Tex., Dallas, 1996. Cert. engr., Greece. Telecom. engr. NEC Am., Irving, Tex., 1996—. Contbr. articles to profl. jours. Tchr. Greek Orthodox Ch., Dallas, 1994-97; pres. Hellenic Cultural Soc. Dalls, 1996-97. Mem. IEEE, Greek Tech. Chamber, Soc. Indsl. and Applied Math. Avocations: reading, teaching greek, bicycling. Office: NEC Am 6535 N State Hwy 161 Irving TX 75039-2402 E-mail: apapakostas@necam.com.

PAPALEO, ANTHONY See FRANCIOSA, ANTHONY

PAPALIA, DIANE ELLEN, human development educator; b. Englewood, N.J., Apr. 26, 1947; d. Edward Peter and Madeline (Borrin) P.; m. Jonathan Finlay, June 19, 1976 (div. 1999); 1 child, Anna Victoria Finlay. AB, Vassar Coll., 1968; MS, W.Va. U., 1970, PhD, 1971. Asst. prof. child and family studies U. Wis., Madison, 1971-75, assoc. prof., 1975-78, prof., 1978-87, coord. child and family studies, 1977-79. Adj. prof. psychology in pediatrics U. Pa. Sch. Medicine, 1987-89. Author (with Sally W. Olds and Ruth D. Feldman): A Child's World: Infancy Through Adolescence, 1975; author: (with others) Human Development, 1978, with others: 9th edit., 2004, Psychology, 1985, 2d edit., 1988; author: (with Harvey Sterns, Cameron J. Camp and Ruth D. Feldman) Adult Development and Aging, 1996, 2d edit., 2002; contbr. articles to profl. jours.; author (with Dana Gross and Ruth Feldman): Child Development: A Topical Approach, 2003. NSF fellow, 1971, Am. Coun. on Edn. fellow, 1979-80; U. Wis. grantee. Fellow: Gerontol. Soc.; mem.: APA, Nat. Coun. Family Rels., Soc. Rsch. in Child Devel., Am. Psychol. Soc., Psi Chi. Home: 316 E 18th St New York NY 10003-2803 E-mail: depapalia@aol.com.

PAPAPETROU, PAULA BARTELLO, special education educator, writer; b. Batavia, N.Y., Mar. 23, 1966; d. Patricia Bartello Lehman and John Michael Bartello; children: Alexander Michael, Kyra Michelle. BS in Exceptional Edn., SUNY, Buffalo, 1994. Cert. tchr. Va., 2000. Varying exceptionalities tchr. Broward County Pub. Schs., Ft. Lauderdale, Fla., 1994—2000; vocat. resource tchr. Forest Pk. Sr. H.S., Woodbridge, Va., 2000—. Author: (autobiography) Fallen On My Knees, 2003. Mem.: Va. Edn. Assn., Counsel for Exceptional Children. Avocation: writing. Home: PO Box 82 Partlow VA 22534 Personal E-mail: paulabartellopapapetrou@publishedauthors.net.

PAPAS, IRENE KALANDROS, English language educator, poet, writer; b. Balt., Mar. 16, 1931; d. Louis and Kounia (Stamatakis) Kalandros; m. Steve S. Papas, Sept. 10, 1952; children: Fotene Stephenie Tina, Barbara Counia. AA with highest honors, Balt. C.C.; BA magna cum laude, Goucher Coll., 1968; MA in English Lang. and Lit., U. Md., 1974, postgrad., 1980—. Lic. theology profl. Tchr./tutor various schs., Balt., 1965—; tchr. theology U. Md. Free Univ., College Park, 1979—; author/pub. Ledger Publs., Silver Spring, Md., 1982—; TV producer Arts and Humanities Prodns., Silver Spring, 1991—. Lectr. in English, philosophy, Montgomery Coll., Goucher Coll.; instr. English Composition, World Literature, U. Md., College Park, 1968—; adj. faculty various colls.; White House duty, 1997—. Author: Irene's Ledger Songs of Deliverance, 1982, Irene's Ledger Song at Sabbatyon, 1986, Small Meditations, Leaves for Healing, 1996; prodr./dir. tv. progs. Election judge, Montgomery County (Md.) Suprs. Bd. of Elections, 90's; tutor in literacy, 1989, 90. Recipient First Prize Arts and Culture Category Smithsonian Inst., 1991; honored 6th Annual Awards Ceremony Montgomery Community, 1991. Mem. AAUP, Internat. Platform Assn., Nat. Poetry Assn., Phi Beta Kappa. Democrat. Greek Orthodox. Avocations: art/iconography, calligraphy, music, needlepoint. Office: PO Box 10303 Silver Spring MD 20914-0303

PAPAVASSILIOU, DIMITRIOS VASSILIOS, chemical engineer, educator; arrived in U.S., 1990; s. Vassilios and Athena Papavassiliou; m. Georgia Kosmopoulou, Aug. 5, 1996; 1 child, Nicholas. Diploma, Aristotle U., Thessaloniki, Greece, 1989; MS, U. Ill., 1993, PhD, 1996. Cert. engr., Tech. Chamber of Greece. Sr. rsch. engr. Mobil Tech. Co., Dallas, 1996—99; asst. prof. U. Okla., Norman, 1999—. Recipient Outstanding Paper award, Am. Soc. of Engring. and Edn., 2002; grantee, NSF, 2000—02, 2002—; Petroleum Rsch. Fund grantee, Am. Chem. Soc., 1999—2001. Mem.: US Nat. Congress Computational Mechanics, Am. Phys. Soc., Soc. Petroleum Engrs., Soc. Indsl. and Applied Math., AIChE (v.p. local sect. 2001—02). Office: U Okla 100 East Boyd SEC T335 Norman OK 73079

PAPAY, FRANCIS ANTHONY, plastic surgeon, researcher; b. Lorain, Ohio, Sept. 24, 1953; s. Frank Steven and Virginia Kay (Plato) P.; m. Patricia Lynn Lake, Dec. 27, 1991 (div. Aug. 1998); m. Michelle Lynn Balsamo, Oct. 28, 2000; children: Francis Lawrence, Anthony Joseph. BA in Chemistry, Zoology cum laude, Ohio U., 1975; MS in Biomed. Engring., Case Western Res. U., 1984, profl. fellows program Weatherhead Sch. Mgmt., 2001; MD, Northeastern Ohio U., Rootstown, 1984. Diplomate Am. Bd. Plastic Surgery, Am. Bd. Otolaryngology, Nat. Bd. Med. Examiners, Am. Bd. Clin. Engrs. Clin. engr. Lake County Meml. Hosp., Willoughby, Ohio, 1976-77; biomed. engr. NASA, Cleve., 1978-79; intern Riverside Meth. Hosp., Columbus, Ohio, 1983-84; intern in gen. surgery Cleve. Clinic Found., 1984-85, resident in otolaryngology, 1985-89, resident in plastic and reconstructive surgery, 1989-91, clin. staff, 1992—, co-dir. craniofacial-occuloplastic surgery, 1992—, head sect. pediat. plastic surgery, 1992—, head sect. craniofacial plastic surgery, 1995—, co-acad. chairperson dept. plastic surgery sch. medicine, 1995—, dir. cleft palate clinic; co-dir. dept. plastic surgery residency program Cleve. Clinic; fellow craniofacial surgery Primary Childrens Med. Ctr., U. Utah, 1991-92. Preceptor facial plastic surgery New Orleans Facial Plastic Surg. Ctr., 1988; founder, pres. N.E. Ohio Tissue Engring. Consortium, 1998—; mem. surg. staff Primary Children's Med. Ctr., Salt Lake City, 1991, Holy Cross Hosp., Salt Lake City, 1991; courtesy staff LDS Hosp., Salt Lake City, 1991; asst. prof. Ohio State U.; with dept. plastic reconstructive surgery Fairview Health Sys., Cleve.; dir. craniomaxillofacial clynic Elyria (Ohio) Health Dept., Lake and Ashtabula Counties, Painesville, Ohio; co-dir. Kaiser Permanente Crani omaxillofacial Clinic, Beachwood, Ohio; vis. prof. Hosp. Clinicas Jose San Martin, Buenos Aires, 1997, Hosp. Clinicias Dept. Pediat. Surgery, Puerto Montt, Chile, 1997; mem. Children's Oncology Svcs. Northeastern Ohio, Inc.; presenter in field. Co-author: (chpt.) The Otolaryngologic Clinics of North America: Advance Techniques for Management of Head and Neck Neoplasms, Vol. 24, 1991, Instructional Courses-Otolaryngology-Head and Neck Surgery, Vol. 4, 1991, Complications of Head and Neck Surgery, 1993, Duane's Clinical Ophthalmology, Vol. 2, 1993; mem. editl. bd. Pediat. Perspectives, 1994—; sect. editor Cleft Palate-Craniofacial Jour., 1994, 98, Jour. Craniofacial Surgery, 1998; contbr. articles to Jour. Craniofacial Surgery, Laryngoscope Jour., Annals Plastic Surgery, Otolaryngolgoy, Head and Neck Surgery, Am. Jour. Ophthalmology, Plastic Reconstructive Surgery Jour., Internat. Jour. Aesthetic Restorative Surgery, Archives Pediat. Adolescent Medicine, Jour. Am. Acad. Dermatology, Cleft Palate Craniofacial Jour., Surg. Forum, Facial Plastic Surgery, Jour. Burn Rehab., Operative Techniques Otolaryngology, Head Neck Surgery, Ear Nose Throat Jour., Otolaryngol. Clinic N.Am., Laryngoscope, Am. Jour. Rhinology, Cleve. Clinic Jour. medicine, Archives Otolaryngology, Ear Nose Throat Jour., Ohio State Med. Jour. Prin. Ambulatory Care. Founding mem. Interplast Ohio, surg. vol. mission, Puerto Viejo, Ecuador, 1990, Santiago, Chile, 1991, Temuco, Chile, 1992, Orsono, Chile, 1992, 94, 95, 96, Puerto Montt, 1995, 96; Nat. judge BF Goodrich Collegiate Inventors Program, Cleve., 1997, 98, 99, 2000, 01; founding mem. Aboutface, Cleve.; trustee Ronald McDonald House, Cleve. Recipient Northeastern Ohio Otolaryngology and Maxillofacial Surgery Rsch. award, 1989, Outstanding Young Men In USA award Jaycees, 1992, Servico Salud Osorno, 1996; Melvin E. Jones Rsch. Found. Meml. scholar, 1981, Maxillofacial Surg. Internat. scholar A-O Synthes, 1990; George and Grace Crile Traveling Surg. fellow U. Basel Kantonspital, 1991, Craniomaxillofacial and Pediat. Plastic Surgery fellow Primary Children's Ctr., 1991-92; grantee Cleve. Clinic Found., 1987-88, 90-96, 98, U. Utah, 1992-93, Calif. Birth Defects Monitoring Program, 1995, NIH, Leibinger Surg., others. Fellow ACS, Am. Acad. Pediat., Am. Acad. Otolaryngology; mem. AAAS, Internat. Coll. Surgeons, Internat. Soc. Craniofacial Surgeons, Lipoplasty Soc. N.Am. (continguing med. edn. com.), Am. Cleft Palate-Craniofacial Assn. (internat. rels. com., publs. com.), Am. Soc. Plastic Reconstructive Surgeons (ednl. tech. com., internat. rels. com., managed care com., rep. young plastic surgeons com.), Am. Rhinologic Soc., Assn. Am. Med. Instrumentation, Am. Bd. Clin. Engrs., Am. Soc. Maxillofacial Surgeons, Utah State Med. Assn., Ohio State Med. Assn. (pres. med. student sect. 1983, coun. 1983, Student Leadership award 1983), Ohio Valley Soc. Plastic Reconstructive Surgeons (pres. 2003—), Ohio Valley Soc. Plastic Surgeons (pres. 2004), Resident Rsch. award 1990), Tissue Engring. Soc., Bur. Children Med. Handicaps, Plastic Surgery Rsch. Coun., No. Ohio Pediat. Soc. (assoc.), Cleve. Med. Soc., Robin Anderson Soc. (founding), A-O Maxillofacial Fellowship Alumni. Republican. Roman Catholic. Achievements include first to perform world's first robotic endoscopic nerve anastomosis for pudenal nerve reconstruction; patents for subcutaneous mandibular bone distractor, pneumatic cranial molding helmet, osseous integrated bone anchor, anti SIDS sleep cradle. Home: 30548 Royal Woods Pl Westlake OH 44145-3771 Office: Cleve Clinic Found 9500 Euclid Ave Cleveland OH 44195-0001 E-mail: papayf@ccf.org.

PAPE, PATRICIA ANN, social worker, consultant; b. Aurora, Ill., Aug. 2, 1940; d. Robert Frank and Helen Louise (Hanks) Grover; children: Scott Allen, Debra Lynn. BA in Sociology, Northwestern U., 1962; MSW, George Williams Coll., 1979. Cert. addictions counselor, Ill.; lic. clin. social worker, sch. social worker, Ill. Pvt. practice family counseling, 1979—; coord. community resources DuPage Probation Dept., Wheaton, Ill., 1977-80; dir. The Abbey Alcoholism Treatment Ctr., Winfield, Ill., 1980-81; prin. Pape & Assocs., Wheaton, 1982—; dir. alcoholism counselor tng. program Coll. of DuPage, Glen Ellyn, Ill., 1982-87. Chgo. affiliate Employee Assistance Program, 1982—; cons. Luth. Soc. Services Ill., 1979-82. Contbr. articles to profl. jours. Mem. alcohol drug task force Ill. Synod Luth. Ch. Am., Chgo., 1985—. Named Woman of Yr., Entrepreneur Women in Mgmt., Oak Brook, Ill, 1986, Social Worker of Yr. Fox Valley Dist., 1998. Mem. Assn. Labor-Mgmt. Adminstrs. Cons. Alcoholism (women's issues com. 1984—), Acad. Cert. Social Workers, Am. Assn. Marriage Family Therapists, Nat. Assn. Soc. Workers, Women in Mgmt. Home: 1330 Shagbark Ln Wheaton IL 60187 Office: Pape & Assocs 618 S West St Wheaton IL 60187-5038

PAPE, STUART M. lawyer; b. Paterson, NJ, Dec. 24, 1948; BA, U. Va., 1970, JD, 1973. Bar: Va. 1973, DC 1980, US Ct. Appeals (6th cir.) 1975, US Supreme Ct. 1976. Law clk. to Hon. Leonard Braman Superior Ct. DC, 1973-74; exec. asst. to commr. FDA, 1979; mng. ptnr. Patton Boggs LLP and predecessors, Washington. Mem. ABA (com. food and drug law, sect. adminstrv. law 1973-2002), Va. State Bar, DC Bar. Address: 2950 Chain Bridge Rd NW Washington DC 20016-3408 Office Phone: 202-457-5240. Business E-Mail: spape@pattonboggs.com.

PAPE, WILLIAM JAMES, II, newspaper publisher; b. Waterbury, Conn., Aug. 14, 1931; s. William B. and Helen (Cronan) P.; m. Patricia Moran, Oct. 15, 1959; children: William B. II, Andrew J. BS, U.S. Naval Acad., 1953; MBA, Harvard U., 1959; LHD (hon.), Teikyo Post U., 1991. Commd. ensign USN, 1953, advanced through grades to lt., 1955, resigned, 1957; asst. treas. Ea. Color Printing Co., Waterbury, 1959-63, pres., treas. Avon, Conn., 1977-87; v.p., asst. treas. Am.-Republican Inc., Waterbury, 1963-64, asst. publisher, comptroller, v.p., treas., 1964-72, pres., 1972—, treas., 1972-98; pub. Republican-Am., 1972—, editor, 1988—; also bd. dirs.; v.p., asst. treas. & dir. Paper Delivery, Inc., 1972—. Bd. dirs. Platt Bros., Waterbury. Bd. dirs. Conn. Coun. Freedom of Info., 1968-88, Conn. Bus. and Industry Assn., 1980-83, Naugatuck Valley Devel. Corp., Regional Action Coun., Waterbury, 1991; bd. dirs. Conn. Citizens for Jud. Modernization, pres., 1973-75; bd. dirs. Waterbury YMCA, 1970-78, trustee, 1972-2001, chmn. trustees, 1976-85; trustee Northeast Utilities, 1974-2001, Greater Waterbury Health Network Inc., 1993-95; mem. Conn. Pub. Expenditure Coun. Inc., 1974-77, dir. Conn. policy and econ. coun., 1994-2000; trustee Teikyo Post U., 1976-96; grants com. Waterbury Found., 1980-87; pub. affairs com. Waterbury Hosp., 1984-90, past trustee; incorporator Conn. Found. for Open Govt. Inc.; active Conn. Legislature Commn. to Study Modernization and Unification of Cts., 1973-75,

Citizens for Better Govt. Through Reorganization, 1977. Mem. Am. Judicature Soc. (assoc. dir. 1975-76), New England Newspaper Assn. (Conn. bd. govs. 1983-87), Conn. Bar Assn. (task force conflict of interest 1979), Conn. Daily Newspaper Assn. (pres. 1970, exec. com. 1971-91), Waterbury C. of C. (exec. com., v.p. 1975, chmn. 1977-79, dir. 1980-2001, vice-chmn. transp. 1981-2001), Navy League U.S. (comms. bd. 1982), Waterbury Club, Madison Beach Club, Highfield, Liverpool Nautical Rsch. Soc. Republican. Roman Catholic. Avocations: sailing, firearms, walking, carpentry. Home: Old Sherman Hill Rd Woodbury CT 06798 Office: Rep-Am PO Box 2090 389 Meadow St Waterbury CT 06722-2090 E-mail: wjpape@rep-am.com.

PAPELL, HELEN GERTRUDE, poet, retired librarian; b. N.Y.C., Apr. 8, 1924; d. Henry and Anna (Gimpel) Sobel; m. Robert Papell, June 1, 1949; 1 child, David H. BA, U. Mo., 1949; MLS, Pratt Inst., 1969; cert. profl. pub. libr., SUNY, 1973. Libr. trainee Bklyn. Pub. Libr., 1967-69, libr., storyteller, puppeteer, sr. libr., supervising libr., 1969-84; libr., cataloger Jewish Women's Resource Ctr. Nat. Coun. Jewish Women, N.Y.C., 1984-98; ret., 1998. Puppeteer in librs., schls., chs., st. fairs, N.Y.C., Bklyn., 1969-84. Author: (poems) Talking with Eve, Leah, Hagar, Miriam, 1996, Caretaker's Mask, 2003; contbg. editor Jewish Women's Lit. Ann. Grantee Poets and Writers, 1991, 93. Mem. Nat. Coun. Jewish Women, Phi Beta Kappa. Avocations: reading judaica, folklore and mysteries, visiting museums, attending plays. Home: 720 W End Ave New York NY 10025-6299

PAPEN, MARY KAY, state senator; Car dealer; Dem. senator dist. 38 N.Mex. State Senate. Mem. pub. affairs com. N.Mex. State Senate, vice chair edn. com. Home: 904 Conway Ave Las Cruces NM 88005 Office: NMex State Senate State Capitol Mail Rm Dept Santa Fe NM 87503 E-mail: senate@state.nm.us.

PAPENFUSE, EDWARD CARL, JR., archivist, state official; b. Toledo, Ohio, Oct. 15, 1943; m. Sallie Fisher; children: Eric, David. BA in Polit. Sci., Am. U., 1965; MA in History, U. Colo., 1967; PhD, Johns Hopkins U., 1973. Assoc. editor Am. Hist. Rev., Washington, 1970-73; asst. archivist Md. Hall of Records, Annapolis, 1973-75, archivist, 1975—, commr. land patents, 1975—. Author: In Pursuit of Profit: The Annapolis Merchants in the Era of the American Revolution, 1975, (with others) Biographical Dictionary of Maryland Legislators, 1635-1789, 1974, (with others) Maryland: A New Guide to the Old Line State, 3d edit., 1999, Doing Good to Posterity, 1995, Maryland State Archives Atlas of Historical Maps of Maryland, 1608-1908, 2003; contbr. articles and revs. to profl. jours. Mem. Johns Hopkins U. Med. Archives. NEH grantee; recipient Disting. Svc. award to State Govt. Nat. Gov.'s Assn., 1985, Marylander of Yr. award Md. Colonial Soc., 1985. Fellow Soc. Am. Archivist, Md. Hist. Soc., Am. Antiquarian Soc. Home: 206 Oakdale Rd Baltimore MD 21210-2520 Office: Md State Archives 350 Rowe Blvd Annapolis MD 21401-1686 Office Phone: 410-260-6401. E-mail: edp@mdsa.net.

PAPER, LEWIS J. lawyer, educator; b. Newark, Oct. 13, 1946; s. Sidney and Dorothy (Nieman) P.; m. Jan Clachko, Sept. 4, 1972; children: Lindsay, Brett. BA, U. Mich., 1968; LLM, Harvard U., 1971; JD, Georgetown U., 1972. Bar: D.C. 1971, N.J. 1975, Md. 1984. Fellow Inst. Pub. Interest Representation Georgetown U. Law Sch., Washington, 1971-72; staff atty. Citizens Comms. Ctr., Washington, 1972-73; legis. counsel to Sen. Gaylord Nelson U.S. Senate, 1973-75; assoc. atty. Lowenstein, Sandler, Brochin, Kohl & Fisher, Newark, 1975-78; asst. gen. counsel FCC, Washington, 1978-79, assoc. gen. counsel, 1979-81; ptnr. Grove Engelberg & Gross, Washington, 1981-86, Keck, Mahin & Cate, 1986-95, Dickstein, Shapiro, Morin & Oshcinsky LLP, Washington, 1995—. Adj. prof. law Georgetown U. Law Sch., Washington, 1983-86. Author: John F. Kennedy: The Promise and the Performance, 1975, 79, Brandeis: An Intimate Biography, 1983, Empire: William S. Paley and the Making of CBS, 1987; contbr. articles to newspapers, mags., and profl. jours. Office: Dickstein Shapiro Morin & Oshinsky LLP 2101 L St NW Washington DC 20037-1526 Office Phone: 202-828-2265. E-mail: paperl@dsmo.com.

PAPERNIK, JOEL IRA, lawyer; b. N.Y.C., May 4, 1944; s. Herman and Ida (Titefsky) Papernik; m. Barbara Ann Barker, July 28, 1972; children: Deborah, Ilana. BA, Yale U., 1965; JD cum laude, Columbia U., 1968. Bar: NY 1969. Assoc. Shea & Gould, N.Y.C., 1968-76, ptnr., 1976-91; ptnr., chmn. corp. and securities dept., mem. mgmt. com. Squadron, Ellenoff, Plesent & Sheinfeld, N.Y.C., 1991-2000; ptnr., chair mergers and acquisitions practice group, mem. policy com. Mintz, Levin, Cohn, Ferris, Glovsky and Popeo PC, N.Y.C., 2000—. Lectr various panels. With 11th Spl. Forces USAR, 1967—73. Mem.: ABA (sect. corp. law), Negotiated Acquisitions Com., NY Tri-Bar Opinion Com., Assn. Bar City NY (mem. securities regulation com. 1992—95, chmn., lectr., mem. corp. law com.), NY State Bar Assn. (lectr. various panels, mem. securities law com.), NY Biotech. Assn. (lectr. various panels), Yale Club. Office: Mintz Levin Cohn Ferris Glovsky and Popeo PC 666 3rd Ave New York NY 10017-4011 Office Phone: 212-692-6774. E-mail: jpapernik@mintz.com.

PAPERT, SEYMOUR AUBREY, mathematician, educator, writer; b. Pretoria, South Africa, Mar. 1, 1928; came to U.S., 1964; s. Jack and Betty P.; m. Androula Christofides, Apr. 10, 1963 (div.); 1 dau., Artemis; m. Sherry Turkle, Dec. 18, 1977 (div.); m. Suzanne Massie, Sept. 2, 1992. BA, U. Witwatersrand, S. Africa, 1949, PhD, 1952, Cambridge U., Eng., 1959. Co-dir. artificial intelligence lab. MIT, Cambridge, 1967-73, dir. Logo Group, 1970-81, prof. applied math., 1968-80, Cecil and Ida Green prof. edn., 1974-80; vis. prof. math. Rockefeller U., N.Y.C., 1980-81; sci. dir. Centre Mondial Informatique et Ressource Humaine, Paris, 1982-83; Lego Prof. Learning Rsch. MIT, Cambridge, Mass., 1990—, prof. program media arts and sci., 1987—. Author: (with Marvin Minsky) Perceptrons, 1969, Artificial Intelligence, 1974, (with McNaughton) Non-Counting Automata, 1971, Mindstorms: Children, Computers..., 1980, The Children's Machine: Rethinking School in the Age of the Computer..., 1992, The Connected Family: Bridging the Digital Generation Gap, 1996; Foundr. The Seymour Papert Inst./The Learning Barn, Blue Hill, ME. Marconi Internat. fellow, 1981; J.S. Guggenheim fellow, 1980; recipient Software Publishers Assn. Lifetime Achievement award, 1994, Computerworld Smithsonian Awd., 1997. Office: The Learning Barn PO Box 387 Blue Hill ME 04614

PAPISH, STEVEN WILLIAM, internist; b. Phila., Oct. 22, 1948; BA, U. Pa., 1970, MD, 1974. Diplomate Am. Bd. Internal Medicine. Intern George Washington U. Hosp., Washington, 1974-75, resident in internal medicine, 1975-78; resident in oncology Dana-Farber Cancer Inst., Boston, 1979-81; fellow in hematology Tufts-New England Med. Ctr., Boston, 1978-79; staff Morristown (N.J.) Meml. Hosp., 1983—. Asst. prof. Columbia U., N.Y.C. Mem. Am. Coll. Physicians, Am. Soc. Clin. Oncology, Am. Soc. Hematology. Office: HemOnc Assocs Northern NJ 261 James St Ste 1B Morristown NJ 07960-6348

PAPKIN, ROBERT DAVID, lawyer; b. New Bedford, Mass., Feb. 26, 1933; s. Barney and Rose (Shuster) P.; m. Rachel Friedberg, Aug. 29, 1965; children: Steven C., Daniel M. AB, Harvard U., 1954, LLB, 1957. Bar: Mass. 1957, D.C. 1964. Legal asst. NRLB, Washington, 1958-61; assoc. Cox, Langford & Brown, Washington, 1963-66, ptnr., 1966-73, Squire, Sanders & Dempsey, Washington, 1973—. Trustee Art Svcs. Internat., 1990—. Served with U.S. Army, 1957-58, 61-62. Mem. ABA, D.C. Bar Assn., Fed. Bar Assn., Internat. Bar Assn., Met. Club Washington D.C., Cosmos Club. Democrat. Jewish. Home: 9702 Leeds Landing Cir Easton MD 21601-5564 Office: Squire Sanders & Dempsey PO Box 407 1201 Pennsylvania Ave NW Washington DC 20004-2491 E-mail: rpapkin@ssd.com.

PAPP, HARRY, science association administrator; Pres. Ariz. Zool. Soc., The Phoenix Zoo, from 1995, now former pres. also: Phoenix Zoo 455 N Galvin Pkwy Phoenix AZ 85008-3431 Office: L Roy Papp and Assoc LLP 2201 E Camelback Rd 227B Phoenix AZ 85016-9028

PAPP, LASZLO GEORGE, architect; b. Debrecen, Hungary, Apr. 28, 1929; came to U.S., 1956; m. Judith Liptak, Apr. 12, 1952; children: Andrea, Laszlo-Mark (dec. 1978). Archtl. Engr., Poly. U. Budapest, 1955; MArch, Pratt Inst., 1960; D of Liberal Arts, Tech. U. Budapest, 1998. Designer Harrison & Abramovitz, Architects, N.Y.C., 1958—63; ptnr. Whiteside & Papp, Architects, White Plains, NY, 1963—67; pres. Papp Architects, P.C., White Plains, 1967—96, chmn., 1996—; exec. dir. Urban Redevel. Commn., Stamford, Conn., 2001—. Adj. prof. U. Debrecen, Hungary, 1999—. Mem. Pres.'s Adv. Com. on Pvt. Sector Initiatives, 1980-85; mem. adv. com. Westchester C.C., 1971-75, Iona Coll., New Rochelle, N.Y., 1982-87, Norwalk State Tech. Coll., 1983-95; v.p. Clearview Sch., 1985-89, pres., 1990-91; mem. Town Coun. New Canaan, Conn., 1993-99. Fellow AIA (reg. dir. 1983-85); mem. Internat. Union Architects (rep. habitat com. 1986-90), N.Y. State Assn. Architects (v.p. 1977-80, pres. 1981), Am.-Hungarian Engrs. Assn. (bd. dirs. 1978-90), Am. Coun. World Fedn. Hungarians (pres. 1993-97, regional pres. 1996-2000), Hungarian Univ. Assn. (pres. 1958-60), Westchester County C. of C. (bd. dirs. 1968-71, vice chmn. bd. for area devel. 1983-89, chmn. bd. dirs. 1989-90), Am.-Hungarian C. of C. (charter 1989—). Home: 1197 Valley Rd New Canaan CT 06840-2428 Office: Urban Redevel Commn 888 Washington Blvd Stamford CT 06901 Personal E-mail: papparch@aol.com.

PAPPAGALLO, MICHAEL V. realty company executive; b. 1958; Grad. summa cum laude, Iona Coll., New Rochelle, N.Y. Sr. mgr. audit group KPMG Peat Marwick; with GE Capital, mgr. fin. bus. devel. team Vendor Fin. Svcs. unit, mgr. fin. reporting and practices, CFO comml. real estate fin. and svcs.; CFO Kimco Realty Corp., New Hyde Park, N.Y., 1997—. Office: Kimco Realty Corp PO Box 5020 3333 New Hyde Park Rd #100 New Hyde Park NY 11042-0020 Fax: (516) 869-9001.*

PAPPALARDO, FAYE, academic administrator; b. Phila. d. Gregory and Helen (Gregory) P. BS, St. Mary's U., 1968; MS, Johns Hopkins U., 1978; MA, Columbia U., 1991, EdD, 1992. Dept. chair fgn. lang. Cath. Girls High Sch., Balt., 1970-72; dean of coll. Bay Coll. Md., Balt., 1972-76; dir. student life C.C. of Balt., 1978-83, dean student affairs, 1983-88, Carroll C.C., Westminster, Md., 1988-91, exec. v.p., 1991—. Cons. Sci. Rsch. Assn., N.Y.C., 1974-76. Bd. dirs. Multiple Sclerosis Soc., Westminster, 1991-93; mem. Md. Tomorrow, Westminster, 1989-90. Recipient fellowship Francisian Community, Paris, 1974. Mem. AAUW, Am. Assn. Women in C.C., Am. Assn. Women in Higher Edn. (treas. 1991—, Outstanding Adminstr. award 1994), Md. Assn. Higher Edn. (treas. 1991—), Md. State Deans of Student Affairs (chairperson 1992-93), Johns Hopkins U. Alumni Assn., Columbia U. Alumni Assn. Roman Catholic. Avocation: reading. Office: Carroll CC 1601 Washington Rd Westminster MD 21157-6944

PAPPAS, BARBARA ESTELLE, Biblical studies educator, author; b. Chgo., July 26, 1941; m. George G. Pappas, Sept. 20, 1964; children: Dheanna Pappas Fikaris, Michele Pappas Glavanovits, Laina Pappas Krabbe. Lay asst. Holy Apostles Ch., Westchester, Ill., 1976—. Sec., lectr. Diocese of Chgo. Religious Edn. Commn., 1982—; founder, dir. Holy Apostles Resource Ctr., Westchester, 1984—. Author: Are You Saved?, The Orthodox Christian Process of Salvation, 4th edit., 1997, The Christian Life in the Early Church and Today, Commentaries on Paul's Epistles to the Corinthians, Vol. I, 2d edit., 2004, Vol. II, 1998, God's Bubbly, Gurgly, Overwhelming, Overflowing Love, 2000. Mem. teenage curriculum com. Greek Orthodox Archdiocese. Mem.: ASCD. Greek Orthodox. Home: 379 Arboretum Cir Wheaton IL 60187 E-mail: ayspappas@msn.com.

PAPPAS, CHARLES ENGELOS, plastic surgeon; b. Phila., May 20, 1946; s. Engelos George and Angelina (Biniaris) Pappas; m. Aprille Pappas; children: Evan, Angela, Chrysten. BA, BS, U. Pa., 1968; MD, Temple U., 1972. Intern, then resident in gen. surgery Johns Hopkins Hosp., Balt., 1972-75; resident in gen. surgery Temple U. Hosp., Phila., 1975-76, resident in plastic surgery, 1976-78, clinical fellow cardiac sugery, 1972-73; clinical fellow transplant Harvard Med. Sch., 1973; chmn. dept. plastic surgery Temple U. Hosp., Phila., 1978-81, clin. assoc. prof. surgery, 1981—; chief dept. plastic surgery Meml. Hosp., Phila., 1986—; clin. assoc. plastic surgery Chestnut Hill Hosp., Phila., 1979—, chief/dir. dept. plastic surgery, 1994—; med. dir. Ft. Washington Surgery Ctr., 1994—. Dir. Inst. for Aesthetic Plastic Surgery, Ft. Washington, Pa., 1985—; chmn. bd. Am. Gaming Industries, 1984—; dir., ptnr. Tristate Quicklube Co., 1982-91, Medars; pres., dir. two carwash cos., Phila., 1989—; med. dir. Fort Washington Surgery Ctr., 1995—, dir., trustee, 1996—; med. dir. Aesthetica, Inc., 1996—; nat. med. dir. Aesthetics Med. Mgmt., Inc., 1996—, med. advisor, 1997—; dir., CEO Spa Aesthetika, 1998—; CEO, dir. Aesthetic Health Care Ctrs., 1999—, SPA Aesthetika, 1999—; founder, CEO Papco Ventures, Inc., 2000--. Contbr. articles to profl. jours. Trustee Germantown Acad., Ft. Washington, 1986—, Commonwealth Nat. Country Club, Horsham, 1988—, Patrons' Charity Found. Fellow ACS, Royal Coll. Surgeons; mem. Am. Soc. Plastic Reconstructive Surgeons (diplomate), Am. Soc. Aesthetic Plastic Surgeons (diplomate), Phila. Soc. Plastic Surgeons (pres. 1990-92). Greek Orthodox. Avocations: golf, tennis, development and investing, skiing. Office: The Aesthetic Health Care Ctr 467 Pennsylvania Ave Ste 202 Fort Washington PA 19034-3420 Personal E-mail: cepmd@att.net.

PAPPAS, CHARLES NICHOLAS, III, dentist, educator; b. Phila., Jan. 14, 1936; s. Charles Nicholas, Jr. and Marie (Pero) Pappas; m. Edith Basedow, Aug. 24, 1974. Student, U. Colo., 1953—55; DDS, Northwestern U., 1959. Assoc. practice dentistry, South Weymouth, Mass., 1962; pvt. practice dentistry Weymouth Heights, Mass., 1962—65; public health dentist Dept. Health and Hosps., Boston, 1965—70; assoc. practice Weymouth, 1965—68, Brookline, Mass., 1969; practicing clin. dentist Harvard U., 1970—71, clin. instr. operative dentistry, 1967—71; clin. rsch. asst. Forsyth Dental Ctr., 1972; asst. prof. restorative dentistry U. Pa., 1972—83; dentist Dept. Pub. Health, City of Phila., 1984—. Clin. instr. Tufts U., 1965. Author: The Life and Times of G.V. Black, 1983, (pamphlet) Self-Control of Tooth Decay, 1967; contbr. articles to profl. publs. Program, fund-raising chmn. Phillips Brooks Club Boston Trinity Ch., 1965—66. Capt. AUS, 1960—62. Recipient Earle Banks Hoyt award for excellence in tchg., 1980. Mem.: AAAS, ADA, Christian Dental Soc., NY Acad. Scis., Pa. Assn. Dental Surgeons, Mass. Dental Soc., Philadelphia County Dental Soc., Harvard Odontological Soc., Yale Libr. Assocs., U.S. Submarine Vets WWII (assoc. Cert. of Appreciation 1982), Goethe Soc. New Eng., English-Speaking Union, 4001 Lit. Union (founder, faculty advisor), New Haven Colony Hist. Soc., Hist. Soc. Pa., Ill. State Hist. Soc., G.V. Black Soc., Northwestern U. of Delaware Valley Club (pres. 1978), Xi Psi Phi, Lambda Chi Alpha. Home: 5723 Charles St Philadelphia PA 19135-3806 Office: City of Phila Dist Health Ctr # 10 Dental Clinic 2230 Cottman Ave Philadelphia PA 19149

PAPPAS, DAVID CHRISTOPHER, lawyer; b. Kenosha, Wis., Mar. 18, 1936; s. theros and Marion Lucille (Piperas) P.; m. Laurie Jean LaCaskey, Nov. 26, 1956 (div. 1969); children: Christopher David, Andrea Lynn; m. Nancy Marie Pratt, June 11, 1983. BS, U. Wis., 1959, JD, 1961. Bar: Wis. 1961, U.S. Dist. Ct. (ea. and we. dists.) Wis. 1965, U.S. Supreme Ct. 1971; lic. master mariner. Asst. corp. counsel Racine County (Wis.), 1961; atty., advisor U.S. Dept. Labor, Washington, 1961-62; staff atty. U.S. Commn. Civil rights, Washington, 1962-63; asst. city atty. City of Madison (Wis.), 1963-65; atty. pvt. practice, Madison, 1965—. Chmn. Madison Mayor's Citizen Adv. Com., 1964-65; pres. Wis. Cup Assn., Madison, 1965; c0-chmn. 2d Congl. Dist. Humphrey for Pres., Madison, 1972. Recipient commendation for Supreme Ct. work Madison County Coun., 1965, commendation resolution City of Madison, 1965. Mem. Wis. Bar Assn., Dane County Bar Assn., Wis. Acad. Trial Lawyers, Am. Assn. Trial Lawyers, Lawyer-Pilot Bar Assn. (master mariner), Gt. Lakes Hist. Soc., Madison Club, South Shore Yacht Club (Milw.). Home and Office: 1787 Strawberry Rd Deerfield WI 53531-9779

PAPPAS, DAVID WAYNE, guidance counselor, consultant; b. Chgo., May 19, 1958; s. Danny and Roselle Pappas. BS in Adminstrn. Justice, So. Ill. U., 1981, M Bus. Edn., 1988; ednl. specialist degree in curriculum and instrn., No. Ill. U., 1993, MEd in Counseling, 1997, EdD in Curriculum Inst. and Supervision, 2001. Cert. tchr., in guidance, gen. supervisory cert., lic. profl. counselor, Ill.; nat. cert. counselor; cert. in scuba diving. Residence hall coord. So. Ill. U., Carbondale, Ill., 1981—84, grad. asst. Sch. Tech. Careers, 1983; tng. specialist Dawson Tech. Inst., Chgo., 1985-92; coord. coop. edn. Chgo. City-Wide Coll., 1987-89, ast. dir. curriculum and tng., 1989-90, dir. Life Skills Employment Awareness Program, 1990-92; dir. opportunities program Harold Washington Coll., Chgo., 1992-94; tchr. tech. Taft H.S., Chgo., 1994-2001, lead tchr. summer sch., 1999; coord. Chgo. Police and Firefighters Tng. Acad., Chgo. Bd. Edn., 1999—, guidance counselor, 2001—; instr. No. Ill. U., DeKalb, 1997—. Cons. Strategies, Inc., Chgo. Author: The History and Development of Correctional Education in the Correctional Institutions of Southern Illinois, 1988, An Investigation of the Personality Types of Chicago Fire Fighters and High School Students Participating in the Chicago Police and Fire Fighters Training Academy, 2001; contbr. articles to profl. jours. Mem. ACA, Am. Sch. Counseling Assn., Ill. Counseling Assn., Phi Delta Kappa, Chi Sigma Iota. Democrat. Roman Catholic. Avocations: international travel, scuba diving, running, swimming, skiing. Home: 700 W Bittersweet Pl Apt 1010 Chicago IL 60613-2385 Office: Chgo Bd Edn 6545 W Hurlbut Chicago IL 60631 Fax: 773-534-1027. E-mail: dwpappas@ix.netcom.com.

PAPPAS, EFFIE VAMIS, language educator, finance educator, writer, poet, artist; b. Cleve., Dec. 26, 1924; d. James Jacob and Helen Joy (Nicholson) Vamis; m. Leonard G. Pappas, Nov. 3, 1945; children: Karen Pappas Morabito, Leonard J., Ellen Pappas Daniels, David James. BBA, Western Res. U., 1948; MA in Edn., Case Western Res. U., 1964, postgrad., 1964-68; MA in English Lit., Cleve. State U., 1986; postgrad., Ind. U. Pa., 1979-86. Cert. elem. and secondary tchr. Ohio. Tchr. elem. schs., Ohio, 1963-70; office mgr. Cleve. State U., 1970-72, adminstr. pub. rels., 1972-73; med. adminstr. Brecksville (Ohio) VA Hosp., 1974-78; lectr. English, econs./bus. mgmt., math., comm., composition Cuyahoga CC, Cleve., 1978-92. Tchg. asst. Case Western Res. U., 1979—80; lectr. bus. comm. Cleve. State U., 1980; participant in sci. and cultural exch. dels. Am. Inst. Chemists, China, 1984, Russia, 89. Feature writer: The Voice, 1970—78, editor, writer: Cleve. State U. newsletter and mag., 1970—73. Cub scout leader Boy Scouts Am., Brecksville, 1960; mem. local coun. PTA, 1965—70; sec. St. Paul's Coun., 1990—91; mem. membership com. St. Paul Ladies Philoptohos, 1990—2004; active Women's Equity Action League, 1995—2003; mem. Greater Cleve. Learning Project; Sunday sch. tchr., mem. choir Brecksville United Ch. of Christ, 1975—76, mem. bd. missions, 1966—67, mem. membership com., 1993; mem. planning com. edn. Case Western Res. U.; mem. 75th Anniversary steering com. Cleve. Coll. Recipient Editor's Choice award for outstanding achievement in poetry, Nat. Libr. Poetry, 1995, 2000; grantee, Cuyahoga CC, 1982. Mem.: AARP, AAUW (legis. chair, del. Ohio meetings 1993—94, del. Ohio Coalition for Change 1993—94, mem. Ohio and Cleve. br. del. Gt. Lakes regional meeting 1994, co-chair Cleve. br. 1994, 1996—97, legis. chair 1997—98, del. to S.W. regional meeting 1995, del. to Internat. Fedn. Univ. Women triennial meeting Stanford U. 1992), NAFE, NAE (named to Nat. Women's Hall Fame), Ohio Edn. Assn. (rep. assembly Columbus 1994, 1999—2001, 2002—03), Nat. Mus. Women in Arts (hon. roll. mem.). Avocations: travel, art, legal studies, theater, correspondence with national and international friends. Home: 8681 Brecksville Rd Brecksville OH 44141-1912

PAPPAS, GEORGE DEMETRIOS, anatomy and cell biology educator, scientist; b. Portland, Maine, Nov. 26, 1926; James and Anna (Dracopoulos) Pappatheodoros; m. Bernice Levine, Jan. 14, 1952; children: Zoe Alexandra, Clio Nicollette. BA, Bowdoin Coll., 1947; MS, Ohio State U., 1948, PhD, 1952; DSc (hon.), U. Athens, Greece, 1988. Vis. investigator Rockefeller Inst., N.Y.C., 1952-54; assoc. in anatomy Coll. Physicians and Surgeons, Columbia U., N.Y.C., 1956-57, asst. prof. anatomy, 1957-63, assoc. prof., 1963-66; prof. anatomy Albert Einstein Coll. Medicine, Yeshiva U., N.Y.C., 1967-77, prof. neurosci., 1974-77, vis. prof. neurosci., 1977-97; prof., head dept. anatomy and cell biology U. Ill. Coll. Medicine, Chgo., 1977-96, prof. cell biology and psychiatry, 1996—. Trustee Marine Biol. Lab., Woods Hole, Mass., 1975-81 Author: (with others) The Structure of the Eye, 1961, Growth and Maturation of the Brain, vol. IV, 1964, Nerve as a Tissue, 1966, The Thalmus, 1966, Pathology of the Nervous System, vol. 1, 1968, Structure and Function of Synapses, 1972, Methodological Approaches to the Study of Brain Maturation and Its Abnormalities, 1974, Advances in Neurology, vol.12, 1975, The Nervous System, vol. 1 The Basic Neurosciences, 1975, Cellular and Molecular Basis of Synaptic Transmission, 1988, also author many conf. procs.; contbr. over 200 articles to profl. jours.; former mem. editorial bd. Anatomical Record, Biol. Bull., Brain Rsch., Jour. Neurocytology, Microstructure, Neurol. Rsch.; patentee method inducing analgesia by implantation of cells releasing neuroactive substances. Arthritis and Rheumatism Found. fellow, 1954-56; recipient career devel. award Columbia U., 1964-66; rsch. grantee NIH Fellow AAAS, N.Y. Acad. Scis., Inst. Medicine Chgo.; mem. Am. Soc. Cell Biology (pres. 1974-75), Am. Assn. Anatomists (chmn. pub. policy com. 1981-82, Henry Gray award 2003), Assn. Anatomy Chmn. (exec. com. 1978-80, pres. 1981-82), Electron Microscopy Soc. Am. (program chmn. 1984-85), N.Y. Soc. Electron Microscopy (pres. 1967-68), Soc. for Neurosci. (pres. Chgo. chpt. 1985-86), Harvey Soc., Internat. Brain Rsch. Orgn., Cajal Club, Sigma Xi. Home: Apt 512 S 680 N Lake Shore Dr Chicago IL 60611 Office: U Ill Psychiat Inst MC 912 1601 W Taylor St Chicago IL 60612-4310 Office Phone: 312-413-4562. E-mail: gdpappas@uic.edu.

PAPPAS, GEORGE FRANK, lawyer; b. Washington, Oct. 5, 1950; s. Frank George and Iora Marie (Stauber) P.; m. Susan Elizabeth Bradshaw, Apr. 25, 1980; children: Christine Bradshaw, Alexandra Stauber. BA, U. Md., 1972, JD, 1975. Bar: Md. 1976, D.c. 1991, u.S. Dist. Ct. Md. 1976, U.S. Dist. Ct. (d.C. cir.) 1986, U.S. Dist. Ct. (we. dist.) Tex. 1993, U.S. Ct. Appeals (4th cir.) 1976, U.S. Ct. Appeals (d.c. cir.) 1984, U.S. Ct. Appeals 9fed. cir.) 1991, U.S. Ct. Appeals (2d cir.) 1993, U.S. Ct. Appeals (6th and 7th cirs.) 1994, U.S. Supreme Ct. 1984, U.S. Ct. of Fed. Claims, 1995. Assoc. H. russell Smouse, Balt., 1976-81, Melnicove, Kaufman, Wiener & Smouse, Balt., 1981-83, prin., 1983-88; ptnr. Venable, Baetjer and Howard, Balt., 1986—. Lectr. Wash. Coll. Law, Am. U., Washington, 1980-84; mem. moot ct. bd., 1974-75; Master of the Bench, Inn XIII, Am. Inns of Ct., 1989; mem. U.S. Dist. Ct. of Delaware Judges' Intellectual property Adv. Com., 1998—; mem. Dist. Judge Edn. Adv. Com. for the Fed. Jud. Ctr., 2001—, chmn. Gov. Commn. on Devel. of Advanced Tech. Bus., 2003—. Founding editor-in-chief Internat. Trade law Jour., 1974-75. Mem. bd. vis. U. Md. Sch. of Law, 2000—. 1st lt. USAF, 1972-76. Mem. ABA, Am. Law Inst. 2002-, Internat. Assn. Def. Counsel, Md. Bar Assn. (chmn. internat. coml. law sect., 1980-81), Am. Intellectual Property Law Assn., U.S. Trademark Assn., Omicron Delta kappa, Phi Kappa Phi, Phi Beta Kappa, L'Hirondelle Club, Balt. Country Club. Republican. Greek Orthodox. Home: 9 Roland Ct Baltimore MD 21204-3550 Office: Venable Baetjer & Howard 2 Hopkins Plz Ste 2100 Baltimore MD 21201-2982 also: 1201 New York Ave NW Ste 1000 Washington DC 20005-6197

PAPPAS, GREGORY, health agency administrator; BS in Natural Scis. magna cum laude, U. Akron, 1974; PhD in Med. Anthropology, MD, Case Western Res. U., 1986. Diplomate Nat. Bd. Examiners. Intern in internal medicine Mt. Sinai Med. Ctr., Cleve., 1986-87; svc. fellow Nat. Ctr. Health Stats., Hyattsville, Md., 1987-89; spl. asst. in med. sociology Nat. Ctr. Health Stats., Ctr. Disease Control and Prevention, Hyattsville, Md., 1989-96; sr. pub. health and population advisor Office of Internat. and Refugee Health, Rockville, Md., 1996-97, assoc. dir. med. and sci. affairs, 1998, acting dir., 1998-99; sr. policy advisor Office of Surgeon Gen., Washington, 1999—. Vis. prof. Sch. Medicine, Kuwait; mem. health policy study group Case Western Res. Sch. Medicine, 1982; undergrad. instr. La Verne Coll., Athens, Greece, 1978; instr. Hellenic Internat. Schs., Athens, 1976-97; mem. thesis com. dept. sociology U. Md.; assoc. prof. Johns Hopkins U., Sch. Hygiene and Pub. Health, 1991—; faculty preventive medicine residency Ctrs. for Disease Control, 1997; mem. Nat. Com. on Vital and Health Stats.; mem. adv. com. NCHS Minority Grants; mem. health stats. adv. panel Am. Hosp. Assn.; mem. instnl. review bd. Nat. Health Exam. Survey; cons. Kaiser Permanente of No. Calif., 1996, Govt. of Spain, 1998; presenter in field. Author: The Magic City: Unemployment in a Working-Class Community, 1989, Health Profile of the People of Pakistan, 1997, Social Science and Medicine, 1997; contbr. articles to profl. jours. Mem. APHA (program devel. bd., Exec. Dir. award 1997), Am. Anthropology Assn. Office: Office of Surgeon Gen 200 Independence Ave SW Washington DC 20201-0004

PAPPAS, JAMES PETE, university administrator; b. Price, Utah, June 30, 1939; s. Pete S. and Dia P. (Metrakis) P.; m. Peggy Ann Kunz, Aug. 30, 1964; children: C. Jennifer, Peter T. AS in Psychology, Coll. Eastern Utah, 1959; BA in Psychology, U. Utah, 1961; MS in Counseling Psychology, Ohio U., 1964; PhD in Clin. Psychology, Purdue U., 1968; cert. in Mgmt., Stanford U., 1979; cert. in adminstrn., Harvard U., 1985. Asst. dir. counseling ctr. U. Utah, Salt Lake City, 1969-72, dir. ctr. for acad. advising, assoc. dean liberal edn., 1975-78, assoc. dean divsn. of continuing edn., 1978-87; prof. ednl. psychology and liberal studies U. Okla., Norman, 1987—, v.p. for univ. outreach; dean Coll. of Continuing Edn., 1994-00, Coll. of Liberal Studies, 2000—. Author: (book) Windows of Opportunity: Preparing University Based Residential Continuing Education for the Twenty-First Century, 1992, The University's Role in Economic Development: From Research to Outreach, 1997; co-author: (workbook) Promotional Techniques, 1987. Mem. Norman Econ. Devel. Coalition, 1996—; state chmn. Utah Endowment for Humanities, 1985-88; pres. Norman Arts and Humanities Coun., 1994-95. Recipient St. Paul award Greek Orthodox Ch. of N. Am., Denver, 1990, Christopher Outstanding Leadership and Bittner Svc. awards U. Continuing Edn. Assn.; inductee Internat. Adult and Continuing Edn. Hall of Fame, 1997. Mem. Am. Assn. Counseling and Devel. (nat. senator 1975-77), Assn. Acad. Affairs Adminstr. (bd. dirs. 1977-78), Adult Edn. Assn. Utah (bd. dirs. 1979-82), Univ. Continuing Edn. Assn. (pres. 1996-97), Nat. Assn. State Univs. and Land Grant Colls. (bd. dirs. 1994-97), Assn. Grad. Liberal Studies Programs (bd. dirs. 2002—). Avocations: reading, cmty. svc., writing, sports, travel. Office: Coll Continuing Edn 1700 Asp Ave Rm 111 Norman OK 73072-6407

PAPPAS, LEAH AGLAIA, civic worker, political consultant; b. Ogden, Utah, Mar. 23, 1936; d. George Thomas and Maria (Haramcs) P. BA, Coll. St. Mary of the Wasatch, 1959. Tchr. Bishop Gorman High Sch., Las Vegas, Nev., 1959-64; with Dist. Atty.'s staff, Las Vegas, 1972-75; tchr. Weber State Coll., Las Vegas, 1985. Civic worker various orgns., including Opera Guild, Heart Fund, City of Hope, March of Dimes, also groups for prevention of blindness, sr. citizens' groups, others, Ogden and Las Vegas, 1955—; cons. numerous polit. campaigns, Ogden, Las Vegas and Boston, L.A., John F. Kennedy campaign, 1959; alt. del. Chgo. Nat. Conv.; vol. Senator Robert Kennedy Campaign, 1968; supr. Senator Edward M. Kennedy Campaign, Boston, 1970, 76, Presdl. Campaign, 1980; campaign worker Gov. Jerry Brown, L.A., 1978, office mgr., Reagan-Bush campaign, 1984, Pres. Bill Clinton, 1996. Greek Orthodox. Home: 1323 Marilyn Dr Ogden UT 84403-0424

PAPPAS, MARJORIE L. library studies educator; b. Adrian, Mich., Oct. 4, 1938; d. Raymond C. Spielman and Adalene E. Dickey, Alfred Dickey (Stepfather); children: David J, Mark J. BS, U. Toledo, 1961; MEd, Miami U., Oxford, Ohio, 1977, PhD, 1987. Sch. libr. Watts Mid. Sch., Centerville, Ohio, 1970—78; dir. tech. and librs. Troy (Ohio) City Schs., 1978—85; asst. prof. Wright State U., Dayton, Ohio, 1986—95; assoc. prof. U. No. Iowa, Cedar Falls, 1995—98, vis. prof. online, 1998—2001; assoc. prof. Ea. Ky. U., Richmond, 2001—04; adj. prof. Mansfield U., Mansfield, Pa., 2004—. Pres., cons. C L Assocs., Inc., Danville, Ky., 1999—2000. Author: (information process model) Pathways to Knowledge, 1997, Searching Electronic Resources, 1998, Pathways to Knowledge and Inquiry Learning, 1998; contbr. articles to profl. jours. Recipient Edgar Dale award, Assn. Ednl. Comm. and Tech., 1995. Mem.: ALA, Ky. Sch. Media Assn., Am. Assn. Sch. Librs. (regional dir. 1993—96), Ohio Ednl. Libr. Media Assn. (life award of merit 2001), Phi Delta Kappa, Delta Kappa Gamma. Office: Mansfield U 426 Cloverdale Dr Danville KY 40422 E-mail: mpappas@mansfield.edu.

PAPPAS, MICHAEL, former congressman; b. New Brunswick, N.J., Dec. 29, 1960; Mem. U.S. House of Reps., Washington, 1996-98. Mem. Nat Security com., Small Bus. com., Govt. Reform and Oversight Com.; vice chmn. Civil Svc. subcom. Govt. Reform and Oversight com.; mem. Caucus on Hellenic Issues; freeholder Somerset County, dep. dir. 1986, 87, 92, 96, freeholder dir., 1998, 93; chmn. Somerset County Bd. Social Svcs., 1986-96; past liaison Somerset County Agriculture Devel. Bd.; mem. Franklin Township Coun., 1982-87, mayor, 1983-84. Trustee Somerset Med. Ctr.; Rep. candidate for Congress in N.J., 1999—. Recipient Disting. Svc. award Somerville Area Jaycees, 1992; named Outstanding Young Citizen, N.J. Jr. C. of C., 1993. Mem. Somerset County 4-H Assn. (Outstanding Svc. award 1994), Franklin Township Lions Club (Citizen of Yr. 1988), Ctrl. Jersey Club of the Deaf, Inc., Order AHEPA.

PAPPAS, MILTON J. venture capitalist; b. Cleve., Nov. 13, 1928; s. John Milton and Helen Stajos Pappas; m. Christine Kanillos, Nov. 7, 1953; children: Jeannine, William. BBA, Case Western Res. U., 1950; LLB, Cleveland Marshall Law Sch., 1956. Bar: Ohio 1956; cert. Inst. Chartered Analysts. Trust investment officer Cleve. Trust Co., 1954-60; fin. analyst Merrill Turben & Co., Cleve., 1960-62; sr. v.p. First of Mich., Detroit, 1962-66; v.p. Drexel, Harrman Ripley, N.Y.C., 1966-70, Euclid Ptnrs., N.Y.C., 1970—. Bd. dirs. IntraLinks, Inc., N.Y.C., Vision RX.com, Inc., White Plains, N.Y., Xanoptix, Inc., Merrimack, NH. Lt. (j.g.) USCG, 1952-54. Mem. N.Y. Venture Capital Forum. Greek Orthodox. Avocations: opera, ballet, theater, travel, jogging. Office: Euclid Ptnrs Corp 45 Rockefeller Plz Ste 3240 New York NY 10111-0999

PAPPAS, PHILIP JAMES, real estate company executive; b. Chgo., Sept. 29, 1954; s. Nicholas James and Ann (Nicholson) P.; m. Ana Lucia Sant'Anna; children: Tiago, Marcelo, Amanda. BA, Shimer Coll., 1975. Mgr. Cook County Hosp., Chgo., 1975-77, purchasing agt., 1977-81; pres. L.G. Properties, Chgo., 1980—, Tiamar Real Estate, 1990—. Docent Chgo. Architecture Found., 1976-78. Pres. Lincoln Park Builders Assn., 1997-99, Lake View Developers, 1988-89; trustee Shimer Coll., 1997-2003. Recipient 1st pl. award for best interior restoration Nat. Trust for Hist. Preservation, 1991. Mem. Nat. Assn. Realtors, Oxford Union Soc. (life), Chgo. Assn. Realtors (Good Neighbor award 1992, 96, 99-2004), Owassippe Staff Assn. Boy Scouts Am. (life). Greek Orthodox. Office: LG Properties 3654 N Lincoln Ave Chicago IL 60613-3536

PAPPAS, SANDRA LEE, state senator; b. Saint Paul, Minn., June 15, 1949; m. Neal Gosman, 1976; 3 children. BA, Met. State U., 1986; MPA, Harvard U., 1994. Mem. Minn. Ho. of Reps., St. Paul, 1984-90, Minn. Senate, St. Paul, 1990—. Part-time coll. instr. Mem. Dem. Farmer Labor Party. Home: 182 Prospect Blvd Saint Paul MN 55107-2136 Office: Minn State Senate 120 State Capitol 75 Martin Luther King Jr Blvd Saint Paul MN 55155-1601

PAPPAS, THOMAS NICHOLAS, insurance brokerage executive, consultant; b. Phila., Dec. 14, 1942; s. Thomas and Marcedes Pappas; m. Carol Ann Pappas; children: Thomas Nicholas Jr., Karen, Suszanne, Debora Pappas German. BS in Mktg., La Salle U., Phila., 1970; Exec. MBA, U. Pa., 1994. Sales rep. comsu,er OaOer Orpdicts Kimberley Clark Corp., Phila., 1966-67; regional sales and mktg. mgr. Xerox Corp., White Plains, Greenwich, Conn., 1968-74, br. sales mgr. Mountainside, N.J., 1974-75, sales mgr., 1975-76, mem. hdqs. mktg. staff Rochester, N.Y., 1976-77, sales rep. Phila., 1977-79; exec. v.p. Users, Inc., Glen Hardie, Pa., 1979-80; ptnr. Winklevoss & Assocs., Phila., 1981-82; mng. prin., sr. v.p., mgr. global sales and mktg. Johnson & Higgins, N.Y.C. and Phila., 1982-98; mem. sr. exec. transition team for merger Johnson & Higgins and Marsh & McLennan, Inc., 1997-98; chmn., CEO TNP Holdings Inc., Radnor, Pa., 1998—. Mem. adv. bd. dirs. Rittenhouse Trust Co. Mem. president's coun. LaSalle U.; trustee Acad. Notre Dame de Namur, Villanova, Pa., 1983-88, chmn. bd. trustees, 1987-88, chmn. endowment com., 1989. Named Man of Yr., Cath. Youth Orgn., 1994, Holy Family Coll., 1999. Mem. Union League Phila. (bd. dirs. 1991-96, v.p. 1994-96, pres. 1997-98, mem. Benson table, chmn. membership com., chmn. membership devel. com. 1991-95), Sunday Breakfast Club, Kindergarten Club, Cross Keys. Home: 105 Rock Rose Ln Radnor PA 19087-3736

PAPPAS, TOM, Olympic track and field athlete; b. Sept. 6, 1976; Attended, Lane Community Coll., Oregon, 1995—97; BA in Recreation & Leisure Studies, U. Tenn., 1997—99. Decathlete Team USA, Sydney Olympic Games, 2000, Team USA, Athens Olympic Games, 2004. Named SEC Outdoor Track Athlete of the Yr., 1999. Achievements include U.S. Outdoor National decathlon champion, 2003; Set new single meet record with 8,784 points. Office: c/o USOC One Olympic Plz Colorado Springs CO 80909*

PAPPERT, GERALD J. (JERRY), state attorney general; m. Ellen Pappert; 2 children. Grad. with honors, Villanova U., 1985; JD, Notre Dame U., 1988. Trial atty. Duane, Morris and Heckscher (now Duane Morris LLP), Philadelphia, Pa., 1988—96; first deputy atty. gen. State of Pa., Harrisburg, Pa., 1996—2003, atty. gen., 2003—. Office: Off of Atty Gen 1600 Strawberry Sq Harrisburg PA 17120*

PAPPS, BRUCE WILLIAM, financial analyst, investment company executive; b. Mt. Kisco, N.Y., Jan. 19, 1962; s. Ernest W. and Annette (Lazration) P. BS in Econs., U. Pa., 1985. CFA Designation, 2000. Pres., CEO Papps Capital Group, Inc., N.Y.C., 1996—. Adj. prof. SUNY, Valhalla, 1996—98. Mentor P.R.I.D.E., Harlem, N.Y., 1996-98. Mem. N.Y. Soc. Securities Analysts (mem. com.), Merrill Lynch Pres.'s Club, Wharton Club. Avocations: sky diving, scuba diving, boating, skiing. Office: Papps Capital Group Inc 67 Wall St Ste 2211 New York NY 10005-3101 Office Phone: 212-488-7259. E-mail: CEO@papps.com.

PAPROCKI, THOMAS JOHN, lawyer, priest; b. Chgo., Aug. 5, 1952; s. John Henry and Veronica Mary (Bonat) P. BA, Loyola U., Chgo., 1974; student Spanish lang. study, Middlebury Coll., 1976, student Italian lang. study, 1987; MDiv, St. Mary of the Lake Sem., 1978; student Spanish lang. study, Instituto Cuannahuac, 1978; Licentiate in Sacred Theology, St. Mary of the Lake Sem., 1979; JD, DePaul U., 1981; JCD, Gregorian U., Rome, 1991; student Polish lang. study, Cath. U. Lublin, Poland, 1989, Jagiellonian U., Cracow, Poland, 2000. Bar: Ill. 1981, U.S. Dist. Ct. (no. dist.) Ill. 1981, U.S. Supreme Ct. 1994. Assoc. pastor St. Michael Ch., Chgo., 1978-83; pres. Chgo. Legal Clinic, 1981-87, 91—; exec. dir. South Chgo. Legal Clinic, 1981-85, bd. dirs., 1987—; adminstr. St. Joseph Ch., Chgo., 1983-86; vice-chancellor Archdiocese of Chgo., 1985-92, chancellor, 1992-2000; adj. faculty Loyola U. of Law, 1999—; pastor St. Constance Parish, 2001—03; Titular Bishop of Vulturara, Auxiliary Bishop of Chgo., Episc. Vicar, Vicariate IV Archdiocese of Chgo., 2003—. Senator Presbyteral senate Archdiocese of Chgo., 1985-87, mem. Presbyteral coun., 1992-2000, mem. Cardinal's cabinet, 1992-2000, sec. coll. consultors, 1992-2000; chmn. incardination com., 1991-2000, chmn. policy devel. com., 1998-2000, chmn. Fgn. Priests Initiative, 1998-2000; asst. to the Gen. Sec., Vatican Synod of Bishops, Spl. Assembly for Am., Rome, 1997, cardinal's del. to profl. rev. bd., 1991-2003, chmn. profl. conduct adminstrv. com., 1991-2002; bd. dirs. Cath. Conf. Ill., 1985-87. Mem. editl. adv. bd. Chgo. Cath. Newspaper, 1984-85; contbr. articles to profl. jours. Bd. dirs. United Neighborhood Orgn., Chgo., 1982-85, S.E. Community Youth Svc. Bd., Chgo., 1985, Ctr. for Neighborhood Tech., Chgo., 1986-87, Chgo. Area Found. for Legal Svcs., 1994-2002; active Chgo. Cmty. Trust Com. on Children, Youth and Families, 1991-2002, Ill. Family Violence Coordinating Coun., 1994—. Recipient Humanitarian award Polish Am. Congress, 1997, Alumni award for Outstanding Pub. Svc., DePaul Coll. of Law, 2001; named Man of Yr., Nat. Advs., 1999. Fellow Leadership Greater Chgo.; mem. Ill. Bar Assn., Chgo. Bar Assn. (bd. mgrs. 1999-2001, Maurice Weigle award 1985), Advs. Soc. (award of merit 1996), Cath. Lawyers Guild, Canon Law Soc. Am., Polish Am. Leadership Initiative (bd. dirs. 2001—), Polish Am. Assn. (bd. dirs. 1998—), The Chgo. Jr. Assn. Commerce and Industry (Ten Outstanding Young Citizens award 1986), Union League Club of Chgo., Pi Sigma Alpha, DePaul U. Alumni Assn. Avocations: hockey, running, reading. Office: Aux Bishop of Chgo 1400 S Austin Blvd Cicero IL 60804

PAPY, FRANK MARIN, III, writer, editor; b. Savannah, Ga., Jan. 31, 1940; s. Frank M. Jr. and Catlain I. Papy; m. Nora M. Maaganck, Sept. 23, 1943; 1 child, Ellie M. At, Armstrong Coll., Savannah, Ga., 1957, U. Ga., Athens, 1958. Cons. Strachan Shipping, Savannah, Ga., 1960; adminstr. Nautica, Inc., Miami, Fla., 1972; instr. Boy Scouts of Am., Keys, Fla., 1976; writer Coastal Cruising mag., Beaufort, NC, 1990; contbg. editor Tropical Isles Pub., N.Y.C., 1992. Commodore Seven Seas Cruising Club, Ft. Lauderdale, Fla. Author: Cruising Guide to Fla. Keys, 1976, Sailing Impressions Ideas Deeds, 2000, Waypoint for Revenge, 2002. Advisor Boy Scouts Am., Fla. Keys, 1976, sailing instr., 1981; group leader George Gurdjieff Studies, Fla. Keys, 1971—. Staff sgt. U.S. Army, 1960—67. Mem.: Sports Writers Guild, Boating Writers Assn. Republican. Episcopalian. Avocations: yachting, philosophy, writing, fishing. Home: 87425 Old Hwy Islamorada FL 33036

PAPYRIN, ANATOLII NIKIFOROVICH, physicist, researcher; b. Novosibirsk, Russia, Apr. 2, 1942; s. Nikifor Vasilievich Papyrin and Kaleria Sergeevna Chirkovskaya; children: Margarita Anatolievna Vartanyan, Veronica Anatolievna Payrina. PhD, State U., Tomsk, Russia, 1971; MS, State Tech. U., Novosibirsk, Russia, 1965. Sr. rschr. K Tech. Corp., Albuquerque, 2000—; sr. rschr. assoc. Penn State U., State Coll., Pa., 1997—2000; visiting prof. McGill U., Montreal, Canada, 1990—91; assoc. prof. State U., Novosibirsk, Russia, 1972—85, prof., 1985—90; sr. scientist, head of lab. ITAM of RAS, Novosibirsk, Russia, 1971—97; rsch. asst. Inst. Nuclear Physics, Novosibirsk, Russia, 1965—71. Coord. Metallurgical Plant, Novosibirsk, Russia, 1986—89; cons. ASB Ind. Inc., Barberton, Ohio, 1996—97, Round Table Group, Inc., Wash., DC, 2001—; mem. Cold Spray Consortium. Author: (book) Supersonic Two-Phase Flows, 1980 (SB of RAS award), Methods of Experimental Physics, 1981; contbr. articles to jour. Mem. Social Coun. Edn., Novosibirsk, Russia, 1981—86. Mem.: ASM Internat. Achievements include invention of gas dynamic spraying method. Avocations: basketball, tennis, music. Office: K Tech Corp 1300 Eubank Blvd SE Albuquerque NM 87123-3336

PAQUET, GARY LEE, elementary school educator; b. Marquette, Mich., Feb. 28, 1963; s. Herbert Russell and Rena Ann McEachern. MusB, No. Mich. U., 1985; MA in Child Devel., Mich. State U., 1995. Music tchr. grades K-5 Algonac (Mich.) Cmty. Schs., 1985—93, tchr. 3d grade, 1993—. Prin. Pte. Tremble Elem. Sch., 2004—. Conductor Rainbow Singers Cmty. Honor Choir, Port Huron, Mich., 1998—99; soloist Schubert Male Chorus, Port Huron, Mich., 1998—2001. Mem.: Algonac Edn. Assn. (bldg. rep. 1996—99, exec. bd. 1998—99, pres. 2001—). Avocation: art. Home: 362 4th St Marysville MI 48040 Office: Algonac Cmty Schs 9541 Phelps Rd Algonac MI 48001 Office Phone: 810-794-3022 1602.

PAQUET, MICHAEL J. academic administrator; m. Barbara D. Gambetta, July 11, 1970; children: Michele L, Michael R. BA magna cum laude, La Salle U., 1970; MA, Pa. State U., 1972. Registrar Coll. Health Profls. Thomas Jefferson U., Phila., 1980—97, asst. dean Coll. Health Profls., 1998—2004, assoc. dean Coll. Health Profls., 2004—. Contbr. book Pennsylvania 1776, articles to profl. jours. Scholar, Pa. State U., 1970—72; McLean Found.scholar, Phila. Evening/Sunday Bull., 1966—70. Mem.: Mid. States Assn. Collegiate Registrars & Officers of Admission (pres. 1996—97), Alpha Sigma Lambda (charter mem. eta tau chpt. 1992), Alpha Eta (sec., treas. tju chpt. 1999).

PAQUETTE, WILLIAM ARTHUR, historian, educator; b. Lawrence, Mass., Aug. 6, 1947; s. Arthur Conrad Paquette and Dorothy Lucille Root; m. Sylvia Lois Kreps, June 14, 1969 (div. 1987). BA, Grove City (Pa.) Coll., 1969; MA, Duquesne U., 1971; PhD, Emory U., 1994. Tchr. Acad. Holy Cross, Kensington, Md., 1972—75, chmn. dept. social sci., 1973—75; from adj. prof. to prof. history Tidewater C.C., Portsmouth, Va., 1975—94, prof., 1994—. Grad. tchg. asst. Duquesne U., Pitts., 1969—71; adj. prof. history Old Dominion U., Norfolk, Va., 1975—78, Spelman Coll., Atlanta, 1983—84, adj. prof., 1989—90; adj. prof. history Ga. Perimeter, Atlanta, 1983—84; adj. prof. edn. Emory U., Atlanta, 1989—90; project historian NEH, 1979—82, 1995—96, 2000—02; reviewer ETS, 1995—; chmn. chancellor's prefix review com. Va. CC. Sys., Richmond, 1998—2000; nat. co-editor history Merlot Project, 2000—; mem. adv. bd. history digital project Gale Group Pubs., 2003—, ProQuest Pubs., 2004—; cons. in field. Author: U.S. Colored Troops from Lower Tidewater in the Civil War, 1992, Encyclopedia of African-American Civil Rights, 1992, Ready Reference: Censorship, 1997, Great Events from History, North America Series, 1997, The War of 1812: An Encyclopedia, 1998, Dictionary of World Biography: 20th Century, 1999, Biographical Encyclopedia of Twentieth Century World Leaders, 1999, Encyclopedia of the U.S. Supreme Court, 2000, Encyclopedia of America's Historic Sites, 2000, Putting the World into World History textbooks, Teaching History, 2001, Great Events: 1900-2001, 2002, World Education Encyclopedia, 2002, World Press Encyclopedia, 2003, A Taste of Merlot: The Multimedia Resources for Historians and Others, Perspectives, 2003; co-author: Instructor's Guide to the Teaching of American History, 1979, Readings in Black and White, 1982, Suffolk: A Pictorial History, 1987, Dictionary of World Biography: Renaissance, 1998, Encyclopedia of North America, 1998, Teaching History, A Journal of Methods, 2001; contbr. articles to profl. jours. Mem. adv. bd. US Com. World Food Day, 1999—; commr. Mus. Fine Arts, Portsmouth, Va., 1997—2002; mem. adv. bd. Ba. Fest. of the Book, 1998—. Fellow Summer fellow, NEH, 1985; grantee Study grant, Tidewater C.C., 1992—93. Mem.: Va. Political Scientists, History of Edn. Soc., Comparative and Internat. Edn. Soc., US Capitol Hist. Soc., Internat. Standing Conf. History Edn., Am. Ednl. Rsch. Assn., Am. Coun. Quebec Studies, Cmty. Coll. Humanities Assn. (v.p. 1991—93, bd. dirs. 1993—97, Disting. Svc. award 1997), Orgn. Am. Historians (com. cmty. coll. 2002—), Am. Hist. Assn. (Nancy Roelker Mentorship com. 1997—2000, chmn. 1999—2000, joint com. adj. 2000—), Mayflower Soc. Va. (asst. historian 1992—93, historian 1993—98, dep. gov. gen. 2004—). Avocations: stamp collecting/philately, photography, travel, genealogy. Office: Tidewater CC 7000 Coll Dr Portsmouth VA 23703 Home: 13565 Filly Ct Gainesville VA 20155 Office Phone: 757-822-2386. Business E-Mail: wpaquette@tcc.edu.

PAQUIN, ANNA, actress; b. Winnipeg, MB Canada, July 24, 1982; d. Brian and Mary Paquin. Actor: (films) The Piano, 1993 (Academy Award best supporting actress, 1993, Golden Globe nomination best supporting actress, 1993), Jane Eyre, 1995, Fly Away Home, 1996, Amistad, 1997, A Walk on the Moon, 1988, Hurly-burly, 1998, Begin the Beguine, 1998, Sleepless Beauty, 1998, A Walk on the Moon, 1999, She's All That, 1999, X-Men, 2000, Almost Famous, 2000, Finding Forrester, 2000, Buffalo Soldiers, 2001, Darkness, 2002, 25th Hour, 2002, X2, X-Men United, 2003, (TV films) Member of the Wedding, 1997, Hercules (voice only), 1988, All the Rage, 1999. Office: Double Happy Talent c/o Gail Cowan PO Box 9585 Wellington New Zealand also: William Morris Agy One William Morris Pl Beverly Hills CA 90212

PAQUIN, EDWARD H., JR., former state legislator, non-profit organization executive; b. Bennington, Vt., Feb. 12, 1953; s. Edward H. Sr. and Alice Marie P.; m. Patricia LaRose, July 4, 1981; 1 child, Katherine Marie. BA, U. Vt., 1975. Various positions including silversmith and factory worker; builder; rep. Vt. Gen. Assembly, Montpelier, 1991—2002; exec. dir. Vt. Protection and Advocacy, Inc., Montpelier, 2002—. Dir. summer camp for low-income rural children CAMP!; bd. dirs. Vt. Ctr. Ind. Living. Recipient Victory award Nat. Rehab. Hosp., 1991. Democrat. Baptist. Home: PO Box 219 Fairfax VT 05454-0219 Office: Vt Protection and Advocacy Inc 141 Main St Ste 7 Montpelier VT 05602

PAQUIN, THOMAS CHRISTOPHER, lawyer; b. Quincy, Mass., Feb. 12, 1947; s. Henry Frederick and Rita Marie (St. Louis) P.; m. Jean Jacqueline O'Neill, Aug. 5, 1972; children: Martha, Edward. BS in Acctg., Bentley Coll., 1969; JD, U. Notre Dame, 1974. Bar: Mass. 1974, U.S. Dist. Ct. Mass. 1976. Tax atty. Coopers and Lybrand, Boston, 1974-76; assoc. Cargill, Masterman & Cahill, 1976, Wilson, Curran & Malkasian, Wellesley, 1976-77; ptnr. Bianchi and Paquin, Hyannis, 1977-98; shareholder, dir. Quirk and Chamberlain, P.C., Yarmouthport, 1998—2001; of counsel Quirk, Chamberlain & Marsh, P.C., 2002—. Bd. dirs., chmn. nominating com. Elder Svcs. Cape Cod and Islands, Inc., Dennis, Mass., 1986-91; bd. dirs., corporator Vis. Nurse Assn. Cape Cod Found., Inc., Dennis, 1988-97; pres. Life Svcs. Inc., 1991-95; bd. dirs. Woodside Cemetery Corp., 1998—, pres., 1999—. Mem. Bass River Golf Commn., Yarmouth, Mass., 1980-83, chmn., 1982-83; chmn. Yarmouth Golf Course Bldg. Com., 1985-89; mem. hearing com. bd. Bar Overseers of the Supreme Jud. Ct., 1989-95; bd. dirs. Project Coach, Inc., 1990-97; conciliator Barnstable Superior Ct., 1992—; trustee, asst. treas. Cape Symphony Orch., 1999—, chmn. fin. com., 2003-04. Fellow Mass. Bar Found.; mem. ABA, Mass. Bar Assn. (del. 1986-87, mem. com. on bicentennial U.S. Constn. 1986-88, fee arbitration bd. 1985-86, chmn. spkrs. and writers subcom. 1986-88), Barnstable County Bar Assn. (chmn. seminar com. 1979-83, mem. exec. com. 1981-84, v.p. 1984-86, pres. 1986-87), Estate Planning Coun. Cape Cod (exec. com. 1985-98, sec. 1991-93, pres.-elect 1993-95, pres. 1995-97), Mass. Conveyancers Assn., Mid-Cape Men's Club (v.p. 1992, pres. 1993), Cummaquid Golf Club (dir. 2003-). Office: Thomas C Paquin Atty at Law 99 Willow St PO Box 38 Yarmouth Port MA 02675-0038 Office Phone: 508-362-8540. E-mail: t.c.paquin@comcast.net.

PARA, GERARD ALBERT, lawyer, real estate broker, consultant; b. Oak Park, Ill., June 27, 1953; s. Bruno Joseph and Bernice Agnes Para; m. Gayle Louise Keegan, Sept. 15, 1979; children: Eric, Teresa. BA with honor, De Paul U., 1973, JD, 1976. Bar: Ill. 1977, U.S. Dist. Ct. (no. dist.) Ill. 1977, U.S. Ct. Appeals (7th cir.) 1977, Fed. Trial Bar. 1984; lic. real estate broker, Ill., 1981. Jud. law clk. Ill Appellate Ct. (1st dist.), Chgo., 1977-78; divsnl. counsel Household Internat. Franchisor Divsns., Prospect Heights, Ill., 1978-85; v.p. Bannockburn (Ill.) Pk. Concepts, Inc., 1986-93; dir. real estate ops., asst. gen. counsel Ben Franklin Stores, Carol Stream, Ill., 1994-96; v.p., gen. counsel DiMucci Devel. Corp., Palatine, Ill., 1996-97; gen. counsel Urban Investment Trust Inc., Chgo., 1998-99; prin. Franchise ESQ.sm, Lincolnshire, Ill., 1999—; arbitrator 19th Jud. Cir., Lake County, Ill., 1999—, 18th Jud. Cir., DuPage County, Ill., 2000—, Cir. Ct. of Cook County, Ill., 2000—; candidate 19th Jud. Cir. Judge, Dem. Party, Lake and McHenry Counties, Ill., 2002. Real estate broker, Long Grove, Ill., 1987—; franchise cons. Elliotts' Off Broadway Deli, Oak Brook, Ill., 1993—. Editor: Medical Malpractice, 1975, Trial Technique, 1975. Asst. coach Little League Buffalo Grove (Ill.) Recreation Assn., 1988-2000; asst. scoutmaster Boy Scouts Am., Long Grove, 1995—. Mem. ABA, Internat. Coun. Shopping Ctrs., Internat. Corp. Real Estate Execs. (bd. dirs. Chgo. chpt. 1999-2002), Chgo. Bar Assn., Internat. Franchise Assn., Coun. Franchise Suppliers. Roman Catholic. Avocations: lap swimming, boating, scuba diving, weightlifting. Office: Franchise ESQ sm 125 Shelter Rd #450 Lincolnshire IL 60069 Office Phone: 847-634-2175. Personal E-mail: franchiseesq@aol.com.

PARADIS, DENIS, Canadian government official, member of parliament; b. St.-Jean-sur Richelieu, Que., Can., Apr. 1, 1949; m. Viviane Crevier; 1 child, Marie-Florence. BComm, U. Ottawa, 1970, LLL, 1975. Bar: Quebec, 1976. Ptnr. Paradis-Lemieuy, Brome-Missisquoi, 1976—; elected to House of Commons, Brome-Missisquoi, 1995—; parliamentary sec. to min. fgn. affairs Govt. of Can., 1999—2001, sec. state (Latin America & Africa) and (Francophonie), 2002—03, min. state (fin. instn.), 2003—. Mem. Fed. Liberal Assn. of Brome-Missisquoi (pres.), Assn. of Lawyers Outside Major Urban Ctrs. (past pres. 1983), Bedford Bar Assn., Bar Assn. of Vt., Bar of Quebec (v.p. 1992, pres. 1993-94), Can. Bar, Fedn. of Law Socs. in Can. Office: House of Commons 353 West Block Ottawa ON Canada K1A OA6*

PARADIS, JUDY, state legislator; b. St. Agathe, Maine, Jan. 17, 1944; m. Ross Paradis, 1970. BS, postgrad., U. Maine. Former mem. Dist. 150 Maine Ho. of Reps., mem. appropriations and fin. affairs coms.; mem. Dist. 1 Maine Senate; tchr. Frenchville, Maine. Chair Senate Haelth and Human Svcs. Com., ranking mem. Agr., Conservation and Forestry Com. Columnist St. John Valley Times. Co-host Maine Dem. Conv., 1998; mem. John Valley Hist. Assn., Maine Women's Lobby; co-pres. State Franco-Am. Conseil. Recipient Disting. Legislator award, 1990; Toll fellow, 1991. Mem. AAUW, Bus. and Profl. Women's Club, Assn. of French Speaking (Parliamentarian, pres. Maine sect. 1997), Optimists. Home: 40 US Route 1 Frenchville ME 04745-6151 Office: Maine State Senate State Capitol 3 State House Sta Augusta ME 04333-0003 Fax: 728-6374. E-mail: rody@nbnet.nb.ca.

PARADIS, WILFRID H. retired historian; b. Manchester, N.H., June 23, 1922; s. Wilfrid Z. Paradis and Alice L. Dugré. MA in History, St. Mary Sem. and U., Balt., 1949; PhD in History summa cum laude, U. Paris, 1952; Dr. Canon Law summa cum laude, Cath. U. Paris, 1953; DDiv (hon.), St. Anselm Coll., Manchester, 1979; DLitt (hon.), Notre Dame Coll., Manchester, 1992.

Lectr. history, various locations, 1952—80; chancellor, jud. rector Diocese of Manchester, 1960—65; advisor 2d Vatican Council, Vatican City, 1962—65; sec. edn. Washington, 1973—80; ret., 1987. Author: (book) Influence des Archévêques de Rouen in Nouvelle France, Catholicism in New Hampshire in 1647-1997 (Nat. award, 2000). Mem. planning bd. Notre Dame Hosp., Manchester, 1960—68; chmn. judicatory leaders N.H. Coun. Chs., 1967; bd. advisors N.H. Coun. of Christians and Jews, 1969—73, N.H. Coun. Chs., 1969—73; bd. dirs. Franklin Pierce Coll., 1970—73; adv. bd. N.H. Coun. World Affairs, 1960—73. With U.S. Army, 1942—45. Recipient Medaille Grand Prix, Soc. Historique Franco Americaine, Boston, 1956, Brotherhood award, N.H. Coun. of Christians and Jews. Mem.: Nat. Cath. Edn. Assn. (bd. dirs. 1974—80). Roman Catholic. Avocations: reading, hiking, travel. Home: 107 Alsace St Manchester NH 03102 Office: Diocese of Manchester PO Box 310 153 Ash St Manchester NH 03105

PARADISE, LOUIS VINCENT, educational psychology educator, university official; b. Scranton, Pa., Apr. 19, 1946; s. Louis Benjamin and Lucille (Bochicchio) P.; children: Christopher, Gabrielle,Victoria. BS, Pa. State U., 1968; MS, Bucknell U., 1974; PhD, U. Va., 1976. Lic. psychologist, profl. counselor; cert. sch. psychologist. Assoc. prof. Cath. U. Am., Washington, 1976-83; prof. edn., chmn. edn. leadership U. New Orleans, 1983-90, dean Coll. Edn., 1990-92, univ. vice chancellor, provost, 1992-94, exec. vice chancellor, provost, 1994—2003, prof. Dept. Ednl. Leadership, Counseling, and Found., 2003—. Author: Ethics in Counseling and Psychotherapy, 1979, Questioning: Skills for the Helping Process, 1979, Counseling in Community College, 1982. 1st lt. U.S. Army, 1968-72. DuPont scholar U. Va., 1974. Mem. APA, ACA (ethics com. 1986-89), Am. Edn. Rsch. Assn., So. Assn. Counselor Edn. (chmn. ethics com. 1988-89), Acad. Counseling Psychology, Chi Sigma Iota (founding chpt. pres. 1985-87). Roman Catholic. Avocations: running, bicycling, music. Office: U New Orleans Dept Ednl Leadership Counseling & Found New Orleans LA 70148-0001 Business E-Mail: louis.paradise@uno.edu.

PARADISE, PAUL RICHARD, writer, editor; b. N.Y.C., July 4, 1950; s. Paul L. and Ann (Ho) P. BA in Journalism, Wash. State U., 1975; MLS, Pratt Inst., Bklyn., 2002. Staff writer T.F.H. Publs., Neptune, N.J., 1977-79; legal indexer Matthew Bender, N.Y.C., 1980-86; free-lance writer, 1988—. Author: Raccoons, 1976, Amazon Parrots, 1978, African Gray Parrots, 1979, Cockatiels, 1987, Trademark Counterfieting, Product Piracy and the Billion Dollar Threat to the U.S. Economy, 1999. Mayors Grad. scholar, 2001—. Mem. Soc. Profl. Journalists. Home: 722 Willow Ave Hoboken NJ 07030-4034 E-mail: paulrpirate@aol.com.

PARADY, FRED, state representative; b. Presque Isle, Maine, July 19, 1955; m. Lisa Skiles Parady. BS, U. Idaho; MS, Mont. State U. Mgr. OCI Wyo.; state rep. dist. 17 Wyo. State Legis., Cheyenne, 1995—. Mem. Rules and Procedure com. Wyo. State Legis., Cheyenne, chmn. mgmt. coun. Mem.: Am. Soc. Safety Engrs., East Jr. High PTO. Republican. Home: 1221 Hilltop Dr Rock Springs WY 82901 Office: Capitol Bldg Wyo State Legis Cheyenne WY 82002

PARAGAS, ROLANDO G. physician; b. Philippines, Apr. 15, 1935; came to U.S., 1959; s. Epifanio Y. and Ester (Guiang) P.; m. Liwayway Galvey, May 5, 1963; children: Suzanne, Richard, Esther, Dawn. AA, U. Philippines, 1953; MD, Far Eastern U., 1958. Physician pvt. practice, Burlington, Iowa, 1968—. Fellow Am. Acad. Pediatrics; mem. AMA, Assn. Philippine Physicians in Am., Iowa Med. Soc. Office: 828 N 7th St Burlington IA 52601-4921

PARAN, MARK LLOYD, retired lawyer; b. Cleve., Feb. 1, 1953; s. Edward Walter and Margaret Gertrude (Ebert) P. AB in Sociology cum laude, Harvard U., 1977, JD, 1980. Bar: Ill. 1980, Mass. 1986, Tex. 1993. Assoc. Wilson & McIlvaine, Chgo., 1980-83, Lurie Sklar & Simon, Ltd., Chgo., 1983-85, Sullivan & Worcester, Boston, 1985-92; pvt. practice Boston, 1992, Euless, Tex., 1992—2002. Mem. ABA, State Bar Tex. Avocations: tornado hunting, severe thunderstorms, photography. Home and Office: 1050 W Ash Ln Apt 1015 Euless TX 76039-2171 Office Phone: 817-267-1400. E-mail: f6tornado@comcast.net.

PARANTHAMAN, MARIAPPAN PARANS, research scientist; s. Sundara Thangappa and Vasantha Devi Mariappa Nadar; m. Sathiya Rajappan, June 10, 1990; children: Nithya, Bhavya. PhD, Indian Inst. Tech., Chennai, 1982—88. Post doctoral rschr. U. Tex., Austin, 1988—91; rsch. assoc. U. Colo., Boulder, 1991—93; sr. rsch. staff mem. Oak Ridge Nat. Lab., Tenn., 1993—. Editor: (jour.) Superconductor Sci. and Tech. Mem.: Materials Rsch. Soc. (corr.; organizer, confs. and workshops 2001—02). Achievements include patents for the RABiTS process to superconducting wires. Home: 1117 Oak Haven Rd Knoxville TN 37932 Office: Oak Ridge Nat Lab Bethel Valley Rd Oak Ridge TN 37831-6100 Office Phone: 865-574-5045.

PARASCOS, EDWARD THEMISTOCLES, engineering consultant; b. N.Y.C., Oct. 20, 1931; s. Christos and Nina (Demitrovich) P.; m. Jenny Morris, July 12, 1978; children: Jennifer Mellissa, Edward T., Jr. BSME, CCNY, 1956, MSME, 1958; postgrad. ops. rsch., NYU, 1964. Registered profl. engr., Calif. Design engr. Ford Instrument, 1957-61; reliability engring. supr. Kearfott divsn. Gen. Precision Inc., 1961-63; staff cons. Am. Power Jet, 1963-64; reliability mgr. Perkin Elmer Corp., 1964-66; dir. system effectiveness CBS Labs., Stamford, Conn., 1966-72; pres. Dipar Cons. Svcs. Ltd., East Elmhurst, N.Y., Lapa Trading Corp.; gen. mgr., prin. reliability engr. engring. Consol. Edison Co., N.Y.C., 1972-95, mgr. transp. and stores environ. affairs, 1995-98, ret., 1998; sr. reliability engring. cons. Morris Cons. Agy., 1998—. Pres., chmn. bd. RAM Cons. Assocs.; pres., 1978-80; chmn. 1st Reliability Engring. Conf. Electric Power Industry, 1974, also 4th and 18th confs.; chmn. bd. Inter-Ram Q Conf. for electric power industry; gen. chmn. 18th Inter-Ramq Conf. for electric power industry; lectr. in field. Fellow Am. Soc. Quality Control (vice chmn. Reliability divsn. 1968-70, sr. mem.); mem. ASME, Soc. Reliability Engrs., Edison Engring. Soc. Home: 30-02 83d St Jackson Heights NY 11370-1919 Office: Morris Consulting Agy 82-18 30th Ave Jackson Heights NY 11370 Personal E-mail: ETP1919@aol.com.

PARATJE, MERCEDES, bank executive; b. Barcelona; m. Sergio Verdu; 1 child, Ariana Verdu. Grad. telecommunications engring., Poly. U. Barcelona, 1981; MA in Labor Rels., U. Ill., 1983, MBA in Fin., 1985. Lic. stockbroker. Engr. N.V. Philips, Barcelona, 1978-81; fin. analyst Ctr. Internat. Fin. Analysis, Princeton, N.J., 1985-87, rsch. mgr., 1987-88; 2nd v.p., investment strategist internat. pvt. bank Chase Manhattan Bank, N.Y.C., 1988-90, 2d v.p., internat. equity analyst, 1990-91; v.p., portfolio mgr. pvt. banking internat. The Chase Manhattan Pvt. Bank, N.Y.C., 1991-94; v.p., global product head equity adv. svcs. Citicorp Securities Pvt. Bank Divsn., 1994-98; chief investment officer Americas pvt. bank divsn. Barclays Bank, N.Y.C., 1998-2000; global head Investment Adv. Svcs., N.Y.C., London, 2000—02; exec. dir. Morgan Stanley Pvt. Wealth Mgmt., 2002—. Co-editor: Worldscope, Industrial, 1988; contbg. researcher: Worldscope, Financial, 1988, International Accounting Trends, 1989; contbr. articles to profl. publs. Mem. European Register Tech. Professions, Nat. Assn. Tech. Engrs. (prize 1981), Sigma Iota Epsilon. Home: 6 Farrand Rd Princeton NJ 08540-6777 Office: Morgan Stanley 1221 Ave of Americas 4 Fl New York NY 10021

PARAVASTU, SWAMY, economist, researcher; s. Ranganayakammal and Jagannatha Swamy Sri Paravastu; m. Padmavathi Alavattam, July 11, 1970; children: Nagini, Ananta Krishna Venkata. MS in econs., Andhra U., Visakhapatnam, India, 1956, MS in stats., 1958; PhD, U. Wis., Madison, 1967. Math. statistician Bur. Labor Stats., 2001—; economist Office Comptr. Currency, Washington, 1995—2001. Assoc. prof. econs. SUNY, 1967—70; prof. econs. Ohio State U., Columbus, 1970—73; sr. economist Fed. Res. Bd., Washington, 1974—95. Recipient Econ. Rsch. Svc. Adminstr. Award, USDA, 1989.

PARAZYNSKI, SCOTT E. astronaut; b. Little Rock, Ark., July 28, 1961; m. Gail Marie Vozzella; 2 children. BS in Biology, Stanford U., 1983, MD with honors, 1989. Intern Brigham and Women's Hosp., 1990; resident in emergency medicine Denver; astronaut NASA, Houston, 1992, crew rep. Astronaut Office Mission Devel. Br., crew rep. Astronaut Office Ops. Planning Br., dep. Astronaut Office ISS Br. Team coach for the Philippines Olympic Winter Games, Calgary, Canada, 1988. Recipient Predoctoral Tng. award in cancer biology, NIH, 1983. Mem.: Aircraft Owners and Pilots Assn., Exptl. Aircraft Assn., Assn. Space Explorers, Wilderness Med. Soc. (Rsch. award 1991), Am. Soc. Gravitational and Space Biology, Aerospace Med. Assn., Am. Alpine Club. Achievements include logged over 2,000 flight hourse in a variety of aircraft; logged over 1.019 hours in space; 20 hours EVA; crew STS-66 (1994), STS-86 Atlantis (1997), STS-95 Discovery (1998) and STS-100 Endeavour (2001). Avocations: mountain climbing, rock climbing, flying, scuba diving, skiing. Office: Astronaut Office/CB NASA Johnson Space Ctr Houston TX 77058

PARBOTEEAH, KAVIRAJ PRAVEEN, finance educator; b. Quatre Bornes, Mauritius, Sept. 7, 1969; s. Balmik and Sita Shakuntala Parboteeah; m. Kyong Ryun Pyun, May 31, 1996; 1 child, Alisha Jade. BSc with honors in Mgmt. Studies, U. of Mauritius, Reduit, 1992; MBA, Calif. State U., Chico, 1994; PhD, Wash. State U., 1999. Asst. prof. Wash. State U., Pullman, 1999—2000; asst. prof. of internat. mgmt. U. of Wis. - Whitewater, 2000—. Faculty co-advisor Sigma Iota Epsilon - U. of Wis. Whitewater, Whitewater, Wis., 2000—. Author: (textbook) Multinational Management: A Strategic Approach; contbr. articles to profl. jours. Mem.: Acad. of Mgmt. Office: University of Wisconsin - Whitewater 800 West Main St Whitewater WI 53190 Office Phone: 262-472-3971. E-mail: parbotek@uww.edu.

PARCELL, JOHN CLEO, music educator; b. Oskaloosa, Iowa, July 17, 1945; s. John Melvin and Verda Louella May Parcell; m. Cathy Kay Hardy, Sept. 30, 1990;; children: Kent Bradley, Khristina Lynn. BS, NE Mo. St U., Kirksville, MO, 1967; MA, Truman St U., Kirksville, MO, 1968; MS, Ctrl. Mo. St U., Warrensburg, MO, 2000; DMA, U. Mo., Kansas City, MO, 1990. DESE-Life Certification Mo., Orff Schulewerk Level J Mo., Elementary Administration-DESE Mo. Band dir. Rich Ctrl. H.S., Olympia Field, Ill., 1967—69, Tipton Cmty. Sch., Tipton, Iowa, 1969—72, Maynard (West Ctrl.), Maynard, Iowa, 1972—73, Carl Junction R-I Schools, Carl Junction, Mo., 1973—73; choir dir. Meml. H.S., Joplin, Mo., 1980—82; music and instrumental music tchr. Joplin R-8, Joplin, Mo., 1982—88; elem. music tchr. Kans. City Sch. Dist., Kansas City, Mo., 1990—; adj. prof. Longview CC, Lee's Summit, Mo., 1992—. Music critic Pk. Forest Star, Park Forest, Ill., 1967—69; trumpet player Chgo. Hgts Symphony, Chicago Heights, Ill., 1967—69; member-european tour Mid Am. Jazz & Concert Band-Coe Coll., Cedar Rapids, Iowa, 1972; member-mexican tour Kans. City Symphony Chorus, Kansas City, Mo., 1988; mem. Mid. Sch. Music Curriculum Committe, Joplin, Mo., 1984, Profl. Devel. Com., Kansas City, Mo., 1990—2000, Kans. City Sch. Dist. Core Curriculum and Textbook Com., Kansas City, Mo., 1999—2000. Camelot cast mem. Joplin Little Theater, Joplin, Mo., 1983—83; asst. condr. Carthage Cmty. Band, Carthage, Mo., 1985—87; mem. Blue Springs Summer Musical Orch., Blue Springs, Mo., 1990—95. Recipient Cowlgill & Blair Incentive Award, SW Mo. Teachers Assoc, 1986, Phi Kappa Phi, Ctrl. Mo. St U., 2000. Mem.: Mo. Music Educators Assn., Music Educators Nat. Conf. Southern Baptist. Avocations: music listening, music listening, landscaping, instrument and vocal music performance. Home: 5433 Appleton Ave Raytown MO 64133 Office: Kansas City School District 12th & McGee Kansas City MO 64109 Personal E-mail: john_parcell2003@yahoo.com.

PARCELLS, BILL (DUANE CHARLES PARCELLS), professional football coach; b. Englewood, N.J., Aug. 22, 1941; m. Judith Parcells; children: Suzy, Jill, Dallas. BA, Wichita State U., 1964. Asst. coach Hastings Coll. (Nebr.), 1964, Wichita State U. (Kans.), 1969, U.S. Mil. Acad., 1966—69, Fla. State U., Tallahassee, 1970—72, Vanderbilt U., Nashville, 1973—74, Tex. Tech U., Lubbock, 1975—77; head coach U.S. Air Force Acad., Colorado Springs, Colo., 1978; asst. coach New Eng. Patriots, NFL, 1980, N.Y. Giants, NFL, 1981—82, head coach, 1983—91; NFL studio analyst NBC Sports, 1991—92; head coach New England Patriots, NFL, 1993—97, NY Jets, 1997—2000, chief football ops., 2000—01; head coach Dallas Cowboys, 2003—. Coach NFL championship team N.Y. Giants, 1986, 90. Office: Dallas Cowboys One Cowboys Pkwy Irving TX 75063

PARCH, GRACE DOLORES, librarian; b. Cleve. d. Joseph Charles and Josephine Dorothy (Kumel) P. BA, Case Western Res. U., 1946, postgrad., 1947-50; B.L.S., McGill U., 1951; M.L.S., Kent State U., 1983; postgrad., Newspaper Library Workshop, Kent State U., 1970, Cooper Sch. Art, 1971-72, API Newspaper Library Seminar, Columbia U., 1971, Coll. Librarianship, U. Wales, 1984, 85. Cert. literacy instr., Ohio. Publicity librarian Spl. Services U.S. Army, Germany, 1951, post librarian, 1952; USAF base librarian, 1953-54; br. librarian Cleveland Heights (Ohio) Pub. Library, 1954-63; asst. head reference div. Va. State Library, Richmond, 1964; dir. Twinsburg (Ohio) Pub. Library, 1965-70; dir. newspaper library Cleve. Plain Dealer, 1970-83; county librarian N.C., 1987-92. Cons. Cath. Library Assn., 1961-64; mem. home econs. adv. com., Summit County, 1969, books/job com., 1968; mem. adv. com. Guide to Ohio Newspapers, 1793-1973, 1971-74; appointed to del. spl. librs. for People-to-People Program in Russia, 1995. Exhibited oil paintings at Cuyahoga Cmty. Coll., 1996, 97; contbr. articles to Plain Dealer, N. Summit Times, Twinsburg Bull., Sun Press; author: Where In the World But in the Plain Dealer Library, 1971; Editor: Directory of Newspaper Libraries in the U.S. and Canada, 1976. Donor coll. scholarship grants at Hayesville, H.S., N.C., 1997. Recipient MacArthur Found. award, 1988, Libr. of Am. award, 1988, Libr. Internat. Woman of Yr. award Internat. Biog. Ctr., Cambridge, Eng., 2000. Mem. McGill U. Alumnae Assn. (sec. 1973), Kent State U. Alumni Assn., ALA (rep. on joint com. with Cath. Library Assn. 1967-70), John Cotton Dana award 1967, Library Pub. Rels. Coun. award 1972), Cath. Library Assn. (co-chmn. 1960-63), Spl. Libraries Assn. (chmn. newspaper library directory com. 1974-76, chmn. pub. relations Cleve. chpt. 1973, chmn. edn. com. newspaper div. 1982-83, mem. edn. com. nominating com. 1984), Ohio Library Assn., Western Res. Hist. Soc., Am. Soc. Indexers, Cleve. Mus. Art Assn., Coll. and Research Librarians, Nat. Micrographic Assn., Women Space, Women's Nat. Book Com., Nat. Trust Hist. Preservation Clubs: Cleve. Athletic, Cleve. Women's City. Roman Catholic. Home: 1533 Regina Ct S Irving TX 75062-4329 *Greatness results in adapting aspects or ideas in other disciplines to one's own specialty.*

PARDAVI-HORVATH, MARTHA MARIA, physicist, educator; b. Budapest, Hungary, Feb. 3, 1940; arrived in US, 1985; d. Elek and Katalin (Sattelberger) Horvath; m. Ferenc Pardavi, July 7, 1967; 1 child, Martha Pardavi. PhD in Physics, Hungarian Acad. Sci., Budapest, 1985, R. Eotvos U., 1988. Rsch. assoc. Hungarian Acad. Sci., Budapest, 1967-75, head lab., 1975-85; rsch. assoc. Ohio State U., Columbus, 1988; vis. prof. NRC, Rome, 1989; prof. George Washington U., Washington, 1989—. Author: Microelectronic Technology, Magnetic Multilayers, Nonlinear Microwave Signal Processing, Magnetic Systems; contbr. articles to profl. jours. Mem.: AAAS, IEEE (chpt. chair 1989), Internat. Soc. Interdisciplinary Study Symmetry (sec.), Am. Phys. Soc., N.Y. Acad. Scis., Sigma Xi. Office: George Washington U Dept ECE 801 22nd St NW Washington DC 20052 Business E-Mail: mpardavi@gwu.edu.

PARDE, DUANE ARTHUR, association executive; BA in Polit. Sci., History, U. Kans. Legis. rsch. asst. Atty. Gen. Office, Topeka, 1986-87; dir. state legis. rsch. Am. Legis. Exchange Coun., Washington, 1989-92; dir. state affairs Coun. Affordable Health Ins., Alexandria, Va., 1992-95; chief of staff Am. Legis. Exchange Coun., Alexandria, 1995-96, exec. dir., 1996—. Bd. adv. Kans. Pub. Policy Inst. Mem. Am. Soc. Assn. Exec. Office: Am Legis Exchange Coun 1129 20th St NW #500 Washington DC 20036-3479

PARDEE, ARTHUR BECK, biochemist, educator; b. Chgo., July 13, 1921; s. Charles A. and Elizabeth B. (Beck) Pardee; m. Ruth Sager (dec.); m. Ann Goodman; children: Michael, Richard, Thomas. BS, U. Calif., Berkeley, 1942; MS, Calif. Inst. Tech., 1943, PhD, 1947; D (hon.), U. Paris, 1993. Merck postdoctoral fellow U. Wis., 1947—49; mem. faculty U. Calif., Berkeley, 1949—61, assoc. prof., 1957—61; NSF fellow Pasteur Inst., 1957—58; prof. biology, chmn. dept. biochem. scis. Princeton (NJ) U., 1961—67, prof. biochemistry, 1961—75, Donner prof. sci., 1966; prof. Dana Farber Cancer Inst. and biochem. pharmacology dept. Harvard Med. Sch., Boston, 1975—. Co-author: Experiments in Biochemical Research Techniques, 1957; editor: Biochemica et Biophysica Acta, 1962—68. Mem. rsch. adv. coun. Am. Cancer Soc., 1967—71; trustee Cold Spring Harbor Lab. Quantitative Biology, 1963—69. Named Princess Takamatu lectr., 1990, hon. faculty mem., Nanjing U., 1999; recipient Young Biochemists travel award, NSF, 1952, Krebs medal, Fedn. European Biochem. Socs., 1973, Rosenstiel award, Brandeis U., 1975, 3M award, Fedn. Am. Socs., Exptl. Biology, 1980, CIIT prize, 1993, Disting. Alumnus award, Calif. Inst. Tech., 1999; fellow, Internat. Inst. for Advanced Studies, 1999. Fellow: AAAS; mem.: NAS (editl. bd. proc. 1971—73, com. on scis. and pub. policy 1973—76), Chem. Industry Inst. Toxicology (Founders award, Boehringer-Mannheim award 1998), Ludwig Inst. Cancer Rsch. (sci. com. 1988—), Japanese Biochem. Soc., Am. Philos. Soc., Am. Soc. Microbiologists, Am. Assn. Cancer Rsch. (pres. 1985—86), Am. Soc. Biol. Chemists (treas. 1964—70, pres. 1980—81), Am. Chem. Soc. (Paul Lewis award 1960). Office: 44 Binney St Boston MA 02115-6013 E-mail: arthur.pardee@afci.harvard.edu.

PARDEE, OTWAY O'MEARA, computer scientist, educator; b. Seattle, June 26, 1920; s. Otway and Mary Gertrude (O'Meara) Pardee; m. Marilynn Lowrie, Aug. 9, 1946; children: Irene, Loraine, Suzanne. BS in Elec. Engring., U. Wash., 1941; PhD in Elec. Engring., Stanford U., 1948. Instr. math. Syracuse U., N.Y., 1948-52, asst. to assoc. prof., 1952-69, dir. Computing Ctr., 1962-69, prof. computer sci., 1969-86, prof. emeritus, 1986—. With USNR, 1944—46. Mem.: IEEE, AAUP (pres. Syracuse U. chpt. 1960), Am. Phys. Soc., Math. Assn. Am., Am. Math. Soc., Assn. Computing Machinery (chmn. Syracuse chpt. 1963), Tau Beta Pi, Sigma Xi. Avocations: camping, photography. Home: 843 Maryland Ave Syracuse NY 13210-2502 Office: Syracuse U Ctr for Sci and Tech Ste 2-175 Syracuse NY 13244-0001 Business E-Mail: oopardee@syr.edu.

PARDEE, SCOTT EDWARD, securities dealer; b. New Haven, Oct. 11, 1936; s. William Durley and Catherine (Eames) P.; m. Aida Milagros Fuentes Tavarez, Jan. 29, 1966; 1 child, Alan Alexander. BA, Dartmouth Coll., 1958; PhD, MIT, 1962. Research asst. Fed. Res. Bank, Boston, 1959-62; teaching asst. in econs. MIT, Cambridge, Mass., 1961-62; research economist Fed. Res. Bank N.Y., N.Y.C., 1962-66, mgr. fgn. dept., 1967-70, asst. v.p. fgn. dept., 1970-74, v.p. fgn. dept., 1974-79; tchr. banking and fin. NYU, 1965-67, Am. Inst. Banking, 1969-72; adj. prof. Grad. Sch. Bus. Columbia U., N.Y.C., 1972-75; dep. mgr. fgn. ops. Fed. Res. System Open Market Account, 1975-79, mgr. fgn. ops., 1979-81; exec. v.p., dir. Discount Corp. N.Y., N.Y.C., 1981-86; dir. Am. Internat. Group, 1982-86; vice chmn. Yamaichi Internat. Am. Inc., N.Y.C., 1986-88, chmn., 1988-95, sr. advisor, 1995-97; sr. lect., exec. dir. Fin. Rsch. Ctr., MIT Sloan Scool of Mgmt., 1997-99; adj. prof. Grad. Sch. of Business, U. Chicago, Chicago, IL, 1997-98; Alan R. Holmes prof. of monetary econs. Middlebury Coll., Vt., 2000—. Bd. dirs. Renaissance Holdings, Ltd. Author: A Study of Inter-City Wage Differentials, 1962. Trustee Woodrow Wilson Fellowship Found., 1994—; mem. Coun. on Fgn. Rels., 1995—. Woodrow Wilson fellow MIT, 1958-59; recipient Dr. Louis M. Spadaro award Fordham U., 1980 Mem. Phi Beta Kappa. Home: 250 South End Ave New York NY 10280-1074 Office: Middlebury Coll Econs Dept Middlebury VT 05753

PARDEN, ROBERT JAMES, engineering educator, management consultant; b. Mason City, Iowa, Apr. 17, 1922; s. James Ambrose and Mary Ellen (Fahey) P.; m. Elizabeth Jane Taylor, June 15, 1955; children— Patricia Gale, James A., John R., Nancy Ann. BS in Mech. Engring, State U. Iowa, 1947, MS, 1951, PhD, 1953. Reg. profl. engr. Iowa, Calif.; lic. gen. contractor Calif. Indsl. engr. LaCrosse Rubber Mills, 1947-50; asso. dir. Iowa Mgmt. Course, 1951-53; asso. prof. indsl. engring. Ill. Inst. Tech., 1953-54; prof. engring. mgmt. Santa Clara U., 1955—, dean Sch. Engring., 1955-82; prin. Saratoga Cons. Group (Calif.), 1982—. Mem. Sec. Navy's Survey Bd. Grad. Edn., 1964 Mem. Saratoga Planning Commn., 1959-61. Served to 1st lt., Q.M.C. AUS, 1943-46. Named to Silicon Valley Engring. Hall of Fame Silicon Valley Engring. Coun., 1993. Mem. ASME (chmn. Santa Clara Valley sect. 1958), Am. Soc. Engring. Edn. (chmn. Pacific N.W. sect. 1960), Am. Inst. Indsl. Engrs. (edn. chmn. 1958-63, dir. ASEE-ECPD affairs 1963-68), Nat. Soc. Profl. Engrs., Engrs. Council Profl. Devel. (dir. 1964-65, 66-69), Soc. Advancement Mgmt., ASEM, Sigma Xi, Tau Beta Pi. Roman Catholic. Home: 19832 Bonnie Ridge Way Saratoga CA 95070-5010 Office: Santa Clara U Sch Engring Santa Clara CA 95053-0001 Office Phone: 408-554-4987. E-mail: bobparden@comcast.net., rparden@scu.edu.

PARDES, HERBERT, psychiatrist, educator, health facility executive; b. Bronx, N.Y., July 7, 1934; s. Louis and Frances (Bergman) P.; m. Judith Ellen Silber, June 9, 1957; children: Stephen, Lawrence, James. BS, Rutgers U., 1956; MD, SUNY-Downstate Med. Center, Bklyn., 1960; DSc (hon.), SUNY, 1990. Straight med. intern Kings County Hosp., 1960-61, intern & resident in psychiatry, 1961-62, 64-66; asst. prof. psychiatry Downstate Med. Ctr., Bklyn., 1968-72, prof., chmn. dept., 1972-75; dir. psychiat. svcs. Kings County Hosp., Bklyn., 1972-75; prof., chmn. dept. psychiatry U. Colo. Med. Sch., 1975-78; dir. psychiat. svcs. Colo. Psychiat. Hosp., Denver, 1975-78; dir. NIMH, Rockville, Md., 1978-84; asst. surgeon gen. USPHS, 1978-84; prof. psychiatry Columbia U., NYC, 1984—, chmn. dept., 1984; dir. Psychiat. Svc. Presbyn. Hosp. (now Columbia Presbyn. Center of NY Presbyn. Hosp.), NYC, 1984-89; dir. NY State Psychiatric Inst., 1984—89; v.p. for health scis., dean faculty medicine Columbia U., NYC, 1989—99; pres., CEO NY-Presbyn. Hosp. and Healthcare Systems, NYC, 2000—. Contbr. articles to med. jours. Pres. sci. bd. Alliance for Rsch. on Schizophrenia and Depression. Capt. M.C., AUS, 1972-74. Named Ann. Hon. Lectr. Downstate Med. Ctr. Alumni Assn., 1972; recipient Alumni Achievement medal, 1980, William Menninger award ACP, 1992, Dorothy Dix award Mental Illness Fedn., 1992, Vester Mark award, 1994, Salmon award, 1996. Mem. Assn. Am. Med. Colls. (chair 1995-96), Am. Psychiat. Assn. (v.p. 1986-88, pres. 1989-90, Disting. Svc. award 1993), Inst. Medicine, Am. Psychoanalytic Assn., Coun. of Deans (adminstrv. bd., chair-elect 1993-94, chair 1994-95), Assoc. Med. Schs. NY (pres. 1995-2000), Phi Beta Kappa, Alpha Omega Alpha. Office: NY Presbyn Hosp Pres and CEOs Office 161 Ft Washington Ave New York NY 10032 also: NY Presbyn Hosp 525 E 68th St New York NY 10021 Office Phone: 212-305-8000. Business E-Mail: pardesh@nyp.org.

PARDIECK, ROGER L. lawyer; b. Seymour, Ind., Mar. 1, 1937; s. Martin W. and Lorna (Wente) P.; m. Mary Ann Pardieck; children: Amy, Andrew, Melissa, Duncan. AB, Ind. U., 1959, LLB, 1963; student, Internat. Grad. Sch., Stockholm, 1960. Bar: Ind. 1963, U.S. Dist. Ct. (so. dist.) Ind. 1964, U.S. Ct. Appeals (7th cir.) 1965; diplomate Am. Bd. Trial Advocates. Tchg. asst. Ind. U., Bloomington, 1963-64; spl. prosecutor Jackson County, Ind., 1964-65; ptnr. Montgomery, Elsner and Pardieck, 1965-84; prin. Pardieck Law Firm, Seymour, Ind., 1985—. Faculty Nat. Inst. Trial Advocacy, Ind.; lectr. in field. Contbr. articles to profl. jours. Bd. dirs. Seymour Girls Club, 1968-72, Seymour C. of C., 1971-75; bd. dirs. Luth. Comty. Home, 1964-82, pres., 1970; trustee Immanuel Luth. Ch., 1977-80, bd. Immanuel Luth. Sch., 1980-83; adv. bd. Ind. U., Purdue U.-Indpls., 1981-83. Fellow Am. Coll. Trial Lawyers, Ind. Trial Lawyers Assn. (bd. dirs. 1969—, pres. 1975), Ind. Coll. Trial Lawyers, Roscoe Pound Found., Ind. Bar Assn.; mem. FBA, ATLA (bd. govs. 1985-88), Ind. State Bar Assn. (bd. govs. 1980-82), Inst. for Injury Reduction (bd. dirs. 1992-95), Nat. Bd. Trial Advocacy, Safety Attys. Fedn. (bd. dirs. 1993-95), Internat. Soc. Primerus Law Firms (bd. dirs. 1995-2004), Am. Bd. Trial Advocates, Trial Lawyers Pub. Justice (IN coord. 1991-), Am. Judicature Soc., Inner Cir. Advocates. Office: 100 N Chestnut St PO Box 608 Seymour IN 47274-0608 Office Phone: 812-523-8686. E-mail: rlp@pardiecklaw.com.

PARDO, GABRIEL, neuro-ophthalmologist, neurologist, researcher; b. Lincoln, Nebr., July 5, 1962; s. Jaime H. and Wilma E. (Tovar) P.; m. Diana E. Hampton; 1 child, Isabela. MD, U. Militar Nueva Granada, Bogota, Colombia, 1986. Resident ophthalmology U. Militar Nueva Granada, Bogota, 1986; fellow neuro-ophthalmology U. Tex., Galveston, 1995; resident neurology U. Okla., Oklahoma City, 1999; vice-dean Med. Sch. U. Militar Nueva Granada, Bogota, 1992-93, asst. prof. ophthalmology, 1992-95, basic scis. sect. chief Med. Sch., 1992; clin. asst. prof. ophthalmology U. Okla., Oklahoma City,

2000—, clin. asst. prof. neurology, 2000—; rschr. Okla. Med. Rsch. Found., Oklahoma City, 2000—01; med. dir. Multiple Sclerosis Ctr. Neurosci. Inst. Mercy Hosp., 2002—. Bd. mem. Nat. Med. Edn. Coun., Bogota, 1992; cons. Coll. Optometry, U. Houston, 1993-95; reviewer Jour. Neurology. Contbr. articles to profl. jours. Mem.: Nat. Multiple Sclerosis Soc. (bd. mem. Okla. chpt.), Okla. State Med. Assn., N.Am. Neuro-ophthalmology Soc., Am. Acad. Neurology, Am. Acad. Ophthalmology, AMA. Office: MS Ctr Okla Mercy Neurosci Inst 4120 W Memorial Rd Ste 108 Oklahoma City OK 73120 Office Phone: 405-936-5648. Business E-Mail: gabriel-pardo@ouhsc.edu.

PARDO, JANETTE M. archivist, librarian; b. Passaic, NJ, May 22, 1970; d. Jesus and Gladys Pardo. BA, Rutgers U., Newark, 1992, MLS, 2001. Libr. Wayne Pub. Libr., NJ, 1995—. Archival cons. Caucus Archival Projects Evaluation Svc., Trenton, NJ, 2001—. Mem.: ALA, Romance Writers Am., Soc. Am. Archivists, Mid-Atlantic Regional Archival Conf. Democrat. Roman Catholic. Avocation: writing. Office: Wayne Pub Libr 461 Valley Rd Wayne NJ 07470 Personal E-mail: jpardo22@yahoo.com.

PARDOLL, PETER MICHAEL, gastroenterologist; b. Bklyn., Oct. 24, 1946; s. Abraham Jacob and Lee (Nyfield) P.; m. Lois, June 29, 1969; children: Todd, Missy, Mindy. MD, Med. Coll. Va., 1971. Diplomate Am. Bd. Internal Medicine, 1974, Am. Bd. Gastroenterology, 1977. Intern U. Miami Affiliated Hosps., 1971-72, resident, 1972-74; fellow gastroenterology U. South Fla., 1974-76; gastroenterologist pvt. practice, St. Petersburg, Fla., 1978—2004; pres. Ctr. Digestive Diseases, St. Petersburg, Fla., 1992—. Bd. dirs. Palms of Pasadena Hosp., v.p. Founder, bd. dirs. Menorah Manor Home for Living, St. Petersburg. Maj. USAF, 1976-78. Gastroenterology fellow U. South Fla., 1974-76. Fellow Coll. Gastroenterology (chmn. com. practice affairs), Am. Coll. Gastroenterology (gov. North Fla. chpt., elected bd. trustees); mem. HCFA (gastroenterology rep., carrier adv. com.), Fla. Gastroenterology Soc. (pres. 1997), Fla. Ind. Physicians Assn. (bd. dirs. region 5), scientific advisory bd., Bovie Med. Ctr., 2003-. Avocations: bicycling, health care activism. Office: Ctr Digestive Diseases 1609 Pasadena Ave S Ste 3-m Saint Petersburg FL 33707-4563 Office Phone: 727-360-4342.

PARDUE, A. MICHAEL, retired plastic and reconstructive surgeon; b. Nashville, June 23, 1931; s. Andrew Peyton and Ruby (Fly) P. BS, U. of the South, 1953; MD, U. Tenn., 1957. Resident in gen. surgery Pittsfield (Mass.) Affiliated Hosps., 1966; resident in plastic surgery N.Y. Hosp./Cornell Med. Ctr., 1968; plastic surgeon A. Michael Pardue, M.D., Thousand Oaks, Calif., 1968-98; ret., 1998. Lt. comdr. USN, 1956-62. Fellow ACS; mem. Am. Soc. Plastic Surgeons, Am. Soc. Aesthetic Plastic Surgery, Calif. Soc. Plastic Surgeons. Episcopalian. Avocations: fly fishing, skiing, golf, horses, African safaris. Home: PO Box 4677 Tubac AZ 85646-4677 Also: 3217 Augusta Dr Bozeman MT 59715-8792

PARDUE, BILL, publishing executive; Grad., Harvard Law Sch. Atty. Wiley, Rein and Fielding, Washington; business exec. Baltimore Sun; journalist, exec. Assoc. Press; editor Denver Post; mktg. dir. The Washington Post; CEO U.S. Corp. and Fed. Markets divsn. Lexis-Nexis, Miamisburg, Ohio, 2000—04; pres., Intelligence Unit Gartner, Inc., Stamford, Conn., 2004—. Office: Gartner Inc 56 Top Gallant Rd Stamford CT 06904

PARDUE, DWIGHT EDWARD, venture capitalist; b. North Wilkesboro, N.C., Aug. 3, 1928; s. Gilbert F. and Nina (Glass) P.; m. Annie Eller, Mar. 24, 1951; children: Richard S., Dwight E. Cert., Clevenger Bus. Coll., 1956. Dir. warehousing Lowe's Co., Inc., North Wilkesboro, 1956-57, store mgr. Sparta, N.C., 1957-59, Richmond, Va., 1959-70, regional v.p. North Wilkesboro, 1970-75, sr. v.p. store ops., 1975-78, exec. v.p. sales and store ops., 1978-86, sr. exec. v.p., 1986-90; pres., investor D. Pardue & Assocs., Wilkesboro, N.C., 1990—. Mem. steering com. Home Ctr. Leadership Coun., Nat. Home Ctr. Home Improvement Congress and Exposition, 1983—86; bd. dirs. Northwestern Nat. Bank, Inc., Wilkesboro, NC, Integrity Fin. Corp., Hickory, NC; chmn. bd. Cmty. Bancshares, Inc., Wilkesboro, 1992—2002. Served with U.S. Army, 1950-52. Mem. Jefferson Landing Golf Club, Masons.

PARDUE, MARY-LOU, biology professor; b. Lexington, Ky., Sept. 15, 1933; d. Louis Arthur and Mary Allie (Marshall) P. BS, William and Mary Coll., 1955; MS, U. Tenn., 1959; PhD, Yale U., 1970; D.Sc. (hon.), Bard Coll., 1985. Postdoctoral fellow Inst. Animal Genetics, Edinburgh, Scotland, 1970-72; assoc. prof. biology MIT, Cambridge, 1972-80, prof., 1980—, Boris Magasanik prof. biology, 1995—. Summer course organizer Cold Spring Harbor Lab., NY, 1971—80; mem. rev. com. NIH, 1974—78, 1980—84, nat. adv. gen. med. scis. coun., 1984—86; sci. adv. com. Wistar Inst., Phila., 1976—2004; mem. health and environ. rsch. adv. com. U.S. Dept. Energy, 1987—94; bd. trustees Associated Univs., Inc., 1995—97; mem. Burroughs Wellcome Adv. Com. on Career Awards in Biomed. Scis., 1996—2000, now bd. dirs.; chair Inst. of Medicine Com. on Biol. Basis of Sex and Gender Differences, 1999—2001. Contbr. articles to profl. jours. Mem. rev. com. Am. Cancer Soc., 1990-93, Howard Hughes Med. Inst. Adv. Bd., 1993-2000. Recipient Esther Langer award Langer Cancer Rsch. Found., 1977, Lucius Wilbur Cross medal Yale Grad. Sch., 1989; grantee NIH, NSF, Am. Cancer Soc. Fellow AAAS, NAS (chmn. genetics sect. 1991-94, coun. 1995-98), Am. Acad. Arts and Sci. (coun. mem. 1992-96); mem. NRC (bd. on biology 1989-95), Genetics Soc. Am. (pres. 1982-83), Am. Soc. Cell Biology (coun. 1977-80, pres. 1985-86), Phi Beta Kappa, Phi Kappa Phi, Sigma Xi. Office: MIT Dept Biology 68-670 77 Massachusetts Ave Dept 68-670 Cambridge MA 02139-4307 Office Phone: 617-253-6741. Business E-Mail: mlpardue@mit.edu.

PAREDES, JAMES ANTHONY, anthropologist, educator; b. N.Y.C., Sept. 29, 1939; s. Antonio Paredes Piñeiro and Mildred Olene (Brown) P.; m. Anna Hamilton, Nov. 25, 1959 (div. 1984); children: J. Anthony Jr., Anna Teresa P. Lesinski, Sara Caroline P. Campbell; m. Elizabeth Dixon Purdum, Aug. 10, 1985 (div. 1994); 1 stepchild, David Joseph Plante; m. Alleen Dimitroff Deutsch, July 24, 2003. BA, Oglethorpe U., 1961; MA, U. N.Mex., 1964, PhD, 1969. Rsch. coord. Upper Miss. Mental Health Ctr., Bemidji, Minn., 1964-67; asst. prof., acting dir. Am. Ind. Studies Bemidji State Coll., 1967-68; community devel. specialist U. Minn. Agrl. Extension Svc., Bemidji, 1967-68; asst. prof. dept. anthropology Fla. State U., Tallahassee, 1969-74, assoc. prof., 1974-78, prof., 1979-99, emeritus prof., 1999—, chmn. dept., 1974-77, 84-90; chief ethnography and Indian affairs S.E. regional office Nat. Park Service, Atlanta, 1999—. Adj. prof. dept. anthropology U. Fla., Gainesville, 1979—; cons. Nat. Marine Fisheries Svc., Galveston, Tex., 1987-88, Bur. Indian Affairs, Washington, 1985, 92, Fed. Recognition Panel, Assn. on Am. Indian Affairs, N.Y.C., 1987-88. Author: Indios de los Estados Unidos Anglosajones, 1992; editor: Anishinabe: Six Studies of Modern Chippewa, 1980, Indians of the Southeastern United States in the Late 20th Century, 1992; co-editor: Classics of Practicing Anthropology: 1978-1998, 2000; co-editor: Anthropologists and Indians in the New South, 2001; author or co-author numerous articles, chpts. in books, revs. Mem. Sci. and Statis. Com., Gulf of Mex. Fishery Mgmt. Coun., Tampa, Fla., 1978-88. Recipient svc. award Poarch Creek Indians, 1990, Woodrow Wilson Found. fellow U. N.Mex., 1961-62; Nat. Inst. Mental Health predoctoral fellow U. N.Mex., 1968-69; Rockefeller Ctr. for Study of So. Culture and Religion fellow, Fla. State U., 1978. Fellow Am. Anthrop. Assn. (exec. bd. 2004—), Soc. for Applied Anthropology (assoc. editor 1983-88, pres. 1993-95); mem. So. Anthrop. Soc. (pres. 1988-89), Fla. Acad. Scis. (sect. chair 1984-85), Sigma Xi (Fla. State U. chpt. pres. 1977-78). Democrat. Avocation: walking. Office: Nat Park Svc SE Region 100 Alabama St SW Atlanta GA 30303-8701 Office Phone: 404-562-3117 ext 638. E-mail: Tony_Paredes@nps.gov.

PAREDES, ROBERT WESLEY, music educator; b. San Diego, Feb. 10, 1948; s. Fernando Napoleon Paredes and Laureta Gay Williams; m. Melody Noel Scherubel, Nov. 2, 2001. MA, U. of Iowa, 1989, PhD, 1990. Instr. U. of Iowa, 1987—91, vis. asst. prof. & dir. of exptl., sic studios, 1991—93; composer, educator, freelance musician, brass and woodwind instrument repairman Iowa City, 1993—2001; adj. asst. prof., jazz studies U. of Iowa, 2000—. Freelance musician, Melbourne, Australia, 1984—86; artist in residence Festival of Improvised Music/Evos Found., Perth, Australia, 1986, Unit One/Exptl. Sch. of the U. of Ill., Champaign, Urbana, 1989—89; composer-adjudicator for the mcknight prize Minn. Composer's Forum, Mpls., 1992; artist in residence/festival de inverno Universidade Fed., Belo Horizonte, Brazil, 1992; composer in residence Meet the Composer: So. Arts Fedn., Nat. Endowment for the Arts & The Ala. State Coun. of the Arts, Birmingham, Ala., 1993. Author (composer): (text) Open Space Mag., Perspectives of New Music, Empty, 1993, After...In...After, 2003; musician (clarinetist): (jazz recording) Out On the Western Plains, (recording) The Bewitched, 1980; musician: (clarinetist, saxophonist) (jazz recording) Blood and Water:, 2000, PHD, Paredes-Hatwich Duo, 2001; musician: (clarinetist, bass clarinetist) John Rapson's Mallicked Simulacrum, 2002; exhibition, xerox art work, Tex. Musicians in Art, 1987, exhibition, xerox art works, Composition as Eco-Sys., 1990; composer (musician): (recording) (On)e for flute and clarinet, 1985; composer: (musician, clarinetist) Forgetting and Remembering for two-channel tape (a multi-track accumulation of improvisations on clarinet, 1986; composer: (electronic music) Speakers, a series of seventeen tape compositions-as-writings/drawings, 1987—93, (electronic music, recording) #16 (Speakers)/Fiesta, 1992, (electronic music recording) #17 (Speakers)/In Every Moment of Decay), 2-channel tape, 1993, (composition for solo cello, recording) Small Writing, 1994. Henry and Parker Pelzer fellow, 1989—90. Mem.: Pi Kappa Lambda. Buddhist. Office: Univ of Iowa Sch of Music 1006 Voxman Hall Iowa City IA 52242 Personal E-mail: parrw@avalon.net.

PARELLA, MARY A. state legislator; b. Bristol, R.I., Feb. 10, 1957; BA, Emmanuel Coll., 1979; M in Cmty. Planning, U. R.I., 1982. Program dir. Pawtucket Sch. Dept.; mem. Bristol Town Coun., 1986-92, R.I. Senate, Dist. 45, Providence, 1992—. Mem. judiciary com., health, edn. and welfare com. and joint com. on vets. affairs, R.I. State Senate. Mem. Bristol Rep. Town Com.; bd. dirs. Self Help, Inc.; chief marshall Bristol 4th of July Celebration, 1995. Mem. Am. Planning Assn. (R.I. sect.), Bristol Jaycees. Home: 259 High St Bristol RI 02809-2222

PARENT, MARY, film company executive; Past agt. trainee ICM; dir. develop. to v.p. prodn. New Line Cinema, 1994—97; sr. v.p. prodn. Universal Pictures, Universal City, Calif., 1997—2000, exec. v.p. prodn., 2000—01, co-pres. prodn., 2001—03, vice chmn., worldwide prodn., 2003—. Office: 100 Universal City Plaza Universal City CA 91608

PARENT, RODOLPHE JEAN, Canadian air force officer, pilot; b. Thurso, Que., Can., June 16, 1937; s. Eugène Jean and Eliane Marie (Raby) P.; m. Michelle Marie Masse, Aug. 10, 1963; children— Stéphane, Nathalie, Cynthia Student, Coll. Militaire Royal de St-Jean, 1958-61; B.Sc., Royal Mil. Coll. Can., Kingston, Ont., 1963. Commd. Royal Can. Air Force, 1958; advanced through grades to brig.-gen., 1984; joined 425 Squadron for ops. on CF-101 aircraft, 1964-69; worked for Directorate of Recruiting and Selection at Nat. Def. Hdqrs., Ottawa, Ont., Can., 1969-71; chief of ops. 433 Tactical Fighter Squadron, Bagotville, 1972-75, Can. Forces Base Bagotville, 1975-76; comdg. officer 433 Tactical Fighter Squadron, 1976-80; asst. dir. personnel careers Nat. Def. Hdqrs., Ottawa, 1980-81; base comdr. Can. Forces Base Lahr, Federal Republic Germany, 1981-83; commandant Coll. Militaire Royal de Saint-Jean, Que., 1983-86; dir. gen. personnel careers other ranks Nat. Def. Hdqrs., Ottawa, 1986-89; def. attaché Paris, 1989-92; ret., 1992. Decorated Order of Mil. Merit, Order of St. John of Jerusalem Roman Catholic. Avocations: hockey, tennis, windsurfing. E-mail: rudy.michelle@sympatico.ca.

PARENTE, RONALDO, business educator, consultant; b. Rio de Janeiro, July 5, 1962; s. José Eduardo Leite and Inez Angélica Couto Parente; m. Glice Lima Parente, Jan. 3, 1992; 1 child, Paulo Eduardo Lima. Degree in civil engring., U. Fortaleza, Brazil, 1986; MBA in Fin., U. Tampa, 1993; PhD in Bus. Adminstrn., Temple U., 2003. Project analyst Banco Nordeste, Fortaleza, 1983—91; pvt. cons. Brazil, 1991—2002; asst. prof. Salisbury (Md.) U., 2002—. Cons. State Govt. Ceará, Brazil, 1994, pvt. bus., Brazil, 1995. Mem.: Acad. Mgmt., Acad. Internat. Bus. Avocations: windsurfing, tennis, sailing, surfing, soccer. Office: Salisbury U Perdue Sch Bus 1101 Camden Ave Salisbury MD 21801

PARENTE, WILLIAM JOSEPH, political science educator; b. Chgo., July 7, 1937; s. Salvatore S. and Genevieve (Rooney) P.; m. Diane Alpern, Nov. 30, 1963; children: Elizabeth, Margaret, William Joseph, Caroline, Rebecca, Catherine, Abigail, Christopher, Natalya. AB cum laude, Xavier U., Ohio, 1961; PhD (Woodrow Wilson fellow, Woodrow Wilson dissertation fellow), Georgetown U., 1970. Woodrow Wilson intern Wilberforce (Ohio) U., 1965-66; asst. prof., chmn. polit. sci. dept. Antioch Coll., 1966-69, assoc. dean faculty, 1969-70; dean Coll. Arts and Scis., U. Scranton, Pa., 1970-85, assoc. prof. polit. sci., 1970-73, prof., 1973—; Fulbright scholar Chulalongkorn U., Bangkok, Thailand, 1985-86, Inst. for Policy Studies, Washington, 1986-87. Mem. nat. Fulbright screening com. for East Asia, Southeast Asia; mem. adv. com. Inst. Internat. Edn.; cons. on world affairs to Peace Corps. Author articles in field. Fellow Inst. Acad. Deans, 1971, Inst. Ednl. Mgmt., Harvard Bus. Sch., 1972, Fulbright fellow, Korea, 1974, Indonesia, 1978, Germany, 1980, Thailand, 1985-86, fellow NEH Seminar, U. Va., 1976, Harvard U., 1985, Columbia U., 1988, George Mason U., Va., 1990, UCLA, 1991, U. Mich., 1992, William and Mary, 1993, U. Iowa, 1994, U. Accra, Ghana, 1996; scholar-diplomat program State Dept., 1970, 73; vis. scholar in humanities NYU, 1989. Fellow Union Experimenting Colls. and Univs., Inst. for Policy Studies, Soc. for Religion in Higher Edn.; mem. Am. Polit. Sci. Assn., Assn. Jesuit Colls. and Univs. (chmn. conf. on internat. edn. 1981-85), Alpha Sigma Nu (nat. sec.-treas. 1979-82, nat. pres. 1983-85), Pi Sigma Alpha, Eta Sigma Phi, Alpha Sigma Lambda, Tau Kappa Alpha, Phi Alpha Theta. Roman Catholic. Home: 1608 Summit Pointe Scranton PA 18508-1034 Office: U Scranton Coll Arts & Sciences Scranton PA 18510 Office Phone: 570-941-7644.

PARESKY, DAVID S. travel company executive; b. Boston, Sept. 27, 1938; s. Paul and Ada (Rudnick) P.; m. Linda Kotzen, Aug. 18, 1963; children: Pamela, Laura, Mark. BA, Williams Coll., 1960; JD, Harvard U., 1963, MBA, 1965. Bar: Mass. Pres., chmn. bd. Crimson Travel Svc., Inc., Cambridge, Mass., 1965-89; pres., CEO, chmn. bd. Thomas Cook Travel, Cambridge, Mass., 1989-94. Mem. Bd. Higher Edn., Boston, 1980; trustee New Eng. Med. Ctr., 1982-83; mem. Bd. Regents of Higher Edn., Boston, 1980-86. Mem. Young Pres. Orgn. (chmn. New Eng. chpt. 1985), Chief Execs. Orgn., Phi Beta Kappa, Fisher Island Club (bd. dirs.).

PARESKY, LINDA K. travel company executive, educator; b. Cambridge, Mass., Mar. 18, 1943; d. Gilbert Milton and Marcia (Brown) Kotzen; m. David S. Paresky, Aug. 18, 1963; children: Pamela, Laura, Mark. BA, Simmons Coll., 1964; MA, Harvard U., 1965; PhD, Boston Coll., 1988; hon. degree, Simmons Coll., 1999, Bay Path. Coll., 2000. Chmn., CEO Travel Edn. Ctr., Cambridge, 1975-98; pvt. investor. V.p. Crimson Travel, Cambridge, 1965-89; co-chmn. Thomas Cook Travel, Cambridge, 1989-94; chair bd. trustees Simmons Coll., Boston, 1994-98; chair bd. dirs. Com. 200 Found., Chgo., 1997-98; bd. dirs. Thryoid Found. Am., Boston, 1994-97. Adv. com. Investment Svcs. and Policy Adv. Com., U.S. Trade Dept., Washington, 1995-2000. Recipient Bus. Leadership award New England Coun., 1994; named Outstanding Woman Entrepreneur, Pres. Reagan, 1986, Top 50 Women Bus. Owners, Nat. Found. Woman Bus. Owners and Working Woman Mag., 1994, Outstanding Bus. Leader award Northwood U., 2001. Mem. Internat. Women's Forum, (Mass. chpt., pres. 1994-96), Travel Bus. Roundtable (policy com.), Acad. Travel and Tourism (adv. bd.), Com. 200. Avocations: travel, sports. Home: 7212 Fisher Island Dr Miami FL 33109-0725 Office: 41212 Fisher Island Dr Miami FL 33109-1253

PARET, PETER, historian; b. Berlin, Apr. 13, 1924; s. Hans and Suzanne Aimée (Cassirer) P.; m. Isabel Harris, Sept. 23, 1961; children: Suzanne Aimée, Paul Louis Michel. BA, U. Calif., Berkeley, 1949; PhD, U. London, 1960, DLitt, 1992; LittD, U. S.C., 1995; HHD, Coll. of Wooster, 1996. Resident tutor, delegacy of extramural studies Oxford U., 1959-60; research assoc. Center of Internat. Studies, Princeton U., 1960-62, 63; vis. asst. prof. U. Calif., Davis, 1962-63, assoc. prof., 1963-66, prof., 1966-69; prof. history Stanford U., 1969-77, Raymond A. Spruance prof. internat. history, 1977-86; Andrew W. Mellon Prof. in humanities Inst. Advanced Study, Princeton, N.J., 1986-97, Andrew W. Mellon Prof. in humanities emeritus, 1997—. Mem. Inst. for Advanced Study, Princeton, 1966-67; fellow Ctr. for Advanced Study in Behavioral Scis., Stanford, Calif., 1968-69; vis. fellow London Sch. Econs., 1972-73; NEH fellow, 1979-80; sr. fellow Hoover Instn., Stanford U., 1988-93. Author: (with John Shy) Guerrillas in the 1960's, 1962, French Revolutionary Warfare from Indochina to Algeria, 1964, Yorck and the Era of Prussian Reform, 1966, Clausewitz and the State, 1976, rev. edit., 1985; The Berlin Secession, 1980, Art as History, 1988, (with Beth Irwin Lewis and Paul Paret) Persuasive Images, 1992, Understanding War, 1992, Imagined Battles, 1997, German Encounters with Modernism, 1840-1945, 2000, An Artist against the Third Reich: Ernst Barlach, 1933-1938, 2003; editor, translator: (with Michael Howard) On War (C. v. Clausewitz), 1976, (with Daniel Moran) Historical and Political Writings (C. v. Clausewitz), 1992; editor: Frederick the Great, 1968, Frederick the Great: A Historical Profile, 1972, Sisyphus or the Limits of Education, 1973, The Age of German Liberation, 1977, Berliner Secession, 1981, Makers of Modern Strategy, 1986, (with Ekkehard Mai) Sammler, Stifter & Museen, 1993. Served with inf. U.S. Army, 1943-46. Decorated Officer's Cross, Order of Merit, Germany. Fellow AAAS, Royal Hist. Soc., Leo Baeck Inst., London Sch. Econs. (hon.); mem. Am. Philos. Soc. (Jefferson medal), Hist. Kom zu Berlin, Soc. for Mil. History (Samuel Eliot Morison medal), Clausewitz Gesellschaft (hon.). Office: Sch Hist Studies Inst Advanced Study Princeton NJ 08540

PARETSKY, SARA N. writer; b. Ames, Iowa, June 8, 1947; d. David Paretsky and Mary E. Edwards; m. S. Courtenay Wright, June 19, 1976; children: Kimball Courtenay, Timothy Charles, Philip William. BA, U. Kans., 1967; MBA, PhD, U. Chgo., 1977. Mgr. Urban Rsch Ctr., Chgo., 1971-74, CNA Ins. Co., Chgo., 1977-85; writer, 1985—. Author: (novels) Indemnity Only, 1982, Deadlock, 1984 (Friends of Am. Writers award 1985), Killing Orders, 1985, Bitter Medicine, 1987, Blood Shot, 1988 (Silver Dagger award Crime Writers Assn., 1988), Burn Marks, 1990, Guardian Angel, 1992, Tunnel Vision, 1994, Hard Time: A V.I. Warshawski Novel, 1999, also numerous articles and short stories. Pres. Sisters in Crime, Chgo., 1986-88; dir. Nat. Abortion Rights Action League Ill., 1987—; mentor Chgo. inner-city schs. Named Woman of Yr. Ms mag., N.Y.C., 1987; recipient Mark Twain award fot disting. contbns. to mid-western lit., 1996. Mem. Crime Writers Assn. (Silver Dagger award 1988), Mystery Writers Am. (v.p. 1989), Authors Guild, Chgo. Network Achievements include being the founder of two scholarships at U. Kans. Address: Sally McCartin Assoc PO Box 432 Millerton NY 12546-0432

PARETTE, HOWARD P. school system administrator, special education educator; b. Pine Bluff, Ark., July 9, 1952; s. Howard Phillips Parette and Marjorie Edith Wright. BS, U. Ark., 1976, MSE, 1979; EdD, U. Ala., 1982. Asst. prof. La. Tech. U., Ruston, La., 1982-84; rsch. assoc. U. Ark. for Med. Scis., Little Rock, 1988-89; asst. prof. U. Ark., Little Rock, 1989-92; prof. Southeast Mo. State U., Cape Girardeau, Mo., 1993-2000, dean Grad. Sch., 2000—02; prof. Ill. State U., Bloomington, 2002—. Coord. Ark. Easter Seal Soc., Little Rock, 1992-93. Author, editor 4 books, 1997-2000; contbr. over 120 articles to profl. jours., chpts. to books. Mem. Am. Assn. Colls. of Tchr. Edn., Coun. for Exceptional Children (newsletter editor 1993-99). Democrat. Methodist. Avocations: running, gardening, weightlifting, fine art. Office: Ill State U Spl Edn Campus Box 5910 Normal IL 61790-5910 E-mail: hpparet@ilstu.edu.

PARFET, DONALD REID, pharmaceutical executive; b. Kalamazoo, Sept. 26, 1952; s. R. Ted and Martha (Gilmore) P.; m. Ann Peelor Van DeWater, July 21, 1973; children: Sydney, Rachel. BA in Econs., U. Ariz., 1975; MBA in Fin., U. Mich., 1977. With Acctg. & Fin. Profl. Devel. Program Upjohn Co., Kalamazoo, 1977-80; mktg. contr. domestic pharm. divsn. Upjohn Co., Kalamazoo, 1980-82, contr. domestic pharm. adminstrn., 1982-85, v.p. adminstrn., 1986-89, sr. v.p. adminstrn., 1989-91, exec. v.p. adminstrn., 1991—; exec. v.p. Upjohn Healthcare Systems, 1985. Contbr. articles to profl. jours. Chmn. adv. coun. U. Mich. Bus. Sch.; active U. Okla. State Ctr. Molecular Medicine, Leadership Edn. & Devel.; bd. dirs. First of Am., Nat. Assn. Mfrs.; chmn. bd. trustees Kalamazoo Coll.; trustee Bronson Hosp., Coun. Mich. Founds. Avocations: sailing, skiing, tennis. Home: 4841 Ridgewood Richland MI 49083-9550 Office: Upjohn Co 7000 Portage Rd Kalamazoo MI 49001-0102

PARHAM, CAROL SHEFFEY, school system administrator; b. Balt. m. William N. Parham, Jr.; children: William N. III, Julie Desai. BA in Social Studies Edn., U. Md.; M in Edn. Guidance and Counseling, postgrad. studies, Johns Hopkins U.; EdD, U. Md. Social studies tchr. Balt. City Schs., personnel specialist, acting staff specialist, personnel assoc.; supr. office personnel Howard County Pub. Schs., 1985-89; dir. personnel Anne Arundel County Pub. Schs., 1989—. Bd. dirs. Anne Arundel Trade Coun., United Way Ctrl. Md.; mem. task force Md. State Dept. Edn.; mem. edn. adv. com. Johns Hopkins U. Sch. Continuing Studies; mem. adv. bd. Leadership Anne Arundel; trustee Western Md. Coll., Mt. Washington Pediat. Hosp. Recipient Outstanding Achievement in Leadership award Md. State Tchrs. Assn., Good Scout award Baltimore Area Coun. Boy Scouts Am., Martin Luther King Peacemaker award, 1998, Kathleen Kennedy Townsend award; named Woman of Yr., Glen Burnie Chpt. Nat. Fedn. Bus. Profl. Women, Md. Supt. of Yr., 1995, Md.'s Top 100 Women, 1996, 98, 99. Mem. Pub. Sch. Supts. Assn. Md., Assn. Sch. Bus. Officials Md. and DC (past pres.), Md. Pers. Assn. (past pres.), Coalition 100 Black Women, Wash. Area Sch. Study Coun. (pres.), Rotary, Delta Sigma Theta. Office: Office of Supt 2644 Riva Rd Annapolis MD 21401-7305

PARHAM, ELLEN SPEIDEN, nutrition educator; b. Mitchells, Va., July 15, 1938; d. Marion Coote and Rebecca Virginia (McNiel) Speiden; m. Arthur Robert Parham, Jr., Dec. 16, 1961; children: Katharine Alma, Cordelia Alyx. BS in Nutrition, Va. Poly. Inst., 1960; PhD in Nutrition, U. Tenn., 1967; MSEd in Counseling, No. Ill. U., 1994. Registered dietitian; lic. clin. profl. counselor. Asst. prof. to prof. nutrition No. Ill. U., DeKalb, Ill., 1966—2004, coord. programs in dietetics, 1981-86, 90—, coord. grad. faculty sch. family, consumer, nutrition scis., 1985-87. Cons. on nutrition various hosps., clins. and bus., Ill., 1980-88; founder, dir. Horizons Weight Control Program, DeKalb, 1983-91; founder, leader "Escaping the Tyranny of the Scale" Group, 1994—; co-chair Nutrition Coalition for Ill., 1989-90; ptnr., mgr. Blue Chicory Arts, 1986—; adj. counselor Ctr. for Counsel, Family Svc. Agy. of DeKalb County. Bd. editors Jour. Nutrition Edn., 1985-90, 97—, Jour. Am. Dietetic Assn., 1991-97; contbr. articles to profl. jours. Recipient Fisher award, No. Ill. U. Coll. Health and Human Svcs., 2001, Sullivan award, 2002. Mem. Am. Inst. Nutrition, Soc. Nutrition Edn., Am. Dietetic Assn. (named Ill. Outstanding Dietetics Educator 2001, Excellence in Dietetics Edn. award 2001), Soc. Nutrition Edn. (treas. 1991-94, chair divsn. nutrition and weight realities 1995-96, chair jour. com. 2002—, Weight Realities Cert. of Achievement 1999), N.Am. Assn. Study Obesity. Avocations: painting in watercolor, gardening, reading.

PARHAM, IRIS ANN, gerontology educator; b. Orange, Tex., Nov. 14, 1948; d. George Kevlin and Nina Mabel Parham; m. Edward Swarbrick, Aug. 9, 1975; 1 child, Erin Elsbeth. BA, U. Tex., 1970; MA, W.Va. U., 1973; PhD, U. So. Calif., 1976. Asst. prof. gerontology Va. Commonwealth U., Richmond, 1976-81, assoc. prof., 1981-91, prof., 1991—. Exec. dir. Va. Geriatric Edn. Ctr. Co-editor: Modular Gerontology Curriculum, 1982, vol. II, 1984, Access, 1990, Resource Guides--Geriatrics, 2990, Gerontological Social Work, 1992, Alcoholism and Aging, 1995, Jour. Social Issues, 1980; spl. editor Jour. Minority Aging. Grantee Adminstrn. on Aging, 1978-79, 79-82, 85-87, Adjusting to Widowhood Va., 2978-79, Temple U., 1983-84, Health Resources and Svcs. Adminstrn., 1985-90, 91-94, 97-01, 00—. Fellow Gerontol. Soc. Am., So. Gerontol. Soc. (treas. 1984-87); mem. APA, Aassn. Gerontology in Higher Edn. (charter fellow), Sigma Xi. Avocation: photography. Office: Va Commonwealth U Med Coll Va Campus Dept Gerontology PO Box 980228 Richmond VA 23298-0228

PARHAM, VALERIE DEFOREST BYRON, artist; b. Cambridge, Mass., Jan. 25, 1953; d. Donald Cameron and Mary deForest Pierce Byron; m. Anthony Bruce Parham, Oct. 30, 1990; children: Victoria deForest, Corrina Bess. Grad., Buckingham Sch., Cambridge, 1968; pvt. classes in painting, 1968—74. Lay missionary Holy Spirit Assn. for Unity of World Christianity, N.Y.C. and Washington, 1974—95. Amb. for peace-Ghana Family Fedn. for World Peace and Unification, N.Y.C., 1974—2000. Vol. Rep. presdl. campaigns. Republican. Home and Studio: Sparrow Art by deForest Byron 36 Upsala St unit #G109 Worcester MA 01601 E-mail: deforestbyron@hotmail.com.

PARHAM-HOPSON, DEBORAH, health administrator; BSN, U. Cin., 1977; MS in Pub. Health, U. NC, 1979, PhD in Pub. Health, 1990. Rear adm. USPHS Commd. Corps.; dep. assoc. adminstr. Health Resources and Svcs. Adminstrn., HIV/AIDS Bur., HHS, 2000—02, acting assoc. adminstr., 2002, assoc. adminstr., 2002—. Office: US Dept Health and Human Svcs Health Resources Svcs Adminstrn 5600 Fishers Ln Rm 7-05 Rockville MD 20857*

PARHAMI, BEHROOZ, engineering educator, consultant; b. Tehran, 1947; s. Salem and Kowkab Parhami; m. Vida Parhami; children: Sepehr, Sepand, Sepideh. PhD, UCLA, 1973. Chartered engr., Engring. Coun. U.K. Acting asst. prof. UCLA, 1973—74; prof. math. and computer sci. Sharif (formerly Arya-Mehr) U. Tech., Tehran, 1974—88; prof. elec. and computer engring. U. Calif., Santa Barbara, 1988—. Author: (book) Computer Appreciation, 1984, Introduction to Parallel Processing: Algorithms and Architectures, 1999, Computer Arithmetic: Algorithms and Hardware Designs, 2000. Fellow: IEEE (chmn. Iran sect. 1977—85, Centennial medal 1984), Brit. Computer Soc.; mem.: Informatics Soc. Iran (pres., editor-in-chief 1979—84, disting. mem. 1985), Assn. for Computing Machinery. Office: U Calif Dept Elec and Computer Engring Santa Barbara CA 93106-9560 Business E-Mail: parhami@ece.ucsb.edu.

PARIAG, HAIMWATTIE RAMKISTODAS, information management administrator; b. Golden Fleece, Guyana, Aug. 31, 1967; came to U.S., 1977; d. Ramkisto Das and Surujpati Ramkistodas; m. Moolchand Pariag. BS in Med. Records Adminstrn., C.W. Post Coll., 1988. Registered health info. mgmt. adminstr. Med. records clk. Mary Immaculate Hosp., Jamaica, N.Y., 1986-87; coder Parkway Hosp., Forest Hills, N.Y., 1987, adminstrv. coord., 1987-88, dir. health info. mgmt. svcs., 1988-91; dir. med. records Massapequa Gen. Hosp., Seaford, N.Y., 1991—; dir. health info. svcs./telecom. Brunswick Hosp. Ctr., Amityville, NY, 2000—01; dir. med. records, privacy officer Parker Jewish Inst. Healthcare and Rehab., Hyde Park, NY, 2001—. Mem. Am. Health Info. Mgmt. Assn., N.Y. Health Info. Mgmt. Assn., L.I. Health Info. Mgmt. Assn., Health Info. Mgmt. Assn. N.Y.C. Democrat. Hindu. Avocations: volleyball, raquetball, tennis.

PARIENTE, BARBARA J. state supreme court chief justice; b. N.Y.C., Dec. 24, 1948; m. Frederick A. Hazouri; 3 children. Grad. with high honors, Boston U., 1970; JD with highest honors, George Washington U., 1973. Bar: Fla. 1973; cert. civil trial lawyer Fla. Bar; cert. Nat. Bd. Trial Advocacy. Law clk. to hon. Norman C. Roettger, Jr. U.S. Dist. Ct. (so. dist.) Fla., 1973-75; assoc. Cone Wagner Nugent, 1975—77, ptnr., 1977—83, Pariente & Silber, P.A., 1983; pvt. practice, 1983—2001; judge U.S. Ct. of Appeals (4th dist.), 1993-97; justice Fla. Supreme Ct., Tallahassee, 1997—, now chief justice. Participant Twenty-First Century Justice Conf.; mem. Jud. Cir. Grievance Com., 1989-92, chair, 1990-92; mem. nominating com. U.S. Ct. Appeals (15th cir.), 1989-94; past faculty mem. Supreme Ct. Justice Tchg. Inst. Contbr. articles to profl. jours. Bd. dirs. Fla. Bar Found.; mentor Take Stock in Children; active Palm Beach County Youth Ct. program, 1997, Cities in Schs. mentoring program, 1993, Temple Judea, Palm Beach County Sephardi Fedn., Jewish Cmty. Ctr., Ballet Fla., Palm Beach County Commn. on Status of Women; vol. judge Palm Beach County Youth Ct. Program; past chair Supreme Ct. Steering Com. on Families and Children in the Courts Fla. Supreme Ct.; liaison Supreme Ct. Task Force on Treatment-Based Drug Courts, 1999—; mem. nat. judges adv. com. Balanced and Restorative Justice Project Dept. Justice. Recipient award for disting. svc. to the arts Palm Beach County Bar Assn., 1987, Civil Litigation Pro Bono award Legal Aid Soc., 1993, Lifetime Achievement award Palm Beach County Jewish Fedn., 1998, Disting. Jud. Svc. award Fla. Coun. on Crime and Delinquency, 2000, Breaking the Glass Ceiling award Jewish Mus. Fla., 2002. Mem. ABA (mem. Coalition for Justice 2000-03, Law Day Speech award 1998), Nat. Assn. Women Judges, Am. Inns. of Ct. (founding mem. Palm Beach County chpt.), Acad. Fla. Trial Lawyers (bd. dirs., chair Spkr.'s Bur. program 1984-87, outreach com. 1991-92, co-chair Workhorse Seminar 1991-92), Assn. Trial Lawyers Am. (vice chair profl. rsch. and devel. dept. 1980-82, chair comml. litig. sect. 1984-85, women's trial lawyer caucus 1986-87; mem. ethics com. 1989-90, conv. planning com. 1992-93), Fla. Assn. Women Lawyers (Lifelong Dedication award 2000), Order of Coif. Office: State Supreme Ct of Florida 500 S Duval St Tallahassee FL 32399-1925 Business E-Mail: supremecourt@flcourts.org.

PARIKH, MIHIR, consumer products company executive; PhD, U. Calif., Berkeley. Varius mgmt. positions IBM, N.Y.C., San Jose, Calif., Hewlett-Packard Labs., Palo Alto, Calif.; pres., CEO ASYST technologies, Inc., Fremont, Calif., 1984—, chmn., 1992—. Contbr. articles to profl. jours. Office: ASYST Technologies Inc 48761 Kato Rd Fremont CA 94538-7313

PARIKH, NIMMI CHANDRA, Physics educator; b. Brookings, SD, Nov. 15, 1967; d. Goraldas Chandulal and Josephine Ann Parikh. BS in Physics, Yale U., 1989; MS in Physics, Cornell U., 1993, PhD in Physics, 1997. Asst. prof. Physics Richard Stockton Coll. N.J., Pomona, 1997—98; assoc. prof. Physics Central Conn. State U., New Britain, 1999—. Rschr. NASA Wallops Flight Facility, Wallops Island, Va., NOAA Mauna Loa Observatory, Hilo, Hawaii. Contbr. articles to jour. Grantee, Nat. Aeronautics and Space Adminstrn., Nat. Sci. Found. Office: Central Conn State Univ Dept Physics and Earth Sci 1615 Stanley St New Britain CT 06050

PARILIS, EDWARD S. physicist, researcher, consultant; b. Balti, Moldova, Jan. 11, 1932; s. Simha I. and Sima P. Parilis; m. Rachel Goodman, Aug. 17, 1990; 1 child, Sergey E. MSc in theoretical physics, Chisinau State U., 1949—54; PhD in Atomic Physics, Inst. Nuclear Physics, Tashkent, 1960. Rschr., head of theoretical physics dept. Inst. of Nuc. Physics, Tashkent, Uzbekistan, 1957—67; head of theoretical physics dept. Arifov Inst. of Electronics, Tashkent, Uzbekistan, 1967—91. Rsch. assoc. Calif. Inst. of Tech., 1991; cons. Phrasor Sci., Duarte, Calif., 1991—95; rschr. Institut de Physique Nucleaire, Orsay, Paris, France (incl. Monaco), 1991—98; cons. Tex. A&M U., 1997—. Author: (book) Atomic Collisions on Solid Surfaces, Elsevier, (over 200 articles in scientific journals) Interaction of atomic particles with solids. Mem. Bohmische Phys. Soc., Los Alamos, N.Mex., 1992. Achievements include development of theories of Auger processes in multiply charged ions, electron and ion emission, atomic scattering, Coulomb explosion sputtering, shock wave biomolecule desorption, cluster effects. Home: 4946 Verdura Ave Lakewood CA 90712 Office: Calif Inst of Tech 200-36 Pasadena CA 91125 E-mail: parilis@caltech.edu.

PARINS, ROBERT JAMES, professional football team executive, judge; b. Green Bay, Wis., Aug. 23, 1918; s. Frank and Nettie (Denissen) P.; m. Elizabeth L. Carroll, Feb. 8, 1941; children: Claire, Andrée, Richard, Teresa, Lu Ann. BA, U. Wis., 1940, LL.B., 1942. Bar: Wis. Supreme Ct. 1942. Pvt. practice, Green Bay, Wis., 1942-68; dist. atty. Brown County, Wis., 1949-50, cir. judge, 1968-82, res. judge, 1982—; pres. Green Bay Packers, Inc., 1982-90, chmn. bd., 1990-92; hon. chmn. bd., 1992-94. Mem.: Wis. State Bar Assn. Roman Catholic.

PARIS, DAVID ANDREW, dentist; b. Milw., Jan. 16, 1962; s. John Baptistia and Geraldine Louella (Grosso) P. BA, UCLA, 1985, DDS, 1989. Oral surgery extern VA, Phoenix, 1989; primary practitioner Aids Project L.A. Dental Clinic, 1990-94; assoc. M. Marchese D.D.S., Sun Valley, Calif., 1990-92, D. Pickrell DMD, West Hollywood, Calif., 1992-94, Dental Arts Assocs., Milw., 1994-95, Family Dental Ctr., Milw., 1994-96; pvt. practice Elm Grove, Wis., 1996—. Mem. ADA, Wis. Dental Assn., Calif. Dental Assn., Acad. Gen. Dentistry, Delta Sigma Delta. Avocations: cello, Italian language. Office Phone: 262-784-7770.

PARIS, DAVID C. academic administrator, political scientist, educator; b. Rochester, N.Y. married; 3 children. Grad., Hamilton Coll., 1971; PhD, Syracuse U. Mem. faculty Hamilton Coll., Clinton, NY, 1979—, James S. Sherman prof. govt., assoc. dean faculty, acting dean faculty, 2000—01, v.p. acad. affairs, dean faculty, 2001—. Author: Ideology and Education Reform: Themes and Theories in Public Education, 1995. Office: Hamilton College 198 College Hill Rd Clinton NY 13323*

PARIS, WAYNE, social worker, researcher; b. Claremore, Okla., Nov. 8, 1949; s. Arch LaVerne and Aileen Rosella (McGraw) P.; m. Donna Marie Lindley, Mar. 20, 1982; 1 child, Joel Michael. BA, Northeastern State U., 1972; MSW, U. Okla., 1979; postgrad., U. Huddersfield, Eng., 2000—. Lic. clin. social worker, Okla. Med. social worker Bapt. Med. Ctr., Oklahoma City, 1979-84; clin. transplant social worker Nazih Zuhdi Transplantation Inst., Oklahoma City, 1985—. Pvt. practice, cons. Wayne Paris & Assocs., Edmond, Okla., 1993—; grant reviewer The Wellcome Trust, London, 1999, Internat. Soc. Heart and Lung Transplantation; vis. prof. Tokyo Inst. Psychiatry, 2001-2002; invited lectr./rsch. cons. U. Huddersfield, 2002. Contbr. Yearbook of Surgery, 1994; Jour. Transplant Coordination, 1996—;: Progress in Transplantation, 2000, invited reviewer Jour. Heart and Lung Transplantation, 1995—, 1999—, 2001—. Rsch. on Social Work Practice, 1999—2003; contbr. articles to med. jours. Mem.: NASW, Internat. Soc. for Heart and Lung Transplantation (co-chair edn. com. nursing and social sci. coun. 2001—02, psychosocial white paper com. 2002—), Soc. for Social work and Rsch. (charter, abstract review com. 2000—02), Soc. for Transplant Social Work (chmn. abstract rev. com. 2000, charter, bd. dirs.). Avocations: coin collecting/numismatics, sailing. Office: Nazih Zuhdi Transplantation Inst 3300 NW Expwy Oklahoma City OK 73112-4418

PARISEAU, PATRICIA, state legislator; b. St. Paul, Aug. 10, 1936; d. James Martin and Mary Margaret (May) Wright; m. Kenneth Edward Pariseau, July 9, 1960; children: Susan M., Douglas C., Penny A., Linda D., Barbara J., Jacqueline. RN, Ravenswood Hosp. Sch. Nursing, Chgo., 1957. Staff nurse Ravenswood Hosp., Chgo., 1957-58, St. Joseph's Hosp., St. Paul, 1958-59, Office of Drs. Roy & Hilker, St. Paul, 1959-60; aide to U.S. Senator Rudy Boschwitz, St. Paul, 1982-88; mem. Minn. Senate from 37th dist., St. Paul, 1989—2002, Minn. Senate from 36th Dist., St. Paul, 2003—. Mem. adv. bd. St. Paul chpt. ARC, 1986-88; vol., officer Minn. Ind. Rep. Com., 1972-83; bd. dirs. Ind. Sch. Dist. 192, Farmington, Minn., 1976-79. Mem. Minn. Waterfowl Assn., Farmington C. of C., Dakota Arts Coun., Ducks Unltd., Eagles Aux., Am. Legion Aux. (sec. Farmington chpt.), VFW Aux., So. Dakota County Sportsmen Club. Avocations: needlecrafts, knitting, drawing, painting, travel. Office: Minn Senate 117 Stat Office Bldg Saint Paul MN 55155-1232

PARISH, JAMES ROBERT, author, cinema historian; b. Cambridge, Mass., Apr. 21, 1944; s. Fred Arthur and Ann Lois (Magilevy) P. BA, U. Pa., 1964, LLB, 1967. Pres. Entertainment Copyright Rsch.Co. Inc., N.Y.C., 1967-68; film reporter, reviewer, interviewer Variety, Motion Picture Daily, 1968-69; entertainment publicist Harold Rand & Co., 1969-70; free-lance writer, publicist, film book cons., film reviewer, novelist, 1970—; acquisition editor Renaissance Books, 1996-99. Author: (with P. Michael) The Emmy Awards: A Pictorial History, 1970, The Fox Girls, 1971, The Great Movie Series, 1971 (with A.H. Marill) The Cinema of Edward G. Robinson, 1972, The Slapstick Queens, 1972, The Paramount Pretties, 1972, (with R. Bowers) The MGM Stock Company, 1973, Actors TV Credits, 1950-72, 73, Good Dames, 1973, (with M.R. Pitts) The Great Spy Pictures, 1973, The RKO Gals, 1973, (with S. Whitney), The George Raft File, 1973, (with M.R. Pitts) Film Directors: A Guide to Their American Pictures, 1974, Hollywood's Great Love Teams, 1974, (with S. Whitney) Vincent Price Unmasked, 1974, The Great Movie Heroes, 1975, (with D. Stanke), The Glamour Girls, 1975, The Debonairs, 1975, (with L. DeCarl) Hollywood Players: The Forties, 1975, (with J. Ano) Liza! (The Liza Minnelli Story), 1975, (with M.R. Pitts) The Great Gangster Pictures, 1975, The Elvis Presley Scrapbook, 1975, (with W. Leonard) Hollywood Players: The Thirties, 1976, (with D. Stanke) The All Americans, 1976, Film Directors: A Guide for Western Europe, 1976, Great Child Stars, 1976, The Jeanette MacDonald Story, 1976, (with D. Stanke) The Leading Ladies, 1977, (with M.R. Pitts) The Great Science Fiction Pictures, 1977, Film Actors Guide: Western Europe, 1977, The Elvis Presley Scrapbook (update), 1977, (with M. Trost) Actors TV Credits: Supplement One, 1977, (with M.R. Pitts) Hollywood on Hollywood, 1978, (with R. Braff et al.) Hollywood Character Actors, 1978, (with G. Mank and D. Stanke) The Hollywood Beauties, 1978, (with W. Leonard) The Funsters, 1979, (with D. Stanke) The Forties Gals, 1980, (with G. Mank) The Hollywood Reliables, 1980, The Great American Movies Book, 1980, (with G. Mank) The Best of MGM, 1981, (with M.R. Pitts) The Great Spy Pictures II, 1986, (with M.R. Pitts) The Great Gangster Pictures II, 1987, (with M.R. Pitts) The Great Western Pictures II, 1988, Black Action Pictures from Hollywood, 1989, (with M.R. Pitts) The Great Science Fiction Pictures II, 1990, (with V. Terrace) Complete Actors TV Credits, 1990, (with M.R. Pitts) Hollywood Songsters, 1990, updated edit., 2002, The Great Cop Pictures, 1990, Prison Pictures from Hollywood, 1991, (with M.R. Pitts) Hollywood's Great Musicals, 1992, (with D. Stanke) Hollywood Baby Boomers, 1992, Prostitution in Hollywood Film, 1992, The Hollywood Death Book, 1992; Let's Talk: America's Favorite Talk Show Hosts, 1993, Gays and Lesbians in Mainstream Cinema, 1993, Hollywood's Celebrity Death Book, updated and expanded, 1994, Ghosts and Angels on the Hollywood Screen, 1995, Today's Black Hollywood, 1995, Pirates and Seafaring Swashbucklers, 1995, The Great Child Stars, 1996, The Unofficial "Murder She Wrote" Casebook, 1997, Rosie: Rosie O'Donnell's Biography, 1997, updated edit., 1998, Whoopi Goldberg: From Poverty to Mega Stardom, 1997, updated edit., 1999, Jason Biggs, 2000, The Hollywood Book of Death, 2001, Gus Van Sant, 2001, Hollywood Bad Boys, 2002, Jet Li, 2002, The Encyclopeida of Ethnic Groups in Hollywood, 2002, Hollywood Divas, 2002, The Hollywood Book of Love, 2003, Whitney Houston, 2003, Steven Spielberg, 2004, The Hollywood Book of Scandals, 2004, Tom Hanks, 2004, Stephen King, 2004, Halle Berry, 2004; assoc. editor: The American Movies Reference Book, 1969, TV Movies, 1969, The Great American Movie Book, 1980. Mem. Phi Beta Kappa. Avocations: docent, reading, writing. Address: 4338 Gentry Ave Unit 1 Studio City CA 91604-1764 E-mail: jrparish@sbcglobal.net. *To succeed in one's ambitions requires an unyielding avoidance of other people's skepticisms.*

PARISH, RICHARD LEE, engineer, consultant; b. Kansas City, Mo., May 31, 1945; s. Charles Lee and Ruth (Duncan) P.; m. Patricia Ann Erickson, June 2, 1968; children: Christie Lynn White, Kerry Anne Parish-Philp. BS in Agrl. Engring., U. Mo., 1967, MS in Agrl. Engring., 1968, PhD, 1970. Registered profl. engr., Ohio. Asst., then assoc. prof. engring. Univ. Ark., Fayetteville, 1969-74; mgr. mech. research and devel. O.M. Scott & Sons Co., Marysville, Ohio, 1974-83; assoc. prof., then prof. La. State U., Baton Rouge, 1983-97; prof. Hammond Rsch. Sta., 1995—. Cons. in equipment patents, equipment safety, product liability, personal injury, design and evaluation; expert witness testimony in agrl. and hort. equipment, patents, 1984—. Contbr. over 100 articles to profl. jours.; patentee in field. Bd. dirs. Agrl. Devel. Found. Recipient Quality award, ITT, 1979, Doyle Chambers award for excellence in rsch., La. State U. Agrl. Ctr., 2001; NSF fellow, 1967—69. Mem. Am. Soc. Agrl. Engrs. (chmn. agrl. chem. application com. 1982-83, chmn. power and machinery divsn. program com. 1986-87, chmn. cultural practices equipment com. 1994-95, chmn. fruit and vegetable prodn. engring. com. 1999-2001), La. Vegetable Growers Assn., Am. Soc. Hort. Sci. Republican. Baptist. Avocations: old tractors, gardening, woodwork, bicycling. Home: 21135 Highway 16 Amite LA 70422-4733 Office: Hammond Rsch Sta 21549 Old Covington Hwy Hammond LA 70403-0533 Office Phone: 985-543-4125. Business E-Mail: dparish@agcenter.lsu.edu.

PARISH, WILLIAM HENRY, lawyer; b. Oakland, Calif., July 28, 1954; s. Harry and Elaine Katherine (Triplett) P.; m. Kathryn Annette, Aug. 14, 1976; children: Michael Erik, Jennifer Christine, Melissa Ann. AA, Hartnell Coll., 1974; BA, Calif. State U., 1977; JD, U. Pacific, 1980. Bar: Calif. 1980, U.S. Dist. Ct. (ea. dist.) Calif. 1980, U.S. Ct. Appeals (9th cir.) 1980, U.S. Supreme Ct. 1990. Assoc. Cavalero, Bray, Geiger & Rudquist, Stockton, Calif., 1980-82, ptnr., 1982-87, Bray, Geiger, Rudquist, Nuss & Parish, Stockton, Calif., 1987; prin. Law Offices of William H. Parish, Stockton, Calif., 1987—96, Parish & Nelson, A Profl. Corp., Stockton, Calif., 1997—2002, Parish & Small, A Profl. Corp., Stockton, Calif., 2003—. Mem. ABA (litigation sect. 1980—), Order of Coif, Am. Heart Assn., San Joaquin County, mem. bd. dirs. (2001-), pres. (2002-). Office: Parish & Small Profl Corp 1919 Grand Canal Blvd Ste A-5 Stockton CA 95207

PARISI, CHERYL LYNN, elementary school educator; b. Hackensack, N.J., Aug. 26, 1955; d. Elza A. and Constance Leah (Sculley) Sockey; m. Albert J. Parisi, Apr. 18, 1981; 1 child, Christopher Thomas. BA, Fairleigh Dickinson U., 1977; postgrad., Columbia U., N.Y.C., 2002—. Cert. tchr., N.J. Piano instr., Bergen County, N.J., 1972-79; art tchr. Meml. Sch., South Hackensack, N.J., 1979-80, Hackensack Mid. Sch., 1980-84, Nellie K. Parker Sch., Hackensack, 1984—. Exhibited in group shows at The Jacob Javits Conv. Ctr., N.Y.C., 1990, The Designer Craftsmen's Gallery, New Brunswick, N.J., 1993, Gloucester County Coll., Sewell, N.J., 1993, Johnson and Johnson Corp., Titusville, N.J., 1993, Arts Coun. Princeton, N.J., 1993, Montclair State U., Upper Montclair, N.J., 1992, 94, named to panel for selection of educators for the NEH seminar Amer. and Brit. Chldrns. Lit., Princeton, 1999. Author and co-dir. of chldrns. musical: Claude Monet: A Bridge to the Past, 1999. Recipient Art Educator Achievement award Fantasy Fund Inc. at the Cathedral of St. John the Divine, N.Y.C., 1992; grantee Hackensack Edn. Found., 1991; grantee Hackensack Small Grants Program, 2003; NEH fellow Princeton U., 1991. Mem. Art Educators N.J. (chairperson 1993 Yr. of the Am. Craft 1991-93, publicity 50th anniversary conf. 1990; pres. Bergen County chpt. 1984-86, Achievement award 1989), Nat. Art Edn. Assn. Avocations: playing the piano, reading. Home: 167 Godwin Ave Wyckoff NJ 07481-2004 Office: Nellie K Parker Sch 261 Maple Hill Dr Hackensack NJ 07601-1497

PARISI, MARITA, artist, art gallery director; b. Bad Kreuznach, Germany, July 29, 1946; came to U.S., 1984; d. William Acker. BA, Wilfred Laurier U., Waterloo, Can., 1968; MEd, U. Toronto, Can., 1969. Tchr. Halton Bd. Edn., Oakville, Ont., Can., 1971-83; pres., owner Nature Art Gallery, Citra, Fla., 1995—. Cons., workshop leader York U., Toronto, 1977-82, tchr., 1978-79. Artist cover N.E. Wildlife Exposition, Albany, N.Y., 1987-89, Smithsonian, 1989; represented in permanent collection N.Y. State Art Mus., Albany, Sundancer Gallery, Cocoa Village, Fla., Amrita Gallery, Poughkeepsie, N.Y., Long Ago and Far Away, Manchester Ctr., Vt.; exhibited in numerous one-woman and group shows. Mem. Ward Found., Md., 1991-92. Rotary Club Can. scholar, 1964, Ont. scholar, 1966; Ministry Edn. Hilroy fellow, Ont., 1983; recipient award in art Washington Project, 1993; named Best of Show, Bonita Springs, Fla., 1995, first in category Mandarin Art Festival, Fla., 1996, Higginbotham award, 1998, Best of Show, Stuart, Fla., 1998, Best of Show, Martin Coun. for Arts, 1999, Award of Excellence, Ft. Lauderdale, 2001. Mem. Ulster Arts Alliance, Empire States Crafts Alliance, Nat. Mus. Am. Indian, So. Vt. Art Ctr. Avocations: photography, wildlife, travel, writing, reading. Home and Office: PO Box 1028 Citra FL 32113

PARISI, PAULA ELIZABETH, writer, photographer, editor; b. N.Y.C., Feb. 27, 1960; d. Alfred John and Patricia Ann (Delucas) P. BA, Rutgers U., 1982; photography classes, Phila. Coll. Art, 1978-82. Reporter TVSM Inc./The Cable Guide, Horsham, Pa., 1982-84; assoc. editor Home Viewer Publs., Phila., 1984-85, mng. editor, 1985-87; home video cable TV, technology editor The Hollywood Reporter, Los Angeles, 1987—, editorial dir., 2000—. Contbr. articles to Billboard, Film & Video Prodn., Mix, Hollywood Reporter, Phila. Inquirer; photographs published in Phila. Inquirer, Washington Jour., Miami Herald, Circus, Us, Sixteen, others. Republican. Roman Catholic. Office: The Hollywood Reporter 5055 Wilshire Blvd Ste 600 Los Angeles CA 90036-4396

PARISOTTO, GLORIA, publishing executive, poet; b. São Paulo, Brazil, July 4, 1938; came to U.S., 1980; d. Luiz and Antonia (Guimarães) P.; m. Onofre Pereira Mendonca, Dec. 13, 1954 (div. 1980); children: Marco Antonio, Marco Tulio, Maria Emilia. Degree in tchg., Inst. Fernando Costa, Prudente, 1954; student, Brazilian Acad. Fine Arts, Rio de Janeiro, 1985. Cert. tchr., Brazil. Tchr. Sch.-Pres. Bernardes, São Paulo, Brazil, 1954-56, Maristas H.S., Parana, P.R., 1954-66; hosp. supr. Sanatory Maringa Ltd., Parana, P.R., 1955-90; pres. Sunrising Publ. Co., N.Y.C., 1991—. Author: Learning Portuguese Without a Teacher, 1991, The Extraterrestrial and the Blue Planet, 1992, My Poems (3 langs.), 1992; (poems) The Flower (Poet of Merit award Am. Poetry Assn. 1990), Mother (Poet of Merit award Internat. Poetry soc. 1991); contbr. poetry to numerous anthologies; one-woman art show at Cricket Club, Miami, U.S., 1981; exhibited art in group shows at Assn. de Criticos y Comentaristas de Arte, Miami, Fla., 1981, Hispanic Heritage Festival, Miami, 1981, Internat. Festival, Nhan-@, 1982, Nouvelle Gailerie, Geneva, Switzerland, 1983, UNESCO, Paris, 1984, Brazilian Artists Show, Rio de Janeiro, 1985, Internat. Expo, N.Y.C., 1986, Internat. Art Expo, Montreal, Que., Can., 1986, Pub. Libr., Gt. Neck, N.Y., 1987 (Excellence medal), Am. Embassy, Brasilia, Brazil, 1987, House of Spain, Rio de Janeiro, 1987, Lever House, N.Y.C., 1987, Mcpl. Gallery, São Paulo, 1989, Lincoln Ctr. Cork Gallery, N.Y.C., 1989, Icaro Gallery, N.Y.C., 1990, Epiphany Gallery, N.Y.C., 1990, Vanderbilt Mus., L.I., N.Y., 1992, Rio Design Ctr. Gallery, 1993 (hon. mention), Portal Gallery, São Paulo, 1993, Who's Who Artists, Edinburgh, Scotland, 1994, IPS's Conv. Art Show, Washington, 1995, Art Show, Capetown, South Africa, 1995, Am. & Internat. Bio Ctr., San Francisco, 1996, Oxford (Eng.) Gallery, 1997. Rep. abroad Brazilian Ecology Assn., Rio de Janeiro, 1988, Pan Am. Writers Assn., Brazilian Acad. Fine Arts, Rio de Janeiro, 1988. Recipient Bronze medal L'Amounier Gallery, Rio de Janeiro, 1981, Hebrew Cmty., Rio de Janeiro, 1981, Silver medal Brazilian Assn. Drawing and Visual Arts, Rio de Janeiro, 1982, Mil. Assn. Art Show, Rio de Janeiro, 1982, Gold medal Internat. Blenal, Rio de Janeiro, 1983, Ho. of Reps., Rio de Janeiro, 1983, Planetarium Gallery, Rio de Janeiro, 1984, Nat. Acad. Fine Arts, Rio de Janeiro, 1985, Palace "Espelho D'Agua", Belem, Portugal, 1986, Civil Police Acad., Rio de Janeiro, 1986, Gold Palette award Exhbn. Brazilian Artists, Salvador, Bahia, Brazil, 1987, Editor's award Nat. Libr. of Poetry, Washington, 1993, 94, Excellentia Order of Merit award, 1995, 1st prize award Famous Poetry Soc., Calif., 1996; semi-finalist nat. contest Internat. Poetry Soc.; named Poet of Merit, Internat. Poetry Assn., Washington, 1990, 91, 92. Mem. Nat. League Am. Pen Women, Inc., Internat. Platform Assn., Writers and Poets Soc., Acad. Am. Poets, Française-Italian Cultural Inst. Avocations: tennis, gym, travel, reading, music. Home and Office: 150 W 56th St Apt 3407 New York NY 10019-3843

PARIZEK, ELDON JOSEPH, geologist, educator, dean; b. Iowa City, Apr. 30, 1920; s. William Joseph and Libbie S. P.; m. Mildred Marie Burger, Aug. 9, 1944; children— Richard, Marianne, Elizabeth, Amy. BS, U. Iowa, 1942, MS, 1946, PhD, 1949. Instr. U. Iowa, 1947-49; asst. prof. geology U. Ga., 1949-54, asso. prof., 1954-56, U. Kansas City, 1956-63; prof. U. Mo., Kansas City, 1963—, chmn. dept. geoscis., 1968-78; dean U. Mo. (Coll. Arts and Scis.), 1979-86. Served with USN, 1942-45. Fellow Geol. Soc. Am.; mem. AAUP, Assn. Mo. Geologists, AAAS, Sigma Xi. Roman Catholic. Achievements include research, numerous publs. on mass wasting, slope failure, underground space, geology of West Mo. Home: 6913 W 100th Shawnee Mission KS 66212 Office: 5100 Rockhill Rd Kansas City MO 64110-2481

PARK, ALICE MARY CRANDALL, genealogist; b. Loda, Ill., Oct. 4, 1901; d. Frederick Adam and Sarah Elizabeth (Clemens) Crandall; m. Lee I. Park, Aug. 29, 1925 (dec. Aug. 24, 1978); children: Lee Crandall, Nancy Park Kern. BS, U. Chgo., 1924. Tchr. U. Chgo. Lab. Sch., 1924-25; genealogy rschr. Washington, 1925—. Author: Park/e/s and Bunch on the Trail West, 1974, rev. edit., 1982, Schenck and Related Families in New Netherlands, 1992, One Crandall Family 1651-1996, 1996, supplement, 1999, Our Immigrant Ancestors from Scotland: George Smith and His Wife, Mary Baird and Their Descendants, 2002. Pres. Falls Church (Va.) PTA, 1941-42, LWV, Fairfax County, Va., 1947-48. Mem. DAR, Nat. Soc. Colonial Dames Am., Nat. Soc. Sons and Daughters of Pilgrims, Nat. Soc. Daughters Am. Colonists, Friends

Holland Soc., Nat. Hubenot Soc., Nat. Soc. U.S. Daughters 1812, Chevy Chase Club, Met. Club Washington, Farmington Country Club Va. Avocations: gardening, travel, cooking, music. Home: #314 4200 Cathedral Ave NW Washington DC 20016-4931

PARK, BARBARA, writer; b. Mt. Holly, NJ, Apr. 27, 1947; m. Richard A. Park, 1969; 2 children. Attended, Rider Coll., 1965—67; BS, U. Alabama, 1969. Author: (children's books) Don't Make Me Smile, 1981, Operation: Dump the Chump, 1982 (Tennessee Children's Choice Book award, 1986), Skinnybones, 1982, Beanpole, 1983, Buddies, 1985 (Parents' Choice award, 1985), Kid in the Red Jacket, 1987 (Library of Congress Book of the Yr., 1987), Almost Starring Skinnybones, 1988, Mother Got Married: and Other Disasters, 1989, Rosie Swanson, 1991, Junie B. Jones and the Stupid Smelly Bus, 1992, Junie B. Jones and Her Big Fat Mouth, 1993, Junie B. Jones and a Little Monkey Business, 1993, Junie B. Jones and Some Sneaky Peeky Spying, 1994, Mick Harte Was Here, 1995, Junie B. Jones and the Yucky Blucky Fruitcake, 1995, B. Jones Loves Handsome Warren, 1996, Junie B. Jones and that Meanie Jim's Birthday, 1996, Junie B. Jones Loves Handsome Warren, 1996, Junie B. Jones has a Monster Under Her Bed, 1997, Junie B. Jones is Not a Crook, 1997, Junie B. Jones is a Party Animal, 1997, Junie B. Jones Smells Something Fishy, 1998, Junie B. Jones is a Beauty Shop Guy, 1998, Psst! It's Me...the Bogeyman, 1998, Junie B. Jones is Almost a Flower Girl, 1999, Junie B. Jones and the Mushy Gushy Valentine, 1999, Junie B. Jones has a Peep in her Pocket, 2000, Junie B. Jones is Captain Field Day, 2001, Junie B. Jones is a Graduation Girl, 2001, Junie B. Jones: First Grader, 2001, Junie B. First Grader: Boss of Lunch, 2002, Junie B. First Grader: Toothless Wonder, 2002, Top Secret, Personal Beeswax: A Journal by Junie B., 2003, Junie B. First Grader: Cheater Pants, 2003, Junie B., First Grader: One-Man Band, 2003. Recipient Young Hoosier award, 1985, Milner award, 1986. Office: c/o Random House 1745 Broadway New York NY 10019*

PARK, BEVERLY GOODMAN, lawyer; b. Boston, Nov. 10, 1937; d. Morris and Mary (Keller) Goodman; divorced; children: Glynis Forcht, Seth, Elyse. BS, Simmons Coll., 1959; MS, Ea. Conn. State U., 1968; JD, Western N.E. Coll. Law, 1998. Bar: Mass. 1998. Asst. dir. comty. svc. Hartford (Conn.) Courant, 1976-79; mayor Borough of Colchester, Conn., 1979-83; lifestyle editor Chronicle, Willimantic, Conn., 1980-82, suburban editor, 1982-84; officer mktg. & comm. U. Conn. Health Ctr., Farmington, 1981-97; pvt. practice juvenile law BGP, 2000—. Selected team mem. radiation exposure info. study Belorussia, 1993; mem. adv. bd. Hosp. News; mem. women's affairs com. U. Conn. Health Ctr. Women's Networking Task Force; mem. Univ. Adminstrv. Staff Coun.; mem. minority awards com. U. Conn. Health Ctr., mem. John N. Dempsey hosp. disaster plan com. Designer: (libr. studies curriculum) Classroom Instruction on the Use of Books and Libraries, 1972; pub.: (ednl. booklets) Have You Made Plans for the Future?, 1977-78; editor of edn. holiday and bridal supplements The Chronicle, 1980-84; editor: U. Conn. Health Ctr. Anniversary Mag., 1986, U. Conn. Health Ctr. Med. Catalog, 1986, (ann. pub.) Salute, 1988, U. Conn. Health Ctr. 30th Anniversary Supplement, 1991. Bd. dirs. Ea. Conn. Found. for Pub. Giving, Norwich, 1990-96; women's club officer Dem. Town Com., Colchester, Conn., 1963-90; active Hadassah, Northampton/Amherst, 1996—, Women's League for Conservative Judaism. Recipient Lifestyle Page award New England Press Assn., 1980, Media Excellence in Covering Human Svcs. award Conn. chpt. NASW, 1982, Ragan Report Arnold's Admirables award for excellence in graphics and typography, 1985, Gold award Healthcare Mktg. Report, 1987, award for video ACS, 1990. Mem. NOW (membership com. Southea. chpt., mem. legis. task force, Meritorious Svc. award Southea. Conn. chpt. 1985), Am. Soc. for Hosp. Mktg. and Pub. Rels., Am. Mktg. Assn., Assn. Am. Med. Colls. (mem. group on pub. affairs), Conn. Hosp. Assn. (participant hosp. pub. rels. conf.), State of Conn. Pub. Info. Coun. (mem. steering com.), Mass. Bar Assn., Hampshire County and Franklin County Bar Assns., New England Hosp. Pub. Rels. and Mktg. Assn. (bd. dirs. 1987, 88). Avocations: swimming, hiking, spending time with grandchildren. Home and Office: 116 N Main St Florence MA 01062-1220 E-mail: parklegal@aol.com.

PARK, BYEONGJU, engineer; b. Jangsung, Korea (South), Nov. 14, 1965; s. Banghyun Park and Sun-Za Cho-Schade; m. Young Shin Kim, Dec. 2, 1995; children: Richard D., Sophia T., Christine F. PhD, U. of Ill., 1994. Engr. Applied Materials, Inc., Santa Clara, Calif., 1994—96; adv. engr. Internat. Bus. Machines, Inc., Hopewell Junction, NY, 1996—. Achievements include 12 US patents and other international patents. Home: 32 Colburn Dr Poughkeepsie NY 12603 Office: International Business Machines Inc 2070 Route 52 B/300-3H9-37 Z/47B Hopewell Junction NY 12533 Personal E-mail: youngbjp@yahoo.com. E-mail: parkbj@us.ibm.com.

PARK, CHAN HO, professional baseball player; b. Kong Ju City, Korea, June 30, 1973; Student, Hang Yan U., Seoul, Korea. Pitcher L.A. Dodgers, 1994—. Achievements include being the first Korean to play in Major Leagues. Address: LA Dodgers 1000 Elysian Park Ave Los Angeles CA 90012-1112

PARK, CHAN HYUNG, cell biologist, physician; b. Seoul, Korea, Aug. 16, 1936; s. Chung Suh and Yoon Sook Yuh; m. Mary Hyungrok Kim, Apr. 16, 1966; 1 child, Christopher Myungwoo. MD, Seoul Nat. U., 1962, MS, 1964; PhD, U. Toronto, 1972. Diplomate in internal medicine and med. oncology Am. Bd. Internal Medicine. Asst. prof. U. Kans. Med. Ctr., 1974-80, assoc. prof., 1980-86, prof., 1986-89; prof., chief divsn. oncology/hematology, dept. internal med. Tex. Tech U. Health Scis. Ctr., 1989—94; dir. Cancer Ctr., Samsung Med. Ctr., Seoul, 1994—2001, cons. physician, 2001—, head divsn. hematology/oncology dept. medicine, 1994-99, cons. physician, 2001—; sr. rsch. scientist The Ctr. for the Improvement of Human Functioning Internat., Inc., Wichita, Kans., 2001—. Transl. novel from German to Korean; mem. editl. bd. Jour. Nutrition, Growth and Cancer, 1986-87; mem. editl. bd. Internat. Jour. Hematology, 1999—; contbr. articles to biomed and sci. jours. Recipient Rsch. Career Devel. award USPHS, NIH, 1979-84. Fellow: ACP; mem.: Am. Soc. Hematology, Internat. Soc. Exptl. Hematology, Am. Soc. Clin. Oncology, Am. Assn. Cancer Rsch. Home: 8814 E Churchill Cir Wichita KS 67206 Office: The Ctr for the Improvement Human Functioning Internat Inc 3100 N Hillside Wichita KS 67219

PARK, CHONG S. computer company executive; BA in Mgmt., Yonsei U.; MA in Mgmt., Seoul Nat. U.; MBA, U. Chgo.; PhD in Mgmt., Nova Southeastern U. Chmn., pres., CEO Axil Computer, Inc., 1993—95; from pres., CEO to vice-chmn. bd. Maxtor, Milipitas, Calif., 1995—98, chmn., 1998—; pres., CEO Hynix Semiconductor Am., Inc., 1996—2000, chmn., 1996—2002; pres., CEO, chmn. Hynix Semiconductor, Inc., 2000—02. Bd. dirs. Dot Hill Sys. Corp., ChipPAC. Office: Maxtor 500 McCarthy Blvd Milpitas CA 95035

PARK, CHUL, aerospace engineer; b. Taegon, Korea, June 8, 1934; came to U.S., 1964; s. Hyung-jin and Har-woon (Ryang) P.; m. Chyon Sue Sohn, Sept. 28, 1962; children: Sora, Pora, Marie. BS, Seoul (Korea) Nat. U., 1957, MS, 1960; PhD, Imperial Coll., London, 1964. Rsch. assoc. NASA Ames Rsch. Ctr., Moffett Field, Calif., 1964-67, aerospace engr., 1967-90, sect. head, 1990-92, staff scientist, 1993—. Author: Nonequilibrium Hypersonic Aerothermodynamics, 1990; patentee in field. Dir. Korean-Am. Music Supporters Assn., Cupertino, Calif., 1989—. 1st lt. Korean Air Force, 1958-61. Recipient Thermophysics award AIAA, 1994 Fellow AIAA (assoc., Thermophysics award 1994). Home: 106 Almond Blossom Ct Los Gatos CA 95032-5101 Office: NASA Ames Research Ctr Mail Stop 230-2 Moffett Field CA 94035

PARK, CHUNG, painter, educator, computer software developer; b. Pusan, Korea, Oct. 27, 1941; s. Byung Ho Park and Jung Sun Im; m. Sue Bok Park, May 9, 1974; children: Paul, Janet Sujean Park. Diploma, Pusan Tchr.'s Coll., 1962; BFA, U. Mich., 1979; MFA, Pratt Inst., 1981. Cert. secondary edn. tchr., Korea. Art prof. Pusan Women's U., Korea, 1984-87, Pusan Nat. U., Korea, 1983-84; instr. painting & drawing Sch. of Visual Arts, N.Y.C., 1990-92, 94—; adj. prof. fine arts Nyack (N.Y.) Coll., 1992-93; asst. adminstr. Upsala Coll., Orange, N.J., 1993-94; exec. dir. Uran Tech., Inc., Palisades Park, N.J., 1994—. Trustee Bd. of Edn., Tenafly, 1997-2000; chmn. Korean-Am. Elected Sch. Bd. Mem. Assembly, 1998-2000; mem. adv. com. N.J. State Dept. Edn., Bilingual Edn., 1998-2000; founder Korean-Am. Youth Ctr. N.J., 1998—, Korean-Am. Parents Assn. N.J., 1998—; exec. dir. Asian Am. Youth and Cultural Ctr., 2000—' apptd. mem. com. human rels. Bergen County, N.J., 2001-. Mem. Coll. Art Assn., Korean-Am. Tchrs. Assn. N.J. (founder), Korean-Am. Contemporary Artists Assn. Greater N.Y. (founder). Office: Uran Tech Inc 15 Bergen Blvd Fairview NJ 07022 Home: 282 American Legion DR Apt 2 Hackensack NJ 07601-2415 E-mail: chungpark@parkchung.com.

PARK, CHUNG IL, retired librarian; b. Chang-won, Korea, Aug. 25, 1938; s. Zung S. and Bong-y (Choo) P.; m. Jung Yoo, Aug. 30, 1969; children: Charlotte, Sue, Andrew. BA, Yonsei U., 1961; MLS, U. So. Calif., L.A., 1971; postgrad., U. Ill., 1975. Libr., mem. faculty Malcolm X Coll., Chgo., 1972—2002; ret., 2002—. Compiler, editor: (books) Best Sellers and Best Choices 1980-83, Best Books by Consensus 1984-88, Advertisement Digest: Library and Information Services, 1979; editor COINT, 1980-88; contbr. articles to profl. jours. Mem. ALA, Am. Fedn. Tchrs. Avocation: automobile travel. Home: 4384 N Indianhead R Hernando FL 34442 E-mail: ci_park@yahoo.com.

PARK, DAVID ALLEN, physicist, researcher; b. N.Y.C., Oct. 13, 1919; s. Edwin Avery and Frances (Paine) P.; m. Clara Justine Claiborne, Aug. 18, 1945; children: Katharine, Rachel, Paul, Jessica. AB, Harvard, 1941; PhD, U. Mich., 1950. Instr. Williams Coll., 1941-44; ops. research on radar countermeasures Harvard U. and Eng., 1944-45; instr. U. Mich., 1950; mem. Inst. Advanced Study, Princeton, 1950-51; mem. faculty Williams Coll., 1952-88, prof. physics, 1960-88, emeritus, 1988—; sr. vis. Cambridge (Eng.) U., 1962-63; vis. lectr. U. Ceylon, 1955-56, 72, Mass. Inst. Tech., 1966; vis. prof. U. N.C., 1964. Author: Quantum Theory, 1964, 3d edit., 1991, Contemporary Physics, 1964, Strong Interactions, 1966, Classical Dynamics and Its Quantum Analogues, 1979, 2d edit., 1990, The Image of Eternity, 1980, (with P.J. Davis) No Way, 1987, The How and the Why, 1988, The Fire Within the Eye, 1997. Fellow Am. Phys. Soc.; mem. Internat. Soc. for Study Time (pres. 1973-76). Office: Williams Coll Dept Physics Williamstown MA 01267

PARK, EDWARD CAHILL, JR., retired physicist; b. Wollaston, Mass., Nov. 26, 1923; s. Edward Cahill and Fentress (Kerlin) P.; m. Helen Therese O'Boyle, July 28, 1951. AB, Harvard U., 1947; postgrad., Amherst Coll., 1947-49; PhD, U. Birmingham, Eng., 1956. Instr. Amherst (Mass.) Coll., 1954-55; mem. staff Lincoln Lab., Lexington, Mass., 1955-57, Arthur D. Little, Inc., Cambridge, Mass., 1957-60, group leader electronic systems Santa Monica, Calif., 1960-64; sr. staff engr., head laser system sect. Hughes Aircraft Co., Culver City, Calif., 1964-68, sr. scientist El Segundo, Calif., 1986-88; mgr. electro optical systems sect. Litton Guidance and Control Systems, Woodland Hills, Calif., 1968-70; sr. phys. scientist The Rand Corp., Santa Monica, 1970-72; sr. scientist R&D Assocs., Marina Del Rey, Calif., 1972-1986, cons., 1986-89; sr. tech. specialist Rockwell Internat., N.Am. Aircraft, Seal Beach, Calif., 1988-94. Contbr. articles to profl. jours.; patentee in field. Served to 1st lt. USAAF, 1943-46. Grantee Dept. Indsl. and Sci. Research, 1953. Fellow Explorers Club (sec. So. Calif. chpt. 1978-79); mem. IEEE, Soc. Archtl. Historians, Acad. Am. Poets, Sigma Xi. Clubs. 20-Ghost (Eng.), BMW Car Club Am., Mercedes Benz Club Am. Democrat. Avocations: music, art, architecture, gardening, classic cars. Home: 932 Ocean Frnt Santa Monica CA 90403-2410

PARK, ELIZABETH HASKELL, librarian, educator; d. Henry Cummings and Lois Ogren Haskell; m. Melburn Robert Park, June 11, 1966; children: Geoffrey Haskell, Carolyne Elizabeth. BA, Stanford U., 1966; MLS, SUNY, Buffalo, 1972; MS, Memphis State U., 1989. Libr. Gardenville Elem. Sch., West Seneca, NY, 1972—73; reference libr. Lansing (Mich.) C.C., 1980—82; asst. bus. libr. Mich. State U., Lansing, 1982—83; reference libr. U. Memphis, 1983—95, head reference dept., 1995—. Co-author: Charging and Collecting Fees and Fines: A Handbook for Libraries, 1998; contbr. articles to profl. jours., chpt. to book. Mem.: ALA, Mich. Libr. Assn., Tenn. Libr. Assn., Assn. Coll. and Rsch. Librs., Kappa Delta Phi, Beta Phi Mu. Office: U Memphis 126 Ned R McWherter Library Memphis TN 38152 Personal E-mail: ehpark@memphis.edu. E-mail: ehpark@memphis.edu.

PARK, GLORIA, family physician, consultant; b. Spokane, Wash., Apr. 13, 1930; d. George Edmund and Nellie Edessa (Dorman) Knowles; m. Orlo Edward Park, Aug. 9, 1952; children: Kevin, Loren, Galen, Diane. BS in Zoology cum laude, Wash. State Coll., 1952; MD, U. Colo., 1955. Cert. Nat. Indian Health Bd. Intern St. Anthony Hosp., Denver, 1955-56; chief outpatient svc. Alaska Native Med. Ctr., Anchorage, 1956-61, acting chief profl. svc., 1961-63, dir. outpatient dept. and field health, 1963-71, asst. dir. svc. unit affairs, 1971-74, dir. ambulatory care, 1974-85, mem. cons. staff family medicine svc., 1985—. Cons. hepatitis program Alaska Native Health Bd., Anchorage, 1986-87; clin. instr. U. Wash., Anchorage, 1978-85. Med. reviewer Alaska Medicine, 1987—. Former mem. Alaska Gov.'s Com. on Edn.; mem. Anchorage Municipality Libr. Bd., 1981-86; life mem. Alaska Coun. on Smoking or Health, 1981—. Recipient recognition award Anchorage Bus. and Profl. Women, 1968, award Nat. Indian Health Bd., 1985, 88, Alumni Achievement award Wash. State U., 1994. Fellow Am. Acad. Family Physicians (com. minority health affairs 1980-85); mem. AMA, Am. Assn. Sr. Physicians, Alaska Acad. Family Physicians (pres. 1981-83), Alaska Med. Assn. (councilor 1984-88), Anchorage Med. Soc. (com. mem.), Alaska Pub. Health Assn. (life), Alaska Heart Assn. (life), Cook Inlet Hist. Soc. (life). Republican. Avocations: travel, fishing, reading, genealogy. Office: Alaska Native Med Ctr 4315 Diplomacy Dr # Mailrm Anchorage AK 99508-5926

PARK, INUCK, economist, researcher; b. Daegu, Korea (South), Oct. 26, 1961; s. Chiho Park and Gapnam Sohn; m. Kyunghwa Jin Lee, Aug. 24, 1987; 1 child, Sunoo Eleanor. PhD, U. Minn., Usa, 1988—93. Lectr., econs. U. Bristol, England, 1993—2000; asst. prof. U. of Pitts., Pitts., 2000—; leverhulme prof. U. of Bristol, England, 2004—. Assoc. editor European Econ. Rev., 2003—. Contbr. articles to prof. jours. 2nd lt., Korea (South), 1987—88. Grantee Rsch. grant, England, Leverhulme Trust. Mem.: Am. Econ. Assn., Econometric Soc. Office: U Pitts 4S01 WW Posvar Hall Pittsburgh PA 15260

PARK, JAMES WALLACE, economics professor; b. Forest, Miss., May 1, 1934; s. Ulric Z. and Estelle Park; m. Martha A. Mayes, June 5, 1958; children: Julia C., Mary J. BS, U. Miss., 1958, M in Bus. Edn., 1959; PhD, U. Ala., 1974. Asst. prof. bus. U. N.Mex., Albuquerque, 1959—68; asst. prof. econs. Miss. U. for Women, Columbus, 1968—70; prof. bus. Jackson (Miss.) State U., 1974—77; prof. econs. Belhaven Coll., Jackson, 1977—2001, prof. emeritus, 2001—. Contbr. articles to profl. jours. Mem. Gov.'s Task Force on Miss. Economy, 1981; pres. Men of Ctrl. Miss. Presbytery, 1981—84. Recipient Tchg. Excellence and Campus Leadership award, Sears-Roebuck Found., 1991. Democrat. Avocation: writing. Home: 107 Pine Hill Dr Forest MS 39074 E-mail: jwmpark@aol.com.

PARK, JANIE C. provost; children: Christopher, Eric. BSN, Baylor U., 1968; MS in Cell and Molecular Biology, Fla. Inst. Tech., 1979, PhD in Cell and Molecular Biology, 1982. Nurse Holmes Regional Med. Ctr., Melbourne, Fla., 1968-69; grad. student tchg. asst. Fla. Inst. Tech., Melbourne, 1977-82, instr. biol. scis., 1982-84, asst. prof. biol. scis., 1984-89, chair preprofl./premed. program, 1986-93, assoc. prof. biol. scis., 1989-93, assoc. dean coll. sci. and liberal arts, 1990-93; dean coll. arts and scis., prof. biol. scis. Mont. State U., Billings, 1993-96, provost, acad. vice chancellor, prof. biol. scis., 1996—. Rsch. dir. Ctr. for Interdisciplinary Rsch. in Aging, 1988-90; rsch. dir. elctron microscopy svcs. Joint Ctr. Advanced Therapy and Biomed. Rsch. Fla. Inst. Tech. and Holmes Regional Med. Ctr., 1991-93; spkr. in field. Contbr. articles to profl. jours. Bd. dirs. St. Vincent's Regional Med. Ctr., Youth Dynamics, Inc.; mem. steering com. Billings Town and Gown; mem. Bldg. a Healthy Cmty. Task Force. Mem. Microscopy Soc. Am., Am. Assn. of State Colls. and Univs., Southeast Electron Microscopy (sessions chair ann. meeting 1991, 92), Soc. for Neurosci., Rocky Mountain Deans' Assn. (ann. meeting organizer 1995), Assn. for Rsch. in Otolaryngology (mem. membership com. 1991-97, chair membership com. 1993-97), Fla. Soc. for Electron Microscopy (v.p. 1983, bd. dirs. 1983-93, session chair ann. meeting 1989-92, pres.-elect 1989, pres. 1990-91, mem. local arrangements com. 1991, meeting registration chair 1990—), Coun. Colls. of Arts and Scis. (session chair ann. meeting 1995), Coun. Arts and Scis. of Urban Univs., Billings Rotary Internat., Leadership Billings Alumni Assn. Office: Mont State U Office Acad Vice Chancellor 1500 N 30th St Billings MT 59101-0245

PARK, JEFFREY BRYAN, controller; b. Tampa, Fla., Nov. 20, 1951; s. William H. Jr. and Mary W. (Pounds) P.; m. Kathaleen Barbara Mace, Feb. 4, 1973; children: Shawn M., Amber M. BS in Acctg., Calif. State U., Sacramento, 1973. Cost analyst Antioch (Calif.) Mill-Crown Zellerbach, 1973-76; planning analyst Crown Zellerbach Corp., San Francisco, 1976-77, fin. analyst, 1977-78; controller Crown Zellerbach Multiwall Bag Div., Antioch, 1978-79, Crown Zellerbach Bogalusa (La.) Mill, 1979-84; group controller Crown Zellerbach Gaylord Container Group, San Francisco, 1985-86; v.p., corp. controller Gaylord Container Corp., Deerfield, Ill., 1986—. Mem. Fin. Exec. Inst. Avocation: golf. Home: 701 Paddock Ln Libertyville IL 60048-3734 Office: Gaylord Container Corp 500 Lake Cook Rd Deerfield IL 60015-5609

PARK, JOHN, finance, investment consultant; b. Seoul, Korea, Nov. 29, 1925; came to U.S., 1949; s. Young-Kee and In-Oak P.; m. Nancy A. King, Dec. 21, 1961 (div. Nov. 1969); children: John K., Ben C.; m. Kwi Yong Lee, Aug. 14, 1990; 1 child, Angela L. AB, Coll. St. Thomas, 1953; MA, U. Nebr., 1955, PhD, 1959. Chmn., dept. econs., bus. Tarkio (Mo.) Coll., 1957-62; sr. prof. econs., bus. Clarkson Coll., Potsdam, N.Y., 1962-65, Northeast Mo. State U., 1965-67; prof. bus. econs. Southwest Mo. State U., 1967-70; chmn., dept. econ., bus. adminstrn. Frostburg (Md.) State U., 1970—93, prof., econs., bus. adminstrn., 1970—78. Investment advisor, Met. Securities Corp., St. Louis, 1966-70. Mem. Am. Econs. Assn., Am. Fin. Assn., Nat. Assn. Securities Dealers, Am. Assn. Polit. Social Scis., Eastern Fin. Assn., Fin. Mgmt. Assn., Alpha Kappa Delta, Pi Gamma Mu. Republican. Methodist. Avocation: classical music. Home and Office: PO Box 3436 451 Beacon Knoll Ln Fort Mill SC 29708-3436

PARK, JOHN J. investment banker; b. Pusan, Korea, June 1, 1964; came to U.S., 1978; s. Bong Hoon and Sun Ok (Kim) Park; m. Jessica Y. Lee, May 30, 1992. BS, MIT, 1986; MBA, NYU, 1991. Analyst W.P. Carey & Co., Inc., N.Y.C., 1987-89, asst. to the chmn., 1989-91, v.p., 1991-94, sr. v.p. fin., 1994—. Mem. Univ. Club. Avocations: tennis, squash, movies. Office: WP Carey & Co Inc 620 5th Ave New York NY 10020-2402*

PARK, JOHN THORNTON, academic administrator; b. Phillipsburg, N.J., Jan. 3, 1935; s. Dawson J. and Margaret M. (Thornton) P.; m. Dorcas M Marshall; June 1, 1956; children: Janet Ernst, Karen Daily. BA in Physics with distinction, Nebr. Wesleyan U., 1956; PhD, U. Nebr., 1963. NSF postdoctoral fellow Univ. Coll., London, 1963-64; asst. prof. physics U. Mo., Rolla, 1964-68, assoc. prof. physics, 1968-71, prof., 1971-2000, prof. emeritus, 2000—, chmn. dept. physics, 1977-83, vice chancellor acad. affairs, 1983-85, 86-91, interim chancellor, 1985-86, 91-92, chancellor, 1992-2000, chancellor emeritus, 2000—. Vis. assoc. prof. NYU, 1970-71; pres. Talema Electronics, Inc., St. James, Mo., 1983-99, Tortran Corp., 1990—; prin. investigator NSF Rsch. Grants, 1966-92; bd. dirs. Mo. Tech. Corp., Jefferson City, Mo., 1994—, Mo. Enterprise, 1990—, Phelps County Bank, 1997—. Contbr. articles to profl. jours. Recipient Most Disting. Scientist award Mo. Acad. Sci., 1994. Fellow Am. Phys. Soc. (mem. divsn. elec. and atomic physics); mem. Am. Assn. Physics Tchrs., Rotary. Methodist.

PARK, JON KEITH, dentist, educator; b. Wichita, Kans., May 26, 1938; DDS, U. Mo., 1964; BA, Wichita State U., 1969; MS in Dental Hygiene Edn., U. Mo., 1971; MS in Oral Pathology, U. Md., 1982; cert. in dental radiology, U. Pa. Sch. Dental Medicine, 1982. Diplomate Am. Bd. Oral and Mixillofacial Radiology. Pvt. practice dentistry, Wichita, 1964-67; chmn. dept. dental hygiene Wichita State U., 1967-72; assoc. prof. oral diagnosis, dir. oral radiology Balt. Coll. Dental Surgery, U. Md., 1972—. Program dir. U. Md. dental externship, 1974-77; lectr. Essex C.C., Harford County C.C.; cons. in radiology VA Hosp., Medix Sch. Dental Assisting; mem. Md. StateRadiation Control Adv. Bd., 1981—; chmn. devel. com. Introduction to Basic Concepts in Dental Radiography, Dental Assisting Nat. Bd., Inc., Am. Dental Assts. Assn., 1991 Editor Am. Acad. Oral and Maxillofacial Radiology Newsletter; patentee pivotal design dental chair. Mem. Ute Pass Hist. Soc. Recipient U. Md. Media Achievement award, 1977, 78. Fellow Am. Coll. Dentists, Am. Acad. Dental Radiology; mem. ADA, Md. State Dental Assn., Balt. City Dental Soc. (ad hoc com. radiation safety, exec. coun.), Am. Acad. Oral Pathology, Am. Acad. Oral and Maxillofacial Radiology (ednl. standards com., editor newsletter), Orgn. Tchrs. oral Diagnosis, Am. Theater Organ Soc., Kans. Dental Hygienists Assn. (hon.), Balt. Music Club, Am. Assn. Dental Schs., Internat. Assn. Dental and Maxillofacial Radiology, Balt. Opera Guild, Engring. Soc. Balt., Met. Opera Guild, Balt. Symphony Orch. Assn., Ute Pass Cmty. Assn., Univ. Club, Omicron Kappa Upsilon, Psi Omega. Episcopalian. E-mail: jpark@umaryland.edu.

PARK, JOON BU, biomedical engineer, researcher, educator; b. Pusan, Republic of Korea, June 20, 1944; arrived in U.S., 1964; s. Sung Sub and Jung Ju (Kim) P.; m. Hyonsook Yoo, Apr. 15, 2000; children: Misun, Yoon Ho, Yoon Il, Lajong. Student, Seoul Nat. U., Republic of Korea, 1962—64; BS, Boston U., 1967; MS, MIT, 1969; PhD, U. Utah, 1972. NIH postdoctoral fellow U. Wash., Seattle, 1972-73; vis. asst. prof. U. Ill., Urbana, 1973-76; asst., assoc. prof. Clemson (SC) U., 1976-81; prof. Tulane U., New Orleans, 1981-83; prof. biomed. engring. U. Iowa, Iowa City, 1983—. Advisor, cons. FDA, Rockville, Md., 1980—. Author: Biomaterials: An Introduction, 1979, 2nd edit., 1992, Biomaterials Science and Engineering, 1984, Biomaterials: Principles and Applications, 2002; contbr. more than 120 articles to profl. jours. Fellow Am. Inst. Med. and Biol. Engring.; mem. Soc. for Biomaterials (founding mem.), Biomed. Engring. Soc., Orthop. Rsch. Soc., NY Acad. Scis. Achievements include 10 patents. Home: 1810 Country Club Dr Coralville IA 52241-1183 Office: Univ Iowa Dept Biomed Engring Iowa City IA 52242 Office Phone: 319-335-5636. Business E-Mail: joon_park@uiowa.edu.

PARK, LEE (LEE PARKLEE), artist; b. Seoul, Republic of Korea; s. Chung-Kun Park and Mil-Hwa Kim; m. Chai Kyung Lim, June 3, 1994. MA, Fla. State U., 1986. Prof. associated academician dept. arts Vinzaglio, Italy, 2002—. Group shows include Shinpara Gallery, LA, Up-Stairs Gallery, LA, Beverly Plz. Hotel, Pacific Mus., Pasadena, Calif., Barnsdall Art Gallery, Hollywood, Calif., Brand XXII The Assn. of Brand Art Ctr., Glendale, Calif., Asia Invitation Art Exhbn., Sejong Cultural Ctr., Seoul, la Peintre Moderne Coreend '93, Paris, Korea-Japan Interchange Exhbn., Tokyo, 1994, Downtown Lives '96 Art Exhbn., LA, City Hall of Paris, 4, Biennale Internat. de Paris, 1994, Musee d'Art Moderne de la Commanderie d'Unet, Paris, 1994, Bridgeport (NY) U., 1995, San Bernardino County Mus., 1995, Kong-Ja Culture Art Exhbn., China, 1995, His Majesty the King's 50th Anniversary Art Exhbn., Thailand, 1996, 1st Venice Ann. Internat. Open Art Exhbn., Venice, 1998, 1st Internat. Biennial Contemporary Art, Perugia, Italy, 1998, Heukyong-gangsung Internat. Art Exhbn., China, 1998, Ting Shao-Kuang Fine Art Ctr., Beverly Hills, Articulture Gallery, Hermosa Beach, Calif., 1998, '99 World Peace Art Exhbn., Sejong Cultural Ctr., Seoul, 1999, The Millennium Art Collection, 2000, Invitational Art Exhbn. Jin-Jiang Gen. Assn. Gallery, Philipines, 2001, Galerie Michelangelo, Las Vegas, 2002, Reasons to Love the Earth, Den Haag, Netherlands, 2002; 2 person shows include Cosmos Gallery, Honolulu, The City of LA Cultural Affairs Dept.; solo exhibits include Modern Art Gallery, LA, Olympic Gallery, LA, Sun Space Gallery, LA, Gallery Nuevo, Pusan, Republic of Korea, Westside Jewish Cmty. Ctr., LA, World Festival of Art Exhbn., Slovenia, Caesars Palace Hotel Michelangelo, Las Vegas, Nev., 49th Toyo Calligraphy Art Assn., Tokyo; publ. artwork in American References, Art of California mag., Artweek mag., The Biweekly Art Jour., Seoul, Artprint mag., Washington, Art Exposure mag., Calif., Ency. of Living Artists mag., Calif., Art 2000, Seoul, Art Diary Internat. 1998-2003, Milan, Italy, Internat. Encyclopaedic Dictionary Modern and Contemporary Art, Ferrara, Italy, 2002-03, Dictionary Internat. Biography Ctr., Cambridge, Eng. Recipient Bronze award Art of Calif., 1993, Gold award

Art Addiction, Stockholm, 1997. Avocations: collecting stamps and antiques, music, reading books, jogging, playing tennis. Home: 1935 S La Salle Ave Apt 31 Los Angeles CA 90018-1627 E-mail: park@b17.com.

PARK, LEE CRANDALL, psychiatrist; b. Washington, July 15, 1926; s. Lee I. and Alice (Crandall) P.; m. Barbara Ann Merrick, July 1, 1953; children: Thomas Joseph, Jeffrey Rawson; m. Mary Woodfill Banerjee, Apr. 27, 1985; stepchildren: Stephen Kumar, Scott Kumar. Grad., Putney Prep. Sch., Vt.; BS in Zoology, Yale U., 1948; MD, Johns Hopkins U., 1952. Diplomate Nat. Bd. Med. Examiners, Am. Bd. Psychiatry and Neurology. Intern medicine Johns Hopkins Hosp., Osler Clinic, Balt., 1952-53; resident psychiatry USN Hosp., Oakland, Calif., 1953-54, Henry Phipps Psychiat. Clinic, Johns Hopkins Hosp., Balt., 1955-59, asst. psychiatrist, 1955-59, staff psychiatrist, 1959—, staff dept. medicine, 1970—, hon. staff dept. medicine, 1991—, dir. psychiat. outpatient svcs. and community psychiatry program, 1972-74, asst. dir. clin. svcs. dept. psychiatry, 1973-74, mem. departmental coun., 1974-76. Fellow psychiatry Johns Hopkins U., 1955-59, faculty in psychiatry, 1959—, assoc. prof., 1971—, physician charge psychiat. svcs. student health svc., 1961-73; vis. psychiatrist Balt. City Hosp., 1960-61; co-prin., prin. investigator NIMH Psychopharmacology Rsch. Br. Outpatient Study of Drug-Set Interaction, 1960-68, co-dir. (with Eugene Meyer) Time-Limited Psychotherapy Rsch. Grant, 1969-73; pvt. practice psychiatry, 1964—; cons. Met. Balt. Assn. Mental Health, 1961-63, Bur. Disability Ins., Social Security Adminstrn., 1964-81; attending staff Seton Psychiat. Inst., 1966-73, exec. bd., 1970-73; staff Sheppard and Enoch Pratt Hosp., 1974—. Co-author: A Primer on Mental Disorders: A Guide for Educators, Families and Students, 2001; contbr. articles and chpts. to profl. jours. and books. Served to lt. M.C., USNR, 1953-55, div. psychiatrist 1st Marine Div., Korea, staff psychiatrist USN Hosp., Camp Pendelton, Calif., 1954-55; mem. Md. Interdisciplinary Coun. for Children and Adolescents, 1978-98, treas., 1980-87. Fellow: AAAS, Am. Psychiat. Assn. (mem. assembly 1983—93, Psychiat. Rsch. Network 1994—, Disting. life fellow); mem.: AAUP, AMA, Johns Hopkins Med. and Surg. Assn., Balt. County Med. Assn., Balt. City Med. Soc., Med. and Chirurg. Faculty Md., Group Therapy Network, N.Y. Acad. Scis., Soc. Psychotherapy Rsch., Md. Psychiat. Soc. (pres. 1978—79), Md. Assn. Pvt. Practicing Psychiatrists, Am. Assn. Pvt. Practicing Psychiatrists, Am. Coll. Neuropsychopharmacology, Am. Soc. Adolescent Psychiatry, Internat. Soc. Study Personality Disorders, Am. Psychosomatic Soc., Md. Found. Psychiatry (bd. dirs. 1995—2003, pres. 2000—03), Nat. Assn. Scholars, Gen. Soc. Colonial Wars, Avery Assn., Denison Soc., Crandall Assn., Van Kouwenhoven-Conover Assn., Van Voorhees Assn., Parke Soc., Nat. Soc. Sons and Daus. of Pilgrims, Gen. Soc. War 1812 (bd. dirs. State of Md. 1997—, officer, surgeon 2000—03, v.p. 2002—04, pres. 2004—), Nat. Huguenot Soc., Descendants Mexican War Vets, Sons Union Vets. Civil War, SAR, Yale Club NYC, Farmington Country Club (Charlottesville, Va.), Met. Club (Washington), Johns Hopkins Club (Balt.), Chevy Chase (Md.) Country Club, Phi Beta Pi. Episcopalian. Achievements include research in borderline and narcissistic conditions, long-term effects of childhood emotional abuse and neglect, psychotherapy; interrelationships of psychotherapy and pharmacotherapy, ethical considerations in clinical research. Home: 308 Tunbridge Rd Baltimore MD 21212-3803 Office: 1205 York Rd Ste 35 Lutherville Timonium MD 21093-6268 Office Phone: 410-321-1276. E-mail: lpark3@jhmi.edu.

PARK, LELAND MADISON, librarian; b. Alexandria, La., Oct. 21, 1941; s. Arthur Harris and Jane Rebecca (Leland) P. Student, McCallie Sch., 1957—59; AB, Davidson Coll., 1963; MLS, Emory U., 1964; postgrad., Simmons Coll., 1968; AdvM in Libr. Sci., Fla. State U., 1973, PhD, 1974. Reference libr. Pub. Libr. of Charlotte and Mecklenburg County, NC, 1964-65; head reference and student pers. Davidson (N.C.) Coll. Libr., 1967-70, asst. dir., 1970-75, dir., 1975—. Cons. coll. cons. network So. Assn. Colls and Schs.; vis. lectr. Emory U., summer 1972; temporary instr. Fla. State U., 1973; libr. cons.; conf. spkr.; chmn. state adv. com. Libr. Svcs. and Constrn. Act, 1975-79; mem. N.C. State Libr. Commn., 1983-85, 87-92, chmn., 1989-92; mem. Davidson (N.C.) Town Appearance Commn., 1986-93, 98—, Hist. Preservation Commn., 1994-96; mem. editl. bd. CHOICE, 2003-. Editor Southeastern Librarian, 1976-78; acad. sect. editor N.C. Libraries, 1972-77; contbr. articles to profl. jours. Mem. Wake County Citizens for Better Librs., N.C., 1965-67; sec. com. libr. affairs Piedmont U. Ctr., 1969-70, chmn., 1970-72; mem. nat. bd. cons. NEH, 1976—; clk. mission com. St. Alban's Episcopal Mission, Davidson, N.C., 1969-72, layreader, 1970-75, treas., 1975-86; bd. dirs. statewide computer libr. resource network NC-LIVE, 1997—. Recipient H.W. Wilson Libr. periodical award, 1979, Alumni Achievement award The McCallie Sch., 1989, Order of Long Leaf Pine presented by N.C. Gov. James G. Martin, 1993. Mem. ALA, Southeastern Libr. Assn. (chmn. coll. and univ. sect. 1976-78, exec. bd. 1976-78), N.C. Libr. Assn. (2d v.p. 1975-77, 1st v.p. 1981-83, pres. 1983-85), Metrolina Libr. Assn. (pres. 1969-71), Mecklenburg County Libr. Assn. (treas. 1969-70), Soc. of Cin. (2d v.p. Ga. Soc. 1982-83), SAR, Mil. Order World Wars, Raleigh Jaycees (chmn. libr. com. 1965-67), Res. Officer Assn., SCV, Soc. Colonial Wars, S.C. Huguenot Soc., Rotary, Beta Phi Mu, Sigma Nu, Omicron Delta Kappa. Home: PO Box 777 235 Ney Circle Davidson NC 28036-0777 Office: Davidson Coll E H Little Libr PO Box 7200 Davidson NC 28035-7200 Office Phone: 704-894-2155. E-mail: lepark@davidson.edu.

PARK, LESLIE DESMOND, health organization executive; b. Chgo., May 23, 1925; s. Andrew Gordon Park and Edith Emily Windsor; m. Jeannette Irene Park; children: Kathy Jean, Pamela Louise, Jane Ann. BA, Northwestern U., 1949, MA, 1950. Tchr. Ill. State Normal U., 1949-54; exec. dir. United Cerebral Palsy, Ill., Bloomington, 1954-58, United Cerebral Palsy of Pa., Harrisburg, 1959-67, United Cerebral Palsy of N.Y.C., 1967-88; chmn., founder Disabled and Alone/Life Svcs. for the Handicapped, Inc., N.Y.C., 1988—. Author: How to be a Friend to the Handicapped; contbr. articles to profl. jours. Founder, dir. The Open Congregation, 1984—; adult bible sch. tchr., 1951—; ordained elder Presbyn. Ch. Lt. (j.g.) USN, 1943-45. Recipient Founder's award The Open Congregation, 1986, Henry Kessler Human Dignity award Kessler Rehab. Inst., 1984, Hon. award Schuylkill County, 1968, Profl. award Oustanding Exec. in Cerebral Palsy Work, 1964, Svc. to Soc. award Northwestern U., 1997; named Hon. Chief, Nigeria. Mem. Am. Acad. for Devel. Medicine, Internat. Cerebral Palsy Soc. Achievements include research in needs of the handicapped in Bahrain, Greece, Nigeria, U.S. Avocations: gardening, hiking, Bible study. Office: Disabled and Alone Life Svcs for Handicapped Inc 352 Park Ave S Fl 11 New York NY 10010

PARK, LINDA SUE, writer; b. Ill. BS in English, Stanford U. Pub. rels. writer major oil co., 1981—83; writer, 1997—. Author: Seesaw Girl, 1999, The Kite Fighters, 2000, A Single Shard, 2001 (Newbery Medal, 2002), When My Name Was Keoko, 2002. Avocations: cooking, travel, movies, crossword puzzles. Office: Clarion Books 215 Park Ave S New York NY 10003

PARK, MARY WOODFILL, information consultant; b. Nevada, Mo., Nov. 20, 1944; d. John Prossor and Elizabeth (Devine) Woodfill; m. Salil Kumar Banerjee, Dec. 29, 1967 (div. 1983); children: Stephen Kumar, Scott Kumar; m. Lee Crandall Park, Apr. 27, 1985; stepchildren: Thomas Joseph, Jeffrey Rawson. BA, Marywood Coll., 1966; postgrad., Johns Hopkins U., 1983, Goucher Coll., 1986. Asst. to dir. U. Pa. Librs., Phila., 1968-69; investment libr. Del. Funds, Phila., 1969-71; investment officer Investment Counselors Md., Balt., 1980-84, 1st Nat. Bank Md., Balt., 1984-85; founder Info. Consultancy, Balt., 1985—. Lectr. Loyola Coll., Balt., 1991-92, Cath. U., 1993. Author: InfoThink—Practical Strategies for Using Information in Business, 1998; editor, contbr. to profl. publs. Vol. Internat. Visitors' Ctr., Balt., 1979-80, 91; del. White House Conf. on Librs.; v.p. bd. dirs. Friends of Goucher Libr., 1988-90; mem. industry applications com. Info. Tech. Bd., State of Md., 1993-96; mem. info. tech. com. of the Tech. Coun., Greater Balt. Com., 1993-98. Named One of Md.'s Top 100 Women, Warfield's Bus. Publn., 1996. Mem.: DAR, MD Women's Health Initiative, Huguenot Soc. Md. (1st v.p. 2003—05), Nat. Huguenot Soc., Md. Found. for Psychiatry (bd. mem. 1998—), Assn. Ind. Info. Profls., Info. Futures Inst., Spl. Librs. Assn. (pres. Md. chpt. 1991—92, v.p. network coord. coun. Sailor project 1993—95, govt. rels. chair 1998—2003, pub. rels. chair 2003—), Nat. Inst. Geneal. Rsch. Alumnae Assn., Nat. Soc. of the Sons and Daus. of the Pilgrims, Nat. Soc. Colonial Dames XVII Century (state rec. sec. 2003—05), Nat. Soc. of U.S. Daus. of 1812 (Md. state rec. sec. 2003—05), Soc. of Daughters of Holland Dames, Descendants of Ancient and Honorable Families of New Netherland, Friends of New Netherlands, Nat. Soc. Dames Ct. Honor, Nat. Soc. Daus. Am. Colonists (Md. state 1st vice regent 2003—05, regent Joppa Trail chpt., corr. sec. 2003—), Three Arts Club Homeland, Hamilton St. Club (bd. dirs. 1989—92). Episcopalian. Office: The Information Consultancy 308 Tunbridge Rd Baltimore MD 21212-3803 E-mail: mwpark@informationconsultancy.com.

PARK, MINSEO, physicist, educator; b. Seoul, Republic of Korea, July 28, 1968; arrived in US, 1991; s. Seungryul and Jungia Park; m. Soohyun Baik; children: Michelle, Joshua. BS in Ceramic Engring., Yonsei U., 1991; MS in Materials Sci., Engring., Iowa State U., 1994; PhD in Materials Sci., Engring., NC State U., 1998. Rsch. asst. prof. NC State U., Raleigh, 2001—03; asst. prof. Auburn (Ala.) U., 2003—. Mem.: Materials Rsch. Soc., Am. Phys. Soc. Home: 2260 E University Dr Apt 5B Auburn AL 36830 Office: Auburn U Dept Physics 303 Allison Lab Auburn AL 36849 E-mail: park@physics.auburn.edu.

PARK, MYUNG KUN, medical educator; b. Suhung, Hwanghae, Republic of Korea, Sept. 30, 1934; arrived in U.S., 1962; s. Jung-Jin and Sonnyu (Lee) Park; m. Issun Kim, Jan. 21, 1967; children: Douglas Kim, Christopher Kim, Warren Kim. Diploma, Seoul (Republic of Korea) Nat. U., 1956, MD, 1960. Asst. prof. U. Kans. Coll. Medicine, Kansas City, 1973-76; assoc. prof. U. Tex. Med. Sch., San Antonio, 1976-83, prof., 1983—; prof., chmn. pediat. Arabian Gulf U. Med. Coll., Bahrain, 1995-98. Author: (book) How to Read Pediatric ECG, 1982, 3d rev. edit., 1992, Pediatric Cardiology for Practitioners, 1984, 4th rev. edit., 2002, The Pediatric Cardiology Handbook, 1991, 3d rev. edit., 2002; contbr. articles to profl. jours. Postdoctoral fellow, NIH, 1965—68, Rsch. fellow, 1971—73, Rsch. grantee, Maternal and Child Health Bur., 1991—95. Fellow: Am. Acad. Pediat., Am. Coll. Cardiology; mem.: Soc. Pediatric Rsch., Sigma Xi. Home: 3318 Buckhaven St San Antonio TX 78230-3956 Office: U Tex Med Sch 7703 Floyd Curl Dr San Antonio TX 78229-3900

PARK, NO-HEE, academic administrator; b. Jan. 30, 1944; m. Yu Bai Yuly, 1969; 1 child, Jennifer. DDS, Seoul Nat. U., 1968, MSD, 1970; PhD, Med. Coll. Ga., 1978; DMD, Harvard U., 1982. Postdoctoral fellow in oral biology and pharmacology Med. Coll. Ga., 1975—78; rsch. assoc., Eye Rsch. Inst. Harvard Med. Sch., Boston, 1978—80, instr., dept. ophthalmology, 1978—82, asst. scientist, Eye Rsch. Inst., 1980—82, assoc. scientist, Eye Rsch. Inst., 1982—83; asst. prof., oral biology and pathophysiology Harvard U. Sch. Dental Medicine, Boston, 1982—83; assoc. prof., oral biology UCLA Sch. Dentistry, L.A., 1984—85, prof., 1985—, assoc. dean rsch., 1997—98, dean, 1998—; assoc. dir. UCLA Dental Rsch. Inst., L.A., 1986—90, dir., 1995—, UCLA Wound Healing Rsch. Ctr., L.A., 1997—. Contbr. articles to profl. jours.; editl. bd. Internat. Jour. Oncology, Electronic Jour. Biotechnology, editor-in-chief Internat. Jour. Oral Biology, ad-hoc reviewer for various publs. Mem.: Internat. Coll. Dentistry, Omicron Kappa Upsilon Dental Soc. Achievements include research in the role of telomerase in oral carcinogenesis, gene therapy for oral cancer, molecular mechanism of replicative senescence in normal human oral keratinocytes and viral and chemical oncogenesis; cellular proto-oncogenes and tumor suppressor genes, cell cycle and DNA repair, and antiviral chemotherapy. Office: UCLA 10833 Leconte Ave Rm 53-038 Los Angeles CA 90095*

PARK, PENNY SHERAN, elementary school educator, writer; b. Tulare, Calif., July 13, 1948; d. Sheridan Lee Roy Harris and Jeanne Avril Lightbody. AA, Coll. of the Sequoias, Visalia, CA, 1968; B in Music Edn., U. of Pacific, 1971; M in Music Edn., U. Calif., Fresno, 1980. Registered music therapist Nat. Assn. Music Therapy, 1971. Music therapist mental health wing Emmanual Hosp., Turlock, Calif., 1971; music therapist Brandel Manor Nursing Home, Turlock, 1971, Kings County Mental Health Day Treatment Ctr., Hanford, Calif., 1971—77; self-employed Hanford, 1977—85; music therapist Lee Richmond Sch. -Spl. Edn., Hanford, 1979—84; resource tchr.- music The Learning Ctr., Hanford, 1984—85; tchr. Hanford Elem. Sch. Dist., 1985—. Consulting music therapist & music educator various, Hanford, 1977—79; program developer Kings County Supt. Schs.-Spl. Edn., 1979—84; chorale instr. Hanford Elem. Sch. Dist., 1985—90; trainer The Activities In Math & Sci. Found.- Fresno (Calif.) Pacific Coll., 1987—92. Author: Five Merry Santas, 1992; editor: Community Treasures, 2000. Mem.: Hanford Elem. Tchrs. Assn., Calif. Tchrs. Assn., Ea. Star (25 year pin 1997). Avocations: writing, reading, music, scrapbooks, computer games. Office: Hanford Elem Sch Dist 741 White St Hanford CA 93232 Business E-Mail: ppark@hesd.k12.ca.us.

PARK, ROY HAMPTON, JR., advertising executive; b. N.C., 1938; s. Roy Hampton and Dorothy Goodwin (Dent) P.; m. Elizabeth Tetlow Parham; children: Elizabeth P. Fowler, Roy H. III. BA in Journalism, U. N.C., 1961; MBA, Cornell U., 1963. Sr. acct. exec., rev. bd. exec., advt. planning dir., J. Walter Thompson Co., N.Y.C. and Miami, 1963-70; v.p. mktg. and account mgmt. Kincaid Advt. Agency divsn. First Union Nat. Bank Corp., Charlotte, N.C., 1970-71; v.p. Park Outdoor Advt., Ithaca, N.Y., 1971-75; v.p. advt. and promotion Park Broadcasting Inc., Ithaca, 1976-81; dir., 1993-95; mng. editor Park Comm. Newsletter, Ithaca, 1976-81; mng. dir. Agrl. Rsch. Advt. Agy., Ithaca, 1976-81; v.p., gen. mgr. Park Outdoor Adv., 1981-84; pres., CEO, dir. Park Outdoor Advt. of N.Y. Inc., 1984—; pres. Outdoor Advt. Coun. N.Y. Inc., 1986-91, chmn., dir., 1992-95; dir., sr. v.p. RHP Inc., 1994-96, RHP Properties Inc., 1994-96. Mem. region I planning bd. Inst. Outdoor Advt., 1984—86. Dir. Boyce Thompson Inst. for Plant Rsch. Inc., 1995-2001, dir., vice chmn. 2002—; trustee, v.p. Park Found. Inc., 1995-2002; trustee Cornell U., 1999—; pres., chmn. Triad Found., 2003—; mem. adv. coun. Cornell U. Johnson Grad. Sch. Mgmt., 1996—, founding mem. alumni exec. com., 1984-88; bd. vis. U. N.C. Sch. Journalism and Mass Comm., 1994—; chmn. Ithaca Assembly Cotillion, 1979-81; dir. pub. rels. Tompkins County Conf. and Tourist Coun., 1976; exec. com. Tompkins County Rep. Fin. Com., 1983-84; chmn. fin. com. MacNeil for Assembly, 1984-86, co-chmn. 1978-82; bd. dirs. Tompkins County Coun. Arts, 1976; chmn. pub. rels. com. United Way Tompkins County, 1973-74, loaned publicity exec., 1977; bd. chmn., publicity dr. Jr. Olympics, 1973-74; dir. pub. rels. United Fund Raleigh, N.C., 1971; fin. com. Spl. Childrn's Ctr., 1979. Mem. Tompkins County C. of C. (chmn. legis. action com. 1976, acting chmn. nominating com. 1976, chmn. sign ordinance com., 1975-76, pub. rels. coun. 1976, Project of Yr. award 1974, Recognition award 1975), Charlotte C. of C. (pub. rels. com. 1970-71), N.C. Soc. of N.Y., Boque Banks Beach Preservation Assn., Ithaca Yacht Club, Ithaca Country Club, Boca Bay Pass Club, Gasparville Inn Beach and Tennis Club. Office: Park Outdoor Advt PO Box 4680 Ithaca NY 14852-4680 Office Phone: 607-257-1477. Business E-Mail: roy.park@parkoutdoor.com.

PARK, SEOK-KYUN, civil engineer, educator; b. Seoul, Oct. 10, 1961; s. Keum-Churl and Chae-Joong (Kim) P.; m. Hyun-Joo Na, May 10, 1985; 1 child, Jeong-Min. BE, U. Hanyang, Seoul, Korea, 1984, M in Engring., 1986; PhD, U. Tokyo, 1996. Asst., tchr. U. Hanyang, Seoul, 1984-86; rschr. Ssangyong Rsch. Ctr., Taejon, 1986-94, sr. rschr., project mgr., 1995-96; postdoctoral fellow U. Tokyo, 1996-97; lectr. Korea Infrastructure Safety and Tech. Corp., Goyang, 1998—; asst. prof. U. Taejon, 1998—. Vis. prof. Ssangyong Rsch. Ctr., Taejon, 1998—; expert advisor Korea Inst. of Contrn. Tech., Seoul, 1998—; cons. prof. Korea Infrastructure Safety and Tech. Corp., Goyang, 1999—; design cons. Adv. Com. of Cheonju City Hall, 1999—; mem. internat. exchange com., U. Taejon, 1999—; hon. supr. Subway Constrn. Hdqs. Taejon City, 2000—; mem. Asian Model Code Com.; exec. sec. study com. smart concrete structures, study com. repair and reinforcement of concrete structures, tech. com. concrete structure instrumentation, 2000; mem. tech. coun. of Chungmam provincial govt., 2001—. Author: Evaluation and Repair of Concrete Structures, 1998, Design and Maintenance of Civil Structures, 2000, Reinforced Concrete Engineering, 2002, Construction Materials, 2002, Diagnosis and Maintenance of Concrete Structures, 2002; contbr. articles to profl. jours., including Jour. Japan Soc. Civil Engrs., INSIGHT (jour. Brit. Inst. Non-Destructive Testing), Concrete Libr. Internat., Jour. Korean Soc. Non-Destructive Testing, Jour. KCI, Jour. KSCE Recipient Best Acad. prize, U. Hanyang, 1981, grand prize, Ssangyong Cement Ind. Co. Ltd., 1993. Mem. Japan Soc. Civil Engrs. (Best Presentation award 1995, 96), Japan Concrete Inst., Korea Concrete Inst. (mem. editl. bd. 1999—, design cons.), Korean Soc. Civil Engrs. (design cons.), Korea Inst. for Structural Maintenance Inspection, Taeduk Sci. Forum. Achievements include patent for ultrasonic measurement system for concrete setting time; radar image processing system for non-destructive evaluation of concrete; composite material of high tenacity and non-retraction grouting material which includes powder of wasted tire and powder of plastic. Home: 115-1401 Nurie APT Wolpyungdong Seo-gu Taejon 302-280 Republic of Korea Office: U Taejon Dept Civil Engring 96-3 Yongwoon-dong Tong-gu Taejon 300-716 Republic of Korea E-mail: skpark@dju.ac.kr.

PARK, SOONG-KOOK, internist, researcher; b. Pyung-Yang, Korea, Aug. 9, 1938; s. Tae-Soo and Wha-Sil (Lee) P.; m. Sine-Ja, Oct. 9, 1965; children: Han-Kil, See-Nae, Han-Sol. BA, MD, Kyung-Pook Nat. U., Daegu, Korea, 1963. Med. diplomate. Surgeon gen. Republic of Korea, 1963-67; hosp. intern Bklyn. Jewish Hosp., 1968-69; resident in internal medicine Grassland Hosp., Valhalla, N.Y., 1969-72; fellow in gastroenterology Lahey Clinic, Boston, 1972-74; chief internal medicine Dongsan Presbyn. Hosp., Daegu, 1974-76; cons. in internal medicine, chief staff Mariana Med. Ctr., Guam, 1977-78; chief internal medicine Bak Hosp., Seoul, Korea, 1978, Dongsan Presbyn. Hosp., Daegu, 1978-90; prof. Keimyung U. Med. Sch., Daegu, 1980—2003, prof. emeritus, 2003—. Supt. Dongsan Med. Ctr., Daegu, 1990—94, Kyungju Dongsan Hosp., Kyungju, Republic of Korea, 1994—96; v.p. for med. affairs Keimyung U., 1996—98; dir. Dongsan Med. Ctr., 1996—98; supt. Andong (Korea) Presbyn. Hosp., 2003—. Elder Sungji Presbyn. Ch., Daegu, 1976—; bd. dirs. YMCA, Daegu, 1980—, chmn., 1999-2001; dist. gov. Y's Men's Internat., Daegu, 1987-88; regional dir. Korea East region Y's Men's Internat., 2001-2002; internat. svc. dir. Internat. Bro. Club, Y's Men's Internat., 2002-2003; comdt. Med. Drs. Soccer Team, Daegu, 1990-94, 96-2003; pres. Korea Christian Hosp. Assn., 1997-98. Mem. Korean Assn. Internal Medicine (councilor 1980—, v.p. 1999), Korean Assn. Gastroenterology (councilor 1980—), Korean Soc. Gastrointestinal Endoscopy (coun. 1988—, pres. 1996), Korean Soc. Gastrointestinal Motility Study (pres. 1993), Am. Coll. Gastroenterology (internat.) N.Y. Acad. Scis. Presbyterian. Avocations: tennis, soccer, choir. Home: Eunhatown 101-1708 Sangin-Dong 42 Dalseo-Ku Daegu 704-370 Republic of Korea E-mail: skpark@dsmc.or.kr.

PARK, STEVE, race car driver; b. Islip, N.Y., Aug. 23, 1967; s. Bob and Dorothy Park. Racecar driver Dale Earnhardt Inc., 1996—. Named Most Popular Driver, NASCAR Featherlite Modified Tour, 1995, one of Top 10 Drivers to Watch, Sports Illustrated, 1997, Rookie of Yr., Busch Series, 1997; recipient 2d pl., NASCAR Featherlite Modified Tour Championship, 1995, 5th pl., GoRacing.com 500, 2000, 4th pl., Cracker Barrel 500, 2000, Chevrolet Monte Carlo 400, 2000, Dover Downs Internat. Speedway, 2000, 3d pl., Checker Auto Parts 500, 2000, 1st pl., Winston Open, 2000, Dura Lube 400, 2001. Avocations: motorcycling, boating, golf. Office: Dale Earnhardt Inc 1675 Coddle Creek Hwy Mooresville NC 28115-8245

PARK, SUNWOO, engineer; s. Chankeun Park and Wolshik Sihn; m. Yehsoon Park; children: Jean, Daniel. BS, MS, Seoul Nat. U., Korea, 1982; PhD, U. Tex., Austin, 1994. Vis. rsch. scientist Ga. Inst. of Tech., Atlanta, 1997—99; project engr. Profl. Svc. Industries, Inc., Fairfax, Va., 1999—2001; sr. rsch. engr. Lendis Corp. @ FHWA, McLean, Va., 2001—. Tech. session chair Engring. Mechanics Conf., Austin, Tex., 2000. Contbr. articles to profl. jours. Recipient Ofcl. Commendation, U.S. Dept. of the Army, 1986. Mem.: ASCE. Office: Fhwa/Tfhrc/Lendis 6800 Georgetown Pike F-127 Mc Lean VA 22101

PARK, THOMAS JOSEPH, biology researcher, educator; b. Balt., June 8, 1958; s. Lee Crandall and Barbara Ann (Merrick) P.; m. Stephanie Suzanne Reynolds, June 22, 1985; 1 child, Nicholas Timothy. BA, Johns Hopkins U., 1982; PhD, U. Md., 1988. Vis. scientist Coll. of France, Paris, 1988-89; rsch. fellow U. Tex., Austin, 1989-94; Alexander von Humboldt rsch. fellow U. Munich, 1994-95; with U. Ill. dept biol. scis., Chgo., 1995—. Contbr. chpt. to book, articles to Jour. Neurosci., Jour. Comparative Psychology, Hearing Rsch., Jour. Neurophysiol. Grantee NIMH, 1986, Nat. Ctr. Sci. Rsch., Paris, 1988, Alexander von Humboldt Found., 1994, NIH, 1996. Mem. AAAS, Soc. for Neurosci., Assn. for Rsch. in Otolaryngology. Office: U Ill at Chgo Dept Biol Scis Chicago IL 60607

PARK, WILLIAM ANTHONY (TONY PARK), lawyer; b. Blackfoot, Idaho, June 4, 1934; s. William Clair and Thelma Edelweiss (Shear) P.; m. Elizabeth Taylor, Aug. 26, 1961 (div.); children: Susan E., W. Adam, Patricia A.; m. Gail Chaloupka, Aug. 6, 1983. AA, Boise Jr. Coll., 1954; BA, U. Idaho, 1958; JD, U. Idaho, 1963. Bar: Idaho 1963. Sole practice, Boise, Idaho, 1963-70, 82-83; atty. gen. State of Idaho, 1971-75; ptnr. Park & Meuleman, Boise, 1975-81, Park & Burkett, Boise, 1983-84, Martin, Chapman, Park & Burkett, Boise, 1984-90, Park, Costello & Burkett, Boise, 1990-93, Park, Redford, Thomas & Burkett, Boise, 1994-97, Park, Thomas, Burkett & Williams, Boise, 1997-99; of counsel Huntley Park (formerly Huntley, Park, Thomas, Burkett, Olsen & Williams), Boise, 1999—. Chmn. Idaho Bicentennial Commn., 1971—77; bd. dirs. ACLU, Idaho, 1996—2000, pres., 1997—99; chmn. Idaho State Dem. Party, 1998—99; bd. dirs. Radio Free Europe/Radio Liberty, Inc., 1977—82, Am. Lung Assn., 1978—90, Am. Lung Assn. of Idaho/Nev., 1976—96, pres., 1991—95, 2002—04, bd. dirs., 1999—. Served with U.S. Army, 1956—58. Recipient Disting. Svc. award. Home: 706 Warm Springs Ave Boise ID 83712-6420 Office: PO Box 2188 Boise ID 83701-2188 Office Phone: 208-345-7800. Business E-Mail: tpark@huntleypark.com. E-mail: gchaloupka@msn.com.

PARK, WILLIAM H(ERRON), financial executive; b. Monongahela, Pa., Sept. 19, 1947; s. William M. and Marjorie (Herron) P.; m. Mary Cornell, June 25, 1977; children: William H., Douglas C. BS in Indsl. Engring. with distinction, Cornell U., 1969, MBA, 1970. Engr. True Temper Corp., Geneva, Ohio, 1970-72; with Price Waterhouse & Co., Boston, 1972-82; exec. v.p., CFO United Asset Mgmt. Corp., Boston, 1982—2001; v.p. The UAM Funds, 1982—2001; pres. and CEO Prizm Capital Mgmt., 2001—. Bd. dirs. No. Light Asset Mgmt.; bd. trustees Eaton Vance Group of Mut. Funds, 2003—. Chmn. Nat. Com. to Preserve Social Security and Medicare, 2000—03; dir. The Chautauqua Found., Inc., 1996—; treas., trustee Tower Sch. in Marblehead, 1982—92; trustee Proctor Acad., 1998—; bd. dirs. Nat. Com. to Preserve Social Security and Medicare, 1997—, Spry Found., 2000—01, The Chautauqua Found., Inc., 1992—. Home: 3 Fort Sewall Ter Marblehead MA 01945-3505 Office: Prizm Capital Mgmt LLC 150 Federal St Boston MA 02110

PARK, WILLIAM LAIRD, agricultural economics educator, consultant, college associate dean; b. Mar. 29, 1931; s. William D. and Ardella (Laird) Park; m. Ann Payne, Aug. 7, 1953; children: Leslie, David W., Wayne I., Andrea, John L. BS, Utah State U., 1957, MS, 1958; PhD, Cornell U., 1963. Dep. chief coop. rels. NY/NJ Milk Mktg. Adminstrn., N.Y.C., 1958—65; assoc. prof. agrl. econs. Rutgers U., New Brunswick, NJ, 1965—68, chmn. dept. agrl. econs. and mktg., 1970—75; sr. agrl. economist Devel. and Resources Corp., Sacramento, 1969—70; chmn. dept. agrl. econs. Brigham Young U., Provo, Utah, 1977—83, prof., 1983—, assoc. dean agr., 1988—98, dir. Agrl. Sta., 1995—98, ret., 1998. Pres. Ag-Econ Rsch. Assocs., Orem, Utah, 1978—; bd. dirs. N.E. Agrl. Econs. Coun., 1972—77; cons. agr., agribus. Author: Estimating Demand and Price Structures by Residual Analysis, 1970; author: numerous bulls., reports on dairy econs., feasibility analysis, internat. econ. devel.; contbr. articles to profl. jours. Cpl. U.S. Army, 1953—55. Mem.: Am. Agrl. Econs. Assn., Western Agrl. Econs. Assn., Phi Kappa Phi, Sigma Xi. Republican. Mem. Lds Ch. Home: 7807 White Pine Way Sandy UT 84094-0256

PARK, WILLIAM WYNNEWOOD, law educator; b. Phila., July 2, 1947; s. Oliver William and Christine (Lindes) Park. BA, Yale U., 1969; JD, Columbia U., 1972; MA, Cambridge U., 1975. Bar: Mass. 1972, DC 1980. Law practice, Paris, 1972-79; prof. law Boston U., 1979—, dir. Ctr. Banking Law Studies, 1990—93. V.p. London Ct. Internat. Arbitration; vis. prof. U. Dijon, France, 1983—84, Inst. U. Hautes Etudes Internat., Geneva, 1983, U. Hong Kong,

1990; mem. appeals tribunal Internat. Holocaust Ins. Claims; arbitrator Claims Resolution Tribunal Dormant Accts., Switzerland, 1998—2002, Internat. Commn. Holocaust Era Ins. Claims. Author: International Chamber of Commerce Arbitration, 3d edit., 2000, International Forum Selection, 1995, International Commercial Arbitration, 1997, Arbitration in Banking and Finance, 1998, Income Tax Treaty Arbitration, 2004; contbr. articles to profl. jours. Trustee Mass. Bible Soc.; sr. warden King's Chapel, Boston. Fellow, Selwyn Coll., Cambridge, Eng., 1975—77. Fellow: Coll. Comml. Arbitrators, Chartered Inst. Arbitrators (U.K.); mem.: ABA (chmn. internat. dispute resolution com.). Home: 36 King St Cohasset MA 02025-1304 Office: Boston U Law Sch 765 Commonwealth Ave Boston MA 02215-1401 Office Phone: 617-353-3149.

PARK, WON KUK, foundation administrator; b. Bukchang Dong, Chung-Ku, Korea, Mar. 24, 1929; s. Jun Seop and Kum Sun (Song) P. BA in Economics, Sungkyunkwan U., Seoul, Korea, 1957; MA in Economics, Am. U., 1960; PhD in Economics, Kyunghee U., Seoul, Korea, 1975; PhD (hon.), Caldwell Coll., 1997. Asst. prof. Duksung Women's Coll., Seoul, Republic of Korea, 1961-63, assoc. prof., 1965-67, v.p., 1965-70, prof., 1967-77, pres., 1970-77, chmn. bd. trustees Daksung Sch. Found., 1979—2001; asst. prof. Kyunghee U., Seoul, Republic of Korea, 1963-65; v.p. Korean Pvt. Ednl. Found., Seoul, Republic of Korea, 1987-90, Korean Assn. for Univ. Found., Seoul, Republic of Korea, 1987-92. Dir. Korean Pvt. Ednl. Found., Seoul, 1978—, Korean Assn. for Univ. Found., 1987—. Chmn. bd. trustees Jungam Found. of Culture in Korea, 2002—. Recipient Choon Kang award, Republic of Korea, 1995. Mem. Korean Sect. World Edn. Fellowship (v.p. 1987—), The Seoul Ctrl. Club of Good Will. Office: D-201 The Sungbookville Ho 330-21 Sungbuk 2-dong Sungbuk-ku Seoul 136-022 Republic of Korea

PARKE, BRIAN, textile company executive; b. Knocknahur, Ireland; Mgmt. trainee J. & L.F. Goodbody Ltd., Clare, Ireland, 1970; various mgmt. positions Snia Ltd., Milan, Italy, and Ireland; sr. prodn. mgr. Lirelle Ltd., Letterkenny, Ireland, 1976-84; with European operation Unifi, 1984—; CEO Unifi Textured Parke, to 1999; pres., COO Unifi, Greensboro, N.C., CEO. Office: Unifi Inc 7201 W Friendly Ave Greensboro NC 27410

PARKE, DAVID WILKIN, II, ophthalmologist, educator, healthcare executive; b. Columbus, Ohio, May 19, 1951; s. David William Parke and Eunice Joyce Erikson; m. Julie Diane Thorne, Sept. 15, 1975; children: David W. III, Laura Thorne, Lindsey Diane. AB, Stanford U., 1973; MD, Baylor Coll. Medicine, 1977. Diplomate Am. Bd. Ophthalmology. Resident in internal medicine Baylor Coll. Medicine, Houston, 1977-78, resident in ophthalmology, 1978-81, fellow in med. retina, 1981-82, asst. prof., 1983-90, assoc. prof., 1990-92; fellow diseases and surgery of the retina and vitreous Med. Coll. of Wis., 1982-83; prof., chair dept. ophthalmology U. Okla., Oklahoma City, 1992—; pres., CEO McGee Eye Inst., Oklahoma City, 1992—. Bd. dirs. Medem, Inc., Ophthalmic Mut. Ins. Co. Active Okla. Econ. Devel. Found., 1992, Okla. Health Ctr. Found., 1992—; trustee Presbyn. Health Found., 1995—, Casady Sch., 1997-2004, vice chair, 1999-2004; mng. dir. Stephenson Laser Ctr., 1996—; bd. mgrs. Okla. Health Alliance, 1995-97; dir. Oklahoma City C. of C. Fellow: Am. Acad. Ophthalmology (assoc. sec. 1983—92, trustee 2000—, sr. sec. for ophthalmic practice 2002—, Honor award 1980, Sr. Honor award 1998); mem.: Vitreous Soc., Retina Soc., Assn. Univ. Profs. Ophthalmology (trustee 1997—2003, pres. 2001—02), Greater Oklahoma City C. of C. (bd. dirs. 1998—99), Alpha Omega Alpha. Office: Dean A McGee Eye Institute 608 Stanton L Young Blvd Oklahoma City OK 73104-5065 E-mail: david-parke@ouhsc.edu.

PARKE, JAMES A. corporate financial executive; BA in history, polit. sci. and economics, Concordia Coll., Minn., 1968. Corp. audit staff GE Capital Svcs., 1973—78, audit adminstr., 1978, v.p. corp. audit staff, 1987, CFO, 2000—, vice chmn., 2002—. Mgr. fin. sect. lighting sys. dept. Gen. Electric Co., 1980; mgr. fin. operation Gen. Electric Credit Corp., 1982, mgr. comml. and indsl. fin. divsn., 82; mgr. lighting fin. lighting bus. group Gen. Electric Co., 1983, sr. v.p., 2002—; mem. Fin. Acctg. Stds. Coun., 1999—2003. Dir. Bldg. with Books, Norwalk CC Found.; bd. regents Concordia Coll. Office: GE Capital Corp 260 Long Ridge Rd Stamford CT 06927

PARKE, MARILYN NEILS, writer; b. Libby, Mont., June 5, 1928; d. Walter and Alma M. Neils; m. Robert V. Parke, Aug. 25, 1951; children: Robert, Richard, Gayle Crawford, Lynn Parke Castle. BA, U. Mont., 1950; MEd, Colo. State U., 1973. Tchr. Poudre R-1, Fort Collins, 1973—. Co-author: (with Sharon Panik) A Quetzalcoatl Tale of Corn, 1992, A Quetzalcoatl Tale of the Ball Game, 1992 (Parent's Choice Gold award paperback of yr. 1992), A Quetzalcoatl Tale of Chocolate, 1994. Mem. Internat. Reading Assn., Soc. Children's Book Writers and Illustrators, Nat. Edn. Assn., Colo. Coun. Internat. Reading Assn. Avocations: gardening, cooking, sports, reading, travel.

PARKE, ROBERT LEON, retired communications executive; b. Jersey City, Aug. 28, 1940; s. Edwin Gager and Alice Elizabeth (Servis) P.; m. Geraldine R. Pavlick, Sept. 2, 1967; children: Cheryl Lynn, Tracy Ann, David Scott. Grad. high sch., Jersey City. Asst. bookkeeper Snow-Kist Frozen Foods, Jersey City, 1964-67; supr. accounts receivable Swift Line Transfer Co., Inc., North Bergen, N.J., 1967-69; contr. Imperial Cartage Co., Inc., Jersey City, 1969-79; mgr. logistic svcs. Vista United Telecommunications, Lake Buena Vista, Fla., 1980-2000; ret., 2000. Corp. sec. Imperial Warehouse Co., Inc., Jersey City, 1968—79, Arbe Transfer Co. Inc., 1968—79; v.p. Cole Foods, Inc., Jersey City, 1968—79. Spl. min. of the eucharist Diocese Orlando, Fla., 1992; vol. Give Kids The World, Kissimmee, Fla., 1992-98; mem. Pemberton Twp. Zoning Bd., Browns Mills, N.J., 1977-79; trustee, bd. dirs. Browns Mills Improvement Assn., 1974-79; life trustee Rebecca Worf Meml. Fund Browns Mills, N.J., Parke Soc., S.E. Milw.; hon. trustee Am. Indian Relief Coun. Recipient Cert. Appreciation Am. Indian Relief Coun., 1996, 97, 98, 99, 2000, hon. trustee, 1999, 2000; recipient spl. recognition award masters degree program in Nat. Security Studies, Grad. Sch. of Georgetown U., 1996; Bob Parke day proclaimed by Twp. of Pemberton, 1979, Customer Appreciation Award GN Netcom/Unex, 1997, Partners in Excellence Award Walt Disney Co., 1997. Mem.: Nat. Assn. Purchasing Mgmt. (scholarship for continued edn., Ctrl. Fla. Most Supportive Mem. 1994, accrediated purchasing practitioner cert. 1998), Nat. Assn. Purchasing Mgmt. Ctrl. Fla. (named scholar), Am. Soc. Notaries, Fla. Notary Assn. (hon.), Nat. Notary Assn., Fla. Sheriffs Assn. (life), Winthrop Soc., Nat. Soc. Sons and Daus. of Pilgrims, Soc. Sons and Daus. Am.'s First Families (life), Soc. Descs. of the Colonial Clergy (life), KC (mem. coun.). Personal E-mail: rlparke828@aol.com. *Everyone can have a dream, but only those that care and show perseverance will achieve success.*

PARKE, TERRY RICHARD, state legislator; b. Pittsfield, Ill., Feb. 21, 1944; m. Joanne Toombs; 2 children. BS, 1970. Mem. Ill. Ho. of Reps. from 44d dist., 1985—. Rep. spokesman ins. com., computer tech. com.; mem. labor com.; mem. consumer protection, environment and energy coms.; co-chmn. Ill. Econ. and Fiscal Commn.; mem. Employee Suggestion Award Bd.; mem. Sec. of State Corp. Acts Adv. Com.; past pres. Elgin Area Life Underwriters. Exec. comm. Bus. and Labor Am. Legis. Exch. Coun. Past Pres. and Nat. Coun. of Ins. Legis.; past pres. N.W. Schaumnurg Assn. Commerce and Industry; bd. dirs., Boy Scouts Northwest Suburban Coun., Girl Scouts Crossroads Coun. Mem. Rotary (past pres. Schaumburg club). Republican. Home: 1572 Rosedale Ln Hoffman Estates IL 60195-2653 Office: 202-N Stratton Build Springfield IL 62706-0001

PARKE, WILLIAM H. communications executive; s. Henry Wellings Parke; m. Penelope Carr Flather; children: William Flather, Andrew Wellings. BA, MSJ, Northwestern U. Dir. corp. comm. and pub. rels. Ill. Tool Works / Signode, Glenview, 1980—87; mgr. fin. comm. and advt. Ameritech, Chgo., 1987—93; dir. fin. comm. Sears, Roebuck and Co., Hoffman Estates, Ill., 1993—2000, Sara Lee Corp., Chgo., 2000—01; sr. comm. cons. Fed. Res. Bank Chgo., 2001—03; dir. fin. comm. Motorola, Inc., Schaumburg, Ill., 2003—. Mem.: Executives' Club Chgo., Pub. Rels. Soc. Am. (dir., Chgo. chpt. 2001—03), Nat. Investor Rels. Soc. (pres., Chgo. chpt. 2000—01), Soc. Colonial Wars, Econ. Club Chgo., The Casino.

PARKEL, JAMES G. former health association administrator; BS in elec. engring., U. Denver; LLD (hon.), Am. Grad. Sch. Internat. Mgmt. Exec. mgmt. IBM Internat. Found., 1961—93; pres.-elect AARP, 2000—02, pres., 2002—04. Chair AARP Andrus Found.; mem. bd. councilors Andrus Gerontology Ctr., U. So. Calif. Mem. Madison Coun. Libr. of Congress; former pres. and CEO Junior Achievement Internat.; former chair Junior Achievement Westchester; former nat. bd. mem. Junior Achievement; bd. dirs. Danbury Hosp., New Fairfield Cmty. Trust, Am. Grad. Sch. Internat. Mgmt. Mem.: Soc. Human Resource Mgmt. (past nat. chair).*

PARKER, ALAN (WILLIAM) (SIR ALAN PARKER), film director, writer; b. London, Feb. 14, 1944; s. William Leslie and Elsie Ellen Parker; m. Annie Inglis, July 30, 1966 (div. 1992); children: Lucy Kate, Alexander James, Jake William, Nathan Charles; m. Lisa Moran, Dec. 16, 2001. Student Brit. schs. Advt. copywriter, 1965—67; dir. TV commls., 1968—78. Author: (screenplay) Melody, 1968; (novels) Bugsy Malone, 1975, Puddles in the Lane, 1977, The Sucker's Kiss, 2003; author, dir.: No Hard Feelings, 1972, Our Cissy, 1973, Footsteps, 1973, Bugsy Malone, 1975 (5 Brit. Acad. awards), Come See the Paradise, 1990; dir.: The Evacuees (Brit. Acad. award, Internat. Emmy award, Press Guild U.K. award), Midnight Express (6 Golden Globe awards, 3 Brit. Acad. awards, 2 Oscar awards), Fame, 1980 (Brit. Acad. award, Golden Globe award, 2 Oscar awards), Shoot the Moon, 1982, Pink Floyd-The Wall, 1982, Birdy, 1984 (Grand Prix Spl. du Jury, Cannes Film Festival), A Turnip Head's Guide to the British Cinema, 1986 (British Press Guild award), Angel Heart, 1987, Mississippi Burning, 1988 (Oscar award), The Commitments, 1991 (4 BAFTA awards), The Road to Wellville, 1994, Evita, 1996 (3 Golden Globe awards), Angela's Ashes, 1999, The Life of David Gale, 2003. Recipient 4 Brit. Acad. awards. Mem.: Acad. Motion Picture Arts and Scis., Dirs. Guild Gt. Britain, Writers Guild Am., Writers Guild Gt. Britain, Dirs. Guild Am., Brit. Film Inst. (chmn. 1997—99), chmn. UK Film Coun. 1999—2004), Brit. Acad. Film and TV Arts. Office: care Michael Wimer Creative Artists Agy 9830 Wilshire Blvd Beverly Hills CA 90212-1804

PARKER, ALAN JOHN, veterinary neurologist, educator, researcher; b. Portsmouth, Eng., Oct. 28, 1944; arrived in U.S., 1969, naturalized, 2002; s. William Barton and Emily (Begley) P.; m. Heather Margaret Nicholson, Oct. 30, 1971; children: Alyxander John, Robert William. B.Sc. with honors, Bristol U., 1966, B.V.Sc. with honors, 1968; MS, U. Ill., 1973, PhD, 1976. Diplomate Am. Coll. Vet. Internal Medicine-Neurology, European Coll. Vet. Neurology. Intern Vet. Coll., U. Calif.-Davis, 1969-70; instr. vet. clin. medicine U. Ill., Urbana, 1970-71, 72-76, asst. prof., 1976-77, assoc. prof., 1977-82, prof., 1982-2000, prof. emeritus, 2001—. Cons. pharm. cos., seminar presenter; cons. in neurology Berwyn Vet. Hosp., Chgo., 1973—, Lake Shore Animal Hosp., Chgo., 1978-03. Contbr. numerous articles to sci. jours., chpts. to books. Active Boy Scouts Am., Champaign, Ill., 1982—; active Presbyn. Ch., Monticello, Ill., 1979—. Recipient Vigil Honor and Founder's award Order of the Arrow, Silver Beaver award Boy Scouts Am.; sci. grantee various orgns., 1972-2000. Mem. AVMA, Am. Animal Hosp. Assn., Brit. Vet. Assn., Ill. State Vet. Assn. Republican. Office: 2845 S Harlem Ave Berwyn IL 60402 E-mail: a-parker@staff.uiuc.edu.

PARKER, ALICE, composer; b. Boston, Dec. 16, 1925; d. Gordon and Mary (Stuart) P.; widowed; children: David, Timothy, Katharine, Mary, Elizabeth. BA, Smith Coll., Northampton, Mass., 1947; MS, Juilliard Sch., N.Y.C., 1949; MusD (hon.), Hamilton U., 1979, Macalester Coll., St. Paul, 1989, Bluffton (Ohio) Coll., 1991, Westminster Choir Coll., Princeton, N.J., 1996. Arranger Robert Shaw Chorale, N.Y.C., 1948-66; artistic dir. Melodious Accord, N.Y.C., 1985—. Tchr., workshop leader Westminster Choir Coll., Princeton, N.J., summers, 1972-98; McDonald chair Emory U., 2003. Composer 4 operas, 35 cantatas, 8 song cycles and numerous anthems and suites. Recipient composer's award ASCAP, 1968—, AGO Disting. Composer of the Yr., 2000, Barlow Endowment, 1992, spl. award Nat. Endowment Arts, 1976, Gottschalk award Pioneer Valley Symphony, 2003. Fellow Hymn Soc., Hymn Soc. Am.; mem. Am. Choral Dirs. Assn., Am. Condrs. Guild, Chorus Am. (Founders award 1994), Am. Music ctr., Sigma Alpha Iota. Office: Melodious Accord Inc Park West Sta PO Box 20801 New York NY 10025-1523

PARKER, ALICE CLINE, computer engineering educator, consultant; b. Birmingham, Ala., Apr. 10, 1948; d. Joseph Kalman Cline and Elizabeth (Wenk) Jebeles; m. Donald Joseph Bebel, Aug. 9, 1980; 1 child, Joseph Cline Bebel. BEE, N.C. State U., 1970; MEE, Stanford U., 1971; PhD, N.C. State U., 1975. Asst. prof. Carnegie-Mellon U., Pitts., 1975-80, U. So. Calif., L.A., 1980-83, assoc. prof., 1983-91, prof., 1991—, computer engring. divsn. dir., 1991-93, acad. senate pres.-elect, 1993-94, vice provost for rsch., dean grad. studies, 1994-96, vice provost rsch. and grad. studies, 1996—97. Cons. Hughes Aircraft, El Segundo, Calif., 1983, Xerox, El Segundo, 1982-83, Aerospace Corp., El Segundo, 1981-91. Contbr. articles to profl. jours. Program chmn. 11th Microprogramming Workshop, Asilomar, Calif., 1978. IBM rsch. grantee, 1981-86, U.S. Army rsch. grantee, 1976-87; NSF fellow, 1970, grantee, 1984; recipient NSF award for women in sci. and engring., 1991. Fellow IEEE; mem. IEEE Computer Soc. (bd. govs. 1994), Assn. Computing Machinery (treas. spl. interest group 1979-83, 83-87, v.p. 1981-83), Stanford Profl. Women. Presbyterian. Office: U So Calif EEB 348 MC 2562 Los Angeles CA 90089-2562

PARKER, ARNOLD JOHN, minister; b. Wis., Oct. 13, 1924; s. Edgar Martin and Grace May Parker; m. Esther-Jean Parker, Aug. 19, 1926; children: Jon, Winifred Parker Jeffers, Claudia Parker Kikuta. Diploma, Moody Bible Inst., Chgo., 1957. Ordained to ministry Conservative Baptist Ch., 1958. Seamen's pastor Chgo. Am. Bible Soc., Chgo., 1954-64, Seamen's Internat. Christian Assn., Wonder Lake, Ill., 1954-64; min. various Bapt. chs., Ill., INd., Wis., Ohio, 1964-90; adminstr., supt. Cmty. Christian Acad., Wisconsin Rapids, Wis., 1990-99. Chaplain Marine Hosp., Chgo. Active in jail visitation in Chgo. and Crown Point, Ind. Republican. Home: Apt 223 2521 10th St S Wisconsin Rapids WI 54494-6391

PARKER, BARRINGTON D., JR., federal judge, lawyer; b. Washington, Aug. 21, 1944; BA, Yale U., 1965, JD, 1969. Bar: N.Y. 1971. Law clk. to Hon. Aubrey E. Robinson, U.S. Dist. Ct. for D.C., Washington, 1969-70; assoc. Sullivan & Cromwell, N.Y.C., 1970-77; ptnr. Parker Auspitz Neesemann & Delehanty, P.C., N.Y.C., 1977-87, Morrison & Foerster, N.Y.C., 1987-94; judge U.S. Dist. Ct. for so. dist. N.Y., White Plains, 1994—2001, U.S. Ct. Appeals (2nd Ct.), NY, 2001—. Bd. dirs., v.p. NAACP Legal Def. and Educational Fund, Inc., 1980—; com. on grievances, com. on civil discovery U.S. Dist. Ct. (so. dist.) N.Y., 1983—; com. on pre-trial phase civil cases U.S. Ct. Appeals (2nd cir.) 1983—. Trustee Governance Inst., Greenwich Acad., South Africa Legal Svcs. and Legal Edn. Project, Inc.; successor trustte an mem. Yale Corp. Mem. ABA, Fed. Bar Coun., Assn. Bar City N.Y. (com. on the judiciary 1978-82, exec. com. 1982-86, nominating com. 1987), Coun. on Fgn. Rels. Office: US Courthouse 300 Quarropas St Rm 633 White Plains NY 10601-4150 also: Thurogood Marshall US Courthouse 40 Foley Square New York NY 10007

PARKER, BRENT MERSHON, retired medical educator, internist, cardiologist; b. St. Louis, July 3, 1927; s. William Bahlmann and Florence (Mershon) P.; m. Martha Shelton, Aug. 1, 1953; children: Martha Parker Burgess, Elizabeth, Margaret. MD cum laude, Wash. U., St. Louis, 1952. Diplomate Am. Bd. Internal Medicine. Intern and asst. resident N.Y. Hosp.-Cornell, N.Y.C., 1952-54; asst. resident, fellow Barnes Hosp., Wash. U., St. Louis, 1954-57; cardiology sect. chief VA Hosp., U. Oreg., Portland, 1957-59; asst. prof. to assoc. prof., co-dir. cardiovascular div., chief adult cardiac catherization Wash. U. Sch. Medicine, St. Louis, 1959-73; prof. medicine U. Mo., Columbia, 1973-89, prof. emeritus, 1989-94, chief of staff, assoc. dean, 1976-82, chief of cardiology, 1983-89. Mem. colloquium faculty Merck, Sharp and Dohme, West Point, Pa., 1980-86. Author or co-author 58 papers in referred jours., 6 book chpts., teaching papers, others. Bd. dirs. St. Louis Heart Assn., 1962-73, v.p. 1972-73; bd. dirs. Mo. Heart Assn., 1965-75, pres. 1970-71. Served with USN, 1945-46. Recipient Arthur Strauss award St. Louis Heart Assn., 1973, 3 teaching awards U. Mo. Sch. Medicine, 1974, 75, 86, Preventive Cardiology Acad. award, Nat. Heart Lung and Blood Inst., 1982-87, Alumni Achievement award Washington Univ. Sch. Medicine, 1992; Brent Mershon Parker professorship estab. in honor U. Mo., 1989. Fellow ACP, Am. Coll. Cardiology (Mo., Kans. council rep. 1973-77), Clin. Cardiology Soc. Am. Heart Assn.; mem. Am. Fedn. Clin. Research, Cen. Soc. for Clin. Research, Alpha Omega Alpha, Sigma Xi. Episcopalian. Avocations: choral singing, jogging, camping, back packing.

PARKER, C. DANIELLE, government agency administrator; b. Columbus, Ohio, Aug. 27, 1975; d. Darrell Jackson and Vicki Lynn Parker. Program mgr. DCI Group, Washington, 2001—03; dir. ops. Missile Def. Advocacy Alliance, Alexandria, Va., 2002—. Mktg. rsch. coord. Sixth Man Mgmt., Nashville, 2001; event coord. Access Nashville, 2001. Mem. MDAA, Alexandria, Va., 2002—03. Liberal. Office: Missile Def Advocacy Alliance Suite 320 100 N Pitt St Alexandria VA 22314 Business E-Mail: dparker@missiledefenseadvocacy.org.

PARKER, CATHERINE SUSANNE, psychotherapist; b. Norwood, Mass., Nov. 4, 1934; d. George Leonard and Hazel Olga (Remmer) P. BA, Bates Coll., 1956; MSW, U. Denver, 1961. cert. social worker, Colo. Social worker Taunton (Mass.) State Hosp., 1956-59, Ft. Logan Mental Health Ctr., Denver, 1961-66, clin. team leader, 1966-72; dir. adult services Western Inst. Human Resources, Denver, 1973-74; pvt. practice psychotherapy Denver, 1974—. Workshop facilitator Arapahoe C.C., 1986-90. Mem. NASW. Avocations: tennis, skiing, fishing, antiques, gardening. Home: 6453 S Downing St Littleton CO 80121-2517 Office: Denver Mental Health 165 Cook St Ste 100 Denver CO 80206-5308

PARKER, CHARLES WALTER, JR., consultant, retired equipment company executive; b. nr. Ahoskie, NC, Nov. 22, 1922; s. Charles Walter and Minnie Louise (Williamson) P.; m. Sophie Nash Riddick, Nov. 26, 1949; children: Mary Parker Hutto, Caroline Parker Robertson, Charles Walter III, Thomas Williamson. BS in Elec. Engring, Va. Mil. Inst., 1947; Dr. Engring. (hon.), Milw. Sch. Engring., 1980. With Allis-Chalmers Corp., 1947-87, dist. mgr., 1955-57, Phila., 1957-58, dir. sales promotion industries group Milw., 1958-61, gen. mktg. mgr. new products, 1961-62, mgr. mktg. services, 1962-66, v.p. mktg. and public relations services, 1966-70, v.p., dep. group exec., 1970-72, staff group exec. communications and public affairs, 1972-87, ret., 1987; prin. Charles Parker & Assocs. Ltd., Milw., 1987—. Founding mem. World Mktg. Contact Group, London; bd. dirs. Internat. Gen. Ins. Corp., Dinermite Corp. Gen. chmn. United Fund Greater Milw. Area, 1975; trustee Boy Scouts Am. Trust Fund, Milw.; bd. dirs., pres. Jr. Achievement; pres. bd. trustees Univ. Sch. Milw., 1978-80; trustee Carroll Coll., Waukesha, Wis.; bd. dirs. Milw. Children's Hosp.; bd. regents Milw. Sch. Engring.; mem. Greater Milw. Com.; chmn. bd. dirs. Milw. Found., 1987-89. Served to capt. AUS, 1943-46, ETO. Decorated Bronze Star. Mem. NAM (dir.), Wis. C. of C. (pres. 1974-76), Sales and Mktg. Execs. Internat. (pres., CEO 1974, 75, Eduardo Rihan Internat. Mktg. Exec. of Yr. award 1979), Wis. Mfrs. and Commerce Assn. (exec. com.), Pi Sigma Epsilon (pres. 1976-77, trustee and chmn. nat. edn. found. 1979-86), Kappa Alpha. Home: 4973 N Newhall St Milwaukee WI 53217-6049 Office: 828 N Broadway Ste 100 Milwaukee WI 53202-3611

PARKER, CHRISTOPHER WILLIAM, lawyer; b. Evanston, Ill., Oct. 26, 1947; s. Robert H. and Dorothy Boynton P.; m. Mary Ann P., Dec. 28, 1984. BA, Tufts U., 1969; JD, Northeastern U., 1976. Bar: Mass. 1977, U.S. Dist. Ct. Mass. 1977, U.S. Dist. Ct. (we. dist.) Tex. 1986, U.S. Ct. Appeals (1st cir.) 1988, U.S. Supreme Ct. 1988. Law clk. to judge U.S. Bankruptcy Ct. Mass. dist., Boston, 1976-77; assoc. Fletcher, Tilton & Whipple, Worcester, Mass., 1977-79; counsel U.S. Trustee, Boston, 1979-81; assoc. Craig and Macauley P.C., Boston, 1982-84, ptnr., 1984-87; counsel Hinckley, Allen, Snyder & Comen, Boston, 1987-88, ptnr., 1989-91, McDermott, Will & Emery, Boston, 1991—. Mem. ABA, Mass. Bar Assn., Am. Bankruptcy Inst. Boston Bar Assn., Comml. Law League. Clubs: Union Boat (Boston). Home: 11 Tophet Rd Lynnfield MA 01940-1616 Office: McDermott Will & Emery 28 State St Boston MA 02109-1775 E-mail: cparker@mwe.com.

PARKER, CLEA EDWARD, retired university president; b. Talisheek, La., Apr. 2, 1927; s. William A. and Lutritia (Davis) P.; m. Peggy Ann Faciane, June 21, 1953; children— Brian, Stephen, Karen, Robin. BA, Southeastern La. U., 1948; M.Ed., La. State U., 1952, Ed.D., 1965. Coach, tchr. Rugby Acad., New Orleans, 1948-50; tchr., prin., supr. instr., dir. curriculum and instrn. St. Tammany Parish Sch. Bd., 1950-67; prof. edn., head dept. student teaching Nicholls State Coll., Thibodaux, La., 1967-68; acting pres. Southeastern La. U., Hammond, 1968, pres., 1968-80, pres. emeritus, 1980—. Liaison La. State Dept. Edn., Higher Edn. and Bds. for Edn. in La., 1986; vis. lectr. La. State U., 1965-69; Past pres. St. Tammany Parish Tchrs. Assn., La. Assn. Supervision and Curriculum Devel.; past pres. elementary dept. La. Tchrs. Assn.; chmn. Pres.'s Council La. Bd. Edn., 1972-73; v.p. Conf. La. Colls. and Univs., 1973-74, pres., 1974-75; pres. elect Gulf South Conf., 1974-75, pres., 1975-76; mem. Steering Com. on Curriculum Devel. and Revision for Career Edn. for State La., 1973; mem. adv. council for State Plan for Career Edn., 1973 Mem. planning com. Gov.'s Conf. on Aging, 1976; v.p. chpt. 15 La. Good Samaritans, 1987-88; bd. dirs. Assn. for Retarded Citizens, pres.-elect, 1981; mem. Zemurray Park Recreation Commn., Hammond, 1992-95; chmn. bd. dirs. Lallie Kemp Meml. Hosp., 1993-94; bd. dirs. Lallie Kemp Med. Ctr., 1994—, chmn., 1994-95. With USCGR, 1945, 93-94. Named Hon. State Farmer La., 1970, Disting. Alumnus of Yr., Southeastern La. U. Alumni Assn., 1977, 91, 92; inductee La. Spl. Olympics Hall of Fame, 1998. Mem. Am. Assn. State Colls. and Univs. (com. on nat. svc. 1972-73, task force on aging 1975-76, 78-79, nominating com. 1977—, state Rep. for La. 1979—, com. agr. renewable resources and rural devel. 1979-80, Svc. to Edn. award 1980), Hammond C. of C., La. Assn. for Sch. Execs., Ozone Ramblers Camping Club (pres. 1988), KC (lectr. 1982, 85, 90-91, chancellor 1983-84, 87—, dep. grand knight 1995-96), Rotary (bd. dirs. Hammond, internat. svc. dir. 1972), Phi Delta Kappa, Kappa Delta Pi. Home: 10 Golden Dr Hammond LA 70401-1010 E-mail: par-fac@earthlink.net.

PARKER, DAVID R. trucking executive; JD, U. Tex.; PhD, Baylor U. Founder, pres. Covenant Transport, Inc., Chattanooga, 1985—, chmn. bd. dirs., CEO, 1994—. Mem.: Am. Trucking Assn. (bd. dirs., exec. com., safety com., audit com.), Truckload Carriers' Assn. (bd. dirs. 1994—). Office: Covenant Transport Inc 400 Birmingham Hwy Chattanooga TN 37419*

PARKER, DEBORAH A. language educator, translator; b. Sioux City, Iowa, Aug. 5, 1962; d. William Henry and Ella Renate Parker. BA German, S.W. Mo. State U., Springfield, 1984; MA German, MEd in Curriculum and Instrn., U. of Mo., Columbia, 1987. German instr. U. Mo., Columbia, 1985—87; English instr. U. Trier, Germany, 1987—90; German instr. Longview CC, Lee's Summit, Mo., 1990—97, U. Mo., Kans. City, 1991—2002, coord. HS/Coll. program, 1993—2003, dir. lang. resource ctr., 1997—2002; German tchr. Lee's Summit North (Mo.) HS, 2002—. Translator articles to profl. jours. Recipient Excellence in Tchg. award, Golden Key Nat. Honor Soc., 2000. Mem.: AAUP, Fgn. Lang. Assn. Mo., Am. Assn. Tchrs. German. Avocations: mountain biking, hiking, backpacking. Office: Lee's Summit N HS 901 NE Douglas Lees Summit MO 64086 Office Phone: 816-986-1499. Business E-Mail: deborah.parker@leesummit.k12.mo.us.

PARKER, DENNIS GENE, former sheriff, martial arts instructor; b. Kansas City, Kans., Jan. 5, 1956; s. Billy Gene and Lola Ruth (Martens) P.; m. Melissa Ann Cox; children: Heatheryn Ruth, Jessica Elise. Student, U. Kans., 1984. Nat. accredited police firearms instr. and expert., police side handle baton instr. Martial arts instr. Northland Tai-Ryuku, Kansas City, Mo., 1974-84; anti-terrorist/hostage rescue specialist ITC CITRO, 1977-78; police cpl. Atchison (Kans.) Dept. Police, 1984-90; estate investigator Am. Rsch. Bur., L.A., 1990; sheriff Atchison County, Kans., 1990-94; instr. martial arts, including Shito-Ryu Okinawate, Tang Soo Do Mu Duk Kwon, Chinese Wu-Shu Chin Na. Bd. dirs. Atchison County Community Corrections; team mem. Atchison County Multidisciplinary Child Protection Team, 1992—; bd. dirs. N.E. Kans. Drug Task Force, Oskaloosa, 1990-91. Bd. dirs. N.E. Kans. Community Action Program, Atchison, 1991—, Atchison Area Drug Task Force, 1993—. Recipient Silver Star for Bravery Am. Police Hall of Fame, 1992, Honor award, 1992, John Edgar Hoover Meml. award Nat. Assn. Chiefs of Police and Police

Hall of Fame, 1993, State of Kans. medals of valor, 1992, 93, Pres.'s Nat. medal of patriotism, 1993, APD Life Saving award and commendation, 1987, knight chevalier medal Am. Police Hall of Fame, 1992, Medal of Valor Atchison County, 1992, U.S. Cold War Recognition award, 2000. Mem. World Black Belt Bur., Sandan-3d Level Black Shito-Ryu Okinawa Te. Baptist. Home and Office: 5125 NW Parkdale Rd Kansas City MO 64151-3205 Office Phone: 816-505-0949. Personal E-mail: d.g.parker@worldnet.att.net.

PARKER, DEREK, architectural firm executive; Chmn., sr. prin. Anshen & Allen Archs. Inc., San Francisco, 1993—; chmn. Anshen Dyer, London. Mem. design rev. com. U. Calif., Berkeley; practicum faculty doctoral program U. Hawaii; adv. faculty for doctoral program Coll. Arch., Ga. Tech.; bd. mem. Ctr. for Health Design; mem. bd. on infrastructure and constructive environment NRC, 2003—. Fellow: AIA, Am. Coll. Healthcare Archs.; mem.: Royal Inst. Brit. Archs. Office: Anshen & Allen Archs Inc 901 Market St San Francisco CA 94103*

PARKER, DIANA LYNNE, restaurant manager, special events director; b. Eureka, Calif., June 21, 1957; d. Carol Dean and Lynne Diane (Havemann) P. BA in English, Humboldt U., 1981, postgrad., 1982-84. Lic. real estate agent, Calif. Retail clk. Safeway, Inc., Eureka, 1977-84; caterer, owner TD Catering, Eureka, 1982-84; asst. buyer Macy's Calif., San Francisco, 1984-85; realtor Mason-McDuffie, Alameda, Calif., 1985-87; host, Rotunda Restaurant Neiman Marcus, San Francisco, 1987-89, asst. mgr. Rotunda Restaurant, 1989—96, dir. spl. events, 1989—96, mgr. dining room Rotunda Restaurant, 1996—. Mem.: San Francisco Visitor and Conv. Bur., Women Chefs and Restaurateurs, Mus. Modern Art, Commonwealth Club Calif. Republican. Avocations: gourmet chef, artist, antique collecting. Office: Rotunda at Neiman Marcus 150 Stockton St San Francisco CA 94108-5807 Office Phone: 415-362-4777.

PARKER, DONALD EDWARD, aeronautics and aerospace educator; b. Chgo., Apr. 6, 1936; s. Kenneth Coldwell and Florence (Wilson) P.; m. Lynn Goodrich, Sept. 27, 1959 (dec. Apr. 1986); children: Katherine, Susan, Geoffrrey, Rebecca; m. Sharon Lynne Parker, Aug. 19, 1987. BA in Psychology and Econs., DePauw U., 1958; PhD in Exptl. Psychology, Princeton U., 1961. Postdoctoral fellow Auditory Rsch. Lab. Princeton (N.J.) U., NIMH, 1961-62; sr. postdoctoral fellow Max Planck Inst., NIMH, Germany, 1965-66; asst. prof. psychology Miami U., Oxford, Ohio, 1966-69, assoc. prof. psychology, 1969-72, prof. psychology, 1972-93, chair dept. psychology, 1977-80, prof. emeritus dept. psychology, 1993—; affiliate prof. otolaryngology U. Wash., Seattle, 1993—. Vis. scientist Space Biomed. Rsch. Inst. NASA, Houston, 1983, 85-87, project scientist pre-flight adaptation trainer project, 1987-89, co-investigator, 1989-94; clin. prof. cmty. medicine Wright State U., Dayton, Ohio, 1984—; assoc. investigator Spatial Orientation Rsch. Project Harry G. Armstrong Aerospace Med. Rsch. Lab. Wright-Patterson AFB, Dayton, 1988-93; assoc. investgator Kodak Immersive Experience Project, Human Interface Tech. Lab., 1994— Contbr. numerous articles to profl. jours. Capt. USAF, 1962-65. Numerous grants NIH, USAF, NASA, 1965—. Mem. Internat. Acad. Astronautics, Barany Soc. Avocation: hiking. Office: Dept Otolaryngology Box 357923 U Wash Seattle WA 98195-7923

PARKER, DONALD FRED, college dean, human resources management educator; b. Oilton, Okla., Nov. 7, 1934; s. Robert Fred Parker and Georgia Marie (Culley) Meek; m. Jo Ellen Dunfee, Apr. 6, 1963; children: Margaret Elizabeth, Emily Lyle. BA in Sociology, U. Okla., 1957; MS in Personnel Adminstrn., George Washington U., 1966; PhD in Human Resource Mgmt., Cornell U., 1974. Commd. ensign USN, 1957, advanced through grades to capt., 1977, staff officer with chief naval ops., 1969-71, comdg. officer, exec. officer, Patrol Squadron Ten Brunswick, Maine, 1974-76, prof. Naval War Coll. Newport, R.I., 1976-78, comdg. officer Navy Personnel Research & Devel. Ctr. San Diego, 1978-80, ret., 1980; asst. prof. Grad. Sch. Bus., U. Mich., Ann Arbor, 1980-84; prof., dean Coll. Commerce and Industry U. Wyo., Laramie, 1984-91; Sara Hart Kimball dean bus., prof. human resources mgmt. Oreg. State U., Corvallis, 1991—2001, dean emeritus, 2004—. Advisor U.S. West Wyo. State Bd. Advisors, Cheyenne, 1986-91; ex-officio dir. Wyo. Indsl. Devel. Corp., Casper, 1987; vis. prof. Acad. Internat. Econ. Affairs, Hsinchu, Taiwan, 1986-91. Author numerous articles, book chpts., case studies. Mem. Acad. of Mgmt. (human resource mgmt. divsn. dir. 1983-85), Midwest Assn. Deans and Dept. Chairs in Bus. (pres.), Western Assn. Collegiate Schs. Bus. (bd. dirs., pres. 1999), Phi Kappa Phi, Beta Gamma Sigma (pres. 1998-2000, past pres. 2000—02). Avocations: jogging, hiking. Home: 4400 NW Honeysuckle Dr Corvallis OR 97330-3355 Office: Oreg State U Coll Bus 200 Bexell Hall Corvallis OR 97331-8527 E-mail: parker@bus.orst.edu.

PARKER, DRUE A. writer, educator; b. Hillsboro, Tex., May 21, 1948; d. Andrew Washington and Para Wright Porter; m. Royce C. Parker. BA, Baylor U., 1969; MA, Ea. N.Mex. U., 1972; EdD, Tex. A&M U., 1981. Tchr. Tex. A&M U., Commerce, Tex., Ralls (Tex.) HS, Richland Coll., Dallas, Collin County C.C., Plano, Tex.; mgr., tech. writer EDS, Plano, Tex.; sr. pubs. cons. Predictive Sys., Dallas; cons. InSource Ptnrs., Plano. Home: 13016 Stillforest Austin TX 78729

PARKER, ELLIS JACKSON, III, lawyer, broadcaster; b. Haleyville, Ala., Oct. 2, 1931; s. Ellis J. and Elizabeth (Funderburg) P.; m. Nancy Elizabeth Bealer; children: Francis Hill, Ellis Stuart. Student, U.S. Mil. Acad., West Point, N.Y., 1953-57; AB, U. Ala., 1958, LLB, 1960, JD, 1961; diploma, Droit Compare, Luxembourg, 1959; cert., Acad. Internat. Law, Hague, The Netherlands, 1960. Bar: Ala. 1960, U.S. Tax Ct. 1960, U.S. Supreme Ct. 1966, D.C. Ct. Appeals 1972, U.S. Ct. Appeals D.C. 1972, Md. Ct. Appeals 1973, U.S. Ct. Claims 1977. Legis. atty. IRS, Washington, 1961-62; chief of staff to U.S. Congressman Grant Ala., 1963-64; pvt. practice, 1964-84; spl. advisor to Pres. Richard Nixon White House, Washington, 1968-69; v.p., counsel Birmingham Broadcasting Co., 1964-83; ptnr. Taylor, Smith & Parker Law Office, Upper Marlboro, Md., 1970-86; prin., owner Ellis J. Parker, Law Office, Washington, 1986—. V.p., sec. Constrn. Components Corp., Upper Marlboro, Md., 1968-72; pres. Washington-Ala. News Reports, Washington, 1980-01; pres. Sta. WNPT-AM-FM, Tuscaloosa, Ala.; v.p. Sta. WLPH, Birmingham, Parker Real Estate, Birmingham, N.B. Devel. Co., Washington; chmn. bd. Blackbelt Broadcasting Co., Selma, Ala.; founding mem. Women's Nat. Bank, Washington; CEO Birmingham Broadcasting Co.; ptnr. Linden Radio Joint Venture, Faunsdale, Ala., 1969-89; bd. dirs. 17th St L.L.C., Bealer-Parker, LLC, Washington. Mem. Presdl. Inaugural Com., inaugural protocol officer V.p. Agnew, 1968; mem. steering com. Rep. Party, Balt., 1972; chmn. bd. trustees Prince George's Hist. and Cultural Trust, Upper Marlboro, 1974; chmn. bd. advisors Prince George's Equestrian Ctr., Upper Marlboro, 1980; founder, pres. bd. dirs. Hospice of Prince George's County, Upper Marlboro, 1982; mem. Upper Marlboro Devel. Com. Mem. IEEE, ABA, FCC Bar Assn., Fed. Bar Assn., Inter-Am. Bar Assn., Ala. Bar Assn., Md. Bar Assn., Nat. Assn. Broadcasters, Ala. Broadcasters Assn., Balt. Coun. Fgn. Affairs, Assn. Grads. U.S. Mil. Acad., Chevy Chase Club, Md. Club, St. Andrews Soc., Met. Club, Ala. Alumni Assn., Scabbard and Blade (chmn. nat. alumni coun.), Pi Kappa Alpha, Sigma Delta Kappa. Home: Chateau Rambouillet 2165 Ibis Island Palm Beach FL 33480 E-mail: eparker124@aol.com.

PARKER, EUGENE LEROY, III, lawyer; b. Arlington, Mass., Oct. 17, 1949; s. Eugene LeRoy Jr. and Jane Gates (Washburn) P.; m. Jo Ann Williams, June 24, 1978; children: Willis Washburn, Jones Griffith, Alden Jackson, Eliza Ann. Student, Hampden-Sydney (Va.), 1969; AB, Rutgers U., 1972; JD, Memphis State U., 1976. Bar: Tenn. 1977. Sole practice, Etowah, Tenn., 1977—. Judge City of Etowah, 1986-95. Regional dir. Am. Youth Soccer Orgn., 1985-95. Mem. Tenn. Trial Lawyers Assn., McMinn County Bar Assn. Republican. Methodist. Avocations: walking, coaching, scout activities, reading, yard work. Home and Office: PO Box 804 Etowah TN 37331-0804

PARKER, EUGENE NEWMAN, retired physicist, educator; b. Houghton, Mich., June 10, 1927; s. Glenn H. and Helen (MacNair) Parker; m. Niesje Meuter, 1954; children: Joyce, Eric. BS, Mich. State U., 1948, DSc (hon.), 1975; PhD, Calif. Inst. Tech., 1951; DHC in Physics and Math. (hon.), U. Utrecht, The Netherlands, 1986; DHC in Theoretical Physics (hon.), U. Oslo, 1991. Instr. math. and astronomy U. Utah, 1951—53, asst. prof. physics, 1953—55; mem. faculty physics U. Chgo., 1955—95, prof. dept. physics, 1962—95, prof. dept. astronomy and astrophysics, 1967—95, prof. emeritus, 1995—. Author: Interplanetary Dynamical Processes, 1963, Cosmical Magnetic Fields, 1979, Spontaneous Current Sheets in Magnetic Fields, 1994. Recipient Space Sci. award, AIAA, 1964, Chapman medal, Royal Astron. Soc., 1979, Gold medal, 1992, Disting. Alumni award, Calif. Inst. Tech., 1980, Karl Schwarzschild award, Astronomische Gesselschaft, 1990, Bruce medal, Astron. Soc. Pacific, 1997, medal, Assn. Internat. Devel. Nice (France) Obs., 1997, Kyoto prize, Inamori Found., 2003, Maxwell prize, plasma physics divsn., Am. Phys. Soc., 2003. Mem.: NAS (H. K. Arctowski award 1969, U.S. Nat. medal of Sci. 1989), Norwegian Acad. Sci. and Letters, Am. Geophys. Union (John Adam Fleming award 1968, William Bowie medal 1990), Am. Astron. Soc. (Henry Norris Russell lectr. 1969, George Ellery Hale award 1978). Achievements include development of theory of the origin of the dipole magnetic field of Earth; prediction and theory of the solar wind and heliosphere; theoretical basis for the X-ray emission from the Sun and stars. Home: 1323 Evergreen Rd Homewood IL 60430-3410 E-mail: parker@odysseus.uchicago.edu.

PARKER, EVERETT CARLTON, clergyman; b. Chgo., Jan. 17, 1913; s. Harry Everett and Lillian (Stern) P.; m. Geneva M. Jones, May 5, 1939; children: Ruth A. (Mrs. Peter Weiss), Eunice L. (Mrs. George Kolczun, Jr.), Truman E. AB, U. Chgo., 1935; BD magna cum laude, Chgo. Theol. Sem., 1943, Blatchford fellow, 1944-45, DD, 1964, Catawba Coll., Salisbury, N.C., 1958; L.H.D., Fordham U., 1978, Tougaloo Coll., 1987; LLD, Coll. St. Elizabeth, 2000. Pastor Waveland Ave. Congl. Christian Ch., 1943; asst. pub. service and war program mgr. NBC, 1943-45; founder-dir. Protestant Radio Commn., 1945-50; lectr. communication Yale Div. Sch., 1946-58, dir. communications research project, 1950-54; dir. Office Communication United Ch. Christ, 1954-83; sr. research assoc., adj. prof. Fordham U., 1983—; founder citizen movement to protect minority rights in media, 1963—. Chmn. broadcasting and film commn. Nat. Coun. Chs., 1969-72, mem. gen. bd., 1966-72; chair Study Commn. on Theology, Edn. and Electronic Media, 1985-87; founder Found. for Minority Interests in Media, 1985—, treas., 1985—, Hispanic Telecommunications Network, 1986-2004; mem. adv. com. on advanced TV svcs., Consumer Adv. Group FCC, 1988-92. Producer-dir.: nat. TV programs including series Off to Adventure, 1956, Tangled World, 1965; originator: series Six American Families, PBS-TV, 1977; Author: Religious Radio, 1948, Film Use in the Church, 1953, The Television-Radio Audience and Religion, 1955, Religious Television, 1961, (with others) Television, Radio, Film for Churchmen, 1969, Fiber Optics to the Home: The Changing Future of Cable, TV and The Telephone, 1989, Social Responsibility of Television in the United States, 1994. Recipient Human Relations award Am. Jewish Com., 1966, Faith and Freedom award Religious Heritage Found., 1966, 77, Alfred I. DuPont-Columbia U. award pub. service in broadcasting, 1969; Roman Cath. Broadcasters Gabriel award pub. service, 1970; Lincoln U. award significant contbn. human relations, 1971; Racial Justice award Com. for Racial Justice, United Ch. Christ, 1973; Ch. Leadership award Council for Christian Social Action, 1973; Public Service award Black Citizens for a Fair Media, 1979, Pioneer award World Assn. for Christian Communication, 1988, Pres.'s award for Ecumenical Leadership Nat. Coun. Chs., 2000, Jacques Ellul award, 2004; Congl. citation, 1993. Mem.: Yale (N.Y.C.). Home: 11 Midland Ave White Plains NY 10606-2828 Office: Fordham University Dept Communications Bronx NY 10458 Office Phone: 718-817-4854.

PARKER, GARY DEAN, manufacturing executive; b. Omaha, Mar. 27, 1945; s. Norman and Dolores (Pierce) P.; m. Joanne Baker, Aug. 27, 1966; children: Jason E., Rodney R. BS in BA, BS in Econs., Nebr. Wesleyan U. Dir. sales Lindsay Mfg. Co., Nebr., 1971-73, v.p. sales-mktg., 1973-76, sr. v.p., 1976-78, exec. v.p., 1978-83, pres., 1983—, dir., 1977—. Pres. Irrigation Assocs., Silver Springs, Md., 1981-82, dir., 1978-83; dir. Irrigation Found. & Research, Silver Springs, 1978— Mem. Nebr. Mfg. Assn. (pres. 1982-83), Delta Omicron Epsilon Lodges: Elks. Office: Lindsay Mfg Co PO Box 156 Lindsay NE 68644-0156

PARKER, GEORGE, retired pen manufacturing company executive; b. Janesville, Wis., Nov. 9, 1929; s. Russell C. and Eleanor (Jackson) P.; m. Nancy E. Bauhan, Aug. 11, 1951; children: George Safford III, Elizabeth, Martha, Patricia. BA, Brown U., 1951, LLD (hon.), 1986; MA, U. Mich., 1952; LLD (hon.), Milton Coll., 1974. With Parker Pen Co., Janesville, 1952-86, from asst. to gen. mgr. Gilman Engring. Co. subs., successively asst. domestic advt. mgr., fgn. advt. mgr., dir. fgn. sales, dir. domestic sales, v.p., gen. mgr., 1958-60, exec. v.p., 1960-66, pres., 1966-77, 81-82, CEO, 1966-80, 81-82, chmn. bd., 1976-86, Manpower Inc., 1976-86; pres., chmn. Caxambas Assocs. of Fla., Inc., 1986—; ret., 1986. Chmn. bd. BANCWIS Corp., 1971-84; bd. dirs. Bank of Wis.; chmn. bd. Moebius Printing Co., Milw., 1992-93; guest lectr. U. Wis., 2002-03. Chmn. Wis. Rep. Fin. Com., 1971-73, state chmn., 1974-76; mem. Nat. Rep. Fin. Com., 1971-73; mem. Rep. Nat. Com., 1974-76; chmn. bd. dirs., CEO Janesville Found.; bd. dirs., pres. Marco Island Taxpayers Assn., 1993-94; fellow Lake Forest Acad.; trustee emeritus Brown U., Beloit Coll.; chmn. emeritus bd. fellows Beloit Coll.; dir. Wis. Acad. Found., 1994-99, v.p., 1996, pres., 1997-99, councillor Wis. Acad., 1998-99; bd. govs. John Carter Brown Libr., 1997-99; dir. Wis. History Found., 1999-2000; coun. mem. Elvehjem Mus. of Art, Madison, Wis., 2001—.

PARKER, GERALD M. osteopath, researcher; b. Olean, N.Y., Nov. 20, 1943; s. Richard and Kathleen (Manwaring) P.; m. Linda Kay Stuart, Dec. 28, 1968; children: Kimberly, Gerald, Cassandra, Kevin. BA, Western Wash. U., 1965; DO, Kirksville Coll. Osteopathy & Surgery, 1969. Intern Art Centre Hosp., Detroit, 1969-70; ptnr. Doctor's Clinic, Amarillo, Tex., 1970. Dir. S.W. Inst. Preventive Medicine, Amarillo, 1978—, Hyperbaric Oxygen Ctr., Amarillo, 1979—; appeared on That's Incredible TV show, 1982. Contbr. articles to profl. jours. Pres. S.W. Amarillo Little Dribblers Assn., 1979—; coach Girls Nat. Champion Basketball Teams, 1981, 83-87, 89. Fellow Am. Acad. Med. Preventics; mem. S.W. Acad. Preventive Medicine (pres. 1980—), Am. Osteo. Assn. Methodist. Avocation: athletics. Office: Doctors Clinic 4714 S Western St Amarillo TX 79109-5950 Office Phone: 806-355-8263.

PARKER, GERALD WILLIAM, internist, health facility administrator, retired military officer; b. Susquehanna, Pa., Oct. 22, 1929; m. Susan Emerson, May 4, 1985. BS, Union Coll., Schenectady, 1951; MD, N.Y. Med. Coll., 1955. Diplomate Nat. Bd. Med. Examiners, Am. Bd. Internal Medicine; lic. physician, N.Y., Tex., D.C. Intern Ellis Hosp., Schenectady, 1955-56; resident internal medicine Wilford Hall, USAF Med. Ctr., San Antonio, 1958-61; resident in gastroenterology Water Reed Army Med. Ctr., Washington, 1965-66; commd. capt. U.S. Air Force, 1956, advanced through grades to brig. gen., 1980, retired, 1986; chair dept. medicine USAF Hosp., Clark AFB, Philippines, 1967-69; chief internal medicine Malcolm Grow USAF Med. Ctr., Andrews AFB, Washington, 1969-70, chair dept. medicine, 1970-72, Wilford Hall USAF Med. Ctr., Lackland AFB, Tex., 1972-75, dir. hosp. services, 1975-77; comdr USAF Hosp., Torrejon Air Base, Spain, 1977-78; dep. dir. med. plans and resources Office of Surgeon Gen. USAF, Washington, 1978-80, dir. med. plans and resources, 1980-81; dir. med. inspection AF Inspection and Safety Ctr., Norton AFB, Calif., 1981-83; dep. surgeon gen. for ops. AF Med. Service Ctr., Brooks AFB, Tex., 1983-85; dir. profl. affairs and quality assurance Office of Surg. Gen., USAF, Washington, 1985-86; dep. dir., chief profl. services King Health Ctr., U.S. Soldiers and Airmens Home, Washington, 1986-97, ret., 1997. Clin. prof. medicine U. Tex. Health Scis. Ctr., San Antonio, 1972-77; adj. prof. Health Care Scis., George Washington Univ., 1987-97; clinical prof. medicine Uniformed Svcs. Univ. of Health Scis., 1988-97. Trustee, Hampshire Country Sch., 2000—; mem. Rindge (N.H.) Planning Bd., 2000—, Rindge Conservation Commn., 2000—04, Rindge Hist. Soc., 2000—; Rindge health officer, 2001—. Decorated Air Force D.S.M. with oak leaf cluster, Legion of Merit with oak leaf cluster, Bronze Star, Air Medal with oak leaf cluster, ACP Laureate award, 1996, Air Force Civilian Outstanding Svc. medal. Fellow ACP; mem. Soc. AF Physicians, Alpha Omega Alpha. Personal E-mail: gengwparker@aol.com.

PARKER, H. LAWRENCE, investor, rancher, retired investment banker; b. Portchester, N.Y., June 16, 1926; s. Raeburn H. and Alice (Lawrence) P.; m. Eleanor Sage, Mar. 3, 1951 (div. 1967); children: Katherine, Richard, Michael, Douglas (dec.); m. Regine Hawes, Nov. 15, 1994. BA, Yale U., 1949. With Morgan Stanley & Co., N.Y.C., 1950—, ptnr., 1959-75, mng. dir., 1975-83, adv. dir., 1984—; pres. Morgan Stanley Can. Ltd., 1976-79, chmn., 1979-84, ret. Mem. adv. bd. on edn. and tng. Sec. Navy, 1985-87; dir. Jupiter (Fla.) Med. Ctr. Found., vice chmn., 2002—. Trustee Green Mountain Valley Sch., Waitsfield, Vt., 1981-91. Served with USMC, 1944-46. Mem. Investment Bankers Assn. Am. (bd. govs. 1966-70, pres. 1969), Nat. Assn. Securities Dealers (gov. 1981-84), Sublette County Hist. Soc. (trustee 1987-91), Blind Brook Club, Augusta (Ga.) Nat. Golf Club, Jupiter (Fla.) Island Club, Seminole Golf Club, Ekwanok Country Club. Home: One Angas Trail Hobe Sound FL 33455 Office Phone: 212-762-8865. E-mail: thepard@aol.com.

PARKER, H. STEWART, biotechnology company executive; BA, MBA, U. Wash. V.p. corp. devel. Immunex, 1981—91; pres., CEO, dir. Targeted Genetics, 1989—. Chmn. bd. CellExSys, Inc. (subs. Targeted Genetics, Inc.), 2000—. Bd. visitors U. N.C.; Arts & Sciences Coun. U. Wash.; bd. dirs. Pilchuck Glass Sch. Recipient Small Bus. Person of the Year for Western Wash., Small Bus. Admin., 2001. Mem.: Biotechnology Industry Orgn. (exec. com., bd. dirs.). Office: Targeted Genetics Corp 1100 Olive Way Ste 100 Seattle WA 98101

PARKER, HARRY JOHN, retired psychologist, educator; b. Sioux City, Iowa, Jan. 18, 1923; AB, Elmhurst Coll., 1947; MA, Northwestern U., 1953, PhD, 1956, postgrad., 1958, Roosevelt U., 1957-58; LittD, Elmhurst Coll., 1990. Lic. psychologist, Okla. Tex.; diplomate bd. cert. in rehab. psychology Am. Bd. Profl. Psychology. Counselor Northwestern U. Counseling Ctr., Chgo., 1952-56, counseling psychologist, 1956-59, asst. dir., 1957-58, dir., 1958-59; pvt. practice counseling psychologist Chgo., 1956-59, 1959-69, 1969—; prof. edn. U. Okla., 1959-69; dir. manpower planning, regional med. program and Sch. Health Related Professions U. Okla. Med. Ctr., Oklahoma City, 1967-69, prof. preventive medicine and pub. health, 1966-69, prof. human ecology, 1969; assoc. dean Sch. Allied Health Scis. U. Tex. Southwestern Med. Ctr., Dallas, 1969-74, prof. phys. medicine and rehab., prof. psychiatry, 1969-90, prof. rehab. sci., 1970-90. Adj. prof. rehab. U. N. Tex., 1990; adj. prof. psychology Ill. Inst. Tech., 1990-96, Tex. Woman's U., 1991-99; adj. prof. allied health edn. U. Tex. Southwestern Med. Ctr., Dallas, 1990-98. Contbr. articles to profl. jours. Served with U.S. Army, 1943-46 Fellow Am. Psychol. Assn.; mem. Southwestern Psychol. Assn. (life), Dallas Psychol. Assn., Tex. Psychol. Assn., Sigma Xi, Phi Delta Phi, Alpha Eta. Address: 318 Hidden Valley Trl Sherman TX 75092-7618

PARKER, HARRY LEE, retired army officer, counselor; b. Birmingham, Ala., Feb. 20, 1944; s. Guy Milburn and Grace (Lee) P.; m. Sheri Lynn Pogue (div. Oct. 1973); children: John Lee, Suzanne Grace, Stephen Scott; m. Melanie Louise Cox, Apr. 20, 1979; 1 child, Christopher Robert. BA, Miss. State U., 1966; MS, Johns Hopkins U., 1980; postgrad., U.S. Army Command & Staff Coll, 1982. Commd. 2d lt. U.S. Army, 1966, advanced through grades to lt. col., 1987; maintenance officer 85th Maintenance Bn., Hanau, Fed. Republic of Germany, 1967-69; commanding officer 143d Engr. Co. and A Co. 34th Engr. Bn., Long Binh, Vietnam, 1969-70; chief plans and ops. div. Dir. of Logistics, Ft. Rucker, Ala., 1971-73; supply and maintenance officer 97th Signal Bn. NATO, Mannehim, Fed. Republic of Germany, 1973-76; asst. materiel officer 8th Maintenance Bn., Grossalheim, Fed. Republic Germany, 1977; tng. evaluator HQ 1st US Army, Ft. Meade, Md., 1978-81; logistics coord. Cuban Task Force, Ft. Indiantown Gap, Pa., 1980; project officer Dept. Def., Project Office, Mobile Electric Power, Washington, 1982-85; exec. officer 193d Support Bn., Ft. Clayton, Panama, 1986-87; chief of maintenance U.S. Army South, Ft. Corozol, Panama, 1987-88; prof. mil. Sci. Army ROTC, Miss. State U., Starkville, Miss., 1988-90; ops. officer 101st area support group, Guardian City, Saudia Arabia, logistics officer, 1st Corps Support Command, XVIII Airborne Corps., Damman, Saudi Arabia (Desert Shield and Desert Storm), 1990-91; career/coop. edn. counselor Ctrl. Fla. CC, Ocala, Fla., 1992-95; educator Seminole County (Fla.) Pub. Sch. Sys., 2000—02; asst. dir. office of vet.'s svcs. U. Ctrl. Fla., Orlando, 2003—; asst. u. registrar U. Ctr. Fla., 2004—. Decorated Bronze Star with oak leaf cluster, Meritorious Svc. medal with two oak leaf clusters, Army Commendation medal with four oak leaf clusters. Mem. Mil. Officers Assn. Am. (life), Am. Legion, Sigma Chi (life). Presbyterian (Elder). Avocations: woodworking, private pilot, scuba, boating, computers. Home: 895 Palmetto St Oviedo FL 32765 E-mail: hleepark@bellsouth.net.

PARKER, HARRY S., III, museum director; b. St. Petersburg, Fla., Dec. 23, 1939; s. Harry S. Parker and Catherine (Baillie) Knapp; m. Ellen McCance, May 23, 1964; children: Elizabeth Day, Thomas Baillie, Samuel Ferguson, Catherine Allan. AB magna cum laude, Harvard U., 1961; MA, NYU, 1966. Exec. asst., adminstrv. asst. to dir. Met. Mus. Art, N.Y.C., 1963-66, exec. asst. to pres., 1966-67, exec. asst. to dir., 1967, chmn. dept. edn., 1967-71, vice dir. edn., 1971-73; dir. Dallas Mus. Art, 1974-87, Fine Arts Mus. San Francisco, 1987—. Mem. Am. Assn. Mus. (v.p.) Assn. Art Mus. Dirs., Century Assn., Bohemian Club. Office: Fine Arts Mus San Francisco 233 Post St Fl 5 San Francisco CA 94108*

PARKER, HENRY GRIFFITH, III, insurance executive; b. Plainfield, N.J., Oct. 27, 1926; s. Henry Griffith and Ruth Martin (Van Auken) P.; m. Audrey Lansing Turner, May 11, 1957; children: Henry Griffith, IV, Elizabeth Wright. AB, Princeton U., 1948; postgrad., U. Pa. Sch. Law. With Chubb & Son, Inc., 1949-97, v.p., 1968-70, sr. v.p., dir., 1971-92, mng. dir., 1986-92; cons. to chmn., 1992-97; v.p. Fed. Ins. Co., 1968-73, sr. v.p., 1973-91; v.p. Vigilant Ins. Co., 1966-91, mgr. internat. div., 1967-84; chmn. Parker Assocs., Madison, N.J., 1997—. Adv. bd. Firemark Global Ins. Fund II, L.P., 1997—, bd. dirs. Alliance Assurance Co. Am., N.Y.C., Sun Ins. Office Am. Inc., N.Y.C.; mem. industry sector adv. com. on svcs. U.S. Dept. Commerce, Washington; bd. dirs. Nat. Fgn. Trade Coun., chmn. declarations com., 1974-81, chmn. ins. com., 1976-81; chmn. internat. policy com. U.S. C. of C., 1970-73; chmn. U.S. del. XII-XIII-XX-XXII-XXII Hemispheric Ins. Conf., Chile, 1969, Paraguay, 1987, Panama, 1985, Buenos Aires, 1989; chmn. Internat. Ins. Adv. Coun., Washington, 1970-73, 85-90, chmn. Internat. Com. Am. Ins. Assn., 1991-93; mem. N.J. Commn. on Internat. Trade, 1986—; chmn. bus. adv. com. bus. coun. UN, 1988—; mem. adv. bd. Liaison Office Peoples Ins. Co. China, 1986-94. Appeared on numerous TV and radio programs; contbr. articles to profl. jours. Chmn. bd. Overlook Hosp., Summit, N.J., 1973-80; trustee Drew U., Madison, 1974—. Lt. (j.g.) USNR, 1944-46. Recipient Internat. Ins. award U.S. C. of C., 1981, Disting. Service award Internat. Ins. Council, 1988. Mem. Nat. Assn. Ins. Commrs. (chmn. internat. adv. com.), Am. Ins. Assn. (chmn. internat. com.), Downtown Assn. Club (N.Y.C.), Princeton Club (N.Y.C.), River Club (N.Y.C.), Devon Yacht Club, Morris County (N.J.) Golf Club, Hillsboro Club (Fla.), Psi Upsilon. Republican. Episcopalian. Office: Parker Assocs 38 East Ln Madison NJ 07940-2652

PARKER, JACK STEELE, retired manufacturing company executive; b. Palo Alto, Calif., July 6, 1918; s. William Leonard and Mary Isabel (Steele) P.; m. Elaine Elizabeth Simons; 1 child, Kaaren Parker Gray. BSME, Stanford U., 1939; DBA (hon.), Southeastern Mass. U., 1970; LLD (hon.), Clark U., 1972, Renssalaer Poly. Inst., 1986. Engr. Western Pipe & Steel Co., San Francisco, 1939-40; marine surveyor Am. Bur. Shipping, Seattle, 1940-42; supt. steel constrn. Todd Shipyards, Houston, 1942-44, supt. outfitting L.A., 1944-46; asst. chief engr. Am. Potash & Chem., Trona, Calif., 1946-50; mgr. separations div. GE, Hanford Works, Wash., 1950-52, div. mgr., v.p. aircraft gas turbines Cin., 1952-57, v.p. corp. rels. N.Y.C., 1957-61, v.p., group exec. aerospace and electronics, 1961-68, vice chmn., exec. officer, dir., 1968-80, dir. emeritus, 1980—. Overseer Hoover Instn., Stanford U., chmn. 1974-76; trustee Monterey Bay Aquarium Found., Heard Mus., Phoenix, Ariz.; hon. trustee Renssalaer Poly. Inst., Troy, N.Y.; bd. dirs. Smithsonian Instn., 1985-91. Fellow AIAA, ASME; mem. NAE, NAS (Pres.'s Circle), The Conf. Bd. (councilor for life, chmn. 1971-73), Aerospace Industries Assn. (chmn. 1966-68, hon. dir.), Augusta (Ga.) Nat. Golf Club, Desert Forest Golf Club,

Desert Mountain Club, Bohemian Club, Boone & Crocket Club, Conquistadores del Cielo, Forest Highlands Club. Avocations: fishing, shooting, golf. Home: 6972 Stage Coach Pass Carefree AZ 85377 Office: GE 260 Long Ridge Rd Stamford CT 06902-1627

PARKER, JAMES AUBREY, federal judge; b. Houston, Jan. 8, 1937; s. Lewis Almeron and Emily Helen (Stuessy) P.; m. Florence Fisher, Aug. 26, 1960; children: Roger Alan, Pamela Elizabeth. BA, Rice U., 1959; LLB, U. Tex., 1962. Bar: Tex. 1962, N.Mex. 1963. With Modrall, Sperling, Roehl, Harris & Sisk, Albuquerque, 1962-87; judge U.S. Dist. Ct. N.Mex., Albuquerque, 1987—2000, chief judge, 2000—03. Mem. Standing Commn. on Rules of Practice and Procedures of U.S. Cts., 1993-99, N.Mex. Commn. on Professionalism, 1986-2004; bd. vis. U. N.Mex. Law Sch., 1996-2004; bd. dirs. Fed. Jud. Ctr. Articles editor Tex. Law Rev., 1961-62. Mem. Fed. Judges Assn., Am. Judicature Soc., Am. Bd. Trial Advocates, N.Mex. Bar Assn. (Outstanding Judge award 1994), Albuquerque Bar Assn. (Outstanding Judge award 1993, 2000), Order of Coif, Chancellors, Phi Delta Phi. Avocations: ranching, fly fishing, running, skiing. Office: US Dist Ct 421 Gold S W 6th Fl Albuquerque NM 87102-2277 Office Phone: 505-348-2220. Office Fax: 505-348-2225. Business E-Mail: jparker@nmcourt.fed.us.

PARKER, JAMES FRANCIS, former air transportation executive, lawyer; b. San Antonio, Jan. 1, 1947; s. Raymond Francis and Libbie Olivia (Dusek) P.; m. Patricia Elaine Lorang, May 15, 1971; children: James, Jennifer. BA with hons., U. Tex., 1969, JD with hons., 1971. Bar: Tex., U.S. Dist. Ct. (ea., we., so. no. dists.) Tex., U.S. Ct. Appeals (5th and 11th cirs.), U.S. Supreme Ct. Law clk. to presiding judge U.S. Dist. Ct., Austin, Tex., 1972-76, asst. atty. gen. State of Tex., Austin, 1976-79; atty. Oppenheimer, Rosenberg, Kelleher & Wheatley, San Antonio, 1979-86; v.p., gen. counsel SW Airlines Co., Dallas, 1986—2001, vice chmn., CEO, 2001—04. Mem. ABA, Tex. Bar Assn. Democrat. Lutheran.*

PARKER, JAMES JOHN, engineering and marketing manager; b. June 16, 1947; s. John J. and Marjorie (Grohmann) P.; m. Mary P. Nash, Oct. 21, 1972; children: Elizabeth Ann, John James, Patricia Mary. BSEE, Marquette U., 1971; BSBA, Elmhurst Coll., 1981; MBA, U. Chgo., 1987. Student engr. Motorola Consumer Products, Franklin Park, Ill., 1968-70, engring. assoc., 1972-74; co-op engr. Warwick Electronics, Niles, 1971-72; sr. engr. R&D Quasar Electronics, Inc., Franklin Park, 1974-76; sr. project engr. Motorola Data Products, Carol Stream, 1976-79, Zenith Electronics Co., Glenview, 1979-82, market rsch. mgr., 1982-85, sect. mgr., 1985-86, program mgr., 1988-95; mgr. displays Zenith Data Sys./Groupe Bull, Buffalo Grove, 1995-96; v.p. mktg. AVC Tech, Niles, 1996-97; product mgr. Visiontek, Gurnee, 1997; dir. product planning Telular, Inc., Vernon Hills, 1997-98; mgr. product mktg. Motorola BCS/SBNS, Schiller Park, 1998—2001; sr. cons. Pro-Team Cons., Palatine, 2001—03; engring. mgr. Graphic Solutions, Inc., 2003—. Faculty Wright Jr. Coll., Chgo., 1975-80. Mem. editl. bd. Electronic Products Mag., 1976-77. Adviser Jr. Achievement, Chgo., 1972-78; treas. I.C. Christian Svc. Commn., 1988-91; vol. Pub. Action to Deliver Shelter, 1987-2000; alderman 5th ward Elmhurst, 1993—; vice-chmn. fin. com. City of Elmhurst, 1995-2003, vice chmn. Pub. Works and Bldg. com., 2003—, vice-chmn. telecom. and tech. adv. group, chmn. pub. works and bldg. com., 2002-. Mem. IEEE Midcon. (vice-chmn. pub. rels. 1979, chmn. spl. exhibits 1981, vice-chmn. spl. exhibits 1983), Delta Mu Delta. Home: 421 Berkley Ave Elmhurst IL 60126-3706 E-mail: jimparker@ameritech.net.

PARKER, JAMES K. corporate lawyer; b. Des Moines, July 21, 1929; s. Kermit Union and Alice J. (Phillips) Parker. BS, UCLA, Los Angeles, Calif.; LLB, U. Calif.-Berkeley, Berkeley, Calif. Counsel Kaiser Industries Corp., Oakland, 1961—68, v.p., asst. chief counsel, 1969—70, v.p., gen. counsel, 1970—77, pres., 1977—78, dir., 1972—80; v.p. Kaiser Cement Corp., 1970—76, Kaiser Steele Corp., 1974—76; v.p., gen. counsel CBS Inc., NYC, 1978—81, sr. v.p., gen. counsel, 1981—87; gen. counsel Advanced Network & Svc., Inc., Elmsford, NY. Office: Advanced Network & Service Inc 100 Clearbrook Rd Elmsford NY 10523-1116

PARKER, JAMES WESLEY, former career naval officer, investment company executive; b. Portsmouth, Va., July 31, 1917; s. Charles Wesley Parker and Dempsey Elizabeth Darden; m. Mary Elizabeth Mara, Oct. 12, 1946; children: Diane Marie Wright, Susan Gertrude Kennelly. BA, Elon U., 1939; MBA, Stanford U., 1951. Registered securities broker, life ins. agent, Calif., real estate agt., Calif., registered fin. cons.; accredited estate planner. Commd. ensign USN, 1940, advanced through grades to capt., 1959, ret., 1962; v.p., gen. mgr. so. divsn. Montgomery Bros., Inc., L.A., 1962—66; dir. comm. Master Charge, Western States Bancard Assn., 1967—70; ops. mgr. Nat. BankAmericard, 1971—73; v.p. Bank of Am., 1974—87, Bank of Calif., 1987—92, Pacific Trust Co., 1992—94, Comerica Bank, 1994—95, Kelmoore Investment Co., Palo Alto, Calif., 1996, exec. v.p., 1997—2002, cons., 2002—03. Bd. dirs. Diablo Valley Estate Planning Coun., Walnut Creek, Calif., 1986-95, Planned Giving Coun. Santa Cruz County, Calif., 1993-94, Tri-Valley Estate Planning Coun., 1989-2002, pres. 1996; mem. Santa Clara County Estate Planning Coun., 1988-2002, Estate Planning Coun. So. Alameda County, 1988-92, Santa Cruz County Estate Planning Coun., 1989-2002, San Mateo County Estate Planning Roundtable, 1989-98, Silicon Valley Planned Giving Coun., 1992-, No. Calif. Planned Giving Coun., 1997-2002, Fin. Planning Forum, 1988-, Peninsula Estate Planning Coun., San Mateo, Calif., 1980-, pres., 1996-98, Tri-Valley Estate Planning Coun., 1996; active East Bay Estate Planning Coun., Oakland, Calif., 1991-, pres. 1997-98; bass Calvarymen Gospel Quartet; big band saxaphonist, clarinetist Elon Coll and USS Kasaan Bay; violinist Norfolk Symphony Orch., 1934-35, Bethel Ch. Orch., San Jose, Calif. Mem. Fin. Planning Assn. (bd. dirs. Silicon Valley chpt. 1997-99), Nat. Assn. Estate Planners Couns., Inst. Cert. Investment Mgmt. Cons., Alameda County Bar Assn. (estate planning probate sect. 1988-93), San Mateo County Bar Assn. (estate planning probate sect. 1983-95), Santa Clara County Bar Assn. (estate planning probate sect. 1988-2002), Pi Gamma Mu, Alpha Pi Delta. Avocations: golf, photography, music. Home: 20278 Kilbride Dr Saratoga CA 95070 Office: Kelmoore Investment Co 2471 E Bayshore Rd # 501 Palo Alto CA 94303

PARKER, JEFFREY SCOTT, law educator; b. Alexandria, Va., Sept. 6, 1952; s. Clarence Franklin and Mary Florence (Partlow) P. B in Indsl. Engring., Ga. Inst. Tech., 1975; JD, U. Va., 1978. Bar: N.Y. 1979, U.S. Dist. Ct. (ea. and so. dists.) N.Y. 1979, U.S. Ct. Appeals (3d cir.) 1981, U.S. Ct. Appeals (2d cir.) 1984, U.S. Supreme Ct. 1984, U.S. Ct. Appeals (fed. cir.) 1985, U.S. Ct. Appeals (4th cir.) 1992, U.S. Ct. Appeals (D.C. cir.) 1997. Assoc. Sullivan & Cromwell, N.Y.C., 1978-86, Sacks Montgomery, N.Y.C., 1986-87; dep. chief counsel U.S. Sentencing Commn., Washington, 1987-88; of counsel Sacks Montgomery, N.Y.C., 1988-90; assoc. prof. law George Mason U Sch. Law, Arlington, Va., 1990-94; prof. George Mason U. Sch. Law, Arlington, Va., 1994—, assoc. dean acad. affairs, 1994-96. Cons. counsel U.S. Sentencing Commn., Washington, 1988-89. Contbr. articles to law revs.; mem. editorial bd. Va. Law Rev., 1976-78. Mem. ABA, Assn. of Bar of City of N.Y., N.Y. State Bar Assn., Am. Law and Econs. Assn., Am. Econs. Assn., Am. Judicature Soc. Office: George Mason U Sch of Law 3401 Fairfax Dr Arlington VA 22201-4411 E-mail: jparke3@gmu.edu.

PARKER, JOANN MAUDIE, freelance/self-employed writer, retired reporter; b. Lodi, Calif., Dec. 17, 1938; d. Charles Edward Gunier and Irene Virginia Goupp-Gunier; m. C.T. Parker, Nov. 3, 1956; children: Barbara Lynn, Candra Ann, Troy Eward. Attended, Delta Coll., 1980—90. Reporter, feature writer Stockton Record, Calif., 1963—70; bookkeeper C.T. Parker Trucking, Lodi, Calif., 1964—93; reporter, feature writer Clements-Lockeford News, 1975—82, Lodi Life & Times, 1979—81; bookkeeper Ordermatic of Calif., Lodi, 1982—93; retired, 1993. Sec., treas. Clements-Lockeford C. of C., 1980—83; v.p. Lodi Writer's Group, 1983—93. Mem.: Lauderdale County Arts Coun. Achievements include raising and showing Rottweiler Dogs 1985-2000; raising and showing Appaloosa & Quarter horses 1970-1990. Home: 320 Joe Barfield Rd Henning TN 38041

PARKER, JOHN HILL, lawyer; b. High Point, N.C., Feb. 1, 1944; s. George Edward and Tullia Virginia (Hill) Parker; m. Lynette Becton Smith, July 7, 1977; children from previous marriage: Alice Lindsey, Elizabeth Shelby(dec.). BA, U. N.C., 1966; JD, U. Tenn., 1969. Bar: N.C. 1969, U.S. Dist. Ct. (ea. dist.) N.C. 1970, U.S. Supreme Ct. 1975. Assoc. Sanford, Cannon, Adams & McCullough, Raleigh, NC, 1969-73; pvt. practice Raleigh, 1974-76; judge N.C. Dist. Ct., Raleigh, 1976-82; ptnr. Cheshire & Parker, Raleigh, 1982—. Instr. judges seminars Inst. Govt., Chapel Hill, NC, 1977—82. Mem. Raleigh Arts Commn., 1981—84, chmn., 1983; parlementarian Wake County Dems., 1971—73. Fellow: Am. Acad. Matrimonial Lawyers (mem. ethics com. 1995—97, pres. N.C. chpt. 1999); mem.: ABA, Wake County Bar Assn., N.C. Acad. Trial Lawyers, N.C. Bar Assn. (editor newsletter family law sect. 1984—86, chmn. 1985—86, 1996—97, CLE family law 1979—, chmn. 1985—87, 1996—98, chmn. ethics com. 1989—90, mem. gen. curriculum com. 1989—2003, mem. trial practice curriculum com. 2004—). Episcopalian. Avocations: travel, backpacking, fishing, reading, music. Home: 1620 Park Dr Raleigh NC 27605-1609 Office: Cheshire & Parker PO Box 1029 133 Fayetteville St Mall Raleigh NC 27601-1356 Office Phone: 919-833-3114. Business E-Mail: John.Parker@Cheshirepark.com.

PARKER, JOHN MALCOLM, management and financial consultant; b. Halifax, N.S., Can., June 13, 1920; came to U.S., 1936, naturalized, 1942; s. Charles Fisher and Mabel (Hennigar) P.; m. Irene Wilson Davis, Oct. 11, 1942 (dec. Nov. 1987); 1 child, Elane Parker Jones; m. Kathryn Harvey Smithey, Apr. 22, 1989. Cert. internal auditor. With Standard Oil Co. N.J., Charlotte, N.C., 1941, Duke Power Co., Charlotte, 1941-42, Do. Bell Tel. & Tel. Co., Charlotte, 1946-50, Atlanta, 1950-68, South Ctrl. Bell Telephone Co., Birmingham, Ala., 1968-83, asst. v.p., gen. internal auditor; pres. Omega Assocs. Inc., 1983 . Commr. gen. assembly Presbyn. Ch. of U.S., 1980, 81. With AUS, 1942-46. Mem. Inst. Mgmt. Accts. (pres. local chpt. 1972-73, nat. dir.), Am. Mgmt. Assn., Inst. Internal Auditors (pres. chpt. 1978-79, dist. dir. 1979-81, regional dir. 1981-83, internat. vice chmn. 1983-84, internat. bd. dirs. 1979-87, v.p. found. 1984-85), Internat. Platform Assn. Republican. Home and Office: 4509 Clairmont Ave S Birmingham AL 35222-4438

PARKER, JOHN MARCHBANK, consulting geologist; b. Manhattan, Kans., Sept. 13, 1920; s. John Huntington and Marjorie Elizabeth (Marchbank) P.; m. Agnes Elizabeth Potts, Mar. 17, 1978; m. Jan Goble, July 18, 1941 (div. 1968); children— Susan Kelly, Elizabeth Douglass, Deirdre Parker, John Eric; m. Nancy Booth, Jan. 24, 1970 (div. 1974). Student U. Minn., 1937, U. Wyo., 1938; B.S., Kans. State U., 1941. Cert. petroleum geologist Am. Inst. Profl. Geologists. Geologist, U.S. Pub. Roads Adminstrn., Alaska Hwy., Can., 1942-43; Field geologist Imperial Oil Ltd., Northwest Ter., Can., 1943-44; dist. geologist Stanolind Oil & Gas Co., Casper, Wyo., 1944-52; v.p. exploration Kirby Petroleum Co., Houston, 1952-74; v.p. exploration Northwest Exploration Co., Denver, 1974-75; cons. geologist Dana Point, Calif., 1975— . Contbr. articles to profl. jours. Recipient Disting. Service in Geology award Kans. State U., 1983. Fellow AAAS, Geol. Soc. Am.; mem. Am. Assn. Petroleum Geologists (pres. 1982-83, adv. council Tulsa 1983-84, Hon. Mem. award), Rocky Mountain Assn. Geologists (explorer of yr. 1979; pres. 1980-81). Home: 25401 Sea Bluffs DR #139 Dana Point CA 92629-2190

PARKER, JOHN OSMYN, management consultant; b. Denver, May 31, 1919; s. George Lindsey and Marie (Bloedorn) P.; m. Judith Fehr, July 20, 1942; children: Craig Steven, John Fehr, Diane, Newton Lindsey. BS in Bus., U. Colo., 1942. Jr. indsl. engr. U.S. Steel Corp., Gary, Ind., 1942-43; mgr. pers. rsch. TWA, Kansas City, Mo., 1945-55; mgmt. cons. Douglas Williams Assocs., N.Y.C., 1955-56; dir. pers. Ctrl. Hudson Gas & Electric Corp., Poughkeepsie, NY, 1956—69, United Hosp., Port Chester, NY, 1969-78; v.p. human resources Mountainside Hosp., Montclair, NJ, 1978-83; mgmt. cons., 1983—. Instr. mgmt. Rutgers U., Ocean County Coll. Author: A Genealogical History of the Parker Family, 1996. Chmn. budget divsn., bd. dirs. United Way, Dutchess County, N.Y., 1963-69; mem. adv. bd. Montclair Salvation Army; pres. Fellowship Club, Presbyn. Ch., 1985, elder, trustee, deacon; mem. Garden State Philharm. Chorus. With U.S. Army, 1943-45, ETO. Mem. Soc. for Human Resources Mgmt. (accredited exec. in pers.), Am. Soc. Tng. Dirs., Am. Mgmt. Assn., Am. Legion (trustee 1990-92, chaplain 1991-95), DAV (comdr. 1988-90, trustee 1990-2003), Rotary (bd. dirs. Rye, N.Y. 1975-78, pres. 1977-78, bd. dirs. Montclair 1978-83, bd. dirs. Ctrl. Ocean, Toms River, N.J. 1985-88, 94-95), Phi Kappa Psi. Republican. Home: Apt C111 50 Lacey Rd Whiting NJ 08759-4113 E-mail: Parker770@msn.com.

PARKER, JOHN R., JR., food products executive, lawyer; V.p., gen. counsel The Coca-Cola Bottling Co. of N.Y., 1993—95; counsel for Nordic and No. Eurasia Divsn. The Coca-Cola Co., 1995; gen. counsel. European group Coca-Cola Enterprises, 1996—99, sr. v.p., gen. counsel, 1999—. Office: Coca-Cola Enterprises 2500 Windy Ridge Pkwy Atlanta GA 30339

PARKER, JOHN VICTOR, federal judge; b. Baton Rouge, La., Oct. 14, 1928; m. Mary Elizabeth Fridge, Sept. 3, 1949; children: John Michael, Robert Fridge, Linda Anne. BA, La. State U., 1949, JD, 1952. Bar: La. 1952. Atty. Parker & Parker, Baton Rouge, 1954-66; asst. parish atty. City of Baton Rouge, Parish of East Baton Rouge, 1956-66; atty. Sanders, Downing, Kean & Cazedessus, Baton Rouge, 1966-79; chief judge U.S. Dist. Ct., Middle Dist. La., Baton Rouge, 1979—. Vis. lectr. law La. State U. Law Sch. Served with Judge Adv. Gen.'s Corps U.S. Army, 1952-54. Mem. ABA, Am. Judicature Soc., Am. Arbitration Assn., La. State Bar Assn. (past mem. bd. govs.), Baton Rouge Bar Assn. (past pres.), Order of Coif, Phi Delta Phi. Clubs: Baton Rouge Country. Lodges: Masons (32 deg.); Kiwanis (past pres.). Democrat. Office: Russell B Long Fed Bldg & Courthouse 777 Florida St Ste 355 Baton Rouge LA 70801-1717

PARKER, JOHN WILLIAM, retired pathology educator, investigator; b. Clifton, Ariz., Jan. 5, 1931; m. Barbara A. Atkinson; children: Ann Elizabeth, Joy Noelle, John David, Heidi Susan. BS, U. Ariz., 1953; MD, Harvard U., 1957. Diplomate Am. Bd. Pathology. Clin. instr. pathology U. Calif. Sch. Medicine, San Francisco, 1962-64; asst. prof. U. So. Calif. Sch. Medicine, L.A., 1964-68, assoc. prof., 1968-75, prof., 1975-98, prof. emeritus, 1998—, dir. clin. labs., 1974-94, vice chmn. dept. pathology, 1985-97, dir. pathology reference labs., 1991-94, assoc. dean sci. affairs, 1987-89, prof. emeritus, 1998—. Co-chmn. 15th Internat. Leucocyte Culture Conf., Asilomar, Calif., 1982; chmn. 2d Internat. Lymphoma Conf., Athens, Greece, 1981; v.p. faculty senate U. So. Calif., 1991-92; bd. dirs. ann. meeting Clin. Applications of Cytometry, Charleston, S.C., 1988-97. Founding editor (jour.) Hematological Oncology, 1982-93; assoc. editor Jour. Clin. Lab. Analysis, 1985-98; co-editor: Intercellular Communication in Leucocyte Function, 1983; founding co-editor (jour.) Communications in Clin. Cytometry, 1993-97; contbr. over 200 articles to profl. jours., chpts. to books. Named sr. oncology fellow Am. Cancer Soc., U. So. Calif. Sch. Medicine, 1964-69, Nat. Cancer Inst. vis. fellow Walter and Eliza Hall Inst. for Med. Rsch., Melbourne, Australia, 1972-73. Fellow Coll. Am. Pathologists, Am. Soc. Clin. Pathologists; mem. Am. Assn. Pathologists, Am. Soc. Hematology, Internat. Acad. Pathology, Clin. Cytometry Soc. (v.p. 1994-95, pres. 1995-97), Phi Beta Kappa, Phi Kappa Phi. Avocations: gardening, reading, hiking.

PARKER, JOSEPH CORBIN, JR., pathologist, educator; b. Richmond, Va., Aug. 1, 1937; s. Joseph Corbin and Alice Cabell (Horsley) P.; m. Patricia Hugh Singleton, June 24, 1961; children: John Randolph, Nancy Jordan. BA, Va. Mil. Inst., 1958; MD, Med. Coll. Va., 1962; MS in Pathology, U. Minn., 1968. Fellow Mayo Clinic, Rochester, Minn., 1963-68; fellow in neuropathology Duke U., Durham, NC, 1968—69, asst. prof., 1969-70, Harvard U., Boston, 1970-71; assoc. prof. U. Ky., Lexington, 1971-75; prof. U. Miami, Fla., 1975-81; assoc. dean, prof. U. Tenn., Knoxville, 1981-86; prof. pathology, chmn. U. Mo., Kansas City, 1986-92; prof. pathology U. Louisville Sch. Medicine, 1996—2002, chmn. Dept. Pathology, 1992—2002, dir. grad. med. edn., 2002—. Bd. dirs. Truman Med. Ctr., Kansas City, Mo., Hosp. Hill Health Svc., Kansas City; cons. in field. Author 4 chpts. in books; contbr. more than 120 articles to profl. jours. Bd. dirs. Multiple Sclerosis Soc., Knoxville, Tenn., 1985, Alzheimers Assn., Kansas City, 1988-91. With Med. Corp, USAR, 1958-67. Recipient 1st Jackson -Hope medal Va. Mil. Inst., 1958; Caldwell award Alzheimers Assn., 1986. Fellow Am. Asns. Neuropathology, Am. Soc. Clin. Pathology, Coll. Am. Pathology, Assn. Clin. Scientists (pres. 2000); mem. So. Med. Assn., Am. Acad. Neurology, Am. Assn. Neurol. Surgeons, Univ. Pathologists (pres. 1993-2001). Republican. Unitarian Universalist. Achievements include discovery of autosomal recessive neonatal adrenal leuko-distrophy, and types of cerebral mycoses at autopsy. Home: 4606 Wolf Creek Pky Louisville KY 40241-5502 Office: U Louisville Sch Medicine Dept Pathology Louisville KY 40292-0001 Office Phone: 502-852-6515.

PARKER, JOSEPH MAYON, retired publishing executive; b. Washington, N.C., Oct. 11, 1931; s. James Mayon and Mildred (Poe) Parker; m. Lauretta Owen Dyer, Mar. 23, 1957; children: Katherine Suzanne, Joseph Wilbur. Student, Davidson Coll., 1949-51; BA, U. N.C., 1953, MPA, 1992; postgrad., Carnegie Inst. Tech., 1955-56. From mgr. print divsn. to pres. Parker Bros., Inc., Ahoskie, NC, 1956—77, pres., CEO, 1977—2001; ret., 2001. Editor, columnist: 5 cmty. newspapers; panelist (TV series) North Carolina This Week, 1986—89. Treas. Chowan Graphic Arts Found., Murfreesboro, NC, 1971—90, pres., 1990—92; mem. Ind. Devel. Commn., 1974—86; dir. Gov.'s Hwy. Safety Program, 1993—2001; vice chmn. N.C. Goals and Policy Bd., Raleigh, 1977—84; pres. Com. of 100, Winton, NC, 1984—87; chmn. Northeastern N.C. Tomorrow, Elizabeth City, 1981—84, sec., 1984—90; mem. Meth. Bd. Pub., 2004—; del. Dem. Nat. Conv., N.Y.C., 1980, mem. platform com., 1988; dist. chmn. N.C. Dem. Ctrl. Com., 1980—82; bd. dirs. Wake Dem. Men, 2004—; trustee Pitt County Meml. Hosp., 1980—88. With U.S. Army, 1953—54, col. USAR, 1954—88. Mem.: Roanoke Island Hist. Assn. (vice-chmn. 1987—89), Nat. Newspaper Assn. (state chmn. 1976—83), N.C. Press Assn., E. N.C. Press Assn. (past pres.), Soc. Profl. Journalists, Eastern N.C. C. of C. (past chmn.), Raleigh Exec. Club, Rotary. Democrat. Methodist. Avocations: golf, reading. Home: 4500 Connell Dr Raleigh NC 27612-5600 Personal E-mail: jpark4173@aol.com.

PARKER, JOYCE WHITE, application developer, educator; b. Seattle, Wash., Feb. 26, 1948; d. Ellison Fred and Olive Joneson White. BS, U. of Wis., Madison, 1966—72. Cert. tchg. learning-disabled NC Dept. of Pub. Instrn., 1993. Educator Maple Tree Learning Ctr., Cherokee, NC, 2000—; tchr. Cherokee Ctrl. Schools, Cherokee, 1993—2000. Author: (computer programs) Maple Tree Multiplication Package and Maple Tree Fraction Package. Bd. mem. NC Agrl. Ext. Agy., Cherokee, 1994—2004. Episcopal. Avocations: computer graphics, reading, gardening, creative cooking, stamp collecting/philately. Home: 3049 Old Number 4 Road Box 562 Cherokee NC 28719 Office: Maple Tree Learning Center 3049 Old Number 4 Road Box 562 Cherokee NC 28719 Office Phone: 828-497-6759. E-mail: jparker@dnet.net.

PARKER, KATHLEEN KAPPEL, state legislator; b. Pitts., Sept. 21, 1943; m. Keith Parker; 2 children. BA, U. Miami, 1968. Tax assessor Northfield Twp., 1979-83; mem. Regional Transp. Authority Bd., 1983-95; del. Ill. and Nat. Rep. Convs., 1988; Northfield Twp. coord. George Bush's Presdl. Campaign, 1988; mem. U.S. Archtl. and Transp. Barriers Compliance Bd., 1991-94; Ill. state sen., 1995—. Mem. Fin. Inst., vice chair Pub. Health and Welfare Coms., Transp. Com., 1995—, chair; co-owner Keith Parker and Assocs., 1985—; pres., bd. dirs. Chgo. divsn. Busch Jewelry Co., 1988-93. Chair Mental Health Task Force. Mem. Northeastern Ill. Planning Coun., Met. Planning Coun. Office: 4104 Timberlane Dr Northbrook IL 60062-6123

PARKER, KEVIN JAMES, electrical engineer, educator; BS in Engring. Sci. summa cum laude, SUNY, Buffalo, 1976; MSEE, MIT, 1978, PhD, 1981. Rsch. assoc. lab. for med. ultrasound MIT, Cambridge, 1977-81; asst. prof. dept. elec. engring. U. Rochester, NY, 1981-85, assoc. prof., 1985-91, assoc. prof. dept. radiology, 1989-91, prof., 1992—, chair, 1992-98, dean sch. engring. & applied scis., 1998—. Com. mem. Internat. Symposium Ultrasound Imaging, 1989—; dir. Rochester Ctr. Biomedical Ultrasound, 1990—. Mem. editl. bd. Ultras. Med. Biology, 1989—; contbr. articles to profl. jours. Named IBM Supercomputing Contest finalist, 1989; recipient Ultrasound Medicine and Biology prize, World Fed., 1991, Outstanding Innovation award, Eastman Kodak Co., 1991; fellow, NIH, 1979; Lilly Tchg. fellow, 1982. Fellow: IEEE, Am. Inst. Ultrasound Medicine (ethics com. 1987—90, stds. com. 1990—93, bd. govs. 1996—99, Joseph P. Holmes Pioneer award 1999); mem.: Acoustical Soc. Achievements include patents in field. Office: Univ of Rochester Sch Engring & Applied Scis Lattimore Bldg Rm 309 Rochester NY 14627-0076

PARKER, KEVIN T. computer company executive; BS in Acctg., Clarkson U. With O'Neil Data Sys., Toshiba Am. Info. Sys., CalComp, Price Waterhouse; contr. sys. product divsn. Std. Microsystems; sr. v.p. fin. and adminstrn. Fujitsu Computer Products Am., 1996—99; sr. v.p., CFO Aspect Comm. Corp., 1999—2000, PeopleSoft, Inc., Pleasonton, Calif., 2000—02, exec. v.p. fin. and adminstrn., CFO, 2002—. Office: PeopleSoft Inc 4460 Hacienda Dr Pleasanton CA 94588*

PARKER, LEONARD S. architect, educator; b. Warsaw, Jan. 16, 1923; came to U.S. 1923; s. Rueben and Sarah (Kollica) Popuch; m. Betty Mae Buegen, Sept. 1, 1948 (dec. 1983); children— Bruce Aaron, Jonathan Arthur, Nancy Anne, Andrew David BArch., U. Minn., 1948; MArch., MIT, 1950. Sr. designer Eero Saarinen Assocs., Bloomfield Hills, Mich., 1950-56; CEO, chmn. bd., pres., dir. design The Leonard Parker Assocs., Mpls., 1957-97; pres., dir. design The Alliance Southwest, Phoenix, 1981-91; chmn. bd. dirs. The Leonard Parker Assocs., Minn., 1997—. Prof. grad. program Sch. Architecture, U. Minn., Mpls., 1959—; pres. Minn. Archtl. Found., 1991. Author: Abandoning the Catalogs, 1979, Rivers of Modernism, 1986, Collaboration-Same Bed, Different Dream? Panel mem. Mpls. City Hall Restoration Com., Am. Arbitration Assn., USAF bd. visitors (chmn.). Served with U.S. Army, 1943-46; ETO Firm has received 84 nat. and regional awards for design excellence. Fellow AIA; mem. Minn. Soc. Architects (pres. 1981, Gold medal 1986, pres. Mpls. chpt. 1979), Tau Sigma Delta. Home: 3936 Willmatt Hl Hopkins MN 55305-5142 Office: The Leonard Parker Assocs 430 Oak Grove St Ste 300 Minneapolis MN 55403-3234

PARKER, MARIETTA, prosecutor; Asst. U.S. atty. Dept. Justice, Kansas City, Mo.; U.S. atty. Dept. Justice, Kansas City, Mo., 1993—. Office: US Attys Office 1201 Walnut St Ste 300 Kansas City MO 64106-2136

PARKER, MARY-LOUISE, actress; b. Ft. Jackson, S.C., Aug. 2, 1964; 1 child, William Atticus. Attended, Bard Coll. Actress: (theatre) Hay Fever, 1987, The Miser, 1988, The Art of Success, 1989, The Importance of Being Earnest, 1989, Prelude to a Kiss, Broadway, 1990-91 (Theatre World award, Clarence Derwent Award, Tony nomination, 1990), Babylon Gardens, 1991, How I Learned to Drive, 1997 (Lucille Lortel Award for outstanding actress, OBIE Award, 1997), Proof, Broadway (Tony award for best actress in a play, 2001);(films) Signs of Life, 1989, Longtime Companion, 1990, Grand Canyon, 1991, Fried Green Tomatoes, 1991, Mr. Wonderful, 1993, Naked in New York, 1994, The Client, 1994, Bullets Over Broadway, 1994, Boys on the Side, 1995, A Portrait of a Lady, 1996, Reckless, 1995, Murder in Mind, 1997, The Maker, 1997, Let the Devil Wear Black, 1998, Goodbye, Lover, 1998, Five Senses, 1999, Pipe Dream, 2002, Red Dragan, 2002, The Best Thief in the World, 2004, others; (TV movies) Too Young the Hero, 1988, A Place for Annie, 1994, Sugartime, 1995, Legalese, 1998, Saint Maybe, 1998, The Simple Life of Noah Dearborn, 1999, Cupid & Cate, 2000, Master Spy: The Robert Hanssen Story, 2002; (TV miniseries) Angels in America, 2003 (Golden Globe for best supporting actress 2004); (TV series) Ryan's Hope, 1975, West Wing, 2001- (Emmy nomination, 2002). Office: William Morris Agy care Scott Henderson 151 S El Camino Dr Beverly Hills CA 90212-2775*

PARKER, MEL, editor; b. N.Y.C., Feb. 11, 1949; s. David Parker and Mollie (Kantorowicz) Lederman; m. Diane Nancy Goldberg, June 27, 1971; children: Emily, David. AB, Rutgers U., 1971; AM in English, NYU, 1973. Editl. rschr. Esquire Mag., N.Y.C., 1973; grad. asst. NYU Dept. English, 1974-77; adj. lectr. CUNY, 1977-78; editor Leisure Books, N.Y.C., 1978-81; sr. editor Playboy Paperbacks, N.Y.C., 1981-82, Berkley Pub. Group, N.Y.C., 1982-85, exec. editor, 1985-86, editor-in-chief, 1986-87; v.p. editor-in-chief Warner Paperbacks, 1987-90, pub., 1990-96; sr. v.p. Warner Books, N.Y.C., 1996-98, sr. v.p., editor-in-chief Book-of-the-Month Club, 1999-2000; editl. dir. Book-

span, 2000—03; pres. Mel Parker Books, LLC, 2004—. Co-chair exec. pub. com. United Jewish Appeal Fedn.; mem. faculty Stanford Pub. Course, 1997-98. Mem. Jerusalem Book Fair Com., 1997—. Mem. Assn. Am. Publs. (chmn. trade exec. com. 1997-99), Book Table, Pub. Lunch Club (sec.-treas. 2000-01, v.p. 2001-02, pres. 2002-03). E-mail: mel.parker@bookspan.com., mel@melparkerbooks.com.

PARKER, MICHAEL (MIKE PARKER), federal agency administrator; b. Laurel, Miss., Oct. 31, 1949; m. Rosemary Prather; children: Adrian, Marisa, Thomas. BA, William Carey Coll., 1970. Operator various businesses; mem. U.S. Congress from 4th Miss. dist., 1989-99; prin. Parker Malvaney Consulting, Brookhaven, Miss., 2000—01; asst. secy. civil works U.S. Dept. Defense, Washington, 2001—. Presbyterian. Office: US Dept Defense Civil Works 108 Army Pentagon Washington DC 20310-0108

PARKER, MICHAEL D. chemicals executive; BSChemE, U. Manchester (Eng.); MBA, Manchester Bus. Sch. With organics R & D Dow Internat., Freeport, Tex., 1968, prodn. engr., field sales position Birmingham, Eng., 1972-75, dist. sales mgr., 1975-77; product mktg. mgr. Epoxy resins Dow Europe, 1977, dir. mktg. inorganic chems., dir. mktg. organic chems., comml. dir. functional products dept., 1983-84; gen. mgr. splty. chems. dept. Dow U.S.A., Midland, Mich., 1984-87, group v.p. chems. and hydrocarbons, 1993-95; comml. v.p. Dow Pacific, Hong Kong, 1987-88, pres., 1988-93; pres., bus. v.p. chems. Dow N.Am., Midland, 1995—96; exec. v.p. Dow Chem. Co., Midland, 1996—2000, pres., CEO, 2000—, also bd. dirs. Bd. dirs. Dow Corning Corp. Bd. dirs. Nat. Legal Ctr. Pub. Interest. Mem. Nat. Assn. Mfrs. (bd. dirs.), Am. Plastics Coun. (bd. dirs.), Am. Chemistry Coun.

PARKER, MICHAEL J. editor, writer, researcher; b. Camden, NJ, Apr. 21, 1959; s. Harry J. and Charlotte D. Parker. BA, Glassboro State Coll., 1981. Mng. editor, regional editor Suburban Newspaper Group, Cherry Hill, NJ, 1980-82; database sketch editor Lehigh Press, Pennsauken, NJ, 1983; copy control editor, assoc. supr. Datapro, Delran, NJ, 1984-95, sr. data quality adminstr., 1996-98; editor Gartner Datapro, Delran, NJ, 1998—, spl. projects U.S. and abroad, 2002—. Article writer, columnist Silent Film Monthly, Silent Film Annual-U.S., Canada, Europe, Far East, 1993-2000; freelance writer, 2001—; cons. to film historians- U.S., Europe; contbr. articles to The Grapevine. Assoc., coord. Homeless Hospitality Network, Merchantville, N.J., 1995-2002; rep. Echelon Mall Ministry, Voorhees, N.J., 1975-76; asst. to clergy First Presbyn. Ch., 1992—; editor promotion, Anthony Griggs Found. for the Advancement of Youth. Recipient cert. Borough of Haddonfield Commrs., 1981, Commendations Maple Shade Bd. of Edn. Avocations: writing to members of the arts (U.S. and overseas), collecting autographed items, exhibits, stamps, coins. Office: Gartner Datapro 600 Delran Pkwy Delran NJ 08075-1255 Business E-Mail: mike.parker@gartner.com.

PARKER, NANCY KNOWLES (MRS. CORTLANDT PARKER), retired publishing executive; b. Buffalo, Aug. 30, 1929; d. Ward Emerson and Barbara Louise (Bull) Knowles; m. Cortlandt Parker, Sept. 8, 1951; children: Elizabeth, Cortlandt, Stephen, Nancy Gray. Student, Chevy Chase Jr. Coll., 1949. Copy girl Washington Evening Star, 1947-49; reporter Newark Evening News, 1949-51; asst. pub. rels. dir. Newark Cmty. Chest, 1951-52; writer Suburban Life mag., Summit, NJ, 1952-55; co-founder, assoc. editor, then editor Observer Tribune, Mendham, NJ, 1955-59; cmty. living editor Recorder Pub. Co., Bernardsville, NJ, 1959-84, v.p., 1960—2002; pub. emeritus, 2002—; editor, pub. New Eng., Finger Lakes, L.I. and Va. Wine Gazettes, 1988—. Pres. Greenvale Vineyards, Portsmouth, R.I. Former trustee Somerset Hills Cmty. Chest, North Jersey Tng. Sch., Totowa, Morris-Somerset chpt. UN Assn., Bonnie Brae Ednl. Ctr., Millington, N.J. Vis. Homemaker Svc. of Somerset County (N.J.); trustee, bd. dirs. Camp Brett-Endeavor, Clinton, N.J., N.J. Hist. Soc., Newark, Morristown (N.J.) Meml. Hosp.; mem. Glen Manor House Com., Portsmouth, R.I. Mem. Bus. and Profl. Women, Nat. Soc. Arts and Letters, Southeastern New Eng. Grape Growers Assn., Jr. League, Pen and Brush N.Y.C., New Eng. Wine Coun. (sec.), Friends of Whitehall, Colonial Dames in Am. (former bd. dirs. R.I. chpt.), Newport (R.I.) Garden Club (bd. dirs., past pres.), English Speaking Union. Home: 582 Wapping Rd Portsmouth RI 02871-5306 Office: Greenvale Farm & Vineyard 582 Wapping Rd Portsmouth RI 02871-5306 also: 17 Morristown Rd Bernardsville NJ 07924-2312 Office Phone: 401-847-3268.

PARKER, NANCY WINSLOW, artist, writer; b. Maplewood, N.J., Oct. 18, 1930; d. Winslow Aurelius and Beatrice (Gaunt) P. BA, Mills Coll., 1952; student, Sch. Visual Art, N.Y.C., Art Students League. Pub. rels. exec. N.Y. Soccer Club, N.Y.C., 1961-63; with RCA, N.Y.C., 1964-67; art dir. Appleton-Century-Crofts, N.Y.C., 1968-70; staff designer Holt Reinhart & Winston, N.Y.C., 1970-73; free lance writer, illustrator, 1974—. Author, illustrator: The Man with the Take-Apart Head, 1974, The Party at the Old Farm, 1975, Mrs. Wilson Wanders Off, 1976, Love from Uncle Clyde, 1977, The Crocodile Under Louis Finneberg's Bed, 1978, The President's Cabinet, 1978, rev. edit., 1991, The Ordeal of Byron B. Blackbear, 1979, Puddums, The Cathcarts' Orange Cat, 1980, Poofy Loves Company, 1980 (ALA Notable Book, 1980), The Spotted Dog, 1980, The President's Car, 1981, Cooper, The McNally's Big Black Dog, 1981, Love from Aunt Betty, 1983, The Christmas Camel, 1983, The United Nations from A to Z, 1985, Working Frog, 1992; co-author: Money, Money, Money, 1995, Locks, Crocs and Skeeters, The Story of the Panama Canal, 1996, Land Ho! Fifty Glorious Years in The Age of Exploration with 12 Important Explorers, 2001; illustrator Oh, A Hunting We Will Go!, 1974, Warm as Wool, Cool as Cotton, The Story of Natural Fibers, 1975, The Goat in the Rug, 1976, Willy Bear, 1976 (Christopher award, 1976), Sweetly Sings the Donkey, 1976, The Substitute, 1977, Hot Cross Buns and Other Old Street Cries, 1978, No Bath Tonight, 1978, My Mom Travels a Lot, 1981 (Christopher award, 1981), Paul Revere's Ride, 1985, General Store, 1988, Aren't You Coming Too?, 1988, Peter's Pockets, 1988, The Jacket I Wear in the Snow, 1989, At Grammy's House, 1990, Black Crow, Black Crow, 1991, When The Rooster Crowed, 1991, Barbara Frietchie, 1992, The Dress I'll Wear to the Party, 1992, Sheridan's Ride, 1993, Here Comes Henny, 1994, The Bag I'm Taking to Grandma's, 1995, We're Making Breakfast for Mother, 1996, The House I'll Build for the Wrens, 1997, I'm Taking a Trip on My Train, 1999, I'm Not Feeling Well Today, 2001, Our Class Took a Trip to the Zoo, 2002. Sec. East 74th St. Block Assn., 1974-83. Recipient various awards, 1974—; Jane Tinkham Broughton fellow, Breadloaf, Vt., 1975. Mem. Author's Guild, Mills Coll. Club of N.Y., Mantoloking Yacht Club. Home: Apt 3R 51 E 74th St New York NY 10021-2717 E-mail: nwparker52@aol.com.

PARKER, OLIVIA, photographer; b. Boston, June 10, 1941; d. Harvey Perley and Barbara Ellen (Churchill) Hood; m. John Otis Parker, Apr. 4, 1964; children: John Otis, Helen Elizabeth. BA, Wellesley Coll., 1963. Tchr. photog. workshops, 1975—. Photographer, 1969—; author: (monographs) Signs of Life, 1978, Under the Looking Glass, 1983, Weighing the Planets, 1987; portfolios of black and white photographs Ephemera, 1977, Lost Objects, 1980; one-woman shows include, Vision Gallery, Boston, 1976, 77, 79, 82, 83, 86, 87, Friends of Photography, Carmel, Calif., 1979, 81, Marcuse Pfeifer, N.Y.C., 1980, 83, George Eastman House, Rochester, N.Y., 1981, Art Inst. Chgo., 1982, Photo Gallery Internat., Tokyo, 1983, 84, 87, Fotografie Forum Gallery, Frankfurt, Germany, 1985, Lieberman and Saul, N.Y.C., 1988, Mus. Photographic Arts, San Diego, 1988, Photographers' Gallery, London, 1990, Brent Sikkema, N.Y.C., 1990, 91, Parco, Tokyo, 1991, ICAC/Weston, Tokyo, 1992, Vision, San Francisco, 1993, Robert Klein, Boston, 1993, 96, 99, Wooster Gardens, N.Y.C., 1996, (with Jerry Uelsmann) Isabella Stewart Gardner Mus., Boston, 1997, Huntington (W.Va.) Mus. of Art, 2000, Lancaster (Pa.) Mus. of Art, 2000, Toledo (Ohio) Art Mus., 2002, Visual Arts Ctr. Coll. of Santa Fe, 2003; group shows include, Mus. Fine Arts, Boston, 1978, 92, 93, 96, 99, Chgo. Art Inst., 1978, Internat. Ctr. Photography, N.Y.C., 1985, 87, Fogg Art Mus. Harvard U., 1989; represented in permanent collections, Mus. Modern Art, N.Y.C., Art Inst. Chgo., Boston Mus. Fine Arts, Victoria and Albert Mus., London, (TV documentary) Africans in America, 1998. Bd. dirs. MacDowell Colony, 1988—; trustee Art Inst. Boston, 1992—. Artists Found. fellow, 1978; recipient Wellesley College Alumnae Achievement award, 1996. Mem. Soc. for Photog. Edn. Clubs: Chilton. Office: Robert Klein 4th Fl 38 Newbury St Fl 4 Boston MA 02116-3210 E-mail: glasslight@mac.com. *I am interested in the way people think about the unknown. New ideas form, the old are shattered, and sometimes old ideas pop up among the new like graffiti on a wall. All is uncertainty and change, but optimists and bingo players are on the look out for moments of perfect knowledge and perfect cards.*

PARKER, PAM, apparel manufacturing company executive; b. San Francisco, 1960; BA, U. Calif., Berkeley; MBA, Stanford U., 1989. Cons. Bain and Co.; co-founder, co-pres. Ariat Internat., Inc., San Carlos, Calif., 1990—. Office: 26 Heritage Dr San Rafael CA 94901-8308 Address: 800 Redfield Pkwy Apt 174 Reno NV 89509-6533

PARKER, PATRICK STREETER, manufacturing executive; b. Cleve., 1929; BA, Williams Coll., 1951; MBA, Harvard U., 1953. With Parker-Hannifin Corp. and predecessor, Cleve., 1953—, sales mgr. fittings div., 1957-63, mgr. aerospace products div., 1963-65, pres. Parker Seal Co. div., 1965-67, corp. v.p., 1967-69, pres., 1969-71, pres. and chief exec. officer, 1971-77, chmn. bd. and chief exec. officer, 1977-84, chmn. bd., 1984-99, pres., 1982-84, also bd. dirs., 1982-99, chmn. emeritus, 1999—. Bd. trustees Case Western Res. U.; With USN, 1954-57. Mem. Union Club, Country Club, Pepper Pike Club. Office: Parker Hannifin Corp 6035 Parkland Bvld Cleveland OH 44124-4141

PARKER, R. JOSEPH, lawyer; b. St. Louis, June 29, 1944; s. George Joseph and Ann Rosalie Parker; m. Theresa Gaynor, Aug. 26, 1967; children: Christa Michele, Kevin Blake. AB, Georgetown U., 1966; JD, Boston Coll., 1969. Bar: Ohio 1969. Law clk. to judge U.S. Ct. Appeals (6th Cir.), Akron, Ohio, 1969-70; assoc. Taft, Stettinius & Hollister, Cin., 1970-78, ptnr. Arbitrator Am. Arbitration Assn., Cin., 1980—; faculty Nat. Inst. for Trial Advocacy, 1990—; faculty advanced trial advocacy program IRS, 1993. Editor Law Rev. Ann. Survey Mass. Law, 1967-69; contbg. author: Fed. Civil Procedure Before Trial-6th Circuit. Bd. dirs. West End Health Ctr., Inc., Cin., 1972-76, Legal Aid Soc. Cin., 1982-85; chmn. bd. dirs. Vol. Lawyers for Poor Found., Cin., 1986-88; master Am. Inn of Court, 1984—. Fellow Am. Coll. Trial Lawyers; mem. Ohio State Bar Assn., Cin. Bar Assn., Cin. Country Club, Order of Coif. Democrat. Roman Catholic. Office: 425 Walnut St Ste 1800 Cincinnati OH 45202-3759 E-mail: parker18002000@yahoo.com.

PARKER, REBECCA BOLLINGER, emergency physician; b. Oct. 22, 1969; MD, Northwestern U. Med. Sch., 1995. Resident in emergency medicine Tex. Tech. U. Health Sci. Ctr., El Paso, coding, billing, and compliance physician, R.E. Thomason Hosp., El Paso, performance improvement dir., asst. med. dir. to med. dir; attending emergency physician Centegra Health Sys., McHenry and Woodstock, Ill.; med. dir. St. Therese Med. Ctr., Waukegan, Ill.; staff physician St. Therese Hosp., Waukegan; clinical asst. prof. emergency medicine Tex. Tech. U., El Paso. Cons. billing and compliance Team Parker LLC, Lake Forest, Ill. Recipient Excellence in Medicine Leadership award, AMA Found., 2004. Mem.: Tex. Coll. Emergency Physicians (Vol. Yr. award, Pres. Leadership award), Ill. Coll. Emergency Physicians, Am. Coll. Emergency Physicians (chair section young physicians). Office: Team Parker LLC 366 E Wisconsin Ave Lake Forest IL 60045 Office Phone: 847-295-3491.

PARKER, RICHARD ALLAN, music educator; b. Springfield, Ohio, Dec. 19, 1944; s. John Edward and Florence Marion Parker; m. Sharon Kay Willis, Aug. 5, 1967; children: Kari Anama, David, Amy Nichols. BS in edn., Wittenberg U., 1962—66; MA in music edn., Ohio State U., 1966—70, PhD in music edn., 1970—74. Music tchr. Northwestern Cmty. Schools, Springfield, Ohio, 1967—69, Delware City Schools, Delaware, Ohio, 1971—74; prof. of music and music edn. Taylor U., Upland, Ind., 1974—. Dir. of music/choir dir. Grace United Meth., Hartford City, Ind., 1975—; elder hostel coord. Taylor U., Upland, Ind., 1994—. Recipient, Pi Lambda Kappa (Music Hon.), 1971, Outstanding Cmty. Citizen, Hartford City, IN, 1982, Outstanding Coll. Music Educator, Ind. Music Educators Assn., 2000; grantee travel grant, J. Howard Pew Trust Found., 1987; Outstanding Music Student Scholarship, Presser Found., 1964—66, Presdl. Fellowship, Ohio State U., 1970. Mem.: Am. Guild of English Handbell Ringers, Music Educators Nat. Conf. (assoc.). Home: 24 S Shamrock Rd Hartford City IN 47348 Office: Taylor University 236 W Reade Av Upland IN 46989 Personal E-mail: raparker6@insightbb.com. E-mail: rcparker@tayloru.edu.

PARKER, RICHARD WILSON, lawyer, retired rail transportation executive; b. Cleve., June 14, 1943; s. Edgar Gael and Pauline (Wilson) P.; m. Helen Margaret Shober, Jan. 3, 1998; children from previous marriage: Brian Jeffrey, Lauren Michelle, Lisa Christine. BA in Econs. cum laude, U. Redlands, 1965; JD cum laude, Northwestern U., 1968. Bar: Ohio 1968, Va. 1974. Assoc. Arter & Hadden, Cleve., 1968—71; asst. gen. atty. Norfolk & Western Ry. Co., Cleve. and Roanoke, Va., 1971-74, asst. gen. solicitor Roanoke, 1974-78, gen. atty., 1978-84, Norfolk So. Corp., 1985-88, sr. gen. atty., 1988-93, asst. v.p. real estate, 1993-99, v.p. properties, 1999-2000, v.p. real estate, 2000—03. Mem. ABA, Va. State Bar, Norfolk-Portsmouth Bar Assn. Presbyterian. Office: 3 Commercial Pl Norfolk VA 23510-2108

PARKER, ROBERT ALLAN RIDLEY, federal agency administrator, astronaut; b. N.Y.C., Dec. 14, 1936; s. Allan Elwood and Alice (Heywood) P.; m. Joan Audrey Capers, June 14, 1958 (div. 1980); children: Kimberly Ellen, Brian David Capers; m. Judith S. Woodruff, Apr. 2, 1981. AB, Amherst Coll., 1958; PhD, Calif. Inst. Tech., 1962. NSF postdoctoral fellow U. Wis., 1962-63, asst. prof., then assoc. prof. astronomy, 1963-74; astronaut NASA, Johnson Space Ctr., 1967-91; dir. policy plan Office Space Flight, NASA Hdqs., Washington, 1991, dir. space ops. utilization program, 1992-97; dir. NASA Mgmt. Office, JPL, Pasadena, Calif., 1997—. Mem. support crew Apollo XV and XVII, mission scientist Apollo XVII, program scientist Skylab program, mission specialist for Spacelab 1, 1983, ASTRO-1, 1990. Mem. Am. Astron. Soc., Phi Beta Kappa. Office: NMO 180 801 JPL 4800 Oak Grove Dr Pasadena CA 91109-8001 E-mail: rparker@nmo.jpl.nasa.gov.

PARKER, ROBERT CHAUNCEY HUMPHREY, clergyman, publishing executive, psychic; b. NYC, Apr. 6, 1941; s. Robert Humphrey and Edith Louise (Corya) P. Student, U. Va., 1960—61, student, 1962—63; diploma, Inst. Psychorientology, Laredo, Tex., 1973. Ordained to ministry Ch. of Antioch-Malabar Rite, 1975. Law clk. Shearman & Sterling, NYC, 1961-62; owner Parker's Pronto-Pups Inc., NYC, 1962-64; asst. to pres. U.S. Packaging, NYC, 1964-66; asst. nat. sales mgr. Elliott Svc. Co. Inc., Mt. Vernon, NY, 1966-67; pres., cons. Lenfield Assocs. & Cons., NYC and Washington, 1967-71; founder, pres. Occult Comm. Corp., NYC, Washington, and Danbury, Conn., 1971-76, New Awareness Corp., London and Mpls., 1973-81; dir., resident min. The Healing Ctr. at St. Patricia's, Inver Grove Heights, Minn., 1975; lectr., min. Ch. of Antioch-Malabar Rite, 1975—; editor New Awareness News, 1975—; founder, pres. Parker/Tofte Comm., Robert Parker Assocs., Minnetonka, Minn., 1977—; pres., CEO Am. Energy & Alcohol Corp., Mpls., 1981-84. Cons. Boat Owners Assn. U.S., Washington, 1967-70, Durance Co., 1994-95; rschr., cons. Am. Marine Corp., Marblehead, Mass.; new product devel., venture capital and cons. investment, banking houses, NYC and Washington, 1967-71; dir., cons. to regional and nat. healing orgns. and publs., 1973-81; pres. Field Harmonics Rsch. Group Inc., 1993-97, New Awareness Spkrs. and Pub. Group, Inc., 1997—; spkr., tchr. numerous orgns. Author: Watergate Flight 553, 1974, Reabsorption Energy, 1975, Finding Your Own Four-Leaf Clover, 1993; author Telsa Newsletter, 1979; editor New Awareness mag., 1973-75, (newsletter) Sunbeams; editor, pub. New Awareness News and Book News, 1977—, New Awareness Computer News, 1995—, psychic/parapsychology internat. trade jours., 1971-75; designer, pub.: Henry's Hilarious One Liners, 1991, Henry's Just a Chuckle, 1992, Henry's Just a Laugh, 1992, Henry's Just a Witticism, 1992; contbr. articles to profl. jours.; guest spkr. various radio, TV and Internet programs, including Dimension, Sta. WCCO-AM-FM; featured on Dimension WCCO-TV (CBS), 1991, 93, Forbes Mag., 1996, Elizabeth Smart Recovery, Sta. WCCO-TV, 2003, Ruth Koscielak Show, Sta. KCCO-AM, 2003, Smart Predictions 100% Correct, 2003; host cable TV program Astrology and Mind, Etc., 1994-96; syndicated columnist. Bd. dirs. Toutorsky Ednl. Found., Washington, 1988-91. Mem. Nat. Press Club (Washington), Internat. Telsa Soc. Inc., Knickerbocker Greys Vet. Corps (NYC), Brownings Sch. Alumni Assn. (NYC), Lenox (Mass.) Sch. Alumni Assn. Avocations: reading, travel. Home and Office: Box 387 Excelsior MN 55331-0387 Office Phone: 952-936-9974. E-mail: rchparker@aol.com.

PARKER, ROBERT ERNSER, lawyer; b. Howell, Mich., Dec. 9, 1938; s. Robert W. and Maxine (Ernser) P.; m. Dona Scott, June 27, 1969 (div. Oct. 1988); children: Robert S., Donald S. BS, Ea. Mich. U., 1967; JD, Oklahoma City U., 1973. Bar: Mich. 1973, U.S. Dist. Ct. (ea. dist.) Mich. 1973, U.S. Ct. Appeals (6th cir.) 1973, Ind. 1987, Wis. 1988. Magistrate 53d Jud. Dist. Ct., Howell, Mich., 1968-72; owner Parker Abstract and Title Co., Howell, Mich., 1969-78; ptnr. Parker & Parker, Howell, Mich., 1973. Arbitrator Nat. Assn. Security Dealers, N.Y. Stock Exch., Nat. Futures Assn., 1983-97. Mayor City of Howell, 1975-76. Mem. Mich. Bar Assn. (com. trial cts. adminstrn. 1982-88), Rep. Assembly of State Bar, Livingston County Bar Assn. (pres. 1987), Rotary (pres. 1990), Masons, Phi Delt aPhi, Sigma Alpha Epsilon. Home: 609 Curzon Ct # 204 Howell MI 48843 Office: Parker & Parker 704 E Grand River PO Box 888 Howell MI 48844-0888 Office Phone: 517-546-4864. Business E-Mail: REParker@Parker-and-Parker.com.

PARKER, ROBERT FREDERIC, university dean emeritus; b. St. Louis, Oct. 29, 1907; s. Charles T. and Lydia (Gronemeyer) P.; m. Mary L. Warner, June 20, 1934; children: David Frederic, Jane Eleanor (Mrs. Howard H. Hush, Jr.). BS, Washington U., St. Louis, 1925, MD, 1929. Diplomate: Am. Bd. Microbiology. Asst. radiology Washington U. Med. Sch., 1929-30, instr. medicine, 1932-33; asst. Rockefeller Inst., 1933-36; mem. faculty Case Western Res. U., 1936—, prof. microbiology, 1954-77, prof. emeritus, 1977—, assoc. dean, 1965-73, dean, 1973-76, dean emeritus, 1976—. Mem. Cleve. Acad. Medicine (past bd. dirs.), Am. Soc. Clin. Investigation, Central Soc. Clin. Research, Am. Acad. Microbiology, Sigma Xi, Alpha Omega Alpha. Achievements include spl. research virus immunology, quantitative aspects virus infection, tissue culture, action of antibiotics. Home: 2181 Ambleside Dr Apt 404 Cleveland OH 44106-7603

PARKER, ROBERT GEORGE, radiation oncology educator, academic administrator; b. Detroit, Mich., Jan. 29, 1925; s. Clifford Robert and Velma (Ashman) P.; m. Diana Davis, June 30, 1977; children by previous marriage: Thomas Clifford, James Richardson. BS, U. Wis., 1946, MD., 1948. Diplomate Am. Bd. Radiology (trustee 1978-90, pres. 1988-90). Intern U. Nebr. Hosp., Omaha, 1948-49; resident in pathology Western Res. U., Cleve., 1949-50; resident in radiology U. Mich., Ann Arbor, 1950, 52-54, instr. in radiology, 1954-55; staff radiotherapist Swedish Hosp. Tumor Inst., Seattle, 1955-58; prof. radiology U. Wash., Seattle, 1958-77; prof. radiation oncology UCLA, 1977—. Lt. USNR, 1950-52. Fellow Am. Coll. Radiology (gold medalist 2001); mem. AMA (radiology residence rev. com.), Am. Soc. Therapeutic Radiologists (pres. 1975-76, gold medalist 1989), Radiol. Soc. N.Am. (bd. dirs. 1984-90, pres. 1991-92, gold medalist 1996), Am. Radium Soc. (bd. dirs. 1988-92, pres. 1992, Janeway medalist 1997). Office: UCLA 200 Ucla Medical Plz Ste B265 Los Angeles CA 90095-8344 Office Phone: 310-825-9304. Business E-Mail: parker@mednet.ucla.edu.

PARKER, SARA ANN, librarian, consultant; b. Cassville, Mo., Feb. 19, 1939; d. Howard Franklin and Vera Irene (Thomas) P. BA, Okla. State U., 1961; M.L.S., Emporia State U., Kans., 1968. Adult svcs. librarian Springfield Pub. Libr., Mo., 1972-75, bookmobile dir., 1975-76; coord. S.W. Mo. Libr. Network, Springfield, 1976-78; libr. developer Colo. State Libr., Denver, 1978-82; state librarian Mont. State Libr., Helena, 1982-88, State Libr. Pa., Harrisburg, 1988-90; Pa. commr. librs., dep. sec. edn. State of Pa., Harrisburg, 1990-95; state libr. State of Mo., Jefferson City, 1995—. Cons. and lectr. in field. Author, editor, compiler in field; contbr. articles to profl. jours. Sec., Western Coun. State Librs., Reno, 1984-88, mem. Mont. State Data Adv. Coun., 1983-88, Mont. Telecommunications Coun., 1985-88, WLN Network Coun., 1984-87, Kellogg ICLIS Project Mgmt. Bd., 1986-88; mem. adv. com. Gates Libr. Initiative, 1998—; mem. OCLC Strategic Directions and Governance Study Adv. Coun., 2000-01. Recipient Pres.'s award, Nature Conservancy, 1989, Friends award, Pa. Assn. Ednl. Comms. and Techs., 1989, Friend of Sch. Librs. award, Mo. Sch. Librs. Assn., 2000, Bohley Libr. Cooperation award, 2001; fellow Inst. Ednl. Leadership, 1982. Mem. ALA, Chief Officers State Libr. Agys. (pres. 1996-98), Mont. Libr. Assn. (bd. dirs. 1982-88), Mountain Plains Libr. Assn. (sec. chmn. 1980, pres. 1987-88). Home: PO Box 554 Jefferson City MO 65102-0554 Office: Mo State Libr PO Box 387 600 W Main St Jefferson City MO 65101-1532

PARKER, SARAH ELIZABETH, state supreme court justice; b. Charlotte, N.C., Aug. 23, 1942; d. Augustus and Zola Elizabeth (Smith) P. AB, U. N.C., 1964, JD, 1969; LHD (hon.), Queens Coll., 1998. Bar: N.C. 1969, U.S. Dist. Ct. (mid., ea. and we. dists.) N.C. Vol. U.S. Peace Corps, Ankara, Turkey, 1964-66; pvt. practice Charlotte, 1969-84; judge N.C. Ct. Appeals, Raleigh, 1985—92; assoc. justice N.C. Supreme Ct., Raleigh, 1993—. Bd. visitors U. N.C., Chapel Hill, 1993—97; pres. Mecklenburg County Dem. Women, Charlotte, 1973; N.C. ct. commr., 1999—; bd. dirs. YWCA, Charlotte, 1982—85. Recipient Disting. Woman of N.C. award, 1997, Woman of Achievement award Nat. Fedn. Women's Clubs, 1997. Mem. ABA, Inst. Jud. Adminstrn., N.C. Bar Assn. (v.p. 1987-88), Mecklenburg County Bar (sec.-treas. 1982-84), Wake County Bar Assn., N.C. Internat. Women's Forum, Women Attys. Assn. (Gwynth David Pub. Svc. award 1986). Episcopalian. Office: NC Supreme Ct PO Box 1841 Raleigh NC 27602-1841

PARKER, SARAH JESSICA, actress; b. Nelsonville, Ohio, Mar. 25, 1965; m. Matthew Broderick May, 1997; 1 child: James. Actress: (theatre) The Innocents, 1976, The Sound of Music, 1977, Annie, 1978, The War Brides, 1981, The Death of a Miner, 1982, To Gillian on Her 37th Birthday, 1983, 84, Terry Neal's Future, 1986, The Heidi Chronicles, 1989, How to Succeed in Business Without Really Trying, 1996, Once Upon a Mattress, 1996—, (films) Rich Kids, 1979, Somewhere Tomorrow, 1983, Firstborn, 1984, Footloose, 1984, Girls Just Want to Have Fun, 1985, Flight of the Navigator, 1986, L.A. Story, 1991, Honeymoon in Vegas, 1992, Hocus Pocus, 1993, Striking Distance, 1993, Ed Wood, 1994, Miami Rhapsody, 1995, If Lucy Fell, 1996, Mars Attacks!, 1996, The First Wives Club, 1996, Extreme Measures, 1996, 'Til There Was You, 1997, The Substance of Fire, 1996, (voice) A Life Apart: Hasidism in America, 1997, Isn't She Great, 1999, Dudley Do-Right, 1999, State and Main, 2000, Life Without Dick, 2001; (TV movies) My Body, My Child, 1982, Going for the Gold: The Bill Johnson Story, 1985, A Year in the Life, 1986, The Room Upstairs, 1987, Dadah Is Death, 1988, The Ryan White Story, 1989, Twist of Fate, 1989, In the Best Interest of the Children, 1992, (TV series) Square Pegs, 1982-83, A Year in the Life, 1987-88, Equal Justice, 1990-91, Sex and the City, 1998-2004 (Best Supporting Actress Golden Globe award 1999, 2000, 01, 02, 04, Emmy nominee for Outstanding Lead Actress 1999-2002, Outstanding Performance by Female Actor in Comedy Series award 2001), (TV pilots) The Alan King Show, 1986; guest appearances The Ben Stiller Show, 1992, The Larry Sanders Show, 1992; co-exec. prodr. Sex and the City. Nat. amb. U.S. Fund for UNICEF. Recipient, Am. Civil Liberties Union award, 1995. Office: Creative Artists Agy care Jane Berliner 9830 Wilshire Blvd Beverly Hills CA 90212-1804*

PARKER, SHEILA, newscaster; Reporter, Orlando, Fla.; anchor Tallahassee; reporter WSAV-TV, Savannah, Ga., 1999—. Avocations: news, travel, reading, college football. Office: WSAV-TV3 1430 E Victory Dr Savannah GA 31404

PARKER, SUSAN BROOKS, healthcare executive; b. Newport, NH, Nov. 7, 1945; d. Ronald Elliott and Elizabeth Louise (Wiggins) P.; m. Allen D. Avery, 1967 (div. 1978); children: Jeffrey Roberts Avery, Mark Brooks Avery. BS in English and French, U. Vt., 1968; MSW/MSP, Boston Coll., 1978. EMT, Vt., 1973-76. Resort hotel mgr., retail buyer Avery Vt. Inns, 1967-75; aftercare psychiatric worker Orange County Mental Health, Bradford, Vt., 1974-76; exec. dir. Grafton County Planning Coun., Lebanon, N.H., 1978-80, N.H. Developmental Disabilities Planning Coun., Concord, N.H., 1980-87; commr. Dept. of Mental Health, Augusta, Maine, 1987-89; assoc. commr. U.S. Social Security Adminstrn., Balt., 1989-93; sec. gen. Rehab. Internat., NYC, 1993—98; sr. adv., interim dir. disability program Internat. Labor Office,

Geneva, 1998—2001; dir. policy and rsch. Office Disability Employment Policy U.S. Dept. Labor, Washington, 2002—. Cons. Nat. Gov.'s Assn., Washington, 1985-86, Office of Health and Devel. Svcs., Washington, 1987; bd. dirs. Nat. Assn. Devel. Disabilities, Washington, 1983-87, Ctrl. NH Mental Health Ctr., Concord, 1985-87, World Com. Disability, Washington, 1997—, Roeher Inst., Toronto, Ont., Can., 1997-2000, Orah.com, Geneva, 2002—, NH Devel. Disabilities Coun., 2002—; bd. dirs. US Coun. for Internat. Disability, Washington; hon. coun. Rehab. Internat. and mem. World Assembly, N.Y. Author: (poetry) Scheme, 1965, Jamaican Collection, 1973; contbr. articles to newspapers and profl. jours. Pres. Parent Tchr. Orgn., Fairlee, Vt., 1972-73; founder and dir. Ford Sayre Ski Program, Dartmouth Coll. Skiway, Fairlee, 1972-76, United Way, Concord, 1983-86; bd. dirs. PTO Rundlett Jr. H.S., Concord, 1982-85; pres. U.S. Coun. for Internat. Rehab., 1993. Recipient Assn. Retarded Citizens Children's Disability Pub. Policy award, 1992, Kathryn C. Arneson award from People to People, 1992, Commr.'s citation for outstanding efforts in developing policy U.S. Social Security Adminstrn., 1992, Commn.'s citation for outstanding exec. leadership, 1993; named Outstanding Alumnae Boston Coll., 1991. Avocations: skiing, gardening, canoeing, reading, movies.

PARKER, SUSAN D. state official, auditor; b. Eva, Ala., Sept. 30, 1955; m. Paul Parker. AS magna cum laude, Calhoun C.C., 1975; BS in Edn. magna cum laude, Athens State Coll., 1977; MA in Counseling magna cum laude, U. Ala., Birmingham, 1979; PhD in Adminstrn. Higher Edn., U. Ala., Tuscaloosa, 1984. Admissions clk., office mgr., dir. job placement, asst. dean Calhoun C.C., 1972-88; asst. to prs. for external affairs, chief devel. officer Athens State Coll., 1988-96; pres. Parker Plus Cons., 1996-98; state auditor State of Ala., Montgomery, 1998—. Past mem. numerous bd. dirs. nonprofit, charitable orgns., including Ala. bd. dirs. Am. Heart Assn.; past pres. county chpts. Am. Heart Assn., Am. Cancer Soc., Leukemia Soc., Boys and Girls Club, C. of C. leadership programs, Mental Health Assn., United Way, Cmty. Unity; former Sunday sch. tchr. 1st Bapt. Ch., Hartselle, Ala. Named One of 10 Outstanding Young Ams., U.S. Jaycees, 1987, One of 10 Outstanding Young Alabamians and Outstanding Citizen of Hartselle, Hartselle Jaycees, Ala.'s Most Outstanding Young Career Woman, Ala. Bus. and Profl. Women's Assn., Outstanding United Way Vol. Morgan County; named to Alumni Hall of Honor, Ala. Coll. Sys. Avocations: walking, golf, travel, fishing. Office: State Auditor's Office PO Box 300200 Montgomery AL 36130-0200 Fax: 334-242-7650. E-mail: sparker@auditor.state.al.us.

PARKER, SUSAN RICHBOURG, historian, consultant; b. St. Augustine, Fla., Sept. 28, 1946; d. James Hartwell Richbourg and Janette Hope Phinney; children: Christopher A., Amanda Parker Struckhoff, Robert Dexter. BA, Fla. State U., 1969; MA, U. Fla., 1991, PhD, 1999. Historian, preservationist State of Fla., St. Augustine, 1987—. Rsch. assoc. Hist. St. Augustine Rsch. Inst., 1999—. Author: The New History of Florida. Chair St. Johns Co. Hist. Resources Bd., St. Augustine, 2000; pres. St. Augustine Hist. Soc., 2004. Mem.: Fla. Hist. Soc. (assoc. Thompson prize 1991, Collins prize 1997), Am. Hist. Assn. (assoc. Beveridge prize 1997). Democrat. Episcopal. Achievements include research in Spanish colonial documents. Avocation: gardening. Home: 1671 Asturias St Saint Augustine FL 32080 Office: Florida Division of Historical Resources 48 King St Saint Augustine FL 32084 Personal E-mail: sparker@aug.com. E-mail: sarpres@aug.com.

PARKER, TERRY S. telecommunications industry executive; Pres. GTE Mobil Comms., GTE Telecommunicatins, 1991—93; sr. v.p. GTE Corp., 1993—96; pres., COO CellStar Corp., Carrollton, Tex., 1995—96, dir., 1995—, CEO, 2001—; pres., CEO Telenetics, 2000—01. Office: Cellstar Corp 1730 Briercroft Ct Carrollton TX 75006*

PARKER, TREY, actor, producer, director; b. Conifer, Colo., Oct. 19, 1969; s. Randy and Sharon Parker. Attended, Colo. Univ. Dir., writer: (films) American History, 1992; prodr., dir., writer, voice of various characters The Spirit of Christmas (also titled Jesus vs. Frosty), 1992; The Spirit of Christmas (also titled Jesus vs. Santa), 1995 (Los Angeles Film Critics Assoc. award for Best Animation, 1997); dir., writer, actor Your Studio and You, 1995; prodr., dir., writer, composer, actor Alfred Packer: The Musical (also titled Cannibal! The Musical), 1996; dir.: For Goodness Sake II, 1996; exec. prodr., dir., writer, creator, composer (TV series) South Park, 1997—, voice of Mr. Mackey, Satan, Randy Marsh, Ned Gerbalnski, Mr. Hankey, Officer Barbrady, and others (CableACE award for Animated Programming Special or Series, 1997, Producers Guild of America Nova award for Television, 1997); prodr., dir., composer, actor: (films) Orgazmo, 1997; composer, actor BASEketball, 1998; prodr., dir., writer, composer (films) South Park: Bigger Longer & Uncut, 1999, voice of Stan Marsh, Eric Cartmanm Satan, Mr. Herbert Garrison, Phillip Niles Argyle and others (Los Angeles Film Critics Assoc. award for Best Music, 1999, New York Film Critics Circle award for Best Animated Film, 1999); exec. prodr.: (films) How's Your News?, 1999—; exec. prodr., writer, creator, composer (TV series) That's My Bush, 2001—; voice of Juan Schwartz: (films) Tales From the Crapper, 2004; voice of William L. Garrison, Counselor Mackey, S.D. Kluger, and others: (films) Christmas in South Park, 2000. Office: c/o Comedy Central 1775 Broadway 10th Fl New York NY 10019*

PARKER, VIRGINIA MARIE, English language educator; b. Boston, Aug. 31, 1950; d. Thomas Gurney Sr. and Marguerite Mary (O'Sullivan) P. BA, Emmanuel Coll., 1972; postgrad. studies in English, Lincoln Coll. U. Oxford, (Eng.) Bread Loaf Sessions, summers 1987-89; MA, Middlebury Coll., 1989. Cert. secondary English tchr., Mass. Vol. Jesuit Vol. Corps N.W., Seattle, 1972-73; tchr. English Blue Hills Regional Tech. Sch., Canton, Mass., 1973—, sch. newspaper advisor, 1973—75. Editl. cons. competency-based vocat. ednl. curriculum Dept. Edn./Occupl. Divsn., Commonwealth of Mass., 1984-88; nat. honor soc. advisor, screening com. mem. William A. Dwyer Chpt., Blue Hills, Canton, 1986-88, 1994-97; mediation trainee, advisor Sch. Mediation Assocs., 1993. Ch. lector, religious educator, youth retreat facilitator various parishes, 1970—; grad. master tchr. program Office of Religious Edn., Archdiocese of Boston, 1977. Mem. NEA, Nat. Coun. Tchrs. English, Mass. Vocat. Assn., Mass. Tchrs. Assn., Blue Hills Ednl. Assn. (sec. 1977-78), Alden Kindred Am. Democrat. Roman Catholic. Avocations: travel, theater-going, beach walking, genealogical research, cemetery haunting. Home: 80 Parks St Duxbury MA 02332-4831 Office: Blue Hills Regional Tech Sch 800 Randolph St Canton MA 02021-1358 E-mail: vparker@bluehills.org.

PARKER, W. DOUGLAS, transportation executive; BA in Econ., Albion Coll., 1984; MBA, Vanderbilt U., 1986. Various positions Am. Airlines; v.p., fin. planning and analysis, v.p., asst. treas. Northwest Airlines; sr. v.p., CFO Am. West Holdings, 1995—99, exec. v.p., corp. group, 1999—2000, pres., COO, 2000—01, chmn., pres., CEO, 2001—. Bd. dirs. Am. West Holdings, 1999—. Office: America West Holdings 111 W Rio Salado Plwy Tempe AZ 85281*

PARKER, WALTER BRUCE, arctic research specialist, consultant; b. Spokane, Wash., Aug. 11, 1926; s. Bruce Velorus and Lucille Kathryn (Chessman) P.; m. Patricia Isabelle Ertman, Jan. 28, 1946; children: Sandra Wassilie, Patrick B., Jeffrey K., Douglas S., Lisa M. BA in History, U. Alaska, Fairbanks, 1964; DSc, U. Alaska, Anchorage, 1998. Air traffic controller FAA, 1946-64, evaluation officer, 1964-66, analyst Washington, 1966-68, planner Anchorage, 1968-70; sr. planner Fed. Field Com. for Alaska, Anchorage, 1970-71; rsch. assoc. U. Alaska, Anchorage, 1971-74; commr. Alaska Dept. Hwys., Juneau, 1974-76; chmn. Alaska Fed./State Land Use Planning Commn., 1976-79; disting. practioner in residence U. Alaska, Anchorage, 1979-80; chmn. Alaska Oil Spill Commn., Anchorage, 1989-90; pres., cons. transp. and telecom. sys. Parker Assocs., Inc., Anchorage, 1971—; commr. U.S. Arctic Rsch. Commn., Anchorage, 1995—2001. Mem. marine bd., com. on advances in pilotage and navigation NRC, 1991-94, North Pacific rsch. bd., 2000-, Oil Spill Recovery Inst.bd., 1999-; chmn. Alaska Hazardous Substance Spill Coun., 1991-95. Author: Alaska and The Law of the Sea, 1974, Alaska People's and Alaska Lands, 1977; contbr. reports to profl. publs. Chmn. Alaska Conservation Soc., Anchorage, 1969-71, Alaska Humanties Forum, Anchorage, 1987-93, Anchorage Parks and Recreation Coun., 1971-74; active Alaska Bd. Fish and Game, Juneau, 1971-74; chmn. Prince William Sound Sci. Ctr., 1996—, chmn.; assemblyman Anchorage Borough, 1971-74. With USN, 1944-46. Mem. Am. Soc. Pub. Adminstrn. (chmn. Alaska chpt. 1971-73). Democrat. Avocations: skiing, dog mushing and breeding, gardening. Home: 3724 Campbell Airstrip Rd Anchorage AK 99504-4422

PARKER, WARREN CAMERON, registrar, small business owner; s. Roy E. and Martha D. Parker; m. Bonnie Parker, June 23, 1979; children: Sarah, Sharon, Samuel, Samantha, Susanna. AA, Mitchell C.C., 1974. Registrar Piedmont Bapt. Coll., Winston-Salem, NC, 1998—2004. Mem.: Phi Theta Kappa. R-Consevative. Baptist. Avocations: reading, playing chess, civil war history, gardening. Office Phone: 336-725-8344 2320. Office Fax: 336-725-5522. E-mail: parkerw@pbc.edu.

PARKER, WILLIAM DALE, management consultant, political and presidential adviser; b. Portsmouth, Va., Apr. 13, 1925; s. Otis Durie and Eva Estelle (Dempsey) P.; m. Frances Ross Jennings, Feb. 2, 1946 (dec.); children: Frances Lea, Elizabeth Dale, Kim Carolyn, Penny Jo Ann, Jacquelyn Susan; m. Boots Lee Farthing, 1968. Student, Coll. William and Mary, 1946; grad. indsl. engring., Internat. Corr. Schs., 1956; student, U. Del., 1959-60, Calif. Western U., 1961-62, U. Calif., 1964, Stetson U., 1969; DSc, James Balmes U., Saltillio, Mex., 1968; PhD in Edn., Fla. Inst., 1970. Layout, process and prodn. engr. GM, Wilmington, Del., 1949-59, asst. dir. salaried personnel pub. rels., 1959-61; mfg. engr., lectr. Gen. Dynamics/Astronautic, San Diego, 1961-64; dir. Internat. Inst. Human Rels., LaJolla, Calif., 1964—; family and marriage counselor Titusville, Fla., 1967-71, Boone, N.C., 1996—; mgmt. cons., v.p. Multiple Services, Inc., Titusville and Boone, 1969—. Bd. dirs., v.p. Spangler TV, N.Y.C., 1969-73; chmn. bd. Travel Internat., Inc., Titusville, 1971-74, presdl. advisor, 1972 76, 72 76, 98 ; v.p. Pictorial Gravesite Creations, Inc., Boone and Titusville, 1989—. Author: Philosophy of a Genius: American Values, Solutions to Family and Marriage Problems, Gutless America, 1973, God Knows I Want to Come Home, 1989, Prose and Poetry-9 to 90, 1990, Geography 101, 1992, A Political Candidate Guide, 1995, A Selection of Writings, 1992-95, 1995, The Parker Family, 1616-1996, 1996, Your Personal Angel, 1997—98; spkr. in field; columnist: Sentinal Newspapers, 1963—64, asst. editor: Campers Illus. Mag., 1964—65, Star Adv., 1968, Insight, 1969—72, Challenge, 1970—, Mountain Times, 1981—84, hon. mem. editl. adv. bd: Am. Biog. Inst., 1975—; patentee Amy Carter peanut dolls, inventor process to keep B/W and color pictures from aging in sunlight. Founder Monroe Park CD, 1951; mem. Wilmington coun. Boy Scouts Am., 1953—55; chmn. Varions Agy. Fund, 1954—60; co-chmn. Del. Dept. CD TV Shows, 1956—57; mem. Middle Atlantic States Conf. Correction, 1956—60; chmn., pres. Del. Md. Pa. Tri-State Hosp. Com., 1957—59; mem. Wilmington Inner City Study Commn., 1957—60; chmn. Del. CD Evacuation Commn., 1958—59, Del. Hwy. Safety Campaign, 1959—60; active PTA; bd. advisors Salvation Army, Va. Tech. U., 1999; friend of the libr. Legacy Soc., 2000; Mem. Nat. Dem. Com., 1980—; ind. candidate for gov. Fla., 1976; mem. Dem. Exec. Com., 1975—77; polit. cons. Congress; advisor to U.S. Pres., 1974—; bd. dirs. Boys and Girls Aid Soc. San Diego, 1962—64; traveler Arctic Circle, 1990, 2000. With USCGR, USN, SSII. Named Del. Outstanding Young Man of Yr., Wilmington/U.S. Jr. C. of C., 1957; recipient Silver award Del. Vol. Bur., 1957, ann. awards Va. Jr. Achievement, inc., 1959; speech award U.S. Jr. C. of C., 1960, Gemini award NASA, 1967, Internat. Disting. Svc. to Humanity award, 1971, Keys to City, wilmington, 1959, 61, 72, Titusville, 1970, Miami, 1973; named Hon. Sheriff, Portsmouth, Va., 1973; named White Ho. Vet., White Ho. Chief Staff, 1997; named on on the Gen. Dynamics-Atlas and on Gemini monuments with Mercury, Gemini and Apollo Spacewalk Hall of Fame, Titusville; papers, books and awards are in Librs. Space Archives, Va. Poly. and State U., Blacksburg. Mem.: SAR, NRA, DAV (life), VFW (life), Wilmington Indsl. Mgmt. Club, Am. Assn. Polit. Consultants, Accomack, Va., First Family of Va. (1616 William Parker), Authors League Am., Mus. of Flight (life), Mensa (life), Nat. Space Soc. (life; charter), Monroe Park Civic Assn. (pres. 1952—53), Universal Space Assn. (co-founder 1992), Vols. Spkrs. Bur. (San Diego), Coll. William and Mary Alumni Soc. (pres., rep.), Authors Guild, Mexican Turf Club, Royal Oak Golf and Country Club, S.Am. Turf Club (life), Masons, Moose (life), Elks (life), Am. Legion (life). E-mail: wm246@webtv.net.

PARKER, WILLIAM H., JR., telecommunications industry executive; b. N.J. BA in Econs., Denison U., 1976; MBA in Fin., Southeastern U., 1981. Customer svc., credit, labor rels. exec. Potomac Elec. Power Co.; sr. mktg. exec. Xerox Corp., Pitney Bowes; founder Washington Cable Supply, Inc., Lanham Seabrook, Md., 1984—. Dir. YMCA, Washington. Office: Washington Cable Supply Inc 4600 Boston Way Ste D Lanham Seabrook MD 20706-4857

PARKER, WILLIAM H., III, federal official; b. Westbrook, Maine, May 4, 1937; s. William H. II and Anne Marney (Delaney) P.; m. Joan Moody Currier, June 17, 1959; children: Laurie Jean, Michael Currier, Suzan Elizabeth, Julie Ann. BS, U. Maine, 1960; MS, Northeastern U., 1966; MEM, U. Detroit, 1981, MBA, 1982; postgrad., Nova U. Diplomate Am. Acad. Environ. Engrs. Project engr. Camp Dresser & McKee, Boston, 1962-72, v.p., 1972-75, E.C. Jordan, Portland, Maine, 1975-77; sr. v.p., reg. mgr. Camp Dresser & McKee, Detroit, 1977-87, bd. dirs., 1982-87; sr. v.p. CDM Fed. Programs Corp., Washington, 1987-88, bd. dirs., 1987-88; dep. asst. sec. Dept. of Def., Washington, 1988-90; dir. environ. health and safety programs, dir. chem programs EG&G Inc., Wellesley, Mass., 1990-98; founder, pres. Global Mgmt. & Tech. Solutions, Wellesley, 1999—. Bd. dirs. Parker Currier Inc., Brunswick, Maine; fin. cons. VMI, treas., pres., 1993—, White River Junction, Vt., 1987-90; presenter Congl. test, 1988-90; keynote speaker tech. and profl. socs., 1988—. Contbr. articles to profl. jours. Mem., chmn. planning bd. Town of Reading, Maine, 1968-73; mem. Town Meeting, Reading, 1969-75, Mcpl. Light Bd., Reading, 1974-75. 1st lt. U.S. Army, 1960-62. Recipient Outstanding Pub. Svc. medal Sec. of Def., 1989, Environ. Svc. award Nat. Def. Industries Assn., 2000. Fellow ASCE; mem. NSPE, Mass. Soc. Profl. Engrs (Young Engr. of Yr. award 1971), Am. Def. Preparedness Assoc., Engring. Socs. New Eng. (New Eng. award 1990), Soc. Am. Mil. Engrs., Nat. Security Industries Assn. (hon.), Water Pollution Control Fedn., Am. Water Works Assn., Mass. Jaycees (Reading) (local pres., state v.p. 1970-72, Econ. Club Detroit, Detroit Club, Sigma Xi, Tau Beta Pi, Alpha Kappa Psi, Beta Gamma Sigma, Phi Kappa Phi, Chi Epsilon. Republican. Roman Catholic. Avocations: reading, writing, travel. Home and Office: 60 Merrimac St #807 Amesbury MA 01913 E-mail: w.parker@mediaone.net.

PARKER, WILMER, III, lawyer, educator; b. Ozark, Ala., Oct. 3, 1951; s. Wilmer and Anne Laura (Ragsdale) P.; m. Rebecca Joy Skillern, Aug. 25, 1984; children: R. Virginia, J. William; m. Beverly Laura Barnard, Dec. 23, 1972 (div. Dec. 1977). BS in Commerce, U. Ala., 1972, MBA, JD, U. Ala., 1975; LLM, Emory U., 1976. Bar: Ala. 1975, Ga. 1976, Fla. 1976, U.S. Dist. Ct. (no. dist.) Ga. 1976, U.S. Tax Ct. 1976, U.S. Ct. Appeals (11th cir.) 1986, U.S. Dist. Ct. (mid. dist.) Ga. 1997. Assoc. Nall, Miller & Cadenhead, Atlanta, 1975-78; trial atty. tax divsn. U.S. Dept. Justice, Washington, 1978-83; asst. U.S. atty. Organized Crime Drug Enforcement Task Force, Atlanta, 1983-97; ptnr. Kilpatrick Stockton LLP, Atlanta, 1997—2002, Gillen Parker & Withers, Atlanta, 2002—. Lectr. trial advocacy Emory U. Law Sch., Atlanta, 1984—. Named Outstanding Trial Atty. Tax Divsn., U.S. Dept. Justice, Washington, 1979; recipient Spl. Commendation award U.S. Dept. Justice, 1985, 87, Superior Performance as Asst. U.S. Atty. Dirs. award, 1986, 94. Mem. ABA, Internat. Bar Assn., Atlanta Bar Assn., Lawyers Club Atlanta. Episcopalian. Office: Gillen Parker & Withers 3490 Piedmont Rd NW Ste 1050 Atlanta GA 30305

PARKES, WALTER, film company executive; b. Bakersfield, Calif. m. Laurie MacDonald, prodr.; 2 children. AB in Anthropology, Yale U.; student, Grad. Sch. Comm., Stanford U. Pres. Amblin Entertainment, 1994—; co-head, dir. motion pictures Dreamworks Pictures, 1995—. Prodr., dir.: (films) The California Reich, 1975 (nominated Acad. Award, spl. citation Cannes Film Festival); prodr.: Volunteers, 1985, True Believer, 1987, Awakenings, 1990 (nominated best picture, 1990), Men in Black, 1997, The Peace Maker, 1997, Gladiator, 2000, Artificial Intelligence, 2001; prodr.: (films) The Time Machine, 2002; prodr.: (films) Minority Report, 2002, Men in Black II, 2002, Road to Perdition, 2002, The Tuxedo, 2002, The Ring, 2002, Catch Me If You Can, 2002; exec. prodr.: (TV series) Birdland, 1994, Men in Black: The Series, 1997; (films) Littler Giants, 1994, To Wong Foo, Thanks for Everything Julie Newmar, 1995, How to Make an American Quilt, 1995, Twister, 1996, The Trigger Effect, 1996, Amistad, 1997, Deep Impact, 1998, Small Soldiers, 1998, Mask of Zorro, 1998; writer: WarGames, 1983 (nominated best original screenplay, 1983); prodr., writer: (films) Sneakers, 1992 (nominated Acad. Award, spl. citation Cannes Film Festival). Office: DreamWorks SKG 1000 Flower St Glendale CA 91201 Office Phone: 818-733-7000. Office Fax: 818-695-7574.

PARKHURST, CAROLYN, writer; b. 1971; BA, Wesleyan U.; MFA in creative writing, Am. U. Author: The Dogs of Babel, 2003 (Best Fiction Book Fort Worth Star-Telegram, 2003, Notable Book New York Times, 2003), (short stories) (included in) North Am. Review, Minn. Review, Hawaii Review, Crescent Review. Office: c/o Douglas Stewart Curtis Brown Ltd 10 Astor Pl New York NY 10003

PARKHURST, CHARLES LLOYD, electronics company executive; b. Nashville, Aug. 13, 1943; s. Charles Albert Parkhurst and Dorothy Elizabeth (Ballou) Parkhurst Crutchfield; m. Dolores Ann Oakley, June 6, 1970; children: Charles Thomas, Deborah Lynn, Jere Loy. Student, Hume-Fogg Tech. Coll., 1959-61; AA, Mesa Community Coll., 1973; student, Ariz. State U., 1973-76. Mem. design staff Tex. Instruments, Dallas, 1967-68; mgr. design Motorola, Inc., Phoenix, 1968-76; pres. LSI Cons., Inc., Tempe, Ariz., 1976-85, LSI Photomasks, Inc., Tempe, 1985-94, Charles Parkhurst Books, Inc., Prescott, Ariz., 1994—; founder, CEO IC Photomask, LLC, Chandler, Ariz., 2002—. CEO IC Photomask, LLC. Designer 1st digital watch chip, 1973. Mem. Rep. Congl. Leadership Coun., Washington, 1988; life mem. Rep. Presdl. Task Force, 1990. Served as cpl. USMC, 1961-64. Mem. Ariz. State U. Alumni Assn. (life), Antiquarian Booksellers Assn. Am. Baptist. Achievements include design of the world's first digital watch chip. Office: Charles Parkhurst Books Inc PO Box 10850 Prescott AZ 86304-0850

PARKHURST, EDWIN WALLACE, JR., healthcare management consultant; b. Waukegan, Ill., June 17, 1943; s. Edwin W. Sr. and Marie Violet (Wolf) P.; m. Grace Ann Dovemuehle, July 6, 1963; children: John Edward, Janet Lynn, Jeanine Marie, Julie Ann. BA, Carthage Coll., 1965; MBA, U. Chgo., 1968. Adminstrv. asst. West Allis (Wis.) Meml. Hosp., 1965—66; asst. dir., asst. prof. U. Mo. Med. Ctr., Columbia, 1968—71; from assoc., prin., to ptnr. Herman Smith Assoc., Hinsdale, Ill., 1971—88; dir. grad. program in health adminstrn. and policy Univ. Chgo., Ill., 2001—03; ptnr. Herman Smith Assoc. divsn. Coopers & Lybrand, Chgo., 1988—93; mng. prin. MEDCO, Inc., Hatboro, Pa., 1997—, PRISM Healthcare Cons., Glen Ellyn, 1993—; assoc., dept. of health studies, lectr. Sch. of Social Svcs. Adminstrn. U. Chgo., dir. grad. program in health adminstrn. and policy, 2001—03. Spkr. in field; bd. dirs. Clin. Benchmaking. Contbr. articles to profl. jours. Bd. dirs., past pres. Lisle (Ill.) Cmty. Dist. 202 Bd. Edn., 1985—; scout leader Boy Scouts Am., Lisle, 1974-93. Named Disting. Alumni, U. Chgo., 1997; recipient Alumni Svc. citation U. Chgo., 1999. Fellow Am. Assn. Healthcare Cons. (bd. dirs., past pres., chair-elect, 2004, Chester A. Minkalis Svc. award 1999); mem. Health Issues Study Soc. (sec.-treas. 1972—), Am. Hosp. Assn., Am. Coll. Healthcare Execs. (cert. healthcare exec., chmn. healthcare cons. com.), Soc. Healthcare Planning and Mgmt., Chgo. Health Exec. Forum. Avocations: fishing, hunting, hiking, camping, photography. Home: 4239 White Birch Dr Lisle IL 60532-1252 Office: PRISM Healthcare Cons 799 Roosevelt Rd # B4s317 Glen Ellyn IL 60137-5908 Office Phone: 630-790-1265. E-mail: eparkhurst@consultprism.com.

PARKHURST, TODD SHELDON, lawyer; b. Evanston, Ill., Mar. 8, 1941; s. Don A. and Ruth Ellen (Sheldon) P.; m. Karen Judy Huckleberry, Sept. 2, 1968 (dec. Sept. 1969); m. Beverly Ann Susler, Aug. 15, 1976. BS in Gen. Engring., U. Ill., 1963; JD, U. Pa., 1966. Bar: Ill. 1968, U.S. Dist. Ct. (no. dist.) Ill. 1968, U.S. Dist. Ct. (ea. dist.) Wis. 1989, U.S. Ct. Appeals (7th cir.) 1977, U.S. Ct. Appeals Fed. Cir. 1978, U.S. Ct. Mil. Appeals, 1968, U.S. Patent and Trademark Office, 1973, U.S. Supreme Ct. 1973. Assoc. Wolfe, Hubbard, Voit & Osann, 1968-72; assoc. and ptnr. Trexler, Wolters, Bushnell & Fosse, Chgo., 1972-84; ptnr. Jenner & Block, Chgo., 1984-87; ptnr., mgr. intellectual property practice Schiff Hardin & Waite, Chgo., 1987-96; ptnr. Gardner, Carton & Douglas, 1996-98, Hill & Simpson, Chgo., 1998-2000; ptnr., mgr. intellectual property practice Holland & Knight, Chgo., 2000—. Adj. prof. John Marshall Law Sch., Chgo., 1980-84, Ill. Inst. Tech.-Chgo. Kent Law Sch., 1989—. Contbr. articles to profl. jours. Mem. Lifeline Pilots, Inc., pres. 1994-96; hearing officer Ill. Pollution Control Bd., 1972-96. Mem. Am. Intellectual Property Law Assn., Licensing Execs. Soc., Chgo. Bar Assn., Patent Law Assn. Chgo., Chgo. Lit. Club (pres. 1989-90), Adventurers Club Chgo. (sec. 1988). Methodist. Avocations: flying, scuba diving, photography, theatrical acting. Home: 260 E Chestnut St Apt 4301 Chicago IL 60611-2474 Office: Holland & Knight 131 S Dearborn Ste 3000 Chicago IL 60603 Office Phone: 312-263-3600. E-mail: tparkhur@hklaw.com.

PARKHURST, WILLIAM MICHAEL, media consultant; b. Manchester, N.H., July 29, 1945; s. John Theodore and Anna Agnes (Padden) P.; m. Doreen Carney, Mar. 16, 1968 (div. July 1975); children: Carolyn; stepchildren: Christopher Katz, Terry Katz. BA, U. N.H., 1970. Newscaster Sta. WLKW Radio, Providence, 1970-73; prodr. Sta. WOR Radio-TV, N.Y.C., 1973-74; assoc. dir. publs. Simon & Schuster, N.Y.C., 1974-77; dir. pub. Putnam Pub. Group, N.Y.C., 1977-80; dir. of publicity Avon Books Hearst Corp., N.Y.C., 1980-81; pres. H.K. Simon Co., Yonkers, N.Y., 1992—, Parkhurst Comm., Inc., N.Y.C., 1981—. Chmn. publicity com. Nat. Book Awards, N.Y.C., 1980-81; lectr. Yale U., New Haven, Conn., 1993—; cons. 20-20 ABC-TV, True Detectives CBS-TV, 1991-93. Author: How to Get Publicity, 1985, rev., 2000, The Eloquent Executive, 1988, True Detectives, 1989. With USN, 1967-69. Mem. Pubs. Publicity Assn. (exec. bd. dirs. 1979-82). Democrat. Avocation: marathons. E-mail: BillParkhurst@Parkhurstcom.com.

PARKIN, GERARD FRANCIS RALPH, chemistry educator, researcher; b. Middlesbrough, Cleveland, Eng., Feb. 15, 1959; s. Ralph and Clementine (Gill) P.; m. Rita K. Upmacis. BA with honors, Oxford (Eng.) U., 1981, MA, 1984, PhD, 1985. NATO/SERC (U.K.) postdoctoral rsch. fellow Calif. Inst. Tech., 1985-88; asst. prof. Columbia U., N.Y.C., 1988-91, assoc. prof., 1991-94; prof., chmn. chemistry dept., 1994—; chmn. dept. chemistry, 1999—2002. Contbr. numerous articles to profl. jours. Recipient Camille and Henry Dreyfus Tchr.-Scholar award, 1991, award in pure chemistry Am. Chem. Soc., 1994, Corday Morgan medal Royal Soc. Chemistry, 1995; A.P. Sloan rsch. fellow; NSF Presdl. faculty fellow, 1992—. Roman Catholic. Achievements include discovery that bond stretch isomerism in an artifact. Office: Columbia U 116th St And Broadway New York NY 10027

PARKIN, JAMES LAMAR, otolaryngologist, educator; b. Salt Lake City, June 2, 1939; s. Elmer Lamar and Mary Ilene (Soffe) Parkin; m. Bonnie Dansie, July 1, 1963; children: Jeffrey, Brett, Matthew, David. BS, U. Utah, 1963, MD, 1966; MS, U. Wash., 1970. Diplomate Am. Bd. Otolaryngology. Resident in otolaryngology U. Wash., Seattle, 1968—72; practice medicine specializing in otolaryngology Salt Lake City, 1972—; chmn. divsn. otolaryngology U. Utah Sch. Medicine, Salt Lake City, 1974—93, prof. surgery, 1981—, acting chmn. dept. surgery, 1984—84, 1993—94, chmn., 1994—96. Pres. med. bd. Univ. Med. Ctr., Salt Lake City, 1983—85, chmn. exec. com. faculty practice orgn., 1994—96, assoc. v.p. health scis., 1996—97, v.p. sch. medicine alumni, 2003—, v.p. med. alumni, 2003—; bd. govs. Utah Med. Ins. Assn., Salt Lake City, 1979—81. Guest editor Ear, Nose and Throat Jour., 1982, assoc. editor Archives of Otolaryngology. Leader Boy Scouts Am.; bishop Ch. of Jesus Christ of Latter-Day Saints, Salt Lake City, 1983—86, stake pres., 1986—96, pres. Eng. London South Mission, 1996—2000. Recipient Honor award, Am. Acad. Otolaryngology, 1980. Fellow: ACS, Am. Neurotology Soc., Am. Soc. Laser Medicine and Surgery, Am. Otol. Soc., Am. Plastic and Reconstructive Surgery, Am. Laryngol, Rhinol. and Otol. Soc.; mem.: Collegium Aesculapium, Collegium Aesculapium (pres.elect 2004), Soc. Otolaryngology-Maxillofacial Surgery (pres. Utah chpt. 1979), Am. Cancer Soc. (pres. Utah chpt. 1984—86), Soc. Univ. Otolaryngologists (pres. 1984—85), Assn. Acad. Depts. Otolaryngology (chmn. nat. faculty survey

com. 1980—90, sec.-treas. 1982—84, pres. 1986—88). Home: 2390 Bernadine Dr Salt Lake City UT 84109-1206 Office: U Utah Health Scis Ctr 50 N Medical Dr Salt Lake City UT 84132-0001

PARKIN, STUART STEPHEN PAPWORTH, materials scientist; IBM fellow IBM Almaden Rsch. Ctr., San Jose, Calif., 1983—. Recipient Internat. prize for new materials Am. Phys. Soc., 1994, C.V. Boys prize Inst. Physics, London, 1991, Inaugural Outstanding Young Investigator award Materials Rsch. Soc., 1991, Europhysics prize Hewlett-Packard, 1997, Indsl. Applications of Physics prize Am. Inst. Physics, 1999-2000; named Innovator of Yr., R&D Mag., 2001. Fellow AAAS, IEEE, Am. Phys. Soc., Royal Soc. London, Inst. Physics (London). Office: IBM Almaden Rsch Ctr K11 D2 650 Harry Rd San Jose CA 95120-6099 E-mail: parkin@almaden.ibm.com.

PARKINS, FREDERICK MILTON, dental educator, university dean; b. Princeton, N.J., Sept. 8, 1935; s. William Milton and Phyllis Virginia (Plyler) P.; m. Carolyn V. Rude; children: Bradford, Christopher, Eric. Student, Carleton Coll., 1953-56; D.D.S., U. Pa., 1960; MSD. in Pedodontics, U. N.C., Chapel Hill, 1965; PhD in Physiology, 1969. Instr. pedodontics U. N.C., 1965-67; asst. prof. pedodontics U. Pa., 1967-68, dir. Dental Aux. Utilization program, chmn. pedodontics, 1968-69; assoc. prof., head pedodontics U. Iowa, Iowa City, 1969-72, prof., head pedodontics, 1972-75; asst. dean acad. affairs U. Iowa (Coll. Dentistry), 1974-75, asso. dean acad. affairs, 1975-79, dir. continuing edn., 1975-77; prof. pedodontics, dean Sch. Dentistry, U. Louisville, 1979-85, prof. pediatric dentistry, 1985—2003, prof. pediatric dentistry emeritus, 2003—. Mem. Hillenbrand Fellowship adv. com. Am. Fund Dental Health, 1980-85; cons. Div. Dental Health USPHS, 1969-72; dental cons., med. staff Children's Hosp. Phila., 1968-71; med. staff Kosair Children's Hosp. Louisville, 1983—; cons., mem. pedodontic adv. com. Council Dental Edn., 1974-80, chmn. pedodontic adv. com., 1978-80, cons. council on legislation, 1978-79; dental cons. Aux. Utilization VA, 1968-69; cons. Bur. Health Resources Devel., 1974-76, Dept. Army, 1980-, numerous others Assoc. editor Jour. Preventive Dentistry, 1973-79, mem. editl. bd., 1980-83; editl. reviewer Jour. Pediatrics, 1969-, Jour. Dental Edn, 1978-, Jour. AMA, 1979-; assoc. editor Jour. Clin. Preventive Dentistry, 1979-84; mem. editl. bd. Jour. Clin. Laser Medicine and Surgery, 1999-; contbr. chpts. to textbooks, articles to profl. publs. Bd. govs. Youth Performing Arts Coun., Louisville-Jefferson County Sch. Dist., 1980-89, pres., 1986-88; bd. govs. Regional Cancer Ctr., U. Louisville, 1979-84, Univ. Hosp., 1979-84; mem. human studies com. U. Louisville, 1988-90. Robert Wood Johnson Congl. fellow Inst. of Medicine, 1977-78; USPHS postdoctoral fellow, 1963-67; NIH grantee, 1971-75; Recipient Earle Banks Hoyt Teaching award, 1969 Fellow AAAS, Am. Acad. Pediat. Dentistry (chmn. rsch. com. 1972-73, Ann. Rsch. award 1968, chmn. advanced edn. com. 1974-75, chmn. dental care programs com. 1978-80); mem. ADA, Am. Coll. Dentistry, Am. Soc. Dentistry for Children (exec. bd. Iowa unit 1969-75, award com. 1973-76, edn. com. 1974-77, chmn. rsch. adv. com. 1973-76), Biophys. Soc., Internat. Assn. Dental Rsch., N.Y. Acad. Dentistry, Ky. Dental Assn. (exec. bd. 1979-84), Am. Assn. Dental Schs. (coun. deans 1979-85, chmn. pedodontics sect. 1976, chmn. continuing edn. sect. 1979, legis. com. 1978-83), Louisville Dental Alumni Assn. (bd. govs. 1979-84), Am. Assn. Dental Rsch. (nat. affairs com. 1978-85), Acad. Laser Dentistry (co-chmn. rsch. and edn. 1997, chair 1998-2003, bd. dirs. 1997-2003, cert. com., T.H. Maiman award for excellence in dental laser rsch.), U.S. Power Squadron (bd. govs. 1987-93, sec. 1989, adminstrv. officer 1990, exec. officer 1991, comdr. 1992), Aircraft Owners and Pilots Assn., Omicron Kappa Upsilon (pres. Wa. chpt. 1991-92), Rotary. Unitarian Universalist. Home: 6424 Marina Dr Prospect KY 40059-8846 Office: U Louisville Sch Dentistry Dept Orth Pediatric & Geriatric Dent Rm 240N Louisville KY 40292 Office Phone: 502-852-1334. E-mail: fmpark01@louisville.edu.

PARKINS, FREDERICK WALLACE EUGENE, environmental services administrator, educator, coroner; b. Ft. Bragg, N.C., Mar. 3, 1967; s. Frederick Wallace Eugene and Carolyn Sealey Parkins; m. Barbara Jean DeAngelis, July 4, 1998; m. Jennifer Lea Johnson, Feb. 23, 1993 (div. Aug. 21, 1995); children: Brandon Louis, Samantha Marie, Michael Connor, Johnathan Daniel. BA, Idaho State U., 1992. Environ. health specialist Health Dept., Pocatello, Idaho, 1992—95; chemist U.S. Army Dugway Proving Ground, Dugway, Utah, 1995—2000; environ. health and safety mgr. ILEX Oncology, San Antonio, Tex., 2000—01; counter-terrorism instr. First Response Group, San Antonio, Tex., 2001—. Author: Elixir The Medieval Quest, The NATO Opposition, Target America Terror at the 2002 Olympics. With USAR, 1989—. Recipient Cert. of Appreciation for preparing San Antonio cmty. to defend against terrorism, Mayor of San Antonio, 2001, Commn. as Adm. in Tex. Navy for assisting comty. in Tex. prepare for acts of terrorism involving the use of weapons of mass destruction, Gov. of Tex., 2003. Achievements include prepared municipal, state, county, and federal first responders in several U.S. states to respond to acts terrorism involving the use of weapons of mass destruction. Personal E-mail: fredparkins@email.com.

PARKINSON, BRADFORD WELLS, astronautical engineer, educator; b. Madison, Wis., Feb. 16, 1935; s. Herbert and Metta Tisdale (Smith) P.; m. Virginia Pinkham Wier, Nov. 26, 1977; children: Leslie, Bradford II, Eric, Ian, Bruce, Jared Bradford. BS, U.S. Naval Acad., 1957; MS, MIT, 1961; PhD, Stanford U., 1966; grad. (disting.), USAF Command and Staff Coll., 1969, Naval War Coll., 1972. Commd. 2d lt. USAF, 1957, advanced through grades to col., 1972; divsn. chief AF Test Pilot Sch., 1966-68; chair dept. astronautics and computer sci. USAF Acad., 1969-71; dir. engring. ABRES, 1972; program mgr. NAVSTAR GPS, 1972-78; ret. USAF, 1978; prof. mech. engring. Colo. State U., Ft. Collins, 1978-79; v.p. advanced engring. Rockwell Internat., Downey, Calif., 1979-80; gen. mgr., v.p. Intermetrics, Inc., Cambridge, Mass., 1980-84; prof. emeritus, assoc. dir. gravity probe-B Stanford (Calif.) U., 1984—; CEO, pres. Trimble Navigation Ltd., 1998-99. Chair adv. coun. JPL NASA; dir. Trimble Navigation Ltd., Sunnyvale, Calif., NTV, Cambridge; chair bd. dirs. Aerospace Corp., El Segundo, Calif. Decorated Def. Superior Svc. medal, AF Commendation medal with oak leaf cluster, Meritorius Svc. medal, Presdl. Unit citation, Bronze Star, Legion of Merit, Air medal with oak leaf cluster; recipient Pub. Svc. award, Disting. Pub. Svc. award, NASA, 1984, Thurlow award Inst. Navigation, 1986, Burka award, 1987, Kepler award, 1991, von Karman Lectureship Am. Inst. of Aeronautics and Astronautics, 1996, Magellan Premium, Am. Philos. Soc., 1997, Gold medal Space Tech. Hall of Fame of U.S. Space Found., 1998, Williams Space medal Soc. Logistics Engrs., 1996. Draper Prize, Nat. Acad. Engring. Fellow AIAA, Royal Inst. Navigation (Gold medal 1983), Inst. Navigation, IEEE (Kirchner award 1986, Pioneer award 1994, Sperry award 1999, Sr. Remo medal); mem. AAS, NAE (Draper Prize, 2003), Internat. Acad. Astronautics, Sigma Xi, Tau Beta Pi. Avocations: hiking, skiing, sailing. Office: Stanford U 4085 Mail Code Stanford CA 94305 Home: 2360 Camino Edna San Luis Obispo CA 93401

PARKINSON, DEL R. music educator, pianist; b. Blackfoot, Idaho, Aug. 6, 1948; s. Douglas R. and Jane (Peck) P.; m. Glenna M. Christensen, Aug. 6, 1986. MusB, Ind. U., 1971, MusM, 1972, MusD, 1975; diploma, Juilliard Sch., N.Y.C., 1977. Asst. prof. Furman U., Greenville, S.C., 1975-76; assoc. prof. Ricks Coll., Rexburg, Idaho, 1977-85; prof. Boise (Idaho) State U., 1985—. Tchr., performer Dixie Festival of the Performing Arts, St. George, Utah, 1986-91; performer Hsu & Parkinson duo pianists, 1986-93, Am. Piano Duo, 1984—, Am. Piano Quartet, 1989-95; pianist Boise Philharmonic, 1988—; faculty Coll. So. Idaho Summer Fest, 1995—. Rec. pianist Am. Piano Quartet, 1992, Am. Piano Duo, 1998, 2004. Fulbright-Hays grantee, London, 1974-75; recipient Gov. of Idaho Excellence award, 1988. Mem. Music Tchrs. Nat. Assn. (master, state chmn.), Nat. Guild Piano Tchrs. (adjudicator), Am. Liszt Soc. (jour. contbr.). Office: Boise State U Dept Of Music Boise ID 83725-1560 Office Phone: 208-426-3300.

PARKINSON, DIAN, actress; Student, Lee Strasberg Studio, Los Angeles. Talk show hostess The Women's Side; appeared on TV shows The Price is Right, The Tonight Show Starring Johnny Carson, Vegas, Bob Hope's Desert Classic, The Bob Hope Christmas Show (Emmy Award Citation); model on cover of Bert Stein, Master of Contemporary Photography, Cosmopolitan mag., commls., posters, billboards, other mags. Named Miss U.S.A. Office: Jo-Ann Geffen & Assocs 3151 Cahuenga Blvd W Suite 235 Los Angeles CA 90068

PARKINSON, HOWARD EVANS, insurance company executive; b. Logan, Utah, Nov. 3, 1936; s. Howard Maughan and Valeria Arlene (Evans) P.; m. Lucy Kay Bowen, Sept. 2, 1960; children: Blake, Gregory, Dwight, Lisa, David, Rebecca. BS, Brigham Young U., 1961; MBA, U. Utah, 1963. CLU. Chartered fin. cons. Mgmt. intern AEC, Richland, Wash., 1963-65; v.p. Belstar, Inc., Rexburg, Idaho, 1965-71, dir., 1966-76, pres., 1971-76; v.p., dir. Grand Targhee Resort, Inc., Rexburg, 1967-69; v.p. Fargo-Wilson-Wells Co., Pocatello, Idaho, 1974-76; equity qualified agt. Equitable Life Assurance So. U.S., Idaho Falls, Idaho, 1977-80, mem. nat. coun. sales group, 1978; dist. mgr. Mass. Mut. Life Ins. Co., Idaho Falls, 1980—; fin. cons. small bus. Bd. dirs. Little League Baseball, 1974-75; coach Little League Basketball, 1975-76; high councilman Rexburg Stake, Ch. of Jesus Christ of Latter-day Saints, 1976-77, bishop, 1977—; mem. Pres.'s Coun., 1988. Recipient Bronze award Mass. Mut. Life Ins. Co., Gold award, 1984. Mem. Million Dollar Roundtable, Toastmasters (past pres.). Republican. Address: Massachusetts Mutual 1970 E 17th St Ste 202 Idaho Falls ID 83404-8048

PARKINSON, JAMES THOMAS, III, investment consultant; b. Richmond, Va., July 10, 1940; s. James Thomas and Elizabeth (Hopkins) P.; m. Molly O. Owens, June 16, 1962 (div. June 1998); children: James Thomas, Glenn Walser; m. Caroline Smith Pyle, Oct. 10, 1998. BA, U. Va., 1962; MBA, U. Pa., 1964. Trainee Chem. Bank, N.Y.C., 1964-66; assoc., corp. fin. dept. Blyth & Co., Inc., N.Y.C., 1968-69; v.p., corp. fin. dept. Clark Dodge & Co., Inc., N.Y.C., 1969—72; pvt. practice investment mgmt. N.Y.C., Va., 1972—85, 1987—; v.p. Pleasantville Advisors, Inc., N.Y.C., 1986-87. Instr. corp. fin. Ind. U., 1966-68. Sr. warden Ch. of Holy Trinity, N.Y.C., 1978-79; trustee Am. Bible Soc., 1980—, Funds, Episcopal Diocese of Va., 2000—; dir. Bowles Fluidics corp., Columbia, Md., 1998—. With AUS, 1966-68. Mem. Univ. Club (N.Y.C.), Va. Country Club. Republican. Episcopalian. Home and Office: PO Box 2247 Middleburg VA 20118-2247

PARKINSON, ROBERT L., JR., medical products executive, health facility administrator; BBA, MBA, Loyola U., Chgo. With Abbott Labs., Abbott Park, Ill., 1976, v.p. European ops., 1990-93, sr. v.p. chem. and agrl. products, 1993-95, pres. internat. divsn., 1995-98, bd. dirs., 1998, pres., COO, 1999-2001; dean Loyola U. Chgo.'s Sch. of Bus. Adminstrn. and Grad. Sch. of Bus., 2002—04; chmn., CEO Baxter Intenat., Inc., 2004—. Chmn. Geneva (Switzerland) Proteomics, 2001. Bd. dirs. Northwestern Mem. Hosp., Northwestern Mem. Found. Office: Baxter Internat Inc One Baxter Pkwy Deerfield IL 60015 Office Phone: 847-948-2000.*

PARKINSON, WILLIAM CHARLES, physicist, researcher; b. Jarvis, Ont., Can., Feb. 11, 1918; came to U.S., 1925, naturalized, 1941; s. Charles Franklin and Euphemia Alice (Johnston) P.; m. Martha Bennett Capron, Aug. 2, 1944; children: Martha Reed, William Reid. BSE, U. Mich., 1940, MS, 1941, PhD, 1948. Physicist Applied Physics Lab., Johns Hopkins U., 1942-46, OSRD, 1943-44; mem. faculty U. Mich., 1947—, prof. physics, 1958-88, prof. emeritus physics, 1988—, dir. cyclotron lab., 1962-77; mem. subcom. nuclear structure NRC, 1959-68; mem. nuclear physics sub panel mgmt. and costs nuclear program, 1969-70; adv. panel physics NSF, 1966-69. Cons. grad. sci. facilities, 1968, chmn. postdoctoral fellowship evaluation panel, 1969, cons. to govt. and industry, 1955— Quondam mem. Trinity Coll., Cambridge, Eng. Recipient Ordnance Devel. award Navy Dept., 1946; Fulbright research scholar Cavendish Lab., Cambridge U., 1952-53 Fellow Am. Phys. Soc.; mem. N.Y. Acad. Scis., Biophys. Soc., Grad. "M" Club (awarded hon. "M" 1991), Sigma Xi, Phi Kappa Phi, Kappa Kappa Psi. Achievements include invention of automatic judging and timing for swim meets, fast neutron spectroscopy using cyclotrons; development of high resolution nuclear spectroscopy with cyclotrons. Home: 1600 Sheridan Dr Ann Arbor MI 48104-4052 Office: Univ Mich Dept Physics Ann Arbor MI 48109 Office Phone: 734-764-3458. E-mail: wcpark@umich.edu.

PARKIN-SPEER, DIANE, English law educator; b. Salt Lake City, Feb. 19, 1941; d. Lorin David and Thora (Bauer) Parkin; m. Richard L. Speer, June 3, 1963; divorced. BA magna cum laude, Lewis & Clark Coll., 1963; MA, Bowling Green State U., 1965; PhD, U. Iowa, 1970. Grad. asst. U. Iowa, Iowa City, 1965-69; prof. English SW Tex. State U., San Marcos, 1969—; rschr. in history English law and rhetoric. Mem. Am. Soc. Legal History, Sixteenth Century Studies Conf., ACLU. Presbyterian. Contbr. articles on English law to profl. jours. Office: Tex State U San Marcos TX 78666

PARKISON, JAMES MAX, trial court administrator, educator; b. Kansas City, Mo., Jan. 12, 1943; s. Amherst Max and Agnes Lorraine (St. George) P.; m. Anne Ruth Hale, Nov. 1, 1969; 1 child, Christopher Hale. BA, Grinnell Coll., 1965; JD, U. Mo., Kansas City, 1968. Bar: Mo. 1968, U.S. Dist. Ct. (ea. dist.) Mo. 1969. Vol. VISTA, 1969-70; staff atty. St. Louis Legal Aid Soc., 1970-71; cts. program chief Mo. Law Enforcement Assistance Coun., Jefferson City, 1971-73; state ct. adminstr. State of Mo. Supreme Ct., Jefferson City, 1973-81; asst. dir. Inst. Jud. Adminstrn., N.Y.C., 1981-83; trial ct. adminstr. Burlington County, State N.J., Mt. Holly, 1983-91; clk. of ct. so. dist. N.Y. U.S. Dist. Ct., N.Y.C., 1991—. Mem. nat. adv. com. Nat. Inst. Law Enforcement and Criminal Justice, Dept. Justice, Washington, 1977-81, nat. adv. com. Inst. for Econ. and Policy Studies, Inc., A Comparative Study of State Ct. Orgns., 1980-83; mem. Nat. State Jud. Info. Sys. Com., 1973-81, chmn. sys. documentation com., 1976-77, mem. long range planning com. and sys. devel. com. Nat. Ctr. for State Cts., Williamsburg, Va., 1976-80; mem. exec. com. Coordinating Coun. of Nat. Ct. Orgns., 1983-84; cons. Koba Assocs., 1975-83; adj. asst. prof. law NYU Sch. Law, 1982-83; adj. assoc. prof. NYU Sch. Pub. Adminstrn., 1983-85; adj. instr. Rutgers Sch. Law, Camden, 1986-91; cons. Asian Coun. for Law and Devel., Colombo, Sri Lanka, Ministry of Justice Sri Lanka, 1982; internat. rapporteur Commn. on Juries, Conf. on Independence of Justice, 1983. Mem. editl. bd. The Justice Sys. Jour., 1983-91; exec. prodr. Little Theatre, Jefferson City, 1980-81, bd. dirs., 1979-81; bd. dirs. Burlington Co. Footlighters, 1986-91. U. Mo.-Kansas City Law Sch. scholar, 1965. Mem. ABA (mem. criminal justice sect. 1981-84), Am. Judicature Soc. (life), Conf. State Ct. Adminstrs. (nat. exec. com. 1976-81, nat. vice chmn. 1978-79, nat. chmn. 1979-80), Internat. Bar Assn. (vice chmn. com. on adminstrn. of justice sect. gen. practice 1982-84), Sigma Delta Chi, Phi Alpha Delta. Methodist. E-mail: jparki@aol.com.

PARKLEE, LEE See PARK, LEE

PARKMAN, CYNTHIA ANN, medical and surgical nurse, nursing educator; b. Mpls., Nov. 7, 1957; d. Byron F. and Carolyn M. (Waltenen) Bray; m. Russell O. Parkman, Mar. 15, 1980; children: Theodore Owen, Thomas Edward, Elizabeth Ann. BSN cum laude, Point Loma Coll., San Diego, 1980; MSN, U. San Diego, 1988. Project nurse Sharp Meml. Hosp., San Diego, 1987-91, clin. nurse specialist, mgr. ambulatory care, program mgr., clin. specialist, 1992-93. Instr. Point Loma Nazarene Coll., San Diego, 1991—92; free-lance writer, 1993—; house supr. Suttr Davis Hosp., 1996—98; educator Mercy Healthcare Sacramento, Calif., 1996—99; asst. prof. Calif. State U., Sacramento, 1997—; cons. quality managed care/leadership. Contbr. articles to profl. jours. Manchester scholar, 1988, grad. fellow, 1987-88. Mem.: ANA, Am. Sociol. Assn., Am. Holistic Nurses Assn., Case Mgmt. Am. Soc., Point Loma Nazarene Coll. Nursing Honor Soc. (charter), Zeta Eta, Zeta Mu, Sigma Theta Tau. E-mail: parkmanc@csus.edu.

PARKS, ALBERT LAURISTON, lawyer; b. Providence, July 18, 1935; s. Albert Lauriston and Dorothy Isabel (Arnold) P.; m. Martha Ann Anderson, Jan. 12, 1961; children: Amy Woodward, George Webster, Reed Anderson. BA, Kent State U., 1958; JD, U. Chgo., 1961. Bar: R.I. 1962, U.S. Dist. Ct. R.I. 1963, U.S. Ct. Appeals (1st cir.) 1966, U.S. Supreme Ct. 1980. Assoc. Hanson, Curran, Parks & Whitman, Providence, 1961-65, ptnr., 1966-2000. Town solicitor No. Kingstown, RI, 1978—80, Jamestown, 1999—2000, 2003—. Fellow: Am. Coll. Trial Lawyers; mem.: ABA, R.I. Bar Assn., Maritime Law Assn., Wickford Yacht Club, Saunderstown Yacht Club. Republican. Episcopalian. Office: 10 Coronado St Jamestown RI 02835 Home: 14 Church Ln North Kingstown RI 02852-5004 Office Phone: 401-423-8900. E-mail: alp@hcpw.com.

PARKS, BLANCHE CECILE, public administrator; b. Leavenworth, Kans., Feb. 2, 1949; d. Nile Eugene Sr. and Fern (Dickinson) Williams; m. Sherman A. Parks Jr.; children: Michael A., Stacy M. BEd, Washburn U., 1971, MEd, 1976, postgrad., 1983-84. Tchr. Topeka Pub. Schs., 1971-76, reading specialist, 1979-84; ins. regulator Kans. Ins. Dept., Topeka, 1984-88; spl. asst. to sec. Kans. Dept. Human Resources, Topeka, 1988-92; real estate lease adminstr. State of Kans., Topeka, 1992—. Pres. Kans. Children's Svc. League, 1990-94, YWCA, Topeka, 1992-94; chmn. Topeka Human Rels. Commn., 1991-93; mem. Topeka Pub. Schs. Found., 1993-94; participant Leadership Topeka, 1994, Leadership Kans., 1994 Named The Outstanding Young Woman of Kans. Jaycee Women, 1984, 85, one of Outstanding Young Women Am., 1985. Mem. Jr. League of Topeka (Gold Rose award 1993), Jack and Jill Am., Kans. C. of C. (leadership award 1985), Links, Phi Kappa Phi, Phi Delta Kappa, Alpha Delta Kappa, Delta Kappa Gamma, (life) Delta Sigma Theta (v.p. 1980-82). Republican. Mem. A.M.E. Ch. Home: 1727 SE 36th Terrace Topeka KS 66605

PARKS, CORRINE FRANCES, insurance company executive; b. Pulaski, Illinois, May 23, 1934; d. Elizabeth (Stanfield) Daniels; m. Charles Robert Parks, July 6, 1957; children: Reginald, Pierre. BA, Chgo. State U., 1976; student, Columbia Coll., 1986—87; MA, Governor's State U., 1981; postgrad., Chgo. U. Sem., 1990—94, Luth. Sem. of Theology; PhD in Philosopy, Bridgewater U. Exec. rep. Marsh and McLennon, Inc., Chgo., 1970—74; account exec. Internat. Ins. Cons., Chgo., 1974—77; mktg. rep. Alexander and Alexander, Chgo., 1977—79; mem. Nat. Coun. S.S. Rep., Chgo., 1981; pres. A, A, and A Ins. Agy., Chgo., 1981—. Radio show host Sta. WBAX-1570 AM, Chgo., 1985—, WYAA Radio; bd. dir. Unity Chgo., Chgo. Urban Day Love Cmty. COGIC, Hazelcrest, Ill. Sec. Englewood Re-devel. Group, Chgo., 1987; rep. State Sun. Sch., N.I. Juris. Mem. Ind., Ill. Ins. Agts., Women in Radio and TV, Chgo. Bd. Underwriters, Nat. Assn. Black Journalists, Chgo. Mus. Sci. and Industry, Chgo. Assn. Black Journalists, Order of Eastern Star (treas. 1983). Democrat. Avocations: theater, singing, golf, reading. Home: 72 Iliad Dr Tinley Park IL 60477 Office: AA and A Mort Assn 450 Prairie St Calumet City IL 60409-1926 also: AA and A Ins Agy 10016 S Western Chicago IL 60643 Office Phone: 708-868-4072., 773-248-9700. Office Fax: 708-868-4785. Personal E-mail: parkscfp@aol.com.

PARKS, DAVID R. heating/air conditioning manufacturing executive; CFO Goodman Mfg., Houston, 2000—. Office: Goodman Mfg 2550 N Loop W Ste 400 Houston TX 77092-8908 Office Fax: (713) 861-2176.

PARKS, DONALD LEE, mechanical engineer, human factors engineer; b. Delphos, Kans., Feb. 23, 1931; s. George Delbert and Erma Josephine (Boucek) P.; m. Bessie Lou Schur, Dec. 24, 1952; children: Elizabeth Parks Anderson, Patricia Parks-Holbrook, Donna, Charles, Sandra. Student, Kans. Wesleyan U., 1948-50; BSME, BSBA, Kans. State U., 1957, MS in Psychology, 1959. Cert. profl. ergonomist. Elem. tchr., 1950-51; with Kans. State U. Placement Svc., 1959-57; human factors engr., sys. engr. Boeing Co., Seattle, 1959-90, sr. specialist engr., 1972-74, sr. engring. supr., 1974-90; pres. D-Square Assocs. Engring. Cons., 1990-95, Venture Worlds, 1995—. Adj. lectr. UCLA Engring. Extension, 1989—; cons., lectr. in field; participant workshops on guidelines in profl. areas, NATO, NSF, Nat. Acad. Sci., NRC. Author over 80 publs., 8 book chpts. Mem. Derby (Kans.) Planning Commn., 1961-62, chmn., 1962; del. King County (Wash.) Rep. Conv., 1972. With AUS, 1952-54. Mem. ASME, APA, Human Factors Soc. (Puget Sound Pres.'s award 1969), Elks. Presbyterian. Home: 6232 127th Ave SE Bellevue WA 98006-3943

PARKS, FREDRICK SCOTT, systems engineer; b. Phoenix, Ariz., Jan. 7, 1961; s. David Walker and Carrie Ellen (Abbott) P.; m. Kimberly Louise Kubeja, May 8, 1993. BS, Rensselaer Poly. Inst., 1982, MS, 1984. Rsch. material physicist DSM, Geleen, The Netherlands, 1982; sr. engr. analyst Anser Inc., Arlington, Va., 1983-93; sr. systems engr. Lockheed Missiles and Space Co., Inc., Sunnyvale, Calif., 1993-96; assoc. systems engr. Steven Myers & Assocs, Newport Beach, Calif., 1996—. Contbr. articles to profl. jours. Emergency Planning Coun. ARC, Arlington, 1985-92. Mem. AIAA, Internat. Coun. Systems Engring., Am. Def. Preparedness Assn. Achievements include development of first detailed system architecture to enable multi-shot theater missile defense doctrine, development of Integrated Theater High Altitude Area Defense system architecture, lead system integrator for ground-based missile defense battle management, command, control and communication. Office: 4695 Macarthur Ct Fl 8 Newport Beach CA 92660-1882

PARKS, GEORGE RICHARD, retired librarian; b. Boston, Apr. 11, 1935; m. Carol A. Richmond; children: Elizabeth, Jennifer, Geoffrey. AB summa cum laude, U. N.H., 1959; MALS, U. Mich., 1962; postgrad., Johns Hopkins, 1959-65; EFM cert. Sch. Theology, U. of the South, 1985. Preprofl. young adult librarian Enoch Pratt Free Library, Balt., 1960-61, ctrl., br. librarian, 1962-65, asst. to asst. dir., 1965-66; asst. dir. for adminstrn., libraries U. Rochester, 1966-68, chief adminstrv. officer, 1968-69; dean of libraries U. R.I., 1969-80; univ. librarian Colgate U., 1980-85, U. So. Maine, Portland, 1985-97; ret., 1997. Lectr. in field, cons. libr. bldg.; cons. antique map collection; mem. exec. bd. Greater Portland Theol. Libr., 1986-88, Maine Community Cultural Alliance, 1992-98; mem. exec. bd. So. Maine Libr. Dist., 1990-97, chmn., 1993. Apptd. Maine State Libr. Commn., 1994-98; asst. treas. St. Ann's Episcopal Ch., 1999—, lay preacher 2001—. Recipient Margaret Mann award U. Mich., 1962; Phillips Exeter Acad. scholar, 1952-54; U. N.H. scholar, 1955-59; Enoch Pratt Free Library scholar, 1961-62; Woodrow Wilson fellow, 1959-60. Mem. ALA, Assn. Coll. Rsch. Librs. (pres. New Eng. chpt. 1975, chmn. nat. conf. 1978, coll. librs. sect. planning com. 1994-96), Consortium R.I. Acad. Rsch. Librs. (chmn. 1972-73), Maine Libr. Assn., New Eng. Libr. Assn. (chmn. planning com. 1992-97, v.p./pres. elect 1995-96, pres. 1996-97, exec. bd. 1997-99), Libr. Adminstrn. and Mgmt. Assn. (exec. bd. bldgs. and equipment sect., libr. bldg. awards com. 1983-85), U. So. Maine Retirees Assn. (exec. bd. 2002—), Phi Beta Kappa, Phi Kappa Phi, Beta Phi Mu. Home: 4 Pierce St Westbrook ME 04092-2331 Personal E-mail: grparks@aol.com.

PARKS, GORDON ROGER ALEXANDER, film director, author, photographer, composer; b. Ft. Scott, Kans., Nov. 30, 1912; s. Jackson and Sarah (Ross) P.; m. Sally Alvis, 1933 (div. 1961); m. Elizabeth Campbell, 1962 (div. 1973); m. Genevieve Young, Aug. 26, 1973 (div. 1979); children by previous marriage: Gordon (dec.), Toni Parks Parsons, David, Leslie. Student pub. schs., Fort Scott, St. Paul; DFA (hon.), Md. Inst., 1968, Fairfield U., 1969; D (hon.), Boston U., 1969; LittD (hon.), Kans. State U., 1970; LHD (hon.), St. Olaf Coll., 1973; DFA (hon.), Colby Coll., 1974; DLit (hon.), MacAlester Coll., 1974; D (hon.), Lincoln U., 1975; HHD (hon.), Thiel Coll., 1976; DA (hon.), Columbia Coll., 1977; DFA (hon.), Rutgers U., 1980, Pratt Inst., 1981; LHD (hon.), Suffolk U., 1982; DFA (hon.), Kansas City Art Inst., 1984; LHD (hon.), Art Ctr. Coll. Design, 1986; DA (hon.), Hamline U., 1987; DFA (hon.), Am. Internat. Coll., 1988; HHD (hon.), Savannah Coll. Art and Design, 1988; D (hon.), U. Bradford, Eng., 1989; DFA (hon.), Rochester Inst. Tech., 1989, SUNY, 1990, R.I. Coll., 1990, Parsons Sch. Design, 1991, Manhattanville Coll., 1992, Coll. New Rochelle, 1992, Skidmore Coll., 1993; LittD (hon.), Montclair State U., 1994. Freelance fashion photographer, Mpls., 1937-42; photographer Farm Security Adminstrn., 1942-43, OWI, 1944, Standard Oil Co., N.J., 1945-48, Life mag., 1948-68; ind. photographer, film maker, 1954—. Color and black and white cons. various motion picture prodns., U.S. and Europe, 1954—. Writer, producer, dir.: The Learning Tree, 1969; dir.: (films) Shaft, 1972, 2000, Shaft's Big Score, 1972, The Super Cops, 1974, Leadbelly, 1976, Odyssey of Solomon Northup, 1984, Moments Without Proper Names, 1986 (Silver medal Internat. Film Festival 1989); creator, composer, dir. Martin, 1990; TV documentary: Diary of a Harlem Family, 1968 (Emmy award); author: Flash Photography, 1947, Camera Portraits: The Techniques and Principals of Documentary Portraiture, 1948, The Learning Tree, 1963, A Choice of Weapons, 1966 (Notable Book award ALA 1966), A

Poet and His Camera, 1968, Whispers of Intimate Things, 1971, Born Black, 1971, In Love, 1971, (poetry) Moments Without Proper Names, 1975, Flavio, 1977 (Christopher award 1978), To Smile in Autumn, 1979, (novel) Shannon, 1981, Voices in the Mirror, 1990, (photography, paint and poetry) Arias in Silence, 1994, Glimpses Toward Infinity, 1996, founder, editorial dir. Essence mag., 1970-73; composer Piano Concerto, 1953, Tree Symphony, 1967, 3 piano sonatas, 1956, 58, 60, modern works for piano and wind instruments, (film scores) The Learning Tree (Libr. Congress Nat. Film Registry Classics film honor, 1989), Shaft's Big Score, The Odyssey of Solomon Northup, Moments Without Proper Names; dir., composer (film) Ballet for Martin Luther King, 1991; poetry: Gordon Parks: A Poet and His Camera, Gordon Parks: Whispers of Intimate Things, In Love, Moments Without Proper Names; traveling exhibits in U.S. and abroad, 1990. Bd. dirs. Schomburg Ctr. for Research in Black Culture, Am. Arts. Alliance, W. Eugene Smith Meml. Fund, Black Tennis and Sports Found., Rondo Ave. Inc., St. Paul; Harlem Symphony Orch., N.Y.C.; mem. adv. com. Kans. Ctr. for the Book; bd. advocates Planned Parenthood Fedn. Am. Inc.; patron N.Y. City Housing Authority Symphony; supporter Apple Corps Theatre, N.Y.C., Quindaro Project, Kans., numerous other civic activities. Decorated Comdr. de l'Ordre des Arts et des Lettres (Republique Francaise); recipient Julius Rosenwald award for photography, 1942, award NCCJ, 1964, awards Syracuse U. Sch. Journalism, 1961, Newhouse citation Syracuse U., 1963, awards Phila. Mus. Art, 1964, awards N.Y. Art Dirs. Club, 1964, 68, Frederic W. Brehm award, 1962, Carr Van Anda Journalism award Ohio U., 1970, Carr Van Anda Journalism award U. Miami, 1964, Pres.'s fellow award R.I. Sch. Design, 1984, Am. Soc. Mag. Photographers award, 1985, Nat. Medal Arts award Commonwealth Mass. Communications, 1988, Kans. Gov.'s medal, 1986, Nat. medal of Arts, 1988, World Press Photo award, 1988, N.Y.C. Mayor's award, 1989, Artist of Merit Josef Sudek medal, 1989, award Internat. Ctr. Photography, 1990; named Kansan of Yr. Sons and Daus. Kans., 1985. Mem. Urban League N.Y., ASCAP, Writers Guild, NAACP (Spingarn award 1972, Hall of Fame 1984), Acad. Motion Pictures Arts and Scis., AFTRA, Am. Inst. Pub. Service, Nat. Urban League Guild, Internat. Mark Twain Soc. (hon.), Newspaper Guild, Assn. Composers and Dirs., Dirs. Guild (nat. dir.), Dirs. Guild N.Y., Am. Soc. Mag. Photographers (Photographer of Yr. award 1960, 85), Nat. Assn. for Am. Coposers and Condrs., Stylus Soc. (hon.), U.S. Tennis Assn. Inc., Am. Film Inst, Kappa Alpha Mu. Clubs: Pen; Black Tennis and Sports Found. (bd. dirs.). Home: 860 United Nations Plz New York NY 10017-1810

PARKS, GRACE SUSAN, bank official; b. N.Y.C., Oct. 14, 1948; d. Marco A. and Gloria (Alvino) Vale; m. Louis Parks, Feb. 14, 1988; 1 child, Adam. BS, Pa. State U., 1970; MA, New Sch. for Social Rsch., 1974; cert. in mgmt., Adelphi U., 1979, MBA, 1980; cert. in entrepreneurship, Hofstra U., 1996. Bus. office rep. N.Y. Tel. Co., Rockville Centre, 1971-74; social worker Children's Aid Soc., N.Y.C., 1974-75; EEO officer Edwin Gould Svcs., N.Y.C., 1976-79; v.p. fin. instns. and global markets Bankers Trust Co., N.Y.C., 1979-92; v.p. compensation human resources Chase Manhattan Bank, 1992-96; pres. Loodie Prodns., Inc., 1996; instr. mgmt. Adelphi U. Grad. Sch. Bus. Adminstrn., 1981—; notary pub. State N.Y., 1978—. Mem. Human Resource Planning Soc., Assn. MBA Execs., Am. Compensation Assn., Wall St. Compensation and Benefits Assn. (chmn. 1994-96, pres. 1993-94), N.Y. Compensation Assn., Adelphi U. Businesswomen's Alumni Assn. (pres. 1980-82).

PARKS, HAROLD RAYMOND, mathematician, educator; b. Wilmington, Del., May 22, 1949; s. Lytle Raymond Jr. and Marjorie Ruth (Chambers) P.; m. Paula Sue Beaulieu, Aug. 21, 1971 (div. 1984); children: Paul Raymond, David Austin; m. Susan Irene Taylor, June 6, 1985; 1 stepchild, Kathryn McLaughlin. AB, Dartmouth Coll., 1971; PhD, Princeton U., 1974. Tamarkin instr. Brown U., Providence, 1974-77; asst. prof. Oreg. State U., Corvallis, 1977-82, assoc. prof., 1982-89, prof. math., 1989—, chmn. dept. math., 2001—04. Vis. assoc. prof. Ind. U., Bloomington, 1982-83. Author: Explicit Determination of Area Minimizing Hypersurfaces, vol. II, 1986, (with Steven G. Krantz) A Primer of Real Analytic Functions, 1992, 2d edit., 2002, (with G. Musser, R. Burton, W. Siebler) Mathematics in Life, Society and the World, 1997, 2d edit., 2000, (with Steven G. Krantz) The Geometry of Domains in Space, 1999, (with Krantz) The Implicit Function Theorem: History, Theory, and Applications, 2002; contbr. articles to profl. publs. Cubmaster Oregon Trail Coun. Boy Scouts Am., 1990-92. NSF fellow, 1971-74. Mem. Am. Math. Soc., Math. Assn. Am., Soc. Indsl. and Applied Math., Phi Beta Kappa. Republican. Mem. Soc. Of Friends. Home: 33194 Dorset Ln Philomath OR 97370-9555 Office: Oreg State U Dept Math Corvallis OR 97331-4605 Office Phone: 541-737-5166. E-mail: parks@math.orst.edu.

PARKS, HEATHER JEWEL, music educator; b. Fla., Dec. 16, 1975; d. James and Victoria Boyce; m. Todd James Parks, Aug. 6, 1996; children: Mackensae Rae, Madison Rose. A in bus., Hyles Anderson Coll., 1998. Sales assoc. Tru-Green Chemlawn, Ill.; music tchr. Temple Christian Sch., Louisville, Tex.; pvt. music tchr. New Song Piano Studio, Louisville. Recipient 1st pl. duet piano competition, Accelerated Christian Edn., 1992, 2d pl. solo competition, 1992. Mem.: Music Teachers Nat. Assn., Carrollton Musich Teachers Assn. Avocations: music, piano, shopping.

PARKS, J. ANNE, state representative, funeral director; b. Greenwood, S.C., July 1, 1955; d. James Lloyd and Julia (Arnold) Parks. BS, Johnson C. Smith U., 1976; grad., Gupton-Jones Sch. Mortuary Sci., 1977. Mortician Parks Funeral Home, funeral dir.; real estate agent; state rep. S.C. Legis., 1997, state rep. dist. 12, 1999—, mem. med., mil., pub. and mcpl. com. Mem. Stop the Violence Com.; budget com. Uniter Way, 1996; mem. Orgn. Concerned Citizens, Greenwood City Coun., 1988—96. Mem.: NAACP, Greenwood C. of C., Epsilon Nu Delta, Delta Sigma Theta. Democrat. Baptist. Home: PO Box 181 Greenwood SC 29648 Office: State Capitol 434D BlattBldg Columbia SC 29211 Address: 232 N Hospital St Greenwood SC 29648 E-mail: JAP@scstatehouse.net.

PARKS, JAMES WILLIAM, II, public facilities executive, lawyer; b. Wabash, Ind., July 30, 1956; s. James William and Joyce Arlene (Lillibridge) P.; m. Neil Ann Armstrong, Aug. 21, 1982; children: Elizabeth Joyce, Helen Frances, James William III. BS, Ball State U., 1978; JD, U. Miami, 1981. Bar: La. 1981, U.S. Dist. Ct. (ea. dist.) La. 1981, U.S. Ct. Appeals (5th and 11th cirs.) 1981. Fla. 1982, U.S. Dist. Ct. (mid. dist. La.) 1982. Atty. Jones, Walker, Waechter, Poitevent, Carrere et al., New Orleans, 1981-83, Foley & Judell, New Orleans, 1983-88, McCollister & McCleary, pc, Baton Rouge, 1988-95; pres., CEO La. Pub. Facilities Authority, Baton Rouge, 1995—. Mem. AICPA, Nat. Assn. Bond Lawyers, La. State Bar Assn., Fla. Bar Assn., Assn. for Gifted and Talented Students, Baton Rouge (treas. 1994-96, pres.-elect 1996-97, pres. 1997-98), Soc. La. CPA (govt. acctg. and auditing com. 1994-95), Nat. Assn. Higher Edn. Facilities Authorities (bd. dirs. 1996-2001, v.p. 1997-99, pres. 1999-2001), Nat. Coun. Health Facilities Fin. Authorities (bd. dirs. 2004—, treas. 2004—), Coun. of Devel. Fin. Agys. (bd. dirs. 2002—), La. Assistive Tech. Access Network (bd. dirs. 2002—). Avocations: travel, computers. Home: 5966 Tennyson Dr Baton Rouge LA 70817-2933 Office: La Pub Facilities Authority 2237 S Acadian Thruway Ste 650 Baton Rouge LA 70808-2380 Office Phone: 225-923-0020. E-mail: jameswparks2@hotmail.com., parks@lpfa.com.

PARKS, JOAN H. research scientist, educator; b. Rochester, N.Y., Mar. 24, 1938; d. Robert Cushman and Fanny Cassidy Hunt; m. John Elton Parks, Sept. 11, 1959 (div. Oct. 1979); children: Gregory, Dana, Leslie. BA, U. Rochester, 1959; MBA, U. Chgo., 1981. Adminstr. kidney stone program U. Chgo., 1981—, rsch. assoc., asst. prof. nephrology program, 1984—. Bd. mem. Litholink Corp., Chgo. Author: Nephro Lithiasis, 1978, 1996; contbr. articles to profl. jours. Avocations: poetry, plays. Office: Univ Chgo Nephrology Sect 5841 S Maryland MC5100 Chicago IL 60637 Home: # 309 1700 E 56th St Chicago IL 60637 Office Phone: 773-702-6171.

PARKS, JOE BENJAMIN, entrepreneur, former state legislator; b. McAlester, Okla., Dec. 17, 1915; s. James Allen and Mary Florence (Youngblood) P.; m. Florence M. Evans, Oct. 25, 1941; children: Anne, Kathryn. BS in Pub. Adminstrn., Okla. State U., 1939. Div. dir. U.S. VA, Washington, 1946-56; spl. asst., cons. U.S. GSA, Washington, 1957-58; mgr. dist. EDP div. RCA Corp., Washington, 1959-65; mgr. Ea. region Dashew Bus. Machines, Arlington, Va., 1966-68; assoc. adminstr. social and rehab. svc. U.S. Dept. Health, Edn. & Welfare, Washington, 1969-73; dir. mktg. govt. systems div. Booz, Allen & Hamilton, Washington, 1974-75; ptnr. Forbes & Parks, Dover, NH, 1976—2002; mem. N.H. State Legislature, Concord, 1985-92, chmn. joint com. on elderly affairs, 1987-92, mem. com. on health, human svcs. and elderly, 1987-90; chmn. subcom. mileage and electronic roll call, 1989-90; vice chmn. legis. adminstrn. com., 1990-91; mem. appropriations com., 1991-92; proprietor Portsmouth (N.H.) Athenaeum, 1992—. Corporator Wentworth Douglas Hosp., Dover, 1980-89; pres. Berr Par, Inc., 1994—. Columnist Nat. Antiques Rev., 1975-77, Boston Globe N.H. Weekly 1987-88, Foster's Daily Democrat (Dover, N.H.), 1988-90; freelance writer, 1990—. Vice-chmn. N.H. State Rep. Com., 1987-88; chmn. Strafford County (N.H.) Reps., 1988; Strafford County campaign mgr. George W. Bush for Pres., 1999-2000; bd. dirs. Coastal Maine Bot. Garden, 2001—. Decorated Bronze Star; recipient Lawmakers award for disting. environ. svc. Sierra Club, 1990, N.H. State award New England Wildflower Soc., 1998; named Norris Cotton Rep. of Yr., 1993; Paul Harris fellow Rotary Internat. Found., 1998. Mem. Am. Rhododendron Soc. (pres. Mass. chpt. 1995-96, Bronze medal 1992, 2003). Congregationalist. Avocation: plant hybridizing. Home and Office: Parkwood Farm 195 Long Hill Rd Dover NH 03820-6108

PARKS, KRISTIN M. pediatrics health nurse, educator and practitioner; b. Lynn, Mass., Feb. 24, 1953; d. James B. and Phyllis (Hannaway) Parks; m. Roderick M. Fuqua, Sept. 10, 1977; children: Sarah, Emily, Abigail. BSN, U. Mass., 1974; MS, Boston U., 1977. RN, Mass.; cert. PNP, ANCC. Staff nurse McLean Hosp., Belmont, Mass.; clin. nurse specialist Beth Israel Hosp., Boston; asst. prof. Massaqoit C.C., 1980-91; prof. Quincy (Mass.) Coll., 1991—, chair assoc. degree prog. in nursing. Mem. ANA, Mass. Assn. RN (MARN), Mass. Assn. for Advancement ADN. Home: 42 Clinton Rd Weymouth MA 02189-3010 E-mail: kparks@quincycollege.edu.

PARKS, LLOYD LEE, oil company executive; b. Kiefer, Okla., Dec. 9, 1929; s. Homer Harrison and Avis Pearl (Motes) P.; m. Mary Ellen Scott, Aug. 20, 1948; children: Connie Jo, Karyn Ann, Rebecca Lee. Student, Okla. State U., 1948-50, Tulsa U., 1950-51, Harvard U. Bus. Sch., 1965. Acct. Deep Rock Oil Corp., 1951-54; chief acct. Blackwell Oil & Gas Co., Tulsa, 1954-60, sec. treas., 1960-62; v.p., controller Amax Oil & Gas Inc., Houston, 1962-67, pres., CEO, 1968—92; v.p. Amax, Inc., 1975-92; pvt. practice oil and gas and real estate imvestment Salado, Tex., 1992—. Served with AUS, 1946-48, 50-51. Mem.: Ind. Petroleum Assn. Am. (dir.), Lions Club, Wildflower Country Club (Temple, Tex.). Republican. Office: PO Box 1021 Salado TX 76571-1021 *Work hard, work smart and believe in yourself. You can and will be successful; if you want to be.*

PARKS, MICHAEL CHRISTOPHER, journalist; b. Detroit, Nov. 17, 1943; s. Robert James and Rosalind (Smith) P.; m. Linda Katherine Durocher, Dec. 26, 1964; children: Danielle Anne, Christopher, Matthew. AB, U. Windsor, Ont., Can., 1965. Reporter Detroit News, 1962-65; corr. Time-Life News Service, N.Y.C., 1965-66; asst. city editor Suffolk Sun, Long Island, N.Y., 1966-68; polit. reporter, foreign corr. The Balt. Sun, Saigon, Singapore, Moscow, Cairo, Hong Kong, Peking, 1968-80; fgn. corr. L.A. Times, L.A., Peking, Johannesburg, Moscow, Jerusalem, 1980-95, dpty. fgn. editor, 1995-96, mng. editor, 1996-97, editor, 1997-2000, v.p., 1996-97, sr. v.p., 1997-98, exec. v.p., 1998-2000; v.p. Times Mirror Co., 1998-2000; prof. Annenberg Sch. Comm. U. So. Calif., L.A., 2000—02, dir. Annenberg Sch. Journalism, 2002—, prof. journalism, 2002—. Disting. fellow Pacific Coun. Internat. Policy, 2000-02, dir. 1998-; dir. L.A. Jewish Jour., 2004-. Recipient Pulitzer Prize, 1987. Mem. Am. Soc. Newspaper Editors, Pacific Coun. on Internat. Policy, Internat. Press Inst., Soc. Profl. Journalists, City Club (L.A.; bd. govs.), Athenaeum (Pasadena, Calif.), Coun. on Fgn. Rels. Office: Annenberg Sch U So Calif Los Angeles CA 90089-0281 Office Phone: 213-740-0638. E-mail: mparks@usc.edu.

PARKS, MICHAEL JAMES, publisher, editor; b. Spokane, Wash., June 3, 1944; s. Floyd Lewis and Marie (McHugh) Parks; m. Janet K. Holter, Aug. 12, 1967; children: Michael J., Gregory F., Sarah M. BA, Seattle U., 1966. Reporter The Seattle Times, 1966—74, fin. editor, 1974—77; pub., editor Marple's Pacific N.W. Newsletter, Seattle, 1977—. Bd. govs. Seattle U. Alumni Assn.; trustee Seattle Rotary Svc. Found. Fellow, Am. Press Inst., N.Y.C., 1973. Mem.: Rotary. Roman Catholic. Avocations: opera, reading, camping, hiking, swimming. Office: Marples NW Newsletter Ste 200 117 W Mercer St Seattle WA 98119-3960 E-mail: info@marples.com.

PARKS, MICHELLE, journalist; b. Fort Smith, Ark., Feb. 17, 1972; d. Mike and Linda Parks. B in Journalism, U. Ark., 1994. Features editor N.W. Ark. Times, Fayetteville, 1994—2000; feature writer The Morning News, Springdale, Ark., 2000—02, Ark. Democrat-Gazette, Springdale, 2002—. Mem.: Nat. Fedn. Press Women (2d pl. in editl. 2001, 3d pl. in spl. articles 2002), Ark. Press Women (h.s. comm. contest dir. 2001—03, Comm. Contest Sweepstakes winner 2001—03), Soc. Profl. Journalists N.W. Ark. (membership chair 2003), Altrusa Internat. (past literacy com. chair 2001—03, Mem. of Yr. 2000). Avocations: reading, cooking, gardening. Home: 1766 Janice Ave Fayetteville AR 72703 Office: Ark Dem-Gazette 2201 S Thompson Ste B Springdale AR 72765 Office Phone: 479-927-5289. Personal E-mail: michelle17@cox-internet.com. E-mail: michelle_parks@adg.ardemgaz.com.

PARKS, PATRICIA JEAN, lawyer; b. Portland, Oreg., Apr. 2, 1945; d. Robert and Marion (Crosby) P.; m. David F. Jurca, Oct. 17, 1971 (div. 1976). BA in History, Stanford U., 1967; JD, U. Pa., Phila., 1970. Bar: N.Y. 1971, Wash. 1974. Assoc. Milbank, Tweed, Hadley & McCoy, N.Y.C., 1970-73, Shidler, McBroom, Gates & Lucas, Seattle, 1974-81, ptnr., 1981-90, Preston, Thorgrimson, Shidler, Gates & Ellis, Seattle, 1990-93; pvt. practice Seattle, 1993-99; spl. counsel Karr Tuttle Campbell, Seattle, 1999—. Active Vashon Allied Arts. Mem.: ABA, Pension Roundtable, Western Pension Conf., Seattle-King County Bar Assn., Wash. Women in Tax, Wash. State Bar Assn. (past pres. tax sect., past chair gift and estate tax com.), Wash. Native Plant Soc., Vashon Athletic Club, Wash. Athletic Club. Avocations: kayaking, hiking, contra dancing, bird watching, Karate. Office: 1201 3rd Ave Ste 2900 Seattle WA 98101-3284 Office Phone: 206-224-8094. Business E-Mail: pparks@karrtuttle.com.

PARKS, ROBERT HENRY, consulting economist, educator; b. New Orleans, Sept. 20, 1924; s. Charles Samuel and Amelia (England) P.; m. Inta Kondrats, Sept. 20, 1958 (div.); children: Karen E., Robert R., Alison J.; m. Annette Fiechter, Dec. 10, 1982 (div.). AB in Econs., Swarthmore Coll., 1949; MA, PhD in Econs., U. Pa., 1958. Economist Econ. Forecasting div. Gen. Electric Co., 1958-61; dir. econ. research Life Ins. Assn. Am., 1961-68; chief economist Maj. Wall St. Investment Firms, 1968-80; pres. Robert H. Parks & Assocs., Inc., N.Y.C., 1980—; cons. to instnl. investment officers; prof. fin. Wharton Sch., U. Pa., 1957—58, Pace U., 1980—. Adj. prof. fin. U. Pa., Baruch Sch., CUNY, Lehigh U. Author: The Witch Doctor of Wall Street, 1996, Unlocking the Secrets of Wall Street, 1998, Prometheus; contbr. articles to profl. jours. Democrat. Home: Scarborough Manor 6M-2 PO Box 307 Scarborough NY 10510

PARKS, ROBERT MYERS, appliance manufacturing company executive; b. Nevada, Mo., July 18, 1927; s. Cecil R. and Marcella (Myers) P.; m. Audrey Lenora Jones, June 18, 1955; children— John Robert, Janet M. Parks Huston. BS, U. Mo., 1949; MBA, Harvard U., 1952. Asst. dept. mgr. Jewett & Sherman Co., Kansas City, Mo., 1949-50; staff cons. Harbridge House, Inc., Boston, 1952; v.p. Electronic Splty. Co., Inc., Los Angeles, 1952-57; founder, chmn. bd. Parks Products, Inc., Hollywood, Calif., 1957—; pres. Generalist Industries, Inc., Hollywood, 1960-73. Chmn. bd. Shaver Corp. Am., L.A., 1965—; lectr. mktg. UCLA Extension divsn., 1960-61. Contbr. articles to profl. jours.; patentee in field. Active YMCA; bd. dirs. Hollywood Presbyn. Med. Center Found., Presbyn. Homes Found.; mem. dean's adv. council U. Mo. Bus. Sch., mayor's task force on L.A. River Cahuenga Pass Coalition. With USNR, 1944-45. Named in his honor Grad. Bus. Sch., U. Mo. Mem. Sales and Marketing Execs. Assn., C. of C., Navy League, World Affairs Council, Calif. Caballeros, Rangers, Vaqueros del Desierto, Los Caballeros, Rancheros Visitadores, E Clampus Vitus, Delta Sigma Pi, Sigma Chi. Clubs: Mason (Shriner), L.A. Breakfast, Braemar Country, Saddle and Sirloin. Presbyterian. Home: 7421 Woodrow Wilson Dr Los Angeles CA 90046-1322 Office: 3611 Cahuenga Blvd Hollywood CA 90068-1205 Office Phone: 323-876-5454.

PARKS, ROGER, food products executive; Grad. in computer sci., U. Houston, 1972. Joined J.R. Simplot Co., Boise, Idaho, 1999, CIO, 2000—. Named one of Premier 100 IT Leaders, Computerworld mag., 2003. Office: JR Simplot One Capital Ctr 999 Main St PO Box 27 Boise ID 83707-0027

PARKS, ROSA LOUISE, civil rights activist; b. Tuskegee, Ala., 1913; Stidemt, Ala. State Coll.; hon. degree, Shaw Coll. Former seamstress and housekeeper, Montgomery, Ala., Detroit, from 1957; office mgr. for Congressman John Conyers, Jr., from 1965; co-founder Rosa and Raymond Parks Inst. for Self-Devel., Detroit, 1987—. Author: Quiet Strength, 1994 Formerly active Montgomery Voters League; mem. youth coun. NAACP, sec. Montgomery br., 1943; active SCLC. Recipient Spingarn medal NAACP, 1970, Martin Luther King Jr. award, 1980, Congl. Gold Medal of Honor, 1999, 31st NAACP Image award for outstanding supporting actress in a drama series for Touched by an Angel, 2000. Office: Rosa & Raymond Park Inst Ste 2200 Cadillac Sq Detroit MI 48226-1002*

PARKS, SUZAN LORI, playwright; b. Fort Knox, KY, 1964; d. Donald and Francis Parks; m. Paul Oscher, 2001. BA, Mount Holyoke Coll., 1985. Guest lecturer Pratt Institute, N.Y.C., 1988, U. Mich., Ann Arbor, Mich., 1990, Yale U., New Haven, 1990—91, NYU, 1990—91; prof. of playwriting Eugene Lang Coll., N.Y.C., 1990; writer-in-residence New School for Social Research (now New School U.), N.Y.C., 1991—92; dir. Theater Projects Calif. Inst. Arts, Valencia, 2000—. Author: (plays) The Sinner's Place, 1985, Betting on the Dust Commander, 1988, Imperceptible Mutabilities in the Third Kingdom, 1990 (Obie award, 1990), Devotees in the Garden of Love, 1992, The Death of the Last Black Man in the Whole Entire World, 1992, The America Play, 1993, Venus, 1996 (Obie award, 1996), In the Blood, 1999, Topdog/Underdog, 2001 (Pulitzer Prize for drama, 2002), (screenplays) Anemone Me, 1990, Girl 6, 1996, (novels) Getting My Mother's Body, 2003. Recipient Rockefeller Foundation grant, 1990, N.Y. Found. for the Arts grant, 1990, Whiting Found. Writers award, 1992, Ford Found. grant, 1995, CalArts/Alpert award, 1996, PEN-Laura Pels award, 2000; fellow MacArthur Found., 2001, Guggenheim Found., 2000; grantee Mary E. Woolley fellowship, 1989, Naomi Kitay fellowship, 1989, Nat. Endowment for the Arts playwrighting fellowship, 1990—91. Office: Calif Inst Arts 24700 McBean Pkwy Valencia CA 91355

PARK SPENCER, KAREN LYNN, architect, jewelry designer; b. Brookville, Pa., Apr. 30, 1963; d. John Joseph Park, Roselyn Ann Park; m. Michael Vincent Spencer. A Specialized Tech., Triangle Tech. Coll., 1986. Cert. interior design 1995, lic. real estate Pa., 1993, cert. kitchen specialist 1988, quality control mfg. housing 1988. Space planner & cad drafter Pace Design, McLean, Va., 1986—86; cad drafter and quality control Strattan Homes, Strattanville, Pa., 1986—88; store planner Penn-Traffic Riverside Engring., DuBois, 1988—95; designer K.T.H. Architects, 1995—96; drafting coord. C-Cor Elecs., State College, 1996—97; mech. engr. D.L. Martin (for Schindler Elevator Corp.), Mercersburg, 1997—98; sr. project mgr. Noelker & Hull Architects, Chambersburg, 1998—2000. Cons. Park Places, Chambersburg, 1995—2002; drafting shadow Riverside Engring., DuBois, 1988—95; real estate Sarvey, Brookville, 1993—94; elec. tech. Strattan Homes, Strattanville, 1987—88. Author: (Poetry) Aspirations of Pen and Thought, 1997 (Editors Choice Award, 1998), Perceptions in Harmony, 1998 (Editors Choice Award, 1999), Dawn of Silence, 1998 (Editors Choice Award, 1999), Last Good-byes, 1998 (Editors Choice Award, 1999), America at the millenium - The Best Poems and Poets of the 20th Century, 2000 (Editors Choice Award, 2001). Vol. Brookville Civic Club, Brookville, 1992—95, Vols. for Charity, DuBois, 1992—95; asst. Girl Scout of Am., Brookville, 1972—76; helper 4-H, Home & Dairy, Brookville, 1971—76; tchr. The Presbyn. Ch. Brookville, Brookville, Pa., 1991—95; facilitator Alpha program The Presby. Ch. Falling Spring, Chambersburg, Pa., 2001—02. Mem.: Order of Ea. Star. Presbyterian. Avocations: poetry, art, swimming, travel. Office Phone: (717) 267-5003. Personal E-mail: www.park-places.com. Business E-Mail: www.park-places.com.

PARKYN, JOHN DUWANE, nuclear engineer; b. La Crosse, Wis., Feb. 20, 1944; s. Lionel Eric and Florence Katrina (Klum) P.; m. Betty Christine Tarnutzer, Aug. 13, 1966; children: Christine Peggy, Sarah Katherine, John Martin. Student, Wis. State U., 1962-64, U. N.Mex., 1968-69; BS in Nuclear Engring. and Physics, U. Wis., 1972. Cert. assessor, Wis.; registered profl. engr., Calif., Wis.; lic. sr. reactor operator; lic. min. United Ch. of Christ. Asst. plant engr. Ohio Med. Products Co., 1966-67; party chief U.S. Geol. Survey, Madison, Wis., 1971-72; asst. ops. gorup Point Beach Nuclear Plant, Two Rivers, Wis., 1972-74; asst. supt. La Crosse Boiling Water Reactor, Genoa, Wis., 1974-82; supt., 1982-95; mem. industry rev. bd. Inst. Nuclear Power Ops.; CEO Great Salt Lake and So. R.R., mem; pres., CEO Nuclear Three Inc. Past chmn. bd. dirs. BAnks Stoddard, BAnk Ferryville; chmn. bd. dirs. Wis. Masonic Home; chmn. bd., CEO Pvt. Fuel storage LLC; dir. River BAnk; past chmn. bd. Mescalero Fuel Storage LLC; v.p. Genoa Fuel Tech Co.; chmn. bd., CEO Great Salt Lake & So. R.R.; mem. investigation com. atty. conduct, mem. atty.'s responsibility investative bd. Wis. Supreme Ct. Mem. Two Rivers City Coun., 1974; mem. Vernon County Bd. Suprs., 1976-94, 2002-, past vice chmn. county bd., mem. fin. com., chmn. human svcs. rev. bd., chn. cmty. options program; assessor Bergen Twp. (Wis.), 1977-79; chmn. Vernon County Libr. Com., 1976—; chmn. pers. com. Vernon County Bd. Equalized Values; chmn. Vernon County Com. for Programs of Aging; past pres. Sch. Dist. of La Crosse, pres.; past pres. Riverland coun. Girl Scouts U.S.A.; past mem. exec. bd. Gateway Area coun. Boy Scouts Am.; advisor, mem. Wis. staff Order of DeMolay; past chmn. Wis. Masonic Home; pres. St. Johns United Ch. Christ; pres. River Rails Inc., Gov. Commn. on Midwest Rail Initiative; vice chmn. Vernon County Jail Study Commn. Mem. Am. Nuclear Soc. (chmn. Wis. sect., mem. nat. planning com.), Nat. Assn. R.R. Passengers (nat. bd. dirs.), Wis. Assn. R.R. Passengers (state pres.), Am. Legion, Wis. Legis. Coun., Masons (past worshipful master Frontier Lodge 45). Home: Pleasant Vly Stoddard WI 54658 Office: La Crosse Boiling Water Reactor RR 1 Genoa WI 54632-9801

PARKYN, JOHN WILLIAM, editor, writer, columnist; b. London, Dec. 7, 1931; came to U.S., 1967; citizen, 1973; s. James R. and Eva M. (Dix) P.; m. Sybil (Judy) Hetherington; 1 child, Elaine. Student, Dulwich Coll., 1943-48. Staff writer Bus. Mag., London, 1954-56; writer-editor Amalgamated Press, London, 1956-58; features editor Woman's Illustrated mag., London, 1958-60; staff writer Internat. Pub. Corp., London, 1960-61; editor Westward mag. Daily News Ltd., London, 1961-64; assoc. editor Daily Telegraph mag., London, 1964-66; features editor King mag. Europress, Ltd., London, 1966-67; assoc. editor Tropic mag. Miami (Fla.) Herald, 1967-69; editor Tropic mag., 1969-77; editor Calif. Today mag. San Jose (Calif.) Mercury News, 1977-83; editor Sunshine: The Mag. of South Fla. Sun-Sentinel Co. (subs. Tribune Co.), Ft. Lauderdale, Fla., 1983-96; columnist S. Fla. Sun-Sentinel, 1997—; exec. editor, sr. writer Vero Beach (Fla.) Mag., 1998—; columnist, feature writer City & Shore mag., 2000—. Cons. Het Parool newspaper, Amsterdam, 1965. Contbr. numerous articles to Am. and European mags. Chmn. Sunday Mag. Editors Conf., Louisville, 1973. With RAF, 1950-52. Recipient Outstanding Use of Editl. Color award Editor & Pub. mag., 1974, 75, 77, Nat. Headliner award, 1976, 79; named Editor Best Weekly Mag. in State Fla. Press Club, 1985-93, 95. Office: 505 Beachland Blvd Ste 1 PMB 275 Vero Beach FL 32963-1798 E-mail: johnparkyn@aol.com.

PARLAMIS, MICHAEL FRANK, civil engineer, construction company executive; b. Bklyn., May 29, 1940; s. Frank Michael and Phyllis (Burnago) P.; m. Marguerite Koskinas, Aug. 21, 1966; children: Franklin, Christine, Alexander. BSCE, BS in Indsl. Mgmt., MIT, 1962; MSCE, Stanford U., 1963. Registered profl. engr., N.Y. Engr. Port Authority of N.Y. and N.J., 1963-64; asst. to chief engr. George A. Fuller Co., N.Y.C., 1964-67; pres. Frank

Parlamis Inc., Bklyn., 1968—, Parlamis Bros. Inc., Bklyn., 1968—, Hermes Constrn. Corp., Bklyn., 1968—; ptnr. City Path LLC, City Jam LLC, 128 MAC LLC, 128 MAPP LLC. Author: CPM/PERT As Basis for Management Information Systems in Building Construction, 1966, Regulation of Building Construction in the City of New York, 1967, Greece and the Panama Canal, 1988. Chmn. expansion program Greek Orthodox Cathedral St. John the Theologian, Tenafly, N.J., 1978—; mem. Leadership 100 of the Greek Orthodox Ch.; Archon of the Ecomenical Patriarcate, Greek Orthodox Ch.; mem. ednl. coun. MIT; trustee Hellenic Heritage Mus., Washington, Frank Parlamis Sr. Citizens Ctr., Jamaica, NY.; founder St. John the Theologian Peace Meml. Gymnasium; exec. dir. St. John the Theologian World Peace Inst.; mem. MIT Com. investigating World Trade Ctr. disaster. Recipient Ellis Island medal of honor, 2002. Mem. Am. Hellenic Progressive Assn., Bklyn. Tech. Rsch. Found. (life), Tau Beta Pi, Chi Epsilon. Republican. Avocations: engineering and religious history, peace advocacy, ecumenical religious activities. Home: 128 Downey Dr Tenafly NJ 07670-3006 Office: 328 Atlantic Ave Brooklyn NY 11201-5804 Office Phone: 718-875-6744. Business E-Mail: parlamis@alum.mit.edu.

PARLE, BERTHA IBARRA, writer; b. El Paso, Tex., Nov. 14, 1947; d. Arnulfo and Bertha (Soto) Ibarra; m. Dennis Jerome Parle, Aug. 16, 1969; children: Joseph, Mónica, Angélica. BA in French, Spanish, U. Tex., El Paso, 1968; MA in Spanish, U. Kans., 1970, H.S. tchg. cert., 1971; postgrad. courses in French, U. Houston, 1990—95. Bilingual tchr. Kans. Remedial Edn. Program, Sharon Springs, 1967, 71, 72; Spanish tchr. Ottawa (Kans.) H.S., 1971-74; ESL instr. North Harris Coll., Houston, 1977-83; modern lang. prof. N. Harris Montgomery C.C. Dist., Houston, 1983-97, head lang. inst., 1997—2002. Cultural cons., sponsor Hispanic students North Harris Coll. and Montgomery Coll., 1983-97, organizer Hispanic cultural events, 1983—, sponsor Cath. Newman Club, 1985-95; lectr., slide show The Nahua Mexica Legacy, 1994-96; participant in field seminars; NEH and Fulbright Ecuador field experience. Poetess; Spanish poetry publ. in Tejidos, Grito al Sol, 1972-94. Hispanic leader St. Leo's Cath. Ch., Houston, 1982-92; del. People to People Am. Program to S. Africa, 2000. Recipient Tchg. Excellence award North Harris Coll., 1997, Excellence award Nat. Inst. for Staff and Orgn. Devel., 1998; Am. Coun. Tchrs. Fgn. Langs. summer scholar U. Montreal, 1999. Mem. AAUW, Am. Coun. Tchrs. Fgn. Langs., Computer Assisted Lang. Instn. Consortium, Am. Assn. C.C. Women, Tex. Fgn. Lang. Assn., Inst. Hispanic Culture., North Harris United Faculty. Avocations: creative writing, study of indigenous language cultures, hispanic students and hispanic issues in the community. Office: North Harris Coll 2700 W W Thorne Dr Houston TX 77073 Office Phone: 281-618-5546. Business E-Mail: bertha.parle@nhmccd.edu.

PARLETTE, LINDA EVANS, state senator; m. Bob Parlette; 2 children. BS in Pharmacy, Wash. State U. Pharmacist; orchardist; Rep. rep. dist. 12 Wash. Ho. of Reps., 1997-2000; Rep. senator dist. 12 Wash. State Senate, 2000—. Mem. agr. and internat. trade, health and long-term care, higher edn. and ways and means coms. Wash. State Senate; chair Nat. Coun. State Legislators' Children, Family and Health Com.; bd. dirs. Wash. State Ag-Forestry Edn. Found. Mem. Lake Chelan United Meth. Ch.; former chair Lake Chelan Sch. Bd.; former mem. Lake Chelan Hosp. Guild. Recipient Trail Blazer award Lewis and Clark Elem. Sch., Margaret Chase Smith award Wash. State Rep. Women, 1995, award Friend of Rural Health Care, 1997-98, Rural Legislator of Yr. award Wash. State Hosp., 2000, Outstanding Legislator award Nat. Fedn. Ind. Bus., 2000. Mem. Wash. State Pharm. Assn., Wash. State Hort. Assn., Wenatchee Rotary (founder Lunch Buddy program). Office: PO Box 40412 106A Irv Newhouse Bldg Olympia WA 98504-0412 Fax: 360-786-7819. E-mail: parlette_li@leg.wa.gov.

PARLIER, GREG H. military officer, engineer; b. San Luis Obispo, Calif., May 10, 1952; s. Merton B. and Kathleen F. Parlier; m. Judy D. Olson, Aug. 30, 1975; children: Jamie Lynn, Timothy Scott, Steven Hugh. BS, U.S. Mil. Acad., 1974; MS, Naval Postgrad. Sch., 1983; MA, Georgetown U., 1988; postgrad., USMC Command and Staff Coll., 1988—89, U. Va., 1992, U.S. Army War Coll., 1995—96. Registered profl. engr., Va.; master parachutist, army strategist, battle staff officer. Vulcan and redeye platoon leader 3-4 ADAR, 82d Airborne Divsn., Ft. Bragg, NC, 1975—76; exec. officer Battery C, 3-4 ADAR, 82d Airborne Divsn., 1976—77, Battery C, 2-71 ADA, 31st ADA Brigade, Republic of Korea, 1977; battery comdr. Battery C, 3-4 ADAR, 82d Airborne Divsn., 1979—81; asst. prof. dept. engring. U.S. Mil. Acad., West Point, NY, 1983—86; chief officer plans U.S. Army Mil. Pers. Ctr., Alexandria, Va., 1986—88, 3-4 ADAR ops. officer, 1989—90, exec. officer, 1990—91; G-3 air def. element XVIII Airborne Corps, Ft. Bragg, 1991—92; bn. comdr. 5-2 ADAR, 69th ADA Brigade, V Corps, Crailsheim and Bamberg, Germany, 1992—94; chief resource plans and analysis divsn. Office of the Chief of Staff U.S. Army, Washington, 1996—98; dir. program analysis and evaluation U.S. Army Recruiting Command, Ft. Knox, Ky., 1998—2002; dir. for transformation U.S. Army Aviation and Missile Command, Redstone Arsenal, Ala., 2002—. Sr. tactical comdr. McKee Barracks, Crailsheim, 1993; vice chmn. Bamberg (Germany) Scholarship Com., 1993—94; mentor Georgetown U. ROTC, Washington, 1996—98. Col. US Army, 1997. Decorated Bronze Star U.S. Army, Legion of Merit; named 8th FLAK, 1st German Mountain Divsn., 1994, Dept. of the Army Rsch. Analyst of the Yr., 1987; recipient German Efficiency Badge (Gold), Bundeswehr (German Army), 1999, 2001, plaque of appreciation, Korean Nat. Assembly, 1978, Can. Parachutist Badge, Can. Forces, 1977, USMC CSC Disting. Grad. and Gen. Clifton B. Cates award, 1989, Jim and Rafer Johnson Outstanding Athlete Award, Kingsburg H.S. Faculty and Coaches, 1970; Nat. Def. Fellow, MIT, 1994—95. Mem.: Mil. Ops. Rsch. Soc. (Grad. Rsch. award 1983, Franz Edelman Prize finalist 2001), Inst. Ops. Rsch. and Mgmt. Scis., 82nd Airborne Divsn. Assn. (life). Avocations: reading, classical music, sports. Home: 230 Fieldridge Ln Harvest AL 35749 Office: US Army Aviation and Missile Command Redstone Arsenal AL Personal E-mail: gparlier@knology.net. E-mail: greg.parlier@redstone.army.mil.

PARLOW, CYNTHIA MARIA, professional soccer player; b. Memphis, May 8, 1978; BS in Nutrition, U. N.C., 1998. Profl. soccer player Atlanta Beat, 2001—03. Mem. U.S. Women's Nat. Soccer Team, 1996—, U.S. Under-20 Nat. Team, Nordic Cup championships, Denmark, 1997, U-16 Nat. Team pool. Named All-ACC and ACC Rookie of Yr., 1995, Soccer Am. Freshman of Yr., 1995, Most Valuable Player, 1995 Under-17 U.S. Youth Soccer nat. tournament, World Cup Champion, 1999; recipient Gold medal, Centennial Olympic Games, 1996, Herman Trophy, Mo. Athletic Club Player of Yr. award, 1997, Silver medal, Sydney Olympic Games, 2000. Achievements include helped U. N.C. to NCAA Championship 1996, 97; 1st-Team All-ACC selection in 1997; named to 1997 NCAA All-Tournament Team. Office: US Soccer Fedn 1801-1811 S Prairie Ave Chicago IL 60616

PARMA, EDWARD SCOTT, engineer, surgeon; b. Montgomery, Ala., May 17, 1963; s. George Edward and Marie Little Parma; m. Victoria Mathison; children: Edward Scott, Catherine Mathison. BS in engring., Auburn U., 1981—86; MBA, U. of Ala. at Birmingham, 1987—93; MD, U. of Ala., Sch. of Medicine, 1994—98. Design engr. SCI Systems, Huntsville, Ala., 1986—90; project engr. So. Rsch. Technologies, Birmingham, Ala., 1990—92; systems engr. Rust Internat., Birmingham, 1992—94; internal medicine resident Bapt. Health Sys., Birmingham, 1998—99; ophthalmology resident Tulane Health Sciences Ctr., New Orleans, 1999—2002; vitreoretinal surgery fellow Retina Specialists of Ala., 2002—. Chief resident Tulane U. Dept. of Ophthalmology, New Orleans, 2001—02. Musician: Ala. All-State Band (First Chair Trumpet State of Ala., 1981); singer: Performed with DisneyWorld Voices of Liberty; contbr. articles to profl. jours. Humanitarian liaison Montgomery Coun. on Aging, Ala., 1981—85; staff mem. Frazer United Meth. Ch., Ala., 1981—85. Mem.: AMA, Jefferson County Med. Soc., La. Med. Soc., Ala. Med. Soc., Am. Acad. Of Ophthalmology, Beta Gamma Sigma, Upsilon Pi Epsilon, Tau Beta Pi, Sigma Pi Epsilon. Methodist. Achievements include design of space computer hardware currently in geosychronous orbit supporting intercontinental ballistic missile tracking; design of in-flight missile computer to process real time tracking video; discovery of genetic mutation causing blindness in a large 3000 member pedigree dating to 1793. Avocations: weightlifting, tennis, music. Office: Retina Specialists Of Alabama 1201 11th St South Birmingham AL 35205

PARMELEE, ARTHUR HAWLEY, JR., pediatric medical educator; b. Chgo., Oct. 29, 1917; s. Arthur Hawley and Ruth Frances (Brown) P.; m. Jean Kern Rheinfrank, Nov. 11, 1939; children: Arthur Hawley III, Ann (Mrs. John C. Minahan Jr.), Timothy, Ruth Ellen. BS, U. Chgo., 1940, MD, 1943. Diplomate Am. Bd. Pediatrics (examiner 1966—). Intern U.S. Naval Hosp., Bethesda, Md., 1943-44; extern Yale Inst. Child Devel., 1947, New Haven Hosp., 1947-48, L.A. Children's Hosp., 1948-49; mem. faculty UCLA Med. Sch., 1951—, prof. pediat., 1967-88, prof. emeritus, 1988, dir. divsn. child devel., 1964-88; mem. Brain Rsch. Inst., 1966-88, Mental Retardation Rsch. Ctr., 1970-88. Rsch. prof. pediat. U. Göttingen, Germany, 1967-68; mem. com. child devel. rsch. and pub. policy NRC, 1977-81; cons. Nat. Inst. Child Health and Human Devel., 1963-70, Holy Family Adoption Svc., 1949-80. Author articles, chpts. in books. Trustee Los Angeles Children's Mus., 1979. Served with USN, 1943-47. Recipient C. Anderson Aldrich award in child devel., 1975; Commonwealth fellow Centre de Recherches Biologiques Neonatales, Clinique Obstetricale Baudelocque, Paris, 1959-60; fellow Ctr. Advanced Study in Behavioral Scis., Stanford U., 1984-85; hon. lectr. Soc. for Developmental and Behavioral Pediat., 1996. Mem. AMA, Am. Pediat. Soc., Soc. Pediat. Rsch., Western Soc. Pediat. Rsch., Am. Acad. Pediat. (chmn. com. sect. child devel. 1966), Assn. Ambulatory Pediat. (mem. coun. 1966-69), Soc. Rsch. in Child Devel. (pres. 1983-85, Disting. Sci. Contbns. to Child Devel. award 1993), Assn. Psychophysiol. Study of Sleep, Los Angeles County Med. Soc., Phi Beta Kappa. Home: 764 Iliff St Pacific Palisades CA 90272-3927 Office: Univ Calif Dept Pediatrics Los Angeles CA 90024

PARMELEE, SCOTT, publishing executive; New Eng. sales rep., Santa Fe; N.Y. mgr. Outside, advt. mgr., 1992—95, assoc. pub., 1995—98, v.p., pub., 1998—. Office: Outside Ste 440 420 Lexington Ave New York NY 10172

PARMELEE, WILLIAM DOUGLAS, financial executive, accountant; b. Providence, Aug. 16, 1957; s. Lyman Malcolm and Dorothy (Baird) P.; m. Luann Moody, Aug. 23, 1980. BSBA, U. N.C., 1979. CPA, N.C. Sr. mgr. Ernst & Young, Raleigh, NC, 1979—88; v.p., contr. Qualex, Inc., Durham, NC, 1988—2000; CFO Nat. Gypsum Co., Charlotte, NC, 2000—. Dir., treas. Carolina Excellence, Inc., Wake Forest, N.C., 1988—. Pres. Theatre in the Park, Raleigh, 1992-93; treas. N.C. Consumers Coun., Chapel Hill, 1987-93; elder, treas. Hudson Meml. Presbyn. Ch., Raleigh, 1986-89; elder Wake Forest Presbyn. Ch., 1991-92. Mem. AICPA, N.C. Assn. CPAs (health care com. 1985-88), Inst. Mgmt. Accts., Fin. Execs. Inst. Mem. AICPA, N.C. Assn. CPA's (health care com. 1985-88). Democrat. Avocations: team sports, gardening, theater, reading fiction, music. Office: Nat Gypsum 2000 Rexford Rd Charlotte NC 28211 E-mail: wdparmelee@nationalgypsum.com.*

PARMELLE, WILLIAM, light manufacturing execdtive; CFO Nat. Gypsum, Charlotte, N.C. Office: National Gypsum 2001 Rexford Rd Charlotte NC 28211 Office Fax: (704) 365-7579.

PARMENTER, ROBERT HALEY, physics educator; b. Portland, Maine, Sept. 19, 1925; s. LeClare Fall and Esther (Haley) P.; m. Elizabeth Kinnecom, Oct. 27, 1951; children: David Alan, Douglas Ian. BS, U. Maine, 1947; PhD, Mass. Inst. Tech., 1952. Mem. staff solid state and molecular theory group Mass. Inst. Tech., 1951-54; guest scientist Brookhaven Nat. Lab., 1951-52; mem. staff Lincoln Lab., 1952-54, RCA Labs, Princeton, NJ, 1954—66, acting head, solid state rsch. group, 1962—65; prof. physics U. Ariz., 1966-96, chmn. dept., 1977-83, prof. emeritus, 1996—. Mem. NASA rsch. adv. com. electrophysics, 1964-68, chmn., 1966-68, mem. rsch. and tech. adv. com. basic rsch., 1966-68; vis. lectr. Princeton (N.J.) U., 1960-61. Served with USNR, 1944-46. Fellow AAAS, Am. Phys. Soc. (chmn. div. condensed matter physics 1967-68); mem. Sigma Xi, Tau Beta Pi. Achievements include predicting the existence of the acoustoelectric effect, the enhancement of the transition temperature of a superconductor by means of tunneling extraction; demonstration of the conditions under which deterministic chaos occurs in quantum mechanical systems. Home: 1440 E Ina Rd Tucson AZ 85718-1175 Office: U Ariz Physics Dept Tucson AZ 85721-0001

PARMER, DAN GERALD, veterinarian; b. Wetumpka, Ala., July 3, 1926; s. James Lonnie and Virginia Gertrude (Guy) P.; m. Donna Louise Kesler, June 7, 1980; 1 child, Dan Gerald; 1 child from previous marriage, Linda Leigh. Student, L.A. City Coll., 1945-46; DVM, Auburn U., 1950. Gen. practice vet. medicine, Galveston, Tex., 1950-54, Chgo., 1959-83; veterinarian in charge Chgo. Commn. Animal Care and Control, 1974-88; med. dir. food protection divsn., disease outbreak control Chgo. Dept. Health, 1988-93, ret., 1993; dir. Cook County Dept. Animal Control and Rabies Control, 1998—. Chmn. Ill. Impaired Vets. Com., 1985-93; mem. Ala. Impaired Vets. Com., 1993-98; chmn. Ill. Wellness Com., 1998—; tchr. Highlands U., 1959; humane officer Elmore County, 1994—; dir. sales for south, southeast and lower midwest Am. Vet. Identification Devices, Norco, Calif., 1993-98, nat. dir. companion animal divsn., 1996—. Pres. Elmore County Humane Soc. Served with USNR, 1943-45, PTO, USAF Vet. Corps, 1954-59. Decorated 9 battle stars; recipient Vet. Appreciation award U. Ill., 1971, commendation Chgo. Commn. Animal Care and Control, 1987, Prestigious Svc. award U. Ill., 2002. Mem.: AVMA (coun. pub. health and regulatory medicine 1990—, nat. com. animal welfare 1999—, nat. com. for impaired vets.), VFW, Ill. State Vet. Med. Assn. (chmn. bd. govs. 2002—), Ill. Acad. Vet. Medicine, Elmore County Humane Soc. (pres. 1994—98), Am. Assn. Zool. Pks. and Aquariums, Am. Assn. Zoo Vets., Nat. Assn. Professions, Ill. Acad. Vet. Practice (pres. 1994), Am. Animal Hosp. Assn. (dir.), South Chgo. Vet. Medicine Assn. (pres. 1965—66), Chgo. Vet. Medicine Assn. (bd. govs. 1969—72, 1974—81, pres. 1982, treas. 1999, Lifetime Merit award 2000), Ill. Vet. Med. Assn. (chmn. civil def. and package disaster hosps. 1968—71, chmn. bd. 2002—, Pres.'s award 1986, Prestigious Spl. Svc. award 2002), Valley Internat. Country Club, Midlothian Country Club, Kiwanis, Shriners, Masons. Achievements include discovery of Bartonellosis in cattle in N.Am. and western hemisphere, 1951; co-development of bite-size high altitude in-flight feeding program USAF. Home: 5704 W 89th St Oak Lawn IL 60453-1222 Office: Cook County Animal Control 10220 S 76th Ave Bridgeview IL 60455-2427 Office Phone: 708-974-6140. Business E-Mail: Dan.Parmer@comcast.net.

PARMET, HERBERT SAMUEL, historian, writer; b. N.Y.C., Sept. 28, 1929; s. Isaac and Fanny (Scharf) P.; m. Joan Kronish, Sept. 12, 1948; 1 child, Wendy. BS, SUNY, Oswego, 1951; MA, Queens Coll., 1957; postgrad., Columbia U., 1958-62. Prof. history Grad. Sch. CUNY, 1968-95, disting. prof. history, 1983-95, prof. emeritus, 1995—. Cons. ABC-TV, N.Y.C., 1983, KERA-TV, Dallas, 1986-91, WGBH-TV, Boston, 1988-91. Author: Aaron Burr: Portrait of an Ambitious Man, 1967, Never Again: President Runs for a Third Term, 1968, Eisenhower and the American Crusades, 1972, The Democrats, 1976, Jack: The Struggles of John F. Kennedy, 1980, JFK: The Presidency of John F. Kennedy, 1983, Richard Nixon and His America, 1990, George Bush: The Life of a Lone Star Yankee, 1997, Presidential Power: From the New Deal to the New Right, 2001. Cpl. U.S. Army, 1952-54. Grantee, NEH, 1987. Fellow Soc. Am. Historians; mem. Am. Hist. Assn., Orgn. Am. Historians, Authors Guild. Avocation: photography. Home: 36 Marsten Ln Hillsdale NY 12529-5816

PARMET, ROBERT DAVID, historian, educator; b. N.Y.C., Dec. 11, 1938; s. Isaac and Fanny (Scharf) Parmet; 1 child, Andrew Charles. BA, CCNY, 1960; MA, Columbia U., 1961, PhD, 1966. Fellow CCNY, 1960-62, lectr., 1962-65; asst. prof. Newark State Coll., Union, N.J., 1965-67, CUNY, Jamaica, N.Y., 1967-70, assoc. prof., 1971-77, chmn. dept. history, 1972-75, prof., 1978—. Author: Labor and Immigration in Industrial America, 1981, rev. edit., 1986; co-author: American Nativism 1830-1860, 1971, rev. edit., 1979; contbr. articles to encys., profl. jours. Fellow, Woodrow Wilson Nat. Found., 1960, CUNY, 1994. Mem.: Labor and Working Class History Assn., Immigration History Soc., Am. Jewish Hist. Assn., So. Hist. Assn., N.Y. Labor Hist. Assn. (mem. exec. bd. 1990), Conn. Hist. Soc., Acad. Polit. Sci., Orgn. Am. Historians, Am. Hist. Assn., Phi Alpha Theta. Democrat. Jewish. Avocations: photography, travel, musical theater, baseball. Home: 1 Highland Pl Great Neck NY 11020 Office: York Coll CUNY 94-20 Guy R Brewer Blvd Jamaica NY 11451 Office Phone: 718-262-2644. Business E-Mail: parmet@york.cuny.edu.

PARMITER, KAREN LYNN, education educator; b. McKeesport, Pa., Jan. 8, 1943; d. William and Helen Wolk Barlow; m. Jon Parmiter, Mar. 20, 1965; children: Mechel Ruth Golenberke, Jon Kyle. BS, Edinboro State U., 1964; MA, Allegheny Coll., 1970; PhD, U. Pitts., 1995. Tchr. Linesville High Sch., Pa., 1964—67, Conneaut Lake High Sch., 1973—79, pvt. tutoring, 1975—79, Conneaut Lake High Sch., 1979—80, Jamestown High Sch., 1981—98; prof. Thiel Coll., Greenville, 1999—. Dept. head, class/club advisor Linesville High Sch., 1964—67, Jamestown High Sch., 1981—98, curricular cons., designer, 1981—98; guest spkr. U. Pitts., 1996. Author: Fulfilling the Prophecies: The Journey of Education, 1999, Life: The Power of Promise, 2001. Program cons. Penn Lakes Girl Scout Troop 365, Conneaut Lake, 2003; participant Daffodil Drive/Cancer Fundraiser Thiel Coll., 2003; vol. tchr. West End. Elem. Sch., Meadville, Pa., 2003. Grantee, Nat. Def. Edn., Elmira Coll., 1965. Mem.: NEA, Pa. State Edn. Assn., Red Hat Soc., Order Ea. Star, Kappa Delta Pi. Democrat. Greek Orthodox. Avocations: writing, reading, travel. Home: 9361 Free Rd Conneaut Lake PA 16316 Office: Thiel Coll 75 Coll Ave Greenville PA 16125 Office Phone: 724-589-2000.

PARMLEY, JAY, political organization administrator; Assoc. in arts, Northeastern A&M Coll.; B in pub. adminstrn., MPA, U. Okla. Fin. dir. Glen Johnson for Congress campaign; mem. DNC Exec. Com., Okla. Dem. Party Exec. Com.; chmn. Young Dems. Am. Nat. Platform Com., 1997; nat. pres. Young Dems. of Am., 1999—2001; chmn. Okla. Dem. Party, 2001—. Asst. to pres. U. Okla., 1993—95; chancellor's student rels. liaison Okla. State Regents for Higher Edn., 1995—97; dir. Okla. City Downtown Coll. Consortium, 1997—2001. Recipient Outstanding Alumnus award, Northeastern Okla. A&M Coll., 2001. Democrat. Office: 4100 N Lincoln Blvd Oklahoma City OK 73105

PARMLEY, RICHARD TURNER, pediatric hematologist, oncologist; b. Madison, Wis., Sept. 10, 1949; BA, U. Va., 1970; MD, Med. U. S.C., 1973. Diplomate in pediatrics and in pediatric hematology/oncology Am. Bd. Pediatrics; diplomate in hematopathology Am. Bd. Pathology. Intern Med. U. S.C., Charleston, S.C., 1973, resident in pediats., 1974-75; fellow in pediat. hematology-oncology St. Jude Children's Rsch. Hosp., Memphis, 1976-77, U. Ala., Birmingham, 1977; clin. fellow in med. oncology bone marrow transplant svc. Fred Hutchinson Cancer Rsch. Ctr., Seattle, 1986; dir. electron microscopy and histology unit inst. dental rsch. U. Ala., Birmingham, 1978-83, assoc. scientist Comprehensive Cancer Cancert Ctr., 1978-83, asst. prof. pediats. and pathology, 1978-82, assoc. prof. pediats., 1982-83; assoc. prof. pediats. and pathology U. Tex. Health Sci. Ctr., 1983-88, prof. pediats., 1988-94; dir. divsn. pediat. hematology/oncology Carolinas Med. Ctr., Charlotte, NC, 1994—2000; clin. prof. pediat. U. N.C., Chapel Hill, 1994—2000; mem. pediat. hematologist-oncology staff Spartanburg (S.C.) Reg. Med. Ctr., 2000—; clin. prof. pediat. Med. Univ. SC, Charleston, 2000—. Mem. Am. Soc. Pediatric Hematology/Oncology, Am. Acad. Pediat., Am. Pediatric Soc., Soc. Pediatric Rsch., Alpha Omega Alpha. Office: Spartanburg Regional Med Ctr Dept Med Edn 101 Eastwood St Spartanburg SC 29303 Office Phone: 864-560-6287. Personal E-mail: rparmley@srmc.com.

PARMLEY, ROBERT JAMES, lawyer, consultant; b. Madison, Wis., Oct. 23, 1950; s. Loren Francis and Dorothy Louise (Turner) P.; m. Debra Paliszewski, Dec. 23, 1982; children: Michelle Hope, Matthew Turner. BA, U. Va., 1972; JD, U. S.C., 1975. Bar: S.C. 1975, Tex. 1976, U.S. Dist. Ct. (so. dist.) Tex. 1976, U.S. Dist. Ct. (we. and no. dists.) Tex. 1980, U.S. Ct. Appeals (5th cir.) 1978, U.S. Tax Ct. 1976, U.S. Supreme Ct. 1980. Staff atty., Vista vol. Tex. Rural Legal Aid, Inc., Alice, 1975-76, mng. atty. Kingsville, 1976-79, sr. staff atty. Kerrville, 1979-81; sole practice Kerrville, 1981—. Mem. State Bar Tex., State Bar S.C., Kerr County Bar Assn. Episcopalian. Office: Ste 615 222 Sidney Baker St S Kerrville TX 78028-5900 Office Phone: 830-896-4900. E-mail: law@ktc.com.

PARMLEY, VAN SAMUEL, retired anesthesiologist; b. Electra, Tex., 1914; s. Tim Hennesy and Madge Parmley; m. Rose Jean Selzer; children: Tim H. II, Martha Lillian Sjogreen. MD, Tulane U., 1939. Cert. anesthesiologist. Intern Charity Hosp., New Orleans, 1939-40; gen. practice, 1945-54; resident in anesthesiology St. Francis Hosp., Wichita, 1954-56; pvt. practice anesthesiology Wichita, Kans., 1956—64; tchr. Project Hope, 1964—65, U. Tex. Med. Sch., Galveston, 1965—77. With U.S. Army, 1940—45. Mem. AMA, Am. Soc. Anesthesiologists, Pan Am. Med. Assn. Republican. Episcopalian.

PARNELL, CALVIN BOYD, JR., agricultural engineering educator; b. Hatch, N.Mex., Apr. 3, 1941; s. Calvin Boyd Sr. and Doris Virginia P.; m. Peggy Ann Hibbs; children: Christopher Boyd, Sarah Elizabeth. BS in Agrl. Engring., N.Mex. State U., 1964; MS in Agrl. Engring., Clemson U., 1965, PhD in Environ. Sys. Engring., 1970. Registered profl. engr., Tex. Regents prof. agrl. engring. U. Tex. A&M, College Station. Cons. Nat. Cottonseed Products Assn., 1977, Bunge Corp., 1978, Jack's Bean Co., 1978, Environ. Control, 1978-80, ADM Milling, 1979, Continental Gin Co., 1981-83, 87-88, Carter Day Co., 1982, Tex. Air Control Bd., 1990-93, Archer Daniels Midland, 1991, 94, Office Tech. Assessment, 1994-95, Task Force on Air Pollution Regulations Advising Sec. of Agr., 1996-98. Contbr. articles to profl. jours., chpts. to books; patentee in field. Pres. Our Saviors Luth. Ch.; coach Little League. Decorated Army Commendation medal; recipient Am. Indsl. Hygiene Paper award, 1987, Superior Svc. award Nat. Cotton Ginners Assn., 1998; grantee in field. Fellow Am. Soc. Agrl. Engrs. (chmn. southwest region 1983-84, past chmn. farm materials handling com. 1978-79, past chmn. environ. air quality com. 1979-79, past chmn. cotton engring. com. 1986-87, chmn. agrl. engrs. regional cotton rsch. project 1983-84, assoc. editor pubs. rev. com., chmn. task force to evaluate cotton mktg. and grading sys. 1986-89, elected to nat. nominating com. 1988-89, Mayfield Cotton engring. award 1989, paper award 1990, 92, outstanding engr. award Tex. section 1992); mem. Nat. Soc. Profl. Engrs., Am. Soc. Engring. Edn. (chmn. agrl. engring. divsn. 1985), Tex. Soc. Profl. Engrs. (outstanding engr. award Brazos chpt. 1985, pres. Brazos Valley chpt. 1986), Air and Waste Mgmt. Assn., Air Pollution Control Assn., Reserve Officers Assn., Blue Key, College Station Kiwanis Club (past pres.), Gamma Sigma Delta (treas. TAMU chpt. 1987-88, sec. 1988-89, pres.-elect 1989-90, pres. 1990-91), Sigma Xi (mem. program com. 1981-84), Phi Kappa Phi, Alpha Epsilon, Sigma Tau. Office: Tex A&M U Dept Agrl Engring 207D Scoates Hill College Station TX 77843-2117

PARNELL, CHARLES L. speechwriter; b. Myrtis, La., Feb. 13, 1938; s. Forrest L. and Dorothy D. (Jones) P. BA, Rice U., 1960; M Bus. and Pub. Adminstrn., Southeastern U., 1977. Commd. ens. USN, 1960, advanced through grades to comdr., 1975, ret., 1987; speechwriter Mead Data Cen., Dayton, Ohio, 1987-89, Nationwide Ins. Co., Columbus, Ohio, 1989-90; exec. speechwriter Miller Brewing Co., Milw., 1990-96; speechwriter, Milw., 1996-98; exec. speechwriter, Dallas, 1998—. Contbr. articles to profl. jours.; frequently quoted in leading speech-related publs.; speeches used as models in 8 college level textbooks in U.S. and Can. Mem. U.S. Naval Inst., Mil. Officers Assn., World Future Soc. Avocations: reading, writing, travel. Home and Office: 1311 Brittany Ln Mansfield TX 76063-4013

PARNELL, FRANCIS WILLIAM, JR., otolaryngologist; b. Woonsocket, R.I., May 22, 1940; s. Francis W. and Dorothy V. (Lalor) P.; m. Diana DeAngelis, Feb. 27, 1965; children: Cheryl Lynn, John Francis, Kathleen Diana, Alison Anne, Thomas William. Student, Coll. Holy Cross, 1957-58; AB, Clark U., 1961; MD, Georgetown U., 1965. Diplomate: Nat. Bd. Med. Examiners, Am. Bd. Otolaryngology. Intern Univ. Hosps., Madison, Wis., 1965-66, resident in gen. surgery, 1966-67, otolaryngology, 1967-70; pvt. practice medicine specializing in otolaryngology San Rafael, Calif., 1972-75, Greenbrae, Calif., 1978—2000; chmn., pres., CEO Parnell Pharms., Larkspur, Calif., 1982—. Cons. corp. med. affairs, 1978-82; corp. med. dir. Becton, Dickinson & Co., Rutherford, N.J., 1976-78; clin. instr. U. Calif. at San Francisco, 1972-75, asst. clin. prof., 1975-76; Alt. del., U.S. Del. 27th World

Health Assembly WHO, Geneva, 1974. Contbr. articles to profl. jours. Candidate Calif. State Assembly, 1988; bd. dirs. Marin Coalition, 1980-96, 97-01, chmn., 1986-87; trustee Ross (Calif.) Sch. Dist., 1981-89; mem. governing bd. Marin Cmty. Coll. Dist., 1995-2003, pres., 1999-2000, 02-03. Maj. M.C. AUS, 1970-72, lt. col. M.C., USAR, 1985-93. Fellow ACS (gov. 1988-94), Am. Acad. Otolaryngology. Home: PO Box 998 Ross CA 94957-0998 Office: 1100 S Eliseo Dr Greenbrae CA 94904-2017 Office Phone: 415-256-1800.

PARNELL, THOMAS ALFRED, physicist; b. Lumberton, N.C., Nov. 24, 1931; s. Johnathan Alfred and Lula Beale (Lashley) P.; m. Elizabeth G. Brite, June 4, 1955; children: Marc Thomas, Gina Ann. BS in Physics, U. N.C., 1954, MS in Physics, 1962, PhD in Physics, 1965. Rsch. adj., dept. physics U. N.C., Chapel Hill, 1962-65; ops. analyst U.S. Air Force Europe, Wiesbaden, W. Ger., 1965-66; asst. prof. physics Marshall U., Huntington, W.Va., 1966-67; physicist NASA-Marshall Space Flight Center, Huntsville, Ala., 1978-99, chief astrophysics br., 1969-98; prin. rsch. scientist U. Ala., Huntsville, 1999—. Mem. editorial bd. Radiation Measurements; contbr. articles to profl. jours. Served to capt. USNR, 1954-91. Recipient Exceptional Sci. Achievement medal, Outstanding Leadership medal NASA, U.S. Antarctic Svc. medal. Mem. Am. Phys. Soc., Monte Sano Club (Huntsville). Home: 907 Corinth Cir SE Huntsville AL 35801-2064

PARNEROS, DEMOS, retail executive; Joined Staples, Inc., Framingham, Mass., 1987, v.p. ops., 1996—99, sr. v.p. ops., 1999—2002, pres. U.S. superstores, 2002—. Office: Staples Inc 500 Staples Dr Framingham MA 01702

PARNES, ANDREW H. financial executive; V.p. fin., treas., CFO Standard Pacific Corp., Costa Mesa, Calif., 1996—. Office: Standard Pacific Corp 15326 Alton Pkwy Irvine CA 92618-2338

PARNES, EDMUND IRA, oral and maxillofacial surgeon, educator; b. Pitts., Apr. 16, 1936; s. David E. and Sara (Engelberg) P.; m. Elizabeth Cameron, Nov. 27, 1977; children: Dana, Mara, Lauren. Student, Vanderbilt U., 1954-55, U. Miami, 1955-56; DMD, U. Pitts., 1960. Diplomate Am. Bd. Oral and Maxillofacial Surgery. Oral surgery intern Jackson Meml. Hosp., Miami, Fla., 1960-61; resident, tchr. fellow in anesthesiology Presbyn. Univ. Hosp., Pitts., 1963-64; sr. resident in oral surgery Ben Taub Gen. Hosp., Houston, 1964-65; pvt. practice oral and maxillofacial surgery, Miami, 1965—. Interim assoc. chief oral surgery Jackson Meml. Hosp., Miami, 1970-72; clin. assoc. prof. U. Miami, 1975—; lectr. in field. Mem. Hist. Preservation Bd., City of Coral Gables, Fla. Capt. U.S. Army, 1961-63. Fellow Am. Coll. Dentists, Am. Assn. Oral and Maxillofacial Surgeons (com. on legis. 1972-73, com. sci. sessions 1979-86, trustee 1991-94, pres.-elect 1994-95, pres. 1995-96), Internat. Coll. Dentists; mem. ADA, Fla. Soc. Oral and Maxillofacial Surgeons (pres. 1974-75), Fla. Dental Assn. (ho. of dels., trustee 1982-95, v.p. 1996, pres.-elect 1998, pres. 1999-2000), S.E. Soc. Oral Surgeons, East Coast Dist. Dental Soc. (chmn. coms. 1980-84, pres. 1981-82), North Dade Dental Soc. (pres. 1971-72), Am. Soc. Dental Anesthesiology (pres. Fla. chpt. 1970), Alpha Omega (pres. 1977-78, regent 1983), Hist. Assn. South Fla. (trustee, bd. dirs. Hist. Mus. South Fla.), Coral Gables Hist. Preservation Bd. (chmn.). Jewish. Office: 8700 N Kendall Dr Ste 221 Miami FL 33176-2206

PARO, JEFF, publisher; b. 1959; married; 2 children. BA in Internat. Afairs and Econs., U. Colo. Various advtg. sales and mktg. positions Sports/Leisure mag. divsn., past nat. sales mgr. Tennis mag./The Tennis Co. NY Times, 1982-95; nat. sales mgr. Times Mirror Mags., Inc., NYC, 1995, pub. Field & Stream mag., Outdoor Life mag, Outdoor Explorer Mag.; group pub. AOL Time Warner's Time4Media; pres. Time's Outdoor Co., 2000—01; sr. v.p. and group pub. dir. PRIMEDIA Enthusiast Media, NY, 2002—. Bd. dir. Nat. Forest Found. Office: Primedia Enthusiast Media 260 Madison Ave New York NY 10016*

PARODE, ANN, lawyer; b. L.A., Mar. 3, 1947; d. Lowell Carr and Sabine Parode. BA, Pomona Coll., 1968; JD, UCLA, 1971. Bar: Calif. 1972, U.S. Dist. Ct. (so. dist.) Calif. 1972, U.S. Ct. Appeals (9th cir.) 1975, U.S. Supreme Ct. 2000. Assoc. Luce, Forward et al, San Diego, 1971-75; gen. counsel, exec. v.p., sec. San Diego Trust & Savs., 1975-94; with First Interstate Bank, 1994—97; campus counsel U. Calif., San Diego, 1997—. Judge pro tem San Diego Mcpl. Ct., 1978-84; campus counsel U. Calif., San Diego, 1997—. Bd. dirs. San Diego Cmty. Found., 1989-97, chmn., 1994-96; bd. dirs. The Burnham Inst., 1995-2001, Girard Found., 1990-. Mem. Calif. Bar Assn. (corp. law com. 1980-83, client trust fund commn. 1986-90, chmn. 1989-90), San Diego County Bar Found. (founder, bd. dirs. 1979-86, 98-2001, pres. 1980-83), San Diego Bar Assns. (bd. dirs. 1977-81, v.p. 1977-78, 80-81, treas. 1979-80), Law Libr. Justice Found. (pres. 1994). Business E-Mail: aparode@ucsd.edu.

PARR, ALBERT CLARENCE, physicist; b. Tooele, Utah, June 22, 1942; s. Trafton Charles and Esther Laura (Schuldheisz) P.; m. Ruth E. Pieplow, Jan. 29, 1966; children: Robin, Trafton. B.S. in Physics, Oreg. State U., 1964, B.S. in Math., 1964; M.S. in Physics, U. Chgo., 1966, Ph.D. in Physics, 1971. Research asst. U. Chgo., 1964-70, research assoc., 1971; assoc. prof. U. Ala., University, 1971-80; physicist Nat. Bur. Standards, Gaithersburg, Md., 1980-86; group leader spectral radiometry Nat. Inst. Standards and Tech., 1986-90, cons. Argonne Nat. Lab, Ill., 1981-86; divsn. chief Optical Tech. Divsn. Nat. Inst. Standards and Tech., 1990—. Contbr. articles to profl. jours. Served as seaman USNR, 1960-66. Cotrell Found. grantee, 1973. Fellow Am. Phys. Soc.; mem. Coun. Optical Radiation Measurement, Commn. Internat. de l'Eclairage (U.S. Nat. Com.), Optical Soc. Am. Lodge: Elks. Avocations: fishing; reading.

PARR, CAROLYN MILLER, federal judge; b. Palatka, Fla., Apr. 17, 1937; d. Arthur Charles and Audrey Ellen (Dunklin) Miller; m. Jerry Studstill Parr, Oct. 12, 1959; children: Kimberly Parr Trapasso, Jennifer Parr Turek, Patricia Audrey Smith. BA, Stetson U., 1959; MA, Vanderbilt U., 1960; JD, Georgetown U., 1977; LLD (hon.), Stetson U., 1986. Bar: Md. 1977, U.S. Tax Ct. 1977, D.C. 1979, U.S. Supreme Ct. 1983. Gen. trial atty. IRS, Washington, 1977-81, sr. trial atty. office of chief counsel, 1982; spl. counsel to asst. atty. gen. tax divsn. U.S. Dept. Justice, Washington, 1982-85; judge U.S. Tax Ct., Washington, 1985-2000, sr. judge, 2001—. Nat. Def. fellow Vanderbilt U., 1959-60; fellow Georgetown U., 1975-76; recipient Spl. Achievement award U.S. Treasury, 1979. Mem. ABA, Md. Bar Assn., Nat. Assn. Women Judges, D.C. Bar Assn. Office: US Tax Ct 400 2nd St NW Washington DC 20217-0002

PARR, GRANT VAN SICLEN, surgeon; b. N.Y.C., Dec. 30, 1942; s. Ferdinand Van Siclen and Helene H. P.; m. Helen Mushat Frye, July 1, 1967; children: Kathleen Gage, Helen Johnston. AB with honors, Wesleyan U., 1965; MD, Cornell U., 1969. Diplomate: Am. Bd. Thoracic Surgery, Am. Bd. Surgery. Intern, resident U. Hosps. of Cleve., 1969-71; resident in surgery U. Ala. Hosps., Birmingham, 1971-74, chief resident in surgery, 1974-75, resident in cardiovascular and thoracic surgery, 1975-77; practice medicine specializing in thoracic surgery Hershey, Pa., 1978-82; mem. staff Presbyn.-U. Pa. Med. Ctr., Phila., 1982-88, chief div. Thoracic surgery, 1984-88, acting chmn. Dept. Surgery, 1988, chief cardiovascular surgery, 1984-88; asst. prof. cardiothoracic surgery M.S. Hershey Med. Center, Hershey, Pa., 1987-88; chief cardiovascular surgery Morristown (N.J.) Meml. Hosp., 1988-97, co-chmn. dept. cardiovasc. scis., 1997—2004, chmn. dept. cardiovasc. medicine, 2004—; asst. prof. Pa. State U., 1978-82; clin. assoc. prof. surgery U. Pa., 1982-89; assoc. prof. clin. surgery Columbia U., 1992—. Chief cardiovasc. surgery Overlook Hosp., 1988—, Morristown Meml. Hosp., 1988-98; chmn. cardiovasc. surgery Atlantic Health Sys., 1998—, trustee, 1998-2004, med. dir. cardiac svcs., 2004—. Contbr. articles on thoracic surgery to med. jours. Fellow Am. Coll. Cardiology, ACS, Am. Coll. Chest Physicians, Phila. Coll. Physicians; mem. AMA, Internat. Cardiovascular Soc., Assn. of Acad. Surgeons, Am. Assn. Thoracic Surgery, Phila. County Med. Soc., Soc. Thoracic Surgeons, Soc. Critical Care Medicine Pa., Thoracic Surg. Soc., John W. Kirklin Soc., Pa. Med. Assn., N.J. Soc. Thoracic Surgery, N.Y. Soc. Thoracic Surgery, Morris County Golf Club, NYU Club, Beverkill Trout Club. Office: 100 Madison Ave Morristown NJ 07960-6136 Office Phone: 973-971-7300. Business E-Mail: gparr@ahsys.org.

PARR, JAMES ALLAN, literature professor; b. Ritchie County, W.Va., Oct. 7, 1936; s. James William and Virginia Alice (Bragg) P.; m. Franciszka Duda, May 4, 1957 (div. 1967): 1 child, Jacqueline; m. Carmen Salazar, Aug. 19, 1968 (div. 1980); m. Patricia Catherine Brinck, June 28, 1985. BA, Ohio U., 1959, MA, 1961; PhD, U. Pitts., 1967. Prof., chmn. Murray (Ky.) State U., 1964-70; prof. U. So. Calif., Los Angeles, 1970-90, U. Calif., Riverside, 1990—. Dir. Nat. Def. Edn. Act Inst., summers, 1966, 67, 69. Author: Don Quixote: An Anatomy of Subversive Discourse, 1988, Confrontaciones calladas, 1990, After Its Kind: Approaches to the Comedia, 1991, Don Quixote, Don Juan and Related Subjects, 2004; editor: Critical Essays on Juan Ruiz de Alarcon, 1972, El Burlador de Sevilla, 1991, On Cervantes: Essays for L.A. Murillo, 1991, Don Quixote, 1998; editor jour. Bull. of the Comediantes, 1973-98. Recipient Phi Beta Kappa award, Ohio U., 1960, Mellon fellowships, U. Pitts., 1961-63, Del Amo fellowship, U. So. Calif., Los Angeles, 1977, 84, 89, Fulbright, 1991. Mem. MLA, Am. Assn. Tchrs. of Spanish and Portuguese, Internat. Assn. Hispanists, Cervantes Soc. Am. (pres.). Avocation: travel. Home: 421 Elmwood Dr Pasadena CA 91105-1358

PARR, ROBERT GHORMLEY, chemistry professor; b. Chgo., Sept. 22, 1921; s. Leland Wilbur and Grace (Ghormley) P.; m. Jane Bolstad, May 28, 1944; children: Steven Robert, Jeanne Karen, Carol Jane. AB magna cum laude with high honors in Chemistry, Brown U., 1942; PhD in Phys. Chemistry, U. Minn., 1947; D (hon.), U. Leuven, 1986, Jagiellonian U., 1996. Asst. prof. chemistry U. Minn., 1947-48; mem. faculty Carnegie Inst. Tech., 1948-62, prof. chemistry, 1957-62, Johns Hopkins U., 1962-74, chmn. dept., 1969-72; William R. Kenan, Jr. prof. theoretical chemistry U. N.C., Chapel Hill, 1974-90, Wassily Hoeffding prof. chem. physics, 1990—. Vis. prof. chemistry, mem. Ctr. Advanced Study, U. Ill., 1962; disting. vis. prof. SUNY, Buffalo, Pa. State U., 1967; vis. prof. Japan Soc. Promotion Sci., 1968, 79, U. Haifa, 1977, Free U., Berlin, 1977, Duke U., 1996-97; Firth prof. U. Sheffield, 1976; Coochbehar prof. Indian Assn. Cultivation of Sci., 1990; Sandoval Vallarta prof. UAM-Iztapalapa, 1992; chmn. com. postdoctoral fellowships in chemistry NAS-NRC, 1961-63; chmn. panel theoretical chemistry Westheimer com. survey chemistry NAS, 1964; mem. coun. Gordon Rsch. Conf., 1974-76, mem. Commn. on Human Resources, NRC, 1979-82; mem. coun. Inst. for Molecular Sci., Okazaki, Japan, 1986-88; bd. trustees Inst. for Fundamental Chemistry, Kyoto, Japan, 1988—. Author: Quantum Theory of Molecular Electronic Structure, 1963, Density-Functional Theory of Atoms and Molecules, 1989, also numerous articles.; Assoc. editor: Jour. Chem. Physics, 1956-58, Chem. Revs, 1961-63, Jour. Phys. Chemistry, 1963-67, 77-79, Am. Chem. Soc. Monographs, 1966-71, Theoretica Chimica Acta, 1966-69, 92-96; Chinese Chem. Letters, 1998—; bd. editors: Jour. Am. Chem. Soc, 1969-77; adv. editorial bd.: Internat. Jour. Quantum Chemistry, 1967—, Chem. Physics Letters, 1967-79. Recipient Outstanding Achievement award U. Minn., 1968, N.C. Disting. Chemist award, 1982; fellow U. Chgo., 1949; research asso., 1957; Fulbright scholar U. Cambridge, Eng., 1953-54; Guggenheim fellow, 1953-54; NSF sr. postdoctoral fellow U. Oxford (Eng.) and Commonwealth Sci. and Indsl. Research Orgn., Melbourne, Australia, 1967-68; Sloan fellow, 1956-60, N.C. award in sci., 1999. Fellow AAAS, Am. Phys. Soc. (chmn. divsn. chem. physics 1963-64); mem. NAS (award in chem. scis., 2004), AAUP, Am. Chem. Soc. (chmn. divsn. phys. chemistry 1978, Irving Langmuir award in chem. physics 1994), Am. Acad. Arts and Sci., Indian Nat. Sci. Acad., Internat. Acad. Quantum Molecular Sci. (pres. 1991-97), Phi Beta Kappa, Sigma Xi, Phi Lambda Upsilon, Pi Mu Epsilon. Home: 701 Kenmore Rd Chapel Hill NC 27514-2019 Office: U NC Dept Chemistry Chapel Hill NC 27599-3290

PARR, ROYSE MILTON, retired lawyer, writer; b. Elk City, Okla., Sept. 11, 1935; s. Clinton Riley and Caroline (Royse) Parr; m. Sheila Ann Harshaw, May 28, 1960; children: Clinton Howard, Reagan Royse. BS, Okla. State U., 1958; JD, U. Tulsa, 1964. Bar: Okla. 1964. Rsch. scout Jersey Prodn. Rsch. Co., Tulsa, 1960-64; atty. Sun Oil Co., 1964-70, White Shield Corp., 1970-71; sec., atty., asst. gen. counsel MAPCO, Inc., Tulsa, 1971-97; gen. counsel, dir. Seminole Pipeline Co., 1989-97. Lectr. in field. Co-author: Glory Days of Summer: The History of Baseball in Oklahoma, 1999, Allie Reynolds: Super Chief, 2002, Native Americans in Sports, 2004. Vice chmn. Tulsa County Election Bd., 1973—97; pres. Ret. Sr. Vol. Program, 1982—83. Served to 1st lt. U.S. Army, 1958—60, capt. USAR, 1960—63. Mem.: ASME, ABA, Soc. Am. Baseball Rsch., Am. Soc. Corp. Secs., Tulsa County Bar Assn., Okla. Bar Assn., Soc. Petroleum Engrs., Oaks Country Club, Phi Delta Phi. Republican. Methodist. E-mail: crashparr@aol.com.

PARR, VIRGINIA HELEN, retired librarian; b. Mansfield, Ohio, May 23, 1937; d. Bernard Franklin and Frances Cole (Downes) P.; m. Marvin E. Lickey, June 14, 1959 (div. 1972); children: Sarah Elizabeth, David Andrew, Rachel Alison; m. Laurence E. Steadman, Nov. 27, 1993. AB, Oberlin Coll., 1959; AM, U. Mich., 1961; MLS, U. Oreg., 1973. English and social studies tchr. Whittier Jr. High Sch., Livonia, Mich., 1961-64; libr. U. Oreg. Libr., Eugene, 1973-79, head edn. and psychology, 1979-80, acting asst. univ. libr. for pub. svcs., 1980-82; head reference, rsch. and instrn. svcs. U. Cin., 1982-89, reference libr., bibliographer, 1989—2002, ret., 2002—. Chair, mem. budget com. Eugene Sch., 1976-79. Founding editor: Behavioral and Social Scis. Libr., 1978; contbr. articles to profl. jours. Bd. dirs. Eugene Jr. Symphony Assn., 1979-82; mem. adv. bd. various mental health groups, Eugene, 1971-79. Mem. Assn. Coll. and Rsch. Librs. of ALA (various offices edn. and behavioral sci. sect. 1977-86, numerous coms. reference and adult svcs. divsn. 1981-92), Beta Phi Mu, Pi Lambda Theta. Democrat. Episcopalian. Avocations: reading, classical music, travel. Home: 5532 S Shore Dr 12F Chicago IL 60637-1990 E-mail: v_parr@sbcglobal.net.

PARRA, DEREK, Olympic athlete; b. San Bernardino, Calif., Mar. 15, 1970; Mem. U.S. Elite Long Track Speedskating Team. Named U.S. Allround Overall Champion, 2000, Allround World Championships Men, 2003; recipient 5000-meter Silver medal, 2002 Olympic Games, 1500-meter Gold medal, ranked 10th in 5000m, World Single Distance Championships, 2003, ranked 5th in 1500m, 2003, ranked #16 in 10000m, 2003. Achievements include set world record for 1500m, Salt Lake City, 2002. Address: US Speedskating P Box 450639 Westlake OH 44145

PARRA, NICOLE M. state representative; b. Bakersfield, Calif., Feb. 3, 1970; BA in Econs., U. Calif., Berkeley, 1992; JD, Cath. U. Columbus, 1998. Dist. dir. U.S. Rep. Cal Dooley, legis. asst., 1992—98, campaign mgr., 2000; field dir. Supr. Pete Parra, 1996; GOTV coord. Calif. Assemblyman Dean Florez, 1998; co-chair Gov.'s Econ. Devel. Subcom., 2000—; mem. Calif. Assembly, 2002—. Alumna Hispanas Organized Polit. Equality, 1998—; adv. bd. San Joaquin Valley Hosp., 2001; mem. San Joaquin Valley Empowerment Initiative; bd. dirs. County, 1999—. Mem.: Latina Leaders Kern. Democrat. Roman Catholic. Office: PO Box 942849 Sacramento CA 94249

PARRA, WILLIAM, administrator; b. San Diego, Sept. 15, 1942; BS, Santa Clara U., 1964; MS, Ga. State U., 1979. CDC pub. health advisor USAID, Washington, 1971-73; CDC sr. pub. health advisor Commonwealth of Puerto Rico Dept. Pub. Health, San Juan, 1973-76; chief tng. edn., divsn. sexually transmitted diseases CDC, Atlanta, 1976-84; program mgmt. officer divsn. communicable diseases WHO, Geneva, 1984-88; dep. dir. Office of HIV/AIDS CDC, Atlanta, 1988-95, acting dep. dir. Nat. Ctr. for HIV, STD and TB prevention, 1995, dep. dir. Nat. Ctr. for Environ. Health, 1996-99; v.p. Am. Soc. Health Assn., Triangle Pk., NC, 2000—02, interim pres., CEO, 2002—. Office: Am Social Health Assn PO Box 13827 Research Triangle Park NC 27709-3827

PARRA-ARANGUREN, GONZALO, judge International Court of Justice; b. Caracas, Venezuela, Dec. 5, 1928; Degree juridical and political studies, Ctrl. U. Venezuela, 1950; degree, Inter-Am. Law Inst., NYU; LLD, Ludwig-Maximilians U., Munich. Prof. Ctrl. U. Venezuela, Caracas, 1956—. Andrés Bello Cath. U., Caracas, 1957—; judge 2d Ct. of 1st Instance Fed. Dist. and State of Miranda, Caracas, 1958-71; 1st assoc. judge Chamber of Cassation Supreme Ct. of Justice, Caracas, 1988-92, alt. judge, 1992—96; judge Internat. Ct. Justice, The Hague, Netherlands, 1996—. Mem. nat. group for Venezuela Permanent Ct. of Arbitration, The Hague, 1985—; arbitrator, Venezuela and abroad; mem. legal adv. com. Ministry of Fgn. Affairs, 1984-96, Nat. Congress, 1990-96; mem. Acad. Polit. and Social Scis. of Caracas, 1966—, pres., 1993-95; mem. Inst. of Internat. Law, 1979—; Venezuelan rep. several sessions of The Hague Conf. on Pvt. Internat. Law. Author books in field; contbr. articles to profl. jours. Office: Internat Ct of Justice Peace Palace 2517 KJ The Hague Netherlands

PARRAMORE, BARBARA MITCHELL, education educator; b. Guilford County, N.C., Aug. 29, 1932; d. Samuel Spencer and Nellie Gray (Glosson) Mitchell; m. Lyman Griffis Worthington, Dec. 23, 1956 (div. 1961); m. Thomas Custis Parramore, Jan. 22, 1966 (dec. Jan. 2004); children: Lisa Gray, Lynn Stuart. AB, U. N.C., Greensboro, 1954; MEd, N.C. State U., 1959; EdD, Duke U., 1968. Counselor, tchr. Raleigh City Schs., 1954-59, sch. prin., 1959-65; prof. dept. of curriculum and instrn. N.C. State U., 1970-96, prof. emeritus, 1996—. Acad. specialist Office Internat. Edn., U.S. Info. Svcs., sec. sch. initative program, The Philippines, 1987. Author: The People of North Carolina, 1972, 3rd edit. 1983. Japan Inst. Social and Econ. Affairs fellow, 1980; N.C. AAUW award for juvenile lit., 1973, Holladay medal for excellence N.C. State U., 1994. Mem. ASCD, N.C. ASCD (pres. 1994-96), N.C. Coun. for Social Studies (pres. 1985-87), Assn. Tchr. Educators, Delta Kappa Gamma, Kappa Delta Pi. Home: 5012 Tanglewood Dr Raleigh NC 27612-3135

PARRESOL, BERNARD ROSS, research biometrician, statistician; b. Washington, Sept. 15, 1953; s. Thomas and Rita Delores P.; m. Lisa Leigh Morton-Barbé, May 5, 1995; children: Sarah Marie Barbé, Christine Pamela Barbé. BS with honors, Mich. State U., 1977; M of Applied Stats., La. State U., 1983, PhD, 1998. Reg. forester, N.C. Br. mgr. James M. Vardaman & Co. Forestry Cons., Shreveport, La., 1977-80; rsch. assoc. dept. explt. stats. La. State U., Baton Rouge, 1983-86; math. statistician USDA Forest Svc., New Orleans, 1986-95, Asheville, N.C., 1996—. Stats. cons. Internat. Inst. Tropical Forestry, Rio Piedras, P.R., 1987-2002; guest lectr. Nanjing (China) Forestry U., 1994, 97, U. de Tras-os-Montes e Alto Douro, Portugal, 1998, 2002, 2003, Universidad Autonoma de Nuevo Leon, Mex., 2001, Universidad de Santiago de Compostela, Spain, 2002, Beijing Forestry U., 2003; adj. prof. U. Fla., 1999-2002. Guest assoc. editor Forest Sci., 1999-2000, assoc. editor Southern Jour. of Applied Forestry, 2002—; contbr. Encyclopedia of Environmetrics; contbr. articles to profl. jours. Officer La. Indian Heritage Assn., 1988-92; mem. organizing com. Nanjing Internat. Wetland Symposium, 2002. Recipient Dir.'s award for internat. programs USDA Forest Svc. So. Rsch. Sta., 2002, Chief's Global Stewardship award USDA Forest Svc., 2003; Rockefeller Found. scholar, 1990; grantee Smithsonian Tropical Rsch. Inst., Panama, 1992, U.S. Office Internat. Coop. and Devel., Chile, 1993; Humanities scholar La. Endowment for Humanities, 2000, 02. Mem. Am. Statistical Assn., Soc. Am. Foresters, Internat. Soc. Tropical Foresters. Avocation: American Indian culture. Office: USDA Forest Svc PO Box 2680 Asheville NC 28802-2680 Office Phone: 828 259 0500. Office Fax: 828 257-4840. Business E-Mail: bparresol@fs.fed.us.

PARRETT, SHERMAN O. lawyer; b. Cin., Jan. 8, 1943; s. Earl and Ruby (Angel) P.; m. Rosalind K. Brooks, Sept. 21, 1985; children: Laura, Samantha. BSEE, U. Cin., 1965; JD with honors, George Washington U., 1969. Bar: Calif. 1970, D.C. 1975, Ariz. 1992. Assoc. Flehr, Hohbach et al., San Francisco, 1970-73; ptnr. Cushman, Darby & Cushman, Washington, 1973-86, Irell & Manella, L.A., 1986-91, Streich Lang, Phoenix, 1991-94, Snell & Wilmer, Phoenix, 1994-98. Address: 2818 SE 19th Ave Cape Coral FL 33904 E-mail: parretts@aol.com.

PARRETT, WILLIAM G. consultant company executive; m. Diane Parrett; six children. BS, St. Francis Coll. Various positions Deloitte & Touche LLP, 1967-77, ptnr. Stamford (Conn.), group mng. ptnr. NY, regional mng. ptnr. Tri-State, bd. dirs., mem. mgmt. com., chmn. Global Fin. Svcs. Industries divsn., 1977-99, mng. ptnr., 1999—; global CEO, sr. ptnr. Deloitte, Touche Tohmatsu, 2003—. Bd. trustee Nat. Adv. Bd. of Nat. Underground Railroad Freedom Center; bd. dirs. Japan Soc., US-Japan Bus. Coun. Trustee Carnegie Hall, co-chair corp. fund, Cath. U. of Am.; treas. Madison Sq. Boys & Girls Club; bd. govs. United Way of Tri-State; pres., chmn. devel. bd. St. Agnes Boys High Sch.; vol. not-for-profit orgns; bd. trustee United Way of Am. Mem. Econ. Club NY, Am. Inst. of Cert. Pub. Accts., Com. to Encourage Corp. Philanthropy (CECP), G100 CEO Forum, Transatlantic Bus. Dialogue (TABD), US Coun.for Internat. Bus. (USCIB), Internat. Councillor for Center for Strategic & Internat. Studies (CSIS). Office: 1633 Broadway New York NY 10019-6754

PARRICK, GERALD HATHAWAY, communications and marketing executive; b. Cushing, Okla., Oct. 27, 1924; s. Gerald H. and Phyllis A. (Sheppard) B.; m. Gail V. Straney, Dec. 5, 1984; children: Gerald Hathaway III, Candace Anne. BJ, U. Mo., 1948. Creative account exec. George Knox & Assoc., Oklahoma City, 1948-51; account exec. Batten, Barton, Durstine & Osborn, San Francisco, 1952-60; account dir. McCann-Erickson, L.A., 1960-67, v.p. Portland, Oreg., 1967-72; dir. comm. Pacific Power Co., Portland, 1972-77, spl. asst. to chmn. bd., 1977-79; pres. Entreepublic Comm., West Linn, Oreg., 1979—, Bailey/Parrick, Inc., Portland, 1981-84, Parrick/Milpacher, Inc., Portland, 1984-85, The Laugh Clinic, Inc., Portland, 1984-90, K-KOR, Inc., 1990-93. Author: A 20th Century Miracle, 1981, Touched by a Miracle, 1997. Mem. Oreg. Advt. Rev. Bd., 1974-75. Capt. AUS, 1943-45, 51-52, ETO. Named Oreg. Advt. Man of Yr., Oreg. Advt. Club, 1971. Mem. Am. Advt. Fedn. (chmn. edn. western region 1973-74), Portland Advt. Fedn. (pres. 1974-75), Toastmasters (pres. 1966-67) (Encino, Calif.), Kappa Tau Alpha. Home: 17185 Carlson Ct Lake Oswego OR 97034-5802

PARRILLO, JOSEPH EDISON, JR., allergist, immunologist, cardiologist; b. Paterson, N.J., Jan. 5, 1947; MD, Cornell U., 1972. Diplomate Am. Bd. Allergy and Immunology, Am. Bd. Internal Medicine, Am. Bd. Cardiology. From intern to resident in medicine Mass. Gen. Hosp., Boston, 1972-74, fellow in cardiology, 1978-80; resident in medicine N.Y. Hosp.-Cornell Med. Ctr., N.Y.C., 1977-78; resident in allergy & immunology and infectious disease Clin. Ctr. Nat. Inst. Allergy and Immunology Disease, Bethesda, Md., 1974-77; med. staff Rush-Presbyn.-St. Lukes Med. Ctr., Chgo.; chief divsn. cardiology and critical care medicine Rush Heart Inst. Mem. Am. Coll. Cardiology, Am. Fedn. Clin. Rsch., Am. Heart Assn., Am. Soc. Clin. Immunology, Am. Coll. Critical Care Medicine, Am. Coll. Chest Physicians, Soc. Critical Care Medicine, Alpha Omega Alpha. Office: Dorrance Bldg, Floor 3 One Cooper Plaza Camden NJ 08103

PARRINELLO, KATHLEEN ANN MULHOLLAND, nursing administrator, educator; b. Syracuse, N.Y., June 26, 1953; d. Bernard Joseph and Mary Catherine (Wicke) Mulholland; m. Richard John Parrinello, June 30, 1973; children: Michael, Jeffrey, Stephen. BS, U. Rochester, 1975, MS, 1983, PhD, 1990. RN, N.Y. Staff nurse U. Rochester (N.Y.)-Strong Meml. Hosp., 1975-78, asst. head nurse, 1976-77, head nurse, 1978-83, assoc. clin. chief, 1983-86, coord. ambulatory care, 1986-88, clin. chief, asst. prof. Sch. Nursing, 1990—; practitioner tchr., asst. prof. Rush Presbyn. St. Luke's Med. Ctr., Chgo., 1988-89. Cons. in nursing U. Wis. Hosps. and Clinics, 1990, 91; prin. investigator State of N.Y. Dept. of Health, 1991. Author pamphlet Arterial Bypass Surgery Patient Booklet, 1981; contbr. articles to profl. publs. Workforce Demonstration grantee N.Y. Dept. Health. Mem. Am. Acad. Ambulatory Nursing Adminstrn. (bd. dirs. 1989-92), Am. Orgn. Nurse Execs., Genesee Valley Nurses Assn., Sigma Theta Tau. Office: Strong Meml Hosp 601 Elmwood Ave Rochester NY 14642-0002

PARRINO, CHERYL LYNN, federal agency administrator; b. Wisconsin Rapids, Wis., Jan. 21, 1954; m. Jack J. Parrino, Sept. 1, 1990; 1 child, George. BBA in Acctg., U. Wis., 1976. Auditor Pub. Svc. Commn. Wis., Madison, 1976-82, dir. utility audits, 1982-86, exec. asst. to chmn., 1986-91, commr., 1991-98, chmn., 1992-98; chmn., CEO Universal Svc. Adminstrv. Co.,

Madison, 1998—. Mem. adv. bd. Bellcore, 1991; vice chmn. bd. dirs. Wis. Ctr. Demand Side Rsch., Madison, 1991-92; chmn. bd. dirs. Wis. Pub. Utility Inst., Madison, 1992-95 Mem. Gov.'s Task Force Gross Receipts Tax, Madison, 1991-92, Gov.'s Task Force Alternative Fuels, Madison, 1992-98, Gov.'s Task Force Clean Air, Madison, 1992-98, Gov.'s Task Force Telecom., Madison, 1993-94. Mem. Nat. Assn. Pub. Utility Commrs. (exec. com. 1991, chmn. comm. com. 1992-98, pres. 1995-96, pres. Gt. Lakes conf. 1996). Republican. Lutheran. Avocations: skiing, tennis, travel. Office: Universal Svc Adminstrv Co 583 Donofrio Dr Ste 201 Madison WI 53719-2096 Fax: (608) 827-8893.

PARRINO, ROBERT, finance educator; b. N.Y.C., Sept. 4, 1957; s. Dominick Paul Parrino and Gertrude (Rainer) Wieczorek; m. Emily Allen Parrino, July 12, 1980. BSChemE, Lehigh U., Bethlehem, Pa., 1979; MBA, Coll. William and Mary, 1980; MS, U. Rochester, 1991, PhD in Fin., 1992. CFA. Sr. analyst Marriott Corp., Bethesda, Md., 1984-85; pres. Sprigg Lane Fin. Corp., Charlottesville, Va., 1985-88; faculty dept. fin. U. Tex., Austin, 1992-96, 97—; faculty U. Chgo., 1996-97. Dir. The Bentley Group, Charlottesville, 1987-88, Hicks, Muse, Tate & Furst Ctr. for Pvt. Equity Fin., Austin, 2000—. Contbr. articles to profl. jours. Capt. U.S. Army, 1981-84, lt. col. USAR. ret. Mem. Assn. for Investment Mgmt. and Rsch. (cand. curriculum com. 1994-99), Am. Econ. Assn., Fin. Mgmt. Assn., Am. Soc. Appraisers 1988-96 (Richmond chpt. treas. 1987-88), Beta Gamma Sigma. Office: McCombs Sch Bus Dept Fin CBA 6 222 U Tex at Austin Austin TX 78712-1179 Office Phone: 512-471-5788. E-mail: parrino@mail.utexas.edu.

PARRIS, MARK ROBERT, former ambassador, policy advisor; b. Mpls. m. Joan Elizabeth Gardner; 2 children. BS magna cum laude, Georgetown U., 1974. With Fgn. Svc., 1972-77, polit. counselor, 1982-85, dir. Office Soviet Union Affairs, 1985-88; dep. chief mission U.S. Embassy, Tel Aviv, 1989-92; spl. asst. pres., sr. dir. Nat. Security Coun., Washington, 1995-97; amb. to Turkey Ankara, 1997—2000; sr. fgn. policy advisor Baker, Donelson, Bearman and Caldwell, Washington, 2000—. Counselor Turkish Rsch. Program The Washington Inst., 2002—; bd. chmn. Am. Friends of Turkey; bd. mem. Am. Turkish Coun. Mem. policy bd. Una Chapman Cox Found., U.S.-Israel Edn. Found. Phi Beta Kappa. Office: Baker Donelson Bearman and Caldwell 6th Fl 555 Eleventh St Washington DC 20004*

PARRIS, SALLY NYE, real estate agent; b. Evanston, Ill., Apr. 5, 1946; d. Harry Gale Nye Jr. and Bettye (Herb) Sollitt; m. Thomas Baxter Parris, Mar. 25, 1988 (div. Sept. 1985); 1 child, Samantha Ross. AA, Bradford Jr. Coll., 1966; BS in Secondary Edn., Northwestern U., 1968; cert. real estate, Conn. Real Estate Inst., Norwalk, 1985. Lic. real estate agt., Conn. Dir. girls phys. edfn. Latin Sch. of Chgo., 1967-68; dir. Greenwich (Conn.) YWCA, 1972-79; English tchr. Inlingua Sch. Langs., Stamford, Conn., 1981-84; real estate agt. Curtis Assocs., Realtors, Greenwich, Conn., 1985—. Chair profl. divsn. United Way, Greenwich, 1995-98, chair real estate sect. profl. divsn., 1993-94, co-chair campaign kickoff Septemberfest, 1985-99, co-chair Greenwich Pro-Am. Lit. Vol. Benefit, 1995—; v.p., bd. dirs. YMCA, Greenwich, 1993—, chair spl. events com., 1994—, co-chair annual campaign, 1998; bd. dirs., benefit chair Cmty. Answers, Greenwich, 1994—; co-chair 350th Yr. parade Town of Greenwich, 1990; mem. benefits com. Literacy Vols., 1991-93. Recipient Vol. Recognition award Literacy Vols. Am., 1996, Town of Greenwich, 1991, United Way of Greenwich, 1985-97, Thomas Shepard award, 1995, 96. Mem. Conn. Assn. Profl. Women, Greenwich Bd. Realtors (advisor pub. rels. 1985-87, grievance com. 1999), Riverside Yacht Club (winter mem., social register 1960—), Greenwich Country Club (paddle tennis com. co-chmn. 1984-86, quar. editor 1982-86). Republican. Episcopalian. Avocations: swimming, racquet sports, golf, sporting clays, needlepoint. Office: Colwell Banker/Curtis Assocs 278 Sound Beach Ave Old Greenwich CT 06870-1626

PARRIS, THOMAS GODFREY, JR., medical facility administrator; b. Phila., Jan. 30, 1937; married. BS, Pa. State U., 1958; M Health Care Adminstrn., U. Pitts., 1965. Adminstrv. resident Homestead (Pa.) Hosp., 1964-65; exec. assoc. to v.p. Assocs. Hosp. Svcs. of N.Y., N.Y.C., 1965-67; asst. adminstr. Hackensack (N.J.) Med. Ctr., 1967-68; assoc. exec. dir. Met. Hosp. Ctr., N.Y.C., 1968-73; adminstr., CEO Women and Infants Hosp. of R.I., Providence, 1973-76, exec. v.p., CEO, 1976-79, pres., CEO, 1979—. Contbr. articles to profl. publs. Active various cmty. orgns. Fellow Am. Coll. Health Care Execs. (regent R.II. 1984-90); mem. Am. Hosp. Assn. (mem. com., del., trustee 1985-88), R.I. Hosp. Assn. (bd. dirs. 1973—, exec. com. 1974-79, chair 1978-79, del. 1979-80). Office: Women & Infants Hosp RI 101 Dudley St Providence RI 02905-2401

PARRIS, THOMAS MARTIN, research scientist, consultant; s. Arthur A and Nina G. Parris, Joan Weisman (Stepmother); m. Victoria Tamas, Dec. 1, 1962; children: David A. Tamas-Parris, Noah M. Tamas-Parris. BS, U. of Mich., 1978—82; MPP, Harvard U., 1988—90. Rsch. scientist Environ. Rsch. Inst. of Mich. (ERIM), Ann Arbor, 1980—88; dir., policy and applied user programs Consortium for Internat. Earth Sci. Info. Network (CIESIN), Washington, 1990—95; environ. resources libr. Harvard U., 1995—2001; rsch. sientist, exec. dir. Boston office ISciences LLC, Jamaica Plain, Mass., 2001—. Contbr. columns in newspapers Bytes of Note, Environment Mag., articles in prof. jours. Characterizing a Sustainability Transition: The Internat. Consensus. Office: ISciences LLC 685 Centre St Ste 207 Jamaica Plain MA 02130 E-mail: parris@isciences.com.

PARRISH, CARL E. artist, educator; b. Cuthbert, Ga., Jan. 21, 1945; s. Carl Edward and Frances Allen Parrish; m. Sarah Carter, Dec. 22, 1966 (div. Dec. 1976); 1 child, Rebecca Carter. AB cum laude, Harvard U., 1967; MA, Emory U., Atlanta, 1972. Head liberal arts dept. Atlanta Coll. of Art, 1997—. Rschr. Helike (Greece) Archeol. Project, 2004. Author: (plays) Jimmy!, 1993. Head protocol Alex. Coliseum, Internat. Olympic Com., Atlanta, 1996. Grantee Rsch. grantee, Atlanta Coll. Art, Sorbonne, 2002, Atlanta Coll. Art, Oxford U., Eng., 2001, Study grantee, Atlanta Coll. Art, Harvard U., 2000. Mem.: Harvard Faculty Club, Harvard Club of Ga. (v.p. membership 1994—96, scholarship com. 1992—95). Avocation: bridge. Office: Atlanta College of Art 1280 Peachtree St NE Atlanta GA 30309

PARRISH, DAVID WALKER, JR., legal publishing company executive; b. Bristol, Tenn., Feb. 8, 1923; BA, Emory and Henry Coll., 1948, LLD, 1978; BS, U.S. Mcht. Marine Acad., 1950; LLB, U. Va., 1951. Pres. The Michie Co., Charlottesville, Va., 1969-89, vice chmn., 1989-96; pub. cons., 1996—. Home: 250 Pantops Mountain Rd Apt 5102 Charlottesville VA 22911 Office: 300 Preston Ave Ste 103 Charlottesville VA 22902-5044 Office Phone: 434-984-4307.

PARRISH, EDGAR LEE, financial services executive; b. Washington, Apr. 11, 1948; s. Frank Jennings Parrish and Lorene (Lomax) Parrish.; m. Katherine Ellen MacLachlan; children: Robert Alexander Wilson, Stephen Edgar MacLachlan. BS in Commerce, U. Va., 1970. Cert. investment mgmt. analyst. Sr. v.p. Wheat, First Securities, Inc., Washington, 1971—79; v.p. Merrill Lynch, Pierce, Fenner & Smith, Inc., Washington, 1979—82, Phila., 1982—85; sr. v.p., fin. cons. Shearson Lehman Bros., Inc., Phila., 1985—87, Washington, 1987—93, mem. chmn.'s coun., 1987—92, mem. dirs. coun., 1986; sr. v.p. investments, Parrish Consulting Group UBS Fin. Svcs., Inc., Washington, 1993—2004, mem. Pacesetter Coun., 1994—2003, managed account cons., 1998—99, sr. managed account cons., 2000—04, Parrish Consulting Group, Merrill Lynch; 1st v.p., sr. fin. advisor Investments, Wash., 2004—. Pres. HESCO Corp., Manassas, Va., 1989—, also chmn. bd. dirs.; arbitrator NYSE. Mem. adv. bd. McIntire Sch. Commerce Univ. Va., 2001—; past chmn. investment com. Nat. Presbyn. Sch., Washington. Capt. USAFR, 1970-76. Mem. U. Va. Alumni Assn. (life), Investment Mgmt. Cons. Assn., Reserve Officers Assn. (life). Democrat. Episcopalian. Home: 4502 Wetherill Rd Bethesda MD 20816-1813 E-mail: edgar_parrish@ml.com.

PARRISH, EDWARD ALTON, JR., electrical and computer engineering educator, academic administrator; b. Newport News, Va., Jan. 7, 1937; s. Edward Alton and Molly Wren (Vaughn) Parrish; m. Shirley Maxine Johnson, Oct. 26, 1963; children: Troy Alton, Gregory Sinton. BEE, U. Va., 1964, MEE, 1966, DScEE, 1968. Registered Tenn., Va. Group leader Amerad Corp., Charlottesville, Va., 1961—64; asst. prof. elec. engring. U. Va., Charlottesville, 1968—71, assoc. prof. elec. engring., 1971—77, prof. elec. engring., 1977—86, chmn. dept. elec. engring., 1978—86; dean, centennial prof. electrical engring. Vanderbilt U., Nashville, 1987—95; pres., prof. elec. and computer engring. Worcester Poly. U., 1995—. Cons. U.S. Army, Charlottesville, Va., 1971—77, ORS, Inc., Princeton, NJ, 1973—74, Sperry Marine Systems, Charlottesville, 1975—76, Hajime Industries Ltd., Tokyo, 1978—84. Contbr. articles to profl. jours. With USAF, 1954—58. Grantee numerous rsch. grants. Fellow: IEEE (bd. dirs. 1990—91, v.p. ednl. activities 1992—93, engring. accreditation commn. 1989—96, exec. com. 1991—96, officer 1993—96, chmn. elect 1994—95, chmn. 1995—96, past chmn. 1996—97, editor-in-chief IEEE Computer 1995—98), ABET (bd. dirs. 2000—); mem.: IEEE Computer Soc. (sec. 1997, v.p. 1978—81, pres. 1988), Tau Beta Pi, Eta Kappa Nu, Sigma Xi. Baptist. Avocations: music, woodworking. Office: Office of Pres Worcester Polytechnic Institue 100 Institute Rd Worcester MA 01609-2247 E-mail: eap@wpi.edu.

PARRISH, FRANK JENNINGS, retired food products executive; b. Manassas, Va., Dec. 29, 1923; s. Edgar Goodloe and Alverda (Jennings) P.; m. Lorene Lomax, Feb. 11, 1944 (div. Apr. 1984); children: Edgar Lee, Julia Lorene; m. Mary Jane Biser, Aug. 25, 1984 Student, Va. Poly. Inst., 1942-43; grad., Indsl. Coll. Armed Forces, 1972. Pres. Manassas Frozen Foods, Inc., 1946—2001; pres., mgr. Cert. Food Buyers Svc., Inc., 1953—2001; pres. First Nat. Acceptance Co., 1966—2001; ret., 2001. V.p. Manassas Ice & Fuel Co. Mem. bus. adminstrn. adv. com. No. Va. Community Coll.; chmn. bd. North Va. coun. Am. Heart Assn., 1987-88; mem. inaugural com., 1961, vice-chmn. inaugural parade com. Maj. USAAF, 1943-46, CBI; ret. brig. gen. comdr. 909th TAC Airlift Group 1969-73, USAF; moblzn. asst. DCS plans and ops. Hdqrs., 1973-79. Maj. USAF, 1943—46, CBI, comdr. USAF, 1969—73, mobilization asst. USAF, 1973—83, ret. brig. gen. USAF, 1983. Decorated Legion of Merit, Air medal. Mem. Nat. Inst. Locker and Freezer Provisioners Am. (past pres., Industry Leadership award 1968), Va. Frozen Foods Assn. (past pres., dir.), Hump Pilots Assn., Va. Assn. Meat Processors (pres. 1986-90), Kiwanis. Methodist (chmn. bd. trustees 1958-66). Home: 9107 Park Ave Manassas VA 20110-4350 *Do unto others as you would have them do unto you.*

PARRISH, JAY See PIFER, ALAN

PARRISH, JILL NIEDERHAUSER, judge; BA, Weber State U., 1982; JD, Yale U., 1985. Bar: Utah 1985, 10th Cir. Ct. Appeals 1987, U.S. Supreme Ct. 2000. Clk. Hon. David K. Winder U.S. Dist. Ct., Utah, 1985; atty. Parr, Wadddoups, Brown, Gee & Loveless, Salt Lake City, 1986—90, shareholder, 1990—95; asst. U.S. atty. Civil Divsn. U.S. Dist. Ct., Utah, 1995—2003; justice Utah Supreme Ct., Salt Lake City, 2003—. Supr. Fin. Litigation Unit U.S. Attys. Office. Mem.: Fed. Bar Assn. (pres.). Office: Utah Supreme Ct PO Box 140210 Salt Lake City UT 84114-0210

PARRISH, JOHN ALBERT, dermatologist, research administrator; b. Louisville, Ky., Oct. 19, 1939; Children: Lynn, Susan, Mark. BA, Duke U., 1961; MD, Yale U., 1965. Diplomate Am. Bd. Dermatology. Medicine intern U. Mich., Ann Arbor, 1965-67; dermatology resident Harvard Med. Sch., Boston, 1969-72; dermatologist Mass. Gen. Hosp., Boston, 1972-87, dir. Wellman labs., 1975—, dir. cutaneous biology rsch. lab. Harvard, 1987—, chief, dermatology; chmn. dermatology Harvard Med. Sch., Boston, 1987—; prof. health sci. & tech. MIT. Dermatology cons. Beth Israel Hosp., Boston, 1973—; elected mem. Inst. of Medicine, 2000. Author: A Doctor's Year in Vietnam, 1972, Dermatology and Skin Care, 1975, Effects of Ultraviolet Radiation on the Immune System, 1983; co-author: Science of Photomedicine, 1982, Photoimmunology, 1983. Lt. Commdr. USN, 1968-89. Decorated Vietnamese Cross Gallantry with gold; recipient Outstanding Gen. Med. Officer award USN, 1969; Dohi lectr. Japanese Soc. Dermatology, 1990. Mem. Am. Soc. Dermatology (photobiology task force 1972—, Marion B. Sulzberger award 1988), Am. Soc. Lasers in Surgery and Medicine (pres. 1987-88), Am. Soc. Photobiology (coun. 1978-82), Soc. Investigative Dermatology (Wm. Montagna award 1982). Achievements include developing novel and safe effective treatment of psoriasis. Office: Mass Gen Hosp Derm Wel 2 55 Fruit St Boston MA 02114-2696

PARRISH, JOHN EDWARD, state appellate judge; b. Lebanon, Mo., June 10, 1940; s. Folie and Thelma (Osborn) P.; m. Claudia Barbee, Sept. 1, 1962; 1 child, Mark Everett. BBA, U. Mo., 1962, JD, 1965. Acct. Arthur Andersen & Co., St. Louis, 1965-66; ptnr. Phillips & Parrish, Camdenton, Mo., 1968-73; prosecuting atty. Camden County, Camdenton, 1969-73; circuit judge State of Mo., Camdenton, 1973-1990, judge Mo. Ct. Appeals (southern dist.), 1990-; mem. State Adv. Group on Juvenile Justice, Jefferson City, Mo., 1981—; Bd. dirs. Lake Regional Health Sys., Osage Beach, Mo., 1977—, pres. 1983-85, 1991-93, 1999-2001. Capt. U.S. Army, 1966-68. Mem. Mo. Bar Assn., Mo. Coun. Juvenile Ct. Judges (pres. 1978-79), Mo. Jud. Conf. (exec. coun. 1980-87, 92-94), Nat. Coun. Juvenile and Family Ct. Judges, Nat. Juvenile Ct. Found Inc. (trustee 1987-90). Mem. Christian Ch. (Disciples of Christ). Office: MO Ct Appeals 300 Hammons Pky Springfield MO 65806 Business E-Mail: john_e_parrish@courts.mo.gov.

PARRISH, LORI NANCE, commissioner; b. Evansville, Ind., July 31, 1948; m. Geoffrey Cohen; children: Gary Brown, Brandi Schmidt. Student, Fla. Atlantic U., 1969, Nova/Davie Cmty. Sch., 1974-75, Broward C.C., Davie, Fla., 1980, Clemson U., 1982, Fla. Atlantic U., 1986; student, Fla. Internat. U., 1988; LHD (hon.), Keiser Coll., 1996; postgrad., U. Ctrl. Fla., 1996—98. Toll operator So. Bell Telephone Co., 1966-68; adminstrv. asst. appraisal and cons. loan dept. Hollywood Fed. Savings and Loan Assn., 1968-72; acct., qualifying agt. Victor Purdo Painting Co., 1972-81; fin. mgr. CRG, Inc., 1982-83; bookkeeper I county and vocational Sch. Bd. Broward County South Plantation H.S., 1983-84; commr. dist. 5 Broward County, Fla., 1988—, chair, 1990-91, 97-98, vice-chair, 1989-90, 96-97, chair, 2001—02. Spl. projects coord. Davie/Cooper City C. of C.; adminstrv. asst. to bldg. ofcl. City of Cooper City, 1972-81; landscape contractor, owner Earthy Interiors; Lake Shore Motel and Swap Shop, Inc., 3290 Sunrise Investments, Inc., 3291 Sunrise Investments, Inc. (dba Swap Shop), Swap Shop Management LLC, 1994—. Adv. bd. Broward County Libr., 1979-85, Mommas and Poppas of Cooper City High, 1982-90, Broward C.C. Women's Programs Adv. Com., 1981-82; chair Cooper City Elem. Sch. Adv. Com., 1980-82, sec., 1979-80; chair South Ctrl. Area Adv. Com., 1982-83, sec., 1981-82; legis. chair Broward County Libr. Adv. Bd., 1982-84; active Broward County Sch. Bd., 1984-88, vice-chair, 1986-87, chair, 1987-88; bd. dirs. Pembroke Pines Human Resource Ctr. Adv. Com., 1984-88, others. Recipient Legislator of Yr. award Broward County Fire Fighters and Paramedics, 1994, Humanitarian of Yr. award Soref Jewish Cmty. Ctr., 1995, award Manatee Survival Found., 1996, Dream Maker award Jr. League Greater Fort Lauderdale, 1996, Jesse Portis Helms award Dolphin Dem. Club, 1996, Par Excellence award Miramar High Cmty. Sch., 1997, Ray Lisanty Meml. award GUARD, 1999, Gracias award Hispanic Unity, 1999, Polit. Leader of Yr. award The Vanguard Chronicle, 1999; named to Broward County Women's Hall of Fame, 1997. Mem. ALA, Southeastern Libr. Assn., Davie/Cooper City Friends of Libr. (founder), Fort Lauderdale Friends of Libr., Broward County Friends of Libr. Office: Office County Commr Govtl Ctr 115 S Andrews Ave Ste 421 Fort Lauderdale FL 33301-1801 also: Dist Office One North University Dr Ste 111-A Plantation FL 33324-2031 E-mail: ldrip01@bellsouth.net., lparrish@broward.org.work.

PARRISH, MARK, health facility administrator; Grad., U. Calif. Various gen. mgmt. and sales positions Foxmeyer, Gen. Med., Bergen Brunswig, Proctor & Gamble; exec. v.p. sales and mktg. Cardinal Health, Inc., 1997—99, exec. v.p. retail sales and mktg., 1999—2001, pres. medicine shoppe internat., 2001—03, group pres. pharm. distbn., 2003—, exec. v.p., 2003—. Office: Cardinal Health Inc 7000 Cardinal Pl Dublin OH 43017

PARRISH, MAURICE DRUE, museum executive; b. Chgo., Mar. 5, 1950; s. Maurice and Ione Yvonne (Columns) P.; m. Gail Marie Sims, Sept. 2, 1978; children: Theodore, Andrew, Brandon, Cara. BA in Arch., U. Pa., 1972; MArch, Yale U., 1975. City planner City of Chgo., 1975-81; architect John Hiltscher & Assocs., Chgo., 1981-83, Barnett, Jones & Smith, Chgo., 1983-84; zoning adminstr. City of Chgo., 1984-87, bldg. commr., 1987-89; dep. dir. Detroit Inst. of Arts, 1989-97, interim dir., 1997-99, exec. v.p., 1999—. Bd. dirs. Arts League of Mich., Detroit, 1994-97, Mosaic Youth Theatre Detroit, 2000—, chmn., 2002—; co-chmn. Mayor's Affordable Housing Task Force, Chgo., 1984-89; chmn. Chgo. Elec. Commn., 1984-89; mem. Chgo. Econ. devel. Commn., 1987-89; pres. St. Philip Neri Sch. Bd., Chgo., 1981-85, South Shore Commn., Chgo., 1982-84. King Chavez Parks fellow U. Mich., 1991, H.I. Feldman fellow Yale U., 1972; Franklin W. Gregory scholar Yale U., 1974, Nat. Achievement scholar U. Pa., 1968. Mem. Am. Assn. Mus., Am. Assn. Mus. Adminstrs., Constrn. Specifications Inst., Lambda Alpha. Avocations: sailing, chess, reading, astronomy. Office: Detroit Inst of Arts 5200 Woodward Ave Detroit MI 48202-4094 E-mail: mparrish@dia.org.

PARRISH, OVERTON BURGIN, JR., pharmaceutical corporation executive; b. Cin., May 26, 1933; s. Overton Burgin and Geneva Opal (Shinn) P. BS, Lawrence U., 1955; MBA, U. Chgo., 1959. With Pfizer Inc., 1959-74; salesman Pfizer Labs., Chgo., 1959-62, asst. mktg. product mgr. N.Y.C., 1962-63, product mgr., 1964-66, group product mgr., 1966-67, mktg. mgr., 1967-68, v.p. mktg., 1969-70, v.p., dir. ops., 1970-71; exec. v.p. domestic pharm. div. Pfizer Pharms., 1971-72; exec. v.p., dir. Pfizer Internat. Divsn., 1972-74; pres., chief operating officer G.D. Searle Internat., Skokie, Ill., 1974-75, pres., chief exec. officer, 1975-77; pres. Worldwide Pharm./Consumer Products Group, 1977-86; pres., chief exec. officer Phoenix Health Care, Chgo., 1987—; chmn., CEO, bd. dirs. Wis. Pharmiacal Co., Inc., 1990-96; co-chmn. Inhalon Pharms., 1991-95, also bd. dirs.; chmn. ViatiCare Fin. Svcs. LLC, 1993—, also bd. dirs.; chmn., CEO, bd. dirs. The Female Health Co., 1996—. Bd. dirs., chair Miicro Inc., 1999—. Author: The Future Pharmaceutical Marketing; International Drug Pricing, 1971. Trustee Mktg. Sci. Inst.; trustee Food and Drug Law Inst., 1979-86, Lawrence U., 1983-87, 98— . Served to 1st lt. USAF, 1955-57. Mem. Beta Gamma Sigma, Phi Kappa Tau. Home: 505 N Lake Shore Dr Chicago IL 60611-3427 Office: Phoenix Health Care 515 N State St Chicago IL 60610- Office Phone: 312-595-9833. E-mail: oparrish@aol.com.

PARRISH, PETER TRASEL, retired civil engineer; b. Phila., June 14, 1930; s. Edward Wetherill and Marie Trasel Parrish. Student, Proctor Acad., 1949—50, Colo. Coll., 1950—55; assoc. engring., Santa Monica C.C., 1958. Tech. illustrator missile divsn. Douglas Aircraft, Santa Monica, Calif., 1956—59; parts compiler RCA, Van Nuys, Calif., 1960; sr. draftsman Mine and Smelter Supply Co., Denver, 1961—68, Joy Mfg. Co., Denver, 1968—72; design draftsman Mac Steel Inc., Commerce City, Colo., 1972—73; draftsman II engring. dept. Waste Water Mgmt., Denver; ret., 1973. Del. for Denver County Rep. Party, Ft. Collins, Colo., 1980; campaign asst. for Federico Pena Dem. Party, Denver, 1982. Mem.: Wheat Ridge Photography Club, Mt. Vernon Country Club, Sigma Chi (tras. Beta Gamma chpt. 1952—53). Democrat. Episcopalian. Avocations: designing cars, photography, golf, tennis. Home: 7150 W 42d Ave Wheat Ridge CO 80033-4861

PARRISH, RICHARD KENNETH, II, medical educator; b. Decatur, Ind., July 18, 1951; s. Richard Kenneth and Cloe Marie (Liniger) P.; m. Marianne Pantin, Oct. 7, 1989; children: Andrés, Felipe, Deanna. BA in Biol. Sci., Ind. U., 1972; MD, Ind. U., Indpls., 1976. Asst. prof. ophthalmology U. Miami (Fla.) Sch. Medicine, 1982-89, assoc. prof., 1989-94, prof., 1994—, chmn. dept. ophthalmology, 1996-99, assoc. dean. med. edn., 2000—; staff surgeon VA Med. Ctr., Miami, 1982-83, 97. Chmn. grad. med. edn. com. Jackson Meml. Hosp., 2000—. Co-author: Clinical Decisions in Glaucoma, 1993, Cirugia de Glaucoma, 2000; editor: U. Miami Bascom Palmer Eye Inst. Atlas of Ophthalmology; mem. editl. bd. Archives of Ophthalmology, 1985—95, Ophthalmic Practice, 1997—, Ophthalmic Surgery and Lasers, 1989—; assoc. editor: Am. Jour. Ophthalmology, 1997—. Mem. Am. Ophthalmol. Soc., Alpha Omega Alpha, Phi Beta Kappa. Avocations: gardening, art collecting. Office: Univ of Miami Sch Medicine Bascom Palmer Eye Inst 900 NW 17th St Miami FL 33136-1119 E-mail: rparrish@med.miami.edu.

PARRISH, STEVEN C. consumer products company executive; BA in Polit. Sci., U. Mo., 1972, JD, 1975. Joined Philip Morris USA, 1990, sr. v.p. external affairs, gen. counsel, 1992—94, sr. v.p. worldwide regulatory affairs, 1994—95; sr. v.p. corp. affairs Altria Group, Inc., N.Y.C., 1995—. Vice chmn. bd. dirs. Safe Horizon; bd. dirs. Stamford Symphony Orch. Office: Altria Group Inc 120 Park Ave New York NY 10017-5592

PARRISH, THOMAS KIRKPATRICK, III, marketing consultant; b. Richmond, Va., May 18, 1930; s. Thomas Kirkpatrick and Sally Cary (Friend) P.; divorced: children: Linn Cary, Wayne Elizabeth, Susan Scott, Thomas Kirkpatrick IV. AB, Princeton U., 1952. Product mgr. Vick Chem. Co., N.Y.C., 1955-58; v.p. Benton & Bowles Advt. Agy., N.Y.C., 1958-65; pres. Am. Chicle Co. div. Warner-Lambert Co., Morris Plains, N.J., 1965-70, Life Savers Inc. div. Squibb Corp., N.Y.C., 1970-73, Lanvin-Charles of Ritz Inc. subs. Squibb Corp., N.Y.C., 1974-76; dir. parent co. Squibb Corp., 1974-77; group dir. new bus. devel. Gillette Co., Boston, 1977-78; exec. v.p. SSC & B, Inc., N.Y.C., 1978-81; sr. assoc. Am. Cons. Corp., 1982-86; prin. The Parrish Co., N.Y.C., 1986—. Mem. N.Y. State Republican Com., 1962-63; bd. dirs. YMCA Ctr. for Internat. Mgmt. Studies, N.Y.C., 1970-85. Served to lt., jr. grade USN, 1952-55. Home: 138 Fiddlers Green Waitsfield VT 05673

PARRISH-PORTER, VALLERIE, controller; b. Baxley, Ga., July 12, 1951; d. Robert and Evelyn (Howell) Parrish; m. Julius Devan Porter, May 8, 1987. BS, So. U., Baton Rouge, La., 1971; MBA, U. Miami, Fla., 1973. Auditor Price Waterhouse & Co., Miami, 1973-77; fin. mgr. Post Newsweek div. Washington Post, Miami, 1977-80; acctg. supr. Schlumberger, Houston, 1981-83, controller, 1983-90, Princeton, N.J., 1990—. Mem. Nat. Assn. Accts., NAACP, Urban League. Avocations: tennis, chess, running, writing.

PARRISH-ST. JOHN, FLORENCE TUCKER, writer, educator, retired government official; b. Greenville, Miss., Nov. 12, 1925; d. Victor Amos and Martha Buchannan (Binkley) Denslow; m. Joseph Nathaniel Tucker Jr., Nov. 9, 1946 (dec. Dec. 1955); children: Joseph Nathaniel Tucker III, Frederick Steven Tucker, James Denslow Tucker; m. Noel Francis Parrish, June 25, 1983 (dec. Apr. 1987); m. Adrian St. John, Jan. 29, 1998. Diploma in piano, Ward-Belmont Coll., Nashville, 1945; studied piano with Michael Field, NYC, 1945—46; B of Music Edn., Delta State U., Cleveland, Miss., 1960; MS in Counseling, U. So. Miss., 1971; EdD in Human Resources, George Washington U., 1983. Tchr. music Gulfport (Miss.) Pub. Schs., 1959-63; recreation therapist VA Hosp., Gulfport, 1964-70; edn. counselor USAF, Miss. and Japan, 1971-74, edn. svcs. officer Kunsan, Republic of Korea, 1974-75; asst. dir. sr. tng. CAP nat. hdqrs., 1975-77; EEO officer DC Dept. Labor, 1977-80; bur. chief complaints processing and adjudication Office EEO, U.S. Geol. Survey, Reston, Va., 1980-82; mgr. human resources Dept. Interior, 1982-84; internat. forum coord. Inspire 85 Pres.'s Com. on Employment of Handicapped, 1985; commr. Alexandria (Va.) Commn. on Aging, 1985-88, chmn. edn. and cultural affairs com., 1985-88, sec., 1987-88; lead scholar pilot project Nat. Coun. Aging. Mem. adv. bd. Inst. Conflict Analysis and resolution George Mason U., 1993—, vice chair adv. bd. Inst. Conflict Analysis and resolution, 1995—97, chmn. adv. bd. Inst. Conflict Analysis and resolution, 1998—2000, adv. bd. mem. emeritus, 2003—. Feature writer on aging issues: Alexandria Gazette-Packet, 1986—92; contbr. articles to profl. jours. Pianist/organist Sr. Living Cmty., The Fairfax, Ft. Belvoir, Va., 2003—. Mem.: Nat. Press Club (sr. rep. NPC trip to China and Hong Kong 1998, events com., chmn. oral history com., presenter 7 panel programs, Vivian award 1998, 1999, 2000, 2002, 2003), Va. Assn. on Aging, World Affairs Coun., Women in Comm., Nat. Tuskegee Airmen Inc. Orgn., Smithsonian Assocs., Friends of Kennedy Ctr., Ret. Officers Assn., Miss. Soc. Washington, Am. Inst. Wine and Food, NATO Def. Coll. Ancients Assn., USAF Assn. (v.p. for cmty. programs Gen. Charles Gabriel chpt. 1991—98, Pres.'s award 1998, Woman of Distinction award

Thomas Anthony chpt.), Washington Opera Guild. Address: Stonehurst 9302 Arlington Blvd Fairfax VA 22031-2503 Home: 9110 Belvoir Woods Pky Apt 118 Fort Belvoir VA 22060-2717 Office Phone: 703-799-4355. E-mail: fpstjohn@msn.com.

PARR-JOHNSTON, ELIZABETH, economy and policy consultant; b. N.Y.C., Aug. 15, 1939; d. Ferdinand Van Siclen and Helene Elizabeth Parr; m. David E. Bond, Dec. 28, 1962 (div. July 1975); children: Peter V.S., Kristina Aline; m. Archibald F. Johnston, Mar. 6, 1982; children: James, Heather, Alexandra, Margaret. BA, Wellesley Coll., 1961; MA, Yale U., 1962, PhD, 1973; postgrad., Harvard U., 1986. Various positions Govt. of Can., Ottawa, Ont., 1973-76, INCO Ltd., Toronto, 1976-79; chief of staff, sr. policy advisor Ministry of Employment and Immigration, Govt. of Can., 1979-80; various positions Shell Can. Ltd., Calgary, Alta., 1980-90; pres. Parr-Johnston & Assocs., Calgary, 1990-91; pres., vice-chancellor Mt. St. Vincent U., Halifax, Nova Scotia, N.S., 1991-96, The U. New Brunswick, Fredericton, Canada, 1996—2002; pres. Parr Johnston Econ. and Policy Cons., Chester Basin, Canada, 2002—. Instr. U. We. Ont., London, 1964—67, U. B.C., Vancouver, 1967—71; vis. scholar Wesleyan U., Middletown, Conn., 1971—72; acad. rsch. assoc. Carleton U., Ottawa, 1972—73; bd. dirs. Nova Scotia Power, Emera Ltd., Bank of Nova Scotia, Social Rsch. and Demonstration Corp., Can. Found. Sustainable Devel. Tech., Can. Millennium Scholarships Found.; spkr. and presenter in field. Mem. editl. bd. Can. Econ. Jour., 1980-83; contbr. articles to profl. jours. Planning chmn. John Howard Soc., 1980—84; mem. policy adv. com. C.D. Howe, 1980—85; mem. Ont. Econ. Coun., 1981—84; bd. dirs. Dellcrest Home, 1980—84, Calgary S.W. Fed. Riding Assn., 1985—91, The Learning Ctr., Calgary, 1989—91, Halifax United Way, 1991—92, North/South Inst., 1992—96, Unity Coun. Humanities, 1993—, Vol. Planning N.S., 1992—93, Social Sci. Human Rsch. Coun., 1995—98, FPI Ltd., 1996—2001, Empire Co., 1994—2002, Symphony Nova Scotia, Nat. Theatre Sch. Recipient Canada 125 medal, Queen's Jubilee medal; Hon. Woodrow Wilson fellow, 1962. Mem. Assn. Atlantic Univs. (chair 1994-96), Assn. Univs. and Colls. in Can. (bd. dirs., mem. exec. com. 1994-96), Women in Acad. Adminstrn. (adv. bd. 1991-96), Calgary Coun. Advanced Tech. (exec. 1990-91), Can. Econs. Assn., Inst. Pub. Adminstrn. Can., Sr. Women Acad. Adminstrs. Can., Assn. Commonwealth Univs. (former mem. exec. com.), Phi Beta Kappa. Anglican. Avocations: golf, sailing, travel. Home: PO Box 219 Chester Basin NS Canada B0J 1K0 Personal E-mail: EPJ@chesterbasin.com.

PARROTT, ANDREW MYLES, research scientist; b. Barrow-in-Furness, Cumbria, UK, Mar. 18, 1973;, US, 2000; s. Myles Edwin and Elizabeth Mary Parrott. BS in chemistry, U. Leeds, 1995, PhD in biology, 1999. Postdoctoral rschr. UMDNJ, Newark, 2000—. Grad. supr. Leeds U., 1996—99, sci. collaboration, 1996—99. Contbr. articles to profl. jours. Leeds U. scholarship, Leeds U., 1995—98, UMDNJ fellowship, 2001—02. Mem.: Am. Assn. for the Advancement of Sci., NY Acad. Sciences. Democrat. Ch. Of Eng. Avocations: movies, chess, soccer, travel. Office: UMDNJ 185 South Orange Ave Newark NJ 07104 Personal E-mail: am_parrott@hotmail.com.

PARROTT, DENNIS BEECHER, retired insurance executive; b. St. Louis, June 13, 1929; s. Maurice Ray and Mai Ledgerwood (Beecher) P.; m. Vivian Cleveland Miller, Mar. 24, 1952; children: Constance Beecher, Dennis Beecher, Anne Cleveland. BS in Econs., Fla. State U., Tallahassee, 1954; postgrad., Princeton U., 1964; MBA, Pepperdine U., 1982. With Prudential Ins. Co. Am., 1954-74, v.p. group mktg., 1971-74; sr. v.p. Frank B. Hall Cons. Co., L.A., 1974—83; v.p. Johnson & Higgins, L.A., 1983-95; exec. v.p. Arthur J. Gallagher & Co., L.A., 1995-98; ret., 1998. Spkr. in field. Chmn. Weekend with the Stars Telethon, 1976-80; chmn. bd. dirs. United Cerebral Palsy/Spastic Children's Found., L.A. County, 1979-82, chmn. bd. govs., 1982-83; bd. dirs. Nat. United Cerebral Palsy Assn., 1977-82, pres., 1977-79; bd. dirs. L.A. Emergency Task Force, 1992; mem. cmty. adv. coun. Birmingham High Sch., Van Nuys, Calif., 1982-85; sect. chmn. United Way, L.A., 1983-84; bd. dirs. The Betty Clooney Found. for Brain Injured, 1986-88; mem. com. to fund an endowed chair in cardiology at Cedars-Sinai Med. Ctr., 1986-88; adv. coun. Family Health Program, Inc., 1986-88; bd. deacons Bel Air Presbyn. Ch., 1990-92, chmn., 1991-92, elder, 1993-96; mem. adv. coun. Blue Cross Calif., 1996-98; chmn. Danny Arnold Meml. Golf Classic at Riviera Country Club benefitting John Wayne Cancer Inst., 1997. 1st lt. AUS, 1951-53. Named Tournament Champion, Sunkist Invitational Golf Tournament, 1995. Mem. Am. Soc. C.L.U.s., Internat. Found. Employee Benefits, Merchants and Mfrs. Assns. 44th Ann. Mgmt. Conf. (chmn. 1986), Employee Benefits Planning Assn. So. Calif., L.A. Club, Woodland Hills Country Club, Jonathan Club (L.A.). Republican. Presbyterian. Home: 17023 Encino Hills Dr Encino CA 91436-4009 Personal E-mail: callparrott@aol.com.

PARROTT, THENA ELIZABETH, nurse educator; b. Amarillo, Tex., Sept. 13, 1950; d. William Duard and Ruth Virginia (Crist) Henry; m. William Jackson Parrott, Dec. 23, 1977; children: William Richard, Cody Spencer. BSN, Baylor U., 1972; MSN, Tex. Woman's U., 1977; PhD in Edn. Curriculum and Instrn., Tex. A&M U., 1993. RN, Tex. Asst. prof. Dallas Bapt. U., 1976-81; part-time charge nurse Dallas Med.-Surg. Hosp., 1979-81; dir. Vocat. Sch. Nursing, Goodall-Witcher Hosp. Found., Clifton, Tex., 1982; part-time home health nurse Girling Health Care, Temple, Tex., 1988-89; faculty/course coord. Ctrl. Tex. Coll., Killeen, 1984-89; staff nurse ICU/CCU, St. Joseph Regional Health Ctr., Bryan, Tex., 1989-97; mem. faculty Blinn Coll., Bryan, 1990-97, ADN program, 1997—, dir. ADN program coord. allied health programs, 1997-2000, divsn. chair, 2000—. Cons. reviewer W.B. Saunders Co., Phila., 1999, J.B. Lippincott, Phila., 1999. Contbr. articles to profl. jours. Sunday Sch. tchr., mem. choir, soloist Northview Bapt. Ch., Bryan, 1989—, Christ's Way Baptist Ch., Bryan, 2000; vol., bd. dirs., program chair, CPR instr.-tr ainer Am. Heart Assn., Bryan, 1975—; mem. Brazos Hist. Commn., Bryan, 1995—. Recipient awards for vol. work. Mem. ANA, Nat. Orgn. for AD Nursing, Nat. League for Nursing, Nat. Soc. DAR (past treas.), Kappa Delta Pi. Republican. Baptist. Avocations: sewing, crafts, gardening, fishing. Office: Blinn Coll ADN Program PO Box 6030 Bryan TX 77805-6030 E-mail: tparrott@blinn.edu.

PARROTT, WANDA SUE, writer, journalist; b. Kansas City, Mo., Feb. 12, 1935; d. William Raymond and Lois Marie (Cain) Childress; m. Edward Anthony Cyriacus Parrott, Dec. 16, 1962 (div. 1971); 1 child, Edward Anthony. AA, Citrus Coll., 1954; journalism cert., L.A. Evening Adult Coll., 1968; PhD in Comms., Colegium Orthogenesis, 1961; DD in Comparative Religion, Universal Life Ch., 1974. Tech. writer aerospace industry, So. Calif., 1965-67; journalist Hearst Corp./L.A. Herald-Examiner, 1967-74, Daily News subs. Chgo. Tribune, 1977-79, Assoc. Valley Publs., 1980-82, Sr. Living Newspapers, 1992-2000. Co-prodr. Golden Words, 1993-2002; co-author: How to Try Your Own Case in Court...And Win!, 1997, There's A Spirit in the Kitchen, 2001; author: Springfield's Version of the Trail of Tears, 2002. Co-founder, prodr. nat. ann. Sr. Poet Laureate Poetry Competition; founder Springfield Writers' Workshop, 1992; founder Amy Kirchener's Angels Without Wings Found. Recipient Gold Kettle award, Salvation Army, 1994—2002. Fellow Ancient Mystical Order Rosae Crucis (master of lodge 1984-85), Springfield Writers' Guild (bd. dirs., past pres.), Mo. Writers' Guild (past sec.-treas.), Book Publicists of So. Calif., Mo. State Poetry Soc. (hon. life).

PARRS, MARIANNE M. paper and lumber company executive; b. N.Y.C. m. Walter Parrs; 3 children. Grad., Brown U. Joined Internat. Paper Co., 1974, sector controller, printing papers, staff v.p., worldwide responsibility tax planning and compliance, CFO, sr. v.p., 1995—99, exec. v.p. adminstrn., info. tech. and human resources, 1999—. Office: Internat Paper Co 2 Manhattanville Rd Purchase NY 10577-2196 Fax: 914-397-1650.

PARRY, ATWELL J., JR., state legislator, retail executive; b. Ogden, Utah, June 14, 1925; s. John Atwell and Nina Virginia (McEntire) P.; m. Elaine Hughes, Feb. 6, 1946; children: Bonnie, Michael, Jay, Donald, David, Delbert, Kent. Student pub. sch., Nampa, Idaho. Salesman King's Packing Co., Nampa, 1947-54, credit mgr., 1954-55; plant mgr. Stone Poultry Co., Nampa, 1955-56; salesman Nestle Chocolate Co., 1956-64; owner, mgr. Melba Foods, Idaho, 1964-82; mem. Idaho Senate, 1981—. Bd. dirs. Western Idaho Tng. Ctr., 1987-90; chmn. Senate Finance Com. and co-chmn. Joint Fin. and Appropriations Com., 1987—; chmn. Idaho State Bd. for Nat. Ctr. for Constl. Studies, 1988-90. Bd. dirs. Alcohol Treatment Ctr., Nampa, 1976-81; mem. Melba City Coun., 1971-74; mem. adv. bd. Mercy Med. Ctr., Nampa, 1976-81. Recipient Silver Beaver award Boy Scouts Am., 1959, Svc. award Mercy Med. Ctr., Outstanding Rep. Legislator in Idajo State award, 1993, Friend of Small Bus. award, 1987-88, 90, 92, Friend of Agrl. award, 1989-90, 91-92, 94-95, Melba Citizen of Yr. award, 1996, Canyon County Rep. Hall of Fame Outstanding Rep., 1998, Support of Scouting award Ore-Ida Coun. Boy Scouts Am., 2000, Silver Medallion award Boise (Idaho) State U., 2000, Spl. Recognition award Idaho Profl. Technician Edn., 2000. Office: State Capitol PO Box 83720 Boise ID 83720-3720

PARRY, DALE D. newspaper editor; BS in Journalism cum laude, Ball State U., Muncie, Ind., 1981. Feature writer Richmond (Ind.) Palladium-Item, 1981-84, Cin. Enquirer, 1984-86; editor Today section The Dallas Morning News, 1987-90; assignment editor The Way We Live sect. Detroit Free Press, 1990-92, dep. features editor, 1992-94, features editor, 1993-96, asst. mng. editor, 1997-2000, dep. mng. editor, 2001—. Mem. Am. Assn. Sun. and Feature Editors. Office: Detroit Free Press 600 W Fort St Detroit MI 48226-2706

PARRY, EDWARD JONES, III, insurance company executive; b. July 21, 1959; BSBA, Bryant Coll., 1981. CPA, Mass. With Price Waterhouse, N.Y.C., 1981-82; mgr. Ernst & Whitney, Providence, 1982-86, Sansiveri, Ryan and Sullivan, Providence, 1986-87; sr. mgr. Price Waterhouse, Providence, 1987-92; v.p., treas. Allmerica Fin., Worcester, Mass., 1992-96, v.p., CFO, 1996—. Office: Allmerica Fin Corp 440 Lincoln St Worcester MA 01653-0001

PARRY, LANCE AARON, newspaper executive; b. Allentown, Pa., Sept. 4, 1947; s. Harwood Clayton Bachman and Iola Mary (Johnson) P.; m. Virginia Eleanor Ford, Apr. 24, 1971; children: Halloran Lee, Christine Ford. BS in English Edn., Kutztown U., 1969; MS in Journalism, W.Va. U., 2003. With Call-Chronicle Newspapers, Allentown, 1970-81, mng. editor, 1979-81; asst. news editor The Phila. Inquirer, 1981-82, systems editor, 1982-84, night news editor, 1984-86, news editor daily edit., 1986-87, news editor Sunday edit., 1987-89, sr. editor/systems and tech., 1989-93, page design dir., 1993-94, features news editor, 1994-96, news editor Sunday edit., 1996-98, features news editor, 1998—. Recipient 1st Place award for front page design Pa. Newspaper Pubs. Assn./Pa. Soc. Newspaper Editors, 1985, 87, 88, Disting. Alumnus award Kutztown U., 1992; Sigma Delta Chi scholar, 1969. Mem. Soc. Profl. Journalists, Pen and Pencil Club. Democrat. Presbyterian. Home: 16 Salisbury Ln Malvern PA 19355-2836 Office: The Phila Inquirer 400 N Broad St Philadelphia PA 19130-4099

PARRY, ROBERT WALTER, chemistry professor; b. Ogden, Utah, Oct. 1, 1917; s. Walter and Jeanette (Petterson) P.; m. Marjorie J. Nelson, July 6, 1945; children: Robert Bryce, Mark Nelson. BS, Utah State Agr. Coll., 1940; MS, Cornell U., 1942; PhD, U. Ill., 1946; DSc (hon.), Utah State U., 1985, U. Utah, 1997. Rsch. asst. NDRC Munitions Devel. Lab. U. Ill., Urbana, 1943-45, tchg. fellow, 1945-46; mem. faculty U. Mich., Ann Arbor, 1946-69, prof. chemistry, 1958-69; Disting. prof. chemistry U. Utah, Salt Lake City, 1969-97, prof. emeritus, 1997—. Chmn. bd. trustees Gordon Rsch. Conf., 1967-68; cons. in field. Founding editor Inorganic Chemistry, 1960-63. Recipient Mfg. Chemists award for coll. tchg., 1972, Sr. U.S. Scientist award Alexander Von Humboldt-Stiftung, West Germany, 1980, First Govs. medal of Sci., State Utah, 1987. Mem. AAAS (chmn. chemistry sect. 1983), Internat. Union Pure and Applied Chemistry (chmn. U.S. nat. com., chmn. com. tchg. chemistry 1968-74), Am. Chem. Soc. (bd. editors jour. 1969-80, dir. 1973-83, pres.-elect 1981, pres. 1982, Disting. Svc. to Inorganic Chemistry award 1965, Disting. Svc. to Chem. Edn. award 1977, Utah award Utah sect. 1978, Priestly medal 1993), Sigma Xi. Achievements include research in structural problems of inorganic chemistry and incorporation results into theoretical models, chemistry of phosphorus, boron and fluorine. Home: 5002 Fairbrook Ln Salt Lake City UT 84117-6205 Office: U Utah Dept Chemistry 315 South 1400 East Salt Lake City UT 84112-0850 Office Phone: 801-581-7022. Business E-Mail: parry@chem.utah.edu.

PARRY, SCOTT BRINK, psychologist; b. Reading, Pa., Sept. 4, 1932; s. George Raymond and Claire (Blackburne) Parry; m. Joan SantAntonio; 1 child, Christiana Claire. BA, Princeton U., 1954; MS, Boston U., 1960; PhD, NYU, 1969. Account exec. Hill & Knowlton, Inc., N.Y.C., 1960-62; editor Harcourt, Brace, Jovanovich, N.Y.C., 1962-64; ptnr. Parry & Robinson, Inc., N.Y.C., 1964-66; mgr. N.Y.C. office Sterling Inst., 1966-71; v.p., pres., chmn. Tng. House, Inc., N.Y.C., Princeton, 1971—; prof. comms. Mercer County (N.J.) C.C., 2000—. Educ. cons. UNESCO, Paris, Nigeria, 1963, Ghana, 64; mem. adv. bd. Training Mag. Lakewood Publs., Mpls., 1988—92; adj. prof. NYU, 1968—74; spkr. convs. and meetings in 17 countries on 6 continents; cons. to more than 50 Fortune 500 cos. Author: (book) The Story of Handbells, 1957, A Handbell Handbill, 1963, From Managing to Empowering, 1993, The Managerial Mirror, 2 vols, 1997, Evaluating the Impact of Training, 1997, Training for Results, 2000, 46 training books; contbr. articles to profl jours and newspapers. Lt U.S. Army, 1957—59. Named Hon Chmn, 25th Anniversary Am Guild English Handbell Ringers, 1979; named to Human Resource Develop Hall of Fame, 1999; recipient Best Training Product Award, Human Resource Exec, 1990, 1994. Mem.: ASTD, Instructional Sys Asn, Int Soc Performance Improvement, Int Fedn Training and Develop Orgns. Republican. Presbyterian. Avocations: music (harpsichord, organ, carillon), collecting and restoring antiques, renovating buildings. Office: Training House 96 Bear Brook Rd Princeton NJ 08540-6246 E-mail: jsparry@erols.com.

PARRY, WILLIAM DEWITT, lawyer; b. Hartford, Conn., June 4, 1941; s. William Brown and Mary Elizabeth (Caton) p.; m. Andrea Hannah Lewis, June 30, 1973; children: Sara, Jessica. BA, U. Mass., 1963; JD, U. Pa., 1966. Bar: N.J. 1987, Pa. 1967, U.S. Dist. Ct. (ea. dist.) Pa. 1974, U.S. Ct. Appeals (3d cir.) 1980, U.S. Ct. Appeals (9th cir.) 1998, U.S. Supreme Ct. 1980. Assoc. Shapiro, Cook & Bressler, Phila., 1966-67; asst. dir. ABA joint com on continuing legal edn. Am. Law Inst., Phila., 1967-73; assoc. Lowenschuss Assocs., Phila., 1973-85; of counsel Weiss, Golden & Pierson, Phila., 1985-88; pvt. practice Phila., 1988; ptnr. Rubin, Quinn, Moss & Patterson, Phila., 1989-93; pvt. practice Phila., 1993—. Author: Understanding and Controlling Stuttering: A Comprehensive New Approach Based on the Valsalva Hypothesis, 1994, 2000; editor U. Pa. Law Rev., 1964-66, The Practical Lawyer, 1967-73. Founder Phila. area chpt. Nat. Stuttering Project, 1985; bd. dirs. Nat. Stuttering Assn., 1996-2002; trustee Unitarian Soc. Germantown, Phila., 1983-86. Mem.: ATLA, ABA, Pa. Trial Lawyers Assn., Phila. Bar Assn., Pa. Bar Assn. Democrat. Avocations: writing, lecturing. Home: 520 Baird Rd Merion Station PA 19066-1302 Office: 1608 Walnut St Ste 900 Philadelphia PA 19103-5451 E-mail: wdparry@aol.com.

PARRY-JONES, RICHARD, automotive executive; b. Wales, 1951; Mech. engrng.(hon.), Univ. Salford, Manchester, 1973; D (hon.), Loughborough Univ., 1995. Apprentice Ford's European Product Devel. Group, 1969; leading role in devel. of the 1981 European Escort Ford Motor Co., 1981, apptd. mgr. small car programs, 1982, v.p. European vehicle ctr., 1994—98, group v.p. global product devel. and quality, 1998—2001, chief tech. officer, 2001—. Vis. prof. Dept. of Aero. and Automotive Engrng. at England's Loughborough U., 2001. Named Exec. Engr.of Ford's Technol. Rsch. in Europe, 1985, Chief Engr. for Vehicle Rngring., 1991, Man of the Yr., Bit. publ. Autocar, 1994, U.S. mag. Automobile, 1997, sr. exec. for Mazda oversight on Nov. 15, 2001; recipient Golden Gear Award, Wash. Motor Press Assn., 2001, Mktg. Statesman of the Yr., Sales and Mktg. Executives of Detroit. Fellow: Inst. of Mech. Engineers, Royal Acad. Engineers. Office: Ford Motor Co One American Rd Dearborn MI 48126-1899

PARRY-SOLA, CHERYL LEE, critical care nurse; b. Bristol, Pa., Oct. 27, 1960; d. Edmund H. and F. Renee (Platt) P. ADN, Bucks County C.C., 1982. RN NJ, CCRN. Formerly asst. head nurse Deborah Heart and Lung Ctr., Browns Mills, NJ; charge nurse med. ICU Holy Spirit Hosp., Camp Hill, Pa., 1995—2002, tng. ctr. coord., 2001—. Office: Holy Spirit Hosp Edn/Tng/Devel 503 N 21st St Camp Hill PA 17011-2288

PARSA, FEREYDOUN DON, plastic surgeon; b. Tehran, Iran, May 20, 1942; came to U.S., 1970; s. Issa and Zahra (Bismark) P.; m. Touri Akhlaghi, June 17, 1972; children: Natalie, Alan, Sean. MD, Lausanne U., Switzerland, 1969. Diplomate Am. Bd. Plastic Surgery. Chief of plastic surgery, prof. surgery U. Hawaii, Honolulu, 1981—. Contbr. articles to profl. jours. Mem. Am. Cancer Soc. Avocation: painting. Office: U Hawaii Sch Med Surg 1356 Lusitana St Honolulu HI 96813-2421 also: U Hawaii 1329 Lusitana St Honolulu HI 96813-2429 Office Phone: 808-526-0303. E-mail: parsaplasticsurgery@yahoo.com.

PARSEGHIAN, GREGORY J. former mortgage company executive; BS, MBA, U. Pa. Mng. dir. First Boston; ptnr. Blackrock Fin. Mgmt., investment mgr.; mng. dir. Salomon Bros.; sr. v.p. Freddie Mac, McLean, Va., 1996—2002, chief investment officer, 1996—2003, exec. v.p., 2002—03, CEO, 2003, pres., 2003.

PARSHALL, GEORGE WILLIAM, chemist, researcher; b. Hackensack, Minn., Sept. 19, 1929; s. George Clarence and Frances (Virnig) Parshall; m. Naomi B. Simpson, Oct. 9, 1954; children: William, Jonathan, David. BS, U. Minn., 1951; PhD, U. Ill., 1954. Rsch. chemist E.I. duPont de Nemours & Co., Wilmington, Del., 1954—65, rsch. supr., 1965—79, dir. chem. sci., 1979—92, cons., 1992—, mem. com. on environ. mgmt. techs., 1994—97; mem. chem. stockpile disposal com. NRC, Washington, 1992—98, mem. non-stockpile com., 1998—99, 2001—. Bd. chem. sci. NRC, Washington, 1983—86; Reilly lectr. Notre Dame U., 1980; Ipatieff lectr. Northwestern U., 1994; mem. sci. adv. bd. Phoenix S&T, 2002—. Author: (book) Homogeneous Catalysis, 1980, Homogeneous Catalysis, 2d rev. edit., 1992; editor: Inorganic Syntheses, 1974, Jour. Molecular Catalysis, 1977—80. Recipient Ballar Inorganic Chemistry medal, U. Ill., 1976. Mem.: NAS, Am. Acad. Arts Scis., Am. Chem. Soc. (award in inorganic chemistry 1983, award leadership in chem. rsch. mgmt. 1989), Inst. Chemists (Chem. Pioneer award 1992, Gold medal award 1995), Guild Episcopal Scholars (treas. 1994—99). Episcopalian. Home: 2504 Delaware Ave Wilmington DE 19806-1220 E-mail: parshallgw@aol.com.

PARSHALL, GERALD, journalist; b. St. Paul, Apr. 24, 1941; s. William Elmer and Evelyn (Steckling) P.; m. Sandra Grant, Dec. 20, 1970. BA, U. Minn., 1963; MA, U. Mich., 1964; grad. fellow, U. Chgo., 1966-67. Reporter York (Pa.) Gazette and Daily, 1968, Balt. Evening Sun, 1968-71; Capitol Hill staff U.S. News & World Report, Washington, 1971-77, sr. editor, 1977-79, asst. mng. editor, 1979-90, sr. writer, 1990-99, contbg. editor, 1999—2004. Mem. Exec. Com. of Periodical Corrs., U.S. Congress, 1974-80, chmn., 1979-80 Served to 1st lt. U.S. Army, 1964-66. Recipient First Page award Washington-Balt. Newspaper Guild, 1971, Silver Gavel award ABA, 1983 Home: 1004 Congress Ln Mc Lean VA 22101-2116 E-mail: gparshall@worldnet.att.net.

PARSKY, BARBARA, utilities executive; BA, Rollins Coll. Various mgmt. positions Gen. Electric Co.; ptnr. Porter Novelli, gen. mgr.; prin., owner; v.p. corp. comms. Edison Internat., Rosemead, Calif., 2002—. Office: Edison International 2244 Walnut Grove Ave Rosemead CA 91770

PARSLEY, HENRY NUTT, JR., bishop, academic administrator; b. Memphis, Tenn. m. Rebecca Knox Allison; 1 child, Henry Nutt III. B in English magna cum laude, U. of the South, 1970; MDiv, Gen. Theol. Sem., N.Y.C., 1973. Asst. rector Trinity Ch., Myrtle Beach, SC, St. Philip's Ch., Charleston, SC; rector St. Paul's Ch., Summerville, SC, Christ Ch., Charlotte, NC; bishop Episcopal Diocese Ala., 1999—; chancellor U. of the South, Sewanee, Tenn., 2003—. Avocations: reading, fishing. Office: Univ of the South 735 University Ave Sewanee TN 37383*

PARSLEY, STEVEN DWAYNE, title company executive; b. Monrovia, Calif., Dec. 31, 1959; BBA magna cum laude, U. Albuquerque, 1985. Lic. agt. to issue title ins. N.Mex. Data processing asst. Orion Corp., Albuquerque, 1978-79; title searcher N.Mex. Title, Albuquerque, 1979; various positions Rio Grande Title Co., Albuquerque, 1979-84, v.p., mgr. title ops., 1984-91, sr. v.p., escrow officer, 1992-94, exec. v.p., 1994-99; pres., shareholder Dona Ana Title Co., Las Cruces, N.Mex., 1999—. Bd. dirs. N.Mex Land Title Trust Fund. Mem. state apptd. Title Ins. Task Force State of N.Mex.; mem. Affordable Housing Round Table. Presdl. scholar, U. N.Mex, 1978. Mem.: Las Cruces Homebuilders Assn. (v.p.), N.Mex Land Title Assn. (past v.p., pres. 1997—98). Avocation: ragtime piano. Home: 746 Oro Viejo Las Cruces NM 88011-8071 Office: Dona Ana Title Co 425 S Telshor Blvd Ste B Las Cruces NM 88011-8237 Office Phone: 505-521-5800. E-mail: ssp1988keys@aol.com., stevep@donaanatitle.com.

PARSONS, ANDREW JOHN, management consultant; b. Kingston, Surrey, Eng., July 22, 1943; arrived in US, 1968; s. S John and Hylda P (Wili) Parsons; m. Carol Ann Iannucci, June 6, 1970; children: Alexandra, Katherine. BA, MA, Oxford U., 1965; MBA, Harvard U., 1970. Acct. exec. LPE/Leo Burnett, London, 1965—68; from strategic planning dir. to v.p. mktg. Prestige Group Ltd. div. Am. Home Products, N.Y.C. and London, 1970-76; v.p. mktg. Kurzweil Computer Products div. Xerox Corp., Cambridge, Mass., 1979-80; assoc. McKinsey & Co., Inc., N.Y.C., 1976-82, prin., 1982-88, dir. consumer industries sector, mktg. ctr., sr. ptnr., 1988-2000; chmn. Kantar Group of WPP, PLC, 2001—03. Underwriting mem Lloyds of London, 1986—; chmn. Gulliver Growth Ptnrs. LLC, 2001—; with McKinsey Adv. Coun., 2001—; adv. bd. aQuantive, Inc., 2002—, Quaero, Inc., 2001—; pres. Smithfield Estates LLC, 2002—; bd. dirs. A.T. Cross Co., eNewsrelease.com, Inc., IXI Corp., ENR, Inc. Contbr. articles to profl jours. Mem. adv. bd. Salvation Army, Greater NY, 1983—, chmn. adv. bd., 1993—97; gov. United Way of Tri-State, 2003—; bd. dirs. United Way, N.Y.C., 1988—; trustee Sarah Lawrence Coll., Bronxville, NY, 1993—2001. Scholar Baker, Harvard Bus Sch, 1970. Mem.: Shelter Harbor Golf Club, Weekapaug Golf Club, Watch Hill Yacht Club, Siwanoy Country Club. Home: 56 Hereford Rd Bronxville NY 10708-5408 Office: McKinsey & Co Inc 55 E 52d St 18th Fl New York NY 10055-0183 Home: 2 Arraquat Rd Westerly RI 02891 E-mail: andrew_parsons@mckinsey.com.

PARSONS, ANNE, performing company executive; m. Donald Dietz; 1 child. BA, Smith Coll., 1980. Staff Nat. Symphony Orchestra, Wash., DC, 1981—83; orchestra mgr. Boston Symphony Orchestra, 1983—91; gen. mgr. Hollywood Bowl, LA, 1991—98, NY City Ballet, 1998—2004; exec. dir. Detroit Symphony Orchestra, 2004—. Fellow Am. Symphony Orchestra League, 1980—81. Office: Detroit Symphony Orchestra Max M Fisher Music Ctr 3711 Woodward Ave Detroit MI 48201

PARSONS, DANIEL LANKESTER, pharmaceutics educator; b. Biscoe, N.C., Sept. 10, 1953; s. Solomon Lankester and Doris Eva (Bost) P. BS in Pharmacy, U. Ga., 1975, PhD, 1979. Asst. prof. pharmaceutics U. Ariz., Tucson, 1979-82; asst. prof. Auburn (Ala.) U., 1982-86, assoc. prof., 1986-91, prof., 1991—, chmn. divsn., 1990—. Cons. Wyeth-Ayerst, Phila., 1989—93, Technomics, Ardsley, NY, 1990—93, Murty Pharm., Lexington, Ky., 1996—99; presenter in field. Author: (with G.V. Betageri and S.A. Jenkins) Liposome Drug Delivery Systems, 1993. Named Disting. Alumni Sandhills Coll., 1990, Tchr. of Yr., Pharmacy Student Coun., 1987, Grad. Faculty Mem. of Yr., Grad. Student Orgn., 1994, Prof. of Yr., Kappa Psi Fraternity, 2000. Mem. Am. Pharm. Assn., Am. Assn. Pharm. Scientists, Phi Kappa Phi, Kappa Psi (advisor 1990-95, nat. grad. devel. com. 1993-95, nat. scholarship com. 1995-99, nat. grand coun. dep. com. 1997—, Svc. award 1990, 95, Advisor award 1992). Achievements include research on plasma protein binding of drugs and effects of perfluorochemical blood substitutes on such binding. Office: Auburn U Sch Pharmacy Auburn AL 36849 Business E-Mail: parsodl@auburn.edu.

PARSONS, DAVID, artistic director, choreographer; b. Ill. Dancer Paul Taylor Dance Co., 1978—87; founder, artistic dir. Parsons Dance Co., 1987—. Choreographer The Envelope, 1984, Sleep Study, 1987, Caught, 1987, Elysian Fields, 1988, Reflections of Four, 1991, A Hiry Night on Bald Mountain, 1991, Bachiana, 1993, Destines, 1993, Ring Around the Rosie, 1993, AEROS, 2000 (Dance Magazine award, 2000, Am. Choreography award 2001);

performed with N.Y.C. Ballet, Berlin Opera, White Oak Dance Project, Paris Opera Ballet, Feld Ballets/NY, Nederlands Dans Theatre, English Nat. Ballet, Hubbard St. Dance Co., and BatSheva Dance Co. of Israel. Choreography fellow Nat. Endowment for the Arts, 1988-89, 95. Office: Parsons Dance Co 229 W 42nd St Ste 800 New York NY 10036

PARSONS, DONALD FRANCIS, lawyer; b. Phila., June 28, 1948; BSEE cum laude, Lehigh U., 1970; MA, 1972; JD, Georgetown ., 1977. Bar: Del. 1977. Law clk. to Hon. James L. Latchum U.S. Dist. Ct. Del., 1977-79; ptnr. Morris, Nichols, Arsht & Tunnell, Wilmington, Del., 1979—. Case and note editor Georgetown Law Jour., 1976-77. Mem. ABA, N.Y. Patent Law Assn., Phila. Patent Law Assn., Am. Intellectual Property Law Assn., Del. Bar Assn. (pres. 1999-2000). Office: Morris Nichols Arsht & Tunnell PO Box 1347 1201 N Market St Wilmington DE 19899-1347 E-mail: dparsons@mnat.com.

PARSONS, DONALD JAMES, retired bishop; b. Phila., Mar. 28, 1922; s. Earl and Helen (Drabble) P.; m. Mary Russell, Sept. 17, 1955; children—Mary, Rebecca, Bradford. BA, Temple U., 1943; M.Div., Phila. Div. Sch., 1946, Th.D., 1951, D.D. (hon.), 1964; postgrad., U. Nottingham, Eng., 1968; D.C.L., Nashotah (Wis.) House, 1973. Ordained priest Episcopal Ch., 1946, consecrated bishop, 1973; curate Immanual Ch., Wilmington, Del., 1946-49; rector St. Peter's Ch., Smyrna, Del., 1949-50; prof. N.T. Nashotah House, 1950-73, pres., dean, 1963-73, Ramsey prof. ascetical theology, 2000—; bishop Diocese of Quincy, Ill., 1973-88. Author: A Life-time Road to God, 1966, In Time with Jesus, 1973, Holy Eucharist: Rite Two, 1976. Episcopalian. Home: 6901 N Galena Rd Apt 111 Peoria IL 61614-3158

PARSONS, EDMUND MORRIS, investment company executive; b. Houston, Oct. 19, 1936; s. Alfred Morris and Virgina (Hanna) P. AB, Harvard U., 1958; MBA, U. Pa., 1961; MS, MIT, 1970. Pres. Fredonia Enterprises, Inc., Houston, Tex., 1990—; fgn. service officer U.S. Dept. State, Washington, 1965-90; 1st sec. Am. Embassy, Mexico City, 1973-76; economist Fed. Res. Bank N.Y., N.Y.C., 1976-77; chief food aid div. U.S. Dept. State, Washington, 1977-80, dir. office devel., 1981-82, dir. office econ. policy, 1983-84; dep. chief mission U.S. Mission to FAO, Rome, 1985-86; dir. Office Ecology and Natural Resources U.S. Dept. State, Washington, 1986-88; dir. Office of Internat. Narcotics Control Programs, 1988-89; min.-counselor for econ. affairs Am. Embassy, Mexico City, 1989-90; pres. Fredonia Enterprises, Inc., Houston, 1990—. Co-chmn. Tropical Forest Task Force, Washington, 1986-88; dep. U.S. rep. UN FAO, Rome, 1985-86; alt. U.S. rep. to environ. program U.S. Del. Nairobi, Kenya, 1987. Capt. USAF, 1962-72. Mem. Am. Fgn. Svc. Assn., Houston Restaurant Assn. (bd. dirs. 1992—), Houston World Affairs Coun. (bd. dirs. 1995—), Consular Corps of Houston (hon.), Houston Hispanic C. of C., Coun. Fgn. Rels. (Houston com.), Univ. Club (Houston). Republican. Methodist. Avocation: geneology. Office: 2727 Fondren Rd Ste 2A Houston TX 77063-4114 Home: 11823 Poplar Creek Dr Houston TX 77077-6118 Personal E-mail: elviaspub@aol.com.

PARSONS, EDWIN SPENCER, clergyman, educator; b. Brockton, Mass., Feb. 16, 1919; s. Edwin Webber and Ethel Faunce (Marsh) P.; m. Eleanor Millard, Nov. 3, 1944; children: William Spencer, Ellen, James Millard, Bradford Delano. AB, Denison U., 1941, D.D., 1967; B.D., Andover Newton Theol. Sch., 1945; D.D., Kalamazoo Coll., 1966; L.H.D., Chgo. Coll. Osteo. Medicine, 1978. Ordained to ministry Am. Baptist Ch., 1944; asst. minister First Bapt. Ch., Newton Centre, Mass., 1945-47; exec. dir. Bapt. Student Found., Inc., Cambridge, Mass., 1947-59; pastor Hyde Park Union Ch., Chgo., 1959-65; assoc. prof. ethics U. Chgo. Div. Sch., 1965-78, prof., 1978-81; dir. ministerial field edn., 1977-79; asst. to dean, 1981-88; dean Rockefeller Meml. Chapel, 1965-79; v.p., dir. New Eng. office Health Resources Ltd., Kansas City, Mo., 1979-89. Cons. dept. ch. and soc. Am. Bapt. Chs. of Mass., 1979-86, also editor Mass. Bapt. News, 1983-85; chmn. strategy and action com., bd. dirs. Mass. Council Chs., 1983-85; adj. prof. Andover Newton Theol. Sch., 1981-85 Author: The Christian Yes or No, 1964; contbr.: Belief and Ethics, 1978. Pres. Council Hyde Park-Kenwood Chs. and Synagogues, 1963; chmn. Abortion Rights Assn. Ill., 1974-79; founder, chmn. Ill. Religious Coalition for Abortion Rights, 1975, Ill. Clergy Consultation Services on Problem Pregnancies, 1971-79; bd. dirs., chmn. clergy adv. com. Planned Parenthood Assn., Chgo., 1977-79; bd. dirs. Hyde Park YMCA, Facing History and Ourselves Nat. Found., 1983-87; bd. govs. Internat. House, Chgo., 1969-79; trustee Packard Manse (Mass.), Bapt. Theol. Union, U. Chgo., 1960-70, 81-96, hon. trustee, 1996—; pres., bd. mgrs. Ministers and Missionaries Benefit Bd., 1975-81; mem. policy council Religious Coalition for Abortion Rights of Mass., 1980-86; sec., treas. Bolton Inst. for Sustainable Future, 1983-87; mem. gen. bd., mem. exec. com., mem. commn. on Christian unity Am. Bapt. Chs., 1963-72, 74-81; bd. dirs. Planned Parenthood League of Mass., 1984-92; interim assoc. dir. Mass Coun. Chs., 1988-89. Democrat. Baptist. Home: 65 Briarwood Cir Apt 300 Worcester MA 01606-1247

PARSONS, ESTELLE, actress, director, theater producer; b. Lynn, Mass., Nov. 20, 1927; d. Eben and Elinor (Mattson) P.; m. Richard Gehman, Dec. 19, 1953 (div. Aug. 1958); children: Martha and Abbie (twins); m. Peter L. Zimroth, Jan. 2, 1983; 1 child, Abraham. BA in Polit. Sci., Conn. Coll. Women, 1949; student, Boston U. Law Sch., 1949-50. Stage appearances include Happy Hunting, 1957, Whoop Up, 1958, Beg, Borrow or Steal, 1960, Threepenny Opera, 1960, Mrs. Dally Has a Lover, 1962, Ready When You Are C.B, 1964, Malcolm, 1965, Seven Descents of Myrtle, 1968, And Miss Reardon Drinks a Little, 1971, Mert and Phil, 1974, The Norman Conquests, 1975-76, Ladies of the Alamo, 1977, Miss Margarida's Way, 1977-78, The Pirates of Penzance, 1981, The Shadow Box, 1994; adapted, dir., performer Orgasmo Adulto Escapes from the Zoo, 1983, The Unguided Missile, Baba Goya, 1989, Shimada, 1992, Grace & Glorie, 1996, The Last of the Thorntons, 2000-01, Morning's At seven, 2002; film appearances include Bonnie and Clyde, 1966; Rachel, Rachel, 1967, I Never Sang for My Father, 1969, Dick Tracy, 1990, Boys On The Side, 1995, Looking for Richard, 1996, That Darn Cat, 1997; TV appearances include Roseanne, 1990—, NBC Today, 1951-56; artistic dir. N.Y. Shakespeare Festival Players, 1986, Actors' Studio, 1997-2003; dir. (Broadway play) Salome, the Reading, 2003. Recipient Theatre World award, 1962-63, Obie award, 1964; recipient award Motion Picture Acad. Arts and Scis., 1967; Recipient Medal of Honor, Conn. Coll., 1969 Home: 924 West End Ave Apt T5 New York NY 10025-3543 *It's in attempting all, that one succeeds.*

PARSONS, HARRY GLENWOOD, retired surgeon; b. San Bernardino, Calif., Mar. 5, 1919; s. Harry Glenwood and Evelen May (Peris) P.; m. Rubyann Kattenhorn, Sept. 28, 1986. AB, Stanford (Calif.) U., 1942, MD, 1946. Diplomate Am. Bd. Surgery, Am. Bd. Thoracic Cardio-Vascular Surgery. Intern Stanford Hosp., San Francisco, 1941-42, Rockor fellow in surg. rsch., 1944-45, asst. resident in surgery, 1945-52, chief resident in surgery, 1952-53, Boyd fellow in thoracic cardiovasc. surgery, 1953-54; asst. clin. prof. surgery Stanford Med. Sch., 1955-65; med. dir., faculty head Weimar (Calif.) Med. Ctr., 1955-72; ret. Capt. M.C. U.S. Army, 1940-44. Fellow ACS; mem. AMA, Western Thoracic Surg. Soc., Placer Nevada County Med. Assn. (pres. 1979), Calif. Med. Assn. (del.), Alpha Omega Alpha. Avocation: flying. E-mail: parsons@neworld.net.

PARSONS, HENRY MCILVAINE, psychologist; b. Lenox, Mass., Aug. 31, 1911; s. Herbert and Elsie Worthington (Clews) P.; m. Renee Oakman, 1938 (div. 1945); 1 son, Jack; m. Marina Svetlova, 1949 (div. 1957); m. Marjorie Thorson, 1957. BA, Yale U., 1933; MA, Columbia U., 1947; PhD, U. Calif., Los Angeles, 1963. Reporter N.Y. Herald Tribune, 1935-42; organizer N.Y. Newspaper Guild, 1942; asst., then lectr. psychology Columbia U., 1947-52; research asso. N.Y. U., 1951-52; supr. Electronics Research Labs., Columbia U., 1952-58; mem. human factors staff Douglas Aircraft Co., Long Beach and Santa Monica, Calif., 1956-58; sr. human factors scientist, br. head System Devel. Corp., Santa Monica and Falls Church, Va., 1958-68; self-employed cons., 1968-69; 70-73; v.p. research Riverside Research Inst., N.Y.C., 1969-70; exec. dir. Inst. Behavioral Research Inc., Silver Spring, Md., 1974-79; pres. Exptl. Coll. of Inst. Behavioral Research, Silver Spring, 1974-80; mgr. human factors projects Human Resources Research Orgn., Alexandria, Va., 1980-83; sr. staff scientist Essex Corp., Alexandria, Va., 1983-90; mgr. Ctr. for Human Factors Rsch. Human Resources Rsch. Orgn., Alexandria, 1990—; adj. prof. Lehigh U., 1983-84. Author: Man-Machine System Experiments, 1972; also chpts. in books, articles in jours. Served with USNR, 1942-45. Fellow AAAS, APA (pres. divsn. 21 1975-76, Franklin V. Taylor award 1992), Human Factors and Ergonomics Soc. (pres. 1968-69, Pres.'s Disting. Svc. award 1993), Washington Acad. Scis., Am. Psychol. Soc.; mem. N.Y. Acad. Scis., Ergonomics Soc., Sigma Xi. Clubs: Century (N.Y.C.); Cosmos (Washington). Home: 1600 S Eads St Apt 1223 Arlington VA 22202 Office: Human Resources Rsch Orgn 66 Canal Center Plz Alexandria VA 22314-1591

PARSONS, IRENE ADELAIDE, management consultant; b. North Wilkesboro, N.C. d. Everett T. and Martha (Minton) P. BS in Bus. Edn. and Adminstrn., U. N.C., 1941, LLD (hon.), 1967; MS in Pub. Adminstrn., George Washington U., 1965. Tchr. Roanoake Rapids (N.C.) High Sch., 1941-42; rep. U.S. Civil Svc. Commn., 1942-43; with VA, 1946-74, asst. adminstr. vets. affairs, dir. personnel, dir. equal employment opportunity, 1965-74; mgmt. cons., 1974—. Exec. com. Pres.'s Study Group Careers for Women. Served to lt. USCGR, 1943-46. Recipient Fed. Woman's Outstanding Achievement award, 1966, Silver Helmet award Amvets, 1971, Career Svc. award Nat. Civil Svc. League, 1972, Disting. Alumni Achievement award George Washington U., 1973; named to Brevard Coll. Hall of Fame, 1984 Mem. Assn. Fed. Woman's Award Recipients (chmn. 1972-76) Address: PO Box 2046 North Wilkesboro NC 28659-2046

PARSONS, JEFFREY ROBINSON, anthropologist, educator; b. Washington, Oct. 9, 1939; s. Merton Stanley and Elisabeth (Oldenburg) P.; m. Mary Thomson Hrones, Apr. 27, 1968; 1 child, Apphia Hrones. BS, Pa. State U., 1961; PhD, U. Mich., 1966. Asst. prof. anthropology U. Mich., Ann Arbor, 1966-71, assoc. prof., 1971-76, prof., 1976—, dir. mus. anthropology, 1983-86. Vis. prof. Universidad Nacional Autonoma de Mexico, 1987; vis. prof. Universidad Buenos Aires, 1994, Univ. Nac de Catamarca, Argentina, 1996, Univ. Nac de Tucuman, Argentina, 1996, Univ. Mayor de San Andres, Bolivia, 1999. Author: Prehistoric Settlement Patterns in the Texcoco Region, Mexico, 1971; (with William T. Sanders and Robert Santley) The Basin of Mexico: The Cultural Ecology of a Civilization, 1979; (with E. Brumfiel) Prehispanic Settlement Patterns in the Southern Valley of Mexico, 1982; (with M. Parsons) Chinampa Agriculture and Aztec Urbanization in the Valley of Mexico, 1985; (with Mary H. Parsons) Maguey Utilization in Highland Central Mexico, 1990; The Production and Consumption of Salt During Postclassic Times in the Valley of Mexico, 1994; (with E. Brumfiel and M. Hodge) The Developmental Implications of Earlier Dates for Early Aztec in the Basin of Mexico, 1996; (with C. Hastings and R. Matos) Rebuilding the State in Highland Peru, 1997; A Regional Perspective on Inca Impact in the Sierra Central, Peru, 1998; (with C. Hastings and R. Matos) Prehispanic Settlement Patterns in the Upper Mantaro-Tarma Drainage, Peru, 2000; The Last Saltmakers of Nexquipayac, Mexico, 2001. Rsch. grantee NSF, 1967, 70, 72-73, 75-76, 81, Nat. Geog. Soc., 1984, 86, 88, 2003. Mem. Am. Anthrop. Assn. (Alfred V. Kidder award 1998), Soc. Am. Archaeology, AAAS, Inst. Andean Rsch., Inst. Andean Studies, Sociedad Mexicana de Antropologia, Sociedad Argentina de Antropologia. Office: Museum of Anthropology U Mich Ann Arbor MI 48109 E-mail: jpar@umich.edu.

PARSONS, JOHN THOREN, manufacturing executive; b. Detroit, Oct. 11, 1913; s. Carl Berger and Edith Charlotte (Thorén) Parson; m. Elizabeth Mae Shaw, Apr. 20, 1940; children: Carl A, John T. II, Robert S., Grant W., David C., Meredith W. Student, Wayne U., 1934; D of Engring. (hon.), U. Mich., 1988; LLD (hon.), Lake Superior State U., 1997. With Parsons Corp., Detroit & Traverse City, Mich., 1928-68, owner Traverse City, Mich., 1954-68, pres., 1956-68, Parsons Co., France, 1959-68; pres., owner The John T. Parsons Corp., Traverse City, Mich., 1968—. Invited lectr., Japan, Germany, Brazil. Recipient Nat. Medal of Tech., U.S. Dept. Commerce, 1985, Jules Marie Jacquard award, AIM Tech., 1968, Disting. Service award, Nat. Tooling and Machining Assn., Citation Soc. Am. Value Engrs., inductee Inventors Hall of Fame, 1993. Fellow: Soc. Mfg. Engrs. (charter, internat. dir. 1992—93, citation 1975); mem.: Detroit Athletic Club. Republican. Lutheran. Achievements include invention of products and mfg. processes. Avocations: music, reading, family. Home and Office: 3950 Sumac Dr Apt 330 Traverse City MI 49684-7016

PARSONS, JOSEPH B. apparel company executive; With Donna Karan Internat., Inc., N.Y.C., 1993—, exec. v.p., chief adminstrv. officer, CFO, chief fin. and ops. officer, 2000—. Office: Donna Karan Internat Inc 550 7th Ave New York NY 10018

PARSONS, LEONARD JON, marketing educator, consultant; b. Pitts., Sept. 1, 1942; s. Leonard J. and Marion Jane (Williams) P.; m. Julia Grieve, Jan. 23, 1965; children: Lorelei, Leonard Jon Jr. BSChemE, MIT, 1964; MS in Indsl. Adminstrn., Purdue U., 1965, PhD in Indsl. Adminstrn., 1968. Asst. prof. Ind. U., Bloomington, 1968-70; assoc. prof. Claremont (Calif.) Grad. Sch., 1970-77; prof. marketing Ga. Inst. Tech., 1977—. Vis. scholar MIT, Cambridge, fall 1973; Fulbright-Hays sr. scholar Cath. U. Leuven, Belgium, spring 1977; vis. prof. INSEAD, France, fall 1984, Norwegian Sch. Mktg., Oslo, fall 1989, UCLA, spring 1990, Advt. Edn. Found., Anheuser Busch, St. Louis, summer 1993, CREER/FUCAM, Belgium, Fall 1995; mem. rsch. and test devel. com. Grad. Mgmt. Admissions Coun., 1988-90. Author: Using Microcomputers in Marketing, 1986; co-author: Marketing Management, 7th edit., 2000, Market Response Models, 2d edit., 2001, others; edtl. bd. Jour. Mktg. Rsch., 1970-80, 83-85, Jour. Bus. Rsch., 1973-79, Jour. Mktg., 1978-80; assoc. editor: Decision Scis., 1976-79; mktg. dept. editor: Mgmt. Sci., 1980-82; contbr. numerous chpts. to books, articles to profl. jours. Recipient first prize rsch. design contest Am. Mktg. Assn., 1971-72. Mem. Am. Mktg. Assn. (mem. adv. bd. mktg. rsch. spl. interest group 1998), Am. Statis. Assn. (chmn. stats. in mktg. sect. 1995), European Mktg. Acad. (mem. exec. com. 1981-84), Theta Delta Chi, Beta Gamma Sigma, Phi Kappa Phi. Office: Ga Inst Tech Dupree Coll Mgmt Atlanta GA 30332-0520 E-mail: len.parsons@mgt.gatech.edu.

PARSONS, MARCIA PHILLIPS, judge; Bankruptcy judge U.S. Bankruptcy Ct. (Tenn. ea. dist.), 6th circuit, Greeneville, 1993—. Office: US Courthouse 101 W Summer St Greeneville TN 37743-4944

PARSONS, MICHAEL J. health facility administrator; BS in Acctg., U. New Orleans; MBA, Pepperdine U. Former sr. v.p., divisional CFO, v.p. fin. Nat. Med. Enterprises (now Tenet); former CFO Ctrl. Group, Columbia/HCA; former COO/CFO Pacific Group; exec. v.p., COO Triad Hosps., Inc., Plano, Tex. Mem.: Fedn. Am. Hosps. (bd. govs.). Office: Triad Hosps 5800 Tennyson Pky Plano TX 75024

PARSONS, PATRICK JEREMY, research scientist, science educator; arrived in U.S.A., 1984; s. Cyril Stanley and Dorothy Ellen Parsons; m. Susan Marie Bieniek, Oct. 7, 1989; children: Kristin Elizabeth, Jeremy Robert. BEd, U. London, 1978, PhD, 1983. Secondary sch. tchr. St. Thomas More Sch., London, 1981—83; vis. fellow NIH, Bethesda, Md., 1984—86; rsch. scientist NY State Dept. Health, Albany, 1986—. Assoc. prof. SUNY, Albany, 1988—. Contbr. numerous articles to profl. jours. Recipient Pangbourne award, Wadsworth Ctr., 1997; grantee Bone Lead Standardization Program, NIH, 2003—. Fellow: Royal Soc. Chemistry. Achievements include research in lead poisoning, analytical chemistry of trace elements.

PARSONS, RHEA FAITH, psychiatrist, educator; BA, Lehman Coll., 1987; MD, NYU, 1992; MA, John Jay Coll. of Criminal Justice, 2001. Resident in psychiatry Albert Einstein Coll. of Medicine, 1996; adj. asst. prof. Mercy Coll., Dobbs Ferry, NY, 1997—2002; asst. prof. Borough Manhattan C.C., N.Y., 2000—; adj. asst. prof. Sch. of Continuing and Profl. Studies NYU, 2001—; intern. Albert Einstein Coll. of Medicine, 1992—96. Presenter in field. Contbr. articles to profl. jours. Mem.: APA. Office: Borough of Manhattan Community College 199 Chambers Street New York NY 10007 Business E-Mail: rparsons@bmcc.cuny.edu.

PARSONS, RICHARD DEAN, communications company executive; b. N.Y.C., Apr. 4, 1948; s. Lorenzo Locklair and Isabelle (Judd) P.; m. Laura Ann Bush, Aug. 30, 1968; children: Gregory, Leslie, Rebecca. Student, U. Hawaii, 1968; JD, U. Ala. Law Sch., 1971; LLD (hon.), Adelphi U., 1990, Medgar Evers Coll., NYC, 1991; LHD (hon.), U. Hawaii, 2003. Bar: NY 1972. Asst. counsel to gov. State of NY, Albany, 1971-73, 1st asst. counsel to gov., 1973-74; dep. counsel to v.p. Office of V.P., Washington, 1975; gen. counsel, assoc. dir. domestic coun. White House, Washington, 1975-77; ptnr. Patterson Belknap Webb & Tyler, NYC, 1979—88; pres., COO Dime Savs. Bank NY, NYC, 1988-90, chmn., CEO, 1990-94; dir. Time Warner, NYC, 1991—, pres., 1995—99; co-COO AOL Time Warner, Inc., NYC, 1999—2002; CEO Time Warner Inc., NYC, 2002—, chmn., 2003—. Bd. dirs. Citigroup, Estee Lauder, Colonial Williamsburg Found., Museum of Modern Art, Howard U., Fed. Nat. Mortgage Assn., Philip Morris Co.; trustee, Rockefeller Brothers Fund. Mem. Presdl. Drug Task Force; mayor-elect transition coun., head, 1993; chmn. Wildcat Svc. Orgn., NYC Econ. Develop. Corp.; bd. dir. NY Zoological Soc., Am. TV & Comm. Inc.; trustee Howard U., Met. Mus. Art. Recipient Disting. Alumnus award, U. Hawaii, 2003. Chmn., Apollo Theatre Found. Avocation: owns winery in Tuscany, Italy. Office: Time Warner Inc 75 Rockefeller Plz New York NY 10019-6990*

PARSONS, RICHARD HUGO, lawyer; b. Okla., June 9, 1936; s. Alfred Richard and Veronica Cecilia (Hugo) Parsons; m. Catherine Ann Logan; children: Karen Ann (Parsons) Voss, Anne Logan (Parsons) Muren, Alfred Richard Parsons II. BA, Bradley U., Peoria, Ill., 1958; JD, Wash. & Lee, Lexington, Va., 1961; Cert., Harvard Law Sch. Bar: Ill., DC. Asst. sec. Chgo. Title and Trust, 1961—68; pvt. practice Peoria, Ill., 1968—95; fed. pub. defender Ctrl. Dist. of Ill., Peoria, 1995—. Commr./trial judge Ill. Ct. of Claims, Springfield, Ill., 1975—95; pres. Ill. Assn. of Criminal Def. Lawyers, 1994, Clarence Darrow Inn of the Am. Inns of Ct., Peoria, Ill.; chmn. Am. Bar Association's Criminal Justice Sect. Amicus Curiae Com., 2000—; dir. Peoria County Bar Assn., Peoria, Ill. Author: Possible Issues for Review in Criminal Appeals, Second Edition; editor: (newsletter) The Back Bencher. Founder City of Peoria St. Patrick's Day Parade, Peoria, Ill., 1981; del. 1972 Dem. Nat. Conv., 1972; pres. Ancient Order of Hibernians, Peoria, Ill., 1981; precinct committeeman Dem. Precinct Committeeman, Peoria, Ill. Mem.: Ill. Assn. of Criminal Def. Lawyers (pres. 1994—95, Lawyer of the Yr. 2000), Nat. Assn. of Criminal Def. Lawyers (life), Mt. Hawley Country Club, Union League Club of Chgo., Sigma Phi Epsilon. Democrat. Roman Catholic. Avocations: tennis, golf, literature, crossword puzzles. Office: Federal Public Defender 401 Main Street - Suite 1500 Peoria IL 61602 E-mail: richard_parsons@fd.org.

PARSONS, TERRY THOMAS, psychotherapist, educator; b. Paris, Tex., Apr. 8, 1947; s. Thomas Anderson and Ruby May (Emmons) Parsons; m. Kathleen Kay Krueger, June 3, 1972; children: Laura Elizabeth Parsons Chester, Adam Thomas. BA in History and Sociology, Tex. A&M U., 1969; ThM, So. Meth. U., 1972, DM, 1977; PhD in Clin. Psychology, Fielding Grad. Inst., 1997. Lic. profl. counselor and marriage and family therapist; ordained min. United Meth. Ch., 1971. Asst. chaplain Presbyn. Hosp., Dallas, 1971—72, dir. drug rsch. and counseling, 1972—73, staff chaplain, 1973—77; min. pastoral care and counseling First United Meth. Ch., Richardson, Tex., 1977—80; pvt. practice psychotherapist Dallas, 1980—. Coord. divsn. family United Meth. Ch.-North Tex. Conf., 1984—88; pres. Interfaith Alliance, Richardson, 1986—88; cons., trainer Network Cmty. Ministries, Richardson, 1986—; cons., adj. faculty So. Meth. U., Dallas, 1989—; developer Commit and Thrive Seminars, Dallas, 1997—. Author: The Intimacy Jungle: How You Can Survive and Thrive in a Lasting Marriage, 2000. Chairperson alumni loyalty fund Perkins Sch. Theology, Dallas, 1988—89; mem. adv. bd. Learning Disabilities Assn., Richardson, 1997—99. Recipient Outstanding Vol. award, Network Cmty. Ministries, 1987, Disting. Svc. award, Perkins Sch. Theology, 1989. Mem.: APA, Am. Group Psychotherapy Assn., Am. Assn. for Marriage and Family Therapy (clin. mem.). Methodist. Achievements include research in sources and stages of mate selection, relationship development and marriage; characteristics of drug overdose patients and supplementary treatment needs. Avocations: baseball, travel, reading, writing, member church choir. Home: 331 E Tyler St Richardson TX 75081 Office: Ste 518 13140 Coit Rd Dallas TX 75240 Office Phone: 972-437-3370.

PARSONS, VINSON ADAIR, retired computer software company executive; b. Frankfort, Ky., Oct. 22, 1932; s. Richard Adair and Nina (Mefford) P.; m. Elizabeth Ann Peltier, June 2, 1956. A.S., Mitchell Coll., 1959; BS, U. Conn., 1960; AMP, Harvard U., 1985. Auditor, Price Waterhouse & Co. (C.P.A.s), Hartford, Conn., 1960-65; controller Pervel Industries Inc., Plainfield, Conn., 1965-70; v.p., controller Akzo Am. Inc., Asheville, N.C., 1970-71, 73-83, v.p., chief fin. officer, 1983-86, System Software Assocs. Inc., Chgo., 1986-89, also bd. dirs.; ret., 1990. Dir. Am. Tape Co., BRIntec Co., Control Tech. Corp. Elected commr. Town of Weaverville Bd. Commrs., 1994-2000. With USN, 1953-57. Mem. Am. Mgmt. Assn., Fin. Execs. Inst., Inst. Mgmt. Accts. (pres. local chpt. 1969-70) Clubs: Asheville Country; University (N.Y.C.); Reems Creek Golf. Home and Office: 15 Preston Ct Weaverville NC 28787-8907

PARSONS, WILLIAM JONATHAN, cardiologist; b. Apr. 3, 1955; married; 3 children. BA, Dartmouth Coll., 1977, MD, 1980. Diplomate Am. Bd. Internal Medicine, Am. Bd. Cardiovascular Diseases, Am. Bd. Nuclear Cardiology, Nat. Bd. Echocardiography. Resident in internal medicine Strong Meml. Hosp. U. Rochester (N.Y.), 1983-85; cardiology fellow Duke U. Med. Ctr., Durham, 1985-88, asst. prof., 1988-91; asst. prof. medicine Southwestern Med. Ctr. U. Tex., Dallas, 1991-93; attending cardiologist Baylor U. Med. Ctr., Dallas, 1993—2001, Rex Hosp., Raleigh, NC, 2001—. Contbr. articles to profl. jours. Gen. med. officer USPHS-IHS, 1981-83. Fellow Am. Coll. Physicians, Am. Coll. Cardiology. Office: Carolina Cardiology Cons 3324 Six Forks Rd Raleigh NC 27609 E-mail: wjpdnp@aol.com.

PART, HOWARD MITCHELL, dean; b. NYC, Apr. 26, 1949; m. Kristine Kunesh-Part. BS, Ohio U.; MD, Ohio State U., 1982. Cert. Am. Bd. Internal Medicine. Intern Ohio State U. Hospitals, Columbus, 1982—83, resident in internal medicine, 1983—85; voluntary faculty mem. Wright State U. Sch. Medicine, Dayton, Ohio, 1986—88, mem. faculty, 1988—, chief of gen. medicine consult svc., dir. internal medicine residency program Dayton VA Med. Ctr., vice chair to chair dept. med. edn., assoc. dean faculty and clin. affairs, 1995—98, acting dean, 1998—99, dean, 1999—. Recipient Dean's Award for Excellence in Med. Edn., Wright State U. Sch. Medicine, 1992. Fellow: Am. Coll. Physicians (Gov.'s Award - Ohio Chpt.). Office: 115 Med Scis Bldg Wright State U 3640 Colonel Glenn Hwy Dayton OH 45435-0001*

PARTAN, DANIEL GORDON, lawyer, educator; b. Gardner, Mass., Aug. 2, 1933; s. Toivo Antero and Lempi Sivia (Adamson) P.; m. Doris Liepmann, June 8, 1957; children: Andrew Stewart, Matthew Alexander, Sarah Ruth, Iliana Maria, Juan Carlos. AB, Cornell U., 1955; LLB, Harvard U., 1958, LLM, 1961. Bar: Mass. 1959. Rsch. assoc. Harvard Law Sch., 1961, Rule of Law Ctr., Duke U. Law Sch., 1962-65; assoc. prof. U. N.D., 1964-65; assoc. prof. law Boston U., 1965-68, prof., 1968—, prof. London Inst., 2003—. Mem. NAFTA dispute settlement roster and binat. dispute panel U.S.-Can. Free Trade Agreement; mem. dispute settlement panel roster World Trade Orgn.; sr. specialist roster U.S. Fulbright Commn.; cons. Dept. State, UN Devel. Program, Am. Acad. Arts and Sci.; pres., chmn. Bd. dirs. UN Assn. Greater Boston, 1969-71, 76-77; chmn. Brookline Selectmen's Com. on Harvard Energy Plant, 1976—; vis. scholar Harvard Law Sch., 1977-78; vis. fellow Cambridge (Eng.) U., 1972; vis. prof. Peking U., Beijing, 2000; Fulbright prof. Tsinghue U. Law Sch., Beijing, 2003. Author: Population in the United Nations System, 1973, Documentary Study of the Politicization of UNESCO, 2 vols., 1975, The International Law Process, 1992, Documents Supplement to the International Law Process, 1999; co-author: Legal Problems of International Administration, 1968, The United States and the International Labor Organization, 1980; co-editor: Corporate Disclosure of Environmental Risks: U.S. and European Law, 1990; contbr. articles to books and jours. Mem. ABA (amicus brief com. sect. internat. law and practice), Bretton Woods Com., Commn. to Study the Orgn. Peace, Am. Law Inst., Acad. Coun. UN System, Am. Soc. Internat. Law, Internat. Law Assn., European Communities Studies Assn., UN Assn., Coalition for a Strong UN, Trade Law Consultative Group, Boston Area Tchrs. Internat. Law (convenor). Office: 765 Commonwealth Ave Boston MA 02215-1401 E-mail: partan@bu.edu.

PARTANEN, CARL RICHARD, biology professor; b. Portland, Oreg., Nov. 23, 1921; s. Emil and Ellen (Engstrom) P.; m. Jane Nelson, June 24, 1961; children: Karen, Kirsten, Richard (dec.) Student, Multnomah Jr. Coll., 1946-48; BA, Lewis and Clark Coll., 1950; MA, Harvard, 1951, PhD, 1954. Am. Cancer Soc. postdoctoral research fellow Columbia, 1954-55; Harvard, 1955-57; research asso. Childrens Cancer Research Found., Boston, 1957-61; asso. prof. biology U. Pitts., 1961-64, prof. biology, 1964-86, chmn. biology, 1964-70, prof. emeritus, 1987—; Research fellow U. Edinburgh, Scotland, 1971-72, U. Nottingham, Eng., 1978-79. Contbr. articles to profl. jours. Served with AUS, 1942-45, ETO. Recipient Distinguished Achievement award Lewis and Clark Coll., 1968 Mem. AAAS, Bot. Soc. Am., Soc. for Devel. Biology, Soc. for In Vitro Biology. Home: 1112 Farragut St Pittsburgh PA 15206-1746 Office: U Pitts Dept Biol Scis Pittsburgh PA 15260 Business E-Mail: partanen@pitt.edu.

PARTEE, BARBARA HALL, linguist, educator; b. Englewood, N.J., June 23, 1940; d. David B. and Helen M. Hall; m. Morriss Henry Partee, 1966 (div. 1971); children: Morriss M., David M., Joel T.; m. Emmon Bach, 1973 (div. 1996); m. Vladimir B. Borschev, 1997. BA with high honors in Math., Swarthmore Coll., 1961; PhD in Linguistics, MIT, 1965; DSc (hon.), Swarthmore Coll., 1989, Charles U., Prague, Czechoslovakia, 1992, Russian State Humanities U., Moscow, 2001. Asst. prof. UCLA, 1965—69, assoc. prof., 1969-73; assoc. prof. linguistics and philosophy U. Mass., Amherst, 1972-73, prof., 1973-90, Disting. Univ. prof., 1990—2003, Disting. Univ. prof. linguistics and philosophy emerita, 2004—, head dept. linguistics, 1987-93; fellow Ctr. for Advanced Study in Behavior Scis., 1976-77. Mem. bd. mgrs. Swarthmore Coll., 1990-2001. Author: (with Stockwell and Schachter) The Major Syntactic Structures of English, 1972, Fundamentals of Mathematics for Linguists, 1979, (with ter Meulen and Wall) Mathematical Methods in Linguistics, 1990, (with Hajicova and Sgall) Topic-Focus Articulation, Tripartite Structures, and Semantic Content, 1998, Compositionality in Formal Semantics: Selected Papers of Barbara H. Partee, 2004; editor: Montague Grammar, 1976; co editor: (with Chierchia and Turner) Properties, Types and Meaning, Vol. I: Foundational Issues, Vol. II: Semantic Issues, 1989, (with Bach, Jelinek and Kratzer) Quantification in Natural Languages, 1995, (with P. Portner) Formal Semantics: The Essential Readings, 2002; mem. editl. bd: Language, 1967-73, Linguistic Inquiry, 1972-79, Theoretical Linguistics, 1971—, Linguistics and Philosophy, 1977—. Recipient Chancellor's medal U. Mass., 1977; NEH fellow, 1982-83; Internat. Rsch. and Exchanges Bd. fellow, 1989-90, 95, Fulbright fellow 2000. Fellow AAAS, NAS (chair anthropology sect. 1993-96), Am. Acad. Arts and Scis., Sigma Xi; mem. Linguistic Soc. Am. (pres. 1986), Am. Philos. Assn., Assn. Computational Linguistics, Royal Netherlands Acad. Arts and Scis. (fgn.). Home: 50 Hobart Ln Amherst MA 01002-1321 Office: U Mass Dept Linguistics Amherst MA 01003 E-mail: partee@linguist.umass.edu. *In college I studied math, Russian, and philosophy, the three subjects I loved best, with no idea of relating them, and ended up ideally prepared for a field that didn't exist then. I'm also grateful for wonderful parents, teachers, students, colleagues, family.*

PARTENHEIMER, ROBERT CHAPIN, emergency physician; b. Springfield, Mass., Feb. 12, 1923, s. Joseph Everad and Leila Ursula (Parker) P.; m. Marion Claire Hill, June 23, 1949 (div. Feb. 1971); children: Barbara Haislip, Robert Hill, Richard Chapin; m. Carol Griffiths, Jan. 1991. BA, Amherst Coll., 1945; MD, Cornell U., 1947. Rotating intern Orange (N.J.) Meml. Hosp., 1947-48; intern in medicine U. Hosp., N.Y.C., 1948-49; resident in internal medicine USPHS, Boston, 1950-52; pvt. practice Summit, N.J., 1954-71; emergency physician Raritan Bay Med. Ctr., Perth Amboy, N.J., 1971-77, 84-90, St. Cloud (Fla.) Hosp., 1994-97, Columbia HCA Rauterson Hosp., Okeechobee, Fla., 1992-96. Lt. comdr. USPHS, 1949-54. Em. N.J. Med. Soc., Union County Med. Soc. Methodist. Avocations: golf, boating, fishing, skiing. Home: 5213 Indian Bend Ln Fort Pierce FL 34951

PARTER, SEYMOUR VICTOR, computer science and mathematics educator; b. Chgo., June 9, 1927; s. Peter and Tillie (Dekovetzky) P.; m. Ruth Ghitman, Oct. 9, 1957; children: Paul Jeffry, David William. BS, Ill. Inst. Tech., 1949, MS, 1951; PhD, N.Y.U., 1958. Staff mem. Los Alamos Sci. Lab., 1951-57; inst. math. Mass. Inst. Tech., 1957-58; asst. prof. math. Ind. U., 1958-60, Cornell U., 1960-62; vis. asst. prof. computer sci. Stanford, 1962-63; asso. prof. computer sci. and math. U. Wis., Madison, 1963-65, prof., 1965—, chmn. computer sci. dept., 1968-70. Mem. NRC adv. com. on math. to Office Naval Research, 1970-72; mem. adv. com. on computing to pres. Stanford, 1969-72; mem. ICASE Sci. Council, 1981-87 Contbr. articles to profl. jours. Mem. Math. Assn. Am., Soc. Indsl. and Applied Math. (vis. lectr. 1969-72, mem. council 1978-80, mng. editor Jour. Numerical Analysis 1977-80, pres. 1981-82), Bd. Math. Scis. (chmn. 1984-86). Home: 5 S Rock Rd Madison WI 53705-4634 E-mail: parter@cs.wisc.edu.

PARTH, FRANK R. consulting company executive, educator; b. Eichendorf, Germany, Aug. 26, 1949; came to U.S., 1952. s. Frank and Erna (Framelsberger) P.; m. Jane Hoppe, Dec. 27, 1974 (div. Jan. 1985); children: Katherine, Frank. BS in Physics, Creighton U., 1972; MS in Physics, U. Wyo., 1978; MS in Sys. Mgmt., U. So. Calif., L.A., 1986; MBA, Peter Drucker Inst., 2000. Design engr. Tex. Instruments, Dallas, 1978-81; asst. tech. dir. Martin-Marietta Space Sys., Long Beach, Calif., 1981-92; pres. InterVolve Mgmt. Sys., Mission Viejo, Calif., 1993-95; dir. sys. engring. Experian, Orange, Calif., 1995-97; mgr. Deloitte & Touche, Santa Ana, Calif., 1997-98; practice mgr. Keane, Inc., Long Beach, 1998-99; v.p. devel. Overstock Market (e-commerce), 2000—01; pres. Project Auditors, LLC, 2001—. Faculty U. So. Calif. Inst. Safety and Sys. Mgmt., L.A., 1993-97, U. Calif. Irvine, 1996—, Claremont Grad. U., 2000—. Contbr. articles to profl. jours. Bd. dirs. Orange County (Calif.) Search and Rescue, 1989-2002, OC Project Mgmt. Inst., 1996—, v.p. membership, 2003, v.p. profl. devel., 2004. Mem. Internat. Coun. Sys. Engring., Mensa Internat. (pres. Orange County chpt. 1993, officer 1994—), Project Mgmt. Inst. (Spkr.'s award 1998). Avocations: sailing, skiing, wine. Home: 21901 Palanca Mission Viejo CA 92692-1012 Office: PO Box 80688 Rancho Santa Margarita CA 92688-0688 Office Phone: 949-452-0578. E-mail: Fparth@projectauditors.com.

PARTHASARATHY, SANJAY, information technology executive; BS in Mech. Engring., Anna U., Madras, India; MS in Mgmt., M in Engring., MIT. From product mgr. to corp. v.p. Microsoft, Redmond, Wash., 1990, corp. v.p. strategy & bus. devel. group. Office: One Microsoft Way Redmond WA 98052-6399

PARTHEMORE, JACQUELINE GAIL, internist, educator, hospital administrator; b. Harrisburg, Pa., Dec. 21, 1940; d. Philip Mark and Emily (Buvit) Parthemore; m. Alan Morton Blank, Jan. 7, 1967; children: Stephen Eliot, Laura Elise. BA, Wellesley Coll., 1962; MD, Cornell U., 1966. Diplomate Am. Bd. Internal Medicine. Resident in internal medicine N.Y. Hosp./Cornell U., 1966-69; fellow in endocrinology Scripps Clinic and Rsch. Found., La Jolla, Calif., 1969-72; rsch. ednl. assoc. VA Hosp., San Diego, 1974-78; staff physician VA San Diego Health Care Sys., 1978-79, asst. chief, med. svc., 1979-83, acting chief, med. svc., 1980-81, chief of staff, 1984—; asst. prof. medicine U. Calif. Sch. Medicine, San Diego, 1974-80, assoc. prof. medicine, 1980-85, prof. medicine, assoc. dean, 1985—. Mem. nat. rsch. resources coun. NIH, Bethesda, Md., 1990-94. Contbr. chapters to books, articles to profl. jours. Mem. adv. bd. San Diego Opera, 1993—; mem. Roundtable and Channel 10 Focus Group, San Diego Millennium Project, 1999; bd. dirs. San Diego Vets. Med. Rsch. Found., 1989—, Nat. VA Rsch. and Edn. Found., 2001—. Recipient Bullock's 1st Annual Portfolio award, 1985, San Diego Pres.'s Coun. Woman of Yr. award, 1985, YWCA Tribute to Women in Industry award, 1987, San Diego Women Who Mean Bus. award, 1999, Excellence in Leadership award Am. Hosp. Assn., 2002. Fellow ACP (gov.-elect Region III 2004), Am. Assn. Clin. Endocrinologists; mem. Endocrine Soc., Nat. Assn. VA Chiefs Staff (pres. 1989-91), Wellesley Coll. Alumnae Assn. (1st v.p. 1992-95), San Diego Wellesley Club (pres. 1997-99), San Diego Herb Soc. (co-pres. 2003-04). Avocations: gardening, reading, sailing, cooking, travel. Office: VA San Diego Healthcare Sys 3350 La Jolla Village Dr San Diego CA 92161-0002 Office Phone: 858-552-7419. Business E-Mail: jparthemore@ucsd.edu.

PARTIDA, GILBERT A. lawyer; b. Nogales, Ariz., July 27, 1962; s. Enrique Gilberto and Mary Lou (Flores) P.; m. Soncee Ray Brown, July 30, 1992. BA with distinction, U. Ariz., 1984; JD cum laude, Pepperdine U., 1987; LLD (hon.), Calif. Western Sch Law, San Diego, 1993. V.p., bd. mem. Partida Brokerage, Inc., Nogales, 1983-91; law clk. Office of Ariz. Atty. Gen., Tucson, 1985; assoc. Gray, Cary, Ames & Frye, San Diego, 1986-89, sr. assoc., 1990-92, chmn. Mex. Practice Group, 1992; pres. Greater San Diego C. of C., 1993-98; pres., CEO Price Smart, San Diego, 1998—. Corp. counsel San Diego Incubator Corp., 1990—. Contbr. articles to profl. jours. Mem. United Way Latino Future Scan Com., 1990; mentor Puente, 1991; leadership tng. mentor Chicano Fedn., 1992; dinner com. Young at Art, 1991; mem. Children's Initiative, 1993, Superbowl Task Force, 1993, San Diego Dialogue, 1993; hon. mem. Sister City, 1993, LEAD, 1993; hon. chair Easter Seals Telethon, 1994; vice chmn. Border Trade Alliance, 1989-91; mem. nat. gala com. HDI Ednl. Svcs., 1990; Calif. state del. U.S.-Mexico Border Govs.' Conf., 1990, 92; exec. com. San Diego Conv. and Visitors Bur. Mem. San Diego County Hispanic C. of C. (chmn. 1991, pres. 1990-91, v.p. 1989-90, internat. com. chair 1989-90, sec. 1989, founding bd. mem. 1988), Consejo Nacional de Maquiladoras, Calif. Hispanic C. of C. (state conv. joint venture com. 1991, spl. projects chair 1991), San Diego/Tijuana Sister Cities Soc. (adv. coun. 1993—), San Diego County Bar Assn. (U.S./Mexico liaison com.), ABA (U.S./Mexico bar liaison com.), Hispanic Alliance for Free Trade, Rotary Club San Diego. Avocations: tennis, running, creative writing. Office: 9740 Scranton RD San Diego CA 92121-1777

PARTIE, DAVID JOHN, language educator; b. Detroit, Mich., Apr. 14, 1944; s. William Richey and Arlene Esther Partie; m. Janice Sue Stanage, June 14, 1975; 1 child, Elizabeth Catherine. BA, U. of Redlands, 1966; postgrad., U. Heidelberg, Germany, 1967—68; MA, UCLA, 1971; MDiv, Talbot Theol. Sem., 1978; MA, U. of So. Calif., 1982, PhD, 1988. C.C. Instr. Credential in German Calif. Cmty. Colleges, 1974, Cert. of Completion, World Travel Counselor Tng. Program Automobile Club of So. Calif., 1981, Apollo Travel Services Tng. Cert. United Airlines, 1982, Qualification Cert. as an ESL Tchr. for Speakers of Japanese Japanese Cross Cultural Ctr./ LA, Calif., 1984, sys. direct access tng. program cert. Ea. Airlines, 88. Tchg. asst. in German UCLA, 1968—70; instr. in German, French, Spanish and English LA Bapt. Coll., Newhall, Calif., 1969—73; instr. in German Santa Monica City Coll., 1974—77; instr. in German and French Biola Coll., La Mirada, Calif., 1974—78; instr. in French and Spanish Baymonte H.S., Santa Cruz, Calif., 1978—79; tchg. asst. in freshman writing U. of So. Calif., 1979—82; tour counselor/world travel agt. Automobile Club of So. Calif., LA, 1979—82; account exec. Agnew Tech-Tran, Woodland Hills, Calif., 1982—84; instr. in ESL and German Berlitz Sch. of Langs., Pasadena, 1984—85; prof. English and modern langs. Liberty U., Lynchburg, Va., 1985—; adj. prof. English Ctrl. Va. C.C., Lynchburg, 1998—. Chair, dept. of modern languages Liberty U., 1985—93, mem., faculty senate, 1989—93, chair, libr. com., 1993—94, editor, sacs report from the com. on orgn. and adminstrn., 1995—95, coord., european travel abroad program, dept. of english and modern languages, 1996—, mem., president's com. on instl. effectiveness, 1996—98, mem. univ. planning com., 1998—99, co-chmn. writer's conf., 1999, mem., adv. bd. for the ctr. for global ministries, 2001—, moderator of the faculty senate, 2002—03, chair, faculty senate exec. com., poetry editor Lamplight, 2003—, chmn. faculty senate, 2003—, mem. pres.' com. on faculty devel. and welfare, 2004—. Actor(cmty. theater): (musical) Fiddler on the Roof, Annie, South Pacific, Annie Warbucks, The Music Man, State Fair, Oklahoma!, (drama) Death of a Salesman, The Crucible, Romeo and Juliet, (coll. theater) The Good Woman of Setzuan (outstanding contbn. to theater at Sweet Briar Coll., 1999), (comedy) Much Ado About Nothing (outstanding contbn. to theater at Sweet Briar Coll., 2000), (musical) The Fantasticks, (film) The Gathering; author: (poetry) Wide Open Mag., The Footstool Rev., 1996, The Penwood Rev., 1997, The Poet's Domain (Hon. Mention, Poet's Choice Award, vol. 13 of The Poet's Domain, 1997), The Anthology of the Poetry Soc. of Va., Scene Mag., Piedmont Poets; contbr. The Flight of Icarus Photographic and Lit. Exhbn. at the Umlauf Sculpture Garden and Mus. Austin, Tex., 1997—98. Roving reader Lynchburg Pub. Schools, 1995—96; tchr. of creative writing Lynchburg Parks and Recreation Dept., 1995—95; forensics judge Va. Orgn. of German Students, Lynchburg, 1997—97; crisis counselor Centinella Valley Hotline, 1977—89, Suicide Prevention Ctr., L.A., 1985, Life Aid, 1988—89; mem. Lynchburg Rep. City Com., Lynchburg, 1988—2000; del. to state polit. conventions Rep. Party, Richmond, Va., 1988—96; legis. liaison to Va. state del. Joyce Crouch Va. Soc. for Human Life, Lynchburg, 1991—92; mem., mission selection com. Heritage Bapt. Ch., Lynchburg, 1991—98, 2003—; student poetry contest judge Poetry Soc. of Va., Williamsburg, 1996—96. Recipient First Pl. In The Serious Poem Category, Lynchburg Poetry Festival, 1987, 1991, 1994, 2000, Karma Deane Ogden Prize for Poetry, Poetry Soc. of Va., 1991, Brodie Herndon Meml. Prize for Poetry, 1997, Carleton Drewry Meml. Prize for Poetry, 2000; Walter Loewy fellow for Grad. Study Abroad, U. of Heidelberg, 1967-68, Chancellor's Tchg. fellow, UCLA, 1966—70. Mem.: Poetry Soc. of Va. (assoc.; regional v.p. 2002), Assn. for the Interdisciplinary Study of the Arts (assoc.), F. Scott Fitzgerald Soc. (assoc.), MLA (assoc.), Alpha Mu Gamma (life). Avocations: travel, athletics, church work, drama, book collecting. Office: Liberty U 1971 University Blvd Lynchburg VA 24502-2269 E-mail: djpartie@liberty.edu.

PARTIN, C. FRED, lawyer; b. Cin., Apr. 9, 1945; s. Charles F. and Marian (Carroll) P.; m. Susan Fischer; children: Amy Beth, Kelly Blythe, Frederick Matthew. BA, U. Ky., 1968; JD, U. Louisville, 1971. Bar: U.S. Dist. Ct. (we. dist.) Ky. 1971, U.S. Dist. Ct. (ea. dist.) Ky. 1973, U.S. Ct. Appeals (6th cir.) 1971, U.S. Supreme Ct. 1976, U.S. Dist. Ct. (so. dist.) Ohio 1983, U.S. Dist. Ct. (mid. dist.) Calif. 1983, U.S. Ct. Appeals (9th cir.) 1984. Asst. U.S. atty. Western Dist Ky., Louisville, 1971-74, 1st asst. U.S. atty., 1975-81; ptnr. Wood, Pedley, Stansbury, Rice & Warner, Louisville, 1974-75, Parker & Partin, Louisville, 1981-84. Recipient spl. award for outstanding achievement U.S. Aty. Gen., Washington, 1974. Republican. Roman Catholic. Home: 3223 Canterbury Ln Louisville KY 40207-3676 Office: 915 Ky Home Life Bldg 239 S 5th St Louisville KY 40202-3213 E-mail: scarymason@aol.com., cfredpartin@justice.com.

PARTINGTON, JAMES WOOD, engineering executive; b. Omaha, Jan. 16, 1939; s. Lee Edward and Carol Virginia (Wood) Parington; m. Barbara Jean Arline, July 15, 1961; children: Jennifer Parington, Kathleen Parington, Mary Elizabeth Parington. BA, U. R.I., 1970; grad., Naval War Coll., 1971. Commd. ensign USN, 1961, advanced through grades to rear adm., 1989; ops. officer Attack Squadron 122, Lemoore, Calif., 1974-77; commdg. officer Attack Squadron 27, Lemoore, 1977-80, Strike Fighter Squadron 125, Lemoore, 1980-82, Naval Air Sta., Lemoore, 1984-86; coord. F/A 18 program Chief Naval Ops., Washington, 1982-84; chief staff Cruiser Destroyer Group 5, San Diego, 1986-87; dir. Naval Aviation Officer Assignments, Washington, 1987-88; comdr. Strike Fighter Wings Atlantic, Jacksonville, Fla., 1988-90, Naval Tng. Ctr., Great Lakes, Ill., 1990-92; v.p., dir. corp. planning Sr. Technologies Inc., 1992-94; pres. Partington and Associates, Lincoln, 1994—, Risel-Bond Instruments, Lincoln, 1998. Decorated Legion of Merit (5), DFC, Air medal (28), Meritorious Svc. medal. Mem.: Naval Order U.S., Assn. Naval Aviation, U.S. Naval Inst. Roman Catholic. Avocations: sailing, tennis, scuba diving. E-mail: jimpartington@aol.com.

PARTLETT, DAVID F. dean, law educator; b. 1947; LLB, Sydney U., 1970; LLM, Mich. U., 1972, 74; SJD, U. Va., 1980. Bar: New South Wales 1971, Australian Cap. Terr. 1978. Vis. asst. prof. U. Ala., 1972-73; legis. officer Australia Atty. Gen.'s Office, 1974—75; dir, rsch. Australian Law Reform Commn., 1975—78; lectr. Australian Nat. U., 1978-80, sr. lectr., 1980-87, assoc. dean, 1982—85; vis. prof. Vanderbilt U., Nashville, 1987-88, prof. law, 1988-2000, acting dean, 1996-97; v.p., dean, prof. Sch. Law Washington & Lee U., Lexington, Va., 2000—. Sparkman Dist. vis. prof. Ala. U., 1986-87. Office: Washington & Lee U Sydney Lewis Hall Lexington VA 24450

PARTNOY, RONALD ALLEN, lawyer; b. Norwalk, Conn., Dec. 23, 1933; s. Maurice and Ethel Marguerite (Roselle) P.; m. Diane Catherine Keenan, Sept. 18, 1965. BA, Yale U., 1956; LL.B., Harvard U., 1961; LL.M., Boston U., 1965. Bar: Mass. 1962, Conn. 1966. Atty. Liberty Mut. Ins. Co., Boston, 1961-65; assoc. counsel Remington Arms Co., Bridgeport, Conn., 1965-70, gen. counsel, 1970-88, sec., 1983-93; sr. counsel E.I. du Pont de Nemours & Co., Wilmington, Del., 1985-95. Served to capt. USNR, 1956-85. Mem.: ABA, Naval Res. Assn. (nat. exec. com. 1981—85, 1997—99, nat. v.p. 1997—99, nat. exec. com. 2001—03, nat. v.p. 2001—03, 3d dist. pres.), U.S. Navy League (pres. Bridgeport coun. 1975—77, Conn. pres. 1977—80, v.p. Empire region 1980—85, nat. dir.), Am. Judicature Soc., Sporting Arms and Ammunition Mfrs. Inst. (chmn. legis. and legal affairs com. 1971—86), Assn. of Yale Alumni (del. 1997—2000), Yale Club of N.Y.C., Harvard Club of Phila., Harvard Club of Boston, Chancery Club. Home: 616 Bayard Rd Kennett Square PA 19348-2504

PARTON, DOLLY REBECCA, singer, composer, actress; b. Sevier County, Tenn., Jan. 19, 1946; d. Robert Lee and Avie Lee (Owens) P.; m. Carl Dean, May 30, 1966. Country music singer, rec. artist, composer, actress, radio and TV personality. Entrepreneur, owner entertainment park Dollywood, established 1985. Radio appearances include Grand Ole Opry, WSM Radio, Nashville, Cass Walker program, Knoxville; TV appearances include Porter Wagoner Show, from 1967, Cass Walker program, Bill Anderson Show, Wilburn Bros. Show, Barbara Mandrell Show; rec. artist, Mercury, Monument, RCA, CBS record cos.; star movie Nine to Five, 1980, The Best Little Whorehouse in Texas, 1982, Rhinestone, 1984, Steel Magnolias, 1989, Straight Talk, 1991; albums include Here You Come Again (Grammy award 1978), Real Love, 1985, Just the Way I Am, 1986, Portrait, 1986, Think About Love, 1986, Trio (with Emmylou Harris, Linda Ronstadt) (Grammy award 1988), 1987, Heartbreaker, Great Balls of Fire, Rainbow, 1988, White Limozeen, 1989, Home for Christmas, 1990, Eagle When She Flies, 1991, Slow Dancing with the Moon, 1993 (Grammy nomination, Best Country Vocal Collaboration for Romeo (with Tanya Tucker, Billy Ray Cyrus, Kathy Mattea, Pam Tillis, & Mary-Chapin Carpenter), (with Tammy Wynette and Loretta Lynn) Honky Tonk Angels, 1994, The Essential Dolly Parton, 1995, Just the Way I Am, 1996, Super Hits, 1996, (with others) I Will Always Love You & Other Greatest Hits, 1996, Hungry Again, 1998, Trio II, 1998, Grass is Blue, 1999 (Grammy award for best bluegrass album), Best of the Best-Porter & Doll, 1999, Halos and Horns, 2002, For God and Country, 2003, Makin' Believe, 2003; appears on song "Creepin' In" with Norah Jones, 2004; composer numerous songs including Nine to Five (Grammy award 1981, Acad. award nominee and Golden Globe award nominee 1981); author: Dolly, 1994. Recipient (with Porter Wagoner) Vocal Group of Yr. award, 1968; Vocal Duo of Yr. award All Country Music Assn., 1970, 71; Nashville Metronome award, 1979; Am. Music award for best duo performance (with Kenny Rogers), 1984; named Female Vocalist of Yr., 1975, 76; Country Star of Yr., Sullivan Prodns., 1977; Entertainer of Yr., Country Music Assn., 1978; People's Choice award, 1980, 88; Female Vocalist of Yr., Acad. Country Music, 1980; Dolly Parton Day proclaimed, Sevier County, Tenn., designated Oct. 7, 1967, Los Angeles, Sept. 20, 1979; recipient Grammy awards for best female country vocalist, 1978, 81, for best country song, 1981, for best country vocal performance with group, 1987; co-recipient (with Emmylou Harris and Linda Ronstadt) Acad. Country Music award for album of the yr., 1987; named to Small Town of Am. Hall of Fame, 1988, East Tenn. Hall of Fame, 1988. Address: RCA 6 W 57th St New York NY 10019-3901 Office: Dollywood Co 1020 Dollywood Ln Pigeon Forge TN 37863-4101*

PARTOYAN, GARO ARAKEL, lawyer; b. Toledo, Dec. 6, 1936; s. Garo and Vartoohi Partoyan; children: Garo Linck, Elizabeth Margaret, Martin Joseph. BS in Chem. Engring., Northwestern U., 1959; JD, U. Mich., 1962; LLM, NYU, 1964. Bar: N.Y. 1963, U.S. Dist. Cts. (so. dist.) N.Y. 1964, U.S. Ct. Claims 1966, U.S. Ct. Appeals (2nd cir.) 1966, U.S. Dist. Ct. (ea. dist.) N.Y. 1968. Ptnr. Curtis, Morris & Safford, N.Y.C., 1962-76; gen. counsel mktg. and tech. Mars, Inc., McLean, Va., 1976-98; pres. Mgmt. of Intellectual Property, Inc., Sarasota, Fla., 1998—. Mem. Dobbs Ferry (N.Y.) Bd. Edn., 1972-76, pres., 1975-76; chmn. Fairfax Citizens Group, Fairfax County, Va., 1988-90. Mem. ABA, Am. Intellectual Property Law Assn., N.Y. Intellectual Property Law Assn., Internat. Trademark Assn. (pres. 1990-91, bd. dirs. 1983—), Intellectual Property Owners (bd. dirs. 1992-99). Avocations: sailing, curling. Office: 4756 Sweetmeadow Cir Sarasota FL 34238 Fax: 941-922-2410. E-mail: partoyanga@aol.com.

PARTRIDGE, BRUCE JAMES, lawyer, educator, writer; b. Syracuse, N.Y., June 4, 1926; arrived in Can., 1969; s. Bert James and Lida Marion (Rice) P.; m. Mary Janice Smith, June 13, 1948 (dec. 1986); children: Heather Leigh, Eric James, Brian Lloyd, Bonnie Joyce; m. May S. Archer, May 28, 1988; stepchildren: Sheila Archer, Laurel Archer. AB cum laude, Oberlin Coll., Ohio, 1946; LLB, Blackstone Coll., Chgo., 1950, JD, 1952; LLB, U. B.C., 1974. Bar: B.C. 1976, N.W.T. 1980. Rsch. physicist Am. Gas Assn., Cleve., 1946-48; bus. mgr. Cazenovia (N.Y.) Coll., 1948—51; bus. mgr., purchasing agt., asst. treas. Rochester Inst. Tech., NY, 1953—58; bus. adminstr. Baldwin-Wallace Coll., Berea, Ohio, 1951-53; v.p. bus. and mgmt. U. Del., Newark, 1958-63; v.p. adminstrn. Johns Hopkins U., Balt., 1963-69; pres. U. Victoria, B.C., Can., 1969-72; assoc. Clark, Wilson & Co., Vancouver, B.C., Can., 1975-78; successively solicitor, mng. solicitor, gen. solicitor, v.p. law and gen. counsel, sec. Cominco Ltd., Vancouver, 1978-88; exec. dir. Baker & McKenzie, Hong Kong, 1988-90; v.p. Pacific Creations, Inc., 1990-92; faculty Camosun Coll., 1992-99. Author: Management in Canada: The Competitive Challenges, 2000; co-author: College and University Business Administration, 1968; chmn. editl. com. Purchasing for Higher Education, 1962; contbr. numerous articles to profl. jours. Chmn. commn. on adminstrv. affairs Am. Coun. on Edn., Washington, 1966-69; mem. Pres.'s Com. on Employment of Handicapped, Washington, 1967-69; mem. adv. coun. Ctr. for Resource Studies, Queen's U., 1983-88; bd. dirs. L'Arche in the Americas, 1984-88; mem. adv. coun. Westwater Rsch. Ctr., U. B.C., 1982-88. Mem. Law Soc. of N.W. Ters., Assn. Can. Gen. Counsel, Def. Rsch. Inst. (product liability com.), Am. Inst. Parliamentarians, Nat. Assn. Parliamentarians. Unitarian Universalist. E-mail: brucepart@telus.ca.

PARTRIDGE, CAROLYN, farmer, state representative; b. Hackensack, N.Y., Jan. 21, 1949; m. Alan C. Partridge; 3 children. BA, NYU, 1971. Farmer; rep. Vt. State Ho. Reps., 1999—. Commr. Windham (Vt.) Regional Planning; mem. Windham (Vt.) Cmty. Orgn., Cultural Heritage Tourism Adv. Coun.; deacon Windham (Vt.) Congl. Ch.; chmn. Windham (Vt.) Sch. Bd.; exec. bd. Windham (Vt.) Regional Planning. Democrat. Protestant. Home: 1612 Old Cheney Rd Windham VT 05359

PARTRIDGE, DAVID EDWARD, secondary school educator; b. Cleve., Ohio, Mar. 5, 1948; s. Wilbur Nolan and Carolyn Agnes Partridge; m. Linda Dugan Partridge, June 19, 1971. BA, Otterbeiu Coll., Westerville, Ohio, 1970; MA, Ind. Univ. of Pa., Ind., Pa., 1978; MEd, Kutztown Univ., Kutztown, Pa., 1983. Tchr. New Albany H.S., New Albany, Ohio, 1970—72, Commodore Perry H.S., Hadley, Pa., 1973—74, Schuykill Haven H.S., Sch. Haven, Pa., 1974—79, Shippensberg H.S., Pa., 1979—80, Wilson Sch. Dist., Westlawn, Pa., 1980—. Editl. advisor John O'Hara Jour., Pottsville, Pa., 1979—81. NEH, Ohio State Univ., 1986, Cornell Univ., 1989, Penn, 1992. Mem.: People for the Am. Way, World Wildlife Fund, Nature Conservancy, Wilson Edn. Assn., Nat. Edn. Assn., Pa. State Edn. Assn., Nat. Resource Defense Coun. Avocations: reading, birdwatching, cross country skiing, music, art. Office: Wilson Sch Dist 2601 Grandview Blvd West Lawn PA 19609

PARTRIDGE, MARK VAN BUREN, lawyer, educator, writer; b. Rochester, Minn., Oct. 16, 1954; s. John V.B. and Constance (Brainerd) P.; m. Mary Roberta Moffitt, Apr. 30, 1983; children: Caitlin, Lindsay, Christopher. BA, U. Nebr., 1978; JD, Harvard U., 1981. Bar: Ill. 1981, U.S. Dist. Ct. (no. dist.) Ill. 1981, U.S. Dist. Ct. (ea. dist.) Mich. 1983, U.S. Ct. Appeals (1st cir) 2003, U.S. Ct. Appeals (4th cir.) 1986, U.S. Ct. Appeals (7th cir.), 1992, U.S. Ct. Appeals (5th cir.) 1993, U.S. Ct. Appeals (3rd cir.) 1998. Assoc. Pattishall, McAuliffe, Newbury, Hilliard & Geraldson, Chgo., 1981-88, ptnr., 1988—. Adj. prof. John Marshall Law Sch., Chgo., 1987—; arbitrator Cook County Mandatory Arbitration Program, 1989-2003; v.p. Harvard Legal Aid Bur., 1980-81; mediator no. dist. Ill. Voluntary Mediation Program, 1997—; panelist World Intellectual Property Orgn., Domain Name Dispute Resolution Svc., 1999—. Author, Guilding Rights Trademarks, Copyright and the Internet, iUniverse, 2003, Contbr. articles to profl. jours.; mem. editl. bd. The Trademark Reporter, 1994-97; adv. bd. IP Litigator, 1995—. Vol. Chgo. Vol.

Legal Svcs., 1983—. Mem. ABA (com. chmn. 1989-91, 94-99), Internat. Trademark Assn. (com. vice chmn. 1996), World Intellectual Property Orgn. (experts panel internet domain name process 1998-99), Am. Intellectual Property Law Assn. (com. chmn. 1989-91, 96-98, bd. dirs. 1998-2001), Intellectual Property Law Assn. Chgo. (com. chmn. 1993-96), Brand Names Ednl. Found. (moot ct. regional chmn. 1994-96, nat. vice-chmn. 1997-98, nat. chmn. 1998-99), Nat. Spkrs. Assn., Legal Club (v.p. 1998, pres. 1999), Lawyers Club Chgo. (pres. 2000, bd. dirs. 2000-01), Union League Club, Harvard Club Chgo., Bagatelle Club. Avocations: writing, music, genealogy, travel, internet. Office: Pattishall McAuliffe Newbury Hilliard & Geraldson 311 S Wacker Dr Ste 5000 Chicago IL 60606-6631 Office Phone: 312-554-8000. E-mail: mpartridge@pattishall.com.

PARTRIDGE, WILLIAM FRANKLIN, JR., lawyer; b. Newberry, S.C., July 16, 1945; s. William F. and Clara (Eskridge) P.; m. Ilene S. Stewart, Aug. 16, 1969; children: Allison, William F. BA in History, The Citadel, 1967; JD, U. S.C., 1970. Bar: S.C. 1970, U.S. Ct. Claims 1971, U.S. Ct. Mil. Appeals 1971, U.S. Tax Ct. 1971, U.S. Supreme Ct. 1973, U.S. Dist. Ct. S.C. 1980. Instr. internat. law Chapman Coll., 1973-74; pub. issue com. S.C. Bar, 1982-83. Lt. Col. USAFR. Mem. Newberry Bar Assn. (pres. 1982-83), Palmetto Club, County of Newberry Club, Cotillion Club, Assn. Citadel Mens Club, Masons, Phi Delta Phi. Democrat. Methodist. Home: 2029 Harrington St Newberry SC 29108-3055 Office: 1201 Boyce St Newberry SC 29108-2705 Office Phone: 803-276-5968.

PARTRIDGE, WILLIAM J. military officer, government agency administrator; b. Saugerties, N.Y. Grad., U.S. Mil. Acad., 1975; MS in Space Systems Engring., Naval Postgrad. Sch. Commd. 2d lt. U.S. Army, 1975, advanced through grades to col.; comdr. 2d Bn., 2d Aviation Regiment, 2d Infantry Divsn., Republic of Korea; battery fire direction control officer, battery exec. officer 1-15th Field Artillery, Ft. Carson; flight platoon leader, ops. officer 62d Aviation Co., Germany; co. comdr., brigade exec. officer 4th Aviation Brigade, Ft. Lewis, Wash.; plans officer U.S. Space Command; brigade exec. officer 4th Aviation Brigade, 4th Infantry Divsn., Ft. Carson; dep. chief of staff for ops. Army Space Command; chief current ops. divsn. Hqrs. U.S. Space Command, Peterson AFB, Colo.; comdr. Army Space Forces U.S. Army Space and Missile Def. Command, Colorado Springs, Colo., 2001—. Decorated Army Meritorious medal with 3 oak leaf clusters, Army Commendation medal with 1 oak leaf cluster, Army Achievement medal with 1 oak leaf cluster. Office: HQ US Army Space Command 350 Vandenberg St Colorado Springs CO 80914-4999

PARULEKAR, MARC SAMIR, music educator; b. Cleve., Apr. 14, 1976; s. Suhas and Billie Jean Parulekar; m. Tracie Carter, June 22, 2002. MusB in Edn., Ohio State U., 1999. Teaching Cert. Ohio State Bd. Edn., 1999. Dir. bands West Jefferson H.S., West Jefferson, Ohio, 1999—2000; dir. band Pickerington (Ohio) H.S., 2003—, Pickerington (Ohio) H.S. North, 2003—. (pickerington h.s. symphonic band) OMEA State Band & District 15 Band Contest (Superior Rating (1), 2001); musical arranger (marching band arrangement) Give it One (By Maynard Ferguson/Arr. Parulekar) (2nd Pl. Richard Heine Arranging Contest (Performed by The Ohio State U. Marching Band), 1997), (marching routine for pickerington h.s.) MACY*S Thanksgiving Day Parade (NYC) (Honor Band (1st Band Unit in Parade), 2001); dir., dir., dir.: OMEA District 15 Band Contest, (Superior Rating (1), 2002). Recipient Eagle Scout, Boy Scouts Am., 1992; Alumni Scholarship, Script Ohio Club, 1997—98. Mem.: Music Educators Nat. Conf., Ohio Music Edn. Assn., Kappa Kappa Psi, Phi Mu Alpha (life; pres. 1997—99). Avocations: ohio state football, travel, music. Office: Pickerington High School North 7880 Refugee Rd Pickerington OH 43147 Home: 9338 Harness Pl Pickerington OH 43147-8386 Personal E-mail: mparulekar@email.com.

PARVIAINEN, SILVE KATARIINA, marketing executive; b. Helsinki, Finland, Aug. 22, 1965; arrived in U.S., 1995; d. Kari Olavi and Tiia Katriina Parviainen; m. Juha Ilmari Seppälä, Sept. 10, 1993; 1 child, Johanna Katariina Seppälä. M in Social Sci., U. Helsinki, 1993, Licentiate of Social Scis., 1997. Trainee Finnish Internat. Devel. Agy., Helsinki, 1989—89, attache, 1991—92; trainee Assn. Internat. des Etudiants en Scis. Economiques et Commerciales, Nat. Devel. Bank, Ltd., Freetown, Sierra Leone, 1990—90; project economist Labour Inst. for Econs. Rsch., Helsinki, 1995—96; rsch. asst. U. Chgo., 1996—97; vis. scholar Kellogg Grad. Sch. Bus., Northwestern U., Evanston, Ill., 1997—98; sr. mktg. analyst Infoworks, Chgo., 1999—2000, mktg. cons., 2000—01; product mgr. Wolfram Rsch., Inc., Champaign, Ill., 2001—03; econ. lectr. U. Ill., Urbana Champaign, 2003—. Contbr. articles to profl. jours. Vice-chmn. Assn. Internat. des Etudiants en Scis. Economiques et Commerciales, U. Helsinki, 1987—88; chmn. Orgn. Econs. Students, Helsinki, 1987—88, vice-chmn., 1986—87. Scholar, Yrjö Jahnsson Found., 1993, 1994, 1997, Finnish Cultural Found., 1995.

PARZIALE, JOHN R. physiatrist; b. N.Y.C., Mar. 3, 1957; m. Mary Frates Parziale. BSc, Brown U., 1979; MD, U. Conn., 1983. Diplomate Am. Bd. Phys. Medicine and Rehab., 1987. Resident, physician Tufts NE Med. Ctr., Boston, 1983—86; chief physiatrist R.I. Hosp., Providence, 1986—93, Univ. Rehab., East Providence, RI, 1997—. Clin. assoc. prof. Brown U., Providence, 1986—. Contbr. articles to profl. jours. Mem.: Assn. Acad. Physiatrists (bd. dirs.), Am. Acad. Phys. Medicine and Rehab. Achievements include patents in field. Office: Univ Rehab Inc 450 Veterans Meml Pkwy East Providence RI 02914 Office Phone: 401-435-2288.

PASACHOFF, JAY MYRON, astronomer, educator; b. NYC, July 1, 1943; s. Samuel S. and Anne (Traub) P.; m. Naomi Schwartz, Mar. 31, 1974; children: Eloise Hilary, Deborah Donna. AB, Harvard U., 1963, AM (NSF fellow), 1965, PhD (NSF fellow, N.Y. State Regents fellow for advanced grad. study), 1969. Rsch. physicist Air Force Cambridge Rsch. Labs., Bedford, Mass., 1968-69; Menzel rsch. fellow Harvard Coll. Obs., Cambridge, Mass., 1969-70; rsch. fellow Hale Obs., Carnegie Instn., Washington, and Calif. Inst. Tech., Pasadena, 1970-72; from asst. prof., dir. Hopkins Obs. to prof. Williams Coll., Williamstown, Mass., 1972—84, Field Meml. prof. of astronomy, 1984—, chmn. astronomy dept., 1972—77, 1991—92, 1997—2001, 2004—. Adj. asst. prof. astronomy U. Mass., Amherst, 1975-77, adj. assoc. prof., 1977-83, adj. prof., 1986-90; vis. colleague and vis. assoc. prof. astronomy Inst. for Astronomy, U. Hawaii, 1980-81; vis. scientist Inst. d'Astrophysique, Paris, 1988; mem. Inst. Advanced Study, Princeton, 1989-90, Harvard-Smithsonian Ctr. for Astrophysics, 1993-94, 2001-02; total and other solar eclipse expdn. leader numerous locations; guest investigator NASA, 1975-79, 1999-2000, 2004—; lectr. in field. Author: Contemporary Astronomy, 1977, 4th edit., 1989, Astronomy Now, 1978, Astronomy: From Earth to the Universe, 1979, 6th edit., 2002, A Brief View of Astronomy, 1986, First Guide to Astronomy, 1988, First Guide to the Solar System, 1990, Journey Through the Universe, 1992; co-author: (with Marc L. Kutner, Naomi Pasachoff) Student Study Guide to Contemporary Astronomy, 1977, (with Kutner, Pasachoff and N.P. Kutner) Student Study Guide to Astronomy Now, 1978; (with M.L. Kutner) University Astronomy, 1978, Invitation to Physics, 1981; (with N. Pasachoff, T. Cooney) Physical Science, 1983, 2d edit., 1990, Earth Science, 1983, 2d edit., 1990; (with D.H. Menzel) A Field Guide to the Stars and Planets, 4th edit., 2000; (with R. Wolfson) Physics, 1987, 3rd edit., 1999 (Extended with Modern Physics, 1989, 3rd edit. 1999), (with N. Pasachoff, R.W. Clark, M.H. Westermann) Physical Science Today, 1987; (with N. Pasachoff and others) Discover Science, 7 vols., 1989; (with Michael Covington) Cambridge Eclipse Photography Guide, 1993; (with Leon Holder and James DeFranza) Calculus, 1994, Single Variable Calculus, 1994, Multivariable Calculus, 1995; (with Edward Cheng, Patrick Osmer and Hyron Spinrad) The Farthest Things in the Universe, 1994; editor (with J. Percy) The Teaching of Astronomy, 1990, (with Leon Golub) The Solar Corona, 1997, rev. edit., 1998, (with Roberta J. M. Olson) Fire in the Sky: Comets and Meteors, the Decisive Centuries, 1998, rev. edit., 1999, Science Explorer: Astronomy, 1998, rev. edit., 2004, Sound and Light, 1999, (with J. Percy) Effective Teaching and Learning of Astronomy, 2004; (with Alex Filippenko) The Cosmos: Astronomy at the New Millennium, 2000, 2d edit., 2003, The Complete Idiot's Guide to the Sun, 2003; assoc. editor: Jour. Irreproducible Results, 1972-94, Annals of Improbable Rsch., 1994—; abstractor from Am. jours. for Solar Physics, 1968-78; cons. editor McGraw-Hill Ency. Sci. and Tech., 1983—; co-editor-in-chief (with S.P. Parker), McGraw-Hill Ency. of Astronomy, 1993; cons. Random House Dictionary, 1983-86, Nat. Geographic Atlas, 5th edit., 1981, 6th edit., 1990; phys. sci. com. World Book Ency., 1989-95, cons., 1996—; contbr. articles to profl. jours. Recipient bronze medal Nikon Photo Contest Internat., 1971, photograph aboard NASA Voyagers, 1977, Dudley award Dudley Obs., 1985; grantee NSF, 1973-75, 79-83, 88—2002, Nat. Geog. Soc., 1973-86, 91—2001, 2004—, Rsch. Corp., 1973-78, 82-88, 2001, Getty Found., 1994-95, NASA, 1999-2000, 2004—. Fellow AAAS (chair sect. D 1987-88, 97-98), Royal Astron. Soc., Am. Phys. Soc. (mem.-at-large thrs. forum edn. 1995-98), Internat. Planetarium Soc.; mem. AAUP (chpt. pres. 1977-80), Internat. Astron. Union (U.S. nat. rep. Commn. tchg. astronomy 1976-2000, chair eclipse working group 1991—, rep. com. tchg. sci. internat. coun. sci. unions 1991-93, v.p. com. on edn. and devel. 2000-2003, pres. 2003—, US nat. liaison commn. on edn. and devel., 2000—), Am. Astron. Soc. (astronomy edn. adv. bd. 1990-97, astronomy news com. 1991-96, rep. 2004—, Edn. prize 2003), Astron. Soc. Pacific, Union Radio Sci., Am. Assn. Physics Tchrs. (astronomy com. 1983-87), Sigma Xi (chpt. pres. 1973-74, 95—, nat. lectr. 1993-97), Phi Beta Kappa. Home: 111 Park Street Williamstown MA 01267-2116 Office: Williams Coll Hopkins Obs 33 Lab Campus Dr Williamstown MA 01267-2565 E-mail: jay.m.pasachoff@williams.edu.

PASAHOW, LYNN H(AROLD), lawyer; b. Ft. Eutiss, Va., Mar. 13, 1947; s. Samuel and Cecelia (Newman) P.; m. Leslie Aileen Cobb, June 11, 1969; 1 child, Michael Alexander. AB, Stanford U., 1969; JD, U. Calif., Berkeley, 1972. Bar: Calif. 1972, U.S. Ct. Appeals (9th cir.) 1972, U.S. Dist. Ct. (no. dist.) Calif. 1973, U.S. Dist. Ct. (ctrl. dist.) Calif. 1974, U.S. Supreme Ct. 1976, U.S. Dist. Ct. (ea. dist.) Calif. 1977, U.S. Ct. Appeals (fed. cir.) 1990. Law clk. judge U.S. Dist. Ct. (no. dist.) Calif., San Francisco, 1972-73; with McCutchen, Doyle, Brown & Enersen, Palo Alto, Calif., 1973—2001; ptnr. Fenwick & West LLP, 2001—. Bd. dirs. Bay Area Biosci. Ctr., 2002—, Boalt Hall Alumni Assn., 2003—; mem. adv. bd. Berkeley Ctr. for Law and Tech., 1998—. Author: Pretrial and Settlement Conferences in Federal Court, 1983; co-author: Civil Discovery and Mandatory Disclosure: A Guide to Effective Practice, 1994; contbr. articles to profl. jours. Mem. ABA, Calif. Bar Assn., Boalt Hall Alumni Assn. (bd. dirs. 2003-). Democrat. Office: Fenwick & West LLP Silicon Valley Ctr 801 California St Mountain View CA 94041 Office Phone: 650-335-7225. Business E-Mail: lpasahow@fenwick.com. *Notable cases include: Amazon.com v. BarnesandNoble.com, duPont vs. Cetus, PCR patent litigation, Elan Pharmaceutical transgenic mouse litigation, Omega Zip Disk litigation, nicotine patch patent litigation, University of California & Vysis v. Oncor FISH litigation.*

PASCAL, AMY, film company executive; b. 1958; BA, U. of Calif., Los Angeles. V.p. of prod. Fox, 1986—87, Columbia, 1987—89, exec. v.p. of prod., 1989—94; pres. of prod. Turner Pictures, 1994—96; pres. Columbia Pictures, Culver City, Calif., 1996-99, chmn., 1999—; vice chmn. Sony Pictures Entertainment, 2002—. Bd. trustees Rand Corp. Office: Columbia Pictures 10202 Washington Blvd Culver City CA 90232-3119*

PASCAL, C(ECIL) BENNETT, classics educator; b. Chgo., May 4, 1926; s. Jack and Goldie (Zeff) P.; m. Ilene Joy Shulman, Feb. 1, 1959; 1 child, Keith Irwin. BA, UCLA, 1949, MA, 1950, Harvard U., 1953, PhD, 1956. Instr. U. Ill., Champaign, 1955-56, Cornell U., Ithaca, N.Y., 1957-60; asst. prof., then assoc. prof. U. Oreg., Eugene, 1960-75, prof. classics, 1975-96, prof. emeritus, 1996—, head dept., various years - 1965-85. Author: Cults of Cisalpine Gaul, 1964; contbr. articles to profl. jours. Active Eugene Bicycle Com., 1971-83. Wwith USN, 1944-46. Traveling fellow, Italy, Harvard U., 1956-57, Fulbright-Hays fellow, Rome, 1967-68. Mem. Am. Philol. Assn., Classical Assn. Pacific N.W. (pres. 1965-66), AAUP, Archeol. Inst. of Am. (past pres., sec. Eugene Soc.) Democrat. Jewish. Avocations: skiing, fly fishing, novel writing. Home: 330 Fulvue Dr Eugene OR 97405-2788 Office: U Oreg Dept Classics Eugene OR 97403 E-mail: cbpasc@darkwing.uoregon.edu.

PASCAL, MARK S. oncologist; b. Newark, 1947; B, Muhlenberg Coll.; MD cum laude, Thomas Jefferson Med. Coll., 1973. Diplomate Am. Bd. Internal Medicine, Am. Bd. Med. Oncology. Intern Cornell U. Med. Ctr., N.Y.C., 1973—74, resident/chief resident in pathology, 1974—76, resident in internal medicine, 1976—77; fellow in med. oncology and hematology Meml. Sloan-Kettering Cancer Ctr., N.Y.C., 1977—79; attending physician Holy Name Hosp., Teaneck, NJ, chief med. oncology/hematology; dir. adult inpatient oncology unit Hackensack (N.J.) Med. Ctr. Adj. attending physician Meml. Sloan-Kettering Cancer Ctr., 1970—; clin. asst. prof. hematology and med. oncology N.Y. Med. Coll. Named one of Top Drs. in N.Y. Metro Area, Castle Connolly, Top Drs. 2003, N.J. Monthly Mag. Mem.: ACP, Am. Soc. Internal Medicine, Oncology Soc. N.J. (exec. com.), Am. Soc. Clin. Oncology. Office: Hackensack U Med Ctr 20 Prospect Ave Ste 400 Hackensack NJ 07601-1962

PASCAL, ROGER, lawyer; b. Chgo., Mar. 16, 1941; s. Samuel A. and Harriet E. (Hartman) P.; m. Martha Hecht, June 16, 1963; children: Deborah, Diane, David AB with distinction, U. Mich, 1962; JD cum laude, Harvard U., 1965. Bar: Ill. 1965, U.S. Dist. Ct. (no. dist.) Ill. 1965, U.S. Ct. Appeals (7th cir.) 1969, U.S. Supreme Ct. 1976, Wis. 1985, U.S. Ct. Appeals (2d, 6th, 9th and 10th cirs.) 186. Assoc. Schiff Hardin LLP, Chgo., 1965-71, ptnr., 1972—. Adj. prof. law Northwestern U. Law Sch., 1994—. Bd. dirs., mem. exec. com. Chgo. Law Enforcement Study Group, 1975-80, pres., 1978-80; pres. Harvard Law Soc. Ill., 1976-78; bd. dirs. ACLU of Ill., 1984—, gen. counsel, 1986—. Recipient Roger Baldwin Lifetime Achiavement award, 2003. Fellow Am. Bar Found.; mem. ABA (antitrust, intellectual property, and litigation sects.),Pub. Interest Law Initiative (bd. dirs. 1989—, v.p. 1995-97, pres. 1997-98), Fund for Justice (v.p., bd. dirs. 1986-97), Chgo. Coun. Lawyers (bd. dirs. 1970-74, 80-84), Chgo. Legal Assistance Found. (bd. dirs. 1985-88), Chgo. Bar Found.(recipient Edward Lewis II Pro Bono Svc. award, 2003), Univ. Club, Met. Club, Phi Beta Kappa. Office: Schiff Hardin LLP 6600 Sears Tower Chicago IL 60606 Office Phone: 312-258-5663.

PASCALE, DANIEL RICHARD, lawyer; b. Racine, Wis., Mar. 22, 1940; s. Domenic and Fannie Colette (Julian) P.; m. Mary Sara McDonald, June 28, 1986; 1 child, Alexander. AB cum laude, Harvard U., 1962; JD, U. Chgo., 1965. Bar: Ill. 1966, U.S. Ct. Appeals (7th cir.) 1967, U.S. Dist. Ct. (no. dist.) Ill. 1969, U.S. Supreme Ct. 1972. Asst. corp. counsel City of Chgo., 1966-72, chief appellate atty., 1972-79, 1st dep. corp. counsel, 1979-84; assoc. Rudnick & Wolfe, Chgo., 1984-87, ptnr., 1987-90; judge Circuit Ct. of Cook County, Ill., 1990-94, 96-98; adminstrv. dir. Adminstrv. Office of Ill. Cts., Chgo., 1995-96; sr. corp. aty. Dean Foods Co., 1999—2002. Bd. dirs. DeKoven Found., Racine, 1986—, The Church Home/Montgomery Pl., 1998-; adv. bd. Art Resources in Teaching, Chgo., 1987-94; v.p. Episcopal Homes Mgmt., Inc., Milw., 1988-94. Mem. ABA, Fed. Bar Assn., Ill. Bar Assn., Chgo. Bar Assn., Justinian Soc., Union League Club Chgo., English-Speaking Union. Independent. Episcopalian.

PASCALE, JANE FAY, pathologist; b. New Haven, Conn., May 20, 1932; d. John Adam and Madeline J. (Pompano) P.; m. Joseph H. Kite Jr., Aug. 6, 1970. BA, Mount Holyoke Coll., 1954; MD, U. Chgo., 1959. Cert. anat. and clin. pathology Am. Bd. Pathology; diplomate Nat. Bd. Med. Examiners. Intern, resident in pathology Yale-New Haven Hosp., 1959-63; NIH-NCI spl. fellow dept. microbiology Yale U. Sch. Medicine, 1963-64; NIH-NCI spl. fellow Inst. de Recherches Scientifiques sur le Cancer, Villejuif, France, 1964-66; asst. in pathology Mass. Gen. Hosp. and Harvard Med. Sch., Boston, 1966-68; asst. prof. clin. pathology Yale U. Sch. Medicine, New Haven, 1968-69; attending pathologist Erie County Med. Ctr., Buffalo, N.Y., 1969-95; clin. asst. prof. pathology SUNY, Buffalo, 1969-90, clin. asst. prof. microbiology, 1991—. Mem. scientific adv. bd. Infectech, Inc., Sharon, Pa., 1995—; scientific del. Citizen Amb. Program People-to-People Internat. Contbr. articles to profl. jours. Recipient Physician's Recognition award AMA, 1981-99. Fellow Am. Soc. Clin. Pathologists, Coll. Am. Pathologists; mem. AMA, N.Y. Acad. Scis., Am. Soc. Cytopathology, Assn. Clin. Scientists. Methodist. Achievements include research in immunopathology of tuberculosis and autoimmune disease.

PASCARELLA, HENRY WILLIAM, lawyer; b. New Haven, Conn., Aug. 15, 1933; s. John Manlio and Mary (Iannotti) P.; m. Tessa Peruzzi, Jan. 28, 1967; children: Averardo, Leonora, Cassandra. BS in Econs., U. Pa., 1955; LLB, Yale U., 1958. Bar: Conn. 1958, U.S. Supreme Ct. 1963. Ptnr. Badger, Fisher, Cohen & Barnett and predecessors, Greenwich, Conn., 1959-73; sr. counsel to Taylor Cooper & Alcorn, Greenwich, Conn., 1978—. Pres., dir. The Timber Trails Corp. Sherman, Conn.; dir. Nine West Group, Inc., 1995-99. Author column, theater critic Greenwich Times, 1964-67. Dir. Planned Parenthood League of Conn., Greenwich coun. Boy Scouts Am., 1990-96. Served to lt. (j.g.) USCG, 1959. Me.m ABA, Greenwich Bar Assn. (pres. 1967), Conn. Bar Assn., Yale Club (N.Y.C.), Belle Haven Club (Greenwich). Home: 675 Steamboat Rd Greenwich CT 06830-7140 E-mail: henry@pascarellalaw.com.

PASCARELLA, PERRY JAMES, author, editor, speaker; b. Bradford, Pa., Apr. 11, 1934; s. James and Lucille Margaret (Monti) P.; m. Carol Ruth Taylor, May 4, 1957; children: Cynthia, Elizabeth. AB, Kenyon Coll., 1956; Coll. William and Mary, William and Mary Coll., 1957; postgrad., George Washington U., 1958. Credit reporter Dun & Bradstreet, Cleve., 1956, 60; from asst. editor to mng. editor Steel mag., Cleve., 1961-69; mng. editor Industry Week mag., Cleve., 1970-71, exec. editor, 1971-86, editor-in-chief, 1986-89; v.p. editorial Penton Pub. Inc., 1989-96. Lectr. in field. Author: Technology-Fire in a Dark World, 1979, Humanagement in the Future Corporation, 1981, The New Achievers, 1984, The Purpose-Driven Organization, 1989, The Ten Commandments of the Workplace, 1996, Leveraging People and Profit, 1998, Christ-Centered Leadership, 1999; co-author: Optimistic Outlooks, 1982, Creating a Global Agenda, 1984, Leadership in a New Era, 1994, The New Bottom Line, 1996. Lt. comdr. USNR, 1957-60. Recipient Disting. Service award Kenyon Coll., 1975, 81, Am. Bus. Press Crain award, 1992; Carnegie scholar, 1952-56 Mem. World Future Soc., U. Akron Inst. for Future Studies (bd. advisors). Presbyterian (elder). Home: 30413 Winsor Dr Cleveland OH 44140-1143

PASCH, ALAN, philosopher, educator; b. Cleve., Dec. 1, 1925; s. P. Jerome and Esther (Broverman) P.; m. Eleanor Kudlich Berna, Dec. 27, 1950; 1 child, Rachel. BA, U. Mich., 1949; MA, New Sch. Social Research, 1952; PhD, Princeton U., 1955; Bamford fellow, 1955-56. Instr. philosophy Ohio State U., 1956-59, asst. prof., 1959-60; assoc. prof. philosophy U. Md., College Park, 1960-67, prof., 1967-97, prof. emeritus, 1997—. Author: Experience and the Analytic, 1958; also articles, revs. Served with AUS, 1944-46, PTO. Mem. ACLU, Am. Philos. Assn. (exec. dir. 1969-72, sec.-treas. Eastern div. 1965-68), Metaphys. Soc. Am., Washington Philosophy Club (pres. 1978-79), Washington Rare Book Group. Office: Dept Philosophy Univ Md College Park MD 20742 Business E-Mail: ap3@umail.umd.edu.

PASCHALL, LEE MCQUERTER, retired communications consultant; b. Sterling, Colo., Jan. 21, 1922; s. Lee McQuerter and Agnes (Woldridge) P.; m. Bonnie Jean Edwards, Oct. 24, 1942; children: Patricia Ann Grillos, Stephen Lee, David Edward. BA, U. Ala., 1957; MA, George Washington U., 1964. Served with U.S. Army, 1940-46; communications engr. Colo. Air N.G., Denver, 1946-51; commd. maj. U.S. Air Force, 1951, advanced through grades to lt. gen., 1974, ret., 1978; ind. cons. Springfield, Va., 1978-81; pres., chief exec. officer Am. Satellite Co., Rockville, Md., 1981-84, chmn., 1984-85. Dir. Gen. Data Comm. Industries. Contbr. numerous articles to profl. publs. Mem. com. rev. nat. communications system initiatives NRC, 1982-88. Decorated Legion of Merit with oak leaf cluster; decorated disting. service medals; recipient Eascon IEEE, 1979 Mem. Armed Forces Comms.-Electronics Assn. (chpt. pres., nat. bd. dirs. Disting. Svc.), Air Force Assn., Phi Beta Kappa. Mem. Christian Ch. (Disciples Of Christ). Home and Office: 1513 Hampton Hills Cir Mc Lean VA 22101-6018

PASCHE, BORIS CLAUDE ROGER, physician; b. Lausanne, Vaud, Switzerland, Aug. 5, 1961; came to U.S., 1989; Rene Charles Edouard and Marina (Guidetti) P. MD, Karolinska Inst., Stockholm, 1986, U. Lausanne, Switzerland, 1987; PhD, Karolinska Inst., Stockholm, 1989. Cert. diplomate, Am. Bd. of Internal Med. 1994, diplomate, Am. Bd. of Medical Oncology 1997, diplomate, Am. Bd. of Hematology 1999, lic. New York State Med. Lic. 1995, Illinois Med. Lic. 2001. Clin. trial dir. Symtonic S.A., Renens, Switzerland, 1983-86, chief sci. officer, 1986—; pres. Symtonic U.S., N.Y.C., 1992-96; rsch. fellow in cardiovascular medicine Harvard Med. Sch., Boston, 1989-92; intern in medicine N.Y. Hosp. Meml. Sloan-Kettering Cancer Ctr., Cornell U. Med. Ctr., N.Y. C., 1992-93, resident in medicine N.Y. Hosp., N.Y.C., 1993-94; fellow in hematology-oncology Meml. Sloan-Kettering Cancer Ctr., N.Y.C., 1994—2000; att. phys. Northwestern Meml. Hosp., Chgo., 2001—; dir. Northwestern U. Cancer Genetics prog., 2002—. Asst. in medicine Clinique Bon Port, Montreux, Switzerland, 1988—2000; asst. physician Meml. Sloan-Kettering Cancer Ctr., Cornell U. Med. Ctr., N.Y.C., 1993—2000; asst. prof. med. Northwestern U., Feinberg Sch. of Med., 2000—. Inventor (with others): chimeric molecule with plaminogen activator activity and affinity for atherosclerotic plaques, method and system for applying low energy emission therapy; author: (books) Non-thrombogenic Properties of Artificial and Biological surfaces, Medecine Homeopathique Moderne; contbg. editor to Jour. Am. Med. Assn., contbr. articles to profl. jours. and chpt. to book. With Swiss Med. Corps., 1980. Recipient Swiss Academic Soc. fellowship, 1983, Lausanne Academic Soc. Rsch. fellowship, 1984-86, Swedish Bd. for Tech. Devel. Rsch. fellowship, 1986-89; Physician Scientist award Nat. Cancer Inst. Mem. AAAS, AMA, Nat. Inst. Electromed. Info., Bioelectromagenetics Soc., European Bioelectromagnetics Soc., Internat. Soc. on Thrombosis and Haemostasis (Young Scientist Merit award 1989, Young Investigator Merit award 1991) Am. Soc. Hematology, Am. Soc. Clinical Oncology, Am. Assn. Cancer Research, Am. Soc. Human Genetics, Am. Heart Assn. (clin. cardiology coun., arteriosclerosis coun.), Am. Fedn. for Clin. Rsch. (Trainee Investigator award 1992), Fellow of the Am. Coll. Physicians (assoc.), mem. Cancer Genetics Panel of the National Comprehensive Cancer Network. Avocations: skiing, windsurfing, classical music, fine arts. Home: 401 East Ontario Street, #4502 Chicago IL 60611 Office: Robert H Lurie Comprehensive Cancer Center Northwestern U Feinberg Sch of Med 676 N St Clair Street Suite 880 Chicago IL 60611

PASCHKE, JERRY BRYAN, lawyer; b. Palmdale, Calif., Aug. 6, 1965; s. Donald Joseph and Diana Marie (Scott) P. BS, St. John's U., Collegeville, Minn., 1988; JD, Hamline U., St. Paul, 1991. Bar: Minn. 1991, Army Ct. Mil. Rev. 1992, U.S. Magistrates Ct. 1993. Commd. 1st lt. U.S. Army, 1992, advanced through grades to capt., 1992; post judge advocate U.S. Army-Sierra Army Depot, Herlong, Calif., 1992-94; brigade trial counsel U.S. Army-Camp Stanley, Uijongbu, South Korea, 1994-95; legal instr. U.S. Army-Ft. Huachuca, Sierra Vista, Ariz., 1995-97, chief criminal law, 1997-98, mil. magistrate, 1995-97; acct. Accts.-On-Call, Mpls., 1998—; adminstrv. law officer USAR, Ft. Snelling, Minn., 1998—. Mem. landlord-tenant hotline Minn. Pub. Interest Rsch. Group, Mpls., 1989; advisor DeMolay, Reno, 1992-94. Decorated Army Commendtion medal, Meritorious Svc. medal. Mem. Masons, Order St. Barbara. Avocations: hiking, chess, travel, bowling. Home: 15 6th St SE Medford MN 55049-7000

PASCHOUD, FRANÇOIS, university educator; b. Jan. 11, 1938; s. Maurice Paschoud and Nelly (Suter) Pascound; m. Anne-Marie Chene, July 24, 1978; children: Jerôme, Ubain. Lic. Letters, U. Lausanne, Switzerland, 1960, LittD, 1967. Mem. Swiss Inst., Rome, 1962—64; Wissenschaftlicher Mitarbelter Thesaurus linguae Latinae, Munich, 1965—67; prof. extraordinarius, ordinarius U. Geneva, 1969—74, 1974—2004; vis. mem. Inst. for Advanced Study Princeton (NJ) U., 1976—77, 1983—84. Author: Roma aeterna, 1967; translator: Commentary of Zosimus I, 1971, II 1 and II 2, 1979, III 1, 1986, III 2, 1989, Historia Agusta V 1, 1996, V 2, 2001. Mem.: Groupe Romand des Etudes Grecques et Latines (pres. 1978—81), Fondation Hardt pour l'étude de l'antiquité Vandoeuvres Geneva (pres. 1996—2003), Soc. Latin Studies Paris, Internat. Fedn. of Socs. of Classical Studies (sec. gen. 1974—2004), Real Academia Barcelona (corr.). E-mail: zosime@bluewin.ch.

PASCIUTO, JOSEPH DORIA, priest; b. Bklyn., N.Y., June 27, 1945; s. Carmine Michael Pasciuto, Rose Marie (Doria) Pasciuto. BA, St. John's U., 1968, MBA, 1981; MDiv, Immaculate Conception Sem., Huntington, N.Y.,

1991; MA in Theology, Immaculate Conception Sem., 1999; theol. studies, Pontifical N.Am. Coll., Vatican City, 2003. Ordination Roman Cath. Diocese Bklyn., 1991. CFO Local 371 AFSCME, N.Y.C., 1981—84; mgr. pers./labor rels Child Welfare Adminstrn., N.Y.C., 1984—87; vicar Our Lady Help of Christians, Bklyn., 1991—99, Our Lady of Hope, Queens, NY, 1999—2000, St. Brendan, Bklyn., 2000—03; adminstr. Holy Cross Roman Cath. Ch., Bklyn., 2003—. Chaplain Boy Scouts Am., Bklyn., 2000—, Internat. Firefighters Assn., N.Y.C., 2001. Mem.: KC (chaplain 1995—, 4th degree L.I. Assembly 2001), Montauk Club. Democrat. Avocations: music, reading, cooking. Home: 106 Petrus Ave Staten Island NY 10312 Office: Holy Cross Roman Cath Ch 2530 Church Ave Brooklyn NY 11226

PASCO, ALLAN HUMPHREY, literature educator; s. Ray Edwin and Bernedine May (Humphrey) P.; m. Dallas Marlene Christiansen, Dec. 29, 1960; children: Schuyler, Teague, Brandt, Chandar. BA, Whitman Coll., Walla Walla, Wash., 1960; MA, Northwestern U., 1961; PhD, U. Mich., 1968. Asst. prof. French U. Chgo., 1967-73; assoc. prof. French Purdue U., West Lafayette, Ind., 1973-79, prof. French, 1979-89; Hall disting. prof. 19th century lit. U. Kans., Lawrence, 1989—. Vis. prof. French UCLA, 1979; editorial bd. Purdue U. Press, 1975-78. Author: The Color Keys, 1976, Novel Configurations, 1987, 2d edit., 1994, Balzacian Montage, 1991, Allusion: A Lit. Graft, 1994, reprinted, 2002, Sick Heroes: French Society and Lit. in the Romantic Age, 1997; editor: Purdue U. Monographs, 1977-87, Summa, 1990—, French Rev., 1989—, Nineteenth-Century French Studies, 1995—, EMF: Studies in Early Modern France, Lingua Romana; co-editor: The Play of Terror in 19th Century France, 1996; contbr. articles to profl. jour. With US Army, 1961-63. Recipient Cramer Teaching award, U. Kans., 1996, 1999, 2000, 2001, 2002; Chancellor's Outstanding Mentor award, 2004; Ctr. for Humanistic Studies fellow Purdue U., 1985, Lilly Libr. summer rsch. fellow, 1976, various rsch. fellow, 1969-88, Hall Ctr. Humanities fellow, U. Kans., 1996. Mem. MLA, Assn. Am. Tchr. of French, Am. Soc. 18th Century Studies, Phi Sigma Iota, Phi Kappa Phi. Lutheran. Office: 1445 Jayhawk Blvd 2053 Lawrence KS 66044-7590 E-mail: apasco@ku.edu.

PASCOE, DONALD MONTE, lawyer; b. Jan. 4, 1935; s. Donald Leslie and Marjorie Lucille (Powers) Pascoe; m. Patricia Hill, Aug. 3, 1957; children: Sarah Lynn, Edward Llewellyn, William Arthur. AB, Dartmouth Coll., 1957; LLB, Stanford U., 1960. Bar: Colo. 1960, Calif. 1961. From assoc. to ptnr. and officer Ireland, Stapleton, Pryor & Pascoe, P.C., Denver, 1960—, also bd. dirs. Exec. dir. Colo. Dept. of Natural Resources, Denver, 1980—83; bd. dirs. G.G. Shaw, Inc. Trustee Webb-Waring Lung Inst., Denver, 1985—91, pres.; commr. Denver Water Bd., 1983—95, pres., 1986—89; chmn. Moffat Tunnel Commn., 1996—98; mem. Rocky Mountain Regional Ctr. Inst. Internat. Edn., 1995—, trustee, 1998—2001, Legal Aid Found. Colo., 2003—, Colo. Sch. Mines, Golden, 1979—81, Iliff Sch. Theology, 2002—. Mem.: ABA, Am. Judicature Soc., Calif. Bar Assn., Colo. Bar Assn., Cactus Club, Law Club Denver, Rotary. Home: 744 Lafayette St Denver CO 80218-3503 Office: Ireland Stapleton Pryor & Pascoe PC 1675 Broadway Suite 2600 Denver CO 80202 Office Phone: 302-623-2700.

PASCOE, PATRICIA HILL, former state legislator; b. Sparta, Wis., June 1, 1935; d. Fred Kirk and Edith (Kilpatrick) Hill; m. D. Monte Pascoe, Aug. 3, 1957; children: Sarah, Edward, William. BA, U. Colo., 1957; MA, U. Denver, 1968, PhD, 1982. Tchr. Sequoia Union H.S. Dist., Redwood City, Calif. and Hayward (Calif.) Union H.S. Dist., 1957-60; instr. Met. State Coll., Denver, 1969-75, Denver U., 1975-77, 81, rsch. asst. bur. ednl. rsch., 1981-82; tchr. Kent Denver Country Day Sch., Englewood, Colo., 1982-84; freelance writer Denver, 1985—; mem. Colo. Senate, Dist. 32, Denver, 1989—93, Colo. Senate, Dist. 34, Denver, 1995—2003; chair minority caucus Colo. Senate, Denver, 1996-2000, chair policy and planning com., 2001, chair edn. com., 2002. Commr. Edn. Commn. of the States, Denver, 1975-82, 2001—. Contbr. articles to numerous publs. and jours. Bd. dirs. Samaritan House, 1990-94, Cystic Fibrosis Found., 1989-93, ACLU of Colo., 2003—; pres. East H.S. Parent Tchr. and Student Assn., Denver, 1984-85; mem. Moore Budget Adv. Com., Denver, 1966-72; legis. chmn. alumni bd. U. Colo., Boulder, 1987-89; del. Dem. Nat. Conv., San Francisco, 1984, N.Y.C., 1992; mem. Denver Woman's Press Club, 1986—, Colo. Arts Coalition, 1988-97, Conflict Ctr. Bd.; bd. dirs. Opera Colo., 1996-2002, ACLU Colo. Mem. Soc. Profl. Journalists, Common Cause (bd. dirs. Denver chpt. 1986-88), Lions Club (dir. 2003—), Phi Beta Kappa. Democrat. Presbyterian.

PASCRELL, WILLIAM J., JR., congressman; b. Paterson, N.J., Jan. 25, 1937; s. William J. Sr. and Roffie (Loffredo) P., m. Elsie Marie Botto; children: William III, David, Glenn. BS, Fordham U., 1959; MA, Montclair State Coll., 1961; postgrad., Fairleigh Dickinson U. Tchr. Jr. High Sch., Clifton, N.J., 1962, Paramus (N.J.) High Sch., 1962-74; adult sch. tchr. Dwight Morrow High Sch., Englewood, N.J., 1969-70; prof. Fairleigh Dickinson U., Madison, N.J., 1963-68; dir. Dept. Pub. Works City of Paterson, 1974-77, dir. Dept. Policy Planning and Mgmt., 1977-87; mem. N.J. Gen. Assembly, 1988-97, chmn. higher edn. com., 1988-97, vice chmn. edn. com., 1988-97, mem. appropriations com., 1988-97; mayor City of Paterson, 1990-97; mem. U.S. Congress from 8th N.J. dist., 1997—; mem. small bus. com., transp. and infrastructure com., homeland sec. com. Pres. Paterson Bd. Edn., 1979-82; campaign coord. Robert A. Roe for Gov., N.J., 1977; regional coord. James Florio for Gov., Hudson County, N.J., 1981; active County Chairmen for Sen. Frank Lautenberg, N.J., 1982—; chmn. Passaic County Democrats, N.J., 1982—. With U.S. Army, 1961-67. Named Man of Yr., Mother Cabrini Soc., 1978, Am. Legion (John Road Post), 1983, St. Gerard's Parish, 1988, Assn. Retarded Citizens, 1991. Mem. N.J. Math. Coalition (bd. govs. 1991—), UNICO (Paterson chpt. Man of Yr., 1981), Italian Sport Club. Democrat. Roman Catholic. Office: US Ho of Reps 1722 Longworth House Office Bldg Washington DC 20515-0001

PASCU, DAN, astronomer; b. Arad, Romania, July 20, 1938; came to U.S., 1941; s. Danila and Maria (Pojar) P.; m. Julia Fay Stephens, Aug. 28, 1965; children: David, Mark, Adam. BS in Astronomy, Case Western Res. U., 1961, MS in Astronomy, 1964; PhD in Astronomy, U. Va., Charlottesville, 1972. Astronomer U.S. Naval Obs., Washington, 1963—. Specialist in planetary satellite studies and solar sys. astrometry. Contbr. rsch. and rev. articles to profl. jours. Recipient NASA Group Achievement award, 1981, 86, Inaugural Newcomb award U.S. Naval Obs., 1983. Mem. Internat. Astron. Union, Am. Astron. Soc., Sigma Xi. Baptist. Achievements include developing techniques for astrometric observation of the planetary satellites; co-discoverer 14th moon of Saturn, Calypso, and recovered 10th moon of Saturn, Janus, 1980. Office: US Naval Obs 3450 Massachusetts Ave NW Washington DC 20392-5420 Office Phone: 202-762-1490. Business E-Mail: pascu.dau@usno.navy.mil.

PASCUAL, CARLOS, marketing professional; b. Malaga, Spain, Nov. 10, 1945; MSEE, U. Madrid, 1968. Mktg. specialist to gen. mgr. Xerox, Spain, 1968-83; dir. Office Systems Divsn. Rank Xerox, London, 1983-86; v.p., gen. mgr. regional opers. Xerox, Stamford, Conn., 1986-91; mng. dir. Rank Xerox, France, 1991-93; pres., gen. mgr. Americas Customer Opers. Xerox, 1995-98; dep. exec. officer Industry Solutions Opers. Xerox Corp., Stamford, Conn., 1998-99, exec. v.p., pres. developing markets opers., 1999—. Bd. dirs. Columbus McKinnon, U.S. C. of C. Office: Xerox Corp 800 Long Ridge Rd Stamford CT 06902-1227

PASCUAL, CARLOS, ambassador; BA in Internat. Rels., Stanford U., 1980; MA in Pub. Policy, Harvard U., 1982. With USAID, South Africa, Mozambique, Washington, project devel. officer, 1983—92, dir., Office of Program Analysis and Coordinatoin for New Ind. States Task Force, 1994—94, dep. asst. adminstr. for Europe and New Ind. States, 1994—95; dir. for Russian, Ukrainian and Eurasian Affairs Nat. Security Coun., 1995—98, spl. asst. to Pres., sr. dir. for Russia, 1998—2000; U.S. amb. to Ukraine, 2000—03; coordinator for U.S. assistance to Europe and Eurasia U.S. Dept. State, 2003—. Office: Dept State Bureau European Eurasian Affairs 2201 C Street NW Washington DC 20520

PASETTI, LOUIS OSCAR, retired dentist; b. Tampa, Fla., Dec. 27, 1916; s. Joseph G. and Carmen (Gonzalez) P.; m. Mary Mendez, Jan. 11, 1942; children: Louis M., Arleen Pasetti Mariotti. BS, U. Fla., 1937; DDS, Emory U., 1941; postgrad., U. Pa., 1978. Capt. U.S. Army, 1942—46; dentist pvt. practice Tampa, Fla., 1947—2002; ret., 2002. Past. pres. Tampa Civitan Club, 1953; past lt. gov. Civitan Clubs of Tampa, 1962; past dep. gov. Civitan Internat., Tampa, 1964; fin. officer Am. Legion Post 248. Named Fla. Dentist of the Yr., Fla. Acad. Gen. Dentistry, 1983; recipient meritorious Svc. award Fla. Acad. Gen. Dentistry, 1989, Disting. Svc. award, 1985. Fellow Acad. Gen. Dentistry (emeritus 2002), Am. Coll. Dentists, Internat. Coll. Dentists, Acad. Dentistry Internat.; mem. ADA, Fla. Dental Assn., Fla. Acad. Gen. Dentistry (pres. 1981, Lifetime Achievement award 1996, mem. emeritus 2002), Tampa Bay Acad. Gen. Dentistry (pres. 1977-78), Elks, Round Table of Civic Clubs of Tampa (sec. 1953), Palma Ceia Golf and Country Club. Democrat. Roman Catholic. Avocations: photography, orchid culture. Home: 10023 Hampton Pl Tampa FL 33618-4227

PASHGIAN, MARGARET HELEN, artist; b. Pasadena, Calif., Nov. 7, 1934; d. Aram John and Margaret (Howell) P. BA, Pomona Coll., 1956; MA in Fine Arts, Boston Univ., 1958; student, Columbia U., 1957. Art instr. Harvard-Newton Program Occidental Coll., 1977-78; artist in residence Calif. Inst. Tech., 1970-71. Grants panelist Calif. Arts Coun., Sacramento, 1993. Artist: solo shows include Rex Evans Gallery, L.A., 1965, 67, Occidental Coll., 1967, Kornblee Gallery, N.Y.C., 1969-72, U. Calif., Irvine, 1975, U. Calif. Santa Barbara, 1976, Stella Polaries Gallery, L.A., 1981, 82, Kaufman Galleries, Houston, 1982, Modernism Gallery, San Francisco, 1983, Works Gallery, Long Beach, Costa Mesa, Calif., 1986, 87, 88, 89, 90, 91, 92, Malka Gallery, L.A., 1997; group exhibitions include Pasadena Art Mus., 1965, Carson Pirie Scott, Chgo., 1965, Calif. Palace of Legion of Honor, San Francisco, 1967, Esther Bear Gallery, Santa Barbara, 1967, 69, Lytton Ctr. of the Visual Arts, L.A., 1968, Salt Lake Art Inst., Salt Lake City, 1968, Mus. Contemporary Crafts, Internat. Plastics Exhibition, 1969, Second Flint (Mich.) Invitational, 1969, Milw. Art Ctr., 1969, U.S.I.S. Mus., N.Y.C., Mus. Contemporary Art, Chgo., 1970, Studio Merconi, Milan, 1970, Calif. Inst. Tech., Baxter Art Galley, 1971, 1980, Calif. Innovations, Palm Springs Dessert Mus., 1981, Calif. Internat. Arts Found. Mus. of Modern Art, Paris, 1982, L.A. Artists in Seoul, Donsangbang Gallery, 1982, An Artistic Conversation, 1931-82, Poland, USA, Ulster Mus., Belfast, Ireland, 1983, Madison (Wis.) Art Ctr., 1994, Calif. State U., Fullerton, 1995, Oakland (Calif.) Mus., 1995, Molly Barnes Gallery, LA, Calif., 2000, Pasadena (Calif.) Mus. Calif. Art, 2002; represented in pub. collections at River Forest (Ill.) State Bank, Atlantic Richfield Co., Dallas, Frederic Weisman Collection, L.A., Security Pacific Bank, L.A., Singapore, Andrew Dickson White Mus. of Art, Cornell U., Ithaca, N.Y., L.A. County Mus. of Art, Santa Barbara Art Mus., Laguna Beach Mus. of Art, Portland (Oreg.) Art Mus. Trustee, Pomona Coll, Claremont, Calif., 1987—; parade judge Tournament of Roses Centennial Parade, Pasadena, 1987; bd. dirs. L.A. Master Chorale, 1992—. NEA grantee, 1986. Home: 731 S Grand Ave Pasadena CA 91105-2424

PASHLER, HAROLD E. psychologist, educator; AB in Logic and Philosophy of Sci., ScB in Psychology magna cum laude, Brown U., 1980; PhD in Psychology, U. Pa., 1985. Asst. prof. dept. psycholgoy U. Calif., San Diego, 1985-90, assoc. prof., 1990-93, prof. dept. psychology, 1993—. Mem. various coms. U. Calif. San Diego; ad hoc reviewer Hong Kong Rsch. Coun., Natural Sci. and Engring. Rsch. Coun., Can., NSF, Behavioral and Neural Scis., USAF Office Sci. Rsch. Life Scis. Program. Assoc. editor Psychonomic Bull. and Rev., 1998—; mem. editl. bd. Perception & Psychophysics, 1988—, Psychol. Rsch., 1989—, Cognitive Psychology, 1992-98, Visual Cognition, 1994—, Psychonomic Bull. and Rev., 1994-97, Am. Jour. Psychology, 1998—; ad hoc reviewer Am. Jour. Psychology, Attention and Performance XII, XIV, Cognition, Cognitive Psychology, Cognitive Sci., Current Directions in Psychol. Sci., Ency. Human Biology, Exptl. Brain Rsch., Jour. Exptl. Psychology: Human Perception and Performance, Jour. Exptl. Psychology: Learning, Memory and Cognition, Memory and Cognition, Nature, Nature Neurosci., Perception, Perception & Psychophysics, Psychol. Rsch., Psychol. Rev., Quarterly Jour. Exptl. Psychology, Spatial Vision, Vision Rsch. Recipient Troland Rsch. award NAS, 1999; NSF grad. fellow, 1981-84, IBM grad. fellow, 1984-85. Fellow Am. Psychol. Soc.; mem. Phi Beta Kappa, Sigma Xi. Office: Dept Psychology 0109 U Calif San Diego La Jolla CA 92093 E-mail: hpashler@ucsd.edu.

PASHMAN, SUSAN ELLEN, writer; b. NYC, Dec. 17, 1942; d. Jonas Charles and Pearl (Steinberg) Greenfield; m. Louis Jonathan Pashman, Sept. 17, 1964 (div. Feb. 1978); children: Joshua, Benjamin. BA, NYU, 1963; JD, Bklyn. Law Sch., 1982. Bar: NY 1983. Tch. fgn. langs. N.Y.C. Pub. Schs., 1963-65; instr. philosophy Adelphi U., Garden City, N.Y., 1965-77; dir. humanities project N.Y. Coun. Humanities, N.Y.C., 1977-79; dean coll. rels. Douglass Coll., New Brunswick, N.J., 1978-79; assoc. atty. Proskauer, Rose, Goetz & Mendelsohn, N.Y.C., 1982-84, Moses & Singer, N.Y.C., 1984-86, Cravath, Swaine & Moore, N.Y.C., 1986-91; freelance writer Sag Harbor, NY, 1991—. Program dir. Pub. Access Continuing Edn., Sag Harbor, 1991—; lectr. philosophy Jewish Ctr. of the Hamptons. Author: The Speed of Light, 1997. Active Jewish Ctr. of the Hamptons. Jewish. Avocations: gardening, cooking, tennis. Home: PO Box 2530 Sag Harbor NY 11963-0116

PASICH, KIRK ALAN, lawyer; b. La Jolla, Calif., May 26, 1955; s. Chris Nick and Iva Mae (Tormey) P.; m. Pamela Mary Woods, July 30, 1983; children: Christopher Thomas, Kelly Elizabeth, Connor Woods. BA in Polit. Sci., UCLA, 1977; JD, Loyola Law Sch., L.A., 1980. Bar: Calif. 1980, U.S. Dist. Ct. (no., so., ea. and cen. dists.) Calif. 1981, U.S. Ct. Appeals (9th cir.) 1982, U.S. Ct. Appeals (1st cir.) 1992. Assoc. Paul, Hastings, Janofsky & Walker, L.A., 1980-88, ptnr., 1988-89, Troop Steuber Pasich Reddick & Tobey, LLP, 1989-2000, Howrey Simon Arnold & White LLP, 2001—03, Pasich & Kornfeld LLP, 2003—. Author: Casualty and Liability Insurance, 1990, 2000, 03; co-author: Officers and Directors: Liabilities and Protections, 1996, 2000, 03, The Year 2000 and Beyond: Liability and Insurance for Computer Code Problems, 2000; contbg. editor: West's California Litigation Forms: Civil Procedure Before Trial, 2000; entertainment law columnist, ins. law columnist L.A. and San Francisco Daily Jour., 1989—; contbr. articles to profl. jours. Active bd. dirs. Nat. Acad. Jazz, L.A., 1988-89, chmn. bd. dirs. Woody Herman Found., L.A., 1989-92, Constnl. Rights Found., 2000; active L.A. City Atty's. Task Force for Econ. Recovery, 1992-93. Named to Calif's. Legal Dream Team as 1 of state's top 25 litigators, Calif. Law Bus., 1992, as one of the nation's top 45 lawyers under age 45, The Am. Lawyer, 1995. Mem. ABA (mem. Task Force on Complex Insurance Coverage Litigation). Home: 10419 Lindbrook Dr Los Angeles CA 90024-3323 Office: 10866 Wilshire Blvd Ste 300 Los Angeles CA 90024 Office Phone: 310-441-8461. Business E-Mail: kpasich@pasichlaw.com.

PASINETTI, PIER MARIA, author; b. Venice, Italy, June 24, 1913; came to U.S., 1946, naturalized, 1952; s. Carlo and Maria (Ciardi) P. Dottore in Lettere, U. Padua, Italy, 1935; PhD in Comparative Lit., Yale U., 1949. Fellow La. State U., 1935-36, U. Calif. at Berkeley, 1936-37; lectr. U. Stockholm, 1942-46; prof. Italian and comparative lit. UCLA, 1949—. Author: L'ira di Dio, 1942, Venetian Red, 1960, The Smile on the Face of the Lion, 1965, From the Academy Bridge, 1970, Suddenly Tomorrow, 1971, Dall' Estrema America, 1975, Il Centro, 1979, Dorsoduro, 1983, Life for Art's Sake: Studies in the Literary Myth of the Romantic Artist, 1985, Melodramma, 1993, Piccole Veneziane Complicate, 1996, Astolfo, 1999; also articles, revs., film scripts. Recipient Fiction award Nat. Inst. Arts and Letters, 1965, Prix Écureuil Li. Etrangère, 1996. Mem. Authors Guild. Clubs: Elizabethan Yale. Office: 1259 Dorsoduro Venice Italy 30123

PASK, SCOTT, set designer; Grad., Yale Sch. Drama. Broadway: Nine, Take Me Out, Amour, Urinetown (Lucille Lortel nom.), Little Shop of Horrors; in London: On an Average Day, Tales from Hollywood, Albert Herring, Pillowman; also appeared at Almeida Theatre, Royal Nat. Theatre, Donmar Warehouse, Opera North, Atlantic Theater Co., The Pub. Theatre, Roundabout Theatre, Yale Rep., South Coast Rep., Ctr. Stage, Williamstown, NY Theatre Workshop, Classic Stage Co., Playwrights Horizons, Chgo. Opera Theater, Bklyn. Acad. Music. Recipient Lucille Lortel award, 1999, Henry Hewes award, Am. Theater Wing, 1999, Bessie award, 2001. Office: 4 Times Sq #15 New York NY 10036-6518

PASKACH, DAVID M. lawyer, food products executive; BS in Acctg., Iowa State U., 1980; JD, U. Ill., 1983. Bar: Iowa, Ill., Minn. Lawyer; corp. atty. Schwan Food, Marshall, Minn., 1989—93, sr. atty., 1993—97, gen. counsel, 1997, v.p. adminstrn., exec. v.p., gen. counsel, 1997—. Maj. USAF. Office: Schwan Food 115 W College Dr Marshall MN 56258

PASKAWICZ, JEANNE FRANCES, pain specialist; b. Phila., Mar. 3, 1954; d. Alex and Lillian (Pyluck) P. BSc, Phila. Coll. Pharmacy; MA, Villanova U., 1973; postgrad., St. Joseph U., 1979; PhD, Kensington U., 1984. Mem. anesthesiology staff Einstein Med. Ctr., Phila., 1990-94, Temple U. Hosp., 1994—; mem. detox./rehab. staff Presbyn. Med. Ctr., Phila., 1984—; house officer Tenet Hosps., Elkins Park, Pa., 1990—; mem. psychiatry staff Hahnemann U. Hosp., Phila., 1984-90; hostage negotiator Office of Mental Health, Phila., 1984-90; mem. surgery/anesthesiology staff Mt. Sinai Hosp., Phila., 1989-91. Bd. dirs. Phila. Coll. Pharmacy, St. Joseph U. Mem. NAFE, Am. Pain Soc., Nat. Parks Conservation Assn., North Shore Animal League, Amvets, DAV Comdrs. Club, Lambda Kappa Sigma.

PASLER, JSNN C. music educator; b. Milw., 1951; BA, Vanderbilt U., 1973; MA, U. Chgo., 1974, PhD, 1981. Prof. U. Calif., LaJolla, 1985—. Vis. asst. prof. U. Va., Chalottesville, 1978—80, U. Cin., 1980; vis. prof. Case Western Res. U., Cleve., 2003—04; co-dir. re-theorizing music U. Calif. Humanities Rsch. Inst., 1993. Co-author (editor): Confronting Stravinsky: Man, Musician and Modernist, 1986; co-author: Time and Mind: Interdisciplinary Issue, The Study of Time VI, 1989, La Musique: du Theorique au Politique, 1990, Tradition and its Fiture in Music, 1991, Music-Cultures in Contact, Convergences and Collisions, 1994, John Cage: Composed in America, 1999, Debussy in Performance, 1999, Western Music and its Others, 2000, Queer Epispdes in Music and Modern Identity, 2002, Concert of Publix: Mitation da la Musicale en Eruope de 1780 - 1914, 2002, Historical Musicology: Sources, Methods, Interpretations, 2004; contbr. articles to profl. jours.; dir.(writer, prodr.): (documentaries) The Great Ceremony to Straighten the World, 1994. Recipient award, NEH, 1985, 1988; fellow, Stanford Humanities Ctr., 1993—94. Mem.: Soc. Ethnomusicology (audio-visual com. 1998—), Am. Musicology Soc. (program com. nat. meeting. 2000—00, chair program com. nat. com. 2003). Office: U Calif Music Dept 0726 La Jolla CA 92093-0326

PASNICU, CORNEL, mathematician, educator; b. Bucharest, Romania, Sept. 6, 1953; arrived in U.S., 1992; s. Tanasa Pasnicu, Xenia Adina Pasnicu; m. Adina Melania Truta; 1 child, Nastasia Laura. BA, U. Bucharest, 1976, MS, 1977, PhD, 1987. Rsch. fellow INCREST (IMAR), Bucharest, Romania, 1980—91; vis. scholar U. Copenhagen, 1991—91; vis. assoc. prof. U. Toronto, Canada, 1992—92; assoc. prof. U. P.R., San Juan, 1992—97, full prof., 1997—. Mem. operator algebras/operator theory panel NSF, Arlington, Va., 2002. Contbr. articles to profl. jours. Recipient S. Stoilov prize, Romanian Acad., 1988; grantee, NSF, 1994—96, 1996—2000, 2001—, Army Rsch. Office, 2000—. Mem.: Am. Math. Soc. Avocations: reading, music, sports. Office: Univ PR Math Dept San Juan PR 00931 Home: L12 Calle 15 San Juan PR 00926 Office Phone: 787-764-0000 4679. Business E-Mail: cpasnic@upracd.upr.clu.edu.

PASQUALE, MICHAEL DAVID, linguist, educator, linguist, consultant; b. Norfolk, Va., Aug. 16, 1973; m. Monica Bolet, June 27, 1998; 1 child, Alexander Michael. BA, Cedarville Coll., 1995; PhD, Mich. State U., 2001. Asst. prof. linguistics Cornerstone U., Grand Rapids, Mich., 2000—. Mem.: TESOL, Linguistic Soc. Am. Office: Cornerstone Univ 1001 East Beltline NE Grand Rapids MI 49525 E-mail: michael_pasquale@cornerstone.edu.

PASQUIER, JOËL, music educator; b. Montmorency, France, Sept. 25, 1943; arrived in Can., 1967; s. Jean and Raymonde (Gourdin) P.; m. Anne Vachon, Nov. 28, 1970; 1 child, Ariane. Grad. in piano and chamber music, Conservatoire Nat. Superieur de Musique, Paris, 1962. Prof. Conservatoire de Musique de St. Germain-en-Laye, France, 1964-65; grad. asst. Sch. Music, Ind. U., Bloomington, 1965-67; tchr. piano U. Laval, Quebec, Canada, 1967—2003, dir., 1988-91. Recording artist ATMA Records. Appeared as solo pianist concert halls, radio, TV, with chamber and symphony orchs. in France, U.S., Can., The Netherlands. Fulbright scholar Ind. U., 1965. Mem. Que. Yacht Club. E-mail: joelpasquier@tv.videotron.ca.

PASRICHA, ATUL, automotive executive; B, U. Delhi; MBA, U. Va. Dir. pension funding Gen. Motors, NY, 1994—95, dir. bus. devel., 1995—96, regional treas. Asia-Pacific ops., 1996—98; asst. treas. Delphi Corp., Troy, Mich., 1998—2000, acting gen. dir. fin. electronics and mobile comm. sector, 2000—01, exec. dir. new markets unit, 2001—02, v.p. mergers acquisitions new markets, 2002—. Recipient Deal of Yr., Project Fin. Mag., 1998. Office: Delphi Corp World Headquarters 5725 Delphi Dr Troy MI 48098-2815

PASS, CAROLYN JOAN, dermatologist; b. Balt., May 14, 1941; d. Isidore Earl and Rhea (Koplowitz) P.; m. Richard Malcolm Susel, June 23, 1963; children: Steven, Gary. BS, U. Md., 1962; MD, U. Md., 1966. Diplomate Am. Bd. Dermatology. Rotating intern USPHS Hosp., Balt., 1966-67; med. resident St. Agnes Hosp., Balt., 1967-68; dermatology resident and fellow U. Md. Sch. Medicine Hosps., 1968-71; pvt. practice specializing in dermatology Balt. and Ellicott City, Md., 1971—. Mem. staff St. Agnes Hosp.; vol. dermatology clinics U. Md., St. Agnes hosps.; asst. clin. prof. dermatology U. Md. Sch. Medicine, 1978—; mem. exec. com. adv. bd. Nat. Program in Dermatology, 1975. Mem. AMA, Med. and Chirurgical Soc. State Md. (del.), Balt. City Med. Soc. (del 1974, pub. rels. com., 1992-94, alternate del. 1994—), Am. Women's Med. Assn., Am. Acad. Dermatology (award exhibit 1970), Soc. Investigative Dermatology, Md. Dermatology Soc. (sec.-treas. 1974-76, pres. 1976-77), U. Md. Sch. Medicine Alumnae Assn. (bd. dirs. 1987—), Woodholme Country Club, Country Garden Club. Jewish. Avocations: gourmet cooking, gardening, art, golf. Home: Timberlane 8410 Park Heights Ave Baltimore MD 21208-1716 Office: Pine Heights Med Ctr 1001 Pine Heights Ave Ste 301 Baltimore MD 21229-5285 Office Phone: 410-525-1515.

PASSAGE, DAVID, diplomat; b. Charlotte, N.C., June 16, 1942; s. John T. and Virginia (Beam) P. BA in Internat. Rels., U. Denver, 1964; MS in Internat. Econs., Georgetown U., 1966; student, Nat. War Coll., Ft. McNair, Washington, 1981-82. With U.S. Dept. State, 1966-99; politico-mil. affairs officer U.S. Embassy, London, 1966; pacification program analyst U.S. Mil. Command, Saigon, Vietnam, 1968; with U.S. State Dept. Ops. Ctr., 1970; officer Secretariat Staff, 1971; special asst. to Asst. Sec. State Politico-Mil. Affairs, 1972-74; pol. officer, 1974-76; spl. asst. to Sec. of State Henry Kissinger U.S. State Dept., Washington, 1976; polit. counselor Am. Embassy, Canberra, Australia, 1977-79; dir. Press Office and Assoc., 1979; from. dep. to acting spokesman U.S. Dept. State, dep. dir. So. African Affairs, 1982-84; dep. chief mission/charge d'affairs U.S. Embassy, 1984-86; dir. Office Regional Affairs Africa Bur., 1986; dir. for Africa, Nat. Security Coun. The White House, Washington, 1989; U.S. amb. to Botswana, 1990-93; polit. adviser to U.S. Spl. Opers. Command MacDill AFB, Fla., 1993-96; dir. Andean affairs Dept. State, Washington, 1996-99; ret., 1999—. Lectr. Nat. War Coll., John F. Kennedy Spl. Warfare Ctr., USAF Spl. Ops. Sch., Armed Forces Staff Coll., others. Contbr. chpt.: Managing Contemporary Conflict, 1996, The U.S. and Colombia, 2000; contbr. articles to profl. jours. Recipient Chuong My Boi Tinh medal (Vietnam), Sec. of State Career chievement Medal, State Dept. Superior Hon. Awd.; Gen. James Doolittle Educator of Yr. Awd., U.S. Air Force Def. Disting. Civilian Svc. medal Dept. Def.; Centennial scholar U. Denver. Avocation: environment and conservation. Home: 2416 Chain Bridge Rd NW Washington DC 20016-3304

PASSAILAIGUE, ERNEST L., JR., state legislator, accountant; b. Columbia, S.C., Nov. 9, 1947; s. Ernest L. and Marie S. Passailaigue; m. Margaret I. Passailaigue; children: Alys Anne, Michelle, Angele, Tori, Jacques. BA, U. S.C.; MA, The Citadel, Charleston, S.C.; Doctorate (hon.), Coll. of Charleston.

CPA, S.C. Assoc. prof. Bapt. Coll., Charleston, 1973-88; sr. ptnr. Passailague, Blanchard & Knight, P.A., CPAs, Charleston, 1984—; mem. S.C. Senate, Columbia, 1989—. Owner Charleston Royals and Rainbows Baseball Team, 1983-87; bd. visitors Charleston So. U., 1990-92. Mem. adv. bd. Commn. on Better Racial Assurance, Sickle Cell Adv. Bd., Charleston, 1991—; mem. Oil Exch. Bldg. Commn., Charleston, 1989-91. Served with S.C. Air N.G., 1969-75. Recipient S.C. Ann. Pub. Svc. award Common Cause, 1991. Mem. S.C. Assn. CPAs (pres. Coastal chpt. 1991-92, state pres. 1992-93), Isle of Palms Exch. Club (past pres.). Democrat. Avocations: Tae Kwon Do, Karate.

PASSANO, E. MAGRUDER, JR., strategic planning consultant; b. Balt., Oct. 2, 1942; s. Edward M. and Mildred P. (Nelson) P.; m. Helen C. Marikle, Sept. 4, 1971; children: Catherine, Tammy, Sarah. BS, Johns Hopkins U., 1967, MA, 1969. With Waverly Inc., Balt., 1965-98, salesman, 1970-73, v.p., 1973-75, v.p. adminstrn., sec., 1975-90, vice chmn., sec., 1990-98; pres., CEO One Waverly LLC, Balt., 1998—. Chmn. Passano Found., Balt., 1982—; pres. Am. Lung Assn., Md., 1982-84; mem. exec. com. Vol. Coun. Equal Opportunity, Balt., 1978-2002, chmn., 1995-2002; bd. dirs. Combined Health Appeal Am., 1994-97; pres. (CHA) Combined Health Agys., Md., 1985-87, chmn. exec. com., 1987-95; pres. 12:30 Club Balt., 1981-83; mem. exec. com. Balt. City Life Mus., 1982-93, v.p. 1987-93; trustee emeritus, 1993-98; mem. adv. coun. Johns Hopkins U. Sch. Profl. Studies in Bus. and Edn., 1984—, exec. chair alumni chpt., 1986-89, chair edn. cmty. devel. iniative, 1995—; mem. Md. Gov.'s Commn. on High Blood Pressure and Related Cardiovascular Risk Factors, 1986-2002; bd. govs. Md. New Directions, Inc., 1987-94; bd. dirs., mem. exec. com. YMCA Ctrl. Md., 1988-96; treas., bd. dirs., chmn. edn. com. Pride of Balt., 1990—; bd. dirs. Ind. Coll. Fund Md., 1994—; bd. vis. Towson State U., 1994—, chmn. 1997-2001, Sch. Medicine U. Md., 1995—; mem. planning com., bd. vis. Md. Bus. Responsive Govt., 1994-2002. With USN, 1963-65. Recipient Prince Hall Bicentennial award Masons, 1975; citations Mayor of Balt., 1976, City of Balt., 1977, Vol. of Yr. award for outstanding svc. to CICHA, 1984-85, Presdl. award for outstanding svc. to Am. Lung Assn. Md., 1985, Outstanding Vol., 1988, Disting. Svc. award Soc. Profl. Journalists, 1987, Outstanding Svc. award Am. Heart Assn., 1988, Outstanding Vol. Svc. award Balt. Assn. Retarded Citizens, 1990, Vol. of Yr./Outstanding Leadership and Dedication award Combined Health Agys., 1991-92, Outstanding Family of the Century, Am. Lung Assn. Md., 2003, Outstanding Bd. Mem., Ind. Coll. Fund Md., 2004. Mem. Purchasing Mgmt. Assn. Md. (chmn. com. 1968-70), Balt. Jaycees (v.p. 1974-76, internat. senator 1975), Greater Balt. Minority Purchasing Coun. (Svc. award 1978), Soc. Colonial Wars (chpt. gov. 1989-91), Johns Hopkins U. Alumni Assn. (pres. Balt. 1984-86, Univ. Heritage award 1987). Democrat. Episcopalian. Home: 3925 Linkwood Rd Baltimore MD 21210-3001 Office: One Waverly LLC 1122 Kenilworth Dr Ste 115 Towson MD 21204-2142 E-mail: passano@worldnet.att.net.

PASSANO, WILLIAM M., III, publishing executive; BS, Roanoke Coll.; MS, Columbia U. Bd. mem., past chmn. Mt. Washington Pediatric Hosp., Balt.; with Williams & Wilkins; CEO, bd. mem. SCP Comms., Inc., N.Y.C., 2001—. Office: SCP Comms 134 W 29th St New York NY 10001*

PASSANTINO, BENJAMIN ARTHUR, business/marketing executive; b. Bklyn., Feb. 26, 1956; s. Anthony Frank and Ann Marie (Ruggerio) Passantino. Mgr. pub. rels. AT&T, NYC, mgr. mktg. comm. and new techs.; pres. B. Arthur Comm., Morristown, NJ, 1984-89; sr. v.p. bus. devel. IMEDIA Creative Corp. Mktg., Morristown, 1989-94, also dir.; mng. ptnr., CEO, Tribeca Global, Inc., Hackettstown, NJ; dir. media and comm. onProject.com, Morristown, NJ, 2000—01; pres. Avid Records, Inc., NYC, 2002—; COO Avid Listener, Inc., NYC, 2002—. Bd. dirs. Dieknowlogist, Inc., NYC, One World Botanicals, Inc., Red Bank, NJ, Lasercomb Am., Inc., NYC, The Perfect Supply Co., Inc., NYC, Imedia, Morristown. Co-author: One with the Flame, NFL Quarterbacks; contbr. articles to mags. Bd. dirs. Am. Cancer Soc., Morristown, Jr. Achievement, Basking Ridge, NJ; mem. Washington Twp. (Morris County) Planning Bd., chairperson econ. devel. com.; trustee Drakestown United Meth. Ch. Mem. IEEE, Internat. Assn. Bus. Communicators, Am. Mktg. Assn., Bus. Profls. of Advt. Assn., Conf. Bd. Office: 375 Mt Prospect Ave Ste 7BE Newark NJ 07104 Office Phone: 201-456-6500. E-mail: bap@avidrecords.com.

PASSANTINO, RICHARD J. architect; b. N.Y.C., Apr. 4, 1934; s. Charles V. and Ruth M. (Defina) P.; m. Erika F. Dethlefs, Sept. 1, 1962; children: Stefan C., Fiona R. BS in Architecture, U. Cin., 1957. Registered arch., D.C., Md., Va., Ga., Miss., Fla., Ky., Mo., N.J., S.C.; cert. Nat. Coun. Archtl. Registration Bds. Rsch. assoc. McLeod, Ferrara, Ensign, Washington, 1960-70; founding prin. Richard J. Passantino, AIA Architects, Bethesda, Md., 1970-80; pres. SAIC Architects, McLean, Va., 1980-90, LEA/Passantino & Bavier, Arlington, Va., 1990-94, Passantino & Bavier subs. Facility Holding Corp. Smyrna, Ga., Bethesda, Md., 1995—. Spkr. to various ednl. instn. in U.S., AIA rep. Union Internat. Archs., 1985-88, nat. chmn. com. architecture edn., 1998; mem. nat. archtl. juries throughout U.S., 1975—. Co-author: Urban Schools in Europe, 1963; contbr. numerous articles to profl. jours.; designer 7 earthquake resistant schs. in So. Italy, 1985-88, Project Dir., for design of multiple U.S. Navy projects in Greece, 11 locations, 1985-89, Early Childhood Ctr., Buffalo, 1995, psychiat. hosp., Leesburg, Va., 1979, Haile Selassie U., Addis Ababa, Ethiopia; designer modifications Am. Consulate Gen., Ecuador, Am. embassies, Papua-New Guinea, The Philippines, Liberia, Ghana, others. Bd. dirs. Nat. Child Rsch. Ctr., Washington, 1969-74. 1st lt. USAF, 1958-60; capt. USAFR, 1960-62. Recipient award for sch. architecture exhbn. Am. Assn. Sch. Bd. Adminstrs., 1984. Mem. v.p. chmn., architecture for edn. 1994), Coun. for Ednl. Facilities Planners (co-recipient Projects of Distinction award 1993), recipient of Coun. of Ednl. Facility Planners Internat., 1996, recipient of the James D, MacConnell award for Ednl. Facility Planning Excellence, Assn. for Childhood Edn. Internat., Assn. Sch. Bus. Ofcls. Internat. (award of excellence 1986), Nat. Hist. Trust, Soc. Am. Mil. Engrs. Avocations: tennis, photography, travel. Office: Passantino & Bavier Archs 2233 Lake Park Dr SE Ste 450 Smyrna GA 30080-8856

PASSARO, PAUL CHARLES, business executive; b. Ridgewood, N.J., June 6, 1967; s. Richard Paul and Barbara (Brown) Passaro; m. Kristi-Anne Tolo, June 25, 1994; children: Peter James, Anne Marie. BA in History cum laude, Williams Coll., Williamstown, Mass., 1989; MBA, U. N.C., 1993. Mcpl. bond trader and salesman Roosevelt & Cross, Inc., N.Y.C., 1989—91; v.p. The Fraser Co., Hilton Head, SC, 1992—94; CFO Pine Needles and Mid Pines Resorts, Southern Pines, NC, 1994—2003; COO EastWest Ptnrs. Club Mgmt., Chapel Hill, NC, 2003—. Bd. dirs. small bus. adv. bd. N.C. Citizens for Bus. and Industry, Raleigh, 1999—2002; v.p. The Toppers, N.Y.C., 1991; founder Habitat for Humanity Charity Golf Classic, Chapel Hill, 1992—2004; mem. fin. com. Trinity Sch., Durham and Chapel Hill, 1999—2002; bd. dirs. Leadership N.C., 1999—; mem. audit com. N.C. Rep. Party, Raleigh, 1999—2003, chmn., 2001—03; alt. del. 2004 Rep. Nat. Conv.; elder Ch. of the Good Shepherd, Durham, 1994—. Mem.: Christmas Fore Moore (treas. 1997—2003, Charity Golf Tourney), Theodore Roosevelt Assn. Republican. Avocations: bible study, golf, reading history, bird hunting. Office: 190 Finley Golf Course Rd Chapel Hill NC 27517 Office Phone: 919-929-0660. E-mail: pcpassaro@yahoo.com.

PASSEY, GEORGE EDWARD, psychology educator; b. Stratford, Conn., Sept. 28, 1920; s. Henry Richard and Elizabeth (Angus) P.; m. Algie Aldridge Ashe, Nov. 18, 1950; children— Richard Ashe, Elizabeth Aldridge, Mary Louise. BS, Springfield Coll., 1942; MA, Clark U., 1947; PhD, Tulane U., 1950. Asst. prof. U. Ala., Tuscaloosa, 1952-55, assoc. prof., 1955-56, 57-59, prof., 1959-63, prof. psychology, chmn. div. social and behavioral scis., 1967-73, prof. engring., 1969-84, Disting. Service prof. psychology, 1984-85, Disting Service prof. emeritus, 1985—; dean U. Ala. (Sch. Social and Behavioral Scis.), 1973-84. Research scientist Lockheed Ga. Co., Marietta, Ga., 1956-57, 63-65, cons., 1965-67; prof. Ga. Inst. Tech., 1965-67 Served with USNR, 1942-46, PTO; with USAF, 1951-52. Fellow Am. Psychol. Assn.; mem. So. Soc. for Philosophy and Psychology, Southeastern Psychol. Assn., Ala. Psychol. Assn., Pine Harbor Golf and Racquet Club, Sigma Xi. Home: 7141 Skyline Dr Pell City AL 35128-6936 *Whatever success I have enjoyed ought to be attributed to the attempt I have made to carry out the admonitions of my parents to make choices only after having appraised the alternatives in terms of their consequences, to weigh ethical considerations above all others, never to demand of others what one is unwilling to give of himself, and to work untiringly for those causes to which one is committed.*

PASSON, RICHARD HENRY, English language educator, former administrator; b. Hazleton, Pa., Aug. 18, 1939; s. Henry Richard and Grace Miriam (Bernstein) P.; m. Margaret Rose Ferdinand, Aug. 14, 1965; children—Michael, Rebecca, Christopher. BA (Bishop Hafey scholar), King's Coll., Pa., 1961; MA, U. Notre Dame, 1963, PhD (NDEA fellow), 1965. From instr. to prof. English U. Scranton, 1964-73, chmn. English dept., 1970-73, fgn. student adviser, 1965-67; dean Coll. Arts and Scis., Creighton U., Omaha, 1973-77; acad. v.p. St. Joseph's U., Phila., 1977-84; provost U. Scranton, Pa., 1984-2000, prof. English, 2000—02, 2004—; interim acad. v.p. St. Joseph's U., Phila., 2002—04. Contbr. articles profl. jours. Recipient grant Nat. Assn. Fgn. Students, 1966 Mem. Modern Lang. Assn., Am. Assn. Higher Edn., Am. Assn. Acad. Deans, Nat. Coun. Tchrs. English. Democrat. Roman Catholic. Office: U Scranton 402 Brennan Hall Scranton PA 18510 Office Phone: 570-941-4327. E-mail: passonr1@scranton.edu.

PASSTY, JEANETTE NYDA, English language educator, writer; b. LA, Calif., Jan. 19, 1947; d. Walter Isaac and Mollie Sarah Nyda; m. Gregory Bohdan Passty, June 18, 1976; 1 child, Benjamin. AA, L.A. Valley Coll., 1966; BA, UCLA, 1968; MA, U. So. Calif., 1974, PhD, 1982. Cert. c.c. instr., Calif. Tchg. asst., lectr., assoc. dir. freshman English program U. So. Calif., 1971-78; lectr. English dept. U. Tex., Austin, 1983-85; vis. asst. prof., adj. assoc. prof. Tex. Luth. U., Seguin, 1983, 85-87; from instr. to asst. prof. St. Philip's Coll., San Antonio, Calif., 1988-92, assoc. prof., 1992—. Lectr. UCLA, U. Tex., Austin, Western Mich. U., U. Louisville, Salisbury State U., Morehead State U., Tex. Tech. U., U. Wales, Bangor; humanities book reviewer CHOICE (ALA Jour.), 1985—86; manuscript reviewer Fairleigh Dickinson U. Press, 1991—; editl. cons. CONNECTIONS: Online Distance Learning Faculty Forum, 2002—. Author: Eros and Androgyny: The Legacy of Rose Macaulay, 1988, The Lion Tells Her Story: A Biography of the Honorable N.P. Brooks Hinton, 1998, Bringing Denis Home: The Hero from Hope, Kansas, 2001; annotator: Alice Crawford's Paradise Pursued, 1995; contbr. articles to encyclopedia and profl. jours.; guest Sta. KSPL Radio in Touch With, 1989; appearance Sta. KENS-TV, 1992; Channel 12 Morehead, KY, 1998; CNN, 1995, Roadside (entr'acte with G.S. Bailey), 2000. Mem. Nat. Abortion Rights Action League, Tex. Abortion Rights Action League, Greenpeace, Environ. Def. Fund, The Nature Conservancy, NOW, Sierra Club, Handgun Control Inc., Orgn. Internat. Conf. on the Holocaust, San Antonio, 2000. Recipient Elizabeth K. Pleasants Tchg. award, U. So. Calif., 1974, letters of appreciation, Lord Bonham-Carter, 1987, HRH Princess Margaret, 1989—90, Oustanding Acad. Book award, ALA, 1989, Women Honoring Women award, Am. Assn. Women in C.C.s, 1997, Katherine Anne Porter Lit. prize, 1999, NISOD Internat. Conf. on Tchg. and Leadership Excellence Award, 2003, St. Philip's Coll. Tchg. Excellence award, 2003—04; Vierling Kersey scholar, L.A. Valley Coll., 1964—66, NEH grantee, Tex. Luth. U., 1986. Mem. AAUW, MLA, Nat. Coun. Tchrs. English, South Ctrl. Soc. 18th Century Studies, Virginia Woolf Soc. Avocations: academic decathlon, taekwondo, arctic travel. Office: St Philip's Coll English Dept 1801 Martin Luther King Dr San Antonio TX 78203-2098 Office Phone: 210-531-3373.

PASSWATER, RICHARD ALBERT, biochemist, author; b. Wilmington, Del., Oct. 13, 1937; s. Stanley Leroy and Mabel Rosetta (King) P.; m. Barbara Sarah Gayhart, June 2, 1964; children: Richard Alan, Michael Eric. BS, U. Del., 1959; PhD, Bernadean U., 1976. Cert. firefighter. Supr. instrumental analysis lab. Allied Chem. Corp., Marcus Hook, Pa., 1959-64; tech. svcs. rep. F&M Sci. Corp., Avondale, Pa., 1965; dir. applications lab. Am. Instrument Co., Silver Spring, Md., 1965-77; dir. Am. Gen. Enterprises, Minn.; former daily broadcaster Sta. WMCA, N.Y.C., 1980-88, Sta. WRNG, Atlanta, 1982-85; rsch. dir. Solgar Nutritional Rsch. Ctr., Berlin, Md., 1978—. Corp. v.p. Solgar Co., Inc.; mem. health, edn., rsch. coun. adv. bd. ICCC, NGO, UN, 2003—; chmn. Worcester County Emergency Planning Com., 1995-96; bd. dirs. Worcester Meml. Hosp., Atlantic Gen. Hosp., River Run Assn.; pres. 1989-92, Subaqueous Exploration and Archeology Ltd.; apptd. Md. State One Md. Com. and the Eastern Shore Econ. Task Force, Md. Gov. Glendenning, 1999, 2000. Author: Guide to Fluorescence Literature, vol. 1, 1967, vol. 2, 1970, vol. 3, 1974, Supernutrition, 1975, Supernutrition for Health Hearts, 1977, Super Calorie, Carbohydrate Counter, 1978, Cancer and Its Nutritional Therapies, 1978, 83, 93, The Easy No-Flab Diet, 1979, Selenium as Food and Medicine, 1980, The Slendernow Diet, 1982, (with Dr. E. Cranton), Trace Elements, Hair Analysis and Nutrition, 1983, The New Supernutrition, 1991, The Longevity Factor, 1993, Cancer Prevention and Nutritional Therapy, 1993, (with Ben Friedrich and Hans Kugler) Heart Health, 1994, Pycnogenol: The Super Protector Nutrient, 1994, Lipoic Acid: The Metabolic Antioxidant, 1995, numerous others; contbg. author: Fire Protection Guide to Hazardous Materials, 1991; editor Fluorescence News, 1966-77, Jour. Applied Health Scis., 1982-83; mem. editl. bd. Nutritional Perspectives, 1978-96, The Body Forum, 1979-80, Jour. Holistic Medicine, 1981-88, VIM Newsletter, 1979—99; contbg. Firehouse Mag., 1988-94, Jour. Applied Nutrition; contbr. over 400 health articles to mags.; co-editor booklet series Your Good Health; sci. adv. and columnist Whole Foods mag.; patentee in field. Bd. dirs. Sci. Documentation Ctr., Dunfermline, Eng.; Am. Found. Firefighter Health and Safety; chief Ocean Pines Vol. Fire Dept., 1984-93; active Emergency Med. Tech.; adviser Nat. Inst. Nutrition Edn.; past adv. bd. Stephen Decatur High Sch., Worcester County Dept. Edn. Cubmaster, 1975-79. Named Citizen of Yr. Ocean Pines, Md., 1987; recipient 5th Ann. Achievement award, 1989, VFW Cert. of Commendation, 1988, Industry award Nat. Inst. Nutritional Edn., 1991, Pres.'s award Nat. Nutritional Foods Assn., 1999; named to Delmarva Fireman's Hall of Fame, 1993. Fellow Internat. Acad. Preventive Medicine, Am. Inst. Chemists; mem. ASTM, AAAS, Am. Chem. Soc., Gerontology Soc., Am. Geriatric Soc., Am. Aging Assn., Internat. Found. Preventive Medicine (v.p.), Internat. Union Pure and Applied Chemistry, Royal Soc. Chemistry (London), Internat. Acad. Holistic Health and Medicine, Capital Chem. Soc., Nutrition Today Soc., Am. Acad. Applid Health Sci. (pres., bd. dirs.), Internat. Found. Preventive Medicine (v.p., dir.), Inst. Nutritional Rsch., N.Y. Acad. Scis., Nat. Fire Protection Assn. (cert. firefighter level III, com. on properties of hazardous chemicals), Pi Kappa Alpha. Office: 11017 Manklin Meadows Ln Berlin MD 21811-9340 E-mail: solgar@dmv.com.

PASSY, CHARLES, arts critic; b. N.Y., Jan. 9, 1964; s. Victor and Beverly (Green) P.; m. Leslie M. Olsen, Dec. 15, 1989; two children: Jacob E., Emma F. BA, Columbia U., 1985. Assoc. Jay K. Hoffman and Assocs., N.Y.C., 1983-87; sr. editor, mng. editor Ovation Mag., N.Y.C., 1988-89; editor Classical Mag., N.Y.C., 1989-91; editor-in-chief Musical Am. Pub., N.Y.C., 1991-92; staff writer The Palm Beach Post, West Palm Beach, Fla., 1992—. Announcer, prodr. WNYC FM, N.Y., 1984-85; entertainment stringer N.Y. Newsday, 1987-92. Author (with others): New Voices: Selected University and College Prize Winning Poems, 1989, The New Grove Dictionary of Jazz, 1988, The New Grove Dictionary of American Music, 1986, The New Grove Dictionary of Music and Musicians, 2d edit., 2001; editor: The Letters of Virgil Thomson, 1988; contbr. numerous articles to publs. in field, The Wall St. Jour., 1999-. Recipient Poetry award Acad. Am. Poets Columbia U., 1985, Criticism awards Soc. Profl. Journalists, 1995, 97, 99, 2001, 03, Fla. Press Club, 1993, Fla. Soc. Newspaper Editors, 1993, 2001, Cox Newspapers, 2001, Am. Assn. Sunday and Feature Editors, 2002; fellow Knight Ctr. for Specialized Journalism, 1993. Home: 180 Bent Tree Dr Palm Beach Gardens FL 33418-3597 Office: Palm Beach Newspapers Inc 2751 S Dixie Hwy West Palm Beach FL 33405-1298 E-mail: chazpbg@aol.com., charles_passy@pbpost.com.

PASTAN, LINDA OLENIK, poet; b. N.Y.C., May 27, 1932; d. Jacob L. and Bess (Schwartz) Olenik; m. Ira Pastan, 1953; children: Stephen, Peter, Rachel. BA, Radcliffe Coll., 1954; MLS, Simmons Coll., 1955; MA, Brandeis U., 1957. Author: (poetry) A Perfect Circle of Sun, 1971, On the Way to the Zoo, 1975, Aspects of Eve, 1975, The Five Stages of Grief, 1978 (Alice Fay di Castagnola award Poetry Soc. Am. 1978), Setting the Table, 1980, Waiting for My Life, 1981, PM/AM: New and Selected Poems, 1982 (Am. Book award nomination 1982), A Fraction of Darkness: Poems, 1985, The Imperfect Paradise, 1988, Heroes in Disguise, 1991, An Early Afterlife, 1995, Carnival Evening: New and Selected Poems, 1968-98 (nat. Book award nomination 1998), The Last Uncle, 2002. Recipient Dylan Thomas Poetry award Mademoiselle, 1958, Virginia Faulkner award Prarie Schooner, 1992, Charity Randall citation Internat. Poetry Forum, 1996, Ruth Lilly Poetry prize, 2003; NEA fellow; grantee Md. Arts Coun.; poet laureate of Md., 1991-95. Jewish. Office: 11710 Beall Mountain Rd Potomac MD 20854-1105 E-mail: lpastan@att.net.

PASTAN, PETER, chef, restaurant owner; Owner, chef Obelisk, Washington; owner Pizzeria Paradiso, Washington. Office: Obelisk 2029 D St NW Washington DC 20036-5948

PASTEN, LAURA JEAN, veterinarian; b. Tacoma, May 25, 1952; d. Frank Larry and Jean Mary (Slavich) Brajkovich. BA in Physiology with distinction, Stanford U., Davis, 1970; BA in Physiology, U. Calif., Davis, 1970, DVM, 1974; postgrad., Cornell U., 1975. Veterinarian Nevada County Vet. Hosp., Grass Valley, Calif., 1975-80; pvt. practice vet. medicine, owner Mother Lode Vet. Hosp., Grass Valley, 1980-96; veterinarian for Morris the 9-Lives cat (of TV comml. fame), 1985-94. Lectr. in field; spokesperson Nat. Cat Health Month; guest Today Show on wildlife, raising and tng. mini horses for guide horses for the blind. Author: Malignant, Tarantula Whisperer, Rocky Point Murders; contbg. author: Rocky Point Murders; pub. video How Smart is Your Puppy?, contbr. monthly newspaper column. Bd. dirs. Aguajito Property Owners Assn., Serrano Ranch Property Owners Assn., Sierra Svcs. for the Blind. Mem.: AOPA, AVMA, ASPCA, Bay Area Vet. Assn., Monterey Bay Vet Assn. (Carmel wildlife ednl. com., vet. coord. Monterey County Animal Disasters), Carmel Wildlife Edn. Com., Citizens Against Raccoon Extermination, Monterey SPCA, Denver Area Med. Soc., Am. Animal Hosp. Assn. (Mother Lode Hosp. cited for excellence), Mother Lode Vet. Assn., Calif. Vet. Med. Assn., Fund Animals Defenders Wildlife, Def. Animals, Inst. Protection Animals, In Def. of Animals, Humane Soc. U.S., Nature Conservancy, Am. Internat. Fund Animal Welfare, Internat. Vet. Med. Assn., Sierra Club, Big Sur Land Trust, Nat. Assn. Underwater Instrs., Rep. Womens Found. (bd. dirs.), Ninety-Nines Pilots Assn., Mensa. Republican. Lutheran. Home and Office: 27479 Schulte Rd Carmel CA 93923-9477 Office Phone: 831-626-7227. E-mail: lpasten@aol.com.

PASTER, HOWARD G. public relations and public affairs company executive; b. N.Y.C., Dec. 23, 1944; BA with honors, Alfred U., 1966; MS in Journalism, Columbia U., 1967. Legis. dir. UAW, 1977-80; exec. v.p. Timmons & Co., 1980-92; asst. to pres. and dir. Office Legis. Affairs White House, Washington, 1993; chmn., CEO Hill and Knowlton, Inc., N.Y.C., 1994—2002; exec. v.p. WPP Group, N.Y.C., 2002—. Office: WPP Group 125 Park Ave 4th Fl New York NY 10017-5529

PASTER, JANICE DUBINSKY, lawyer, former state legislator; b. St. Louis, Aug. 4, 1942; BA, Northwestern U., 1964; MA, Tufts U., 1967; JD, U. N.Mex., 1984. Bar: N.Mex. 1984. Atty. in pvt. practice, 1984—; mem. N.Mex. State Senate from 10th dist., 1988-96. Democrat. Home and Office: 5553 Eakes Rd NW Albuquerque NM 87107-5529

PASTERNAC, ANDRÉ, cardiologist, educator; b. Toulouse, France, July 22, 1937; came to Can., 1971, naturalized, 1978. s. Jacques and Régine P. Adv. math., Lyceé Henri IV, Paris, 1956; BA in Polit. Sci., Toulouse U., 1963, MD Med. Sch., 1968; grad. in Mgmt. Program, Columbia U., 2000. Cert. Ins. and Disability Assessment U. Montreal, 2002. Intern Toulouse Univ. Hosp., 1962-63, resident, 1963-64, Edouard-Herriot Hosp., Lyon, France, 1965-66; Fulbright scholar in cardiology Harvard U., 1968-71; research fellow Peter Bent Brigham Hosp., Boston, 1968-69; Milton fellow Children's Hosp., Boston, 1969-71; fellow in cardiology Toronto (Ont., Can.) U., 1971-72; staff cardiologist Montreal (Que., Can.) Heart Inst., 1972—; asst. prof. medicine U. Montreal, 1972-78, clin. assoc. prof., 1978—, clin. prof. medicine, 1994—. Vis. lectr. U. Liège (Belgium), 1977, U. Madrid, 1977, U. Warsaw, 1979, 83; cons. Harley St. Clinic, Cromwell Hosp., Wellington Hosp., London; vis. assoc. prof. McGill U., Montreal, 1975-76; medico-legal and ins. expert U. Montreal, 2002. Contbr. articles to profl. jours. Bd. dirs. Heart-Brain Rsch. Found. Inc., NYC, Cardiostat Inc., Montreal, Cardiostat USA Inc., West Palm Beach, Fla. Am. Field Svc. grantee, Oreg., 1954-55. Mem. French Cardiac Soc., European Soc. Cardiology, Canadian Cardiovasc. Soc., Am. Coll. Cardiology, Am. Heart Assn., Internat. Soc. Heart Rsch., Am. Fedn. Clin. Rsch., NY Acad. Scis. Research in stress-related myocardial ischemia and dysfunction, mitral valve prolapse, cardiovascular drugs, cardiomyopathies, catecholamines, neuroendocrine control of the heart, stress and the heart, prevention of cardiovascular disease. Home: Port Royal 1455 Sherbrooke St W # 703 Montreal QC Canada H3G 1L2 Office: Montreal Heart Inst 5000 Belanger E Montreal QC Canada H1T 1C8 Office Phone: 514-376-3330. E-mail: andre.pasternac@sympatico.ca.

PASTERNACK, DAVID, chef; Ptnr., exec. chef Esca, N.Y.C. Office: Esca 402 W 43d St New York NY 10036-6322

PASTERNACK, ROBERT FRANCIS, chemistry professor; b. N.Y.C., Sept. 20, 1936; 2 children. BA, Cornell U., 1957, PhD in Chemistry, 1962. Research assoc. in chemistry U. Ill., Champaign, 1962-63; from asst. to prof. chemistry Ithaca Coll., N.Y., 1963-66, Charles A. Dana Endowed prof. chemistry, 1976-82; Edmund Allen prof. chemistry Swarthmore Coll., Pa., 1984—. Invited speaker seminars, colls., univs., nat., internat. meetings, confs. including Bioinorganic Chem., Italy, Portugal, Gordon Rsch. Confs., Spanish Royal Soc. Chem., many others; lectr. series Nankai U., China, U. Messina, Italy; mem. adv. com. Rsch. Corp.; mem. sci. & art com. Franklin Inst.; co-organizer, chmn. workshop on rsch. at undergrad. instn. NSF, mem. undergrad. curriculm chem.; vis. prof., vis. rschr. U Messina, U. Paris, Nakai, Rome, King's Coll., London, Fritz Haber Inst., Berlin, Doshisha U., Kyoto; co-developer A Unified Lab. Program; initiator, chmn. C.P. Snow Lectr. Series. Author, co-author more than 100 sci. publs. Mem. com. on sci. and the arts Franklin Inst., 1992-98. Grantee NSF, 1965-66, 69-72, 77-78, 83-84, 86-94, 95—2003, Petroleum Rsch. Fund, 1967-74, 86-88, NIH, 1971-89, 2001—, Monsanto Corp., 1986-92, Rsch. Corp., 1974-75, 78-79, 84-85, Danforth Assocs., 1978-84, Camille and Henry Dreyfus Found., 1981, 95, NATO, 1979, 88-89, 95-96; recipient Camille and Henry Dreyfus Tchg./Scholar award, 1987-89, NSF Manpower Improvement award, King's Coll., U. London, 1977-78, Commemorative medal for sci. contbns. U. Catania, 1994; NSF sci. faculty fellow U. Rome, 1968-70. Mem. AAAS, Am. Inst. Chemists (Hon. Scroll award 1998), Am. Chem. Soc. (award for rsch. at an undergrad. instn. 2001), N.Y. Acad. Sci., Sigma Xi. Office: Swarthmore Coll Dept Chemistry Swarthmore PA 19081 Office Phone: 610-328-8559. Business E-Mail: rpaster1@swarthmore.edu.

PASTERNACK, ROBERT HARRY, school psychologist; b. Bklyn., Nov. 30, 1949; s. William and Lillian Ruth (Levine) P.; m. Jeanelle Livingston, Apr. 10, 1980; children: Shayla, Rachel. BA, U. South Fla., 1970; MA, N.Mex. Highlands U., 1972; PhD, U. N.Mex., 1980. Dir. Eddy County Drug Abuse Program, Carlsbad, N.Mex., 1972-73; adminstrv. intern U.S. Office Edn., Washington, 1975-76; exec. dir. Villa Santa maria, Cedar Crest, N.Mex., 1976-78; clin. dir. Ranchos Treatment Ctr., Taos, N.Mex., 1978-79; sch. psychologist N.Mex. Boys Sch., Springer, 1980—, supt., 1991; pres. Ensenar Health svcs., Inc., Taos, 1980—; CEO Casa de Corazon, Taos, N.Mex., 1994-98; state dir. spl. edn. N.Mex. State Dept. Edn., Santa Fe, 1998—. Instr. N.Mex. Highlands U., Las Vegas, 1980—, U. N.Mex., Albuquerque, 1980—; cons. N.Mex. Youth Authority, Santa Fe, 1988—, N.Mex. Devel. Disabilities Bur., Santa Fe, 1986—, various sch. dists.; state dir. spl. edn., N.Mex., 1998—; asst. sec. spl. edn. and rehab. svcs. U.S. Dept. Edn., 2001—. Author: Growing Up: The First Five Years, 1986; contbr. articles to profl. publs. Pres., bd. dirs. Children's Lobby, N.Mex., 1978, N.Mex. Spl. Olympics, 1986-88, Child-Rite, Inc., Taos, 1990; mem. Gov.'s Mental Health Task Force, Albuquerque, 1988—. Mem.: N.Mex. Coun. on Crime and Delinquency, Nat. Alliance Mentally Ill, Correctional Edn. Assn., Nat. Assn. Sch. Psychologists. Avocations: tennis, racquetball, skiing, cooking. Home and Office: 6235 5th St NE Apt 14 Washington DC 20002

PASTERNACK, STEFAN ALAN, psychiatrist, psychoanalyst; b. Jersey City, Nov. 5, 1939; BA, Cornell U., 1961; MD, Georgetown U., 1965. Diplomate in psychiatry Am. Bd. Neurology and Psychiatry; lic. physician, D.C., Md. Resident in psychiatry U. Cin. Gen. Hosp., 1966-69; psychiat. cons. North Cmty. Mental Health Ctr., Washington, 1971-97; asst. prof. psychiatry Georgetown U. Sch. Medicine, Washington, 1971-79, assoc. clin. prof. psychiatry, 1979-86, clin. prof. psychiatry, 1986—, co-dir. advanced studies prog. in psychiatry/psychoanalysis, 1995—. Pvt. practice psychiatry and psychoanalysis, Washington, 1978—. Editor: Violence and Victims, 1975; contbr. articles to profl. jours. Bd. dirs. Nat. Capital Med. Found., Washington, 1973-76, Forum for Psychoanalytic Study of Film, Washington, 1989—. Lt. comdr. USN, 1969-71. Fellow: Am. Psychiat. Assn. (life); mem.: Washington Psychiat. Soc. (mem. coun. 1987—99), Am. Psychoanalytic Assn., Cosmos Club. Avocations: motorboating and yachting, piano, writing. Office: 2121 Wisconsin Ave NW Ste 280 Washington DC 20007-2297 E-mail: sp39@aol.com.

PASTERNAK, GAVRIL WILLIAM, neurologist, neuropharmacologist; b. Bklyn., June 29, 1947; m. Sandra F. Pasternak, Nov. 12, 1977; children: Katie, David, Anna. BA, Johns Hopkins U., 1969, MD, 1973, PhD, 1975. Diplomate Am. Bd. Psychiatry and Neurology. Asst. mem. Meml. Sloan Kettering Cancer Ctr., N.Y.C., 1979-85, assoc. mem., 1985-89, mem., 1989—; asst. prof. Cornell U. Med. Coll., N.Y.C., 1979-83, assoc. prof., 1983-89, prof., 1989—. Bd. scientific counselors Nat. Inst. on Drug Abuse, 1987-92. Editor: The Opiate Receptors; co-editor: Analgesics: Neurochemical Behavioral and Clinical Perspectives; contbr. numerous articles to profl. jours.; patentee in field. Recipient Boyer Young Investigator award Meml. Sloan Kettering Cancer Ctr., N.Y.C., 1987, Millenium prize Norwegian U. Sci. and Tech., 2002. Fellow Am. Acad. Neurology (S. Weir Mitchell award 1980); mem. AAAS, Am. Neurol. Assn., N.Y. Acad. Scis. (conf. com.), Soc. Neurosci., Johns Hopkins Soc. Scholars, Phi Beta Kappa. Office: Memorial Sloan Kettering 1275 York Ave New York NY 10021-6094

PASTERNAK, KENNETH D. trading company executive; b. 1954; BA, SUNY, New Paltz, 1976. Sr. v.p., ltd. ptnr., trading rm. mgr. Spear Leeds & Kellogg/Troster Singer, 1979-94; co-founder Roundtable Ptnrs., LLC and Knight Securities; pres., CEO, trading rm. supr. Knight Securities; pres., CEO, dir. Knight Trading Group, Inc. (previously Knight/Trimark Group), Jersey City. Named one of 1999 N.J. Ernst & Young Entrepreneur of Yr. in Emerging Entrepreneur of Yr. category. Office: 23d Fl 525 Washington Blvd Jersey City NJ 07310

PASTERNAK, PATRICIA A. writer, freelance/self-employed newswriter; b. Albany, NY, Mar. 6, 1948; d. Charles Aloysius Teator and Victoria Patricia Remkus; m. Peter E. Pasternak, July 24, 1989; m. Francis L. Kizlinski, Aug. 19, 1967 (div. July 7, 1981); children: Michael F. Kizlinski, Jason A. Kizlinski, Rebecca D. Kizlinski, Stephanie E. Kizlinski. BA in English, Siena Coll., Loudonville, 1994—99. Writer The Evangelist, Albany, NY; freelance writer. Mktg. com. Dominican Spiritual Life Ctr., Niskayuna, NY, 2003. Mem.: Cath. Press Assn., NY Press Assn. (First Pl. Feature Article, The Greenville Press 1999). Democrat. Catholic. Avocations: reading, quilting.

PASTIN, MARK JOSEPH, association executive; b. Ellwood City, Pa., July 6, 1949; s. Joseph and Patricia Jean (Camenite) Pastin; m. Joanne Marie Reagle, May 30, 1970 (div. Mar. 1982); m. Carrie Patricia Class, Dec. 22, 1984 (div. June 1990); m. Christina M. Brecto, June 15, 1991. BA summa cum laude, U. Pitts., 1970; MA, Harvard U., 1972, PhD, 1973. Asst. prof. Ind. U., Bloomington, 1973-78, assoc. prof., 1978-80; founder, bd. Compliance Resource Group, Inc., 1983—; chmn., CEO, pres. Coun. Ethical Orgns., Alexandria, Va., 1986—; prof. mgmt., dir. Ariz. State U., Tempe, 1988-92, prof. emeritus, 1996—; chair Health Ethics Trust, 1995—. Mem. adv. bd. Aberdeen Holdings, San Diego, 1988-90; dir. Learned Nicholson, Ltd., 1990-91; bd. Japan Am. Soc. Phoenix, Found. for Ethical Orgns.; cons. GTE, Interim Healthcare, 1997-2000, U.S. Dept. Edn., 2002, Tex. Instruments, MicroAge Computers, Med-Tronic, Blood Sys., Inc., Opus Corp., GTE, NyNex, Am. Express Bank, Kaiko Bussan Co., Japan, Arex Co., Japan, Century Audit Co., U.S. Dept. Edn., Japan, Scottsdale Meml. Hosp., Consanti Found., Lincoln Electric Co., Tenet Healthcare, The Williams Co.; vis. faculty Harvard U., 1980; invited presenter Australian Inst. Mgmt., Nippon Tel. & Tel., Hong Kong Commn. Against Corruption, 1984, Young Pres.'s Orgn. Internat. U., 1990, Nat. Assn. Indsl. & Office Parks, 1990, ABA, 1991, Govt. of Brazil, 1991. Author: Hard Problems of Management, 1986 (Book of Yr. Armed Forces Mil. Comtrs. 1986, Japanese edit. 1994), Power by Association, 1991, The Hotline Handbook, 1996, Planning Forum, 1992; editor: Public-Private Sector Ethics, 1979; mem. editl. bd. Report on Medicare Compliance; pub. Pastin Report on Best Compliance Practices, 1998—, Guerin Lect. on Philanthropy, 1996. Founding bd. mem. Tempe Leadership, 1985-89; bd. mem. Ctr. for Behavioral Health, Phoenix, 1986-89, Tempe YMCA, 1986—, Valley Leadership Alumni Assn., 1989-92; mem. Clean Air Com., Phoenix, 1987-90. Nat. Sci. Found. fellow, Cambridge, Mass., 1971-73; Nat. Endowment for the Humanities fellow, 1975; Exxon Edn. Found. grant, 1982-83. Mem.: Found. Ethical Orgns. (chmn. 1988, pres.), Am. Soc. Assn. Execs. (invited presenter 1987—97), Mt. Vernon Country Club, Harvard Club D.C., Phi Beta Kappa, Golden Key. Avocations: golf, running. Office: 214 S Payne St Alexandria VA 22314-3530 Home: 7205 Regent Dr Alexandria VA 22307-2044 Office Phone: 703-683-7916. Personal E-mail: councile@aol.com.

PASTOOR, ROBERTUS ANTONIUS, academic administrator; b. Maastricht, The Netherlands, Jan. 6, 1953; arrived in U.S., 1961; s. Johannes Pastoor and Maria Van der Pas; m. Ann Marie Lynch, June 8, 1985; children: Thomas Lynch-Pastoor, Tully Lynch-Pastoor, Marijka Lynch-Pastoor. BS in History and Edn., Mount St. Mary's Coll., Emmitsburg, Md., 1976; MEd in Counseling, McDaniel Coll., Westminster, Md., 1979; EdD in Ednl. Leadership, U. Mont., Missoula, 2003. Asst. dean of students Mount St. Mary's Coll., Emmitsburg, Md., 1979—81, assoc. dean of students, 1981—83, dean of students, 1983—87, v.p. student affairs, 1987—95; v.p. student life Carroll Coll., Helena, Mont., 1985—2002; v.p. student affairs U. San Diego, 2002—. Chair, bd. dirs. St. Johns Lit Inst. at Prospect Hall, Frederick, Md., 1977—79; pres., bd. dirs. ASACCU, 1998—2003. Vol. Project Concern, Inc., Vienna, Va., 1968—71. Mem.: Assn. Student Affairs at Cath. Colls., ACPA, NASPA. Democrat. Roman Catholic. Avocations: tennis, music, reading. Home: 11909 Sunshine Peak Ct San Diego CA 92131 Office: U San Diego 5998 Alcala Park San Diego CA 92120

PASTOR, EDWARD, congressman; b. Claypool, Ariz., June 28, 1943; m. Verma Mendez; children: Yvonne, Laura. BA, Ariz. State U., 1966, JD, 1974. Mem. Maricopa County Bd. Suprs., Phoenix, 1976-91; mem. U.S. Congress from 4th Ariz. dist. (formerly 2nd), Washington, 1991—; mem. appropriations com., steering & policy com. Democrat. Office: Ho Reps 2465 Rayburn HOB Washington DC 20515

PASTOR, JENNIFER, sculptor; b. Hartford, 1966; BFA, Sch. Visual Arts, 1988; MFA in Sculpture, UCLA, 1992. One-woman shows include Richard Telles Fine Art, 1994, Studio Guenzani, Milan, Italy, 1995, Mus. Contemporary Art, Chgo., 1996, exhibited in group shows at Regen Projects, L.A., 1993, Richard Telles Fine Art, 1994, Studio Guenzani, Milan, 1996, La. Mus. Modern Art, Humlebaek, Denmark, 1997, Whitney Mus. Am. Art, N.Y.C., 1997, Mus. Modern Art, San Francisco, 1997, others. Louis Comfort Tiffany grantee, 1995. Office: c/o Richard Telles Fine Art 7380 Beverly Blvd Los Angeles CA 90036-2501

PASTOR, MILLIE A. interior designer, consultant; d. Martin Joseph and Bessie B. Kloka; m. Robert Henry Pastor, Sept. 29, 1951; children: Robert Henry, George H., Patricia C., Karen M. BSN, RN, Mercy Coll., 1951. Founder, pres. Pastor Interiors, Inc., Bloomfield Hills, Mich., 1965—. Cons. URI, Nashville; cons., spkr., mem. nat. women's bd. Northwood Inst. Pres., Project Hope, 1973-75. Commr. Mich. Am. Recolution Bicentennial, 1972-78; bd. dirs. March of Dimes, 1980-82, Christ Child Soc., 1960-68, Mich. Artrain, Women's Com. of Detroit Symphony Orch., Mich. Opera, Ford Hospice, I.F.D.A., Henry Ford Hospice Health Sys.; pres. Am. Lung Assn., Southeastern Mich., 1980-83; active Boys and Girls Club Met. Detroit; active Mich. Opera Theatre, Mich. Cancer Found.; trustee Henry Ford Hospice Health Sys. Cmty. Care, 2000—; active Cystic Fibrosis Found., ARC, Equestrian Order of Holy Sepulchre Fan Club. Recipient Outstanding Contbn. award March of Dimes, 1977-79, Outstanding Fund Raising Vol. award Nat. Soc. Fund Raising Execs., 1982, Matilda R. Wilson award Boys & Girls Club, 1998; named Woman of Yr., Boys Town Italy, 1980. Mem. Internat. Furnishings and Design Assn. (v.p., Image Maker award Mich. chpt. 1979), Detroit Zool. Soc., Founders Soc., Legatus (pres. Detroit chpt. 2003-04). Republican. Office Phone: 248-851-0754.

PASTOR, PETER, history professor; b. Budapest, Hungary, Mar. 4, 1942; s. Steven Pastor and Julia Brown; m. Tatiana Kobishcha, Sept. 12, 1975; 1 child, Tatiana Anaïs. BA, CUNY, 1964; MA, NYU, 1965, PhD, 1969. Asst. prof. history Monmouth Coll., West Long Branch, NJ, 1969—71, Montclair (N.J.) State U., 1971—76, assoc. prof. history, 1976—82, prof. history, 1982—. Pub. Ctr. for Hungarian Studies and Publs., Inc., Wayne, NJ, 1998—. Author: Hungary Between Wilson and Lenin, 1976; editor: Revolutions and Interventions in Hungary and Its Neighbor States, 1918-1919, 1988. Decorated Mid. Cross of the Hungarian Republic; grantee, IREX, 1978. Home: 47 Cecilia Dr Wayne NJ 07470-4649 Office: Montclair State U Normal Ave Montclair NJ 07043 Office Phone: 973-655-7564.

PASTOR, STEPHEN DANIEL, chemistry educator, researcher, consultant; b. New Brunswick, NJ, Feb. 15, 1947; s. Stephen and Irene (Bors) P.; m. Joan Ordemann, Apr. 3, 1971 (div. 1979); 1 child, Melanie; m. Joanne Behrens, July 13, 1985 (div. 1990). BA in Chemistry, Rutgers U., 1969, MS in Chemistry, 1978, PhD in Chemistry, 1983. Chemist Nat. Starch and Chem. Corp., Bridgewater, NJ, 1972-79; rsch. group leader CIBA-Geigy Corp., Ardsley, NY, 1979-84, rsch. mgr., 1985-87; group leader Ctrl. Rsch. Labs. CIBA-Geigy Ag, Basel, Switzerland, 1987-89, rsch. fellow Ardsley, 1989-90, rsch. mgr., 1990-97, sr. rsch. fellow, 1997—2003; cons. Mayhill, N.Mex., 2003—. Asst. adj. prof. Pace U., Pleasantville, NY, 1984—, assoc. adj. prof., 1989-93, adj. prof., 1994—. Contbr. articles to profl. jours.; 103 patents in field. 1st lt. U.S. Army, 1969-71. Fellow, CIBA-Geigy Ag, 1998—2003. Mem. Am. Chem. Soc. (Westchester sect. Disting. Scientist award 1997). Achievements include research on organophosphorous and organosulfur chemistry, conformational analysis, germanium chemistry, organometallic chemistry, asymmetric synthesis, homogeneous catalysis. Home: PO Box 195 Mayhill NM 88339-0195

PASTORE, DONNA LEE, physical education educator; BA in Phys. Edn., U. Fla., 1981, MA in Phys. Edn., 1983; PhD, U. So. Calif., 1988. Instr. Pa. State U., Beaver, Pa.; asst. prof. Sch. Health Ohio State U., assoc. prof. Advisor Sports Mgmt. Club. Editl. bd. Jour. Sport Mgmt.; rev. Strategies. State coord. Nat. Girls and Women in Sport Day, 1992. Recipient NAGWS Linds to to Leadership award, 1982, NAGWS Rsch. award, 1983, Mabel Lee award, 1995. Mem. Ohio AHPERD (chair rsch. sect. higher edn., v.p.-elect sports sci. divsn., eastern dist. bylaws & oper. code com.), N. Am. Soc. Sports Mgmt. Office: Ohio State U Sch Phys Activity and Ednl Svcs 455 Larkins Hall 337 W 17th Ave Columbus OH 43210 E-mail: pastore.3@osu.edu.

PASTORE, WILLIAM M. insurance company executive; BS in Bus., MBA, L.I. U. Various positions Citibank, N.Y.C., divsn. exec. Nat. Servicing. Orgn.; sr. v.p. CIGNA HealthCare, Phila., 1995, pres., 1999—. Office: CIGNA HealthCare 1 Liberty Pl 1650 Market St Philadelphia PA 19192-0001

PASTOREK, MARCIA JAMBU, language educator, writer; d. Orlando Jambu and Lerocelier Rodriguez; m. Guy Michel Pastorek, Oct. 19, 1984; m. Gary Paul Sarrat, Sept. 0, 1970 (div. Dec. 0, 1982); children: Jon Pierre, Gary Paul Sarrat, Rene Charles, Remi Gerard, Scott Joseph Sarrat. BA in French, La. State U., 1966—70. Second Language Specialist Nicholls State U., La., 1982. Bilingual tchr. New Orleans Pub. Schools, 1971—72; french tchr. Ferncrest Sch., New Orleans, 1976—77; lang. arts tchr. St. Dominic Sch., New Orleans, 1977—78; french tchr. Rummel H.S., New Orleans, 1978—91; dir. lang. programs Lang. Odyssey, New Orleans, 1996—97; french tchr. Trinity Episcopal Sch., New Orleans, 1991—; cons./story writer Prog. Languages, New Orleans, 2002. Evaluator Ind. Schools Assn. SW, Mex. City, 1996—96; dir. french immersion camp Trinity Episcopal Sch., New Orleans, 1996—98; student european travel group leader Ednl. Travel Companies, 1979—2001; creative writing camp for children Trinity Episcopal Sch., New Orleans, 2000—00. Author (also director): (plays) La Chasse Galerie, Acadie; author: (collection) Contes Quebecois; prodr.: (cd) A Trinity Christmas; author: (short stories) The Secret of the Animals and other stories; contbr. articles. France exhibit co-chairman La. Children's Mus., New Orleans, 1998; children's soiree music chmn. Hermann-Grima Ho., New Orleans, 1997—2000; cons. on cajun culture La. Children's Mus., New Orleans, 2000—02. Fgn. Lang. fellowship, Nat. Endowment for the Humanities, 1995, Faculty grant, Trinity Episcopal Sch., 1996, 2000, Tchg. Mini-grant, La. Fgn. Lang. Teachers Assn., 1999, Presdl., La. State U., 1966—70, Emily Blake scholarship, 1968—69, Writers Conf., Highlights Found., 2001, Fgn. Lang. Asst., La. State U., 1970. Mem.: ASCD, Soc. of Children's Book Writers and Educators, Am. Coun. on Tchg. Fgn. Languages, La. Fgn. Lang. Teachers Assn., Am. Assn. Teachers of French (state pres. 1980—81), Nat. Network for Early Lang. Learning (exec. treas. 1998—2002), Phi Kappa Phi, Alpha Phi (vice-president 1969—70, Spirit Award, Best to Wear the Bordeaux 1969, 1970). R-Consevative. Catholic. Avocations: jazzercise, reading, tennis, travel. Office: Trinity Episcopal Sch 1315 Jackson Ave New Orleans LA 70130

PASTOREK, NORMAN JOSEPH, facial plastic surgeon; b. Moline, Ill., Feb. 8, 1939; s. Joseph Andrew and Rose (Faurone) P.; m. Janice Marie Gloss, Apr. 27, 1986; children: Kate Haviland, Kelly Taylor. AB, Augustana Coll., 1960; MD, U. Ill., Chgo., 1964. Diplomate Am. Bd. Otolaryngology. Intern San Francisco Gen. Hosp., 1964-65; resident U. Ill. Hosps., Chgo., 1965-69; pvt. practice medicine specializing in facial plastic surgery N.Y.C; clin. asst. prof. N.Y. Hosp. Cornell Med. Coll., 1971-83, dir. div. facial plastic surgery dept. otolaryngology, 1977—, clin. assoc. prof., 1983-91, clin. prof., 1991—; clin. prof. dept. otolaryngology NYU Sch. Medicine, 2003—. Examiner Am. Bd. Otolaryngology, 1971, 91-93; mem. bd. surgen dirs. Manhattan Eye, Earr and Throat Hosp., N.Y.C., 2001. Author: Blepharoplasty, 1983, 3d edit., 1994; editor: Aesthetic Facial Surgery, 1990; editor for beauty: Archives of Facial Plastic Surgery, 1999. Lt. comdr. USN, 1969-71. Fellow Am. Acad. Otolaryngology, Am. Bd. Otolaryngology (examiner 1991—), Am. Acad. Facial Plastic and Reconstructive Surgery (v.p. eastern region 1982-86, pres.-elect 1989-90, pres. 1990-91, pres. founders club 1996—), ACS; mem. Alpha Omega Alpha. Republican. Episcopalian.

PASTOREK, PAUL G. federal agency administrator; Undergrad., Loyola U., 1976, JD, 1979. Former ptnr. Adams and Reese, New Orleans; gen. counsel NASA, Washington, 2002—. Pres. La. State Bd. Elem. and Secondary Edn., 2000—; mem. various state bds. and commns. Office: NASA Hdqrs Mail Code A 300 E St SW Washington DC 20546

PASTORES, GREGORY MCCARTHY, pediatrician, medical geneticist, researcher; b. Bklyn., Sept. 4, 1959; s. Jovito Camara and Annie Harrington (McCarthy) P. BS in Biology, U. St. Thomas, 1979, MD, 1983. Diplomate Am. Bd. Pediat., Am. Bd. Med. Genetics in Clin. Genetics and Clin. Molecular Genetics. Resident in pediat. Mt. Sinai Med. Ctr., N.Y.C., 1986-89; fellow med. genetics Mayo Clinic Found., Rochester, Minn., 1989-91; fellow med. and molecular genetics Mt. Sinai Sch. Medicine, N.Y.C., 1991-92, instr. pediatrics, genetics, 1992-93, asst. prof. human genetics and pediatrics, 1993-97; asst. prof. neurology and pediatrics NYU Sch. Medicine, N.Y.C., 1997—2004, assoc. prof. neurology and pediatrics, 2004—. Roman Catholic. Home: 215 W 90th St Apt 6G New York NY 10024-1224 Office: NYU at Rivergate 493 E 34th St 2d Fl New York NY 10016 Office Phone: 212-263-8344. Business E-Mail: gregory.pastores@med.nyu.edu.

PASTORES, STEPHEN M. internist; b. N.Y.C., Sept. 5, 1958; s. Jovito Camara and Annie McCarthy Pastores; m. Maria Teresa Desancho; children: Steven Michael, Monica Cristina. MD, Lyceum Northwestern Coll. Medicine, Philippines, 1982. Diplomate Am. Bd. Internal Medicine, Am. Bd. Pulmonary Disease, Am. Bd. Critical Care Medicine. Resident Met. Hosp. Ctr., 1989; attending critical care physician Montefiore Med. Ctr., Bronx, NY, 1993—96; dir. emergency svcs. Dept. VA Med. Ctr., Bronx, 1996—99, asst. dir. surg. ICU, 1996—99; assoc. attending critical care physician Meml. Sloan-Kettering Cancer Ctr., N.Y.C., 1999—, dir. critical care rsch. and critical care fellowship program, 1999—. Editor: (book) ICU Bedside Technology, 2000; contbr. articles to profl. jours. Fellow: ACP (2000-Present), Am. Coll. of Critical Care Medicine, Am. Coll. Chest Physicians (1997-Present). Office: Meml Sloan-Kettering Cancer Ctr 1275 York Ave M-210C New York NY 10021 Business E-Mail: pastores@mskcc.org.

PASTRICK, HAROLD LEE, aeronautical engineer; b. Ambridge, Pa., June 28, 1936; s. Samuel and Mary (Makara) P.; m. Vivienne Lee Nusser Heinricher, June 3, 1961; children: Tracy Lee, Gregory Harold, Michael Joseph Samuel. BSEE, Carnegie-Mellon U., 1958; postgrad., Rutgers U., 1959-61, CCNY, 1961-63, U. Ala. Huntsville, 1964-66, 68-73; student, MIT, summers 1961-63; MS in Aeronautics & Astronautics, Stanford U., 1967, engr. in Aeronautics & Astronautics, 1972; PhD in Engring., Calif. Western U., 1977. Registered prof. engr., Ala. Metallurgical engring. aide Jones & Laughlin Steel Corp., Aliquippa, Pa., 1955-56; asst. engr., designer Am. Bridge Divsn., U.S. Steel Corp., Ambridge, 1957; electronics engr. Avionics Divsn., U.S. Army Signal R&D Labs., Ft. Monmouth, N.J., 1958-63; aerospace engr., Inertial Systems Team Missile R&D Labs., Redstone Arsenal, Ala., 1963-64; tech. dir. Army Inertial Guidance & Tech. Ctr., Redstone Arsenal, 1964-66; project engr. Inertial Guidance Br., Redstone Arsenal, 1967-71; rsch. aerospace engr. Guidance & Control Br., Redstone Arsenal, 1971-73; group leader Terminal Homing Missile Analysis, Redstone Arsenal, 1973-79; staff specialist, asst. to dir., land warfare Office of Under Sec. Def., Rsch. and Engring., Washington, 1979-80; chief, guidance and control analysis U.S. Army Missile Command, Redstone Arsenal, Ala., 1980-81; v.p. engring. Control Dynamics Co., Huntsville, 1981-83; asst. v.p., engring. analysis divsn. Sci. Applications Internat. Corp., Huntsville, 1983-86; v.p. theater missile def. and system analysis operation, 1986-91; corp. v.p., gen. mgr. SRS Technologies, Huntsville, 1991—. Acting pres. and COO SRS Techs., 1994, mem. corp. exec. mgmt. com., 1991—, mem. profit sharing and 401(k) com., 1993—; lectr. Sch. of Sci. and Engring., U. Ala., Huntsville, 1967-83; lectr. dept. continuing edn. George Washington U., 1985-87; engring. seminar dir. Applied Tech. Inst., Frankfurt, Germany, 1984, Singapore, 1986; tech. tng. dir. Tech. Tng. Corp., Tel Aviv, 1988; lectr. Advanced Tech. Internat., Ltd., London, 1985; guidance and control cons. various labs Dept. of Def., Washington, 1971-2001; lectr., rsch. advisor Southeastern Inst. Tech., Huntsville, 1978-84; lectr., seminar leader Guidance and Control Technologies, U.S., Europe, Asia, Mex., 1980-94. Contbr. over 120 articles to profl. jours. Chmn. combined fed. campaign ARDEC United Way, Redstone Arsenal, 1976; mem. Huntsville Econ. Devel. Com., 1994; chmn. indsl. contbns. Armed Forces Week C. of C. Huntsville-Madison County, 1993—96, 1999, vice chmn. mil. affairs. com., 1994—95, chmn. mil. affairs com., 1996; program chmn. tech. and bus. symposium and exhbn. Huntsville, 1994—95; gen. chmn., 1995—96; chmn. adv. com., 1997—98; founding trustee Ala. Constn. Village Found., 2001—; mem. All-Peoples Meml. for All Vets., Madison County, 2001—; mem. elec. and computer engring. adv. bd. The Citadel, Charleston, SC, 2001—; pres. St. Michael's Serbian Orthodox Ch., 2002—, Greek Orthodox Ch., 1967, 1973, chmn. planning com., 1993—2000. Capt. U.S. Army, 1958—64. Recipient Eminent Engr. Disting. Tau Beta Pi, 1998. Fellow: AIAA (assoc.; vice-chmn. Huntsville chpt. 1979, guest editor Jour. Guidance and Control 1981, missile tech. com. 1989—91); mem.: Ala. Acad. Sci. (vice chmn. 1978—79, engring. chmn. 1979—81), Inst. Navigation, Assn. U.S. Army, IEEE (sr.; chpt. program chmn. 1972—73), Soc. Computer Simulation, Am. Def. Preparedness Assn. (vice-chmn. Huntsville chpt. 1974—75), Huntsville Assn. Tech. Socs. (adv. com. 1997—98, pres. 1998—99, chmn.), Redstone Golf Club, Greenwhyche Club (v.p. 1979), Heritage Club, Rotary (sec. 1994—95, pres.-elect. 1995—96, pres. 1996—97, asst. gov. dist. 6860 1997—2000, dist. task force dir. 2000—01), Greater Huntsville Rotary Found. (dir. internat. svc. 1992—94, CEO 1998—2000). Achievements include pioneering hardware in the loop simulations for testing laser semi-active guided missiles. Avocations: golf, weight tng., choral music, reading, running. Home: 2624 Trailway Rd SE Huntsville AL 35801-1474 Office: SRS Technologies 500 Discovery Dr NW Huntsville AL 35806-2810 E-mail: hpastrick@stg.srs.com.

PASTUCH, BORIS MAX See MAX, BUDDY

PASULA, ANGELA MARIE, lawyer; b. Michigan City, Ind., Oct. 2, 1956; d. Edward Joseph Pasula and Theresa Jeanette (Stella) Hack; m. David Mark Prusa, June 19, 1982. BA in Polit. Sci. cum laude, Western Mich. U., 1977; JD, Valparaiso U., 1980. Bar: Mich. 1980. Asst. pros. atty. Kalamazoo (Mich.) Prosecutors Office, 1980-82, Berrien County Prosecutors Office, Niles, Mich., 1982—. Office: Berrien County Prosecutors Office 1205 Front St Niles MI 49120-1627

PASUPULETI, VENUMADHAV, business executive, consultant; b. Hyderabad, India, Mar. 24, 1969; s. Srinivas Rao and Rama Kumari P.; m. Marilyn L. Miller, May 7, 1992; 1 child, Teja. Grad., Bur. of Data Processing Sys., Hyderabad, 1985; student, Wright State U., 1988-92. Info. tech. cons., 1984-93; mgr. Info. Horizons, Parsippany, N.J., 1993-95; exec. v.p. Globe Tech. Exch., Dayton, Ohio, 1995; COB/CEO Megasoft, Dayton, 1995—. Pres. Indian Student Assn. Wright State U., Dayton, 1989-92; vol. India Literacy Project, Dayton, 1990-95, Ohio India Project, Dayton, 1990-95, Project Outreach, Dayton, 1999--, Day of Caring, Dayton, 1990-95; coun. mem. Dayton Minority Supplier Devel. Coun., 1997—. Mem. IEEE, South Ctrl. Ohio Minority Bus. Coun. (coun. mem. 2000—), Assn. for Computing Machinery, Math. Assn. of Am., Dayton Area C. of C., Beavarcreek C. of C. Office: Megasoft PO Box 20271 Dayton OH 45420-0271 Office Phone: 937-554-7479. Business E-Mail: c.e.o@megasoft.us.

PASURKA, CARL A., JR., economist; b. Elgin, IL, Sept. 15, 1953; s. Carl A. Pasurka, Sr., Lorraine Pasurka. AA, Harper Jr. Coll., Palatine, Ill., 1973; BS, No. Ill. U., 1975; MS, PhD, U. Ill., 1981. Vis. asst. prof. dept. econs. So. Ill. U., Carbondale, 1981—85, vis. asst. prof. dept. fin., 1983; asst. prof. dept. econs. Loyola U., Chgo., 1985—92; economist U.S. EPA, Washington, 1992—. V.p. Chgo. Energy Economists, 1988—89, pres., 1989—90, bd. advisors, 1990—91. Assoc. editor: Jour. Environ. Econs. and Mgmt., 1994—96; contbr. chapters to books, articles to profl. jours. Grantee, U.S. EPA, 1991—92. Mem.: Internat. Input-Output Assn., Productivity Analysis Rsch. Network, Assn. Environ. and Resource Economists, Am. Econs. Assn. Home: 320 23rd St S Apt 623 Arlington VA 22202-3806 Office: EPA 1301 Constitution Ave NW Washington DC Business E-Mail: PASURKA.CARL@EPA.GOV.

PASVOLSKY, RICHARD LLOYD, parks, recreation, and environment educator; b. Englewood, NJ, Feb. 16, 1924; s. Valentine and Ellen Isabel (Stoughton) P.; m. Jo Anne Evans, June 16, 1968. BEd, Panzer Coll., 1950; MA in Edn., NYU, 1955; D in Recreation, Ind. U., 1973. Asst. supt. recreation City of Rutland, Vt., 1951-53; supt. recreation City of Montpelier, Vt., 1953-55; dir. parks and recreation Twp. of Parsippany-Troy Hills, NJ, 1955-62; asst. prof. outdoor and environ. edn. NJ State Sch. Conservation, Branchville, NJ, 1962-71; assoc. prof. edn. Ramapo Coll. NJ, Mahwah, NJ, 1972-84, coach archery, 1973-84; adj. prof. Kean Univ., Union, NJ, 1985—. Instr. archery, dir. dance and recreation World Archery Ctr., Pomfret, Conn., 1964-92; dir. NJ State Coll. divsn. Nat. Archery Assn., 1978-84. Advisor to choreographer, cons. prodn. office closing ceremonies Statue of Liberty Centennial Celebration, 1986; rec. artist: Square Dances, 1961, 91, mag. articles, 1954-66; columnist Lines About Squares, 1983—. Instr. dance camp staff Lloyd Shaw Found., 1981—, bd. dirs., 1982-88; bd. trustees Sussex County Sr. Legal Resources Ctr., 1992-94. With U.S. Army, 1943-46, ETO. Recipient Alumni award Panzer Coll. NJ, 1979, Spl. Alumni award, 1987; named to Ramapo Coll. Athletic Hall of Fame, 1993, Lakewood (NJ) HS Hall of Fame, 1998. Mem. AAHPERD (Recreator of Yr. Ea. Dist. 1977), NJ Alliance Health, Phys. Edn., Recreation and Dance, Callers Coun. NJ,

Callerlab, Phi Delta Kappa. Avocations: calling square dances, ballroom dancing, skiing, golf, tennis. Home: 31 Newton Ave Branchville NJ 07826-4203 Office: Kean U NJ Phys Edn Dept Union NJ 07083

PATAKI, ANDREW, bishop; b. Palmerton, Pa., Aug. 30, 1927; Student, St. Vincent Coll., St. Procopious Coll., Lisle, Ill., Sts. Cyril and Methodius, Byzantine Cath. Sem., Grigorian U., Rome. Ordained priest Roman Cath. Ch., 1952. Apptd. aux. bishop of Passaic, N.J. Byzantine Cath. Diocese, 1983; bishop of Parma (Ohio) Diocese of Passaic, NJ, 1984—96, bishop, 1996—. Home: 445 Lackawanna Ave West Paterson NJ 07424-2969

PATAKI, GEORGE E. governor; b. Peekskill, N.Y., June 24, 1945; m. Elizabeth (Libby) Rowland; children: Emily, Teddy, Allison, George Owen. BA, Yale U., 1967; JD, Columbia U. Sch. Law, 1970. Mayor City of Peekskill, NY, 1981—84; elected mem. State Assembly, N.Y., 1985-92, State Senate, NY, 1993—95; assoc. Law Firm of Dewey, Ballantine, Bushby, Palmer & Wood, 1970-74; ptnr. Law Firm Plunckett & Jaffe, P.C., N.Y.C., White Plains, Albany and Peekskill, 1974-89; co-proprietor Pataki Farm, Peekskill, N.Y.; gov. State of NY, 1995—. Advanceman Friends of Rockefeller Team, 1970; upstate campaign coord. Com. to Elect Gov. Wilson, 1974; mem. Peekskill Rep. City Com., 1974—, chmn. 1977-83; mem. N.Y. State Rep. Com., 1980-85. Republican. Address: Office of the Gov Exec Chambers/State Capitol Albany NY 12224

PATAKY, PAUL ERIC, ophthalmologist; b. Phila., May 19, 1945; s. Andrew and Helen (Koffler) P.; m. Aimee Janet Margoles, June 13, 1971; Meryl Corinne, Lisa Ann. BS, Trinity Coll., 1966; MD, Pa. State U., 1971. Diplomate Am. Bd. Ophthalmology. Resident ophthalmology Mass. Eye and Ear Infirmary, Boston, 1972-76; asst. in ophthalmology Harvard Med. Sch., Boston, 1976-79; ophthalmologist Dedham (Mass.) Med. Assocs., 1976-79, Paul E. Pataky M.D. P.A., Boynton Beach, Fla., 1979—. Chmn. dept. surgery Bethesda Meml. Hosp., Boynton Beach, 1988-89; pres. med. staff, 1990-91, chmn. credentials chmn., 1992-93, chmn. surg. care com., 1993-97. Named One of Am.'s Top Ophthalmologists 2004-05, Consumer Rsch. Coun. Am., 2004. Fellow Am. Acad. Ophthalmology; mem. Fla. Soc. Ophthalmology, AMA, Pan-Am. Assn. Ophthalmology, Palm Beach County Med. Soc., Fla. Med. Assn. Avocations: travel, fine art. Office: 2623 S Seacrest Blvd Ste 102 Boynton Beach FL 33435-7531 Office Phone: 561-734-5056. E-mail: ppataky2@earthlink.net.

PATANKAR, SUNIL NARAYAN, research scientist; b. Mumbai, Maharastra, India, June 11, 1959; s. Narayan S. and Usha N. Patankar; m. Madhavi S. Jadhav, Apr. 23, 1965; children: Aishwarya S., Ameya S. PhD, Indian Inst. of Tech., 1983—89. Rsch. fellow Nanyang Technol. U., Singapore, 1997—2000; vis. scientist U. Idaho, 2000—. Rsch. engr. Thapar Corp. R & D Ctr., Patiala, India, 1993—97. Mem.: Am. Soc. of Metals. Achievements include patents pending for. Home: 458 Taylor Ave # 6 Moscow ID 83843 Office: University of Idaho Mclure Bldg Moscow ID 83844-3026 Personal E-mail: mspatankar@hotmail.com. E-mail: pata1630@uidaho.edu.

PATCHETT, ANN, writer; b. Los Angeles, Calif., 1963; BA, Sarah Lawrence College. Writer-in-residence Allegheny Coll., 1989—90; vis. asst. prof. Murray State U., 1992. Author: (novels) The Patron Saint of Liars, 1992 (James A. Michener/ Copernicus award for a book in progress, 1990, TV movie, 1997), Taft (also screenplay), 1994 (Janet Heidinger Kafka prize for the best work of fiction, 1994), The Magician's Assistant, 1997 (Nashville Banner Tennessee Writer of the Year Award), Bel Canto, 2001 (PEN/Faulkner prize, 2002), (non-fiction) Truth & Beauty, 2004; contbr. articles The New York Times Magazine, Chicago Tribune, Boston Globe, Vogue, GQ, Elle, Gourmet. Fellow Bunting Fellowship, Mary Ingrahm Bunting Institute at Radcliffe College, 1993, Guggenheim, 1994; grantee Residential fellowship, Fine Arts Work Ctr., Provincetown, Mass., 1990. Mailing: c/o HarperCollins Publishers 10 East 53rd Street New York NY 10022*

PATCHETT, ARTHUR ALLAN, medicinal chemist, pharmaceutical executive; b. Middletown, N.Y., May 28, 1929; s. Arthur Allan and Anna Gertrude (Vossler) P.; m. Lois Rhoda Mc Neil, Aug. 18, 1962; Thomas John, Steven Edward. BA, Princeton U., 1951; PhD, Harvard U., 1955; DSc (hon.), Bloomfield Coll., 2001. Rsch. assoc. NIH, Bethesda, Md., 1955-57; rsch. chemist Merck Rsch. Labs., Rahway, N.J., 1957-62, dir. synthetic chem. rsch., 1962-69, sr. dir. synthetic chem. rsch., 1969-71, sr. dir. new lead discovery, 1971-76, exec. dir. new lead discovery, 1976-88, v.p. exploratory chemistry, 1988-95, v.p. medicinal chemistry, 1995-2000, cons., 2000—. Contbr. over 170 papers to profl. jours., sci. confs. Named to, N.J. Inventors Hall of Fame, N.J. Inst. Tech., 1990; recipient Discoverers award, Pharm. Mfrs. Assn., 1992, Smissman Bristol-Myers Squibb award, 2001. Fellow AAAS; mem. Am. Chem. Soc. (chmn. div. medicinal chemistry 1971, E.B. Hershberg Important Discoveries in Medicinally Active Substances award 1993, Alfred Burger award in medicinal chemistry 2002). Achievements include 180 U.S. patents (co-holder); co-inventor antihypertensive drug Vasotec; key contbr. to discovery of cholesterol lowering drug Mevacor.

PATCHIN, REBECCA J. anesthesiologist, educator, administrator; b. Detroit, Dec. 8, 1949; d. Robert Ira and Doris J. (Hubert) P.; m. Carl W. Anderson, 1988. ASN, Pacific Union Coll., 1969; BSN, Walla Walla Coll., 1971; MD, Loma Linda U., 1989. Diplomate in anesthesiology and pain mgmt. Am. Bd. Anesthesiology. Resident in internalmedicine Loma Linda (Calif.) U. Med. Ctr., 1989-90, resident in anesthesiology, 1990-93, fellow in pain mgmt. dept. anesthesiology, 1993-94; asst. prof. anesthesiology Loma Linda U., 1994—; assoc. med. dir. Ctr. for Pain Mgmt., Loma Linda, 1995—. Presenter in field. Contbr. abstracts to profl. jours. Mem. AMA (mem. credentials com. 1986—, mem. awards com. bd. trustees 1988-89, del. ho. of dels. 1990—, mem. reference com. 1994—, chair coun. on med. edn. 2002-03, trustee 2003—), Internat. Anesthesiology Rsch. Soc., Internat. Assn. for Study of Pain, Am. Soc. Anesthesiology, Am. Pain Soc., Am. Soc. Regional Anesthesia, Am. Acad. Pain Medicine, Calif. Soc. Anesthesiology (del. resident component 1991-93, mem. com. on young physicians 1994—96, chair com. on young physicians 1996—), Calif. Med. Assn. (mem. reference com. 1988, trustee 1991-93, mem. com. on health professions and licensure 1992—, chair com. on health professions and licensure 1993-96, mem. coun. on legislation 1995-96, chair coun. on legislation 2000—), So. Calif. Cancer Pain Initiative, Riverside County Med. Assn. (sec.-treas 2002, pres. 2004), San Bernardino County Med. Soc. Office Phone: 951-413-0200.

PATE, BROOKS, chemist; BS, U. Va., 1987; PhD, Princeton U., 1992. NRC postdoctoral fellow Nat. Inst. Stds. and Tech., Gaithersburg, Md., 1992—93; prof. chemistry U. Va., Charlottesville, 1993—. Recipient CAREER award, NSF, 1996. Office: U Va Dept Chemistry McCormick Rd Charlottesville VA 22903

PATE, JACK D. publishing executive; m. Debbie Pate; 3 children. B in Comm. Media, Indiana U. Pa., 1982. Customer svc. rep. to retail advt. dept. intern The Pitts. Press, 1979—82; positions in retail and classified advt. sales The Hollywood Sun Tattler, Fla., circulation sales mgr.; classified advt. mgr. Evansville (Ind.) Courier & Press, 1989—93, advt. dir., 1993—98, dir. sales and mktg., 1998—2000, pres., pub., 2004—, San Angelo Std.-Times, Tex., 2000—04. Office: Evansville Courier & Press 300 E Walnut St Evansville IN 47702-0268*

PATE, JACQUELINE HAIL, retired data processing company executive; b. Amarillo, Tex., Apr. 7, 1930; d. Ewen and Virginia Smith (Crosland) Hail; children: Charles (dec.), John Durst, Virginia Pate Edgecomb, Christopher. Student, Southwestern U., Georgetown, Tex., 1947-48; grad., Real Estate Inst., 1998. Exec. sec. Western Gear Corp., Houston, 1974-76; adminstr., treas., dir. Aberrant Behavior Ctr., Personality Profiles, Inc., Corp. Procedures, Inc., Dallas, 1976-790; mgr. regional site svcs. programs Digital Equipment Corp., Dallas, 1979-92; ret., 1992. Realtor Keller Williams Realty, Austin, Tex., 1996—. Active Austin Bd. Realtors, PTA, Dallas, 1958-73. Mem. Daus. Republic Tex. (treas. French Legation state com. 1996). Methodist. Home: 6501 Brush Country #118 Austin TX 78749

PATE, JAMES LAVERT, lawyer; b. Shreveport, La., Feb. 16, 1952; s. Barney Fain and Mary Elizabeth (Stancil) P.; m. Andrea Carol Cofer, Nov. 7, 1975; children: Allison, Erin, Caitlin. BS, La. State U., 1975; JD, Loyola U., New Orleans, 1979. Bar: La. 1979, U.S. Dist. Ct. (ea., mid. and we. dists.) La. 1979. Assoc. Bailey & Leininger, New Orleans, 1979-80; ptnr. Onebane, Donohoe, Lafayette, La., 1982-87, Laborde & Neuner, Lafayette, 1987—. Bd. mem. Acadiana Safety Assn., Lafayette, 1987—. Mem. ABA, Am. Arbitration Assn., La. Bar Assn., La. Assn. Def. Counsel, Def. Rsch. Inst. Republican. Episcopalian. Office: Laborde and Neuner 1 Petroleum Ctr 1001 W Pinhook Rd Lafayette LA 70503-2407

PATE, JAMES LEONARD, oil company executive; b. Mt. Sterling, Ill., Sept. 6, 1935; s. Virgil Leonard and Mammie Elizabeth (Taylor) Pate; m. Donna Charlene Pate, Oct. 23, 1955; children: David Charles, Gary Leonard, Jennifer Elizabeth. Prof. econs. Monmouth (Ill.) Coll., 1965—68; sr. economist Fed. Res. Bank Cleve., 1968—72; chief economist B.F. Goodrich Co., Akron, Ohio, 1972—74; asst. sec. Dept. Commerce, Washington, Ohio, 1974—76, spl. adviser to White House, 1976, sr. v.p. fin., 1976; v.p. fin. Pennzoil Co., Houston, Ohio, 1976—89, exec. v.p., 1989, exec. v.p., COO, 1990, CEO, 1990, also chmn. bd.; chmn. Pennzoil-Quaker State Co., Houston, 1994—. Contbr. articles to profl. jours. and textbooks. Bd. govs. Rice U.; mem. Senated Monmouth Coll.; bd. dirs. Am. Petroleum Inst., Nat. Petroleum Coun. Fellow: Royal Econ. Soc.; mem.: Pi Gamma Mu. Republican. Office: Pennzoil Co 700 Milam Houston TX 77002-2805

PATE, JOHN GILLIS, JR., financial consultant, accounting educator; b. Chattanooga, Jan. 27, 1928; s. John Gillis Pate and Iona Estelle (Bowman) Pate Ketchman; m. Daphne Mae Davis, Feb. 8, 1946; children: John Gillis III, Daphne Iona, Donna Gay. Student, U. Tampa, 1947-48; AA with highest honors, U. Fla., 1950; BS cum laude, Fla. State U., 1953, MS, 1958; PhD, Columbia U., 1968. CPA, S.C. Mgr. Grocery Concession, Albany, Ga., 1944-45, Variety Store, Panama City, Fla., 1946-47; asst. to CPA Standard Brands, Inc., Birmingham, Ala., 1951-53; acctg. supervisory trainee Birmingham, Ala., 1953-54; grad. asst. Fla. State U., Tallahassee, 1957-58; asst. to CPA Pensacola, Fla., 1956-58; CPA, 1958; asst. prof. U. Ga., Athens, 1958-60; lectr. Columbia U., N.Y.C., 1961-64; asst. prof. Bernard M. Baruch Coll. of CUNY, 1963-69; prof. acctg. U. Tex.-El Paso, 1969-85, U. S.C., Spartanburg, 1988-93. Cons. resource person fin. and human resources Charles Lea Ctr., Spartanburg, 1988—, dir. Internal Audit and Spl. Projects, 1994-2002. Author: Index C.P.A. Exams and Unofficial Answers, 1974-81; co-author: Accounting Trends and Techniques, 1967-88, Index to Accounting and Auditing Services, 1971; contbr. articles to ann. profl. publs. Tither, Coronado Bapt. Ch., El Paso, 1969-86, Buck Creek Bapt. Ch., Spartanburg, 1987—; cons. Alderman of El Paso, 1982, County Councilman of Spartanburg, 1991-98. With lt. j.g. USN, 1955-56. Columbia U. fellow, 1960; Earhart Found. fellow, 1960, Am. Acctg. Assn. fellow, 1960, Found fellow, 1961-62; recipient Haskins and Sells award, 1960. Mem. AICPA (cons. 1961-88), Am. Acctg. Assn., Moose, Masons, Shriners, Beta Alpha Psi, Beta Alpha Chi. Republican. Home and Office: 106 Lori Cir Spartanburg SC 29303-5527

PATE, MICHAEL LYNN, lawyer; b. Ft. Worth, Tex., July 9, 1951; s. J.B. and Mary Anna (Hable) P.; m. Barbara Ann Linch, May 28, 1977. AA, Schreiner Coll., 1971; BS, Tex. Wesleyan Coll., 1973; JD, U. Tex., 1975. Bar: Tex. 1976, D.C. 1983, U.S. Tax Ct. 1986, U.S. Supreme Ct. 1987. Adminstrv. asst. to Senator Sherman, counsel natural resources com. Tex. Senate, 1976-77; adminstrv. asst. to Lt. Gov. Bill Hobby, Austin, Tex., 1977-79; legis. asst. Senator Bentsen, Washington, 1979-81, legis. dir., 1981-86; ptnr., head Washington office Bracewell & Patterson, Washington, 1986—. Trustee Schreiner U. Mem. ABA, Tex. Bar Assn., D.C. Bar Assn. Democrat. Methodist. Avocations: basketball, tennis, golf. Office: Bracewell & Patterson 2000 K St NW Ste 500 Washington DC 20006-1872 Office Phone: 202-828-5800. E-mail: mpate@bracepatt.com., michael.pate@bracewell.com.

PATE, PAUL DANNY, mayor; b. Ottumwa, Iowa, May 1, 1958; s. Paul Devern and Velma Marie (McConnell) P.; m. Jane Ann Wacker, July 15, 1978; children: Jennifer Ann, Paul Daniel III, Amber Lynn. AA in Bus., Kirkwood Coll., 1978; cert. fin. mgmt. program, U. Pa., 1990. Exec. dir. Jr. Achievement, Cedar Rapids, Iowa, 1978-82; pres. PM Systems Corp., Cedar Rapids, 1982—; senator Iowa State Senate, Des Moines, 1989-93; Sec. of State State of Iowa, 1994-98; mayor City of Cedar Rapids, 2002—. Chmn. Iowa Young Reps., Des Moines, 1989-93, Recipient Guardian Small Bus. award Nat. Fedn. Independent Bus., 1990; named Young Entrepreneur of Yr. U.S. Small Bus. Adminstrn., Iowa, 1988, Alumnus of Yr. Kirkwood Coll., Cedar Rapids, 1990. Republican. Methodist. Avocation: water-skiing. Home: 6801 Bowman Ln NE Cedar Rapids IA 52402-1575 Office: PM Sys Corp 850 Robins Rd Hiawatha IA 52233-1320

PATE, ROBERT HEWITT, JR., counselor educator; b. Abingdon, Va., Apr. 5, 1938; s. Robert Hewitt and Esther Frances (Kirk) P.; m. Ellen O'Neal Pope, Dec. 11, 1960; children: Robert Hewitt III, Mary Ellen Pate Barton. AB, Davidson Coll., 1960; MEd, U. Va., 1965; PhD, U. N.C., 1968. Lic. prof. counselor, Va. Marketer Sinclair Refining Co., Abingdon, Va., 1960-61, 63-64; counselor St. Andrews Presbyn. Coll., Laurinburg, N.C., 1965-66; prof. counselor edn. U. Va., Charlottesville, 1968—, interim dean, 1994-95, assoc. dean, 1995—. Mem. adj. faculty Fed. Exec. Inst., Charlottesville, 1978—. Author: Being A Counselor, 1983. Elder local Presbyn. ch. 1st lt. U.S. Army 1961-63. Mem. Am. Counseling Assn., Va. Counselors Assn. (pres. 1983-84), Nat. Bd. Cert. Counselors (chair 1996-97). Avocation: reading. Home: 552 Dryden Pl Charlottesville VA 22903-4666 Office: Curry Sch Dean's Office 405 Emmet St S PO Box 400260 Charlottesville VA 22904-4260

PATE, THOMAS LOWELL, manufacturing executive; b. Lutie, Okla., Nov. 10, 1926; s. George Lewey and Francis Lula (Humphrey) Pate; m. Thelma Christine Mankin, June 26, 1996; children: Gwendolyn, Carla. BS, Southeastern State Teachers Coll., 1947—48. Adv. to Star Builder Coun. Star Mfg. Co., Okla. City, 1963—80; owner Pate Constrn. Co., Wilburton, Okla., 1960, Patco Mfg. Co., Wilburton, Okla., 1966, Began Liquidating Const. and Mfg. Co., Wilburton, Okla., 1980—84, Pate Enterprises, Wilburton, Okla., 1984—. Organizer of S.T.O.P. Okla. City, 1990; pres. C of C, 1980; organizer and first chmn. Okla. for Integrity in Govt., 1993—2003. Cpl., 1944—46, Manila, Philippines. Mem.: Nat. Fedn. of Ind. Bus. Republican. Bapt. Avocations: archaeology, genealogy, hunting, fishing, history. Home: 2307 E Main Wilburton OK 74578

PATE, VIRGINIA FRANCES, artist, educator; b. Athens, Tex., Dec. 16, 1927; BA, U. Evansville, 1974; MA in Edn., Psychology, Southwestern Bapt. Theol. Sem., 1976. Cert. art instr., 1994, Grumbacher cert. instr., 1997. Artist, owner Pate Art and Ceramics, Stanville, Ky., 1977-82, owner, artist Ft. Worth, 1982-88; owner, artist, art instr. PATE Art Studio/Gallery, Lehigh, Fla., 1988—. One-woman shows include First Nat. Bank, Pikeville, Ky., 1980, Cultural Ctr., Prestonsburg, Ky., 1980, PATE Art Studio/Gallery, Lehigh, Fla., 1980-03, PATE Fine Art Gallery, Irving, Tex., 2003—, Tessier Galleries, Paris, Limoges, France, 1996—; group exhibits include S.W. Fla. Art Coun., Ft. Myers, 1994, Charlotte County Art Guild, Punta Gorda, Fla., 1995, Lee County Art Alliance, Ft. Myers, 1997, Robb & Stucky, Fort Myers, Fla., 1999, Am. Impressionist Soc. Nat. Exhibit, 2000 (award, charter/signature mem.), Spring Festival, Lehigh, Fla., 2001 (awards); represented in permanent collections France, Germany, Can., U.S. Office Phone: 972-254-7200. E-mail: patefineart@comcast.net.

PATE, WILLIAM, telecommunications industry executive; grad. in Journalism, grad. in Comm., Ga. State U. Pub. rels. specialist Goodwill Industries, ARC; prodr. advt. and mktg. programs S.E. Dairy Assn.; with Knapp Inc., Atlanta; supr. domestic and internat. advt. and pub. rels. MCI; v.p. advt. and Pacific rels. BellSouth Corp., Atlanta, 1997—. Chmn. Atlanta Conv. and Visitors Bur., The Chick-Fil-A Peach Bowl; mem. bd. trustees Ga. State U.; bd. dirs. Alliance Theatre Co., The Ad Coun. Recipient Ad Campaign of Yr. for Gramercy Press campaign, Advt. Age mag., Campaign of Yr. award for Chatsford, Am. Mktg. Assn. Mem.: Pub. Rels. Soc. Am., Assn. Nat. Advertisers, Am. Advt. Fedn. Office: BellSouth Corp 1155 Peachtree St NE Atlanta GA 30309-3610

PATE, WILLIAM PATRICK, city manager; b. Duplin County, N.C., July 30, 1962; s. William Atlas and Bonny Lou (O'Leary) P.; m. Sandra Martin, Aug. 17, 1985; children: William Glenn, Andrew Patrick. BA in Polit. Sci. and Religion, U. N.C., 1984, MPA, 1986. Budget and evaluation analyst intern City of Winston-Salem, N.C., 1985-86, budget and evaluation analyst, 1986-87, lead budget and evaluation analyst, 1987; budget and rsch. mgr. City of Greensboro, N.C., 1987-90, budget and evaluation dir., 1990-99; asst. city mgr. City of High Point, N.C., 1999—. Inst. of Govt. intern N.C. Office Coastal Mgmt., Raleigh, N.C., 1984; rsch. asst. U. N.C., Chapel Hill, 1984-85. Mem. Chmns. Soc. United Way of High Point, 1998—; mem. Leadership Greensboro, 1993-99, Leadership High Point, 2000—; elder, clk. session Faith Presbyn. Ch., Greensboro; mem. Salem Presbyn. World Ministries Cluster, 1997-99. Recipient Disting. Svc. award Alpha Phi Omega, 1984. Mem. Internat. City Mgrs. Assn., Am. Soc. Pub. Adminstrn. (pres. Piedmont Triad chpt. 1994), Gov. Fin. Officers Assn. U.S. and Can. (exec. bd. 1998-2004, nat. com. on govtl. budgeting and mgmt. 1993-98, nat. com. on debt and fiscal policy 1998-2001, pres. 2002-03, Disting. Budget Presentation award reviewer, Disting. Budget Presentation award 1992-98), N.C. Local Govt. Budget Assn. (bd. dirs. 1990-92, 95, 1st v.p. 1992-93, pres. 1993-94), N.C. City/County Mgrs. Assn., U. N.C. MPA Alumni Assn. (program chmn. 1992, pres-elect 1993, pres. 1994, Scholarship award 1985), U. N.C. Gen. Alumni Assn. (bd. dirs. 1994-95), Kiwanis Club. Presbyterian. Home: 4509 Calabria Ct High Point NC 27265-9595 Office: City of High Point PO Box 230 High Point NC 27261-0230 E-mail: pat.pate@ci.high-point.nc.us.

PATÉ-CORNELL, MARIE-ELISABETH LUCIENNE, management and engineering educator; b. Dakar, Senegal, Aug. 17, 1948; arrived in U.S., 1971; d. Edouard Pierre Lucien and Madeleine (Tournissa) Paté; m. C. Allin Cornell, Jan. 3, 1981; children: Phillip Cornell, Ariane Cornell. Eng. Degree, Inst. Polytechnique de Grenoble, France, 1971; MS in Ops. Rsch., Stanford U., 1972, PhD in Engring.-Econ. Systems, 1978. Asst. prof. in civil engring. MIT, 1978-81; asst. prof. indsl. engring. Stanford (Calif.) U., 1981-84, assoc. prof. indsl. engring., 1984-91, prof. indsl. engring., 1991—, chmn. dept. indsl. engring., 1997-99, chmn. dept. mgmt. sci. and engring., 2000—. Cons. Electric Power Rsch. Inst., 1995, SRI Internat., 1993, Atty. Gen. of N.Mex., 1995, Halliburton, 2000, Swiss Re, 2002; mem. adv. coun. NASA, 1995—98; mem. Marine Bd. NRC, 1995—97; mem. Army Sci. Bd., 1995—97, Air Force Sci. Bd., 1998—2002, Calif. Coun. on Sci. and Tech., 2000—, Pres.'s Adv. Bd. on Fgn. Intelligence. Contbr. numerous articles to profl. jours. Numerous rsch. grants. Mem.: Nat. Acad. Engring. (councilor 2001—), Inst. for Mgmt. Scis., Ops. Rsch. Soc. Am., Soc. for Risk Analysis (councilor 1985—86, pres. 1995). Avocations: tennis, swimming, chess, music. Home: 110 Coquito Way Menlo Park CA 94028-7404 Office: Stanford U Dept Mgmt Sci and Engring Stanford CA 94305 E-mail: mep@leland.stanford.edu.

PATEL, AJAY, dean; m. Aparna Patel; 2 children. BS, St. Joseph's Coll., India; MBA, U. Balt.; PhD, U. Ga. Faculty appointments U. Mo., Bentley Coll.; faculty mem. Babcock Grad. Sch. Mgmt., Wake Forest U., 1993, Babcock rsch. prof. fin., 2001—, interim dean, 2003—04, dean, 2004—. Office: Babcock Grad Sch Mgmt Wake Forest Univ PO Box 7659 Winston Salem NC 27109-7659 Office Phone: 336-758-5575. E-mail: ajay.patel@mba.wfu.edu.

PATEL, ANIL S. biomedical engineer, researcher, medical products executive; b. Baroda, India, June 28, 1939; came to U.S., 1961; s. Shankerbhai S. and Gangaben T. Patel; children: Ravi, Sunil; m. Asha Rairkar, Aug. 22, 1992. BS, U. Baroda, 1960; MS, Purdue U., 1963; PhD, Northwestern U., 1966; postgrad., Stanford U., 1993. Sr. rsch. scientist Baxter Travenol Labs. Inc., Morton Grove, Ill., 1968-74; chief scientist Cavitron Corp., N.Y.C., 1974-79; chief scientist, mgr. advanced prodcts rsch. Cooper Vision Sys. divsn. Cooper Vision Inc. (formerly Cavitron Corp.), Irvine, Calif., 1979-83, Bellevue, Wash., 1983-86; dir. advanced product rsch., chief scientist Cooper Vision CILCO divsn. Cooper Cos., Inc., Bellevue, 1986-89; dir. rsch. intraocular lens Alcon Labs., Inc., Ft. Worth, 1989-92, sr. dir. rsch. surg. products, 1993-2000, v.p. rsch. surg. products, 2001—02; cons. Global Healthcare, Seattle, 2003—. Contbr. articles to profl. jours.; patentee in field. Organizer Highland Park (Ill.) Chess Club, 1970-74, White Plains (N.Y.) Chess Club, 1974-77. Recipient free passage from India to U.S., Indian Ministry Sci. and Cultural Affairs, 1961; NIH postdoctoral fellow Northwestern U., 1966-67. Fellow Am. Soc. Laser Medicine and Surgery (founder); mem. AAAS, IEEE, Assn. for Advancement Med. Instrumentation (chmn. infrared warmers and incubators stds. com. 1978-80, pulmonary function devices-spirometer stds. subcom. 1978-80), Am. Nat. Stds. Inst. (com. intraocular lenses std. 1988-94, viscoelastic ophthalmic devices 1992—, apptd. tech. expert del. U.S.A. tech. adv. group Internat. Stds. Orgn. tech. com. 1992—), Am. Soc. Cataract and Refractive Surgery, Assn. Rsch. in Vision and Ophthalmology, Internat. Soc. Refractive Keratoplasty, Soc. Biomaterials, Sigma Xi. Office Phone: 206-525-9765. Personal E-mail: anilasha@aol.com.

PATEL, ANJANA, education educator, consultant; b. Navsari, India, Mar. 5, 1974; d. Maganlal R and Vina M Patel; m. Nitan A Patel, May 12, 1996. BA, U. Regina, 1996; MSc, Gannon U., 1999. Behavioral specialist Human Svc. Cons., Phila.; mental health clinician UDMNJ, Cherry Hill, NJ; sr. intake counselor United Behavioral Health, Phila.; adj. faculty Rowan U., Glassboro, NJ. Mem.: Am. Psychol. Assn. Home: 8 BIrkdale Ct Westampton NJ 08060

PATEL, BHARAT, financial executive; b. Wednesbury, West Midlands, Eng., Oct. 29, 1965; came to U.S., 1981; s. Maganbhai and Shantaben Patel; m. Naynitaben Bharatbhai, Feb. 14, 1990; children: Pritesh, Kunal. AS, Heald Bus. Coll., San Francisco; BS, Golden Gate U. Chmn. bd. dirs. API San Francisco, 1993—; CEO Patelco Investments, Brit. V.I., 1990—. Contbr. articles to profl. publs. Law enforcement cadet Calif. Peace League Activities, San Francisco, 1986; mem. coun. Calif. Dem. Assn., Modesto, 1998. Recipient award Internat. Fedn. for Bus., 1987, Amateur Athletic Assn., Eng., 1998. Mem. Golden Gate Hotel Assn. (bd. dirs. 1989-94). Avocations: travel, reading, playing cricket, movies, teaching. Office: Apt 2 1130 Mulberry St Ukiah CA 95482-6342

PATEL, CHANDRA KUMAR NARANBHAI, communications company executive, educator, researcher, entrepreneur; b. Baramati, India, July 2, 1938; came to U.S., 1958, naturalized, 1970; s. Naranbhai Chaturbhai and Maniben P.; m. Shela Dixit, Aug. 20, 1961; children: Neela, Meena. B.Engring., Poona U., 1958; MS, Stanford U., 1959, PhD, 1961. Mem. tech. staff Bell Telephone Labs., Murray Hill, N.J., 1961-93, head infrared physics and electronics rsch. dept., 1967-70, dir. electronics rsch. dept., 1970-76, dir. phys. rsch. lab., 1976-81, exec. dir. rsch. physics and acad. affairs div., 1981-87, exec. dir. rsch., materials sci., engring. and acad. affairs div., 1987-93; trustee Aerospace Corp., L.A., 1979-88; vice chancellor rsch. UCLA, 1993-2000, prof. dept. physics and astronomy, dept. chemistry, 2000—, prof. dept. elec. engring., 2000—; chmn., CEO Pranalytica, Inc, Santa Monica, Calif., 2001—. Mem. governing bd. NRC, 1990-91; bd. dirs. Newport Corp.; chmn. bd. Calif. Accuwave Corp., 1994-98; founder, chmn. bd. Pranalytica, Inc., Santa Monica, Calif.; co-founder Photuris, Inc. Contbr. articles to tech. jours. Chmn. Calif. Biomed. Found., 1994-2000; mem. exec. bd. Calif. Healthcare Inst., 1995-2000; mem. L.A. Regional Tech. Alliance, 1997—. Recipient Ballantine medal Franklin Inst., 1968, Coblentz award Am. Chem. Soc., 1974, Honor award Assn. Indians in Am., 1975, Founders prize Tex. Instruments Found., 1978, award N.Y. sect. Soc. Applied Spectroscopy, 1982, Schawlow medal Laser Inst. Am., 1984, Thomas Alva Edison Sci. award N.J. Gov., 1987, William T. Ennor Manufacturing Technology award ASME, 1995, Nat. Medal of Sci., 1996. Fellow AAAS, IEEE (Lamme medal 1976, medal of honor 1989, Millennium medal 2000), Am. Acad. Arts and Scis., Am. Phys. Soc. (coun. 1987-91, exec. com. 1987-90, George E. Pake prize 1988, pres. 1995), Optical Soc. Am. (Adolph Lomb medal 1966, Townes medal 1982, Ives medal 1989), Indian Nat. Sci. Acad. (fng.); mem. NAS (coun. 1988-91, exec. com. 1989-91), NAE (Zworykin award 1976), Gynecol. Laser Surgery Soc. (hon.),

Am. Soc. for Laser Medicine and Surgery (hon.), Third World Acad. Scis. (assoc.), Calif. Biomed. Found. (pres. 1994-2000), Calif. Healthcare Inst. (exec. com. 1995-2000), Sigma Xi (pres. 1994-96). Office: Pranalytica Inc 1101 Colorado Ave Santa Monica CA 90401 E-mail: patel@pranalytica.com.

PATEL, HOMI BURJOR, apparel company executive; b. Bombay, June 28, 1949; s. Burjor Ratan and Roshen Burjor (Marfatia) P.; married; children: Neville H., Cyrus H., Natasha E. BS in Stats., U. Bombay, 1973; MBA in Fin. and Mktg., Columbia U., 1975. Exec. asst. to pres. Corbin Ltd., N.Y.C., 1976, dir. mktg., 1978; with subs. Hartmarx Corp., Chgo., 1979—; v.p., gen. mgr. Fashionaire Apparel Inc., Chgo., 1979-81; exec. v.p. Austin Reed of Regent St., Chgo., 1981-82, M. Wile and Co., Buffalo, 1982-84; pres., chief exec. officer M. Wile & Co., Johnny Carson Apparel, Intercontinental Apparel, Buffalo, 1984—; group exec. v.p. Hartmarx Mens Apparel Group Corp., Buffalo, 1987-91, chmn., ceo Chgo., 1991-92; pres., COO Hartmarx Corp., Chgo., 1992—, bd. dirs., 1994—2001, CEO, 2002—. Mem. Clothing Mfrs. Assn. Am. (bd. dirs. 1984—, chief labor negotiator for U.S. tailored clothing industry), Univ. Club N.Y., Chgo. Club. Office: Hartmarx Corp 101 N Wacker Dr Fl 23 Chicago IL 60606-1718

PATEL, HOMI K. automotive executive; B in Mech. Engring., U. Baroda, India, 1963; M in Indsl. Engring., U. Tenn., 1966; MS in Mgmt., MIT, 1979. Process engr. GM, Dayton, Ohio, 1968; plant mgr. Delco Products, Kettering, Ohio, 1979—81, Rochester, NY, 1981—83; gen. mfg. mgr. GM, Saginaw Divsn., 1984—86; dir. steering sys. bus. unit GM, 1986; gen. mgr. Delco Remy Divsn., Anderson, Ind., 1987—91; gen. mgr. Saginaw divsn. GM, 1991—93; gen. mgr. GM Powertrain, Pontiac, Mich., 1993; v.p. GM, 1994—. Office: GM Corp Box 300 300 Renaissance Ctr Detroit MI 48265-3000

PATEL, KIRAN, manufacturing executive; BEE; MBA, U. Tenn. CPA. With Cummins Inc., 1974—2001; exec. v.p. Solectron Corp., Milpitas, Calif., 2001—, CFO, 2001—. CFO iMotors, 2000. Mem.: Fin. Exec. Inst., Tenn. Soc. CPAs, Am. Inst. CPAs. Office: Solectron Corp 777 Gibraltar Dr Milpitas CA 95035

PATEL, MARILYN HALL, judge; b. Amsterdam, N.Y., Sept. 2, 1938; d. Lloyd Manning and Nina J. (Thorpe) Hall; m. Magan C. Patel, Sept. 2, 1966; children: Brian, Gian. BA, Wheaton Coll., 1959; JD, Fordham U., 1963. Bar: N.Y. 1963, Calif. 1970. Mng. atty. Benson & Morris, Esq., N.Y.C., 1962-64; sole practice N.Y.C., 1964-67; atty. U.S. Immigration and Naturalization Svc., San Francisco, 1967-71; sole practive San Francisco, 1971-76; judge Alameda County Mcpl. Ct., Oakland, Calif., 1976-80, U.S. Dist. Ct. (no. dist.) Calif., San Francisco, 1980—; now chief judge U.S. Dist. Ct. for No. Dist. Calif., San Francisco, 1998—. Adj. prof. law Hastings Coll. of Law, San Francisco, 1974-76 Author: Immigration and Nationality Law, 1974; also numerous articles Mem. bd. visitors Fordham U. Sch. Law. Mem. ABA (litigation sect., jud. adminstrn. sect.), ACLU (former bd. dirs.), NOW (former bd. dirs.), Am. law Inst., Am. Judicature Soc. (bd. dirs.), Calif Conf. Judges, Nat. Assn. Women Judges (founding mem.), Internat. Inst. (bd. dirs.), Advs. for Women (co-founder), Assn. Bus. Trial Lawyers (bd. dirs.). Democrat. Avocations: piano playing; travel. Office: US Dist Ct PO Box 36060 450 Golden Gate Ave Ste 36052 San Francisco CA 94102-3482

PATEL, MULCHAND SHAMBHUBHAI, biochemist, researcher; b. Sipor, India, Sept. 9, 1939; came to U.S., 1965; s. Shambhubhai J. and Puriben (Patel) P.; m. Kankuben M. Patel; children: Sumitra, Yashomati, Mayank. BS, Gujarat U., 1961; MS, U. Baroda, 1964; PhD, U. Ill., 1968. Asst. prof. pediat. rsch. Sch. Medicine Temple U., Phila., 1970-72, rsch. asst. prof. medicine, 1972-75, rsch. asst. prof. biochemistry, 1970-75, rsch. assoc. prof. biochem. medicine, 1975-78; assoc. prof. biochemistry Sch. Medicine Case Western Res. U., Cleve., 1978-86, prof., 1986-93; prof., chmn. biochemistry SUNY, Buffalo, 1993-98, assoc. dean biomed. rsch. edn., 1999—, prof., 1999—2004, disting. prof., 2004—. Mem. NIH biochem. study sect. 2, 1984-88; mem. editl. bd. Jour. Biol. Chem., 1991-97, 99-2004. Contbr. articles to profl. jours. Recipient gold medal in biochemistry U. Baroda, 1973, Fulbright Rsch. Scholar award to India, 1987; prin. investigator, rsch. grantee NIH. Mem. Am. Soc. for Biochemistry and Molecular Biology, Am. Soc. Nutritional Scis. Office: SUNY-Dept Biochemistry Sch Medicine 140 Farber Hall 3435 Main St Buffalo NY 14214-3001 Office Phone: 716-829-3074. Business E-Mail: mspatel@buffalo.edu.

PATEL, PIYUSH HIRJIBHAI, communications executive; b. Pipar-Khared, Gujarat, India, July 16, 1964; M in Engring., U. Wis. Various tech. and mgmt. roles Intel, Sun Microsystems, MIPS Sys., QED; founder, CEO YAGO Sys., 1996-98; chmn., CEO Cabletron, sr. v.p. worldwide engring. Office: 36 Industrial Way Rochester NH 03867-4296

PATEL, SUNIT, telecommunications industry executive; Treas. MFS Comm., Inc., 1994—97, MCI WorldCom, 1997—2000; CFO, co-founder Looking Glass Networks, Inc., 2000—03; group v.p., CFO Level 3 Comm., Inc., Broomfield, Colo., 2003—. Office: Level 3 Comm 1025 Eldorado Blvd Broomfield CO 80021

PATEL, VINOD MOTIBHAI, accountant; b. Kilosha, Tanzania, Mar. 1, 1944; came to U.S., 1971; s. Motibhai R. and Lalitaben M. (Lalitaben C.) P.; m. Surekha J. Patel, Dec. 6, 1969; children: Chirag, Roshni. BComm., U. Baroda, India, 1964. Chartered acct., India; CPA, Md. Acct. Dalal, Desai & Kumana, Bombay, 1964-70, Bellman, Atlas & Co., London, 1970-71, Garbelman, Winslow & Co., Upper Marlboro, Md., 1971-79; prin. Vinod M. Patel, CPA, Jacksonville, Fla., 1979—. Mem. AICPA, Md. Assn. CPA's, Inst. Chartered Accts. India. Hindu. Home and Office: 11262 Saint Augustine Rd Jacksonville FL 32257-1142

PATEL, VIRENDRA CHATURBHAI, mechanical engineer, educator; b. Mombasa, Kenya, Nov. 9, 1938; arrived in U.S., 1969, naturalized, 1975; s. Chaturbhai S. and Kantaben N. (Rai) Patel; m. Manjula Patel, May 29, 1966; children: Sanjay, Bindiya. BSc with honors, Imperial Coll., London, 1962; PhD, Cambridge (Eng.) U., 1965; Doctor honoris causa, Tech. U. Civil Engring., Bucharest, Romania, 1994. Sr. asst. in rsch. Cambridge U., 1965-69; vis. prof. Indian Inst. Tech., Kharagpur, 1966; cons. Lockheed Ga. Co., Marietta, 1969-70; mem. faculty U. Iowa, Iowa City, 1971—, prof. mech. engring., 1975—, chmn. div., 1976-82, chmn. mech. engring., 1978-82, U. Iowa Found. Disting. prof., 1990—, Edwin B. Green chair in hydraulics, 2000—; research engr. Iowa Inst. Hydraulic Rsch., 1971—, dir., 1994—; hon. prof. Dharamsinh Desai Inst. Tech., 2002—; dir. Ctr. for Computer Aided Design, 2003—. Mem. Iowa Gov. Sci. Adv. Coun., 1977—83; mem. resistance com. Internat. Towing Tank Conf., 1978—87; vis. prof. U. Karlsruhe, Germany, 1980—81, Ecole Nationale Superieure de Mechanique, Nantes, France, 1984, Nantes, 96; jubilee prof. Chalmers Inst. Tech., Goteborg, Sweden, 1988; dir. Ctr. for Computer Aided Design, 2003—; cons. in field. Author: (book) Three Dimensional Turbulent Boundary Layers, 1972; contbr. articles to profl. jours.; assoc. editor: AIAA Jour., 1987—90. Recipient Sr. Scientist award, Alexander von Humboldt Found., 1980, 1993. Fellow: ASME (Fluids Engring. award 1997), AIAA (assoc.); mem.: Soc. Naval Archtl. Marine Engrs., Am. Soc. Engring. Edn., Pi Tau Sigma, Sigma Xi. Home: 60 Kennedy Pkwy Iowa City IA 52246-2780 Office: IIHR Hyrdoscience and Engring U Iowa 404 Hydraulics Laboratory Iowa City IA 52242-1585 E-mail: v-c-patel@uiowa.edu.

PATERIK, FRANCES SUE, secondary school educator, actress; b. Bloomington, Ill., Feb. 10, 1953; d. Francis LaVerne and Magaline Wilken. Student, Am. Cons. Music, Chgo., 1976—78, N.W. Ind. Opera Co., 1980, Hinsdale Opera Co., Ill., 1981; BA, MA, Western Ill. U., 1984. Tchg. asst. Western Ill. U., Macomb, 1982—84; music tchr. Cardinal Cmty. Schs., Eldon, Iowa, 1985—89, Johnston (Iowa) Cmty. Schs., 1990—94; music/performing arts tchr. Colfax (Iowa)-Mingo Cmty. Sch., 1995—2002, Merrill Middle Sch., Des Moines, 2002—. Dir. handbell choir First Christian Ch., Des Moines, 1996—2000; soprano soloist Des Moines Concert Singers, 1989—, Des Moines Choral Soc., 2002—. Actress: (various comedic roles) Ingersoll Dinner Theatre; Playhouse; Drama Workshop; Stage West. Mem.: Iowa Choral Dirs. Assn., Am. Choral Dirs. Assn., Music Educators Nat. Conf., Nat. Wildlife Fedn., Sierra Club. Democrat. Avocations: gardening, animal welfare, dance. Office: Des Moines Pub Schs Des Moines IA 50312

PATERNO, JOSEPH VINCENT, college football coach; b. Bklyn., Dec. 21, 1926; s. Angelo Lafayette and Florence (de LaSalle) P.; m. Suzanne Pohland, May 12, 1962; children: Diana Lynne, Mary Kathryn, David, Joseph Vincent, George Scott. BA, Brown U., 1950, LL.D., 1975. Asst. football coach Pa. State U., 1950-66, head football coach, 1966—. Author (with Bernard Asbell): The Paterno Principle, 1989; Paterno: By the Book, 1989. Served with AUS, 1945-46. Named Coach of Yr. Walter Camp Football Found., 1972, Coach of Yr. Washington Touchdown Club, 1973, 86, Coach of Yr. Football Writers Assn. Am.,1968, 78, 82, 86; coached Nat. Collegiate Champions, 1982, 86, Named Sports Illustrated's 1986 Sportsman of the Yr. Mem. Am. Football Coaches Assn. (dir., Coach of Yr. awards 1968, 78, 82, 86). Ranked 4th in All-Time Divsn. IA Coaching Victories, 1st among active coaches. Office: Pa State U 101D Bryce Jordan Ctr University Park PA 16802-7101

PATERON, ROBERT G. architecture educator; BA in Criminal Justice, Fla. Atlantic U., 1984, MPA in Growth Mgmt., 1985; PhD, U. N.C., 1993. Assoc. prof. U. Tex. Sch. Arch., Austin, assoc. dean for rsch. and ops., dir. Grad. Program in Cmty. and Regional Planning. Mem. numerous state and regional planning adv. bds. and task forces; edn. found. mem., awards chair Tex. APA Bd.; contbr. Tex. APA Conf. Faculty Fellow in Social Sci. Rsch. Applied to Hazards and Disasters, NSF. Office: Univ Tex Austin Sch Arch 1 University Sta Stop B7500 Austin TX 78712*

PATERSON, BASIL ALEXANDER, lawyer; b. N.Y.C., Apr. 27, 1926, s. Leonard J. and Evangeline (Rondon) P.; m. Portia Hairston, 1953; children: Daniel, David. BS, St. John's Coll., 1948; JD, St. John's U., 1951. Bar: N.Y. 1952. Ptnr. Paterson, Michael, Dinkins and Jones, N.Y.C., 1956—77, Meyer, Suozzi, English & Klein, P.C., Mineola, NY, 1983—; mem. N.Y. State Senate, 1965-70, dep. mayor for labor rels. City of N.Y., 1978; sec. of state State of N.Y., 1979-82. Pres. Inst. Mediation and Conflict Resolution, 1971-77; chmn. 2d Jud. Screening Com., 1985-95; assoc. chmn. N.Y. State Sentencing Guidelines Com.; commr. Port Authority N.Y. and N.J., 1989-95; mem. commn. to promote confidence in judicial elections, 2003-. Bd. dirs. St. Benedict's Day Nursery, 1999—, vice chmn. Dem. Nat. Com., 1972-78, mem., 1972-78; chmn. KeySpan Found., 2003—. Recipient Eagleton Inst. Politics award, Disting. Svc. award Guardians Assn. N.Y. Police Dept., City Club N.Y. award, Black Expo award, Excellence medal St. John's U., Kibbe award CUNY. Roman Catholic. Office: Meyer Suozzi English & Klein PC 1505 Kellum Pl Ste 3 Mineola NY 11501-4824

PATERSON, DAVID J. paper company executive; b. Washington, Aug. 15, 1954; BS, Cornell U., 1976; MBA, U. Mich., 1978. Mktg. analyst Continental Forest Industries, 1978—79, supr. fibre supply, 1979—80, shift foreman, 1980—82, mgr. quality control, 1982—83; sales mgr. containerboard S.W. Forest Industries, 1983—87; export sales mgr. containerboard Ga.-Pacific Corp., Atlanta, 1987—88, dir. export pulp sales, 1988—92, dir. pulp sales and mktg., 1992—94, v.p. sales and mktg. pulp and bleached bd., 1994—95, v.p. market pulp and recycling ops., 1995—96, v.p. market pulp, 1996—2000, v.p. electronic commerce, 2000, sr. v.p. comm. papers, 2000—01, pres. paper, 2001, pres. paper and bleached bd., 2001, exec. v.p. pulp and paperboard, 2001—03, exec. v.p. and pres. bldg. products, 2003—. Bd. mem. Rsch. Atlanta, Inc.; mem. ISAC12 U.S. Dept. Commerce. Mem.: Japan-Am. Soc. Ga. Office: Ga-Pacific Corp 55 Park Pl Atlanta GA 30303

PATERSON, DAVID LESLIE, epidemiologist; arrived in U.S., 1997; s. Brian and Robin Paterson; m. Susan Mary Bellamy, Sept. 22, 1990; children: Matthew David, Alexander John. MB, BS, U. Queensland, Brisbane, 1988. Med. resident Princess Alexandra Hosp., Brisbane, 1989—92; infectious diseases registrar Royal Brisbane Hosp., Brisbane, 1993—95; infectious disease physician Sullivan, Nicolaides and Ptnrs., Brisbane, 1996; vis. rschr. U. Pitts. Med. Ctr., Pitts., 1997—99, dir. antibiotic mgmt. program, assoc. prof. dept. medicine, 2001—; dir. infectious diseases U. Pitts. Med. Ctr. - Italy/ISMETT (Inst. Mediterraneo per Trapiant e ad alta Specializzione), Palermo, Italy, 1999—2001; chief transplant infectious diseases U. Pitts. Med. Ctr., 2003—. Contbr. articles to profl. jours. Fellow: Royal Coll. Pathologists Australasian, Royal Australasian Coll. Physicians; mem.: Am. Soc. Microbiology (Merck Irving S. Sigal Meml. award for significant rsch. in microbiology and infectious diseases 2000). Office: Univ Pitts Med Ctr Falk Clini 3601 5th Ave Pittsburgh PA 15213 Personal E-mail: patersond@msx.dept-med.pitt.edu. E-mail: patersond@msx.dept-med.pitt.edu.

PATERSON, KATHERINE WOMELDORF, writer; b. Huaiyin, China, Oct. 31, 1932; came to U.S., 1940; d. George Raymond and Mary Elizabeth (Goetchius) Womeldorf; m. John Barstow Paterson, July 14, 1962; children: Elizabeth Polin, John Barstow, David Lord, Mary Katherine Nah-he-sah-pe-che-a. AB, King Coll., Bristol, Tenn., 1954; post grad., Kobe Sch. Japanese Lang., 1957-60; MA, Presbyn. Sch. Christian Edn., 1957; MRE, Union Theol. Sem., 1962; LittD. (hon.), King Coll., Bristol, Tenn., 1978; LHD (hon.), Otterbein Coll., 1979; LittD (hon.), St. Mary's of the Woods, 1981, Washington and Lee U., 1982, U. Md., 1982, Shenandoah Coll., 1982; LHD, Washington and Lee U, 1982, Norwich U., 1990, Mount St. Vincent U., Halifax, N.S., Can., 1994; LittD, Hope Coll., 1997; DLitt (hon.), Prebyn. Coll., 2002. Tchr. Lovettsville Elem. Sch., Va., 1954-55; missionary Presbyn. Ch., Japan, 1957-61; master sacred studies and English Pennington Sch. for Boys, NJ, 1963-65. Author: The Sign of the Chrysanthemum, 1973, Of Nightingales That Weep, 1974, The Master Puppeteer, 1976, Bridge to Terabithia, 1977, The Great Gilly Hopkins, 1978, Angels and Other Strangers, 1979, Jacob Have I Loved, 1980, Rebels of the Heavenly Kingdom, 1983, Come Sing, Jimmy Jo, 1985, (with John Paterson) Consider the Lilies, 1986, Park's Quest, 1988, The Tale of the Mandarin Ducks, 1990, The Smallest Cow in the World, 1991, Lyddie, 1991, The King's Equal, 1992, Who Am I?, 1992, Flip-Flop Girl, 1994, A Midnight Clear: Stories for the Christmas Season, 1995, A Sense of Wonder, 1995, The Angel and the Donkey, 1996, Jip: His Story, 1996, Marvin's Best Christmas Present Ever, 1997, (with John Paterson) Images of God, 1998, Parzival, 1998, Celia and the Sweet, Sweet Water, 1998, Preacher's Boy, 1999, The Wide-Awake Princess, 2000, The Field of the Dogs, 2001, Marvin One Too Many, 2001, The Invisible Child, 2002, The Same Stuff as Stars, 2002; translator: The Crane Wife, 1981, The Tongue-Cut Sparrow, 1987. US nominee for Hans Christian Andersen award, 1979, 89, 97; recipient Nat. Book award, 1977, 79, Newbery medal, 1978, 91, Newbery honor, 1979, New Eng. Book award New Eng. Booksellers Assn., 1982, Union medal Union Theol. Sem., 1992, Scott O'Dell award for hist. fiction, 1997, May Hill Arbuthnot Lectr. award, 1997, Hans Christian Andersen award, 1998, Lion award NY Pub. Libr., 1998, Literary Light award Boston Pub. Libr., 2000, Living Legend award Libr. of Congress, 2000, Jefferson cup Va. Libr. Assn., 2000, Vt. Gov.'s award for excellence in arts, 2001. Mem. Authors Guild, Children's Book Guild Washington. Democrat. Office: Clarion Books 215 Park Ave S New York NY 10003-1603

PATERSON, PAUL CHARLES, retired private investigator, security consultant; b. Bethlehem, Pa., Dec. 31, 1927; s. Thomas and Ida (Weiss) P.; m. Estelle Marie Nabors; children: Linda Ann, Thomas Scott, Terry Maurice Leard. Grad., Inst. Applied Sci., Chgo., 1950. Jr. credit analyst Bethlehem Steel Corp., Pa., 1947-50; inspector claim spec., claim dir., field supr. Equifax Svcs., Inc., Allentown, Pa., 1953-61, field claim supr. St. Louis, 1961-63, regional claims mgr. Phila., 1963-71, spl. claim sales, sales exec.-claims Atlanta, 1971-89; pvt. investigator, pres. Paterson Investigations, Inc., Douglasville, Ga., 1989-2001. Editor CFE newsletter The Ga. Examiner, 1994-95. With U.S. Army, 1950-53. Mem. VFW, Am. Legion, Life, Accident and Health Claims Assn. Phila. (life, pres. 1969-70), Mktg. Ins. Claims Assn. (life, v.p. 1985—, pres. 1989-90), So. Loss Assn., Nat. WWII Meml. Assn. (charter), Atlanta Claims Assn., Ga. Assn. Profl. Pvt. Investigators (chair ethics com. 1999, treas. 2000), Assn. Cert. Fraud Examiners (cert., past pres. Ga. chpt. 1990, 93, bd. dirs. 1991-92, faculty 1995-96, bd. regents 1996, Disting. Achievement award 1994, 95, Regent Emeritus, life mem.), Criminal Investigation Divsn. Agts. Assn. Inc., Ga. Sheriffs' Assn., Ga. Claims Assn., Ga. Fire Investigators Assn., Ret. Mil. Police Assn. (assoc.), Am. Legion, Chapel Hills Golf Club. Republican. Avocations: golf, music, swimming, physical conditioning. Home: 5235 Stilesboro Rd NW 215 Kennesaw GA 30152-3968 E-mail: paulpaterson@earthlink.net.

PATERSON, RICHARD DENIS, financial executive; b. Ottawa, Ont., Can., Oct. 13, 1942; m. Antoinette Paterson; children: Christopher, Russell, Kathlyn, Victoria, Connor. B in Commerce, Concordia U., Montreal, Que., Can., 1964. Auditor Coopers & Lybrand, Montreal, 1964-67; acct. Genstar Corp., Montreal, 1967-69; dir. fin. and adminstrn. Indussa Corp. (subs. Genstar Corp.), N.Y.C., 1969-73; v.p., comptroller Genstar Corp., Montreal and San Francisco, 1973-83, sr. v.p., CFO San Francisco, 1983-87; exec. v.p. Genstar Investment Corp., San Francisco, 1987-95; mng. dir. Genstar Capital LP, San Francisco, 1996—. Bd. dirs. Installs Inc., Am. Pacific Enterprises, Inc.; chmn. Andros Inc., Woods Equipment Co. Mem. Order Chartered Accts. Que. Office: Genstar Capital LP Four Embarcadero Ctr Ste 1900 San Francisco CA 94111-4191 E-mail: rpaterson@gencap.com.

PATERSON, ROBERT E. trading stamp company executive; b. Kearny, N.J., Nov. 30, 1926; s. Robert McKinley and Ethel (Brookes) P.; m. Eileen Josephine Connolly; children: Carol, Joan, Robert, Richard, Donald, Jeffrey. MBA, Columbia U., 1971. Sr. v.p. fin., treas. The Sperry & Hutchinson Co., Inc., N.Y.C., 1952-87, also bd. dirs. Mem. Nat. Assn. Accts., 1954-89, nat. treas., 1985-88; bd. dirs. Govt. Obligations Fund, 1986-87. Elected mem. Borough Coun., 1991-98, 2002-04, coun. pres., 1995-98, 2002. Served with U.S. Army, 1944-45, PTO.

PATHAK, DOROTHY RYBACZYK, epidemiologist, biostatistician; b. Dlugosiodlo, Warsaw, Poland, Nov. 26, 1947; d. Henryk M. and Anna Bobowska Rybaczyk; m. Pramod K. Pathak, Dec. 6, 1969; children: Bogdan A., Leszek A., Anna D. PhD, U. of N.Mex, 1975; MS, Harvard Sch. of Pub. Health, 1983. Asst. prof. U. of N.Mex, Albuquerque, 1975—86, assoc. prof., 1986—94; vis. asst. prof. Harvard Med. Sch., Boston, 1982—83; vis. scholar Stanford U., Calif., 1988—88; assoc. prof. Mich. State U., E. Lansing, 1995—98, prof., 1998—; vis. scholar Harvard Sch. of Pub. Health, Boston, 2001—02. Author: (editl.) Cancer Causes and Control, (article) Am. Jour. of Epidemiology, Internat. Jour. of Cancer. Mem. Zdrowie Plus Inc. NFP-Breast Cancer Survivors Club, Chgo. Grantee Breast Cancer in Women of Polish Ancestry, Nat. Cancer Inst., 1997—, Improved Follow-up of Breast Abnormalities Through Comprehensive Breast Care in Women 40 Years and Older, Dept. of Def., 1998—2001, Breast Cancer: Gene-Diet Interactions in Polish Women, Nat. Cancer Inst., 2002—. Mem.: Am. Statis. Assn., Soc. for Epidemiologic Rsch. Home: 3947 Belding Ct Okemos MI 48864 Office: Mich State Univ 4660 S Hagadorn Rd East Lansing MI 48824 E-mail: pathak@msu.edu.

PATHE, PETER, information technology executive; BS in Engring. & Applied Sci., Calif. Inst. Tech.; MS, MIT. From mgr. to corp. v.p. Microsoft, Redmond, Wash., 1991, corp. v.p. Office: One Microsoft Way Redmond WA 98052-6399

PATIENT, WILLIAM F. chemicals executive; V.p. sales and mktg. Borg-Warner Chemicals, v.p. mfg.; pres. Borg-Warner Chemicals Europe; sr. v.p. BF Goodrich Company, pres. Geon Vinyl divsn.; CEO Geon (now PolyOne Corp.), 1993—99; chmn. PolyOne Corp., 2003—. Bd. dir. Navistar Internat. Corp. Bd. dir. Wash. U.; chmn. of bd. Cleve. State U. Found. Office: 33587 Walker RD Avon Lake OH 44012-1145

PATINKIN, HUGH M. retail executive; b. 1950; BA, Tufts U.; JD, U. Chgo. Atty. Sidley & Austin; from asst. sec. to pres., CEO Whitehall Jewellers, Inc., Chgo., 1979—89, pres., 1989—, CEO, 1989—, bd. dir. Office: Whitehall Jewellers Inc 155 North Wacker Dr Chicago IL 60606*

PATINKIN, MANDY, actor, singer; b. Chgo., Nov. 30, 1952; s. Lester and Doris (Sinton) P.; m. Kathryn Grody, June 15, 1980. Student, U. Kans., 1970-72, Juilliard Sch. Drama, 1972-74. Actor N.Y. Shakespeare Festival, 1975-81; plays include Hotspur in Henry IV, Part 1, Hudson Guild, N.Y.C., Rebel Women, Hamlet, Leave it to Beaver is Dead, Savages; (Broadway) Evita (Tony award 1980), Shadow Box, Sunday in the Park with George, 1984, The Knife, 1987, The Winter's Tale, 1989, Mandy Patinkin in Concert: Dress Casual, 1989, The Secret Garden, 1991, Man of La Mancha, 1996, Forbidden Broadway, 1999, The Wild Party, 2000; (films) The Big Fix, 1978, Last Embrace, 1979, French Postcards, 1980, Night of the Juggler, 1980, Ragtime, 1981, Yentl, 1983, Daniel, 1983, Maxie, 1985, The Princess Bride, 1987, The House on Carroll Street, 1988, Alien Nation, 1988, Dick Tracy, 1990, The Doctor, 1991, True Colors, 1991, The Music of Chance, 1993, Life with Mikey, 1993, Squanto: A Warrior's Tale, 1994, Men with Guns, 1997, Lulu on the Bridge, 1998, The Adventures of Elmo in Grouchland, 1999, Piñero, 2001; (TV appearances): That Thing on ABC, That Second Thing on ABC, Taxi, Midnight Special, (TV series) Chicago Hope, 1994-95, 1999-2000 (Emmy award, 1995), Dead Like Me, 2003-; TV movies include Charleston, 1979, Sunday in the Park with George, 1986, Broken Glass, 1996, The Hunchback, 1997, Strange Justice, 1999, NTSB: The Crash of Flight 323, 2001; albums: Mandy Patinkin, 1984, Sunday in the Park with George, 1986, Dress Casual, 1990, Oscar and Steve, 1995, Experiment, 1994, Mamaloshen, 1998, Kidults, 2001. Recipient Music Achievement award Drama League, 1989. Mem. AFTRA, Screen Actors Guild, Actors Equity Assn. Office: United Talent Agy care Adam Isaacs 9560 Wilshire Blvd Ste 500 Beverly Hills CA 90212-2427 also: care Dodger Touring Ltd 501 Broadway Ste 2015 New York NY 10036*

PATINKIN, TERRY ALLAN, physician; b. Oak Park, Ill., Feb. 1, 1950; s. Lester D. and Marcella Jaqueline (Steynburg) P.; m. Sandra Lee Friedman, Apr. 21, 1985; children: Jonathan, Zachary. BS, U. Ill., 1971; MD, U. Calif., San Francisco, 1975; MPH in Health Care Mgmt., Harvard U., 1996. Diplomate Am. Bd. Emergency Medicine, Am. Bd. Family Medicine; cert. physician exec. Intern, resident in family practice U. Calif. San Francisco/Natividad Med. Ctr., Salinas, Calif., 1975-78, assoc. dir. family medicine residency program, 1978-90; dir. emergency dept. Natividad Med. Ctr., Salinas, 1985-91, dir. continuing med. edn., 1978-91, dir. undergrad. edn., 1978-90, emergency physician, 1979-91, Sturdy Meml. Hosp., Attleboro, Mass., 1991-94; dir., chmn. emergency dept. Roger Williams Hosp., Providence, 1994-99, Landmark Med. Ctr., Woonsocket, RI, 2000—02; med. dir. urgent care East Boston Neighborhood Health Ctr., 2002—. Asst. clin. prof. U. Calif., San Francisco, 1981-88, assoc. clin. prof., 1988-91; clin. asst. prof. Stanford U., 1990-93; asst. clin. prof. Brown U., Providence, 1995—, Boston U., 1999—. Fellow AMA, Am. Coll. Emergency Physicians; mem. Am. Coll. Physician Execs., Mass. Coll. Emergency Physicians, Mass. Med. Soc., U. Ill. Alumni Assn. (life), U. Calif. San Francisco Alumni Faculty Assn. Office: 10 Gove St East Boston MA 02128 Office Phone: 617-568-4639.

PATINO, DOUGLAS XAVIER, foundation, government agency, and university administrator; b. Calexico, Calif., Apr. 11, 1939; s. Jose Luis and Maria Teresa (Seymour) P.; m. Barbel Wilma Hoyer, Aug. 13, 1970; 1 child, Viktor Xavier. AA, Imperial Valley Coll., 1960; BA, Calif. State U., San Diego, 1962, MA, 1966; PhD, U.S. Internat. U., 1972. Deputy dir. Sacramento (Calif.) Concilio, Inc., 1968-69; v.p. student affairs U. So. Colo., Pueblo, 1973-75; dep. dir. for planning and rev. svc. br. to dir. Calif. Employment Devel. Dept., dir.; sec. Calif. Health & Welfare Agy., 1975-83; dir. Ariz. Dept. of Econ. Security, Phoenix, 1983-87; pres., chief exec. officer Marin Community Found., Larkspur, Calif., 1987-91; pres. New Partnership Found. and Patino Group, San Rafael, Calif., 1991-93; vice chancellor Calif. State U. Sys., Long Beach, 1993—2002; prof. social welfare Calif. State U., L.A., 1998—. Commr. W.T. Grand Found., 1986—88, Enterprize for the Ams., Washington, 1994—; trustee C.S. Mott Found., Flint, Mich., 1995—, Calif. Wellness Found., Woodland Hills, 1997—; bd. dirs. Marguerite Casey Found.; chair, treas. Hispanics in Philanthropy, 1993. Mem. Sec. of U.S. Dept. of Labor Task Force, Ariz., 1985-86, Staff Adv. Com. of the Human Resource Com., Nat. Gov. Assn., Washington, 1983-86; bd. dirs. Calif. Leadership, Santa Cruz, Calif., 1985-95, No. Calif. Grantmakers, 1990-91, Ariz. Assn. Bus., 1984;

chair U.S. Savs. Bond Dr. for State of Calif., 1982; trustee Nat. Hispanic U., Oakland, Calif., 1987-90, Hispanic Community Fund, San Francisco, 1989-95, bd. dirs. Calif. Sch. Profl. Psychology, 1989-94, Coun. on Found., Washington, 1990-96, Found. Ctr., N.Y., 1993; pres. Calif. State U. Found. Recipient The Monty Disting. Alumni award San Diego State U., 1997, Simon Bolivar award for cmty. leadership award Hispanic Cmty. Found. and Bay Area United Way, 1996, Azteca award Human Devel. Corp., 1991, Leadership award Nat. Concilors of Am. and United Way of Bay Area, 1990, Disting. Performance award, Nat. Alliance of Bus., Washington, 1985, Superior Svc. Mgmt. award, Am. Soc. Pub. Adminstrn., 1985, Humanitarian award, Los Padrinos, Inc., 1981, Small and Minority Bus. award for the State of Calif. 1982, Disting. Alumni award, Calif. Jr. Community Coll. Assn., Sacramento, 1982, Silver Spur award, Nat. Fedn. of Charros in Guadalajaro, Jalisco, Mex., 1974, Calif. Community Svc. award, Former Gov. Ronald Reagan, Sacramento, 1973; named to 100 Most Influential Hispanics, Hispanic Bus., 1995, 97. Mem. Am. Pub. Welfare Assn. (bd. dirs., Leadership award 1987), Rotary, 1987-93. Office: The Patino Group Sacramento CA 95822 E-mail: dpatino604@earthlink.net.

PATMAN, PHILIP FRANKLIN, lawyer; b. Atlanta, Nov. 1, 1937; s. Elmer Franklin and Helen Lee (Miller) P.; m. Katherine Sellers, July 1, 1967; children: Philip Franklin, Katherine Lee. BA, U. Tex., 1959, LLB, 1964; MA, Princeton U., 1962. Bar: Tex. 1964, U.S. Supreme Ct. 1970, U.S. Dist. Ct. (so. dist.) Tex. 1971, U.S. Dist. Ct. (we. dist.) Tex. 1975. Atty. office of legal adviser Dept. State, Washington, 1964-67; dep. dir. office internat. affairs HUD, Washington, 1967-69; pvt. practice Austin, Tex., 1969—. Contbr. articles to legal jours. Ofcl. rep. of Gov. Tex. to Interstate Oil Compact Commn., 1973-83, 87-91. Woodrow Wilson fellow, 1959. Fellow Tex. Bar Found. (life); mem. ABA, State Bar Tex., Tex. Ind. Prodrs. and Royalty Owners Assn., Tex. Oil and Gas Assn., Tex. Law Rev. Assn., Austin Club, Headliners Club, Westwood Country Club, Rotary, Phi Beta Kappa, Phi Delta Phi. Office: Patman & Osborn 515 Congress Ave Ste 1704 Austin TX 78701-3503 Office Phone: 512-476-3529.

PATMORE, KIMBERLY S. financial services executive; BBA, U. Toledo. CPA, Colo. With Ernst & Young; joined First Data Corp., Inglewood, Colo., 1992, exec. v.p., CFO, 2000—. Mem. Gov.'s Commn. on Sci. and Tech., Colo. Bd. dirs. Coors Tek, Girls Scouts, Family Tree Found. Office: First Date Corp 6200 S Qubec St Inglewood CA 90301

PATMOS, ADRIAN EDWARD, retired dean; b. Paterson, NJ, June 29, 1914; s. Adrian and Myra (Van Splinter) P.; m. Pearl Van Den Heuvel, Apr. 25, 1942; children: Adrian Edward III, Bruce Douglas. BA magna cum laude, NYU, 1935, MA, 1936; LLD, Wittenberg U., 1996; postgrad., Am. U., 1936—37. Asst. prof. econs. Wittenberg U., 1938-47, assoc. prof., head dept., 1947-50, prof. econs., 1950—, head dept., 1950-64, dir. mgmt. devel. program, 1952-79, eve. sessions, 1952-78; dean Wittenberg U. (Sch. Community Edn.), 1955-79, prof. and dean emeritus, 1979—. Jr. accountant Def. Plant Corp., Curtiss-Wright Corp., 1943; vis. instr. Ohio Wesleyan U., 1944; spl. field rep. NLRB, 1946; vis. lectr. econs. N.Y.U., 1946-48; vis. prof. econs. USAF Inst. Tech., 1949-50; cons. Clark C.C., 1982-84, Urbana U., 1983-94. Mem. Springfield City Firemen's Pension Bd., 1948-53; mem. Springfield City Planning Bd., 1953-58; chmn. Clark County Health Facilities Planning Com., 1965-66, City commr., Springfield, Ohio, 1958-62, mayor, 1960-62; Trustee United Way, Springfield and Clark County, 1960-74; trustee Clark Tech. Coll., 1965-78, chmn., 1969-71, trustee emeritus, 2004—; trustee Springfield Cmty. Hosp., 1975-84, Elderly United, 1979-92. Recipient Wittenberg award for meritorious svc. to univ., 1964, Silver Knight award Nat. Mgmt. Assn., Sta. WIZE award for outstanding cmty. svc., Cmty. Svc. award C. of C., 1979, award of distinction Bd. of Realtors, Outstanding Svc. in Cmty. Labor-Mgmt. Relationships award Fed. Mediation Svc., citation as one of Ohio's foremost educators Ohio Senate, Medal of Honor for leadership in liberal arts edn., 1987; named Jr. Achievement Hall of Fame laureate, 1996; NYU Penfield fellow, 1937-38. Mem. Ohio Coll. Assn. (pres. adult edn. sect. 1959-60), Am. Econs. Assn., Kiwanis (Disting. Svc. to Cmty. award), Phi Beta Kappa, Phi Gamma Delta, Blue Key. Baptist.

PATNAUDE, WILLIAM EUGENE, architect; b. Sanger, Calif., Sept. 24, 1937; s. Eugene Joseph Patnaude and Vera Mae (Giles) Patnaude Fagan; m. Mary Esther Simerly, Aug. 22, 1971 (div. 1987); children: Nathaniel, Matthew BArch, U. Calif., Berkeley, 1961; postgrad., Calif. State U., Fresno, 1968-72. Registered arch., Calif., Wash., Idaho, Nev., Colo., Utah, Ariz., Mont., Ind., Nebr., Ohio, N.Y., N.J. Draftsman, arch. Robert Stevens Assoc., Santa Cruz, Calif., 1963-66; arch. Llewelyn Davies, Weeks & Ptnrs., London, 1966, Allen Y. Lew, Fresno, Calif., 1967-69, assoc., 1969-74; v.p., arch. Lew & Patnaude, Inc., Fresno, Calif., 1978-84, pres., 1985—. Instr. Calif. State U., Fresno, 1968-81 Constn. arbitrator Am. Arbitration Assn., 1976-96; chair ctrl. area plan citizen's adv. com. City of Fresno, 1991-93, chair gen. plan update com., 1994-97; bd. dirs. Fresno Arts Ctr., 1971-74, Fresno County Alliance for the Arts, 1986-88, 91-94. With USNR, 1961-63. Recipient Award of Merit, Calif. Hist. Preservation Conf., Orange County, 1983; Award of Excellence, Woodwork Inst. Calif., 1982 Fellow AIA (nat. dir. 1983-85, pres. Calif. Coun. 1982, San Joaquin chpt. 1978, Awards of Excellence, 1972-95); mem. Constrn. Specifications Inst. (pres. Fresno chpt. 1977). Democrat. Avocations: photography, fine wines. Home: 4190 N Van Ness Blvd Fresno CA 93704-4213 Office: Lew & Patnaude Inc 1050 S St Fresno CA 93721-1497 E-mail: billp@osufresno.edu.

PATNER, MARSHALL, lawyer, educator; b. Chgo., Apr. 15, 1931; s. Saul and Rose (Dobkin) P.; B.S., U. Wis., 1953; J.D., U. Chgo., 1956; postgrad. U. Edinburgh (Scotland), 1953; m. Irene Herman, July 11, 1954; children—Andrew, Joshua, Seth. Bar: Ill. 1956, Calif. 1975. Practice in Chgo.; gen. counsel Bus. and Profl. People for the Pub. Interest, 1969-74; lectr. law Wilberforce (Ohio) U., 1974; U. Ill. Chgo. Circle Campus, Stanford, U. Calif. at Berkeley, U. Puget Sound. Institutor Chgo. Law Enforcement Study Group, 1970; ptnr. Orlikoff, Flamm & Patner, Chgo., 1983— . Served with AUS, 1957. Recipient Civil Liberties award Ill. div. ACLU, 1972, ann. service award Chgo. Newspaper Guild, 1974, Silver Circle award excellence in teaching U. Ill. Chgo. Campus, 1974. Author: Criminal Trial and Appellate Guide, 1974; Appointed Counsel's Guide for Criminal Appeals, 1968. Pioneer exptl. introductory law course to help minority students improve qualifications for law sch. Office: Orlikoff Flamm & Patner 200 S Michigan Ave Chicago IL 60604-2402

PATON, BOB, theater director, writer; s. Robert Paton and Teresa Filippone; m. April N. Hopkins; children: Craig R., Trevor K. BA, Swarthmore Coll., 1950; MA, Middlebury Coll., 1969. Cert. N.Y. State Dept. Edn. Freelance tchr., writer, actor various locations, 1950—58; sch. tchr. Kingston (N.Y.) H.S., 1958—70; real estate owner Woodstock, NY, 1970—89; founder, artistic dir. Outreach Theatre, Inc., N.Y.C., 1989—. Author: For Our Children's Sake, 2003; artistic dir.: Theatre of Dreams, 1991—2003. With U.S. Army, 1945—46. Avocations: reading, singing, acting, dance. Home: 1219 77 St Brooklyn NY 11228

PATON, DAVID, ophthalmologist, educator; b. Balt., Aug. 16, 1930; s. Richard Townley and Helen (Meserve) P.; m. Diane Johnston Brokaw, Mar. 9, 1985; 1 child from previous marriage, D. Townley. BA, Princeton U., 1952; MD, Johns Hopkins U., 1956; DSc (hon.), Bridgeport U., 1984, Princeton U., 1985. Diplomate Am. Bd. Ophthalmology. Intern Cornell Med. Sch.-N.Y. Hosp., 1956-57; rsch. fellow in ophthalmology NIH, Bethesda, Md., 1957-59; resident Wilmer Inst., Johns Hopkins Sch. Medicine, Balt., 1959-64; assoc. prof. Wilmer Inst., 1964-71; asst. prof. Johns Hopkins Sch. Medicine, 1964-71; prof., chmn. dept. ophthalmology Baylor Coll. Medicine, Houston, 1971-82, prof. emeritus ophthalmalogy, 1998—; med. dir. King Khaled Eye Specialist Hosp., Riyadh, Saudi Arabia, 1982-84; chmn., chief med. officer OcuSystems, Inc., Greenwich, Conn., 1985-87; prof. Cornell U. Coll. Medicine, 1986-92; chmn., program dir. dept. ophthalmology Cath. Med. Ctr. of Bklyn. and Queens, 1986-92. Founder Project ORBIS, Inc., N.Y.C., 1971, med. dir., 1971-87; founder, bd. pres. The EXCEL Found., 1989-99; mem. com. med. sci. USIA, 1991-94; bd. dirs. Eye Bank for Sight Restoration, N.Y.C., One World Sight Project, Southhampton Hosp., 1998—2003, East Hampton Healthcare Found., 1998—; bd. pres. World Eye Orgn., Hong Kong, 1999—; mem. med. adv. bd. Johns Hopkins Sch. Pub. Health, 1988-2003. Author of several books; contbr. articles to profl. jours. Named honoree Manhattan League Helen Keller Svcs. for the Blind, 2002; recipient Royal Decoration 3d Order, Royal Decoration 2d Order, Jordan, Pres.'s Citizen medal, 1987, Legion of Honor, France, Johns Hopkins Disting. Alumnus award, 2005; scholar Markle scholar in acad. medicine, 1967—72. Fellow Am. Acad. Ophthalmology (sec. continuing edn. 1977-82, 1st v.p. 1982, Honor award 1975, Sr. Honor award 1992), ACS (bd. govs. substitute 1972-73); mem. Am. Bd. Ophthalmology (chmn. 1982), Assn. Univ. Profs. Ophthamology (trustee 1978-81), Md. Ophthalmol. Soc. (pres. 1969-70), Pan Am. Assn. Ophthalmology (coun. 1973-75). Home: PO Box 5015 East Hampton NY 11937-6096 E-mail: dpaton1@aol.com.

PATON, LELAND B. investment banker; b. Worcester, Mass., Nov. 30, 1943; s. Andrew John and Anne Louise (Kehoe) P.; m. Nancy Carlon Nation, May 13, 1978;children: Scott Bartlett, Mark Grosvenor, Elisabeth Anne. Asst. sec. New England Mcht. Nat. Bank, Boston, 1965-69; with Prudential Bache Securities Inc. Prudential Securities Inc., 1969—; mgr. N.Y. instl. sales, N.Y.C., 1976-77; dir.mktg., 1977-82; pres. Capital Markets Group, 1986—; also bd. dirs.; mem. operating com. Prudential Securities Inc., chief adminstrv. officer, pres. adminstrv. group, 1997—. Exchange ofcl. Am. Stock Exchange; bd. dirs. Chgo. Bd. of Options Exchange. Bd. dirs. Riverdale Country Sch. Mem. N.Y. Stock Exchange, Securities Industry Assn. (chmn. mktg. com. 1981, bd. dirs.), Securities Ind. Inst. (bd. dirs.), Am.Mktg. Assn., Bond Club, N.Y., Apawamis Club, Harvard Club, Mid-Ocean Club, Long Cove Club. Office: Prudential Securities Inc One Seaport Plz New York NY 10292-0134

PATON WALSH, JILL, writer; b. London, Apr. 29, 1937; d. John Llewelyn and Patricia (Dubern) Buss; m. Antony Edmund Paton Walsh, Aug. 5, 1961; Children: Edmund, Margaret, Clare. Author: Hengest's Tale, 1966, The Dolphin Crossing, 1967, Fireweed, 1969, (World Book Festival award 1970), Wordhoard, 1969, Goldengrove 1972, Farewell Great King, 1972, Toolmaker, 1973, The Dawnstone, 1973, The Emporer's Winding Sheet, 1974 (Whitbread prize 1974), The Huffler, 1975, The Island Sunrise: Preshistoric Culture in the British Isles, 1975, Unleaving, 1976 (Boston Globe, Horn Book award 1976), Children of the Fox: Crossing to Salamis, 1977, The Walls of Athens, 1978, Persian Gold, 1978, A Chance Child, 1978, The Green Book, 1981, Babylon, 1982, Parcell of Patterns, 1983 (Universe prize 1984), Lost and Found, 1984, Gaffer Samson's Luck, 1984 (Smarties Grand prix 1984), Lapsing, 1985, A School for Lovers, 1989, Birdy and the Ghosties, 1990, "Grace", 1991, Matthew and the Sea Singers, 1992, When Grandma Came, 1992, The Wydham Case, 1993, Knowledge of Angels, 1994, A Piece of Justice, 1995, Connie Came to Play, 1995, Thomas and the Tinners, 1995, The Serpentine Cave, 1997, When I Was Little Like You, 1997, (with Dorothy L. Sayers) Thrones, Dominations, 1998, A Desert in Bohemia, 2000, (with Dorothy L. Sayers) A Presumption of Death, 2002. Fellow Royal Soc. of Lit. (CBE award 1996). Address: care David Higham Assocs 5-8 Lower John St Golden Sq London W1R 3PE England

PATRIC, JASON, actor; b. June 17, 1966; s. Jason and Linda Gleason Miller. Actor: (films) include The Lost Boys, 1987, The Beast, 1988, After Dark, My Sweet, 1990, Denial Loon, 1991, Rush, 1991, Geronimo-An American Legend, 1993, The Journey of August King, 1995, Sleepers, 1996, Incognito, 1997, Speed 2, 1997, Friends and Neighbors, 1998, 3 Days of Rain, 2000, Narc, 2002, The Alamo, 2004;(TV movies) Toughlove, 1985. Office: United Talent Agy care David Schiff 9560 Wilshire Blvd Ste 500 Beverly Hills CA 90212-2427

PATRICK, BRENDA JEAN, educational consultant; b. Dallas, Aug. 24, 1955; d. Gene Everett and Peggy Rose Patrick; children: Michael Everett, Tray Riley. BS in Elem. Edn., Tex. A&M U., Commerce, 1981, MS, 1984, postgrad., 1989—. Cert. Tex. Edn. Agy. Tchr. Garland Ind. Sch. Dist., 1982-87, acad. coach, 1983-86; with Austin Acad. for Excellence, 1987-88; program coord., master cons. Region 10 Edn. Svc. Ctr., 1988—. Coord. Tchr. Expectation Student Achievement; trainer Devel. Capable People; trainer of trainers Profl. Devel. and Appraisal Sys.; developer, presenter workshops and seminars in field. Author: Better Teaching, Texas Secretary. Past bd. dirs. Dallas Arboretum's Fan Club. Recipient Tex. History Tchr. award Daus. of Republic of Tex., Am. History Tchr. award DAR; named Vol. with a Heart, YWCA. Mem. Tex. PTA (hon. life), Tex. Staff Devel. Coun., Phi Delta Kappa.

PATRICK, CHARLES WILLIAM, JR., lawyer; b. Monroe, N.C., Oct. 9, 1954; s. Charles William and Louise (Nisbet) P.; m. Celeste Hunt, June 5, 1976; children: Laura Elizabeth, Charles William III. BA magna cum laude, Furman U., 1976; JD, U. S.C., 1979. Bar: S.C. 1979, U.S. Dist. Ct. S.C. 1981, U.S. Ct. Appeals (11th cir.) 1981, U.S. Ct. Appeals (10th cir.) 1983, U.S. Ct. Appeals (4th cir.) 1986. Law clk. to presiding judge 9th Cir. Ct. State of S.C., Charleston, 1979—80; assoc. Ness, Motley, Loadholt, Richardson and Poole and predecessor firm Blatt and Fales, Charleston, 1980—2002, 1980—84, ptnr., 1984—2002, Richardson, Patrick, Westbrook & Brickman, LLC, Charleston, 2002—. Exec. editor S.C. Law Review, 1978; contbr. articles to profl. jours. Mem. ABA, Assn. Trial Lawyers Am., S.C. Assn. Trial Lawyers, Trial Lawyers for Pub. Justice, Nat. Order Lion (comdr.), Phi Beta Kappa. Democrat. Presbyterian. Avocations: boating, skiing, jogging. Home: 38 Church St Charleston SC 29401-2742 Office: Richardson Patrick Westbrook & Brickman LLC PO Box 879 174 East Bay St Charleston SC 29402-0879 Office Phone: 843-727-6500. Business E-Mail: cpatrick@rpwb.com.

PATRICK, CRAIG, professional hockey team executive; b. Detroit, May 20, 1946; s. Lynn P.; m. Sue Patrick; children— Erin, Cory, Ryan MBA, U. Denver. Hockey player Calif. Golden Seals, 1971-74; hockey player St. Louis Blues, 1974-75, Kansas City, 1975-76, World Hockey Assn., Minn., 1976-77, Washington Capitals, 1977-79; v.p., gen. mgr. N.Y. Rangers, N.Y.C., 1981-86; dir. athletics and recreation Univ. Denver, 1987-89; gen. mgr., exec. v.p. Pitts. Penguins, 1989—. Achievements include being capt., U.S. Nat. Team, World Championships, Moscow, 1979; asst. mgr. and asst. coach U.S. Olympic Hockey Team, 1980. Office: Pitts Penguins Civic Arena 66 Mario Lemieux Pl Pittsburgh PA 15219-3501

PATRICK, DAN, sportscaster; b. May 15, 1957; married; 2 children. BA in Broadcasting, U. Dayton, 1979. Morning sports and news reporter WTUE Radio, Dayton, Ohio, 1979-81; weekend sports anchor, reporter WDTN-TV, Dayton, Ohio, 1981-83, CNN, 1983-89; sports dir. WKLS, Atlanta, 1987-91; reporter weekday sports Laser 103, Milw., 1989-91, WLVQ-AM, Columbus, 1989-91; anchor, reporter SportsCenter ESPN, Bristol, Conn., 1989—; reporter weekday sports KSEG, Sacramento, 1991. Guest host ABC Good Morning Am., 1996. Recipient Sports Emmy award for studio host, 1998. Office: ESPN Inc Comms Dept ESPN Plz 935 Middle St Bristol CT 06010-1099

PATRICK, DEVAL LAURDINE, lawyer; b. Chgo., July 31, 1956; s. Laurdine Kenneth and Emily Mae (Wintersmith) P.; m. Diane Louise Bemus, May 5, 1984; children: Sarah Baker, Katherine Wintersmith. AB cum laude, Harvard Coll., 1978, JD, 1982, Dist. Columbia Law Sch., 1994, Morris Brown Coll., 1996, Curry Coll., 1997, Clark U., 1999, New Eng. Sch. of Law, 1999, Suffolk U., 2000, Northeastern U., 2002. Bar: Calif. 1983, D.C. 1985, Mass. 1987, U.S. Dist. Ct. Mass. 1987, U.S. Dist. Ct. (cen. dist.) Calif. 1983, U.S. Ct. Appeals (1st and 5th cirs.) 1984, U.S. Ct. Appeals (9th and 11th cirs.) 1984, U.S. Supreme Ct. 1988. Law clk. to Hon. Stephen Reinhardt U.S. Ct. Appeals (9th cir.), L.A., 1982-83; asst. counsel NAACP Legal Def. Fund, N.Y.C., 1983-86; ptnr. Hill & Barlow, Boston, 1986-94; asst. atty. gen. civil rights divsn. U.S. Dept. Justice, Washington, 1994-97; ptnr. Day, Berry & Howard, Boston, 1997-99; v.p., gen. counsel Texaco Inc., White Plains, N.Y., 1999-2001; exec. v.p., gen. counsel The Coca-Cola Co., Atlanta, 2001—04. Herman Phleger disting. vis. prof. Stanford Law Sch., 1997; lectr. Boston Coll. Sch. Law, 1997, Harvard Law Sch., 1998; mem. various corp. bd. dirs.; bd. overseers Harvard U., 1998—2003; dir. UAL Corp., 1997-2001, Reebok Internat. Ltd., 2001-, Coca-Cola Enterprises Inc., 2001-2004. Dir., mem. exec. com., chmn. New Eng. steering com. NAACP Legal Def. and Edn. Fund., Inc., 1991-94, vice chmn. Mass. Jud. Nominating Coun., 1991-93; trustee, mem. exec. com. Milton Acad., 1985-97; overseer WGBH, 1993-94; trustee Nathan Cummings Found., 1998-2000, Ford Found., 2000--. Recipient George Leisure award Harvard Law Sch., 1981; Rockefeller Traveling fellow, 1978. Mem. ABA (numerous bds. and coms.), Mass. Bar Assn., Mass. Black Lawyers Assn., Boston Bar Assn. (coun. mem. 1993), Harvard Alumni Assn. (dir. 1993-96). Avocations: squash, cooking, gardening.

PATRICK, DONALD LEE, social scientist, health services researcher; b. Eugene, Oreg., Sept. 23, 1944; s. Lawrence Leonard and Marie Esther (Bell) P.; m. Shirley Anne Alexander Beresford, May 31, 1980; children: Alistair Lawrence Beresford, Mira Yvonne Bell. AB with distinction, Northwestern U., 1966; MSPH, Columbia U., 1968, PhD, 1972. Rsch. assoc. U. Calif., San Diego, 1970-72; lectr. Yale U., New Haven, 1972-76; sr. lectr. U. London, 1976-82; assoc. prof. U. N.C., Chapel Hill, 1982-87; prof. and dir. social and behavioral scis. program U. Wash., Seattle, 1987—. Adj. prof. sociology, U. Wash., 1988—, dept. rehab. medicine, 1987—. Author: Health Status and Health Policy, 1993; editor: Sociology as Applied to Medicine, 1976, Disablement in Community, 1989. Mem. APHA (mem. coun. 1993-96), Spina Bifida Assn. Am. (chair profl. adv. bd. 1990-93, Pres.' award 1995), Internat. Soc. for Quality of Life Rsch. (pres. 1994-96, Pres. award 2001), Inst. Medicine. Democrat. Unitarian Universalist. Avocations: gardening, music, travel. Home: 5427 43rd Ave W Seattle WA 98199-1061 Office: U Wash PO Box 357660 Seattle WA 98195-7660

PATRICK, ERLINE M. federal agency administrator; BA in Biology, Talladega Coll., 1960; MEd in Urban Edn., U. Hartford, 1971, 6th yr. cert. adminstrn. and supervision, 1974; PhD, U. Conn., 1992. Secondary sch. math. and sci. tchr., Pa., N.C. and Conn., 1960-71; vice prin. Hartford (Conn.) Bd. Edn., 1971-78, prin., 1978-84; exec. asst. program devel. Sys. Mgmt. Am. Corp., Arlington, Va., 1984-85; profl. staff mem. U.S. Senate Small Bus. Com., Washington, 1985-89; assoc. adminstr. minority small bus. devel. program U.S. Small Bus. Adminstrn., Washington, 1989-91, dir. office program rev., 1991-94, agy. liaison to Dept. HUD for Pres.' Empowerment Initiative, 1994, dep. assoc. adminstr. small bus. devel. ctrs., 1994-95, asst. adminstr. OEO Civil Rights, 1995—. Contbr. articles to profl. jours. Corporator Hartford Sem. Found., 1978—; active various civic and charitable orgns. NSF grantee Columbia U., 1963, Franklin and Marshall Coll., 1965; Nat. Edn. Policy fellow George Washington, 1978-79; apptd. Adm. Great Navy of State of Nebr., 1989-91; recipient Svc. award Nat. Urban League, 1981, citations for Outstanding Ednl. Leadership, City of Hartford and State of Conn., 1982-84, Disting. Alumni award U. Hartford, 1978-84, Charlotte Jazz Club award, 1962, various trade assn. awards for leadership and svc., 1989—. Mem. NAACP, Exec. Women in Govt., Greater Washington Talladega Alumni Assn. (pres. 1993—). Address: 417 S 96th St Omaha NE 68114-4968

PATRICK, GEORGIA O'BRIEN LAKAYTIS, communications executive; b. Dallas, July 2, 1945; d. Jack Dallas and Jane (Childs) O'Brien; m. Thomas Donald Patrick, Oct. 23, 1981. BJ, U. Mo., 1967. Tech. writer Mo. Regional Med. Programs, Columbia, Kansas City, 1967-69; with Ctr. for Student Life, U. Mo., Columbia, 1969-76; comm. dir. Am. Assn. Family and Consumer Sci., Washington, 1976-81; exec. v.p. The Communicators, Inc., Washington, 1981-92, CEO, 1992—. Founder Internat. Managed HealthCare Inst., 1996; Washington office dir. TeckSkills Edgia, 1999—; Washington bur. chief Profl. Cert. Mag., 2001—;; co-founder, pres. Cert. Profls. Internat., 2003; cons. and leader seminars and workshops for nat. and internat. orgns.; expert on Internet relevance to nat. assns. Contbr. articles to profl. jours. Mem.: Nat. Orgn. Competency Assurance, Greater Washington Soc. Assn. Execs. (Leadership Team), Am. Soc. Assn. Execs. Office: The Communicators Inc 10072 Vista Ct Myersville MD 21773-8138 Office Phone: 301-293-3350. E-mail: georgia@communicators.com.

PATRICK, H. HUNTER, judge; b. Gasville, Ark., Aug. 19, 1939; s. H. Hunter Sr. and Nelle Frances (Robinson) P.; m. Charlotte Anne Wilson, July 9, 1966; children: Michael Hunter, Colleen Annette. BA, U. Wyo., 1961, JD, 1966. Bar: Wyo. 1966, U.S. Dist. Ct. Wyo. 1966, Colo. 1967, U.S. Supreme Ct. 1975. Mcpl. judge City of Powell (Wyo.), 1967-68; sole practice law Powell, 1966-88; atty. City of Powell, 1969-88; justice of the peace County of Park, Wyo., 1971-88; bus. law instr. Northwest C.C., Powell, 1968-98; dist. judge State of Wyo. 5th Jud. Dist., 1988—; drug ct. judge Park County, Wyo., 2001—. Mem. Wyo. Dist. Judges Conf., sec.-treas., 1993-94, vice chair, 1994-95, chair, 1995-96. Editor: Bench Book for Judges of Courts of Limited Jurisdiction in the State of Wyoming, 1980-90. Dir. cts. Wyo. Girls State, Powell, 1982-85, 89-99; elder, deacon, moderator of deacons Powell Presbyn. Ch., 1997; mem. Wyo. Commn. Jud. Conduct & Ethics, 1997-2003; judge, chair mgmt. com. Park County Drug Ct., 2001—. Recipient Wyo. Crime Victim Compensation Commn. Judicial award, 1995. Fellow Am. Bar Found. (life), Wyo. Jud. Adv. Coun.; mem. ABA (Wyo. state del. to ho. of dels. 1994-2001, Wyo. del. jud. adminstrn. divsn., exec. com. nat. conf. trial ct. judges representing Wyo., Colo., Kans., Nebr., N.Mex. 1996-2000, bd. govs. 2001-04, Pub. Svc. award for ct.-sponsored Law Day programs 1990, 92), Wyo. Bar Assn. (Cmty. Svc. award 1999, Ann. Pub. Svc. award 1999), Colo. Bar Assn., Park County Bar Assn. (sec. 1969-70, pres. 1970-71), Wyo. Assn. Cts. Ltd. Jurisdiction (pres. 1973-80), Wyo. Dist. Judges Conf. (chair 1996), Am. Judicature Soc. (bd. dirs.). Avocations: photography, travel, fishing, reading, writing. Home: PO Box 941 Powell WY 82435-0941 Office: PO Box 1868 Cody WY 82414-1868 E-mail: hpatrick@parkco.wtp.net., hpatrick@wir.net.

PATRICK, HUGH TALBOT, economist, educator; b. Goldsboro, N.C., Feb. 22, 1930; s. Talbot and Paula (Miller) P.; children: Stephen, Matthew, Catherine. BA, Yale U., 1951; MA in Far Eastern Studies, U. Mich., 1955, MA in Econs., 1957, PhD in Econs., 1960; MA (hon.), Yale U., 1968; PhD (hon.), Lingnan U., 2000. Econ. analyst U. S. Govt., 1951-52; lectr. econs. U. Mich., 1958-60; asst. prof. econs. Yale U., New Haven, 1960-64, assoc. prof., 1964-68, prof. Far Eastern econs., 1968-84; dir. Yale U. Econ. Growth Ctr., 1976-79, 80-83; R.D. Calkins prof. internat. bus. Columbia U., N.Y.C., 1984—2001, prof. emeritus, 2001—. Vis. prof. U. Bombay, 1961-62; mem. Japan-U.S. Econ. Rels. Group, 1978-81, U.S. Com. for Pacific Econ. Coop.; dir. Ctr. on Japanese Econ. and Bus., Columbia U., 1986—. Editor: Japanese Industrialization and Its Social Consequences, 1976, Japanese High Technology Industries-Lessons and Limitations of Industrial Policy, 1986; contbr. chpt. and co-editor (with Henry Rosovsky): Asia's New Giant-How the Japanese Economy Works, 1976; contbr. chpt., co-editor (with Masahiko Aoki): The Japanese Main Bank System: Its Relevance for Developing and Transforming Economies, 1994, co-editor (with Larry Meissner): Pacific Basin Industries in Distress: Structural Adjustment and Trade Policy in Nine Industrialized Economies, 1991 (Masayoshi Ohira Meml. prize 1992), (with Yung Chul Park) The Financial Development of Japan, Korea and Taiwan: Growth, Repression and Liberalization, 1994, (with Takeo Hoshi) Crisis and Change in the Japanese Financial System, 2000. Ford Found. fellow 1957-58; grantee Am. Coun. Learned Socs., 1962; Guggenheim fellow, 1964-65; Fulbright rsch. prof., 1964-65; Fulbright-Hays NDEA fellow, 1969-68; Assn. Asian Studies Disting. lectr., 1977. Mem. Japan Soc. (dir. 1973-79, 81-2000), Social Sci. Rsch. Coun. (dir., chmn. 1985-88), Pacific Trade and Devel. Confs. (chmn.). Democrat. Office: Columbia U 320 Uris Hall 3022 Broadway New York NY 10027-6945 Office Phone: 212-854-3497.

PATRICK, JAMES DUVALL, JR., lawyer; b. Griffin, Ga., Dec. 28, 1947; s. James Duvall and Marion Wilson (Ragsdale) P.; m. Cynthia Hill, Jan. 19, 1991. BS in Indsl. Mgmt., Ga. Inst. Tech., 1970; JD, U. Ga., 1973. Bar: Ga. 1973, U.S. Dist. Ct. (mid. dist.) Ga. 1973, U.S. Dist. Ct. (so. dist.) Ga. 1983, U.S. Ct. Appeals (5th cir.) 1974, U.S. Ct. Appeals (11th cir.) 1981, U.S. Tax Ct. 1985, U.S. Supreme Ct. Assoc. Cartledge, Cartledge & Posey, Columbus, Ga., 1973-74; ptnr. Falkenstrom, Hawkins & Patrick, Columbus, 1975, Falkenstrom & Patrick, Columbus, 1975-77; sole practice Columbus, 1977—. Instr. bus. law Chattahoochee Valley C.C., Phenix City, Ala., 1975-77; instr. paralegal course Columbus Coll., 1979, 84; del. U.S./China Joint Session on Trade, Investment, and Econ. Law, Beijing, 1987, Moscow Conf. on Law and Bilateral Econ. Rels., Moscow, 1990; U.S. del. U.S./Cuba Law Initiative, Havana, 2000. Mem. Hist. Columbus Found., Mayor's Comn. for the

Handicapped, 1987-88; local organizer, worker Joe Frank Harris for Gov. Campaign, Columbus, 1982; bd. dirs. Columbus Symphony Orch., 1988-94. Mem. ATLA, ABA, Am. Judicature Soc., State Bar Ga., Ga. Trial Lawyers Assn., Columbus Lawyers Club, Columbus Kappa Alpha Alumni Assn. (sec.), Civitan (bd. dirs. 1975-77), Country Club of Columbus, Georgian Club (Atlanta), Buckhead Club, Chattahouchee River Club, Phi Delta Phi, Kappa Alpha. Methodist. Office: PO Box 2745 Columbus GA 31902-2745

PATRICK, JANE AUSTIN, association executive; b. Memphis, May 27, 1930; d. Wilfred Jack and Evelyn Eudora (Branch) Austin; m. William Thomas Spencer, Sept. 11, 1952 (div. Apr. 1970); children: Duke Anthony-Spencer Austin, ToniLee Candice Spencer; m. George Milton Patrick, Oct. 1, 1971 (dec. July 2002). Student, Memphis State U., 1946-47; BSBA, Ohio State U., 1979. Svc. rep. So. Bell Tel. and Tel., Memphis, 1947-52; placement dir. Mgmt. Pers., Memphis, 1965-66; pers. dir. E & E Ins. Co., Columbus, Ohio, 1966-69; Ohio exec. dir. Nat. Soc. for Prevention of Blindness, Columbus, 1969-73; regional dir. Ohio and Ky. CARE and MEDICO, Columbus, 1979-87; v.p. Career Execs. of Columbus, 1987-91; owner, pres. Patricks Distbn., 1994—. Lectr., cons. in field. Author of poetry. Mem. choir 1st Cmty. Ch., Columbus, 1972--, bd. dirs. Ohio State U. Med. Ctr. Svc. Bd.; bd. dirs. Columbus Coun. on World Affairs, 1980-92, sec., 1983-91, chmn. devel. com.; chmn. pers. com. Ohio Hunger Task Force, 1989-90; founder Ctrl. Ohio Lions Eye Bank. Recipient commendation Nat. Soc. Prevention Blindness, commendation Ctrl. Ohio Lions Eye Bank, 1973, Svc. award plaque Upper Arlington Pub. Schs., 1986. Mem. Non-Profit Orgn. Mgmt. Inst. (pres.), Nat. Soc. Fund-Raising Execs. (cert., nat. dir., v.p.), Pub. Rels. Soc. Am. (cert., membership com. chairperson), Ohio State Med. Ctr. Svc. Bd. (bd. dirs.), Ins. Inst. Am. (cert.), Mensa Internat., Columbus Dental Soc. Aux. (historian and publicity chair), Alpha Gamma Delta (undergrad. editor Gamma Zeta chpt.), Epsilon Sigma Alpha (pres.). Home: 434 Fountain Lake Dr Memphis TN 38120-1832 Personal E-mail: gnjp27@aol.com.

PATRICK, JANET CLINE, personnel company executive, b. San Francisco, June 30, 1934; d. John Wesley Patrick and Edith Bertha (Corde) Cline; m. Robert John Patrick Jr., June 13, 1959 (div. 1988); children: John McKinnon, Stewart McLennan, William Robert. BA with distinction, Stanford U., 1955; postgrad., U. Calif.-Berkeley, 1957, George Washington U., 1978—82. English tchr. George Wash. H.S., San Francisco, 1957, K.D. Burke Sch., San Francisco, 1957—59, Berkeley Inst., Brooklyn, 1959—63; placement counselor Wash. Sch. Secs., Wash., 1976—78, asst. dir. placement, 1978—81; mgr. Med. Pers. Svc. Med. Soc., D.C., 1981—89; pres. Med. Personnel Svcs., Inc., Washington, 1989—. Editor, co-pub. The Medical Bulletin of North Virginia, 1997—. Chmn. area 2 planning com. Montgomery County Pub. Schs., Md., 1974—75; mem. vestry, corr. sec. Christ Ch., Kensington, Md., 1982—84, vestry, sr. warden, 1984—85, vestry, chmn. ann. giving com., 1986—89; chmn. Long-range planning com., 1989—92, sec., 1992—93, jr. warden, 1994, co-chair captain campaign, 1996; finance com. Montgomery County Pvt. Industry Coun., 1994. Mem.: Met. D.C. Med. Group Mgmt. Assn., Jr. League (Wash.), Phi Beta Kappa. Republican. Episcopalian. Office: Med Personnel Svcs Inc 1707 L St NW Ste 250 Washington DC 20036-4215 Home: 7800 Glenbrook Rd Bethesda MD 20814-1302

PATRICK, JOHN JOSEPH, social sciences educator; b. East Chicago, Ind., Apr. 14, 1935; s. John W. and Elizabeth (Lazar) P.; m. Patricia Grant, Aug. 17, 1963; children— Rebecca, Barbara AB, Dartmouth Coll., 1957; Ed.D., Ind. U., 1969. Social studies tchr. Roosevelt High Sch., East Chicago, 1957-62; social studies tchr. Lab. High Sch., U. Chgo., 1962-65; research assoc. Sch. Edn., Ind. U., Bloomington, 1965-69, asst. prof., 1969-74, assoc. prof., 1974-77, prof. edn., 1977—, dir. social studies devel. ctr., 1986—, dir. ERIC clearinghouse for social studies, social sci. edn., 1986—2003. Bd. dirs. Biol. Scis. Curriculum Study, 1980-83; ednl. cons. Author: Progress of the Afro-American, 1968, The Young Voter, 1974; (with L. Ehman, Howard Mehlinger) Toward Effective Instruction in Secondary Social Studies, 1974, Lessons on the Northwest Ordinance, 1987; (with R. Remy) Civics for Americans, 1980, rev. edit. 1986; (with Mehlinger) American Political Behavior, 1972, rev. edit. 1980, (with C. Keller) Lessons on the Federalist Papers, 1987; America Past and Present, 1983; (with Carol Berkin) History of the American Nation, 1984, rev. edit., 1987; Lessons on the Constitution, 1985, James Madison and the Federalist Papers, 1990, How to Teach the Bill of Rights, 1991, Ideas of the Founders on Constitutional Government: Resources for Teachers of History and Government, 1991, Young Oxford Companion to the Supreme Court of the United States, 1994, Founding the Republic: A Documentary History, 1995, (with Gerald Long) Constitutional Debates on Freedom of Religion: A Documentary History, 1999, (with Richard M. Pious and Donald A. Ritchie) The Oxford Essential Guide to the U.S. Government, 2000, The Bill of Rights: A History in Documents, 2002. Bd. dirs. Law in Am. Soc. Found., 1984-88, Social Sci. Edn. consortium, 1984—; mem. Gov.'s Task Force on Citizenship Edn., Ind., 1982-87; active Ind. Commn. on Bicentennial of U.S. Constn., 1986-92; bd. dirs. Coun. for the Advancement of Citizenship, Nat. History Edn. Network, 1994-96; mem. Natr. Coun. for History Standards, 1991-94. Recipient John W. Ryan award for disting. svc. in internat. programs and studies, Ind. U., 2002. Mem. ASCD, Nat. Coun. Social Studies, Social Sci. Edn. Consortium (v.p. 1985-87), Coun. for Basic Edn., Am. Polit. Sci. Assn., Am. Hist. Assn., Orgn. Am. Historians, Phi Delta Kappa. Home: 1209 E University St Bloomington IN 47401-5045 Office: Ind U 2805 E 10th St Bloomington IN 47408-2601

PATRICK, JULIAN EARNEST, vocalist; b. Meridian, Miss., Oct. 26, 1927; s. Julian Patrick and Margueretta Jean Lewis. BMus, Cin. Conservatory, 1950; DMus, Rocky Mountain Coll., Billings, Mont., 1995; student of voice, Cornelius L. Reid. Music faculty U. Wash., Seattle. Singer (chorus, small roles): Trinity Episc. Ch., Broadway musicals, TV, radio, night clubs, 1952—63; singer: Opera cos. and concerts, N.Y.C., Dallas, San Francisco, Vienna, Paris, Strasbourg, Amsterdam, other internat. venues, 1965—, various CDs, (Operas) (premiers) Of Mice and Men, 1970, Casanova's HomeComing, 1985, Dream of Valentino, 1991, numerous others. Avocation: gardening. Home: 1511 Magnolia Way W Seattle WA 98199 Office: U Wash Sch Music Box 353450 Seattle WA 98195

PATRICK, MICHELE MARY, government official; b. Phila., Apr. 18, 1963; d. George Robert and Mary Elizabeth (Pristic) P. BA with honors in Econs., La Salle U., 1985; M in Govt. Adminstrn., U. Pa., 1990. Intern Phila. Water Dept., 1987; intern, asst. to exec. dir. Global Interdependence Ctr., Phila., 1988-89; intern, asst. to dep. dir. Phila. Fin. Dept., 1989, asst. to fin. dir., 1990; asst. mng. dir. City of Phila., 1990-91, 93-96; speechwriter to U.S. Senator Frank R. Lautenberg, 1996-97; speechwriter to Hon. Donna Shalala U.S. Sec. Health and Human Svcs., 1997—. Speaker in field. Author: Haunted Prague; co-author: sect. of Municipal Dept. Handbook; trivia writer Merit Inds., Bensalem, Pa., 1993-95; monthly columnist Global Stamp News, 1994-96. Recipient Fulbright fellowship, U.K., Bd. Fgn. Scholarships, Washington, 1985, Nat. Resource fellowship, Pacific-Asian Mgmt. Inst., U. Hawaii, 1984, Lindback award, La Salle U., Phila., 1985, Pa. Forensic Assn., State Championships, 1982, 83, 85, Nat. Forensic Assn. Nat. championship, 1985, Meyerson fellowship, U. Pa., Phila., 1987, Pres. Classroom scholarship, Pres. Classroom for Young Ams., Washington, 1982, James and Helen Hovorka scholarship, Coun. Higher Edn., Brookfield, Ill., 1982, 83, 84. Mem. Amnesty Internat., Am. Friends of Czech Republic, Fulbright Alumni Assn., Omicron Delta Epsilon. Avocations: historical travel, classical music, british and russian studies.

PATRICK, PAMELA ANN, research consultant; b. Dallas, June 10, 1963; d. Gene Everett and Peggy Rose (Tanzy) P. AAS, Eastfield Coll., 1982; BA in English, Tex. A&M U.-Commerce, 1987, MS in Edn., English, 1988. Tex. provisional cert. 1990. Sales clk. Sears, Mesquite, 1982-84; substitute tchr. various Ind. Sch. Dists., Tex., 1988—. Contbr. articles to profl. jours. Mem. UDC, DAR, Daus. Republic Tex., Daus. Union Vets. Civil War, Dallas County Heritage Soc., Dallas Geneal. Soc., Nat. Trust for Historic Preservation, Dallas Hist. Soc., Green County Hist. Geneal. Soc., Snyder Kennedy Cemetery Preservation Soc. (pres.), Robert Morris Hist. Soc. (pres.), Humane Soc. U.S., DAV Aux., Phi Delta Kappa, Sigma Tau Delta. Republican. Methodist. Avocations: photographer, gardener, genealogist, corvette enthusiast. Home: PO Box 870668 Mesquite TX 75187-0668

PATRICK, RICHARD M. professional hockey team executive; b. Victoria, B.C., Can., Oct. 20, 1946; married; 3 children. Ed., Dartmouth Coll., Am. U. Washington. Exec. v.p. Washington Capitals Hockey Team, Landover, Md.; now pres, gov. Washington Capitals, 1992—. Office: Washington Capitals MCI Center 601 F St NW Washington DC 20004-1605

PATRICK, ROBERT, playwright; b. Kilgore, Tex., Sept. 27, 1937; s. Robert and Beulah (Goodson) O'Connor. Author numerous plays produced off-off Broadway, off-Broadway, Broadway, also abroad including Robert Patrick's Cheep Theatricks (23 plays), 1972, Simultaneous Transmissions, 1973, Play-By-Play, 1975, The Golden Circle, 1975, Kennedy's Children, 1975, Let Me Tell It To You, Dr. Paroo, 1976, One Man, One Woman (6 plays), 1978, T-Shirts, 1979, Mutual Benefit Life, 1980, Mercy Drop and Other Plays (5 plays), 1980, My Cup Ranneth Over, 1984, Big Sweet, 1985, Untold Decades (7 plays), 1988, Drowned Out, 1990, Connie, 1991, Michaelangelo's Models, 1994, Bread Alone, 1994, The Trial of Socrates, 1994, Evan on Earth, 1995, Hollywood at Sunset, 2004, Pouf Positive (CD), 1996; author: (novels) Temple Slave, 1986, Echo, 1990, (book on CD) Film Moi, 2003, (films) Resident Alien, 1990, The O Boys Documentary, 1999; teleplays include: High Tide, 1994, Robin's Hoods, 1995, Ghost Story, 1997, (essay) Film Moi, 1999; contbr. poems, articles, stories to profl. jours. Rockefeller grantee, 1974, N.Y. State CAPS grantee, 1975; recipient Show Bus. Best Playwright award 1968-69, Glasgow Citizens' Theatre Best World Playwright award, 1974, Omni-Act One award, 1975, Robbie award, 1976, Founders award Internat. Thespians Soc., 1980, Blue is for Boys weekends in Manhattan, 1983, 86, Lifetime Achievement award for Gay Playwriting Robert Chesley Found., 1996. Home: 1837 N Alexandria Ave Apt 211 Los Angeles CA 90027-4068 E-mail: rbrtptrck@aol.com. *No object or action has any meaning except that given to it by a writer. Writers create the consciousness of humanity, which in turn creates our world. Writers write the world.*

PATRICK, RUTH (MRS. RUTH HODGE VAN DUSEN), limnologist, diatom taxonomist, educator; b. Topeka, Kans. d. Frank and Myrtle (Jetmore) Patrick; m. Charles (IV) Hodge, July 10, 1931; 1 child, Charles (V). BS, Coker Coll., 1929; MS, U. Va., 1931, PhD, 1934; LLD (hon.), Coker Coll., 1971; LHD (hon.), Chestnut Hill Coll, 1974; DSc (hon.), Beaver Coll., 1970, PMC Colls., 1971, Phila. Coll. Pharmacy and Sci., 1973, Wilkes Coll., 1974, Cedar Crest Coll., 1974, U. New Haven, 1975, Hood Coll., 1975, Med. Coll. Pa., 1975, Drexel U., 1975, Swarthmore Coll., 1975, Bucknell U., 1976, Rensselaer Poly. Inst., 1976, St. Lawrence U., 1978, U. Mass., 1980, Princeton U., 1980, Lehigh U., 1983, U. Pa., 1984, Temple U., 1985, Emory U., 1986, Wake Forest U., 1986, U. S.C., 1989, Clemson, 1989, Glassboro State Coll., 1992. Assoc. curator microscopy dept. Acad. Natural Scis., Phila., 1939-47; curator Leidy Micros. Soc., 1937-47, curator limnology dept., 1947—, chmn. limnology dept., 1947-73; occupant Francis Boyer Research Chair Acad. Natural Scis., Phila., 1973—, chmn. bd. trustees, 1973-76, hon. chmn. bd. trustees, 1976—; lectr. U. Pa., 1950-70, adj. prof., 1970—; guest Fellow of Saybrook Yale, 1975. Participant Am. Philos Soc. limnology expdn. to Mexico, 1947, leader Catherwood Found. expdn. to Peru and Brazil, 1955; del. gen. assembly Internat. Union Biol. Scis., Bergen, Norway, 1947; bd. dirs. E.I. Du Pont, Pa. Power and Light Co.; chmn. algae com. Smithsonian Oceanographic Sorting Ctr., 1963—68; mem. panel on water blooms Pres. Sci. Adv. Com., 1966; mem. panel on water resources and water pollution Gov.'s Sci. Adv. Com., 1966; mem. nat. tech. adv. com. on water quality requirements for fish and other aquatic life and wildlife Dept. Interior, 1967—68; mem. citizen's adv. coun. Pa. Dept. Environ. Resources, 1971—73; mem. hazardous materials adv. com. EPA, 1971—74, exec. adv. com., 1974—79; chmn. com.'s panel on ecology, 1974—76; mem. Pa. Gov.'s Sci. Adv. Coun., 1972; mem. exec. adv. com. nat. power survey FPC, 1972—75; mem. coun. Smithsonian Instn., 1973—; mem. Phila. Adv. Coun., 1973—76; mem. energy R&D adv. coun. Pres.s Emergy Policy Office, 1973—74; mem. adv. coun. Renewable Nat. Resources Found., 1973—76, Elecric Power Rsch. Found., 1973—77; mem. adv. com. for rsch. NSF, 1973—74; mem. gen. adv. com. ERDA, 1975—77; mem. adv. bd. Sec. Energy, 1975—89; mem. com. on human resources NRC, 1975—76; trustee Biological Abstracts, 1974—76; mem. adv. coun. dept. biology Princeton U., 1975—80; mem. com. on sci. and arts Franklin Inst., 1978—; mem. univ. coun. com. Yale Sch. Forestry and Environ. Studies, 1978—80; mem. sci. adv. coun. World Wildlife Fund-US, 1978—80; trustee Aquarium Soc., Phila., 1951—58, Henry Found.; bd. dirs. Wissahickon Valley Watershed Assn.; bd. govs. Nature Conservancy; bd. mgrs. Wistar Inst. Anatomy and Biology. Author: (series of volumes) Rivers of the United States Vol. 1, 1994, Rivers of the United States Vol. 2, 1997, Chemical and Physical Characteristics Vol. 3, 1995, Rivers of Atlantic and Eastern Gulf Drainage Vol. 4, The Mississipi River and Major Tributaries; co-author (with C.W. Reimer): Diatoms of the United States Vol. 1, 1966, Vol. II, Part 1, 1975; co-author: (with others) (books) Ground Water Contamination in the United States, 1983, 2nd edit.; co-author: (with others) (book) Surface Water Quality: Have the Laws Been Successful?, 1992; mem. editorial bd.with C. W. Reimer: sci. jours. Science, 1974—76, mem. editorial bd.: sci. jours. American Naturalist; contbr. articles over 150 to profl. jours. Recipient Disting. Dau. of Pa. award, 1952, Richard Hopper Day Meml. medal, Acad. Nat. Scis., 1969, Gimbel Phila. award, 1969, Gold medal, YWCA, 1970, Lewis L. Dollinger Pure Environment award, Franklin inst., 1970, Pa. award for excellence in sci. and tech., 1970, Eminent Ecologist award, Ecol Soc. Am., 1972, Phila. award, 1973, Gold medal, Pa. State Fish and Game Protective Assn., 1974, Internat. John and Alice Tyler Ecology award, 1975, Gold meda;, Phila. Soc. for Promoting Agr., 1975, Pub. Svc. award, U.S. Dept. Interior, 1975, Iben award, Am. Water Resources Assn., 1976, Outstanding Alumna award, Coker Coll., 1977, Francis K. Hutchinson medal, Garden Club of Am., 1977, Golden medal, Royal Zool. Soc., Antwerp, 1978, Green World award, N.Y. Bot. Garden, 1979, Hugo Black award, U. Ala., 1979, Sci award, Gov. Pa., 1988, Founders award, Soc. Environ. Toxicology and Chemistry, 1982, Environ. Regeneration award, Rene DuBois Ctr., 1985, Disting. Citizen award, Pa., 1989, Excellence award, N. Am. Benthological Soc., 1993, Benjamin Franklin medal, Am. Philosophical Soc., 1993, U.S. medal of svc., Pres. Bill Clinton, 1996, Nat. medal for sci., 1997, Nat. Wetlands award, 2000, Sci. Edn. Ctr. named in her honor, U. S.C., 1989. Fellow: AAAS (com. environ. alternatives 1973—74); mem.: Internat. Phycol. Soc., Am. Inst. Biol. Scis., Ecol. Soc. Am., Am. Soc. Naturalists (pres. 1975—76), Am. Soc. Limnology and Oceanography (Lifetime Achievement award 1996), Am. Soc. Plant Taxonomy, Internat. Soc. Plant Taxonomists, Internat. Limnological Soc., Phycol Soc. Am. (pres. 1954), Bot. Soc. Am.. (mem. Darbarker prize com. 1956, Merit award 1971), Am. Acad. Arts and Scis., Assn. Metro. Sewage Agys. (Environ. award 1995), Am. Philos. Soc. (Benjamin Franklin Outstanding Sci. Achievement award 1993), Nat. Acad. Enginrg. (com.environ. engr. study explicit criteria for power plant siting 1973), Nat. Acad. Scis. (chmn. panel com. on pollution 1966, mem.environ. measures panel com. remote sensing earth resources survey 1973—74, mem. nominating com. 1973—75, mem. com. sci. and public policy 1973—77), Water Pollution Control Fedn. (hon.), Soc. Study Evolution, Sigma Xi. Presbyterian. Office: Acad Natural Scis 19th at Benjamin Franklin Pkwy Philadelphia PA 19103 Office Phone: 215-299-1098. Business E-Mail: Patrick@acnatsci.org.

PATRICK, STEPHEN C. consumer products company executive; Joined Colgate-Palmolive Co., N.Y.C., 1982, CFO, 1996—. V.p. Fin. Acctg. Found.; bd. dirs. Arrow Electronics, 2003—. Office: Colgate-Palmolive Co 300 Park Ave New York NY 10022-7499

PATRICK, SUSAN D. government agency administrator; B in English, Colo. Coll.; M in Comm. Mgmt., U. So. Calif. Dir. distance learning campus Old Dominion U.; coord. Digital State Survey 2002 State of Ariz.; dep. dir. Office Edn. Tech. U.S. Dept. Edn., Washington. Office: US Dept Edn Rm FB6-7E208 400 Maryland Ave SW Washington DC 20202

PATRICK, THOMAS H. investment company executive; b. 1944; BA, Rutgers U., 1965; MBA, U. Pitts., 1966. Equity rsch. analyst Mellon Nat. Bank, 1966-68; prin. Sears, Chgo., 1970-72; with White Weld & Co., 1972-79; chief fin. officer, exec. v.p. Life Investors Inc., Cedar Rapids, Iowa, 1979-81; mng. dir. Merrill Lynch Capital Mkts., 1982-89; exec. v.p. equity mkts. group Merrill Lynch & Co. Inc.; CFO Merril Lynch & Co. Inc., 1989—90; exec. v.p., CFO Merrill Lynch & Co. Inc., N.Y.C., 2000—02; exec. vice-chmn., 2002—03.

PATRICK, VICTOR PHILLIP, lawyer; b. Lake Forest, Ill., Jan. 7, 1958; s. Rodger Ralph Patrick and Phyllis Elaine Bachler; m. Elizabeth Fletcher, Aug. 9, 1985; children: Kathryn Elaine, Stephen James, Diane Elizabeth, Marie Christine, Thomas Grant, John Wallace, Daniel Victor. AB in Politics magna cum laude, Princeton U., 1982; JD cum laude, Harvard U., 1985. Bar: D.C. 1986, N.Y. 1986, U.S. Ct. Appeals (10th cir.) 1986. Law clk. U.S. Ct. Appeals 10th Cir., Denver, 1985-86; assoc. Cleary, Gottlieb, Steen & Hamilton, Washington, 1986-88, 92-94, Brussels, 1988—91; from asst. gen. counsel to v.p., sec. and dep. gen. counsel Honeywell Internat. Inc. (formerly AlliedSignal Inc.), Morristown, NJ, 1994—97, 1999—2002, Torrance, Calif., 1997—99; sr. v.p., gen. counsel, sec. Walter Industries, Inc., Tampa, Fla., 2002—. Mem. ABA. Mem. Lds Ch. E-mail: vpatrick@walterind.com.

PATRICK, WILLIAM HARDY, JR., wetland biogeochemist, educator, laboratory director; b. Johns, Miss., Nov. 9, 1925; s. William Hardy and Alma (Webb) P.; m. Ruth Martin, Dec. 21, 1951; children: Terry Lynn, William Hardy, Carol Ann, Henry Carr. BS, La. State U., 1950, MS, 1951; PhD, La State U., 1954; D.Honoris Causa, U. Ghent (Belgium), 1979. Asst. prof. agronomy dept. La. State U., Baton Rouge, 1953-56, assoc. prof., 1956-61, prof., 1961-76, prof. marine scis., 1977-78, Boyd prof. marine scis., 1978—; dir. Wetland Biogeochemistry Inst., Baton Rouge. Moore lectr. in ecology U. Va., 1985, York lectr. U. Fla., 1989, cons. numerous govt., indsl. orgns. Contbr. articles to sci. jours. Organizer, dir. La. Methodist World Hunger Scholarship Program, Baton Rouge, 1979— . Served with AUS, 1944-46. Grantee numerous research orgns., 1963—; recipient Lifetime Achievement award Soc. Wetland Scientists, 2002, Nat. Wetland award Environ. Law Inst., 2002. Fellow AAAS, Am. Soc. Agronomy, Soil Sci. Soc. Am. (Internat. award 1992, Rsch. award 1993, Disting. Svc. award 2004); mem. Sigma Xi, Phi Kappa Phi. Republican. Methodist. Home: 888 Dubois Dr Baton Rouge LA 70808-5008 Office: Louisiana St Univ Wetland Biogeochemistry Baton Rouge LA 70803-0001 Office Phone: 225-578-6424. E-mail: wpatric@lsu.edu.

PATRON, JUNE EILEEN, former government official; b. N.Y.C., May 15; d. Irving B. and Mollie Patron. BA in Govt. with honors, Clark U., Worcester, Mass., 1965; MA, Am. U., 1967. With U.S. Dept. Labor, 1966-95, dir. Black Lung benefits program, 1976-79, asst. adminstr. pension and welfare benefit programs, 1979-84, assoc. dir. pension and welfare benefit programs, 1984-88, dir. program svcs., 1988-95; ret., 1995. Mem. Sr. Exec. Svc.; ind. contractor, mgmt. cons., 1997—. Vol. alumni admissions program Clark U., 1998—. Van Ness Neighborhood Network, 2003—. Recipient various awards Dept. Labor. Mem. Nat. Assn. Ret. Fed. Employees, Sr. Execs. Assn. Home: 3001 Veazey Ter NW Washington DC 20008-5454 E-mail: jpdcny@aol.com.

PATROUCH, JOSEPH FRANCIS, history professor; b. Cin., July 12, 1960; s. Joseph Francis and Ruth Marie Patrouch; m. Felice Lifshitz, May 15, 1994; m. Barbara Maier, 1985 (div. 1993); children: Quinn Bellamy Patrouch Lifshitz, Daniel Alexander Joseph. BA, Boston U., 1982; MA, U. of Calif., 1985, PhD, 1991. Asst. prof. Dept. of History, Fla. Internat. U., Miami, 1991—97, assoc. prof., dir. grad. studies, 1997—. Guest rschr. Max Planck Gesellschaft, Potsdam, 1995, GWZO Leiezis, 2001; pres. south fla. chpt. Fulbright Assn., Miami, Fla., 2000—; guest prof. U. Vienna, 2004. Author: (historical monograph) A Negotiated Settlement: The Counter-Reformation in the Habsburg Province of Upper Austria, 2000. Fellow Fulbright Rsch. Grant, Vienna, Inst. for Internat. Edn., 1999; Fulbright Student Grant, Linz, Austria, Coun. on Internat. Exch. of Students, 1988. Mem.: Soc. for Ct. Studies, Fruehe Neuzeit Interdisziplinaer, Soc. for Austrian and Habsburg History, European History Sect., So. Hist. Assn., Sixteenth Century Studies Conf., Am. Cath. Hist. Assn., Am. Folklore Soc., Fulbright Assn. (chpt. pres. 2000—), Am. Hist. Assn., Am. Assn. for the Advancement of Slavic Studies (assoc.). Roman Catholic. Office: Fla Internat U Dept History University Park Miami FL 33199 Office Phone: 305-348-3768. E-mail: patrouch@fiu.edu.

PATSTONE, CHERYL, public relations executive; b. Boston, May 4, 1955; d. Harold E. and Anna M. Brown; m. Walter Patstone, Nov. 10, 1979. BA in Econs. and French, Tufts U., 1977. Sr. economist, editor electronic bus. forecast Cahners Pub. Co., San Jose, Calif., 1977-87; mgr. pub. rels. Nat. Semiconductor Corp., Santa Clara, Calif., 1987-91, Marcom team leader comm. and computing group, 1991-96, dir. product pub. rels., 1996-99, dir. strategic Marcom programs, 1999—; v.p. comm. Autoweb.com, Inc., Santa Clara, 2000—; dir. corp. comm. Atheros Comms., Inc., Sunnyvale, Calif., 2001—. Mem. Internat. Assn. Bus. Communicators, No. Calif. Bus. Mktg. Assn. (bd. dirs., v.p. programs 1999-2000). Office: Atheros Comms 529 Almanor Ave Sunnyvale CA 94085 E-mail: cheryl@atheros.com.

PATTANAIK, PRASANTA KUMAR, economics professor; b. Cuttack, Orissa, India, Apr. 5, 1943; s. Kshetramohan and Krishnapriya (Mohanty) P.; m. Geeta Mohanty, June 11, 1968; 1 child, Swaha. BA (hons.), Utkal U., India, 1963; MA, U. Delhi, India, 1965; PhD, U. Delhi, 1968. Asst. prof. econ. Harvard U., 1968—70; rsch. fellow Nuffield Coll., Oxford, England, 1970—71; vis. fellow U. Delhi, 1971—72, reader in econ., 1972, prof. econs., 1972—75; prof. LaTrobe U., Bundoora, Vic., Australia, 1975-77; prof. econs. So. Meth. U., Dallas, 1977-78; prof. math and econs. U. Birmingham, 1978—; prof. econs. U. Calif., Riverside, 1991—. Author: Voting and Collective Choice, 1971, Strategy and Group Choice, 1978; co-editor: Social Choice and Welfare, 1983, mng. editor: Social Choice and Welfare, 1984-; assoc. editor: Journ. Econ. Theory, 1975-; numerous articles, chpts. to books. Recipient Mahalanobis Meml. Nat. award Indian Econometric Soc., 1986. Fellow Econometric Soc. Avocation: literature.

PATTEN, BERNARD MICHAEL, neurologist, writer, educator; b. N.Y.C., Mar. 23, 1941; s. Bernard M. and Olga (Vaccaro) P.; m. Ethel Doudine, June 18, 1964; children: Allegra, Craig. AB summa cum laude, Columbia Coll., 1962; MD, Columbia U., 1966. Med. intern N.Y. Hosp. Cornell Med. Ctr., N.Y.C., 1966-67; resident neurologist Columbia Presbyn. Med. Ctr., N.Y.C., 1967-69, chief resident neurologist, 1969-70; assoc. prof. neurology Baylor Coll. Medicine, Houston, 1973-95; ret., 1995. Asst. chief med. neurology NIH, Bethesda, Md., 1970-73; mem. med. bd. Nat. Myasthenia Gravis Found., 1973—, Nat. AmyoTrophic Lateral Sclerosis Found., 1982—, Nat. Myositis Assn., 1995—; invited faculty Rice U., 1999—; faculty Women's INst. Houston. Author: One or Two Things I Remember About Her, 1999, Tristan and Iseult: Modern Version, 2000, Investment Pearls for Modern Times Expressed in Meter and in Rhymes, 2000, The Great Cotzias, 2001, Ascent to Heaven, 2001, Quia Imperfectum, 2001, Truth, Knowledge or Bull: How to Tell the Difference, 2004, The Blood of a Million Christs, 2004; contbr. more than 200 articles to profl. jours. With USPHS, 1970-73. Rsch. grantee NIH, pvt. founds., nat. health orgns. Fellow ACP, Royal Coll. Physicians, Tex. Neurol. Soc. Achievements include discoverer (with others) L-Dopa for Parkinson's disease; pioneered use of immune suppression for myasthenia gravis, diagnosis and treatment of medical and neurologcal complications of breast implants. Home: 1019 Baronridge Dr Seabrook TX 77586-4001 E-mail: DADPATTEN@aol.com.

PATTEN, BETSEY LELAND, state legislator; b. Newton, Mass., Apr. 26, 1945; m. Richard C. Patten; 1 child. Student, Kings Coll. State rep. N.H. Ho. Reps., chmn. mcpl. and county govt. com. Chmn. Joint Legis. Com. on Adminstrv. Rules, Assessing Standards Bd., Carroll County Rep. Com., 1996—; mem. state exec. com. N.H. State Rep. Party, 1996—. Home: HC62 Box 415 46 Patten Hill Rd Center Harbor NH 03226 E-mail: rcpatten@worldpath.net.

PATTEN, CHARLES ANTHONY, management consultant, retired manufacturing company executive, author, publisher; b. Allentown, Pa., May 12, 1920; s. Charles Henerie and Mae (Doyle) P.; m. Kathleen Marie Breene, Jan. 6, 1951 (dec. 1999); children: Charles Anthony Jr., Amy Elizabeth Goddard,

Nancy Kathleen Hansen. BSM.E., Lehigh U., 1942. With Joy Mfg. Co., 1947-63, works mgr., 1956-63; v.p. mfg. White Motor Corp., 1963-68, Colt Industries, 1968-69; With Dravo Corp., Pitts., 1942-47, 69-85, gen. mgr. engring. works div., 1970-71, corp. v.p., gen. mgr. engring. works div., 1971-75, corp. group v.p., chief exec. officer Dravo Mfg. Group, 1975-81, corp. sr. v.p., mem. corp. policy com., chief exec. officer Dravo Mfg. Group, 1981-83, corp. sr. v.p., asst. to pres. and chief exec. officer, mem. exec. com., 1984-85; pres. C.A. Patten Enterprises, 1985—. Bd. dirs., v.p. Dravo (Can.) Ltd., 1975-85; dir., pres. Dravo-Okura Co. Ltd., 1974-79; dir. Dravo Mfg. (Can.) Ltd., 1975-83, Tru Weld Grating Inc., 1983-85; v.p. Dravo Internat., Inc., 1974-85; adv. com. Nat. Mgmt. Assn., 1973-85; chief devel. officer Western Pa. Model RR. Mus., 2001-, corp. mem., Am. Mgmt. Assn., 1954-85 Seminar spkr. in field, contbr. publs. Trustee Ohio Valley Gen. Hosp., McKees Rocks, Pa., 1975-82, Marietta (Ohio) Coll., 1979-89, emeritus trustee, 1989—; bd. dirs. Vocat. Rehab. Ctr. of Allegheny County, 1972-79, Jr. Achievement of S.W. Pa., 1975-80, Sherwood Oaks Residents Assn., 2003—. Recipient Silver Knight of Mgmt. award Nat. Mgmt. Assn., 1976. Mem. ASME, Neville Island Mfrs. Assn. (pres. 1975-85), Am. Arbitration Assn. (panel of arbitrators, 1989-95), Shipyard Steering Com. of Am. Waterways Operators, Inland Waterways Am. Bur. of Ships, Duquesne Club Republican. Roman Catholic. Home and Office: 204 Norman Dr Cranberry Township PA 16066-4233 Office Phone: 724-776-8204. E-mail: cpatten512@aol.com. *The successful manager is a time-oriented goal setter. Without waiting for others to ask, envisions things that should happen and thinks through possible paths to reach the goals. When the goals are reached, is quick to laud and praise people for their accomplishments.*

PATTEN, DUNCAN THEUNISSEN, ecologist educator; b. Detroit, Oct. 13, 1934; s. Marc T. and Doris (Miller) P.; m. Eva Chittenden, July 27, 1957; children: Michael, Marc, Robin, Scott. BA, Amherst Coll., 1956; MS, U. Mass., Amherst, 1959; PhD, Duke U., 1962. Asst. prof. ecology Va. Poly. Inst., Blacksburg, 1962-65, Ariz. State U., Tempe, 1965-67, assoc. prof., 1967-73, prof., 1973-95, prof. emeritus, 1995—, dir. ctr. environ. studies, 1980-95. Rsch. prof. Mont. State U., 1995—. Contbr. articles to profl. jours. Fellow AAAS, Ariz.-Nev. Acad. Sci.; mem. Ecol. Soc. Am. (bus. mgr. 1979-95), Brit. Ecol. Soc., Soc. Range Mgmt., Am. Inst. Biol. Scis., Soc. Wetland Scientists (pres. 1996-97), Am. Water Resource Assn., Am. Geophys. Union, Soc. Conservation Biology, Sigma Xi. Office: Mont State U Big Sky Inst Box 173490 Bozeman MT 59717-3490 Office Phone: 406-994-2784. Personal E-mail: dtpatten@starband.net. Business E-Mail: dtpatten@montana.edu.

PATTEN, LANNY RAY, industrial gas industry executive; b. St. Joseph, Mo., July 31, 1934; s. E.L. and Sarah Catherine (Langner) P.; m. Ann Rogers Hall, Oct. 26, 1957; children: David, John, Jeffrey, Mark. BS in Engring., Iowa State U., 1956; AMP, Harvard U., 1976. Net sr. v.p. gases and equipment Air Products and Chems., Inc., Allentown, Pa., 1960—90; pres., COO Airgas Inc., Radnor, Pa., 1990-91; founder, pres. CylServ, Inc., West Conshohocken, Pa., 1992—. Chmn. Lehigh U. Parents Assn., Bethlehem, Pa., 1977—90. Officer USAF, 1957—60. Recipient PACE award for Engring. Achievement Iowa State U., 1990, Friend of Lehigh award, 1991. Mem. SAR (officer), Pa. Soc. SR (bd. dirs.), Compressed Gas Assn. (exec. bd. dirs. 1977-91), Internat. Oxygen Mfg. Assn. Allentown C. of C. (exec. bd. dirs. 1978-82), Phila. Country Club, Union League of Phila., Kappa Sigma (Alumni Hall of Fame). Republican. Episcopalian. Avocations: baseball, golf, reading. Home: 1306 Club House Rd Gladwyne PA 19035-1006

PATTEN, RICHARD E. not-for-profit developer, director; b. Seattle, May 17, 1953; s. Donald Wesley and Lorraine Louise (Kienholz) P.; m. Monica Rose Bourg, Mar. 20, 1976; children: Richard Douglas, Wesley Bourg, Melinda Rose. BA, U. Wash., 1976. Exec. v.p. Microfilm Svc. Co., Seattle, 1976—84, gen. mgr., 1985—87, chmn. bd., 1988—90; pres. Express Pers. Svc., Seattle, 1990—2002; exec. dir. Am. Family Bus. Inst., 2002—. Candidate for U.S. Ho. of Reps., 1982; deacon Bethany Bapt. Ch., Seattle, 1983-86; co-chmn. fin. com. Wash. State Billy Graham Crusade, 1990-91; chmn. Wash. State Coalition toEliminate Death Tax. Mem. Nat. Micrographics Assn. (pres. N.W. chpt. 1979-80, bd. dirs. 1978-79), Assn. Image and Info. Mgmt. (chmn. svc. co. 1987), Assn. Records Mgrs. and Adminstrs., Wash. Athletic Club, Rotary (bd. dirs. 1996-98). Republican. Baptist. Home: 7012 NE 161st St Kenmore WA 98028-4265

PATTEN, ROBERT LOWRY, English language educator; b. Oklahoma City, Apr. 26, 1939; s. Charles H. and Helen (Lowry) P.; m. Faith L. Harris, June 12, 1960 (div. 1974); children: Jocelyn S., Christina S. BA, Swarthmore Coll., 1960; MA, Princeton U., 1963, PhD, 1965. Lectr. Bryn Mawr (Pa.) Coll., 1964-66, asst. prof. English, 1966-69; asst. prof. Rice U., Houston, 1969-71, assoc. prof., 1971-76, prof. English, 1976-96, chair, dept. of English, 1991-92, master Grad. House, 1992-95, Lynette S. Autrey prof. humanities, 1996—. Pres. PEN S.W., Houston, 1989-92. Author: Charles Dickens and His Publishers, 1978, George Cruikshank's Life, Times and Art, vol. 1, 1992, vol. 2, 1996 (best biography of the decade Guardian); editor: (book by Charles Dickens) Pickwick Papers, 1972, George Cruikshank: A Revaluation, 1974, 2d edit., 1992, (with John O. Jordan) Literature in the Marketplace, 1995; editor SEL: Studies in English Lit., 1978-84, 90—. Bd. dirs. Cultural Arts Coun., Houston, 1979-80, Tex. Com. for the Humanities, 1979-80; pres., bd. dirs. Houston Ctr. for the Humanities, 1976-84. NEH fellow, 1968-69, 77-78, 87-88; Guggenheim fellow, 1980-81; Nat. Humanities Ctr. fellow, 1987-88; Nat. Gallery of Art Assoc., 1988-89. Mem. AAUP, MLA, PEN Am. Ctr., Dickens Fellowship, Dickens Soc., Soc. for the History of Authorship, Reading and Pub. (bd. dirs. 1992-2003, treas. 1997-2003, v.p. 2003-), Coun. Editors of Learned Jours., Phi Beta Kappa (pres. Beta chpt. Tex. 1991-94, 97-2002, bd. dirs. Houston chpt. 1997—2000, adv. dir. 2000-03, senator 2002-03, Couper scholar, 2004—). Episcopalian. Avocations: travel, opera. Office: Rice U Dept English MS 30 PO Box 1892 Houston TX 77251-1892 Office Phone: 713-348-4697. E-mail: patten@rice.edu.

PATTEN, RONALD JAMES, university dean; b. Iron Mountain, Mich., July 17, 1935; s. Rudolph Joseph and Cecelia (Fuse) Pataconi; m. Shirley Ann Bierman, Sept. 5, 1959; children: Christine Marie, Cheryl Ann, Charlene Denise. BA, Mich. State U., 1957, MA, 1959; PhD, U. Ala., 1963. Acct. Price Waterhouse & Co., Detroit, 1958; instr. No. Ill. U., 1959-60; asst. prof. U. Colo., 1963-65; assoc. prof. Va. Poly. Inst. and State U., 1965-67, prof., 1967-73, head dept. accounting, 1966-73; dir. research Financial Accounting Standards Bd., Conn., 1973-74; dean Sch. Bus. Adminstrn., U. Conn., Storrs, 1974-88; chief of party-Eastern Caribbean Arthur D. Little Internat., 1988-89; dean Coll. Commerce and Kellstadt Grad. Sch. Bus. De Paul U., Chgo., 1989-99; dean Ritsumeikan Asia Pacific U. Grad. Sch. Mgmt., Beppu, Japan, 2003—. Individual investors adv. com. N.Y. Stock Exch., 1993-98; cons. in field. Contbr. chapters to books, articles to profl. jours. Bd. dirs. U.S. com. UNICEF, Chgo., 1996—99. Recipient Nat. Quartermaster award Nat. Quartermaster, Assn., 1956; Earhart Found. fellow, 1962-63. Mem. AICPA, Am. Acctg. Assn., Inst. Mgmt. Accts., Acad. Internat. Bus. (Internat. Dean of Yr. award 1987), Internat. Assn. for Acctg. Edn. and Rsch., Ill. Coun. Econ. Edn. (Chgo., trustee 1989—, chmn. bd. trustees 1997-2000), Pacioli Soc., Internat. Trade and Fin. Assn., dir. 1998-2000, West Towns Chorus, Heidelberg Club Internat., Scabbard and Blade, Golden Key, Beta Gamma Sigma (mem. bd. govs. 1975-90, nat. sec.-treas. 1980-82, nat. v.p. 1982-84, nat. pres. 1984-86), Beta Alpha Psi (bd. dirs. 1992-94), Delta Sigma Pi, World Assn. for Case Method Rsch. and Application, Adv Bd., 1998-, Phi Kappa Phi, Delta Mu Delta. Avocations: hiking, softball, golf, travel, singing. Home: 334 N Montclair Ave Glen Ellyn IL 60137-5253 E-mail: rpatten@depaul.edu.

PATTEN, THOMAS HENRY, JR., management, human resources educator; b. Cambridge, Mass., Mar. 24, 1929; s. Thomas Henry and Lydia Mildred (Lindgren) Patten; m. Rosalie Medina, May 23, 2002. AB, Brown U., 1953; MS, Cornell U., 1955, PhD, 1959. Dir. program planning Ford Motor Co., Dearborn, Mich., 1957-65; prof. mgmt. and sociology U. Detroit, 1965-67; prof. orgnl. behavior and personnel mgmt. Sch. Labor and Indsl. Relations, Mich. State U., E. Lansing, 1967-84; prof. mgmt. and human resources Calif. State Poly. U., Pomona, 1984—2003, prof. emeritus, 2003—. Cons. in field. Author: The Foreman: The Forgotten Man of Management, 1968, Manpower Planning and the Development of Human Resources, 1971, OD-Emerging Dimensions and Concepts, 1973, A Bibliography of Compensation Planning and Administration, 1960-1974, 2d rev. edit., 1981, 3d rev. edit., 1987, Pay: Employee Compensation and Incentive Plans, 1977, Classics of Personnel Management, 1979, Organizational Development Through Teambuilding, 1981, A Manager's Guide to Performance Appraisal, 1982, Fair Pay: The Managerial Challenge of Comparable Job Worth and Job Evaluation, 1988, Exercises for Developing Human Resources Management Skills, 1996. Served with USMC, 1946-51. Mem. ASTD (chmn. orgn. devel. div. 1972), Indsl. Rels. Rsch. Assn. (chpt. pres. 1970-71), Am. Sociol. Assn., Internat. Pers. Mgmt. Assn., Internat. Indsl. Rels. Assn., Inst. Applied Behavioral Sic., Am. Compensation Assn. Home: 2540 King Way Claremont CA 91711-1719 Office: Calif State Poly U Dept Mgmt & Human Resources 3801 W Temple Ave Pomona CA 91768-2557 E-mail: thpatten@csupomona.edu. *Human values come first.*

PATTEN, VALERIE LYNN, lawyer; b. L.A., Apr. 8, 1950; d. Russell Carl and Donna D. Patten; 1 child, Elizabeth Nicole Wood. AB, Stanford U., 1972; MFA, San Jose State U., 1981; JD, Georgetown U., 1992. Bar: Calif. 1992. Legal intern Washington Area Lawyers for the Arts, 1990—90; law clk. Garfinkle & Assocs., Washington, 1990—92; staff atty. Legal Advocates for Children and Youth, San Jose, Calif., 1992—93; assoc. atty. Law Offices of Robert L. Hoover, San Jose, 1994—96; pvt. practice Law Offices of Valerie L. Patten, Palo Alto, Calif., 1996—. Freelance writer Bay Area (Calif.) Art Publ., 1980—84; writer arts & entertainment Palo Alto (Calif.) Weekly, 1982—84; instr. art dept. U. Mont., Missoula, 1984—84; lectr. continuing edn. art dept. legal issues for artists San Jose State U., Calif., 1993; referral atty., lectr. Calif. Lawyers for the Arts, San Francisco, 1993—; asst. prof. art dept. San Francisco State U., 1994—95; atty. mem. Graphic Artists Guild, 1997—; presenter, continuing edn. seminar on custody and visitation in Calif. Nat. Bus. Inst., Eau Claire, Wis., 2003. One-woman shows include DeSaisset Mus., Pro Arts Gallery, Oakland, Henry Art Gallery, Seattle, exhibited in group shows at Am. Acad. and Inst Arts and Letters, N.Y. (selected for Hassam and Speicher fund Purchase Exhbn., 1983). Pro tem judge Superior Ct. Santa Clara County, San Jose, 1999—, property divsn. mediator, 1998—2001; pro bono panel mem. Santa Clara County Bar Assn. Law Found., San Jose, 1993—; vol. tchr. Prisoners' Info. Svcs., Palo Alto, 1977—84; vol. atty. Pro Bono Project, San Jose, 2002—; bd. mem., sec. Young Audiences San Jose, 1998—2001; bd. mem. DanceVisions, Palo Alto, 1993—. Recipient Am. Jurisprudence award, Lawyers Coop. Pub., 1991; Charles Warren Kendrick Meml. scholar, Stanford U., 1968—72. Mem.: San Mateo County Bar Assn. (family law sect. 2003—), Calif. State Bar Assn., ABA (family law sect. 1992—), Santa Clara County Bar Assn. (family law sect. com. 1995—), State Bar Calif. Episcopalian. Avocations: painting, art history, hiking. Home: 1528 Rosita Rd Pacifica CA 94044 Office: Law Offices Valerie L Patten Ste 7 744 San Antonio Rd Palo Alto CA 94303 Office Phone: 650-855-9570. E-mail: valpatten@prodigy.net.

PATTENAUDE, RICHARD LOUIS, university administrator; b. Seattle, Feb. 22, 1946; s. Joseph Arthur and Alice June (Vrooman) P.; m. Michele Arlen Stevenson, May 31, 1975; children: Lauren, Lisa, Dylan, Joshua. BA with honors in Econs., San Jose State U., 1968; PhD in Polit. Sci., U. Colo., 1974. Asst./assoc. prof. Drake U., Des Moines, 1974-80, assoc. dean liberal arts, 1976-80; asst. v.p. acad. affairs SUNY-Binghamton, 1980-82, assoc. v.p., 1982-86; v.p. acad. affairs; prof. polit. sci. Ctrl. Conn. State U., New Britain, 1986-91; pres., prof. polit. sci. U. So. Maine, Portland, 1991—. Cons. in field; panelist, presenter various nat. higher edn. meetings. Contbr. numerous articles to profl. jours., chpts. to books in field. Commr. Occupational and Licensing Commn., Iowa, 1978-80; mem. Gov.'s Com. Efficiency, 1979; mem. adv. coun. planning dept. City of Binghamton, 1984-1986; bd. dirs. Broome County United Way, 1985, Greater Hartford Red Cross, 1991-93, Mercy Hosp., Portland, 1992-94, Portland Symphony Orch., Maine Devel. Found., 1991-97, Maine Sci. & Tech. Found., 1992-98, Portland Mus. Art, 1993-99, Pmt. Symphony 1998-, Maine Med. Ctr., 2002-, Inst. Civic Leadership, 1992-94, Greater Portland United Way, Maine Med. Ctr., 2002—. With U.S. Army, 1969-71, Vietnam. Fanny W. Ames scholar, 1965; Title II fellow, 1970. Mem. Assn. Instl. Rsch. and Planning Officers (v.p. 1983-84, pres. 1984-85), Am. Assn. State Colls. and Univs. (state rep. 1995—, bd. dirs. 1999—2003), Greater Portland C. of C. Office: U So Maine Office of Pres 707 Law Building 96 Falmouth St Portland ME 04103-9300 Address: U So Maine PO Box 9300 Portland ME 04104-9300 Office Phone: 207-780-4480. Business E-Mail: pattenau@usm.maine.edu.

PATTERSON, ANNE BREVARD WOODS, ambassador; b. Ft. Smith, Ark., 1949; m. David R. Patterson; children: Edward, Andrew. BA in Econs., Wellesley Coll.; postgrad., U. N.C. With U.S. Fgn. Svc., 1973—, econ. officer, 1974-77, desk officer, analyst for Ctrl. Am., trade specialist, econ. counselor, 1984-88, polit. counselor U.S. Mission to UN Geneva, dir. Office of Andean Affairs, 1991-93, dep. asst. sec. for Ctrl. Am. and the Caribbean, 1993-95, prin. dep. asst. sec. for inter-Am. affairs, 1995—97, amb. to El Salvador, 1997-2000, amb. to Colombia Bogota, 2000—03; dep. US rep. UN, NYC, 2004—. Recipient Superior Honor award Dept. of State, 1981, 88, Meritorious Honor award, 1977, 83, Presdl. award, 1993. Office: UN 799 UN Plz 11th Fl New York NY 10017-3505 Fax: 278-6011.*

PATTERSON, AUBREY BURNS, JR., banker; b. Grenada, Miss., Sept. 25, 1942; s. Aubrey Burns and Elizabeth (Staten) P.; m. Ruby Kathryn Clegg, Dec. 12, 1964; children: Aubrey B. III, Clayton H., Jennifer L. BBA, U. Miss., 1964; MBA, Mich. State U., 1969. With Bancorp South (formerly Bank of Miss.), Tupelo, 1972—, pres., 1983-99, chmn., chief exec. officer, 1990—. Chmn., CEO BancorpSouth, Inc. Former chmn. bd. dirs. Salvation Army, Tupelo, 1978—; bd. dirs. Cmty. Devel. Found., chmn. bd., 1994-95; bd. dirs. Columbia Theol. Sem., Decatur, Ga., Fin. Svs. Roundtable, Presbyn. Ch. U.S.A. Found., New Covenant Trust Co., Bankers' Roundtable; vice-chmn. CREATE, Inc.; bd. dirs. Miss. Econ. Coun., Jackson, 1986—, chmn., 1994; chmn. bd. dirs. North Miss. Health Svcs. Inc., 1987—, also exec. com.; bd. dirs. Miss. Partnership Econ. Devel.; moderator St. Andrews Presbytery Presbyn. Ch. USA; chmn., bd. dirs. U. Miss. Found.; laureate Miss. Bus. Hall of Fame; bd. dirs. Journal Pub. Co.; mem. exec. com. Miss. Pub. Edn. Forum. Capt. USAF, 1965-72. Decorated Air Force Commendation medal, Meritorious Svc. medal, Nat. Def. Svc. medal. Mem. ABA (govt. rels. coun.), Am. Bankers Assn. (chmn. 2002-, U. Miss. Hall of Fame), Miss. Bankers Assn. (pres. 1995—), Soc. Internat. Bus. Fellows, Conf. of State Bank Supr., Bankers Adv. Coun. (chmn.), Tupelo Country Club, Univ. Club, Kiwanis (pres. Tupelo 1987), Beta Gamma Sigma, Beta Alpha Psi. Presbyterian. Office: BancorpSouth PO Box 789 Tupelo MS 38802-0789

PATTERSON, BEVERLY ANN GROSS, not-for-profit fundraiser, consultant, social services administrator; b. Pauls Valley, Okla., Aug. 5, 1938; d. Wilburn G. Jack and Mildred E. (Steward) Gross; m. Kenneth Dean Patterson, June 18, 1960 (div. 1976); children: Tracy Dean Patterson, Nancy Ann Patterson-McArthur, Beverly Jeanne Patterson-Wertman. AA, Modesto (Calif.) Jr. Coll., 1958; BA in Social Sci., Fresno (Calif.) State U., 1960; M in Community Counseling, Coll. Idaho; postgrad., Stanislaus State Coll., Turlock, Calif., U. Idaho, Boise (Idaho) State U. Cert. secondary tchr., Calif., Idaho, lic. real estate agt., Idaho. Secondary tchr., Ceres and Modesto Calif., Payette and Weiser Idaho, Ontario Oreg., 1960-67; dir. vol. svcs. mental retardation and child devel. State of Idaho, 1967-70, cons. dir. vol. svcs. health and welfare, 1970-72; dir. Ret. Sr. Vol. Program, Boise, 1972-74; exec. dir. Idaho Nurses Assn., Boise, 1974-76; community svcs. adminstr. City of Davis, Calif., 1976-78; dir. devel. and fundraising Mercy Med. Ctr., Nampa, Idaho, 1978-85; exec. dir. St. Alphonsus Med. Ctr. Found., Boise, 1985-87; dir. devel. and gift planning Idaho Youth Ranch, Boise, 1989-94; fund devel. cons. Mercy Housing, Nampa, Idaho, 1994-96, Pratt Ranch Boys Home, Emmett, Idaho, 1994-96, Northwest Childrens Home, Lewiston, Idaho, 1994-96, Idaho Spl. Olympics, Boise, 1994-95, Idaho Found. for Parks and Lands, Boise, 1994-95, St. Vincent de Paul, Inc., Boise, 1995-96, Nampa Shelter Found., Inc., 1994-95, Turning Point Inc., Nampa, 1994-95, Port of Hope Treatment Ctr. Inc., Boise, 1994-97, Idaho Theater for Youth, Inc., Boise, 1995-96, Boise Tennis Coalition, Inc., 1995-2000, El Ada Cmty. Action Ctr., Boise, 1995, Hemophilia Found. Idaho, 1995-96, Boise YWCA, 1996, Marsing (Idaho) Sch. Dist., 1996-98. Founder Fellowship Christian Adult Singles, Boise, 1974; cons., exec. dir. Boise Hotline, 1988-90; co-dir. ACOA workshop leader Child Within Concepts, Inc., Boise, 1987—; cons. coord. Rural Hosp. Edn. Consortium, 1988; cons. hosp. fund devel. and cmty. resources Gritman Meml. Hosp., Moscow, Idaho, 1987-88; cons., conf. coord. State of Idaho, 1987-88; counsel Adult Children of Alcoholics, 1991; pres. Nonprofit Solutions, Inc., Boise, 1995—; co-dir. Child Within Concepts, Inc., Meridian, 1996—; cmty. resource devel. specialist Idaho Dept. Health and Welfare, 1997-2000, United Way Portland, 2000; chmn., pres. Creative Solutions P.A., 2000—; grant writing cons. sch. dist. # 3JT, Oreg., Tillamook Sch. Dist., Oreg., Banks Sch. dist., Oreg., North West Regional Ednl. Svcs. Dist., Oreg. Author poetry; contbr. articles to profl. jours. Coord. Idaho Golf Angels Open Pro-Am Tournament, Boise, 1989-91; founding exec. v.p. Coll. Fund for Students Surviving Cancer, 1993-96; bd. dirs. Arthritis Found., Idaho, 1984-86, Idaho Mental Health Assn., 1978-97; founder Ctrl. Vol. Bur., Boise, 1971. Named Idaho Statesman Disting. Citizen, 1985. Mem. Nat. Assn. for Hosp. Devel. (accredited, treas. 1980, accreditation chmn. 1984-86, conf. chmn. 1982, 85), Assn. Healthcare in Philanthrophy (accredited), Nat. Soc. Fund Raising Execs., Idaho Devel. Network, Choices in Giving, Inc. Avocations: golf, family activities. Address: 9451 N Polk Ave Portland OR 97203-1630

PATTERSON, CARLY, Olympic athlete; b. Baton Rouge, Feb. 4, 1988; d. Ricky and Natalie. Mem. TOPS Nat. Team, 1996, 1997, U.S. Nat. Gymnastics Team, 2000—; gymnast Team USA, Athens Olympic Games, 2004. Achievements include mem. U.S. World Championships Gold medal team, 2003; Silver medal, all-around, World Championships, 2003; won Visa Am. Cup Championship by winning all four events, 2004; Gold medal, all-around, Athens Olympic games, 2004; mem. U.S. Women's Silver medal Gymnastics team, Athens Olympic games, 2004. Office: c/o USOC One Olympic Plz Colorado Springs CO 80909*

PATTERSON, CHAN, food service executive; Dir., prin. instr. Everyday Gourmet, Jackson, Miss. Featured on Miss. Morning (WJTV), recipes appeared in nat. mags. Mem.: Internat. Assn. Culinary Profls., Am. Inst. Wine and Food. Office: Everyday Gourmet 1625 E County Line Rd Jackson MS 39216

PATTERSON, CHARLES DAROLD, librarian, educator; b. Wahpeton, N.D., Aug. 8, 1928; s. Charles Irwin and Inez Fern (Slagg) P. BSc, Bemidji State U., 1950; MA, U. Minn., 1956; MusM, W.Va. U., 1964; advanced cert., U. Pitts., 1968, PhD, 1971. Tchr. music Fargo (N.D.) Pub. Schs., 1950; jr. reference libr. U. Minn. Librs., 1954-55; head libr. Bemidji (Minn.) State U., 1955-58; dir. librs., asst. prof. Glenville (W.Va.) State Coll., 1958-62; asst. prof. W.Va. U., 1962-66; instr. Grad. Sch. Libr. and Info. Scis. U. Pitts., 1966-71, asst. prof., 1971-72; assoc. prof. Sch. Libr. and Info. Sci. La. State U., Baton Rouge, 1972-78, prof., 1978-93, prof. emeritus, 1993—. Del. La. Gov.'s Conf. on Libr. and Info. Svcs., 1978. Author: Analysis of Library of Congress Music Subject Headings, 1971, JEL Cumulative Index, 1979, supplement, 1982, (with D.G. Davis) ARBA Guide to Library Science Literature, 1987, Letters from the Far East, 2003; editor W.Va. Libraries, 1963-66; mem. editl. bd. Jour. of Edn. for Librarianship, 1975-79, editor, 1980-84; editor Jour. Edn. for Libr. and Info. Sci., 1984-88; asst. editor Reference Svcs. Rev., 1986-93; contbr. articles to profl. jours. Served with U.S. Army, 1950-52. Recipient La. State U. Faculty Excellence award, 1984, ALA/Beta Phi Mu award, 1989. Mem. ALA (chmn. scholarship jury 1972-73), W.Va. Libr. Assn. (chmn. coll. and univ. libr. sect. 1960-61, exec. bd. 1960-61, 64-66), Assn. Coll. and Rsch. Librs. (pres. Tri-state chpt. 1972), Assn. Am. Libr. Schs. (exec. bd. 1980-88), La. Libr. Assn., Southeastern Libr. Assn., AAUP (pres. chpt. 1985-86), Am. Guild Organists (dean chpt. 1985-86), Pitts. Bibliophiles, Univ. Chamber Music Soc. (pres., dir. 1979-80), La. Sinfonietta (exec. bd. 1994—), Beta Phi Mu. (dir.-at-large 1982-85). Methodist. Home: 1480 Kenmore Ave Baton Rouge LA 70808-1130 also: Birchmont Beach Bemidji MN 56601 Office: La State U Sch Libr And Info Sci Baton Rouge LA 70803-0001 *When one is confident in his own mind that he has, with given abilities, done his very best, then perhaps he has paid for his niche in eternity.*

PATTERSON, CHARLES ERNEST, lawyer; b. Rockford, Ill., Jan. 4, 1941; s. Alvin Maurice and Helen Mae (Mitchell) P. A.B. cum laude, U. Kans., 1963; J.D. with distinction U. Mich., 1966. Bar: Mo. 1966, U.S. Dist. Ct. (we. dist.) Mo. 1966, U.S. Ct. Mil. Appeals 1968, U.S. Supreme Ct. 1969, U.S. Ct. Appeals (8th cir.) 1971, Calif. 1985, U.S. Dist. Ct. (cen., no. dists.) Calif. 1985. Assoc. Watson, Ess, Marshall & Enggas, Kansas City, Mo., 1966-74, ptnr., 1974-85; ptnr. Lillick, McHose & Charles, Los Angeles; chmn. exec. com. 1987—; now ptnr. Pillsbury Madison & Sutro, L.A.; chmn. various coms. Def. Research Inst., 1978—; bd. govs. Legal Aid of Western Mo., 1978-80; mem. bench/bar com. Western div. Mo. Ct. Appeals, 1983—, 16th Jud. Cir. Ct. Mo., 1983—; mem. fed. practice com. U.S. Dist. Ct. (we. dist.) Mo. 1983— . Contbr. articles to profl. jours. Bd. dirs. Boys Clubs Greater Kansas City, Inc., 1974-78, Dismas House Kansas City, 1978-84, Mo. Assn. for Ex-Offenders, 1976-79, YMCA, 1976-79; v.p. Heart of Am. Rugby Football Union, Kansas City, 1976-78; pres. Pre Trial Diversion Services, Inc., Kansas City, 1976-78, Kansas City Vietnam Vets. Meml. Fund, 1984—; mem. bd. Kansas City Arts Council, 1984, Mo. Boys Town, Kansas City, 1983-84. Served to capt. USMC, 1966-69; Vietnam. Decorated Bronze Star medal with Combat V, Vietnamese Cross of Gallantry with Palm, Vietnamese Medal of Honor. Mem. ABA (ho. of dels. 1984—), Mo. Bar (bd. govs. 1978-84, pres. 1983-84, Award of Merit 1984, Jud. Conf. award 1984), Kansas City Bar Assn., Lawyers Assn. Kansas City, Western Mo. Def. Lawyers Assn. (pres. 1981-82), Mo. Orgn. Def. Lawyers (bd. dirs. 1984-85), Internat. Assn. Ins. Counsel. Clubs: Kansas City, Carriage (Kansas City, Mo.). Office: Pillsbury Madison & Sutro 725 S Figueroa St Ste 1200 Los Angeles CA 90017-5443

PATTERSON, CHRISTOPHER NIDA, lawyer; b. Washington Courthouse, Ohio, Apr. 17, 1960; s. Donis Dean and JoAnne (Nida) O.; m. Vicky Patterson; children: Travis, Kirsten. BA, Clemson U., 1982; JD, Nova U., 1985. Bar: Fla. 1985, U.S. Dist. Ct. (mid. dist.) Fla. 1985, U.S. Ct. Mil. Rev. 1986, U.S. Ct. Mil. Appeals 1987, U.S. Dist. Ct. (ea. dist.) Va. 1987, U.S. Supreme Ct. 1990, U.S. Ct. Appeals (11th cir.) 1992, U.S. Dist. Ct. (no. dist.) Fla. 1992, U.S. Dist. Ct. (so. dist.) Tex. 1995; cert. criminal trial lawyer Fla. Bar. and Nat. Bd. Trial Advocacy. Pros. Fla. State Attys. Office, Orlando, Fla., 1985; spl. asst. U.S. Atty. U.S. Dist. Ct. (ea. dist.) Va., 1987-90; ptnr. Patterson & Hauversburk, Panama City, Fla., 1992—. Adj. prof. law Gulf Coast Coll.; mem. Fla. Supreme Ct. Mediators Qualifications Bd.; family law mediator Fla. Supreme Ct., dependency law mediator, county ct. mediator, mem. mediators qualifications bd.; mediator County Ct.; on-air legal analyst Nex Media-WYOO-FM. Author: Queen's Pawn, 1996, Treasure Trove, 1997; contbr. Nat. DAR Mag., Fla. Defender mag. Chancellor St. Thomas Episcopal Ch. Capt. JAGC, U.S. Army, 1986-92, Desert Storm. Recipient U.S. Army Chief of Staff award for legal excellence, 1989, Guardian ad litem commendation, Fla. Supreme Ct., 1999. Mem. ABA, ATLA, FBA, SAR, NACDL (life), Am. Coll. Barristers, Fla. Assn. Criminal Def. Lawyers, Acad. Fla. Trial Lawyers, Assn. Fed. Def. Attys., Fla. Acad. Profl. Mediators, Fla. Bar Spkrs. Bur. (criminal law sect., mil. law standing com., del. 11th cir. jud. conf. 1999, Pro Bono Svc. award, nominee Jefferson award for pub. svc. 1999), Bay County Bar Assn., The Ret. Officers' Assn., Christian Legal Soc., Am. Legion, Fellowship of Christian Athletes, Nat. Triathlon Fedn., Soc. Colonial Wars, Mil. Order Fgn. Wars. Episcopalian. Avocations: athletics, triathlons. Office: PO Box 9474 415 Beckrich Rd Ste 290 Panama City Beach FL 32417

PATTERSON, COLLIS DELANO, secondary school educator; b. Balt., Aug. 29, 1950; s. William Phillip Patterson and Lucille Mini Patterson-Wheeler. BS, Towson U., 1973; MEd, Loyola Coll., Balt., 1988. Cert. tchr. grades 5-12 Md. State Dept. Edn. Tchr. Balt. City Schs., 1973—. Instr. Sojourner-Douglass Coll., Balt., 1990—92. Editor: Dr. Samuel L. Banks Speaks, 1995. Vol. Am. Friends, Balt., 1978—. Grantee Geography grant, Md. Geog. Alliance, Balt., 1988, Tchg. grant, NEH, Washington, 1990. Mem.: Third World Coalition (rep. 1995—98, Honor award 1997), Am. Friends Svc. Com. (clk. 1978—). Democrat. African Methodist. Avocations: gardening, collecting.

PATTERSON, DEB, women's college basketball coach; Grad., Rockford Coll., 1979. Asst. coach, recruiting coord. No. Ill. U., 1986-91; asst. coach So. Ill. U., 1991-92; top asst. coach, recruiting coord. Vanderbilt U., 1992-96; head

coach Kans. State U., 1996—. Asst. coach 1997 World U. Games; women's sr. nat. team asst. coach USA Invitational Tournament of Champions, 1997. Named Women's Coll. Basketball Coach of the Yr. Kans. Basketball Coaches Assn., 1997, Coach of Yr. Ill. H.S. Assn., 1985, Conf. Coach of Yr., 1985, 86. Office: Kansas State U 1800 College Ave Manhattan KS 66502-3308 Fax: 785-532-6093.

PATTERSON, DONALD EUGENE, research scientist; b. El Paso, Tex., Feb. 7, 1958; s. Donald M. Patterson and Beverly Lee (Viles) McElroy; m. Mary Jane Ingram, May 6, 1989. BS, U. Tex., 1982, MS, 1984; MA, Rice U., 1987, PhD, 1989. Rsch. scientist Rice U., Houston, 1989-91; sr. rsch. scientist Houston Advanced Rsch. Ctr., The Woodlands, Tex., 1989-93, TSA, Inc., The Woodlands, 1991-95; sr. scientist SI Diamond Tech. Inc., Houston, 1991-95, dir. R & D, 1995-96; edn. supr. ITT Tech. Inst., Houston, 1996-97; prin. scientist Sys. & Processes Engrng. Corp., Austin, Tex., 1997-98; founder, sr. v.p. product devel. Extreme Devices, Inc., Austin, 1998—2003; sr. scientist Nanohmics, Inc., Austin, 2004—. Contbr. articles to profl. jours. Recipient Harry B. Weiser award, Rice U., 1988; Grad. fellow, 1984, VFW Voice Democracy scholar, 1974, Davis and Bertha Green scholar, 1982, Grad. scholar, U. Tex. El Paso, 1983. Mem.: SID, AAAS, Am. Chem. Soc., Sigma Xi, Phi Kappa Phi. Achievements include patents in field. Home: 4728 Interlachen Ln Austin TX 78747 Office: Nanohmics Inc 6201 E Olfort St 100 Austin TX 78741 Office Phone: 512-389-9990. Business E-Mail: dpatterson@nanohmics.com.

PATTERSON, DONALD LEE, music educator; b. Colorado Springs, Colo., Aug. 14, 1947; s. Thurman Alvin and Bernice Eileen (May) P.; m. Janet Louise Andrews, Feb. 19, 1971. MusB, U. Denver, 1969; MusM, Manhattan Sch. Music, 1972; MusD, U. North Tex., 1977. Staff accompanist Harlem Sch. Arts, N.Y.C., 1970-72, Manhattan Sch. Music, N.Y.C., 1970-72; instr. music Angelo State U., San Angelo, Tex., 1972-74; tchg. fellow U. North Tex., Denton, 1974-76; prof. music U. Wis., Eau Claire, 1976—, Maxwell Schonfeld disting. prof., 2002—03. Co-author: Vincent Persichetti: A Bio bibliography, 1989; author: One Handed: A Guide to Piano Music for One Hand, 1999, (sound rec.) EDUCO, Inc., Contemporary Rec. Soc. Mem. Am. Liszt Soc., Music Tchrs. Nat. Assn. (cert.), Recs. for Contemporary Rec. Soc., Educo, Hemera Music, Kappa Kappa Psi, Phi Mu Alpha Sinfonia, Pi Kappa Lambda. Home: 3504 W Country Club Ln Altoona WI 54720-1055 Office: U Wis Music Dept Eau Claire WI 54702 E-mail: patterdl@uwec.edu.

PATTERSON, DONALD ROSS, lawyer, educator; b. Sept. 9, 1939; s. Sam Ashley and Marguerite (Robinson) P.; m. Peggy Ann Schulte, May 1, 1965; children: D. Ross, Jerome Ashley, Gretchen Anne. BS, Tex. Tech U., 1961; JD, U. Tex., 1964; LLM, So. Meth. U., 1972. Bar: Tex. 1964, U.S. Ct. Claims 1970, U.S. Ct. Customs and Patent Appeals 1970, U.S. Ct. Mil. Appeals 1970, U.S. Supreme Ct. 1970, U.S. Dist. Ct. (ea. dist.) Tex. 1982, U.S. Ct. Appeals (5th cir.) 1991, U.S. Ct. Appeals (D.C. cir.) 1994; bd. cert. in immigration and naturalization law, Tex. Commd. lt. (j.g.) USN, 1964, advanced through grades to lt. comdr., 1969; asst. officer in charge Naval Petroleum Res., Bakersfield, Calif., 1970-72; staff judge adv. Kenitra, Morocco, 1972-76; officer in charge Naval Legal Svcs. Office, Whidbey Island, Wash., 1976-79; head mil. justice divsn., Subic Bay, The Philippines, 1979-81; ret. USN, 1982; pvt. practice Tyler, Tex., 1982—. Former instr. U. Md., Chapman Coll., U. LaVerne, Tyler Jr. Coll., Jarvis Christian Coll., U. Tex., Tyler. Mem. East Tex. Estate Planning Coun. Mem. Coll. of State Bar of Tex., Tex. Bar Assn., Smith County Bar Assn., Am. Immigration Lawyers Assn., Masons, Rotary (past pres.), Shriners, Toastmasters (past pres.), Phi Delta Phi. Republican. Baptist. Home: 703 Wellington St Tyler TX 75703-4666 Office: 777 S Broadway Ave Ste 106 Tyler TX 75701-1648 Office Phone: 903-592-8186. E-mail: oneworld2gether@cs.com.

PATTERSON, DOUG, state representative; b. Kansas City, Mo., June 13, 1940; m. Dorothy Patterson; children: Emily, Jessie. BA, U. Mo., 1970, JD, 1973. With Mo. Nat. Guard, 1969—75; atty., 1973—; mem. Kans. Ho. of Reps., 2000—. Mem. City Coun., Leawood, Kans., 1993—97; bd. dirs. Oxford Pks., 1985—87. Mem.: Rotary (pres. 1997). Republican. Methodist. Office: 174-W State Capitol 300 SW 10th Ave Topeka KS 66612 Address: 12712 El Monte Leawood KS 66211

PATTERSON, DOUGLAS MACLENNAN, finance educator; b. Jan. 16, 1945; s. Thomas and Ruth (MacLennan) P.; m. Sara Louise Lucas; children: Cara Beth, John Douglas. BSEE, U. Wis., 1968, MBA, 1972, PhD, 1978. Elec. engr. Westinghouse Electric, Balt., 1968-71; asst. prof. U. Mich., Ann Arbor, 1976-80, Va. Tech., Blacksburg, 1980—, dir. PhD program in fin., 1991-95, assoc. prof., 1986-98, prof., 1998—. Vis. prof. U. Calif., Santa Barbara, 1989; vis. scholar U. Tex., Austin, 1994; presenter numerous seminars; participant Fin. Time Series Conf., Isaac Newton Inst. for Math. Scis., Cambridge, Eng., 1998. Co-author: A Nonlinear Times Series Workshop: A Tool Kit for Detecting and Identifying Nonlinear Serial Dependence; contbr. articles to profl. jours. Mem. ad hoc com. Detroit Area Hosp. Assn., 1978-79. Recipient Tchg. Excellence award Va. Tech., 1983; U. Mich. fellow, 1979; USN grantee, 1984, 85, 90. Mem. Am. Fin. Assn., Am. Econ. Assn., Fin. Mgmt. Assn., Beta Gamma Sigma. Methodist. Home: 702 Crestwood Dr Blacksburg VA 24060-6006 Office: Va Poly Inst Dept Finance 0221 Blacksburg VA 24061 Office Phone: 540-231-5737.

PATTERSON, EDWARD, investment banker; b. N.Y.C., Oct. 16, 1920; s. Arthur C. and Evelyn (Crimmins) P.; m. Joan Metzger, Jan. 10, 1947 (div. 1972); children: Patricia Kean, Lucinda, Elizabeth, Christina P. Fay. BA, Yale U., 1943. Mem. N.Y. Stock Exch., N.Y.C., 1950-56; exec. v.p. Allen & Co., N.Y.C., 1956—, also bd. dirs. Dir. Teleprompter, 1980-82 Guest writer News Leader, Richmond, W.Va.; contbr. articles to N.Y. Times. Trustee Citizens Budget Commn., N.Y.C., 1957-80; trustee Garvan Collection, Yale U., 1968; mem. Fordham U. Council, N.Y.C., 1975; mem. Cardinal's Com. of the Laity. Lt. USNR, 1942-46, ETO. Mem.: Deepdale (Manhasset, N.Y.) (pres. 1970-75); Piping Rock (Locust Valley, N.Y.); Friendly Sons of St. Patrick. Roman Catholic. Office: Allen & Co 711 5th Ave Fl 8 New York NY 10022-3111

PATTERSON, EDWARD PALMER, retired physical scientist; b. Kansas City, Kans., Sept. 5, 1921; s. Sidney Edward and Dura (Palmer) P.; m. Eula Mae Bennett, Oct. 15, 1945; children: Nona Marie, Wilma Jean Patterson Graham. BS in Metall. Engring., U. Mo., Rolla, 1944, MS in Metall. Engring., 1947, prof. degree of engring., 1957. Registered profl. engr., Kans. Instr. Nat. Sch. Aeronautics, Kansas City, Mo., 1947-50; metall. engr. Boeing Airplane Co., Wichita, Kans., 1950-51; sr. rsch. engr. GM Corp., Kansas City, Kans., 1951-52; sr. staff engr. White Motors Co., Cleve., 1952-54; sr. engr. Westinghouse Elec. Co., Kansas City, Mo., 1954-59; sr. staff rschr. Cessna Aircraft Corp., Wichita, 1959-60; project engr., project leader Bendix Corp./Allied Signal Corp., Kansas City, Mo., 1960-87; ret., 1987. Vol. Hospice Mesquite Med. Ctr., 1997-98, Nat. Hospice Orgn., Dallas, 1998. With USAF, 1944-46. Mem. AIME, Am. Soc. Materials Internat., Am. Rocket Soc., Am. Phys. Soc., Masons (master, York Rite Cross of Hon. & Red Cross of Constantine, High Priest), Knights of Kadosh (comdr. 1968). Republican. Mem. Lds Ch. Achievements include discovery of the unitron, basic command unit for life and non-life; established new values for the Planck time, mass, and length; calculated the speed of gravity. Home: 3513 Bermuda Dr Rowlett TX 75088-5364 E-mail: unitron9@attbi.com.

PATTERSON, EDWIN, minister; b. Andalusia, Ala., Sept. 6, 1921; s. Walter Levi and Kate Edline (Aughtman) P.; m. Margaret Alice Hall, May 14, 1966. Degree, Brennan Bus. Sch., 1940; postgrad., Samford U., 1950-57. Ordained to ministry So. Bapt. Conv., 1947. Pastor various chs., Ala., 1947—; including Hopewell Bapt. Ch., 1949-67, Harmony Bapt. Ch., Andalusia, 1967-80, Searight Bapt. Ch., Dozier, Ala., 1980—; acct. C.G. Tomberlin, M.D., Andalusia, 1985—. Mem. bd. regents Liberty U., Lynchburg, Va. Home: 407 Lakeview Dr Andalusia AL 36420-3542 Office: PO Box 486 Andalusia AL 36420-1209 Office Phone: 334-222-5673. *In Him, we live and move and have our being. Therefore, my heart's desire is to honor Christ in all things, for He is the way, the truth, and the life.*

PATTERSON, ELIZABETH JOHNSTON, retired congresswoman; b. Columbia, SC, Nov. 18, 1939; d. Olin DeWitt and Gladys (Atkinson) Johnston; m. Dwight Fleming Patterson, Jr., Apr. 15, 1967; children: Dwight Fleming, Olin DeWitt, Catherine Leigh. BA, Columbia Coll., 1961; postgrad. in polit. sci., U. S.C., 1961, 62, 64; LLD (hon.), Columbia Coll., 1987; D Pub. Svc. (hon.), Converse Coll., 1989, M in Liberal Arts, 1999; LLD (hon.), Wofford Coll., 1999. Pub. affairs officer Peace Corps, Washington, 1962-64, VISTA, OEO, Washington, 1965-66; D Pub. Svc. Head Start and VISTA, OEO, Columbia, 1966-67; tri-county dir. Head Start, Piedmont Community Actions, Spartanburg, S.C., 1967-68; mem. Spartanburg County Coun., 1975-76, S.C. State Senate, 1979-86, 100th-102nd Congresess from 4th S.C. dist., 1987-93; dir. continuing edn., converse II program Converse Coll., 1993—2003; ret. Adj. prof. Spartanburg Meth. Coll., 1993-2001. Trustee Wofford Coll., 1978-90; bd. dirs. Charles Lea Ctr., 1978, Spartanburg Coun. on Aging; pres. Spartanburg Dem. Women, 1968; v.p. Spartanburg County Dem. party, 1968-70, sec., 1970-75, pres. 2004-; trustee Columbia Coll., 1991-2003; chmn., bd. dirs. Bethlehem Cmty. Ctr., 1998—; bd. dirs. S.C. Ind. Colls. and Univs., 1995-99. Mem. Bus. and Profl. Women's Club, Alpha Kappa Gamma. Democrat. Methodist. E-mail: lizjpatterson@charter.net.

PATTERSON, ELLMORE CLARK, banker; b. Western Springs, Ill., Nov. 29, 1913; s. Ellmore Clark and Harriet Emma (Wales) P.; m. Anne Hyde Choate, Sept. 28, 1940; children: Michael Ellmore, Arthur Choate, Robert Ellmore, David Choate, Thomas Hyde Choate. Grad., Lake Forest Acad., 1931; BS, U. Chgo., 1935. With J. P. Morgan & Co., Inc., N.Y.C., 1935-39, 39-41, 46-59, v.p., 1951-59; exec. v.p. Morgan Guaranty Trust Co. N.Y. (merger J.P. Morgan and Guaranty Trust Co.), 1959-65, dir., chmn. exec. com., 1967-68, pres., 1969-71, chmn., 1971-77, chmn. exec. com., 1970. With Morgan Stanley & Co., 1939; chmn. dirs. adv. coun. Morgan Guaranty Trust Co.; mem. Presdl. Com. on Fin. Structure and Regulation, 1970-72. Bd. mgrs. Meml. Hosp. Cancer and Allied Diseases, N.Y.C.; Sloan-Kettering Inst. Cancer Center, N.Y.C., U. Chgo., Mass. Inst. Tech. Served from ensign to lt. comdr. USNR, 1941-46. Mem. Meadowbrook Club, Piping Rock Club, Jupiter Island Club (Hope Sound, Fla.), Fishers Island Country Club, Seminole Golf Club (Palm Beach, Fla.). Episcopalian. Office: 1 Chase Manhattan Plz Fl 36 New York NY 10005-1401

PATTERSON, EUGENE CORBETT, retired editor, publisher; b. Valdosta, Ga., Oct. 15, 1923; s. William C. and Annabel (Corbett) P.; m. Mary Sue Carter, Aug. 19, 1950; 1 child, Mary Patterson Fausch. Student, North Ga. Coll., Dahlonega, 1940-42; AB in Journalism, U. Ga., 1943; LL.D., Tusculum Coll., 1965, Harvard U., 1969, Duke U., 1978, Stetson U., 1984, Ind. U., 1990; Litt.D., Emory U., 1966, Oglethorpe Coll., 1966, Tuskegee U., 1966, Roanoke Coll., 1968, Mercer U., 1968, Eckerd Coll., 1977, U. South Fla., 1986, Dillard U., 1992, Colby Coll., 1994, North Ga. Coll. & State U., 1999. Reporter Temple (Tex.) Daily Telegram and Macon (Ga.) Telegraph, 1947-48; mgr. for S.C. United Press, 1948-49, N.Y. night bur. mgr., 1949-53, mgr. London bur., also chief corr. U.K., 1953-56; v.p., exec. editor Atlanta Journal-Constitution, 1956-60; editor Atlanta Constitution, 1960-68; mng. editor Washington Post, 1968-71; prof. polit. sci. Duke U., 1971-72; editor, pres. St. Petersburg (Fla.) Times, 1972-84, chmn., chief exec. officer, 1978-88, editor emeritus, 1988—; editor, pres. Congl. Quar., Washington, 1972-86, chmn., chief exec. officer, 1978-88. Chmn. bd., chief exec. officer Fla. Trend mag., 1980-88, Ga. Trend mag., 1984-88, Ariz. Trend mag., 1986-88, Governing mag., 1987-88; Modern Graphic Arts, Inc., 1978-88, Poynter Inst. Media Studies, 1978-88, Poynter Fund, 1978-88. Author: The Changing South of Gene Patterson, 2002. Vice chmn. U.S. Civil Rights Commn., 1964-68; mem. Pulitzer Prize Bd., 1973-84; trustee ASNE Found., 1981-84, U. Ga. Found., 1982-88, North Ga. Coll. Found., 1991-93, Am. Press Inst., Reston, Va., 1983-88, Duke U., 1988-94, Fla. Bar Found., 1992-93, LeRoy Collins Ctr. for Pub. Policy, 1990-93. Decorated Silver Star, Bronze Star with oak leaf cluster in 10th Armored Divsn., Gen. Patton's 3rd Army; recipient Pulitzer prize for editl. writing Columbia U., 1967, William Allen White Nat. Citation award U. Kans., 1980, Elijah Parish Lovejoy award Colby Coll., 1994; inducted into Fla. Newspaper Hall of Fame Fla. Press Assn., 1997. Fellow Soc. Profl. Journalists; mem. Am. Soc. Newspaper Editors (pres. 1977-78), St. Petersburg Yacht Club. Home: Snell Isle 1967 Brightwaters Blvd NE Saint Petersburg FL 33704-3007 E-mail: Ecp1015@aol.com.

PATTERSON, GRACE LIMERICK, library director; b. N.Y.C., Nov. 21, 1938; d. Robert and Frieda (Zeiontz) Limerick; m. Joseph Nathaniel Patterson (dec.); children: Lorrayne Carole, Joseph Nathaniel Jr. BA in Sociology, Edn., CUNY, 1971; MLS, Columbia U., 1975; MS in Comm., Coll. New Rochelle, 1989. Cert. libr. N.J. Exec. dir. Manhattanville Community Outreach, N.Y.C., 1971-74; br. and outreach svcs. Paterson (N.J.) Pub. Libr., 1975-79; media specialist II Passaic County C.C., Paterson, 1979-81; coord. outreach svcs. Irvington (N.J.) Pub. Libr., 1981-84; assoc. prof. libr. Rockland C.C., Suffern, N.Y., 1984-89; libr. dir. Hudson County C.C., Jersey City, 1989—. Editor jours. in field. Exec. bd. dirs. IFLA/CPRT, sec.-treas., 1996—; vol. Ridgewood (N.J.) Schs., 1981-83; Ridgewood Centennial Com. First Night, 1993; bd. dirs. Freedom To Read Found., 2002--; mem. coun. of deans Dirs. of N.J. Colls. and Univs. Librs., 2002--. Named among Phenomenal Women of Jersey City, 2002; U.S. Dept. Edn. fellow, 1974-75. Mem. ALA (com., chairperson Black Caucus pub. rels. 1990-92), Am. Coll. and Rsch. Librs., N.J. Libr. Assn. Avocations: photography, oral history, travel, geneology, public speaking. Office: Hudson County CC 25 Journal Sq Jersey City NJ 07306-4012 E-mail: gpatterson@mail.hudson.cc.nj.us.

PATTERSON, JAMES, former mayor; b. San Mateo, Calif., Feb. 18, 1948; m. Sharon LeTourneau, 1968; children: B.J., Jason, Lindsay. BA in Polit. Sci. summa cum laude, Calif. State U., Fresno, 1992. Radio broadcasting exec. Sta. KIRV-AM, Fresno, Calif., 1968—; mayor City of Fresno, 1993—2000; now consultant Valley Investment Group. Mem. San Joaquin River Conservancy, Calif. Ten Largest Cities Mayor's Coalition, 1993—; vice chair Fresno County Transp. Authority; bd. mem. Fresno County Coun. Govts.; chmn. NO on Measure H Com., 1989, Criminal Justice and Law Enforcement Commn., 1990-91; vice chmn. YES on Measure E Com., 1988; mem. Human Rels. Commn., City of Fresno, 1987-91; bd. dirs. Leadership Fresno Alumni Assn., 1989-91, Fresno County YFC/Campus Life, 1984-88. Mem. Fresno City and County C. of C. (chmn. local govt. affairs com. 1990-91, bd. dirs. FRESPAC 1990-91, city budget rev. com. 1989-91, privatization task force 1988-89, charter sect. 809 rev. task force 1987-88).

PATTERSON, JAMES BRENDAN, JR., writer, former advertising agency executive; b. Newburgh, N.Y., Mar. 22, 1947; s. Charles H. and Isabelle (Morris) P. BA, Manhattan Coll., 1969; MA, Vanderbilt U., 1970. With J. Walter Thompson Co., N.Y.C., 1971—96; chmn. J. Walter Thompson U.S., 1990—96. Author: (novels) The Thomas Berryman Number, 1976 (Edgar Allen Poe award Mystery Writers Am.), Season of the Machete, 1977, The Jericho Commandment, 1979, Virgin, 1980, Black Market, 1986, The Midnight Club, 1989, Along Came a Spider, 1993, Kiss the Girls, 1995, Hide and Seek, 1995, Jack and Jill, 1996, Miracle on the 17th green, 1996, See How They Run, 1997, Cat and Mouse, 1997, When the Wind Blows, 1998, Pop! Goes the Weasel, 1999, Black Friday, 2000, Cradle and All, 2000, Roses are Red, 2000, 1st to Die, 2001, Suzanne's Diary for Nicholas, 2001, Violets are Blue, 2001, 2nd Chance, 2002, The Beach House, 2002, Four Blind Mice, 2002, The Jester, 2003, The Lake House, 2003, The Big Bad Wolf, 2003, Sam's Letters To Jennifer, 2004. Recipient 6 Clio awards, 1983; recipient Effie awards, 1983. Mem. Phi Beta Kappa. Mailing: c/o Author Mail Little, Brown and Co 1271 Ave of the Americas New York NY 10020*

PATTERSON, JAMES E. economist, author, speaker; b. Ft. Belvoir, Va., Jan. 1, 1955; s. James G. and Helen L. Patterson; m. Sheryl Rene Alexander; children: James H., Alexandra Baker. BS, Auburn U., 1977, MS in Econs., 1980. Economist Dept. Agrl. Econs., Auburn, Ala., 1978—80; sys. analyst Ind. Employment Security Divsn., Indpls., 1981—84; economist /statistician U.S. Dept. of Commerce, Washington, 1984—87; economist USDA, Washington, 1987—92, diplomat/fgn. svc. officer, 1992—98; freelance writer Washington, 1999—. Prof. Grad. Sch., USDA, Washington, 1989—91; adj. prof. No. Va. C.C., Woodbridge, 1987; instr./ cons. Fairfax County Adult Edn. Dept., Fairfax, Va., 1985—87. Author: (newspaper column) Washington Scene, 1995; contbr. articles to mags. Mem. Rep. Nat. Com.; mem. precinct com. Marion County Rep. Party, Indpls., 1982—83. Named to Outstanding Young Men of Am., 1989; recipient Spl. Svc. award, U.S. Dept. Commerce, 1986, Productivity award, 1987, Performance award, 1989, Presdl. Point of Light, USDA, 1992, certs. from. Mem.: Alpha Zeta (sec., treas., VP 1988—92). Republican. Episcopal. Achievements include being profiled in New York Times, Wall Street Journal, The Washington Times and The Foreign Service Journal, others. Avocations: coin collecting/numismatics, reading, golf, tennis, horseback riding.

PATTERSON, JAMES HARDY, entertainer, conductor, musician, educator, arranger, composer; b. Kingston, Ga., Oct. 12, 1935; s. Hardy and Laura (Cargile) P.; m. Lois Gartrell; children: Adonica Patterson Carson, Phillippa G. AB, Clark Coll., 1957; MusM, U. Mich., 1965; postgrad., Atlanta U., 1962, U. Wis., Lacrosse, 1978. Tchr., dept. chmn. (ret.) Fulton County Bd. Edn., Atlanta, 1957-84; instr. to asst. prof., dir. Jazz Orch. Clark Atlanta U., 1962—; entertainer Motown Band, Detroit, 1962-73; profl. condr. Freda Payne Show, Fairmont Hotel, Atlanta, 1975; musician Atlanta Pops Orch., 1970—; leader James Patterson Jazz Quartet, Atlanta and abroad, 1960—. Profl. musician Lionel Hampton and Dizzy Gillespie Small Group, Duke Pearson's Big Band, Ringling Bros., Barnum and Bailey Circus, Ice Shows, Broadway mus. including Sophisticated Ladies, 1970; substitute, extra, soloist Atlanta Symphony, 1971; music panelist Ga. Coun. for the Arts, Atlanta, 1986—, Bur. Cultural Affairs, Atlanta, 1986—; cons. Fulton County Arts Coun., Atlanta, 1987; mem. adv. bd. So. Music Conf., Atlanta. Composer music including Song for Mr. H.P., 1976, Reminiscence, 1986; author: Jazz And the Young Black Audience, 1982; asst. project dir. film In Search of Imporvision, The Essence of Virtuosity in Jazz, 1983; performer "Gillespiana" IAJE Conv., 1996; performed Montreux, Switzerland, Northsea, Den Hague, Holland, Umbria Jazz Festival, Perugia, Italy, Grande Parade du Jazz, Nice, France, Kool Jazz Festivals, Avery Fisher, Lincoln Ctr., IAJE Conv., Atlanta; performed at Trumped Awards, CNN; author essay. Served with 7th U.S. Army Band, 1958-60, Germany. Named one of Outstanding Young Men of Am., 1970; recipient Bronze Jubilee award Sta. WETV, 1983, Paul Mitchell Cmty. Jazz awards Sta. WRFG, Lifetime Achievement in Jazz award, 2001. Mem. AAUP, ASCAP, NARAS (nat. edn. com.), Nat. Flute Assn., Internat. Assn. Jazz Educators, N.Am. Saxophone Alliance World Saxophone Congress, Atlanta Fedn. Musicians (v.p. 1994—, bd. dirs. 1969—), Internat. Double Reed Soc., Internat. Clarinet Soc., Duke Ellington Soc., Optimists, YMCA, Alpha Phi Alpha. Democrat. Methodist. Home: 413 Fielding Ln SW Atlanta GA 30311-2020 Office: Clark Atlanta U James P Brawley Fair St SW Atlanta GA 30314

PATTERSON, JAMES MILTON, marketing specialist, educator; b. DeQueen, Ark., Oct. 15, 1927; s. Charles Edward and Phoebe Allene (Steel) P.; m. Della Jeanne Hays, July 3, 1964; children— J. Marshall, Julia M.; children by previous marriage— Robert T., Donald A. BS, U.S. Mcht. Marine Acad., 1948; MBA (Teagle Found. fellow), Cornell U., 1954, PhD (Ford Found. dissertation fellow), 1961. Third mate Esso Shipping Co., 1948-52; instr. in bus. adminstrn. Northwestern U., 1957-60; lectr. Center for Programs in Govt. Adminstrn., U. Chgo., 1959; asst. prof. mktg. Ind. U., 1960-63, assoc. prof., 1963-69, prof., 1969—, chmn. dept. mktg., 1972-78, assoc. dir. Poynter Ctr., 1980, acting dir., 1981, co-sec. U. Faculty Coun., pres. Bloomington Faculty Coun.; dir. Ind. U. Inst. for Advanced Study, 1994-97. Bd. dirs. Inst. Advanced Study; cons. petroleum mktg.; expert witness on antitrust and mktg. Author: Marketing: The Firm's Viewpoint, 1964, Highway Robbery: An Analysis of the Gasoline Crisis, 1974, Competition Ltd.: The Marketing of Gasoline, 1972. With USNR, 1945-48. Mem. Assn. for Practical & Profl. Ethics. Democrat. Home: 1303 Dreams Landing Way Annapolis MD 21401-1035 Office: Ind U Inst Advanced Study Bloomington IN 47405 E-mail: tartan33@aol.com.

PATTERSON, JAMES RANDOLPH, physician; b. Lancaster, Pa., Jan. 30, 1942; m. Linda Lewis Patterson, Nov. 22, 1969. AB, U. Pa., 1964; MD, Columbia U., 1968. Diplomate Nat. Bd. Med. Examiners, Am. Bd. Internal Medicine, Subsplty. of Pulmonary Disease. Pulmonary and critical care specialist The Oreg. Clinic, Portland, 1975—; clin. prof. medicine Oreg. Health Scis. U., Portland, 1978—. Mem. Am. Bd. Internal Medicine, Phila., 1995—, sec.-treas., 2002--; trustee Collins Med. Trust, Portland, Oreg., 1992—, chair subsplty. bd. pulmonary disease, 1998-2002. Contbr. numerous articles to profl. jours. Recipient Class of 1964 award U. Pa., Van Loan award Am. Lung Assn. Oreg., 1990, Meritorious Achievement award Oreg. Health Scis. U., 1991; named Class Pres. Coll. Physicians and Surgeons of Columbia U., 1968, Tchr. of Yr. Providence Med. Ctr., Portland, Oreg., 1976, Internist of Yr., 1983, Best Doctors in Am., 1992—, Consumers Guide to Top Doctors, 2002-. Mem. AMA, Am. Thoracic Soc., Am. Coll. Chest Physicians, Oreg. Lung Assn., North Pacific Soc. of Internal Medicine, Pacific Interurban Clin. Club, Multnomah County Med. Soc., Oreg. Med. Assn., Oreg. Soc. Critical Care Medicine. Office: The Oregon Clinic 507 NE 47th Ave Ste 103 Portland OR 97213-2236 Office Phone: 503-215-2300. Business E-Mail: jpatterson@orclinic.com.

PATTERSON, JAMES WILLIS, pathology and dermatology educator; b. Takoma Park, Md., Dec. 29, 1946; s. James Clark and Helen (Hendricks) P.; m. Julie Wyatt, Dec. 30, 1989; 1 child, James Wyatt. BA, Johns Hopkins U., 1968; MD, Med. Coll. Va., 1972. Diplomate Am. Bd. Dermatology, Am. Bd. Dermatopathology, Nat. Bd. Med. Examiners; recert. in dermatology. Fellow dermatopathology Armed Forces Inst. Pathology, Washington, 1979—80; clin. instr. dermatology U. Colo. Med. Ctr., Denver, 1980—82; rotating intern in medicine Med. Coll. Va., Richmond, 1972-73, resident in dermatology, 1973-76, assoc. prof. pathology and dermatology, 1982-89, prof., 1989-92, dir. dermatopathology, 1982-92; with Dermatology Assocs. of Va., 1992-96, Va. Dermatopathology Svcs., Richmond, 1992-96; clin. prof. pathology Med. Coll. of Va., 1992—; prof. pathology and dermatology U. Va., 1996—. Cons. in pathology McGuire VA Hosp., Richmond, 1982-92; cons. in pathology and dermatology Kenner Army Hosp., Ft. Lee, Va., 1982-95. Author: Dermatology: A Concise Textbook, 1987; contbr. over 100 articles on dermatology and pathology to med. jours.; asst. editor Jour. Cutaneous Pathology, 1989-94. Mem. nat. alumni schs. com. Johns Hopkins U., 1986—. With M.C., U.S. Army, 1976-82, col. Res. (ret.). Recipient Stuart McEwen award Assn. Mil. Dermatologists, 1980, 82. Fellow: ACP, Am. Soc. Dermatopathology (sec.-treas. 2001—), Am. Acad. Dermatology; mem.: Va. Dermatol. Soc. (sec.-treas. 1984—88, v.p. 1988—89, pres. 1989—90), Johns Hopkins U. Alumni Assn. (pres. ctrl. Va. chpt. 1989), Res. Officers' Assn. (life), Colonnade Club (bd. govs. 2004—), Tau Epsilon Phi (life). Republican. Presbyterian. Avocations: american history, baseball, golf.

PATTERSON, JEFFERY ALLEN, business owner; b. Albertville, Ala., Sept. 17, 1961; Children: Tamara Jesse, Madeline Paige and Victoria Autumn (twins). Founder, pres. Marshall County Young Dem., Albertville, 1996; exec. com. mem. Marshall County Democratic Club, 1999; Masons; v.p. Lions Club, Albertville, 1999, pres., 2000; mem. Albertville C. of C., Guntersville C. of C., Boaz C. of C., Sand Mt. Saddle Club, Beulah vol. Fire Dept., Marshall County Bd. of Realtors; Albertville Future Farmers of Amer. (pres. 1978-79); Marshall County Bd. of Realtors; pres. Albertville Jaycees, 2000; elected constable Marshall County, 1996; formed Marshall County Sheriffs Posse, CAP, 2000. Recipient Senate award, 1997, Alabama Jr. C. of C. Outstanding Young Alabamian award, 1998, commendation Marshall County Citizen of Yr. Com., 1997, Knights of Kings Heroes, DAR award, 1999. Home: 1201 Jane St Albertville AL 35950-5910 Office: 1201 Jane St Albertville AL 35950-5910 E-mail: jpatterson@jp.com.

PATTERSON, JEFFREY A. real estate company executive; Sr. fin. analyst Real Estate Investment Group Met. Life Ins. Co.; exec. v.p. The Prime Group, Inc., 1989—97; from exec. v.p. to pres. Prime Group Realty Trust, Chgo., 1997—2003, pres., 2003—, chief investment officer, 1997—. Mem.: Nat. Assn. Real Estate Investment Trusts, Urban Land Inst. (assoc.). Office: Prime Group Realty Trust 77 West Wacker Dr Ste 3900 Chicago IL 60601*

PATTERSON, JOHN C. clinical psychology researcher; b. Asheville, N.C. BS in Psychology, MS in Psychology, Stephen F. Austin State U.; PhD in Psychology, Tex. A&M U., 1981. Resident in psychology Wilford Hall USAF

Med. Ctr., San Antonio, 1981; staff psychologist, maximum security unit Rusk State Psychiatric Hosp., Tex.; unit dir. USAF Sch. Aerospace Medicine; chief, aerospace clin. psychology function USAF Aeromed. Consultation Svc., 1985—. Faculty mem. USAF Sch. Aerospace Medicine and U. Tex. Health Sci. Ctr., San Antonio (Psychiatry); internat. vis. lectr. in aeromed. neuropsychiatry; cons. in aerospace clin. psychology and neuropsychology evaluation; mem. NASA In-House Working Group on Astronaut Selection; cons. NASA. Contbr. over 30 articles to profl. jours.; rschr. in psychological factors associated with heart disease, aircrew and astronaut selection, spatial disorientation, aviator cognitive funcitoning, and airsickness; presenter in field. Recipient Armstrong Lab. Dirs. award for Rsch. 1993. Mem. APA, Aerospace Med. Assn. (Raymond F. Longacre award 1995), Am. Soc. Clin. Hypnosis, Internat. Neuropsychology Soc., AF Soc. for Clin. Psychologists, Bexar County Psychol. Assn. Office: USAF FECN SAM 2507 Kennedy Cir Brooks AFB TX 78235-5117*

PATTERSON, JOHN DE LA ROCHE, JR., lawyer; b. Schenectady, N.Y., July 8, 1941; s. John de la Roche Sr. and Jane C. (Clay) P.; m. Michele F. Demarest, Nov. 28, 1987; children: Daniel C., Sara R., Amy C. BA, Johns Hopkins U., 1963; LLB, Harvard U., 1966. Bar: Mass. 1968. Vol. Peace Corps, Chad, 1966-67; assoc. Foley, Hoag & Eliot, Boston, 1967-73, ptnr., 1974—, exec. com., 1989-97. Chmn. Kodaly Ctr. Am. Inc., Newton, Mass., 1977-87. Mem. ABA, Boston Bar Assn. Democrat. Avocations: sailing, tennis, travel, reading. Office: Foley Hoag LLP 155 Seaport Blvd Boston MA 02210- Office Phone: 617-832-1144. E-mail: jpatters@FoleyHoag.com.

PATTERSON, JOSEPH FLANNER, JR., surgeon, anesthesiologist; b. New Bern, N.C., Feb. 12, 1917; MD, Harvard U., 1942. Diplomate Am. Bd. Surgery, Am. Bd. Anesthesiology. Intern Abington (Pa.) Meml. Hosp., 1942-43; resident in neurol. surgery Med. Coll., Va., 1946-47; resident in surgery Lankenau Hosp., Phila., 1947-50; resident in anesthesiology N.C. Meml. Hops., Chapel Hill, 1961-63; fellow in anesthesiology Children's Hosp. Med. Ctr., Boston, 1963-64; staff anesthesiology dept. Balt. City Hosp., 1964-66, N.C. Meml. Hosp., Chapel Hill, 1966-77; surveyor Joint Commn. Accreditation Hosps., Chgo., 1978-90; prof. emeritus Univ. N.C., Chapel Hill, 1977—. Mem. Am. Acad. Pediat., Am. Soc. Anesthesiologists, N.C. Surg. Assn. E-mail: jpatterson@earthlink.net.

PATTERSON, JULIA, state legislator; m. Pat Patterson; children: Alex, Erin, Caitlin. BS in Soc. and Justice, Wash. State U.; BA in English cum laude, U. Wash. Mem. Wash. Legislature, Olympia, 1997—, chair mem. state and local govt. com., mem. human svcs. and corrections com., mem. transp. com., mem. Gov.'s com. on alcohol, tobacco and drug prevention, mem. substance abuse adv. com., mem. Gov.'s Coun. on Substance Abuse, mem. substance abuse prevention adv. com. Mem. Wash. Coun. for the Prevention of Child Abuse and Neglect; bd. dirs. Judson Park Ret. Cmty.; past mem. King County Human Svcs. Roundtable; vol. Highline Sch. Dist.; mem. Valley View PTA. Mem. LVW, Wash. Coun. on Aging, Audubon Soc. Democrat. Office: 422 John Cherberg Bldg Olympia WA 98504-0001

PATTERSON, LILLIAN STANTON, curator; b. Alexandria, Va., June 22, 1927; d. N. Howard and Esther Naomi (Gray) Stanton; m. Edward Lloyd Patterson, June 27, 1956 (dec. Feb. 1979); children: Marilyn Esther Patterson Stevens, Valerie Lisa. BA in Social Studies, Storer Coll., 1950; postgrad., Am. U., 1951-52, U. Va., Alexandria, 1967, 69, 70. Cert. tchr., Va. Field dir. N.W. Fla. coun. Girl Scouts U.S., Pensacola, 1954-56; substitute tchr., 1952-67; travel counselor, mus. specialist City of Alexandria, 1976—; travel counselor Va. State Travel, 1981-82; state asst. to Congressman Stan Parris Alexandria, 1983-86; adminstrv. asst. McEnearney Assoc. Realtors, 1986-92; mus. specialist Alexandria Black History Mus., 1992—. Bd. dirs. Arlington (Va.) Vets. Meml. YMCA, Alexandria Civic Symphony Orch., Alexandria Cmty. Y, Alexandria Human Rels. Coun., Alexandria United Way, Project Discovery; bd. dirs., sec. Alexandria Vol. Bur.; v.p. MacArthur Sch. PTA; v.p., then pres. Alexandria Cmty. Mental Health Ctr. Adv. Bd.; pres. Quettes of No. Va.; charter mem., treas., v.p. Alexandria-Mt. Vernon chpt. Jack & Jill of Am., Inc.; pres. Semin. Civic Assn.; mem., ch. historian Shiloh Bapt. Ch. Recipient Outstanding Cmty. Svc. award United Way of Nat. Capitol Area, 1980, Cmty. Svc. award Hopkins House Assn., 1981, Cmty. Svc. award Alexandria Br. NAACP, 1998, Recipient Women-to-Women, Making a Difference award The Alexandria Commn. for Women Salute to Women Awards, 2001. Mem. Seminary Hill Assn., Inc. (bd. dirs.). Avocation: genealogy. Home: 1034 Woods Pl Alexandria VA 22302-3014 Office: Alexandria Black Mus 902 Wythe St Alexandria VA 22314-1823

PATTERSON, NEAL L. information systems company executive; BS in Fin., MBA, Okla. State U. Sys. cons., mgr. Arthur Andersen & Co., Kansas City, Mo.; co-founder, CEO, chmn. bd. dirs. Cerner Corp., Kansas City, Mo., 1979—. Trustee Midwest Rsch. Inst.; mem. steering com. Coun. Growing Cos. Named Entrepreneur of Yr., Ernst & Young, 1991. Mem. Health Execs. Network. Office: Cerner Corp 2800 Rockcreek Pkwy Ste 601 Kansas City MO 64117-2521

PATTERSON, ORLANDO, sociologist; b. Jamaica, June 5, 1940; came to U.S., 1970. s. Charles A. Patterson and Almina Morris; m. Nerys Wyn Thomas, Sept. 5, 1965 (div. 1994); children: Rhiannon, Barbara; m. Anita Haya Goldman, Aug. 12, 1995. BS, U. of the West Indies, 1962; PhD, London Sch. of Econs., 1965; MA, Harvard U., Harvard, 1971; LHD (hon.), Trinity Coll., Conn., 1992. Asst. lectr. U. of London, London Sch. Econs. and Polit. Sci., 1965-67; lectr. U. of West Indies, 1967-70; vis. lectr. Harvard U., Cambridge, Mass., 1970-71, Allston Burr sr. tutor, 1971-73, prof. sociology, 1971-93, John Cowles prof. sociology, 1993—. Vis. mem. Inst. Advanced Study, Princeton, N.J., 1975-76; vis. fellow, Wolfson Coll., Cambridge U., 1978-79; Phi Beta Kappa vis. scholar, 1988-89; mem. tech. advisory com. to prime min. and govt. of Jamaica, 1972-74, sp. advisor to prime min. of Jamaica, 1973-80. Author: (novels) The Children of Sisyphus, 1964 (1st prize Dakar Festival Negro Arts 1966), An Absence of Ruins, 1967, Die the Long Day, 1972, (nonfiction) The Sociology of Slavery, 1967, Ethnic Chauvinism, 1977, Slavery and Social Death, 1982 (co-winner Ralph Bunche award Am. Polit. Sci. Assn. 1983), Freedom; vol. 1, Freedom in the Making of Western Cluture, 1991 (Nat. Book award Nat Book Found. 1991), The Ordeal of Integration: Progress and Resentment in America's Racial Crisis, 1997, Rituals of Blood: Consequences of Slavery in Two American Centuries, 1999; contbr. Stories from the Caribbean, 1965. Recipient UCLA medal, 1992; Guggenheim fellow, 1978-79. Fellow Am. Acad. Arts and Scis.; mem. Am. Sociol. Assn. (citation for disting. contbn. to scholarship 1983). Office: Harvard U Dept Sociology William James 520 33 Kirkland St Cambridge MA 02138-2044

PATTERSON, OSCAR, III, university program administrator; b. July 25, 1945; s. Oscar Jr. and Frances (Killian) P.; m. Kathy E. Gibson, June 6, 1966 (div. Apr. 1979); 1 child, Elizabeth Anne Patterson Cassel; m. Julie Ann Holmes, Dec. 28, 1990. BA, Pfeiffer U., 1967; MFA, U. Ga., 1973; PhD, U. Tenn., 1982. Asst. prof. architecture and fine arts Auburn (Ala.) U., 1972-75; chairperson BFA in Theatre program Western Carolina U., Cullowhee, N.C., 1975-79; dir. telecom. U. N.C., Pembroke, 1984-88; chair comm. and visual arts U. North Fla., Jacksonville, 1998—. Juvenile probation officer Cleveland Ct. Sys., Shelby, N.C., 1967-68; gen. mgr., news dir. WNCP-TV, N.C., 1984-98. Contbr. articles to profl. jours.; host pub. tv program, 1989-98. U.S. Army, 1968-75, Vietnam. Mem. AEJMC, Soc. Profl. Journalists, Phi Kappa Phi. Republican. Avocations: historical reenactment, beach exploration. Home: 248 Patrick Mill Cir Ponte Vedra Beach FL 32082-4013 Business E-Mail: opatters@unf.edu.

PATTERSON, PAIGE, church administrator, former seminary president; b. Tex, 1942; s. T.A. Patterson; m. Dorothy Jean Kelley; 2 children. BA, Hardin-Simmons U., Abilene, Tex.; ThD in Theology, ThD in Theology, New Orleans Sem. Ordained to ministry Bapt. Ch. Min. various chs.; pres. Criswell Coll., Dallas, 1975-92, Southeastern Bapt. Theol. Sem., Wake Forest, N.C., 1992-98, So. Bapt. Conv., So. Ea. Bapt. Sem., Nashville, 1998—2003, Southwestern Bapt. Theol. Sem., Fort Worth, Tex., 2003—. Office: Southwestern Bapt Theol Sem 2001 W Seminary Dr PO Box 22040 Fort Worth TX 76122-0040*

PATTERSON, PERRY WILLIAM, publishing company executive; b. Lancaster, Pa., Nov. 18, 1949; s. William and Helen (Bergmark) P.; m. A. Kimball Harrill, Mar. 3, 1984; children: Reed W., Amy M. BS in Econs., U. Hartford, 1972; MA, U. Mass., 1974; MBA, Rutgers U., 1983. From econ. analyst to dir. econs. Cahners Pub. Co., 1974-81; economist, asst. dir. Ctr. Internat. Bus. Cycle Rsch. Rutgers U., 1981-83; dir. corp. R&D Gordon Publs., Inc., 1984-88; dir. prod. devel. Faulkner & Gray, 1988-89; v.p. group pub., bd. dirs. Inst. Mgmt. and Adminstrn. (a Bur. Nat. Affairs Inc. co.), N.Y.C., 1989—; founder, pres. IBC, 1988—. Designer aerospace proudcts mag., 1986—, newsletters; contbg. editor Bus. Mktg., 1982-91; contbr. articles to profl. jours. Mem. Am. Econ. Assn., Nat. Assn. Bus. Economists, Bus. Profl. Advt. Assn., Am. Bus. Press (rsch. com.). Home: 259 Forest Ave Glen Ridge NJ 07028-1728 Office: Inst Mgmt and Adminstrn 29 W 35th St Fl 5 New York NY 10001-2221 E-mail: ppatterson@ioma.com.

PATTERSON, PEYTON R. bank executive; b. Weisbaden, Germany; m. Thomas Patterson; 1 child. Degree in Polit. Sci., European Inst. Study, 1977; AB in Polit. Sci., Kenyon Coll., 1978; MBA in Mktg., George Washington U., 1983. From asst. v.p. group product mgr. retail deposit products to v.p. Corestates Fin. Corp., Phila., 1983—85, v.p., 1985—89; from v.p. group product mgr. to sr. v.p. Chemical Banking Corp., N.Y.C., 1989—90, sr. v.p., 1990—95; sr. v.p., dir. nat. fin. svcs. group Chase Manhattan Bank, N.Y.C., 1995—96; exec. v.p., gen. mgr. consumer fin. svcs. Dime Bank Corp., N.Y.C., 1996—2001; chmn., pres., CEO New Haven (Conn.) Savings Bank, 2002—. Co-chmn. Greater N.Y. March of Dimes; mem. Regional Leadership Coun., Arts Coun. Greater New Haven; bd. dirs. United Way. Named One of 25 Most Powerful Women in Banking, U.S. Banker Mag., 2003; Rockefeller fellow, 2000—01, Henry Crown fellow, Aspen Inst. Office: New Haven Savings Bank 195 Church St New Haven CT 06510

PATTERSON, RICHARD NORTH, novelist, writer, lawyer; b. Berkeley, Calif., Feb. 22, 1947; s. Richard Wallace and Marjorie Frances (North) P.; m. Laurie Anderson, Apr. 13, 1993; children: Shannon Heath, Brooke North, Katherine Amber, Adam Chandler, Chase Kenyon, Stephen Thomas Blunt. BA History, Ohio Wesleyan U., 1968; JD, Case Western Reserve, 1971. Bar: Ohio, 1971, D.C., 1973, Ala., 1975, Calif., 1984. Asst. atty. gen. State of Ohio, 1971-73; with divsn. enforcement SEC, Washington, 1973-75, San Francisco, Calif., 1878-81; assoc. atty. Berkowitz, Lefkovits & Patrick, Birmingham, Ala., 1975-77, ptnr., 1978; assoc. McCutchen, Doyle, Brown & Enerson, San Francisco, Calif., 1985-87, ptnr., 1987-93, of counsel, 1993-94. Author: The Lasko Tangent, 1979, The Outside Man, 1981, Escape the Night, 1983, Private Screening, 1985, Degree of Guilt, 1993, Eyes of a Child, 1995, The Final Judgement, 1995, Silent Witness, 1997, No Safe Place, 1998, Dark Lady, 1999, Protect and Defend, 2000, Balance of Power, 2003. Bd. dirs. Family Violence Prevention Fund, Common Cause, Brady Campaign to Prevent Gun Violence, National Partnership for Women and Families. Named Man of Yr., WWRAP, 2001; recipient Edgar Allan Poe award for best 1st novel, Mystery Writers Am., 1979, Grand Prix de Literateur Policiere, 1995, Pres.'s award for Disting. Alumni, Case Western Res. U., 1997, Maggie award, Planned Parenthood, 2001.

PATTERSON, RICKEY LEE, clergyman; b. Indpls., Sept. 24, 1952; s. William Irving and Wanda (Calbert) P.; m. Sharon Rose Leonard, May 4, 1974; children: Rachel L., Rickey L. BA, Ind. U., 1976; postgrad., U. Miami, 1976-80; ThM, Internat. Bible Inst. and Sem., 1983; ThD, Christian Leadership U., 1995; PhD, Miami Christian U., 1997. Cert. pvt. pilot FAA. Pres. Pat-Cat Enterprises, Inc., Miami, 1977-81; pastor, 1972—; founder, pres. Jesus Students Fellowship, Inc., 1973—; pastor, 1979—; radio broadcast spkr., 1978—; dir. J.S.F. Cassette Ministries, 1978—; pres. Jesus Fellowship, Inc., 1981—, Miami Christian U., 1982—; with Metanet Mktg. Grp., Inc., 1993—; CEO, Churches Dot Network, 1995—, Christian Internet Radio Network, 1996—, Christian Internet TV Network, 1997—; travel agt. Global Travel Internat., 2002—. Ordained to minstry Internat. Conv. Faith Chs. and Ministers, Inc., 1980; coll. unit dir., Northwestern Mutual Life Ins. Co., Milw., 1980-83; founder, supt. Jesus fellowship Christian Sch., 1983—, CEO, pres., Metanet Mktg. Grp., Inc., pres. Dade County Pvt. Sch. Sys., Inc., 1983—; instr. Bible, Ind. U., 1973-76; instr. Bible, U. Miami, 1976—, also guest lectr., dept. religion; pres. Miami Bible Inst., 1984—, pres., Christian Internet Radio; guest lectr. Miami North Community Correctional Ctr., Dade County Correctional Inst., Fed. Inst. Corrections; adv. Miami chpt. Women Aglow, 1980-82; campus minister Ind. U., Miami, Fla. internat. U., Miami-Dade C.C., U. P.R.; exec. bd. mem. Internat. Congress of Local Chs., 1988—; dir. Christian Benefactor, 1990—, charter mem. Rep. Presdl. Task Force; sustaining mem. Rep. Nat. Com.; bd. govs. Am. Coalition Traditional Values, 1984—. Mem. Bur. Bus. Practice, Aircraft Owners and Pilots Assn., Nat. Audubon Soc., Am. Entrepreneurs Assn., Inst. Cert. Fin. Planners, Am. Security Counc., U.S. Senatorial Club, Zool. Soc. Fla., Adult Congregate Living Facility (pres. Naples chpt. 1988-90), Christian Booksellers Assn., Nat. Assn. Life Underwriters, Am. Mktg. Assn., Full Gospel Businessman's Fellowship Internat. Coalition of Local Chs. (mem. exec. bd. 1988-99), Ind. U. Alumni Assn., Sigma Pi. Editor: Spirit of Life Mag., 1980-82; chief editor: Miami Jour., 1984—. Home and Office: 9775 SW 87th Ave Miami FL 33176-2954 Office Phone: 305-595-5314. E-mail: reurick@jf.org.

PATTERSON, ROBERT ARTHUR, physician, health care consultant, retired health care company executive, retired air force officer; b. Palestine, Ill., Sept. 3, 1915; s. Robert Bruce and Nera (McColpin) P.; m. Judith Scheirer, May 15, 1961; children: Mary Kay, Elaine Alice Mills, Robert Arthur II, Victoria Patterson Goodrum. Student, U. Ill., 1933-35; MD, U. Louisville, 1939. Diplomate: aerospace medicine Am. Bd. Preventive Medicine. Intern Detroit Receiving Hosp., 1939-40; joined Mich. N.G., 1940; commd. USAAF, 1946; advanced through grades to lt. gen. USAF, 1972; rated chief flight surgeon and command pilot; assigned U.S. and ETO, 1940-45; assigned, 1945-63; dep. dir. plans and hospitalization Office Surgeon Gen., USAF, Washington, 1963-65, dir. plans and hospitalization, 1965-68; surgeon Hdqrs. USAFE, Lindsey Air Sta., Germany, 1968-71, Hdqrs. SAC, Offutt AFB, 1971-72; surgeon gen. USAF, 1972-75, ret., 1975; health care cons. Arlington, Va., 1975; sr. v.p. sci. affairs Baxter Travenol Labs., Inc., Deerfield, Ill., 1976-86, health care cons., 1987—. Decorated D.S.M. with oak leaf cluster, Legion of Merit with two oak leaf clusters, Air Force Commendation medal; recipient citation of honor Air Force Assn., citation of distinction Fed. Hosp. Execs., citation of distinction Am. Hosp. Assn. Fellow Am. Coll. Preventive Medicine, Aerospace Medicine Assn., Am. Coll. Physician Execs. (founder); mem. Assn. Mil. Surgeons (pres. 1972), AMA, Am. Acad. Med. Dirs., Ret. Officers Assn., Soc. Mil. Cons. to Armed Forces, Soc. Armed Forces Med. Labs. Scis., NIH Alumni, U. Ill. Alumni Assn., Aircraft Owners and Pilots Assn., Order Daedalians, Assn. for Advancement of Med. Instrumentation, Exptl. Aircraft Assn., Deutsch Kurzhaar Verband, N.A. Versatile Hunting Dog Assn., Uniformed Services U. Health Scis. Alumni Assn., Air Safety Found., Mid-America (Chgo.), Cen. Fla. Conservation and Hunt (Lake Wales, Fla.), Yacht and Country (bd. govs., 1993-95, pres., 1996-97, Stuart, Fla.), Sunshine Gun, Yacht (Stuart), Willoughby Golf Club (Stuart). Home and Office: Yacht & Country Club 3474 SE Fairway E Stuart FL 34997-6160

PATTERSON, ROBERT EDWARD, lawyer; b. L.A., Sept. 14, 1942; s. Ellis Elwood and Helen (Hjelte) P.; m. Christina Balboni, Oct. 2, 1971; 1 child, Victor Ellis. BA, UCLA, 1964; JD, Stanford U., 1972, grad. bus. exec. program, 1986; vis. scholar, Amos Tuck School Dartmouth Coll., 1998. Bar: Calif. 1972. Sr. counsel Squire Sanders & Dempsey LLP, Palo Alto, Calif., 1972—. Bd. dirs. Procyte Corp., Peninsula Equity Ptnrs., Ctr. for Pvt. Equity, Amos Tuck Sch., Dartmouth Coll., Sumida Corp., HK Pharmaceuticals, Inc, Synzyme Techs., LLC, Calif. State Parks Found., Acuity Ventures, Capital Pacific Devel., Inc., DermoZyme Corp., Transierra Corp., Calif. Airlines; adv. bd. Borealis Ventures. Bd. dirs. John Ernest Found. Lt. comdr. USN, 1964-69. Mem. Palo Alto Club, Menlo Circus Club, Bohemian Club, Band of Angels. Democrat. Office: Squire Sanders & Dempsey 600 Hansen Way Ste 100 Palo Alto CA 94304-1043 Office Phone: 650-843-3372. E-mail: rpatterson@ssd.com.

PATTERSON, ROBERT EUGENE, insurance company executive; b. Lancaster, Pa., June 13, 1932; s. Blanchard S. and Lydia L. (Wert) P.; m. Dorothy J. Shenk, May 26, 1951; children: Craig Robert, Tracy Ann. BS in Econs. magna cum laude, Franklin and Marshall Coll., 1959; postgrad., Temple U., 1960, Harvard U., 1977. CPA, D.C. With Armstrong World Industries, Lancaster, 1950-69, Hamilton Watch Co., Lancaster, 1969-71; v.p. fin., treas. K-D Mfg. Co., Lancaster, 1971-76, dir., officer and dir. subs., 1972-76; sr. v.p. fin., CFO, Blue Shield, Camp Hill, Pa., 1976-95, sr. v.p. cons., 1996-97; chief investment officer Commonwealth of Pa., 1997—. Vice chmn., sec., corp. sec., bd. dirs. Healthguard of Lancaster, Inc.; bd. dirs. Millerville Univ. Found. Served with U.S. Army, 1952-54. Mem. Fin. Execs. Inst. (chpt. pres., area dir., nat. v.p.), Inst. Mgmt. Accts., AICPAs, Pa. Soc. CPAs, Meadia Heights Country Club, Hamilton Club. Episcopalian. Office: Commonwealth of PA Treasury Dept 121 Finance Building Harrisburg PA 17120-0018

PATTERSON, ROBERT HOBSON, JR., lawyer; b. Richmond, Va., Jan. 30, 1927; s. Robert Hobson and Margaret S. (Sargent) P.; m. Luise Franklin Wyatt, June 15, 1952 (dec.); children— India, Robert Hobson, Margaret. B.A., Va. Mil. Inst., 1949; LL.B., U. Va., 1952. Bar: Va. 1952, U.S. Ct. Appeals (4th cir.) 1953, U.S. Supreme Ct. 1955. Assoc. McGuireWoods LLP, Richmond, 1952-56, ptnr., 1956—, sr. ptnr., chmn. exec. com., 1978-89, chmn., 1984-89. Pres. bd. visitors Va. Mil. Inst., 1975; pres. Va. Home for Boys, 1975. Served with USNR, 1945-46. Fellow Am. Coll. Trial Lawyers, Am. Bar Found., Va. Mil. Inst. Alumni Assn. (pres. 1963-65), Commonwealth Club, Country Club of Va. Republican. Episcopalian. Office: McGuireWoods LLP 1 James Ctr 901 E Cary St Richmond VA 23219-4057

PATTERSON, ROBERT HUDSON, research library consultant; b. Alexandria, La., Dec. 11, 1936; s. Hubert Hudson and Beth (Jones) P.; m. Diana E. Sellers; 1 child, Jennifer Bookhart Peters. BA, Millsaps Coll., Jackson, Miss., 1958; MA, Tulane U., 1963; M.L.S., U. Calif., Berkeley, 1965. Mem. profl. staff Tulane U. Libr., New Orleans, 1965-69, 73-76, asst. dir. collection devel., 1973-76; head spl. collections cataloging U. Tex., Austin, 1970-73; dir. librs. U. Wyo., Laramie, 1976-81, U. Tulsa, 1981-98. Chmn. exec. bd. Wyo. State Libr. Adv. Com., 1976-81; mem. bd. Okla. State Libr. Adv. Com., 1981-84; mem. adv. coun. Bibliog. Ctr. for Rsch., Denver, 1978-81; past mem. exec. bd. S.E. La. Libr. Network; bd. dirs. Amigos Bibliog. Coun., 1983-86; cons. NEH, Harry Ransom Humanities Rsch. Ctr., U. Tex., Austin. Editor Conservation Adminstrn. News, 1979-93; contbr. articles to profl. jours. Pres. Western Conservation Congress, 1981-82. Sr. fellow CLR/UCLA, 1989. Fellow Internat. Boswell Inst.; mem ALA (various offices), Okla. Libr. Assn. (various offices). E-mail: rpatterson1@austin.rr.com.

PATTERSON, ROBERT PORTER, JR., federal judge; b. N.Y.C., July 11, 1923; s. Robert Porter and Margaret (Winchester) P.; m. Bevin C. Daly, Sept. 15, 1956; children: Anne, Robert, Margaret, Paul, Katherine. AB, Harvard U., 1947; LLB, Columbia U., 1950. Bar: N.Y. 1951, D.C. 1966. Law clk. Donovan, Leisure, Newton & Lumbard, N.Y.C., 1950-51; asst. counsel N.Y. State Crime Commn. Waterfront Investigation, 1952-53; asst. U.S. atty. Chief of Narcotics Prosecutions and Investigations, 1953-56; asst. counsel Senate Banking and Currency Com., 1954; assoc. Patterson, Belknap, Webb & Tyler, N.Y.C., 1956-60, ptnr., 1960-88; judge U.S. Dist. Ct. (so. dist.) N.Y., 1988—. Counsel to minority select com. pursuant to house resolution no. 1, Washington, 1967; mem. Senator's Jud. Screening Panel, 1974-88, Gov.'s Jud. Screening Panel, 1975-82, Gov.'s Sentencing Com., 1978-79. Contbr. articles to profl. jours. Chmn. Wm. T. Grant Found., 1974-94, Prisoners' Legal Services N.Y., 1976-88; dir. Legal Aid Soc., 1961-88, pres., 1967-71; chmn. Nat. Citizens for Eisenhower, 1959-60, Scranton for Pres., N.Y. State, 1964; bd. mgrs. Havens Relief Fund Soc., 1994—, Millbrook Sch., 1966-78, Vera Inst. Justice, 1981-99, New Sch. for Social Rsch., 1986-94, George C. Marshall Found., 1987-93; mem. exec. com. Lawyers Com. for Civil Rights Under Law, 1966-88; mem. Goldman Panel for Attica Disturbance, 1972, Temporary Commn. on State Ct. System, 1971-73, Rockefeller U. Council, 1986-88, exec. com. N.Y. Vietnam Vets. Meml. Commn., 1982-85, Mayor's Police Adv. Com., 1985-87. Served to capt. USAAF, 1942-46. Decorated D.F.C. with cluster, Air medal with clusters. Mem. ABA (ho. of dels. 1976-80), N.Y. State Bar Assn. (pres. 1978-79), Assn. Bar City N.Y. (v.p. 1974-75), N.Y. County Lawyers Assn., Am. Law Inst., Am. Judicature Soc. (bd. dirs. 1979). Republican. Episcopalian. Home: Fair Oaks Farm 1657 Route 9D Cold Spring NY 10516-3543 Office: US Dist Ct So Dist NY US Court House 500 Pearl St New York NY 10007-1316

PATTERSON, ROGER LEWIS, psychologist; b. Opelika, Ala., Oct. 30, 1939; s. Homer Lee and Ruby (White) P.; m. Maritza Nunez de Gracia, Dec. 21, 1967; children: Anne Marie, Richard Allen. BA, Auburn U., 1963, MS, 1965; PhD, Fla. State U., 1971. Coord. clin. rsch. Camarillo/UCLA Rsch. Unit, 1969-72; psychologist and dir. day treatment Mental Health Ctr. of Escambia County, Pensacola, Fla., 1972-73; psychology U. Ala. and Montgomery Police Dept., 1974-75; prof. faculty Fla. Mental Health Inst., Tampa, 1975-84, prof., chmn. dept. aging and mental health, 1977-84; adj. assoc. prof. dept. psychology U. South Fla., 1977-84, clin. assoc. prof. dept. psychiatry Coll. Medicine, 1982-84; assoc. project dir. Suncoast Gerontology Ctr., 1984; dir. geriatric psychosocial rehab. program VA Med. Ctr., Tuskegee, Ala., 1984-86; clin. coord. combined adult day healthcare and day treatment VA Outpatient Clinic, Daytona Beach, Fla., 1986—. Internat. speaker in field. Author, editor books; contbr. chpts. to books, articles to profl. jours. Mem. APA, Am. Bd. Med. Psychotherapists (profl. adv. coun.), Behavior Therapy and Rsch. Soc. (clin. fellow). Office: VA Outpatient Clinic 1900 Mason Ave Daytona Beach FL 32117-5103 E-mail: rpatterson@cfl.rr.com.

PATTERSON, RONALD PAUL, publishing company executive, clergyman; b. Ashland, Ohio, Dec. 4, 1941; s. Donald Edward and Mildred (Niswender) P.; m. Marlene Pfahler, Sept. 1, 1962; children: Paul Edward, Mark Loren. BA, Malone Coll., 1963; MDiv, United Theol. Sem., Dayton, Ohio, 1967; MA, Syracuse U., 1970; DD, Cen. Meth. Coll., 1988. Ordained to ministry United Methodist Ch., 1967. Editor youth publs. Otterbein Press, Dayton, 1964-68; assoc. editor The Upper Room, Nashville, 1970-74; editor Word Books, Waco, Tex., 1974-77; editorial dir. Abingdon Press, Nashville, 1977-88; book editor United Meth. Ch. Pub. House, 1977-88, v.p., 1984-88, sr. editor Ch. Resources, 1988-92; pub., CEO UMR Comm., Inc., Dallas, 1992—. V.p. Religious Pub. Rels. Coun. Nashville, 1970-74; jr. coll. instr. creative writing, Waco; leader writers' workshops Author: (with others) The Kyle Rote Story, 1975; editor: Come On, Let's Pray, 1972; compiler: The Coming of Easter, 1973; founding editor Alive Now! devotional publ.; editorial dir. Quar. Rev., 1980-87; contbr. articles to mags. Tchr. Tenn. State Prison, Nashville, 1984-88; mem. exec. bd. Perkins Sch. Theology, 1996—; charter mem. Perkins Circle. Recipient George Washington Honor medal Nat. Freedom Found., Valley Forge, Pa., 1960, Paul M. Hinkhouse award Religious Pub. Rels. Coun., N.Y.C., 1973; named Communicator of Yr., Dallas/Ft. Worth chpt. Religion Comm. Coun., 2004; named one of Outstanding Young Men Am., 1972. Mem. Am. Acad. Religion, Religion Pub. Group, Christian Publs. Assn., Southeastern Pubs. Assn. (exec. com. 1985-88), Pubs. Assn. of South (treas.), Evang. Christian Pubs. Assn. (bd. dirs. 1987-88), Protestant Ch.-owned Pubs. Assn. (bd. dirs., chmn. biennial planning com. 1999—), Internat. Pubs. Assn. World Meth. Coun., Hogan Quality Roundtable (Dallas), CEO Inst., Dallas Press, Rotary. Democrat. Methodist. Avocations: bicycling, refinishing furniture, golf. Home: 555 Church St Dallas TX 37219-2328 Office: 2400 Lone Star Dr Dallas TX 75212-6309 Personal E-mail: rppater@aol.com.

PATTERSON, RONALD R(OY), management consultant; b. Baton Rouge, Mar. 4, 1942; BS, U. Houston, 1965; MS, Trinity U., San Antonio, 1973. Asst. adminstr. U. Tex. Med. Br., Galveston, 1972-75; asst. v.p. Hosp. Affiliates Internat., Nashville, 1975-81; chief oper. officer Affiliated Hosp. Systems, Houston, 1981-82; sr. v.p. Republic Health Corp., Dallas, 1982-88; pres. Miller Patterson Inc., Plano, Tex., 1988-89; ind. healthcare mgmt. cons. Plano, 1989-90; sr. v.p. Harris Meth. Health System, Ft. Worth, 1990-91; exec. v.p.,

COO Champion Healthcare Corp., Houston, 1991-96; exec. v.p., pres. healthcare ops. Paracelsus Healthcare Corp., Houston, 1996-99; pres. R. Patterson Assocs., Inc., 1999—. Bd. dirs. Tarrant County Hosp. Dist., 2001—, sec., 2002—; bd. chair Metrowest Health Plan, 2002—04, Tex. Health Facilities Devel. Corp., 2002 . Fellow Am. Coll. Healthcare Execs. (life), Tex. Hosp. Assn. (vice-chmn. multi-hosp. constituency 1987), Fedn. Am. Health Sys. (bd. govs. 1996-99, bd. dirs., sec. 1997-99). Office: R Patterson Assocs Inc PO Box 1826 Keller TX 76244-1826 Office Phone: 817-498-1842.

PATTERSON, SALLY JANE, government affairs consultant; b. Ontario, Calif., May 28, 1948; d. James Lowell and Barbara Verle (Griffin) Swain; 1 child, Robert Elias Sandoval. BA, Calif. State U., Fullerton, 1970, MA, 1974. Adminstrv. asst. Congressman Jerry Patterson, U.S. House of Reps., Washington, 1978-81; v.p. Pub. Response Assocs., Washington, 1981-87, Hamilton & Staff, Washington, 1987-90; v.p. pub. affairs Planned Parenthood Fedn. of Am., N.Y.C., 1990-93; internat. cons. Mgmt. Systems Internat., Washington, 1993—; v.p. Wagner & Assocs. Pub. Affairs Cons., Inc., N.Y.C., Washington, 1994-99; pres. Radiant Comms. Inc., 2000—. Cons. Nat. Dem. Inst., Washington, 1994—. Author: Supporting Democracy in The Newly Independent States of The Former Soviet Union, 1994, Women in Government Relations: 20 Years of Vision, Leadership, Education and Networking, 1995, Pursuing a Paradox: Public Attitudes vs. Public Action on Campaign Finance Reform, How does Congress Approach Population and Family Planning Issues?, 1999. Trainer Nat. Women's Campaign Fund. Recipient Gold Key award PR Soc. Am., 1992; named one of 74 Women Shaping Am. Politics, Campaigns and Elections, 1993. Mem. Women in Govt. Rels., Inc. (disting. mem., chair leader found. 1985 87, v.p. 1987-88, pres. 1988-89), Coun. Excellence in Govt. (prin.), NARAL (chair, bd. dirs.). Democrat. Episcopalian. Office: Radiant Comms Inc 2121 K St NW Ste 800 Washington DC 20037-1829

PATTERSON, SAMUEL C. political science educator; b. Omaha, Nov. 29, 1931; s. Robert Foster and Garnet Marie (Jorgensen) P.; m. Suzanne Louise Dean, June 21, 1956; children— Polly Ann, Dean Foster, Grier Edmund BA, U. S.D., 1953; MS, U. Wis., 1956, PhD, 1959. Asst. prof. polit. sci. Okla. State U., Stillwater, 1959-61; asst. prof. U. Iowa, Iowa City, 1961-64, assoc. prof., 1964-67, prof., 1967-85, Roy J. Carver prof., 1985-86; prof. Ohio State U., Columbus, 1986-98, prof. emeritus, 1998—. Vis. prof. U. Wis., 1962, U. Okla., 1968-78, U. Essex, Colchester, Eng., 1969-70, U. S.D., 2001. Author: (with others) Representatives and Represented, 1975, A More Perfect Union, 4th edit., 1989; co-author: The Legislative Process in the United States, 4th edit., 1986, Comparing Legislatures, 1979; editor: American Legislative Behavior, 1968; co-editor: Comparative Legislative Behavior: Frontiers of Research, 1972, Handbook of Legislative Research, 1985, Political Leadership in Democratic Societies, 1991, Parliaments in the Modern World, 1994, Great Theatre: The American Congress in the 1990s, 1998, Senates: Bicameralism in the Contemporary World, 1999; editor Am. Jour. Polit. Sci., 1970-73; co-editor Legis. Studies Quar., 1981-85; mng. editor Am. Polit. Sci. Rev., 1985-91. Served with U.S. Army, 1953-55 Recipient Disting. Scholar award Ohio State U., 1990; fellow social Sci. Rsch. Coun., 1961, 67, Guggenheim, 1984-85; vis. fellow Brookings Instn., 1984-85, Ctr. Advanced Study in Behavioral Scis., 1993-94; Fulbright Bologna chair, 1995. Mem. Internat. Polit. Sci. Assn., Am. Polit. Sci. Assn. (Frank J. Goodnow award, 2000), Midwest Polit. Sci. Assn. (pres. 1980-81), Phi Beta Kappa, Phi Kappa Phi, Pi Sigma Alpha. Personal E-mail: patpat851@aol.com.

PATTERSON, SETH MATTHEW, music educator; s. Ronald M and Marilyn E Patterson; m. Katie Roxanne Partain, July 21, 2001. MusB, Samford U., 2000, MusM in Edn., 2002. Music Education (K-12) Ohio, 2002, Music Education (P-12) Ala., 2002. Instr. horn Homewood Mid. Sch., Ala., 2000—01; weekend, asst. night mgr. Samford U. Libr., Birmingham, Ala., 2001—02; grad. asst. Samford U., 2001—02; dir. music Lucas Local Sch. Dist., Lucas, Ohio, 2002—. Recipient John Phillip Sousa award, Northmont H.S., 1995. Mem.: Ohio Music Educators Assn., Music Educators Nat. Conf., Phi Kappa Phi, Phi Mu Alpha Sinfonia. Personal E-mail: smpatter@samford.edu.

PATTERSON, STEVE, professional basketball team executive; b. Beaver Dam, Wis., Sept. 21, 1957; BBA with honors, U. Tex., 1980, JD, 1984. Bar: Tex. 1984. Gen. mgr., profl. basketball team counsel Houston Rockets, 1984-89, profl. basketball mktg. exec. group ticket sales, mgr., bus. ops. exec., gen. mgr., 1989-94; pres. profl. hockey team Houston Aeros, 1994-97; pres. Arena Oper. Co., Houston, 1995-99; exec. v.p. Houston NFL Holdings, 1997—2003; pres. Portland Trail Blazers, 2003—. Exec. v.p. Houston Texans Office: Portland Trail Blazers Ste 200 One Center Ct Portland OR 97227 E-mail: steve.patterson@blazers.com.

PATTERSON, W. MORGAN, college president; b. New Orleans, Oct. 1, 1925; s. E. Palmer and Jess Margaret (Wood) P.; m. Ernestine North, June 10, 1948; children: W. Morgan, II, Jay North BA, Stetson U., 1950, D.D. (hon.), 1979; M.Div., New Orleans Baptist Theol. Sem., 1953, Th.D., 1956; postdoctoral, Oxford U., 1965-66, 72-73. Prof. ch. history New Orleans Bapt. Theol. Sem., 1956-59; prof. ch. history, David T. Porter prof. ch. history, dir. grad. studies So. Baptist Theol. Sem., Louisville, 1959-76; dean acad. affairs Golden Gate Bapt. Theol. Sem., Mill Valley, Calif., 1976-84; pres. Georgetown Coll., Ky., 1984-91; asst. to pres. Coll. of Ozarks, Mo., 1994—. Vis. prof. Midwestern Bapt. Theol. Sem., Kansas City, Mo., La. Coll., Pineville, 1991—92, Golden Gate Bapt. Theol. Sem., Mill Valley, Calif., 1992—94, 1997, 2003—04, Fla. Bapt. Theol. Coll., 1998—99, New Orleans Bapt. Sem., 1995, 96, 99-2000, Okla. Bapt. U., 1997; vis. scholar Campbellsville U., Ky., 2000—03; chmn. hist. commn. So. Bapt. Conv., Nashville, 1969—72; honored guest 2d Vatican Coun., Rome, 1965. Author: Baptist Successionism: A Critical View, 1969; co-editor: Professor in the Pulpit, 1963; contbr., editor: Ency. Southern Baptists; book rev. editor Review and Expositor, 1965-70 Served as flight officer USAF, 1943-46 Recipient Disting. Alumnus award Stetson U., 1992, Disting. Svc. award for outstanding contbn. to Bapt. history Hist. Commn., So. Bapt. Conv., 1993; Am. Assn. Theol. Schs. fellow, 1965-66. Mem. Am. Soc. Ch. History, So. Bapt. Hist. Soc. (pres. 1979-80), William H. Whitsitt Bapt. Heritage Soc., Conf. on Faith and History, Commn. on Bapt. Heritage of Bapt. World Alliance. Avocations: travel, stamp collecting/philately, collecting books. Home: 7 Pierce Dr Novato CA 94947-4450

PATTERSON, WILLIAM BROWN, dean, history professor; b. Charlotte, N.C., Apr. 8, 1930; s. William Brown and Eleanor Selden (Miller) P.; m. Evelyn Byrd Hawkins, Nov. 27, 1959; children: William Brown Patterson, Evelyn Byrd Donatelli, Lucy Patterson Murray, Emily Patterson Higgs. BA, U. South, 1952; MA, Harvard U., 1954, PhD, 1966, cert. ednl. mgmt., 1982; BA, Oxford (Eng.) U., 1955, MA, 1959; MDiv, Episc. Div. Sch., Cambridge, Mass., 1958. Ordained to ministry Episcopal Ch. as deacon, 1958, as priest, 1959. Asst. prof. history Davidson (N.C.) Coll., 1963-66, assoc. prof., 1966-76, prof. history, 1976-80, U. of South, Sewanee, Tenn., 1980—, dean Coll. Arts and Scis., 1980-91; Francis S. Houghteling prof. hist., 2001. Author: (with others) Discord, Dialogue, and Concord, 1977, This Sacred History: Anglican Reflections for John Booty, 1990, King James VI and I and the Reunion of Christendom, 1997; mem. bd. editors St. Luke's Jour. Theology, Sewanee, 1982-90; contbr. numerous articles to profl. jours. Trustee U. South, 1968-71; mem. internat. adv. com. U. Buckingham, Eng., 1977-93; pres. So. Coll. and Univ. Union; organizer Associated Colls. of South, 1988-89. Danforth Found. grad. fellow, 1952, Mellon Appalachian fellow U. Va., 1992-93, rsch. fellow NEH, 1967, Folger Shakespeare Libr., Washington, 1975, Inst. for Rsch. in Humanities, U. Wis., Madison, 1976, Newberry Libr., Chgo., 1979; Rhodes scholar, 1953. Mem. Am. Hist. Assn., Am. Soc. Ch. History (Albert C. Outler prize for best book in ecumenical ch. history 1999), N.Am. Conf. on Brit. Studies, Eccles. History Soc. Eng., Royal Hist. Soc. Eng., Renaissance Soc. Am., So. Hist. Assn., Soc. for Values in Higher Edn., Episcopal Div. Sch. Alumni/ae Assn. (mem. exec. com. 1984-87), Phi Beta Kappa, Beta Theta Pi. Avocations: gardening, tennis. Home: 195 N Carolina Ave Sewanee TN 37375-2040 Office: U of South Dept History 735 University Ave Sewanee TN 37383-0001 Business E-Mail: bpatters@sewanee.edu.

PATTERSON, WILLIAM ROBERT, retired lawyer; b. Wathena, Kans., Feb. 25, 1924; s. George Richard and Jessie (Broadbent) P.; m. Lee Rhyne, Aug. 16, 1947; children: Martha, Robert, Elizabeth. Student, U. Rochester, 1943-44; AB, Lenoir-Rhyne Coll., 1947; LL.B. with distinction, Duke U., 1950. Bar: Ga. 1951, D.C. 1962. Asso. firm Sutherland, Asbill & Brennan, Atlanta, 1950-58, partner, 1958—; trustee Ga. Tax Conf., 1980-83, pres., 1980-82. Lectr. in field. Mem. bd. visitors Duke U. Law Sch., 1973-87, chmn., 1977-87, life mem., 1987—; trustee Pace Acad., Atlanta, 1958-89, trustee emeritus, 1989—; mem. devel. bd. Lenoir-Rhyne Coll., 1976-79, trustee, 1980-89; elder Trinity Presbyterian Ch., Atlanta. With USN, 1942-46. Fellow Am. Coll. Mortgage Attys. (bd. regents 1993-99, pres. 1997-98); mem. ABA, Ga. State Bar, Atlanta Bar Assn., D.C. Bar Assn., Am. Coll. Real Estate Lawyers (bd. govs. 1987-90), Am. Law Inst., So. Fed. Tax Inst. (trustee 1957-90, adv. trustee 1990—, pres. 1974-75, chmn. 1975-76), Atlanta Tax Forum (trustee 1977-83, pres. 1981-82), Order of Coif, Cherokee Town and Country Club, Commerce Club, Peachtree Club. Home: 2939 Rivermeade Dr NW Atlanta GA 30327-2039 Office: Sutherland Asbill & Brennan First Union Pla 23d Fl 999 Peachtree St NE Ste 2300 Atlanta GA 30309-3996

PATTERSON, WILLIAM T. writer; b. Findlay, Ohio, July 18, 1933; s. Arthur Dunn Patterson; m. Carol Diane Rockett, Jan. 14, 1968 (div. Mar. 29, 1984); children: Rita, Karen, Sheri. BA, Ohio State U., 1953. Author: (biography) The Farmer's Daughter Remembered. Pres. Pvt. Investigator Assn. Calif., 1967, Guide Dogs of the Desert, 1974—79. Recipient Best Syndicated Pet Column in Newspapers, Dog Writer's Assn. of Am., 1980. Avocation: photography. Home: Box 71235 Las Vegas NV 89170 Personal E-mail: wtpatterson@earthlink.net

PATTERSON DEHN, CATHLEEN, pediatrics administrator; b. Akron, Feb. 25, 1958; d. James Edward and Doris Elizabeth (Boyd) P.; m. James Keith Dehn, June 27, 1981. BSN, U. Akron, 1980; MSN, Case Western Res. U., 1988; MA Applied Psychology, NYU, 1995, postgrad., 1995—. RN, N.Y.; cert. PNP, ANCC. Nurse technician Children's Med. Ctr. Akron, 1979-80, staff nurse, 1980-81; pediatric and advanced clin. nurse, asst. head nurse, clin. nurse specialist Rainbow Babies and Children's Hosp., Cleve., 1981-91, edn. coord., 1991-93; PNP, project coord. divsn. nursing, NYU The Child Health Ctr., Brooklyn, 1994-96; PNP dept. pediat. Inst. for Neurology and Neurosurgery Beth Israel Med. Ctr., N.Y.C., 1996 2000; case mgr. dept. pediats. St. Vincent's Hosp. and Med. Ctr., N.Y.C., 2001—. Lectr., clin. instr. Frances Payne Bolton Sch. Nursing, Case Western Res. U., Cleve., 1990-93; mem. adj. faculty divsn. nursing NYU, 1994-96; project coord. Dance Cleve., 1990-91; regional instr. Neonatal Resuscitation Program, Am. Heart Assn., Am. Acad. Pediatrics. Exec. prodr. videos: Getting to Know the Unique Behavioral Capabilities of the Newborn, 1987, One Step at a Time: A Family's Guide to the Neonatal Intensive Care Unit, 1991. Co-founder Sick Kids Need Involved People, Cleve., 1987; team-walk capt. March of Dimes, Cleve., 1989-92 (Edn. grantee 1991); mem. Nat. Mus. Women in Arts. Recipient Samuel E. and Rebecca Elliott award for Cmty. Svc. Case Western Res. U., 1988; named One of Outstanding Young Women of Am., 1988; Fed. Profl. Nurse Trainee scholar, 1986-87. Mem. APA, Am. Ednl. Rsch. Assn., Kappa Delta Pi, Sigma Theta Tau, Pi Lambda Theta. Avocations: health outcomes research, teaching, educational evaluation. Home: 1 University Pl Apt 10L New York NY 10003-4518

PATTESON, CHARLES LYNN, musician, retired music educator; b. Dallas, Mar. 20, 1923; s. James Nelson and Eula Lee (Jolly) P.; children: Lisa Ann Patteson Kennedy, Charles Lynn Jr. BA, Tex. Christian U., 1948. Band dir. Poly. High Sch., Ft. Worth, 1948-50, Handley High Sch., Ft. Worth, 1948-50; owner TV store Ft. Worth, 1951-61; band dir. McLean Mid. Sch., Ft. Worth, 1961—84; leader Charlie Patteson Dance Orch., Ft. Worth, 1950—. Composer (band) March 200, 1974; (orch.) Two Minute Waltz, 1976, Fantasy, 1991, Paris In June, October in London, November in Rome, Starlight Waltz, Opus in Eb, Dreamer's Waltz, Stardust Waltz, Meadowbrook Waltz, Swinging at the Starlight, others. With USAF, 1943-46. Recipient ten 1st place Concert Competition award (dir. McLean Middle Sch. Band), Ft. Worth., 1974-84. Mem. Am. Fedn. Musicians, Musician's Fed. Credit Union (life, v.p.), Lions, Elks, Masons, Shriners (50 yr. mem., 1st chair clarinet in band 1950-91). Republican. Avocations: water-skiing, recording, music arranging. Home: 5101 Westhaven Dr Fort Worth TX 76132-2036 E-mail: clpatteson@aol.com.

PATTILLO, MANNING MASON, JR., academic administrator; b. Charlottesville, Va., Oct. 11, 1919; s. Manning Mason and Margaret (Camblos) P.; m. Martha A. Crawford, June 8, 1946; children: Manning Mason III (dec.), Martha Crawford, John Landrum. Student, Johns Hopkins U., 1937-38; BA with highest honors, U. of South, 1941, DCL, 1993; student, U. Calif. at Berkeley, 1941-42; AM, U. Chgo., 1947, PhD, 1949; LLD, LeMoyne Coll., 1967, St. John's U., 1968, Oglethorpe U., 1994; LHD, U. Detroit, 1968, Coll. New Rochelle, 1967, Park Coll., 1973; LittD, St. Norbert Coll., 1967. From instr. to assoc. prof. higher edn. U. Chgo., 1949-56; assoc. dir. Lilly Endowment, Inc., Indpls., 1956-60, exec. dir. for edn., 1961-62; dir. Danforth commn. on ch. colls. and univs., 1962-66; assoc. dir. The Danforth Found., 1964-66, v.p., 1966-67; pres. The Found. Center, N.Y.C., 1967-71; adj. prof. N.Y. U., 1968-71; dir. spl. projects U. Rochester, 1972-75; pres. Oglethorpe U., Atlanta, 1975-88, chancellor, 1988—. Cons. in field; tech. asst., then assoc. sec. commn. on colls. and univs. North Ctrl. Assn. Colls. and Secondary Schs., 1948-56; cons. USAF Acad., 1952, Phillips Exeter Acad., 1974; chmn. IBM Incentive awards com., 1970-75; adv. com. Brookings Instn., 1970-71; vis. prof. Inst. Higher Edn., U. Ga., 1988-90; bd. dirs. Fidelity Nat. Bank. Author: (with D.M. Mackenzie) Church Sponsored Higher Education in the United States, 1966, (with D.M. Mackenzie) Eight Hundred Colleges Face the Future, 1965, Private Higher Education in the United States, 1990, The Episcopal Church: Diagnosis and Reform, 1989; contbr. articles to profl. jours. Mem. pres.'s adv. coun. Wellesley Coll., 1969-72; trustee Seabury Press, Japan Internat. Christian U., 1970-72, Le Moyne Coll., 1970-83, Sacred Heart U., 1968-75, U. of South, 1984-88, St. Martin's Episc. Sch.; bd. dirs., interim pres., chmn. Atlanta Coll. Art, 1984-95, Howard Sch.; trustee Greater Rochester Cmty. Found., 1973-75, pres., 1975; trustee, chmn. Nat. Coun. on Philanthropy, 1968-80; trustee, chmn. bd. trustees Park Coll., 1967-74; bd. visitors Salvation Army Coll. for Officer Tng., 1997—; provost St. Mary's Coll. of Md., 1975; bd. visitors Kanuga Confs., Inc.; pres., life trustee Ga. Found. for Ind. Colls., 1977—; chmn. Univ. Center in Ga., 1978-79; pres. Assn. Pvt. Colls. and Univs. of Ga., 1980-81; trustee, chmn. Ga. Spl. Olympics; trustee, mem. exec. com. Nat. Assn. Ind. Colls. and Univs., Ind. Coll. Funds of Am., 1982-86; co-dir. Coll. Cons. Network, So. Assn. Colls. and Schs., 1988-96; mem. De Kalb County Cmty. Rels. Commn.; chmn. De Kalb Cmty. Coun. on the Aging; mem. commn. on colls. and steering com. on revision accrediting procedures So. Assn. Colls. and Schs.; vice-chmn bd. and life trustee, Woodruff Arts Ctr.; mem. adv. coun. ARC. With AUS, 1942-46. Mem.: English Speaking Union (dir., pres. br., nat. bd. dirs.), Guild of Scholars, Nat. Assn. Ind. Schs. (bd. dirs.), Assn. for Higher Edn., Nat. Assn. Scholars, Country Day Sch. Headmasters Assn. U.S. (hon.), DeKalb C. of C. (dir., chmn.), Atlanta Hist. Soc., Am. Anglican Coun. (chmn. Atlanta chpt.), High Mus. of Art, Phi Beta Kappa Assn. of Atlanta (pres., chmn., fellow nat. soc.), Kappa Sigma, Omicron Delta Kappa. Episcopalian (vestryman, sr. warden, mem. cathedral chpt., diocesan council, standing com.). Clubs: Century (N.Y.C.); Commerce, Capital City. Lodge: Rotary.

PATTIS, MARK R. publishing company executive; b. Chgo., Mar. 15, 1953; BS in Econs. with hons., Swarthmore Coll.; postgrad. studies, U. Chgo., London Sch. Econs., Sorbonne, Paris. Banker Chase Manhattan Bank, Am. Nat. Bank, Chgo.; staff Marmon Group; exec. NTC/ Contemporary Publ. Co., Lincolnwood, Ill., 1977—, pres., CEO, 1996-2000, Next Chpt. Holdings, Highland Park, Ill., 2000—. Recipient Palmes Academiques award Govt. of France, 1993, Electronic Book award of excellence, Sony, 1994; nominated for Watson fellowship. Mem. Chgo. Book Clinic, U.S. Electronic Book Publ. Com. (co-chmn 1991-95), Multimedia and Electronic Book Internat. Com. (vice chmn.). Office: Next Chpt Holdings Ste 205 600 Center Ave Highland Park IL 60035

PATTIS, S. WILLIAM, publishing executive; b. Chgo., July 3, 1925; s. William Robert and Rose (Quint) P.; m. Bette Z. Levin, July 16, 1950; children: Mark Robert, Robin Quint Himovitz. BS, U. Ill., 1949; postgrad., Northwestern U., 1949-50. Exec. v.p., pub. United Bus. Publs., 1949-59; chmn., CEO 3M/Pattis, 1959-88; pres. NTC Pub. Group, Lincolnwood, Ill., 1961-96, Next Chapter Holdings, L.P., Highland Park, Ill., 1996—; dir. P-B Comm., Winnetka, Ill., 1978-98; vice-chmn. Profl. Media Group, Norwalk, Conn., 1999—. Bd. dirs. 1st Colonial/Highwood; mem. book and libr. com. USIA, Washington, 1986—89, chmn., 1989—93; mem. exec. com. Pub. Hall of Fame, 1987—2000; chmn. U.S.-USSR Bilateral Media Confs., Washington and Moscow, 1990—91. Mem. Pres.'s Coun. Youth Opportunity, 1968-70; bd. dirs. Photography Youth Found., 1968-70, Expt. in Internat. Living, 1970, Inst. Human Creativity, 1983—, Fund for Am.'s Libraries, 1996-99; vice chmn. bd. dirs. Annenberg Ctr. for Health Scis., 1991—, vice chmn., 1996-99; trustee Eisenhower Med. Ctr., Rancho Mirage, Calif., 1989—, exec. com. mem., 1996—, chmn. investment com., 2000-03; trustee Am. Coun. Tchrs. Russian, 1992-96; bd. dirs. Nat. Security Edn. Act, Washington, 1993-94; lord of manor, Kirkbride, Eng., 1989—. Recipient Human Rels. award Am. Jewish Com., 1971, Paul Simon award Ctrl. States Conf. on Tchg. Fgn. Langs., 1992. Mem. Standard Club (Chgo.), Club Internat. (Chgo.), Northmoor Country Club (Highland Park, Ill.), Tamarisk Country Club (Rancho Mirage). Home and Office: Next Chpt Holdings Port Clinton Sq 600 Central Ave Highland Park IL 60035-3211 Home (Winter): 70843 Tamarisk La Rancho Mirage CA 92270 Office Phone: 847-432-8700. E-mail: bpattis@nextchapterholdings.com.

PATTON, ALTON DEWITT, electrical engineering consultant; b. Corpus Christi, Tex., Feb. 1, 1935; s. Alton G. and Civilia Louise (Taylor) P.; m. Nancy Jo Elder, Mar. 1, 1959; children: Elizabeth, Carolyn. BEE, U. Tex., 1957; MEE, U. Pitts., 1961; PhD in Elec. Engring., Tex. A&M U., 1972. Registered profl. engr., Tex.; diplomate Am. Bd. of Forensic Engring. and Tech. Engr. Westinghouse Electric Corp., Pitts., 1957-65; prof. elec. engring. dept. Tex. A&M U., College Station, 1965-79, 82-2000, head elec. engring. dept., 1992-96, Brockett prof., 1986, Dresser prof., 1987, dir. Electric Power Inst., 1976-79, 85-92; rsch. fellow Tex. Engring. Expt. Sta., College Station, 1985, dir. Ctr. for Space Power, 1987-92; pres. Associated Power Analysts Inc., College Station, 1973—. Mem. panel for assessment of NIST Elec. and Electronics Engring. Lab., 1995-2000, NRS. Contbr. articles to elec. engring. jours., 1960—. V.p. Emerald Forest Home Owners Assn. Fellow IEEE (life, tech. com., aerospace policy com., prize paper award 1975, 94, Richard Harold Kaufmann award 2000); mem. NSPE. Republican. Presbyterian. Avocations: fishing, hunting, photography, stamp and coin collecting. Home: 8411 Spring Crk College Station TX 77845-4608 Office: Associated Power Analysts Inc 303 Anderson St College Station TX 77840-3114 Office Phone: 979-696-0010. Business E-Mail: adpatton@tca.net. E-mail: adewittpatton@msn.com.

PATTON, ANTWAN ANDRE (BIG BOI), vocalist; b. Savannah, Ga., Feb. 1, 1975; 1 child, Jordan Alexus. Performer Outkast, 1992—. Singer: (albums) Southernplayalisticadillacmuzik, 1994, ATLiens, 1996, Aquemini, 1998, Stankonia, 2000 (Grammy awards: Best Rap Album, 2001, Best Rap Performance By A Duo Or Group for song "Ms Jackson", 2001), Big Boi and Dre Present...Outkast, 2001 (Grammy award: (with Killer Mike) Best Rap Performance By A Duo Or Group for song "The Whole World", 2002), Speakerboxxx/The Love Below, 2003 (Grammy awards: Album Of The Yr., 2003, Best Urban/Alternative Performance for song "Hey Ya!", 2003, Best Rap Album, 2003). Office: La Face 3350 Peachtree Rd Atlanta GA 30326*

PATTON, BRUCE M. law educator, management consultant; b. Terre Haute, Ind., Oct. 14, 1956; s. William Eugene and Carol Ann P.; m. Diana McLain Smith, Oct. 21, 1994. AB, Harvard U., 1977, JD, 1984. Bar: Mass. Co-founder, assoc. dir. Harvard Negotiation Project, Cambridge, Mass., 1979-84, dep. dir., 1984—; co-founder, assoc. dir. Program on Negotiation at Harvard Law Sch., Cambridge, Mass., 1983—2002; co-founder, ptnr. Vantage Partners, LLC, Cambridge, 1997—. Co-founder, prin. Conflict Mgmt. Inc., Cambridge, 1984—; co-founder, dir. Conflict Mgmt. Group, Cambridge, 1984-2000; Thaddeus R. Beal lectr. Harvard Law Sch., Cambridge, 1985-99. Co-author: The Mainstream of Alegbra and Trigonometry, 2d edit., 1980, Getting To Yes, 2d edit., 1991, Difficult Conversations, 1999; contbr. articles to profl. jours. Fellow: Coll. of Trial Mediators (hon.). Avocations: squash, hiking, tennis. Office: Harvard Negotiation Project Pound Hall 524 Harvard Law Sch Cambridge MA 02138 also: Vantage Ptnrs Brighton Landing W Ste 350 10 Guest St Boston MA 02135 E-mail: bpatton@post.harvard.edu.

PATTON, CARL ELLIOTT, physics educator; b. San Antonio, Sept. 14, 1941; s. Carl Elliott and Geraldine Barnett (Perry) Patton. BS, MIT, 1963; MS, Calif. Inst. Tech., 1964, PhD, 1967. Sr. scientist Raytheon Co., Waltham, Mass., 1967-71; assoc. prof. physics Colo. State U., Ft. Collins, 1971-75, prof., 1975—. IEEE Magnetics Soc. Disting. lectr., 1993, sec.-treas. 2003-04. Editor-in-chief IEEE Transactions on Magnetics, 1987-91. Recipient Lifetime Achievement award, Magnetics Soc., 2003. Fellow IEEE (Third Millenium medal 2000), Am. Phys. Soc. (chair topical group on magnetism and its applications 1998-99). Office: Colo State Univ Dept Physics Fort Collins CO 80523-0001

PATTON, CARL VERNON, academic administrator, educator; b. Coral Gables, Fla., Oct. 22, 1944; s. Carl V. and Helen Eleanor (Benkert) Patton; m. Gretchen West, July 29, 1967. BS in Cmty. Planning, U. Cin., 1967; MS in Urban Planning, U. Ill.-Urbana, 1969, MS in Pub. Adminstrn., 1970; MS in Pub. Policy, U. Calif.-Berkeley, 1975, PhD in Pub. Policy, 1976. From instr. to prof. U. Ill., 1968—83, dir. Bur. of Urban and Regional Planning Rsch., 1977—79, prof., chmn. dept., 1979—83; prof., dean Sch. Architecture and Urban Planning U. Wis., Milw., 1983—89; v.p. acad. affairs, prof. polit. sci., geography and urban planning U. Toledo, 1989—92; pres. Ga. State U., Atlanta, 1992—. Author: Academia in Transition, 1979; co-author: The Metropolitan Midwest, 1985; co-author: (with David Sawicki) Basic Methods of Policy Analysis and Planning, 1986, rev. 2d edit., 1993 Chinese translations, 2001, 2002; co-author: (with Kathleen Reed) Guide to Graduate Education in Urban and Regional Planning, 1986, 1988; editor: Spontaneous Shelter: International Perspectives and Prospects, 1988; co-editor (with G. William Page): Quick Answers to Quantitative Problems: A Pocket Primer, 1991; assoc. editor: Jour. of Planning Edn. and Rsch., 1983—87, editl. bd.: Habitat International, 1993—99, Intertrade and Investment (formerly Atlanta Internat. Mag.), 1993—2000; contbr. articles to profl. jours. Chmn. Cmty. Devel. Commn., Urbana, 1978—82; mem. Civic Design Ctr., Milw., 1983—87, City of Milw. Art Commn., 1988—89, Toledo Vision, 1989—92, City of Toledo Bd. Cmty. Rels., 1990—92; chair Centennial Olympic Park Area Inc., 1998—2000, Ctrl. Atlanta Progress, 2000—03; mem. Ga. Rsch. Alliance, Atlanta Convention and Vis. Bur., Woodruff Art Ctr., Fox Theatre; chair Grady (Hosp.) Healthcare, Inc., 1998—2000, Atlanta Reg. Consortium for Higher Edn., 1998—; mem. Ga. Coun. on Econ. Edn., Atlanta Neighborhood Devel. Partnership, U.S. Disabled Athletes Fund Bd.; fellow U. Ill. Ctr. for Advanced Studies, 1973—74; bd. dirs. chair The Atlanta Downtown Partnership, 1997—2000. Fellow, NIMH, 1973—75. Fellow: Am. Inst. Cert. Planners; mem.: Met. Atlanta C. of C., Assn. Collegiate Schs. of Planning (v.p. 1985—87, pres. 1989—91), Am. Planning Assn. Avocation: racquetball, photography, travel. Home: 250 Park Ave West NW # 908 Atlanta GA 30313 Office: Ga State U PO Box 3999 Atlanta GA 30302-3999 Office Phone: 404-651-2560.

PATTON, DENNIS DAVID, radiologist, educator; b. Oakland, Calif., Aug. 4, 1930; s. Owen and Norma Rose (Barnes) P.; m. Pamela Ruth Patton, Feb. 14, 1965 (div. Jan. 1992); children: James Patrick, William Christopher. Cert., Heidelberg (Germany) U., 1951; AB in Physics, U. Calif., Berkeley, 1953; MD, UCLA, 1959. Diplomate Am. Bd. Radiology, Am. Bd. Nuc. Medicine. Mgr. biomed. group Planning Rsch. Corp., L.A., 1959-68; asst. prof. radiology U. Calif., Irvine, 1968-70; prof. radiology Vanderbilt U., Nashville, 1970-75, U. Ariz., Tucson, 1975—2000, prof. emeritus, 2000—. Author: (slide set) History of Nuclear Medicine, 1980; translator: Hist. of Nuclear Med. in Europe, 2002; co-author: Imaging for Medicine, 1980, Public Exposure from Nuclear Medicine Procedures, 1996; composer: Elegy for Orchestra, 1999.

Recipient Top Man award City of Santa Monica, Calif., 1961, U.S. Sr. Scientist award Alexander von Humboldt Found., Germany, 1985; disting. fellow Am. Coll. Nuc. Medicine, 1975. Fellow Am. Coll. Nuc. Physicians (del.), Am. Coll. Radiology; mem. Soc. Nuc. Medicine (historian), Am. Bd. Radiology (examiner, Disting. Svc. award 2000), Am. Bd. Nuc. Medicine (life), Alexander von Humboldt Assn. of Am. (bd. dirs., treas.), Med. Soc. of U.S. and Mex., European Assn. Nuc. Medicine. Republican. Methodist. Avocations: history of medicine, composing, travel, languages, stamp collecting/philately. Office: 6133 Ascot Dr Oakland CA 94611 Office Phone: 415-771-5700. Personal E-mail: dpatton50@hotmail.com.

PATTON, DIANA LEE WILKOC, artist, educator; b. New Rochelle, N.Y., June 28, 1940; d. August E. and Meta Diane (Neuburg) Wilkoc; m. Gardner C. Patton, Aug. 10, 1963; children: Michael, Talryn, Shawn. AB cum laude, Brown U., 1962; postgrad., Pan-Am. Art Inst., 1962-63. Svc. mgr. Lord and Taylor, N.Y.C., 1962-63; tchr. adult edn., Mountain Lakes, N.J., 1972-74, Somerville, N.J., 1978-82, Jointure for Cmty. Adult Edn., 1982—. Artist in watercolors, pen and ink and acrylics; creator jewelry; card designer. One-woman and group shows N.E. U.S., Perth, Australia, 1977, spl. bicentennial exhibit, Trenton, N.J., 1976, Rutgers U., 1980, Brookdale Coll., 1982, Camden County Coll., 9186, Moris County Coll., 1988, Bergen Mus. Arts and Scis., 1987, 88, 90, 91, Princeton Med. Ctr., 1993, 94, 96, Madison Gallery--Morristown Hosp., 2001, 03, Salmagundi Club, N.Y.C., 2002; one-woman show SAA Pluckemin Galleries, 1998; represented in pvt. and pub. collections in U.S., Australia, N.Z., Germany, Luxembourg, Japan, Eng.; designer ofcl. poster N.J. Festival Ballooning, 1990, Arc Challenge Races, 1993, 94; instr. in field; developer art appreciation courses for children and adults; toymaker, 1973-76. Winner bronz medal in watercolor Nat. Mystic (Conn.) Outdoor Art Festival, 1977, Mayor's purchase prize Franklin Twp., 1976, Tri-State Watercolor award Somerset County Coll., 1978, Best in Show award Raritan Valley Art Assn., 1978, 94, award Garden State Watercolor Soc., 1979, 84, 85, 1st, 2d and Best in Show award Somerset and Westfield Art Assns. shows, 1st place for profl. watercolor Plainfield Tri-State Arts Festival, 1983, 85, 87, 96, 2001, N.E. Art Festival, Caldwell Coll., 1990, 95, Tewksbury award, 1990, 2d place in watercolor Internat. Miniature Art Show, Washington, 1983, Best in Show and Grumbacher award Caldwell State show, 1984, 1st place Carrier Clinic Tri-State, 1984, Grumbacher bronze award, 1984, Grumbacher silver award, 1985, 88, 94, watercolor award Artists League Ctrl. N.J. Show, Cornelious Lowe Mus., 1986, Winsor-Newton award Am. Artists Proleague, 1987, Robert Simmons award, 1989, Basking Ridge Environ. Ctr. award, 1994, Best in Show award N.J. State Juried, Piscataway, 1988, 2d place N.J. Miniature Art Soc., 1989, 1st Pro award Raritan Valley, 1992, 93, 1st mixed media award Basking Ridge Environ. Ctr., 1994, award Essex Watercolor Club, 1999, Grumbacher Gold award Essex Watercolor Club, 2000, 1st Pro award Bridgewater Arts, 2001, 03; artist-in-residence grantee Middlesex Librs., 1983-92, watercolor demonstrator, 1983—; TV appearances State of Arts-N.J., 1986, Midday (spl. art shows), 1986, TKR, 1995; Elisha Benjamin scholar Brown U., 1960. Mem. Garden State Watercolor Soc. (writer, editor 1994—), Miniature Art Soc., Washington, N.J. Watercolor Soc., AAUW (life, various offices 1963-73), Art Assn. Raritan Valley (pres. 1980-82, writer, editor newsletter 1993—), Art Assn. Somerset, Art Assn. North Haven (Maine), Essex Watercolor Club, Am. Artists Profl. League, Bee Sharps Square Dance Club. Presbyterian. Home: 497 Stony Brook Dr Bridgewater NJ 08807-1945 Office Phone: 907-722-3355. E-mail: diana@dianapatton.com.

PATTON, FRANCES ANNE, lawyer; b. Jan. 14, 1917; d. Peter Mathew and Frances Helen (Lovrenic) Basar; m. Earl Richard Patton, Apr. 20, 1945 (div. Oct. 1963); 1 child, John Michael. LLB, Columbus U. (now Cath. U. Am.), 1940, LLM, 1941. Bar: D.C. 1940, U.S. Dist. Ct. D.C. 1940, U.S. Ct. Appeals (D.C. cir.) 1940, U.S. Supreme Ct. 1944. With U.S. Dept. Interior, Washington, 1938—95; spl. asst. to dir. Office Hearings and Appeals, Arlington, Va., 1970—82, spl. counsel to dir., 1982—95; pvt. practice DC, 1996—. Recipient Superior Performance award, Dept. Interior, 1966, Meritorious Performance award, 1968, Spl. Achievement award, 1980. Roman Catholic. Home: 3725 Macomb St NW Apt 112 Washington DC 20016-3841

PATTON, GREGORY KENNETH, management educator; b. Sheridan, Wyo., Dec. 20, 1960; s. Philip Kenneth and Martha Jane Patton; m. Amy E. Wenzel, July 30, 2000; children: Christopher Kenneth, Gentina Leigh. BA, Northwestern Coll., Orange City, Iowa, 1984; MBA, U. S.D., Vermillion, 1993; PhD, U. Iowa, Iowa City, 2002. Rsch. asst. bus. rsch. bur. U. S.D., Vermillion, 1992—93; instr. economics Buena Vista Coll., Storm Lake, Iowa, 1993—95; grad. tchg./rsch. assitant U. Iowa, Iowa City, 1995—2000; asst. prof. of mgmt. U. N.D., Grand Forks, 2000—. Retail store mgmt. Duckwall-ALCO Stores, Inc., Abilene, Kans., 1984—92; adj. instr. Northwestern Coll., Orange City, Iowa, 1993—95, Western Iowa Tech. CC, Sioux City, Iowa, 1994—95. Contbr. articles to profl. jours. Mem. Chamber of Commerce, Alliance, Nebr., 1988—92; second v.p. Kiwanis, Alliance, Nebr., 1989—92; com. mem. parish health ministries Bethel Luth. Ch., Grand Forks, ND, 2004. Recipient Superior Instrn. and Noteworthy Devotion to the Advancement of Students, Quo Vadis Chpt. of Mortar Bd., 2003, Vol. of Yr., The YMCA of Alliance, Nebr., 1992; Rsch. Grant, Small Bus. Devel. Ctr. N.D., 2003. Mem.: APA, Soc. for Indsl. and Orgnl. Psychology, Acad. of Mgmt. (assoc. Scholarly Achievement award (Human Resources divsn.) 2002), Beta Gamma Sigma. Avocations: running, architecture. Office: Univ ND Box 8377 Grand Forks ND 58202 E-mail: gregory_patton@und.nodak.edu.

PATTON, JACK THOMAS, family practice physician; b. Rogers, Ark., Feb. 18, 1941; s. Jack Marcus and Jewell Selah (Pense) P.; m. Lynette Anne Carr, Sept. 2, 1960; children: Robert, John, Mark, Christopher. BA in History, Calif. State U., Long Beach, 1963; MD in Medicine, U. So. Calif., L.A., 1967; MA in Bib. Studies, Mennonite Brethren Bib. Sem., Fresno, Calif., 1980; MA in History, Calif. State U., Fresno, 1993. Cert. Bd. Med. Examiners, Calif., Hawaii. Intern Tripler Army Med. Ctr., Honolulu, 1967-68; resident in gen. practice Walson Army Hosp., Ft. Dix, N.J., 1968-70; med. supt. Nazarene Hosp., Papua New Guinea, 1973-80; chmn. family practice dept. Sharp Rees-Stealy, San Diego, 1981-86; chmn. occupational medicine Kaiser Permanente, Fresno, 1986-87; assoc. med. dir. Sharp Rees-Stealy, San Diego, 1987-92; med. dir. Summer Inst. Linguistics, Papua New Guinea, 1993-94; with family practice dept. Sharp Rees-Stealy Med. Group, San Diego, 1994-97, Northwest Med. Group, Fresno, Calif., 1997—; chmn. dept. family practice St. Agnes Med. Ctr., 2002—. Family practice residency liaison Tripler Army Med. Ctr., Honolulu, 1972-73; chief medicine, dep. commr. Schofield Army Med. Clinics, Wahiawa, Hawaii, 1970-72; lectr. Calif. State U., Fresno, 1978-79, Pt. Loma Nazarene Coll., 1982-85, San Jose Christian Coll., 1997—. Mem. med. sch. support Salerni Collegium, U. So. Calif. Sch. Medicine, 1967-85; lectr. Ch.-Mission Inst., Mennonite Brethren Bib. Sem., 1984-92; sec. S.E. Asian task force Mennonite Brethren Ch. Fresno, 1990-93. Maj. U.S. Army, 1966-73. Mackenzie scholar U. So. Calif. Sch. Medicine, 1966-67; decorated Meritorious Svc. medal. Fellow Am. Acad. Family Physicians; mem. Am. Bd. Family Practice (diplomate), Calif. Acad. Family Physicians, Royal Soc. Medicine (assoc., London). Avocations: history, travel, hiking. Home: 1566 S Adler Ave Fresno CA 93727-5101 Office: 4770 W Herndon Ave Fresno CA 93722-8401 Office Phone: 559-271-6308.

PATTON, JAMES RICHARD, JR., lawyer; b. Durham, N.C., Oct. 27, 1928; s. James Ralph and Bertha (Moye) P.; m. Mary Margot Maughan, Dec. 29, 1950; children: James Macon, Lindsay Fairfield. AB cum laude, U. N.C., 1948; postgrad., Yale U., 1948; JD, Harvard U., 1951. Bar: D.C. bar 1951, U.S. Supreme Ct. 1963. Attache of Embassy; spl. asst. to Am. ambassador to, Indochina, 1952-54; with Office Nat. Estimates, Washington, 1954-55; atty. Covington & Burling, Washington, 1956-61; founding ptnr., chmn. exec. com. Patton Boggs, LLP, Washington, 1962—. Lectr. internat. law Cornell Law Sch., 1963-64, U.S. Army Command and Gen. Staff Coll., 1967-68; Mem. Nat. Security Forum, U.S. Air War Coll., 1965, Nat. Strategy Seminar, U.S. Army War Coll., 1967-70, Global Strategy Discussions, U.S. Naval War Coll., 1968, Def. Orientation Conf., 1972; mem. Com. of 100 on Fed. City, Washington; mem. adv. council on nat. security and internat. affairs Nat. Republican Com., 1977-81; bd. dirs. Security Nat. Bank (Wash.), Signet, N.A., Madeira Sch., Greenway, Va., 1975-81, Lawyers Com. for Civil Rights Under Law, Washington, Legal Aid Soc. Washington; mem. Industry Policy Adv. Com. for Trade Policy Matters, 1984-87; mem. visiting com. Ackland Art Mus. U. N.C., 1987—, Nat. Coun. Anderson Ranch Arts Ctr., 1987—. Adv. coun. mem. Johns Hopkins U. Sch. Advanced Internat. Studies, 1989-92; nat. bd. dirs. Aspen Mus., 1987-90; nat. coun. mem. Whitney Mus., 1992—; bd. dirs., exec. com. Nat. Mus. Natural History, Smithsonian, 1992—; bd. dirs. Smithsonian Nat. Bd., 1999—; trustee Aspen Music Festival and Sch., 1993—. Fellow U.N.C. Wilson Library, 1996—. Mem. ABA (past com. chmn.), Inter-Am. Bar Assn. (past del.), Internat. Law Assn. (past com. chmn.), Am. Soc. Internat. Law (treas., exec. coun.), Washington Inst. Fgn. Affairs, Nat. Gallery (collectors com. 1988-91), Gerrard Soc., Met. Club (Washington), Phi Beta Kappa, Alpha Epsilon Delta.

PATTON, JOSEPH DONALD, JR., management consultant; b. Washington, Pa., Jan. 4, 1938; s. Joseph Donald and Priscilla Ann (Johnson) P.; m. Susan Oertel, June 3, 1967; children: Jennifer Ann, Joseph Donald III. BS in Phys. Scis. and Math. Edn., Pa. State U., 1959; MBA in Mktg., U. Rochester, N.Y., 1970. Registered profl. quality engr., Calif.; cert. profl. logistician; cert. quality engr.; cert. reliability engr. Tchr. Aschaffebburg (W.Germany) Am. Sch., 1963-64; with Xerox Corp., Rochester, 1964-75, mgr. field engring., 1975-93; CEO Patton Cons., Inc., Rochester, N.Y., 1993—, Hilton Head, SC, 1993—. Chmn., Mgmt. Metrics Svcs., Inc., 1996-2001; mem. adj. faculty Rochester Inst. Tech., SUNY, Geneseo. Author 8 textbooks; contbr. over 200 articles to profl. jours. Capt. U.S. Army, 1959-63. Recipient Leadership and Svc. award Pa. State U. Coll. Edn., 1999. Fellow Am. Soc. Quality Control (reliability and maintainablity tech. award 1982), Soc. Logistics Engrs. (Sole Armitage medal 1980, 82, 97); mem. Instrument Soc. Am. (sr.), Assn. Field Svc. Mgrs. (publs. award 1981), Nat. Assn. Svc. Mgrs. (life cert. svc. exec.). Republican. Presbyterian (elder). Office: Patton Consultants Inc 36 Blue Heron Pt Hilton Head Island SC 29926-1209 Office Phone: 843-689-6650. Personal E-mail: JDPatton@aol.com.

PATTON, JUNE ODESSA, writer, consultant, educator, researcher; d. Joe Edward Patton and Nancy Odessa Britt. BA, MA, Roosevelt U., Chgo.; PhD, postgrad., U. Chgo. Tchg. asst. U. Ill., Chgo.; rsch. assoc. U. Chgo.; vis. prof. Governors State U., University Park, Ill.; instr. Roosevelt U., Chgo.; instr. Lab. H.S. U. Chgo., testing asst., rsch. assoc.; program officer Nat. Endowment for Humanities, Washington; prof. Governors State U., University Park, Ill. Midwestern regional dir. Assn. Black Women Historians, Washington, acting-nat. membership chairperson; cons. Harcourt Brace Jovanovich, Inc., N.Y.C.; cons. Africans in Am. WGBH, Boston; cons. Chgo. Dodo chpt. Tuskegee Airmen, Chgo.; cons. North Ctrl. Assn. of Colls. and Schs., Commn. on Higher Edn., Chgo.; program chair 75th ann. meeting Assn. for Study of African Am. Life and History, Washington; treas. and nat. membership chair Assn. of Black Women Historians, Washington; adv. reviewer Jour. African Am. History, Washington, mem. editl. bd.; exec. coun. Assn. for Study of African Am. Life and History, Washington; treas. Women's Edn. Network, Chgo.; cons. Chgo.'s west side project Ill. Humanities Coun. Contbr. biographical American National Biography, biographical Encyclopedia of African-American Educators, biographical Black Women in the United States: An Historical Encyclopedia, educational Harcourt Brace Jovanovich Resource Guide for Multicultural Classroom; author: (book review) History of Education Quarterly; contbr. book The Closing Door: Conservative Policy and Black Opportunity; author: (documentary essay) The Journal of Negro History; contbr. articles to profl. jours. Charles Hubbard Judd centennial planning com. U. Chgo., 1975—78; rschr. and edl. US-Africa Partnership for Bldg. Stronger Communities, Albany, NY, 1999—2003; com. mem., Katherine Dunham golden anniversary tribute festival Inst. for Intercultural Comm., Chgo.; bd. dirs. Catalyst for Youth, Chgo., 1973—78; cons. and spkr. Chgo. Humanities Festival, 1999—2002, DuSable Mus., Chgo., 1987—2002, Harold Wash. Libr. Reading Group, Chgo., 1999—2002; cons. and judge Chgo. Metro History Fair, Chicago, Ill., 1982—91; cons. and spkr. Ill. Humanities Coun., Chgo., 1984—91; bd. dirs. African Am. Geneal. Soc. of Chgo., 1979—89; bd. dirs., George E. Kent Meml. and Scholarship Fund U. Chgo., 1982—87; com. mem. Women's Com. for 1992 Chgo. World's Fair, 1990—91; planning com., Ill. and Chgo. Salute to Katherine Dunhamgo State of Ill. and City of Chgo., 1982—83; planning com. City of Chgo.'s women's history week City of Chgo., 1982—83; advisor Chgo. Film Symposium, 1975—78. Recipient Achievement award, NAACP, 1980, Chairman's Cert. of Appreciation, Nat. Endowment for Humanities, 1993, Faculty Excellence award, Govs. State U., 1997 and 2000, Students Cert. of Appreciation, 1997 and 1998; scholarship, State of Ill., 1965-1967, Roosevelt U. Grad. Grant-in-Aid, Roosevelt U., 1967-1968, PhD assistantship, U. Ill., 1968-69; 1969-70 (unable to accept), Ednl. fellowship, U. Chgo., 1970-71, Contingency grant, 1972, Ford Found. fellowship, The Ford Found., 1972, Nat. Dissertation Yr. Fellow, Ford Found., 1974-75; 1975-1976, Carter G. Woodson Disting. Scholar-In-Residence, Assn. for Study of African Am. Life and History, 1991—94, Adminstrv. fellowship, State of Ill., 1991-1992 (unable to accept), Profl. Devel. grant, Govs. State U. Alumni Assn., 2001. Mem.: So. Hist. Assn. (life), Orgn. of Am. Historians (life), Assn. of Black Women Historians (life; treas. and nat. membership chair 1993—95), Assn. for Study of African Am. Life and History (life; exec. coun. 1993—2000). Avocations: tennis, white water rafting, bicycling, travel, golf. Office: Govs State Univ 1 University Pky University Park IL 60466-3165 E-mail: j-patton@govst.edu.

PATTON, LAURIE LOUISE, religious studies educator, writer; b. Boston, Mass., Nov. 14, 1961; d. Anthony Seavey and Christine Card Patton. BA, Harvard U, Cambridge, Mass, 1983; MA, U of Chgo., Chgo., Ill, 1985, PhD, 1991. Asst. prof. Bard Coll., Annandale, 1991—96, Emory U., Atlanta, 1996—98, assoc. prof., 1998—2003, full prof., 2003, chair dept. religion, 1999—, Winship Disting. Rsch. prof., 2003—. ACLS, fellowship selection com. Am Coun. of Learned Societies, New York, NY, 2000—02; academic adv. bd. Carlos Mus., Atlanta, 2000—; mem. exec. bd. Am. Soc. Study of Religion, 2001—; academic task force Am. Acad. Religion, Atlanta, 2003—. Editor: Authority, Anxiety Canon; Myth & Method; Jewels of Authority; Notes from a Mandala; author: Myth as argument (DeGruyter Press), 1996, Bringing the Gods to Mind, 2003, Fires Goal: Poems from a Hindu Year; translator: The Bhagavad Gita, 2004. Exec. bd. Atlanta Interfaith Alliance, Atlanta, 2001—; edn. com. Ahavath Achim Synagogue, Atlanta, 2002—. Grantee rsch., Am. Inst. of Indian Studies/Pure, India, 1992, Nat. Endowment for the Humanities/Pure, India, 1995, Fulbright, Jerusalem, 1999, Fulbright, India, 2003—. Fellow: Am. Coun. Learned Socs., Gustafson Seminar (dir. 1999—2002); mem.: South Asia/Am. Acad. Religion (secretary 1998—2001), Humanities Coun. (chair 2000—03). Democrat. Judaism. Avocations: embroidery, photography. Home: 366 Southerland Terr Atlanta GA 30307 Office: Emory Univ Dept of Religion 537 Kilgo Circle Atlanta GA 30322-0001

PATTON, MARY KNOX, mathematician, educator; b. Minneapolis, Minn., Jan. 11, 1943; d. Raymond I and Mary Elizabeth Swartout; m. James William Patton, June 19, 1965; 1 child, Charles Christopher. BA, Ind. U., 1965; MA, Sangamon State U., 1978. Math instr. Springfield H.S., Ill., 1966—69; math instr. and dept. head Griffin H.S., Springfield, Ill., 1978—85; part-time math instr. Lincoln Land C.C., Springfield, 1978—85; math instr. U. of Ill. at Springfield (previously Sangamon State U.), 1985—. Mem. Ill. Articulation Com., Springfield, Ill., 2001—; initiated and organized Expanding Your Horizons in Math and Sci., Springfield, 1986—93; grantee Sci. Literacy, Charleston, Ill., 1992—93. Reviewer (textbook) Discrete Mathematics, Using and Understanding Mathematics, (computerized math program) Interactive math. Find drivers for Meals on Wheels Red Cross, Springfield, Ill., 1995—2003, driver for Meals on Wheels, 1995—2004; elder First Presbyn. Ch., Springfield, Ill., 1999—2004. Recipient Creative Excellence, Nat. U. Continuing Edn. Orgn., 1991; grantee grant, U of Ill., 1995—99. Mem.: Math. Assn. of Am., Nat. Coun. of Teachers of Math., Ill. Coun. of Teachers of Math. Presbyterian. Avocations: camping, history, exercise, gardening. Office: U Ill at Springfield One University Plaza Springfield IL 62703-5407 Office Phone: 217-206-7451. Business E-Mail: patton.mary@uis.edu.

PATTON, NICKI, former political organization executive; BA, MA, U. Ky. Childcare cons.; campaign worker Ky. Dem. Party, 1996-98, exec. dir., 1998-99, chmn., 2000—02. Chair Early Childhood Task Force, Govt. of Ky., 1999—. Office: Early Childhood Task Force 700 Capital Ave Ste 100 Frankfort KY 40601

PATTON, PAUL E. former governor; b. Fallsburg, Ky., May 26, 1937; m. Judi Patton; 4 children. BS in mech. engring., U. Ky., 1959. Dep. sec. transp. State of Ky., 1979; judge-exec. Pike County, 1981; lt. gov., sec. econ. devel., pres. senate State of Ky., Frankfort, 1991-95, gov., 1995—2003. Served on Ky. Crime Commn., Ky. Tourism Commn., Task Force for Workplace Literacy; former mem. Prichard Com. for Acad. Excellence; chmn. Econ. Devel. and Commerce Com.; co-chair Task Force on Transp., Nat. Gov's. Assn.; chmn. Edn. Commn. of the States; former chmn. Southern Regional Edn. Bd., Southern Growth Policies Bd.; former exec. com. mem. Southern Gov's. Assn.; former chmn. Southern Tech. Coun.; mem. Appalachian Regional Commn., Southern States Energy Bd. Mem. bd. overseers Bellarmine Coll., bd. trustees Pikeville Coll.; chmn. Ky. Dems., 1981-83; del. Dem. Nat. Conv.; served numerous terms Pike County Dem. Exec. Com. Democrat.

PATTON, RAY BAKER, financial consultant, real estate broker; b. Jan. 24, 1932; s. Dwight Lyman Moody and Opal (Hembre) P.; m. Gloria Ruth Chambers, June 6, 1954; children: David Baker, Dayna Erin. BA, U. Okla., 1955, MRCP, 1960, MAPA, 1969. Asst. dir. planning San Joaquin, Calif., 1959-61; dir. planning City of Norman, Okla., 1961-65, Oklahoma City, 1965-67, St. Louis County, Mo., 1967-71; pres. Creative Environs., Inc., Clayton, Mo., 1972-74; prin. Raymond B. Patton & Assocs., Ballwin, Mo., 1975-81; investment broker, ins. planner A.G. Edwards & Sons, Inc., Clayton, 1981-83; fin. planning coord., dir. seminars E.F. Hutton & Co., Inc., St. Louis, 1983-84; securities prin. Westport Fin. Group, Inc., St. Louis, 1984-86; securities products coord., agy. edn. coord., fin. planner Equitable Fin. Cos., St. Louis, 1986-91; bus. and fin. cons. Mo. Automotive Svc. Assn., St. Louis, 1991-93; broker, sales assoc. Coldwell Banker Real Estate, Chesterfield, Mo., 1994-95. Pres. Patton Real Estate, Inc., 1975-81, Success Power, Inc., St. Louis, 1975-81, chmn. bd., CEO, 1989-93; dir. pub. works and planning, health commr., zoning enforcement officer City of Des Peres, Mo., 1977-79; zone mgr. Investors Diversified Svc.'s, Chesterfield, 1980-81; securities prin. The Patton Fin. Group, Inc., St. Louis, 1984-86; chmn. bd., CEO Body Works, St. Louis, 1989-93; faculty mem. Nat. Inst. Farm and land Brokers, 1971-76; motivational spkr.; cons. in field. Contbr. articles to profl. jours. Scoutmaster St. Louis Area coun. Boy Scouts Am., 1976-80, vice chmn. adult tng., 1977-83; mem. Christian Bus. Men's Com., Chesterfield; mem. adv. bd. Cleveland County (Okla.) Child Welfare, 1963-64; min. music Ballwin, 1978-83, choir cir. E. Free Ch., Ladue, Mo., 1986; vol. tutor OASIS, 1994-96, vol., 1997-99; former choir dir. E. Free, Manchester, Md.; tutor O.A.S.I.S. Parkway, S.D., 1993-96; instr., area coord. Crown Mins., 1989-94. Served with USMC, 1955-58. Named Outstanding Mcpl. Employee State of Okla., 1963, Woodbage staff Outstanding Adult Scout Leader Pioneer Dist. Boy Scouts Am., 1978, 79; recipient IDS Mercury award, 1980, A.G. Edwards & Sons Crest award, 1982, Outstanding Exec. award E.F. Hutton, 1983, Blue Chip award, 1983, designated fin. advisor award, 1984. Mem. Am. Inst. Cert. Planners, Am. Inst. Planners (pres.-elect Mo., Kans., Okla. chpt. 1957, co-founder St. Louis Metro sect. 1969), Inst. Cert. Fin. Planners, Internat. Platform Assn., Internat. Assn. Fin. Planners, Eagle Scout Assn. (life), Fellowship Christian Fin. Advisors, Crown Ministries (instr. 1991-94), Lambda Chi Alpha (pres. 1953-54). also: 2612 87th Ter E Palmetto FL 34221-8374 Home: 2612 87th Ter E Palmetto FL 34221-8374

PATTON, RICHARD WESTON, retired mortgage company executive; b. Evanston, Ill., Sept. 26, 1931; s. Robert Ferry and Sue Buckley P.; m. Lynda A. Kruse, Feb. 2, 1971; 1 child, Robert Weston BA, Amherst Coll., 1954. Sales engr. Thermo Fax Sales Corp., Chgo., 1958-60; account exec. Nat. Mortgage Investors, Inc., Chgo., 1960-61, sales mgr. Pasadena, Calif., 1962-66, asst. v.p., 1966-67, v.p., 1967-69, exec. v.p., 1969-73, pres., chief exec. officer, dir., 1973-84, vice-chmn. bd., 1984-90; pres. Richard W. Patton Enterprises, Pasadena, 1990—. Pres., chmn. exec. com., dir. Ocean Park Restaurant Corp., Santa Monica, Calif., 1977-88; dir. Cenfed Bank, Cenfed Fin. Corp. Bd. dirs. Pasadena Boys' Club, 1963-66, Opera Assocs., 1984-90; mem. steering com. Amherst Coll. Capital Fund Drive, 1963-66. 1st lt. USMCR, 1955-58. Mem. Amherst Coll. Alumni Assn. (bd. dirs. 1963—2001, pres. 1977-79, 86-89), Overland Club (sec., bd. dirs.), Kroenstadt Ski Club (past pres.). Office: Rich W Patton Enterprises 3644 San Pasqual St Pasadena CA 91107-5419

PATTON, SHARON F. museum director; BA, Roosevelt U., 1966; MA, U. Ill., 1969; PhD in Art History, Northwestern U., 1980. Mem. faculty U. Houston, 1976—79, U. Md., 1979—85; dir. art galleries Montclair State Coll., NJ, 1986—87; chief curator Studio Mus., N.Y.C., 1988—91; assoc. prof. art history U. Mich., Ann Arbor, 1991—98, dir. Ctr. for Arfoamerican and African Studies, 1996—98; prof. art Oberlin Coll., 1998—2000; mem. adv. bd. Nat. Mus. African Art, Washington, 2000—, dir., 2003—. Author: Memory and the Metaphor, the Art of Romare Bearden, 1991, African-American Art, 1998 (Choice Outstanding Book of Yr. award); contbr. articles to publs. in field. Mem. Rapid Transit Pub. Art Commn., Cleve., ArtTable, Cleve.; mem. visual arts jury Cleve. Arts Prize, 2000—02; mem. African Am. adv. coun. and Acquisition adv. com. Cleve. Art Mus. Mem.: Assn. Art Mus. Dirs., Am. Assn. Museums. Office: Nat Mus African Art Smithsonian Instn MRC 708 PO Box 37012 Washington DC 20013-7012

PATTON, STEVEN TODD, research physicist; b. Springfield, Ohio, May 29, 1961; s. Loren Edwin and Lola Maxine Patton; m. LaGina Jodi Ferryman, Feb. 10, 1988; 1 child, Travis Ischmael Ray. PhD, Ohio State U., Columbus, Ohio, USA, 1998. Rsch. physicist, tribologist U. Dayton Rsch. Inst., Ohio, 1998—. Contbr. articles to profl. jours. Mem.: Soc. of Tribologists and Lubrication Engrs. (chmn. 2001—02). Achievements include discovery of mechanisms governing friction and wear in sliding contacts. Home: 3314 Eastham St Springfield OH 45503-1708 Office: Univ Dayton Rsch Inst 300 College Pk Dayton OH 45469-0168 Office Phone: 937-255-5791. Business E-Mail: steve.patton@wpafb.af.mil.

PATTON, STUART, biochemist, educator; b. Ebenezer, N.Y., Nov. 2, 1920; s. George and Ina (Neher) P.; m. Colleen Cecelia Lavelle, May 17, 1945; children— John, Richard, Gail, Thomas, Mary Catherine, Patricia, Joseph. BS, Pa. State U., 1943; MS, Ohio State U., 1947, PhD, 1948. Chemist Borden Co., 1943-44; rsch. fellow Ohio State U., Columbus, 1946-48; faculty Pa. State U., University Park, 1949-80, prof., 1959-80, Evan Pugh rsch. prof. agr., 1966-80; adj. prof. neurosis. Sch. Medicine U. Calif., San Diego, 1981—99; ret., 1999. Vis. scientist Scripps Instn. Oceanography; cons. in field. Author: (with Robert Jenness) Principles of Dairy Chemistry, 1959; (with Robert G. Jensen) Biomedical Aspects of Lactation, 1975; Milk: Its Remarkable Contribution to Human Health and Well-Being, 2004. Lt. (j.g.) USNR, 1944-46. Recipient Borden award chemistry milk Am. Chem. Soc., 1957, Agrl. and Food Chemistry award, 1975, Alexander von Humboldt sr. scientist award, 1981, Macy-Gyorgy award Internat. Soc. for Rsch. on Human Milk and Lactation, 1997, Distinguished Alumnus award, Pa. State U., 2002, Distinguished Svc. award Am. Dairy Sci. Assn., 1999, fellow Pa. State Alumni Assn., 2001. Fellow Am. Dairy Sci. Assn.; mem. Am. Chem. Soc., Am. Soc. Biochemistry and Molecular Biology, Am. Soc. Cell Biology. Home and Office: 6208 Avenida Cresta La Jolla CA 92037-6510 E-mail: spatton@ucsd.edu.

PATTON, THOMAS EARL, lawyer; b. Nov. 25, 1940; s. Thomas E. and Alice F. (Rodarmel) P.; m. Patricia Mann, Aug. 12, 1965 (dec.); m. Barbara Wood, Sept. 21, 1974; 1 child, David Earl AB, Cath. U. Am., 1962, JD summa cum laude, 1965. Bar: N.Y. 1966, D.C. 1966, Va. 1982. Assoc. Sullivan & Cromwell, N.Y.C., 1965-69; mem. Williams Connolly & Califano, Washington, 1970-75; asst. gen. counsel U.S. Dept. Energy, Washington, 1977-78; ptnr. Schnader, Harrison, Segal & Lewis, Washington, 1979-94. Disting. lectr. Cath. U. Am., 1970-90, 95—, bd. regents; nat. arbitrator Am. Arbitration Assn.; bd. dirs. Elcotel, Inc., IXI, Inc., Vanguard Found. Author: Securities Litigation, 1989, Federal Procedure Casebook, 1990; contbr. articles to profl. jours.; editor in chief Cath. U. Am. Law Rev. Mem. Washington World Affairs Coun., 1980—. Mem. ABA, D.C. Bar (founder and chair litigation sect.), Cosmos Club. Roman Catholic. Office: Tighe Patton Armstrong Teasdale 1747 Pennsylvania Ave NW Washington DC 20006-4688

PATTON, THOMAS EDWARD, artist, educator; b. Sacramento, Calif., May 17, 1954; s. Edward Clyde and Joan (Dall) P. BFA, San Francisco Art Inst., 1976; MA, U. New Mex., 1977, MFA, 1982. Instr. Millersville (Pa.) State

Coll., 1979, New Mex. Inst. Mining & Tech., Socorro, 1981-82, Skidmore Coll., Saratoga Springs, N.Y., 1982-83; prof. U. Mo., St. Louis, 1983—. Author: (monograph) The Isolation and Intrusion Series, 1979, (catalogue) New Views: Photgaphs from Two Continents, 1985; one-man shows include Blue Sky Gallery, Portland, Oreg., 1982, U. N.Mex. Art Mus, 1982, Brockton (Mass.) Art Mus., 1984, UCLA, 1987, Mitchell Mus., Mt. Vernon, Ill., 1991, Kansas City Art Inst., 1994; exhibited in group shows at San Francisco Mus. Modern Art, 1985, St. Louis Art Mus., 1989, Mus. Photographic Art, San Diego, 1991, Downey Mus. Art, 1992, Wright State U., 1994; represented in public collections at Australia Nat. Gallery, Milw. Art Mus., Okland Mus., Portland Art Mus., Seattle Art Mus., St. Louis Art Mus., San Francisco Mus. Modern Art, U. N.Mex. Recipient Visual Artists fellowship NEA, Washington, 1990-91, James D. Phelan award, 2001-02. Mem. Soc. for Photographic Edn. Office: Calif State U Chico CA 95929 Business E-Mail: tpatton@csuchico.edu.

PATTON, THOMAS JAMES, sales and marketing executive; b. Cleve., Nov. 2, 1948; s. Michael Anthony and Delores (Bammerlin) P.; m. Thomasina Bernadette Cavallaro, Aug. 9, 1969; children: Thomasina, Thera V. A in Transp., Cleve. State U., 1971, BA in Mktg., 1973; BA, SUNY, Empire State, 1994. CLU; ChFC; registered health underwriter; registered employee benefit cons. Ins. salesman Manulife, Cleve., 1972-75, Mass. Mut., Cleve., 1976-80, Patton Ins. Assn., Inc., Avon Lake, Ohio, 1976—; ins. cons. Diversified Benefit Plans, Inc., Avon Lake, 1978-93, dir. sales and mktg., 1993—; pres. commerce Benefits Group, Inc. and Ins. Mktg. Group, Inc., 1995; prin. Cmty. Health Ptnrs., Ltd., Ill., 1994. Pres. Commerce Benefits Group, Inc.; cons. Regional Sch. Consortium, Lorain County, Ohio, 1986—, County of Lorain, 1984—, City of Lorain, 1986—, County of Lorain, 1984—, City of Lorain, 1984—; prin. Comty. Health Ptnrs. Ltd.; bd. Italian Cultural Found.; founder 1-888 Ohiocomp w/c MCO-Ohio, 1997; co-founder VocRehabOne, Ltd., w/c Vocat. Rehab. Co. Pres. Lake Erie Rate Coun., Cleve., 1970-71; mem. Lorain County Dem. Ctrl. Com., Avon Lake, Ohio, 1986—; mem. com. Cleve. Leukemia Soc., 1985; bd. dirs. Villa Serena Sr. Housing, St. Francis Soc., Italian Cultural Found.; bd. trustees Found. Am. Coll., Bryn Mawr, Pa., 2002—. Mem. Nat. Assn. Life Underwriters, Profl. Ins. Agts. Assn., Cert. Profl. Ins. Agts. Soc., Soc. Benefit Plan Adminstrn., Lorain County Life Underwriters, Irish Heritage, Order Italian Sons and Daus., Profl. Assn. Dive Instrs./Nat. Assn. Underwater Instrs. (SCUBA diving instr.). Roman Catholic. Avocations: fishing, skin and scuba diving, photography. Office: Commerce Group PO Box 900 Elyria OH 44036-0900 Office Phone: 440-930-7500. Business E-Mail: tompatton@thecommercegroup.com.

PATTY, ANNA CHRISTINE, retired elementary school educator, tax specialist; b. Atlanta, Aug. 25, 1937; d. Henry Richard and Gertrude Johnson; children: Robert E., C. Wayne Jr., Christine E. BS in Math., U. Ga., 1959; MA in Curriculum and Instrn., Va. Poly. Inst. and State U., 1991. Cert. tchr., Va. Mgr. Steak and Ale Restaurants, Inc., Dallas, 1982-84; bus. mgr. Nova Plaza Corp., Charlotte, N.C., 1984-86; asst. mgr. WoodLo, Inc., Charlotte, 1986-87; food activity mgr. Army and Air Force Exch. Svc., Schweinfurt, Germany, 1987-89; substitute tchr. Montgomery County Schs., Christiansburg, Va., 1989-91; rsch. asst. Va. Poly. Inst. and State U., Blacksburg, 1990-91; mid. sch. tchr. math. and sci. Hampton (Va.) City Schs., 1991-93, mid. sch. tchr. sci., 1993-97, mid. sch. tchr. Advancement Via Individual Determination, 1997-98; tax preparer Christiansburg, Va., 2001—. Mem. NSTA/APST Summer Inst., U.Md., 1992, NSTA Summer Inst., Sci. and Tech., SUNY, Stoney Brook, N.Y., 1995; EXCEL coach Christopher Newport U., 1993-95. With Operation Path Finders, Sandy Hook, N.J., 1994. Mem. NEA, Va. Educators Assn., Nat. Sci. Tchrs. Assn. (summer inst. participant 1992), Va. Middle Sch. Assn., Va. Sci. Tchrs., Nat. Coun. Tchrs. Math. Democrat. Unitarian Universalist. Avocations: hiking, camping, herbs, wine tasting, cooking. Home: 470 Summit Ridge Rd Christiansburg VA 24073-4446 E-mail: annajpatty@hotmail.com.

PATTY, CLAIBOURNE WATKINS, JR., lawyer; b. Cleve., Feb. 19, 1934; s. Claibourne Watkins and Eleanor (Todd) P.; m. Barbara Benton, May 4, 1968; children— Claibourne Watkins III, William Jordan. BA, U. of South, 1955; JD, U. Ark., 1961. Bar: Ark. 1961. Law clk. U.S. dist. judge, Ft. Smith, 1961-63; pvt. practice Little Rock, 1963-68; asst. ins. commr. State of Ark., 1968-69; trust officer Union Nat. Bank of Little Rock, 1969-77; asst. dean U. Ark. Sch. Law, Little Rock; also exec. dir. Ark. Inst. for Continuing Legal Edn., 1977-86; law clk. 2d Div. Chancery Ct., Pulaski County, 1986-89; of counsel Gruber Law Firm, North Little Rock, 1989-2001; prin. Patty Law Firm, North Little Rock, 2001—. Lectr. law Ark. Sch. Law, 1965; bd. dirs., chmn. Pulaski County Legal Aid Bur., 1966-69; mem. com. on civil practice Ark. Supreme Ct., 1998—. Bd. dirs., pres. Family Svc. Agy. of Ctrl. Ark., 1976-81, 86-93, 99—; bd. dirs., pres. Good Shepherd Ecumenical Retirement Ctr., 1975-2002; bd. dirs. Am. Diabetes Assn., Ark. Affil., 1996—, Ark. Gerontol. Soc. 1996—; mem. Ark. adv. com. U.S. Commn. on Civil Rights, 1985-89. With AUS, 1955-57. Mem.: Phi Alpha Delta, Beta Theta Pi. Office: Patty Law Firm 315 N Broadway St North Little Rock AR 72114-5379 Office Phone: 501-375-5061. Personal E-mail: clairgpm@swbell.net.

PATTY, WILLIAM ROBERT, secondary school educator, principal; b. El Paso, Tex., July 31, 1940; s. Jim Lane and Blanche Helen Patty; m. Sandra Jean Marlin, June 4, 1972 (dec. June 2001); 1 child, Mary Madeline. BS, U. Tex., El Paso, 1969. Cert. elem. and secondary tchr., Tex. Tchr., coach Dolphin Terrace Sch., El Paso, 1966-85; tchr., asst. prin., track coach N.E. Christian Acad., El Paso, 1985-90, 92—. Diabetes edn. asst. VA Clinic, El Paso, 1999—. Track coach Northeast Christian Acad., El Paso, 1963-89; V.p. PTA, El Paso, 1969-71. With USAF, 1958-59. Mem. DAV, Am. Legion. Baptist. Avocations: coins, fast pitch softball. Home: 3409 Volcanic El Paso TX 79904

PATTYN, SUE, publishing executive; b. Sept. 1, 1958; Mem.: Guides for Living LLC. Home: 7363 Nebraska Way Longmont CO 80504-8419 Office: PO Box 1104 Longmont CO 80502-1104 Office Phone: 303-702-1254.

PATULOT, JUN J. R. insurance company executive; b. Manila, Oct. 30, 1947; came to U.S., 1975; s. Silvino M. and Sotera P. Patulot; m. Connie Castro, Sept. 2, 1950; children: Patrick, Aires. BS in Fgn. Svc., Lyceum of Philippines, Manila, 1968; postgrad. in Law, San Sebastian Coll., Manila, 1972; postgrad. in Mgmt. and Supervision, Seattle C.C., 1980. Fgn. svc. staff officer Ministry of Fgn. Affairs, Manila, 1970-74, Philippine Consulate Gen., Seattle, 1975-84; spl. supr. Gt. Am. Res. Ins. Co., Seattle, 1985-87; exec. sales dir. Surety Life Ins. Co., Seattle, 1987-91; mng. gen. agt. N.W. Life Assurance of Am., Belligham, Wash., 1991—, Conseco Life Ins. and Investing Brokerage, Carmel, Wash., 2001—. Pvt. practice ins. brokerage, Seattle, 1987—. Recipient Nat. Sales Achievement award Nat. Assn. Life Underwriters, Nat Quality award Life Ins. Mktg. and Rsch. Assn. Mem. Million Dollar Round Table. Office: Jun Patulot & Co 1415 2nd Ave Ste 1701 Seattle WA 98101-2042 Home: 11813 SE 75th Pl Newcastle WA 98056-1768 E-mail: junpatulot@hotmail.com.

PATUREAU, ARTHUR MITCHELL, chemical engineer, consultant; b. Beaumont, Tex., Nov. 22, 1913; m. Clara Davis, Dec. 24, 1934. BSChemE, U. Tex., 1943, postgrad., Pa. State U., 1946. Chief process engr. Gasoline Plant Constrn. Co., Corpus Christi, Tex., 1944-46, McCarthy Chem. Co., Houston, 1946-48; chief application engr. Fisher & Porter Co., Hatboro, Pa., 1948-50; cons. reactor coolant controls Nautilus nuc. submarine Westinghouse Atomic Power Divsn., Pitts., 1950-53; chief application engr. chem. industry Brown Instrument Divsn., Phila., 1953-55; western sales mgr. Barksdale Valves, L.A., 1955-74; western divisional mgr. Pa. Indsl. Chem. Co., L.A., 1974-75; divisional mgr. Hercules, Inc., L.A., 1973-75; cons. to chem. industry Temple, Tex., 1975—; pres. Artgraphics, Inc., 1975—. Editor: (tech. book) Resins in Rubber, 1975; contbg. author to Ency. Chem. Engring.; contbr. articles to profl. jours. Mem. engring. fund adv. coun. U. Tex. Coll. Engring., 1970—75. Mem. AIChE, L.A. Rubber Group, Rotary. Episcopalian. Avocations: art work, camping, travel, computer work. Home and Office: Apt 8107 1810 Marlandwood Rd Temple TX 76502-2842 Fax: 254-899-1342. Personal E-mail: artpatu@aol.com.

PATURIS, E(MMANUEL) MICHAEL, lawyer; b. Akron, Ohio; s. Michael George and Sophia (Manos) P.; m. Mary Ann Toompas, Febr. 28, 1965. BS, U. N.C., 1954, JD with honors, 1959. Bar: N.C. 1959, D.C. 1969, Va. 1973; CPA. Acct., Charlotte and Wilmington, N.C., 1960-63; assoc. Poyner, Geraghty, Hartsfield & Townsend, Raleigh, N.C., 1963-64; atty. advisor Chief Counsel's Office, Washington, 1964-66, sr. trial atty. Richmond, Va., 1966-69; ptnr. Reasoner, Davis & Vinson, Washington, 1969-78; sole practitioner Alexandria, 1978—. Acctg. lectr. U. N.C., Chapel Hill, 1959-60; acctg., econs. lectr. N.C. State U., Raleigh, 1963-64; business law lectr. George Mason U., Fairfax County, Va., 1978-79. Mem. bd. editors U. N.C. Law Rev. With U.S. Army, 1954-56. Recipient U. N.C. Law Sch. Block award, 1959. Mem.: Washington Golf and Country Club, Beta Gamma Sigma, Phi Beta Kappa. Home: 6326 Stoneham Ln Mc Lean VA 22101-2345 Office: Law Offices of E Michael Paturis 431 N Lee St Alexandria VA 22314-2301 Office Phone: 703-836-2501. Personal E-mail: michael@paturis.com.

PATZ, ARNALL, ophthalmologist; b. Elberton, Ga., June 14, 1920; s. Samuel and Sarah (Berman) P.; m. Ellen B. Levy, Mar. 12, 1950; children: William, Susan, David, Jonathan. BS, Emory U., 1942, MD, 1945; DSc (hon.), U. Pa., 1982, Emory U., 1985, Thomas Jefferson U., 1985; MLA, Johns Hopkins U., 1998, LHD (hon.), 2001. Pvt. practice, Balt., 1951-70; faculty Johns Hopkins Sch. Medicine, 1955—, prof., 1973—; William Holland Wilmer prof., chmn. dept. ophthalmology, dir. Wilmer Ophthal. Inst., 1979-89, disting. svc. prof. ophthalmology, 2001. Mem. Nat. Diabetes Adv. Bd., 1977-80. First recipient Edward Lorenzo Holmes award Inst. Medicine Chgo., 1954, 1st Helen Keller prize Helen Keller Rsch. Found., 1994; Sight-Saving award D.C. Soc. Prevention Blindness, 1954, E. Mead Johnson award Am. Acad. Pediatrics, 1956, Albert Lasker award Am. Pub. Health Assn., 1956, 1st Seeing Eye Rsch. Prof. Ophthalmology award, 1970, Derrick Vail medal Ill. Soc. Prevention Blindness, 1981, Jules Stein award Rsch. to Prevent Blindness, 1981, David Rumbough Sci. award Juvenile Diabetes Found. Internat., 1983, Merit award Retina Rsch. Found., 1983, 1st Issac C. Michaelson award Israel Acad. Scis. and Humanities, 1986, Paul Henkind lectureship Macula Soc., 1989, Pisart award Lighthouse Internat., 2001, Spl. award for Lifetime Contbn. in Vision Rsch., Prevention of Blindness and Low Vision, Assn. for Edn. and Rehab. of Visually Impaired, 2002, Person of Vision award Md. Soc. for Sight, 2004, Presdl. medal freedom, 2004; named to Ophthalmology Hall of Fame, Am. Soc. Cataract and Refractive Surgery, 2002. Mem. AMA (Billings silver medal 1973), Am. Acad. Ophthalmology (honor award 1973, Sr. Honor award 1981, Edward Jackson Meml. lectr. 1982, pres.-elect 1986, pres. 1987, Life Achievement award 1998), Assn. for Rsch. in Vision and Ophthalmology (Friedenwald Meml. award 1980, Weisenfeld award 1993), Nat. Soc. Prevention of Blindness (v.p. 1981—, 1st Disting. Scientist award), Am. Ophthal. Soc. (Howe medal 1991), Balt. City Med. Soc., Md. Soc. Prevention Blindness (past pres.), Pan-Am. Assn. Ophthalmology, Md. Soc. Eye Physicians and Surgeons. Home: 2A Slade Ave Baltimore MD 21208-5214 Office: Johns Hopkins Med Insts Wilmer Eye Inst 600 N Wolfe St Baltimore MD 21287-0005

PATZ, EDWARD FRANK, retired lawyer; b. Balt., Aug. 25, 1932; s. Maurice A. and Violet (Furman) P.; m. Betty Seldner Levi, Nov. 18, 1956; children— Evelyn Anne, Edward Frank, Thomas L. BS, U. Md., 1954, LLB, 1959. Bar: Md. 1959, U.S. Dist. Ct. Md. 1959, U.S. Ct. Appeals (4th cir.) 1959, U.S. Supreme Ct. 1980. Ptnr. Weinberg and Green and predecessor firms (now merged into Sau Ewing), Balt., 1959-97; ret., 1997. Bd. dirs. Jewish Family and Children's Service, 1965-71; regional bd. dirs. NCCJ; pres. Suburban Club Balt. County, 1977-79; bd. trustees, exec. com. Flagler Ecumenical Social Svcs. Ctr., Inc., 1999-2002. Mem.: Hammock Dunes Club. Home: 39 Island Estates Pkwy Palm Coast FL 32137-2203 E-mail: efpatz@pcfl.net.

PATZAKIS, MICHAEL J. orthopaedic surgeon, educator; b. Campbell, Ohio, Nov. 6, 1937; m. Susan Patzakis, 1961; children: Michele, Theresa, John, Peter. BA, Ohio State U., 1959, MD, 1963. Diplomate Am. Bd. Orthopaedic Surgery. Intern L.A. County-USC Med. Ctr., 1963-64, resident, 1964-68; fellow rheumatoid surgery U. Colo. Med. Ctr., 1968-69; instr. U. So. Calif. Sch. Medicine, 1967-68, asst. prof., 1969-75, assoc. prof., 1975-88, prof., 1988—, interim chmn., 1990-91, chmn., 1991—. The Vincent and Julia Meyer chair, 1996—; chief orthop. surgery U. So. Calif. Univ. Hosp., 2000—, L.A. County-U. So. Calif. Med. Ctr., 2000—. Instr. U. Colo., 1968-69; vis. prof. U. Calif., Irvine, 1969, 70, Case Western Res. U., 1976, Cleve. Clinic, 1976, U. Tex., Dallas, 1977, UCLA, 1977, Northwestern U., 1981, Stanford U., 1981, Northeastern Ohio Sch. Medicine, 1983, U. Calif., San Diego, 1985, Drew Med. Sch., L.A., 1988, Martin Luther King Drew Med. Sch., 1989, Athens Hellenic Trauma Soc., 1990, Walter Reed Army Med. Ctr., Washington, 1996, U. Thessalia, Greece, 1998, many others; mem. med. and sci. com. Arthritis Found. So. Calif., 1974-80; lectr., presenter, cons. in field. Assoc. editor Jour. Clin. Orthopaedics and Related Rsch., 1979—, guest editor, 1983, 84; assoc. editor, mem. editl. bd. Contemporary Orthopaedics, 1980— Mem. festival com. St. Anthony's Greek Orthodox, Pasadena, Calif., 1970—, festival chmn., 1971, dir. youth program, 1971-84, mem. ch. bldg. com., 1976-81; basketball commr. Greek Orthodox Youth League So. Calif., 1984-84; active AXIOS Found. of Worthiness-Greek Ams. So. Calif., 1984—; bd. dirs. L.A. Concert Open, 1994—. Named Greek Orthodox Person of the Yr., So. Calif. St. Nectarios Ch., Covina, Calif., 1986; rsch. grantee Am. Arthritis Found., 1968-69, Eli Lilly and Co., 1970-71, 71-72, 72-73, 73-74, 76-77, Bristol Myers Co., 1971-72, Galaxo, 1984, Merck-Germany, 1984, Merrell-Dow, 1987-88, Miles Lab., 1990, R.W. Johnson, 1994, Genetics Inst., 1993-94, 94-95, Abbott Labs., 1996—, Merck Rsch. Labs., 1998-99, Synercid, 1998—, 98—, 99—, others. Mem. AAUP, Am. Acad. Orthopaedic Surgeons (faculty summer inst. 1980-84, mem. com. on evaluation 1986—), Am. Orthopaedic Assn., Assn. Bone and Joint Surgeons, Am. Rheumatism Assn., Western Orthopaedic Assn. (program chmn. 1983-84), Hellenic-Am. Med. Soc. (bd. dirs. 1982-86, Physician of Yr. 2000), Acad. Orthopaedic Soc (mem.-at-large 1995-97), Musculoskeletal Infection Soc. (pres. 1992-93), Calif. Orthopaedic Assn., Calif. Med. Assn., Hippocratic Orthopaedic Soc., L.A. County Med. Assn., U. So. Calif. Grad. Orthopaedic Soc. (program chair 1977-86, pres. 1988-89), Wilson Bost Interurban Club (com. mem. So. Calif. chpt. 1992—), Alpha Epsilon Delta (pres. 1958-59). Office: LA County & USC Med Ctr GNH 3900 1200 N State St Los Angeles CA 90033-1029

PAUGH, PATRICIA LOU, business consultant; b. Pitts., Oct. 30, 1948; d. Marshall Franklin and Helen Jeanne (Graham) P. BA in English, Columbia U., 1982. Adminstrv. asst. Katz, Robinson, Brog & Seymour, N.Y.C., 1972-75; office mgr. Michael D. Martocci, N.Y.C., 1975-80; adminstrv. mgr. O'Melveny & Myers, N.Y.C., 1982-85, Latham & Watkins, N.Y.C., 1985-88; mgr. Nationwide Legal Svcs., N.Y.C., 1988-89; mgr. legal adminstrn. Aluminum Co. of Am., Pitts., 1990-93; ptnr. Domestic & Overseas Countertrade and Consulting Svcs., Ltd., 1986—; pres. Domestic & Overseas Trading Corp., Pitts., 1993—; mng. dir. Gen. Comml. Svcs., Ltd., 1994—. Mem. Am. Mgmt. Assn., Pitts. C. of C. Republican. Episcopalian. Office: 20F 320 Fort Duquesne Blvd Pittsburgh PA 15222-1133 Home: 2403 Charlemagne Circle Pittsburgh PA 15237

PAUKEN, THOMAS WEIR, venture capital executive, mediator; b. Victoria, Tex., Jan. 11, 1944; s. Thomas N. and Patricia (Weir) P.; m. Ida Ayala; children: Thomas II, Michelle, Angela, Elizabeth, Daniel, Victoria, Monica. AB in Polit. Sci., Georgetown U., 1965, postgrad., 1966-67; JD, So. Meth. U., 1973. Bar: Tex., 1975. White House staff asst., dep. dir. White Ho. fellows, Washington, 1970-71; pvt. practice atty. Dallas, 1974-80; dir. ACTION, Washington, 1981-85; pres. Sta. KRZI-Radio, Waco, Tex., 1985-86; v.p., corp. counsel Garvon, Inc., Dallas, 1986-91; pres. TWP, Inc., Dallas, 1991—. Bd. dirs. Tutogen Med., Inc., TOR Minerals, Inc. Author: The Thirty Years War - The Politics of the 60s Generation, 1994. Mem. Reagan transition team Counsel's Office, Washington, 1980-81; Tex. Rep. State chmn., 1994-97. 1st lt. U.S. Army, 1967-70, Vietnam. Recipient Drug Edn. Leadership award PRIDE, 1985, Dir.'s award U.S. Office of Personnel Mgmt., 1985; Weaver fellow 1965. Mem. State Bar Tex. Roman Catholic. Avocation: reading. Office Phone: 214-378-9340. Business E-Mail: twpauken@garven.viyu.net.

PAUKER, STEPHEN GARY, internist, cardiologist; b. N.Y.C., Nov. 21, 1942; s. Carl J. and Helen (Yurdin) P.; m. Susan Perlmutter, Sept. 2, 1967; children: Sheridan Joanna, Scott Gregory. AB magna cum laude, Harvard U., 1964, MD magna cum laude, 1968. Diplomate Am. Bd. Internal Medicine. Asst. prof. medicine Tufts U., Boston, 1972-78, assoc. prof. medicine, 1978-83, vice chmn. clin. affairs dept. medicine, 1995—; chief divsn. clin. decision making New Eng. Med. Ctr., Boston, 1980-97; prof. medicine Tufts U., 1983—, chief divsn. Med. Info. Scis., 1986-97. Vis. rsch. scientist Lab. for Computer Sci. MIT, Cambridge, 1980—. Contbr. 100 chpts. to med. texts, 105 articles to profl. jours. Recipient Bausch and Lomb Sci. award, 1960, Mass. Med. Soc. award, 1968. Fellow ACP (master), Inst. Medicine, Am. Coll. Cardiology, Am. Heart Assn., Am. Coll. Med. Informatics, Coun. on Clin. Cardiology; mem. AMA, Soc. Med. Decision Making (founder, pres. 1987-88, Disting. Career award 1995, Disting. Svc. award 1994), Aesculapian Soc., Assn. Am. Physicians, Am. Soc. Clin. Investigation, Am. Assn. Artificial Intelligence, Am. Fedn. Clin. Rsch., Am. Med. Informatics Assn., Am. Soc. Clin. Hypnosis, Boylston Med. Soc., New Eng. Cardiovascular Soc., New Soc. Clin. Hypnosis, Alpha Omega Alpha. Home: 77 Loring Rd Weston MA 02493-2454 Office: New Eng Med Ctr 750 Washington St # 302 Boston MA 02111-1526

PAUL, ALIDA RUTH, arts and crafts educator; b. San Antonio, May 30, 1953; d. Richard Irving and Anne Louise (Holman) Paul. B.S. in Edn., Southwest Tex. State U., 1975; M.Ed., U. Houston, 1984. Cert. tchr., Tex. Tchr. art and crafts Houston Ind. Sch. Dist., 1975—. Republican. Episcopalian. Home: 16830 Grampin Dr Houston TX 77084-1945

PAUL, AMY, lawyer; b. Santa Monica, Calif. d. Philip and Elaine P.; m. Mark A. Czeplel. Student, UCLA, 1990; JD cum laude, U. San Diego Law Sch., 1993. Bar: Calif.; U.S. Ct. Appeals (9th cir.). Assoc. bus. and tech. group Brobeck Phleger & Harrison LLP, 1993-95; dir. contracts and legal affairs Advanced Fibre Comm., Inc., Petaluma, Calif., 1995-99, v.p., gen. counsel, corp. sec., 1999—. Office: AFC Advanced Fibre Comm 9 Willowbrook Ct Petaluma CA 94954-6507

PAUL, ANDREW MITCHELL, private equity investor; b. N.Y.C., Feb. 10, 1956; s. John William and Bobba Lorraine (Ice) P.; m. Margaret Rae Batchelor, Sept. 19, 1987. BA, Cornell U., 1978; MBA, Harvard U., 1983. Mktg. rep. IBM Corp., N.Y.C., 1978-81; assoc. Hambrecht & Quist Venture Capital Co., San Francisco, 1983-84; gen. ptnr. Welsh, Carson, Anderson & Stowe, N.Y.C., 1984—. Bd. dirs. Centennial Healthcare Inc., Atlanta, Accredo Health, Memphis, also pvt. cos. Mem. Nat. Venture Capital Assn., N.Y. Venture Capital Assn., Bronxville Field Club, Siwanoy Country Club, Hudson Nat. Golf Club., Roaring Fork Club, Aspen., Blind Brook Country Club, Commanderie de Bordeaux, Chevaliers du Tastevin. Avocations: golf, skiing, biking, travel. Home: 283 Pondfield Rd Bronxville NY 10708-4936 Office: Welsh Carson Anderson & Stowe 320 Park Ave New York NY 10022-6815

PAUL, ANDREW ROBERT, defense and legislative consultant; b. N.Y.C., Aug. 14, 1938; s. Andrew B. and Maria (Filotas) P.; m. Britt-Marie Hagelbrant, Feb. 6, 1988. AB in French, Dartmouth Coll., 1960; MS in Fgn. Svc., Georgetown U., 1967. Dir. govt. rels. Motorola, Inc., Washington, 1968-75, Paramount Communications, Washington, 1975-90; sr. v.p. Satellite Broadcasting and Communications Assn., Alexandria, Va., 1990—2001; def. and legis. cons. Mem. GATT adv. com. on Intellectual Property, Washington, 1988-94; mem. adv. com. MS in Fgn. Svc. program Georgetown U., Washington, 1981—. Presdl. campaign advance man Rep. Nat. Com., 1964; pres. chpt. XI Spl. Forces Assn., Washington, 1981-82; chmn. Alternative House Crisis Intervention Ctr., Vienna, Va., 1983-84. Capt. U.S. Army, 1960-65. Roman Catholic. Home: 1013 Heather Hill Ct Mc Lean VA 22101-2024

PAUL, ARA GARO, university dean; b. New Castle, Pa., Mar. 1, 1929; s. John Hagop and Mary (Injejikian) P.; m. Shirley Elaine Waterman, Dec. 21, 1962; children: John Bartlett, Richard Goyan. BS in Pharmacy, Idaho State U., 1950; MS, U. Conn., 1953, PhD in Pharmacognosy, 1956. Cons. plant physiology Argonne (Ill.) Nat. Lab., 1955; asst. prof. pharmacognosy Butler U., Indpls., 1956-57; faculty U. Mich., Ann Arbor, 1957—, prof. pharmacognosy, 1969—; dean U. Mich. Coll. Pharmacy, 1975-96, dean emeritus, Hans W. Vahlteich prof. pharmacognosy, 2001—. Vis. prof. microbiology Tokyo U., 1965-66; mem. vis. chemistry faculty U. Calif., Berkeley, 1972-73; del. U.S. Pharmacopeial Conv., 1980, 90; scholar-in-residence Am. Assn. Colls. Pharmacy, 1996; bd. grants Am. Found. Pharm. Edn., 1997—, chmn., 1999, co-chmn. endowment com., 2002—, bd. dirs., 2003—; mem. organizing com. Millennial World Congress Pharm. Scis., 1996-2000; mem. FIP Found., 2000—, chmn. bd. trustees, 2001—. Contbr. articles to profl. jours. Recipient Outstanding Tchr. award Coll. Pharmacy, U. Mich., 1969, Outstanding Alumnus award Idaho State U., 1976, Profl. Achievement award Coll. Pharmacy, Idaho State U., 1990; G. Pfeiffer Meml. fellow Am. Found. Pharm. Edn., 1965-66, Disting. Svc. Profile award Am. Found Pharm. Edn., 1992; fellow Eli Lily Found., 1951-53, Am. Found. Pharm. Edn., 1954-56, NIH, 1972-73. Fellow AAAS; mem. Am. Pharm. Assn., Am. Soc. Pharmacognosy, Acad. Pharm. Scis., Am. Assn. Colls. Pharmacy, Am. Assn. Pharm. Scientists, Phi Lambda Upsilon, Sigma Xi, Phi Delta Chi, Phi Sigma Kappa, Rho Chi. Home: 1415 Brooklyn Ave Ann Arbor MI 48104-4496 Office: U Mich Coll Pharmacy Ann Arbor MI 48109-1065 E-mail: arapaul@umich.edu.

PAUL, ARTHUR, artist, graphic designer, illustrator, art and design consultant; b. Chgo., Jan. 18, 1925; m. Beatrice Miller, Dec. 24, 1949 (div. 1973); children: William Warren, Fredric; m. Suzanne Seed, Mar. 8, 1975; 1 stepdaughter, Nina. Student, Inst. Design, 1947-51. Vice-pres., art dir. HMH Pub. Co., Playboy, Chgo., 1953-82; also sr. art dir., corp. art dir. Playboy mag.; pres. Art Paul Design; freelance artist Chgo., 1984—. Lectr. in field. Free lance illustrator, designer, 1951-53; designer 1st issue: Playboy mag, 1953, Playboy Rabbit symbol, 1953; one-man shows include Etc. Gallery, 1949, 500D Gallery, 1965, U. Ill., 1965, Chgo. Cultural Ctr., 1997-98; organizer, exhibitor: travelling exhbn. Beyond Illustration-The Art of Playboy; museums, Europe, Asia, U.S., 1971-73, Can., 1976-77; author: Vision-Art Paul, 1983, Art of Playboy, 1986, Sex Appeal, 2000; designer PBS-TV title Sence of Humor for humorous feature film presentations on Chgo. Public Television; prodn. design cons. (PBS-TV movie) Who Am I This Time?. Trustee Chgo. Mus. Contemporary Art, 1970-86; apptd. trustee by Gov. of Ill. to Ill. Summer Sch. of Arts, 1987—. With USAAF, 1943-46. Recipient numerous art awards, including Outstanding Achievement in Trademark Design for Playboy Mag. award Soc. Typographic Arts, 1970, Polycube award Art Dirs. Club Phila., 1975, Art Direction Mag. award, 1975, Gold medal for Chgo. Film Festival poster Art Dirs. Club N.Y., 1980, Top Midwest Mktg. award Playboy TV Subscription Ad, 1979, 82, Gold medal for exhbn. Beyond Illustration City of Milan, 1971, Profl. Achievement award IIT Inst. Design Alumni Assn., 1983; Art Inst. scholar, 1943; named to Art Dirs. Hall of Fame, 1986. Mem. Alliance Graphique Internat. *Design is more than a sense of order for me. It is beauty and common sense. To draw, to paint and to look at art is in the fabric of my life. I enjoy working with ideas and seeing them develop into a reality, after which I am fortunate enough to learn whether they have performed as intended.*

PAUL, CAROL ANN, retired academic administrator, biology educator; b. Brockton, Mass., Dec. 17, 1936; d. Joseph W. and Mary M. (DeMeulenaer) Bjork; m. Robert D. Paul, Dec. 21, 1957; children: Christine, Dana, Stephanie, Robert. BS, U. Mass., 1958; MAT, R.I. Coll., 1968, Brown U., 1970; EdD, Boston U., 1978. Tchr. biology Attleboro (Mass.) High Sch., 1965-68; asst. dean., mem. faculty biology North Shore Community Coll., Beverly, Mass., 1969-78; master planner N.J. Dept. for Higher Edn., Trenton, 1978-80; assoc. v.p. Fairleigh Dickinson U., Rutherford, N.J., 1980-86; v.p. acad. affairs Suffolk Community Coll., Selden, N.Y., 1986-94, prof. biology, 1994-98; ret. Faculty devel. cons. various colls., 1979-98, title III evaluator, 1985-98. Author: (lab. manual and workbook) Minicourses and Labs for Biological Science, 1972 (rev. edit., 1975); (with others) Strategies and Attitudes, 1986; book reviewer, 1973-77, 94-98. V.p. LWV, Beverly, 1970—74, Cranford, NJ, 1982—83; alumni rep. Brown U., 1972—92; mem. Cape Cod Area LWV, 2001—03; mem. bd. dirs. YMCA of Cape Cod, 2004—, bd. dirs., clk. of bd.,

1998—2003. Commonwealth Mass. scholar, 1954-58; recipient Acad. Yr. award NSF, 1968-69, Proclamation for Leadership award Suffolk County Exec., 1989. Mem.: AAUW, AAWCC, AAHE, Nat. Coun. for Staff (nat. exec. bd. 1979—80), Profls. and Orgn. Developers (planning com. 1977—79), Brown Alumni Club of Cape Cod (bd. dirs. 2001—, sec. 2001—), Pi Lambda Theta, Phi Theta Kappa. Roman Catholic. Avocation: swimming. Address: 26 Martin Circle Winslowe's View at Pine Hills Plymouth MA 02360

PAUL, CHARLES S. motion picture and television company executive; b. 1949; BA, Stanford U., 1971; JD, U. Santa Clara, 1975. Law clk. U.S. Supreme Ct., 1975-76; with Cooley Castro Huddleson & Tatum, 1976-79, Atari Inc., 1979-85, sr. v.p., gen. counsel, pres. coin-operated games div., 1983-85; with MCA, Inc., Universal City, Calif., 1985-96, v.p., pres. MCA Enterprises div., 1986-89, exec. v.p., 1989, also bd. dirs., 1985-96; chmn., founder Sega Game Works, Universal City, Calif., 1996—. Office: Universal Studios MCA 1024 N Orange Dr Los Angeles CA 90038-2318

PAUL, DONALD LEE, oil company executive, geophysicist; b. Los Angeles, Apr. 15, 1946; s. Glenn Arthur and Nell May Paul. B.S., MIT, 1967, M.S., 1969, Ph.D., 1975. Research geophysicist Chevron Research, LaHabra, Calif., 1975-79; sr. research geophysicist Chevron Geoscis., Houston, 1979-80; sr. exploration geophysicist Chevron USA, New Orleans, 1980-82; staff geophysicist Chevron Corp., Houston, 1982; div. geophysicist Chevron USA, Denver, 1982-84; Supr. seismic rec. sect. Chevron Oil Field Research, La Habra, Calif., 1984-85, mgr. geophysics div., 1985-90, v.p., exploration rsch., 1990-92, pres., Chevron Petroleum Tech. Co., 1992-94, v.p., Chevron Can. Resources Ltd., 1994-96, v.p., tech. & environ. affairs, Chevron Corp., 1996-2001 v.p., tech., chief tech. officer, ChevronTexaco Corp., San Francisco, 2001-. Mem. Soc. Exploration Geophysicists, Am. Assn. Petroleum Geologists. Democrat. Office: ChevronTexaco Corp 575 Market St 39th Fl San Francisco CA 94105

PAUL, DONALD W. audiologist; b. Lincoln, R.I., Apr. 11, 1947; m. Leslie Christine Paul, June 8, 1968; children: Geoffrey, Jon. BS, Boston U., 1973, MS, 1975. Cert. audiologist. Instr. Bridgewater (Mass.) State Coll., 1979-81, Northeastern U., Boston, 1977-82; dir. Boston City Hosp., 1977—92; pvt. practice North Easton, Mass., 1992—98; dir. audiology (mobile) svcs. Boston Guild for Hard of Hearing, Boston, 1998—. Cons. Health Dr., Newton, Mass., 2001—. Fellow: Am. Acad. Audiology; mem.: Am. Indsl. Hygiene Assn., Acoustical Soc. Am., Coun. on Accreditation of Occupl. Hearing Conservationists, Am. Speech Lang. Hearing Assn. Home: 44 Baltic Ave North Easton MA 02356-2104

PAUL, EDWARD, chemistry professor; b. Newark, N.J., July 16, 1944; s. Albert and Sylvia Paul; life ptnr. Janis Brewer, June 6, 1970; children: Katherine, Jean Paul Goodman. PhD, U. of Oreg., 1970. Prof. of chemistry Stockton Coll., Pomona, NJ, 1972—. Office: Stockton Coll NAMS - Box 195 Pomona NJ 08240 Office Phone: 609-652-4543.

PAUL, EVE W. retired lawyer; b. N.Y.C., June 16, 1930; d. Leo I. and Tamara (Sogolow) Weinschenker; m. Robert D. Paul, Apr. 9, 1952; children: Jeremy Ralph, Sarah Elizabeth. BA, Cornell U., 1950; JD, Columbia U., 1952. Bar: N.Y. 1952, Conn. 1960, U.S. Ct. Appeals (2nd cir.) 1975, U.S. Supreme Ct. 1977. Assoc. Botein, Hays, Sklar & Herzberg, N.Y.C., 1952-54; pvt. practice Stamford, Conn., 1960-70; staff atty. Legal Aid Soc., N.Y.C., 1970-71; assoc. Greenbaum, Wolff & Ernst, N.Y.C., 1972-78; v.p. legal affairs Planned Parenthood Fedn. Am., N.Y.C., 1979—91, v.p., gen. counsel, 1991—2003; ret., 2003. Bd. dirs. Ctr. Advancement of Women, Inc. Contbr. articles to profl. jours. Trustee Cornell U., Ithaca, N.Y., 1979-84; mem. Stamford (Conn.) Planning Bd., 1967-70; bd. dirs. Stamford LWV, 1960-62. Harlan Fiske Stone scholar Columbia Law Sch., 1952. Mem.: ABA, Stamford/Norwalk Regional Bar Assn., Assn. Bar of City of N.Y., Conn. Bar Assn., Phi Kappa Phi, Phi Beta Kappa. E-mail: evewpaul@aol.com. *The ability to plan the number and timing of my children has made it possible for me to enjoy career, marriage and family.*

PAUL, FRANK WATERS, mechanical engineer, educator, consultant; b. Jersey Shore, Pa., Aug. 28, 1938; BSME, Pa. State U., 1960, MSME, 1964; PhD in Mechanical Engring., Lehigh U., 1968. Registered profl. control engr., Calif. Control engr. Hamilton Standard div. United Techs. Corp., 1961-64; instr. mechanical engring. Lehigh U., Bethlehem, Pa., 1964-68; asst. prof. mechanical engring. Carnegie-Mellon U., Pitts., 1968-73, assoc. prof., 1973-77, Clemson (S.C.) U., 1977-79, prof., 1979-83, McQueen Quattlebaum prof., 1983—. Cons. numerous cos. including Westinghouse Electric, 1969, 82-83, Alcoa Rsch. Labs., 1976-80, State of N.J., Dept. Higher Edn., 1986, Dunlop Sports, Inc., 1988, BPM Tech.; hon. prof. engring. Hull U. Eng., 1990-93; Dora Jones vis. prof. of electronic engring., 1993; vis. prof. mech. engring. U. Newcastle Upon Tyne, Eng., 1999-00; dir. Ctr. for Advanced Mfg., 1982-99; lectr. to colls. and univs., U.S. and abroad. Contbr. chpt. to books and articles to IEEE Control Systems mag., Jour. of Engring. for Industry (ASME), Jour. of Dynamic Systems Measurement and Control (ASME), and other scholarly publs. Sabbatical United Techs. Rsch. Ctr., 1985-86, Hull U., 1993. Fellow ASME (participant and paper reviewer Dynamic Systems and Control divsn. 1968—, chmn. panel on robotics 1985-87); mem. Am. Soc. Engring. Educators, Soc. Mech. Engrs. (charter mem. Robotics Internat.), Pi Tau Sigma, Tau Beta Pi, Sigma Tau, Sigma Xi. Achievements include patents related to manufacturing automation. Office: Clemson U Fluor Daniel Bldg Rm 204 Clemson SC 29634-0001 E-mail: fwpaul@clemson.edu.

PAUL, HERBERT MORTON, lawyer, accountant, taxation educator; b. N.Y.C. s. Julius and Gussie Paul; m. Judith Paul; children: Leslie Beth, Andrea Lynn. BBA, Baruch Coll.; MBA, LLM, NYU; JD, Harvard U. Ptnr. Touche Ross & Co. (predecessor Deloitte Touche), N.Y.C., assoc. dir.-tax, dir. fin counseling; mng. ptnr. Herbert Paul, P.C., N.Y.C., 1983—. Prof. taxation, trustee NYU. Author: Ordinary and Necessary Expenses; editor: Taxation of Banks; adv. tax editor The Practical Acct.; mem. adv. bd. Financial and Estate Planning, Tax Shelter Insider, Financial Planning Strategist, Tax Shelter Litigation Report; bd. dirs. Partnership Strategist, The Business Strategist; cons. Profl. Practice Mgmt. Mag.; mem. panel The Hot Line; advisor The Partnership Letter, The Wealth Formula; cons. The Insider's Report for Physicians; mem. tax bd. Business Profit Digest; cons. editor physician's Tax Advisor; bd. fin. cons. Tax Strategies for Physicians; tax and bus. advisor Prentice Hall; contbg. editor. Jour. of Accountancy; mem. editl. bd. Family Bus. Advisor. Trustee NYU, mem. bd. overseers Grad. Sch. Bus.; mem. com. on trusts and estates Rockefeller U.; trustee Alvin Alley Am. Dance Theatre, Assoc. Y's of N.Y.; mem. accts. divsn. Fedn. Philanthropies; mem. adv. bd. Family Bus. Advisor. Mem. NYU Alumni Assn. (pres., bd. dirs.). Mem. ABA, Inst. Fed. Taxation (adv. com. chmn.), Internat. Inst. on Tax and Bus. Planning (adv. bd.), Assn. Bar City N.Y., NYU Tax Soc. (pres.), Bur. Nat. Affairs-Tax Mgmt. (adv. com. on exec. compensation), Am. Inst. CPAs (com. on corp. taxation), Tax Study Group, N.Y. County Lawyers Assn., N.Y. State Soc. CPAs Dir. (chmn. tax div. com. on fed. taxation, gen. tax com., furtherance com., com. on rels. with IRS, bd. dirs.), Nat. Assn. Accts., Assn. of Bar of City of N.Y., Accts. Club of Am., Pension Club, Nat. Assn. Estate Planners (bd. dirs.), N.Y. Estate Planning Coun. (bd. dirs.), N.Y. C. of C. (tax com.), Grad. Sch. Bus. of NYU Alumni Assn. (pres.), NYU Alumni Assn. (pres.). Clubs: Wall St., City Athletic (N.Y.C.), Inwood Country. Office: Herbert Paul PC 450 7th Ave Ste 3000 New York NY 10123 Office Phone: 212-752-3700.

PAUL, HERMAN LOUIS, JR., valve manufacturing company executive; b. N.Y.C., Dec. 30, 1912; s. Herman Louis and Louise Emilie (Markert) P.; student Duke, 1931-32, Lehigh U., 1932-33; m. Janath Powers (dec. Jan. 1996); children— Robert E., Charles Thomas, Herman Louis III. Power plant engr. Paul's Machine Shop, N.Y.C., 1935-43; pres., chief engr. Paul's Machine Shop, N.Y.C., 1943-48; v.p., chief engr. Paul Valve Corp., East Orange, N.J., 1948-54; pres., chief engr. P-K Industries, Inc., North Arlington, N.J., 1954-59; v.p., dir. research Gen. Kinetics, Englewood, N.J., 1959-62; engring. cons., N.Y.C., 1962-65; v.p., dir. Hydromatics, Inc., Bloomfield, N.J., 1965-67; with P.J. Hydraulics, Inc., Myerstown, Pa., 1967—, pres., chief engr., 1968-80, dir. and stockholder, 1980-81; pres. Flomega Industries, Inc., Cornwall, Pa., 1982—; cons. to Metal Industries Devel. Center, Taiwan, 1979; engring. cons. valves and complimentary equipment, 1980—; valve cons. Continental Disc Corp., Kansas City, Mo., 1980-98. Vice chmn. Nat. UN Day Com., 1977, 78, 79, 80. Mem. ASME, Instrument Soc. Am., Am. Soc. Naval Engrs., The Navy League, The Naval Inst. Club: Heidelberg Country (Bernville, Pa.), Quentin (Pa.) Riding. Patentee in field. Home: RD 5 370 Dogwood Ln Lebanon PA 17042-9503

PAUL, JAMES CAVERLY NEWLIN, law educator, retired dean; b. Chestnut Hill, Pa., Apr. 30, 1926; s. William Allen Butler and Adelaide Sims (Newlin) P.; m. Margaret Morris Clausen, June 25, 1948; children: Nicholas Newlin, Martha Morris, Adelaide Sims. BA, Princeton U., 1948; JD, U. Pa., 1951. Bar: Pa. bar 1952. Legal sec. to Chief Justice U.S., 1951-53; asst. prof. U. N.C., 1953-55; asst. dir. Inst. Govt., U. N.C., 1953-55; prof. law, dir. Inst. Legal Research, U. Pa., 1955-63; prof. law, dean and founder of faculty of law Haile Selassie U., Ethiopia, 1963-67, v.p. acad. affairs, 1967-69; exec. v.p. Ednl. and World Affairs, N.Y.C., 1969-70; dean Sch. Law, Rutgers U., Newark, 1970-74, prof. law, 1970-96, Newhouse scholar in law, 1984-88, William J. Brennan prof., 1988-96; exec. sec., trustee Internat. Ctr. for Law in Devel., N.Y.C., 1974—. Founding mem., sec.-treas. Internat. Third World Legal Studies Assn., N.Y.C., 1980—96; adj. prof. Columbia U., 1973—95; cons. US Peace Corps, 1961—62, Constl. Commn. Transitional Govt. of Ethiopia, 1992—95, UN Devel. Programme, 1994—96; commr. Internat. Eritrean-Ethioplan Claims Commn., The Hague, 2001—. Author: Rift in the Democracy, 1951, (with others) Federal Censorship, 1961, Ethiopian Constitutional Development, 1969, Lawyers in the Third World, 1981, The International Context of Rural Poverty in the Third World, 1986, Incorporating Human Rights Into the World Summit for Social Development, 1995. Candidate for U.S. Congress from 9th Dist. Pa., 1958; del. Dem. Nat. Conv., 1960. Served with USNR (Amphibious forces), 1943-46, PTO. Recipient Spl. medal for distinguished service to the devel. of law and univ. edn. in Ethiopia, Emperor Haile Sellassie 1st, 1969; Eisenhower Exch. fellow, Africa, 1960. Mem. Am., N.J., Pa. bar assns., Internat. Third World Legal Studies Assn. (sec.-treas. 1980-96), Order of Coif. Clubs: Princeton (N.Y.C.). Home: 1352 Chancellor Pt Trappe MD 21673-1540 Office: 15 Washington St Newark NJ 07102-3105 *My life in law and teaching about law gives satisfaction because it enables me to direct my energies towards thinking about social justice, individual dignity, and the possibilities of attaining more of the conditions enabling these ideals. But that satisfaction is tempered by constant realization of my own frailities and the failure everywhere of people, particularly those most fortunately endowed, to be guided by principled thinking.*

PAUL, JAMES WILLIAM, lawyer; b. Davenport, Iowa, May 3, 1945; s. Walter Henry and Margaret Helene (Hillers) P.; m. Sandra Kay Schmid, June 15, 1968; children: James William, Joseph Hillers. BA, Valparaiso U., 1967; JD, U. Chgo., 1970. Bar: N.Y. 1971, U.S. Ct. Appeals (2d cir.) 1971, U.S. Dist. Ct. (so. and ea. dists.) N.Y. 1972, U.S. Supreme Ct. 1977, U.S. Ct. Appeals (6th cir.) 1981, Ind. 1982, U.S. Dist. Ct. (no. dist.) Ind. 1982, U.S. Claims Ct. 1989, U.S. Dist. Ct. (ea. dist.) Mich. 1989, U.S. Ct. Appeals (fed. cir.) 1991. Assoc. Rogers & Wells, N.Y.C., 1970-78, ptnr., 1978—. Officer Musica Sacra, Inc., 1972-81 Bd. dirs. Turtle Bay Music Sch., Am. Luth. Publicity Bur., Wartburg Found., chmn. bd. 2004—. Recipient Disting. Alumnus award, Valparaiso U., 1994. Mem. ABA (antitrust sect. ins. com.), Assn. Bar City N.Y. (com. on legal and jud. ethics, com. on civil ct.), Fed. Bar Council. Democrat. Home: 360 E 72nd St Apt A-710 New York NY 10021-4755 also: 5 Curtis Dr Sherman CT 06784-1220 Office: Clifford Chance US LLP 31 W 52nd St New York NY 10019-6131

PAUL, KENNETH, newspaper editor; b. N.Y.C., June 7, 1948; s. Samuel D. and Rose (Markoff) P.; m. Sevara Jeleva, Dec. 5, 1993; 1 child, Kathryn Hannah. BA in English, Dartmouth Coll., Hanover, N.H., 1969; spl. diploma in social studies, Oxford (Eng.) U., 1973. Tchr. Concord (N.H.) H.S., 1969-71; dep. European editor L.A. Times/Washington Post News Svc., London, 1972-73; reporter, news editor Riverside (Calif.) Press Enterprise, 1973-76; specialists editor, copy editor, asst. nat. and day nat. editor Newsday, NY, 1976—87; mng. editor N.Y. Observer, N.Y.C., 1987-91; editor The Litchfield County Times, New Milford, Conn., 2002, Housatonic Pubs., New Milford, 2001—02; editor-in-chief Manhattan Media, N.Y.C., 2002—. Office: Manhattan Media 63 W 38th St Ste 206 New York NY 10018

PAUL, LES, entertainer, inventor; b. Waukesha, Wis., June 9, 1915; s. George and Evelyn (Stutz) Polfuss; m. Mary Ford; children: Lester, Gene, Colleen, Robert, Mary. Student pub. schs., Waukesha. Appeared on numerous radio programs throughout Midwest, in 1920's and 1930's, formed Les Paul Trio, 1936—37, and appeared with Fred Waring, N.Y.C, appeared on first television broadcast with an orch. from NBC, N.Y.C., 1939; mus. dir: WJJD and WIND, 1941; appeared with Mary Ford on own television show, Mahwah, N.J., 1953—57, host Edison 100th Anniversary of invention of phonograph at Edison Home, West Orange, N.J, 1977, numerous TV, club appearances especially Fat Tuesday's, N.Y.C, recs. include Lover and Brazil, 1948, Nola, 1949, Goofus, 1950, Tennessee Waltz, 1950, Little Rock Getaway, 1950, Mockin' Bird Hill, 1951, Just One More Chance, 1951, Walkin' and Whistlin' Blues, 1951, How High The Moon, 1951 (Hall of Fame award 1979), Smoke Rings, 1952, The World's Waiting For The Sunrise, 1952, Tiger Rag, 1953, Meet Mr. Callaghan, 1953, Jazz Me Blues, 1952, Vaya Con Dios, 1954, Chester and Lester, 1976 (Grammy award), Guitar Monsters, 1977 (Grammy nominee), The Legend and the Legacy, 1991, The Best of the Capitol Masters with Mary Ford, 1992, The Guitar Artistry of Les Paul, Greatest Hits!, 1994. Served with Armed Forces Radio Service, World War II. Named to Grammy Hall of Fame Les Paul and Mary Ford, 1977, Rock 'N' Roll Hall of Fame, 1988, Wis. Performing Artists Hall of Fame, 1990; recipient Grammy Achievement award for contbns. to rec., musical instruments industry. Mem.: SAG, ASCAP, AFTRA, Am. Fedn. Musicians, Audio Engring. Soc. Achievements include first to multi-track tape recorder; inventing 1st 8-track tape recorder; inventing sound-on-sound recording; creating Les Paul electric solid body guitars; consultant, Gibson Guitar Corp., Nashville. Address: Columbia Records Sony Music Entertainment 550 Madison Ave Fl 24 New York NY 10022-3211 *To be successful requires hard work, determination, a positive attitude, believing in one's self, a God given talent and luck.*

PAUL, LOIS, public relations company executive; BA in Journalism summa cum laude, Temple U.; MS in Computer Info. Systems, Bentley Coll. Former sr. editor/software Computerworld; former exec. editor/features, founding mem. PC Week; founder, pres. Lois Paul & Ptnrs., Burlington, Mass., 1986—. Chmn. Bentley Coll. Grad. Sch. Mktg. Adv. Coun; bd. on Fleishman-Hillard, 2000. Recipient Disting. Sch. of Comm. and Theater Alumnus award Temple U. Office: Lois Paul and Ptnrs 150 Presidential Way Woburn MA 01801-1179

PAUL, NORMAN LEO, psychiatrist, educator; b. Buffalo, N.Y., July 5, 1926; s. Samuel Joseph and Tannie (Goncharsky) P.; m. Betty Ann Byfield, June 6, 1951 (dec. May 1994); children: Marilyn, David Alexander; m. Janet Athos, Aug. 16, 2002. MD, U. Buffalo, 1948. Fellow pharmacology U. Cin. Coll. Medicine, Ohio, 1949-50; resident psychiatry Mass. Mental Health Ctr., Boston, 1952-55; fellow child psychiatry James Jackson Putnam Children's Ctr., Boston, 1957-59, Mass. Gen. Hosp., Boston, 1958-59; chief psychiatrist Day Hosp. Mass. Mental Health Ctr., Boston, 1960-64; dir. conjoint family therapy Boston State Hosp., 1964-65, cons. in family psychiatry, 1965-70; assoc. clin. prof. dept. neurology Boston U. Sch. Medicine, 1977—. Cons. Mental Health Ctr., Alaska Native Hosp., Anchorage, 1967-68; cons. in family psychiatry Boston VA Hosp., 1967-71, Mass. Soc. for the Prevention of Cruelty to Children, Boston, 1993—; vis. family therapist St. George's Med. Sch., London, 1996-97; lectr. in psychiatry Harvard Med. Sch., Boston, 1976-2003; faculty assoc. Mgmt. Analysis Corp., Cambridge, Mass., 1979-82; presenter paper Internat. Conf. on Telemedicine and Telecare, London, 1996. Family therapist: (tv documentary) PBS-Trouble in the Family, 1965 (George Foster Peabody award 1965); co-author A Marital Puzzle, 1977, 86, German edit., 1987, French edit., 1995, Chinese edit., 1997. Sponsor Mass. Orgn. to Repeal Abortion Laws, Boston, 1965-70; chair Audio Unit of Child Devel. and Mass Media, White House Conf. on Children and Youth, Washington, 1970; bd. trustees Cambridge (Mass.) Coll., 1977-89; bd. dirs. Let's Face It, 1990—, Ctr. for Family Connections, 1998—2002. Capt. USAF, 1950-52. Recipient Edward A. Strecker, M.D. award for young psychiatrist of yr., 1966, Cert. of Merit, Mass. Coun. on Family Life, Boston, 1967, Cert. of Commendation, Mass. Assn. for Mental Health, Boston, 1967, Disting. Achievement award Soc. for Family Therapy and Rsch., Boston, 1973, Lifetime Achievement award Mass. Assn. for Marriage and Family Therapy, 1998, Disting. Svc. award Physician Health Svcs., 1998. Fellow Royal Soc. Medicine, Am. Psychiat. Assn. (life); mem. Am. Assn. Marriage and Family Therapy (bd. dirs. 1983-86), Am. Family Therapy Assn. (v.p. 1982-83, Disting. Contbn. award 1984), Assn. for Rsch. in Nervous and Mental Disorders, Group for the Advancement Psychiatry (chair com. on the family 1982-84). Avocations: study of codes, travel. Office: 394 Lowell St Ste 6 Lexington MA 02420-2549 Office Phone: 781-863-0048. E-mail: npaul@aol.com.

PAUL, OGLESBY, cardiologist, educator; b. Villanova, Pa., May 3, 1916; s. Oglesby and Laura Little (Wilson) P.; m. Marquerite Black, May 29, 1943 (dec. Jan. 1979); children: Rodman, Marquerite; m. Jean Lithgow, Jan. 17, 1981. AB, Harvard Coll., 1938; MD, Harvard Med. Sch., 1942. Intern Mass. Gen. Hosp., Boston, 1942-43, resident, 1946-48; prof. medicine Northwestern U., Evanston, Ill., 1963-77; sr. physician emeritus Brigham & Womens Hosp., Boston, 1977—; prof. medicine emeritus Harvard Med. Sch., Boston, 1977—. V.p. health scis. Northwestern U., Evanston, 1974-75; dir. admissions Harvard Med. Sch., Boston, 1977-82. Author: Take Heart, 1986, The Caring Physician, 1991. Pres. Am. Heart Assn., Dallas, 1960-61. Lt. USNR. Home: 10 Longwood Dr Apt 322 Westwood MA 02090-1142 Office: Harvard Med Sch Countway Libr 10 Shattuck St Boston MA 02115-6011 Personal E-mail: oleypaul@aol.com.

PAUL, PETER, science administrator; PhD in Exptl. Nuclear Physics, U. Freiburg, 1959. Prof. dept. physics Stony Brook U., 1960—92, disting. svc. prof. dept. physics, 1992—98, cheif physics dept., 1986—90, 1996—98; dep. dir. sci. & tech. Brookhaven Nat. Lab., NY, 1998—. Contbr. articles to profl. jours. Fellow: Am. Phys. Soc. (Alexander von Humboldt Sr. Scientist award 1983). Office: Brookhaven Nat Lab PO Box 50000 Upton NY 11973*

PAUL, PETERSON T. savings and loan association executive; b. Provo, Utah; BS, Brigham Young U.; MBA, PhD, U. Utah. From dir. portfolio mgmt. to exec. v.p. and COO Freddie Mac, McLean, Va., 1989—2003, exec. v.p., 2003—, COO, 2003—. Office: Freddie Mac 8200 Jones Branch Drive Mc Lean VA 22102-3110

PAUL, RICHARD R. military officer; BSEE, U. Mo., Rolla, 1966; MSEE, Air Force Inst. of Tech., 1971; disting. grad., Squadron Officer Sch., 1975, Air Command and Staff Coll., 1980, Naval War Coll., 1984. Commd. 2d lt. USAF, 1967, advanced through grades to maj. gen., 1995; nuclear safety engr. Air Force Weapons Lab., Kirtland AFB, N.Mex., 1967-69; missile trajectory engr. 544th Aerospace Reconnaisance Tech. Wing, Offutt AFB, Nebr., 1971-72; command and control project officer Hdqs. Strategic Air Command, Offutt AFB, 1972-76; command and control mgr. Hdqs. USAF, Washington, 1976-79; staff scientist Joint Strategic Target Planning Staff, Offutt AFB, 1980-83; dep. comdr. for advanced tech., electronic sys. divsn. Hanscom AFB, Mass., 1984-88; comdr. Wright Lab., Wright-Patterson AFB, Ohio, 1988-92; dir. sci. and tech. Hdqs. Air Force Materiel Command, Wright-Patterson AFB, 1992-97; comdr. Air Force Rsch. Lab., Wright-Patterson AFB, 1997—. Decorated Legion of Merit with oak leaf cluster. Office: AFRL/CC 1864 4th St Wright Patterson Afb OH 45433-7130

PAUL, RICHARD WRIGHT, lawyer; b. Washington, May 23, 1953; s. Robert Henry Jr. and Betty (Carey) P.; m. Paula Ann Coolsaet, July 25, 1981; children: Richard Haven, Timothy Carey, Brian Davis. AB magna cum laude, Dartmouth Coll., 1975; JD, Boston Coll., 1978. Bar: Mich. 1978, U.S. Dist. Ct. (ea. dist.) Mich. 1978, U.S. Ct. Appeals (6th cir.) 1982, U.S. Supreme Ct. 1989, U.S. Dist. Ct. (we. dist.) Mich. 1991. Assoc. Dickinson, Wright, Moon, Van Dusen & Freeman, Detroit, 1978-85, ptnr., 1985—. Case evaluator Wayne County Cir. Ct., Oakland County Dist. Ct. Co-author, Barbarians At The Gate: Daubert Two Years Later, 1995; contbr. articles to profl. publs. Trustee Bloomfield Village Assn., Birmingham, Mich., 2001-04; sec., 2003-04, bd. dirs. Little League, Birmingham, 2000-. Mem. ABA, State Bar of Mich. (treas. litig. sect. 1998-99, sec. litig. sect. 1999-2000, chmn. elect litig. sect. 2000-01, chairperson litigation sect. 2001-02, mem. representative assembly 2004—), Def. Rsch. Inst., Detroit Met. Bar Assn., Mich. Def. Trial Counsel, Dartmouth Lawyers Assn., Oakland County Bar Assn., Assn. Def. Trial Counsel, Alumni Coun. Dartmouth Coll., Dartmouth Detroit Club (pres. 1980—). Avocations: tennis, bicycling. Business E-Mail: rpaul@dickinson-wright.com.

PAUL, ROBERT, lawyer; b. N.Y.C., Nov. 22, 1931; s. Gregory and Sonia (Rijock) P.; m. Christa Holz, Apr. 6, 1975; 1 child, Gina. BA, NYU, 1953; JD, Columbia U., 1958. Bar: Fla. 1958, N.Y. 1959. From assoc. to ptnr. Paul Landy Beiley & Harper, P.A., Miami, 1964-94; ptnr. Sacher Zelman Van Sant Paul Beiley Hartman & Waldman, P.A., Miami, 1964-94; counsel Republic Nat. Bank, Miami, 1967-95; chmn. internat. affiliation of law firms TerraLex, 1990—. Past pres. Fla. Philharm., Inc., 1978-79; trustee U. Miami. Mem. ABA, N.Y. Bar Assn., Fla. Bar Assn., Fla. Zool. Soc. (past pres.), French-Am. C. of C. of Miami (pres. 1986-87). Home: 700 Alhambra Cir Coral Gables FL 33134-4808 E-mail: rpaul@terralex.com.

PAUL, ROBERT ARTHUR, steel company executive; b. N.Y.C., Oct. 28, 1937; s. Isadore and Ruth (Goldstein) P.; m. Donna Rae Berkman, July 29, 1962; children: Laurence Edward, Stephen Eric, Karen Rachel. AB, Cornell U., 1959; JD, Harvard U., 1962, MBA, 1964. With Ampco-Pitts. Corp. (formerly Screw & Bolt Corp. Am.), 1964—, v.p., 1969-71, treas., 1973-79, exec. v.p., 1972-79, pres., COO, 1979-94, pres., CEO, 1994—2004, dir., 1969—, chmn., CEO, 2004—. Pres., bd. dirs. Louis Berkman Co.; bd. dirs. Nat. City Corp., ECHO Real Estate Svs.; gen. ptnr. Romar Trading Co.; instr. Grad. Sch. Indsl. Adminstrn. Carnegie Mellon U., 1966-69; trustee emeritus Cornell U. Bd. trustees H.L. and Louis Berkman Found., U. Pitts. Med. Ctr. Sys.; trustee, pres. Fair Oaks Found.; trustee Jewish Healthcare Found. Pitts., U. Pitts. Mem. ABA, Mass. Bar Assn., Harvard Club (N.Y.), Concordia Club, Pitts. Athletic Club, Duquesne Club, Williams Country Club, Laurel Valley Golf Club. Republican. Jewish. Office: Ampco-Pitts Corp 600 Grant St Pittsburgh PA 15219-2702 Office Phone: 412-456-4400. Personal E-mail: rpaul@ampcopgh.com.

PAUL, ROBERT CAREY, lawyer; b. Washington, May 7, 1950; s. Robert Henry and Betty Jane (Carey) P. AB, Dartmouth Coll., 1972; JD, Georgetown U., 1978. Assoc. Milbank, Tweed, Hadley & McCloy, N.Y.C., 1978-85; ptnr. Dechert Price & Rhoads, N.Y.C., 1986-89, Kelley Drye & Warren, Brussels, 1989-93; counsel Rockefeller & Co., Inc., N.Y.C., 1995—2003; cons. N.Y.C., 2003—. Home: 310 E 46th St Apt 19E New York NY 10017-3029 E-mail: rpaul@aviaamerica.com.

PAUL, ROBERT DAVID, management consultant; b. N.Y.C., Nov. 1, 1928; s. Joseph Wolf and Freda (Sturm) P.; m. Eve Weinschenker, Apr. 9, 1952; children: Jeremy Ralph, Sarah Elizabeth. BS in Engring., U. Mich., 1950. Administrv. asst. Martin E. Segal Co., N.Y.C., 1950; naval architect Gibbs & Cox, N.Y.C., 1951; with The Segal Co., N.Y.C., 1953—, pres., 1967-76, vice chmn., 1977-91, chmn., 1991-94, dir., 1994-99, ret. chmn., 2000—. Trustee Employee Benefit Rsch. Inst., Washington, 1978-94, fellow, 1994; fellow Human Resource Policy Inst., Boston U. Sch. Mgmt.; bd. dirs. Wiss, Janney, Elstner Assocs., Northbrook, Ill., Empire Blue Cross Blue Shield. Contbr. articles to profl. jours. Cpl. U.S. Army, 1951-53. Mem. Soc. Human Resources Mgmt., Am. Compensation Assn., Internat. Found. Employee Benefit Plans (past chmn. corp. com.), Univ. Club. Avocations: naval and mil. history, jazz piano. Office: The Segal Co 1 Park Ave New York NY 10016-5802 E-mail: rpaul@segalco.com.

PAUL, ROLAND ARTHUR, lawyer; b. Memphis, Jan. 19, 1937; s. Rol and Hattye (Mincer) P.; m. Barbara Schlesinger, June 10, 1962; children: Deborah Lynn, Arthur Eliot. BA summa cum laude, Yale U., 1958; LL.B. magna cum laude, Harvard U., 1961. Bar: N.Y. 1962, Mich. 1978, Conn. 1989. Law clk. to judge U.S. Ct. Appeals, 1961-62; fgn. affairs officer, spl. asst. to gen.

counsel Dept. Def., 1962-64; assoc. firm Cravath, Swaine & Moore, N.Y.C., 1964-69; counsel fgn. relations subcom. security commitments U.S. Senate, 1969-71; assoc. firm Simpson Thacher Bartlett, N.Y.C., 1971-73; v.p., gen. counsel Howmet Corp., Greenwich, Conn., 1976-2000, Howmet Internat. Inc., 1997-2000; v.p., gen. counsel, dir. Pechiney Corp., Greenwich, Conn., 1984-95; counsel Day, Berry & Howard, Stamford, Conn., 2000—03, Ivey, Barnum & O'Mara, Greenwich, 2003—. Author: American Military Commitments Abroad. Mem. ABA, Coun. Fgn. Rels. Home: 8 Ellery Ln Westport CT 06880-5202

PAUL, RON, congressman; b. Pitts., Aug. 20, 1935; m. Carol Paul; five children. Grad., Gettysburg Coll., Duke U. Sch. Medicine. Pvt. practice medicine; mem. U.S. Congress from 14th Tex. dist., 1977-85, 97—; mem. joint econ. com. Mem. fin. svcs. com., internat. rels. com. Author: Challenge to Liberty, The Case for Gold, others. With USAF. Recipient Taxpayer's Best Friend award, National Taxpayers Union, Mises Inst. Groseclose Prize and Leadership award, Leadership award Coalition for Peace Through Strength, Disting. Svc. award Am. Constl. Action, Torch Freedom award Young Conservatives Tex., Guardian Freedom award Young Am. Freedom. Republican.

PAUL, RONALD L. paper company executive; b. Pollock, La., June 11, 1943; BS in Edn., La. Coll., 1966. Plant supt. Maxwell Lumber Co., Pollock, 1966—71, Georgia-Pacific Corp., New Waverly, Tex., 1971—73; mill mgr., plant supt. La.-Pacific Corp., 1973—75, ops. mgr. so. divsn., 1975—81, gen. mgr. so. divsn., 1981—87, v.p. corp. ops., gen. mgr. so. divsn., 1994—95; pres. Kirby Forest Industries, Inc., 1987—94; v.p. bldg. products, engring. and tech. Ga. Pacific Corp., Atlanta, 1995—96, v.p. structural panels and bldg. products engring., 1996—97, exec. v.p. wood products and distbn., 1997—2002, exec. v.p. wood products, 2002—. Mem. adv. bd. Auburn U. Sch. Human Scis.; active Cancer Fund Assn. Mem.: SFPA (bd. dirs.), APA-The Engineered Wood Assn. (trustee). Office: Georgia-Pacific Corp 133 Peachtree St NE Atlanta GA 30303

PAUL, RONALD NEALE, management consultant; b. Chgo., July 22, 1934; s. David Edward and Frances (Kusel) P.; m. Nona Maria Moore, Dec. 27, 1964 (div. Oct. 1981); children: Lisa, Karen, Brenda; m. Georgeann Elizabeth Lapkoff, Apr. 10, 1982. BS in Indsl. Engring., Northwestern U., 1957, MBA, 1958. Asst. to pres. Victor Comptometer Co., Chgo., 1958-64; cons. Corplan, Chgo., 1964-66; pres. Technomic Inc., Chgo., 1966—. Mng. ptnr. L/P Ptnrs., Chgo., 1978-84; bd. dirs. Summit Restaurants, Salt Lake City, 1990-96. Co-author: The 101 Best Performing Companies in America, 1986, Winning the Chain Restaurant Game, 1994. Mem. Am. Mktg. Assn., Am. Mgmt. Assn., Planners Forum, Pres.'s Assn., Product Devel. Mgmt. Assn., Beta Gamma Sigma. Avocations: reading, racquetball. Office: Technomic Inc 300 S Riverside Plz Ste 1940 Chicago IL 60606-6613 Office Phone: 312-876-0004. Business E-Mail: rpaul@technomic.com.

PAUL, RONALD STANLEY, research institute executive; b. Olympia, Wash., Jan. 19, 1923; s. Adolph and Olga (Klapstein) P.; m. Margery Jean Pengra, June 5, 1944; children: Kathleen Paul Crosby, Robert S., James N. Student, Linfield Coll., 1940-41, Reed Coll., 1943-44, Harvard U., 1945; BS, U. Oreg., 1947, MS, 1949, PhD, 1951. Physicist, research mgr. Gen. Electric Co., Richland, Wash., 1951-64; asso. dir. Battelle N.W. Labs., Richland, 1965-68, dir., 1971-72, Battelle Seattle Research Ctr., 1969-70; v.p. ops. Battelle Meml. Inst., Columbus, Ohio, 1973-76, sr. v.p., 1976-78, exec. v.p., 1978-81, pres., 1981-87, chief exec. officer, 1984-87, assoc. trustee, 1986-92. Lectr. modern physics Ctr. for Grad. Studies, Richland, 1951-62; IAEA cons. to, Japan, 1962. Contbr. articles to profl. jours. Trustee Linfield Coll., 1970-73, Denison U., 1982-88, Oreg. Mus. Sci. and Industry, 1971-72, Columbus Ctr. Sci. and Industry, 1973-87, Columbus Cancer Clinic, 1974-87, Columbus Children's Hosp. Research Found., 1975-87, Franklin U., 1987; trustee Pacific Sci. Ctr., 1969-74; v.p. exec. bd. Cen. Ohio council Boy Scouts Am., 1976-87; mem. exec. bd. of fellows Seattle-Pacific Coll., 1970-73; bd. overseers Acad. for Contemporary Problems, 1971-75; mem. nat. adv. bd. Am. U., 1982-86, Ohio State U. Found., 1985-87; bd. dirs. Edward Lowe Found., 1985-98, advisor, trustee emeritus, 1999—. Served with USAAF, 1943-46. Recipient Silver Beaver award Boy Scouts Am., 1986 Mem. Am. Phys. Soc., Am. Nuclear Soc., Sigma Xi, Sigma Pi Sigma, Pi Mu Epsilon. Republican. Presbyterian. Home: 7706 173rd St SW Edmonds WA 98026-5018

PAUL, STEPHEN HOWARD, lawyer; b. Indpls., June 28, 1947; s. Alfred and Sophia (Nahmias) P.; m. Deborah Lynn Dorman, Jan. 22, 1969; children: Gabriel, Jonathan. AB, Ind. U., 1969, JD, 1972. Bar: Ind. 1972, U.S. Dist. Ct. (so. dist.) Ind. 1972. Assoc. Baker & Daniels, Indpls., 1972-78, ptnr., 1979—, chmn. mgmt. com., 2004. Mem. bd. visitors Ind. U. Sch. Law, Bloomington. Editor in chief Ind. U. Law Jour., 1971. Pres. Belle Meade Neighborhood Assn., Indpls., 1974-78; v.p., counsel Brentwood Neighborhood Assn., Carmel, Ind., 1985-88, pres., 1988-91. Mem. ABA (state and local tax com. 1985—, sports and entertainment law com.), Am. Property Tax Counsel (founding mem.), Ind. State Bar Assn., Order of Coif. Office: Baker & Daniels 300 N Meridian St Ste 2700 Indianapolis IN 46204-1782 Office Phone: 317-237-0300.

PAUL, THOMAS FRANK, lawyer; b. Aberdeen, Wash., Sept. 23, 1925; s. Thomas and Loretta (Ounstead) P.; m. Dolores Marion Zaugg, Apr. 1, 1950; children: Pamela, Peggy, Thomas Frank. BS in Psychology, Wash. State U., 1951; JD, U. Wash., 1957. Bar: Wash. 1958, U.S. Dist. Ct. (no. and so. dist.) Wash. 1958, U.S. Ct. Appeals (9th cir.) 1958, U.S. Supreme Ct. 1970, Oreg. 2004. Ptnr., shareholder, pres. LeGros, Buchanan & Paul, Seattle, 1958—. Lectr. on admiralty and maritime law; bd. advisors U. San Francisco Law Jour., 1996—2002; mem. mediation and arbitration panel U.S. Dist. Ct. Seattle. Mem.: ATLA, ABA (chmn. com. on admiralty and maritime litig. 1982—86), Am. Judicature Soc., Asia Pacific Lawyers Assn., Am. Arbitration Assn., Transp. Lawyers Assn., Wash. Def. Trial Lawyers, Def. Rsch. Inst., Wash. State Trial Lawyers Assn., Maritime Law Assn. U.S.A., Million Dollar Advocates Forum, Propeller Club. Republican. Home: 1323 Willard Ave W Seattle WA 98119-3460 Office: LeGros Buchanan & Paul 701 5th Ave Ste 2500 Seattle WA 98104-7051 Office Phone: 206-623-4990. E-mail: tpaul@legros.com.

PAUL, VIVEK, information technology executive; b. India; B in Engring., BITS, Pilani, India; MBA, U. Mass. With PepsiCo Inc., 1982—85, Bain & Co., Boston, 1985—89, GE, 1989—99; vice chmn., CEO Wipro, 1999—. Mem. adv. bd. Stanford U. Radiology Dept. Vol., bd. mem. local chpt. Jr. Achievement. Mem.: Calif. C. of C. (bd. mem., vice chmn. tech. com.), Silicon Valley Indus Entrepreneurs Orgn. (charter). Avocations: swimming, running, bridge.

PAUL, WILLIAM, physicist, researcher; b. Deskford, Scotland, Mar. 31, 1926; came to U.S., 1952; s. William and Jean (Watson) P.; m. Barbara Anderson Forbes, Mar. 28, 1952; children: David, Fiona. MA, Aberdeen U., Scotland, 1946; PhD, Aberdeen U., 1951; A.M. (hon.), Harvard U., 1960; D Honoris Causa, Paris, 1994. Asst. lectr., then lectr. Aberdeen U., 1946-52; mem. faculty Harvard U., 1953—, Gordon McKay prof. applied physics, 1963-91, Mallinckrodt prof. applied physics, 1991—2000, prof. physics, 1980-2000, Mallinckrodt rsch. prof. applied physics, 2000—04, rsch. prof. physics, 2000—04, Mallinckrodt prof. applied physics emeritus, prof. applied physics emeritus, 2004—. Professeur associé U. Paris, 1966-67; cons. solid state physics, 1954—; Ripon prof., Calcutta, 1984 Author: Handbook on Semiconductors: Band Theory and Transport Properties, 1982; co-editor: Solids Under Pressure, 1963, Amorphous and Liquid Semiconductors, 1980, Physics of Semiconductor Materials and Applications, 1986, High Pressure in Semiconductor Physics, Vols. 1 and 2, 1998. Carnegie fellow, 1952-53; Guggenheim fellow, 1959-60; Humboldt awardee, 1990; fellow Clare Hall Cambridge U., 1974-75. Fellow Am. Phys. Soc., Brit. Inst. Physics, N.Y. Acad. Scis., Royal Soc. Edinburgh; mem. AAUP, Sigma Xi. Home: 57 Dartmouth Ct Bedford MA 01730 Office: Harvard U Pierce Hall Cambridge MA 02138 Business E-Mail: paul@deas.harvard.edu.

PAUL, WILLIAM DEWITT, JR., artist, educator, photographer, videographer, museum director; b. Wadley, Ga., Sept. 26, 1934; s. William DeWitt and Sonoma Elizabeth (Tinley) P.; m. Dorothy Hefling, Sept. 2, 1962; children: Sarah Elizabeth, Barbara Susan, Dorothy Ann. Student, Emory U., summer 1952, U. Rome, summer 1953, Ga. State Univ., Atlanta, 1953—; B.F.A., Atlanta Art Inst., 1955; AB, U. Ga., 1958, M.F.A., 1959. Instr. art and art history Park Coll., Parkville, Mo., 1960-61; dir. exhbns., instr. art history Kansas City (Mo.) Art Inst., 1959-64, curator study collections, asst. prof. art, 1964-65; coordinator basic courses dept. art, asst. prof. art U. Ga., Athens, 1965-67; curator Ga. Mus. Art, assoc. prof. art, 1967-69, dir., asso. prof., 1969-80, prof., 1997—2002, gen. Sandy Beaver tchr. prof., 2000—02, prof. emeritus, 2002—. Lectr. Boston, L.A., New Orleans, San Antonio, Memphis, Birmingham; chmn. visual arts rev. panel Ga. Council for Arts and Humanities, 1976-77; v.p. Arts Festival Atlanta, 1982, 84, 85, trustee, 1982-93; guest artist Arts Festival Atlanta, 1987; mem. parents council Randolph-Macon Woman's Coll., Lynchburg, Va., 1986-87. Exhibited in one man shows at Ga. Mus. Art, 1959, Atlanta Art Assn., 1959, Unitarian Gallery, Kansas City, 1960, Palmer Gallery, Kansas City, 1965, Heath Gallery, Atlanta, 1976, Hunter Mus. Art, Chattanooga, 1976, Forum Gallery, N.Y.C., 1977, Madison (Ga.) Morgan Cultural Ctr., 1980, Columbus (Ga.) Mus. Arts and Scis., 1980, Macon (Ga.) Mus. Arts and Sci., 1980, Banks Haley Gallery, Albany, Ga., 1980, Augusta Richmond County (Ga.) Mus., 1980, Heath Gallery 1982, Moon Gallery, Berry Coll., Rome, Ga., 1983, Bathhouse Gallery, Atlanta, 1987, MIA Gallery, Seattle, 1988, Valencia C.C., Orlando, Fla., 1991, Gasperi Gallery, New Orleans, 1993, Contemporary Arts Ctr., New Orleans, 1994; numerous site-specific installations, 1986-97; exhibited group shows, New Arts Gallery, Atlanta, 1961, Kansas City Art Inst., 1960-64, Park Coll., 1960, Mulvane Art Ctr., Topeka, 1965, Palazzo Venezia, Rome, 1984, Elaine Benson Gallery, Bridgehampton, L.I., N.Y., 1986, Dulin Gallery Art, Knoxville, Tenn., 1986, 1987 Atlanta Biennale, Nexus Contemporary Art Ctr., Atlanta, Valencia C.C., Orlando, 1988, Greg Kucera Gallery, Seattle, 1992, King Plow Arts Ctr., Atlanta, 1994, Leslie-Lohman Found., N.Y.C., 1995, Mus. Fine Arts, Tallahassee, 1996, Art Ctr., Miami Beach, Fla., 1997, Lebanon Valley Coll., Annville, Pa., 1998, others; represented in permanent collections Gen. Mills, Inc., Mpls., Hallmark Cards, Kansas City, Little Rock Arts Ctr., Ga. Mus. Art, U. Ga., The Kinsey Inst., Ind. U., Calif. State U., Tom of Finland Found. Ford Found. faculty enrichment grantee, 1978; recipient numerous awards for paintings. Mem. Am. Fedn. Arts (trustee 1969-81), Coll. Art Assn., Am. Assn. Museums (council 1981), Lovis Corinth Meml. Found., Ga. Alliance Arts Edn. (dir. 1975-77), Phi Kappa Phi. Home: 150 Bar H Ct Athens GA 30605-4702 Office: 4900 Barnett Shoals Rd Athens GA 30605 E-mail: bpaul@uga.edu.

PAUL, WILLIAM ERWIN, immunologist, researcher; b. Brooklyn, June 12, 1936; s. Jack and Sylvia (Gleicher) Paul; m. Marilyn Heller, Dec. 25, 1958; children: Jonathan M. Carmel, Matthew E. BA summa cum laude, Bklyn. Coll., 1956; MD cum laude, State U. N.Y., Bklyn., 1960, DSc (hon.), 1991; PhD (hon.), Hebrew U., Jerusalem, 2003. Intern, asst. resident Mass. Meml. Hosp., Boston, 1960—62; clin. assoc. Nat. Cancer Inst., NIH, Bethesda, Md., 1962—64; post doctoral fellow, instr. N.Y. Univ. Sch. Medicine, N.Y.C., 1964—68; sr. investigator lab. immunology Nat. Inst. Allergy and Infectious Diseases, NIH, Bethesda, Md., 1968—70, chief lab. immunology, 1970—; dir. office of AIDS rsch. NIH, Bethesda, Md., assoc. dir. AIDS rsch., 1994—97. Mem. sci. adv. bd. Suntory Pharm. Rsch. Lab.; chmn. selection com. Irene Diamond Fund Professorship in Immunology; exec. com. bd. dir. Aaron Diamond AIDS Rsch. Ctr.; Sackler sr. prof. Tel Aviv U., Israel; adj. prof. U. Pa., 2002—. Adv. editor Jour. Exptl. Medicine, 1974—; editor: Ann. Rev. Immunology, Volumes 1-22, 1983—, Fundamental Immunology, 1984; assoc. editor Cell, 1985—96, transmitting editor Internat. Immunology, 1989—96, corr. editor Procs. Royal Soc. Series B, 1989—93, mem. editl. bd. Molecular Biology of Cell, 1990—93; contbg. editor: Procs. NAS U.S.A., 1992—94; editor: Immunity, 2003—, Fundamental Immunology, 5th edit., 2003; mem. editl. bd. Procs. NAS U.S.A., 2004—; contbr. numerous articles to sci. journals. Mem. sci. adv. bd. Trudeau Inst. With USPHS, 1962—64, with USPHS, 1975—96. Recipient Founders' prize, Tex. Instruments Found., 1979, Alumni medal, SUNY Downstate Med. Ctr., 1981, Disting. Svc. medal, USPHS, 1985, Life Sci. Award, 3M, 1988, Tovi, Comet, and Wallerstein prize, CAIR Inst., Bar Ilan U., 1992, 6th ann. Excellence Award in Immunologic Rsch., Duke U., 1993, Alumni Honors, Bklyn. Coll., 1994, Abbott Labs. Award in Clin. and Diagnostic Immunology, Am. Acad. Microbiology, 1998. Fellow: Am. Acad. Arts and Sci.; mem.: NAS, Assn. Am. Physicians, Am. Assn. Immunologist (pres. 1986—87), Scandinavian Soc. Immunology (hon.), Am. Soc. Clin. Investigation (pres. 1980—81), Inst. Medicine NAS. Office: NIH Bldg 10 Rm 11n311 Bethesda MD 20892-0001 Business E-Mail: wepaul@nlh.gov.

PAUL, WILLIAM GEORGE, lawyer; b. Pauls Valley, Okla., Nov. 25, 1930; s. Homer and Helen (Lafferty) P.; m. Barbara Elaine Brite, Sept. 27, 1963; children: George Lynn, Alison Elise, Laura Elaine, William Stephen. BA, U. Okla., 1952, LL.B., 1956. Bar: Okla. bar 1956. Pvt. practice law, Norman, 1956; ptnr. Oklahoma City, 1957-84; with Crowe & Dunlevy, 1962-84, 96—; sr. v.p., gen. counsel Phillips Petroleum Co., Bartlesville, Okla., 1984-95; ptnr. Crowe & Dunlevy, Oklahoma City, 1996—. Assoc. prof. law Oklahoma City U., 1964-68; adv. bd. Martindale Hubbell, 1990—. Author: (with Earl Sneed) Vernon's Oklahoma Practice, 1965. Bd. dirs. Nat. Ctr. for State Cts., 1993-99, Am. Bar Endowment, 1986—; trustee Nat. Constitution Ctr., 2000—. 1st lt. USMCR, 1952-54. Named Outstanding Young Man Oklahoma City, 1965, Outstanding Young Oklahoman, 1966, Okla. Hall of Fame, 2003. Fellow Am. Bar Found. (chmn. 1991), Am. Coll. Trial Lawyers; mem. ABA (bd. govs. 1995—, pres. 1999), Okla. Bar Assn. (pres. 1976), Oklahoma County Bar Assn. (past pres.), Nat. Conf. Bar Pres. (pres. 1986), U. Okla. Alumni Assn. (pres. 1973), Order of Coif, Phi Beta Kappa, Phi Delta Phi, Delta Sigma Rho. Democrat. Presbyterian. Home: 13017 Burnt Oak Rd Oklahoma City OK 73120-8919 Office: Crowe & Dunlevy 20 N Broadway Ave Ste 1800 Oklahoma City OK 73102-8273 Office Phone: 405-239-6676.

PAUL, WILLIAM MCCANN, lawyer; b. Cambridge, Mass., Feb. 9, 1951; s. Kenneth William and Mary Jean (Lamson) P.; m. Janet Anne Forest, Feb. 25, 1984; children: Emily L'Engle, Andrew Angwin, Elizabeth Seton. Student, U. Freiburg, Fed. Republic of Germany, 1971-72; BA, Johns Hopkins U., 1973; JD, U. Mich., 1977. Bar: D.C. 1978, U.S. Dist. Ct. D.C. 1978, U.S. Ct. Claims 1984, U.S. Ct. Appeals (4th cir.) 1980, U.S. Ct. Appeals (fed. cir.) 1983, U.S. Tax Ct. 1990. Law clk. to judge U.S. Ct. Appeals (5th cir.), Austin, Tex., 1977-78; assoc. Covington & Burling, Washington, 1978-87, ptnr., 1987-88, 89—; dep. tax legis. counsel U.S. Treasury Dept., 1988-89. Mem. ABA (asst. sec. tax sect. 1995-97, sec. 1997-99, coun. mem. 1999-2002), D.C. Bar Assn., Am. Law Inst., Am. Coll. Tax Counsel, Order of Coif. Presbyterian. Home: 5604 Chevy Chase Pkwy NW Washington DC 20015-2520 Office: Covington & Burling PO Box 7566 1201 Pennsylvania Ave NW Washington DC 20004-2401 E-mail: wpaul@cov.com.

PAUL, YVONNE C. retired elementary school educator; b. Chgo., July 9, 1934; d. Reuben Douglas Adams and Gladys Winters Bacot; m. William Ralph Paul, Nov. 13, 1962; adopted children: Vanessa, Jonathan. BA, U. Ill., Chgo., 1956; MA in Counseling, San Francisco State U., 1976, MA in Adminstrn., 1983. Classroom tchr. Chgo. Pub. Schs., 1956-59; sch. tchr. Dep. Schs. Europe, Eritrea, East Africa, 1959-60, Stuttgart/Ludwigsburg, Germany, 1960-62; dir. pre-sch. AFB, Killeen, Tex., 1962-63; classroom tchr. Jericho (N.Y.) Sch. Dist., 1964-65; sch. tchr. middle grades Balt. County Schs., Towson, Md., 1965-69; vice prin., tchr. Pittsburg (Calif.) Unified Sch. Dist., 1969-99; ret., 1999. Resource mgr., reading and sci. leadership; classroom tchr., lead math., leader Pittsburg Unified Sch. Dist., 1969-99. Cadet leader Girl Scouts Am., Killeen, 1962; hosp. vol. Killeen Gen. Hosp., 1963; Parent's Booster Club. Technol. Edn. Contra Costa Sch. grantee Alameda/Contra Costa Office Edn., Hayward, Calif., 1985; grant writer awards Technol. Edn. Contra Costa. Mem. No. Calif. Math. Assn., Assn. Calif. Sch. Adminstrs., Artist Guild, Phi Delta Kappa. Roman Catholic. Avocations: writing for publication, reading, gardening, interior design, children's science theater. Home: 488 Lakeview Dr Brentwood CA 94513-5070

PAULEY, BRUCE FREDERICK, history professor; b. Lincoln, Nebr., Nov. 4, 1937; s. Carroll Righter and Blanche Marie (Hulsebus) P.; m. Marianne Barbara Utz, Dec. 21, 1963; children: Mark Allan, Glenn Hamilton. BA, Grinnell Coll., 1959; MA, U. Nebr., 1961; PhD, U. Rochester, 1966. Instr. history Coll. of Wooster (Ohio), 1964-65, U. Nebr., Lincoln, 1965-66; asst. prof. history U. Wyo., Laramie, 1966-71; from assoc. prof. to prof. history U. Ctrl. Fla., Orlando, 1971—, chmn. faculty senate, 1978-79. Vis. prof. history U. Nebr., Lincoln, 2002; cons., expert witness war crimes divsn. Can. Justice Dept., 1998-99. Author: The Habsburg Legacy, 1867-1939, 1972, Hahnenschwanz und Hakenkreuz: Steirischer Heimatschutz und österreichischer Nationalsozialismus, 1918-1934, 1972, Hitler and the Forgotten Nazis: A History of Austrian National Socialism, 1981, Der Weg in den Nationalsozialismus: Ursprünge und Entwicklung in Österreich, 1988, From Prejudice to Persecution: A History of Austrian Anti-Semitism, 1992 (Charles Smith prize So. Hist. Assn. best book European history, 1992, best book Austrian studies Austrian Cultural Inst., 1993), Eine Geschichte des österreichischen Antisemitismus: Von der Ausgrenzung zur Auslöschung, 1993, Hitler, Stalin and Mussolini: Totalitarianism in the Twentieth Century, 1997, 2d edit., 2003. Chmn. parents' adv. com. Oviedo (Fla.) High Sch., 1981-82. Fulbright fellow, 1963-64, rsch. fellow NEH, 1972, 87. Mem.: Soc. Austrian and Habsburg Historians, German Studies Assn. (exec. com. 1986—89), Am. Hist. Assn. Avocations: traveling to historical sites, photography, golf. Office: U Ctrl Fla Orlando FL 32816-1350 Office Phone: 407-823-2224. Business E-Mail: bpauley@pegasus.cc.ucf.edu.

PAULEY, JANE, television journalist; b. Indpls., Oct. 31, 1950; m. Gary Trudeau; 3 children. BA in Polit. Sci, Ind. U., 1971; D of Journalism (hon.), DePauw U., 1978. Reporter Sta. WISH-TV, Indpls., 1972—75; co-anchor WMAQ-TV News, Chgo., 1975—76, The Today Show, NBC, N.Y.C., 1976—90; from co-anchor to corr. NBC News, N.Y.C., 1976—; prin. writer, reporter NBC Nightly News, 1980—82, substitute anchor, 1990—2003; co-anchor Early Today, NBC, 1982—83; prin. corr. Real Life With Jane Pauley, NBC, 1991; co-anchor Dateline NBC, N.Y.C., 1992—99, prin. anchor, 1999—2003; anchor Time & Again MSNBC, 1999—2003. Mem. adv. bd. Childrens Health Fund, Internat. Coun. Freedom From Hunger; bd. dirs. Pub. Edn. Needs Civic Involvement in Learning. Named Broadcaster of Yr., Internat. Radio and TV Soc., 1986, Best in Bus., Washington Journalism Rev., 1990; named to Broadcasting and Cable Hall of Fame; recipient Emmy award, Edward R. Murrow award, Gabriel award, Nancy Susan Reynolds award, Maggie award, Humanitas award, Commendation award, Am. Women in Radio and TV, Gracie Allen award, Clarion award, Assn. for Women in Comm., Wilbur award, Religious Pub. Rels. Coun., Salute to Excellence award, Nat. Assn. Black Journalists, Leonard Zeidenberg First Amendment award, Radio TV News Dirs. Found., Paul White award, NTNDA. Fellow: Soc. for Profl. Journalists (hon. chair Jane Pauley task force on mass comm. edn.).

PAULEY, SHIRLEY STEWART, religious organization executive; b. Boston, Sept. 13, 1938; d. Charles Norris and Nellie Consuelo (Yorke) Stewart; m. Edward Haven Pauley, May 29, 1964; children: David Stewart, Deborah Jeanne. BA, Gordon Coll., 1960; postgrad., Ariz. State U., 1961, Boston U., 1963. Sec./receptionist Atwell Co., Boston, summer 1956; sec., typist Kelley Girl, Boston, 1956-60; asst. office mgr. Radiator Chem. Corp., Scottsdale, Ariz., 1960-62; sec., clerical worker GM, Westwood, Mass., 1962-64; v.p. Truth Alive Ministries, Dallas, 1995—. Spkr. At Large, Boston, 1956-60; Sunday sch. tchr. Blaney Meml. Bapt. Ch., Boston, 1956-60; choir dir. Sherwood Bapt. Ch., Phoenix, 1961-62, co-youth dir., 1961; co-youth dir. Blaney Meml. Ch., Boston, 1964-66; mem. book store com. Prestonwood Bapt. Ch., Dallas, 1994—; messenger Bapt. Gen. Conv. Tex., Ft. Worth, 1996. Republican. Avocations: photography, reading, music. Office: Truth Alive Ministries PO Box 794945 Dallas TX 75379-4945

PAULEY, STANLEY FRANK, manufacturing executive; b. Winnipeg, Man., Can., Sept. 19, 1927; came to U.S., 1954, naturalized, 1961; s. Daniel and Anna (Tache) P.; m. Dorothy Ann Ruppel, Aug. 21, 1949; children: Katharine Ann, Lorna Jane. B.E.E., U. Man., 1949. With Canadian Industries Ltd., Kingston, Ont., 1949-53, sr. engring. asst., 1952-53; controls designer Standard Machine and Tool Co. Ltd., Windsor, Ont., 1953-54; prodn. supt. E.R. Carpenter Co., Richmond, Va., 1954-57, pres., 1957-83, chmn., CEO, 1983-94; chmn., CEO, Carpenter Co. (formerly E.R. Carpenter Co.), Richmond, 1994—, also bd. dirs. Bd. dirs. Carpenter Co. of Can., Carpenter de Mexico, Carpenter Plc., Carpenter S.A., Carpenter Gmbh, Old Westbury Venture Capital Fund LLC. Trustee Va. Mus. Found., Va. Mus. Fine Arts. Mem. Commonwealth Club, Country Club of Va. Republican. Presbyterian. Home: 314 St Davids Ln Richmond VA 23221-3708 Office: Carpenter Co 5016 Monument Ave Richmond VA 23230-3620 E-mail: Stan.Pauley@carpenter.com.

PAULHUS, NORMAN GERARD, JR., aerospace engineer; b. Washington, May 19, 1950; s. Norman Gerard and Kathryn Frances (Schwartz) P. BS Aerospace Engring. with high honors, U. Md., 1970; graduate (hon.), USCG Chief Petty Officers' Acad., 2003. Transp. intern U.S. Dept. Transp., Washington, 1970-71, aerospace engr. Office of Sec., 1971-72, gen. engr., 1972-82, dep. dir. Office Tech. and Planing Assistance, 1982-87, program devel. officer Rsch. and Tech., 1987-91, sr. tech. advisor Office Rsch. and Tech. Transfer, 1991—2002; transp. specialist Fed. Highway Adminstrn., 2002—. Editor: (with D. McKelvey and D. Ewing) Procs. of 4th Nat. Conf. Rural Pub. Transp., 1979, Technology Sharing, 1979, (with A. Brecher, R. Stevens and others) Effective Global Transportation in the Twenty-First Century, 1999; contbr. articles to profl. jours. Recipient Sec.'s award U.S. Dept. Transp., 1974, Meritorious Achievement award, 1979, Spl. Achievement award, 1984, Superior Achievement award, 1989, Cert. Appreciation, Coun. Stat Govts., 1990, Way to Go award Dept. Transp., 1991, Cert. Appreciation, USCG Commandant, 1991, Sec.'s Find Good and Praise It award, 1999, Exemplary Achievemnt (Eagle) award, 2000, Commandant's Pub. Svc. medal USCG, 2002; named hon. chief petty officer, 2003. Mem. AAAS, Nat. Space Inst., U.S. Naval Inst., Navy League U.S., Planetary Soc., Inst. Noetic Scis., Tau Beta Pi, Sigma Gamma Tau, Phi Kappa Phi. Roman Catholic. Home: 18816 Muncaster Rd Rockville MD 20855-1430 Office: 400 7th St SW Washington DC 20590-0001 Office Phone: 202-493-3491. Personal E-mail: otterx@erols.com. Business E-Mail: norman.paulhus@fhwa.dot.gov.

PAULHUS, THOMAS A. social studies educator; b. Paterson, N.J., Oct. 8, 1953; s. Albert Richard and Shelby Ann Paulhus; m. Mary C. Fedigan, Aug. 28, 1988 (div. 1996). BA, Heidelberg Coll., Tiffin, Ohio, 1975; MA, Seton Hall U., 2002. Cert. tchr. social studies, N.J. Cons. The Triad Group, Boston, 1984-90, Toma Assocs., Little Falls, N.J., 1990—; tchr. Blessed Sacrament, Paterson, N.J., 1999—, asst. prin., 2002—. Mem.: Kappa Delta Pi. Democrat. Roman Catholic. Avocation: golf. Home: 275 6th Ave NW Paterson NJ 07524 E-mail: tpaulhusgr6@hotmail.com.

PAULIKAS, GEORGE ALGIS, retired physicist; b. Pagegiai, Lithuania, May 14, 1936; came to U.S., 1949, naturalized, 1955; s. George and Olga (Pacas) P.; m. Joan Marie Gross, Sept. 7, 1957; 1 child, Nancy Marie. BS in Engring. Physics, U. Ill., Chgo. and Urbana, 1957, MS (univ. fellow 1957-58), 1958; PhD in Physics (NSF fellow 1958-61), U. Calif., Berkeley, 1961. With Aerospace Corp., El Segundo, Calif., 1961-98; ret., head space particles and fields dept., 1968, dir. space scis. lab., 1968-81, v.p. labs., 1981-85, sr. v.p. devel., 1985-89, sr. v.p. programs, 1989-94, exec. v.p., 1992-98. Mem. various ad hoc coms. NAS, 1970, 73, 79, 80, ann., 1984—87, 1991—92, 1999—2002, 2004, mem. com. solar and space physics, 1977—80; mem. adv. coun. geophysics U. Calif., 1973—75, exec. com. space scis. lab., 1978—81; mem. sci. adv. bd. USAF, 1975—82, 1991—95; cons. Lawrence Berkeley Lab., 1961—66, Office Space Scis., NASA, 1975—82, Los Alamos phys. divsn. adv. com., 1983—96, Naval Rsch. Adv. Com., 1984—86, Naval Studies Bd., 1989—95, Inst. Def. Analysis, 1998—; mem. def. space tech. com. NRC, 1987—92; mem. NAS/NRC Space Studies Bd., 1999—, vice chair, 2003—. Author papers in field; asso. editor: Jour. Geophys. Research, 1972-75. Trustee Calif. Sci. Ctr., 1994-2000, Boy Scouts Am., L.A., 1996-2000. Recipient Aerospace Corp. Trustees Disting. Achievement award, 1980, Meritorious Civilian Svc. award USAF, 1982, 95, U. Ill. Alumni Disting. Engring. award,

1992, Nat. Reconnaissance Office Gold Medal, 1998; named U. Ill. (Navy Pier) Hall of Fame, 1996. Fellow AIAA (chmn. tech. com. space sci. and astronomy 1976-77), Am. Phys. Soc.; mem. Am. Geophys. Union, Sigma Xi. Home: 1537 Addison Rd Palos Verdes Estates CA 90274 Office Phone: 310-336-7076. E-mail: george.a.paulikas@aero.org.

PAULIN, AMY RUTH, civic activist, consultant; b. Bklyn., Nov. 29, 1955; d. Ben and Alice Lois (Roth) P.; m. Ira Schuman, May 25, 1980; children: Beth, Sarah, Joseph. BA, SUNY, Albany, 1977, MA, 1978, postgrad., 1979—. Instr. SUNY, Albany, 1978, Queens (N.Y.) House of Detention, 1979; fundraiser United Jewish Appeal Fedn., N.Y.C., 1979-83; dir. devel. Altro Health & Rehab., Bronx, N.Y., 1983-86; fundraising cons. N.Y.C., 1986-88; pres. LWV, Scarsdale, N.Y., 1990-92, Westchester, N.Y., 1992-95; trustee Scarsdale (N.Y.) Village, 1995-99; exec. dir. My Sisters' Place, 1999—. Mem. adv. coun. Family Ct.; co-chair woman Westchester Womens Agenda, Westchester Dept. Social Svcs.; mem. adv. com. Fund for Women & Girls; bd. dirs. Mid. Sch. PTA,, 1995-97, Westchester Coalition for Legal Abortion, Scarsdale Open Soc. Assn., 1992-95, United Jewish Appeal Fedn. Scarsdale Women's Campaign; v.p. Westchester Children's Assn.; troop leader Girl Scouts U.S., 1992-96; mem. Town Club Edn. Com., 1983-89; mem. Scarsdale Bowl com., 1992-95, chair, 1994-95; mem. Scarsdale Japanese Festival, 1992-93; mem. Westchester Women's Equality Day, 1987-92; mem. nominating com. Heathcote Neighborhood Assn., 1991-92; bd. advisors Westchester County Found., 1994—; mem. Scarsdale Village Youth Bd., 1992-95; mem. U.S. legislators task force on families at risk Westchester County Bd., 1994—; mem. Updating Voting Equipment Com., 1994; mem. Tobacco Free Westchester, 1993-95, chair 1995—; co-chair Parent Tchr. Coun. Sch. Budget Study, 1991-94; planning chair Kids Base Bd., 1992-95, dir. 1992-94chair parking and traffic subcom. Village Downtown Devel. Com., 1994-95; mem. Westchester Commn. Campaign Fin. Reform, Westchester Commn. Child Abuse, 1996-87; exec. com. Westchester Mcpl. Offcls. Assn., 1996-97; adv. com. Jr. League, 1996-99. Named Westchester County Woman of Yr., 1995, Bridge Fund award, 1998, Women's Health NNetwork Ann. award, 1999. Mem. LWV (bd. dirs. women and children's issues Westchester chpt., dir. social policy N.Y. state), State Communities Aid Assn. (econ. securities com.), N.Y. State Pub. Health Assn. (bd. dirs. Lower Hudson Valley chpt.), N.Y. State Coalition Choice, New Yorkers Against Gun Violence (bd. dirs.). Avocations: swimming, dance. Home: 12 Burgess Rd Scarsdale NY 10583-4410

PAULISON, R. DAVID, federal agency administrator; b. Miami; BA, Fla. Atlantic U.; postgrad., Harvard U. Rescue firefighter, lt., battalion comdr., dist. chief ops., divsn. chief, asst. chief, deputy dir. adminstrn. Miami-Dade Fire Rescue Dept., chief, 1992—2001; adminstr. U.S. Fire Adminstrn., Fed. Emergency Mgmt. Agy., Emmitsburg, Md., 2001—. Office: FEMA 16825 S Seton Ave Emmitsburg MD 21727

PAULISSEN, JAMES PETER, retired pediatrician, county official; b. Chgo., Aug. 14, 1928; s. Joseph Edward and Louise Catherine (Muno) P.; m. Lorraine Antoinette Polly, Sept. 11, 1954; children: Linda, Steven, Mark, Daniel. Student, Loyola U., 1946-49, MD cum laude, 1953; MPH, Johns Hopkins U., 1966. Diplomate Am. Bd. Pediat. Intern Milw. County Hosp., 1953-54; resident Milw. Children's Hosp., 1957-58; practice medicine specializing in pediats. Wauwatosa Children's Clinic, Wis., 1959-65; pediat. fellow Johns Hopkins U., 1965—66; chief Bur. Maternal and Child Health Ill. Dept. Pub. Health, Springfield, 1966-70, chief Divsn. Family Health, 1970-76; exec. dir. DuPage County Health Dept., Wheaton, Ill., 1976-93. Bd. dirs., mem. exec. com. Suburban Cook-DuPage Health Sys. Agy., Oak Park, Ill., 1976-82; bd. dirs., past pres. Comprehensive Health Coun. Met. Chgo., 1977-87; dir. Sr. Home Sharing, Inc., Wheaton, 1981-83; mem. Ill. Commn. on Children, 1971-85, vice chmn., 1983-85; chmn. Ill. Perinatal Adv. Com., 1981-84, mem., 1981-92; mem. Ill. Sch. Health Adv. Com., 1982-93, Gov.'s Adv. Coun. on Devel. Disabilities, 1973-76, Ill. Med. Determinations Bd., 1985-93; vice chmn. Ill. Pub. Health Advisors, 1988-91; mem. adv. bd. divsn. Svcs. Crippled Children U. Ill., 1986-94; trustee DuPage County Med. Found., 1976-82, 86-92, 99—, treas. 2002—; bd. dirs. DuPage Cmty. Clinic, 1993—, Cmty. Nursing Svc. of DuPage, 1993-99, vice chair, 1997-99; mem. cmty. health com. Ctrl. DuPage Health Sys., 1993-98; del. White House Conf. for Children, 1970. Capt. USAF, 1954-56. Recipient Dir.'s award for Sustained Excellence Ill. Dept. Pub. Health, 1988, Ill. Pediatrician of Yr. award, 1992, Humanitarian award DuPage County Health Planning Coun., 1994. Fellow Am. Acad. Pediats. (exec. com. Ill. chpt. 1978-81, sec. 1988-92), APHA, Am. Coll. Preventive Medicine; mem. Ill. Pub. Health Assn. (pres. 1977-78, Disting. Svc. award 1983), Ill. Assn. Maternal and Child Health (pres. 1975-76). Avocation: model railroading. Home: 28w660 Hawthorne Ln West Chicago IL 60185-2472

PAULL, MATTHEW H. food service executive; BA, M in Acctg., U. Ill. Ptnr. Ernst & Young; with McDonald's Corp., 1993—, v.p. corp. tax, sr. v.p., fin., 1999—2001, exec. v.p., 2001—04, CFO, 2001—, sr. exec. v.p., 2004—. Adv. dir. bd. dirs. McDonalds Corp., 1999—2000, mem. chmns. coun., mem. Japan Bd., 2002—03; mem. adv. coun. Fed. Res. Bank, Chgo.; bd. dirs. Best Buy Co., Inc. Active Kohl Children's Mus., Chgo. Symphony Orch.; trustee Ravinia Festival Assn.; bd. mem. Loyola Ronald McDonald House. Office: McDonalds Corp McDonalds Plaza Oak Brook IL 60523

PAULL, RICHARD ALLEN, geologist, educator; b. Madison, Wis., May 20, 1930; s. Ethra Harold and Martha (Schaller) P.; m. Rachel Kay Krebs, Mar. 6, 1954; children: Kay Marie, Lynn Ellen, Judith Ann. BS, U. Wis., 1952, MS, 1953, PhD, 1957. Party chief Pan Am. Petroleum Co., 1955-57; research group leader Jersey Prodn. Research Co., 1957-62; mem. faculty U. Wis.-Milw., 1962-97, chmn. dept. geol. scis., 1962-66, prof., 1966-97, prof. emeritus, 1997—. Cons. in field, 1966— Author books, papers in field. Colo. vol. Naturalist Roxborough State Park; co-exec. sec. NAGT/USGS/AASG-Coop. Summer Field Tng. Program, 1994-99. Served with USAF, 1953-55. Hon. curator Milw. Museum; recipient Amoco Distinguished Teaching award, 1975 Fellow Geol. Soc. Am. (chmn. ann. meeting 1970, tech. program com. 1970, 77, membership com. 1977-80, chmn. 1980); mem. Am. Assn. Petroleum Geologists (chmn. sci. fair award com. 1980, membership com. 1981-87, vis. petroleum geologists com. 1982-87, pub. affairs com. 1982-85), Soc. Econ. Paleontologists and Mineralogists, Nat. Assn. Geology Tchrs. (v.p. 1976-77, pres. 1977-78), Am. Geol. Inst. (governing bd. 1977-79, sec. and exec. com. 1986-88), Nature Conservancy, Sigma Xi. Home: 1657 W Canal Ct Littleton CO 80120-4515 Personal E-mail: rocdox@comcast.net.

PAULOSE, ANIL CHIRAMEL, financial market data/trading systems software infrastructure consultant; b. Kerala, India, Aug. 24, 1965; came to U.S., 1989; s. C.J. Paulose; m. Lata Anil. BS in Electronics, Bangalore (India) U., 1988; MS in Computer Engring., La. State U., 1992. Software arch. IGT, Reno, Nev., 1992-94; mem. tech. staff Tibco Software Inc., Palo Alto, Calif., 1994-96; prin. cons. J.P. Morgan, N.Y.C., 1996-98, Greenwich (Conn.) Capital, 1998-2001; sr. architect Bloomberg Tradebook LLC, N.Y.C., 2001—. Cons. bus. strategy Sharp Decisions Inc., N.Y.C., 1997-2000; founder, pres. Marketcube Inc., N.J., 1999-2001, epasse.com, N.J., 2000—. Inventor tibscript/passage software architecture framework. Mem. World Future Soc., N.Y. Acad. Scis. E-mail: anil@chiramel.com.

PAULS, JANICE LONG, state legislator; m. Ron Pauls. BS, Sterling (Kans.) Coll., 1973; JD, U. Kans., 1976. Rep. dist. 102 Kans. Ho. of Reps., mem. Judiciary, rules and regulations, transp., corrections and juvenile justice coms. Democrat. Home: 1634 N Baker St Hutchinson KS 67501-5621 Office: Kans Ho of Reps State Capitol Topeka KS 66612

PAULSEN, ANNE M. state legislator; B.S., Framingham State Coll.; M.A., Boston State Coll. Mem. Belmont School Committee, 1976—85, Belmont Board of Selectmen, 1986—92, Mass. Ho. of Reps., 1993—. Address: State House Rm 22 Boston MA 02133

PAULSEN, FRANK ROBERT, college dean emeritus; b. Logan, Utah, July 5, 1922; s. Frank and Ella (Ownby) P.; m. Marye Lucile Harris, July 31, 1942; 1 son, Robert Keith; m. Lydia Ransier Lowry, Nov. 1, 1969. BS, Utah State U., 1947; MS, U. Utah, 1948, Ed.D., 1956; Kellogg Found. postdoctoral fellow, U. Oreg., 1958; Carnegie Found. postdoctoral fellow, U. Mich., 1959-60. High sch. prin., Mt. Emmons, Utah, 1948-51; supt. schs. Cokeville, Wyo., 1951-55; from asst. prof. to assoc. prof. edn. U. Utah, 1955-61; prof. edn., dean Sch. Edn. U. Conn., 1961-64; dean Coll. Edn. U. Ariz., Tucson, 1964-84, dean emeritus, prof. emeritus higher edn., 1984—. Scholar-in-residence Fed. Exec. Inst., Charlottesville, Va., 1970; Disting. prof. edn. U. Bridgeport, summer 1972; dir. Am. Capital Growth Fund, Am. Series Portfolio Stock Co., Houston, Am. Gen. Equity Fund, Am. Capital Bond Fund, Am. Capital Convertible Securities Fund, Am. Capital Exch. Fund, Am. Series Portfolio Co., Am. Capital Income Trust; exec. com. New Eng. Coun. Advancement Sch. Adminstrn., 1960-64; trustee Common Sense Trust Co., Houston. Author: The Administration of Public Education in Utah, 1958, Contemporary Issues in American Education, 1966, American Education: Challenges and Images, 1967, Changing Dimensions in International Education, 1968, Higher Education: Dimensions and Directions, 1969, also numerous articles. Trustee Joint Council Econ. Edn., 1962-70; v.p., dir. Southwestern Coop. Ednl. Lab., 1965-67; bd. dirs. Nat. League for Nursing, 1967-69, mem. com. on perspectives, 1966-72; dir., chmn. exec. com. ERIC Clearinghouse on Tchr. Edn., 1968-70; bd. dirs. Tucson Mental Health Center, 1968-70. Served with AUS, 1942-46, PTO. Mem. Aerospace Med. Assn., Am. Assn. Sch. Adminstrs., Am. Acad. Polit. and Social Sci., Utah Acad. Letters, Arts and Scis., Ariz. Acad., Am. Assn. Colls. Tchrs. Edn. (Conn. liaison officer 1962-64, mem. studies com. 1962-68, dir.), Ariz. Assn. Colls. Tchr. Edn. (pres. 1972-80), AAAS, Am. Ednl. Research Assn., Kappa Delta Pi, Pi Sigma Alpha, Pi Gamma Mu, Phi Delta Kappa. Lodges: Rotary.

PAULSEN, JAN, clergyman, church administrator; b. Narvik, Norway, Jan. 5, 1935; came to Eng., 1968. s. Reidar A. and Alfhild K. (Kirstensen) P. m. Kari Trykkerud, July 1, 1955; children: Laila, Jan-Rune, Rein Andre. BA, Andrews U., Berrien Sprgs., Mich., 1957, MA, 1958, MDiv, 1962; PhD in Theol., Tubingen U., W. Ger., 1972. ordained to ministry Seventh-Day Adventist Ch. Minister Seventh-Day Adventist Ch., Arendal, Norway, 1959-61, Haugesund, Norway, 1959-61; lectr. Bekwai Tchr. Tng. Coll., Ghana, 1962-64; lectr., coll. pres. Adventist Coll. West Africa, Ilishan, Nigeria, 1964-68; lectr. Newbold Coll., Bracknell, Eng., 1968-76, pres., 1976-80; gen. sec. Seventh-Day Adventist Ch. Hdqrs. for No. Europe, St. Albans, Hertsforde, Eng., 1980-83, 1983-95; v.p., gen. coun. Seventh day Adventist Ch., Silver Sprg., Md., 1995-99, pres., 1999—. Author: When the Spirit Descends, 1977; contbr. articles to varous jours. Recipient Charles E. Weninger Award for Outstanding Achievement, Pacific Union Coll., 2000. Office: Seventh-day Adventist Church World Headquarters 12501 Old Columbia Pike Silver Spring MD 20904-6601*

PAULSEN, SERENUS GLEN, architect, educator; b. Spooner, Wis., July 27, 1917; s. Serenus Justin and Edna Anne (Dalton) P.; m. Virginia C. Habel, Jan. 26, 1944; children: Thomas J., Nancy Lee (Mrs. John Marshall). Student, U. Ill., 1938-42; B.Arch. cum laude, U. Pa., 1947; Diploma in Architecture and City Planning, Royal Acad. Art, Stockholm, 1948. With Carroll, Grisdale & Van Alan (Architects), Phila., 1946-47, Eero Saarinen & Assos., Bloomfield Hills, Mich., 1949-51, 53-57; chief designer Reisner & Urbahn (Architects), N.Y.C., 1951-52; archtl. coordinator Knoll Assos., N.Y.C., 1952-53; prin. Glen Paulsen Assos., Birmingham, Mich., 1958-69; prin., v.p. Tarapata-MacMahon-Paulsen Assos., Inc. (Architects), Bloomfield Hills, 1969-77; pres. Cranbrook Acad. Art, head dept. architecture, 1966-70; prof., chmn. Masters Program in Architecture U. Mich., 1976-78, Emil Lorch prof. architecture, 1982-85, prof. emeritus, 1985—. Mem. Nat. Com. on Urban Planning and Design, 1971-72; archtl. commn. U. Wash., Seattle, 1968-76 (Recipient 3d prize Bi-Nat. Competition for Design Rainbow Center Plaza, Niagara Falls, N.Y. 1972). Gov. emeritus Cranbrook Acad. Art. Served with C.E. USAAF, 1942-46. Fellow AIA (honor awards Detroit chpt. for Shapero Hall of Pharmacy 1965, Our Shepherd Lutheran Ch. 1966, Ford Life Sci. Bldg. 1967, Birney Elementary Sch., Detroit 1971, Fed. Bldg., Ann Arbor, Mich. 1978, gold medal for 1980 Detroit chpt.); mem. Mich. Soc. Architects, (Robert F. Hastings award 1985). Home: 1101 Silver Maples Dr Chelsea MI 48118-1187

PAULSEN, VIVIAN, magazine editor; b. Salt Lake City, May 10, 1942; d. Paul Herman and Martha Oline (Blattmann) P. BA, Brigham Young U., 1964, postgrad., 1965, U. Grenoble, France, 1966. Cert. tchr., Utah. Tchr. French Granite Sch. Dist., Salt Lake City, 1966-67; assoc. editor New Era mag., Salt Lake City, 1970-82; mng. editor Friend mag., Salt Lake City, 1982—. Am. Field Service scholar, 1959; grad. fellow Brigham Young U., 1964-66 Republican. Mem. Ch. of Jesus Christ of Latter-day Saints Office: The Friend 50 E North Temple # F23 Salt Lake City UT 84150-0002

PAULSON, BERNARD ARTHUR, oil company executive, consultant; b. Lakeview, Mich., July 12, 1928; s. Arthur Bernard and Genevieve Talbard (Bushley) P.; m. Joan Lee Curtiss, Dec. 4, 1954; children: James, Joseph (dec.), Ann, Thomas (dec.), Bernadette, Patricia, Steven. BS in Chem. Engring., Mich. State U.-East Lansing, 1949. Registered profl. engr., Tex. Process engr. Mid-West Refineries Inc., Alma, Mich., 1949-57; plant mgr. Kerr-McGee Corp., Cleve. and Wynnewood, Okla., 1957-66; v.p. Coastal States Petrochemical, Corpus Christi, Tex., 1966-71, Koch Industries Inc., St. Paul and Wichita, 1971-88, cons. Corpus Christi, Tex., 1988-94; pres. Koch Refining Co., Wichita, 1981-88; chmn. bd. dirs. The Automation Group Inc.; chmn., CEO The Inspection Group Inc. CEO Tor Minerals Internat., 1997, also bd. dirs; dir. Orion Refining Corp., 1999—. Chmn., pres. Cleve. Area Hosp. Corp., 1962; bd. dirs. Ada Wilson Hosp. Found., Dirscoll Hosp. Found., Coastal Bend Cmty. Found.; pres. Corpus Christ Bd. Trade; commr. Port of Corpus Christi Authority, sec., 1997. 1st lt. USAF, 1955-57. Recipient Claud R. Erickson Disting. Alumnus award Mich. State U., 1994. Mem. AIChE (fuels and petrochem. award 1989), Nat. Petroleum Refiners Assn., Refining Am. Petroleum Inst., Wichita Area C. of C. (bd. dirs.), Bd. Trade, Corpus Christi Town Club (bd. dirs.), Elks. Home and Office: Tor Minerals 3 Ocean Park Dr Corpus Christi TX 78404-1600

PAULSON, BOYD COLTON, JR., civil engineering educator; b. Providence, Mar. 1, 1946; s. Boyd Colton and Barbara (McKinstry) P.; m. Jane Margaret Kingdon, Feb. 12, 1970; children: Jeffrey Boyd, Laura Jane. BS, Stanford U., 1967, MS, 1969, PhD, 1971. Asst. prof. U. Ill., Urbana, 1972-73; asst. prof., assoc. prof. civil engring. Stanford (Calif.) U., 1974, prof., 1984-89, Ohbayashi prof. engring., 1989-91, Charles Leavell prof. civil engring., 1991—. Mem. civil engring. adv. com. NSF, 1983-84; mem. U.S. Nat. Com. on Tunneling, 1986-89; mem. com. on constrn. superconducting supercollider in Tex., NAS, 1988-89; presenter in field. Author: Computer Applications in Construction, 1995; co-author: Professional Construction Management, 1978, 2d edit., 1984, 3d edit., 1992; also articles. Bd. dirs. Peninsula Habitat for Humanity, 1996—2002, Mid-Peninsula Housing Coalition, 1999—. Fellow Humboldt Found., Munich, 1983, Brit. Coun., Glasgow, Scotland, 1990-91, Fulbright fellow, 1990-91. Mem. ASCE (chmn. constrn. divsn. 1986-87, Huber Rsch. prize 1980, Constrn. Mgmt. award 1984, Peurifoy Rsch. award 1993), Am. Soc. for Engring. Edn., Urban Land Inst., Nat. Acad. Constrn. Achievements include research in human-computer systems for project management, in analytical modeling and simulation of construction operations, in tunneling in urban environments, in low-cost housing. Office: Stanford U 4020 Civil Engring Stanford CA 94305-4020

PAULSON, DONALD ROBERT, chemistry professor; b. Oak Park, Ill., Sept. 6, 1943; s. Robert Smith and Florence Teresa (Beese) P.; m. Elizabeth Anne Goodwin, Aug. 20, 1966; children: Matthew, Andrew. BA, Monmouth Coll., 1965; PhD, Ind. U., 1968. Asst. prof. chemistry Calif. State U., Los Angeles, 1970-74, assoc. prof., 1974-78, prof., 1979—, chmn. dept., 1982-90. Vis. prof. U. B.C., Vancouver, Can., 1977-78, U. Sussex, Brighton, Eng., 1984-85. Author: Alicyclic Chemistry, 1976; contbr. articles to profl. jours. Named Outstanding Prof., Calif. State U., Los Angeles, 1978, 84, 96. Mem. Am. Chem. Soc., Chem. Soc. (London), InterAm. Photochem. Soc., Nat. Assn. Sci. Tchrs., Sigma Xi. Democrat. Episcopalian. Avocations: photography, hiking, soccer. Home: 497 E California Blvd Apt 203 Pasadena CA 91106-3789 Office: Calif State U Dept Chemistry 5151 State University Dr Los Angeles CA 90032-4226 Office Phone: 323-343-2332. Business E-Mail: dpaulso@calstatela.edu.

PAULSON, GWEN O. GAMPEL, government relations consultant; b. Detroit, Mar. 16, 1945; d. Maurice V. and Lilyan Victor; div.; children: Jill Susan, Mindy Beth; m. Jerome A. Paulson, July 2, 1989. BA, Mich. State U., 1966; MA, Wayne State U., 1974; postgrad., U. Mich., 1981. Lectr. Oakland U., Mich., 1979—80, U. Mich., Ann Arbor, 1981; legis. asst. U.S. Rep. Pete Stark, Washington, 1982—85; mem. profl. staff, ways and means health subcom. U.S. Ho. of Reps., Washington, 1985—89; v.p. for health Capitol Assocs., Washington, 1989—90; pres. Congl. Cons., Washington, 1990—. Author: Women and the Structure of Society, 1984. Edward S. Beck fellow U. Mich., Ann Arbor, 1978-79; Rackham Dissertation grant U. Mich., Ann Arbor, 1980. Mem. Women in Govt. Rels., Bus. and Profl. Women, Fedn. Am. (co-chair 1999-2001), Am. League Lobbyists, Greater Washington Soc. Assn. Execs., Phi Alpha Theta, Tau Sigma. Avocations: collecting contemporary glass, travel, history, politics, reading. Office: Congl Cons LLC 1113 N Howard St Alexandria VA 22304-1627 E-mail: gwencc@comcast.net.

PAULSON, HENRY MERRITT, JR., (HANK PAULSON), venture capitalist, investment company executive; b. Palm Beach, Fla., Mar. 28, 1946; s. Henry Merritt and Marianna (Gallaeur) P.; m. Wendy Judge, Sept. 6, 1969; children: Henry Merritt III, Amanda Clark. BA in English, Dartmouth Coll., 1968; MBA, Harvard U., 1970. Staff asst. to the asst. sec. def. (comptroller) Pentagon, Dept. Def., Washington, 1970-72; staff asst. to the Pres. Domestic Council, The White House, Washington, 1972-73; assoc. Goldman Sachs & Co., Chgo., 1974-77, v.p., 1977-82, ptnr. investment banking dept., 1982—, ptnr. in charge investment banking Midwest region, 1984-90; mgmt. com. co-head investment banking div., vice chmn., COO, 1994—98; CEO, chair Goldman Sachs & Co., Chgo., 1999—. Bd. dirs. NY Stock Exch., Peregrine Fund Inc.; mem. exec. com. N.Y.C. Investment Fund. Mem. adv. bd. J.L. Kellogg grad. sch. of mgmt.; chmn. adv. bd. Tsinghua U. Sch. Econs. and Mgmt.; mem. governing bd. Indian Sch. Mgmt. NCAA Scholar Athlete, 1967; named to 1st team All-Ivy, All New Eng., All-East; New Eng. Football Coaches' Selection as Outstanding Coll. Lineman, Div. I, New England, 1967 Mem. The Commercial Club (Chgo.), The Econ. Club (Chgo.), Chgo. Club, Phi Beta Kappa. Republican. Mem. Christian Science Ch. Avocations: skiing; fishing; canoeing; tennis. Office: Goldman Sachs Group 85 Broad St New York NY 10004-2434*

PAULSON, JAMES MARVIN, engineering educator; b. Wausau, Wis., Jan. 1, 1923; s. Gustav Victor and Susanna (Dracy) P.; m. Marjorie Beulah Burton, May 11, 1946; children— Vicki Rae, Michael James. BS in Civil Engring, The Citadel, 1947; MS in Civil Engring, Ill. Inst. Tech., 1949; PhD, U. Mich., 1958. Registered profl. engr., Mich. Draftsman Wausau Iron Works, 1946; engr. Charles Whitney Cons. Engr., Milw., 1948-49; faculty Wayne State U., Detroit, 1949—, prof., 1961-85, chmn. dept. civil engring., 1967-72, assoc. dean Coll. Engring., 1973-83, prof. emeritus, 1985—. V.p. Civil Engrs., Inc., 1954—; cons. in field. Served with AUS, 1943; Served with USMCR, 1943-46. Mem. ASCE (life), Mich. Soc. Profl. Engrs. (life), Am. Soc. for Engring. Edn., Sigma Xi, Tau Beta Pi, Chi Epsilon. Presbyterian. Home: PO Box 23 Greenbush MI 48738-0023

PAULSON, JEROME AVROM, pediatrician; b. Balt., July 31, 1949; s. Robert R. and Edna (Brenner) P.; m. Susan Miller, 1973 (div. 1986); m. Gwen Victor Gampel, July 2, 1989. BS in Biochemistry, U. Md., 1971; MD, Duke U., 1974. Diplomate Am. Bd. Pediatrics, Nat. Bd. Med. Examiners. Resident in pediatrics Johns Hopkins Hosp., Balt., 1974-76, Sinai Hosp., Balt., 1976-77, fellow in ambulatory pediatrics, 1977-78; asst. prof. pediatrics Case Western Res. U., Cleve., 1978-86; dir. sci. rsch. and pub. policy devel. Joseph P. Kennedy Jr. Found., Washington, 1986-87; dir. pediatrics Regional Inst. for Children and Adolescents, Rockville, Md., 1987-89; clin. assoc. prof. pediatrics Georgetown U., Washington, 1987—; exec. dir. Research!America, Alexandria, Va., 1989-90; assoc. prof. medicine (formerly healthcare scis.) George Washington U., Washington, 1990—2002, assoc. prof. pediats., 1991—, fellow Ctr. Health Policy Rsch., 1991—98, assoc. prof. prevention and cmty. health, 1997—, assoc. rsch. prof. environ. and occupl. health, 2003—; co-dir. Mid-Atlantic Ctr. for Children's Health and the Environment George Washington U. Med. Ctr., 2000—. Mem. conf. on methodology and std. definitions for childhood injury rsch. Nat. Inst. Children & Human Devel., 1989; health adv. com. Congressman James Moran, 8th Congl. Dist., Va., 1992—94; mem. benefits working group Nat. Drinking Water Adv. Coun. EPA, 1989—99; adv. Health Pages, 1994—97; spl. asst. to dir. Nat. Ctr. for Environ. Health, Ctrs. for Disease Control, Washington, 1999—2001; Soros advocacy fellow Children's Environ. Health Network, 2000—02; bd. dirs. Crative Glass Ctr. Am. Author: Pediatrics: Review for New National Boards, 2000; contbr. articles to profl. jours., chpts. to books. Profl. adv. bd. Nat. Safety Town Ctr., Cleve., 1981-85; bd. dirs., pres. James Renwick Alliance, Washington, 1986-93, 95-98; bd. dirs. Jewish Social Svcs. Agy Greater Washington, 2002—. Recipient Cert. for Ednl. and Pub. Policy Activity, Ohio State Senate/Ho. of Reps., 1985; Robert Wood Johnson Health Policy fellow, 1985-86, Soros Advocacy fellowship 2000-02. Fellow Am. Acad. Pediatrics; mem. Ambulatory Pediatric Assn. Jewish. Avocation: collecting contemporary american crafts. Office: CP & A Foggy Bottom 2141 K St NW # 401 Washington DC 20037-1866 Office Phone: 202-833-4543. Business E-Mail: jpaulson@cnmc.org.

PAULSON, KENNETH ALAN, editor; b. Chgo., Dec. 3, 1953; s. Knut Norman and Helen Elizabeth (Beardsley) P.; m. Peggy Jean Foot, June 12, 1976; children: Carrie Ann, David. BA in Journalism, U. Mo., 1975; JD, U. Ill., 1978. Bar: Ill., 1978, Fla. 1979. Reporter, bur. chief Fort Myers News-Press, Fla., 1978—80; metro editor to mng. editor Courier-News, Bridgewater, NJ, 1980—84; founding staff member USA Today, McLean, Va., 1982; editor Green Bay Press-Gazette, Wis., 1985—86; spl. asst./chief of staff to chmn. Gannett Co., 1986—88; exec. editor Florida Today, Brevard County, 1988—92; exec. editor, v.p. news Gannett Suburban Newspapers, White Plains, NY, 1992—96; exec. dir. 1st Amendment Ctr. Vanderbilt U., Nashville, 1997—2004; sr. v.p. Freedom Forum, Arlington, Va., 1997—2004; editor USA Today, McLean, Va., 2004—. Adj. prof. Vanderbilt U. Law Sch.; host TV show Speaking Freely. Office: USA Today 7950 Jones Beach Dr Mc Lean VA 22108 Home: 2791 Centerboro Dr Apt 178 Vienna VA 22181

PAULSON, LORETTA NANCY, psychoanalyst; b. L.A., Nov. 5, 1943; d. Frank Morris and Rose (Kaufman) Fargo; m. Maurice Krasnow; 1 child, Kira. BA, U. So. Calif., 1966; MS in Social Work, Columbia U., 1969; cert. psychoanalyst, C.G. Jung Inst., N.Y.C. Cert. clin. social worker, N.Y., Conn., N.J. Pvt. practice psychoanalysis, N.Y.C., 1976—. Vice.- chmn. CGJ Inst. Tng. Bd. Mem. NASW (diplomate in clin. social work), Internat. Assn. for Analytical Psychology (past del., bd. dirs.), N.Y. Assn. for Analytic Psychology (past pres., past chair program com.), Conn. Soc. Clin. Social Work (com. on psychoanalysis), C.G. Jung Inst. Address: 334 W 86th St Apt 1A New York NY 10024-3130

PAULSON, PAUL JOSEPH, advertising executive; b. White Plains, N.Y., Sept. 25, 1932; s. Paul and Ann (Loughlin) P.; m. Kathryn P. Keeler, June 30, 1962; children: Thomas, Mark, Kathryn, John, Clifford. BSBA, Ohio State U., 1954; MBA, U. Pa., 1959. With Compton Advt. Inc., N.Y.C., 1959-78, mgmt. supr., 1965-78, sr. v.p., 1968-78, also dir.; pres., dir. Doyle Dane Bernbach Inc., N.Y.C., 1978-83; pres., chief exec. officer Isidore & Paulson, Inc., N.Y.C., 1983-93; chmn., pres., CEO Paulson & Co. Mktg. Svcs., Greenwich, 1993—. Chmn. Mktg. Exec. Networking Group, 2000—03; mem. Ohio State U. Alumni Adv. Coun., 1982—; pres. coun. mem. Ohio State U., 1993—. Author: Fundamentals of Consumer Goods Marketing, 1966. Chmn. Christmas for Underprivileged Children, N.Y.C., 1963—. Served to lt. (j.g.) USNR, 1955-58, MTO, ETO. Mem. Wharton Grad. Bus. Sch. Alumni Assn. (pres. N.Y.C. club 1963-65, dir. 1972—), Ohio State U. Alumni Assn., Wharton Grad. Bus. Sch., Milbrook Owners Assn. (pres.). Clubs: N.Y. (dir.), Milbrook, Sigma Chi. Roman Catholic. Home: 45 W Brother Dr Greenwich CT 06830-6726

PAULSON, PETER JOHN, librarian, publishing company executive; b. N.Y.C., Jan. 30, 1928; s. Peter John and Lillian Agnes Elaine (Neuman) P.; m. Josephine C. Bowen, Dec. 5, 1953 (dec. June 2002); children: David (dec. Apr. 1997), Debora. B.Social Scis. cum laude, CCNY, 1949; MA in History, Columbia, 1950; MA in L.S, SUNY, Albany, 1955. Library asst. N.Y. State

Library, Albany, 1952-55, head, gift and exchange sect., 1955-65, head catalog sect., 1965-66, prin. librarian tech. services, 1966-71, dir., 1972-85; exec. dir. OCLC Forest Press, 1985-98. Adj. asst. prof. library sci. State U. N.Y. at Albany, 1960-71; Adv. com. Ohio Coll. Library Center, 1970-71; adv. council to pub. printer depository libraries, 1972-77, chmn., 1975-77, com. fed. depository library service N.Y. State, 1960-70, chairperson, 1960-70; bd. dirs. Capital Dist. Libr. Coun., Nat. Info. Standards Orgn., N.E. Document Conservation Ctr. Mem. ALA (chmn. com. on legislation 1980-82, pres. state library agy. sect. 1982-83), N.Y. Library Assn. (pres. 1975), Hudson-Mohawk Library Assn. (v.p. 1964), SUNY-OCLC Network (governing bd. 1980-82), Phi Beta Kappa. Home: 24 Tillinghast Ave Albany NY 12204-2312 Office Phone: 518-465-3103.

PAULSTON, CHRISTINA BRATT, linguistics educator; b. Stockholm, Dec. 30, 1932; arrived in US, 1951; d. Lennart and Elsa Bratt; m. Rolland G. Paulston, July 26, 1963; children: Christopher-Rolland, Ian Rollandsson. BA, Carleton Coll., 1953; MA in English and Comparative Lit., U. Minn., 1955; Ed.D., Columbia U., 1966. Cert. tchr., Minn. Tchr. Clara City and Pine Island High Schs., Minn., 1955-60, Am. Sch. of Tangier, Morocco, 1960-62, Katrineholm Allmanna Laroverk, Katrineholm, Sweden, 1962-63, East Asian Library, Columbia U., N.Y.C., 1963-64; asst. instr. Tchrs. Coll., Columbia U., 1964-66; instr. U. Punjab, Chandigarh, India, summer 1966, Pontificia Universidad Catolica Del Peru, Lima, 1966-67; cons. Instituto Linguistico de Verano, Lima, 1967-68; asst. prof. linguistics U. Pitts., 1969-75, prof., 1975-99, prof. emerita, tchg. pro bono, 1999—, asst. dir. English Lang. Inst., 1969-70, dir. English Lang. Inst., 1970-97, acting dir. Lang. Acquistion Inst., fall 1971, acting chmn. dept. gen. linguistics, 1971-75, chmn., 1975-89. Apptd. internat. advisor in sociolinguistics to Summer Inst. of Linguistics, 1997. Author numerous books and articles on linguistics. Recipient research award Am. Ednl. Research Assn., 1980; Fulbright-Hays grantee, Uruguay, 1985. Mem. Assn. Tchrs. English to Speakers of Other Langs. (2d v.p., conv., chmn. 1972, exec. com. 1972-75, rsch. com. 1973-75, 78-80, chmn. 1973-75, 1st v.p. 1975, pres. 1976), Linguistics Soc. Am. (com. linguistics and pub. interest 1973-77), Internat. Assn. Tchrs. of English as a Fgn. Lang., Am. Coun. on Tchg. of Fgn. Langs., MLA (exec. com. lang. and soc. 1975-76), Ctr. Applied Linguistics (trustee 1976-81, exec. com. 1980, publs. com. 1981, rsch. com. 1981). Democrat. Episcopalian. Office: U Pitts Linguistics Pittsburgh PA 15260 Office Phone: 412-624-5900.

PAULU, FRANCES BROWN, retired international center administrator; b. Hastings, Minn., June 22, 1920; d. Thomas Andrew and Florence Ida (Tuttle) Brown; m. Burton Paulu, June 29, 1942; children: Sarah Leith Paulu Boittin, Nancy Jean Paulu Hyde, Thomas Scott. BA magna cum laude, U. Minn., 1940. Case worker Family Welfare Assn., Mpls., 1943—45; interviewer County Health and Welfare Coun., Mpls., 1963; sch. social worker Project Head Start, Mpls., 1966; program dir. Minn. Internat. Ctr., Mpls., 1970—72, exec. dir., 1972—89; mem. tourism adv. com. City of Mpls., 1976—83; mem. adv. coun. Minn. World Trade Ctr., 1984—86. Pres. UN Rally, 1970—72; chmn. Mpls. Charter Commn., 1972—74; dir. Minn. World Trade Week, 1977—81; del. Nat. Coun. World Affairs, Taipei-Manila, 1988; coord. Voices from Around the World, 1996—2000; bd. dirs. Urban Coalition of Mpls., 1967—70; sec. Becketwood Coop., 2001—04; mgmt. team Minn. Awareness Project, 1982—89; participant Intercultural Comm. Project Japan, 1974; dir. Elder Learning Inst., 1995—2000. Fellow, U. Min. Sch. Social Work, 1942—44; DeWitt Jennings Payne scholar, 1939—40. Mem.: LWV (pres. Mpls. chpt. 1967—69), Nat. Coun. Internat. Visitors (officer, mem. exec. com. 1975—81, leader fact-finding team N. Africa, Mid. East, India 1978, conf. chair 1989), Alliance Française (bd. dirs. 1991—94), People to People Internat. (Disting. Membership award 1987), UN Assn. Minn. (mem. adv. coun. 1979—92, 1996—, sec. 1994—96), U. Minn. Women's Club (pres. 1992—94), Phi Beta Kappa, Lambda Alpha Psi, Alpha Omicron Pi. Home: 4300 W River Pkwy Apt 444 Minneapolis MN 55406-3681 E-mail: paulu005@umn.edu.

PAULUS, ELEANOR BOCK, professional speaker, author; b. N.Y.C., Mar. 12, 1933; d. Charles William Bock and Borghild (Nelson) Garrick; m. Chester William Paulus Jr., Sept. 6, 1952; children: Chester W. III, Karl Derrick, Diane Paulus Henricks. Student, Smith Coll., 1952-53. Owner, founder Khan-Du Chinese Shar-Pei, Somerset, N.J., 1980—; dir. Pet Net, Santa Fe, N.Mex., 1992—; co-owner, CFO Am. Dream TV Prodns., Washington, 1993—; co-owner, exec. prodr. Capitol Ideas, 1995-2001, Pierre Salinger's Round Table, 1997; pets and animals columnist www.goodnewsbroadcast.com, 2000—. Lectr., cons. on Chinese Shar-Pei and canine health, 1980—; internat. con., lectr. on pet care and health. Author: Health Care Handbook for Cats, Dogs and Birds, The Proper Care of Chinese Shar-Pei; contbr. articles to mags. and jours. including Dog Fancy, chpts. to books, including The World of the Chinese Shar-Pei; creator, prodr. World of Dogs, 1996—. Dir. bd. trustees Rutgers Prep. Sch., Somerset, 1970-76, v.p. bd. trustees, 1976-81, pres. PTA, 1966-76; chmn. Raritan River Festival, New Brunswick, N.J., 1980-91. Named Woman of Yr., City of New Brunswick, 1982. Mem. Dog Writers Am. Assn., Dog Fanciers N.Y.C., Bonzai Clubs Internat., Koi Internat. N.Y., Raritan Valley Country Club, Chinese Shar-Pei Club of Am. (v.p. 1982-86, bd. dirs. east sect. 1980-82, Humanitarian award 1986). Avocations: travel, dog related activities, gardening. Home: 321 Skillman Ln Somerset NJ 08873-5325 Office: E B Paulus 20 Sutton Pl S # 5A New York NY 10022-4165

PAULUS, MICHAEL JOHN, government official, bank executive, economist; b. Port Washington, Wis., Feb. 18, 1957; s. John Peter and Elizabeth Jane (Streff) P.; m. Christine H. Kwon, Apr. 29, 2000; 1 child, Alexandra. BA, U. Wis., Milw., 1980; cert., U. Freiburg, Fed. Republic Germany, 1979-80; M Internat Affairs, Columbia U., 1982. Economist Fed. Res. Bank, N.Y.C., 1982-85, sr. fgn. exchange trader, 1985-87, dep. chief fgn. exchange trader, spl. asst., 1987-88, mgr., chief fgn. exchange trader, 1988-90; v.p. capital markets group 1st Nat. Bank Chgo., 1990—92; v.p. treasury dept. Dresdner Bank, N.Y.C., 1992-94; v.p., mgr. instnl. mktg. desk Bank of Am., N.Y.C., 1994-97, v.p., mgr. sales and mktg., 1997-98, prin., mgr. mktg. and bus. devel. U.S. Fgn. Exch., 1998-2000; dep. asst. sec. for fed. fin. U.S. Dept. Treasury, Washington, 2000—01; mng. dir. head of U.K. investor sales, fgn. exch., global rates and currencies Citigroup, N.A., London, 2001—. Fgn. Student scholar U. Freiburg, 1979; Sch. of Internat. Affairs fellow Columbia U., 1980-81, Internat. fellow Columbia U., 1981; recipient U.S. Dept. Treasury exceptional Svc. award, 2001. Mem. Mortar Bd., Phi Beta Kappa, Phi Kappa Phi. Roman Catholic. Avocations: sports, history. Office: Citigroup Ctr Canada Square, Canary Wharf London E14 5LB England Home: 106 Sussex Mansions 65-69 Old Brompton Rd London SW7 3JT England Fax: 44 0 207 986 1345. E-mail: michaelj.paulus@yahoo.com., michael.paulus@citigroup.com.

PAULUS, NORMA JEAN PETERSEN, lawyer; b. Belgrade, Nebr., Mar. 13, 1933; d. Paul Emil and Ella Marie (Hellbusch) Petersen; m. William G. Paulus, Aug. 16, 1958; children: Elizabeth, William Frederick. LL.B., Willamette Law Sch., 1962; LL.D. (hon.), Linfield Coll., 1985; LittD (hon.), Whitman Coll., 1990; LHD (hon.), Lewis & Clark Coll., 1996. Bar: Oreg. 1962. Sec. to Harney County Dist. Atty., 1950-53; legal sec., 1953-55; sec. to chief justice Oreg. Supreme Ct., 1955-61; of counsel Paulus and Callaghan, Salem; mem. Oreg. Ho. of Reps., 1971-77; sec. of state State of Oreg., Salem, 1977-85; supt. pub. instrn., 1990-99; of counsel Paulus, Rhoten & Lien, 1985-86. Mem. Oreg. exec. bd. U.S. West, 1985-97; adj. prof. Willamette U. Grad. Sch., 1985; mem. N.W. Power Planning Com., 1986-89. Mem. adv. com. Def. Adv. Com. for Women in the Svc., 1986, Nat. Trust for Hist. Preservation, 1988-90; trustee Willamette U., 1978—; bd. dirs. Oreg. Grade Instn. Sci. and Tech., 1985-2001, Edn. Commn. States, 1991-99, Coun. Chief State Sch. Officers, 1995-98, Nat. Assessment Governing Bd., 1996-99, Oreg. Garden Found., 1997—, Oreg. Coast Aquarium, 1999—; bd. dirs., adv. bd. World Affairs Coun. Oreg., 1997—; overseer Whitman Coll., 1985—; bd. cons. Marion-Polk Boundary Commn., 1970-71; mem. Presdl. Commn. to Monitor Philippines Election, 1986; dir. Oreg. Hist. Soc., 2001—. Recipient Disting. Svc. award City of Salem, 1971, LWV, 1995, Path Breaker award Oreg. Women's Polit. Caucus, 1976; named One of 10 Women of Future, Ladies Home Jour., 1979, Woman of Yr. Oreg. Inst. Managerial and Profl. Women, 1982, Oreg. Women Lawyers, 1982, Woman Who Made a Difference award Nat. Women's Forum, 1985; Eagleton Inst. Politics fellow Rutgers U. Mem. Oreg. State Bar, Nat. Order Women Legislators, Women Execs. in State Govt., Women's Polit. Caucus Bus. and Profl. Women's Club (Golden Torch award 1971), Delta Kappa Gamma. Home: 1209 SW 6th Ave Apt 201 Portland OR 97204-1023

PAULY, JOHN EDWARD, anatomist, educator; b. Elgin, Ill., Sept. 17, 1927; s. Edward John and Gladys (Myhre) P.; m. Margaret Mary Oberle, Sept. 3, 1949; children: Stephen John (dec.), Susan Elizabeth, Kathleen Ann, Mark Edward. BS, Northwestern U., 1950; MS, Loyola U., Chgo., 1952, PhD, 1955. Grad. asst. gross anatomy Stritch Sch. Medicine, Loyola U., 1953-54; rsch. asst. anatomy Chgo. Med. Sch., 1952-54, rsch. instr., 1954-55, instr. in gross anatomy, 1955-57, assoc. in gross anatomy, 1957-59, asst. prof. anatomy, 1959-63, asst. to pres., 1960-62; assoc. prof. anatomy Tulane U. Sch. Medicine, 1963-67; prof., head dept. anatomy U. Ark. for Med. Scis., Little Rock, 1967-83, prof., head dept. physiology and biophysics, 1978-80, vice chancellor for acad. affairs and sponsored rsch., 1983-92, assoc. dean Grad. Sch., 1983-92, prof. anatomy, 1992-95, prof. emeritus, 1995—. Flight instr. Ctrl. Flying Svc., Little Rock, 1997—2002; tech. adviser Ency. Brit. Films, 1956; mem. safety and occupl. health study sect. Nat. Inst. Occupl. Safety and Health, Ctr. for Disease Control, 1975—79; vis. prof. faculty medicine Kuwait U., 1993, 94; vis. prof. anatomy U. Nev., 1996; chief of staff Ark. wing Civil Air Patrol, 2002—. Author: (with Hans Elias) Human Microanatomy, 1960, 3d edit. 1966, (with Elias and E. Robert Burns) Histology and Human Microanatomy, 1978; editor: (with Lawrence E. Scheving and Franz Halberg) Chronobiology, 1974, (with Heinz von Mayersbach and Lawrence E. Scheving) Biological Rhythms in Structure and Function, 1981, The American Association of Anatomists, 1888-1987. Essays on the History of Anatomy in America and a Report on the Membership Past and Present, 1987, (with Lawrence E. Scheving) Advances in Chronobiology, 1987, (with Dora K Hayes and Russel J. Reiter) Chronobiology: Its Role in Clinical Medicine, General Biology and Agriculture, 1990; editor Am. Jour. Anatomy, 1980-92; co-mng. editor Advances in Anatomy, Embryology and Cell Biology, 1980-95; mem. adv. editl. bd. Internat. Jour. Chronobiology, 1973-83; contbr. articles to profl. jours. Chief of staff, mission pilot, instr. pilot and check pilot Ark. Wing Civil Air Patrol, 2002. With USNR, 1945—47. Recipient merit certificates AMA, 1953, 59; Bronze award Ill. Med. Soc., 1959; Lederle Med. Faculty award, 1966 Fellow AAAS; mem. Am. Assn. Anatomists (sec.-treas. 1972-80, pres. 1982-83, Centennial award 1987, Henry Gray award 1995), So. Soc. Anatomists (pres. 1971-72), Assn. Anatomy Chmn. (sec.-treas. 1969-71), Am. Physiol. Soc., Internat. Soc. Chronobiology, Pan-Am. Assn. Anatomy, Internat. Soc. Electrophysiol. Kinesiology, Internat. Soc. Steriology, Consejo Nacional de Profesores de Ciencias Morfologicas (hon.), Sigma Xi, Sigma Alpha Epsilon. Roman Catholic. E-mail: pauly.d@sbcglobal.net.

PAUP, MARTIN ARNOLD, real estate and securities investor; b. Seattle, Aug. 30, 1930; s. Clarence Jacob and Emaline Ethel (Lodestein) P.; m. Mary Jean Iske, Apr. 4, 1959; children: Barbara Ann Paup Soriano, Jennifer Marie, Elizabeth Paup-Byrnes. BS, U. Wash., 1952. Indsl. engr. Boeing Airplane Co., Seattle, 1954-60; owner Coopers Unfinished Furniture, Seattle, 1960-63; claims rep. Unigard Ins., Seattle, 1963-66; asst. benefits mgr. Equitable Life Assurance, Seattle, 1966-85; owner Paup Ventures, Seattle, 1974—, Paup Investment Co., Seattle, 1963—, Ella Paup Properties, Seattle, 1963—. Bd. dirs. Denny Regrade Property Owners' Assn., Seattle, Denny Regrade Bus. Assn., Seattle, First Ave. Assn., Seattle. Seattle Dept. Community Devel. grantee, 1980. Mem. Greenwood C. of C., Seattle Opera Guild. Democrat. Roman Catholic. Avocations: opera, travel, lit., history.

PAUP, THOMAS, retail department store executive; CFO Montgomery Ward & Co., Chgo. Office: Montgomery Ward & Co 1 Wards Plz 535 W Chicago Ave Chicago IL 60671

PAUPP, TERRENCE EDWARD, research associate, educator; b. Joliet, Ill., Aug. 10, 1952; s. Edward Theodore and Mary Alice (Combs) P. BA in Social Scis., San Diego State U., 1974; ThM, Luth. Sch. Theology, 1978; JD, U. San Diego, 1990. Instr. philosophy San Diego City Coll., 1983-86, Southwestern Coll., Chula Vista, Calif., 1980-83; law clerk Sch. Law U. San Diego, 1987-88; law clerk Office of Atty. Gen., San Diego, 1988-89; rsch. assoc. Frank & Milchen, San Diego, 1989, Dougherty & Hildre, San Diego, 1990-95; sr. rsch.-assoc. Inst. for Ctrl. and Ea. European Studies, San Diego State U., 1996-98; sr. policy analyst Nuc. Age Peace Found., Santa Barbara, Calif., 2001—. Cons. Cmty. Reinvestment Act, San Diego, 1993-95; sr. rsch. assoc. Inst. Ctrl. and Ea. European Studies San Diego State U., 1994-95; adj. faculty in criminal justice and polit. sci. Nat. U.; cons., contbr. Inst. for Policy Studies, Washington, Interhemispheric Resource Ctr., N.Mex., The Ctr. of Concer, Washington, Global Exch., San Francisco. Author: Achieving Inclusionary Governance: Advancing Peace and Development in First and Third World Nations, 2000; contbr. articles to law jours. Appointed National Chancellor of the USA Internat. Assn. of Educators for World Peace, 2001; cons. Neighborhood House 5th Ave., 1994—95, PBS Frontline documentary The Nicotine Wars, 1994, Bethel Baptist Ch., 1994—95. Mem. ATLA, N.Y. Acad. Scis. Democrat. Lutheran. Avocation: tennis. Home: 1426 Monroe Ave San Diego CA 92116-3931 E-mail: tpaupp@aol.com.

PAUTROT, JEAN-LOUIS JACQUES, literature and language professor; b. Lillebonne, France, Oct. 18, 1954; came to U.S., 1984; BA in English, Caen U., France, 1983; MA in French, Washington U., St. Louis, 1986; PhD, Wash. U., St. Louis, 1992. Prof. French St. Louis U., 2003—. Author: La Musique Oubliée, 1994; composer songs, guitar pieces. Office: Modern Langs St Louis U 221 N Grand Blvd Saint Louis MO 63103-2006 Office Phone: 314-977-2496.

PAVALON, EUGENE IRVING, lawyer; b. Chgo., Jan. 5, 1933; m. Lois M. Frenzel, Jan. 15, 1961; children: Betsy, Bruce, Lynn. BSL, Northwestern U., 1954, JD, 1956. Bar: Ill. 1956. Sr. ptnr. Pavalon, Gifford, Laatsch & Marino, Chgo., 1970—. Adj. prof. Northwestern U. Sch. Law; mem. com. on discovery rules Ill. Supreme Ct., 1981—; lectr., mem. faculty various law schs. Author: Human Rights and Health Care Law, 1980, Your Medical Rights, 1990; contbr. articles to profl. jours., chpts. in books. Mem. bd. overseers Inst. Civil Justice, Rand Corp., 1993-99; mem. vis. com. Northwestern U. Law Sch., 1990-96. Capt. USAF, 1956-59. Fellow Am. Coll. Trial Lawyers, Internat. Soc. Barristers, Internat. Acad. Trial Lawyers, Roscoe Pound Found. (life mem., pres. 1988-90); mem. ABA, Chgo. Bar Assn. (bd. mgrs. 1978-79), Ill. Bar Assn., Ill. Trial Lawyers Assn. (pres. 1980-81), Trial Lawyers for Pub. Justice (founding mem., v.p. 1991-92, pres.-elect 1992-93, pres. 1993-94), Assn. Trial Lawyers Am. (parliamentarian 1983-84, sec. 1984-85, v.p. 1985-86, pres.-elect 1986-87, pres. 1987-88, bd. trustees endowment 2003, pres. 2004—), Am. Bd. Profl. Liability Attys. (diplomate), Am. Bd. Trial Advocates, Inner Circle of Advocates, Chgo. Athletic Assn., Std. Club. Home: 1540 N Lake Shore Dr Chicago IL 60610-6684 Office: Pavalon Gifford et al 2 N La Salle St Chicago IL 60602-3702 Office Phone: 312-419-7400. E-mail: pavalon@pglmlaw.com.

PAVAROTTI, LUCIANO, lyric tenor; b. Modena, Italy, Oct. 12, 1935; s. Fernando and Adele (Venturi) Pavarotti; m. Adua Veroni, Sept. 30, 1961; children: Lorenza, Cristina, Giuliana; m. Nicoletta Mantovani, Dec. 13, 2003; 1 child, Alice. Diploma magistrale, Istituto Magistrale Carlo Sigonio, 1955; studies with, Arrigo Pola, Ettore Campogalliani. Formerly tchr. elem. schs.; salesman ins. Singer: (Operas) (debut) as Rodolfo in La Bohème, 1961, (roles) Edgardo in debut Lucia di Lammermoor, 1963, the Duke in debut Rigoletto, 1961, Rodolfo in La Bohème, 1963, Tonio in debut The Daughter of the Regiment, 1966, (appeared) Lucia di Lammermoor, 1965, (Am. debut) Miami, Fla., 1965; performer (numerous): European performances including Italy, Vienna Staatsoper, Paris; performer: with San Francisco Opera, 1967; singer: (Operas) (debut) Met. Opera, 1968; appeared (Operas) The Daughter of the Regiment, Met. Opera, 1971, Elisir d'Amore, 1973, La Bohème, Chgo. Opera, 1973, La Favorita, San Francisco Opera, 1973, Il Trovatore, 1975, Bellini I Puritani, Met. Opera, 1976, Ponchielli La Gioconda, San Francisco Opera, 1979, Aida, 1981, Mozart, Idomeneo, Met. Opera, 1982, Verdi, Ernani, Met. Opera, 1983, Tosca, Met. Opera, 1995, numerous internat. performances La Scala, Milan, Hamburg, Teatro Colon, Buenos Aires, Australian Opera, Sydney, concert series of Am. and internat. cities Carnegie Hall, 1973, Buenos Aires, Moscow, Beijing, Hong Kong, Tokyo, including arena concerts Madison Square Garden, 1984, and major cities in America, Europe, South America, appeared (films) Yes, Giorgio, 1983, established Opera Co. Philadelphia/Luciano Pavarotti Vocal Competition, 1980, rec. artist Winner Concorso Internationale, Reggio Emilia, 1961, Amore, 1992, Pavarotti and Friends, 1993, Ti Amo-Puccini's Greatest Love Songs, 1993, Pavarotti and Friends 2, 1995, appeared (PBS TV spl. TV series) (with Placido Domingo & Jose Carreras) The Three Tenors, 1994. Named Artist of Yr. Gramophone, 1992; recipient Grammy award, 1981, 1988. Office: care Herbert Breslin 119 W 57th St New York NY 10019-2303

PAVELICH, DANIEL L. retired account, tax management consulting executive; CEO BDO Seidman LLP, Chgo.; ret., 1999. Office: BDO Seidman LLP Two Prudential Plaza 130 E Randolph St Fl 2800 Chicago IL 60601-6300

PAVELKA, ELAINE BLANCHE, mathematics professor; b. Chgo. d. Frank Joseph and Mildred Bohumila (Seidl) P. BA, MS, Northwestern U.; PhD, U. Ill. With Northwestern U. Aerial Measurements lab., Evanston, Ill.; tchr. Leyden Cmty. H.S., Franklin Park, Ill.; prof. math. Morton Coll., Cicero, Ill. Invited prof. Internat. Congress on Math. Edn., Karlsruhe, Germany, 1976. RecipientSci. Talent award Westinghouse Electric Co. Mem. Am. Edn. Rsch. Assn., Am. Math. Assn. 2-Yr. Colls., Am. Math. Soc., Assn. Women in Math., Can. Soc. History and Philosophy of Math., Ill. Coun. Tchrs. Math., Ill. Math. Assn. C.C., Math. Assn. Am. Math. Action Group, Ga. Ctr. Study and Tchg. and Learning Math., Nat. Coun. Tchrs. Math., Sch. Sci. and Math. Assn., Northwestern U. Alumni Assn., U. Ill. Alumni Assn., Am. Mensa Ltd., Intertel, Sigma Delta Epsilon, Pi Mu Epsilon. Home: PO Box 7312 Westchester IL 60154-7312

PAVETTI, FRANCIS JAMES, lawyer; b. New Haven, Dec. 14, 1931; s. Frank and Ellen (Dawson) P.; m. Sally Thomas, July 5, 1958; 1 child, Leah Thomas. BS, U. Conn., 1953; JD cum laude, Boston coll., 1959. Bar: Conn. 1959, U.S. Dist. Ct. Conn. 1960, U.S. Ct. Appeals (2d cir.) 1966, U.S. Supreme Ct. 1966. Law clk. to judge U.S. Ct. Appeals (2d cir.), Conn., 1959-60; lawyer, arbitrator and mediator New London, Conn. Commr. from Conn. Nat. Conf. Commrs. on Uniform State Laws; chair drafting com. Revised Uniform Arbitration Act, State Adminstrv. Procedure Act; judge advocate Navy League; judge advocate, arbitrator N.Y. Stock Exch. Mem. Conn. Dem. State Ctrl. Commn., 1968-72; founding trustee, corp. sec., gen. counsel Eugene O'Neill Theater Found., 1964—; trustee emeritus, vice-chair, treas. Cmty. Found. of S.E. Conn., 1982-97. Mem. ABA, Conn. Bar Assn. (chmn. planning and zoning law sect. 1983-86), Fed. Bar Council (v.p., sec. 1974-80), Navy League. Clubs: Players (N.Y.C.). Democrat. Roman Catholic. Office: Law Offices Francis J Pavetti 18 The Strand Waterford CT 06385 Office Phone: 860-442-9408. E-mail: pavetti@aol.com.

PAVIA, GEORGE M. lawyer; b. Genoa, Italy, Feb. 14, 1928; s. Enrico L. and Nelly (Welisch) P.; m. Ellen Salomon, June 15, 1952; children— Andrew, Alison; m. 2d, Antonia Pearse, Dec. 2, 1976; children— Julian, Philippa. B.A., Columbia U., 1948, LL.B., 1951; postgrad. U. Genoa, 1954-55. Bar: N.Y. 1951, U.S. Supreme Ct. 1956, U.S. Dist. Ct. (so. and ea. dists.) N.Y. 1956. Assoc., Fink & Pavia, N.Y.C., 1955-65; sr. ptnr. Pavia & Harcourt, N.Y.C., 1965— . Served to capt. JAGC, U.S. Army, 1951-54. Mem. ABA, Internat. Law Soc., Consular Law Soc. Home: 18 E 73rd St New York NY 10021-4130 Office: 600 Madison Ave New York NY 10022-1615

PAVIET-HARTMANN, PATRICIA, chemist, researcher; b. Cormeilles, France, June 8, 1964; came to U.S., 1997; d. Roland Jean and Josette Juliette (Camus) Paviet; m. Thomas Hartmann, Apr. 27, 1996; 1 child, Josephine Caroline. BS, U. Nice, France, 1986, MS, 1988; PhD in Chemistry, U. Paris XI, 1992. Rsch. scientist Commissariat a l'Energie Atomique, Cadarache, France, 1990-92; postdoctoral fellow Lawrence Livermore Nat. Lab., Livermore, Calif., 1992-93; mem. staff Forschungszentrum, Karlsruhe, Germany, 1993-97, Los Alamos Nat. Lab., 1997—2003. Project leader in actinide chemistry, 2000—03; sr. scientist adv. MOX project Framatome ANP, Inc., 2003—. Contbr. articles to profl. jours.; patentee in field. Mem. Am. Chem. Soc., Am. Nuclear Soc. Roman Catholic. Avocations: painting, piano, languages (french, english, german, italian, spanish). Office: Los Alamos Nat Lab Environ Sci MS A141 Carlsbad NM 88220 Home: 6738 Thornton Oaks Ct Charlotte NC 28270 Office Phone: 704-382-1213. E-mail: Patricia.PavietHartmann@framalome-anp.com.

PAVIN, COREY ALLEN, professional golfer; b. Oxnard, Calif., Nov. 16, 1959; Winner Mastercard Colonial, 1996. Mem. Ryder Cup Team, 1991, 93, 96; mem. Pres.'s Cup, 1994, 96. PGA Tour top U.S. golfer, leading money winner, 1991, 6th on PGA Tour 1992; Tour Wins include: Houston Coca-Cola Classic, 1984, Colonial Nat. Invitation Tournament, 1985, Hawaiian Open, 1986, 87, Greater Milw. Open, 1986, Bob Hope Chrysler Classic, 1987, 91, Tex. Open, 1988, Bell South Atlanta Golf Classic, 1991, Honda Classic, 1992, L.A. Open, 1994, Nissan Open, 1995, U.S. Open, 1995, Mastercard Colonial, 1996. Address: care PGA Tour 112 Tpc Blvd Ponte Vedra Beach FL 32082-3046

PAVLAKOS, ELLEN TSATIRI, sculptor; b. Athens, May 25, 1936; d. Andrew and Katherine (Fliskanopoulou) Tsatiri; m. Andrew George Pavlakos, Nov. 2, 1952; children: James, John Andrew. Student, Arsakeion, Athens, 1952, Norton Sch. Art, West Palm Beach, Fla., 1975-79, Nat. Acad. Design, N.Y.C., 1980-81. Solo shows include Brevard Art Mus., 1981, Hess Galleries, Allentown, Pa., 1983, Cultural Ctr. Athens, 1990, 5th Ave. Art Gallery, Melbourne, Fla., 1994, 98; group shows include Le Salon des Nations, Paris, 1984, Nat. Exhbn. of Contemporary Realism in Art, Springfield, Mass., 1984, Springville Mus. Art, Utah, 1985, Capitol Gallery, Fla. Dept. Cultural Affairs, Tallahassee, 1988, Outstanding Am. Women Artists Invitational, Sarasota, 1993, Chamber of fine Arts and Min. of Edn. and Civilization Symposium, Nicosia, Cyprus, 1994, Mus. of Art and Sci., Melbourne, 1996, Appleton Mus. Art, Ocala, Fla., 1997, Sculpture '97, Thessaloniki, Greece, 1997, Dunedin (Fla.) Fine Arts Ctr., 1998, Orlando City Hall Gallery, 1998, 621 Gallary, Tallahassee, Fla., 1999, Lee County Alliance of the Arts, Fort Myers, Fla., 1999, La. State U., Shreveport, 2000, Mt. Dora (Fla.) Art Ctr., 2000, U. Fla. Arts Ctr., Gainesville, 2001, DeLand (Fla.) Mus. Art, 2001, Oceola Art Ctr., Kissimmee, 2002, Visual Arts Ctr. of NW Fla., Panama City, Fla., 2002, Brevard Mus. of Arts and Sci., Melbourne, Fla., 2002, Gadsen Arts Ctr., Lake Wales, Fla., 2004, Atlantic Ctr. for the Arts at Harris, 2004; bronze sculpture commd. The Harry T. Moore Monument, Titusville Social Svcs. Ctr., 1985, wall relief Knowledge, Brevard Libr., 1993, bronze sculpture Mother Earth, Penakotheke, Athens, 1990, painting Interlude, Penakotheke, Hydrostone sculpture The Flame Keeper, Kennedy Space Ctr., Fla., 1992, Stephen Girard relief Girard Coll., Phila., 1999, Welcoming Christ, bronze sculpture, Holy Name of Jesus CH., Fla., 2004. Recipient best of Show award Brevard Art Mus., 1980; grantee Brevard County Art in Pub. Places, 1990, 93. Mem. Acad. Artists Assn., Medalic Sculpture Assn., Chamber of Visual Arts in Greece, Ten Women in Art. Greek Orthodox. Avocations: art collecting, gardening. Studio: 331 Coral Way W Indialantic FL 32903-4401

PAVLEY, FRAN J. state representative; b. LA, Nov. 11, 1948; m. Andy Pavley; children: Jennifer, David. BA, Calif. State U., Fresno, 1970; MA, Calif. State U., 1985. Cert. tchr. Calif. Mem. Calif. Assembly, 2000—. Founder Agoura Hills Disaster Response Team, 1987—; adv. com., bd. Santa Monic Mountains Conservancy, 1990—; coastal commn. State of Calif., 1995—2000; councilmember, mayor Agoura Hills, Calif., 1981—97. Democrat. Office: PO Box 942849 Rm 3126 Sacramento CA 95814 Address: 6355 Topanga Canyon Blvd Ste 205 Woodland Hills CA 91367-2108

PAVLICK, PAMELA KAY, nurse, consultant; b. Topeka, Aug. 16, 1944; d. Cy Pavlick and June Lucille Dull. Diploma in nursing, St. Luke's Hosp., Kansas City, Mo., 1966; BA in Psychology magna cum laude, U. North Fla., 1982, MS in Health Adminstrn. summa cum laude, 1987. RN, Mo., Ill., Fla.; cert. ins. rehab. specialist; lic. rehab. providor, Fla., Ga. Clin. instr. St. Luke's Hosp., Kansas City, 1966—70; instr. lic. practical nursing Springfield (Ill.) Sch. Bd., 1970—72; nursing supr. Jacksonville Beach (Fla.) Hosp., 1972—74;

pub. health nurse State of Fla., Ocala, 1974—76; dir. nursing Upjohn Health Care, Jacksonville, Fla., 1976—77, mem. adv. com.; med. rep. Travelers Ins. Co., Jacksonville, 1977—84; rehab. cons. Aetna Life & Casualty, Jacksonville, 1985—, rep. nurse cons. adv. coun., 1988—90. Mem. ANA., Am. Assn. Rehab. Nurses, Nat. Assn. Rehab. Providers, Phi Kappa Phi. Republican. Episcopalian. Avocation: boating. Home: 14023 Tontine Rd Jacksonville FL 32225-2025 Office: Aetna Life & Casualty PO Box 2200 Jacksonville FL 32203-2200 Office Phone: 904-221-7811.

PAVLIK, JAMES WILLIAM, chemistry professor; b. Chgo., Sept. 22, 1937; s. Victor William and Rose (Jaros) P.; m. children— Claire, David, Anne AB, Carthage Coll., 1959; MS, Va. Poly. Inst. and State U., 1961; PhD, George Washington U., 1970. Asst. prof. chemistry Haile Sellasie I U., Addis Ababa, Ethiopia, 1967-69; research scientist George Washington U., Washington, 1969-70; from asst. prof. to assoc. prof. chemistry U. Wis., River Falls, 1970-74; prof. chemistry Worcester Poly. Inst., Mass., 1974—. Cons. in field Contbr. articles to profl. jours. Recipient Award for Outstanding Teaching, Worcester Poly. Inst., 1981 Mem. Am. Chem. Soc., Inter-Am. Photochem. Soc., Sigma Xi Home: 11 Sawyer Rd Northborough MA 01532-1353 Office: Dept Chemistry Worcester Poly Inst Institute Rd Worcester MA 01609-2706 Office Phone: 508-831-5283.

PAVLIK, JOHN MICHAEL, performing arts association executive; b. Melrose, Iowa, Dec. 3, 1939; s. Michael and Suzanna (Majersky) P.; m. Susan Catherine Haysel, Aug. 14, 1971; children: Paige, Blythe. BA, U. Minn., 1963. Reporter Jour.-Times, Racine, Wis., 1964-66, Sun-Telegram, San Bernardino, Calif., 1966; news writer Pacific Telephone, L.A., 1966-68; asst. dir. pub. rels., dir. pub. rels., then v.p. Assn. Motion Picture and Television Producers, L.A., 1968-79; exec. adminstr. Acad. Motion Picture Arts and Scis., Beverly Hills, Calif., 1979-82; exec. dir. Motion Picture and Television Fund, Woodland Hills, Calif., 1982-88; prin. John M. Pavlik Co., Thousand Oaks, Calif., 1988-89; dir. endowment devel. Acad. Found./Acad. Motion Picture Arts and Scis., Beverly Hills, 1989-92; dir. comm. Acad. Motion Picture Arts and Scis., Beverly Hills, Calif., 1992—. Mem. pub. rels. coordinating com. Acad. Motion Picture Arts and Scis., 1969-82; exec. com. L.A. Film Devel. Com., 1974-85, v.p., 1977-78; spl. cons. Calif. Motion Picture Coun., L.A., 1974-79; instr. U. So. Calif. Sch. of Journalism, 1994-96. Bd. dirs. Permanent Charities Com. of Entertainment Industries, L.A., 1979-84. Mem. Acad. Motion Picture Arts and Scis., Assn. Film Commrs. Internat. (adv. bd. 1988-94, chmn. ad hoc com. on exec. mgmt. 1988-89), Conejo Future Found., Hollywood C. of C. (bd. dirs. 1979-85, Walk of Fame com. 1985-89), Soc. of L.A. Pub. Rels. Counselors, Air Force Office of Pub. Affairs Western Region (adv. bd. 1998—). Avocations: reading, photography, travel. Office: Acad Motion Picture Arts and Scis 8949 Wilshire Blvd Beverly Hills CA 90211-1972

PAVLOVICH, JOHN STEPHEN, civil engineer; s. Stephen and Helen Pavlovich; 2 children. B.Engring., Stevens Inst. Tech., Hoboken, N.J., 1972; MS in Engring., Purdue U., West Lafayette, Ind., 1973; MBA, Rutgers U., Newark, 1978. Registered profl. engr., N.J. Civil engr. II N.J. Dept. Transp., Trenton, 1973; project engr. Barton-Aschman, Washington, 1974—75, Raymond, Parish & Pine, Tarrytown, NJ, 1975—78; mgr. tech. programs Tri-State Regional Planning Commn., N.Y.C., 1978—81; dir. planning N.Y. Met. Transp. Coun., N.Y.C., 1981—85; sr. project mgr. Edwards and Kelcey, Morristown, NJ, 1985—. Chmn. intermodal facilities com. Transp. Rsch. Bd., 1991—96, sec., 1985—91; instr. Rutgers U., Piscataway, 1986—96, Piscataway, 2000—01. Contbr. articles to profl. jours. Fellow Urban Mass Transp. Adminstrn. fellow, U.S. Dept. Transp., 1972—73. Mem.: Inst. Transp. Engrs. (mem. Blue Ribbon Panel on improving how a street works for all users 1983—84). Roman Catholic. Avocations: tennis, swimming. Office: Edwards and Kelcey Inc 299 Madison Ave Morristown NJ 07962

PAVONY, WILLIAM H. retail executive, consultant; b. Bklyn., Mar. 1, 1940; s. Harry and Mollie (Leibel) Pavony; m. Geraldine Rice, June 10, 1961; 1 child, Sheryl. BBA cum laude, Hofstra U., 1960. CPA, N.Y., Tex. Mgr. Arthur Andersen & Co. Inc., N.Y.C., 1960-73; group sr. v.p. Purolator Svcs. Inc., New Hyde Park, N.Y., 1973-75; v.p., contr. Purolator Inc., Piscataway, N.J., 1975-78; sr. v.p. Zale Corp., Dallas, 1978-85; sr. v.p. fin., chief fin. officer Alexander's Inc., N.Y.C., 1985-88, exec. v.p., chief fin officer, 1988-89; exec. v.p. adminstrn. The Kobacker Co., Columbus, Ohio, 1989-93; also bd. dirs.; exec. v.p. Arthur Rutenberg Homes, Clearwater, Fla., 1993-94; CFO Color Tile, Inc., Ft. Worth, 1994-95; pres. Pavony Assocs., Corona Del Mar, Calif., 1995-99, Newport Coast, Calif., 1999, 2001—; exec. bus. cons. The Netplex Group, Newport Coast, Calif., 1999-2001; pres. Pavony Assocs., Newport Coast, 2001—. Treas., bd. dirs. Tex. Vis. Nurses Assn., Dallas, 1984-85. Mem AICPA, Fin. Execs. Internat. (past bd. dirs. North Tex. chpt., sec. Columbus chpts.), N.Y. Soc. CPAs, Inst. Mgmt. Accts. Home: 5 Adriana Newport Coast CA 92657-1224 Office Phone: 949-497-8026. Personal E-mail: Bpavony@aol.com.

PAWELCZYK, JAMES A. astronaut, educator; b. Buffalo, N.Y., Sept. 19, 1960; s. Joseph A. and Rita M. Pawelczyk; m. Ruth A. Anderson; 2 children. D of Pub. Svc.(hon.), Tex. Coll. of Osteo. Medicine, Fort Worth, Tex.; BA in Biology, BA in Psychology, U. Rochester, 1982; MS in Physiology, Pa. State U., 1985; PhD in Physiology, U. of North Tex., Denton, 1989. Postdoctoral fellow in cardiovasc. neurophysiology U. Tex. Southwestern Med. Ctr., 1989—92; vis. scientist dept. anaesthesia Rigshospitalet, Copenhagen, 1990; asst. prof. medicine cardiology U. Tex. Southwestern Med. Ctr., 1992—95; dir. autonomic and exercise physiology labs. Inst. Exercise and Environ. Medicine, Presbyn. Hosp. Dallas, 1992—95; asst. prof. bioengring. U. Tex. Southwestern Med. Ctr., 1995; asst. prof. physiology and kinesiology Pa. State U., University Park, 1995—; astronaut, payload specialist NASA, STS-90 (Neurolab), Houston, 1996—98. Rsch. scientist U.S. Olympic Swimming Trials, 1984. Co-editor: Blood Loss and Shock, 1994; contbr. articles to profl. jours., chapters to books. Recipient Predoctoral tng. award, NIH, 1988—89, Rsch. award, Tex. chpt. Am. Coll. Sports Medicine, 1988, Postdoctoral tng. award, NIH, 1989—92, Young Investigator award, Life Scis. Project Divsn., NASA Office of Life and Microgravity Sci. Applications, 1994, Space Flight medal, NASA, 1998. Mem.: Soc. Neurosci., Am. Coll. Sports Medicine, Am. Physiol. Soc., Am. Heart Assn. Avocations: bicycling, swimming, woodworking, stamp collecting/philately, outdoor activities. Address: Astronaut Office/CB NASA Johnson Space Ctr Houston TX 77058

PAWELEC, WILLIAM JOHN, retired electronics company executive; b. Hammond, Ind., Feb. 15, 1917; s. John and Julia (Durnas) P.; m. Alice E. Brown, May 30. 1041 (dec. Dec. 1970); children: William John, Betty Jane Pawelec Conover; m. June A. Shepard, Nov. 27, 1976 (div. June 1980). BS in Acctg., Ind. U., 1939. Statistician Ind. Bd. Accounts, 1939-41; with RCA, 1941-81, mgr. acctg. and budgets internat. divsn., 1957-61, contr. internat. divsn., 1961-68, corp. mgr. internat. fn. ops. and controls, 1968-75, mgr. corp. acctg., 1975-77, dir. internat. acctg., 1977-81, ret., 1981. Contr. RCA Internat., Ltd., Electron Ins. Co., 1977, RCA Credit Corp., 1979; ret., 1981. Active Westfield United Fund, 1967—. Mem. Nat. Assn. Accts. (past nat. v.p.), Watchung Power Squadron, N.J. C. of C., Commerce and Industry Assn. N.Y., Stuart Cameron McLeod Soc., Ind. U. Alumni Assn. (pres. N.J. chpt.), Echo Lake Country Club, Beta Gamma Sigma, Sigma Epsilon Theta. Office: 46 Witherspoon Ct Morristown NJ 07960-2734

PAWL, RONALD PHILLIP, neurosurgery educator; b. Chgo., July 26, 1935; s. Phillip Joseph and Ruby Helen (Graham) P.; m. Mary M. Rohner, July 11, 1959; children: Mary, Linda, Diane, Julie, Matthew, Michael. BS in Neurosurgery, Loyola U., Chgo., 1957, MD, 1961. Diplomate Am. Bd. Neurol. Surgery. Intern Resurrection Hosp., 1961-62; resident in gen. surgery and orthopedics Hines VA Hosp., 1962-63; resident in neurology and neurosurgery U. Ill., Chgo., 1963-66, asst. prof. neurosurgery, 1968-73; asst. chief neurosurgery Tripler Army Med. Ctr., Honolulu, 1966-68; assoc. prof. neurosurgery U. Ill., Chgo., 1973—; dir. pain treatment ctr. Lake Forest (Ill.) Hosp., 1978—. Pres. Am. Bd. Pain Medicine, 1995, residency rev. com. chmn., 1997—. Author: Chronic Pain Primer, 1979; editor Seminars in Neurology, 1989; editor Clin. Jour. Pain, 1988—, Surg. Neurology, 1994—, Clin. Rev. of Pain, 1997—, Currant Rev. of Pain, 1995—; contbr. articles to profl. jours. Capt. U.S. Army, 1966-68. Named Physician of Yr., Ill. Masonic Med. Ctr., Chgo., 1973. Mem. Ctrl. Neurosurg. Soc. (pres. 1979), Midwest Pain Soc. (pres. 1986), Am. Acad. Pain Medicine (treas. 1990), Ill. Neurosurg. Soc. (pres. 1982). Roman Catholic. Office: 900 N Westmoreland Rd Lake Forest IL 60045-1674 Office Phone: 847-535-6132. E-mail: ron@pawl.com.

PAWLENTY, TIMOTHY J. governor; b. South St. Paul, Minn., Nov. 27, 1960; m. Mary Elizabeth Anderson, 1987; 1 child. BA, JD, U. Minn. Chmn. Eagan Planning Comm., 1988-89; mem. Minn. Ho. of Reps. St. Paul, 1993—2002; gov. State of Minn., St. Paul, 2003—. Active Eagan city coun., 1990-92. Fannie Gilbertson Coll. scholar. Republican. Office: Office of the Gov 130 State Capitol 75 Rev Dr Martin Luther King Jr Blvd Saint Paul MN 55155

PAWLEY, CARL JOHN, laser engineer, physicist; b. Milw., Feb. 28, 1956; s. James Arthur and Janet (Vogel) P.; m. Kimberly Moran, June 29, 1985; children: Conor M., Kathryn E. BSEE, Purdue U., 1977; MS in Applied Physics, UCLA, 1982, PhD in Applied Physics, 1986. Scientist Sci. Applications Internat. Corp., McLean, Va., 1986-88, Naval Rsch. Lab., Washington, 1989—. Mem. Joint Ctrl. Diagnostics Team, Livermore, Calif., 1998—. Contbr. articles to profl. jours. Mem. Am. Phys. Soc. (spkr. divsn. plasma physics 1986, 96). Democrat. Roman Catholic. Avocations: hiking, sports, science fiction. Office: Naval Rsch Lab 4555 Overlook Ave SW Washington DC 20375-0001

PAWLEY, RAY LYNN, retired zoological park consultant, real estate developer; b. Midland, Mich., Nov. 7, 1935; s. Lynn Richard and Alice Marie (Skelton) P.; m. Ethel Marie Condon, Feb. 19, 1955 (div. 1974); children: Ray Allyn, Shanna Sue, Cynthia Ann, Dawn Marie, Brandon Earl, Dareen Joy; m. Hedda P. Saltz, Mar. 16, 1997. Student, Mich. State U., 1954—57. Asst. curator, lectr. Black Hills Reptile Gardens, Rapid City, SD, summers 1952-53; owner, adminstr. Reptile Exhibit, St. Ignace, Mich., 1957-59; animal coord. Marlin Perkin's Wild Kingdom (Don Meier Prodns.), Chgo., 1961-62; zoologist Lincoln Park Zool. Gardens, Chgo., 1961-64; curator Brookfield (Ill.) Zoo, 1964-97; ret., 1997. Formerly assoc. dept. zoology Field Mus. Natural History, Chgo.; internat. zoo and conservation cons., Russia, Latvia, Mex., Kenya, China, Ecuador, Galapagos Islands; past instr. herpetology Field Mus., Coll. of DuPage, Triton Coll.; assoc. zoologist Moscow Zool. Pk., Russia; info. resource for fed. and state wildlife agys.; lectr., cons. in field. Contbr. over 100 articles to profl. jours. and popular mags.; co-creator money bench Chgo. Children's Mus. Past v.p. Ill. Endangered Species Protection Bd., Springfield; liaison Endangered Species Tech. Adv. Com., Springfield. Mem. Am. Zoo Assn. (3 Outstanding Svc. awards), Chgo. Acad. Scis. (life), Chgo. Herpetological Soc. (life), Mensa. Achievements include first to create several new live animal exibit concepts; discovery of and documented parthenogenisis in snakes; first discovery and recording of Goliath frog calls. Avocations: hiking, archaeology, art, mechanics, paleontology. Home and Office: PO Box 218 Hinsdale IL 60522-0218 Business E-Mail: raypawley@core.com.

PAWLICZKO, GEORGE IHOR, academic administrator; b. Rochester, N.Y., Oct. 26, 1950; s. Roman and Irene Olha (Zubryckyj) P.; m. Ann Maria Lencyk, June 10, 1978. BA, St. John Fisher Coll., 1972; MA, Fordham U., 1974, MBA, 1986, PhD, 1989. Admissions counselor Fordham U., Bronx, N.Y., 1977-78, asst. dean Grad. Sch. of Bus. N.Y.C., 1978-81; asst. to pres., dir. mgmt. info. systems Marymount Coll., Tarrytown, N.Y., 1981-82; exec. dir. N.Y. Inst. Credit, N.Y.C., 1982-94, The Global Inst. Fin. and Banking (formerly Am. Inst. Banking Greater N.Y.), N.Y.C., 1994—. Trustee St. Andrew's Ch., Hamptonburgh, N.Y., 1986-2002. Mem. Shevchenko Scientific Soc., Beta Gamma Sigma, Phi Alpha Theta. Office: The Global Inst Fin and Banking 80 Maiden Ln New York NY 10038-4811 Office Phone: 212-480-3200.

PAWLIK, JAMES DAVID, lawyer, historian; b. Cleve., May 26, 1958; s. Eugene Joseph and Eleanor Therese Marie (Gorzelanczyk) P. BA cum laude, Ohio State U., 1980, MA, 1991; JD cum laude, Harvard U., 1983. Bar: Calif. 1984, Ohio 1990, U.S. Dist. Ct. (no. dist.) Calif. 1984, U.S. Dist. Ct. (ctrl. and ea. dists.) Calif. 1986, U.S. Dist. Ct. (no. and so. dists.) Ohio 2001, U.S. Ct. Appeals (9th cir.) 1985, U.S. Ct. Appeals (6th cir.) 1994, U.S. Supreme Ct. 2002. Intern Dept. Def., Washington, 1980; assoc. Chandler, Wood, Harrington & Maffly, San Francisco, 1983-87, ptnr., 1988-89; teaching assoc. Ohio State U., 1990-91; pvt. practice Law Offices of James D. Pawlik, Cleve., 1991-93; ind. contractor Gallagher, Sharp, Fulton & Norman, Cleve., Ohio, 1992-93; jud. law clk. to Hon. Robert J. Krupansky U.S. Ct. Appeals (6th cir.), Cleve., 1993—. Instr. history and polit. sci. Cuyahoga C.C., Parma, Ohio, 1993—; instr. dept. polit. sci. Lourdes Coll., Sylvania, Ohio, 1993; co-founder, co-owner Vicar Sauce Co. Ltd., 2000—; reader AP European history exams U. Neb., Lincoln, 2003; adj. instr. dept. polit. sci. Baldwin-Wallace Coll., Berea, Ohio, 2004—. Mem. staff Harvard Internat. Law Jour., 1981-83. Campaign mgr. for city coun. candidate, Westerville, Ohio, 1977; bd. trustees Midpark H.S. Alumni Assn., 1999—, vice chair, 2000—. William Green Meml. scholar 1979, Kosciuszko scholar 1989-91; Ohio State U. fellow, 1989-90; named Midpark H.S. Acad. Hall of Fame, 1997. Mem. Fed. Bar Assn., Mensa, Ohio State U. Alumni Assn., Harvard Alumni Assn., Ohio State U. Undergrad. Student Govt. Alumni Assn., Berea Fine Arts Club, Cleve. Coun. World Affairs, City Club Cleve., Rock Hall of Fame and Mus.,Phi Beta Kappa, Phi Kappa Phi, Phi Alpha Theta. Office Phone: 216-357-7182. Personal E-mail: jdpesq_546@msn.com.

PAWLITSCHEK, DONALD PAUL, business consultant; b. Heron Lake, Minn., Aug. 5, 1941; s. Paul P. and Marion (Erickson) P.; student Southwest Tech. Inst., 1960, Mankato State Coll., 1965-66; m. Korrine Kunerth, Oct. 9, 1965; children: Andrew, Jennifer, Heidi, Sarah, Benjamin. Farmer, Heron Lake, 1967-73; pres. Dundee Steel Inc., 1973-75, Alpha Prime Inc., Heron Lake, 1975-80, Prime Ventures, Inc., 1980—; dir. Am. Search and Referral Co. Served with AUS, 1960. Mem. Nat. Assn. Fin. Cons., Am. Entrepreneurs Assn., Am. Legion. Conservative. Roman Catholic. Club: Elks. Patentee livestock flooring. Home and Office: Prime Ventures Inc RR 1 Box 144A Lake Crystal MN 56055-9700

PAWLOSKY, MARK A. broadcast executive; b. 1957; married. Reporter Wall St, Jour., several others; chief editor MSN News; exec. prodr. MSNB-C.com; v.p., editor-in-chief Onvia.com, 1999—2001; editor-in-chief Microsoft MSN MoneyCentral, 2001—. Office: MSN Money Central 1 Microsoft Way Redmond WA 98052

PAWLSON, LEONARD GREGORY, physician; b. Victoria, Tex., 1943; MD, U. Pitts., 1969; MPH, U. Wash., 1976. Diplomate Am. Bd. Internal Medicine. Intern, affiliate hosps. Stanford U., 1969-70, resident in medicine, 1970-71; fellow in endocrinology U. Wash., 1973-75, Robert Wood Johnson clin. scholar, 1975-76; asst. prof. medicine and health care scis. George Washington U., Washington, 1976-80, assoc. prof. med. and health care scis., 1980-85, prof. health care scis., medicine, and health svcs. mgmt. and policy, 1985-99, assoc. chmn. dept. health care scis., 1978-90, Mudoch head prof. preventive medicine, 1995-99, acting chmn., 1987-90, chmn., 1990-98, sr. assoc. v.p. for health affairs, 1998-99, clin prof. healthcare scis., medicine and health scis. mgmt., 2000—; attending physician George Washington Hosp., Washington, 1976—; exec. v.p. Nat. Com. for Quality Assurance, 2000—. Dir. Inst. for Health Policy, Outcomes and Human Values, 1995-99; vis. scholar Am. Assn. Med. Colls., 1997-98. Robert Wood Johnson health policy fellow, 1986-87; bd. dirs. Bon Secours Hosp. System, 1993—, U.S. Soliders and Airmans Home, 1992—, Med. Faculty Assocs., 1990-99. Mem. ACP, Am. Geriatrics Soc. (past pres. and chmn. bd., editor law and pub. policy sect. Jour. Am. Geriatrics Soc.); mem. Soc. Gen. Internal Medicine (past bd. dirs.), Assn. Tchrs. Preventive Medicine (chair pub. policy com.). Office: George Washington U Med Ctr Dept Health Care Scis 2150 Pennsylvania Ave NW Washington DC 20037-3201

PAWSEY, STUART FREDERICK, structural engineer, retired; b. London, Apr. 20, 1939; came to U.S., 1964; s. Joseph Lade and Greta Lenore (Nicoll) P.; m. Glenda Jean Powell, Dec. 14, 1968; children: Chris, Warwick. BS, U. Sydney, Australia, 1959; B in Engring., U. Sydney, 1961; MS, U. Calif., Berkeley, 1967; PhD, U. Calif., 1970. Reg. profl. engr., Calif. Structural engr. McDonald, Wagner & Priddle, Sydney, 1961-64; asst. prof. Middle East Tech. U., Ankara, Turkey, 1970-72, U. New South Wales, Sydney, 1972-75; structural engr. P.M.B. Engring., San Francisco, 1975-82, Bechtel Corp., San Francisco, 1982-2000, ret., 2000. Mem. ASCE. Home: 1127 Fresno Ave Berkeley CA 94707-2519 E-mail: pawsey@comcast.net.

PAXON, L. WILLIAM, former congressman; b. Buffalo, Apr. 29, 1954; s. Leon W. and Mary P. (Sellers) P.; m. Susan Molinari, July 3, 1994; children: Susan Ruby, Katherine Mary. BA, Canisius Coll., 1977. Mem. Erie County Legis., N.Y., 1978-82, N.Y. State Assembly, 1983-89, 101st-105th Congresses from 31st (now 27th) N.Y. dist., 1989-98; chair Nat. Rep. Congrl. Com.; mem. com. on commerce; lobbyist Akin, Gump, Strauss, Hauer & Feld, 1999—. Roman Catholic. Office: Akin Gump Strauss Hauer & Feld Ste 400 1333 New Hampshire Ave NW Washington DC 20036-1564

PAXSON, RICHARD, newspaper editor; Editor Va. news desk, Va. weeklies The Washington Post, 1993-99, dep. editor Metro Sect., 1999—. Office: The Washington Post 1150 15th St NW Washington DC 20071-0002

PAXSON, WILLIAM H. architectural firm executive; Ptnr. Davis Brody Bond, 1979—. Mem. peer rev. design charette Edward A. Garmatz Fed. Bldg., U.S. Courthouse, Balt. Participant Nat. Endowment for the Arts Fed. Design improvement Program. Office: David Brody Bond LLP 315 Hudson St 9th Fl New York NY 10013

PAXTON, BILL, actor, writer, director; b. Ft. Worth, May 17, 1955; s. John Lane and Mary Lou (Gray) P; m. Louise Newbury. Student, NYU; studies with Stella Adler, Vincent Chase. Actor: (feature films) Mortuary, 1981, The Lords of Discipline, 1982, Streets of Fire, 1983, Impulse, 1983, Weird Science, 1984, Terminator, 1984, Commando, 1985, Aliens, 1985 (Saturn award Acad. of Sci. Fiction, Fantasy, and Horror Films 1986), Near Dark, 1986, Pass the Ammo, 1987, Next of Kin, 1989, The Last of the Finest, 1990, Navy Seals, 1990, Predator 2, 1990, One False Move, 1992, Hurricane, 1992, The Vagrant, 1992, Indian Summer, 1993, Boxing Helena, 1993, Tombstone, 1993, True Lies, 1994, Frank and Jesse, 1994, Apollo 13, 1995, Twister, 1995, Evening Star, 1996, The Last Supper, 1996, Traveler, 1996 (also prodr.), Titanic, 1997, A Simple Plan, 1998, Mighty Joe Young, 1998, U-571, 2000, Vertical Limit, 2000, Frailty, 2001 (also dir.), Spy Kids 2: Island of Lost Dreams, 2002, Resistance, 2003, Spy Kids 3-D: Game Over, 2003, Ghosts of the Abyss, 2003, Club Dread, 2004, Thunderbirds, 2004; (TV movies) Deadly Lessons, 1983, The Atlanta Child Murders, 1985, An Early Frost, 1985, (TV mini-series) Fresno, 1986, (TV series) The Hitch-Hiker, 1986, A Bright Shining Lie, 1998; dir. (theatrical short) Fish Heads, 1982 (Spl. Award Melbourne Film Festival 1982); prodr., co-author (theatrical short) Scoop, 1983. Mem. Screen Actors Guild. Address: Banner Entertainment c/o Bryan Swardstorm 8000 W Sunset Blvd Los Angeles CA 90046-3909*

PAXTON, GLENN GILBERT, composer; b. Chgo., Dec. 7, 1931; s. Glenn G. and Florence A. (Nosek) P.; m. Leslie H. Davis, Dec. 8, 1962; children: Alexandra, Eben. BA, Princeton U., 1953. Freelance composer Broadway, opera, TV and film, 1959—. Composer: (theater prodns.) First Impressions, 1959, The Adventures of Friar Tuck, 1983 (Pulitzer prize nomination 1984), W.R. and Daisy, 2003, (opera) Monticello, 2000, (film) When the Legends Die, 1972, (concert pieces) Four Character Pieces for Piano, 1962, Sara's Diary, 9/11, 2003, The Evening Sing, 1981, (TV movies) Charlie and the Great Balloon Chase, 1981, Vital Signs, 1986, Dark Night of the Scarecrow, 1981, Isobel's Choice, 1981, The Two Worlds of Jenny Logan, 1979, The Clone Master, 1978, (TV shows) Amazing Stories, 1986, Willa Cather's America, 1976, Andy Rooney Takes Off, 1983, An American Christmas: Words and Music, 1971, The Hill Country: Lyndon Johnson's Texas, 1967, The Stately Ghosts of England, 1968, Barry Goldwater's Arizona, 1968, New World Visions, 1984, The American Image, 1969, others; (TV Special) Which Mother Is Mine, (1980 Emmy nominee) (multi-media) Walking Home, 1991; (CD) Prairie Indigo, 1995. Served to lt. (j.g.) USCG, 1953-56. Mem. ASCAP, Dramatists Guild, Am. Music Ctr., Am. Fedn. Musicians. Home and Office: 230A Saddle Ln Ojai CA 93023-4204 Office Phone: 805-640-9449. Personal E-mail: gpaxton@alumni.princeton.edu.

PAXTON, ROBERT OWEN, historian, educator; b. Lexington, Va., June 15, 1932; s. Matthew W. and Nell B. (Owen) P.; m. Sarah Plimpton, Dec. 9, 1983 BA, Washington and Lee U., 1954, LittD (hon.), 1974; BA, Oxford (Eng.) U., 1956, MA, 1961; PhD, Harvard U., 1963; DHL (hon.), SUNY, Stony Brook, 1994; DL (hon.), U. Caen, France, 1994; DL, DL, U. Lyon, France, 2003. Instr. history U. Calif., Berkeley, 1961-63, asst. prof., 1963-67; asso. prof. SUNY, Stony Brook, 1967-69; prof. history Columbia U., 1969—, chmn. dept., 1980-82, dir. Inst. on West Europe, 1991-95. Author: Parades and Politics at Vichy, 1966, Vichy France: Old Guard and New Order, 1940-44, 1972, 2d edit., 2001, Europe in the Twentieth Century, 1975, 4th edit., 2001, French Peasant Fascism, 1997, Anatomy of Fascism, 2004; co-author: Vichy France and the Jews, 1981, 2d edit., 1995; co-editor: De Gaulle and the U.S., 1995. Served with USNR, 1956-58. Decorated comdr. Ordre National des Arts et des Lettres (France), officer Ordre Nat. du Mérite (France); recipient Scholarly Distinction award Am. Hist. Soc., 1998; Rhodes scholar, 1954-56; Am. Coun. Learned Socs. fellow, 1974-75; Rockefeller Found. fellow, 1978-79; German Marshall Fund fellow, 1986. Fellow Am. Acad. Arts and Letters; mem. Am. Philos. Soc., Linnaean Soc. N.Y. (pres. 1978-80). Home: 460 Riverside Dr Apt 72 New York NY 10027-6801 Office: Columbia U Dept History New York NY 10027 E-mail: rop1@columbia.edu.

PAYACK, PAUL JJ, marketing executive; b. Morristown, N.J., Jan. 3, 1950; BA in Comparative Lit., Harvard U., 1974, cert. advanced study in fine arts, 1983. Asst to pres., asst. dir. admissions Newbury Coll., Boston, 1975-78; tech. writer Digital Equipment Corp., Maynard, Mass., 1978-79, Wang Labs., Lowell, Mass., 1980-82; mktg. mgr., sales promotion Apollo Computer Inc. (now Hewlett-Packard Workstations), Chelmsford, Mass., 1982-87; corp. dir., mktg. Unisys Corp., Blue Bell, Pa., 1987-90; v.p., global comm. A.C. Nielsen, Unit of Dun & Bradstreet, Northbrook, Ill., 1990-93; dir., worldwide network mktg. The Network Systems Corp.(acquired by StorageTek 1995), Mpls., 1994-95; v.p. corp. mktg. Intersolv, Rockville, Md., 1995-96; sr. v.p. strategic mktg. Intelliguard Software, Dublin, Calif., 1997; v.p. worldwide mktg. Legato Sys., Mountainview, Calif., 1998-99; chmn., pres., wordman yourDictionary.com, Pleasanton, Calif., 2000—. Cons., lectr. Babson Coll., GM/Hughes, Fed. Res. Bank of N.Y., Shandwick, Bunting's Window TV show, Bus. Week's Digital Economy, CIO conf.; adjunct prof. Babson Coll., Harvard U., Mass State Coll., Univ. of Tex. Author: A Ripple in Entropy, 1973, The Star-Tales Cycle (Solstice 1-3), 1979, Children of the Mind, 1984, (short stories) Mythomania, 1978, Shortest Tomas, 1980, A Plague of Darkness, 1997, (autobiography) A Brief Note on Metafiction, 2000, Anatomical Plates, 1989, The Wind Turbine Studies, 2000, The Pacific Plates, 1999, The Paris Plates, 1999, The End of Empire, 1999, Children of the Mind, 1983, The Perspective Series, 1986, The Land of Orth, 1977, Unexpected Twill Series, 1976, The Book of Hours, 1986, (play) Worlds to Shatter, Shattered Worlds, 1983; contr. articles to profl. jours. including PARIS Rev., New Letters, Creative Computing & Blvd. Office: Your Dictionary dot com 3825 Hopyard Rd Ste 275 Pleasanton CA 84588 E-mail: pjjp@post.harvard.edu.

PAYACK, PETER, poet, writer, artist, educator; b. Mortistown, N.J., Jan. 3, 1950; s. Peter Paul and Florence (Marcello) P.; m. Monica Elizabeth Hynes, June 5, 1981; children: Michael, Peter Paul. BA, Cath. U. Am., 1972; postgrad., Harvard U., 1992-94. Asst. prof. Berklee Coll. Music, Boston, 1997—. Adj. vis. lectr. U. Mass., Lowell, 1987—; founder, pres. Speculative Poetics, Cambridge, Mass., 1976—; contbg. editor Creative Computing, Morristown, N.J., 1977-87; artist-in-residence MIT, Cambridge, 1982, 84, 86; mem. art adv. com. Internat. Space Sta., NASA. Author: (poetry and prose poems) No Free Will in Tomatoes, 1988, Blanket Knowledge, 1997; contbt. poems, prose poems and short stories to more than 1000 publs. including The Paris Rev., The N.Y. Times, Asimov's Sci. Fiction Rev., Readers Digest, Boston Globe, Cornell Rev., also textbooks and anthologies; inventor, innovator. Recipient The Rhysling award Sci. Fiction Poetry Assn., 1979,

Commendation, State of Mass., 1985, Commendation, City of Cambridge, 1995, 96, 98, 98, Youth Sports award Galluccio Assocs., 1998. Avocations: running (20 marathons), ancient and zen philosophy, metrology, collecting antiques, coaching youth sports. Home: 65 Highland Ave Cambridge MA 02139-1039 Office: Berklee Coll Music 1140 Boylston St Boston MA 02215-3631

PAYARD, FRANCOIS, food service executive; b. Nice, France; With Au Nid de Friandises, Riviera, France; pastry chef La Tour d'Argent, Paris, 1988; pastry chef under Alain Senderens Lucas Carton, 1989; pastry chef Le Bernardin, N.Y.C., 1990; pastry chef with chef Daniel Boulud Restaurant Daniel, 1993; pastry chef, owner Payard, N.Y.C., 1997—. Named Pastry Chef of Yr., James Beard Assn., 1995, Bon Appétit Food & Entertainment Awards, 1998. Office: Payard 1032 Lexington Ave New York NY 10021

PAYMENT, KENNETH ARNOLD, lawyer; b. Aug. 6, 1941; s. Arnold F. and Eleanor J. (Kinsey) Payment; m. Jane A. Conrad, Aug. 16, 1996; children: Simone, Elise, Ryan. BS, Union Coll., 1963; LLB, Cornell U., 1966. Bar: NY 66, U.S. Dist. Ct. (we. dist.) NY 67, U.S. Ct. Appeals (2d cir.) 68, U.S. Supreme Ct. 89. Assoc. Wiser, Shaw, Freeman, Van Graafeiland, Harter & Secrest, Rochester, 1966—75; ptnr. Harter, Secrest & Emery, Rochester, 1975—. Instr. Rochester Inst. Tech., 1969, U. Rochester, 1970, Cornell U. Law Sch., Ithaca, NY, 1971—72. Mem.: ABA, Best Lawyers in Am. (bus. litigation 1989—, antitrust 2003), Rochester C. of C., Monroe County Bar Assn. (trustee), NY State Bar Assn. (chmn. constrn. and suretyship divsn. 1978), Cornell Club. Home: 268 Harmon Rd Churchville NY 14428-9518 Office: Harter Secrest & Emery 1600 Bausch & Lomb Place Rochester NY 14604-2006 Office Phone: 585-231-1227.

PAYN, CLYDE FRANCIS, technology company executive, consultant; b. Auckland, New Zealand, Jan. 17, 1952; came to U.S., 1973; s. Phillip Francis and Ngaire Eunice P.; m. Betsy Ann Dannels, June 17, 1978; children: Tamara, Brittany, Erik. Cert., Auckland Inst. Tech., 1971; MBA, Vanderbilt U., 1980. Tech. mgr. Carborundum (N.Z.) Ltd., Auckland, 1968-73; mem. product application tech. staff Carborundum Co., Niagara Falls, N.Y., 1973-78; mgr. product mktg. Universal Abrasives, Phila., 1978-80; bus. mgr., catalyst advocate Johnson Matthey, Inc., Phila., 1980-84; pres. Catalyst Cons., Inc., Phila., 1984—2004, CEO Catalyst Group, Phila., 1988—. Pres. Hideaway Hill Civic Assn., Maple Glen, Pa., 1988, 89. Mem. AIChE, Am. Chem. Soc., Catalysis Soc., Comml. Devel. Assn., Chem. Mktg. Rsch. Assn., Polymer Mfg. Engrs. Assn. Achievements include development of new process technology, catalyst and product development for petroleum, petrochemical, chemical, polymer, pharmaceutical, fine chemical and environ. industries. Office: The Catalyst Group Inc PO Box 637 Spring House PA 19477-0637 Fax: 215-628-2267. E-mail: cfp@catalystgrp.com.

PAYNE, ANCIL HORACE, retired broadcasting executive; b. Mitchell, Oreg., Sept. 5, 1921; s. Leslie L. and Pearl A. (Brown) P.; m. Valerie Dorrance Davies, Apr. 6, 1959; children: Anne Sparrow, Alison Louise, Lucinda Catherine. Student, Willamette U., 1939-41, U. Oreg., 1941, U. Notre Dame, Ohio State U., 1943; BA, U. Wash., 1947; postgrad., U. Wash., 1950-51; hon. PhD, Willamette Univ., 1991. Adminstrv. asst. to congressman, Washington, 1949-52; gen. mgr. Martin Van Lines, Anchorage, 1952-56; mgr. Frontiers-Oreg. Ltd., Portland, Oreg., 1956-59; asst. v.p. bus. div. King Broadcasting Co., Seattle, 1959-63, v.p., 1963-70, exec. v.p., 1970-71, pres., 1971-87. Chmn. bd. affiliates NBC, 1975-80. Mem. Oreg. Bd. Higher Edn., 1966-70; bd. trustees Whitman Coll,. 1985-90; Lt. (j.g.) USNR, 1942-45, PTO. Fellow Phi Beta Kappa; mem. Monday Club, Rainier Club, Alpha Delta Sigma. Episcopalian. Office: Ancil H Payne & Assocs 1107 1st Ave Apt 606 Seattle WA 98101-2944

PAYNE, DANIEL HAROLD (HAROLD PAYNE), real estate developer, small business owner; b. Caddo Mills, Tex., Jan. 12, 1921; s. Flavy Malone and Sally Ella Payne; m. Wanda Louise Lyday, Aug. 3, 1941; 1 child, Kyle Steven. At, Tex. A&M, Commerce, 1940—41; grad., Tex. Real Estate Sch., Dallas, 1971. Sales J.C. Penney, Greenville, Tex., 1940—41, A&P Grocery, Greenville, 1940—41; office and credit mgr. Firestone Tire Co., Ft. Worth, 1941—42; office mgr. Guy F. Atkinson Co., Denison, 1942—43; co-owner Payne Bros. Super Markets, 1945—55; owner Payne's Famous Furniture Village, Caddo Mills, Tex., 1955—90, Payne Magnavox Ctr., Garland, Tex., 1960—61, Harold Payne Land Sales & Devel., Caddo Mills, Tex., 1970—. Adv. bd. Tex. Retail Grocery Assn., Dallas, 1951—55; bd. mem. State Nat. Bank, Caddo Mills, 1972—99; adv. mem. Tex. Retail Furniture Assn., Dallas, 1967—88. Contbr. articles to trade periodicals. Pres. Lions Club Internat., Caddo Mills, Tex., 1955—56; treas. Hunt County Fair Bd., Greenville, 1966—, publicity chmn., 1966—87; public spkr. civic, military and ch. groups in Tex. and Okla., 1963—83; mem. Inner Cir. Senate Com. Rep. Party, Washington, 2000—; elder Faith Bible Ch., Caddo Mills, Tex.; bd. mem. and publicity chmn. Sky Ranch Christian Youth Camp, Van, 1962—63; founding mem. 390th Bomb Group Meml. Mus., Tucson. 2d lt. USAF, 1942—45, ETO. Recipient Advt. award, Tex. Furniture Assn., 1969, Nat. Sales award, Nat. Furniture Assn., 1976, numerous manufacturers' sales awards. Mem.: Hunt County Freedom Forum (chmn. 1957—63, chmn. of bd. 1959—81), Masons (32 degree 1973). Republican. Avocations: youth work, civic activities, church, scouting, athletics.

PAYNE, DAVID EMER, university administrator; b. Salt Lake City, Mar. 29, 1944; s. John W. and Sara (Harris) P.; m. Grettle Haglund, Nov. 17, 1973; children: Sara, John, Samuel, Daniel, James, David. BS, Brigham Young U., Provo, Utah, 1968; MS, U. N.C., 1970, PhD, 1972. Asst. prof. U. Iowa, Iowa City, 1972-76; assoc. prof. U. N.D., Grand Forks, 1976-80, prof., 1980-81; fellow Am. Coun. Edn., New Orleans, 1981-82; dean social sci. S.E. Mo. State U., Cape Girardeau, 1982-88; v.p. acad. affairs Sangamon State U., Springfield, Ill., 1988-89, Emporia (Kans.) State U., 1989-96, Sam Houston State U., Huntsville, Tex., 1997—. Vis. prof. U. Iceland, Reykjavik, 1974-75. Contbr. articles to profl. jours. Dist. commr. Boy Scouts Am. Am. Coun. Edn. fellow, 1981-82, Bush Found. sr. fellow, 1982. Mem. Coun. Fellows Am. Coun. Edn., Am. Sociol. Assn., C. of C., Renaissance Group (exec. bd. dirs.), Alliance of Univs. for Democracy (exec. bd. dirs., v.p.), Rotary, Sigma Xi. Mem. Lds Ch. Home: 837 Elkins Lk Huntsville TX 77340-7322 Office: Sam Houston State U Huntsville TX 77340 Office Phone: 936-294-1001. E-mail: payne@shsu.edu.

PAYNE, DONALD M. congressman; b. Newark, July 16, 1934; BA, Seton Hall U. Freeholder Essex County, 1973-78; ins. co. exec., prior to 1989; former v.p. computer forms mfr.; mem. Newark Mcpl. Coun., 1982-89, U.S. Congress from 10th N.J. dist., 1989—; mem. internat. rels. com. edn. and workforce com. Chmn. World YMCA Refugee and Rehab. Com., 1973-81; pres YMCA's of USA. Democrat. Office: US Ho of Reps 2209 Rayburn House Office Bldg Washington DC 20515-0001 also: 50 Walnut St Ste 1016 Newark NJ 07102-3506

PAYNE, ERIC ALAN, physician; b. Hattiesburg, Miss., Mar. 23, 1962; s. Charles and Essie (Crumpton) Payne; m. Lisa Bourgeois, Jan. 29, 2000; 1 stepchild, Erin Elizabeth Rossignol. BS, Morehead State U., 1985; MD, U. Ky., 1994. Diplomate Am. Bd. Internal Medicine. Intern U. Ky. Coll. Medicine, Lexington, 1994—95; resident in internal medicine La. State U. Med. Ctr., New Orleans, 1995—97; physician C & M Med. Svc., Metairie, La., 1997—, The Schumacher Group, Lafayette, La., 2000—03; physician, med. dir. Gaylord Family Med. Ctr., Bogalusa, La., 2001—03; physician NES Healthcare Group, Toledo, 2003—; internist family med. clinic St. Tammany Parish Hosp., Franklinton, La., 2004—. Dir. emergency dept. Riverside Med. Ctr., Franklinton, 2000—01; med. dir. Bur. Emergency Med. Svc., EMT Basic Edn. La. Tech. Coll., Bogalusa, 2001—; med. adv. bd. CHD Meridian Healthcare, Latham, NY, 2002—03, nat. pharmacy and therapeutic com., 2002—03. Dep. coroner Washington Parish, La., 2002—; med. dir. Washington Parish Comm. Dist., 2002—; infectious disease officer Bogalusa Cmty. Med. Ctr., 2002; reserve dep. Washington Parish Sheriff's Dept., 2002—; med. dir. Washington Parish Dist. 1 and 9 Vol. Fire Dept., 2002—; chmn. Washington Parish Chpt. Am. Heart Assn., 2003. Mem.: ACP, AMA (Physicians Recognition award 2001), Am. Soc. Internal Medicine, La. State Med. Soc., Washington Parish Med. Soc. Republican. Avocations: scuba diving, hunting, target shooting, travel, fishing. Home and Office: 711 Riverside Dr Franklinton LA 70438

PAYNE, FRANCES ANNE, literature educator, researcher; b. Harrisonburg, Va., Aug. 28, 1932; d. Charles Franklin and Willie (Tarvin) P. BA, B.Mus., Shorter Coll, 1953; MA, Yale U., 1954, PhD, 1960. adj. fellow St. Anne's Coll., Oxford Eng. Instr. Conn. Coll., New London, 1955-56, U. Buffalo, 1958-60, lectr., 1960, asst. prof., 1960-67; assoc. prof. SUNY, Buffalo, 1967-75, prof. English and medieval lit., 1975—. Adj. fellow St. Anne's Coll., Oxford, Eng., 1966—. Author: King Alfred and Boethius, 1968; Chaucer and Menippean Satire, 1981. Contbr. articles to scholarly publs. AAUW fellow, Oxford, 1966-67; Research Found. grantee SUNY Central, Oxford, 1967, 68, 71, 72; recipient Julian Park award SUNY-Buffalo, 1979. Mem. Medieval Acad. Am., New Chaucer Soc., Internat. Soc. Anglo-Saxonists, Pi Kappa Lambda Office: SUNY-Buffalo 306 Clemens Hall Buffalo NY 14260-4600 Office Phone: 716-645-2575 2557. E-mail: fapayne@buffalo.edu.

PAYNE, FRED J. physician, educator; b. Grand Forks, N.D., Oct. 14, 1922; s. Fred J. and Olive (Johnson) P.; m. Dorothy J. Peck, Dec. 20, 1948; children: Chris Ann Payne Graebner, Roy S. William F., Thomas A. BS, U. Pitts., 1948, MD, 1949; MPH, U. Calif., Berkeley, 1958. Diplomate Am. Bd. Preventive Medicine. Intern St. Joseph's Hosp., Pitts., 1949-50; resident Charity hosp., New Orleans, 1952-53; med. epidemiologist Ctr. Disease Control, Atlanta, 1953-60; prof. tropical medicine La. State U. Med. Ctr., New Orleans, 1961-66; dir. La. State U. Internat. Ctr. for Med. Rsch. and Tng., San Jose, Costa Rica, 1963-66; exec. sec. 3d Nat. Conf. on Pub. Health Tng., Washington, 1966-67; epidemiologist Nat. Nutrition Survey, Bethesda, Md., 1967-68; chief pub. health professions br. NIH, Bethesda, 1971-74; med. officer, sr. rsch. epidemiologist Nat. Inst. Allergy and Infectious Diseases, 1974-78; asst. health dir. Fairfax County (Va.) Health Dept., 1978-94; dir. HIV/AIDS case mgmt. program, 1988-94; cons. epidemiologist, 1994—; med. advisor Ams. for Sound AIDS Policy, 1996 , Childrens AIDS Fund, 1997—. Clin. prof. La. State U., 1966-79; cons. NIH, 1979-81; leader WHO diarrheal disease adv. team, 1960. Contbr. articles to profl. jours. Served with AUS, 1942-46, 49-52. Decorated Combat Medic Badge. Fellow Am. Coll. Preventive Medicine, Am. Coll. Epidemiology; mem. AAAS, AMA, Am. Soc. Microbiology, Internat. Epidemiology Assn., Soc. Epidemiol. Rsch., USPHS Commd. Officers Assn., Sigma Xi. Office: PO Box 16433 Washington DC 20041 Office Phone: 703-471-8750. E-mail: jjiyd@ibm.net., fdpayne6@email.msn.com.

PAYNE, GERALD OLIVER, retired elementary education educator; b. East St. Louis, Ill., July 17, 1930; s. Amos Oliver and Suzanne Louise (Goussery) P.; m. Nancy Louise Ecklund, Aug. 8, 1959; children: Paul Clifton, Christopher Amos, Scott Eric, Miriam Louise, Susan Jeannette. BA, Yale U., 1953; MusB, U. Dubuque, Iowa, 1957; PhD, U. Wis., 1969. Tchr. pub. schs., Aspen, Colo., 1959-61; tchr. pub. schs. Madison, 1961-65; coord. fgn. langs., 1964-69; asst. dir. curriculum, 1967-69; assoc. prof. edn. SUNY, Buffalo, 1969-71, prof. edn., 1971-86, chmn. dept. curriculum and supervision, 1975-78, coord. cert. advanced studies in adminstrn. and supervision, 1969-75, 78-86, assoc. chmn. dept. elem. edn. and reading, 1985-86; chmn. dept. edn. and psychology Warren Wilson Coll., N.C., 1986-90, chmn. div. social sci. and profl. studies, 1987-90; tchr. Hendersonville (N.C.) County Schs., Hendersonville, N.C., 1990-96. Contbr. articles to profl. jours. Chmn. troop com. Greater Niagara Frontier coun. Boy Scouts Am., Lewiston, N.Y., 1974-76, scoutmaster, 1976-79; advisor Explorer Post, 1979-83, Order of Arrow, 1978-83; elder 1st Presbyn. Ch., Lewiston, 1978-83, 1st Presbyn. Ch., Hendersonville, N.C., 1991-94; leader Stephen Ministries. Mem. NEA (life), Western N.Y. Yale Alumni Assn. (mem. schs. com. 1972-83, dir. 1977-83), Nat. Middle Sch. Assn., Assn. for Supervision and Curriculum Devel., Phi Delta Kappa (exec. com. 1978-81, sec. 1985-86, pres.-elect 1986) Republican. Home: 158 Dunroy Dr Hendersonville NC 28739-6260 E-mail: ridgemou@bellsouth.net.

PAYNE, GLORIA MARQUETTE, business educator; b. Elkins, W.Va., Dec. 21, 1923; d. Anthony and Roselyn Marquette; m. Carl Wesley Payne, Mar. 6, 1950; 1 child, Mary Debra Payne Moore. BA, MHL (hon.), Davis and Elkins Coll.; MA, W.Va. U.; PhD, U. Pitts., 1975; postgrad., NYU Fashion Inst. Tech. Cert. designed appearance cons. Sec. Equitable Ins. Co., Elkins, 1943-44; tchr., dept. head Spencer (W.Va.) H.S., 1944-45; prof. bus. Davis & Elkins Coll., Elkins, 1945-93; image cons. Elkins, 1988-93; bus. cons., 1970-93; mgr. Elkins Wallpaper Shop, 1945-65; owner Merle Norman Cosmetic Studio, Elkins, 1950-56. Dir. tchr. workshops W.Va. U., Marshall U., State Dept. Edn., Charleston, W.Va., summers; dir. machine shorthand workshops for tchrs. throughout the U.S.; dir. designer appearance World Modeling Assn., N.Y.C., 1989—; instr. modeling Davis & Elkins Coll., 1980-93. Author: A Methods Class is Interesting and Challenging, 1970, The Oak or the Pumpkin; mem. editl. bd. Nat. Assn. of Business Teachers Edn. Pub., 1993, 94; contbr. articles to profl. jours. Chair Bi-Centennial, City of Elkins; dir. Elkins Fair, City of Elkins; pres. St. Brendans Parish; judge Mountain State Forest Festival Parades, 1988-94; rep. Region I at Dallas Nat. Conv., 1994 (one of five nat. finalists); div. chair bus., econs., and tourism. Recipient Outstanding Prof. award Sears-Roebuck Co., Lois Latham award for Excellence in Tchg., Cmty. Svc. award Elkins C. of C., 1992, Outstanding Educator award BPW, 1997, WVBEA, W.Va. Vocat. Assn., 1994, 97, Region I award for Outstanding Vocational Educator, Outstanding Collegiate Tchr. Bus. award, 1997, 1st recipient James S. McDonnell Found. Fully Endowed Acad. Chair in Bus. and Econs.; named Educator of Yr., W.Va. Women's Club, Outstanding Educator AAUW, Randolph County C. of C. Citizen of Yr., 1998. Mem. Am. Bus. Writers Assn., W.Va. Edn. Assn. (past pres., Outstanding Prof., Outstanding Svc. award, Outstanding Bus. Educator award), Tri-State Bus. Edn. Assn. (historian, outstanding svc. award, Tchr.-Educator of the South award 1991), World Modeling Assn. (v.p. 1988-95, modeling award 1989), Designed Appearance U.S. (dir. 1990-98), W.Va. Bus. Edn. Assn. (award 1977, 85, 94, 97), Bus. & Profl. Women's Orgn., W.Va. C. of C., The Fashion Club (advisor), Beta Sigma Phi (advisor), Beta Alpha Beta (advisor), Pi Beta Phi, Phi Beta Lambda (advisor). Democrat. Roman Catholic. Avocations: flower arranging, modeling. Home: 301 Davis St Elkins WV 26241-4030 Office: Davis & Elkins Coll 100 Sycamore St Elkins WV 26241-3996

PAYNE, HARRY CHARLES, historian, educator; b. Worcester, Mass., Mar. 25, 1947; BA, MA, Yale U., 1969, PhD, 1973, MPhil, 1970; degree (hon.), Hamilton Coll., 1988, Colgate U., 1989, Williams Coll., 1993, Amherst Coll., 1994, U. of the South, 1997. Mem. faculty Colgate U., Hamilton, NY, 1973—82, prof. history, 1982—85; provost, acting pres. Haverford Coll., Pa., 1985—88; pres. Hamilton Coll., Clinton, NY, 1988—93, Williams Coll., Williamstown, Mass., 1994—99, Woodward Acad., College Park, Ga., 2000—. Contbr. scientific papers. Bd. dirs. Barnard Coll. Fellow Overseas fellow, Churchill Coll., Cambridge U., Eng., 1977. Mem.: Am. Coun. Edn., Am. Soc. 18th-Century Studies (pres. 1984—85, Article prize 1977). Office: Woodward Acad 1662 Rugby Ave College Park GA 30337-2199

PAYNE, HARRY MORSE, JR., architect; b. Norwood, Mass., Nov. 3, 1922; s. Harry Morse and Edna May (Beardsley) P.; m. Helen Marion Beasley, Aug. 29, 1946; children: Harry Morse, Thomas Beasley, Amelia Morse. Student, Boston Archtl. Center, 1946-49, MIT, 1949-50. Draftsman William G. Upham, Norwood, 1946-47; designer William Riseman Assos., Boston, 1947-49, Harry J. Korslund, Norwood, 1949-51, William Hoskins Brown, Boston, 1951-52; designer, prin. dir. The Architects Collaborative, Cambridge, Mass., 1952-86, pres., 1975-77, emeritus, 1986—, Boston Archtl. Center, 1963-65, 71-73; asst. prof. Harvard U. Grad. Sch. Design, 1954-63. Prin. works include U.S. Embassy, Athens, Greece, U. Baghdad, Iraq, Temple Israel, Boston, Quincy Sch., Boston, Nauset Regional H.S., Cape Cod, Mass.; author: The Survey System of the Old Colony, 1985, Name Change--Paine to Payne, 1992, Cape Cod Land Strategy, 1994, New England 17th Century Land Strategy, 1997, America's Stonehenge As Architecture, 1998, Payne Paine Family—England and Cape Cod, 1999, The Ordering of Towns: Massachusetts Bay Colony 17th Century Land Strategy, 2002. Served with USN, 1943-46. Recipient Cascieri Lectureship in Humanities medal, Boston Archtl. Ctr., 2002. Fellow AIA; mem. Soc. Archtl. Historians, N.E. Antiquities Rsch. Assn., Boston Soc. Architects, Mass. State Assn. Architects, New Eng. Hist. and Geneal. Soc., The Colonial Soc. Mass., Mass. Soc. Genealogists (pres. 1986-88), Lincoln Hist. Soc. (pres. 1990-92). Home: 303 Winthrop Terr Bedford MA 01730

PAYNE, HOWARD JAMES, retired insurance company executive; b. Des Moines, Iowa, Oct. 22, 1940; s. James W. and Wilma F. (Kever) P.; m. Mary J. Kellam, June 8, 1963; children: Scott D., Steven M. MBA, U. Iowa, 1986. CPCU; assoc. in underwriting, assoc. in mgmt. Underwiter Allied Ins. Co., Des Moines, 1963-70, br. underwriting mgr. Phoenix, 1973-75, asst. br. mgr. Santa Rosa, Calif., 1975-77; casualty underwriting mgr. Am. States Ins. Co., Indpls., 1970-73; asst. v.p. underwriting Lumberman's Mut. Ins. Co., Mansfield, Ohio, 1977-80; asst. v.p., underwriting mgr. Hastings (Mich.) Mutual Ins. Co., 1980-82; v.p. underwriting John Deere Ins. Co., Moline, Ill., 1982-86, v.p., regional mgr., 1986-90; v.p. credit ins. mgr. John Deere Ins. Co, Des Moines, 1990-93; v.p., spl. program mgr. John Deere Transp., Brookfield, Wis., 1993-99. Ins. instr. Am. States Ins. Co., Indpls., 1971-73, CPCU chpt., Phoenix, 1973-75; ins. instr., adviser C.C. Mansfield, Ohio, 1978-80; pres. Am. States Credit Union, Indpls., 1973. Mem.: CPCU Soc. Republican. Avocations: tennis, physical fitness, reading. Home: 12 Spring River Ln Cherokee Village AR 72529

PAYNE, JAMES RICHARD, environmental chemist; b. Anaheim, Calif., Sept. 3, 1947; s. Theodore L. and Laura P. (Schutz) P.; m. Marinee J. Pavlovich, June 29, 1968; children: Clayton Bennett, Taylor Sierra. BA with honors, Calif. State U., Fullerton, 1969; PhD, U. Wis., 1974. Chemist in engring. coll. unit N.Am. Rockwell Corp., Downey, Calif., 1968-69; tchg. asst., rsch. asst., and NIH predoctoral fellow U. Wis., Madison, 1969-74; postdoctoral scholar Woods Hole (Mass.) Oceanographic Inst., 1974-75; asst. rsch. chemist U. Calif. Bodega Marine Lab., Bodega Bay, 1975-78; sr. chemist, asst. v.p., v.p. Sci. Applications Internat. Corp., La Jolla, Calif., 1978-91; sr. v.p., dir. rsch. SOUND Environ. Svcs., Inc., Carlsbad, Calif., 1991-96; mgr. chem. tech. br. Ogden Environ. & Energy Svcs. Co., Inc., San Diego, 1996; founder J.R. Payne Environ. Cons., $Drlsbad, 1997; pres. Payne Environ. Cons., Inc., Encinitas, 1998—, 1998—. Mem. exec. sci. and tech. coun. Sci. Applications Internat. Corp., La Jolla, 1985-91; mem. NAS/NRC Marine Bd.: Com. on Effectiveness of Oil Spill Dispersants, Washington, 1985-88. Co-author: Fate and Weathering of Petroleum Spills in the Marine Environment: A Literature Review and Synopsis, 1980, Petroleum Spills in the Marine Environment: The Chemistry and Formation of Water-in-Oil Emulsions and Tar Balls, 1985, Oil Spill Dispersants: Mechanisms of Action and Laboratory Tests, 1993; contbr. over 25 articles to profl. jours. Achievements include participant in two NAS/NRC studies and coms. on oil pollution in the marine environment and the use of oil spill dispersants; research on oil weathering, oil/ice interactions, remediation of hazardous waste sites. Home: 1651 Linda Sue Ln Encinitas CA 92024-2427 Office: Payne Environ Cons Inc Ste 201 317 N El Camino Real Encinitas CA 92024 Fax: 760-942-1036. E-mail: jamesrpayne@compuserve.com.

PAYNE, JEAN L. writer; b. Quincy, Mass., Jan. 13, 1932; d. Louis Pierre and Blanche Istella Lemire; m. Gregory D. Payne, June 28, 1954 (dec. Aug. 6, 1968); children: Douglas, Dwight. BA, Bates Coll., Lewiston, ME, 1953; postgrad., U. Maine, 1957. Office worker Oldtown H.S., Old Town, Maine, 1946—49; bus. asst. Morin's, Old Town, 1948—49; speech asst. Bates Coll., Lewiston, 1950—53; ins. writer Aetna Life Ins., Hartford, 1953—54; educator/libr. Lewiston H.S., Lewiston, 1954—55; libr., acquisitions Bates Ladd Libr., Lewiston, 1970—90; writer Free-lance Writer, Lewiston, 2002—. Mem.: Women's Lit. Union (pres. 1967), Art/Lit. Club (pres. 2002), LA Coll. Club (pres. 1956). Independent. Avocation: poetry. Home: 94 Marble Street Lewiston ME 04240-5344

PAYNE, JOHN ROSS, rare books, archives and photographs appraisal consulting company executive, library science educator; b. Clarksville, Tex., Dec. 4, 1941; BA, Tex. Christian U., 1963; MLS, North Tex. State U., 1967. Successively acting dir., asst. to dir., assoc. libr. for acquisitions, assoc. libr. for ops., rsch. assoc. Harry Ransom Humanities Rsch. Ctr. U. Tex., Austin, 1969-85, prof. Grad. Sch. Libr. and Info. Sci., 1988-89, 91-93, tchr. course in rare books and lit. manuscripts; dir. Payne Assocs., 1978—. Author: A Bibliography of W. H. Hudson, 1977, Modern British Fiction: An Exhibit, 1972; co-author: (with Elizabeth Johnson) Katherine Mansfield: An Exhibit, 1973, (with Adrian Goldstone) A Bibliographical Catalogue of John Steinbeck, 1975; contbr. articles to profl. jours. Lilly fellow Ind. U., 1967-68. Mem. ALA, Am. Soc. Appraisers (state dep. dir.), Appraisers Assn. Am., Soc. Am. Archivists (hon., speaker at Atlanta meeting 1988), Manuscripts Soc., Tex. Libr. Assn., Tex. State Hist. Assn., Book Club of Tex., Tex. and Southwestern Collectors' Assn., Grolier Club, Book Collectors of L.A. Address: 2309 Camino Alto Austin TX 78746-2404 E-mail: payne@payne-associates.com.

PAYNE, LADELL, retired college president; b. Birmingham, Ala., Dec. 6, 1933; s. Clyde Ladell and Martha Gerusia (McBrayer) P.; m. Mary Jean Taylor, Aug. 23, 1954; children: Lisa, Jennifer BA with honors, Samford U., 1955; MA in English, La. State U., 1956; PhD in English, Stanford U., 1966; LittD, Samford U., 1996; DHL, Randolph-Macon Coll., 1998. From instr. to prof. English, chmn. dept. lit. and presdl. asst. Claremont McKenna Coll., Calif., 1960-79; pres. Randolph-Macon Coll., Ashland, Va., 1979-97, prof. emeritus, 1997—, pres. emeritus, 1998—. Fulbright lectr. U. Vienna, Austria, 1971-72; nat. cons. Ctr. for Study So. Culture, U. Miss., Oxford, 1980—; adminstrv. assoc. Am. Coun. on Edn., Washington, 1979, mem. nat. panel, comm. on women in higher edn., 1981-97; founding mem. pres.'s commn. Nat. Collegiate Athletic Assn., 1984-97. Author: Thomas Wolfe, 1969, Black Novelists and the Southern Literary Tradition, 1981; contbr. articles on William Faulkner, Robert Penn Warren, Thomas Wolfe, and Ellen Glasgow to profl. jours. Mem. Va. bd. dirs. NCCJ, 1980-92, chmn. Va. region, Richmond, 1982-85; trustee, mem. exec. com. The Collegiate Schs., Richmond, 1986-89; bd. dirs. Music in the Mountains, Nevada City, Calif., 2000-02. NEH fellow, 1973. Mem. Nat. Assn. Ind. Colls. and Univs. (bd. dirs. 1990-93), Coun. on Postsecondary Accreditation (bd. dirs. 1991-93), Pi Kappa Phi, Phi Beta Kappa. Methodist. Avocation: classical music.

PAYNE, LESLIE (LES PAYNE), newspaper editor, columnist, author, journalist; b. Tuscaloosa, Ala., July 12, 1941; s. Thomas and Josephine Payne; m. Violet S. Cameron; children: Tamara Olympia, Jamal Kenyatta, Haile K. BA, U. Conn., 1964, LittD (hon.), 2003; degree (hon.), Medgar Evers Coll., LI U. Reporter Newsday, Melville, NY, 1969-73, copy editor, mag. editor, 1973, minority affairs specialist, 1974-77, nat. corr., 1977-81, nat. editor, 1981-85, asst. mng. editor, assoc. mng. editor, 2000—01, dep. mng. editor for nat., sci., and internat. news, 2001—03, NY editor, 2003—; columnist Tribune Media Services. Judge Pulitzer Prize Selection Com., 1983, 84, 2000 Emmy Blue-Ribbon Panel, Acad. TV Arts and Scis., 1981, 82, 96; inaugural prof. for the David Laventhol Chair, Columbia U. Grad. Sch. Journalism, 1998; has appeared on numerous TV and radio shows. Author: Life and Death of the Symbionese Liberation Army, 1976; co-author: Heroin Trail, 1974. Served to capt. U.S. Army, 1963-69 Decorated Bronze Star; recipient Pulitzer prize, 1974, Tobenkin award, Columbia U., 1978, World Hunger Media award, UN, 1983, Award for Best Commentary, UPI, 1984, Citation for Column Writing, Am. Soc. Newspaper Editors, 1986, 3 Unity awards for investigative reporting, Lincoln U., Journalism prize, Howard U., Cable Ace Award, 1990, numerous other awards. Mem. Nat. Assn. Black Journalists (pres. 1981-83, Commentary Award, 1987, 88), Com. to Protect Journalists, Internat. Press Inst. Avocations: painting; softball; mountain climbing. Office: Newsday Inc 235 Pinelawn Rd Melville NY 11747-4250*

PAYNE, MARGARET ANNE, lawyer; b. Aug. 10, 1947; d. John Hilliard and Margaret Mary (Naughton) P. Student, Trinity Coll., Washington, 1965-66; BA magna cum laude, U. Cin., 1969; JD, Harvard U., 1972; LLM in Taxation, NYU, 1976. Bar: N.Y. 1975, U.S. Dist. Ct. (so. dist.) N.Y. 1975, Calif. 1979, U.S. Dist. Ct. (so. dist.) Calif. 1979. Assoc. Mudge, Rose, Guthrie, and Alexander, N.Y.C., 1972-75, Davis, Polk and Wardwell, N.Y.C., 1976-78, Seltzer, Caplan, Wilkins and McMahon, San Diego, 1978-79, Higgs, Fletcher and Mack, San Diego, 1980-82, ptnr., 1983-90, of counsel, 1991—. Adj. prof. grad. tax program U. San Diego Sch. Law, 1979-89, Calif. Western Sch. Law,

San Diego, 1980-82; judge pro tem Mcpl. Ct., San Diego Jud. Dist., 1983, 92. Bd. dirs. Artist Chamber Ensemble, Inc., 1983-86, Libr. Assn. La Jolla, Calif., 1983-86, San Diego County Crimestoppers, Inc., 1993-95, San Diego Crime Commn., 1994-95, St. Augustine's H.S., 1994-95, San Diego Hist. Soc., 1993-95. Mem. ABA, Calif. State Bar Assn., San Diego County Bar Assn., Mortar Bd., Guidon Soc., Charter 100, Phi Beta Kappa. Office: Higgs Fletcher & Mack 401 W A St Ste 2600 San Diego CA 92101-7913 Office Phone: 619-595-4292.

PAYNE, MARY LIBBY, retired judge; b. Gulfport, Miss., Mar. 27, 1932; d. Reece O. and Emily Augusta (Cook) Bickerstaff; m. Bobby R. Payne; children: Reece Allen, Glenn Russell. Student, Miss. U. for Women, 1950-52; BA in Polit. Sci. with distinction, U. Miss., 1954, LLB, 1955. Bar: Miss. 1955. Ptnr. Bickerstaff & Bickerstaff, Gulfport, 1955-56; sec. Guaranty Title Co., Jackson, Miss., 1957; assoc. Henley, Jones, & Henley, Jackson, Miss., 1958-61; freelance rschr. Pearl, Miss., 1961-63; solo practitioner Brandon, Miss., 1963-68; exec. dir. Miss. Judiciary Commn., Jackson, 1968-70; chief drafting & rsch. Miss. Ho. Reps., Jackson, 1970-72; asst. atty. gen. State Atty. Gen. Office, Jackson, 1972-75; founding dean, assoc. prof. Sch. Law Miss. Coll., Jackson, 1975-78, prof., 1978-94, scholar in residence, prof. emerita, 2003—; judge Miss. Ct. Appeals, Jackson, 1995—2001; ret., 2001. Mem. bd. disting. alumnae Miss. U. Women, 1988—2000. Contbr. articles to profl. jours. Founder, bd. dirs. Christian Conciliation Svc., Jackson, 1983-93; bd. dirs. Exchange Club's Child Abuse Prevention Ctr. of Jackson, 1999-2001; counsel Christian Action Com. Rankin Bapt. Assn., Pearl, 1968-92; advisor Covenant Ministerial Fellowship, 1995-2002. Named Miss. Coll. Lawyer of Yr., Miss. Coll. Sch. Law Alumni Assn., 1998, Outstanding Woman Lawyer, Miss. Women Lawyers Assn., 1999, Susie Blue Buchanan award, Women in Profession Com. of Miss. Bar, 2000; recipient Book of Golden Deeds award, Pearl Exch. Club, 1989, Excellence medallion, Miss. U. Women, 1990, Woman of Yr. award, Miss. Assn. Women Higher Edn., 1989, Power of One award, Miss. Govs. Conf., 1996, Disting. Jurist award, Miss. State U., 2004. Fellow Am. Bar Found.; mem. Miss. Bar Found., Christian Legal Soc. (nat. bd. dirs. 1992-2001, Skeeter Ellis Svc. to Law Students award 1999, Lifetime Achievement award 2002). Baptist. Avocations: public speaking, travel, needlepoint, sewing, reading.

PAYNE, MARY LOUISE, music educator, musician; d. Nicholas and Helen Mae Square; m. John Charles Payne, June 25, 1977; children: Christopher Michael, Timothy Andrew, Bethany Marie. MusB cum laude, Baldwin-Wallace Coll. Conservatory of Music, 1975; MusM, Ind. U. Sch. Music, 1977. 2nd clarinet Am. Wind Symphony, Pitts., 1976—76; prin. clarinet Wheaton Symphony, 1979—87, Wheaton Mcpl. Band, 1995, 2nd-5th clarinet, 1978—79, 1989—98; prin. clarinet Northbrook Symphony, 1980—82; clarinet Five Winds Quintet, Glen Ellyn, 1980—84; clarinet w/position rotation wind ensemble Coll. of DuPage, 1982—84, instr. music theory, music appreciation, 1997—98; prin. clarinet Fox Valley Symphony, Aurora, 1985—98; music tchr. pvt. studio, Wheaton, Ill., 1989—; clarinet Blaser Quintet, Joliet, 1993—96; co-acting prin. clarinet Elmhurst Symphony, 1996—97; prin. clarinet New Philharm., Glen Ellyn, 1997—. Featured artist clarinet soloist Fox Valley Symphony, Aurora, Ill., 1991—91, 1995—95, Wheaton Mcpl. Band, 1994—94, 1997—97, Met. Youth Symphony Orch., Romeoville, 2002—02, New Philharm., Glen Ellyn, 2002—02, Glen Ellyn Children's Chorus, 1998—98; clarinet adjudicator Ill. Music Educator Assn., Chgo., 2002—02, Naperville, 1997—97; adj. instr. clarinet, saxophone Lewis U. Music Dept., Romeoville, 1994—; participant Selected Clarinet Summit, 2004. Named Outstanding Musician of Yr., Mu Phi Epsilon Mu Phi Chpt., 1974. Mem.: Internat. Clarinet Assn., Glen Ellyn Wheaton Musicians' Club (assoc.; publicity chmn. 1993—95). Avocations: needlepoint, hiking, sketching, painting, tai chi. Home: 756 Barry Ave Wheaton IL 60187 E-mail: mlpayne@intergate.com.

PAYNE, MAXWELL CARR, JR., retired psychology educator; b. Nashville, Feb. 9, 1927; s. Carr and Mary Evans (Tarpley) P.; m. Juanita Campbell, Oct. 17, 1958; children: Maxwell Carr III, Elizabeth Campbell McKinney, Mary Allison Klausner. AB, Vanderbilt U., 1949; AM, Princeton U., 1950, PhD, 1951. Rsch. assoc. U. Ill., Urbana, 1951-54; asst. prof. psychology Ga. Inst. Tech., Atlanta, 1954-60, assoc. prof., 1961-65, prof., 1965-90, ret., 1991. Cons. Lockheed-Ga. Co., Marietta, 1963; testing dir. Aircrew Ctr., Am. Insts. Rsch., Atlanta, 1960-75; faculty Atlanta Sch. Art, 1970; mem. Ga. State Bd. Examiners of Psychologists, 1970-74. Contbr. articles to profl. jours. Sunday Sch. tchr. Northside United Meth. Ch., Atlanta, 1989—. With USNR, 1944-46. Recipient Disting. Tchr. award Ga. Inst. Tech., 1970. Fellow AAAS; mem. Am. Psychol. Assn., Ga. Psychol. Assn. (Cert. of Merit), Southeastern Psychol. Assn., So. Soc. Philosophy and Psychology (treas. 1971-74, pres. 1985-86), Ga. Inst. Tech. Faculty Club (pres. 1970), Phi Beta Kappa, Sigma Xi, Phi Kappa Phi, Omicron Delta Kappa, Beta Theta Pi. Avocation: gardening. Home: 3035 Farmington Dr NW Atlanta GA 30339-4704

PAYNE, MEREDITH JORSTAD, physician; b. St. Louis, Feb. 7, 1927; d. Louis Helmar and Cleone Gladys (Branian) Jorstad; m. Spencer Payne, 1948 (div. 1959); m. James McGarity, 1965 (div. 1977); children: Maureen Meredith, James Louis. AB, Washington U., St. Louis, 1947, MD, 1950; MBA, Lindenwood U., 1999. Diplomate Am. Bd. Surgery, Am. Bd. Plastic Surgery. Intern gen. surgery St. Louis City Hosp., 1950-51, asst. resident surgery, 1951-54; chief surg. resident Roswell Park Meml. Hosp., Buffalo, 1954-55; chief plastic surgery resident Allentown (Pa.) Gen. Hosp., 1955-57; clin. instr. surgery Washington U. Med. Sch., 1957-70; vis. surgeon Homer G. Phillips Hosp., St. Louis, 1957-70; staff St. Luke's, St. Louis and Bethesda, 1957—, St. Mary's, 1988—; chief plastic surgery Vets. Hosp., 1986-98; assoc. prof. plastic surgery (clin.) St. Louis U. Sch. Medicine, St. Louis, 1986—. Med. dir. Unity Clft Palate Clinic; asst. dir. Bethesda Delworth Nursing Home, 1997—2001; attending physician Concentra Med. Ctrs., 1994—. Contbr. articles to profl. jours. Fellow ACS; mem. AMA, Am. Soc. Plastic and Reconstructive Surgery, Mo. Med. Assn. (del., councillor 1988X), St. Louis Met. Med. Soc. (councillor 1983-86, sec. 1998-99, v.p. 1999-00), Am. Cleft Palate Assn., Roswell Park Surgery Assn., So. Med. Assn., Washington U. Med. Alumni Assn., Am. Geriatrics Soc., Midwestern Assn. Plastic Surgeons, Pan Am. Med. Assn., City Hosp. Alumni Assn., Soc. Head and Neck Surgeons, St. Louis Area Soc. Plastic Surgeons (pres. 1990-93), City Hosp. Alumni Assn. (v.p. 1995-97, pres. 1997-99), Mo. Assn. Plastic and Reconstructive Surgery (treas. 1995X, v.p. 1997, pres. 1998), St Louis Surg. Soc. (v.p. 1998), AMWA (treas. St. Louis chpt. 1995), Order Eastern Star, Zonta (St. Louis pres. 1968-69), College Club (bd. dirs. St. Louis 1983-85). Avocations: skiing, tennis, sewing, knitting, gardening. Home: 7314 Westmoreland Dr Saint Louis MO 63130-4240

PAYNE, MICHAEL DAVID, English language educator; b. Dallas, Jan. 17, 1941; s. Fred G. Payne and Jocie Marie (Kirkham) Lundberg; children: Jeffrey, Jennifer, Albert, Edward. Student, U. Calif.-Berkeley, 1958-59, 61; BA, So. Oreg. Coll., 1962; PhD, U. Oreg., 1969. Tchr. English, Medford (Oreg.) Sr. High Sch., 1962-63; instr. English, U. Oreg., Eugene, 1963-69; asst. prof. to prof. English, Bucknell U., Lewisburg, Pa., 1969—, chmn. dept. history, 1980-82, chmn. dept. English, 1982-88, 92-94, chair faculty, 2000—04, Presdl. prof., 1982-86, John P. Crozer prof. English lit., 1986—; dir. Bucknell Univ. Press, 1972-76; assoc. editor Bucknell Rev., 1970-85, editor, 1985-88. Author: Irony in Shakespeare's Roman Plays, 1974, Reading Theory, 1993, Reading Knowledge, 1997; editor: Contemporary Essays on Style, 1969, Shakespeare: Contemporary Critical Approaches, 1979, Text, Interpretation, Theory, 1985, Self, Sign and Symbol, 1986, Perspective, 1986, Criticism, History and Intertextuality, 1987, New Interpretations of American Literature, 1987, The Senses of Stanley Cavell, 1988, Dictionary of Cultural and Critical Theory, 1996, Renaissance Literature: An Anthology, 2003, Life.after.theory, 2003; gen. editor Bucknell Lectures in Lit. Theory, 1990-95. Recipient Lindback award for disting. teaching, 1976, Disting. Svc. award CEA, 1988, Profl. Achievement award, 1993; Folger Shakespeare Libr. fellow, 1973, NEH fellow, 1974, Bucknell Alumni fellow, 1978-79. Mem.: MLA, Children's Lit. Assn., Coll. English Assn., Inst. Romance Studies (U. London), Johnson Soc. London, Phi Beta Kappa (hon.). Home: 24 Water St Lewisburg PA 17837-1562 E-mail: payne@bucknell.edu.

PAYNE, MICHAEL LEE, association management executive; b. Monroe, N.C., Aug. 6, 1948; s. Robert H. and Martha (Brooks) P. BA in History, U. S.C., 1970, BA in Journalism, 1971; BA in Polit. Sci., 1972. Program dir. Coastal Plains Reg. Commn., Washington, 1972-75; dir. fed. rels. Office Coastal Zone Mgmt. NOAA, Washington, 1975-80; investment specialist Econ. Dirs. Adminstrn. U.S. Dept. Commerce, Washington, 1980-82; dep. to asst. sec. for congl. affairs Office of Sec. U.S. Dept. Commerce, Washington, 1982-84; sr. exec. v.p.,mng. dir. Smith-Bucklin Assoc., Washington, 1984—. Bd. dirs. Smith-Bucklin Assoc., PCMA, CEIR, INCON; mem. worldwide adv. bd. Hilton; presenter to hospitality industry. Author: Complete Guide to Non-Profit Management, 1993; contbr. numerous articles to profl. publs. Mem. Am. Soc. Assn. Execs., Profl. Conv. Mgrs. Assn., Meeting Profls. Internat. Avocations: travel, tennis, fishing, handball, biking. Office: Smith-Bucklin Assoc 2025 M St NW # 800 Washington DC 20036-3309

PAYNE, PAULA MARIE, minister; b. Waukegan, Ill., Jan. 13, 1952; d. Percy Howard and Annie Maude (Canady) P. BA, U. Ill., 1980; MA, U. San Francisco, 1986; MDiv, Wesley Theol. Sem., 1991, postgrad., 1995—. Ordained to ministry United Meth. Ch., 1990. Chaplain for minority affairs Am. U., Washington, 1988-89; chaplain, intern NIH, Bethesda, Md., 1989-90; pastor Asbury United Meth. Ch., Charles Town, W.Va., 1990—. Supt. ch. sch. United Meth. Ch., Oxon Hill, Md., 1989-90; mem. AIDS task force Wesley Theol. Sem., Washington, 1988-89; mem. retreat. com. Balt. Conf., 1990—; chair scholarship com. Asbury United Meth. Ch., 1990—. Bd. dirs. AIDS Task Force Jefferson County, Charles Town, 1991—, Cmty. Ministries, Charles Town, 1991—; formerly N.H. state v.p. Ch. Women United, now pres.; mem. ethics com. Concord Hosp. Tech. sgt. USAF, 1984-88; chaplain Army N.G., Md., 1994-96, Mass. 2001; chaplain USAFR, 1997. Maj. Air N.G. Recipient Cert. of Recognition, Ill. Ho. of Reps., 1988, 20th Century award of Achievement Internat. Biog. Ctr., Cambridge, Eng., 1993, 1st Five Hundred, Cambridge, 1994, Citizen's citation, City of Balt., 1994, others; Ethnic Minority scholar United Meth. Ch., 1988-89, Brandenburg scholar, 1988-89, Tadlock scholar, 1989-90, Calvary Fellow scholar Calvary United Meth. ch., 1989-90. Mem. AAUW, U. Ill. Alumni Assn. (bd. dirs. 1987-88), Alpha Kappa Alpha (pres. local chpt. 1974-76, v.p. 1973). Republican. Home: 39 Nathan Ellis Hwy Mashpee MA 02649-3267 E-mail: revpmpumc@msn.com., revpmpumc@hotmail.com. *Education can be as deep as the ocean.*

PAYNE, RICHARD HAROLD, university research administrator; b. Lowell, Mass., Apr. 30, 1941; s. Calvin Lee and Helen Josephine (Hennessey) P.; m. Harriett Gean Rowan, Feb. 4, 1961 (dec. Feb. 1977); children: James Richard, Deloria Linn; m. Kathy Leigh Freydenfeldt, Mar. 20, 1978. ABJ, U. Ga., 1965, MA, 1966, PhD, 1970. Asst. prof. polit. sci. The Citadel, Charleston, S.C., 1966-72; prof. polit. sci. Sam Houston State U., Huntsville, 1972—, chair dept., 1972-99, assoc. v.p. rsch. and grad. studies, 1999—. Editor Tex. Jour. Polit. Studies, 1988-90; contbr. articles to profl. jours. Bd. dirs. Tex. Rsch. Inst. for Environ. Studies, Huntsville, 1991-97; mem., vol. positions Boy Scouts Am., Huntsville and Houston, 1974-94. Mem. Aubudon Soc. (pres. Huntsville chpt. 1978-79, 84-85), Tex. Ornithol. Soc., Okla. Ornithol. Soc., Am. Birding Assn. (bd. dirs. 1998—, pres. 1999—), Internat. Ecotourism Soc., Ecotourism Assn. Australia, Nat. Coun. Univ. Res. Adminstrs., Policy Studies Orgn., S.W. Assn. for Can. Studies, Western Social Sci. Assn., Wildlife Mgmt. Inst., Watchable Wildlife, Inc. (vice chmn. bd. dirs. 1999—), Phi Kappa Phi, Pi Sigma Alpha, Kappa Tau Delta, Phi Eta Sigma. Avocations: birding, camping, hiking. Office: Sam Houston State U Office Rsch and Sponsored Huntsville TX 77341

PAYNE, ROGER LEE, geographer; b. Winston-Salem, N.C., Oct. 26, 1946; s. Irvin Lee and Gladys Odel (Binkley) P.; m. Sara Lucinda Parker, Aug. 16, 1970 (div. Feb. 1992); 1 child, Jennifer Nicole; m. Anne F. Remen, June 11, 1995. BA, East Carolina U., 1969, MA, 1972. Geographer, chief geog. names U.S. Geol. Survey, Reston, Va., 1974—; instr. geography and history Pan Am. Inst./U.S. Geog. Survey, 1989—; exec. sec. U.S. Bd. Names, U.S. Geol. Survey, Washington, 1990—. Instr. East Caroline U., Greenville, N.C., 1969-71, George Washington U., Washington, 1977-90, George Mason U., Fairfax, Va., 1979-83, 98—, Benjamin Franklin U., Washington, 1985-87; del. UN, N.Y.C., 1987—, instr., 1995—; mem. scientist exch. Geol. Survey, Beijing, 1989; instr. Nat. Black Colls., Howard U., 1985; book reviewer AAAS, 1975—; mem. Antarctica Sci. Field Program, 1999-2000; cons. in field. Author: Urban Development in South Africa, 1972, Place Names of Outer Banks, 1985, Manuals on Auto Names, 1987, 89, 97; coord., editor: (book series) National Gazetter U.S., 1982—; contbr. articles to profl. jours. Chmn. E. Carolina Blood Dr., Greenville, 1969. Lt. USAF, 1970-72. Recipient Guy Buzzard award Gamma Theta Upsilon, 1970; Superior Svc. award Geol. Survey, 1988, Outstanding Achievement award, 1997. Fellow Explorers Club; mem. Assn. Am. Geographers (various coms. 1969-95, pres. mid-Atlantic divsn. 1981-82, treas., sec.), Am. Name Soc. (pres. 1989), Am. Nat. Std. Inst. (rep. 1986—), Cosmos Club. Avocation: hiking. Home: 47762 Hammerstone Way Sterling VA 20165-4769 Office: US Geol Survey 523 National Ctr 12201 Sunrise Valley Dr Reston VA 20192-0523 E-mail: rpayne@usgs.gov.

PAYNE, ROGER SEARLE, zoology researcher and administrator, conservationist; b. N.Y.C., Jan. 29, 1935; m. Katy Boynton, 1960 (div. 1985); children: John, Holly, Laura Sam; m. Lisa Harrow, Aug. 18, 1991. AB in Animal Behavior, Harvard U., 1957; PhD, Cornell U., 1961. Rsch. zoologist Inst. for Rsch. in Animal Behavior N.Y. Zool. Inst., N.Y.C., 1968-71; asst. prof. biology Rockefeller U., N.Y.C., 1968-71; founder, pres. Ocean Alliance, Lincoln, Mass., 1971—. Author: Among Whales, 1995; host (TV documentary) In the Company of Whales, 1992 (series) Ocean Planet, 1994-95; co-writer, co-dir. (film) Whales, 1995. Co-recipient Albert Schweitzer medal Animal Welfare Inst., 1980; recipient Joseph Wood Krutch medal Humane Soc. U.S., 1989, Lyndhurst prize Lyndhurst Found., 1984; genius grantee John D. and Catherine T. MacArthur Found., 1984, Global 500 award UN, 1988; knighted, Netherlands, 1977. Home: 2141 Biscuit Hl South Woodstock VT 05071-9530 Office: Ocean Alliance 191 Weston Rd Lincoln MA 01773-4516 E-mail: rpayne@oceanalliance.org.

PAYNE, ROY STEVEN, judge; b. New Orleans, Aug. 30, 1952; s. Fred J. and Dorothy Julia (Peck) P.; m. Laureen Fuller, Sept. 8, 1973; children: Julie Elizabeth, Kelly Kathryn, Alex Steven, Michael Lawrence. BA with distinction, U. Va., 1974; JD, La. State U., 1977; LLM, Harvard U., 1980. Bar: La. 1977, U.S. Dist. Ct. (we. dist.) La. 1980, U.S. Ct. Appeals (5th cir.) 1980, U.S. Supreme Ct. 1983. Law clk. to judge U.S. Dist. Ct., Shreveport, La., 1977-79; assoc. Blanchard, Walker, O'Quin & Roberts, Shreveport, 1980-83, ptnr., 1984-87; U.S. Magistrate judge We. Dist. La., Shreveport, 1987—. Instr. New Eng. Sch. Law, Boston, 1979-80. Contbr. articles to profl. jours. Chmn. Northwest La. Legal Svcs. Assn., Shreveport, 1984-85. Mem. 5th Cir. Bar Assn., 5th Cir. Jud. Coun. (magistrate judges com. 1992—), La. State Bar Assn. (editl. bd. Forum jour., 1983-87, legal aid com.), Fed. Magistrate Judges Assn. (circuit dir. 2003—), Shreveport Bar Assn., La. Assn. Def. Counsel (bd. dirs. 1987), Harry V. Booth Am. Inn of Ct. (pres. elect 1994-95, pres. 1996-98), Order of Coif, Rotary, Phi Kappa Phi, Phi Delta Phi. Republican. Methodist. Home: 12494 Harts Island Rd Shreveport LA 71115-8505 Office: US Courthouse 300 Fannin St Ste 4300 Shreveport LA 71101-3122 E-mail: roy_payne@lawd.uscourts.gov.

PAYNE, R.W., JR., lawyer; b. Norfolk, Va., Mar. 16, 1936; s. Roland William and Margaret (Sawyer) P.; m. Gail Willingham, Sept. 16, 1961; children: Darrell, Preston, Darby, Clinton. BA in English, U. N.C., 1958, LLB, 1961, Stetson U., 1962. Bar: Fla. 1963, U.S. Dist. Ct. (so. dist.) 1964, U.S. Ct. Appeals (11th cir.) 1965, U.S. Supreme Ct. 1970. Assoc. Roney & Beach, St. Petersburg, Fla., 1963-64, Nichols, Gaither, Beckham, Colson & Spence, Miami, Fla., 1964-67; ptnr. Spence, Payne, Masington, Miami, 1967-95, Payne, Leeds, Colby & Robinson, P.A., Miami, 1995-97; pvt. practice Miami, 1997, 98; ptnr. McLuskey, McDonald & Payne, P.A., Miami, 1999-2001; lawyer R.W. Payne Jr. P.A., Miami, 2001—. Presenter numerous profl. convs. and seminars. Contbr. articles to legal jours., legal edn. books. Mem. Ottawa Roughriders, Can. Football League, fall 1958; capt. football team U. N.C., 1957, bd. dirs., v.p. alumni bd., 1984-92, bd. dirs. ednl. found., 1988-92; bd. dirs. Chem. Dependency Tng. Inst.; past pres. Coral Gables (Fla.) Sr. H.S. Athletic Boosters Club; past bd. dirs. Coral Gables War Meml. Youth Ctr., bd. trustees 1st United Meth. Ch. Coral Gables; past mem. gov.'s coun. on phys. fitness and sports, Fla.; past assoc. mem. Jr. Orange Bowl Com. With USMC, 1959. Fellow Am. Coll. Trial Lawyers, Internat. Acad. Trial Lawyers; mem. ABA, ATLA, Am. Bd. Trial Advocates, Fla. Bar Assn., Acad. Fla. Trial Lawyers (past mem. bd. govs.), Dade County Bar Assn. (past bd. dirs.), Dade County Trial Lawyers Assn. (founder, past pres.), Bankers Club, Miami Club, Univ. Club, Coral Reef Yacht Club, Order of Golden Fleece, Order of Old Well, Sigma Chi, Phi Delta Phi. Avocations: boating, golf, diving. Office: RW Payne Jr Apt 1503 2645 S Bayshore Dr Miami FL 33133 Office Phone: 305-285-5199. E-mail: paynerw@bellsouth.net.

PAYNE, SIDNEY STEWART, retired archbishop; b. Fogo, Nfld., Can., June 6, 1932; m. Selma Carlson, 1962; children: Carla Ann, Christopher Stewart, Robert Clement, Angela Marie Louise. BA, Meml. U., St. John's, Nfld., 1958; lic. of theology, Queen's Coll., St. John's, 1958; BDiv, Gen. Synod, 1968; DDiv (hon.), King's Coll., Halifax, N.S., Can., 1981. Ordained priest Anglican Ch., 1958, bishop, 1978, archbishop, 1990. Deacon Mission of Happy Valley, Goose Bay, Labrador, Nfld., Can., 1957-65; rector Parish of Bay Roberts, Nfld., Can., 1965-70, Parish of St. Anthony, Nfld., 1970-78, 1976-78; bishop Diocese of Western Nfld., 1978-90, archbishop of Western Nfld. and Met. Eccles. Province of Can., 1990-97; ret., 1997. Pres. Diocesan Synod, chmn. exec. com., mem. ex-officio diocesan coms.; pres. Provincial Synod, Provincial Coun.; chair Provincial House of Bishops; mem. long range planning com., ministry com., mem. nat. exec. coun. Partners in World Mission, Stewardship and Fin. Devel. Com.; mem. Anglican/Roman Cath. Bishops' Dialogue, Can.; active Provincial and Nat. House of Bishops. Mem. Internat. Grenfell Assn. (past bd. dirs.). Anglican. Avocations: reading, walking, gardening, cross country skiing. Home: PO Box 2255 R R 1 Stn Main Corner Brook NF Canada A2H 2N2 E-mail: stewart.payne@nf.sympatico.ca.

PAYNE, THOMAS H. market research company executive; Pres., CEO Market Facts, Inc., Arlington Heights, Ill., 1996—. Office: Market Facts Inc 3040 W Salt Creek Ln Arlington Heights IL 60005-1085

PAYNE, THOMAS L. university official; b. Bakersfield, Calif., Oct. 17, 1941; s. Harry LeRoy and Opal Irene (Ansel) P.; m. S. Alice Lewis, Feb. 1, 1963; children: Jacob, Joanna. AA in Liberal Arts, Bakersfield (Calif.) Jr. Coll., 1962; BA in Zoology, U. Calif., Riverside, 1965, MS in Entomology, 1967, PhD in Entomology, 1969. Asst. prof. entomology and forest sci. Tex. A&M U., College Station, 1969-73, assoc. prof., 1973-78, prof., 1978-87, rsch. coord. USDA so. pine beetle program, 1974-78; prof. entomology, head dept. Va. Poly. and State U., Blacksburg, 1987-92; dir. Ohio Agrl. R & D Ctr., Wooster; assoc. dean rsch., assoc. v.p. agrl. adminstrn. Ohio State U. Coll. Agr., Wooster, 1993—99; vice chancellor, dean agr., food and natural resources. U. Mo. Coll. Agr., Columbia, 1999—. Sec. protection sect. Nat. Planning Conf. for Rsch. in Forestry and assoc. Rangelands, 1977; bd. dirs. Urban Pest Control Rsch. Ctr. Endowment Fund, 1988—; dean's rep., ex officio mem. Va. Pesticide Control Bd., 1989—; vis. prof. Forest Zoology Inst., U. Freiburg, Germany, 1978. Editor: (with Birch and Kennedy) Mechanisms in Insect Olfaction, 1986; mem. editorial bd. Jour. Ga. Entomol. Soc., 1979-83; co-editor Jour. Insect Behavior, 1987—; contbr. chpts. to books. Pres., co-founder Brazos County Firefighters Assn., 1979-81; v.p., co-founder Precinct 2 Vol. Fire Dept., 1979-80, pres., 1982-86; author grant to build Edge Tex. Sr. Citizens Ctr., 1979; mem. Friends of Blacksburg Master Chorale. Recipient numerous awards, 1976—, including cert. of appreciation for svc. as rsch. coord. expanded so. pine beetle rsch. USDA, 1976, 78, 80, rsch. award Tex. Forestry Assn., 1977, awards Am. Registry Profl. Entomologists, 1979, Alexander von Humboldt Stiftung sr. U.S. scientist award, 1982, Faculty Disting. Achievement award in rsch. Assn. Former Students Tex. A&M U., 1985, A.D. Hopkins award for outstanding rsch.-adminstrn. in forest entomology, 1991; Volkswagenwerk fellow U. Freiburg, 1978. Mem. AAAS, Entomol. Soc. Am. (CIBA-GEIGY agrl. recognition award 1982), Internat. Soc. Chem. Ecology, Internat. Chemoreception Workshop on Insects, Internat. Union Forest Rsch. Orgns., Nat. Corn Growers Assn., So. Forest Insect Work Conf., Va. Agribus. Coun., Va. Agrl. Chem. and Soil Fertility Assn., Va. Hort. Soc. (exec. coun. 1989), Va. Corn Growers Assn., Va. Soybean Assn., Va. Pest Control Assn, Western Forest Insect Work Conf., Coll. Agr. and Life Scis. Agr. Faculty Assn., Sigma Xi, Gamma Sigma Delta. Office: Univ Missouri Coll Agr Food/Nat Resource 2-69 Agrl Bldg Columbia MO 65211-0001 E-mail: cafnr@missouri.edu.

PAYNE, TYSON ELLIOTT, JR., retired insurance executive; b. Dallas, May 25, 1927; s. Tyson Elliott and Winnie Claris (Denman) P.; m. Billie Jane Spears, Aug. 28, 1948; children: David Tyson, Sally Jane. B.J., U. Tex., 1949. CLU, ChFC. Sports editor Lufkin (Tex.) News, 1949-51, Tyler (Tex.) Courier Times, 1951-53; with Am. Nat. Ins. Co., Galveston, Tex., 1953-88, v.p. health ins. ops. St. Louis, 1965-1970, v.p. mktg. Galveston, 1970-86; pvt. practice ins. agt. Austin, Tex., 1987-88; exec. v. p., dir. Sch. of Ins. & Fin. Svcs. at U. Houston, 1988-92; ret., 1992. Elder Presbyn. Ch. With USNR, 1945-46. Home: 8110 Cardin Dr Austin TX 78759-8704 E-mail: tpaynejr@aol.com.

PAYNE, WILLIAM D. assemblyman; b. Newark, N.J., July 8, 1932; children: Eric, Lisa, Gina, Kristi. BA in polit. sci., Rutgers U., 1959. Commr., vice chmn. Essex County Improvement Authority, 1980—86; commr., chmn. Newark Housing Authority, 1986—89; campaign mgr. Congressman Donald M. Payne, 1988—; candidate for mayor Newark, 1994; campaign mgr. Assemblyman Craig A. Stanley, 1995; assemblyman N.J. Gen. Assembly, 1998—; dep. majority conf. leader, 2002—. Founder, pres., CEO UrbanData Sys., Inc., 1969—88; exec. dir. One to One/N.J. Sch.-Centered Mentoring Orgn., 1992—94; mkt. devel. cons., chief of staff Assemblyman Craig Stanley, Irvington, NJ, 1996—97; prin. William Payne & Assocs. Mem. N.J. Congl. Award Coun., 1995—; small bus. adv. coun. N.Y. Fed. Res. Bank. Office: 40 Clinton St Ste 200 Newark NJ 07102 E-mail: AsmPayne@njleg.org.

PAYNE, WILLIAM P. communications executive; married; 2 children. PhD, U. Ga. Atty. pvt. practice; pres. Olympic Organizing Com.; pres., CEO Atlanta Com. Olympic Games; vice chmn. NationsBank Corp., 1997; chmn. Orchestrate.com Premiere Techs., Inc., Atlanta, 1998—. Bd.d irs. Jefferson Pilot Corp., Cousins Properties, Inc., ACSYS, Inc., ILD Telecomm., Inc., WebMD, Inc. Athletic bd. dirs. U. Ga. Office: Premiere Techs Inc 3399 Peachtree Rd NE Atlanta GA 30326-1120

PAYNTER, HARRY ALVIN, retired trade association executive; b. Miami, Ariz., July 22, 1923; s. Harry and Mabel Vera (Moore) P.; m. Betty Clarice Wilkins, Dec. 3, 1944; children: Harry Alvin, Steven Wilkins, Barbara Elizabeth, Susan Moore. BS, Okla. State U., 1948; MBA, Harvard U., 1954; postgrad., Air Command and Staff Coll., 1957, Armed Forces Staff Coll., 1961, Nat. War Coll., 1969. Commd. 2d lt. AC U.S. Army, 1943; advanced through grades to col. USAF, 1968; service as flight comdr. 8th Air Force, World War II and Berlin airlift; asst. air attache (Am. embassy), Karachi, Pakistan, 1958-60, air attache Quito, Ecuador, 1965-67, 1969; prof. aerospace studies Dartmouth, 1967-68; ret., 1970; mng. dir. Gas Appliance Mfrs. Assn., Inc., N.Y.C., 1970-73, pres. Arlington, Va., 1973-88. Decorated D.F.C., Air medal with 3 oak leaf clusters, Purple Heart, Joint Services Commendation medal with oak leaf cluster U.S.; Abdon Calderon Ecuador; recipient Am. Bankers award, 1947; named Ecuador Hon. Command Pilot. Mem. Can. Gas Assn. (life), Guild Ancient Supplers (hon.), Am. Soc. Gas Engrs. (hon.), Air Force Assn., Ret. Officers Assn., Am. Soc. Assn. Execs., Nat. Press Club. Phi Kappa Phi. Presbyterian. Home: 1416 N Inglewood St Arlington VA 22205-2735

PAYNTER, VESTA LUCAS, pharmacist; b. Aiken County, S.C., May 29, 1922; d. James Redmond and Annie Lurline (Stroman) Lucas; m. Maurice Alden Paynter, Dec. 23, 1945 (dec. 1971); children: Sharon Lucinda, Maurice Alden, Doyle Gregg. BS in Pharmacy, U. S.C., 1943. Lic. pharmacist. Owner, pharmacist Cayce Drug Store, S.C., 1944-52, Dutch Fork Drug Store, Columbia, S.C., 1955-60, The Drug Ctr., Cayce, 1963-81; pharmacist Lane-Rexall, Columbia, 1952-55; dist. pharmacist S.C. Dept. Health and Environ. Control, Columbia, 1983-90, ret., 1990. Vol. pharmacist Free Med. Clinic, Columbia, 1987-90. Named Preceptor of Yr., Syntex Co./Student Body of U.

S.C., 1981. Fellow S.C. Pub. Health Assn., S.C. Pharm Assn., 5th Dist. Pharm. Assn.; mem. CBI VA Assn. (assoc.), 14th Air Force Assn. (assoc.), Order Eastern Star, White Shrine of Jerusalem, Am. Legion Aux. (Post 130). Baptist. Avocations: travel, art, oenology, Lowery organ. Home: 2351 Vine St Cayce SC 29033-3000 Personal E-mail: MPaynter@sc.rr.com.

PAYRI, JOEL, pharmaceutical marketing executive; b. Sidi-Bel-Abbes, Algeria, Nov. 29, 1961; s. Rene and Marie P. DVM, Nat. Vet. Sch., Toulouse, France, 1985, diploma of anatomo-pathology, 1988; diploma of med. stats., U. Paris VI, 1989; MBA, INSEAD, Fontainebleau, France, 1991. Pvt. vet. practice, St. Gaudens, France, 1985-86; study dir. Searle Rsch. and Devel., Sophia Antipolis, France, 1986-87; head exptl. cardiology Rhone Poulenc Sante, Vitry sur Seine, France, 1988-90; mktg. mgr. Pharmuka-Rhone Poulenc, Paris, 1991-92; worldwide product mgr. Taxotere Rhone Poulenc Rorer, Paris, 1992-96; internat. mktg. dir. GlaxoSmithkline, London, 1996—2001; v.p. internat. Biogen Idec, Paris, 2001—. Surg. asst. Nat. Vet. Sch., Toulouse, 1984-85; pres. new mgmt. team Rhone Poulenc Sante, Paris, 1989-91; interviewer INSEAD MBA cands. Biogen Idec, Paris, 1995—. Author: Telemetry and Gastric pH Measurements, 1985 (gold medal 1985); contbr. to websites and pubs. for Internat. Herpes Alliance. Capt. French Army, 1987-90, Paris. Grantee Ministry Agr., 1985. Mem. Am. Social Health Assn., Infectious Disease Soc. Am. Home: La petite Ourse Anse de Maldorme Bouches du Rhone 13007 Marseilles France Office: Biogen 55 Av Des Champs Pierreux 92012 Nanterre France Fax: 33-147-217535. E-mail: joel_payri@biogen.com.

PAYSON, MARTIN F. lawyer; b. Bklyn., Dec. 25, 1940; m. Rhoda Shapiro, Oct. 8, 1961; children: Jacqueline, Marla. BBA, CCNY, 1961; JD, Bklyn. Law Sch., 1966. Bar: N.Y. 1967, Pa. 1989, U.S. Ct. Appeals (1st cir.) 1971, U.S. Ct. Appeals (2d and 3d cirs.) 1968, U.S. Ct. Appeals (4th cir.) 1969, U.S. Supreme Ct. 1970. Gen. ptnr. Jackson Lewis L.L.P. (formerly Jackson, Lewis, Schnitzler & Krupman), White Plains, NY, 1967—. Lectr. in field. Contbr. articles to various publs. With U.S. Army, 1961-62. Mem. N.Y. State Bar Assn. (labor and employee rels. sects.), Soc. for Human Resource Mgmt. Avocations: photography, bicycling, model railroading, gardening. Office: Jackson Lewis LLP One N Broadway White Plains NY 10601 E-mail: Paysonm@JacksonLewis.com.

PAYTON, BENJAMIN FRANKLIN, college president; b. Orangeburg, S.C., Dec. 27, 1932; s. Leroy Ralph and Sarah (Mack) P.; m. Thelma Louise Plane, Nov. 28, 1959; children: Mark Steven, Deborah Elizabeth. BA, S.C. State U., 1955; BD (Danforth grad. fellow 1955-63), Harvard U., 1958; MA, Columbia U., 1960; PhD, Yale U., 1963; LLD (hon.), Eastern Mich. U., 1972; LHD (hon.), Benedict Coll., 1972; LittD (hon.), Morgan State U., 1974, U. Md., 1987; LLD, Morris Brown Coll., 1975, Lehigh U., 1990; LLD (hon.), S.C. State U., 2001. Asst. prof. sociology of religion and social ethics Howard U., Washington; also dir. Howard U. (Community Rsch.-Svc. Project, 1963-65; exec. dir. dept. social justice and Commn. on Religion and Race Nat. Coun. Chs. of Christ in U.S.A., 1965-67; pres. Benedict Coll., Columbia, S.C., 1967-72; program officer higher edn. and rsch. Ford Found., 1972-81; pres. Tuskegee (Ala.) U., 1981—. Mem. nat. rev. bd. Ctr. for Cultural and Tech. Exch. between U.S. and Asia; mem. commn. on Pre-Coll. Edn. in Math., Sci. and Tech. NSF; edn. advisor to V.P. George Bush during Seven-Nation Tour of Africa, 1982; team leader U.S. Presdl. Task Force on Agrl. and Econ. Devel. to Zaire; bd. dirs. AmSouth Bancorp.; mem. vis. com. dept. humanities MIT, 1988—90; vis. com. bd. overseers Harvard U., 1989—95. Author: (with Dr. Seymour Melman) A Strategy for the Next Stage in Civil Rights: Metropolitan-Rural Development for Equal Opportunity, 1966. Mem. nat. commn. on higher edn. issues Am. Coun. Edn.; bd. dirs. Ala. Shakespeare Festival. Named South Carolinian of Yr., statewide TV-Radio, 1972; recipient Billings prize, 1st Pl., Harvard U., 1957, Gold medal award, Napoleon Hill Found., 1987, Benjamin E. Mays award, 1988, Centennial Alumnus award, S.C. State U., 1988. Mem. NAACP, Am. Soc. Scholars, Soc. for Religion, Higher Edn. (dir.), Assn. Governing Bds. (pres.'s adv. coun.), Phi Beta Kappa, Alpha Phi Alpha, Alpha Kappa Mu, Sigma Pi Phi. Home: Grey Columns 399 Old Montgomery Rd Tuskegee AL 36083-1519 Office: Office Pres Tuskegee U Tuskegee AL 36088

PAYTON, GARY DWAYNE, professional basketball player; b. Oakland, Calif., July 23, 1968; m. Monique Payton; children: Raquel, Gary Dwayne, Julian. Grad., Oreg. State U., 1990. Drafted NBA, 1990; guard Seattle Supersonics, 1990—2003, Milwaukee Bucks, 2003, L.A. Lakers, 2003—04, Boston Celtics, 2004—. Author: (novels) Confidence Counts, 1999. Founder Gary Payton Foundation, 1996—. Named NBA All-Star, 1994—98, 2000—01, NBA Defensive Player of the Year, 1996; named to All-Am. 1st team, The Sporting News, 1990, NBA All-Def. 1st team, 1994—2001, All-NBA 1st team, 1998, 2000, All-NBA 2nd team, 1995—97, 1999; recipient Gold Medal, Atlanta Olympic Games, 1996, Sydney Olympic Games, 2000. Office: c/o Boston Celtics 151 Merrimac st Boston MA 02114*

PAYTON, GARY E. astronaut; b. Rock Island, Ill., June 20, 1948; BS in Astronautical Engring., USAF Acad., 1971; MS in Astronautical and Aeronautical Engring., Purdue U., 1972; grad. Pilot Tng., Craig AFB, Ala., 1973. Commd. 2d lt. USAF, 1971, advanced through grades to maj.; instr. pilot Craig AFB; spacecraft test contr. Cape Canaveral AFS, Fla., 1976—80; astronaut NASA, Houston. Achievements include logged over 1,080 hours in different aircraft; logged over 73 hours in space; payload specialist STS-51C Discovery (1985). Office: Astronaut Office/CB NASA Johnson Space Ctr Houston TX 77058

PAYTON, JOHN, lawyer; b. Dec. 27, 1946; BA, Pomona Coll., 1973; JD, Harvard U., 1977. Law clk. to Hon. Cecil F. Poole U.S. Dist. Ct., Northern Dist. Calif.; corp. counsel D.C., 1991—94; ptnr. Wilmer, Cutler & Pickering. Mem.: D.C. Bar (pres. 2001—02). Office: Wilmer Cutler & Pickering 2445 M St NW Washington DC 20037

PAYTON, MARK EDWARD, statistician, educator; b. Sioux City, Iowa, Sept. 2, 1964; s. Homer Bill and Naomi Ruth Payton; m. Deanna Gail Corley, Mar. 7, 1992; children: Riley Jacob, Mackenzie Leigh. BS in Edn., S.W. Mo. State U., 1986; MS, Okla. State U., 1988, PhD, 1991. Asst. prof. dept. stats. Okla. State U., Stillwater, 1991—96, assoc. prof., 1996—2001, prof., 2001—. Presenter in field. Mem. editl. bd.: BioScience, 2001—; contbr. articles to profl. jours. Fellow: Royal Statis. Soc.; mem.: Am. Statis. Assn. (chpt. pres. 1992—93), Centennial Rotary Club, Mu Sigma Rho (nat. pres. 1997—2000). Office: Okla State Univ Dept Stats MSCS 301 Stillwater OK 74078

PAYTON, ROBERT See PROUD, ROBERT

PAYTON, ROGER, logistics company executive; CEO, Pickfords Indsl. Ltd. (subs. NFC plc), 1982-84, Merchants Home Delivery Svcs. Inc. (subs. NFC plc), 1985-87, 91-95, Allied Van Lines Inc. (subs. NFC plc); pres., CEO, Internat. Logistics Ltd., Hillside, Ill., 1996-99. Address: Ste 150 13952 Denver West Pky Golden CO 80401-3171

PAYTON, THOMAS WILLIAM, corporate finance consultant executive; b. Toronto, Ont., Can., Sept. 7, 1946; With Can. Imperial Bank of Commerce, Toronto; dir. Bramalea Ltd., Toronto, 1981-82, v.p., 1982-88, sr. v.p., 1988-90, sr. v.p., treas., 1991-93; dir. Cadillac Fairview, Inc., 1994-95; pres. Sunnybrook Properties Inc., 1997-2000, DelLyn Advisors Inc., 1993—; v.p. Hawthorne Realty Advisors Inc., 2003—. E-mail: dellynadvinc@aol.com.

PAYTON-ROBINSON, CONSTANCE MARIAN, educational consultant, writer; b. Las Vegas, Mar. 14, 1942; d. J. Lowell Payton and Maxine Key; children: S. Robyn Hamilton, Rhett, Tom Harris. A in Art, Lubbock Christian U., 1962; BS in Edn., Abilene Christian U., 1964, M cum laude (hon.) in Human Comm., 1990. Tchr. 5th grade Tatum Elem., N.Mex., 1964—65; tchr. 3d grade Houghtling Elem., Ketchikan, Ark., 1965—66; tchr. trainable and emotionally disturbed Ketchikon, 1969—70; with Hobbs H.S., 1989—96; with real estate Hobbs, N.Mex., 1991—; tutoring coord. N.Mex. Coll., Hobbs, 1996—. Author: This Day of Love, 1978, The Secret Hope, 1978, Song in My Heart, 1985, Time for Love, 1991, (short stories) Christian Women-Family Reunion, (devotional mag.) Power for Today; dir.: (10 prodns.) Cmty. Theatre, 1988—; actor: Lettice and Lovage, 1996—. Named Outstanding Women of Yr., Jr. Svc. League, 1976. Mem.: AAUW (local and state officer 1968—69), Coll. Reading and Learning Assn. (pres. 2002—04). Avocations: writing, art. Home: 5701 N Dal Paso Hobbs NM 88242

PAYTON-WRIGHT, PAMELA, actress; b. Pitts., Nov. 1, 1941; d. Gordon Edgar and Eleanor Ruth (McKinley) Payton Wright; m. David Arthur Butler, May 8, 1978 (div. 1989); 1 child, Oliver Dickon Hedley. Grad., St. Mary's Jr. Coll., 1961; BA, Birmingham So. Coll., 1963; postgrad., Royal Acad. Dramatic Arts, London, 1963-65. Theatre debut Diary of a Scoundrel, 1965, Broadway debut The Show-Off, 1968, Broadway appearances Exit The King, The Cherry Orchard, 1968, Jimmy Shine, 1969, The Crucible, 1972, Mourning Becomes Electra, 1972, All Over town, 1975, Glass Menagerie, 1976, Romeo and Juliet, 1977, A Streetcar Named Desire, 1988, Night of the Iguana, 1988, M. Butterfly, 1988-90, Something Unspoken, 1995, Long Day's Journey Into Night, 2003, Off-Broadway appearances The Effect of Gamma Rays on Man-In-The Moon Marigolds, 1970-71, Jesse and the Bandit Queen, 1975, The Seagull, 1980, Don Juan, 1982, Hamlet, 1982, Mrs. Warren's Profession, 1992, The Replacement, 1995, Richard III, 'Til the Rapture Comes, 1998, What You Get and What You Expect, 2000, Fifth of July, 2003, Duet, 2004, The Day Emily Married, 2004, regional theater appearances Skin of Our Teeth, 1972, Aimee, 1973, Othello, Troilus and Cressida, As You Like It, 1976, Lunch Girls, 1977, Summerfolk, 1978, The Greeks, 1982, The Misanthrope, 1982, Tobacco Road, 1984, Passion, 1984-85, Cat on a Hot Tin Roof, 1985, Little Eyolf, 1985, On the Verge, 1986, Our Town, 1987, The Road to Mecca, 1990, Picnic, 1991, The Way of the World, 1991, Quartermaine's Terms, 1993, Misalliance, 1993, Six Degrees of Separation, 1993, Ghosts, 1994, Sea Gull, 1994, The Show-Off, 1995, The Rivals, 1996, Touch of the Poet, 1996, Glass Menagerie, 1997, Voir Dire, 1997, She Stoops to Conquer, 1997, Blithe Spirits, 1998, Transit of Venus, 1998, Seagull, 1999, Long Day's Journey Into Night, 1999, Sweet Bird of Youth, 1999, A Fair Country, 2000, Philadelphia Story, 2001, Long Days Journey Into Night, 2002, Seascape, 2002, Outward Bound, 2002, others, film appearances At the Dark End of the Street, 1980, Going in Style, 1981, Starlight, 1985, My Little Girl, 1985, Ironweed, 1987, The Freshman, 1989, In Dreams, 1999, TV appearances Look Homeward Angel, 1972, The Haunting of Rosalind, 1973, The Prodigal, Brother to Dragons, 1973, The Adams Chronicles, 1976. Nominee Emmy, 1972, Lucille Lortel, 2003; recipient Fulbright award, 1963, Spl. medal, Edmund Gray prize for high comedy, Herbert Beerbohm Tree citation, Royal Acad. Dramatic Art, 1963—65, Obie award, 1970, 1975, 1976, Clarence Derwent award, Variety Critics' Poll citation, 1970, Drama Desk award, 1972, Best Actress citation, Dallas Theater Critics' Forum, 1994, Balt., 1997, Dean Goodman award, 1999, Joseph Jefferson award, 1996; Fox Grant fellow, 1999. Mem. Actors Equity Assn., AFTRA, Screen Actors Guild. Episcopalian. Office: Bauman & Assocs 250 W 57th St New York NY 10019-3741

PAZ, GEORGE, accountant; b. St. Louis, Aug. 27, 1955; s. Geronimo and Collen May (Hart) P.; m. Georgene Marie Wade, July 27, 1974; children: Stacy, Kelly, Rebecca. BSBA, U. Mo., St. Louis, 1982. CPA, Mo. Jr. acct. Gen. Am., St. Louis, 1980-82, sr. acct., 1982-83, acctg. adminstr., 1983-85, tax planning analyst, 1985-87, dir. tax planning, 1987—. Bd. dirs. Gen. Am. Employees Fed. Credit Union, 1985—. Fellow Life Office Mgmt. Assn.; mem. Am. Inst. CPA's, Mo. Soc. CPA's. Lutheran. Avocations: golf, running, softball. Office: Gen Am Life Ins Co 700 Market St Saint Louis MO 63101-1829 Home: 587 Tennyson Dr Wheaton IL 60187-7604

PAZ, HAROLD LOUIS, dean, educator, internist; b. N.Y.C., Jan. 3, 1955; BA in Biology and Psychology, U. Rochester, 1977, MD, 1982; MS in Life Sci. Engring., Tufts U., 1979. Diplomate subspecialty in pulmonary medicine Am. Bd. Internal Medicine. Intern in internal medicine Northwestern U. Med. Ctr., Chgo., 1982—83, resident in internal medicine, 1983—85, chief med. resident, 1985—86; instr. clin. medicine Northwestern U., Chgo., 1985—86; fellow in pulmonary and critical care Johns Hopkins U., Balt., 1986—88, fellow in environ. health scis., 1986—88; asst. prof. medicine Hahnemann U., Phila., 1988—92, asst. prof. anesthesia, 1989—92, assoc. dean grad. med. edn., 1992—94, assoc. prof. medicine, 1992—94, dir. med. ICU, 1988—94, assoc. hosp. med. dir., 1992—94, dir. Ctr. for Clin. Outcomes, 1992—94; med. dir., assoc. dean for clin. affairs U. Medicine and Dentistry N.J. Robert Wood Johnson Med. Sch., New Brunswick, 1994—95, assoc. prof. medicine, 1994—2003, dean, 1995—, prof. medicine, 2003—; CEO U. Medicine and Dentistry N.J. Robert Wood Johnson U. Med. Group, New Brunswick, 1995—. Editor: Jour. Undergrad. Rsch., 1976, Med. Staff News newsletter, 1992—94; cons.: Annals Internal Medicine, Clin. Immunology and Immunopathology, Chest, Intensive Care Medicine, Physician Execs., N.Y. State Med. Jour., mem. editl. bd.: Jour. Disease Mgmt. and Clin. Outcomes, 1996—, Chest, 1998—2003. Recipient Disting. Svc. award, Motolinsky Rsch. Found., 1998, Cmty. Leaders of Distinction award, County C. of C., 1999; Eudowood fellow, Johns Hopkins U., 1987—88, U. Rochester scholar, 1979. Fellow: ACP, Am. Coll. Chest Physicians; mem.: AMA, Laennec Soc. (pres. 1994—95), Philip Drinker Soc. for Critical Care (pres. 1992—94), Am. Thoracic Soc. Office: UMDNJ Robert Wood Johnson Med Sch 125 Paterson St New Brunswick NJ 08901-1962

PAZANDAK, CAROL HENDRICKSON, liberal arts educator; b. Mpls. d. Norman Everard and Ruth (Buckley) Hendrickson; m. Bruce B. Pazandak (dec. 1986); children: David, Bradford, Chris, Eric, Paul, Ann; m. Joseph P. O'Shaughnessy, May 1991 (dec. Feb. 2000). PhD, U. Minn., 1970. Asst. dir. admissions U. Minn., Mpls., 1970-72, asst. dean liberal arts, 1972-79, asst. to pres., 1979-85, office of internat. edn., acting dir., 1985-87, asst. prof. to assoc. to prof. liberal arts, 1970-96, prof. emerita, 1996—; ptnr. Hollrad-Pers. Consulting, Reykjavik, Iceland, 1999—. Vis. prof. U. Iceland, Reykjavik, 1984, periods in 1983, 86-99; vis. rsch. prof. U. Oulu, Finland, 1993; exec. sec. Minn.-Iceland Adv. Com., U. Minn., 1984—; cons. U. Iceland, 1983-98; co-chair Reunion of Sisters-Minn. and Finland Confs., 1986-98; sec. Icelandic Assn. of Minn., 1995-97. Editor: Improving Undergraduate Education in Large Universities, 1989. Past pres. Minn. Mrs. Jaycees, Mpls. Mrs. Jaycees; formerly bd. govs. St. John's Preparatory Sch., Collegeville, Minn.; former bd. trustees Coll. of St. Teresa, Winona, Minn. Recipient Partnership award for contbn. to advancing shared interests of Iceland and Am., 1994, Recognition award U. Iceland, 2002, Recognition award yrs. collaboration Iceland and U. Minn., 2002; named to Order of the Falcon, Govt. of Iceland, 1990, Coll. Liberal Arts Alumna Notable Achievement, 1995, Pres.'s Club, U. Minn., 1996. Mem. APA, Waikoloa Village Outdoor Cir. Home: 4505 Harry's Ln Dallas TX 75229 Office: U Minn N 218 Elliott Hall 75 E River Rd Minneapolis MN 55455-0280 E-mail: carolpz@umn.edu.

PAZOUR, DON, publishing executive; Pres. Miller Freeman, Inc., San Francisco. Office: c/o Miller Freeman Inc 600 Harrison St San Francisco CA 94107-1387

PAZUNIAK, GEORGE, lawyer; b. Phila., Jan. 15, 1952; s. Roman and Natalia Pazuniak; m. Maria Bilynsky, Aug. 3, 1974; children: Maksym, Andriy, Markian. BA, Temple U., 1973; JD, Duke U., 1975. Bar: Del. 1976. Lectr. law Widener U. Sch. Law, Wilmington, Del., 1979-80; v.p. Assn. Patent Law Firms, Washington, 1997-99. Cons. Smolosky, Inc., 1978—. Home: 216 Sorrel Dr Wilmington DE 19803 Office: 1220 N Market St Wilmington DE 19801-2535 Office Fax: (302) 658-5614. E-mail: gp@cblhlaw.com.

PCHELNIKOV, YURIY NIKITICH, microwave engineer; s. Nikita Ignat and Marija Nikolay Pchelnikov; m. Raisa Mark Dymshits, Jan. 4, 1972; children: Georgij Yuriy, Alexandr Yuriy. M, Moscow High Engring. Sch., Russia, 1952; PhD, Ctrl. Radio-Engring. Inst., Russia, 1957; Deng Sciences, Ctrl. Radio-Engring. Inst., 1971. Minor scientist Ctrl. Radio-Engring. Inst., Moscow, 1953—57, sr. scientist, 1957—61, head of laborotory, 1961—71; head of faculty, microwave, quantum devices Moscow State U., Electronics and Math., Moscow, 1971—91, prof., 1991—96; sr. scientist MTS Sys. Corp., Sensors Divsn., Cary, NC, 1996—2004, SloWaves Inc., Cary, NC, 2004—. Head of projects Moscow State U., Electronics and Math., 1971—96; cons. Sci. Applications Internat. Corp., San Diego, 2004—. Author: Traveling-Wave Tubes Theory and Amplification Calculation, Microwave Electronics, Radio-Wave Elements on Slow-Wave Structures, Calculation of Traveling Tubes Gain, Calculation and Design of Slow-Wave Structures; contbr. articles numerous profl. jours. Recipient 2 Honor Diplomas, USSR Ministry of High Edn., 1976-1991, 3 Honor Diplomas, USSR Soc. of Radio-Electronics, 1975 - 1991, 2 Signs of Excellent Prof., USSR Ministry of High Edn., 1984- 1991, Sign of Excellent Inventor, 1986; Jucovskiy stipendia, USSR Ministry of High Edn., 1950-1952. Mem.: IEEE. Achievements include patents for 13 RF patents in microwave, 5 US patents in radio-frequency measurements, 178 USSR cerified inventions. Home: 104 Drexelbrook Ct Cary NC 27519 Office: MTS Sys Corp 30001 Sheldon Dr Cary NC 27513 Office Phone: 919-303-6212. Business E-Mail: yupchel@slowaves.com.

P. DIDDY, See COMBS, SEAN

PEABODY, ARLENE L. HOWLAND BAYAR, retired, nurse; b. Deposit, NY, June 26, 1931; d. Burt and Olive (Oralls) Howland; m. Atilla C. Bayar, Dec. 8, 1956 (div.); m. Norman R. Peabody, Feb. 1, 1975 (dec.); children: Tildy Anne Bayar Sparrow, Carol A. Digilio; m. Robert A. Ehlers, Feb. 15, 2003. Diploma, Ridley's Sec. Sch., Binghamton, N.Y., 1949, Binghamton Sch. Practical Nursing, 1970, Harrisburg Hosp. Sch. Enterostomal Therapy, 1971; AAS, Empire State Coll., 1985; BS in Edn., SUNY, Oneonta, 1990. RN, N.Y.; cert. therapeutic touch practitioner, natural force healing practitioner, enterostomal nurse. Sec. pres.'s office Cornell U., Ithaca, NY, 1949—55; exec. sec. Rudolph Lang, Office Execs. Assn. N.Y. and Prestige Expositions Inc., N.Y.C., 1955—69; enterostomal therapy nurse M.I. Bassett Hosp., Cooperstown, NY, 1972—89; pvt. practice enterostomal therapy nurse Oneonta, NY, 1989—2002. Spkr. in field. Vol. Am. Cancer Soc., 1972-2002, Catskill Area Hospice, 1990-02, Glimmerglass Opera, 1975-2002; bd. dirs. Del. Heritage Inc., 1996-2002; trustee Unitarian Universalist Soc.; active Storytelling Cir. of Oneonta, Oneonta Concert Assn., Oneonta Contradance. Mem. AARP (bd. dirs. 1986-2002), N.Y. State Hist. Assn., Delaware County Hist. Assn., Wound Ostomy and Continence Nurses Soc., United Ostomy Assn. (N.Y. state field svcs. rep.), Order Ea. Star. Avocations: heirloom quilting, traditional folk music, couturier clothing, costuming, dance. Home: 13511 Pebblebrook Dr Houston TX 77079-6023

PEABODY, WILLIAM TYLER, JR., retired paper manufacturing company executive; b. Melrose, Mass., Mar. 17, 1921; s. William Tyler and Dorothy (Atkinson) P.; m. Florence Marshall, July 27, 1946 (dec. June 18, 1993); children: Carol Peabody Mathews, William Tyler III, Janet Peabody Barrow, Marshall R.; m. Kay Nolan Giffen, Sept. 18, 2000. AB cum laude, Harvard U., 1942, postgrad. Grad. Sch. Arts and Scis., 1946-47, LLB, 1949. Bar: NY 1950. Asso. firm Root, Ballantine, Harlan, Bushby & Palmer, N.Y.C., 1949-54; with law div. Scott Paper Co., Phila., 1954-62, 67-85, asst. to gen. mgr. Everett, Wash., 1962-67, asst. sec., 1965-71, corp. sec., 1971-83, asst. sec., 1983-84, ret., 1985. Pres. Knollwood Terrace Civic Assn., Carle Place, NY, 1952-53; pres. Carle Place Taxpayers Assn., 1953-54; bd. dirs. Nether Providence Cmty. Assocs., Inc., Wallingford, Pa., 1969-75, pres., 1969-70, operator neighborhood social svcs. ctr.; bd. dirs. Ethel Mason Day Care Ctr., Wallingford, 1976-81, pres., 1979-80; vestryman St. Mary's Episc. Ch., Carle Place, NY, 1952-54; vestryman, jr. warden Trinity Episc. Ch., Everett, Wash., 1965-67; chmn. Rose Valley Folk, 1977-78; bd. dirs. Helen Kate Furness Free Libr., Wallingford, 1984-87, v.p., 1986-87; bd. dirs. Chester-Wallingford chpt. ARC, 1991-98, 99—, exec. com., 1992-98, 2000—, 1st vice chmn., 1994-95, chmn., 1995-98, sec., 2000—; bd. dirs. Everett, Wash. Area C. of C., 1965-67; Snohomish County Family Counseling Svc., Everett, 1962-67, pres., 1965; pres. Wallingford, Pa. Swim Club, 1960-61. Lt. USNR, 1942-46. Mem. ABA, Am. Soc. Corp. Secs. (dir. 1977-81, pres. Middle Atlantic group 1976-77), Harvard Club (Phila., sch. com. 1959-62, 76-90). Home: 971 Putnam Blvd Wallingford PA 19086-6762

PEABODY, WILLIAM W., JR., publishing executive; b. Mpls., July 21, 1956; s. William W. and Ellen Karen Peabody. BA, U. Notre Dame. Mgr. Stanford Publ. Course, Palo Alto, Calif.; prod. mgr. Simon & Schuster, N.Y.C., Crown Publ. Group, N.Y.C.; v.p. prod. dir. Penguin Group USA, N.Y.C. Home: 37 Wellesley St Maplewood NJ 07040

PEACE, H. W., II, oil company executive; b. Clinton, Okla., May 21, 1935; s. Herman Wilbern and Bernice (Mitchell) P.; m. Norma June Williams; children: Hugh William, Susannah Lee. BS in Geology, U. Okla., 1959, MS in Geology, 1964; postgrad., U. S.W. La., 1968. Jr. geologist Union Oil Co. Calif., Houston, 1964-65, area geologist Lafayette, La., 1965-70, geologist dist. exploration Oklahoma City, 1970-77, mgr. Rocky Mountain exploration Casper, Wyo., 1977-80; mgr. divsn. exploration Cotton Petroleum Corp., Tulsa, 1980-83; v.p. exploration Hadson Petroleum Corp., Oklahoma City, 1983-85, exec. v.p., COO, 1985-88, also bd. dirs.; exec. v.p., COO Mosswood Oil and Gas Co., Oklahoma City, 1985-88, Anadarko Supply Co., Oklahoma City, 1986-88, also bd. dirs.; mng. ptnr. EXAD, Oklahoma City, 1988-91; pres., CEO, dir. Panhandle Royalty Co., Oklahoma City, 1991—; pres., CEO Wood Oil Co. subsidiary Panhandle Royalty Co., 2001—. Mgmt. com. PLC Energy Data, LLC, 1994—2001; bd. dirs. OIL Law Recs. Corp. Dir. sch. geology adv. com. U. Okla., Norman, 1984—, vice chmn. 1988-89, chmn. 1989-90, exec. com. 1990—. Lt. USN 1959-63, capt. USNR, 1963-82, ret. list 1995. Mem. Am. Assn. Petroleum Geology (rep. del. or alt. 1984—), Soc. Exploration Geophysicists, Soc. Econ. Paleontologists and Mineralogists, Petroleum Assn. Wyo. (v.p. 1979-80), Tulsa Geol. Soc., Oklahoma City Geol. Soc. (chmn. profl. affairs 1976-77), Naval Res. Assn., Cherokee Hills Homeowners Assn. (pres. 1971-73), Fieldstone Homeowners Assn. (pres. 1983), Navy League, Okla. Corp. Commn. (mem. royalty adv. com. 1998—), Civitan Lodge. Republican. Avocations: golf, swimming, hiking. Office: Panhandle Royalty Co 5400 N Grand Blvd Ste 210 Oklahoma City OK 73112-5688 Office Phone: 405-948-1560.

PEACE, JOHN T. religious studies educator; b. Tunneltown, Pa., Aug. 6, 1930; s. John and Deane Peace; m. Mary Louise Dawson, Aug. 25, 1953; children: David, Rebecca, Thomas. AB, Thiel Coll., 1952; MDiv, Gettysburg Luth. Sem., 1955. Cert. Congl. clergyman Mass.; tchr. Pa., Fla. Sr. min. East Congl. Ch., Milton, Mass., 1963—65, People's Ch., Dover, Del., 1970—71; faculty Mercersburg (Pa.) Acad., 1971—85, chmn. dept. religion, 1980—84; owner Spkr.'s Bur., 1985—. Presenter in field. V.p. Franklin County Bd. Assistance, Pa., 1980—85. Recipient First prize ann. poetry contest, Poets of the Palm Beaches, 1998. Mem.: Congl. UCC (ret. clergyman), Free and Accepted Masons. Democrat. Avocation: writing.

PEACOCK, A(LVIN) WARD, textile company executive; b. Durham, N.C., June 17, 1929; s. Erle Ewart and Vera Louise (Ward) P.; m. Barbara Sheppard White, July 2, 1955; children: Alvin Ward, Stephen White, Nancy Lay. BS in Commerce, U. N.C., 1950; MBA, Harvard U., 1952. Asst. to v.p. Erwin Mills, Inc., Durham, 1953-55, sec., 1957-62, sec.-treas., 1962-64; v.p. Dixie Yarns, Inc., Chattanooga, 1964-76, sr. v.p., 1976-81, Springs Industries, Fort Mill, S.C., 1981-86, exec. v.p., 1986-92. Bd. dirs. Palmetto Seed Capital Corp.; regional dir. First Wachovia Corp., Charlotte, N.C., 1988-92. Trustee Holston Conf. Colls., Tenn., 1968-79, Sci. Mus. Charlotte, 1990-94; bd. dirs. Chattanooga Meml. Hosp., 1979-81, Charlotte Symphony, 1990-94, Greater Carolinas chpt. ARC, 1988-94; dir. Allied Arts Fund, 1978-81, Metrolina Food Bank, 1994-2003; mem. Chattanooga Wastewater Regulation Bd., 1978-81. 1st lt. USAF, 1955-57. Mem. Tenn. Mfrs. Assn. (chmn. bd. dirs. 1980-81), Chattanooga Mfrs. Assn. (pres. 1968-69), Am. Textile Mfrs. Inst., Univ. Club, River Hills Club, Phi Beta Kappa, Alpha Kappa Psi, Sigma Nu. Republican. Methodist. Home: 6618 Seton House Ln Charlotte NC 28277-4520

PEACOCK, CHARLES H. agricultural studies educator; From asst. to assoc. prof. turfgrass sci. U. Fla., extension turfgrass specialist; sr. agronomist Anheuser-Busch Co.; prof. Agriculture N.C. State U., Raleigh. Fellow Nat. Assn. Colls. Tchrs. Agriculture 1992. Office: N C State U Dept Crop Sci Williams Hall 1215 PO Box 7620 Raleigh NC 27695-7620

PEACOCK, CHRISTOPHER A. former real estate company executive; b. 1946; Student, Wellington Coll., Berkshire, Eng. With Jones Lang Wooten (now Jones Lang LaSalle Inc.), 1972—2004, ptnr., 1974, former mem. exec.

bd. continent of Europe, mng. ptnr. continent of Europe, chmn. leasing agy., 1992-96, European CEO, 1996-97, internat. CEO, 1997-99, pres., dep. CEO, COO, chmn. mgmt. exec. com., dir., 1999—2002, CEO, 2002—04. Fellow Royal Instn. Chartered Surveyors.*

PEACOCK, ERLE EWART, JR., surgeon, lawyer, educator; b. Durham, N.C., Sept. 10, 1926; s. Erle Ewart and Vera Louise (Ward) P.; m. Mary Louise Lowrey, Apr. 17, 1954; children: James Lowrey, Susan Louise, Virginia Gayle. Cert. in Medicine, U. N.C., 1947, BS, 1990, JD, 1999; MD, Harvard U., 1949. Bar: N.C. 1993. Intern, asst. resident surgery Roosevelt Hosp., N.Y.C., 1949-51; from asst. resident gen. surgery U. N.C. Hosps., Chapel Hill, 1953-54, chief resident gen. surgery, 1954-55; resident in plastic surgery Barnes Hosp., St. Louis, 1955-56; mem. faculty dept. surgery U. N.C., Chapel Hill, 1956-69, prof. surgery, head divsn. plastic surgery, 1965-69; prof., chmn. dept. surgery U. Ariz., Tucson, 1969-77; prof. surgery Tulane U., New Orleans, 1977-82; pvt. practice surgery Chapel Hill, 1982-93; vis. prof. surgery U. Va., Charlottesville, 1988-97; clin. prof. surgery U. N.C., Chapel Hill, 1996—. Chief hand surgery Valley Forge Army Hosp., Phoenixville, Pa., 1951-53. Author: Wound Repair, 1977, 3d edit., 1982; assoc. editor: Am. Jour. Surgery, 1967—, Surgery Yearbook, 1970-89, Plastic and Reconstructive Surgery, 1972-78; asst. editor: Jour. Surg. Rsch., 1970-76. Served with U.S. Navy, 1945-46; served to capt. M.C. U.S. Army, 1951-53. Recipient Yandell medal Louisville Surg. Soc., 1972, McGraw medal Detroit Surg. Soc., 1973, Disting. Svc. award U. N.C., 1979, Jacob Markowitz award Acad. Surg. Rsch., 1993, Lifetime Achievement award Wound Healing Soc., 1994. Mem. AAAS, ACS, ABA, Womack Sur. Soc. (pres. 1979-80), Soc. U. Surgeons (treas. 1965-68), Plastic Surgery Rsch. Coun. (pres. 1966), Am. Surg. Assn., Am. Bd. Plastic Surgery (pres. 1976), Am. Bd. Gen. Surgery, Am. Assn. Plastic Surgeons (Clinician of Yr. 1985), Am. Soc. Surgery Hand, Internat. Soc. Surgeons, So. Surg. Assn., Am. Coll. Legal Medicine, Rotary, Alpha Omega Alpha. Republican. Methodist. Home and Office: 645 Rock Creek Rd Chapel Hill NC 27514-6714 Office Phone: 919-967-0347. E-mail: eepeacockmd@aol.com.

PEACOCK, GEORGE ROWATT, retired life insurance company executive; b. Lakeland, Fla., Aug. 27, 1923; s. Robert and Annie Keane (Rowatt) P.; m. Virginia Jenkins, June 7, 1952; 1 child, Robert George. BA, U. Fla., 1948, postgrad., 1948-49, U. N.C., 1949-50, 51, Ind. U., summers 1966, 67. With Equitable Life Assurance Soc. U.S., 1952-88, v.p., head real estate dept., 1974-77, sr. v.p., head equities sector, 1977-80, sr. v.p., head real estate sector, 1980-84; chmn., chief exec. Equitable Real Estate Investment Mgmt., Inc., 1984-88; pres., chief exec. officer Carluke Inc., 1988—2002. Past pres. Planters Redevel. Corp., St. Louis, 1984-87; trustee Equitable Life Mortgage & Realty Investors, 1981-83; emeritus mem. adv. bd. govs. Wharton Real Estate Ctr., U. Pa., 1985—. Author papers in field. Trustee Urban Land Inst., 1982-88; bd. dirs. Urban Land Found., 1994-99; bd. govs. Ctrl. Atlanta Progress, 1984-86. With USAAF, 1942-45, with USAF, 1950-51. Decorated Purple Heart. Mem. Am. Soc. Real Estate Counselors, Urban Land Inst., Am. Inst. Real Estate Appraisers, Real Estate Bd. N.Y. (past gov.), Phi Beta Kappa, Phi Kappa Phi, Phi Gamma Delta. Democrat. Office: GR Peacock PO Box 420979 Atlanta GA 30342

PEACOCK, JAMES DANIEL, lawyer; b. Moorestown, N.J., Dec. 19, 1930; s. L. Lawrence and Esther H. Peacock; m. Joan Peacock, June 14, 1953; children: Elizabeth Holcomb, Martha McLaughlin, Margaret Mae Daly, Mary Anne Freidman. AB, Duke U., 1952; LLB, U. Md., 1957. Bar: M. 1957, U.S. Ct. Appeals (4th cir.) 1959, U.S. Dist. Ct. Md. 1957, U.S. Supreme Ct. 1976. Of counsel Semmes Bowen & Semmes, Balt., 1957-97. Trustee Sheppard and Enoch Pratt Hosp., Towson, Md., 1964-97, chmn., 1993-97, assoc. trustee, 1998—. Fellow Am. Coll. Trial Lawyers (state chmn. 1985-86, adj. state chmn. 1992-93), Am. Bar Found., Md. Bar Found. Home: 105 Bonnie Hill Rd Baltimore MD 21204-4209

PEACOCK, JUDITH ANN See ERWIN, JUDITH

PEACOCK, LAMAR BATTS, retired physician; b. Albany, Ga., Sept. 21, 1920; s. Herbert A. and Helen Marian (LeVan) P.; m. Jane Bonner, June 7, 1947; children: Helen Lee (Mrs. Richard Paul Wade), Linda Jane (Mrs. Mathew Gossage), Lamar Bonner. BA, Emory U., 1941; MD, Med. Coll. Ga., 1946. Diplomate: Am. Bd. Internal Medicine. Intern Univ. Hosp., Augusta, 1946-47, resident, 1947-48; fellow internal medicine U. Va. Hosp., Charlottesville, 1948-49; resident Univ. Hosp., Augusta, 1949-50; practice medicine specializing in internal medicine and allergy Atlanta, 1950-91. Mem. staff St. Joseph's Hosp., Crawford Long Hosp., Piedmont Hosp., Grady Meml. Hosp., Hughes Spalding Pavilion, Northside Hosp., All Atlanta, Cobb Gen. Hosp., Austell, Ga., Douglasville (Ga.) Hosp.; instr. internal medicine Ga. Bapt. Hosp., Atlanta, 1950-58, chief medicine, 1958-72; mem. faculty Emory U. Sch. Medicine, Atlanta, 1950—, asst. clin. prof. medicine, 1962—; instr. internal medicine Sch. Dentistry, 1958— Chief med. br., health services Atlanta Met. Area Civil Def., 1960-63; mem. Ga. Pub. Health Assn., 1967-69, Ga. Bd. Health, 1966-72, Ga. Vocational Rehab. Council, 1973—; Pres. trustees Med. Coll. Ga. Found., 1963. Recipient Physicians Physician award, MCG, 1984. Fellow ACP, Am. Coll. Allergy, Asthma and Immunology (nat. pres. 1972-73), Am. Acad. Allergy, Asthma and Immunology; mem. AMA, Am. Heart Assn., Ga. Heart Assn., Am. Soc. Internal Medicine, Ga. Soc. Internal Medicine, 5th Dist. Med. Soc., Ga. Thoracic Soc., Med. Assn. Atlanta (prs. 1965), Med. Assn. Ga. (1st v.p. 1966-67), Southeastern Allergy Assn. (pres. 1963-64), So. Med. Assn., Cherokee Town and Country Club. Episcopalian. Home: 3120 Verdun Dr NW Atlanta GA 30305-1940 Personal E-mail: strutjbp@webtv.net.

PEACOCK, MARILYN CLAIRE, primary education educator; b. Harvey, Ill., Aug. 2, 1952; d. Carmen Anthony and Helen Elaine (Welch) R. AA with high honors, Thornton C.C., 1972; BS in Edn. with high honors, Ill. State U., 1974; MEd, Nat.-Louis U., 1990. Cert. K-9, Ill. Tchr. kindergarten Primary Acad. Ctr., Markham, Ill., 1976-91, tchr. K-3, 1991—. Ill. State scholar, 1969. Mem. Ill. Edn. Assn. (assn. rep. 1976-88), Kappa Delta Pi, Phi Theta Kappa. Republican. Avocations: music, travel. Home: 2447 Clyde St Homewood IL 60430-3103 Office: Acad Ctr 3055 W 163rd St Markham IL 60426-5626 Personal E-mail: mcrpeacock@hotmail.com.

PEACOCK, MARY WILLA, magazine editor; b. Evanston, Ill., Oct. 23, 1942; d. William Gilbert and Mary Willa (Young) P. BA, Vassar Coll., 1964. Assoc. lit. editor Harper's Bazaar mag., N.Y.C., 1964-69; staff editor Innovation mag., N.Y.C., 1969-70; editor in chief, co-founder Rags mag., N.Y.C., San Francisco, 1970-71; co-founder, features editor Ms. mag., N.Y.C., 1971-77; pub., pres. Rags mag., N.Y.C., 1977-80; sr. editor Village Voice, N.Y.C., 1980-85, style editor, 1985-89; editor-in-chief Model mag., N.Y.C., 1989—, editorial cons., 1991—; fashion dir. Lear's Mag., N.Y.C., 1992-93; dep. editor In Style Mag., 1993-94, Mirabella mag., 1994-95; cons., 1995—. Internat. editor InStyle; writer and cons. in field.

PEACOCK, MOLLY, poet, educator; b. June 30, 1947; d. Edward Frank and Pauline Ruth (Wright) P. BA magna cum laude, Harpur Coll., Binghamton, N.Y., 1969; MA with hons., Johns Hopkins U., 1977. Adminstr., lectr. in english SUNY, Binghamton, 1970-76; instr. english Friends Sem., N.Y.C., 1981-92; poet-in-residence Bucknell U., 1993-94, Cathedral St. John the Divine, 2000. Author: And Live Apart, 1980, Raw Heaven, 1984, Take Heart, 1989, Original Love, 1995, Paradise, Piece by Piece, 1998, How To Read A Poem and Start A Poetry Circle, 1999, The Private I: Privacy in A Public World, 2001, Cornucopia: New and Selected Poems, 2002, The Shimmering Verge: A One-Woman Show in Poems, 2003; contbg. writer House and Garden mag., 1996-2001; contbr. poems to The New Yorker, The New Republic, The Nation. Danforth Found. fellow, 1970, Yaddo fellow, 1980, 82, 89, Ingram Merrill Found. fellow 1981, 86, Lila Wallace/Woodrow Wilson fellow 1994, 95, 96, 2001; grantee Creative Artists Pub. Svc. Program, 1977, N.Y. Found. for Arts, 1985, NEA, 1991; Regents scholar U. Calif., Riverside, 1998. Mem. PEN, Poetry Soc. Am. (governing bd. 1988—, pres. emeritus). Home: 109 Front St E #1041 Toronto ON M5A 4P7 Canada also: 109 Front St Apt 1041 Toronto ON Canada M5A 4P7 E-mail: peacockmol@aol.com.

PEACOCK, NEIL T. engineer; b. Sept. 15, 1960; s. R. Norman Peacock and Alma L. Goetcheus; m. Susan Benes, Aug. 27, 1995; 1 child, Kevin G. BS, U. Colo., 1983. Devel. engr. HPS Corp., Boulder, Colo., 1984—86; development engr. MKS Instruments, Boulder. Contbr.: technical handbook/reference Handbook of Vacuum Science and Technology; contbr. articles to profl. jours. Mem.: Am. Vacuum Soc. (chmn. vacuum techology divsn. 1994—95, vacuum tech. rep. to iuvsta 2001—04). Achievements include patents for enhanced ignition of cold cathode vacuum gauges; patents pending for improved degassing of hot cathode ionization gauges. Office: MKS Instruments 5330 Sterling Dr Boulder CO 80301

PEACOCK, PENNE KORTH, ambassador; b. Hattiesburg, Miss., Nov. 3, 1942; m. Fritz-Alan Korth, Dec. 15, 1965 (div. 1997); children: Fritz-Alan Jr., Maria Korth Chieffalo, James Frederick; m. Andrew Peacock, Sept. 21, 2002. Student, U. Tex., 1960—64. Sr. Washington assoc., client liaison and rep. trust and estate div. Sotheby's, 1986-89; amb. to Mauritius, Port Louis, 1989-92; pres. Firestone and Korth Ltd., Washington, 1993-97; commr. US Adv. Commn. Pub. Diplomacy, 1997—. Bd. dir. Chevy Chase Bank, 1993—; rep. Sotheby's Internat., 1997—; adv. com. Sydney (Australia) Cancer Ctr., 2003—. Co-chmn. Am. Bicentennial Presdl. Inauguration, Washington, 1988—99; mem. adv. bd. Washington Ballet, 2002—; mem. adv. com. Sydney Cancer Ctr.; bd. dirs. Hillwood Mus. and Gardens; counselor Meridian Internat. Ctr.; bd. dirs. Coun. of Am. Ambs., 1994—. Mem.: Assn. for Diplomatic Studies and Tng. (bd. dir. 1996—). Office: 11 Gladswood Gardens Double Bay 2028 NSW Australia

PEAK, HOWARD W. former mayor; b. Tokyo, Dec. 31, 1948; m. Margie Bratten. BA in History, U. Tex., 1974, MA in Urban Studies/Environ. Mgmt., 1975. Councilman City of San Antonio, 1993-97, mayor, 1997—99. Owner Land Devel. Svcs.; instr. urban adminstrn. grad. program Trinity U.; former instr. land use planning Southwest Tex. State U.; former v.p. Trans Tex. Interests, Inc.; former mem. planning dept. City of San Antonio. Bd. dirs. Alamo Area Coun. Govts.; chmn. transp. steering com. Met. Planning Orgn.; mem. mcpl. solid waste adv. coun. Tex. Natural Resources Conservation Commn.; mem. standing coms. water, annexation, airport noise abatement, city/county, state initiatives, ethics, military, policy & planning, joint land use study, planning commn. San Antonio City Coun.; past chmn., mem. planning commn. City of San Antonio; former vice chmn. bd. govtl. affairs North San Antonio C. of C.; former mem. airport noise abatement adv. com. City of San Antonio, water consolidation study task force; past mem. resource/technical team Greater San Antonio Area Citizens Com. on Water; former mem. steering com. South Bexar County Water Project. Formerly with U.S. Army. Recipient Merit award Tex. chpt. Am. Inst. Planners, 1978. Mem. Am. Planning Assn. (Merit award Tex. chpt. 1984, Pres.'s award 1996, Dir.'s award San Antonio sect.), Tex. Soc. Architects (hon.). Avocations: classic car restoration, long-distance running. Home: 410 Oakleaf Dr San Antonio TX 78209-2928

PEAKE, JAMES BENJAMIN, military career officer; b. St. Louis, June 18, 1944; m. Janice Peake; children: Kimberly, Thomas. BS, U.S. Mil. Acad., 1966; MD, Cornell U., 1972; grad., U.S. Army War Coll., 1988. Commd. 2nd lt. inf. U.S. Army, 1972, advanced through grades to lt. gen., 1995; gen. surgery resident Brooke Army Med. Ctr., Ft. Sam Houston, asst. chief cardiothoracic surgery; staff gen. surgeon, chief gen. surgery clinic DeWitt Army Hosp., Ft. Belvoir, Va.; dep. comdr. for clin. svcs. Tripler Army Med. Ctr., Honolulu; comdr. 18th Med. Command and 121st Evacuation Hosp. U.S. Army, Seoul, Korea, dep. dir., profl. svcs. chief, cons. Office Surgeon Gen., commdg. gen. 44th Med. Brigade/Corps Surgeon XVIII Airborne; commdg. gen. Madigan Army Med. Ctr./N.W. Health Svc. Support Activity, Tacoma, Wash.; dep. comdr. U.S. Army Med. Command, 1996-97; installation comdr. U.S. Army, Ft. Sam Houston, 1996; comdr. U.S. Army Med. Dept. Ctr. and Sch., 1996-2000, U.S. Army Med. Command, Fort Sam Houston, TX, 2000—. Presenter in field. Contbr. articles to profl. jours. Decorated Order of Mil. Med. Merit, Silver Star, Def. Superior Svc. medal, Legion of Merit with three oak leaf clusters, Bronze Star with V device and oak leaf cluster, Purple Heart with oak leaf cluster, Meritorious Svc. medal with two oak leaf clusters, Air medal, Joint Svc. Commendation medal, Army Commendation medal with V device and oak leaf cluster, Humanitarian Svc. medal, Armed Forces Expeditionary medal, Joint Meritorious Unit award with oak leaf cluster. Fellow ACS, Soc. Thoracic Surgeons, Am. Coll. Cardiology; mem. Korean Med. Assn. (hon.), Assn. Mil. Surgeons U.S., Soc. Med. Cons. of the Armed Forces. Office: US Army Med Command 2050 Worth Rd Ste 3 Fort Sam Houston TX 78234-6003

PEALE, RUTH STAFFORD (MRS. NORMAN VINCENT PEALE), religious leader; b. Fonda, Iowa, Sept. 10, 1906; d. Frank Burton and Anna Loretta (Crosby) Stafford; m. Norman Vincent Peale, June 20, 1930; children: Margaret Ann (Mrs. Paul F. Everett), John Stafford, Elizabeth Ruth (Mrs. John M. Allen). AB, Syracuse U., 1928, LLD, 1953; LittD, Hope Coll., 1962; LHD (hon.), Judson Coll., 1988. Tchr. math. Cen. High Sch., Syracuse, NY, 1928—30; nat. pres. women's bd. domestic missions Ref. Ch. Am., 1936-46; sec. Protestant Film Commn., 1946-51; chmn. Am. Mother's Com., 1948-49; pres., editor-in-chief, gen. sec., CEO, chmn. bd. dirs., chmn. emeritus Guideposts Peale Ctr. for Christian Living, 1940—; nat. pres. bd. domestic missions Ref. Ch. in Am., 1955-56; mem. bd. N. Am. Missions, 1963-69, pres., 1967-69; mem. gen. program council Ref. Ch. in Am., 1968—; mem. com. of 24 for merger Ref. Ch. in Am. and Presbyn. Ch. U.S., 1966-69; v.p. Protestant Council N.Y.C., 1964-66; co-founder, pub. Guideposts, N.Y.C., 1945—, pres., 1985-92, chmn. bd., 1999—2003, chmn. emeritus, 2003—; pres. Fleming H. Revell, Tarrytown, N.Y., 1985-92. Appeared on: (nat. TV program) What's Your Trouble, 1952—68; author: I Married a Minister, 1942, The Adventure of Being a Wife, 1971, Secrets of Staying in Love, 1984, A Lifetime of Positive Thinking, 2001; founder, pub. (with Dr. Peale) Guidepost mag., 1945—, co-subject with husband (film) One Man's Way, 1963. Named N.Y. State Mother of Yr., 1963, Disting. Woman of Yr., Nat. Art Assn., Religious Heritage Am. Ch. Woman of Yr., 1969, Woman of Yr., AAUW, 2000; recipient Cum Laude award Syracuse U. Alumni Assn. N.Y., 1965, Honor Iowans award Buena Vista Coll., 1966, Am. Mother's com. award for religion, 1970, Disting. Svc. award Coun. Chs., N.Y.C., 1973, Disting. Citizen award Champlain Coll., 1976, Disting. Svc. to Cmty. and Nation award Gen. Fedn. Women's Clubs, 1977, Horatio Alger award, 1977, Religious Heritage award, 1979, joint medallion with husband Soc. for Family of Man, 1981, Soc. Family of Man award, 1981, Alderson-Broaddus award, 1982, Marriage Achievement award Bride's mag., 1984, Gold Angel award Religion in Media, 1987, Adela Rogers St. John Roundtable award, 1987, Disting. Achievement award Am. Aging, 1987, Paul Harris award N.Y. Rotary, 1989, Leader's award Arthritis Found. Dutchess County, 1992, Dave Thomas Well Done! award, 1994, Norman Vincent Peale award for positive thinking, 1994, Master of Influence award, 1995, The Leadership award Worldwide Leadership Coun., 1998, Cert. for Disting. Svc., N.Y. State Fedn. Women's Clubs, 1999, Light award CANDL Found., 2000, Woman of Distinction awd RCA Women, 2001. Mem. Blanton-Peale Inst. (bd. exec. com.), Am. Bible Soc. (trustee 1948-93, hon. trustee 1993—, bd. dirs.), Nat. Bible Assn. (bd. dirs.), United Bible Soc., Interch. Ctr. (bd. dirs. 1957-92, chmn. 1982-90), Nat. Coun. Chs. (v.p. 1952-54, gen. bd.; treas. gen. dept. United Ch. Women, vice chmn. broadcasting and film commn. 1951-55, program chmn. gen. assembly 1966), N.Y. Fedn. Women's Clubs (chmn. religion 1951-53, 57-58), Home Missions Coun. N.A. (nat. pres. 1942-44, nat. chmn. migrant com. 1948-51), Internat. Platform Orgn. (bd. govs. 1994-2000), Cmty. Action Network (adv. bd. 1998—), Wainwright House (hon. trustee, advisor 2001), PEO, Sorosis (pres. 1953-56, hon. pres.), Alpha Phi (Frances W. Willard award 1976). Republican. Office: Peale Ctr Christian Living 66 E Main St Pawling NY 12564-1409 Office Phone: 845-855-5000. Business E-Mail: rpeale@guideposts.org.

PEAPPLES, GEORGE ALAN, retired automotive executive; b. Benton Harbor, Mich., Nov. 6, 1940; s. Arthur L. and Kathleen C. (Peters) Peapples; m. Rebecca Dean Sowers, June 27, 1962; children: Lucia Christine, Sarah Bouton. BA in Econs., U. Mich., 1962, MBA in Fin., 1963. Fin. analyst GM Corp., Detroit, 1964-68, fin. analyst treas. office N.Y.C., 1968—72, dir. capital analysis and investment, 1972—73, asst. divsn. comptr. Delco Moraine divsn. Dayton, Ohio, 1973-75, asst. treas. bank rels. Detroit, 1975-77, asst. comptr., 1980-82; v.p. fin. mgr. GM Can. Ltd., Oshawa, 1982-84; group dir. strategic bus. planning Chevrolet-Pontiac-Can. group GM Corp., Warren, Mich., 1984-86; v.p. GM Corp., pres., gen. mgr. GM Can. Ltd., Oshawa, 1986-94; v.p. pub. policy GM Corp., Washington, 1994-99; ret., 2000; asst. sec. of Navy U.S. Dept. Def., 1977-80. Bd. dirs. The Ark. Recipient Disting. Pub. Svc. award, Washington, 1980. E-mail: gapeapples@aol.com.

PEAR, CHARLES E., JR., lawyer; b. Macon, Ga., June 18, 1950; s. Charles Edward and Barbara Jane P.; m. Linda Sue King; children: Jennifer Sue, Charles Edward III, Stephanie Sue. BA, U. Hawaii, 1972 with honors; JD, U. Calif., Berkeley, 1975. Bar: Hawaii 1976, Fla. 1977, Colo. 1994, U.S. Ct. of Appeals (9th cir.). Assoc. Rush, Moore, Craven, Sutton, Morry & Beh, Honolulu, 1976-77, of counsel, 1987-90; assoc., ptnr. Carlsmith & Dwyer, Honolulu, 1977-82; ptnr. Burke, Sakai, McPheeters, Bordner & Gilardy, Honolulu, 1983-87; vis. prof. law and computers U. British Columbia, 1990-93; of counsel Holland & Hart, Denver, 1993-96; counsel, ptnr. McCorriston, Miller, Mukai, MacKinnon, Honolulu, 1996—. Mem. Hawaii Real Estate Commn. com. on condominium and resort real estate legis., 1978-79; spl. counsel to consumer protection com. Hawaii State Ho. of Reps., 1981-82; chair real property and fin. svcs. sect. Hawaii State Bar Assn., ABA. Editor-in-Chief Hawaii Conveyance Manual II, 1987; editor Hawaii Commercial Real Estate Manual, 1988; bd. editors Hawaii Inst. of Continuing Legal Edn.; co-author: Nat. Assn. of Real Estate Licensing Law Officials and Nat. Timesharing Coun. Model Timesharing Act, 1981-82; contbg. author: Winning With Computers, 1992, Hawaii Real Estate Manual, 1997; lectr. in field, 1981—. Mem. ABA .

PEARCE, BETTY MCMURRAY, manufacturing company executive; b. Hastings, Nebr., Oct. 11, 1926; d. Frank Madry and Sereta (Mudd) McMurray; BS in Aerospace, U. Tex., Austin, 1949; 1 child, Karen A. Harsley. Draftsman, Koch & Fowler, Civil Engrs., Dallas, 1945-47; with Ling Temco Vought-Aircraft Products Group-Aircraft Maintenance and Support Group, Dallas, 1949—, project engr., 1955-77, engrng. project mgr., 1977-83, dir. engrng., 1983-89, engrng. mgr. advanced sys. concepts, 1989-90; program mgr. PAMPA 2000, 1990-92; ret., 1992; dir. LTV Fed. Credit Union, v.p. LTV Mgmt. Club; cons. Active Aux. St. Joseph's Hosp.; pres. St. Andrews Catholic Ch. Coun., Fort Worth, 1977-78; mem. Bishop's Adv. Coun. Fort Worth Diocese, 1980-87, chmn. svc. com., 1980-81, pres., 1981-82, 84-85; mem. Allied Cmtys. of Tarrant, 1982—. Mem. AIAA, Tech. Mktg. Soc. Am. Home: 3613 W Biddison St Fort Worth TX 76109-2704

PEARCE, CHRISTIE PATRICIA, professional soccer player; b. Broward County, Fla., June 24, 1975; m. Chris Rampone, Nov. 9, 2001. BS in spl. edn., Monmouth U., N.J., 1997. Mem. N.Y. Power, WUSA, 2001—; soccer player, defender U.S. Women's Nat. Team, 1997, mem. World Cup championship team, 1999. Founding player N.Y. Power, WUSA, 2001. Named First Team All-Mid-Atlantic Region, 1995, 1996, Player of Yr., N.E. Conf., 1995, 1996. Office: US Soccer Fedn 1801 S Prairie Ave Chicago IL 60616

PEARCE, DONALD JOSLIN, retired librarian; b. Southampton, Eng., May 31, 1924; came to U.S., 1949, naturalized, 1952; s. Alfred Ernest and Constance May (Jeffrey) P.; m. June Inez Bond, Dec. 7, 1946; children—Kristin, Kim. Student, Sch. Oriental and African Studies, U. London, 1942-43; AB, George Washington U., 1953; MS in L.S, Cath. U. Am., 1954. Part-time library asst. U.S. Dept. Agr., 1949-54; student asst. George Washington U. Library, 1950-53; circulation librarian Denison U., 1954-56; staff Ohio State U. Library, 1956-59, asst. acquisition librarian, 1958-59; head librarian, asst. prof. U. N.D., 1959-69, chief bibliographer, 1969-73, asst. dir. libraries, 1973-75, asst. prof. Oriental philosophy, 1969-75; library dir., asst. prof. philosophy U. Minn., Duluth, 1975-88, ret., 1988. Chmn. staff orgn. round table Ohio Library Assn., 1958-59 Served with Brit. Army, 1943-47. Mem. ALA, N.D. Library Assn. (pres. 1965-67), Minn. Library Assn. (sec. 1978-80, v.p. 1985, pres. 1986), Assn. Coll. Reference Librarians, Mountain Plains Library Assn. (v.p. 1968-69), Buddhist Assn., Phi Beta Kappa, Beta Phi Mu. Home: 70 E St Marie St Apt 127 Duluth MN 55803 E-mail: dpearce@d.umn.edu.

PEARCE, DRUE, government official, former state legislator; b. Fairfield, Ill., Apr. 2, 1951; d. H. Phil and Julia Detroy (Bannister) P.; m. Michael F.G. Williams; 1 child, Tate Hanna Pearce-Williams. BA in Biol. Scis., Ind. U., 1973; MPA, Harvard U., 1984; cert. exec. program Darden Sch. Bus., U. Va., 1989. Sch. tchr., Clark County, Ind., 1973-74; curator of edn. Louisville Zoo, 1974-77; dir. Summerscene, Louisville, 1974-77; asst. v.p., br. mgr. Alaska Nat. Bank of the North, 1977-82; legis. aide to Rep. John Ringstad Alaska Ho. of Reps., Juneau, 1983, mem., 1984-88, minority whip, 1986; mem. Alaska Senate, chmn. com. oil and gas, mem. exec. com. energy coun., 1989-90, chmn. com. labor and commerce, mem. exec. coms. western state conf., coun. state govts., energy coun., 1991-92, co-chmn. senate fin., chmn. energy coun., vice chmn. com. energy, nat. coun. state govts., 1993-94, mem. select com. legis. ethics and legis. coun., 1993—, pres. senate, mem. exec. com. energy coun., vice chmn. senate coms. resources and rules, 1995-96, co-chmn. com. senate fin., mem. exec. com. energy coun., vice chmn. com. senate judiciary, 1997—98. Senate pres., 1995-96, 99-2000, senate rules chmn., 2001; ptnr. 4150 Co., Anchorage and Kotzebue, Alaska, 1983-2002, Cloverland N., Anchorage, 1993—; resources cons. Arctic Slope Regional Corp., Anchorage, 1987-91, 95-96; sr. adv. Sec. Interior for Alaska Affairs, 2001-. Former bd. dirs. Alaska Women's Aid in Crisis, Anchorage Econ. Devel. Coun., Alaska Aerospace Devel. Corp., Alaska Spl. Olympics, Gov.'s Bd. Mem. DAR, Commonwealth North, Resource Devel. Coun., Alaska Miners Assn., Alaska Fedn. Rep. Women, Aircraft Owners & Pilots Assn., U.S. Trotting Assn. Republican. Home: 221 E Seventh Ave #313 Anchorage AK 99501 Office: Office of the Secretary Dept of the Interior 1849 C St NW MS 6020 Washington DC 20240- Office Phone: 202-208-4177.

PEARCE, HARRY JONATHAN, lawyer; b. Bismarck, N.D., Aug. 20, 1942; s. William R. and Jean Katherine (Murray) P.; m. Katherine B. Bruk, June 19, 1967; children: Shannon Pearce Baker, Susan J., Harry M. BS, USAF Acad., Colorado Springs, Colo., 1964; JD, Northwestern U., 1967; Degree in Engrng. (hon.), Rose-Hulman Inst. Tech., 1997; LLD (hon.), Northwestern U., 1998. Bar: N.D. 1967, Mich. 1986. Mcpl. judge City of Bismarck, 1970-76, U.S. magistrate, 1970-76, police commr., 1976-80; sr. ptnr. Pearce & Durick, Bismarck, 1970-85; assoc. gen. counsel GM, Detroit, 1985-87, v.p., gen. counsel, 1987-92, exec. v.p., gen. counsel, 1992-94, exec. v.p., 1994-95, vice chmn., 1996—2001; chmn. Hughes Electronics, El Segundo, Calif., 2001—. Bd. dirs. GM Corp., Hughes Electronics Corp., GM Acceptance Corp., Delphi Automotive Sys. Corp., Alliance of Automobile Mfrs. of Marriott Internat. Inc., Econ. Strategy Inst., Theodore Roosevelt Medora Found., MDU Resources Group, Inc., Nat. Def. U. Found., Detroit Investment Fund. Mem. law bd. Sch. Law, Northwestern U.; mem. bd. visitors U.S. Air Force Acad.; chmn. Product Liability Adv. Coun. Found.; founding mem. minority counsel demonstration program Commn. on Opportunities for Minorities in the Profession, ABA; chmn. The Sabre Soc., USAF Acad.; trustee Howard U., U.S. Coun. for Internat. Bus., New Detroit, Inc.; mem. The Mentor's Group Forum for U.S.-European Union Legal-Econ. Affairs, The Conf. Bd., Network of Employers for Traffic Safety's Leadership Coun., Pres.'s Coun. on Sustainable Devel., World Bus. Coun. for Sustainable Devel., World Economic Forum Coun. Innovative Leaders in Globalization. Capt. USAF, 1964-70. Named Michiganian of Yr., The Detroit News, 1997; Hardy scholar Northwestern U., Chgo., 1964-67, recipient Alumni Merit award, 1991. Fellow Am. Coll. Trial Lawyers, Internat. Soc. Barristers; mem. Am. Law Inst. Avocations: amateur radio, woodworking, sailing. Office: Hughes Electronics 200 N Sepulveda Blvd El Segundo CA 90245

PEARCE, HERBERT HENRY, real estate company executive; Student, New Haven Coll.; LLD (hon.), U. New Haven, 1980; LHD (hon.), Albertus Magnus Coll., 1988. Various mgmt. positions A.C. Gilbert Co., New Haven, Conn., 1935-57; chmn., CEO H. Pearce Real Estate Co., North Haven, Conn., 1958—. Hon. chmn. YMCA Fund Raising Project; mem. Yale New Haven Hosp. Devel. Com.; nominations com. U. New Haven; bd. dirs. Nation Conf. Christians and Jews; mem. adv. bd. South Ctrl. Jr. Achievement; chmn. United Way Loaned Exec. Com.; chmn. mktg. and rsch. Conn. Regional Econ. Devel. Coun.; advisor Eli Whitney Mus. on A.C. Gilbert Project. Recipient Cmty.

Leadership award Greater New Haven C. of C., Greater New Haven Realtor of Yr. award, Outstanding Achievement award Nat. Jr. Achievement Orgn., Humanitarian award Hunger Relief and Devel., Inc., YMCA Cmty. Leadership award; inducted into Jr. Achievement Free Enterprise Hall of Fame. Fellow Berkeley Coll. (assoc.), Yale U. (assoc.); mem. Conn. Assn. Realtors (past pres.), Greater New Haven Bd. Realtors (past pres.), Quinnipiack Club, New Haven Country Club, Mory's Assn., Kiwanis. Office: H Pearce Real Estate Co 393 State St North Haven CT 06473-3115

PEARCE, JOHN Y. lawyer; b. New Orleans, Mar. 26, 1948; s. John Young II and Marina (Harris) P.; m. Marjorie Pamela Doyle, May 22, 1971 (div.); children: Andrea Elizabeth, Roger Wellington; m. Julia Evans Reed, May 10, 2003. BA, La. State U., 1973, JD, 1976. Bar: La. 1977, U.S. Dist. Ct. (ea., mid. and we. dists.) La., U.S. Ct. Claims, U.S. Ct. Appeals (5th and 11th cirs.). Assoc. Doyle, Smith & Doyle, New Orleans, 1977-79, ptnr., 1979-80, mng. ptnr., 1980-84; ptnr. Montgomery, Barnett, Brown, Read, Hammond & Mintz, New Orleans, 1984—2003, mng. ptnr., 2003—. Pres. New Orleans Legal Assistance Corp., 1999—2002, S.E. La. Legal Svcs. Corp., 2002—. Sgt. U.S. Army, 1969—71. Mem.: ABA (ho. of dels. 1998—2003), New Orleans Bar Assn. (pres. 1997—98, exec. com.), La. Bar Assn. (chmn. mineral law sect. 1994—95). Republican. Episcopalian. Office: Montgomery Barnett Brown Read Hammond & Mintz 1100 Poydras St New Orleans LA 70163-1101 E-mail: jpearce@monbar.com.

PEARCE, PATSY BEASLEY, elementary education educator; b. Dunn, N.C., Apr. 13, 1945; d. Marvin Franklin and Christine (Bryant) Beasley; m. Robert Michael Cole, Aug. 15, 1970 (div.); 1 child, Matthew Bryant Cole; m. Elwood Glenn Pearce, Mar. 1, 1980. BSEd, E. Caroline U., 1966. Cert. collegiate profl., Va. Primary tchr., 1st and 2d grade Va. Beach (Va.) City Schs., 1966-75; primary tchr., 1st. and 3rd grade Jasper County Schs., Hardeeville, S.C., 1976-78; tchr., 4th grade Campbell County Schs., Lynchburg, Va., 1979; kindergarten tchr. Aesop Acad., Portsmouth, Va., 1981-84; primary tchr., 1st grade Chesapeake (Va.) City Schs., 1984—2001, ret., 2001. Mem. social studies adoption com. Chesapeake City Schs., 1996-98, colleague mentor, 1997-98, Pizza Hut Book-It chairperson, 1997-2001; United Way chair, 1995-97; sch. rep. Chesapeake Reading Coun., 1986-95, colleague mentor, 1988-90; equity tutor Camelot Elem. Sch., Chesapeake, 1994, grade level chmn., 1990-95, coop. tchr., 1990-91; mem. tech. tng. Va. Stds. Learning Tng., 1999-2001, 2001. Sunday sch. tchr. Cradock United Meth. Ch., Portsmouth, Va., 1982, worship com. chmn. 1990-91, Acolyte chmn., 1984-89; vacation Bible sch. tchr. Thail United Meth. Ch., Virginia Beach, 1969; com. chmn., treas. Cub Scout Pack 251, Portsmouth, Va., 1980-91; roundtable commr. Merrimac Dist. Boy Scouts Am., Portsmouth, 1989-90, dist. chmn. Scouts Ann. Mall Show and Pinewood Derby Race, 1987-89; children's choir dir. Kempsville Ch. of Christ, Virginia Beach, 1979-80. Named Camelot's Tchr. of Yr., 1995-96. Mem. NEA, Va. Edn. Assn., Chesapeake Edn. Assn., Chesapeake Reading Coun., Internat. Reading Coun., PTA (corr. sec. 1997-98). Avocations: gardening, needlework crafts, travel, granddaughter. Home: 2233 Ferndale Rd Chesapeake VA 23323-5016

PEARCE, PAUL FRANCIS, retired aerospace electronics company executive; b. Boston, Sept. 17, 1928; s. George Hamilton and Marie Louise (Duval) P.; m. Gilda Troisi, Apr. 11, 1953; children: Janet, Theresa, Diane. BSEE (Edwards scholar), MIT, 1950; MS, Mass. Inst. Tech., L.A., 1952; postgrad. (Hughes fellow), U. Calif., Los Angeles, 1957-58, U. So., Calif., 1958-59, Inst. Mgmt. Northwestern U., 1966. Project engr. Trans-Sonics, Inc., Burlington, Mass., 1952-55; sect. head application engring., strategic systems Hughes Aircraft Co., Culver City, Calif., 1955-59; with Lockheed Electronics Co., Plainfield, N.J., 1959-67, gen. mgr. div. mil. systems, 1964-65, v.p., gen. mgr., 1965-67; v.p., div. mgr. Tele-Dynamics div. AMBAC Industries, Inc., Ft. Washington, Pa, 1967-74; group v.p. comml. and aerospace electronics group AMBAC Industries, Inc., Carle Place, N.Y., 1973-80; pres. James G. Biddle Co., Blue Bell, Pa., 1980-93, ret. Bd. dirs. AVO Internat. Ltd., 1987-91. Mem. Armed Forces Communications and Electronics Assn. (pres. 1969-71), Inst. Nav., Delaware Valley Mfrs. Assn. (sr. vice chmn. 1987-89, chmn. 1990-92—), Greater Phila. C. of C., Ft. Washington Indsl. Park Mgmt. Assn. (gov. 1973-74), Sigma Xi. Clubs: Mfrs'. Golf and Country (Oreland, Pa.) (handicap chmn. 1987-90), St. David's Golf Club (Wayne, Pa.). E-mail: pfpearce@att.net.

PEARCE, RICHARD LEE, lawyer; b. Racine, Wis., Apr. 11, 1959; s. John Wallace and Betty Jane P.; m. Cynthia Diane Davis, June 11, 1983; 1 child, Melissa Lauren. BS in Chemistry, U. S.C., 1981, JD, 1984. Bar: S.C. 1984, U.S. Dist. Ct. S.C. 1985, U.S. Ct. Appeals (4th cir.) 1985. Law clk. to resident cir. judge Edward B. Cottingham, 1984-85; assoc. Fox, Zier, Burkhalter & Verenes, Aiken, S.C., 1985-86; ptnr. Toole & Toole, Aiken, 1986-96; asst. pub. svcs. dir., legis. liaison S.C. Bar, 1996-98; city solicitor, staff atty. City of Aiken, 1998—. Instr. Am. Banking Inst., Nat. Advocacy Ctr., Nat. Dist. Attys. Assn.; guest lectr., adj. instr. U. S.C., Aiken; legal advisor Bd. Zoning Appeals, Hist. Preservation Commn., Neighborhoods Com., City Dept. Dirs., Bldg. Code Bd. Appeals, Pks. Commn.; bd. dirs. Leadership Aiken County Class of 2003, 2003—, Hitchcock Health Svcs., 2004—; adv. bd. Soc. Prevention of Cruelty to Aminals, 2000-01; mem. spl. commn. on domestic violence, S.C. Atty. Gen.; mem. U.S. Dept. Justice Operation Cease Fire. Emcee Sch. Bd. Acad. Tournament, Aiken, 1986; bd. dirs. Tri-Devel. Ctr., Aiken, 1985-86; spl. events com. Downtown Aiken Devel. Corp.; fundraiser com. Am. Cancer Soc., 1985-2000, Am. Heart Assn., 2000-01; legal advisor Children's Place, Inc.; judge mock trial high sch. competition, 1991-96; trustee Aiken, Barnwell, Bamberg, and Edgefield Libr. Sys.; organizer, coord. Aiken Youth Ct.; active Ptnrs. in Friendship, Sister Cities, Orvieto, Italy and Schoalhaven, Australia, Mex./S.C. Govt. Study Exchange Seminars, Internat. Youth Exchange. Mem. S.C. Bar Assn. (ho. of dels. 1989-95, pro bono program 1989-97, resolution of fee disputes bd., lawyers' fund for client protection, task force on justice for all, ethics adv. com., unauthorized practice law com., co-editor Legis. Update, editor Ethics Adv. Opinion Summaries, coord. annual jud. evaluation, sec. govtl. law sect.), Aiken County Bar Assn. (pres. 1990-92), Aiken C. of C. (legal liaison 1986), Internat. Mcpl. Lawyers Assn., Nat. Dist. Attys. Assn., S.C. Solicitors Assn., Leadership Aiken County (bd. dirs. 2003—, disting. grad. 2003), Rotary Internat. (bd. dirs. 1994-96, pres.-elect 1994-95, pres. 1995-96, group study exch. coord., chair internat. group study exch. hosting teams from Gt. Britain, Wales, Brazil, Argentina, Japan, W.I., Australia, India, dist. 7750 group study exch. com., alternate team leader, dist. 7750 to dist. 9320 South Africa team, Aiken-Llandrindod, Wales, U.K., Exch. Program, Paul Harris fellow, Sustaining Paul Harris fellow), Omicron Delta Kappa, Hitchcock Woods Axe Club. Presbyterian (vice-chair bd. deacons 1999-2000, chair 2001-02). Avocations: antique phonographs/records, camping, outdoor activities, historical research, bicycling. Office: City of Aiken PO Box 1177 Aiken SC 29802-1177 Office Phone: 803-642-7654. E-mail: rpearce@aiken.net.

PEARCE, ROBERT BRENT, agricultural studies educator; BS, U. Calif., 1963; MS, Va. Polytechnic Inst., 1965, PhD, 1967. Prof. agr. Iowa State U., Ames, prof. agr. emeritus, 1999—. Fellow Nat. Assn. Colls. Tchrs. Agriculture, 1992. Office: Iowa State U Dept Agronomy 120 Agronomy Ames IA 50011-0001

PEARCE, RONALD, retired cosmetic company executive; b. Apr. 29, 1920; s. Fernley Charles and Medora Kate (Lissenden) P.; m. Olive Stacey, Apr. 4, 1942; children: David Fernley, Jane Ryding Robertson. Cambridge matriculation, Lindisfarne Coll., Ruabon, North Wales, U.K., 1937. Chief cashier Westminster Bank, Croydon, Eng., 1947-48; comml. officer Brit. Consulate, Dallas, 1949-52; v.p. World Gift Co., Dallas, 1953-63, Nelson Electronics, Dallas, 1963-68; stockbroker Walston & Co., Dallas, 1968-73; dir. purchasing Mary Kay Cosmetics, Inc., Dallas, 1973-85; pres. Global Water Techs., Inc., 1992-95; chmn. bd. Alpha Aqua, 1996—, Concha Holdings LTD, 2002—. Chmn. bd. Dallas Lighthouse for the Blind, 1987. Flight lt. RAF, 1940-46. Republican. Episcopalian. Home: 5455 La Sierra Dr Apt 1014 Dallas TX 75231

PEARCE, STEVE, congressman; b. Lamesa, Tex., Aug. 23, 1947; m. Lea Pearce. BBA, N.Mex. State U.; MBA, Ea. N.Mex. U. Owner, operator Lea Fishing Tools; mem. N.Mex. State Ho. Reps., 1996—2002, chmn. Rep. Caucus; congressman 2nd Dist. N.Mex. U.S. Ho. Reps., 2003—. With USAF. Republican. Office: 1408 Longworth House Office Bldg Washington DC 20515-3102

PEARCEY, LYNNE G. university dean, nursing educator; ADN, Paducah Jr. Coll., 1967; BSN with distinction, Eastern Ky. U., 1974; MSN, U. Ky., 1975, PhD in Ednl. and Counseling Psychology, 1982. Instr. Midway (Ky.) Coll., 1975-77, U. Ky., Lexington, 1977-79; asst. prof. dept. nurisng U. West Fla., Pensacola, 1981-82; assoc. prof., chmn. cmty.-mental health dept. U. South Ala. Coll. Nursing, Mobile, 1982-89; assoc. dean, prof. U. N.C., Greensboro, 1989-90, acting dean, prof., 1990-91, dean Sch. Nursing, prof., 1991—. Adj. prof. anesthesia Bowman Gray Sch. Medicine of Wake Forest U., Winston-Salem, N.C., 1990— Contbr. articles to profl. jours. Mem. ANA, Nat. League for Nursing, So. coun. on Collegiate Edn. for Nursing (bd. dirs. 1993-95, mem. nominating com. 1995-96, membership com. 1995-97), Am. Assn. for Higher Edn., Am. Assn. Colls. of Nursing, Ala. State Nurses Assn. (outstanding nurse educator 1984), Mobile County Nurses' Socj. (excellence in profl. nursing 1985), Sigma Theta Tau. Office: U NC Sch Nursing Office of Dean PO Box 26172 Greensboro NC 27402-6172

PEARL, B. MICHAEL, business owner; b. Cleve., July 21, 1957; s. Raymond Albert and Adele Gertrude (Waxman) P.; m. Patricia Marie Marotta, Oct. 7, 1978; 1 child, Tyler Michael. Cert. pers. cons. Gen. mgr. Pearl Carpet Stores, Cleve., 1979-82, exec. v.p. J.D. Brown & Assocs., Cleve., 1982-89; pres., owner The Pearl-Waxman Co., Chagrin Falls, Ohio, 1990—; founder, mng. ptnr. Cruises on Sail Travel, LLC, Chagrin Falls, 1994—. Columnist, Two if By Sea DCI Comm., 2001—. Editor Aware - The Jour. for Inner Devel., 1983-89; author: The Path and the Power, 1988; columnist Chagrin Valley Times, Solon Times and Geauga Times, 1995-2001; talk show host: Becoming Aware, 1989-90. Exec. dir. The A.W.A.R.E. Found., Cleve., 1985-89; mem. spkrs. Bur., 1982—; faculty advisor Cleve. Clinic Ctr. for Health Edn., Rocky River, Ohio, 1986—. Recipient No. Ohio's 88 Most Interesting People, Cleve. Mag., 1988, Spkr. award Masonic Srs., Cleve., 1997, Circolo d'Amici Platinum award, Costa Cruise Lines, Captain's award, Norwegian Cruise Line. Mem. Greater Cleve. Assn. Pers. Cons. (membership chmn. 1985-87), Chagrin Valley C. of C. (corp. sponsor), Cruise Lines Internat. Assn., Vacation.com. Avocations: travel, theater, food and wine, antique collecting, parapsychology.

PEARL, HARVEY, rehabilitation psychologist; b. N.Y.C., July 11, 1930; s. Louis and Blanche (Birnbaum) P.; m. Dorothy Morrison, June 20, 1953; children: Stuart Ray, Lesley, Andrea. BS, NYU, 1953, MA, 1957; PhD, Syracuse U., 1970. Tchr. indsl. arts Pub. Schs. Elizabeth (N.J.), 1955-56; workshop supr. United Cerebral Palsy Assn., Roosevelt, N.Y., 1956-58; workshop dir. Jewish Vocat. Service, Cin., 1958-61; dir. work tng. center Assn. Retarded Children, Rochester, N.Y., 1961-63; asst. exec. dir. Consol. Industries Greater Syracuse (N.Y.), 1965-96, rehab. cons., 1996—. Instr. Cornell U., Ithaca, NY, 1970—; cons. Social Security Adminstrn., 1962—2000. Author: (with A. Speiser, A. Stanjec) Bibliography of Work Evaluation in Vocational Rehabilitation, 1966; Comparison of Personal Values and Worker Assessments of Work Evaluators in Rehabilitation and Industrial Settings, 1970. Pres. Jewish Family Service Bur., 1974-82; adv. council Cazenovia Coll., 1977—, Occupational Edn., Syracuse City Sch. Dist., 1971—. Served with U.S. Army, 1953-55. Recipient citation of merit Syracuse U. Sch. Social Work, 1972; cert. rehab. counselor. Mem. Nat. Rehab. Assn., Am. Counseling Assn., Am. Rehab. Counseling Assn., Nat. Career Devel. Assn., Am. Psychol. Assn., Am. Wine Soc. Home and Office: 227 Wellington Rd De Witt NY 13214-2225 E-mail: hndpearl@worldnet.att.net.

PEARL, JUDEA, computer scientist, educator; b. Tel-Aviv, Sept. 4, 1936; U.S. citizen; married; 3 children. BSc, Israel Inst. Tech., 1960; MSc, Newark Coll. Engring., 1961; PhD in Elec. Engring., Poly. Inst. Bklyn., 1965. Rsch. engr. Dental Sch., NYU, 1960-61; mem. tech. staff RCA Rsch. Labs., 1961-65; dir. advanced memory devices Electronic Memories, Inc., Calif., 1966-69; prof. Sch. of Engring./Dept. Computer Scis. UCLA, 1969—. Instr. Newark Coll. Engring., 1961; cons. Rand Corp., 1972, Integrated Sci. Corp., 1975, Hughes Aircraft, 1989. Recipient Outstanding Achievement award RCA Labs., 1965, Rsch. Excellence award, ISCAI, 1999. Fellow IEEE, Am. Assn. Artificial Intelligence (Classical Paper award 2000, Lakatos award 2001), Acad. Engring. (mem. 2002, ACM-AAA1 Allen Newell award, 2003); corr. mem. Nat. Acad. Engring, 2002. Office: UCLA Dept Computer Sci 4532 Boelter Hl Los Angeles CA 90095-0001

PEARL, LAURENCE DICKSON, retired federal government executive; b. Phila., Mar. 2, 1934; s. Simon and Dorothy (Lichtig) P.; m. Ruth Switzer, Dec. 22, 1959 (div. Apr. 1972); children: Natasha, Lisa Talbott, Thomas Simon; m. Anne Womeldorf, Dec. 20, 1972. AB, Antioch Coll., 1955; postgrad., Harvard U., 1955-56; LLB, Yale U., 1959. Bar: D.C. 1959, U.S. Supreme Ct. 1983. Assoc. Trammell, Rand & Nathan, Washington, 1960-61; rsch. assoc. George Washington U., Washington, 1961; atty., advisor HUD, Washington, 1961-67, exec. asst. to gen. counsel, 1967-69, spl. asst. to asst. sec. for equal opportunity, 1969-72, dir. program standards and data analysis, 1972-74, dir. program compliance, 1974-86, dir. program standards and evaluation, 1986-98; ret., 1998. Pres. Capitol Hill Restoration Soc., Washington, 1990-92. Ford Found. fellow, 1955-56. Mem. Am. Bar Assn., Sr. Execs. Assn. (pres. HUD chpt. 1990-91). Avocations: music, gardening, cross country skiing.

PEARL, NANCY LINN, librarian; b. Detroit, Mich, Jan. 12, 1945; d. Sidney and Anne Linn; m. Joseph Harold Pearl; children: Eily Raman, Katie. MLS, U. Mich., 1967. Exec. dir. Washington Ctr. Book Seattle Pub. Lib., 1993—; head collection devel. Tulsa City County Libr., Okla. Author: Now Read This: A Guide to Mainstream Fiction, 1978-1998, 1999, Now Read This II: A Guide to Mainstream Fiction, 1990-2001, 2002, (book) Book Lust: Recommended Reading for Every Mood, Moment and Reason, 2003. Named Fiction Reviewer of Yr., Libr. Jour. Magazine, 1998; recipient Allie Beth Martin award, Pub. Libr. Assn., 2001, Open Book award, Pacific Northwest Writer's Conf., 1997, Humanities Washington award, 2003. Office: Seattle Pub Libr 800 Pike St Seattle WA 98101 Office Fax: 206 386 4672. Business E-Mail: nancy.pearl@spl.org.

PEARLMAN, JERRY KENT, electronics company executive; b. Des Moines, Mar. 27, 1939; s. Leo R. Pearlman; married; children: Gregory, Neal. BA cum laude, Princeton U., 1960; MBA, Harvard U., 1962. With Ford Motor Co., 1962-70; v.p. fin. dir. Behring Corp., 1970-71; from contr. to chmn. Zenith Electronics Corp., Glenview, Ill., 1971-95. Bd. dirs. Smurfit-Stone Container Corp, Ryerson-Tull Corp., Nanophase Techs., Evanston Northwestern Healthcare. Bd. dirs. Northwestern U. Office: 21 Linden Ave Wilmette IL 60091-2837 E-mail: jpearl@northwestern.edu.

PEARLMAN, LOUIS JAY, aviation and entertainment company executive; b. Flushing, N.Y., June 19, 1954; s. Herman and Reenie (Nevler) P. BA, Queens Coll., 1976; MBA, Century U., 1980; Degree in Sales Mgmt., SUNY, Buffalo, 1980; PhD in Bus. Adminstrn., Century U., 1983. Pres. Commuter Helicopter Corp., N.Y.C., 1974-75; pres., COO Trans Continental Airlines, Inc., N.Y.C., 1975—, Trans Continental Records, Orlando, Fla., 1991—; chmn. Trans Continental Talent, Inc., 2002—. Gen. mgr. U.S. Westdeutsche Luftwerbung GmbH, N.Y.C., 1976-85; chmn., pres., CEO Airship Internat. Ltd., N.Y.C., 1982—, bd. dirs., 1985—; pres., CEO Trans Continental Records, Inc., 1992—; pres. Backstreet Boys, Inc., 1993-99; chmn. Natural Prodns. LLC, 2001-; CEO Chippendales, Inc., 1996-2000, Entertainment Internat. Ltd., 1997—, Planet Airways Inc., 1998—, bd. dirs.; cons. Queens Coll., CUNY, 1977—. Author: Survey and Analysis of the Airline Industry, 1983; song writer. Active Mitchell-Linden Civic Assn., Flushing, 1980-82, Kissimmee (Fla.) Mcpl. Airport, 1985—. Recipient Govs. award NARAS, 2000. Mem. U.S. Power Squadron, Wings Club (disting., recipient Lighter-than-Air award 1987), Lighter-than-Air Soc. (hon.), Young Entrepreneurs Am., Young Millionaires Club, Internat. Air Transport Assn., Blimp Port U.S.A. (pres. 1987—), Friar's Club (N.Y.C.). Avocations: flying airplanes, helicopters and blimps, swimming, bowling, music, boating. Office: Trans Continental Cos Inc Trans Continental Bldg 127 W Church St Ste 350 Orlando FL 32801 Office Phone: 407-345-0004.

PEARLMAN, PETER STEVEN, lawyer; b. Orange, N.J., June 11, 1946; s. Jack Kitchener and Tiela Josephine (Fine) P.; m. Joan Perlmutter, June 19, 1969; children: Heather, Christopher, Megan. BA, U. Ill., 1967; JD, Seton Hall U., 1970. Bar: N.J. 1970, U.S. Dist. Ct. N.J. 1970, U.S. Dist. Ct. (so. dist.) N.Y. 2003, U.S. Dist. Ct. S.D., 2003, U.S. Dist. Ct. N.Y., 2003, U.S. Tax Ct. 1973, U.S. Supreme Ct. 1974, U.S. Ct. Appeals (2d cir.) 1981, U.S. Ct. Appeals (3d cir.) 1983, U.S. Ct. Appeals (7th cir.) 1985, U.S. Ct. Appeals (D.C. cir.) 1998, U.S. Ct. Appeals (4th cir.) 1999, U.S. Ct. Claims 2000; cert. civil trial atty., 1982. Assoc. Cohn & Lifland, Esquires, Saddle Brook, N.J., 1970-72; ptnr. Cohn, Lifland, Pearlman, Herrmann & Knopf, Saddle Brook, 1972—. Lectr. Nat. Inst. Trial Advocacy, Hempstead, N.Y., 1988—; active trial advocacy program Widener Law Sch.; adj. faculty mem. trial advocacy program Hofstra Law Sch.; master C. Willard Heckel Inn of Ct.; guest lectr. appellate advocacy Roger Williams Law Sch., 1995—; mem. panel arbitrators Am. Arbitration Assn.; lectr. for Inst. Continuing Legal Edn. for State of N.J. Mem. ABA, ATLA, N.J. Bar Assn. Home: 9 Harvey Dr Short Hills NJ 07078-1122 Office: Cohn Lifland Pearlman Herrmann & Knopf 1 Park 80 Plz W Ste 4 Saddle Brook NJ 07663-5808 Office Phone: 201-845-9600. E-mail: psp@njlawfirm.com.

PEARLMAN, RONALD ALAN, lawyer, educator; b. Hamilton, Ohio, July 10, 1940; AB with honors, Northwestern U., 1962, JD cum laude, 1965; LL.M. in Taxation, Georgetown U., 1967. Bar: D.C. 1991, U.S. Tax Ct. 1969, U.S. Supreme Ct. 1968. Atty. office chief counsel IRS, Washington, 1965—69; assoc. Thompson & Mitchell, St. Louis, 1969—70, ptnr., 1970—83; dep. asst. sec. for tax policy Dept. Treasury, Washington, 1983—84, asst. sec. tax policy, 1984—85; ptnr. Bryan, Cave, McPheeters & McRoberts (now Bryan Cave), St. Louis, 1986—88; chief of staff joint com. on taxation U.S. Congress, Washington, 1988—90; ptnr. Covington & Burling, Washington, 1991—99; prof. Georgetown U. Law Ctr., Washington, 1999—. Ind. trustee Eaton Vance Mut. Funds, 2003—; vis. prof. Georgetown U. Law Ctr., Washington, 1998, Harvard U. Law Sch., Cambridge, Mass., 2002; adj. prof. Sch. Law Wash. U., St. Louis, 1972—83; vis. instr. Sch. Law U. Va., Charlottesville, 1995—98; mem. BNA Tax Mgmt. Adv. Bd., 1986—88, 1993—; participant ednl. seminars. Mem. bd. editors Northwestern U. Law Rev.; contbr. articles to various publs. Trustee Am. Tax Policy Inst., 1998—, pres., 2003—. Fellow Am. Coll. Tax Counsel; mem. ABA (vice chair govt. rels. 1997-99, chair govt. rels. com. 1996-97, mem. coun., tax sect. 1986-88), Am. Law Inst. (tax adv. group, cons. pass-through entities project and tax integration project), Order of Coif. Office: Georgetown U Law Ctr 600 New Jersey Ave NW Washington DC 20001-2022 Office Phone: 202-662-9882. Business E-Mail: pearlman@law.georgetown.edu.

PEARLMAN, SAMUEL SEGEL, lawyer, educator; b. Pitts., May 28, 1942; s. Merle Maurice and Bernice Florence (Segel) P.; m. Cathy Schwartz, Aug. 16, 1964; children: Linda P. Kraner, Caren E. AB, U. Pa., 1963, LLB magna cum laude, 1966. Bar: Pa. 1966, Ohio 1967, U.S. Ct. Appeals (3d cir.) 1967. Law clk. U.S. Dist. Ct. for Ea. Dist. Pa., Phila., 1966-67; assoc. Burke, Haber & Berick, Cleve., 1967-72, prin., 1973-86, Berick, Pearlman & Mills, Cleve., 1986-99; ptnr. Squire, Sanders & Dempsey L.L.P., Cleve., 2000—. Lectr. law Case Western Res. U. Sch. Law, 1978-82; mem. registration com. Ohio Div. Securities, 1979-89; adv. dir. Midland Title Security, Inc.; trustee Realty ReFund Trust, N.Y. Stock Exch., 1990-98. Author: Cases, Forms and Materials for Modern Real Estate Transactions, 1978, 82. Mem. ABA, Ohio Bar Assn., Greater Cleve. Bar Assn. (chmn. securities law sect. 1985-86), Order of Coif. Republican. Jewish. Office: Squire Sanders & Dempsey 4900 Key Tower 127 Public Sq Ste 4900 Cleveland OH 44114-1304 Office Phone: 216-479-8500. E-mail: spearlman@ssd.com.

PEARLMAN, STEVEN JAY, otolaryngologist, educator, surgeon; b. NYC, 1956; BA in biology magna cum laude with high honors, Brandeis U., 1978; MD, Mt. Sinai Sch. of Medicine, 1982. Cert. Am. Bd. Otolaryngology-Head and Neck Surgery, 1987, Am. Bd. Facial Plastic and Reconstructive Surgery. Resident gen. surgery Mt. Sinai Med. Ctr., NYC, 1982-83, resident otolaryngology-head and neck surgery, 1983-87; fellow facial plastic surgery St. Luke's Roosevelt Hosp., NYC, 1987-88, otolaryngologist, assoc. dir., head and neck surgery; attending surgeon Lenox Hill Hosp., NY, Manhattan Eye Ear and Throat Hosp., NY. Asst. prof. clin. otolaryngology, Columbia U. Hosp. Ctr. of Physicians and Surgeons; tchr. facial plastic surgery, Columbia U. Med. Sch. and NY Eye and Ear Infirmary. Contbr. to numerous medical and sci. publs., to chpts. in books.; appeared on nat. and local television talk and news programs (including CNN, WABC, Eyewitness News, Good Day NY, The Food Network, Fox-Channel 5, Montel Williams Show, and performed "live" face lift on CNBC's "The Real Story".). Pro bono surgeon Face to Face; pro bono facial reconstructive surgeon Nat. Domestic Violence Project. Mem. AMA, Am. Acad. Otolaryngology-Head and Neck Surgeons, Am. Acad. Facial Plastic and Reconstructive Surgery (past eastern region v.p. and nat. com. chmn.) NY State Med. Soc., NY Facial Plastic Surgery Soc. (founding pres. 1993-). Office: Head & Neck Surgery Group 425 W 59th St New York NY 10019-1128 also: 521 Park Ave New York NY 10021-8140 Office Phone: 212-262-4444., 212-223-8300. Office Fax: 212-644-8655., 212-523-6364. E-mail: PearlmanS@aol.com.*

PEARLSTEIN, PAUL DAVIS, lawyer; b. Berlin, NH, Jan. 3, 1938; s. Victor and Sophia (Davis) Pearlstein; m. Patricia Hurston, June 1964 (div.); children: Laura Sue, David Seth; m. Marilyn Mills, Jan. 11, 1981; children: Adam Lowell, Susanna Lee. AB, U. Pa., 1959; LLB, U. Va., 1962. Bar: Va. 1962, D.C. 1963, Md. 1990, U.S. Supreme Ct. 1970, cert.: Comml. Law League, Am. Arbitration Assn. (arbitrator), Nat. Assn. Securities Dealers, Am. Bd. of Cert. (bus. bankruptcy specialist). Atty. HUD, Washington, 1964-66; adminstr. contrn. and purchasing activities Cafritz Co. and affiliated cos., Washington, 1966-68; pvt. practice Washington, 1968-96; ptnr. Pearlstein & Jacques, Washington, 1989—, Pearlstein & Assocs., Washington, 1997—. Chair adv. rules com. U.S. Bankruptcy Ct. D.C., Washington; bankruptcy trustee Washington and Va., 1973—90; spkr. in the field. Editor, contbg. author: Real Estate Practice in DC, Md. and Va., 1995, contbg. author, editor: articles and books revs. to legal jours. Mandolinist, guitarist Takoma Mandoleers, 1971—, Orgn. Anacostia Rowing and Scullings, Coun. Ct. Excellence; bd. dirs., sec. Met. Washington, DC Trial Lawyers Found., 1991—96; bd. dirs. DC shpt. Am. Diabetes Assn., 1987—89; bd. dirs., treas. Anacostia Comty. Boathouse Assn., 2002—; pres. brotherhood Washington Hebrew Congregation, 1974—75, bd. mgrs., 1979—85; mem. inter group rels. com. Jewish Cmty. Coun., 1973—90. Capt. U.S. Army, 1962—64. Fellow: Am. Bar Found.; mem.: ABA (real property and probate sects.), D.C. Land Title Assn. (v.p. 1989—90), Washington Estate Planning Coun., Washington Assn. Realtors, Jud. Conf. D.C. cir., Bar Assn. D.C. (chmn. real property law com. 1976—78, pres. rsch. found., Chmn. of the Yr. 1977, Spl. Projects award 1987). Democrat. Avocations: kayaking, outrigger canoeing, mandolin, guitar, rowing. Office: Ste 505 1730 Rhode Island Ave NW Washington DC 20036-3101 Fax: 202-223-8737. E-mail: merraul@aol.com.

PEARLSTEIN, PHILIP, artist; b. Pitts., May 24, 1924; s. David and Libbie (Kalser) P.; m. Dorothy Cantor, Aug. 20, 1950; children: William, Julia, Ellen. BFA, Carnegie Inst. Tech., 1949; MA, NYU, 1955. Instr. Pratt Inst., 1959-63; vis. critic Yale U., 1962-63; from asst. prof. to prof. art dept. Bklyn. Coll., 1963-88, disting. prof. emeritus; pres. Am. Acad. Arts Letters, 2003—. Shows include Tanager Gallery, NYC, 1955, 59, Peridot Gallery, NYC, 1956, 57, 59, Allan Frumkin Gallery, NYC, 1962, 63, 65, 67, 69, 72, 74, 76, 78, 80, 83, Frumkin Gallery, Chgo., 1960, 65, 69, 73, 75, 80, 81, Hirschl & Adler Mod., N.Y.C., 1985, 88, 91, 92, 93, Robert Miller Gallery, NYC, 1995, 96, 97, 2001, Kansas City Art Inst., 1962, Ceeje Gallery, 1965, 66, Reed Coll., 1965, 79, Galerie Thelen, Cologne, Germany, 1972, Galleri Ostergren, Malmo, Sweden, 1972, Galerie Kornfeld, Zurich, Switzerland, 1972, Staatliche Museen-Kupferstichkabinett, Berlin, 1972, Kunstverein, Hamburg, Germany, 1972, Editions La Tortue, Paris, 1973, Donald Morris Gallery, Detroit, 1973, 76, 80, 94, Gimpel Fils Ltd., London, 1975, 79, Marianne Friedland Gallery, Toronto, Ont., Can., 1975, 81, Springfield (Mo.) Art Mus., 1978, 95, Harkus

Krakow Gallery, Boston, 1978-79, Myers Fine Arts Gallery, SUNY, Plattsburg, 1979, Galerie Jöllenbach, Cologne, Germany, 1979, 89, Carnegie-Mellon U., Pitts., 1979, Assoc. Am. Artists, 1980, FIAC, Paris, 1980, Brooke Alexander Gallery, 1980, 81, Ringling Mus. Art, Sarasota, Fla., 1981, San Antonio Mus. Art, 1981, (Retrospective) Milw. Art Mus., The Bklyn. Mus., The Pa. Acad. Fine Arts, Phila., The Toledo Mus. Art, 1983-84, Carnegie Inst. Mus. Art, Pitts., 1982, Brody's Gallery, Washington, 1983, Images Gallery, Toledo, 1984, Galerie Rudolph Zwirner, Cologne, Germany, 1989, 91, Compass Rose Gallery, Chgo, 1991, Printworks Gallery, Chgo., 1990, Condeso Lawler Gallery, NYC, 1991, P.S. 1, NY, 1992, Butler Art Inst, Youngstown, Ohio, 1992, Il Politico, Rome, 1997, Simon Capstick Dale, London, 1998, Daniel Templon, Paris, 1998, The Armory, West Palm Beach, Fla., 1998, Galerie Charlotte Moser, Geneva, 1999, U. Haifa Mus, Israel, 2002, U. Art Gallery, IN State U., 2003 Fulbright fellow to Italy, 1958-59; Guggenheim fellow, 1971-72; Nat. Endowment for the Arts grantee, 1968, NAD assoc., 1983. Mem.: Am. Acad. Arts, Letters. (grantee 1992).

PEARLSTEIN, SEYMOUR, artist; b. Bklyn., Oct. 14, 1923; s. Morris Lazarus and Anna (Bassiur) P.; m. Toby Tessie Rubinstein, Mar. 21, 1943; children: Judith Helene, Lawrence Jonathan. Cert., Pratt Inst., Bklyn., 1950, Art Students League N.Y., 1954; student of Jack Potter. Owner, illustrator, designer Sy Pearlstein Advt. Art Studio, N.Y.C., 1946-71; artist-painter rep. by Far Gallery, N.Y.C., 1969-81; prof. N.Y.C. Tech. Coll., CUNY, Bklyn., 1971-94, prof. emeritus, 1994—, chmn. art and advt. design dept., 1985-88. One-man shows Silvermine Guild of Artists, New Canaan, Conn., 1973, Far Gallery, 1973, 75, 78, Klitgord Ctr., N.Y.C., C.C., 1974, De Mers Gallery, Hilton Head, S.C., 1975, Adelphi U., Garden City, N.Y., 1979, Grace Gallery, N.Y.C. Tech. Coll., 1992; group shows A.M. Sachs Gallery, N.Y.C., 1971, Springfield (Mo.) Art Mus., 1971, Am. Acad. Arts and Letters, N.Y.C., 1975, 76, 77, NAD, N.Y.C., 1986, 87, 89, 91, 92, Butler Inst. Art, Ohio, 1975, Ball State U., Queens Mus., N.Y.C., 1978, 81, Dept. State Art in Embassies Program, N.Y. Hist. Soc., 1981, Colo. Heritage Mus., Denver, 1981, 82, 86, Am. Watercolor Soc., N.Y.C., Ingber Gallery, N.Y.C., 1985, Audubon Artists, N.Y.C., 1990, 92, 97, Allied Artists Am., N.Y.C., 1991, 95, 2002, Nat. Arts Club, N.Y.C., 1989, Grace Gallery, N.Y.C. Tech. Coll., CUNY, 1998, 99, 2000, others; represented in permanent collections Mus. N.Mex., Santa Fe, Mint Mus. Art, Charlotte, N.C., NAD, N.Y.C., Fine Arts Gallery, San Diego, Adelphi U., Queens Mus., N.Y.C., Munson-Williams-Proctor Inst., Utica, N.Y., N.Y.C. Tech. Coll., Bklyn. Served with AUS, 1942-46. Recipient Gold medal Nat. Acad. Design, 1969, Hassam Fund Purchase award Am. Acad. Arts and Letters, 1969, 77, Gold medal of honor Nat. Arts Club, 1970, Ranger Fund Purchase award NAD, 1971, 82, Gold medal Soc. Illustrators, 1972, Nat. Inst.-Am. Acad. Arts and Letters grant, 1975 Mem. NAD (sec. coun.) 1980-84, W.H. Leavin prize 1985), Am. Watercolor Soc. (bd. dirs. 1979-80, Watercolor U.S.A. award 1971), Art Students League of N.Y. (life), Allied Artists Am. (bd. dirs. 1976-79, E. Lowe award 1969, gold medal 1980, George Tweed Meml. award 1989, 92), Audubon Artists (bd. dirs. 1986-89, 91-93, Grumbacher award 1971, Fabri medal 1980), Alliance Figurative Artists (c0chmn. 1976-77), Profl. Staff Congress. Home: 52 Dartmouth St Forest Hills NY 11375-5142 Office: NYC Tech Coll AD Dept CUNY 300 Jay St Brooklyn NY 11201-1909 Personal E-mail: sntp52@aol.com.

PEARLSTINE, NORMAN, editor; b. Phila., Oct. 4, 1942; s. Raymond and Gladys (Cohen) Pearlstine. AB, Haverford Coll., 1964; LLB, U. Pa., 1967. Staff reporter Wall Street Jour., Dallas, Detroit, L.A., 1968—73, Tokyo bur. chief, 1973—76; mng. editor Asian Wall Street Jour., Hong Kong, 1976—78; exec. editor Forbes Mag., L.A., 1978—80; nat. news editor Wall Street Jour., N.Y.C., 1980—82; editor, pub. Wall Street Jour./Europe, Brussels, 1982—83; mng. editor, v.p. Wall Street Jour., N.Y.C., 1983—91, exec. editor, 1991—92; pres., CEO Friday Holdings, L.P., N.Y.C., 1993—94; editor-in-chief Time Inc., N.Y.C., 1995—. Pres. Atsuko Chiba Found.; bd. councilors USC Annenberg Sch. Comm.; bd. mem. Com. to Protect Journalists, 2004—. Recipient Editor of Yr. award, Nat. Press Found., 1989. Mem.: ABA, Japan Soc., Coun. Fgn. Rels., N.Y. Hist. Soc. (former chmn.), D.C. Bar Assn. (trustee). Office: Time Inc 1271 Avenue Of The Americas New York NY 10020-1300

PEARSALL, GEORGE WILBUR, materials scientist, mechanical engineer, educator, consultant; b. Brentwood, NY, July 13, 1933; s. Milo Dickerson and Margaret Elizabeth (White) P.; m. Patricia Louise Stevens, Oct. 11, 1962. B. Metall. Engring., Rensselaer Poly. Inst., 1955; Sc.D. (Am. Soc. Metals fellow), MIT, 1961. Registered profl. engr., NC. Rsch. engr. Dow Chem. Co., Midland, Mich., 1955-57; rsch. asst. MIT, 1959-60, asst. prof. metallurgy, 1960-64; assoc. prof. mech. engring. Duke U., 1964-66, prof., 1966-81, prof. mech. engring. and materials sci., 1981—2001, prof. pub. policy studies, 1982—2001, acting dean Sch. Engring., 1969-71, dean, 1971-74, 82-83, prof. emeritus, 2001—. Trustee Triangle Univ. Ctr. for Advanced Studies, 1976-92, chmn. exec. com., 1983-88; dir. Duke-IBM Product Safety Inst., 1979-90. Author: (with W.G. Moffatt and J. Wulff) The Structure and Properties of Materials, 1964; mem. editl. bd. Jour. Products Liability, 1977-96, Proceedings of the IEEE, 1994-96; contbr. articles to profl. jour. Served with AUS, 1957. Mem. ASME (Triodyne Safety Award 2001), Am. Soc. Metals (life), Phi Lambda Upsilon, Tau Beta Pi, Pi Tau Sigma. Home: 2941 Welcome Dr Durham NC 27705-5555

PEARSALL, SAMUEL HAFF, III, landscape ecologist, geographer, foundation administrator; b. Nashville, Sept. 2, 1949; s. Sam H. Jr. and Margaret Isabelle (Ikard) P.; m. Patricia Davenport, July 1973 (div. 1978); 1 child, Rachel Claire; m. Linda Louise Parrish, Sept. 4, 1982; 1 child, Paul Samuel. BS, U. Tenn., 1942; M of Prof. Studies, Cornell U., 1982; PhD, U. Hawaii, 1993. Exec. dir. Coastal Resources Ctr., Bar Harbor, Maine, 1975-77; program dir. Natural Areas and Natural Heritage Survey Tenn. Dept. Conservation, Nashville, 1978-81, dir. Ecol. Svcs. divsn., 1982-85; dir. Pacific Sci. The Nature Conservancy, Honolulu, 1989-91, dir. sci. and stewardship Durham, NC, 1992-99, dir. sci. and Roanoke River Project, 2000—. Adj. faculty U. N.C., 1993—, Nicholas Sch. Environment Duke U., 1999—, founder Pacific Sci. program The Nature Conservancy, 1989, founding mem. conservation com., 1994-96, Ecoregions working group, 1996-97; mem. So. Blue Ridge Ecoregional Planning Team, 1996-97; leader Mid-Atlantic Coastal Plain Ecoregional Planning Team, 1997—; founding mem. Ga.-Pacific/Nature Conservancy Roanoke Ecosys. Partnership, 1995-97; mem. sci. and tech. adv. com. Albermarle-Pamlico Nat. Estuarihe Program, 2004—. Author: Terrestrial Coastal Environments and Tourism in Western Samoa, 1993, (with others) Wildlife Conservation Evaluation Methods in U.S., 1985; contbr. more than 30 nature conservation articles to profl. jours.; sole author conservation databases on 10 Pacific island countries, 1988—. Bd. dirs. Tenn. Environ. Coun., Nashville, 1980-85, Natural Areas Assn., Rockford, Ill., 1984-87, Bend, Oreg., 97-2000, treas., 1999-2000; counselor Conservation Trust for N.C., 1993-98; founder Tenn. Protection Planning Com.; student fellow East-West Ctr., 1985-90. Recipient Hodgson award Assn. Am. Geographers, 1988, Wiens award U. Hawaii, 1993, Conservation by Design award Nature Conservancy, 2003. Achievements include research in nature conservation, adaptive ecosystem management and landscape ecology in Western Samoa and North Carolina, coastal climate change and sea level rise in North Carolina; co-author FERC Lic. Settlement among Dominion Generation, Inc. and stakeholders at Lake Gaston and Roanoke Rapids dams. Home: 1307 Chaney Rd Raleigh NC 27606-2736 Office: Nature Conservancy Ste 209/One University Pl 4705 University Dr Durham NC 27707 Office Phone: 919-403-8558. Business E-Mail: sampearsall@tnc.org.

PEARSE, WARREN HARLAND, obstetrician and gynecologist, association executive; b. Detroit, Mich., Sept. 28, 1927; s. Harry Albridge and Frances (Wressell) P.; m. Jacqueline Anne Langan, June 15, 1950; children: Kathryn, Susan, Laurie, Martha. BS, Mich. State U., 1948; M.B., MD, Northwestern U., 1950. Intern. Univ. Hosp., Ann Arbor, Mich., 1950-51; resident obstetrics and gynecology, 1951-53, 55-56; practice medicine specializing obstetrics and gynecology, 1956-58; mem. faculty U. Nebr. Med. Ctr., Omaha, 1959-71, Found. prof., chmn. dept. obstetrics and gynecology, 1962-71, asst. dean, 1963-71, mem. residency rev. com. obstetrics and gynecology, 1968-93; dean Med. Coll. Va., Richmond, Va., 1971-75; exec. dir. Am. Coll. Obstetrics and Gynecology, 1975-93; cons., 1993—; editor Women's Health Issues, Washington, 1993—. Chmn. rsch. adv. group Maternal Child Health Svc., Health Sci. Mental Health Adminstrn., HEW, 1967—; cons. family planning Office Econ. Opportunity, 1970—. Author: (with V.L. Seltzer) Primary Health Care for Women, 1999; contbr. chpts., articles tech. lit. Served from 1st lt. to capt. AUS, 1953-55. Mem. Am. Coll. Obstetrics and Gynecology (dist. sec., treas. 1964-68, vice chmn. 1968-71), Am. Gynecology Soc., Soc. Gynecology Investigation, Assn. Profs. Gynecology and Obstetrics (sec., treas. 1969—), Alpha Omega Alpha. Office: American College of Obs & Gyns 409 12th St SW Washington DC 20024-2125 Home: #5005 10450 Lottsford Rd Bowie MD 20721-3301

PEARSON, ANDRALL EDWIN, food service executive; b. Chgo., June 3, 1925; s. Andrall E. and Dorothy M. (MacDonald) P.; m. Joanne Pope, Mar. 2, 1951; 1 dau., Jill Lee. BS, U. So. Calif., 1944; MBA, Harvard U., 1947. Mktg. mgr. Standard Brands, Inc., N.Y.C., 1948-53; assoc. to prin. McKinsey & Co., Inc., N.Y.C., 1953-70, dir., 1965-70; exec. v.p. PepsiCo, Inc., Purchase, NY, 1970-71, pres., 1971—84; prof. Harvard Bus. Sch., 1985—93; oper. ptnr. Clayton, Dubilier & Rice, 1993—97; CEO, chmn. Tricon Restuarants (now Yum Brands!, Inc.), 1997—2001. Bd. dirs. Pepsi Co., 1971—96; dir., mem. exec. com. May Co. Dept. Stores; bd. dirs. Comml. Credit Corp., Hasbro Inc., Munford Inc., Citigroup; founding chmn. Yum Brands!, Inc., 1997—. Contbr. articles profl. jour., chpt. in handbook. Trustee Wesleyan U., 1977—83; trustee N.Y.U. Med. Sch., Good Samaritan Med. Ctr., Palm Beach, Fla. Lt. (j.g.) USNR, 1943—46. Mem. Ref. Ch. of Bronxville (elder). Clubs: Harvard Bus. Sch. of N.Y. (N.Y.C.) (dir.), Bronxville Field (N.Y.C.), Blind Brook (N.Y.C.); Longwood Cricket (Boston). Office: Yum! Brands Inc 1441 Gardiner Ln Louisville KY 40213

PEARSON, CHARLES THOMAS, JR., lawyer, director; b. Fayetteville, Ark., Oct. 14, 1929; s. Charles Thomas and Doris (Pinkerton) P.; m. Wyma Lee Hampton, Sept. 9, 1988; children: Linda Sue, John Paddock. BS, U. Ark., 1953, JD, 1954; postgrad., U.S. Naval Postgrad. Sch., 1959; A.M., Boston U., 1963. Bar: Ark. bar 1954. Practice in, Fayetteville, 1963—. Dir. officer N.W. Comms., Inc., Dixieland Devel., Inc., Jonlin Investments, Inc., World Wide Travel Svc., Inc., Okliania Farms, Inc., N.W. Arl. Land & Devel., Inc., Garden Plaza Inns, Inc. Word Data, Inc., M.P.C. Farms, Inc., Fayetteville Enterprises, Inc., NWA Devel.Co., Delta Comm., Inc.; past. dir., organizer N.W. Nat. Bank. Adviser Explorer Scouts, 1968—; past pres. Washington County Draft Bd.; past pres. bd. Salvation Army. Served to comdr. Judge Adv. Gen. Corps USNR, 1955-63. Mem. ABA, Ark. Bar Assn., Washington County Bar Assn., Judge Advs. Assn., N.W. Ark. Ret. Officers Assn. (past pres.), Methodist Men (past pres), U. Ark. Alumni Assn. (past dir.), Sigma Chi (past pres. N.W. Ark. alumni, past chmn. house corp.), Alpha Kappa Psi, Phi Eta Sigma, Delta Theta Phi. Clubs: Mason (32 deg., K.T., Shriner), Moose, Elk, Lion, Metropolitan. Republican. Methodist. Office: 9 N College Ave Fayetteville AR 72701-5301 Office Phone: 479-521-4300. E-mail: tpesq1101@aol.com.

PEARSON, CLARENCE EDWARD, management consultant, educator; b. Chgo., Apr. 22, 1925; s. Edward and Irene (Silander) P.; m. June Waldhe, Apr. 21, 1951 (dec. 1967); 1 child, Scott (dec.); m. Laurie Norris, Apr. 25, 1995. BS, No. Ill. U., 1950; MPH, U. N.C., 1952. Instr. Mt. Prospect (Ill.) Pub. Schs., 1950-51; dir. health edn. DuPage County Health Dept., Wheaton, Ill., 1952-55; chief health edn. St. Louis Health Dept., 1955-57; dir. health and hosps. Health and Welfare Council, St. Louis, 1957-61; dir. health and safety Met. Life Ins. Co., N.Y.C., 1961-87. Prof. edn. Columbia Tchrs. Coll., 1975—; pres. Universal Health Concepts, N.Y.C., 1984-87; Coun. Internat. Health, Washington, 1981-84; chmn. Profl. Exam. Svc., N.Y.C., 1996-99; v.p. Peter Drucker Found. for Nonprofit Mgmt., 1994-96; adv. bd. C. Everett Koop Inst.; bd. overseers Dartmouth Med. Sch., 1992-96, 99—; adj. prof. cmty. health Rober Wood Johnson Med. Sch., 1996—; pres., CEO Nat. Ctr. for Health Edn., 1997—; sr. adv. Who office, U.N. Co-author: Managing Health Promotion, 1982; co-editor: (with C. Everett Koop) Critical Issues in Global Health, 2000; contbr. chpts. to books. Co-chmn. Scandinavian-Ams. for Rockefeller presdl. campaign, N.Y., 1968; co-dir. Salzburg Seminar Spl. Session: Critical Issues in Global Health. Served as staff sgt. U.S. Army, 1943-46. Recipient Disting. Career award APHA, Washington, 1981, Gold Medal for Achievement, Columbia U., N.Y.C., 1984, Internat. Health award Asia Pacific Consortium, Honolulu, 1984, Porter Prize, Pitts. Health Ctr., 1986, Disting. Alumni award Sch. Pub. Health, U. N.C., 2001. Fellow APHA (governing coun. 1970-78, pres. conf. emeritus members 2002—, Internat. Health Lifetime Achievement award), AARP (bd. dirs. 2002—), Advt. Coun. (adv. bd.), The Univ. Club (N.Y.C.). Home: 530 E 23rd St New York NY 10010-5022 Office Phone: 212-254-3309. Personal E-mail: nyvikings@aol.com. Business E-Mail: pearsonc@un.org.

PEARSON, CONRAD E. financial services executive; b. Edmonton, Alta., Can., Sept. 1, 1951; came to U.S., 1960; s. Hilding A. and Elva Rose (Land) P.; m. Barbara Anne Schroeder; children: Cameron, Nicole, Morgan, Everett. Cert. in Mid. East Studies, BA in Polit. Sci., Portland State U., 1973; MA in Internat. Affairs, Johns Hopkins U., 1975. Polit. risk analyst Shell Oil, Houston, 1977-78; mgr. Chase Manhattan Bank, N.Y.C., 1979-80; pres. Risk Insights, N.Y.C., 1980-82; co-owner Pearson Fin. Group, Portland, Oreg., 1982—. Pres. Tigard (Oreg.) Coalition Chs., 1983—. Mem. Tigard C. of C. (chmn. bd. dirs. 1994-95), Rotary (pres. Tigard club 1992). Lutheran. Avocation: poetry writing. Office: Pearson Fin Group 5665 SW Meadows Rd Ste 120 Lake Oswego OR 97035-3130 Home: 4375 Southshore Blvd Lake Oswego OR 97035-5511

PEARSON, DAVID PETRI, chemist; b. Oct. 24, 1926; s. Brewer Petri and Laura Alvine (Johnson) P.; m. Patricia Margaret Cowan, June 4, 1949; children: Kathryn A., James P., Rebecca L., Kristine R., Judith G. BA in Chemistry, Reed Coll., 1949; MS in Phys. Chemistry, Oreg. State U., 1953; PhD in Phys. Chemistry, U. So. Calif., 1960. Rsch. chemist Phillips Petroleum Co. (AEC), Idaho Falls, Idaho, 1957-62, Bartlesville, Okla., 1962-69; lectr. in chemistry Portland State U., 1969-71; asst. prof. chemistry So. Oreg. State Coll., Ashland, 1971-72; rsch. assoc. Oreg. Grad. Ctr., Beaverton, 1972-74; sr. chemist Portland Gen. Electric Co., 1975-87, ret., 1987. Patentee in field. Cpl. USAAF, 1946-47. Mem. Am. Chem. Soc. (treas. Portland sect. 1979-82, chmn. 1983). Clubs: Am. Alpine, Idaho Alpine (sec. Idaho Falls 1961, pres. 1962). Republican. Presbyterian. Home: 6324 SW Radcliffe St Portland OR 97219-5749

PEARSON, FORD G. automotive executive; CFO Frank Consolidated Enterprises Inc., Des Plaines, Ill., exec. v.p., COO. Office: Frank Consolidated Enterprises Inc 666 Garland Pl Des Plaines IL 60016-4725

PEARSON, GARY DEAN, dentist; b. Rockford, Ill., Dec. 25, 1952; s. Miles Addison and Pauline (Hammond) P.; m. Marcea Lou Schlenske, Dec. 4, 1981 (div. 1989); 1 child, Grant Addison; m. Menchu Nagal Caperocho, Apr. 22, 2000; 1 child, Mia Caperocho. BS cum laude, Rockford Coll., 1974; DDS, U. Ill., Chgo., 1978. Lic. dentist, Ill., Mich., N.H., Wis., Ariz. Pvt. practice dentistry, Rockton, Ill., 1978-93; group practice dentistry Tucson, 1993—; dentist in charge Prin. Fin. Group's Dental-Net Group Dental Ctr., 2000—; dental dir. Luth. Med. Ctr. Tucson Cmty. Clinic, 2001—; cons. faculty dept. surgery Luth. Med. Ctr., Bklyn., 2002—. Recipient Gen. Assembly Scholarship, State of Ill., 1977. Mem. Am. Dental Assn., Ill. State Dental Soc., Winnebago County Dental Soc., U. Ill. Alumni Assn., Rockton C. of C., Phi Theta Kappa. Clubs: Rockford Coll. Alumni. Lutheran. Avocations: flying, photography, motorcycling, tennis, basketball. Home: 5622 N Placita Paisaje Tucson AZ 85750-6078 Office: Dental Net Group 1057 N Kolb Rd Tucson AZ 85710-1328

PEARSON, GERALD LEON, food company executive; b. Mpls., June 24, 1925; s. Perry and Lillian (Peterson) P.; m. Beverly Mary Schultz, Nov. 10, 1946; children: Steven, Perry, Liecia. Grad., Trimont (Minn.) High Sch., 1943. Treas. Trimont Packing Co., 1946-52; v.p. Spencer Foods, Iowa, 1952-68, pres., chief exec. officer, 1969-80, chmn. bd., chief exec. officer, 1972-80; chmn. Beef Specialists of Iowa Inc., 1983-94. Bd. dirs. Graffaloy, Inc.; chmn., CEO World Champions of Golf Inc.; owner Brooks Golf Club, Okoboji, Iowa. Pres. Pearson Art Found.; bd. dirs. Bethany Coll., Lindsborg; commr. Nat. Mus. Am. Art-Smithsonian Instn., 1995-99; founder Internat. Ctr. for Jazz Found. With USN, 1943-46. Mem. Swedish Royal Roundtable, Swedish Council Am. (bd. dirs.). Home: Desert Highlands # 444 10040 E Happy Valley Rd Scottsdale AZ 85255-2395 Office: Brooks Golf Club PO Box 948 Okoboji IA 51355-0948 Office Phone: 712-332-7300. E-mail: bud.pearson@worldnet.att.net.

PEARSON, GREGORY DAVID, publisher, media specialist; b. Douglas, Ariz., Apr. 28, 1944; s. William Howard and Ruthanna (Knoff) P.; m. Myrna G. Pearson, May 22, 1972 (div. 1984); m. Della Griffith, June 22, 1989; 1 child, Ashley Brooke Klein. BA, DePauw U., 1966. V.p. Rust Comm., Richmond, Va., 1977-81, Capitol Broadcasting Co., Raleigh, N.C., 1982; sr. v.p. mktg. and advt. S&K Famous Brands, Richmond, Va., 1983-89; pres. Media Buying Assocs., Midlothian, Va., 1990-97; owner, pub., editor Chesterfield Observer, Midlothian, Va., 1995—. 2d v.p. bd. dirs. Brandermill Cmty. Assn., 2000—01; pres. bd. dirs. Chesterfield Sr. Softball Assn., 2002—03. Capt. USAF, 1966—71. Mem. Richmond Ad Club (bd. dirs. 1985-87). Office: Chesterfield Observer PO Box 1616 Midlothian VA 23113-1616 Office Phone: 804-744-9200. E-mail: editor@chesterfieldobserver.com.

PEARSON, HENRY CLYDE, retired judge; b. Ocoonita Lee County, Va., Mar. 12, 1925; s. Henry James and Nancy Elizabeth (Seals) P.; m. Jean Calton, July 26, 1956; children: Elizabeth, Frances, Timothy Clyde. Student, Union Coll., 1947-49; LLB, U. Richmond, 1952. Bar: Va. 1952, U.S. Ct. Appeals (4th cir.) 1957, U.S. Supreme Ct. 1958. Sole practice, Jonesville, Va., 1952-56; asst. U.S. atty. Western Dist. Va., Roanoke, 1956-61; ptnr. Hopkins, Pearson & Engleby, Roanoke, 1961—70; so. states presdl. campaign mgr. Nelson A. Rockefeller, 1964; judge U.S. Bankruptcy Ct. Western Dist. Va., Roanoke, 1970-98; ret., 1998. Participant Va. Continuing Edn. Seminars; mem. adv. com. fed. rules bankruptcy procedure; mem. Va. Ho. of Reps., 1954-56, Va. Senate, 1968-70; Republican nominee Gov. of Va., 1961. Editl. bd. Am. Survey Bankruptcy Law, 1979. Served with USN, 1943—46, PTO. Mem. Va. State Bar, ABA, Va. Trial Lawyers Assn., Assn. Trial Lawyers Am., Am. Judicature Soc., Am. Judges Assn., Fed. Bar Assn., Delta Theta Phi, Tribune Jefferson Senate, Am. Legion, VFW, Masons, Shriners. Methodist. Office: 1910 Mcvitty Rd Salem VA 24153-7406

PEARSON, JAMES BOYD, JR., electrical engineering educator; b. McGehee, Ark., June 3, 1930; s. James Boyd and Lydia Frances (Lacey) P.; m. Marian Scarborough, Feb. 16, 1957; children: Sarah, Jane, Carol, Catherine, Susan, Joanne. BSEE, U. Ark., 1958, MSEE, 1959; PhD, Purdue U., 1962. Asst. prof. electrical engring. Purdue U., Lafayette, Ind., 1962-65; assoc. prof. Rice U., Houston, 1965-70, prof., 1970-79, J.S. Abercrombie prof., 1979-99, J.S. Abercrombie prof. emeritus, 1999—. Served to capt. USAR, 1952-55. Fellow IEEE. Office: Rice Univ Dept Elec/Computer Engring PO Box 1892 Houston TX 77251-1892

PEARSON, JENNIE SUE, retired government administrator; b. Washington, Jan. 26, 1928; d. Orville Louis and Jennie (Rogers) Ganbin; m. Eugene Ryder Pearson, Feb. 3, 1945 (div. 1955); 1 child, Ronald Eugene. AA, Frederick (Md.) C.C., 1987. Title examiner Md. Motor Vehicle Adminstrn., Glen Burnie, 1970-74, title advisor, 1975-80, title supr., 1980-84, asst. br. mgr., 1984-91; ret., 1991. Pres. Rebekah Assembly Md., 1968-69, Internat. Assn. Rebekah Assemblies, Winston-Salem, N.C., 1973-74; v.p. Citizens Nursing Home Aux. Vols., 1997-98, pres., 1999—; vice chmn. bd. dirs. Md. Odd Fellows Home, 1991-92; mem. Srs. and Law Enforcement Together Coun.-Frederick City Police Dept.; mem. adv. bd. Inst. Learning in Retirement Frederick Cmty. Coll., bd. dirs.; trustee Schuyler Colfax Mus., Winston Salem, N.C.; bd. dirs. Frederick C.C. Found., Inc., Md. Sr. Citizens Hall Fame, 2003. Recipient Outstanding Alumni award for significant contbns. Coll. Mission and Alumni Assn., 1991, 98, Meritorious Jewel Rebekah Assembly of Md. Outstanding Svc. in Fraternal Order and Cmty., Vol. of Month, Frederick Sr. Mag.; inductee Md. Sr. Citizens Hall of Fame, Inc. Mem. AARP (pres. Frederick chpt. 1997-99, Andrus award pin for vol. cmty. svc. 2003), Frederick C.C. Alumni Assn. (pres. 1991-98), Montgomery County Agrl. Ctr., Inc. (life), Frederick County Commn. for Women, Rebekah Lodge (past noble grand mem. 1997-98, Meritorious Jewel award 2000), Frederick Woman's Civic Club, Inc. (mem. com. 1992-2003), Md. Sr. Citizens Hall of Fame, Inc. (bd. dirs. 2003), 1902 Club. Republican. Methodist. Avocations: volunteer work, travel, ice skating, walking.

PEARSON, JIM BERRY, JR., human resources specialist; b. Wichita Falls, Tex., Sept. 25, 1948; s. Jim Berry and June Louise (Young) P.; m. Cynthia Ann Medlin, Nov. 9, 1985 (div. Jan. 1999). Cert. mediator. Community organizer VISTA, Pitts., 1969-71; youth dir. East Liberty YMCA, Pitts., 1971-72; aide, therapist technician Austin (Tex.) State Sch., 1972-80; labor organizer Comm. Workers Am., Austin, 1980-90; employee resource officer Austin State Hosp., 1990-96; human resource dir. Capital Area State-Operated Cmty. MHMR Svcs., Austin, 1996-97; human resources dir. Bluebonnet Trails Cmty. Mental Health/Mental Retardation Ctr, Round Rock, Tex., 1997-2001; employee rels. specialist Tex. Dept. Mental Health and Mental Retardation, Austin, 2001—03, Tex. Health and Human Svcs. Commn., Austin, 2003—. Exec. bd. rep. Communications Workers Am./Tex. State Employees Union, Austin, 1987-90; trustee Austin Cen. Labor Coun. AFL-CIO, Austin, 1983-84. Vol. AFL-CIO Polit. Action Com., 1980—; del. founding conv. Labor Party, 1996. Recipient Vols. in Politics award Nat. ALF-CIO, Washington, 1984, Peacemaker award Travis County Dispute Resolution Ctr., 1993. Mem. Comm. Workers Am./Tex. State Employees Union Local 6186 (founding mem.). Avocation: pre-colombian archaeology. Home: 1118 Mclain St Taylor TX 76574-2343 Office: Tex Dept Mental Health and Mental Retardation PO Box 12668 909 W 45th St Austin TX 78711-2668 Office Phone: 512-419-2305. Personal E-mail: dzul@texas.net. Business E-Mail: jim.pearson@hhsc.state.tx.us.

PEARSON, JOHN EDWARD, lawyer; b. Jamaica, N.Y., Aug. 20, 1946; s. Stanley Charles and Rose Margaret (Manning) P.; m. Laura Marie Johannes, Dec. 28, 1968; children: Laura Rose, Jack. BA, Manhattan Coll., 1968; JD, St. John's U., 1972. Bar: N.Y. 1973, Fla. 1981, U.S. Dist. Ct. (so. dist.) N.Y. 1977, U.S. Dist. Ct. (so. dist.) Fla. 1982, U.S. Ct. Appeals (11th cir.) 1982, U.S. Ct. Appeals (5th cir.) 1982. Assoc. Sage, Gray, Todd & Sims, N.Y.C., 1972-78, ptnr., 1979, Miami, Fla., 1980-87, Hughes, Hubbard & Reed, Miami, 1987-91, 94-98, counsel, 1998—2002; ptnr. Hughes, Hubbard & Reed, N.Y.C., 1992-93. Author jour. article (Best Article award 1971). With USMCR, 1968-69. Mem. ABA, Fla. Bar Assn., N.Y. State Bar Assn., Assn. Bar City N.Y., Dade County Bar Assn., N.Y. County Lawyers Assn., Greater Miami C. of C. (trustee). Republican. Roman Catholic. Avocations: sailing, running. Home: 180 Harbor Dr Key Biscayne FL 33149-2409 E-mail: jep8436@aol.com.

PEARSON, JOHN YEARDLEY, JR., lawyer; b. Norfolk, Va., July 23, 1942; BA, Washington & Lee U., 1964; JD, U. Va., 1971. Bar: Va. 1971. Atty. Willcox & Savage P.C., Norfolk. Mem editl. bd.: Va. Law Rev., 1969-71. Fellow Am. Coll. Trial Lawyers; mem. ABA (litig. sect.), Internat. Assn. Def. Counsel, Order of Coif. Office: Willcox & Savage PC 1800 Bank of America Ctr Norfolk VA 23510-2197

PEARSON, KELLY JEANNE, education educator; b. Porterville, Calif., Mar. 10, 1970; d. Othel Lee and Marcia Jeanne Pearson; m. Tan Zhang, Apr. 4, 1969. AA, Porterville Coll., 1987—89; BS, Calif. State U., 1991—93; MS, Utah State U., 1993—95; PhD, U. of Oreg., 1995—2000. Asst. prof. Math. Dept, Murray State U., Murray, Ky., 2000—; grad. tchg. fellow Math. Dept, U. of Oreg., Eugene, Oreg., 1995—2000. Contbr. articles. Recipient Frank Anderson Excellence in Tchg., Math. Dept, U. of Oregeon, 1999. Mem.: Am. Math. Soc. Office: Murray State University Mathematics Dept Murray KY 42071 E-mail: kelly.pearson@murraystate.edu.

PEARSON, KEVIN, health facility administrator; Pres. Med-Index (divsn. Medicode Inc.); CFO Medicode Inc., COO; sr. mgr. Ernst & Young, San Francisco; CEO health intelligence divsn. Ingenix, Unitedhealth Group, Inc., Minnetonka, Minn., 1990—2003, CEO, 2003—. Office: Unitedhealth Group Ctr 9900 Bren Rd E Minnetonka MN 55343

PEARSON, LARRY LESTER, journalism educator; b. Sioux Falls, S.D., Sept. 27, 1942; s. Lester Loren and Lois Ursula (Cochran) P.; m. Alice Marie Simons, Sept. 15, 1979; children: Gregory Eric, Hillary Yvette, Andrew Todd. BA cum laude, U. Minn., 1964, PhD, 1990; MA, U. Wis., 1969. Newsman UPI, Mpls., 1962-63; newsman Daily American, Rome, 1964-65; instr. Journalism Sch., U. Wis., 1965-67; with Mpls. Tribune, 1967-85, wire editor, 1970-72, news editor, 1972-82, Mpls. Star & Tribune, 1982; with Anchorage Daily News, 1996—. Asst. prof. U. Alaska, Anchorage, 1985-92, assoc. prof., 1992-99, dir. Ctr. for Info. Tech., 1990-92; spl. cons. to Alaska Ho. Com. on Telecomm., 1985-90; propr. Online Design, 1995—. Home: 2410 E 16th Ave Anchorage AK 99508-2906 E-mail: design@alaska.net.

PEARSON, MICHELLE LINE, private school educator, not-for-profit fundraiser; b. Marin, Calif., Dec. 9, 1968; d. Robert E. and Lina V. Howe; m. Kirk D. Pearson, June 18, 1994; children: Connor L., Alex J., Andrew D. BA, Mary Wash. Coll., Fredericksburg, Va., 1992. Cert. tchg. Va., 1992, lic. profl. tchg. Colo., 2004. Tchr. Woodland Acad., Montross, Va., 1992—94, Annunciation Sch., Denver, 1995—. Dir. of hist. preservation Annuncaition Parish, Denver, 1996—; edn. cons., Broomfield, Colo., 1999—. Author: (collection of lessons) White House History in the Classroom (White Ho. History Fellowship in Pre-Collegiate Edn., 2003), (lesson collection) The Wright Brothers, (educational video insert) Tour of the White House. Bd. commr. Mamie Dowd Eisenhower Libr., Broomfield, Colo., 2004—; coord. restoration and preservation of sacred places Archdiocese of Denver/Annunciation Parish, Denver, 1999; faith action steering com. Hist. Denver, Denver. Recipient Mem.- US All Tchr. Team, Gannett Newspapers/USA Today, 1997, Classroom Connection Outstanding Tchr., Xcel Energy Found., 1998-2004; fellow Fulbright Tchr. Meml. Fund, IIE/FMF, 1997, William B. Hosokawa Fellowship, Japan Am. Soc., 2002; grantee Environ. Edn. in the Classroom, nat. Cath. Sch., 1999, Colo. Hist. Soc. Grants, Colo. Hist. Soc., 1998-2003, Ben and Jerry's Found., 1999; scholar Constn. Rights Found. Program Scholarship, CRF, 2003, White Ho. Seminar Travel Scholarship, White Ho. Hist. Soc., 2000, Japan Studies Leadership Scholarship, Freeman Found., 1998; White Ho. Fellowship, White Ho. Hist. Soc., 2003. Mem.: Nat. Coun. for History Edn., Orgn. of Am. Historians, Colo. Coun. of the Internat. Reading Assn. Liberal. Catholic. Avocations: travel, reading, quilting. Office: Annunciation Sch 3536 Lafayette St Denver CO 80020

PEARSON, PAUL DAVID, lawyer, arbitrator, mediator; b. Boston, Jan. 22, 1940; s. Bernard J. and Ruth (Bayla) Horblit; m. Carol A. Munschauer; children: David Todd, Lisa Kari, Grant M. BA, Bucknell U., 1961; LLB, U. Pa., 1964. Bar: Mass. 1966, NY 1987. Staff atty., tech. assoc. lab. cmty. psychiatry dept. psychiatry Med. Sch. Harvard U., Boston, 1966-68; assoc. Snyder Tepper & Berlin, Boston, 1968-71; ptnr., 1971-77; ptnr., chmn. family law dept. Hill & Barlow, 1977-87; ptnr. chmn. family law dept. Hodgson, Russ, LLP, Buffalo, 1987—96; of counsel Sullivan Oliverio & Gioia, 1996—. Lectr. Mass. Con. Legal Edn., New Eng. Law Inst., dept. psychiatry SUNY Sch. of Medicine, Buffalo, 1989—; instr. law and mental health Boston Psychoanalytic Soc. and Inst., 1975-87; lectr. in law, mental health, alternative dispute resolution. Contbr. articles to profl. jour. and interdisciplinary publ. Founding mem. Alliance for Dispute Resolution, 1996, Buffalo Collaborative Law Coun., 2002; bd. dir. Jewish Cmty. Ctr. Greater Buffalo, 1991-96, Am. Jewish Com. Buffalo, 1991—, pres., 1995-97, nat. bd. govs., 1997—; bd. dir. Arts Coun. Buffalo and Erie County, 1992-99; legal coord. Parent Edn. And Custody Effectiveness program NY 8th jud. dist.; pres., trustee, legal counsel Wayland (Mass.) Townhouse; trustee Family Counseling Svc. (region West); mem., chmn., clk. Wayland Zoning Bd. Appeals, 1970-80; v.p., counsel Arts Wayland Found., 1982-87; vis. fellow Woodrow Wilson Found., 1985-87, Mass. Gov. Spl. Commn. on Divorce, 1985-87. Capt. Mil. Police Corps USAR. Fellow Am. Acad. Matrimonial Lawyers (pres., bd. mgr. Mass); mem. Mass. Bar Assn. (chmn. family law sect.), Assn. Conflict Resolution (advanced practitioner), NY State Coun. on Divorce Mediation, Assn. Family and Conciliation Ct., Boston Bar Assn. (family law com., legis. chmn.), NY Bar Assn. (family law com., ADR com.), Erie County Bar Assn. (chmn. alternative dispute resolution com. 1992-96, family law com., judiciary com.),Am. Bar Assn. sections of Dispute Resolution & Family Law (chair, ADR and Family Function Comm.) Home: 605 Lebrun Rd Amherst NY 14226-4232 Office: 600 Main Place Tower Buffalo NY 14202-3706 Office Phone: 716-854-5300. Office Fax: 716-854-5299. Business E-Mail: ppearson@soglawny.com.

PEARSON, PAUL HAMMOND, physician; b. Bolenge, Belgian Congo; s. Ernest B. and Evelyn (Utter) P. BS, Northwestern, 1944, B.Medicine, 1946, MD, 1947; M.P.H., UCLA, 1963. Diplomate: Am. Bd. Pediatrics. Intern Los Angeles County Gen. Hosp., 1946-47; resident Cin. Children's Hosp., 1949-51; fellow convulsive disorders and electroencephalography Johns Hopkins Hosp., Balt., 1951-53; resident in child psychiatry U. B.C., Can., 1976-77; practice medicine specializing in pediatrics L.A., 1953-62; chief mental retardation br. USPHS div. chronic disease, 1963-65; asst. dir. mental retardation program Nat. Inst. Child Health and Human Devel., NIH, 1965-66; spl. asst. to surgeon gen. USPHS, 1966-67; C.L. Meyer prof. child health, prof. pub. health and preventive medicine, dir. Meyer Children's Rehab. Inst., 1967-81, McGaw prof. adolescent medicine, dir. adolescent medicine, 1982-89, prof. emeritus dept. pediatrics, 1989—; mem. grad. faculty U. Nebr. Coll. Medicine, Omaha, 1967—, med. dir. Univ. Hosp. Eating Disorder Program, 1983-89, sr. cons. Univ. Hosp. Eating Disorder Program, 1989—. From instr. to asst. clin. prof. U. So. Calif. Med. Sch., 1953-62; from assoc. clin. prof. pediatrics to clin. prof. pediatrics Georgetown U. Sch. Medicine, Washington, 1963-67; Cons., mem. profl. services program com. United Cerebral Palsy Assn., 1969-72, mem. nat. awards com., 1971; Am. Acad. Pediatrics liaison rep. to Am. Acad. Orthopedic Surgery, 1969-73; apptd. to Nat. Adv. Council Services and Facilities for Developmentally Disabled Dept. Health. Edn. and Welfare, 1971-75; councilor Accreditation Council Facilities for Mentally Retarded, Joint Commn. on Accreditation Hosps., 1973-74; fellow adolescent medicine Boston Children's Hosp. Med. Center, 1981 Cons. editor: Am. Jour. Mental Deficiency, 1970-72; Contbr. articles to profl. jours. Mem. com. on accessible environments Nat. Acad. Scis., 1974-77. Served to capt. MC AUS, 1947-49. Mem. Am. Acad. Pediatrcs (com. on children with handicaps 1969-75, com. sect. on child devel. 1974—), Am. Assn. Mental Deficiency, Nat. Assn. for Retarded Children, Greater Omaha Assn. for Retarded Children (dir.), Am. Pub. Health Assn., Am. Acad. Cerebral Palsy and Developmental Medicine (exec. com. 1971-76, chmn. sci. program com. 1972-74, sec. 1974-77, mem. research and awards com. 1977-78, pres. 1981-82, bd. dirs. 1982-84), Assn. Univ.-Affiliated Facilities (exec. com. 1973—, v.p. 1974-75, pres. 1975-76, dir. 1971-78), Soc. Adolescent MedicineAlpha Omega Alpha. Home: 3247 N Boulder Cyn Mesa AZ 85207-1846 Office: U Nebr Med Ctr Dept Pediatrics Omaha NE 68198-0001

PEARSON, PAUL HOLDING, insurance company executive; b. Worcester, Mass., Feb. 14, 1940; s. Malcolm D. and Myra L. (Holding) P.; m. Judith N. Howe, July 13, 1958 (div. June 1974); children: Scott D., Todd E.; m. Anne Beck, July 26, 1974. BA in Bus. and Econs., U. Maine, 1961. C.L.U., 1971. Jr. life underwriter State Mut. Am., Worcester, 1961-63, life underwriter, 1963-67, sr. life underwriter, 1967-69; dir. life underwriting Security Mut. Life Ins. Co., Binghamton, N.Y., 1969, 2d v.p. underwriting, 1970, v.p., 1971-75, sr. v.p. ins. services div., 1975-79, exec. v.p., 1979-81, pres., 1981-96, chief exec. officer, 1987-97; chmn. Security Mutual Life Ins. Co. of N.Y., Binghamton, 1996-97. Chmn., CEO, bd. dirs. SML Properties corp., Binghamton, Security Equity Life Ins. Co., Binghamton, 1987-93; vice chmn. Generalife, 1997-99. Trustee, treas. Lourdes Meml. Hosp., Binghamton, 1978-92; mem. SUNY Found., Binghamton, 1982-89; trustee, chmn. fin. com. Elmira Coll., 1983-87; bd. dirs. Broome C.C. Found., 1982-91, pres. 1985-86; pres. New Industries for Broome, Binghamton, 1985-95, N.Y. State Bus. Devel. Coun., 1987-96; bd. dirs. Valley Devel. Found., 1987-91, Bus. Coun. N.Y., 1988-97, Am. Coun. Life Ins., 1990-96; bd. dirs., treas. Fiddlesticks C.C., 2002-; bd. dirs., treas. Fiddlesticks CC, 2002-. Mem. Assn. for Advanced Life Underwriting, Nat. Assn. Life Underwriters, Broome County C. of C. (bd. dirs. 1980-88, chmn. 1986), Binghamton C/C Live Wire Club. Office Phone: 239-768-0162.

PEARSON, R. SCOTT, investment advisor, editor; b. Putnam, Conn., Aug. 27, 1961; s. Walter Donald and Elsa Viola (Swanson) P. BA, Samford U., 1985; MBA, U. South Fla., 1992. Editor Pearson Investment Letter, Dover, Fla., 1990-98; instr. fin. U. South Fla., Tampa, 1993-95, 2002; counselor Consumer Credit Counseling Svcs., Tampa, 1996-98; editor, pub. Investor's Value View, Winter Park, Fla., 1999—; instr. fin. Webster U., Altamonte Springs, Fla., 1999—; investment advisor Value View Fin. Corp., Winter Park, 1999—, 2002. Market commentator Investor's TV News Mag., Orlando Fla., 1999-2000; columnist Englewood Sun-Herald/Venice Gondolier, Fla., 1997-2000. Mem. Fla. Fedn. Young Reps. (platform com. chair 2000-01, mem. Orange County chpt.), Greater Orlando C. of C. Christian. Avocations: tennis, skiing, travel, music, beach. Office: Value View Fin Corp Ste 2000 2254 Winter Woods Blvd Ste B Winter Park FL 32792-1928 E-mail: ValueView@aol.com.

PEARSON, RALPH GOTTFRID, chemistry professor; b. Chgo., Jan. 12, 1919; s. Gottfrid and Kerstin (Larson) P.; m. Lenore Olivia Johnson, June 15, 1941 (dec. June 1982); children: John Ralph, Barry Lee, Christie Ann. BS, Lewis Inst., 1940; PhD, Northwestern U., 1943. Faculty Northwestern U., 1946-76, prof. chemistry, 1957-76, U. Calif., Santa Barbara, 1976-89, prof. emeritus, 1989—. Cons. to industry and govt., 1951— Co-author 5 books. Served to 1st lt. USAAF, 1944-46. Recipient Chemical Pioneer award Am. Inst. Chemists, 1995; Guggenheim fellow, 1951. Mem. Am. Chem. Soc. (Midwest award 1966, Inorganic Chemistry award 1969), Nat. Acad. Sci., Phi Beta Kappa, Sigma Xi, Phi Lambda Upsilon (hon.) Lutheran. Achievements include being originator prin. of hard and soft acids and bases.

PEARSON, RICHARD JOSEPH, archaeologist, educator; b. Kitchener, Ont., Can., May 2, 1938; s. John Cecil and Henrietta Anne (Wallwin) P.; m. Kazue Miyazaki, Dec. 12, 1964; 1 child, Sarina Riye. BA in Anthropology with honours, U. Toronto, 1960; PhD, Yale U., 1966. Asst. prof., then assoc. prof. archaeology U. Hawaii, 1966-71; mem. faculty U. B.C., Vancouver, 1971-2000. Conf. chmn. Internat. Jomon Conf., 2003. Author: The Archaeology of the Ryukyu Islands, 1969, Higashi Ajia no Kodai Shakai to Kokogaku, 1984, Windows on the Japanese Past, Studies in Archaeology and Prehistory, 1986, Ancient Japan, 1992; contbr. articles to profl. jours. Guggenheim fellow. E-mail: pearsonrj@shaw.ca.

PEARSON, ROBERT GREENLEES, writing services company executive; b. Kansas City, Mo., Feb. 19, 1917; s. Ridley Stillson and Agnes (Greenlees) P.; m. Laura Gray Betsy Dodge, Jan. 3, 1945; children— Bradbury, Wendy, Robert Ridley. AB with honors, U. Kans., 1938. Mgr. corp. pub. rels. Shell Oil Co. (N.Y. Head Office), 1938-71; v.p. pub. rels. Council Better Bus. Bur. (N.Y. Hdqrs.), 1971-73; writer pub. affairs dept. Mobil Oil Corp., N.Y.C., 1973-74; sr. advisor Alcoholics Anonymous World Services, Inc., N.Y.C., 1974-85; pres. Robert Pearson Assocs., Writing Svcs., Riverside, Conn., 1985—. Bd. dirs. Nat. Safety Council; pres. Fairfield County (Conn.) Council on Alcoholism, 1962 Author: Oil for Victory, 1946, The J.C. Nichols Chronicle, 1994; contbr. articles to profl. jours. Served to lt. comdr. USNR, 1941-45. Mem.: Riverside (Conn.); Yacht, Dutch Treat. Congregationalist. Home and Office: 38 Fox Hollow Rd Bellevue ID 83313

PEARSON, ROBERT LAWRENCE, executive recruiter; b. Chgo., Apr. 19, 1939; s. Jonas Peter and Caroline Margaret (Reilly) P.; m. Norma Eloise Dale, April 27, 1963; children: Jill C., Keith D. BSEE, Mich. State U., 1961; MS magna cum laude, MIT, 1963. Cons. McKinsey and Co., Inc., Chgo., 1964-68; v.p. Raymond James and Assoc., St. Petersburg, Fla., 1968-70; pres. Pearson Wade and Co., Inc., Ft. Lauderdale, Fla., 1970-71, Pearson, Inc., Racine, Wis., 1971-81; exec. dir. Russell Reynolds Assoc., Inc., Dallas, 1981-83; mng. dir. Lamalie Assoc., Inc., Dallas, 1984-89, chmn., 1989-94; pres. Lamalie Amrop Internat., Dallas, 1994-98, chmn., CEO, 1994—99; CEO Pearson Ptnrs. Internat., Inc., 1999—; mem., bd. dirs., CFO Tatum Inc., 1999—2003; mem. bd. dirs. Pentagon Techs. Inc., 2000—, Baird Capital Ptnrs. Inc., 2000—. Mem. fund raising com. Dallas Mus. of Art, 1983-85; mem. Dallas Mus. Natural History, 1985—, bd. dirs., 1988-90; mem. YMCA, Dallas; speech writer Gov.'s Campaign, Chgo., 1968. Contbr. articles to profl. jours. Mem. MIT Enterprise Forum, Dallas C. of C., Phi Delta Theta (pres. 1959-61), Tower Club (Dallas), MIT (Dallas), Gilda's Club (founding sponsor), Dallas Nat. Golf Club. Republican. Episcopalian. Avocations: squash, jogging, deep sea fishing, hunting, marathon running. Home: 3843 Maplewood Ave Dallas TX 75205-2828 Office: Pearson Ptnrs Internat Inc Ste 1480 8080 Central Expwy Dallas TX 75206

PEARSON, ROGER, organization executive; b. London, Aug. 21, 1927; s. Edwin and Beatrice May (Woodbine) P.; m. Marion Primrose Simms, June 3, 1959; children: Edwin, Sigrid, Emma, Rupert BS with honors, U. London, 1951, MS, 1954, PhD, 1969. Chmn. Pakistan Tea Assn., 1963-64; mng. dir. Octavius Steel & Co. of Pakistan Ltd., Chittagong, East Pakistan, 1959-65; chmn. Plummer Bros., Ltd., Chittagong, East Pakistan, 1959-65, Chittagong Warehouses, Ltd., Chittagong, East Pakistan, 1960-65; chmn. dept. sociology and anthropology Queens Coll., Charlotte, N.C., 1970-71; chmn. dept. anthropology U. So. Miss., Hattiesburg, 1971-74; dean acad. affairs, dir. research Mont. Coll. Mineral Sci. Tech., Butte, 1974-75; exec. dir. Council for Econ. and Social Studies, Washington, 1975—. Author: Eastern Interlude, 1954, Introduction to Anthropology, 1978, Anthropological Glossary, 1985, Race, Intelligence and Bias in Academe, 1991, Shockley on Eugenics and Race, 1992, Heredity and Humanity, 1996, Cultural Anthropology, 2002; editor: Ecology and Evolution, 1982, (jour.) Social Polit. and Econ. Studies, 1976—. Trustee, Benjamin Franklin U., Washington, 1984-87. Served to lt. Brit. Indian Army, 1945-48. Mem. Oriental Club, Reform Club (London), Army and Navy Club (Washington). Office: Coun Econ and Social Studies 1133 13th St NW Washington DC 20005-4203

PEARSON, ROGER LEE, library director; b. Galesburg, Ill., Dec. 7, 1940; s. Clifford Emmanuel and Lillian Louise (Fisher) P. BA, Knox Coll., 1963; MA in Sociology, U. Nebr.-Omaha, 1968; MA in Library Sci., Rosary Coll., 1974. Vol. U.S. Peace Corps, Brazil, 1964-66; extension service supr. Brown County Libr., Green Bay, Wis., 1974-75; system adminstr. Nicolet Libr. System, Green Bay, 1976-77; exec. dir. South Central Libr. System, Madison, Wis., 1977-81; dir. Corpus Christi Pub. Librs., Tex., 1981-84, Naperville (Ill.) Pub. Librs., 1984-95, Sonoma County Libr., Santa Rosa, Calif., 1996-2001; interim dir. Spokane (Wash.) Pub. Libr., 2001; interim libr. dir. Coll. of Marin, Kentfield, Calif., 2002; interim dist. libr. Dixon (Calif.) Pub. Libr., 2002—03; interim dir. Kans. City (Mo.) Pub. Libr., 2004. Lectr. Grad. Sch. Libr. and Info. Sci., Dominican U., River Forest, Ill., 1991-95. Mem. ALA, AARP, Train Riders Assn. Calif., Calif. Libr. Assn., Wine Libr. Assocs. Sonoma County. Avocations: power walking, travel research, train travel. Home: 1451 Country Manor Dr Santa Rosa CA 95401

PEARSON, RONALD DALE, retail food stores corporation executive; b. Des Moines, 1940; married. BS in Bus. Adminstrn., Drake U., 1962. With Hy-Vee Food Stores, Inc. (name changed to Hy-Vee, Inc. in 1996), Chariton, Iowa, 1962—; pres. Hy-Vee, Inc., Chariton, Iowa, 1983—, chmn., pres., & CEO, 1989—2001, chmn., CEO, COO, 2001—. Dir. Beverage Mfrs., Inc., Civic Ctr. Cts., Inc. Office: Hy-Vee Inc 5820 Westown Pkwy West Des Moines IA 50266-8223

PEARSON, RONALD EARL, educator, researcher; b. Worcester, Mass., Dec. 21, 1944; s. Earl Leon and Hilma (Dahlberg) P.; m. Joanne Miller, June 19, 1965; children: Stacey Lynne, Thomas Alan. BS, U. Mass., 1966; MS, Iowa State U., 1970, PhD, 1971. Rsch. geneticist USDA/ARS, Beltsville, Md., 1971-79; assoc. prof. Va. Poly. Inst. and State U., Blacksburg, 1979-84, prof., 1984—. Cons. Holstein Assn. Am., Brattleboro, Vt., 1986-91, Select Sires, Inc., Plain City, Ohio, 1987—, Jersey Catile Club, Reynoldsburg, Ohio, 1990—, vis. scientist dept. animal breeding Wageningen Agrl. U., 1994-95. Contbr. articles to profl. jours. Elder Northside Presbyn. Ch., Blacksburg, 1984-87; chair budget and fin. com. Presbytery of the Peaks, Lynchburg, Va., 1989-91, chair div. adminstrn., 1992. Recipient Rsch. award Nat. Assn. Animal Breeders, 1992. Mem. Am. Dairy Sci. Assn. (J.L. Lush Animal Breeding Rsch. award 1994). Avocation: raising dairy cattle. Office: Va Polytech Inst & State U Dept Dairy Sci 2100 Litton Reaves Hall Blacksburg VA 24061-0315

PEARSON, SELA, poet, speaker; b. Bklyn., Aug. 10, 1952; d. Thomas Turner and Thelma (Brown) Razor; m. Nassar Anwar Jonathan (dec.). BS, St. Joseph's Coll., Bklyn., 1988. LPN. Psychiat., pediat. nurse Syosset (N.Y.) Hosp., 1974-78; sales agent Combined Life Ins. Co. N.Y., Albany, 1978-80; med., surg. nurse Bapt. Med. Ctr., Bklyn., 1980-86; nurse counselor Riker's Island Prison Hosp., Queens, N.Y., 1986-88; clinic nurse St. Christopher Ottilie, Queens, 1988-90; intensive case mgr. AIDS Ctr. Queens County, 1990-92; quality assurance, utilization rev. nurse Vanderbilt U. Med. Ctr., Nashville, Tenn., 1992-94; program dir. Boys and Girls Club, Franklin, Tenn., 1994-95; spkr., writer, nurse Akanke Creations, Brentwood, Tenn., 1996—; ind. health contractor Clayton County Crisis Unit, 1997-98; nurse Phoenix Program FHC of Nashville, 1998-99; nurse Murci Homes, 1999—. Cons. Murphy Alternative Ctr., Nashville, 1996, Serendipity House, Nashville, 1996, Family and Ednl. Adv. Assocs., Inc., Nashville, 1996, Growing In Grace Leadership Sch., Nashville, 1996; storyteller, presenter poetry recitals; ind. contractor Crisis Group Home, Riverdale, Ga., Antara Ctr. Faculty mem., 2004. Author: New York Poetry Foundation Anthology, 1986, Beyond the Stars, 1995 (Editors Choice 1995), Sela's Sounds of Silence, 1995, A Soulful Journey, 2000; performer (video) A Soulful Journey, 1995, The Magic of Peace, 1996, Our Voices, 1996; author numerous poems; contbr. articles to profl. jours., mags. Vol. Williamson County Libr., Franklin, 1995—, Boys and Girls Club, Franklin, 1996—, TPAC; bd. dirs. Nashville Peace Action, 1996—; mem. New Gospel Singers Choir, 1995—; storytelling del. to South Africa People to People Amb. Programs, Invited Women in Soc. rep., Egypt, 2000—; mem. Coun. for the Written Word. Recipient Vol. Svc. award Berksheire Nursing Ctr., West Babylon, N.Y., 1977. Mayor's award for svc. in cmty. in the arts, 2001; icluson of poem Faith to Wm. Kings Regl. Art Ctr., 1999, Cmty. Svc. award Edith Taylor Langster, Ho. of Reps., 54th Dist., 2003. Mem. Nat. Spkrs. Assn., Brentwood Early Risers Toastmasters (v.p. membership 1996—, various awards), Tenn. Writers Alliance, Harpeth Storytelling Group, Nat. Storytelling Assn., Internat. Soc. Poets (Poets Choice award 1995, Internat. Poet of Merit award 1995), Tenn. Writers Group Franklin, Tenn. Assn. Perpetuation Preservation Storytelling, Ga. Writers Group, Creative Artists Tenn., Tenn. Spkrs. Assn., Women Vision Enhancing Network (cert., dir. pub. rels.), Cherokee Wolf Clan (tribal coun. mem.). Avocations: piano playing, travel, reading. Address: PO Box 111341 Nashville TN 37222-1341 Office Phone: 615-365-3187. E-mail: serenityrises@aol.com.

PEARSON, THOMAS ARTHUR, epidemiologist, educator; b. Berlin, Wis., Oct. 21, 1950; married; 2 children. BA, Johns Hopkins U., 1973, MD, MPH, Johns Hopkins U., 1976, PhD in Epidemiology, 1983. Fellow in cardiology Johns Hopkins Sch. Medicine, Balt., 1981-83, from asst. prof. to assoc. prof. medicine, epidemiology, 1983-88; prof. epidemiology Columbia U., 1988-97, prof. medicine, 1995-97; dir. Mary Imogene Bassett Rsch. Inst., 1988-97; prof. medicine, Jane Forbes Clark chair in health rsch. Columbia U., N.Y.C., 1995-97; Kaiser prof., chair Sch. Medicine U. Rochester, N.Y., 1997—. Chmn. monitoring bd. CARDIA project Nat. Heart, Lung and Blood Inst., 1987—; mem. rsch. com. Md. Heart Assn., 1986-88; chmn. data safety monitoring bd. HIT trial VA, 1994-98; commr. Md. Coun. Phys. Fitness, 1985-88; mem. clin. applications and prevention commn. NIH, 1987-91, chmn., 1990-91. Mem. ACP, Am. Heart Assn. (nat. rsch. com. 1987-92, coun. epidemiology 1987—, vice chmn. 1994-95, chmn. 1996-98), Am. Fedn. Clin. Rsch., Am. Coll. Epidemiology, Am. Coll. Preventive Medicine, Am. Coll. Cardiology (prevention com.), Soc. Epidemiol. Rsch. (rsch. prize 1978). Achievements include research in the etiology and pathogenesis of atherosclerosis. Office: U Rochester Sch Medicine Dept Cmty Preventive Med 601 Elmwood Ave Rochester NY 14642-0001 Office Phone: 585-275-2191.

PEARSON, TIMOTHY ALFRED, newspaper circulation executive; b. Meriden, Conn., May 29, 1955; s. Howard Lukens and Fran (Felchner) P BS, So. Ill. U., Carbondale, 1977. Circulation mgr. motor rt. and single copy sales The Columbian, Vancouver, Wash., 1992-94; dir. circulation The Sentinel, Howard Publs., Carlisle, Pa., 1994-95; mgr. sales devel. Ctrl. Maine Newspapers divsn. Guy Gannett Inc., Augusta, 1995-96; sales and mktg. mgr. So. Conn. Newspapers divsn. Times-Mirror, Stamford, 1996-98; circulation sales mgr. Hartford (Conn.) Courant, 1998; dir. mem. sales and svc. Seacoast divsn. Dow Jones, Inc., Portsmouth, NH, 1998—2001; with Times Herald-Record, Middletown, NY, 2001—02; dir. sales and mktg. Gazette Newspapers, Schenectady, NY, 2002—. Contbr., spkr. Anti-Defamation League World of Differnce Diversity Project, New Haven, 1996—. Mem. Dem. Nat. Com., Washington, 1972—. Mem. Nat. Wildlife Fedn., Nature Conservancy, Sierra Club, New Eng. Assn. Circulation Execs., N.Y. State Circulation Mgrs. Assn. Episcopalian. Avocations: travel, history, native american studies. Office: Daily Gazette 2345 Maxon Rd Ext Schenectady NY 12301

PEARSON, W. ROBERT, former ambassador; b. Bells, Tenn., June 28, 1943; s. Marion Robert and Louise (Wilson) P.; m. Margaret Coplin, June 20, 1975; 1 child, Matthew. BA, Vanderbilt U., 1965; LLB, U.Va., 1968. Vice consul U.S. Consulate Gen., Auckland, New Zealand, 1976-78; staff asst./Conf. Asia Bur. Dept. of State, Washington, 1978-79, Chinese lang. tng. officer Washington and Taiwan, 1979-81; polit. officer U.S. Embassy, Beijing, 1981-83; dep. dir. Ops. Ctr. Dept. of State, Washington and Taiwan, 1983-85; dep. exec. sec. Nat. Security Coun., Washington, 1985-87; dept. asst. sec. gen. NATO, Brussels, 1987-90; dep. exec. sec. Dept. of State, Washington and Taiwan, 1990-91, exec. sec., 1991—93; dep. permanent rep. to US mission NATO, 1993—97; dep. chief of mission US Embassy, France, 1997—2000; amb. to Turkey Dept. of State, 2000—03; chmn., bd. fgn. svc. US Dept. State, Washington, 2003—. Mem. Internat. Inst. of Strategic Studies. Office: Harry S Truman Bldg 2201 C St NW Rm 6218 Washington DC 20520

PEARSON, WALTER DONALD, editor, columnist; b. Pittsfield, Mass., Feb. 5, 1916; s. Edgar C. and Edna (Scott) P.; divorced; children: Florence, Donald, Sharon; m. Elsa Swanson (dec.); 1 child, Richard Scott. Student, Dartmouth Coll., 1941-43. Advt. salesman, 1935-41; securities broker Charles A. Day Co., Boston, 1947-55; founder, owner, mgr. First New Eng. Securities Co., Inc., Southbridge, Mass., 1955-71; now owner, editor Pearson Investment Letter, Dover, Fla.; ptnr. Pearson Capital Inc.; fin. columnist World Intelligence Rev., CDL Report, Nationalist Times; free-lance columnist various publications; fin. advisor, investment mgr. Author: Investing for the Millions, 1990, Bridge Made Easy, 1995 With inf. U.S. Army, 1943-45, ETO. Decorated Bronze star, Croix de Guerre (France), Combat Infantry badge. Home: 1628 White Arrow Dr Dover FL 33527-5741 Office Phone: 813-659-2560. Personal E-mail: PearsonCap@aol.com.

PEARSON, WALTER HOWARD, marine biologist, researcher; b. Troy, N.Y., Mar. 25, 1946; s. Howard Stevenson and Mazel Mott (Brownhill) P.; m. Cynthia-Ruth Egan, June 16, 1972 (div. Oct. 1989); children: Kristin Turnbull, Jeffrey Mott; m. Terri L. Sumner, Nov. 28, 1992. BS in Biology, Bates Coll., 1967; MS in Biology, U. Alaska, 1970; PhD in Oceanography, Oreg. State U., 1977. Fishery biologist, rschr. Nat. Marine Fisheries Svc., Sandy Hook Lab., Highlands, N.J., 1975-78; sr. rsch. scientist Battelle Marine Rsch. Lab., Sequim, Wash., 1978-88, tech. group leader marine scis. lab., 1988-91, mgr. tech. devel. program, 1991-93, sr. rsch. scientist, 1993-95, staff rsch. scientist, 1995-97, staff scientist, 2000—02, assoc. dir. Marine Scis. divsn., 2002—. Program dir. environ. studies program Western Wash. U., Port Angeles Ctr., 1993-98; head marine environ. rsch. ctr. Environ. Rsch. and Wildlife Devel. Agy., Abu Dhabi, United Arab Emirates, 1998-2000; tech. leader large multidisciplinary studies of oil spill effect. Contbr. articles on behavior of marine organisms and effects of pollution and human activity to jours. Sgt. U.S. Army, 1969-71. NSF grantee, 1967-69. Mem.: AAAS, Soc. Environ. Toxicology and Chemistry, Am. Fisheries Soc. Episcopalian. Avocations: hiking, canoeing. Home: 332 Viewcrest Ave Port Angeles WA 98362 Office: Battelle Marine Scis Lab 1529 W Sequim Bay Rd Sequim WA 98382-8415 Office Phone: 360-681-3661. Business E-Mail: walter.pearson@pnl.gov.

PEARSON, WILLIAM ROWLAND, retired nuclear engineer; b. New Bedford, Mass., Sept. 30, 1923; s. Rowland and Nellie (Hilton) P.; BS, Northeastern U., 1953; postgrad. U. Ohio, 1960; m. Arlene Cole Loveys, June 14, 1953 (dec.); children: Denise, Robert, Rowland, Nancy. Engr., Goodyear Atomic Corp., Portsmouth, Ohio, 1953-63, Cabot Titania Corp., Ashtabula, Ohio, 1963-64; supr. United Nuclear, Wood River, R.I., 1964-72; sr. engr. Nuclear Materials and Equipment Co., Apollo, Pa., 1972-74; engr. U.S. Nuclear Regulatory Commn., Rockville, Md., 1974-90, ret., 1990. Served with USNR, 1942-45. Decorated Air medal. Mem. AAAS, Am. Nuclear Soc., Am. Inst. Chem. Engrs. (chmn. 1966-67). Republican. Baptist. Clubs: Masons, Elks. Home: 60 Meeting Hill Rd Hillsboro NH 03244-4856

PEASBACK, DAVID R. recruiting company executive; 1 child, Jennifer. BA, Colgate U., 1955; LL.B., U. Va., 1961. Mgmt. trainee Proctor & Gamble, N.Y.C., 1955-56; assoc. Covington & Burling, Washington, 1961-64; litigation counsel Litton Industries, Inc., Beverly Hills, Calif., 1965-67; v.p. Bangor Punta Ops., Greenwich, Conn., 1968-71; assoc. Heidrick and Struggles, N.Y.C., 1972-76, ptnr., 1976-88, pres., CEO, 1983-87; vice-chmn., CEO Canny, Bowen, Inc., N.Y.C., 1988-98, chmn., CEO, pres., CEO, 1998—. Served as sgt. USMC, 1956-58 Office: Canny Bowen Inc 280 Park Ave Fl 30 New York NY 10017-1216

PEASE, DAVID GORDON, artist, educator; b. Bloomington, Ill., June 2, 1932; s. Gordon A. and June (Stephens) P.; m. Julie Jensen, Mar. 29, 1956; children: Lisa Kay, Kerry Susan. BS, U. Wis., 1954, MS, 1955, M.F.A., 1958. Instr. audio visual ctr. Mich. State U., 1958-60; mem. faculty Tyler Sch. Art, Temple U., Phila., 1960-83, prof., 1970-83, chmn. painting dept., 1968-77, dean, 1977-83; prof. of painting Yale U. Sch. Art, New Haven, 1983-2000, Street prof., dean emeritus, 2000—, dean, 1983-96, dir. grad. studies/painting, 1997-2000. Vis. faculty mem. Yale U. Summer Sch. Music and Art, 1970-72, Ohio State U., spring 2001. One-man shows include Baylor U., 1972, U. Wis., 1972, Pa. Acad. Fine Arts, 1977, Terry Dintenfass Inc., N.Y.C., 1969, 71, 76, Phila. Art Alliance, 1961, 70, Vassar Coll., 1999, Ohio State U., 2001; group exhbns. include Carnegie Internat., Pitts., 1961, Corcoran Biennial, Washington, 1961, 63, Whitney Annual, N.Y.C., 1963; represented in permanent collections Whitney Mus. Am. Art, Phila. Mus. Art, Pa. Acad. Fine Arts, Des Moines Art Center, Pa. State U., U. Wis., Temple U., Hallmark Cards Inc., Columbia Pictures, Yale U. Art Gallery, others. Trustee Louis Comfort Tiffany Found., 1988-97, 98—; bd. trustees Lyme Acad. Coll. Fine Arts, 1999—. With U.S. Army, 1955-57. Recipient William A. Clark award Corcoran Biennial, 1963, Lindbeck Found. Disting. Teaching award, 1968, Disting. Alumni award U. Wis., 1991; Guggenheim Found. fellow, 1965-66; Tiffany Found. grantee, 1975-76 Mem. Assn. Ind. Colls. Art and Design (trustee 1992-96). Home: 95 Thankful Stow Rd Guilford CT 06437-2529 E-mail: david.pease@yale.edu.

PEASE, EDWARD A, former congressman; b. Terre Haute, Ind., May 22, 1951; BA with distinction, Ind. U., 1973, JD cum laude, 1977; past postgrad. in English, Ind. State U. Past city atty. City of Brazil, Ind.; past gen. counsel Ind. State U., v.p. univ. advancement, 1993; past ptnr. Thomas Thomas & Pease; senator Ind. Gen. Assembly, 1980-92, past chmn. senate jud. com., past chmn. Ind. commn. trial cts., past chmn. Ind. code revision commn.; mem. U.S. Congress from 7th Ind. dist., 1997—2001, mem. jud. com., mem. transp. and infrastructure com. Past mem. adv. coun. on nat. coun. Boy Scouts Am., chmn. com. Nat. Order of Arrow. Recipient numerous awards Boy Scouts Am. Mem. Nat. interfraternity Conf. (bd. dirs.), Pi Kappa Alpha (nat. dir. alumni affairs, chpt. advisor, nat. pres.). Republican.*

PEASE, GERALD, state legislator; b. Hardin, Mont., July 21, 1954; m. Maria Pease. Cert., Missoula VoTech. Rancher; hwy. constrn. worker; Dem. rep. dist. 6 Mont. Ho. of Reps., 1997-98. Trustee Lodge Grass Sch. Bd.; mem. Ptnrs. in Policy Making, Parents Lets Unite for Kids. Office: PO Box T Lodge Grass MT 59050-0556

PEASE, STACEY LYN, music educator; d. Richard Nellis and Vicki Lyn Thompson; m. Cameron Len Pease. MusB, Miami U., Oxford, Ohio, 1999. Principle flutist, piccoloist West Chester (Ohio) Symphony, 1999—2002, libr., 2000—02; music tchr. Heritage Elem., West Chester, 2000, Adena Elem., West Chester, 2000—. Author: (musical) Shake Rattle and Roll, 2001; editor: Tales of Temples and Tombs, 2000. Mem. crisis com., West Chester, 2000—, PTO, West Chester, 2000—; dir. Pride Club, West Chester, 2003—, student coun. sponser, 2003—04. Mem.: NEA, Lakota Edn. Assn., Ohio Music Educators Conf., Music Tchrs. Nat. Conf. Avocations: flute, piccolo, coaching cheerleading, designing musicals for elementary children. Office: Adena Elem Sch 9316 Minuteman Way West Chester OH 45069 E-mail: stacey.pease@latoktaonline.com.

PEASE-PRETTY ON TOP, JANINE B. community college administrator; b. Nespelam, Wash., Sept. 17, 1949; d. Benjamin and Margery Louise (Jordan) Pease; m. Sam Vernon Windy Boy, July 30, 1975 (div. Jan. 1983); children: Rosella L. Windy Boy, Sam Vernon Windy Boy; m. John Joseph Pretty On Top, Sept. 15, 1991. BA in Sociology, Anthropology, Ctrl. Wash. U., 1970; MEd, Mont. State U., 1987, EdD, 1994; HHD (hon.), Hood Coll., 1990; LLD (hon.), Gonzaga U., 1991; DHL (hon.), Teikyo/Marycrest U., 1992; EdD (hon.), Whitman Coll., 1993; HHD (hon.), Rocky Mountain Coll., 1998. Dep. dir. Wash. State Youth Commn., Olympia, 1971; tutor student svcs. Big Bend C.C., Moses Lake, Wash., 1971-72, upward bound dir., 1972-75; women's counselor Navajo C.C., Many Farms, Ariz., 1972; dir. adult & continuing edn. Crow Ctrl. Edn. Commn., Crow Agy., Mont., 1975-79; ednl. cons. Box Elder, Mont., 1979-81; dir. Indian career svc. Ea. Mont. Coll., Billings, 1981-82; pres. Little Big Horn Coll., Crow Agency, 1982—. Exec. com. Am. Indian Higher Ednl. Consortium, Washington, 1983—; bd. dirs. Am. Indian Coll. Fund, N.Y.C., 1988—; sec. Indian Nations at Risk U.S. Dept. Edn., Washington, 1990-91, collaborator task force, 1990-91; 2d vice chmn. Nat. Adv. Coun. Indian Edn., Washington, 1994—. Chmn. Bighorn County Dem. Ctrl. Com., Hardin, Mont., 1983-88; mem. coun. First Crow Indian Bapt. Ch., 1989—; bd. dirs. Ctr. for Rocky Mountain West, 1998—; chmn. Mont. State Reappt. an dDistructing Commn., 1999—. MacArthur fellow John D. & Catharine MacArthur Found., 1994. Mem. Nat. Indian Edn. Assn. (Indian educator of yr. 1990), Mont. Assn. Chs. (bd. dirs. 1997—), Crow Tribe Nighthawk Dance Soc. Office: Little Big Horn Coll PO Box 370 Crow Agency MT 59022-0370

PEASLEE, JAMES M. lawyer; b. Scranton, Pa., Sept. 1, 1952; s. Robert Victor and Jean (Mark) P. BA, MA, Yale U., 1973; JD, Harvard U., 1976; LLM in Taxation, NYU, 1979. Bar: N.Y. 1977. Assoc. Cleary, Gottlieb, Steen & Hamilton, N.Y.C., 1976-84, ptnr., 1984—. Office: Cleary Gottlieb Steen & Hamilton 43d Fl 1 Liberty Plz Fl 43D New York NY 10006-1404

PEASLEE, JANICE L. state legislator, agricultural products executive; b. Auburn, Maine, Jan. 20, 1935; m. Bert H. Peaslee; five children. Co-owner Peaslee's Vt. Potatoes; mem. Vt. Ho. of Reps., Montpelier, 1989—. Mem. govt. ops. com., clk. transp. com., Vt. Ho. Reps; mem. state bd. trustees, Rep. state exec. com., state legis. com. Former town auditor, former pres., mem. Essex County Sch. Bd.; chmn. Coos-Essex Com. for Agrl. Awareness. Mem. Farm Bur., Eastern Star, 4-H Club (orgn. leader), Conn. Valley Sno-Riders. Home: PO Box 12 Guildhall VT 05905-0012 Office: Vt House of Reps Office of House Mems Montpelier VT 05602

PEASLEE, MARGARET MAE HERMANEK, zoology educator; b. Chgo., June 15, 1935; d. Emil Frank and Magdalena Bessie (Cechota) Hermanek; m. David Raymond Peaslee, Dec. 6, 1957; 1 dau., Martha Magdelena Peaslee-Levine. AA, Palm Beach Jr. Coll., 1956; BS, Fla. So. Coll., 1959; med. technologist, Northwestern U., 1958, MS, 1964, PhD, 1966. Med. technologist Passavant Hosp., Chgo., 1958-59; med. technologist St. James Hosp., Chicago Heights, Ill., 1960-63; asst. prof. biology Fla. So. Coll., Lakeland, Fla., 1966-68; asst. prof. of biology U. S.D., Vermillion, SD, 1968-71, assoc. prof., 1971-76, prof., 1976, acad. opportunity liaison, 1974-76; prof., head dept. zoology La. Tech. U., Ruston, La., 1976-90, assoc. dean, dir. grad. studies and rsch., prof. biol. scis. Coll. Life Scis., 1990-93; v.p. for acad. affairs U. Pitts. at Titusville, Titusville, Pa., 1993—. Contbr. articles to profl. jours. Fellow AAAS; mem. AAUP, Am. Inst. Biol. Scis., Am. Soc. Zoologists, S.D. Acad. Sci. (sec.-treas. 1972-76), N.Y. Acad. Scis., Pa. Acad. Sci., La. Acad. Sci. (sec. 1979-81, pres. 1983), Sigma Xi, Phi Theta Kappa, Phi Rho Pi, Phi Sigma, Alpha Epsilon Delta. Office Phone: 814-827-4473. Business E-Mail: peaslee@pitt.edu.

PEAT, RANDALL DEAN, defense analysis company executive, retired air force officer; b. Chicago, July 6, 1935; s. Thomas R. and Lulu M. (Ray) P.; m. Joyce Enid Hunter, Sept. 15, 1956; children— Brian James. Sondra Lee Peat Gadell BS in Journalism, Medill Sch. Journalism Northwestern U., Evanston, Ill., 1956, MS in Journalism Mgmt., 1957. Commd. officer U.S. Air Force, 1957, advanced through ranks to maj. gen.; pilot, instr. Strategic Air Command, Westover AFB and Clinton-Sherman, Okla., 1958-66; asst. air attache Am. Embassy, Djakarta, Indonesia, 1967; pilot Pacific Command Airborne Command Post, Hickam AFB, Hawaii, 1968-70; staff officer 7th Air Force, Saigon, Vietnam, 1971, Hdqrs. U.S. Air Force, Pentagon, D.C., 1972-75, SHAPE, Belgium, 1976-79, Hdqrs. U.S. Air Force, Pentagon, D.C., 1980-81; dep. dir. plans Office Joint Chief of Staff, Pentagon, D.C., 1982-84; asst. chief of staff ops. Supreme Hdqrs. Allied Powers Europe, Belgium, 1984-87; chief of staff Strategic Air Command, Offutt AFB, Nebr., 1987-89; v.p. R&D Assocs., Europe, 1989—2002. Decorated Air medal, Bronze Star, Meritorious Service medal, Def. Superior Service medal, Def. Disting. Service medal; Republic of Vietnam Cross of Gallantry with Palm, Republic of Vietnam Campaign medal Mem. Daedalians (vice flight capt. 1976), Air Force Assn., Pi Alpha Mu Avocations: cooking; hiking; painting; British mystery writers. Home: 28 Likely Rd Santa Fe NM 87508

PEAVY, HOMER LOUIS, JR., real estate executive, accountant; b. Okmulgee, Okla., Sept. 4, 1924; s. Homer Louis and Hattie Lee (Walker) P.; m. children: Homer Martin, Daryl Mark. Student, Kent State U., 1944-49; grad., Hammel-Actual Coll., Ohio, 1962. Sales supr. Kirby Sales, Akron, Ohio, 1948-49; sales mgr. Williams-Kirby Co., Detroit, 1949-50; area distributor Peavy-Kirby Co., Phila., 1953-54; salesman James L. Peaby Realty Co., Akron, 1964-65; owner Homer Louis Peavy Jr., Real Estate Broker, Akron, 1965—; pvt. practice acctg. Akron, 1962—. Fin. aid officer Buckeye Coll., Akron, 1982. Author: Watt Watts, 1969; poet: Magic of the Muse, 1978, P.S. I Love You, 1982; contbr. poetry to Am. Poetry Anthology, 1983, New Worlds Unlimited, 1984, Treasures of the Precioys Moments, 1985, Our World's Most Cherished Poems, 1985; songs: Sh..Sh, Sheree, Sheree, 1976, In Akron O, 1979; teleplay: Revenge, 1980. Bd. dirs. Internat. Elvis Gold Soc., 1978—; charter mem. Statue of Liberty-Ellis Island Found., 1984, Nat. Am. Indian, U.S. Holocaust Meml. Mus.; mem. Nat. Trust Hist. Preservation, Ohio Hist. Soc., Preservation/N.C., Japanese Am. Nat. Mus.; charter mem. USS Constn. Recipient Am. Film Inst. Cert. Recognition, 1982, Merit cert. World Poetry 10th ann. contest, 1985, Golden Poet award World of Poetry, 1985, 87-89. Mem. NAACP (mem.-at-large), Ohioana Libr. Assn., Internat. Black Writers Conf., Acad. Am. Poets, Poetry Soc. Am., Smithsonian Nat. Assocs., Manuscript Club Akron, Ohio Theatre Alliance, Kent State U. Alumni Assn. Democrat. Home and Office: 1160 Cadillac Blvd Akron OH 44320-2858

PEAY, J.H. BINFORD, III, retired army officer; b. Richmond, Va., May 10, 1940; m. Pamela Jane Pritchett; children: James, Ryan. BS, Va. Mil. Inst., 1962; MA, George Washington U., 1975; grad., U.S. Army Command and Gen. Staff Coll., U.S. Army War Coll. Commd. 2d lt. U.S. Army, 1962, advanced through grades to gen., 1993, ret., 1997, commd. gen., 101st Airborne Divsn., 1989—91, vice chief staff, 1993; comdr. in chief U.S. Ctrl. Command, MacDill AFB, Fla., 1994-97; ret., 1997; chmn. bd., CEO, Allied Def. Group, 2001—03; supt. Va. Mil. Inst., 2003—. Served in Viet Nam, 1967-68, 71-72, Desert Storm, 1991. Decorated Silver Star, Legion of Merit with oak leaf cluster, D.S.M. with three oak leaf clusters, Def. D.S.M., Purple Heart, Bronze Star medal with three oak leaf clusters. Home: 412 VMI Parade Lexington VA 24450-2115

PECA, MICHAEL, professional hockey player; b. Toronto, Ont., Can., Mar. 26, 1974; Center Vancouver Canucks, 1993—95, Buffalo Sabres, NC, 1995—2000; player NY Islanders, 2001—, Team Canada Olympic Hockey Team, 2002. Recipient Gold medal, Can. Team World Jr. Championships, 1994, Can. Games, Olympic Games, 2002. Office: New York Islanders 1535 Old Country Rd Plainview NY 11803-5014

PECANO, DONALD CARL, automotive manufacturing executive; b. L.A., Dec. 2, 1948; s. Domenick Lawrence and Carlotta Noble (Martello) P.; m. Sandra Ann Tuminello, Apr. 26, 1969; children: Julia Ann, Melissa Ann, Donald Carl. BS in Acctg, Pa. State U., 1970; MBA in Mktg., Youngstown State U., 1981. CPA, Pa.; cert. mgmt. acct., cert. fin. mgr. Contr. Atlas Guard Svc. subs. SERVISCO, East Orange, N.J., 1974-76; asst. to pres. SERVISCO, Hillside, N.J., 1976-77; v.p. fin. Columbus Svcs., Inc. subs. SERVISCO, New Castle, Pa., 1977-82; dir. fin. East Mfg. Corp. and subs. cos., 1982-88, v.p. fin. and adminstrn., 1988-99, also mem. exec. com., exec. v.p., CFO, 1999—; v.p. fin. Intermodal Techs. Inc., 1991—. Bd. dirs. Intermodal Techs. Inc. Weatherhead fellow Case Western Res. U., 1995. Republican. Roman Catholic. Office: 1871 State Route 44 Randolph OH 44265 *Placing the best interests of the company ahead of your own is ultimately in your own best interest.*

PECCARELLI, ANTHONY MARANDO, lawyer; b. Newark, Apr. 12, 1928; s. Adolph and Mary (Marano) P.; m. Mary Dearborn Hutchison, Dec. 23, 1953; children: Andrew Louis, David Anthony, Laura Elizabeth. BS, Beloit Coll., 1952; JD, John Marshall Law Sch., 1959; M in Jud. Studies, U. Nev., 1990. Bar: Ill. 1961, U.S. Dist. Ct. (no. dist.) Ill., U.S. Supreme Ct. Supr. real estate and claims Gulf Oil Corp., Chgo., 1956-61; asst. state's atty. DuPage County, Wheaton, Ill., 1961-65; first asst. state's atty. DuPage County State's Atty., Wheaton, Ill., 1965-69; mem.-del. Ill. Constnl. Conv., Springfield, 1969-70; exec. dir. Ill. State's Atty. Assn., Elgin, 1970-71; ptnr. Barclay, Damisch & Sinson, Chgo., 1971-79; assoc. cir. judge 18th Jud. Cir. Ct., Wheaton, 1979-82, cir. judge, 1982-93, chief judge, 1989-93, presiding judge domestic rels. divsn., 1982-83, presiding judge law divsn., 1987-89, chief judge, 1989-93; justice 2nd dist. Ill. Appellate Ct., Wheaton, 1993-94; state's atty. DuPage County, Wheaton, Ill., 1995-96; assoc., of counsel Ottosen Trevarthen Britz Kelly & Cooper, Ltd., Wheaton, Ill., 1996—. Exec. Conflict Resolution Ltd.; chair Ill. Jud. Conf. Ill. Supreme Ct., Springfield, 1987-89. Contbr. articles to profl. jours. Bd. dirs., treas. DuPage Coun. for Child Devel.; bd. dirs. Ctrl. DuPage Pastoral Counseling Ctr.; chair Wheaton Com. for Jud. Reform, 1962; trustee Midwestern U., 1993—, vice chmn., bd. trustees 1997-99. Cpl. USMC, 1946-48. Mem. DuPage County Bar Assn. (pres. 1972-73), DuPage County Legal Assistance Fedn. (pres. 1973-74), DuPage County Lawyer Referral Svc. (pres. 1972). Office Phone: 630-682-0085.

PECHILIS, WILLIAM JOHN, lawyer; b. Brockton, Mass., May 13, 1924; s. John and Kaleroe (Karmeris) P.; m. Kay Dillon, June 7, 1958; children: Julie W., Karen P., John D. BA, Harvard U., 1946, LLB, 1951. Bar: Mass. 1951. Law clk. to assoc. justice Supreme Judicial Ct., Boston, 1951-52; assoc. Goodwin Procter LLP, Boston, 1952-61, ptnr., 1961-94, of counsel, 1995—. Trustee Concord (Mass.) Acad., 1978-80, Wang Inst. Grad. Studies, Tyngsboro, Mass., 1979-87, Wang Ctr. for Performing Arts, 1983—, Anatolia Coll., Boston, 1984-91; mem. fin. com. Weston, Mass., 1972-74. With USNR, 1943-46, PTO. Fellow Am. Coll. Trust and Estate Counsel; mem. ABA, Mass. Bar Assn., Boston Bar Assn., Harvard Club, Weston Golf Club, Woods Hole Golf Club, Phi Beta Kappa. Avocation: golf. Home: 59 Jericho Rd Weston MA 02493-1209 Office: Goodwin Procter LLP Exchange Pl Boston MA 02109-2881

PECHUKAS, DIANA GISOLFI **See GISOLFI, DIANA**

PECHUKAS, PHILIP, chemistry professor; b. Akron, Ohio, Oct. 30, 1942; s. Alphonse and Evelyn (Grebenak) P.; children: Rolf Birkhoff, Maria Berenson, Sarah Landau, Fiona Veronese, Amy Hayes. BS, Yale U., 1963; PhD, U. Chgo., 1966. Asst. prof. chemistry Columbia U., N.Y.C., 1967-72, assoc. prof., 1972-78, prof., 1978—, chmn. dept. chemistry, 1984-87. Contbr. articles to profl. jours. Fellow Nat. Bur. Standards, 1966-67, Alfred P. Sloan Found., 1970-74, J.S. Guggenheim Found., 1975, Haverford Coll., 1985; Rockefeller Found. resident fellow Bellagio Study Ctr., 2000. Fellow AAAS, Am. Phys. Soc.; mem. Am. Chem. Soc. (chmn. theoretical chemistry subdivision 1985-86), Humboldt Sen. Scientist, 1993-94. Office: Columbia Univ Dept Chemistry 3000 Broadway New York NY 10027-6941 E-mail: pechukas@chem.columbia.edu.

PECHURA, CONSTANCE MARY, foundation official; BS, Va. Commonwealth U., 1980; PhD, Uniformed Svcs. U. Health Scis, 1987. Lab. asst. dept. pharmacology Med. Coll. Va., Richmond, 1977-79, rsch. asst. dept. surgery, divsn. neurosurgery, 1979-81; staff fellow NIH-NINDS, 1987-88; sr. program officer Inst. Medicine, Washington, 1989-98, dir. divsn. neurosci. & behavioral health, 1994-98; sr. program officer Robert Wood Johnson Found., Princeton, N.J., 1998—. Contbr. chpts. to books and articles to profl. jours. Bd. dirs., trainer, counselor Richmond Hotline, 1975-78; dir., counselor Rape Crisis Outreach, Richmond, 1976-78; mem., chair bd. dirs. Student Pugwash, Washington, 1995-2000. Office: Robert Wood Johnson Found PO Box 2316 Rte 1 and College Rd E Princeton NJ 08543-2316

PECK, ABRAHAM, editor, writer, educator, media consultant; b. N.Y.C., Jan. 18, 1945; s. Jacob and Lottie (Bell) Peckolick; m. Suzanne Wexler, Mar. 19, 1977; children: Douglas Benjamin, Robert Wexler. BA, NYU, 1965; postgrad., CUNY, 1965-67; cert. in advanced exec. program, Northwestern U., 1997. Engaged in cmty. organizing and tutoring, 1962-64; with N.Y.C. Welfare Dept., 1965-67; free-lance writer, 1967—; writer, organizer Chgo. Action Youth Internat. Party, 1968; editor Chgo. Seed, 1968-70; treas. Seed Pub., Inc., 1968-70; mem. coordinating com. Underground Press Syndicate, 1969; assoc. editor Rolling Stone mag., San Francisco, 1975-76, contbg. editor, 1976-2001; cons. various mags., 1984—; ednl. cons. Asian Sources Media Group, Hong Kong, Manila, 1989-97; editl. co-auditor Advanstar Comm., 1999—; strategic content cons. Putman Media, 2003—04; feature writer Chgo. Daily News, 1977-78; with features dept. Chgo. Sun-Times, 1978-81; from asst. prof. to prof. Medill Sch. Journalism Northwestern U., Evanston, Ill., 1981—2001, Theodore R. & Annie Laurie Sills prof. journalism, 2001—, dir. mag. programs Media Mgmt. Ctr., 2002—. Editor, co-founder Sidetracks, alt. newspaper supplement, Chgo. Daily News, 1977—78; critic at large Sta. WBBM, 1979—82; mem. exec. com. mag. divsn. Assn. Edn. Journalism and Mass Communication, 1987—89, 1992—96, 2003—04, pres., 1994—95; mem. adv. bd. Academe mag., AAUP, 1990—2000, Heartland Jour., 1990—2002, Technos, 1992—, Chgo. chpt. Asian Am. Journalists Assn., 2002—; chair ethics subcom. Am. Bus. Media, 2002. Editor: (book) Dancing Madness, 1976; author: Uncovering the Sixties: The Life and Times of the Underground Press, 1985, 1991; consulting editor, contbr.: The Sixties, 1977, contbr.: The Eighties: A Look Back, 1979, Voices From the Underground, 1993. With U.S. Army, 1967. Recipient Mag. Divsn. Educator of Yr., Assn. Edn. Journalism and Mass Comm., 2003—04. Office: Northwestern U Medill Sch Journalism 1845 Sheridan Rd Evanston IL 60208-0815 Office Phone: 847-491-2068. Business E-Mail: a.peck@northwestern.edu.

PECK, ANDREA SUE, writer, educator; d. Morton and Malvene Phyllis Peck. BA in Psychology, U. Mich., Ann Arbor, 1976; MA in Comm., Kent State U., Ohio, 1984. Prodn. asst. WVIZ Pub. TV, Parma, Ohio, 1985—86; asst. prodr. Cuyahoga CC, Cleve., 1986—88, coord., sr. edn., 1992—96, editor, writer, 1996—99, asst. prof., 1999—. Cons. Carpenters Union, Cleve. Contbr. chapters to books, articles to profl. jours. Mem.: Assn. for Psychol. Type. Avocations: yoga, skiing, hiking. Office: Cuyahoga CC 11000 Pleasant Valley Rd Parma OH 44130

PECK, ANDREW JAY, federal judge; b. 1953; AB, Cornell U., 1974; JD, Duke U., 1977. Bar: N.Y. 1978, U.S. Dist. Ct. (so. dist.) N.Y., U.S. Ct. Appeals (2d thru 11th cirs.), U.S. Supreme Ct. Law clk. to Hon. Paul Roney, U.S. Ct. Appeals for 5th Circuit, St. Petersburg, Fla., 1977-78; from assoc. to counsel Paul, Weiss, Rifkind, Wharton & Garrison, N.Y.C., 1978-95; magistrate judge for so. dist. N.Y., U.S. Dist. Ct., N.Y.C., 1995—, chief magistrate judge for so. dist. N.Y., 2004—. Adj. prof. Cardozo Law Sch. Editor Duke Law Jour., 1976-77. Mem. ABA, Fed. Magistrate Judges Assn., Mystery Writers Am. Inc. (exec. v.p.), Order of Coif. Office: 1370 US Courthouse 500 Pearl St New York NY 10007-1316 Office Phone: 212-805-0036.

PECK, AUSTIN H., JR., lawyer; b. Pomona, Calif., Dec. 25, 1913; s. Austin H. and Helen (Templeton) P.; m. Jean Albertson, Nov. 9, 1939 (dec. Aug. 1997); children: Julie (dec.), Francesca, Lisa; m. Janice Galloway, Apr. 3, 1998 (dec. May 2001); m. Carolyn P. Amory, May 2, 2004. AB with distinction, Stanford, 1935, JD, 1938. Bar: Calif. 1938. Practiced in, L.A., from 1938; mem. Latham & Watkins, 1946-76, of counsel, 1976-92. Mem. nat. coun. House Ear Inst. Mem. ABA, Calif. Bar Assn., L.A. Bar Assn., Calif. Club, L.A. Country Club, Birnam Wood Club (Montecito, Calif.), Valley Club (Montecito), Zeta Psi, Phi Delta Phi. Home: 2108 Forge Rd Santa Barbara CA 93108-2262 Office: 633 W 5th St Los Angeles CA 90071-2005

PECK, CAROLE, food service executive; m. Bcrnard Cabernet. Student, Culinary Inst. Am.; apprentice with Fernand Granger, Le Pavillon. Exec. chef Hilton Head Sea Pines Plantation Resort, Fisher Island, Miami, Fla., Cafe Greco, N.Y.C.; opened Carole Peck's restaurant, Hunt Hill Farms, Conn.; owner, chef Good News Cafe, Woodbury, Conn. Selected chef Julia Child Cookbook Awards. Named one of Nation's Top Young Chefs, Food Arts mag., 1992, 1994; named to honor roll of eight chefs from around the country, Eating Well mag., 1994. Avocation: collecting American folk art. Office: Good News Cafe 694 Main St South Woodbury CT 06798

PECK, CAROLYN, professional basketball coach; b. Jefferson City, Tenn. BA in Comm., Vanderbilt U., 1988. Mktg. cons., Nashville; salesperson; profl. basketball player Nippondenso Corp., Japan, 1991-93; asst. coach U. Tenn., U. Ky., 1995-96, Purdue U., West Lafayette, Ind., 1996-97, coach, 1997-98; head coach, gen. mgr. Orlando (Fla.) Miracle, 1999—. Asst. coach USA Jones Cup team, 1997. Named AP Coach of the Yr., 1999, IKON/WBCA Div. I Nat. Coach of the Yr., 1999. Office: Orlando Miracle Two Magic Pl 8701 Maitland Summit Blvd Orlando FL 32810-5915

PECK, CHARLES EDWARD, retired construction and mortgage executive; b. Newark, Dec. 1, 1925; s. Hubert Raymond and Helen (White) P.; m. Delphine Murphy, Oct. 15, 1949; children: Margaret Peck Iovino, Charles Edward, Katherine Peck Koustmer, Perry Anne Peck Flanagan. Grad., Phillips Acad., 1943; student, MIT, 1944; BS, U. Pa., 1949; PhD in Pub. Svc. (hon.), Univ. Md. Univ. Coll., 1995. With Owens-Corning Fiberglas Corp., 1949-81, from sales mgr. home bldg. products to exec. v.p., 1975-81; co-chmn. The Ryland Group, Columbia, Md., 1981-82, chmn., CEO, 1982-91; dir. The Delaware Group of Funds, 1991-2000; sec. Enterprise Homes, Inc., 1992-2000, New Homes by Enterprise, Inc., 2000-01; ret., 2001. Statutory vis. com. U.S. Nat. Bur. Standards, 1972-77; adv. com. Fed. Nat. Mortgage Assn., 1977-78, 85-86; vis. com. MIT-Harvard Joint Ctr. for Urban Studies; chmn. Prodrs. Adv. Forum, 1977-81; mem. nat. adv. bd. Way Sta., 2004—. Vis. com. Harvard U. Grad. Sch. Design, 1981-86; chmn. Howard County United Way Campaign, Md., 1987; chmn. Cmty. Partnerships, 1991-94; bd. dirs. Nat. Inst. for Urban Wildlife, 1986-90, United Way Ctrl. Md., 1987-91, Howard County Gen. Hosp., 1988-94, NAHB Rsch. Found., 1989-92, Alliance to End Childhood Lead Poisoning, 1990-93, Meml. Hosp. Found., 2004—; adv. bd. U. Md. Engring. Sch., 1990-2003, Continuing Edn. Johns Hopkins U., 1988-91; policy adv. bd. Harvard Joint Ctr. Housing Studies, 1984-94; chancellor's adv. com. U. Md. Sys., 1988-2001, chmn., 1988-99; chmn. Univ. Md. Found., 1990-94, bd. dirs., 1990—; bd. visitors U. Md. Ctr. Environ. Sci., 2001—; exec. fellow Kennedy Sch., Harvard U., 1990-92; chmn. Affordable Housing Initiative, Columbia, Md., 1990-92; bd. overseers U. Md., College Park, 1994-97; bd. visitors Sch. Law U. Md., Balt., 1996-2004; vis. com. U. Md. Univ. Coll., 1997—; bd. dirs. Ctr. for Grant Devel., 1994-98, Victory '94 com. Md. State Rep. party, chmn. election inquiry funding com., 1994-95; chmn. Children of Separation and Divorce Ctr., 1995-2000; pres. adv. coun. Washington Coll., Chestertown, Md., 1997—, chmn., 2000—; mem. Commn. on Future, Howard C.C. bd. visitors, 1999-2002; mem. Howard County Delta Project; pres. Peck Family Found., 1992—; co-chmn. Smart Growth Forum, 2001; bd. dirs. Columbia Festival of Arts, Md., 1988-91, 2002-03. Mem. U.S. C. of C. (bd. dirs. 1975-81), Ohio C. of C. (bd. dirs. 1975-81), Depression and

Related Affective Disorders Assn. (pres. 1986-89, bd. dirs. 1986-2000, pres. 1993-94), Talbot Country Club, City Club, Ctr. Club, Caves Valley Golf Club, Phi Gamma Delta. Home and Office: 6855 Pea Neck Rd Saint Michaels MD 21663-2725 Office Phone: 410-745-3205. Personal E-mail: tpeck@toad.net.

PECK, DALLAS LYNN, retired geologist; b. Cheney, Wash., Mar. 28, 1929; s. Lynn Averill and Mary Hazel (Carlyle) P.; m. Tevis Sue Lewis, Mar. 28, 1951 (dec.); children: Ann, Stephen, Gerritt; m. Carmella M. Benson, Apr. 29, 1995. BS, Calif. Inst. Tech., 1951, MS, 1953; PhD, Harvard U., 1960. With U.S. Geol. Survey, 1954-95, asst. chief geologist, office of geochemistry and geophysics, 1967-72, geologist, geologic div., 1972-77, chief geologist, 1977-81, dir., 1981-93, geologist, 1993-95, emeritus scientist, 1995—. Mem. Lunar Sample Rev. Bd., 1970-71; chmn. earth scis. adv. com. NSF, 1970-72; vis. com. dept. geol. scis. Harvard U., 1972-78; mem. Earthscis. Adv. Bd., Stanford U., 1982-93; chmn. com. earth scis. Fed. Coord. Coun. Sci., Enring. and Tech., 1987-92; mem. sci., tech. com. UN Decade for Nat. Disaster Reduction, 1992-94. Recipient Meritorious Svc. award Dept. Interior, 1971, Disting. Svc. award, 1979; Presdl. Meritorious Exec. award, 1980, Disting. Alumni award Calif. Inst. Tech., 1985, Ian Campbell medal Am. Geol. Inst., 1994. Fellow AAAS (pres. sect. E 1996-97), Geol. Soc. Am., Am. Geophys. Union (pres. sect. volcancology, geochemistry and petrology 1976-78). Home: 2524 Heathcliff Ln Reston VA 20191-4225 Office Phone: 703-648-6448. E-mail: dpeck@usgs.gov.

PECK, DANIEL FARNUM, chemical company executive; b. Port Jervis, N.Y., Aug. 6, 1927; s. John Flint and Frances Ann (Farnum) P.; m. Ardyce Chase Hoover, July 14, 1951 (dec. July 1979); children: Cheryl H. Gerber, Daniel Farnum Jr., Lauric A. Peck Perry; m. Barbara Ann Gunning Gillinder, Sept. 5, 1980. BSChemE, Clarkson U., 1950. Field engr. Rsch. Corp., Bound Brook, N.J., 1950-51; process devel. engring. supr. Nat. Starch and Chem. Corp., Plainfield, N.J., 1951-55, prodn. dept. head, 1955-60, divsn. supt. Indpls., 1960-67, plant and mfg. mgr. Meredosia, Ill., 1967-72, dir. mfg., 1972-76, divsn. v.p., 1976-80, corp. v.p., 1980-84, group v.p., 1984-89, ret., 1989, also bd. dirs. Bridgewater, N.J. Mem. Envelope Mfrs. Assn., Soc. Chem. Industry, Adhesive Mfrs. Assn., Adhesive Sealant Coun. (pres. edn. found., bd. dirs.). Avocations: boating, golf, bridge, hunting, fishing.

PECK, DARRYL, software company executive; Degree, NYU, 1977, Columbia U., 1986. Gaffer various, 1979—89; pres. Inline Software, 1989—94, pres., CEO Cyberian Outpost, Kent, Conn., 1995—99, chmn., founder, 1999—. Office: Cyberian Outpost 25 N Main At PO Box 636 Kent CT 06757-1512 E-mail: dpeck@outpost.com.

PECK, DIANNE KAWECKI, architect; b. Jersey City, June 13, 1945; d. Thaddeus Walter and Harriet Ann (Zlotkowski) Kawecki; m. Gerald Paul Peck, Sept. 1, 1968; children: Samantha Gillian Gildersleeve, Alexis Hilary. BArch, Carnegi-Mellon U., 1968. Architect P.O.D. R&D, 1968, Kohler-Daniels & Assocs., Vienna, Va., 1969-71, Beery-Rio & Assocs., Annandale, Va., 1971-73; ptnr. Peck & Peck Architects, Occoquan, Va., 1973-74, Peck Peck & Williams, Occoquan, Va., 1974-81; corp. officer Peck Peck & Assocs., Inc., Woodbridge, Va., 1981—. CEO interior design group Peck Peck & Assocs., 1988—; mem. archtl. rev. bd. Prince William County, 1998—, chair 2000—. Work pub. in Am. Architecture, 1985. V.p. Vocat. Edn. Found., 1976; chmn. architects and engrs. United Way, Indsl. Devel. Authority of Prince William, 1976, vice chair, 1977, mem. 1975-79, chmn. Prince William County Arch-Rev. Bd., 2001-04, mem., 2004—; mem. Health Sys. Agy. of No. Va., commendations 1977, Washington Profl. Women's Coop.; developed rsch. project Architecture for Adolescents, 1987-88; mem. inaugural class Leadership Am., 1988, Leadership Greater Washington D.C. Coun. Metrication, 1992—, D.C. Hist. Preservation League, Rep. Nat. Com. Recipient commendation Prince William Bd. Suprs., 1976, State of Art award for Contel Hdqrs. design, 1985, Best Middle Sch. award Coun. of Ednl. Facilities Planners Internat., 1989, Creativity award Masonry Inst. Md., 1990, First award, 1990, Detailing award, 1990, Govt. Workplace award for renovations of Dept. of Labor Bldg., 1990, Creative Use of Materials award Inst. of Bus. Designers, 1991, 1st award Brick Inst. Md., 1993, award Brick Inst. Va., 1994, Bull Elephant award Prince William County Young Reps., 1995, Detailing & Craftsmanship award Washington Builder's Congress, 1998; winner Archtl. Design Competition Vis. Pavillion Bur. Engraving and Printing, 2002; named Best Instl. Project Nat. Comml. Builders Coun.; subject of PBS spl.: A Success in Howard Co. Mem. Soc. Am. Mil. Engrs., Prince William C. of C. (bd. dirs.), Soroptimist Club. Roman Catholic. Research on inner-city rehab., adolescents and the ednl. environ. Office: 2050 Old Bridge Rd Woodbridge VA 22192-2447 Office Phone: 703-690-3121. Personal E-mail: dpeck@peckpeck.com.

PECK, EDWARD LIONEL, retired foreign service officer, corporate executive; b. Los Angeles, Mar. 6, 1929; s. Alexander George and Rae (Lee) P.; m. Heather Dianne Hicks-Beach, Jan. 20, 1957 (div. July 1971); m. Ann Day Slevin, May 5, 1974; children: Heather Anne, Brian Michael, Thomas William, Julia Katherine BS, UCLA, 1956; MBA, George Washington U., 1973. Joined Fgn. Service Dept. State, Washington, 1957, intelligence specialist, 1968-71, spl. asst., 1971-74; econ. counselor U.S. Embassy, Cairo, 1974-77; chief of mission U.S. Interests Sect., Baghdad, Iraq, 1977-80; dir. Office of Egyptian affairs Washington, 1980-82; ambassador U.S. Embassy, Nouakchott, Mauritania, 1983—85; dep. dir. Vice Pres.' Task Force on Combatting Terrorism, 1985-86; dir. Office of Career Transition, 1986-88; ret., 1989; pres. Fgn. Svcs. Internat., 1989—; exec. sec. Am. Acad. Diplomacy, 1989-92. Trainer, lectr., cons. on fgn. affairs, internat. bus., 1990—; dir. polit. tradecraft program Nat. Fgn. Affairs Tng. Ctr., Arlington, Va., 1991-96; sr. assoc. Global Bus. Access Ltd., Washington, 1991—; Woodrow Wilson vis. fellow, 1993—. Bd. dirs. Ams. for Middle East Understanding, 1999—; chmn. Coun. for the Nat. Interest Found., 2001-03. Served to capt. U.S. Army, 1946-49, 50-52 Recipient Meritorious Honor award Dept. State, 1967, 73, 77, 79, Superior Honor award Dept. State, 1974, 88, Wilbur J. Carr award, 1989; Rivkin award Am. Fgn. Svc. Assn., 1973 Home and Office: 106 Grafton St Bethesda MD 20815-3426

PECK, ELLIE ENRIQUEZ, retired state administrator; b. Sacramento, Oct. 21, 1934; d. Rafael Enriquez and Eloisa Garcia Rivera; m. Raymond Charles Peck, Sept. 5, 1957; children: Reginaldo, Enrico, Francisca Guerrero, Teresa, Linda, Margaret, Raymond Charles, Christina. Student polit. sci., Sacramento State U., 1974. Tng. svcs. coord. Calif. Divsn. Hwys., Sacramento, 1963-67, tech. and mgmt. cons., 1968-78; expert examiner Calif. Pers. Bd., Sacramento, 1976-78; tng. cons. Calif. Pers. Devel. Ctr., Sacramento, 1978; spl. cons. Calif. Commn. on Fair Employment and Housing, Sacramento, 1978; cmty. svcs. rep. U.S. Bur. of Census, No. Calif. counties, 1978-80; project dir. Golden State Sr. Discount Program, 1980-83; dir. spl. programs Calif. Lt. Gov., 1983-90; ret., 1990; pvt. cons., 1990—. Project dir. SSI/QMB Outreach Project, 1993-94; cons., project dir. nat. sr. health issues summit Congress Calif. Srs. Edn. and Rsch. Fund, 1995; project dir. various post-White House Conf. on Aging seminars and roundtables, 1995-97; coord. Calif. Sr. Legis., 2000-03; exec. dir. SMART Coalition Calif., 1997—2004. Mem. editl. adv. bd. Latino Jour. Mag., 1996—2002. Campaign workshop dir. Chicano/Latino Youth Leadership Conf., 1982—; chmn. ethnic minority task force Am. Diabetes Assn., 1988—90; steering com. Calif. Self-Esteem Minority Task Force, 1990—93; v.p. Comision Femenil Nacional, Inc., 1987—90; del. Dem. Nat. Conv., 1976, White House Conf. Aging, 1995—2004; mem. exec. bd. Calif. Dem. Ctrl. Com., 1977—95, mem., 1997—2001; bd. dirs. Sacramento/Sierra Am. Diabetes Assn., 1989—90; trustee Stanford Settlement Inc., Sacramento, 1975—79; bd. dirs. Sacramento Emergency Housing Ctr., 1974—77, Sacramento Cmty. Svcs. Planning Coun., 1987—90, Calif. Advs. for Nursing Home Reform, 1990—96, Calif. Human Devel. Corp., 1995—2003. Named Outstanding Advocate on Aging Issues, Calif. State Senate, 1998, Dem. Yr., Sacramento County Dem. Com., 1987; recipient Outstanding Cmty. Svc. award, Comunicaciones Unidos de Norte Atzian, 1975, 1977, Vol. Svc. award, Calif. Human Devel. Corp., 1998, Outstanding Svc. award, Chicano/Hispanic Dem. Caucus, 1979, Vol. Svc. award, Calif. Human Devel. Corp., 1981, Outstanding Advocate award, Calif. Sr. Legis., 1988—89, Meritorious Svc. to Hispanic Cmty. award, Comite Patriotico, 1989, Cert. Recognition, Sacramento County Human Rights Commn., 1991, Tish Sommers award, Older Women's League/Joint Resolution Calif. Legislature, 1993, Latino Eagle award in govt., 1994, Mentor Yr. award, Latina Leadership Network, 2002, Outstanding Vol. Svs. Throughout Yrs. award, Calif. Sr. Legislature, 2003. Mem. Hispanic C. of C., Older Women's League, Nat. Coun. Silver Haired Legislators, Nat. Coun. La Raza, Latina Leadership Network (Mentorship award 2002). Home and Office: 101 Simmons Way Folsom CA 95630

PECK, FRED NEIL, economist, educator; b. Bklyn., Oct. 17, 1945; s. Abraham Lincoln and Beatrice (Pikholtz) P.; m. Jean Claire Ginsberg, Aug. 14, 1971; children: Ron Evan, Jordan Shefer, Ethan David. BA, Binghamton (NY) U., 1966; MA, SUNY, Albany, 1969; PhM, NYU, 1984; PhD, Pacific Western U., 1984; MS in Edn., Coll. New Rochelle, 1993. Lectr. SUNY, Albany, 1969-70; research asst. N.Y. State Legislature, Albany, 1970; sales and research staff Pan Am. Trade Devel. Corp., N.Y.C., 1971; v.p., economist The First Boston Corp., N.Y.C., 1971-88; mng. dir. Sharpe's Capital Mkt. Assocs. Inc., N.Y.C., 1988-89; pres., chief economist Hillcrest Econs. Group, N.Y.C., 1989-93; dir. edn. The Ednl. Advantage, Inc., New City, N.Y., 1990-95; dir. Robert F. Kennedy Acad., N.Y.C. Dept. Edn., 1998—. Adj. prof. Hofstra U., Hempstead, NY, 1975, Mercy Coll., 2004—, Touro U., 2004—; lectr. NYU, 1982; faculty New Sch. for Social Rsch., NYC, 1974-94; coord. ednl. tech. NYC Bd. Edn., 1990-98. Author, editor: Handbook of Securities of U.S. Government, 1972-86. Mem. ASCD, Am. Econ. Assn., Ea. Econ. Assn., Econometric Soc., Nat. Assn. Bus. Economists, Am. Statis. Assn., Coun. Exceptional Children, Doctorate Assn. of N.Y. Educators, Beta Gamma Sigma (hon. soc.), Phi Delta Kappa. Lodges: Knights Pythias, Knights Khorassan. Democrat. Jewish. Office: Robert F Kennedy Acad 420 E 12th St New York NY 10009-4019 Office Phone: 212-420-4763. Personal E-mail: docfnp@bigfoot.com. E-mail: fpeck@nycboe.net. *March in one place long enough and eventually you will wind up leading the parade of progress...No one grows old. When you tire of learning, of experiencing new things you are old.*

PECK, GARNET EDWARD, pharmacist, educator; b. Windsor, Ont., Can., Feb. 4, 1930; s. William Crozier and Dorothy (Marentette) P.; m. Mary Ellen Hoffman, Aug. 24, 1957; children: Monique Elizabeth, Denise Anne, Philip Warren, John Edward. BS in Pharmacy with Distinction, Ohio No. U., 1957; MS in Indsl. Pharmacy, Purdue U., 1959, PhD, 1962. Sr. scientist Mead Johnson Research Center, 1962-65, group leader, 1965-67; assoc. prof. indsl. and phys. pharmacy Purdue U., West Lafayette, 1967—73, prof., 1973—2003, dir. indsl. pharmacy lab., 1975—, assoc. dept. head, 1989-96, prof. emeritus, 2003—. Cons. in field. Contbr. articles to profl. jours. Mem. West Lafayette Mayor's Advisory Com. on Community Devel., 1973-; mem. West Lafayette Citizen's Safety Com., 1974-81; mem. West Lafayette Park Bd., 1981-, pres., 1983-96. Served with U.S. Army, 1951-53. Recipient Lederle Faculty award Purdue U., 1976 Fellow APHA, AAAS, Am. Inst. Chem., Am. Assn. Pharm. Scientists; mem. Am. Chem. Soc., Acad. Rsch. and Sci. (Sidney Riegelman award 1994), Am. Assn. Colls. Pharmacy, Cath. Acad. Sci. (founding mem.), KC, Knight of Holy Sepulchre, Sigma Xi, Rho Chi, Phi Lambda Upsilon, Phi Kappa Phi, Phi Sigma Lambda, Phi Lambda Sigma. Roman Catholic. Office: Purdue U Sch Pharmacy & Pharm Scis Dept Industrial & Physical Pharm West Lafayette IN 47907 Business E-Mail: gepeck@pharmacy.purdue.edu.

PECK, H. DANIEL, literature educator; b. Milw., July 15, 1940; s. Henry Edward and Carmen (Barbulesco) P.; m. Patricia B. Wallace, Apr. 3, 1982; 1 child, Jennifer Peck; stepchildren: Christopher Wallace, Matthew Wallace. BA, Ohio Wesleyan U., 1962; MA, U. Iowa, 1971, PhD, 1974. Asst. prof. to assoc. prof. U. Calif., Santa Barbara, 1972-80; assoc. prof. Vassar Coll., Poughkeepsie, NY, 1980-83, prof. lit., 1983—, John Guy Vassar chair, 1999—. Dir. Am. culture program Vassar Coll., Poughkeepsie, NY, 1980—83, founding dir. environ. studies program, 2000—03. Author: Thoreau's Morning Work, 1990, A World by Itself: The Pastoral Moment in Cooper's Fiction, 1977; editor: The Green American Tradition, 1989, New Essays on the Last of the Mohicans, 1992, World's Classics edit. Fenimore Cooper's Deerslayer, 1993, A Year in Thoreau's Journal: 1851, 1993, Thoreau's A Week on the Concord and Merrimack Rivers, 1998, Mark Twain's The Adventures of Tom Sawyer, 2003; contbr. Columbia Lit. History of the U.S., 1988, Health Anthology of Am. Lit., 1996—. Am. Coun. Learned Socs. fellow, 1977-78; NEH sr.fellow, 1984, 94; Georgia O'Keeffe Mus. Rsch. Ctr. fellow, 2002. Mem. MLA (chmn. div. 19th Century Am. lit. 1986), Am. Studies Assn., New Eng. Am. Studies Assn. (coun. 1991-93), Assoc. for Study Lit. of Environ. (editl. bd., 1995—), John Burroughs Assoc. (bd. dir. 1994-2001). Home: 26 Sunrise Ln Poughkeepsie NY 12603-4213 Office: Vassar Coll Box 226 Poughkeepsie NY 12604-0226 E-mail: peckd@vassar.edu.

PECK, KENNETH E. lawyer; b. Carson City, Nev., June 20, 1950; s. Donald Leon and Thelma Louise (Robinson) P.; m. Katherine Louise Weeks, Oct. 20, 1973; children: Jason Z., Jennifer D., Joy H., Jessica K. BA in Polit. Sci. cum laude, U. Colo., 1971; MA in Pub. Adminstrn., U. Va., 1975; JD, Georgetown U., 1979. Bar: Colo. 1979, U.S. Dist. Ct. Colo. 1979, U.S. Ct. Appeals (10th cir.) 1980, U.S. Supreme Ct. 1983. Rsch. analyst Va. Hwy. Rsch. Coun., Charlottesville, 1972-73; budget and mgmt. analyst Prince Georges County Schs., Upper Marlboro, Md., 1974-76; chief legis. asst. U.S. Rep. Paul Trible, Washington, 1977-79; atty. Holland & Hart, Denver, 1979-83, Hopper & Kanouff, Denver, 1983-85, Phelps, Singer & Dunn, Denver, 1985-90, Law Firm of Kenneth E. Peck, Denver, 1990-98, Bushell & Peck, L.L.C., Denver, 1999—. Mem. nat., regional and state adv. councils SBA, 1981-86; mem. bd. appeals U.S. Dept. Edn., Washington, 1982-84; profl. lobbyist Colo. Legis., Denver, 1983-84; nat. commr. of econ. policy 1986 White House Conf. on Small Bus. Asst. campaign mgr. Jim Tate for Congress, Fairfax, Va., 1976; bd. dirs. Jefferson County Srs.' Resource Ctr., Wheatridge, Colo., 1982-88; pres. Arvada Rep. Club, Colo., 1982; mem. bd. mgrs. Northwest YMCA, Arvada, 1982-88. William McIntyre fellow U. Va., 1971-72; law fellow Georgetown U. Law Ctr., 1976-77. Mem. ABA (litigation sect., various coms.), Colo. Bar Assn. (various coms.), Colo. Assn. Comml. Industry (chmn. small bus. legis. com. 1983-85), Denver Bar Assn. (various coms.). Republican. Mem. Ch. of Christ. Avocations: golf, hiking, coaching youth sports. Home: 10935 W 68th Ave Arvada CO 80004-2744

PECK, LEONARD WARREN, JR., lawyer; b. El Paso, Tex., June 3, 1948; s. Leonard Warren and Perry Elizabeth (Lewis) Peck; m. Johanna Lee Blaschke, July 23, 1976; 1 child, Margaret Elizabeth. AB, Harvard U., 1970; JD, U. Tex., 1973. Bar: Tex. 1973, US Dist. Ct. (so. dist.) Tex. 1980, US Dist. Ct. (ea. dist.) Tex. 1980, US Dist. Ct. (we. dist.) Tex. 1980, US Dist. Ct. (no. dist.) Tex. 1984, US Ct. Appeals (11th cir.) 1981, US Supreme Ct. 1980. Analyst Tex. Gov.'s Office, Austin, 1974—75; cons. Atty. Gen. Tex. Office, Austin, 1976—80, asst. atty. gen., 1981; dir. R & D Tex. Dept. Corrections, Huntsville, Tex., 1981—82, legal counsel, 1982—2002. Trustee Tri-County MHMR Svcs., 1985—. Home: 489 Elkins Lk Huntsville TX 77340-7312

PECK, LOUIS MOSES, editor; b. N.Y.C., Apr. 16, 1951; s. Seymour and Susan (Lustig) P.; m. Nancy Jean Schwerzler, Sept. 5, 1987. BA in Am. History, Brown U., 1973. Govt. and politics reporter Frankfort (Ind.) Times, 1974-76, Poughkeepsie (N.Y.) Jour., 1976-78; regional corr. Gannett News Svc., Washington, 1978-82, congl. and polit. corr., 1983-87; editor Campaigns and Elections, Washington, 1988-89; freelance writer editor Washington, 1989-91; editor Congress Daily, Washington, 1991—; editor-in-chief Nat. Jour.'s Tech. Daily, 2000—. Vis. instr. Medill Sch. Journalism, Northwestern U., Washington, 1988, 90. Editorial cons.: Reform and Reality: The Financing of State and Local Campaigns, 1990, Financing Politics: Money, Elections and Political Reform, 1991. Mem. Washington Ind. Writers. Office: Nat Jour 1501 M St NW Washington DC 20005-1700 E-mail: lpeck@nationaljournal.com.

PECK, MALCOLM CAMERON, educational exchange specialist; b. Boston, Apr. 4, 1939; s. Wilfred Cameron and Ruth Lorriaux (Murdoch) P.; m. Adelaida Boquilon Ravelo, Dec. 30, 1972; 1 child, John Cameron. AB, Harvard U., 1961, AM, 1966; MA, Tufts U., 1963, MALD, 1964, PhD, 1970. Instr. U. Chattanooga (now U. Tenn.), 1967-68; postdoctoral fellow Harvard U., Cambridge, Mass., 1969-70; asst. to the pres., dir. programs Middle East Inst., Washington, 1970-81; Arabian peninsula affairs analyst U.S. Dept. State, Washington, 1981-83; program officer Meridian Internat. Ctr., Washington, 1984-2000, sr. program officer, 2000—. Pres., bd. dirs. nat. com. to Honor the 14th Centennial of Islam, Washington, 1979-83. Author: The United Arab Emirates: A Venture in Unity, 1986, Historical Dictionary of the Gulf Arab States, 1997; contbr. articles to profl. jours. Pres. Ch. of the Holy City, 1998-00. NDFL fellowship U.S. Govt., 1964-65; postdoctoral fellowship Harvard U., 1969-70. Mem. Middle East Studies Assn., Middle East Inst. (resident fellow 1983), Philippine Arts, Letters, and Media Coun. (sec. 1995—), Soc. for Gulf Arab Studies (co-founder, sec. 1987—). Democrat. Avocations: bicycling, music, reading. Home: 3118 1st St N Arlington VA 22201-1033 Office: Meridian Internat Ctr 1624 Crescent Pl NW Washington DC 20009-4004 E-mail: mpeck@meridian.org.

PECK, MARYLY VANLEER, retired academic administrator, chemical engineer; b. Washington, June 29, 1930; d. Blake Ragsdale and Ella Lillian (Wall) VanLeer; m. Jordan B. Peck, Jr., June 15, 1951; children: Jordan B. III, Blake VanLeer, James Tarleton VanLeer, Virginia Ellaine.; m. 2d, Walter G. Ebert, Sept. 3, 1983 (dec. June 1990); m. 3d Edwin L. Carey, Apr. 13, 1991. Student, Ga. Inst. Tech., 1948, 55-58, Duke U., 1947-48; B.Ch.E., Vanderbilt U., 1951; MSE., U. Fla., 1955, PhD, 1963. Chem. engr. Naval Research Lab., Washington, 1951-52; chem. engr. Med. Field Research Lab., Camp LeJeune, N.C., 1952; asso. research and instr. U. Fla., Gainesville, 1953-55; chem. engr., research asso. Ga. Tech. Expt. Sta., Atlanta, 1956-58; lectr. Ga. State Coll., Atlanta, 1957-58; lectr. math. East Carolina Extension, Camp Lejeune, 1959; sr. research engr. Rocketdyne div. N.Am. Aviation Co., 1961-63; self-employed as lectr., 1963; assoc. prof. Campbell Coll., Buie's Creek, N.C., 1963-66, prof., 1966; acad. dir. St. John's Episcopal Sch., Upper Tumon, Guam, 1966-68; chmn., prof. phys. scis. U. Guam, Agana, 1968-73, dean Coll. Bus. and Applied Tech., 1973-74, dean Community Career Coll., 1974-77; pres. Cochise Coll., Douglas, Ariz., 1977-78; systems planning analyst Urban Pathfinders, Inc., Balt., 1978-79; dean undergrad. studies U. Md. Univ. Coll., College Park, 1979-82; pres. Polk Community Coll., Winter Haven, Fla., 1982-97, pres. emeritus, 1997—; headmaster All Saints' Acad., 1997-99. Cons. in field. Founder, pres. Guam Acad. Found., 1972-77; bd. dirs. Cochise Coll. Found., 1977-78; charter bd. dirs. Turnaround Inc., 1987-91, chmn. 1990-93; bd. dirs. United Way Ctrl. Fla., 1986-95, vice-chmn., 1992, chair elect, 1993, chmn. 1994; founding mem. Prince George's Ednl. TV Cable Coalition; mem. Prince George's Cable TV Ednl. Adv. Group, 1980-82, Polk County Coun. Econ. Edn., 1982; sec. Polk C.C. Found., 1982-97; mem. Polk County Coord. Coun. Vocat. Edn., 1982-91, PRIDE Adv. Coun.; vice-chmn. Fla. Job Tng. Coord. Coun., 1983-87, Fla. Edn. Fund Bd., 1988-93; active Girls Inc. Bd., 1992—, pres., 2000-2001; trustee All Sts.' Acad. 1994-2002; mem. Vanguard Sch. Fdn. Bd., 2001-; bd. dirs. Theater Winter Haven, 2000—, chair, 2002-03. Named Disting. Alumnus U. Fla., 1992, Woman of Distinction, 1997, Woman of Distinction Girls Scouts U.S.A., 1994; fellow NSF, 1961-63; recipient She Knows Where She's Going award Girls Inc. of Winter Haven, 1995, Cmty. Svc. award Jr. League Winter Haven, 2002. Fellow Soc. Women Engrs. (nat. v.p. 1962-63); mem. AAUW, AIChE, Am. Chem. Soc., NSPE, Am. Assn. for Higher Edn., Am. Assn. Cmty. and Jr. Colls., Am. Assn. Univ. Adminstrs., Rotary (pres.-elect 2003-04, centennial pres. 2004—), Sigma Xi, Tau Beta Pi, Chi Omicron Gamma, Phi Kappa Phi, Delta Kappa Gamma. Episcopalian. Home: 1290 Howard Ter NW Winter Haven FL 33881-3158 E-mail: mpeck@tampabay.rr.com.

PECK, MERTON JOSEPH, economist, educator; b. Cleve., Dec. 17, 1925; s. Kenneth Richard and Charlotte (Hart) P.; m. Mary McClure Bosworth, June 13, 1949; children— Richard, Katherine, Sarah, David. AB, Oberlin Coll., 1949; AM, Harvard U., 1951, PhD, 1954; AM (hon.), Yale U., 1963. Teaching fellow, instr. econs. Harvard U., Boston, 1951-55, asst., then assoc. prof. bus. adminstrn., 1956-61; asst. prof. econs. U. Mich., Ann Arbor, 1955-56; dir. systems analysis Office Sec. Def., Washington, 1961-63; prof. econs. Yale U., New Haven, 1963—81, chmn. dept., 1968—74, 1977—84, acting dean sch. of orgn. and mgmt., 1986—88, Thomas DeWitt Cuyler prof., 1981—, prof. emeritus, 2002. Mem. Council Econ. Advisers, Exec. Office of Pres., 1968-69; cons. in field, 1954— Author: (with others) The Economics of Competition in the Transportation Industries, 1959, Competition in the Aluminum Industry, 1945-58, 1961, (with F. Scherer) The Weapons Aquisition Process, An Economic Analysis, 1962, (with others) Technological Change, Economic Growth and Public Policy, 1967, Federal Regulation of Television, 1973; editor The World Aluminum Industry in a Changing Energy Era, 1988; co-editor: What Is To Be Done? Proposals for the Soviet Transition to the Market, 1991, Competitiveness, The Impact of Public Policy, 1992; contbr. (with others) articles to profl. jours. With AUS, 1944-46. Mem. Am. Econ. Assn., Am. Assn. U. Profs., Lawn Club, Yale Club. Home: 27 Temple Ct New Haven CT 06511-6820 Office: Dept Econs Yale U PO Box 208268 New Haven CT 06520-8268 Office Phone: 203-432-3558.

PECK, MIRA P. lawyer; b. Minsk, USSR, Mar. 31, 1946; d. Wolf and Zofia (Wlaznik) Paszko; m. David O. Peck, May 15, 1971; children: Lena Ruth, Benjamin Jay. BEChemE, RMIT Univ., Australia, 1972; MS in Indsl. Adminstrn., Union Coll., 1976; JD, Rutgers U., 1984. Bar: N.J. 1984, U.S. Dist. Ct. N.J. 1984. Tchr. sci. Victoria Edn. Dept., 1971-72; process engr. GAF Corp., Rensselaer, N.Y., 1974-77; design engr. BASF Corp., Parsippany, N.J., 1977-80, product mgr., 1980-86, mgr. corp. strategic planning, 1986-92, v.p. tech. purchasing Mount Olive, N.J., 1993-2000; pvt. law practice Denville, N.J., 1984—. Mem., counsel Protect Wildlife Water and Woods, Denville, 1987—; mem. Mus. Modern Art, N.Y.C. Mem. ABA, NOW, N.J. Bar Assn., Am Inst. Chem. Engrs., Am. Humanist Assn., Amnesty Internat., Simon Wiesenthal Ctr., So. Poverty Law Ctr. Democrat. Avocations: art, writing, music, hiking, bicycling.

PECK, PAUL LACHLAN, minister; b. Glens Falls, N.Y., Sept. 11, 1928; s. Paul Lee and Caroline Jeannette (Stanton) Peck; children: Paul Barrett, Kathryn Elizabeth, Gretchen, Kole W. BS, U. Conn., 1952; ThD, Bernadean U., 1976; MEd, Westfield State Coll., 1983. Ordained to ministry Truth Ctr., 1972. With Proctor and Gamble Co., Watertown, N.Y., 1956-60; dir. deferred giving programs Syracuse (N.Y.) U., 1960-68, v.p., 1968-70, Fairleigh-Dickinson U., N.J., 1970-71, Manhattan Coll., Bronx, N.Y., 1971-75; founder, pastor Arete' Truth Ctr., San Diego, 1975—. Author: Footsteps Along the Path, 1978, Inherit the Kingdom, 1978, Milestones of the Way, 1978, Freeway to Health, 1980, Freeway to Work and Wealth, 1981, Freeway to Human Love, 1982, Freeway to Personal Growth, 1982, Your Dreams Count, 1990, Heroic Love Poems, 1990. Bd. dirs. Girl Scouts U.S.A., Syracuse, 1967-70; trustee, bd. dirs. Erickson Ednl. Found., 1970-75; vol. chaplain Auburn (N.Y.) State Prison, 1967-68; mem. chaplains' coun. Syracuse U., 1960-70; co-founder suicide and drug abuse prevention program Syracuse U., 1968-71, Fairleigh-Dickinson U., 1970-71, Manhattan Coll., 1971-75. Staff sgt. USNG, 1947-50. Mem. Internat. New Thought Alliance, SAR, Rotary, Knights of Malta (svc. award 1973), Masons, Shriners, Spiritual Frontiers Fellowship. Avocations: golf, book collecting.

PECK, RALPH BRAZELTON, civil engineering educator, consultant; b. Winnipeg, Man., Can., June 23, 1912; (parents Am. citizens); s. Orwin K. and Ethel Indie (Huyck) Peck; m. Marjorie Elizabeth Truby, June 14, 1937; children: Nancy Jeanne Peck Young, James Leroy. D in Civil Engring., Rensselaer Poly. Inst., 1937; postgrad., Harvard U., 1938; D Eng. (hon.), Rensselaer Poly. Inst., 1974; DSc (hon.), Laval U., 1987. Registered Ill., structural engr., Ill., civil engr., Calif. Structural detailer Am. Bridge Co., Ambridge, Pa., 1937; asst. subway engr. City of Chgo., 1939—43; chief engr. testing Holabird & Root, Scioto Ordnance Plant, Marion, Ohio, 1943; research asst. prof. soil mechanics U. Ill., Champaign-Urbana, 1943—48, research prof. found. engring., 1948—57, prof. found. engring., 1957—74, prof. emeritus, 1974—. Cons. in field. Author (with K. Terzaghi and G. Mesri): Soil Mechanics in Engineering Practice, 1948, 3rd edit., 1996; author: (with T.H. Thornburn and W.E. Hanson) Foundation Engineering, 1953, 2d edit., 1973, Judgment in Geotechnical Engineering: The Professional Legacy of Ralph B. Peck, 1984; contbr. articles to profl. jours. Named to Hall of Fame, Renssalaer Poly. Inst., 1998; recipient Disting. Civilian Svc. award, Dept. of Army, 1973, Moles Non-mem. award, 1973, Nat. Medal Sci., Pres. Gerald Ford, 1974, Golden Beaver award, 1983, Disting. Svc. award, Deep Founds Inst., 1984, Merit award, Am. Cons. Engrs. Coun., 1988. Fellow: Geol. Soc. Am. (sr.); mem.: NSPE (award 1972), ASCE (hon.; nat. dir. 1962—65, Norman medal 1944, Wellington prize 1965, Terzaghi award 1969, Washington award 1976,

Pres.'s award 1986, John Fritz medal 1987, Rickey medal 1988, Outstanding Projects and Leaders award 2001), NAE, Internat. Soc. Soil Mechanics and Geotech. Engring. (pres. 1969—73), Am. Acad. Arts and Scis., Mexican Soc. Soil Mechanics (hon.), Japanese Soc. Soil Mechanics (hon.), Southeast Asian Soc. Soil Mechanics (hon.), Phi Kappa Phi, Tau Beta Pi, Chi Epsilon, Sigma Xi. Home: 1101 Warm Sands Dr SE Albuquerque NM 87123-4328

PECK, RAYMOND CHARLES, SR., behavior research specialist, consultant; b. Sacramento, Nov. 18, 1937; s. Emory Earl and Margaret Helen (Fiebiger) P.; m. Ellie Ruth Enriquez, sept. 5, 1957; children: Teresa M. Peck Montijo, Linda M. Peck Heisler, Margaret V. Peck Henley, Raymond C., Christina M. Peck Reich. BA in Psychology, Calif. State U., Sacramento, 1961, MA in Exptl. Psychology, 1968. Rsch. analyst Calif. Dept. Motor Vehicles, Sacramento, 1962-71, sr. rsch. analyst, program mgr., 1971-80, rsch. program splst. II, 1980, 81-84, acting, chief rsch., 1980-81, chief rsch., 1984-2000; pres. R.C. Peck & Assocs., 2000—; sr. rsch. scientist Pacific Inst. for Rsch. and Evaluation, 2004—. Chmn. com. on operator regulation Transp. Rsch. Bd., NAS, 1976-82; statis. cons. in field. Past editl. adv. bds. Traffic Safety Evaln. Rsch. Review, Alcohol, Drugs and Driving; mem. editl. bds. Jour. Safety Rsch., Accident Analysis and Prevention; contbr. articles to profl. jours. Recipient Met. Life award of honor. Nat. Safety Coun., 1970, Met. Life cert. of comendation Nat. Safety Coun., 1972, A.R. Lauer award Human Factor Soc., 1981, Award of Honor, Award of Merit, Nat. Hwy. Traffic Safety Adminstrn., 1982. Mem. APHA, AAAS, Am. Statis. Assn. Am. Assn. Automotive Medicine, Internat. Coun. Alcohol, Drugs and Traffic Safety, Human Factors Soc., Soc. Epidemiologic Rsch., Transp. Rsch. Bd. (emeritus mem.). Democrat. Home and Office: 101 Simmons Way Folsom CA 95630 Office Phone: 916-989-5628.

PECK, RICHARD WAYNE, novelist; b. Decatur, Ill., Apr. 5, 1934; s. Wayne Morris and Virginia (Gray) P. Student, Exeter (Eng.) U., 1954-55; BA, DePauw U., 1956; MA, So. Ill. U., 1959; DHL, DePauw U., 1999. Mem. faculty Sch. Edn., Hunter Coll., 1965-71. Lectr. in field; adj. prof. libr. sci. La. State U., 1996—. Author: books for adolescents, including Are You in the House Alone?, 1977 (Edgar Allen Poe award 1977), Father Figure, 1978, Secrets of the Shopping Mall, 1979, Remembering the Good Times, 1986, Never Met, 1989, Anonymously Yours, 1991, Strays Like Us, 1998, A Long Way from Chicago, 1999 (Newbery silver medal, Nat. Book Award finalist), Those Summer Girls I: A Year Down Yonder, 2000 (Newbery award), Fair Weather, 2001, The River Between Us, 2003; (Blossom Culp series) The Ghost Belonged to Me, 1975, Ghosts I Have Been, 1987, Blossom Culp and the Sleep of Death, 1994, Dreadful Future of Blossom Culp, 2001; (poetry anthology) Sounds and Silences, 1970; (novels for adults) New York Time; Contbr. articles on architecture and local history to N.Y. Times. Asst. dir. Council Basic Edn., Washington, 1969-70. Served with U.S. Army, 1956-58. Recipient Nat. Prize for Young People's Lit., ALA, 1990, Newbery Gold medal, 2000, Nat. Humanities medal, 2001; fellow English-Speaking Union fellow, Jesus Coll., Oxford (Eng.) U., 1973. Mem. Authors Guild, Authors League, Delta Chi. Republican. Methodist. Home: 155 E 72nd St New York NY 10021-4371

PECK, ROBERT A. newspaper publisher, state legislator; b. Riverton, Wyo., Oct. 7, 1924; s. LeRoy E. and Elvira Eugenia (Sostrom) P.; m. Cordelia S. Peck, Oct. 5, 1949 (dec. Feb. 1996); children: Christopher, George, Steven. BA, U. Wyo., 1949. Pub. The Riverton Ranger, 1949—; mem. Wyo. Senate, Dist. 26, Cheyenne, 1991—. Pres. Central Wyo. Coll. Bd., Riverton, 1966-81; sec. CWC Found., Riverton, 1968—. Staff sgt. U.S. Army, 1943-46, ETO. Mem. Soc. Profl. Journalists, Masons, Phi Beta Kappa. Republican. Methodist. Office: The Riverton Ranger 421 E Main PO Box 993 Riverton WY 82501-0993 Office Phone: 307-856-2244. E-mail: bpeck@wyoming.com., ranger@wyoming.com.

PECK, ROBERT DAVID, educational foundation administrator; b. Devil's Lake, N.D., June 1, 1929; s. Lester David and Bernice Marie (Peterson) P.; m. Lylia June Smith, Sept. 6, 1953; children: David Allan, Kathleen Marie. BA, Whitworth Coll., 1951; MDiv, Berkeley (Calif.) Bapt. Div. Sch., 1958; ThD, Pacific Sch. Religion, 1964; postgrad., U. Calif., Berkeley, 1959-60, 62-63, Wadham Coll., Oxford U., Eng., 1963. Music tchr. pub. schs., Bridgeport, Wash., 1954-55; prof., registrar Linfield Coll., McMinnville, Oreg., 1963-69; asst. dir. Ednl. Coordinating Coun., Salem, Oreg., 1969-75; assoc. prof. Pacific Luth. U., Tacoma, 1976-79, U. Puget Sound, Tacoma, 1977; v.p. John Minter Assocs., Boulder, Colo., 1979-81, Coun. Ind. Colls., Washington, 1981-84; adminstrv. v.p. Alaska Pacific U., Anchorage, 1984-88; pres. Phillips U., Enid, Okla., 1988-94, chancellor, 1994-95; chmn. The Pres. Found. for Support of Higher Edn., Washington, 1995—; sr. assoc. InterEd, Phoenix, 1998—. Pres. Phillips U. Ednl. Enterprises Inc., 1994-95; cons. Higher Edn. Exec. Assocs., Denver, 1984—; owner Tyee Marina, Tacoma, 1975-77; yacht broker Seattle, 1977-79. Author: Future Focusing: An Alternative to Strategic Planning, 1983, also articles. Dem. county chmn., McMinnville, 1968, Dem. candidate for state Ho. of Reps., McMinnville, 1969; pres. McMinnville Kiwanis, 1965-69. Cpl. Signal Corps, U.S. Army, 1952-54. Carnegie Corp. grantee, 1982, 84. Mem. Okla. Ind. Coll. Assn. (sec. 1989—). Mem. Christian Ch. Avocations: sailing, sculpting. E-mail: robertpeckb@cs.com.

PECK, ROBERT MCCRACKEN, naturalist, science historian, writer; b. Phila., Dec. 15, 1952; s. Frederick William Gunster and Matilda (McCracken) P. BA in Art History, Princeton U., 1974; MA, U. Del., 1976. Dir. Pocono Lake (Pa.) Preserve Nature Ctr., 1971, 72; asst. to dir. Natural History Mus. Acad. Natural Scis., Phila., 1976-77, spl. asst. to pres., 1977-82, acting v.p. Nat. History Mus., 1982-83, fellow, 1983—, curator Art and Artifacts, 2000—, editor sci. publs., 2001—, sr. fellow, libr., 2003—; tech. dir. Bartram Heritage Study U.S. Dept. Interior and Bartram Trail Conf., Atlanta and Montgomery, Ala., 1977-78. Cons. BBC, Eng., 1987-92; bd. dirs. Phila. Conservationists, Natural Lands Trust, Phila., Libr. Co. of Phila., Phila. City Inst.; mng. editor Frontiers, 1979-82, editor Proceedings of The Acad. of Natural Scis., 2001-04; lectr. in field. Author: A Celebration of Birds: The Life and Art of Louis Agassiz Fuertes, 1982, Headhunters and Hummingbirds: An Expedition Into Ecuador, 1987, Wild Birds of America: The Art of Basil Ede, 1991, Land of the Eagle: A Natural History of North America, 1991, German edit., 1992; author: (with others) John James Audubon in the West: The Last Expedition, 2000, William Bartram's Travels, 1980, John Cassin's Illustrations of the Birds of California, Texas, Oregon, British and Russian America, 1991; author: (forward) The Birds of America by John James Audubon, 1985; editor: Bartram Heritage Report, 1978; author (with others), editor: Philadelphia Wildflowl Exposition Catalog, 1979; contbr. chpts. to books, articles to mags. and newspapers including The New York Times. Recipient Richard Hopper Day Meml. award Acad. Natural Scis. of Phila., 1991, Wyck-Strickland award for contbns. to cultural life of Phila., 2003; Eleanor Garvey fellow in printing and graphic arts Houghton Libr., Harvard U., 1995; Yale Ctr. for Brit. Art fellow, 1997. Fellow Royal Geog. Soc., Explorers Club (various coms. 1983—, Explorers award 1988); mem. Soc. History of Natural History, Sigma Xi. Achievements include discovery of a new species of frog, Eleutherodactylus pecki; research in orthoptera indigenous to the Caribbean; status of invasive African Desert Locust in the West Indies; the Orinoco River and its tributaries, botanical, entomological, ichthyological, herpetological and malacological specimens for the Smithsonian Institution and the Academy of Natural Sciences; participation in expeditions which discovered several new species of fish in Guyana Shield, Venezuela; discovery of (with others) several new species of amphibians and insects; current projects include biological and cultural research in Mongolia, the natural history illustrations of Edward Lear; research in 19th century exploration. Office: Acad Natural Scis 1900 Benjamin Franklin Pkwy Philadelphia PA 19103-1195 Office Phone: 215-299-1138. Business E-Mail: peck@acnatsci.org.

PECK, ROBERT STEPHEN, lawyer, educator; b. Bklyn., Dec. 11, 1953; s. Irwin and Edith Rose (Welt) P.; m. Terre Garcia; 1 child, Zachary Madison. BA in Polit. Sci., George Washington U., 1975; JD, Cleve.-Marshall Law Sch., 1978; postgrad., NYU, 1978; LLM, Yale U., 1990. Bar: N.Y. 1979, U.S. Dist. Ct. (so. and ea. dists.) N.Y. 1979, D.C. 1989, U.S. Ct. Appeals (11th cir.) 2004, U.S. Supreme Ct. 2002. Congl. aide U.S. Ho. of Reps., Washington, 1972-74; divsn. dir. Automated Correspondence, Washington, 1974-75; law clk. to presiding justice Cleve. Mcpl. Ct., 1976; editor Matthew Bender & Co., N.Y.C., 1977-78; legal dir. Pub. Edn. Assn., N.Y.C., 1978-82; staff dir. ABA, Chgo., 1982-87, Washington, 1987-89; jud. fellow U.S. Supreme Ct., 1990-91; legis. counsel ACLU, 1991-95; adj. prof. Am. U., Washington, 1991—, George Washington U., Washington, 2000—; dir. legal affairs Assn. Trial Lawyers Am., 1995-98, sr. dir. legal affairs, 1998—2003; pres. Ctr. for Constl. Litigation, 2001—. Legal advisor Freedom to Read Found., Chgo., 1986-2002, exec. com. bd. trustees, 1987-90, 93-97, pres., 1988-90, v.p., trustee, 1993-97; bd. dirs. Nat. Constl. Ctr., 1990-93; bd. overseers RAND Inst. Civil Justice, 2001—; mem. lawyers com. Nat. Ctr. for State Cts., 2002—; lectr. on constl. law, legal ethics. Author: We the People, 1987, The Bill of Rights and the Politics of Interpretation, 1991, Libraries, the First Amendment and Cyberspace, 1999; co-author: Speaking and Writing Truth, 1985; editor: Understanding the Law, 1983, Blessings of Liberty, 1986, To Govern A Changing Society, 1990; contbr. numerous articles on constl. law to law revs. Mem. N.Y. State Edn. Adv. Bd., Albany, N.Y., 1979-81; bd. dirs. Nat. Com. on Pub. Edn. and Religious Liberty, 1995-97, Ams. for Religious Liberty, 1995-2000, Citizens for Constitution, 1997—; nat. chair Lawyers for Librs., 1996-2002; chair legal adv. com. Nat. Ctr. for Sci. Edn., 1996-2000; mem. first amendment adv. coun. Media Inst., 1996—. NEH grantee 1983, 85. Mem.: ABA (chmn. pub. election law com. 1983—85, 1987—90, vice chmn. access to justice com. 1997—98, program chmn. consumer and personal rights litigation com. 1997—2000, chmn. 1998—99, chmn. first amendment com. 1999—, chmn. appellate adv. com. 2001—02, chmn. com. Am. Law Inst. and Uniform Laws 2002—03, spl. advisor Commn. on 21st Century Judiciary 2002—03, mem. governing coun. tort, trial and ins. law sect. 2003—, chmn. 20/20 vision task force 2004—), U.S. Supreme Ct. Fellows Alumni Assn. (pres. 2004—). Democrat. Jewish. Avocations: tennis, music, travel. Office: Ctr for Constl Litigation 1050 31st St NW Washington DC 20007-4499 Business E-Mail: robert.peck@cclfirm.com.

PECK, SUSAN NELL, pediatric nurse; b. Dayton, Ohio, July 21, 1951; d. D. Bradley and Helen Louise (DePree) P. BSN, Northeastern U., Boston, 1974; MSN, U. Va., 1981. Cert. registered nurse practitioner. Sr. staff nurse Tufts-New Eng. Med. Ctr., Boston, 1974-79; staff nurse U. Va. Med. Ctr., Charlottesville, 1980-81, grad. teaching asst., 1980-81; clin. nurse specialist in gastroenterology The Children's Hosp. of Phila., 1981—. V.p. profl. edn. Delaware Valley chpt. Crohn's and Colitis Found. Am., Phila., 1992—. Contbr. articles to profl. jours.; author videotape: Facts From Your Friends, 1991. Bd. dirs. Phila. chpt. Am. Liver Found., 1988—. Named Woman of the Yr., Crohn's and Colitis Found. of Am., 1995, Nurse Profl. of Yr., Am. Liver Found., 1997; inducted into Northeastern U. Nursing Hall of Fame, 1998. Mem. ANA, Nat. Assn. Pediatric Nurse Practitioners and Assocs., Soc. Gasteroenterology Nurses and Assocs. (editl. bd. 1986-92), Assn. Pediatric Gastroenterology and Nutrition Nurses (founder, sec.-treas. 1989-94, sec. 1994-95, treas. 1996), Sigma Theta Tau. Avocations: travel, reading. Office: Childrens Hosp of Phila 34th And Civic Center Blvd Philadelphia PA 19104

PECK, THOMAS, newspaper publishing executive; BS in Acctg., U. Conn.; MS Wharton Sch. Bus., U. Pa. CPA. Audit mgr. and computer audit specialist Ernst & Young, 1969—75; v.p. fin. and adminstrn. Orba Corp., 1975—83; contr. and chief acctg. officer Esprit Systems, 1983—85; v.p. PRD Property Devel., 1985—89; asst. v.p. Mac Andrews & Forbes, 1989—90; CFO Daily News, L.P., 1990—, U.S. News & World Report, Fast Company Media Group, LLC. Office: NY Daily News Office of the CFO 450 W 33rd St Fl 3 New York NY 10001-2681

PECK, WILLIAM ARNO, internist, educator, dean, academic administrator; b. New Britain, Conn., Sept. 28, 1933; m. Patricia Hearn, July 10, 1982; children by previous marriage: Catherine, Edward Pershall, David Nathaniel; stepchildren: Andrea, Elizabeth, Katherine. AB, Harvard U., 1955; MD, U. Rochester, N.Y., 1960; DSc (hon.), U. Rochester, 2000. Intern, then resident in internal medicine Barnes Hosp., St. Louis, 1960-62; fellow in metabolism Washington U. Sch. Medicine, St. Louis, 1963; mem. faculty U. Rochester Med. Sch., 1965-76, prof. medicine and biochemistry, 1973-76, head divsn. endocrinology and metabolism, 1969-76; John E. and Adaline Simon prof. medicine, co-chmn. dept. medicine Washington U. Sch. Medicine, St. Louis, 1976-89; physician in chief Jewish Hosp., St. Louis, 1976-89; prof. medicine and exec. vice chancellor med. affairs, dean sch. medicine, pres. univ. med. ctr. Washington U., St. Louis, 1989—2003, Wolff disting. prof., dean emeritus and dir. ctr. for health policy, 2003—. Chmn. endocrinology and metabolism adv. com. FDA, 1976-78; chmn. gen. medicine study sect. NIH, 1979-81; chmn. Gordon Conf. Chemistry, Physiology and Structure of Bones and Teeth, 1977, Consensus Devel. Conf. on Osteoporosis, NIH, 1984; co-chmn. Workshop on Future Directions in Osteoporosis, 1987; chmn. Spl. Topic Conf. on Osteoporosis, U.S. FDA, 1987; bd. dirs. Angelica Corp., Allied Healthcare Products, Hologic, TIAA-CREF Trust Co. Editor Bone and Mineral Rsch. Anns., 1982-88. Pres. Nat. Osteoporosis Found., 1985-90. Served as med. officer USPHS, 1963-65. Paul Harris fellow Rotary Found., 2001; recipient Lederle Med. Faculty award, 1967, Career Program award NIH, 1970-75, Commr.'s Spl. citation FDA, 1988, Humanitarian award Arthritis Found. Ea. Mo., 1995, Crohn's and Colitis Fedn. Am., 1999, Founders award Nat. Osteoporosis Found., 1996, Huntington Disease Soc. Am. award, 2002, Juvenile Diabetes Rsch. Found. Lifetime Achievement award, 2003, Internat. Brotherhood award Bikur Cholim Hosp., Jerusalem, 2003. Fellow AAAS, ACP; mem. Internat. Bone & Mineral Soc., Royal Soc. Medicine, Am. Assn. Clin. Endocrinologists, Am. Geriatrics Soc., Am. Soc. Biochemistry & Molecular Biophysics, Am. Soc. Bone and Mineral Rsch. (councilor 1978-81, pres.-elect 1982-83, pres. 1983-84), Am. Soc. Clin. Investigation, Am. Soc. Internal Medicine, Assn. Am. Med. Colls. (coun. deans adminstrv. bd. 1992—, chmn. 1996-97, chair elect 1997-98, chair 1998—, immediate past chair 1999), Assn. Am. Physicians, Endocrine Soc., Orthopaedic Rsch. Soc., Soc. Med. Adminstrs., St. Louis Metro. Med. Soc., St. Louis Soc. Internal Medicine (pres. 1986), Inst. Medicine Nat. Acad. Sci., Washington U. Health Adminstrn. Program Alumni Assn. (hon.), Research! Am. (vice chair 1999—), Pi Theta Epsilon (hon.), Sigma Xi, Alpha Omega Alpha (bd. dirs 1992-95). Home: 32 Huntleigh Downs Saint Louis MO 63131 Office: Washington U Sch Medicine #1 Brookings Dr Box 1133 Saint Louis MO 63130

PECK, WILLIAM HENRY, museum curator, art historian, archaeologist, author, lecturer; b. Savannah, Ga., Oct. 2, 1932; s. William Henry Peck and Mildred (Bass) Peck Tuten; m. Ann Amelia Keller, Feb. 2, 1957 (dec. 1965); children: Alice Ann, Sarah Louise; m. Elsie Holmes, July 8, 1967; 1 child, William Henry IV. Student, Ohio State U., 1950-53; BFA, Wayne State U., 1960, MA, 1961. Jr .curator Detroit Inst. Arts, 1960-62, asst. curator, 1962-64, assoc. curator, 1964-68, curator ancient art, 1968—, acting chief curator, 1984-88, sr. curator, 1988—2004. Lectr. art history Cranbrook Acad. Art, Bloomfield Hills, Mich., 1963-65; vis. lectr. U. Mich., Ann Arbor, 1970; adj. prof. art history Wayne State U., Detroit, 1966—; excavations in Egypt, Mendes, 1964-66, Precinct of Mut, Karnak, 1978—. Author: Drawings from Ancient Egypt, 1978, The Detroit Institute of Arts: A Brief History, 1991, Splendors of Ancient Egypt, 1978; co-author: Ancient Egypt: Discovering its Splendors, 1978, Mummies, Diseases and Ancient Cultures, 1980, also articles. With U.S. Army, 1953-55. Recipient award in the arts Wayne State U., 1985; Ford Motor Co. travel grantee, 1962; Am. Rsch. Ctr. Egypt fellow, 1971; Smithsonian Instn. travel grantee, 1975. Mem. Archaeol. Inst. Am., Am. Rsch. Ctr. Egypt, Internat. Assn. Egyptologists, Soc. Study Egyptian Antiquities, Am. Assn. Mus., Oriental Inst.-U. Chgo. Democrat. Episcopalian. Avocations: origami, performance of early music, collecting T.E. Lawrence material. Office: 1901 Orleans Detroit MI 48207-2718 E-mail: whpeck@yahoo.com.

PECKENPAUGH, ROBERT EARL, investment advisor; b. Potomac, Ill., July 17, 1926; s. Hilery and Zella (Stodgel) P.; m. Margaret J. Dixon, Sept. 21, 1945; children: Nancy Lynn, Carol Sue, David Robert, Daniel Mark, Jeanne Beth, Douglas John. Student, Ind. U., 1946-47; BS, Northwestern U., 1949, MBA with distinction, 1952. Chartered fin. analyst. With First Nat. Bank Chgo., 1949-52; pres. Security Suprs., Inc., Chgo., 1952-73; v.p. Chgo. Title & Trust Co., 1973-77; pres. Hotchkiss & Peckenpaugh, Inc., Chgo., 1977-84; v.p. Morgan Stanley Asset Mgmt. Inc., 1984-86, Morgan Stanley & Co., Inc., Chgo., 1986-91; pres. Peckenpaugh Asset Mgmt. Inc., Chgo., 1991—. Chmn., Evang. Covenant Ch. of Hinsdale, Ill., 1981-84. Served with USNR, 1944-46. Mem. Investment Analyst Soc. Chgo. (pres. 1963-64), Mid-Day Club, Hinsdale Golf Club. Home: 429 S County Line Rd Hinsdale IL 60521-4724 Office: Peckenpaugh Asset Mgmt 429 S County Line Rd Hinsdale IL 60521-4724

PECKER, DAVID J. magazine publishing company executive; b. N.Y.C., Sept. 24, 1951; m. Karen Balan, Oct. 31, 1987. BBA, postgrad., Pace U. CPA, N.Y. Sr. auditor Price Waterhouse & Co.; mgr. fin. reporting Diamandis Communications, Inc., N.Y.C., 1979, dir. fin. reporting, dir. acctg., asst. contr., 1983; COO, CFO, exec. v.p. pub. Hachette Mags., Inc., N.Y.C., 1990-91, pres., COO, 1991-92, pres. and CEO, 1992-99; chmn., CEO Am. Media Inc., 1999—, pres., CEO, COO, 1999—. Mem. Fashion Group's Internat. Adv. Bd., The N.Y. City Partnership Com.; mem. bd. dirs. The Madison Square Boys & Girls Club. Bd. dirs. Pace U., N.Y.C., Drug Enforcement Agents Found., 1995—. Mem. Am. Mgmt. Assn. Office: Am Media Inc 600 East Coast Ave Lake Worth FL 33464-0001

PECKHAM, DONALD, computer company executive; b. Aberdeen, S.D., Feb. 8, 1932; s. Donald Seth and Crystal (Maytum) P.; m. Jeanette G. Mackenzie, June 20, 1967 (div. Jan. 1995); children: Dean, Deanna Jean. BSEE, U. Wash., 1957; MSEE, Calif. Inst. Tech., 1958. Engr. Hughes Aircraft Co., Culver City, Calif., 1957-60; sr. engr. Nortronics divsn. Northrup Corp., Hawthorne, Calif., 1960-61, rsch. scientist Nortronics divsn., 1965-67, tech. dir. Aircraft divsn., 1985-92; v.p. Digitek Corp., Inglewood, Calif., 1961-63, v.p., gen. mgr. L.A., 1963-65; mem. staff Decade Computer Corp., Huntington Beach, 1967-71; mgr. software Pertec Computer Corp., Santa Ana, Calif., 1971-81; mgr. software tools CXC Corp., Irvine, Calif., 1981-85; instr. U. So. Calif., 1960-61; pres. Modern Computer, Carlsbad, Calif., 1992-2001, Modern.net, Oceanside, Calif., 2001—. With USN, 1950-54. Mem. IEEE, Assn. Computing Machinery, Tau Beta Pi. Home and Office: Unit 85 3890 Vista Campana S Oceanside CA 92057-8160 also: Unit 85 3890 Vista Campana S Oceanside CA 92057-8160 E-mail: donaldpeckham@msn.com.

PECKHAM, ELLEN, artist, poet; b. Rochester, NY, Sept. 28, 1938; d. Walter Fredrick and Florence Albertina (Schmanke) Stoepel; m. Anson Wheeler Peckham, Sept. 10, 1976. Exhibitions include Atelier A/E Enterprises, NYC, 1994—, Instituto Cultural Peruano Norteamericano, Peru, 1997—, Art Internat., NYC, 1998, Boston Printmakers, 1999—, Katonah (NY) Mus., 1999—, Collage/Assemblage Soc., NYC, 2000—02, Brand Libr. and Art Ctr., Glendale, Calif., 2001—, Springfield (Mo.) Art Mus., 2001, Stocker Ctr., Elyria, Ohio, 2001, U. Richmond, Va., 2002, N.W. Arts Coun./Ill. Arts Coun., Woodstock, Ill., 2002, Sothebys, NY, 2002, Pacific States Biennial, Hilo, Hawaii, 2002, No. Ariz. U., Flagstaff, 2002, Multisensory Hera Gallery, Warwick, RI, 2003, Solarplate Traveling Exhibits, NY and Mass., 2003, Zimmerli Mus., Rutgers U., NJ, 2004, Robert Blackburn Printmaking Workshop, NY, 2004;, author numerous poems. Avocations: gardening, theater. Office Phone: 212-620-8103.

PECKHAM, EUGENE ELIOT, judge, lawyer; b. Stamford, Conn., Aug. 11, 1940; s. Joseph E. and Margaret (Nabors) P.; m. Judith Alice Chamberlain, Dec. 19, 1964; children: Margaret, Joseph, Elizabeth. BA with honors, Wesleyan U., Middletown, Conn., 1962; JD, Harvard U., 1965. Bar: N.Y. 1965, Fla. 1981, U.S. Tax Ct. 1974, U.S. Ct. Appeals (2d cir.) 1975, U.S. Dist. Ct. (no. dist.) N.Y. 1965. Assoc. Hinman, Howard & Kattell, Binghamton, N.Y., 1965-72, ptnr., 1972-2000; surrogate judge Broome County, N.Y., 2001—; acting justice N.Y. Supreme Ct. (6th jud. dist.), 2003—. Instr. Broome C.C., Binghamton, 1968-69, Am. Coll. Life Underwriters, Bryn Mawr, Pa., 1969-70, Am. Coll. Property and Casualty Underwriters, Bryn Mawr, 1970-71; adj. lectr. SUNY, Binghamton, 1972-77, adj. asst. prof., 1977-81, adj. assoc. prof., 1981-87, adj. prof. acctg., 1987—; vis. lectr. Cornell U., Ithaca, N.Y., 1978, adj. prof., 1984. Author: Warren's Heaton Surrogate's Courts, Federal and New York Estate Taxes, vol., revised, 1988, 89, Bender's Federal Tax Service " Income Taxation of Estates & Trusts", 1989; mem. bd. editors Warren's Heaton on Surrogate Courts, 2001-; contbr. articles to profl. jours. Peace Corps vol. tchr. Santa Maria U., Arequipa, Peru, 1966-67, treas. Joint Legis. Adv. Com. on Estates, Powers and Trusts Law and The Surrogates Ct. Procedure Act, 1990—; pres. Binghamton Girls Club, N.Y., 1974-76, bd. dirs., 1970-77; chmn. bd. Binghamton Boys and Girls Club, 1977, trustee, 1987-2000, chmn. bd. trustees, 1996-2000; bd. dirs. A. Lindsay and Olive B. O'Connor Found., 1982—, Dr. G. Clifford and Florence B. Decker Found., 1984-2001; bd. dirs. Comty. Found. South Ctrl. N.Y., 1996-2002; mem. trust fund. com. Broome County United Way, N.Y., 1979-94; pres. SUNY Found., Binghamton, 1977-79, bd. dirs., 1975-82; bd. dirs. Estate Planning Coun. So. Tier, 1983-87, treas., 1983, sec., 1984, v.p., 1985, pres., 1986; bd. dirs. Samaritan Counselling Ctr. So. Tier, Inc., 1982-87, v.p., 1986, pres., 1987; co-chmn. sta. WSKG-TV auction, 1983; treas. Roberson Ctr. Arts & Scis., 1980, bd. dirs., 1977-80, 87-95; bd. dirs. Twin Tier Home Health, Inc., 1990-97, v.p., 1991-93, pres., 1993-95; chmn. Broome County Cmty. Ambassador Project, 1970-71; mem. Broome Bd. Ethics, 1985-89, chair, 1999-2000; mem. Broome County Arena Bd., 1987-89; deacon 1st Presbyn. Ch., Binghamton, 1971-74, moderator, 1974, elder, 1975-78, 87-90, trustee, 1980-83, 92-95; exec. com. Broome County Rep. Com., 1980-83, 96-2000, co-chmn. fin. com., 1982-83, vice chmn., 1996-2000; pres. Broome County Young Rep. Club, 1969-70. Recipient SUNY-Binghamton Alumni Recognition award, 1984. Fellow Am. Coll. Trust and Estate Coun.; mem. N.Y. State Bar Assn. (exec. com. trusts and estates sect. 1980-84, 86-92, treas. 1986, sec. 1987, chmn. elect 1988, chmn. 1989, tax sect. 1972-2000, chmn. spl. commn. on alt. sources funding legal svcs. 1976-78, action unit 6 1984-86, ethics com. 1979-82, bd. editors N.Y. State Bar Jour. 1998—, v.p. 1999-2002, ho. dels. 1990-94, 95-2002), Fedn. Bar Assns. 6th Jud. Dist. (pres. 1984-85), Broome County Bar Assn. (chmn. prepaid legal ins. com. 1976-80, ethics com. 1981-87, chmn. jud. rating com. 1988-90). Home: 1 Stonecrest Ct Binghamton NY 13903 Office: Broome County Surrogate Ct PO Box 1766 Binghamton NY 13902-1766

PECKHAM, MICHAEL JOHN, academic administrator; b. Pontypool, Wales, Aug. 2, 1935; s. William Stuart and Gladys Mary (Harris) P.; m. Catherine Stevenson King, Oct. 7, 1958; children: Alexander, Daniel, Robert Shannan. BA MA, St. Catharine's Coll., Cambridge, Eng., 1956; MB BChir, U. Coll. Med. Sch., London, 1959; Dr. Honoris Causa, U. Franche Compte, Besancon, France, 1991, Cath. U. Leuven, Belgium, 1993; DSc (hon.), Loughborough U. Tech., Eng., 1992, Exeter U., 1996. Rsch. scholar Inst. Gustav Roussy, Paris, 1965-67; lectr., sr. lectr. Inst. Cancer Rsch., London, 1967-73, prof. radiotherapy Royal Marsden Hosp., 1974-86, dean, 1984-86; dir. Brit. Postgrad. Med. Fedn., London, 1986-90; dir. R & D Dept. of Health, London, 1991-95; dir. Sch. Pub. Policy U. Coll., London, 1996—. Civilian cons. Royal Navy, 1974-86. Editor: Oxford Textbook of Oncology, 1995; editor-in-chief European Jour. Cancer, 1990-94, (with M. Marinker) Clin. Futures' 1998; contbr. rsch. papers to profl. publs. Capt. RAMC, 1959-65. Hon. fellow St. Catharine's Coll., Cambridge, 1998. Fellow Royal Coll. Radiologists, Royal Coll. Physicians, Royal Coll. Pathologists, Royal Coll. Surgeons; mem. NAS Inst. Medicine (fgn. assoc.), European Soc. Therapeutic Radiology and Oncology (pres. 1984-85), Brit. Oncol. Assn. (pres. 1986-88), Fedn. European Cancer Socs. (pres. 1989-91). Avocation: painting. Office: U Coll London Sch Pub Pol 29/30 Tavistock Sq London WC1H 9EZ England E-mail: m.peckham@ucl.ac.uk.

PECKOL, JAMES KENNETH, consulting engineer; b. Cleve., Oct. 24, 1944; s. William John and Elinor Elizabeth (Bustard) P.; children: Erin, Robyn. BS Engring., Case Inst. Tech., 1966; MSEE, U. Wash., 1975, PhDEE, 1985. Cons. GE, Raytheon, Ling Temco Vought, RCA, Boeing Co., 1966-72; sr. staff engr. indsl. products bus. unit John Fluke Mfg. Co., Seattle, 1972-83, sr. staff engr. automated systems bus. unit, 1983-86, sr. staff engr. MR&D Bus. unit, 1986-93; founder Oxford Cons., Edmonds, Wash., 1987—. Affiliate asst. prof. dept. elec. engring., affiliate asst. prof. dept. computers and software sys. U. Wash., Seattle, 1984-87, 95—, prof. dept. elec. engring., 1997—; sr. lectr., assoc. prof. dept. elec. engring. U. Aberdeen, Scotland, 1987; lectr. dept. math. and sci. Shoreline C.C., Seattle, 1989—; lectr. dept. computer sci. Edmonds (Wash.) C.C., 1992—; assoc. prof. dept. engring./computer sci. U. Nantes, Frances, 1993, 96; mem. computer sci. and elec. engring. curriculum adv. bd. Wash. State U., 1990—; lectr. various confs. and univs. Contbr. articles to

profl. jours.; patentee in field. Mem. IEEE, Am. Assn. Artificial Intelligence, Assn. Computing Machinery, Tau Beta Pi. Home and Office: Oxford Cons Ltd 859 14th St SW Edmonds WA 98020-6611

PECKOLICK, ALAN, painter, photographer, graphic designer; b. N.Y.C., Oct. 3, 1940; s. Charles and Belle (Binenbaum) P.; m. Jessica Margot Weber, June 3, 1984. AAS, Pratt Inst., Bklyn., 1968. Art dir. McCann-Erickson, 1964-68; graphic designer Herb Lubalin, 1968-72; v.p., creative dir. Lubalin, Smith, Carnase, Inc., N.Y.C., 1972-74, LCS & P Design Group, Inc., N.Y.C., 1974-76; pres. Lubalin Peckolick Assoc., N.Y.C., 1976-81, Pushpin, Lubalin, Peckolick, N.Y.C., 1981-86, Peckolick and Ptnrs., N.Y.C., 1986-89; design dir. Addison Design Cons., N.Y.C., 1989-91; chmn. Peckolick Inc., N.Y.C., 1991—; painter, 2000—. Bd. advisors Designworld mag., Victoria, Australia, 1983—, Herb Lubalin Study Ctr., N.Y.C.; lectr. Pratt Inst., Parsons Sch. Design, Sch. Visual Arts, also various orgns. Co-author, designer Herb Lubalin Graphic Designer, 1986; exhibitions include Sony Gallery, Tokyo, 1989, one-man shows include, N.Y.C., 2000, 2002, Key West, Fla., 2001, 2003, 2004, Salamagundi Club Invitational, 2002, Gallery 468, N.Y.C., 2002, Agora Gallery, 2003, Photo Dist. Gallery, 2004, Fales Libr. at NYU, 2004. Bd. dirs. Glaucoma Found., 1993, Whale Conservation Inst., 1994. Recipient awards AIGA, Art Directors Club awards. Mem. N.Y. Art Dirs. Club (6 gold medals, over 50 awards), N.Y. Type Dirs. Club (bd. dirs.), Alliance Graphique Internationale, Art Dirs.Club Bergen (Norway) (hon.). Avocations: sculpting, collecting art and prints, cooking, travel, photography. Home: 30 E 10th St New York NY 10003-6202

PECORA, ANDREW LOUIS, hematologist; b. Newark, 1957; B magna cum laude, Seton Hall U., MD, U. Medicine and Dentistry N.J., 1983. Diplomate Am. Bd. Internal Medicine, Am. Bd. Hematology, Am. Bd. Med. Oncology. Intern N.Y. Hosp.-Cornell Med. Ctr., N.Y.C., 1983—84, resident in internal medicine, 1984—86; fellow in hematology and oncology Meml. Sloan Kettering Cancer Ctr., N.Y.C.; asst. dir. adult stem cell/bone marrow transplantation program Hackensack (N.J.) Univ. Med. Ctr., 1990—93, chief, program dir., 1993—, dir. stem cell collection and storage svc., 1993—. Clin. asst. hematology/oncology Hackensack Univ. Med. Ctr.; clin. asst. prof. medicine U. Medicine and Dentistry N.J. Med. Sch.; chmn. bone marrow transplant coordinating com. and protocol adv. com. Cancer Inst. N.J. Bd. dirs. Hackensack Univ. Med. Ctr. IPA. Named one of Top Drs. in N.Y. Metro Area, Castle Connolly, Top Drs. 2003, N.J. Monthly Mag. Office: No NJ Cancer Ctr Hackensack U Med Ctr 20 Prospect Ave Ste 400 Hackensack NJ 07601-1962

PECSOK, ROBERT LOUIS, chemist, educator; b. Cleve., Dec. 18, 1918; s. Michael C. and Katherine (Richter) P.; m. Mary Bodell, Oct. 12, 1940 (dec. Apr. 1996); children: Helen Pecsok Wong, Katherine, Jean Pecsok Nagle, Michael, Ruth Pecsok Hughes, Alice Pecsok Tominaga, Sara Pecsok Lima; m. Marcella Beeman, Apr. 23, 1997. SB summa cum laude, Harvard U., 1940, PhD, 1948. Prodn. foreman Procter & Gamble Co., Balt., 1940-43; instr. chemistry Harvard U., 1948; asst. prof. chemistry U. Calif., L.A., 1948-55, assoc. prof., 1955-61, prof., 1961-71, vice-chmn. dept., 1965-70; prof., chmn. dept. U. Hawaii, Honolulu, 1971-80, dean natural scis., 1981-90. Sci. adviser FDA, 1966-69. Author: Principles and Practice of Gas Chromatography, 1959, Analytical Methods of Organic and Biochemistry, 1966, Modern Methods of Chemical Analysis, 1968, 2d edit., 1976, Modern Chemical Technology, 1970, rev. edit. 1989, Physicochemical Applications of Gas Chromatography, 1978. Lt. USNR, 1943-46. Recipient Tolman medal, 1971; Guggenheim fellow, 1956-57, Petroleum Rsch. Fund Internat. fellow, 1963-64. Mem. Am. Chem. Soc., Am. Inst. Chemists, Phi Beta Kappa, Alpha Chi Sigma, Phi Lambda Upsilon. Home: 13903 Amber Sky Ln San Diego CA 92129-3101

PEDDICORD, ROLAND DALE, lawyer; b. Van Meter, Iowa, Mar. 29, 1936; s. Clifford Elwood and Juanitas Irene (Brittain) P.; m. Teri Linn O'Dell; children: Erin Sue, Robert Sean. BSBA with honors, Drake U., 1961, JD with honors, 1962. Bar: Iowa 1962; cert. civil trial specialist Nat. Bd. Trial Advs. Asst. atty. gen. State of Iowa, 1962-63; assoc. Steward, Crouch & Hopkins, Des Moines, 1962-65; ptnr. Peddicord, Wharton, Spencer & Hook, Des Moines, 1965—. Lectr. in law Drake U., 1962-68; lectr. law Coll. Osteo. Medicine, Des Moines, 1965-72 Editor and chief Drake Law Rev., 1961-62 Past mem. nat. bd. dirs., nat. coun. YMCA of U.S.A., past vice chmn. nat. bd.; bd. dirs., past chmn. Greater Des Moines YMCA, 1968-89. With USMC, 1954-57. Mem. ABA, ATLA, Iowa Bar Assn., Polk County Bar Assn., Iowa Trial Lawyers Assn., Iowa Acad. Trial Lawyers, Am. Bd. Trial Advs. (mem. nat. bd., past pres. Iowa chpt.). Republican. Methodist. Office: 405 6th Ave Ste 700 Des Moines IA 50309-2415 also: Peddicord Wharton Spencer & Hook PO Box 9130 Des Moines IA 50306-9130 Office Phone: 515-243-2100 ext. 515. Business E-Mail: Dale.Peddicord@Peddicord-Law.com.

PEDDIE, IAN A. language educator; b. Wolverhampton, England, Jan. 14, 1965; arrived in U.S., 1992; s. Alexander McKay and Kathleen Mary Peddie. BA with honors, U. Bradford, Eng., 1992; MA, Ill. State U., 1996, U. Rochester, 1998, PhD, 2002. Asst. prof. modern Brit. and Am. lit., popular culture W. Tex. A&M U., Canyon, 2002—. Contbr. articles to profl. jours. Mem.: Ctr. Working Class Studies, Modern Lang. Assn. Avocations: chess, rugby, history. Office: West Tex A&M Univ Canyon TX 79016 E-mail: ipeddie@mail.utamu.edu.

PEDDY, LISA LYNN, secondary school educator; b. Muskogee, Okla., Nov. 29, 1969; d. David P. and Linda S. Peters; m. Jack T. Peddy Jr., May 31, 1997. BS, Okla. State U., 1993. Cert. English tchr. Okla. English tchr. Muskogee H.S., 1993—. Bd. dirs. Muskogee Literacy Coun., 2002—. Mem.: NEA, Okla. Edn. Assn., Delta Kappa Gamma. Avocations: reading, acting, sports. Office: Muskogee HS 3200 E Shawnee Rd Muskogee OK 74403

PEDEN, JAMES ALTON, JR., lawyer; b. Gainesville, Fla., Apr. 24, 1944; s. James Alton and Frances Merle (Wilson) P. BA summa cum laude, U. Miss., 1966, JD, 1970; postgrad., U. Bristol, England, 1966-67. Bar: Miss. 1970, U.S. Dist. Ct. (no. and so. dists.) Miss., U.S. Ct. Appeals (5th cir.) 1970, U.S. Supreme Ct. 1973. Staff asst. to Sen. John C. Stennis U.S. Senate, Washington, 1964-65; assoc. Stennett, Wilkinson & Ward (now Stennett, Wilkinson & Peden), Jackson, Miss., 1970-73, ptnr., 1973—. Staff asst. to lt. gov. State of Miss., Jackson, 1972-75; services officer Miss. Senate, Jackson, 1972-75; staff judge adv. Miss. Air N.G., Jackson, 1974-99; judge Miss. Ct. Mil. Appeals, 2004—; mem. Miss. Gov.'s Jud. Nominating Com., 1980-83. Mem. Leadership Jackson, 1991-92; co-pres. Millsaps Arts and Lecture Series, 2004—. Col. Miss. Air N.G., 1968-99. Named Fulbright scholar, 1966-67; Inst. Politics in Miss. fellow, 1971-72. Fellow Miss. Bar Found.; mem. ABA (fellow young lawyers divsn.), Miss. Bar Assn. (pres. young lawyers sect. 1978-79, 2d v.p. 1979-80, pres. fellows young lawyers 1989-90), Hinds County Bar Assn., Supreme Ct. Hist. Soc., Miss. Law Inst. (chmn. 1979). Baptist. Avocations: american and military history, baseball, basketball. Office: PO Box 13308 Jackson MS 39236-3308 Office Phone: 601-982-3330. Business E-Mail: jpeden@swplaw.net.

PEDEN, KEITH J. human resources specialist; b. Mich., May 1950; BA, Western Mich. U.; MA, Ea. Mich. U. Human resources staff Honeywell, Prime Computer; dir. worldwide compensation, benefits and human resources info. systems Lotus Devel. Corp.; dir. benefits, compensation, human resources mgmt. systems Raytheon Co., Lexington, Mass., 1993—97, v.p., dep. dir. human resources initiatives, 1997—2001, sr. v.p. human resources, 2001—. Office: Raytheon Co 141 Spring St Lexington MA 02421

PEDEN, LYNN ELLEN, marketing executive; b. L.A., Mar. 1, 1946; d. Orlan Sidney and Erna Lou (Harris) Friedman; m. Ernest Peden, Aug. 1994. Student, UCLA, 1963-65, 71-72, Willis Bus. Coll., 1965-66, Fin. Schs. Am., 1982, Viewpoints Inst., 1970-71. Office mgr. Harleigh Sandler Co., L.A., 1965-67; customer svc. Investors Diversified Svcs., West L.A., Calif., 1968-76; exec. sec. McCulloch Oil Corp., West L.A., 1976; mgr. publs. Security 1st Group, Century City, Calif., 1976-80; office mgr. Morehead & Co., Century City, 1980-81; dir. mktg., mgr. customer svc. Inst. Mktg. Svcs., Santa Monica, Calif., 1981-82; v.p. Decatur Petroleum Corp., Santa Monica, 1982-83; asst. v.p., broker svcs., dir. Angeles Corp., L.A., 1984-87; asst. to pres. Pacific Ventures, Santa Monica, 1988-90, La Grange Group, West L.A., 1990-95; property mgmt. asst. Desert Resort Mgmt., Palm Desert, Calif., 1997-99, bus. mgr., 1999—. Fin. and ins. writer; contbr. poetry to UCLA Literacy Mag., 1964. Mem. Migi Car Am. Club (sec., newsletter editor). Home: 78580 Villeta Dr La Quinta CA 92253-3856

PEDERSEN, DARLENE DELCOURT, publishing executive, psychotherapist; b. Westbrook, Maine; 1 child, Jorgen David. BSN, U. Conn., 1967; postgrad., U. B.C., 1974-75; MSN, U. Pa., 1997. RN Pa., N.J., N.Y., cert. clinical specialist in adult psychiatric and mental health nursing, ANCC. Various nursing positions, psychiat.-comty health, 1967-79; assoc. editor JB Lippincott Co., Phila., 1979-84; acquisition editor WB Saunders Co., Phila., 1984-88, v.p., editor in chief, 1988-91, sr. v.p., editorial dir. books divsn., liaison to London office, 1991-95; domestic and internat. pub. cons. Phila., 1995—; psychotherapist pvt. practice Glen Mills, Pa., 1997—. Team leader Northwestern Human Svcs. Delaware County, 1998—99; dir. PsychOptions, 2000—; v.p. content ops. MedCases, Phila., 2000—03; exec. editor Thomson Physicians World, 2003—04; mng. editor FA Davis Co., Phila., 2004—. Author: Canadian Nurse, 1976; co-author: (book) Basic Nursing Skills, 1977; acquisition editor: book Saunders Manual of Medical Practice. Mem.: ANA, Internat. Soc. Traumatic Stress Studies, U.S. Dressage Fedn., Inc., Am. Orthopsychiat. Assn., Internat. Platform Assn., Assn. Profl. Comm. Cons., Manuscript Soc., Forum Exec. Women, Internat. Soc. Psychiat. Mental Health Nurses, Med. Mktg. Assn., Assn. Am. Pubs., Med. Mktg. Assn., Am. Med. Writers Assn., Am. Med. Pubs. Assn., Am. Group Psychotherapy Assn., Am. Psychiat. Nurses Assn., Am. Group Psychotherapy Assn., Montgomery County C. of C., Emily's List, U. Pa. Faculty Club, Sigma Theta Tau (Xi chpt.). Avocations: autograph and art collection, travel, francophile, french music, reading. Office: FA Davis Co 1915 Arch St Philadelphia PA 19103 Office Phone: 215-568-2270. E-mail: ddped@aol.com.

PEDERSEN, GEORGE J. engineering company executive, computer support company executive; b. 1935; Student, Rutgers U., 1952—53. Contracts mgr. VitroLabs, West Orange, NJ, 1953—68; with Mantech Internat. Corp., Fairfax, Va., 1968—; now chmn. bd., CEO., pres. ManTech Internat. Corp. Office: ManTech Internat Corp 12015 Lee Jackson Hwy Ste 300 Fairfax VA 22033-3300

PEDERSEN, KAREN SUE, electrical engineer; b. Indianola, Iowa, Apr. 27, 1942; d. Donald Cecil and Dorothy Darlene (Frazier) Kading; m. Wendell Dean Pedersen, May 6, 1961; children: Debra Ann Pedersen Schwickerath, Michael Dean. AA, Grand View Coll., Des Moines, 1975; BSEE, Iowa State U., 1977; MBA, Bentley Coll., Waltham, Mass., 1989. Registered profl. engr., Mass., Iowa, Ill. Engr. Iowa Power & Light Co., Des Moines, 1978-80, rate engr., 1980-84; sr. rsch. engr. Boston Edison Co., Boston, 1984-87, sr. engr., 1987-94, prin. rsch. analyst, 1994-98; sr. engr. MidAmerican Energy Co., Davenport, Iowa, 1998—. Ops. chmn. Old South Ch., Boston, 1989-98. Mem. IEEE (chmn. Iowa ctrl. sect. 1983-84, sec. Iowa-Ill. sect. 2003), NSPE (v.p. 1999-2000, v.p. North Ctrl. region 2001-03), Mass. Soc. Profl. Engrs. (pres. 1992-93), Eta Kappa Nu. Republican. Congregationalist. Office: MidAmerican Energy Co 106 E 2nd St # D Davenport IA 52801-1502 Personal E-mail: kspedersen@midamerican.com.

PEDERSEN, KNUD GEORGE, economics educator, academic administrator; b. Three Creeks, Alta., Can., June 13, 1931; s. Hjalmar Neilsen and Anna (Jensen) P.; m. Joan Elaine Vanderwarker, Aug. 15, 1953 (dec. 1988); children: Greg, Lisa; m. Penny Ann Jones, Dec. 31, 1988. Diploma in Edn., Provincial Normal U., 1952; BA, U. B.C., 1959; MA, U. Wash., 1964; PhD, U. Chgo., 1969; LLD (hon.), McMaster U., 1996; DLitt (hon.), Emily Carr Inst. of Art and Design, 2003; LLD (hon.), Simon Fraser U., 2003. Asst. prof. econs. of edn. U. Toronto; asst. prof. econs. of edn., assoc. dir. U. Chgo., 1970-72; dean, assoc. prof., then prof. U. Victoria, B.C., 1972-75, acad. v.p., prof., 1975-79; pres., vice-chancellor, prof. Simon Fraser U., Vancouver, B.C., 1979-83; pres., prof. U. B.C., Vancouver, 1983-85; pres., vice-chancellor U. Western Ont., London, Can., 1985-94, prof. econs. of edn., 1985-96; interim pres. U. No. B.C., 1995; founding pres., vice-chancellor Royal Roads U., 1995-96; chancellor U. No. B.C., 1998—2004; bd. govs. Emily Carr Inst. Art and Design, 2004—. Bd. dirs. Assn. Univs. and Colls., Canada, 1979—84, chmn., Canada, 1989—91; bd. dirs. Vancouver Bd. Trade, 1983—85; pres. Can. Club Vancouver, 1983—84; mem. coun. trustees Inst. for Rsch. on Pub. Policy, Ottawa, Ont., Canada, 1983—89; chmn. Coun. Ont. Univs., 1989—91. Author: The Itinerant Schoolmaster, 1972; contbr. chpts. to books, numerous articles to profl. jours. Decorated officer Order of Can., Order of Ont., Order of B.C.; recipient 125th Anniversary of Confedn. of Can. medal, Queen's Jubilee medal; fellow Ford Found., 1965-68, Can. Coll. Tchrs., 1977, Royal Soc. for Encouragement of Arts, 1984; also 11 major scholarships. Mem., Min. Advanced Edn. Adv. Com; mem. Semiahmoo Golf and Country Club, Loo Mis Trail Golf and Country Club. Avocations: golf, fishing, gardening, cooking, carving. E-mail: pedersen@sfu.ca.

PEDERSEN, LEE G. chemistry educator; b. Oklahoma City, June 15, 1938; s. Leonard Melnot Pedersen and Naomi Shinn; m. Barbara L. Pedersen; children: Lars, Kurt. B in Chemistry, U. Tulsa, 1961; PhD in Chemistry, U. Ark., 1965. From asst. prof. to prof. chemistry U. N.C., Chapel Hill, 1967—, now M.A. Smith prof. chemistry. Cons. NIEHS, Research Triangle Park, N.C., 1985—. Author: Problems in Quantum Chemistry and Physics, 1974. NSF fellow, Columbia U., N.Y.C., 1965-66, NIH fellow Harvard U., Boston, 1966-67. Office: Dept Chemistry U NC Chapel Hill CB 3290 Chapel Hill NC 27599 Office Phone: 919-962-1578.

PEDERSEN, PAUL BODHOLDT, psychologist, educator; b. Ringsted, Iowa, May 19, 1936; BA in History and Philosophy, U. Minn., 1958, MA in Am. Studies, 1959; ThM, Luth. Sch. Theology, Chgo., 1962; MA in Ednl. Psychology, U. Minn., 1966; PhD in Asian Studies, Claremont (Calif.) Grad. Sch., 1968. Asst. prof. dept. psychoednl. studies, psychologist U. Minn., Mpls., 1971-75; sr. fellow Culture Learning Inst. East-West Ctr., Honolulu, 1975-76, sr. fellow coord., 1975-76; assoc. prof. dept. psychoednl. studies, psychologist U. Minn., 1975-79, higher edn. coord., 1976-77; sr. fellow Culture Learning Inst. East-West Ctr., 1979-81; prof., chmn. dept. counselor edn. Syracuse (N.Y.) U., 1982-90, prof. edn. dept. counseling and human svcs., 1989—95, adj. prof. dept. internat. rels., 1993—95, prof. emeritus, 2000—; prof. counseling edn. U. Ala., Birmingham, 1996-2001. Vis. lectr. Nommensen U., Medan, Sumatra, Indonesia, 1962—65, U. Malaya, 1969—71; vis. prof. dept. psychology U. Hawaii, 1978—81, 2000—; spkr. in field. Author numerous books, chpts. in books, articles to profl. jours.; mem. editl. bd. Am. Jour. Multicultural Counseling and Devel.; editl. advisor Jour. Profl. Psychology, Jour. Simulation and Games, Internat. Jour. Intercultural Rels. Sr. Fulbright fellow Nat. Taiwan U., Taipei, 1999-2000. Mem. APA, Am. Assn. Counseling and Devel. Internat. (mem. rels. com., editl. bd. Jour. Counseling and Devel., editor Internationally Speaking newsletter, mentor media com.), Internat. Assn. for Cross Cultural Psychology, Internat. Coun. Psychologists, Soc. Intercultural Tng. and Rsch. (exec. com., program chairperson 1977, chairperson Pacific Com. 1977, pres. 1978-80, editl. bd. Jour. Intercultural Rels.). Home: 1330 Ala Moana Blvd Apt 1306 Honolulu HI 96814-4221 Office Phone: 808-589-2662.

PEDERSEN, PAUL MARK, sportswriter, educator, columnist; b. Stratten, Nebr., Sept. 21, 1970; s. Harold Clifford and Cassandra Sue Pedersen; m. Jennifer Lynn Estes, May 31, 1991; children: Hallie Susannah, Zack Paul, Brock Victor. AA in Bibl. Studies, Hobe Sound Bible Coll., Hobe Sound, Fla, 1990; BSBA, Palm Beach Atlantic U., West Palm Beach, Fla., 1992; MA in History, U. Ctrl. Fla., Orlando, 1997; MA in Bus. Comm. and Pub. Rels., Emerson Coll., Boston, Mass., 1993; PhD in Sport Mgmt., Fla. St. U., Tallahassee, Fla., 2000. Lic. FCC Broadcasting Fed. Comm. Commn./Washington, 1993. Sportswriter, agate clk. Palm Beach Post, West Palm Beach, Fla., 1996—98; comm. instr. Palm Beach Atlantic U., West Palm Beach, Fla., 1997—98; sports corr. Palm Beach Post, West Palm Beach, Fla., 1998—2002; grad. tchg., rsch. asst. Fla. State U., Tallahassee, 1988—2000, sport mgmt. instr., 2001—01; asst. prof. sport mgmt. Bowling Green State U., Bowling Green, Ohio, 2001—03; asst. prof. sport mgmt. Palm Beach Atlantic U., West Palm Beach, Fla., 2003—. Editl. rev. bd. mem. Cyber Jour. of Sport Views and Issues, Houston, 1999—2001; presider Fla. AAHPERD Conf., Orlando, Fla., 2000; book rev. editor Academic Athletic Jour., Tallahassee, 2001—02; sports mktg. cons. Bd. Ads Dot Com, Kansas City, Kans., 2001; faculty advisor Sport Mgmt. Alliance, Bowling Green, Ohio, 2002—03; reviewer 2004 Hawaii Internat. Conf. on Edn., Honolulu, 2003—03; faculty advisor Sport Mgmt. Club, West Palm Beach, Fla., 2003—04; sports bus. columnist Treasure Coast Bus. Jour., Stuart, Fla., 2003. Author: (songs) (books) Build It and They Will Come: Arrival of the Tampa Bay Devil Rays, 1997; contbr. chapters to books; author: (books) Bobby Bowden: Win by Win, 2003; contbr. articles to profl. jour. Staff vol. Fat Tire Festival, Tallahassee, 1999, Fla. Archery Assn. Championships, Tallahassee, 1999, FHSAA Winter Soccer Finals, Tallahassee, 1999. Recipient Outstanding BS Grad., Palm Beach Atlantic U., 1992. Mem.: North Am. Soc. for Sport Mgmt., Sport Mktg. Assn., Fla. Alliance for Health, Phys. Edcucation, Recreation, and Dance (president-sport 2003—04), Phi Kappa Phi, Phi Alpha Theta. Home: 4264 SE Cocoplum Pl Stuart FL 34997 Office: Palm Beach Atlantic Univ 901 South Flagler Dr West Palm Beach FL 33416-4708 Personal E-mail: paul_pedersen@pba.edu. Business E-Mail: paul_pedersen@pba.edu.

PEDERSEN, PEDIE, physiology educator; b. Milan, Tenn., Apr. 12, 1948; d. E.E. and Bettye M. Pedersen. BA, Rhodes Coll., 1970; MS, U. Ala., 1972; BS, U. New Orleans, 1977; PhD, Tulane U., 1986. Tchr. biology Holy Name Sch. and Chapelle H.S., New Orleans, 1978-81; vis. instr., postdoctoral fellow Tulane U., New Orleans, 1986-87; asst. prof. physiology Delgado C.C., New Orleans, 1987-91, assoc. prof., 1991—. Author: Human Anatomy and Physiology: Lecture Outlines and Self Tests I and II, 1995. Mem. Human Anatomy and Physiology Soc., Sweet Adelines, Sigma Xi. Office: Delgado Cmty Coll 615 City Park Ave New Orleans LA 70119 Office Phone: 504-483-4426.

PEDERSEN, RICHARD FOOTE, diplomat and academic administrator; b. Miami, Ariz., Feb. 21, 1925; s. Ralph Martin and Gertrude May (Foote) P.; m. Nelda Newell Napier, May 9, 1953; children: Paige Elizabeth, Jonathan Foote, Kendra Gayle. BA summa cum laude, Coll. of Pacific, 1946; MA, Stanford U., 1947; PhD, Harvard U., 1950; LLD (hon.), George Williams Coll., 1964, U. of Pacific, 1966; DHL (hon.), Am. U., Cairo, 1997. Teaching fellow, tutor Harvard U., Cambridge, Mass., 1949-50; with UN econ. and social affairs Dept. State, Washington, 1950-53; adviser econ. and social affairs U.S. Mission to UN, N.Y.C., 1953—55, adviser polit. and security affairs, 1956-59, sr. advisor polit. and security affairs, 1959-64, minister, counselor, 1964-66, ambassador, sr. adviser to U.S. rep., 1966-67; ambassador, dep. U.S. rep. UN Security Coun., N.Y.C., 1967—69; counselor Dept. State, 1969-73; ambassador to Hungary, 1973-75; sr. v.p. internat. U.S. Trust Co., 1975-78; pres. Am. U., Cairo, 1978-90; dir. internat. programs Calif. Poly Pomona U., 1990-95. Mem. adv. bd. Nat. Coun. U.S.-Arab Rels., 1985—; trustee Consortium for Internat. Devel., 1990—95; mem. adv. bd. Ctr. Near Eastern Studies UCLA, 1996—99; adv. bd. Sch. Internat. Studies, U. Pacific, 1997—. Mem. Nat. Coun. YMCAs, 1961-73; bd. dirs. Ctr. for Civic Edn., 1995—, Physicians for Peace, 1988-90; mem. Fulbright bd., Egypt, 1980-82, adv. bd. Fulbright Cultural Enrichment Program, So. Calif., 1991—2001. With AUS, 1943-45 ETO. Recipient Sumner Peace prize Harvard U., 1950, Outstanding Alumnus award U. Pacific, 1962, Order of Sacred Treasure, Gold and Silver Star, Govt. of Japan, 1987; named One of 10 Outstanding Young Men, U.S. Jr. C. of C., 1956; awarded Order of Scis. and Arts, first class Govt. of Egypt, 1990. Mem. Coun. Fgn. Rels., Am. Soc. Internat. Law, L.A. World Affairs Coun., Am. Fgn. Svc. Assn., Mid. East Inst., Oriental Inst., UN Assn. Am., Internat. Assn. Univ. Pres., Pacific Coun. Internat. Policy, Asia Soc. Clubs: Harvard (N.Y.); Cosmos (Washington). Democrat. Congregationalist. Avocations: swimming, tennis, egyptology, local history. Home: 2503 N Mountain Ave Claremont CA 91711-1545 E-mail: rfpdrsn@earthlink.net.

PEDERSEN, WESLEY NIELS M. public relations and public affairs executive; b. South Sioux City, Nebr., July 10, 1922; s. Peder Westergaard and Marie Gertrude (Sorensen) P.; m. Angeline Kathryn Vavra, Oct. 17, 1948; 1 son, Eric Wesley. Student, Tri-State Coll., Sioux City, Iowa, 1940-41; BA summa cum laude, Upper Iowa U.; postgrad. in Russian, George Washington U., 1948—59. Editor, writer Sioux City Jour., 1941-50; corr. N.Y. Times, Life, Time, Fortune, 1948-50; editor Dept. State, 1950—52, fgn. svc. officer, 1960-63; fgn. affairs columnist, roving corr., counselor summit meetings and fgn. ministers confs. USIA, 1952—60, chief, worldwide spl. publs. and graphics programs, 1963-69; chief Office Spl. Projects, Washington, 1969-78, Office Spl. Projects, Internat. Comm. Agy., 1978-79; v.p. Fraser Assocs., pub. rels., Washington, 1979-80; dir. comm. and pub. rels. Pub. Affairs Coun., Washington, 1980—. Lectr. creative comm. Upper Iowa U., 1975; chmn., Europe, Ambassadorial Internat. Affairs Seminar, Fgn. Svc. Inst., 1975; lectr. internat. pub. rels. Pub. Rels. Inst., Am. U., 1976; lectr. bus. and mgmt. divsn. NYU, 1976-78; cons. pub. rels., editl. and design; del. founding sessions 1st Amendment Congress, Phila. and Williamsburg, Va., 1980, exec. com., 1980. Columnist: (as Paul L. Ford) The World Today, 1952-60; (as Benjamin E. West) Behind the Curtain, 1952-60; White House Report, 1966-69 (as Wesley Pedersen), Washington Report-Pub. Rels. Jour., 1980-85; author: Mr. President: Lyndon B. Johnson, 1964, Legacy of a President, 1964, Journey to the Pacific, 1965, Mr. President: Richard M. Nixon, 1969, American Heroes of Asian Wars, 1969; co-author: Effective Government Public Affairs, 1981; editor: The Imam's Story, 1961, Escape at Midnight and Other Stories (Pearl S. Buck), 1962, Exodus From China (Harry Redl), 1962, Macao, 1962, The Dividing Line (Arturo Gonzalez), 1962, China's Men of Letters (K.E. Priestley), 1963, Children of China (Pearl S. Buck and Margaret Wylie), 1963, Destination the Moon (William Howard), 1964, Man on the Moon, 1964, Nine From Little Rock, 1964, To the Moon and Beyond, 1965, Bounty From the Land, 1965, Workers Paradise Lost (Eugene Lyons), 1967, The Americans and the Arts (Howard Taubman), 1969, The Dance in America (Agnes de Mille), 1969, Getting the Most From Grassroots Public Affairs Programs, 1980, Computer Applications in Public Affairs, 1984, Cost-Effective Management for Today's Public Affairs, 1984, Making Community Relations Pay Off: Tools and Strategies, 1988, Winning at the Grassroots: How to Succeed in the Legislative Arena by Mobilizing Employees and Other Allies, 1989, Leveraging State Government Relations, 1990, Managing the Business-Employee PAC, 1992, Adding Value to the Public Affairs Function, 1994, Winning at the Grassroots (with Tony Kramer), 2000, Managing the Corporate Political Action Committee, 2001; Pub. Affairs Rev. Mag., 1980-86, 2000, 01, 02, 03, 04, Impact newsletter on nat. and internat. pub. affairs, 1980—; contbr. to The Commissar, 1972, Informing the People: A Public Affairs Handbook, 1981, The Practice of Public Relations, 1984, 2d edit., 2003; mem. editl. bd. Pub. Rels. Quar., 1975—, Washington editor, Pub. Rels. Quar., 1998—, Fgn. Svc. Jour., 1975-81; mem. adv. bd. Pub. Rels. News, 1991-98; author scripts Uncle Walter's Doghouse radio show, 1938; contbr. articles to profl. jours. Founding chmn. bd. dirs. Nat. Inst. for Govt. Pub. Info. Rsch., Am. U., 1977-80. Served with USAAF, 1943-46. Recipient 2 awards A.P. Mng. Editors Assn., Iowa, 1949, Meritorious Svc. award USIA, 1963, Superior Svc. award USIA, 1964, Presdl. commendation, 1964, 70, 1st prize Fed. Editors Assn., 1970, 74-75, Agy. Dir.'s citation USIA, 1965, 74, 78, Soc. Tech. Comm., 1974-76, Gold award Internat. Newsletter Conf., 1982, Silver award, 1985, Eddi award for design excellence Editor's Workshop, 1983, Gold Circle award Am. Soc. Assn. Execs., 1983-89, 97-2000, Ten Cool award Am. Soc. Assn. Execs., 2001, Editors' Forum award, 1988-90, 94-96, Assn. Trends award, 1989-2003, Great Assn. Communicator award, Assn. Trends, 1999, Best of Century Comm. award, Assn. Trends, 2001, spl. citation Assn. Trends, 2001, Trends award, 2002, Silver and Gold awards, 2004, Grand prize Internat. Ann. Report Conf., 1989, Gold award 1997, Comm. Concepts awards, 1989-2004, Grand Comm. Concepts awards, 1992, 95, 2000, 02, 04, MerComm awards, 1990-2000, Nat. Media Conf. award, 1989, 90, Internat. Acad. Comm. Arts and Scis. award, 1994-98, 2000, Grand prize, 1995, awards Printing and Graphic Assn., 1987, 91, 96-97, 2000, Excell award Soc. of Nat. Assn. Publishers, 2000, Judges award 2000; named Most Outstanding Info. Officer in Exec. Br. Govt. Info. Orgn., 1975, Ky. Col. and Adm. Nebr. Navy, 1984. Mem. DAV, Am. Fgn. Svc. Assn., Am. Legion, Internat. Assn. Bus. Communicators (Communicator of Yr. Washington chpt. 1978, various awards 1973, 76-78, 84, 90, 94-2003, Winners' Circle awards dist. III 1996-2003), Nat. Assn. Govt. Communicators (pres. 1978-79, Communicator of Yr. 1977, Disting. Svc. award 1978), Pub. Rels. Soc. Am. (mem. Counselor's Acad. 1980—, chmn. 1st Amendment task force 1980-81, co-recipient Thoth award 1980-81, 94, twin Thoth awards 1995-97, 2003, Thoth awards 1998-2003,

Bronze Anvil award 2000), Am. Soc. Profl. Communicators (Colonial award 2002, Masters award 2004), World Affairs Coun., Soc. Profl. Journalists, The Acad. Polit. Sci., Fgn. Svc. Club, Nat. Press Club, Overseas Press Club. Episcopalian. Home: 4701 Willard Ave Apt 1007 Chevy Chase MD 20815-4622 Office: Pub Affairs Coun 2033 K St NW Ste 700 Washington DC 20006-1019 Office Phone: 202-872-1790. Personal E-mail: wesped@comcast.net. Business E-Mail: wpedersen@pac.org. *Keenness of mind and an abundance of luck, it is said, are the key ingredients of personal success. The truth be told, however, I've performed only one act of brilliance in my lifetime: the selection of my parents. But I've had an enormous amount of good fortune, a fact manifestly clear to anyone who has ever met my wife, my son and my granddaughters. They, thank goodness, chose me.*

PEDERSEN, WILLIAM FRANCIS, lawyer; b. N.Y.C., Apr. 4, 1943; s. William F. and Priscilla S. (Auchincloss) P.; m. Ellen L. Frost, Feb. 2, 1974; children: Mark Francis, Claire Ellen. BA, Harvard U., 1965, LLB, 1968. Bar: Mass. 1969, D.C. 1978. Assoc. Ropes & Gray, Boston, 1969-72; staff atty. EPA, Washington, 1972-75, dep. gen. counsel, then assoc. gen. counsel, 1976-85; staff counsel Senate Com. on Govt. Ops., Washington, 1975-76; lectr. Harvard Law Sch., 1985-86; of counsel Perkins Coie, Washington, 1987—89, ptnr., 1989-94, Shaw, Pittman, Potts & Trowbridge, Washington, 1994-2001; pvt. practice Washington, 2001—. Vis. prof. Law Sch., U. Mich., 1997-98. Contbr. articles to profl. jours. Mem. ABA (standing com. on environ. law 1987-89). Republican. Episcopalian. Office: William F Pedersen PLLC Ste 800 1752 N St NW Washington DC 20036 E-mail: bill.pedersen@billpedersen.com.

PEDERSON, GORDON ROY, state legislator, retired military officer; b. Gayville, S.D, Aug. 8, 1927; s. Roy E. and Gladys F. (Masker) P.; m. Betty L. Ballard, Mar. 8, 1955; children: James D., Carol A. Pederson Niemann, Nancy G. Pederson Holub, Gary W. Student, Yankton Coll., 1948-50, Fla. State U., 1963; advanced course, Infantry Sch., 1958-59. Drafted U.S. Army, 1945-47, commd. 2nd lt., 1952, advanced through grades to lt. col., 1967, served CONUS World War II, platoon leader 17th infantry regiment, 7th infantry divsn., 1953-54, served Korean War, 1950-54, rifle co. commdr. 10th mountain divsn., 1955-58, instr., dir. instrn. U.S. Army Jungle Warfare Tng. Ctr., 1961-63, comdr. post, 1963-64, 1st brig., 1st infantry divsn., 1965—66, dir. tng. hdqs. G3, Ft. Leonard Wood, 1966—68; advisor Ministry of Nat. Def., Rep. China on Taiwan, 1969-70; retired U.S. Army, 1970; rep. S.D. Ho. Reps., Pierre, 1977-99, 2001—; operator Dairy Queen, Wall, S.D., 1990-95. Chmn. transp. com. S.D. Ho. Reps., 1979-93, vice chair state affairs com., 1996-98, vice chair commerce com., 1998, chmn. budget audit com., 2001-2002, chmn. transp. com., 2002—. Del. S.D. Rep. Conv., 1974-78, 80, 82, 84, 86, 88, 90, 92, 94, 96, 98, 2000, 02, 04, Nat. Rep. Conv., 1976, 80, 84, 88, 92, 96, 2000, 04; bd. dirs. Legis. Rsch. Coun., 1988, 90, 92, 96, 98, 2001-02. Decorated Bronze Star, Medal of Merit, U.S. Presdl. Unit Citation, Rep. Korea Presdl. Unit Citation, Rep. Vietnam Presdl. Unit Citation, Combat Infantry Badge with Star, Legion of Merit, Air Medal with 2 Oak Leaf Clusters, Army Accomodation medal with 2 oak leaf clusters, Cross of Gallantry with Palm, Republic Vietnam. Mem. VFW, DAV, Am. Legion, Retired Officers Assn., Wall C. of C., Internat. Lions Club, Sons of Norway. Lutheran. Home: PO Box 312 116 W 7th St Wall SD 57790 Office: SD Ho of Reps State Capitol Bldg Pierre SD 57501 Business E-Mail: rep.gordonpederson@state.U.S.S.D. E-mail: bpers@GWTC.net.

PEDERSON, LINDA LUE, epidemiologist, researcher; d. Richard and Lucy (Kouyoumjian) Johnson; m. David R. Pederson, June 12, 1965 (div. 1983); children: Ingrid, Erica, Kristen; m. Frederick D. Hamilton, Dec. 8, 2002. BA, Brown U., 1964; MA, Inst. Child Behavior & Devel., U. Iowa, 1966; PhD, U. Western Ont., London, Can., 1980. Tchr. devel. psychology U. Western Ont., 1968-73, rsch. asst. dept. medicine, 1973-76, tchg. asst. dept. epidemiology and preventive medicine, 1978, asst. prof. dept. medicine, 1980-84, assoc. prof. dept. epidemiology and biostats., 1984-93, prof., 1993-95, prof. cmty. health and preventive medicine, 1995-99, dir. rsch., 1995—. Assoc. dir. Drew-Meharry-Morehouse Consortum Cancer Ctr., 1996-97; sr. staff fellow Office on Smoking and Health, CDC. Contbr. articles over 140 and revs. to sci. publs. Recipient numerous grants, fellowships and scholarships. Avocations: exercise, cats, music. Office: 23 Deerpath Rd Chalfont PA 18914

PEDERSON, RENA, newspaper editor; b. San Angelo, Tex. children: Gregory Gish, Grant Gish. B in Journalism with honors, U. Tex., 1969; M in Journalism, Columbia U., 1970. With UPI, AP; with Washington Bur. Houston Chronicle; with Dallas Morning News, 1973—, Fed. beat, city hall, features, TV critic, editl. writer, op-ed editor, v.p., editl. page editor, 1986—2002, editor-at-large, 2002—. Mem. Pulitzer Prize Bd., 1989—. Author: What's Missing? Inspirtation for Women Seeking Faith and Joy in Their LIves, 2003; co-author (with Lee Smith): What's Next? Women Redefining Their Dreams in the Prime of Life, 2001. Named one of Most Powerful Women in Tex., Tex. Monthly Mag.; recipient award, Headliners Club, Dallas Press Club, AP Mng. Editors. Mem.: Am. Soc. Newspaper Editors, Coun. on Fgn. Rels., Nat. Conf. Editl. Writers (former pres.). Methodist. Office: The Dallas Morning News PO Box 655237 508 Young St Dallas TX 75265

PEDERSON, SALLY, lieutenant governor; b. Muscatine, Iowa, Jan. 13, 1951; d. Gerald and Wineva Pederson; m. James A. Autry, Feb. 6, 1982; children: Rick, Jim Jr., Ronald. Grad., Iowa State U., 1973. With Meredith Corp., 1973-84; sr. food editor Better Homes & Gardens mag.; lt. gov. State of Iowa, 1999—. Pres. Polk County Health Svcs.; bast bd. trustees Nat. Alliance for Autism Rsch.; pres. bd. trustees Autism Soc. Iowa; founding pres. The Homestead Living and Learning Ctr. for Adults with Autism; past cmty. bd. svcs. includes Des Moines Cmty. Playhouse, Very Spl. Arts Iowa, YWCA Aliber Child Care Ctr., YMCA Ctr. Br.; parent rep. Heartland AEA Autism Steering Com.; mem. Iowa State Spl. Edn. Adv. Bd; bd. dirs. Blank Children's Hosp., Mid-Iowa Health Found.; gov.'s appointee State Spl. Edn. Adv. Panel. Democrat. Office: Office of Lt Governor State Capitol Bldg Des Moines IA 50319-0001

PEDERSON, TONY WELDON, newspaper editor; b. Waco, Tex., Oct. 27, 1950; s. Lloyd Moody and Ida Frances (Walker) P.; m. Julianne Kennedy, Mar. 21, 1974 BA, Baylor U., 1973; MA, Ohio State U., 1976. Sports writer Waco (Tex.) Tribune, Tex., 1970-73; sports writer Houston Chronicle, 1974-75, copy editor, 1976-80, sports editor, 1980-83, mng. editor, 1983-99; exec. editor and sr. v.p. Houston Chronicle, 2000—. Adj. faculty U. Houston, 1977-79 Mem. Houston Com. Fgn. Rels. Mem. Nat. AP Mng. Editors Assn., Tex. AP Mng. Editors Assn. Methodist. Avocations: golf, reading. Office: Houston Chronicle Pub Co 801 Texas St Houston TX 77002-2996

PEDERSON, WILLIAM CHRISTOPHER, plastic surgeon; b. Texas City, Tex., July 15, 1952; s. Alton Curtis and Lucy Vernor (Windham) P.; m. Cynthia Lea Anderson, June 17, 1978; children: Liv, Anton, Candice. BA, U. Tex., 1974, MD, 1978. Hand fellow U. Louisville, 1984; rsch. fellow Duke U. Med. Ctr., Durham, N.C., 1985; microsurgery rsch. fellow St. Vincent's Hosp., Melbourne, 1986; asst. prof. plastic surgery Duke U. Med. Ctr., Durham, 1087-89; chief of plastic surgery U. Tex. Health Sci. Ctr., San Antonio, 1989—. Contbr. articles to profl. jours. Bd. dirs. C.E. Homeowner's Assn., San Antonio, 1990—. Fellow ACS (assoc.); mem. Am. Soc. Plastic and Reconstructive Surgery, Am. Assn. Hand Surgery, Am. Soc. Reconstructive Microsurgery.

PEDERSON, WILLIAM DAVID, political scientist, educator; b. Eugene, Oreg., Mar. 17, 1946; s. Jon Moritz and Rose Marie (Ryan) P. BS in Polit. Sci., U. Oreg., 1967, MA in Polit. Sci., 1972, PhD in Polit. Sci., 1979. Tchg. asst. polit. sci. dept. U. Oreg., Eugene, 1975-77; instr. govt. dept. Lamar U., Beaumont, Tex., 1977-79; asst. prof. polit. sci. dept. Westminster Coll., Fulton, Mo., 1979-80; asst. prof., head polit. sci. and pre-law Yankton Coll. U. S.D., 1980-81; prof., Am. Studies Chair, dir. Internat. Lincoln Ctr. La. State U., Shreveport, 1981—; program analyst NIH, Bethesda, Md., summer 1973; assoc. prof. jr. state program Am. U., Washington, summer 1984; prof. jr. state program Georgetown U., 1997—2002; rsch. assoc. Russian and East European Ctr./U. Ill., Urbana, summers 1982—; founding dir. Washington semester La. State U., Shreveport, 1982-91, 96—, with Presdl. Conf. Series, 1992—, with ann. Abraham Lincoln lecture series/Am. Studies program, 1982—. Mem. nat. adv. com. Presdl. commn. on the Bicentennial of Abraham Lincoln, 2002—. Editl. staff writer: The Times, Shreveport, 1990; columnist: Red Rooster, 2002; author: The Rating Game in American Politics, 1987; editor: The Barberian Presidency, 1989, Morality and Conviction in American Politics, 1990, Congressional-Presidential Relations: Governmental Gridlock, 1991, Great Justices of the U.S. Supreme Court: Ratings and Case Studies, 1993, 2d edit., 1994, Lincoln and Leadership: A Model for a Summer Teachers Inst., 1993, Abraham Lincoln: Sources and Style of Leadership, 1994, Abraham Lincoln: Contemporary, 1995, 2d edit., 1996, FDR and the Modern Presidency: Leadership and Legacy, 1997, Lincoln Forum: Abraham Lincoln, Gettysburg and the Civil War, 1999, George Washington's Image in American Culture, 2001, George Washington and the Origins of the American Presidency, 2000, George Washington: Foundations of Leadership and Character, 2001, Franklin D. Roosevelt and the Shaping of American Culture, 2001, Franklin D. Roosevelt and Congress, 2001; The New Deal and Public Policy, 1998; co-editor: Grassroots Constitutionalism, 1988; editor The Polit. Sci. Educator, 1996-98, Abraham Lincoln Abroad, 1998—; co-editor Jour. Contemporary Thought, 1997—; guest editor: Quarterly Jour. Ideology, 1994; founding editor Washington Semesters and Internships, 1998—, Internat. Abraham Lincoln Jour., 2000—, Classic Cases in American Constitutional Law, 2001, Franklin D. Roosevelt and the Transformation of the Supreme Court, 2003, Franklin D. Roosevelt and Abraham Lincoln, 2003, Franklin D. Roosevelt and the Shaping of the Modern World, 2003, Leaders of the Pack: Polls and Case Studies of Great Supreme Justices, 2003; contbr. articles to profl. jours.; founder La. Lincolnator, 1994. Mem. Mayor's Comm. on the Bicentennial U.S. Constn., 1987; active Barnwell Ctr., Shreveport, 1984, Am. Rose Soc., Shreveport, 1982. With U.S. Army, 1968-70. Recipient Tng. award NIH, 1973, Outstanding Prof. award Westminster Coll. 1980, La. State U., 1984, 2001-02, Cultural Olympiad award, 1995, Page Shreveport Rose Shreveport Times Jour., 1995; grantee La. State U., 1982, La. Endowment for Humanities, 1987, 93, 95-97; NEH fellow, 1981-85. Fellow Am. Polit. Sci. Assn., Am. Judicature Soc.; mem. Abraham Lincoln Assn. (mem. bd. dirs. 1994, Achievement award 1994, dir. conf. in the south, 1992, dir. 1st summer Inst. on Abraham Lincoln, 1993, grantee 1992, 93), Ctr. Study Presidency, Internat. Soc. Polit. Psychology, Washington Semesters and Internship Assn., Internat. Lincoln Assn. (bd. dirs. 1994-95, pres. 1990-93, chair bd. dirs. 1998—), La. Hist. Assn. (bd. dirs. 2001-04), White House Studies (bd. dirs. 2004—). Office: La State U Internat Lincoln Ctr One University Pl BH Shreveport LA 71115-2301 Office Phone: 318-797-5349. E-mail: wpederso@pilot.lsus.edu.

PEDHIRNEY, GAYLAND, food products company executive; Pres., CEO, Wash. Beef Inc., Toppenish, 1996—. Bd. dirs. United Way Yakima County. Mem. Nat. Meat Assn. (bd. dirs.).

PEDINI, EGLE DAMIJONAITIS, radiologist; b. Kaunas, Lithuania, July 22, 1943; d. Vytautas and Elena Damijonaitis; m. Kenneth Pedini, June 4, 1966; children: David Durand, Julian Adam. BA cum laude, MD, Boston U., 1967. Diplomate Am. Bd. Radiology. Intern St. Elizabeth's Hosp., Brighton, Mass., 1967-68; resident in radiology Boston City Hosp., 1968-71; radiologist St. John's Hosp., Lowell, Mass., 1972, Chelmsford (Mass.) X-Ray, 1979-80, Amesbury (Mass.) Hosp./Amesbury Health Ctr., 1973-98, New Eng. Meml. Hosp./Boston Regional Med. Ctr., Stoneham, Mass., 1973-98, Anna Jacques Hosp., Newburyport, Mass., 1973-98. Ptnr. NE Radiology Assocs., Brockton, Mass., 1980-98; chief radiology Anna Jacques Hosp., Newburyport, Mass., 1984, Amesbury Hosp., 1988, 89, 90. Founder, bd. dirs. Andover Sch. Montessori, Mass., 1974-79; parent ann. fundraising com. Phillips Exeter (N.H.), 1985, 86, 87. Mem. Am. Coll. Radiology, Mass. Radiol. Soc., New Eng. Roentgen Ray Soc., Stonehorse Yacht Club, Chatham Women's Club, Garden Club Harwich.

PEDINI, KENNETH, radiologist; b. Hartford, Conn., Mar. 19, 1940; s. Daniel Victor and Elizabeth Catherine Pedini; m. Egle Damijonaitis; children: David D., Julian A. AB in Philosophy, Trinity Coll., 1962; MD, Boston U., 1966. Diplomate Nat. Bd. Med. Examiners, Am. Bd. Radiology. Resident in radiology Boston City Hosp., 1967-70, chief resident in radiology, 1969-70, jr. staff radiologist, 1970-71, U. Hosp., Boston, 1970-71; ptnr. Shawsheen Radiology, Andover, Mass., 1971-98; sr. radiologist Lawrence (Mass.) Gen. Hosp., 1971—, dir. radiology, 1976-87; sr. radiologist Melrose (Mass.)-Wakefield Hosp., 1971-99, chief radiologist, 1993-97, emeritus staff, 1999; pres. L & M Radiology Inc, Andover, Mass., 1994-98. Bd. trustees Lawrence Gen. Hosp., 1984-89, fin. com., 1986—. Mem. Townwide Water Quality Mgmt. Task Force, 2001—; trustee Lawrence Gen. Hosp. Health Enterprises, Inc., 1990—93; mem. fin. com. Lawrence Gen. Regional Health Sys., 1996—; mem. alumni adv. com. Trinity Coll., 1995; co-founder Andover Sch. Montessori, 1975—. Fellow Am. Coll. Radiology (councilor 1979-81); mem. New England Roentgen Ray Soc., Mass. Radiol. Soc. (pres. 1985-86, pres.-elect 1984-85, v.p. 1983-84, exec. com. 1977-87), Mass. Med. Soc., Stonehorse Yacht Club, Algonquin Club. Personal E-mail: wychview@aol.com.

PEDLEY, JOHN GRIFFITHS, archaeologist, educator; b. Burnley, Eng., July 19, 1931; arrived in U.S., 1959, naturalized, 2002; s. George and Anne (Whitaker) Pedley; m. Mary Grace Sponberg, Aug. 30, 1969. BA, Cambridge (Eng.) U., 1953, MA, 1959; postgrad. (Norton fellow), Am. Sch. Classical Studies, Athens, Greece, 1963-64; PhD, Harvard U., 1965. Loeb rsch. fellow in classical archaeology Harvard U., Cambridge, Mass., 1969-70; asst. prof. classical archaeology and Greek U. Mich., Ann Arbor, 1965-68, assoc. prof., 1968-74, acting chmn. dept. classical studies, 1971-72, 75-76; dir. Kelsey Mus. Archaeology, 1973-86, prof., 1974—2002, prof. emeritus, 2002—. Guest scholar J. Paul Getty Mus.; mem. staff excavations, Sardis, Turkey, 1962—64, Pylos, Greece, 1964; co-dir. excavations, Apollonia, Libya, 1966—68; field dir. Corpus Ancient Mosaics, Tunisia, 1972—73; co-prin. investigator excavations, Carthage, North Africa, 1975—79; dir. excavations, Paestum, Italy, 1982—85, Paestum, 1993, Paestum, 95, Paestum, 1997—98; vis. scholar UCLA, 1989; resident in archaeology Am. Acad., Rome, 1990. Author: (book) Sardis in the Age of Croesus, 1968, Sardis in the Age of Croesus, reprint, 1999, Ancient Literary Sources on Sardis, 1972, Greek Sculpture of the Archaic Period: The Island Workshops, 1976, Paestum: Greeks and Romans in Southern Italy, 1990, Greek Art and Archaeology, 1992, Greek Art and Archaeology, 3d edit., 2002; co-author: Apollonia, the Port of Cyrene, 1977, The Sanctuary of Santa Venera at Paestum, Vol. 1, 1993, Corpus des Mosaiques de Tunisie, Vol. III, 1996; editor: New Light on Ancient Carthage, 1980; co-editor: Studies Presented to GMA Hanfmann, 1971. Fellow Am. Coun. Learned Socs., 1972—73, NEH, 1986; grantee, Am. Philol. Soc., 1979, Nat. Endowment Arts Mus., 1974, 1977, 1979, 1980, NEH, 1967, 1975, 1983, 1984. Home: 1720 Morton Ave Ann Arbor MI 48104-4522 Office: Dept Classical Studies Univ Mich Ann Arbor MI 48109 E-mail: jpedley@umich.edu.

PEDLEY, LAWRENCE LINDSAY, lawyer; b. Hopkinsville, Ky., May 27, 1932; s. Gracean McGoodwin and Elizabeth (Lindsay) Pedley; m. Ellen Mack, Oct. 9, 1957 (div. 1981); children: Lawrence Lindsay Jr., David M., Joan Elizabeth; m. Jill Flick, 1981 (div. 1991); 1 child, Jill Katharine; m. Wanda Polk, Feb. 3, 1995. BA, The Citadel, S.C., 1955; JD, Yale U., 1959. Bar: Ky. 1959, Fla. 1980, U.S. Dist. Ct. Ky. 1959, U.S. Ct. Appeals (6th cir.), 1975, U.S. Supreme Ct. 1981. Prin. atty. Ky. Dept. of Hwys., Frankfort, 1960; v.p. Nat. Industries, Louisville, 1964-66; gen. counsel, v.p., dir. Life Ins. Co. Ky., Louisville, 1966-69; ptnr. Goldberg & Pedley, Louisville, 1970-80, Pedley, Zielke, Gordinier and Pence, Louisville, 1980—. Owner Exec. Express, Louisville, 1969—80. Capt. JAGC, 1967. Mem. ABA, Ky. Bar Assn., Fla. Bar Assn., Filson Club, Harmony Landing Country Club, Pendennis Club. Office: Pedley Zielke Gordinier and Pence 2000 Meidinger Tower 462 S 4th Ave Louisville KY 40202-2512 Office Phone: 502-589-4600.

PEDLEY, TIMOTHY ASBURY, IV, neurologist, educator, researcher; b. Phoenix, Aug. 31, 1943; s. Timothy Asbury Pedley III and Mary Adele (Newcomer) Melis; m. Barbara S. Koppel, Mar. 17, 1984. BA, Pomona Coll., 1965; MD, Yale U., 1969. Cert. neurology, electroencephalography, clin. neurophysiology; diplomate Am. Bd. Psychiatry and Neurology. Intern Stanford U. Hosp., 1969-70; resident in neurology Stanford U., 1970-73, postdoctoral fellow, 1973-75, asst. prof. neurology, 1975-79; from assoc. prof. neurology to prof., vice chmn. Columbia U., 1979-98, Henry and Lucy Moses prof., chmn. neurology, 1998—; neurologist-in-chief Columbia U. Med. Ctr., N.Y.C., 1998—. Dir. comprehensive epilepsy ctr. Columbia U. Med. Ctr., 1983-97. profl. adv. bd. Epilepsy Found Am., 1984-98, chmn. profl. adv. bd., 1985-87, pres. bd. dirs., 1991-93, chmn. 1993-95. mem. rev. com. NIH Nat. Inst. Neurol. and Chronic Diseases and Strokes, 1985-89, chmn., 1988-89; various adv. coms. NIH/NINDS, 1990-98; vis. fellow in exptl. neurology Inst. Psychiatry, London, 1978-79; mem. merit rev. bd. neurobiology rsch., VA, 1992-96, chmn., 1995-96; vis. prof. various univs., U.S. and abroad. Editor-in-chief: Epilepsia, 1993—2001; contbr. articles to profl. jours. Fellow AAAS, N.Y. Acad. Medicine; Recipient various honors and awards. Fellow Am. Acad. Neurology (sec. bd. trustees 2003—), Am. Electroencephalographic Soc. (pres. 1989-90, bd. dirs. 1981-85); mem. Am. Neurol. Assn. (coun. 1992-94, treas. 1995-98, first v.p. 2003—04), Am. Epilepsy Soc. (treas. 1980-83, pres. 1991-92), N.Y. Clin. Surg. Soc., Soc. for Neurosci., N.Y. Med. and Surg. Soc., Internat. League Against Epilepsy (exec. com. 1994-2002), Vidonian Club, Yale Club, Shenorock Shore Club (Rye, N.Y.), Alpha Omega Alpha. Office: The Neurological Inst 710 W 168th St New York NY 10032-2603 Fax: 212-305-6978. E-mail: tap2@columbia.edu.

PEDOTO, GERALD JOSEPH, supplier quality specialist; b. Jersey City, Jan. 5, 1948; s. Salvatore Joseph and Rosalie (Benigno) P.; m. Karen Sue Knutty, June 28, 1975; children: Deborah Louise, Donald Lee, Timothy Scott. BS, Bowling Green (Ohio) State U., 1970; MBA, U. Akron, 1976. Cert. mgr., quality engr., quality auditor. Trainee indsl. engring. Timken Co., Canton, Ohio, 1970, assoc. indsl. engr., 1972-73, supervisory candidate, 1973-74, foreman product inspection, 1974-75, supr. indirect labor, 1975-80, supr. heat treatment, 1980-82, sr. product acceptence engr., 1982-96, sr. supplier quality engr., 1996-97, prin. supplier quality advancement analyst, 1997—2004, supplier quality advancement specialist, 2004—. Active United Way, YMCA fund dirs.; region and automotive divsn. councilor. With U.S. Army, 1970-72. Mem. Nat. Mgmt. Assn., Assn. MBA Execs., Am. Soc. for Quality (bd. dirs. 1992-2000), Alpha Tau Omega, Beta Gamma Sigma, Omicron Delta Kappa. Home: 1188 Salway Ave SW North Canton OH 44720-3471 Office: The Timken Co GNW-35 1835 Dueber Ave SW Canton OH 44706-2798 E-mail: gerald.pedoto@timken.com.

PEDOWITZ, MARK, broadcast executive; b. Bklyn., 1953; m. Carolyn Martin. BA in history, Rockford Coll.; JD, John Marshall Law Sch. Atty. MCA Inc., 1979—80; v.p. bus. affairs Reeves Entertainment Group/Alan Landsburg Prodns., 1980—85; v.p. bus. affairs, gen. counsel Landsburg Co., 1985—98; sr. v.p. bus. affairs and adminsrn. MGM/UA TV Prodn. Group, 1987—91; sr. v.p. bus. affairs and contracts ABC, 1991; exec. v.p. ABC Entertainment Group Walt Disney Co., pres. Touchstone TV, 2004—, exec. v.p. ABC Entertainment TV Group, 2004—. Mem.: Hollywood Radio and TV Soc. (past mem. exec. bd.), Acad. TV Arts and Scis. (found bd. dirs., past mem. exec. bd.). Office: Touchstone TV 500 S Buena Vista St Burbank CA 91521*

PEDREIRA, MARK ALAN, education educator; b. Syracuse, N.Y., May 10, 1964; s. Frank Alan and Anita Marie Pedreira. MA, U. of Md., 1987, PhD, 1994. Vis. prof. of english Chonbuk Nat. U., Democratic Peoples Republic of Korea, 1994—95; preceptor, dept. of eng. Boston U., 1996—98; assoc. prof. of english U. of PR, Rio Piedras Campus, San Juan, 1999—. Author: (jour. rev.) Essays in Criticism, (jour. article) 1650-1850: Ideas, Aesthetics, and Inquiries in the Early Modern Era. Office: U of Puerto Rico U Sta PO Box 22586 San Juan PR 00931 E-mail: mpedreira@attglobal.net.

PEDROTTI, LENO STEPHANO, physics educator; b. Zeigler, Ill., May 21, 1927; s. Celeste Louis and Dolores (Galeaz) P.; m. Wilma Jean Sullivan, June 23, 1951; children— Daro Stephano, Michael Louis, Sandra Maria, Laura Jean, Catherine Ann, Leno Matthew, Mary Ann, John Owen. BS in Edn, Ill. State U., 1949; MS in Physics, U. Ill., 1951; PhD, U. Cin., 1961. Teaching asst. U. Ill., Urbana, 1949-51; prof. physics, chmn. dept. Air Force Inst. Tech., Wright-Patterson AFB, Ohio, 1951-82, prof. emeritus, 1982—; cons., editor Ctr. Occupational Rsch. & Devel., Waco, Tex., 1975-82, sr. v.p., 1982—. Presenter in field, 1982—; author, editor, lectr. laser and electro-optics Engring. Tech., Inc., Waco, 1978—; mem. indsl. adv. com. laser electro-optics program Cin. Tech. Coll., 1981-82; tech. cons. Univ. Eye Surgeons, Inc., Ohio State U., 1979-82; mem. exec. com. joint svcs. optical program Optical Scis. Ctr., U. Ariz., 1975-82. Author: Principles of Technology, 1986, Introduction to Optics, 1987, rev. edit., 1993, Applied Mathematics, 1988, Optics and Vision, 1998; contbg. author: Technical Prep Associate Degree: A Win/Win Experience, 1991, The Science Technology, Society Movement, 1993; contbr. articles to profl. jours. Fellow Faculty fellow, NSF, 1959. Fellow Optical Soc. Am.; mem. Am. Nuclear Soc., Am. Phys. Soc. (vice chmn. then chmn. Ohio sect. 1974-76), Laser Inst. Am. (bd. dirs. 1974-84), Am. Assn. Physics Tchrs., Am. Soc. Engring. Edn., Am. Vocat. Assn. (Outstanding Mem. award 1988 vocat. instrnl. materials affiliate Ednl. Exhibitor Assn.-SHIP citation for outstanding commitment to vocat.-tech. edn. 1994), Nat. Coun. Tchrs. Math., Sigma Xi, Tau Beta Pi (Outstanding Tchr. award 1961, 62, 63, 68), Sigma Pi Sigma. Home: 11006 Trailwood Dr Waco TX 76712-3131 Office: CORD 601 Lake Air Dr Waco TX 76710-5841 Office Phone: 254-772-8756.

PEEBLER, CHARLES DAVID, JR., venture capital executive; b. Waterloo, Iowa, June 8, 1936; s. Charles David and Mary E. (Barnett) P.; m. Susie Jacobs, June 5, 1958 (div. 1977); children: David Jacobs, Mark Walter; m. Tonita Worley, Nov. 12, 1979; 1 child, Todd Whitney. Student, Drake U., 1954-56. Asst. to exec. v.p. J.L. Brandeis & Sons, Omaha, 1956-58; with Bozell, Jacobs, Keyon & Eckhardt (formerly Bozell & Jacobs), 1958—, v.p., mem. plans bd., 1960-65, pres. mid-continent ops., 1965-67, pres., CEO, 1967-86, CEO, 1986-97; pres. True North Comms., Inc., NYC, 1997—99, chmn. emeritus, 1999—; chmn. bd., CEO True North Diversified Cos. Group, 1999—; mng. dir. Plum Holdings, L.P., NYC. Bd. dirs. Valmont Industries, Veon, Dreamlife.com., youbet.com, Am. Tool Hotline, mPulse (chmn.), Corp. Fulfillment Inc., Presspoint. Hon. chmn. bd., dirs. Am. Craft Mus.; bd. dirs. Drake U., Juvenile Diabetes Found. Internat., NYC Partnership; mem. corp. com. Central Park Conservancy; mem. adv. bd. Naomi Berrie Diabetes Ctr. Columbia Presbyn. Med. Ctr. Home: 435 E 52nd St New York NY 10022-6445 Office: True North Comms Inc 40 W 23rd St New York NY 10010-5215*

PEEBLES, ALLENE KAY, manufactured housing company executive; b. Waukegan, Ill., Feb. 9, 1938; d. Allan Laverne and Kathryn Bernice (McGill) Sedlmayr; m. William Ross Peebles, July 9, 1960; children: Ross William, Robb Allan, Raymond John, Renda Kay (Mrs. Christopher Sivak). BS with high honors, U. Wis., 1960, MS, 1967; grad., Realtors Inst., 1968. Cert. home economist. Tchr. Horicon (Wis.) High Sch., 1960-61, Oconomowoc (Wis.) High Sch., 1961-67; freelance writer, 1967-70; v.p. Luxury Homes, Inc., Watertown, Wis., 1970-93, Land Devel. Plus Devel. Inc., Watertown, 1970—; co-developer Hidden Meadows Condominium Community, Watertown, 1976-96; gen. ptnr. W and A Elderly Housing Ltd. Partnership, Watertown, 1988—; pres. Housing Am., Inc., 1991—. Gen. ptnr. Sunrise Housing Ltd. Ptnrship., 1990—; builder new and rehab low-income housing, 1983—. Active Wis. Gov.'s Conf. on Family, 1980, long range planning team, 1996—; membership chmn. Boy Scouts Am., 1984—90; chmn. Ams. Abroad Am. Field Svc., Oconomowoc, 1982—87; del. Wis. Rep. Conv., 1997—; chmn. adminstrv. bd. United Meth. Ch., Oconomowoc, 1974—77, 1996—99, lay leader, 2000—03, pres. United Meth. Women, 2002—, chmn. family ministry Wis. Conf., del. to Wis. conf., 2000—03. Recipient Dist. award of Merit Potawatomi Area coun. Boy Scouts Am., 1986. Mem.: AAUW (pres. Oconomowoc br. 1981—83, pres. Oconomowoc 1983—85, officer's bd. 1984—93, fin. advisor 1995—2002), NAFE, Wis. Assn. Family and Consumer Scis. (state bd. 1999—, state housing chmn. 2000—02), Met. Builders Assn. Greater Milw., Internat. Fedn. Home Economists (USA internat. del. 1997—), Wis. Manufactured Housing Assn. (bd. dirs. 1979—90, chmn. bd. 1985—88, Mem. of Yr. award 1986), Wis. Builders Assn., Waukesha Bd. Realtors, Wis. Assn. Realtors, Am. Assn. Family and Consumer Scis., Nat. Assn. Realtors, Wis. Home Economists in Bus. (state chmn. 1987—88, internat. rep. 1998—2000, Home Economist in Bus. of Yr. 1987), Internat. Profl. and Bus. Women, Nat.

Assn. Home Builders, Nat. Home Economists in Bus. (internat. com. 1985—87, regional U.S. advisor 1990—92), Wis. Home Econs. Assn. (parliamentarian 1988—90), Am. Home Econs. Assn., Phi Lambda Theta, Kappa Omicron Nu, Phi Upsilon Omicron, Phi Kappa Phi. Republican. Avocation: writing. Home: 37788 Mapleton Rd Oconomowoc WI 53066 Office: Housing Am Inc W1140 Marietta Ave Ixonia WI 53036-9748 E-mail: peebles@execpc.com.

PEEBLES, CAROL LYNN, immunology researcher; b. Wellington, Kansas, Jan. 20, 1941; d. Harry Alexander and Phyllis Dorothy (Pyle) Pebbles. BA, Kans. State Coll., Pitts., 1962, MS, 1964. Cert. in med. tech. St. Francis Hosp., Wichita, Kans., 1965. Med. technologist St. Francis Hosp., Wichita, Kans., 1965—74; lab. supr. allergy and immunology Scripps Clinic and Rsch. Found., La Jolla, Calif., 1974—77; lab. supr. rheumatology lab. U. Colo. Health Sci. Ctr., Denver, 1977—82; sr. rsch. asst. auto-immune disease ctr. Scripps Clinic and Rsch. Found., La Jolla, Calif., 1982—2001; scientist Inova Diagnostics, Inc., San Diego, 2001—. Author workshop manual; contbr. articles to sci. publications. Mem. Am. Coll. Rheumatology, AAAS, Am. Soc. Micro-biology, Am. Soc. Clin. Lab. Sci., Am. Soc. Clin. Pathology. Avocation: photography. Office: Inova Diagnostics Inc 10180 Scripps Ranch Blvd San Diego CA 92131-1234 Office Phone: 858-586-9900. Business E-Mail: cpeebles@inovadx.com.

PEEBLES, CHRISTOPHER SPALDING, anthropologist, educator, dean, academic administrator; b. Clearwater, Fla., May 26, 1939; s. Frederick Thomas and Corinne deGarmendia (Stephens) P.; m. Laura Ann Wisen, Oct. 6, 1993. AB, U. Chgo., 1963; PhD, U. Calif., Santa Barbara, 1974. Asst. prof. U. Windsor, Ont., Can., 1970-74; asst. curator U. Mich., Ann Arbor, 1974-81; prof. prehistory U. Amsterdam, The Netherlands, 1981-82; prof. Ind. U., Bloomington, 1983—, dean acad. computing, assoc. v.p., 1992—. Author: Excavations at Moundville, 1974, Representations in Archaeology, 1992. With USAF, 1956-60. Mem. Cosmos Club. Avocation: flying. Office: Ind U Glenn A Black Lab 423 N Fess Bloomington IN 47408-3800 Office Phone: 812-855-9544. Business E-Mail: peebles@indiana.edu.

PEEBLES, E(MORY) B(USH), III, lawyer; b. Hattiesburg, Miss., May 3, 1943; s. E.B. Jr. and Lee (Baldwin) P.; m. Celeste H. Hodges; children: E.B. IV, Catharine Celeste, Thomas Hill. BA, Vanderbilt U., 1965, JD, U. Ala., 1967. Bar: Ala. 1967, U.S. Dist. Ct. (so. dist.) Ala., U.S. Ct. Appeals (5th and 11th cirs.), U.S. Supreme Ct. Assoc. Armbrecht, Jackson, DeMouy, Mobile, Ala., 1967-72, ptnr., 1972—. Bd. dirs. South Ala. area bd. Am. South Bank. Mem. Ala. Securities Commn., 1989-93; chmn. sports com. Mobile Area C. of C., 1988-90; bd. dirs. Am.'s Jr. Miss Orgn., Mobile, 1983-90; active Mobile area coun. Boy Scouts Am., 1979—; mem. Sr. Bowl Com., Mobile, 1978—; chmn. trustees Maritime Mus. of Mobile; bd. trustees United Way, Mobile, 2003--; bd. dirs. Mobile Area Conv. and Visitors Bur., 2003--. Mem. ABA (chmn. fin. svcs. com., tort and ins. practice sect. 1989-90, comml. fin. svcs. com. bus. law sect. 1984—), Ala. Bar Assn., Maritime Law Assn. U.S., Southea. Admiralty Law Inst., Internat. Bar Assn., Am. Soc. Internat. Law, Inter-Am. Bar Assn., Ala. Law Inst. (mem. governing coun. 1975—, corp. law com., letters of credit com.), Mobile Touchdown Club (pres. 1987-88), Mobile Area C. of C. (bd. dirs. 2000—). Office: 1300 Riverview Plz Mobile AL 36602

PEEBLES, LUCRETIA NEAL DRANE, policy and administration educator; b. Atlanta, Mar. 16, 1950; d. Dudley Drane and Annie Pearl (Neal) Lewis; divorced; 1 child, Julian Timothy. BA, Pitzer Coll., 1971; MA, Claremont Grad. Sch., 1973, PhD, 1985. Special edn. tchr. Marshall Jr. High Sch., Pomona, Calif., 1971-74; high sch. tchr. Pomona High Sch., 1974-84; adminstr. Lorbeer Jr. High Sch., Diamond Bar, Calif., 1984-91; prin. Chapparal Mid. Sch., Moorpark, Calif., 1991-92, South Valley Jr. High Sch., Gilroy, Calif., 1992—95; asst. prof. dept. edn. Spelman Coll., Atlanta, 1995—97; asst. prof. Coll. Edn. U. Denver, 1997—. Co-dir. pre-freshman program, Claremont (Calif.) Coll., 1974; dir. pre-freshman program, Claremont Coll., 1975; cons., Claremont, 1983—. Author: Negative Attendance Behavior: The Role of the School, 1985, Teaching Children Proactive Responses to Media Violence, 1996, Validating Children: A Collaborative Model, 1996, The Challenge of Leadership in Charter Schools, 2000, Charter School Equity Issues: Focus on Minority and At-Risk Students, 2000, Millennial Challenges for Educational Leadership: Revisiting Issues of Diversity, 2000. Active Funds Distbn. Bd.-Food for All, 1987—, Funds Distbn. Task Force-Food for All, 1986; mem. Adolescent Pregnancy Childwatch Task Force. Named Outstanding Young Career Woman Upland Bus. and Profl. Women's Club, 1978-79; Stanford U. Sch. Edn. MESA fellow, 1983, NSF fellow Stanford U., 1981, Calif. Tchrs. Assn. fellow, 1979, Claremont Grad. Sch. fellow, 1977-79, fellow Calif. Edn. Policy Fellowship Program, 1989-90; recipient Woman of Achievement award YWCA of West Edn., 1991. Mem. Assn. Calif. Sch. Adminstrs. (Minigrant award 1988), Assn. for Supervision and Curriculum Devel., Nat. Assn. Secondary Sch. Principals, Pi Lambda Theta. Democrat. Am. Baptist. Home: 2080 Shoreline Loop #270 San Ramon CA 94583-3269

PEEBLES, PEYTON ZIMMERMANN, JR., electrical engineer, educator; b. Columbus, Ga., Sept. 10, 1934; s. Peyton Zimmermann Peebles Sr. and Maida Erlene Dials; m. Barbara Ann Suydam, Sept. 6, 1969; children: Peyton Zimmermann III, Edward Arlen. BSEE, Evansville Coll., 1957; MSEE, Drexel Inst., 1963; PhD, U. Pa., 1967. Design engr. RCA, Moorestown, N.J., 1958-64, systems engr., 1966-69; prof. U. Tenn., Knoxville, 1969-75, 76-81; vis. prof. U. Hawaii, Honolulu, 1975-76; prof. U. Fla., Gainesville, 1981-84, 90-96, assoc. chmn., 1984-90, prof. emeritus, 1996—. Cons. in field. Author: Communication System Principles, 1976, Probability, Random Variables and Random Signal Principles, 1980, 4th edit., 2001, Digital Communication Systems, 1987; prin. author: Principles of Electrical Engineering, 1991, Radar Principles, 1998; contbr. articles to profl. jours.; patentee in field. Capt. USAFR, 1957-61. David Sarnoff fellow, 1964-66. Fellow IEEE (life); mem. Sigma Xi, Eta Kappa Nu, Tau Beta Pi, Sigma Pi Sigma, Phi Beta Chi. Methodist. Avocations: fishing, painting, woodworking. Office: U Fla Dept Elec& Computer Engring Gainesville FL 32611 Business E-Mail: ppeeb@ece.ufl.edu.

PEEDE, WAYNE CARROLL, small business owner; b. Kinston, N.C., Sept. 9, 1975; s. Wayne Carrol and Charlene Thurman Peede. Owner Ea. Theatrical, Kinston, NC, 1994—; ptnr. PC Sense, Kinston, NC, 2003—04; tech. dir./ bd. Grainger-Hill Performing Arts Ctr., Kinston, NC, 1995—. Fundraiser chair Grainger-Hill Performing Arts Ctr., Kinston, NC, 2001—. Prodr.: (multiple fundraising shows). Tech./media dir. Tanglewood Ch. of God, Kinston. Home: 2702 Carey Rd Kinston NC 28504 Office: Eastern Theatrical 2702 Carey Rd Kinston NC 28504 Office Phone: 252-521-6110. Personal E-mail: wpeede@aol.com. E-mail: wpeede@aol.com.

PEEK, JEFFREY M. corporate financial executive; BA in internat. affairs, Woodrow Sch. of Princeton U., 1969; MBA, Harvard Bus. Sch., 1972. With Merrill Lynch, 1983—2002; exec. v.p. Merrill Lynch & Co., Inc., 1997—2001; pres. Merrill Lynch Investment Managers, 1997—2001; vice chmn. Credit Suisse First Boston LLC, 2002—03; pres., COO CIT Group, 2003—04; pres., CEO CIT Group Inc., Livingston, NJ, 2004—. Former exec. mgmt. com. mem. Merrilly Lynch & Co.; bd. mem. CIT; mem. bd. dirs. Travelers Property Casual Corp. Office: CIT Group 1 CIT Dr Livingston NJ 07039*

PEEK, WILLIAM DEWITT, JR., music educator; b. Plainfield, NJ, Mar. 21, 1954; s. William D. and Barbara D. Peek. BA, Hamilton Coll., 1977; MusM, Westminster Choir Coll., 1994. Choral dir. Packer Collegiate Inst., Bklyn., 1984—88, Newark (N.J.) Boys Chorus Sch., 1989—92; tchr., performing arts chair Portledge Sch., Locust Valley, NY, 1995—. Music dir. Musical Theater; pianist Grand Picnic, Bklyn. Swing Ensemble; music dir. First Unitarian Congl. Soc., Bklyn., organist. Contbr. Encyclopedia of American History: The Development of the Industrial United States, 2003. Mem.: Nassau Music Educators Assn., NY State Sch. Music Assn., Am. Guild Organists, Music Educators Nat. Conf., Am. Choral Dirs. Assn. Home: 63 Lindbergh Street Locust Valley NY 11560 Personal E-mail: wdpeek@aol.com.

PEEL, HARRIS, art gallery owner, retired diplomat; b. Decatur, Ill., Nov. 14, 1923; s. Wilbur David Peel and Ruth Harris; m. Margaret Backus, Oct. 11, 1946 (dec. Nov. 1990); children: Susan Harris, Jane Peel Fuller, David Harris. BS, Columbia U., 1950; MS, George Washington U., 1967. Editor War Dept., Frankfurt, Germany, 1946; writer Holiday Mag., Europe, 1947-48; fgn. svc. officer U.S. Dept. State and USIA, various locations, 1950-74; owner Peel Gallery Fine Art, Danby, Vt., 1976—. Author: (book) History of 254th Infantry Regiment, 1945. Advisor on psychol. warfare U.S. Army and USN, Ft. Bragg, N.C., 1971-74. Cpl. U.S. Army, 1943-45. Decorated Bronze star with oak leaf cluster U.S. Army, 1945, Disting. Civilian Svc. medal U.S. Army; 4-yr. scholar Chgo. Tribune, 1941. Mem. Vt. Assn. Galleries (pres. 1978-98), Overseas Press Club. Avocation: astronomy. Home: 1 Peel Rd Danby VT 05739 Office: Peel Gallery Peel Rd Danby VT 05739 E-mail: hpeel@earthlink.net.

PEEL, MARK, chef, restaurant owner; b. Calif. m. Nancy Silverton; children: Vanessa, Benjamin, Oliver. Student, U. Calif., Santa Barbara, Calif. Poly. U. Former apprentice Ma Maison, L.A.; former mem. staff La Tour d'Argents, Moulin de Mougins; former sous chef Michael's, Santa Monica, Calif.; former mem. staff Chez Panisse, Berkeley, Calif.; head chef Spago, Hollywood, Calif., 1985—89; co-owner, chef Campanile, L.A., 1989—. Author (with Nancy Silverton): Mark Peel and Nancy Silverton at Home, Two Chefs Cook for Family and Friends, The Food of Campanile. Nominee Best Am. Chef, Calif., James Beard Found., 1990, 1995, 1996; named Restaurateur of Yr., So. Calif. Restaurant Writers, 1995; named one of Best New Chefs, Food & Wine Mag., 1989. Office: Campanile 624 S La Brea Ave Los Angeles CA 90036

PEELE, ANNE MARIE, government relations administrator; b. Durham, NC, June 30, 1968; d. Robert Louis and Brabara (Davis) P. BA, N.C. A&T State U., 1996; MPA, N.C. Ctrl. U., 1996; MBA, High Point (N.C.) U., 2003. Cert. human resources mgr. Legis. asst., com. clk. N.C. Ho. of Reps., Raleigh, 1993—2001; employment recruiter Triangle Communities, Durham, 2000—01; v.p. govt. rels. Durham C. of C., 2002—. Mem. multi-jurisdictional adv. bd. City of Durham, 2001—. Mem. ASPA, Soc. Human Resources Mgmt., Am. Polit. Sci. Soc., Nat. Black MBA Assn., Nat. Forum Black Pub. Adminstrs., Internat. City/County Mgmt. Assn., Multi Jurisdictional Adv. Bd. Transporatation. Home: 3601-F Highgate Dr Durham NC 27713 Office: Durham C of C PO Box 3829 300 W Morgan St Ste 1400 Durham NC 27702

PEELE, KATHERINE N. architect; BArch (summa cum laude), NC State U., 1988. With Boney, PLLC, Raleigh, NC, 1988—, dir. Raleigh office, 1992—, COO, 2002—. Sch. constrn. support com. Wake County Pub. Sch. Sys. Fellow: AIA (pres. 2000, chair com. arch. edn. 2001, adv. bd. nat. com. arch. edn.); mem.: NC Ednl. Facility Planners (pres. 1999). Office: 5511 Capital Ctr Dr Ste 105 Raleigh NC 27606 Office Phone: 919-851-9393. E-mail: knp@booneyarchitects.com.

PEELE, ROGER, hospital administrator; b. Elizabeth City, N.C., Dec. 24, 1930; s. Joseph Emmett and Catherine (Groves) P.; m. Diana Egan, June 15, 1963 (dec.); children: Amy, Rodney, Holly; m. Gail Nelson Oct. 15, 1992. AB, U. N.C., 1955; MD, U. Tenn., 1960. Cert. adminstrv. psychiatry, 1970 cert. forensic psychiatry, 1982. Intern St. Elizabeths Hosp., Washington, 1960-61, resident in psychiatry, 1961-64, tng. officer, 1964-67, chief of service William A. White div., 1967-69; dir. Area D Community Mental Health Center, 1969-73, asst. supt., 1974-75, 77-79, acting supt., 1975-77, chmn. dept. psychiatry, 1979-95. Clin. prof. George Washington U., 1979—; asst. dir. NIMH, 1978-79; chief clin. officer D.C. Commn. on Mental Health, 1987-91; med. dir. Northern Va. Mental Health Ctr., 1996-98; attending George Washington U., 1998-2001; chief psychiatrist Montgomery County, Md. Contbr. articles on clin., forensic and adminstrv. issues in Am. psychiatry to profl. jours. Served with USAF, 1950-53. Superior Service award HEW, 1967. Fellow Am. Coll. Psychiatry, Am. Psychiat. Assn. (speaker 1986-87, Adminstr. of Yr. 1989); mem. AMA, D.C. Med. Soc., Am. Assn. Psychiat. Adminstrs. (past pres.), Group for Advancement Psychiatry, Med. Soc. St. Elizabeth's Hosp. (past pres.), Fed. Physicians Assn. (past pres.). Episcopalian. Home: 8002 Lions Crest Way Gaithersburg MD 20879-5637 Office Phone: 301-580-7662. Personal E-mail: RogerPeele@aol.com. *A key to effective treatment is not to allow the seductiveness of logic to narrow one's observations.*

PEELER, BOB, lieutenant governor; b. Gaffney, South Carolina, 1952; s. Smith and Sally (Bratton) P.; m. Bett (Carter); children: Caroline, Robert, Jr. V.p. Peeler's Milk Now Peeler Bros. Dairy, Cattle Co.; former chmn. Cherokee County Sch. Bd., S.C. State Bd. Edn.; lt. gov. State of S.C., 1995—. Founding mem. Advancement Bd. Coll. Commerce, Clemson Univ. Mem. S.C. Dairy Assn. (past pres.),;Cherokee County C. of C. (past pres.); Sertoma Internat. (life); Rotary (Gaffney chpt.); Masons; York Rite. Republican. Methodist.

PEELER, STUART THORNE, petroleum industry executive and independent oil operator; b. Los Angeles, Oct. 28, 1929; s. Joseph David and Elizabeth Fiske (Boggess) P.; m. Sylvia Frances Townley, Nov. 5, 1985. BA, Stanford U., 1950, JD, 1953. Bar: Calif. 1953. Ptnr. Musick, Peeler & Garrett, L.A., 1958-73; with Santa Fe Internat. Corp., Orange, Calif., 1973-81, v.p., sec., assoc. gen. counsel, 1973-74, sr. v.p., gen. counsel, dir., 1975-81; vice-chmn. bd., chmn. exec. com. Supron Energy Corp., 1978-82; chmn. bd., CEO Statex Petroleum, Inc., 1982-89; chmn., pres., CEO Putumayo Prodn. Co., Tucson, 1989—. Bd. dirs. Chieftain Internat. Inc. Trustee J. Paul Getty Trust, 1963-99; mem. U.S. Tuna Team, 1957-67, capt., 1966. Served with U.S. Army, 1953-55. Decorated Army Commendation medal. Mem. AIME, State Bar Calif., Am. Judicature Soc., Theta Chi, Phi Delta Phi, Skyline Country Club. Republican. Congregationalist. Office: PO Box 35852 Tucson AZ 85740-5852 Fax: 520-544-0632.

PEELER, WILLIAM JAMES, lawyer; b. Highland Park, Mich., Nov. 27, 1927; s. Herb and Beulah (Wells) P.; m. Nancy Jean Bradley, Dec. 26, 1949; children: Nannette Peeler Bradley, Jeana Peeler Hosch, Jacqueline Peeler Safstrom. LLB, Cumberland U., 1952. Bar: Tenn. 1952. Ptnr. Porch, Peeler, Williams & Thomason, Waverly, Tenn., 1952—; gen. counsel New Life Found., Burns, Tenn., 1983—. Mem. Tenn. Ho. of Reps., 1959-63; majority leader Tenn. Senate, 1967-75; trustee Cumberland U., Lebanon, Tenn., 1985—. Fellow Am. Coll. Trial Lawyers, Tenn. Bar Found.; mem. Am. Judicature Soc., ABA, Tenn. Bar Assn., Humphreys County Bar Assn., Masons (32 deg.), Shriners, Elks, Cumberland Club, City Club, Capitol Club, Jefferson Club Louisville. Democrat. Mem. Ch. of Christ. Home: 2351 Ogden Rd Waverly TN 37185 Office: Porch Peeler Williams & Thomason 102 S Court Sq Waverly TN 37185-2198

PEEPLES, MARY LOUISE, music educator, musician; d. John Henry Kapp and Louise (Brown) Bowles; m. Wade A. Peeples, June 30, 1982. MusB cum laude, Salem Coll., Winston-Salem, 1971; MusM, Eastman Sch. Music, Rochester, N.Y., 1973; pvt. organ study, Marie-Claire Alain, Paris, 1974—76. Instr. music Salem Coll., Winston-Salem, 1973—74; asst. organist/choirmaster St. George's Anglican, Paris, 1974; organist St. Mary's Cath. Ch., Paris, 1975; prof. music Judson Coll., Marion, Ala., 1976—98; organist/choirmaster St. Paul's Episc. Ch., Selma, Ala., 1983—97; asst. organist/choirmaster Episc. Cathedral, Birmingham, Ala., 1997—98; organist, choirmaster First Christian Ch., Winston-Salem, 1998—. Clinician Episc. Diocese, Birmingham, 1985, Moravian Music Festival, Winston-Salem, 1984; clinician, recitalist Ala. Music Tchrs. Assn., Montgomery, 1979, 83, 94; mem. liturgy/music com. State of Ala.; harpsicordist Carolina Chamber Symphony; organ recitals include St. Louis des Invalides, Paris, Delta Omicron Internat. Conv., St. Thomas Ch., NYC. Recipient Thompson Tchg. award, Judson Coll. Mem.: Am. Hymn Soc., Am. Choral Dirs. Assn., N.C. Music Tchrs. Assn. (bd. dirs., organ chair 1999—), Music Tchrs. Nat. Assn. (cert.). Moravian Ch. Office: First Christian Ch 2320 Country Club Rd Winston Salem NC 27104

PEEPLES, RUFUS RODERICK, JR., (RODDY PEEPLES), farm and ranch news radio broadcaster; b. Tehuacana, Tex., July 3, 1932; s. Rufus Roderick and Josephine (Gray) P.; m. Bettimae Scrivener, Aug. 8, 1953; children: James Roderick, Deidre Lynn. BA, Tex. A&M Coll., 1953. Farm dir. KADA Radio, Ada, Okla., 1953-56, KGNO Radio, Dodge City, Kans., 1956-59, KLIK Radio, Jefferson City, Mo., 1959; assoc. farm dir. KWFT Radio, Wichita Falls, Tex., 1959-64; sr. farm broadcaster, former owner Voice of S.W. Agt. Radio Network, San Angelo, Tex., 1964—. Mem. adv. bd. Tex. Agrl. Lifetime Leadership Program, College Station, 1987—, West Tex. Boys Ranch, San Angelo, 1966—. Named Man of Yr. in Tex. Agr., Tex. Assn. County Agrl. Agts., 1984, Disting. Alumnus, Coll. Agr. and Life Scis. Tex. A&M U., 1995; recipient Ann. Comms. award, Tex. Profl. Agrl. Workers, 1982, Tex. Farm Bur. Agr. Journalism award, 1997. Mem.: Nat. Assn. Farm Broadcasters (pres. 1982, Farm Broadcaster of Yr. 1992, Farm Broadcasters Hall of Fame 2001). Republican. Methodist. Avocations: flying, music, photography.

PEEPLES, WILLIAM DEWEY, JR., mathematics professor; b. Bessemer, Ala., Apr. 19, 1928; s. William Dewey and Thelma Jeannette (Chastain) P.; m. Katie Ray Blackerby, Aug. 30, 1956; children: Mary Jeannette, William Dewey III, Gerald Lewis, Stephen Ray. *Sister, Sarah Jeannette Peeples, taught. Daughter, Mary Jeannette, married Gene Paul Branham. Grandsons were Joel William, Aaron Ray, Paul, Cameron, and great-grandsons Allen and Andrew. Gene is a network systems manager. Son, William D. III, computer systems architect, married Amelia Hart. Son, Rev. Gerald Lewis, is pastor at New Bethel Southern Baptist Church., married Donna Harris and had granddaughter, Katlyn Marie. Son, Stephen Ray, second vice president and acturary, married Kathy Beam and had grandchildren Samantha Leigh and Jordan Karl. Sister-in-law, Carolyn Blackerby, married Milton Adams. Brother-in-law, Edwin Blackerby, married Linda Moore and had children Brandon, Leigh Dale, Bonnie and Jeb.* BS, Samford U., 1947; MS, U. Wis., 1949, PhD, U. Ga., 1951. Rsch. mathematician Ballistics Rsch. Lab., Aberdeen, Md., summer 1951; mem. faculty Samford U., Birmingham, Ala., 1951-56, prof. math., 1959-95, head dept., 1967-95; prof. emeritus, 1995, mem. faculty Auburn U., 1956-59. Cons. Hayes Internat. Corp. Co-author: Modern Mathematics for Business Students, 1969, Finite Mathematics, 1974, Modern Mathematics with Applications to Business and the Social Sciences, 4th edit, 1986, Finite Mathematics with Applications to Business and the Social Sciences, 1981, 2d edit., 1987; Contbr. articles to profl. publs. Served to 1st lt. AUS, 1954-56. Mem. Am. Math. Soc., Math. Assn. Am., Nat. Council Tchrs. Math., Ala. Coll. Tchrs. Math. (pres. 1969), Sigma Xi, Pi Mu Epsilon, Phi Kappa Phi (pres. 1977), Lambda Chi Alpha. Baptist (deacon, chmn. 1986). Club: Mason (Shriner). Home: 419 Poinciana Dr Birmingham AL 35209-4129 E-mail: wdpeeples@peoplepc.com.

PEER, GEORGE JOSEPH, metals company executive; b. St. Louis, Aug. 26, 1925; s. George J. and Melba (Rahning) P.; m. Mary Jane Hazlewood, Feb. 14, 1948; children— Linda, Gary, Steven, Scott. BS, Purdue U., 1945, MS, 1948; postgrad., Advanced Mgmt. Program, Harvard, 1967. Operating supr. Republic Steel Corp., Canton, Ohio, 1948-54; various sales positions to v.p. sales Basic, Inc., Chgo., Cleve., 1954-63; v.p. marketing Handy & Harman, N.Y.C., 1963-71, dir., 1971-75, group v.p. precious metals, 1972-75; chmn., pres., chief exec. officer Multi-Metal Wire Cloth, Inc., 1975-88; pres. Holyoke Wire Cloth Co., 1975-88, Multi-Wedge Corp., 1976-88, United-Holyoke Corp., 1980-86; pres., chief exec. officer Liquid-Solids Separation Corp., 1988-93, dir., 1988-96; retired. Bd. dirs. Handy & Harman Refining Group Inc.; chmn. Phillips Steel Fabricators, Inc., 1989-93. Chmn. bd. Lucas Milhaupt, Inc., Cudahy, Wis., 1967-75. Served with USNR, 1943-46, 51-53. Mem. Landings Club (Savannah, Ga.), Cornell Club of N.Y., Tau Beta Pi, Kappa Delta Rho. Republican. Congregationalist. Home: 9 Springpine Ln Savannah GA 31411-3080

PEER, LARRY HOWARD, literature educator; b. Ogden, Utah, Jan. 2, 1942; s. Howard Harvey and Edna Celina (Baron) P.; m. Janet Priday; 9 children. BA, Brigham Young U., 1963, MA, 1965; PhD, U. Md., 1969. From asst. to assoc. prof. U. Ga., Athens, 1968-75; assoc. prof. Brigham Young U., Provo, Utah, 1975-78, prof., 1978—. Acting head dept. comparative lit. U. Ga., Athens, 1973-74, Brigham Young U., Provo, 1978-81; pres. Western Regional Honors Coun., 1978-79; exec. dir. Am. Conf. on Romanticism, 1992—. Author: Beyond Haworth, 1984, The Reasonable Romantic, 1986, The Romantic Manifesto, 1988. Mem. MLA, Am. Comparative Lit. Assn. (exec. officer 1988-94), Am. Soc. for Aesthetics, Rocky Mountain Soc. for Aesthetics (pres. 1986-87), Internat. Byron Soc., Internat. Brontë Soc. Mem. Lds Ch. Avocation: travel. Office: Brigham Young U Comparative Lit Dept Provo UT 84602

PEERMAN, DEAN GORDON, magazine editor; b. Mattoon, Ill., Apr. 25, 1931; s. Staley Jacob and Irene (Monen) P. BS with highest distinction, Northwestern U., 1953; postgrad., Cornell U., 1953-54; B.D., Yale, 1959; D.D., Kalamazoo Coll., 1967. With Christian Century Found., 1959—; copy editor Christian Century mag., 1959-61, assoc. editor, 1961-64, mng. editor, 1964-81, exec. editor, 1981-85, sr. editor, 1985-98, contbg. editor, 1998—. Author: (with M.E. Marty) Pen-ultimates, 1963, (with Marty, L.M. Delloff, J.M. Wall) A Century of The Century, 1987; editor: Frontline Theology, 1967; co-editor: (with Marty) New Theology 1-10, 1964-73, A Handbook of Christian Theologians, 1965, enlarged edit., 1984, (with Alan Geyer) Theological Crossings, 1971; contbg. author: Chile: Under Military Rule, 1974; editor, contbr. Faithful Witness, 2002. Active Chgo. community theater groups. Recipient award for distinction in lay ministry within the church Yale Div. Sch., 1995. Mem. ACLU, Fellowship of Reconciliation, Amnesty Internat., Chgo. Religious Leadership Network on Latin Am., Phi Beta Kappa. Democrat. Baptist. Office: Christian Century Mag 104 S Michigan Ave Ste 700 Chicago IL 60603-5901 Office Phone: 312-263-7510 ext. 236.

PEET, AMANDA, actress; b. Jan. 11, 1972; d. Charles and Penny Peet. BA in History, Columbia U., 1994. Actor: (TV series) Law & Order, 1995, Central Park West, 1995—96, The Single Guy, 1996, Spin City, 1997, Seinfeld, 1997, Jack & Jill, 1999, Partners, 1999; (TV films) Ellen Foster, 1997, Date Squad, 2001; (films) Animal Room, 1995, She's the One, 1996, One Fine Day, 1996, Virginity, 1996, Grind, 1997, Touch Me, 1997, Sax and Violins, 1997, 1999, 1998, Southie, 1998, Playing by Heart, 1998, Origin of the Species, 1998, Simply Irresistible, 1999, Jump, 1999, Two Ninas, 1999, Body Shots, 1999, Isn't She Great?, 2000, The Whole Nine Yards, 2000, Takedown, 2000, Whipped, 2000, Saving Silverman, 2001, High Crimes, 2002, Changing Lanes, 2002, Igby Goes Down, 2002, Whatever We Do, 2003, Identity, 2003, Something's Gotta Give, 2003, The Whole Ten Yards, 2004. Office: The Gersh Agy Ste 201 232 N Canon Dr Beverly Hills CA 90210

PEET, CHARLES D, JR., lawyer; b. N.Y.C., Sept. 3, 1935; s. Charles D and Margaret Louise (Sherman) P.; children: Alisa, Amanda. BA, Yale U., 1957; JD, Harvard U., 1960. Bar: N.Y. 1962. Assoc. Milbank, Tweed, Hadley & McCloy, N.Y.C., 1960-68, ptnr., 1969-98; of counsel Freshfields Bruckhaus Deringer LLP (and predecessor firm), N.Y.C., 1998—. Mem. Assn. Bar N.Y.C. Office: Freshfields Bruckhaus Deringer LLP 520 Madison Ave Fl 34 New York NY 10022-4213 E-mail: charles.peet@freshfields.com.

PEET, PHYLLIS IRENE, women's studies educator; b. Winnipeg, Man., Can., Mar. 3, 1943; came to the U.S., 1948; d. Harold Parsons and Gladys Mae (Riley) Harrison; m. Thomas Peter Richman, June 14, 1963 (div. 1969); m. Charles Francis Peet, Sept. 9, 1972. BA in Art, Calif. State U., Northridge, 1972; MA in Art History, U. Calif., L.A., 1976, PhD in Art History, 1987. Sec. L.A. County Supr. Kenneth Hahn, 1960-68; assoc. in art history L.A. County Mus. Art, 1974-75; asst. dir., curator Grunwald Ctr. for the Graphic Arts, U. Calif., L.A., 1975-78; Am. art scholar High Mus. Art, Atlanta, 1984-90; instr. women's studies Monterey (Calif.) Peninsula Coll., 1986—, dir., instr. women's programs/women's studies, 1989—. Dirs.' adv. com. The Art Mus. of Santa Cruz County, 1981-84, 89-94; vis. lectr. Calif. State U., Fresno, 1984; program coord. conf. Inst. for Hist. Study, San Francisco, 1987; lectr. bd. studies in art U. Calif. Santa Cruz, 1991-95. Author, co-curator, editor, compiler: (book and exhbn.) The American Personality: The Artist Illustrator of Life in the United States, 1860-1930, 1976; author, curator: (book and exhbn.) American Women of the Etching Revival, 1988; co-author: American Paintings in the High Museum of Art, 1994; contbr. articles to profl. jours. including Am. Nat. Biography, Fitzroy Dict. of Women Artists, 1997, Dict. Literary Biography, 1998. Vol., activist Dem. Party, L.A., 1960-66, Peace and

Freedom Party, L.A., 1967-71; vol. Dem. Party Candidates, Santa Cruz, Calif., 1979-96, Santa Cruz Action Network, 1980-85; mem. nominating com. Girl Scouts of Am., Monterey Bay, 1991-93. Rockefeller Found. fellow U. Calif. LA, 1978-80, Dickson grantee U. Calif. LA, 1981-82; recipient Women Helping Women award Soroptimists, Monterey and Carmel, Calif., 1991, 95, Allen Griffin for Excellence in Edn. award Cmty. Found. Monterey County, 1993, Quality of Life award Econ. Devel. Corp., Monterey, 1994; named Tchr. of Yr., Tchrs. of Tomorrow, 2004. Mem.: NAACP, ACLU, NOW, AAUW, Western Assn. Women Historians, Inst. for Hist. Study, Nat. Women's Studies Assn., Planned Parenthood, Monterey Bay Women's Caucus for Art (founder, bd. dirs. 1988—93), Women's Internat. League for Peace and Freedom. Avocations: print collecting, photography. Office: Womens Programs Monterey Peninsula Coll 980 Fremont St Monterey CA 93940-4704 Office Phone: 831-646-4276. Business E-Mail: ppeet@mpc.edu.

PEET, RICHARD CLAYTON, lawyer, consultant; b. N.Y.C., Aug. 24, 1928; s. Charles Francis and Florence L. (Isaacs) P.; m. Barbara Jean McClure, Mar. 17, 1956 (div. July, 1988); children: Victoria Clementine, Alexandra Constance, Elizabeth Erica, Clarissa Barbara. JD, Tulane U., 1953. Bar: La. 1955, D.C. 1955. Law clk. Melvin M. Belli, San Francisco, 1954; with The Calif. Co., Standard Oil of Calif., 1955; atty. appellate sect. Lands div. Dept. Justice, Washington, 1956; asst. to gen. counsel Dept. Commerce, 1957; legis. asst. Republican policy com. U.S. Senate, 1958; legis. asst. U.S. Senate minority leader William F. Knowland, 1958; asso. counsel House Judiciary Com., 1959-62; asso. minority counsel House Pub. Works Com., 1969-74; pres. Citizens for Hwy. Safety, 1978-84; practiced in Washington, 1962-68; prin. Richard Clayton Peet & Assos., 1972—; ptnr. Anderson, Pendleton, McMahon, Peet & Donovan, 1977-80, Anderson, Peet & Co., 1980-84. Pres., mng. dir. Lincoln Rsch. Ctr., 1965-72; v.p. Oil East Corp., 1978-83. Author: Goals for a Constructive Opposition, 1966; contbg. editor: Congressional Digest, 1960-61, Jour. Def. and Diplomacy, 1983-86, Senate Rep. Week, 1991; (weekly radio show) Across the Aisle, 1992; composer: song Stand Up For America, 1971 (George Washington medal Freedom's Found. 1971), A Monologue With God, 1996, Remembrance House. Chmn. bd. Workshop Library on World Humor; Rep. candidate Pres. of U.S., 1999-2000. With U.S. Army, 1946-47, with USAFR, 1950-55. Nominated for Rockefeller Public Svcs. Awd. Mem. Phi Delta Phi, Pi Kappa Alpha. Achievements include conceiving Highway Safety Act of 1973 with Cong. Wm. Harsha, OH, establishing road safety improvement programs, created (with congress) Natl. Bicentennial Highway Safety Year to promote, organized and chaired (with Pres. Ford) White House Conf. on Highway Safety, 1976, Rep. candidate for U.S. Pres., 1999-2000. Home: Remembrance House Inc Ste 186-184 4200 Wisconsin Ave NW Washington DC 20016 E-mail: Dick079@aol.com.

PEETA, SRINIVAS, civil engineering educator, consultant; arrived in U.S., 1988; s. Koteswara Rao Chinna and Jhansi Laxmi (Tata) Peeta; m. Uma Devi Kambalapadu, June 8, 1995. BTech, Indian Inst. Tech., Madras, 1988; MS, Calif. Inst. Tech., Pasadena, 1989; PhD, U. Tex., Austin, 1994. Asst. prof. Purdue U., West Lafayette, Ind., 1994—2000, assoc. prof., 2000—. Mem. transp. network modeling com. Nat. Rsch. Coun., Washington, 1994—, chair route choice and spatial behavior subcom., 1998—, mem. travel behavior and values com., 2002—. Contbr. articles to profl. jours.; assoc. editor: Networks and Spatial Econs., 1999—, guest editor:, 2001; mem. editdl. adv. bd. Transp. Rsch., Part B, 2004—; mem. editl. adv. bd.: Intelligent Transp. Sys. Jour., 2002—. Recipient CAREER Award, NSF, 1997, Transp. Sci. Best Dissertation award, Ops. Rsch. Soc. Am., 1994, Wansik Excellence in Rsch. award, Sch. Civil Engring. Purdue U., 2004. Mem.: ASCE, Internat. Fedn. Automatic Control (mem. tech. com. transp. sys. 2000—), Internat. Assn. Travel Behavior Rsch., Inst. Opers. Rsch. and Mgmt. Sci., Tau Beta Pi, Omega Rho, Sigma Xi. Achievements include research in traveler information systems, disaster management, infrastructure systems, and traffic modeling. Office: Purdue Univ Sch Civil Engring 550 Stadium Mall Dr West Lafayette IN 47907 Business E-Mail: peeta@purdue.edu.

PEFANIS, HARRY, manufacturing executive; b. Buffalo, 1957; Grad., U. Okla., 1979. Exec. v.p. All American, LLC, Houston, 1998, pres., COO, 1999—. Office: 333 Clay St Houston TX 77002

PEFLEY, NORMAN GORDON, corporate financial executive; b. Eugene, Oreg., Dec. 15, 1955; s. Gordon Vergne Pefley and Jean Pefley (Lee) Hawley; m. Emma Ginete Lacuesta, July 5, 1986. BA, U. Calif., Davis, 1977; MA, Johns Hopkins U., 1979; MBA, U. Chgo., 1981; MA, Golden Gate U., 2001. CFA. Rsch. analyst Chgo. Bd. Options Exch., 1981-83; sr. fin. analyst Bank of Am., San Francisco, 1983-89, v.p., 1989-99. Referee Jour. Futures Markets, N.Y.C., 1984-87. Mem.: ASTD, The Security Analysts of San Francisco, Internat. Soc. Performance Improvement, CFA Inst., Toastmasters Internat., Omicron Delta Epsilon, Delta Phi Alpha, Phi Beta Kappa. Avocation: foreign languages.

PEGRAM, J.J. architectural firm executive; CEO, mgr., designer Pegram Assocs., Inc., Myrtle Beach, S.C. Office: Pegram Assocs Inc PO Box 7448 Myrtle Beach SC 29572-0012

PEHLIVANOV, NONKO DIMITROV, gastroenterologist, researcher; b. Sliven, Bulgaria, Aug. 25, 1961; came to U.S., 1997; s. Dimitar Noykov and Bogdana Georgieva Pehlivanov; m. Daniela Nikolaeva Mitreva, Feb. 16, 1985; 1 child, Plamena. MD, Med. Acad., Sofia, Bulgaria, 1985, specialist in internal medicine, 1991, specialist in gastroenterology, 1993. Asst. prof. Transport Med. Inst., Sofia, 1987-97; rsch. assoc. U. Va., Charlottesville, Va., 1997; postgrad. fellow U. Calif., San Diego, 1998-99; rsch. assoc. U. Kans. Med. Ctr., 1999—2002; asst. dir. Motility Lab, 2002—. Contbr. rsch. articles and studies to profl. jours.; patentee in field. Mem.: Am. Motility Soc., Am. Gastroenterol. Assn. Avocation: classical music. Office: U Kans Med Ctr Dept Pediat Mail Stop 4006 Miller Bldg 2 3901 Rainbow Blvd Kansas City KS 66061 E-mail: npehl@hotmail.com., npehlivanov@kumc.edu.

PEI, IEOH MING, architect; b. Canton, China, Apr. 26, 1917; arrived in U.S., 1935, naturalized, 1954; s. Tsu Yee Pei and Lien Kwun Chwong; m. Eileen Loo, June 20, 1942; children: Ting Chung, Chien Chung, Li Chung, Liane. BArch, MIT, 1940; MArch, Harvard U., 1946; DFA (hon.), U. Pa., 1970, Rensselaer Poly. Inst., 1978, Carnegie Mellon U., 1980, U. Mass., 1980, Brown U., 1980, NYU, 1980, Dartmouth Coll., 1991, Northeastern U.; LLD, Chinese U., Hong Kong, 1970, Pace U.; LHD, Columbia U., 1980, U. Colo., 1982, U. Rochester, 1982, U. Hong Kong, 1990, Am. U., Paris, 1990. Practice architecture, N.Y.C., 1939—42; asst. prof. Harvard Grad. Sch. Design, 1945—48; dir. archtl. divsn. Webb & Knapp, Inc., 1948—55; with Pei Cobb Freed & Partners (formerly I.M. Pei & Ptnrs., I.M. Pei & Assocs.), N.Y.C., 1955—96; now ind. arch. N.Y.C., 1996—. Prin. works include Mile High Ctr., Denver, Nat. Ctr. Atmospheric Rsch., Boulder, Colo., planning projects include, S.W. Washington Redevelopment Plan, prin. works include Dallas City Hall, John Fitzgerald Kennedy Libr., Boston, Can. Imperial Bank Commerce Complex, Toronto, Overseas Chinese Banking Corp. Ctr., Singapore, Dreyfus Chemistry Bldg., MIT, East-West Ctr. U. Hawaii, Honolulu, Mellon Art Ctr. and Choate Rosemary Hall Sci. Ctr., Wallingford, Conn., Univ. Plz., NYU, Johnson Mus. Art Cornell U., Ithaca, N.Y., Washington Sq. East, Phila., Everson Mus. Art, Syracuse, N.Y., Nat. Gallery Art, East Bldg., Washington, Wilmington Tower, Raffles City, Singapore, West Wing Mus. Fine Arts, Boston, expansion and modernization of Louvre Mus., Paris, Morton H. Meyerson Symphony Ctr., Dallas, MIT Arts and Media Ctr., Jacob K. Javits Conv. Ctr., N.Y.C., Fragrant Hill Hotel, Beijing, Tex. Commerce Tower, Houston, Bank of China, Hong Kong, Creative Artists Agy., Beverly Hills, Calif., Guggenheim Pavilion, Mount Sinai Med. Ctr., N.Y.C., Rock n' Roll Hall of Fame and Mus., Cleve., Mus. Modern Art, Athens, Greece, Miho Mus. of Art, Shiga, Japan, Bilbao (Spain) Estuary Project, Four Seasons Hotel, N.Y.C., others, planning projects include, S.W. Washington Redevelopment Plan, Govt. Ctr. Redevelopment Plan, Boston, Oklahoma City Downtown Redevelopment Plan, Bedford Stuyvesant Super Block, Bklyn., master plan Columbia U. Mem. Nat. Def. Rsch. Com., Princeton, NJ, 1943—45, Nat. Coun. Humanities, 1966—70, Nat. Coun. on Arts, 1981—84. Recipient Thomas Jefferson Meml. medal for Architecture, 1976, gold medal for architecture, Am. Acad. Arts and Letters, 1979, Nat. Arts Club Gold medal of honor, 1981, Mayor's award of Honor for Art and Culture, N.Y.C., 1981, La Grande Medaille D'or L'Académie d'Architecture, 1981, Pritzker Architecture prize, 1983, Medal of Liberty, 1986, Medal of French Legion of Honor, 1988, Nat. Medal of Art, 1988, Praemium Imperiale, Japan Art Assn., 1989, UCLA Gold medal, 1990, Colbert Found. first award for excellence, 1991, Excellence 2000 award, 1991, Freedom medal, 1993; fellow MIT traveling, 1940, Wheelwright, Harvard U., 1951. Fellow: AIA (Medal of Honor N.Y. chpt. 1963, Gold Medal 1979), ASID (hon.); mem.: NAD, Urban Design Coun., Royal Inst. Brit. Architects, Am. Acad. and Inst. Arts and Letters (chancellor 1978—80), Am. Acad. Arts and Scis., Nat. Inst. Arts and Letters (Arnold Brunner award 1961). Office: care Pei Cobb Freed & Ptnrs 600 Madison Ave New York NY 10022-1615

PEI, LOWRY CHENG-WU, education educator, writer; b. Chgo., Sept. 24, 1946; s. Ching Pong Pei and Marjorie Nelle Lowry; m. Vaughn Jelly Sills, June 6, 1993; m. Sarah Abrams (div.); children: Matthew Abrams, Matthew Braden Sills, Dylan Eliyahu Sills. BA in English, Harvard U., 1963—67; MA in English, Stanford U., 1967—69, PhD in English, 1972—75. Asst. prof. of English U. of Calif., San Diego, 1974—78; preceptor in expository writing Harvard U., 1978—85; prof. of English Simmons Coll., Boston, 1985—. Author: Family Resemblances, 1984. Home: 20 Bellevue Ave Cambridge MA 02140 Office: Simmons Coll 300 The Fenway Boston MA 02115 Business E-Mail: pei@simmons.edu.

PEI, ZJ, engineer, educator, researcher; m. Su Liu, Nov. 15, 1986; children: Linda, Kevin. BS, Zhengzhou Inst. Tech., 1982; MS, Beijing Inst. Tech., 1984; PhD in Mech. Engring., U. Ill., 1995. Process engr. MEMC Electronic Materials, Inc., St. Peters, Mo., 1996—98; mech. engr. GE Panametrics, Waltham, Mass., 1998—99; rsch. scientist Strasbaugh, Inc., 1999; application engr. St-Gobain Abrasives, Inc., Worcester, Mass., 1999—2000; instr. mfg. engring. Kans. State U., Manhattan. Contbr. articles various profl. jours. Mem.: Soc. Mfg. Engrs., ASME, Am. Soc. for Engring. Edn., American Society for Precision Engineering. Achievements include patents for rotary ultrasonic disk grinding and semiconductor wafer manufacturing methods. Office: Kansas State U 237 Durland Hall Manhattan KS 66506 Office Phone: 785-532-3436. E-mail: zpei@ksu.edu.

PEIFFER, RANDEL AARON, agricultural sciences educator, researcher; b. Ligonier, Pa., Aug. 4, 1944; s. Tony and Emma E. (Leighty) P. BS, Delaware Valley Coll., 1968; MS, Pa. State U., 1970, PhD, 1976. Rsch. asst. prof. Del. State U., Dover, 1986; asst. prof. Del. State Coll., Dover, 1986-93, assoc. prof., 1993—. Vis. prof. Farmers Home Adminstrn. Advisor carpentry adv. com. Vocat. Tech. Sch., Kent County, Del., 1987—; mem. Del. Agr. Mus., Dover, 1986—; mem. tech. com. NE-SARE, 1994—. Recipient First Pl. Sci. Poster in Plant and Soil Sci., 9th Biennial Rsch. Symposium, Assn. Rsch. Dirs. 1890 Land-Grant Colls. and Univs., Atlanta, 1992—. Mem. Am. Soc. Agronomy, Crop Sci. Soc. Am., Fraternal Order Police, Silver Lake Fishing Club (editor newsletter Dover chpt. 1984—). Achievements include research inforage management and utilization, biological control of gypsy moth in urban forest and crop ecology. Office: Del State U Dept Agr Natural Resources Dover DE 19901 E-mail: rpeiffer@desu.edu.

PEIPERL, ADAM, kinetic sculptor, photographer; b. Sosnowiec, Poland, June 4, 1935; arrived in US, 1953, naturalized, 1958; s. Jacob and Fanny (Alster) P.; m. Martha Rose Dorf, June 15, 1958; children: Maury, Laurence, Linda. Grad., Cours Complementaire Gen, Paris, 1952; BS in Chemistry, George Washington U., 1957; postgrad., Pa. State U., 1959. Cons. in Russian sci. lit. Libr. Congress, Washington, 1959-61, 66-67; chemist Nat. Bur. Standards, Washington, 1961-63; sci. translator Am. Inst. Physics, NYC, 1973-94, Plenum Pub., 1993-98. One-man shows include Balt. Mus. Art, 1969, Pa. Acad. Fine Arts, 1969, Marlborough Gerson Gallery, NYC, 1969, Smithsonian Mus. History and Tech., 1972, Phila. Art Alliance, 1978; group shows include Washington Gallery Modern Art, 1968, Corcoran Gallery Art, 1968, Kent State U., McKay Art Inst., San Antonio, 1969, NASA Manned Spacecraft, Houston, 1970-71, Nat. Mus. Am. Art, 1972-82, Meml. Art Gallery, U. Rochester, 1978, Foster Harmon Galleries Am. Art, Sarasota, Fla., 1982-83, Artworks Gallery, Santa Barbara, Calif., 1989, Art of the Sixties, Fred Jones Jr. Mus. of Art, U. Okla., 2002, Pa. Acad. Fine Arts, 2004; represented in permanent collections Pa. Acad. Fine Arts, Mus. Boijmans-Van Beuningen, Rotterdam, Netherlands, Hirshhorn Mus. and Sculpture Garden; with choreographer Denise Vale collaboration involving projections of sculpture video, U. Okla., 2003. Home: 1135 Loxford Ter Silver Spring MD 20901-1130

PEIPERT, JAMES RAYMOND, journalist; b. Alton, Ill., Nov. 15, 1942; s. Lawrence George and Virginia Pauline (Sieve) P.; m. Mary Ellen Finney, Aug. 1, 1970; children: Benjamin, Matthew, Thomas. BA, So. Ill. U., 1965. Reporter, editor AP, Chgo., 1965-68, N.Y.C., 1968-70, corr. Moscow, 1970-74, London, 1974-80, news editor Johannesburg, South Africa, 1980-81, East Africa bur. chief Nairobi, Kenya, 1981-86; nat.-fgn. editor Fort Worth Star-Telegram, 1986-2001, mem. editl. bd., 2001—. With U.S. Army, 1965-67. Roman Catholic. Avocations: bicycling, maintaining 1967 mustang, reading. Office: Fort Worth Star Telegram PO Box 1870 Fort Worth TX 76101-1870 E-mail: jpeipert@star-telegram.com.

PEIRANO, LAWRENCE EDWARD, civil engineer; b. Stockton, Calif., May 13, 1929; s. Frank Lloyd and Esther Marie (Carigiet) P.; m. Mary Ellen Alabaster, July 26, 1952; children: Thomas Lawrence, Ellen Marie. BSCE, U. Calif., Berkeley, 1951, MSCE, 1952. Registered profl. engr., Calif.; diplomate Am. Acad. Environ. Engrs. Assoc. civil engr. Calif. Div. Water Resources, 1952-53; with Kennedy Engrs., Inc., San Francisco, 1955-94, project mgr., 1960-79, v.p., chief environ. engr., 1974-79; dir. ops. Kennedy/Jenks Engrs., Inc., San Francisco, 1979-86; sr. v.p., regional mgr. Kennedy/Jenks/Chilton, Inc., San Francisco, 1986-90; exec. v.p., chief tech. officer Kennedy/Jenks Cons., Inc. (formerly Kennedy Engrs., Inc.), San Francisco, 1990-94, also bd. dirs., chmn. bd., 1972-94; ret., 1994. Spl. lectr. san. engring. U. Calif., Berkeley, 1976. Served in U.S. Army, 1953-55, Korea, Okinawa. James Monroe McDonald scholar, 1950-51; recipient Trustees' citation U. Calif., Berkeley, 1996. Fellow ASCE (life); mem. Water Environ. Fedn., U. Calif. Alumni Assn., Sierra Club, Tau Beta Pi, Chi Epsilon. Republican. Roman Catholic. Home: 3435 Black Hawk Rd Lafayette CA 94549-2326 *Focus on serving clients and rewards will follow.*

PEIRCE, JAMES WALTER, secondary school educator, historian; b. Aug. 8, 1933; s. Kenneth Adelbert and Helen Virginia Peirce; m. Nancy Anne Kratovil, Apr. 14, 1962; 1 child, Mark Andrew. Cert. social studies tchr., secondary prin. Md. History tchr., adminstr. Prince George's County Bd. Edn., Upper Marlboro, Md., 1957—. Vol. fireman Chillum-Adelphi (Md.) Fire Dept., 1960—65; vol. ranger Pasapsco River Valley State Pk., Ellicott City, Md., 1991—99. Author: Pasapsco Valley Mill Sites, 1995, Four Hundred Years of Dicken, 2001, (poems) History of Post #28, 1997, The People Call it Chesapeake, 1999, History of the Prince George's Council of the American Legion, 2003. Life mem. Md. Congress of Parents and Tchrs., 1976—. With USN, 1951—56. Named Outstanding Educator of Am., Acad. Am. Edn., 1974; recipient Outstanding Svc. award, Prince George County. Mem.: U. Md. Alumni Assn., Am. Legion (life; historian 1995—). Republican. Avocations: history, genealogy, research, poetry, writing. Home: 5900 Whaleboat Dr Clarksville MD 21029

PEIRCE, KAREN PATRICIA, education educator; b. Providence, July 12, 1971; d. Raymond Fales and Patricia Kay Peirce. ABH, Rollins Coll., 1993; MA, Carnegie Mellon U., 1997. Peer writing cons. Rollins Coll. Writing Ctr., Winter Pk, Fla., 1990—93; Fulbright English tchg. asst. Korean Am. Edn. Commn., Ulsan, 1993—94; pub. rels. asst. Embassy of the Republic of Korea, Washington DC, 1995—96; rsch. asst. Carnegie Mellon U., Pittsburgh, Pa., 1996—97; English instr. The Sawyer Sch., Warwick, RI, 1997—98; upper divsn. English tchr. Berkeley Prep. Sch., Tampa, Fla., 1998—2001; grad. assoc. in tchg. U. of Ariz., 2001—. Mem.: Rhetoric Soc. Am., Internat. Writing Center Assn., Conf. on Coll. Composition and Comm., Nat. Coun. Teachers in English. Home: 6651 North Campbell Ave #205 Tucson AZ 85718

PEIRCE, NEAL R. journalist; b. Phila., Jan. 5, 1932; s. J. Trevor and Miriam deS. (Litchfield) P.; m. Barbara von dem Bach-Zelewski, Apr. 18, 1959; children: Celia, Andrea, Trevor. BA, Princeton U., 1954; postgrad., Harvard U., 1957-58. Polit. editor Congl. Quar., 1960-69; co-founder, contbg. editor Nat. Jour., Washington, 1969-97. Cons. and commentator elections CBS News, 1962, 67-76, NBC News, 1964-66; lectr. in field; syndicated newspaper columnist Washington Post Writers Group; chmn. The Citistates Group; mem. faculty Salzburg (Austria) Seminar, 1980, 84, 97; 1st Weinberg prof. Princeton U.'s Woodrow Wilson Sch. Pub. and Internat. Affairs, 1992. Author: The People's President, 1968, 2d edit., 1981, The Megastates of America, 1972, The Pacific States of America, 1972, The Mountain States of America, 1972, The Great Plains States America, 1973, The Deep South States of America, 1974, The Border South States, 1975, The New England States, 1976, The Mid-Atlantic States of America, 1977, The Great Lakes States of America, 1980, The Book of America: Inside Fifty States Today, 1983, Citistates: How Urban America Can Prosper in A Competitive World, 1993, Breakthroughs: Recreating The American City, 1993; Corrective Capitalism, 1987; editor Peirce Report series on 21 regions' Citistate futures starting with Phoenix Republic and Gazette, 1987. Founder, chmn. S.W. Neighborhood Assembly, Washington, 1963-65; mem. exec. com. Nat. Civic League, 1990-95; trustee German Marshall Fund U.S., 1987-97. With CIC, U.S. Army, 1954-57. Fellow Woodrow Wilson Internat. Center Scholars, 1971-74 Fellow Nat. Acad. Pub. Adminstrn.; mem. Newfound Lake Region Assn. (v.p. 1989-92), Phi Beta Kappa. Episcopalian. Home and Office: 1101 Mayhew Tpke Bristol NH 03222-5109 E-mail: npeirce@citistates.com.

PEIRIS, SUHITHI MAHESICA, research chemist; b. Colombo, Sri Lanka, Nov. 23, 1965; d. Suran A. and Marguerite M. Peiris; m. Brett M. Goodman, Apr. 28, 2001. BS with honors, U. Mich., 1991; PhD in Inorganic Chemistry, U. Chgo., 1996. Postdoctoral fellow U. Chgo., 1996-97; staff scientist Nova Rsch. Inc., Alexandria, Va., 1997-98; rsch. chemist Naval Rsch. Lab., Washington, 1998-2000, Naval Surface Warfare Ctr., Indian Head, Md., 2000—. Contbr. articles to profl. jours. Sci. fair judge, Washington, 1999, Indian Head, 2000. Recipient Outstanding Young Scientist award, Gordon Rsch. Conf., 2000. Mem. Am. Chem. Soc. Avocations: swimming, reading. E-mail: peirisSM@ih.navy.mil.

PEIRSOL, AARON, Olympic athlete; b. Irvine, Calif., July 23, 1983; s. Tim Hartig and Wela Peirsol. Student, U. Texas. Swimmer U.S. Olympic Team, Sydney Olympic games, 2000, U.S. Olympic Team, Athens Olympic games, 2004. Named NCAA Swimmer of the Yr., 2003. Silver medal, 200m backstroke, Sydney Olympic games, 2000, Gold medal, 200m backstroke, World Championships, 2001, Gold Medal, 100m, 200m backstroke, 400m relay, Pan American games, 2002, Gold Medal, 100m backstroke, 200m backstroke, 4x100m medaly relay, Athens Olympic Games, 2004, Holds world record in the 200m backstroke (long and short course meters), mem. Gold Medal U.S. 400m medley relay team, World Championships, 2003, Gold Medal, 200m backstroke, World Championships, 2003, Youngest American (age 15) to break two minutes in 200m backstroke. Office: c/o USA Swimming One Olympic Plaza Colorado Springs CO 80909*

PEISCH, ALICE HANLON, state legislator; BA, Smith Coll.; JD, Suffolk U. Law Sch. Town clerk Wellesley, 2000—03; state rep. Mass. House, 2003—. Bd. dirs. Wellesley Edn. Found., 1999—; bd. overseers Newton-Wellesley Hosp., 1996—; mem. League of Women Voters of Wellesley, 1986—; bd. mem. Senior Living, Inc., 2001—; mem. Wellesley Svc. League, 1988—. Democrat. Office: Rm 26 State House Boston MA 02133

PEISER, JOHN GEORGE, accountant, consultant; b. Chgo., June 2, 1944; m. Liora Rappaport, June 29, 1969; children: Daniela Jacqui, Gary Dean. BSc, U. Witwatersrand, South Africa, 1965, BSc (hon.), 1969; M in Bus. Leadership, U. South Africa, Pretoria, 1977. CPA; cert. valuation analyst. Researcher Nat. Inst. for Pers. Rsch., Johannesburg, South Africa, 1966-69; various mgmt. positions Lindsay Saker, Johannesburg, South Africa, 1970-76, bd. dir. pers., 1976 -78; mgr. human resource planning & devel. Fox & Jacobs, Dallas, 1978-83, regional sales dir., 1984-85; pres. Sidran, Inc., Dallas, 1985-90; CPA, ptnr., exec. cons. Peiser & Peiser, CPAs, Dallas, 1990-93; ptnr., exec. cons. bus. valuations Goldin Peiser & Peiser, CPAs, L.L.P., Dallas, 1993—. Bd. dirs. Solomon Schechter Acad. Dallas, chmn., 1984-86. Bd. dirs. Shearith Israel Congregation, Dallas, 1983-86, Zionist Orgn. Am., Dallas; pres. Yavneh Acad. of Dallas, 1993-97, pres. Zionist Mvmt./Bnai, Zion, 1998-2002; bd. dirs. Dallas Area Torah Assn., 2003-. Mem. AICPA, Am. Inst. Tng. and Devel., Nat. Assn. Cert. Valuation Analysts, Tex. Soc. CPA, Inst. Personnel Rsch. (branch chair, 1974-75). Avocations: reading, squash, tennis, bridge, travel. Office: 17742 Preston Rd Dallas TX 75252

PEISER, ROBERT ALAN, financial executive; b. N.Y.C., Apr. 17, 1948; s. Donald Edward and Natalia (Phillips) Peiser; children: Karyn, Brian, Craig, Scott. BA, U. Pa., 1969; MBA, Harvard U., 1972. Dir. corp. fin. TWA, N.Y.C., 1972-77, sr. v.p. fin., CFO, 1983-86, exec. v.p. fin., CFO, 1994-96; treas. Hertz Corp., N.Y.C., 1977-80; staff v.p., treas. ops. RCA Corp., N.Y.C., 1980-81; v.p., treas. Trans World Corp., N.Y.C., 1981-83; sr. v.p., CFO ALC Comm. Corp., Birmingham, Mich., 1986-88; sr. v.p. fin., CFO Borman's Inc., Detroit, 1988-89; pres., CEO Orange-Co. Ic., Bartow, Fla., 1989-92; with BBK, Ltd., Southfield, Mich., 1992-94; vice chmn., CEO FoxMeyer Drug Co., Carrollton, Tex., 1996; pres., CEO Western Pacific Airlines, Colorado Springs, Colo., 1996-98; chmn. CVSI, Inc., Bedford, Mass., 1998-99; chmn., CEO Vitality Beverages, Tampa, Fla., 1999—. Bd. dirs. Ascent Assurance, Inc., Microware, Inc., Tampa Bay Partnership. Trustee Mich. chpt. Leukemia Soc. Am. Mem. Birmingham Athletic Club, The Wyndgate Country Club. Office: Ste 2000 400 N Tampa St Tampa FL 33602 Home: PO Box 9 Sugar Land TX 77487-0009

PEITHMAN, ROSCOE EDWARD, physicist, educator; b. Hoyleton, Ill., Feb. 26, 1913; s. Edward Henry Peithman and Sarah Jane Smith; m. Laura Jane Davenport, Apr. 3, 1936 (dec. Oct. 13, 1987); children: Ann Davenport, Stephen Edward. BS, So. Ill. U., 1935; MS, U. of Ill., 1939; EdD, Oreg. State U., 1955. Tchr. various HS, Ill., 1935—42; prof. of physics Humboldt State U., Arcata, Calif., 1946—77, chmn. Divsn. of phys.PscienSess., 1960—69, dean Sch. Scis., 1969—70, emeritus prof. of physics, 1977—. Academic senator Calif. State U. Sys., Calif., 1963—66. Lt. comdr. USNR, 1942—73. Fellow: Am. Men and Women of Sci. (life); mem.: Am. Assn. of Physics Tchrs. Avocation: amateur radio. Home: 2704 Sunny Grove Ave Mckinleyville CA 95519-7912 E-mail: W6BME@cox.net.

PEITLER, ARTHUR JOSEPH, mayor, lawyer; b. N.Y.C., Dec. 2, 1948; s. Arthur Joseph and Dorothy Virginia Peitler; m. Mary Elizabeth Fitzpatrick, July 1, 1972; children: Daniel Joseph, Maureen Elizabeth, James Fitzpatrick. BS, St. Johns U., Jamaica, N.Y., 1970, MBA, 1973; JD, U. Conn., 1983. Bar: Conn. 1983, U.S. Dist. Ct. Conn. 1984. Acctg. mgr. J.C. Penney Co., N.Y.C., 1970-75; fin. analyst AMF, White Plains, N.Y., 1975-78; fin. mgr. Timex, Middlebury, Conn., 1978-83; pvt. practice, New Milford, Conn., 1983-95; mayor Town of New Milford, 1995—. Pres. New Milford Bar Assn., 1987. Treas., asst. treas. New Milford Jaycees/Conn. Jaycees, 1975-78; vice chmn. Childrens Ctr. Inc., New Milford, 1984-95; treas. Merryall Ctr. for Arts, New Milford, 1986—; chmn. Rep. Town Com., New Milford, 1988-89, 93-95; active Fin. Coun. St. Francis, New Milford, 1990-94. Roman Catholic. Office: Town of New Milford 10 Main St New Milford CT 06776-2831

PEIXOTO NETO, JOSE ULYSSES, internist, researcher; b. Crato, Ceará, Brazil, Aug. 29, 1930; s. Adérito de Aquino Silva and Adelite Alencar Peixoto; m. Maria Isolda Teles Cartaxo, May 23, 1958; children: Jose Ulysses Peixoto Filho, Eunice Ulysséia Peixoto Maia, Jorge André Cartaxo Peixoto. 1st degree, State Coll. Goias, Brazil, 1942, postgrad., 1942-49; 2d degree, St. John Coll., Fortaleza, Brazil, 1949; postgrad., Fed. U., Recife, Brazil, 1955; Laurel, Cearense Med. Ctr., 1994. Med. resident St. Michael Hosp., Rio de Janeiro, 1956; intern St. Anthony Hosp., Iguatú, Ceará, 1957; founder Social Providence, Crato, Ceará, 1958-64; attendent St. Frances Hosp., Crato, 1958-69; founder St. Michael Hosp., Crato, 1967-93, pres., dir., 1983-93, internist, researcher, 1993—; founder Faculty of Law, Crato, 1977-78. Lectr. faculty of medicine The Fed. U. of Ceará, 1976—. Recipient Good Svc. award Lyons

Club, 1992, Laurel Cearense Med. Ctr., 1994, Cert. Merit Health Care Profls. Juazeiro North Profl. Health Assn., 1998, Gold Medal of Profl. Merit, Ceara Estate Regional Coun. Medicine, 1999, Plaque of profl. merit Cariri sect. Coun. of Ceara, 2002. Fellow Brazilian Med. Assn. (specialist); mem. AAAS, ACP, Brazilian Soc. Clin. Medicine (specialist), N.Y. Acad. Sci. Roman Catholic. Avocations: reading, walking in woods, cinema, farming.

PEKER, ELYA ABEL, artist; b. Moscow, June 15, 1937; came to U.S. 1972; s. Aba Z. and Frieda I. (Warshavsky) P.; m. Katrina Friedman, May 19, 1977; 1 child, Benjamin E. Diploma of Artist for Theater Decoration, Art Inst., Moscow, 1956. Comml. artist, N.Y.C., 1972-88. One-man shows include Nakhamkin Fine Art Gallery, N.Y.C., 1980-85; exhibited in group shows in Basel, Switzerland, Hong Kong, others; represented in permanent collections of Kennedy-Onassis family, Emil Wolf, Frank L'Angella, Campbell family, Benjamin family, others; contemporary flower and still-life poster series published 1991, reproductions published worldwide. Mem. Am. Biog. Inst. (dep. gov., order internat. ambs., Gold Record Achievement 1995, 20th Century Achievement award 1995, Internat. Cultural Diploma Honor 1996), Internat. Platform Assn., Licensing Industry Merchandiser's Assn. Home: 1610 E 19th St # 297-196 Brooklyn NY 11229

PÉLADEAU, MARIUS BEAUDOIN, art and history consultant, retired museum director; b. Boston, Jan. 27, 1935; s. Marius and Lucienne (Beaudoin) P.; m. Mildred L. Cole, Feb. 26, 1972. BA cum laude, St. Michael's Coll., 1956; MS, Boston U., 1957; MA, Georgetown U., 1962. Assoc. editor Public Utilities Fortnightly, Washington, 1962-66; adminstrv. asst., press sec. to U.S. Congressman J. P. Vigorito, Washington, 1967-72; dir. Maine League Hist. Socs. and Mus.'s, Monmouth, 1972-76, William A. Farnsworth Library and Art Mus., Rockland, Maine, 1976-87; gen. mgr. The Theater at Monmouth, Maine, 1989; cons. in field, 1990—. Author: The Verse of Royall Tyler, 1968, The Prose of Royall Tyler, 1972, Chansonetta: The Life and Photographs of Chansonetta Stanely Emmons, 1858-1937, 1977, Charles Daniel Hubbard, 1876-1951: American Impressionist, 1996, John Francis Sprague: Chronicler of Maine History, 1998, Burnished Rows of Steel: The Role of Vermont Troops at the Battle of Gettysburg, July 1-3 1963, 2002. Trustee Mus. Glass and Ceramics, 1983-2003; guest curator L.C. Bates Mus., Hinckley, Maine, 1993-2000. Fellow Co. Mil. Historians; mem. Vt. Hist. Soc. Democrat. Roman Catholic. E-mail: peladeau@gwi.net.

PELAGALLI, JAMES A. surgeon; b. Bedford, Ohio, Mar. 10, 1931; MD, Loyola U. - Stritch Sch. Med., 1955. Diplomate Am. Bd. Surgeons. Intern St. Vincent Charity Hosp., Cleve., 1955-56, resident, 1956-57, 59-62; surgeon Parma Comm. Gen. Hosp., Ohio, U.S. Army Med. Corp., 1957-59. Fellow Am. Coll. Surgeons; mem. AMA. Office: 3666 Forest Run Dr Richfield OH 44286-9408

PELAVIN, DIANE CHRISTINE, small business owner; m. Sol H. Pelavin, Aug. 14, 1966. BA, So. Ill. U., 1965; MS, San Jose (Calif.) State U., 1979. Tchr., 1965—68; planning analyst EPRI, Palo Alto, Calif., 1977—78; rsch. analyst NTS Rsch. Corp., Durham, NC, 1978—82; v.p., co-founder Pelavin Assocs., Inc., Washington, 1982—94; pres., co-founder Chesapeake Inst., Washington, 1991—94; sr. v.p. Am. Insts. for Rsch., 1994—. Contbr. articles to profl. jours. U. Chgo. fellow, 1966, NSF fellow, 1968. Mem. Am. Edn. Rsch. Assn. Office: 1000 Thomas Jefferson St NW Washington DC 20007-3835

PELAVIN, SOL HERBERT, research company executive; b. Detroit, Dec. 16, 1941; s. Norman J. and Alice A. Pelavin; m. Diane Christine Blakemore, Aug. 14, 1966; 2 children. BA in Math., U. Chgo., 1965, MAT in Math., 1969; MS in Stats., Stanford U., 1974, PhD candidate in mathematical models of edn. research, 1975. Tchr. pub. schs., 1965-70. teaching rsch. asst. Stanford (Calif.) U., 1972-74; cons. Rand Corp., Santa Monica, Calif., 1975; policy analyst SRI Internat., Menlo Park, Calif., 1975-78; exec. officer NTS Research Corp., Durham, N.C., 1978-82; pres. Pelavin Assocs., Inc., Washington, 1982-94; exec. v.p., COO Am. Inst. Rsch., 1994-2001, pres., CEO, 2001-; dir. Data Analysis and Tech. Support Ctr., Washington, 1989-93, Policy Analysis Support Ctr., Washington, 1993—; expert witness to U.S. Congress, 1977, 79, Cabinet briefing, 1983; cons. Frank, Bernstein, Conway and Goldman, Balt., 1980-81; dir. Ednl. Analysis Ctr., Washington, 1982-85. Author: (with P. Barker) A Study of the Generalizability of the Results of Standardized Achievement Tests, 1976, (with J.L. David) Research on the Effectiveness of Compensatory Education Programs: A Reanalysis of Data, 1977, (with others) Federal Expenditures for the Education of Children and Youth With Special Needs, 1981, (with D.C. Pelavin) An Evaluation of the Fund for the Improvement of Postsecondary Education, 1981, 83, (with others) Evaluation of the Commodity Supplemental Food Program, 1982, An Evaluation of the Bilingual Education Evaluation, Dissemination and Assessment Centers, 1984, A Study of a Year-Round School Program, 1978, Teacher Preparation: A Review of State Certification Requirements, 1984, Analysis of the National Availability of Mathematics and Science Teachers, 1983, Minority Participation in Higher Education, 1988, Changing the Odds, 1990, others; contbr. articles to profl. jours. NSF fellow U. Chgo., 1968-69; Cuneo fellow Stanford U., 1973. Mem. Am. Ednl. Research Assn., Am. Psychol. Assn. Democrat. Jewish. Office: American Inst Rsch 1000 Thomas Jefferson Washington DC 20007-3500 E-mail: spelavin@air.org.

PELC, KAROL IGNACY, engineering and technology management educator, researcher; b. Czestochowa, Poland, July 29, 1935; came to U.S., 1985; s. Stanislaw Pelc and Kamilla (Hecko) Pelc-Kosna; m. Ryszarda Lidia Ryglewicz, Sept. 24, 1959; 1 child, Dariusz. MScEE, Tech. U. Wroclaw, Poland, 1958, PhD in Econs., 1976; PhD in Electronics, U. Uppsala, Sweden, 1968. Prodn. & engring. mgr. Energopomiar Co., Wroclaw, 1960-65; rsch. asst. dept. electronics U. Uppsala, 1961-62; assoc. dir. divsn. Inst. Electric Power Industry, Wroclaw, 1966-68; founder, dir. Forecasting Rsch. Ctr., Wroclaw, 1971-81; electronic design engr. Rsch. Inst. Tech. U. Wroclaw, 1957-60, rsch. dir., 1968-77, lectr., dir. Jelenia Gora Coll. br., 1982-85; prof. Mich. Technol. U., Houghton, 1985—; dir. Ctr. for Technol. Innovation, Leadership & Entrepreneurship, 2001—02. Vis. prof. Indian Inst. Tech., Bombay, 1981, Stevens Inst. Tech., Hoboken, N.J., 1993, U. Sci. and Tech., Beijing, 2002; vis. scholar Japan Ctr. for Mich. Univs., Hikone, 1992; mem. innovation task force Internat. Inst. for Applied Sys. Analysis, Laxenburg, Austria, 1983-84; chmn. forecasting seminar Polish Acad. Scis., Warsaw, 1974-81; v.p. divsn. Soc. Mgmt. and Orgn., Wroclaw, 1979-80. Author: Planning of Research and Development, 1981; co-author: Technological Challenges, 1999, Technology Strategies and Forecasts, 2003; mem. editl. bd. U.S. R&D Mgmt., Eng., Transformations, Poland; contbr. over 100 articles to scholarly jours.; patentee in field. Recipient Excellence in Rsch award, Internat. Assn. for Mgmt. of Tech., 2004. Mem. Internat. Assn. Mgmt. Tech., Internat. Assn. for Rsch. and Devel. Mgmt., Engring. Mgmt. Soc. of IEEE. Roman Catholic. Avocations: classical music, tourism, cross country skiing, bicycling, swimming. Office: Mich Technol Univ Sch Bus & Econ Houghton MI 49931

PELFREY, D. PATTON, lawyer; b. Ky., 1941; BA, Calif. State U., L.A., 1963; JD, U. Louisville, 1968. Bar: Ky. 1968. Trial atty. region 9 NLRB, Cin., 1968-72; mem. Frost Brown Todd LLC, Louisville, 1972—. Prof. labor law sch. law U. Louisville. Fellow Coll. Labor and Emloyment Lawyers; mem. ABA (sect. labor and employment law), Ky. Bar Assn. (labor sect.), Louisville Bar Assn. (mem. labor com. 1983—), Delta Theta Phi. Office: Frost Brown Todd LLC 400 W Market St Ste 3200 Louisville KY 40202-3363

PELHAM, JUDITH, health system administrator; b. Bristol, Conn., July 23, 1945; d. Marvin Curtis and Muriel (Chodos) Pelham; m. Jon N. Coffee, Dec. 30, 1992; children: Rachel Welch, Molly, Edward. BA, Smith Coll., 1967; MPA, Harvard U., 1975. Various govt. postions, 1968-72; prin. analyst Urban Systems, Cambridge, Mass., 1972-73; dir. devel. and planning Roxbury Dental and Med. Group, Boston, 1975-76; asst. to dir. for gen. medicine and ambulatory care Peter B. Brigham Hosp., Boston, 1976-77, asst. dir. ambulatory care, 1977-79; asst. v.p. Brigham and Women's Hosp., Boston, 1980-81; dir. planning and mktg. Seton Med. Ctr., Austin, Tex., 1980-82, pres., 1982-92, CEO, 1987-92; pres., CEO Daughters of Charity Health Svcs., Austin, 1987-92, Mercy Health Svcs., Farmington Hills, Mich., 1993—2000, Trinity Health (merger of Mercy Health Svcs. and Holy Cross Health Sys.), Novi, Mich., 2000—. Bd. dirs. Amgen, Cath. CEO Healthcare Connection; cons. Robert W. Johnson Found., 1979—80; mem. mgmt. bd. Inst. for Diversity in Health Mgmt., 1994—97; chair Coalition for Non-Profit Healthcare, 1997—2000, exec. com., 1997—2002; mem. Healthcare Rsch. and Devel. Inst., 1998—, bd., 2003—. Contbr. articles to profl. jours. Trustee A. Shivers Radiation Therapy Ctr., Austin, 1982—92, Marywood Maternity and Adoption Agy., 1982—86; bd.dirs. Quality of Life Found., Austin, 1985, Austin Rape Crisis Ctr., adv. bd. mem., 1986—88; bd. dirs., trustee League House, 1992—93, Seton Fund, 1982—93, Greater Detroit Area Health Coun.; mem. Gov.'s Job Tng. Coordinating Coun., 1983—85; mem. adv. coun. U. Tex. Social Work Found., 1983—85; charter mem. Leadership Tex., Austin, 1983—93. Recipient Leadership award, YWCA Austin, 1986. Fellow: Am. Hosp. Assn., Am. Coll. Healthcare Execs. (bd. dirs. 1987—95); mem.: Cath. Health Assn. (sec., treas. 1982—95, com. on govt. rels. 1984—91, chair fin. com. 1992—95, bd. dirs. 1987—95), Tex. Conf. Health Facilities (bd. dirs. 1985—89, pres. 1988), Austin Area Rsch. Orgn., Tex. Hosp. Assn. (various couns. 1982—87). Office: Trinity Health 27870 Cabot Dr Novi MI 48377

PELHAM, TOM, commissioner; Commr. fin. and mgmt. dept. Vt. State Fin. and Mgmt. Dept., Montpelier, 2000—. Office: Vt State Fin and Mgmt Dept Pavilion Office Bldg 109 State St Montpelier VT 05609-0001

PELIKAN, JAROSLAV JAN, history professor; b. Akron, Ohio, Dec. 17, 1923; s. Jaroslav Jan and Anna (Buzek) P.; m. Sylvia Burica, June 9, 1946; children: Martin, Michael, Miriam. Grad. summa cum laude, Concordia Jr. Coll., Ft. Wayne, Ind., 1942; BD, Concordia Theol. Sem., St. Louis, 1946; PhD, U. Chgo., 1946; MA (hon.), Yale U., 1961; DD (hon.), Concordia Coll., Moorehead, Minn., 1960, Concordia Sem., 1967, Trinity Coll., Hartford, Conn., 1987, St. Vladimir's Orthodox Theol. Sem., 1988, Victoria U., Toronto, 1989, U. Aberdeen, Scotland, 1995; LittD (hon.), Wittenberg U., 1960, Wheeling Coll., 1966, Gettysburg Coll., 1967, Pacific Luth. U., 1967, Wabash Coll., 1988, Jewish Theol. Sem., 1991; HHD (hon.), Providence Coll., 1966, Moravian Coll., 1986, Jewish Theol. Sem., 1991; LLD (hon.), Keuka Coll., 1967, U. Notre Dame, 1979, Harvard U., 1998, U. Regina, 1998; LHD (hon.), Valparaiso U., 1966, Rockhurst Coll., 1967, Albertus Magnus Coll., 1973, Coe Coll., 1976, Cath. U. Am., 1977, St. Mary's Coll., 1978, St. Anselm Coll., 1983, U. Nebr.-Omaha, 1984, Tulane U., 1986, Assumption Coll., 1986, LaSalle U., 1987, Carthage Coll., 1991, U. Chgo., 1991, So. Meth. U., 1992, SUNY, Albany, 1993, Fla. Internat. U., 1997; LHD (hon.), U. Pa., 2004, St. Tikhan's Orth. Sem., 2004; ThD (hon.), U. Hamburg, 1971, St. Olaf Coll., 1972, Charles U., Prague, 1999; STD, Dickinson Coll., 1986; DSc in Hist., Comenius U., Bratislava, 1992; ScD (hon.), Loyola U., Chgo., 1995. Faculty Valparaiso (Ind.) U., 1946-49, Concordia Sem., St. Louis, 1949-53, U. Chgo., 1953-62; Titus Street prof. eccles. history Yale U., 1962-72, Sterling prof. history, 1972-96, William Clyde DeVane lectr., 1984-86, dir. div. humanities, 1974-75, chmn. Medieval studies, 1974-75, 78-80, dean Grad. Sch., 1973-78; Joseph chair Boston Coll., 1996-97; prof. Annenberg Sch. U. Pa., 1998-2001; Disting. Vis. Scholar Libr. Congress, Washington, 2001—02. Vis. prof. Boston Coll., 1996-97, Annenberg Sch. Comm., U. Pa., 1998—; Gray lectr. Duke U., 1960, Ingersoll lectr. Harvard U., 1963, Gauss lectr. Princeton U., 1980, Jefferson lectr. NEH, 1983, Richard lectr. U. Va., 1984, Rauschenbusch lectre. Colgate-Rochester Divinity Sch., 1984, Gilson lectr. U. Toronto, 1985, 98, Hale lectr. Seabury-Western Sem., 1986, Mead-Swing lectr. Oberlin Coll., 1986, Gross lectr. Rutgers U., 1989; adv. bd. Ctr. Theol. Inquiry, 1984-90; mem. coun. The Smithsonian Instn., 1984-90; US chmn. US Czechoslovak Commn. on Humanities and Social Scis., 1987-92; scholarly dir. instns. of democracy project Annenberg Found Trust, Sunnylands, 2002—. Author: From Luther to Kierkegaard, 1950, Fools for Christ, 1955, The Riddle of Roman Catholicism, 1959 (Abingdon award 1959), Luther the Expositor, 1959, The Shape of Death, 1961, The Light of the World, 1962, Obedient Rebels, 1964, The Finality of Jesus Christ in an Age of Universal History, 1965, The Christian Intellectual, 1966, Spirit Versus Structure, 1968, Development of Doctrine, 1969, Historical Theology, 1971, The Christian Tradition, 5 vols., 1971-89, Scholarship and Its Survival, 1983, The Vindication of Tradition, 1984, Jesus through the Centuries, 1985, The Mystery of Continuity, 1986, Bach Among the Theologians, 1986, The Excellent Empire, 1987, The Melody of Theology, 1988, Confessor Between East and West, 1990, Imago Dei, 1990, Eternal Feminines, 1990, The Idea of the University: A Reexamination, 1992, Christianity and Classical Culture, 1993, Faust the Theologian, 1995, The Reformation of the Bible/ The Bible of the Reformation, 1996, Mary through the Centuries, 1996, The Illustrated Jesus Through the Centuries, 1997, What Has Athens to do with Jerusalem?, 1997, Divine Rhetoric, 2001, Credo, 2003, Interpreting the Bible and the Constitution, 2004; editor, translator: Luther's Works, 22 vols., 1955-71, The Book of Concord, 1959; editor: Makers of Modern Theology, 5 vols., 1966-68, The Preaching of Chrysostom, 1967, Interpreters of Luther, 1968, Twentieth-Century Theology in the Making, 3 vols., 1969-70, The Preaching of Augustine, 1973, The World Treasury of Modern Religious Thought, 1991, Sacred Writings, 7 vols., 1992; (with Valerie Hotchkiss) Creeds and Confessions of Faith in the Christian Tradition, 3 vols., 2003; mem. editl. bd. Collected Works of Erasmus, Classics of Western Spirituality, Evangelisches Kirchenlexikon, Emerson's Nature, 1986, The World Treasury of Modern Religious Thought, 1990; departmental editor Ency. Britannica, 1958-69; adminstrv. bd. Papers of Benjamin Franklin; chmn. publs. com. Yale U. Press, 1979-90, 92—, v.p. bd. govs., 1988—; contbr. articles to profl. jours. Pres. 4th Internat. Congress for Luther Research, 1971, New Eng. Congress on Grad. Edn., 1976-77. Recipient Abingdon award, 1959; Pax Christi award St. John's U., Collegeville, Minn., 1966, Colman J. Barry award, 1995; John Gilmary Shea prize Am. Cath. Hist. Assn., 1971, nat. award Slovak World Congress, 1973, religious book award Cath. Press Assn., 1974, Christian Unity award Atonement Friars, 1975, Bicentennial award Czechoslovak Soc. Arts and Scis., 1976, Wilbur Cross medal Yale U. Grad. Sch. Assn., 1979, Profl. Achievement award U. Chgo. Alumni Assn., 1980, Shaw medal Boston Coll., 1984, Comenius medal Moravian Coll., 1986, Alumnus of Yr. award U. Chgo. Div. Sch., 1986, Bicentennial medal Georgetown U., 1989, award for excellence Am. Acad. Religion 1989, Umanità award Newberry Libr., 1990, Jacques Barzun award Am. Acad. for Liberal Edn., 1997, Festschriften: Schools of Thought in the Christian Tradition, 1984, The Unbounded Community, 1996; sr. fellow Carnegie Found. for Advancement Tchg., 1982-83. Fellow Medieval Acad. Am. (councillor, Haskins medal 1985); mem. Am. Hist. Assn., Am. Soc. Ch. History (pres. 1965, Achievement award 1998), Internat. Congress Luther Rsch. (pres. 1971), Am. Acad. Arts and Scis. (v.p. 1976-94, pres. 1994-97), Am. Philos. Soc. (councillor 1984-87, Moe prize 1997), Am. Acad. Polit. and Social Sci. (pres. 2000—), Coun. Scholars of Libr. of Congress (founding chmn. 1980-83), Elizabethan Club, Mory's, Phi Beta Kappa (senator United chpts. 1985-90). Home: 156 Chestnut Ln Hamden CT 06518-1604

PELIZZO, RICCARDO, political scientist; b. Verona, Italy, Dec. 31, 1971; arrived in U.S., 1997; s. Carlo Pelizzo and Vittoria Elisabetta Benedetti. Laurea, U. Bologna, Italy, 1995; diploma, Sch. Adv. Internat. Studies, Bologna, 1997; MA in Polit. Sci., Johns Hopkins U., 2002, PhD in Polit. Sci., 2004. Polit. scientist Johns Hopkins U., Balt.; asst. prof. polit. sci. Singapore Mgmt. U. Cons. World Bank, 2002. Author: Tre e Mezzo, 2004. Bd. dirs. Azienda Municipalizzata di Igiene Ambientale, Verona, 1994-96. Recipient Vincent Wright ann. meml. prize, 2004. Roman Catholic. Office: Singapore Mgmt U Sch Econs 469 Bukit Timah Rd Singapore 259756 Singapore Home: 22 Newton Rd # 8-10 Amaryllisville Singapore

PELIZZONI, VIRGINIA MATKO, writer, editor, consultant; b. East Orange, N.J., July 2, 1951; d. Edward Martin and Dorothy (Pohorelli) Matko; m. Joseph A. Pelizzoni, May 10, 1975. BA in Journalism and Art, Rutgers U., 1973; postgrad., Union County Tech. Inst., 1974, DuCret Sch. of the Arts, Plainfield, N.J., 1980. Pub. rels. asst. Mutual Benefit Life Ins. Co., Newark, 1973-75, publs. supr., 1975-84, comms. mgr., 1984-85; pub. rels. dir. Welkind Rehab. Hosp., Chester, N.J., 1985-87; prin., owner VMP Comm., Warren, N.J., 1987—. Contbr. articles to profl. pubs. Mem. pub. rels. com. Am. Cancer Soc., Somerset County, Raritan, N.J., 1997-98. Recipient First Pl. award United Way of Tri-State, 3 awards for merit Life Advertisers Assn., award of excellence Bus. Mktg. Assn. of N.J., Internat. Assn. of Bus. Communicators, 2 awards of excellence, 3 1st pl. U.S. Savs. Bond campaign newsletter awards U.S. Dept. Treasury, 1st pl. award editl. writing, 2 awards of merit newsletters. Mem. Internat. Assn. of Bus. Communicators. E-mail: vpelizzo@bellatlantic.net.

PELL, ARTHUR ROBERT, human resources specialist, consultant, author; b. N.Y.C., Jan. 22, 1920; s. Harry and Rae (Meyers) P.; m. Erica Frost, May 19, 1946; children— Douglas, Hilary. AB, NYU, 1939, MA, 1944; PhD, Calif. Coast U., 1977; diploma, Cornell U., 1943. Personnel dir. Eagle-Electric Mfg. Co., Long Island City, N.Y., 1946-50, North Atlantic Constructors, N.Y.C., 1950-53; v.p. Harper Assos., Inc., N.Y.C., 1953-75; cons. Human Resources Mgmt., Hempstead, N.Y., 1975—. Adj. assoc. prof. mgmt. NYU Sch. Continuing Edn., 1962-84, St. John's U. Coll. Bus. Adminstrn., 1971-76; lectr. Baruch Sch. Bus. and Pub. Adminstrn. Coll. City N.Y., 1948-67. Author: (with W.B. Patterson) Fire Officer's Guide to Leadership, rev. edit., 1963, Placing Salesmen, 1963, Placing Executives, 1964, Police Leadership, 1967, How to Get the Job You Want After 40, 1967, Recruiting and Selecting Personnel, 1969, (with M. Harper) Starting and Managing an Employment Agency, 1970, Recruiting, Training and Motivating Volunteer Workers, 1972, Be a Better Employment Interviewer, 1972, rev. edits., 1978, 86, 94, The College Graduate Guide to Job Finding, 1973; (with Wilma Rogalin) Women's Guide to Executive Positions, 1975; (with Albert Furbay) College Student's Guide to Career Planning, 1975; (with Dale Carnegie Assocs.) Managing Through People, 1975, rev. edits., 1978, 1987, Choosing a College Major: Business, 1978, Enrich Your Life: The Dale Carnegie Way, 1979, The Part Time Job Book, 1984, Making the Most of Medicare, 1987, rev. edit., 1990, (with George Sadek) Resumes for Engineers, 1982, Resumes for Computer Professionals, 1984, How to Sell Yourself on an Interview, 1982, The Job Finder's Kit, 1989, Getting the Most from Your People, 1990, Diagnosing Your Doctor, 1991, The Supervisor's Infobank, 1994, The Complete Idiot's Guide to Managing People, 1995, 3d edit., 2003, The Pocket Idiot's Guide to One Minute Management, 1999, The Complete Idiot's Guide to Team Building, 1999, The Complete Idiot's Guide to Recruiting The Right Stuff, 2000, The Complete's Idiot Guide to Human Resources Management, 2001, (with Franklin C. Ashley) Embracing Excellence, 2001; editl. cons. for revision Dale Carnegie's How to Win Friends and Influence People, 1981; author syndicated feature The Human Side; contbr. articles to profl. jours. With AUS, 1942-46. Office: 400 High Point Dr Apt 101 Hartsdale NY 10530-1125 E-mail: arpell22@optonline.net.

PELL, CLAIBORNE, former senator; b. N.Y.C., Nov. 22, 1918; s. Herbert Claiborne and Matilda (Bigelow) P.; m. Nuala O'Donnell, Dec. 1944; children: Herbert Claiborne III, Christopher T. Hartford, Nuala Dallas Yates, Julia L.W. Student, St. George's Sch., Newport, R.I.; AB cum laude, Princeton U., 1940; AM, Columbia U., 1946; 51 hon. degrees. Enlisted USCGR, 1941; served as seaman, ensign North Atlantic sea duty, Africa, Italy; hospitalized to, 1944; instr. Navy Sch. Mil. Govt., Princeton, 1944-45; capt. USCGR; ret.; on loan to State Dept. at San Francisco Conf., 1945, State Dept., 1945-46, U.S. embassy, Czechoslovakia, 1946-47; established consulate gen. Bratislava, Czechoslovakia, 1947-48; vice consul Genoa, Italy, 1949; assigned State Dept., 1950-52; v.p., dir. Internat. Rescue Com.; senator from R.I., 1961-96; U.S. del. to UN, 97—. Ranking minority mem. Fgn. Rels. Com., Labor and Human Resources Subcom. on Edn., Arts, and Humanities; mem. Rules and Adminstrn. Com., Joint Com. on Libr. and Congl. Intern Program, Senate Dem. Policy Com.; U.S. del. Internat. Maritime Consultative Orgn., London, 1959, 25th Gen. Assembly, 1970; disting. vis. prof. Salve Regina U., Newport, R.I., 1997—. Author: Megalopolis Unbound, 1966, (with Harold L. Goodwin) Challenge of the Seven Seas, 1966, Power and Policy, 1972. Hon. bd. dirs. World Affairs Council R.I.; trustee St. George's Sch.; trustee emeritus Brown U.; Cons. Democratic Nat. Com., 1953-60; exec. asst. to chmn. R.I. State Dem. Com., 1952-54; chmn. R.I. Dem. Fund drive, 1952, Dem. nat. registration, chmn., 1956, co-chmn., 1962; chief delegation tally clk. Dem. Nat. Conv., 1956, 60, 64, 68. Decorated knight Crown of Italy, Grand Cross Order of Merit Italy, Red Cross of Merit Portugal, Legion of Honor France, comdr. Order of Phoenix Greece, Grand Cross Order of Merit Liechtenstein, Grand Cross Order of Christ Portugal, Order of Henry the Navigator, Portugal, Grand Cross Order of N. Star Sweden, Grand Cross of Merit Knights of Malta, Grand Officer of Merit Luxembourg, Grand Comdr. Lebanon; recipient Caritas Elizabeth medal Cardinal Franz Koenig, Grand decoration of honor in silver with sash Austria, Gold medal of St. Barnabas (Cyprus), recipient Pres.'s Fellow award R.I. Sch. Design, medal Nat. Order of Cedar, Hugo Grotius Commemorative medal The Netherlands, recipient Harold W. McGraw, Jr. Prize in Education, McGraw-Hill, 1988. Mem. Soc. Cin. Clubs: Hope (Providence); Knickerbocker (N.Y.C.), Racquet and Tennis (N.Y.C.), Brook (N.Y.C.); Metropolitan (Washington); Travellers (Paris); Reading Room (Newport); White's (London). Democrat. Episcopalian. *I have a seven word definition of my job and of my life: "Translate ideas into events, and help people.".*

PELL, JONATHAN LAURENCE, artistic administrator; b. Memphis, Oct. 20, 1949; s. Burton Marshall and Eleanor (Leopold) P. BA, U. So. Calif., 1971. Interior designer Gene Morse Assocs., Wichita, Kans., 1971-77; mgr. Internat. Artists Mgmt., N.Y.C., 1977-79, Robert Lombardo Assocs., N.Y.C., 1979-80; TV producer Sta. WNET, N.Y.C., 1980-83; dir. publicity John Curry Skating Co., N.Y.C., 1983; prodr. Jerome Kern Centennary Gala Town Hall, N.Y.C., 1984; dir. artistic administration The Dallas Opera, 1984—. Vocal competition judge Met. Opera Nat. Coun. Auditions, Pavarotti Competition, George London Awards, Ctr. for Contemporary Opera, Dallas Opera Guild, Denver Lyric Opera Guild, Ft. Worth Opera, Marguerite McCammon Competition, San Antonio Opera Guild, Richard Tucker Award, others; tchr. master classes for young singers Opera Am., Nat. Opera Assn., Can. Opera Co., S.W. Chpt. NATS, Performing Arts Assistance Corp., U. North Tex., Internat. Sch. Performing Arts, Amarillo Opera, So. Meth. U.; host Dallas Opera Radio Hour, WRR, 1994—97, Inside the Dallas Opera, WRR, 2004—; advisor singer svcs. com. Opera Am.; lectr. on opera Crystal Cruises. Bd. dirs., chmn. nat. auditions com., mem. award selection com. Richard Tucker Music Found.; mem. adv. bd. Awards Recognizing Individual Artistry; advisor to singer svcs. com. Opera Am. Office: Dallas Opera Campbell Ctr I LBI-11 8350 N Central Expy Ste 210 Dallas TX 75206-1601 Office Phone: 214-443-1043.

PELL, SIDNEY, epidemiologist; b. N.Y.C., Dec. 13, 1922; m. Lola May, July 2, 1950. MBA, CCNY, 1952; PhD, U. Pitts., 1956. Biostatistician E.I. Du Pont de Nemours and Co., Wilmington, Del., 1955-76, mgr. epidemiology sect., 1976-82, sr. cons., 1982-85; epidemiology cons. Wilmington, 1985—. Epidemiology cons. Del. Divsn. Pub. Health, Dover, 1986-95. Contbr. articles to New Eng. Jour. Medicine, Jour. Occupational Medicine, Jour. AMA. With U.S. Army, 1943-45, ETO. Recipient Merit in Authorship Hon. Mention, Inds. Med. Assn., 1959. Fellow Am. Coll. Epidemiology, Am. Heart Assn., Am. Pub. Health Assn., Delta Omega. Home: 1416 Emory Rd Wilmington DE 19803-5120 E-mail: pell104@aol.com.

PELL, TERENCE J. legal association administrator; BA, Haverford Coll., 1976; JD, Cornell Law Sch., 1981; PhD, U. Notre Dame, 1996. Atty. Arent, Fox, Kintner, Plotkin & Kahn; dep. asst. sec. for civil rights U.S. Dept. Edn., 1985—88; gen. counsel, chief of staff Office of Nat. Drug Control Policy; sr. counsel Ctr for Individual Rights, Washington, 1997—2000, pres., 2000—. Office: Ctr for Individual Rights 1233 20th St NW Ste 300 Washington DC 20036*

PELLA, MILTON ORVILLE, retired science educator; b. Wilmot, Wis., Feb. 13, 1914; s. Charles August and Ida Marie (Pagel) P.; m. Germaine Marie Reich, Dec. 9, 1944. B.E., Milw. State Tchrs. Coll., 1936; MS, U. Wis., 1940, PhD, 1948. Tchr. sci. and math. Wyler Mil. Acad., 1937-38; tchr. elementary sch. Delavan Pub. Schs., 1938-39; tchr. sci. U. Wis. High Sch., 1939-42; prof. sci. edn. U. Wis., Madison, 1946-80; prof. emeritus, 1980—; With Fgn. Ednl. Service, Turkey, 1959, 1961, 62, 1963, 64, 65, 66, 68, 1967, 1969, 1968, 69, 1971-81. Author: Physical Science for Progress, 3d edit, 1970, Science Horizons— The Biological World, (with Branley and Urban), 1965-70. Served

with AUS, 1942-46. Fellow AAAS; mem. Ctrl. Assn. Sci. and Math. (pres. 1955), Nat. Assn. for Rsch. in Sci. Tchg. (pres. 1966), Nat. Sci. Tchrs. Assn. (dir. 1950, 60), Masons. Home: 6209 Mineral Point Rd Madison WI 53705-4652

PELLECCHIA, JOHN MICHAEL, lawyer; b. Orange, N.J., Dec. 6, 1958; BA, Lafayette Coll., 1980; JD cum laude, Tulane U., 1983. Bar: N.J. 1983, U.S. Dist. Ct. N.J. 1983, U.S. Supreme Ct. 1994. Assoc. Pitney, Hardin, Kipp & Szuch, Morristown, N.J., 1983-86; asst. counsel to gov. Thomas H. Kean State of N.J., Trenton, 1986-88; ptnr. Riker, Danzig, Scherer, Hyland & Perretti, LLP, Morristown and Trenton, 1988—. Mem. mgmt. com. Riker, Danzig, Scherer, Hyland & Perretti LLP, Morristown and Trenton, 1995-98; jud. extern to fed. dist. ct. judge, U.S. Dist. Ct., New Orleans, 1982-83; sr. fellow Tulane Law Sch., 1982-83; bd. dirs. Proformance Ins. Co.; mem. N.J. Supreme Ct. Com. on Tax Ct., 1993-96, 2000—; mem. bus. and fin. svcs. task force of Gov. Whitman's Econ. Master Plan Commn., 1994. Trustee, v.p. Leukemia Soc. Am. North Jersey chpt., 1991—; trustee N.J. Shakespeare Festival, 1996—, Schiff Natural Lands Trust, 2002—. Vol. of Yr., Leukemia Soc. Am. North Jersey chpt., 1994. Office: Riker Danzig Scherer Hyland & Perretti LLP Hdqrs Plaza One Speedwell Ave Morristown NJ 07962-1981

PELLEGRENE, THOMAS JAMES, JR., editor, researcher; b. Wilmington, Del., Dec. 26, 1959; s. Thomas J. and MaryBelle (McGowan) P.; m. Pamela Heinecke, Apr. 5, 1986. BS in Journalism, Northwestern U., 1981, MS in Journalism, 1982. Staff writer Ft. Wayne (Ind.) Journal-Gazette, 1982-87, bus. editor, 1987-95, asst. metro editor, 1995-98, mgr. news techs., 1998—. Mem. Soc. Profl. Journalists, Spl. Librs. Assn. Office: Fort Wayne Journal-Gazette 600 W Main St Fort Wayne IN 46802-1408 E-mail: tpellegrene@jg.net.

PELLEGRINI, ROBERT J. psychology educator; b. Worcester, Mass., Oct. 21, 1941; s. Felix and Teresa (Di Muro) P.; 1 child, Robert Jerome. BA in Psychology, Clark U., 1963; MA in Psychology, U. Denver, 1966, PhD in Social Psychology, 1968. Prof. San Jose (Calif.) State U., 1967—. Rsch. assoc. U. Calif., Santa Cruz, 1989-90; pres. Western Inst. for Human Devel., San Jose, 1985—. Author: Psychology for Correctional Education, Bringing Psychology to Life; contbr. articles to profl. jours. Recipient Warburton award for scholarly excellence, 1995, Disting. Tchr. of Yr. award Western Psychol. Assn., 1996. Mem. Phi Beta Kappa. Office: San Jose State U Dept Psychology 1 Washington Sq San Jose CA 95192-0001

PELLEGRINO, EDMUND DANIEL, internist, educator, retired academic administrator; b. Newark, June 22, 1920; s. Michael J. and Marie (Catone) Pellegrino; m. Clementine Coakley, Nov. 17, 1944; children: Thomas, Virginia, Michael, Andrea, Alice, Leah. BS, St. John's U., 1941, DSc (hon.), 1971; MD, NYU, 1944; 39 hon. degrees. Diplomate Am. Bd. Internal Medicine. Intern Bellevue Hosp., N.Y.C., 1944—45, asst. resident medicine, 1948—49; resident medicine Goldwater Meml. Hosp., N.Y.C., 1945—46; fellow medicine NYU, 1949—50; supervising Tb physician Homer Folks Hosp., Oneonta, NY, 1950—53; dir. internal medicine Hunterdon Med. Center, Flemington, NJ, 1953—59, med. dir., 1955—59; prof., chmn. dept. medicine U. Ky. Med. Center, 1959—66; prof. medicine SUNY, Stony Brook, 1966—72, v.p. for health scis., dir. Health Scis. Center, 1968—73, dean Sch. Medicine, 1968—72; v.p. health affairs U. Tenn. System; chancellor U. Tenn. Med. Units, Memphis, 1973—75; prof. med. Yale U., New Haven, 1975—78; pres. Yale-New Haven Med. Center, 1975—78, Cath. U. Am., Washington, 1978—82, prof. philosophy and biology, 1978—82; John Carroll prof. medicine and med. ethics Georgetown U., Washington, 1982—; dir. Kennedy Inst. Ethics, Washington, 1983—88; dir. Ctr. for Advanced Study Ethics Georgetown U., Washington, 1988—94, dir. Ctr. for Clin. Bioethics, 1991—, acting chief Divsn. Gen. Internal Medicine, 1993—94, chief Gen. Internal Medicine, 1995. Founding editor: Jour. Medicine and Philosophy, 1983—. With USAF, 1946—48. Master: ACP; fellow: N.Y. Acad. Medicine; mem.: Inst. Medicine NAS, AMA, Am. Clin. and Climatol. Assn., Assn. Am. Physicians. Office: Georgetown U Ctr for Clin Bioethics Washington DC 20007

PELLEGRINO, STEPHEN CHARLES, civilian military employee; b. Bangor, Maine, Apr. 7, 1967; m. Nicole Springer. BSCE, Pa. State U., 1989; MS in Ops. Rsch., Naval Postgrad. Sch., 1996. Supply officer USMC, Okinawa, Japan, 1990—94; ops. analyst Installations and Logistics Dept., Spl. Projects and Analysis Hdqs. Marine Corps, Washington, 1996—99, activity based costing program mgr., 1999—2000, ABC/M (activity based costing/mgmt.) program mgr. Washington, DC, 2001—; sr. cons. Grant Thornton, LLP, Vienna, Va., 2000—01. Maj. USMC, 1990—2000. Decorated Navy and Marine Corps Achievement medal USMC, Meritorious Svc. medal. Mem.: NRA, Assn. for Psychol. Type, Marine Corps Assn. Office: Hdqs Marine Corps I&L (LR) 2 Navy Annex Rm 3305 Washington DC 20380-1775 E-mail: pellegrinosc@hqmc.usmc.mil.

PELLEGROM, DANIEL EARL, international health and development executive; b. Three Rivers, Mich., May 29, 1944; s. Francis Robert and Regina Elizabeth (Valentine) P.; m. Sally Margaret Stukenbroeker, Nov. 30, 1968; children: Daniel, Jr., Benjamin, Sara. BA, Western Mich. U., 1966; MDiv, Union Theol. Seminary, 1969. Ordained to ministry, Presbyn. Ch., 1970. Dir. coll. programs Planned Parenthood Fedn., N.Y.C., 1969-71; exec. dir. Memphis Planned Parenthood, 1971-75, Md. Planned Parenthood, Balt., 1975-85; pres. Pathfinder Internat., Watertown, Mass., 1985—. Chair bd. dirs., mem. exec. com. InterAction, Washington; bd. dirs. Brush Found., Cleve., Planned Parenthood League Mass., Boston. Bd. dir. World Neighbors, Oklahoma City; Mem. Gov.'s conf. on children and youth State of Md., Balt., 1978-80; assoc. sch. hygiene and pub. health Johns Hopkins U., Balt., 1984-85. Recipient Leadership award Greater Balt. Com., 1983-84, UN Population award Pathfinder Internat., 1996, Internat. award Nat. Family Planning and Reproductive Health Assn., 1997. Mem. APHA. Democrat. Avocations: baseball, travel, hiking. Home: 48 Bound Brook Rd Newton MA 02461-2036 Office: Pathfinder Internat 9 Galen St Ste 217 Watertown MA 02472-4523 E-mail: dpellegrom@pathfind.org.

PELLETIER, ARTHUR JOSEPH, state legislator, data processing executive, educator; b. Dec. 13, 1946; s. Joseph Telesphor and Elsie Jane (Dillon) P.; m. Marsha Lynn Mingle, May 19, 1973; 1 child, John. Diploma, N.H. Vocat. Tech. Inst., 1966; BA, Kans. State U., 1970, MS, 1972. Asst. to dir. Kans. State U. Divsn. Contbg. Edn., Manhattan, 1971-74; tchr. drafting Portsmouth (N.H.) H.S., 1974-86; tchr. computer programming McIntosh Coll., Dover, NH, 1982-84; assoc. prof. N.H. Vocat.-Tech. Coll., Stratham, 1986-87; kitchen designer Area Kitchen Ctr., Portsmouth, 1987; mem. N.H. Ho. of Reps., 1993—. Mem. legis. sci., tech. and energy com., N.H. Ho. Reps., 1993-96, 2003—, mem. legis. edn. com., 1997-2000; co-founder N.H. Coalition for Edn.; mem. Dover Ready to Learn Task Force, 1995-2001; mem. evaluation and review com., Dover Schs., curriculum com., 1997-2001, facilities com., 1997-98; bd. advs. Hub Family Support Ctr., 1996-97. Mem. Partnership Healthier Cmty., 1995-97, Ams. for Non-Smoker's Rights, 1996—. Mem. World Future Soc., Friends of Dover Libr. Avocations: radio-controlled model aircraft, tennis, photography. Home: 94 Back River Rd Dover NH 03820-4411

PELLETIER, DAVID, Olympic athlete, ice skater; b. Sayabec, Que., Can., Nov. 22, 1974; Profl. figure skater, Canada. Recipient (with Jamie Salé) 2d pl. pairs, Can. Nat. Championships, 1999, 1st pl., 2000, 2001, 2002, ISU Four Continents, 2000, 2001, Skate Am., 2000, 2001, Sears Figure Skating Open, 2000, ISU Grand Prix Finals, 2001, ISU Grand Prix Final, 2002, World Championships, 2001, Skate Can., 2001, Gold medal, 2002 Olympic Games, (with Jamie Sale) Partners of the Yr. award, 30th Ann. Can. Sports awards, 2003. Office: Skate Canada 865 Shefford Rd Gloucester ON K1J 1H9 Canada

PELLETIER, LOUIS CONRAD, surgeon, educator, health facility administrator; b. Montreal, Que., Can., Mar. 15, 1940; s. Conrad L. and Lucienne (Rochette) P.; m. Louise Montpetit, June 26, 1965; children: Conrad R., Marie-Helene. BA, Brébeuf Coll., Montreal, 1959; MD, U. Montreal, 1964, MBA, 1996. Resident in cardiovascular and thoracic surgery U. Montreal, 1964-70, chmn. dept. surgery, 1986-94; rsch. asst. Mayo Clin. Found., Rochester, Minn., 1970-72; mem. dept. surgery Maisonneuve-Rosemont Hosp., Montreal, 1972-76, Sacré-Coeur Hosp., Montreal, 1972-80, Montreal Heart Inst., 1979—2000, head dept. surgery, 1979-87; dir. rsch. Ctr. Sacre-Coeur Hosp., 1998—2002; pres. Cardianove, Inc., 1998—; dir. med. affairs Sacrè-Coeur hosp., 2000—02; cons. in health adminstrn. and mgmt. of emergency wards, 2002—. Contbr. articles to profl. jours. Mem. adminstrv. bd. College Stanislas, Montreal, 1979-86, Que. Heart Found., 1980-84, regional healthcare bd., 1991-92, Hotel-Dieu Hosp., 1993-95. Recipient Young Investigator's award Am. Coll. Cardiology, 1972; Med. Rsch. Coun. Can. scholar U. Montreal, 1973-78. Fellow Royal Coll. Physicians and Surgeons Can.; mem. ACS, Association des Medecins de Langue Francaise du Canada, Can. Med. Assn., Royal Coll. Can., Assn. Cardiovascular and Thoracic Surgery Que., Can. Cardiovascular Soc., Montreal Cardiac Soc., Clin. Rsch. Club Que., Soc. Thoracic Surgeons, Can. Assn. Clin. Surgeons, Sociedad de Cardiocirujanos, Coun. on Cardiovasular Surgery, Am. Heart Assn., Internat. Soc. for Heart Transplantation, Can. Soc. Cardiovascular and Thoracic Surgeons, Am. Assn. Thoracic Surgery, Am. Surgical Assn. Roman Catholic. Avocations: skiing, bicycling.

PELLETIER, MARSHA LYNN, secondary school educator, poet; b. Mt. Pleasant, Mich., July 29, 1950; d. Eugene Russell and Mary Ellen (Edde) Mingle; m. Arthur Joseph Pelletier, May 19, 1973; 1 child, John Frederick. BS in Home Econs. and Edn., Kans. State U., 1971, MS in Edn. Guidance and Counseling, 1972. Lic. real estate broker N.H. Conf. coord., guidance counselor Kans. State U., Manhattan, 1971-73; tchr. home econs. Franklin (Mass.) HS, 1974, Exeter (N.H.) HS, 1974-75, Barrington (N.H.) Mid. Sch., 1975-81, Pentucket Regional Jr. HS, West Newbury, Mass., 1981-82; realtor assoc. Century 21 Ocean and Norword Realty, Portsmouth, NH, 1983-86; tchr. interior design, cons. U. N.H., Durham, 1986-87; tchr. family and consumer sci. Dover (N.H.) Mid. Sch., 1983—2001; tchr. Dover HS, 2001—; mem. legis. adminstrn. com. N.H. Ho. of Reps., Concord, 1992—94, 1996—2002; ind. real estate broker Dover, 1986-2000. Bd. dirs. N.H. State Profl. Bd. Stds., 1999—; assessor Nat. Bd. Profl. Tchg. Stds., 2001; tchr. assessor Nat. Tchrs. Bd. Cert., 2002—. Author: (poems) Arriving at the Crossroads, 2003; costume dir. & designer: Guys and Dolls, 2004. Bd. dirs. Dover Adult Learning Ctr., 1995—98; mem. Health Task Force, Dover, Concord, 1993—94, Cornerstone Dancers, Dover Friends of Pub. Libr., 1996—, bd. supt. adv. com., 2001—03, poetry judge, 2003—04; trustee St. John's Meth. Ch., 1995—97. Mem.: NEA (local pres., negotiator, v.p., membership chair, mem. leadership exec. com., bldg. rep. 1979—, N.H. del. to nat. conv.), Seacoast Writers Assn., Nat. Coalition Consumer Econ., Alpha Delta Kappa (v.p., historian, altruistic chmn. 1984—89). Democrat. Avocations: gardening, aerobics, poetry, sewing, cooking. Home: 94 Back River Rd Dover NH 03820-4411

PELLETIER, SANDRA MAUREEN, mathematician, educator; b. Orange, Calif., June 17, 1952; d. Raymond Hobert Ziegler and Shirley Mae Prather; m. Michael Jon Pelletier, Aug. 24, 1979; children: Joshua, Michelle, Alissa. BA magna cum laude, So. Calif. Coll., Costa Mesa, 1976. Cert. math tchr. State of Calif. Adj. math. tchr. So. Calif. Coll., Costa Mesa, 1981—86; math. tchr. Iao Sch., Wailuku, Hawaii, 1986—87, Coastal Christian Sch., Arroyo Grande, Calif., 1987—92; math. tchr., dept. head Maranatha H.S., Pasadena, Calif., 1992—. Mem.: Calif. Math. Coun., Math. Assn. Am. Republican. Home: 1507 N Viewcrest Azusa CA 91702 Office: Maranatha HS 1610 E Elizabeth Pasadena CA 91104 Office Phone: 626-720-8141. Business E-Mail: s_pelletier@maranatha_hs.org.

PELLETT, JON MICHAEL, lawyer; b. Orlando, Fla., Nov. 16, 1961; s. Milton Francis and Jean Ellen (Avery) P.; m. Karen Walker, July 21, 1984 (div. Sept. 1990). BS in Biology, U. Ctrl. Fla., Orlando, 1984, BS in Stats., 1985; JD, Fla. State U., 1993. Bar: Fla. 1995, U.S. Dist. Ct. (mid. dist.) Fla. 1996. Legal trainee Dept. Bus. and Profl. Regulation, Tallahassee, 1993-95; staff atty. Agy. for Health Care Adminstrn., Tallahassee, 1995-96; assoc. Freeman, Hunter & Malloy, Tampa, Fla., 1996-2000, Barr, Murman, Tonelli et al, Tampa, 2000—. Vol. guardian ad litem Guardian ad Litem Program, Tallahassee, 1991-95; mem. Coun. for Licensure Enforcement and Regulation, 2003—. Bd. dirs. Friends of Arboretum, Orlando, 1998-2003. Mem. ABA, ATLA, Hillsborough County Bar Assn. Avocations: racquetball, beach volleyball. Office: Barr Murman Tonelli Et Al 201 E Kennedy Blvd Ste 1750 Tampa FL 33602-5829 Office Phone: 813-223-3951.

PELLI, CESAR, architect; b. Tucuman, Argentina, Oct. 12, 1926; arrived in U.S., 1952, naturalized, 1964; s. Victor V. and Teresa S. Pelli; children: Denis G., Rafael A. BArch cum laude, U. Tucuman, 1949; MS in Architecture, U. Ill., 1954. Assoc. firm Eero Saarinen & Assocs., 1954-64, Daniel, Mann, Johnson & Mendenhall, 1964-68, Gruen Assocs. Inc., L.A., 1968-77, Cesar Pelli & Assocs., New Haven, Conn., 1977—; dean Sch. Architecture, Yale U., New Haven, 1977-84. Works include Pacific Design Ctr. and Expansion, LA (Honor award So. Calif. chpt. AIA 1976), US Embassy, Tokyo, Mus. Modern Art Expansion, NYC, World Fin. Ctr. and Winter Garden, NYC (Bard award 1992), Cleve. Clinic (Honor award AIA 1986), Herring Hall, Rice U., Houston (Honor award AIA 1986), Carnegie Hall Tower, NYC (Honor award AIA 1994, Design award AIA/Conn. 1991), Boyer Ctr. Molecular Medicine Yale U. (Design award AIA/Conn. 1991), Bank of Am. Corp. Ctr., Charlotte, NTT Corp. Hdqrs., Tokyo (Design award AIA/Conn. 1997), New Terminal, Washington Nat. Airport (Design award AIA/Conn. 1998, NE Design award 1999, Design for Transp. award 2000), Aronoff Ctr. for the Arts, Cin. (USITT Honor award 1996, Design award AIA/CIN 1996, Design award AIA/Conn. 1997), Petronas Towers, Kuala Lumpur, Malaysia (Design award AIA/Conn. 1999, NE Design award 2000, Honor award AIA 2000), Frances Lehman Loeb Art Ctr. Vassar Coll., poughkeepsie, N.Y. (Design award AIA/Conn. 1996), Internat. Fin. Ctr., Hong Kong, Nat. Mus. Contemporary Art, Osaka, Japan, Performing Arts Ctr. Greater Miami, Fla., Mpls. Ctrl. Libr.; editor Yale Seminars on Architecture, 1981-82; author Observations for Young Architects, 1999. Fellow AIA (Firm award 1989, named to top ten list of living Am. archs. 1991, Gold medal 1995); mem. NAD (Arnold M. Brunner Meml. prize 1978), Am. Acad. Arts and Letters (academician), Internat. Acad. Architecture (academician). Office: Cesar Pelli Assocs Pub Rels 1056 Chapel St New Haven CT 06510-2402 E-mail: mailroom@cesar-pelli.com.

PELLI, LEEMOUR, artist; b. NYC, Feb. 25, 1964; parents Moshe and Dalia Pelli. BA, Hebrew U. Jerusalem, 1986; MA, Hunter Coll., 1989; BFA, Sch. Visual Arts, 1994. One-person shows include, Artcore Gallery, Toronto, 2000, U. Ctrl. Fla. Art Gallery, 2003, Nikolai Fine Art, NY, The Pierro Gallery, South Orange, NJ, Annina Nosei Gallery, N.Y.C., 2004, exhibited in group shows at Matthew Izzo Gallery, Pa., Paul Rodgers Gallery, NYC, 2003, Riva Gallery, N.Y.C., 2004. Home: 45 University Pl #2 New York NY 10003

PELLICONE, WILLIAM, artist, sculptor, architect, writer; b. Phila., Apr. 12, 1915; s. Emilio and Amelia (Practico) P.; m. Marle Guzzette, July 1964 (div. 1992); m. Ilka Bartel, Aug. 5, 1992. Student, Temple U., Pa. Acad. Fine Arts. Lectr. art Phila. Parkway Mus., Queens Settlement, N.Y., U. Iowa, Iowa City, Delaware Sch. Sys., Converse Coll., S.C., Ednl. Alliance, N.Y. One-man shows include Allen Stone Gallery, N.Y., Beryl Lush Gallery, Phila., Trylon Gallery, Southampton, N.Y., Capricorn Gallery, Bethesda, Md., Opus 127 Gallery, Soho, N.Y.C., Harpers Coll., Binghamton, N.Y., Phoenix Gallery, N.Y., Creighton Univ., Nebr., Gallery East, East Hampton, N.Y., Frederick Spratt Gallery, San Jose, Calif., Cheltenham (Pa.) Gallery, Goodman Gallery, South Hampton, N.Y., Woodmere (Pa.) Mus., Frederick Spratt Gallery, San Jose; group shows include Allan Stone Gallery, N.Y., Egan Gallery, N.Y., Alan Gallery, N.Y., Betty Parsons Gallery, N.Y., Tanager Gallery, N.Y., Phoenix Gallery, N.Y., M & L Gallery of Fine Art, N.Y., Arsenal Gallery, N.Y., Camino Gallery, N.Y., Trylon Gallery, N.Y., March Gallery, N.Y., Capricorn Gallery, Bethesda, Md., Brata Gallery, N.Y., Art Alliance, Phila., Landmark Gallery, N.Y., Tenth St. Days, N.Y., Profile Gallery, N.Y., Noho Gallery, N.Y., Gallery East, East Hampton, N.Y., Marie Pellicone Gallery, N.Y., Parish Mus., Southampton, N.Y., Elaine Benson Gallery, Bridgehampton, N.Y., Belanthi Gallery, A Retrospective, Bklyn., Lombardi Gallery, Retrospective, Austin, Tex., 1997; represented in permanent collections, including Met. Mus. Art, N.Y.C., Boston Mus., Smithsonian Inst., Washington, Am. Broadcasting Collection, Iowa Mus., Iowa City, Bayonne (N.J.) Mus., Martin-Rathburn Gallery, San Antonio. With Merchant Marines, 1943-45, France. Grantee Barnes Found., Temple U., Pa. Acad. Fine Arts, Greek Govt., others; exhibited first in Pa. Acad. Fine Arts, Phila. Republican. Avocations: musician, sailing, carpentry, writing. Home and Office: 101 Myers Creek Rd Dripping Springs TX 78620-3302

PELLITTERI, JOHN STEVEN, psychologist, therapist, educator; b. Bklyn., Feb. 19, 1964; s. Horace Mario and Lorraine (LoNano) Pellitteri; m. Leda Sabio, June 21; children: Alexander Rafael, Maya Paloma. BS in Music Edn., NYU, 1985, MA in Music Therapy, 1988; MEd in Psychol. Counseling, Columbia U., 1993; PhD in Counseling Psychology, NYU, 1999. Lic. psychologist N.Y., 2000, cert. sch. counselor N.Y., 1998, lic. music educator N.Y., 1985, cert. music therapist Am. Music Therapy Assn., 1988, martial arts instr. 1985-96. Music tchr. Leif Ericson Day Sch., Bklyn., 1986—87; crisis counselor Postgraduate Ctr. for Mental Health, N.Y.C., 1986—89; music therapist Northside Ctr. for Child Devel., N.Y.C., 1987—91; sch. counselor Archdiocese Drug Prevention Program, Bronx, NY, 1991—93; clin. supr. and music therapist Heartsong Music Therapy Program, Bronxville, NY, 1993—2000; pvt. psychotherapy practice Bklyn., 2000—. Program dir. Queens Coll. City U. N.Y., Flushing, NY, 2000—, asst. prof. Queens Coll., 1998—; cons. Bay Ridge Prep. Sch., Bklyn., 2000—02; mem. adv. bd. N.Y.C. (N.Y.) Bd. Edn., 2001—03; bd. dir. Heartsong Music/Art Therapy Program, 2000—05. Contbr. articles to profl. jours. Recipient Student Rschr. award, NYU, 1994; scholar, 1983—85. Mem.: Am. Psychol. Assn., World Martial Arts Assn. Avocations: martial arts, music, marathon running. Office: Queens College City Univ NY 65 30 Kissena Blvd Flushing NY 11367 E-mail: jpellitt@qcl.qc.edu.

PELLO, MARK JOEL, surgeon, educator; b. N.Y.C., 1949; MD, Jefferson Med. Coll., 1975. Resident gen. surgery Cooper Med. Ctr., Camden, N.J., 1975-79; resident colon and rectal surgery William Beaumont Hosp., Royal Oak, Mich., 1979-80; surgeon Cooper Hosp., Camden, U. Med. Ctr., Camden. Assoc. prof. clin. surgery U. Medicine and Dentistry N.J.-Rutgers. Mem. ACS, AMA, Am. Soc. Colon and Rectal Surgeons, Med. Soc. N.J., N.J. Soc. Colon and Rectal Surgeons. Office: Ste 411 Three Cooper Plaza Camden NJ 08103-1438

PELLOCK, JOHN DAVID, chemist, educator; b. Passaic, NJ, June 17, 1966; s. John and Jane Adrianne Pellock; m. Chrystal Dawn Sparks, Aug. 2, 1997; 1 child, Olivia Ileana. AA in Gen. Edn., Merced Coll., 1985; BS in Chemistry, Calif. State U., Turlock, 1988; MS in Chemistry, Calif. State U., Fresno, 1993. Chemistry educator C.C. of So. Nev., Henderson. Contbr. chpt. to book. Recipient Academic Instr. award of Merit for Western Region, Internat. Assn. of Gen. Motors Automotive Svc. Edn. Programs, 2003. Mem.: Am. Chem. Soc. Office: CC of So Nev 700 College Drive H3C Henderson NV 89015-8464 E-mail: jd_pellock@ccsn.nevada.edu.

PELLS, RICHARD H. historian, educator; b. Kansas City, Mo., Nov. 6, 1941; m. Molly Dougherty, Oct. 2, 1999. BA, Rutgers U., 1963; PhD, Harvard U., 1969. Lectr. Harvard U., Cambridge, Mass., 1968—71; from asst. to full prof. U. Tex., Austin, 1971—. Author: Radical Visions & American Dreams, 1973, The Liberal Mind in a Conservation Age, 1985, Not Like Us, 1997. Named chaired prof., Fulbright, Bonn, Germany, 1997—99; fellow, Wilson Ctr., Washington, 1985—86, Guggenheim, 1993—94. Office: Dept History Univ Tex Austin TX 78712

PELOFSKY, JOEL, lawyer; b. June 23, 1937; s. Louis J. and Naomi (Hecht) Pelofsky; m. Brenda L. Greenblatt, June 19, 1960; children: Mark, Lisa, Carl. AB, Harvard U., 1959; LLB, Harvard Law Sch., 1962. Bar: Mo. 62, U.S. Dist. Ct. (we. dist.) Mo. 62, U.S. Ct. Appeals (8th cir.) 68, U.S. Ct. Appeals (10th cir.) 70. Law clk. to judge U.S. Dist. Ct. (we. dist.) Mo., 1962—63; mem. Miniace & Pelofsky, Kansas City, Mo., 1965—80; asst. pros. atty. Jackson County, Mo., 1967—71; mem. Kansas City (Mo.) City Coun., 1971—79; judge U.S. Bankruptcy Ct. Western Dist. Mo., Kansas City, 1980—85; ptnr. Shughart, Thomson & Kilroy P.C., Kansas City, 1986—95; U.S. Trustee Ark., Mo., Nebr., 1995—2003; of counsel Spencer, Fane, Britt and Browne, LLP, Kansas City, Mo., 2003—. Intermittent lectr. in law U. Mo.; mem. Region I Law Enforcement Assistance Adminstr. Mem. adv. bd. Urban League, Kansas City, Mo.; chmn. human resource devel. com. Mo. Mcpl. League; bd. dirs., mem. exec. com. Truman Med. Ctr., Kansas City, Mo., pres. bd., 1988—90, chmn. bd., 1990—92; pres., trustee JVS, 2000—04; mem. Kansas City (Mo.) Sch. Bd., 2002—; bd. dirs. Greater Kansas City Mental Health Found. Lt. U.S. Army, 1963—65. Mem.: ABA, Am. Coll. Bankruptcy, Comml. Law League, Kansas City Met. Bar Assn., Mo. Bar. Office: 1000 Walnut Ste 1400 Kansas City MO 64106-2140 Office Phone: 816-292-8189. E-mail: jpelofsky@spencerfane.com.

PELOFSKY, STAN, neurosurgeon, educator; b. Brklyn., N.Y. MD, U. Okla. Intern U. Hosp./Okla. Health Scis. Ctr., Oklahoma City, resident. Chief neurosurgery St. Anthony's Hosp., Oklahoma City; asst. prof. neurosurgery Okla. Meml. Hosp., Oklahoma City; attending physician Mercy Health Ctr., Oklahoma City, Integris, Oklahoma City, Okla. Spine Hosp., Oklahoma City, Bone and Joint Hosp., Oklahoma City, VA Hosp., Oklahoma City, Okla. Children's Hosp., Oklahoma City. Contbr. chpts. in books, articles to profl. jours. Commd. USN, 1967, Vietnam. Recipient Gubernatorial Appt. to Sate of Okla. Adv. Coun. on Traumatic Spinal Cord and Traumatic Brain Injury. Mem.: Okla. State Neurol. Surgery Soc. (pres.), Ctrl. Okla. Coun. Hosp. Med. Staffs (pres.), Am. Assn. Neurol. Surgeons (pres. 2000—, sec. bd. dirs., chair Coun. of State Neurosurg. Socs., governance com., task force on med. edn.). Office: Neurosci Specialists 4120 W Memorial Rd Ste 300 Oklahoma City OK 73120-9322

PELOSI, HAYDEE, sculptor; b. Buenos Aires, Nov. 27, 1942; d. Oriondo Pelosi and Maria Ester Repp; m. Donald G. Pullum, Nov. 10, 2000. A, N.Y. U., 1963; B, SICC, 1972; student, Am. U., Cairo, 1975; D (hon.), Belgeano U., Buenos Aires, 1983. Interpreter Associated Press, N.Y.C., 1960—62; street artist N.Y.C., 1960—69; corr. Tankian Pub., N.Y.C., 1976—82; sculptor, 1987—. Author: How to Create in Clay, 2001. Mem.: Debary Art League (dir. programs 2003—, v.p. 1999—2002), Phi Theta Kappa. Democrat. Unitarian. Avocations: reading, tennis, painting. Home: 2050 Greenview Dr Deltona FL 32725 Office: Debary Art League 37 Keeble Ave Debary FL 32713

PELOSI, MARCO ANTONIO, obstetrician and gynecologist; b. Lima, Peru, Oct. 5, 1942; came to the U.S., 1968; m. Luisa Garcia-Pacheco, 1962; children: Marco, Carla, Monica. BS, U. Peruana Mayor de San Marcos, Lima, 1962; MD, U. Peruana Cayetano Heredia, Lima, 1968. Cert. Am. Bd. Ob-Gyn. Intern Navy Med. Ctr., Lima, 1967-68; intern dept. ob-gyn. U. Medicine and Dentistry of N.J., Martland Hosp., Newark, 1968-69; resident dept. ob-gyn. CMDNJ-NJMC/Martland Hosp., Newark, 1969-72, fellow oncology dept. ob-gyn., 1972-74; pvt. practice, 1975—. Instr. dept. ob-gyn. UMDNJ-N.J. Med. Sch., Newark, 1972-75, clin. asst. prof., 1975-80, 80—; clin. asst. prof. dept. ob-gyn. Hahnemann Med. Coll. Phila., Pa., 1980—; attending physician dept. ob-gyn. UMDNJ-N.J. Med. Sch., Newark, 1972—, Bayonne (N.J.) Hosp., 1974—, St. Joseph Hosp., Paterson, N.J., 1974—, St. Elizabeth Hosp., Elizabeth, N.J., 1979-87, Meadowlands Hosp., Secaucus, N.J., 1979—, Greenville Hosp., Jeresey City, N.J., 1980—; dir. dept. ob-gyn. Bayonne (N.J.) Hosp., 1987—; presenter; pres. Bayonne Hosp. Med. Staff, 1996—. Contbr. chpts. to books and articles, abstracts to profl. jours. Recipient 1st prize The Female Patient's 1st Annual Photo Contest, The Female Patient Mag., 1988, Physician's Recognition award AMA, 1979, 81, 84, 87, 90, 93, 96, 99, Sci. Exhibit Recognition award, Sci. Exhibit Achievement award 83rd Annual Sci. Assembly, So. Med. Assn., Washington, 1989, Physician's Recognition award Med. Soc. N.J., 1999. Fellow: ACOG (Philip F. Williams award 1972, Cont. Edn. award 1972, 1979, 1982, 1984, 1987, 1990, 1993, 1996, 1999, 2nd prize winner film festival 1999), ACS, Am. Inst. Ultrasound in Medicine, N.J. Ob-Gyn. Soc., Am. Fertility Soc., Internat. Coll. Surgeons; mem.: Med. History Soc. N.J., Royal Soc. Medicine, Am. Assn. Gynecol. Laparoscopists (1st place surg. videos 1996, winner Golden Laparoscope award 1996, Golden Laparoscope award 2001, 3rd place best surg. video 1997, first place/Golden Laparoscope award best surg. video 1998, award best surg. video 2001, 2002),

Internat.Soc. Physician Historians, Am. Assn. History Medicine, Med. Collectors Assn., Gynecol. Urology Soc., Pan Am. Cancer Cytology Soc., Am. Soc. Cytology, Passaic County Med. Soc., N.J. Med. Soc., N.J. Med. Soc., Soc. Laparoendoscopic Surgeons, Soc. Minimally Invasive Surgery, Am. Soc. Porfs. Ob-Gyn. Office: Pelosi Womens Med Ctr 350 Kennedy Blvd Bayonne NJ 07002-1313

PELOSI, NANCY, congresswoman; b. Balt., Mar. 26, 1940; d. Thomas J. D'Alesandro Jr.; m. Paul Pelosi; children: Nancy Corinne, Christine, Jacqueline, Paul, Alexandra. Grad., Trinity Coll., 1962—62. Former chmn. Calif. State Dem. Com., 1981; committeewoman Dem. Nat. Com., 1976, 80, 84; fin. chmn. Dem. Senatorial Campaign Com., 1987; mem. U.S. Congress from 5th Calif. dist., 1987-93, U.S. Congress from 8th Calif. dist., 1993—; mem. appropriations com., intelligence com.; mem. House Dem. Whip, 2002; Ho. Dem. Leader, 2002—. Democrat. Office: 2371 Rayburn House Office Bldg Washington DC 20515

PELOSO, JOHN FRANCIS XAVIER, lawyer; b. N.Y.C., Oct. 7, 1934; s. Rocco C. and Victoria P.; m. Elizabeth Byrne Peloso, Oct. 7, 1961; children: Alycia, John, Matthew. BA, Fordham U., 1956, LLB, 1960. Bar: N.Y. 1960, U.S. Dist. Ct. (so. dist.) N.Y. 1962, U.S. Ct. Appeals (2nd cir.) 1967, U.S. Supreme Ct. 1968. Law clk. to judge U.S. Dist. Ct. (so. dist.) N.Y., 1960-61; asst. U.S. Atty. U.S. Atty.'s Office, N.Y.C., 1961-65; assoc. Carter Ledyard & Milburn, N.Y.C., 1965-70; chief trial counsel NYRO-SEC, N.Y.C., 1970-75; ptnr. to chmn. Sage Gray Todd & Sims, N.Y.C., 1975-87; ptnr. to mng. ptnr. Morgan, Lewis & Bockius, LLP, N.Y.C., 1987-95, 95-99, sr. counsel, 2000—. Adj. prof. law Fordham Law Sch., 2000—; spkr. in field. Contbr. articles to profl. jours. Capt. inf. USAR, 1956-64. Mem. ABA (sect. corp., banking and bus. law, com. fed. regulation securities 1975—, com. bus. and corp. litig., chair subcom. securities litig. 1993-99, litig. co-chmn. com. securities 1983-87, com. on liaison with jud. 1987-88, coun. 1989-91, co-chmn. com. trial evidence 1994-95, co-chmn. task force on the ind. lawyer 1995-99), Assn. Bar of City of N.Y. (arbitration com. 1970-73, fed. legis. com. 1975-78, fed. cts. com. 1982-86), Nat. Assn. Securities Dealers (nat. panel arbitrators 1975—, nat. arbitration com. 1982-85), CPR Inst. for Dispute Resolution (Disting. Neutral). Office: Morgan Lewis & Bockius LLP 101 Park Ave Fl 44 New York NY 10178-0060 Office Phone: 212-309-6240. Business E-Mail: jpeloso@morganlewis.com.

PELOSO, PAUL MICHAEL, medical educator; b. Hamilton, Ont, Can., Jan. 10, 1958; s. Dino F and Donna Marie Peloso; m. Marie Lise Riley, Oct. 5, 1960; children: Nicholas John, Oliver Michael. BA, McMaster U., 1981, BSc, 1980; MSc, U. Toronto, 1994; MD, U. Calgary, 1985. Diplomate Am. Bd. Internal Medicine. Prof. internal medicine U. Saskatoon, Canada, 1994—2000; med. cons. VA Hosp., Iowa City, 2001—; assoc. prof. internal medicine U. Iowa Health Care, 2001—; adj. prof. epidemiology U. Iowa, 2003—. Sci. secreatriate WHO Task Force on Mild Traumatic Head Injury, Edmonton, Alta., Canada, 1998—. Contbr. articles to profl. jours. Recipient Rsch. award, Pan Am. League Against Rheumatism, 1998; grantee Multi Ctr. Osteoarthritis Trial, NIH, 2001-2005, Aerobic Exercise vs. Stretching and Strengthening vs. Edn. in Osteoarthritis of the Hip, Can. Arthritis Soc., 1998-2000; Rsch. scholar, Inst. for Work and Health, 1993-1994, Arthritis Soc. Rsch. scholar, Can. Arthritis Soc., 1992-1993, Arthritis Soc. Clin. fellow, 1990-1991. Fellow: Royal Coll. of Physicians and Surgeons of Can.; mem.: ACP-ASIM, Ctrl. Soc. for Clin. Rsch., Osteoarthritis Rsch. Soc., Can. Rheumatology Assn., Am. Pain Soc., Am. Coll. of Rheumatology. Avocations: coaching youth hockey, ice hockey. Office: U Iowa Health Care Room E 330 GH 200 Hawkins Dr Iowa City IA 52242 Home: 4533 Via Rio Thousand Oaks CA 91320-6850 E-mail: paul-peloso@uiowa.edu.

PELTASON, JACK WALTER, foundation executive, educator; b. St. Louis, Aug. 29, 1923; s. Walter B. and Emma (Hartman) P.; m. Suzanne Toll, Dec. 21,1946; children: Nancy Hartman, Timothy Walter H., Jill K. BA, U. Mo., 1943, MA, 1944, LLD (hon.), 1978; AM, Princeton U., 1946, PhD, 1947; LLD (hon.), U. Md., 1979, Ill. Coll., 1979, Gannon U., 1980, U. Maine, 1980, Union Coll., 1981, Moorehead (N.D.) State U., 1980; LHD (hon.), 1980, Ohio State U., 1980, Mont. Coll. Mineral Scis. and Tech., 1982, Buena Vista Coll., 1982, Assumption Coll., 1983, Chapman Coll., 1986, U. Ill., 1989. Asst. prof. Smith Coll., Mass., 1947-51; asst. prof. polit. sci. U. Ill., Urbana, 1951-52, assoc. prof., 1953-59, dean Coll. Liberal Arts and Scis., 1960-64, chancellor, 1967-77; vice chancellor acad. affairs U. Calif., Irvine, 1964-67, chancellor, 1984-92; pres. U. Calif. System, Oakland, 1992-95, Am. Coun. Edn., Washington, 1977-84; prof. emeritus dept. politics and soc. U. Calif., Irvine, 1995—2003; pres. Bren Found., 1997—2003; ret., 2003. Cons. Mass. Little Hoover Commn., 1950 Author: The Missouri Plan for the Selection of Judges, 1947, Federal Courts and the Political Process, 1957, Fifty-eight Lonely Men, 1961, Understanding the Constitution, 15th edit., 2000, orig. edition, 1949, (with James M. Burns) Government By the People, 1952, 20th edit., 2003; contbr. articles and revs. to profl. jours. Recipient James Madison medal Princeton U., 1982 Fellow Am. Acad. Arts and Scis.; mem. Am. Polit. Sci. Assn. (coun. 1952-54), Phi Beta Kappa, Phi Kappa Phi, Omicron Delta Kappa, Alpha Phi Omega, Beta Gamma Sigma. Home: 18 Whistler Ct Irvine CA 92612-4069 Office: U Calif Dept Politics & Society Social Sci Plz Irvine CA 92697-0001 E-mail: jwpeltas@uci.edu.

PELTO, GRETEL H. nutritional anthropologist, educator; b. Mpls., May 6, 1940; d. Isaac L. and Deana (Harris) Hoffman; m. Pertti J. Pelto, July 27, 1968 (div. Dec. 1995); children: Jonathan, Dunja, Ari; m. Jean-Pierre Habicht, June 13, 1997. Student, Bennington Coll., 1957—60; BA, U. Minn., 1963, MA, 1967, PhD, 1970; DSc (hon.), U. Helsinki, 1996. Clin. assoc. U. Conn. Sch. Medicine, Farmington, 1970-74; asst. prof. anthropology U. Conn., Storrs, 1974-77, prof. nutritional scis., 1977-92; scientist, child health divsn. WHO, Geneva, 1992-98; prof. nutritional scis. Cornell U., Ithaca, NY, 1998—. Mem. adv. bd. divsn. diarrheal disease control WHO, 1987-92; mem. adv. bd. subcom. on maternal and infant nutrition NAS, Washington, 1980-83; cons. UN U., Washington and Tokyo, 1985, Population Coun., NYC, 1980-82. Co-author: Anthropological Research, 1978, Community Assessment of Natural Food rces of Vitamin A; co-editor: Nutritional Anthropology, 2000. Bd. dirs. Parent-Child Rsch. Ctr. for Eastern Conn., 1974-79; mem. task force Hartford (Conn.) Area Health Edn. Ctr., 1980-82; mem. adv. com. Travelers Ctr. on Aging, Hartford, 1988-89. Fulbright grantee, 1984; hon. rsch. fellow U. Birmingham, Eng., 1994-97; U.S. AID rsch. grantee, Mex., 1982-87. Fellow Soc. for Applied Anthropology; mem. Soc. for Internat. Nutritional Rsch. (bd. dirs. 1989-92), Coun. on Nutritional Anthropology (pres. 1982-84, v.p. 1998-2000), Am. Soc. Nutritional Scis. (mem. long range planning com. 2001-, coun. mem. 2004-), Soc. for Med. Anthropology (bd. dirs. 1980-82). Avocations: photography, cooking. Home: 129 Eastlake Rd Ithaca NY 14850-9700 Office: Cornell U Div Nutritional Sci MVR 3M1 Ithaca NY 14853 Office Phone: 607-255-6277. Business E-Mail: gp32@cornell.edu.

PELTON, JAMES RODGER, librarian; b. St. Louis, Mar. 21, 1945; s. Norman C. and Leona V. (Schulte) P.; m. Sandra Lee Birdsell, Mar. 29, 1969; children: Joni Lee, Vicki Sue. BA, U. Mo., 1967, MLS, 1969. Br. libr. Scenic Regional Libr., Union, Mo., 1968-71; adminstr. Daniel Boone Regional Libr. - Columbia Ctr., Columbia, Mo., 1971-78; cons. La. State Libr., Baton Rouge, 1978-80; dir. Shreve Meml. Libr., Shreveport, La., 1980-. Mem. ALA, La. Libr. Assn. Home: 3201 Old Mooringsport Rd Shreveport LA 71107-3926 Office: 424 Texas St Shreveport LA 71101-3522 Office Phone: 318-226-5870.

PELTON, M. LEE, academic administrator; B magna cum laude, Wichita U., 1974; D, Harvard U., 1984. Tchg. fellow, English instr. Harvard U., 1980—86; sr. tutor Winthrop Ho., 1986; dean of student to dean of coll. Colgate U., 1986—91; dean of coll., adj. prof. Dartmouth Coll., 1991—98; pres. Willamette U., 1998—. Mem. bd. Oregon Ind. Coll. Fund, 1998—, Oregon Ind. Coll. Assn., 1998—; bd. overseers Harvard U., 2000; mem. Commn. on Minorities in Higher Edn., 2000—02. Mem.: Governor's Commn. on Financing Higher Edn. (Ore.), President's Coun. of Nat. Collegiate Athletic Assn. (Div. III), Nat. Assn. of Ind. Colleges and Universities (com. on policy analysis and pub. rels. 2000—03), Am. Coun. on Edn., Am. Assn. of Higher Edn. Office: Willamette U 900 State St Salem OR 97301

PELTON, RUSSELL GILBERT, retired lawyer; b. Monticello, N.Y., July 23, 1914; s. William and May (Morgan) P.; m. Marion Gosart, Dec. 14, 1940; children: William, Marjorie, Marilyn Pelton Barringer. BS, Syracuse U., 1935; JD, George Washington U., 1944. Bar: D.C. 1944, N.Y. 1947, U.S. Supreme Ct. 1948, U.S. Dist. Ct. N.Y. 1947; U.S. Dist. Ct. (fed. dist.). Ptnr. Darby & Darby, N.Y.C., 1945-56; sr. v.p. N.Am. Philips Corp., N.Y.C., 1956-75; exec. v.p. U.S. Philips Corp., N.Y.C., 1968-75; of counsel Rogers, Hoge & Hills, N.Y.C., 1976-78; organizer, mgr. Patent Law Office in U.S. Siemens of Germany, White Plains, NY, 1979—83. Officer, dir. Tech. Container Corp., N.Y.C., 1977-95; former dir. Ferroscube Corp., Savgerties, N.Y., Polyseal Corp., N.Y.C.; lectr. Practising Law Inst., 1953-69; arbitrator, mediator Am. Arbitration Assn., 1985—. Patentee in field. V.p. Siwanoy coun. Boy Scouts Am., 1948-53; v.p. Rye Neck Bd. Edn., Mamaroneck, N.Y., 1952-62; mem. Zoning Bd. Appeals, 1966-70; town justice, 1970-85; trustee Syracuse U., 1967-73. Served with Signal Corps, U.S. Army, 1941-45. Mem. ABA, Am. Patent Law Assn. (past chmn. antitrust com.), N.Y. State Bar Assn. (ethics com., Iola com.), N.Y. Patent Law Assn. (past bd. govs.), State Magistrates Assn., County Magistrates Assn. (treas., v.p., pres.), Westchester County Bar Assn. (dir., chmn. ethics com., alternative dispute resolution com.), Assn. Bar City N.Y. (patent com.), IEEE, Am. Radio Relay League, Aircraft Owners and Pilots Assn., Wings Club, Cloud Club, Winged Foot Golf Club, Waccabuc Country Club, Masons, Elks. Home: 3 Oxford Rd Larchmont NY 10538-1428

PELTON, RUSSELL MEREDITH, JR., lawyer; b. Chgo., May 14, 1938; BA, DePauw U., 1960; JD, U. Chgo., 1963. Bar: Ill. 1963, U.S. Supreme Ct. 1979. Assoc. Peterson, Ross, Schloerb & Seidel, Chgo., 1966-72, ptnr., 1972-90, Oppenheimer, Wolff & Donnelly, Chgo., 1990-2000, Chgo. mng. ptnr., 1992-95, 98-2000; ptnr. Ross & Hardies, Chgo., 2000—03, McGuire-Woods LLP, Chgo., 2003—. Co-founder, gen. counsel Chgo. Opportunities Industrialization Ctr., 1969—83; gen. counsel Delta Dental Plan Ill., 1979—96, Am. Assn. Neurol. Surgeons, 1983—. Pres. Wilmette Jaycees, 1970; chmn. Wilmette Sch. Bd. Caucus, 1970-71; Wilmette Dist. 39 Bd. Edn., 1972-80; bd. dirs. Wilmette United Way, 1980-86, campaign chmn., 1983-85, pres., 1985-86; Wilmette Zoning Bd. Appeals, 1989-2000, chmn., 1990-2000. Served to capt. USAF, 1963-66. Mem.: ABA, Soc. Trial Lawyers, Chgo. Bar Assn., Ill. Bar Assn., Ill. State Dental Soc. (hon.), Plaza Club (chair 2003—). Office: McGuireWoods LLP 77 W Wacker Dr Ste 4100 Chicago IL 60601-1815 Office Phone: 312-750-8652. E-mail: rpelton@mcguirewoods.com.

PELTON, WALTER EUGENE, information technology executive, mathematician, physicist; s. Clarence Elijah and Mary Hartman Pelton; children: Denel Renee' Pugh, Steven James. Student, Calif. Inst. Tech., 1957—60. Rsch. engr. autonetics divsn. N.Am. Rockwell, Anaheim, Calif., 1961—63; tech. specialist Filtors, Inc., Port Washington, NY, 1963—64; head circuits dept. Whittaker Controls, North Hollywood, Calif., 1964—65; owner, mgr., tech. cons. C.E.I. Co., Canoga Park, Calif., 1965—67; design specialist, exec. staff Am. Data Systems, Canoga Park, 1967—69; owner, mgr., tech. cons. Gen. Consulting, Corona, Calif., 1970—80, Dallas, 1981—86; software engr. Ilex Systems, Inc., Milpitas, Calif., 1995; head R&D Hand Held Products, Inc., Charlotte, NC, 1987—94; sr. RF design engr. GRE Am., Belmont, Calif., 1996; sr. design engr. analog and digital integrated circuits Sierra Rsch. and Tech., Mountain View, Calif., 1996—98; PhD advisor Northwestern Poly. U., Fremont, Calif., 1998—2000; CEO Agnitio Techs., Inc., Fremont, 2000—; pres. Faster Fourier Transforms, Inc., Fremont, 2000—. Cons. in field. Mem.: Am. Math. Assn. Achievements include patents for Low Power Optical Sensing and Decoding of Data; Sample Integrated Fourier Transform; invention of Rotational Fourier Transform; Special Case Processing Paradigm; Modern Switching Power Supply; development of Integrated Circuit with Jack Kilby et al; Multilayer Printed Circuit Team Physicist; First Solid-State Boiler Controller for Ship; Deep Space Low-Power Data Theory; research in Sliding Aperture Fourier Transform. Personal E-mail: walter@alumni.caltech.edu.

PELTZ, PAULETTE BEATRICE, corporate lawyer; b. Bklyn., May 30, 1954; BA, SUNY, Binghamton, 1976; JD, Am. U., 1979. Bar: D.C. 1980, Va. 1982, Md. 1986. Atty. U.S. EPA, Washington, 1979-83; assoc. Mahn, Franklin & Goldenberg, Washington, 1983-85, Deso, Greenberg & Thomas, P.C., Washington, 1985-87; corp. gen. counsel Western Devel. Corp., Washington, 1987-91; v.p. and corp. gen. counsel Mills Corp., 1992-94; sr. v.p., gen. counsel Charter Oak Ptnrs., 1994—. Office: Charter Oak Ptnrs 8000 Towers Crescent Dr Ste 950 Vienna VA 22182-6208

PELTZER, DOUGLAS LEA, semiconductor device manufacturing company executive; b. Clinton, Iowa, July 2, 1938; s. Albert and Mary Ardelle (Messer) P.; m. Nancy Jane Strickler, Dec. 22, 1959; children: Katharine, Eric, Kimberly. BA, Knox Coll., 1960; MS, N.Mex. State U., 1964; MBA, U. Phoenix, 1990. Rsch. engr. Gen. Electric Co., Advanced Computer Lab., Sunnyvale, Calif., 1964-67; large scale integrated circuit engr. Fairchild Camera & Instrument, Rsch. & Devel. Lab., Palo Alto, Calif., 1967-70, bipolar memory divsn. Mountain View, Calif., 1970-83, tech. dir., 1977-83; v.p. tech. ops. Trilogy Systems Corp., Cupertino, Calif., 1983-85; pres. Tactical Fabs, Inc., Cupertino, Calif., 1985-89; v.p. process devel. Chips and Techs. Inc., Cupertino, Calif., 1989-92; pres., CEO Camlan, Inc., San Jose, Calif., 1992-94; staff Chip Express, Santa Clara, Calif., 1994-98; prin. Corp. Tech. Devel., Santa Clara, Calif., 1994—, Ft. Lauderdale, Fla., 1994—. Inventor, patentee in field. NSF fellow, 1962-63; recipient Sherman Fairchild award for tech. excellence, 1980, Semiconductor Equipment and Materials Inst. award, 1988; Inventor of Yr. award Peninsula Patent Law Assn., 1982. Mem. IEEE, Sigma Pi Sigma. Home: 340 San Marco Dr Fort Lauderdale FL 33301

PELTZMAN, SAM, economics professor; b. Bklyn., Jan. 24, 1940; s. Benjamin Raphael and Ceil (Heller) P.; m. Nancy Virginia Bradney, Sept. 7, 1952; children: Shira Malka, Talya Rose. BBA, CCNY, 1960; PhD, U. Chgo., 1965. Prof. econs. UCLA, 1964-73; sr. staff economist Coun. Econ. Advisers, Washington, 1970-71; prof. econs. grad. sch. bus. U. Chgo., 1973-87, Sears, Roebuck prof., 1987-2001, dir. George J. Stigler Ctr. Study of Economy and the State, 1992—, Ralph and Dorothy Keller disting. svc. prof., 2001—. Vis. fellow Inst. for Advanced Study Hebrew U., Jerusalem, 1978; dir. CMP Industries LLC, 1995—; mem. coun. acad. advisers Am. Enterprise Inst., 1995—. Author: Political Participation and Government Regulation, 1998; co-author: Public Policy Toward Mergers, 1967; editor Jour. Law and Econs.; contbr. articles to profl. jours. Mem. Am. Econ. Assn., Mt. Pelerin Soc. Jewish. Office: U Chgo Grad Sch Bus 1101 E 58th St Chicago IL 60637-1511 Office Phone: 773-702-7457. E-mail: s-peltzman@uchicago.edu.

PELZ, CAROLINE DUNCOMBE, retired educational administrator; b. White Plains, N.Y. d. David Sanford and Helena (Ebert) Duncombe; m. Edward Joseph Pelz, July 11, 1942; children: Caroline Pelz Elbow, Margaret L. (dec.), Patricia Pelz Hart, Sanford M. AB, Barnard Coll., 1940. Adjustments supr. R.H. Macy & Co., N.Y.C., 1940-42; admissions interviewer Barnard Coll., 1960-63; alumni sec. Allen-Stevenson Sch., N.Y.C., 1967-70, admissions asst., 1969-70; adminstrv. asst. Ednl. Records Bur., N.Y.C., 1970-72; dir. admissions Grace Ch. Sch., N.Y.C., 1972-87; ret. Trustee Barnard Coll., 1963-67. Recipient Columbia U. Alumni Fedn. medal, 1991. Mem. Barnard Coll. Alumnae Assn. (pres. 1963-66). Republican. Episcopalian. Home: PO Box 395 Berlin NY 12022-0395

PELZ, ROBERT LEON, lawyer; b. N.Y.C., Nov. 18, 1918; s. Leon S. and Fanny M. (Berk) P.; m. Mary Jane Gips, Feb. 11, 1949; children: Kathryn Louise, Robert Leon Jr. AB, Columbia U., 1939, JD, 1942. Bar: N.Y. 1942. Since practiced in, N.Y.C.; ptnr. Hess Segall Guterman Pelz Steiner & Barovick, 1953-86, Loeb and Loeb, N.Y.C., 1986-2000. Life trustee, former v.p. Fedn. Jewish Philanthropies; bd. dirs., former chmn. bd. dirs. Fedn. Jewish Philanthropies Svc. Corp.; past trustee Coll. Pharm. Scis. Columbia U.; former chmn. bd. trustees Am. Jewish Com. Capt. AUS, WWII. Office: Loeb and Loeb 345 Park Ave Fl 18 New York NY 10154-1895

PEMBER, JOHN SCOTT, poet; b. Jackson Heights, N.Y., June 3, 1940; s. Gordon Franklin and Marion Louise (Burt) P.; m. Patricia Ann Farley, Nov. 10, 1965; 1 child, John Scott Jr. BA, Trenton State Coll., 1963; EdM, Rutgers U., 1979, postgrad., 1979-81, 88, U. Va., 1987. Cert. secondary tchr., N.J. Tchr. Hammarskjold Jr. H.S., East Brunswick, N.J., 1963-69, East Brunswick H.S., 1969-94, Rutgers U., New Brunswick, N.J., 1992; vis. poet Geraldine R. Dodge Found., Morristown, N.J., 1994—; tchr. Green Mountain Coll. Acad., Poultney, Vt., 2000—. Journalism evaluator Columbia U., N.Y.C., 1993-94; mem. poetry adv. bd. Geraldine R. Dodge Found., 1986-94; panelist Piscataway (N.J.) Pub. TV, 1992; presenter, cons. in field. Author: Rope to the Barn, 1993 (Poetry award), (anthology) Under a Gull's Wing, 1996; contbr. poetry to lit. jours. Docent Pember Mus. Natural History, Granville, N.Y., 1996—. Grantee East Brunswick Bd. Edn., 1972, 90-93; Va. Coun. on Arts fellow, 1987; recipient Gov.'s award for outstanding tchg. N.J. Bd. Edn., 1992. Mem. Acad. Am. Poets, Am. Philatelic Soc., Equinox Poetry Soc. Manchester, Vt., Poets' House, Kappa Delta Pi. Avocations: stamp collecting/philately, golf, reading, cinema. Home: 276 Dorset West Rd Dorset VT 05251-9426 also: PO Box 185 Dorset VT 05251-0185

PEMBERTON, BRADLEY POWELL, lawyer; b. Ft. Scott, Kans., June 15, 1952; s. Howard Duane and Juanita Lucille (Powell) P.; m. Kathleen Frances Querrey, May 22, 1976 (div. Feb. 1984); m. Lori Scott, June 18, 1994. BSBA, U. Mo., Columbia, 1974; JD, U. Mo., Kansas City, 1977. Bar: Mo. 1977, U.S. Dist. Ct. (we. dist.) Mo. 1981, U.S. Tax Ct. 1981; CPA, Mo. Tax acct. Alexander Grant & Co., Kansas City, Mo., 1977-79; shareholder Polsinelli, Shalton & Welte, Kansas City, 1979—; also bd. dirs. Kansas City. Active Vol. Atty. Project, Kansas City, 1984—; bd. dirs. Synergy House Inc., Kansas City, 1985-88, Youth Vol. Corps of Am., 1991—, March of Dimes, 1995—. Mem. ABA, Internat. Entrepreneurs Coun. (bd. dirs.), Mo. Bar Assn., Kansas City Bar Assn., AICPAs, Mo. Soc. CPAs, Kansas City C. of C. Avocations: tennis, golf, water-skiing, skiing, private aviation. Home: 5806 W 131st St Shawnee Mission KS 66209-3639 Office: Polsinelli Shalton Welte Sweltlaws PC 700 W 47th St Ste 1000 Kansas City MO 64112-1805 Office Phone: 816-753-1000. Business E-Mail: bpemberton@pswslaw.com.

PEMBROOK, RICHARD CHARLES, internist, cardiologist; b. Lincoln, Nebr., May 12, 1930; MD, U. Minn., 1963. Intern USPHS Hosp., Balt., 1963-64; resident U. N.Mex. Hosps., Albuquerque, 1965-67, U. Mo. Hosps., Columbia, 1967-68, Maine Med. Ctr., 1971-72; asst. med. dir. Las Vegas (N.Mex.) Med. Ctr., 1991—2001; self-employed, 2003—. Clin. asst. prof. medicine U. N.Mex. Sch. Medicine, 1995—2001. Fellow: ACP, Am. Heart Assn. Address: 876 Middlebridge South Kingstown RI 02879 E-mail: r.pembrook@cox.net.

PENA, ANTONIO FRANCISCO (TONY PENA), professional athletics coach; b. Monte Cristy, Dominican Republic, June 4, 1957; m. Amaris Pena; children: Tony, Jennifer Amaris. Profl. baseball player Pitts. Pirates, Nat. League, 1980-86, St. Louis Cardinals, 1986-89, Boston Red Sox, 1989—93, Cleveland Indians, 1994—97; mgr. Astros AAA farm club, New Orleans, 1997—2001; mgr. Kansas City Royals, 2002—. AL Mgr. of the Year, 2003. Player Major League All-Star Game, 1982, 84; winner Gold Glove. Office: Kansas City Royals One Royal Way Kansas City MO 64129

PEÑA, ELIZABETH, actress; b. Elizabeth, N.J., Sept. 23, 1961; d. Mario Peña and Margarita Toirac. Grad., Sch. Performing Arts. Actor: (plays) Rome and Juliet, Antigone, Blood Wedding, Night of the Assassins, Italian-American Reconciliation, Cinderella, Act One and Only; (films) El Super, 1979, Times Square, 1980, They All Laughed, 1981, Crossover Dreams, 1984, Down and Out in Beverly Hills, 1985, La Bamba, 1986, Batteries Not Included, 1987, Vibes, 1988, Blue Steel, 1989, Jacob's Ladder, 1990, The Waterdance, 1991, Across the Moon, 1992, Free Willy II, 1994, Dead Funny, 1995, Lone Star, 1996, The Pass, 1997, Strangeland, 1997, Rush Hour, 1998, Seven Girlfriends, 1999, Imposter, 2000, Tortilla Soup, 2001, Ten Tiny Love Stories, 2001, Zig-Zag, 2001, Keep Your Distance, 2003, Sueño, 2003, How the Garcia Girls Spend Their Summer, 2003; dir.: The Brothers Garcia, 2002; actor: Down in the Valley, 2004; (TV films) Fugitive Among Us, 1992, It Came From Outer Space II, Contagious, 1996, Dead Man's Gun, 1997, Aldrich Ames: America Betrayed, 1998, Border Line, 1999, Hollywood Dead Moms Society, 2003; (TV miniseries) Drug War: The Camarena Story, The Invaders; (TV series) Saturday Night Live, Hillstreet Blues, Cagney and Lacey, Dellaventura, I Married Dora, 1987—, Shannon's Deal, Tough Cookies, Resurrection Blvd., 2000—02; actor, actor: (TV series) Boston Public, 2003, C.S.I. Miami, 2003; dir.: (plays) Celebrando La Diferencia, 1992; (TV series) Resurrection Blvd., 2002. Mem.: AFTRA, SAG, Dirs. Guild Am., Actors' Equity Assn. Office: Paradigm care Joel Rudnick 10100 Santa Monica Blvd Fl 25 Los Angeles CA 90067-4003

PEÑA, FEDERICO FABIAN, retired federal official; b. Laredo, Tex., Mar. 15, 1947; s. Gustavo J. and Lucille P.; m. Ellen Hart, May 1988. BA, U. Tex., Austin, 1969, JD, 1972. Bar: Colo. 1973. Ptnr. Pena & Pena, Denver, 1973-83; mayor City and County of Denver, 1983-91; pres. Peña Investment Advisors, Inc., Denver, 1991-93; sec. U.S. Dept. of Energy, Washington, 1993-98, U.S. Dept. Transp., Washington, 1993-97, U.S. Dept. Energy, Washington, 1997-98; sr. advisor Vestar Capital Ptnrs., Denver, 1998-00; mng. dir. Vestar Capital Partners, Denver, 2000—. Assoc. Harvard U. Ctr. for Law and Edn., Cambridge, Mass.; mem. Colo. Bd. Law Examiners. Mem. Colo. Ho. of Reps., 1979-83, Dem. leader, 1981. Named Outstanding House Dem. Legislator, Colo. Gen. Assembly, 1981. Roman Catholic.

PENA, GUILLERMO ENRIQUE, lawyer; b. Miami Beach, Fla., Aug. 16, 1963; s. Gustavo A. and Rosa Amelia (LeRiverend) P.; m. Jacqueline Torre, Sept. 11, 1993; children: Austin Jake, Allison Lee. BBA, Austin Peay State U., Clarksville, Tenn., 1988; JD, Fla. State U., 1991. Bar: Fla. 1991, U.S. Dist. Ct. (no. and so. dists.) Fla. 1991, U.S. Ct. Appeals (11th cir.) 1991, U.S. Supreme Ct. 1996; cert. in criminal trial law Criminal Trial Law Found., Middle Dist. of Fla., 1998, Dist. of Utah, 1999, Western Dist. of Tex., 1998. Assoc. Boehm, Brown, Rigdon & Seacrest, P.A., Tallahassee, 1990-92, Raia & Preira, Miami Beach, Fla., 1992-95, Jeffrey S. Weiner, P.A., Miami, Fla., 1995-96; pvt. practice Miami, 1996—. Guest judge U. Miami Sch. Law-Moot Ct. Camp, 1996—99; adj. prof., bus. law U. Miami. Young pres. Mt. Sinai Hosp., Miami Beach, Fla. Sgt. U.S. Army, 1984—86. Recipient Recognition award Legal Svcs. Greater Miami, 1996, Pro Bono Svc. award Dade County Bar Assn., Miami, 1995, Young Pres. Mt. Sinai Hosp., 1999. Mem. ABA (criminal justice sect.), Cuban Am. Bar Assn. (Pro Bono Project 1996), Nat. Assn. Criminal Def. Lawyers, Am. Judicature Soc., Am. Inns of Ct. (barrister), Fla. Assn. Criminal Def. Lawyers, Fla. Bar (cert. as specialist in criminal law), Young Pres. Club. Office: 444 Brickell Ave Ste 51 Miami FL 33131-2407 Office Phone: 305-377-1119. E-mail: gepena@yahoo.com.

PEÑA, JUAN JOSÉ, interpreter; b. Hagerman, N.Mex., Dec. 13, 1945; s. Rosa Peña; m. Petra Cervantes, Dec. 22, 1974 (div. 1982); children: Federico Ezequiel, Margarita María Blea. BA, N.Mex. Highlands U., 1968, MA, 1972, postgrad. With Albert Garcia Gen. Contr., Las Vegas, N.Mex., 1955-67; tchg. asst. N.Mex. Highlands U., Las Vegas, Nev., 1971-72, prof. Spanish, Chicano studies, 1972-78; teaching asst. U. N.Mex., Albuquerque, 1978-79; attendant N.Mex. State Mental Hosp., Las Vegas, Nev., 1982-83; staff and supervisory interpreter US Dist. Ct. N.Mex., Albuquerque, N.Mex., 1983—. Head Raza Unida del to PLO in Lebanon, 1981, head negotiator with Iranians for release of 2 Chicanos and 1 Indian; supr ct. interpreters and reporters sect. US Dist. Ct. N.Mex.; co-chmn. Cuatro-Centennial Com., Inc.; mem. exec. com. N.Mex. Human Rights Coalition. Author collection of poetry: Angustias y Remembranzas; contbr. articles to profl. jour.; author play: Canto a La Raza, 1978. Pres. Dads Against Discrimination, Albuquerque, 1993—; chmn. bd. trustees No. N.Mex. Legal Svc., Las Vegas, 1972-81; mem. exec. com. Ind. Socialist Parties of Latin Am.; exec. commn. N.Mex. Human Rights Coalition; vice chmn. Barelas Cmty. Devel. Corp.; Barelas rep. Hist. Neighborhoods Alliance; mem. cmty. coun. on equity Albuquerque Pub. Sch.; mem. N.Mex. Cmty. Loan Fund; bd. dir. Albuquerque Downtown Action Team, N.Mex. Land Grant Forum; mem. textbook rev. commn. N.Mex. Dept. Edn., mem. bilingual edn. adv. com.; commr. N.Mex. Textbook Selection Commn., 2001—; nat. sec. Am. GI Forum of US, 2000-01, 2003-2004; v.p. Cmty. Enrichment Svc. Orgn., Inc.; bd. dir., bd. trustees Nat. Hispanic Cultural Ctr. N.Mex., 2003—; vice chmn., Hispano Round Table N.Mex., 1999-2003, chmn. 2003-2004; v.p. Cmty. Enrichment Svcs. Orgn., Inc.; bd. dir., bd. trustees Nat. Hispanic Cultural Ctr. N.Mex., U. N. Mex. Coll. Edu. Advancement Coun.; mem. adv. com. U.

N.Mex Coll. Edn.; nat. sec. Am. GI Forum, 2003-, chmn. N. Mex. Voter Registration Project. Decorated Bronze Star; recipient Human Rights award City of Albuquerque Human Rights Bd., N.Mex. State Coun. Profile of Courage award Vietnam Vets. Am., 1995, N.Mex. Nat. Guard Cinco de Mayo award, 1995, Hispanics for U N.Mex. Achievement award, 1999, Human Rights award Albuquerque Human Rights Bd., 2000. Bd. dir. Albuquerque Downtown Action Team; mem. N.Mex. Translator and Interpreters Assn. (pres. 1984-86), Nat. Assn. Judiciary Interpreters (sec. 1986-88), Nat. Partido Raza Unida (pres. 1976-81), N.Mex. Partido Raza Unida (pres. 1972-75, 77-78), Vietnam Vets. Am. (vice chmn. chpt. 1993—), Vietnam Vets. N.Mex., Am. GI Forum (Albuquerque chpt. 1 comdr. 1993—, vice comdr. 1997-98, sec.), N.Mex. GI Forum (comdr. 1996), Univ. of N.Mex. Sch. of Ed. Adv. comm. mem., Nat. Assn. Chicano Studies (founding mem.), N.Mex. Chicano Studies Assn. (pres. 1972-78), Hispanic Round Table of N.Mex. (chmn. 1995, 98), Barelas Neighborhood Assn. (pres.), Hist. Neighborhoods Assn., Barelas Cmty. Devel. Corp. (rep.), Phi Sigma Iota. Democrat. Roman Catholic. Avocations: weight lifting, swimming, ice skating, hiking, camping. Home: 1115 9th St SW Albuquerque NM 87102-4027 Office: US Dist Ct Dist NMex 333 Lomas Blvd NW Albuquerque NM 87102-2272 E-mail: jpena71@comcast.net., jjp3000@aol.com.

PENA, MARIA GEGES, academic services administrator; b. Torrance, Calif., Nov. 27, 1964; d. Nicholas John and Dina Connie (Vengel) Geges; m. Vicente Gregorio Pena, June 22, 1991. AA, El Camino Coll., 1985; BA, U. Calif., San Diego, 1987; MS, San Diego State U., 1989, postgrad., Claremont Grad. Sch., 1990—, Western State U., 1995—. Peer counselor El Camino Coll., Torrance, Calif., 1982-85; peer advisor U. Calif., San Diego, 1985-87, vice chancellor student affirmative action rsch. intern, 1986-87, outreach asst. disabled student svcs., 1986-89; coord. student svcs. Mira Costa Coll., Oceanside, Calif., 1989—. Contbr. articles to profl. jours. Mem. Calif. Assn. Postsecondary Educators of Disabled. Democrat. Greek Orthodox. Avocations: law, education, cd collecting, collecting beatles memorabilia. Office: Mira Costa Coll 1 Barnard Dr Oceanside CA 92056-3820

PENA, MODESTA CELEDONIA, retired principal; b. San Diego, Tex., Mar. 3, 1929; d. Encarnacion E. and Teofila (Garcia) P. BA, Tex. State Coll. for Women, 1950, MA, 1953. Cert. sch. supr., prin., supt., Tex. Tchr. English San Diego H.S., 1950-76; asst. supt. curriculum and instrn. San Diego Ind. Sch. Dist., 1976-80; gifted edn. resource tchr. William Adams Jr. H.S., Alice, Tex., 1980-83, asst. prin. for instrn., 1983-88; ret., 1988. Faculty Bee County Coll., 1975-76. V.p. San Diego PTA, 1963; charter mem. Duval County Hist. Commn., 1975—; reporter Duval Co. Hist. Com., 1988—; chmn. Com. to Establish Local Pub. Libr., 1993; trustee Duval County-San Diego Pub. Libr., pres., 1993-98, mem., 1999—, dir. Duval County literacy program, 1994—; cmty. rep. site-based dist. mgmt. com. San Diego Ind. Sch. Dist., 1995-97. Newspaper Fund Inc. fellow, 1964; recipient Adolfo Arguijo Day award, 1990; named Outstanding Sr. of Duval County, Grayfest, 1992; named to San Diego Hall of Honor, 1995. Mem. Tex. State Tchrs. Assn. (local unit rec. sec. 1952-53, 63-64, 1st v.p. 1957-58, 66-67, pres. 1961), Delta Kappa Gamma (rec. sec. chpt. 1972-74, 1st v.p. 1974-76, pres. 1976-78, chpt. parliamentarian 1984-88, 2003-2004, 2004-2006, state com. constn./bylaws 1979-81, state com. Eula Lee Carter Meml. Fund, 1987-89, area coord., 1989-1991, state com. pers. 1991-93, state rec. sec. 1993-95, state com. nominations 1995-97, chmn. 1997-99, state conv. chair 1999-2000, state com. necrology 2001-03, state com. ceremonials 2003-05, Chpt. Achievement award 1985, Internat. Golden Gift award 1994, State Achievement award 1996, Internat. Mem. in Print award 2002), Phi Delta Kappa (treas. chpt. 1978-79, rec. sec. chpt. 1983-84). Home: PO Box 353 306 W Gravis Ave San Diego TX 78384-2604

PENA, RAYMUNDO JOSEPH, bishop; b. Corpus Christi, Tex., Feb. 19, 1934; s. Cosme A. and Elisa (Ramon) P. DD, Assumption Sem., San Antonio, 1957. Ordained priest Roman Cat. Ch., 1957. Asst. pastor St. Peter's Ch., Laredo, Tex., 1957—60, St. Joseph's-Our Lady of Fatima, Alamo, Tex., 1960—63, Sacred Heart, Mathis, Tex., 1963—67, Christ the King and Our Lady of Pillar Parishes, Corpus Christi, 1967—69; pastor Our Lady of Guadalupe Parish, Corpus Christi, 1969—76; v.p. Corpus Christi Diocesan Senate of Priests, 1970—76; aux. bishop San Antonio, 1976—80; bishop El Paso, 1980—95, Brownsville, Tex., 1995—. Mem. secretariat Prep. Synod of Bishops for Am., 1996—97; Synodal Father Synod of Bishops for Am., 1995. Mem.: U.S. Conf. Cath. Bishops (chmn. bishops' com. for Hispanic affairs 1987—90, bishops' com. for ch. in L.Am. 1994—97, 2000). Roman Catholic. Home: 741 Bowie Alamo TX 78516 Office: PO Box 2279 Brownsville TX 78522-2279 Office Phone: 956-542-2501. Business E-Mail: rjpena@cdob.org.

PENA, RICHARD, lawyer; b. San Antonio, Feb. 13, 1948; s. Merced and Rebecca (Trejo) P.; m. Carolyn Sarah Malley, May 25, 1979; 1 stepchild, Jason Charles Schubert. BA, U. Tex., 1970, JD, 1976. Bar: Tex. 1976, Colo. 1986. Pvt. practice, Austin, Tex., 1976—. Instr. bus. law St. Edwards U., Austin, 1983, Austin C.C., 1981-82; broker Tex. Real Estate Commn., 1980—; sports editor Austin Light, 1982. Bd. dirs. Ctr. for Battered Women, Austin, 1979-82, Austin Assn. Retarded Citizens, 1980-82; chmn. Austin Travis County Mental Health/Mental Retardation Pub. Responsibility Com., 1979-84; chmn. pvt. facilities monitoring com. Austin Assn. Retarded Citizens, 1981; bd. dirs. Boys Club of Austin, 1987-88; chair Homeless Task Force Austin, 1999—. Named one of Outstanding Young Men of Am., 1982. Fellow Tex. Bar Found. (sustaining life; trustee 1994, sec., treas. 1994, vice-chmn. 1995, chmn. 1996); mem. ABA (ho. dels., nominating com. 1998—, immigration bono com. 2000—, vice chair credentials com. 2001, state del. 2002), Am. Bar Found. (bd. dirs. 2000, fellows officer 2003—), Nat. Conf. Bar Pres. (exec. com. 2001-03), State Bar Tex. (bd. dirs. Dist. 9 1991-94, exec. com. 1992—, chmn. minority representation com. 1991-92, chair James Watson Inn 1997-98, pres. 1998-99, chmn. profl. devel. com. 1991-92, policy manual com. 1993, fed. jud. appts. com. 1984-86, opportunities for minorities in the profession com. 1990-91, mem. advt. rev. com., pres.-elect 1997, pres. 1998-99), Travis County Bar Assn. (trustee lawyer referral svc. 1984-85, bd. dirs. 1986-88, sec. 1988, pres. 1990-91, chmn. jud. screening com. 1987, chmn. 1988-89, ins. com. 1988, 89, chmn. law day banquet com. 1988-89, lawyer referrel svc. com. 1983-84, trustee 1984-86, membership com. 1989), Capitol Area Mex. Am. Lawyers (pres. 1985, Outstanding Hispanic Lawyer Austin 1989), Legal Aid Soc. Ctrl. Tex. (bd. dirs. 1984), Austin Young Lawyers Assn., Tex. Trial Lawyers Assn., Austin C. of C. (Leadership Austin 1985-86). Democrat. Home: 107 Top O The Lake Dr Austin TX 78734-5234 Office: 2028 E Ben White #220 Austin TX 78741 Office Phone: 512-327-6884. Personal E-mail: richard@rpena73.com.

PENACHIO, ANTHONY JOSEPH, JR., psychotherapist, hypnotherapist, behavioral therapist; b. Stamford, Conn., Apr. 3, 1953; 1 child, Ariana. Cert. in psychotherapy, Am. Sch. Med. Hynotherapy, 1978; DD, Aquarian Ch. of Jesus, 1978; PSD, Neotharian Sch. of Philosophy, 1980. Cert. clin. registered med. hypnotherapist, psychotherapist, behavioral therapist, biomed. electronics, personal and bus. coach, psychophysiologist, personal coach; ordained counseling min. Aquarian Ch.; diplomate Am. Psychotherapy Assn. Counseling min., exec. dir. Inst. Clin. Tricotomy, Stamford, 1978—. Author, emotional investment profiler Wall St., corp. and govt.; lectr., radio and cable TV talk show seminar presenter. Contbr. articles profl. jour., corp. and govt. Mem. Am. Coun. Hypnotherapist-Psychotherapist (bd. examiners), NY Acad. Sci. (lectr.).

PENBERTHY, STANLEY JOSIAH, JR., publisher; b. Des Moines, Sept. 3, 1921; s. Stanley Josiah and Beatrice Ann (Voith) P.; m. Dorothea Oehmke, July 7, 1945; 1 child, Robert Bruce. Student, Drake U., Des Moines, 1940-43. Engaged in broadcasting WJR, Detroit, 1941-56; freelance radio, TV, motion picture, actor, narrator, 1956—95. V.p. Fed. I-D Equipment Corp., Dearborn, Mich., 1951-62; pres. Publishers, Inc., Detroit, 1976-99. Author, prodr., narrator nat. radio series These Were Our Presidents, 1975; contbr. Mich. Sesquintennial hist. articles; author: Living Under Cover, Episodes of Life and other Relatives, Cottage Industry, The Photographs of William A. Roeser: A Talent Unfulfilled, . . .From the Golden Tower of the Fisher Building. Past mem. bd. dirs. Sleeping Bear Dunes Citizens Coun., Traverse City, Mich., 1968-72, Cass Park Area Devel. Corp., City of Detroit, 1989; pres. Heritage Village Condominium Assn.; trustee Detroit Masonic Temple Assn.; mem. Founders Soc. Detroit Inst. Arts. Mem. AFTRA (past dir.), Adcraft Club Detroit, Detroit Execs. Assn. (dir.), Am. Film Inst., Detroit Prodrs. Assn., Broadcast Pioneers, Screen Actors Guild, Masons (33rd degree), Alpha Tau Omega (past alumni pres.). Home: 35560 Heritage Ln Farmington MI 48335-3136

PENCE, HOBERT LEE, physician; b. Campton, Ky., July 14, 1941; s. Bruce Elmer and Elva (Banks) P.; m. Marsha Lee Sweet, June 29, 1962; children: Robert, Ryan, Stefanie. BS, Ohio State U., Columbus, 1963, MD, 1968. Residency Walter Reed Gen. Hosp., Washington, 1969-71, fellowship in allergy and clin. immunology, 1971-73; pvt. practice pvt. practice, Louisville, 1975—. Asst. clin. prof. medicine U. Louisville, 1976-81, assoc. clin. prof. medicine, 1981—; assoc. clin. prof. Pediat. U. Louisville, 1995—. Contbr. articles to profl. jours. V.p. Jefferson County Med. Soc., Louisville, 1984-86; pres. Greater Louisville Allergy Soc., 1990-92. Major U.S. Army, 1969-75. Fellow ACP, Am. Acad. Allergy Asthma and Immunology, Am. Coll. Allergy and Immunology; mem. Southeastern Allergy Assn. (1st v.p., pres. elect, pres. 1996). Avocations: golf, tennis, reading. Office: Kentuckiana Allergy 9113 Leesgate Rd Louisville KY 40222-5003

PENCE, IRA WILSON, JR., material handling research executive, engineer; b. Pontiac, Mich., June 18, 1939; s. Ira Wilson and Fern Elizabeth (Fraser) P.; m. JoAnna Springer, Sept. 5, 1959; children: Ira W. III, Teresa Ann, Deidre Lynn. BS, U. Mich., 1962, MSEE, 1964, PhD, 1970. Rsch. engr. Willow Run Labs., Ypsilanti, Mich., 1960-67, Dow Lab., Ann Arbor, Mich., 1967-70, GE, Schenectady, N.Y., 1970-80, engring. mgr. Charlottesville, Va., 1980-83; v.p. engring. Unimation, Inc., Danbury, Conn., 1983-87; dir. MHRC Ga. Inst. Tech., Atlanta, 1987-97, dir., pres. Intelligent Integrated Info. Sys., 1999—. Cons. Superior Motor, Hartford, 1987-89; bd. dirs. Wesley Found.; mem. adv. coun. Westinghouse, Pitts., 1983-87, treas. Wesley Comm. Ctrs., Inc., 1999-2003; dir. 21iii.com, 2000—04; exec. pres. Intelligent Integrated Info. Sys., 1999—. Editor: Progress in Material Handling and Logistics, 1988; Material Handling for 90's, 1990. Trustee United Meth. Ch., 1988—, Camp Wesley, Inc. 1998— (treas. 2003-). Recipient New Product of Yr. award Innovation Today, 1985. Mem. IEEE (sr., sect. chmn. 1978), ASME (Materials Handling Engring. divsn. chair 1994). Republican. Methodist. Avocations: cabinet making, golf. Office: Ga Inst Tech 765 Ferst Dr Atlanta GA 30332-0001 Office Phone: 770-435-3183. Office Fax: 770-435-0493. Business E-Mail: ipence@isye.gatech.edu.

PENCE, JEAN VIRGINIA (JEAN PENCE), retired real estate broker; d. William Roscoe and Sophie Cottrell; m. Robert Albert Pence, June 14, 1947; children: Marjorie Pence Tuinstra, Robert J. Grad., Realtors Inst., Ill. Assn. Realtors. Cert. in real estate Central YMCA Coll., 1976. Sales assoc. William Knight Co., Realtors, LaGrange, Ill., 1962—70, sales mgr., 1970—76; pres. Pence & Co., Realtors, LaGrange, Ill., 1976—86; freelance writer Sun City Center, Fla., 1999—. Chmn. LaGrange Go-Getters Com. Channel 11 WTTG, Chgo., 1973—74. Author: (genealogy) The Cottrell Adventure With the Wright Connection, (novel) The Apprentice Angel, short stories. Sec. bd. deacons St. Andrew Presbyn. Ch., Sun City Center, 2003—. Mem.: DAR (vice regent Clearwater chpt. 1984—86), Women's Coun. Realtors (pres. West suburban chpt. 1979—81), DuPage Bd. Realtors, LaGrange Bd. Realtors (sec.-treas. 1973—75, dir. multiple listing service 1978, chmn. profl. standards com. 1985—86), Nat. Assn. Realtors, Coterie (pres. 1982—83), LaGrange Park Woman's (sec. 1967—68), Pierre Chastain Family Assn. (press chmn. 1998—2001). Congregationalist.

PENCE, MICHAEL RICHARD, congressman; b. Columbus, Ind., June 7, 1959; m. Karen; three children. Grad., Hanover Coll., 1981; JD, Ind. U. Sch. Law, 1986. Atty, 1986—91; host The Mike Pence Show, Indpls., 1992—99; mem. U.S. Ho. of Reps. from 2nd Ind. dist., 2001—. Named Asst. Majority Whip; mem. Congressional judiciary com. House Agriculture; House Internat. Relations Com. Republican. Office: 1605 Longworth House Bldg Washington DC 20515

PENCE, ROBERT DUDLEY, biomedical research administrator, hospital administrator; b. Hillsboro, Ohio, June 16, 1928; s. Glenn Roush and Mildred (Wright) P. BA cum laude, Miami U., Oxford, Ohio, 1950; postgrad., U. Montpellier, France, 1950-51. Mktg. rep. Tex. Petroleum Co., West Africa, 1956-58; mgr. lab. and office svcs. Sloan-Kettering Inst. for Cancer Rsch., N.Y.C., 1958-68; bus. mgr., cancer rsch. inst. New Eng. Deaconess Hosp., Boston, 1968-72, adminstr. Shields Warren Radiation Lab., 1970-78, asst. dir., 1972-86, adminstrv. dir., cancer rsch. inst., 1974-88, adminstrv. dir. Shields Warren Radiation Lab., 1978-88, dir. div. of rsch., 1986-88, cons., 1988—. Field liaison fellow ACS, Chgo., 1981-88. Pres. Am. Cancer Soc., Brookline, Mass. Served to lt. (j.g.) USN, 1951-55. Fulbright scholar, Montpellier, 1950. Mem. Assn. Community Cancer Ctrs. (del.), Internat. Union Against Cancer (U.S. standing com.), Assn. Am. Cancer Insts., Soc. Rsch. Adminstrs. (charter), Nat. Coun. Univ. Rsch. Adminstrs., Nat. Tumor Registrars Assn. (advisor 1980—), Tumor Registrars Assn. New Eng. (bd. dirs. 1975—), Phi Beta Kappa. Home: 30 Driftwood Cir Norwood MA 02062-5505

PENCE, STEPHEN BEVILLE, lieutenant governor; b. Dec. 22, 1953; m. Ruth Ann Cox; 5 children. BS, Ea. Ky. U., 1976, MBA, 1978; JD, U. Ky., 1981; PhD (hon.), Eastern Kentucky U., 2004. Asst. atty. gen. State of Ky., 1981—82; assoc. Taustine and Post, 1987—88, Borowitz and Goldsmith, 1988—90; ptnr. Sheffer and Hoffman, 1995—96, Pedley, Zielke, Gordinier and Pence, Louisville, 1996—2001; U.S. Atty. We. Dist. Ky U.S. Dept. Justice, 2001—03; lt. gov Commonwealth of Ky., 2003—. JAG Corps U.S. Army, 1982—87. Recipient Ky Bar Assn.'s Outstanding Lawyer award, 1995. Office: 700 Capitol Ave Ste 142 Frankfort KY 40601*

PENCEK, CAROLYN CARLSON, treasurer, educator; b. Appleton, Wis., June 13, 1946; d. Arthur Edward and Mary George (Notaras) Carlson; m. Richard David Pencek, July 10, 1971; children: Richard Carlson, Mallory Barbara Rowlinds. BA in Polit. Sci., Western Coll., 1968; Ma in Polit. Sci., Syracuse U., 1975; EdD, Temple U., 1999. Investment analysts asst. Bankers Trust Co., N.Y.C., 1969-71; substitute tchr. Lackawanna Trail Sch. Dist., Factoryville, Pa., 1971-81; instr. polit. sci. Keystone Coll., La Plume, Pa., 1972-73; USGS coding supr. Richard Walsh Assocs., Scranton, Pa., 1975-76; instr. polit. sci. Pa. State U., Dunmore, 1976-77; treas. Creative Planning Ltd., Dunmore, 1988—. Bd. trustees Lourdesmont Sch., Clarks Summit, Pa., 1989-2004, v.p., 2000-04. Bd. dirs. Lackawanna County Child and Youth Svcs., Scranton, 1981—, pres., 1988-90, v.p. 2004—; founding mem., sec. Leadership Lackawanna, 1982-84; bd. dirs. N.E. Pa. Regional Tissue and Transplant Bank, Scranton, 1984-88, Vol. Action Ctr., Scranton, 1986-91; founding mem. Women's Resource Ctr. Assn., Scranton, 1986—, pres., 1986-87; v.p. sch. improvement coun. Lackawanna Trail Sch. Dist., 1995-96, sec., 1996-97; mem. adv. bd. Pa. State U., Worthington Scranton, 1998—. Named Vol. of Yr. nominee, Vol. Action Ctr., 1985; Temple U. fellow, Phila., 1991-92. Mem. AAUW (sec. 1973-75, state sel. com. 1979-81), Assn. Jr. Leagues Internat. (area II coun. mem. 1978-79), Jr. League Scranton (v.p. 1980, pres. 1981-83, Margaret L. Richards award 1984), Philharmonic League (v.p. 1976, pres. 1977). Episcopalian. Home: RR 2 Box 2489 Factoryville PA 18419-9649 Office: Creative Planning Ltd 1100 Dunham Dr Dunmore PA 18512-2653 Personal E-mail: spot717@aol.com.

PENDER, MICHAEL ROGER, engineering consultant; b. Feb. 18, 1926; s. Horace Gibson and Lilian Frances (Higgins) P.; m. Francina Joan Krosschell, June 4, 1949; children: Michael Roger, Jr., William J., Robin Jane, Richard A., John A. AB, Dartmouth Coll., 1949, MS in Civil Engring., 1950. Registered profl. engr., Fla., NY, NH; diplomate Am. Acad. Environ. Engrs. Project engr. Madigan-Hyland, Inc., L.I., NY, 1950-60; dir. state exhibits NY World's Fair, Flushing, 1960-65; commr. pub. works Town of Hempstead (NY), 1966-77, Nassau County, Mineola, NY, 1978-82; supt. pub. works Village of Valley Stream (NY), 1982-85; tech. advisor NY State Assembly, Albany, 1985-86; cons. engr. Boyle Engring. Corp., Sarasota, Fla., 1987—. Exec. dir. World's Fair Collectors Soc., 1968—. Contbr. articles to profl. jours. Treas. Town of Hempstead Local Devel. Corp., 1967-86, Town of Hempstead Ind. Devel. Agy., 1973-86, Nassau County Local Devel. Corp., 1978-83; mem. adv. bd. Sarasota County Pub. Utilities, 1986-87; chmn. adv. bd. Solid Waste Mgmt., 1992—, Sarasota County Water & Sewer, 1995—; ruling elder Pine Shores Presbyn. Ch., Sarasota. Sgt. U.S. Army, 1945-46. Named Profl. Engring. Mgr. of Yr., NY State Soc. Profl. Engrs., 1979. Fellow ASCE (life), Inst. Transp. Engrs. (life), Fla. Engring. Soc.; mem. NSPE (life, v.p. 1982-84), Am. Pub. Works Assn. (life, pres. 1984-85, chmn. Suncoast br. 1993-94, named one of Top Ten Pub. Works Ofcls. in U.S. 1973), Dartmouth Club of Sarasota (pres. 1991-93), Sarasota Sister Cities Assn. (treas. 1990-2001), Am. Water Works. Assn. (life), Univ. Club L.I. (pres. 1985-86), Rotary (pres. Sarasota Bay 1992-93). Republican. Presbyterian. Avocation: photographing railroad depots. Home: 6639 Waterford Ln Sarasota FL 34238-2639 Office: Worlds Fair Collectors Soc PO Box 20806 Sarasota FL 34276-3806 Personal E-mail: wfcs@aol.com.

PENDER, NANCY, newscaster; b. Concord, Calif., 1960; BBus in mktg. with honors, Sacramento State U. Freelance reporter, LA and San Francisco; dep. press sec. Calif. Assembly Spkr. Willie J. Brown, Jr.; with KCRL-TV, Reno, Orange County Newschannel, Calif., KMST-TV, Monterey, KJEO-TV, Fresno, KCOY-TV, Santa Maria; morning news anchor KUSI-TV, San Diego; weekend news anchor and reporter WFLD-TV, Chgo., 1997—. Office: WFLD-TV 205 N Mich Ave Chicago IL 60601

PENDERECKI, KRZYSZTOF, composer, conductor; b. Debica, Poland, Nov. 23, 1933; s. Tadeusz and Zofia P.; m. Elzbieta Solecka; children: Lukasz, Dominique. Grad., State Acad. Music, Krakow, 1958; student, Arthur Malawski and Stanislaw Wiechowicz; Dr. honoris causa, U. Rochester, St. Olaf Coll., Northfield, Minn., Cath U., Leuven, Belgium, U. Bordeaux, France, Georgetown U., Belgrade U., Madrid U., Spain, Adam Mickiewicz U., Warsaw U., Poland, 1993, U. Catolica Argentina, Buenos Aires, 1994, Acad. Music, Cracow, 1994, Acad. Music, Warsaw, 1994, U. Glasgow, 1995, Beijiung Conservatory, 1998, U. Pitts., 1999. Prof. composition Krakow State Sch. Music, 1959-65, Folkwang Hochschule für Musik, Essen, Fed. Republic Germany, 1966-68; composer-in-residence Sch. Music, Yale U., alternate years; guest condr. London Symphony Orch., Polish Radio Orch., Berlin Philharm. Orch. Composer: Psalms of David for chorus and percussion, 1958, Emanations for 2 string orchs., 1959, Strophes for soprano, narrator and 10 instruments, 1959, Dimensions of time and silence, 1959-61, Anaklasis, 1959-60, Threnody for the Victims of Hiroshima, 1960, Psalmus for tape, 1961, Polymorphia, 1961; Fluorescences, 1961, Stabat Mater, 1962, Canon, 1962, Sonata for cello and orch., 1964, St. Luke Passion, 1965, De Natura Sonoris I, 1966, Dies Irae, 1967, Capriccio for violin and orch., 1967, Capriccio for cello Solo, 1968; opera The Devils of Loudun, 1968-69; Utrenja for double chorus, soloists and orch., 1969-71, Cosmogony, 1970, Utrenja II-Resurrection, 1971, Actions for jazz ensemble, 1971, Partita for harpsichord, 4 solo instruments and orch., 1971-72, Cello Concerto, 1967-72; for double chorus, soloists and orchestra Ecloga VIII for 6 male voices, 1972; Symphony 1, 1972-73, Canticum Canticorum Salomonis for 16 voices and chamber orch., 1970-73, Magnificat, 1973-74, When Jacob Awoke for orch., 1974, Violin Concerto, 1976-77, Paradise Lost (rappresentazione), 1976-78, (Christmas) Symphony No. 2, 1980, Te Deum, 1979-80, Lacrimosa, 1980, Agnus Dei for a cappella chorus, 1981, Cello Concerto No. 2, 1982, Requiem, 1983, Concerto per Viola, 1983, Polish Requiem, 1983-84, The Black Mask, 1986, Der Unterbrochene Gedanke, 1987, Adagio, 1989, Ubu Rex, 1991, Sinfonietta for orchestra, 1990-91, Symphony No. 5 for orchestra, 1991-92, Partita for orchestra, rev. edit., 1991, Flute concerto, 1992-93, Quartet for Clarinet and String Trio, 1993, Divertimento per Cello solo, 1994, Violin Concerto No. 2, 1992-95, Agnus Dei, 1995, Symphony No. 3, Seven Gates of Jerusalem, 1997, Hymn to St. Daniel, 1997, Hymn to St. Adalbert, 1997, Credo, 1998, Sonata No. 2 for violin and piano, 2000, Sextet for violin, viola, piano, clarinet, and french horn, 2000, also other works; prin. guest condr. NDR Symphony Orch., Hamburg, and MDR Symphony Orch., Leipzig; artistic dir. Casals Festival, PR. Recipient 1st prize for Strophes Polish Composers Assn., 1959, UNESCO award, Fitelberg prize and Polish Ministry Culture award all for Threnody, 1960, Krakow composition prize for Canon, 1961, grand prize State N. Rhine-Westphalia for St. Luke Passion, 1966, Pax prize Poland, 1966, Jurzykowski prize Polish Inst. Arts and Scis., 1966, Sibelius award, 1967, Prix d'Italia, 1967-68, Polish 1st Class State award, 1968, Gottfried von Herder prize, 1977, prix Arthur Honegger, 1978, Sibelius prize Wihouri Found., 1983, Wolf Found. prize, 1987, 3 Grammy awards, Gamma prize Acad. Rec. Arts and Scis., 1988, Manuel de Falla Gold medal Accademia de Bellas Artes, Granada, 1989, Das Grosse Verdienstkreuz des Verdienstordens der Bundesrepublik Deutschland, 1990, 2 Grammy nominations, 1992, Grawermeyer Music award, 1992, Österreichische Ehrenzeichen für Wissenschaft und Kunst, 1994, 2 Primetime Emmy awards, 1995, 96, Crystall award, Davos, 1997, 2 Grammy awards, 1999, Musikpreis Duisburg, 1999, Cannes Classical award Composer of Yr., 2000, Principe de Asturias, 2001; grantee several founds., govts., insts. Mem. AAAL (hon.), Royal Acad. Mus. London (hon.), Nat. Acad. of Santa Cecilia (Rome) (hon.), Royal Swedish Acad. Music, Acad. of Kuenste West Berlin (extraord. mem.), Nat. Acad. of Bellas Artes (Buenos Aires) (corr.), Internat. Acad. Philosophy and Art (Berne), Nat. Acad. Scis., Belles-lettres et Arts (Bordeaux), Acad. Scientiarium et Artium Europaea (Salzburg), L'Ordre de Saint Georges de Bourgogne (officer, Brussels), Am. Acad. Arts and Letters, Bay. Acad. des Schönen Künste. Achievements include creating original notational system allowing aleatory freedom for performer within sects. of precise duration. Home: ul Cisowa 22 30229 Cracow Poland Office: ICM Artists Ltd c/o Jenny Vogel 8942 Wilshire Blvd Beverly Hills CA 90211-1934 also: Panstwowa Wyzsza Szkola Muzyczna ul Starowislna 31 038 Cracow Poland also: Am Daubhaus 6 D 55276 Oppenheim Germany Fax: 49-6133/92 63 56.

PENDERGEST, KEVIN W. insurance company executive; married; 4 children. BS in Acctg., U. Dayton. Acct. Ernst & Young; with Deloitte Haskins & Sells, 1981—89; from v.p., CFO to exec. v.p., CFO GranCare Inc., 1990—91, exec. v.p., CFO, 1991—95; prin., owner Strategic Alliance Network, 1995—2002; exec. v.p., CFO Sun Healthcare Group, 2002—. Office: SunHealthcare Group 101 Sun Ave NE Albuquerque NM 87109

PENDERGHAST, THOMAS FREDERICK, business educator; b. Cin., Apr. 23, 1936; s. Elmer T. and Dolores C. (Huber) P.; m. Marjorie Craig, Aug. 12, 1983; children: Brian, Shawna, Steven, Dean, Maria. BS, Marquette U., 1958; MBA, Calif. State U., Long Beach, 1967; D in Bus. Adminstrn., Nova U., 1987. Cert. in data processing. Sci. programmer Autonetics, Inc., Anaheim, Calif., 1960-64; bus. programmer Douglas Missile & Space Ctr., Huntington Beach, Calif., 1964-66; computer specialist N.Am. Rockwell Co., Huntington Beach, Calif., 1966-69; asst. prof. Calif. State U., Huntington Beach, Calif., 1969-72; prof. Sch. Bus. and Mgmt. Pepperdine U., L.A., 1972—; spl. adviser Commn. on Engring. Edn., 1968; v.p. Visual Computing Co., 1969-71; founder, pres. Scoreboard Animation Systems, 1971-77; exec. v.p. Microfilm Identification Systems, 1977-79; pres. Data Processing Auditors, Inc., 1981—. Data processing cons. designing computer system for fin. health and mfg. orgns., 1972—; mem. Orange County Blue Ribbon Com. on Data Processing, 1973; mem. Orange County TEC Policy Bd., 1982-87; mgmt. and organization devel. cons. Assn. Psychological Type, 1993—. Author: Entrepreneurial Simulation Program, 1988, Journey to Couples' Conflict Resolution Using Game Theory, 1999. Served to lt. USNR, 1958-60. Mem. Users of Automatic Info. Display Equipment (pres. 1966). Home: 17867 Bay St Fountain Valley CA 92708-4443 E-mail: tpenderg@pepperdine.edu.

PENDERGRAFT, JANICE GAYLE, volunteer; b. San Antonio, Mar. 9, 1950; d. Janice Gayle and John Joseph Pendergraft(Stepfather); m. Pete E. Kraus, Nov. 3, 1973 (dec. Aug. 3, 1987); 1 child, Heather Kraus; m. John Joseph Pendergraft, June 18, 1988. Cert. dental asst., L.A. Coll. Med. and Dental Assts., San Bernardino, Calif., 1969. Cert. dental asst. Vol. M.A.D.D., San Bernardino, 1995—, Ronald McDonald House, Loma Linda, Calif., 1998—. Author poetry. Active Yucaipa Edn. Bd., Calif., 1980—98. Recipient several poetry awards, 1998—2002. Office: Ronald Mcdonald House Barton Rd Loma Linda CA 92353

PENDERGRASS, EWELL DEAN, communications executive; b. Houston, Dec. 24, 1945; s. Ewell Burl and Mary LaVerne (Sharp) P.; m. Linda Jo Williams, 1973; children: William Dean, Douglas Aaron, Nagaya Jo. AAS, Westark C.C., 1979. Comm. technician Murdock Comm., Ft. Smith, Ark.,

1966-73; electronics technician City of Ft. Smith, Ft. Smith, 1973—, now electronics supr.; co-owner LED Comms., 1975—. Broadcast engr. Sta. KWHN, 1972-73, Sta. KFSA, 1975-76; mem. Ark. Dept. Pollution and Ecology Wastewater Licensing Bd.; mem. Ark. Licensing Commn. Mem. Am. Water Works Assn., Ark. Water Works and Pollution Control Assn. (chmn. Western dist. dir.), Border Amateur Radio Club (prs. 1974-75). Democrat. Methodist. Home: 1106 Country Meadow Ln Cedarville AR 72932-9524 Office: 3900 Kelley Hwy Fort Smith AR 72904-5610 Office Phone: 479-784-2334. E-mail: edpbub@cs.com.

PENDERGRASS, GLEN, construction executive; Pres. Perry Homes, Houston, 1997—. Office: Perry Homes PO Box 34306 Houston TX 77234-4306

PENDERGRASS, HENRY PANCOAST, radiologist, nuclear medicine physician; b. Bryn Mawr, Pa., Jan. 29, 1925; s. Eugene Percival and Rebecca (Barker) P.; m. Carol Lowe Dodson, Aug. 27, 1960 (dec. Aug. 1993); children: Sharon (dec. Aug. 1993), Lisa (dec. Aug. 1993), Deborah, Margaret; m. Carol Minster Roberts, Oct. 2, 1994. Student, U.S. Naval Acad., 1944-46; AB, Princeton U., 1948; MD, U. Pa., 1952; MPH, Harvard U., 1969. Diplomate: Am. Bd. Radiology, Am. Bd. Nuclear Medicine. Intern Pa. Hosp., 1952—53; resident Hosp. U. Pa., 1953—56; mem. staff and faculty U. Pa. Med. Sch. and Univ. Hosp., Phila., 1956—58, U. Pa. Med. Sch. & U. Hosp., 1960—61; clin. asst. in neuroradiology Inst. Neurology Queen Sq., London, 1959-60; mem. staff and faculty Harvard U. Med. Sch. and Mass. Gen. Hosp., Boston, 1958-59, 61-76; prof. radiology Vanderbilt U. Sch. Medicine, Nashville, 1976-95, prof. emeritus, 1995—, vice chmn., 1976-89; adj. prof. radiology U. Pa. Sch. Medicine, Phila., 1996—. Mem. editorial bd. Am. Family Physician, 1980-94, Jour. Digital Imaging, 1987-96; contbr. chpts. to books, articles to med. jours. Mem. cancer control rev. com. Nat. Cancer Inst., 1975-79; Bd. dirs. state and local div. Am. Cancer Soc., 1976-85; mem. Project Hope Med. Mission, Peru, 1962; trustee Harpeth Hall Sch., Nashville, 1983-88. With U.S. Army, USN, 1943-46. Am. Cancer Soc. grantee, 1956-57; Nat. Cancer Inst. grantee, 1957-58; Nat. Inst. Neurol. Disease and Blindness grantee, 1959-60; Nat. Inst. Gen. Med. Scis. grantee, 1968-69. Fellow: AMA (sect. coun. on radiology 1979—99, chair 1997-99, sect. on med. schs. 1979—99, sec. 1986—97, mem. ho. of dels. 1986—99, specialty and svc. sect. 1986—99, grad. med. edn. adv. com. 1994—97, chair 1996, Gold medal 1994), Tenn. Radiol. Soc. (exec. com. 1984—88, pres.-elect then pres. 1985—86, Disting. Svc. award 1993), Soc. Magnetic Resonance in Medicine, Soc. Thoracic Imaging, Mid. Tenn. Radiol. Soc. (pres. 1984—85), Tenn. Med. Assn., Am. Soc. Emergency Radiology, Radiol. Soc. N.Am. (bd. dir. 1972—77, chmn. 1975—76, pres.-elect then pres. 1977—78, appointee to AMA ho. dels. 1986—97, sec.-treas. 1988—90, trustee RSNA rsch. and edn. found., Gold medal 1984), Nashville Acad. Medicine (chmn. com. on ethics 1981—82), Mass. Med. Soc. (counselor 1968—76), Mass. Radiol. Soc. (v.p. 1967—68, 1975—76, sec.-treas. 1985—94), Assn. U. Radiologists, Ea. Radiol. Soc. (sci. program chmn. 1964, pres. 1968—72, trustee 1968—72), Coun. on Med. Specialty Socs., Brit. Inst. Radiology, Am. Roentgen Ray Soc., Am. Coll. Radiology (life; coun. steering com. 1968—73, bd. chancellors 1977—81, appointee to AMA ho. of dels. 1997—99, coun., Gold medal 2002); mem.: Cap & Gown Club (Princeton, NJ), Merion Golf Club, Belle Meade Country Club, Merion Cricket Club, Amateur Ski Club NY, Delta Psi, Sigma Xi.

PENDERGRASS, TEDDY (THEODORE D. PENDERGRASS), musician; b. Phila., Mar. 26, 1950; m. Karin Michelle Still, June 20, 1987; children: Tisha, Ladonna, Teddy. Student public schs. Drummer for various groups, 1966-69; Singer, lead singer Harold Melvin & Blue Notes, 1969-75; solo artist, 1975—; pres. Teddy Bear Enterprises, Phila. Squire, Memphis. Albums include: Life Is a Song Worth Singing, 1978, Teddy, 1979, T.P., 1980, Live Coast to Coast, 1980, It's Time for Teddy, 1981, Teddy Pendergrass, 1982, This One's For You, 1982, Heaven Only Knows, 1983, Greatest Hits, 1984, Love Language, 1984, Workin' It Back, 1985, Joy, 1988, Truly Blessed, 1991, A Little More Magic, 1993, You & I, 1997, Greatest Hits, 1998, This Christmas, 1998, (with Harold Melvin & The Blue Notes) Teddy Live Coast to Coast, 1994. Recipient civic and pub. service awards., Image award NAACP, 1973, 80, Black Achievement award Ebony Mag., 1979, award outstanding mus. contbn. Afro-Am. Hist. Mus., 1983, award of merit City of Detroit, 12 gold and 7 platinum albums; recipity Keys to Cities, Lakeland (Fla.), Detroit, Savannah (Ga.), Memphis; named New Artist of 1977 for Top Pop Album Billboard Mag. Address: The Right Stuff EMI Music Distbn 21700 Oxnard St Ste 700 Woodland Hills CA 91367-3617

PENDLETON, MARY CATHERINE, foreign service officer; b. Louisville, June 15, 1940; d. Joseph S. and Katherine R. (Toebbe) Pendleton. BA, Spalding Coll., 1962; MA, Ind. U., 1969; cert., Nat. Def. U., 1990; D (hon.), U. N. Testemitanu, Moldova, 1994. Cert. secondary tchr. Ky. Tchr. Presentation Acad., Louisville, 1962-66; vol. Peace Corps, Tunis, Tunisia, 1966-68; employment counselor Ky. Dept. for Human Resources, Louisville, 1969-75; gen. svcs. Am. Embassy, Khartoum, Sudan, 1975-77, counsular officer Manila, 1978-79, adminstrv. officer Bangui, Central African Republic, 1979-82, Lusaka, Zambia, 1982-84; post mgmt. officer Dept. of State Bur. European and Can. Affairs, Washington, 1984-87; adminstrv. counselor Am. Embassy, Bucharest, Romania, 1987-89; dir. adminstrv. tng. divsn. Fgn. Svc. Inst., Arlington, Va., 1990-92; ambassador Am. Embassy, Chisinau, Moldova, 1992-95, adminstrv. counselor Brussels, 1995-98; consul gen. U.S. Consulate Gen., Montreal, 1998-2001; mgmt. counselor Am. Embassy, Cairo, 2001—04; diplomat in residence U. Memphis, 2004—. Bd. dirs. Cairo Am. Coll., 2001—04, Am. Sch. Bucharest, 1987—89. Named to, Hon. Order Ky. Cols., 1988. Democrat. Roman Catholic. Avocations: family history research, outdoor activities. Office: U Memphis Dept Polit Sci CL 421 Memphis TN 38152 Business E-Mail: mpendltn@memphis.edu.

PENDLETON, MILES STEVENS, JR., diplomat; b. Montclair, NJ, Mar. 22, 1939; s. Miles Stevens and Lucille (Bond) P.; m. Elisabeth Morgan, Aug. 13, 1967; children: Constance Morrow, Nathaniel Palmer. BA magna cum laude, Yale U., 1961; MPA, Harvard U., 1967; diploma, Nat. War Coll., 1980. Tchr. Ghana Secondary Sch., Koforidua, 1962-63, Adisadel Coll., Cape Coast, Ghana, 1963-64; vice consul Am. Embassy, Tel Aviv, 1968-70, polit. and econ. officer Bujumbura, Burundi, 1970-72; watch officer Ops. Ctr. Dept. State, Washington, 1972-73, staff officer Secretariat Staff, 1973-74, spl. asst. to Dep. Sec. of State Office Dep. Sec., 1974-76, dep. dir. Office of No. European Affairs, 1980-82, dir. Office of Israel and Arab-Israel Affairs, 1982-83, exec. asst. to under sec. of state for polit. affairs, 1983-85, dir. Office of Ecology and Terrestrial Conservation, 1995-97; polit. officer U.S. Mission to NATO, Brussels, 1976-79; min.-counselor for polit. affairs Am. Embassy, London, 1985-89, min., counselor for polit. affairs Paris, 1989-93; prof. strategy Indsl. Coll. Armed Forces Nat. Def. U., Washington, 1993-95. Mem. Am. Fgn. Svc. Assn., North Haven (Maine) Yacht Club, Met. Club (Washington), Phi Beta Kappa. Avocations: sailing, reading. Home: 3410 Lowell St NW Washington DC 20016-5023 Office Phone: 202-363-2601.

PENDLETON, MOSES ROBERT ANDREW, dancer, choreographer; b. St. Johnsbury, Vt., Mar. 28, 1949; s. Nelson Augustus and Mary Elizabeth (Patchel) P. BA, Dartmouth Coll., 1971. Co-founder, dir. dancer, choreographer Pilobolus Dance Theater, Washington, Conn., 1971—; founder, artistic dir. Momix Dance Theater, Washington, 1980—. Tchr., artist-in-residence at univs throughout U.S., 1997; tchr., condr. workshops. Choreographer, dancer numerous works including Pilobolus, 1971, Anendrom, 1972, Walklyndon, 1972, Ocellus, 1972, Ciona, 1973, Monkshood's Farewell, 1974, Untitled, 1975, Eve of Samhain, 1977, Alraune, 1975, Lost in Fauna, 1976, Shizen, 1977, Bonsai, 1978, Day Two, 1981, Elva, 1987, Debut C, 1988, Accordion, 1989, Fantasy on a Variation on a Theme, 1989; choreographer Am. premiere of Jean Coeteau's Les Marie de la tour Eiffel, 1988; actor, dancer: (film) Pilobolus and Joan, 1974; choreographer: Erik Satie Festival, Paris Opera, 1978, The Elatesse for Romania Gymnastic Federation, Opus Cactus, 1999; co-choreographer: Molly's Not Dead, 1978; choreographer: (for Pilobolus Dance Theater) Day Two 1981, Stabat Mater, 1985, Carmina Burana Side II, 1985; Joffrey Ballet Relache, 1980, Closing Ceremonies 1980 Winter Olympics, Berlin Opera Tutuguri, 1981, Moses Pendleton Presents Moses Pendleton, 1982, Ballet de Nancy, France, Pulcinella, 1985, (for Momix Dance Theater) E.C., 1982, Skiva, 1984, Kiss Off Spiderwoman, 1986, Spawning, 1986, Venus Envy, 1986, Medusa, 1986, Preface to Preview, 1986, excerpts from Gifts from the Sea, 1986, (opera for Spoleto Festival) Platee, 1987, White Widow, 1990, Passion, 1991, Table Talk, 1992, Baseball, 1995, Jonas et Latude, 1995, Orbit, 1996, Tvv, 1996, Sputnik, 1997; created show Centennial Fiat in Torino, Italy, 1999. Recipient Edinburgh Fringe Festival Scotman's award, 1973, Berlin Critic's prize, 1975, Gov.'s award Conn. Commn. on Arts, 1978, Positano Choreographic award, 1999; Nat. Endowment for Arts grantee, 1975-76; Guggenheim fellow in choreography, 1977. Democrat. Office: Momix PO Box 1035 Washington Depot CT 06793-0035*

PENDLETON, PEGGY A. state legislator, nurse education consultant; b. Lackawana, N.Y., Feb. 9, 1946; m. Robert Pendleton; 2 children. AA, U. So. Maine; student, Ea. Maine Med. Ctr. Sch. Nursing. Nurse edn. cons.; mem. Dist. 31 Maine Senate, Augusta, 1996—. Chair state and loval govt. com. Maine State Senate, marine resources com., joint select com. on R&D. Mem. Kiwanis. Democrat. Home: 110 Holmes Rd Scarborough ME 04074-9788 Office: Maine State Senate 3 State House Sta Augusta ME 04333-0003

PENDLETON, ROBERT GRUBB, pharmacologist; b. Kansas City, Mo., Apr. 24, 1939; AA, Kansas City Jr. Coll., 1959, AB in Chemistry, U. Mo., 1961; PhD in Pharmacology, U. Kans., 1966. Sr. scientist SmithKline and French, Phila., 1966-67, assoc. sr. investigator, 1967-69, sr. investigator, 1969-74, asst. dir., 1974-79, assoc. dir., 1977-80, dir. pharmacology, 1980-81; dir. gastroenterology Merck, West Point, Pa., 1981-86; sr. dir. biology Rper Ctrl. Rsch., King of Prussia, Pa., 1986-90; dir. pharmacology Sepracor, Marlborough, Mass., 1991—96; assoc. prof. Temple U., Phila., 1993—. Lab. sci. cons. Office Surgeon Gen., U.S. Army, Washington, 1989—96, Ft. Detrick, Md., 1996—99; lectr. pharmacology Thomas Jefferson U., 1991—; chief sci. officer Biopharm Cons., 1996—. Col. U.S. Army. Decorated Legion of Merit. Mem.: Soc. Armed Forces Med. Lab. Scientist, Am. Chem. Soc. (divsn. med. chemistry), Am. Soc. Pharmacology Exptl. Therapy. Achievements include patents for dopamine receptor agonists (SK&F 38393); PNMT inihibitors; discovery of new drugs to activate dopamine reactors in CNS and kidney; new drugs to inihibit epinephrine biosynthesis PNMT in adrenal gland and CNS; new drugs to block histamine receptors insurmountably including Pepcid; tricyclic antidepressants act in CNS to decrease gastric acid secretion; role of CCK in gut; new approaches to treat ischemia via rightward shifts of hemoglobin/oxygen dissocation curve; research in role of catecholamines in developmental biology and Parkinson's disease; pharmacology of chiral molecules including Xopenex. Avocation: ballroom dancing. Home and Office: 1312 Sumneytown Pike Lower Gwynedd PA 19002-1303

PENDLETON, YVONNE, astrophysicist; m. Dale Cruikshank; two children. BS in Aerospace Engring., MS in Aeronautics and Astronautics; PhD in Astrophysics, U. Calif., Santa Cruz, 1987. Astrophysicist Ames Rsch. Ctr., Moffett Field, Calif., infrared observational astronomer, Planetary Systems Branch. Avocations: reading, scuba diving, tennis, piano playing. Office: Ames Rsch Ctr Moffett Field CA 94035

PENDLEY, DONALD LEE, association executive; b. Jersey City, Nov. 5, 1950; s. Donald L. and Loretta M. (Purcell) P.; m. Donna Lynn Meade, Oct. 14, 1984; 1 child, Katelyn. BA, Montclair State Coll., 1972; MA, Syracuse U., 1974. Reporter/rewriter The Herald-News, Passaic, N.J., 1969-72; reporter The Dispatch, Union City, N.J., 1973; writer Keep America Beautiful, Inc., N.Y.C., 1974-75, comm. dir., 1976-78, v.p. comm. program devel., 1979-84; sr. v.p. comm. Greater Newark C. of C., 1985-86; dir. pub. rels. Internat. Coun. Shopping Ctrs., N.Y.C., 1987-92; exec. dir. N.J. Hospice and Palliative Care Orgn., Scotch Plains, N.J., 1993-97, pres., 1997—. Creator, dir. theatre composer series William Carlos Williams Ctr., 1987-91; creator, dir. SRO Cabaret Series, 1991-99. Pres. State Repertory Opera, South Orange, N.J., 1981-85, 92-99, Ars Musica Chorale, Englewood, N.J., 1979-81; mem. steering com. Coun. of States, 1999—2003, chmn. 2000—03; bd. dirs. Nat. Hospice Orgn., 2000—03; pres. Cmty. Health Charities of NJ, 2003—. Recipient Award of Excellence Am. C. of C. Execs. 1986, Gold Key awards, Pub. Rels. News, 1982, 86. Mem. PRSA (accredited, sec.-treas. assn. sec. 1989-90, vice-chmn. assn. sect. 1990-91, chmn. 1991-92), Am. Soc. Assn. Execs. (cert., Gold Circle award 1988, comm. sect. coun. 1994-96, dean Sch. Pub. Rels. 1998-2000), Am. Mensa, Ltd. (nat. devel. officer 1985-89, 96-2003, regional tng. officer 1989-93), Intertel. Avocations: music, photography. Home: 32 Hamilton Rd Glen Ridge NJ 07028-1109

PENDLEY, KEVIN, communication media executive; Bur. chief Bridge News, Chgo., 1996—. Office: Bridge News 30 S Wacker Dr Ste 1810 Chicago IL 60606-7404

PENDLEY, WILLIAM TYLER, naval officer, international relations educator; b. Paris, Ky., June 21, 1936; s. Louis Tyler and Virginia Lorene (Poplin) P.; m. Anne Carroll Cooke, Dec. 13, 1958; children: Stephen Tyler, Robert Randolph, Lisa Carroll, Leslie Brooks. BS in Engring., U.S. Naval Acad., 1958; MA, Am. U., Washington, 1965. Commd. ensign USN, 1958, advanced through grades to rear adm., 1983; comdg. officer Patrol Squadron 45, Jacksonville, Fla., 1975-76; ops. officer Patrol Wing 11, U.S. Atlantic Fleet, Jacksonville, 1976-78, comdr., 1979-81; exec. sec. for joint chief of staff matters Chief Naval Ops., Washington, 1978-79, planner for joint chief of staff matters, 1981-82, dir. plans policy and strategy divsn., 1985-86; exec. asst. to comdr. in chief U.S. Pacific Fleet, Pearl Harbor, Hawaii, 1982-83; comdr. patrol wings U.S. Atlantic Fleet, Brunswick, Maine, 1983-85; commdr. Naval Forces Korea, Seoul, 1986-89; sr. mem. UN Mil. Armistice Commn., 1986-89; dir. strategic plans and policy USCINCPAC, Camp H. M. Smith, Hawaii, 1989-91; dep. asst. sec. def. for East Asia and Pacific affairs Dept. Def., Washington, 1992-93; prof. internat. rels. Air War Coll., Maxwell AFB, Ala., 1993-98. Lectr. and cons., 1998—; fellow Georgetown U. Leadership Seminar, Washington, 1985. Co-author: Nuclear Coexistence, 1994; contbr. articles to profl. jours. Decorated Def. D.S.M. with oak leaf cluster, Legion of Merit with 4 gold stars; named hon. Ky. Col., 1975; recipient Def. medal for disting. pub. svc., 1993. Mem. Phi Kappa Phi, Pi Gamma Mu. Methodist. Avocations: flying, golf, tennis, skiing. Home: 10 Walden Ln Bluffton SC 29909 Office Phone: 843-705-2334. E-mail: pendleyw@aol.com.

PENDZIWIATR, WILLIAM J. music educator; b. Bklyn., Dec. 6, 1949; s. Charles Roman and Caroline Francis Pendziwiatr; m. Laverne Ann Kindler, Dec. 14, 1974; 1 child, Jennifer. MusB, State U Coll., Fredonia, NY, 1971; MusM ed., Marywood U, Scranton, PA, 1995; MSc in edn., Wilkes U., 2003. Cert. tchg. K-12, elem. ed. Tchr. Crestwood Sch. Dist., Mountaintop, Pa. Sec. Plum Ridge Acad., Inc., Nescopeck, Pa., treas. Recipient Citation of Excellence, PA Music Ed., 2002. Mem.: PA Music Ed. Assoc. (assoc.; pres. dist. 9 2004). Achievements include wrote and dir. four HS plays; inducted into the Buffalo Music Hall of Fame as a member of the musical group United Sound. Home: 54 Overlook Rd Nescopeck PA 18635 Office: Crestwood Sch Dist 281 S Mountain Blvd Mountaintop PA 18707 Office Phone: 570-474-6782.

PENELAS, ALEX, mayor; b. Miami, Fla., 1961; m. Lilliam Penelas; children: William, Christopher. BA in Polit. Sci. summa cum laude, Biscayne Coll. now St. Thomas U.; JD cum laude, U. Miami, 1985; LLD (hon.), St. Thomas U. Counsel Shutts & Bowen; councilman City of Hialeah, Hialeah, 1987—90; mem. Miami-Dade Bd. County Commrs.; mayor Miami-Dade, Fla., 1996—. Active Dem. Nat. Com.; bd. dirs. March of Dimes, Fla. League Cities. Named Top Ten Outstanding Young Ams., U.S. Jr. C. of C., Person of the Yr., Miami Boys and Girls Club; recipient Outstanding Svc. award, Nat. Transp. Safety Bd., Excellence in Govt. award, Nat. Assn. Hispanic Pub. Adminstrs. and Fedn. Black Employees, Outstanding Cmty. Leadership award, Greater Miami Jewish Fedn., Woodrow Wilson award for pub. svc., Abraham Lincoln award. Mem.: KC. Office: Stephen P Clark Ctr 29th Fl 111 NW 1st St Miami FL 33128

PENFIELD, PAUL LIVINGSTONE, JR., electrical engineering educator; b. Detroit, May 28, 1933; s. Paul Livingstone and Charlotte Wentworth (Gilman) P.; m. Martha Elise Dieterle, Aug. 24, 1956 (dec. Apr. 1988); children: David Wesley, Patricia Jane, Michael Baldwin; m. Barbara Jean Buehrig Lory, July 22, 1989. BA, Amherst Coll., 1955; ScD, MIT, 1960. Asst. prof. elec. engring. MIT, Cambridge, 1960-64, assoc. prof., 1964-69, prof., 1969—, head dept. elec. engring. and computer sci., 1989-99. Author: Frequency-Power Formulas, 1960, MARTHA User's Manual, 1971; co-author: Varactor Applications, 1962, Electrodynamics of Moving Media, 1967, Tellegen's Theorem and Electrical Networks, 1970. Sr. postdoctoral fellow NSF, 1966-67. Fellow IEEE (chmn. Boston sect. 1971-72, Darlington award 1985, Centennial medal 1984, Golden Jubilee award 1999); mem. Nat. Acad. Engring., Am. Phys. Soc., Assn. for Computing Machinery, Audio Engring. Soc., Sigma Xi. Avocation: field identification of ferns and fern hybrids. Office: MIT Dept EECS Cambridge MA 02139

PENG, LIANG-CHUAN, mechanical engineer; b. Taiwan, Feb. 6, 1936; came to U.S., 1965, naturalized, 1973; s. Mu-Sui and Wang-Su (Yang) P.; m. Wen-Fong Kao, Nov. 18, 1962; children: Tsen-Loong, Tsen-Hsin, Lina, Linda. Diploma, Taipei Inst. Tech., 1960; MS, Kans. State U., 1967. Registered profl. engr., Tex., Calif. Project engr. Taiwan Power Co., 1965—66; asst. engr. Carlson & Sweatt, N.Y.C., 1966—67, Pioneer Engrs., Chgo., 1967—68; mech. engr. Bechtel, San Francisco, 1969—71; sr. specialist Nuc. Svcs. Co., San Jose, Calif., 1971—75; sr. engr. Brown & Root, Houston, 1975; stress engr. Foster Wheeler, Houston, 1976; staff engr. AAA Technologists, Houston, 1977; prin. engr. M.W. Kellogg, Houston, 1978—82; pres., owner Peng Engring., Houston, 1982—. Instr. U. Houston; condr. piping tech. seminars. Developer: (computer programs) SIMFLEX. Chmn. South Bay Area Formosan Assn., 1974, No. Calif. Formosan Fedn., 1975. Mem. ASME, NSPE. Buddhist. Home: 3010 Manila Ln Houston TX 77043-1312 Business E-Mail: lcpeng@pipestress.com.

PENGRA, R. RENE, lawyer; b. 1967; BA, U. Wyo., 1988; JD, NYU, 1993. Bar: Ill. 1995, N.Y. 2000. Law clk. to Hon. David B. Sentelle U.S. Ct. Appeals, D.C. Cir., 1993; with Sidley Austin Brown & Wood, Chgo., 1993—, ptnr., 2002—. Office: Sidley Austin Brown and Wood Bank One Plz 10 S Dearborn St Chicago IL 60603

PENHOET, EDWARD, medical association administrator, biochemicals company executive, former dean; b. Oakland, Calif., Dec. 11, 1940; AB, Stanford U., 1963; PhD, U. Wash., 1968. Dean Sch. Pub. Health U. Calif., Berkeley, 1998—2002, dean emeritus, 2002—; sr. dir., Sci. & Higher Education Gordon and Betty Moore Found., 2002—. Bd. dirs., sr. adv. to CEO Chiron Corp. Mem.: Inst. Medicine. Office: Chiron Corp 4560 Horton St Emeryville CA 94608-2900

PENICHEIRO, TICHA NUNES, professional basketball player; b. Portugal, Sept. 18, 1974; d. Joao Penicheiro. Degree comm. and interdisciplinary studies, Old Dominion. Profl. basketball player Sacramento Monarchs, 1998—. Named 3d Rookie of Yr., 1998, All-WNBA 1st Team, 1999, All-WNBA 2nd Team, 2001. Mem.: Portuguese Nat. Team. Avocation: music. Office: Arco Arena 1 Sports Pkwy Sacramento CA 95834 Business E-Mail: monarchs@arcoarena.com.

PENICK, ELIZABETH C. psychologist; b. New Orleans, July 17, 1934; d. Rawley M. Penick and Marie G. Sells. BA, Newcomb Coll., 1957; MS, Tulane U., 1960; PhD, Washington U., St. Louis, 1975. Diplomate clin. psychology Am. Bd. Profl. Psychology. Prof. dept. psychiatry Kans. U. Med. Ctr., Kansas City, 1980—, dir. divsn. psychology. Rsch. grantee Nat. Assn. Alcohol Abuse and Alcoholism, Washington, 1980-97. Mem. APA, Kans. Psychol. Assn. (dir.). Home: 12231 Charlotte Kansas City MO 64146 Office: Kans U Med Ctr Dept Psychiatry 3901 Rainbow Blvd Kansas City KS 66160 E-mail: epenick@kumc.edu.

PENIKETT, ANTONY DAVID JOHN, negotiator, writer, politician; b. Nov. 14, 1945; s. Erik John Keith and Sarah Ann (Colwell) P.; m. Lula Mary Johns, 1974 (div. 1997); children— John Tahmoh, Sarah Lahlil, Stephanie Yahsan Exec. asst. to nat. leader New Dem. Party, Ottawa, Ont., Canada, 1975-76, nat. pres., 1981-85, fed. councillor, 1973—, leader Whitehorse, Canada, 1980—, campaign mgr., 1972; alderman City of Whitehorse, Canada, 1977-79; elected mem. Yukon Legis. Assembly, 1978-95, opposition leader, 1982-85, 92-95, elected premier Yukon Terr., 1985-92; sr. policy advisor Govt. of Sask., 1995-97; dep. min. negotiations Ministry of Fin. and Corp. Rels., Govt. of B.C., Victoria, 1997-2000; dep. min. labor Ministry of Fin., Govt. of B.C., Victoria, 2000—01; propr. Tony Penikett Negotiations Inc., Vancouver, Canada, 2001—. Author (film): The Mad Trapper, 1972; La Patrouille Perdue, 1974. Office: Tony Penikett Negotiations INc PO Box 2494 Vancouver BC V6B 3W7 Canada

PENISTEN, GARY DEAN, entrepreneur; b. Lincoln, Nebr., May 14, 1931; s. Martin C. and Jayne (O'Dell) P.; m. Nancy Margaret Golding, June 3, 1951; children: Kris D., Janet L., Carol E., Noel M. BS in Bus. Adminstrn., U. Nebr., Omaha, 1953; LLD (hon.), Concordia Coll., 1993. With Gen. Electric Co., 1953-74, mgr. group fin. ops. power generation group, 1973-74; asst. sec. navy fin. mgmt., 1974-77; sr. v.p. fin., chief fin. officer, dir. Sterling Drug Inc., N.Y.C., 1977-89; sr. v.p. fin., health group Eastman Kodak Co., N.Y.C., 1989-90. Chmn. bd. dirs. Acme United Corp. Mem./corp. adv. bd. U. Nebr. Coll. Bus., Omaha. Recipient Disting. Public Service award Navy Dept., 1977; Alumni Achievement citation U. Nebr., Omaha, 1975. Mem. Fin. Execs. Inst., Navy League of U.S., Army and Navy Club (Washington), Rotary, Union League (N.Y.), Ft. Lauderdale (Fla.) Country Club, White Eagle Golf Club (Naperville). Republican. Unitarian Universalist. Home and Office: 1409 Aberdeen Ct Naperville IL 60564-9787 Office Phone: 630-978-7093. Personal E-mail: asnfm@aol.com.

PENKAVA, ROBERT RAY, radiologist, educator; b. Virginia, Nebr., Jan. 30, 1942; s. Joseph Evert and Velta Mae (Oviatt) P.; m. Kathy Bennett Secrest, Apr. 6, 1973; children: Ashley Secrest, J. Carson Bennett. AB BS, Peru State Coll., Nebr., 1963; MD, U. Nebr., Omaha, 1967. Intern Lincoln Gen. Hosp., Nebr., 1967-68; resident Menorah Med. Cen., Kansas City, 1968-71; chief resident Menorah Med. Ctr., Kansas City, 1970-71; adj. faculty U. Mo., Kansas City, 1970-71; staff radiologist Ireland Army Hosp., Ft. Knox, Ky., 1971-72, chief, dept. radiology & nuclear med., 1972-73; staff radiologist Deaconess Hosp., Evansville, Ind., 1973-99; mem. faculty U. So. Ind., Evansville, 1973—; assoc. faculty Ind. U. Coll. Med., Bloomington, 1973—; med. dir. Sch. Radiol. Tech. U. So. Ind., Evansville, 1978—; dep coroner Vanderburgh County, 1991—; med. dir. Deaconess Breast Ctr., 1999—. Chmn. So. Ind. Health Sys., 1980-83; pres. Vanderburgh County Med. Soc. Svc. Bur., 1979—; mem. roentgen soc. liaison com. Ind. Bd. Health, 1968. Author numerous articles on med. ultrasound, nuclear med., angiography, and computed tomography. Chmn. profl. div. United Way of So. Ind., 1983; bd. dirs. S.W. Ind. Pub. Broadcasting, 1978-84, S.W. Ind. PSRO, 1982; v.p. Mesker Zoo Found., bd. dirs., 1991-95; mem. Evansville Pub. Safety Bd., 2000—. Maj. U.S. Army, 1971-73. Named Sci. Tchr. of Year, Lewis & Clark Jr. High Sch., 1963. Mem. AMA, Evansville Med. Radiol. Assn. (treas. 1987-98), Am. Soc. Breast Disease, Internat. Soc. Clin. Dosimetry, Tri-State Radiology Assn. (pres.), Vanderburgh County Med. Soc. (pres.), Physicians Svc. Bur. (treas.), Magnetic Resonance Imaging, Inc. (treas. 1995-98), Am. Coll. Radiology, Radiol. Soc. N.Am., Am. Roentgen Ray Soc., Am. Inst. Ultrasound in Medicine, Soc. Cardiovascular and Interventional Radiology. Avocations: golf, boating, flying. Office: 520 Mary St Ste #140 Evansville IN 47710

PENLAND, JOHN THOMAS, retired import and export and development companies executive; b. Guntersville, Ala., Mar. 31, 1930; s. James B. and Kathleen (Bolding) P.; m. Carolyn Joyce White, May 30, 1961; children— Jeffrey K., Mark A., Michael J. BA, George Washington U., 1957. Vice pres., dir. Rouse, Brewer, Becker & Bryant, Inc., Washington, 1957-63; staff mem. SEC, Washington, 1963-67; pres., dir. INA Trading Corp., Phila., 1968-69; v.p. INA Security Corp., Phila., 1967-69; from v.p. to pres. Shareholders Mgmt. Co., L.A., 1969—75; v.p. Shareholders Capital Corp., L.A., 1972-73; v.p., dir. several mut. funds managed by Shareholders Mgmt. Co., 1970-75; pres., chmn., CEO, HMO Internat. and its subs., L.A., 1975; founder, pres., chmn. Pendlar Corp., Atlanta, 1977-97; chmn., pres. Bella Vista Developers, Inc., Albuquerque, 1977-98; chmn. CompuComp Corp., Atlanta, 1977-81; chmn.,

pres. Fran Stef Corp., N.Y.C., 1982-89; pres., chmn. Engineered Products Corp., Dandridge, Tenn., 1983-90; founder, chmn., CEO Am. Accessories Inc., Covington, Ga., 1983-98; founder, pres., chmn. United Am. Products Corp., Dandridge, 1983-89; founder, chmn. Chamisa Properties, Inc., Albuquerque, 1988-94, Glorieux Ltd., Atlanta, 1988-96, Ga. Ptnrs. Ltd., Covington, 1988-94, Premier Trading Internat., Inc., Atlanta, 1989—98, Chamisa Enterprises, Inc., Covington, 1990—2001; founder, mng. ptnr. Ft. Hill Ptnrs., Knoxville, Tenn., 1990-93; chmn. Einson Freeman & Detroy Corp., Fair Lawn, N.J., 1978-83; founder, dir., pres. West Point Contract Packaging, Inc., Martinsville, Va., 1991-98; founder, mng. ptnr. Harbor View, Ltd., Fernandina Beach, Fla., 1992-94; founder, chmn. West Point Tech. Assembly, Inc., Winston-Salem, NC, 1993—2002; dir., pres. BKP Industries, Inc., Monroe, Ga., 1995-97. With U.S. Army, 1948—55. Republican. Episcopalian. Home: PO Box 549 Social Circle GA 30025-0549

PENLEY, JULIE ANNE, psychologist, educator; b. Chicago, Ill., July 13, 1967; d. John and Marcheta Isabelle Dietzen; m. Howard Lawson Penley. PhD, U. Tex., 2001. Tchg. asst. U. Tex., El Paso, 1995—96, rsch. asst., 1996—2001; instr. Dona Ana C.C., Sunland Park, N.Mex., 1999; part-time instr. El Paso C.C., 2000—02, full-time instr., 2002—; evaluation coord. U. Tex., El Paso, 2001—02. Mem.: APA, Soc. Behavioral Medicine, Am. Edn. Rsch. Assn., Am. Evaluation Assn. Lutheran. Office: El Paso Community Coll PO Box 20500 El Paso TX 79998-0500

PENLEY, LARRY EDWARD, management educator; b. Bristol, Va., Feb. 9, 1949; s. William Edward and June (Caudill) P.; m. Yolanda Elva Sanchez, Nov. 25, 1977; children: Jonathan Andrew, Josephine Anna. BA, Wake Forest U., 1971, MA, 1972; PhD, U. Ga., 1976. Assoc. dean U. Tex., San Antonio, 1980-85; vis. prof. ITESM, Monterey, Mex., 1977, Universidad de Carobobo, Valencia, Venezuela, 1978; prof., chmn. dept. Ariz. State U., Tempe, 1985—, chair dept of mgmt., 1985-90; dean Coll of Bus., Ariz. State U., 1985-90. Contbr. articles to profl. jours.; mem. editorial rev. bd. Borderlands Jour., 1985—. Mem. Acad. Mgmt. (chmn. div. program 1986), Southwestern Council Latin Am. Studies, Internat. Communication Assn., Am. Soc. Personnel Adminstrn., Acad. Internat. Bus. mem. bd. dirs., Greater Phoenix Coun., Well Fargo Bank, Ariz., mem. bd. Adv.Inroads Ariz.,First Interstate Svs. Marketing., mem. Fin. Co. Coun. Diocese of Phoenix. Democrat. Roman Catholic. Home: 14052 S 24th Way Phoenix AZ 85048-9002 Office: Ariz State U Office of The Dean Coll Business Tempe AZ 85287

PENLIDIS, ALEXANDER, chemical engineering educator; b. Kozani, Greece, Feb. 12, 1957; Diploma in engring., U. Thessaloniki, 1980; PhD in Chem. Engring., McMaster U., 1986. Rsch. assoc. Polymer Prodn. Techs., McMaster Inst., Can., 1985-86; from asst. prof. to assoc. prof. chem. engring. U. Waterloo, Ontario, Can., 1986-90, assoc. prof., 1990-95, prof., 1995—, assoc. dir. Inst. Polymer Rsch., 1990-95, dir., 1995—, assoc. dean rsch. & grad. studies, faculty engring., 1998—2004. Can. rsch. chmn. in poly. engring., 2002; cons. in field. Founding co-editor Polymer Reaction Engring. Jour., 1990-2003. Fellow Chem. Inst. Can., Can. Acad. Engring.; mem. AIChE, Am. Chem. Soc., Can. Soc. Chem. Engring. Office: Univ Waterloo Inst Polymer Rsch Chem Engring Dept Waterloo ON Canada N2L 3G1 Office Phone: 519-888-4567 x 6634. E-mail: penlidis@cape.uwaterloo.ca.

PENN, ARTHUR HILLER, film and theatre director; b. Phila., Sept. 27, 1922; s. Harry and Sonia Penn; m. Peggy Maurer, Jan. 27, 1955; children: Matthew, Molly. Student, Black Mountain Coll., Asheville, N.C., U. Perugia, Florence, Italy, Actors Studio, Los Angeles; studied with Michael Chekhov. Pres. Actors Studio. Worked in TV, 1951-53; dir. plays for Broadway theatre including Golden Boyu, Hunting Cockroaches, The Miracle Worker (Tony award 1960), All The Way Home, Toys in the Attic, Two for the Seesaw, Wait Until Dark, Sly Fox, Monday After the Miracle; films include The Left-Handed Gun, 1957, The Miracle Worker, 1962, Mickey One, 1964, The Chase, 1965, Bonnie and Clyde, 1967, Alice's Restaurant, 1969, Little Big Man, 1971, Night Moves, 1975, The Missouri Breaks, 1976, Four Friends, 1981, Target, 1985, Dead of Winter, 1987, Penn & Teller Get Killed, 1989, TV films The Portrait, 1993, Lumiere et Compagnie, 1995, Inside, 1996; co-dir. film Visions of Eight; exec. prodr. Law and Order; TV appearances: Beastmaster, 1989; episode dir. 100 Centre Street, 2001. Served with inf. U.S. Army, World War II. Address: Bell & Co PC 535 5th Ave Fl 21 New York NY 10017-3610

PENN, AUDREY S. federal agency administrator; BA, Swarthmore Coll., Pa., 1956; MD, Columbia U., NYC, 1960. Intern, asst. resident Bronx Mcpl. Hosp. Ctr., Albert Einstein Coll. Medicine, 1960—62; asst. resident in neurology, Neurol. Inst. Columbia Presbyn. Med. Ctr., NYC, 1962—64, neurologist; asst. and instr. in neurology Coll. Physicians and Surgeons, Columbia U., NYC, 1964, prof. neurology; from instr. to assoc. prof. neurology U. Pa., Phila., 1967—73; dep. dir. Nat. Inst. Neurol. Disorders and Stroke, dep. and acting dir., 1995—. Bd. dirs. Am. Bd. Psychiatry and Neurology, 1975—82, exec. com, 1981—82; mem. immunological soc. study sect. NIH, 1982—86; mem. rev. panel for rsch. tng. fellowships Howard Hughes Med. Inst., 1989—91, chair rev. panel, 1992—94; mem. nat. adv. neurol. disorders and stroke coun. NIH, 1992—95. Mem.: AAAS, Assn. Rsch. in Nervous and Mental Disease, Harvey Soc., Am. Acad. Neurology, Am. Neurol. Assn. (pres. 1994). Office: Nat Inst Neurol Disorders & Stroke Bldg 31 8A52 31 Center Dr Bethesda MD 20892-2540 Office Phone: 301-496-3167.

PENN, LEE, information technology consultant, journalist; b. Midland, Tex., Jan. 19, 1953; s. Rhesa and Dorothy Penn. BA, Harvard U., 1976; MBA, MPH, U. Calif., Berkeley, 1986. Freelance journalist Oregon mag. and others, Portland, 1975-79, San Francisco, 1998—; rsch. asst. Kaiser Permanente Ctr. for Health Rsch., Portland, 1979-83; sys. planner Alta Bates Corp., Berkeley, 1985—86; sr. fin. analyst St. Mary's Hosp., San Francisco, 1987; mgr. assoc., cons. JDA/SAIC, San Francisco, 1992-96; prin. Penn Cons., San Francisco, 1988—. Mem. adj. faculty, lectr. Goden Gate U., San Francisco, 1990-98. Contbr. articles to profl. jours. and mags., including Jour. Ambulatory Care Mgmt., also chpts. to books. Vestryman, chmn. fin. com., mem. search coms. Episcopal Parish St. John the Evangelist, San Francisco, 1989-94. Edgar F. Kaiser Sr. fellow U. Calif., 1983-84, Regents fellow, 1984-85. Mem. IEEE Computer Soc., Soc. Profls. in Healthcare, Am. Coll. Health Care Execs., Phi Beta Kappa. Office: Penn Cons 131 Corwin St Ste 3 San Francisco CA 94114-2343 Office Fax: 415-255-1381. E-mail: leepenn@aol.com.

PENN, LINDA, computer animator; m. Billy Penn; 4 children. B in Home Econs., M in Home Econs., East Tex. State U. From field office staff to East Tex. regional mgr. U.S. Senator Phil Gramm; Head Start Program specialist in adminstrn. for children and families U.S. Dept. Health and Human Svcs., 1992—, Regional Head Start Edn. specialist, regional rep. Region VI, 2001—. Office: US Dept HHS Ste 1124 1307 Young St Dallas TX 75202

PENN, SEAN, actor; b. Burbank, Calif., Aug. 17, 1960; s. Leo and Eileen (Ryan) P.; m. Madonna Louise Ciccone, Aug. 16, 1985 (div.); m. Robin Wright Penn, 1996; 2 children: Dylan Frances, Hopper Jack. Appearances include (Broadway debut) Heartland, others include Slab Boys, Hurlyburly, 1988; (films) Taps, 1981, Fast Times at Ridgemont High, 1982, Bad Boys, 1983, Crackers, 1984, Racing with the Moon, 1984, The Falcon and the Snowman, 1985, At Close Range, 1986, Shanghai Surprise, 1986, Colors, 1988, Judgment in Berlin, 1988, Casualties of War, 1989, We're No Angels, 1989, State of Grace, 1990, Carlito's Way, 1993, Dead Man Walking, 1995 (Golden Globe award nominee for best actor, 1995, Best Actor award Berlin Film Festival, 1996, Acad. award nominee for best actor, 1996), She's So Lovely, 1997, Loved, 1997, The Game, 1997, U Turn, 1997, Hugo Pool, 1997, The Thin Red Line, 1998, Hurly Burly, 1998, As I Lay Dying, 1998, Up at the Villa, 2000, Before Night Falls, 2000, The Weight of Water, 2000, I Am Sam, 2001, It's All About Love, 2003, Mystic River, 2003, (Golden Globe for best dramatic actor, 2004, Acad. award for best actor, 2004, Golden Satellite award, 2004, London Critics Circle Film awards, 2004, Screen Actors Guild Award nomination for best actor, 2004), 21 Grams, 2003; dir., writer: The Indian Runner, 1991; dir., prodr., writer: The Crossing Guard, 1995; prodr., dir.: The Pledge, 2001; (TV movie) The Killing of Randy Webster, 1981. Office: Ste 2500 2049 Century Park E Los Angeles CA 90067-3127*

PENN, STANLEY WILLIAM, journalist; b. NYC, Jan. 12, 1928; s. Murray and Lillian (Richman) P.; m. Esther Aronson, July 12, 1952; children—Michael, Laurel. Student, Bklyn. Coll., 1945-47; B. Journalism, U. Mo., 1949. With Wall St. Jour., 1952-90; investigative reporter N.Y. bur., 1957-90. (Co-recipient Pulitzer prize for nat. reporting 1967). Home: 380 Riverside Dr New York NY 10025-1858 Personal E-mail: estan380@hotmail.com.

PENNANT-REA, RUPERT LASCELLES, banker, economist; b. Harare, Zimbabwe, Jan. 23, 1948; came to Britain, 1966; s. Peter Athelwold and Pauline Elizabeth (Creasy) Pennant-Rea; m. Louise Greer, Oct. 3, 1970 (div. 1976); m. Jane Trevelyan Hamilton, Aug. 18, 1979 (div. 1986); children: Emily Trevelyan, Rory Marcus; m. Helen Jay, June 24, 1986; 1 child, Edward Peter. B.A. with honors, Trinity Coll., Dublin, 1970; M.A., U. Manchester, 1972. Economist, Confedn. Irish Industry, Dublin, 1970-71, Gen. and Mcpl. Workers Union, Eng., 1972-73, Bank of Eng., 1973-77; journalist The Economist, London, 1977-93, editor, 1986-93; dep. gov. Bank of Eng., London, 1993-95; chmn. Plantation and General Investments, London, 1997—, chmn. The Stationery Office, London, 1996—. Author: Gold Foil, 1979; The Pocket Economist, 1983; The Economist Economics, 1986. Recipient Wincott prize for fin. journalism Wincott Found., London, 1984. Mem. Ch. of Eng. Clubs: Marylebone Cricket, Reform (London), Harare (Zimbabwe). Avocations: music; tennis. Office: The Stationery Office 51 Nine Elms Lane London SW8 5DR England

PENNELL, DANIEL MARK, researcher; b. Valparaiso, Ind., July 14, 1971; s. Lawrence Foster Pennell and Nancy Lea Rogan. BA, Ind. U., Bloomington, Ind., 1989—93, MA, 1997—99, MLS, 1999—2001. Bibliographer for Russian, east European, and Germanic studies U. of Pitts., Pitts., 2001—; asst. slavic bibliographer Ind. U., Bloomington, Ind., 1996—2001; program mgr. for edn. US Peace Corps., Saratov, Russia, 1995—96. Asst. dir. Inst. for the Study of Russian Edn., Bloomington, Ind., 1996—98; reviews editor Slavic and East European Info. Resources, Pitts., 2003—, Balkan Academic News, Pitts., Politics and Societies, 2004—. Author: (article) New Approaches to Balkan History, (annotated bibliography) Romanian Studies: An Annotated Guide to Bibliographies, Encyclopedias, and Handbooks. Fellow Fgn. Lang. Area Studies Fellowship, Ind. U., 1997-2000. Mem.: Southeastern European Studies Assn., Soc. for Romanian Studies, Am. Libr. Assoication, Am. Assn. for the Advancement of Slavic Studies, Phi Beta Kappa. Achievements include development of Slavic, East European, and Germanic Studies Research Collections; research in Modern Russian and Eastern European History. Home: 3564 Beechwood Blvd Pittsburgh PA 15217 Office: University of Pittsburgh 3960 Forbes Avenue G-20X Hillman Library Pittsburgh PA 15260 E-mail: pennell@pitt.edu.

PENNELL, DANNY JOE, social worker; b. Aug. 31, 1945; s. Donald Louis and Lela Geneva (Murray) P.; m. Janis Evelyn Reynolds, Dec. 26, 1984; children: Joel, Jason, Jaime, Chad, Colter. BA, U. Ill., 1970, MSW, 1972. Social worker Dept. Child and Family Svcs., Danville, Ill., 1971-72, social worker supr. Rockford, Ill., 1972-74; instr. Rockford Coll., 1977-78; pres., CEO Goldie B. Floberg Ctr., Rockton, Ill., 1974—. Exec. dir. Found. Ft. Lewis Coll., Durango, Colo., 1986-87; bd. dirs. Winnebago County Child Protection Assn., Rockford, 1974-76; bd. dirs., mem. legis. affairs com., chmn. mental health devel. disabilities com., spl. edn. com. Child Care Assn. Ill., Springfield, Ill., 1980—; mem. child welfare adv. com. Ill. Dept. Children and Family Services; mem. devel. disabilities adv. com. Dept. Mental Health, mem. children's svcs. subcom.; cons. in field. Bd. dirs., v.p. H.O.P.E. Found., 2001—. Grantee Ill. Dept. Children and Family Svcs., 1970-72. Mem. Nat. Soc. Fund Raising Execs. (bd. dirs., sec. 1984-85, v.p. 1986-87), Nat. Soc. Fund Raising Dirs. (pres. bd. dirs. 1988, v.p. 1987, v.p. 1986, bd. mem. various coms. 1984, 85), Am. Assn. Mental Deficiency, Nat. Assn. Retarded Citizens, Coordinating Council for Handicapped Children, Nat. Assn. Devel. Disabilities Mgrs., Roscoe C. of C. (bd. dirs. 2000—). Home: 12080 N Ledges Dr Roscoe IL 61073-9600 Office: Goldie B Floberg Ctr PO Box 346 Rockton IL 61072-0346 Office Phone: 815-624-8431. Personal E-mail: dpenn58@aol.com.

PENNELL, WILLIAM BROOKE, lawyer; b. Mineral Ridge, Ohio, Oct. 28, 1935; s. George Albert and Katherine Nancy (McMeen) P. AB, Harvard U., 1957; LLB cum laude, U. Pa., 1961; m. Peggy Polsky, June 17, 1958; children: Katherine, Thomas Brooke. Bar: NY 1963, US Dist. Ct. (so. dist.) NY 1964, US Dist. Ct. (ea. dist.) NY 1964, US Ct. Appeals (2d cir.) 1966, US Ct. Claims 1966, US Tax Ct. 1967, US Supreme Ct. 1967. Clk. US Dist. Ct., (so. dist.) NY, NYC, 1961-62; assoc. Shearman & Sterling, NYC, 1962-71, ptnr., 1971-91. Recent case editor U. Pa. Law Rev., 1960-61. Bd. govs. Bklyn. Heights Assn., 1964-74, pres., 1969-71; chmn. bd. Willoughby House Settlement, 1972-95. Served with US Army, 1957. Fellow Salzburg Seminar Am. Studies, 1965. Mem. Rembrandt Club. Home and Office: PO Box 249 Canaan NY 12029-0249

PENNELLO, GENE ANTHONY, statistician; b. Huntsville, Ala., Nov. 23, 1962; s. Julian Joseph and Betsy Pennello; m. Chung-Chin Sun, Sept. 18, 1993; children: Julian, Chelsie. BS in Computer Sci. & Math., BS in Statis., U. Calif., Davis., 1985, MS in Statis., 1989; PhD in Statis., Oreg. State U., 1993. Math. statis. Food and Drug Adminstrn., Rockville, Md., 1998—. Lectr. George Washington U., 1996-97. Author: Atlas of Cancer Mortality: 1950-1994, 1999; contbr. articles to profl. jours. Postdoctoral fellow Nat. Cancer Inst., Bethesda, Md., 1994-98. Mem. Am. Statis. Assn. Republican. Roman Catholic. Avocations: origami, tennis. Office: Food & Drug Adminstrn 1350 Piccard Dr Rockville MD 20850 E-mail: gxp@cdrh.fda.gov.

PENNER, KEITH, former Canadian government official; b. Sask., Can., May 1, 1933; BA, U. Alberta, Can., 1955; MDiv, Toronto U., 1959; MEd, U. Ottawa, Can., 1971. Secondary sch. tchr., Dryden, Ont., Can., 1961-68; mem. parliament Cochrane-Superior, Ont., 1968-88; mem. Can. Transp. Agy., Ottawa, 1988—2003; pres. dispute resolution Keith Penner & Assocs., Ottawa, 2003—. Past parliamentary sec. to Min. of State for Sci. and Tech., past parliamentary sec. to Min. of Indian Affairs and No. Devel., past chmn. Standing Com. on Indian Affairs and No. Devel.; vis. fellow Sch. of Polit. Sci., Queen's U., 1987-88. Fellow: Chartered Inst. of Transport. Office: Ottawa ON Canada Office Phone: 613-828-3067. E-mail: keith.penner@disputers.ca.

PENNER, RUDOLPH GERHARD, economist, educator; b. Windsor, Ont., Can., July 15, 1936; s. Jacob Gerhard P. and Agnes (Dyck) Bremsteller; m. Alice Braeker, June 27, 1959; children: Eric, Brian. Vis. asst. prof. Princeton U., 1965-66; sr. staff economist Council Econ. Advisers, Washington, 1970-71; prof. U. Rochester, N.Y., 1970-75; asst. dir. econ. Office Mgmt. and Budget, Washington, 1975-77; resident scholar Am. Enterprise Inst., Washington, 1977-83; dir. Congl. Budget Office, Washington, 1983-87; dep. asst. sec. econ. HUD, Washington, 1973-75; sr. fellow Urban Inst., Washington, 1987-92; dir. econ. studies KPMG Peat Marwick, Washington, 1992-97; sr. fellow Urban Inst., Washington, 1997—. Washington editor BCA Pubs., Montreal, 1987; author: (with Alan Abramson) Broken Purse Strings, 1988, (with Isabel Sawhill and Timotny Taylor) Updating America's Social Contract, 2001. Mem. Nat. Economist Club (chmn. 1980-81, pres.), Am. Econ. Assn., Nat. Tax Assn., Nat. Assn. Bus. Economists (bd. dirs.), Manpower Demonstration Rsch. Corp. (bd. dirs.). Republican. Mennonite. Office: Urban Inst 2100 M St NW Washington DC 20036-3310 Office Phone: 202-261-5212.

PENNER, STANFORD SOLOMON, engineering educator; b. Unna, Germany, July 5, 1921; arrived in U.S., 1936, naturalized, 1943; s. Heinrich and Regina (Saal) P.; m. Beverly Preston, Dec. 28, 1942; children: Merilynn Jean, Robert Clark. BS, Union Coll., 1942; MS, U. Wis., 1943, PhD, 1946; Dr. rer. nat. (hon.), Technische Hochschule Aachen, Germany, 1981. Rsch. assoc. Allegany Ballistics Lab., Cumberland, Md., 1944-45; rsch. scientist Standard Oil Devel. Co., Esso Labs., Linden, NJ, 1946; sr. rsch. engr. Jet Propulsion Lab., Pasadena, Calif., 1947-50; mem. faculty Calif. Inst. Tech., 1950-63, prof. divsn. engring., jet propulsion, 1957-63; dir. rsch. and engring. divsn. Inst. Def. Analyses, Washington, 1962-64; prof. engring. physics, chmn. dept. aerospace and mech. engring. U. Calif., San Diego, 1964-68, vice chancellor for acad. affairs, 1968-69, dir. Inst. for Pure and Applied Phys. Scis., 1968-71, dir. Energy Ctr., 1973-91. Bd. dirs. Optodyne Corp.; U.S. mem. adv. group aero. rsch. and devel. NATO, 1952-68, chmn. combustion and propulsion panel, 1958-60; mem. adv. com. engring. scis. USAF-Office Sci. Rsch., 1961-65; mem. subcom. on combustion NACA, 1954-58; mem. rsch. adv. com. on air-breathing engines NASA, 1962-64; mem. coms. on gas dynamics and edn. Internat. Acad. Astronautics, 1969-80; nat. lectr. Sigma Xi, 1977-79; chmn. fossil energy rsch. working group Dept. Energy, 1978-82, chmn. advanced fuel cell commercialization working group, 1993-95; mem. assembly engring. NAE, 1978-82; chmn. NAS-NRC U.S. Nat. Com. IIASA, 1978-82; mem. commn. engring. tech. sys. NRC, 1982-84; spl. guest Internat. Coal Sci. Confs., 1983, 85, 87, 89, 91; mentor Def. Sci. Studies Group, 1985-93; chmn. studies mcpl. waste incineration NSF, 1988-89, Calif. Coun. Sci. Tech., 1992; pub. info. adv. com. Nat. Acad. Engring., 1994-98, Independent Commn. on Environ. Edn., 1995-97, Environ. Literacy Coun., 1998—; sci. adv. bd., San Diego County, 1997-, chair, 2004—; divsn. advisor, bds. of the divsn. on engring. and phys. scis. The Nat. Acads., 2001—. Author: Chemical Reactions in Flow Systems, 1955, Chemistry Problems in Jet Propulsion, 1957, Quantitative Molecular Spectroscopy and Gas Emissivities, 1959, Chemical Rocket Propulsion and Combustion Research, 1962, Thermodynamics, 1968, Radiation and Reentry, 1968; sr. author: Energy, Vol. I (Demands, Resources, Impact, Technology and Policy), 1974, 81, Energy, Vol. II (Non-nuclear Energy Technologies), 1975, 77, 84, Energy, Vol. III (Nuclear Energy and Energy Policies), 1976; editor: Chemistry of Propellants, 1960, Advanced Propulsion Techniques, 1961, Detonations and Two-Phase Flow, 1962, Combustion and Propulsion, 1963, Advances in Tactical Rocket Propulsion, 1968, In Situ Shale Oil Recovery, 1975, New Sources of Oil and Gas, 1982, Coal Combustion and Applications, 1984, Advanced Fuel Cells, 1986, Coal Gasification: Direct Applications and Syntheses of Chemicals and Fuels, 1987, CO2 Emissions and Climate Change, 1991, Commercialization of Fuel Cells, 1995, Advanced Nuclear Techs., 1998; assoc. editor Jour. Chem. Physics, 1953-56; founding editor Jour. Quantitative Spectroscopy and Radiative Transfer, 1960-92, Jour. Def. Rsch., 1963-67, Energy (The Internat. Jour.), 1975-98; sect. editor Energy and Power Systems, Ency. Phys. Sci. and Tech., 1998-2002. Recipient spl. award People-to-People Program, pub. svc. award U. Calif., San Diego, N. Manson medal Internat. Colloquia on Gasdynamics of Explosions and Reactive Systems, 1979, internat. Columbus award Internat. Inst. Comm., Genoa, Italy, 1981, disting. assoc. award U.S. Dept. Energy, 1990, Edward Teller award for def. of freedom, 1997, Rockwell medal, 2003. Fellow Am. Phys. Soc., Optical Soc. Am., AAAS, N.Y. Acad. Scis., AIAA (dir. 1964-66, past chmn. com., G. Edward Pendray award 1975, Thermophysics award 1983, Energy Systems award 1983), Am. Acad. Arts and Scis.; mem. Nat. Acad. Engring., Internat. Acad. Astronautics, World Level Hall of Fame for Engring., Sci. and Tech., Am. Chem. Soc., Sigma Xi. Home: 5912 Avenida Chamnez La Jolla CA 92037-7402 Office: U Calif San Diego 9500 Gilman Dr La Jolla CA 92093-0411 Office Phone: 858-534-4284. Business E-Mail: spenner@ucsd.edu.

PENNEY, CHARLES RAND, lawyer, civic worker, world traveler; b. Buffalo, July 26, 1923; s. Charles Patterson and Gretchen (Rand) P. BA, Yale U., 1945; JD, U. Va., 1951; DFA (hon.), SUNY, 1995. Bar: Md. 1952, NY 1958, U.S. Supreme Ct. 1958. Law sec. to U.S. Dist. Ct. Judge W.C. Coleman, Balt., 1951-52; dir. devel. office Children's Hosp., Buffalo, 1952-54; sales mgr. Amherst Mfg. Corp., Williamsville, N.Y., 1954-56, also; Delevan Electronics Corp., East Aurora, N.Y.; mem. firm Penney & Penney, Buffalo, 1958-61; pvt. practice, Niagara County, N.Y., 1961—. Numerous contemporary art collection exhbns. include Mus. Modern Art, NYC, 1962, Whitney Mus. Am. Art, NYC, 1963, 79, 80, Burchfield-Penney Art Ctr., 1973, 92-2003, Meml. Art Gallery, Rochester, 1976, 78, 83, 88, U. Iowa, 1978, Columbus (Ohio) Gallery Fine Arts, 1976, 78. Hon. life trustee Burchfield-Penney Art Ctr.; adv. bd. Found. Study of Arts and Crafts Movement at Roycroft; hon. bd. dirs. Buffalo-Lille/France Assn., Inc. 2d lt. U.S. Army, 1943-46. Recipient Pres.'s Disting. Svc. award Buffalo State Coll., 1991, Disting. Svc. to Culture award Coll. Arts and Scis., SUNY, Potsdam, 1983; named Disting. fellow Cultural Studies of the Burchfield-Penney Art Ctr., 1994, Outstanding Individual Philanthropist, Nat. Soc. Fund Raising Execs. Western NY, 1996, Individual Patron of the Arts award Buffalo and Erie County Arts Coun. and Buffalo C. of C., 1997, Citation for Outstanding Achievements and Svc. to Lockport Cmty., NY State Assembly, 1997; awarded Key to City of Lockport, 1997; inductee Lockport Hist. Walk of Fame, 1999. Fellow The Explorers Club; mem. AARP, YWCA Niagra (life), Albright-Knox Art Gallery Buffalo (life), Buffalo Mus. Sci. (Life), Buffalo and Erie County Hist. Soc. (life, Red Jacket award 2000), Niagara County Hist. Soc. (life), Old Ft. Niagara (life), Buffalo Soc. Artists (hon. trustee), Hist. Lockport (life), Landmark Soc. Western NY (life), Am. Ceramic Cir., Hist. Lewiston (life), Friends of U. Rochester Librs. (life) Meml. Art Gallery U. Rochester (hon. bd. mgrs., hon. life), Winslow Homer Soc. of Dirs. Cir. (hon. life), Smithsonian Instn. (benefactors cir.), Rochester Hist. Soc. (life), Am. Hist. Print Collectors Soc. (life), Burchfield Homestead Soc. (hon. life), Charles E. Burchfield Nature and Art Ctr., Archives Am. Art, Mark Twain Soc. (hon.), U. Rochester's Pres.'s Soc. (hon. life), U. Iowa's Pres.'s Club (hon. life), Va. Law Found., Nat. Geog. Soc. (life), World's Fair Collectors Soc., Hist. Soc. of Tonawandas (life), Pres.'s Cir. Buffalo State Coll. (hon. life), Buffalo State Alumni Assn. (life), Yale Sailing Assocs., Yale Glee Club Assocs., Peanut Pals, Grolier Club, Pan Am. Expo Collectors Soc., Buffalo Indsl. Heritage Com., Roycrofters-at-Large Assn. (life), Arctic Cir. Club, Order of the Alaska Walrus, Automobile Club (Lockport), Niagara County Antiques Club (hon.), Rochester Art Club (hon. life), Chi Psi, Phi Alpha Delta. Office: 538 Bewley Building Lockport NY 14094-2944 E-mail: charliepenney@aol.com. *I have tried to strive for excellence in whatever I undertake, be it small or large. What success I may have achieved has required initiative, imagination, and dedication to the task at hand. Satisfaction comes from the hard work that leads to an objective. In all that I do I adhere to the Golden Rule and to fairness, honesty, and understanding in human relationships. I try to maintain a sense of humor at all times. And I enjoy living in a small community because it is from such areas that the strength of America comes.*

PENNEY, GEOFF, finance company executive; b. England; m. Linda Penney; children: Neill, Daniel, Leslie. BA, PhD in organic chemistry, St. John's Coll. Sr. v.p. mng. dir. Bankers Trust Co., NY and London; sr. v.p. Fidelity Investments, Boston; head of fin. products and internat. tech. Charles Schwab, 1997—98, exec. v.p., 1998—, CIO, 2001—. Mem. exec. com. Charles Schwab Corp.; bd. dirs. Keynote Systems. Office: Charles Schwab 101 Montgomery St San Francisco CA 94104

PENNEY, SHERRY HOOD, university president, educator; b. Marlette, Mich., Sept. 4, 1937; d. Terrance and B. Jean (Stoutenburg) Hood; m. Carl Murray Penney, July 8, 1961 (div. 1978); children: Michael Murray, Jeffrey Hood; m. James Duane Livingston, Mar. 30, 1985. BA, Albion Coll., 1959, LLD (hon.), 1989; MA, U. Mich., 1961; PhD, SUNY, Albany, 1972; hon. degree, Quincy Coll., 1999. Vis. asst. prof. Union Coll., Schenectady, N.Y., 1972-73; assoc. higher edn. N.Y. State Edn. Dept., Albany, 1973-76; assoc. provost Yale U., New Haven, 1976-82; vice chancellor acad. programs, policy and planning SUNY System, Albany, 1982-88; acting pres. SUNY, Plattsburgh, 1986-87; chancellor U. Mass. Boston, 1988-95; pres. U. Mass. Sys., Boston, 1995; chancellor U. Mass. Boston, 1996-2000, endowed prof., 2001—. Chmn., bd. dirs. Nat. Higher Edn. Mgmt. Sys., Boulder, Colo., 1985-87; mem. commn. on higher edn. New Eng. Assn. Schs. and Colls., Boston, 1979-82, Mid. States Assn. Schs. and Colls., Phila., 1986-88; mem. commn. on women Am. Coun. Edn., Washington, 1979-81, commn. on govt. rels., 1990-94; bd. dirs. NSTAR (Boston Edison Co.), 1990—, Carnegie Found. for Advancement of Teaching, 1994-2002. Author: Patrician in Politics, 1974; editor: Women and Management in Higher Education, 1975; contbr. articles to profl. jours. Nat. adv. com. Nat. Initiative for Women in Higher Edn., 2001—; mem. Internat. Trade Task Force, 1994—96; mem. exec. com. Challenge to Leadership, 1988, chair, 1995—98; mem. Mid-Am. adv. bd. HERS, 1992—, Mary Baker Eddy Libr., Boston, 2001—; trustee Berkeley Div. Sch., Yale U., 1978—82, John F. Kennedy Libr. Found., 1988—2001; bd.

dirs. Albany Symphony Orch., 1982—88, U. Mass. Found., 1988—2000, Mcpl. Rsch. Bur., Boston, 1990—2001, New Eng. Coun., 1990—2000, Greater Boston C. of C., 1989—2002, Met. Affairs Coalition, chair, 1999—2001; bd. overseers New Eng. Aquarium, 1990—; bd. dirs. Greater Boston One to One Leadership Coun., 1990—2000, NASULGC Commn. Urban Affairs, 1990—2000, The Ednl. Resource Inst., chair, 1996—; bd. dirs. The Environ. Bus. Coun., 1991—97; bd. visitors WEIU, 2002—. Recipient Disting. Alumna award Albion Coll., 1978, Disting. Citizen award for racial harmony Black/White Boston, 1994, Am. Coun. on Edn./Nat. Identification Program Mass. Leadership award, 1995, New Eng. Women's Leadership award, 1996, Pinnacle award for Lifetime Achievement Greater Boston C. of C., 1998, Abigail Adams award, Mass. Women's Polit. Caucus, 2003. Mem. Orgn. Am. Historians, St. Botolph Club, Comml. Club (Boston). Unitarian Universalist. Office: U Mass Boston 100 Morrissey Blvd Boston MA 02125-3300 Office Phone: 617-287-3890. Business E-Mail: sherry.penney@umb.edu.

PENNIMAN, NICHOLAS GRIFFITH, IV, retired newspaper publisher; b. Balt., Mar. 7, 1938; s. Nicholas Griffith Penniman III and Esther Cox Lony (Wight) Keeney; m. Linda Jane Simmons, Feb. 4, 1967; children: Rebecca Helmle, Nicholas G. V. AB, Princeton U., 1960; MA, Washington U., 1999. Asst. bus. mgr. Ill. State Jour. Register, Springfield, 1964-69, bus. mgr., 1969-75; asst. gen. mgr. St. Louis Post-Dispatch, 1975-84, gen. mgr., 1984-86, pub., 1986-99; sr. v.p. newspapers ops. Pulitzer Pub. Co., 1986-99; pres., CEO Pulitzer Comm. Newspapers Inc., 1997-99; chmn. bd. Penniman & Browne, Inc., Balt., 2001—. Chmn. Downtown St. Louis, Inc., 1988-90, Mo. Health and Ednl. Facilities Adminstrn., 1982-85, Ill. State Fair Bd., Springfield, 1973-75, Parks and Open Space Task Force St. Louis 2004, 1996-2000; pres. Caring Found. for Children, 1988-91, Forest Park Forever, 1991-93, St. Louis Sports Com., 1992-93, Gateway Parks and Trails 2004, 1999—; Trustee St. Louis Country Day Sch., 1983-86, Nat. Recreation Found., 2003—, Mercantile Libr. of St. Louis, 1997-2000, Nat. Recreation Found., 2003-; bd. dirs. Mo. Coalition for the Environment, 1997-2000, Randall Rsch. Ctr., Pineland, Fla., 2001—, Friends of Rookery Bay, 2004—, Vt. River Conservancy, 2002—; bd. chair Am. Rivers, 2004—. With U.S. Army, 1962—67. Mem.: Elkridge Club, Lake Champlain Yacht Club, Noonday Club (pres. 1994), Grey Oaks Country Club. Home: 611 Portside Dr Naples FL 34103-4118 E-mail: ngpiv@aol.com.

PENNIMAN, W. DAVID, information scientist, educator, consultant; b. St. Louis, Dec. 19, 1937; s. William Leon and Laura Mae (Van Winkle) P.; m. Charlotte Ann Meder, Mar. 17, 1973; children: Kara, Rachel, John; 1 child by previous marriage, Jessica. BS in ME, U. Ill., 1960, MS in Journalism, Communications, 1962; PhD in Communication Theory, Ohio State U., 1975. Registered profl. engr., Ohio. Assoc. dir. engring. publs. U. Ill. Coll. Engring., Urbana, 1965-66; research scientist info. systems Battelle Columbus Labs., Columbus, Ohio, 1966-69, assoc. mgr. info. systems, 1969-77; research scholar Internat. Inst. Applied Systems Analysis, Laxenburg, Austria, 1977; mgr. research Online Computer Library Ctr., Dublin, Ohio, 1978-79, dir. software devel., 1979-82, v.p. planning and research, 1982-84; dir. libraries and info. systems AT&T Bell Labs., Murray Hill, N.J., 1984-90, dir. info. svcs. group, 1990-91; pres. Coun. on Libr. Resources, Inc., Washington, 1991-95; dir. Ctr. for Info. Studies, 1995-99; prof. sch. of Info. Scis. Univ. Tenn., 1995-99; private cons., 1999—2001; prof. sch. informatics U. Buffalo, Buffalo, 2001—, dean sch. informatics, 2001—. Chmn. Engring. Info. Inc., N.Y.C., 1983-91; governing com. Forest Press Inc., Albany, N.Y., 1985-88; adv. com. info. sci. Rutgers U., 1982-91. Author numerous book chpts. and articles in profl. jours. Advisor United Way, Columbus, 1981-83. Served with U.S. Army, 1963-65. Named Tech. Person of the Yr. Columbus Tech. Council, 1982, U.S. Del. to Internat. Inst. for Applied Systems Analysis, 1977. Fellow AAAS; mem. IEEE (sr.), Am. Soc. Info. Sci. (pres. 1988-89), Assn. for Computing Machinery. Avocations: antique automobiles, hiking. Office: U Buffalo Sch of Informatics Buffalo NY 14260 Office Phone: 716-645-6481 x1176. Business E-Mail: penniman@buffalo.edu.

PENNINGER, FRIEDA ELAINE, retired English language educator; b. Marion, N.C., Apr. 11, 1927; d. Fred Hoyle and Lena Frances (Young) P. AB, U. N.C., Greensboro, 1948; MA, Duke U., 1950, PhD, 1961. Copywriter Sta. WSJS, Winston-Salem, N.C., 1948-49; asst. prof. English Flora Macdonald Coll., Red Springs, N.C., 1950-51; tchr. English Barnwell, S.C., 1951-52, Brunswick, Ga., 1952-53; instr. English U. Tenn., Knoxville, 1953-56; instr., asst. prof. Woman's Coll., U. N.C., Greensboro, 1956-58, 60-63; asst. prof., assoc. prof. U. Richmond (Va.), 1963-71; chair., dept. English Westhampton Coll., Richmond, 1971-78; prof. English U. Richmond, 1971-91, Bostwick prof. English, 1987-91; ret., 1991. Author: William Caxton, 1979, Chaucer's "Troilus and Criseyde" and "The Knight's Tale": Fictions Used, 1993, (novel) Look at Them, 1990; compiler, editor: English Drama to 1660, 1976; editor: Festschrift for Prof. Marguerite Roberts, 1976. Fellow Southeastern Inst. of Mediaeval and Renaissance Studies, 1965, 67, 69. Democrat. Presbyterian. Home: 2701 Camden Rd Greensboro NC 27403-1438

PENNINGER, SAMUEL A., JR., consumer products company executive; Founder Serologicals Corp., Atlanta, 1971, pres., 1983-93, chmn. bd. dirs., 1993—. Mem. Am. Blood Resource Assn. (past bd. dirs.), Am. Assn. Blood Banks. Office: Serologicals Corp 5655 Spalding Dr Norcross GA 30092-2504

PENNINGTON, CHAD, professional football player; b. Knoxville, Tenn., June 26, 1976; m. Robin Pennington. Degree, Marshall Coll., 2000. Quarterback N.Y. Jets, 2000—. Mailing: 1000 Fulton Ave Hempstead NY 11550*

PENNINGTON, RANDY KEITH, music educator; b. Tucson, Ariz., July 2, 1956; s. Bobby Ray and Marian Sue Pennington; m. Suzanne Jane Carter, June 8, 1964; children: Brock Robert, Keith Carter. MusB in edn., MA in music, Calif. State U.; Doctorate in musical arts, U. Ariz. Dir. of choral activities Adams State Coll., Alamosa, Colo.; spl. asst. to chancellor NC Sch. of the Arts, Winston-Salem, NC; dir. of choral studies No. Ky. U., Highland Heights, Ky., 1994—. Dir., music ministry St. Joseph Ch., Crescent Springs, Ky. Mem.: Am. Choral Dir. Assn. (Ky. chair jazz show choir repertoire and standards 2001—03, Colo. chair coll. U. repertoire and standards 1991—94, Colo. membership chair 1989—91), Music Educators Nat. Conf. (Ky. festival commn. 1999—2003). Office: No Ky U Music Dept Nunn Dr Highland Heights KY 41009 Office Phone: 859-572-5286. Office Fax: 859-572-6076.

PENNINGTON, RICHARD J. police chief; m. Renee Pennington; 1 child. BA, American U.; MA, U. Dist. Columbia. Asst. police chief Met. Police Dept., Washington, 1993—94; chief of police New Orleans Police Dept., 1994—2002, Atlanta Police Dept., 2002—. Office: Atlanta Police Dept 675 Ponce De Leon Ave Atlanta GA 30308*

PENNINGTON, ROBERT EDGAR, music educator; b. West Line, Mo., Nov. 27, 1931; s. William Ray Pennington, Edna Marie Johnson. BMus, Northwestern U., 1953, M in Music, 1955, DMus, 1966. Instr. Howard Coll., Birmingham, Ala., 1955—56; prof. piano Drury Coll., Springfield, Mo., 1959—65, West Chester (Pa.) U., West Chester, 1966—. Mem.: Mo. Music Tchrs. Assn. (editor notes 1962—63), Music Tchrs. Nat. Assn., Pi Kappa Lambda. Avocation: Travel. Office: West Chester Univ West Chester PA 19383 Home: 121 W Miner St #2W West Chester PA 19382-3238 Office Phone: 610-436-2640. Office Fax: 610-436-2873. Business E-Mail: rpennington@wcupa.edu.

PENNINGTON, WAYNE D. science educator; b. Rochester, Minn., Dec. 19, 1950; s. Stanley Robert and Shirley Heckart Pennington; m. Laura Leah Leitermann, Aug. 9, 1953; children: Matthew William, Keith Eliot. AB, Princeton U., 1972; MS, Cornell U., 1976; PhD, U. Wis., 1979. Prof. dept geol. and mining engring. and scis. Mich. Technol. U., Houghton, 1994—2003, prof., chair dept. geological and mining engring. and scis., 2003—; asst. prof. dept. geol. scis. U. Tex., 1979—85; advanced sr. rsch. geophysicist Marathon Oil Co., Littleton, Colo., 1985—94. 1st v.p. Soc. Exploration Geophysicists, Tulsa, 2002—03. Office: Michigan Tech U Dept Geol Engring Houghton MI 49931 Office Phone: 906-487-2531. E-mail: wayne@mtu.edu.

PENNISI, LIZ, women's health nurse; b. Bklyn., Nov. 20, 1953; d. Alexander and Marjorie (Soviero) Perillo; m. Stephen Crain Pennisi, Jan. 17, 1976; children: Stephen, Scott, Greg. Diploma, Beth Israel Sch. Nursing, N.Y.C., 1974. RN, N.Y.; cert. ambulatory women's health nurse. Staff nurse Montefiore Hosp., Bronx, N.Y., 1974-75; mem. staff Beth Israel Med. Ctr., N.Y.C., 1975-77; office nurse Martin Kurman, M.D., N.Y.C., 1977-80, Adam Romoff, M.D. and Suzanne Yale, M.D., P.C, 1984—. Mem. AWHONN. Avocations: tennis, horseback riding, reading. Office: Drs Romoff and Yale 768 Park Ave New York NY 10021-4153 E-mail: liz@exgen.net.

PENNISTEN, JOHN WILLIAM, computer scientist, actuary, linguist; b. Buffalo, Jan. 25, 1939; s. George William and Lucy Josephine (Gates) P. AB in Math. and Chemistry with honors, Hamilton Coll., 1960; postgrad., Harvard U., 1960-61, U.S. Army Lang. Sch., 1962-63; MS in Computer Sci. with honors, N.Y. Inst. Tech., 1987; cert. in taxation, NYU, 1982; cert. in profl. banking, Am. Inst. of Banking of Am. Bankers Assn., 1988.; cert. Asian Langs., NYU, 1992. Actuarial asst. New Eng. Mut. Life Ins. Co., Boston, 1965-66; asst. actuary Mass. Gen. Life Ins. Co., Boston, 1966-68; actuarial assoc. John Hancock Mut. Life Ins. Co., Boston, 1968-71; asst. actuary George B. Buck Cons. Actuaries, Inc., N.Y.C., 1971-75, Martin E. Segal Co., N.Y.C., 1975-80; actuary Laiken Siegel & Co., N.Y.C., 1980; cons. Bklyn., 1981—; timesharing and database analyst banklink corp. cash mgmt. div. Chem. Bank N.Y.C., 1983-85; programmer analyst Empire Blue Cross and Blue Shield, N.Y.C., 1986-88, Mt. Sinai Med. Ctr., N.Y.C., 1988-89, French Am. Banking Corp. (subs. Banque National de Paris), N.Y.C., 1989; sr. programmer analyst Dean Witter Reynolds, Inc., N.Y.C., 1989-92; computer specialist for software N.Y.C. Dept. Fin., 1992—97; sr. cons. Pinkerton Computer Cons., Inc., N.Y.C., 1997-99; tech. officer J.P. Morgan Chase & Co., N.Y.C., 1999—2003; computer specialist N.Y.C. Dept. Fin., 2003—. Enrolled actuary U.S. Fed. Pension Legis. Bklyn., 1976—. Contbr. articles to profl. jours. With U.S. Army, 1961-64. Fellow: Soc. Actuaries; mem.: IEEE Computer Soc., MLA, AAAS, Harvard Grad. Soc., Am. Friends of Covent Garden, Bklyn. Heights Assn., Nat. Ry. Hist. Soc., Am. Chem. Soc., Math. Assn. Am., Nat. Model R.R. Assn. (life), Ry. and Locomotive Hist. Soc. (life), Am. Math. Soc., Assn. Computational Linguistics, Linguistic Soc. Am., Am. Assn. Artificial Intelligence, Assn. Computing Machinery, Met. Opera Guild, Am. Legion, Phi Beta Kappa. Home: 135 Willow St Brooklyn NY 11201-2255 Office Phone: 718-403-4233.

PENNOCK, DONALD WILLIAM, retired mechanical engineer; b. Ludlow, Ky., Aug. 8, 1915; s. Donald and Melvin (Evans) P.; B.S. in M.E., U. Ky., 1940, M.E., 1948; m. Vivian C. Kern, Aug. 11, 1951; 1 son, Douglas. Stationary engring., constrn. and maintenance Schenley Corp., 1935-39; mech. equipment design engr. mech. lab. U. of Ky., 1939; exptl. test engr. Wright Aero. Corp., Paterson, N.J., 1940, 1941, investigative and adv. engr. to personnel div., 1941-43; indsl. engr. Eastern Aircraft, div. Gen. Motors, Linden, N.J., 1943-45; factory engr. Carrier Corp., Syracuse, N.Y., 1945-58, sr. facilities engr., 1958-60, corporate material handling engr., 1960-63, mgr. facilities engring. dept., 1963-66, mgr. archtl. engring., 1966-68, mgr. facilities engring. dept., 1968-78. Staff, Indsl. Mgmt. Center, 1962, midwest work course U. Kan., 1959-67. Mem. munitions bd. SHIAC, 1950-52; trustee Primitive Hall Found., 1985—. Elected to Exec. and Profl. Hall of Fame, 1966. Registered profl. engr., Ky., N.J. Fellow Soc. Advancement Mgmt. (life mem., nat. v.p. material handling div. 1953-54); mem. ASME, NSPE, Am. Material Handling Soc. (dir. 1950-57, chmn. bd., pres. 1950-52), Am. Soc. Mil. Engrs., Am. Mgmt. Assn. (men. packaging council 1950-55, life mem. planning council), Nat. Material Handling Conf. (exec. com. 1951), Found. N.Am. Wild Sheep (life), Internat. Platform Assn., Tau Beta Pi. Protestant. Mng. editor Materials Handling Engring. (mag. sect.), 1949-50; mem. editorial adv. bd. Modern Materials Handling (mag.), 1949-52. Contbr. articles to tech. jours. Contbg., cons. editor: Materials Handling Handbook, 1958. Home: 24 Pebble Hill Rd Syracuse NY 13214

PENNOCK, ELIZABETH H. retired music educator; b. Nashville, Ind., Nov. 7, 1932; d. Joseph Strattan and Ada Lammott Haines; widowed; children: Robert Tatnall, Mary H. Sears. BA, Earlham Coll., 1954. Music and home econ. tchr. Fairview Sch., Falmouth, Ind., 1954—56; sec. Cornell U., Ithaca, NY, 1956, 1958; music and home econ. tchr. Newfield Cent. Sch., NY, 1956—58; home econ. tchr. Massapequa HS, NY, 1958—59, Parkside Jr. HS, Massapequa, 1959—60; music tchr. Amityville Union Free Sch., NY, 1960—61; tchr. Holt Pub. Sch., Mich., 1963—64; food supr. Pa. State U., State College, 1966—67; music tchr. Four Indian Cath. Sch., Pune, India, 1968—72, Bellefonte Area Sch. Dist., Pa., 1973, Penns Valley Area Sch. Dist., Spring Mills, Pa., 1973—96, pvt. studio, State College, 1973—. Pianist Friends Meeting, State College, 1976—93, music com., 1976—2004; sch. music organizer Pa. Music Tchr., State College, 1980. Photographer Pa. State Alumni Assn. Calendar, 1993; photo exhibition, Foxdale Gallery, 1994, Centre Cmty. Hosp., 1994; photographer (photograph) Town & Gown mag., State College, 1993, PA Mag., 1994—2003 (3rd place honorable mention, 1997, honorable mention, 2001), Clearwater News, 1996—2004, Shawnee Press Brochure, 1996, A Photographic Celebration, State College, 1995, State College Film Ctr., 2000 (3rd place and honorable mention, 2000). Bd. mem. Foxdale Retirement Home, State College, 2003—; photographer Clearwater Conservancy Cent. Pa., State College, 1999, 2003—04; chmn. children's day music program Festival Arts, State College, 1985. Recipient Judges' Choice, "Color Slide", New England Camera Club Conf., 1997; grantee Music Tchr. Projects Assistance Program, Pa. Music Tchr. Assn., 1979. Mem.: Photographic Soc. Am. (travelette chmn. 2002, chmn. small club bulletin 2001), Pa. Assn. Sch. Retirees, Music Educators Nat. Conf. Quaker. Achievements include organized "Parent Tchr. Orgn." in St. Joseph's Sch., Pune India, 1971. Avocations: photography, poetry, travel, interior decorating, recorder consort playing. Home: 1325 E Park Hills Ave State College PA 16803

PENNOYER, F. DOUGLAS, dean; b. Port Angeles, Wash., Mar. 19, 1947; s. Fredrick Douglas Pennoyer and Virginia Pennoyer; m. Joann Alice Steinhauer, Aug. 17, 1968; children: Heather Alice Kooiman, Rachel Elaine McClelland, Amanda Joy, Timothy Douglas. PhD Anthropology, Wash. State U., Pullman, 1975; MA Anthropology, Wash. State U., 1972; BA in Social Sci. Edn., Western Oreg. Univ., Monmouth, 1969. Dean, sch. of intercultural studies Biola U., La Mirada, Calif., 1998—; sr. pastor Free Meth. Ch., Snohomish, Wash., 1991—98; dir., intercultural inst. Seattle Pacific U., 1983—91; sr. fulbright U. of Philippines, Iloilo, 1983—83; exec. dir. Small Tribes Org. of Western Washingotn, Sumner, 1975—82; rsch. fulbright Ateneo de Manila, Philippines, 1974—75. Anthrop. cons. Snoqualmie Tribe of Indians, Redmond, Wash., 1984—97. Editor: (regal book) Wrestling With Dark Angels, (book) Caring for the Harvest Force; author: (anthropological journal articles) Journals: Folk, Anthropolos, Philippine Quarterly of Culture and Society, Philippine Sociological Review, etc.; exhibition of photographs, Philippine Portraits: Faces of Tribal People at Charles and Emma Frye Museum, Seattle, WA; author: (linguistic monograph) Inati: The Hidden Negrito Language of Panay. Rev. fin. plans Am. Indian Devel. Corp., Albuquerque, 1980—83. Fellow Anthropology rsch. with primitive tribe, Wenner-Gren Found. for Anthrop. Rsch., 1973, Nat. Def. Fgn. Lang. Fellowship, Cornell U., 1972, Dissertation Fellow, NIMH, 1974-75; grantee US Seafood Sales Mission to Japan, Dept. of Commerce, 1980. Mem.: Am. Anthrop. Assn. Achievements include discovery of a Philippine language previously thought extinct. Home: 15439 Tetley Street Hacienda Heights CA 91745 Office: Biola University 13800 Biola Ave La Mirada CA 90639 Office Phone: 562-906-4577. Personal E-mail: dpennoyer@aol.com.

PENNOYER, PAUL GEDDES, JR., lawyer; b. N.Y.C., Feb. 11, 1920; s. Paul G. and Frances (Morgan) P.; m. Cecily Henderson, Feb. 5, 1949; children: Jennifer, Deirdre, Paul T., Sheldon K., William M. BS, Harvard U., 1942, LLB, 1948. Bar: N.Y. 1949, U.S. Dist. Ct. (so. and ea. dists.) N.Y. 1952, U.S. Supreme Ct. 1972, U.S. Ct. Appeals (2d cir.) 1964, U.S. Ct. Appeals (4th cir.) 1986, U.S. Ct. Appeals (11th cir.) 1987. Assoc. Bingham Englar Jones & Houston, N.Y.C., 1949-55, ptnr., 1955-63, Chadbourne & Parke, N.Y.C., 1963-89; of counsel, 1989—. Trustee Frick Collection, 1975—2002, trustee emeritus, 2003—; trustee L.I. U., 1975-85, Morgan Meml. Park, 1970—, North Shore Wildlife Inc., 1980—. Lt. USN, 1942-45. Decorated Navy Cross, Air Medal, USN; recipient Outstanding Cmty. award KC, 2003, 04. Mem. ABA, N.Y. State Bar Assn., Assn. Bar City N.Y., N.Y. Bar found., Am. Coll. Trial Lawyers, Air Force Assn. (named Outstanding Mem. Yr. 2004), N.Y. Yacht Club. Republican. Episcopalian. Office: Chadbourne & Parke 30 Rockefeller Plz New York NY 10112 Office Phone: 301-585-0081.

PENNOYER, ROBERT M. lawyer; b. N.Y.C., Apr. 9, 1925; BA, Harvard U., 1946; LL.B., Columbia U., 1950. Bar: N.Y. 1951, U.S. Supreme Ct. 1971. Asst. U.S. atty. criminal div. So. Dist., N.Y., 1953-55; asst. to gen. counsel Office of Sec. of Def., Dept. Def., Washington, 1955-57, spl. asst. to asst. sec. of def. for internat. security affairs, 1957-58; ptnr. Patterson, Belknap, Webb & Tyler, N.Y.C., 1962-95, of counsel, 1995—. Trustee Carnegie Instn., Washington, 1968-79, John Merck Fund, 1982—, Mrs. Giles Whiting Found., 1970—, Met. Mus. Art, 1966—, Pierpont Morgan Libr., 1969—, Columbia U., 1982-88, Boyce Thompson Inst. for Plant Rsch., Cornell U., 1974-97, Inst. Democracy Studies, 1999-2002. Lt. (j.g.) USNR, PTO, 1944-46. Mem. ABA, N.Y. State Bar Assn., Assn. Bar City N.Y., Century Assn. Office: Patterson Belknap Webb & Tyler Rm 2200 1133 Ave of the Americas New York NY 10036-6731 E-mail: rmpennoyer@pbwt.com.

PENNY, PAUL BALDWIN, landscape artist; b. Lawrence, Kans., July 27, 1925; s. Myrl Nuzum and Addie (Underwood) P.; m. Virginia Rae Albury, Nov. 20, 1949; children: Alan Dean, Michael Paul, Gary Russell, Christopher Ray, Melissa Lynn Penny Swanson. Student, Bethany Coll., 1948-49; BFA in Drawing and Painting, U. Kans., 1952. Prodn. illustrator, engring. educator Boeing Aircraft, Wichita, 1952-55; supt. Penny Ready-Mix Concrete Co., 1955-60. Oil painting tchr. Adult Edn.; guest lectr. H.S. Art Class. One-man shows include Muchnic Gallery, Atchison, Agriculture Hall of Fame, Bonner Springs, Whitsitt Hall Gallery Pittsburg State U., Kans.; juried exhbns. include Bert Nash Mental Health Quarters, Lawrence Art Guild Ann. Show, 2003 (3d pl. award); interviewed on Sta. KTWU-TV, 2001; featured in documentary As Time Goes By, Sunflower Cablevision, 1997. Instnl. rep. Boy Scouts Am., Lecompton, Kans.; mem. website Post Rock Opportunities Found., 1997-99, Kans. Originals Market, Wilson. Mem. Lawrence Art Guild (exhbn. mem., contbr. paintings to ann. art auction). Avocations: swimming, fishing, camping, nature walks, historial record. Home: 638 Ohio St Lawrence KS 66044-2356

PENNY, ROGER PRATT, management executive; b. Buffalo, July 13, 1936; s. George Albert and Louise (Mings) P.; m. Judith Stevens, Aug. 25, 1957; children: David, Sarah, Julia. BA in Adminstrv. Engring., Union Coll., 1958; grad., Wharton Bus. Sch., 1993. Registered profl. engr., N.Y., Ind., Pa. From supt. to sr. mgr. Bethlehem Steel Corp., Lackawanna, N.Y., 1958-83, gen. mgr. Burns Harbor, Ind., 1983-87; sr. v.p. Bethlehem (Pa.) Steel Corp., 1987-92, bd. dirs., bd. dirs., pres., COO, 1992—, vice chmn., 1999-2001. Mem. United Way, Buffalo, 1960-82; chmn. campaign United Way Porter County, Valparaiso, Ind., 1986; mem. Orchard Park Town Bd., 1970-82; mem. adv. bd. Purdue U., West Lafayette, Ind., 1985-86, Bus. Sch., Valparaiso U., 1986; bd. dirs. Minsi Trails coun. Boy Scouts Am., Lehigh Valley, Pa., 1988—, pres., 1996; trustee St. Luke's Hosp. Mem. Am. Iron and Steel Inst., Assn. Iron and Steel Engrs., Valparaiso C. of C. (dir. 1985-86), Orchard Park C. of C., Buffalo C. of C., Sand Creek Club (pres. 1983-86), Buffalo Soccer Club (pres., sec. 1960-75), Saucon Valley Country Club. Republican. Episcopalian. Office: Martin Tower 1170 8th Ave Rm 101 Bethlehem PA 18016-7600

PENROD, MARIAN PENUEL, retired school librarian; b. Statesville, Tenn., May 11, 1930; d. Hayden L. Penuel and Zoie L. Cunningham; m. William T. Penrod, Jr., June 8, 1954 (div. Oct. 1979); children: Cheryl Anne Penrod Puryear, Paula Wynn, Laura Lynn Penrod Moseng. BS, Middle Tenn. State Coll., 1952; M of Religious Edn., Carver Sch. Missions and Social Work, 1955; EdM, U. Miami, 1958. Cert. specialist in pastoral care Pastoral Counseling Ctrs. Tenn., Inc., 2002. Tchr. Parma (Mich.) Elem., 1953—54, Golden Pond (Ky.) Elem., 1955—57, West Jackson (Tenn.) Bapt., 1965—66; tchr., libr. Madison County, Jackson, 1967—69; tchr. Dyer County, Dyersburg, Tenn., 1969—70; sch. libr. Murfreesboro (Tenn.) City Schs., 1972—98; ret. Baptist. Avocations: choral groups, pastoral care training and ministry.

PENROSE, CHARLES, JR., professional society administrator; b. Phila., Oct. 9, 1921; s. Charles and Beatrice (d,Este) P.; m. Ann Lucille Cantwell, Apr. 17, 1943; children: James, Thomas, John. Grad., Episcopal Acad., Overbrook, Pa., 1940. Exec. sec. Newcomen Soc. N.Am. (N.A.), Phila., 1946-48; dist. sales mgr. Fitchburg Paper Co., Mass., 1948-50, 52-53; from sales mgr. to v.p. sales A.M. Collins Mfg. Co., Phila., 1953-55; sales mgr. A.M. Collins divsn. Internat. Paper Co., N.Y.C., 1955; asst. to sales mgr. fine paper and bleached bd. divsn., 1956-57; sr. v.p., CEO Newcomen Soc. in N.Am., Downingtown, Pa., 1957-61, also bd. dirs.; pres., CEO Newcomen Soc. U.S., 1961-87, chmn., 1987-89, chmn. emeritus, 1989—; sr. v.p. N. Am. Newcomen Soc., London, 1957-89, hon. v.p., 1989—. Pres., CEO Newcomen publs. in N. Am., Inc., 1958-61, trustee, 1948-61; pres., dir. Rocaton, Inc., Darien, Conn., 1960-61. Author: They Live on a Rock in the Sea The Isles of Shoals in Colonial Days, 1957. Sec., asst. treas. Chester County Investment Fund Assn., Phila., 1959-64; v.p. Brit. Am. Ednl. Found., Inc., N.Y.C., 1968-70, pres., 1970-75, trustee, 1968-81; trustee Stanley Mus., Kingfield, Maine, 1995-2000; sec. Stanley Mus., Maine, 1996-98, 1999-2000, trustee. Capt. USAAF, 1940-46, PTO; capt. U.S. Army, 1950-2. Mem. Most Venerable Order Hospice of St. John of Jerusalem (London). Mem. Newcomen Soc. U.S., Newcomen Soc. London, Royal Soc. Arts (Benjamin Franklin fellow 1980), Pilgrims of U.S., First Troop Phila. City Calvary (hon.), Nat. Inst. Social Scis., Soc. Am. Historians, Marine Hist. Assn., N.H. Hist. Soc., Mt. Washington Obs., Sandwich (N.H.) Hist. Soc. (trustee 1992-94, v.p. 1994-98), Chi Psi Omicron. Clubs: Tokeneke (Darien); Tamworth Outing (N.H.); Wonalancet Outdoors (N.H.). Republican. Episcopalian. also: 11 Mansfield Ave Darien CT 06820-4714 Home: 81 Mansfield Ave Darien CT 06820 Office Phone: 203-655-4504.

PENROSE, CYNTHIA C. retired health care consultant; b. Manila, Philippines, Nov. 24, 1939; d. Douglas Lee Lipscomb Cordiner and Jane (Sturgeon) Edises; m. Douglas Francis Penrose, July 11, 1959 (div. 1981); children: Vicki Flores, Lee Douglas; m. Alan Harrison Magazine, Aug. 30, 1984. BA, U. Calif., Berkeley, 1963; MBA, U. Santa Clara, 1977. Cert. social svcs. V.p., dir. employment Resource Ctr. for Women, Palo Alto, Calif., 1973-78; bus. planner Raychem Corp., Menlo Park, Calif., 1979; adminstrv. mgr. Electric Power Rsch. Inst., Palo Alto, 1979-83; sr. ptnr. MB Assocs., Washington, 1983-88; dir. ops. Utility Data Inst., Washington, 1984-85, Randmark, Inc., 1986-87; coord. market devel. for Mid-Atlantic states Kaiser Found. Health Plan, Washington, 1987-88, asst. to assoc. regional mgr., 1988-94; market planner MetraHealth, Vienna, Va., 1995; exec. staff asst. United HealthCare, Vienna, 1995, dir. strategic planning, splty. cos., 1996-97; dir. spl. projects MetraComp subs. United HealthCare, Vienna, 1995, v.p. regulatory affairs and compliance, 1997-99; ptnr. Penrose Mag. LLC, 2000—01; ret., 2001. Bd. dirs., treas. Unique Enterprises, Washington, 1985-87; sec. Wesley Property Mgmt. Co., 1987-89; bd. dirs. Wesley Housing Devel. Corp., 1988-89. Chair vol. com. Habitat for Humanity, No. Va., 2002—03, bd. dirs., 2003—, chair Restore adv. coun., 2004—; mem. Affirmative Action Adv. Com., Palo Alto, 1975—76; bd. dirs., sec. Am. Hospice Found., 1995—97, treas., 1998—2000; bd. dirs. Nat. Inst. for Med. Options, 1999—2001; bd. dirs., v.p. LWV, Berkeley and Palo Alto, 1966—73; chmn. program adv. com. Resource Ctr. for Women, Palo Alto, 1980—83; bd. dirs. HFHNV, 2003—. Mem. Peninsula Profl. Women's Network (v.p. 1981-82), U. Calif. Alumni Assn., AAUW (Bicentennial br. sec. 1986-88), Capitol Area Soc. Healthcare Planning and Mktg., Nat. Capital Healthcare Execs., LWV. Democrat. Episcopalian. Avocations: swimming, nutrition and health, reading. Home and Office: 322 S Fayette St Alexandria VA 22314-5903 E-mail: ccpenrose@comcast.net.

PENSADO, OSVALDO, research scientist; b. Xalapa, Veracruz, Mex., May 31, 1971; s. Faustino Pensado and Ana María Rodríguez; m. Esperanza Ortiz-Pensado; children: Diego children: Edna. BS in Physics and Math., U. de las Américas, 1994; PhD in Engring. Sci., Pa. State U., 1998. Asst. prof. Univ. Veracruzana, Xalapa, Mexico, 1995; rsch. asst. Pa. State Univ., Univ. Pk., 1995; rsch. engr. Southwest Rsch. Inst., San Antonio, 1999—2002, sr. rsch. scientist, 2002—. Contbr. rsch. articles to sci. jours. Mem.: Materials Rsch. Soc., Electrochem. Soc. Avocation: playing soccer and tennis. Office: S W Rsch Inst 6220 Culebra Rd San Antonio TX 78238 Business E-Mail: opensado@swri.org.

PENSE, ALAN WIGGINS, metallurgical engineer, academic administrator; b. Sharon, Conn., Feb. 3, 1934; s. Arthur Wilton and May Beatrice (Wiggins) P.; m. Muriel Drews Taylor, June 28, 1958; children: Daniel Alan, Steven Taylor, Christine Muriel. B.Metall. Engring., Cornell U., 1957; MS, Lehigh U., 1959, PhD, 1962. Research asst. Lehigh U., Bethlehem, Pa., 1957-59, instr., 1960-62, asst. prof., 1962-65, asso. prof., 1965-71, prof., 1971-96, chmn. dept. metallurgy and materials engring., 1977-83, assoc. dean Coll. Engring. and Applied Scis., 1984-88, dean, 1988-90, v.p., provost, 1990-96, prof. emeritus, 1996—. Assoc. dir. Ctr. Advanced Tech. for Large Structural Systems NSF, 1986-89; cons. adv. com. on reactor safeguards NRC, 1965-86; rsch. engr., 1997—; cons. Lehigh U., 1997—. Author: (with D. Henkel) Structure and Properties of Engineering Materials, 5th edit, 2001; also articles. Recipient Robinson award Lehigh U., 1965, Stabler award, 1972, Hillman award 1997, Materials Sci. and Engring. Disting. Alumni award, 2002; Danforth fellow, 1974-86. Fellow Am. Soc. Metals, Am. Welding Soc. (William Spraragan award 1963, Adams Membership award 1966, Jennings award 1970, Adams lectr. 1980, William Hobart medal 1982, Plummer lectr. 1995); mem. ASTM, Am. Soc. Engring. Edn. (Western Elec. award 1986), Internat. Inst. Welding, Nat. Acad. Engring. Republican. Evang. Congregationalist (bd. trustees Evang. Sch. Theology). Home: 2586 Lynhurst Dr Bethlehem PA 18017-3940 Office: The ATLSS Rsch Ctr 117 Atlss Dr Bethlehem PA 18015-4728 Office Phone: 610-758-6104. Business E-Mail: awp0@lehigh.edu. *Achievement of significant goals in our life must be balanced by the quality of that life itself, for what we are is as important as what we do.*

PENSHORN, JOHN S. health facility administrator; Stock analyst Piper Jaffray; dir. Capital Markets Comm. and Strategy, Unitedhealth Group, Inc., Minnetonka, Minn., 1998—. Office: Unitedhealth Group Ctr 9900 Bren Rd E Minnetonka MN 55343

PENSINGER, JOHN LYNN, lawyer; b. Hagerstown, Md., June 5, 1949; s. Linford Snider and Marguerite Joan (McNeal) P.; m. Eileen Sue Howard, Nov. 7, 1972. BA, U. Md., 1971; JD, U. Balt., 1976; LLM, George Washington U., 1987. Bar: Md. 1976, D.C. 1977, U.S. Ct. Claims 1977, U.S. Tax Ct. 1977, U.S. Dist. Ct. Md. 1978, U.S. Dist. Ct. D.C. 1978, U.S. Ct. Appeals (4th cir.) 1978, U.S. Ct. Mil. Appeals 1978, U.S. Ct. Appeals (D.C. cir.) 1978, U.S. Customs Ct. 1979, U.S. Supreme Ct. 1980, U.S. Ct. Internat. Trade 1981, U.S. Ct. Appeals (fed. cir.) 1982, U.S. Ct. Appeals (5th cir.) 1986, U.S. Ct. Appeals (3d cir.) 1988, U.S. Army Ct. Mil. Rev. 1989. Mgr. E.M. Willis & Sons, Washington, 1977-79; pvt. practice Rockville, Md., 1978-79; atty. Amalgamated Casualty Ins. Co., Washington, 1979-86; asst. gen. counsel Legal Svcs. Corp., Washington, 1986-88, sr. litigation counsel, 1988-95; atty. Office Justice Programs, U.S. Dept. Justice, 1995-96, assoc. gen. counsel, 1996—. Mem. ABA, Am. Soc. Internat. Law, Fed. Bar Assn., Med. Bar Assn. Roman Catholic. Home: 4 Stratton Ct Rockville MD 20854-6227

PENSIS, HENRI BRAM, music educator, conductor; b. Luxembourg, Mar. 18, 1927; came to U.S., 1940; s. Henri Paul and Marielouise (Deltgen) P.; m. Patricia Adams Robinson, June 14, 1951; children: Henri Paul, Claude Norris. Student, Morningside Coll., 1944-45; MusB, Northwestern U., 1950, MusM, 1951, postgrad., 1952. Conductor Chamber Orch., Evanston, Ill., 1947-51; prof., chair music dept. Salem (W.Va.) Coll., 1952-55; asst. prof., conductor orch. Cen. Meth. Coll., Fayette, Mo., 1955-65; prof., conductor emeritus U. Wis., Oshkosh, 1965-95; music dir., conductor, mem. exec. com. Oshkosh Symphony Orch., 1967-96, music dir. laureate, 1998. Guest conductor Radio Luxembourg Symphony Orch., 1964, 72, 76, 78, 82, 84, 88; conducted Orchestre Philharmonique de Luxembourg Gala Concert in honor of father's death anniversary, October 1998; mus. dir., condr. CD: 20th Century Contrasts, 2002. Condr.: CD 20th Century Contrasts, Miramar Sinfonietta (One of Best CDs for 2002, Audiophile Audition). Recipient Key to City of Oshkosh, 1976, cert. of appreciation U.S. Amb. to Luxembourg, 1976, cert. of commendation Gov. of Wis., 1988, Outstanding Svc. award Assn. Wis. Symphony Orchs.; Henri B. Pensis Day declared in his honor, 1988, Maestro Pensis Week declared in his honor, 1996; selected as an influential citizen The Oshkosh Northwestern, 1993. Mem. Assn. Wis. Symphony Orchs. (exec. com. 1976—, past pres.; hon. life mem., Outstanding Svc. award 2002), Am. Symphony Orch. League (hon.), Conductors Guild, Grand Ducal Inst. Arts and Letters Luxembourg, Phi Mu Alpha Sinfonia (life), Pi Kappa Lambda. Avocations: photography, collecting records, stereo equipment. E-mail: hbpensis@northnet.north.

PENSKAR, MARK HOWARD, lawyer; b. Detroit, Mar. 4, 1953; s. Sol Leonard and Frances (Rosenthal) P.; m. Carol Ann Stewart, Aug. 7, 1977; children: David, Rebecca. BA, U. Mich., 1974, M in Pub. Policy, 1975, JD cum laude, 1977. Bar: Calif. 1977, U.S. Dist. Ct. (no. dist.) Calif. 1977, U.S. Dist. Ct. (ea. and ctrl. dists.) Calif. 1983, U.S. Dist. Ct. (so. dist.) Calif. 1988, U.S. Ct. Appeals (9th cir.) 1987, U.S. Tax Ct. 1993. Assoc. Pillsbury, Madison and Sutro, San Francisco, 1977-84, ptnr., 1985-96; sr. bus. litig. atty. Pacific Gas and Electric Co., San Francisco, 1996—, sect. head comml. and contracts sect., 2001—. Mediator Superior Ct. early settlement program, San Francisco; mediator and early neutral evaluator U.S. Dist. Ct. Alternative Dispute Resolution Program; bd. dirs. Legal Aid Soc. of San Francisco Employment Law Ctr. Mem. ABA, San Francisco Bar Assn., Commonwealth Club, Phi Gamma Delta (past pres. Bay Area grad. chpt.). Avocations: camping, golf, wine collecting, fishing. Home: 29 E Altarinda Dr Orinda CA 94563-2415 Office: Pacific Gas & Electric Co Law Dept B30A PO Box 7442 San Francisco CA 94120-7442 E-mail: MHP5@pge.com.

PENSKE, ROGER S. manufacturing and transportation executive; b. 1937; married. Grad., Lehigh U., 1958. With Alcoa Aluminum, Pitts., 1958-63, George McKean Chevrolet, Phila., 1963-65; prin. Penske Corp., Red Bank, N.J., pres., chmn. bd.; chmn. bd. dirs., pres., CEO Penske Transp. Inc., Detroit; chmn. bd. dirs., pres. Pa. Internat. Raceway, Nazareth, 1986—; CEO Detroit Diesel Corp., chmn. bd. dirs.; pres. Competition Tire West, inc., Brooklyn, Mich.; chmn., CEO United Auto Grp. Chmn. bd. dirs. Penske Truck Leasing Corp., Penske Speedway, Inc., Detroit, Penske Automotive Group, Detroit, Outer Drive Holidays, Inc., Detroit, D Longo, Inc., El Monte, Calif.; sec. Ilmore Engring., Inc., Redford, Mich. Office: Penske Corp 8801 N Haggarty Rd Ann Arbor MI 48107*

PENSKY, CAROL, political organization administrator; Past nat. chair Womens Leadership Forum/Democratic Nat. Com., Washington; past treas. Democratic Nat. Com., Washington. Office: Womens Leadership Forum 430 S Capitol St SE Washington DC 20003-4024

PENSO, CHRISTINE ARETY, obstetrician-gynecologist; b. Ft. Lauderdale, Fla., Feb. 5, 1952; BS, Fla. Atlantic Univ., 1974; MD, U. Miami, 1979. Diplomate Am. Bd. Ob-Gyn., Am. Bd. Maternal and Fetal Medicine. Intern Jackson Meml. Hosp., Miami, 1979-80, resident ob-gyn., 1980-83, fellow maternal and fetal medicine, 1983-85; fellow in ultrasound and prenatal diagnosis Yale-New Haven (Conn.) Hosp., 1995-96; mem. staff St. Elizabeth's Hosp., Boston. Mem. ACOG, Am. Inst. Ultrasound in Medicine, Soc. Maternal-fetal Med., Internat. Soc. Ultrasound in Ob-gyn.

PENSON, EDWARD MARTIN, management consulting company executive; b. N.Y.C., Aug. 30, 1927; s. Michael and Cecile (Cohan) P.; m. Georgann Ellen McCune, June 25, 1975; children: Jeffery, Albert, Cynthia. BA cum laude, U. Fla., 1950, PhD, 1955; MA, Ohio U., 1951. Prof. communication Ohio U., Athens, 1955-75, dean, 1965-68, v.p., 1969-75; pres., prof. Salem State Coll., Mass., 1975-78; prof., chancellor U. Wis.-Oshkosh, 1978-89, chancellor emeritus, 1989—; pres. Penson Assocs., Inc., Tallahassee, 1989—. Cons. Royal McBee, Litton Industries, Ohio Credit Union, Battelle Meml. Inst., 1963-66, U. Nev., 1980-81, OshKosh B'Gosh, Inc., 1987, Akron U., 1988, 300 univs. and sys., 1989—; bd. dirs. Valley Bank, Wis. Contbr. numerous articles to profl. jours., chpts. to books. Bd. dirs. Assn. Retarded Citizens, Salem, Mass., 1975-78; bd. dirs. Econ. Devel. Council, North Shore, Mass., 1976-78, Ohio student loan commr., Columbus, 1971-75. Mem. Communication Assn. Am., Internat. Communication Assn., Am. Assn. State Colls. and Univs., Nat. Assn. Student Personnel Adminstrs., Sigma Alpha Eta, Phi Kappa Phi, Alpha Lambda Delta, Psi Chi, Rotary (Salem, Mass. and Oshkosh, Wis.). Home and Office: 924 Summerbrooke Dr Tallahassee FL 32312-6729

PENTELÉNYI, THOMAS JOHN, neurosurgeon; b. Budapest, Hungary, Feb. 25, 1939; s. László and Anna Maria (Bohuniczky) P.; m. Mary P. Pálfalvy, Dec. 19, 1947; children: Marianne, Kinga. MD, Semmelweiss Medical Sch., Budapest, 1963, specialist of surgery, 1967; specialist of neurosurgery, Haynal Imre Univ., Budapest, 1974; PhD, Hungarian Acad. of Scis., 1978. Resident of surgery Szovetség Hosp., Budapest, 1964-66, Bajcsy Hosp., Budapest, 1966-68; resident of neurosurgery Nat. Inst. of Traumatology, Budapest, 1968-73, scientific co-worker, 1974-86, head of neurosurgery, 1986-96; prof., chmn. of neurosurgery Nat. Inst. of Traumatology, Haynal Imre Univ., Budapest, 1987-96; head, chmn. dept. neurosurgery Nat. Inst. of Traumatology, Budapest, 1986—; prof. of neurotraumatology Semmelweis U., Budapest, 1986—. Pres. Internat. Conf. on Lumbar Fusion and Stabilization/ICLFS Movement, Budapest, 1995—; internat. adv. bd. Paraplegia and Spinal Cord, 1992—, editl. bd. Clinical Neuroscience, 1992—; vis. prof. U. Chgo. Med. Sch., 1990, U. Tenn., 1989, Temple U., Phila., 1990, Thomas Jefferson U., Phila., 1990, U. Calif., Davis, 1990, U. Calif., Sacramento, 1990, U. Xaveriana, Bogota, Columbia, 1990; coord. Ctrl.-European Internat. Brain Injury Data-Base, 1997—; sr. cons. bd. Memphis Neuroscis. Ctr., 1989-96; head Hungarian-Japanese Intergovtl. Neurotrauma Sci. Rsch. Project. Hungarian coord. Ctrl. European Internat. Brain Injury Data Base. Recipient Highest Medical Profl. award Min. of Health, 1987, Budapest, Felicitation Medalist of Indian Neurology Soc., 1994. Mem. WHO (steering com.), World Fedn. Neurosurg. Socs. (neurotraumatology com., chmn. subcom. edn.), Internat. Med. Soc. of Paraplegia, Scientific Program Com. (coun. mem.), European Fedn. Neurol. Soc. (scientist panel 1994—), Euroacad. Multidisciplinary Neurotramatology (exec. com.), Hungarian Spine Soc. (pres. 1993-95), U. Padova (hon.), Purkinje Med. U. (hon.), N.Y. Acad. Scis. (diploma), Indian Neurology Soc. (hon.). Avocations: music, philosophy, fine arts, history of family, ethical problems. Office: Nat Inst of Traumatology Dept Neurosurgery VIII Fiumei ut 17 1081 Budapest Hungary E-mail: pentelenyi@freemail.hu., otri@axelero.hu.

PENTERMAN, CAROL A. opera company executive; b. Lincoln, Nebr., June 18, 1955; BMus, U. Nebr., 1977; MM in Voice and Opera, Coll. Cons. Music, 1981. Performer, 1981-84; prodn. stage mgr. Lyric Opera, Kansas City, Mo., 1985-95, Des Moines Metro Opera, Des Moines, 1985-95, Opera Carolina, 1985-95, New Orleans Opera, 1985-95, Balt. Opera, 1985-95; exec. dir. Nashville Opera, 1995—. Recipient achievement award Frist Found. Mem. Opera Am., Am. Guild of Musical Artists. Home: 5500 Cottonport Dr Brentwood TN 37027-7640 Office: Nashville Opera Ctr 3628 Trousdale Dr Ste D Nashville TN 37204-4523

PENTKOWSKI, RAYMOND J. principal; Former supt. Battenkill (Vt.) Valley Supervisory Union, Addison-Rutland (Vt.) Supervisory Union; formerly prin. Ludlow (Vt.) Elem. Sch.; prin. Poultney (Vt.) Elem. Sch. Named state finalist Nat. Supt. of Yr. award, 1989. Office: PoultneyElem Sch Poultney VT 05764 Office Phone: 802-287-5212. Business E-Mail: Ray.Pentkowski@rswsu.org.

PENZ, CARLA MARIA, biologist, researcher; b. Porto Alegre, Brazil, Oct. 17, 1961; d. Isolde Renate and Rubem Paulo Penz; m. Philip James DeVries, July 20, 1987. BS, Biol. Scis. Inst., U. Fed. do Rio Grandedo Sul, 1983; MS, U. Fed. so Rio Grande do Sul, 1988; PhD, U. Tex., 1996. Curator Milw. Pub. Mus., Milw., 2000—, sect. head invertebrate zoology, 2003—. Contbr. articles to profl jours. Grantee Rsch. grant, NSF, Smithsonian Tropical Rsch. Inst., CNPq, 1984 -89 -92 -94 -95 -96 -98 2001 -03, grant, Nat. Sci. Found. Systematics and Populatin Biology Program, 2003; Pre-doctoral fellow, Conselho Nat. of Desenvolvimento Sci. Tech., 1984—86, Pre-doctoral fellow, Rsch grant, 1989—93, Rsch. grant, Percy Sladen Found., 1992, Field Rsch. grant, Inst. Latin Am. Studies, 1992, Doctoral Dissertation Improvement grant, Nat. Sci. Found., 1994—95, Pre-doctoral fellow, Smithsonian Tropical Rsch. Inst., 1995, Field Rsch. grant, U. Tex. Dept. Zoology, 1996, grant, Nat. Sci. Found. Systematics and Populatin Biology Program, 1998, 1998. Mem.: Soc. Systematic Biologists. Achievements include research in Butterfly Systematics. Office: Milw Pub Mus 800 West Wells St Milwaukee WI 53233 E-mail: flea@mpm.edu.

PENZER, MARK, lawyer, writer; b. Bklyn., Nov. 22, 1932; s. Ed and Fay (Weinberg) P.; m. Eileen Malen, Aug. 12, 1962; children: Matthew, Nicole; m. Nydia A. Rey, Nov. 25, 1984. BBA, CCNY; JD, Fordham U. Bar: N.Y. 1968, D.C. 1973, Fla. 1982, U.S. Dist. Ct. (ea. dist.) N.Y. 1976, U.S. Dist. Ct. (so. dist.) Fla. 1991; cert. instr. DMA, 1986. Free-lance writer, 1950-83; editorial asst. Hearst mags., N.Y.C., 1955, asst. editor, 1956, assoc. editor, 1957-66; columnist N.Y. Jour.-Am., 1960-62; editor in chief Rudder mag., 1967-69, editorial dir., 1970-74; editor in chief True, 1970-73, editor at large, 1973-75; pub., editor in chief Jour. Energy Medicine, 1978-81; Medicare hearing officer Miami, Fla., 1981-82; pres. Success Internat., Inc., Coral Gables, Fla., 1984-85; adj. prof. bus. and tech. writing Fla. Internat. U., small bus. mgmt., U. Miami, 1986-89; pres. Heroica, Inc., Miami Lakes, Fla., 1989-90; pvt. practice Law Offices of Mark Penzer, Hialeah and Miami Lakes, Fla., 1991—. Tchr. creative writing Dade County Off Campus Edn. Author: The Motorboatman's Bible, 1965, The Powerboatman's Bible, 1977; asst. editor: The Path of Least Resistance, 1989, Do It!, 1991. Served with AUS, 1953-55. Mem. Hialeah-Miami Lakes Bar Assn. (pres. 1990-92). Office Phone: 305-828-6400. E-mail: mpenz@aol.com.

PENZIAS, ARNO ALLAN, astrophysicist, technology consultant, research scientist, information systems specialist; b. Munich, Apr. 26, 1933; arrived in U.S., 1940, naturalized, 1946; s. Karl and Justine (Eisenreich) Penzias; m. Sherry Chamove Levit, Aug. 2, 1996; children: David Simon, Mindy Gail, Laurie Shifra. BS in Physics, CCNY, 1954; MA in Physics, Columbia U., 1958, PhD in Physics, 1962; DHC (hon.), Observatoire de Paris, 1976; ScD (hon.), Rutgers U., 1979, Wilkes Coll., 1979, CCNY, 1979, Yeshiva U., 1979, Bar Ilan U., 1983, Monmouth Coll., 1984, Technion-Israel Inst. Tech., 1986, U. Pitts., 1986, Ball State U., 1986, Kean Coll., 1986, U. Pa., 1992, Ohio State U., 1988, Iona Coll., 1988, Drew U., 1989, Lafayette Coll., 1990, Columbia U., 1990, George Washington U., 1992, Rensselaer Univ., 1992, U. Pa., 1992, Bloomfield Coll., 1994, Rankin Tech. U., 1997, Hebrew Union Coll., 1997, Oxford U., 2002. Mem. tech. staff Bell Labs., Holmdel, NJ, 1961—72, head radiophysics rsch. dept., 1972—76, dir. radio research lab., 1976—79, exec. dir. rsch., communications scis. div., 1979—81, v.p. rsch., 1981—85; v.p., chief scientist Lucent Technologies, 1995—98, sr. tech. adv., 1998—2000; venture ptnr. New Enterprise Assocs., 1997—. Bd. dirs. Alien Tech. Corp.; sr. advisor New Enterprise Assocs., 1997—98; adj. prof. earth and scis. SUNY, Stony Brook, 1974—84, Univ. Disting. lectr., 1990; lectr. dept. astrophys. Scis. Princeton U., 1967—72, vis. prof., 1972—85; rsch. assoc. Harvard Coll. Obs., 1968—80; Edison lectr. U.S. Naval Rsch. Lab., 1979; Kompfner lectr. Stanford U., 1979; Gamow lectr. U. Colo., 1980; Jansky lectr. Nat. Radio Astronomy Obs.1983, 1983; Michelson Meml. lectr., 85; Grace Adams Tanner lectr., 87; Klopsteg lectr. Northwestern U., 1987; grad. faculties alumni Columbia U., 1987—89; Regents' lectr. U. Calif., Berkeley, 1990; Lee Kuan Yew Disting. vis. Nat. U. Singapore, 1991; mem. astronomy adv. panel NSF, 1978—79, mem. indsl. panel on sci. and tech., 1982—92, disting. lectr., 1987; affiliate Max-Planck Inst. for Radioastronomy, 1978—85; chmn. Fachbeirat, 1981—83; rschr. in astrophysics, info. tech., its applications and impacts. Patentee auction-based selection of telecom. carriers, participant tracking in conference call, computer-based transportation system, fraud prevention in calling cards, identifying telephone extensions in residence environment, double-encrypted identity verification sys.; author: Ideas and Information Managing in a High-Tech World, 1989, Harmony-Business, Technology and Life After Paperwork, 1995; editl. bd. Ann. Rev. Astronomy and Astrophysics, 1974—78, AT&T Bell Labs. Tech. Jour., 1978—84, chmn., 1981—84, assoc. editor Astrophys. Jour., 1978—82, contbr. over 100 articles to tech. jours. Bd. overseers U. Pa. Sch. Engring. and Applied Sci., 1983—86; mem. vis. com. Calif. Inst. Tech., 1977—77; mem. Com. Concerned Scientists, 1975—, vice chmn., 1976; mem. adv. bd. Union of Couns. for Soviet Jews, 1983—95; bd. dirs. Coun. on Competitiveness, 1989—92; bd. trustees Trenton (N.J.) State Coll., 1977—79. With U.S. Army, 1954—56. Named to N.J. Lit. Hall of Fame, 1991; recipient Herschel medal, Royal Astron. Soc., 1977, Nobel prize in Physics, 1978, Townsend Harris medal, CCNY, 1979, Newman award, 1983, Joseph Handleman prize in the scis., 1983, Grad. Faculties Alumni award, Columbia U., 1984, Achievement in Sci. award, Big Bros. Inc., N.Y.C., 1985, Priestly award, Dickinson Coll., 1989, Pender award, U. Pa., 1992, N.J. Sci. and Tech. medal, 1996, Internat. Eng. Cons. Fell. award, 1997, Indsl. Rsch. Inst. medal, 1998. Mem.: AAAS, NAS (Henry Draper medal 1977), IEEE (hon.), NAE, World Acad. Arts and Sci., Internat. Astron. Union, Am. Phys. Soc. (Pake prize 1990), Am. Astron. Soc. Office: New Enterprises Assocs 2490 Sand Hill Rd Menlo Park CA 94025-6940

PENZIEN, JOSEPH, structural engineering educator; b. Philip, S.D., Nov. 27, 1924; s. John Chris and Ella (Stebbins) P.; m. Jeanne Ellen Hunson, Apr. 29, 1950 (dec. 1985); children: Robert Joseph, Karen Estelle, Donna Marie, Charlene May; m. Mi-jung Park, June 16, 1988. Student, Coll. Idaho, 1942—43; BS, U. Wash., 1945; ScD, MIT, 1950. Staff Sandia Corp., 1950—51; sr. structures engr. Consol. Vultee Aircraft Corp., Fort Worth, 1951—53; asst. prof. U. Calif. at Berkeley, 1953—57, assoc. prof., 1957—62, prof. structural engring., 1962—88, prof. emeritus, 1988—; dir. Earthquake Engring. Rsch. Ctr., 1968—73, 1977—80. Cons. engring. firms; chief tech. adv. Internat. Inst. of Seismology and Earthquake Engring., Tokyo, Japan, 1964-65; chmn. bd. Ea. Internat. Engrs., Inc., 1980-90, Internat. Civil Engring. Cons., Inc., 1990—. NATO Sr. Sci. fellow., 1969 Fellow Am. Acad. Mechanics; hon. mem. ASCE (Walter Huber Rsch. award, Alfred M. Freudenthal medal, Nathan M. Newmark medal, Ernest E. Howard award), Earthquake Engring. Rsch. Inst. (hon., Hausner medal), IAEE (hon.), EERI (Alfred E. Alquist award, Dist. Lectr. 2000); mem. Am. Concrete Inst., Structural Engrs. Assn. Calif., Seismol. Soc. Am., Nat. Acad. Engring. Home: 800 Solana Dr Lafayette CA 94549-5004 Office: Int Civil Engr Cons Inc 1995 University Ave Berkeley CA 94704 Office Phone: 510-841-7328.

PEON, ROBERTO, telecommunications industry executive; b. Mexico City, Mex. BA in Bus. Adminstrn., Ctrl. Coll.; postgrad. Drake U. Mktg. dir. Contel Cellular, Inc.; product mgmt. InteCom, Inc.; v.p. L.Am. Bellsouth Internat.; pres. ops. Bellsouth Internat., CEO BCP Telecomm., Brazil, 1997—2000; chief mktg. officer Bellsouth Corp., Atlanta, 2000—. Mem. telecomm. adv. bd. Compaq; mem. adv. bd. MedShare Internat. Co-chmn. Ams. Gateway Strategy, Atlanta; bd. dirs. Ga. Dept. Trade and Tourism. Office: Bellsouth Corp 1155 Peachtree St NE Atlanta GA 30309-3610

PEOPLES, CAROLYN Y. federal agency administrator; b. Md. BS in Fin., U. Balt., 1982, MBA, 1984. Mgr. St. Andrews House, Balt., 1977—80; program adminstr. for aging divsn. Cath. Charities, Balt., 1980—85, adminstr. housing aging divsn., 1985—90, property mgr. aging divsn., 1980—90, dir. ops. for the housing divsn., 1990—99; founder, CEO Jeremiah Housing Svcs., Inc., 1999—2001; asst. sec. for fair housing and equal opportunity HUD, Washington, 2002—. Pres. edn. com. Beacon Inst.; trustee Mid-Atlantic Nonprofit Health and Housing Assn.; bd. govs. U. Balt. Mem.: Am. Assn. of Homes and Svcs. for the Aging (mem. hos. of dels.). Office: US Dept HUD 451 7th St SW Washington DC 20410

PEOPLES, CRYSTAL D. state legislator; 1 child, Rashaun. BS in Elem. Edn., M in Student Adminstrn., Buffalo State Coll. Legislator 7th Dist. Erie Co., 1993—2002; state rep. N.Y. House, 2003—. Chair Erie Co. Legislature Fin. Com. Democrat. Office: 792 E Delavan Ave Buffalo NY 14215

PEOPLES, JOHN ARTHUR, JR., former university president, consultant; b. Starkville, Miss., Aug. 26, 1926; s. John Arthur and Maggie Rose (Peoples) P.; m. Mary E. Galloway, July 13, 1951; children: Kathleen, Mark Adam. BS, Jackson State U., 1950; MA, U. Chgo., 1951, PhD, 1961. Tchr. math. Froebel Sch., Gary, Ind., 1951-58; asst. prin. Lincoln Sch., Gary, 1958-62; prin. Banneker Sch., Gary, 1962-64; asst. to pres. Jackson (Miss.) State U., 1964-66, v.p., 1966-67, pres., 1967-84; Trustees disting. prof. Univs. Ctr. of Jackson, 1984-85; asst. to pres. SUNY, Binghamton, 1965-66; cons. in higher edn., 1985—. Lectr. summers numerous univs. and colls. Contbr. articles to profl. jours. Active Boy Scouts Am.; bd. govs. So. Regional Edn. Bd.; bd. visitors Air U.; adv. com. U.S. Army Command and Gen. Staff Coll.; mem. Commn. Excellence Am. Assn. State Colls. and Univs.; bd. commrs. Jackson Airport Authority. Served with USMCR, 1944-47. Recipient Disting. Am. award Nat. Football Found., Presdl. citation, Lifetime Achievement award Nat. Black Coll. Alumni Found., 1993—; named to Southwestern Athletic Hall of Fame. Mem. Am. Council Edn. (chmn. dir. 1975), Am. Assn. Higher Edn. (dir. 1971-74), NEA, Miss. Tchrs. Assn., Jackson C. of C. (econ. council), Alpha Kappa Mu, Phi Kappa Phi, Phi Delta Kappa, Omega Psi Phi (Man of Year, Sigma Omega chpt. 1966), Sigma Pi Phi. Lodges: Masons (33 deg.).

PEPE, FRANK A. cell and developmental biology educator; b. Schenectady, May 22, 1931; s. Rocco and Margherita (Ruggiero) P. BS, Union Coll., 1953; PhD, Yale U., 1957. Instr. anatomy U. Pa., Phila., 1957-60, assoc. in anatomy, 1960-63, asst. prof., 1963-65, assoc. prof., 1965-70, prof., 1970-92, chmn. dept. anatomy, 1977-90, prof. cell. and devel. biology, 1992-96, emeritus prof., 1996—. Editor: Motility in Cell Function, 1979. Recipient Rsch. Career Devel. award USPHS, 1968-73, Raymond C. Truex Disting. Lecture award Hahneman U., 1988. Fellow AAAS; mem. Am. Assn. Anatomists, Am. Chem. Soc., Biophys. Soc., Microscopy Soc. Am., Sigma Xi. Home: 4614 Pine St Philadelphia PA 19143-1808 E-mail: fpepe@cellbio.med.upenn.edu.

PEPE, LOUIS ROBERT, lawyer, educator; b. Derby, Conn., Mar. 7, 1943; s. Louis F. and Mildred R. (Vollaro) P.; m. Carole Anita Roman, June 8, 1969; children: Marissa Lee, Christopher Justin, Alexander Drew. B in Mgmt. Engring., Rensselaer Poly. Inst., 1964, MS, 1967; JD with distinction, Cornell U., 1970. Bar: Conn. 1970, U.S. Dist. Ct. Conn. 1970, U.S. Ct. Appeals (2d cir.) 1971, U.S. Supreme Ct. 1975, U.S. Ct. Claims 1978. Assoc. Alcorn, Bakewell & Smith, Hartford, Conn., 1970-75, ptnr., 1975-82; sr. ptnr. Pepe & Hazard, Hartford, 1983—. Adj. assoc. prof. Hartford Grad. Ctr., 1972-87; adj. prof. U. Conn. Law Sch., 2000—. Active New Hartford Housing Authority, 1971-72, New Hartford Planning Zoning Commn., 1973-84, chmn., 1980-84, New Hartford Inland Wetlands Commn., 1975-78; dean's adv. coun. Cornell Law Sch., 1990—; dir. Greater Hartford Legal Aid Found., 1993—, pres., 1999-2001. 1st lt. U.S. Army, 1964-66. Decorated Army Commendation medal. Fellow Am. Bar Found., Conn. Bar Found., Am. Coll. Constl. Lawyers, Am. Coll. Trial Lawyers; mem. ABA, Am. Bd. Trial Advocates, Conn. Bar Assn. (chmn. constrn. law sect. 1989-92, chmn. standing com. on professionalism 2000-2003, v.p. 2003-2004, pres.-elect, 2004—, chmn. probono com. 2003-2004, Conn. Trial Lawyers Assn., Hartford County Bar Assn., Phi Kappa Phi. Home: 3 Metacom Dr Simsbury CT 06070-1851 Office: Pepe & Hazard Goodwin Sq Hartford CT 06103-4300 E-mail: lpepe@pepehazard.com.

PEPE, STEPHEN PHILLIP, lawyer; b. Paterson, N.J., Oct. 30, 1943; s. Vincent Attilio and Emma (Opletal) P.; m. Catherine B. Hagen, Dec. 8, 1990. BA, Montclair (N.J.) State U., 1965; JD, Duke U., 1968. Bar: Calif. 1969, U.S. Dist. Ct. (no., so., ea. and cen. dists.) Calif. 1975, U.S. Ct. Appeals (9th cir.) 1975, U.S. Sup. Ct. 1978. Assoc. O'Melveny & Myers, L.A., 1968-75, ptnr., 1976—, chmn. lab. and employment law dept., 1989-92. Co-author: Avoiding and Defending Wrongful Discharge Claims, 1987, Privacy in the Work Place, 1993, Corporate Compliance Series: Designing an Effective Fair Hiring and Termination Compliance Program, 1993, The Law of Libel & Slander, 1994; co-editor: Guide to Acquiring and Managing a U.S. Business, 1992, Calif. Employment Law Letter, 1990-94. Bd. visitors Duke Law Sch., 1992-96; bd. trustees Montclair State U. Found., 1991; bd. govs. Coll. of Labor and Employment Law, 1996—, pres., 2000—; pres. Inst. Indsl. Rels. Assn., 1989-91; bd. advisors UCLA Sch. Medicine, 2001--. With USAR, 1969-75. Fellow Coll. of Labor and Employment Law, 1996—. Mem. Am. Hosp. Assn. (labor adv. com. 1975-90), The Employers Group (bd. dirs., chmn. legal com. 1989-93), Calif. Club (chmn. employee rels. com. 1980—). Democrat. Roman Catholic. Avocations: wine collecting, wine making, wine judging, vineyard owner. Office: O Melveny & Myers 610 Newport Center Dr Newport Beach CA 92660-6419

PEPELEA, KIMBERLI RAE, case manager; b. Clinton, Ind., Sept. 14, 1963; d. Charles W. and Sally Luft; m. Rockie Gene Pepelea, Sr., Jan. 19, 1990. AA, Southeastern C.C., West Burlington, Iowa, 1999; BA in Psychology and Criminal Justice, Iowa Wesleyan Coll., 2001. Cert. activity dir. Nurses aide Clinton (Ind.) Nursing Home, 1982-87; asst. activity dir. BMC Klein Unit, Burlington, Iowa, 1992-98; case mgr. Hamilton Ctr., Rockville, Ind., 2002. Avocations: cross-stitch, computers.

PEPER, CHRISTIAN BAIRD, lawyer; b. St. Louis, Dec. 5, 1910; s. Clarence F. and Christine (Baird) Peper; m. Ethel C. Kingsland, June 5, 1935 (dec. Sept. 1995); children: Catherine K. Peper Larson(dec.), Anne Peper Perkins, Christian B.; m. Barbara C. Pleiter, Jan. 25, 1996. AB cum laude, Harvard U., 1932; LLB, Washington U., 1935; LLM, Yale U., 1937. Bar: Mo. 1934. Pvt. practiced, St. Louis; of counsel Blackwell Sanders Peper Martin LLP, St. Louis. Lectr. Washington U. Law Sch., St. Louis, 1943—61; ptnr. A. G. Edwards & Sons, 1945—67; pres. St. Charles Gas Corp., 1953—72; bd. dirs. El Dorado Paper Bag Mfg. Co., Inc. Editor: (book) An Historian's Conscience: The Correspondence of Arnold J. Toynbee and Columba Cary-Elwes, 1986. Mem. vis. com. Harvard Div. Sch., 1964—70. Sterling fellow, Yale U., 1936. Mem.: ABA, East India Club (London), St. Louis Bar Assn., Mo. Bar Assn., Harvard Club, Noonday Club, Univ. Club, Order of Coif, Phi Delta Phi. Roman Catholic. Home: 1454 S Mason Rd Saint Louis MO 63131-1211 Office: Blackwell Sanders Peper Martin LLP 720 Olive St Saint Louis MO 63101-2338 Business E-Mail: cpeper@blackwellsanders.com.

PEPONIS, HAROLD ARTHUR, insurance agent, broker; b. Chicago, Dec. 12, 1928; s. Arthur Harold and Ethel (Karambis) P.; m. Toula H. (Preketes), Mar. 1, 1952 (dec. Dec. 1984); one child, Arthur Harold II; m. Aphrodite E. (Stavros), May 26, 1990. BS, Loyola U., Chgo., 1950, postgrad., 1991. Treas. Plaza Cleaners and Dyers, Inc., Chgo., 1950—58; owner Exch. Cleaners, Chgo., 1958—63, Park West Plaza Cleaners, Chgo., 1963—69; ins. agt. Aetna Life and Casualty, Lisle, Ill., 1969—95; ind. broker Registered Rep., Evanston, Ill., 1995—; ptnr. lecture series, pub. co. Images of Orthodoxy; instr. religion Plato Acad., Chgo., 1998—99. Pres. Tesera Assoc., Evanston, Ill., 1973—; dir. Faith Net, Inc., 2003-. Mem. editl. bd. Christianity and Arts mag., 1996-98; columnist Coyote Chronicle Newsletter, 2003-. Pres. parish coun. United Greek Orthodox Ch. of Chgo., 1963—64, Annunciation Cathedral, 1991—92, 1994; archon Order of St. Andrew, Greek Orthodox Ch., state comdr., 1994—2001, regional comdr., 2001—. Recipient Medal of St. Paul, Greek Orthodox Archdiocese, 1999. Mem. Pan Arcadian Fedn. Am. (nat. pres. Chgo. 1963-64), Du Page Life Underwriters Assn; bd. dir. 2626 North Lakeview Condominium Assn., 2004-. Home: 2626 N Lakeview Apt 2503 Chicago IL 60614-1821 Office: 2956 Central St Evanston IL 60201-1246 Office Phone: 847-866-9370.

PEPPAS, NIKOLAOS ATHANASSIOU, chemical and biomedical engineering educator, consultant; b. Athens, Greece, Aug. 25, 1948; s. Athanassios Nikolaou Peppas and Alice Petrou Rousopoulou; m. Lisa Brannon, Aug. 10, 1988; children: Katherine, Alexander. Diploma in Engring., Nat. Tech. U., Athens, 1971; ScD, MIT, 1973; D honoris causa, U. Parma, Italy, 1999, U. Ghent, Belgium, 1999, U. Athens, 2000. Asst. prof. chem. engring. Purdue U., West Lafayette, Ind., 1976 78, assoc. prof., 1978-81, prof., 1981—2002, Showalter Disting. prof. of chem. and biomed. engring., 1993—2002; prof. chem. engring. U. Tex., Austin, 2003—, prof. biomed. engring., 2003, prof. pharmaceutics, 2003—, Fletcher S. Pratt disting. prof., 2003—. Vis. prof. U. Geneva, 1982-83, Calif. Inst. Tech., Pasadena, 1983, U. Paris, 1986, Hoshi U., Japan, 1994, Hebrew U., Jerusalem, 1994, U. Naples, 1995, Free U. Berlin, 2001, Complutense U. Madrid, 2001; adj. prof. U. Parma, Italy, 1987; cons. in field; mem. adv. bd. several cos. Author: Biomaterials, 1982, Hydrogels in Medicine and Pharmacy, 1987, One Hundred Years of Chemical Engineering, 1989, Pulsatile Drug Delivery, 1993, Biopolymers, 1993, Superabsorbent Polymers, 1994, Biomaterials for Drug and Cell Delivery, 1994, Polymer/Inorganic Interfaces, 1995, Physicochemical and Cellular Foundations of Biomaterials, 2004; contbr. over 900 articles and over 300 abstracts to jours. Active Austin Symphony Orch., Transfiguration Orthodox Ch. Austin. Recipient APV medal, Herbert McCoy award Purdue U., 2000. Fellow: AIChE (chmn. materials divsn. 1988—90, dir. bioengring. divsn. 1994—97, bd. dirs. 1999—2002, Materials Engring. Sci. award 1984, Bioengring. award 1994, Best Paper award 1994), Am. Phys. Soc., Italian Soc. Medicine and Scis., Am. Phys. Soc., Am. Assn. Pharm. Scientists (Rsch. Achievements Pharm. Tech. award 1999, Dale Wurster award 2002), Am. Inst. Med. Biol. Engrs., Soc. Biomaterials (pres.-elect 2002, pres. 2003—04); mem.: Biomed. Engring. Soc. (Best Rsch. award 2002), Polymer Pioneer, Am. Soc. Engring. Edn. (AT&T award 1982, Curtis McGraw award 1988, G. Westinghouse award 1992), Soc. Biomaterials (Clemson award 1992), Controlled Release Soc. (pres. 1987—88, Founders award 1991, Eurand award 2002), N.Y. Acad. Scis., Am. Chem. Soc. (Newsmaker of Yr. award 2002), Sigma Xi. Avocations: linguistics, opera, rare maps, classical record collecting, wine collecting. Office: U Tex Dept Chem Engring Austin TX 78712 Office Phone: 512-471-6644. E-mail: peppas@che.utexas.edu.

PEPPEL, MICHAEL E. computer company executive; BA, U. Notre Dame. Money desk mgr. Edward J. DeBartolo Corp., 1987-90; dir., CFO Diversified Data Products, Inc., 1990-96; v.p., CFO Miami Computer Supply Corp., Dayton, Ohio, 1996—. Office: Miami Computer Supply 3001 W Tech Blvd Miamisburg OH 45342-0824 Fax: 937-291-8298.

PEPPER, ALLAN MICHAEL, lawyer; b. Bklyn, July 5, 1943; s. Julius and Jeanette (Lasovsky) P.; m. Barbara Benjamin, Aug. 30, 1964; children—Leslie Anne, Joshua Benjamin, Adam Richard, Robert Benjamin BA summa cum laude, Brandeis U., 1964; LL.B. magna cum laude, Harvard U., 1967. Bar: N.Y. 1968, U.S. Dist. Ct. (so. and ea. dists.) N.Y. 1968, U.S. Ct. Appeals (2d cir.) 1968, U.S. Supreme Ct. 1988. Law clk. U.S. Ct. Appeals for 2d Circuit, NYC, 1967-68; assoc. Kaye, Scholer, Fierman, Hays & Handler LLP, NYC, 1968-74; ptnr. Kaye, Scholer LLP, NYC, 1975—. Lectr. in field. Exec. com., assoc. nat. chmn. Brandeis U. Alumni Fund, 1979-82, nat. chmn., 1982-85, chmn. 25th reunion gift com., 1989, devel. com., trustee, 1982-85, pres., councillor, 1980—, 35th reunion gift com., 1999; trustee Brandeis U., 1985-95, sec., 1992-93, budget and fin. com., 1988-95, chmn. com. strategic plan, 1990-91, acad. affairs com., 1985-92, student life and phys. facilities com., 1985-89, vice-chmn. ad hoc by-laws com., 1988-89, long range planning com., 1989-91, chmn. audit com., 1991-95, exec. com., 1990-91; bd. dir. Styles Brook Homeowners Assn., 1990—, exec. com., 1994—, 2d v.p., 2002—; mem. nominating com. Edgemont Sch. Bd., 1992-93; trustee Edgemont Sch. Found., 1994-2002, 2003-; 30th reunion gift com. Harvard Law Sch., 1996-97, class agt., 1998-2001. Recipient Henry Jones-Golda Meier Bnai Brith Youth Services award, 1986, LI Press Valedictory medal, 1960; Felix Frankfurter scholar Harvard U. Law Sch., 1964-65; Louis D. Brandeis hon. scholar Brandeis U., 1964 Mem. ABA, Assn. of Bar of City of N.Y. (law firm mgmt. com. 1987-91, litig. com, 1998-2001), N.Y. State Bar Assn. (comml. and fed. litig. sect., vice chmn. com. on discovery 1993-97), Brandeis U. Alumni Assn. (exec. com. 1982-87, alumni giving strategic planning com., 1992, Alumni Svc. award 1988), Phi Beta Kappa (LI Alumni award 1960), B'nai B'rith (pres. Henry Jones Lodge 1982-84, Westchester-Putnam coun. 1982-85, bd. gov. dist. 1, 1985-86). Democrat. Jewish. Office: Kaye Scholer 425 Park Ave New York NY 10022-3506 E-mail: apepper@kayescholer.com.

PEPPER, DAVID M. physicist, educator, writer, inventor; b. LA, Mar. 9, 1949; s. Harold and Edith P.; m. Denise Danyelle Koster, Mar. 19, 1992. BS in Physics summa cum laude, UCLA, 1971; MS in Applied Physics, Calif. Inst. Tech., 1974, PhD in Applied Physics, 1980. Mem. tech. staff Hughes Rsch. Labs., Malibu, Calif., 1973-87, sr. staff physicist, 1987-91, head nonlinear and electro-optic devices sect., 1989-91, sr. scientist, 1991-94; sr. rsch. scientist HRL Labs. (formerly Hughes Rsch. Labs.), Malibu, 1994—2004; rsch. scientist Malibu Scientific, 2004—. Adj. prof. math. and physics Pepperdine U., Malibu, 1981—; adv. panel NSF, Washington, 1997; panel on advanced signal processing U. Va., 1999; mem. Def. Sci. Rsch. Coun., U.S. Govt., Washington, 1999; presenter in field. Co-author: Optical Phase Conjugation, 1983, Laser Handbook, Vol. 4, 1985, Optical Phase Conjugation, 1995, Spatial Light Modulator Technology, 1995, CRC Handbook of Laser Science and Technology, 1995; contbr. over 250 articles to profl. jours. and tech. pubs. Mem. Sons and Daughters of 1939 Club, 2d Generation of Martyrs Meml., Mus. Holocaust. Recipient Rudolf Kingslake award Soc. Photo-Optical Instrumentation Engrs., 1982, Publ. of Yr. award Hughes Rsch. Lab., 1986, Patent award HRL Labs., 1997-2004; NSF trainee Calif. Inst. Tech., 1971; Howard Hughes fellow Hughes Aircraft Co., 1973-80. Fellow Optical Soc. Am. (conf. chair 1996-2001, adv. bd. topical conf. on nonlinear optics, Hawaii 1996, 98, 2000, invited tutorial meeting laser ultrasound 2001); mem. AAAS, IEEE (guest editor, assoc. editor, program com. US Cleo laser 1997-2001, instr. laser tech. 1994-2000, invited tutorial laser tech. 2001, European CLEO laser conf. program com. 2003), SPIE (guest editor, conf. co-chmn. 1998-2000), NY Acad. Scis., Am. Phys. Soc., Laser Inst. Am., Internat. Coun. Sci. Unions (com. on sci. and tech. in developing countries), Sigma Xi (v.p. 1986-87, chpt. pres. 1987-88, 90-92), Sigma Pi Sigma. Jewish. Achievements include 32 U.S. patents, 20 patents pending, and a top 10 cited paper of all time in the Opt. Soc. Am. Tech. Journal "Optics Letters". Avocations: classical music, travel, sports, astronomy. Office: Malibu Photonics P O Box 126 Malibu CA 90265-0126 E-mail: dmpepper@charter.net. *Personal philosophy: We all have a profound, meaningful purpose and mission in life—the challenge is to identify, appreciate, realize and embrace our dreams and goals.*

PEPPER, DOTTIE, professional golfer; b. Saratoga Springs, N.Y., Aug. 17, 1965; Student, Furman University. Top ranked player LPGA Tour, 1992. 3 time NCAA All-American; recipient Rolex Player of the Year Award, 1992; recipient Vare Trophy, 1992; leading money winner LPGA, 1992. Achievements include winning tournaments including Mazda Classic, 1989, Crestar Classic, 1990, Nabisco Dinah Shore, 1992, Sega Women's Championship, 1992, Welch's Classic, 1992, Sun-Times Challenge, 1992, LPGA Leading Money Winner, 1992, Wendy's Three-Star Challenge, 1992, PING/Welch's Championship, 1995, JC Penney/LPGA Skins Game, McCall's LPGA Classic, wom four tournaments: Rochester Internat., ShopRite LPGA Classic, Friendly's Classic and Safeway LPGA Golf Champ., 1996, 24 tournaments earning $293,652, 1997, tied 2nd at Rochester Internat., tied 3rd at Star Bank LPGA Classic, tied fourth at ShopRite LPGA Classic, 1997, Solheim Cup, 1998, Nabisco Dinah Shore, 1999. Address: care LPGA 100 International Golf Dr Daytona Beach FL 32124-1082

PEPPER, J. STANLEY, construction company executive; BA, Monmouth Coll. Various positions Pepper Cos., Chgo., 1968-91, pres., COO, 1991-93, CEO, 1993—.

PEPPER, JOHN ENNIS, JR., academic administrator; b. Pottsville, Pa., Aug. 2, 1938; s. John Ennis Sr. and Irma Elizabeth (O'Connor) P.; m. Frances Graham Garber, Sept. 9, 1967; children: John, David, Douglas, Susan BA, Yale U., 1960; PhD (hon.), Mt. St. Joseph Coll., St. Petersburg (Russia) U., Xavier U. Staff asst. Procter & Gamble Co., Cin., 1963-64, asst. brand mgr., 1964-66, brand mgr., 1966-68, copy supr., 1968-69, brand promotion mgr., 1969-72, advt. mgr. bar soap and household cleaning products divsn., 1972-74, gen. mgr. Italy subs., 1974-77, divsn. mgr. internat., 1977-78, v.p. packaged soap and detergent divsn., 1978-80, group v.p. bar soap and household cleaning products divsn., 1980-81, group v.p. Europe, 1981-84, exec. v.p. U.S. bus., 1984-86, pres. U.S. Bus., 1986-90, pres. internat. bus., 1990-95, chmn. bd., chief exec., 1995-99; chmn. Proctor & Gamble Co., Cin., 1999—2002, exec. com. of bd., 2000—03; v.p. fin. and adminstrn. Yale U., New Haven, 2004—. Bd. dirs. Xerox Corp., Motorola, Inc., Boston Scientific Corp. Chmn. U.S. Advisory Com. for Trade Policy and Negotiations; co-chair Devel. campaign, mem., exec. com. Nat. Underground Railroad Freedom Ctr.; group chmn. Cin. United Appeal Campaign, 1980; bd. trustees Xavier U., 1985-89, mem. exec. com., 1989; trustee Cin. Coun. World Affairs, Cin. Art Mus., Ctr. Strategic & Internat. Studies, Christ Ch. Endowment Fund; fellow Yale Corp.; gen. chmn. United Way Campaign, 1994; mem. Gov.'s Edn. and Bus. Advisory Group, State of Ohio; mem. adv. coun. Yale Sch. Mgmt.; mem. schs. com. Cin. Bus. Com.; co-chmn., mem. exec. com. Cin. Youth Collaborative; mem. Total Quality Leadership steering com.; mem., bd. dirs. United Negro Coll. Fund; former v.p. Am. C. of C., Brussels, Belgium (1981-84); former mem. Cin. Symphony Bd. (1979-81), Cin. Art Mus. Served to lt. USN, 1960-63. Mem. Am. Soc. Corp. Execs., Grocery Mfrs. Am., Nat. Alliance Businessmen (chmn. communication com.), Partnership for a Drug-Free Am., Soap and Detergent Assn. (bd. dirs.), The Bus. Coun., Bus. Roundtable, Yale Club, Queen City Club, Commonwealth Club, Comml. Club (former pres.). Office: VP Fin and Adminstrn Yale Univ New Haven CT 06520*

PEPPERS, JERRY P. lawyer; b. Cleve., Mar. 8, 1946; s. Jerry P. and Katherine M. Peppers; m. Sue E. Schafer, June 14, 1969; children: Amy E., Erica K., Christina A., Michele S. BBA, Ohio U., 1968; JD, Duke U., 1971. Bar: N.Y. 1972, U.S. Dist. Ct. (so. dist.) N.Y. 1972, U.S. Ct. Appeals (2nd cir.) 1972. Assoc. Pillsbury Winthrop LLP, N.Y.C., 1971-81, ptnr., 1982—. Bd. dirs. Firth Rixson, Inc., Rochester, NY, Monroe Forgings, Inc., Rochester, Viking Metall. Corp., Reno; mem. N.Am. pension com. The Morgan Crucible Co., Windsor, England. Editor (booklet): Outline of Mergers and Acquisitions in the United States, 15th edit., 2003. Trustee emeritus, mem.alternative investment com. Ohio Univ. Found., Athens, 1991—; trustee Scarsdale Youth Soccer Club, Inc.; bd. dirs. Atheneum Venture Fund, Athens, 1996—; com. mem. Fields for Kids. Mem.: ABA, Soc. Automotive Engrs., Assn. Bar City NY, Internat. Bar Assn., India House, Fox Meadow Tennis Club (Scarsdale, NY). Avocation: coaching soccer. Office: Pillsbury Winthrop LLP 1 Battery Park Plz New York NY 10004-1490 Office Phone: 212-858-1205. Business E-Mail: jpeppers@pillsburywinthrop.com.

PEPYNE, EDWARD WALTER, lawyer, psychologist, former educator; b. Springfield, Mass., Dec. 27, 1925; s. Walter Henry and Frances A. (Carroll) P.; m. Carol Jean Dutcher, Aug. 2, 1958; children— Deborah, Edward, Jr., Susan, Byron, Shari, Randy, David, Allison, Jennifer, Jaymie Page. BA, Am. Internat. Coll., 1948; MS, U. Mass., 1951, Ed.D., 1968; postgrad., NYU, 1952-55; prof. diploma, U. Conn., 1964; JD, Western New Eng. Coll., 1978. Bar: Mass. 1978, U.S. Supreme Ct. 1981. Prin., tchr. Gilbertville Grammar Sch., Hardwick, Mass., 1948-49; sch. counselor West Springfield High Sch., Mass., 1949-53; instr. NYU, 1953-54; supt. schs. New Shoreham, R.I., 1954-56; asst. prof. edn. Mich. State U., 1956-58; sch. psychologist, guidance dir. Pub. Sch. System, East Long, Mass., 1958-62; lectr. Westfield State Coll., 1961-65; dir. pupil services Chicopee Pub. Sch., 1965-68; assoc. prof. counselor edn. U. Hartford, West Hartford, Mass., 1968-71, prof., 1971-85, dir. Inst. Coll. Counselors Minority and Low Income Students, 1971-72, dir. Div. Human Services, 1972-77; cons. Aetna Life & Casualty Co., Hartford, 1962-75; hearing officer Conn. State Bd. Edn., 1980-99; exec. dir. Sinapi Assocs., 1959-78; pvt. practice, Ashfield, Mass., 1978—. Co-author: Better Driving, 1958; assoc. editor: Highway Safety and Driver Education, 1954; chmn. editorial com.: Man and the Motor Car, 5th edit., 1954; contbr. numerous articles to profl. jours. Chief Welfare Svcs. Civil Def., Levittown, N.Y., 1953-54; chmn. Ashfield Planning Bd., Mass., 1979-83; moderator Town of Ashfield, 1980-81, town counsel, Charlemont, Mass., 1983-84; mem. jud. nominating coun. Western Regional Com., 1993-99; mem. Mohawk Regional Sch. Com., 1999-2000. Mem. ABA, APA, Mass. Bar Assn., Mass. Acad. Trial Attys., Am. Pers. and Guidance Assn., New Eng. Pers. and Guidance Assn. (bd. dirs.), New Eng. Ednl. Rsch. Orgn. (pres. 1971), Am. Assn. Sch. Adminstrs., Am. Ednl. Rsch. Assn., Mt. Tom Amateur Radio Assn., Franklin County Amateur Radio Club, Elks, Kiwanis (pres. 1988-89, lt. gov. div. 12, 1991-92), Masons (master 1994-96), Shriners, Phi Delta Kappa. Office: PO Box 345 134 Ashfield Mountain Rd Ashfield MA 01330-9505 Home: 3808 Airport Rd Newport VT 05855-9187 Personal E-mail: pepyne@earthlink.net.

PERA, MCCALL, newscaster; B in Broadcast News, U. Ga. Intern WSB-TV, Atlanta; anchor, reporter CNN Affiliate, Athens, Ga.; weekend reporter, spl. projects prodr. WSAV-TV, Savannah, Ga., 1999—2003; weekend reporter, anchor WUPN-TV, Winston-Salem, 2003—. Recipient two Ga. Associated Press Broadcast awards for spot news coverage. Office: WUPN-TV 3500 Myer Lee Dr Winston Salem NC 27101

PERADOTTO, JOHN JOSEPH, classics educator, editor; b. Ottawa, Ill., May 11, 1933; s. John Joseph and Mary Louise (Giacometti) P.; m. Noreen Doran, Aug. 29, 1959 (div. 1982); m. Marlene Rosen, Aug. 29, 1992; children: Erin, Monica, Noreen, Nicole. BA, St. Louis U., 1957, MA, 1958; PhD, Northwestern U., 1963. Instr. classics and English Western Wash. U., Bellingham, 1960-61; instr. Georgetown U., 1961-63, asst. prof. classics, 1963-66, SUNY, Buffalo, 1966-69, asso. prof., 1969-73; prof., chmn. classics U. Tex., Austin, 1973-74; prof. classics SUNY-Buffalo, 1974-2000, Andrew V.V. Raymond prof. classics, 1984-99, Disting. tchg. prof., 1990-2000, Disting. tchg. prof. emeritus, 2000—, chmn. dept., 1974-77, dean div. undergrad. edn., 1978-82. Benedict Disting. vis. prof. Carleton Coll., 2003; Martin lectr. Oberlin Coll., 1987; dir. summer seminar for coll. tchrs. NEH, 1976, for secondary sch. tchrs., 1984; vis. scholar winter quarters U. Calif., San Diego, 2000—. Author: Classical Mythology: An Annotated Bibliographical Survey, 1973, Man in the Middle Voice: Name and Narration in the Odyssey, 1990, also articles and revs.; founding assoc. editor: Arethusa, editor-in-chief:, 1974—95, mem. bd. editors: SUNY Press, 1978—81; editor: SUNY Press Classical Series, 1981—2000, Classical Literature and Contemporary Literary Analysis, 1977, Women in the Ancient World, 1978, 1983, Studies in Latin Literature, 1984, Under the Text; co-editor: Population Policy in Plato and Aristotle, 1975, The New Archilochus, 1976, Augustan Poetry Books, 1980, Indo-European Roots of Classical Culture, 1980, Vergil: 2000 Years, 1981, Texts and Contexts: American Classical Studies in Honor of J.P. Vernant, 1982, Semiotics and Classical Studies, 1983, Audience-oriented Criticism and the Classics, 1986, Herodotus and the Invention of History, 1987, Gonimos: Neoplatonic and Byzantine Studies Presented to L.G. Westerlink at 75, 1988, The Challenge of Black Athena, 1989, Pastoral Revisions, 1990, Reconsidering Ovid's Fasti, 1992, Bakhtin and Classical Studies, 1993, Rethinking the Classical Canon, 1994, Horace: 2000 Years, 1995, The New Simonides, 1996, The Iliad and its Contexts, 1997. Fellow Center for Hellenic Studies, 1972-73; recipient Chancellor's award for teaching excellence State U. N.Y., 1975, Disting. Retiring Editor award Coun. of Editors of Learned Jours., 1995. Mem. Am. Philol. Assn. (dir. 1974-77, pres. 1990), Classical Assn. Atlantic States (exec. com. 1976-78). Office: Dept Classics State U Ny Buffalo NY 14261-0011 Office Phone: 716-645-2154 ext. 115. E-mail: peradott@buffalo.edu.

PERAHIA, MURRAY, pianist; b. NYC, Apr. 19, 1947; m. Naomi Shohet, 1980; 2 children. MS, Mannes Coll. Music; student, Jeannette Haien, Artur Balsam, Mieczyslaw Horszowski; Doctorate (hon.), U. of Leeds, United Kingdom. Appeared with Berlin Philharm., Chgo. Symphony Orch., English Chamber Orch., Boston Symphony Orch., N.Y. Philharm., Cleve. Orch., LA Philharm., Phila. Orch., others; performed with Budapest, Guarneri and Galimir string quartets; performer, artistic dir.: Aldeburgh Festival, 1983-89; apptd. prin. guest condr. Acad. St. Martin in the Fields, 2000; past participant: Marlboro Music Festival; tours in U.S., Can., Europe and Japan; recs. for SONY Classical; 1st Am. to record the Complete Mozart Concertos as condr. with English Chamber Orch., recorded complete Beethoven concertos with Haitink concertgebouw Orch. Recipient Kosciusko Chopin prize, 1965, Avery Fisher prize, 1975, Gramophone Record award, 1997, Grammy award, 1999, 2003, maj. awards including Leeds Competition, 1972. Office: c/o Edna Landau IMG 825 7th Ave New York NY 10019-6014

PERALTA, JOSEPH SORIANO, financial planner; b. Davao City, Philippines, Mar. 11, 1962; came to the U.S., 1984; s. Edward Embry and Rosamar Marfori (Soriano) P.; m. Leslie Sison-Aquino. BS in Commerce with honors, BA in Econs., De La Salle U., 1983; grad. profl. edn. program, Coll. for Fin. Planning, 1992. CFP; registered prin. series 24, registered rep. series 7; enrolled agt., lic. to practice before IRS; cert. sr. advisor. Gen. mgr. RSP Enterprises, Davao City, 1983-84; market rsch. supr. Sheer Communications, Albertson, N.Y., 1985-86; dir. fin. Apex Health Svcs./Kidney Ctr. of Vernon, Tex., 1987-89; CFP FFP Securities, Inc., Orange, Calif., 1990—; pres. Retirement Distbn. and Wealth Mgmt. Strategies, Inc., 1998—, founder, pres. Co-author: Econometric Investigation of the Debt Service Capacity of the Philippines, 1982, Role of Government in the Development of Private Investment Houses, 1983. Mem. Fin. Plannig Assn., Calif. Soc. Enrolled Agts. Democrat. Roman Catholic. Avocations: reading, travel, performing arts, basketball, swimming. Home: 737 Lakewood Pl Pasadena CA 91106-3923 Office: Retirement Distbn and Wealth Mgmt Strategies Inc 2501 E Chapman Ave Ste 230 Fullerton CA 92831-3108

PERANICH, DIANE C. state legislator; b. Biloxi, Miss., Jan. 11, 1940; m. A. John Peranich. State legislator Miss. Ho. of Reps., Jackson, 1988—. Vice chmn. banks and banking com. Miss. Ho. of Reps., mem. apportionment and elections, appropriations, county affairs and transp. coms. Active State Exec. Commn. Miss. Dem. Party; bd. dirs. Crimestoppers; adv. coun. constitution study com. State Bd. of Econ. Devel. Home: 25176 Le Chene Dr Pass Christian MS 39571 Office: State Capitol Bldg Rm 400 E PO Box 1018 Jackson MS 39215-1018

PERATA, DON, state legislator; Tchr. Alameda County Pub. Schs., 1966-81; supr. Alameda County, 1986-94; mem. Calif. State Assembly, 1997-98, chmn. rules com., 1997, chmn. pub. safety com., 1998, majority leader, 1998; mem. Calif. State Senate, 1998—. Democrat. Office: State Capitol Rm 4061 Sacramento CA 95814 also: 1515 Clay St # 2002 Oakland CA 94612-1499

PERCHIK, BENJAMIN IVAN, operations research analyst; b. Passaic, N.J., May 3, 1941; s. Morris and Frances (Antman) P.; m. Ellen Mae Colwell, Aug. 25, 1963 (dec. Oct. 1993); children: Joel, Dawn; m. Mary L. Westcott, Jan. 25, 1994 (div. Mar. 1997). BA, Rutgers U., 1964; postgrad., N.Y. Inst. Tech., 1964-65. Quality control rep. E.R. Squibb Corp., New Brunswick, N.J., 1964-67; edn. specialist Signal Sch., Ft. Monmouth, N.J., 1967-74, Armor Sch., Ft. Knox, Ky., 1974-75, ops. rsch. analyst, 1975-78, HQ TRADOC, Ft. Monroe, Va., 1978-80, Army Material Command, Alexandria, Va., 1980—2004; exec. officer USAREUR ORSA Cell, Alexandria, Va., 1988-90, chmn. supervisory com. credit union, 1985-88, 91—. Cons. Delta Force, Carlisle Barracks, Pa., 1982-84, Internat. Policy Inst., 1983-85, World Future Soc., 1982—; nat. coord. Mansa investment SIG, 1983—; coord. econ. forecasting group Met. Washington Mensa, 1983-99; chmn. security com. Watergate at Landmark, 1985-88; chmn. supervisory com. Commonwealth One FCU, 1992—. Author: ADP Program and Repair, 1972; writer, editor, pub. internat. newsletter Speculation and Investments, 1983—. Chmn. credit com. ComonWealthOne fed. Credit Union, 1982-85; vol. Crisis Link Hot Line; mentor offender aide and restoration Arlington County; sec. Wharf Cluster Bd., 2002—. Mem. Inst. Mgmt. Scis., Ops. Rsch. Soc. Am., Nat. Integrative Health Congress (treas.), Prayer Vigil for Earth (treas.), Wharf Cluster Assn. (sec.), Coast Guard Auxilary. Office: 5001 Eisenhower Ave Alexandria VA 22333-0001 Personal E-mail: perchikb@aol.com. Business E-Mail: perchikb@hqamc.army.mil.

PERCUS, JEROME KENNETH, physicist, researcher; b. N.Y.C., June 21, 1926; s. Philip M. and Gertrude B. (Schweiger) P.; m. Ora Engelberg, May 20, 1965; children: Orin, Allon. BSE.E., Columbia U., 1947, MA, 1948, PhD, 1954. Instr. elec. engring. Columbia U., N.Y.C., 1952-54; asst. prof. Stevens Inst. Tech., Hoboken, N.J., 1955-58; assoc. prof. NYU, N.Y.C., 1958-65, prof. physics, 1965—. Dir. Nat. Biomed. Research Found. Author: (book) Many-Body Problem, 1963, Kinetic Theory and Statistical Mechanics, 1969, Combinatorial Methods, 1971, Combinatorial Methods in Developmental Biology, 1977, Mathematical Methods in Developmental Biology, 1978, Mathematical Methods in Enzymology, 1984, Lectures on the Mathematics of Immunology, 1986, Mathematics of Genome Analysis, 2001; editor: (Jours.) Pattern Recognition, Jour. Statis. Physics. With USN, 1944-46. Recipient Pregel Chemistry Physics award N.Y. Acad. Scis., 1975, Joel Henry Hildebrand award in the Theoretical and Exptl. Chemistry of Liquids, Am. Chem. Soc., 1993, Pattern Rec. Soc. award, 1992. Fellow AAAS, Am. Phys. Soc.; mem. Am. Math. Soc., Sigma Xi. Office: NYU 251 Mercer St New York NY 10012-1110 Office Phone: 212-998-3130. Business E-Mail: percus@cims.nyu.edu.

PERCY, LEE EDWARD, motion picture film editor; b. Kalamazoo, Feb. 10, 1953; s. Richard Noyes and Helen Louise (Sheffield) P. Student, Goodman Sch., Chgo., 1971, Juilliard Sch., 1972; AB, U. Calif., Santa Cruz, 1977. Radio news reporter McGovern Campaign, Chgo., 1972; cons. Kjos Pub. Co., Chgo., 1973-74; dir. VisArt, Ltd., San Francisco, 1977; ind. film editor L.A., 1978—.

Editor: (films) Re-Animator, 1984, Kiss of the Spiderwoman, 1985 (Acad. award Best Actor), Slam Dance, 1987, Checking Out, 1988, Blue Steel, 1989, Reversal of Fortune, 1990 (Acad. award Best Actor), Year of the Gun, 1991, Single White Female, 1992, Against the Wall, 1993 (Eddie award, 1995, nominated for Cable ACE award), Corrina, Corrina, 1994, Kiss of Death, 1995, Before and After, 1996, Desperate Measures, 1997, "54", 1998, Boys Don't Cry, 1999 (Acad. award Best Actress), The Center of the World, 2001, Lift, 2001, The Believer, 2001 (winner Sundance Film Festival), Our Lady of the Assassins (La Virgen de los Sicarrios), 2001, Murder by Numbers, 2002, Maria Full of Grace, 2003 (Sundance Film Festival Audience award, Best Actress at Venice Film Festival), A Home at the End of the World, 2004, A Love Song for Bobby Long, 2004. Mem. Am. Cinema Editors, Acad. of Motion Picture Arts and Scis., Motion Picture Editor's Guild.

PERDEW, JOHN PAUL, physics educator, condensed matter and density functional theorist; b. Cumberland, Md., Aug. 30, 1943; BS, Gettysburg Coll., 1965; PhD, Cornell U., 1971. Postdoctoral fellow U. Toronto, 1971-74, Rutgers U., New Brunswick, N.J., 1974-77; prof. physics Tulane U., New Orleans, 1977—, chair physics dept., 1991—94, 2001—03. Vis. scientist Nordita, Copenhagen, Argonne Nat. Lab., ETH Zurich, ITP Santa Barbara, Naval Rsch. Lab., Washington; invited lectr. more than 68 internat. confs. Contbr. more than 190 sci. articles to profl. jours. NSF Rsch. grantee, 1978—, Petroleum Rsch. Fund grantee 1998-2000; recipient Tulane LAS award for excellence in rsch., 1990. Fellow Am. Phys. Soc.; mem. Am. Chem. Soc., Am. Assn. Physics Tchrs., Internat. Acad. Quantum Molecular Sci., Phi Beta Kappa. Office: Tulane U Dept Physics New Orleans LA 70118 E-mail: perdew@tulane.edu.

PERDIKOU, KIM, information technology executive; BSc. Comp. Sci. and Operational Rsch., Paisley U., Scotland; MA Info. Systems, Pace U. Dir. Network Svcs. Knight Ridder; VP, CIO Women.com Networks, Inc., 1999—2000; CIO Juniper Networks, Inc., Calif., 2000—. Office: Juniper Networks Inc 1194 N Mathilda Ave Sunnyvale CA 94089

PERDUE, BEVERLY E. lieutenant governor, geriatric consultant; b. Grundy, Va., Jan. 14, 1948; d. Alfred P. and Irene E. (Morefield) (dec.) Moore; m. Robert W. Eaves, Jr.; children: Garrett, Emmett. BA, U. Ky., 1969; MEd, U. Fla., 1974, PhD, 1976. Pvt. lectr., writer, cons., 1980-86; pres. The Perdue Co., New Bern, N.C., 1985—; rep. N.C. State Gen. Assembly, Raleigh, 1986-90; senator N.C. Gen. Assembly, Raleigh, 1990-2001; lt. gov. State of N.C., 2001—. Bd. dirs. Nations Bank, New Bern. Bd. dirs. N.C. United Way, Greensboro, 1990-92; exec. mem. N.C. Dem. Party, Raleigh, 1989—; mem. N.C. travel bd. Nat. Conf. State Legislators. Named Outstanding Legislator, N.C. Aging Network, 1989, 92, 100 to Watch, Dem. Leadership Coun. 2003; Toll fellow Nat. Conf. State Legislators, Lexington, Ky., 1992. Mem. Nat. Coun. on Aging, Bus. and Profl. Women, Rotary. Democrat. Episcopalian. Office: Hawkins-Hartness House 310 North Blount Street Raleigh NC 27603 E-mail: bperdue@ncmail.net.*

PERDUE, CHARLES L., JR., social sciences educator, language educator; b. Panthersville, Ga., Dec. 1, 1930; s. Charles L. Sr. and Eva Mae (Samples) Perdue; m. Nancy J. Martin; children: Martin Clay, Marc Charles, Kelly Scott, Kevin Barry(dec.). Student, North Ga. Coll., 1948-49, Santa Rosa (Calif.) Jr. Coll., 1953; AB in Geology, U. Calif., Berkeley, 1958, postgrad., 1958-59; MA in Folklore, U. Pa., 1968, PhD in Folklore, 1971. Engring. writer Convair Astronautics, Vandenberg AFB, Calif., 1959-60; geologist, mineral classification br. U.S. Geol. Survey, Washington, 1960-67; asst. prof. English dept. U. Va., Charlottesville, 1971-72, asst. prof. English, sociology and anthropology depts., 1972-73, from asst. prof. to assoc. prof. English and anthropology depts., 1973—92, prof., 1992—. Cons. in field. Author (with others): (book) Weevils in the Wheat: Interviews with Virginia Ex-Slaves, 1976; author: Outwitting the Devil: Jack Tales from Wise country, Virginia, 1987, Pig's Foot Jelly and Persimmon Beer: Foodways from the Virginia Writers' Project, 1992; author: (with Nancy J. Martin-Perdue) Talk About Trouble: A New Deal Portrait of Virginians in the Great Depression, 1996; contbr. articles to profl. jours. With U.S. Army, 1951—54. Recipient award for Outstanding Book Using Oral History, Nat. Oral History Assn., 1997; Univ. Predoctoral fellow, U. Pa., 1967—71, Wilson Gee Inst. Rsch. grantee, U. Va., 1974, 1975, Rsch. grantee, NEH, 1980—81, 1984. Mem.: Va. Folklore Soc. (archivist, editor 1974—89, archivist 1990—94, archivist, pres. 1995—96, archivist 1997—), Nat. Coun. Traditional Arts (bd. dirs. 1971—87, pres. 1973—79), Mid. Atlantic Folklore Assn. (founding mem., bd. dirs.), Am. Folklore Soc. (exec. bd. 1980—83, book rev. editor jour. 1986—87). Office: U Va Dept Anthropology PO Box 400120 Charlottesville VA 22904-4120 E-mail: clp5a@virginia.edu.

PERDUE, DIANA S. mathematician, educator; d. James C. Perdue and Renate E. Perdue-Davenport; life ptnr. Toni R. Davis, Jan. 1, 1998. BA, Belmont U., 1988; MAT, Jacksonville U., 1991; PhD, U. Va., 1997. Dir. Edward Waters Coll., Jacksonville, Fla., 1989—90; tech. trainer Lockheed Martin, Rsch. Triangle Pk., NC, 1998—99; asst. prof. math. edn. West Tex. A&M U., Canyon, 1999—2003; assoc. prof. math. edn. Va. State U., Petersburg, 2003—. Adj. faculty Jacksonville U., 1980—91, U. Va., Charlottesville, 1991—97. Author of poems. Mem.: Rsch. Coun. Math. Learning, Math. Assn. Am., Nat. Coun. Tchrs. Math., Mensa. Democrat. Mem. United Ch. Of Christ. Avocations: kayaking, reading, white-water rafting. Office: Va State U Math Dept 1 Hayden Dr Petersburg VA 23806 Office Phone: 804-524-5437. E-mail: dperdue@vsu.edu.

PERDUE, FRANKLIN P. retired poultry/agricultural products executive; b. Md., 1920; m. Mitzi Henderson Ayala, July 1988. With Perdue Farms Inc., 1953—88, chmn. exec. com., Perdue Inc. subs. Perdue Farms Inc., Salisbury; chair exec. com. bd. dirs. Perdue Farms, Inc. Address: Perdue Farms PO Box 1656 Horsham PA 19044-6656*

PERDUE, GEORGE (SONNY PERDUE), governor, state legislator; b. Perry, Ga., Dec. 20, 1946; m. Mary; children: Leigh, Lara, Jim, Dan. PhD in Vet. Medicine, U. Ga. Mem. Ga. Senate (dist. 18), Atlanta, 1990—2002; pres. pro tem; mem. appropriations, ethics, rules, reapportionment coms.; also fin. and pub. utilities, health and human svcs. coms.; former chmn. higher edn., def. conversion com.; co-chair joint commn. legis. info. mgmt.; gov. State of Ga., Atlanta, 2003—. Capt. USAF, 1971-74, Vietnam. Democrat. Baptist. Office: Office of the Gov 203 State Capitol Atlanta GA 30334

PERDUE, JAMES A. food products executive; b. 1949; BS, Wake Forest U., 1973; MA in Marine Biology, Southeastern Mass. U., 1976; PhD in Fisheries, U. Wash., 1983. With U. Md., Cambridge, 1976-78; chmn. bd. Perdue Transp., Inc., Salisbury, Md., 1983—, Perdue Farms Inc., 1983—, CEO, chmn. bd., 1991—. Office: Perdue Farms Inc 31149 Old Ocean City Rd Salisbury MD 21804

PERDUE, KAREN, state agency administrator; BA in Biology, Stanford U., 1978. Reporter, photographer Fairbanks (Alaska) Daily News-Miner, 1969-74; editor River Times, Fairbanks, 1974-75; foreman, expeditor Teamsters Union, Alaska Pipeline, 1975-76; health planner Tanana Chiefs Conf., Fairfanks, 1977; instr., counselor Stanford (Calif) Med. Ctr., 1978; rsch. dir. Fairbanks Town and Village Assn., 1978-79; legis. aide/press sec. U.S. Senator Ted Stevens, Washington, 1979-80; spl. asst. to lt. gov. Terry Miller State of Alaska, 1980-82; dir. Divsn. of Cmty. Devel., Dept. of Cmty. and Regional Affairs, Juneau, 1982-85; dep. commr. Dept. of Health and Social Svcs., Juneau, 1985-90; cons., ptrn. Northern Rsch. and Planning, 1991—; commr. Alaska Dept. of Health and Social Svcs., 1995—. Office: Health & Social Svcs Dept Office Commr PO Box 110601 Juneau AK 99811-0601 E-mail: karen_perdue@health.state.ak.us.

PERDUNN, RICHARD FRANCIS, management consultant; b. Trenton, N.J., Dec. 12, 1915; s. Francis R. and Edith (Nogle) P.; m. Eugenia E. Morel, June 7, 1941; 1 child, Justine Reneau; m. Doris D. Andrus, Jan. 30, 1993. BS, Lehigh U., 1939; postgrad. student, U. Pitts., 1939-40, Johns Hopkins, 1941-42. With U.S. Steel Co., also Glenn L. Martin, 1939-43, supt. machine and assembly, 1941-43; partner Nelson & Perdunn (engrs. and cons., also); v.p. Penco Corp., 1947-49; with Merck & Co., 1949-54, mgr. adminstrn., 1951-54; with Stevenson, Jordan & Harrison (mgmt. engrs.), N.Y.C., 1954-68, exec. v.p., 1962-64, pres., 1964-68; pres., chief exec. officer Bachman-Jacks, Inc., Reading, Pa., 1968-71; sr. v.p. Golightly Internat., N.Y.C., 1971—, also dir. Chmn. Perdunn Assocs., Inc., 1979—, dir. West Point & Annapolis Text Book Pub. Co., 1948—, Indsl. Edn. Films Inc., 1966—, Eldun Corp., 1964—, Security Nat. Bank, Newark, 1964—, Surburban Life Ins. Co., 1966—, Mainstem Inc., 1965—, Greenhouse Decor Inc., 1961—, Neuwirth Mut. Fund Inc., 1975—; Lectr. on finance and mfg. in, U.S., Can., Eng., Sweden. Assoc. editor: Systems and Procedures Quar, 1948-51; Contbr. articles to profl. publs. Bd. dirs. Inst. Better Confs., Internat. Inst. Bus. Devel., Inst. Urban Affairs, People Care, Inc.; dir. finance Assn. Help for Retarded Children. Served with USAAF, 1942-47. Mem. N.Y.C. C. of C., Council Econ. Devel., Am. Mgmt. Assn., AIM (pres.'s council), Newcomen Soc. N.Am., Systems and Procedures Assn. Am., Soc. Advanced Mgmt. Address: Perdunn % J P Kovacs PO Box 700 New Vernon NJ 07976-0700

PEREL, JAMES MAURICE, pharmacology and psychiatry educator, researcher; b. Buenos Aires, Mar. 30, 1933; came to U.S., 1947, naturalized, 1954; s. Aria and Bella (Silverberg) P.; m. July 18, 1959 (div. 1971); 1 child, Allan B.; m. Audrey Feldman, Apr. 9, 1972; children: Alissa A., Stephen M. BS, CUNY, 1956; MS, NYU, 1961, PhD, 1964. Nuclear chemist N.Y. Naval Shipyard Lab., Bklyn., 1956-58; assoc. rsch. scientist NYU, Goldwater Meml. Hosp., N.Y.C., 1964-67; asst. prof. medicine and chemistry Emory U., Atlanta, 1967-70; asst. prof. psychiatry, pharmacology Columbia U. Coll. Physicians and Surgeons, N.Y.C., 1970-76; assoc. prof. clin. pharmacology, chief psychiat. rsch. N.Y. State Psychiat. Inst., N.Y.C., 1976-80; chief clin. pharmacology VA Med. Ctr. Highland Drive, Pitts., 1979-83; prof. psychiatry U. Pitts. Sch. Medicine, 1980—2001, acting chmn. dept. pharmacology, 1985-88, prof. pharmacology, 1980—, prof. emeritus psychiatry, 2001—; dir. clin. pharmacology Western Psychiat. Inst. and Clinic, Pitts., 1980—; prof. grad. neurosci., 1988—; postdoctoral fellow in clin. pharmacology NIH and NYU, 1964-67. Lectr. chemistry CUNY, 1963-67; assoc. rsch. scientist N.Y. State Psychiat. Inst., 1970-76; cons., mem. grant-awarding study sects. NIH, NIMH. Mem. editorial bd. Psychopharmacology, Neuropsychobiology, Therapeutic Drug Monitoring, Focus on Schizophrenia and Bipolar Disorders; contbr. over 400 articles to sci. jours., chpts. to books. Recipient Founders Day award NYU, 1974, Julius Koch Meml. award Rho Chi, 1983; named Psychopharmacologist of Yr., U. Toronto, 1993; predoctoral fellow NSF, 1958-60; numerous rsch. grants, including NIH, NIMH, Founds. Fund for Rsch. in Psychiatry, pharm. cos., pvt. founds. Fellow Am. Inst. Chemists; mem. Am. Soc. Clin. Pharmacology and Therapeutics, Am. Soc. Pharmacology and Exptl. Therapeutics, Am. Chem. Soc., Internat. Assn. Therapeutic Drug Monitoring and Clin. Toxicology, Soc. for Biol. Psychiatry, Sigma Xi. Jewish. Achievements include discovery of several widely-used pharmacotherapeutic agents. Office: U Pitts Sch Medicine 3811 Ohara St Pittsburgh PA 15213-2593 E-mail: pereljm@upmc.edu., pereljm@pitt.edu.

PERELLA, JOSEPH ROBERT, investment banker, securities company executive; b. Newark, Sept. 20, 1941; s. Dominic A. and Agnes P.; m. Amy Gralnick, Jan. 20, 1974 BS, Lehigh U., 1964; MBA, Harvard U., 1972. C.P.A., N.Y. Pub. acct. Haskins & Sells, NYC, 1964-70; cons. Internat. Bank for Reconstruction & Devel., Washington, 1971; assoc. The First Boston Corp., NYC, 1972-74, asst. v.p., 1974-75, v.p., 1975-78, mng. dir., 1978-88; chmn. Wasserstein, Perella & Co., NYC, 1988—2001; head, investment banking div. Morgan Stanley & Co., Inc., NYC, 1997—2000, chmn.,institutional securities, 2000—. Trustee Lehigh U. Office: Wasserstein Perella & Co 31 W 52nd St Fl 7 New York NY 10019-6163 also: Morgan Stanley & Co Inc 1585 Broadway New York NY 10036 Office Phone: 212-761-4000.

PERELLE, IRA B. psychologist, educator; b. Mt. Vernon, NY, Sept. 16, 1925; s. Joseph Yale and Lillian (Schaffer) P.; m. Diane A. Granville, 1982; 1 child, Jessica Eve. Student, U. Tex., 1943; grad. in elec. engring, R.C.A. Inst., 1951; student, Iona Coll., 1952—53; BS, Fordham U., 1969, MS, 1970, PhD, 1972. Prodn. mgr. Arden Jewelry Case Co., 1946-49; became chief engr. Westlab Electronic Service Engrs., 1949; ptnr. Westlab, 1954; pres. Westlab, Inc., 1955-64, chmn. bd., 1956; pres. Westchester Research and Devel. Labs., 1953-65; exec. dir. Interlink, Ltd., 1966—; dir. Atlantic Research Inst., 1975—. Cons. higher edn. divsn. U.S. Dept. of Edn., 1994—; cons. ednl. research Fordham U., Catholic U. of P.R., Bayamon (P.R.) Central U., World U., San Juan, P.R., John Jay Coll., N.Y.C., Rockland C.C., N.Y.; rsch. cons. So. Westchester County Bd. Coop. Ednl. Services; stats. cons. City of Mt. Vernon (N.Y.), Reader's Digest, Pleasantville, N.Y., GT&E Inc., CUNY; devel. dir. Animal Behavior Soc.; served as expert witness for N.Y. State Tax Ct.; assoc. Columbia U. Seminars; prof. dept. psychology NYU; prof. dept. bus. and econs., dept. psychology Mercy Coll., Dobbs Ferry, N.Y.; prof. Grad. Sch. Bus., L.I. U.; adj. prof. SUNY-Purchase, Fordham U., N.Y.C.; vis. prof. Fairleigh Dickenson U.; faculty adv. com. Mercer County Coll., 1969-73; conf. leader Nat. Conf. Ednl. Tech., 1971-73. Author: A Practical Guide to Educational Media for the Classroom Teacher, 1974; also articles; research on laterality for evolutionary biology. Discoverer Perelle Phenomenon, psychology-attention. Mem. staff Civil Def., 1954-74; bd. dirs. Mid-Hudson Inst., Dobbs Ferry, N.Y. Served as radio instr. USAAF, 1943-45. With USAAF, 1943—45. Mem. IEEE, AAAS, N.Y. Zool. Soc., Assn. Ednl. Communication and Tech., N.Y. State Ednl. Communication Assn., Audio Engring. Soc., Acoustical Soc. Am., Am. Inst. Physics, Am. Psychol. Assn., Am. Ednl. Rsch. Assn., Am. Statis. Assn., Animal Behavior Soc., Am. Genetic Soc., N.Y. Acad. Scis. Office: Mercy Coll Dept of Psychology & Bus Econ Dobbs Ferry NY 10522 Office Phone: 914-674-7486. Business E-Mail: iperelle@mercy.edu.

PERELMAN, MICHAEL A, education educator, psychologist; s. Marshall "Buddy" and Estherann Perelman; m. Jane Terker Perelman; children: Matthew H.T., Grant Aaron. BA, U. Wis., Madison, Wis., 1971; MS, Columbia U., N.Y., 1973, MPhil, 1975, PhD, 1976. Diplomate AASECT Certified: Sex Therapist, Sex Supervisor, Sex Educator Am. Assn. of Sex Educators, Counselors, and Therapists, lic. psychologist NY, registered Health Svc. Providers in Psychology Nat. Register of Health Svc. Providers, cert. AGPA Certified Group Therapist Nat. Registry of Cert. Group Psychotherapists. Chief intern in med. psychology Duke U. Med. Ctr., Durham, NC, 1973—74; fellow Payne Whitney Clinic, NY Hosp., Cornell U. Med. Ctr., N.Y., 1976—77; co-dir., human sexuality program Payne Whitney Clinic, Dept. of Psychiatry, NY Presbyn. Hosp., Weill Cornell Med. Ctr., N.Y.; clin. assoc. prof. of psychology in psychiatry, reproductive medicine, and urology Weill Med. Coll. of Cornell U., N.Y.; sr. cons. psychologist/sex therapist NY Ctr. for Human Sexuality; Dept. of Urology, Columbia U., Columbia Presbyn. Med. Ctr., N.Y.; clin. psychologist in pvt. practice Dr. Michael A. Perelman & Assoc., N.Y.; cons., speaker's bur. Bayer/Glaxo SmithKline Pharml., New Haven, 2001—, Proctor & Gamble, Ohio, 2001—; cons. speaker's bur. Johnson & Johnson, NJ, 2001—; cons., speaker's bur. Lilly/ICOS, Indianapolis, Ind., 2001—, Johnson & Johnson, Raritan, NJ, Pfizer Corp., N.Y., 1997—, TAP Pharml., Deerfield, Ill., 1999—, Pharmacia Corp., Kalamazoo, 1999—; cons. HBO, N.Y., 1998—2001. Bd. of directors Internat. Acad. of Eclectic Psychotherapy, 1990—91; cons. editor Jour. of Sex Edn. and Therapy, 1978—81, Jour. of Integrative & Eclectic Psychotherapy, 1990—92; dept. editor, sex therapy today Contemporary Urology, 1994—97; judge Nat. Acad. of Arts & Sciences, Los Angeles, Calif., 1989; cons. editor Jour. of Sex and Marital Therapy; us cialis ed adv. bd. Lilly/ICOS; vardenafil primary care adv. bd. Bayer/GlaxoSmithKline; us cialis mental health adv. bd. Lilly/ICOS; bd. of dir. Soc. for Sex Therapy and Rsch., 1981—84, Am. Assn. of Sex Educators, Counselors and Therapists, 1983—87; ed adv. bd. TAP Pharml.; bd. of dir. Tango Comm., 1996—97. Contbr. articles to prof. jour., chapters to books. Recipient Apptd. by Chancellor to the Human Rights Commn. of the U. Wis., U. Wis., 1969-1971; scholar, Ill. State Scholarship, 1967; Pub. Health Svc. Fellowship, NIMH, 1971-1975. Fellow: Internat. Acad. of Eclectic Psychotherapists; mem.: Am. Assn. of Sex Educators, Counselors and Therapists (chairperson, task force on certification 1983—87), Am. Assn. of Sex Educators, Counselors and Therapists (long range planning com. 1981—82), Am. Group Psychotherapy Assn., Manhattan Psychol. Assn., Soc. for the Exploration of Psychotherapy Integration, Soc. for Sex Therapy and Rsch., NY Soc. of Clin. Psychologists, NY State Regional Psychol. Assn., Soc. for the Sci. Study of Sex, Assn. for the Advancement of Behavior Therapy, Internat. Soc. for Study of Women's Sexual Health, Internat. Soc. for Sexual Impotence Rsch. (ISSIR), Internat. Acad. of Sex Rsch., Assn. of Med. Sch. Professors of Psychology, Am. Urol. Assn., APA, Sexual Medicine Soc. of N.Am., Phi Kappa Phi. Office: Dr Michael A Perelman & Assoc 70 East 77th St Ste 1C New York NY 10021-1811 Office Phone: 212-570-5000. E-mail: perelman@earthlink.net.

PERELMAN, RONALD OWEN, diversified holding company executive; b. Greensboro, N.C., 1943; s. Raymond and Ruth (Caplan) P.; m. Claudia Cohen; 4 children. BA, U. Pa., 1964; MBA, Wharton Sch. Fin., 1966. With Belmont Industries Inc., 1966-78; chmn., chief exec. officer, dir. MacAndrews & Forbes Holdings Inc., Wilmington, Del., 1983—; chmn., chief exec. officer MacAndrews & Forbes Group Inc. (subs.), N.Y.C., 1978—; chmn., chief exec. officer, dir. Revlon Group Inc. (subs. MacAndrews & Forbes Group Inc.), N.Y.C., 1985—, Revlon Inc. (subs.), N.Y.C., 1985—; also chmn. Nat. Health Labs. Inc., La Jolla, Calif., 1985—, Andrews Group Inc., N.Y.C., 1985—; pres. Solomon R. Guggenheim Mus., N.Y.C., 1995—. Jewish. Office: Revlon Group Inc 625 Madison Ave Fl 8 New York NY 10022-1894 also: Solomark Guggenheim Mus 1071 5th Ave New York NY 10128-0173

PERENCHIO, ANDREW JERROLD, film and television executive; b. Fresno, Calif., Dec. 20, 1930; s. Andrew Joseph and Dorothea (Harvey) P.; m. Robin Green, July 16, 1954 (div.); children: Candace L., Catherine M., John Gardner; m. Jacquelyn Claire, Nov. 14, 1969 (div.); m. Margaret McHugh, 1987. BS, UCLA, 1954. V.p. Music Corp. Am., 1958-62, Gen. Artists Corp., 1962-64; pres., owner theatrical agy. Chartwell Artists, Ltd., L.A., from 1964; chmn. bd. Tandem Prodns., Inc. and TAT Communications Co., L.A., 1973-83; pres., CEO Embassy Pictures, L.A., 1983—85; pres. Chartwell Partnerships Group, L.A.; chmn., CEO Univision Communications, 1992—. Promoter Muhammad Ali-Joe Frazier heavyweight fight, 1971, Bobby Riggs-Billie Jean King tennis match, 1973. Served to 1st lt. USAF, 1954-57. Mem.: Bel-Air Country (Los Angeles); Westchester (N.Y.) Country; Friars (N.Y.C.). Office: Univision Communications 1999 Ave Of Stars Ste 3050 Los Angeles CA 90067-4611*

PERERA, LAWRENCE THACHER, lawyer; b. Boston, June 23, 1935; s. Guido R. and Faith (Phillips) P.; m. Elizabeth A. Wentworth, July 5, 1961; children: Alice V. Perera Lucey, Caroline F. Perera Barry, Lucy E., Lawrence Thacher, Jr., Perera Adams. BA, Harvard U., 1957, LL.B., 1961. Bar: Mass. 1961, U.S. Supreme Ct. 1973. Clk. Judge R. Ammi Cutter, Mass. Supreme Jud. Ct., Boston, 1961-62; assoc. Palmer & Dodge, Boston, 1962-69, ptnr., 1969-74; judge Middlesex County Probate Ct., East Cambridge, Mass., 1974-79; ptnr. Hemenway & Barnes, Boston, 1979—. Mem. nat. coun. Hon. Nat. Jud. Coll., Reno, prof., pres. Mass. CLE, Inc., 1988-90; trustee Mass. Investors Inst., 1981—; trustee, vice chmn. Boston Found., 1981-1996. Chmn. Boston Fin. Commn., 1969-71; overseer Boston Lyric Opera; chmn. bd. overseers Boston Opera Assn.; chmn. Back Bay Archtl. Commn., 1966-72; trustee emeritus Sta. WGBH Ednl. Found., Boston Athenaeum, Wang Ctr. Performing Arts. Fellow Am. Acad. Matrimonial Lawyers, Am. Coll. Trust and Estate Counsel; mem. ABA, Am. Bar Found., Am. Law Inst., Mass. Bar Assn., Mass. Bar Found., Boston Bar Assn., Boston Bar Found. Home: 18 Marlborough St Boston MA 02116-2101 Office: 60 State St Boston MA 02109-1800

PERES, JUDITH MAY, journalist; b. Chgo., June 30, 1946; d. Leonard H. and Eleanor (Seltzer) Zurakov; m. Michael Peres, June 27, 1972; children: Dana, Avital. BA, U. Ill., 1967; M Studies in Law, Yale U., 1997. Acct. exec. Daniel J. Edelman Inc., Chgo., 1967-68; copy editor Jerusalem (Israel) Post, 1968-71, news editor, 1971-75, chief night editor, 1975-80, editor, style book, 1978-80; copy editor Chgo. Tribune, 1980-82, rewriter, 1982-84, assoc. fgn. editor, 1984-90, nat. editor, 1990-95, nat./fgn. editor, 1995-96, specialist writer, 1997—; Yale Law fellow, 1996-97. Recipient Media award, U. Mich., 2000. Office: Chicago Tribune 435 N Michigan Ave Chicago IL 60611-4066 Office Phone: 312-222-4330. Business E-Mail: jperes@tribune.com.

PERESS, MAURICE, symphony conductor, musicologist; b. N.Y.C., Mar. 18, 1930; s. Haskell Ben Ezra and Elka (Tygier) P. BA, N.Y.U., 1951; postgrad., Mannes Coll. Music, NYU Grad. Sch. Musicology. Asst. condr. Mannes Coll. Music, 1957-60; music dir. NYU, 1958-61; asst. condr. New York Philharmonic, 1961-62; music dir. Corpus Christi (Tex.) Symphony, 1961-74, Austin Symphony, 1970-72, Kansas City Philharm., 1974-80; dir. Bur. Indian Affairs pilot project Communication through Music, 1968; faculty Queens Coll., 1969-70, 83—; mus. dir. world premiere Bernstein Mass, J.F. Kennedy Center, Washington, 1971. Pub.: musical adaptation and devel. Ellington Opera, Queenie Pie; orchestrations: Ellington, New World 'a Comin', Black Brown and Beige, Bernstein West Side Story Overture; reconstrn. Gershwin's "Strike Up the Band", 1929, Paul Whiteman's Historic Aeolian Hall concert of 1924 (recorded Musical Heritage Soc.), Duke Ellington's First Carnegie Hall concert, 1944; George Antheil's 1927 Carnegie Hall "Ballets Mécanique" concert (recorded Musical Heritage Soc.); James Reese Europes Clef Club concert, 1912, First "All Negro" concert composed and performed by African Ams. in Carnegie Hall; author: Some Music Lessons for American Indian Youngsters, 1968; contbr. articles profl. jours. Served with AUS, 1953-55. Named Millicent James fellow NYU, 1955; Mannes Coll. scholar, 1955-57. Mem. ASCAP, Conductor's Guild, The Friends of Earl Robinson (pres.), Dvorak Am. Soc. (bd. dirs.), Am. Soc. for Jewish Music (bd. dirs.). Jewish. Home: 310 W 72nd St New York NY 10023-2675

PERETSMAN, NANCY B. investment banker; b. Worcester, Mass., Mar. 27, 1954; d. George Peretsman and Norma (Burofsky) O'Haire. AB with hons., Princeton U., 1976; MPPM, Yale, 1979. V.p. Blyth, Eastman, Dillon & Co., N.Y.C., 1979—83; dir., head of media group Salomon Bros., N.Y.C., 1983—95; exec. v.p., mng. dir. Allen & Co., N.Y.C., 1995—. Bd. mem. Charter Comm., Inc. Charter trustee, Princeton U., 1976—.*

PEREY, RON, lawyer; b. Cleve., Feb. 2, 1943; s. John Perecinsky and Anne (Nagy) Disman; 1 child, Page Suzanne; m. Janice Ash, Aug. 19, 1995. BA in Polit. Sci., Miami U., Oxford, Ohio, 1965; JD cum laude, Ohio State U., 1968. Bar: Wash. 1968, U.S. Dist. Ct. (we. dist.) Wash. 1968, U.S. Ct. Appeals (9th cir.) 1973, U.S. Supreme Ct. 1985. Assoc. Reed McClure, Seattle, 1968-71, ptnr., 1971-82, Perey & Smith, Seattle, 1982-86, Perey Langley, Seattle, 1986-92; owner Law Offices of Ron Perey, Seattle, 1992—. Lectr. in field of personal injury and trial practice. Contbr. articles to profl jours. Fellow Roscoe Pound Found.; mem. ATLA (state del. 1989-90), ABA (litigation sect.), King County Bar Assn. (chmn. med.-legal com. 1989-90), Wash. State Trial Lawyers Assn. (bd. govs. 1983-85, 89-91), Am. Bd. Trial Advs. (diplomate; nat. bd. rep. 1996—, treas. 1998, v.p. 1999), Wash. State Bar Assn. (bd. govs. 1994-97), Damage Attys. Round Table. Democrat. Avocations: travel, reading, weightlifting, tennis, hiking, jogging. Office: Market Place Tower 2025 1st Ave Ste 250 Seattle WA 98121-2147

PEREYRA-SUAREZ, CHARLES ALBERT, lawyer; b. Paysandu, Uruguay, Sept. 7, 1947; arrived in U.S., 1954, naturalized, 1962; s. Hector and Esther (Enriquez-Sarano) Pereyra-Suarez; m. Susan H. Cross, Dec. 30, 1983. BA in History magna cum laude, Pacific Union Coll., 1970; postgrad., UCLA, 1970-71; JD, U. Calif., Berkeley, 1975. Bar: Calif. 1975, DC 1980. Staff atty. Western Ctr. Law and Poverty, Inc., LA, 1976; trial atty. civil rights divsn. U.S. Dept. Justice, Washington, 1976—79, asst. U.S. atty., criminal divsn. LA, 1979—82; sr. litig. assoc. Gibson, Dunn & Crutcher, LA, 1982—84; pvt. practice LA, 1984—86, 1998—; ptnr. McKenna & Cuneo, LA, 1986—95, Davis Wright Tremaine, LA, 1995—98. Democrat. Avocations: tennis, jogging, travel. Office Phone: 213-623-5923.

PEREZ, ANTONIO M. consumer products company executive; b. Spain; BSEE, Madrid U. Corp. v.p., mem. exec. coun., pres. consumer bus. Hewlett-Packard Co., pres., CEO inkjet imaging bus., 1995—99; pres., CEO Gemplus Internat., 2000—01; pres., COO Eastman Kodak Co., Rochester, NY, 2003—. Chmn. bd. dirs. Previo (formerly Stac Software); bd. mem. Adobe Sys. Office: Eastman Kodak Co 343 State St Rochester NY 14650

PEREZ, AUGUST, III, architectural firm executive; Ptnr. Perez, Ernst, Farnet Archs., New Orleans. Office: Perez Ernst Farnet Archs 909 Poydras St Ste 2250 New Orleans LA 70112-1097

PEREZ, CARLOS F. health facility administrator; BS, Hobart Coll., 1974; MPA, NYU, 1974-76. Administrv. intern Kings County Hosp., NYU Med. Ctr., Bronx Psychiat. Ctr., 1973-75; adminstrv. asst. to dep. commr. N.Y.C. Dept. Health, 1975-76; adminstrv. resident Met. Hosp. Ctr., N.Y.C., 1975-77; night-weekend adminstr. Bronx Psychiat. Ctr., 1975-77; assoc. dir. Queens Hosp. Ctr., Jamaica, N.Y., 1977-78; sr. mental health program analyst Health and Hosp. Corp., N.Y.C., 1981-83; dep. area administr. N.Y. State Dept. Health, 1983-89, dir. hosp. surveillance, 1988-89, area adminstr. N.Y.C. Office Health Sys. Mgmt., 1988-95, v.p. for network devel. mental health divsn., 1995—; sr. v.p., exec. dir. N.Y.C. H.H.C. Bellevue Hosp., 1997—. Presenter numerous papers. Recipient Peter B. Schwab Meml. trust fund scholarship, 1973-74, 75-76; Martin Luther King fellow, 1974. Mem. Nat. Assn. Health Svcs. Execs., Hispanic Assn. Health Svcs. Execs., Assn. Univ. Programs in Hosp. Adminstrn., P.R. Health Svcs. Fedn. Office: Bellevue Hosp Ctr 462 1st Ave New York NY 10016-9196

PEREZ, DIANNE M. medical researcher; b. Cleve., Dec. 13, 1959; BA in Chemistry and Biology with honors, Coll. of Wooster, 1982; PhD in Chemistry, Calif. Inst. Tech., 1988. Grad. rsch. asst. dept. chemistry Calif. Inst. Tech., Pasadena, 1982—87, grad. tchg. asst. introductory chemistry and biochemistry, 1982—87; sr. rsch. scientist Specialty Labs., Inc., Santa Monica, Calif., 1987—88; fellow dept. eye rsch. Doheny Eye Inst., L.A., 1988—89; fellow dept. heart and hypertension rsch. Cleve. Clinic Found., 1989—91, rsch. assoc. dept. cardiovasc. biology, 1992—93, project scientist dept. molecular cardiology, 1993—95, mem. asst. staff dept. molecular cardiology, 1996—. Coord. Molecular Cardiology's Protein Group Seminar Series Cleve. Clinic Found., 1994—95, supr. DNA Synthesis Core Facility Rsch. Inst., fellow's rep. Dept. Heart and Hypertension Rsch. to Divsn. Com.; adj. asst. prof. dept. pharmacology U. Ky., Lexington, 1994—; manuscript referee Molecular Pharmacology, Circulation Rsch., Cardiovasc. Rsch., Jour. Pharmacology and Exptl. Therapeutics, Gene, Biochemistry; lectr. in field. Contbr. articles to profl. jours.; patentee in field. Recipient Nat. Rsch. Svc. award, NIH, 1991; grantee Glaxo, 1994—; scholar Lubrizol, Coll. of Wooster, 1980. Mem.: AAAS, Am. Soc. Biochemistry and Molecular Biology, Am. Chem. Soc. (cert.), Am. Heart Assn. (Established Investigator award 1996), Am. Soc. Pharmacology and Therapeutics, Sigma Xi, Iota Sigma Pi, Phi Beta Kappa.

PEREZ, EDDIE A. mayor; b. Corozal, PR, 1957; arrived in U.S., 1969; m. Maria Perez; 2 children. AAS in Liberal Arts, Capital Cmty. Coll.; BA in Econs., Trinity Coll. Assoc. v.p. cmty. and govt. rels. Trinity Coll.; mayor City of Hartford, Hartford, Conn., 2002—. Exec. dir., chmn. Southside Instns. Neighborhood Alliance, Inc. (SINA); vol. VISTA, 1978; founder, dir. O.N.E./C.H.A.N.E., Inc., North Hartford; dir. program MASH (Make Something Happen), Urban League Greater Hartford, Conn. Puerto Rican Forum; former commr. Met. Dist.; established teen pregnancy program Breaking the Cycle; MetroHartford Regional Econ. Alliance. Office: 550 Main St Hartford CT 06103

PEREZ, EDITH R. lawyer; BA, U. Calif., Davis, 1976; JD, U. Calif., Berkeley, 1980. Bar: Calif. 1982. Vis. atty. Sergio Augusto Malta Advogados, Rio de Janeiro, Pablo Martinez Cano y Asociados, Mexico City; with Latham & Watkins, L.A., 1984—. Mem. adv. com. on women in svcs. U.S. Dept. Def.; mem. bd. dirs. Hugh O'Brian Youth Leadership Found., Nat. Conf. Christians and Jews, Cmty. Enhancement Corp., Mex.-Am. Legal Def. and Ednl. Fund, ARC, Latino Mus. History, Art and Culture; bd. regents Loyola Marymount U.; mem. adv. coun. on equal opportunity to CEO of So. Calif. Edison; mem. Calif. Gov.'s Task Force on Diversity and Outreach. V.p. L.A. Bd. Recreation and Pks. Commrs., 1994—95; pres. L.A. Bd. Police Commrs., 1997—99; mem. bd. dirs. Nat. Recreation Found., Ctr. for Study of L.A., Loyola Marymount U., Oakwood Sch. Named one of 25 Up-and-Coming Attys. Who Are Making a Difference in Calif., L.A. Daily Jour., 1994, 100 Most Influential Hispanics in U.S., Hispanic Bus. Mag., 1996; recipient Bringing Up Daughters Differently award, NOW Legal Def. and Edn. Fund, 1996, Redesigning Policing award, Nat. Ctr. for Women and Policing, 1997, Cmty. Commitment award, Calif. Latino Civil Rights Network, 1998, Women of Achievement award, Anti-Defamation League, 1998, Legal Svcs. award, Mex.-Am. Legal Def. and Ednl. Fund., 1998, Twice a Citizen award, L.A. Police Res. Found., 1999. Mem.: ABA, Mex. Am. Bar Assn., L.A. County Bar Assn., Calif. State Bar Assn. Office: Latham and Watkins LLP 633 W Fifth St Ste 4000 Los Angeles CA 90071

PEREZ, FRANCISCO, JR., music educator; b. Chula Vista, Calif., Feb. 11, 1975; s. Francisco Perez, Sr. and Guadalupe Perez; m. Cynthia Agold, June 19, 2004. MusB in Trombone Performance, U. of So. Calif., L.A., 1997, MusB in Music Edn., 1998, MusM in Edn., M.M.Ed., 2003. Profl. clear single subject tchg. credential - in music Calif., Kodály Cert. Level I Orgn. of Am. Kodály Educators. Band dir. Bellflower (Calif.) H.S., 1998—2001, Ganesha H.S., Pomona, Calif. Clinician, lectr., Calif.; freelance musician, Calif.; lectr. Calif. Music Educator's Conf., 2001. Recipient David Falconner scholarship for rsch. in the Kodály Method of Tchg., U. of So. Calif., 1996, Outstanding Collegiate award, Calif. Music Educator's Assn., 1998. Mem.: Calif. Band Dir.'s Assn., Calif. Tchr.'s Assn., Internat. Trombone Assn., So. Calif. Band Dir.'s Assn. (assoc.), Blue Key, Phi Kappa Phi, Pi Kappa Lambda. Presbyterian. Avocations: travel, computers, music. Office: Ganesha H S 1151 Fairplex Dr Pomona CA 91768 Office Phone: 909-397-4400. Office Fax: 909-629-4069. E-mail: fperez@alumni.usc.edu.

PEREZ, GABRIEL FELAN, music educator; s. Eduardo A. and Estella H. Perez. MusB, Sam Houston State U., 1993. Chorister Houston Grand Opera, 1993—99; music tchr. Northbrook H.S., Houston, 1995—2001; vocal tchr. Hastings-on-Hudson (N.Y.) H.S., 2002—. Arts in edn. coord. Hastings Sch. Dist., Hastings-on-Hudson, 2003—. Mem.: NYSSMA. Avocations: opera, travel, museums, walking, performing arts.

PEREZ, JEAN-YVES, engineering company executive; b. 1945; Ingenieur Civil Engring., Ecole Centrale des Arts et Manufactures, Paris, 1967; MS, U. Ill., 1970. With Soletanche Enterprise, 1971-72; pres., CEO Woodward-Clyde Group, Inc., Denver, 1967-70, 73-97; exec. v.p. URS Greiner Woodward Clyde, Denver, 1998—. With French Air Force, 1970-71. Office: URS 4582 S Ulster St Ste 600 Denver CO 80237-2635

PEREZ, JORGE LUIS, retired manufacturing executive; b. Jaguey Grande, Matanzas, Cuba, Nov. 29, 1945; came to U.S., 1960; s. Adalberto Aquileo and Esther Mireya (Haedo) P.; children: Jorge Alejandro, Ricardo Javier, Ruben Luis. BS in Commerce & Engring. Sci., Drexel U., 1969, MBA, 1981. Jr. indsl. engr. IBM Corp., East Fishkill, N.Y., 1969-70, assoc. indsl. engr., 1970-71, sr. assoc. indsl. engr., 1972-75, staff indusl. engr., 1976-77, ops. rsch. analyst Princeton, N.J., 1977-80, fin. program adminstr. Franklin Lakes, N.J., 1980-82, mgr. production control Boca Raton, Fla., 1983-85, project mgr. div., 1986-88, program mgr., 1988-92, ret., 1992. Pres. Presch. Mgmt., Inc., 1999; ind. cons. Eclipse Group. Author: (manuals) Machine Tooling, Transportation Forecasting, Workload Planning, Measurement, 1972-81. Exec. com. Palm Beach (Fla.) County Rep. Party, 1989; pres., bd. dirs. Palm Beach Farm Workers Coun., 1989. Mem. Am. Prodn. & Inventory Control Soc. (v.p. membership com. 1984-85), Inst. Indsl. Engrs. (sr. mem., pres. 1974-75, excellence award, 1975). Republican. Roman Catholic. Avocations: boating, fishing, scuba diving, reading. Home and Office: 1678 New Haven Point Ln Royal Palm Beach FL 33411 E-mail: jlph55@aol.com.

PEREZ, JOSE RAFAEL, JR., lawyer; b. Victoria de las Tunas, Oriente, Cuba, May 14, 1955; s. Jose Rafael Perez and Yolanda Ramona Sosa; m. Joan Anne Terp, Dec. 9, 1984; children: Alexander Rafael, Gabriella Susanna. BA in History, St. Mary's U., San Antonio, 1977, MA in History, 1980; JD, Tex. So. U., 1985. Cert.: Tex. Bd. Legal Specialization (immigration and nationality law) 1993, bar: Tex. Shareholder Quan, Burdette & Perez, PC, Houston, 1986—. Spkr. in field; consular liaison with U.S. consulate Tex. Am. Immigration Lawyers Assn., Ciudad Juarez, Mexico, 1997—99. Pres. Immigration Counseling Ctr., Houston, 1996—. Mem.: Am. Immigration Assn. (spkr.). Avocations: reading, exercise. Home: 6111 Riverview Way Houston TX Office: Quan Burdette and Perez PC 5177 Richmond Ave Ste 800 Houston TX 77056 Office Phone: 713-625-9231. E-mail: jperez@quanlaw.com.

PEREZ, JOSEPHINE, psychiatrist, educator; b. Tijuana, Mex., Feb. 10, 1941; came to the U.S., 1960, U.S. citizenship, 1968. BS in Biology, U. Santiago de Compostela, Spain, 1971, MD, 1975. Nuc. medicine technician, EEG technician, supr. Electrographic Labs., Encino, Calif., 1963—69; clerkships in internal medicine, gen. surgery, otorhinolaryngology, dermatology and venereology Gen. Hosp. of Galicia, Spain, 1972-75; resident in gen. psychiatry U. Miami, Jackson Meml. Hosp. and VA Hosp., Miami, Fla., 1976-78; practice medicine specializing in psychiatry, marital and family therapy, individual psychotherapy Miami, 1979—. Emergency room physician Miami Dade Hosp., 1975; attending psychiatrist Jackson Meml. Hosp., 1979—, asst. dir. adolescent psychiat. unit, 1979-83; mem. clin. faculty U. Miami Sch. Medicine, 1979—, clin. instr. psychiatry, 1979—. Mem. AMA (Physicians' Recognition award 1980, 83, 86, 89, 98, 2000, 01), Am. Assn. for Marital and Family Therapy (cert. clin. mem., treas. 1982-84, pres.-elect 1985-87, pres. 1987-89), Am. Psychiat. Assn., Am. Med. Women's Assn., Assn. Women Psychiatrists, Fla. Psychiat. Soc., South Dade Women Physicians Assn. Office: 420 S Dixie Hwy Ste 4A Coral Gables FL 33146-2228 Office Phone: 305-666-7766.

PEREZ, LEYANEE C. nutritionist, consultant; b. Habana, Cuba, Dec. 7, 1966; d. Andres and Teresa Perez; m. Guillermo Jose Cuevas, Mar. 9, 1996; 1 child, Fernando J. Cuevas. AA, Miami Dade C.C., 1989, BS, Fla. Internat. U., 1992. Cert. RDLD Am. Dietetic Assn. Nutritional specialist NutriSystem, Miami, 1990—92; cons. dietitian Med. Offices Miami Lakes, Miami, 1992—95; clin. dietitian Cedars Med. Ctr., Miami, 1993—95, Hialeah Hosp., Miami, 1995—96; cons. dietitian and corp. mem. Nutrition & Wellness Consultants, Miami, 1995—99; regional cons. to chief clin. cons. Integrated Health Svcs., Miami, 1996—2001; owner, mgr., dietician The Floridian Day Spa Salon & Nutritional Inst., Miami, 2001—. Author: The Ultimate Diet - A Journey into the new Millennium. Mem.: Am. Fedn. Astrologers, Am. Dietetic Assn. R-Conservative. Avocations: reading, writing, astrology. Office: The Floridian Day Spa 7160 W 20th Ave Ste M 133 Hialeah FL 33016

PEREZ, LOUIS ANTHONY, radiologist; b. N.Y.C., June 11, 1939; s. Salvatore Lawrence and Valvadina Rose (Ruscillo) P.; divorced, 1988; children: Lisa, Gregg, Nicole; m. Patricia Ann McVey, May 19, 1990; 1 child, Kelsey. BEE, Manhattan Coll., 1962; MD, SUNY, Bklyn., 1966. Diplomate Am. Bd. Radiology (oral examiner), Am. Bd. Nuclear Medicine. Chief nuclear medicine Misericordia Hosp., Bronx, 1973-75; cons. Manhattan Coll., Radiology Inst., Riverdale, N.Y., 1974-81; chief nuclear medicine Norwalk (Conn.) Hosp., 1975-82; dir. radiology Lawrence Hosp., Bronxville, N.Y., 1982—; asst. clin. prof. radiology Columbia U. Coll. Physicians and Surgeons, N.Y.C., 1995—. Contbr. articles to profl. jours., chpts. to books. Lt. comdr. USN, 1963-77. Grantee, Am. Cancer Soc., 1968-70, USPHS, 1974-75. Fellow Am. Coll. Radiology; mem. Soc. Nuclear Medicine (trustee 1985-89, 92—, chmn. sci. subcom. 1988—, chpt. pres. 1982), Am. Coll. Physician Execs., N.Y. State Med. Soc., Explorers Club, Alpine Club. Republican. Roman Catholic. Office: Diagnostic Imaging Svcs Bronxville 700 White Plains Rd Ste 244 Scarsdale NY 10583-5063 also: Northeast Radiology No Westchester Hosp Ctr 400 E Main St Mount Kisco NY 10549

PEREZ, LUCILLE C. NORVILLE, medical association administrator, pediatrician; BA, Manhattanville Coll., Bklyn., N.Y., 1974; MD, N.Y. Med. Coll., 1979. Pres. Nat. Med. Assn., Washington, 2001—; assoc. dir. ctr. for substance abuse, prevention, mental health svcs. adminstrn. Dept. Health & Human Svcs., Washington, 2001—. Asst. prof. Mount Sinai Sch. Medicine; assoc. prof. clin. pediat. SUNY Health Sci. Ctr., Bklyn., St. George's Sch. Medicine, Grenada, West Indies; lectr. in field. Recipient Spl. Achievement award, Congl. Black Caucus, Disting. Svc. award, Sec. Health & Human Svcs. Mem.: AMA, Nat. Med. Assn., Medico-Chirurgical Soc. of D.C., Acad. Pediat. Office: Nat Med Assn 1012 Tenth St NW Washington DC 20001

PEREZ, PAUL IGNATIUS, lawyer; b. Cuba; Bachelor, Jacksonville U.; Master, U. Fla.; grad. in Law, George Washington U. Asst. U.S. atty., Jacksonville, Fla., 1988—92; fed. criminal def. atty. Booth, Arnold & Perez, Jacksonville, Fla., 1994—2002; U.S. atty. Mid. Dist. Fla., 2002—. Office: Mid Dist Fla 400 N Tampa St Ste 3200 Tampa FL 33602 Office Phone: 813-274-6000.

PEREZ, ROSIE, actress; b. Bklyn. d. Ismael Serrano and Lydia Perez. Dramatic appearances include: (TV) 21 Jump Street, WIOU, Rosie Perez Presents Society's Ride, 1993, Happily Ever After: Fairy Tales for Every Child, 1995, Subway Stories: Tales From The Underground, 1997, (film) Do the Right Thing, 1989, White Men Can't Jump, 1992, Night on Earth, 1992, Untamed Heart, 1993, Fearless, 1993 (Acad. award nom. Best Supporting Actress 1994), It Could Happen To You, 1994, Somebody to Love, 1995, A Brother's Kiss, 1997, Perdita Durango, 1997, 24-Hour Woman, 1998, Louis and Frank, 1998, The Road to El Dorado, 2000, (TV series) House of Buggin, 1995. Office: Parks Palmer Turner & Yemenidjian c/o Diane Schroeder 1990 S Bundy Dr Ste 600 Los Angeles CA 90025-5291

PEREZ, SYLVIA, newscaster, reporter; married; 2 children. B, U. Okla. Sch. of Journalism. Reporter KRPC-TV, Houston, Denver, Lawton, Okla.; weekend anchor and reporter WLS-TV, Chgo., 1989—, med. reporter, anchor 11am news. TV journalist with prodr. Holly Grisham HealthBeat, WLS-TV (Silver Dome award, 2001), TV journalist with prodr. Christine Tressel Desktop Doctors (Peter Lisagor award, 2002). Office: WLS-TV 190 N State St Chicago IL 60601

PEREZ, TONY, former baseball player; b. Ciego De Avila, Cuba, May 14, 1942; arrived in U.S., 1960; Profl. baseball player Cin. Reds, 1960—76, Montreal Expos, Canada, 1976—79, Boston Red Sox, 1979—82, Phila. Phillies, Cin. Reds, mgr., 1993; spl. asst. gen. mgr. Fla. Marlins, Miami, 1993—. Named to Baseball Hall of Fame, 2000. Office: Fla Marlins 2269 NW 199th St Opa Locka FL 33056-2664

PEREZ, WILLIAM D. chemical company executive; Pres. SC Johnson & Son, Inc., Racine, Wis., 1993-97, pres., CEO, 1997—. Office: SC Johnson & Son Inc 1525 Howe St Racine WI 53403-5011

PEREZ ARJONA, EIMIR ARIEL, neurosurgeon, researcher; b. Panama City, Panama, May 17, 1968; s. Nicolas Camilo Perez and Rita Omaira Arjona; m. Sadith Alicia De La Cruz, June 24, 1999; children: Hanameel, Eimir Manuel. BS, BA, Pedagogic Inst., Las Cumbres, Panama City, 1985; MD, U. Panama, Panama City, 1993. Cert. in neurosurgery Panama Ministry of Health. Med. intern Ministry of Health, Panama City, 1993—95; med. officer staff emergency and trauma Social Security Hosp., Panama City, 1995—96, residency in neurosurgery David, Panama, 1997—2000, neurosurgery staff, 2002—03; med. officer staff emergency and trauma Paitilla Med. Ctr., Panama City, 1997; resident in neurosurgery Wayne State U., Detroit Med. Ctr., Detroit, 2000—02; mem. neurosurgery staff Mae Lewis Med. Ctr., David, 2002—03. Editor in chief web page U.S./Can. chpt. Latin Am. Fedn. Neurosurgery, 2003—; assoc. editor web page Neurosurgical Instrumentation and Innovations in Biotechn. sect. World Fedn. Neurosurg. Soc., 2003—; mem. peer rev. group, advisor to the editor Neurol. Rsch. jour., Wilton, Conn., 2000—, book reviewer, 2000—; peer rev. group Med. Sci. Monitor jour., Alberston, NY, 2003—, Psychline, Chgo., 2001—; presenter, spkr. in field; mem. Med. Commn. of High Level for Acts of Transference of Panama Canal, Spl. Commn. to Hannover, Germany; rep. 1st Nat. Young Leadership Meeting, Pedagogic Inst., Panama City, Panama. Contbr. articles to profl. jours., chpt. to book. Mem.: Internat. Soc. for Prevention of Child Abuse and Neglect (assoc.), Mich. State Med. Soc. (assoc.), Wayne County Med. Soc. (assoc.), Mich. Assn. of Neurol. Surgeons (assoc.), Latin Am. Fedn. Neurosurgery (assoc.), World Fedn. on Neurosurg. Socs. (assoc.). Achievements include research in child abuse found for the first time the description of the full syndrome of child abuse late outcome; arteriovenous malformation study (ONYX); smart brain retractor; first to full clinical syndrome, type of fractures (Computer Modeling Fractures), and intracranial-ophtalmic consequences associated to a baseball assault injury in a study of 90 patients; development of cerebral vessels and aneurysm using a technique named Stereolythography, for er understanding of intraarterial flow and microanatomy; computer model (Finite Element Analysis) to represent cranial bone prosthesis and cranial fixation devices, analyzing in vitro the cranial behaviour under stress forces; research in carotid occlussive surgery study (COSS); balloon prophylactic angioplasty in cerebral vasospasm (BPAV); Acculink for revascularization of carotids in high risks patients; Boston Scientific EPI: a carotid stenting trial for high risk surgical patients; cerebral aneurysm trial. Avocation: martial arts instructor. Home: 31115 Huntley Square East Apt 621 Beverly Hills MI 48025 Office: Harper Professional Office Building 4160 John R Suite 930 Detroit MI 48201 Personal E-mail: sadith_eimir@hotmail.com.

PEREZ-CRUET, JORGE, physician, psychopharmacologist, psychophysiologist, psychiatrist, educator, addictionologist, geropsychiatrist; b. Santurce, P.R., Oct. 15, 1931; s. Jose Maria Perez-Vicente and Emilia Cruet-Burgos; m. Anyes Heimendinger, Oct. 4, 1958; children: Antonio, Mick, Graciela, Isabelle. BS magna cum laude, U. P.R., 1953, MD, 1957; diploma in psychiatry, McGill U., Montreal, Que., Can., 1976. Diplomate Am. Bd. Psychiatry and Neurology, Nat. Bd. Med. Examiners, Am. Bd. Geriat. Psychiatry; lic. Can. Coun. Med. Examiners, Med. Coun. Canada; cert. in quality assurance; cert. CHPQ by HQCB; cert. specialist in psychiatry RCPC, 1976. Rotating intern Michael Reese Hosp., Chgo., 1957-58; fellow in psychiatry Johns Hopkins U. Med. Sch., 1958-60, instr., then asst. prof. psychiatry, 1962-73; psychiatrist neurophysiology and psychosomatic lab. Walter Reed Army Inst. Rsch., Washington, 1960—62, cons., 1963-65; rsch. assoc. lab. chem. pharmacology NHI, NIH, Bethesda, Md., 1969-71; med. dir. USPHS adult psychiatry sect. lab. clin. sci. NIMH, Bethesda, 1971-73; psychiatry resident diploma course in psychiatry McGill U. Sch. Medicine, Montreal Gen. Hosp., 1973-76, Montreal Children's Hosp., 1975; prof. psychiatry, cief psychopharmacology lab. U. Mo.-Mo. Inst. Psychiatry, St. Louis, 1976—78; chief psychiatry svc. San Juan (P.R.) VA Hosp., pharmacy and therapeutic com., 1978-92; also prof. psychiatry U. P.R. Med. Sch., 1978-92; prof. psychiatry U. Okla. Health Sci. Ctr., Oklahoma City VA Med. Ctr., 1992—. Spl. cons. NASA, Moffettfield, Calif., 1965-69; cons. divsn. narcotic addition and drug abuse NIDA, 1972-73; mem. drug adv. com. FDA/NIDA, 1976-80, mem. pharmacy and therapeutic com., 1992—; local organizer Internat. Coll. Neuropsychiatry, San Juan, P.R., 1986, CINP, 1986; spl. advisor mental health P.R. Senate, P.R. sec. health, 1989; prin. investigator NASA biosatellite project JH Sch. Med., 1963-65.; staff psychiatrist mental health svcs., VAMC, Oklahoma City, 1992—, med. dir. opivid treatment program, 2001--. Editor: Catholic Physicians Guild Archiocese of Okla., 1997-98. Mem. Rep. Nat. Com., 1995; mem. Eisenhower Commn., 2001. Capt. M.C. USAR, 1960-62; sr. surgeon USPHS, 1969-71, med. dir., 1971-73. Recipient Coronas award, 1957, Ruiz-Arnau award, 1957, Diaz-Garcia award 1957, Geigy award, 1975, 76, AMA Recognition award 1971, 76, 81, Horner's award 1975, 76, Pavlovian award, 1978, Recognition cert. VA Svc. awards and commendations, 1980-98, Senate of P.R., 1986, Cert. of Merit Gov. of P.R., 1986, Cert. Recognition, Sec. Health, San Juan, Puerto Rico, Appreciation plaque Fifth World Congress of IRMA, Manila, Philippines, Eisenhower Commn., 1995. Disting. fellow APA (life); fellow Interam. Coll. Physicians and Surgeons, Royal Coll. Physicians and Surgeons Can. (sr., cert.), Am. Psychiat Assn. (life, disting. life fellow, 2003); mem. Am. Coll. Med. Quality, Am. Physiol. Soc., Am. Coll. Psychiatrists, Pavlovian Soc., Am. Fedn. Clin. Rsch., Am. Fedn. Med. Rsch., Am. Assn. Geriat. Psychiatry, Am. Soc. Clin. Pharmacology and Therapeutics, Am. Soc. Pharmacology and Exptl. Therapeutics, Am. Soc. Addiction Medicine (cert. 1998), Am. Acad. Addiction Psychiatry (dir. Area VIII, 2002), Soc. Neurosci., Am. Coll. Med. Quality, Nat. Assn. Healthcare Quality, Internat. Soc. Rsch. Aggression, Okla. Psychiat. Assn., Am. Soc. Clin. Psychopharmacology, Menninger Found., Charles F. Menninger Soc., Okla. Assn. Health Care Quality, Alumni, UPR Sch. Med., Johns Hopkins Med. Surg. Inst., NIH Alumni (life), McGill, Okla. Hist. Soc. Republican. Roman Catholic. Home: 3304 Rosewood Ln Oklahoma City OK 73120-5604 Office: Oklahoma City VA Med Ctr 921 NE 13th St Oklahoma City OK 73104-5007 Fax: 405-270-1566. E-mail: jperezcrue@aol.com.

PEREZ-CRUET, MICK JORGE, neurological surgeon, educator; b. Washington, May 3, 1961; s. Jorge Fortunato and Anyes Lilly (Heimendinger) Perez-Cruet; m. Donna Jeanne Roggenbuck, July 9, 1994; children: Kristin Magdalene, Joshua Michael, Rachel Elizabeth, David Gabriel. BA, Grinell Coll., 1983; MSc in Chemistry, U. South Fla., 1986; MD, Tufts U., 1991. Intern surg. svc. Baylor Coll. Medicine, Houston, 1991-92, resident in neurosurgery, 1992-97; attending neurosurgery, v. chmn. Wilford Hall Med. Ctr., San Antonio, 1997—2001; spinal fellow Rush U./CINN, Chgo., 2001—02; asst. prof., dir. minimally invasive spine surgery Rush U., Chgo., 2002—03; assoc. dir. Inst. Spine Care/CINN; dir., spinal surgery Mich. Head and Spine Inst., 2003—. Prin. investigator clin. trials; presenter in field; appointee Coun. State Neurosurg. Socs., 1997, chmn. young physicians com., chmn. workforce com., corr. sec.; chmn. workforce com., scientific adv. bd. Neospine; chmn. workforce com., scientific adv. bd., cons. CBYON; publs. com. CNS. Editor: (textbooks) Outpatient Spinal Surgery, An Anatomical Approach to Minimally Invasive Spine Surgery; asst. editor: Neurosurgery News; contbr. chapters to books, articles to profl. jours. Chmn. class reunion Tufts Sch. Medicine, 1995-96; dir. class fund Grinnell Coll., 1999—. Air Force Health Professions scholar, 1987-91. Mem. AMA, ACS, AAAS, Congress Neurol. Surgeons, Am. Assn. Neurol. Surgeons, Mass. Med. Soc., Tex. Med. Assn., Maj. USAF Med. Corp, Fla. Acad. Sci., Am. Fedn. Clin. Rsch., Mich. Med. Soc., Sigma Xi (grantee 1985). Avocations: hunting, fishing, scuba diving, underwater photography, biking. Office: Mich Head and Spine Inst 22250 Providence Dr Ste 300 Southfield MI 48075 Office Phone: 248-440-2162. E-mail: perezcruet@yahoo.com.

PEREZ-GELABERT, DANIEL ERNESTO, biologist; b. Santo Domingo, Dominican Republic, May 10, 1963; s. Socrates Osiris Perez and Maria Ramona Gelabert; m. Lucrecia Herminia Rodriguez, Aug. 24, 1991; 1 child, Elisa Michelle Perez. BS, Universidad Autonoma de Santo Domingo, Santo Domingo, Dominican Republic, 1988; MS, U. of Rochester, N.Y., 1991; PhD, The U. of Chgo., 1994. Postdoctoral fellow Nat. Cancer Inst., FCRDC, Frederick, Md., 1995—98; contr. Nat. Mus. of Natural History, Smithsonian Instn., Washington, 1999—2000, rsch. assoc. in entomology, 2000—. Contbr. articles to profl. jours. Grantee Biol. Survey and Inventory, NSF, 2001—04. Home: 5714 Ridgway Ave Rockville MD 20851 Office: National Museum of Natural History 10th St and Constitution Ave Washington DC 20560 Office Phone: 202-357-2834. Office Fax: 202-786-2894. E-mail: perez.daniel@nmnh.si.edu.

PÉREZ-MONFORTI, JESSICA L. social sciences educator, researcher; b. Islip, NY, Feb. 6, 1976; d. Steven K. and Maryann Monforti. BS, Fla. State U.; MA, PhD, Ohio State U. Rschr. FSU Survey Rsch. Lab, Tallahasse, Fla., 1995—97; intern Dept. of Edn. Legis. and Cabinet Affairs, Tallahasse, Fla., 1995—97; instr. Ohio State U., 1999—2001; adj. instr. U. of South Fla., Tampa, 2001; asst. prof. Mercer U., Macon, Ga., 2001—. Mem. family selection com. Habitat Humanity, Columbus, Ohio, 1997—2000; founder, adv. Hispanic and Latin Am. Student Union, Macon, Ga., 2001—. Recipient hon. mention, Ford Found., 1998, GSARA award, Ohio State U., 1999; grantee, So. Scholarship Found., 1996. Mem.: Western Polit. Sci. Assn., So. Polit. Sci. Assn., Midwest Polit. Sci. Assn., Am. Polit. Sci. Assn., Nat. Assn. of Black Polit. Scientists, Alpha Psi Lambda (v.p. 1998—99).

PEREZ-REYES, EDWARD, molecular physiologist; b. Cheverly, Md., Feb. 18, 1957; s. Mario Perez-Reyes and Maria Gispert; m. Emilia Aranda Ripoll, June 15, 1984 (div. June 1989); m. Deborah Lynn Benuska, Apr. 13, 1991. PhD, U. Colo., 1986. Technician Nat. Inst. Environ. Health Scis., Research Triangle Park, N.C., 1978-80; postdoctoral fellow Baylor Coll. Medicine, Houston, 1986-91, asst. prof., 1991-92, Loyola U. Med. Ctr., Maywood, Ill., 1993-98, assoc. prof., 1998-99, U. Va., Charlottesville, 1999—. Contbr. articles to profl. jours. Recipient Nat. Rsch. Svc. award NIH, 1988, Estab-

lished Investigatorship award Am. Heart Assn., 1996; fellow NSF, 1980. Mem. Biophys. Soc. Achievements include molecular biophys. characterization of dihydropyridine sensitive L-type and T-type calcium channels. Office: 1300 Jefferson Park Ave Charlottesville VA 22908-0735

PÉREZ-RIVERA, FRANCISCO (FRANK RIVERA), writer; b. Vertientes, Cuba, Oct. 3, 1938; came to U.S., 1968, naturalized, 1974; s. Francisco Daniel Pérez and María Eloísa Rivera. BA, Camagüey Coll., Cuba, 1955; MA in Romance Langs., U. Munich, 1967. Newsman, script writer Bavarian Radio, Munich, 1964-68; newsman AP, N.Y.C., 1968-92, arts and entertainment editor, 1992—; dir. Spanish programs for lang. labs., 1987. Author: (poetry) Constructions, 1979; (novel) Bells Over the Prairies, 1986, (short stories) Cuban Short Stories, 1992; (short stories) Varadero and Other Cuban Short Stories, 1998; co-author: Introduction to Spanish Literature, 1982, short stories in the anthologies New Cuban Storytellers (in Spanish), 1961, Cuba: Nouvelles et contes d'aujourd'hui, 1985, Narrative and Liberty: Cuban Tales of the Dispersion, 1996, Prosa moderna del mundo hispánico, 1997; author, narrator audio books The Golden Age of Spanish Literature, 2002. Grantee German Academic Exchange Svc., Munich, 1961-67; fellow Cintas Found., N.Y., 1980; 1st prize short story Círculo de Escritores y Poetas Latinoamericanos, N.Y., 1997, Internat. Short Story award Círculo de Cultura Panamericano, N.J., 1997. Home: 212 E 77th St Apt 1G New York NY 10021-2111 Office: AP 50 Rockefeller Plz New York NY 10020-1605

PÈREZ-RODRIGUEZ, JUAN ESTEBAN, II, (ESTEBAN DE LARES), journalist, writer, historian, researcher; b. Lares, Puerto Rico, Sept. 23, 1944; arrived in U.S., 1987; s. Juan Esteban Pèrez and Rosa Louisa Rodríguez; m. Aurea Nivia Torres-Bonilla, June 1, 1978; children: Elsie Celinés, Josué Esteban III. BS in Secondary Edn., Catholic U., P.R., 1972; post grad., Dept. of Edn., P.R. Cert. tchr. Spanish Dept. Edn. Govt. of P.R., 1973, tchr. social studies Dept. Edn. Govt. of P.R., 1973, lic. tour guide Dept. of Tourism Govt. of P.R., 1972. Tchr. Dept. of Edn., PR, 1968—75; historian PR, 1967—87; tour guide Tourism Dept., 1975—87; prodr. and broadcaster WABE, PR, 1975—78, WIVA, PR, 1975—78, WGDL, PR, 1988—89; journalist newspapers and mag., 1966—. Founder and pres. Lares Hist. Soc., PR, 1981—83, Lares Hist. Mus., 1982; founder and editor Revista Rescoldo mag., 1982, Revista Cordillera mag., 1983; organizer nat. festivals. Author: PEQUEñeces, A Galope Por La Montaña, Las Aventuras De Yarì, El Coquì, Abalario De Cuentecillos Chuscos Para Una Cabuya, Dimensiones, Dialogando Contigo, De El ArcÓn De Mis Recuerdos, Manual Para Vivir En Un Mundo Conocido, Burundanga. Lds. Home: 1117 W Fourth St Lorain OH 44052

PEREZ-STABLE, ELISEO, medical educator; Prof. medicine U. Calif., San Francisco. Mem. Evidence Based Practice Ctr. U. Calif. San Francisco, Stanford U. Office: U Calif San Francisco Box 0320 A405 San Francisco CA 94143: Evidence Based Practice Ctr Stanford U Redwood Bldg T246 Stanford CA 94305-5405 E-mail: eliseops@medicine.ucsf.edu.

PERHACH, JAMES LAWRENCE, pharmaceutical company executive; b. Pitts., Oct. 26, 1943; s. James Lawrence and Elizabeth Louise (Hoffman) P.; m. Judith Irene Selter, Apr. 15, 1967; children: Laura Anne, Amy Elizabeth. BS, U. Dayton, 1966; MS, U. Pitts., 1969, PhD, 1971. Sr. scientist dept. pharmacology Mead Johnson Rsch. Ctr., divsn. Bristol Myers, 1971—74, sr. investigator dept. biol. rsch., 1974—76, sr. rsch. assoc. dept. biol. rsch., 1976—77, sr. rsch. assoc. dept. pathology and toxicology, 1977—78, prin. rsch. assoc. dept. pathology and toxicology, 1978—80; from dir. pharmacology to dir. biol. rsch. to dir. clin. investigation Wallace Labs. Divsn. Carter-Wallace, Inc., Cranbury, NJ, 1980—87, v.p. clin. pharmacology and pharmacokinetics, 1987—2001; sr. dir. clin. pharmacology Purdue Pharma, L.P., 2001—04; sr. dir. Forest Rsch. Inst., CNS Therapeutic Area, 2004—. Vis. asst. prof. dept. pharmacy practice and adminstrn. Coll. Pharmacy Rutgers U., 1993—; adj. prof. toxicology Phila. Coll. Pharmacy and Sci., 1981-87; assoc. faculty Evansville Ctr. Med. Edn., Ind. U., 1973-80; lectr. grad. physiology U. Evansville, 1973-79; mem. adv. bd. clin. rsch. ctr. U. Medicine and Dentistry N.J. Robert Wood Johnson Med. Sch., 1995—; mem. Drug Utilization Rev. Coun., State of N.J., 1983-2003, med. pharmacologist, 1983, sec., 1984, chmn., 1985-87; mem. substance abuse com. Tri-State Area Health Planning Coun., Evansville, 1972-75; mem. addictions mem. edn. program Evansville Ctr. for Med. Edn., 1972-78. Fellow: Am. Coll. Clin. Pharmacology; mem.: AAAS, Drug Info. Assn., N.Y. Acad. Sci., Soc. Neurosci., Soc. Exptl. Biology and Medicine, European Soc. Toxicology, Am. Coll. Toxicology, Am. Soc. Clin. Pharmacology and Therapeutics, Sigma Xi. Achievements include research in drug discovery, elucidation of mechanism of action and safety evaluation of new therapeutic agents. Home: 1406 Barclay Blvd Lawrenceville NJ 08648-5887 Office: Forest Rsch Inst Harbor Side Fin Ctr Plaza V Jersey City NJ 07311 Office Phone: 201-427-8465. Business E-Mail: james.perhach@frx.com.

PERHACS, MARYLOUISE HELEN, musician, educator; b. Teaneck, N.J., June 15, 1944; d. John Andrew and Helen Audrey (Hosage) P.; m. Robert Theodore Sirinek, Jan. 27, 1968 (div. Jan. 1975). Student, Ithaca (N.Y.) Coll., 1962-64; BS, Juilliard Sch., 1967, MS, 1968; postgrad., Hunter Coll., 1976, St. Peter's Coll., Jersey City, N.J., 1977. Cert. music tchr., N.Y., N.J. Instr. Carnegie Hall, N.Y.C., 1966-69; program developer, coord., instr. urban edn. program Newburgh (N.Y.) Pub. Sch. System, 1968-69; adj. prof. dept. edn. St. Peter's Coll., Jersey City, 1976-92; tchr. brass instruments Indian Hills High Sch., Oakland, N.J., 1976; tchr. Jersey City Pub. Schs., 1976-77, N.Y.C. Pub. Sch., Bronx, 1980-84; pvt. tchr. Cliffside Park, N.J., 1976—; vocal music tchr. East Rutherford, N.J., 1990; tchr. music Bergen County Spl. Svcs. Sch. Dist., 1990-91; tchr. gen. music Little Ferry (N.J.) Pub. Schs., 1991-92; tchr. mid. sch. instrumental Paramus (N.J.) Pub. Schs., 1993-94; tchr. vocal music West New York (N.J.) Pub Schs., 1995—. Tchr. music summer enrichment program, West New York, NJ, 1999, 2000, summer instrumental music program Park Ridge (N.J.) H.S., 1995, 96, Waldwick Concert Band, 2003-04; tchr., singer, trumpeter Norwegian Caribbean Lines, 1981-82, Jimmy Dorsey Band, Paris and London, 1974; music and edn. lecture cir., 1992—. Singer with Original PDQ Bach Okay Chorale, 1966, Live from Carnegie Hall Recordings, 1970, St. Louis Mcpl. Opera, 1970, Ed Sullivan Show, 1970; singer, dancer, actress (Broadway shows) Promises, Promises, 1969-71, Sugar, 1971-72, Lysistrata, 1972; trumpeter (Broadway shows) Jesus Christ Superstar, 1973, Debbie!, 1976, Sarava!, 1979, Fiddler on the Roof, Lincoln Ctr., 1981, Sophisticated Ladies, 1982; writer, host series on women in music Columbia Cable/United Artists, 1984; recordings: Carnegie Hall Live, Avery Fisher Hall, Lincoln Ctr. Cons. to cadette troop Girl Scouts U.S., Jersey City, 1967-68, Bergen County N.J. Coun., 1995—. Mem. NEA, AFTRA, Actors Equity Assn., Am. Fedn. Musicians (mem. theatre com. local 802 N.Y.C. 1972—, chmn. 1973), Music Educators Nat. Conf., N.J. Music Educators Assn., N.J. Sch. Music Assn., N.J. Edn. Assn., Internat. Women's Brass Conf. (charter mem.), Internat. Trumpet Guild, Mu Phi Epsilon. Democrat. Episcopalian. Avocations: cats, cake decorating, food sculpting, horticulture, sewing. Home and Office: 23 Crescent Ave Cliffside Park NJ 07010-3003

PERHAM, LEN, communications executive; BSEE, Northeastern U., 1968. Various mgmt. positions AMD, Western Digital; pres., CEO Optical Info. Systems, Inc. (divsn. Exxon Enterprise), IDT, Santa Clara, Calif., 1983-99, also bd. dirs. Bd. dirs. IDT. Office: 2975 Stender Way Santa Clara CA 95054-3214

PERHAM, ROY GATES, III, industrial psychologist; b. Hackensack, N.J., Apr. 22, 1958; s. Roy Gates Jr. and Titania Joan (Robbitts) P. BA with honors, Bates Coll., 1980; MS, Stevens Inst. Tech., 1982, PhD, 1989. Intern Sen. Edmund S. Muskie, Washington, 1978; psychometrician Lab. Psychol. Studies Stevens Inst. Tech., Hoboken, N.J., 1981-83, instr., 1985, adj. asst. prof., 1990—, Fairleigh Dickinson U., Rutherford, N.J., 1986; sr. assoc. AAI Orgnl. Performance Cons., Florham Park, N.J., 1990-94; assessment projects mgr. Tech. Employee Selection and Tng. Inc., Hasbrouck Heights, N.J., 1995—. WordStar coord. N.Y. Computer Soc., N.Y.C., 1985-88. Chmn. Juvenile Conf. Com., Hasbrouck Heights and Wood-Ridge, N.J., 1985-95; mem. N.J. State Juvenile Delinquency Commn., Trenton, N.J., 1988-91; county exec.'s rep. Bergen County Youth Svcs. Commn., 1990—, chair, 1994-96; chair Bergen County Task Force on Youth Violence, 1993—; asst. Bergen County Exec. for Juvenile Justice, N.J., 1999—; mem. N.J. Juvenile Justice and Delinquency Prevention Adv. Com., 2001—. Named Citizen of Yr., Lions Club of Hasbrouck Heights, N.J., 1988. Mem. APA, Am. Psychol. Soc., Met. N.Y. Assn. for Applied Psychology, Soc. for Indsl./Orgnl. Psychology, Inc., Phi Beta Kappa, Psi Chi. Home: 269 Raymond St Hasbrouck Heights NJ 07604-1723 Office: Technical Employee Selection & Tng Inc The Profl Bldg 248 Blvd Hasbrouck Heights NJ 07604 E-mail: Rperham@compuserve.com.

PERIBERE, JEROME A. agricultural products executive; M in Bus. Econs. and Fin., Inst. D'Etudes Politiques, Paris. With Dow Chem. Co., 1977—, regional mktg. mgr. Eastern Europe, 1982—85, regional mgr. Middle East and Africa, 1985—88, dir. European agr. bus., 1988—89, comml. dir. agr. bus. Europe, 1989—93, global comml. dir., 1993—97, global leader, Weed Mgmt. Global Bus. Unit. European Trade area, 1998—2002, global leader agr. chems., 2002—04; corp. strategy leader Dow AgroScis., 1997—98, pres., CEO, 2004—. Mem. bd. BioCrossroads. Office: Dow AgroScis LLC 9330 Zionsville Rd Indianapolis IN 46268

PERICAK-VANCE, MARGARET A. health facility administrator; b. Buffalo, June 28, 1951; m. Jeff Pericak-Vance; 1 child. PhD in Med. Genetics, Ind. U., 1978. Dir., chief sect. med. genetics dept. medicine Duke Ctr. for Human Genetics, Duke U., Durham, NC. Named to Century Club: 100 People to Watch as We Move to the Next Millennium, Newsweek Mag., 1997. Mem.: Inst. Medicine, 2004, Am. Coll. Med. Genetics (founding fellow, bd. cert. PhD med. geneticist). Office: Duke U Med Ctr Ctr for Human Genetics Box 3445 Durham NC 27710

PERICH, TERRY MILLER, secondary school educator; b. Greensburg, Pa., Sept. 22, 1948; s. Miller and Eleanor Ann (Schmuck) P.; m. Kathleen Ann Ferrari, July 26, 1975. BA in Elem. Edn., Edinboro U., 1970; elem. cert., Pa. State U., 1973; Masters equivalency degree, U. Pitts., 1994; postgrad., Carlow Coll., 1994. Trained student assistance profl., Pa.; cert. tchr. elem. edn. Tchr. sci. and math. Penn Trafford Schs., Harrison City, Pa., 1970—. Mentor, tchr. Tchr. Enhancement Inst. St. Vincent Coll., Latrobe, Pa.; selected tchr. Watershed Restoration St. Vincent Coll., Latrobe. County committeeman Dem. Party, Penn Twp., Pa., 1994—; lion tamer Bushy Run Lions Club, Claridge, Pa., 1993—, 3rd v.p., 1995, 2d v.p., 1996, 1st v.p., 1997—. Recipient Commendation, Pres.-elect Clinton, Student Assistance Program award for working with students at risk St. Vincent Coll. Prevention Projects, 1991. Mem. NEA, ASCD, PACE, Nat. Sci. Tchrs. Assn., Pa. Tchrs. Edn. Assn., Pa. Sci. Tchrs. Assn., Westmoreland County Assn. Student Assistance Profls. (bd. dirs. 1992-94, mem. Westmoreland county student assistance team 1995-96, 96-97), Penn Trafford Edn. Assn. (exec. bd. dirs. 1990-91). Roman Catholic. Avocations: travel, education. Home: 13 Rizzi Dr Irwin PA 15642-8902 Office: Penn Mid Sch PO Box 368 Watt Rd Claridge PA 15623 E-mail: middie22@aol.com.

PERIN, DONALD WISE, JR., former association executive; b. Newton, Mass., Feb. 28, 1915; s. Donald Wise and Beatrice Franklin (Cobb) P.; m. Jean Newcomb Mulcahy, Dec. 5, 1942 (dec. Feb. 2003); children: William Kirk, Betsy Cobb, Donald Wise. Student, Norwich U., 1932-34; BA, Columbia U., 1936. With Gt. Am. Indemnity Co., N.Y.C., 1936-50, asst. sec., 1946-50; asst. sec.-treas. Nat. Assn. Ins. Agts., N.Y.C., 1950-54; v.p. Alexander & Co., Chgo., 1954-63, Great Am. Ins. Co., N.Y.C., 1964-69; dir. research Ind. Ins. Agts. of Am., N.Y.C., 1970-79, exec. v.p., 1979-81, exec. v.p. emeritus, 1981. Served with U.S. Army, 1940-46, PTO. Mem. Am. Soc. Assn. Execs., Soc. C.P.C.U.'s, Sigma Alpha Epsilon. Republican. Home: 2523 Monument Ave Bennington VT 05201-9347

PERINE, MAXINE HARRIET, retired reading educator; b. Worth County, Mo., May 11, 1918; d. Robert Rozwell and Della Dale (Martin) P. BS in Edn., Ctrl. Mo. State U., 1944; MA, Columbia U., 1954, profl. diploma, 1960, EdD, 1977. Tchr. Worth County Schs., Mo., 1935-44, Kansas City Pub. Schs., 1944-59, reading cons., 1959-64; editor Holt, Rinehart, Winston, N.Y.C., 1964; mem. faculty U. Mich., Flint, 1964-86, tchr. specializing in reading, ret., 1986; ret., 1988. Vis. scholar Columbia U., 1978; program chair World Congress of Reading, Dublin, 1982; spkr. Nat. Coun. Tchrs. English, Honolulu, 1967, World Congress Reading, Hamburg, Fed. Republic Germany, 1978, Hong Kong, 1984, World Congress for the Gifted, Manila, The Philippines, 1983; invited spkr. in field. Author; editor in field:. Mem. Internat. Reading Assn., Kappa Delta Pi (chpt. founding counselor 1980—, internat. com. constn. and bylaws 1982-84), Delta Kappa Gamma (Woman of Distinction 1972). Presbyn.

PERINGTON, PHILIP, management investment company executive; BA, U. Colo., 1976, cert. paralegal, 1989. Pres. Restaurant Devel. Corp., Denver, 1968-73, Harrington-Miller Co., Denver, 1973—. Regional task officer Clinton-Gore Regional Issues, 1996; chmn. Colo. State Dem. Party. Recipient Gov.'s award State of Wyo., 1991. Mem. Assn. State Dem. Chairs (chmn. 1996—). Office: Harrington Miller Co 731 Sherman ST Denver CO 80203

PERINI, JENNIFER MARY, television producer; b. Newton, Mass., Apr. 20, 1963; d. David Bonfiglio and Eileen Louise (Callahan) Perini; m. James Joseph Cunningham, July 18, 1998; children: Meave, Liliana, Fineas. BA, Harvard U., Cambridge, Mass., 1985; MFA, UCLA Film Sch., 1993. Asst. producer NBC Sports, NYC, 1987—88; v.p. Warner Bros., Calif., 1993—97; head creative affairs Image Movers/DWSL, Calif., 1997—2002; pres. Everyman Pics, Calif., 2002—. Co-chair fund raising Harvard U. Class of 1983; bd. dirs. David B. Perini Jr. Quality of Life Clinic, Boston; adv. bd. UCLA Producers' Program. Recipient Sports Emmy for Olympic Games Coverage, Emmy Com., 1988.

PERIQUITO, PAULO F.M.O. manufacturing executive; Formerly with ITT Data Svcs., São Paulo, Brazil; contr. manufactured product divsn. Alcoa, 1983—84, from gen. mgr. to dir. distbn. bus. unit, 1984—88, dir. all bus. units, 1988—89, CFO Latin Am., bd. dirs. Mex., 1989—91, v.p. corp. planning, human resources and quality, CEO Grupo Aluminio subs., 1991—94, exec. v.p., bd. dirs. Latin Am., 1994—96; exec. v.p., pres. Latin Am. Whirlpool Corp. Office: Whirlpool Corp 2000 N M-63 Benton Harbor MI 49022

PERITO, ROBERT MICHAEL, political scientist; b. Denver, June 27, 1942; s. Michael and Alice Perito; m. Patricia Perito, Sept. 30, 1967 (dec. Jan. 2003); children: Robert, Samantha. BA, U. Denver, 1964; MA, George Mason U., Fairfax, Va., 2000. Vol. U.S. Peace Corps, Nigeria, 1965—67; fgn. svc. officer Dept. State, Washington, 1967—95; dir. ICITAP, Dept. Justice, Washington, 1996—2001; sr. fellow U.S. Inst. Peace, Washington, 2001—. Diplomat in residence SIS, Am. U., Washington, 2003—; adj. prof. George Mason U., Fairfax, 1998—2003; vis. lectr. Princeton U., NJ, 2003. Author: Where is the Lone Ranger: The Search for Post-Conflict Security, 2003, American Experience with Police in Peace Operations, 2002; contbr. articles to profl. jours. Recipient Pres.'s Meritorious Honor award, USG, 1992. Avocations: hiking, running. Home: 311 Oak Knoll Terr Rockville MD 20850 Office: US Inst of Peace 1200 17th St NW Washington DC 20076

PERKEL, ROBERT SIMON, photojournalist, educator; b. Jersey City, Apr. 23, 1925; s. Louis Leo and Flora Sonia (Levin) Perkel. BS, NYU, 1948; MS, Barry U., 1964; postgrad., Columbia U. Owner, operator Gulfstream Color Labs., Miami Beach, Fla., 1955-61; graphics instr. Dade County Pub. Schs., 1962-66; freelance photojournalist, 1967—. Rep. News Events Photo Svc., Ft. Lauderdale, Fla.; instr. photography Broward CC, 1982—92; rep. Patch Comm., Titusville, Fla., 1985—88; pub. Biograph/Comm., North Miami Beach, Fla., 1987—90. Contbr. photos stories and photographs to numerous mags. and indsl. trade publs.; exhibitions include Met. Mus. and Art Ctr., Coral Gables, Fla., Mus. Fine Arts, Boston. Former publicity dir. Coun. Internat. Visitors Greater Miami. With U.S. Army, 1943—46, ETO. Recipient Cmty. Spirit award, Zonta Club Greater Miami, 1980, Found. medal, Nat. Press Photographers Found., 2000. Mem.: VFW (life), DAV (life; trustee Jack Schwartz chpt., past comdr. Miami Beach-Surfside chpt., nat. citation for disting. svc. 1969, nat. svc. plaque 2000), Nielsen Media Rsch., Nat. Press Photographers Assn. (life), Barry U. Alumni Assn., Steamship Hist. Soc. Am. Found. (life; S.E. Fla. chpt.), NYU Alumni Fedn. (Leadership award for 1982-1983 fund campaign), World Ocean and Cruise Liner Soc., Am. Legion, Order of the Flame, Alpha Mu Gamma. Home: 3619 NE 207th St Apt 2107 Aventura FL 33180-3805

PERKIN, GORDON WESLEY, international health executive; b. Toronto, Ont., Can., Apr. 25, 1935; came to U.S., 1962; s. Irvine Boyer and Jean (Laing) P.; m. Elizabeth Scott, Dec. 21, 1957; children: Scott, Stuart. MD, U. Toronto, 1959. Asst. dir. clin. rsch. Ortho Rsch. Found., Raritan, N.J., 1962-64; assoc. med. dir. Planned Parenthood Fedn. Am., N.Y.C., 1964-66; program advisor Ford Found., N.Y.C., 1966-67, regional program advisor Bangkok, 1967-69, Rio de Janeiro, 1973-76, program officer Mexico City, 1976-80; project specialist Ministry Fin. and Econ. Planning, Accra, Ghana, 1969-70; cons. WHO, Geneva, 1971-73; pres. Program for Appropriate Tech. in Health, Seattle, 1980-99; dir. reproductive and child health program Bill and Melinda Gates Found., 1999—2003, sr. fellow, 2003—. Affiliate prof. pub. health, U. Wash., Seattle; mem. Global Health Coun. Contbr. numerous articles to profl. jours. APHA fellow, 1970. Mem. Planned Parenthood Fedn. Am. (bd. dirs. 1983-89), Planned Parenthood Seattle-King County (bd. dirs. 1982-96, mem. exec. com. 1983-86), Planned Parenthood Western Wash. (bd. dirs. 1996—), NAS (com. mem. 1987-90), Alan Guttmacher Inst. (bd. dirs. 1985-90), Assn. Reproductive Health Profls., Alpha Omega Alpha. Office: Bill & Melinda Gates Found PO Box 23350 Seattle WA 98102-0650

PERKIN, HAROLD JAMES, retired social historian, educator; b. Nov. 11, 1926; s. Robert James and Hilda May (Dillon) P.; m. Joan Griffiths, July 3, 1948; children: Deborah Jane, Julian Robert. BA with 1st class distinction, Cambridge U., 1948, MA, 1952. From asst. lectr. to lectr. social history Manchester U., 1951-65; sr. lectr. Lancaster U., 1965-67, prof. social history, 1967-84, dir. ctr. social history, 1975-84, vis. prof., 1984-97, prof. emeritus, 1997—; prof. history Northwestern U., Evanston, Ill., 1985-97, prof. higher edn., 1987-97, prof. emeritus, 1997—. Vis. fellow Princeton U., 1979-80; fellow Nat. Humanities Ctr., N.C., 1982-83; hon. prof. U. Wales, Cardiff, 1997—. Author: The Origins of Modern English Society, 1780-1880, 1969, new edit., 2002, Key Profession: The History of the Association of University Teachers, 1969, New Universities in the U.K., 1969, The Age of the Railway, 1970, The Age of the Automobile, 1976, The Structured Crowd, 1980, Professionalism, Property and English Society since 1880, 1981, The Rise of Professional Society: England since 1880, 1989, new edit., 2002, Higher Education and English Society, Japanese transl., 1993, The Third Revolution: Professional Elites in the Modern World, 1996, The Making of a Social Historian, 2002. With RAF, 1948-50. Recipient Gold medal Nat. Inst. Ednl. Rsch., Tokyo, 1982; maj. scholar Cambridge U., 1945-48; John S. Guggenheim fellow, 1989-90. Fellow Royal Hist. Soc.; mem. Social History Soc. U.K. (life v.p., founder 1976), Econ. History Soc., History of Edn. Soc., Assn. Univ. Tchrs. (pres. 1970-71). Home: 106 St Mary's Mansions St Mary's Terr London W2 1SZ England E-mail: hjperkin@borwicks.demon.co.uk.

PERKIN, RONALD MURRAY, pediatrician, educator; b. Denver, July 31, 1948; s. Robert Murray and Marion Kathryn (Thompson) P.; m. Susan Renee Sheer; children: Matthew Murray, Jeffrey Jay, Nickolas James, Thomas Mitchell, Benjamin Sheer, Savannah Paige. BS in Engring., U. Colo., 1970; postgrad., Johns Hopkins U., 1970-71; MD, U. South Fla., 1976; MA, Loma Linda Univ., 1997. Diplomate Am. Bd. Pediatrics. Resident in pediatrics Children's Med. Ctr., Dallas, 1976-79, fellow in pediatric intensive care, 1979-81, asst. dir. pediatric intensive care, 1981; clins. asst. prof. pediatrics U. Tex. Health Sci. Ctr. Southwestern Med. Sch., Dallas, 1981; asst. adj. prof. pediatrics U. Calif. Sch. Medicine, San Diego, 1982-84, co-dir. pediatric intensive care, 1982-84; dir. pediatric ICU attending physician Childrens Hosp. Orange (Calif.) County Hosp., 1984-88; attending physician newborn ICU St. Joseph's Hosp., Orange, 1984-88; assoc. prof. pediatrics Loma Linda Univ., 1988-90, prof. pediatrics, 1990-2000; prof., chmn. dept. pediats. Brody Sch. Medicine, East Carolina U., Greenville, NC, 2000—. Cons. Naval Hosp., San Diego, 1983-84; asst. adj. prof. pediatrics U. Calif., Irvine, 1984-88; dir. pediatric intensive care fellowship program U. Calif. Irvine and Children's Hosp. Orange County, 1984-88; mem. critical care adv. com., critical care council, Extra Corporeal Membrane Oxygenation found. So. Calif., emergency dept. com., ethics com., ethics cons. svc. critical care com., resident evaluation sub-com., respiratory care com.; dir. pediatrics critical care Loma Linda Univ. Children's Hosp., 1988-2000, assoc. chair pediatrics Sch. Medicine, 1993-2000; lectr. in field. Editor: (with others) Brain Insults in Infants and Children: Pathophysiology and Management; Emergency Management of the Critically Ill Child; Pediatric Hosp. Medicine: A Textbook of Inpatient Care, 2003; reviewer Capistrano Press, Ltd., 1982-84, Jour. Pediatrics, 1982—; contbr. numerous articles and to profl. jours. Served with USN, 1971-73. Recipient student awards U. South Fla. Coll. Medicine, faculty awards U. Calif., Irvine, Lange Ann. award Lange Book Co., 1974; Mosby scholar Mosby Book Co., 1975-76. Fellow Am. Acad. Pediatrics, Am. Coll. Critical Care Medicine; mem. Soc. Critical Care Medicine, Calif. Children Svcs. (adv. com. rev. pediatric ICU's 1986-2000). Office: 3E-142 Brody Med Scis Bldg Greenville NC 27858-4354 Fax: 252-816-3292. E-mail: perkinr@mail.ecu.edu.

PERKINS, ANTHONY B. editor-in-chief, writer, educator; b. Dec. 6, 1957; Student, U. Calif., Davis, Calif. V.p. bus. devel. Silicon Valley Bank; founder, CEO Upside Pub. Co.; founder, CEO, editor-in-chief Red Herring Comms., 1993—2003; founder Always On, Woodside, Calif., 2003—, editor-in-chief, 2003—. Commentator CNN Fin. Network Digital Jam show, CNN, CNBC, ZDTV's News programs, Silicon Spin, European Bus. News; spkr. in field. Contbr. guest columns for various industry pubs.; co-author: The Internet Bubble. Founding chmn. Churchill Club, Palo Alto, Calif.; mem. bd. dirs. Am. Entrepreneurs Econ. Growth, Wash. Named one of the top ten tech./bus. journalists, Mktg. Computers mag. Office: Red Herring Communications 185 Berry St Ste 4700 San Francisco CA 94107-1768

PERKINS, ARTHUR LEE, SR., retired principal, real estate broker, insurance agent; b. Denham Springs, La., Feb. 24, 1935; s. Joe I. and Elma (Jackson) P.; m. Nora L. Johnson, Dec. 20, 1958; children: Arthur Jr., Michael, Jeffrey, Tonya. BS, So. U., Baton Rouge, 1957, MEd, 1965, postgrad., 1972. Cert. secondary edn. tchr., La.; lic. ins. agt., real estate broker, La. Prin. West Livingston H.S., Denham Springs, La., 1957-70; tchr., prin. Albany (La.) H.S., 1970-98; ret., 1998; real estate broker State of La., 1972—; ins. agt. Profl. Inc., Baton Rouge, 1997—. Treas. local chpt. NAACP, Denham Springs, 1993—; mem. Livingston Parish Voters League, Denham Springs, 1954—, treas.; commr. Recreation and Parks, Denham Springs, 1980-96, La. H.S. Athletic Assn., Baton Rouge, 1995-97; councilman City of Denham Springs, 1975-91, 95—. 2nd lt. U.S. Army, 1957-58, capt. 951st Ref. Co., 1957-72, ret. lt. col. USNG, 1988. Mem. Capital City Lodge (3d D. award 1968), Kappa Alpha Psi (lt. stratugus 1984—). Democrat. Protestant. Avocation: hunting. Home: 906 Hatchell Ln Denham Springs LA 70726-2621

PERKINS, BRADFORD, history educator; b. Rochester, NY, Mar. 6, 1925; s. Dexter and Wilma (Lord) P.; m. Nancy Nash Tucker, June 18, 1949 (dec.); children: Dexter III, Matthew Edward, Martha Nash. James Bradford (dec.). AB, Harvard U., 1946, PhD, 1952. From instr. to asso. prof. history U. Calif. at, Los Angeles, 1952-62; prof. history U. Mich., 1962-97, chmn. dept., 1971-72, 80-81, prof. emeritus, 1997—. Commonwealth Fund lectr. Univ. Coll., London, Eng., 1964; vis. prof. history Brandeis U., 1970, Ecole des Hautes Etudes en Sciences Sociales, Paris, 1983; Albert Shaw lectr. Johns Hopkins U., 1979; mem. council Inst. Early Am. History and Culture, 1968-71; program dir. Nat. Endowment for Humanities Fellowships in Residence for Coll. Tchrs., 1974-75 Author: The First Rapprochement: England and the United States, 1795-1805, 1955, Youthful America, 1960, Prologue to War: England and the United States, 1805-1812, 1961, Causes of the War of 1812, 1962, Castlereagh and Adams: England and the United States, 1812-1823, 1964, The Great Rapprochement: England and the United States, 1895-1914, 1968, The Creation of a Republican Empire, 1993. Served with AUS, 1943-45, ETO. Decorated Bronze Star.; Recipient Bancroft prize, 1965, Disting. Faculty award U. Mich., 1986; Warren fellow, 1969-70; Faculty Rsch. fellow Social Sci. Rsch. Council, 1957-60; Guggenheim fellow, 1962-63 Mem. Am. Hist. Assn., Soc. Am. Historians, Orgn. Am. Historians

(coun. 1969-72), Soc. Historians Am. Fgn. Rels. (coun. 1967-72, pres. 1974, Graebner award 1992), Mass. Hist. Soc., Am. Antiquarian Soc. Home: 827 Asa Gray Dr # 458 Ann Arbor MI 48105 Business E-Mail: bperkins@umich.edu.

PERKINS, CHARLES, III, newspaper editor; b. Brockton, Mass., July 25, 1952; s. Charles II and Barbara Perkins; m. Linda C. Burroughs, Jan. 4, 1985. BA, Dartmouth Coll., 1975. Editor Journal-Opinion, Bradford, Vt., 1977-78; reporter, editor The Union Leader and N.H. Sunday News, Manchester, 1978-81; Sunday editor N.H. Sunday News, Manchester, 1981-84; mng. editor The Union Leader and N.H. Sunday News, Manchester, 1984-92, exec. editor, 1992—, v.p. editl., 2000—. Office: PO Box 9555 Manchester NH 03108-9555

PERKINS, CHARLES THEODORE, real estate developer, consultant; b. Houston, Aug. 16, 1967; s. Charles Abraham and Mary Margaret Perkins. Attended, St. John's Coll., Santa Fe, 1985-86; AB in Psychology, AB in French, Washington U., St. Louis, 1989; MBA, Institut Superieur Des Affaires/Groupe HEC Paris, 1994; postgrad. The Wharton Sch., U. Pa., 1994-95. Lic. broker, N.Y. Asset mgr. A. David Schwarz, III, Inc., Houston, 1989-93; pres. CTP Interests, Inc., Houston, 1991—; projet mgr. Washington Sq. Ptnrs., N.Y., 1995—, The Arete Group, N.Y., 1995—; mng. dir. Plymouth Ptnrs. Ltd., 1997—. Broker's lic. Tex. Real Estate Commn., Austin, 1991—. Dir. Washington Crew Classic Regata, St. Louis, 1989; founding coach Rice U. Crew, Houston, 1990; lic. judge referee U.S. Rowing Assn., 1991—, level I coach, 1991—. Recipient Prix De L'excellence BDE, Groupe HEC-ISA, Paris, 1994. Mem. The Penn Club of N.Y., N.Y. Sports Club, Mensa. Episcopalian.

PERKINS, DANA STELA, pharmacologist, research scientist; b. Hateg, Romania, Oct. 12, 1965; d. Stelica Corbeanu and Victoria Mandica. PhD, U. Md., 2002. Immunologist Cel-Sci Corp., Balt., 1996—98; rsch. scientist EntreMed, Inc., Rockville, Md., 2002—03; microbiologist US Dept. of Commerce, Washington, 2003—04; sr. rsch. scientist Calspan-UB Rsch. Ctr., Inc., 2004—. Spkr. in field. Reviewer Jour. Cellular and Molecular Medicine, Phila., 2002—; contbr. articles to profl. jours. Recipient Nat. Collegiate Inventors Competition award, USPTO and Nat. Inventors Hall of Fame, 2001, Chpt. award, Soc. Neurosci. and Eli Lilly Co., 2002, 1st pl. 2d Ann. Rsch. Paper Contest for Grad. Students, Am. Soc. Microbiology, 2002. Mem.: Sci. Adv. Bd. Achievements include patents pending for anti-apoptotic activity of herpes simplex virus type 2 gene ICP10 PK. Home: 4005 Cordell Ct Bowie MD 20715 Office Phone: 202-478-3428. Personal E-mail: doctordana@comcast.net.

PERKINS, DWIGHT HEALD, economics professor; b. Chgo., Oct. 20, 1934; s. Lawrence Bradford and Margery (Blair) P.; m. Julie Rate, June 15, 1957; children: Lucy Fitch, Dwight Edward, Caleb Blair. BA, Cornell U., 1956; AM, Harvard U., 1961, PhD, 1964. From instr. to assoc. prof. Harvard U., Cambridge, Mass., 1963-69, prof. econs., 1969-81, assoc. dir. East Asian Rsch. Ctr., 1973-77, chmn. dept. econs., 1977-80, H.H. Burbank prof. polit. economy, 1981—, dir. Asia Ctr., 2002—; dir. Harvard Inst. Internat. Devel., Cambridge, 1980-95. Trustee China Med. Bd., 1995—, chair, 2000—; cons. permanent subcom. on investigations U.S. Senate, 1974-80; H.M. Jackson vis. prof. Chinese studies U. Wash., 1985, Phi Beta Kappa lectr., 1992-93, Faculty Salzburg seminar, 1996; lectr. Fulbright tchg. policy program, Vietnam, 1997-2004; mem. Internat. Adv. Group to Prime Min. of Papua, New Guinea, 1991-92, 2000-02; cons. Korea Devel. Inst., 1972-80, Govt. Malaysia, 1968-69. Author: (with M. Halperin) Communist China and Arms Control, 1965, Agricultural Development in China, 1368-1968, 1969, Market Control and Planning in Communist China, 1966, China: Asia's Next Economic Giant?, 1986, (with E.S. Mason and others) The Economic Modernization of Korea, 1980, (with S. Yusuf) Rural Development in China, 1984, (with M. Gillis and others) Economics of Development, 1983, 5th edit., 2001; editor: China's Modern Economy in Historical Perspective, 1975, (with M. Roemer) Reforming Economic Systems in Developing Countries, 1991, (with J. Stern and others) Industrialization and the State: The Korean Heavy and Chemical Industry Drive, 1995; (with others) Assisting Development in a Changing World, 1997, Industrialization and the State: The Changing Role of the Taiwan Government in the Economy, 1945-1998, 2001, Innovative East Asia: The Future of Growth, 2003. Vis. com. Far Ea. studies U. Chgo., 1973-77; bd. govs. East-West Ctr., Honolulu, 1979-82; co-moderator Aspen Inst. Seminar on Korea, Colo., 1980-83. Lt. (j.g.) USNR, 1956-58. Fgn. Area Tng. fellow Ford Found., N.Y., 1958-62; NSF Sci. Faculty fellow Tokyo, 1968-69. Mem. Am. Philos. Soc., Assn. Asian Studies, Assn. Comparative Econ. Systems (pres. 1999-2000), Am. Econ. Assn., Phi Beta Kappa. Home: 64 Pinehurst Rd Belmont MA 02478-1504 Office: Harvard Univ Dept Econs Cambridge MA 02138-5781 Office Phone: 617-495-2110. Business E-Mail: dwight_perkins@harvard.edu.

PERKINS, EDWARD J. diplomat; b. Sterlington, La., June 8, 1928; m. Lucy Liu; children: Katherine, Sarah. Student, U. Calif., Lewis and Clark Coll.; BA, U. Md., 1967; MPA, U. So. Calif., 1972, DPA, 1978; studied French, Fgn. Service Inst., 1983; LLD (hon.), U. Md., 1990, St. John's U., 1990, Lewis and Clark Coll., 1988; LHD (hon.), Winston-Salem State U., 1990, Bowie State Coll., 1993; HHD (hon.), St. Augustine Coll., 1991, Beloit Coll., 1990, U. So. Calif., 1995. Chief of pers. Army and Air Force Exch. Svc., Taipei, Taiwan, 1958-62, dep. chief Okinawa, Japan, 1962-64; chief pers. and adminstrn. Army and Air Force Exchange Service, Okinawa, Japan, 1964-66; asst. gen. svcs. officer Far East bur. AID, 1967-69, mgmt. analyst, 1969-70; asst. dir. for mgmt. U.S. Ops. Mission to Thailand, 1970-72; staff asst. Office of Dir. Gen. Fgn. Svc., 1972, personnel officer, 1972-74; adminstrv. officer Bur. Near Eastern and South Asian Affairs, 1974-75; mgmt. analysis officer Office Mgmt. Ops., Dept. State, 1975-78; counselor for polit. affairs Accra, Ghana, 1978-81; dep. chief of mission Monrovia, Liberia, 1981-83; dir. Office of West African Affairs, Bur. African Affairs, Dept. State, 1983-85; U.S. amb. to Liberia, 1985-86; U.S. amb. to South Africa, 1986-89; dir. gen., dir. pers. Fgn. Svc., Dept. of State, Washington, 1989-92; U.S. rep. to UN N.Y.C., 1992-93; U.S. amb. to Australia Canberra, 1993-96. William J. Crowe prof. and exec. dir. Internat. Programs Ctr., U. Okla., Norman 1996-; mem. adv. bd. Inst. Internat. Pub. Policy, 1997-; mem. adv. coun. Univ. Office of Internat. Programs, Pa. State U., 1997; mem. White House Adv. Com. on Trade Policy and Negotiations, 2003-. Contbr. articles to profl. publs.; editor (with David Boren) Preparing American's Foreign Policy for the 21st Century, 1999, with (Joseph Ginat) Palestinian Refugees: Traditional Positions and New Solutions, 2001, (with David Boren) Democracy, Morality, and the Search for Peace in America's Foreign Policy, 2002, (with Joseph Ginat and Edwin G. Corr) Middle East Peace Process: Vision Versus Reality, 2002. Trustee Lewis and Clark Coll., 1994—, Woodrow Wilson Nat. Fellowship Found., 1999—; bd. govs. Joint Ctr. for Polit. and Econ. Studies, 1996-2003; mem. steering com. Ctr. for Australian and New Zealand Studies, Georgetown U., 1996—; bd. Cranlana Programme; bd. visitors Nat. Def. U., 2002-. Recipient Presdl. Meritorious Svc. award, 1987, Presdl. Disting. Svc. award, 1989, Meritorious Honor award AID, 1967, Disting. Alumni award U. So. Calif., 1991, Achievement award So. U., 1991, award for outstanding svc. as fgn. svc. officer Una Chapman Cox Found., 1989, Living Legend award The Links, Inc., 1989, Statesman of Yr. award George Washington U., 1992, Superior Honor award Dept. of State, 1983, Dir. Gen.'s cup Dept. of State, 2001; honoree U. Okla. chpt. Beta Gamma Sigma, 1998. Fellow Nat. Acad. Pub. Adminstrn.; mem. VFW, ASPA, Navy League, Am. Polit. Sci. Assn., Fgn. Policy Assn. (ambassadorial fellow), Internat. Studies Assn., Coun. on Fgn. Rels., Am. Acad. Diplomacy, Am. Consortium Internat. Pub. Adminstrn., Am. Fgn. Svc. Assn., Am. Legion, Ctr. Study of Presidency, Chester A. Arthur Soc., Pub. Svc. Comm., World Affairs Couns. Okla. and Washington, Am. Acad. Diplomacy, Pacific Coun. on Internat. Policy, Assn. for Diplomatic Studies and Tng. (bd. dirs. 1998—), Kappa Alpha Psi (Laurel Wreath award 1993, C. Rodger Wilson Leadership Conf. award 1990, Disting. Svc. award 1989, Outstanding Achievement award for Fgn. Svc. 1986), Phi Kappa Phi. Office: U Okla Internat Programs Ctr 339 W Boyd St Rm 400 Norman OK 73019-5144

PERKINS, FRANK OVERTON, university official, marine scientist; b. Fork Union, Va., Feb. 14, 1938; s. Frank Otie and Mary Ella (Hughes) P.; m. Beverly Anne Weeks. BA, U. Va., 1960; MS, Fla. State U., Tallahassee, 1962, PhD, 1966. Marine scientist Va. Inst. Marine Sci., Coll. William and Mary, Gloucester Point, 1966-69, sr. marine scientist, 1969 77, asst. dir., 1977-81, dir., dean Sch. Marine Sci., 1981-91, prof. marine sci., 1991-97; asst. v.p. rsch. and grad. edn. U. Hawaii, Honolulu, 1997—. Baptist. Home: 7519 Olowalu Pl Honolulu HI 96825-2950 Office: U Hawaii 223 Crawford Hall Honolulu HI 96822

PERKINS, GEORGE, educator, writer; b. Lowell, Mass., Aug. 16, 1930; s. George Burton Perkins and Gladys Beatrice Jones; m. Barbara Miller Perkins, May 9, 1964; children: Laura, Suzanne, Alison. AB, Tufts U., 1953; MA, Duke U., 1954; PhD, Cornell U., 1960. Instr. Wash. U., St. Louis, 1957—60; asst. prof. Baldwin-Wallace Coll., Berea, Ohio, 1960—63, Fairleigh Dickinson U., Rutherford, NJ, 1963—66; lectr. U. Edinburgh, Scotland, 1966—67; prof. Ea. Mich. U., Ypsilanti, 1967—2001. Author, editor: The American Tradition in Literature, The Reader's Encyclopedia of American Literature, others. Fellow Inst. for Advanced Studies in the Humanities, U. Edinburgh, 1981; Sr. Fulbright scholar Australia Coun. for Internat. Exch. of Scholars, 1989. Avocations: travel, tennis, literature, basketball. Home: 1316 King George Blvd Ann Arbor MI 48108-3212 E-mail: george.perkins@emich.edu.

PERKINS, GEORGE HOLMES, architectural educator, architect; b. Cambridge, Mass., Oct. 10, 1904; s. George Howard and Josephine (Schock) P.; m. Georgia Hencken, June 3, 1933; children— Gray H., Jennifer H. Student, Phillips-Exeter Acad., 1920-22; AB, Harvard U., 1926, M.Arch., 1929; LL.D., U. Pa., 1972. Instr. architecture U. Mich., 1929-30; instr. architecture Harvard, 1930-36, asst. prof., 1936-39, asso. prof., 1939-42, Norton prof. regional planning, chmn. dept., 1945-51; dean, chmn. dept. architecture Grad. Sch. Fine Arts, U. Pa., 1951-71, prof. architecture and urbanism, 1971—; practicing architect and city planner, 1933—. Asst. regional rep., acting dir. urban devel. div. Nat. Housing Agy., 1942-45; cons. Brit. Ministry of Town and Country Planning, 1946, UN, 1946, 55 56; cons. to Govt. Turkey, 1958-60, Balt. Redevel. Authority, Cambridge Redevel. Authority, Worcester Redevel. Authority.; Mem. Cambridge Planning Bd., 1950-51; dir. Phila. Housing Assn., 1951-56, pres., 1953-56; dir. Citizens Council City Planning, 1951-54; chmn. Phila. Zoning Commn., 1955-58, Phila. City Planning Commn., 1958-68; dir. Phila. Port Corp., Old Phila. Devel. Corp., Phila. Indsl. Devel. Corp. Author: Comparative Outline of Architectural History, 1937; editor: Jour. Am. Inst. Planners, 1950-52; contbr. articles to profl. jours. Mem. Phila. Commn. Higher Edn.; Trustee Fairmount Park Art Assn., 1965— . Fellow A.I.A. (chancellor coll. fellows 1964-66); mem. Am. Inst. Planners, Am. Soc. Planning Ofcls., Nat. Assn. Housing Ofcls., World Soc. Ekistics; hon. corr. mem. Royal Inst. Architects Can. Clubs: The Country (Brookline); Franklin Inn (Phila.), Rittenhouse (Phila.), Philadelphia Cricket (Phila.), Art Alliance (Phila.); Century (N.Y.C.). Home: 82 Bethlehem Pike Philadelphia PA 19118-2821

PERKINS, HERBERT ASA, hematologist, educator; b. Boston, Oct. 5, 1918; s. Louis and Anna (Robinson) P.; m. Frances Snyder, Sept. 2, 1942; children: Susan, Deborah, Dale, Karen, Ronnie. AB cum laude, Harvard U., 1940; MD summa cum laude, Tufts U., 1943. Intern Boston City Hosp., 1944, resident, 1947-48; practice medicine specializing in transfusion medicine; clin. instr. Stanford Med. Sch., 1953-57, asst. clin. prof., 1957-58; hematologist Open Heart Surgery Team, Stanford Hosp., San Francisco, 1955-58, Jewish Hosp., St. Louis, 1958-59; dir. rsch. Irwin Meml. Blood Ctrs. (now Blood Ctrs. of the Pacific), San Francisco, 1959-78, med. and sci. dir., 1978-90, exec. dir., 1987-91, pres., 1991-93, sr. med. scientist, 1993—. Asst. prof. medicine Washington U., St. Louis, 1958-59, U. Calif., San Francisco, 1959-66, assoc. prof., 1966-71, clin. prof., 1971—. Co-editor: Hepatitis and Blood Transfusion, 1972. Maj. M.C., U.S. Army, 1944-47. Mem. AAAS, Am. Assn. Blood Banks (chmn. sci. adv. com. 1972-73, chmn. stds. com. 1968-71, chmn. com. on organ transplantation and tissue typing 1970-80, bd. dirs. 1982-86), Am. Soc. Hematology, Internat. Transfusion Soc., Am. Soc. Histocompatibility and Immunogenetics (pres. 1985-86), Nat. Marrow Donor Program (chair bd. dirs. 1995-96, chmn. com. on stds. 1987-94, chmn. fin. com. 1987-94). Home: 520 Berkeley Ave Menlo Park CA 94025-2323 Office: Blood Ctrs of the Pacific 270 Masonic Ave San Francisco CA 94118-4417 E-mail: hperkins@bloodcenters.org.

PERKINS, HOMER GUY, manufacturing executive; b. New Haven, Oct. 23, 1916; s. Frank W. and Emily (Oesting) P.; m. Dorothy C. Stock, Jan. 24, 1942; children: Maribeth Perkins Grant, Homer Guy Jr., Hazel Mary Perkins Adolphson, Dorothy Catherine, Caroline Ann, Faith Elizabeth Perkins Crotteau, Ruth Emily Perkins Sico. BA in Internat. Rels., Yale U., 1938; LLD (hon.), Westfield (Mass.) State Coll., 1977. With Enesco Group, Inc. (formerly Stanhome, Inc.), Westfield, 1939—, v.p., 1965-66, exec. v.p., 1966-70, pres., CEO, 1970-78, chmn., 1978-81. Treas. Stanley Park of Westfield, 1949—; pres. Citizens Scholarship Found., Easthampton, Mass., 1966-67, Easthampton Cmty. Chest, 1960-61; chmn. fin. com., bd. dirs. Western Mass. coun. Girl Scouts U.S., 1966-69; mem. devel. com. Clarke Sch. Deaf, Northampton, 1965-68; mem. fin. com. Town of Easthampton, 1962-70, chmn. fin. com., 1967-68; dir. Frank Stanley Beveridge Found., Westfield, 1956-95, pres., 1966-87; trustee Cooley Dickinson Hosp., Northampton, 1963-70, 84-92, chmn. bd. trustees, 1989-91; pres. bd. trustees Northampton Sch. for Girls, 1964-73; bd. dirs. Porter Phelps Huntington Found., Hadley, Mass., 1960-92, Guild of Holy Child, Westfield, 1969-76; mem. bd. overseers Williston Acad., Easthampton, 1961-64, Old Sturbridge (Mass.) Village, 1970-76; v.p. bd. trustees Williston-Northampton Sch., 1970-75, pres., 1975-78; dir. The Lathrop Communities, 2000, chair fin. com., 2001. With USAAF, 1942-46. Mem. Direct Selling Assn. (chmn. 1975, bd. dirs., mem. Hall of Fame), Paperweight Collectors Assn. (pres. 1991-95), Lions (past pres. Easthampton club). Home: 8 Carol Ave Easthampton MA 01027-1904

PERKINS, HUEL DAVIS, academic administrator; b. Baton Rouge, La., Dec. 27, 1924; s. John Earl Perkins, Sr. and Velma Davis Perkins; m. Thelma Ovella Smith; 1 child, Huel Alfred. BS, So. U., Baton Rouge, LA, 1947; MusM, Northwestern U., 1951, PhD, 1958. Dean coll. of arts & humanities So. U., Baton Rouge, 1968—78; from asst. vice chancellor for academic affairs to spl. asst. to chancellor La. State U., Baton Rouge, 1980—98, spl. asst. to the chancellor, 1998—. Vis. faculty Havard U., Boston, 1968; chmn. alpha phi alpha edn. found. Alpha Phi Alpha Frat., Balt., 1986—92; nat. chmn. scholars selection com. Coca Cola Found., Atlanta, 1996; invited participant Caribbean-American Scholars Exch. Program, Port-au-Prince, Haiti, 1974; mem. Pres. Clinton's Commn. on Black Coll. and U., Washington, 1994—96. Composer: (musical composition) Southern U. Fight Song, 1953, (songs) Alpha Phi Alpha Sweetheart Song, 1974; book reviewer: Black World Mag., 1973. Pres. Capital Area United Way; torch bearer U.S. Olympics, Baton Rouge, 1995. Named one of 100 Most Influential African Americans, Ebony Mag., 1993; recipient Brotherhood Award, Nat. Conf. of Christian and Jews, 1986, 100 Most Influential African Americans, Ebony Mag., 1994; fellow Humanities fellowship, Nat. Endowment for the Humanities, 1972, Huel D. Perkins Doctoral fellowship, La. State U., 1995; grantee Tchr. grant, Danforth Found., 1957. Mem.: Am. Soc. of Composers, Authors and P:ub., Omicron Delta Kappa, Pi Kappa Lambda, Sigma Pi Phi (grand sire archon 1992—94), Alpha Phi Alpha (chmn. edn. found. 1986—92). Democrat. Baptist. Avocations: tennis, reading, opera. Home: 1923 79th Avenue Baton Rouge LA 70807 Office: Louisiana State University Baton Rouge LA 70803 Personal E-mail: huelperkins@cox.net. Business E-Mail: hperkins@lsu.edu.

PERKINS, JACK EDWIN, lawyer; b. Portola, Calif., May 25, 1943; s. Charles James and Vira Almena (Wing) P.; m. Barbara Kay Nielson, Jan, 18, 1969; children: Jill Christy, Kelli Anne. BA, San Jose State Coll., 1966; JD, Hastings Coll. Law, 1972. Bar: Calif. 1972, D.C. 1989. Asst. U.S. atty., Dept. Justice, San Francisco, 1973-74, staff atty. criminal divsn. Washington, 1972, 74-76, staff atty. Office Legis. Affairs, 1976-80, legis. counsel, 1980-86, dep. asst. atty. gen., 1986-90; chief adminstrv. hearing officer Exec. Office for Immigration Rev., Falls Church, Va., 1990—. Served to capt. USMC, 1966-69, Vietnam. Recipient John Marshall award Dept. Justice, 1986. Avocations: tennis, jogging, racquetball. Office: Exec Office Immigration Rev 5107 Leesburg Pike Ste 2519 Falls Church VA 22041-3234

PERKINS, JAMES WOOD, lawyer; b. New Bedford, Mass., Oct. 14, 1924; s. Ralph Chamberlain and Louise Bartlett (Allen) P.; m. Margaret Neale Heard, Feb. 3, 1951; children: Charles H., James A., George H. AB, Havard U., 1945, JD, 1948; MTS, Harvard Div. Sch., 1996. Bar: Mass. 1948, U.S. Dist. Ct. Mass. 1948. Engr. Sylvania Electric Products, Inc., Salem, Mass., 1944-45; assoc. Palmer & Dodge LLP, Boston, 1948-54, ptnr., 1955-91, mng. ptnr., 1986-89, of counsel, 1992—. Mem. ABA (chmn. sect. local govt. law 1970-71, sect. del. 1974-78), Nat. Assn. Bond Lawyers (pres. 1985-86).

PERKINS, JIM C. automotive executive; V.p. Hendrick Automotive Group, Charlotte, NC, 1996—97, CEO, pres., 1997—. Office: C/O Hendrick Automotive Group 6000 Monroe Rd Ste 100 Charlotte NC 28212-6178

PERKINS, JOHN ALLEN, lawyer; b. New Bedford, Mass., Sept. 13, 1919; s. Ralph Chamberlain and Louise Bartlett (Allen) P.; m. Lydia Bullard Cobb, Sept. 9, 1944; children: John A., Susan W., Robert C., William B. AB, Harvard U., 1940, LL.B., 1943. Bar: Mass. Of counsel Palmer & Dodge LLP, Boston; clk. Social Law Library, 1961-83; grad. researcher Univ. Coll., Oxford U., 1978. Bd. dirs. Greater Boston Legal Services, Inc., 1972-91. Author: The Prudent Peace— Law as Foreign Policy, 1981; contbr. articles to profl. jours. Mem. Dedham (Mass.) Sch. Com., 1959-65, chmn., 1963-65, town counsel, Dedham, 1971-72. Mem. Am. Law Inst., Am. Coll. Trust and Estate Counsel, Mass. Bar Assn. (dir. 1973-75), Internat. Acad. Estate and Trust Law (exec. coun. 1990-94), Boston Bar Assn. (council 1972-75, v.p. 1981-82, pres. 1982-84). Home: 100 Newbury Court Ste 610 Concord MA 01742-5835 Office: Palmer & Dodge LLP 111 Huntington Ave at Prudential Ctr Boston MA 02199-7613

PERKINS, JOSEPH S. medical association administrator; Past corp. retirement mgr. Polaroid Corp.; v.p. AARP, Washington, 1994-96, pres.-elect, 1996-98, pres., 1998-2000. Mem. bd. fin. com., nat. legis. coun., bus. partnerships adv. coun. AARP, trustee Andrus Found. Bd., past vice chair; past mem. exec. com., bd. fin. com., bd. com. human resources, trustee investment program, group health ins. trust, bd. observer pension/welfare trust AARP; bd. councilors Ethel Percy Andrus Gerontology Ctr., U. So. Calif.; mem. bd. Operation ABLE (Abilities Based on Long Experience); mem. adv. coun. Foster Grandparent Program Greater Boston; past mem. Pension Benefit Guaranty Corp. Adv. Com.; past bd. dirs. Alzheimer's Assn., Internat. Soc. Retirement Planning; past founding mem., pres. New England Retirement Planners Coun.; past vol. Project RAP; formerly indsl. engr. Office: AARP 601 E St NW Washington DC 20049-0003

PERKINS, LAWRENCE BRADFORD, JR., architect; b. Chgo., Jan. 13, 1943; s. Lawrence Bradford and Margery Isabella (Blair) P.; m. Phyllis Barbara Friedman, Sept. 11, 1966; children: Rachael Naomi, Judith Eve, Rebecca Abigail. BA, Cornell U., 1967; MBA, Stanford U., 1969; BArch, CCNY, 1976. Registered architect, N.Y., Conn., Md., Ohio, Ill., Conn., Pa., Mass., Ill., N.J., Ga., Fla., Mo., Ariz., Tex. Pres. Perkins Eastman Archs., N.Y.C., 1983—, Omnidata Svcs., N.Y.C., 1971-73; mng. ptnr. Llewelyn-Davies Assocs., N.Y.C., 1973-77, Perkins & Will, N.Y.C., 1977-81; ptnr. Attia & Perkins, N.Y.C., 1981-83. Author: Design of K-12 Schools; contbr. chpts. to books and articles to profl.jours. Bd. dirs. Castle Gallery Coll. New Rochelle, N.Y., 1985—, Settlement Housing Fund, N.Y.C., 1991—, Helen Keller Internat., N.Y.C., 1993—, various other Scarsdale village bds. and coms.; chmn. bd. Hudson Planning Group. Fellow AIA (mem. various coms.), Am. Inst. Cert. Planners, Cornell U. Coun., Epsilon Assn. (pres. 1993-96). Home: 4 Rectory Ln Scarsdale NY 10583-4314 Office: Perkins Eastman Archs 115 5th Ave New York NY 10003-1004

PERKINS, LEEMAN LLOYD, music educator, musicologist; b. Salina, Utah, Mar. 27, 1932; s. Milton Lloyd and Ida Margaret (Johnson) P.; m. Marianne Suzanne Contesse, Nov. 14, 1956; children: Eric Raymond, Bruce Philippe, Marc Christian (dec.), Patrick Thierry. BFA, U. Utah, 1954; PhD, Yale U., 1965. Instr. Boston U., 1964, Yale U., 1964-67, asst. prof., 1967-71, dir. undergraduate studies in music history, 1969-70; assoc. prof. music history, coord. for musicology U. Tex., Austin, 1971-75, grad. adv. for musicology, 1976; prof. music Columbia U., N.Y.C., 1976—2003, prof. emeritus, 2003—, chmn. dept music, 1985-90. Instr. advanced seminar in Medieval History, Smith Coll., 1968; vis. assoc. prof. music Columbia U., 1975; vis. prof. Boston U., 1978; dir. NEH Summer Seminar, 1977. Editor: Johannes Lheritier Opera Omnia, 1969, (with Howard Garey) The Mellon Chansonnier, 1979, Music in the Age of the Renaissance, 1999; gen. editor: Masters and Monuments of Renaissance Music, 1978—. Chmn. grad. musicology com., Columbia U., 1980-84, 1993-96, 97-2001. Sgt., 7th Army Symphony, U.S. Army, 1957-59. Recipient James Morris Whiton Fund award Yale U., 1965, The Otto Kinkeldey award Am. Musicological Soc., 1980, la Médaille de la Ville de Tours, 1997; Trumbull Coll. fellow Yale U., 1966-71, Lewis-Farmington fellow Yale U., 1962-63, Morse fellow Yale U., 1967-68, Am. Coun. Learned Soc. fellow, 1973-74, NEH fellow, 1979, 1984-85, French Archival Scis. fellow Newberry Libr. Center for Renaissance Studies, 1991; Martha Baird Rockefeller grantee, 1963-64, Paul Mellon Found. grantee, 1972, Am. Coun. Learned Soc., 1972, 82, U. Tex. grantee, 1975, Mem. Am. Musicological Soc. (chmn. program com. 1979, bd. dirs. 1980-81, adv. bd., 1985-86, chmn. ad hoc sub com., 1985-86, exec. com. delegate, 1989-92, mem. fellowship com. 1995-98), Internat. Musicological Soc., The Renaissance Soc. of Am., Phi Beta Kappa, Phi Kappa Phi. Mem. Lds Ch. E-mail: LLP1@columbia.edu.

PERKINS, LUCIAN, photographer; Grad., U. Tex. Intern The Washington Post, 1979, now staff photographer. Founder InterFoto (U.S./Russian photography orgn.). Author: (photography book) Runway Madness, 1998. Named Newspaper Photographer of Yr., Pictures of Yr. competition, 1993; recipient Pulitzer prize for explanatory journalism, 1995, Pulitzer prize for feature photography, 2000, Photo of Yr. award, World Press, 1996. Office: The Washington Post 1150 15th St NW Washington DC 20071-0002

PERKINS, MARK L. university chancellor; b. Richmond, Va., Oct. 13, 1948; m. Carolyn J. Snider; children: Patricia, Diana. BA in Psychology, St. Andrews Presbyn. Coll., 1972; MA, U. Ga., 1974, PhD in Psychometrics and Stats., 1976. With divsn. of pers. Gov.'s Office Commonwealth of Va., 1972-73; rsch. assoc., instr. U. Ga., Athens, 1973-76; various positions Old Dominion U., Norfolk, Va., 1976-86, exec. asst. to pres. for policy and planning, assoc. prof., 1981-82, assoc. exec. v.p., prof., 1982-86; v.p. for adminstrn., prof. Calif. State U., Stanislaus, Turlock, 1986-91, exec. v.p., prof., 1991-94; chancellor, prof. U. Wis., Green Bay, 1994—. Environ. mgmt. cons., 1990-95. Contbr. articles to profl. jours. Trustee Green Bay Symphony, 1995—; bd. dirs. Downtown Green Bay, Inc., 1996—, Weidner Ctr. Presents Inc., 1994—; trustee Calif. State U. Stanislaus Found., 1986-94, treas., 1986-94; mem. adv. coun. St. Vincent Hosp., 1994—. Named to Outstanding Young Men of Am., 1978. Mem. APA, Am. Ednl. Rsch. Assn., Am. Assn. for Higher Edn., Am. Assn. State Colls. and Univs., Soc. for Coll. and Univ. Planning, Green Bay Area C. of C./Ptnrs. in Edn. (exec. bd. 1996—), Green Bay Downtown Rotary Club, Phi Eta Sigma, Phi Kappa Phi, Kappa Delta Pi, Phi Delta Kappa. Avocations: running, racquetball, music. Office: U Wis Green Bay 2420 Nicolet Dr Green Bay WI 54311-7003

PERKINS, NANCY JANE, industrial designer; b. Phila., Nov. 5, 1949; d. Gordon Osborne and Martha Elizabeth (Keichline) P. Student, Ohio U., 1967-68; BFA, U. Ill., 1972. Indsl. designer Peterson Bednar Assocs., Evanston, Ill., 1972-74, Deschamps Mills Assos., Bartlett, Ill., 1974-75; dir. graphic design Cameo Container Corp., Chgo., 1975-76; indsl. design cons. Sears Roebuck & Co., Chgo., 1977-88; cons. indsl. design, 1988—. Lectr. CUNY, 1995; founder Perkins Design Ltd., Anna Wagner Keichline Gallery, Bellefonte, Pa.; adj. prof. grad. design seminar U. Ill. Chgo., 1982, 88, 91, 93, adj. instr. undergrad. design, 1984, 88, 91, 93; adj. instr. Ill. Inst. Tech., 1987, 91; vis. assoc. prof. Carnegie-Mellon U., 1991; juror annual design rev. Indsl. Design mag., 1986; mem. tech. rev. com. Ben Franklin Partnerships, 1991—; keynote spkr. several major U.S. design groups; spkr. Design in Am. symposium, Nagoya, Japan, 1989. Contbg. author: Design and Feminism, 1999; featured in Bard Grad. Ctrs.' Exhibit, N.Y.C., 2000; contbr. articles to

profl. jours.; patents in field. Co-leader Cadette troop DuPage County coun. Girl Scouts U.S., 1978-79. Recipient Outstanding Alumni award U. Ill. Alumni Jour., 1981, Goldsmith award, 1992; profiled in Indsl. Design mag., 1986, Feminine Ingenuity (by Anne L. Macdonald), 1992, Dun & Bradstreet Reports, 1993; profiled The Phila. Inquirer Mag., 1994; featured in Chgo. Athenaeum "33 plus 20", 1993, Pratt Manhattan Gallery, N.Y.C., 1994. Fellow Indsl. Designers Soc. Am. (treas. Chgo. chpt. 1977-79, vice chmn. 1979-80, chmn. 1981, mem. dist. membership com. 1982, mem. ann. conf. com. 1983, mem. publs. com. 1985-86, dir.-at-large 1987-88, v.p. Midwest dist. 1989-90, nat. sec.-treas. 1991-92, del. Internat. Coun. of the Socs. Indsl. Design 1989, dist. conf. speaker Mideast, 1993, Midwest, 2000, co-founder women's sect. 1992). Office Phone: 888-223-5211. Personal E-mail: njperkins@earthlink.net.

PERKINS, NANCY LEEDS, lawyer; b. Washington, June 19, 1956; d. Roswell Burchard and Joan (Titcomb) P. AB, Harvard U., 1979, M in Pub. Policy, JD, Harvard U., 1987. Bar: Pa. 1988, D.C. 1989, U.S. Dist. Ct. D.C. 1990. Jud. clk. U.S. Dist. Ct. (ea. dist.) N.Y., Bklyn., 1987-88; spl. counsel Arnold & Porter, Washington, 1988—. Contbr. articles to profl. jours. Recipient Pro Bono svc. award Internat. Human Rights Law Group, 1990. Democrat. Avocation: tennis. Office: Arnold & Porter 555 12th St NW Washington DC 20004-1206

PERKINS, NORRIS LYNWOOD, III, (TERRY PERKINS), columnist and writer; b. Smithfield, N.C., Nov. 3, 1947; s. Norris Lynwood Jr. and Mildred Mary (Brate) P.; m. Zoe Katherine Annis, May l, l982; children: Molly, Drew. Student, U. N.C., 1965—68; AB in English Lit., So. Ill. U., Edwardsville, 1970, postgrad., 1971—75, So. Ill. U., 2002—. Store mgr. Streetside Records, St. Louis, 1975—81, mgr. retail ops., 1981—83; music columnist Riverfront Times, St. Louis, 1983—2003; music reviewer, feature writer St. Louis Post-Dispatch, 1984—. Freelance bus. and tech. writer, prodr. bus. meetings and promotional events, St. Louis, 1988—; contbg. writer (websites) Office-.com, All About Jazz, 1999—; prodr. Busch Creative Svcs., St. Louis, l985-87; tech. writer McDonnell Douglas Fed. Health Systems Co., St. Louis, l987-88. Editor Sou'wester, 1972-76; non-profit orgn. music edn. for disadvantaged children. Nat. coord. Music for Life Alliance, 2003—. Episcopalian. Avocations: baseball, reading. Home and Office: 32 Orchard Ln Saint Louis MO 63122-6945 Office Phone: 314-533-9900. E-mail: tperkins01@charter.net.

PERKINS, RAYMOND LAMONT, retired government official; b. New Rochelle, N.Y., Apr. 8, 1924; s. Raymond Lamont and Dorothy Marie (Porter) P.; m. Margaret Johnson, Aug. 25, 1946; children: Deborah, Doriane, Amy. AB, U. Denver, 1946, LLB, 1948. Bar: Colo. Pvt. practice, Springfield, Colo., 1949-54; fgn. svc. officer Dept. State, various locations, 1954-86; ret., 1986. Lmem. Fgn. Svc. Grievance Bd., Washington, 1990-2000. Contbr. articles to profl. jours. County atty. Baca County, Colo., 1949-54, dep. dist. atty., 1949-52. Capt. USAR. Mem. Kiwanis. Methodist. Home: 1304 Tannery Cir Midlothian VA 23113 E-mail: rperkpeg@aol.com.

PERKINS, RICHARD D(ALE), police official, state legislator; b. Boulder City, Nev., Nov. 15, 1961; s. Daniel Kenneth and Shirley Joan (Williams) P.; m. Terri Perkins, Feb. 24, 1989; children: Nicole, Stephanie, Brian, Ashley, Rikki. Student, U. Nev., Las Vegas, 1979—; grad., FBI Nat. Acad., 1995. Police officer Henderson (Nev.) Police Dept., 1984-91, sgt., 1991-95, capt., 1995—; state assemblyman Nev. Legis., Carson City, 1993—, majority floor leader, 1996—. Mem. adv. bd. McCaw Sch., Henderson, 1996—; mem. Nev. Sentencing Adv. Commn., 1995-97, Indsl. Adv. Panel, Henderson, 1996; v.p. Henderson Dem. Club, 1992—; mem. chmn.'s coun. Big Bros.-Big Sisters; bd. dirs. Safe House Domestic Violence Shelter; mem. adv. bd. Nev. Ptnrs. against ALS. Recipient Meritorious award Clark County Dist. Atty., 1991, Silver State Citizen award Nev. Atty. Gen., 1991, Freshman Legislator of Yr. award Nev. Conf. Police/Sheriffs, 1993, Excellence award Nev. Trial Lawyers, 1995, Counc. of State Govmts. Toll Fell., 1997, Amer. Swiss Found. Young Political Leader, 1997, Leadership Las Vegas Grad., 1998. Avocations: competetive sports, travel, reading, hunting, fishing. Office: Henderson Police Dept 223 Lead St Henderson NV 89015-7328 Home: 328 Fife St Henderson NV 89015-2700

PERKINS, RICHARD P. pilot; s. Paul C. and Louise W. Perkins; m. Kim Miracle Perkins, June 26, 1992. BS in History, U.S. Naval Acad., 1982. Lic. airline tansport pilot Fed. Aviation Adminstrn., 1997. Commd. 2d lt. USMC, 1982, advanced through grades to capt., 1993; col. USMCR, 1993—, served in Operation Desert, served in Iraqi Freedom; pilot Fedex Corp., Memphis, 1995—. Mem. Pilots for Kids, Okla. City, 1997—; fellow Christian Found. for Children and the Aging, Kansas City, 1999—. Mem.: Patriarchal Order of Holy Cross (knight). Avocation: philathopic. Home: 39 Central Sq Keene NH 03431

PERKINS, ROGER ALLAN, lawyer; b. Port Chester, N.Y., Mar. 4, 1943; s. Francis Newton and Winifred Marcella (Smith) P.; m. Katherine Louise Howard, Nov. 10, 1984; children: Marshall, Morgan, Matthew, Justin, Ashley. BA, Pa. State U., 1965; postgrad., U. Ill., 1965-66; JD with honors, George Washington U., 1969. Bar: Md. 1969, Mass. 1975. Trial atty. Nationwide Ins. Co., Annapolis, Md., 1969-72; assoc. Arnold, Beauchemin & Huber, PA, Balt., 1973; from assoc. to ptnr. Goodman & Bloom, PA, Annapolis, 1973-76; ptnr. Luff and Perkins, Annapolis, 1976-78; pvt. practice Anapolis, 1978—. Temp. adminstrv. hearing officer Anne Arundel County, 1984—; asst. city atty., Annapolis, 1980-82; atty. Bd. Appeals of City of Annapolis, 1986-2003; mem. Appellate Jud. Nominating Commn., 1995—. Editl. adv. bd. Daily Record, 1996-97. Mem. Gov.'s Task Force on Family Law, 1991-94; adv. coun. on family legal need of low income persons MLSC, 1991; coach youth sports. Fellow Am. Acad. Matrimonial Lawyers, Am. Bar Found., Md. Bar Found. (bd. dirs. 1992-95); mem. ABA (ho. dels. 1991-93, 94-96, standing com. on solo and small firm practitioners 1993-97, chair 1996-97), Md. State Bar Assn. (pres. 1992-93, treas. 1988-91, bd. govs. 1985-87, chair membership com. 2002—, chair spl. com. on lawyer profl. responsibility 1994-95, family and juvenile law sect. coun. 1983-89, chair 1987-88), Anne Arundel County Bar Assn. (pres. 1984-85). Home: 503 Bay Hills Dr Arnold MD 21012-2001 Office: The Courtyards 133 Defense Hwy Ste 202 Annapolis MD 21401-8907 E-mail: roger@perkinslaw.com.

PERKINS, RONALD DEE, geologist, educator; b. Covington, Ky., May 18, 1935; s. Stanley E. and Pauline L. (Green) P.; m. Beverly L. Hughes, June 8, 1957; children— Lisa, Debra. BS, U. Cin., 1957; MS, U. N.Mex., 1959; PhD in Geology, Ind. U., 1962. Research geologist Shell Devel. Co., Houston, 1962-63, project leader Coral Gables, Fla., 1963-68; mem. faculty Duke U., Durham, N.C., 1968—, prof. geology, 1975-2000, chmn. dept., 1978-90, prof. emeritus, 2000—. Cons. to industry. Author numerous papers in field. NSF grantee, 1969-80 Mem. Internat. Assn. Sedimentologists, Soc. Econ. Paleontologists and Mineralogists (sec.-treas. 1978-82), Geol. Soc. Am., Am. Assn. Petroleum Geologists. Office: Duke U Dept Geology West Campus Old Chemistry Bldg Durham NC 27708 E-mail: rperkins@duke.edu.

PERKINS, ROSWELL BURCHARD, lawyer; b. Boston, May 21, 1926; AB cum laude, Harvard U., 1945, LLB cum laude, 1949; LLD, Bates Coll., 1988. Bar: Mass. 1949, N.Y. 1949. Assoc. Debevoise, Plimpton & McLean, N.Y.C., 1949-53; ptnr. Debevoise & Plimpton and predecessor firm, N.Y.C., 1957-96; of counsel, head rep. office Debevoise & Plimpton LLC, Moscow, 1997-01. Asst. sec. U.S. Dept. HEW, 1954-56; counsel to Gov. Nelson A. Rockefeller State of N.Y., 1959; asst. counsel spl. subcom. Senate Commerce Com. to investigate organized crime in interstate commerce, 1950; chmn. N.Y.C. Mayor's Task Force on Transp. Reorgn., 1966; mem. Pres.'s Adv. Panel on Pers. Interchange, 1968, chmn. adv. com. Medicare Adminstrn. Contracting, Subcontracting HEW, 1973-74; dir. Fiduciary Trust Co., N.Y., 1963-2000; trustee Bowery Savs. Bank, 1975-82; mem. legal com. to bd. dirs. N.Y. Stock Exch., 1995-2000. Editor Harvard Law Rev., 1948-49. Mem. N.Y. Lawyers Com. Civil Rights, 1970-73; mem. nat. exec. com., 1973-1980, co-chmn. 1973-75; mem. adv. coun. Woodrow Wilson Sch. Pub. and Internat. Affairs, Princeton U., 1967-69; bd. dirs. The Commonwealth Fund, 1974-97, Sch. Am. Ballet, 1974-85, chmn. bd. 1976-80; dir., sec. N.Y. Urban Coalition, 1967-74; trustee Pomfret Sch., 1961-76; The Brearley Sch., 1969-75; dir. Salzburg Seminar Am. Studies, 1970-80; mem. overseers vis. com. Kennedy Sch. Govt., Harvard U., 1971-77, Harvard and Radcliffe Colls., 1958-64, 1971-77, Davis Ctr. for Russian and Eurasian Studies, 2000—. Recipient Spl. Merit citation Am. Judicature Soc., 1989, Harvard Law Sch. Assn. award, 1994, 50 Yr. award Fellows of ABA, 2002. Mem. ABA (commn. on law and economy, 1975-79, mem. ho. of dels. 1980-93), N.Y. State Bar Assn., Assn. of the Bar of the City of N.Y. (chmn. spl. com. on fed. conflict of interest laws 1958-60). Harvard Alumni Assn. (pres. 1970-71), Am. Law Inst. (mem. coun. 1969, pres. 1980-93, chmn. coun. 1993—), Am. Arbitration Assn. (bd. dirs. 1966-71), Russian Inst. Dirs. (mem. expert coun. 2002-), Ind. Dirs. Assn. (mem. adv. com. Russia 2002-). Home: 1120 5th Ave New York NY 10128-0144 Office: Debevoise & Plimpton 919 3rd Ave 46th Fl New York NY 10022-3902 E-mail: rbperkins@debevoise.com.

PERKINS, RUSSELL ALEXANDER, publisher, consultant; b. N.Y.C., July 31, 1958; s. Thomas F. and Helen P.; m. Susan Chew, Sept. 20, 1991. BA, Sarah Lawrence Coll., 1982. Assoc. editor NBC Pub., N.Y.C., 1982-83; editor Thomas Pub., N.Y.C., 1983-85; cons. AT&T, Morristown, N.J., 1985; pres. Morgan-Rand Pubs., Phila., 1986-94; group pres. N.Am. Pub. Co., Phila., 1994-96; v.p. Legal Comm., Ltd., Phila., 1996-97; pres. Dorland Healthcare Info., Phila., 1998—. Bd. dirs. Univenture Group, Inc., Phila., Charter Info. Corp., Phila., Ctr. for Healthcare Info., Newport Beach., Calif., BizViz Internet Analytics Inc., Phila. Author: (book) Directory Publishing, 1986, InfoCommerce, 1999; columnist The Morgan Report newsletter. Mem. Assn. Info. Mgrs., Info. Mktg. Roundtable, Phila. Pubs. Group, Phila. Book Clinic, Info. Industry Assn., Union League Phila. Office: Infocommerce Group Inc 2 Bala Plz Ste 300 Bala Cynwyd PA 19004 E-mail: rperkins@infocommercegroup.com.

PERKINS, WILLIAM CLINTON, manufacturing executive; b. Decatur, Ill., Mar. 7, 1920; s. Glen Rupert and Frances Lola (Clinton) P.; m. Eunice Cagle, Sept. 7, 1939 (div. 1954); stepchildren: William Rea Cagle, Howard Christy Cagle; 1 child, Clinton Colcord; m. Lillian Wuollet, Sept. 7, 1955 (div. 1965); m. Shirley Thomas, Oct. 24, 1969. BS Mil. Sci. and Meteorology, U. Md., 1954; MS in Bus. and Pub. Adminstrn., Sussex Coll., Eng., 1975. Commd. USAF, 1943—73, advanced through grades to col.; with Ship Sys. divsn. Litton Ind., Culver City, Calif., 1973—75; dir. material Hughes Aircraft Co., Tehran, Iran, 1974—78; mgr. internat. s/c Northrop Corp., Dhahran, Saudi Arabia, 1979—81; dir. materiel CRS, Riyadh, Saudi Arabia, 1981—83; head major subcontracts Lear Ziegler Corp., Santa Monica, Calif., 1984—88; pres., chmn. bd., CEO Snowtech, Inc., L.A., 1984—. Bd. dirs. Ice Village Ctrs., Inc., L.A., Forefront Industries, Maywood, Calif. Bd. dirs. World Children's Transplant Fund, L.A., 1987-95; mem. Mayor's Space Adv. Com., L.A., 1970-74; mem. Aerospace Hist. Com. Aerospace Hist. Soc., L.A., 1988-, Mus. of Flying, 1998—. Mem. AIAA (sec. chmn. 1970), Ret. Officers Assn. (pres. 1992-95), Military Officers Assn. of Am. (chpt. pres. 2003-), Soc. for Non-destructive Testing (program chmn. 1973), Aerospace Hist. Soc., Am. Soc. Quality Control, Am. Meterol. Soc., Sigma Alpha Epsilon (alumni chpt. pres. 1974-76). Avocations: golf, scuba diving, sailing, flying, gardening. Home: 8027 Hollywood Blvd Los Angeles CA 90046-2510 Personal E-mail: snowtech@pacbell.net.

PERKINS, WILLIAM H., JR., retired finance company executive; b. Rushville, Ill., Aug. 4, 1921; s. William H. and Sarah Elizabeth (Logsdon) P.; m. Eileen Nelson, Jan. 14, 1949; 1 child, Gary Douglas. Ed., Ill. Coll. Pres. Howlett-Perkins Assos., Chgo. Mem. Ill. AEC, 1963-84, sec., 1970-84; apptd. by Pres. to adv. bd. Nat. Armed Forces Mus., Smithsonian Instn., 1964-82. Sgt.-at-arms Democratic Nat. Conv., 1952, 56, del.-at-large, 1964, 68, 72; spl. asst. to chmn. Dem. Nat. Com., 1960; mem. Presdl. Inaugural Com., 1961, 65, 69, 73. Served with U.S. Army, 1944-46. Mem. Ill. Ins. Fedn. (pres. 1965-84), Ill. C. of C. (chmn. legis. com. 1971), Chgo. Assn. Commerce and Industry (legis. com., Raoul Wallenberg Humanitarian award 1993), Sangamo Club, Masons, Shriners. Methodist. Home: 52 N Cowley Rd Riverside IL 60546-2042

PERKINS-CARPENTER, BETTY LOU, fitness company executive; b. Jan. 22, 1931; d. Edward C. and Bertha M. (Loeser) Kalmn; m. Floyd F. Perkins, Jan. 31, 1951 (div. 1979); children: Cheryl Lee Perkins, F. Scott Perkins; m. Marcellus Chipman Carpenter, Oct. 10, 1981 (dec. 2002). BS in Phys. Edn. Adminstrn., Empire State Coll., N.Y., 1979; MS in Early Childhood Edn. Adminstrn., Nova U., 1983; postgrad., Kennedy Western U. Cert. gerontology St. John Fischer Coll. Tchr., coach Rochester YWCA, NY, 1954—59, Perkins Swimming Sch., Penfield, N.Y., 1959-64; pres. Perkins Swim Club, Inc., Rochester, 1959—94, Penfield Fit By Five, Inc., Rochester, 1969-97, Child Fitness Prodns., Inc. d/b/a Sr. Fitness Prodns., Rochester, 1983—. Coach U. Rochester, 1965—75; diving coach Olympic Games, Montreal, Canada, 1976; mem. adv. com. Cmty. Savs. Bank, Rochester, 1976—79; cons. European sports facilities, 1969—83; mem. adv. com. N.Y. State Task Force Phys. Fitness and Sports, 1978—82; mem. adv. bd. O.A.S.I.S.; bd. dirs. U.S. Olympic Diving Com., 1976—80, Wesley Group, Arthritis Found. Genesee chpt., 1995—; affiliated with Pres.'s Coun. Phys. Fitness and Sports, 1986—89, 1995—; exercise cons. U. Rochester Pepper Study, 1992—95. Author: (book) The Fun of Fitness--A Handbook for the Senior Class, 1988, How to Prevent Falls--Introducing the Balance System, 1989, Stretching in Bed to Look and Feel Better, 1999; Am. editor: book Teaching Babies to Swim, 1979; contbr. articles to profl. jours.; exec. prodr.: audio-visual instrnl. materials. Past vice-chmn., bd. dirs. Regional Coun. on Aging; past co-chmn. Monroe County Coun. for Elders. With USAF, 1949—51. Named Sports Woman of the Yr., U.S. Olympic Diving Commn., 1979, Citizen of the Yr., Rotary, 1988, Health Fitness Leader, Rochester Small Bus. Person of the Yr., 1990, Citizen of the Yr., Lions Club, 1995; named to Monroe County Athletes Hall of Fame, Rochester, 1979, Frontier Field Walk of Fame, 1999, Nat. Swim Sch. Hall of Fame, 1999; recipient Gold medal, Inst. Achievement of Human Potential, Brazil, 1973, Mike Malone Meml. Diving award, 1977, Cady Diving award, 1977, Honor award, ARC, 1991, Lifespan-Hero award, 2001, Sportswoman of The year - Life time Achievment award, 2003. Mem.: U.S. Diving Assn. (life; numerous offices), Nova U. Alumnae Assn., Oak Hill Country Club, Order Eastern Star (life), Sigma Phi Omega (Alpha Lamda chpt.). Republican. Avocations: swimming, cross country skiing, reading, travel. Office: Senior Fitness Inc 1780 Penfield Rd Penfield NY 14526-2104 Office Phone: 585-586-7548.

PERKINSON, ROBERT REPS, social studies educator; b. Cheney, Wash., June 17, 1969; s. Robert Ronald and Elizabeth Fly Perkinson; m. Carol Kieko Matteson; 1 child, Amika Nyshie Shafali Matteson. BA, U. Colo., Boulder, 1994; MA, Yale U., 1997, PhD, 2001. Asst. prof. U. Hawaii, Honolulu, 2000—. Recipient C. Vann Woodward award, So. Hist. Assn., Atlanta, Calif., 2001. Office: Am Studies 1890 East West Rd Moore 307 Honolulu HI 96822

PERKINSON, ROBERT RONALD, psychologist, consultant; b. Richmond, Va., Aug. 8, 1945; s. Gordon Archibald and Sarah (Haskins) P.; m. Elizabeth Godfrey Fly, July 27, 1968 (div. 1984); children: Robert Reps, Nyshie Page, Shane William; m. Angela Kaufman, Sept. 20, 1991. BS, Colo. State U., 1968; MS, Ea. Wash. State U., 1970; PhD, Utah State U., 1974. Lic. psychologist, S.D.; cert. chem. dependency counselor level III, S.D.; nat. cert. gambling counselor; nat. cert. alcohol and drug counselor; lic. marriage and family counselor, S.D. Juvenile ct. psychologist, Cedar City, Utah, 1971-72; psychologist in pvt. practice Jackson, Wyo., 1974-83; dir. psychol. svcs. Western Wyo. Mental Health Assn., Jackson, 1977-78, psychologist, 1983—; psychologist, clin. dir. Keystone Treatment Ctr., 1988—. Cons. in field; chief psychologist Grand Teton Nat. Pk., Teton County Sheriff's Office and Police Dept. Copyrights: The Yellowstone Park Game, The Good Health Game, The Grizzly Control Team, Communication from God, Chemical Dependency Counseling, The Mystics, God Talks CD, Peace Will Come CD, The Treatment of Pathological Gambling: A Step By Step Approach. Author: Chemical Dependency Counseling: A Practical Guide, 1997, The Chemical Dependency Treatment Planner, 1998, God Talks to You, 2000, The Addiction Treatment Planner, 2001, Chemical Dependency Counseling: A Practical Guide, 2d edit., 2002, The Alcoholism and Drug Abuse Patient Workbook, 2003, The Gambling Addiction Patient Workbook, 2003, Treating Alcoholism: Helping Your Clients Find the Road to Recovery, 2004; contbr. articles to profl. jours. Mem. APA, S.D. Psychol. Assn., S.D. Chem. Dependency Assn., Biofeedback Soc. Am. (bd. dirs. Wyo. br.), Wyo. Bd. Psychologist Examiners (pres. 1997, bd. dirs. S.D. coun. problem gambling), Nat. Registere of Health Svc. Providers in Psychology. Address: PO Box 159 Canton SD 57013-0159 Personal E-mail: perk@iw.net.

PERKOFF, GERALD THOMAS, physician, educator; b. St. Louis, Sept. 22, 1926; s. Nat and Ann (Schwartz) Perkoff; m. Marion Helen Maizner, June 7, 1947; children: David Alan, Judith Ilene, Susan Gail. MD cum laude, Washington U., 1948. Intern Salt Lake City Gen. Hosp., 1948—49, resident, 1950—52; from instr. to asso. prof. medicine U. Utah, 1954—63; chief med. service Salt Lake VA Hosp., 1961—63; from assoc. prof. to prof. medicine Washington U. Sch. Medicine, St. Louis, 1963—79; chief Med. Svc., St. Louis City Hosp., 1963—68; prof. preventive medicine and pub. health, dir. divsn. health care rsch. Med. Svc. St. Louis City Hosp., 1968—79; Curators prof. and assoc. chmn. dept. family and cmty. medicine and prof. medicine U. Mo., Columbia, 1979—91, Curators prof. emeritus, 1991—, co-dir. program health care and human values, 1984—85. Chmn. nat. adv. com. Robert Wood Johnson Clin. Scholars Program, 1989—96; founder, dir. Med. Care Group Washington U., 1968—70. Contbr. articles to profl. jours. Career rsch. prof. neuromuscular diseases Nat. Found. Neuromuscular Diseases, 1961; dep. dir. Robert Wood Johnson Found. Generalist Physician Initiative, 1991—. Jr. asst. surgeon USPHS, 1953—54. Fellow Henry J. Kaiser Sr. fellow, Ctr. Advanced Studies in Behavioral Sci., 1976—77, 1985—86; scholar John and Mary R. Markle scholar med. sci., 1955—60. Mem.: Inst. Medicine (Nat. Acad. Scis.), Assn. Am. Physicians, Soc. Tchrs. Family Medicine, Am. Soc. Clin. Investigation. Home: 1300 Torrey Pines Dr Columbia MO 65203-4826 Office: U Mo Sch Medicine Dept Family & Community Medicine M228 Med Scis Columbia MO 65212-0001

PERKOVIC, ROBERT BRANKO, retired international management consultant; b. Belgrade, Yugoslavia, Aug. 27, 1925; came to U.S., 1958, naturalized, 1961; s. Slavoljub and Ruza (Pantelic) P.; m. Jacquelyn Lee Lipscomb, Dec. 14, 1957; children: Bonnie Kathryn, Jennifer Lee. MS in Econs, U. Belgrade, 1954; B.F.T., Am. Grad. Sch. Internat. Mgmt., 1960; grad. Stanford exec. program, Stanford U., 1970. Auditor Gen. Foods Corp., White Plains, N.Y., 1960-62, controller Mexico City, 1962-64; dir. planning Monsanto Co., Barcelona, Spain, 1964-67, dir. fin., 1967-70, dir. fin. planning-internat., 1970-71, asst. treas., 1971-72, 1972-74; corp. treas. Fiat-Allis Inc. & BV, Deerfield, Ill., 1974-78; v.p., treas. TRW Inc., Cleve., 1978-88; pres. RBP Internat. Cons., Cleve., 1988—. Former dir. U.S. Bus. Coun. for Southeastern Europe, Inc. Active Cleve. Commn. on Fgn. Relations. Inc. Served with Yugoslavian Army, 1944-47. Mem. Fin. Execs. Inst., Cleve. Treas. Club (past bd. dirs., pres.), Latin Am. Bus. Assn. (co-founder), Mayfield Village (Ohio) Racquet Club. Office: RBP Internat Cons 26 Pepper Creek Dr Cleveland OH 44124-5248

PERKOWITZ, SIMON (SY), architect, architectural firm executive; AA in Architecture, L.A. City Coll., 1968; BS in Archtl. Engring., Calif. Polytech. State U., 1971. Registered architect Oreg., Nev., Ga.; lic. architect Calif., profl. engr., Calif. V.p. Mackel Assocs., L.A., 1966-79; prin., exec. v.p. Musil Perkowitz Ruth, Inc., 1979—, pres., CEO, 1998—. Chmn. City of Palos Verdes Estates (Calif.) Planning Commn. Mem. AIA, NSPE, Internat. Coun. Shopping Ctrs. (so. Calif. planning com.), Nat. Soc. Archtl. Engrs., Calif. C. of C. Office: Perkowitz & Ruth Architects Inc 111 W Ocean Blvd Ste 2100 Long Beach CA 90802-4653*

PERKOWSKI, JAN LOUIS, language, literature and folklore educator; b. Perth Amboy, N.J., Dec. 29, 1936; m. Liliana Asenova Daskalova, May 24, 1989. AB magna cum laude, Harvard U., 1959, AM, 1960, PhD, 1965. Asst. prof. U. Calif., Santa Barbara, 1964-65; assoc. prof. U. Tex., Austin, 1965-74; prof. U. Va., Charlottesville, 1974—. Author: A Kashubian Idiolect in U.S., 1969, Vampires, Dwarves & Witches Among the Ontario Kashubs, 1972, Vampires of the Slavs, 1976, Gusle & Ganga Among the Hercegovinians of Toronto, 1978, The Darkling-A Treatise on Slavic Vampirism, 1989; contbr. over 65 articles to profl. jours. Grantee, fellow Ford Found., Harvard U., Kościuszko Found., U. Tex., Am. Philos. Soc., Nat. Mus. Man, U. Va., NEH, Kennan Inst., I.R.E.X., Fulbright, others. Mem. Am. Assn. for the Advancement of Slavic Studies, Am. Assn. Tchrs. of Slavic and East European Langs., Am. Assn. S.E. European Studies, Bulgarian Studies Assn. Office: U Va Dept Slavic Langs & Lits 109 Cabell Hall Charlottesville VA 22903 Office Phone: 434-924-3540.

PERL, HAROLD, pediatrician; b. July 24, 1950; m. Esther Jayde Strauss, June 18, 1972; children: Ari, Sharona, Gil, Doniel. BA, Yeshiva Coll., 1972; MD, Albert Einstein Coll Medicine, 1975. Diplomate Am. Bd. Pediatrics, cert. in neonatal and perinatal medicine. Intern, resident Montefiore Hosp. and Med. Ctr., N.Y.C., 1975-78; dir. neonatology Hackensack (N.J.) U. Med. Ctr., 1991—; co-dir. SIDS Ctr. N.J. Mem. biomed. ethics com. Hackensack U. Med. Ctr., 1985—. Mem. health profls. adv. com. March of Dimes, No. N.J., 1982-97. Office: Hackensack U Med Ctr 30 Prospect Ave Hackensack NJ 07601-1912 E-mail: hperl@humed.com.

PERL, MARTIN LEWIS, physicist, educator, chemical engineer; b. N.Y.C., June 24, 1927; children: Jed, Anne, Matthew, Joseph. B in Chem. Engring., Poly. Inst. Bklyn., 1948; PhD, Columbia U., 1955; ScD (hon.), U. Chgo., 1990. Chem. engr. Gen. Electric Co., 1948—50; asst. prof. physics U. Mich., 1955—58, assoc. prof., 1958—63; prof. Stanford, 1963—. Author: High Energy Hadron Physics, 1975, Reflections on Experimental Science, 1996; contbr. articles on high energy physics and on relation of sci. to soc. to profl. jours. With U.S. Mcht. Marine, 1944—45, with U.S. Army, 1946—47. Recipient Wolf prize in Physics, 1982, Nobel prize in Physics, 1995. Fellow: Am. Phys. Soc.; mem.: NAS, Am. Acad. Arts and Scis. Home: 3737 El Centro Ave Palo Alto CA 94306-2642 Office Phone: 650-926-2652. Business E-Mail: martin@sluc.stanford.edu.

PERLBERG, JULES MARTIN, lawyer; b. Chgo., Jan. 28, 1931; s. Maurice and Louise Mae (Schonberger) P.; m. Dora Ann Morris, Dec. 22, 1968; children: Julia, Michael. BBA with high distinction, U. Mich., 1952, JD with high distinction, 1957. Bar: Ill. 1958, D.C. 1964; C.P.A., Ill. Acct. Arthur Andersen & Co., Chgo., 1954-55; faculty U. Mich. Law Sch., Ann Arbor, 1957-58; assoc. Sidley & Austin and predecessor firm, Chgo., 1958-65, ptnr., 1966-98, sr. counsel, 1998—. Mem. Glencoe (Ill.) Bd. Edn., 1980-87, pres., 1985-86; bd. dirs. Juvenile Diabetes Found., Chgo., 1981-2001, v.p. 1983-85, treas., 1988-90, 96-98; exec. bd. Am. Jewish Com., Chgo., 1978-88, v.p., 1981-83; trustee New Trier Twp. Schs., 1987-91, pres., 1989-91; class co-chairperson parents com. Duke U., 1992-94. 1st lt. U.S. Army, 1952-54. Recipient Gold medal Ill. Soc. C.P.A.s, 1955 Mem. ABA, Chgo. Bar Assn., Lawyers Club, Mid-Day Club (Chgo.), Std. Club. Clubs: Legal, Law; Mid-Day (Chgo.); Standard. Home: 568 Westley Rd Glencoe IL 60022-1071 Office: Sidley Austin Brown & Wood Apt 605 425 W Surf St Chicago IL 60657-6139

PERLE, EUGENE GABRIEL, lawyer; b. NYC, Dec. 21, 1922; s. Philip and Simme (Meschenberg) P.; m. Ellen Carlotta Kraus, Nov. 26, 1953 (dec. 1964); 1 child, Elizabeth Anne Perle; m. Ruth Friedberg Lerner, May 23, 1972 (div. 1977); m. Patricia Fitzpatrick Sinnott, Jan. 24, 1981. BA, Queens Coll., 1943; JD, Yale U., 1949. Bar: NY 1950, Conn. 1995. Assoc. Cravath, Swaine & Moore, NYC, 1949-53; asst. counsel NY State Moreland Commn. Investigation Harness Racing, NYC, 1953-54; assoc. Gordon, Brady, Caffrey & Keller, NYC, 1954-56; assoc. gen. atty. Time Inc., NYC, 1956-66, pub. counsel, 1966-73, v.p. law, 1973-80, corp. v.p. law, 1980-85; counsel Proskauer & Rose, NYC, 1985-92, Chapman & Fennell, 1992-94; mem. Ohlandt, Greeley, Ruggiero & Perle, Stamford, Conn., 1995-97, sr. counsel, 1998—. Co-author: Perle & Williason Publishing Law, 1988-2004; mem. editl. bd. Yale Law Jour., 1948-49; mem. adv. bd. Bur. Nat. Affairs Patent, Trademark and Copyright Jour., 1972-86; contbr. to Bull. Copyright Soc. USA. Trustee Baron deHirsch Fund, 1959-87, hon. trustee, 1988—; commr. Nat. Commn. New Technol. Uses Copyrighted Works, 1975-78; bd. dirs. NY Sch. Circus Arts, Inc.,

1979-87, Am. Arbitration Assn., 1979-84; justice of peace City of Norwalk, Conn., 1960-63. Lt. USNR, 1943-46. Mem. ABA (chmn. copyright divsn. 1970-71, 86-87, chmn. com. copyright new tech. 1971-73, chmn. com. econs. profession 1976, coun. patent, trademark copyright sect. 1979-83, governing bd. forum com. comms. law 1979-85, chmn. related fields future devels. divsn. forum com. entertainment sports industries 1979), Copyright Soc. USA (trustee 1962-64, 69-70, 71-74, pres. 1976-78, hon. trustee 1978—), US Trademark Assn. (bd. dirs. 1969-72, 74-77, v.p. 1972-73), Assn. Bar City NY, Sunningdale Country Club, Century Assn., Banyan Golf Club of Palm Beach. Democrat. Office: Ohlandt Greeley Ruggiero & Perle One Landmark Sq Stamford CT 06901 Office Phone: 203-327-4500. E-mail: egperle@ix.netcom.com., egperle@ogrp.com.

PERLE, GEORGE, composer; b. Bayonne, N.J., May 6, 1915; s. Joseph and Mary (Sanders) Perlman; m. Laura Slobe, 1940; m. Barbara Philips, Aug. 11, 1958 (dec.); children: Kathy, Annette; 1 stepchild, Max Massey; m. Shirley Gabis Rhoads, June 6, 1982; stepchildren: Paul Rhoads, Daisy Rhoads. MusB, DePaul U., 1938; MusM, Am. Conservatory of Music, 1942; PhD, NYU, 1956. Faculty U. Louisville, 1949-57, U. Calif., Davis, 1957-61, Juilliard Sch. Music, 1963, Yale U., 1965-66, U. So. Calif., summer 1965, Tanglewood, summers 1967, 80, 87; from asst. prof. to prof. CUNY, 1961-85, prof. emeritus, 1985—; composer-in-residence San Francisco Symphony, 1989-91. Vis. Birge-Cary prof. music SUNY, Buffalo, 1971-72; vis. prof. U. Pa., 1976, 80, Columbia U., 1979, 83; vis. Ernest Bloch prof. music U. Calif., Berkeley, 1989; vis. disting. prof. music NYU, N.Y.C., 1994. Author: Serial Composition and Atonality 1962, 6th edit., 1991, Twelve-Tone Tonality, 1977, 2d edit., 1996, The Operas of Alban Berg, vol. 1, 1980, vol. 2, 1985, The Listening Composer, 1990, The Right Notes, 1995, Style and Idea in the Lyric Suite of Alban Berg, 1995, 2d edit., 2001, contbr. articles in Am., fgn. mus. jours.; composer: Pantomime, Interlude and Fugue, 1937, Little Suite for Piano, 1939, Two Rilke Songs, 1941, Sonata for Solo Viola, 1942, Three Sonatas for Clarinet, 1943, Piano Piece, 1945, Hebrew Melodies for Cello, 1945, Lyric Piece for Cello and Piano, 1946, Six Preludes for Piano, 1946, Sonata for Solo Cello, 1947, Solemn Procession for Band, 1947, Sonata for Piano, 1950, Three Inventions for Piano, 1957, Quintet for Strings, 1958, Wind Quintet I, 1959, Sonata I for Solo Violin, 1959, Wind Quintet II, 1960, Fifth String Quartet, 1960-67, Three Movements for Orchestra, 1960, Monody I for flute, 1960, Music for The Birds of Aristophanes, 1961, Monody II for double bass 1962, Serenade I for Viola and Chamber Ensemble, 1962, Three Inventions for Bassoon, 1962, Sonata II for Solo Violin, 1963, Short Sonata for Piano, 1964, Solo Partita for Violin and Viola, 1965, Six Bagatelles for Orch., 1965, Concerto for Cello and Orch., 1966, Wind Quintet III, 1967, Serenade II for Chamber Ensemble, 1968, Toccata for Piano, 1969, Suite in C for Piano, 1970, Fantasy-Variations for Piano, 1971, Sonata Quasi una Fantasia for Clarinet and Piano, 1972, Seventh String Quartet, 1973, Songs of Praise and Lamentation for chorus and orch. 1974, Six Etudes for Piano, 1976, 13 Dickinson Songs, 1978, Concertino for Piano, Winds, and Timpani, 1979, A Short Symphony, 1980; Ballade for Piano, 1981, Sonata a quattro, 1982, Serenade III for Piano and Chamber Ensemble, 1983, Six New Etudes for Piano, 1984, Wind Quintet IV, 1984, Sonata for Cello and Piano, 1985, Sonatina for Piano, 1986, Sonata a cinque, 1986, Dance Fantasy for Orch., 1986, Lyric Intermezzo for fifteen players, 1987, Lyric Intermezzo for piano, 1987, New Fanfares for brass ensemble, 1987, Sinfonietta, 1987, Windows of Order for string quartet, 1988, Sextet for winds and piano, 1988, Concerto for Piano and Orch., 1990, Sinfonietta II, 1990, Concerto No. 2 for Piano and Orch., 1992, Adagio for Orch., 1992, Transcendental Modulations (commd. for 150 anniversary N.Y. Philharmonic), 1993, Phantasyplay for Piano, 1994, Duos for French horn and string quartet, 1995, Six Celebratory Inventions for Piano, 1995, Critical Moments for Six Players, 1996, Chansons Cachées for Piano, 1997, Musical Offerings for Piano (left hand alone), 1998, Brief Encounters for string quartet, 1998, Nine Bagatelles for Piano, 1999, Critical Moments (2) for Six Players, 2001, Triptych for Solo Violin and Piano, 2003. Served with AUS, 1943-46, ETO, PTO. Recipient Nat. Inst. Arts and Letters award, 1977, Pulitzer prize, 1986; Guggenheim fellow, 1966-67, 74-75, MacArthur fellow, 1986; grantee Am. Council Learned Socs., 1968-69, Nat. Endowment for the Arts, 1978-79, 85. Fellow Am. Acad. Arts and Scis.; mem. Am. Musicol. Soc., ASCAP (Deems Taylor award 1973, 78, 81), Am. Acad. Arts and Letters. E-mail: gxperle@aol.com.

PERLE, RICHARD NORMAN, former government official; b. N.Y.C., Sept. 16, 1941; s. Jack Harold and Martha Gloria P.; m. Leslie Joan Barr, July 31, 1977; 1 child, Jonathan Barr. BA, U. So. Calif., 1964; postgrad. in econs., U. London, 1962-63; MA, Princeton U., 1967. Asst. sec. internat. security policy Dept. Def., Washington, 1981-87; prof. staff mem. subcom. nat. security Senate Com. on Govt. Ops., Washington, 1970-72; profl. staff mem. committee on armed services U.S. Senate, Washington, 1969-80; resident fellow Am. Enterprise Inst. for Pub. Policy Rsch., Washington, 1987—; chmn. Def. Policy Bd., Washington, 2001—03. Office: Am Enterprise Inst Pub Policy Rsch 1150 17th St NW Washington DC 20036-4603

PERLEGOS, GEORGE, electronic executive; BS Electrical Engring., 1972. Pres., CEO, chmn. Atmel Corp., San Jose, 2002—. Office: Atmel Inc 2325 Orchard Pkwy San Jose CA 95131-1034

PERLESS, ELLEN, advertising executive; b. N.Y.C., Sept. 9, 1941; d. Joseph B. and Bertha (Messinger) Kaplan; m. Robert L. Perless, July 2, 1965. Student, Smith Coll., 1958-59; BA, Bard Coll., 1962. Copywriter Doyle, Dane Bernbach, N.Y.C., 1964-70, Young & Rubicam, N.Y.C., 1970-74, creative supr., 1974-76, v.p., creative supr., 1977, v.p., assoc. creative dir., 1978, sr. v.p., assoc. creative dir., 1979-84; v.p., assoc. creative dir. Leber Katz Ptnrs., 1984-85, sr. v.p., creative dir., 1986-87; sr. v.p., sr. creative dir. Foote Cone & Belding, N.Y.C., 1987-93, sr. v.p., group creative dir., 1994—2002; sr. v.p., sr. creative dir. Euro RSCG Life Becker, N.Y.C., 2003—04. Author: (poetry) Riverside 4, Approach, Margie. Recipient Clio awards, Andy awards, awards Art Dirs. Club N.Y., N.Y. Festivals, One Club. Home: 37 Langhorne Ln Greenwich CT 06831-2611 E-mail: ellen@perless.com.

PERLESS, ROBERT L. sculptor; b. NYC, Apr. 23, 1938; s. Meyer and Ethel (Glassman) Perless; m. Ellen R. Kaplan, July 2, 1965. Student, U. Miami, Fla., 1955-59. One-man shows include Bodley Gallery, N.Y.C., 1968, 1970, Galerie Simonne Stern, New Orleans, 1969, Bernard Danenberg Gallery, N.Y.C., 1970—72, Bonino Gallery, 1976, exhibited in group shows at Bodley Gallery, 1970, Whitney Mus., 1970, Forum Gallery, N.Y.C., 1975, Bonino Gallery, 1975, Houston Gallery, Aldrich Mus., Ridgefield, Conn., 1978, 1987, 1994, 1997—98, Taft Mus., Cin., 1980, Stamford (Conn.) Mus., 1989, Bruce Mus., Greenwich, Conn., 1989, 2001, André Emmerich's Top Gallant Farm, 1991—96, Greenwich Art Soc., 2000, Sculpture Now, Stockbridge, Mass., 2003, Art Omi Internat. Arts Ctr., NY, Represented in permanent collections Whitney Mus., Aldrich Mus., Chrysler Mus., Norfolk, Va., Okla. Art Ctr., Oklahoma City, Phoenix Art Mus., Stamford Mus., Bard Coll., Annandale-on-Hudson, N.Y., Bucknell U., Lewisburgh, Pa., City of Corpus Christi, Tex., City of Palm Desert, Calif., Syracuse Hancock Internat. Airport, Miami U., Oxford, Ohio, Rusk Inst., NYC, Salt Lake C.C., Town of Port Chester, NY, U. Conn., Storrs, U. No. Iowa, Cedar Falls. Mem.: Sculptors Guild. Address: 37 Langhorne Ln Greenwich CT 06831-2611

PERLGUT, MARK RALPH, public relations executive; b. New Brunswick, N.J., Oct. 4, 1942; s. Louis Eliot and Mildred Ruth (Shapiro) P.; m. Phyllis Norma Hershon, May 21, 1946; children: Lauren, Andrew. AB in History, Rutgers U., 1964; MS in Journalism, Columbia U., 1965. Investigative reporter Atlantic City (N.J.) Press, 1965-67; nat. and local reporter N.Y. Times, 1967-72; assoc. editor McGraw-Hill Inc., 1973-77; dir. new ventures Instnl. Investor, Inc., 1977-78; editl. mgr., personal speechwriter Donald T. Regan Merrill Lynch & Co., Inc., 1978-80; sr. policy writer N.Y. Stock Exch., Inc., 1980-82; v.p., dir. policy comms. Chem. Bank, 1982-84, v.p., dep. head of corp. comms. divsn., 1984-85; pres. Mark Perlgut Pub. Rels., 1985-87; v.p., editorial dir., account group supr. Fin. Rels. Bd., Inc., 1987-90; pres. Perlgut Pub. Rels., Inc., 1990-96, Investor Rels. Co. N.Y., 1992-96; sr. v.p., mng. dir. investor rels. divsn. Lobsenz Stevens, Inc., N.Y.C., 1996-99; exec. prin., mng. dir., investor rels. Publicis Dialog, N.Y.C., 1999—2001; mng. dir. Stern & Co. Comm., N.Y.C., 2001—02; pres. Perlgut Group Comms., N.Y.C., 2002—. Author: Electricity Across the Border: The U.S.-Canadian Experience, 1978. Chmn. Fair Harbor (N.Y.) Community Assn., 1980-82. Recipient 1st pl. award Fin. World Ann. Report Competition, 1st pl. award ARC awards Ann. Report Competition, 1989. Mem. Nat. Investor Rels. Inst. Office: 230 W 41st St New York NY 10036 E mail: mark@perlgutgroup.com.

PERLIK, WILLIAM R. lawyer; b. Pitts., May 20, 1925; s. Charles A. and Teresa Anna (Kraft) P.; m. Annabel Virginia Shanklin, June 16, 1949; children— Ronald A., Lynn C. BA, Oberlin Coll., 1948; JD, Yale U., 1951; LLD (hon.), Oberlin Coll., 2000. Bar: D.C. 1952, Va. 1955, U.S. Supreme Ct. 1974. Law clk. to judge U.S. Ct. Appeals, Washington, 1951-52; assoc., then ptnr. Cox Langford Stoddard & Cutler, Washington, 1952-62; ptnr., of counsel Wilmer Cutler & Pickering, Washington, 1962-98; adj. prof. politics and econs. Oberlin Coll., Ohio, 1973-1997. Trustee, chmn., mem. exec. com. Oberlin Coll., 1980-2000; pres. Va. Sch. Bd. Assn., 1971-72; mem. and chmn. Fairfax County Sch. Bd., Va., 1964-72; pres. Fairfax County Fedn. Citizens Assns., 1958. Served with U.S. Army, 1943-46; ETO. Recipient Edn. award Fairfax Edn. Assn., 1960; Citizen of Yr. award Washington Evening Star, 1961 Mem. ABA, Phi Beta Kappa. Avocations: music, gardening. Home: 1249 Daleview Dr Mc Lean VA 22102-1538 Office: Wilmer Cutler & Pickering 2445 M St NW Washington DC 20037-1487

PERLIN, ARTHUR SAUL, chemistry professor; b. Sydney, N.S., Can., July 7, 1923; s. Benjamin and Eva (Gaum) P.; m. Ruth Laurel Freedman, Nov. 18, 1950; children: Anna, Louise, Deborah, Myra, David BSc, McGill U., Can., 1944, MSc, 1946, PhD, 1949. Rsch. officer Nat. Rsch. Council Can., Ottawa, Ont., Can., 1948-67; E.B. Eddy prof. chemistry McGill U., Montreal, Que., Can., 1967-91, prof. chemistry emeritus, 1991—; rsch. scientist Pulp and Paper Rsch. Inst. Can., Montreal, Que., 1967—. Contbr. articles to profl. jours., chpts. to books; patentee in field Fellow Royal Soc. Can., Chem. Inst. Can.; mem. Am. Chem. Soc. (C.S. Hudson award 1979) Office: McGill U Dept Chemistry Montreal QC Canada H3A 2K6 Office Phone: 514-398-6188.

PERLIN, SEYMOUR, psychiatrist, educator; b. Passaic, N.J., Sept. 27, 1925; s. Samuel and Fanny (Horowitz) P.; m. Ruth Joan Rudolph, Aug. 21, 1958; children: Jonathan Brian, Steven Michael, Jeremy Francis. Student, Johns Hopkins U., 1943-44; BA summa cum laude, Princeton U., 1946; MD, Columbia U., 1950; grad., Washington Psychoanalytic Inst. Diplomate Am. Bd. Psychiatry and Neurology. Intern Univ. Hosp., Ann Arbor, Mich., 1951-52; resident N.Y. State Psychiat. Inst., 1950-51, 53-54, Manhattan State Hosp., 1952; practice medicine specializing in psychiatry and psychoanalysis Bethesda, Md., 1954-59, Stanford, Calif., 1959-60, N.Y.C., 1960-63, Balt., 1964-72, Bethesda, 1974—; chief div. psychiatry Montefiore Hosp., 1960-63; dir. clin. care and tng. Henry Phipps Psychiat. Clinic, Johns Hopkins Hosp., 1964-72; sr. research scholar Ctr. for Bioethics, Kennedy Inst., Georgetown U., Washington, 1974-78; clin. prof. psychiatry UCLA Sch. Medicine, 1973-74, George Washington U. Sch. Medicine, 1974-76, prof. to prof. emeritus, 1977-97, 97—, also dir. residency tng., 1977-93; lectr. psychiatry Columbia U., 1963-64; assoc. prof. psychiatry Johns Hopkins Sch. Medicine, 1964-65, prof., 1966-72, dep. chmn. dept. psychiatry and behavioral scis., 1969-72; program dir. Fellowship Program in Suicidology, 1967-72; adv. council Univ. health services Princeton, 1970-82. Vis. fellow Princeton U., 1973, Oxford U., 1974; Joseph P. Kennedy fellow medicine, law and ethics, 1974-75; chief sect. psychiatry Lab. Clin. Sci., NIMH, 1955-59, mem. clin. program-project com., 1967-70; fellow Ctr. Advanced Study in Behavioral Scis., 1959-60; chmn. mental health study sect. B, div. research grants NIH, 1964-66; cons. Community Mental Health Services, Md. Dept. Mental Hygiene, 1964-72; chmn. bd. dirs. Youth Suicide Nat. Ctr., 1985-87. Cons. editor: Jour. Suicide and Life Threatening Behavior, 1970-89; editorial bd.: Johns Hopkins Med. Jour, 1970-72; editor: Handbook for the Study of Suicide; co-editor: Ethical Issues in Death and Dying; contbr. numerous articles to med. jours. Served with USNR, 1944-46, with USPHS, 1954-58. Recipient Meirhoff award in pathology, 1950, Bicentennial Silver medal for achievement in psychiatry, 1967, both Coll. Phys. and Surg. Columbia. Fellow Am. Psychiat. Assn. (named Disting. Life fellow 2003); mem. Am. Coll. Psychiatry, Washington Psychoanalytic Soc., Med. Soc. D.C., Washington Psychiat. Soc., Am. Assn. Suicidology (pres. 1969-70, Dublin award 1978, ann. lectureship in suicidology in his name George Washington U. 1995), Phi Beta Kappa. Home and Office: 5125 Westbard Ave Bethesda MD 20816-1413

PERLIS, MICHAEL STEVEN, magazine publisher; b. Feb. 12, 1953; s. Sanford and Vivian (Lee) P.; m. Marilyn Dunlap, May 5, 1979; children: Morgan, Steve. BA in Psychology, Syracuse U., 1976. Mktg. dir. Bretton Woods (N.H.) Resort, 1976-78; exec. dir. Mt. Washington Valley C. of C., North Conway, N.H., 1978-80; pub. N.H. Profiles mag., N.Eng. Guide Rumford Nat. Graphics, Concord, N.H., 1980-81; v.p., pub. New Eng. Pubs., Camden, Maine, 1981-82, pres., 1982-84; pub. spls. Rodale Press, Inc., Emmaus, Pa., 1984-85, pub. Runners World mag., 1985-86, group pub., 1986-87; pres. Internat. Data Group, Peterborough, N.H., 1987-89; sr. v.p., pub. Playboy Enterprises, Chicago, 1989-90, sr. v.p., pres. - pub. group, 1990-92, exec. v.p., pres. - pub. group, 1992-94; pub. GQ Mag., 1994—96; COO, pres. TVSM Inc., N.Y.C., 1996—98; pres., CEO Ziff Davis Pub., 1998—2000; mng. ptnr. Softbank Capital Ptnrs., N.Y.C., 1998—. Mem. Mag. Pubs. Am., Young Pres. Org. Office: Softbank Capital Ptnrs 461 5th Ave 15th Fl New York NY 10017

PERLMAN, B. ARTHUR, lawyer; b. Denver, July 22, 1959; s. L.H. and Marie (Stearns) P.; m. Joanne Marie Jakicic, Feb. 14, 1987. BA, U. Denver, 1981; JD, Southwestern U., 1985. Bar: Colo. 1985, U.S. Bankruptcy Ct. 1987, U.S. Dist. Ct. Colo. 1987. Assoc. Duran & Duran, Denver, 1986-88, Hyatt Legal Svcs., Lakewood, Colo., 1988-90, Dodd, Scott, & Stockton, Lakewood, 1990-91, Kurtz & Peckham, Denver, 1991-92; 13th jud. dist. atty. Ft. Morgan, Colo., 1993; sole practitioner Littleton, Colo., 1993—. Atty. coach Abe Lincoln mock trial, Denver, 1988, 89, 90. Mem. Colo. Trial Lawyers Assn., Colo. Criminal Def. Bar, Nat. Assn. of Counsel for Children, Nat. Assn. Criminal Def. Lawyers, Phi Alpha Theta, Phi Sigma Iota. Democrat. Jewish. Avocations: model clipper ship building, coin collecting/numismatics, american history. Office: PO Box 620086 Littleton CO 80162-0086 Office Phone: 303-933-0835. E-mail: avocat@myblueliht.com.

PERLMAN, BARRY STUART, electrical engineering executive, researcher; b. Bklyn., Dec. 5, 1939; s. Harold Wallace and Jane (Cohen) P.; m. Carolyn Amelia Francis; 1 child, David Matthew. BEE, CCNY, 1961; MSEE, Poly. U. N.Y., 1964; PhD in Electrophysics, Poly. Inst. N.Y., 1973. Mem. tech. staff, comms. lab. RCA Corp., N.Y.C., 1961-68; mem. tech. staff RCA Labs., Princeton, N.J., 1968-81, mgr. microwave rsch. lab., 1981-86, head design automation rsch., 1986-88; chief microwave photonic devices br. Electronics and Power Source Directorate, Army Rsch. Lab., Ft. Monmouth, N.J., 1988-95; dir. electronics divsn. Phys. Scis. Directorate, Army Rsch. Lab., Ft. Monmouth, 1995-96; chief RF and electronics divsn. Sensor and Electron Devices Directorate, Army Rsch. Lab., Ft. Monmouth and Adelphi, Md., 1996-97; R&D Engring. Ctr. staff Comm.-Electronics Command, Ft. Monmouth, 1997-98, chief applied comm., 1998-99; assoc. dir. for tech., prin. scientist Intel and Info Directorate, 1999—2002; assoc. dir., DARPA liaison office RDEC Hdqrs., 2002—03; assoc. dir. CERDEC, RDECOM, 2003—. Pres., mem. bd. dirs. INTEREX, Los Altos, Calif., 1981—83; rep. adv. group on electron devices, chmn. subpanel on RF Components Office of Undersec. of Def.; chmn. Computational Electronics and Nanoelectronics tech. area HPCMO, 1995—, program mgr. modeling and simulation Electronic Battlefield Environ. Portfolio, 2000—, chmn. Darpa Working Group, program mgr., agent Nanomechanical Array Signal Processors, MTO; mem. sys. study team, modeling/simulation team DARPA, agt. Intelligent RF Front End Program and tech. Agile Efficient Microsystems Program, 1999—2002; mem. NASA/JPL adv. com. for SATCOM "sys. on a chip" U. Mich.; mem. tech. adv. bds. UCLA; mem. ind. adv. bd. Computer Applications to Electromagnetics Edn. NSF and U. Utah, 1990—94, MIMICAD Ctr., U. Colo., 1989—95; mem. adv. bd. Elec. Engring./WAMI U. So. Fla.; mem. ind. adv. bd. Wireless Commns. N.J. Inst. Tech.; Ctr. prof. microwave/lightwave engring. Drexel U., Phila., 1992—; mem. computational tech. area adv. panel CTAAP; advisor NJ Nanotech. Consortium; mem. R&D Coun. N.J.; mem. ind. adv. bd. U. Hawaii, Manoa, 2003—, Purdue U. Editor: Advances in Microwaves, 1974; mem. editl. bd. Wiley Jour. MW.MMW CAD, 1992—; contbr. articles to profl. jours.; patentee in field. Bd. dirs. YMCA, Princeton, 1975-78; pres. Home Owners Assn., E. Windsor, N.J., 1976-78; instr. Am. Heart Assn., N.J., 1978-82; chief rescue squad, E. Windsor, 1978-82. Fellow: IEEE (awards and advancement com. 1987—95, tech. program chair Sarnoff Symposium 1999—2002); mem.: Comm., Antennas & Propagation, Automated RF Techniques Group (treas. 1984—88, v.p. 1990—91), Cirs. and Sys., Ultrasonics, Ferroelectrics and Frequency Control, Microwave Theory and Tech. Soc. of IEEE (IMS tech. program com. 1980—, editl. bd. chmn. CAD com. MTT-1 1985—92, MTT adcom. 1990—94, chmn. Intersoc. Liaison 1995—97, MTT adcom. 2002—, chmn. meetings and symposia com. 2002—). Avocations: woodworking, photography, pistol/rifle target competition, gardening, gourmet cooking. Office: Army Comm-Electronics Ctr RDEC Hdqrs AMSRD CER TSP Bldg 2700 Fort Monmouth NJ 07703-5000 Business E-Mail: barry.perlman@us.army.mil.

PERLMAN, BURTON, judge; b. Dec. 17, 1924; s. Phillip and Minnie Perlman; m. Alice Weihl, May 20, 1956; children: Elizabeth, Sarah, Nancy, Daniel. BE, Yale U., 1945, ME, 1947; LLB, U. Mich., 1952. Bar: Ohio 1959, N.Y. 1953, Conn. 1952, U.S. Dist. Ct. (so. and ea. dists.) N.Y. 1954, U.S. Dist. Ct. (so. dist.) Ohio 1959, U.S. Ct. Appeals (2d cir.) 1953, U.S. Ct. Appeals (6th cir.) 1959. Assoc. Armand Lackenbach, N.Y.C., NY, 1952—58; pvt. practice Cin., 1958—61; assoc. Paxton and Seasongood, Cin., 1961—67; ptnr. Schmidt, Effton, Josselson and Weber, Cin., 1968—71; U.S. magistrate U.S. Dist. Ct. (so. dist.) Ohio, 1971—76, U.S. bankruptcy judge, 1976—. Chief bankruptcy judge so. dist. Ohio, 1986—93; adj. prof. U. Cin. Law Sch., 1976—. Served with U.S. Army, 1944—46. Mem.: ABA, Cin. Bar Assn., Am. Judicature Soc., Fed. Bar Assn. Office: US Bankruptcy Ct Atrium 2 8th Fl 221 E 4th St Cincinnati OH 45202-4124

PERLMAN, DAVID, science editor, journalist; b. Balt., Dec. 30, 1918; s. Jess and Sara P.; m. Anne Salz, Oct. 15, 1941 (dec. 2002); children: Katherine, Eric, Thomas. AB, Columbia U., 1939, MS, 1940. Reporter Bismarck (N.D.) Capital, 1940; reporter San Francisco Chronicle, 1940-41, reporter, sci. editor, 1952-77, city editor, 1977-79, assoc. editor, sci. editor, 1979—; reporter New York Herald Tribune, Paris, N.Y.C., 1945-49; European corr. Colliers mag. and New York Post, 1949-51. Regents prof. human biology U. Calif., San Francisco 1974; vis. lectr. China Assn. Sci. and Tech., Beijing, Chengdu and Shanghai, 1983; sci. writer in residence U. Wis., 1989. Contbr. articles to major mags. Founding dir. Squaw Valley (Calif.) Community of Writers; dir. Alan Guttmacher Inst., 1990-99; trustee Scientists Inst. for Pub. Info., 1986-94; chmn. pub. svc. award com. Nat. Sci. Bd., 1998-2001. Served with inf. USAAF, 1941-45. Recipient Atomic Indsl. Forum award, 1975, AAAS Sci. Writing award, 1976, Exploratorium award 1977, Ralph Coates Roe medal ASME, 1978, Margaret Sanger Cmty. Svc. award, 1981, Fellows' medal Calif. Acad. Scis., 1984, Career Achievement award Soc. Profl. Journalists, 1989, Glenn T. Seaborg award Internat. Platform Assn., 1993, Sustained Achievement award for sci. journalism Am. Geophys. Union, 1997, U. Calif. San Francisco medal, 2000, Columbia U. Journalism award, 2000, San Francisco Med. Soc. award for disting. med. reporting, 2000, Grady-Stack award for sci. journalism Am. Chem. Soc., 2001, John Wesley Powell award U.S. Geol. Survey, 2004; Poynter Inst. fellow Yale U., 1984, Carnegie Corp. fellow Stanford U., 1987. Fellow Calif. Acad. Scis.; mem. AAAS (adv. bd. Science-81-86 mag., com. Pub. Understanding of Sci. 1985-90), Coun. for Advancement Sci. Writing (pres. 1976-80), Nat. Assn. Sci. Writers (pres. 1970-71, Disting. Sci. Journalism award 1994), Astron. Soc. Pacific (dir. 1976-78), Sigma Xi. Office: San Francisco Chronicle 901 Mission St San Francisco CA 94103-2905 Business E-Mail: dperlman@sfchronicle.com.

PERLMAN, HARVEY STUART, lawyer, educator; b. Lincoln, Nebr., Jan. 17, 1942; s. Floyd Ted and Rosalyn (Lashinsky) P.; m. Susan G. Unthank, Aug. 27, 1966; children: Anne, Amy. BA, U. Nebr., 1963, JD, 1966. Bar: Nebr. 1966, Va. 1980. Teaching fellow U. Chgo. Law Sch., 1966-67; mem. faculty U. Nebr. Sch. Law, 1967-74, prof., 1972-74; prof. law U. Va., Charlottesville, 1974-83; dean law U. Nebr., Lincoln, 1983—; exec. dir. Nebr. Commn. on Law Enforcement. Author: (with Edmund Kitch) Legal Regulation of the Competitive Process, 1972, 79, 86; asso. editor: Jour. Law and Human Behavior, 1974-86. Named Ida Beam Distinguished Vis. Prof. Law, U. Iowa, 1981-86. Mem. Am. Bar Assn., Nebr. Bar Assn., Law-Psychology Assn., Am. Law Inst. Office: U Nebr Coll Law Lincoln NE 68588

PERLMAN, ITZHAK, violinist; b. Tel Aviv, Aug. 31, 1945; arrived in U.S., 1958; s. Chaim and Shoshana P.; m. Toby Lynn Friedlander, 1967; children: Noah, Navah, Miriam, Leora, Ariella. Student, Tel Aviv Acad. Music; studied with Ivan Galamian & Dorothy DeLay, Juilliard Sch.; student, Meadowmount Sch. Music.; hon. degree in music, Tufts U., 1986; Degree (hon.), Harvard U., Yale U., Brandeis U., Roosevelt U., Yeshiva U., Hebrew U. Appeared with numerous orchs. including N.Y. Philharm., Cleve. Orch., Phila. Orch., Nat. Symphony Orch., Berlin Philharm., English Chamber Orch., London Symphony, London Philharm., Royal Philharm., BBC Orch., Vienna Philharm., Israel Philharm.; founder Perlman Music Program, N.Y., 1998—; prin. guest condr. Detroit Symphony, 2001—; participant numerous music festivals including Ravinia Festival, Tanglewood Music Festival, Aspen Music Festival, Israel Festival, Wolf Trap Summer Festival; recital tours U.S., Can., S.Am., Europe, Israel, Australia, Far East; recorded for Angel, London, RCA Victor, DG, Telarc, Teldec, Sony. Albums include Vivaldi: The Four Seasons, 1977 (Grammy award best classical performance 1977), Beethoven: Sonatas For Violin And Piano, 1978 (Grammy award best chamber music performance 1978), Brahms: Concerto For Violin In D, 1978 (Grammy award best classical album 1978), The Spanish Album, 1980 (Grammy award best classical performance 1980), Brahms: Violin And Cello Concerto In A Minor, 1980 (Grammy award best classical performance 1980), Berg: Violin Concerto/Stravinsky: Violin Concerto In D, 1980 (Grammy award best classical performance 1980), Music For Two Violins, 1980 (Grammy award best chamber music performance 1980), Isaac Stern: 60th Anniversary Celebration, 1981 (Grammy award best engineered recording 1981, Grammy award best classical performance 1981), Tchaikovsky: Piano Trio In A Minor, 1981 (Grammy award best chamber music performance 1981), Elgar: Violin Concerto In B Minor, 1982 (Emmy award best classical performance 1982), Chausson: Violin Concerto, 1984, An Isaac Stern Vivaldi Gala, 1985, Beethoven: The Complete Piano Trios, 1987 (Grammy award best chamber music performance 1987), Bach: Double Concerto, 1987, Mozart Violin Concertos Nos.1 & 2, 1987 (Grammy award best classical performance 1987), Paganini & Giuliani: Duos for Violin and Guitar, 1987, The Italian Album, 1989, Brahms: The 3 Violin Sonatas, 1990 (Grammy award best small ensemble performance 1990), Dvorák In Prague: A Celebration, 1994, Bach: Violin Concertos, 1995, The American Album: Works Of Bernstein, Barber, Foss, 1995 (Grammy award best instrumental soloist performance with orch. 1995), Cinema Serenade, 1997, John Williams Greatest Hits 1969-1999 Cinema Serenade 2, 1999, Classic Yo-Yo, 2001, Classic Perlman: Rhapsody, 2002; appeared in PBS documentary Fiddling for the Future, 1998 (Emmy award outstanding cultural music-dance program 1999); TV specials Perlman in Russia, 1992 (Emmy award outstanding classical program 1992), Itzhak Perlman: In the Fiddler's House, 1996 (Emmy award outstanding cultural music-dance program 1996). Founder Perlman Music Program, 1995. Recipient Leventritt prize, 1964, Medal of Liberty, 1986, Nat. Medal of Arts, 2000, Kennedy Ctr. Honor, 2003; named Musician of Yr., Musical Am., 1981; inductee Am. Classical Music Hall of Fame, 2001. Address: IMG Artists 825 7th Ave New York NY 10019-6014*

PERLMAN, JERALD LEE, lawyer; b. Baton Rouge, Feb. 25, 1947; s. Ralph Robert and Carol Mayer (Herzberg) P.; m. Francine Evonne McKelvey, May 8, 1984; children: Louise, Lee, Kevin. BA, Washington & Lee U., 1969; JD, La. State U., 1972. Bar: La. 1972, Tex. 1994, U.S. Dist. Ct. (we. dist.) La. 1972, U.S. Dist. Ct. (ea. and we. dists.) Ark. 1991, U.S. Ct. Appeals (5th cir.) 1977, U.S. Supreme Ct. 1990. Assoc. Blanchard, Walker, O'Quin & Roberts, Shreveport, La., 1972-76, ptnr., 1976-83, Walker, Tooke, Perlman & Lyons, Shreveport, 1983-94; regional office chief litigation divsn. La. Dept. Justice, Shreveport, 1994—. Assoc. editor La. State U. Law Rev., 1971-72. Bd. dirs. Broadmoor Southside YMCA, Shreveport, 1984-88, vice chmn., 1986, chmn., 1987; bd. dirs. Shreveport Met. YMCA, 1987; bd. dirs. NW La. chpt. ACLU,

1987-93. Capt. USAR, 1972. Named to La. State U. Law Ctr. Hall of Fame. Mem. La. Bar Assn. (com. on uniform court rules 1998-2002), Shreveport Bar Assn., La. Assn. Def. Counsel (bd. dirs. 1979-81), Order of Coif, Phi Beta Kappa, Omicron Delta Kappa. Jewish. Avocations: tennis, reading. Office: La Dept Justice Litigation Divsn 330 Marshall St Ste 777 Shreveport LA 71101-3016

PERLMAN, JON ARTHUR, plastic surgeon; b. N.Y.C., Dec. 17, 1948; MD, Cornell U., 1973. Diplomate Am. Bd. Plastic Surgery. Intern Mass. Gen. Hosp., Boston, 1973—74, resident in surgery, 1974—78; resident in plastic surgery UCLA Med. Ctr., 1978—80; pvt. practice plastic surgery Beverly Hills, Calif., 1980—. Attending plastic surgery Cedars-Sinai Med. Ctr., L.A.; chief divsn. plastic surgery Brotman Med. Ctr., 1985—; asst. clin. prof. plastic surgery UCLA Med. Ctr.; featured plastic surgeon ABC's Extreme Makeover. Mem.: L.A. Soc. Plastic Surgeons, Calif. Soc. Plastic Surgeons, Am. Soc. Plastic Surgeons, Am. Soc. Aesthetic Plastic Surgeons. Office: 414 N Camden Dr 8th Fl Beverly Hills CA 90210

PERLMAN, LAWRENCE, retired business executive, corporate director, consultant; BA, Carleton Coll., 1960; JD, Harvard U., 1963. Bar: Minn. 1963. Law. clk. for fed. judge, 1963; assoc., ptnr. Fredrikson & Byron, Mpls., 1964-75; gen. counsel, exec. v.p. U.S. pacing ops. Medtronic, Inc., Mpls., 1975-78; sr. ptnr. Oppenheimer, Wolff & Donnelly, Mpls., 1978-80; exec. Control Data Corp. (now Ceridian Corp.), 1980—2000, CEO, 1990—92, chmn., CEO, 1992—2000; ret., 2000. Dir., chmn. Seagate Tech., 1989-2000; bd. dirs. Carlson Cos., Inc., The Valspar Corp.; chmn. Arbitron Inc.; trustee Carleton Coll. Bd. dirs. Walker Art Ctr.; regent Univ. of Minn., 1993-95; chmn. 21st Century Workforce Commn., 1999-2000. Address: 343 Union Plaza 333 Washington Ave N Minneapolis MN 55401

PERLMAN, MARK, economist, educator; b. Madison, Wis., Dec. 23, 1923; s. Selig and Eva (Shaber) P.; m. Naomi Gertrude Waxman, June 7, 1953; 1 child, Abigail Ruth Williams. BA, MA, U. Wis., 1947; PhD, Columbia, 1950. Asst. prof. U. Hawaii, 1951-52, Cornell U., 1952-55; asst. prof., then assoc. prof. Johns Hopkins U., 1955-63; prof. econs., history and pub. health U. Pitts., 1963-94, chmn. dept., 1965-70, univ. prof., 1969-94, univ. prof. emeritus, 1994—. Vis. Fulbright prof. U. Melbourne, Australia, 1968; co-chmn. Internat. Econ. Assn. Conf. on Econs. of Health in Industrialized Nations, Tokyo, Japan, 1973, Conf. on Orgn. and Retrieval Econs. Data, Kiel, West Germany, 1975; vis. fellow Clare Hall U. Cambridge, 1977; ofcl. visitor faculty econs. and politics, U. Cambridge, 1976-77; co-chmn., co-editor Internat. Congress on Health Econs., Leyden, The Netherlands, 1980; mem. Princeton Inst. Adv. Study, 1981-82; adj. scholar Am. Enterprise Inst., 1981—; Österreichischer Länderbank Joseph Schumpeter prof. Technische Universität, Vienna, 1982; disting. vis. scholar Beijing Chinese Nat. Acad. Social Scis., 1983; Rockefeller Found. resident scholar Villa Serbelloni, Bellagio, Como, Italy, 1983; vis. prof. Inst. für Weltwirtschaft U. Kiel, 1987, U. Augsburg, 1992, U. Chemnitz, 1996; mem. Internat. Com. for Documentation in the Social Scis., UNESCO, 1988-94, exec. com. 1993-94. Author: Judges in Industry: A Study of Labor Arbitration in Australia, 1954, Labor Union Theories in America, 1958, 2nd edit., 1978, The Machinists: A New Study in American Trade Unionism, 1961, Democracy in the I.A.M., 1962; author: (with T.D. Baker) Health Manpower in a Developing Economy, 1967; author: The Character of Economic Thought, Economic Characters, & Economic Institution, 1996, Festschrift: Editing Economics: Essays in Honour of Mark Perlman, 2001; author: (with Bela Gold, et al) Techonological Progress and Insutraial Leadership: The Growth of the U.S. Steel Industry, 1900-1970, 1984; author: (with Charles R. McCann, Jr.) Pillars of Economic Understanding: Ideas & Traditions, 1998, Pillars of Economic Understanding: Factors and Markets, 2000; editor: Human Resources in the Economy, 1963; editor: (with Reuben E. Slesinger and Asher Isaacs) Contemporary Economics and Selected Readings, 1967; author (with Benjamin Chinitz and Charles Levin): Spatial, Regional, and Population Economics: Essays in Honor of Egar M. Hoover, 1972; editor (with Norval Morris): Law and Crime: Essays in Honor of Sir John Barry, 1972; editor: Economics of Health and Medical Care, 1974, The Organization and Retrieval of Economic Knowledge, 1977; editor: (with G.K. MacLeod) Health Care Capital: Competition and Control, 1978; editor: (with Arnold Heertje) Evolving Technology and Market Structure: Studies in Schumpeterian Economics, 1990; editor: (with Klaus Weiermair) Studies in Economic Rationality: X-Efficency Examined and Extolled. Essays Written in the Tradition of and to Honor Harvey Leibenstein, 1990; editor: (with C.E. Barfield) Capital Markets and Trade: The United States Faces a United Europe, 1991; editor: (with N.H. Ornstein) Political Power and Social Change: The United States Faces a United Europe, 1991; editor: (with C.E. Barfield) Industry, Services, and Agriculture: The U.S. Faces a United Europe, 1991; editor: (with F.M. Scherer) Entrepreneurship, Technological Innovation, and Economic Growth: Studies in the Schumpeterian Tradition, 1992; editor: (with Yuichi Shionoya) Innovations in Technology, Industries, and Institutions, 1994, Schumpeter in the History of Ideas, 1994; editor: (with Ernst Helmstadter) Behavioral Norms, Technological Progress, and Economic Dynamics: Studies in Schumpeterian Economics, 1996; editor: (with Kenneth Arrow, Enrico Colombatto, and Christian Schmidt) The Rational Foundations of Economic Behaviour, 1996; editor: (with Francisco Louca) Is Economics an Evolutionary Science?, 2000; editor: Cambridge Surveys of Economic Institutions and Policies, 1991—96, articles, essays on health, population change, econ. devel., orgn. econ. knowledge and methodology, econ. productivity, history of econ. discipline; cons. editor, later editl. cons. (USIA publ.) Portfolio on Internat. Econ. Perspectives, 1972—83, mng. co-editor Jour. Evolutionary Econs., 1989—96, corr. Am. editor Revue d'Economie Politique, 1990—, series editor Great Economists of the World, 1990—96; series editor: Cambridge Surveys of Economic Lit., 1977—94; editor: Cambridge Surveys of Economic Literature, 1977—94. With U.S. Army, 1943—46. Social Sci. Rsch. Coun. fellow, 1949-50; Ford Found. fellow, 1962-63; Fulbright lectr. Melbourne U., 1968 Fellow: History Econs. Soc. (hon.; v.p. 1979—80, pres. elect 1983—84, pres. 1984—85); mem.: J.A. Schumpeter Gesellschaft (editor 1986—96), Verein fuer Sozial-Politik, Ausschuss fuer Dogmengeschichte, Royal Econ. Soc., Am. Econ. Assn. (founding and mng. editor Jour. Econ. Lit. 1968—81), European Assn. History Econ. Thought Soc. (hon.), Athenaeum (London), Phi Beta Kappa. Jewish. Home: 302 Fox Chapel Rd Apt 414 Pittsburgh PA 15238-2337 Business E-Mail: mperlman@pitt.edu.

PERLMAN, MATTHEW SAUL, lawyer; b. Washington, Aug. 30, 1936; s. Jacob and Helen (Aronson) P.; m. Julia Gertrude Hawks, June 22, 1966; children— Penelope Leah, Deborah Jane, Sarah Louise, Jacob Henry AB, Brown U., 1957; LLB, Harvard U., 1960. Bar: D.C. 1960, Md. 1960, U.S. Supreme Ct. 1965. Atty. Air Force Gen. Counsel's Office, Washington, 1960-65; mem. Armed Services Bd. of Contract Appeals, Washington, 1965-67; gen. counsel Pres.' Commn. on Postal Orgn., Washington, 1967; asst. gen. counsel Dept. Transp., Washington, 1967-69; ptnr. Arent, Fox, Kintner, Plotkin & Kahn, Washington, 1969—2001, arbitrator, 2002—. Mem. Pres. Reagan's Transition Team for GSA, Washington, 1980-81; mem. adv. bd. Fed. Contracts Report, Washington, 1970-97; overseas corr. Internat. Constn. Law Rev., London, 1983—. Contbr. articles to profl. jours. Pres. Civic Assn. River Falls, Potomac, Md., 1975-77; mem. Montgomery County Md. Citizens Adv. Commn. for Rock Run AWT Plant, 1979-85. Served to capt. USAF, 1960-63 Mem. ABA (pub. contracts sect.), Fed. Bar Assn., Cosmos Club. Republican. Jewish. Home: 10517 Stable Ln Potomac MD 20854-3867 Office: Arent Fox Kintner Plotkin & Kahn 1050 Connecticut Ave NW Ste 500 Washington DC 20036-5303 Office Phone: 202-857-6279. E-mail: perlmanm@arentfox.com., mspjgp@comcast.net.

PERLMAN, RICHARD E. medical software company executive; BS in Econs., U. Pa.; MBA, Columbia U. Founder, pres. Compass Ptnrs., Atlanta; chmn., CFO, treas. InfoCure, Atlanta, 1998—. Office: InfoCure 1765 The Exchange SE Ste 500 Atlanta GA 30339-2087

PERLMAN, RICHARD WILFRED, economist, educator; b. Mt. Vernon, N.Y., Dec. 15, 1923; s. Uriel and Annie (Feitelberg) P.; m. Irma Lowenthal, Sept. 18, 1949; children: Abel, David, Laura, Jennifer. AB, Cornell U., 1947; PhD, Columbia U., 1953. Asst. prof. econs. Adelphi U., Garden City, N.Y., 1953-57, assoc. prof., 1957-64; prof. econs. U. Wis., Milw., 1964-97, prof. emeritus, 1997—, chmn. dept., 1965-68, 74-77; NRC prof. Brookings Instn., 1958-59. Fulbright lectr. Inst. Politecnico Nacional, Mexico City, 1964, Autonomous U. Madrid, 1972 Author: Economics of Education, 1973, Labor Theory, 1969, Economics of Poverty, 1976, (with others) An Anthology of Labor Economics, 1972, Economics of Unemployment, 1984, Issues in Labor Economics, 1989, Sex Discrimination in the Labor Market, 1994. Mem. President's Com. on EEO, 1963. Rsch. fellow U. Melbourne, Australia, 1985, hon. rsch. fellow U. Birmingham, 1990-93, sr. fellow, 1993-; Fulbright rsch. scholar, Australia, 1987, rsch. scholar Victoria U. Tech., Australia, 1997. Mem. Am. Econ. Assn., Indsl. Relations Research Assn., Phi Beta Kappa. Home: 3341 N Summit Ave Milwaukee WI 53211-2930 E-mail: irmucha@msn.com.

PERLMUTH, WILLIAM ALAN, lawyer; b. N.Y.C., Nov. 21, 1929; s. Charles and Roe (Schneider) P.; m. Loretta Kaufman, Mar. 14, 1951; children: Carolyn, Diane. AB, Wilkes Coll., 1951; LLB, Columbia U., 1953. Bar: N.Y. 1954. Assoc. Cravath, Swaine & Moore, N.Y.C., 1955-61; ptnr. Stroock & Stroock & Lavan, N.Y.C., 1962—. Editor Columbia U. Law Rev., 1952-53. Trustee Aeroflex Found., N.Y.C., 1965—, City Ctr. 55th St. Theater Found., 1995—, Harkness Found. for Dance, N.Y.C., 1976—, Sch. Am. Ballet, 1997—, Wilkes U., Wilkes-Barre, Pa., 1980—, Weininger Found., 1985—, NYU Hosps. Ctr., 1994—, Hosp. for Joint Diseases Orthopaedic Inst., N.Y.C., 1980—, chmn. bd. trustees, 1994—. Mem. N.Y. State Bar Assn., Assn. of Bar of City of N.Y. Jewish. Home: 880 5th Ave New York NY 10021-4951 Office: Stroock & Stroock & Lavan 180 Maiden Ln Fl 34 New York NY 10038-4982 Office Phone: 212-806-5860.

PERLMUTTER, ALVIN HOWARD, television and film producer; b. Poughkeepsie, N.Y., Mar. 24, 1928; s. Fred and Jennie (Albert) P.; children: James F., Stephen H., Tom W. Student, Colgate U., 1945-47; BA, Syracuse U., 1949. Dir. pub. affairs Sta. WNBC, also Sta. WNBC-TV, N.Y.C., 1957-59; program mgr. Sta. WNBC-TV, 1959-61; exec. producer Nat. Ednl. TV, 1961—; v.p. news documentaries NBC, from 1975; pres. Alvin H. Perlmutter Inc., N.Y.C.; instr. TV news and pub. affairs NYU, 1957, Fairleigh Dickinson U., 1962; pres., CEO, Sunrise Media LLC, N.Y.C., 1997—. Cons. John and Mary Markle Found., Pub. Agenda Found.; chmn. Dore Schary Awards for film and TV, Anti-Defamation League. Producer: series Assignment America; Great American Dream Machine, Consumer Reports Presents, Money Matters, Cover Story, Black Journal; various spl. programs including: Native Land, The Primal Mind, Adam Smith's Money World series, Family Computing series, Priceless Treasures of Dresden, The Perpetual People Puzzle; exec. producer: Report From Philadelphia, The Secret Government, The Power of Myth, Muslims (PBS spl. documentary). Chair Dore Schary awards, Anti-Defamation League; bd. dirs. N.Y. Open Ctr., Citizens for Ind. Pub. Broadcasting, Rockland Ctr. for the Arts. 1st lt. AUS, 1950-53. Recipient various citations and awards including 6 Emmy awards, Peabody award, Robert Kennedy award. Mem. Acad. TV Arts and Scis. (gov. N.Y. chpt., nat. trustee, chmn. awards com. 1968), Assn. Pub. TV Producers (chmn. 1969) Clubs: Overseas Press (N.Y.C.), University, Coffee House, The Econ. Club of N.Y.C. Home: 200 Central Park South New York NY 10024-3615 Office: 45 W 45th St New York NY 10036-4602

PERLMUTTER, DAVID H. physician, educator; b. Bklyn., May 11, 1952; s. Herman Arthur and Ruth (Jacobs) P.; m. Barbara Ann Cohlan, Feb. 7, 1981; children: Andrew, Lisa. BA, U. Rochester, 1974; MD, St. Louis U., 1978. Intern then resident in pediatrics U. Pa. Sch. Medicine, Phila., 1978-81; fellow in pediatric gastroenterology Harvard U. Sch. Medicine, Boston, 1981-84, instr. pediatrics, 1983-85, asst. prof. pediatrics, 1985-86; Donald Strominger prof. of pediatrics Washington U. Sch. Medicine, St. Louis, 1986-89, prof. cell biology, physiology, 1989—. Editor: Pediatric Rsch., 1990—; editl. bd. Gastroenterology, 1990—; dir. divsn. gastrology and nutrition and pediatrics; contbr. articles to profl. jours. Recipient Established Investigator award Am. Heart Assn., 1987, Rsch. Scholar award Am. Gastroent. Assn., 1985, RJR Nabisco Co., 1986. Mem. Soc. Pediatric Rsch. (coun. rep. 1990—), Am. Soc. Cell Biology, Am. Soc. Clin. Investigation.

PERLMUTTER, DIANE F. marketing executive; b. N.Y.C., Aug. 31, 1945; d. Bert H. and Frances (Smith) P. Student, NYU Grad. Sch. of Bus., 1969—70; BA in English, Miami U., Oxford, Ohio, 1967. Writer sales promotion Equitable Life Assurance, N.Y.C., 1967-68; bus. adminstr. de Garmo, Inc., N.Y.C., 1968-69, asst. account exec., 1969-70, account exec., 1970-74, v.p., account supr., 1974-76; mgr. corp. advt. Avon Products, Inc., N.Y.C., 1976-79, dir. comm. Latin Am., Spain, Can., 1979-80, dir. brochures, 1980-81, dir. category merchandising, 1981-82, group dir. motivational comm., 1982-83, group dir. sales promotion, 1983-84, v.p. sales promotion, 1984, v.p. internat. bus. devel., 1984-85, area v.p. Latin Am., 1985, v.p. advt. and campaign mktg., 1985-87, v.p. U.S. operational planning, 1987; cons. N.Y.C., 1987-88; sr. v.p. Burson-Marsteller, N.Y.C., 1988-90, exec. v.p., mng. dir. consumer products, 1991-93, bd. dirs., 1992—, co-chief oper. officer, 1993-94, chief oper. officer, 1994-96, chmn. mktg. practice/U.S., 1996-98. Vice chmn., CEO Cohn & Wolfe, N.Y.C., 1998—2000; CEO Gilda's Club Worldwide, 2001—; chair ann. meeting Direct Selling Assn., Washington, 1982; v.p. Nat. Home Fashions League, N.Y.C., 1975—76; adj. instr. SUNY/ Fashion Inst. Tech., 1992—; vice chmn. Columbia-Greene Hosp. Found., 2000—; vice chmn., bd. dirs. Olana Partnership, 2000—03; bd. dirs. Double L.P. Industries, Inc. Bd. dirs. Hudson Opera House, 2002—. Named to YWCA Acad. Women Achievers, 1996. Mem.: Women in Comm., Advt. Women of N.Y., Pub. Rels. Soc. Am., Women's Econ. Round Table (bd. dirs. 1998—2000), Miami U. Alumni Assn. (pres., chair 1986), The Women's Forum (bd. dirs. 1998—2000, pres. 2002—04), YMCA of Greater N.Y. (bd. dirs. 1996—2003), Publicity Club N.Y. (bd. dirs. 1994—96), Beta Gamma Sigma. Avocation: interior design. Office: Gilda's Club Worldwide 322 8th Ave 14th Flr New York NY 10001 Business E-Mail: dperlmutter@gildasclub.org.

PERLMUTTER, DONNA, music critic, dance critic; b. Phila. d. Myer and Bessie (Krasno) Stein; m. Jona Perlmutter, Mar. 21, 1964; children: AAron, Matthew. BA, Pa. State U., 1958; MS, Yeshiva U., 1959. Music and dance critic L.A. Herald Examiner, 1975-84; contbr. L.A. Times, 1984—, N.Y. Times, 1994—. Dance critic Dance Mag., NYC, 1980—; music critic Opera News, NYC, 1981-98, Ovation Mag., NYC, 1983-89, Hollywood Reporter, 2001—, L.A. City Beat, 2003—, NY Mag., 1995—, L.A. Mag., 1996—, Daily News, L.A., 1996-97, New Times, L.A., 1997-2002, Performing Arts Mag., 1996-2002; panelist, spkr. in field. Author: Shadowplay: The Life of Antony Tudor, 1991. Recipient Deems Taylor award for excellence in writing on music ASCAP, 1991. Mem. Music Critics Assn. Home: 10507 Le Conte Ave Los Angeles CA 90024-3305 Business E-Mail: jperl@ucla.edu.

PERLMUTTER, JACK, artist, lithographer; b. NYC, Jan. 23, 1920; s. Morris and Rebecca (Schiffman) P.; children: Judith Faye, Ellen. MA, PhD in Fine Arts. Staff Dickey Gallery, D.C. Tchrs. Coll., 1951-68, dir., 1962-68, prof. art; prof. art, chmn. printmaking dept. Corcoran Gallery Art, Washington, 1960-82; resident artist St. Olaf Coll., Minn., Gibbs Art Gallery, Charleston, S.C., Mus. Sch. Art, Greenville, S.C. Vis. prof. art U. Costa Rica, San Jose, 1983; Fulbright research prof. painting and printmaking Tokyo U. Arts, 1959-60; art cons. Pres.'s Com. to Hire Handicapped; curator exhibits Cosmos Club, Washington. NASA artist for: 1st Saturn V moon rocket, Apollo 6, Apollo 16, Orbiter Columbia (space shuttle), Voyager II; contbg. editor: Art Voices South, 1979-80, Art Voices, 1980-82; one-man shows include Balt. Mus. Art, Brandeis U., Corcoran Gallery Art, Dintenfass Gallery, NYC, Makler Gallery, Phila., Smithsonian Inst., Yoseido Gallery, Tokyo, C. Troup Gallery, Dallas, Nat. Acad. Scis., 1981, Arts Club Washington, 1981, Annapolis, Md., 1982, galleries in Amsterdam, Rotterdam, The Hague and Costa Rica; exhibited in group shows in U.S., Switzerland, Yugoslavia, Europe, S.Am., Can.; represented in permanent collections Bklyn. Mus., Cin. Mus. Art, Carnegie Inst. Art, Corcoran Gallery Art, Library Congress, Met. Mus. Art, NYC, Nat. Gallery Art, Washington, Phila. Mus. Art, Walker Gallery, Mpls., Nat. Mus. Modern Art, Tokyo, U.S. Embassies in Bucharest, Budapest, Bonn, Dublin, London, Prague, Tokyo, others. Recipient awards for paintings and prints from Balt. Mus. Art, Libr. Congress, Corcoran Gallery Art, Butler Inst. Arts, Smithsonian Inst., Soc. Am. Graphic Artists, First Internat. Exhbn. Fine Arts in Saigon, Mus. Fine Arts in Saigon, Mus. Fine Art, Boston, others. Fellow Internat. Inst. Arts and Letters; mem. Soc. Am. Graphic Artists. Clubs: Cosmos (Washington; curator paintings and prints). Achievements include having prints, drawings and biog. data in Art Archives Am. Studio: Apt 2201 9707 Old Georgetown Rd Bethesda MD 20814 Personal E-mail: perltone@aol.com.

PERLMUTTER, JEROME HERBERT, communications specialist; b. N.Y.C., Oct. 17, 1924; s. Morris and Rebecca (Shiffman) P.; m. Evelyn Lea Friedman, Sept. 19, 1948; children: Diane Muriel, Sandra Pauline, Bruce Steven. AB cum laude, George Washington U., 1949; MA, Am. U., 1957. Chief editor svc., prodn. editor NEA, Washington, 1949-50; editor in chief Jour. AAHPER, Washington, 1950-51; editor Rural Elec. News, REA, USDA, Washington, 1951-53; publ. writer Agrl. Rsch. Svc., 1953-56; chief, editor br. Office Info., 1956-60; sec. Outlook and Situation Bd., 1960-62; chief econ. reports Econ. Rsch. Svc., 1960-62; chief div. pub. and reprodn. svcs. U.S. Dept. State, Washington, 1962-79; pres. Perlmutter Assocs., 1979—. Writing cons. CSC, 1956, World Bank, 1967—; communication cons. European Investment Bank, Can. Internat. Devel. Agy., Inter-Am. Devel. Bank, Internat. Monetary Fund; faculty agr. grad. sch. U. Md., also Fgn. Svc. Inst.; pub. cons. White House Conf. on Children and Youth, 1971. Author: A Practical Guide to Effective Writing, 1965; Contbr. articles profl. jours. Coord. fed. graphics Nat. Endowment for Arts, 1972-79, graphic designer, conv. of maj. polit. com., 1980. With USNR, 1943-46. Recipient award U.S. Jr. C. of C., 1963, Editors Choice award Nat. Libr. Poetry. Mem. Am. Assn. Agr. Coll. Editors, Assn. Editl. Bus. (bd. dirs.), Fed. Editors Assn., Am. Farm Econ. Assn., Soc. Tech. Comm. (bd. dirs.), Md. Literacy Coun., Soc. Profl. Journalists, Phi Beta Kappa, Phi Eta Sigma, Artus. Home: 15111 Glade Dr Silver Spring MD 20906-1542

PERLMUTTER, LEONARD MICHAEL, concrete construction company executive; b. Denver, Oct. 16, 1925; s. Philip Permutter and Belle (Perlmutter) m. Alice Love Bristow, Nov. 17, 1951; children: Edwin George, Joseph Kent, Cassandra Love. BA, U. Colo., 1948, postgrad., 1948-50. Ptnr. Perlmutter & Sons, Denver, 1947-58; v.p. Prestressed Concrete of Colo., Denver, 1952-60; pres. Stanley Structures, Inc., Denver, 1960-83, chmn. bd., 1983-87; dir. Colo. Nat. Bankshares, Inc.; adj. prof. Grad. Sch. Pub. Affairs U. Colo., Denver, 1987—; chief exec. officer Econ. Devel. Gov.'s Office State of Colo., 1987-88. Chmn. bd. Colo. Open Lands, 1989. Chmn. bd. U. Colo. Found., Boulder, 1979-81; dir. Santa Fe Opera Assn., N.Mex., 1976-85; v.p. Santa Fe Fedn., 1979-87; chmn. bd. Nat. Jewish Hops.-Nat. Asthma Ctr., Denver, 1983-86; pres. Denver Symphony Assn., 1983-84, chmn. bd., 1985; trustee Midwest Rsch. Inst., 1989—; pres. Nat. Jewish Ctr. for Immunology and Respiratory Medicine, 1991-93. Recipient Humanitarian Am. Jewish Com., 1981 Mem. Prestressed Concrete Inst. (pres. 1977, dir. 1973-74) Clubs: Rolling Hills Country (Golden) (pres. 1966-68). Home: 15125 Foothill Rd Golden CO 80401-2044 Office: LAP Inc 1515 Arapahoe St Denver CO 80202-3150

PERLMUTTER, LOUIS, investment banker, lawyer; b. Cambridge, Mass., Oct. 3, 1934; s. Kermit H and Rachel P (Ehrlich) Perlmutter; m. Barbara Patricia Sondik, Dec. 11, 1966; children: Kermit, Eric. BA, Brandeis U., 1956, LHD (hon.), 1995; JD, U. Mich., 1959. Bar: Mass 1959, NY 1961. Law practice, N.Y.C., 1960-65; asst. to pres. New Eng. Industries, N.Y.C., 1965-67; pres. Octagon Assocs., N.Y.C., 1967-75; sr. v.p. White Weld, N.Y.C., 1975-78; mgn. dir. Merrill Lynch, White Weld, N.Y.C., 1978; exec. mng. dir. Lazard Freres & Co. LLC, N.Y.C., 1978-99, ltd. mng. dir., 2000—. Contbr. articles to profl jours. Bd. dirs. Charles H. Revson Found.; bd. dirs., treas. World Fedn. UNA; chmn. bd. trustees Brandeis U., Waltham, Mass., 1988—95, Am. Jewish Congress, N.Y.C., 1988—94; bd. dirs., chmn. exec. com. UN Assn. USA, 1993—96; com. visitors U. Mich. Law Sch.; bd. fellows Harvard Med. Sch.; adv. bd. Fgn. Affairs, Medis Techs.; mem. adminstrv. coun. Blaustein Inst. Advancement Human Rights. Recipient Human Rels. award, Am. Jewish Com., 1995, Pub. Svc. award, Phoenix H.S., 1999, Israel Policy Forum Tribute Dinner, 2001. Mem.: Coun. on Fgn. Rels. Home: 39 E 79th St New York NY 10021-0216 Office: Lazard 30 Rockefeller Plz New York NY 10112-5900

PERLMUTTER, NORMAN, finance company executive; b. 1934; BS, U. Ill., 1956. With Greenbawm Mortgage Co., Chgo., 1959-66, Heitman Fin. Svcs. Ltd., Chgo., 1966—, chmn., CEO, 1966—99; mng. ptnr. Snowmass Land Co., 1988—. Chmn. bd. mgrs. Internat. Airport Ctrs., 1994, MainStreet Am., 2000; dir., chmn. exec. com. Prime Retail, Inc.; dir. chmn. compensation com. Chris Craft Industries, Inc.; dir., mem. compensation, audit and investment coms. United TV, Inc.; dir. Eisenhower World Affairs Inst.; trustee Milton Acad. With USN, 1956—59. Named One of 40 Real Estate Visionaries, Nat. Real Estate Investor; named to, Chgo. Bd. Realtors Hall of Fame, 1991, 1998. Office: Heitman Fin Ltd 191 N Wacker Dr #2500 Chicago IL 60606-1615

PERLOFF, CAREY, performing company executive, theater director, playwright; children: Lexie, Nicholas. B.A. in classics and comparative lit., Stanford U., 1980. Artistic dir. Classic Stage Co., N.Y.C, 1986—92; faculty, Tisch School of the Arts N.Y.U., 1986—92; artistic dir. Am. Conservatory Theater Found., San Francisco, 1992—. Playwright, dir.: The Colossus of Rhodes, 2001. Recipient Obie award for Artistic Excellence, The Village Voice, 1988; Fulbright Fellow, Oxford, 1981. Mem.: Phi Beta Kappa. Office: Am Conservatory Theater Found 30 Grant Ave San Francisco CA 94108-5800

PERLOFF, MARJORIE GABRIELLE, English and comparative literature educator; b. Vienna, Sept. 28, 1931; d. Maximilian and Ilse (Schueller) Mintz; m. Joseph K. Perloff, July 31, 1953; children: Nancy Lynn, Carey Elizabeth. AB, Barnard Coll., 1953; MA, Cath. U., 1956, PhD, 1965. Asst. prof. English and comparative lit. Cath. U., Washington, 1966-68, assoc. prof., 1969-71, U. Md., 1971-73, prof., 1973-76; Florence R. Scott prof. English U. So. Calif., LA, 1976—; prof. English and comparative lit. Stanford (Calif.) U., 1986—, Sadie Dernham prof. humanities, 1990—, prof. emerita, 2000. Vis. prof. U. Utah, 2002; scholar-in-residence U. So. Calif., 2004—. Author: Rhyme and Meaning in the Poetry of Yeats, 1970, The Poetic Art of Robert Lowell, 1973, Frank O'Hara, Poet Among Painters, 1977, 2nd edit., 1998, The Poetics of Indeterminacy: Rimbaud to Cage, 1981, 2d edit., 1999, The Dance of the Intellect: Studies in the Poetry of the Pound Tradition, 1985, 2d edit., 1996, The Futurist Moment: Avant-Garde, Avant-Guerre and the Language of Rupture, 1986, 2d edit., 2003, Poetic License: Essays in Modern and Postmodern Lyric, 1990, Radical Artifice: Writing Poetry in the Age of Media, 1991, Wittgenstein's Ladder: Poetic Language and the Strangeness of the Ordinary, 1996, Frank O'Hara, 2d edit., 1998, Poetry On and Off the Page: Essays for Emergent Occasions, 1998, Twenty-first Century Modernism, 2001, The Vienna Paradox, 2004; editor: Postmodern Genres, 1990; co-editor: John Cage: Composed in America, 1994; contbg. editor: Columbia Literary History of the U.S., 1987; contbr. preface to Contemporary Poets, 1980, A John Cage Reader, 1983. Guggenheim fellow, 1981-82, NEA fellow, 1985; Phi Beta Kappa scholar, 1994-95. Fellow Am. Acad. Arts and Scis.; mem. MLA (exec. coun. 1977-81, Am. lit. sect. 1993—, 2d v.p. 2004-), Comparative Lit. Assn. (pres. 1993-94, mem. adv. bd. Libr. of Am.), Lit. Studies Acad. Home: 1467 Amalfi Dr Pacific Palisades CA 90272-2752 Office: Stanford U Dept English Stanford CA 94305 E-mail: mperloff@earthlink.net.

PERLOFF, ROBERT, psychologist, educator; b. Phila., Feb. 3, 1921; s. Myer and Elizabeth (Sherman) P.; m. Evelyn Potechin, Sept. 22, 1946; children: Richard Mark, Linda Sue, Judith Kay. AB, Temple U., 1949; MA, Ohio State U., 1949, PhD, 1951; DSc (hon.), Oreg. Grad. Sch. Profl. Psychology, 1984; DLitt (hon.), Calif. Sch. Profl. Psychology, 1985. Diplomate Am. Bd. Profl. Psychology. Instr. edn. Antioch Coll., 1950-51; with pers. rsch. br. Dept. Army, 1951-55, chief statis. rsch. and cons. unit., 1953-55; dir. R & D Sci. Rsch. Assocs., Inc., Chgo., 1955-59; vis. lectr. Chgo. Tchrs. Coll., 1955-56; mem. faculty Purdue U., 1959-69, prof. psychology, 1964-69; field assessment officer univ. Peace Corps Chile III project, 1962; Disting. Svc. prof. bus. adminstrn. and psychology U. Pitts. Joseph M. Katz Grad. Sch. Bus., 1969-90, Disting. Svc. prof. emeritus, 1991—; dir. rsch. programs U. Pitts. Grad. Sch. Bus., 1969-77; dir. Consumer Panel, 1980-83. Bd. dirs. Book Ctr.; adv. com. assessment exptl. manpower R & D labs. NAS, 1972-74; mem. rsch. rev. com. NIMH, 1976-80, Stress and Families rsch. project, 1976-79; cons. in field. Contbr. articles to profl. jours.; editor Indsl. Psychologist, 1963-65,

Evaluator Intervention: Pros and Cons; book rev. editor Personnel Psychology, 1952-55; co-editor: Values, Ethics and Standards Sourcebook, 1979, Improving Evaluations; bd. consulting editors Jour. Applied Psychology; bd. advs. Archives History Am. Psychology, Psychol. Svc. Pitts., Recorded Psychol. Jours.; guest editor Am. Psychologist, 1972, Edn. and Urban Soc., 1977, Profl. Psychology, 1977; adv. editor Contemporary Psychology, 1994—. Bd. dirs., v.p. Sr. Citizens Svc. Corp., Calif. Sch. Profl. Psychology; bd. dirs. Greater Pitts. chpt. ACLU, sec., 1997-98; chmn. nat. adv. com. Inst. Govt. and Pub. Affairs, U. Ill., 1986-89, sec. nat. adv. com., 1997—; mem. adv. com. Cornell Inst. for Rsch. on Children, 2002—. Decorated Bronze Star; named in his honor, Robert Perloff Grad. Rsch. Assistantship in Inst. Govt. and Pub. Affairs, U. Ill., 1990, in his honor, Robert Perloff Career Achievement award, Knowledge Utilization Soc., 1991; recipient Legacy award, Greater Pitts. Psychol. Assn., 2001, Hist. Preservation award, City of Pitts., 2002. Fellow: APA (mem.-at-large exec. com. divsn. consumer psychology 1964—67, coun. reps. 1965—68, pres. divsn. 1967—68, chmn. sci. affairs com., divsn. consumer psychology 1968—69, edn. and tng. bd. 1969—72, mem.-at-large exec. com. divsn. consumer psychology 1970—71, coun. reps. 1972—74, dir. 1974—82, chmn. fin. com., treas. 1975—84, chmn. investment com. 1977—82, pres. 1985, adv. bd., bd. sci. affairs 1994—96, task force Intelligence and Intelligence Tests, author column Std. Deviations in jour., pres. address selected as one of 50 over 50 yrs.), AAAS, Ea. Psychol. Assn. (dir. 1977—80, pres. 1980—81); mem.: Coun. of Sci. Soc. (found. alumnus, pres. 1998—), Knowledge Utilization Soc. (pres. 1993—95), Soc. Psychologists in Mgmt. (pres. 1993—94, Disting. Contbn. to Psychology Mgmt. award 1989), Am. Evaluation Assn. (pres. 1977—78), Am. Psychol. Found. (v.p. 1988—89, pres. 1990—92, trustee 1995—98, Lifetime Achievement in Psychology Gold Medal award 2000), Assn. for Consumer Rsch. (chmn. 1970—71), Pa. Psychol. Assn. (Disting. Svc. award 1985), Internat. Assn. Applied Psychology, Am. Psychol. Soc., Phi Beta Kappa, Psi Chi, Beta Gamma Sigma, Sigma Xi (pres. U. Pitts. chpt. 1989—91). Home: 815 Saint James St Pittsburgh PA 15232-2112 Business E-Mail: rperloff@katz.pitt.edu. *Experiment. Innovate responsibly. Take risks judiciously. Do not shrink from new ventures for fear of failure. No one is immune from adversity. The hallmark of a successful achieving person is his or her ability to snap back after misfortune, and to benefit from and not be immobilized by failure.*

PERLONGO, DANIEL JAMES, composer, educator; b. Gaastra, Mich., Sept. 23, 1942; s. James and Camille (Fittante) P. Mus.B. in Composition, U. Mich., 1964, Mus.M., 1966; Corso di Perfezionamento, Accademia di S. Cecilia, Rome, 1968. Assoc. prof. music Indiana (Pa.) U., 1968—. Composer (for orch.) Myriad, 1968, Ephemeron, 1972, Concertino, 1980, Lake Breezes, 1990, Concerto for Piano and Orchestra, 1992, Shortcut from Bratislava for Piano and Orch., 1994, Sunburst for Clarinet and Orch., 1995, Two Movements, 1996, Millennium Overture, 2000, Symphony No. 1, Millennium Voyage, 2001, (chamber orch.) Variations 1973, Voyage, 1975, Ariadne's Thread for string orchestra, 2002, (chamber music) Improvision for Four, 1965, Improvisation 2, 1966, Eufonia, poetica e sonora, 1966, (string trio) Intervals, 1967, (ensemble pieces) Movement for 8 Players, 1967, Semblance for string quartet, 1969-70, String Quartet II, 1983, (percussion quartet) For Bichi, 1968, Movement in Brass, 1969, (various works) Process 7, 5, 3 for 6 in 12, for flute, oboe, clarinet, 3 percussions, 1969, Tre Tempi for flute, oboe, clarinet, violin, cello, 1971, Fragments for flute and cello, 1972, Structure, Semblance and Tune for tuba and percussion, 1973, (wind ensemble) Changes, 1970, (violin) Violin Solo, 1971, (double bass) Episodes, 1966, (for oboe, clarinet and bassoon) Ricercar, 1976, (solo piano) Piano Sonata, 1965, Suite for Piano, 1988, Serenade, 1977, First Set, 1990, (saxophone quartet) Aureole, 1978, (brass quintet) Summer Music, 1979, (solo bass clarinet) Soliloquy, 1980, (soprano voice and piano) Six Songs, 1980, (solo organ) Tapestry, 1981, (winds, percussion and piano) Montalvo Overture, 1984, (piano and woodwind quintet) A Day At Xochimilco, 1987, (trombone and organ) Novella, 1988, (mezzo soprano, violin, clarinet and piano) By Verse Distills, 1989, (wind ensemble) Preludes and Variations, 1991, (horn and harp) Arcadian Suite, 1993, (cello and piano) Poppies with Butterflies, 1997, (woodwind quintet) Groznjan Souvenir, 1998, (violin, cello, piano) Breezes at Yellow Creek, 1999, Aubade, Morning Songs, for wind trio and string trio, 2002, Sunday Afternoon at the Ghost Ranch for Violin, Trumpet and Alto Sax, 2002. Fulbright fellow Italy, 1966; Italian Govt. grantee, 1967; recipient Joseph Bearns prize Columbia U., 1966; Rome prize, 1971, 72; award Nat. Inst. Arts and Letters, 1975, Internat. Double Reed Soc. prize, 1979, New Music for Young Ensembles prize, 1979, Nebr. Sinfonia prize, 1981; Nat. Endowment Arts grantee, 1981, 95; Guggenheim fellow, 1982. Office: Indiana U of Pa 101 Cogswell Hall Music Dept Indiana PA 15705-0001

PERLOV, DADIE, management consultant; BA, NYU, 1950; postgrad., Adelphi U., 1963, Vanderbilt U., 1973. Cert. assn. exec., N.Y. Exec. dir. ops. Open City, N.Y.C., 1962-64; field svcs. dir. Nat. Coun. Jewish Women, N.Y.C., 1968-74; exec. dir. N.Y. Libr. Assn., N.Y.C., 1974-81, Nat. Coun. Jewish Women, N.Y.C., 1981-90; founder, prin. Consensus Mgmt. Group, N.Y.C. and Indpls., 1989—. Cons. HEW 1975-76; pres.-elect Internat. Coun. Libr. Assn. Execs., 1979-80; exec. mem. Conf. of Pres., 1981-90; strategic planner, lectr., merger facilitator; bd. devel., structure/governance, ops., audits mgmt. cons. ABA, Am. Bankers Assn., ALA, Nat. Assn. Home Builders, Am. Coll. Healthcare Execs., Nat. Assn. Ind. Insurers, and more than 500 other maj. trade and profl. assns. Co-author: The Ultimate Association Diet: How to Stay Fit and Trim in the 21st Century; author monthly column Dear Dadie for Assoc. Trends; contbr. articles to profl. jours. Mem. N.Y. Zool. Soc., 1959—, adv. bd. Nat. Inst. Against Prejudice and Violence, 1985-89; bd. visitors Pratt Inst., Bklyn., 1980-84; bd. dirs. Pres. Coun. on Handicapped, 1981—; facilitator Nursing Summit, 1994, 2004. Recipient Recognition award N.Y. Libr. Assn., 1978, BUDDY award NOW Legal Def. and Edn. Found., 1989, cert. N.Y. State Legislature, 1978; named N.Y. State Exec. of Yr., 1980, One of Am.'s 100 Most Important Women, Ladies' Home Jour., 1988. Fellow Am. Soc. Assn. Execs. (cert. 1978, evaluator 1980-91, bd. dirs. 1987-90, bd. found. 1990-92, Excellence award 1983); mem. LWV (chpt. pres. 1960-62), N.Y. Soc. Assn. Execs, (pres. 1985, Outstanding Assn. Exec. 1989, Outstanding Svc. award 1991), Global Perspectives in Edn. (bd. dirs.), Nat. Orgn. Continuing Edn. (coun.), Audubon Soc., N.Y. Citizens Coun. on Librs. (bd. dirs. 1981-84), Am. Arbitration Assn. (mem. panel). Avocations: writing, mycology, history, music, art. Fax: 212-874-8068.

PERLOW, GILBERT J(EROME), physicist, editor; b. N.Y.C., Feb. 10, 1916; s. David and Esther (Germane) P.; m. Mina Rea Jones. AB, Cornell U., 1936, MA, 1937; PhD, U. Chgo., 1940. Instr. physics U. Minn., Mpls., 1940-41; physicist Naval Ordnance Lab., Washington, 1941-42, Naval Rsch. Lab., Washington, 1942-52; rsch. assoc. physics dept. U. Minn., Mpls., 1952-53; assoc. physicist Argonne (Ill.) Nat. Lab., 1953-57, sr. physicist, 1957—; editor Jour. Applied Physics Am. Inst. Physics/Argonne Nat. Lab., 1970-73, editor Applied Physics Letters, 1970-90, consulting editor Applied Physics Letters, 1990-2000. Vis. assoc. prof. physics U. Wash., Seattle, 1957; vis. prof. German univs., Munich, Berlin; exch. physicist AERE Harwell, Berkshire, Eng., 1961. Contbr. over 70 articles to profl. jours., also chpts. to books; author numerous U.S. patents. Recipient Alexander von Humboldt award Alexander von Humboldt Found., Tech. U. Munich, 1972. Fellow Am. Phys. Soc.; mem. Chgo. Corinthian Yacht Club (life mem., commodore 1974). Avocations: sailing, woodworking, painting. Home: 4919 Northcott Ave Downers Grove IL 60515-3434 Office: Argonne Nat Lab Physics Divsn 9700 Cass Ave Argonne IL 60439-4803 E-mail: perlow@megsinete.net.

PERLSTEIN, WILLIAM JAMES, lawyer; b. N.Y.C., Feb. 7, 1950; s. Justin Sol and Jane (Goldberg) P.; m. Teresa Catherine Lotito, Dec. 20, 1970; children: David, Jonathan. Student, London Sch. Econs., 1969-70; BA summa cum laude, Union Coll., 1971; JD, Yale U., 1974. Bar: Conn. 1974, D.C. 1976, U.S. Dist. Ct. D.C. 1977, U.S. Ct. Appeals (D.C. cir.) 1978, U.S. Supreme Ct. 1993, N.Y. 2000. Law clk. to judge Marvin Frankel U.S. Dist. Ct., N.Y.C., 1974-75; assoc. Wilmer, Cutler & Pickering, Washington, 1975-82, ptnr., 1982—, mem. mgmt. com., 1995—, chmn., 1998—. Mng. editor Yale Law Jour., 1973-74; contbg. author The Workout Game, 1987. Dir. Neighborhood Legal Svcs. program. Mem.: Am. Bar Found., Am. Coll. Bankruptcy (gen. counsel), Am. Law Inst., Am. Bankruptcy Inst. (chmn. legis. com. 1986—89, bd. dirs. 1989—93, 1997—), ABA (bus. bankruptcy com 1983—, v.chmn. executory contracts subcom. of bus. bankruptcy com. 1988—90, bankruptcy cts. subcom. 1990—97, chmn. legislation subcom. 1997—), Phi Beta Kappa. Jewish. E-mail: wperlstein@wilmer.com.

PERMAN, JAY ALLAN, pediatrician, educator; b. Chgo., Aug. 14, 1946, s. Max and Rose (Fishbein) P.; m. Andrea Merle Mittelman, Aug. 31, 1969; children: Corey, Marissa, Chad, Saranne. BA, Northwestern U., 1968, MD, 1972. Resident Northwestern U., Children's Meml. Hosp., Chgo., 1972-75; asst. prof. pediatrics U. Calif., San Francisco, 1977-82, assoc. prof., 1982-84; dir. pediatric gastroenterology and nutrition Johns Hopkins U., Balt., 1984-96, assoc. prof. pediatrics, 1984-92, prof., 1992-96; pres. Johns Hopkins Pediatrics at Home, Balt., 1992-96; Jessie Ball du Pont prof., chmn. dept. pediatrics Med. Coll. Va./Va. Commonwealth U., Richmond, 1996-99; prof., chmn. dept. pediats., chief of pediat. med. sys. U. Md. Sch. Medicine, Balt., 1999—2004; dean U. Ky. Coll. Medicine, 2004—; v.p. clin. affairs Chandler Med. Ctr., 2004—. Contbr. articles to profl. jours. and chpts. to books. Trustee Har Sinai Congregation, Balt., 1987-90. Grantee NIH, numerous pvt. founds. and industry. Mem. N.Am. Soc. for Pediatric Gastroenterology and Nutrition (pres. 1988-90). Avocations: walking, singing. Office: U Md Med Ctr 22 S Greene St # N5E17 Baltimore MD 21201-1544 E-mail: Jperman@peds.umaryland.edu.

PERMUT, STEPHEN ROBERT, physician, lawyer; b. Olympia, Wash., Sept. 24, 1945; s. Max L. and Ruth E. (Epstein) P.; m. Marylene Quiambao, Apr. 20, 1974; children: Laura Q., Irene Q. AB, U. Pa., 1967; MD, Temple U., 1972; JD, Widener U., 1985. Bar: Pa. 1985. Program dir. St. Francis Hosp., Wilmington, Del., 1976-85; med. dir. Blue Cross and Blue Shield of Del., Wilmington, 1985-90; special counsel Saul, Ewing, Remick & Saul, Phila., 1990-93; v.p. med. affairs St. Francis Hosp., Wilmington, 1993 96; prof., chmn. dept. family and cmty. medicine Temple U., Phila., 1994—, asst. dean academic affiliations, 1999—. Pres. Children's Bur. Del., Wilmington, 1986-89. Fellow ACP, Am. Acad. Family Physicians, Am. Coll. Legal Medicine, Coll. Physicians Phila.; mem. ABA, AMA (coun. legislation 1999—, vice chmn. task force on E&M Coding 1999—), Pa. Bar Assn., New Castle County Med. Soc. (bd. trustees 1979—), Med. Soc. Del. (bd. trustees 1979—, v.p. 1990-91, pres.-elect 1991-92, pres. 1992-93, Disting. Svc. award 1987, Pres.'s award 1989). Home: 32 Beethoven Dr Wilmington DE 19807-1923 Office: 3400 N Broad St Philadelphia PA 19140-5104

PERMUTH, JAIME, artist, educator; b. Guatemala, Jan. 15, 1968; s. Mario Permuth and Bertha Ostrowiak; m. Jennifer Dodge, Nov. 6, 1971. BA in Psychology and Eng. Lit., Hebrew U., Jerusalem, 1990; MFA in Photography, Sch. of Visual Arts, N.Y., 1994. Instr. Internat. Ctr. Photography, N.Y.C., 1998; tchg. artist Ctr. for Creative Ageing, Brooklyn, NY, 2000—. Artist in residence Cabras Project, San Miguel de Allende, Mexico, 1998—2008, Longwood Arts Project, N.Y.C., 2000—01, Centro de Investigaciones Regionales Mesoamericano, Antigua Guatemala, Guatemala, 2003; adj. prof. SUNY, New Paltz, NY, 2001; adj. prof. art Kean U., Union, NJ, 2002—03; adj. prof. photography New Sch. U., N.Y.C., 2003—; tchg. artist Ctr. for Creative Aging, Bklyn., 2000—. Represented in permanent collections Mus. City of New York, exhibitions include Queens Theatre in the Park, Mus. Modern Art, Queens Mus. Art, El Mus. del Barrio, Bklyn. Mus. Art, Museo Nacional de Arte Moderno, Guatemala, Represented in permanent collections Brooklyn Mus. of Art, Ploaroid Corp. Recipient, Jewish Mus., N.Y., 2003; grantee, Fuji Photo Film USA, Inc., 1999, Daniele Agostino Found., 1999—2000; vis. scholar Polaroid Collections grant, Polaroid Corp., 1998. Personal E-mail: kaxlan@aol.com.

PERMUTT, SOLBERT, physiologist, physician; b. Birmingham, Ala., Mar. 6, 1925; s. Harry and Rachel (Damsky) P.; m. Loretta Paul, Jan. 17, 1952; children— Nina Rachel, Thomas Joshua, Lisa Ellen. MD, U. So. Calif., 1949. Intern U. Chgo. Clinics, 1949-50, resident medicine, 1952, research assoc. dept. anatomy, 1950-52; resident medicine Montefiore Hosp., N.Y.C., 1954-56; fellow medicine and environmental medicine Johns Hopkins Med. Sch., 1956-58; chief div. cardiopulmonary physiology Nat. Jewish Hosp., Denver, 1958-61; asst. prof. physiology Sch. Medicine, U. Colo., 1960-61; mem. faculty Sch. Hygiene and Pub. Health, Johns Hopkins, 1961, prof. environ. health sci., 1965—; prof. medicine Johns Hopkins U. Sch. Med., 1972—, dir. respiratory div. dept. medicine, 1972-81, prof. anesthesiology, 1978—; head physiology div., environ. health sci. John Hopkins Sch. Hygiene and Pub. Health, 1976-79; dir. pulmonary div. Francis Scott Key Med. Ctr. (John Hopkins Med. Instn.), 1981-87, dir. pulmonary rsch., div. pulmonary medicine, 1986-87, dir. rsch. div. pulmonary and critical care medicine, 1988-98; assoc. dir. Johns Hopkins Asthma and Allergy Ctr., 1990—. Cons. space sci. bd. Nat. Acad. Sci., 1966-67, mem. com. effects atmospheric contaminants human health, 1968-70; mem. project com. Heart and Lung Program, NIH, 1970-74; mem. sci. adv. council Children's Asthma Research Inst. and Hosp., Denver, 1973-75; mem. expert panel Nat. Inst. Allergy and Infectious Diseases, 1972-74; mem. nat. adv. com. for Cal. Primate Research Center, 1972-75; vice chmn. council on cardiopulmonary diseases Am. Heart Assn., 1974-75, chmn., 1976—, mem. research com., 1979-85; nat. adviser Aspen Lung Confs., 1974—; mem. pulmonary disease adv. com. HHS and NIH, 1979-83. Mem. editorial bd. publs. Am. Physiol. Soc. Circulation Research, 1965—, La Revue Française des Maladies Respiratoires, 1975—; contbr. articles to profl. jours. Served with U.S. Army, 1943-46, 53-54. Recipient Gold medal Am. Coll. Chest Physicians, 1977, Louis and Artur Lucian award McGill U., 1980; fellow Nat. Found. Infantile Paralysis, 1956-58 Mem. Am. Lung Assn. (George Wills Comstock award 1988, Edward Livingston Trudeau medal 1992), Cardiovascular System Dynamics Soc., Am. Med. Assn. (reference panel for diagnostic and therapeutic tech. assessment-DATTA), Assn. Am. Physicians, Johns Hopkins Med. and Surg. Assn., Md. Soc. Med. Rsch., Am. Thoracic Soc., Am. Physiol. Soc., AAAS, Am. Heart Assn. (Citation for Disting. Svc. to Rsch. 1979-84, Disting. Achievement award Cardiopulmonary Coun. 1986). Home: 2303 Sulgrave Ave Baltimore MD 21209-4405 Office Phone: 410-550-2512. Business E-Mail: spermutt@jhmi.edu.

PERNA, MARIE IMMACULATE, retired physical education educator; b. Middletown, N.Y., Sept. 23, 1942; d. Ralph and Caroline Margaret (Cosco) D'Onofrio; m. Donald Perna, July 31, 1965; children: Donna, Debbie, Anne. BS in Health and Phys. Edn., Ithaca (N.Y.) Coll., 1964. Coord. Accessible RI. Author: Dare To Dream, 2001. Mem.: Nat. Multiple Sclerosis Soc. (gov. rels. com. (Long Island chpt.) 1999—2001, Achievement award 2000, 2003). Avocations: golf, bridge, movies. Home: 425 Meshanticut Valley Pkwy #305 Cranston RI 02920

PERNA, MICHAEL LEWIS, language educator; b. Hampton, Va., Oct. 3, 1941; s. Michael Archangel and Rita M. (Kocher) Perna. AB, Wash. Coll., Chestertown, Md., 1963; MA, Duke U., PhD, 1977. Spanish tchr. St. Mary's County Schs., Chaptico, Md., 1964—68; instr. Spanish U. N.C., Chapel Hill, 1968—70, Duke U., Durham, NC, 1970—73; acting asst. prof. U. Va., Charlottesville, 1973—76; Spanish tchr. The Tandem Sch., Charlottesville, 1977—78; asst. prof. Spanish U. Maine, Orono, 1978; assoc. prof. Romance langs. Hunter Coll., N.Y.C., 1979—. Editor, contbr.: Twentieth-Century Spanish Poets, 1991; Dictionary of Literary Themes and Motifs, 1988. Mem., activist Harlem Peacemakers, N.Y.C., 1986—96; chair South Africa com. Ch. of Heavenly Rest, N.Y.C., 1987—92; mem., activist Episcopal Peace Fellowship, Chgo., 1981—. Recipient Summer Rsch. Stipend, U. Va., 1976; grantee Hunter Coll. grant award: Presdl. Initiatives in Tchg. and Learning, 2003—04; scholar, Md. State Senate, 1959—63. Mem.: Am. Assn. Tchrs. Spanish and Portuguese, Northeast Modern Lang. Assn. (exec. dir. 1988—90). Episcopalian. Avocations: camping, music, sailing. Home: 161 E 91 St New York NY 10128 Office: Hunter Coll Dept Romance Langs 695 Park Ave New York NY 10021 Office Phone: 212-772-5120. Business E-Mail: mperna@hunter.cuny.edu.

PERNER, DARLENE E. special education educator, consultant, editor; b. Chgo., Dec. 1, 1948; d. LaVerne Perner; m. Lance C. Nielsen, Aug. 3, 1976; 1 child, Jaron M. Nielsen. BA in Fine Arts, Knox Coll., 1970; MEd. in Curriculum Devel. and Urban Edn., SUNY, Buffalo, 1972, MS in Spl. Edn., 1973; EdD in Spl. Edn., U. B.C., 1986. Permanent sch. prin. cert. N.B., Can., permanent tchr.'s cert. N.B., Can., permanent tchr. cert. N.Y. Art and elem. tchr. Chgo. Pub. Schs., 1970—71; spl. edn. tchr. West Seneca (N.Y.) Devel. Ctr., 1973—78; instr. SUNY, Buffalo, 1978; asst. prof. U. N.B., Fredericton, 1980—81; ednl. cons. N.B. Dept. Edn., Fredericton, 1981—82, cons., 1986 93, rsch. and policy devel. cons., 1993—96, rsch. and policy analyst, 1996—98; supr. Sch. Dist. 20, St. John, 1982—86; assoc. prof. Bloomsburg U. of Pa., 1998—. Author: (curriculum guide) Changing Teaching Practices Using Curriculum Differentiation to Respond to Student's Diversity, (curriculum instruction) Implementing Inclusive Edn., Paris: OECD, 2001; co-author: How to Use Differentiated Instrn. with Students with Develop. Disabilities in the Gen. Edn. Classroom, 2002; contbr. chapters to books; author: (curriculum guide) UNESCO, 2001—. Grantee, Ednl. Rsch. Inst. of B.C., 1979—80, N.B. Dept. of Advanced Edn. and Labour's Job Experience for Tomorrow, 1995, 1997; Can. Works grantee, 1985. Mem.: TASH (assoc.), Am. Assn. on Mental Retardation (assoc.), Northea. Ednl. Rsch. Assn. (assoc.; co-editor newsletter 1999—2002), Coun. for Exceptional Children (assoc.; program proposal reviewer 2001—, pres. chpt. # 365 1999—, newsletter editor divsn. devel. disabilities 2000—). Avocations: vegetarian cooking, organic gardening, travel, running, reading. Office: Bloomsburg U of Pa 400 E 2nd St Bloomsburg PA 17815 E-mail: dperner@bloomu.edu.

PERNICIARO, CHARLES VINCENT, dermatologist, educator, entrepreneur; b. New Orleans, June 15, 1957; s. Ernest Gabriel and Phereby Sheppard Perniciaro; children: Jamie Lynn, Kelly Gabrielle. BS, U. La., Lafayette, 1979; MD, La. State U., New Orleans, 1983. Diplomate Am. Bd. Dermatology, Am. Bd. Dermatology and Pathology. Staff physician Ochsner Clin. of Baton Rouge, La., 1987-90; sr. assoc. cons. and staff dermatologist Mayo Clinic, Jacksonville, Fla., 1990-93, cons., staff dermatologist and dermatopathologist, 1993-99; pvt. practice dermatology Brunswick, Ga., 1999—, Neptune Beach, Fla., 1999—. Pres., CEO Holiday Lighting Concepts, Inc., 1996-2000; lectr., presenter in field; adj. clin. assoc. prof. pathology U. Fla. Shands Jacksonville Med. Ctr., 1999-2001. Contbr. articles to profl. jours. Founder, bd. dirs. S.W. La. Skin Cancer Found., 1987. Recipient Resident-in-Tng. award So. Med. Assn., 1994, Outstanding Paper award Noah Worcester Dermatol. Soc., 1993, First Place Poster award 17th Internat. Colloquium Dermatopathology, 1996; named one of Best Doctors, 2000-04, How to Find the Best Fla. Doctors, 2000, Am. Top Physicians, 2003. Fellow: Am. Soc. Dermatopathology (chmn. membership com., bd. dirs. 2000—01), Am. Acad. Dermatology (com. on preventive dermatology 1988 90, task force on dermatologic oncology 1990—93, environ. coun. 1994—96, adv. coun. 1995—2001); mem.: So. Med. Assn. (vice chair sect. dermatology 1995—96, chair-elect 2001—03), Fla. Soc. Dermatology (bd. dirs. 1998—, chmn. membership com. 1999—2002, v.p. 2002—03, pres. 2003—04), Jacksonville Dermatology Soc. (sec.-treas. 1995, pres. 1996, webmaster 2003—), Lions (charter, bd. dirs. Ponte Vedra Beach 1997—98). Avocations: tennis, computers. Home: 514 Midway St Neptune Beach FL 32266 Office: Brunswick Dermatology Clinic 3008 E Park Ave Brunswick GA 31520-4241

PERNOT, GUILLERMO, chef, restaurant owner; Chef de cuisine Treetops Restaurant, Phila., Vega Grill; exec. chef, co-owner Pasión!, Phila., 1998—. Author: Ceviche, 2001 (Best Single Subject Cookbook award, 2001). Named Chef to Watch, Phila. Mag., 1998, Chef of Yr., Esquire Mag., 1999, Best Chef Mid-Atlantic, 2001; named one of Best New Chefs, Food & Wine Mag., 1998, 10 Rising Stars, Restaurant Hospitality, 1998; recipient James Beard award, 2001. Office: Pasion! 211 S 15th St Philadelphia PA 19102-3804 Office Phone: 215-875-9895. Personal E-mail: lgpernot@aol.com.

PERO, PERRY R. investment company executive; CFO Northern Trust Corp., Chgo., 1988—, sr. exec. v.p., vice chmn., 1999—. Office: Northern Trust Corp 50 S Lasalle St Chicago IL 60675-1006

PEROSCH, TONY ANTHONY GEORGE, corporate executive, consul; b. Zagreb, Croatia, Jan. 21, 1930; arrived in Venezuela, 1948; s. Ante Perosch; m. Maria Rosaria De Stefano De Spagna, Aug. 6, 1969; 1 child, Albert. Student, Cen. U. Venezuela, 1959. V.p. Yard, C.A., Caracas, Venezuela, 1959-66; dir. Salta, C.A., Caracas, 1966-83; v.p. Aero Charter, C.A., Caracas, 1972-83; pres. Omni Aviation, C.A., Caracas, 1978-84; chmn. bd. Gruppo Omni, Caracas, 1984—; hon. consul R.S.F. of Yugoslavia, Monte Carlo, Monaco, 1989—. Bd. dirs. Fabrica De Aviones, C.A., Caracas. Bd. dirs. Fed. Sec. Nat. Def., Belgrad, 1983, Fed. Dir. Supply and Procurement. Recipient Golden Star, Govt. of Yugoslavia, 1988. Mem. Caracas Country Club, Aero Club. Democrat. Roman Catholic. Avocations: tourist pilot, golf, swimming.

PEROT, H. ROSS, JR., real estate developer, former sports team executive; b. Arlington, Tex. m. Sarah Fullinwider, 1984. B in Bus. Adminstrn., Vanderbilt U., 1981. With Petrus Oil Co., Okla., 1981-83; mng. ptnr. The Perot Group, 1983—; owner Hillwood Devel., Dallas, 1980—. With USAFR. Office: Hillwood Devel 12377 Merit Dr Ste 1700 Dallas TX 75251-2256*

PEROTTI, ROSE NORMA, lawyer; b. St. Louis, Aug. 10, 1930; d. Joseph and Dorothy Mary (Roleski) Perotti. BA, Fontbonne Coll., St. Louis, 1952; JD, St. Louis U., 1957. Bar: Mo. 1958. Trademark atty. Sutherland, Polster & Taylor, St. Louis, 1958-63, Sutherland Law Office, 1964-70, Monsanto Co., St. Louis, 1971-85, sr. trademark atty., 1985-91, assoc. trademark counsel, 1991-94, trademark counsel, 1994-96, Polster, Lieder, Woodruff & Lucchesi, 1996—. Honored with dedication of faculty office in her honor, St. Louis U. Sch. Law, 1980. Mem. ABA, Mo. Bar, Bar Assn. Met. St. Louis, Am. Judicature Soc., Friends St. Louis Art Mus., Mo. Bot. Garden. Office: Polster Lieder Woodruff & Lucchesi 12412 Powers Court Dr Ste 200 Saint Louis MO 63131-3615 Office Phone: 314-238-2401. Business E-Mail: rperotti@patpro.com.

PEROTTO, GREGORY TODD, public relations professional; b. Pitts., July 13, 1974; s. Richard Daniel and Linda Lou Perotto. BA in Bus. Adminstrn. and Mktg., U. Puget Sound, 1996. Advt. intern Esco Corp., Portland, Oreg., 1992-95, Ad Mark Svcs., Seattle, 1995; mktg. coord. Simon Mktg., Oak Brook Terrace, Ill., Seattle, summer 1995; corp. comms. mgr. Esco Corp., Portland, 1996-99; tactical marketing coordinator ESCO Corporation, 1999; e-commerce marketing manager ESCO Steel Distrubtion, 2000; sr. account exec. KVO Pub. Rels./Fleishman-Hillard, 2000. Mem. Internat. Assn. Bus. Communicators, Pub. Rels. Soc. Am., Puget Sound Mktg. Assn. (dir. publicity), Portland Advt. Fedn., Phi Kappa Phi. Democrat. Lutheran. Avocations: scuba diving, travel, hiking, biking. Office: KVO Pub Rels 200 SW Market St Ste 1400 Portland OR 97201 E-mail: greg_perotto@kvo.com., gtperotto@excite.com.

PERPER, MICHAEL JOSEPH, federal agency administrator; b. Washington, Mar. 5, 1941; s. Harold Perper; 2 children. BBA in Acctg. and Fin., George Washington U., 1962, M in Hospital Svcs. Adminstrn., 2000; JD, Washington Coll. Law, 1966; MBA, Am. U., Washington, 1969; M in Resource Mgmt. and Internat. Rels., Indsl. Coll. Armed Forces, 1991. Lic. realtor, Md., Va. Sr. tax. atty. IRS, Washington, 1967—81; exec. asst. to U/sec. DOE, Washington, 1982—87, dir. internat. affairs, 1991-95; dir. Internat. Programs Emergency Ops., Washington, 1987-89; cons. on homeland security and transp. security issues Contingency Mgmt. Svcs., Washington, 1987—; prof. Indsl. Coll. Armed Forces, Nat. War Coll., Washington, 1989-91; capt. USCG, N.Y., 1995-96. Bd. dirs. Nat. Children's Hosp., Washington, Econ. & Trade Devel. Com. Contbr. articles to profl. jours. Active Landlord Tenant Commn., 1989, orgns. for disabled vets.; fundraiser Am. Cancer, 1995-, Mem. DAV (cert. appreciation), VA (cert. appreciation), Heart, Lung and Diabetes Assn., Am. Legion, Nat. War Coll. Alumni Assn., Phi Alpha Delta. Avocations: collecting sports memorabilia, art, painting, golf, civic activities. Home: 9408 Woodburn Bridge Rd Potomac MD 20854-2421 Office: DOE 1000 Independence Ave SW Washington DC 20585

PERRAULT, JACQUES, biology professor; b. Montreal, Quebec, Can., June 25, 1944; s. Jean-Paul and Irene (Girard) P.; m. Katherine Hampton Rhodes, May 4, 1996; 1 child, Juliette. BSc, McGill U., 1964; PhD, U. Calif., San Diego, 1972. Asst. prof. dept. microbiology and immunology Washington U. Sch. Medicine, St. Louis, 1977-84; assoc. prof. biology San Diego State U.,

1984-87; prof. dept. of biology prof., 1987—. Contbr. articles to profl. jours. Recipient Research Career Devel. award, NIH, 1980-85; grantee, NIH, NSF, March of Dimes Defects Found., 1977—. Mem. AAAS, Am. Soc. Microbiology, Am. Soc. Virology, Gen. Soc. for Microbiology. Avocation: karate (shotokan japanese style). Office: San Diego State U Dept Biology San Diego CA 92182 E-mail: jperrault@sunstroke.sdsu.edu.

PERREAULT, WILLIAM DANIEL, JR., business administration educator; b. N.Y.C., Apr. 7, 1948; s. William Daniel Sr. and Barbara Louise (Peckham) P.; m. Pamela Pittard, May 27, 1972; children: Suzanne Elizabeth, William Daniel III. BS, U. N.C., 1970, PhD, 1973. Asst. prof. U. Ga., Athens, 1973-76, U. N.C., Chapel Hill, 1976-79, assoc. prof., 1979-81, prof., 1981-83, Hanes prof., 1983-88. Vis. prof. Stanford (Calif.) U., 1986-87, assoc. dean, 1988-92. Kenan prof., 1988—; vis. prof. Cambridge (Eng.) U., 1997. Co-author: Essentials Marketing, 2003, The Marketing Game, 2001, Basic Marketing, 2002; editor: Jour. Mktg. Rsch., 1982-85; contbr. articles to profl. jours. Chmn. adv. com. Bur. Census, Washington, 1982-86. Mem. Am. Mktg. Assn. (v.p. 1986, 95, bd. dirs. 1986-89, 94-95, Odell award 1985, Disting. Educator award 1997, Churchill award 1997), Acad. Mktg. Sci. (Outstanding Edn. award 1995), Decision Scis. Inst. (coun. 1977), Assn. Dir. Consumer Rsch. Conf. (chmn. 1976—), Mktg. Sci. Inst. (trustee 1989-94), Phi Beta Kappa. Republican. Presbyterian. Office: U NC CB 3490 Mccoll Bldg Chapel Hill NC 27599-3490

PERRELLA, ANTHONY JOSEPH, electronics engineer; b. Boulder, Colo., Sept. 16, 1942; s. Anthony Vincent and Mary Domenica (Forte) Perrella; m. Pamela Smith, July 19, 1980; 1 child, Kathleen. BS, U. Wyo., 1964, postgrad., 1965, U. Calif., San Diego, 1966-67, U. Calif., Irvine, 1968-70. Flight engr. U.S. Naval Tng. Devices Ctr., San Diego, 1965-67; rsch. engr. Collins divsn. Rockwell Internat. (formerly Collins Radio Co.), Newport Beach, Calif., 1967-69, electromagnetic interference and TEMPEST group head, 1969-74, supr., 1974-75, mgr., 1975-77, mgr. sys. integration, 1977, mgr. space comm. sys., 1977-78; sr. mem. tech. staff ARGOSys. Inc., Sunnyvale, Calif., 1978-81, program mgr., 1978-81, dep. dept. mgr. EW sys., 1980-83, divsn. EW staff engr., 1983-84, dept. mgr., 1984-87, Sun Microsys. Inc., Mountain View, Calif., 1987-89; prin. A. J. Perrella-Cons., Las Vegas, Nev., 1989—. V.p. R & D Things Unlimited, Inc., Laramie, Wyo., 1965—72, pres., 1972—75; bd. dirs., v.p. Columbian Credit Union, 1994—97. Bd. dirs. Bay Area Found. Mentally Retarded Children, 1994—2002, treas., 1996—2002; bd. dirs. Columbian Retirement Home, Inc., 1999—2002. Mem.: AAAS, IEEE, N.Y. Acad. Scis., Am. Mgmt. Assn., KC, Assn. Old Crows (treas. San Jose chpt. 1992—93, sec. 1993—94, dep. dist. 22 1993—94, v.p. 1994—95, dist. 21 1994—97, pres. 1995—96, Calif. dist. sec. 1996—2000, trustee 1996—, Calif. youth dir. 1997—98, 2000—01, Calif. dist. master 2000—02, Calif. ch. dir. 2001—02, dir. Nev. shining armor 2003—04, Nev. state advocate 2004—), Tau Kappa Epsilon. Roman Catholic. Office: 2550 Garcia Ave Mountain View CA 94043-1109 Home: 22 Cascade Lake St Las Vegas NV 89148-2791

PERRELLA, JAMES ELBERT, former manufacturing company executive; b. Gloversville, N.Y., May 30, 1935; s. James E. and A. Irene (Ferguson) P.; m. Diane F. Campesi; 1 child, Joy. BSME, Purdue U., 1960, MSIM, 1961. Gen. mgr. Centac div. Ingersoll-Rand Co., Mayfield, Ky., 1972-75, gen. mgr. Air Compressor Group Woodcliff Lake, N.J., 1975-77, corp. v.p., pres. Air Compressor Group, 1977-82, exec. v.p., 1982-92, pres., 1992—, chmn., CEO, 1993-99, chmn., 1999-2000, also dir. Bd. dirs. Becton Dickinson and Co., Milacron Inc., ArvinMeritor Inc., Bombardier Inc. Named Disting. Alumnus Sch. Mech. Engring., Purdue U., 1982; named Disting. Alumnus Krannert Mgmt. Sch., Purdue U., 1982 Office: Ingersoll-Rand Co 200 Chestnut Ridge Rd Woodcliff Lake NJ 07677-7700

PERRENOD, DOUGLAS ARTHUR, engineer, astronaut; b. Sept. 13, 1947; s. George Edward and Eunice Lillian (Cohn) P. Student, Fla. Inst. Tech., 1968-72; BA in Interdisciplinary Sci., U. South Fla., 1973; postgrad., Calif. State U., 1982—; grad. engr. mgmt. cert. program, Calif. Inst. Tech., 1987; bioenvironmental engr., USAF Sch. Aerospace Medicine, 1992. Cert. glider flight instr. FAA; cert. sci. rsch. diver Am. Acad. Underwater Scis. Engr. trainee NASA Kennedy Space Ctr., Fla., 1969-73; quality control engr. Pelletech Corp., Fontana, Calif., 1976-77; electronics specialist Gen. Telephone Co., San Bernardino, Calif., 1977-79; aerospace and project engr. Rockwell Internat., Downey, Calif., 1979-85, Lockheed Corp., Ontario, Calif., 1986-87, Lockheed Engring. Mgmt. Svc. Co., 1987, Eagle Engring., 1988—89, Eagle Tech. Svcs., 1989—92; program mgr., scientist for advanced sci. and tech. rsch. USAF-NASA, 2000—. Aviation cons., owner-founder Flight Unltd., Long Beach, Calif.; rsch.-flight test pilot; mission pilot, project engr. Flight Level 500 High Altitude Soaring Project Astronauts of Soaring; dep. dir. Tex. EquuSearch, 2001—. Developed concept for and co-authored unprecedented Inter-agency agreement between USAF and NASA for exchange of advanced environmental technology, 1994; designer telescope mount for 1st astronomy obs. Fla. Inst. Tech., 1969. Vol. mem. Orange County Human Svcs. Agy., 1981-86; active Big Bros. of Am., 1978. Lt. col. USAFR, 1994. Recipient Amelia Earhart award CAP, 1968, Manned Flight Awareness Apollo 11 medallion NASA, 1971, 1st Shuttle Flight Achievement award NASA, 1981, Aerospace Maintenance Officer of Yr. award USAFR, 1979, Symons Wave Meml. award, 1988, Hon. Aquanaut award Aquarius Undersea Rsch. Ctr., 2001, 1st prize Great Annual Fish Count Digital Photo Contest, 2002; named to Engr. Honor Roll, Rockwell Internat., 1982, 83, 85. Mem. AIAA, Assn. Mil. Surgeons U.S., Res. Officers Assn., Officers Assn., Air Force Assn., Soc. Flight Test Engrs., Assoc. Glider Soc. of So. Calif., Long Beach Navy Aero. Club.

PERRET, GARY WILLIAM, priest, educator; b. Sioux City, Iowa, May 20, 1947; s. William Joseph and Geraldine Marie (Maurice) Perret. BA in Secondary Edn., U. Ariz., Tucson, 1970; ThM, St.Mary's U., San Antonio, Tex, 1991. Asst. pastor St, Albert the Great, Compton, Calif., 1976—77; asst. pastor St. Joseph, Granite City, Ill., 1977—78; dir. vocations Misssionaries of Holy Family, Overland, Mo., 1978—82; pastor St. Joseph, Granite City, 1982—86; dir. adult religious edn. Our Lady of Guadalupe, Seguin, Tex., 1986—92, St. Joseph Parish, Donna, Tex., 1993—96, Brownsville (Tex.) Diocese, 1993—96. Dir. R.C.I.A. Various Parishes, San Antonio, 1986—92; instr. sacred scriptures Parishes and Diocese, Tex. Valley, 1993—96. Mem.: KC. Home: 3601 E Seneca Tucson AZ 85716

PERRET, GERARD ANTHONY, JR., orthodontist; b. New Orleans, Feb. 13, 1959; s. Gerard A. and Marie M. (Gamino) P.; m. Catherine J. McMahon, 1996; 1 child, Caroline Marie. BS in Chemistry, U. N.C., 1981; DDS, La. State U., 1986, cert. orthodontics, 1989. Clin. asst. prof. La. State U. Sch. Dentistry, New Orleans, 1986-87; pvt. practice dentistry Lakeside Dental Group, Metairie, La., 1986-87; pvt. practice orthodontics Jacksonville, Fla., 1989-91, Tampa, Fla., 1991—; founder, pres. Orthogap, Inc., Tampa, 1993—, Rodent Realty, Inc., 2001—. Patentee in field. Active mem. New Tampa Cmty. Coun.; chmn. New Tampa Rotary Found., Inc., 2003—04. Mem. ADA, Am. Assn. Orthodontists, Fla. Assn. Orthodontists, Hillsborough County Dental Soc., Hillsborough County Dental Rsch. Clinic, So. Assn. Orthodontists, Rotary (pres. New Tampa chpt. 1997-98), Omicron Kappa Upsilon. Avocations: sailing, fishing, music, golf. Home: 16014 Penwood Dr Tampa FL 33647-1137 Office: 15283 Amberly Dr Tampa FL 33647 Office Phone: 813-977-2828.

PERRICONE, CHARLES, former state legislator; b. Oct. 10, 1960; Student, Kalamazoo Coll., Western Mich. U.; DPS (hon.), W. Mich. U. Rep. Mich. State Dist. 61, 1995—; spkr. of the house Lansing, 1999—2001; pres., CEO New Era Consulting. Vice chair tax policy com.; mem. corrections com., house oversight and ethics com., legis. coun.; asst. Rep. leader. Recipient Champion of Commerce, Mich. Chamber of Commerce, Guardian of Small Business, Nat. Fed. of Ind. Bus. Republican. Home: 5630 E Butler Rd Dowling MI 49050-9756

PERRICONE, NICHOLAS V. dermatologist; b. New Haven, Conn., June 23, 1948; BA, U. New Haven, 1970; MD, Mich. State U., East Lansing, 1982. Diplomate Am. Bd. of Dermatology, 1996. Intern in pediat. Yale U. Sch. Medicine, New Haven, 1982—83; resident in dermatology Henry Ford Med. Ctr., Detroit, 1983—86; chmn. Internat. Symposium on Aging Skin, Conn., 1997—; physician Dermatology and Dermatol. Surgery, Meriden, Conn., 1986—2002; chief of dermatology State Vet.'s Hosp., Rocky Hill, Conn., 1987—95; clin. instr. of dermatology Yale U. Med. Sch., New Haven, 1988—97, asst. clin. prof. of dermatology, 1997—2002; adj. prof. Coll. of Human Medicine, Mich. State U., East Lansing, 2002—. Author: (non-fiction book) The Perricone Prescription (NY Times #1 Bestseller, 2002), (chapter in textbook) The Basic Principles and Practice of Anti-Aging Medicine and Age Management for the Aesthetic Surgeon and Physician, (non-fiction book) The Perricone Prescription Personal Journal, The Wrinkle Cure (NY Times #1 Bestseller, 2002); contbg. editor: Jour. Geriatric Dermatology, 1997—, mem. editl. bd.: Archives of Gerontology and Geriatrics, 2000—; contbr. articles to profl. jours. Specialist level 4 Army Mil. Police, 1970—76. Recipient Eli Whitney award, Conn. Intellectual Property Law Assn., 2001, Norman E Clark, Sr. Lecture award, Am. Coll. for Advancement in Medicine, Crystal Communicator award, PBS, 2001, Annenberg Cir., Dermatology Found., 2001. Fellow: Internat. Soc. of Tropical Dermatology, Am. Bd. of Dermatology, N.Y. Acad. Scis., Am. Coll. of Nutrition; mem.: AAAS, Soc. of Investigative Dermatology, New Haven County Med. Assn., Conn. State Med. Soc., Am. Acad. of Dermatology, Conn. Dermatology & Dermatologic Surgery Soc., Assn. of Am. Physicians and Surgeons, Oxygen Soc., Nutrition Rsch. Acad. Achievements include patents for Treatment of Rosacea using Lipoic Acid; Treatment of skin damage using polyenylphosphatidylcholine; Stabilized ascorbyl compositions; Treatment of scar tissue using lipoic acid; Topical administration of catecholamines and related compounds to subcutaneous muscle tissue using percutaneous penetration enhancers; Razor comfort strip with alpha hydroxy acid additive; Lipoic Acid In Topical Compositons; Topical compositions and methods for treatment of skin damage and aging using catecholamines and related compounds; Method and compositions for topical application of ascorbic acid fatty acid esters for treatment and/or prevention of skin damage; Method and compositions for treatment and/or prevention of skin damage and aging; Method and compositions for topical application to the skin of tocotrienols for prevention and/or treatment of skin damage; Treatment of Skin Damage using Olive Oil Polyphenols; Method for treating and prevention of sunburn and sunburn damage to the skin; Method and compositions for topical application to the skin for prevention and/or treatment of radiation-induced skin damage; Method for the topical treatment of psoriasis; Method for the topical treatment and prevention of pseudofolliculitis barbae; Skin Whiteners containing Hydroxytetronic Acid; Electronic Muscle Stimulator Glove; Electronic Muscle Stimulator Finger Tip Triplet; Electronic Stimulator Finger Tip; Treatment of Acne using Lipoic Acid; Topical Scar Treatments using Alkanolamines; Treatment of Skin Damage using Conjugated Linoleic Acid and Ascorbyl Fatty Acid Esters. Office: NV Perricone MD Ltd 377 Research Pkwy 1E Meriden CT 06450

PERRIER, BARBARA SUE, artist; b. Akron, Ohio, Oct. 7, 1937; d. Willis Austin and Mary Gladys (Campbell) Bibler; m. David John Perrier, July 14, 1956 (div. Nov. 1972); children: David John Jr., Kenneth James, Mark Richard. AA in Comml. Art, AA in Liberal Arts, Ventura Coll., 1991. Artist Anointed Brush Studio, Oxnard, Calif., 1987—. Author: Go Hard into the Wind & Waves: Biography of Faustino Rico, 2003; one-woman shows at Columbia Arts Ctr., Vancouver, Wash., 1988, Gallery Los Olivos, 1993, Victor Valley Mus. Art, 2003; exhibited in group shows at Santa Paula Soc. of Arts 3d Annual Fall Show, 1992, Gloria Dei Art Show, Camarillo, Calif., 1991, 92, 13th Annual Nat. Bald Eagle Conf. Art Show, 1992, 53d Annual City of Santa Paula Art Show, 1989, 5th Annual Buenaventura Art Assn. Art Show, Ventura, 1988, Westlake Village 15th Annual Art Show, 1988, Oct. West Wildlife Art Show, Burbank, Calif., 1993, Decoy & Wildfowl Carvers Wildlife Art Show, 1994, Spectacular Monuments Art Show, 1994, Fallbrook Nature Conservancy Art Show, 1995, 96, October West Wildlife Art Show, 1995, numerous others; exhibited in corp. collections at Impact Ministries, Redmond, Wash., The Kid's Pl., Roseburg, Oreg., Trinity, Redding, Calif., Vista, Marina Del Rey, Calif., Century 21 Gold Coast, Port, Hueneme, Calif., Divine Love Internat. Ch., Nigeria, Africa, numerous others. Named to Wildlife Artist Assn. Hall of Fame, 1999. Mem. Calif. Gold Coast Watercolor Soc. (charter, pres. 1992), So. Calif. Wildlife Artist Assn. (pres. 1995, 96), Ventura County Artist Guild. Baptist. Avocations: camping, travel, photography. Home and Office: Anointed Brush Studio 1451 Fathom Dr Oxnard CA 93035-2334 Office Phone: 805-984-1736.

PERRIMAN, WENDY KAREN, poet, educator; b. Stamford, England, July 9, 1958; d. David Wathen Blower and Heather Boulton Unwin; m. Steven Ralph Perriman, Aug. 8, 1981; 1 child. BA, U. Lancaster, Eng., 1979; postgrad. Cert. Edn., U. Bristol, Eng., 1980; MA, Drew U., 2000, MPhil, 2001, PhD, 2003. Probationary tchr. Eastbrook Comprehensive Sch., London, 1980-81; English and drama tchr. Cornwall Sch., Dortmund, West Germany, 1981-83, King's Sch., Gutersloh, West Germany, 1983-85; acting head English and drama Weston Park Girls' Sch., Southampton, England, 1989-92; head drama, asst. head English Bitterne Park Sch., Southampton, 1992-94; freelance poet Madison, NJ, 1994—; adj. asst. prof. English Drew U., Madison, NJ, 2002—. Pub., editor Inka Publs., N.J., 1996—; adj. asst. prof. English Drew U., Madison, NJ, 2002-. Author: Collected Experience, 1996, Show and Tell, 1997, Free Fall, 1998. Mem. MLA, Poetry Soc. Am., Acad. Am. Poets, Modern Poetry Assn. Office: Inka Publs PO Box 53 Madison NJ 07940-0053

PERRIN, EDWARD BURTON, health services researcher, biostatistician, public health educator; b. Greensboro, Vt., Sept. 19, 1931; s. J. Newton and Dorothy E. (Willey) P.; m. Carol Anne Hendricks, Aug. 18, 1956; children: Jenifer, Scott. BA, Middlebury Coll., 1953; student in Stats., Edinburgh (Scotland) U., 1953—54; MA in Math. Stats., Columbia U., 1956; PhD, Stanford U., 1961. Asst. prof. dept. biostats. U. Pitts., 1959-62; asst. prof. dept. preventive medicine U. Wash., Seattle, 1962-65, assoc. prof., 1965-69, prof., 1969-70, prof., chmn. dept. biostats., 1970-72, prof. dept. health svcs., adj. prof. dept. biostats., 1975-98, chmn. dept., 1983-94, prof. emeritus, 1999—; hon. prof. West China U. of Med. Scis., Szechwan, China, 1988-98; overseas fellow Churchill Coll., Cambridge U., 1991-92; sr. scientist Seattle Vets. Affairs Med. Ctr., 1994—2001. Clin. prof. dept. cmty. medicine and internat. health Sch. Medicine, Georgetown U., Washington, 1972—75; dep. dir. Nat. Ctr. for Health Stats., HEW, 1972—73, dir., 1973—75; rsch. scientist Health Care Study Ctr. Battelle Human Affairs Rsch. Ctr., Seattle, 1975—76, dir., 1976—78, Health & Population Study Ctr. Battelle Human Affairs Rsch. Ctr., 1978—83; sr. cons. biostats. Wash./Alaska regional med. programs, 1967—72; biometrician VA Co-op Study on Treatment of Esopageal Varices, 1961—73; mem. epidemiology & disease control study sect. NIH, 1969—73; chmn. health svcs. rsch. study sect. HEW, 1976—79; chmn. health svcs. R & D field program rev. panel VA, 1988—91; chmn. health svcs. info steering com. State of Wash., 1993—94; mem. nat. adv. coun. Agy. for Health Care Policy & Rsch. Dept. HHS U.S. Govt., 1994—97; mem. com. on nat. stats. NRC, 1994—2000, NAS, 1994—2000; chmn. sci. adv. com. Med. Outcomes Trust, 1994—99. Contbr. articles on biostats., health svcs. and population studies to profl. publs.; mem. editl. bd.: Jour. Family Practice, 1978-90, Pub. Health Nursing, 1992-98. Mem. tech. bd. Milbank Meml. Fund, 1974-76, Health Svcs. and Outcomes Rsch. Methodology, 1999-. Recipient Outstanding Svc. citation HEW, 1975; Fulbright scholar 1953-54. Fellow AAAS, APHA (Spiegelman Health Stats. award 1970, program devel. bd. 1971, chmn. stats. sect. 1978-80, governing coun. 1983-85, stats. sect. recognition award 1989), Am. Statis. Assn. (mem. adv. com. to divsn. statis. policy 1975-77); mem. Assn. Health Svcs. Rsch. (pres. 1994-95, bd. dirs. 1991-2000), Inst. Medicine of NAS (chmn. membership com. 1984-86, mem. bd. on health care svcs. 1987-96, forum health stats. 1994-95, chmn. com. on clin. evaluation 1990-93), Biometrics Soc. (pres. Western N.Am. Region 1971), Sigma Xi, Phi Beta Kappa. Home: 4900 NE 39th St Seattle WA 98105-5209 Office: U Wash Dept Health Svcs PO Box 358853 Seattle WA 98195-8853 Office Phone: 206-524-9410. E-mail: perrin@u.washington.edu.

PERRIN, JAMES KIRK, lawyer; b. Saginaw, Mich., Feb. 10, 1940; s. Robert Wallace and Elizabeth (Kirk) P.; m. Harriet Halteman, June 12, 1962; children: Mark, Rob, Jane, Jim. BA, Ohio Wesleyan U., 1962; JD, U. Mich., 1965. Bar: Ill. 1965, U.S. Dist. Ct. (no. dist.) Ill. 1965, U.S. Ct. Appeals (7th cir.) 1976, U.S. Supreme Ct. 1977. Assoc. McKenna Storer Rowe White & Haskell, Chgo., 1965-70, ptnr., 1970-75; founding ptnr. Haskell & Perrin, Chgo., 1975—, sr. ptnr., 1989—. Contbr. over 30 articles to profl. jours.; spkr. in field. Commr. Deerfield (Ill.) Plan Commn., 1970-72. Mem. ABA (trial techniques com., task force on delay in litigation), Internat. Assn. Def. Counsel, Am. Bd. Trial Advocates, Soc. Trial Lawyers, Ill. Assn. Def. Trial Counsel, Phi Beta Kappa. Office: Ste 2650 150 S Wacker Dr Chicago IL 60606-4206

PERRIN, MICHAEL WARREN, lawyer; b. Cameron, Tex., Nov. 10, 1946; s. Frank W. and Mary Ann (Green) P.; m. Melinda Elizabeth Hill, Aug. 9, 1969; children: Elizabeth, Carter, Hunter. BS, U. Tex., Austin, 1969, JD, 1971. Bar: Tex. 1972, U.S. Dist. Ct. (no., ea., we. and so. dists.) Tex., U.S. Ct. Appeals (5th and 11th cirs.), U.S. Supreme Ct. Assoc. Vinson & Elkins, Houston, 1972-73; assoc. Fisher, Roch & Gallagher, Houston, 1973-76; ptnr. Fisher, Gallagher, Perrin & Lewis, Houston, 1976-91; sole practice Houston, 1991-96; ptnr. King & Spalding, Houston, 1996—. Fellow Am. Coll. Trial Lawyers, Internat. Acad. Trial Lawyers, Internat. Soc. Barristers; mem. Am. Bd. Trial Advocates, Am. Bar Found., Houston Young Lawyers Assn. (sec. 1974-75), Tex. Young Lawyers Assn. (dir. 1976-78, chmn. bd. 1978-79), Houston Trial Lawyers Assn. (pres. 1987-88), Tex. Trial Lawyers Assn. (pres. 1989-90), Tex. Bar Found. (Houston chpt.), U. Tex. Devel. bd. Methodist.

PERRIN, ROBERT, editorial consultant, writer; b. Ann Arbor, Mich., Aug. 21, 1925; m. Barbara J. Groom, June 25, 1949; children: Stephen, Jennifer Perrin Hummel. BS, U. Minn., 1945. Reporter United Press Assn., Detroit, 1948-49, Detroit Free Press, 1949-55; adminstrv. asst. U.S. Senate, Washington, 1955-66; asst. dir. U.S. Office Econ. Opportunity, Washington, 1966-68, dep. dir., 1968-70; v.p. Mich. State U., East Lansing, 1970-79; vice-chancellor SUNY System, Albany, 1979-85; exec. v.p. Tchrs. Ins. and Annuity Assn.-Coll. Retirement Equities Fund, N.Y.C., 1987-92; cons. Dept. State, 1993-94. Author: Piggy's Luck and More Tales of Evildoing, 1998, Keeping in Practice, 2001; contbr. articles to mags., newspapers. Mem. U.S.-Mex. Commn. on Border Devel., Washington, 1967-68. Lt. USNR, 1943-46, PTO. Fellow Reid Found., 1954; Pulitzer prize nominee Detroit Free Press, 1956. Home: 2435 Emerald Lake Dr East Lansing MI 48823-7256

PERRINE, RICHARD LEROY, environmental engineer, educator; b. Mountain View, Calif., May 15, 1924; s. George Alexander and Marie (Axelson) P.; m. Barbara Jean Gale, Apr. 12, 1945; children: Cynthia Gale, Jeffrey Richard. AB, San Jose State Coll., 1949; MS, Stanford U., 1950, PhD in Chemistry, 1953. Cert. environ. profl., 1987. Research chemist Calif. Research Corp., La Habra, 1953-59; assoc. prof. UCLA, 1959-63, prof. engring. and applied sci., 1963-92, prof. emeritus, 1992—, chmn. environ. sci. and engring., 1971-82; prin. Aspen Environ. Group, 1990-93. V.p. Sage Resources, 1988-91; cons. environ. sci. and engring., energy resources, flow in porous media; mem. Los Angeles County Energy Commn., 1973-81; mem. adv. council South Coast Air Quality Mgmt. Dist., 1977-82; mem. air conservation com. Los Angeles County Lung Assn., 1970-84; mem. adv. com. energy div. Oak Ridge Nat. Lab., 1987-90; mem. policy bd. William D. Ruckelshaus Inst. Environ. and Natural Resources U. Wyo., 1994—. Editor in chief The Environ. Profl., 1985-90. Served with AUS, 1943-46. Recipient Outstanding Engr. Merit award in environ. engring. Inst. Advancement Engring., 1975; ACT-SO award in field of chemistry West Coast region NAACP, 1984. Fellow AAAS; mem. Am. Chem. Soc., Soc. Petroleum Engrs., Am. Inst. Chem. Engrs., Can. Inst. Mining and Metallurgy, N.Am. Assn. Environ. Edn., Nat. Assn. Environ. Profls. (cert.), Air and Waste Mgmt. Assn., Assn. Environ. Engring. and Sci. Profs., Sierra Club, Wilderness Soc., Audubon Soc., Sigma Xi, Tau Beta Pi, Phi Lambda Upsilon. Home: 22611 Kittridge St West Hills CA 91307-3609 Office: Univ Calif Engring Bldg I Rm 3066D Los Angeles CA 90095-0001 E-mail: rperrine@ucla.edu.

PERRIS, TERRENCE GEORGE, lawyer; b. L.A., Oct. 18, 1947; s. Theodore John Grivas and Penny (Sfakianos) Perris. BA magna cum laude, U. Toledo, 1969; JD summa cum laude, U. Mich., 1972. Bar: Ohio 1972, U.S. Tax Ct. 1982, U.S. Ct. Fed. Claims 1983, U.S. Supreme Ct. 1983. Law clk. to judge U.S. Ct. Appeals (2d cir.), N.Y.C., 1972-73; law clk. to Justice Potter Stewart U.S. Supreme Ct., Washington, 1973-74; assoc. Squire, Sanders & Dempsey LLP, Cleve., 1974-80; ptnr. Squire, Sanders & Dempsey, Cleve., 1980—. V.p., trustee SS&D Found., Cleve., 1984—; nat. coord. Taxation Practice Area, 1987—, mgmt. com., 1996—2000; chmn. Cleve. Tax Inst., 1993; vis. prof. law U. Mich., 1996; adj. prof. Case Western Res. U., Cleve., 2001—; lectr. in field. Vis. com. U. Mich. Law Sch., 1986—. Capt. U.S. Army, 1974. Mem.: ABA, Tax. Club Cleve., Supreme Ct. Hist. Soc., Cleve. Bar Assn., Ohio Bar Assn. (subchtp. C of internal revenue code task force), Pres.'s Club, Union Club Cleve., Club Cleve., U. Mich. Club Cleve., Order of Coif, Phi Kappa Phi. Republican. Eastern Orthodox. Avocation: landscape gardening. Office: Squire Sanders & Dempsey LLP 4900 Key Tower 127 Public Sq Cleveland OH 44114-1216 E-mail: tperris@ssd.com.

PERRITT, HENRY HARDY, JR., law educator; b. Little Rock, Ark., Dec. 30, 1944; s. Henry Hardy and Margaret Frances (Floyd) P. SB in Engring., MIT, 1966, SM in Mgmt., 1970; JD, Georgetown U., 1975. Bar: Va. 1976, Pa. 1977, D.C. 1981, Md. 1995, Ill. 1998, U.S. Supreme Ct. 1981, U.S. Ct. Appeals (3d cir.) 1979, U.S. Ct. Appeals (2d cir.) 1979, U.S. Ct. Appeals (6th cir.) 1983. Sr. sales planner Lockheed Corp., Marietta, Ga., 1968-71; exec. sec. Cost of Living Coun., Washington, 1972-75; legis. analyst U.S. Dept. Commerce, 1971-72; mem. staff White House, Washington, 1975; dep. undersec. U.S. Dept. Labor, Washington, 1975-76; gen. counsel labor Conrail, Phila., 1976-81; prof. law Villanova U., Phila., 1981—97, dir. Villanova Ctr. for Info. Law and Policy, 1992-99, dir. Project Bosnia, 1996-99; dean Kent Coll. of Law, Chgo., 1997—2002, prof. law, 1997—. Cons. atty. Morgan, Lewis & Bockius, Washington, 1981-90, Conrail, 1981-90; apptd. vice chmn. Coal Commn., U.S. Sec. of Labor, 1990; mem. computer sci. and telecom. bd. Nat. Rsch. Coun. Author: Employee Dismissal Law and Practice, 1984, 4th edit., 1997, Labor Injunctions, 1986, How to Practice Law with Computers, 1988, Employee Benefits Claims Law and Practice, 1989, Workplace Torts Rights and Liabilities, 1990, Americans with Disabilities Act Handbook, 1990, 3d edit., 1998, Trade Secrets: A Practitioner's Guide, 1994, Law and The Information Superhighway, 1996, 2d edit., 2001; contbr. articles to profl. jours. Dem. nominee for U.S. Congress 10th Dist. Ill., 2002. Mem. ABA (chmn. com. on R.R. and airline labor law 1983-86, chmn. com. on regulatory initiatives and info. tech., adminstrv. law sect., co-vice chmn. dispute resolution com., adminstrv. law sect. 1987-90, sec. labor and employment sect. 2000-01), Assn. Am. Law Schs. (chmn. sect. on law and computers 1991), Coun. on Fgn. Rels. (bd. dirs. Chgo. 2001-), Econ. Club. Democrat. E-mail: hperritt@kentlaw.edu.

PERRON, BRANDON ALAN, private investigator, director; AS in criminal justice, C.C. of the Air Force, Ala., 1988; BS in criminal justice adminstrn., Columbia So. U., Ala., 2002. Bd. cert. criminal def. investigator, criminal def. investigation tng. coun. Dir. investigations Investigative Support Specialist Inc., Stuart, Fla., 1989—; nat. dir. Criminal Def. Investigation Tng. Coun., Stuart, Fla., 2000—. Tng. dir. 19th Jud. Circuit Pub. Defender, Ft. Pierce, Fla., 1994—; adj. faculty Indian River C.C., Ft. Pierce, Fla., 1998—. Author: (textbook) Uncovering Reasonable Doubt, 1998, (novel) The Quest For Truth, 2004 (Editors Choice, 2004). Sgt. USAF, 1985—89. Named Investigator of Yr., Nat. Assn. of Investigative Specialists, 2003, 2004; named one of Top 10 Pvt. Investigators in U.S., Pvt. Investigator Mag., 1998. Mem.: Fla. Assn. of Lic. Investigators, Nat. Assn. of Legal Investigators (moderator 2001—04). Office: Investigative Support Specialist Inc 800 E Ocean Blvd Ste D Stuart FL 34994 Office Phone: 772-288-1485. E-mail: bperron@aol.com.

PERRONE, NICHOLAS, mechanical engineer, business executive; b. Apr. 30, 1930; B. Aero. Engring., Poly. Inst. Bklyn., 1951, MS, 1953, PhD, 1958. Research asst., then assoc. applied mechanics Bklyn. Poly. Inst., 1951-58; asst. prof., then assoc. prof. Pratt Inst., 1958-62; sr. scientist Structural Mechanics br. Office Naval Research, Washington, 1962-67, acting head dept., 1967-68, dir. program, 1968-69, 71-82; pres. CASA Gifts Inc., 1983-85; dep. to pres. Advanced Tech. and Research Inc., 1986-87; pres. Perrone Forensic Cons. Inc., 1987—. Lectr. civil engring. Cath U. Am., 1962-64, adj. prof., 1965-91; spl. research fellow NIH, Georgetown U., 1969-70; participant numerous

workshops, confs., symposia; lectr. in field. Contbg. author: Biodynamics, 1980; editor or co-editor numerous monographs; editorial adv. bd.: Advances in Engrng. Software, Computers and Structures, Engineering Fracture, Pressure Vessels and Piping; contbr. numerous articles to profl. jours. Fellow AAAS, ASME, Am. Acad. Mechanics, mem. ASCE, AIAA, N.Y. Acad. Sci., Am. Soc. Engrng. Edn., Soc. Automotive Engrs., Soc. Mfg. Engrs. Address: 8 Cherry Ln Newtown Square PA 19073-3949 E-mail: NickPerrone@aol.com., nicolasperrone@comcast.net.

PERROT, PAUL NORMAN, museum director; b. Paris, July 28, 1926; came to U.S., 1946, naturalized, 1954; s. Paul and K. Norman (Derr) P.; m. Joanne Stovall, Oct. 23, 1954; children— Paul Latham, Chantal Marie Claire, Jeannine, Robert. Student, Ecole du Louvre, 1945-46, N.Y. U. Inst. Fine Arts, 1946-52. Asst. The Cloisters, Met. Mus. Art, 1948-52; asst. to dir. Corning (N.Y.) Mus. Glass, 1952-54, asst. dir. mus., 1954-60, dir., 1960-72; editor Jour. Glass Studies, 1959-72; asst. sec. for mus. programs Smithsonian Instn., Washington, 1972-84; dir. Va. Mus. Fine Arts, 1984-91, Santa Barbara Mus. Art, 1991-94, mus. cons., 1995—. Lectr. glass history, aesthetics, museology; past v.p. Internat. Coun. Mus. Found.; past pres. N.E. Conf. Mus.; past pres. Internat. Centre for Study of Preservation and Restoration of Cultural Property, Rome, mem. coun., 1974-88. Author: Three Great Centuries of Venetian Glass, 1958, also numerous articles on various hist. and archael. subjects. Former trustee Winterthur Mus.; former trustee, treas. Mus. Computer Network; former mem. Internat. Cons. Com. for the Preservation of Moenjodaro; former chmn. adv. com. World Monuments Fund; former chmn. vis. com. Getty Conservation Inst. Mem. Am. Assn. Mus. (past v.p., coun. 1967-78), N.Y. State Assn. Mus. (past pres.), Internat. Assn. History Glass (past v.p.) Corning Friends of Library (past pres.), So. Tier Library System (past pres.). E-mail: paulnperrot@cs.com.

PERRUCCI, ROBERT, sociologist, educator; b. N.Y.C., Nov. 11, 1931; s. Dominic and Inez (Mucci) P.; m. Carolyn Land Cummings, Aug. 4, 1965; children: Mark Robert, Celeste Ann, Christopher Robert, Alissa Cummings, Martin Cummings. BS, SUNY, Cortland, 1958; MS (Social Sci. Research Council fellow), Purdue U., Ph.D., 1962. Asst. prof. sociology Purdue U., West Lafayette, Ind., 1962-65, asso. prof., 1965-67, prof., 1967—, head dept., 1978-87. Vis. Simon prof. U. Manchester (Eng.), 1968-69; Bd. dirs. Ind. Center on Law and Poverty, 1973-76 Author: Sociology, 1983, Circle of Madness, 1974, Divided Loyalties, 1980, The Triple Revolution, 1971, Profession Without Community, 1968, The Engineers and the Social System, 1968, Mental Patients and Social Networks, 1982, Plant Closings: International Context and Local Consequences, 1988, Networks of Power, 1989, Japanese Auto Transplants in the Heartland: Corporatism and Community, 1994, The New Class Society, 1999, Science Under Siege?, 2000, The New Class Society: Goodbye American Dream, 2003; editor: The American Sociologist, 1982—84, Social Problems, 1993-96, Contemporary Sociology, 2000-2005; contbr. articles to profl. jours. Served with USMC, 1951-53. Recipient grants, NSF, 1966—68, 1976—78, NIMH, 1969—72, Sloan Found., 2002—05. Mem. Am. Sociol. Assn., Soc. Study Social Problems (dir. 1980-83, v.p. 1996-97, pres. 1999—), N. Central Sociol. Assn. (pres. 1973-74) Home: 305 Leslie Ave West Lafayette IN 47906-2411 Office: Dept Sociology Purdue U West Lafayette IN 47907

PERRY, ANTHONY FRANK, entertainment company executive, printing company executive, graphic designer; b. L.A., Oct. 23, 1965; s. Frank Guy and Verna Dean Perry. Artist Thunderbird Printing Co., Inc., Reno, Nev., 1983-87; pres., chief exec. officer T-Bird Entertainment, Inc., Reno, 1987-91; mktg. dir. Thunderbird Printing and Screening Inc., Reno, 1991-92; pres., CEO Perri Entertainment Svcs., Inc., Reno, 1992—; pres. Internat. Touring Pers. Assn., 2001—. Tour pass security designer Rolling Stones World Tour, 1989-90, Billy Joel Storm Front Tour, 1990, New Kids on the Block, 1990-91, Jimmy Buffett Chameleon Caravan, 1994, Billy Joel River of Dreams, 1994, ZZ Top Antenna World Tour, 1994; designer credentials for San Francisco 49ers, 1995-2000; founder Knotty Baker Pretzel Co.; promoter Big Bang New Years Party, 1987-91; founder Webcarvers Am. Interactive Devel. Co.; creator StreetMagic web site and products. Author: The Expert from Out of Town, Sometimes I Forgot to Look Both Ways; lighting designer Sheep Dip Show, Reno Hilton, 1986, 87, 89; designer tour logo Doobie Brothers and Foreigner Tour 1994; designer Michael Jackson History World Tour, 1996-97, U2 World Tour; credential mfr. for Rolling Stones Bridges to Babylon World Tour, 1997-98, Pavarotti Tour 2000, Rolling Stones No Security Tour, 1999. Mem. Nev. Repertory Co., 1983-89. Recipient Lifetime Achievement award Reed H.S. Theatre Dept., 1983. Mem. Reno Advt. Club, Rotary Internat. Roman Catholic. Office: Perri Entertainment Svcs Inc PO Box 11852 Reno NV 89510-1852

PERRY, BARRY W. manufacturing executive; s. Antone and Adelaide Perry; m. Janice G. Perry. With GE; group v.p., gen. mgr. latex specialty polymers divsn. Rhone-Poulenc, 1991—93; group v.p., gen. mgr. pigments and additives group Engelhard Corp., 1993—97, pres., 1997—2001, CEO, 1997—, chmn., 2001—. Bd. dirs. Arrow Electronics Inc. Office: 101 Wood Ave Iselin NJ 08830

PERRY, BLAIR LANE, lawyer; b. Oct. 2, 1929; s. Elwyn Lionel and Ruth Hubbard (Kelley) Perry; m. Margaret James, July 4, 1959; children: Jennifer E., Andrew B.; m. Theodora Pearson, Mar. 29, 1998. BA, Williams Coll., 1951; LLB, Harvard U., 1957. Bar: Mass. 1957, U.S. Dist. Ct. Mass. 1958, U.S. Dist. Ct. (no. dist.) Tex 1978, U.S. Ct. Appeals (1st cir.) 1958, U.S. Supreme Ct. 1971. Assoc. Hale and Dorr, Boston, 1957—63, jr. ptnr., 1963—68, sr. ptnr., 1968—90; of counsel Fish & Richardson, Boston, 1991—2002. Contbr. articles to profl. jours. With USMC, 1951—53. Mem.: ABA, Boston Patent Law Assn., Mass. Bar Assn. Home and Office: 193 Dromoland Ln Barnstable MA 02630-1804

PERRY, BURTON LARS, retired pediatrician; b. Midland, Mich., Dec. 8, 1931; s. Willard Russell and Myrl Alice (Jacobsen) P.; m. Nancy Fawn Towsley, Aug. 24, 1956; children: Ellen, Willard. BS, U. Mich., 1953, MD, 1960. Diplomate Am. Bd. Pediats.; sub-bd. pediat. cardiology. Physician U. Mich., Ann Arbor, 1960-78, Childrens Hosp. Mich., Detroit, 1978-97. 1st lt. infantry, U.S. Army, 1954-56. Home: 1416 Dicken Dr Ann Arbor MI 48103-4417 Office: Childrens Hosp Mich 3901 Beaubien St Detroit MI 48201-2119

PERRY, CATHERINE D. judge; b. 1952; BA, Univ. of Okla., 1977; JS, Wash. Univ. Sch. of Law, 1980. Sec., law clk. Gillespie, Perry & Gentry, Sentinel, Okla., 1970, 77-78; with Armstrong, Teasdale, Kramer & Vaughn, St. Louis, 1980-90; magistrate judge U.S. Dist. Ct. (Mo. ea. dist.), 8th circuit, St. Louis, 1990-94; dist. judge U.S. Dist. Ct. (ea. dist.), 8th circuit, St. Louis, 1994—. Mem. Fed. Magistrate Judges Assn., Nat. Assn. of Women Judges, Am. Bar Assn., Mo. Bar Assn., Bar Assn. of Metropolitan St. Louis, Women Lawyers Assn. of Greater St. Louis. Office: US Courthouse 1114 Market St Rm 319 Saint Louis MO 63101-2038

PERRY, CHRIS NICHOLAS, retired advertising executive; b. Pitts., Dec. 25, 1945; s. Nicholas and Georgia (Demas) P.; Kathleen Clarke, June 19, 1971; children: Damien, Adam, Dana. BA, U. Pitts., 1968. With Youngstown (Ohio) Steel, 1968-70; creative supr. Ketchum Communications, Pitts., 1970-74; pres., creative dir. Hedding, Perry, Davis Inc., Charlotte, N.C., 1974-76; v.p., creative dir. Fahlgren & Swink Advt., Marion, Ohio, 1976-79, Meldrum and Fewsmith Communications, Inc., Cleve., 1979-82, sr. v.p. creative services, 1982-85, exec. v.p. creative services, 1985-86, pres., chief operating officer, 1986-87, chmn., chief exec. officer, creative dir., 1987-98, also bd. dirs. Mem. bd. disting. judges and advisors The N.Y. Festivals, 1988—. Recipient numerous awards for creative excellence. Mem. Am. Assn. Advt. Agys. (sec.-treas. cen. region 1990-91, chmn. 1992-93), Cleve. Advt. Club, Cleve. Soc. Communicating Arts (pres. 1985-87, Disting. Communicator award 1991), The Hermit Club, Columbia Hills Country Club, The Union Club, Firestone Country Club.

PERRY, CYNTHIA SHEPARD, federal agency administrator; Grad., Ind. State U.; EdD, U. Mass. Chief edn. and human resources Africa Bus. USAID, 1982—86; ambassador, 1986—89, 1990—93; dir. internat. investment adv. svcs. FCA Corp., Houston, 1996—2001; U.S. dir. African Devel. Bank, Abidjan, Cote d'Ivoire, 2001 . N. counsel gen., Senegal. Office: African Devel Bank 01 BP 1387 Abidjan 01 Cote d'Ivoire

PERRY, DAVID, priest; Ecumenical officer Nat. Episcopal Ch., N.Y.C. Office: Episcopal Ch Ctr 815 2nd Ave New York NY 10017-4503

PERRY, DOUGLAS, opera singer; B.M., Wittenberg U.; MA, Ball State U. Made debut as Don Basilio in Marriage of Figaro, with N.Y.C. Opera; appeared as King Kaspar in: Amahl and the Night Visitors; appeared as Timothy in: Help! Help! The Globolinks; appeared as Guillot in: Manon; Dancing Master and Brighella in: Ariadne auf Naxos; Met. Opera debut as scientist/first mate in: The Voyage (Philip Glass); European debut with Netherlands Opera as Mahatma Gandhi in Satyagraha (Philip Glass); appeared as analyst in A Quiet Place (Bernstein), La Scala and Vienna Stadtsoper, as Sailor 1, Scientist 3, Traveler 2 world premier Corvo Bronco, Teatro Camõ, Lisbon, Portugal, Teatro Real, Madrid; featured soloist on tours and recs. with Gregg Smith Singers and Camerata Singers; performed with Sante Fe Opera, also performed with Ft. Worth Opera, Chatauqua Opera, N.Y.C. Opera, Opera Co. of Boston, Houston Grand Opera, Balt. Opera., Miami Opera, Chgo. Lyric Opera, Seattle Opera, San Francisco Opera, Opera Co. Phila.; recs. include Satyagraha, Songs from Liquid Days, A Quiet Place, Mother of Us All. Address: 170 W End Ave New York NY 10023-5401 Office: Pinnacle Arts Mgmt 889 9th Ave Ste 1 New York NY 10019-0999

PERRY, E. EUGENE, communication educator; b. Martins Ferry, Ohio, Dec. 25, 1957; s. Edwin Ray and Sally Lou (Youst) P. BS in Edn., Ohio U., 1979; MDiv, U. Dubuque, 1982, MA in Comms., 2000. Instr. N.E. Iowa C.C., Peosta, 1989—. Substitute tchr. Dubuque Cmty. Schs., 1982-85; advisor drama and speech dept. Western Dubuque Cmty. Schs., Epworth, Iowa, 1989-91; contest judge Iowa H.S. Speech Assn., 1986-02. Author: (plays) It Works for Everybody Else, 1984, Wanted: A Cook, 1990, Just a High School Play, 1991, Once Upon a Beginning, 1994, (textbook) Articulate: a practical handbook for public speakers, 2000; contbr. articles to profl. jours. Chmn. play-selection com. Barn Cmty. Theater, Dubuque, 1981-83; active Dubuque County Dem. Cen. Com., 1984-87, 89-91, office mgr. hdqrs., 1984; del. County Dem. Conv., Dubuque, 1984, 86, 90; del., sec. 2d Dist. Dem. Conv., 1984, 86, 90; mem. 5 Flags City Civic Ctr. Commn., Dubuque, 1989-92, chmn., 1991-92; founding bd. dirs. Dubuque County Habitat for Humanity, 1991; sec., bd. dirs. Dubuque Fine Arts Players, 1993-96; mem. Cmty. Devel. Commn., Dubuque, 1992-94; mem. rezoning rev. com. Dubuque Cmty. Sch. Dist., 1996-97. Individual Artist grantee Iowa Arts Coun., 1993, 96. Home: 1510 Kehl Ct #3 Dubuque IA 52003 Business E-Mail: perryg@nicc.edu.

PERRY, ESTON LEE, real estate and equipment leasing company executive; b. Wartburg, Tenn., June 16, 1936; s. Eston Lee and Willimae (Heidle) P.; m. Alice Anne Schmidt, Oct. 21, 1961; children: Julie Anne, Jeffrey John, Jennifer Lee. BS, Ind. State U., 1961. With Oakley Corp., 1961—, dir., 1965—. Corp. officer Ind. State Bank, Terre Haute, 1975-80; pres. One Twenty Four Madison Corp., Terre Haute, 1979—, also bd. dirs., chmn. bd., 1981—; bd. dirs. Fifth Third Bank of Ind. Bd. dirs. Salvation Army, Terre Haute, 1975-91, mem. exec. adv. bd., 1979-87; bd. dirs. Vigo County Dept. Pub. Welfare, 1979-82, Jr. Achievement Wabash Valley, 1980-86; bd. dirs. United Way of Wabash Valley, 1984-89, chmn. fund campaign, 1984, bd. dirs. United Way of Ind., 1984-90, v.p., 1986, pres., 1988-89; trustee Oakley Found., 1970—; bd. dirs. Terre Haute Symphony Orch., 1984-87, Ind. State U. Found., 1988—, Goodwill Industries of Terre Haute, 1984-97, Leadership Terre Haute, 1984-88, Cen. Eastside Assocs., 1984-88, pres., 1984-85; mem. exec. com. Ind. State U. Found., 1990-94; bd. dirs. City of Terre Haute Hulman Links Commn., pres., 1986-91; mem. President's Assocs., Ind. State U., adv. bd.; bd. overseers Sheldon Swope Art Gallery of Terre Haute, 1984-87; bd. assocs. Rose Hulman Inst. Tech., 1986—. Served with U.S. Army, 1955-57. Mem.: Sycamore Athletic Scholarship Fund (Ind. State U.), C. of C. Terre Haute (bd. dirs. 1984—93, vice chmn. 1986—88, chmn. 1990), Jaycees Terre Haute (v.p. 1967—69), ESPFL of Terre Haute (hon.), Aviation Trades Assn., Air Safety Found., Aircraft Owners and Pilots Assn., Wabash Valley Pilots Assn., Strawberry Hill Cannoneers, Aero Club of Terre Haute, Country Club of Terre Haute (bd. dirs.), Elks, Lions (pres. Terre Haute 1983—84), Lambda Chi Alpha. Home: 25 Bogart Dr Terre Haute IN 47803-2401 Office: 8 S 16th St Terre Haute IN 47807-4102 E-mail: bperry@oakleyusa.com.

PERRY, GEORGE, neuroscientist, educator; b. Lompoc, Calif., Apr. 12, 1953; s. George Richard and Mary Arlene (George) P.; m. Paloma Aguilar, May 21, 1983; children: Anne, Elizabeth. AA in Liberal Arts, Allan Hancock Coll., Santa Maria, Calif., 1973; BA in Zoology with hons., U. Calif., Santa Barbara, 1974; PhD in Marine Biology, U. Calif., San Diego, 1979. Postdoctoral fellow Baylor Coll. Medicine, Houston, 1979-82; from asst. prof. to prof. pathology Case Western Res. U., Cleve., 1982-94, prof., 1994—, interim chmn. dept., 2001—; prof. dept. chemistry & biochemistry U. Alaska, Fairbanks, 2001—. Tchg. asst. U. Calif., San Diego, 1977, Stanford U., 1978—79; mem. task force on Alzheimer's disease Ohio Gov., 1987, 90; mem. sci. adv. bd. Familial Alzheimer's Disease Rsch. Found., 1988—; mem., chair neurol. scis. study sect. NIH, Bethesda, Md., 1989—95; vis. scholar Sci.-by-Mail, 1991—94; cons. Nymox, Inc., Panacea Pharms., Inc., Prion Devel. Labs., Voyager, Takada Pharm., Alzheimer Rsch. Forum; spkr. in field; mem. numerous rev. bds. nationally/internationally. Author: The Neuronal Cytoskeleton, 1992; co-author: (chpt.) Muscle and Cell Motility, 1982, Membranes in Growth and Development, 1982, Electron Microscopy and Alzheimer's Disease, 1986, Banbury Report 27, Molecular Neuropathology of Aging, 1987, Advances in Behavioral Biology, 1987, Fidia Research Series, 1988, Progress in Clinical and Biological Research: Alzheimer's Disease and Related Disorders, 1989, 93, International Congress Series: Molecular Biology and Genetics of Alzheimer's Disease, 1990, Neuroscience Year, 1992, Amyloid and Amyloidosis, 1993, Dementia in Parkinson's Disease, 1994, Non-Neural Cells in Alzheimer's Disease, 1995, Alzheimer's Disease: Aetiological Mechanism and Therapeutic Possibilities, 1996; editor-in-chief Jour. Alzheimer's Disease, 1998—; guest editor Clin. Neurosci., 1993; editor Biomed. Jour., 1994-95; assoc. editor Am. Jour. pathology, 1994-2000; assoc. editor Microscopy Rsch. and Technique; mem. editl. bd. Am. Jour. Pathology, 1992—, Alzheimer Disease and Associated Disorders, 1994—, Alzheimer's Disease Rev., 1995-98, Jour. Alzheimer's Disease,1997—, Jour. Exptl. Neurol., 1997-99, Molecular Chem. Neuropathology, 1997-99, Jour. Neural Transmission, 1998—, Investigational Drugs Jour., 1998—, Brain Pathology, 1999—, Jour. Molecular Neurosci., 1999-2001, Antioxidant and Redox Signaling, 2000-2002, Research Signal Post, 2000—, Lab. Investment, 2000-, Brain Rsch., 2002-, Current Medicinal Chemistry, 2002—, Neurobiology of Lipids, 2003—, Jour. Biomed. Biotechnique, 2002—, Pathology, 2003—; reviewer Acta Neuropathol., Alan Liss Publ. Co., Am. Jour. Pathol., Ann Neurol, others; contbr. articles to Experimental Cell Rsch., Jour Cell Biology, Jour. Leukocyte Biology, Devel. Biology, Brain Rsch., Am. Jour. Pathology, Jour. Neurosci., European Jour. Cell Biology, Nature, Annals Neurology, Lancet, Acta Neuropathology, Jour. Neurochemistry, Neurosci. Letters, Hepatology, Jour. Hirnforsch, Cancer Letters, Neuroreport, Med. Hypotheses, Nature Medicine, Neurodegeneration, Brain Rsch. Protocols, others. Pres. Serra Club, 1995-97. Tng. corps. USAR, 1972—74, U. Calif. Santa Barbara. Recipient Bausch and Lomb medal, 1971, Rsch. Career Devel. award, NIH, 1988—93, Career Devel. award, 1988, Temple award, Alzheimer's Assn., 1999, Disting. American of Portuguese Ancestry award, Portuguese-Am. Hist. Found., Inc., 2001, Mensch award, Alzheimer Rsch. Forum, 2003, Cmty. Svc. award, Cleve. Area Chpt. Alzheimer's Assn., 2004; fellow Kennecott Copper, 1974—75, Muscular Dystrophy Assn., 1980—82, Philip Morris, USA, 2003—; grantee NIH, 1985—, grantee, Am. Health Assistance Found., 1988—90, 1997—99, Alzheimer's Assn., 1989—90, 1998—, Belgian Nat. Found. Sci. Rsch., 1994—, Neurogeriatrics Fund., 1995—96, 1997—, Britton Fund, 1996. Fellow AAAS; mem. AAUP (exec. com. 1996—, membership chair 1996-98, v.p. 1998-99, pres. 1999—), Am. Soc. Cell Biology (fellow 1992), Electron Microscopy Soc. N.E. Ohio (treas. 1986-88, trustee 1988-90, pres. 1990-91), Soc. Neurosci., Am. Assn. Neuropathologists (awards com. 1992-93, 95-2002, chmn. 2001-2002, internat. congress neuropathology concilator 1995-2000, sec.-treas. 2003—), Am. Soc. Investigative Pathology (BioInfo Net 1996—, program com. 1998-2001), Oxygen Club, Soc. Neuroscientists Africa, Am. Soc. Neurochemistry, Am. Inst. Biol. Scis., Mitochondrion Rsch. Soc., U.S. and Can. Acad. of Pathology, Hispanic Med. Assn. (com. on status of Portuguese in medicine and sci.), Am. Assn. Univ. Professors, Soc. for Neuroscience, Cleve. Soc. Pathologists, Am. Inst. Biological Sci., Internat. Coll. Geriatric Psychoneuropharmacology, Univ. Assn. Rsch. and Edn. in Pathology, Sigma Xi. Democrat. Roman Catholic. Home: 2500 Eaton Rd University Heights OH 44118-4339 Office: Case Western Res U Inst Path 2085 Adelbert Rd Cleveland OH 44106-2622 E-mail: george.perry@case.edu.

PERRY, GEORGE LEWIS, research economist, consultant; b. N.Y.C., Jan. 23, 1934; s. Lewis G. and Helen L. (Couloumbis) P.; m. Jean Marion West, 1956; children: Elizabeth, Lewis G., George A.; m. 2d, Dina Needleman, 1987. BS, MIT, 1954, PhD, 1961. Editor Brookings Papers on Econ. Activity, 1970—; columnist L.A. Times, 1981-93. Bd. dirs. State Farm Mut. Automobile Ins. Co., Bloomington, Ill., Dreyfus Mut. Funds, N.Y.C.; co-dir. Brookings Panel Econ. Activity. Author: Unemployment, Money Wage Rates and Inflation, 1966, Curing Chronic Inflation, 1978, Economic Events, Ideas and Policies, 2000; contbr. articles to profl. jours. With USAF, 1955—57. Mem. Am. Econs. Assn. Office: Brookings Instn 1775 Massachusetts Ave NW Washington DC 20036-2103

PERRY, GEORGE WILLIAMSON, lawyer; b. Cleve., Dec. 4, 1926; s. George William and Melda Patricia (Arther-Holt) P. BA in Econs., Yale U., 1949; JD, U. Va., 1953. Bar: Ohio 1953, D.C. 1958, U.S. Supreme Ct. 1958, U.S. Ct. Appeals (D.C. cir.) 1959. Atty. U.S. Dept. Justice, Washington, 1954-56; assoc. Roberts and McInnis, Washington, 1957-59; atty. assoc. counsel Com. on Interstate Fgn. Commerce, U.S. Ho. Reps., Washington, 1960-65; atty., advisor ICC, Washington, 1965-68; assoc. dir. devel. Yale U., New Haven, 1968-70; trust officer The No. Trust Co., Chgo., 1970-71; dir. tax rsch. Pan Am. World Airways, N.Y.C., 1973-75; hearing officer Indsl. Commn. Ohio, Cleve., 1978-81; sole practice Cleve., 1981—. With U.S. Army, 1945-46. Mem. Soc. Cin. in State of Conn., Ancient and Hon. Artillery Co. (mem. Boston-hereditary), Phi Delta Phi, Chi Delta Theta.

PERRY, GEORGE WILSON, oil and gas company executive; b. Pampa, Tex., July 18, 1929; s. Frank M. and Ruth (Ingersoll) P.; m. Patricia Carberry Bowen, 1950; children: Sally Jett Perry Pemrick, Susan Jeanne Perry Bynder-Schrier, Virginia Anne Perry Haynie, Tobe Jackson Perry. BS in Petroleum Engring., U. Tulsa, 1952. Registered profl. engr., Tex. Engr. Stanolind Oil & Gas Co., Oklahoma City, 1952—53, Parker Drilling Co., Tulsa, 1953—54, Holm Drilling Co., Tulsa, 1954—55; mgr. Mobil Oil, Victoria, Tex., 1955—61, drilling engr. Lake Charles, La., 1955—61, Paris, 1961—68, Anaco, Venezuela, 1968—72, 1972—73, Tehran, Iran, 1973—74, Stavanger, Norway, 1974—78, New Orleans, 1978—79; exec. v.p. Loffland Bros. Co., Tulsa, 1979—89; pres., CEO Gas Well Properties, Inc., Dallas, 1989—. Mem. Delta Tau Delta. Avocation: astronomy. Office: Gas Well Properties Inc PO Box 795302 5995 Summerside Dr Dallas TX 75248-9992 E-mail: gperry@airmail.net.

PERRY, HAROLD OTTO, dermatologist; b. Rochester, Minn., Nov. 18, 1921; s. Oliver and Hedwig Clara (Tornow) P.; m. Loraine Thelma Moehnke, Aug. 27, 1944; children— Preston, Oliver, Ann, John. AA, Rochester Jr. Coll., 1942; BS, U. Minn., 1944, MB, 1946, MD, 1947; MS, Mayo Grad. Sch. Medicine, 1953. Diplomate Am. Bd. Dermatology with spl. competence in dermatopathology. Intern Naval Hosp., Oakland, Calif., 1946-47; resident in dermatology Mayo Grad. Sch. Medicine, 1949-52; practice medicine specializing in dermatology Rochester, 1953-86; mem. staff Mayo Clinic, 1953-86, mem. emeritus staff, 1987—; instr., asst. prof., assoc. prof. Mayo Med. Sch., 1953-86, prof., 1978-83, Robert H. Kieckhefer prof. dermatology, 1978-83, head dept. dermatology, 1975-83, emeritus prof. dermatology, 1987—. Civilian cons. dermatology to surgeon gen. USAF, 1979-99. Contbr. articles to med. jours. and, chpts. to books. With USNR, 1943-45, 46-49. Inducted into Rochester (Minn.) C.C. Alumni Hall of Fame, 1993; recipient Disting. Alumnus award Mayo Found., 1995. Mem. AMA, Am. Acad. Dermatology (pres. 1981, Sulzberger internat. lectr. 1986, Gold Medal for visionary leadership 1998), Am. Dermatol. Assn. (bd. dirs. 1985-89, pres. 1989-90), Am. Bd. Dermatology (bd. dirs. 1979-90, v.p. 1989, pres. 1990), Noah Worcester Dermatol. Soc. (pres. 1969), Minn. Dermatol. Soc. (pres. 1967), Chgo. Dermatol. Soc., Internat. Soc. Tropical Dermatology, Minn. Med. Assn.; hon. mem. French Dermatol. Soc., Spanish Acad. Dermatology, Brazilian Dermatol. Soc., Ga. Dermatol. Soc., Iowa Dermatol. Soc., Korean Dermatol. Soc., Bolivar Soc. Dermatology, Jacksonville Dermatol. Soc., N.Am. Clin. Dermatol. Soc., Pacific Dermatol. Assn. Home: 3625 SW Bamber Valley Rd Rochester MN 55902 Office: Mayo Clinic Emeritus Staff Ctr 10th Fl Plummer Bldg Ctr Rochester MN 55905-0001

PERRY, HELEN, medical/surgical nurse, secondary school educator; b. Birmingham, Ala., Mar. 4, 1927; d. Van Mary Ellenol (Thornton) Curry; m. Charlie Pitts, May 1960 (div.); 1 child, Charlenia Pitts; m. George Perry (dec. 1989); children: Hattie Mae(dec.), George Jr., Bishop, Jose Sr. Student, LaSalle Extension U., Chgo., 1968, Georgetown U., 1979; Doctorate/Mayanuis Mosaic Soc., Duke Univ., San Antonio, 1979. Cert. paramedic; LPN. Tchr. Wenona HS City Bd. Edn., Birmingham, 1977—. Notary pub., Ala., 1975—; home health nurse U. Ala. Birmingham Hosp., 1988—; math. and reading tutor Princeton Elem. Sch., 2004. Trustee Nat. Crime Watch, 1989; mem. adv. bd. Am. Security Coun., Va., 1969—91; mem. Coalition for Desert Storm; others; vol. ARC, Birmingham, 1970—; mem. crime watch Am. Police, Washington, 1989; mem. Hall of Fame Pres. Task Force, Washington, 1983—91, Image Devel. Adv. Bd.; nominee Nat. Rep. Com., Washington, 1991, 1992; selected VIP guest del. Rep. Nat. Conv., Houston, 1992; life mem. Rep. Presdl. Task Force, Washington, 1992; mem. Jefferson Com., 2001; mem. adv. bd. Nat. Congl. Com., Washington; mem. fin. com. fundraiser Middleton for Congress Campaign, 1994, Dist. # 59 Bd. Reps.; mem. exec. com. Jefferson County Rep., chairperson legis. dist. 52; chair Harriet Tubman Rep. Com.; del. Commonwealth of Ky. So. Rep. Leadership Conf., 2000; min. Greater Emmanuel Temple Holiness Ch., Birmingham, 1957—, ordained elder, vice champion mother bd.; mem. Nat. Law Enforcement Assn., 1989. Nominee Presdl. Election Registry, Rep. Presdl. Task Force, 1992; named Good Samaritan, Law Envforcement Officers; recipient award, Ala. Sheriff Assn., 1989, Navy League, 1989—91, cert. of appreciation, Pres. Congl. Task Force, 1990, Rep. Nat. Com., 1994, Diamond award, U.S.A. Serve Am., 1992, Rep. Presdl. award, Legion of Merit, 1994, Royal Proclamation, Royal Highness Kevin, Prince Regent of Hutt River Province, 1994, Royal Ceremonial jewel, Svc. award, Ala. Bd. Nursing, Outstanding Sr. Citizen's cert. of recognition. Mem.: Ala. Nurses Assn., Nat. Assn. Unknown Players, Nat. Rep. Women Assn., LaSalle Ext. U. Alumni (life). Avocations: singing, writing, speaking, reading, planting flowers. Home: 2021 10th Ave S Apt 513 Birmingham AL 35205-2716

PERRY, I. CHET, petroleum company executive; b. Phila., Jan. 18, 1943; s. Irving Chester Sr. and Erma Jackson (McNeil) P.; m. Eve Evenson Perry; 1 child, London Schade. BA in Psychology, Bus., Lake Forest Coll., 1965. Lic. real estate broker, Ill. Sr. mgmt. trainee British Overseas Airways Corp., London, Eng., 1968-69; owner Itec Internat. Ltd., Barrington, Ill., 1970—, Itec Refining & Mktg. Co., Ltd., Barrington, 1970—, CEO, mng. dir., 1986—. Lt. U.S. Army, 1965-68, Vietnam. Decorated Bronze Star, Purple Heart. Mem. Am. Petroleum Inst., European Petrochem. Assn., Barrington Bd. Realtors (bd. dirs. 1974-78), Forest Grove Club, Barrington Tennis Club. Republican. Mem. Soc. Of Friends. Avocations: tennis, photography. Home: 3 Porter School Rd Barrington Hills IL 60010 Office Phone: 847-304-4700. Business E-Mail: chetperry@itecref.com.

PERRY, J. WARREN, health sciences educator, administrator; b. Richmond, Ind., Oct. 25, 1921; s. Charles Thomas and Zona M. (Ohler) Perry. BA, DePauw U., 1944; postgrad., Harvard U., 1948—49; MA, Northwestern U., 1952, PhD, 1955; DSc (hon.), D'Youville Coll., 1990, Med. Coll. Ohio, 1996, DePauw U., 1998. Instr. St. John's Mil. Acad., Delafield, Wis., 1944—47;

counselor, asst. prof. psychology U. Ill.-Chgo., 1953—56; dir. prosthetic-orthotic edn., asst. prof. orthopaedic surgery Northwestern U. Med. Sch., 1957—61; lectr. psychology U. Chgo., 1957—61; asst. chief div. tng. Vocat. Rehab. Adminstrn., HEW, 1961—64, dep. asst. commr. research and tng., 1964—66; prof. health scis. adminstrn. SUNY-Buffalo, 1966—95, founding dean Sch. Health Related Professions, 1966—77, dean and prof. emeritus, 1985—. Mary E. Switzer Meml. lectr., Dallas, 1977, Lexington, 91; mem. Task Force for Legislation for Allied Health Professions, 1966—67; com. edn. allied health professions and svcs., coun. med. edn. AMA, 1968—73; nat. adv. com. Am. Dietetic Assn., 1970—75, chmn., 1972—75; nat. rev. com., regional med. programs HEW, 1969—72; mem.steering com. on manpower policy for primary care bd. health promotion and disease prevention Inst. of Medicine-NAS, 1981—83, sr. advisor com. to study role allied health, com. to study med. manpower in VA, 1988—91; spl. med. adv. com. VA, 1974—77; mem. task force on manpower for prevention Fogarty Internat. Inst., NIH, 1975—76; mem. acad. planning com. Mass. Gen. Hosp. Founding editor Jour. Allied Health, 1972—78, editor emeritus, 1985—; contbr. articles to profl. jours. Mem. Legacy Soc.; charter mem. Cmty. Found. for Greater Buffalo, 1998—; patron of the arts Coun. of Buffalo and Erie County, 2000; bd. dirs., dir. com. opera edn. Lyric Opera Guild, Chgo., 1957—61; chmn. acad. divsn. dr., coun. trustees Buffalo Philharm. Orch., 1987—93; bd. dirs. Goodwill Industries, Buffalo, 1969—76; trustee Cmty. Music Sch. Buffalo, 1977—80; adv. bd., v.p. Sisters of Charity Hosp., Buffalo, 1969—87, pres., 1986—88; bd. visitors U. Pitts., 1977—80; coun. trustees D'youville Coll., Buffalo, 1978—88, trustee emeritus, 1989—95; bd. dirs. Am. Lung Assn. Western N.Y., 1975—92, pres., 1983; bd. dirs. ARC, Buffalo, Artpark State Performing Arts Ctr., Lewiston, NY, 1986—96, Am. Lung Assn. N.Y.State, 1981—85, exec. com., 1989—92; chmn. N.Y. State Coalition Smoking or Health, Albany, NY, 1987—91; trustee Theodore Roosevelt Inaugural Site Found., 1987, pres., 1991—94; bd. advisors Buffalo Coun. on World Affairs, 1987—88; trustee Buffalo Opera Co., 1989—94, chmn. opera adv. coun., 1995—97. Named Outstanding Individual Philanthropist, Nat. Soc. Fundraising Execs. Western N.Y., 1992, Ky. Col., 1969, Nebr. Admn., 1964, Man of the Yr., Opera Found. Buffalo, Inc., 2000, J. Warren Perry Disting. Author award in his honor, Jour. Allied Health, Perry Scholarship in his honor, U. Buffalo Found., J. Warren Perry Outstanding Vol. Leadership award in his honor, Western N.Y. chpt. ALA, J. Warren Perry Meml. lectr. in his honor, SUNY, Buffalo, Buffalo Philharmonic Chorus, 2003; recipient Sustained Superior Svc. award, HEW, 1965, Disting. Svc. award, Am. Orthotics-Prosthetics Assn., 1966, Buffalo Opera Co., 1995, Chancellor's award for adminstrv. svc., SUNY, 1977, 1st Allied Health Leadership award, 1988, Disting. Author award, Jour. Allied Health, 1978, Cert. of Merit, AMA, 1979, Pres. Cir. Pin, Buffalo State Coll., 1993, 50th Anniversary Alumni citation, De Pauw U., 1994, Outstanding Svc. award, Theodore Roosevelt Inaugural Site Found., 1994, Theodore Roosevelt Exemplary Citizenship award, 1997, Brotherhood/Sisterhood award in health, NCCJ Western N.Y., 1995, Christmas Seal Hall of Fame award, ALA N.Y. State, 1995, Disting. Citizenship award, Mayor of Buffalo, 1995, Patron of the Arts award, Arts Coun. of Buffalo and Erie County, 2000, Alumni Achievement award, SUNY-Buffalo, 2000, Wisdom award of honor, 1999, Humanitarian award, Coordinated Care Assn. Buffalo, 2002, Clara Barton award, ARC (Greater Buffalo chpt.), 2004; fellow Wisdom Hall of Fame fellow, Wisdom Soc., 1999; Perry Lecture Hall, D'Youville Coll. named in his honor, 2004. Fellow: Assn. Schs. of Allied Health Professions (pres. 1969—70, Cert. of Merit 1977, Pres.'s award 1978, Honors of Soc. award 1984); mem.: Nat. Rehab. Assn., Am. Pers. and Guidance Assn., Am. Dietetics Assn. (hon.), APA, Phi Beta Kappa, Delta Tau Delta, Phi Delta Kappa (pres. 1955). Home: 83 Bryant St Apt 5A Buffalo NY 14209-1831

PERRY, JACQUELIN, orthopedic surgeon; b. Denver, May 31, 1918; d. John F. and Tirzah (Kuruptkat) P. BE, U. Calif., LA, 1940; MD, U. Calif., San Francisco, 1950; DSc (hon.), U. So. Calif., 1996. Intern Children's Hosp., San Francisco, 1950-57; resident in orthop. surgery U. Calif., San Francisco, 1951-55; orthop. surgeon Rancho Los Amigos Hosp., Downey, Calif., 1955—, chief stroke svc., 1972-75; chief pathokinesiology Rancho Los Amigos Med. Ctr., 1961—; mem. faculty U. Calif. Med. Sch., San Francisco, 1966—, clin. prof., 1973—; mem. faculty U. So. Calif. Med. Sch., 1969—, prof. orthop. surgery, 1972—, dir. polio and gait clinic, 1972—. Disting. lectr. for hosp. for spl. surgery and Cornell U. Med. Coll., NYC, 1977-78; Packard Meml. lectr. U. Colo. Med. Sch., 1970; Osgood lectr. Harvard Med. Sch., 1978; Summer lectr., Portland, 1977; Shands lectr.; cons. USAF; guest spkr. symposia; cons. Biomechanics Lab. Centinela Hosp., 1979—. Served as phys. therapist U.S. Army, 1941-46. Recipient Disting. Svc. award Assn. Rehab. Facilities, 1981, Pres.'s award, 1984, Isabelle and Lenard Goldensen award for tech. United Cerebral Palsy Assn., 1981, Jow Dowling award, 1985, Profl. Achievement award UCLA, 1988, Milton Cohen award Nat. Assn. Rehab., 1993, Tribute Pres. award Ruth Jackson Orthop. Soc., 2004; named Woman of Yr. for Medicine in So. Calif. LA Times, 1959, Alumnus of Yr. U. Calif. Med. Sch., 1980, Physician of Yr. Calif. Employment Devel. Dept., 1994; Jacquelin Perry Neuro Trauma Inst. Rancho Clin. Bldg. named in her honor, 1996. Mem. AMA, Am. Acad. Orthop. Surgeons (Kappa Delta award for rsch. 1977, orthop. rsch. svc., 1976), Am. Orthop. Assn. (Shands lectr. 1988), Western Orthop. Assn., Calif. Med. Soc., LA County Med. Soc., Am. Phys. Therapy Assn. (hon. Golden Pen award 1965), Am. Acad. Orthotists and Prosthetists (hon.), Scoliosis Rsch. Soc., LeRoy Abbott Soc., Am. Acad. Cerebral Palsy, Gait & Clin. Movement Analysis Soc. (mem. emeritus, Lifetime Achievement award 2000), Orthop. Rsch. Soc. (Shands award 1998, 99). Home: 12319 Brock Ave Downey CA 90242-3503 Office: Rancho Los Amigos Med Ctr 7601 Imperial Hwy Downey CA 90242-3456 E-mail: pklab@larei.org.

PERRY, JAMES ALFRED, environmental scientist, consultant, science educator, department chairman; b. Dallas, Sept. 27, 1945; BA in Fisheries, Colo. State U., 1968; MA, Western State Coll., 1973; PhD, Idaho State U., 1981. Sr. water quality specialist Idaho Div. Environ., Pocatello, 1974-82; area mgr. Centrac Assocs., Salt Lake City, 1982; H.T. Morse disting. prof. water quality U. Minn., St. Paul, 1982—, head dept. fisheries, wildlife, conservation biol., 2000—, dir. natural resources policy and mgmt., 1985—2002, dir. grad. studies in water resources, 1988—92, 1999—2001; dep. dir. AID-funded Environ. Tng. Project for Ctrl. and Ea. Europe, 1992-96; spl. asst. to dean grad. sch. U. Minn., St. Paul, 1996-2000. Vis. scholar Oxford U., Green Coll., England, 1990—91; cons. in field. Author: Water Quality Management of a Natural Resource, 1996, Ecosystem Management for Central and Eastern Europe, 2001; editor: Jour. Natural Resources and Life Scis. Edn.; mem. editl. bd. Mitigation and Adaptation Strategies for Global Change. Charter mem. Leadership Devel. Acad., Lakewood, Minn., 1988; bd. dirs. Minn. Ctr. for Environ. Advocacy, 1995--. Recipient Richard C. Newman Art of Tchg. award, 1998, Morse-Alumni award, 1999, Outstanding Svc. award U. Minn., 2001, CISW award, 2003; ACOP/ESCOP nat. leadership fellow, 1995-96, CIC acad. leadership fellow, 2000-01; PALI fellow, 2003—. Fellow: Am. Inst. Fish Resource Biology; mem.: The Soc. for Conservation Biology, The Wildlife Soc., Am. Fisheries Soc., N.Am. Benthol. Soc. (exec. bd. Albuquerque 1990—91), Internat. Soc. Theoretical and Applied Limnology, Internat. Water Resources Assn., Am. Water Resources Assn., Minn. Acad. Scis. (bd. dirs. 1987—90), Gamma Sigma Delta (merit award 2001), Xi Sigma Pi, Sigma Xi. Office: U Minn Dept Fisheries Wildlife and Conservation Biology 204 Hodson Hall 1980 Folwell Ave Saint Paul MN 55108-1037 Office Phone: 612-625-4717. Business E-Mail: jperry@umn.edu.

PERRY, JAMES FREDERIC, philosophy educator, writer; b. Washington, Jan. 21, 1936; s. Albert Walter and Helene Anna Maria (Neumeyer) P.; m. Sandra Jean Huizing, Feb. 18, 1957 (div. May 1972); children: Sandra Elaine, James Frederic Jr., Bartholomew; m. Roberta Schofield, June 6, 1984. Student, Princeton U., 1953-56, Marietta (Ohio) Coll., 1958-60; BA with honors in Philosophy, Ind. U., 1962, PhD in Philosophy of Edn., 1972. NDEA fellow in philosophy U. N.C., 1962—65; instr. N.C. State U., Raleigh, 1965-66; Univ. fellow Ind. U., 1971, adj. lectr., 1972-75; prof. philosophy Hillsborough Community Coll., Tampa, Fla., 1975-97, hons. prof. philosophy, 1997—. Adj. prof. philosophy U. South Fla., 2000—. Author: Random, Routine, Reflective, 1989; contbr. articles to profl. jours. Precinct committeeman Dem. Party, Tampa, 1988-2004. Mem. AAUP (pres. Fla. conf. 1986-89, chair com. "A" on acad. freedom 1989-2002), C.C. Humanities Assn. (so. divsn. exec. bd. 1981-89), Am. Philos. Assn., Fla. Philos. Assn. (pres. 2004—), Internat. Soc. Philos. Enquiry, Internat. Congress for Critical Thinking and Moral Critiques (founding mem. S.E. coun. 1991), World Congress Philosophy (Boston 1998, Istanbul 2003), Princeton Alumni Assn. of Fla. Suncoast (sec. 1983-86, pres. 1986-95), Mensa, Authors Guild, Textbook and Acad. Authors Assn., Nat. Collegiate Honors Coun. Avocations: travel, foreign travel, genealogy. Office: Hillsborough C C PO Box 10561 Tampa FL 33679-0561 Office Phone: 813-253-7357. Business E-Mail: jperr@hccfl.edu.

PERRY, JEAN LOUISE, dean; b. Richland, Wash., May 13, 1950; d. Russell S. and Sue W. Perry. BS, Miami U., Oxford, Ohio, 1972; MS, U. Ill., Urbana, 1973, PhD, 1976. Cons. ednl. placement office U. Ill., 1973-75; adminstrv. intern Coll. Applied Life Studies, 1975-76, asst. dean, 1976-77, assoc. dean, 1978-81, asst. prof. dept. phys. edn., 1976-81; assoc. prof. phys. edn. San Francisco State U., 1981-84, prof., 1984-90, chair, 1981-90; dean Coll. of Human and Community Scis. U. Nev., Reno, 1990—. Named to excellent tchr. list U. Ill., 1973-79. Mem. AAHPERD (fellow research consortium, pres. 1988-89), Am. Assn. Higher Edn., Am. Ednl. Research Assn., Nat. Assn. Phys. Edn. in Higher Edn., Nat. Assn. Girls and Women in Sports (guide coordinator, pres.), Delta Psi Kappa, Phi Delta Kappa. Home: 3713 Ranchview Ct Reno NV 89509-7437 Office: U Nev Coll Human Cmty Scis 136 Reno NV 89557-0001 Office Phone: 775-784-6975.

PERRY, JEANINE, state representative; b. Apr. 3, 1942; married; 2 children. BEd, U. Toledo. State rep. dist. 49 Ohio Ho. of Reps., Columbus, 1998—, ranking minority mem., transp. and pub. safety com., mem. agr. and natural resources, econ. devel. and tech., homeland security engrng. and archtl. design, and human svcs. and aging coms., mem. natural resources, parks and recreation subcom. Councilwoman Toledo City Coun., 1993—98. Named Legislator of Yr., Point Place Bus. Assn., 1999; recipient Outstanding Svc. award, Toledo PTA Pub. Schs. Mem.: U. Toledo Alumni Assn., Friends of the Libr., Fraternal Order of Police Aux., Toledo Power Squadron (hon.), Ohio PTA (life). Democrat. Office: 77 S High St 10th fl Columbus OH 43215-6111

PERRY, JOSEPH N. bishop; b. Chgo., Apr. 18, 1948; Ordained priest Roman Cath. Ch., 1975. Pastor All Sts. Parish, Milw.; episcopal vicar Vicariate VI; consecrated aux. bishop, 1998; aux. bishop Archdiocese of Chgo., 1998—. Roman Catholic. Office: PO Box 733 South Holland IL 60473-0733

PERRY, KENNETH WALTER, retired integrated oil company executive; b. Shamrock, Tex., Feb. 24, 1932; s. Charles Bowman and Sunshine Virginia (Grady) P.; m. Mary Dean Sudderth; children: Mary Martha Ernst, Kathryn Virginia. BSME, U. Okla., 1954. Sales engr. Mid-Continent Oil Well Supply Co., 1954-55; with Cosden Oil & Chem. Co., Big Spring, Tex., from 1957, jr. engr., 1957-59, project engr., 1959-60, chem. salesman, 1960-64, chem. products mgr., 1964-65, mktg. mgr., then v.p. mktg., 1965-69, v.p. chems., 1969-72, sr. v.p., 1972-76, pres., from 1976; group v.p. Am. Petrofina, Inc., Dallas, 1976-85, sr. v.p., 1985—89, pres., CEO, 1989, vice chmn., bd. dirs., 1989-92; CEO Nimir Petroleum Co. Ltd., Dallas, 1992-96; ret., 1992. CEO United Commerce Bank, Highland Village, Tex., 1990—91. Mem. bd. govs. Dallas Symphony Orch., 1987-93; bd. dirs. Dallas Coun. World Affairs, 1980; mem. engring. com. U. Okla. Aerospace, Nuclear, 1982; bd. dirs. Colo. Mcpl. Water Dist., 1972; bd. visitors Coll. Engring., U. Okla., 1990—. 1st lt. USASC, 1955-57. Mem. Am. Petroleum Inst. (bd. dirs. 1986-90), Nat. Petroleum Coun., Nat. Petroleum Refiners Assn. (chmn. petrochem. com. 1984-87), Ctr. Strategic and Internat. Studies, 25-Yr. Clubs, Petroleum Industry Club, Petrochem. Industry Club, Northwood Club, Dallas Petroleum Club.

PERRY, L. TOM, religious organization administrator, merchant; b. Aug. 5, 1922; s. Tom and Nora Sonne Perry; m. Virginia Lee (dec. 1974); 3 children; m. Barbara Dayton, 1976. BS, Utah State U. Ass. to the Twelve, 1972—74; mem. Quorum of the Twelve Ch. of Jesus Christ of LDS, Salt Lake City, 1974—; chmn. ZCMI, Salt Lake City. With USMC, WWII, PTO. Office: LDS Ch 50 E North Temple Salt Lake City UT 84150-0002

PERRY, LEE ROWAN, retired lawyer; b. Chgo., Sept. 23, 1933; s. Watson Bishop and Helen (Rowan) P.; m. Barbara Ashcraft Mitchell, July 2, 1955; children: Christopher, Constance, Geoffrey. BA, U. Ariz., 1955, LLB, 1961. Bar: Ariz. 1961. Since practiced in, Phoenix; clk. Udall & Udall, Tucson, 1960-61; mem. firm Carson, Messinger, Elliott, Laughlin & Ragan, 1961-99. Mem. law rev. staff, U. Ariz., 1959-61. Mem. bd. edn. Paradise Valley Elem. and H.S. Dists., Phoenix, 1964-68, pres., 1968; mem. bd. edn. Osborn Elem. Sch. Dist., Phoenix, 2002; bd. dirs. Osborn Sch. Dist. Found., 2003—; treas. troop Boy Scouts Am., 1970-72; mem. Ariz. adv. bd. Girl Scouts U.S.A., 1972-74, mem. nominating bd., 1978-79; bd. dirs. Florence Crittenton Services Ariz., 1967-72, pres., 1970-72; bd. dirs. U. Ariz. Alumni, Phoenix, 1968-72, pres., 1969-70; bd. dirs. Family Service Phoenix, 1974-75; bd. dirs. Travelers Aid Assn. Am., 1985-89; bd. dirs. Vol. Bur. Maricopa County, 1975-81, 83-86, pres., 1984-85; bd. dirs. Ariz. div. Am. Cancer Soc., 1978-80, Florence Crittenton div. Child Welfare League Am., 1976-81; bd. dirs. Crisis Nursery for Prevention of Child Abuse, 1978-81, pres., 1978-80; Ariz. dir. Devereux Found., 1996-2000, vice chmn. 1996-98. 1st lt. USAF, 1955-58. Mem. State Bar Ariz. (conv. chmn. 1972), Rotary (dir. 1971-77, 95-96, pres. 1975-76, West Leadership award 1989), Ariz. Club (bd. dirs. 1994-2002, pres.-elect 1997-98, pres. 1998-99), Phoenix Country Club, Phi Delta Phi, Phi Delta Theta (pres. 1954). Republican. Episcopalian. Home: 106 N Country Club Dr Phoenix AZ 85014-5443 E-mail: leeperry@mac.com.

PERRY, LEWIS CURTIS, historian, educator; b. Somerville, Mass., Nov. 21, 1938; s. Albert Quillen and Irene (Lewis) P.; m. Ruth Opler, June 5, 1962 (div. 1970); 1 child, Curtis Alan; m. Elisabeth Israels, Nov. 26, 1970; children: Susanna Irene, David Mordecai. AB, Oberlin Coll., 1960; MS, Cornell U., Ithaca, N.Y., 1964; PhD, Cornell U., 1967. Asst. prof. history SUNY, Buffalo, 1966-72, assoc. prof., 1972-78; prof. Ind. U. Bloomington, 1978-84; Andrew Jackson prof. history Vanderbilt U., 1984-99, dir. Am. Studies, 1992-95; John Francis Bannon prof. history St. Louis U., 1999—. Ampart lectr. U.S. Info. Service, India and Nepal, 1986, France, 1989; vis. prof. U. Leeds, 1988-89; vis. Raoul Wallenberg fellow Rutgers U., 1991-92; chair Frederick Douglass prize jury, Gilder Lehrman Ctr., 2003-04. Author: Radical Abolitionism, 1973, reissue, 1995, Childhood, Marriage, and Reform, 1980, Intellectual Life in America, 1984, 2nd edit. 1989, Boats Against the Current, 1993, 2nd edit., 2002; co-author: Patterns of Anarchy, 1966, Antislavery Reconsidered, 1979; co-editor Moral Problems in American Life, 1998; editor: Jour. Am. History, 1978-84, American Thought and Culture Series, 1985—. Pres. Unitarian-Universalist Ch., Bloomington, Ind., 1983-84; mem. Ralph Waldo Emerson prize com. Phi Beta Kappa, 1997-99, chair, 1999. N.Y. State Regents fellow, 1965-66, Am. Coun. Learned Socs. fellow, 1972-73, Nat. Humanities Inst. fellow, 1975-76, John Simon Guggenheim Found. fellow, 1982, NEH fellow, 1987-88. Mem.: Soc. Historians Early Am. Republic, Am. Hist. Assn., Orgn. Am. Historians (editor 1978—84, exec. bd. 1996—99). Office: St Louis U Dept History 3800 Lindell Blvd Saint Louis MO 63108 Business E-Mail: perryl@slu.edu.

PERRY, LOUIS BARNES, retired insurance company executive; b. Los Angeles, Mar. 4, 1918; s. Louis Henry and Julia (Stoddard) P.; m. Genevieve Patterson, Feb. 8, 1942; children: Robert Barnes, Barbara Ann, Donna Lou. BA, UCLA, 1938, MA, 1940, PhD, 1950; fellow in econs., Yale U., 1941; LL.D., Pacific U., 1964; L.H.D., Whitman Coll., 1967, Linfield Coll., 1981; D.C.S., Willamette U., 1977. Teaching asst. UCLA, 1940-41, research teaching asst., 1946-47; faculty Pomona Coll., 1947-59, asst. to pres., 1955-57, prof. econs., 1957-59; pres. Whitman Coll., Walla Walla, Wash., 1959-67; v.p., treas. Standard Ins. Co., Portland, Oreg., 1967-68, exec. v.p., 1968-71, pres., 1972-83, chmn., 1983-85, also bd. dirs. Investment counselor, broker Wagenseller & Durst, L.A., 1951-59; rsch. coord. So. Calif. Rsch. Coun., 1952-54; cons. Carnegie Survey Bus. Edn., 1957-58. Author: (with others) Our Needy Aged, 1954, A History of the Los Angeles Labor Movement, 1963; Contbr. (with others) articles to profl. jours. Mem. Oreg. Bd. Higher Edn., 1975-87, pres., 1975-80. Served to maj. AUS, World War II; lt. col. Res. Mem. Am. Coll. Life Underwriters (trustee 1972-81), Rotary, Phi Beta Kappa, Beta Gamma Sigma, Phi Delta Kappa, Pi Gamma Mu, Alpha Gamma Omega, Artus. Methodist. Home: 1585 Gray Lynn Dr Walla Walla WA 99362-9282 *In looking back over the years, an unspoken and oftentime subliminal guiding principle has been to reach beyond one's realistic grasp. This concept coupled with an interest in treating others as one would like to be treated has made it possible to react to new challenges. Successfully meeting the latter has provided a varied career in a number of different fields of activity.*

PERRY, LUKE (COY LUTHER PERRY III), actor; b. Fredericktown, Ohio, Oct. 11, 1966; s. Coy Sr. and Ann Perry; m. Minnie Sharp, Nov. 18, 1993 (div.); children: Jack, Sophie. Actor: (TV series) Loving, 1987, Another World, 1989, Beverly Hills, 90210, 1990—95, (dir. episode Fortune Cookie), 1998—2000, (voice) The Simpsons, 1989, Spin City, 1996, Johnson County War, 2002, (voice): (TV miniseries) Mortal Kombat: The Animated Series, 1995, The Incredible Hulk, 1996, Robin Cook's Invasion, 1997; (TV films) Riot, 1997, Indiscreet, 1998, (voice) The Night of the Headless Horseman, 1999, Jeremiah, 2002, Johnson County War, 2002; (films) Terminal Bliss, 1992, Buffy the Vampire Slayer, 1992, The Webbers, 1993, For Our Children, 1993, 8 Seconds, 1994, Vacanze di Natale 95, 1995, Normal Life, 1996, American Strays, 1996, The Fifth Element, 1997, Lifebreath, 1997, Last Breath, 1998, Storm, 1998, The Florentine, 1999, The Heist, 1999, Blue Light Special, 1999, Attention Shoppers, 2000, The Enemy, 2001, Dirt, 2001, Luxury of Love, 2001, Fogbound, 2002, Down the Barrel, 2003, (Broadway performance) Rocky Horror Picture Show, 2001, (TV guest appearances) Parker Lewis Can't Lose, 1992, The Simpsons, 1993, Biker Mice From Mars, 1994, 1995, Spin City, 1997, Family Guy, 2000. Office: Nigro Karlin & Segal 10100 Santa Monica Blvd Los Angeles CA 90067-4003*

PERRY, MALCOLM BLYTHE, biologist, researcher; b. Birkenhead, Cheshire, Eng., Apr. 26, 1930; s. Cyril A. and Hilda P. (Blythe) Perry; m. Eileen M. Perry, Aug. 10, 1956 (dec. Nov. 1981); children: Sara Jane, Judith Anne; m. Philomena C. Kingsley, July 25, 2001. B.Sc., U. Bristol, Eng., 1953; PhD, U. Bristol, 1956, D.Sc., 1969. Banting rsch. fellow Queen's U., Kingston, Canada, 1955, asst. prof., 1956-60, R.S. McLaughlin research prof., 1960-62; sr. resch. officer Nat. Rsch. Coun., Ottawa, 1962—81, prin. rsch. officer, 1981—. Scientist U. Cambridge, Eng., 1969, U. Paris, 1979; prof. U. Ottawa, 1982 Contbr. articles to profl. jours. Fellow Royal Soc. Can., Royal Inst. Chemistry; mem. Can. Soc. Microbiology (award 1991), Am. Soc. Microbiology. Home: 769 Hemlock Rd Ottawa ON Canada K1K 0K6 Office: NRC 100 Sussex Dr Ottawa ON Canada K1A 0R6 Office Phone: 613-990-0837. E-mail: malcolm.perry@nrc.ca.

PERRY, MALCOLM OLIVER, vascular surgeon; b. Allen, Tex., Sept. 3, 1929; BA, U. Tex., 1951; MD, U. Tex., Dallas, 1955. Diplomate Am. Bd. Surgery, Am. Bd. Gen. Vascular Surgery. Intern Letterman Army Hosp., San Francisco, 1955-56; resident in surgery Parkland Meml. Hosp., Dallas, 1958-62; fellow in vascular surgery U. Calif., San Francisco, 1962-63; asst. prof. surgery U. Tex., Dallas, 1962-67, assoc. prof. surgery, chief vascular surgery, 1967-71, prof. surgery, chief vascular surgery, 1971-74; prof. surgery U. Wash., Seattle, 1974-77; prof. surgery, chief vascular surgery Cornell U. Med. Coll., N.Y.C., 1978-87, Vanderbilt U. Sch. Medicine, Nashville, 1987-91; chief vascular surgery Tex. Tech U. Health Scis. Ctr., Lubbock, 1991-95; prof. surgery Southwestern Med. Sch., Dallas. Capt. USAF, 1955-58; major Tex. Air N.G., 1960-66. Home: RR 2 Box 830 Jacksonville TX 75766-9815 Office: U Tex Dept Surgery Southwestern Med Sch 5323 Harry Hines Blvd Dallas TX 75390-7208 also: St Paul Med Ctr Dept Surgery 5939 Harry Hines Blvd Dallas TX 75235-6246

PERRY, MARGARET, librarian, writer; b. Cin., Nov. 15, 1933; d. Rufus Patterson and Elizabeth Munford (Anthony) P. AB, Western Mich. U., 1954; Cert. d'etudes Francaises, U. Paris, 1956; MSLS, Cath. U. Am., 1959. Young adult and reference libr. N.Y. Pub. Libr., N.Y.C., 1954-55, 57-58; libr. U.S. Army, France and Germany, 1959-63, 64-67; chief circulation U.S. Mil. Libr., West Point, N.Y., 1967-70; head edn. libr. U. Rochester, N.Y., 1970-75, asst. prof., 1973-75, assoc. prof., 1975-82, asst. dir. librs. for reader svcs., 1975-82, acting dir. librs., 1976-77, 80; univ. libr. Valparaiso U., Ind., 1982-93; ret., 1993. Mem. Task Force on Coop. Edn., Rochester, 1972; freelance writer Mich. Land Use Inst., 1995-01. Author: A Bio-bibliography of Countee P. Cullen, 1903-1946, 1971, Silence to the Drums: A Survey of the Literature of the Harlem Renaissance, 1976, The Harlem Renaissance, 1982, The Short Fiction of Rudolph Fisher, 1987; also numerous short stories; contbr. articles to profl. jours. Bd. dirs. Urban League, 1978-80 Recipient 1st prize short story contest Armed Forces Writers League, 1966; 2d prize Frances Steloff Fiction prze, 1968, 1st prize short story Arts Alive, 1990, 2d prize short story Willow Rev., 1990; seminar scholar Schloss Leopoldskron, Salzburg, Austria, 1956, 3d prize short story West Shore C.C., Scottville, Mich., 1995. Mem. ALA. Democrat. Roman Catholic. Avocations: violin and viola, collecting book marks, gardening, reading, travel. Home: 8 Muriel St Ithaca NY 14850 Office Phone: 607-257-3997. E-mail: mperry515@yahoo.com.

PERRY, MATTHEW, actor; b. Williamstown, Mass., Aug. 19, 1969; Actor Friends, 1994—2004. Appeared on TV series including Boys Will Be Boys, Sydney, Growing Pains; TV movies include Deadly Relations, Call Me Anna, Dance 'Til Dawn, Parallel Lives, 1994; films include A Night in the Life of Jimmy Reardon, 1988, She's Out of Control, 1989, Getting In, 1994, Fools Rush In, 1997, Edwards and Hunt: The First American Road Trip, 1997, Almost Heroes, 1998, Three to Tango, 1999, The Whole Nine Yards, 2000, Serving Sarah, 2002, The Whole Ten Yards, 2004; film writer: Imagining Emily, 1999; TV guest appearances include Silver Spoons, 1982, Family Ties, 1982, Charles in Charge, 1984, The Tracey Ullman Show, 1987, Highway to Heaven, 1984, Empty Nest, 1988, Who's The Boss, 1984, Beverly Hills, 90210, 1990, Dream On, 1990, The John Larroquette Show, 1993, Caroline in the City, 1995; theater debut Sexual Perversity in London, 2003.*

PERRY, MATTIE LAVORA, writer, web site designer, editor; b. Cleveland, Ohio, Nov. 19, 1961; d. Rudolph and Mattie Mae (Causey) Perry; m. Cedric Jean Richardson, Nov. 28, 1992; children: Nia Dawn Perry-Richardson, Jarod Chad Perry-Richardson, Jahci Joy Perry-Richardson stepchildren: William Davis Richardson, Sonya Boyd Richardson, Ameer Richardson, Rebecca Richardson. BS, Cleve. State U., 1993—95. Staff writer and editor Am. Greetings, Cleve., 1995—2002; author East Cleve., Ohio, 2003—. Author: (greeting cards) Juvenile and Conventional Cards (Am. Greetings Creative Excellence award - Juvenile & Conventional Cards, 1999), (short story) Forgiving (Best of Ohio Writers Contest Hon. Mention, 1998, Cleve. Free Times Fiction Contest Hon. Mention, 1996), (children's chapter book) Taneesha's Treasures of the Heart (selected for Annual Poet's and writers League of Greater Cleveland, 2004), Wu-lung & I-lung Children's Story Book, 2003 (Norio Saneshige award, 2003, ADDY award, Am. Advertisers Fed., 2003); editor: (calendar) Fulfilling the Dream: An African-American Almanac, 365 Days of Healthy Living, (greeting card line) In Rhythm (Am. Greetings Creative Excellence award - Concept Innovation, 2000). Recipient East Cleve. Volunteerism award, East Cleve. City Coun., 2001. Mem.: Internat. Assn. of Web Masters and Designers, Cleve. Writers of Colour, Soc. of Children's Books Writers & Illustrators, Poets' & Writers' League of Greater Cleve., Cleve. State U. Alumni Assn., Pi Lamda Theta, Internat. Honor Soc. in Edn., Golden Key Nat. Honor Soc. Nichiren Buddhist, Soka Gakkai International (Sgi-Usa). Achievements include first in-house African-American greeting card writer in the world's largest greeting card company; author of first children's book featuring an African American buddhist family; author of first children's book featuring American buddhists of African descent to be included in curriculum of public schools in the African nation of Zambia; author of first children's book featuring American buddhists of African descent to be listed on the reading list of Ohio's (Cleveland)largest school district; author of first children's book featuring American buddhists of African descent to be read by children in the nations of Kenya, South Africa, Zambia and Mali, Cameroon, Uganda, Namibia, Malaysia. Avocations: walking, reading, travel, cooking, music. Personal E-mail: lavora@fortunechildbooks.com.

PERRY, SIR MICHAEL (SIR MICHAEL SYDNEY PERRY), industrialist; b. Eastbourne, Sussex, Eng., Feb. 26, 1934; s. Sydney Albert and Jessie Kate (Brooker) P.; m. Joan Mary Stallard, Oct. 18, 1958; children: Carolyn Clare, Deborah Anne, Andrew John William. MA, St. John's Coll., Oxford,

U.K., 1957. From mem. staff to chmn. Unilever PLC, London, 1957—92, chmn., 1992—96, Dunlop Slazenger Group Ltd., London, 1996—2001, Centrica PLC, London, 1997—2004; v.p. Liverpool Sch. Tropical Medicine, England, 2001—. Non-exec. dir. Bass Plc, London; chmn. Japan Trade Group, London, 1985 98; dep. chmn. Bass PLC, 1991-2001; non exec. dir. Marks & Spencer Ltd., 1996-2001; chmn. Shakespeare Globe Trust, 1993, chmn.; v.p., then pres. Liverpool (Eng.) Sch. Tropical Medicine, 1993-2001; non exec. dir. Brit. Gas, 1992, 1997; mem. supervisory bd. Royal Ahold, 1997-2004; pres. Mktg. Coun.; chmn. faculty bd. Oxford U., 2001-. Decorated Knight Bachelor; decorated comdr. Brit. Empire, knight grand cross Brit. Empire; award GBE double knighthood, 2002. Mem. Oriental Club. Avocations: golf, music. E-mail: perryalfrick@aol.com.

PERRY, MICHAEL CLINTON, physician, medical educator, academic administrator; b. Wyandotte, Mich., Jan. 27, 1945; s. Clarence Clinton and Hilda Grace (Wigginton) P.; m. Nancy Ann Kaluzny, June 22, 1968; children: Rebecca Carolyn, Katherine Grace. BA, Wayne State U., 1966, MD, 1970; MS in Medicine, U. Minn., 1975. Diplomate Am. Bd. Internal Medicine, Am. Bd. Hematology, Am. Bd. Oncology. Intern in internal medicine Mayo Grad. Sch. Medicine, Rochester, Minn., 1970-71, resident, 1971-72, fellow, 1972-75; instr. Mayo Med. Sch., Rochester, 1974-75; asst. prof. U. Mo., Columbia, 1975-80, assoc. prof., 1980-85, prof., 1985—, chmn. dept. medicine, 1983-91, sr. assoc. dean, 1991-94, Nellie A Smith chair oncology, dir. div. hematology/oncology, 1994—. Prin. investigator Cancer and Leukemia Group B, Nat. Cancer Inst., Chgo., 1982—, exec. com., 1982-84, 1987-90. Author, co-author 30 book chpts.; editor: Toxicity of Chemotherapy, 1984, The Chemotherapy Source Book, 1992, 96, Comprehensive Textbook of Thoracic Oncology, 1996; contbr. articles to profl. jours. Recipient Faculty Alumni award U. Mo., Columbia, 1985, Disting. Alumnus award Wayne State U., 1995, Disting. Oncologist of Yr. award So. Assn. Oncology, 2000. Fellow ACP; mem. Am. Soc. Hematology, Am. Soc. Clin. Oncology, Cen. Soc. Clin. Research, Am. Soc. Internal Medicine (Young Internist of Yr. 1981), Sigma Xi, Alpha Omega Alpha. Home: 1112 Pheasant Run Columbia MO 65201-6254 Office: U Mo-Columbia 516 Ellis Fischel Cancer Ctr 115 Business Loop 70 W Columbia MO 65203-3244 E-mail: perrym@health.missouri.edu.

PERRY, MICHAEL S. biotechnology company executive; With Syntex Corp., Schering Plough Corp., Bio Rsch. Labs., Warner Lambert/Parke Davis, Sandoz/Novartis Pharms., 1994—97; pres., CEO SyStemix Inc., 1997—2000, Genetic Therapy, Inc., 1998—2000; head R&D Baxter Global BioPharms., 2000—02; pres., CEO Pharsight Corp., Mountain View, Calif., 2002—. Office: Pharsight Corp 800 W El Camino Real St #200 Mountain View CA 94040

PERRY, MICHAEL WILEY, editor, writer; b. Greenville, Ala., Mar. 21, 1948; s. Thomas Clarence and Reba Avant Perry. BS in elec. engring., Auburn U., 1966—72; Masters in Theology, Dallas Theol. Sem., 1972—76. Editor Inkling Books, Seattle, 1999—. Contbr.; editor: The C. S. Lewis Readers Ency. (ECPA Biography award, 1999), On the Lines of Morris' Romances, The Manhood of the Master, Eugenics and Other Evils, Chesterton Day by Day, Theism and Humanism by Arthur J. Balfour, Dachau Liberated, The Pivot of Civilization in Historical Perspective, The Life of Toussaint L'Overture, Across Asia on a Bicycle, More to William Morris. Office: Inkling Books 6528 Phinney Ave N Seattle WA 98103 E-mail: editor@inklingbooks.com.

PERRY, NANCY ESTELLE, psychologist; b. Pitts., Oct. 30, 1934; d. Simon Warren and Estelle Cecelia (Zaluski) Reichard; children: Scott, Karen, Elaine. BS, Ohio State U., 1956, MA in Psychology, 1969, PhD in Psychology, 1973. Nurse various locations, 1956-63; psychologist Pub. Schs., Columbus, Ohio, 1970-72; human devel. specialist Madison County (Ohio) Schs., 1972-75; pvt. practice clin. psychology; cons. psychology, 1975-80; tchr. U. Wis. Sch. Nursing, Milw., 1980-88, Milw. Devel. Ctr., 1980-83; pvt. practice Assoc. Mental Health Svcs., 1983-87, Glendale Clinic for Stress Mgmt. and Mental Health Clinics, 1987-98, Cambridge Group, 1999—; pvt. practice life transitions therapy Milw. and Santa Fe, 1999—. Mem. faculty Wis. Profl. Schs.; adj. faculty U. Wis., Milw. Ohio Dept. Edn. grantee, 1973-76. Bd. dirs. Youth Shelters & Family Svcs., Santa Fe. EPDA fellow Ohio State U., 1973; Ohio Dept. Edn. grantee, 1973-76. Fellow Internat. Soc. Study of Dissociation (sec.-treas. 1995-98), Wis. Psychol. Assn.; mem. APA, Am. Soc. Clin. Hypnosis, Am. Assn. Marriage and Family Therapists. Office: 355 E Palace Ave Santa Fe NM 87501 Home: 47 Avenida Frijoles Santa Fe NM 87507-3431 Office Phone: 505-955-1995.

PERRY, NELSON ALLEN, retired radiation safety engineer, radiological consultant; b. Louisville, Mar. 26, 1937; s. Leslie Irvin and Sue Helen (Harris) P.; m. Sarita Sue Cornn, Apr. 28, 1956; children: Melody S. Doyle, Kimberly D. Horne. AS, Campbellsville (Ky.) Coll., 1954; BS, U. Louisville, 1961; MS, U. Okla., 1966. Cert. hazard control mgr., hazart material mgt.; lic. med. physicist, Tex. Assoc. prof. Ind. Christian U., Indpls., 1974-76; asst. prof. Ind. U., Indpls., 1971-75; instr. Ind. Voc. Tech. Coll., Indpls., 1968-76; health physicist Michael Reese Hosp., Chgo., 1966-68; radiation safety officer St. Francis Hosp., Beech Grove, Ind., 1968-76, Ind. U., Indpls., 1971-74, U. South Ala., Mobile, 1976—, assoc. prof., 1981—2001; radiol. cons. Perry Radiol. Cons., Inc., 1974—2001. Radiol. cons., 1974—. Contbr. articles to profl. jours. Named Ky. Col., 1964; USPHS trainee, 1965-66. Mem. Am. Assn. Physicists in Medicine, Health Physics Soc., Ala. Health Physics Soc. (sec. 1977-79, pres. 1980-81). Republican. Baptist. Avocation: collecting miniatures. Office: U South Ala 257 Csab Mobile AL 36688-0001

PERRY, RALPH BARTON, III, lawyer; b. N.Y.C., Mar. 17, 1936; s. Ralph Barton Jr. and Harriet Armington (Seelye) P.; m. Mary Elizabeth Colburn, Sept. 2, 1961; children: Katherine Suzanne, Daniel Berenson. AB, Harvard U., 1958; LL.B., Stanford U., 1963. Bar: Calif. 1964. Assoc. and mem. Keatinge & Sterling, Los Angeles, 1963-68; mem. firm Graven Perry Block Brody & Qualls, Los Angeles, 1968—. Bd. dirs. Planning and Conservation League, 1968—, Coalition for Clean Air, 1961—, pres. 1972-80, 85-88. Served with U.S. Army, 1956-58. Mem. ABA (ho. of dels. 1975-95), State Bar Calif., LA County Bar Assn., Lawyers Club LA County (gov. 1968-82), Nat. and Internat. Wildlife Fedns., Sierra Club, LA Athletic Club Home: 296 Redwood Dr Pasadena CA 91105-1339 Office: Graven Perry 523 W 6th St Ste 723 Los Angeles CA 90014-1223 Office Phone: 213-680-9770. E-mail: rbp3@earthlink.net.

PERRY, RANDALL A. business executive; b. Furstenfeldbruk, Germany, Nov. 18, 1955; s. Norman Francis and Elfriede Dorothea (Wachter) P.; m. Donna A. Perry, Apr. 9, 1994; 1 child, Christopher; m. Helen A. Perry, Dec. 11, 1977 (div. Dec. 1992); children: Lea, David, Jonathan, Timothy. BSBA, Kennesaw U., 1981. Dir. reimbursement and legis. affairs Healthdyne, Inc., Marietta, Ga., 1983-85, Abbey Health Care, Inc., Fountain Valley, Calif., 1985-88; dir. reimbursement devel. Genentech, Inc., South San Francisco, Calif., 1988-93. Biotech. industry rep. Am. Legis. Exchange Coun., Washington, 1990-93; dir. customer devel. Janssen Pharm., Titusville, N.J., 1993-94; v.p. reimbursement Mckesson/HDS, Scottsdale, Ariz., 1994-96; v.p. bus. devel. Bergen Brunswig/ICS, Addison, Tex., 1996-99; prin. Med. Comm. Techs., Atlanta, 1999—. Author: Biopharmaceuticals in Transition, 1990. With USAF, 1973-75. Mem. Nat. Assn. of Med. Equipment Suppliers (bd. dirs. 1983-88), Health Industry Distributors Assn. (co-chmn. health care reform com. 1985-88), Biotech. Industry Orgn. (co-chmn. health care reform com. 1989-93), Republican. Avocations: skiing, mountain biking, rollerblading. Home: 234 Picketts Lake Dr Acworth GA 30101-4787

PERRY, RICHARD C. financier; b. 1955; m. Lisa Perry. BA, Wharton Sch. U. Pa., 1977; MBA, NYU. Equity trader Goldman, Sachs & Co., 1977—88; founder, chmn., CEO Perry Capital LLC, 1988—. Chmn. bd. FTD Corp.; dir. Radio & Records, Inc. Bd. trustees Facing History and Ourselves, Allen-Stevenson Sch., Milton Academy, Harlem Children's Zone; mem. Wharton Undergrad Exec. Bd. Office: Perry Capital LLC 599 Lexington Ave Fl 36 New York NY 10022-7649 Office Phone: 212-583-4000.*

PERRY, RICK, governor; b. Paint Creek, Tex., Mar. 4, 1950; m. Anita Thigpen; children: Griffin, Sydney. B.Animal Sci., A&M U., 1972. Farmer/rancher; mem. Tex. Ho. of Reps., 1985-90, mem. appropriations and calendars com.; commr. of agr. State of Tex., 1991-98, lt. gov., 1999-2000, gov., 2000—. Active Boy Scouts Am. Capt. USAF, 1972-77 Named One of the Most Effective Legislators, Dallas Morning News, 1989. Mem. Am. Legion. Republican. Methodist. Office: Office of Governor 1100 San Jacinto PO Box 12428 Austin TX 78711

PERRY, ROBERT (BOB PERRY), construction executive; CEO Perry Homes, Houston, 1997—. Office: Perry Homes PO Box 34306 Houston TX 77234-4306

PERRY, ROBERT MICHAEL, engineering company executive; b. N.Y.C., Dec. 5, 1931; s. Jerome and Rose P.; m. Frances Diane Gross, Feb. 2, 1957; children— Karen, David, Janice. BSE., U. Mich., 1953; postgrad., Columbia U., 1955-57. Engr. Dames & Moore (Cons. Engrs.), L.A., 1955-60, assoc., 1960-65, ptnr., 1965-75, mng. ptnr., 1975-79, CFO, 1980-96, dir., 1981-98, exec. v.p., 1992-99; chmn., CEO, pres. RMP Inc., Palos Verdes Estates, Calif., 1999—. Pres., dir. RMP Inc., 1972—; bd. dirs. Locus Techs., Trinity Cons., SWCA Inc. Served with C.E. U.S. Army, 1953-55. Mem., life, ASCE (dir., treas. N.Y. sect. 1964-68). Office: RMP Inc 2376 Via Victoria Palos Verdes Estates CA 90274

PERRY, RONALD, lawyer; b. Pitts., Feb. 20, 1952; s. Joseph E. and Margaret (Majhan) P.; m. Deborah Lauer, July 19, 1975; children: Meredith Lyn, Erin Michelle. BA in Polit. Sci., Ind. U., Pa., 1974; JD, Western New Eng. U., 1978; LLM in Taxation, Temple U., 1982. Bar: Pa. 1978, U.S. Dist. Ct. (mid. dist.) Pa. 1979, U.S. Tax Ct. 1980, U.S. Supreme Ct. 1984. Pvt. practice, York, Pa., 1978-82; ptnr. Carn, Vaughn & Perry, York, 1982-85, Countess, Gilbert, Andrews, York, 1985—. Asst. dist. atty., York County, 1982-85. Pres. Self-Help Counseling, York, 1978-84; bd. dirs. West York (Pa.) Sch. Dist., 1983-85, York County Jr. Achievement, 1998-2004, dir. White Rose Invitational track and Field Meet, 1998-2001; solicitor West York Zoning Bd., 1987-88; chmn. Manchester Twp. Planning Commn., 1992-98; pres. York County Literacy Coun., 1992-98; bd. dirs. Jr. Achievement York County. Mem. ABA, Pa. Bar Assn., York County Estate Planning Coun. (bd. dirs. 1986-91), Rotary Club. Avocation: music. Office: Countess Gilbert Andrews 29 N Duke St York PA 17401-1204 Office Phone: 717-848-4900.

PERRY, STEPHEN CLAYTON, manufacturing executive; b. Atlanta, Feb. 9, 1942; s. Clayton Henry and Elizabeth Hill (Staples) P.; m. Bonnie Janet Bentley, Nov. 27, 1965; 1 child, Beverly Elizabeth. B in Indsl. Engring., Ga. inst. Tech., 1964; MBA, Harvard U., 1968; PhD, George Washington U., 1998. Indsl. engr. Union Carbide Corp., Columbia, Tenn., 1964; sys. analyst metals and controls divsn. Tex. Instruments, Attleboro, Mass., 1967; with Exxon Corp., 1968-86; gen. mgr. Toledo Scale Corp. subs. Reliance Electric Co., Worthington, Ohio, 1984-89; pres. Toledo Scale Corp. (subs. Ciba-Giegy), 1989-90; pres., CEO Esco Hand Tools, Inc., 1990; instr. George Washington U., 1991-94, 99; pres. mfg. divsn. Leucadia, Inc., 1995-98; prof. Gardner-Webb U., 1999—2002, interim dean Sch. Bus., 2002, Dover Found. chair bus. adminstrn., 2002; instr. U. N.C., Charlotte, 2003; prof. fin. Wofford Coll., Spartanburg, SC, 2003—. Mem. engring. adv. bd. Ga. Tech., 1996-2001. Bd. dirs. Ctr. Sci. and Industry, Columbus, Ohio, 1984-89; mem. Berkeley Heights Twp. (N.J.) Com., 1977-79; dep. mayor, police commr., 1978, mayor, 1979; mem. Clemson U. Pres.'s Adv. Coun., 1990-93; dir., trustee Mars Hill Coll., 1997-99; adv. bd. Mars Hill Coll., 1999—. Home: 152 Lakemont Dr Shelby NC 28150-8326 E-mail: sct05323548@earthlink.net.

PERRY, TROY D. clergyman, religious organization administrator; divorced; 2 children; m. Phillip Ray De Blieck, July 16, 2003. Student, Midwest Bible Sch.; D in Ministry (hon.), Samaritan Coll., L.A.; D in Human Svcs., Sierra U., Santa Monica, Calif.; DDiv (hon.), Episcopal Div. Sch., Cambridge, Mass. Former pastor Ch. of God of Prophecy, Santa Ana, Calif.; founder, moderator Universal Fellowship Met. Cmty. Chs., L.A. Rep. Met. Community Chs. and gay and lesbian rights movement numerous TV shows including 60 Minutes, Phil Donahue, The Mike Douglas Show; author: The Lord is My Shepherd and Knows I'm Gay, Don't Be Afraid Anymore, 1991, (video) God, Gays and The Gospel: This is Our Story; contbg. editor Is Gay Good? Mem. Los Angeles County Commn. Human Rels.; del. 1st White House Conf. on AIDS, 1993; del. 1st White House Conf. on Hate Crimes, 1997; trustee Chgo. Theol. Sem., 2002—. Recipient Humanitarian award Gay Press Assn., Equality award Human Rights Campaign, 1996. Mem. Universal Fellowship Ch. Office: Universal Fellowship Met Comm Chs 8704 Santa Monica Blvd Fl 2 West Hollywood CA 90069-4548 Office Phone: 310-360-8640 ext. 211. E-mail: revtroyperry@mccchurch.org.

PERRY, WALTER LEO, information scientist, operations research specialist; m. Stella Claire Pepin, July 23, 1960; children: Stephanie Lynne Berlin, Geoffrey Scott, Jodie Lee VanDuren, Christopher Jerome, Kimberly Claire. AB in math. and econ., Northeastern U., 1958—63; MBA, Tulane U. Grad. Sch. of Bus., 1969—71; MS in ops. rsch., Tulane U. Sch. of Engring., 1969—71; PhD, George Mason U. Sch. of Info. Tech. and Engring., 1985—91. Sr. info. scientist RAND, Washington, 1984—; adj. prof. George Mason U., Fairfax, Va., 1984—99; adj. prof.lectr. George Wash. Grad. Sch. of Elec. Engring. and Computer Sci., 1992—; exch. scientist Centre for Defence Analysis, West Byfleet, England, 1994—96. Adj. prof., sch. of mgmt. George Mason U., Fairfax, Va., 1997; asst. prof. math. U.S. Mil. Acad., West Point, NY, 1978—81. Author: (book) Disjointed War: Military Operations in Kosovo, 1999, Exploring Information Superiority: A Methodology for Measuring the Quality of Information and its Impact on Shared Awareness, Measures of Effectiveness for the Information-Age Army, Disjointed War: Military Operations in Kosovo, 1999, Response to Warning: Decisionmaking on Strategic Force Readiness, Operational Control of Republic of Korea (ROK) and US Forces in Korea: Issues and Requirements, Measures of Effectiveness for the Information-Age Navy, Measures of Effectiveness for the Information-Age Army; contbr. articles to profl. jours. Lt. col. U.S. Army, 1964—84, US and Overseas. Recipient Knox award for Def. Acquisition, Dept. of Def., 1975. Mem.: Inst. of Elec. and Electronic Engineers (corr.), Math. Assn. of Am. (corr.), Mil. Ops. Rsch. Soc. (corr.), Armed Forces Comm. and Electronics Assn. (assoc.). Roman Catholic. Avocations: church choir, woodworking, antiquarian book collecting, amateur artist. Office: Rand 1200 South Hayes St Arlington VA 22202

PERRY, WILLIAM JAMES, education educator, former federal official; b. Vandergrift, Pa., Oct. 11, 1927; s. Edward Martin and Mabelle Estelle (Dunlap) Perry; m. Leonilla Green, Dec. 29, 1947; children: David, William, Rebecca, Robin, Mark. BS in Math., Stanford U., 1949, MS, 1950; PhD, Pa. State U., 1957. Instr. math. Pa. State U., 1951—54; sr. mathematician HRB-Singer Co., State College, Pa., 1952—54; dir. electronic def. labs. GTE Sylvania Co., Mountain View, Calif., 1954—64; founder & pres. ESL, Inc., Sunnyvale, Calif., 1964—77; tech. cons. Dept. Def., Washington, 1967—77, under sec. def. for research and engring., 1977—81; mng. dir. Hambrecht & Quist (investment bankers), San Francisco, 1981—85; chmn. Tech. Strategies & Alliances, Menlo Park, Calif., 1985—93; prof., co-dir. Ctr. for Internat. Security and Arms Control Stanford U., 1989—93; appt. Dep. Sec. Def. Pentagon, Washington, 1993—94, appt. Sec. Def., 1994—97; prof. engring.-econ. sys. and ops. rsch. Stanford (Calif.) U., 1997—, sr. fellow, Hoover Inst., 1997—, co-dir., Preventive Defense Project, 1997—; chmn. Global Tech. Ptnrs. With U.S. Army, 1946—47. Recipient Def. Disting. Svc. medal, U.S. Govt., 1980, 1981, Achievement medal, Am. Electronics Assn., 1980, Forrestal medal, 1994, Henry Stimson medal, 1994, Arthur Bueche medal, NAE, 1996, Eisenhower award, 1996, Presdl. Medal Freedom, 1997, Outstanding Civilian Svc. medals, U.S. Army, 1997, USN, 1997, USAF, 1997, USCG, 1997, NASA, 1981, Def. Intelligence Agy., 1997; fellow sr. fellow, Inst. Internat. Studies, Stanford U., 1997—. Mem.: bd. dirs., Anteon Internat. Corp. Office: Stanford University CISAC Encina Hall Stanford CA 94305 Fax: 650-725-0920. E-mail: wjperry@aol.com.

PERRY, WILLIAM JOSEPH, food processing company executive; b. Sacramento, Calif., Nov. 4, 1930; s. Joseph Nasciemeto and Jennie (Nunez) P.; m. Beverly Ann Styles, Dec. 9, 1956 (div. May 1981); children: Katherine, Bill Jr., Kathleen, Barbara; m. Leslie Z. Blumberg, June 30, 1986. BS, U. Calif., Berkeley, 1953; MBA, U. So. Calif., 1995. Quality control supr. Stokely Van Camp, Oakland, Calif., 1953-54; plant mgr. Safeway Stores, Brookside div., Grandview, Wash., 1954-61, Gallo Winery, Modesto, Calif., 1961-62; gen. mgr. Bocca Bella Olive Assoc., Wallace, Calif., 1962-65; v.p. Early Calif. Ind., L.A., 1965-74, Fairmont Foods, Santa Ana, Calif., 1974-75; pres. Cal Agra Ind., Stockton, Calif., 1975-76; exec. v.p. Food Brokers Internat., L.A., 1976—; pres., co-owner G.F.F., Inc., L.A., 1981—. Dir. G.F.F., Inc., L.A., 1981—, Food Brokers, Inc., L.A., 1976—, Cozad & Assoc. Ad Agy., Encino, Calif., 1985-87. Wrestling com., dir. protocol, L.A. Olympic Com., 1981-84; dir. Nat. Kidney Cancer Assn., 1999. Mem. Nat. Food Brokers Assn., Assn. of Dressings and Sauces, Product Mktg. Assn., Nat. Single Svc. Assn., Am. Chem. Soc., Calif. League Food Processors (dir. 1997), U. Calif. Alumni Assn., U. So. Calif. Alumni Assn., L.A. Athletic Club. Republican. Roman Catholic. Avocations: tennis, photography, bicycling, amateur sports associations. Home: 3700 Brigantine Cir Thousand Oaks CA 91361-3816 Office: 145 N Willow City Of Industry CA 91746-2118

PERRY-CAMP, JANE, music educator, pianist; b. Durham, N.C., Oct. 5, 1936; d. Harold Sanford and Margrid (Hagelberg) Perry; m. John Barton Camp, Aug. 20, 1960 (div. Sept. 1970); m. Harold Anthony Schiffman, June 10, 1978. AB magna cum laude, Duke U., 1958; MusM in Piano Performance, Fla. State U., Tallahassee, 1960, PhD in Music Theory, 1968; studied piano with, Edward Kilenyi, Ernst von Dohnanyi. Asst. prof. music Brevard C.C., Cocoa, Fla., 1968-69; faculty St. Petersburg (Fla.) Coll., 1969 73; asst. prof., assoc. prof. Sweet Briar (Va.) Coll., 1974-80; assoc. prof., prof. Sch. Music, Fla. State U., Tallahassee, 1980-96, prof. emeritus, 1996—, Orpheus chair musicology, 1999. Mem. adv. bd. Fla. State U., Music Theory Soc., Tallahassee, 1982-88; bd. dirs. Fla. State U. Friends of Libr., Tallahassee, 1985-87. Pianist: (CDs) Schiffman: Spectrum, My Ladye Jane's Booke: Eighteeen Fugues and Postludes for Piano, 1996, Concerto for Piano and Orchestra, 1999, (LPs) Fantasy for Piano, 1986, Chamber Concertino for Piano and Double Wind Quintet, 1987; contbr. articles to profl. jours. and anthologies. Fellow NEH, Paris, London, 1973-74; faculty fellow Sweet Briar Coll., 1979-80; recipient rsch. grants Fla. State U. Found., 1985-86, Internat. Rsch. and Exch. Bd., Krakow, Poland, 1986. Mem. Am. Soc. 18th Century Studies (pres. 1991-92), SE Am. Soc. 18th Century Studies (pres. 1987-88), Mozart Soc. Am. (bd. dirs. 1996-2001), Internat. Soc. Study of Time, Am. Musicol. Soc., Coll. Music Soc. Avocations: gardening, hiking, needlework (knitting, crocheting, sewing). Home: 2304 Don Andres Ave Tallahassee FL 32304-1313 E-mail: jperrycp@mailer.fsu.edu.

PERRYMAN, GERALD F., JR., retired career officer, defense company executive; BS, Tex. A&M U., 1970; grad., Squadron Officer Sch., 1973; MBA, U. N.D., 1979; disting. grad., Air Command and Staff Coll., 1984; grad., Nat. Def. U., 1989. Commd. 2d lt. USAF, 1970, advanced through grades to maj. gen., 1997; comdr. Minuteman intercont. ballistic missile combat crew Grand Forks AFB, N.D., 1977-80; exec. to chief of staff Hdqs. SAC, Offutt AFB, Nebr., 1982-83; missile staff officer strategic divsn. ops. directorate Hdqs. USAF, Washington, 1984-85, dep. mil. asst. to Sec. of Air Force, 1985-86; asst. dep. comdr. for ops. 90th Strategic Missile Wing, Frances E. Warren AFB, Wyo., 1986-88; chief nuclear and missile divsn., plans and policy director. Hdqs. U.S. European Command, Stuttgart, Germany, 1989-91; vice comdr. 341st Missile Wing, Malmstrom AFB, Mont., 1991-92; chief missile ops. divsn., ops. directorate Hdqs. Air Combat Command, Langley AFB, Va., 1992-93; comdr. 91st Missile Wing, Minot AFB, N.D., 1993-95, 21st Space Wing, Peterson AFB, Colo., 1995-96; dir. ops. Hdqs. Air Force Space Command, Peterson AFB, Colo., 1996-97; comdr. 14th Air Force, component comdr. USAF Space Ops., U.S. Space Command, Vandenberg AFB, Calif., 1997-99; comdr. Aerospace Command & Control and Intelligence Surveillance and Reconnaissance Ctr., Langley AFB, Va., 1999—2001; asst. dep. chief of staff, comm. and information Hdqs. US Air Force, Washington, 2001—01; lead exec., ISR Strategic Bus. Area Team Raytheon Co., McKinney, Tex., 2003—. Decorated Def. Superior Svc. medal, Legion of Merit with oak leaf cluster, Meritorious Svc. medal with 4 oak leaf clusters. Office: ISR Strategic Business Raytheon Company 2501 W University Dr Mc Kinney TX 75071*

PERRYMAN, LANCE, dean; DVM in Vet. Medicine, Washington State U., 1970; MS, Ohio State U., 1973; PhD in Vet. Sci., Washington State U., 1975. Dean Colo. State U., Coll. Vet. Medicine and Biomed. Scis., 2001—; asst. prof. Washington State U. Coll. Vet. Medicine, 1975—78, assoc. prof., 1978—84, assoc. dean for rsch. and grad. studies, 1989—94, dir. Animal Health Rsch. Ctr., 1989—94; head of dept., prof. dept. microbiology, pathology, and parasitology N.C. State U. Coll. Vet. Medicine, 1994—2001. Named Disting. Vet. Immunologist of Yr., Am. Assn. Vet. Immunologists, 1999. Mem.: AAAS, Colo. Vet. Med. Assn., Am. Vet. Medicine Assn., Am. Soc. for Microbiology, Am. Assn. Immunologists, Am. Coll. Vet. Pathologists. Office: Colo State U Coll Vet Medicine & Biomed Scis 1601 Campus Delivery Fort Collins CO 80523-1601

PERRY-WIDNEY, MARILYN (MARILYN PERRY), international finance and real estate executive, television producer; b. N.Y.C., Feb. 11, 1939; d. Henry William Patrick and Edna May (Bown) Perry; m. Charles Leonidas Widney (dec. Sept. 1981). BA, Mexico City Coll., 1957. Pres. Marilyn Perry TV Prodns., Inc., N.Y.C., 1970—, C.L. Widney Internat., Inc., N.Y.C., 1977—. Mng. dir. Donerail Corp., N.Y.C., 1980-88, Lancer, N.Y.C., 1980-88, Assawata, N.Y.C., 1980-88. Prodr., host TV program Internat. Byline, series of more than 100 documentaries on the UN; host 80 radio and 200 pages on Internet series regarding environ. and devel. issues; author: (reference book) Leaders of the World, 2003; contbr. pages on environ. and devel. issues to radio and Internet sites; internat. byline-mem. nations UN exec. com. HNCA, 1998, PBS, in S.C., N.C., Ga., Tenn. Bd. dirs. UN After Sch. Program; ambassadorial candidate Pres. Bush., 1989. Recipient U.S. Indsl. Film Festival award, CINE Golden Eagle award, Bronze medal Internat. Film & TV Festival of N.Am., Bronzenen Urkinde, Berlin, award for superior quality Intercom-Chgo. Internat. Film Festival, Knights of Malta Trophy award for superior programming from Min. of Tourism, Internationales Tourismus award Film festival, Vienna, Manhattan Cable Ten Year award for continuous programming, citations from former pres. Ford and Carter, King Hussein Jordan, Pres. Clinton, pres. Maumoon Gayoon, Maldives, pres. Jacques Chirac, France. Mem. UN Corrs. Assn., UN After Sch. Programs, Rep. Presdl. Task Force (charter, journalist). Avocations: music, travel, antiques. Home: 211 E 70th St Apt 3A New York NY 10021-5206

PERSAUD, ANDREA NANDINI, dermatologist; b. Berbice, Guyana, July 11, 1969;, US, 1975; d. Roy Bhagwat and Sheila Persaud. BA, CUNY-Queens Coll., 1990; MD, Mt. Sinai Sch. Medicine, 1996. Lic. NY State. Med. intern NYU Med. Ctr./Bellevue Hosp., NYC, 1996—97; dermatopharmacology fellow NYU, Dept. Dermatology, NYC, 1997—99, Mt. Sinai Sch. Medicine, Dept. Dermatology, NYC, 1999—2001, dermatology resident, 2001—04; dermatologist Sadick Aesthetic Surgery & Dermatology, N.Y.C., 2004—. Spkr. in field. Contbr. articles to jour., chapters to books; reviewer (journ.) Am. Jour. Clinical Dermatology (JAAD), 2004. Mem.: Nat. Psoriasis Found., Am. Acad. Dermatology. Achievements include research in using imiquimod 5% cream for actinic keratosis that helped enabled imiquimod to be approved by FDA to treat actinic keratosis. Office Phone: 212-772-7242.

PERSAUD, TRIVEDI VIDHYA NANDAN, anatomy educator, researcher, consultant; b. Port Mourant, Berbice, Guyana, Feb. 19, 1940; arrived in Canada, 1972; s. Ram Nandan and Deen (Raggy) P.; m. Gisela Gerda Zehden, Jan. 29, 1966; children: Indrani Uta and Sunita Heidi (twins), Rainer Narendra. MD, Rostock U., Germany, 1965, DSc, 1974; PhD in Anatomy, U. West Indies, Kingston, Jamaica, 1970. Intern, Berlin, Germany, 1965-66; govtl. med. officer, 1966-67; lectr., sr. lectr. anatomy dept. U. West Indies, 1967-72; assoc. prof. anatomy dept. U. Man., Winnipeg, 1972-75, prof., 1975—, prof. ob-gyn., reproductive scis., 1979-99, prof. emeritus, 1999—, prof. pediatrics and child health, 1989—, prof., chmn./head dept. human

anatomy & cell sci., 1977-93, dir. Teratology Rsch. Lab., 1972-97. Cons. in teratology, Children's Centre, Winnipeg, 1973—; mem. sci. staff Health Scis. Centre, Winnipeg, 1973—. Author, editor 22 med. textbooks, including: Early History of Human Anatomy: From Antiquity to the Beginning of the Modern Era, 1984, (with others) Basic Concepts in Teratology, 1985, Environmental Causes of Human Birth Defects, 1991, History of Human Anatomy: The Post-Vesalian Era, 1997, (with K.L. Moore) The Developing Human, 7th edit., 2003, Before We Are Born, 6th edit., 2003; rev. Medical Embryology, 6th edit., 2003; contbr. numerous chpts. to books, over 200 articles to profl. jours. Recipient Carveth Jr. Scientist award Can. Assn. Pathologists, 1974, Albert Einstein Centennial medal German Acad. Scis., 1975, Dr. & Mrs. H.H. Saunderson award U. Manitoba, 1985, 12th Raymond Truex Disting. Lectureship award Hahnemann U., 1990, Queen Elizabeth II Golden Jubilee medal Govt. Can., 2003. Fellow Royal Coll. Pathologists of London; mem. Can. Assn. Anatomists (pres. 1981-83, J.C.B. Grant award 1991), Am. Assn. Anatomists, Teratology Soc., European Teratology Soc. Office: U Man Dept Anatomy & Cell Sci 730 William Ave Winnipeg MB Canada R3E OW3 Office Phone: 204-789-3333. Business E-Mail: persaud@ms.umanitoba.ca.

PERSAVICH, WARREN DALE, diversified manufacturing company executive; b. Cleve., Dec. 15, 1952; s. Nick and Sophie (Makris) P.; m. Anita Geraldine Zeleznik, Oct. 12, 1974; children: Nicholas, Katherine. BBA, Kent State U., 1975. CPA, Ohio. Staff acct. Price Water House, Cleve., 1975-76; asst. contr. Banner Industries Inc., Cleve., 1976-79, contr., 1979-86, treas., 1986-88, v.p., treas., 1988-90; sr. v.p., chief fin. officer Banner Aerospace Inc., 1990-98, sr. v.p., chief oper. officer, 1998-99; pres. Banner Aerospace Distbn. Group, 2000—. Mem. AICPA, Ohio Soc. CPAs. Republican. Office: Banner Aerospace Inc 45025 Aviation Dr Ste 400 Dulles VA 20166-7514

PERSCHBACHER, PETER WESLEY, environmental scientist, educator; b. Davenport, Iowa, Nov. 15, 1946; s. Wesley Adolph and Margaret Pohly P.; m. Virginia Brady, Feb. 14, 1986. BS, U. Mich., 1968; MS, Auburn U., 1975; PhD, Tex. A&M U., 1985. Rsch. assoc. U. N.C. Inst. Marine Sci., Morehead City, N.C., 1975-79; grad. rsch. asst. Tex. A&M U., Baytown, 1980-85; Aquaculture Trainer-Peace Corps Rsch. Planning Inst., Ft. Pierce, Fla., 1983; aquaculture biologist Caribbean Marine Rsch. Ctr., Lee Stocking Island, Bahamas, 1985; aquaculture advisor Harza Engring. Internat., Mymensingh, Bangladesh, 1986-87; rsch. biologist Agrl. Rsch. Svc., USDA, Tishomingo, Okla., 1989-93; assoc. prof. U. Ark., Pine Bluff, 1993—. Cons. KTAADIN, Newton, Mass., Norwegian Govt., Trondheim, Norway. Author: Recirculation-Aeration Bibliography for Aquaculture, 1993; editor, contbg. author: Small Scale Aquaculture, 2003; contbg. author: Third National Reservoir Symposium, 1997, Am. Chem. Soc. symposium in Agr., 2002, Third World Fisheries Congress, Beijing, 2000; contbr. article to N.Am. Jour. Aquaculture (named to top ten papers of 1998), others. Chair Clean and Beautiful Commn. Bd., Pine Bluff, 2000; mem. Racial Harmony Task Force, Pine Bluff, 1996—98; organizer and co-chair Environ. Fair Grace Episcopal Ch., Pine Bluff, 1997, 1999, 2001, 2003; organizer and chair Waste Mgmt. and Splty. Animal Prodn. Workshops, U. Ark., 1999, Sustainable Aquaculture Session World Aquaculture Soc., Tampa, Fla., 1999; chair Rural Life Conf., U. Ark., 2003, small-scale Aquaculture Spl. Session World Aquaculture Soc., San Diego, 2002. Grantee Mgmt. of Environmentally-Derived Off-Flavors in Warmwater, USDA, Stoneville, Miss., 1995-2000, USDA-CSRS, 1999-2004. Mem. Am. Fisheries Soc., Am. Inst. Fisheries Rsch. Biologists, World Aquaculture Soc., Asian Fisheries Soc., Sigma Xi, Xi Sigma Pi. Democrat. Episcopalian. Avocations: native orchids, palms. Office: Univ Ark at Pine Bluff Mail Slot 4912 Pine Bluff AR 71601 E-mail: pperschbacher@uaex.edu.

PERSCHBACHER, REX ROBERT, dean, law educator; b. Chgo., Aug. 31, 1946; s. Robert Ray and Nancy Ellen (Beach) P.; children: Julie Ann, Nancy Beatrice. AB in Philosophy, Stanford U., 1968; JD, U. Calif., Berkeley, 1972. Bar: Calif. 1972, U.S. Dist. Ct. (no. dist.) Calif. 1973, U.S. Dist. Ct. (so. dist.) Calif. 1979, U.S. Ct. Appeals (9th cir.) 1980, U.S. Dist. ct. (ea. dist.) Calif. 1985. Law clk. to judge U.S. Dist. Ct. (no. dist.) Calif., San Francisco, 1973-74; asst. prof. law U. Tex., Austin, 1974-75; assoc. Heller, Ehrman, White & McAuliffe, San Francisco, 1975-78; asst. prof. law U. San Diego, 1978-79, assoc. prof. law, 1980-81; mem. faculty Inst. on Internat. and Comparative Law, London, 1984—; acting prof. law U. Calif., Davis, 1981-85, prof., 1988—, assoc. dean, 1993-98, dean Law Sch., 1998—. Dir. clin. edn. Univ. Calif., Davis, 1981-93, acad. senate, law sch. rep., 1989-91; vis. prof. law Univ. Santa Clara (Calif.), summer 1986. Co-author: California Civil Procedure and Practice, 1996, California Legal Ethics, 2nd edit., 1997, Problems in Legal Ethics, 4th edit., 1997, Cases and Materials on Civil Procedure, 3d edit., 1998; contbr. articles to legal jours. Bd. dirs. Legal Svcs. of No. Calif., 1990-96. Mem. ABA, Calif. Bar Assn., Am. Assn. Law Schs., Inn of Ct. Democrat. Avocation: travel. Office: UC Davis Sch Law Dean Office 400 Mrak Hall Dr Davis CA 95616

PERSCHE, HENRY-PETER, art consultant, artist; b. Bklyn., Nov. 21, 1940; s. Henry-Peter and Marie (Gramegna) P. BFA, U. Buffalo, 1973, postgrad., 1973-74, Coll. St. Rose, 1993-94. Installation dir. for artist Ellsworth Kelly, Spencertown, N.Y., 1966-93; archivist, asst., 1966-93. Installation cons. for artist Ellsworth Kelly exhins. at Sidney Janis Gallery, Loe Castelli gallery, Blum/Helman gallery, N.Y.C., 1996-93, Mus. Modern Art, N.Y.C., 1973, Mus. Nat. d'Art Moderne, Paris, 1980, Stedelijk Mus., Amsterdam, 1979, Kunsthalle, Baden Baden, Germany, 1979, Mus. Nat. d'Art Moderne, Paris, 1980. Exhibited in group shows Albany (N.Y.) Inst. Art, 1973, Albright-Knox Art Gallery, Buffalo, N.Y., 1973. Poll inspector Dem. Party, Ghent, N.Y., 1994-95. With fin. corps. U.S. Army, 1963-66. Mem. Mus. Modern Art (N.Y.C.), Met. Mus. Art, Guggenheim Mus., Whitney Mus. Am. Art, Gottschee Heritage Assn., Gottscheer Relief Assn. Democrat. Roman Catholic. Avocations: collecting art publications, stamps, and photographs, travel, music. Home: 127 Oak St Hawley PA 18428-1039

PERSELL, CAROLINE HODGES, sociologist, educator, author, researcher, consultant; b. Ft. Wayne, Ind., Jan. 16, 1941; d. Albert Randolph and Katherine (Rogers) Hodges; m. Charles Bowen Persell III, June 17, 1967; children: Patricia Emily, Stephen David. BA, Swarthmore Coll., 1962; MA, Columbia U., 1967, PhD, 1971. Sr. assoc., then nat. coord. Nat. Scholarship Svc. and Fund for Negro Students, N.Y.C., 1962-66; project dir. Bur. Applied Social Rsch., N.Y.C., 1968-71; asst. prof. NYU, 1971-76, assoc. prof., 1976-86, prof., 1986—, dir. grad. studies dept. sociology, 1984-87, chair dept. sociology, 1987-93, Robin Williams Disting. lectr., 1993-94. Author: Education and Inequality, 1977, Understanding Society, 1984, 3d edit., 1990; author: (with Cookson) Preparing for Power, 1985, Making Sense of Society, 1992; author: (with Maisel) How Sampling Works, 1996; assoc. editor: Tchg. Sociology, 1983—85, Sociology of Edn., 1991—95, Gender & Society, 1992—95; contbr. articles to profl. jours. Carnegie scholar Advancement of Tchg., 2000-01; grantee Fund for Improvement of Postsecondary Edn., 1989-92, NSF Equipment Fund, 1993-96; recipient Faculty Devel. award NSF, 1978-79, Women Educators' Rsch. award, 1978. Mem.: Sociologists for Women in Soc., Ea. Sociol. Soc. (pres. 1995—96), Am. Ednl. Rsch. Assn., Am. Sociol. Assn. (chair sect. 1983—84, chmn. publs. com. 1987—89, chair sect. 1988—89, v.p. 2004—). Avocations: violin, gardening, opera, sports. Office: NYU Dept Sociology 269 Mercer St New York NY 10003-6633 Office Phone: 212-998-8350. E-mail: chp1@nyu.edu.

PERSELLIN, ROBERT HAROLD, physician; b. Fargo, N.D., July 3, 1930; s. James Harry and Bessie (Hoffman) P.; m. Bonnie Feibleman, June 27, 1957 (dec. 1983); children: Kathleen, Jamie; m. Diane Cummings, June 14, 1986 BS, Northwestern U., 1952, MD, 1956, MS, 1959. Diplomate: Am. Bd. Internal Medicine, Am. Bd. Rheumatology. Intern Charity Hosp., New Orleans, 1956-57; resident in internal medicine Northwestern U. Med. Center, 1957-60; fellow in rheumatology Southwestern Med. Sch., 1962-64; asst. prof. medicine U. Oreg. Med. Sch., 1964-68; prof. medicine, head div. rheumatology U. Tex. Health Sci. Ctr., San Antonio, 1968—81, prof. family practice, 1993—2003. Cons. rheumatology VA Hosps., U.S. Army, Internat. Med. Corps, Kosovo and Republic of Moldova; vis. prof. rheumatology Kingstown Med. Coll.; vis. scholar Corpus Christi Coll., Cambridge U., 1979-80; vis. scientist Strangeways Rsch. Lab., Cambridge. Contbr chpts. to books, articles to profl. jours. Bd. dirs. San Antonio Chamber Music Soc., 1970-75, 80-96, pres., 1983-85; bd. dirs. Friends of Strings, 1972-75, San Antonio Bot. Soc., 1985-87; Dem. precinct committeeman Washington County, Oreg., 1966-68. Served to capt. M.C. U.S. Army, 1960-62. Fellow ACP, Am. Coll. Rheumatology (exec. com. mem.); mem. Arthritis Found. (chmn. med. and sci. com. South Ctrl. Tex. chpt.), Heberden Soc., Am. Fedn. Clin. Rsch., So. Soc. Clin. Investigation, Tex. Rheumatism Assn. (pres.), Nat. Soc. Clin. Rheumatology, Mex. Rheumatology Soc. (hon.). Office: 635 E Olmos Dr San Antonio TX 78212-2504

PERSHAN, RICHARD HENRY, lawyer; b. N.Y.C., Jan. 4, 1930; s. Benjamin and Sadie (Aronowsky) P.; m. Kathryn Schaefler, June 11, 1952; children: Lee S., Richard H. Jr., Pamela P. Hochman, Julia B. BA, Yale U., 1951, LLB, 1956. Bar: N.Y. 1956, U.S. Supreme Ct.1969. Assoc. Davis, Polk & Wardwell, N.Y.C., 1956-60; ptnr. Finch & Schaefler, N.Y.C., 1960-85, LeBoeuf, Lamb, Greene & MacRae, N.Y.C., 1986-94, of counsel, 1995—. Counsel Mcpl. Art Soc., N.Y.C., 1965-70, Fine Arts Fedn., N.Y.C., 1975-80. Served to 1st lt. USAF. Fellow Am. Coll. Trust and Estate Counsel (author, editor, articles and studies 1960—); mem. Assn. of Bar of City of N.Y., Yale Club (N.Y.C.), N.Y. Croquet Club. Democrat. Avocations: croquet, weightlifting. Home: 1435 Lexington Ave New York NY 10128-1625 Office: LeBoeuf Lamb Greene & MacRae 125 W 55th St New York NY 10019-5389 Office Phone: 212-424-8523. E-mail: rpershan@yahoo.com., rpershan@llgm.com.

PERSHING, DAVID WALTER, chemical engineering educator, researcher; b. Anderson, Ind., Oct. 2, 1948; s. Walter L. and Treva B. (Crane) P.; m. Lynn Marie Kennard, Apr. 9, 1977; 1 child, Nicole. BSChemE, Purdue U., 1970; PhDChemE, U. Ariz., 1976. Rsch. asst. Exxon Prodn. Rsch., Houston, 1969; project engr. EPA, 1970-73; asst. prof. chem. engring. U. Utah, Salt Lake City, 1977-82, assoc. prof., 1982-85, prof., 1985—, assoc. dean Grad. Sch., 1983-87, dean Coll. Engring., 1987-98, v.p., 1998-99, sr. v.p. acad. affairs, 2000—; asst. to pres. Reaction Engring. Inc., Salt Lake City, 1990—. Vis. scientist Internat. Flame Rsch. Found., Ijmuiden, The Netherlands, 1972-73; vis. assoc. prof. chem. engring. U. Ariz., Tuscon, 1976-77; cons. Energy and Environ. Rsch. Ctr., Irvine, Calif., 1974-90, Acurex Corp., Mountain View, Calif., 1974-79, Kennecott Corp., Salt Lake City, 1979-81, Nat. Bur. Standards, Washington, 1976-78, Geneva Steel, 1989-95; assoc. dir. Engring. Rsch. Ctr., NSF, 1986-97. Contbr. articles to profl. publs.; patentee in field. Maj. USPHS, 1970-73. Recipient Disting. Teaching award U. Utah, 1982, Disting. Rsch. award U. Utah, 1990; grantee NSF, PYI, 1984-90. Mem. Am. Inst. Chem. Engrs., Combustion Inst. Methodist. Office: U Utah Coll Engring 201 Presidents Cir Rm 205 Salt Lake City UT 84112-9007 Office Phone: 801-581-5057. Business E-Mail: david.pershing@utah.edu.

PERSHING, ROBERT GEORGE, telecommunications company executive; b. Battle Creek, Mich., Aug. 10, 1941; s. James Arthur and Beulah Francis P.; m. Diana Kay Prill, Sept. 16, 1961 (div. Jan. 1989); children: Carolyn, Robert; m. Charlene Jean Reed Wallis, Mar. 18, 1989 (div. Dec. 1995). BSEE, Tri-State Coll., 1961. Comm. engr. Am. Elec. Power, Ind., N.Y. and Ohio, 1961-69; design supr. Wescom, Inc., Ill., 1969-74; dir. engring. Tellabs, Inc., Lisle, Ill., 1974-78; pres., CEO Teltrend, Inc., St. Charles, Ill., 1979-89, chmn. bd., 1979-88; CEO DKP Prodns., Inc., St. Charles, Ill., 1986-89; exec. cons. Teltrend, St. Charles, Ill., 1979-93; asst. treas. Magnekopy, inc., Villa Park, Ill. Bd. dirs. TI Investors, Inc.; advisor entrepreneurial studies U. Ill.; engring. cons. Recipient Chgo. Area Small Bus. award, 1986., INC 500 awards, 1987, 88. Mem. IEEE. Office: PO Box 3377 Show Low AZ 85902 Office Phone: 928-537-8952. E-mail: rpershing@frontiernet.net.

PERSINGER, DEL LOUIS, pharmaceutical company executive; b. Whiting, Iowa, Aug. 2, 1949; s. Ardell L. and Doris L. Persinger; m. Mary L. Tabor, Sept. 16, 1984; children: Christopher, Benjamin Hammerschlag, Sarah Hammerschlag. BSChemE with distinction, Iowa State U., 1971, MS in Journalism and Mass. Comm., 1975; MBA in Fin., Am. U., 1990. Refinery process engr. Exxon Co., Baton Rouge, 1971-73; environtl. and pub. affairs mgr. Am. Petroleum Inst., Washington, 1975-89, sr. assoc. refining, 1989-92, dep. dir. mfg., distbn. and mktg., 1992-94, dir. mgmt. and budget, 1994-96; v.p. fin. ops. Pharm. Rsch. and Mfrs. of Am., Washington, 1996—; pres., CEO PhRMA Found., Washington, 1999—. Bd. trustees, past pres. Bethesda Jewish Congregation, 1992—. Mem. Fin. Execs. Inst., Am. Soc. of Assn. Execs., Am. Found. for Pharm. Edn. (bd. dirs. 1999—), Phi Kappa Phi, Tau Beta Pi, Omega Chi Epsilon. Office: Pharm Rsch and Mfrs of Am 1100 15th St NW Ste 900 Washington DC 20005-1763

PERSOFF, NEHEMIAH, actor, artist; b. Jerusalem, Aug. 2, 1919; came to U.S., 1929; s. Samuel and Puah (Holman) P.; m. Thia Persov; children: Jeffrey Jonathan, Dan Deckel, Perry Erez, Dahlia. Student, Hebrew Tech. Inst., N.Y.C., 1934-37. Ind. stage, screen and TV actor, 1945—. Actor: (Broadway prodns.) Sundown Beach, Galileo, Richard the 3d, King Lear, Peer Gynt, Peter Pan, Reclining Figure, Flahooly, Montserrat, Tiger at the Gate, Only in America, (local, regional prodns.) Fiddler on the Roof, Man of La Mancha, Oliver, I'm Not Rappaport, 1988, Death of a Salesman (Stratford, Ont.), Two, Drinking America, Rosebloom, Dybbuk (Best Actor L.A. Critics 1975), Glass Menagerie (Israeli prodn.), Volpone, Of Mice and Men, (films) In Search of the Real Jesus, The Harder They Fall, The Wrong Man, This Angry Age, Men in War, Some Like It Hot, Al Capone, Green Mansions, The Commancheros, The Greatest Story Ever Told, Voyage of the Damned, Yentl, The Hook, The Last Temptation of Christ, Twins, numerous TV shows including For Whom the Bell Tolls (Sylvania award for best supporting actor 1958), The Big Knife, Alfred Hitchcock Presents, Rawhide, Twilight Zone, The Untouchables, The Wild, Wild West, I Spy, Gunsmoke, Police Story, Columbo, Barney Miller, Six Million Dollar Man, Delta House, Littlest Hobo, Magnum P.I., Hotel, Adderly; (TV miniseries) The French Atlantic; (one-man show) Aleichem Sholem-Sholem-Alecheim, 1971 (L.A. Critics award, San Francisco Critics Circle award 1979); paintings exhibited at George Krevsky Fine Arts, San Francisco, Seago Gallery, Cambria, Calif. With U.S. Army, 1942—45. Jewish. E-mail: thiap@thegrid.net.

PERSON, ANDREA MEREDITH, application developer; b. Phoenix, Ariz., Feb. 2, 1974; d. Ted Wilmer and Sheryl Elizabeth Person. BA in english, U. Md., Adelphi, 2000—02. Tech. support rep. MRIS, Rockville, Md., 2000—. Missionary LDS Ch., Los Angeles, Calif., 1996—97. Scholar Dean's Scholarship, U. Md., 2001, 2002. Mem.: Phi Kappa Phi, Sigma Tau Delta, Alpha Sigma Lambda, Phi Theta Kappa. Liberal. Mormon. Avocations: snorkeling, travel, swimming, singing, writing. Personal E-mail: andiperson@hotmail.com.

PERSON, CURTIS S., JR., state legislator, lawyer; b. Nov. 27, 1934; married; 6 children. BS, Memphis State U., 1956; LLB, U. Miss., 1959. Chief legal officer Juvenile Ct. Memphis and Shelby County; former mem. Tenn. Ho. Reps.; mem. Tenn. Senate, 1968—, Senate Rep. whip, 1973-76, minority caucus chmn., 1976-82. Chmn. Senate Judiciary com. 95th-103d Gen. Assemblies. Pres. Memphis-Shelby County Mental Health Assn., 1969-73, Handicapped Inc., 1972-74; chmn. Memphis Commn. Drug Abuse, 1970-71; charter pres. Memphis State Tiger Rebounders; past trustee Memphis State U.; exec. committeeman St. Jude's Memphis Open Golf Classic; co-chmn. Shelby County Legis. Del., 1973-74, vice chmn., 1970, 75, 76, 85-88; chmn. Shelby Rep. Del., 1977, 83-84; mem. adv. bd. Jr. League Memphis, 1995-98; vice chmn. Select Com. Children and Youth, 1997-2002, ex officio Senate Mem., Juvenile Justice Reform Commn., 1998. Named Memphis and Tenn. Outstanding Young Man of Yr., Jaycees, 1969, Outstanding Legis. of Yr., Govt. Leader Against Drunk Driving, Tenn. MADD, 1988, Legis. of Yr., Tenn. Alcohol and Drug Assn., 1988, Legislator of Yr. Tenn. Juvenile Svcs. Yr., 2001; recipient Liberty Bell Freedom award Memphis/Shelby County Bar Assn., 1969, Tenn. Adv. of Yr. Handicapped Children, 1978, Outstanding Svc. Children award Tenn Coun. Juvenile Ct. Judges, 1981, Pres.' Svc. award Tenn. Juvenile Ct. Svcs. Assn., 1981, Americanism award Memphis Civitan Club, 1986, Disting. Svc. award County Ofcls. Assn. Tenn., 1989, Cmty. Svc. award Tenn. Med. Assn., 1989, Eagle award Eagle Forum, 1994, Bill Bates Legis. award United Tenn. League, 1994, Champion for Children award Tenn. Assn. Child Care, 1995, Outstanding Legis. award County Ofcls. Assn. Tenn., 1996, Tenn. Juvenile Svcs. Assn. Pres. Svc. award, 1997, Tenn. Trial Lawyers Assn. Legis. of Yr. award, 1997, Shelby County Rep. Party Chmn. of Yr. award, 1999, Am. Lung Assn. Tenn. Legis. of Yr. award, 1999, Tenn. Task Force Against Domestic Violence Outstanding Legis. of Yr. award, 1999, Tenn. Dispensing Opticians Assn. Legis. of Yr. award, 2000, award Tenn. Juvenile Ct. Svcs. Assn., 2001, Spl. Honor Elvis Presley Meml. Martial Arts Hall of Fame, 2002, Lifetime Achievement award Defenders of Freedom, 2002, Animal Advocacy award Metro Animal Svcs., 2002, Legislator of Yr. award Tenn. Trial Lawyers Assn., 2003; named Legislator of Yr. Tenn. Devel. Dists., 2003, Hon. Fellow and Legislature of Yr., Opticians Assn. Am., 2003. Office: War Meml Bldg Rm 308 Nashville TN 37243 Office Phone: 615-741-2419. E-mail: sen.curtis.person@legislature.state.tn.us.

PERSON, EVERT BERTIL, newspaper and radio executive; b. Berkeley, Calif., Apr. 6, 1914; s. Emil P. and Elida (Swanson) P.; m. Ruth Finley, Jan. 26, 1944 (dec. May 1985); m. 2d, Norma Joan Betz, Mar. 12, 1986. Student, U. Calif., Berkeley, 1937; LHD, Calif. State Univs., 1983, Sonoma State U., 1993. Co-publisher, sec.-treas. Press Democrat Pub. Co., Santa Rosa, Calif., 1945-72, editor, 1972-73, pres., pub., editor-in-chief, 1973-85; sec.-treas. Finley Broadcasting Co., Santa Rosa, 1945-72, pres., 1972-89, Kawana Pubs., 1975-85; pub. Healdsburg Tribune, 1975-85; prin. Evert B. Person Investments, Santa Rosa, 1985—. Pres. Person Properties Co., Santa Rosa, 1945-70; v.p. Finley Ranch & Land Co., Santa Rosa, 1947-72, pres., 1972-79; pres. Baker Pub. Co., Oreg., 1957-67, Sebastopol (Calif.) Times, 1978-81, Russian River News, Guerneville, Calif., 1978-81; pres. publ. Kawana Pubs., 1978-85; mem. nominating com. AP, 1982-84, mem. auditing com., 1984-85 Bd. dirs Empire Coll., Santa Rosa, 1972-98, Sonoma County Taxpayers Assn., 1966-69, San Francisco Spring Opera Assn., 1974-79; bd. dirs. San Francisco Opera, 1986-95, v.p., 1988-95; pres. Calif. Newspaperboy Found., 1957-58; chmn. Santa Rosa Civic Arts Comm., 1961-62; pres. Santa Rosa Sonoma County Symphony Assn., 1966-68, Luther Burbank Meml. Found., 1979, Santa Rosa Symphony Found., 1967-77; adv. bd. Santa Rosa Salvation Army, 1959-67; commodore 12th Coast Guard Dist. Aux., 1969-70; trustee Desert Mus., Palm Springs, 1987-92, v.p. Nat. Bd. Canine Companions, Inc., 1989-92. Decorated Knight of the Holy Sepulchre. Mem. Calif. Newspaper Pubs. Assn. (pres. 1981-82), Internat. Newspaper Fin. Execs. (pres. 1961-62), Bohemian Club, Sonoma County Press Club, Santa Rosa Golf and Country club, The Springs Club, Santa Rosa Rotary (past pres.), Masons (33 degree, Legion of Merit), Shriners. Roman Catholic. Home: 775 White Oak Dr Santa Rosa CA 95409-6155 Office: The Oaks 1400 N Dutton Ave Ste 12 Santa Rosa CA 95401-4644

PERSON, PHILIP, biomedical consultant, biochemist, dentist; b. N.Y.C., Aug. 6, 1919; s. Barney and Lena (Spindel) P.; m. Bertha Paula Kaufman, Mar. 14, 1953; children: Sarah, Naomi, Matthew. BS, CUNY, 1940; DDS, NYU, 1946; MS, Rutgers U., 1951, PhD, 1952. Lic. dentist. Chief dental research lab. VA Med. Ctr., Bklyn., 1954-86; vis. prof. biochemistry Boston U. Sch. Grad. Dentistry, 1964-74; sr. vis. investigator systematics-ecology Marine Biol. Lab., Woods Hole, Mass., 1966-72; spl. research fellow (NIH) Inst. for Muscle Research, Woods Hole, 1967-68; adj. prof. oral biology Columbia U. Sch. Dental and Oral Surgery, N.Y.C., 1969-73; adj. prof. biochemistry and periodontics NYU Coll. Dentistry, N.Y.C., 1977—; dir. oral health studies Research Testing Labs., Little Neck, N.Y., 1986—; biomed. cons. Little Neck, 1986—. Mem. NIH Dental Study Sect., Bethesda, Md., 1963-66; cons. NIDR, NIAMD (NIH), Bethesda, 1963-80, Radiation and Solid State Lab., NYU, N.Y.C., 1965-68, dental health, marine biology WHO, Geneva, 1967-68, Coun. on Dental Therapeutics, ADA, Chgo., 1984-89. Editor: Metabolism of Oral Tissues, 1962, Biology of the Mouth, 1968. Investigator Biocore, Mission of Apollo 17, NASA, Ames Research Ctr., Moffet Field, Calif., 1973. Capt. USAR, 1952-54. Fellow AAAS, Am. Inst. Chemists, N.Y. Acad. Sci., The Harvey Soc. Office: 13787 75th Rd Flushing NY 11367-2815

PERSON, ROBERT JOHN, financial management consultant; b. Mpls., Mar. 7, 1927; s. Otto Carl and Alice Kathryn (Kasper) P.; m. Jeanette Haines, Mar. 11, 1948; 1 dau., Julie Ann. BBA, U. Minn., 1947; MS, Columbia u., 1953. Financial analyst Equitable Life Assurance Soc. U.S., N.Y.C., 1947-53; asst. v.p. bus. devel. met. banking dept. Bankers Trust Co., N.Y.C., 1953-64; v.p. bus. devel. div. Union Bank, Los Angeles, 1964-67; v.p., dir. mktg. Bank of Calif., San Francisco, 1967-70; sr. v.p. Central Nat. Bank of Chgo., 1970-72, 1st v.p., 1973-76, Central Nat. Chgo. Corp., 1973-76; v.p., regional mgr. Lester B. Knight & Assos., Inc., San Francisco, 1976-77; dir. bank cons. Coopers & Lybrand, San Francisco, 1977-80, partner-in-charge, nat. dir. bank cons. Chgo., 1980-89; exec. v.p. RJP Assocs., Inc., Stockton, Calif., 1989-92. Instr. salesmanship sch. pub. relations N.Y. Bankers Assn., 1960-63; instr. mktg. research Stonier Grad. Sch. Banking, Rutgers U., 1964-65, 73, 75-77, Brown U., 1964; instr. Agrl. Lending Sch., Ill. Bankers Assn., 1973-76, Nat. Comml. Lending Sch., Am. Bankers Assn., 1973-76, Sch. Bank Adminstrn., U. Wis., 1982-85, Nat. Grad. Trust Sch., Northwestern U., 1982-84, Southwestern Grad. Sch. Banking, 1983-84; Vice chmn. mgmt. effectiveness com. Community Fund Chgo. Treas. Sch. Bd., Huntington, N.Y., 1957-59; Bd. dirs. Am. Cancer Soc., Chgo.; chief crusader Crusade of Mercy. Served to lt. comdr. USNR, 1944-46, ret. Recipient Florence McNeil Stanley award Columbia, 1953 Mem. Am. Bankers Assn., Bank Mktg. Assn., Am. Mgmt. Assn. (mktg. planning council), Mgmt. Centre-Europe (fin. mgmt. adv. com. 1971—), Sales and Mktg. Execs. Internat., Stockton Symphony Assn. (bd. dirs. 1989-92), Beta Gamma Sigma. Clubs: Eastward Ho (Cape Cod); Stockton Golf and Country (Calif.). Lodges: Elks. Republican. Presbyterian. Home: 14406 W Trading Post Dr Sun City West AZ 85375-5791 also: PO Box 3659 2734 Ponderosa Cir Pinetop AZ 85935-3659

PERSON, RUTH JANSSEN, academic administrator; b. Washington, Aug. 27, 1945; d. Theodore Armin and Ruth Katherine (Mahoney) Janssen. BA, Gettysburg (Pa.) Coll., 1967; AMLS, U. Mich., 1969, PhD, 1980; MS in Adminstrn., George Washington U., 1974. Head of reference/asst. prof. Thomas Nelson C.C., Hampton, Va., 1971-74; lectr. U. Mich., Ann Arbor, 1975-79, coord. of continuing edn., 1977-79; asst. prof. Cath. U., Washington, 1979-85, assoc. prof., 1985-86, assoc. dean Sch. of Libr. and Info. Sci., 1983-86; dean Coll. Libr. Sci. Clarion (Pa.) U., 1986-88; assoc. vice chancellor U. Mo., St. Louis, 1988-93; v.p. for acad. affairs Ashland (Ohio) U., 1993-95; v.p. acad. affairs, prof. bus. adminstrn. Angelo State U., San Angelo, Tex., 1995-99; chancellor, prof. bus. Ind. U., Kokomo, Ind., 1999—. Reviewer U.S. Dept. Edn., Washington, 1987-89, 92; trustee Pitts. Regional Libr. Ctr., 1986-88; chair publs. com. Assn. of Coll. and Rsch. Librs., Chgo., 1986-90; cons. United Way, Alexandria, Va., 1985; cons.-evaluator North Ctrl. Assn., 1993-95, 2000—; nat. vis. com. Southwest Ctr. Advanced Tech. Edn., 1996-98; Health Profs. Edn. Adv. Com.; faculty workload com. Tex. Higher Edn. Coord. Bd., 1998-99; Higher Edn. Info. Sys. Com.; mem. adv. bd. KeyBank, 1999-2001; bd. dirs. Steak n Shake Co. Co-editor: (book) Academic Libraries: Their Role and Rationale in Higher Education, 1995; editor: (book) The Management Process, 1983; editl. bd. Coll. & Rsch. Librs., 1990-96; contr. articles to profl. jours. Mem. Strategic Planning Task Force, Ashland C. of C., 1994; bd. dirs. Alternatives for Living in Violent Environs., Inc., St. Louis, 1992-94, San Angelo Cultural Affairs Coun., 1998-99; commr. Commn. for Women, Anne Arundel County, Md., 1984-86; mem. Citizens Adv. Bd., Clarion, Pa., 1986-88; mem. Olivette, Mo. Human Rels. Commn., 1992-94, San Angelo Bus. and Profl. Women's Club, 1995-99, pres.-elect, 1996-97, pres., 1997—; mem. bldg. design oversight com. San Angelo Mus. Fine Arts, 1995-99; mem. com. Cactus Jazz Festival, 1995-99; bd. dirs. San Angelo Bus. and Edn. Coalition, 1997-99, San Angelo Cultural Affairs Coun., 1998-99; bd. dirs. Ind. Tech. Partnership, 2001-03, YWCA, Kokomo, 2000-02, Workforce Investment Bd., 2002—; mem. adv. bd. St. Joseph's Hosp., 2000, Ind. SDBC, 2002—; trustee Howard County Pub. Libr., 2002—, Ind. Campus Compact (pres bd. 2003-). Fellow Am. Coun. Edn., 1990, Harvard Inst. Ednl. Mgmt., 1989, Rackham fellow U. Mich., 1976; ACE fellow Ariz. Bd. Regents, 1990-91; recipient Washington Woman award Washington Woman mag., 1986. Mem.: ALA (com. on accreditation 1993—97), Am. Assn. State Colls. and Univs. (mem. profl. devel. com. 2001), Howard County C. of C. (women's bus. coun. 2000—), Coun. for the Preservation of Anthropol. Records (bd. dirs.), Am. Assn. Univ. Adminstrs. (bd. dirs. 1993—95, v.p. elect 2001—, pres. 2003—), Beta Gamma Sigma, Phi Alpha Theta, Kappa Delta Pi, Pi Lambda Theta, Beta Phi Mu, Psi Chi. Lutheran. Avocations: piano, herb gardening, antiques, cooking, sailing. Office: Ind U Kokomo PO Box 9003 2300 S Washington St Kokomo IN 46904 Office Phone: 765-455-9225.

PERSONETTE, LOUISE METZGER (SISTER MARY ROGER METZGER), mathematics educator; b. Indpls., Dec. 21, 1925; d. Frank Alexander and Frances Lee Ann (Durham) Metzger; m. Marlen William Personette, Dec. 9, 1967 (div. Dec. 1985); 1 stepson: Lyle Scott. BS in Elem. Edn., Athenaeum of Ohio, 1952; MEd, Xavier U., 1964. Nun St. Francis Convent, Oldenburg, Ind., 1942—67; elem. tchr. Cath. Schs., Cin., 1945-56, secondary math tchr. Middletown, Ohio, 1957-63, Evansville, Ind., 1964-65, Hamilton, Ohio, 1966-67; elem. tchr. Kent (Wash.) Schs., 1968-72, math specialist, 1973-82; math cons. greater Seattle Schs., 1983—; GED instr. Muckleshoot Indian Tribe, Auburn, Wash., 1998—2000. Dir. Heatherhill Edn. Ctr., Kent, 1982—, Homework House, Kent, 1987—90; adj. instr. Seattle Pacific U., 1975—95, City U., Seattle, 1975—95; SAT prep. math tutor, 2002—. Co-author: S.O.S. Story Problems, 1980. Mem. Nat. Coun. Tchrs. Math., Math. Assn. Am., Washington State Math Coun., Puget Sound Coun. Tchrs. Math., New Horizons. Home and Office: Heatherhill Education Ctr 11830 SE 263rd Ct Kent WA 98030-8407 E-mail: louisamath@msn.com.

PERSONS, FERN, actress; b. Chgo., July 27, 1910; d. John William and Alpha Valeska (Solberg) Ball; m. Max I. Persons, Oct. 17, 1935 (dec. Nov. 1971); 1 child, Nancy Janice Persons Rockafellow. BA, Kalamazoo Coll., 1931; BFA, Carnegie-Mellon U., 1933. Faculty mem. speech and drama Ferry Hall, Lake Forest, Ill., 1934-35. V.p. SAG, L.A., 1977-81, nat. bd., 1982-98. Appeared in (films) Prelude to a Kiss, Straight Talk, Curly Sue, Field of Dreams, Hoosiers, Risky Business, Class, Grandview U.S.A., On the Right Track, The Golden Gloves Story, (tv feature films and series) Mario and the Mob, Hard Knox, The Impostor, Under the Biltmore Clock, The Chicago Story, Jack and Mike, Jon Sable, ER, Early Edition, also in regional theatre prodns., 1972-95. Recipient Otto Kahn prize Carnegie-Mellon U., Pitts., 1933; Fern Persons Day in Chgo. named in her honor Mayor Richard M. Daley, Chgo., July 27, 1999. Mem. AFTRA (bd. mem., v.p.), AAUW (scholar 1927), Zeta Phi Eta (v.p. 1971, Disting. Svc. award 1994). Democrat. Methodist. Avocations: travel, reading, walking, gardening, theater. Home: 2700 Woodland Rd Evanston IL 60201-2034

PERSSON, ERLAND KARL, electrical engineer, engineering executive; b. Soderala, Sweden, Oct. 9, 1923; arrived in U.S., 1949, naturalized, 1953; m. Elaine Darm; children: Ann Monn, Eric. BSEE, U. Minn., 1955. Registered profl. engr., Minn. Prin. engr. Gen. Mills, Mpls., 1956-61; v.p. engring. Electro-Craft Corp., Hopkins, Minn., 1961-72, v.p. R & D, 1972-83, sr. v.p., chief tech. officer, 1983-86; pres. Erland Persson Co., Mpls., 1987—. Contbr. articles to profl., chapters to books. Mem. mech. engring. adv. com. U. Minn.; bd. dirs. Minn. High Tech. Coun., 1984—86, mem., 1987. Fellow: IEEE (life; mem. indsl. drives com.); mem.: Audio Engring. Soc. (founder midwest chpt. 1974), Eta Kappa Nu. Achievements include patents in field. Office: 216 Janalyn Cir Minneapolis MN 55416-3321 Office Phone: 763-377-1663.

PERSSON, RONNY ANDERS, accountant, historian; b. Helsingborg, Skane, Sweden, Nov. 19, 1945; s. Oscar Valfrid and Ellen Valborg Persson; m. Eva Gunilla Lindqvist, Oct. 5, 1968; children: Mikael, Thomas, Annika. Economy, Nicolai, 1971. Chief acct. Byggprodukter, Helsingborg, 1970-73, Bilakarna, Helsingborg, 1973-80, Bjuvs Congregation, Bjuv, Sweden, 1980—. Founder, mgr. R.P. Company Service, Bjuv, 1981-85, R.P. Trading, Bjuv, 1985—. Founder Internat. Peace, Economy and Ecology, Bjuv, 1982. Mem.: Thoreau Soc. USA. Environ. Party. Avocations: reading, sports, natural medicine, politics, world history. Home: Sommaren 8A 267 33 Bjuv Sweden E-mail: ronnypersson56@hotmail.com.

PERTH, ROD, network entertainment executive; b. L.A. s. Milford Robert Martinson and Phyllis (Hove) Perth; m. Jill Sunderland, Apr. 27, 1974; children: Chelseah, Lauren, Eric. BS in Mgmt., San Jose State U., 1966. V.p., gen. mgr. spot sales CBS TV, N.Y.C., 1974—86; v.p., station mgr. WBBM-TV, Chgo., 1986—89; sr. v.p. late night non-network programming CBS-TV, L.A., 1989—94; pres. entertainment USA Network, L.A., 1994—95; pres. HRTS, L.A., 1995—99, Jim Henson T.V. Account exec. KNXT, L.A., 1968—71; ea. mgr. spot sales CBS, N.Y.C., 1971—74, dir. midwest spot sales, Chgo., 1974—76; dir. sales KMOX-TV, St. Louis, 1976—79; bd. dirs. HRTS. Contbr. L.E.A.R.N. program, L.A., 1995, Alliance for Children, L.A., 1996; bd. mem. State St. Coun., Chgo., 1988. Lt. j.g. USN, 1968—74. Named Man of Yr., Alliance for Children, L.A., 1996. Mem.: Hollywood (Calif.) Radio and TV Soc. (pres. 1995—). Avocations: skiing, motorcycling, photography. Office: Jim Henson Television 1416 N Labrea Ave Hollywood CA 90068

PERTHOU, ALISON CHANDLER, interior designer; b. Bremerton, Wash., July 22, 1945; d. Benson and Elizabeth (Holdsworth) Chandler; m. A. V. Perthou, III, Sept. 9, 1967 (div. Dec. 1977); children: Peter T. R., Stewart A. C. BFA, Cornish Coll. Arts, 1972. Pres. Alison Perthou Interior Design, Seattle, 1972—, Optima Design, Inc., Seattle, 1986-89; treas. Framejoist Corp., Bellevue, Wash., 1973-90; pres. Classics: Interior Design and Constrn., Inc., 1988—. Cons. bldg. and interiors com. Children's Hosp., Seattle, 1976—; guest lectr. U. Wash., Seattle, 1980—81. Mem. procurement com. Patrons N.W. Cultural and Charitable Orgn., 1985—, mem. antiques com., 1991—; trustee Cornish Coll. Arts, Seattle, 1973—80, sec. exec. com., 1975—77. Mem.: Am. Soc. Interior Design, Sunset Club, Seattle Tennis Club (mem. house and grounds com. 1974—75). Office: 563 Lake Washington Blvd E Seattle WA 98112-4226 Fax: 206-322-2335. Office Phone: 206-322-7909.

PERTSCHUK, LOUIS PHILIP, pathologist, consultant; b. London, July 4, 1925; s. Isaac M. and Rose Pertschuk; m. Andrea Roberts, June 28, 1985; children: Eric, Shawn, Brandy. AB, NYU, 1946; DO, Phila. Coll. Osteo. Medicine, 1950. Diplomate Am. Bd. Pathology. Instr. Downstate Med. Ctr./SUNY, Bklyn., 1974-75, asst. prof., 1975-79, assoc. prof., 1979-86, prof., 1986—. Cons. Corning (N.Y.) Glass Works, 1982-86, Zeus Sci. Co., 1982-94, Abbott Labs., 1982-92, Lifecodes Corp., 1989-93, Oncor, Inc., Gaithersburg, Md., 1994-96, Internat. Bioimmune Sys., Great Neck, N.Y., 1994-96, BioGenex, San Ramon, Calif., 1996-99. Author: Immunocytochemistry for Steroid Receptors, 1990; editor: Localization of Putative Steroid Receptors, 1985. Served with U.S. Army, 1943-46. NCI/NIH grantee, 1979, 82, 85, 92. Fellow Coll. Am. Pathologists, Am. Soc. Clin. Pathologists; mem. AAAS, Am. Assn. Pathologists, Internat. Acad. Pathology, N.Y. Acad. Sci., Histochem. Soc. Achievements include identification of steroid hormone binding sites in human neoplasms by histochemical and immunohistological techniques. Office: SUNY Health Sci Ctr at Bklyn 450 Clarkson Ave # 25 Brooklyn NY 11203-2056

PERTZ, DOUGLAS A. engineering executive; BS in Mech. Engring., Purdue U., 1975. Various exec. positions Caterpillar, Inc., Hong Kong, Malaysia, Singapore, Onan Corp.; group v.p. Danaher Corp.; pres., CEO Culligan Water Technologies, Inc., 1995-98; pres., COO IMC Global Inc., Northbrook, Ill., 1998-99, pres., CEO, officer, dir., 1999—. Office: IMC Global Inc 2100 Sanders Rd Northbrook IL 60062-6139

PERTZSCH, EVELYN MARIA, civic worker; b. La Crosse, Wis., Nov. 6, 1932; m. Dayton Irving Pertzsch, July 5, 1952; children: Patti Pertzsch Virnig, Peggy Pertzsch Chaudhry, Anne Pertzsch Cadd, Kathryn. Reading tutor vol., coord. Onalaska (Wis.) Pub. Schs., 1974-77. Chmn. La Crosse County Housing Authority, 1988—92, La Crosse County chpt. Am. Cancer Soc., 1992—94, pres., 1994—96; past v.p. Wis. PTA; chmn. Book Study Club, Onalaska Libr.; past pres. Onalaska Pub. Libr. Commn.; dir. internal edn. Centering Onalaska Orgn.; mem. sch. bd. Onalaska Pub. Schs., 2000—; chmn. Sias Libr. Trust Fund, 1999—; clk. Onalaska County Pub. Schs., 2003—; alt. delegate Rep. Nat. Convention, Detroit, 1980; pres. La Crosse County Rep. Party, 1994—96. Named Pertzsch Manor, elderly manor, named in her honor, Onalaska, 1994; recipient award for dedicated svc., La Crosse County Rep. Party, 1986, Campbell award, Wis. Rep. Com., 1976—2003, svc. award, 1995—97, Cultural Dir. award, Sons of Norway, 1986, Literacy award, Midwest Reading Coun., 1989, Women of Achievement award, Miss Onalaska Pageant, 1998, 15 Yr. Recognition award, Riverland Girl Scouts, First Lady award, Lacrosse County Rep. Party, 2003. Mem.: Learning in Retirement (v.p. 2002, pres. 2004), Sons of Norway, Wis. PTA (life). Home: 229 2d Ave N Onalaska WI 54650 E-mail: epertzsch@aol.com.

PERU, RAMIRO G. metal products executive; BS in Bus. Adminstrn., U. Ariz.; postgrad., Duke U. Acct. western contrs. dept. Phelps Dodge Corp., 1979, various positions in acctg. and fin., 1979-87, contr. Phelpd Dodge Minign Co., 1987, asst. contr., v.p. Phelps Dodge Mining Co., 1993, v.p., treas., 1995, sr. v.p., 1997, sr. v.p. orgn. devel. and info. tech., CFO, 1999—. Office: Phelps Dodge Corp 1 N Central Ave Phoenix AZ 85004-4414

PERUGGI, REGINA S. academic administrator; b. NYC; BA in Sociology, Coll. New Rochelle; MBA, NYU; EdD, Columbia U. Drug abuse counselor, N.Y.C.; dir. Community Learning Ctr. York Coll. CUNY, 1974-84, with office of acad. affairs, 1984-86, assoc. dean for adult and continuing edn., 1986-90; pres. Marymount Manhattan Coll., NYC, 1990—2001, Ctrl. Park Conservancy, NYC, 2001—04, Kingsborough Cmty. Coll., CUNY, 2004—. Past chair N.Y. State Adult Leanring Svcs. Adv. Coun.; past pres. Continuing Edn. Assn. N.Y.; active N.Y. State Coun. on Vocat. Edn., N.Y. State Lit. Coun. Office: Kingsborough Cmty Coll 2001 Oriental Blvd Brooklyn NY 11235-2398

PERWIN, JEAN SHAPIRO, lawyer; b. Boston, June 26, 1949; d. Leon Nathan and Rose Selma (Kurhan) S.; m. Joel Stephen Perwin, Aug. 23, 1970; children: Amanda Julia, Samuel Harris. BA, Sarah Lawrence Coll., 1971; JD, Boston Coll., 1975. Bar: Mass. 1975, D.C. 1976, Fla. 1981. Counsel commerce, consumer and monetary affairs subcom. U.S. Ho. Reps., Washington, 1975-78; counsel oversight of govt. mgmt. subcom. U.S. Senate, Washington, 1978-80; counsel Spl. Asst. to Pres. for Consumer Affairs, Washington, 1980-81; assoc. Seiler and Seiler, PA, Miami, Fla., 1982-85, Stugin and Gamner, Miami, 1985-87; pvt. practice Miami, 1987—. Author: (book) Electronic Copyright, 1996; co-author: (book) The Artist's Friendly Legal Guide, 1988. Mem. majority coun. Emily's List, Washington, 1986—. Mem. Internat. Trademark Assn., Fla. Bar (computer law com. 1994—, chair entertainment, arts and sports sect. 1991). Office: 25 SE 2nd Ave Ste 1144 Miami FL 33131-1607

PERZEL, JOHN MICHAEL, state legislator; b. Phila., Jan. 7, 1950; s. Michael Joseph and Susan Mary (Delatour) P.; m. Sheryl Stokes; children: Andrew, David, John Jr., Samuel. AA, Enterprise State Jr. Coll., 1972; student, Temple U., 1973; BS, Troy State U., 1975; postgrad., Auburn U. Ward chmn. Rep. Com., 1975—, ward leader, 1979—; mem. Pa. Ho. of Reps., Harrisburg, 1978—, majority leader, chmn. rules com., 1995—, appropriations com., chmn. Rep. policy com., ho. spkr., 2003—. Active Consumer Action of the N.E. Mem. Sandybord Civic Assn., KC, Optimists, Moose. Republican. Address: Pa Ho of Reps 110 Main Capitol Bldg House Box 202020 Harrisburg PA 17120-2020

PESCARINO, RICHARD ANGELO, mathematician, educator; b. Rome, N.Y., Nov. 20, 1968; s. Phil and Nancy Pescarino; m. Catherine Lynn Miller, May 16, 1998; children: Luke Angelo, Joseph Edward. M, So. Ill. U., 2000. Statistician, data analyst Wash. U., St. Louis, 1999—2001; instr. St. Louis C.C., Ferguson, Mo., 2001—. Youth min. helper Assumption Ch., O'Fallon, Mo., 2002—03. Gordon T. Chamness scholar, So. Ill. U., 1998—99. Mem.: Mo. Coun. Tchrs. Math. (assoc.). R-Liberal. Roman Catholic. Office: St Louis Cmty Coll 3400 Pershall Rd Ferguson MO 63135 E-mail: rpescarino@stlcc.edu.

PESCH, ELLEN P. lawyer; BA, Barat Coll., 1986; JD, John Marshall Law Sch., 1989; LLM, DePaul U., 1991. Bar: Ill. 1989, U.S. Dist. Ct. (no. dist.) Ill. With Sidley Austin Brown & Wood, Chgo., 1989—, ptnr., 2001—. Mem.: ABA, Internat. Swaps and Derivatives Assn., Stable Value Investment Assn. Office: Sidley Austin Brown and Wood Bank One Plz 10 S Dearborn St Chicago IL 60603

PESCH, LEROY ALLEN, physician, educator, health and hospital consultant, business executive; b. Mt. Pleasant, Iowa, June 22, 1931; s. Herbert Lindsey and Mary Clarissa (Tyner) P.; children from previous marriage: Christopher Allen, Brian Lindsey, Daniel Ethan; m. Donna J. Stone, Dec. 28, 1975 (dec. Feb. 1985); stepchildren: Christopher Scott Kneifel, Linda Suzanne Kneifel; m. Gerri Ann Cotton, Sept. 27, 1986; 1 child, Tyner Ford. Student, State U. Iowa, 1948—49, Iowa State U., 1950—52; MD cum laude, Washington U., St. Louis, 1956. Intern Barnes Hosp., St. Louis, 1956-57; rsch. assoc. NIH, Bethesda, Md., 1957-59; asst. resident medicine Grace-New Haven Hosp., New Haven, 1959-60; clin. fellow Yale Med. Sch., New Haven, 1960-61, instr. medicine, 1961-62, asst. prof. medicine, 1962-63, asst. dir. liver study unit, 1961-63; assoc. physician Grace-New Haven Hosp., 1961-63; assoc. prof. medicine Rutgers U., New Brunswick, N.J., 1963-64, prof., 1964-66, chmn. dept. medicine, 1965-66; assoc. dean, prof. medicine Stanford Sch. Medicine, 1966-68; mem. gen. medicine study sect. NIH, 1965-70, chmn., 1969-70; dean, dir. univ. hosps. SUNY, Buffalo, 1968-71; dep. asst. sec. manpower HEW, 1970-72, spl. cons. to sec. for health, 1970-75; prof. div. biol. scis. and medicine U. Chgo., 1972-77; prof. pathology Northwestern U., 1977-79; health and hosp. cons.; chmn., chief exec. officer Health Resources Corp. Am., 1981-84; chmn. bd. dirs. Republic Health Corp., 1985-88; chmn., chief exec. officer The Bora Health Group, Seattle, 1987-92; pres. Genus Tech. Corp., 1987—; chmn., chief exec. officer The Pesch Group Cos., Sun Valley, Idaho, 1989—. Contbr. articles on internal medicine to profl. jours. Bd. dirs. Buffalo Med. Found., 1969-72, Health Orgn., Western N.Y., 1968-71, Joffrey Ballet, N.Y.C., 1980—; trustee Michael Reese Hosp. and Med. Ctr., Chgo., 1971-76, pres., CEO, 1971-77; mem. exec. bd. Auditorium Theatre Coun., Chgo.; trustee W. Clement and Jessie V. Stone Found.; mem. adv. com. Congl. Awards; pres. Pesch Found. Sr. asst. surgeon USPHS, 1957-59. Mem. AAAS, Am. Assn. Study of Liver Diseases, Am. Fedn. Clin. Rsch., Am. Soc. Biol. Chemists, Quadrangle Club, Acapulco Yacht Club, Sigma Xi, Alpha Omega Alpha. E-mail: allenp@cox-internet.com.

PESCI, JOE, actor; b. Newark, N.J., Feb. 9, 1943; m. Martha Haro (div.); m. Garrett Warren; 1 child, Tiffany. Film appearances include Death Collector, 1976, Raging Bull, 1980, I'm Dancing as Fast as I Can, 1982, Easy Money, 1983, Dear Mr. Wonderful, 1983, Eureka, 1983, Once Upon a Time in America, 1984, Tutti Dentro, 1984, Man On Fire, 1987, Moonwalker, 1988, Backtrack, 1988, Lethal Weapon II, 1989, Goodfellas (Acad. award Best Supporting Actor, 1991, D.W. Griffith Award, 1990), Home Alone, 1990, The Super, 1991, JFK, 1991, Lethal Weapon III, 1992, Home Alone II, 1992, The Public Eye, 1992, My Cousin Vinny, 1992, A Bronx Tale, 1993, With Honors, 1994, Jimmy Hollywood, 1994, Casino, 1995, Gone Fishin, 1997, 8 Heads in a Duffel Bag, 1997, Lethal Weapon 4, 1998; appeared in TV series Half Nelson, 1985.*

PESEC, DAVID JOHN, data systems executive; b. Cleve., Apr. 19, 1956; s. Rudolph J. and Martha C. (Kessler) P. BS, Cleve. State U., 1988; MBA, U. Phoenix, 1999; PhD, Trinity Coll., 2000. Pvt. practice cons., Cleve., 1976-78; programmer Champion Svc. Corp., Cleve., 1978; sr. sys. programmer United Tel. of Ohio, Mansfield, 1978-89; dir. devel. Broderick Data Sys., Mansfield, 1989-97; prin. cons. Keane, Inc., Independence, Ohio, 1997-2000; pres. Pesec Creative Mgmt., Inc., Mansfield, Ohio, 2000—. Adj. prof. Ashland U., 2001—, Am. Intercontinental U., 2001—; bd. dirs. Park Ave. Pets., Inc. Bd. dirs. ARC, Mansfield, 1989—, Mansfield Emergency Svc., 1986; assoc. pastor Cornerstone Grace Brethren Ch., 1995—; life mem. Rep. Nat. com., 1991—, Rep. Senatorial Inner Circle, 1991—. Recipient Senatoral medal of freedom, 1996. Mem. Am. Mgmt. Assn., Assn. Computing Machinery, Intercity Radio Club (pres. 1987-90), NRA, Gideons (v.p. 1992), Profl. Photographers. Republican. Mem. Grace Brethren Ch. Avocations: flying, auto racing. Office: Pesec Creative Mgmt Inc 1633 Hickory Ln Mansfield OH 44905-2945 E-mail: dpesec@pesecreativemanagement.com.

PESERIK, JAMES E. electrical, controls and computer engineer, consultant, forensics and safety engineer, fire cause and origin investigator; b. Beloit, Wis., Sept. 30, 1945; s. Edward J. and G. Lucille Peserik; m. Elaine L. Peserik, May 6, 1972. BSEE, U. Wis., 1968; MS, St. Joseph's U., 1990. Registered profl. engr., registered profl. land surveyor; cert. fire and explosion investigator, cert. fire investigation instr.; diplomate Am. Coll. Forensic Examiners. Development and instrumentation engr. Square D Co., Milw., 1968-71; product engr. I-T-E Imperial Corp., Ardmore, Pa., 1971-72; project engr. Harris-Intertype Corp., Easton, Pa., 1972-74; elec. engr. Day & Zimmerman, Inc., Phila., 1974-76; pvt. practice Coopersburg, Pa., 1976—; sr. elec. engr. S.T. Hudson Engrs., Inc., Phila., 1980-81. Mem. adv. coun. Swenson Skills Ctr., Phila., 1990-95. Treas. Salford Fraconia Joint Parks Commn., Montgomery County, Pa., 1980-83. Mem. IEEE (sec. indsl. applications group Phila. chpt. 1980, chmn. 1981, chmn. Lehigh Valley computer sect. 1999—), NSPE, Pa. Soc. Profl. Engrs., Del. Assn. Profl. Engrs. (external affairs com. 1995—), Nat. Fire Protection Assn., Internat. Assn. Arson Investigators, Nat. Assn. Fire Investigators. Office: PO Box 181 Coopersburg PA 18036-0181 Office Phone: 215-234-8901. E-mail: jepeserik@enter.net.

PESETSKY, DAVID MICHAEL, linguist; b. Iowa City, Iowa, Jan. 26, 1957; s. Irwin and Bette Pesetsky; m. Janis Melvold; children: Benjamin, Jonathan. BA summa cum laude, Yale U., 1977; PhD, MIT, 1982. Asst. prof. linguistics U. So. Calif., L.A., 1982—83; assoc. prof. linguistics U. Mass., Amherst, 1983—88; Ferrari P. Ward prof. modern langs. and linguistics MIT, Cambridge, 1988—. Adv. bd. NSF, Divsn. Social, Behavioral and Econ. Scis., Washington, 1998—2000; com. visitors to linguistics program NSF, 1999—99, linguistics program rev. panel, 1990—93, vis. prof. Linguistic Soc. Am. Summer Inst., 1983, 96, 97, 99, 2003, LOT Grad. Sch. Linguistics, Netherlands, 1993—2000, Netherlands, 2000; vis. lectr. worldwide; editl. boards Linguistic Inquiry, Rivista di Grammatica Generativa, Natural Lang. Semantics, Oxford Surveys in Syntax, English Linguistics, Lang. Acquisition. Author: (scientific monograph) Zero Syntax, Phrasal Movement and its Kin; contbr. articles to profl. jours. Cons. for English lang. arts curriculum framework Dept. Edn., Mass., 1996. Recipient Ednl. Partnership award, Portsmouth Bd. Edn., N.H., 1998; fellow, Internat. Rsch. and Exchanges Bd., 1979—80; grantee, NSF, 1991—96. Mem.: AAAS (sect. member-at-large 1995—95, coun. del. 1996—99), Linguistic Soc. Am. (com. on lang. k-12 curriculum 2003—), Generative Linguists of Old Worlds (keynote spkr. 2003 2003), Phi Beta Kappa. Achievements include research in the nature of syntactic case marking and its relation to tense systems (with E.Torrego); established the existence and distinctness of three types of syntactic movement operations. Avocations: violin, chamber music. Office: MIT Dept Linguistics & Philos E39-237 Cambridge MA 02420 E-mail: pesetsk@mit.edu.

PESHKIN, MURRAY, physicist; b. Bklyn., May 17, 1925; s. Jacob and Bella Ruth (Zuckerman) P.; m. Frances Julie Ehrlich, June 12, 1955; children—Michael, Sharon, Joel. BA, Cornell U., 1947, PhD, 1951. Instr., then asst. prof. physics Northwestern U., 1951-59; physicist, then sr. scientist Argonne (Ill.) Nat. Lab., 1959—, assoc. dir. physics div., 1972-83. Fellow Weizmann Inst. Sci., Rehovoth, Israel, 1959-60, 68-69; sr. scientist SciTech Mus., Aurora, Ill., 1991—. Served with AUS, 1944-46. Home: 838 Parkside Ave Elmhurst IL 60126-4813 Office: Argonne Natl Lab Argonne IL 60439 Business E-Mail: peshkin@anl.gov.

PESHKIN, SAMUEL DAVID, lawyer; b. Des Moines, Oct. 6, 1925; s. Louis and Mary (Grund) P.; m. Shirley R. Isenberg, Aug. 17, 1947; children: Lawrence Allen, Linda Ann. BA, State U. Iowa, 1948, JD, 1951. Bar: Iowa 1951. Ptnr. Bridges & Peshkin, Des Moines, 1953-66, Peshkin & Robinson, Des Moines, 1966-82. Mem. Iowa Bd. Law Examiners, 1970—. Bd. dirs. State U. Iowa Found., 1957—, Old Gold Devel. Fund, 1956—, Sch. Religion U. Iowa, 1966—. Fellow Am. Bar Found., Internat. Soc. Barristers; mem. ABA (chmn. standing com. membership 1959—, ho. of dels. 1968—, bd. govs. 1973—), Iowa Bar Assn. (bd. govs. 1958—, pres. jr. bar sect. 1958-59, award of merit 1974), Inter-Am. Bar Assn., Internat. Bar Assn., Am. Judicature Soc., State U. Iowa Alumni Assn. (dir., pres. 1957) Office Phone: 480-607-3136.

PESIN, ELLA MICHELE, journalist, public relations professional; b. North Bergen, N.J., Aug. 29, 1956; d. Edward and Helene Sylvia (Rattner) P. BA, Sarah Lawrence Coll., 1978. Press rep. CBS-TV News and Entertainment, N.Y.C., 1978-80; publicist Newsweek Mag., N.Y.C., 1980-81; freelance journalist N.Y.C., 1982-85; publicist Universal Studios MCA Inc., L.A., 1982-83; with publicity and mktg. NBC-TV News, N.Y.C., 1985-86; media exec. Burson Marsteller Pub. Rels., N.Y.C., 1986-87; prin. Pesin Pub. Rels., 1987—. Contbg. editor Cable Age mag., TV Radio Age mag., Advt. Forum, Facts Figures & Film, Advt. Compliance Svc.; syndicated newspaper columnist. Active Israel Bonds/United Jewish Appeal, N.Y.C., Rudolph Giuliani for N.Y.C. Mayor campaign. Mem. Pub. Rels. Soc. Am., Women in Comm., Publicity Club N.Y., Healthcare Pub. Rels. and Mktg. Soc. Avocations: photography, sculpture, modern dance, tennis, skiing. Home and Office: 303 E 83rd St Apt 27J New York NY 10028-4323 E-mail: eem75p@aol.com.

PESKIN, CHARLES, physicist, researcher; b. N.Y.C., Apr. 15, 1946; AB, Harvard U., 1968; PhD in Physics, Albert Einstein Coll. Med., 1972. Prof. math N.Y.U., 1973—. Elected mem. Inst. of Medicine, 2000. McArthur Found. fellow 1982. Mem. Nat. Acad. Sci. Office: Courant Inst 251 Mercer St New York NY 10012-1185

PESKOV, VLADIMIR DMITRIEVICH, physicist, educator, consultant; b. Karaganda, Russia, Jan. 30, 1947; s. Dmitri S. and Olga D. (Petrova) P.; m. Tatiana R. Zabotina, May 3, 1973; children: Dmitri, Tatiana. MS in Physics, Phys. and Tech. Inst., Moscow, 1971; PhD in Physics, USSR Acad. Sci., Moscow, 1976, DSc, 1981. Rschr. Inst. Phys. Problems, Moscow, 1971-76, sr. rschr., 1976-97, leading scientist, 1981-97, prof., 1998; chief scientist Inst. of Applied Mechanics, Russian Acad. Sci., 1997—2000; assoc. scientist European Ctr. for Nuclear Rsch., Geneva, 1986-92; application physicist II Fermi Nat. Accelerator Lab., Batavia, Ill., 1992-95; invited prof. Coimbra (Portugal) U., 1995-98; NRC sr. rsch. assoc. Marshall Space Ctr., Huntsville, Ala., 1995-98; guest prof. Royal Inst. Tech., 1998—. Mem. adv. bd. several internat. confs.; org. com. Internat. Conf. Imaging 2000, 2003, Stockholm; mem. neutron time of flight experiment European Orgn. for Nuclear Rsch. Contbr. more than 100 articles to profl. jours. including Nuclear Instruments and Methods, Soviet Physics JETF, Jour. Physics. Participant Internat. Meeting on Chem. Disarmament, Rome, 1989, Internat. Forum di Amore, Italy, 1991, Internat. Meeting Our Nature, Italy, 1991. Recipient Prize of World Fedn. of Scientists, World Lab./Italian Physics Soc., 1993-2002. Mem. Am. Phys. Soc., Italian Phys. Soc. Achievements include invention of device for magnetic field measurement of landing spacecraft, position sensitive gas scintillating detector; invention of new detector and methods for radiation measurement and med. imaging; some of them, for example detectors with gaseous and solid photocathodes are now widely used in experimental techniques; discovery of new type of plasma instability, connected to accumulation of excited atoms and molecules, a flux-induced breakdown, cathode excitation effect. Office: Stockholm Physics Ctr Particle Physics Grp KTH Phys Dept S-10691 Stockholm Sweden

PESMEN, SANDRA (MRS. HAROLD WILLIAM PESMEN), editor; b. Chgo., Mar. 26, 1931; d. Benjamin S. and Emma (Lipschultz) Zuckerman; m. Harold W. Pesmen, Aug. 16, 1952; children: Bethann, Curtis. BS, U. Ill., 1952. Reporter Radio and Community News Service, Chgo., 1952-53; wire editor Champaign-Urbana (Ill.) Courier, 1953; reporter, feature writer Lerner Chgo. N. Side Newspapers, 1953-55; stringer corr. Wayne (Mich.) Eagle, 1958-61; reporter, feature writer Chgo. Daily News, 1968-78; features editor Crain's Chgo. Business mag., 1978-89; corp. features editor Crain Communications, Inc., 1989-95; tchr. feature writing Northwestern U. Evening Sch., 1972-81. Author: Writing for the Media, 1983, Dr. Job's Complete Career Guide, 1995; editor: Career News Service; author syndicated column Dr. Job, 1985—. Recipient Golden Key award Ill. Mental Health Dept., 1966, 71, award Inst. Psychoanalysis, 1971, Penny Mo. award, 1978, Stick o'Type award Chgo. Newspaper Guild, 1978, award AP, 1975, Peter Lisagor award Soc. Profl. Journalists, 1991; inductee Chgo. Journalism Hall of Fame, 1997. Home: 2811 Fern Ave Northbrook IL 60062-5809 E-mail: drjob@voyager.net.

PESNER, CAROLE MANISHIN, art gallery owner; b. Boston, Aug. 5, 1937; m. Robert Pesner (dec. 1983); children: Ben, Jonah; m. Martin Cherkasky, 1995 (dec. 1997). BA, Smith Coll., 1959. Asst. dir. Kraushaar Galleries, Inc., N.Y.C., 1959-86, dir., 1986-90, pres., 1991—. Author, editor

publs., catalogues in field. Mem. Art Dealers Assn. Am., Internat. Fine Print Dealers Assn. Office: Kraushaar Galleries Inc 724 5th Ave New York NY 10019-4106 Office Phone: 212-307-5730. Business E-Mail: info@kraushaargalleries.com.

PESOLA, GENE RAYMOND, physician, educator; b. Hancock, Mich, Oct. 21, 1952; s. Raymond Lloyd and Helen Eleanor Pesola; m. Helen Rostata, Jan. 5, 1991; children: Gene Richard, Glen Raymond, Gary Roger. BS in Biology magna cum laude, Mich. Technol. U., Houghton, 1974; MD, Wayne State U., 1979; MPH in Biostats. magna cum laude, Columbia U., 1998. Diplomate Am. Bd. Internal Medicine, also sub-bds. pulmonary medicine and critical care medicine; cert. BCLS, ACLS, ATLS, PALS. Intern Harlem Hosp., NYC, 1979-80; resident U. Tenn. Affiliated Hosps., Memphis, 1980-82; fellow in pulmonary medicine Mt. Sinai Hosp. and Affiliates, NYC, 1982-84; fellow in critical care medicine Meml. Sloan-Kettering Cancer Ctr., NYC, 1984-85, rsch. fellow, 1985-87; asst. prof. medicine and anesthesia Albert Einstein U., Bronx, NY, 1988-89; attending physician Mt. Vernon Emergency Room, NY, 1989-90; rschr. cell/molecular pharmacology and exptl. therapeutics Med. U. SC, Charleston, 1991-94; attending physician critical care and emergency medicine N.Y. Cmty. Hosp., Bklyn., 1989—; attending physician dept. emergency medicine St. Vincent's Hosp., NYC, 1994—2000; asst. prof. emergency medicine NY Med. Coll., 1995-2000, assoc. prof. emergency medicine, 2000; assoc. attending physician Divsn. Pulmonary and Critical Care Medicine, Harlem Hosp./Columbia U., NYC, 2001—; assoc. clin. prof. medicine Columbia U., NYC, 2001—; co-prin. investigator ACRN, NYC, 2001—. Mem. editl. bd. Academic Emergency Medicine, 2002—; assoc. editor Internet Jour. Asthma, Allergy, and Immunology, 2002—; contbr. chpts. to books, numerous articles to profl. jour.; reviewer for numerous jours. including CHEST, Catheterization and Cardiovascular Interventions, Annals of Emergency Medicine, The Lancet, Academic Emergency Med. Recipient various awards; grantee Am. Fedn. Clin. Rsch., 1992; Pharm. Mfr. Found. fellow, 1992-94.

PESOLA, WILLIAM ERNEST, restaurant management executive; b. Marquette, Mich., Mar. 2, 1945; s. Ernest Ensio and Janice Mary (LeDuc) P.; m. Kathleen Mary Deschaine, July 9, 1966; children: Christie Lynn, Laurie Anne. BS, No. Mich. U., 1968, MS, 1971. Route driver Coca Cola Co., Marquette, 1963-68; tchr. Gwinn (Mich.) Schs., 1968-78, pub. Sch. News, 1969; pres. Pesola Mgmt., Marquette, 1974—, Humboldt Ridge, Marquette, 1977—; treas. Elite Bar, Inc., Marquette, 1978—; v.p., dir. Marquette Cablevison, 1981-85; pres. Upper Peninsula Big Boy, Marquette, 1990—. Cons. cable TV, 1985—, Bresnan Comm., 1984—. Pres. Gwinn Edn. Assn., 1975-77; regional pres. Upper Peninsula Edn. Assn., 1977-78; mem. Marquette City Commn., 1977-81. Mem. NEA, Marquette Econ. Club, Mich. Edn. Assn., Marquette C. of C. (Exemplary Citizen award 1990), Rotary. Roman Catholic. Home: 1026 N Front St Marquette MI 49855-3514 Office Phone: 906-228-7200. E-mail: bepesola@chartermi.net.

PESSIN, JEFFREY E. physiology educator; b. N.Y.C., Jan. 2, 1953; s. Al Pessin; m. Rene Debra Bronner, June 23, 1975; children: Jacob, Lauren, Melanie. BA in Chemistry, MA in Chemistry, CUNY, 1975; PhD in Biochemistry, U. Ill., 1980; postgrad., U. Mass., 1980. Grad. rsch. asst. U. Ill., Urbana, 1975-80; asst. prof. physiology U. Iowa, Iowa City, 1983-88, assoc. prof., 1988-91, prof., 1991—, assoc. dir. Diabetes and Endocrinology Rsch. Ctr., 1991—. Contbr. articles to Molecular and Cellular Biology, Endocrinology. Basil O'Connor rsch. scholar March of Dimes Birth Defects Found., 1987-90; grantee NIH, 1988-93. Mem. AAAS, NIH (mem. metabolism study sect. 1989-93), Am. Chem. Soc., Am. Diabetes Assn. (R & D award 1985-87, rsch. award 1995), Sigma Xi. Office: U Iowa Dept Physiology and Biophysics Bowman Sci Bldg 5-530 Iowa City IA 52242 Home: 51 Woodchuck Hollow Ct Port Jefferson NY 11777-2093

PESTA, BEN W., II, lawyer, writer; b. Hagerstown, Md., Oct. 15, 1948; s. Ben W. and Ethel Irene (Kirkpatrick) P.; m. Monique Raphel High, Dec. 24, 1987; 1 stepchild, Nathalie Carroll. AB, UCLA, 1969; JD, U. Calif., Berkeley, 1972. Bar: U.S. Supreme Ct., U.S. Ct. Appeals, U.S. Dist. Ct., Calif. Assoc. pub. Weider Health & Fitness, Woodland Hills, Calif., 1984-90; pvt. practice law L.A. Contbr. Esquire, Playboy, Rolling Stone, Sport, TV Guide, Cosmopolitan,L.A. Times, L.A. Style mags. and profl. jours. Capt. USAF., 1973. Office: Ste 1250W 10010 Santa Monica Blvd Los Angeles CA 90067-5803

PESTANA, CARLOS, surgeon, retired dean, educator; b. Tacoronte, Tenerife, Canary Islands, Spain, June 10, 1936; came to U.S., 1968, naturalized, 1973; s. Francisco and and Blanca (Suarez) P.; m. Myrna Lorena Serrato, Aug. 25, 1966; children— Becky Elizabeth, George Byron. BS, Nat. U. Mex., 1952, MD, 1959; PhD in Surgery, U. Minn., 1965. Intern St. Mary of Nazareth Hosp., Chgo., 1959-60; resident Mayo Clinic, Rochester, Minn., 1961-65; surgeon Hosp. 20 de Noviembre Mexico City; asst. prof. surgery Nat. U. Mex., 1966-67, U. Tex. Med. Sch. at San Antonio, 1968-70, asso. prof., 1970-74, prof., 1974—, asso. dean for acad. devel., 1971-73, asso. dean for student affairs, 1973-86, assoc. dean acad. affairs, 1986-97, clin. prof. surgery, 1998-2000, prof. emeritus, 2000—. Recipient Edward John Noble Found. award, 1965, Piper Prof. award Minnie Stevens Piper Founds., 1972, Nat. Golden Apple award Am. Med. Student Assn., 1999. Mem. Alpha Omega Alpha (Robert J. Glaser Disting. Tchr. award 1997). Home: 10123 N Manton Ln San Antonio TX 78213-1932 Office: 7703 Floyd Curl Dr San Antonio TX 78284-6200

PESTELLO, FRED P. academic administrator; BA in Sociology, John Carroll U.; MA in Sociology, PhD in Sociology, U. Akron. Joined U. Dayton, Ohio, 1984, prof. sociology, assoc. dean, 1997—2001, sr. v.p. for ednl. affairs and provost, 2001—. Office: Office of the Provost Univ Dayton 300 College Park St Marys Hall 212 Dayton OH 45469-1634*

PESTILLO, PETER JOHN, auto parts company executive, lawyer; b. Bristol, Conn., Mar. 22, 1938; s. Peter and Ruth (Hayes) P.; m. BettyAnn Barraclough, Aug. 29, 1959; children: Kathleen, Karen, Kerry. BSS, Fairfield (Conn.) U., 1960; LLB, Georgetown U., 1963. Bar: D.C. 1964. Mgr. union relations planning Gen. Electric Co., N.Y.C., 1968-74; v.p. employee relations B.F. Goodrich Co., Akron, Ohio, 1974-80; v.p. labor relations Ford Motor Co., Dearborn, Mich., 1980-85, v.p. employee relations, 1985-86, v.p. employee and external affairs, 1986—90, v.p. corp. rels. and diversified businesses, 1990—93, exec. v.p. corp. rels., 1993, vice chmn., chief of staff; chmn. Visteon Corp., Dearborn, 2000—, CEO, 2000—04. Mem. adv. bd. United Found., Detroit. Mem. Am. Arbitration Assn. (dir.), U.S. C. of C. (labor relation com.), D.C. Bar, Bus. Roundtable, Labor Policy Assn., Nat. Assn. Mfgs., UBA. Office: Visteon Corp 17000 Rotunda Corp Dearborn MI 48120

PESUT, DANIEL J. nursing educator; b. DeKalb, Ill., Dec. 12, 1951; s. George D. and Donna M. Pesut; m. Susan E. Ziel, Aug. 28, 1981; children: Elliott, Erin. BSN, No. Ill. U., 1975; MSN, U. Tex., San Antonio, 1977; PhD, U. Mich., 1984. RN, Ind.; cert. specialist. Assoc. prof. U. Mich. Sch. Nursing, Ann Arbor, 1978-81; dir. nursing William S. Hall Psychiat. Inst., Columbia, 1984-87; assoc. prof. U. S.C., Columbia, 1987-93; prof., dept. chair environ. health Ind. U. Sch. Nursing, Indpls., 1997—. Author: Clinical Reasoning: The Art and Science of Critical and Creative Thinking, 1999. Fellow Am. Acad. Nursing; mem. Sigma Theta Tau (pres. 2003-2005, Creativity award 1993). Avocations: piano, travel, reading. Home: 14144 Blue Heron Dr Carmel IN 46033 Office: Ind Univ Dept Environ Health Sch Nursing Indianapolis IN 46204 E-mail: dpesut@iupui.edu.

PESZKE, MICHAEL ALFRED, psychiatrist, writer; b. Deblin, Poland, Dec. 19, 1932; s. Alfred Bartlomiej and Eugenia Halina (Grebocka) Peszke; m. Alice Margaret Sherman, Sept. 20, 1958; children: Michele Halina Olender, Michael Alexander. BA, Trinity Coll., Dublin, Ireland, 1956; MB, BCh, BAO, Dublin U., 1956. Cert. Bd. cert. psychiatrist. Staff psychiatrist Yale Student Health Svc., New Haven, 1961-64; asst. prof. sch. medicine U. Chgo., 1964-68; cons. psychiatrist Wesleyan U., Middletown, Conn., 1968-70; asst. prof. Sch. Medicine U. Conn., Farmington, 1970-73, assoc. prof., 1973-80, prof. psychiatry, 1980-90; clin. prof. U. Md. Sch. Medicine, Balt., 1991-99; chief Psychiatry Svc. Perry Point (Md.) VA Med. Ctr., 1990-98, co-coord. R&D, 1998-99. Dir. psychiat. clin. svcs. John Dempsey Hosp. U. Conn. Health Ctr., Farmington, 1983—87; chief VA Med. Ctr., Newington, Conn., 1987—90; ind. rschr., 1999—; chmn. adv. com. to the endowed chair of Polish and Polish Am. studies Ctrl. Conn. State U., 2001—; advisor Am. Polish Adv. Coun. Author: Involuntary Treatment of the Mentally Ill: The Problem of Autonomy, 1975, Battle for Warsaw, 1939-44, 1995, Poland's Navy: 1918-1945, 1999; co-author (edited by L.A. Pervin, L.R. Reik, W. Dalrymple): The College Drop-out and the Utilization of Talent, 1966; co-author: (edited by J. Zusman, E. Bertsch) The Future of Psychiatric State Hospitals, 1975; contbr. Advisor Am. Polish Adv. Coun., 2003—. Fellow: APA (life; disting.); mem.: Polish Inst. Arts and Scis. Am., Inc., Am. Coll. Psychiatrists, Royal United Svc. Inst. (London), Soc. for Mil. History, Stonington Harbor Yacht Club.

PETAK, WILLIAM JOHN, systems management educator; b. Johnstown, Pa., June 23, 1932; s. Val Andrew and Lola Agatha (Boroski) P.; m. Ramona Janet Cayuela, Dec. 28, 1957; children: Elizabeth Ann Petak-Aaron, William Matthew, Michael David. BS in Mech. Engring., U. Pitts., 1956; MBA, U. So. Calif., 1963, DPA, 1969. Engr. Northrop Corp., Hawthorne, Calif., 1956-59; test engr. Wyle Labs., El Segundo, Calif., 1959-63; we. regional mgr. Instrument div. Budd Co., Phoenixville, Pa., 1963-69; v.p., dir. J.H. Wiggins Co., Redondo Beach, Calif., 1969-81; prof. systems mgmt. U. So. Calif., L.A., 1982-98, exec. dir. Inst. Safety and Sys. Mgmt., 1987-98, prof. policy, planning and devel., 1998—. Chmn. earthquake mitigation com. Nat. Com. on Property Ins., Boston, 1990-92; mem. com. on natural disasters NRC, Washington, 1985-91, mem. U.S. nat. com. for the decade for natural disaster reduction, 1989-92. Co-author: Natural Hazard Risk Assessment and Public Policy, 1982, Politics and Economics of Earthquake Hazard Reduction, 1986, Disabled Persons and Earthquake Hazards, 1988; editor spl. issue Pub. Adminstrn. Rev., 1985. Commr. County of Los Angeles, 1994—; mem. policy bd. So. Calif. Earthquake Prep. Project, L.A., 1986-92; trustee Marymount Coll., Palos Verdes, Calif., 1974—. Sgt. U.S. Army, 1950-52. Mem. Soc. for Risk Analysis, Earthquake Engring. Rsch. Inst., Am. Soc. for Pub. Adminstrn., Sigma Xi. Republican. Roman Catholic. Avocations: skiing, fishing, hiking. Office: U So Calif MC 0626 Sch Policy Planning & Devel Los Angeles CA 90089-0001

PETCHENEV, ALEX, scientist; b. St. Petersburg, Russia, May 3, 1956; arrived in the U.S., 1993; BS, Poly. U., St. Petersburg, 1977, MS, 1979, PhD, 1987. Engr. Mekhanobr-Tekhnika, St. Petersburg, 1978-85, scientist, 1985-92; engr. Bently Nevada Corp., Minden, Nev., 1993-94, scientist, 1994—. Mem. ASME, Russian Engring. Acad. (fgn.). Office: Bently Nevada Corp 1711 Orbit Way Bldg 1 Minden NV 89423-4114 E-mail: alex.petchenev@bently.com.

PETCHESKY, ROSALIND POLLACK, political scientist, educator, social sciences educator; b. Bay City, Tex., Aug. 16, 1942; BA, Smith Coll., 1964; MA, Columbia U., 1966, PhD, 1974. Prof., polit. sci. and women's studies, Hunter Coll. CUNY, 1987—, head, women's studies program, Hunter Coll., 1987—91. Bd. dirs. Women's Environ. and Develop. Orgn., 2000—. Author: The Individual's Rights and the International Organization, 1966, Abortion and Women's Choice: The State, Sexuality and Reproductive Freedom, 1984 (Joan Kelly Meml. prize Am. Hist. Assn., 1984), Abortion and Women's Choice: The State, Sexuality and Reproductive Freedom, 2d edit., 1990; co-editor: Negotiating Reproductive Rights: Women's Perspectives Across Countries and Cultures, 1998; serves governing bd. Jour. Reproductive Matters. Founder, first internat. coord. Internat. Reproductive Rights Rsch. Action Group. Fellow, MacArthur Found., 1995. Office: CUNY Hunter Coll Dept Polit Sci Hunter West 1726 695 Park Ave New York NY 10021-5024 Office Phone: 212-772-5500., 212-772-5682. E-mail: rpetches@igc.org.*

PETE, ERIC E. claims representative, writer; b. Seattle, Oct. 1, 1968; s. Earl Joseph Pete and Edna Mae Bushnell; m. Marsha Bluin; 1 child, Chelsea. BS, McNeese State U., 1993. Assoc. in mgmt., assoc. in claims, sr. claims law assoc. Claim rep. State Farm Cos., 1994—; owner E-fect Pub., Harvey, La., 2000—. Author: (novels) Real for Me, 2000, Someone's In the Kitchen, 2002. With U.S. Army, 1987—89. Mem.: Internat. Assn. Spl. Investigative Units, Young Leadership Coun. Greater New Orleans, Black Writers Alliance, Toastmasters Internat., Delta Sigma Pi. Avocations: reading, travel, dance, weightlifting, art. Office: PO Box 2425 Harvey LA 70059-2425 Business E-Mail: heyeric@att.net.

PETER, ARNOLD PHILIMON, lawyer, business executive; b. Karachi, Pakistan, Apr. 3, 1957; came to U.S., 1968; s. Kundan Lal and Irene Primrose (Mall) P. BS, Calif. State U., Long Beach, 1981; JD, Loyola U., L.A., 1984; MS, Calif. State U., Fresno, 1991. Bar: Calif. 1985, U.S. Dist. Ct. (ea., so., no. and cen. dists.) Calif. 1986, U.S. Ct. Appeals (9th cir.) 1989, U.S. Ct. Appeals (11th cir.) 1990. Law clk. appellate dept. Superior Ct., L.A., 1984-85, U.S. Dist. Ct. (ea. dist.) Calif., Fresno, 1986-88; assoc. Pepper, Hamilton & Scheetz, L.A., 1988-89, McDermott, Will & Emery, P.A., L.A., 1989-90, Cadwalader, Wickersham & Taft, L.A., 1990-91; labor and employment counsel City of Fresno, Calif., 1991-94; atty. Littler Mendelson, L.A., 1999—. V.p. legal and bus. affairs Universal Studios, Hollywood, Calif., 1994—; adj. prof. law San Joaquin (Calif.) Sch. Law, 1993—; adj. prof. law Calif. State U., Fresno, 1993—, acad. inquiry officer, 1993—. Contbr. articles to profl. jours. Mem. L.A. 2012 Olympic Bd. Com. Mem. ABA, L.A. County Bar Assn. (mem. conf. of dels., com. on fed. cts.), Calif. State Bar Assn. (chmn. com. on fed. cts., chmn. exec. com. labor and employment law sect.), L.A. Athletic Club. Friars Club. Office: Universal Studios 100 Universal City Plz Universal City CA 91608 Home: 2112 Graham Ave #B Redondo Beach CA 90278-2028

PETER, BERNARD GEORGE, lawyer; b. Balt., July 28, 1949; S. Bernard George and Ella (Galvin) P.; m. Ellen Cherobina Carosselli; children: Kyle, Jared. AB, Coll. Holy Cross; JD, U. Md. Bar: Md. 1969, Ill. 1974. Lawyer, asst. sec. C.F. Industries, Inc., Long Grove, Ill., 1974-78; assoc. gen. counsel Joslyn Corp., Chgo., 1978-80; asst. gen. counsel Marshall Field & Co., Chgo., 1980-84; atty./cons. William M. Mercer Inc., Chgo., 1984-89; atty./sr. cons. Alexander & Alexander Cons. Group, Chgo., 1989-94; atty., sr. cons. Watson Wyatt and Co., Chgo., 1994—. Bd. dirs. John T. Galvin, Inc., Balt., treas., 2000. Contbr. articles to profl. jours. Usher St. Mary's Ch., Lake Forest, 1983—; recruiter high sch. athletes. Mem. Ill. State Bar Assn. (com. mem. sect. coun. corp. law), Chgo. Bar Assn. (vice-chmn. corp. law depts. 1988-90), John Purdue Club. Avocations: Purdue U. sports, swimming, tennis. Home: 622 Timber Ln Lake Forest IL 60045 Office: Watson Wyatt Co 191 N Wacker Dr Ste 2100 Chicago IL 60606-1615

PETER, GREGORY A. sociology educator; b. Eau Claire, Wis., Aug. 19, 1970; s. Richard F. and Virginia C. Peter; m. Cathy Lynn Tschida, Aug. 21, 1992; children: Jordynn Catherine, Darby Camille. BA, U. Wis., 1992; MS (hon.), Iowa State U., 1997, PhD, 2000. Rsch. asst. North Ctrl. Regional Ctr. for Rural Devel., Ames, Iowa, 1995—97; asst. prof. of sociology James Madison U., Harrisonburg, Va., 2000—03, U. Wis. Fox Valley, Menasha, 2003—. Chair of tech. writing com. Shenandoah Valley RC&D, Woodstock, Va., 2002—; cons. Shenandoah Resource Conservation and Devel., Woodstock, 2002—, Rockingham County Planning Commn., Harrisonburg, Va., 2002—; usda/sbir panel mem. USDA/Small Bus. Info. Rcsh., Washington, 2001—; sociology club adviser James Madison U., Harrisonburg, 2001—. Author: (book) Farming for Us All, (book chpt.) Country Boys, (journal article) Journal of Extension; contbr. articles to profl. jours. (Outstanding Earth Team Vol. of the Yr., 2002, Outstanding Grad. Student Paper award, 1996). Invited spkr. Rockingham County Planning Commn., Harrisonburg, 2002—03. Mem.: Rural Sociol. Soc. (assoc.), Alpha Kappa Delta (assoc.; adviser 2001—03), Gamma Sigma Delta (assoc.), Sigma Xi (assoc.), Alpha Phi Omega (assoc.; adviser 2001—03). Green Party. Avocations: family, bicycling, hiking, writing, community service. Office: U Wis Fox Valley Dept Anthropology/Sociology 1478 Midway Rd Menasha WI 54952 Office Phone: 920-832-2655. E-mail: gpeter@uwc.edu.

PETER, PHILLIPS SMITH, lawyer; b. Washington, Jan. 24, 1932; s. Edward Compston and Anita Phillips (Smith) P.; m. Jania Jayne Hutchins, Apr. 8, 1961; children: Phillips Smith Peter Jr., Jania Jayne Hutchins Stone. BA, U. Va., 1954, JD, 1959. Bar: Calif. 1959. Assoc. McCutchen, Doyle, Brown, Enerson, San Francisco, 1959-63; with GE (and subs.), various locations, 1963-94, v.p. corp. bus. devel., 1973-76, v.p., 1976-79, v.p. corp. govtl. rels., 1980-94; counsel, head govt. rels. dept. Reed Smith Shaw & McClay, Washington, 1994—. Chmn. bd. govs. Bryce Harlow Found., 1990-92, bd. dirs. Mem. editl. bd. Va. Law Rev., 1957-59. Trustee Howard U., 1981—89; bd. dirs., exec. com. Nat. Bank of Washington, 1981—86; v.p. Fed. City Coun., Washington, 1979—85; bd. dirs. Carlton, 1987—90, 1995—98, pres., 1995—96; bd. dirs. Tudor Place Found., 1999—, v.p., 2001—02, pres., 2002—03. Mem. Calif. Bar Assn., Order of Coif, Wee Burn Club, Ea. Yacht Club, Farmington Country Club, Landmark Club, Congl. Country Club, Georgetown Club, Chevy Chase Club, Carlton Club (bd. dirs. 1990-98), Coral Beach and Tennis Club, Johns Island Club, The Windsor Club, Omicron Delta Kappa. Episcopalian. Home: 10805 Tara Rd Potomac MD 20854-1341 Address: Johns Island 1000 Beach Rd, 690 Ocean Rd & 10656 Eton Way Vero Beach FL 32963-3429 Office Phone: 202-414-9258. Business E-Mail: ppeter@reedsmith.com.

PETER, RICHARD ECTOR, zoology educator; b. Medicine Hat, Alta., Can., Mar. 7, 1943; s. Arthur E. and Josephine (Wrobleski) P.; m. Leona L. Booth, Dec. 27, 1965; children: Jason E., Matthew T.B. BSc with honors, U. Atla., 1965; PhD, U. Wash., 1969. Postdoctoral fellow U. Bristol, Eng., 1969-70; asst. prof. U. Alta., Edmonton, 1971-74, assoc. prof., 1974-79, prof., 1979—, chmn. dept. zoology, 1983-89, 90-92, dean of sci., 1992—2002; v.p. Alta. Rsch. Coun., 2002—. Contbr. over 300 papers to sci. publs. Recipient Outstanding Leadership in Alberta Sci. award Alberta Sci. and Tech. Leadership Awards Found., 1998, Excellence in Mentoring award U. Alberta, 2002; named Disting. Biologist, Can. Coun. Univ. Biology Chairmen. Fellow AAAS, Royal Soc. Can.; mem. Can. Soc. Zoology (pres. 1991-92), Endocrine Soc., Internat. Soc. Neuroendocrinology, Can. Coun. of Univ. Biology Chmn. (pres. 1986-87), Internat. Fedn. Comparative Endocrinol. Socs. (pres. 1989-93, Pickford medal 1985), Canadian Conf. of Deans of Sci., 1995-96 (pres.), Western Can. Univs. Marine Scis. Soc. (pres. 2001-02). Office Phone: 780-450-5205. E-mail: peter@arc.ab.ca.

PETERA, ANNE PAPPAS, state official; b. Richmond, Va., Feb. 13, 1950; d. Evangel Thomas and Margaret Theresa (McGuire) Pappas; m. Ronald Petera, Sept. 15, 1968; 1 child, Paul Evangel. BS, Va. Commonwealth U., 1980; grad., Realtors Inst. Br. officer Ctrl. Fidelity Bank, Richmond, 1972-79; asst. v.p. Signet Bank, Richmond, 1979-85; sales assoc. Hermitage Realty, Richmond, 1985-92; assoc. broker Napier Old Colony, Richmond, 1992-95, Bowers, Nelms & Fonville & Jefferson-Jones, Richmond, 1995-96; chair Va. Dept. Alcoholic Beverage Control, 1996-97; sec. Commonwealth of Va., 1998—2002; chief of staff to Atty. Gen. of Va., 2002—. Mem. faculty Richmond Assn. Realtors Sch. Real Estate, 1991-96; bd. visitors Va. Commonwealth U., 2001—, vice rector, 2003—. Vice-chmn. Hanover (Va.) County Rep. Com., 1990-92, chmn., 1992-94; chmn. 1st Congl. Dist., Rep. Party Va., Richmond, 1994-98, budget dir., 1996-98, treas. 1998-2001; mem. Rep. Nat. Com., 2001—. Named Disting. Achiever, Richmond Assn. Realtors, 1986, 87, 89, 90, 91, 92, 93, 94. Mem. Nat. Alcohol Beverage Control Assn. (dir. 1996-98), Nat. Assn. Realtors, Nat. Assn. Bank Women. Republican. Roman Catholic. Avocations: golf, reading, travel. Office: Office of the Atty Gen 900 E Main St Richmond VA 23219-2725 also: Old Finance Bldg PO Box 2454 Richmond VA 23218-2454 E-mail: annepetera@aol.com.

PETERLE, TONY JOHN, zoologist, educator; b. Cleve., July 7, 1925; s. Anton and Anna (Katic) P.; m. Thelma Josephine Coleman, July 30, 1949; children: Ann Faulkner, Tony Scott. BS, Utah State U., 1949; MS, U. Mich., 1950, PhD (univ. scholar), 1954; Fulbright scholar, U. Aberdeen, Scotland, 1954-55; postgrad., Oak Ridge Inst. Nuclear Studies, 1961. With Niederhauser Lumber Co., 1947—49, Macfarland Tree Svc., 1949—51; rsch. biologist Mich. Dept. Conservation, 1951—54; asst. dir. Rose Lake Expt. Sta., 1955—59; leader Ohio Coop. Wildlife Rsch. unit U.S. Fish and Wildlife Svc., Dept. Interior, 1959—63; asso. prof., then prof. zoology Ohio State U., Columbus, 1959—89, prof. emeritus, 1989, chmn. faculty population and environ. biology, 1968—69, chmn. dept. zoology, 1969—81, dir. program in environ. biology, 1970—71; liaison officer Internat. Union Game Biologists, 1965—93; chmn. internat. affairs com., mem. com., ecotoxicology co-organizer XIII Internat. Congress Game Biology, 1979—80; propr. The Iron Works, 1989—. Pvt. cons., 1989—; mem. com. rev. EPA pesticide decision making Nat. Acad. Scis.-NRC; mem. vis. scientists program Am. Inst. Biol. Scis.-ERDA, 1971-77; mem. com. pesticides Nat. Acad. Scis., com. on emerging trends in agr. and effects on fish and wildlife; mem. ecology com. of sci. adv. council EPA, 1979-87; mem. research units coordinating com. Ohio Coop. Wildlife and Fisheries, 1963-89; vis. scientist EPA, Corvallis, 1987. Author: Wildlife Toxicology, 1991; editor: Jour. of Wildlife Mgmt., 1969-70, 84-85, 2020 Vision Meeting the Fish and Wildlife Conservation Challenges of the 21st Century, 1992. Served with AUS, 1943-46. Named Internat. Scientists of Yr., 2002. Fellow AAAS, Am. Inst. Biol. Scis., Ohio Acad. Sci.; mem. Wildlife Disease Assn., Wildlife Soc. (regional rep. 1962-67, v.p. 1968, pres. 1972, Leopold award 1990, hon. mem. 1990, Profl. award of merit North Ctrl. sect. 1993), Nat. Audubon Soc. (bd. dirs. 1985-87), Ecol. Soc., INTECOL-NSF panel U.S.-Japan Program, Xi Sigma Pi, Phi Kappa Phi. Home: 4072 Klondike Rd Delaware OH 43015-9513 Office: Ohio State U Dept Ecology Evolution and Organismal Bi 1735 Neil Ave Columbus OH 43210-1220

PETERLIN, BORIS MATIJA, physician; b. Ljubljana, Slovenia, July 4, 1947; came to U.S., 1961; s. Anton and Leopoldina (Leskovic) P.; m. Anne Scheel-Larsen, July 21, 1984; children: Anton Alexander, Sebastian Bogomir. BS, Duke U., 1968; MD, Harvard U., 1973. Diplomate Am. Bd. Internal Medicine, Am. Bd. Rheumatology. Intern, resident Stanford (Calif.) Univ. Hosp., 1973-75, sr. resident, 1977-78; fellow in rheumatology, immunology Stanford (Calif.) U. Hosp., 1978-81; asst. prof. U. Calif., San Francisco, 1981-88, assoc. prof., 1988-94, prof., 1994—; asst. investigator HHMI, Bethesda, Md., 1984-89, assoc. investigator, 1989-95, investigator, 1995—2002. Vis. prof. U. Ljubljana, 1998—. Contbr. articles to Nature, Cell, Genes and Development, others. Lt. commdr. USPHS, 1975-77. Rosalind Russell Arthritis scholar U. Calif.; recipient Alexander von Humboldt prize, 1995. Fellow Am. Soc. for Clin. Investigation; mem. Am. Assn. Immunology, Am. Fedn. Clin. Rsch., Am. Soc. for Microbiology, Am. Coll. Rheumatology, Assn. Am. Physicians, Phi Beta Kappa, Phi Lambda Upsilon. Democrat. Roman Catholic. Achievements include diagnosis of bare lymphocyte syndrome; discovery of mechanism of action of HIV Nef and Tat proteins; fundamental studies in replication of HIV. Home: 14 Hill Point Ave San Francisco CA 94117-3603 Office: U Calif San Francisco-HHMI 3D And Parnassus San Francisco CA 94143-0001

PETERMAN, DONNA COLE, communications executive; b. St. Louis, Nov. 9, 1947; d. William H. Cole and Helen A. Morris; m. John A. Peterman, Feb. 7, 1970. BA in Journalism, U. Mo., 1969; MBA, U. Chgo., 1984. Mgr. employee comm. Sears Merchandise Group, Chgo., 1975-80; affairs and mktg. comm. Seraco Real Estate, Chgo., 1980-82; dir. corp. comm. Sears, Roebuck and Co., Chgo., 1982-85; sr. v.p., dir. corp. comm. Dean Witter Fin. Svcs. Group, N.Y., 1985-88; sr. v.p., mng. dir. Hill and Knowlton, Inc., Chgo., 1988-94, exec. v.p. N.Y.C., 1994-96; sr. v.p., dir. corp. comm. Paine Webber Group, Inc., N.Y.C., 1996-2000; mng. dir., regional head comms. and mktg. The Americas, UBS Americas Inc., 2000—03; sr. v.p., dir. corp. comm. PNC Fin. Svcs. Group Inc., 2003—. Media chair DeKalb County Comm., Ga., 1975; media dir., Mo. Atty. Gen., 1971, Rep. Govs. Conf., 1974; copywriter Govt. of Mo., 1971. Chmn. bd. trustees Securities Industry Found. for Investor Edn. Mem. Pub. Rels. Soc. Am., Arthur Page Soc., Pub. Rels. Seminar, Edgewood Country Club, Palmetto Pines Country Club, The Rivers Club, The Wise Men. Republican. Roman Catholic. Avocations: tennis, golf, sailing, skiing, bridge. Office: The PNC Fin Svcs Group Inc 1 PNC Plaza 249 5th Ave Pittsburgh PA 15222-2707

PETERMANN, HANS JÜRGEN, research scientist; b. Vienna, Feb. 2, 1942; MA in German, Calif. State U., 1971; PhD in Physics, 2d Phys. Inst., Vienna, Austria, 1976; PhD in Botany (hon.), Bot. Inst., Berlin, Germany, 1980. Prof. phys. scis. Coll. of Desert, Palm Desert, Calif.; rsch. scientist Palm Springs, Calif., 1991—. Chmn., sr. v.p. Galaxy Energy Sys., Inc. Author: The Esoteric

Sciences, vol. 1, 2d edit., 2001, vol. 2, 2d edit., 2003, Esoteric Curiosities of Plant Kingdom, vol. 2, 2d edit., 2003, Gravitation, Matter and Space Travel, 2d edit., 2002; patentee in field. With US Army, 1963-66. Achievements include development of hydrogen generator to make vehicles, boats and ships operate with water and hydrogen, cold fusion power plants; construction of 600-650 m.p.h. maglev train system in Nevada and California. Avocations: hiking, tennis, scuba diving, mountain climbing, swimming. Office: PO Box 4513 Palm Springs CA 92263-4513 Office Phone: 760-778-4254.

PETERS, ALAN, anatomy educator; b. Nottingham, Eng., Dec. 6, 1929; came to U.S., 1966; s. Robert and Mabel (Woplington) P.; m. Verona Muriel Shipman, Sept. 30, 1955; children: Ann Verona, Sally Elizabeth, Susan Clare. BSc, Bristol (Eng.) U., 1951, PhD, 1954. Lectr. anatomy Edinburgh (Scotland) U., 1958-66; vis. lectr. Harvard, 1963-64; prof., chmn. dept. anatomy and neurobiology Boston U., 1966-98, Waterhouse prof., 1998—. Anatomy com. Nat. Bd. Med. Examiners, 1971-75; mem. neurology B Study sect. NIH, 1975-79, chmn., 1978-79; affiliate scientist Yerkes Regional Primate Rsch. Ctr., 1984—. Author (with S.L. Palay and H. deF Webster): The Fine Structure of the Nervous System, 1970, The Fine Structure of the Nervous System, 3rd edit., 1991; author: Myclination, 1970; contbr. articles to profl. jours.; mem. editl. bd.: Anat. Record, 1972—81, Jour. Comparative Neurology, 1981—97, Neurocytology, 1972—89, 1993—, Cerebral Cortex, 1990—, Studies of Brain Function, Anat. and Embryology, 1989—92; editor (with E.G. Jones): (book series) Cerebral Cortex, 1984—2000; exec. prodr.(with B. Payne): Cat Visual Cortex, 2001. Served to 2d lt. Royal Army Med. Corps, 1955-57. Recipient Javits neurosci. investigator award NIH, 1986; Henry Gray award, 1998. Mem. Anat. Soc. Gt. Britain and Ireland (Symington prize anatomy 1962, overseas mem. coun. 1969), Assn. Anatomy Chmn. (pres. 1976-77), Am. Anat. Assn. (exec. com. 1986-90, pres. 1992-93, Henry Gray award 1998), Am. Soc. Cell Biology, Soc. Neurosci., Internat. Primatological Soc., Cajal Club (Harman lectr. 1990, Cortical Discoverer award 1991). Home: 16 High Rock Cir Waltham MA 02451-2207 Office: Boston U Sch Medicine Dept Anatomy and Neurobiology 80 E Concord St Roxbury MA 02118-2307 Office Phone: 617 638 4235.

PETERS, ARNOLD STEVENS, legal association administrator, mechanical engineer; b. Des Moines, Apr. 25, 1934; s. Paul F. and Lodema (Johnson) Peters; m. Beverly Beverly Ann (div. 1979); children: Caren P., Paula J. AA, Contra Costa Jr. Coll., Concord, Calif., 1955. Quality control insp. Colo. Fuel and Iron, Oakland, Calif., 1959—60; assistance divsn. supt. Cyclone Fence Co., Oakland, 1960—64; plant mgr. Dowman Products, Berkeley, Calif., 1964—65; indsl. engr. Oliver Tire and Rubber, Oakland, 1965—66; fin. adv. A.D. Gordon Co., Oakland, 1966—68; owner A.S. Peters Assoc., Hayward, Calif., 1969—87. Author: WWII Veterans Pension, 1999, Eden Township Hosital, 2004. With U.S. Army, 1956—58. Avocations: football, golf. Home: 3525 Lyon Ave #20A Oakland CA 94601 Office Phone: 510-436-4704.

PETERS, AULANA LOUISE, lawyer, former government agency commissioner; b. Shreveport, La., Nov. 30, 1941; d. Clyde A. and Eula Mae (Faulkner) Pharis; m. Bruce F. Peters, Oct. 6, 1967. BA in Philosophy, Coll. New Rochelle, 1963; JD, U. So. Calif., 1973. Bar: Calif., 1974. Sec., English corr. Publimondial, Spa, Milan, Italy, 1963-64, Fibramianto, Spa, Milan, 1964-65, Turkish del. to Office for Econ. Cooperation & Devel., Paris, 1965-66; adminstrv. asst. Office for Econ. Cooperation & Devel., Paris, 1966-67; assoc. Gibson, Dunn & Crutcher, L.A., 1973-80, ptnr., 1980-84, 88—; commr. SEC, Washington, 1984-88. Bd. dirs. 3M Corp., Merrill Lynch & Co., Mobil Corp., Northrop Grumman, Callaway Golf Co. Recipient Disting. Alumnus award Econs. Club So. Calif., 1984, Washington Achiever award Nat. Assn. Bank Women, 1986, Critics Choice award nat. Women's Econ. Alliance, 1994, Women in Bus. award H0llywood C. of C., 1995. Mem. ABA, State Bar of Calif. (civil litigation cons. group 1983-84), Los Angeles County Bar Assn., Black Women Lawyers Assn. L.A., Assn. Bus. Trial Lawyers (panelist L.A. 1982), Women's Forum, Washington. Office: Gibson Dunn & Crutcher 333 S Grand Ave Ste 4400 Los Angeles CA 90071-3197

PETERS, BARB WATERMAN, artist, educator; b. Topeka, Nov. 3, 1944; d. L.E. Clifton Bailey and Gertrude Minnie McFarland; m. John Herman Waterman, Dec. 21, 1965 (div. Dec. 1985); m. Larry Dean Peters, May 30, 1986. BFA, Washburn U., 1973; MFA, Kans. State U., 1998. Adj. instr. Washburn U., Topeka, 1985—88, adj. asst. prof., 1989—96, 1999—2001; grad. tchg. asst. Kans. State U., Manhattan, 1997—98, temporary asst. prof., 2004—, asst. prof. painting, 2004—. Mus. specialist edn1. svcs. Mulvane Art Mus., Topeka, 1987; faculty advisor Washburn Art Students Assn., Topeka, 1994-96; guest curator Water Marks exhbn. Mulvane Art Mus., Topeka, 1995-96; exhbn. juror in field; spkr., reviewer in field. One-woman shows include Bedyk Gallery, Kansas City, Mo., 1983, 88, Collective Art Gallery, Topeka, 1988-90, 96-97, 1999-2000, 2002-2004, Yost Gallery-Highland (Kans.) C.C., 1989, 95, Art Craft Gallery, Denver, 1994-95, 97, Fourth St. Gallery, Kansas City, 1997, Michael Cross Gallery, Kansas City, 1999-2000, Wichita Ctr. Arts, 2001, Kanas Artist Gallery, Mulvane Art Mus., 2002; group shows include Holman Art Gallery-Trenton State Coll., 1979, N.Mex. Art League, Albuquerque, 1980, Nat. Soc. Painters, N.Y., 1980 (Michael Engle Meml. award), Ball State U. Art Gallery, Muncie, Ind., 1981, Portsmouth (Va.) Cmty. Ctr., 1982, Nelson-Atkins Mus., Kansas City, 1982, Owensboro (Ky.) Mus. Fine Art, 1982 (award), Joslyn Art Mus., Omaha, 1988, others, Women's Conf., Beijing, 1995, Jan Weiner Gallery, Kansas City, 1995, The Columbian Art Gallery, Wamego, Kans., 1997, 2002, Topeka and Shawnee County Pub. Libr., 1997, 2002, Strecker Gallery, Manhattan, Kans., 1999-2000, Cedar Rapids (Iowa) Mus. Art, 1997, Wichita Ctr. for the Arts, 2000, 02, Birger Sandzen Gallery, Lindsborg, Kans., 2001, U. Kans. Art and Design Gallery, 2002, Strecker-Nelson Gallery, Manhattan, Kans., 2002, Mulvane Art Mus., Topeka, 2003, Emporia Art Ctr., Kans., 2003, Gallery of Framewoods, Topeka, 2004; visual artist Andrew J. and Georgia Neese Gray Theatre, Washburn U., 1999--; contbr. articles to profl. jours. Vol. art gallery Topeka and Shawnee County Pub. Libr., 1986—; panelist Kans. Arts Commn., Kans. Presswomen, 1990—; bd. dirs. Arts Coun. Topeka, 2002-04, Raymer Soc., 2004—; mem. ad hoc com. Kans. Arts Commn., 2002-04, mem. fellowship selection panel, 2004; mem. ad. hoc com. Topeka Cmty. Found., 2002-03. Recipient Outstanding Achievement award, Am. Inst. Banking, Topeka, 1977, assistantship in lithography, Kans. Arts Commn., 1981, Woman of Distinction in the Arts award, Kaw Valley Girl Scouts, Topeka, 1996, Artist's Residency award, The Raymer Soc., 2001—04, Cert. of Recognition Outstanding Contributions, State Kans., 2003. Mem. Nat. Mus. Women in the Arts, Chgo. Artists' Coalition, Kansas City Artists Coalition, St. Louis Artists Guild, Mulvane Art Mus., Lawrence Art Ctr., Libr. Friends of Art Topeka and Shawnee County Pub. Libr., The Collective (charter, treas. 1987-89, v.p. 1990-94, 99-00, pres. 2001-04, newsletter editor 2000—), Friends of Art Bd. Beach Mus. Art (collections com. 1997—), Kans. Citizens for Arts, Kans. Author's Club (mem. J. Donald Coffin award selection com., workshop presenter 2004 conv.), Raymer Soc. (bd. dirs.), Assn. Cmty. Arts Agencies of Kansas, Manhattan Arts Ctr. Avocations: reading, writing, travel. Home: 2223 SW Knollwood Dr Topeka KS 66611-1623 E-mail: barbara.r.peters@att.net.

PETERS, BERNADETTE (BERNADETTE LAZZARA), actress; b. Queens, N.Y., Feb. 28, 1948; d. Peter and Marguerite (Maltese) Lazzara. Student, Quintano Sch. for Young Profls., N.Y.C. Ind. actress, entertainer, 1957—. Appeared on TV series All's Fair, 1976-77; frequent guest appearances on TV; (films) The Longest Yard, 1974, Silent Movie, 1976, Vigilant Force, 1976, W.C. Fields and Me, 1976, Silent Movie, 1976, The Jerk, 1979, Heartbeeps, 1981, Tulips, 1981, Pennies from Heaven, 1981 (Golden Globe award best actress), Annie, 1982, Slaves of New York, 1989, Pink Cadillac, 1989, Impromptu, 1991, Alice, 1990, Anastasia (voice), 1997, Cinderella, 1997, Snow Days, 1999, Prince Charming, 2001, Bobbie's Girl, 2002, A Few Good Years, 2002, It Runs in the Family, 2003; (TV movies) Cinderella, ABC-TV, 1997, Holiday in Your Heart, 1997; (stage appearances) This is Google, 1957, The Most Happy Fella, 1959, Gypsy, 1961, Curly McDimple, 1967, Johnny No-Trump, 1967, George M!, 1968 (Theatre World award, 1968), Dames at Sea, 1968 (Drama Desk award, 1968), La Strada, 1969, On the Town, 1971, Tartuffe, 1972, Mack and Mabel, 1974, Sally and Marsha, 1982, Sunday in the Park with George, 1983-85 (Tony nom., 1983), Song and Dance, 1985-86 (Drama League award best actress, 1985, Tony award best actress, 1986, Drama Desk award best actress, 1986), Into the Woods, 1987, The Goodbye Girl, 1992-93, Annie Get Your Gun 1998-1999 (Tony award best actress, 1999, Outer Critics Circle award best actress, 1999, Drama Desk award best actress, 1999), Gypsy, 2003-; TV mini-series The Odyssey, 1997; rec. artist: (MCA Records) Bernadette Peters, 1980, Now Playing, 1981; CD's include I'll Be Your Baby Tonight, Angel Records, 1996 (Grammy nomination), Sondheim Etc: Bernadette Peters Live at Carnegie Hall, Angel Records, 1997 (Grammy nom.), solo concert Radio City Music Hall, 2002. Recipient Hasty Pudding Theatrical award, 1987 Woman of Yr. award, Sara Siddons Actress of Yr. award, 1993-94, Actors Fund medal for artistic achievement, 1999; named Woman of Yr., Police Athletic League, 1999; named to Theatre Hall of Fame. Office: William Morris Agency c/o Jeff Hunter 1325 Ave of the Americas 15th Fl New York NY 10019*

PETERS, CAROL ANN, secondary school educator; b. Ashtabula, Ohio, Feb. 12, 1946; d. Leonard Jay and Anniece Edna Hawkins; m. Robert Lewis Peters, June 12, 1971; children: Brian Jay, Sharon Lynne. BS in Edn., Kent State U., 1968; ESL cert., U. Houston, 1990; postgrad., S.W. Tex. State U., 1999—. Cert. secondary edn. Tex. Tchr. Fairport (Ohio) Exp Village Sch. Dist., 1968—71; substitute tchr. Spring Branch Ind. Sch. Dist., Houston, 1972—74, tchr., 1987—93; substitute tchr. San Marcos (Tex.) Ind. Sch. Dist., 1993—94; tchr. Wackenhut Corrections Corp., Lockhart, Tex., 1994—96; tutor, owner Village Sensei, Maxwell, Tex., 1998—; tchr. cons. Nat. Evaluation Sys., Inc., Austin, Tex., 2000—. Mem. San Marcos H.S. campus improvement team San Marcos Cons. Ind. Sch. Dist., 1999—2002, mem. facilities task force, 2000—02. Troop leader, svc. unit officer Girl Scouts USA, Houston, 1981—93; organizer Ams. Promise Youth Summit City of San Marcos, Tex., 1998—99, youth commr., 1998—. Mem.: NEA, TESOL, Internat. Dyslexia Assn., San Marcos Area and Hispanic C. of C. (edn. com.), Tex. PTA (life), Lions Internat. (youth outreach chair). Roman Catholic. Avocations: bridge, playing piano and organ, camping, landscaping, writing. Home: 36 Mill St Maxwell TX 78656 Office: Village Sensei 36 Mill St Maxwell TX 78656

PETERS, CAROL ANN DUDYCHA, counselor; b. Ripon, Wis., Dec. 23, 1938; d. George John and Martha (Malek) Dudycha; m. Milton Eugene Peters, Aug. 27, 1960. AB, Wittenberg U., 1960, MEd, 1963; leadership devel. cert., Ctr. for Creative Leadership, Greensboro, N.C., 1986; postgrad., U. Toledo, 1973-97, U. Findlay, 1997-99. Lic. profl. counselor, Ohio; nat. cert. counselor, nat. cert. career counselor Nat. Bd. Cert. Counselors, Inc.; cert. basic critical incident stress mgmt. Internat. Critical Incident Stress Found., 1999. Tchr. Springfield (Ohio) City Schs., 1960-62, Mad River-Green Local Schs., Springfield, 1962-63; counselor Napoleon (Ohio) Area Schs., 1963-70, Findlay City Sch., Ohio, 1970-2000; field counselor Career Relocation Corp. Am., Armonk, 1992-95, 98-99; sr. lectr. U. Findlay, 1999—2002. Cons., prin. Peters and Peters, Findlay, 1979—; leader Creative Edn. Found., Buffalo, 1980-91, colleague, Hadley, Mass., 1985—; founder ednl. corp. Career Info. Bur. Hancock County, 1974. Pres. Big Bros./Big Sisters Hancock County, 1982-83; bd. dirs. Citizens Opposing Drug Abuse (C.O.D.A.), Findlay, 1982—; advisor, leader Hancock Addictions Prevention for Youth (H.A.P.P.Y.), 1985-91; mem. Hancock County Community Devel. Found. Edn. Com., 1990-93, Findlay/Hancock County Am. 2000 New Sch. Design Team, 1991-92; mem. Hancock County Crisis Response Team, 1991-97, 99—; mem. assets/needs assessment com. United Way, 1997-98; mem. Findlay Juvenile Diversion Task Force, 1997-98 Named One of Outstanding Young Women of Am., 1967; named Outstanding Woman in Edn., Bus. and Profl. Women, 1983; recipient Outstanding Citizenship award The Lincoln Ctr., Findlay, 1989, Meritorious Svc. award Big Bros./Big Sisters Hancock County, 1988. Mem. ACA, AAUW (Findlay br.), NEA (life), Nat. Career Devel. Assn., Ohio Ret. Tchrs. Assn. (life), Ohio Counseling Assn., Findlay-Hancock County C. of C. (sec. edn. com. 1984-90), Ohio Career Devel. Assn. Lutheran. Avocations: sailing, flower arranging, cooking.

PETERS, CHARLES A, electronics executive; married; 5 children. B in mech. engring., Cornell U.; MBA, Harvard U. Engring. coop. student Emerson Elec. Co., 1975—78; corp. planning, mgmt. positions Emerson Electric Co., 1978; sr. exec., v.p. Emerson Elec. Co., 2000—. Office: Emerson Electric Company 8000 W Florissant Ave Saint Louis MO 63136

PETERS, CHARLES GIVEN, JR., editor; b. Charleston, W.Va., Dec. 22, 1926; s. Charles Given and Esther (Teague) P.; m. Elizabeth Bostwick Hubbell, Aug. 3, 1957; 1 child, Christian Avery. BA in Humanities, Columbia U., 1949, MA in English, 1951; LLB, U. Va., 1957; LLD (hon.), U. Charleston, 1979. Bar: W.Va. 1957, DC 1981. Atty. Peters, Merrick, Leslie & Mohler, Charleston, 1957-61; mem. W.Va State Legislature, Charleston, 1960-62; dir. evaluation Peace Corps, Washington, 1962-68; founder, editor in chief The Washington Monthly, 1968—2001; pres. Understanding Govt., 1999—. Delacorte lectr. Columbia U. Grad. Sch. Journalism, 1990, 2003, Times-Mirror David Laventhol vis. prof., 2002; pub. scholar Woodrow Wilson Internat. Ctr. for Scholars, 2002-03. Author: How Washington Really Works, 1980, Tilting at Windmills, 1988; editor: (with Taylor Branch) Blowing the Whistle, 1972, (with James Fallows) The System, 1975, (with Michael Nelson) The Culture of Bureaucracy, 1977, (with Jonathan Alter) Inside the System, 5th edit., 1985. Mgr. John F. Kennedy campaign, Kanawha County, W.Va., 1960. Served with inf. US Army, 1944-46. Named West Virginian of Yr., Charleston Gazette-Mail, 1980, Poynter fellow, Yale U., 1980; named to Hall of Fame, Am. Soc. Mag. Editors, 2001; recipient Columbia Journalism award, 1978, Richard S. Clurman award, 1996, Carr Van Anda award, 2003. Democrat. Presbyterian. Office: Washington Monthly Co 733 15th St NW Washington DC 20005

PETERS, CHARLES WILLIAM, research and development company manager; b. Pierceton, Ind., Dec. 9, 1927; s. Charles Frederick and Zelda May (Line) P.; m. Katharine Louise Schuman, May 29, 1953; 1 child, Susan Kay; m. 2d, Patricia Ann Miles, Jan. 2, 1981; children: Bruce Miles Merkle, Leslie Ann Merkle Sanaie, Philip Frank Merkle, William Macneil Merkle. AB, Ind. U., 1950; postgrad. U. Md., 1952-58. Supervisory rsch. physicist Naval Rsch. Lab., Washington, 1950-71; physicist EPA, Washington, 1971-76; mgr. advanced systems EATON-Consol. Controls Corp., Springfield, Va., 1976-89, v.p. Nuclear Diagnostic Systems, Inc., Springfield, Va, 1989-92, cons. Am. Tech. Inst., 1993—. With U.S. Army, 1945-47. Mem. IEEE, AAAS, Am. Phys. Soc. Home and Office: 5235 N Whispering Hills Ln Tucson AZ 85704-2510

PETERS, DAVID ALLEN, mechanical engineering educator, consultant; b. East St. Louis, Ill., Jan. 31, 1947; s. Bernell Louis and Marian Louise (Blum) P.; children: Michael H., Laura A., Nathan C. BS in Applied Mechanics, Washington U., St. Louis, 1969, MS in Applied Mechanics, 1970; PhD in Aeros. and Astronautics, Stanford U., 1974. Assoc. engr. McDonnell Astronautics, 1969-70; rsch. scientist Army Aeronautics Lab., 1970-74; asst. prof. Washington U., 1975-77, assoc. prof., 1977-80, prof. mech. engring., 1980-85, chmn. dept., 1982-85; prof. aerospace engring. Ga. Inst Tech., Atlanta, 1985-91; dir. NASA Space Grant Consortium Ga. Inst. Tech., Atlanta, 1989-91; dir. Ctr. for Computational Mechanics Washington U., 1992—, prof. dept. mech. engring., 1991—, chmn. dept. mech. engring., 1997—, McDonnell Douglas prof. engring., 1999. Contbr. 100 articles to profl. jours. Recipient sci. contbn. award NASA, 1975, 76. Fellow AIAA, ASME, Am. Helicopter Soc. (jour. editor 1987-90); mem. Am. Soc. for Engring. Edn., Internat. Assn. for Computational Mechanics (charter), Am. Acad. Mechs., Pi Tau Sigma (gold medal 1978). Baptist. Home: 7629 Balson Ave Saint Louis MO 63130-2150 Office: Wash U Dept Mech Engr Campus Box 1185 Saint Louis MO 63130

PETERS, DENNIS GAIL, chemist; b. L.A., Apr. 17, 1937; s. Samuel and Phyllis Dorothy (Pope) P. BS cum laude, Calif. Inst. Tech., 1958; PhD, Harvard U., 1962. Mem. faculty Ind. U., 1962—, prof. chemistry, 1974—, Herman T. Briscoe prof., 1975—. Co-author textbooks, contbr. articles profl. jours. Woodrow Wilson fellow, 1958-59; NIH predoctoral fellow, 1959-62; vis. fellow Japan Soc. for Promotion Sci., 1980; recipient Ulysses G. Weatherly award disting. teaching Ind. U., 1969, Disting. Teaching award Coll. Arts and Scis. Grad. Alumni Assn. Ind. U., 1984, Nat. Catalyst award for Disting. Teaching Chem. Mfrs. Assn., 1988, Henry B. Linford award The Electrochem. Soc., 2002; grantee NSF. Fellow Ind. Acad. Sci., Am. Inst. Chemists; mem. ACS (grantee, Div. of Analytical Chemistry award for excellence in teaching 1990, James Flack Norris award 2001). Home: 1401 S Nancy St Bloomington IN 47401-6051 Office: Dept Chemistry Ind U Bloomington IN 47405 Office Phone: 812-855-9671. Business E-Mail: peters@indiana.edu.

PETERS, DOUGLAS ALAN, medical-legal consultant, health law attorney; b. Portsmouth, Va., Oct. 4, 1968; s. Terrance Gene and Pamela (Haffner) P. BA in Philosophy, Va. Poly. Inst. and State U., 1992; BSN summa cum laude, James Madison U., 1995; JD, U. Md., Balt., 2003. RN Md.; cert. case mgr., legal nurse cons. Photojournalist CVNI/The Greene County Record, Stanardsville, Va., 1992; nursing asst. Rockingham Meml. Hosp., Harrisonburg, Va., 1993-95; clin. nurse Bapt. Hosp., Pensacola, Fla., 1995-96; nurse mgr. quality assurance Escambia County Jail Infirmary, Pensacola, 1996-97; case mgr./U.R. Total Health Care, Balt., 1997-98; case mgr. Blue Cross/Blue Shield of Md., Balt., 1998-2000, appeals analyst, 2000—01, sr. appeals analyst, 2001—04; jud. law clk. 23d Jud. Cir., W.Va., 2004—. Vol. hospice unit Rockingham Meml. Hosp., 1994-95; vol. Tourette Syndrome Assn., 1996-2000. Mem.: ABA (health law sect.), Montgomery County Med. Res. Corps, Am. Assn. Legal Nurse Cons., Md. State Bar Assn., Montgomery County Bar Assn., Balt. City Bar Assn., Alley Cat Allies, Phi Alpha Delta, Sigma Theta Tau, Alpha Chi Sigma. Avocations: Civil War history, darts, biomedical ethics. E-mail: dapeters2004@yahoo.com.

PETERS, DOUGLAS CAMERON, mining engineer, geologist; b. Pitts., June 19, 1955; s. Donald Cameron and Twila (Bingel) P. BS in Earth and Planetary Sci., U. Pitts., 1977; MS in Geology, Colo. Sch. Mines, 1981, MS in Mining Engring., 1983. Technician, inspector Engring. Mechanics Inc., Pitts., 1973-77; rsch. asst. Potential Gas Agy., Golden, Colo., 1977-78; geologist U.S. Geol. Survey, Denver, 1978-80; cons. Climax Molybdenum Co., Golden, 1981-82; mining engr., prin. investigator U.S. Bur. Mines, Denver, 1984-96; owner Peters Geoscis., Golden, 1996—. Bur. rep. to Geosat Com., 1984-95; program chmn. GeoTech Conf., Denver, 1984-88, mem. long range planning subcom., 1989-92, gen. chmn., 1991; engr. in tng. #11800, Colo., profl. geologist, Wyo., #367, Pa., #2365, Washington, #396. Author: Physical Modeling of Draw of Broken Rock in Caving, 1984, bur. mines articles and reports; editor COGS computer contbns., 1986-90, Geology in Coal Resource Utilization, 1988-91, Atlas of Coal Geology, 1999, Remote Sensing for Site Characterization, 2000; assoc. editor: Computers & Geosciences, 1991-2000; contbr. articles to profl. jours.; guest editor various jours.; dep. editor: Natural Resources Research, 1999—. Recipient award Am. Inst. Profl. Geologists, 1984, 85, 86, Appreciation award, 1987, Spl. award Denver Geotech Com., 1988, Appreciation award, 1989. Mem. Am. Inst. Profl. Geologists (sec. Colo. sect. 1997, pres. elect 1998, pres. 1999), Am. Assn. Petroleum Geologists (hon. charter mem., astrogeology com. 1984-2000, pub. com. 1995—, div. environ. geoscis. 1993-, Energy Mineral divsn. v.p. 1990-91, pres. 1991-92, chmn. pubs. com. 1990-98, remote sensing com. 1990—, Cert. Merit 1992, 93, 99, 2003, Pres.'s award 1993, Disting. Svc. award 1994, hon. mem. award 2004, assoc. editor Search and Discovery 2000—, dep. editor Natural Resources Rsch. 2001—), Am. Soc. Photogrammetry and Remote Sensing, Nat. Space Soc., Computer Oriented Geol. Soc. (charter, com. chmn. 1983-95, pres. 1985, dir. 1986, contbg. editor newsletter 1985-96), Assn. Exploration Geochemists, Geol. Soc. Am., Rocky Mountain Assn. Geologists, Soc. Mining Metallurgy and Exploration, Planetary Soc., Space Studies Inst., Denver Mining Club. Republican. E-mail: petersdc@petersgeo.com.

PETERS, DOUGLAS SCOTT, health care executive; b. Columbus, Ohio, Nov. 2, 1943; s. Edward Alvin and Jane (Appleman) P.; m. Karen Ann Jones, June 19, 1965; children: Brian Edward, Laura Kathleen. BS, Ohio State U., 1965; MHA with distinction, U. Mich., 1967. Assoc. dir. U. Mich. Hosp., Ann Arbor, 1969-74; dir. U. Nebr. Hosps. and Clinics, Omaha, 1974-77; exec. dir. Henry Ford Hosp., Detroit, 1977-83, pres. ceo., 1983-87; exec. v.p. Henry Ford Healthcare Corp., Detroit, 1983-87; pres. ceo. Main Line Health, 1991—. Cons. PanAm. Health Orgn., Washington, 1971-73; asst. prof. dept. med. and ednl. adminstrn. U. Nebr., 1974-77. Bd. dirs. New Detroit, Inc., 1985—; co-chmn. Multiple Sclerosis Testimonial Dinner, Detroit, 1985; big bro. Big Bros./Big Sisters, Omaha, 1975. Served to lt. USNR, 1967-69. Fellow Am. Coll. Healthcare Execs. (regent 1984); mem. Young Pres. Orgn., Mich Hosp. Assn. (bd. dirs.), Frontiers in Health Services Mgmt. (mem. editorial bd. 1983), mem. The Pennsylvania Soc, Amer. Hosp. Assoc. Regency Policy Bd, Foster G. McGaw Prize Review Panel, AHA, 1989-; Katahdin Medical and Philosophical Soc., 1992-; Amer. Healthcare Sys. Risk Purchasing Grp, 1993-; Amer. Healthcare Sys. Insur. Assoc., 1993-; bd of dirs: Healthshare Inc., 1988-; Amer. Healthcare Sys., 1991-; The Philadelphia Contributionship, 1992-; Amer. Red Cross, 1992-; First Fidelity Bank, 1994-; Radnor Education Found., 1994-; Amer. Heart Assoc., 1995. Republican. Office: Main Line Health 130 S Bryn Mawr Ave Bryn Mawr PA 19010-3121

PETERS, EDWARD MURRAY, history professor; b. New Haven, Conn. BA, Yale U., 1963, MA, 1965, PhD, 1967. Instr. English and history Quinnipiac Coll., Hamden, Conn., 1964-67; asst. prof. history U. Calif., San Diego, 1967-68, U. Pa., Phila., 1968-70, assoc. prof., 1970-81, Henry Charles Lea prof. history, 1981—, curator Henry Charles Lea Library, 1968—; vis. prof. Cath. U. Leuven, Belgium, 1992, 2004. Vis. prof. history Yale U., 1998, 2001-02. Author: The Shadow King, 1970; author: (with A.C. Kors) Witchcraft in Europe, 1100-1750, 1972, 2d edit., 2000; author: Europe: The World of the Middle Ages, 1977, The Magician, The Witch and The Law, 1978, Europe and the Middle Ages, 1983, 4th edit., 2003, Torture, 1985, expanded edit., 1996, Inquisition, 1988, Limits of Thought and Power in Medieval Europe, 2001, (TV series) The World of the Middle Ages, 1974, The World Around the Revolution, 1977, also articles, revs. and introductions; editor, transl. (series) The Middle Ages, 1970—95, (with Jeanne Krochalis) The World of Piers Plowman, 1975; editor: Heresy and Authority in Medieval Europe, 1980. Served with AUS, 1956-59. Woodrow Wilson fellow, 1963-64, dissertation fellow, 1966-67, hon. Sterling fellow, 1966-67, ACLS fellow, 1981-82, Guggenheim fellow, 1988-89. Fellow Medieval Acad. Am., Royal Hist. Soc.; mem. Am. Hist. Assn., Medieval Acad. Am., Am. Soc. Legal History, Maiestas, Iuris Canonici Medii Aevi Consociatio, Soc. Jean Bodin, Dante Soc. Am., Renaissance Soc. Am. Office: U Pa Dept History Philadelphia PA 19104-6228 E-mail: empeters@sas.upenn.edu.

PETERS, ELIZABETH, media organization director; Degree in film, U. Tex. Dir. Austin (Tex.) Film Soc., 1995—98; exec. dir. Assn. Ind. Video and Filmmakers, Inc., N.Y.C., 1999—; pub. The Ind. Film & Video Monthly, 1999—. Tchr. prodn. classes. Prodr., dir. Women's Action Coalition, asst. editor (documentary) The Maine Coast, (feature film) Office Space. Office: Assn Ind Video & Filmmakers Inc 304 Hudson St 6th Fl N New York NY 10013 Business E-Mail: elizabeth@aivf.org.

PETERS, ELIZABETH ANNE, nutrition educator; b. Hebron, Ill., June 9, 1940; d. Tibbetts and Ruby Marie (Giddens) Rolls; B.S., U. Ill., 1962, MEd, 1967; postgrad. U. Ill., 1970-74, Iowa State U., 1974, Northwestern U., 1980, 86. Tchr., dept. chair Bremen High Sch., Midlothian, Ill., 1962-65; asst. buyer Carson Pririe Scott, Chgo., 1965-66; tchr. Waller High Sch., Chgo., 1965-67, Evanston (Ill.) High Sch., 1967-70; instr., coordinator food service adminstrn. and hotel mgmt. Coll. DuPage, Glen Ellyn, Ill., 1970-75; clin. dietitian U. Chgo. Hosps. and Clinics, 1975; asst. restaurant mgr. Hyatt Regency, Chgo., summer 1980; prof., coordinator hospitality mgmt. program foodsvc. sanitation program and nutrition Chicago City-Wide Coll., 1975-92, chair campus com. for evaluation of baccalaureate transfer programs; pres. faculty Chgo. City Wide Coll., prof. foodsvc. sanitation and nutrition, 1992-97; cons. bds. health, No. Ill. U. adv. com., judge various food contests; mem. Chgo. Council on Fgn. Relations; pres. Near North chpt. Lyric Opera; trustee, treas. Three Arts Club Chgo. Recipient Nat. Restaurant Assn. Fellowship award, 1980; Master Tchrs. Seminar Fellowship award, 1974; Nat. Leadership Devel. Fellowship award, 1975. Registered Dietitan. Mem. Nat. Restaurant Assn., Ill. Restaurant Assn., Chgo. Restaurant Assn., Am. Dietetic Assn. (dietetic tech. com.), Ill. Dietetic Assn., Chgo. Nutrition Assn., Ill. Nutrition Com. (program chair), Chgo. Dietetic Assn. (dir.), Soc. Nutrition Edn., Inst. Food Technolo-

gists, Restaurant Women's Club Chgo. (dir.), Am. Pub. Health Assn., Coun. on Hotel-Restaurant Edn., Flossmoor Country Club, Lake Geneva Yacht Club, Canyon Club. Office: 30 E Lake St Chicago IL 60601-2403 Home: 515 Victoria Ln Wood Dale IL 60191-1896

PETERS, ELLEN ASH, judge, retired Supreme Court chief justice; b. Berlin, Mar. 21, 1930; came to U.S., 1939, naturalized, 1947; d. Ernest Edward and Hildegard (Simon) Ash; m. Phillip I. Blumberg; children: David Bryan Peters, James Douglas Peters, Julie Haden Dreisch. BA with honors, Swarthmore Coll., 1951, LLD (hon.), 1983; LLB cum laude, Yale U., 1954, MA (hon.), 1964, LLD (hon.), 1985, U. Hartford, 1983, Georgetown U., 1984, Conn. Coll., 1985, N.Y. Law Sch., 1985; HLD (hon.), St. Joseph Coll., 1986; LLD (hon.), Colgate U., 1986, Trinity Coll., 1987, Bates Coll., 1987, Wesleyan U., 1987, DePaul U., 1988; HLD (hon.), Albertus Magnus Coll., 1990; LLD (hon.), U. Conn., 1992, U. Rochester, 1994, Detroit Mercy Coll. Law, 2001. Bar: Conn. 1957. Law clk. to judge U.S. Circuit Ct., 1954-55; assoc. in law U. Calif., Berkeley, 1955-56; prof. law Yale U., New Haven, 1956-78, adj. prof. law, 1978-84; assoc. justice Conn. Supreme Ct., Hartford, 1978-84, chief justice, 1984-96; judge trial referee Superior Ct., Hartford, 2000—. Author: Commercial Transactions: Cases, Texts, and Problems, 1971, Negotiable Instruments Primer, 1974; contbr. articles to profl. jours. Bd. dirs. Nat. Ctr. State Cts., 1992—96, chmn., 1994; bd. mgrs. Swarthmore Coll., 1970—81; trustee Yale-New Haven Hosp., 1981—86, Yale Corp., 1986—92; mem. conf. Chief Justices, 1984—, pres., 1994; hon. chmn. U.S. Constl. Bicentennial Com., 1986—91; mem. Conn. Permanent Commn. on Status of Women, 1973—74, Conn. Bd. Pardons, 1978—80, Conn. Law Revision Commn., 1978—84; bd. dirs. Hartford Found., 1997—2002. Recipient Ella Grasso award, 1982, Jud. award Conn. Trial Lawyers Assn., 1982, citation of merit Yale Law Sch., 1983, Pioneer Woman award Hartford Coll. for Women, 1988, Disting. Svc. award U. Conn. Law Sch. Alumni Assn., 1993, Raymond E. Baldwin Pub. Svc. award Quinnipiac Coll. Law Sch., 1995, Disting. Svc. award Conn. Law Tribune, 1996, Nat. Ctr. State Cts., 1996; named Laura A. Johnson Woman of Yr. Hartford Coll., 1996. Mem. ABA, Conn. Bar Assn. (Jud. award 1992, Spl. award 1996), Am. Law Inst. (coun.), Am. Acad. Arts and Scis., Am. Philos. Coun. Office: Superior Ct 95 Washington St Hartford CT 06106-4431 Office Fax: 860-548-2887.

PETERS, EVELYN JOAN, artist; b. Anchorage, Alaska, Mar. 25, 1927; d. Algernon Sidney Jones and R. Lee (Bartholf) Jones-Lange; m. Curtis Gordon Chezem, Sept. 29, 1945 (div. Oct. 1956); children: Joanne Lee Chezem, David Gordon Chezem; m. Frederick William Peters Jr., May 30, 1958. Student, U. Oreg., 1945-50, Oreg. State Coll., 1955-56. Pvt. sec. Pub. Svc. Commn., Las Vegas, Nev., 1957-58; tech. sec. Los Alamos (N.Mex.) Nat. Lab., 1958-70; sr. sec. EG&G, Los Alamos, 1970-71. Chmn. bd. dirs. Buchanan Arts and Crafts, Inc., Buchanan Dam, Tex., 1980, 86. One-woman shows include Frame Corner Gallery, Farmington, 1996, San Juan Coll., 1998, invitational retrospective St. Francis Newman Ctr., Silver City, N.Mex., 1994, exhibited in group shows at Inn of Loretto, Santa Fe, 1982, Capital Rotunda, Austin, Tex., 1983, Golub Gallery, Steamboat Springs, Colo., 1985, Cowtown Invitational, Ft. Worth, 1987, Safari Park Hotel, Nairobi, Kenya, 1990 (Artistic Expressions award, 1990, Gold medal, 1990), St. John's Coll., Cambridge, Eng., 1992 (Bronze medal, 1992), Western N.Mex. U., Silver City, 1993, Sixth Bear River Western Hist. Art Exhbn., Craig, Colo., 1994, Fed. Hall Mus., N.Y.C., 1994, 1997, Ann. COGAP Exhbn., Governor's Island, N.Y., 1994 (George Gray award, 1993), Apples, Aspen and Art, Cedaredge, Colo., 1995 (Most Popular Painting), Western and Wildlife Art Show, Estes Park, Colo., 1995, Sheraton-on-the-Park Hotel, Sydney, Australia, 1995, Colo. Indian Market, Denver, 1995, Art Concepts Gallery, Tacoma, Wash., 1997, Keble Coll., Oxford, Eng., 1997, Sunwest Bank, Farmington, 1997, Rotunda Canon Office Bldg., U.S. Ho. of Reps., Washington, 1997, Alpine Holiday, Ouray, Colo., 1997, 1999, 2000, Durham (Eng.) Art Gallery, Arts for the Parks, 2000, Represented in permanent collections Aviation Heritage Mus., Anchorage, Daystar Found., Oklahoma City, Eleanor Bliss Ctr. Arts, Steamboat Springs, Marble Falls Depot Mus., Mus. N.W. Colo., Craig, Nat. Gallery Rural Art, Bonner Springs, Kans., Pioneer and R.R. Mus., Temple, Tex., San Juan Coll., Farmington, N.Mex., USCG, art, numerous mags., books, calendars and catalogs. Pres. Highland Arts Guild, Marble Falls, Tex., 1977, 90, 2d v.p., 1989; sec. Highland Lakes Arts Coun., Marble Falls, 1986. Recipient Marine Safety award Olin-Matheson, 1968, cert. of appreciation USCG Aux., 1969, 70, 1st and purchase award Kiwanis Art Competition, Granbury, Tex., 1983, 2d Pl. award Tex. Women Western Artists Show, Cresson, Tex., 1983, 2d and 3d pl. awards Llano Rodeo Art Show, 1986, 1st pl. award 9th Nat. Small Painting Western Show, 1987, 1st and purchase award Gt. Am. Art Competition, 1988, Most Popular Painter award 3d Ann. Invitational Art Show, Waco, Tex., 1988, Best of Show award Bear Valley Hist. Art Show, Craig, 1989, Best of Show, 1st Watercolor, 1st Oil, 1st Sculpture, Highland Lakes Arts Competition, Kingsland, Tex., 1991, Internat. Woman of Yr. in art Internat. Biog. Ctr., 1991-92, Most Popular Painting award Western Colo. Ctr. for Arts, 1996, Purchase award NWNMAC, Farmington, 1997, Purchase award Ouray Coll. 39th Ann. Art Exhibit, 1999, choice award 8th Ann. Nat. Christian Art Show, San Juan Coll., Farmington, N.Mex., 2000, Top 200 Arts for the Parks, 2000, 1st pl. Gateway Regional Art Show, Farmington, N.Mex., 2000, Internat. Peace prize United Cultural Conf., 2003, award NAPA exhbn. Williams Art Gallery and Mus., Birkhead, Eng., 2004, numerous others. Mem. N.W. N.Mex. Arts Coun., signature mem. Nat. Acrylic Painters Assn. (bd. dirs. 2002—, invitation cover award 5th Internat. Open Exhibit 2000), ofcl. Coast Guard Artist, 1987—, Salmagundi Club, 1989-95, World Found. of Successful Women (charter mem.), Nat. Oil and Acrylic Painters Assn., Nat. Soc. Painters in Casein and Acrylic (assoc.), Digital Fine Art Soc. N.Mex., Am. Biog. Inst. Rsch. Assn. (life, dep. gov. 1989, Gold Cup 1993, Medal of Honor 1992, Woman of Yr. 1994, 95), World Inst. of Achievement (life, Excellence as Painter award 1988), N.W. N.Mex. Arts Coun. (acting exec. dir. 1998-2003, Internat. Peace prize United Cultural Conv. 2003), Rio Ranche Art Assn. (charter), Rio Grande Art Assn. Avocations: gardening, photography, reading, travel. Office Phone: 505-892-2324. E-mail: petersart@sprynet.com.

PETERS, F. WHITTEN, lawyer, former federal official; BA magna cum laude, Harvard U., 1968; disting. grad., Naval Officer Candidate Sch., Newport, R.I., 1969; MS with distinction, London Sch. Econs., 1973; JD magna cum laude, Harvard U., 1976. Bar: D.C., U.S. Dist. Ct. (D.C.), U.S. Dist. Ct. (Md.), U.S. Ct. Appeals (D.C., 3rd, 11th cirs.), U.S. Ct. Appeals for the Armed Forces, U.S. Ct. Fed. Claims, U.S. Tax Ct. Res. officer Fleet Intelligence Ctr. Atlantic USN, Norfolk, Va., 1969-72; Frank Knox Traveling Fellow Harvard U., Cambridge, Mass., 1972-73; pres. Harvard Law Rev., 1975-76; law clk. to Hon. J. Skelly Wright U.S. Ct. Appeals (D.C. cir.), Washington, 1976-77; law clk. to Hon. William J. Brennan Jr. U.S. Supreme Ct., Washington, 1977-78; assoc. Williams & Connolly Law Firm, Washington, 1978-84, ptnr., 1984-95; prin. dep. gen. counsel Dept. Def., Washington, 1995-97, undersecretary of the Air Force, 1997-98, acting sec. of the Air Force, 1997—99, sec. of the Air Force, 1999—2001; ptnr. Williams & Connolly Law Firm, Washington, 2001—; vice chmn. Commn. on the Future of U.S. Aerospace Industry, 2001—. Recipient Sears prize, Harvard Law Sch., Navy Meritorious Unit commendation, Nat. Def. Svc. medal. Fellow ABA. Office: Williams & Connolly 725 Twelfth St NW Washington DC 20005 Office Phone: 202-434-5440. Business E-Mail: wpeters@wc.com.

PETERS, FRANK ALBERT, retired chemical engineer; b. Washington, June 3, 1931; s. Charles Albert and Dorothy Lynette (Paine) P.; m. Carol Beattie Taylor, Feb. 25, 1955; children: Thomas, June, Erick, Victor. BSChemE, U. Md., 1955. Devel. engr. Celanese Corp. Am., Cumberland, Md., 1955-58; chem. Engr. U.S. Bur. Mines, College Park, Md., 1958-66, project leader, 1966-70, rsch. supr., 1970-77, chief process evaluation Washington, 1977-94, ret., 1994. Contbr. over 20 articles to profl. jours. Avocations: photography, model railroading. Home: 12311 Glen Mill Rd Potomac MD 20854-1928

PETERS, FREDERICK WHITTEN, lawyer; b. Omaha, Aug. 20, 1946; s. Jordan Holt and Elizabeth (O'Bryant) P.; children: Mary Irvin, Elizabeth Holt, Margaret Etheridge. BA magna cum laude, Harvard U., 1968; MS with distinction, London Sch. Econs., 1973; JD magna cum laude, Harvard U., 1976. Bar: D.C. 1978, U.S. Dist. Ct. D.C. 1978, U.S. Dist. Ct. Md., 1994, U.S. Ct. Appeals (3d and D.C. cirs.) 1979, U.S. Ct. Claims 1981, U.S. Ct. Appeals (11th cir.) 1986, U.S. Ct. Mil. Appeals 1993. Law clk. to Hon. J. Skelly Wright U.S. Ct. Appeals (D.C. cir.), Washington, 1976-77; law clk. to justice William J. Brennan U.S. Supreme Ct., Washington, 1977-78; assoc. Williams & Connolly, Washington, 1978-84, ptnr., 1984-95, 2001—; prin. dep. gen. counsel Dept. of Defense, 1995-97, undersec., acting sec. USAF, 1997-99, sec. USAF, 1999-2001; ptnr. Williams & Connolly LLP, Washington, 2001—. Legal ethics com. DC Bar, 1988-94, chmn. rules rev. com., 1991-96; rules com. US Ct. Mil. Appeals, 1993-95. Pres. Harvard Law Rev., 1975-76. Bd. dirs. Cleveland Park Hist. Soc., Washington, 1986-91, 2001-02, Washington Area Lawyers for the Arts, 1987-93, Air Force Enlisted Found., 2001—, Air Force Aid Soc., 2002—; adv. com. on streamlining procurement laws DOD, 1991-93, vice chmn. adv. com. on future of US aerospace industry, 2001-2002. Lt. USNR, 1969-72. Fellow Am. Bar Found.; mem. ABA. Democrat. Episcopalian. Avocations: sailing, computer science, golf. Home: 735 S Union St Alexandria VA 22314-3889 Office: Williams & Connolly 725 12th St NW Washington DC 20005 Office Phone: 202-434-5440. E-mail: wpeters@wc.com.

PETERS, GORDON BENES, retired musician; b. Oak Park, Ill., Jan. 4, 1931; s. Arthur George and Julia Anne (Benes) P.; children: Rénee Kemper, Erica Kemper. Student, Northwestern U., 1949-50; Mus.B., Eastman Sch. Music, 1956, Mus.M., 1962. Founder, dir. Marimba Masters, 1954—59; percussionist Rochester (NY) Philharm. Orch., 1954—59; prin. percussionist, asst. timpanist Grant Park Symphony Orch., Chgo., 1955-58; mem. faculty Rochester Bd. Edn., 1956-57, Geneseo State Tchrs. Coll., 1957-58; acting prin. percussionist Rochester Philharm., NY, 1958-59; prin. percussionist and assoc. prin. timpanist Chgo. Symphony Orch., 1959—2001; condr., adminstr. Civic Orch. Chgo., 1966-87; condr. Elmhurst Symphony Orch., 1968-73; ret., 2001. Instr. percussion instruments Northwestern U., 1963-68, lectr., 1991; guest conductor Bangor (Maine) Symphony, 1993. Author, pub. The Drummer: Man, 1975, rev., 2003; arranger-pub. Marimba Ensemble arrangements; composer-pub.: Swords of Moda-Ling; editor: percussion column Instrumentalist mag, 1963-69; contbr. articles to profl. jours. Bd. dirs. Pierre Monteux Sch., Hancock, Maine, 1965-95. With U.S. Mil. Acad. Band, 1950-53. Recipient Pierre Monteux disciple award conducting, 1962, Prin. Timpani chair named GBP, Chgo. Youth Symphony Orch., 2000. Mem. Percussive Arts Soc. (pres. 1964-67, Hall of Fame 2004), Am. Symphony Orch. League, Condrs. Guild (treas., exec. com. 1979-82, 86-90), Japan Xylophone Assn. Home (Winter): 824 Hinman Ave Evanston IL 60202-5906 Home (Summer): PO Box 403 Hancock ME 04640-0403

PETERS, GREGORY A. technology company executive; BBA, Rhodes Coll. CPA. Pres., CEO Logic Works, Inc., Princeton, N.J., Vignette, Austin, Tex., 1998—2002, chmn. bd., 2002—. Office: Vignette Bldg 3 901 S MoPac Expressway Austin TX 78746

PETERS, HENRY AUGUSTUS, neuropsychiatrist; b. Oconomowoc, Wis., Dec. 21, 1920; s. Henry Augustus and Emma N. P.; m. Jean McWilliams, 1950; children— Henry, Kurt, Eric, Mark. BA, MD, U. Wis. Prof. dept. neurology and rehab. medicine U. Wis. Med. Sch., Madison, emeritus prof., 1996—. Mem. med. adv. bd. Muscular Dystrophy Assn. Served to lt. M.C. U.S. Navy. Fellow A.C.P.; mem. Wis. Med. Assn., Am. Acad. Neurology, Am. Psychiatric Assn. Clubs: Rotary. Office: 600 Highland Ave Madison WI 53792-0001

PETERS, HOWARD NEVIN, foreign language educator; b. Hazleton, Pa., June 29, 1938; s. Howard Eugene and Verna P.; m. Judith Anne Griessel, Aug. 24, 1963; children: Elisabeth Anne, Nevin Edward. BA, Gettysburg Coll., 1960; PhD, U. Colo., 1965. Asst. prof. fgn. langs. Valparaiso (Ind.) U., 1965-69, assoc. prof., 1969-75, dir. grad. divsn., 1967-70, acting dean Coll. Arts and Scis., 1970-71, assoc. dean Coll. Arts and Scis., 1971-74, dean Coll. Arts and Scis., 1974-81, prof. fgn. langs., 1975—, prof. fgn. langs. and lits., chair dept. fgn. langs. and lits., 1994—95, prof. emeritus fgn. langs. and lits., 1995—. Author (poetry) Espejo De Son, 1997. NDEA fellow, 1960-63 Mem. Midwest MLA, Phi Beta Kappa, Sigma Delta Pi, Phi Sigma Iota. Lutheran. Home: 860 N Cr 500 E Valparaiso IN 46383 Office: Meier Hall Rm 113 Valparaiso U Valparaiso IN 46383 E-mail: howard.peters@valpo.edu.

PETERS, JACQUELINE MARY, secondary school educator; b. Milw., Oct. 6, 1947; d. Arnold Martin and Rosalie Ellen (Mulherin) Fladoos; divorced; children: Casey Martin, Ann Marie. Student, Clarke Coll., Dubuque, Iowa, 1965-67; BA, Calif. State U., Long Beach, 1970; MA in History and Tchg., LaVerne (Calif.) U., 1973. Reading tchr. Chaffey H.S., Ontario, Calif., 1971-78, tchr. phys. edn., 1976-78, English tchr., 1978-90, tchr. history, 1990—. Mentor AAUW, cmty. schs., 1997-99. State rep. Trans Nat. Golf Assn., 1963-75; bd. dirs. Cmty. Challenge Grants, Ontario, 1996-00. Named to Sports Hall of Fame, Dubuque Sr. H.S., 1996; Med-Cal grantee, 1996, Project Yes grantee, 1997-99. Mem. AAUW (bd. dirs., br. pres. 1995-99, Edn. Foun. Gift Honoree 1998), Calif. Tchrs. Assn. Republican. Roman Catholic. Avocations: golf, fly fishing, pysanka, poetry, bridge. Office: Chaffey HS 1245 N Euclid Ave Ontario CA 91762-1923 Home: PO Box 1825 Upland CA 91785-1825

PETERS, JAMES C. retail executive; Various operating positions Office Depot, 1994—97; exec. v.p. US Stores, 1997—98; pres. US Retail Staples, 1998—2000; pres., COO Ross Stores, Newark, Calif., 2000—; also. bd. dirs. Office: Ross Stores 8311 Central Ave Newark CA 94560-3433

PETERS, JANICE C. cable company executive; b. Harlan, Ky., Apr. 23, 1951; m. Mike Peters; 2 children. BS, Wayne State U., 1972; MBA in Mgmt., Stanford U., 1989. Customer svc. rep. Mich. Bell, 1973-78; with AT&T Corp., Chgo., 1978-85, U.S. West, Denver, Seattle, London, from 1985, MediaOne, Englewood, Colo., CEO, pres., 1997—. Bd. dirs. Primus. Office: c/o MediaOne 188 Inverness Dr W Englewood CO 80112

PETERS, JOHN DOUGLAS, lawyer, artist; b. Dover, NH, Jan. 23, 1948; s. John Philip Peters, Helen Irene Hurst; m. Christine K. Consales, June 23, 1973. BA, U. NH, 1971; JD, U. Toledo, 1975. Exec. dir. PSRO 4th Ohio Area PSR Coun., Toledo, 1974—75; shareholder Charfoos & Christensen, P.C., Detroit, 1975—. Legal dir. Mich. Med. Schs. Coun. of Deans, Ann Arbor, 1978—80; lectr. law U. Toledo, 1978—88; assoc. prof. Sch. Medicine Wayne State U., Detroit, 1978—; cons. Georgetown U. Inst. for Health Policy, Washington, 1989, Office of Tech. Assessment, Washington, 1992—96, Robert Wood Johnson Found., Washington, 1994—98. Author: (book) Anesthesiology and the Law, 1983, Obstetrics/Gynecology and the Law, 1984, The Law of Medical Practice in Pennsylvania and New Jersey, 1984, Social Security Disability Claims, 2004, The Law of Medical Practice in Michigan, 1981; editor: Legal and Ethical Aspects of Treating Terminally Ill Patients, 1982; contbr. articles to profl. jours. Bd. dirs. Am. Lung Assn., Detroit, 1978—83, Vis. Nurse Assn., Detroit, 1987—96, Preservation Wayne, 1992—. Avocations: Persian textiles, folk art, collecting and studying antiquities. Office: Charfoos and Christensen PC 5510 Woodward Ave Detroit MI 48202 Office Phone: 313-875-8080.

PETERS, KRISTEN MICHELE, psychologist, researcher; d. Lawrence Stephen and Nancy Caputo Peters. BA in Psychology and Mgmt., Boston (Mass.) Coll., 1996; MSchology in Edn., Fordham U., 2000, diploma in Sch. Psychology, 2002. Cert. sch. psychologist Nat. Assn. Sch. Psychology, 2002, N.Y., 2002, N.J., 2004. Resource rm. tchr. Seton Ctrs. Paul IV HS, Fairfax, Va., 1996—97; asst. tchr. First Friends Preschool, N.Y., 1998—99; sch. psychologist Sacred Heart Primary and Secondary Schs. Fordham U., Bronx, NY, 1999—2004, supr. Rosa A. Hagin Sch. Consultation and Early Childhood Ctrs., 2002—03; intern Dept. of Child and Adolescent Psychiatry Mt. Sinai Med. Ctr., N.Y., 2000—01; intern Scarsdale (N.Y.) Union Free Sch. Dist., 2001—02. Co-coordinator Student Affiliates in Sch. Psychology, N.Y., 1997—2001; student rep. Divsn. Psychol. and Ednl. Svcs. Fordham U., 1997—2001, co-coordinator Grad. Student Adv. Coun., 1999—2001, mem. coms., 1997—2001; adj. prof. Met. Coll. N.Y., N.Y., 2002, Fordham U., 2002. Co-author: Encyclopedia of Creativity, 1999; editor: Sch. Psychology Early Childhood Newsletter, 1998—2003; contbr. articles to profl. jours. Named to The Big East Academic All-Star Team, 1994—95; scholar, Barnes and Nobles Bookstores, 2000, Paul R. Hanna Laureate scholarship, Kappa Delta Phi Ednl. Found., 2002. Mem.: APA, NASP, N.Y. Assn. Early Childhood and Infant Psychology, N.Y. Assn. Sch. Psychologists, N.Y. State Psychol. Assn., Phi Delta Kappa, Phi Kappa Phi, Kappa Delta Phi.

PETERS, LEO FRANCIS, environmental engineer; b. Melrose, Mass., Aug. 14, 1937; s. Joseph Leander and Mary Gertrude (Phalen) Peters; m. Joan Catherine Anderson, May 20, 1961; children: Elizabeth M., Susan J., Carolyn A., Jennifer L. BSCE, Northeastern U., Boston, 1960, MSCE, 1966; postgrad., Harvard U., 1989. Registered profl. engr., Mass., N.H., diplomate, Am. Acad. Environ. Engrs. Jr. engr. N.Y. Dept. Transp., Albany, 1960-61; chief engr. John M. Cashman, Weymouth, Mass., 1961-62; project engr. Metcalf & Eddy, Inc., Boston, 1962-65, Weston & Sampson, Boston, 1965-67, assoc., 1967-70, ptnr., 1970-76; exec. v.p. Weston & Sampson Engrs., Inc., Boston, 1976-82, pres., CEO Wakefield and Peabody, Mass., 1982-99, chmn., 1999—2002, chmn. emeritus, 2002—. Treas. Engring. Ctr., 1991—93; mem. corp. Northeastern U., Boston, 1992—, dir. nat. coun., 1993—; treas. Engring Ctr. Edn. Trust, 1992—94, chmn., 1994—95. Clk., mem. Melrose (Mass.) Planning Bd., 1969—91; mem. Conservation Commn., 2003—, Design Selection Bd. Commonwealth of Mass.; bd. dir. Environ. Bus. Coun. New Eng., 1997—2002. Named Outstanding Civil Engr., Northeastern U. Civil Engring. Alumni, Young Engr. of the Yr., Mass. Soc. Profl. Engrs.; recipient Environ. Merit award, Environ. Bus. Coun. New Eng., Leadership award, Engring. Ctr., 2001. Fellow: Am. Coun. Engring. Cos.; mem.: ASCE (life), Coun. Engring. Couns. New Eng. (pres. 1990—91), Water Environ. Fedn., Boston Soc. Civil Engrs. (hon.), New Eng. Water Works Assn. (hon.; pres. 1989—90), Am. Pub. Works Assn., Am. Water Works Assn. Roman Catholic. Home: 187 E Emerson St Melrose MA 02176-3534 Office: Weston & Sampson Engrs Inc 5 Centennial Dr Peabody MA 01960-7985 E-mail: leopeters@comcast.net.

PETERS, LEON, JR., engineering educator; b. Columbus, Ohio, May 28, 1923; s. Leon P. and Ethel (Howland) Pierce; m. Mabel Marie Johnson, June 6, 1953; children: Amy T. Peters Thomas, Melinda A. Peters Todaro, Maria C. Cohee, Patricia D., Lee A., Roberta J. Peters Cameruca, Karen E. Peters Ellingson. BSE.E., Ohio State U., 1950, MS, 1954, PhD, 1959. Asst. prof. elec. engring. Ohio State U., Columbus, 1959-63, assoc. prof., 1963-67, prof., 1967-93, prof. emeritus, 1993—, assoc. dept. chmn. for rsch., 1990-92, dir. electro sci. lab., 1983-94. Contbr. articles to profl. jours. Served to 2d lt. U.S. Army, 1942-46, ETO. Fellow IEEE Home: 2087 Ellington Rd Columbus OH 43221-4138 Office: Ohio State U Electrosci Lab 1320 Kinnear Rd Columbus OH 43212-1156 Office Phone: 614-292-6153. Business E-Mail: peters.6@osu.edu.

PETERS, LEROY RICHARD, materials management consulting company executive; b. Milw., June 26, 1943; s. LeRoy Edwin and Eleanor Hedwig (Bensing) Peters; m. Barbara Jean Hackney, Nov. 18, 1964 (div. July 1970); 1 child, Neal; m. Nancy Elizabeth Till, July 17, 1971; children: Richard, Brenda, Eric, Linda. BS, U. Wis., 1966; Grad., U.S. Army/Command and, Gen. Staff Coll., Ft. Leavenworth, Kans., 1977. Cert. fellow in prodn. and inventory mgmt. Inventory supr. Bucyrus Erie, Erie, Pa. and Pocatello, Idaho, ach3-76; inventory mgr. Am. Microsystems, Pocatello, 1976-78; prodn. mgr. Worthington Compressor, Buffalo, N.Y., 1978-80; mfg. mgr. St. Regis WPM Div., Denver, 1980-82; materials mgr. Robinson Brick Co., Denver, 1982-86; prodn. mgr. Merritt Equipment Co., Denver, 1986-89; instructional designer Martin Marietta, Denver, 1989-90; sr. cons. J.D. Edwards, Denver, 1990-93; sr. cons. mgr. AMX Internat., 1993-97; v.p. The Thompson Group, 1997-98; CEO, Enterprise Resource Mgmt., Inc., 1998—. Editorial com.: Aerospace and Defense Dictionary, 1990; contbr. articles to profl. jours. Scoutmaster Boy Scouts Am., Denver, 1989, cubmaster, 1988, outdoor chmn., Denver, 1990; dist. capt. Adams County Colo. Reps., Denver, 1986. Col. U.S. Army, 1966-94, Vietnam, Desert Storm. Decorated Legion of Merit, Bronze Star, Meritorious Svc. medal, Army Commendation medal. Fellow Am. Prodn. and Inventory Control Soc. (bd. dirs. region VI 1990—, pres. Colo. chpt. 1989-90); mem. Am. Def. Preparedness Assn., Moose. Lutheran. Avocations: fishing, reading, music, photography, geology. Home: 1468 W 111th Ave Northglenn CO 80234-3397

PETERS, LINDA S. musician, music educator; b. Erie, Pa., Aug. 13, 1952; d. Willard and Della Amale Smith; m. Rocky Grant Peters, Apr. 25, 1997; 1 child, Patrick Harold Allyn. MusB and Tchr. Certification, Mansfield State Coll., 1974; MS in Music, Mansfield U., 1989. Vocal music tchr. Wyalusing (Pa.) Area Elem. Schs., 1975—77; piano instr. 171 Cedar Arts Ctr., Corning, NY, 1978—80; freelance accompanist Sayre, Pa., 1978—94; head preschool tchr. The Barclay Sch., Towanda, Pa., 1983—86; piano instr. Fletcher's Pianos and Organs, Horseheads, NY, 1989—2000; music dir. Big Flats (N.Y.) First Presbyn. Ch., 1993—; piano instr. 171 Cedar Art Ctr., 2004. Accompanist/adjudicator N.Y. State Sch. Music Assn. Festivals, Elmira, 2000—. Musician: (audio tape) Ivory Treasures; musician: (pianist) (audio cd) Classics & Jazz. Session elder Big Flats First Presbyn. Ch., 2002—. Mem.: Music Tchrs. Nat. Assn., N.Y. State Music Tchrs. Assn. (advt. and publicity chairperson 2000—), Am. Fedn. Musicians of the U.S. and Can. Achievements include Winner/Penn State Ragtime Piano Competition; Accompanist at the National Federation of Music Clubs National Convention; Established Fletcher's Showcase of Music Piano Competition, now in its 10th year. Avocations: running, watercolor painting, jewelry designing. Office: 171 Cedar Arts Ctr Studio G Corning NY 14830 Personal E-mail: fingers8@infoblvd.net.

PETERS, MARY E. federal agency administrator; m. Terry Peters; 3 children. B, U. Phoenix; attended govt. program for state & local govt., Harvard U. Dir. Ariz. Dept. Transp., 1985—2001; fed. hwy. adminstr. U.S. Dept. Transp., Washington, 2001—. Past bd. dirs. Project Challenge, Nat. Guard; past chair adv. bd. Hwy. Expansion Loan Program; mem. Gt. Ariz. Develop. Authority; past mem. Growing Smarter Commn. Named Women of Yr., Women's Transp. Seminar; named one of Most Influential Person in Ariz. Transp., Ariz. Bus. Jour. Mem.: We. Assn. State Hwy. Transp. Officials, Am. Assn. State Hwy. Officials (past chair standing com. on planning, assest mgmt. task force, reauthorization steering com. 2001). Office: US Dept Transp Fed Hwy Adminstrn 400 7th St SW Washington DC 20590

PETERS, MAX STONE, chemical engineer, educator; b. Delaware, Ohio, Aug. 23, 1920; s. Charles Clinton and Dixie Mae (Stone) P.; m. Laurnell Louise Stephens, June 29, 1947; children— Margaret Dixie, M. Stephen. BS in Chem Engring, Pa. State U., 1942, MS, 1947, PhD (Shell Oil Co. grad. fellow 1949-51), 1951. Registered profl. engr., Pa., Colo. Prodn. supr. Hercules Powder Co., 1942-44; research asst. Pa. State U., 1946-47; tech. plant supr. George I. Treyz Chem. Co., 1947-49; mem. faculty U. Ill., 1951-62, prof. chem. engring., 1957-62, head dept., 1958-62; dean engring. U. Colo., 1962-78, prof. chem. engring., 1978-87, chmn. dept., 1981-85, emeritus prof. chem. engring., emeritus dean engring., 1987—. Adv. com. engring. div. NSF, 1962-66; chmn. Pres.'s Nat. Medal Sci. Com., 1969-70, Colo. Environ. Commn., 1970-72 Author: Elementary Chemical Engineering, 1954, rev. edit., 1984, Plant Design and Economics for Chemical Engineers, 1958, rev. edit. 1968, 80, 91, 2003; cons. editor: McGraw-Hill series chem. engring, 1960-87. Served with AUS, 1944-46. Recipient Merit award Am. Assn. Cost Engrs., 1969; Distinguished Alumnus award Pa. State U., 1974; Distinguished Alumnus award U. Colo., 1971; Phillips Lecture award Okla. State U., 1980 Mem. Nat. Acad. Engring., Am. Inst. Chem. Engrs. (dir. 1961-64, pres. 1968, Founders award 1974, Lewis award 1979), Am. Soc. Engring. Edn. (chmn. chem. engring. div. 1962, sec. engring. coll. adminstrn. council 1965-67, George Westinghouse award 1959, Lamme award 1973, Merry Field award 1985), Am. Chem. Soc. (adv. bd. jour. 1956-59), Am. Assn. Cost Engring., Sigma Xi, Alpha Chi Sigma, Phi Eta Sigma, Phi Lambda Upsilon, Tau Beta Pi, Sigma Tau. Achievements include research in biomass, kinetics, mechanisms. Home: 4875 Sioux Dr No 004 Boulder CO 80303

PETERS, MELODIE M. state legislator; b. Springfield, Mass., July 22, 1947; m. Earl Peters; two children: Troy, Lalisa. Grad. sch. nursing, Winthrop Cmty. Hosp. Mem. Dist. 20 Conn. Senate, Hartford, 1993—; nurse Quaker

Hill, Conn. Mem. adv. bd. Conn. Occupational Health Clinic, Conn. Legis. Task Force on Safety in Workplace; chair Waterford Dem. Town Com. Office: Conn State Senate 210 Capitol Ave Hartford CT 06106-1535

PETERS, MERCEDES, psychoanalyst; b. N.Y.C. BS, L.I. U., 1945; MS, U. Conn., 1953; tng. in psychotherapy, Am. Inst. Psychotherapy, 1960-70; PhD in Psychoanalysis, Union Inst., 1989. Cert. in psychoanalysis Am. Exam. Bd. Psychoanalysis, mental health cons. Sr. psychotherapist Cmty. Guidance Svc., 1960-75; staff affiliate Postgrad. Ctr. for Mental Health, 1974-76; pvt. practice psychoanalysis and psychotherapy, Bklyn., 1961—; tchr., supr. psychoanalytic psychotherapy at various psychotherapeutic tng. ctrs., 1975—; cons. to advanced tng. program Jewish Bd. Family and Children's Svcs., 2000—. Contbr. articles to profl. jours. Past bd. dirs. Brookwood Child Care Assn. Fellow: Am. Orthopsychiat. Assn.; mem.: NASW, LWV, NAACP, Postgrad. Psychoanalytic Soc., Nat. Assn. Advancement Psychoanalysis (bd. dirs., chair UN com.), Wednesday Club. Office: 142 Joralemon St Brooklyn NY 11201-4709 Office Phone: 718-875-9874.

PETERS, MICHAEL MORGAN, playwright, consultant, theater director, theater critic, educator; b. New London, NH, Aug. 21, 1948; s. Allen Clifford Peters and Lee Susan Bortas. At, U. Calif., Berkeley, 1966—68; AA, Santa Barbara (Calif.) City Coll., 1977; BA, Humboldt State U., Arcata, Calif., 1982. Steel constrn. Disney World, Orlando, Fla., 1973; arts adminstr. Whole Earth Arts, Santa Barbara, Calif., 1974—77; oceanographer asst. U. So. Calif., L.A., 1978—79; freelance theatrical designer, dir. Calif., 1982—87; mng. dir. Studio One Theatre, Oakland, Calif., 1983; instr. Calif. Inst. Arts, Valencia, 1988—90; lighting designer Redding (Calif.) Conv. Ctr., 1994—97; freelance theatre critic, reporter, 1992—. Bd. dir. Tehama Actors Guild, Red Bluff, Calif., 1983—85; cons. designer Red Bluff HS, 1983—87; theatre cons. Shasta CC, Redding, 1983. Author: (plays) As You Might Like It, 1984, (screenplays) Dust, 1984, (novels) Lawrence of Vietnam, 1984. Sgt. USAF, 1968—72, Vietnam. Mem.: Calif. Scholarship Fedn. (life). Democrat. Presbyterian. Achievements include led drive to build Performing Arts Ctr. in Red Bluff, Calif; designed and manufactured animation tables for Disney Sch. Animation, 1989. Avocations: painting, history, travel. Home and Office: 360 Chestnut Ave Red Bluff CA 96080

PETERS, MICHAEL P. former mayor; m. Jeannette Peters; 3 children. Former firefighter City of Hartford; former owner small bus. Hartford; mayor City of Hartford, 1993—2001. Former chmn Hartford Civic Ctr. Commn., Hartford Redevel. Agy.; former mem. Bushnell Park Found.; founder Hartford Thomas Hooker Day Parade and Festival; mktg. com. Downtown Coun.; mem. Am. Leadership Forum, Dem. Town Com.; vol. neighborhood baseball and football teams; bd. dirs. Cedar Hill Cemetery. Democrat.

PETERS, MILTON EUGENE, educational psychologist; b. Anderson, Ind., July 22, 1938; s. Olen A. and Dorothy LaVerne (Lambert) P.; m. Carol Ann Dudycha, Aug. 27, 1960. BA, Wittenburg U., 1960; M in Div., Hamma Sch. Theology, 1963; MA, Bowling Green State U., 1965; PhD, U. Toledo, 1975. Lic. psychologist, Ohio. Pastor Luth. Ch. Am., 1966-69; instr. psychology Defiance (Ohio) Coll., 1969-70, Bluffton (Ohio) Coll., 1970-72; tchr., rsch. asst. U. Toledo, 1973-75, prof., 1975-76; dir. instl. rsch., asst. prof. psychology U. Findlay, Ohio, 1976-85, assoc. prof. psychology, 1985-89, prof., 1989—. Cons., lectr. in field; ednl. rschr. Contbr. articles to profl. and religious jours. Mem. APA, Am. Assn. Univ. Prof. (pres. U. Findlay), Midwestern Psychol. Assn., Creative Edn. Found. (colleague), Findlay Beacon Club, Fostoria Power Squadron. Home: 1130 Country Club Dr Findlay OH 45840-6342 Office: 1000 N Main St Findlay OH 45840-3653 Office Phone: 419-424-4523. E-mail: peters@findlay.edu.

PETERS, R. JONATHAN, lawyer, manufacturing executive; b. Janesville, Wis., Jan. 6, 1927; m. Ingrid H. Varvayn, 1953; 1 dau., Christina. BS in Chemistry, U. Ill., 1951; JD, Northwestern U., 1954. Bar: Ill. 1954. Chief patent counsel Englehard Industries, 1972-82, Kimberly-Clark Corp., Neenah, Wis., 1982-85; gen. counsel Lanxide Corp., Newark, Del., 1985-87; pvt. practice Chgo., 1985—. Served with CIC, U.S. Army, 1955-57. Patentee in field. Mem. ABA, Am. Intellectual Property Law Assn., Lic. Execs. Soc., Assn. Corp. Patent Counsel, North Shore Golf (Menasha, Wis.), Masons, Scottish Rite, Shriners.

PETERS, RALPH EDGAR, architectural firm executive, engineering executive; b. Harrisburg, Pa., Feb. 20, 1923; s. George Edward and Rebecca Flavia (Michener) P.; m. Roberta Jane Shaffer, June 12, 1948; children: Sheila Jane, Gail Marie, Ralph Jr., Bret Edward. Student, U. Pa., 1942; BA in Bus. Adminstrn., Pa. State U., 1948. From payroll supt. to asst. budget supr. Pa. State U., 1948-52; chief acct., pers. officer Haller, Raymond & Brown, State College, Pa., 1952-54; from contr. to CEO and chmn. bd. Benatec Assocs., Inc. (formerly Berger Assocs., Inc.), Camp Hill, Pa., 1954—. Chmn. bd. advisors Pa. State U., Harrisburg, 1979—; chmn. bd. dirs. Holy Spirit Hosp., Camp Hill, 1982—; past pres. Tri-County United Way, Harrisburg, 1978—; chmn. Pvt. Industry Coun., Harrisburg, 1982-87. With U.S. Army, 1943-45, ETO, 1952-53, Korea. Recipient Cmty. Svc. award Salvation Army, 1980, Disting. Pennsylvanian award Greater Phila. C. of C., 1981, Catalyst award Capital Region Econ. Devel., 1992, James Skelly award for exceptional svcs. to the hwy. program Associated Constructors of Pa., 1993, Alexis de Tocqueville Humanitarian award United Way, 1999; named Transp. Adv. of Yr., Pa. Hwy. Info. Assn., 1994; finalist Ctrl. Pa. Entrepreneur of Yr., 1996; Paul Harris fellow Rotary Internat., 1997. Mem. Pa. C. of C. (bd. dirs., transp. com. chmn. 1972-90), Harrisburg Area C. of C. (pres., chmn. 1979-83), Ams. for Competitive Enterprise Sys. (pres. 1981-83), Cumberland County Transp. Authority, Susquehanna Valley Regional Airport Authority, Lions, Masons, Pa. Jaycees (pres. 1955-56, nat. v.p. 1956-57), Delta Sigma Pi. Lutheran. Office: Benatec Assocs Inc 200 Airport Rd New Cumberland PA 17070-2467 Office Phone: 717-901-7055. Business E-Mail: rpeters@benatec.com.

PETERS, RALPH FREW, investment banker; b. Mineola, N.Y., Mar. 21, 1929; s. Ralph and Helen Louise (Frew) P.; m. Ann Marie Haberski, Dec. 31, 1997; children from previous marriage: Louise Frew, Jean Reid, Ralph Frew, Melvyn T., Richard Clayton. BA, Princeton U., 1951; postgrad., Stonier Grad. Sch. Banking, Rutgers U., 1962. With Corn Exchange Bank & Trust Co., 1947-52; chmn. bd., dir. Discount Corp. N.Y., N.Y.C., 1955-93. Bd. dirs. Van Eck Funds. Served with USNR, 1948-55. Mem. Anglers Club, Leash Club, North Woods Club. Episcopalian.

PETERS, RALPH IRWIN, JR., biology professor, researcher; b. Tulsa, June 30, 1947; s. Ralph I. and Margenelle P.; m. Marsha A. Lerenberg; 1 child, Caitlin Louise. BS, U. Tulsa, 1969; PhD, Wash. State U., 1975. NIH pre-doctoral trainee Wash. State U., Pullman, 1971-75; rsch. assoc. Tex. A&M U., College Station, 1975-76; NIH post-doctoral fellow Wash. State Coll. of Vet. Medicine, Pullman, 1976-77; asst. prof. Bates Coll., Lewiston, Maine, 1977-80; from asst. to assoc. prof. Wichita (Kans.) State U., 1980-89; prof., chmn. Lynchburg (Va.) Coll., 1989-93; clin. assoc. prof., dir. office analysis and planning U. Mo. Sch. Dentistry, Kansas City, 1993—. Reviewer West Pub. Co., 1983-84, Worth Pubs., 1985, NSF, 1987, Internat. Jour. of Comparative Psychology, 1988. Contbr. articles and abstracts to profl. jours. With U.S. Army, 1969-71. Summer rsch. fellow USAF, 1987; rsch. grantee NSF, USAF, also others. Mem.: AAAS, Mid-Am. Assn. for Instnl. Rsch., Am. Dentl Edn. Assn., Internat. Brain Rsch. Orgn., Soc. for Neurosci., Sci. Rsch. Soc. Office: U Mo Sch Dentistry 650 E 25th St Kansas City MO 64108-2716

PETERS, RALPH MARTIN, academic administrator; b. Knoxville, Tenn., May 9, 1926; s. Tim C. and Alma (Shannon) P.; m. Lorraine Daniel, 1949; children— Teresa, Marta. BS, Lincoln Meml. U., 1949; MS, U. Tenn., 1953, EdD, 1960. Tchr. pub. schs. Lincoln Meml. U., 1956-63, prof., dept. chmn., v.p., 1956-63, 92-97, interim pres., 1997-98; prof. edn., dean students, dean Grad. Sch. Tenn. Tech. U., Cookeville, 1963-89, dean emeritus, 1989. Editor publs. Served with Armed Forces, World War II. Mem. Phi Kappa Phi, Phi Delta Kappa, Omicron Delta Kappa. Clubs: Rotary. Baptist. Home: PO Box 3231 Cookeville TN 38502-3231

PETERS, RAYMOND EUGENE, historian, writer; b. New Haven, Aug. 24, 1933; s. Raymond and Doris Winthrop (Smith) P.; m. Millie Mather, July 14, 1978 (div. Nov. 1983); life ptnr. Mamie L. Romero, 1986—. Student, San Diego City Coll., 1956-61; cert., Lumbleau Real Estate Sch., 1973, Southwestern Coll., Chula Vista, Calif., 1980, Cert. quality assurance engr. Founder, pub. Silhouette Pub. Co., San Diego, 1960-75; co-founder, news dir. Sta. XEGM, San Diego, 1964-68; news dir. Sta. XERB, Tijuana, Mex., 1973-74; founder, chief exec. officer New World Airways, Inc., San Diego, 1968-77; co-founder, exec. vice chmn. bd. San Cal Rail, Inc.-San Diego Trolley, San Diego, 1974-77; founder, pres., CEO Ansonia Sta., micro systems, San Diego, 1986—. Cons. on multimedia and electronic commerce sys., 1995—; amb. Sycuan Casino & Resort, 2000—; co-founder, dir. S.E. Cmty. Theatre, San Diego, 1960-68; commr. New World Aviation Acad., Otay Mesa, Calif., 1971-77; co-founder New World Internat. Trade and Commerce Commn., Inc., 1991-94, New World Airways Inc, 1968-77. *Raymond has four decades of notable accomplishments including author, "Black Americans in Aviation," (Reference: Tuskegee Airmen). A Sequel "Eagles Don't Cry" is based on a 1961 Supreme Court decision. In 1968, he co-founded New World Airways, Inc. (the first jet powered transcontinental airline ever under direction and operation by African Americans). He also co-founded San Cal Rail, Inc., America's first black owned railroad company with an Amtrack contract (Reference: Federal Railroad Administration, 1974-1975). Raymond's history is VHS tape documented on the Cox Cable/Time Warner TV Show "Heart of San Diego." He is represented nationwide as a public speaker, writer, and lecturer.* Author: Black Americans in Aviation, 1971, Profiles in Black American History, 1974, Eagles Don't Cry, 1988; founder, pub., editor Oceanside Lighthouse, 1958-60, San Diego Herald Dispatch, 1959-60. Co-founder, bd. dirs. San Diego County Econ. Opportunity Commn., 1964-67; co-founder Edn. Cultural Complex, San Diego, 1966-75; co-founder, exec. dir. S.E. Anti-Poverty Planning Coun., Inc., 1964-67; mem. U.S. Rep. Senatorial Inner Circle Com., Washington, 1990—; mem. bus. adv. bd. Value Add Reseller, 1995; ambassador Sycuan Casino and Singing Hills Golf Resort, 2000-2003 With U.S. Army, 1950-53, Korea. Decorated (2) Bronze Svc. stars, UN medal. Mem. Am. Soc. Quality Control, Nat. City C. of C., Afro-Am. Micro Sys. Soc. (exec. dir. 1987—), Negro Airmen Internat. (Calif. pres. 1970-75, nat. v.p. 1975-77), Tuskegee Airmen (charter, bd. dirs. Benjamin O. Davis San Diego chpt. 1995—), Internat. Platform Assn., U.S. C. of C., Greater San Diego Minority C. of C. (bd. dirs. 1974—, past chmn. bd.), Masons (most worshipful grand master, supreme coun.), Shriners (Al Kadosh Disting. Cmty. Svc. award 1975). Republican. Avocations: creative writing, golf, world history. Home: Meadowbrook Estates # 245 8301 Mission Gorge Rd Santee CA 92071-3500 Personal E-mail: ansonia@cox.net.

PETERS, RAYMOND ROBERT, bank executive; b. Concord, Calif., Sept. 14, 1942; s. Robert V. and Pegi M. (Carr) P.; m. Nancy Tsai; children: Angel, Ray, Matthew. BBA, U. Oreg., 1964. Head customer securities Bank of Am., San Francisco, 1969-71, Eurocurrency and fgn. exch. mgr. London, 1971-72, San Francisco, 1972-76, sr. v.p., head offshore funds, 1985-86, exec. v.p., 1987-92; group exec. v.p., treas. Bank Am. Corp., San Francisco, 1992-98, Charlotte, 1998-2001; mng. sr. ptnr. RNR-MAP, Zephyr Cove, Nev., 2001—. Mem. fgn. exch. com. N.Y. Fed. Res. Bank, 1978-87, chmn., 1984-85; mem. Chgo. Merc. Exch., 1987-2001; mem. Chgo. Bd. Trade, 1987-2001; cons. on internat. interest rate risk mgmt., fgn. currency, offshore banking matters, U.S. regulators, fgn. ctrl. banks, and pension and investment funds mgmt. Office: RNR-MAP PO Box 11879 Zephyr Cove NV 89448 E-mail: RRPETERS@aol.com.

PETERS, RICHARD SPENCER, musician; b. San Antonio, Tex., Feb. 2, 1951; s. Alva Spencer and Lucy Alma Peters; m. Nellie Julia Cruz, June 16, 1990; children: Matthew, Brittany. BA, music edn., U. of So. Miss., Hattiesburg, MS, 1973; MA, music, Miss. Coll., Clinton, MS, 1984. Band dir. Mt. Olive Attendance, Mt. Olive, Miss., 1973—75; band dir./supr. Brookhaven H.S., Brookhaven, Miss., 1975—78; head band dir. Mendenhall H.S., Mendenhall, Miss., 1978—85, Newton City Schools, Newton, Miss., 1985—87; asst. band dir. Mission Ind. Sch. Dist. Ctr., Mission, Tex., 1987—91, McAllen Ind. Sch. Dist., McAllen, Tex., 1991—92; dist. music coord. East Ctrl. Ind. Sch. Dist., San Antonio, Tex., 1992—. Mem., adv. bd. US Achievement Acad., Huntsville, Ala., 1980—85, Salvation Army, McAllen, Tex., 1989—91. Contbg. editor: Bandworld Mag. Vol. Salvation Army, San Antonio, Tex., 1992; choir mem. Cornerstone Ch., 1996. Recipient Outstanding Educator, 1985, outstanding young man of Am., 1987, Who's Who Among Am. Teachers, 1998. Mem.: Tex. Music Administrators Conf., Nat. Fedn. Interscholastic Music Assn., Detroit Concert Band Assn., Percy Grainger Soc., Assn. of Tex. Profl. Educators, Nat. Band Assn., Tex. Bandmasters Assn., Tex. Music Educators Assn. Avocations: golf, remote control models. Home: 715 Arch Stone San Antonio TX 78258 Office: East Central Music Department 7173 Fm 1628 San Antonio TX 78263 E-mail: rsp6577@aol.com.

PETERS, ROBERT K. dean, newscaster, newswriter, journalist; b. Tyler, Tex., June 2, 1941; s. Robert K. and Ruth Bailey Peters; m. Judy D. Loden, Feb. 23, 1980; children: Jonathan W., Anne E. AA, Tyler Jr. Coll., 1961—; BA, Tex. Christian U., 1962; M in History, Stephen F. Austin State Coll., 1964; PhD, U. Tex., 1977. Staff writer, weather, and sci. Tyler Courier Times Telegraph, 1962—; newsreader weather KTBB Radio Sta., Tyler, 1962—; dean univ. studoes Tyler Jr. Coll., 1966—; observer, sta. keeper Nat. Weather Svc., Tyler, 1992—. Dir. bd. dirs. Horizon, Tyler, 1977—; trustee Tyler Mus. Art, 1999—. Author: Texas from Annexation to Succession: 1846-1861, 1977, Practicing Texas Politics, Instructor Resource Manual, 1994, 1995, 1997, 1998, 2000, 2001, 2003. Mem. Tex. Coun. Workforce and Econ. Competitiveness, Austin, 1999—2003, N.E. Tex. State Sub-Commrs. Revision, Austin, 1973—74, Tex. Commn. Blind Bd., Austin, 1985—91, 1999—2004, Tex. Coun. Disabilities, Austin, 1990—91, City of Tyler Rev. Bd., 1990—94, Tex. Planning Coun. Disabilities, Austin, 1991—93. Recipient Piper Prof. award, Piper Found., San Antonio, 1993, Nat. Weather Svc. Cooperating Observer award, Nat. Weather Svc., Shreveport, La., 2002. Mem.: Tex. State Hist. Soc., So. Hist. Soc., Orgn. Am. History, Am. Hist. Soc. Republican. Episcopalian. Avocations: reading, cooking. Home: 3813 Brookwood Tyler TX 75701 Office: Tyler Jr Coll 1400 E 5th St Tyler TX 75711 Fax: 903-510-2708. E-mail: rpet@tjc.edu.

PETERS, ROBERT WAYNE, pension fund administrator; b. LaPorte, Ind., Jan. 2, 1950; s. Harry Carl and Dorothy May (Fischer) P.; m. Frances Kay Cooley, Aug. 21, 1971; children: Carolyn Marie, Angela Lynn. BA, Purdue U., 1972. CLU. Mgr. pension adminstrn. Gen. Life Ins. Corp., Milw., 1973-75; dir. qualified plan devel. Cen. Life Assurance Co., Des Moines, 1976-84; v.p. individual ops. First Farwest Ins. Co., Portland, Oreg., 1984-90; pres. CAF Enterprises, Inc., Portland, 1990—. Lectr. various govt. agys. Contbr. articles to profl. jours. Mem. N.W. Vintage Thunderbird (v.p. 1988, pres. 1989-90, exec. bd. 1991, sec. 1992-93, 97-2002, treas. 1995-96, sec.-treas. 2000), N.W. Car Collectors Assn. (treas. 2002-04). Avocations: reading, woodworking, vintage thunderbirds, gourmet cooking. Office: CAF Enterprises Inc PO Box 1529 Tualatin OR 97062-1529

PETERS, ROBERT WOOLSEY, architect; b. Mpls., Mar. 24, 1935; s. John Eugene and Adelaide Elizabeth (Woolsey) P. BArch., U. Minn., 1958; MArch., Yale U., 1964. Registered architect, N.Mex. Participating assoc. Skidmore Owings & Merrill, Chgo., 1961-74; dir. design Schaefer & Assocs., Wichita, Kans., 1975-76; ptnr. Addy & Peters, Albuquerque, 1979-82; owner, sole proprietor Robert W. Peters AIA Architect, Albuquerque, 1985—. Exhibited work Centre Georges Pompidou, Paris, 1980, U. Art Mus., Albuquerque, 1982, 92, Albuquerque Mus., 1988; contbr. articles to Century Mag., Progressive Architecture, House & Garden, House Beautiful, also others. Recipient honor awards N.Mex. Soc. Architects, 1980-83, 86, 87, 92, HUD, 1980; 5th Nat. Passive Solar Conf., Amherst, Mass., 1981. Fellow AIA; mem. Contemporary Art Soc. N.Mex. (bd. dirs., pres.), Yale N.Mex. Democrat. Roman Catholic. Fax: (505) 898-4689.

PETERS, ROBERTA, soprano; b. N.Y.C., May 4, 1930; d. Sol and Ruth (Hirsch) Peters; m. Bertram Fields, Apr. 10, 1955; children: Paul, Bruce. Ed. privately; Litt.D., Elmira Coll., 1967; Mus. D., Ithaca Coll., 1968, Colby Coll., 1980; L.H.D., Westminster Coll., 1974, Lehigh U., 1977; D.F.A., St. John's U., 1982; LittD, Coll. New Rochelle, 1989; MusD, U. R.I., 1992, Fla. Atlantic U., 1997. Author: Debut at the Met; singer: (Operas) Met. Opera debut as Zerlina in Don Giovanni, 1950, recorded numerous operas, (appeared motion pictures including) Tonight We Sing, 1996, frequent appearances radio and TV, (stage appearances include) The King and I, 1973, Bittersweet, Merry Widow, The Sound of Music, Royal Opera House, Vienna State Opera, Munich Opera, West Berlin Opera, Salzburg Festival, The White House, debuts at festivals in Vienna and Munich, premiered Ani M'amin, Carnegie Hall, 1973, concert tours in U.S., Soviet Union, Scandinavian countries, Israel, China, Japan, Taiwan, South Korea, (debut) Kirov Opera, sang at Bolshoi Opera (1st Am. recipient Bolshoi medal). Trustee, bd. dirs. Carnegie Hall; trustee Ithaca Coll.; dir. Met. Opera Guild; chmn. Nat. Inst. Music Theater, 1991—; apptd. by Pres. Bush to Nat. Coun. Arts, 1991; overseer Colby Coll., Bklyn. Coll. Performing Arts Ctr.; past chair Nat. Cystic Fibrosis Found.; active Israel Bonds, AIDS rsch. Named Woman of Yr., Fedn. Women's Clubs, 1964; recipient honored spl. ceremony on 35th anniversary with Met. Opera Co., 1985, Nat. Medal of Arts, Pres. Clinton, 1998. Avocation: tennis. Office: ICM Artists Ltd 40 W 57th St Fl 16 New York NY 10019-4098 *I believe that life is a series of just one darn thing after another. If we can learn that, we can expect, meet, and solve our problems.*

PETERS, SARAH WHITAKER, art historian, writer, lecturer; b. Kenosha, Wis., Aug. 17, 1924; d. Robert Burbank and Margaret Jebb (Allen) Whitaker; m. Arthur King Peters, Oct. 21, 1943; children: Robert Bruce, Margaret Allen, Michael Whitaker. BA, Sarah Lawrence Coll., 1954; MA, Columbia U., 1966; student, L'Ecole du Louvre, Paris, 1967-68; diplome, Ecole des Trois Gourmandes, Paris, 1968; PhD, CUNY, 1987. Freelance critic Art in Am., N.Y.C. Lectr.-in-residence Garrison Forest Sch., Owings Mills, Md.; adj. asst. prof. art history C.W. Post, U. L.I.; lectr. Bronxville (N.Y.) Adult Sch., Internat. Mus. Photography, 1979, Tufts U., 1979, Madison (Wis.) Art Ctr., 1984, Meml. Art Gallery, Rochester, N.Y., 1988, 91, Caramoor Mus., Katonah, N.Y., 1988, Yale U. Art Gallery, New Haven, Conn., 1989, The Cosmopolitan Club, N.Y.C., 1977, 91, Sarah Lawrence Coll., Bronxville, 1992, The Phillips Collection, Washington, 1993, Mpls. Inst. Arts, 1993, Whitney Mus. Am. Art, Champion, 1994, U. Wis., Parkside, 1994, Nat. Mus. Wildlife Art, Jackson Hole, Wyo., 1995, The Georgia O'Keeffe Mus., Santa Fe, 1997, Bronxville Pub. Libr., 1998, Weatherspoon Art Mus., Greensboro, NC, 2003, Amon Carter Mus, Ft. Worth, 2003, Vassar Coll., 2003, Pa. Acad. Fine Arts, Phila., 2004. Author: Becoming O'Keeffe: The Early Years, 1991, 2d edit., 2001, Pattern of the Past: A Kenosha Memoir, 2001; contbr. essays to Portraits of American Women, 1991, The Dictionary of Art, 1996, Frames of Reference; Works from the Whitney Museum of American Art, 1999, American Art Review, 2003; TV appearances include: BBC, London, The Late Show, 1993, A&E Network Biography series on Georgia O'Keeffe, 2004; radio interview: Art Today, Australia Broadcasting Corp., 1999; contbr. articles to profl. jours. Mem. Coll. Art Assn., Bronxville Field Club, The Cosmopolitan Club. Avocations: horseback riding, rock climbing, tennis, cooking. Home: 14 Village Ln Bronxville NY 10708-4806

PETERS, STEPHEN PAUL, medical educator; b. Johnstown, Pa., Apr. 26, 1949; m. Diane H. Henley. BA magna cum laude, Yale U., 1971; PhD in Biochemistry, U. Pitts., 1976, MD cum laude, 1978. Diplomate Nat. Bd. Med. Examiners, Am. Bd. Internal Medicine, Am. Bd. Pulmonary Disease. Intern, asst. resident in internal medicine Johns Hopskins Hosp., Balt., 1978-80; fellow in medicine Johns Hopkins U. Sch. Medicine, Balt., 1980-83, asst. prof., 1982-86, dir. pulmonary consultation svc., 1983-86; assoc. prof. dept. medicine Thomas Jefferson U., Jefferson Med. Coll., Phila., 1986—2002, assoc. dir. divsn. critical care, pulmonary allergic and immunologic diseases, 1986—2002, acting dir. divsn. critical care, pulmonary, allergic and immunologic diseases, 2003, dir. rsch. divsn. pulmonary medicine and critical care, 1989—2003, prof. divsn. pulmonary medicine and critical care, 1984—2003; prof. dept. medicine Wake Forest U.-Bapt. Med. Ctr., 2003—; dir. rsch. sect. on pulmonary and critical care, allergy and immunology diseases Ware Forest U. Health Scis. Ctr., 2003—. Hosp. staff Johns Hopskins Hosp., 1982-86, Good Samaritan Hosp., Balt., 1982-86, Francis Scott Key Med. Ctr., Balt., 1983-86, Thomas Jefferson U. Hosp., Phila., 1986-2003, Jefferson Park Hosp., Phi.a, 1989-94; VA merit rev. bd. Respiration Study Sect., 1991, 97—; spl. rev. com. NIH, Nat. Inst. of Allergy and Infectious Diseases, 1991, 97; prof. dept. medicine Wake Forest U., 2003—; dir. rsch. sect. on pulmonary and critical care medicine Wake Forest U. Health Sci. Ctr., 2003—. Author: Practical Enzymology of the Spingolipidoses, 1977, Year Book of Pulmonary Disease, 1986-91, Clinical Studies in Medical Biochemistry, 1987; mem. editl. bd. Jour. of Allergy and Clin. Immunology, 1988-93, Respiratory Medicine, 1991—, Audio Forum on Asthma, 1998, Respiratory Digest, 1999—, Respiratory Rsch., 2000—, MD Consult, Pulmonary and Critical Care Medicine, 2001—; contbr. numerous articles to profl. jours. Med. scientists scholar, Ins. Med. Scientist scholarship Fund, Mass. Life Ins. Co., 1975-78; recipient numerous rsch. grants. Fellow ACP, Am. Acad. Allergy and Immunology, Coll. of Physicians of Phila., Am. Coll. of Chest Physicians; mem. Am. Thoracic Soc. (program com. allergy, immunology and inflamation sect. 1992—), Am. Assn. of Immunologists, Soc. for Leukocyte Biology, Pa. Thoracic Soc. (rsch. rev. com. 1990—), Am. Lung Assn. (rsch. rev. com. 1990-94), Sigma Xi. Office: Wake Forest Univ Ctr for Human Genomics Med Ctr Blvd Winston Salem NC 27157 Home: Stephen P Peters Md 4510 Chinaberry Ln Winston Salem NC 27106-4290 E-mail: stephen.p.peters@mail.tju.edu, sppeters@triad.rr.com.

PETERS, THOMAS J, management consultant, writer; b. Baltimore, 1942; m. Susan Peters; 2 children. BCE, MCE, Cornell U.; MBA, PhD, Stanford U.; degree (hon.), U. San. Fran., Rhodes Coll., State U. Mgmt., Moscow, 2004. Sr. drug abuse adv. White House, 1973—74; with McKinsey & Co., 1974—81, ptnr., 1979—81; founder Tom Peters Group, Palo Alto, Calif., 1981—. Co-author (with Robert H. Waterman Jr.): In Search of Excellence: Lessons in America's Best-Run Companies, 1982 (Named one of Top Three Business Books of the Century, 1999); co-author: (with Nancy Austin) A Passion for Excellence: The Leadership Difference, 1985; author: Thriving on Chaos: Handbook for a Management Revolution, 1987, Liberation Management: Necessary Disorganization for the Nanosecond Nineties, 1992, The Pursuit of Wow! Every Person's Guide to Topsy-Turvy Times, 1994, The Tom Peters Seminar: Crazy Times Call for Crazy Organizations, 1994, The Circle of Innovation: You Can't Shrink Your Way to Greatness, 1997, The Brand You 50: Or: Fifty Ways to Transform Yourself from an Employee into a Brand That Shouts Distinction, Commitment, and Passion!, 1999, Re-Imagine! Business Excellence in a Disruptive Age, 2003. Navy Seabee USN, 1966—70, Vietnam. Named Second in Top 50 Business Intellectuals, Accenture's Inst. for Strategic Change, 2002. Fellow: Soc. Quality and Participation, Internat. Customer Svc. Assn., World Productivity Assn., Internat. Acad. Mgmt. Office: Tom Peters Company 101 Commerce Blvd Loveland OH 45140

PETERS, WILLIAM, author, producer, director; b. San Francisco, July 30, 1921; s. William Ernest and Dorothy Louise (Wright) P.; m. Mercy Ann Miller, Oct. 12, 1942 (div. 1968); children: Suzanne Peters Payne, Geoffrey Wright, Jennifer Peters Johnson, Gretchen Peters Daniel; m. Helene Louise Yager White, May 31, 1987. BS, Northwestern U., 1947. Account exec. pub. relations J. Walter Thompson Co., Chgo., 1947-51; mem. fiction staff Ladies' Home Jour., 1951-52; article editor Woman's Home Companion, N.Y.C., 1952-53; freelance writer, Pelham, N.Y., 1953-62; producer CBS Reports, CBS News, N.Y.C., 1962-66; freelance writer, film dir. and TV producer/exec. producer N.Y.C., 1966-82; dir. Yale U. Films, New Haven, 1982-89; freelance writer, film dir., TV producer/exec. producer Guilford, Conn., 1990—. Author: American Memorial Hospital--Reims, France: A History, 1955, Passport to Friendship--The Story of the Experiment in International Living, 1957, The Southern Temper, 1959; author: (with Mrs. Medgar Evers) For Us, The Living, 1967; author: A Class Divided, 1971, A More Perfect Union, A Class Divided: Then and Now, 1987; prodr., writer, dir. (CBS Reports documentaries) Mississippi and the 15th Amendment, 1962, Storm Over the Supreme Court, Parts II and III, 1963 (George F. Peabody award, Golden Gavel award ABA), The Priest and the Politician, 1963, Filibuster--Birth Struggle of a Law, 1964, Segregation: Northern-Style, 1964, co-prodr. After Ten Years: The Court and the Schools, 1964 (Nat. Sch. Bell award NEA), (ABC News documentaries) Africa (East Africa), 1967 (Peabody award, NATAS award), Southern Accents--Northern Ghettos, 1967 (nominee for writing achievement Writers

Guild Am.), The Eye of the Storm, 1970 (George Foster Peabody award, Cine Golden Eagle award, Cath. Broadcasters Assn. Gabriel award, Am. Film Festival Blue Ribbon, Saturday Rev. TV award, hon. mention Monte Carlo TV Festival, Nat. Media awards of the Am. Psychol. Found.), An Echo of Anger, 1976, Suddenly an Eagle, 1976, Death of a Family (Writers Guild Am. award), A Bond of Iron, 1982, A Class Divided, 1985 (Emmy award, Sidney Hillman award, Cine Golden Eagle award), others, prodr., dir., writer Bill Moyer's Jour. (PBS), S.C. Ednl. TV Network; exec. prodr.: Boswell's London Journal, 1984; contbr. numerous articles to mags., jours. Co-founder North Shore Citizens Com., 1946, bd. dirs., 1946-51; co-founder Pelham Com. Human Relations, 1963, vice chmn., 1963-65, chmn., 1965-66. Served to capt. USAAF, 1942-45, ETO. Decorated Air medal with 2 oak leaf clusters D.F.C.; recipient Benjamin Franklin mag. award, 1954, Peabody TV award, 1963, 1970, 1976, Golden Gavel award, ABA, 1963, Sch. Bell award, NEA, 1964, Emmy award, Sidney Hillman award, 1985, Lincoln Univ. awards (2), Howard Blakeslee award, Am. Heart Assn., Intergroup Rels. award, Adelphi chpt. B'nai B'rith women and Anti-Defamation League of Phila. Mem. Dirs. Guild Am., Writers Guild Am. Democrat. Home: 3108 Long Hill Rd Guilford CT 06437-3619 Office Phone: 203-457-1744.

PETERS, WILLIAM FRANK, art educator; b. Oakland, Calif., Nov. 8, 1934; s. Clifford Leslie and Gladys Fay (Parrish) P.; m. Patricia Ann Redgwick, June 3, 1956 (div. 1973); 1 child, David William. B. Art Edn. with honors, Calif. Coll. Arts & Crafts, 1961; postgrad., various schools, various locations. Cert. spl. secondary art edn. life, gen. jr. high life. Summer campus art dir., instr. Richmond (Calif.) Unified Sch. Dist., 1961-66, Sch. of Fine Arts, Mt. Diablo Unified Sch. Dist., Concord, Calif., 1967-74; instr. Liberty Union H.S. Dist., Brentwood, Calif., 1961—, chmn. arts & crafts dept., 1976-91, curriculum cons., 1995—. Dist. rep. Pacific Art Assn., East Contra Costa County, Calif., 1967-70, Calif. Art Assn., East Contra Costa County, 1970-74; accreditation team mem. Western Assn. Schs. and Colls., Albany, Calif., 1981; film evaluator Contra Costa County Schs., 1965-84; art cons. Exhibited in group shows at Contra Costa County Fair (oil painting Best of Show 1968, watercolor Best of Show 1990, Collage Best of Show, 1999, 1st pl. photography 1987-95, 98-2004, Open Photography Overall Most Popular award 2001, 1st place short story 2003, 2004), Delta Art Show, Antioch, Calif. (1st pl. jewelry 1979), Festival of Color, Concord, Calif. (1st pl. ceramic 1963). Fundraiser United Crusade, Brentwood, Calif., 1980-83; publicity vol. East Contra Costa County Soroptimist Club, East County Rape/Crisis Ctr., Kappa Beta, John Marsh Meml. Assn., Knightsen 4-H, Delta Rotary Club, Delta Recreation Dept., Oakley Women's Club, Town of Byron, others. Named Contra Costa County Tchr. of Yr. AAUW, 1981; postgrad scholar Calif. Coll. of Arts and Crafts, 1962-63. Mem. NEA, Calif. Tchrs. Assn., Liberty Edn. Assn. (v.p., chmn. salary com., chmn. evaluation com., chmn. pers. policies com., chmn. scholarship com.), Delta Art Assn. (past bd. dirs.), Brentwood C. of C. (dir. Brentwood Christmas decorations 1968-94). Democrat. Avocations: painting, photography, reading, poetry, sports. Office: Liberty Union HS Dist 929 2d St Brentwood CA 94513-1335

PETERS, WILLIAM P. oncologist, educator, science administrator, dean; b. Buffalo, Aug. 26, 1950; m. Elizabeth Zentai; children: Emily, Abigail, James. BS, BS, BA, Pa. State U., 1972; MPhil, PhD, Columbia U., 1976, MD, 1978; postgrad., Harvard U., 1984; MBA, Duke U., 1990. Diplomate Am. Bd. Internal Medicine, Am. Bd. Med. Oncology. Prof. medicine Duke U. Med. Ctr., Durham, N.C., 1993-95, assoc. dir. for clin. ops. Duke Comprehensive Cancer Ctr., 1994-95, dir. bone marrow transplant program, 1984-95; pres., CEO, Mich. Cancer Found., Detroit, 1995—2001; pres., dir., CEO Karmanos Cancer Inst., Detroit, 1995—2001; assoc. dean for cancer programs Wayne State U., Detroit, 1995—2001, prof. oncology, medicine, surgery and radiation oncology, 1995—; disting. chair of oncology Wayne State U., Detroit, 2002—; pres., dir., CEO CETAID, Karamanos Cancer Inst., 2001—; pres. Inst. for Strategic Analysis and Innovation, Detroit Med. Ctr., 2001—. Sr. v.p. for cancer svcs. Detroit Med. Ctr., 1995-2001. Office: Karmanos Cancer Inst Rm 437 HWCRC 110 E Warren Ave Detroit MI 48201-1312

PETERSCHECK, WALTER HERMANN, chemical engineer; b. Rockenhausen, Germany, June 25, 1943; came to U.S., 1977; s. Walter Ludwig and Auguste (Gass) P.; m. Vicki Thureson, June 28, 1969 (div. June 1987); m. Erika Peterscheck-Volk, Dec. 27, 1996; children: Walter John, Hermann Karl, Robert Ludwig. BS in Chem. Engring., Inst. of Tech., Darmstadt, 1968; MS in Chemistry/Chem. Engring., Tech. U. Berlin, 1973. Cert. of designation European Engr. R&D engr. Amoco Chem., Naperville, Ill., 1969-71; process design engr. Lummus Tech. Ctr., Broomfield, N.J., 1973-76; process and project mgr. Lurgi, Frankfurt, Germany, 1977-83; v.p. tech. and ops. VerTech Treatment Sys., Denver, Baarn, Netherland, 1984-93; pres., CEO Euro-US, Inc., Longmont, Colo., 1994—; pres. Peterscheck & Soehne, GmbH, Rockenhausen, Germany, 1995—. Cons. European Commn.; advisor new tech. Mannesmann Demag, Duesseldorf, Germany, 1994—. Contbr. articles to profl. jours.; patentee (30) in field. Recipient Mannesmann Fed. award for best environ. process Fed. Republic of Germany. Fellow Am. Inst. Chem. Engrs. (local chair), Verein Deutscher Ingenieure (local chair); mem. Planetary Soc. Achievements include patent and reutilization of 1200m below ground reaction vessle for waste treatment of liquids and slurries as apparatus; processes for the environmental industries of various kinds are patented and in use. Address: Euro-Us Inc Apt 314 14052 E Tufts Dr Aurora CO 80015 Office: Euro-US Inc 10509 Appaloosa Pl El Paso TX 79924-2021

PETERSDORF, ROBERT GEORGE, physician, medical educator, academic administrator; b. Berlin, Feb. 14, 1926; s. Hans H. and Sonja P.; m. Patricia Horton Qua, June 2, 1951; children: Stephen Hans, John Eric. BA, Brown U., 1948, DMS (hon.), 1983; MD cum laude, Yale U., 1952; ScD (hon.), Albany Med. Coll., 1979; MA (hon.), Harvard U., 1980; DMS (hon.), Med. Coll. Pa., 1982, Brown U., 1983; DMS, Bowman-Gray Sch. Medicine, 1986; LHD (hon.), N.Y. Med. Coll., 1986; DSc (hon.), SUNY, Bklyn., 1987, Med. Coll. Ohio, 1987, Univ. Health Scis., The Chgo. Med. Sch., 1987; DSc (hon.), St. Louis U., 1988; LHD (hon.), Ea. Va. Med. Sch., 1988; DSc (hon.), Sch. Medicine, Georgetown U., 1991, Emory U., 1992; DSc (hon.), Tufts U., 1993; DSc (hon.), Mt. Sinai Sch. Medicine, 1993, George Washington U., 1994; other hon. degrees. Diplomate Am. Bd. Internal Medicine. Intern, asst. resident Yale U., New Haven, 1952—54; sr. asst. resident Peter Bent Brigham Hosp., Boston, 1954—55; fellow Johns Hopkins Hosp., Balt., 1955—59; chief resident, instr. medicine Yale U., 1957—58; asst. prof. medicine Johns Hopkins U., 1958—60, physician, 1958—60; assoc. prof. medicine U. Wash., Seattle, 1960—62, prof., 1962—79, chmn. dept. medicine, 1964—79; physician-in-chief U. Wash. Hosp., 1964—79; pres. Brigham and Women's Hosp., Boston, 1979—81; prof. medicine Harvard U. Med. Sch., Boston, 1979—81; dean, vice chancellor health scis. U. Calif.-San Diego Sch. Medicine, 1981—86; clin. prof. infectious diseases Sch. Medicine Georgetown U., 1986—94; pres. Assn. Am. Med. Colls., Washington, 1986—94, pres. emeritus, 1994—; prof. medicine U. Wash., 1994—, disting. prof., sr. advisor to dean, 1998—; disting. physician Vets. Health Adminstrn., Seattle, 1995—98, sr. physician, 1998—. Cons. to surgeon gen. USPHS, 1960—79; cons. USPHS Hosp., Seattle, 1962—79; mem. spl. med. adv. group VA, 1987—94. Editor: Harrison's Principles of Internal Medicine, 1968—90; contbr. numerous articles to profl. jours. With USAAF, 1944—46. Named Disting. Internist of 1987, Am. Soc. Internal Medicine; recipient Lilly medal, Royal Coll. Physicians, London, 1978, Wiggers award, Albany Med. Coll., 1979, Robert H. Williams award, Assn. Profs. Medicine, 1983, Keen award, Brown U., 1980, Disting. Svc. award, Baylor Coll. Medicine, 1989, Scroll of Merit, Nat. Med. Assn., 1990, 2d Ann. Founder's award, Assn. Program Dirs. in Internal Medicine, 1991, Flexner award, Assn. Am. Med. Coll., 1994. Master: ACP (pres. 1975—76, Stengel award 1980, Disting. Tchr. award 1993, Laureate award Wash. chpt.); fellow: AAAS, Execs. Assn. (hon.); mem.: Assn. Am. Physicians (pres. 1976—77, Kober medal 1996), Inst. Medicine of NAS (councillor 1977—80), Rainier Club, Cosmos Club. Home and Office: 8001 Sand Point Way NE C71 Seattle WA 98115

PETERSEN, ANNE C.(CHERYL), foundation administrator, educator; b. Little Falls, Minn., Sept. 11, 1944; d. Franklin Hanks and Rhoda Pauline (Sandwick) Studley; m. Douglas Lee Petersen, Dec. 27, 1967; children: Christine Anne, Benjamin Bradfield. BA, U. Chgo., 1966, MS, 1972, PhD, 1973. Asst. prof., rsch. assoc. Dept. Psychiatry U. Chgo., 1972-80, assoc. prof., rsch. assoc., 1980-82; prof. human devel., head Dept. Individual and Family Studies Pa. State U., University Park, 1982-87, dean Coll. Health and Human Devel., 1987-92, prof. health and human devel., 1987-92; dean grad. sch., v.p. for rsch. throughout state U. Minn., Mpls., 1992-94, prof. adolescent devel. and pediatrics, 1992-96; dep. dir., COO NSF, Arlington, Va., 1994-96; sr. v.p. programs W.K. Kellogg Found., 1996—. Vis. prof., fellow Coll. Edn., R&D Psychology, Roosevelt U., Chgo., 1973-74; cons. Ctr. for Health Adminstrn. Studies U. Chgo., 1976-78, Ctr. for New Schs., Chgo., 1974-78, Robert Wood Johnson Found. Mathtech, Inc., 1987-89; coord. clin. rsch. tng. program Michael Reese Hosp. and Med. Ctr., Chgo., 1976-80, dir. Lab. for Study of Adolescence, 1975-82; faculty Ill. Sch. for Profl. Psychology, 1978-79; statis. cons. Coll. Nursing U. Ill. Med. Ctr., 1975-83; assoc. dir. health program MacArthur Found., 1980-82, also cons. health program, 1982-88; chair sr. adv. bd. NIMH, 1987-88; nat. adv. mental health coun. NIH, 1997—; trustee Nat. Inst. Statis. Scis., 1998—. Author: Sex Related Differences in Cognition Functioning: Developmental Issues, 1979, Promoting Adolescent Health: A Dialog on Research and Practice, 1982, Firls at Puberty: Biological and psychosocial Perspectives, 1983, Brain Maturation and Cognitive Development: Comparative and Cross Cultural Perspectives, 1991, Narrowing the Margins: Adolescent Unemployment and the lack of a social role, 1991, Grofit: A Fortran Program for the Estimation of Parameters of a Human Growth Curve, 1972, Girls at Puberty: Biological and Psychosocial Perspectives, 1983, Adolescence and Youth: Psychological Development in a Changing World, 1984, Youth Unemployment and Society, 1994, Transitions Through Adolescence: Interpersonal Domains and Context, 1996; reviewer Jour. Youth and Adolescence, 1975-80, Devel. Psychology, 1979—, Sci., 1979—, Jour. Edn. Psychology, 1979—, Child Devel., 1980—, Jour. Edn. Measurement, 1980, Ednl. Rschr., 1980, Am. Ednl. Rsch. Jour., 1981—, Jour. Mental Imagery, 1982-92, Sex Roles, 1984—; cons. editor Psychology of Women Quar., 1978-82, assoc. editor, 1983-86; adv. editor Contemporary Psychology, 1985-86; mem. editl. bd. various profl. jours.; contbr. chpts. to books and articles to profl. jours. Bd. overseers Lewis Coll., Ill. Inst. Tech., 1980-82; mem. adv. bd. longitudinal data archive project Murray Ctr., Radcliffe Coll., 1985-91, mem. sci. adv. bd., 1983-91 Fellow: APA (chmn. task force on reproductive freedom 1979—81, program chmn. 1981—82, chmn. task force on long range planning 1986—89, pres. divsn. 7 1992—93), AAAS; mem.: NAS (nat. forum on future children and their families 1987—91, chmn. panel on child abuse and neglect 1991—93, mem. forum on adolescence Inst. of Medicine 1997—2000, chair bd. on behavioral, cognitive and sensory scis. 1997—), Soc. for Rsch. on Adolescence (pres. 1990—92, past pres. 1992—94, chmn. nominations com. 1992—94), Acad. Europaea, Psychometric Soc., Behavior Genetics Assn., Assn. Women in Sci. (bd. dirs. 1996—2000), Am. Ednl. Rsch. Assn. (various offices), Internat. Soc. for the Study of Behavioral Devel. (coun. mem. 1995—, pres.-elect 2002—04), Inst. for Medicine. Home: 3715 Blackberry Ln Kalamazoo MI 49008-3333

PETERSEN, ARNE JOAQUIN, chemist; b. L.A., Jan. 27, 1932; s. Hans Maria Theodore and Astrid Marie (Pedersen) Petersen; m. Sandra Joyce Sharp, Aug. 12, 1961; children: Christina Lynn, Kurt Arne. AA, Compton Coll., 1957; BS, Calif. State U., Long Beach, 1959; BA, U. Calif., Irvine, 1975. Lic. comml. pilot. Chemist, scientist Beckman Instruments, Inc., Fullerton, Calif., 1959-62, engr., scientist, 1962-65, project, sr. project engr., 1965-74; project/program mgr. clin. divsn. Beckman Clin. Ops., Fullerton/Brea, Calif., 1974-80; ops. mgr. Graphic Controls Corp., Irvine, 1980-82; engr./rsch. and devel. mgr. Carle Instruments Chromatography, Anaheim, Calif., 1982-84; ops. mgr. Magnaflux/X-Ray Devel., L.A., 1984-85; rsch. and devel. dir., new products Am. Chem. Systems, Irvine, Calif., 1985-86; rsch. assoc. U. Calif., Irvine, 1987-88; ind. cons., contractor, sales real estate investment, 1989—. Career guidance counselor U. Calif., Irvine, 1976; co-founder Cak, Inc., 2001. Contbr. articles and sci. papers in field to profl. jours. Exec. svc. A.I.D. Internat. Exec. Svc. Corps, Egypt, 1993—94; vol. F.I.S.H., Costa Mesa, Newport Beach, Calif.; basketball coach Boys-Girls Club, Newport Beach, 1975—78; baseball coach Newport Beach Parks, 1975—78; adv. com. Newport/Costa Mesa Sch. Bd., 1974—75. Mem.: AAAS, AMA, Am. Chem. Soc., Biomed. Engring. Soc., U. Calif. Univ. Club (bd. dirs.), Chi Gamma Iota (pres. compton coll. 1956), Kappa Sigma (founder Calif. State U., Long Beach chpt.). Achievements include patents in field. Avocations: flying, photography, travel, bridge, surfing. Personal E-mail: AJPetersen@earthlink.net.

PETERSEN, BARRY REX, news correspondent; b. Norfolk, Va., Jan. 14, 1949; s. Kermit and Mavis Lucille (Sutton) P.; m. Sandra H. Petersen, June 7, 1971 (div. Dec. 1984); children: Emily Jensine, Juliette Rose; m. Jan Chorlton, Feb. 14, 1985. BS in Journalism, Northwestern U., 1970, MS in Journalism, 1972. Sports columnist Sidney (Mont.) Herald, 1964-66; city hall reporter Arlington Heights (Ill.) Day, 1968-69; columnist, copy editor Chgo. Today, 1970-71; pub. Daily Northwestern, Evanston, Ill., 1970-71; reporter Milw. (Wis.) Jour., 1971-72; investigative reporter Sta. WITI-TV, Milw., 1972-74; reporter, anchor Sta. WCCO-TV, Mpls., 1974-78; corr. CBS News, L.A., 1978-81, San Francisco, 1981-85, Tokyo, 1986-88, Moscow, 1988-90, London, 1991-95, Tokyo, 1995—. Pres. AFRTA, Milw., 1973-74; Josephine B. and Newton N. Minow vis. prof. in communications Northwestern U., Evanston, Ill., 1991. Recipient Investigative Reporting award Wis. Press Assn., 1973, Nat. Emmy award, 1994, 97, World gold medal radio breaking news N.Y. Festivals, 1999. Mem. Fgn. Corrs. Club Japan. Lutheran. Avocations: sailing, travel, internat. real estate. Office: CBS News/Tokyo 524 W 57th St New York NY 10019-2924 also: CBS News 5-3-6 Akasaka Minato-ku Tokyo 107 Japan Office Phone: 212-975-3019.

PETERSEN, CATHERINE HOLLAND, lawyer; b. Norman, Okla., Apr. 24, 1951; d. John Hays and Helen Ann (Turner) Holland; m. James Frederick Petersen, June 26, 1973 (div.); children: T. Kyle, Lindsay Diane; m. Lester E.R. Doty, Apr. 17, 2004. BA, Hastings Coll., 1973; JD, Okla. U., 1976. Bar: Okla. 1976, U.S. Dist. Ct. (we. dist.) Okla. 1978. Legal intern, police legal advisor City of Norman, 1974-76; sole practice Norman, 1976-81; ptnr. Williams Petersen & Denny, Norman, 1981-82; pres. Petersen Assocs., Inc., Norman, 1982—. Adj. prof. Oklahoma City U. Coll. Law, 1982, U. Okla. Law Ctr., 1987; instr. continuing legal edn. U. Okla. Law Ctr., Norman, 1977, 79, 81, 83, 84, 86, 89-95; instr. Okla. Bar Assn., ABA, Am. Acad. Matrimonial Lawyers. Bd. dirs. United Way, Norman, 1978-84, pres., 1981; bd. dirs. Women's Resource Ctr., Norman, 1975-77, 82-84; mem. Jr. League, Norman, 1980-83, Norman Hosp. Ayx., 1982-84; trustee 1st Presbyn. Ch., 1986-87. Named among Outstanding Okla. Women of 1980s, Women's Polit. Caucus, 1980, Outstanding Young Women of Am., 1981, 83. Fellow Am. Acad. Matrimonial Lawyers (pres. Okla. chpt. 1990-91, bd. govs. 1991-95); mem. ABA (family law sect., faculty Family Law Inst. 1993—), Cleveland County Bar Assn., Okla. Bar Assn. (chmn. family law sect. 1987-88), Phi Delta Phi. Republican. Home: 4716 Sundance Ct Norman OK 73072-3900 Office: PO Box 1243 314 E Comanche St Norman OK 73069-6009

PETERSEN, DAVID A. state legislator, financial advisor; b. Mesa, Ariz., Sept. 20, 1950; m. Patti Briggs; 8 children. Student, Ariz. State U., 1971-73, U. Phoenix, 1993. Fin. svcs. advisor, 1976—; mem. Ariz. Senate, Dist. 29, Phoenix, 1994—; mem. edn. com., family svcs. com., Rep. whip Ariz. State Senate. Leader Boy Scouts Am. Republican. Mem. Lds Ch. Office: State Capitol Bldg 1700 W Washington St # 213 Phoenix AZ 85007-2812 also: 623 N Miller St Mesa AZ 85203-7229 E-mail: dpeterse@azleg.state.az.us.

PETERSEN, DAVID L. lawyer; AA, Concordia Jr. Coll., Milw., 1963; BA, Concordia Sr. Coll., Ft. Wayne, Ind., 1965; JD, Valparaiso U., Ind., 1968. Bar: Wis. 1968, U.S. Dist. Ct. (ea. dist.) Wis. 1969, U.S. Ct. Appeals (7th cir.) 1972, U.S. Supreme Ct. 1988, Fla. 1989. Ptnr. Quarles & Brady, Milw. and Naples, Fla., 1968—. Author: Wisconsin Condominium Law, 1988, 98, 2003; editor Valparaiso U. Law Rev., 1967-68; contbr. articles to profl. jours. Mem. Greater Milw. Com. Cmty. Devel., 1983; bd. dirs. Goals for Greater Milw. 2000, 1982, Broward Com. of 100; mem. nat. adv. bd. Nat. Ctr. for Missing and Exploited Children, Washington, Adam Walsh Children's Fund, Palm Beach, Fla.; dir. Boys and Girls Club Collier County. Lt. col., instr. pilot USAF/Wis. Air N.G., 1970-90. Mem. ABA, Wis. Bar Assn., Milw. Bar Assn., Fla Bar Assn., Broward County Bar Assn., Palm Beach County Bar Assn., Collier County Bar Assn., Am. Coll. Real Estate Lawyers, Milw. Yacht Club, Palm Beach Yacht Club. Office: Quarles & Brady LLP 1395 Panther Ln Naples FL 34109 also: Quarles & Brady LLP 411 E Wisconsin Ave Ste 2550 Milwaukee WI 53202-4409

PETERSEN, DONALD SONDERGAARD, lawyer; b. Pontiac, Ill., May 14, 1929; s. Clarence Marius and Esther (Sondergaard) P.; m. Alice Thorup, June 5, 1954; children: Stephen, Susan Petersen Schuh, Sally Petersen Riordan. Student, Grand View Coll., 1946-48; BA, Augustana Coll., Rock Island, Ill., 1951; JD, Northwestern U., 1956. Bar: Ill. 1957. Assoc. Norman & Billick and predecessors, Chgo., 1956-64, ptnr., 1965-78; counsel Sidley & Austin, Chgo., 1978-80, ptnr., 1980-93, ret., 1993. Pres. Chgo. Exhibitors Corp., Chgo., 1972-85. Bd. dirs. Mount Olive Cemetery Co. Inc., Chgo., 1972-90; bd. dirs. Augustana Hosp., 1983-87, The Danish Home, 1976—; bd. dirs. Luth. Gen. Hosp., Park Ridge, Ill., 1968—, chmn., 1979-81, 89-91; bd. dirs. Luth. Gen. Health System and predecessors, Park Ridge, 1980-95, chmn., 1980-81, 83-85; bd. dirs., chmn. Parkside Health Mgmt. Corp., Parkside Home Health Svcs., 1985-88. With U.S. Army, 1951-53. Mem. Chgo. Bar Assn., Ill. State Bar Assn. Clubs: Union League (Chgo.). Home: 241 N Aldine Ave Park Ridge IL 60068-3009 Office: 55 W Monroe St Ste 2200 Chicago IL 60603-5008

PETERSEN, DOUGLAS ARNDT, financial consultant; b. Albert Lea, Minn., Sept. 18, 1944; s. Arndt H. and Helen L. (Slater) P.; m. Winnifred K. Taylor, Aug. 14, 1964 (div. July 1970); children: Scott, Jennifer; m. Cynthia L. Schnabel, June 14, 1975; 1 child, Christopher. BS in Edn., Mankato State U., 1966, postgrad., 1966—68. Youth dir. Mankato (Minn.) YMCA, 1965-68; tchr. Mankato State U., 1965-68; exec. dir. YMCA Camp Christmas Tree, Mound, Minn., 1968-72; asst. exec. dir. West Suburban YMCA, Minnetonka, Minn., 1968-72; exec. dir. Eastside YMCA, Mpls., 1972-75; program/fin. devel. dir. Eastside Neighborhood Svc., Mpls., 1975-79; asst. exec. dir. Mpls. Red Cross, 1979-89; dir. major/planned gifts ARC Nat. Staff, Mpls., 1989-91; pres./chief exec. officer/cons. D.A. Petersen Assocs., Mpls., 1992—. Mem. St. Anthony/New Brighton Found. (chair 1988-92), YMCA Am. (pres. APD 1974), ARC (pres. MFDDC 1988-89). Lutheran. Avocations: travel, community service, scuba, canoeing, backpacking. Home: 3216 Skycroft Dr Minneapolis MN 55418-2552 Office: PO Box 18415 Minneapolis MN 55418-0415 E-mail: dapa2@comcast.net.

PETERSEN, EDWARD SCHMIDT, retired physician; b. Chgo., Nov. 19, 1921; s. William F. and Alma C. (Schmidt) P.; m. Zoe Andre Bakeeff, June 11, 1944; children: Catherine Petersen Mack, Edward B. Student, Harvard U., 1942, MD, 1945. Diplomate Am. Bd. Internal Medicine. Intern St. Luke's Hosp., Chgo., 1945-46, med. practice, 1951-53; resident in medicine U. Chgo., 1948-51; asst. dir. profl. svcs. VA Rsch. Hosp., Chgo., 1953-54; from asst. to assoc. dean, assoc. prof. Northwestern U. Med. Sch., Chgo., 1954-72, asst. dir. to dir. divsn. undergrad. med. edn., AMA, 1972-88, ret., 1988. Chair Midwest group on student affairs Assn. Am. Med. Colls., Washington, 1967-69; pres. Inst. Medicine, Chgo., 1976; chair com. on hosps. and clinics Ill. Dept. Pub. Aid,Chgo., 1961-70; bd. dirs. Hull House, Chgo., 1962-70; mem. sci. adv. com. Mcpl. TB Sanitarium, Chgo., 1970-74. Capt. Med. Corps., AUS, 1946-48. Fellow ACP; mem. AMA (co-sec. liason com. on med. edn. 1976-87), Geneva Lake Assn. (bd. dirs. 1975-99). Lutheran. Avocation: environmental and historical restoration. Home: W4268 Southland Rd Lake Geneva WI 53147-3957

PETERSEN, JAMES L. lawyer; b. Bloomington, Ill., Feb. 3, 1947; s. Eugene and Cathryn Theresa (Hemmele) P.; m. Helen Louise Moser, Nov. 20, 1971; children: Christine Louise, Margaret Theresa. BA, Ill. State U., 1970; MA, U. Ill., Springfield, 1973; JD magna cum laude, Ind. U., 1976. Bar; Ind. 1976, Fla. 1980, U.S. Dist. Cts. (no. and so. Ind.), U.S. Ct. Appeals (7th cir.), U.S. Supreme Ct. Admissions officer U. Ill., Springfield, 1970-71, asst. to v.p., 1971-72, registrar, 1972-73; assoc. Ice Miller, Indpls., 1976-83, ptnr., 1983—. Pres. United Cerebral Palsy of Ctrl. Ind., 1981-83, pres. Found., 1988-90, Stanley K. Lacy Leadership Series participant. Mem. ABA, Fla. Bar Assn., Ind. Bar Assn., Am. Coll. Trial Lawyers, Intl. Franchise Assn. (bd. mem. Symposium Organizing Cmte., 2003-04), Ind. Assn. Defense Couns. (past co-chair, Prods. Liability Cmte; elected 1997 Diplomat), The Business Council, Inc., Ill. State U. Alumni Assn. (pres. 1990-92), Ind. U. Law Alumni Assn. (bd. dirs. 1992—, pres. 1998-99), Ind. U. Bd. Visitors 1998-99, Order of Coif. Home: 11827 Sea Star Dr Indianapolis IN 46256-9400 Office: Ice Miller PO Box 82001 One American Sq Indianapolis IN 46282

PETERSEN, JANET, state representative; b. DesMoines, Aug. 1, 1970; BA, U. No. Iowa; MA, Drake U. Constituency coord. 1992 Clinton-Gore Campaign; comm. specialist Am. Heart Assn.; sr. account exec. Strategic Am.; mem. Iowa Ho. Reps., DesMoines, 2001—, mem. commerce and regulation com., mem. econ. devel. com., mem. appropriations com., mem. edn. com., mem. local govt. com. Active Beaverdale Neighborhood Assn., Walnut Hills Meth. Ch.; bd. mem. DesMoines Arts Festival, United Way Ctrl. Iowa, Women in Pub. Policy, Polk County Housing Trust Fund. Democrat. Office: State Capitol East 12th and Grand Des Moines IA 50319 also: 1346 47th St Des Moines IA 50311

PETERSEN, JEAN SNYDER, association executive; b. N.Y.C., Oct. 16, 1931; d. Peter Eugene and Helyn Brownell (Parker) Snyder; m. Elton Reed Petersen, Sept. 16, 1954; children— Bruce Brownell, Craig Reed. Student, N.Y. U., 1949-51; degree fgn. banking, Am. Inst. Banking, 1952. Fgn. credit investigator Chase Nat. Bank Hdqrs., N.Y.C., 1952-56; nat. exec. dir. Assn. Children and Adults with Learning Disabilities (name changed to Learning Disabilities Assn. of Am.), Pitts., 1972—. Mem. exec. com., treas. Jr. League, Pitts.; bd. dirs. Found. for Children with Learning Disabilities, N.Y.C., Children's Hosp., Pitts., Music for Mt. Lebanon, Vocat. Rehab. Ctr., Pitts.; bd. dirs., v.p., mem. exec. com. Assn. Retarded Citizens Pa.; ptnr. UN Internat. Yr. of Disabled; ruling elder Presbyn. Ch.Assn. Retarded Citizens Pa.; mem. exec. com. Pat Buckley Moss Nat. Children's Charity Found; chmn. bd. dirs. Masonic Learning Ctrs. for Children. Recipient Sustainers award Jr. League, 1977, Recognition award, 1975, Pres.'s award, 1978 Mem. AAUW, Meeting Planners Internat. (treas.), Am. Soc. Assn. Execs. Republican. Presbyterian. Home: 343 Shadowlawn Ave Pittsburgh PA 15216-1239 Office: 4156 Library Rd Pittsburgh PA 15234-1349 Fax: (412) 5634537.

PETERSEN, JOHN D. academic administrator; m. Carol Petersen; 2 children. BS in Chemistry, UCLA, 1970; PhD in Inorganic Chemistry, U. Calif., Santa Barbara, 1975. Asst. prof. chemistry Kans. State U., 1975—80; head dept. chemistry, assoc. dean rsch. Coll. Scis. Clemson (S.C.) U., 1983—93; prof. chemistry, dean Coll. Sci. Wayne State U., 1994—2000; provost, exec. v.p. univ. affairs U. Conn., Storrs, 2000—04; pres. U. Tenn., 2004—. Mem.: Nat. Assn. State Universitites and Land Grant Colleges (exec. com. for chief academic officers), Coun. Chem. Rsch., Am. Chem. Soc. Office: U Tenn Office of Pres 800 Andy Holt Tower Knoxville TN 37996-0180

PETERSEN, JOHN LAURENS, future research and strategic planner; b. Omaha, July 11, 1943; s. J. Allan and Evelyn R. P.; m. Diane Carter, July 22, 1967; 1 child, John Carter Laurens. BSEE, John Brown U., 1966. Asst. to the pres. Embosograph Display Mfg., Chgo., 1971-72; assoc. Richard S. Latham & Assocs., Chgo., 1972-74; v.p. Family Concern, Inc., Chgo., 1974-79; pres. Petersen & Assocs., Chgo., 1979-90; pres., founder The Arlington (Va.) Inst., 1989—. Co-chmn. Nat. Security Group, Washington, 1987-88; adj. fellow Ctr. for Strategic and Internat. Studies, Washington, 1987-91; mem. vis. com. Ctr. for East Asian Studies, U. Chgo., 1987-90; assoc. scholar Fgn. Policy Rsch. Inst., Phila., 1988; lectr. Joint Mil. Intelligence Coll., Def. Intelligence Agy., 1994—; vis. lectr. Internat. Space U., Stockholm, 1995; vis. prof. Indsl. Coll. Armed Forces, Nat. Def. U., 1995. Author: The Road to 2015: Profiles of the Future, 1994 (Outstanding Acad. Book of 1995), Out of the Blue: Wildcards and Other Big Future Surprises, 1997. Ill. state chmn. Gary Hart for Pres. Campaign, 1984, mem. exec. fin. com., 1984; elected del., vice chmn. Ill. Delegation to Dem. Nat. Conv., 1984; del. candidate Dem. Nat. Conv., 1988. Comdr. USNR, 1962-83. Recipient Writing award U.S. Naval Inst., 1994. Mem. Assn. Naval Aviation (life, former nat. trustee), Aircraft Owners and Pilots Assn., Exptl. Aircraft Assn., Global Bus. Network, U.S. Navy Meml.

Found. (vice chmn. bd. dirs. 1992-2001), Soc. for Sci. Exploration, World Future Soc. (bd. dirs.), Assn. Profl. Futurists. Avocations: flying, building an airplane. Office: The Arlington Inst 1501 Lee Hwy Arlington VA 22209-1109

PETERSEN, JONATHAN WILLIAM, marketing professional, writer; b. Racine, Wis., Sept. 4, 1955; s. James John George and Betty Louise; m. Beth Peterson, June 2, 1979; children: Matthew, Andrew, Sarah, Rachel. Diploma in broadcast comms., Moody Bible Inst., Chgo., 1976; BA in Mass Comms., U. Wis., La Crosse, 1978. Cert. eMarketer 2001. Classical music dir. Radio Sta. WLSU-FM, LaCrosse, Wis., 1977-78; announcer, writer Radio Sta. WIHS-FM, Middletown, Conn., 1979-80; program dir., news dir., announcer, writer Radio Sta. KTIG-FM, Pequot Lakes, Minn., 1980-84; religion news editor UPI Radio Network, Washington, 1984-86; media rels. dir. Zondervan, Grand Rapids, Mich., 1986—96, strategic mktg. dir., 1996—99; adminstr. Internet Mktg., 1996—2001; mktg. dir. Zondervan ChurchSource, 1999—2001; dir. Internet. mktg. Zondervan, 2001—. Print/Web news editor Christian Emergency Network, 2003—; seminar leader, Nat'l Religious Broadcasters Convention Washington, 1986, 94; freelance cons., news prodr., writer, Grand Rapids. Creator, developer UPI's Religion Svc. (radio network), 1984-86, Zondervan Radio Network, 1991, Zondervan Press Syndicate, 1992, Zondervan E-Mail Alert Svc., 1996; author: News Department Manual, 1982, Zondervan Author Guide to Book Promotion, 1994, Zondervan Author/Speaker Directory, 1995, Evangelical Christian Publishers Assocation Reporter's Sourcebook, 1995, Zondervan On-Air Copy Book, 1995; columnist Religious Broadcasting mag., 1991-98; contbr. articles to profl. jours. Judge N.Y. Festivals Internat. Radio Awards. Silver Angel, Religion In Media, 1985-86, Honorable Mention, Pub. Rel. Soc. Am. W. Mich. chpt., 1986; recipient Finalist award Internat. Galaxy Awards, 1991, Gold award Internat. Mercury Awards, 1991, Silver award N.Y. Festivals Internat. Radio Competition, 1992, Finalist award cert. of excellence Creativity in Pub. Rels. Awards, 1993, Crystal Award of excellence The Communicator awards, 1996. Mem. eMarketing Assn., Publishers' Publicity Assn., Religion Newswriters Assn., Radio-TV News Dir. Assn., Evang. Press Assn., The Religion Pub. Group, Religious Publicists Network, Soc. Profl. Journalists, Internat. Assn. Bus. Communicators. (past v.p. membership West Mich. chpt., judge dist. 4 Silver Quill awards), Toastmasters (area speech contest winner 1999, Competent Toastmaster award 1999). Evangelical Covenant. Avocations: racquetball, music. Office Phone: 616-698-3417. E-mail: jonathan.petersen@zondervan.com.

PETERSEN, KEVIN, federal agency administrator; b. LeMars, Iowa, Oct. 4, 1951; BS in Aerospace Engring., Iowa State U., 1974; MS, UCLA, 1976; postgrad. in Engring., Stanford U. Rsch. engr. Dryden Flight Rsch. Ctr. NASA, Houston, 1971—74, aerospace engr., 1974, chief flight controls sect., 1982—85, chief engr., 1985—86, chief vehicle tech. br., 1989—90, acting dir., 1998—99, dir., 1999—. Office: Dryden Flight Rsch Ctr PO Box 273 Edwards CA 93523-0273

PETERSEN, KITT MIA FALCK, medical scientist; b. Neastved, Denmark, Mar. 30, 1958; came to the U.S., 1990; d. Bjarne Peter Falck and Jytte Sonja Petersen; m. Gerald Israel Shulman, July 4, 1994. BS, N. Zahle's Gymnasieskole, Copenhagen, 1978; MD, U. Copenhagen, 1985. Intern/resident U. Hosps. Copenhagen, 1985-87; Kandidatstipendiat U. Copenhagen, 1987-89, sr. Kandidatstipendiat, 1989-92; postdoctoral fellow Yale U., New Haven, 1989-92, assoc. rsch. scientist, 1992-97, rsch. scientist, 1997-98, asst. prof. Sch Medicine, 1998—2004, asst. dir. Gen. Clin. Rsch. Ctr., 2001—03, assoc. prof. Sch. Medicine, 2004—. Recipient grant U. Copenhagen, 1986, 89-92, Henry Christian award, 1997, 98, Young Investigator award Novartis, 2002, ROI, N.H., 2003. Mem. Am. Fedn. for Med. Rsch., Am. Physiol. Soc., Am. Diabetes Assn. (Rsch. award 2000), Danish Med. Soc., Soc. for Patient Related Rsch., Juvenile Diabetes Assn. Avocations: ballet, photography, writing. Office: Yale U Sch Medicine TAC S263 300 Congress Ave New Haven CT 06520-8020 E-mail: kitt.petersen@yale.edu.

PETERSEN, MARTIN EUGENE, curator; b. Grafton, Iowa, Apr. 21, 1931; s. Martin S. and Martha Dorothea (Paulsen) P. BA, State U. Iowa, 1951, MA, 1957; postgrad., The Hague (Netherlands), 1964. Curator San Diego Mus. Art, 1957-96; advisor Olaf Wieghorst Mus., El Cajon, Calif., 1996—. Extension instr. U. Calif., 1958, lectr., 1960 Author art catalogues, books, articles in field. Served with AUS, 1952-54. Mem. So. Calif. Art Historians. Home: 2003 Bayview Heights Dr Spc 138 San Diego CA 92105-5537

PETERSEN, MARTIN ROSS, public affairs executive; b. Bakersfield, Calif., Aug. 14, 1944; s. Peter Arthur and Valerie A. (Swink) P.; m. Geri Gottuso, Nov. 12, 1987; children: Kaitlin Jean, Alexander Ross. BA in Govt., Calif. State U., Sacramento, 1969. Asst. dir. govtl. affairs Calif. State U. and Colls., Sacramento, 1967-72; adminstr. divsn. consumer svcs. Calif. Dept. Consumer Affairs, Sacramento, 1972-75; dir. Office External Liaison The White House Office Consumer Affairs, Washington, 1975-77, 83-85; pres. Knauer & Assocs., Inc., Washington, 1977-83; dir. corp. pub. affairs and N.J. ops. adminstrn. Playtex Products, Inc., Allendale, 1985—. Exec. v.p. Trade Net, Washington, 1981-85; chmn. Washington Legis. Group, 1984-85; mem. bd. govs. Ramapo (N.J.) State Coll., 2001—. Editor: Auto Imports, 1979; founding editor Customer Relationship Mgmt., 1980-82. Pub. mem. Voluntary Effort To Contain Health Care Costs in Am., Chgo., 1977-80; sec. subcom. on consumer affairs Rep. Nat. Com., Washington, 1979-80; mem. transition team and inaugural com. Reagan-Bush White House, Washington, 1981; v.p. Nat. Coalition for Consumer Edn., Washington, 1981-91; v.p. Oakland (N.J.) Rep. Club, 1990, 2001; councilman Borough of Oakland, 1991-2002; author, vol. in pub. svc. Consumer Product Safety Commn., 1977. With USAF, 1962-66. Mem. Soc. Consumer Affairs Profls. in Bus. (nat. bd. dirs. 1979-83, 98—2002, exec. com. 1980-83, 99—2002, pres. D.C. chpt. 1977-78, Outstanding Leader of Yr. award 1985), Am. League Lobbyists, Govt. Affairs Profls. (N.Y.C.), Am. Soc. Quality, Internat. Facility Mgmt. Assn., Internat. Bus. Comm. Assn. Home: 10 Wichita Path Oakland NJ 07436-3818 Office: Playtex Products Inc 75 Commerce Dr Allendale NJ 07401-1600 E-mail: martin.petersen@usa.net.

PETERSEN, MAUREEN JEANETTE MILLER, management information consultant, former nurse; b. Evanston, Ill., Sept. 4, 1956; d. Maurice James and M. Joyce (Mielke) Miller; m. Gregory Eugene Petersen, July 7, 1984; children: Trevor James, Tatyana Brianne. BS in Nursing cum laude, Vanderbilt U., 1978; MS in Biometry and Health Info. Systems, U. Minn., 1984. Nurse U. Iowa Hosps. and Clinics, Iowa City, 1978—82; research asst. Sch. Nursing, U. Minn., Mpls., 1982—83; mgr. Accenture, Mpls., 1984—2001; sr. mgr. clin. systems Park Nicollet, Eden Prairie, Minn., 2003—. Mem.: Project Mgmt. Inst. (proj. mgmt. profl.), Mensa. Methodist. Avocation: travel. Home: 1050 County Rd C2 W Roseville MN 55113-1945 Office: Park Nicollet 7905 Golden Triangle Dr Eden Prairie MN 55344 E-mail: peters1050@aol.com., petema@parknicollet.com.

PETERSEN, RICHARD HERMAN, federal agency administrator, aeronautical engineer; b. Quincy, Ill., Oct. 9, 1934; s. Herman Hiese and Nancy (Getty) P.; m. Joandra Windsor Shenk, Sept. 15, 1959; children: Eric Norman, Kristin. BS in Aero. Engring., Purdue U., 1956, Dr. Engring. (hon.), 1986; MS in Aeronautics, Calif. Inst. Tech., 1957; D in Pub. Service (hon.), George Washington U., 1987; DSc (hon.), Coll. of William and Mary, 1992. Rsch. engr. NASA Ames Rsch. Ctr., Moffett Field, Calif., 1957-63, aerospace engr., 1963-65, 66-70, br. chief, 1970-73, div. chief, 1975-80; aerospace engr. NASA, Washington, 1965-66; exec. Nielsen Engring. & Rsch. Inc., Mountain View, Calif., 1973-75; dep. dir. NASA Langley Research Ctr., Hampton, Va., 1980-85, dir., 1985-91; assoc. adminstr. Aeronautics and Space Tech. NASA Hdqrs., Washington, 1991-93, retired, 1993; aerospace cons., 1993—. 1st lt. USAF, 1957-60. Recipient Disting. Alumnus award Purdue U., 1980, Meritorious Exec. award U.S. Pres., 1982, Disting. Exec. award U.S. Pres., 1989; Sloan exec. fellow Stanford U., 1973. Fellow AIAA (bd. dirs. 1984-90, Sylvanus A. Reed Aeronautics award 1991), Nat. Acad. Engring. Republican. Avocations: golf, skiing. Home and Office: 352 Dunemere Dr La Jolla CA 92037-5311

PETERSEN, RICHARD JOHN, small business owner, educator; s. Richard J. Petersen and Audrey Marie Morris; m. Mildred Costas Petersen, May 24, 1975 (div. 1996); children: Cecily Francis, Derick Anthony. Diploma in bus. adminstrn., Mercy Coll., Bronx, 1980. Cert. N.Y.C. Bd. of Educators, 1985. Computer operator First Nat. City Bank, N.Y.C., 1968—72; mgmt. Organization of United Reg. Svcs., Bklyn., 1972—79, Superior Care, N.Y.C., 1980—82; tchr., volley ball coach N.Y.C. Bd. of Edn., N.Y.C., 1982—88; owner, operator STAT Bldg., Bklyn., 1988—; assoc. dean evening adminstrn. Blake Bus. Sch., N.Y.C., 1995—97; mgmt. United Home ATT / Home Care, Bklyn., 1997—2000. Author: (poems) The Last Hurrah, 1985, Why God Made Paraplegics, 1999 (1st Pl., 1999). Cubmaster, scoutmaster troup III Boy Scouts of Am., Bklyn., 1979—82. With U.S. Army, 1969—71, Vietnam. Decorated Commendation medal U.S. Army Vietnam. Mem.: Orgn. Eagle Scouts, All Cmtys. Arts Inc. Democrat. Roman Catholic. Avocations: poetry, photography, entrepreneurship, web programming, bid wisk. Home: 1381 E 48th St Brooklyn NY 11234 Office: Stat Billing 1381 E 48th St Brooklyn NY 11234 Office Phone: 718-258-5474.

PETERSEN, ROBERT ALLEN, pediatric ophthalmologist; b. N.Y.C., Dec. 30, 1933; s. Harold Marinus and Elinor Louise (Buckley) P.; m. Veronica Margiana Stinnes, Dec. 22, 1956; children: Anne, Catherine, John. BS, CUNY, 1955; MD, Columbia U., 1959, DrMedSc, 1964. Diplomate Am. Bd. Ophthalmology. Med. resident Presbyn. Hosp., N.Y.C., 1959-61; USPHS postdoctoral fellow Columbia U. Coll. Physicians and Surgeons, N.Y.C., 1961-62; USPHS preclin. trainee Howe Lab. of Ophthalmology, MEEI, Boston, 1962-63; resident in ophthalmology Mass. Eye and Ear Infirmary, Boston, 1963-66; instr. in ophthalmology to asst. prof. Harvard Med. Sch., Boston, 1970—; assoc. in Ophthalmology to sr. assoc. Children's Hosp., Boston, 1966—. Contbr. over 40 articles to profl. jours. Cons., vision task force Mass. Dept. Pub. Health, 1981-85. Major U.S. Army, 1967-69, South Vietnam. Various rsch. grants NIH, 1961-63, 94—. Fellow Am. Acd. Ophthalmology, Am. Acad. Pediatrics; mem. Am. Assn. for Pediatric Ophthalmology and Strabismus (bd. dirs. 1974-76, edn. com. 1987-93, Costenbader Lectureship com. 1993-96, 97-2000, chair 1995-96, 99-2000, chair site selection com. 1995-97), New Eng. Ophthal. Soc. Mem. Soc. Of Friends. Achievements include rsch. on the genetics of reinoblastoma; first to describe optic nerve hypoplasia in the children of diabetic mothers, to describe eye findings in a variety of systemic anomalies. Office: Children's Hosp 300 Longwood Ave Boston MA 02115-5737 E-mail: robert.petersen.tch@harvard.edu.

PETERSEN, ROBERT R. brokerage house executive; b. Nebr. m. Doris Petersen. Pres. Nat. Grain Trade Coun., Washington, 1983—2000; CEO and pres. Kans. City Bd. Trade, Mo., 2000—. Office: Kans City Bd Trade 4800 Main St Ste 303 Kansas City MO 64112

PETERSEN, STEVEN E. neuroscientist, educator, health facility administrator; BA in Anthropology, U. Mont., Missoula, 1974; PhD in Biology, Calif. Inst. Tech., 1982. Prof. neurology, psychology and radiology, chief neuropsychology Washington U. Sch. Medicine, St. Louis, 1985—; postdoctoral position Nat. Eye Inst. Office: Washington U Sch Medicine Campus Box 8111 660 S Euclid Saint Louis MO 63110

PETERSEN, ULRICH, geology educator; b. Negritos, Peru, Dec. 1, 1927; s. Georg and Harriet (Bluhme) P.; m. Edith Martensen, Apr. 27, 1952 (dec. Aug. 1978); children: Erich, Armin (dec.), Heidi.; m. Eileen Bourque, June 19, 1982. Mining Engr., Escuela Nacional de Ingenieros, Lima, Peru, 1954; MA, Harvard U., 1955, PhD, 1963. Geologist Instituto Geológico del Peru and Instituto Nacional de Investigación y Fomento Mineros, 1946-51; geologist Cerro de Pasco Corp., Peru, 1951-54, asst. chief geologist, 1956-57, chief geologist, 1958-63; lectr. Harvard, 1963-66; assoc. prof. Harvard U., 1966-69, prof. mining geology, 1969-81, Harry C. Dudley prof. econ. geology, 1981-95; cons. geologist, 1963—; prof. emeritus, 1996—. Named comendador de la orden al Merito por Servicios Distinguidos Peru, 1968; recipient A. von Humboldt rsch. award, 1992-93, 2003-04. Mem. Soc. Econ. Geologists (pres. 1988-89), Geol. Soc. Am., Soc. Geologica del Peru (hon.) Home: 414 Marsh St Belmont MA 02478-1109 Office: 20 Oxford St Cambridge MA 02138-2902 E-mail: ulrichp@aol.com.

PETERSEN, WILLIAM OTTO, lawyer; b. Chgo., Nov. 28, 1926; s. William Ferdinand and Alma Schmidt P.; m. Jane Browne, Nov. 25, 1978. AB cum laude, Harvard U., 1949, LLB, 1952. Bar: Ill., 1952. Atty. No. Trust. Co., Chgo., 1952-55; ptnr. Vedder, Price, Kaufman & Kamholz, Chgo., 1955-2001, of counsel, 2001—. Mem. exec. bd. Ct. Theatre, 1992-97; mem. vis. to U. Chgo. Libr., 1992—; bd. dirs. Chgo. Youth Ctrs., 1958—, pres., 1971, 72; bd. dirs., v.p. Luther I. Replogle Found., Chgo. and Washington, 1986—. With USN, 1944-46. Mem. ABA, Ill. State Bar Assn., Chgo. Bar Assn. (chmn. corp. law com. 1976), Racquet Club of Chgo. (pres. 1981, 82), Univ. Club, Lake Geneva (Wis.) Country Club, Lake Geneva Yacht Club, Caxton Club. Lutheran. Home: 1120 N Lake Shore Dr Chicago IL 60611-1036

PETERSEN, WOLFGANG, film director; b. Emden, Germany, Mar. 14, 1941; Asst. state dir. Ernst Deutsch Theatre, Hamburg, Fed. Republic Germany. Dir.: (films) Eine-der Andere, 1967, Ich nicht, 1969, I Will Kill You, 1971, One or the Other of Us, 1973, Enemy Mine, 1985, (TV) Tatort-Blechschaden, 1971, Tatort-Strandgut, 1972, Anna und Toto, 1972, Van der Valk und die Reichen, 1973, Smog, 1973 (Prix Futura award 1975), Tatort-Jagdrevier, 1973, Tatort-Nachtfrost, 1974, Aufs Kreuz gelegt, 1974, Stellenweise Glatteis, 1975, Stadt im Tal, 1975, For Your Love Only, 1976, Hans im Glück, 1976; dir., writer: (TV) Vier gegen die Bank, 1976, Planübung, 1977, Black and White Like Day and Night, 1978, Das Boot, 1981, (films) The Consequence, 1977, Das Boot (Acad. award nomination Best Adapted Screenplay 1981), NeverEnding Story, 1984; dir., prodr.: In the Line of Fire, 1993, Outbreak, 1995, Air Force One, 1997, The Perfect Storm, 2000; dir., writer, prodr.: Shattered, 1991. Office: Creative Artists Agy care Rand Halston 9830 Wilshire Blvd Beverly Hills CA 90212-1804

PETERSEN-FREY, ROLAND, manufacturing executive; b. Hamburg, Germany, Aug. 17, 1937; arrived in US, 1958; s. Georg and Erna (Coltzau) Petersen-Frey; m. Pamela Susan Mobley, Feb. 2, 1993; children: Martin, Anya, Daniel. BA in Fin., CUNY, 1967, MA in Fin., 1970. Asst. v.p. Mfrs. Hanover, N.Y.C., 1961-70; v.p. gen. mgr. Rusch Inc., N.Y.C., 1970-75; CEO, chmn. bd. dirs. Inmed Corp., Atlanta, 1975-89; chmn. bd. Burrellco, Inc., Atlanta, 1989-90; pres., chmn., CEO A4, Inc., Atlanta, 1997—. Bd dirs Albert Int, Gainesville, Ga.; chmn bd dirs A4, Inc, Alpharetta, Ga.; mng ptnr Bunter Holdings Ltd, Atlanta, chmn bd dirs. With U.S. Army, 1959—61. Fellow: Inst Dirs. Republican. Avocations: tennis, hiking, swimming. Office Phone: 770-521-8877. Business E-Mail: r.frey@a4inc.com.

PETERSON, ALFRED EDWARD, family physician; b. Bridgeport, Conn., Mar. 23, 1922; s. Carl Emil Rudolf and Elin Maria (Lindholm) P.; m. June Meadows, May 27, 1944; children: Christina, Elin, Martha, Amy. BA, Dartmouth Coll., 1946; MD, U. Vt., 1950. Diplomate Nat. Bd. Med. Examiners. Intern Binghamton (N.Y.) City Hosp., 1950-51; pvt. practice, Binghamton, N.Y., 1952—; a founding mem. Chenango Bridge Med. Group. Sch. physician Chenango Forks (N.Y.) Ctrl. Schs., 1953-94. Bd. dirs. Chenango Emergency Squad, Binghamton, 1980-85, Robert W. Smith Found., Rotary Club, 1980—; bd. dirs. med. records Broome C.C., Binghamton, 1988—. Capt. USAAF, 1943-45. Fellow Am. Acad. Family Physicians; mem. AMA, N.Y. State Med. Soc., Broome County Med. Soc., N.Y. State Acad. Family Physicians. Democrat. Avocations: cabinet making, environmental and animal welfare causes, travel, history. Office: Chenango Bridge Med Group 1290 Upper Front St Binghamton NY 13901-1043

PETERSON, ANDREA LENORE, law educator; b. L.A., July 21, 1952; d. Vincent Zetterberg and Elisabeth (Karlsson) P.; m. Michael Rubin, May 29, 1983; children: Peter Rubin, Eric Rubin, Emily Rubin. AB, Stanford U., 1974; JD, U. Calif., Berkeley, 1978. Bar: Calif., 1979, U.S. Dist. Ct. (no. dist.) Calif., 1979. Law clk. to Judge Charles B. Renfrew U.S. Dist. Ct. (no. dist.) Calif., San Francisco, 1978-79; lawyer Cooley, Godward, Castro, Huddleson & Tatum, San Francisco, 1979-80; law clk. to Justice Byron R. White U.S. Supreme Ct., Washington, 1980-81; lawyer Heller, Ehrman, White & McAuliffe, San Francisco, 1981-83; prof. law Boalt Hall U. Calif., Berkeley, 1983—. Contbr. articles to profl. jours. Office: U Calif Sch Law Boalt Hall Berkeley CA 94720

PETERSON, ANN SULLIVAN, physician, health care consultant; b. Rhinebeck, N.Y., Oct. 11, 1928; AB., Cornell U., 1950, M.D., 1954; M.S. (Alfred P. Sloan fellow 1979-80), M.I.T., 1980. Diplomate Am. Bd. Internal Medicine. Intern, Cornell Med. Div.-Bellevue Hosp., N.Y.C., 1954-55, resident, 1955-57; fellow in medicine and physiology Meml.-Sloan Kettering Cancer Ctr., Cornell Med. Coll., N.Y.C., 1957-60; instr. medicine Georgetown U. Sch. Medicine, Washington, 1962-65, asst. prof., 1965-69, asst. dir. clin. research unit, 1962-69; assoc. prof. medicine U. Ill., Chgo., 1969-72, asst. dean, 1969-71, assoc. dean, 1971-72; assoc. prof. medicine, assoc. dean Coll. Physicians and Surgeons, Columbia U., N.Y.C., 1972-80; assoc. prof. medicine, assoc. dean Cornell U. Med. Coll., N.Y.C., 1980-83; assoc. dir. div. med. edn. AMA, Chgo., 1983-86, dir. div. grad. med. edn., 1986-89; v.p. mgmt. cons. corp., 1989-93; ind. cons., Chgo., 1993—; mem. bd. regents Uniformed Svcs. U. of Health Scis., 1984-90. John and Mary R. Markle scholar, 1965-70. Fellow ACP; mem. Mortar Board, Alpha Omega Alpha, Alpha Epsilon Delta. Contbr. articles to med. jours.

PETERSON, ARTHUR LAVERNE, foundation administrator; b. Glyndon, Minn., June 27, 1926; s. John M. and Hilda C. (Moline) P.; m. Connie Lucille Harr, June 14, 1952 (dec. July 26, 2003); children: Jon Martin, Rebecca Ruth, Donna Harr, Ingrid Bliss; m. Mary Kinum, Sept. 12, 2003. AB, Yale U., 1947; MSPA, U. So. Calif., 1949; postgrad., U. Chgo., 1949-50; PhD, U. Minn., 1962; LLD, Lebanon Valley Coll., 1988. Mem. Wis. State Legislature, 1951-55; from instr. to asst. prof. polit. sci. U. Wis., Eau Claire, 1954-60; assoc. prof. to prof. polit. sci. Ohio Wesleyan U., Delaware, 1961-65, 70-80; pres. Am. Grad. Sch. Internat. Mgmt., Phoenix, 1966-70; dean spl. programs Eckerd Coll., St. Petersburg, Fla., 1980-84, dir. Acad. Sr. Profls., 1987-94; pres. Lebanon Valley Coll., Annville, Pa., 1984-87; pres., CEO Ctr. for the Study of the Presidency, 1997-99; Scott prof. leadership Rocky Mountain Coll., Billings, Mont., 1999—2002; mem. Mont. Ho. Reps., 2001—; pres. Thomas Wathen Found. Acad., Riverside, Calif., 2002—. Bd. dirs. Arnold Industries; asst. to chmn. Rep. Nat. Com., Washington, 1960-61; founding dir. Ctr. Internat. Bus., L.A., 1969-70; cons. Novin Inst. Polit. Affairs, Tehran, Iran, 1973; exec. dir. Fla. Assn. Colls. and Univs., 1988—. Author: McCarthyism: Ideology and Foundations, 1962; co-author: Electing the President, 1968; contbr. articles to profl. jours. Chmn. Ohio Civil Rights Commn., 1963-65; dep. chmn. Republican Nat. Com., 1965-66; mem. Ohio Ethics Commn., 1976-80. Capt. USMC, 1951-52, Korea Citizenship Clearing House Nat. Faculty fellow, 1960; recipient citation for excellence Sigma Phi Epsilon, 1977, Marshall award Ohio Wesleyan Students, 1979. Mem. Am. Polit. Sci. Assn., Am. Judicature Soc. (dir. 1975—), Soc. Polit. Enquiries (pres. 1985—), Acad. Polit. Sci., Rotary, Masons, Pi Sigma Alpha (dir. 1972—), Phi Mu Alpha Sinfonia, Omicron Delta Kappa Republican. Mem. United Ch. of Christ. Avocations: sailing, flying, music. Home: 26555 Chambers Ave Sun City CA 92586-2132 E-mail: apeter333@aol.com. *Give the most you can give, of what you are and what you believe, both talent and treasure - where you are - now!.*

PETERSON, BARBARA ANN BENNETT, history educator, television personality; b. Portland, Oreg., Sept. 6, 1942; d. George and Hope Bennett; m. Frank Lynn Peterson, July 1, 1967. BA, BS, Oreg. State U., 1964; MA, Stanford U., 1965; PhD, U. Hawaii, 1978; PhD (hon.), London Inst. Applied Rsch., 1991, Australian Inst. Coordinated R, 1995. From prof. history to prof. emeritus U. Hawaii, 1967—95, prof. emeritus, 1995—; prof. history Oreg. State U., 2000—03. Prof. Asian history and European colonial history and world problems Chapman Coll. World Campus Afloat Semester At Sea, 1974, European overseas exploration, expansion and colonialism U. Colo., Boulder, 1978, Modern China, Modern East Asia, The West in the World U. Pitts., 1999; assoc. prof. U. Hawaii-Manoa Coll. Continuing Edn., 1981; Fulbright prof. history Wuhan (China) U., 1988-89; Fulbright rsch. prof. Sophia U., Japan, 1967; rsch. assoc. Bishop Mus., 1995-98; lectr. Capital Spkrs., Washington, 1987—; prof. world civilization Hawaii State Ednl. Channel, U. Hawaii Sys., 1993-97; adj. fellow East-West Ctr., Honolulu, 1998-99; prof. history U. Pitts. Semester at Sea, fall 1999; adj. prof. Hawaii Pacific U.; adj. fellow East-West Ctr., Hawaii, 1998-99. Co-author: A Woman's Place is in the History Books, Her Story: A Curriculum Guide for American History Teachers, 1980; author: America in British Eyes, 1988, John Bull's Eye on America, 1995, Sarah Childress Polk, First Lady of Tennessee and Washington, 2002 (nominated for Pulitzer prize 2003, Avery O. Craven award 2003, Merle Curti award 2003, Albert J. Beveridge award 2003), Emalani, 2003; editor: Notable Women of Hawaii, 1984, (with W. Solheim) The Pacific Region, 1990, 91, American History: 17th, 18th and 19th Centuries, 1993, America: 19th and 20th Centuries, 1993, Notable Women of China, 2000 (nominated for Pulitzer prize 2001), Hawaii in the World, 2000; assoc. editor Am. Nat. Biography, 1998 (Dartmouth medal); contbr. articles to profl. publs. Participant People-to-People Program, Eng., 1964, Expt. in Internat. Living Program, Nigeria, 1966; chmn. 1st Nat. Women's History Week, Hawaii, 1982; pres. Bishop Mus. Coun., 1993-94; active mem. Hawaii Commn. on Status of Women; fundraiser local mus. and children's activities. Fulbright scholar, Japan, 1967, sr. tchg. Fulbright scholar, China, 1988-89; NEH-Woodrow Wilson fellow Princeton U., 1980; recipient state proclamations Gov. of Hawaii, 1982, City of Honolulu and Hawaii State Legis., 1982, Outstanding Tchr. of Yr. award Wuhan (China), U., 1988, Woman of Yr. award, 1991; inducted into the Women's Hall of Fame, Seneca Falls, N.Y., 1991; co-champion Hawaii State Husband and Wife Mixed Doubles Tennis Championship, 1985. Fellow: World Lit. Acad. (Eng.); mem.: AAUW, Am. Studies Assn. (Hawaii chpt. pres. 1984—85), Women in Acad. Adminstrn., Hawaii Found. History and Humanities (mem. editl. bd. 1972—73), Fulbright Assn. (founding pres. Hawaii chpt. 1984—88, mem. nat. steering com. chairwomen ann. conf. 1990, pres. 1998—99), Am. Hist. Assn. (mem. numerous coms., nominated Albert J. Beveridge award 2003), Maison Internat. des Intellectuals, Phi Kappa Phi, Pi Beta Phi (mem. mortar bd.). Avocations: writing, cooking, fund raising for charity and children's organizations and museums, gardening, travel. Office: East West Ctr Burns Hall 1601 East West Rd Honolulu HI 96848-1601 also: Oreg State U History Dept 306 Milam Hall Corvallis OR 97331 E-mail: fandbpeterson@aol.com.

PETERSON, BART, mayor; m. Amy Minick; 1 child, Meg. Grad., Purdue U., 1980; JD, U. Mich., 1983. Atty. Ice Miller Donadio & Ryan, Indpls.; from exec. asst. for environ. affairs to chief of staff Ind. Gov. Evan Bayh, 1989-95; pres. Precedent Cos., 1995; mayor City Indpls., 2000—. Bd. mem. Ind. Nature Conservancy, Regenstrief Found. Office: 2501 City-County Bldg 200 E Washington St Indianapolis IN 46204-3307 Office Phone: 317-327-4622., 317-327-3601. Office Fax: 317-327-3980. E-mail: mayor@indygov.org.

PETERSON, BOB, real estate company executive; Student, U. N.C. With Arthur Rubloff Co., Chgo., 1974—79; founder Peterson Properties, 1979—96; with Carr Am., 1996—99; exec. v.p. brokerage and corp. svcs. Carter & Assocs., Atlanta, 2001—. Office: Carter & Assocs 1275 Peachtree St NE Atlanta GA 30309*

PETERSON, BRIAN F. agricultural products supplier; BS in Econometrics, Oreg. State U. Pres. ADM bioproducts divsn. Archer Dnaiels Midland Co., 1995—99, v.p., 1996—99, pres. ADM protein specialities divsn., 1999, group v.p., mng. dir. ADM Internat. Ltd., 1999—2003, sr. v.p. corp. affairs, 2003—. Office: Archer Daniels Midland Co 4666 Faries Pkwy Decatur IL 62526

PETERSON, CARL ERIC, metals company executive, banker; b. Wareham, Mass., Apr. 8, 1944; m. Frances Harkness, Sept. 7, 1966; children: Robin, Alec Harkness. BA, Brown U., 1966; MA, U. Pa., 1971. With R.I. Hosp. Trust Nat. Bank, Providence, 1971-82; with Engelhard Corp., Iselin, N.J., 1982-85, Dryvit System, Inc., West Warwick, R.I., 1986, Gerald Metals, Inc., Stamford, Conn., 1987—2002.

PETERSON, CHARLES GORDON, retired lawyer; b. Lansing, Mich., May 21, 1926; s. Russell V. and Edna E. (Jones) P.; m. Clara Elizabeth Parmelee, Mar. 8, 1947; children— Wendy, Pamela, Christopher BS, Columbia U. Sch. Gen. Studies, 1954; LL.B., Columbia U. Sch. Law, 1956. Bar: N.Y., 1957. Legal assoc. Beekman & Bogue, N.Y.C., 1956-67; mem. Gaston & Snow, N.Y.C., 1967-91; of counsel Reid & Priest, N.Y.C., 1991-93; ret., 1993. Trustee The Riverside Ch., N.Y.C., 1968-80, 82-89, mem. bd. deacons, 1960-68; pres. Lincoln Guild Housing Corp., N.Y.C., 1961-62, 84-87, v.p., 1987-89, 94-96, bd. dirs., 1961-62, 84-89, 94-96. Mem. Phi Beta Kappa. Republican. Mem. United Ch. of Christ. Avocations: piano, reading, travel. Home: 303 W 66th St Apt 20ee New York NY 10023-6330

PETERSON, CHARLES HAYES, lawyer; b. St. Louis, May 8, 1938; s. Edmund Herbert and Dorothy Marie (Brennan) P.; m. Auli Irene Ahonen, Nov. 28, 1981; children: Mika, Charles, Michael, Katja. BS, U.S. Naval Acad., 1960; MBA, Stanford U., 1971, JD, 1974. Commd. midshipman USN, 1956, advanced through grades to capt., resigned, 1969; with USNR, 1969-89, ret., 1998; counsel Gen. Electric, San Jose, Calif., 1973-79; divsn. counsel Syracuse, NY, 1980-83; v.p. COGEMA, Inc., Washington, 1983-87; pres. NUEXCO Trading Co., Washington, 1987-95; of counsel Morgan, Lewis & Bockius, LLP, 1995—2001; ptnr. Shaw Pittman, Washington, 2001—. Recipient Meritorious Service medal State of Calif., 1986. Mem. Calif. and Washington Bar Assns. Lutheran. Office: Shaw Pittman 2300 N Street NW Washington DC 20037 Office Phone: 202-663-8083. Office Fax: 202-663-8007.

PETERSON, CHARLES MARQUIS, medical educator; b. N.Y.C., Mar. 8, 1943; s. Charles William and Elisabeth (Marquis) P.; m. Karen Pielop, Dec. 26, 1996; children: Caroline, Elisabeth. BA in cum laude, Carleton Coll., 1965; MD, Columbia Coll., 1969. Intern Harlem Hosp., N.Y.C., 1969-70, resident, 1970-73, chief resident, 1972-73; guest investigator, asst. physician Rockefeller U., N.Y.C., 1971-73, assoc. physician, 1973-78, asst. prof., 1973-78, assoc. prof., 1978-84; clin. prof. medicine U. So. Calif., L.A., 1985-98; program dir. blood diseases program Nat. Heart, Lung and Blood Inst., NIH, Bethesda, Md., 1998—. Vis. clin. fellow Columbia Coll. Physicians and Surgeons, 1970-73; asst. vis. physician Harlem Hosp., 1973-84; cons. pediatrics Cornell U. Med. Ctr., 1975-84; assoc. attending medicine Beth Israel Med. Ctr., 1976-84; lectr. Mt. Sinai Sch. Medicine, 1977—; adj. assoc. prof. dept. medicine Cornell U. Med. Ctr., 980-84; assoc. attending physician dept. medicine N.Y. Hosp., 1980-84; attending physician in medicine Cottage Hosp., Santa Barbara, Calif., 1984-98; dir. rsch., med. dir. Sansum Med. Rsch. Found., 1984-96, sr. scientist, 1997-98; dir. diabetes Endocrine Clinic, Santa Barbara County, 1989-98; CEO, Sansum Med. Rsch. Found., 1995-96; program dir. Blood Diseases Program Nat. Heart Lung Blood Inst., NIH. Author: Self Monitoring of Blood Glucose: A Physician's Guide, 1981, Take Charge of Your Diabetes, 1982, Diabetes Management in the 80's, 1982; co-author: The Diabetes Self-Care Method, 1990, A Touch of Diabetes, 1991, Vivere con il Diabete, 1992, and many others; mem. editorial bd. Diabetes Care, 1980-84, Diabetes in the News, 1985—, Diabetes News Bureau, 1985—, Diabetes Profl., editor-in-chief, 1988-91, Diabetic Nephropathy/Jour. of Diabetic Complications, 1982-91; contbr. numerous articles to Prensa Medica, Jour. Lab. and Clin. Medicine, New England Jour. Medicine, Annals of Internal Medicine, Archives of Neurology, Blood, Jour. Nat. Med. Assn., Am. Jour. Obstetrics and Gynecology, many others. Mem. med. adv. bd. Cooley's Anemia Vols., 1975-84; bd. mem. Diabetes Control Found., 1980-88; dir. Diabetes Self Care Program, 1978-84, med. dir., 1981-84; bd. mem. Leake and Watts, 1978-84, Gifts for Life, 1986-89; bd. dirs. Sports Tng. Inst., 1984-86, others. Fellow ACP; mem. AAAS, Am. Chem. Soc., Am. Diabetes Assn., Am. Fedn. Clin. Rsch., Am. Med. Writers Assn., Am. Soc. Clin. Investigation, Am. Soc. Hematology, Am. Soc. Pharmacology and Experimental Therapeutics, Coun. Biology Editors, Diabetes and Pregnancy Study Group West (founder), N.Y. Acad. Scis., Rsch. Soc. Alcoholism, Soc. Experimental Medicine and Biology, Am. Med. Writers Assn., Am. Diabetes Assn. (founding bd. mem. Santa Barbara chpt. 1988-98, pres. 1991-92), Sigma Xi. Home: 11920 Glen Mill Rd Potomac MD 20854-1919 Office: 6701 Rockledge Dr # 7950 Bethesda MD 20817-1813 E-mail: petersoC@gwgate.nhlbi.nih.gov.

PETERSON, COLEMAN HOLLIS, former retail store executive; b. Birmingham, Ala., Apr. 6, 1948; s. George Bell and Doris Mae (Wilson) P.; m. Shirley Ann Hardy, May 31, 1975; children: Rana, Collin. BA in English Lit., Loyola U., Chgo., 1972, MS in Indsl. Rels., 1977. Mgmt. trainee Osco Drug, Inc., Oakbrook, Ill., 1972-74, coll. recruiter, 1974-75, dir. coll. recruiting, 1975-77, mgr. recruit and devel., 1977-78, dist. personnel officer, 1978-79; regional personnel mgr. Venture Stores, Inc., Chgo., 1979-82, v.p. orgn. devel. O'Fallon, Mo., 1982-84, sr. v.p. human resources, 1984—94; exec. v.p., human div. Wal-Mart Stores, Inc., Bentonville, Ark., 1994—2004. Mem., bd. dirs. J.B. Hunt Transport Services, Inc., 2004—. Bd. mem. Urban League Met. St. Louis, United Way Greater St. Louis. Recipient Meritorious Svc. award United Negro Coll. Fund, St. Louis, 1986. Mem. Kappa Alpha Psi (life). Avocations: jogging, creative writing, music.

PETERSON, COLLIN C. congressman; b. Fargo, N.D., June 29, 1944; children: Sean, Jason, Elliott. BA in Bus. Adminstrn. and Acctg., Moorhead State U., 1966. CPA, Minn. Senator State of Minn., 1976-86; mem. U.S. Congress from 7th Minn. dist., 1991—; mem. agrl. com., subcoms. gen. farm commodities, specialty crops and natural resources, livestock, environ. credit and rural devel.; mem. permanent select Com. Intelligence, 2001—; mem. govt. ops. com., chmn. subcom. employment housing and aviation; mem. resource conservation com., rsch. and forestry subcom., livestock, dairy and poultry subcom., govt. reform and oversight com.; nat. econ. growth com., nat. resources and regulatory affairs com.-ranking minority mem., vet. affairs com. With U.S. Army N.G., 1963-69. Mem. Am. Legion, Ducks Unltd., Elks, Sportsmen's Club, Rural Caucus, Mainstream Forum, Cormorant Lakes Sportsmen Club, Congl. Sportsmen's Caucus, Mainstream Forum, Congl. Rural Caucus. Democrat. Office: US Ho of Reps 2159 Rayburn Hob Washington DC 20515-0001 also: Dist Office 714 Lake Ave Ste 107 Detroit Lakes MN 56501

PETERSON, DAVID FREDERICK, government agency executive; b. Washington, Apr. 4, 1937; s. Victor Henry and Alice Augusta (Vogle) P.; m. Laurie A. Cadigan, June 11, 1988. AB, Harvard U., 1959; LL.B., Cornell U., 1962. Bar: D.C. 1963. With Metromedia Inc., N.Y.C. and Los Angeles, 1963—70; exec. dir. consumer info. ctr. GSA, Washington, 1970—76, dir. consumer affairs, 1976—82, assoc. archivist for mgmt. Nat. Archives and Records Service, 1982—83; asst. archivist for Fed. Records Ctrs. Nat. Archives and Records Adminstrn., Washington, 1983—96; asst. archivist Presdl. Librs., 1996—2001; ret., 2001. Served with U.S. Army, 1963 Home: 1417 NE High Hammock Ct Jensen Beach FL 34957-6507

PETERSON, DAVID MAURICE, plant physiologist, research leader; b. Woodward, Okla., July 3, 1940; s. Maurice Llewellyn and Katharine Anne (Jones) P.; m. Margaret Ingegerd Sundberg, June 18, 1965; children: Mark David, Elise Marie. BS, U. Calif., Davis, 1962; MS, U. Ill., 1964; PhD, Harvard U., 1968. Rsch. biologist Allied Chem. Corp., Morristown, N.J., 1970-71; plant physiologist U.S. Dept. Agr.-Agrl. Rsch. Svc., Madison, Wis., 1971—; from asst. to full prof. U. Wis., Madison, 1971—. Capt. U.S. Army, 1968-70. Fellow AAAS; mem. Am. Soc. Plant Biologists (editorial bd. 1984-86), Am. Assn. Cereal Chemists (assoc. editor 1988-91), Crop Sci. Soc. Am. (assoc. editor 1975-78). Office: USDA Cereal Crops Rsch Unit 501 Walnut St Madison WI 53726 E-mail: dmpeter4@wisc.edu.

PETERSON, DAVID ROBERT, lawyer, former Canadian government official; b. Toronto, Dec. 28, 1943; s. Clarence and Laura Marie (Scott) P.; m. Shelley Peterson, Jan. 16, 1974; children: Benjamin David, Chloe Matthews, Adam Drake Scott BA, U. Western Ont., 1964; LLB, U. Toronto, 1967; LLD (hon.), U. Ottawa, Am. U. of Caribbean, U. Tel Aviv, U. Toronto. Bar: Ont. 1969, Queens counsel 1981. Chmn., pres. C.M. Peterson Co. Ltd., 1969-75, Cambridge Acceptance Corp., 1969-75; M.P. Ont. Parliament, Canada, 1975—; leader Ont. Liberal Party, 1982; premier Province of Ont., 1985-90; chmn. Cassels Brock & Blackwell LLP, Toronto, 1991—. Bd. dirs. Rogers Comms., Ltd., Nat. Life Assurance Co., Industrielle-Alliance Life Assurance Co., BNP Paribas (Can.), Rogers AT&T Wireless, others; founding chmn. Chpts. Inc., Cassels-Pouiliot Noriega. Leader of the ofcl. opposition party, Liberal Party, Ont., 1982-85; dir. Legal Svcs., Yorkville; mem. Kidney Found. Can., Ont., Cystic Fibrosis Found. Fellow McLaughlin Coll., 1985; appointed Knight of Order of Legion of Honor, Govt. France, 1994; recipient Ordre de la Pléiade, Internat. Assembly French-Speaking Parliamentarians, 1995. Mem. Law Soc. U.C., Young Pres. Orgn., London C. of C., London Hunt Country Club, London Racquets Club, Can. Club, Toronto Raptors Basketball Club Inc. (founding chmn.). Mem. United Ch. Of Christ. Avocations: theater, riding, jogging, skiing, tennis. Office: Cassels Brock Blackwell LLP 40 King St W Ste 2100 Toronto ON Canada M5H 3C2

PETERSON, DELAINE CHARLES, lawyer, bank executive; b. Villisca, Iowa, July 28, 1936; s. Reuben Merrill and Margaret Helena (Sederquist) P.; m. Marcia Joan Hitchcock, Aug. 18, 1962; children: Robert, Paul, Janet. BBA, U. Iowa, 1963, JD, 1966. Bar: Iowa 1966. Asst. trust officer Security Nat. Bank, Sioux City, Iowa, 1966-73, mgr. trust dept., 1974-82, sr. v.p., 1983-92, sr. v.p., chief trust officer, 1992—2001; assoc. atty. Corbett Anderson Law Firm, Sioux City, 2001—. Bd. dirs. Siouxland Easter Seals, Sioux City, 1983-91, St. Luke's Health Systems, Inc., 1987-2000, chmn. 1989-91; bd. dirs. St. Luke's Regional Med. Ctr., chmn. 1988-89; bd. dirs. St. Luke's Coll. Nursing and Health Scis., 1991-2000, chmn., 1991-93; trustee Prarie Gold coun. Boy Scouts Am., 1987—, pres., 1989-92; mem. Iowa Coll. Found., 1975-85; com. mem. Morningside Coll. Found., 1989-95. Mem. ABA, Iowa Bar Assn., Woodbury Bar Assn., Iowa Trust Assn. (pres. 1978), Rotary (pres. 1984), Masons (past master 1988). Republican. Methodist. Office: Corbett Anderson Law Firm 423 Sixth St Ste 400 Sioux City IA 51101

PETERSON, DONALD FRED, physiologist, educator; b. Great Bend, Kans., Aug. 4, 1941; s. Donald F. and Mary K. (Doerr) P.; m. Bonnie Jean Campbell, July 30, 1967; children: Corilynn, Bailey, Ronald. Student, U. Sorbonne, Paris, 1962-63; BS in Zoology, Kans. State U., 1965, PhD in Physiology, 1970. Postdoctoral fellow U. Utah Med. Ctr., Salt Lake City, 1969-71; instr. U. Tex. Health Sci. Ctr., San Antonio, 1971-73, asst. prof., 1973-77, assoc. prof., 1977-78, Oral Roberts U. Med. Ctr., Tulsa, 1978-88, prof., chmn. physiology, 1988-90; prof., chmn. physiology Kirksville (Mo.) Coll. Osteo. Medicine, 1990—. Mem. extra-curricular task force Kirksville (Mo.) Sch. Dist., 1995, pres. Kirksville Boosters, 1994-95. Recipient Rsch. Career Devel. award NIH, 1976. Fellow Am. Physiol. Soc.; mem. Am. Heart Assn. (chmn. Mo. peer rev. com. 1995-96, chmn. Mo. rsch. com. 1996-97, bd. dirs. and exec. com. Mo. affil. 1996-98, bd. dirs. Heartland affiliate 1998-2000, Heartland rsch. com. 1997-2000, Mo. pub. advocacy com., 2001-), Sigma Xi. Mem. Ch. of Christ. Avocations: road-running races, triathlons, gardening. Home: 2201 Crestline Dr Kirksville MO 63501-5709 Office: Kirksville Coll Osteo Med Dept Physiology 800 W Jefferson St Kirksville MO 63501-1443 Office Phone: 660-626-2309. Business E-Mail: fpeterson@atsu.edu.

PETERSON, DONALD K. telecommunications executive; b. Worcester, Mass. m. Maureen Mack; children: Janine, Daniel. BSME, Worcester Poly. Inst., 1971; MBA, Darmouth Coll., 1973. CLU, ChFA. Sr. analyst State Mutual Life Assurance Co., Worcester, 1973-76; with Northern Telecom, 1976-94; pres. NORTEL Comm. Sys., Inc., Nashville, 1994-95; CFO AT&T Comm. Svcs. Group, 1995-96; exec. v.p., CFO Lucent Technologies, Inc., Murray Hill, N.J., 1996-2000; pres., CEO, vice chmn. Avaya, Inc., Basking Ridge, N.J., 2000—. Bd. dirs. Reynolds & Reynolds, Dayton, Ohio. Active various repertory theaters, Inroads, Inc., Dallas United loaned exec. programs; bd. trustees Worcester Poly. Inst., Lucent Found. Avocations: Karate, travel, woodworking. Office: Avaya Inc 211 Mount Airy Rd Basking Ridge NJ 07920

PETERSON, DONALD MATTHEW, insurance company executive; b. Mt. Vernon, N.Y., Dec. 22, 1936; s. Cornelius J. and Catherine M. (Carney) P.; m. Patricia A. Frusciante, Sept. 10, 1960; children: Daniel, Linda, David, Debra, James. BA in Econs., LaSalle U., 1958. CLU; ChFC; FSA, MAAA, EA, RHU. Actuarial analyst Met. Life, N.Y.C., 1958-63; actuarial assoc. N.Am. Co. for Life and Health, Chgo., 1963-66; chmn. bd. dirs. Trustmark Ins. Co., Lake Forest, Ill., 1966—. Bd. dirs. Trustmark Ins. Co., Trustmark Life Ins. Co., Star Mktg. and Adminstrs., InfoTrust Coresource. Bd. dirs. Glenview (Ill.) Pub. Schs., 1973-76, Lake County (Ill.) United Way, 1989-96, Glenview Dist. 34 Found., 1990-93, Lake Forest Hosp., 1992-2001, Ill. Life Ins. Coun., 1990-94, Barat Coll., 1994-2001, Lake Forest Grad. Sch. Mgmt., 1995-2001. Mem. NALU, Nat. Assn. Health Underwriters, Am. Acad. Actuaries, Health Ins. Assn. Am. (bd. dirs. 1992-99), Am. Coun. Life Ins. (bd. dirs. 1995-98), Econ. Club Chgo., North Shore Country Club, Conway Farms Golf Club, Pelican Nest Golf Club, Exec. Club. Republican. Roman Catholic. Avocations: golf, curling, swimming, running. Office: Trustmark Ins Co 400 N Field Dr Lake Forest IL 60045-4809

PETERSON, DONALD ROBERT, magazine editor, vintage automobile consultant; b. Sandstone, Minn., Apr. 1, 1929; s. Martin Theodore and Margaret Mildred (Dezell) P.; m. Lois Taylor, Dec. 31, 1951 (div. 1975); children: Wyatt A., Winston B., Whitney C. (dec.), Westley D., Webster E.; m. Edie Tannenbaum, Aug. 31, 1975; 1 child, Ryan Kerry. Student, U. Minn., 1947-50; BS, Gustavus Adolphus Coll., 1952. Asst. underwriter Prudential Ins. Co. Am., Mpls., 1953-64; chief health underwriter North Central Life, St. Paul, 1964-66; pres. 1st State Bank Murdock, Minn., 1967-73, EDON, Inc., Roswell, Ga., 1974—; editor Car Collector mag., Roswell, 1977-91, editor emeritus, 1992—; v.p., dir. Classic Pub. Inc., Atlanta, 1979-97. Contbr. chpt. to book. Councilman, City of Murdock, 1968-72, mayor, 1972-74; del. State Republican Conv., 1970-72; treas. Swift County Rep. Com., 1970-73. Served with U.S. Navy, 1946-47. Recipient citation for disting. service Classic Car Club Am., 1965, Hemmings Motor News Hobby Hero Award, 2002. Mem. Internat. Soc. Philos. Enquiry, Swift County Bankers Assn. (pres. 1970-73), Soc. Automotive Historians, Am. Legion, Mensa (pres. Ga. chpt. 1976-78), Milestone Car Soc., Classic Car Club Am. (chpt. pres. 1959, 60, 63, nat. bd. dirs. 1978-81, 97—), Rolls-Royce Owners Club, Antique Automobile Club, Vet. Motor Car Club Am., Packard Club, Cadillac-La Salle Club, Lincoln and Continental Owner's Club, Horseless Carriage Club Am. Republican. Avocations: automobile collecting, internat. traveling. Home: 1400 Lake Ridge Ct Roswell GA 30076-2869 Office Phone: 770-993-5622.

PETERSON, DONALD ROBERT, psychologist, educator, university administrator; b. Pillager, Minn., Sept. 10, 1923; s. Frank Gordon and Ruth (Friedland) P.; m. Jean Hole, Feb. 10, 1952 (div.); children: Wendy, Jeffrey, Roger, Lisa; m. Jane Snyder Salmon, Dec. 21, 1974. BA, U. Minn., 1948, MA, 1950, PhD, 1952. Mem. faculty U. Ill., Urbana, 1952-75, prof. clin. psychology, 1963-75, head div. clin. psychology, 1963-70, dir. Psychol. Clinic, 1961-70, dir. D. Psychology program, 1970-75; dean Grad. Sch. Applied and Profl. Psychology Rutgers U., New Brunswick, 1975-89. Pres. Nat. Coun. Schs. of Profl. Psychology, 1981-83. Author: The Clinical Study of Social Behavior, 1968, Educating Professional Psychologists, 1997; co-author: Close Relationships, 1983; also articles; editor Jour. Abnormal Psychology, 1970-72. With AUS, 1943-46. Mem. N.J. Psychol. Assn., Am. Psychol. Assn. (awards for disting. contbns. to practice of psychology 1983, disting. contbns. to edn. and tng. 1989) Office: Rutgers U Grad Sch Applied & Profl Psychology Piscataway NJ 08854-8085 E-mail: drpeters@rci.rutgers.edu.

PETERSON, DONN NEAL, forensic engineer; b. Northwood, ND, Jan. 1, 1942; s. Emil H. and Dorothy (Neal) Peterson; m. Lorna Jean Kappedal, July 8, 1962 (div. July 1966); m. Donna Sue Butts Daiker, Aug. 26, 1967; children: Barbara Daiker, Elizabeth Plamondon, Phoebe Prathap, Phaedra, Rosalind Ward. BSME, U. N.D., 1963; MSME, U. Minn., 1972. Registered profl. engr.; cert. forensic engr., Internat. Inst. Forensic Engring. Scis. Advanced engring. courses student GE, Evendale, Ohio, 1963-66; systems engr. GE Aircraft Engine Group, Evendale, Ohio, 1963-70; prin. Donn N. Peterson & Assocs., Mpls., 1971-74; pres. Donn N. Peterson & Assocs., Inc., Mpls., 1974-85, Peterson Engring., Inc., Mpls., 1985—. Instr. GE Edn. Program, 1968-69; presenter State Bd. of Registration, Mpls., 1980; seminar leader Minn. Fedn. Engring. Socs., Mpls., 1990-91; speaker, expert witness in field. Del. Minn. 6th Dist. Rep. Conv., Brooklyn Park, Minn., 1982. Fellow Am. Acad. Forensic Scis. (sect. chmn. 1989-90, Founders award 1991), Nat. Acad. Forensic Engrs. (v.p. 1996, sr. v.p. 1997-98); mem. ASME (Young Engr. of Yr. 1976, state chmn. 1979-80), NSPE, Profl. Engrs. in Pvt. Practice (state pres. 1987-88, Svc. award 1988), Soc. Automotive Engrs., Rotary (sec. Brooklyn Park chpt. 1990-93, v.p. 1993-94, pres.-elect 1994-95, pres. 1995-96, Svc. award 1992), Brooklyn Park C. of C. (city hwy. 610 corridor com. 1992-94). Lutheran. Achievements include devel. of successful math. models to simulate jet engine transient performance and wave dynamics in gas flow, computer simulations for vehicle and occupant dynamics during collisions. Home: 15720 15th Pl N Plymouth MN 55447-2405 Office: PO Box 47565 Plymouth MN 55447-0565 Office Phone: 763-258-2704.

PETERSON, DONNA RAE, gerontologist; b. Wichita, Kans., Aug. 29, 1948; d. Raymond Houston and Edna Brooks (Waddell) Hobbs; m. William E. Peterson, Nov. 7, 1993; 1 child, Shauna Layne Reed. Student, Wichita State U., 1968—70; BS in Mgmt., N.W. Christian Coll., 1996, MA in Interdisciplinary Studies Gerontology, 2000. Adminstrv. asst. postgrad. edn. Med. Sch. U. Kans., Wichita, 1974-80; activity coord. continuing med. edn. Wesley Med. Ctr., Wichita, 1980-84; mgr. support svcs. 9th dist. Farm Credit Svcs., Wichita, 1984-88; sales and mktg. mgr. Amb. Travel, Eugene, Oreg., 1988-93; mktg. dir. Peterson Design Devel., Eugene, 1993-95; pres. Davinci Designs, Eugene, 1996-2000; owner 2nd Half Dynamics, 2000—; dir. Alzheimer's program Sunwest Mgmt., Inc., 2002—04; owner 2nd Half Dynamics, 2000—; adult/elder specialist Life ERA/Working Solutions United Health Group, 2004—. Cons. Jr. League Wichita, 1983, Plancon, Inc., Martinsville, NJ, 1987-88, Changing Creatively, 1997; continuing edn. instr. Lane C.C., 2000—; mem. adv. bd. Lane C.C. Ctr. for Leisure and Learning, 2000—. Mem. Wichita Conv. and Visitors Bur., 1987; mem. events com. Wichita Festivals, Inc., 1987; mem. Eugene Conv. and Visitors Bur., 1988—; mem. Eugene Airport Commn., 1991—, chmn., 1992-93; bd. dirs. Campus Life, chmn., 1993-94; mem. steering com. Eugene Celebration, 1991-94, Oreg. Women Bus. Owners Conf., 1997; bd. pres. Of Coun. for Bus. Edn., 1999-2000. Mem. AAUW, Am. Mktg. Assn. (pres. S.W. chpt. 1991—, pres. 1992-94, bd. dirs.), Soc. Travel Agt. in Govt., Adminstrv. Mgmt. Soc., Forum for Exec. Bus. Women, Gt. Plains Bus. Adminstrn. Group, Assn. Travel Exec., Eugene C. of C. (bus. devel. com. 1990-91), The Gerontol. Soc. Am. (student mem. campus rep. 1999), Alzheimers Assn. (Oreg. chpt., edn. com., 2002-), Eugene High Ground Assn. (chmn.), Delta Gamma Alumni Assn. Republican. Avocations: decorating, writing, skiing, water-skiing, camping. Home: 1460 Olive St Apt 32 Eugene OR 97401-3991 Personal E-mail: gerovision@aol.com.

PETERSON, DOUGLAS ARTHUR, physician; b. Princeton, N.Y., Sept. 13, 1945; s. Arthur Roy William and Marie Hilma (Anderson) P.; m. Virginia Kay Eng., June 24, 1967; children: Rachel, Daniel, Rebecca. BA, St. Olaf, 1966; PhD, U. Minn., 1971, MD, 1975. Postdoctoral fellow U. Pitts., 1971-72; intern Hennepin County Med. Ctr., Mpls., 1975-76, resident in medicine, 1976-78; physician Bloomington Lake Clinic, Mpls., 1978-82; staff physician Mpls. VA Med. Ctr., 1992—, chief compensation and pension, 1992—2001, emergency physician, 2001—. Asst. prof. U. Minn., 1985—; flight surgeon Operation Iraqi Freedom, 2003-04. Bd. dirs. Rolling Acres Home, Victoria, Minn., 1985-2000. Col. M.C., USAR, also 2003-04, Iraq. Mem.: AAAS, Am. Coll. Emergency Physicians. Achievements include introduction of concept of reductive activation of receptors. Home: 5008 Queen Ave S Minneapolis MN 55410-2207 Office: VA Med Ctr One Veterans Dr Minneapolis MN 55417 Office Phone: 612-725-2000. E-mail: douglas.apeterson@us.army.mcu.

PETERSON, DOUGLAS PETE (PETE PETERSON), ambassador, retired congressman; b. Omaha, Nebr., June 26, 1935; m. Carlotta Ann Neal (dec.); children: Michael, Paula, Douglas (dec.); m. Vi Peterson. Grad., Nat. War Coll., 1975; BA, U. Tampa, 1976; postgrad., U. Ctrl. Mich., 1977. Commd. USAF, 1954, advanced through grades to col., ret., 1980; exec. CRT Computers, 1984-90; mem. faculty Fla. State U., 1985-90; mem. 101st-104th Congresses from 2nd Fla. Dist., 1991-96; mem. appropriation com.-energy and water, agrl.; amb. to Vietnam, 1997—2001; pres. Peterson Internat., Inc., 2001—. Founder, CEO The Alliance for Safe Children. Prisoner of war, Vietnam. Mem.: VFW, Am. Legion. Roman Catholic. Office: 27 Bowen St Camberwell VIC 3124 Australia

PETERSON, E. ANNE, federal agency administrator; married; 3 children. MD, Mayo Med. Sch.; MPH, Emory U. Cert. bd. cert. gen. preventive medicine and pub. health, lic. Va., Ga., Minn., Zimbabwe. Resident Emory U.; commr. health State of Va., 1998—2001; asst. adminstr. bur. global health USAID, Washington, 2001—. Cmty. devel., pub. health tng. and AIDS prevention, Kenya, Zimbabwe. Office: USAID RRB 1300 Pennsylvania Ave NW Washington DC 20523-3900

PETERSON, EDWARD ADRIAN, lawyer; b. St. Louis, May 19, 1941; s. Adrian J. and Virginia (Hamlin) P.; m. Catherine Frances Younghouse, Dec. 17, 1960; children: Kristin, Kendra. BSBA, Washington U., St. Louis, 1963; LLB, So. Methodist U., 1966. Bar: Tex. 1966, U.S. Dist. Ct. (no. and so. dists.) Tex. Instr. bus. law and acctg. Midwestern U., Wichita Falls, Tex., 1966-67; assoc. Schenk & Wesbrooks, Wichita Falls, 1966-67, Newman & Pickering, Dallas, 1967-72; ptnr. Moore & Peterson, Dallas, 1972-89, Winstead Sechrest & Minick P.C., Dallas, 1989—. Spkr. in field. Contbr. articles to legal jours. Bd. dirs. Leukemia Soc., 1970-71, North Tex. Commn., 1992-96, South Dallas/Fair Park Trust Fund, 1992, Tex. Ch. Extension Fund, Tex. Dist., Tex. Dist. Luth. Ch. Mo. Synod. Fellow Am. Coll. Mortgage Attys., Tex. Bar Found. (life), Coll. State Bar Tex.; mem. ABA, Am. Coll. Real Estate Lawyers (title ins. com., common interest com.), State Bar Tex., Tex. Coll. Real Estate Attys., Dallas Bar Assn., Phi Alpha Delta, Sigma Alpha Epsilon. Lutheran. Home: Ste 617 2808 McKinney Ave Dallas TX 75204-2562 also: 131 Hilton Head Island Dr Mabank TX 75147-9325 Office: Winstead Sechrest & Minick PC 5400 Renaissance Tower 1201 Elm St Dallas TX 75270-2199 Office Phone: 214-745-5642. Business E-Mail: epeterson@winstead.com.

PETERSON, EDWIN J. retired judge, mediator, law educator; b. Gilmanton, Wis., Mar. 30, 1930; s. Edwin A. and Leora Grace (Kitelinger) P.; m. Anna Chadwick, Feb. 7, 1971; children: Patricia, Andrew, Sherry. BS, U. Oreg., 1951, LLB, 1957. Bar: Oreg. 1957. Assoc. firm Tooze, Kerr, Peterson, Marshall & Shenker, Portland, Oreg., 1957-61, mem. firm, 1961-79; assoc. justice Supreme Ct. Oreg., Salem, 1979-83, 91-93, chief justice, 1983-91; ret., 1993; disting. jurist-in-residence, adj. instr. Willamette Coll. of Law, Salem, 1994—. Chmn. Supreme Ct. Task Force on Racial Issues, 1992-94; standing com. on fed. rules of practice and procedure, 1987-93; bd. dirs. Conf. Chief Justices, 1985-87, 88-91; founder Understanding Racism Found., 1998; mem. Oreg. Joint Bench-Bar Commn. on Professionalism, 1996-, chair, 1996-97. Chmn. Portland Citizens Sch. Com., 1968-70; vice-chmn. Young Rep. Fedn. Orgn., 1951; bd. visitors U. Oreg. Law Sch., 1978-83, 87-93, chmn. bd. visitors, 1981-83; pres., bd. dirs. Understanding Racism Found., 1999-2002. 1st lt. USAF, 1952-54. Mem. Oreg. State Bar (bd. examiners 1963-66, gov. 1973-76, vice chmn. profl. liability fund 1977-78), Multnomah County Bar Assn. (pres. 1972-73), Phi Alpha Delta, Lambda Chi Alpha. Episcopalian. Home: 3365 Sunridge Dr S Salem OR 97302-5950 Office: Willamette Univ Coll Law 245 Winter St SE Salem OR 97301-3916 Office Phone: 503-375-5399. E-mail: epeterso@willamette.edu.

PETERSON, ERIC H. lawyer, energy executive; m. Tonya Peterson; 2 children. BA, JD, So. Meth. U. Ptnr. Worsham Forsythe & Wooldridge; sr. v.p., gen. counsel DTE Energy, Mich.; exec. v.p., gen. counsel TXU, Dallas, 2002—. Presbyterian. Office: TXU Energy Plz 1601 Bryan St Dallas TX 75201

PETERSON, ERLE VIDAILLET, retired metallurgical engineer; b. Idaho Falls, Idaho, Apr. 29, 1915; s. Vier P. and Marie (Vidaillet) P.; m. Rosemary Sherwood, June 3, 1955; children: Kent Sherwood, Pamela Jo. BS in Mining Engring., U. Idaho, 1940; MS in Mining Engring., U. Utah, 1941. Tech. advisor Remington Arms Co., Salt Lake City, 1941-43; constrn. engr. plutonium plant duPont, Hanford, Wash., 1943-44, R & D engr. exptl. sta. Wilmington, Del., 1944-51, plant metallurgist heavy water plant Newport, Ind., 1951-57, rsch. metallurgist metals program Balt., 1957-62, prin. project engr. USAF contracts, 1962-68, devel. engr. Wilmington, 1969-80; ret., 1980.

Patentee in field; contbr. articles to profl. jours. Candidate for State Senate-Am. Party, Wilmington, 1974; com. chmn. Boy Scouts Am., Wilmington, 1975-78; treas. Local Civic Assn., Wilmington, 1977-79. Rsch. fellow U. Utah, 1940. Mem. Am. Soc. Metallurgists Internat., Del. Assn. Profl. Engrs. Republican. Avocations: lapidary, jewelry making, gardening. Home: PO Box 74 Rigby ID 83442-0074 *It matters not that you grow up on homestead and graduate from a country high school in a class of five during a great depression. With persistence and dedication toward your objectives, you can achieve goals that appear impossible.*

PETERSON, ERLEND DEAN, dean; b. St. George, Utah, Nov. 24, 1940; s. Dean Andrew and Lyle (Evans) P.; m. Colleen Dawn Keith, Dec. 5, 1968; children: Kristin, Sheri, Deborah, Deanne, Rebecca, Andrew. BS, Brigham Young U., 1967, MS, 1971, EdD, 1985. From registration officer to dean admissions and records Brigham Young U., Provo, Utah, 1968-87, asst. prof. ednl. leadership, 1990—, dean admissions and records, 1990—; LSD mission pres. to Norway, 1988-90; assoc. David M. Kennedy Ctr., 1985—, asst. prof. Ednl. Leadership, 1990—. Bd. dirs. Utah Higher Edn. Assistance Authority, Salt Lake City, Am.-Norwegian Hist. Soc., Northfield, Minn., 1996-99; lectr. and cons. in field. Contbr. articles to profl. jours. Chair, bd. dirs. United Way Utah County, Provo, 1991-94 (chair fund raising campaign 1994-95); coord. Utah Statehood Centennial Ambassadorial Visits Program, Utah, 1995-96. Recipient Norwegian Order Merit and Knight First Class award King Harald of Norway, Oslo, 1997. Mem. Am. Assn. Collegiate Registrars Admissions Officers (Utah chpt., Pacific chpt.). Republican. Mem. Lds Ch. Home: 1121 S 350 W Orem UT 84058-6769 Office: Brigham Young U PO Box 21111 Provo UT 84602-1111

PETERSON, ERLING WINSTON, religion educator; b. Ray, N.D., Jan. 22, 1921; s. Christian Frederic Peterson and Lydia Aemilia Megow; m. Elizabeth June Zorn, 1945; children: Thomas, Susan, Timothy, Bruce. BA magna cum laud, North Ctrl. Coll., 1943; MDiv, Evang. Theological, 1946; MA, U Wis., 1950; EdD, No. Ill. U, 1969. Pastor Badger Cristian Fellowship, Badger, Wis., 1946—51, First Evang. Ch., Kenosha, Wis., 1951—56, Windsor Union Congregational, Windsor, Wis., 1956—60, Dane Evang. and Reformed, Dane, 1958—60; assoc. prof. North Ctrl. Coll., Naperville, Ill., 1960—70; prof. U Indpls., 1970—86, prof. emeritus, 1986—; assoc. pastor Friedens United Ch. of Christ, 1986—91, 1998—2003. Moderator Madison Assoc. United Ch. of Christ, Madison, Wis., 1959—60; pres. Naperville Coun. Chs., Naperville, Ind., 1969—70; adv. bd. Indpls. Shakespeare Festival, Indpls., 1979—84; pres. Indpls. Shakespeare, 1979—84; adv. bd. Indpls. Coll. English Assoc., Indpls., 1980—83, pres., 1980—83. Contbr. What Every English Tchr. Should Know, 1965. Bd. mem. Indpls. Girls Club, 1979—83. Recipient Travel Scholarship, English Speaking Union, 1974. Avocations: reading, golf. Home: 1937 E Lawrence Ave Indianapolis IN 46227

PETERSON, FRANCIS, physicist, educator; BEE, Rensselaer U., 1964; PhD, Cornell U., 1968. Prof. physics dept. Iowa State U., Ames, prof. emeritus, 2003—. Recipient Disting. Svc. Citation award, 1993. Mem. Am. Assn. Physics Tchrs. Address: 669 El Tango La Casa Venice FL 34287-2501

PETERSON, FRANKLIN DELANO, lawyer; b. Braham, Minn., Nov. 11, 1932; s. John Erick and Myrtle M. (Anderson) P.; m. Beverly Ann Crabb, Aug. 2, 1958; children: Heidi, Durward, Heather. Student, Augsburg Coll., 1950-51; BA, St. Cloud State Coll., 1955; LLB, William Mitchell Coll. Law, 1961. Bar: Minn. 1961. Field claims adjuster Farmers Mut. Ins. Co., St. Paul, 1955-57; asst. dist. claims mgr. Minn. Farmers Ins. Group, Mpls., 1957-62; sole practice Kenyon, Minn., 1963—. Atty. City of Kenyon, 1964-82; v.p. Kenyon Devel. Corp., bd. dirs.; sec. Tri-Valley Constrn. Co., Kenyon, bd. dirs. Chmn. Goldwater for Pres. campaign, Village of Kenyon Reps., 1964, Goodhue County LeVander for Gov., 1966, Goodhue County Reps, 1969-70; sec. Goodhue Selective Service Bd., 1968—; pres. Mineral Springs Chem. Dependency Ctr., 1974-85; mem. Kenyon Pub. Sch. Bd. Edn., 1976-82, treas. 1980-82, Kenyon Booster Club (charter), v.p. 1983; mgr. mgr. Kenyon Legion Baseball, 1979—; bd. dirs. Kenyon Roseview Apts., 1967—, pres. 1985—. Served with USAF, 1950-52. Mem. ABA, Minn. Bar Assn. (jud. dist. del., pres. 1st dist. 1979-80), Goodhue County Bar Assn., Minn. Assn. Plaintiffs Attys., Nat. Assn. Claimants Counsel, Sons of Norway (pres. Kenyon lodge 1969), Kenyon Comml. Club, Kenyon Country Club (pres. Osman Shrine Clowns 1993), Masons, Shriners, Lions (pres. Kenyon chpt.), royal Order Jesters, Ct. of St. Paul and Shriner Clowns. Lutheran. Home: RR Box B Kenyon MN 55946 Office: 634 2nd St Kenyon MN 55946-1334

PETERSON, FRED MCCRAE, retired librarian; b. Mpls., Dec. 29, 1936; BA, U. Minn., 1958, MS, 1960; PhD in L.S., Ind. U., 1974. Asst. to dir. Iowa State U. Library, 1961-64, head catalog dept., 1964-67, asst. dir. library, 1967-69, assoc. dir. library, 1969-70; with Catholic U. Am., Washington, 1970-82, asst. prof., assoc. chairperson, 1973-77, acting dir. libraries, 1977-78, dir., 1978-82; univ. librarian Ill. State U., Normal, 1982-96, univ. libr. emeritus, 1996—. Mem. ALA, Ill. Libr. Assn. (past pes., Libr. of Yr. award 1994). Home: 32792 Via Malaga San Juan Capistrano CA 92675-4455

PETERSON, G. P. "BUD", academic administrator; b. Prairie Village, Kans. BS in Mech. Engrng. and Math., Kans. State U., 1975, MS in Engrng., 1980; PhD, Tex. A&M U., 1985. Engrng. prof. Tex. A&M U., 1981—2000; provost Rensselaer Poly. Inst., Troy, NY, 2000—. Editor (N.Am.): Jour. Exptl. Thermal and Fluid Scis.; assoc. editor: ASME Jour. Heat Transfer, AIAA Jour. Thermophysics and Heat Transfer, Internat. Jour. Heat and Fluid Flow, Microscale Thermophysical Engrng.; contbr. articles to profl. jours. Recipient Best Paper award, AIAA, 1990, award for outstanding mgmt., NSF, 1994, Ralph James and the O. L. "Andy" Lewis awards, ASME, Dow Outstanding Young Faculty award, ASEE, Pi Tau Sigma Gustus L. Larson Meml. award, ASME, Thermophysics award, AIAA, Meml. award, ASME, Sustained Svc. award, AIAA; fellow, Tex. Engrng. Expt. Sta., 1986, 1988; sr. fellow, 1989. Mem.: Phi Kappa Phi, Sigma Xi, Tau Beta Pi, Pi Tau Sigma. Office: Rensselaer Poly Inst Office of the Provost 110 8th St Troy NY 12180-3590*

PETERSON, GALE EUGENE, historian; b. Sioux Rapids, Iowa, May 23, 1944; s. George Edmund and Vergene Elizabeth (Wilson) P. BS, Iowa State U., 1965; MA, U. Md., 1968, PhD, 1973. Instr. dept. history U. Md., College Park, 1971-72, Cath. U. Am., Washington, 1972-73; prin. investigator Gregory Directory project Orgn. Am. Historians, Bloomington, Ind., 1973-75; instr. dept. history Purdue U., West Lafayette, Ind., 1975-76; dir. U.S. Newspaper Project, Orgn. Am. Historians, Bloomington, Ind., 1976-78; exec. dir. Cin. Hist. Soc., 1978-96, exec. dir. emeritus, 1996—; exec. dir. Ohio Humanities Coun., 1998—. Author: (with John T. Schlebecker) Living Historical Farms Handbook, 1970, Harry S Truman and the Independent Regulatory Commissions 1945-52, 1985. Mem. Cin. Bicentennial Commn., 1983-88. Mem. Orgn. Am. Historians (treas. 1993-2003), Am. Assn. State and Local History, Am. Hist. Assn., Am. Assn. Mus., Assn. Midwest Museums (v.p.-at-large 1993-95, exec. v.p. 1995-96, pres. 1996-98), Nat. Coun. on Pub. History (bd. dirs. 1992-95). Office: Ohio Humanities Coun Ste 1620 471 E Broad St Columbus OH 43215-3857 E-mail: galep@one.net.

PETERSON, GARY ANDREW, agronomics researcher; b. Holdrege, Nebr., Apr. 30, 1940; s. Walter Andrew and Evelyn Christine (Johnson) P.; m. Jacquelyn Charlene Flick, June 18, 1965; children: Kerstin, Ingrid. BS, U. Nebr., 1963, MS, 1965; PhD, Iowa State U., 1967. Research assoc. agronomy Iowa State U., Ames, 1964-67; prof. U. Nebr., Lincoln, 1967-84; prof. soil and crop scis. Colo. State U., Ft. Collins, 1984—, head dept. soil and crop scis., 2003—. Assoc. editor AGronomy Jour., 1979-81, tech. editor, 1981-83, editor, 1984-89, editor-in-chief, 1991-96; contbr. articles to profl. jours. Fellow Am. Soc. Agronomy (Ciba-Geigy Agr. Achievement award 1974, Agronomic Achievement award-Soils 1990), Soil Sci. Soc. Am. (Applied Rsch. award 1987); mem. Soil Conservation Soc. Am. Republican. Avocations: reading, hiking, skiing. Office: Colo State U Dept Soil Crop Scis Fort Collins CO 80523-0001 Office Phone: 970-491-6501. Business E-Mail: gary.peterson@colostate.edu.

PETERSON, GARY J, retail executive; Gen. mgr. WalMart, 1984—85; dir. of distbn. and transp. systems, 1985—88; sr. v.p. Carter, Hawley, Hale Stores, 1988—91; sr. v.p. of operation svcs. Thrifty Drug Stores, 1991—93; COO Southeast Frozen Foods, LP, 1993—96; exec. officer, COO Blockbuster Entertainment, 1996—2000; pres., COO OfficeMax, 2000—.

PETERSON, GENE DAVID, music educator; b. Milw., Apr. 27, 1974; s. Larry Robert and Mary Lydia Peterson. MusB in Performance - Conducting, Chapman U., Orange, Calif., 1999. Tchg. credential Calif. Choral dir. 1st Bapt. Ch., Anaheim, Calif., 1997—99, Moraga Valley Presbyn. Ch., Moraga, Calif., 2000—03. Recipient USC Book Award for Leadership, U. of So. Calif., 1992. Mem.: Calif. Music Educator's Assn. (Bay Sect. choral rep. 2002—03), Am. Choral Dirs. Assn. (Nat. Choral Conducting Competition award 1999). Office: Campolindo H S 300 Moraga Rd Moraga CA 94556 Office Phone: 925-376-5986. Office Fax: 925-376-6189. E-mail: gpeterson@acalanes.k12.ca.us.

PETERSON, GEORGE F. retired insurance company executive, writer; b. Racine, Wis., June 04; s. George Edwin Peterson and Anna Zetterquist; m. Evelyn Marie Peterson, Dec. 29, 1959. Student, Carthage Coll., 1945—48; BA, Ariz. State U., 1949. Mng. ptnr., co-pub. Opportunities Pub. Co., Racine, 1949—50; mkt. rsch. dir., circulation dir. Watson Publs., Chgo., 1955—58; circulation dir., rsch. mgr. Am. Aviation Pub. Co., Washington, 1958—62; editor, pub. Astrosci. News, Washington, 1962—64; mgmt. cons. Alexander Proudfoot Co., Chgo., 1964—66; field exec. Blue Cross of Fla., Inc., St. Petersburg, 1968—84; freelance writer Holiday, Fla., 1984—. Co-founder, CEO Inst. Cons. Engrs., Chgo., 1956—58; CFO Corp. Treas. Anchor Det. Co., Bristol, Va., 1962—64. Editor, pub.: Sci. Newsletter, 1964; author (as Lane Stevenson): (novel) To Las Vegas With Love, 2002, Searching for Krisztina, 2004. Bd. dirs. Health Sys. Agy., Fla., 1980—83; former mem. Fla. Health Sys. Agy. With Med. Corp U.S. Army, 1950—52. Recipient Pub.'s Achievement award, Washington, 1960, Cert. of Recognition, Sec. of Def. William Cohen, 2000. Avocations: astronomy, cosmology, particle physics, string theory physics. Home and Office: 3538 Burntwood Ct Holiday FL 34691

PETERSON, GERALD ALVIN, physics educator; b. Chesterton, Ind., Apr. 12, 1931; s. Gustaf Albert and Esther Josephine (Carlson) P.; m. Doris Lee DeJonge, Dec. 22, 1953; children— Curtis Mark, Thomas Andrew, Anna Beth. BS, Purdue U., 1953, MS, 1955; PhD, Stanford U., 1962. Lectr. Yale U., New Haven, 1962-64; asst. prof., 1964-67; research scientist Inst. voor Kernphysisch Onderzoek, Amsterdam, 1967-68; assoc. prof. physics U. Mass., Amherst, 1968-73, prof., 1973-2000, prof. emeritus, 2000—. Vis. prof. U. Mainz, Fed. Republic Germany, 1975, Japan Soc. Promotion Sci., 1972, 89; U.S.-Israel Binat. Sci. Found. vis. prof. Tel Aviv U., 1983; cons. in field. Contbr. articles to profl. jours. Served with U.S. Army, 1955-57. NATO fellow, 1969, U.K. sr. rsch. fellow, 1970. Fellow Am. Phys. Soc. (chmn. New Eng. sect. 1996); mem. Sigma Xi. Congregationalist. Achievements include research in electron scattering and nuclear structure. Home: 10 Old Briggs Rd Leverett MA 01054-9759 Office: U Mass Nuclear Physics Grad Rsch Ctr Amherst MA 01003 Office Phone: 413-545-2008. Business E-Mail: peterson@physics.umass.edu.

PETERSON, GLEN RAYMOND, protective services official; b. Williamsport, Pa., July 1, 1951; s. Earl Carl and Naomi May Peterson; m. Diane Elizabeth Bosch, June 14, 1973; 1 child, Douglas Darby. BA in social sci., Lock Haven State, 1973. Admin. police officer Lock Haven (Pa.) State Coll., 1973—75; probation parole officer State of Va., Chesterfield, 1975—80; correction officer fed. US Bur. of Prisons, Petersburg, Va., 1980—81; dir. comm. corrections Chesterfield County, Chesterfield, 1981—. Pres. Va. Jaycees Salem Works, Chesterfield. Mem.: Va. Comm. Criminal Justice Assn. (pres. 1990—, Outstanding Dir. 1998, Outstanding Svc. award 1995). Achievements include development of local comm. criminal justice program to include parental release, local probation, day reporting center; domestic violence resource ctr. Avocations: fishing, hunting, hiking, reading. Office: Community Corrections Svc PO Box 40 Chesterfield VA 23832 E-mail: petersong@chesterfield.gov.

PETERSON, H(ARRY) WILLIAM, chemicals executive, consultant; b. Yokohama, Honshu Island, Japan, Mar. 9, 1922; came to U.S., 1924; s. Harry William and Alice (Mateer) P.; m. Doris Jane Howe, Apr. 27, 1946; children: Robert, Christine Fitzpatrick, Janet McMillan. BA in Chemistry and Botany, Colgate U., 1946; postgrad., Princeton U., 1949-50, U. Del., 1982-83. Lic. capt. U.S. inland waters U.S. Coast Guard. Researcher, developer ESSO Standard Oil Co., Bayway, N.J., 1946-51; various positions Enjay Chem. Co., N.Y.C., 1951-65; coord. world-wide chem. Gulf Oil Corp., Pitts., 1965-67; gen. mktg. mgr. Gulf Oil-Eastern Hemisphere, London, 1967-71; corp. v.p. chem. mktg., corp. v.p. mktg. Gulf Oil Can. Ltd., Montreal, Que., Can., 1971-77; CEO chems. divsn., corp. v.p. Golfoil Can., Montreal, Quebec, Can., 1971-77; chief operating officer Corpus Christi Chem. Co., Wilmington, Del., 1971—; mng. dir. Food Machinery & Chem. Corp. Internat. Chems., Phila., 1979-80; internat. cons. Bozman, Md., 1980—. Patentee in field. Leader Young Christians Assn., 1st Bapt. Ch., Somerville, N.J., 1948-53; lay speaker, mem. adminstrn. bd. Riverview Charge, United Meth. Ch.; chaplain Mil. Order Purple Heart. With USMC, 1942-46, PTO. Decorated Purple Heart, two battle stars. Fellow Am. Inst. Chemists; mem. Am. Chem. Soc. (emeritus). Avocations: writing, philosophy, religion. Home and Office: 1257 Marywood LN Apt 219 Richmond VA 23229-6060

PETERSON, JAMES KENNETH, manufacturing executive; b. Sioux City, Iowa, Oct. 17, 1934; s. David Winfield and Beulah Lillian (Johnson) P.; m. Nanette Kay Olin, Feb. 2, 1957; children: Kimberly, Kristin, David. BA in Econs, Mich. State U., 1956. R & D engr. Reynolds Metals Co., Richmond, Va., 1957-59, sales rep., 1959-61, dist. sales mgr., 1961-65, regional sales mgr., 1965-67, asst. to exec. v.p., 1968, mktg. dir., 1969-71; dir. nat. account sales The Continental Group, Stamford, Conn., 1971, gen. mgr. sales, 1972-73, div. gen. mgr., 1974-78, v.p., corp. officer, 1974-80, v.p., gen. mgr. global bus. devel., 1979; pres., COO, Ludlow Corp., Needham, Mass., 1980-82, also bd. dirs.; pres., CEO, dir. Graphic Packaging Corp., Paoli, Pa., 1982-89; pres., CEO, Peterson Group, Easton, Md., 1989—. Bd. dirs. Jenard Co., Graphic Packaging Corp., South Chester Tube Co. Served to 1st lt. U.S. Army, 1957. Mem. Merion Golf Club, Merion Cricket Club, Talbot Country Club. Home: 27779 Waverly Rd Easton MD 21601-8121

PETERSON, JAMES LINCOLN, museum executive; b. Kewanee, Ill., Nov. 12, 1942; s. Reinold Gustav and Florence Josephine (Kjellgren) P.; m. M. Susan Pepin, Aug. 15, 1964; children: Hans C., Erika C. BA, Gustavus Adolphus Coll., 1964; PhD, U. Nebr., 1972. Sci. tchr. pub. schs., Ill. and Minn., 1964-68; research asst. U. Nebr., Lincoln, 1968-72; research assoc. U. Wis., Madison, 1972-74; staff ecologist Nat. Commn. Water Quality, Washington, 1974-75; v.p. research Acad. Nat. Scis., Phila., 1976-84, v.p. devel., 1982-84; pres. Sci. Mus. Minn., St. Paul, 1984—. Bd. dirs. Ea. Pa. chpt. Nature Conservancy, Phila., 1982-84, Downtown Coun., St. Paul, 1986-93, Keystone (Colo.) Ctr., 1989-93; mem. St. Paul Riverfront Commn., 1987-91; mem. adv. com. U. Minn. Coll. Biol. Scis., 1989-95. Mem. Assn. Sci. Mus. Dirs., Assn. Sci. and Tech. Ctrs. (pres. 1993-95), Sci. Mus. Exhibit Collaborative (pres. 1986-89), St. Paul C. of C. (bd. dirs. 1985-89), Informal Club. Office: Sci Mus Minn 30 10th St E Ste N Saint Paul MN 55101-2265

PETERSON, JAMES ROBERT, engineering psychologist; b. St. Paul, Apr. 16, 1932; s. Palmer Elliot and Helen Evelyn (Carlson) P.; m. Marianna J. Stockvig, June 26, 1954; 1 child, Anne Christine. BA in Psychology cum laude, U. Minn., 1954, MA in Exptl. Psychology, 1958; PhD in Engrng. Psychology, U. Mich., 1965. Devel. engr. Honeywell Inc., 1961-65, sr. devel. engr., 1965-67, staff engr., 1967-90, sr. project staff engr., 1990-93, retired, 1993. Honeywell sponsor rep. Shuttle Student Involvement Program, 1982, 84. Contbr. articles to profl. jours. With USMC, 1954-57, USMCR, 1957-62. Mem. Human Factors and Ergonomics Soc. (life), Air & Space Mus. (charter), Smithsonian Inst., Masons. Achievements include invention of Apollo translation hand controller; participation in development work in all U.S. Manned Space Programs (Mercury, Gemini, Apollo, Lunar Excursion Module, Manned Orbiting Laboratory, Space Shuttle and Space Sta.) as member/manager of associated human factors groups. Home: 3303 San Gabriel St Clearwater FL 33759-3341 Personal E-mail: bpeteputt@aol.com.

PETERSON, JAMES ROBERT, retired writing instrument manufacturing executive; b. Momence, Ill., Oct. 28, 1927; s. Clyde and Pearl (Deliere) P.; m. Betty Windham, May 12, 1949; children: Richard James, Lynn Peterson Anderson, Susan Peterson Hanske, John Windham. Student, St. Thomas Coll., 1945, Iowa State U., 1945-46, U. Colo., 1946, Northwestern U., 1946; BS in Mktg. cum laude, U. Ill., 1952; grad. exec. MBA program, Stanford U., 1967. With Pillsbury Co., Mpls., 1952-76, brand mgr. grocery products, 1953-57, brand supr. flour, 1957-61, dir. mktg., 1961-66, v.p. mktg., 1966-68; v.p., gen. mgr. Grocery Products Co., 1968-71, group v.p. consumer cos., 1971-73, pres., dir., 1973-76; exec. v.p., dir. R.J. Reynolds Industries, Inc., Winston-Salem, N.C., 1976-82; pres., chief exec. officer, dir. Parker Pen Co., Janesville, Wis., 1982-85. Dir. Dun & Bradstreet Corp., N.Y.C., 1977-98, Waste Mgmt., Inc., Oak Brook, Ill., 1980-98, IMS. Health, Inc., Westport, Conn., 1996-98. Former mem. bd. dirs. Boy Scouts Am., past pres. Viking coun.; mem. bd. regents St. Olaf Coll., 1974-91. Lt. USN, 1945-50. Recipient Bronze Tablet award U. Ill. Mem. Pilgrims of U.S., Tequesta Country Club, Bear Path Golf & Country Club, Beta Gamma Sigma. Methodist. Address: 17750 Beach Rd Unit 505 Tequesta FL 33469-2863 Office Phone: 561-747-4610. Personal E-mail: jrsonpeter@aol.com.

PETERSON, JAMES SCOTT (JIM PETERSON), Canadian government official; b. Ottawa, Can., 1941; married Heather Peterson. BA, LLB, U. We. Ont.; Diploma, L'Acad. de Droit Internat., The Hague and La Sorbonne; DCL, McGill U.; LLM, Columbia U. Mem. faculty of law U. Toronto, 1974-79; elected mem. of parliament Willowdale, 1980—; chair Cambridge Acceptance Corp. Ltd., 1984-87; chair standing com. on fin. Minister of State, Minister of Justice, 1993-97; sec. of state Internat. Fin. Instns., Ottawa, 1997—2002; min. internat. trade Govt. of Canada, Ottawa, 2003—. Legal counsel and cons. UN. Office: Office of the Min for Internat Trade 515S Ho of Commons Rm 359 West Block K1A 0A6 Ottawa ON Canada*

PETERSON, JANE WHITE, nursing educator, anthropologist; b. San Juan, P.R., Feb. 15, 1941; d. Jerome Sidney and Vera (Joseph) Peterson; 1 child, Claire Marie. BS, Boston U., 1968; M in Nursing, U. Wash., 1969, PhD, 1981. Staff nurse Visiting Nurse Assn., Boston, 1964-66; prof. Seattle U., 1969—, dir. nursing home project, 1990-92, chair pers. com., 1988-90; chair dept. Community Health and Psychiat. Mental Health Nursing, 1987-89. Sec. Coun. on Nursing and Anthropology, 1984-86; pres. Wash. League Nursing, Seattle, 1988-90; pres. bd. Vis. Nurses Svcs., Seattle, 1988-90; contbg. cons. CSI Prodn., Okla., 1987; cons. in nursing WHO/U. Indonesia, Jakarta, fall 1989, Myanmar (Burma), Yangon, winter 1995, Beijing, 1995. Contbr. articles to profl. jours., chptrs. to books. Co-owner (with Robert Colley) North End Train Ctr., Seattle; mem. Seattle Art Mus., 1986—. Fellow: Soc. for Applied Anthropology; mem. Am. Anthropological Assn., Soc. for Med. Anthropology, Nat. League for Nursing, Am. Ethological Soc. Office: Seattle U Sch Nursing Broadway and Madison Seattle WA 98122

PETERSON, JILL SUSAN, elementary school educator; b. Richland, Wash. July 26, 1946; d. Clarence Edward and Doris Edeline (Ostby) Lange; m. Wallace Peterson Jr., Aug. 10, 1968 (dec. Jan. 1991); 1 child, Dawn Sa Ra. BA, Pacific Luth. U., 1968; MA, U. St. Thomas, 1984; post grad., Augsburg Coll., U. Minn., U. St. Thomas, U. Calif., Irvine. Tchr. Little Can. Elem. Sch., 1968—74; title I tutor Red Oak Elem., St. Paul, 1975—79; lead tchr. Sand Creek Elem., Mpls., 1979—88, Andover Elem., Mpls., 1988—. Adj. instr. multicultural edn. Hamline U., 1995—99; instr. Seeking Ednl. Equity and Diversity, 1995—. Human rights commr. City Arden Hills, Minn., 1987—90; pres. Children of the World, 1995—99; vol. Ctr. for Victims of Torture, Mpls., 2000—; Women in Soc. del. to Brazil People to People Ambassador Program, 2003; mem. coun. Roseville Luth. Ch., Minn., 1986—88, 1994—96. Recipient Award of Excellence, Minn. Elem. Sch. Prin. Assn., 1992. Mem.: NEA, Anoka-Hennepin Edn. Minn., Edn. Minn., Alpha Delta Kappa (pres. Alpha Omicron chpt. 1993—94, Regional Scholar of Merit 1994, Tchr. Outstanding Performance 2000). Avocations: reading, swimming, travel, volunteering. Home: 3061 Highpointe Curve Roseville MN 55113 Office: Andover Elem Sch 14950 Hanson Blvd NW Andover MN 55304

PETERSON, JOHN E. congressman; b. Titusville, Pa., Dec. 25, 1938; s. Axel Benjamin and Mary Elizabeth (Baker) P.; m. Saundra June Watson, 1968; children: Richard D., Florence Waychoff. Student, Pa. State U. Owner retail food market, Pleasantville, Pa., 1958-84; mem. Pa. Ho. of Reps., 1977-84, Pa. State Senate, 1984-96, U.S. Congress from 5th Pa. dist., 1997—; mem. appropriations com., resources com. Former mem. nat. adv. coun. U.S. Small Bus. Adminstrn.; mem. Pub. Health and Welfare Com., now chmn.;active PENNVEST Bd., Pa. Hardwoods Devel. Coun.; sec. Ctr. Rural Pa. Former dist. asst. U.S. Congressman Albert Johnson; mem. regional adv. coun. Pitts. Cancer Inst.; former lay leader Pleasantville United Meth. Ch., former chmn. pastoral parish com.; bd. advisors Foxview Manor, Inc.; mem. adv. bd. U. Pitts., Titusville and Bradford campuses; mem. adv. coun. Ind. U. of Pa. Culinary Sch.; active Pa. Trauma Ctr. Found., Venango County Indsl. Bd. Served U.S. Army. Recipient John Heinz Meml. award; Presdl. Distinction medal U. Pitts. at Bradford, Recognition award Pa. Acad. Family Physicians, Appreciation award, Better Life award Pa Health Care Assn., Guardian of Small Bus. award Nat. Fedn. Ind. Bus., Spl. Achievement award Pa. Bar Assn., Elected Officials award Pa. Home Health Assn., 1994; named Senator of Yr., Pa. Jewish Coalition, Legislator of Yr., Pa. Assn. County Human Svc. Adminstrs., 1993, Pa. Home Health Care Assn., 1993. Mem. Titusville Area C. of C. (past pres.), Pleasantville Parent-Tchr. Assn. (past pres.), Lions. Republican. Methodist. Home: PO Box 295 248 N Main St Pleasantville PA 16341-9776 Office: US Ho of Reps 123 Cannon Ho Office Bldg Washington DC 20515-0001

PETERSON, JOHN LEONARD, lawyer, judge; b. Butte, Mont., Sept. 11, 1933; s. Roy victor and Lena Pauline (Umhang) P.; m. Jean Marie Hollingsworth, June 10, 1957; children: Michael R., John Robert, Carol Jean. BA in Bus., JD, U. Mont., 1957. Bar: Mont. 1957, U.S. Supreme Ct. 1964, U.S. Ct. Appeals (9th cir.) 1974, U.S. Tax Ct. 1978. Assoc. McCaffery, Roe, Kiely & Joyce, 1957-63; ptnr. McCaffery & Peterson, 1963-79; sole practice Butte, 1979-85. Part-time U.S. bankruptcy judge, 1963-85; U.S. bankruptcy judge, Mont., 1985—; bd. govs. Nat. Conf. Bankruptcy Judges, 1989-92. Mem. Mont. Bd. Regents Higher Edn., 1975-82; del. Dem. Nat. Conv., 1968. Mem. Nat. Conf. Bankruptcy Judges, Mont. Bar Assn., Silver bow County Bar Assn., Butte Country Club. Democrat. Lutheran. Office: US Dist Ct Chief Bankruptcy Judge 215 Fed Bldg Butte MT 59701

PETERSON, JOHN WILLARD, composer, music publisher; b. Lindsborg, Kans., Nov. 1, 1921; s. Peter Ephraim and Adlina Mary (Nelson) P.; m. Marie Alta Addis (Feb. 11, 1944); children: Sandra Lynn Peterson Catzere, Candace Kay Peterson Strader, Pamela Lee Peterson Cruse. Student, Moody Bible Inst., 1947-48; MusB, Am. Conservatory Music, 1952; MusD (hon.), John Brown U., 1967; DD (hon.), West Bapt. Sem., 1970; DFA (hon.), Grand Canyon U., 1979. Radio broadcaster Sta. WMBI, Chgo., 1950-55; editor in chief, pres. Singspiration, Inc., Grand Rapids, Mich., 1955-71, exec. composer Carefree, Ariz., 1977-83; pres. Good Life Prodns., Scottsdale, Ariz., 1977-83, John W. Peterson Music Co., Scottsdale, 1983-88. Bd. dirs. Gospel Films, Inc., Muskegon, Mich. Co-author: (autobiography) The Miracle Goes On, 1976; composer works include numerous cantatas, musicals, gospel songs, hymns and anthems. 1st lt. USAAF 1942-45, CBI. Decorated Air medal; recipient Sacred Music award Nat. Evang. Film Found., 1966, Music Achievement award Christian Artists, 1985; Honor Cert. Freedoms Found., 1975; winner Internat. Gospel Composition of Yr., Soc. European Stage, Authors and Composers, 1986, Ray DeVries Ch. Music award, 1996; inductee Gospel Music Hall of Fame, 1986. Mem. ASCAP, Hump Pilots Assn. Home: 11668 N 80th Pl Scottsdale AZ 85260-5650 Office Phone: 480-483-3306.

PETERSON, JON A. education educator; b. Columbus, Ohio, Sept. 21, 1935; s. Alvah and Helen (Hoff) Peterson; m. Mary Jane Eaker, Aug. 31, 1963; children: Sarah, Andrew. BA in History, Swathmore Coll., 1957; MA in Am. History, Ohio State U., 1959; PhD in Am. History, Harvard U., 1967. Lectr. history Queens Coll., CUNY, Flushing, 1966—67, asst. prof. history, 1967—81, assoc. prof. history, 1982—2001, prof. history, 2002—. Chair dept. history Queens Coll. CUNY, Flushing, NY, 1990—94, grad. advisor dept. history, 2000—03. Author: The Birth of City Planning in the United States: 1840-1917, 2003, (study manual) A Research Guide to the History of the Borough of Queens, 1987. Mem.: OAH, AHA, Soc. Archl. Hist., Soc. for Am. City & Regional Planning History, Urban History Assn. Home: 11 Baker Hill Rd Great Neck NY 11023

PETERSON, JULIE, public information officer; b. Ft. Dodge, Iowa; m. John P. Wesley; 2 children. BA, St. Olaf Coll., Northfield, Minn.; MA, Sarah Lawrence Coll. Previously in edn.; mem. Vt. Legislature; with Office of Gov. of Vt., 1991—, now chief of staff, 1991—. Office: Office of the Gov 109 State St Montpelier VT 05609-0001

PETERSON, KAREN L. information technology manager; b. Memphis, Tenn., July 21, 1963; d. Duane Sheldon Peterson and Peterson Nina; 1 child, Karl Glastad. BS in Math and Computer Sci., U. Tex. at Dallas, Richardson, 1985. IT mgr. Cyrix Corp., Richardson, 1994—96; IT supr. DSC Comm., Plano, Tex., 1988—94; program mgr. Lucent Technologies, Mesquite, Tex., 1996—99; v.p., rsch. dir. Gartner, Inc., Stamford, Conn., 1999—. Mem. editl. adv. bd. Achieving Supply Chain Excellence through Tech., San Francisco, 2001—; mem. comml. industry team Office of Sec. of Def., Dept. Def., Washington, 2002—. Mem.: Am. Prodn. and Inventory Control Soc. Office: Gartner Inc 56 Top Gallant Rd Stamford CT 06904 Personal E-mail: klp75248@yahoo.com. E-mail: karen.peterson@gartner.com.

PETERSON, KATHERINE H. federal agency administrator, former ambassador; b. Pasadena, CA; Student, Nat. War Coll.; BA, U. Calif., Santa Cruz. Mem. staff Foreign Svc., 1976, Bureau of African Affairs, Washington; deputy chief of mission Amer. Embassy, Windhoek, Namibia, 1993—96; U.S. ambassador to Lesotho U.S. Dept. State, Washington, 1998—2001; dir. Fgn. Service Inst., Washington, 2001—. Office: Fgn Service Inst 4000 Arlington Blvd Washington DC 22204-1500*

PETERSON, KENNETH ALLEN, SR., superintendent, retired; b. Hammond, Ind., Jan. 20, 1939; s. Chester E. and Bertha (Hornby) P.; B.Ed. cum laude, Chgo. State U., 1963; M.S., Purdue U., 1970; NSF grantee U. Iowa, 1964-65; postgrad. U. Ill., 1977-81; Vanderbilt U.; m. Marilyn M. Musson, Jan. 3, 1961; children: Kimberly, Kari, Kenneth Allen Jr. Tchr., Markham (Ill.) Sch. Dist. 144, 1961-67; prin. Brookwood Sch., Glenwood (Ill.) Sch. Dist. 1967, 1967-77, prin. Hickory Bend Sch., 1977-78, dir. spl. edn., 1978-80, asst. supt. schs., 1981-83, ret. supt schs., 1983-94; prof. Govs. State U., 1994—, now emeritus superintendent of schools; mem. No. Ill. Planning Commn. for Gifted Edn. Chmn. Steger (Ill.) Bicentennial Commn., 1976; vice chmn. Ashkum dist. Boy Scouts Am., 1981-83, lodge advisor, sect. advisor, exec. bd., area advisor Vigil honor mem. Order of Arrow Calumet council Boy Scouts Am.; v.p. Calumet Coun. Boy Scouts of Am., 1989—; program com. South Cook County council Girl Scouts U.S.A., 1971-73, 80-81, mem. fin. com., 1981-86, also bd. dirs., nat. del.; mem. Steger Community Devel. Commn. Recipient Order of Arrow Service nat. founders award, Silver Beaver award, Dist. award of merit Boy Scouts Am., Disting. Svc. award Nat. Order of Arrow. Mem. ASCD, Coun. Exceptional Children, P.T.A. (life), Am. Assn. Sch. Adminstrs., Kappa Delta Pi. Republican. Lutheran. Home: 3208 Phillips Ave Steger IL 60475-1161 Office: Coll of Edn Governors State Univ University Park IL 60466

PETERSON, KEVIN BRUCE, newspaper editor, publishing executive; b. Kitchener, Ont., Can., Feb. 11, 1948; s. Bruce Russell and Marguerite Elizabeth (Hammond) P.; m. Constance Maureen Bailey, Feb. 11, 1975 (dec. May 1975); m. Sheila Helen O'Brien, Jan. 9, 1981 BA, U. Calgary, Alta., Can., 1968. Chief bur. Calgary Herald, 1972-75, city editor, 1976-77, news editor, 1977-78, bus. editor, 1978, mng. editor, 1978-86, editor, asst. pub., 1986-87, gen. mgr., 1987-88, pub., 1989-96; sr. counsel GPC Comms., 1999—. Pres. Canadian Univ. Press, Ottawa, Ont., Can., 1968-69; dir. New Directions for News. Harry Brittain Meml. fellow Commonwealth Press Union, London, 1979 Mem. Can. Mng. Editors (bd. dirs. 1983-87), Am. Soc. Newspaper Editors, Horsemen's Benevolent and Protective Assn., Alta. Legis. Press Gallery Assn. (v.p. 1971-76), Can. Daily Newspaper Assn. (bd. dirs. 1990-96, vice chmn., treas 1992, chmn. 1993-96), Alta. Theatre Projects (bd. dirs. 1996—, v.p. 1998—), Calgary Ctr. for Non-Profit Mgmt. (bd. dirs. 1998—), Calgary Petroleum Club, Ranchmen's Club, 100-t-1 Club, (Arcadia, Calif.) Avocations: thoroughbred horse racing; art collecting.

PETERSON, LARRY JAMES, medical educator, oral surgeon; b. Winfield, Kans., Apr. 23, 1942; m. Susan Bartlett; children: Brie, Tucker. BS, U. Kans., 1964; DDS cum laude, U. Mo., Kans. City, 1968; MS, Georgetown U., 1971. Diplomate Am. Bd. Oral and Maxillofacial Surgery. Oral surgery resident Georgetown U. Sch. Dentistry, Washington, 1968-71; active staff Eugene Talmadge Meml. Hosp., Augusta, Ga., 1971-75, John N. Dempsey Hosp., Farmington, Conn., 1975-82, Ohio State U. Hosp., Columbus, 1982—, Children's Hosp., Columbus, 1982—; asst. prof. oral surgery Med. Coll. Ga. Sch. Dentistry, Augusta, 1971-74, assoc. prof. oral surgery, 1974-75; assoc. prof. oral and maxillofacial surgery U. Conn. Sch. Dental Medicine, Farmington, 1975-81; program dir. oral and maxillofacial surgery residency U. Conn. Affiliated Program, Farmington, 1980-82; prof. oral and maxillofacial surgery U. Conn. Sch. Dental Medicine, Farmington, 1981-82; prof., chmn. oral and maxillofacial surgery and pathology Ohio State U. Coll. Dentistry, Columbus, 1982—. Adv. com. Am. Bd. Oral and Maxillofacial Surgeons 1980-86, assoc. subject leader 1982-84, subject leader 1984-86. Editor: (textbook) Contemporary Oral and Maxillofacial Surgery, (multi-vol. ref. book) Principles of Oral and Maxillofacial Surgery; contbr. over 40 articles to profl. jours., 25 chpts. to books; editor oral surgery sect. Clinical Dentistry, 1981-87, oral and maxillofacial surgery sect. Oral Surgery, Oral Medicine, Oral Pathology, 1992—, editor-in-chief 1993—; editl. bd. Jour. Oral and Maxillofacial Surgery 1991-92; presenter in field. Recipient awards Am. Coll. Dentists, 1984, Internat. Coll. Dentists, 1992; Mosby scholar 1968. Fellow Am. Dental Soc. of Anesthesiology; mem. ADA (cons., oral and maxillofacial surgery site visitor, commn. on dental accreditation 1985-91, nat. dental bd. test constrn. com. oral and maxillofacial surgery 1985-90, nat. dental bd. part II restructuring com. 1987-92, cons. coun. on dental therapeutics 1980-92), Am. Assn. of Oral and Maxillofacial Surgeons (rsch. adv. com. 1976-79, test constrn. com. 1978-91, com. on scientific sessions 1991-94, com. on residency edn. and tng. 1992—, del. Ho. Dels. 1991-94), Internat. Assn. for Dental Rsch., Am. Assn. Dental Schs., Acad. of Osteointegration, Assn. for Acad. Surgery, Surg. Infection Soc., Alliance for Prudent Use of Antibiotics, Ohio Dental Assn., Ohio Soc. Oral and Maxillofacial Surgeons, Great Lakes Soc. Oral and Maxillofacial Surgeons, Columbus Dental Soc., Sigma Xi, Omicron Kappa Upsilon. Office: Ohio State U Coll Dentistry Dept Oral and Max Surgery 305 W 12th Ave Columbus OH 43210-1267

PETERSON, LESLIE RAYMOND, barrister; b. Viking, Alta., Can., Oct. 6, 1923; s. Herman S. and Margaret (Karen) P.; m. Agnes Rose Hine, June 24, 1950; children: Raymond Erik, Karen Isabelle. Student, Camrose Luth. Coll., Alta., McGill. U., Can., London U.; LLB, U. B.C., Can., 1949; LLD (hon.), U. B.C., 1993, Simon Fraser U., Can., 1965; EdD, Notre Dame U., Nelson, Can., 1966; diploma tech. (hon.), B.C. Inst. Tech., 1994. Bar: B.C. 1949; called to Queens Counsel, 1960. Pvt. practice barrister, Vancouver, 1949-52; with Peterson & Anderson, 1952, Boughton & Co., 1953—55; mem. B.C. Legislature for Vancouver Centre, 1956—63, Vancouver-Little Mountain, 1966; min. of edn., 1956-68; min. of labour, 1960-71; atty. gen., 1968-72; bd. govs. U. B.C., Vancouver, 1979-83, chancellor, 1987-93. Bd. dirs. Can. Found. Econ. Edn., Inst. Corp. Dirs. Can., West Vancouver Found., Inst. for Pacific Ocean Sci. and Tech., Peterson Bus. Consultants Inc.; trustee Peter Wall Inst. for Advanced Studies; chmn. U. B.C. Found., 1990—96. Bd. dirs. Portland unit Shriners Hosp. for Children, 1994-96; past bd. dirs. Western Soc. of Rehab., YMCA, Victoria B.C.; past pres. Twenty Club; hon. mem. Vancouver Jr. C. of C.; former v.p. Normanna Old People's Home; founding mem. Convocation, Simon Fraser U. and U. Victoria; hon. dep. French Nat. Assembly, Paris; hon. commr. labor State of Okla.; gov. Downtown Vancouver Assn. With Can. Army, 1942-46, ETO. Recipient Disting. Alumnus award Camrose Luth. Coll., 1980. Fellow: Royal Soc. Arts; mem.: Internat. Assn. Govt. Labour Ofcls. (chmn. standing com., Can. mins. of edn. 1965—66), Law Soc. B.C., Vancouver Bar Assn., Wesbrook Soc. of U. B.C. (chmn. 1987), Union Club (Victoria), Terminal City Club (pres. 1991—92), Scandinavian Bus. Men's Club (past pres.), Order of Can., Venerable Order of Saint John (comdr.), Order of B.C., Freemason (potentate Gizeh Temple Shrine 1988), Order of St. Lazarus (knight comdr.). Avocations: skiing, golf, fishing, tennis. Home: 814 Highland West Vancouver BC Canada V7S 2G5 Office: Boughton Peterson Yang Anderson 595 Burrard St Ste 1000 PO Box 49290 Vancouver BC Canada V7X 1S8 E-mail: lpeterson@boughton.ca.

PETERSON, LINDA ELLEN, lawyer; b. Kearny, N.J., Feb. 8, 1960; d. Walter Raymond and JoAnn Evelyn Peterson; m. Domenic James Valentine, Oct. 2, 1988 (div. Apr. 1991); m. Nicholas Joseph Mango, Aug. 17, 1996; 1 child, Jessica Lynn Mango. BA with honors, Rutgers U., 1983; JD, Pace U., 1987. Bar: N.J. 1987. Law clk. to Hon. Bruce A. Gaeta, Hackensack, N.J., 1987-88; asst. county counsel Bergen County Counsel, Hackensack, 1988-91; asst. dep. pub. defenders Passaic County Pub. Defenders, Paterson, N.J., 1991-93, Bergen County Pub. Defenders, Hackensack, 1993—. Vol. St. Catherine's Parish, Ringwood, N.J.1995—. Ranking scholar Pace U., 1986. Mem. Nat. Assn. Criminal Def. Lawyers, N.J. State Bar. Methodist. Avocations: dance, yoga, antiques, gardening, moutain biking. Office: Office Pub Defender 60 State St Hackensack NJ 07601-5469

PETERSON, LOUIS ROBERT, retired consumer products company executive; b. Racine, Wis., Nov. 11, 1923; s. Edward J. and Effie (Buenning) P.; m. Marian Francis Barber, Nov. 22, 1947; children: Karen Jean, Kathleen Alice, Jill Ann. Student, Utah State Agrl. Coll., U. Wis.-Racine. With Johnson Wax Co., Racine, Wis., 1947—, sales rep., 1970-72, v.p. household sales, 1972-76, exec. v.p. U.S. consumer products, ptnr. in office of the chmn., 1976-80, exec. v.p. internat. consumer products, 1980-86. Past pres., bd. dirs. Racine Area United Way.; bd. dirs. St. Mary's Med. Ctr. With U.S. Army, 1943-46. Mem. Northwestern U. Assocs., Conf. Bd. (internat. coun.), Internat. C. of C. (U.S. coun. internat. bus.), Somerset Club (Racine, Wis.), Pinnacle Peak Country Club (Scottsdale, Ariz.). Republican. Roman Catholic. Home: 1219 Sweetbriar Ln Hartland WI 53029

PETERSON, LOWELL, cinematographer; b. L.A., Feb. 1, 1950; s. Lowell Stanley and Catherine Linda (Hess) P.; m. Deanna Rae Terry, Aug. 2, 1981. Student, Yale U., 1968; BA in Theater Arts, UCLA, 1973. Asst. cinematographer, Hollywood, Calif., 1973-83; camera operator, 1983-92; dir. photography, 1992—. Asst. cinematographer various prodns. including Blind Ambition, 1979, Hawaii Five-O, 1979-80, White Shadow, 1980-81, Lou Grant, 1981-82, Two of a Kind, 1982, Remington Steele, 1982-83, Something About Amelia, 1983; camera operator various prodns. including Tourist Trap, 1979, Newhart, 1983, Scarecrow and Mrs. King, 1983-85, Children in the Crossfire, 1984, Stranded, 1986, Knots Landing, 1986-87, 89-92, Like Father Like Son, 1987, Star Trek: The Next Generation, 1987-89, Coupe de Ville, 1990, Show of Force, 1990; dir. photography Knots Landing, 1992-93, Second Chances, 1993-94 (Am. Soc. Cinematographers award nomination), Galaxy Beat, 1994, Hotel Malibu, 1994, Lois and Clark, 1995, The Client, 1995-96, Moloney, 1996-97, Four Corners, 1998, Profiler (Am. Soc. Cinematographers award nomination), 1998-99, Ryan Caulfield, 1999, Bedazzled (2d Unit), 2000, Bubble Boy (2d Unit), 2001, Just Ask My Children, 2001 (Am. Soc. Cinematographers award nominee); contbr. articles to Film Comment, 1974, Internat. Photographer, 1984—. Mem. Acad. TV Arts and Scis. (bd. govs. 2001—), Am. Soc. Cinematographers, Soc. Motion Picture and TV Engrs., Internat. Cinematographers Guild, L.A. Music Ctr. Opera League, Friends of UCLA Film Archive, U.S. Chess Fedn. Home and Office: 1845 Butler Ave Apt 112 Los Angeles CA 90025-5495 E-mail: lowell@peterson.net.

PETERSON, MARJORIE, former mayor; b. Chisholm, Minn., Aug. 16, 1924; d. Martin and Catherine Mihelich Champa; m. Andrew Levchak, July 6, 1946 (dec. Mar. 2, 1975); children: Carol, Andrea, Richard, Lisbeth; m. Walter C. Peterson, Sept. 25, 1976. Bookkeeper Ford Sales & Svc., Chisholm, Minn.; dental asst. Office of Dr. J.E. Hoffman, Chisholm, 1960—65; podiatrist asst. Office of Dr. Larson, Hibbing, Minn., 1967; divsn. sec. Fin. Programs, Hibbing, 1967—74; mem. city coun. City of Chisholm, 1977—85, ofcl., 1989—95, mayor, 1996—98. Mem. Pub. Utilities Bd., Chisholm. Contbr. poetry to anthologies. Pres. Range Assn. Sch. and City, Chisholm; chmn. Chisholm-Hibbing Airport Authority, Hibbing, 1991—2001; v.p. bd. dirs. Mus. Mining, 2002; mem. Friends of Libr.; bd. dirs. League Minn. Cities, St. Paul, 1984. Recipient C.C. Ludwig award, League Minn. Cities, 1984, Silver award, World of Poetry, 1990, Golden Poet award, 1998, Famous Poet, Famous Poet Soc., 2000. Mem.: Moose. Democrat. Roman Catholic. Achievements include being first woman elected to City Council in Chisholm, and first woman elected as mayor. Avocations: reading, volunteer work, travel, cards. Home: 405 7th St NW Chisholm MN 55719

PETERSON, MARK BRADLEY, lawyer; b. Mpls., Aug. 16, 1957; s. C. Donald and Gretchen Elaine (Palen) P.; m. Teresa Mahoney, 1990; children: Stephen James, John Donald, David Michael. BA magna cum laude, St. Olaf Coll., 1979; JD, U. Minn., 1982. Bar: Minn. 1982, U.S. Dist. Ct. Minn. 1983, U.S. Ct. Appeals (8th cir.) 1991, U.S. Supreme Ct. 1992. Law clk. Hennepin County Dist. Ct., Mpls., 1982-83, Meagher & Geer, Mpls., 1983—84; with Popham, Haik, Schnobrich & Kaufman, Ltd., Mpls., 1984—95; assoc. Plunkett, Schwartz, Peterson, P.A., 1995-2000; with Moss & Barnett, P.A., Mpls., 2000—; adjunct prof. William Mitchell Coll. Law, 1994-95. Deacon Christ Presbyn. Ch., Edina, Minn., 1988-91, elder, 1993-97; bd. dirs. Cystic Fibrosis Found., Mpls., 1991-96; mem. Minn. Internat. Ctr., Mpls.; bd. dirs. Hennepin County Vol. Lawyers Network, 1994-98; bd. dirs. Southdale YMCA, 1999-2002. Mem. ABA, Minn. Bar Assn., Hennepin County Bar Assn., Golden Key, Phi Beta Kappa. Avocations: skiing, sailing, golf. Office: Moss & Barnett PA 4800 Wells Fargo Ctr Minneapolis MN 55402-4129 Fax: (612) 339-6686. E-mail: Petersonm@moss-barnett.com.

PETERSON, MARK F. business educator; b. Phila., May 23, 1953; s. Eugene F. Jr. Peterson, June R. Peterson; m. Susan M. Mende; children: Janice M., Daniel F. BA, Duke U., 1975; PhD, U. Mich., 1979. Prof. mgmt. Tex. Tech. U., Lubbock, 1985—96; Internet Coast Adams prof. mgmt. Fla. Atlantic U., Boca Raton, 1996—. John R. Galvin vis. prof. Fletcher Sch. Law and Diplomacy, Tufts U., 2002—03. Editor: Handbook of Organizational Culture and Climate, 2001 (Outstanding Academic Title, ALA, 2001), Jour. Orgnl. Behaviors, 2001, Jour. Internat. Bus. Studies, 2004—. Presbyterian. Office: Fla Atlantic U Coll Bus Dept Mgmt Boca Raton FL 33431 Office Phone: 561-297-3669. Business E-Mail: mpeterso@fau.edu.

PETERSON, MARY L. state agency official; BA in English, Carleton Coll., 1972; MA in Tchg. in Edn. and English, Duke U., 1974; postgrad., U. Utah, 1977-80. Tchr. English, New Canaan (Conn.) Sch. Dist., from 1973, Brighton Ctrl. Sch. Dist., Rochester, N.Y., Davis County Sch. Dist., Kaysville, Utah, until 1977; rsch. asst. in cultural founds. and ednl. adminstrn. U. Utah, Salt Lake City, 1977-79; prin. St. Nicholas Elem. Sch., Rupert, Idaho, 1979-81; cons. Nev. Dept. Edn., Carson City, 1981-92, dep. supt. instrnl., rsch. and evaluative svcs., 1992-94, supt. pub. instrn., 1994—. Assessor Nev. Assessment Ctr., Nat. Assn. Secondary Sch. Prins.; mem. accreditation team N.W. Assn. Schs. and Colls.; trainer Tchr. Effectiveness for Student Achievement, Correlates Effective Schs.; facilitator Assisting Change in Edn.; mem. state team Nat. Coun. for Accreditation Tchr. Edn. Asst. editor: Work, Family and Careers (C. Brooklyn Derr), 1980; contbr. to profl. publs. Scholar Carleton Coll., Duke U. Mem. Phi Kappa Phi, Delta Kappa Gamma. Office: Nev Dept Edn Capitol Complex 700 E 5th St Carson City NV 89701-5096

PETERSON, MARY N. state representative, lawyer; b. Buffalo, Apr. 3, 1960; m. Barrett Peterson; 4 children. BA summa cum laude in Govt., St. Lawrence U., 1982; JD, Northwestern U., 1985. Atty.; state rep. State of Vt., 2003—. Chair Williston Selectboard, 2001—; mem. Taft Corners Task Force, Future Develop. Com., Williston Sch. Growth Planning Com.; past mem. Williston Planning Commn., Williston Conservation Commn., Colchester Planning Commn.; mem. Williston Fed. Ch. Mem.: Vt. League of Cities and Towns (bd. dirs.). Democrat. Avocations: skiing, canoeing, camping. Office: 2588 N Williston Rd Williston VT 05495 E-mail: marypeterson@adelphia.net.

PETERSON, MAX RUPERT, JR., chemist, researcher; b. Sampson County, N.C., May 26, 1945; s. Max Rupert Sr. and Mary Lily (Peterson) P.; m. Bonnie Fay Farrell, July 20, 1969; children: Karen Fay, Kathryn Hope. BS in Chemistry, Campbell U., 1966; PhD in Organic Chemistry, N.C. State U., 1971. Tchg. asst. N.C. State U., Raleigh, 1966-70, vis. assoc. prof., 1980-82; instr. Campbell U., Buies Creek, NC, 1970-71, asst. prof., 1971-75, assoc. prof., 1975-87; sr. rsch. chemist RTI Internat., Research Triangle Park, NC, 1987—. Cons. Natural Energy Rsch., Inc., Lillington, N.C., 1978-80, Geotech. Engring., Raleigh, 1975. Contbr. numerous articles to profl. jours. and ency., chpt. to book. Named Outstanding Educator in Am., Acad. Am. Educators, 1974-75. Mem. Am. Chem. Soc., Air and Waste Mgmt. Assn., Sigma Xi, Phi Kappa Phi. Baptist. Achievements include research in chemical method development for pollutants in environmental media, evaluation and validation studies related to measurement of pollutants in fine particles (PM2.5), stationary source emissions, ambient air, indoor air, hazardous and other wastes, and commercial formulations. Home: 116 Braintree Ct Cary NC 27513-3117 Office: Research Triangle Inst 3040 Cornwallis Rd PO Box 12194 Durham NC 27709-2194

PETERSON, MERRILL DANIEL, history educator; b. Manhattan, Kans., Mar. 31, 1921; s. William Oscar and Alice Dwinell (Merrill) P.; m. Jean Hymphrey, May 24, 1944 (dec. Nov. 1995); children: Jeffrey Ward, Kent Merrill. Student, Kans. State U., 1939-41; AB, U. Kans., 1943; PhD in History of Am. Civilization, Harvard U., 1950. Teaching fellow Harvard U., Cambridge, Mass., 1948-49; instr., then asst. prof. history Brandeis U., Waltham, Mass., 1949-55; asst. prof., bicentennial preceptor Princeton U., N.J., 1955-58; mem. faculty Brandeis U., Waltham, Mass., 1958-62, dean students, 1960-62; Thomas Jefferson Found. prof. U. Va., Charlottesville, 1962-87, prof. emeritus, 1987—, chmn. dept. history, 1966-72, dean faculty Arts and Scis., 1981-85; Mary Ball Washington prof. Am. History University Coll., Dublin, Ireland, 1988-89; vol. Peace Corps, Armenia, 1997. Scholar in residence Bellagio Study Ctr., 1974; faculty Salzburg Seminar in Am. Studies, 1975; Lamar lectr. Mercer U., 1975; Fleming lectr. La. State U., 1980; lectr. at 20 European univs., 40 Am. colls. and univs. Author: The Jefferson Image in the American Mind, 1960 (Bancroft prize, Gold medal Thomas Jefferson Meml. Found.), Major Crises in American History, 2 vols., 1962, Democracy, Liberty and Property: The State Constitutional Convention Debates of the 1820s, 1966, Thomas Jefferson and the New Nation: A Biography, 1970, James Madison: A Biography in His Own Words, 1974, Adams and Jefferson: A Revolutionary Dialogue, 1976, Olive Branch and Sword: The Compromise of 1833, 1982, The Great Triumvirate: Webster, Clay and Calhoun, 1987; editor: Thomas Jefferson: A Historical Profile, 1996, The Portable Thomas Jefferson, 1975, Thomas Jefferson Writings, 1984, Thomas Jefferson: A Reference Biography, 1986, The Virginia Statute for Religious Freedom: Its Evolution and Consequences in American History, 1988, Visitors to Monticello, 1989, Lincoln in American Memory, 1994 (History finalist, Pulitzer prize, PBK Book award U. Va.), Coming of Age with the New Republic, 1938-1950, 1999, The John Brown Legend Revisited, 1859-2000, 2002, Starving Armenians: America and the Armenian Genocide. 1915-1930 and After, 2004. Bd. dirs. Thomas Jefferson Found.; chmn. Thomas Jefferson Commemoration Commn., 1993-94. Guggenheim fellow, 1962-63, Ctr. for Advanced Study in Behavioral Scis. fellow, 1968-69, NEH and Nat. Humanities Ctr. fellow, 1980-81; recipient 20th Anniversary award Va. Found. for Humanities, 1994, Nat. First Freedom award First Freedom Coun., 1997. Fellow Am. Acad. Arts and Scis.; mem. Am. Hist. Assn., Am. Antiquarian Soc., Mass. Hist. Soc., Phi Beta Kappa. Home: 250 Pantops Mountain Rd Apt 6 Charlottesville VA 22911-8600 Office Phone: 434-972-2346.

PETERSON, MILLIE M. state senator; b. Merced, Calif., June 11, 1944; BS, U. Utah, 1979, MSW, 1984. Mem. Utah Senate, Dist. 12, Salt Lake City, 1991—. Susa Young Gates Award, 1998. Mem. NASW. Democrat. Address: 7131 W 3800 S West Valley City UT 84128-3416 Office: Senate House 319 State Capitol Salt Lake City UT 84114 E-mail: mpeter7131@aol.com.

PETERSON, NAD A. retired lawyer; b. Mt. Pleasant, Utah, 1926; m. Martha Peterson, 1948; children: Anne Carroll (Mrs. Stanford P. Darger, Jr.), Christian, Elizabeth (Mrs. Henry G. Ingersoll), Robert and Lane (twins). AB, George Washington U., 1950, JD, 1953. Bar: D.C. 1953, Calif. 1960, U.S. Supreme Ct. 1958. Law practice, Washington, 1953-60; sec., asst. gen. counsel Dart Industries, L.A., 1960-67; chief counsel Fluor Corp., 1967-73, gen. counsel, 1973-79, v.p. law, 1979-82, sr. v.p. law, 1983-84, sr. v.p., sec., 1984-93; sr. v.p., gen. counsel San Diego Gas & Electric Co., 1993-95. With USNR, PTO, 1944-46. Mem. ABA, Calif. Bar Assn., Phi Delta Phi. Home: PO Box 9101 Rancho Santa Fe CA 92067-4101

PETERSON, NANCY, special education educator; AS, Webster State Coll., 1963; BS in Elem. Edn. magna cum laude, Brigham Young U., 1964, MS in Ednl. Psychology, 1966, PhD in Ednl. Psychology, 1969. Instr. in tchr. edn. Brigham Young U., Provo, Utah, 1966-69; asst. prof. edn. dept. spl. edn. U. Kans., Lawrence, 1969-74, dir. spl. edn. classes for handicapped children Clin. Tng. Ctr., 1969-89, project dir. head start tng., 1973-74, coord. edn. univ. affiliated facility Clin. Tng. Ctr., 1969-74, coord. pers. tng. programs in mental retardation, 1973-76, assoc. prof. edn., 1974-88, project dir. pers. tng. programs, 1986-93, prof. edn. dept. spl. edn., 1988—, dept. chair, 1994—. Rsch. sci. Bur. Child Rsch., U. Kans., 1969—; prin. investigator for Kans. U. Kans. Early Childhood Rsch. Inst., 1977-82 Recipient J.E. Wallace Wallin award Internat. Coun. Exceptional Children, 1993. Office: U Kans Dept Spl Edn 3001 Dole Bldg Lawrence KS 66045-0001

PETERSON, OSCAR EMMANUEL, pianist; b. Montreal, Que., Can., Aug. 15, 1925; s. Daniel and Olivia (John) P. Studied with Paul deMarky; LLD (hon.), Carleton U., 1973, Queen's U., 1976, Concordia U., 1979, McMaster U., 1981, U. of Victoria, 1981, U. Toronto, 1985, U. B.C., 1994; DMus (hon.), Mount Alison, N.B., 1980, U. Laval, 1985; LittD (hon.), York U., 1982; D.F.A. (hon.), Northwestern U., Evanston, Ill., 1983, Niagara U., 1996; MusD (hon.), U. Laval, 1985. Founder Advanced Sch. Contemporary Music, Toronto; former chancellor York U., 1991-94. Chancellor emeritus York U., 1994, leader seminars, 1994—; composer, writer. Began music career on weekly radio show, then with Johny Holmes Orchestra, Can., 1944-49; recorded with RCA Victor Records; appeared with Jazz at the Philharmonic, Carnegie Hall, 1949; toured the U.S. and Europe, 1950—; leader trio with Ray Brown, Irving Ashby, later Barney Kessel, Herb Ellis, Ed Thigpen, Sam Jones, Louie Hayes, concert appearances with Ella Fitzgerald, Eng., Scotland, 1955; appeared Stratford (Ont.) Shakespeare Festival, Newport Jazz Festival; recorded and performed solo piano works, 1972—; toured USSR, 1974, recordings with Billie Holiday, Fred Astaire, Benny Carter, Count Basie, Roy Eldridge, Lester Young, Ella Fitzgerald, Niels-Henning Orsted Pederson, Dizzy Gillespie, Harry Edison, Clark Terry; composer: Canadiana Suite, Hymn to Freedom, Fields of Endless Day, City Lights, Begone Dull Care, (with Norman McLaren) salute to Johann Sebastian Bach, music for films Big North and Silent Partner; author: Jazz Exercises and Pieces: Oscar Peterson New Piano Solos; numerous TV specials. Decorated officer Order of Canada, 1972, companion, 1984; recipient award for piano Down Beat mag. 13 times, Metronome mag. award, 1953-54, Edison award, 1962, Award of merit City of Toronto, (1st mention) 1973 (2d mention 1983), Diplome d'honneur Can. Conf. of the Arts, 1975, Grammy award 7 times, Olympic Key to Montreal, The Queen's medal, 1977, Genie Film award for film score The Silent Partner, 1978, Grand-Prix du Disques for Night Child album, 1981, Canadian Band Festival Award, 1982, Juno Hall of Fame award, 1982, George Peabody medal Peabody Conservatory of Music, Balt., 1987, Volunteer award Roy Thompson Hall, Toronto, 1987, Can. Club Arts and Letters award, N.Y.C., 1987, Officer in Order of Arts and Letters, France, 1989, Chevalier Order of Que., 1991, Lifetime Achievement Toronto Arts Award, 1991, appointed Order of Ontario, 1992, Lifetime Achievement Gov. Gens. award, 1992, Glenn Gould prize,

1993, Gemini Film award, 1993, Three-Key award Bern Internat. Jazz Festival, 1995, NARAS Grammy award for Lifetime Achievement, 1997, Loyola medal, 1997, Carnegie Hall Anniversary medal, Charlie Parker bronze medal, Ville de Salon de Provence medal, Award of Thanks, Mexico City; 12-time jazz poll winner Playboy mag.; named number one (piano) Jazz and Pop, Readers Poll 1968, 85; named to U. Calif. at Berkeley Hall of Fame, 1983, Contemporary Keyboard Hall of Fame, 1983; Oscar Peterson Day proclaimed by Baltimore, Oreg., 1981, 83; Oscar Peterson Scholarship founded in his honor Berklee Sch. of Music, Boston, 1982. Avocations: fly fishing, photography, astronomy. Office: Regal Recs Ltd 2421 Hammond Rd Mississauga ON Canada L5K 1T3

PETERSON, OSLER LEOPOLD, lawyer; b. Mpls., Oct. 19, 1946; s. Osler Luther and Delores (Kealy) P.; m. Sandra Ann Freeto, Jan. 2, 1971 (div. Dec. 1983); m. Deborah Jean Bero, July 30, 1989. BA, Brown U., 1969; JD cum laude, Suffolk U., 1976. Bar: Mass. 1976, U.S. Dist. Ct. Mass. 1976. Pvt. practice, Newton, Mass., 1976-84; ptnr. Freeto, Peterson & Scoll, Newton, 1984—. Bd. dirs. Riverside Cmty. Care (formerly Neww Ctr., Inc.), 1976-96, clk., 1978-84, pres., 1984-89; bd. dirs. Lasell Coll. (formerly Lasell Jr. Coll.), 1983-97, 98—, clk., 1984-91; bd. dirs. Lasell Village, Inc., 1990—, chmn., 1992-2000; bd. mem. Medfield Zoning Bd. Appeals, 1993-2000;, Beth Israel Deaconess Hosp.-Needham Campus, 2001—; selectman Town of Medfield, 2000—, chair, 2002-03. Mem. ABA, ATLA, Mass. Bar Assn., Mass. Conveyancers Assn. Home: 10 Copperwood Rd Medfield MA 02052-1034 Office: Freeto Peterson & Scoll 580 Washington St Newton MA 02458-1416 also: 66 North St PO Box 358 Medfield MA 02052-0358 Office Phone: 617-969-1500., 508-359-9190. E-mail: osler.peterson@verizon.net.

PETERSON, PAMELA CARMELLE, English language educator; b. Bakersfield, Calif., Sept. 24, 1954; d. Bob Eugene and Carmelita Denyse (Coodey) York; m. Robert Leroy Peterson, Feb. 9, 1979; children: Aimee, Sara, Matthew, Hannah. AA, Bakersfield Coll., 1992; BA in History, Calif. State U., Bakersfield, 1994. Exec. adminstr. Kern Bldg. Materials, Bakersfield, 1973-95; prin. Rosewall Christian Acad., Bakersfield, 1994 ; prin., tchr. Dynasty Christian Schs., Bakersfield, 1995-97; instr. ESL Calif. State U., Bakersfield, 1997—; instr. English Santa Barbara (Calif.) Bus. Coll., 1998—. Pres. bd. Dynasty Christian Schs., 1995; exec. sec. bd. dirs. Kern Bldg. Materials, 1983-95. Mem. Assn. Christian Schs., Inc., Assn. Christian Sch. Adminstrs., Phi Alpha Theta (sec. 1994-95, v.p. 1995-96). Avocations: history, reading, needlecrafts, gardening, baking. Home: 6309 Juniper Rd Lake Isabella CA 93240-2529 Office: Rosewail Christian Acad 7850 White Ln # E149 Bakersfield CA 93309-7689 Office Phone: 760-549-0098. E-mail: rcateach@aol.com.

PETERSON, PATTY, radio personality; d. Willie and Jeanne Arland Peterson; m. Stuart Paster; 4 children. Radio show host Sta. WCCO Radio, Mpls., 1997—. Singer: (albums) The More I See You. Recipient 7 time Minn. Music award winner for Best Female Vocalist and Best Group. Office: WCCO 625 2nd Ave S Minneapolis MN 55402 Mailing: PO Box 390697 Minneapolis MN 55439-0697

PETERSON, PETER G. investment company executive; b. Kearney, Nebr., June 5, 1926; s. George and Venetia P.; m. Sally H., May 1953 (div. 1979); children: John, Jim, David, Holly, Michael; m. Joan Ganz Cooney, Apr. 26, 1980. BS, Northwestern U., 1947; MBA, U.Chgo., 1951; PhD (hon.), Colgate U., George Washington U., Northwestern U., Georgetown U., U. Rochester, New School U., Southampton Coll. at L.I. Exec. v.p. Market Facts, Chgo., 1948-52; v.p. McCann Erickson, Chgo., 1952-58; pres. Bell and Howell, Chgo., 1961—63, exec. v.p., 1961—63, chmn. & CEO, 1963-71; asst. to Pres. of US for Internat. Econ. Affairs Washington, 1961-63; sec. of commerce US Govt., 1972-73; CEO, chmn. bd. Lehman Bros. and Lehman Bros., Kuhn, Loeb, Inc., NYC, 1973-84; chmn. & co-found. The Blackstone Group, 1985—. Chmn. Fed. Res. Bank NY, 1999-2003; founding pres. The Concord Coalition co-chmn, The Conf. Bd. Comm. on Publ. Trust and Pvt. Enterprise. Author: Running on Empty: How the Democratic and Republican Parties Are Bankrupting Our Future and What Americans Can Do About It, Gray Dawn: How the Coming Age Wave Will Transform America--and the World, Will America Grow Up Before it Grows Old, Facing Up: How to Rescue the Economy from Crushing Debt and Restore the American Dream; editor: Readings in Market Organization and Price Policies; co-author: On Borrowed Time: How The Growth In Entitlement Spending Threatens America's Future. Founding mem. Bi-Partisan Budget Appeal; pres. The Concord Coalition; trustee Commn. for Econ. Devel., Mus. Modern Art, NYC; bd. dir. Pub. Agenda. Recipient Outstanding Service award Phoenix House, NYC, 1976, Stephen Wise award Am. Jewish Congress, 1981, U. Chgo. Alumni medal, 1983, Man of Vision award, 1994, Nebraskalander award, 1994, Harvard Bus. Sch. Leadership award, 2004, Coro N.Y. Leadership award, 2004; named to Pres. Clinton's Bi-Partisan Comm. on Entitlement Reform, 1994. Mem. Coun. on Fgn. Rels. (chmn. bd. 1985—), Inst. Internat. Econ. (chmn. bd 1980), Nat. Bur. Econ. Rsch. (trustee), Japan Soc., Blind Brook Club (Purchase, NY), Deepdale Club (Manhasset, NY), Maidstone Club (Easthampton, NY), Chgo. Club, River Club, Links, Augusta Nat. Club, Friar's Head Golf Club (Riverhead, NY), Burning Tree (Washington), Quail Valley Golf Club, Atlantic Club, Windsor Club. Republican. Home: 435 E 52nd St Apt 11G New York NY 10022-6445 Office: The Blackstone Group 345 Park Ave Ste 3101 New York NY 10154-0004

PETERSON, PHILLIP KEITH, physician, clinical investigator; b. Chgo., Feb. 10, 1943; s. Frank Martin and Ann dorothea (Engwall) P.; m. Karin Enette Sundquist, June 3, 1967; children: Kirstin, Per. BA, St. Olaf Coll., 1965; MD, Columbia U., 1970. Asst. prof. medicine U. Minn., Mpls., 1977-80, assoc. prof., 1980-85, prof., 1986—, dir. internat. med. edn. and rsch. program, 1998—; dir. infectious diseases Hennepin County Med. Ctr., Mpls., 1984—; dir. Inst. on Brain and Immune Disorders Mpls. Med. Rsch. Found., Mpls., 1998—; dir. divsn. infectious diseases and internat. medicine, dept., medicine U. Minn. Med. Sch., 2002—. Editor Internat. Jour. Antimicrobial Agts., 1993-99; author med. textbooks; contbr. articles to profl. jours. Grantee NIH, 1986—. Mem. Mpls. Med. Rsch. Found. (pres. 1995-00), Internat. Immunocos. Host Soc. (past pres.). Avocations: travel, angling, hiking, reading, gardening. Home: 4822 Russell Ave S Minneapolis MN 55410-1913 Office: Hennepin County Med Ctr Dept Medicine 701 Park Ave Dept Medicine Minneapolis MN 55415-1623 Office Phone: 612-873-2877. E-mail: peter137@umn.edu.

PETERSON, RALPH RANDALL, engineering executive; b. Hayti, Mo., Oct. 12, 1944; s. James Tony and Helen Irene (Webb) P.; m. Betty Shoemaker, Nov. 7, 1964; children: Jamie Marie Jones, Jeffrey Scott. BSCE, Oreg. State U., 1969; MS in Environ. Engring., Stanford U., 1970; AMP in Bus., Harvard U., 1991. Registered profl. engr., Oreg., Wash., Colo. Engring. aide Johnson, Underkofler & Briggs, Boise, Idaho, 1962—63; surveyor Smith, Keyes, & Blakely, Caldwell, Idaho, 1963—64; with Chronic & Assocs., Boise, Idaho, 1964—65; various project devel. and dept. mng. roles CH2M Hill Cos., Corvallis, Oreg., 1965-78, v.p. indsl. process divsn., 1978-87, sr. v.p., tech. dir. Denver, 1987-90, CEO, 1990—. Bd. dirs. Std. Ins. Co., Portland, Oreg.; bd. advisors Constrn. Industry Pres. Forum, Washington, 1994—; co-chair Nat. Congress Advancement of Minorities in Environ. Professions, Atlanta, 1993-94; industry co-chair tech. for sustainable future White House Office Sci. and Tech. Policy, 1995-96. Bd. dirs. Stapleton Devel. Corp., Denver, 1994—, World Trade Ctr., Denver, 1990—; corp. patron Smithsonian Instn. Corp. Patron. Recipient Colo. Gov.'s award for internat. trade devel., 1995. Mem. ASCE, Am. Water Works Assn., Water Environment Fedn., Colo. Environ. Bus. Assn. (co-chair 1993—), Oreg. State U. Alumni Assn. (bd. dirs. 1992—). Avocations: skiing, camping, fishing, performing arts. Office: CH2M Hill 9191 S Jamaica St Englewood CO 80112

PETERSON, RANDALL THEODORE, law educator, law librarian; b. Sioux City, Iowa, Aug. 27, 1944; s. Theodore Melvin and Ilean Grace (Wendrich) Peterson; m. Judith Ashcroft, Aug. 24, 1967; children: Kristen, Randall, Heidi, Travis, Robert, Quinn. Student, Dixie Coll., 1962—63; BS, Brigham Young U., Provo, Utah, 1968, MLS, 1974; JD, U. Utah, 1972. Asst. law libr. Brigham Young U., Provo, Utah, 1972—74, assoc. law libr., 1974—77; asst. prof. law and dir. libr. svcs. John Marshall Law Sch., Chgo., 1977—86, assoc. prof. law and dir. libr. svcs., 1986—90, assoc. prof. law, 1990—. Mem.: ABA. Mem. LDS Ch. Office: John Marshall Law Sch 315 S Plymouth Ct Chicago IL 60604-3968 E-mail: 7rtp@jmls.edu.

PETERSON, RICHARD HERMANN, retired history educator; b. Berkeley, Calif., Jan. 16, 1942; s. William Martin and Dorothy Jeane (Heyne) P.; m. Nora Ann Lorenzo, June 21, 1970; 1 child, Nina Elizabeth. AB, U. Calif., Berkeley, 1963; MA, San Francisco State U., 1966; PhD, U. Calif., Davis, 1971. Calif. community coll. teaching credential. Asst. prof. history Ind. U., Kokomo, 1971-76; instr. social studies Coll. of Redwoods, Ft. Bragg, Calif., 1976-78; assoc. prof. history San Diego State U., 1978-82, prof. history, 1982-96, prof. emeritus, 1996—; freelance writer, 1996—. Author: Manifest Destiny in the Mines, 1975, The Bonanza Kings, 1977, 91, Bonanza Rich, 1991; book rev. editor Jour. of San Diego History, 1978-82, editl. cons., 1980-82; contbr. articles to profl. jours., book revs., websites, newspapers. Judge for papers Internat. History Fair, San Diego, Tijuana, Mex., 1983-88. Faculty Summer fellow Ind. U., 1975, 76, San Diego State U., 1980, Meritorious Performance and Prof. Promise award, 1989; rsch. grantee Sourisseau Acad., 1977, Am. Assn. State/Local History, 1988, 1st Pl. award in History Poetry Contest, Distant Frontier Press, 2001, 2d Pl. award Showcase Writers Contest, San Diego, 2003; named Golden Poet of Yr., World of Poetry, 1987-89. Mem. Mining History Assn., Calif. Hist. Soc., Western History Assn. Avocations: golf, gardening, poetry, travel. Home: 7956 Lake Adlon Dr San Diego CA 92119-3117 Office Phone: 619-464-7935.

PETERSON, RICHARD WILLIAM, retired judge, lawyer; b. Council Bluffs, Iowa, Sept. 29, 1925; s. Henry K. and Laura May (Robinson) P.; m. Patricia Mae Fox, Aug. 14, 1949; children: Katherine Ilene Peterson Sherbondy, Jon Eric, Timothy Richard. BA, U. Iowa, 1949, JD with distinction, 1951; postgrad., U. Nebr.-Omaha, 1972-80, 86. Bar: Iowa 1951, U.S. Dist. Ct. (so. dist.) Iowa 1951, U.S. Supreme Ct. 1991, U.S. Ct. Appeals (8th cir.) 1997. Pvt. practice law, Council Bluffs, 1951—; U.S. commr. U.S. Dist. Ct. (so. dist.) Iowa, 1958-70. U.S. magistrate judge U.S. Dist. Ct. (so. dist.) Iowa, 1970-99; nat. faculty Fed. Jud. Ctr., Washington, 1972-82; emeritus trustee Children's Square, U.S.A.; verifying ofcl. Internat. Prisoner Transfer Treaties, Mexico City, 1977, La Paz, Bolivia, 1980-81, Lima, Peru, 1981. Author: The Court Moves West: A Study of the United States Supreme Court Decision of Appeals from the United States Circuit and District Court of Iowa, 1846-1882, 1988, West of the Nishnabotna: The Experiences of Forty Years of a Part-Time Judicial Officer as United States Commissioner, Magistrate and Magistrate Judge, 1958-1998, 1998; co-author: (with George Mills) No One is Above the Law: The Story of Southern Iowa's Federal Court, 1994; contbr. articles to legal publs. Bd. dirs. Pottawattamie County (Iowa) chpt. ARC, state fund chmn., 1957-58; state chmn. Radio Free Europe, 1960-61; dist. chmn. Trailblazer dist. Boy Scouts Am., 1952-55; mem. exec. coun. Mid-Am. Coun., 1976—. With inf. U.S. Army, 1943-46. Decorated Purple Heart, Bronze Star; named Outstanding Young Man Council Bluffs C. of C., 1959 Fellow Am. Bar Found. (life); mem. ABA, Am. Judicature Soc., Iowa Bar Assn. (chmn. com. fed. practice 1978-80, probate and trust coun. and sect. 1997—, Disting. Cmty. award 2004), Pottawattamie County Bar Assn. (pres. 1979-80), Fed. Bar Assn., Inter-Am. Bar Assn., Supreme Ct. Hist. Soc., Fed. Magistrate Judges Assn. (pres. 1978-79), Iowa Conf. Bar Assn. (pres. 1985-87), Hist. Soc. of U.S. Cts. Eighth Jud. Cir. (pres. 1989-99, ct. historian U.S. Dist. Ct. S.D. and Iowa 2000-), Kiwanis (pres. Council Bluffs chpt. 1957), Masons, Phi Delta Phi, Delta Sigma Rho, Omicron Delta Kappa. Republican. Lutheran. Home: 1007 Arbor Ridge Cir Council Bluffs IA 51503-5000 Office: PO Box 248 25 Main Pl Ste 200 Council Bluffs IA 51503-0790

PETERSON, ROBERT ALLEN, marketing educator; b. N.Y.C., Mar. 25, 1944; s. Robert A. and Carrol D. (Collins) P.; m. Diane S. Femrite, June 18, 1966; children: Jeffrey, Jennifer, Matthew. BS, U. Minn., 1966, MS, 1968, PhD, 1970. Asst. prof. mktg. U. Tex., Austin, 1970-73, assoc. prof., 1973-77, prof., 1977—, John T. Stuart chair, 1985—, chmn. dept. mktg. adminstrn., 1983-85, assoc. dean for rsch., 2002—04. Prin. Group Seven Assocs., Austin Author: Marketing Research, 1982, 2d edit., 1988; co-author: Modern American Capitalism, 1990, Strategic Marketing, 10th edit., 2004; editor: Jour. Mktg. Rsch., 1985-88, Jour. Acad. Mktg. Sci., 1991-94; mem. editorial bd. Jour. Mktg., Internat. Mktg. Rev. Recipient rsch. award AMA, 1988, Charles Hurwitz fellow, 1983—. Fellow Southwestern Mktg. Assn. (pres. 1977-78), Am. Mktg. Assn. (v.p. 1980-81), Acad. Mktg. Sci. (bd. govs. 1982-86, chmn. 1994-98, pres. 2000-02), Am. Inst. Decision Scis. (dir. 1974-75). Lutheran. Office: Univ Texas Dept Mktg Austin TX 78712

PETERSON, ROBERT AUSTIN, manufacturing company executive retired; b. Sioux City, Iowa, July 5, 1925; s. Austen W. and Marie (Mueller) P.; m. Carol May Hudy, May 17, 1952; children: Roberta, Richard., Bruce. BS, U. Minn., 1946, BBA, 1947. Credit mgr. New Holland Machine div. Sperry Rand Corp., Mpls., 1952-61; from credit mgr. to treas. Toro Co., Mpls., 1961-70, v.p., treas. internat. fin., 1970-83; v.p. fin., pres. Toro Credit Co., 1983-93. Chmn. Prior Lake Spring Lake Watershed Dist., 1970-80; chmn., bd. dirs. Prior Lake Bd. Edn., 1965-71; chmn. Scott County Republican Party, 1969-70; bd. dirs. Scott Carver Mental Health Center, 1969-73, Minn. Watershed Assn., 1972-76. Served to ensign USNR, 1943-46. Mem. Prior Lake Yacht Club (bd. dirs.).

PETERSON, ROBERT B. petroleum company executive; b. Regina, Sask., Can. BSc in Chem. Engring., Queen's U., Kingston, Ont., Can., 1959, MSc in Chem. Engring., 1961. Various prodn. positions Imperial Oil Ltd. and affiliates, Can. and U.S., 1960-81, dir., 1984, COO, 1985; pres. and dir. Esso Resources, Calgary, Alta., Can., 1981, dir., pres. & CEO, 1982; exec. v.p., COO Imperial Oil Ltd., Toronto, 1988-92, chmn., 1988-92, chmn., CEO, pres., 1994—. Bd. dirs. Royal Bank Can., C.D. Howe Inst., Bus. Coun. Nat. Issues. Gov. Jr. Achievement Can., Can. Olympic Found.; past chmn. The Conf. Bd. Can. Mem. Assn. Profl. Engrs. Geologists and Geophysicists of Alta. Office: Imperial Oil Ltd 111 St Clair Ave W Toronto ON Canada M5W 1K3

PETERSON, ROBERT L. meat processing executive; b. Nebr., July 14, 1932; married; children: Mark R., Susan P. Student, U. Nebr., 1950. With Wilson & Co., Jim Boyle Order Buying Co.; cattle buyer R&C Packing Co., 1956—61; cattle buyer, plant mgr., v.p. carcass prodn. Iowa Beef Processors, 1961—69; exec. v.p. ops. Spencer Foods, 1969—71; founder, pres., chmn., CEO Madison (Nebr.) Foods, 1971—76; group v.p. carcass divsn. Iowa Beef Processors, Inc. (name now IBP, Inc.), Dakota City, Nebr., 1976—77, pres., COO, 1977—80, CEO, 1980—81, co-chmn. bd. dirs., 1981—82, CEO, CFO, 1980—, chmn., CEO. Served with Q.M.C. U.S. Army, 1952—54. Mem.: Sioux City Country Club. Office: IBP Inc 800 Stevens Port Dr Dakota Dunes SD 57049-5005

PETERSON, ROBERT SCOTT, electrical engineer; b. McKeesport, Pa., Mar. 24, 1930; s. William James and Emma Elizabeth (Scott) P.; m. Betty Louise Oleska, Aug. 11, 1962 (dec. 1995). BSEE, Pa. State U., 1952; MSEE, U. Pitts., 1961. Lic. prof. engr., Pa. Sr. application, design engr. Westinghouse Elec., Pitts., 1952-63, devel. engr. Buffalo, 1963-85, Pitts., 1985-89, AEG Automation Corp., Pitts., 1989-94; cons. engr. CDI-Ctrl. Corp., Pitts., 1994—. Holder 30 U.S. patents. Coach Midget Football League, McKeesport, 1953-55. With U.S. Army, 1955-57. Mem. IEEE, N.Y. Acad. Scis., Assn. Iron Steel Engrs. Achievements include patents in field. Avocations: gardening, woodworking, painting, dance, sports. Home and Office: 719 Heathergate Dr Pittsburgh PA 15238-1000 Office Phone: 412-767-4690.

PETERSON, ROBIN TUCKER, marketing educator; b. Casper, Wyo., July 31, 1937; s. Walfred Arthur and Mary Lurene Peterson; m. Marjorie K. Greenwald, June 25, 1963; children: Timothy, Kimberly. BS, U. Wyo., 1959, MS in Bus., 1961; PhD, U. Wash., 1967. Mem. faculty Idaho State U., Pocatello, 1963-73; prof. mktg., head mktg. dept. St. Cloud (Minn.) State U., 1973-76, N.Mex. State U., Las Cruces, 1976—. Fulbright lectr., Yugoslavia, 1973; vis. scholar Ea. Mont. State Coll., 1985; Sunwest Fin. Svcs. Disting. Centennial prof. N.Mex. State U., 1991, 92; Norwest Disting. prof. N.Mex. State U., 1999, Wells Fargo Disting. prof., 2002; vis. lectr. Nirma Inst. Ahmedabad, India, 1999, Chiang Moi U., Thailand, 2000; Fulbright lectr. Kathmandu U., Nepal, 2001. Author: Marketing-A Contemporary Introduction, 1976, Forecasting, 1976, edit., 1983, Personal Selling, 1977, Marketing in Action, 1977, Lernbook Marketing, 1984, Marketing: Concepts and Decision Making, 1987, Principles of Marketing, 1989, Argentina, 1990, Managing the Distributor Sales Network, 1990, Business Forecasting, 1992, Getting New Products to Market Rapidly, 1994; exec. editor Bus. Forecaster, 1993-94; editor Jour. Bus. and Entrepreneurship, 1994-98; contbr. articles to profl. publs. Served with USAR, 1962-63. Fellow Assn. Small Bus. Entrepreneurship; mem. Am. Mktg. Assn., Sales and Mktg. Execs. Internat., Acad. Mktg. Sci. (pres. 1977-78, 80-82), Am. Arbitration Assn. (Outstanding Educators Am. award), S.W. Small Bus. Assn. (pres. 1983-84, Outstanding Mktg. Educators award, Outstanding Educator, Assn. of Small Bus., 2002), S.W. Mktg. Assn., Western Mktg. Educators, Las Cruces C. of C., Las Cruces Sales and Mktg. Club, Beta Gamma Sigma, Phi Kappa Psi, Alpha Kappa Psi, Alpha Mu Alpha. Republican. Presbyterian. Home: 4350 Diamondback Dr Las Cruces NM 88011-7539 Office: NMex State U PO Box 5280 Las Cruces NM 88003-5280 Office Phone: 505-646-5748. Business E-Mail: ropeters@nmsu.edu.

PETERSON, ROBYN GAYLE, museum curator; b. San Francisco, Jan. 17, 1958; BA, UCLA, 1979; MA, U. Wis., 1982, PhD, 1987. Goldsmith, 1974-80; collections acquisition asst. social studies bibliographer Meml. Libr./U. Wis., 1984-86; curator of collections The Rockwell Mus., Corning, N.Y., 1988-99; dir. collections and rsch. Turtle Bay Exploration Park, Redding, Calif., 1999—. Author: American Frontier Photography, 1993, Edward Borein, 1997, Warp and Weft: Cross-cultural Exchange in Navajo Weavings, 1997, Transforming Trash: Bay Area Fiber Art, 2000; contbg. author: Allgemeines Künstlerlexikon, 1998—; editor/contbr.: Collector's Choice Review: Masterpieces of Glassmaking; Frederick Carder and the Steuben Glass Works, 1993, Brilliance in Glass: The Lost Wax Glass Sculpture of Frederick Carder, 1993, Journey to Justice: The Wintu People and the Salmon, 2002, The Other Side of the Looking Glass: The Glass Body and Its Metaphors, 2003, Bug-Eyed: Art, Culture, Insects, 2004; mng. editor: Frederick Carder and Steuben Glass: American Classics (Thomas P. Dimitroff), 1998; contbr. articles to profl. jours.; peer reviewer IMLS. Mem. Coll. Art Assn., Soc. Advancement of Scandinavian Studies, Glass Art Soc., Am. Assn. Mus. Office: Turtle Bay Exploraton Park PO Box 992360 Redding CA 96099-2360 E-mail: rpeterson@turtlebay.org.

PETERSON, RODNEY DELOS, retired mediator, economist; b. Sioux Falls, S.D., Nov. 10, 1932; s. Severin Ingvald and Vera (Blow) P.; m. Evelyn Koubsky, Dec. 26, 1965; children: Douglas, Russell, Stuart. BA, Huron (S.D.) Coll., 1958; MS in Econs, S.D. State U., 1959; PhD in Econs. and Bus. Orgn, U. Nebr., 1964; JD, U. Denver, 1982. Instr. U. Nebr., Lincoln, 1959-64, vis. asst. prof. agrl. econs., summers 1964-66; instr. adult edn. U. Omaha, part-time 1963-64; asst. prof. econs. Cen. Wash. State U., Ellensburg, 1964-65; asst. prof., then assoc. prof. U. Idaho, Moscow, 1965-68; mem. faculty Colo. State U., Ft. Collins, 1968-91, prof. econs., 1971-91, mediation officer, 1985-91, prof. emeritus, 1991; economist Fla. Dept. Commerce, 1991-96, Fla. Dept. Labor, 1996-98; dir. Ctr. Econ. Edn. Colo. State U., 1976-77. Vis. prof. Simon Fraser U., Vancouver, B.C., Can., 1974-75. Author: Student Guide to Accompany Our Changing Economy, 1976, Economic Organization in Medical Equipment and Supply, 1973, Political Economy & American Capitalism, 1991; contbr. numerous articles to profl. jours. NSF fellow, summers 1971, 73, expert witness personal injury and antitrust cases. Mem. Am. Econ. Assn., Midwest Econs. Assn., Sigma Xi, Delta Sigma Pi, Beta Gamma Sigma, Omicron Delta Epsilon (regional dir. 1975-76) Home: 8479 Manderston Ct Fort Myers FL 33912-6613

PETERSON, ROGER, community bank executive, retired international investment banker, retired manufacturing executive, retired Air Force officer; b. Chgo., June 7, 1929; s. Milton Albert and LaVergne Geraldine (Andelin) P.; m. Sally Ann Alder, Apr. 25, 1952; children: Bruce Roger, Dale Alder, Drew Alan. BS in Acctg., UCLA, 1955; MS in Mgmt., U. Colo., 1964; grad., Air Command and Staff Coll. Air U., Ala., 1965; grad. Exec. Program for Internat. and Nat. Security, J.F. Kennedy Sch. Govt., Harvard U., 1983. Joined USAF, 1955, advanced through grades to maj. gen., 1981, pilot, 1956-61, mgr. tactical missile site constrn., 1961; air officer comdg. 11th Cadet Squadron, Air Force Cadet Wing USAF Acad., 1961-64; asst. sec. Joint Chiefs of Staff and NSC matters for Hdqrs. Pentagon, 1965-68; transport pilot USAF, Vietnam, 1968, asst. chmn. U.S.-Japan Joint Com., Adminstrn. of Status of Forces Agreement, 1968-73, chief program cost, dir. budget, 1973-76, chief plans, comptroller of Air Force, 1976-78, dir. mgmt. analysis, 1978-79, dir. programs, asst. chief of staff for research and devel., 1979-81; asst. dir. plans, policies and programs Def. Logistics Agy., Alexandria, Va., 1981-82, dep. dir., 1982-83; asst. dep. chief staff for logistics and engring. Hdqrs. USAF, Washington, 1983-84; pres., chief exec. officer advanced tech. factory, 1984-85; strategic planner United Techs. Corp., 1985-88; v.p., chief oper. officer Sikorsky Support Svcs. Inc., 1988-90; exec. asst. to mng. ptnr. O'Connor & Assocs., 1990-92; mng. dir. global ops. and svcs. Swiss Bank Corp., Zurich, 1992-96, chief of staff Chgo., 1996-99, br. mgr. Chgo., 1996-99; mng. dir. UBS A.G. (formerly Swiss Bank Corp.), NY, 1996-99, UBS AG, N.Y.C., 1999—2001; mng. dir. mktg. and strategic planning SunSouth Bank, Dothan, Ala., 2002—. Decorated D.S.M., Legion of Merit, Air medal with oak leaf cluster, Joint Service Commendation medal, Air Force Commendation medal with two oak leaf clusters Mem. Air Force Assn., Beta Gamma Sigma, Sigma Iota Epsilon Presbyterian. Achievements include designing and negotiating consolidation of U.S. Air Force bases in Tokyo, 1970-73; negotiating mil. and civil aviation agreement for return of Okinawa to Japan; created global bus. mgmt. system for Swiss Bank Corp. Home: 1602 Deerpath Rd Dothan AL 36303-2173 Office: SunSouth Bank 108 Jamestown Blvd Dothan AL 36302 *Always with honor.*

PETERSON, RONALD R. health service administrator; b. New Brunswick, NJ, 1948; m. Elizabeth Rooney; children: Joey, Susie. MA in Hosp. Adminstrn., Johns Hopkins U., Balt., 1970. Adminstrv. resident Johns Hopkins U., Balt., 1973, adminstr. Henry Phipps Psychiatric Clinic, 1974, adminstr. cost improvement program, 1975, adminstr. Children's Ctr., 1978, adminstr. Balt. City Hosps., 1982, exec. v.p., COO Johns Hopkins Health Sys., 1995, acting pres. Hopkins Hosp. and Health Sys., 1996, pres., John Hopkins Health Sys., 1997—. Mem. bus. adv. coun., Balt.; vol. ARC, United Way, Am. Heart Assn. Mem. Md. Hosp. Assn. (mem. exec. com.), Md. C. of C. Office: Johns Hopkins Hosp 600 N Wolfe St Baltimore MD 21287-0005 also: Johns Hopkins U 720 Rutland Ave Baltimore MD 21205-2109*

PETERSON, RONALD ROGER, lawyer; b. Chgo., July 27, 1948; married; children: Elizabeth G., Ronald W. AB, Ripon, 1970; JD, U. Chgo., 1973. Bar: Ill. 1974, U.S. Dist. Ct. (no. dist.) Ill. 1974, U.S. Ct. Appeals (7th cir.) 1974, U.S. Dist. Ct. (ea. dist.) Wis. 1975, U.S. Dist. Ct. (no. dist.) Ind. 1978, U.S. Dist. Ct. (cen. dist.) Ill. 1980, U.S. Dist. Ct. (we. dist.) Mich. 1999, U.S. Ct. Appeals (8th cir.) 1984, U.S. Ct. Appeals (6th cir.) 1990, U.S. Ct. Appeals (9th cir.) 1996, U.S. Ct. Appeals (3rd cir.) 2001. Ptnr. Jenner & Block, Chgo., 1974—; commd. 2d lt. U.S. Army, 1968, advanced through grades to 1st lt., 1973, ret., 1978, with mil. intelligence, 1968-78. Mem. ABA, Chgo. Bar Assn., Internat. Soc. Insolvency Practitioners, Comml. Law League, Am. Bankruptcy Inst., Am. Coll. Bankruptcy Lawyers, U.S. Supreme Ct. Hist. Soc. Avocation: skiing. Office: Jenner & Block 1 E Ibm Plz Fl 4000 Chicago IL 60611-7603 Office Phone: 312-923-2981. Business E-Mail: rpeterson@jenner.com.

PETERSON, ROY MARTIN, JR., environmental scientist; b. Inglewood, Calif., May 14, 1947; s. Roy Martin and Peggy (Rowett) Peterson. BA in Biology and Environ. Studies, U. of Calif., Santa Cruz, 1971; MS in Zoology (Ecology), U. of Ill., 1974; PhD in Ecology (Physiol.), U. of Calif., Davis, 1988. Rsch. assoc. U. of Calif., Davis, 1975—84; postdoctorate U. of Oxford, England, 1988—89; assoc. in agr. expt. sta., postgrad. rschr. U. of Calif., Davis, 1989—90, postgrad. rschr., 1990—91; environ. scientist Calif. Dept. of Water Resources, Sacramento, 1992—. Contbr. articles to profl. jours. Sunday sch. tchr. St Martin Episcopal Ch., Davis, Calif., 1996—2000; bd. dirs. No. Calif. chpt. Retinitus Pigmentosa Nat. Found., Sacramento, 1979—80. Mem.: AAAS, Sigma Xi. Episcopalian. Avocations: gemstone lapidary, photography.

Home: 2808 Mallorca Ln Davis CA 95616 Office: Calif Dept Water Resources 1725 23rd St Ste 220 Sacramento CA 95816 Office Phone: 916-445-6153. Personal E-mail: rmpeterson3@sbcglobal.net. E-mail: rpeterso@water.ca.gov.

PETERSON, RUSSELL WILBUR, former association executive, former state governor; b. Portage, Wis., Oct. 3, 1916; s. John Anton and Emma (Anthony) P.; m. E. Lillian Turner, June 30, 1937 (dec. Apr. 28, 1994); children: Russell Glen, Peter Jon, Kristin, Elin; m. June B. Jenkins, Oct. 21, 1995. BS, U. Wis., 1938, PhD, 1942, LL.D. (hon.), 1984; D.Sc. (hon.), Williams Coll., 1975, Butler U.; DSc (hon.), Springfield Coll., Stevens Inst. Tech., 1979, Gettysburg Coll., 1980, Alma Coll., 1981, Ohio State U.; D.Sc. (hon.), SUNY-Syracuse; DSc (hon.), Northland Coll., Fairleigh Dickinson U., 1981; LLD (hon.), Monmouth Coll., 1982, Salisbury State U., 1988; LHD, Meadville-Lombard Theol. Sch., 1992; DHL, Colby-Sawyer Coll., 2000. With E. I. DuPont de Nemours & Co., Inc., 1942-69, rsch. dir. textile fibers dept., 1954-55, 56-59, merchandising mgr. textile fibers, 1955-56, dir. new products divsn. textile fibers, 1959-62, dir. R & D divsn. devel. dept., 1963-69; chmn. exec. com. Textile Research Inst., Princeton, N.J., 1959-61, chmn. bd. dirs., 1961-63, fellow, 1969; gov. State of Del., 1969—73; chmn. exec. com. Nat. Commn. Critical Choices for Am., 1973; chmn. U.S. Council on Environ. Quality, 1973-76; pres. Nat. Audubon Soc., 1979-85; mem. Nat. Commn. Critical Choices for Am., 1973-74; dir. Office Tech. Assessment, U.S. Congress, 1978-79. Pres. New Directions, 1976-77; regional v.p. Nat. Mcpl. League, 1968-78; chmn. Edn. Commn. States, 1970; chmn. com. nuclear energy and space tech. So. Govs. Conf., 1970-71; chmn. Nat. Adv. Commn. on Criminal Justice Standards and Goals, 1971-73; chmn. com. law enforcement, justice and pub. safety Nat. Govs. Conf., 1970-73; v.p. Council State Govts., 1970-71; chmn. adv. bd. Solar Energy Research Inst., 1979-83; vis prof. Dartmouth Coll., 1985, Carleton Coll., 1986, U. Wis., Madison, 1987; chmn. Centennial Internat. Symposium, Nat. Geog. Soc., 1986-88. Author: Oral History, Russell W. Peterson, 1995, Rebel with a Conscience, 1999, Delaware Heritage Series, 1999, Patriots, Stand Up!, 2004, (CD) We Can Save the Earth, 2000; contbr. articles to profl. jours. Chmn. Del. River Basin Commn., 1971-72; founding chmn. Bio-Energy Coun., 1976-78; bd. dirs. World Wildlife Fund, 1976-82, Population Action Internat., 1973-97, Alliance to Save Energy, 1979-93, Global Tomorrow Coalition, 1981-91, chmn., 1981-87; regional councillor Internat. Union Conservation Nature and Natural Resources, 1981-88, v.p., 1984-88; mem. Pres.'s Commn. on Accident at Three Mile Island, 1979; pres. Nat. Audubon Soc., 1979-85, Internat. Coun. Bird Preservation, 1982-90; chmn. Ctr. on Consequences of Nuclear War, 1983-87; vice-chmn. Better World Soc., 1985-90, pres., 1985-87; vis. com. John F. Kennedy Sch. Govt., 1979-85; Goodwill amb. UN Environ. Program, 1984-2002, world environ. prize com., 1989-2002; mem. Gov. Cuomo's Environ. Adv. Bd., 1985-94; adv. bd. Pace U. Sch. Law, 1988-98, Earth Island Inst., 1988-2002; chmn. bd. Earth Lobby, 1992-96; co-chmn. gov.'s task force on rejuvenating Wilmington waterfront, 1992-95; exe. com. Del. Riverfront Devel. Corp., 1995—. Decorated Order of Golden Ark (The Netherlands); Disting. fellow U. Del., 2000; recipient Ann. award NCCJ, 1966, Gold medal World Wildlife Fund, 1971, Ann. award Comml. Devel. Assn., 1971, Gold Plate award Nat. Acad. Achievement, 1971, Audubon award Nat. Audubon Soc., 1977, Frances K. Hutchinson medal Garden Club Am., 1980, Spl. Recognition award Population Reference Bur., 1983, Robert Marshall award Wilderness Soc., 1984, Nat. Conservation medal DAR, 1989, Human and Civil Rights award Del. Human Rights Commn., 1989, Spl. Recognition award Del. State Human Rels. Commn., 1989, Environ. Law Inst. award, 1990, Dr. Martin Luther King, Jr. Citation, Mt. Joy Meth. Ch., 1991, Ann. award Am. Civil Liberties Found. Del., 1992, Lawrence Solid Waste award Assn. N.Am., 1993, Kiwanis Cmty. Svc. award, 1993, Lifetime Achievement award Global Tomorrow Coalition, 1994, Lifetime Achievement award League of Conservation Voters, 1995, Del. Nature Soc., 1997, Liberty Bell award Del. State Bar Assn., 1998, Green Century award Resource Renewal Inst., 1999, Spl. Recognition award Med. Soc. Del., 2000, Samual Baxter Meml. award Water Resources Assn., 2002, Presdl. medal Del. State U., 2003, Holmes Weatherly award Unitarian-Universalist Assn., 2004; Paul Harris fellow Rotary Internat., 2002; named Conservationist of Yr., Nat. Wildlife Fedn., 1972, Swedish-Am. of Yr., Vasa Order of Am. In Sweden, 1982, Lifetime Achievement award Creative Grandparenting, 1999, NAACP, 1999; Del. refuge named in his honor Russell W. Peterson Wildlife Refuge, 2000; bronze statue in his honor on Wilmington Waterfront, 2002. Fellow Am. Inst. Chemists (hon.), AAAS (past bd. dirs.); mem. Am. Ornithologists Union, Linnaean Soc., Fedn. Am. Scientists, Am. Chem. Soc. (Parsons award 1974), Del. Acad. Sci., U.S. Assn. for Club of Rome, Cosmos Club (Cert. of Appreciation 2001), Phi Beta Kappa, Sigma Xi (Proctor prize 1978), Phi Lambda Upsilon, Phi Kappa Phi. Unitarian Universalist. Address: 11 E Mozart Dr Wilmington DE 19807-1942

PETERSON, SOPHIA, international studies educator; b. Astoria, N.Y., Nov. 24, 1929; d. George Loizos and Caroline (Hofstetter) Yimoyines; m. Virgil Allison Peterson, Dec. 28, 1951; children: Mark Jeffrey, Lynn Marie. BA, Wellesley (Mass.) Coll., 1951; MA, UCLA, 1956, PhD, 1969; DHL (hon.), Wheeling Jesuit U., 1997. Instr. Miami U., Oxford, Ohio, 1961-63; with W.Va. U., Morgantown, 1966—, assoc. prof., 1972-79, prof., 1979-97, prof. emerita, 1997—, dir., internat. studies maj., 1980-92. Dir. W.Va. Consortium for Faculty & Course Devel. in Internat. Studies, Morgantown, 1980-97, founding dir., 1997—. Author: monograph Monograph Series in World Affairs, 1979. Recipient gold medal semi-finalist CASE Prof. of Yr. award Coun. for Advancement and Support of Edn., 1987, Outstanding Tchr. award W.Va. U., W.Va. U. Coll. Arts and Scis., 1988, finalist Prof. of Yr. award W.Va. Faculty Merit Found., 1991, Heebink award for disting. state svc. W.Va. U., 1984. Mem. W.Va. Polit. Sci. Assn. (pres. 1984-85). Democrat. Avocations: sailing, travel. Home: 849 Vandalia Rd Morgantown WV 26501-6247 Office: WVa U Dept Polit Sci Morgantown WV 26506

PETERSON, STEPHEN JOSEPH, internist; b. Bellerose, N.Y., Mar. 17, 1953; s. Robert Francis and Veronica Mae (Burns) P. BS in Biology, Fairfield U., 1975; MD, Cebu Drs. Coll. Medicine, Cebu City, The Philippines, 1982. Diplomate Am. Bd. Internal Medicine, 1985. Intern internal medicine N.Y. Med. Coll., Met. Hosp. Ctr., 1982—83; resident to chief resident internal medicine N.Y. Med. Coll., 1983—86, dir. medicine clerkship, 1994—2003; assoc. program dir. Met. Hosp. Ctr., NYC, 1986—88; dep. dir. dept. medicine Lincoln Med. & Mental Health Ctr., Bronx, 1988—93; attending physician Westchester Sq. Hosp Med. Ctr., Bronx, 1993—94; dir. internal medicine residency tng. program Westchester Med. Ctr., Valhalla, 1994—, chief gen. internal medicine, 1994—. Bd. dirs. St. Agnes Hosp., White Plains, NY, 1995—2003; asst. prof. medicine NY Med. Coll., 1986—96, assoc. prof. clin. medicine, 1996—99, adj. prof. pharmacology, 2001—; mem. med. edn. coms. N.Y. Med. Coll., Westchester Med. Ctr.; prof. clin. medicine NY Med. Coll., 1999—, vice chmn. dept. medicine, 2002—. Contbr. articles to profl. jours. Recipient Advisor award Med. Explorers Boy Scouts Am., 1986, 88. Mem. AMA, ACP (gov. Hudson Valley region 2004—), Clerkship Dirs. Internal Medicine, Assn. Program Dirs. Internal Medicine, Assoc. Chiefs Gen. Internal Medicine, Soc. Gen. Internal Medicine. Rep. Roman Cath. Avocations: singing, exercise. Office: NY Med Coll Munger Pavillion # 256 Valhalla NY 10595 Office Phone: 914-493-8370. E-mail: stephen_peterson@nymc.edu.

PETERSON, THOMAS CHARLES, minister, pastoral counselor and therapist; b. San Francisco, Mar. 16, 1955; s. Roy Joseph and Grace Jeannette (Burns) P.; m. Melody Rose Clarkson, Aug. 17, 1985; children: Shannon Nicole, Chad Michael. BA, Living Word Sem., Maryland Heights, Mo., 1986; MS, Carolina Christian U., Linwood, N.C., 1990; postgrad., U. Bibl. Studies, Bethany, Okla., 1990; PhD in Counseling Psychology, Carolina U. Theology, Charlotte, N.C., 1995. Ordained to ministry Full Gospel Assemblies, 1984, Internat. Conf. Faith Ministries, 1986, Assn. Evang. Assemblies, 1989; lic. pastoral counselor and temperament therapist, Wash. Elder, tchr. Joy of Lord Fellowship, Buckley, Wash., 1980-81, By His Word Christian Ctr., Tacoma, 1982-88; assoc. pastor Valley Christian Ctr., Sumner, 1988-89; founder, pres. Joyful Life Ministries, Tacoma, 1985-92; pastoral staff Victory Bible Ch., Tacoma, 1992-96; dir., chancellor, acad. dean Tacoma Christian Life Sch. of Theology, Tacoma, 1993-96; pastor Resurrection Christian Life Ctr., Tacoma, 1996—. Chaplain Tacoma Police Dept., 1988-90, Tacoma Gen. Hosp., 1988—; dir. Inst. for Personal Devel., Tacoma, 1991. Mem. Critical Incident Stress Mgmt. Team, Tacoma Gen. Hosp., 1997—. Sgt. USAF, 1973-77. Mem. Nat. Christian Counselors Assn. (profl. clin. mem.). Am. Assn. Christian Counselors (founding mem.), Internat. Assn. Christian Clin. Counselors, U.S. Chaplaincy Assn., United Assn. Christian Counselors. Republican. Office: Resurrection Life Ministries Internat PO Box 98198 Tacoma WA 98498-0198 Home: 2212 143rd St Ct S Spanaway WA 98387-9025 *The human potential is limited only by our ability to believe.*

PETERSON, VICTOR LOWELL, aerospace engineer, consultant; b. Saskatoon, Sask., Can., June 11, 1934; came to U.S., 1937; s. Edwin Galladet and Ruth Mildred (McKeeby) P.; m. Jacqueline Dianne Hubbard, Dec. 21, 1955; children: Linda Kay, Janet Gale, Victor Craig. BS in Aero. Engring., Oreg. State U., 1956; MS in Aerospace Engring., Stanford U., 1964; MS in Mgmt., MIT, 1973. Rsch. scientist NASA-Ames Rsch. Ctr., Moffett Field, Calif., 1956-68, asst. chief hypersonic aerodyns., 1968-71, chief aerodyns. br., 1971-74, chief thermo and gas dynamics div., 1974-84, dir. aerophysics, 1984-90, dep. dir., 1990-94; pvt. mgmt. cons., 1994—. Mem. nat. adv. bd. U. Tenn. Space Inst., Tullahoma, 1984-94. Contbr. numerous articles to profl. jours. Treas. Woodland Acres Homeowners Assn., Los Altos, Calif., 1978—. Capt. USAF, 1957-60. Recipient medal for outstanding leadership NASA, 1982; Alfred P. Sloan fellow MIT, 1972-73. Fellow AIAA. Republican. Methodist. Achievements include development of numerical aerodynamic simulation system for aerospace, of method for reconstructing planetary atmosphere structure from accelerations of body entering atmosphere, of theory for motions of tumbling bodies entering planetary atmospheres. Home: 484 Aspen Way Los Altos CA 94024-7100 E-mail: vlpeterson@att.net. *Achievements in life are maximized by creating visions of success and focussing relentlessly on successful accomplishment of intermediate objectives.*

PETERSON, WALLACE CARROLL, SR., economics professor; b. Omaha, Mar. 28, 1921; s. Fred Nels and Grace (Brown) P.; m. Eunice V. Peterson, Aug. 16, 1944 (dec. Nov. 1985); children: Wallace Carroll Jr., Shelley Lorraine; m. Bonnie B. Watson, Nov. 11, 1988 (dec. Oct. 1996). Student, U. Omaha, 1939-40, U. Mo., 1940-42; BA in Econs. and European History, U. Nebr., 1947, MA in Econs. and European History, 1948, PhD in Econs. and European History, 1953; postgrad., Handelshochschule, St. Gallen, Switzerland, 1948-49, U. Minn., 1951, London Sch. Econs. and Polit. Sci., 1952. Lic. pilot. Reporter Lincoln (Nebr.) Jour., 1946; instr. econs. U. Nebr., Lincoln, 1951-54, asst. prof., 1954-57, assoc. prof., 1957-61, prof., 1962—, chmn. dept. econs., 1965-75, George Holmes prof. econs., 1966-92; George Holmes prof. econs. emeritus, 1992—; v.p. faculty senate U. Nebr., Lincoln, 1972-73, pres. faculty senate, 1973-74; S.J. Hall disting. vis. prof. U. Nev., Las Vegas, 1983-84. Author: The Welfare State in France, 1960, Elements of Economics, 1973, Our Overloaded Economy: Inflation, Unemployment and the Crisis in American Capitalism, 1982, Market Power and the Economy, 1988, Transfer Spending, Taxes and the American Welfare State, 1991, Income, Employment and Economic Growth, 8th edit., 1996, Silent Depression: The Fate of the American Dream, 1994; co-author: (with F.R. Strobel) The Coming Class War: Power, Conflict and the Consequences of Middle Class Decline, 1998, The Social Security Primer: What Every Citizen Should Know, 1999, Pylon! The Omaha Air Races, 1931-1934, 2002. Mem. Nebr. Dem. Cen. Com., 1968-74, vice-chmn., chmn. Nebr. Polit. Accountability and Disclosure Commn., 1977-80; chmn. Nebr. Coun. Econ. Edn., 1976-77. Capt. USAAF, 1942-46. Recipient Champion Media award for Econ. Understanding, 1981; Fulbright fellow, 1957-58, 64-65; Mid-Am. State Univs. honor scholar, 1982-83. Mem. ACLU, AAUP (pres. Nebr. 1963-64, nat. coun.), Assn. for Evolutionary Econs. (pres. 1976, Veblen-Commons award 1991), Am. Econs. Assn., Midwest Econs. Assn. (pres. 1968-69), Mo. Valley Econ. Assn. (pres. 1989), Assn. Social Econs. (pres. 1992, Thomas F. Devine award 1995), Fedn. Am. Scientists, Antique Aircraft Assn., Aircraft Owners and Pilots Assn., Exptl. Aircraft Assn., Nat. Assn. R.R. Passengers. Office: U Nebr Dept Econs CBA Lincoln NE 68588-0489 Office Phone: 407-472-2319. E-mail: wcpeterson@mindspring.com.

PETERSON, WALTER FRITIOF, academic administrator; b. Idaho Falls, Idaho, July 15, 1920; s. Walter Fritiof and Florence (Danielson) P.; m. Barbara Mae Kempe, Jan. 13, 1946; children: Walter Fritiof III, Daniel John. BA, State U. Iowa, 1942, MA, 1948, PhD, 1951; HHD (hon.), Loras Coll., 1983; LHD (hon.), Clarke Coll., 1991; DHum (hon.), U. Dubuque, 1997. Asst. prof. history, chmn. dept. history Milw. Downer Coll., 1952-57, assoc. prof. history, chmn. social sci. div., 1957-64; assoc. prof. history Lawrence U., Appleton, Wis., 1964-67, prof. history, Alice G. Chapman libr., 1967-70; pres. U. Dubuque, 1970-90, chancellor, 1990—2000, chancellor emeritus, 2000. Regional tng. officer Peace Corps, 1965-68; cons. history Allis-Chalmers Mfg. Co., 1959-75, Secura Ins. Group, 1968-92, Wm. C. Brown Pub. Co., 1981-92, bd. dirs. Editor: Transactions of Wis. Acad. Scis., Arts and Letters, 1965-72, The Allis-Chalmers Corporation: An Industrial History, 1977, A History of Wm. C. Brown Cos., 1994, A History of Hawkeye Bancorporation, 1996. Advisor Templeton Prize for Progress in Religion, 1986-91; bd. dirs. Finley Hosp., pres., 1983-84; chmn. Finley Health Found., 1986-95, Finley Health Found. Hall of Fame, 2000; bd. dirs. Dubuque Symphony Orch., Dubuque Art Assn., Jr. Achievement, Nat. River Hall of Fame, 1984; chmn. Iowa Assn. Coll. and Univ. Pres., 1975-76; chmn. Iowa Coll. Found., 1982-83; chair Grand Opera House Found., 1998—. With USAAF, 1942-45, PTO. Recipient Dubuque 1st Citizen award, 1990, Disting. Civic Svc. award, 1991, Benjamin Franklin award Nat. Soc. Fundraising Execs., 1994, Paul Harris fellowship, Duduque Rotary Club, 1993; named to Dubuque Bus. Hall of Fame, 1990 Mem. Iowa Assn. Ind. Colls. and Univs. (chmn. 1988-89), Dubuque County Hist. Soc. (bd. dirs.), Dubuque Golf and Country Club, Phi Alpha Theta, Kappa Delta Pi, Phi Delta Kappa.

PETERSON, WAYNE TURNER, composer, pianist; b. Albert Sea, Minn., Sept. 3, 1927; s. Leslie Jules and Irma Thelma (Turner) Peterson; m. Harriet Christiansen, 1948 (div. 1978); children: Alan, Craig, Drew, Grant. BA, U. Minn., 1951, MA, 1953; postgrad., Royal Acad. Music, London, 1953—54; PhD, U. Minn. Instr. music U. Minn., 1955—59; asst. prof. music Chico (Calif.) State U., 1959—60; prof. music San Francisco State U., 1960—91, prof. emeritus, 1991—. Vis. prof. composition U. Ind., Bloomington, 1992, Stanford U., 1992—94; artist in residence Briarcombe Found., Bolinas, Calif., 1983; vis. artist Am. Acad. in Rome, 1990. Composer: Allegro for String Quartet, 1952, Introduction and Allegro, 1953, Free Variations for Orch., 1954—58, Can Death Be Sleep, 1955, Earth, Sweet Earth, 1956, (cappella chorus) Cape Ann, 1957, Three Songs for Soprano and Piano, 1957, (cappella chorus) Psalm 56, 1959, Cape Ann, 1957, Exaltation, Dithyramb and Caprice, full orch., 1959—60, An e e cummings Triptych, 1962, Tangents for flute, clarinet, horn and violin, 1963, An e e cummings Cantata, 1964, Fantasy Concertante for violin and piano, 1965, Reflections, ballet, full orch., 1965, Metamorphosis for Wind Quintet, 1967, Phantasmagoria for flute, clarinet, double bass, 1968, Cataclysms, full orch., 1968, Clusters and Fragments for string orch., 1969, Ceremony After a Fire Raid, Soprano and piano, 1969, Sinfonia and Canticle for baritone voice and organ, 1969, Capriccio for Flute and Piano, 1973, Transformations for String Quartet, 1974, Trialogue for violin, cello and piano, 1975, Diatribe for violin and piano, 1975, Encounters mixed ensemble of mini instrument, 1976, Rhapsody for Cello and Piano, 1976, An Interrupted Serenade for flute, harp and cello, 1978, Dark Reflections (cycle of 4 songs for high voice, violin and piano), 1980, Mallets Aforethought (symphony for percussion ensemble), 1981, Sextet for flute, clarinet, percussion, harp, violin and cello, 1982, Doubles for 2 flutes and 2 clarinets, 1982, Debussy Song Cycle transcribed for voice and small orch., 1983, String Quartet, 1983—84, Ariadne's Thread for harp, flute, clarinet, horn, percussion and violin, 1985, Transformations for chamber orch., 1986, Duo for viola and cello, 1986—87, Trilogy for Orch., 1987, Labyrinth for flute, clarinet, violin and piano, 1987, The Widening Gyre for full orch., 1991, The Face of the Night, the Heart of the Dark for full orch., 1991 (Pulitzer prize for music, 1992), Mallets Aforethought percussion symphony revision, 1991, String Quartet # 2, 1992, Diptych, fl, cl, pec., po, rn, vc, 1992, Janus, mixed ensemble of ten instruments, 1993, Duo for Violin and Piano, 1993, And the Winds Shall Blow, a fantasy for saxophone quartet, symphony winds, brass and percussion, 1994, Theseus for smaller orch., Vicissiyude (fl, cl, perc, po vn, vc), 1995, A Robert Herrick Motley (5 a capella choruses), Windup Saxophone Quartet, Peregrinations (solo clarinet), 1996; recs. with Mercury Records, Desto Records, Arch Records, Grenadilla Records, Koch Internat. CRI, Innova, Foghorn, Centur, San Francisco Chamber Singers, recs. commds. Am. Music Ctr., 1959, Virtuosi of San Francisco, 1968, Unitarian Ch., 1969, Paul Mason, Inc., 1974, 1987, NEA Consortium Commn., 1982, Charles Wuorinen and San Francisco Symphony, 1985, Am. Composers Symphony, Inc., 1987, San Francisco Symphony, 1991, Gerbode Found., 1990, Koussevitzky Found., 1990, Fromm Music Found., 1992, Philharm. Orch. of Freiburg in Breisgau, Germany, 1993, U. Minn., 1995, Neel the Composer (Consortium, Comm.), 1996, Allen Blustine, 1996. Named Fulbright scholar, Royal Acad. Music, 1953—54, Guggenheim fellow, 1989—90, Djerassi Found. fellow, 1989—91; recipient 11th Ann. Norman Fromm Composer's award, 1982, Meritorious Svc. award, Calif. State U. Sys., 1984, Top award, Am. Harp Soc., 1985, Composer's award, Am. Acad. and Inst. Arts and Letters, 1986; grantee, NEA, 1976. Home: 140 S Lake Merced Hls San Francisco CA 94132-2935 Office: San Francisco State U Dept Mus 1600 Holloway Ave San Francisco CA 94132-1722

PETERSON, WILLIAM CANOVA, architect; b. Cleve., Nov. 3, 1945; m. Anne Lee Deitz Vassar, June 3, 1967 (div. Nov. 1981); children: Lisa Peterson Thompson, Amanda Peterson Courtney; m. Patricia Hill, July 4, 1985. BArch, Va. Poly. Inst. and State U., 1968; postgrad., Va. Commonwealth U., 1975-77. Registered architect, Va.; cert. Nat. Coun. Archtl. Registration Bds. Project mgr. R.P. Fox Architects, Newark, Del., 1970-73, Highfill & Assocs., Richmond, Va., 1973, Wright, Jones & Wilkinson, Richmond, 1973-79; pres. Canova Assocs. Arch., Mechanicsville, Va., 1979—. Chmn. Bldg. & Code Appeals Bd., King William County, Va., 1997—; mem. Housing Task Force, Hanover County, Va., 1992; mem. exec. UVB Sr. PGA, Richmond, 1984. 1st lt. U.S. Army, 1968-70. Mem. AIA, Assn. of Cons. for Liturgical Space, Constrn. Specifications Inst. (bd. dirs. 1985-87, 88-90), Greater Richmond C. of C., Hanover County Rotary (pres. 1981-82, Paul Harris fellow). Roman Catholic. Office: Canova Assocs Arch PO Box 429 7277 Hanover Green Dr Mechanicsville VA 23111-1764 Office Phone: 804-746-1558. E-mail: canova-arch@erols.com.

PETERSON, WILLIAM GEORGE, lawyer; b. Minn., Sept. 30, 1944; s. Henry Gaufin and Grace Marie (Reker) P.; m. Ann Ophoven; children: Emily Marie, Elizabeth Ann. B.A., U. Minn., 1966, J.D., U. Pitts., 1969. Bar: Minn. 1969, U.S. Dist. Ct. Minn. 1970, U.S. Ct. Appeals (8th cir.) 1976, U.S. Supreme Ct. 1976, Wis. 1983. Spl. asst. atty. gen. State of Minn., St. Paul, 1969-78; sole practice, Bloomington, Minn., 1978-80; ptnr. Peterson & Lange, Bloomington, 1980-81; owner Peterson & Assocs., Bloomington, 1981-97, Peterson Law Office, P.A., 1997-; instr. hotel and restaurant law Normandale C.C., Bloomington, 1981-87; referee Hennepin County Conciliation Ct., Mpls., 1982—; arbitrator ins. claims Am. Arbitration Assn., 1988—. Contbr. articles to profl. jours. Bd. dirs. Viking Coun. Boy Scouts Am., 1981-84, Minn. Valley YMCA; chmn. Hennepin County Ind. Republicans, Mpls., 1984-90; mem. Minn. Legislature, 1978-82, Bloomington City Merit Bd., 1983-96. Recipient Silver Beaver award Boy Scouts Am., 1981, Legis. Excellence award Minn. Legis. Evaluation Assembly, 1981. Mem. ABA, Minn. State Bar Assn., Minn. Trial Lawyers Assn. Roman Catholic. Home: 4103 Overlook Cir Minneapolis MN 55437-3540 Office: Law Office 3601 Minnesota Dr Ste 800 Minneapolis MN 55435 Office Phone: 952-921-5818. E-mail: petersonlaw@visi.com.

PETH, HOWARD ALLEN, lawyer, educator; b. Calif., Apr. 20, 1955; s. Howard Allen and Diane Marie (Munyan) P.; m. Gloria Gene Stockton, Aug. 9, 1992; children: Andrew Howard, Rachel Gloria. BA, U. Calif., San Diego, 1980; MD, U. Santiago, 1984; JD, U. Mo., 1991. Bar: Calif. 1993, U.S. Ct. Appeals (9th cir.) 1993, U.S. Ct. Claims, U.S. Ct. Appeals (fed. cir.) 1993, U.S. Dist. Ct. (so. dist.) Calif. 1993, U.S. Supreme Ct. 1997; diplomate Am. Bd. Internal Medicine, Am. Bd. Emergency Medicine; lic. physician, Calif., Mo., Wis. Asst. prof. U. Mo. Sch. Medicine, Columbia, 1997—. Fellow Am. Coll. Legal Medicine; mem. AMA, ABA (health law sect.), ACP, Am. Coll. Emergency Physicians. Republican. Episcopalian. Office: U Mo Hosp and Clinic One Hospital Dr Columbia MO 65212 Home: PO Box 357 Osage Beach MO 65065-0357 Business E-Mail: pethh@health.missouri.edu. E-mail: hpethmdjd@aol.com.

PETHEL, STANLEY ROBERT, composer, music educator; b. Gainesville, Ga., Feb. 3, 1950; s. Jack Charles and Eva Coleen (Henderson) P.; married, 1973; children: Mary Ellen, Robert Russell, Joseph Charles. MusB, U. Ga., 1972, MFA, 1973; student, Peabody Coll., summer 1974; D of Mus. Arts, U. Ky., 1981. Band dir. Clark County Schs., Athens, Ga., 1972-73; assoc. prof. music Berry Coll., Rome, Ga., 1973—. Writer: (cantatas) Christ is Born, 1980, He Came in Love, 1985, There's a Song on the Air, 1987, (mus.) Timothy, 1984, Birthday of the King, 1990, Go Tell It On the Mountain, 1991, Bethlehem Joy, 1991, A Risen Savior, 1992, Lord of Glory, 2002, Praise the Risen Lord, 2000, The Perfect Christmas, 2001, Three Kings, 2004. Music dir. Calvary Bapt. Ch., Rome, 1974-83, Garden Lakes Bapt. Ch., Rome, 1983—. Recipient ASCAP award, 1984-91. Mem. Internat. Trombone Assn., Music Educators Nat. Conf., Ga. Music Educators Assn. Avocation: sports. Office: 91 Berry College Rome GA 30149-0001

PETHICK, CHRISTOPHER JOHN, physicist; b. Horsham, Sussex, Eng., Feb. 22, 1942; s. Richard Hope and Norah Betty (Hill) P. BA, Magdalen Coll., Oxford (Eng.) U., 1962, DPhil, 1965. Fellow Magdalen Coll., Oxford U., 1965-70; research assoc. U. Ill., Urbana, 1966-68, research asst. prof., 1968-69, assoc. prof. physics, 1970-73, prof. physics, 1973-95, Nordita, Copenhagen, 1975—. A.P. Sloan research fellow, 1970-72. Fellow Am. Phys. Soc.; mem. European Phys. Soc. Office: Nordita Blegdamsvej 17 DK-2100 Copenhagen Denmark

PETILLON, LEE RITCHEY, lawyer; b. Gary, Ind., May 6, 1929; s. Charles Ernest and Blanche Lurene (Mackay) P.; m. Mary Anne Keeton, Feb. 20, 1960; children: Andrew G., Joseph R. BBA, U. Minn., 1952; LLB, U. Calif., Berkeley, 1959. Bar: Calif. 1960, U.S. Dist. Ct. (so. dist.) Calif. 1960. V.p. Creative Investment Capital, Inc., L.A., 1969—70; corp. counsel Harvest Industries, L.A., Calif., 1970—71; v.p., gen. counsel, dir. Tech. Svcs. Corp., Santa Monica, Calif., 1971—78; ptnr. Petillon & Davidoff, L.A., 1978—92, Gipson Hoffman & Pancione, 1992—93; pvt. practice Torrance, Calif., 1993—94; ptnr. Petillon & Hansen, Torrance, Calif., 1994—2003, Petillon & Hiraide LLP, Torrance, 2004—. Co-author: R&D Partnerships, 2d edit., 1985, Representing Start-Up Companies, 1992, 11th edit., 2003; contbr. chapters to books. Chmn. Neighborhood Justice Ctr. Com., 1983-85, Middle Income Co., 1983085; active Calif. Senate Commn. on Corp. Governance, State Bar Calif. Task Force on Alternative Dispute Resolution, 1984-85; chmn. South Bay Sci. Found., Inc.; vice-chmn. Calif. Capital Access Forum, Inc.; dir., legal counsel ACE-Net.org, Inc. Recipient Cert. of Appreciation L.A. City Demonstration Agy., 1975, United Indian Devel. Assn., 1981, City of L.A. for Outstanding Vol. Svcs., 1984, Outstanding Vol. award Torrance C. of C., 2000, Small Bus. Adv. of Yr. award Torrance C. of C., 2001; named Small Bus. Adv. of Yr. Calif. C. of C., 2001. Mem.: ABA (venture capital and pvt. equity com.), Los Angeles County Bar Assn. (trustee 1984—85, alt. dispute resolution sect. 1992—94, bus. and corp. law sect. 2000—, chmn. law tech. sect., Griffin Bell Vol. Svc. award 1993), Los Angeles County Bar Found. (bd. dirs.), Calif. State Bar Assn. (pres., Pro Bono Svcs. award 1983). Avocations: backpacking, reading, music, painting. Home: 1636 Via Machado Palos Verdes Estates CA 90274-1930 Office: Petillon & Hiraide LLP 21515 Hawthorne Blvd Ste 1260 Torrance CA 90503-6503 Office Phone: 310-543-0500. E-mail: lpetillon@corplawp-h.com.

PETINGA, CHARLES MICHAEL, transportation executive; b. Atlantic City, July 9, 1946; s. Thomas Joseph and Rose Marie (Merindino) P.; m. Velna Mae McVicker, June 7, 1969; children: Scott, Jeffery. BS in Geology, Geography, U. Wis., Superior, 1969. Ops. supr. Schneider Transport, Inc., Green Bay, Wis., 1973-74, prodn. mgr., 1974-76, safety dir., 1976-79; dir. safety Schneider Nat., Inc., Green Bay, 1979-82, dir. risk mgmt., 1982-87; gen. mgr. Petinga Candy Co., Atlantic City, 1987-89; sr. v.p., midwest practice leader Transp. Industry, Appleton, Wis., 1989-2000; exec. v.p. Smith Transport Inc., Roaring Spring, Pa., 2003—. Cons. local charitable groups, Green Bay,

1985-88; preactice leader freight/logistics Global Transp. Industry; adviser, cons. Small Bus. Execs., Green Bay, 1989; mem. worker compensation task force Wis. Motor Carriers, Madison, 1991; nat.-internat. spkr. at univs., bus. schs., vocat. schs. and high schs.; speaker to motor carrier assns., bd. directors, and industry mgmt. groups, nat. and state assns. Co. liaison Green Bay United Way, 1985, 86. With U.S. Army, 1971-73. Mem. Wis. Coun. Safety Supprs., Nat. Safety Mgmt. Soc., Wis. Motor Carriers Assn., Risk and Ins. Mgmt. Soc., Nat. Safety Coun., Am. Trucking Assn. Avocations: martial arts, physical fitness, weightlifting. Office: Marsh Global Transp Group 59 Park Pl Appleton WI 54914-8230

PETIT, PARKER HOLMES, health care corporation executive; b. Decatur, Ga., Aug. 4, 1939; s. James Percival and Ethel (Holmes) P.; m. Janet Lewis; children: William Wright, Patricia Monique, Meredith Katherine. BS in Mech. Engring., Ga. Inst. Tech., 1962, MS in Engring. Mechanics, 1964; MBA, Ga. State U., 1973. Engr. Gen. Dynamics Corp., Fort Worth, Tex., 1966-67; engring. project mgr. Lockheed-Ga. Co., Marietta, 1967-71; pres., founder, chief exec. officer Healthdyne, Inc., Marietta, 1971—. Bd. dirs. Atlantic S.E. Airlines, Inc., Atlanta, Healthdyne Technologies, Inc., Atlanta, Healthdyne Info. Enterprises, Inc., Marietta, Ga., Matria Healthcare, Inc., Marietta, Logility Corp., Atlanta, Intelligent Sys., Norcross, Ga. Author: Primer on Composite Materials, 1968; patentee in field Chmn. bd. dirs. Sudden Infant Death Syndrome Alliance, Washington, 1986; active nat. adv. coun. Emory U. Med. Sch., Coun. fellows for the Emory, Ga. Tech. Biomed. Tech. Rsch. Ctr.; bd. dirs. Ga. Rsch. Alliance, 1995. 1st lt. U.S. Army, 1964-67. Recipient Humanitarian award La SocieteFrancaise de Bienfaisance, 1981; mem. Tech. Hall of Fame of Ga.; mem. Ga. Tech. Acad. Disting. Alumni, 1994; Internat. Bus. fellow, 1986. Mem. Health Industry Mfrs. Assn., Cobb County C. of C. (bd. dirs. 1980-82), Atlanta C. of C. (bd. dirs. 1997—), Pi Kappa Phi. Republican. Methodist. Avocations: flying, painting, golf, tennis. Office: Healthdyne Inc 1850 Parkway Pl SE Marietta GA 30067-4439

PETITAN, DEBRA ANN BURKE, elementary school educator, counselor, design engineer, writer; b. Chgo., Mar. 12, 1932; d. James Marcellus and Susan Florence (Hines) Burke; m. Kenneth Charles Petitan, Aug. 9, 1952; 1 child, Susan Florence. AA, Wilson Jr. Coll., Chgo., 1951, N.Y. Inst. Photography, 1952; BS in Primary Edn., Chgo. State U., 1956, MS in Indsl. Edn., 1967; DSc in Applied Sci. and Tech., London Inst. Tech., 1971; postgrad., U. Wis., Bradley U., U. Calif., U. Ill.; grad., Inst. Children's Lit., West Redding, Conn., 1991; cert. in Childrens' Portraiture, North Light Art Sch., 1997. Tchr. Chgo. Bd. Edn., 1958-71, guidance counselor, 1976-84, now tchr., cons.; nat. dir. edn. Nation of Islam, 1971-75; design engr. Fed. Sign and Signal Corp., Chgo., 1975-76; CEO, owner Petitan's Creative Projects, Inc. Nat. adv. bd. Nat. Right to Work Orgn., 1976-85; cons. ednl. devel., 1978; computer libr. cons.; owner, CEO, Fayzah's Fin. Svcs., Instrn. Svcs. in Trading and Investing, Fayzah's Creative Projects, Inc.; ednl. cons. tech. analysis and chart reading stock market; participant summer writing festival U. Iowa, 1991. Photographer VISTA News, 1969-70; writer children's lit.; author curriculum introducing computer-aided design techniques in the pub. schs., 1965. Cmty. svc. rec. sec. 9600 Block Club; navigator, pub. rels. officer IL wing Squadron 8, capt. CAP, 1953—56; chmn. Career Women for Johnson/Humphrey, Chgo., 1965; dir. Christian edn. Trinity United Ch. Christ, Chgo., 1978—81, family counselor, 1978—81; organizer, leader family counseling ministry, lic. lay Eucharistic min. Episcopal Ch. St. Edmund, Chgo. Episc. Diocese, 1989. Named Woman of Yr. Iota Phi Lambda, 1978; recipient 250 Hr. medal Ground Observer Corps, 1952, 25 Yr. Service medal Chgo. Bd. Edn., 1987. Mem. Off-Campus Writer's Workshop (editor newsletter), Soc. of Children's Book Writers, Am. Contract Bridge League, Am. Bridge Assn. (life master, rec. sec.), Children's Reading Roundtable, Green River Writers, Epsilon Pi Tau. Achievements include introduction of Computer Aided Design curriculum to field of education. Office: Fayzah's Analytical Guidance Svc Chicago IL 60628 E-mail: drdap1@ameritech.net.

PETITO, MARGARET L. foundation administrator; b. Dallas, Sept. 28, 1950; d. Jacob Charles and Eileen (Shank) Loehr; m. John Haven Petito, 1978 (div. 1984); children: John Christian Robert, David Nelson. BA, So. Meth. U., 1972. Mem. Action/Vista Program U.S. Govt., Middlesex, NY, 1972—74; dir., curator Oliver House Mus., Penn Yan, NY, 1975—77; staff asst. Williams & Jensen, P.C., Washington, 1986—89; dir. fed. rels. Chambers Devel. Co., Inc., 1989—92; dir. fed. affairs DSSI-U.S. Biotech., Washington, 1992—94; cons., dir. pub. affairs Embassy Ecuador, Govt. Ecuador, Washington, 1994—96; prin. Petito & Assocs., Washington, 1994—. Dir. external events Internat. Cancer Alliance, Bethesda, Md., 1996—97, Sch. of Bus., Georgetown U., Washington, 1998—99; pres., exec. dir. Friends of Rule of Law in Ecuador, Inc., 2001—. Spl. legis. advisor Drugwatch Internat., Chgo., 1993—; mem. Women's Coun. Energy and Environ., Washington, 1990—94; bd. dirs. Nyumbani Orphanage for Kenyan Children with AIDS, Washington, 1989—99; dir. Marshall Ho. Mus., Lambertville, NJ, 1980—82; mem. task force Women in Govt. Rels., Washington, 1990—96; founder, co-chair Forum for Environ., Washington, 1989—91; pres. Cultural Partnership of the Ams., Washington, 1999—. Mem.: Tex. State Soc., Tex. Breakfast Club. Roman Catholic. Avocations: squash, needlepoint, fishing. Home and Office: Friends of Rule of Law in Ecuador Inc 6008 34th Pl NW Washington DC 20015-1607 E-mail: mlp3@starpower.net.

PETITTO, LAURA-ANN, cognitive neuroscience educator; b. New York, NY; m. Kevin Dunbar; children: Eva-Molly Dunbar, Annafaye Dunbar, Maaraluisa Dunbar. PhD, EdD, Harvard U., 1984. Rsch. project coord. & primary tchr. of project nim chimpsky Columbia U., NYC, 1973—76; staff lectr. NY Soc. for the Deaf, NYC, 1978—79; asst. prof., dept of psychology McGill U., Montreal, 1983—89, assoc. prof., dept of psychology, 1989—99, full prof., dept of psychology, 1999—2001; full prof. Dartmouth Coll., Dept. Edn., Dept. Psychology, Hanover, NH, 2001—; chmn., dir. of cognitive neuroscience lab. for lang. & child devel. Dartmouth Coll., Dept. Edn., Dept. Psychology, 2001—. Rschr. in neurolinguistics lab. for am. sign lang. The Salk Inst. for Biol. Studies, San Diego, 1980—85; rsch. scientist, McDonnell-pew ctr. for cognitive neuroscience Montreal Neurol. Inst., 1983—2001, rsch. scientist, 1983—2001; prof. of psychology and dir. of cognitive neuroscience lab. for lang., sign, & cognition McGill U., Montreal, Quebec, Canada, 1983—2001. Contbr. articles to profl. jours., chapters to books. Recipient Natural Sciences and Engring. Rsch. Coun. of Can. Career Develop. award, NSERC, Can., 1985—95, Young Psychologist award, APA, 1988, Outstanding Tchg. & Sci. Achievements award, Golden Key Nat. Hon. Soc., 1997, Pub. achievement award, Boys Town Med. Ctr. (in assn. with the U. of Nebr.), 1997; fellow The John D. and Catherine T. MacArthur Found., Postdoctoral fellowship, USA, 1983—84; grant, Social Sciences and Humanities Rsch. Coun. of Can., 2000—03, 1997—2000, Guggenheim fellowship, The John Simon Guggenheim Meml. Found., 1998, Maj. Rsch. grant, The Spencer Found., 2000—03, MNI, Brain Scanning Ctr. grant, Montreal Neurol. Inst., Brain Imaging Ctr., 2000—. Mem.: AAAS, Soc. for Rsch. in Child Devel., Soc. for Neuroscience, Can. Deafness Rsch. & Tng. Inst. Coop. Coun. (assoc.; exec. adv. com. mem. 1983—2003). Office: Dartmouth Coll Dept Edn 103 Raven House Hanover NH 03755 E-mail: laura-ann.petitto@dartmouth.edu.

PETOK, SAMUEL, retired manufacturing company executive; b. Detroit, Aug. 12, 1922; s. Harry and Jennie (Weingarten) P.; m. Fayne Joyce Myers, June 26, 1952; children— Carol, Seth, Michael. BA in History, Wayne State U., Detroit, 1945; postgrad., Medill Sch. Journalism, Northwestern U., 1946. Reporter Detroit Free Press, 1946-50; account exec. McCann Erickson, 1950-52; pub. relations exec. Chrysler Corp., 1952-70; Vice pres. public relations and advt. White Motor Corp., Cleve., 1971-76; dir. communications automotive ops. Rockwell Internat. Co., Troy, Mich., 1976-77, corp. staff v.p. public relations Pitts., 1977-78, v.p. communications, 1978-82, sr. v.p. communications, mem. mgmt. com., 1982-88; retired. Former trustee Arthur W. Page Soc.; trustee Hist. Soc. Princeton. Recipient Page One award Newspaper Guild Detroit, 1948 Mem. Pub. Rels. Soc. Am. (Silver Anvil award 1964), Internat. Pub. Rels. Assn., Overseas Press Club Am., The Old Guard of Princeton, Nassau Club, Cherry Valley Country Club.

PETORAK, BRYAN THOMAS, music educator, musician; b. Rockville Centre, NY, Oct. 16, 1977; s. Thomas and Barbara Jean Petorak. BFA, LI U., 1995—99, MA, 1999—2001. Cert. Vocology Nat. Ctr. for Voice and Speech, 2001. Pvt. music instr. Self employed, Long Island, 1997—; voice adjudicator NY State Sch. Music Assn., 2000—; magnet lead tchr. Miami-Dade County Schools. Young artist in residence Dicapo Opera Theater, New York City, 2001—; guest artist Gt. Neck Ho., 2002. Cantor St. Gerard Majella Ch., Hollis, NY, 2000—02. Recipient Semi- Finalist Ea. Region, Nat. Assn. of Teachers of Singing, 2001, Outstanding Musician award, West Hempstead Rotary Club, 1995; Grad. Tchg. Assistantship, LI U., 1999, 2000, 2001, H. H. Born award of excellence, 1998. Mem.: The Voice Found., NY Viola Soc., NY State Sch. Music Assn., Nat. Assn. of Teachers of Singing (assoc.). D-Liberal. Russian Orthodox Christian. Home: 900 W Ave Apt 1505 Miami FL 33139-5218 Personal E-mail: petorak@aol.com.

PETOSA, JASON JOSEPH, publisher; b. Des Moines, Iowa, Apr. 26, 1939; s. Joseph John and Mildred Margaret (Cardamon) P.; m. Theodora Anne Doleski, Aug. 12, 1972; 1 son, Justin James. Student, Marquette U., 1957-59, St. Paul Sem., 1959-63, 65-67, Colegio Paolino Internationale, Rome, 1963-65. Asso. editor Cath. Home Mag., Canfield, Ohio, 1965-67, editor, 1968; dir. Alba House Communications, Canfield, 1968-71; with Office of Radio and TV, Diocese of Youngstown, Ohio, 1969-71; dir. pub. relations, instr. Alice Lloyd Coll., Pippa Passes, Ky., 1971-76; writer, cons. Bethesda, Ohio, 1976-79; pres., pub. Nat. Cath. Reporter, Kansas City, Mo., 1979-85; v.p., gen. mgr. Towsend-Kraft Pub. Co., Liberty, Mo., 1985-86; pres., pub. Steadfast Pub. Co., Kansas City, 1986—. Bd. dirs. David (Ky.) Sch., 1973-79; mem. Mayor's UN Day Com., Kansas City. Mem. Kansas City Direct Mktg. Assn., UN Assn. (bd. dirs. Met. Kansas City chpt., pres. 2000). Roman Catholic. Office: 19 W Linwood Blvd PO Box 410265 Kansas City MO 64141-0265 Office Phone: 816-561-4561. E-mail: jasonpetosa@steadfastpublishing.com.

PETRAEUS, DAVID HOWELL, career military officer; b. Cornwall, N.Y., Nov. 7, 1952; s. Sixtus and Miriam Sweet (Howell) P.; m. Hollister Knowlton, July 6, 1974; children: Anne, Stephen. BS, U.S. Mil. Acad., 1974; grad., U.S. Army Command and Gen. Staff Coll., Ft. Leavenworth, Kans., 1983; M in Pub. and Internat. Affairs, Princeton U., 1985, PhD, 1987. Commd. 2d lt. U.S. Army, 1974, advanced through grades to lt. gen., 2004; platoon leader, adjutant 1-509th Inf. (Airborne), Vicenza, Italy, 1975-78; co. comdr., ops officer, aide-de-camp 24th Inf. divsn., Ft. Stewart, Ga., 1979-82; asst. prof. internat. relations Dept. Social Scis., U.S. Mil. Acad., West Point, N.Y., 1985-87; mil. asst. to supreme allied comdr. Europe, 1987-88; bn. and brigade ops. officer 3rd infantry divsn. U.S. Army, 1988-89, aide-de-camp to chief of staff, asst. divsn. comdr. for operations, 82nd Airborne divsn., chief of staff, XVIII Airborne Corps.; asst. chief of staff for military ops. SFOR (Sarajevo) Joint Hdqs. Centre, Allied Command Europe, 2001—02; comdr., 101st Airborne Divsn. U.S. Army, Ft. Campbell, Ky., 2002—04; chief Office of Security Transition, Iraq, 2004—. Mem. Inter-Univ. seminar on Armed Forces and Soc. Author: The American Military and the Lessons of Vietnam, 1987; contbr. to: Strategy, Democracy, and Vietnam, 1987; co-editor: NATO At Forty, 1989; contbr. articles to profl. jours. Mem. Council on Fgn. Relations, Acad. Polit. Sci., Assn. U.S. Army, Phi Kappa Phi. Clubs: Army-Navy (Arlington, Va.). Presbyterian. Avocations: distance running, writing.*

PETRAKIS, HARRY MARK, author; b. St. Louis, June 5, 1923; s. Mark E. and Stella (Christoulakis) P.; m. Diane Perparos, Sept. 30, 1945; children: Mark, John, Dean. Student, U. Ill., 1940-41, LHD (hon.), 1971, Gov.'s State U., 1980, Hellenic Coll., 1984, Roosevelt U., 1987, Am. Coll. Greece, 2004. Freelance writer, tchr., lectr.; tchr. workshop classes in novel, short story; McGuffey vis. lectr. Ohio U., Athens, 1971; writer-in-residence Chgo. Pub. Library, 1976-77, Chgo. Bd. Edn., 1978-79; Kazantzakis Prof. San Francisco State U., 1992. Author: Lion at My Heart, 1959, The Odyssey of Kostas Volakis, 1963, Pericles on 31st Street, 1965 (nominated for Nat. Book award), The Founder's Touch: The Life of Paul Galvin of Motorola, 1965, A Dream of Kings, 1966 (Nat. Book award nomination), The Waves of Night, 1969, Stelmark: A Family Recollection, 1970, In the Land of Morning, 1973, The Hour of the Bell, 1976, A Petrakis Reader, 28 Stories, 1978, Nick the Greek, 1979, Days of Vengeance, 1983, Reflections on a Writer's Life and Work, 1983, Collected Stories, 1986, Ghost of the Sun, 1990, Tales of the Heart, 1999, Twilight of the Ice, 2003, The Orchards of Ithaca, 2004; writer (films) A Dream of Kings, 1969, Picture Windows, 1995; contbr. short stories to mags. including, Atlantic Monthly, Sat. Eve. Post, Harper's Bazaar, Country Beautiful. (Story included in Prize Stories, also O. Henry Award 1966). Recipient awards Friends of Am. Writers, Friends of Lit., Soc. Midland Authors, Carl Sandburg award, Ellis Island medal of honor, 1995, O'Henry award; named Kazantzakis chair in Modern Greek Studies San Francisco State U., 1992. Mem. Authors Guild, PEN, Writers Guild Am.-West. Address: Dune Acres 80 East Rd Chesterton IN 46304-1035 Personal E-mail: hmp801@comcast.net. *"...The older I become, the more clearly I see that there is a stunning purity in the writing of a book that I cannot achieve in my own life with its frailty and desperation. The work takes over with a life of its own. In those moments, I wouldn't trade writing with all its loneliness and sometimes with its pain, for any other profession in the world.*

PETRAKIS, NICHOLAS LOUIS, epidemiologist, oncologist, medical researcher, educator; b. San Francisco, Feb. 6, 1922; s. Louis Nicholas and Stamatina (Boosalis) P.; m. Patricia Elizabeth Kelly, June 24, 1947; children: Steven John, Susan Lynn, Sandra Kay. BA, Augustana Coll., 1943; BS in Medicine, U. S.D., 1944; MD, Washington U., St. Louis, 1946. Intern Mpls. Gen. Hosp., 1946-47; physician, researcher U.S. Naval Radiol. Def. Lab., San Francisco, 1947-49; resident physician Mpls. Gen. Hosp., 1949-50; sr. asst. surgeon Nat. Cancer Inst., USPHS, San Francisco, 1950-54; asst. research physician Cancer Research Inst., U. Calif., San Francisco, 1954-56; asst. prof. preventive medicine U. Calif. Sch. Medicine, San Francisco, 1956-60, assoc. prof., 1960-66, prof., 1966-91, chmn. dept. epidemiology and internat. health, 1978-88, prof. emeritus, 1991—; prof. epidemiology U. Calif. Sch. Pub. Health, Berkeley, 1981-91. Assoc. dir. G.W. Hooper Edn., U. Calif., San Francisco, 1970-74, acting dir., 1974-77, chmn. dept. epidemiology and internat. health, 1979-89; co-dir. Breast Screening Ctr. of No. Calif., Oakland, 1976-81; cons. Breast Cancer Task Force, Nat. Cancer Inst., Bethesda, Md., 1972-76; chmn. Biometry & Epidemiology Contract Rev. Com., Bethesda, 1977-81; mem. bd. sci. counselors, div. cancer etiology Nat. Cancer Inst., Bethesda, 1982-86; mem. scientific adv. com. Calif. State Tobacco-Related Disease Rsch. Program, 1991-93; cons. U. Crete Sch. Medicine, Heraklion, Greece, 1984; bd. dirs. No. Calif. Cancer Ctr., 1991. Contbr. over 200 research papers on breast cancer, med. oncology and hematology. Eleanor Roosevelt Internat. Cancer fellow Am. Cancer Soc., Comitato Reserche Nucleari, Cassacia, Italy, 1962; U.S. Pub. Health Service Spl. fellow Galton Lab., U. London, 1969-70; recipient Alumni Achievement award Augustana Coll., Sioux Falls, S.D., 1979, Axion award Hellenic-Am. Profl. Soc. of Calif., San Francisco, 1984, Lewis C. Robbins award Soc. for Prospective Medicine, Indpls., 1985, Otto W. Sartorius, MD, award from Susan Love MD Breast Cancer Found., 2001. Mem. Am. Soc. Preventive Oncology (founding, pres. 1984-85, Disting. Achievement award 1992), Soc. for Prospective Medicine (founding), Am. Assn. Cancer Rsch., Am. Epidemiol. Soc., Am. Soc. Clin. Investigation, Am. Bd. Preventive Medicine (cert.). Home: 335 Juanita Way San Francisco CA 94127-1657 Office: U Calif Sch Medicine Dept Epidemiology & Biostats Box 0560 MU420W San Francisco CA 94143-0001 Office Phone: 415-476-2001. E-mail: petrakis@ix.netcom.com.

PETRALIA, RONALD SEBASTIAN, entomologist, neurobiologist; b. Lawrence, Mass., Nov. 7, 1954; s. Samuel and Rosalie (Zanfagna) P. BS in Entomology summa cum laude, U. Mass., 1975; PhD in Entomology and Biology, Tex. A&M U., 1979. Rsch. asst. Tex. A&M U., College Station, 1975-79, rsch. assoc., 1979-80; asst. prof. biology St. Ambrose Coll., Davenport, Iowa, 1980-85; rsch. fellow dept. anatomy George Washington U., Washington, 1985-90; sr. staff fellow Nat. Inst. Deafness and Other Comm. Disorders, NIH, Bethesda, Md., 1991-97, staff scientist, 1997—. Presenter in field. Contbr. chpts. to books: Excitatory Amino Acids, 1992, The Mammalian Coclear Nuclei: Their Role in Neuroendocrine Function, 1996, The Ionotropic Glutamate Receptors, 1997, Ionotropic Glutamate to Receptors in the CNS, 1999, Handbook of Chemical Neuroanatomy: Glutamate, 2000; contbr. articles to profl. jours. Mem. AAAS, Chesapeake Soc. Microscopy (coun. mem., newsletter editor, past pres.), Soc. Neurosci., Entomol. Soc. Am., Microscopy Soc. Am., Assn. Rsch. Otolaryngology, Cambridge Entomol. Club, Sigma Xi. Roman Catholic. Home: 3 Pooks Hill Rd Apt 218 Bethesda MD 20814-5404 Office: NIDCD NIH Rm 50/4142 9000 Rockville Pike Bethesda MD 20892-8027 Business E-Mail: petralia@nidcd.nih.gov.

PETRANEK, STEPHEN LYNN, editor; b. Washington, Aug. 19, 1944; s. Chester J. and Mabel Oleta (Mercer) P.; m. Barbara Ergas, 1983. Student, U. Okla., 1962-63; BS, U. Md., 1970; postgrad., U. Mo., 1970-71. Editor-in-chief The Diamondback, U. Md., 1969-70; reporter Democrat and Chronicle, Rochester, N.Y., 1972, financial writer, 1972-73, asst. Sunday editor, 1973; editor Upstate mag., 1974-75, 1975-77, Tropic Mag. The Miami Herald, 1977-78; dep. editor Washington Post Mag., 1978-81, mng. editor, 1982-90; sr. editor LIFE mag., 1990-96; editor-in-chief This Old House mag., 1996-98, Discover mag., 1999—. Author: newspaper series Decline and Fall of Stirling Homex, 1972. Recipient John Hancock award for fin. writing, 1972, Bus. Journalism award U. Mo., 1973, Frank Tripp Newswriting award, 1973 Mem. Sigma Delta Chi, Kappa Tau Alpha, Omicron Delta Kappa, Pi Delta Epsilon. Mem. United Ch. of Christ. Home: 10 Deepwood Dr Chappaqua NY 10514-2414 Office: DISCOVER Mag 114 5th Ave Fl 15 New York NY 10011-5604 E-mail: stephen.petranek@disney.com.

PETRASH, JEFFREY MICHAEL, lawyer; b. Cleve., Dec. 14, 1948; s. Robert Anthony and Naomi Marjorie (Close) P.; 1 child, Michael Stewart. AB, U. Mich., 1969, JD, 1973. Bar: Mich. 1974, D.C. 1975, Md. 1997. Assoc. Dickinson, Wright, McKean, Cudlip & Moon, Detroit, 1973-75, Hamel, Park, McCabe & Saunders, Washington, 1975-78; from assoc. to ptnr. Dickinson, Wright, Washington, 1978-99; sr. counsel Am. Gas Assn., Washington, 2000—. Capt. U.S. Army, 1973-74. Mem. Soc. Barristers. Episcopalian. Avocation: sailing. Home: 6606 Hillandale Rd Bethesda MD 20815-6406 Office: 400 N Capitol St NW Washington DC 20001-1511

PETRAUSKAS, HELEN O. automobile manufacturing company executive; b. 1944; married. BS, Wayne State U., 1966, JD, 1971. Chemist, group supr. Sherwin-Williams Co., 1966-71; various positions Ford Motor Co., Dearborn, Mich., 1971-79, asst. dir. emissions and fuel economy cert., 1980-82, exec. dir. environ. and safety engring and rsch. staff, 1982-83, exec. dir. engring. and tech. staff, 1983, corp. v.p. environ. and safety engring., 1983—2001; ret., 2001. Office: 1 American Rd Dearborn MI 48126-2701

PETREQUIN, HARRY JOSEPH, JR., foreign service officer; b. Ste. Genevieve, Mo., July 1, 1929; s. Harry Joseph and Crescentia Ellen (Bechter) P.; m. Katharine McDonnell Drouin, Oct. 7, 1980; children: John Andrew, Marc Christopher, Paul Nicholas. AB, Westminster Coll., 1950; B of Fgn. Trade, Am. Grad. Sch. Internat. Mgmt., 1954; postgrad., Johns Hopkins U., 1960; MA, Tufts U., 1970. Joined U.S. Fgn. Svc., 1955; assigned AID and predecessor agys., 1955—; dep. dir. S.E. Asia Regional Econ. Devel. Office, Thailand, 1970-74; U.S. coord. Senegal River Basin Authority, Dakar, 1975-76; dir. ASEAN and South Pacific Affairs, 1977-80; dir. program devel. and evaluation staff Bur. Internat. Orgn. Affairs State Dept., 1980-81; dep. dir. AID Mission, Morocco, 1981-85; coord. AID Sr. Mgmt. Course, 1985-86, Indsl. Coll. of the Armed Forces, 1986-87; faculty dept. nat. security policy Nat. War Coll., Washington, 1987-89; internat. devel. cons. Black Mountain, N.C., 1989—. Adj. prof. polit. sci. Warren Wilson Coll., Swannanoa, NC, 1993-94; faculty U. NC Coll. Srs., 1995—. Lt. (j.g.) USCGR, 1951-53, Comdr. Ready Res., 1973. Recipient Superior Honor award AID, 1979, State Dept. Superior Honor award, 1981, Comdrs. award for Civilian Svc., Dept. of the Army, 1989. Mem. Soc. Internt. Devel., World Federalist Assn. (nat. bd. dirs.), Am. Fgn. Svc. Assn., UN Assn. U.S., Acad. Polit. Sci., Cousteau Soc., Common Cause, Inst. Noetic Scis., World Future Soc., Amnesty Internat., Coast Guard Combat Vets Assn., Greenpeace, Vets. for Peace, The Land Inst., Phi Alpha Theta.

PETRI, DANIEL C. communications executive; Pres. global systems Bell Atlantic, 1997, pres. internat. telecomms.; pres. internat. Europe/Asia Verizon Wireless (formerly Bell Atlantic), 2000—. Office: Verizon Comms 1095 Ave of the Americas New York NY 10036

PETRI, THOMAS EVERT, congressman; b. Marinette, Wis., May 28, 1940; s. Robert and Marian (Humleker) P.; m. Anne Neal, Mar. 26, 1983; 1 child, Alexandra. BA in Govt., Harvard U., 1962, JD, 1965. Bar: Wis. 1965. Law clk. to presiding justice U.S. Dist. (we. dist.) Wis., Madison, 1965-66; vol. Peace Corps, Somalia, 1966-67; aide White House, Washington, 1969-70; dir. crime and drug studies Pres.'s Nat. Adv. Coun. on Exec. Orgn., 1969; pvt. practice Fond du Lac, Wis., 1970-79; mem. Wis. State Senate, Madison, 1973-79, U.S. Congress from 6th Wis. dist., Washington, 1979—; mem. edn. and workforce com., trans. and infrastructure com. Editor: National Industrial Policy: Solution or Illusion, 1984. Republican. Lutheran. Avocations: reading, swimming, hiking, biking, skiing. Office: US Ho of Reps 2462 Rayburn Bldg Washington DC 20515-0001

PETRICK, ALFRED, JR., mineral economics educator, consultant; b. Mt. Vernon, N.Y., Dec. 30, 1926; s. Alfred and Ruth (Updike) P.; m. Ruth Goodridge, Jan. 2, 1956; children: Elizabeth, Andrew Wayne. BS, BA, Columbia U., 1952, MS, 1962; MBA, Denver U., 1966; PhD, U. Colo., 1969. Registered profl. engr., Colo. Sales engr. Ingersoll Rand Co., N.Y.C., 1953-54; project engr. U.S. AEC, Grand Junction, Colo., 1954-57; mining engr. Reynolds Metals Co., Bauxite, Ark., 1957-61, 1957-61; mineral economist U.S. Bur. Mines, Denver, 1963-70; Coulter prof. Colo. Sch. Mines, Golden, 1970-84, emeritus prof., 1984—; dir. Petrick Assocs., Evergreen, Colo. Author: Economics International Development, 1977, Economics of Minerals, 1980, Preparacion y Evaluacion, 1982. Mem. com. tech. aspects strategic materials Nat. Acad. Sci., Washington, 1973-76, mem. com. surface mining and reclamation, 1979. Served with USAF, 1945-47, PTO. Fulbright research scholar U. Otago, Dunedin, New Zealand, 1986; recipient Edn. award Instituto Para Funcionarios De Las Industrias Minera y Siderurgica, Mexico City, 1981; recipient Service award Office Tech. Assessment, U.S. Congress, 1981. Mem. AIME (chmn. council econs. 1977-78, Henry Krumb lectr. 1986, service award), Profl. Engrs. Colo. Presbyterian. Home: 5544 S Hatch Dr Evergreen CO 80439-7233 Office: Colo Sch Mines Golden CO 80401 E-mail: peta33@comcast.net.

PETRICK, ERNEST NICHOLAS, mechanical engineer, researcher; b. Pa., Apr. 9, 1922; s. Aurelius and Anna (Kaschak) P.; m. Magdalene Simcoe, June 13, 1946; children: Deborah Petrick Healey, Katherine, Denise, Victoria Petrick Kropp. BS in Mech. Engring, Carnegie Inst. Tech., 1943; MS, Purdue U., 1948, PhD, 1955. Registered profl. engr., Mich. Faculty Purdue U., 1946-53; dir. heat transfer research Curtiss-Wright Corp., Woodridge, N.J., 1953-56; chief advanced propulson systems Curtiss-Wright Research divsn., Quehanna, Pa., 1957-60; chief research engr. Kelsey-Hayes Co., Detroit, 1960-65; chief scientist, tech. dir. U.S. Army Tank-Automotive Command, Warren, Mich., 1965-82; chief scientist, dir. engring. labs. Gen. Dynamics, 1982-87; engring. cons., 1987—; panel mem. combat vehicles NATO, 1973-82; mem. adv. bd. on basic combustion research NSF, 1973; chmn. advanced transp. systems com. White House Energy Project, 1973; mem. adv. com. NSF-RANN research program Drexel U. Coll. Engring., 1976-78; mem. Army Sci. Bd., 1983-89; cons. Air Force Studies Bd. NRC, 1991-93, cons. Def. Sci. Bd., 1994-95; cons. NAS, 1997—99, 2001—03, Bd. Army Sci. and Tech. Rev. NAS Naval Studies Bd., 2003; adj. prof. engring. Wayne State U., Detroit, 1972-82, U. Mich., Ann Arbor, 1982-83. Contbr. articles on transp., ground vehicles, propulsion and project mgmt. to profl. jours. Lt., chief engr. destroyer USNR, 1942—46, WWII. Recipient certificate of achievement U.S. Army, 1967, Outstanding Performance awards, 1970, 71, 76, 82, Outstanding Mech. Engring. award Purdue U., 1991; named Disting. Engring. Alumnus Purdue U., 1966. Mem. Soc. Automotive Engrs. (nat. dir. 1978-80), Am. Def. Preparedness Assn. (chmn. land warfare survivability divsn. 1990-95, Silver medal 1992, Recognition award 1992), Assn. U.S. Army, Sigma Xi, Pi Tau Sigma. Home: 1540 Stonehaven Rd Ann Arbor MI 48104-4150 Office: ENP Cons 1540 Stonehaven Rd Ann Arbor MI 48104

PETRICK, JOSEPH ANTHONY, small business owner, management consultant, educator; b. Pueblo, Colo., Dec. 31, 1946; s. Joseph John and Hermina Emma Petrick; m. Kimberly Marie Weber, Sept. 22, 1984. BA in Philosophy, Colo. State U., 1968; PhD, Pa. State U., 1972; MBA, U. of Cin., 1990. Cert. Human Resources Certification Inst., Wash., D.C., 1993. Asst. prof. of philosophy Coll. of Charleston, SC, 1972—75; assoc. prof. and head of philosophy dept. No. Ky. U., Highland Heights, Ky., 1975—82; asst. dean So. Ohio Coll., Fairfield, Ohio, 1982—84; head off-Campus Bus. Wilmington (Ohio) Coll., 1984—87; prof. U. of Cin., 1987—89; prof. of mgmt. Wright State U., Dayton, Ohio, 1989—. Prin., owner Orgnl. Ethics Assocs., Cin., 1992—, Performance Leadership Assocs., Cin., 1996—, Integrity Capacity Assocs., Cin., 2002—; bd. dirs. Human Resources Cert. Inst. Author: Total Quality in Managing Human Resources, 1995, Total Quality and Organization Development, 1997, Management Ethics: Integrity at Work, 1997, Managing Project Quality, 2002. Baldrige quality award examiner U.S. Dept. of Commerce, Washington, 1998—2000; examiner Ohio Quality Award for Excellence, Dayton, 1999—2000. Recipient Innovation in Bus. Edn. Group award, Midwestern Deans of U.S. Bus. Schs., 1998; fellow, Pa. State U., 1969—71, Woodrow Wilson Nat. Found., 1971—72, Malone Arabic Studies fellow, U.S. Arab Rels. Inst., 1995. Mem.: Midwestern Soc. for Human Resources and Indsl. Rels. (pres. 1996—97), Soc. for Human Resource Mgmt., Acad. of Mgmt., U.S. Assn. for Small Bus. and Entrepreneurship (v.p. individual entrepreneurship 1994—95), Am. Philos. Assn., Sigma Iota Epsilon, Beta Gamma Sigma. Democrat. Avocations: travel, reading, films, dance, golf. Home: 3505 Arborcrest Court Cincinnati OH 45236 Office: Wright State University 3640 Colonel Glenn Hwy Dayton OH 45435 E-mail: joseph.petrick@wright.edu.

PETRICK, MICHAEL JOSEPH, journalism educator; b. Antigo, Wis., Sept. 6, 1942; BS, U. Wis., Milw., 1965, MS, 1967; PhD, U. Wis., Madison, 1970. News editor Milw. South Times Star, 1966-67; disting. teaching fellow U. Wis., Madison, 1969-70; from asst. to assoc. prof. U. Md., College Park, 1970-78; copy editor Evening Star, Washington, 1974-75; chairperson dept. journalism Ctrl. Mich. U., Mt. Pleasant, 1978-84, prof., 1984-2000, prof. emeritus, 2000—. Writing and editing coach Ctrl. Mich. Newspapers, 1984-85; writing and reporting coach Greenville (Mich.) Daily News, 1997-99; chair bd. in control of student media Ctrl. Mich. U., 1997-99. Co-author: Using the Mass Media, 1975; contbr. articles to profl. jours. Mem. Md.-Del.-D.C. Press Assn. (chmn. freedom of info. com. 1972-73), Soc. Profl. Journalists (campus chpt. adviser 1970-99), Nat. Coun. Editl. Writers, Assn. for Edn. in Journalism and Mass Communication. Home: PO Box 6 Mount Pleasant MI 48804-0006 Office: PO Box 6 Mount Pleasant MI 48804-0006 E-mail: michael.petrick@cmich.edu.

PETRICOFF, M. HOWARD, lawyer, educator; b. Cin., Dec. 22, 1949; s. Herman and Neoma P.; m. Hanna Sue, Aug. 11, 1974; children: Nicholas, Eve. BS, Am. U., 1967-71; JD, U. Cin., 1971-74; M in Pub. Adminstrn., Harvard U., 1980-81. Bar: Ohio, U.S. Ct. Appeals (D.C. cir.) 1977, U.S. Ct. Appeals (10th cir.) 1985, U.S. Ct. Appeals (6th cir.) 1989, U.S. Supreme Ct. 1989. Asst. city law dir. City of Toledo (Ohio), 1975-77; asst. atty. gen. Ohio Atty. Gen. Office, Columbus, 1977-82; ptnr. Vorys, Sater, Seymour & Pease, Columbus, 1982—. Adj. prof. law Capital U. Law Sch., Columbus, 1991—. Contbr. articles to profl. jours. Reginald Heber Smith Found. fellow Washnigton, 1974-75. Mem. Ohio Bar Assn., Columbus Bar Assn., Ohio Oil and Gas Assn. Office: Vorys Sater Seymour & Pease PO Box 1008 52 E Gay St Columbus OH 43215-3161

PETRIDES, GEORGE ATHAN, ecologist, educator; b. N.Y.C., Aug. 1, 1916; s. George Athan and Grace Emeline (Ladd) P.; m. Miriam Clarissa Pasma, Nov. 30, 1940; children: George H., Olivia L., Lisa B. BS, George Washington U., 1938; MS, Cornell U., 1940; PhD, Ohio State U., 1948; postdoctoral fellow, U. Ga., 1963-64. Naturalist Nat. Park Service, Washington and Yosemite, Calif., 1938-43, Glacier Nat. Park, Mont., 1947, Mt. McKinley Nat. Park, Alaska, 1959; game technician W.Va. Conservation Commn., Charleston, 1941; instr. Am. U., 1942-43, Ohio State U., 1946-48; leader Tex. Coop. Wildlife Unit; assoc. prof. wildlife mgmt. Tex. A. and M. Coll., 1948-50; assoc. prof. wildlife mgmt., zool. and African studies Mich. State U., 1950-58, prof., 1958—; research prof. U. Pretoria, S. Africa, 1965; vis. prof. U. Kiel, Germany, 1967; vis. prof. wildlife mgmt. Kanha Nat. Park, India, 1983; del. sci. confs. Warsaw, 1960, Nairobi and Salisbury, 1963, Sao Paulo, Aberdeen, 1965, Lucerne, 1966, Varanasi, India, Nairobi, 1967, Oxford, Eng., Paris, 1968, Durban, 1971, Mexico City, 1971, 73, Banff, 1972, Nairobi, Moscow, The Hague, 1974, Johannesburg, 1977, Sydney, 1978, Kuala Lumpur, 1979, Cairns, Australia, Mogadishu, Somalia, Peshawar, Pakistan, 1980. Participant NSF Expdn., Antarctic, 1972, FAO mission to, Afghanistan, 1972, World Bank mission to, Malaysia, 1975 Author: Field Guide to Trees and Shrubs, 1958, 2d edit., 1972, Field Guide to Eastern Trees, 1988, 98, Field Guide to Western Trees, 1992, 98, First Guide to Trees, 1993, Trees of the California Sierra Nevada, 1996, Trees of the Pacific Northwest, 1998, Trees of the Rocky Mountains and Intermountain West, 2000, Trees of the American Southwest, 2000; editor wildlife mgmt. terrestrial sect. Biol. Abstracts, 1947-72; contbr. articles to biol. publs. Served to lt. USNR, 1943-46. Fulbright research awards in E. Africa Nat. Parks Kenya, 1953-54; Fulbright research awards in E. Africa Nat. Parks Kenya, Uganda, 1956-57; N.Y. Zool. Soc. grantee Ethiopia, Sudan, 1957; N.Y. Zool. Soc. grantee Thailand, 1977; Mich. State U. grantee Nigeria, 1962; Mich. State U. grantee Zambia, 1966; Mich. State U. grantee Kenya, 1969; Mich. State U. grantee Africa, 1970, 71, 73, 81; Mich. State U. grantee Greece, 1974, 83; Mich. State U. grantee Iran, 1974; Mich. State U. grantee Botswana, 1977; Mich. State U. grantee Papua New Guinea, Thailand, 1979; Iran Dept. Environment grantee, 1977; Smithsonian Instn. grantee India and Nepal, 1967, 68, 75, 77, 83, 85; World Wildlife Fund grantee W. Africa, 1968 Mem. Am. Ornithologists Union, Am. Soc. Mammalogists, Wildlife Soc. (exec. sec. 1953), Wilderness Soc., Am. Comm. Internat. Wildlife Protection, Ecol. Soc., Fauna Preservation Soc., E. African Wildlife Soc., Internat. Union Conservation Nature, Zool. Soc. So. Africa, Sigma Xi. Presbyterian. Home: 4895 Barton Rd Williamston MI 48895-9305 Office: Mich State U Dept Botany East Lansing MI 48824 E-mail: petrides@msu.edu.

PETRIE, BRUCE INGLIS, lawyer; b. Washington, Nov. 8, 1926; s. Robert Inglis and Marion (Douglas) P.; m. Beverly Ann Stevens, Nov. 3, 1950 (dec. Oct. 1993); children: Laurie Ann Roche, Bruce Inglis, Karen Elizabeth Medsger. BBA, U. Cin., 1948, JD, 1950. Bar: Ohio 1950, U.S. Dist. Ct. (so. dist.) Ohio 1951, U.S. Ct. Appeals (6th cir.) 1960, U.S. Supreme Ct. Assoc. Kunkel & Kunkel, Cin., 1950-51, Graydon, Head & Ritchey, 1951-57, ptnr., 1957—. Exec. prodr. (sch. video) Classical Quest, 2000; author: How To Get the Most Out of Your Lawyer, 2002; contbr. articles to legal jours. Mem. bd. Charter Com. Greater Cin., 1952—; pres. Charter Rsch. Inst., 2000—03; mem. bd. edn. Indian Hill Exempted Village Sch. Dist., 1965—67, pres., 1967; mem. adv. bd. William A. Mitchell Ctr., 1969—86; mem. Green Areas adv. com. Village of Indian Hill, Ohio, 1969—80, chmn., 1976—80; mem. Ohio Ethics Com., 1974—75; founder Parents as Tchrs. Metro Housing Authority Commn., 1991—; a prin. advocate merit selection judges Ohio; trustee, mem. bd. Seven Hills Neighborhood Houses' Inst. for Learning in Retirement; mem. bd. Hamilton County Good Govt. League; organizer Late Gt. Lakes Book Distbn. project, global vol. tchr. China, 2003, 2004; elder, trustee, deacon Knox Presbyn. Ch.; bd. dirs. Murray Seasongood Good Govt. Fund, 1975—, chmn., 1989—; bd. dirs. Nat. Civic League, Cin. Vol. Lawyers for Poor Found., Linton Music Series, Amernet Chamber Music Soc.; co-founder Sta. WGUC-FM; mem. WGUC-FM Cmty. Bd., 1974—, chmn., 1974—76. Recipient Pres.'s award U. Cin., 1976, Disting. Alumnus award, 1995. Fellow: Am. Bar Found.; mem.: ABA, Ohio State Bar Assn. Found. (Outstanding Rsch. in Law and Govt. award 1986, Charles P. Taft Civic Gumption award 1988, Ohio Bar medal 1988), Am. Law Inst., Nat. Civic League (coun. 1984—, Disting. Citizen award 1985), Am. Judicature Soc. (dir., Herbert Lincoln Harley award 1973), Cin. Bar Assn. (pres. 1981, Trustee's award 2000), Ohio Bar Assn., Cin. Country Club, Univ. Club, Cincinnatus Assn., Lit. Club, Order of Coif. Avocations: tennis, squash, woodworking, writing, horticulture, music. Home: 2787 Walsh Rd Cincinnati OH 45208-3428 Office: Graydon Head & Ritchey 1900 Fifth 3d Ctr 511 Walnut St Ste 1900 Cincinnati OH 45202-3157

PETRIE, DONALD JOSEPH, banker; b. N.Y.C., Sept. 2, 1921; s. John and Elizabeth (Thomson) P.; m. Jane Adams, Aug. 27, 1949; children: R. Scott, Anne, Elizabeth, Douglas, Susan. BBA, Manhattan Coll., 1950. Personnel mgr. Otis Elevator Co., N.Y.C., 1951-59; personnel dir. Brown Bros. Harriman & Co., N.Y.C., 1959-68; exec. v.p. U.S. Trust Co., N.Y.C., 1966-79; sr. v.p. Marine Midland Bank, N.Y.C., 1979-86, Drake Beam Morin Inc., N.Y.C., 1986-90; chmn., chief exec. officer Webster Corp., N.Y.C., 1990—. Lectr. Baruch Sch. Bus., Coll. City N.Y., 1955-58; pres., chmn. exec. and fin. coms., dir. Webster Apts., N.Y.C., 1973—; adj. prof. mgmt. Hofstra U., Hempstead, N.Y., 1986-93. Author: Explaining Pay Policy, 1969, Handling Employee Questions About Pay, 1976. Capt. USAAF, 1942-46. Mem. N.Y.C. Partnership and C. of C. (chmn. mgmt. edn. and adv. com. 1964-98). Home: 11 Fairview Ave Great Neck NY 11023-1462 Office: 419 W 34th St New York NY 10001-1596

PETRIE, FERDINAND RALPH, illustrator, artist; b. Hackensack, N.J., Sept. 17, 1925; s. Archibald John and Bessie (Rutherford) P.; m. Phyllis C. Haddow, Oct. 19, 1951; children: Beth, David. Advt. cert., Parson's Sch. Design, N.Y.C., 1949; student, Art Students League, 1947-49, Famous Artists Course in Illustration, 1958-59. Illustrator J. Gans Assos., N.Y.C., 1950-69. Free lance illustrator, artist, 1969—, owner, Petrie Gallery, Rockport, Mass., 1971-95; represented in permanent collections, U.S. Supreme Ct., Smithsonian Instn., Washington, Indpls. Mus. Art; designer U.S. commemorative stamp design, 2 Zaire commemorative stamps, 1980, USN, USCG, The Salvation Army; Author: Drawing Landscapes in Pencil, 1979; illustrator: The Drawing Book, 1980, The Color Book, 1981, The Alkyd Book, 1982, The Watercolorists Guide to Painting Trees, 1983, The Watercolorists Guide to Painting Skies, 1984; The Watercolorists Guide to Painting Water, 1985, Painting Nature in Watercolor, 1990. Served with U.S. Maritime Service, 1943-46. Mem. Artists Fellowship, Rockport Art Assn., Am. Artists Profl. League, N.J. Watercolor Soc. Presbyterian. Address: 51 Vreeland Ave Rutherford NJ 07070-2227

PETRIE, GREGORY STEVEN, lawyer; b. Seattle, Feb. 25, 1951; s. George C. and Pauline P.; m. Margaret Fuhrman, Oct. 6, 1979; children: Kathryn Jean, Thomas George. AB in Polit. Sci and Econs., UCLA, 1973; JD, Boston U., 1976. Bar: Wash. 1976, U.S. Dist. Ct. (we. dist.) Wash. 1976. Adminstr. Action/Peace Corps, Washington, 1973, Fed. Power Commn., Washington, 1974; assoc. Oles Morrison et al, Seattle, 1976-80; ptnr. Schwabe Williamson Ferguson & Burdell, Seattle, 1981-94; mng. shareholder Krutch Lindell Bingham Jones & Petrie, Seattle, 1994—. Mem. Seattle-King County Bar Assn., Profl. Liability Architects and Engrs., Wash. Athletic Club. Avocations: woodworking, skiing. Office: Krutch Lindell Bingham Jones & Petrie 1420 Fifth Ave Ste 3150 Seattle WA 98101 Office Phone: 206-682-1505. E-mail: gsp@nwlink.com.

PETRIE, RICHARD ALLEN, retired lawyer, tax consultant; b. Milw., Oct. 11, 1930; s. Elmer Jacob and Ella Emma (Hass) P.; m. Helen Ann Brunner, July 31, 1965; children: Paula Erin Schmidt, Brenda Marie Williams. BS in Bus. Adminstrn. magna cum laude, Marquette U., U. Wis., Milw., 1953; LLM cum laude, U. Wis., 1956. Assoc. Paul P. Lipton, Milw., 1956-71; ptnr. Lipton & Petrie, Milw., 1971-74; shareholder Lipton & Petrie, Ltd., Milw., 1974-80, Meldman, Case & Weine, Ltd., Milw., 1980-85, Mulcahy & Wherry, S.C., Milw., 1986-91, Richard A. Petrie, S.C., Milw., 1991—2002. Tax cons. Reinhart, Boerner, Van Deuren, Norris & Rieselbach, SC, Milw., 1991—2001. Co-author: Federal Taxation Practice and Procedure, 4th edit., 1992; bd. editors Wis. Law Rev., 1954-56; contbr. articles to profl. jours. Mem. ABA, State Bar Wis., Order of the Coif. Avocations: reading, golf, gardening, bowling.

PETRIE, WILLIAM, physicist, researcher; b. Victoria, B.C., Can., Dec. 30, 1912; s. James and Amelia (Robertson) P.; m. Isabelle Ruth Chodat, May 8, 1944; children: Heather Louise (dec.), Douglas Bruce. BA, U. B.C., Vancouver, Can., 1938; A.M., Harvard U., 1941, PhD, 1944. Assoc. prof. U. Sask., Saskatoon, Can., 1945-51; chief ops. research Def. Research Bd., Ottawa, Ont., Can., 1954-60, dep. chmn., 1966-68, chief Can. def. research staff London, 1968-71. Sci. advisor Apollo Energy, Victoria, 1981-83; mem. numerous sci. bds. and coms. Author: The Story of the Aurora Borealis, 1963, Guide to Orchids of North America, 1981; also numerous articles Recipient Centennial medal Govt. of Can., 1967, numerous research grants and contracts Fellow Royal Soc. Can. Avocations: gardening, fishing. Home: 306-2300 Henry Ave Rural Rt 4 Sidney BC Canada V8L 2B2

PETRIE, WILLIAM MARSHALL, psychiatrist; b. Louisville, Oct. 19, 1946; s. Garner McReynolds and Claire (Samuels) P.; children: Christopher W., Ellen M., Shelley M.; m. Lori L. Molchin, Oct. 1, 1994. BA, Vanderbilt U., 1968, MD, 1972. Research psychiatrist NIMH, Rockville, Md., 1975-77; asst. prof. dept. psychiatry Vanderbilt Med. Ctr., Nashville, 1977-81, assoc. prof., 1981-82, assoc. clin. prof., 1982-87, clin. prof., 1992—; pvt. practice psychiatry Psychiat. Cons., P.C., Nashville, 1982—, pres., 1996—. Clin. instr. Georgetown U. Med. Ctr., 1975-77; cons. psychopharmacology rsch. br. NIMH, 1977-80; rschr. in geriatric psychopharmacology; med. dir. memory Study Ctr., 1987—; chmn. of psychiatry, Parthenon Pavilion, 1994-96; bd. trustees Centennial Mutual Ctr., 1994—, vice-chmn. bd. trustees, 1998—; pres. Columbia Psychiat. Care Network, 1997—. Mem. editorial bd. Gen. Hosp. Psychiatry, 1995—, Audio Digest Psychiatry, 1996-99; author numerous articles and book chpts. on psychopharmacology and geriatric psychiatry. Fellow Am. Psychiat. Assn. (pres. mid. Tenn. dist. br. 1986-87); mem. AMA, Tenn. Med. Assn., Am. Assn. Geriatric Psychiatrists, Am. Coll. Psychiatrists, Tenn. Psychiat. Assn. (pres. 1999-2000). Democrat. Methodist. Office: Psychiat Cons PC 310 25th Ave N Nashville TN 37203-1515 Office Phone: 615-250-6780.

PETRIK, GERD, pharmaceutical executive; b. Brno, CSR, Czechoslovakia, Apr. 13, 1943; came to U.S., 1993; s. Wilhelm and Ingeborg (Bittner) P.; m. Feli Schueller, July 10, 1971; children: Sharon, Wendy. Pharmacist, Free U. Berlin, 1968. Pres. Dr. Will Inc., Karlsruhe, Germany, 1968-70; product mgr. Pfizer, Illertissen, Germany, 1970-73; head rsch. Helopharm, Berlin, 1973-85, pres., owner, 1985—. Pres. Berlin Pharm. Assn., 1990-93; owner over 25 rsch. and devel. med. cos., worldwide, 1995—. Inventor chem. compounds. Pres. Harness Racing Assn., Berlin, 1992-96. Named hon. consul Bangladesh, 1986-90, hon. gen. consul, Panama, 1990-94; scholar Columbia U., 1995-97. Roman Catholic. Avocations: harness racing (german champion, world record holder), golf, tennis, classic car collector. Home: 1538 N Casey Key Rd Osprey FL 34229-9770 E-mail: gpetrik@comcast.net.

PETRILA, JOHN PHILIP, health law educator; b. Terre Haute, Ind., June 25, 1951; s. John Joseph and Patricia Ann (McCrisaken) P.; m. Amelia Ann Thompson, Oct. 18, 1953; 1 child, Patrick John. BA, St. Joseph's Coll., Renssalaer, Ind., 1973; JD, U. Va., 1976, LLM, 1977. Bar: Va. 1976. Fellow in mental health law U. Va. Law Sch., Charlottesville, 1976-78; asst. atty. gen. State of Mo., Jefferson City, 1978-79; dir. forensic svcs. Mo. Mental Hygiene Dept., Jefferson City, 1979-81; dep. counsel N.Y. Office Mental Health, Albany, 1981-87, counsel, dep. commr., 1987-92; chmn. dept. mental health law and policy Fla. Mental Health Inst./ U. South Fla., Tampa, 1992—. Mem. mental health planning coun. State of Fla., 1993-95, mem. steering com. on managed behavioral health care, 1996; mem. Fla. Gov.'s Task Force on Medicaid Reform, 1996; interim dir. Statewide Pub. Guardianship Office, 2000—. Co-author: Psychological Evaluations for the Courts: A Handbook for Mental Health Professionals and Attorneys, 1987, 2d edit., 1997, Law and Mental Health Professionals: Florida, 1996, Mental Health Services: A Public Health Perspective, 1996; contbr. articles to profl. jours. Mem. Keel Club Hillsborough County United Way, Tampa, 1993—. Recipient Cmty. Svc. award Sch. Social Work U. South Fla., 1995, Saleem Shah award for contbn. to forensic mental health, 1999. Avocations: biking, sailing. Office: U South Fla 13301 Bruce B Downs Blvd Tampa FL 33612-3807

PETRILLI, RALPH CLEMENT, finance company executive; s. Clemente and Mary Theresa Petrilli; divorced; 1 child, Cythia Marie. BS, Duquesne U., 1952. Pres., owner Petrilli Econ. Studies, Sacramento, 1953—56; ops. mgr. Bel Air Mkts., Sacramento, 1955—59; pres., owner Petrilli Real Estate Co., Sacramento, 1958—87; pres., co-owner Choctaw Crode Corp., Marina Del Rey, Calif., 1971—; pres., owner Petrilli and Assoc., Marina Del Rey, 1971—93, Transworld Oil Co., Marina Del Rey, 1973—91; v.p. Variety Internat. Actores, Century City, Calif., 1973—87; mng. ptnr. Eco-Burn Co., Marina Del Rey, 1973—78; pres., co-owner Gemini Capital Formation Group, Bala Cynwyd, Pa., 1991—; lectr., cons. in field. Fundraiser NIAPAC, Phila., 1993—. With USNR, 1944—45. Mem.: Nat. Italian Am. PAC. Avocations: hiking, physical fitness. Office: Gemini Capital Formation Group 555 E City Line Ave Bala Cynwyd PA 19004 Office Fax: 610-660-9460. Personal E-mail: ralphpetrilli@hotmail.com.

PETRILLO, LEONARD PHILIP, retired corporate securities executive, lawyer; b. Toronto, Ont., Can., June 20, 1941; s. Philip Ralph and Bernice Petrillo; m. Linda née Hodgson; children: Larissa, Matthew, Stefanie, Ann-Marie, Karen. BSc, U. Toronto, 1964; LLB, Osgoode Hall Law Sch., Toronto, 1967. Bar: Ont. 1969. Ptnr. Robinson & Petrillo, 1969-79; corp. counsel Seel Enterprises Ltd., 1979-81; gen. counsel Toronto Stock Exch., 1981, v.p., gen. counsel, corp. sec., sec. to bd. dirs., 1984—2003.

PETRILLO, NANCY, public relations executive; CFO, exec. v.p. Edelman Pub. Rels. Worldwide, Chgo. Office: Edelman Pub Rels Worldwide 200 E Randolph St Fl 63D Chicago IL 60601-6436

PETRIN, JURIJ, pharmaceutical company executive; b. Ljubljana, Slovenia, Feb. 10, 1956; came to U.S., 1994; s. Ernest and Mira Petrin; m. Vilma Petrin, June 27, 1979; children: Anze, Ziva, Vesna. MD, U. Ljubljana, 1979. Diplomate Am. Bd. Internal Medicine. Intern U. Ljubljana Med. Ctr., Slovenia, 1979-81, resident, 1983-87, staff physician, 1983-92, ZD Ribnica, Slovenia, 1981-83; rsch. fellow U. Mich. Med. Ctr., Ann Arbor, Mich., 1987-88; med. dir. Ea. Europe Bristol-Myers Squibb, Munich, N.J., Germany, 1992-94, exec. dir. internat. regulatory affairs Princeton, N.J., 1994-96, v.p. intercontinental regulatory sci., 1996—. Asst. prof. internal medicine U. Ljubljana Med. Sch., 1989-91; presenter in field. Author: Emergency Medicine Manual, 1988, 89, 90; contbr. over 40 articles to profl. publs. Mem. ACP, Am. Acad. of Pharm. Physicians, Am. Soc. of Hypertension, Internat. Soc. of Hypertension, Interam. Soc. of Hypertension. Office: Bristol Myers Squibb Rte 206 & Provinceline Rd Princeton NJ 08543

PETRINI, DAVID J. bank executive; Audit mgr. Providian Fin. Corp., 1986-88, controller, 1988-90, v.p., 1990-94, sr. v.p., Sr. Fin. Officer, 1994-97, sr. v.p., CFO, 1997-98, exec. v.p., CFO, 1998—. Office: Providian 201 Mission St San Francisco CA 94105

PETRINI, FABRIZIO, computer science researcher; b. Foligno, Italy, May 26, 1964; m. Mariella DiGiacomo, June 22, 1997; 1 child, Alessandro DiGiacomo. Laurea in computer sci., U. Pisa, Italy, 1990, PhD in Computer Sci., 1997. Rsch. fellow Hewlett Packard Labs, Pisa, 1990-93, U. Oxford, U.K., 1999; mem. tech. staff Los Alamos (N.Mex.) Nat. Lab., 1999—. Grantee Enidata, 1990; Marie Curie fellowship European Cmty., 1997; recipient Excellence award Nat. Nuc. Security Agy., 2002, Def. Program award ASCI Q Integration Team, 2003. Mem. IEEE, Computer Soc. Office: Los Alamos Nat Lab MSB256 CCS-3 Los Alamos NM 87545 Office Phone: 505-665-2969. E-mail: fabrizio@lanl.gov.

PETRINOVICH, LEWIS FRANKLIN, psychology educator; b. Wallace, Idaho, June 12, 1930; s. John F. and Ollie (Steward) P. BS, U. Idaho, 1952; PhD, U. Calif., Berkeley, 1962. Asst. prof. San Francisco State Coll., 1957-63; from assoc. to prof. SUNY, Stony Brook, 1963-68; prof. U. Calif., Riverside, 1968-91, chmn. psychology, 1968-71, 86-89, prof. emeritus, 1991—. Author: Understanding Research in Social Sciences, 1975, Introduction to Statistics, 1976, Human Evolution, Reproduction and Morality, 1995, Living and Dying Well, 1996, Darwinian Dominion: Animal Welfare and Human Interests, 1999, The Cannibal Within, 2000; editor: Behavioral Development, 1981, Habituation, Sensitization and Behavior, 1984; cons. editor Behavioral and Neural Biology, 1972-90, Jour. Physiol. and Comparative Psychology, 1980-82, Jour. Comparative Psychology, 1983-90, Board of Dir., Eastman Medical Products; Cymed Corp., 2000-. Fellow Am. Psychol. Assn., Am. Psychol. Soc., Calif. Acad. Scis., Human Behavior and Evolution Soc., Western Psychol. Assn.; mem. Am. Ornithological Union (elected), Animal Behavior Soc., Sigma Xi, bd. dirs. Eastman Med. Products, Cymed Corp., 2000-, Friends of Big Band Jazz, 2003-. Home: 415 Boynton Ave Berkeley CA 94707-1701 Office: U Calif Riverside Psychology Dept Riverside CA 92521-0001

PETRO, JAMES MICHAEL, state attorney general; b. Cleve., Oct. 25, 1948; s. William John and Lila Helen (Janca) P.; m. Nancy Ellen Bero, Dec. 16, 1972; children: John Bero, Corbin Marie. BA, Denison U., 1970; JD, Case Western Res., 1973. Bar: Ohio 1973, U.S. Dist. Ct. (no. dist.) Ohio 1974, U.S. Ct. Appeals (6th cir.), U.S. Supreme Ct. Spl. asst. U.S. senator W.B. Saxbe, Cleve., 1972-73; asst. pros. atty. Franklin County, Ohio, 1973-74; asst. dir. law City of Cleve., 1974; ptnr. Petro & Troia, Cleve., 1974-84; dir. govt. affairs Standard Oil Co., Cleve., 1984-86; ptnr. Petro, Rademaker, Matty & McClelland, Cleve., 1986-93, Buckingham, Doolittle & Burroughs, Cleve., 1993-95; auditor State of Ohio, 1995—2003, atty. gen., 2003—. Mem. city coun. Rocky River, Ohio, 1977-79, dir. law, 1980; mem. Ohio Ho. of Reps., Columbus, 1981-84, 86-90; commr. Cuyahoga County, Ohio, 1991-95. Mem. ABA, Ohio State Bar Assn., Cleve. Bar Assn. Republican. Methodist. Home: 1933 Lake Shore Dr Columbus OH 43204-4963 Office: 30 E Broad St Columbus OH 43266 Office Phone: 614-466-4320. Business E-Mail: jpetro@ag.state.oh.us.

PETROCELLI, A. F. hotel executive; With United Capital, 1975, chmn., CEO, 1987, pres., 1991; chmn., CEO, pres. Prime Hospitality Corp., Fairfield, N.J., 1998—. Pres., chmn., CEO United Capital Corp.; bd. dirs. Metex Corp., Nathan's Famous, Inc., Philips Internat. Realty Corp., Boyar Value Fund, Inc. Office: Prime Hospitality Corp PO Box 2700 700 Route 46 E Fairfield NJ 07004-1532

PETROKUBI, MARILYN, film company executive, researcher, film producer, writer; d. Stephen Joseph and Mary L. (Butchkosky) P.; m. Robert A. Lieberman; 1 child, Matthew Alexander. BA, Upsala Coll., 1973; MLS, Rutgers U., 1974. Reference librarian Livingston (N.J.) Pub. Library, 1974-75, Phillipsburg (N.J.) Free Pub. Library, 1975-78; freelance researcher, producer, 1979—; pres., exec. producer TimeSteps Prodns., Inc., West Orange, N.J., 1987—. Library systems cons., 1979—. N.J. State Council on the Arts grantee, 1977. Mem. Media Comms. Assn. Internat., N.Y. Women in Film and TV. Avocations: gardening, hiking, skiing, ice skating, biking. Office: TimeSteps Prodns Inc 2 Glenside Dr West Orange NJ 07052-4709

PETRONE, JOHN R. music educator, composer; b. Youngstown, Ohio, Dec. 26, 1932; s. Angelo R. and Mary C. Petrone; m. Diane Rupple Petrone, Oct. 18, 1987; m. Margaret Adams Petrone, Apr. 12, 1958 (div. Feb. 20, 1986); children: Nicolette, Jennifer, John, Margaret, Michael, Susan. MusB, Youngstown Coll., 1958; MusM, Duquesne U., 1963; PhD in music composition, Conservatoire Musique La Lille, France, 1982. Cert. permanent tchg. cert. Ohio, 1980. Dir. music St. Mary's HS, Warren, Ohio, 1957—58; elem. music supr. Cath. Diocese of Youngstown (Ohio), 1958—60; music dir. Cardinal Mooney HS, Youngstown, Ohio, 1960—65; music dir., specialist Willoughby (Ohio) Eastlake Schs., 1965—84; ret. state of Ohio tchr., 1984; adj. faculty Ursuline Coll., Pepper Pike, Ohio, 1986—. Composer (arranger and conductor): The Flight of Apollo Eleven, 1979; composer: (arranger, music dir.) Augustine, 1980, Mr. Jingeling, 1981, Care Bears, 1982; composer: NASA/Higbees Christmas show, 1983, (songs) Goin' Baroque, 1977, Haydn Seek, 1979, Disco-Tinued, 1979, Also Sprach Whatsisname. With spc. svcs. USAF, 1951—54, Korea. Recipient Outstanding Secondary Educator of Am., 1974, Martha Holden Jennings Scholar, 1975—76. Mem.: ASCAP, Am. Fedn. Musicians, Simfonia, Kappa Delta Pi, Phi Mu Alpha. Roman Catholic. Avocation: car racing. Home: 7325 Chardon Rd Kirtland OH 44094

PETRONE, WILLIAM FRANCIS, pediatrician, microbiologist, corporate executive; b. Bklyn., Sept. 12, 1949; s. Arthur Carmen and Helen (Kenny) P.; m. Kathleen Anne Baron, Aug. 25, 1979; children: William Gaetano, Katherine Bridget, Jason Daniel. BA, U. Conn., 1972; MS, U. Mass., 1974; PhD, U. R.I., 1978; MD, U. South Ala., 1984. Diplomate Am. Bd. Pediatrics, Pediatric Emergency Medicine, Gen. Pediatrics. Rsch. assoc. Coll. Medicine U. South Ala., Mobile, 1978-80; resident in pediat. Orlando (Fla.) Regional Med. Ctr., 1984-85, W.Va. Univ. Med. Ctr., 1985-87; emergency rm. physician, pediat. emergency svcs. Mercy Hosp., Springfield, Mass., 1987—. Pres. Med. Simulation Software, Cmty. Pediat. Assoc. Contbr. articles on inflamation and white blood cell function to sci. jours. Fellow Am. Acad. Pediat., Am. Coll. Emergency Physicians; mem. AAAS, AMA, N.Y. Acad. Scis., Sigma Xi. Roman Catholic. Office: Mercy Hosp Emergency Unit PO Box 9012 Springfield MA 01102-9012

PETROPOULOS, EVANGELOS, former health institute director, educator, researcher; b. Athens, Greece, Jan. 14, 1935; arrived in U.S., 1965; s. Anastassios P. and Metaxia P. Petropoulos; m. Panayota E. Tzela, Nov. 12, 1964; children: Anna, Anastassios. MD, U. Athens, 1959, PhD in Exptl. Medicine, 1964, PhD in Endocrinology, U. Calif., San Francisco, 1970; MD (hon.), Med. U. Sofia, Bulgaria, 2003. Spl. NIH fellow U. Calif., San Francisco, 1968—73; attending physician in endocrinology Evangelisnos Med. Ctr., Athens, 1973—75; prof., head dept. physiology U. Zimbabwe Med. Sch., Harare, 1975—82, prof., dean, 1982—85, prof. physiology, 1986—88; dir. Inst. Internat. Health, prof. physiology Mich. State U., E. Lansing, 1988—2002, dir., prof. emeritus, 2003—. Mem. com. regional office Africa WHO, Brazzaville, Republic of the Congo, 1982—85; mem. com. Commonwealth Secretariat, London, 1984—85; cons. African health policies World Bank, Washington, 1991. Contbr. articles and monographs to profl. jours. Lt. Med. Corp. Greek Air Force, 1960—63. Grantee, NIH, 1968, 1972, 1994, 1996, 1999, 2001; Internat. fellow in health, Kellogg Found., 1986—90. Mem.: NY Acad. Scis., Am. Physiol. Soc. Christian Orthodox. Achievements include research in etiology of Balkan endemic nephropathy in Bulgaria, Serbia and Romania. Avocations: classical music, church chanting, farming, underwater fishing, history of medicine. Home: 11 Nichols Ln Peabody MA 01960 Office: Inst Internat Health Mich State U B-301 W Fee Hall East Lansing MI 48824-1315

PETROSKI, HENRY, engineer educator, writer; b. NYC, Feb. 6, 1942; s. Henry Frank and Victoria Rose (Grygrowych) P.; m. Catherine Ann Groom, July 15, 1966; children: Karen Beth, Stephen James. B Mech. Engring., Manhattan Coll., 1963, DP (hon.), 2003; MS, U. Ill., 1964, PhD, 1968; DSc (hon.), Clarkson U., 1990; DHL (hon.), Trinity Coll., Hartford, Conn., 1997; DSc (hon.), Valparaiso U., 1999. Registered profl. engr., Tex.; chartered engr., Inst. of Engrs. of Ireland. Instr. U. Ill., Urbana, 1965-68; asst. prof. U. Tex., Austin, 1968-74; engr. Argonne (Ill.) Nat. Lab., 1975-80; assoc. prof. civil engring. Duke U., Durham, N.C., 1980-87, prof., 1987-93, Aleksandar S. Vesic prof., 1993—, prof. history, 1995—, chmn. dept. civil and environ. engring., 1991-2000, dir. grad. studies, 1981-86. Author: To Engineer is Human, 1985, Beyond Engineering, 1986, The Pencil, 1990, The Evolution of Useful Things, 1992, Design Paradigms, 1994 (Best Book award in engring., Am. Assn. U. Presses, 1994), Engineers of Dreams, 1995, Invention by Design, 1996, Remaking the World, 1997, The Book on the Bookshelf, 1999, Paperboy, 2002, Small Things Considered, 2003, Pushing the Limits, 2004; writer, presenter: documentary To Engineer is Human, 1987, columnist: Am. Scientist, 1991—, ASEE Prism, 2000—. Fellow NEH, 1987-88, Nat. Humanities Ctr., 1987-88, Guggenheim fellow, 1990-91; recipient Outstanding Engring. Grad. award Manhattan Coll., 1992, Alumni award for disting. svc. Coll. Engring. U. Ill. at Urbana-Champaign, 1994. Fellow ASCE (Civil Engring. History and Heritage award 1993), ASME (Ralph Coats Roe medal 1991), Am. Acad. Arts and Sci., Inst. Engrs. Ireland, NAE, Soc. History Tech., The Moles (hon.), Sigma Xi, Tau Beta Pi. Office: Duke U Sch Engring Durham NC 27708-0287

PETROU, DAVID MICHAEL, marketing and communications executive; b. Washington, Nov. 3, 1949; s. John and Bebe (Koch) P. BA, U. Md., 1971; MA, Georgetown U., 1973. Assoc. dir. publicity Random House-Ballantine Books, N.Y.C., 1973-75; asst. prodr. Salkind Orgn., London, 1975-78; asst. dir. promotional devel. Warner Bros., L.A., 1978-79; dir. spl. projects Jos. P. Kennedy Jr. Found., Washington, 1980-83; pres., COO Eisner, Petrou & Assoc., Washington, 1986—. Author: Crossed Swords, 1977, The Making of Superman, 1978; sr. editor: Regardie's mag., 1983-84. Mem. nat. fundraising com. Dukakis for Pres., Washington, 1988; mem. bd. U. Md. Ctr. Performing Arts, 1996—; mem. adv. bd. Washington Men's Camerata, 1996—. Woodrow Wilson fellow U. Md., 1971. Mem. Am. Film Inst.'s 2d Decade Coun. (chmn. of bd. 1992-96), Found. for Comty. Mental Health (bd. dirs. 1984—), Choral Arts Soc. Washington (bd. dirs. 1996—). Democrat. Jewish. Avocations: choral singing, music, tennis, film and film criticism. Office: Eisner Petrou & Assoc Inc 927 15th St NW Ste 900 Washington DC 20005-2340

PETROVICH, DOROTHY, elementary school educator; b. N.J., July 14, 1931; d. Nicholas and Freida (Kleva) Frantin; m. Walter Petrovich, Aug. 22, 1954; children: David, Amy. BS, Jersey City State Tchrs. Coll., 1953. Cert. Newspaper Inst. of Am., 1949, The Inst. Children's Lit., 1996. Tchr. Bd. Edn., Middletown, N.J., 1953-54; substitute tchr. various schs., 1954-70; remedial math. tchr. Monmouth Beach (N.J.) Bd. Edn., 1970-72, 1st-4th grade tchr., 1972-91, ret., 1991. Editorial asst. to Socialist Republic, winner writing awards, cons. to editorial bd. internat. mag. Mem. N.J. Edn. Assn., NEA, Monmouth Beach Edn. Assn. (sec.-treas.). Home: 165 S Manor Ct Wall NJ 07719-3658

PETRUS, ROBERT THOMAS, internet business owner, real estate investor; b. Manchester, Conn., 1957; s. John Joseph and Geraldine Petrus; m. Laura Lee Waggoner, Nov. 22, 1986; children: Elizabeth Ashley, Nicholas Kent. BA with honors, Trinity Coll., Hartford, Conn., 1979. Mgmt. intern Aetna Life & Casualty Co., Hartford, 1979-82, sr. adminstr. data processing ops., 1982-85, cons. Tech. Ctr., 1985-90; pres. Omoo Distbn. Corp., Mansfield, Conn., 1990—; v.p. Cogitore, Inc., 1990—. Author: Get Organized!, 1991. Chmn. Conn. Youth for Pres. Ford, 1976; com. mem. Big Bros.-Big Sisters, Hartford, 1982-83; loaned exec. Greater Hartford United Way-Combined Health Appeals Campaign, 1985. Recipient ofcl. citation Conn. Ho. of Reps., 1985. Mem. Phi Beta Kappa, Pi Gamma Mu, Mu Alpha Theta. Republican. Avocations: photography, golf, skiing. Office: ODI-Omoo Distbn Inc 27 Wormwood Hill Rd Ste 101 Mansfield Center CT 06250-1135 E-mail: rpetrus@quixnet.net.

PETRUSH, JOHN JOSEPH, lawyer; b. Rochester, Pa., Oct. 15, 1942; s. Joseph Anthony and Helen Rosemarie (Klucarich) P.; children: John Joseph, Joshua Laurence. AB cum laude, Princeton U., 1964; LLB, Stanford U., 1967. Bar: Calif. 1967, Pa. 1970. Assoc. Bernard Petrie, San Francisco, 1967-68; law clk. to judge Common Pleas Ct. Beaver County, Pa., 1969; assoc. Buchanan, Ingersoll, Rodewald, Kyle & Buerger, Pitts., 1970-75; pvt. practice Beaver, Pa., 1976—. Mem. Beaver Town Coun., 1973-88; bd. dirs. Beaver County unit Am. Cancer Soc., 1976-90, United Way of Beaver County, 1986-92; trustee Beaver Area Sch. Dist. Edn. Found. With USMCR, 1961-63. Mem. ABA, ATLA, Pa. Bar Assn., Pa. Trial Lawyers Assn. (bd. govs. western chpt. 1984-90), Allegheny County Bar Assn., Beaver County Bar Assn. (treas. 1987-2002). Republican. Home: 331 Wilson Ave Beaver PA 15009-2323 Office: 348 College Ave Beaver PA 15009-2209 E-mail: john.j.petrush@verizon.net.

PETRUSKI, JENNIFER ANDREA, speech and language pathologist; b. Kingston, NY, Jan. 28, 1968; d. Andrew Francis and Judith (Cruger) Petruski. BS, SUNY, Buffalo, 1990, MSEd, 1992. Cert. tchr. speech-hearing handicapped N.Y., lic. speech-lang. pathology N.Y. Speech-lang. pathologist Kingston (N.Y.) City Schs., 1992—, student rev. team facilitator, 2002—04, clin. fellowship yr. supr., 2004—; clin. practicum supr. SUNY, New Paltz, 1995—2004. Cooperating tchr. SUNY, New Paltz, 1995—2002; ind. contr. speech svcs. Ulster County, 1997; cooperating tchr. Coll. St. Rose, 1997, 2004; summer sch. tchr. New Paltz Sch. Dist., 2002, clin. fellowship year supr., 2004—05. Mem.: Bd. Regional Assn. Pres., N.Y. State Speech-Lang. and Hearing Assn., Am. Speech and Hearing Assn. (award for continuing edn. 2004—), Speech and Hearing Assn. Hudson Valley (corr. sec. 1995—98, newsletter editor 1995—2002, membership com. 1995—2002, treas. 1997, pres. 1999—2000, nominating com. 1999—2000, membership chmn. 2000—02, legis. chmn. 2000—04, website adminstr. 2001—, historian 2001—, continuing edn. adminstr. 2002, program com. 2003, newsletter com. 2003—04), Bd. Regional Presidents (membership chair 2000—02, pub. info. chair 2003—04). Home: PO Box 88 Hurley NY 12443 E-mail: jpetruski@aol.com.

PETRUZZI, CHRISTOPHER ROBERT, business educator, consultant; b. Peoria, Ill., July 28, 1951; s. Benjamin Robert and Mary Katherine (Urban) P.; m. Georgina Sailer, June 20, 1992; 1 child, Lillian Caroline. BA, Wabash Coll., 1972; MBA, U. Chgo., 1974; PhD, U. So. Calif., 1983. Lectr. bus. U. Wis., Milw., 1975-77; cons. H.C. Wainwright, Boston, 1978-79; lectr. U. So. Calif., 1978-81; prof. bus. U. Pa., Phila., 1981-84; prof. acctg. NYU, 1984-89, Calif. State U., Fullerton, 1989—. Pres. ECON Investment Software, San Clemente, Calif., 1987-2000; pres. Euronet Securities Corp., N.Y.C., 2000-2001, Smart Execution LLC, 2001-. Earhart fellow, 1972-73, U. Chgo. fellow, 1974-76. Libertarian. Christian. Office: Ste 302B 629 Camino de los Mares San Clemente CA 92673 Home: 1527 Via Tulipan San Clemente CA 92673

PETRY, RUTH VIDRINE, principal; b. Eunice, La., Jan. 20, 1947; d. Adea and Ruth Alice (Fox) Vidrine; m. Carson Clinton Petry, June 19, 1976. BA, La. Coll., 1971; MEd, McNeese State U., 1984. Cert. tchr., La. Tchr. jr. high sch. Jefferson Davis Parish, Jennings, La., 1970-72; tchr. high sch. St. Tammany Parish, Mandeville, La., 1972-73, Jefferson Parish, Gretna, La., 1973-81; tchr. jr. high Acadia Parish, Crowley, La., 1981-90; tchr. lang. arts Crowley Jr. High Sch., 1981-90, master tchr. assessor La. State Dept. Edn., Lafayette, 1990-91; tchr. Crowley Mid. Sch., 1991-94, instrnl. asst., 1994-95; exec. dir. Assoc. Profl. Educators of La., Baton Rouge, 1995-96; asst. prin. Rayne (La.) H.S., 1996—2001, principal, 2001—. Writing assessment coord. Crowley Jr. High Sch., 1984-85, mem. faculty insvc. team, 1986-89, chmn. spelling bee, 1983-90, 92-93, co-chmn. interim self study Crowley Jr. High Sch. So. Assn., 1985-86; mem. state selection com. for La. Tech. of Yr., Students of Yr., 1992-93; mem. Tchr. Evaluation Revision Panels, I, III, IV, 1992-93, Prin.'s Evaluation State Com., 1993; presenter workshops in field. Co-sponsor Nat. Jr. Hon. Soc., 1984-90; mem. La. Gov.-Elect's Edn. Transition Team, 1991-92; mem. La. Goals 2000 steering com. on sch. governance and accountability, 1994-95, mem. sch. fin. commn., 1999-2000. Named Crowley Jr. High Tchr. of the Yr., 1985-86. Mem. ASCD, Assn. Profl. Educators La. (pres. Acadia chpt. 1988-92, mem. dist. VII state exec. bd., 1990-91, state pres.-elect 1991-92, state pres. 1992-94), Nat. Assn. Secondary Sch. Prins., La. Assn. Sch. Execs., La. Assn. Prins., La. Assn. for Retarded Citizens, Delta Kappa Gamma (chpt. pres. 1988-90, state leadership scholar 1993), Phi Delta Kappa. Republican. Baptist. Avocations: music, reading, sewing. Home: 206 Bruce St Lafayette LA 70503-6102

PETRYSHYN, WALTER ALEXIS, otolaryngologist; b. N.Y., 1922; m. Helen A. Pronczak, 1946. MD, SUNY, 1945. Diplomate Am. Bd. Otolaryngology. Intern Lenox Hill Hosp., N.Y.C., 1945-46; resident otolaryngology NYU Bellevue Med. Ctr., N.Y.C., 1948-51; fellow otolaryngology NYU Med. Sch., N.Y.C., 1948. Med. dir. Deafness Rsch. Found., 1984—91. Capt. M.C. U.S. Army, 1946—48. Fellow ACS, Am. Acad. Otolaryngology Head and Neck Surgery; mem. AMA, Am. Triol. Assn.

PETRYSHYN, WOLODYMYR V. retired mathematician; b. Murovane, Ukraine, Jan. 22, 1929; arrived in U.S.A., 1950; s. Vasyl and Maria Petryshyn; BA, Columbia U., 1953, MS, 1954, PhD, 1961. Assoc. prof. math. U. Chgo., 1964—67; prof. math. Rutgers U., New Brunswick, NJ, 1967—96, ret., 1996. Dir. Math.-Physics Sect. Shevchenko Sci. Soc., N.Y.C. Author: Generalized Topological Degree and Semilinear Equations, 1995. Recipient M. Krylov award, Acad. Scis. Ukraine, 1992; grantee, NSF, 1964—86. Mem.: Ukrainian Acad. Sci. in Kiev. Achievements include first to establishing a new branch of mathematics, the A-proper mapping theory. Home: 10 Jackson Drive Cranford NJ 07016

PETSKO, GREGORY ANTHONY, chemistry and biochemistry scientist educator; b. Washington, Aug. 7, 1948; s. John and Mary (Santoro) P.; m. Carol Bannister Chamberlain, July 3, 1971 (div. 1982). BA, Princeton U., 1970; DPhil, Oxford U., 1973. Instr. Wayne State U. Med. Sch., Detroit, 1973-75, asst. prof., 1975-78; assoc. prof. MIT, 1979-85, prof. chemistry, 1985-90; Lucille P. Markey prof. biochemistry and chemistry Brandeis U., Waltham, Mass., 1990-96, Gyula & Katica Tauber prof. biochemistry & pharmacodynamics, 1997—, dir. Rosenstiel Basic Med. Scis. Rsch. Ctr., 1994—. Founding scientist, cons. Arqule, Inc., Medford, 1993-2001. Editor. Jour. Protein Engring., 1988-2003. Recipient Sr. Scientist award Alexander von Humboldt Found., 1989, Max Planck prize Max Planck Gesellschaft, 1992, Sr. Scientist award Ellison Med. Rsch. Found., 1998, Lynen medal Nature Mag., 2001; Rhodes scholar Oxford U., 1970; Alfred P. Sloan fellow MIT, 1978, Danforth fellow 1980, Guggenheim fellow 1995. Mem. NAS, Inst. of Medicine, Am. Acad. Arts and Scis., Am. Crystallographic Assn. (Siddhu award 1981), Am. Chem. Soc. (Pfizer award 1987), Biophys. Soc., Am. Soc. Biochemistry and Molecular Biology, Am. Soc. Microbiology. Avocations: writing essays, poetry and fiction, hiking, travel, old movies, sports cars. Home: 8 Jason Rd Belmont MA 02478-3129 Office: Brandeis U Mail Stop 029 Rosenstiel Ctr Waltham MA 02454-9110 E-mail: petsko@brandeis.edu.

PETT, JOHN LYMAN, banker; b. Erie, Pa., Dec. 7, 1948; s. Peter Paul and Dorothy (Rhoades) P. BS, Gannon U., 1971; MBA, DePaul U., 1977; postgrad., Harvard Bus. Sch., 1989. Asst. dir. acctg. and adminstrn. Constrn. Engring. div. Continental Can Co., Chgo., 1974-77; comml. v.p. and lending officer Mfrs. & Traders Trust Co., Buffalo, 1977-79, unit mgr. Mid. Market Lending, 1979-84, exec. v.p., chief credit officer, 1984—. Mem., cons. Erie County Fiscal Res. Com., Buffalo, 1984-86. Capt. USMC, 1971-74. Mem. Robert Morris Assocs., Am. Bankers Assocs., Wanakah Country Club (Hamburg, N.Y.). Republican. Roman Catholic. Avocations: golf, running, reading. Office: M&T Bank Corp 1 M&T Plaza Buffalo NY 14203

PETT, TIMOTHY, finance educator, management consultant; b. Utica, N.Y., Jan. 26, 1964; m. Katherine Steiner, Dec. 31, 2003; 1 child, Krisitn. BBA, St. Leo Coll., St Leo, Fla., 1989; MBA, Memphis State U., 1992; PhD in Bus. Adminstrn., U. of Memphis, 1998. Asst. prof. Wichita State U., Kans., 1996—2004, assoc. prof. and Hayes fellow in bus., 2004—. Recipient 40 Under 40 - 2002, Wichita Bus. Jour., 2002; fellow Hayes Family fellow, Wichita State U., 2004—; grantee Entrepreneurship Rsch. Assoc. grantee, Ctr. for Entrepreneurship - Devlin, 2002—. Mem.: Strategic Mgmt. Soc., Acad. of Mgmt., World Trade Coun. of Wichita (assoc.). Office: Wichita State University 1845 Fairmount Ave Barton School Wichita KS 67260-0088 E-mail: tim.pett@wichita.edu.

PETTEE, DANIEL STARR, retired neurologist; b. N.Y.C., Feb. 15, 1925; s. Allen Danforth and Helen Marien (Starr) P.; m. Dimetra Marie Peters, June 24, 1961; children: William, Margaret, Allen. BA, Yale U., 1951; MD, Columbia U., 1955. Diplomate Am. Bd. Psychiatry and Neurology, 1965, Am. Bd. Clin. Neurophysiology, 1984. Rotating internship Strong Meml. Hosp. U. Rochester, N.Y., 1955-57, residency neurology, 1957-62; neurologist pvt. practice, Rochester, N.Y., 1962-96; clinic dir. Rochester (N.Y.) Area Multiple Sclerosis Chpt., Rochester, N.Y., 1962-76; assoc. clin. prof. neurology U. Rochester (N.Y.) Sch. Medicine, 1978-96, emeritus assoc. clin. prof., 1996-97, emeritus clin. prof. neurology, 1997—; clin. assoc. dept. neurology Strong Meml. Hosp., Rochester, 1978-96; head neurology div. dept. medicine The Genesee Hosp., Rochester, 1972-96; pres. Genesee Neurol. Assocs., Rochester, 1974-96. Mem. bd. dirs. Rochester (N.Y.) Area Multiple Sclerosis Chpt., 1970-76. Contbr. articles to profl. jours. Mem., singer Rochester Oratorio Soc., 1955—78, bd. dirs., 1960—61. Recipient Purple Heart, Bronze Star U.S. Army, 1944, Bronze Hope Chest for Svc. award Rochester (N.Y.) Area Multiple Sclerosis Chpt., 1976. Mem. N.Y. Acad. Sci., Rochester Acad. Sci. (astronomy sect. 1989-98, bd. dirs. astronomy sect. 1993-94), Denver Astron. Soc. Home: 6652 Starlight Dr Morrison CO 80465

PETTENGILL, GORDON H(EMENWAY), physicist, researcher; b. Providence, Feb. 10, 1926; s. Rodney Gordon and Frances (Hemenway) P.; m. Pamela Anne Wolfenden, Oct. 28, 1967; children: Mark Robert, Rebecca Jane. BS, MIT, 1948; PhD, U. Calif., Berkeley, 1955. Staff mem. Lincoln Lab. MIT, Lexington, 1954-63, 65-68, prof. planetary physics, dept. earth, atmospheric and planetary scis. Cambridge, 1971—2001, dir. Ctr. Space Rsch., 1984-90; assoc. dir. Arecibo (P.R.) Obs., 1963-65, dir., 1968-71. Served with inf., Signal Corps AUS, 1944-46. Decorated Combat Inf. badge; recipient Magellanic Premium, Am. Philos. Soc., 1994. Fellow Am. Geophys. Union (Whipple award 1995, Charles A. Whitten award 1997); mem. AAAS, Am. Phys. Soc., Am. Astron. Soc., Internat. Astron. Union, Internat. Radio Sci. Union, Nat. Acad. Sci., Am. Acad. Arts and Sci. Achievements include pioneering several techniques in radar astronomy for describing properties of planets and satellites; discovering 59-day rotational period of planet Mercury. Office: MIT 77 Massachusetts Ave Rm 37-582D Cambridge MA 02139-4307

PETTERCHAK, JANICE A. researcher, writer, editor; b. Springfield, Ill., Sept. 15, 1942; d. Emil H. and Vera C. (Einhoff) Stukenberg; m. John J. Petterchak, Oct. 5, 1963; children: John A., Julie Gilmour, James. AA, Springfield Coll., 1962; BS, Sangamon State U., 1972, MA, 1982. Supr. hist. markers Ill. State Hist. Soc., Springfield, 1973-74, asst. exec. dir., 1985-87; curator photographs Ill. State Hist. Libr., Springfield, 1974-79, assoc. editor, 1979-83, rep. local history svcs., 1983-85, libr. dir., 1987-95. Project dir. NEH/Ill. newspaper cataloging project. Author: Mapping a Life's Journey: The Legacy of Andrew McNally III, 1995, Jack Brickhouse: A Voice for All Seasons, 1996, Researching and Writing Local History in Illinois: A Guide to the Sources, 1987, Taming the Upper Mississippi, 2000; To Share: The Heritage, Legend and Legacy of Nathan Cummings, 2000, Out To Sea Again: A Naval Armed Guard in World War II, 2002, Lone Scout: W.D. Boyce and American Boy Scouting, 2003; editor: Illinois History: An Annotated Bibliography, 1995; assoc. editor Illinois Historical Jour.; contbr. articles to profl. jours. Grantee NEH, 1987-95. Mem. Ill. State Hist. Soc., Stephen A. Douglas Assn., Sangamon County Hist. Soc. (bd. dirs. 1991-94, 99-2002, 2004-, v.p. 1996-97, pres. 1995-96), Soc. of Midland Authors. Home: 11381 Mallard Dr Rochester IL 62563-8011 E-mail: petterchak@biogwriter.com.

PETTERSEN, KEVIN WILL, investment company executive; b. Yonkers, N.Y., July 4, 1956; s. Kjell Will and Marilyn Ann (Stevens) Pettersen; m. Mary Elizabeth Murphy, Aug. 30, 1981; children: Kelly Elizabeth, Erin. Diploma academia, Chaminade, Mineola, N.Y., 1974; BA in Econs., SUNY, Stony Brook, 1978. Buyer JC Penney Co., Inc., N.Y.C., 1979-82; nat. sales mgr. Randa Corp., Inc., N.Y.C., 1982-83; dir. sales Wemco, Inc., N.Y.C., 1983-86; mng. dir., sr. v.p. D.H. Blair & Co., Inc., N.Y.C., 1986-89; exec. v.p. Brean Murray, Foster Securities, Inc., N.Y.C., 1989-90; v.p., br. mgr., corp. officer A.G. Edwards and Sons, Inc., Glen Cove, N.Y., 1990—. Cons. Oncor Inc., Gaithersburg, Md., 1987—93, Wedding Info. Network, Inc., Omaha, 1987—91; fin. adviser European banking ins. and investment industry, 1987—95; mem. All Am. team Am. Funds Group, 1990—94, mem. pres. club, mem. Alliance Premier coun.; mem. pres. coun. A. G. Edwards, mem. Million Dollar Club, mem. chmn.'s coun., 1998; mem. pres.'s adv. coun. Rochester Funds; mem. exec. coun. Oppenheimer Funds Group. Mem. Oyster Bay Supr.'s Adv. Com. Crime, 1993—95; basketball coach Cath. Youth Orgn. Girls Team, 1998—2001; del. Rep. Planning Com.; bd. dirs. Harbour Green L.I. Assn., 1990—94, pres., 1991. Recipient Outstanding Character award, Chaminade, 1974. Mem.: Chaminade Wall St. Assn., Chaminade Torch Club, Swan Lake Country Club, Green Harbour Beach Club (bd. dirs. 1994—98, treas. 1999). Republican. Roman Catholic. Avocations: golf, skiing, boating. Home: 280 Bay Dr Massapequa NY 11758-8142 Office: AG Edwards and Sons Inc 51 Glen St Glen Cove NY 11542-2738 Office Phone: 516-656-5566.

PETTERSEN, KJELL WILL, stockbroker, consultant; b. Oslo, June 19, 1927; came to U.S., 1946, naturalized, 1957; s. Jens Will and Ragna O. (Wickstrom) P.; m. Marilyn Ann Stevens, Aug. 16, 1952; children: Thomas W., Maureen, Kevin W., Maryann, Kathleen. Student, Zion Theol. Sch., 1945-49, N.Y. Inst. Finance, 1955-56. Mgr. A.M. Kidder & Co., N.Y.C., 1954-64; sr. v.p., sec., dir. Halle & Stieglitz, Fillor Bullard Co., Inc., 1964-73; sr. v.p., dir. mktg. Parrish Securities, Inc., N.Y.C., 1973-74; cons. Loeb, Rhoades & Co., N.Y.C., 1974-79; mng. dir. Prudential Securities, N.Y.C., 1979-89; pres. Arbitration Recovery Cons., Marco, Fla., 1992-93; vice chmn. Noddings Investment Group, Inc., Oakbrook Terrace, Ill., 1993-95; mem. City Coun., Marco Island, Fla., 1997—2002, chmn., 2001—02. Dir. Ski for Light Inc., Mpls., Creative Arts Rehab. Ctr. Inc., N.Y.C. Dem. candidate N.Y. State Assembly, Nassau County, 1962; past dir. Guadalupe Ctr., Marco YMCA; pres. Quest for Peace Internat.; co-chmn. Marco Island Celebration 2000. Mem. Nat. Assn. Security Dealers (bd. arbitrators), N.Y. C. of C., Norwegian-Am. C. of C. (dir. Guadalope Ctr.), Scandinavian Found., Bankers Club of Am., Norwegian Club (N.Y.C.), Rotary. Home: 350 Rockhill Ct Marco Island FL 34145-3860 Personal E-mail: marcokjell@aol.com.

PETTERSEN, THOMAS MORGAN, accountant, finance executive; b. Poughkeepsie, N.Y., Nov. 9, 1950; s. Olsen Thomas and Reva Frances (Palmer) P. BS, U. Albany, 1973. CPA, N.Y. Sr. acct. Arthur Andersen and Co., N.Y.C., 1973-76; sr. ops. auditor Gulf and Western Inc., N.Y.C., 1977, fin. analyst, 1978; adminstr. auditing NBC, N.Y.C., 1979, mgr. auditing Burbank, Calif., 1980, dir. auditing, 1981-88, dir. acctg. systems and ops. analysis, 1988-90; v.p. fin. and adminstrn. Data Dimensions, Inc., Culver City, Calif., 1991-92; cons. Westwood One, Inc., Culver City, 1992-93; CFO Computer Image Sys., Inc., Torrance, Calif., 1993-97; dir. corp. fin. DeCrane Aircraft Holdings, Inc., El Segundo, Calif., 1997-2000; bus. cons., 2000—. Mem. AICPA, Fin. Execs. Internat. Republican. Roman Catholic. Avocations: sports, travel. Home: 217 1st Pl Manhattan Beach CA 90266-6503

PETTERSON, MARGO, artist; b. L.A., Jan. 12, 1944; d. Edmund and Helen Smolinski; m. Richard M. Petterson, Apr. 14, 1962; 1 child, Sandra. AA, San Bernardino Valley Coll., 1981; student, Cuesta Coll., 1982-83. Asst. libr. San Bernardino County, Big Bear Lake, Calif., 1975-81; med. records clk. San Luis Obispo (Calif.) Gen. Hosp., 1981-83; adminstrv. asst. Donez Real Estate, Big Bear Lake, 1984-90; owner Petterson's Bear Valley Saw Shop, Big Bear Lake, 1983—; artist Margo Petterson/The Feminine West, Big Bear Lake, 1986—. Instr. Beverly Hills (Calif.) Art Guild, 1997-98, Orange (Calif.) Art Guild, 1998, Corona (Calif.) Art League, 1999, Huntington Beach (Calif.) Art Guild, 1999; dir. publicity Women Artists of the West. Pub. limited edit. lithographs, 1990—; contbr. painting to Art of American West, 1998. Sec. City Spirit, Big Bear Lake, 1977; pres. Big Bear Lake Art Assn., 1977-78, treas., 1979-80, 84-86; fundraiser United We Stand Am., Big Bear Lake, 1992; bd. dirs. Friends of the Libr., Big Bear Lake. Recipient 3d Pl. award George Phippen Meml., 1989, Best of Show, 1st Pl. Big Bear Lake Art Assn., 1992, Excellence in Artisty Ed and Maxine Runci Meml. award, 1993, Best of Show award Snake River Showcase, 1995, 2d Pl. award Calif. State Fair, 2002. Mem. Calif. Art Club, Women Artists of the West, Oil Painters of Am., Soroptimist Internat. Avocations: reading, camping, cooking. E-mail: MargoFemWest@msn.com.

PETTEWAY, SAMUEL BRUCE, college president; b. Fayetteville, N.C., July 18, 1924; s. Walter Bernard and Margaret Maysie (Cole) P.; m. Eleanor Glenn Sugg, Nov. 27, 1948; children— Margaret Petteway Small, Samuel Bruce. BS, N.C. State U., 1949, MEd, 1966, EdD, 1968. Gen. mgr. Homeowners Ins. and Realty Co., 1960-63; engring. tech. dept. chmn., dean occupational and transfer programs, dir. evening programs Lenoir County Community Coll., 1963-68; pres. Coll. of the Albemarie, Elizabeth City, N.C., 1968-75, N.C. Wesleyan Coll., Rocky Mount, 1975-86. Prof. Va. Poly. Inst. and State U., 1973-75, East Carolina U., 1994-99; pres. Philanthropic Cons., Inc., Kinston, N.C., 1986-96; sec. Coll. Mgmt. Svcs., Inc., Raleigh, N.C., 1989; lic. amateur radio operator, 1992—. Pres. chpt. Am. Cancer Soc., 1960-61, Boys' Club Lenoir County, 1987-91, Westminster Homeowners Assn., 1997; bd. dirs. Rocky Mount Acad., 1979-80, Triangle East, Inc., 1985-86, Cypress Glen Retirement Home, chmn. 1996; chmn. deferred giving com. N.C. Meth. Found., 1979-86; chmn. coun. on ministries 1st United Meth. Ch., Rocky Mount, 1980-81, Westminster United Meth. Ch., 1989-90, chmn. bd. trustees, 1994-99, chmn. adminstrv. bd., 2001-03; chmn. bd. trustees Art Edn. Found., 1980; mem. Nash County Bd. Health, 1985-86; bd. trustees

United Meth. Retirement Homes, Inc., 1996-99; treas. Meth. Home for Children, 1997-2002. Named Tar Heel of Week News and Observer, 1975, Today's Outstanding N.C. Citizen WNCT-TV, 1975; NSF fellow U. Ill., 1963 Mem. Nat. Assn. for Hosp. Devel., N.C. Assn. Colls. and Univs., N.C. Conf. United Meth. Ch. (chmn. bd. trustees 1973-79), Nat. Soc. Fund Raising Execs. (cert.), Rocky Mount C. of C. (bd. dirs. 1980-84), Rotary (scholarship com. dist. 7730 1995-2004), Phi Kappa Phi, Theta Alpha Phi. Clubs: Benvenue Country, Galaxy Social; Kinston Country. Lodges: Rotary (pres. 1980-81, bd. dirs. Kinston chpt. 1988-92). Republican. Office: 708 Westminster Ln Kinston NC 28501-2770

PETTIBON, RAYMOND, video artist; b. Tucson, June 10, 1957; BA, UCLA, 1977. One-man shows include Semaphore Gallery, NYC, 1986, Feature Gallery, NYC, 1989, 90, 93, Richard/Bennett Gallery, LA, 1990, 91, Robert Berman Gallery, LA, 1991, Galerie Rudiger Schottle, Munich, 1991, Massimo de Carlo Arte Contemporanea, Milan, Italy, 1991, N.A.M.E. Gallery, Chgo., 1991, Feature Gallery, NYC, 1991, Galerie Marc Jancou, Zurich, Switzerland, 1992, Galerie Metropol, Vienna, Austria, 1992, 94, Esther Schipper Galerie, Cologne, Germany, 1992, Matrix Gallery, U. Calif. Berkeley, 1992, Air de Paris, Nice, France, 1992, Univ. Galleries, Ill. State U., Normal, 1993, Regen Projects, LA, 1993, 95, 98, Jack Hanley Gallery, San Francisco, 1993, Galerie Beaumont, Luxembourg, 1994, Galeria Ramis Barquet, Garza, Mex., 1994, Ynglingagatan, Stockholm, Sweden, 1995, 14/16 Verneuil, Paris, 1995, Contemporary Fine Arts, Berlin, 1995, 98, Galeria Massimo De Carlo, Milan, 1995, Kunsthalle Bern, Switzerland, 1995, David Zwirner Gallery, NYC, 1995, 97, Tramway, Glasgow, Scotland, 1996, Taka Ishii Gallery, Tokyo, 1996, Meyer Kainer, Vienna, 1998, The Renaissance Soc., Chgo., 1998, The Drawing Ctr., NYC, 1999, Phila. Mus. Art, 1999, Galerie Meyer Kainer, Vienna, 1999; exhibited in group shows at Whitney Mus. Am. Art, NYC, 1997-98, 98-99, Sudwestdeutsche Landesbank, Stuttgart, Germany, 1997, Galerie Tanya Rumpff, Haarlem, The Netherlands, 1998, 11 Duke Street Ltd., London, 1998, The Parrish Art Mus., Southampton, NY, 1998, Laguna Art Mus., 1999, Austin Mus. Art, 1999, David Swirner, NY, 2000, numerous others. Mailing: David Zwirner Gallery 43 Greene St New York NY 10013*

PETTIBONE, PETER JOHN, lawyer; b. Schenectady, NY, Dec. 11, 1939; s. George Howard and Caryl Grey (Ketchum) P.; m. Jean Kellogg, Apr. 23, 1966; children: Stephen, Victoria. AB summa cum laude, Princeton U., 1961; JD, Harvard U., 1964; LLM, NYU, 1971. Bar: Pa. 1965, D.C. 1965, N.Y. 1968, U.S. Supreme Ct. 1974, Russia (fgn. legal cons.) 1995. Lectr. Heidelberg (Fed. Republic Germany) U., 1965-67; assoc. Cravath, Swaine & Moore, N.Y.C., 1967-74, Lord Day & Lord, Barrett Smith, N.Y.C., 1974-76, ptnr. N.Y.C. and Washington, 1976-94, Patterson, Belknap, Webb & Tyler LLP, N.Y.C. and Moscow, 1994-99, Hogan & Hartson LLP, N.Y.C. and Moscow, 2000—. Pres. 1158 Fifth Ave. Corp., N.Y.C., 1991-94; pres. North Ferry Co., Shelter Island, N.Y., 1987-90; bd. dirs., vice-chmn. N.Y. State Facilities Devel. Corp., N.Y.C., 1983-89. Editor USSR Legal Materials, Columbia U., 1990-92. Trustee, treas. Hosp. Chaplaincy Inc., N.Y.C., 1980-86, Civitas, N.Y.C., 1984-92; mem. Coun. Fgn. Rels., 1993—; trustee Union Chapel, Shelter Island, N.Y., 1990—, CEC Internat. Ptnrs., 1996-2002; bd. dirs., vice chmn. Geonomics Inst., Middlebury, Vt., 1991-98; mem. vestry Ch. of Heavenly Rest, N.Y.C., 1987-93; mem. Nat. Adv. Coun. Harriman Inst. Columbia U., 1996—; mem. Russia com. Episcopal Diocese of N.Y. Capt. U.S. Army, 1965-67, Heidelberg, Germany. Mem. ABA, Assn. Bar City N.Y. (chmn. com. on CIS affairs 1991-94), U.S.-USSR Trade and Econ. Coun. Inc. (U.S. co-chmn. legal com. 1980-92), U.S.-Russia Bus. Coun. (bd. dirs.), Soc. of Cin., Anglers Club N.Y.C., N.Y. Yacht Club, Shelter Island Yacht Club, Moscow Country Club, Amateur Ski Club N.Y. (pres. 1980-82), Canterbury Choral Soc. (pres. 1983-84), Phi Beta Kappa. Episcopalian. Home: 1158 5th Ave New York NY 10029-6917 also: 10 Wesley Ave Shelter Island Heights NY 11965 Office: Hogan & Hartson LLP 875 3rd Ave New York NY 10022 Office Phone: 212-918-3510. Business E-Mail: pjpettibone@hhlaw.com.

PETTIGREW, ANTONIO, Olympic athlete; b. Macon, Ga., Nov. 3, 1967; m. Cassandra Pettigrew. Winner Gold Medal World Championship, 1997; placed 2nd nats., 1998; placed 5th 400 meter final World Championships, 1999; co-winner Gold Medal 4X400 relay, 2000. Ptnr. DMH Enterprises, Raleigh, NC. Recipient Visa U.S.A. Humanitarian Athlete of the Yr. award. Office: USA Track and Field Team One RCA Dome Ste 140 Indianapolis IN 46225

PETTIGREW, CAROLYN LANDERS, theological school official, minister; b. Columbus, Ohio, Sept. 30, 1945; d. Wayman and Mary Gerldine (Lambert) Landers; m. Grady L. Pettigrew, Jr., Jan. 27, 1968; children: Dawn Karima, Grady Landers. BSc in Edn., Ohio State U., 1967; MDiv, Meth. Theol. Sch., Delaware, Ohio, 1987; postgrad., Washington Theol. Union, 1991—, United Theol. Sch., Dayton, Ohio. Ordained to ministry United Ch. of Christ, 1988; lic. speech and hearing therapist, Ohio. Youth min., dir. Christian edn. 1st Congl. Ch., Columbus, 1983-86; assoc. chaplain Grant Med. Ctr., Columbus, 1987-90; ednl. asst. to acad. dean for MA in alcohol and drug abuse ministry and continuing edn. Meth. Theol. Sch., 1990-94. Trustee United Ch. of Christ House, Chautauqua, N.Y., 1990—, Chautauqua Inst. Arts, 1990-94; chmn. new clergy orientation Met. Area Ch. Bd., Columbus, 1990-91, co-convenor drug abuse task force; sec., tchr. gifted children's program Ohio Wesleyan U.; speaker in field; faculty Ea. Union Bible Coll., 1998—; planning team U.S. Atty. Gen. Drug Abuse Task Force, 1990-94. Compiler, author: African American Spirituality: A Bibliography, 1991. Mem. women's bd. Martin Luther King Ctr. for Performing Arts, Columbus, 1987—; mem. docent alumni group Columbus Mus. Arts; mem. women's agenda on human svcs. Ohio Gov.'s Task Force, Columbus, 1990—; mem. Chgo. Conf. Spiritual Renewal Task Force; exec. bd. United Ch. Christ, Cleve., 1997—. Recipient 11 Kudos, Grant Med. Ctr., 1987-90, Humanitarian award Columbus chpt. Alpha Kappa Alpha, 1990. Mem. Women's Theol. Group, Cen. S.E. Assn. United Ch. of Christ (chair dept. Christian edn. 1985-90), Jr. League Columbus, Zora Lit. Club (founder, convenor), Ladies of Lambda. Home: 1801 E 12th St Apt 301 Cleveland OH 44114-3530 Office: Meth Theol Sch Delaware OH 43015-0931

PETTIGREW, JO ARNOLD, educational association administrator; MA in Speech and Drama, North Tex. State U.; EdD in Ednl. Adminstrn., Okla. State U. asst. exec. dir. Okla. State Sch. Bds. Assn., 1983—95; exec. dir. United Suburban Schs. Assn., 1996—. Bd. dirs. S.W. Ednl. Lab., Austin, Tex., 2002—, sec. bd. dirs., 2003—. Mem.: Okla. Edn. Coalition. Office: SEDL 211 E 7th St Austin TX 78701-3281

PETTIGREW, L. EUDORA, retired academic administrator; b. Hopkinsville, Ky., Mar. 1, 1928; d. Warren Cicero and Corrye Lee (Newell) Williams; children: Peter W. Woodard, Jonathan R. (dec.). MusB, W.Va. State Coll., 1950; MA, So. Ill. U., 1964, PhD, 1966; PhD honoris causa, U. Pretoria, South Africa, 2002, Holy Family Coll., 2002. Music/English instr. Swift Meml. Jr. Coll., Rogersville, Tenn., 1950-51; music instr., librarian Western Ky. Vocat. Sch., Paducah, 1951-52; music/English instr. Voorhees Coll., Denmark, S.C., 1954-55; dir. music and recreation therapy W.Ky. State Psychiatric Hosp., Hopkinsville, 1956-61; research fellow Rehab. Inst., So. Ill. U., Carbondale, 1961-63, instr., resident counselor, 1963-66, coordinator undergrad. ednl. psychology, 1963-66, acting chmn. ednl. psychology, tchr. corps instr., 1966; asst. prof. to assoc. prof. dept. psychology U. Bridgeport, Conn., 1966-70; prof., chmn. dept. urban and met. studies Coll. Urban Devel. Mich. State U., East Lansing, 1974-80; assoc. provost, prof. U. Del., Newark, 1981-86; pres. SUNY Coll. at Old Westbury, 1986-98. Cons. for rsch. and evaluation Hall Neighborhood House Day Care Tng. Project, Bridgeport, 1966-68, U.S. Ea. Regional Lab., Edn. Devel. Ctr., Newton, Mass., 1967-69; coordinator for edn. devel., 1968-69; cons. Bridgeport Public Schs. lang. devel. project, 1967-68, 70; Lansing Model Cities Agy., Day Care Program, 1971; U. Pitts., 1973, 74, Leadership Program, U. Mich. and Wayne State U., 1975, Wayne County Pub. Health Nurses Assn., 1976, Ill. State Bd. Edn., 1976-77; assoc. prof. U. Bridgeport, 1970, Ctr. for Urban Affairs and Coll. of Edn., Mich. State U., East Lansing, 1970-73; trustee L.I. Community Found.; program devel. specialist Lansing Public Schs. Tchr. Corps program, 1971-73; coord. workshop Conflict Resolution The Woman's Role in Our World, 4th Internat. UN Conf. on Women, Beijing, China, 1995; lectr. in field; condr. workshops in field; mem. adv. com. Economists Allied for Arms Reduction, 1996; guest spkr. Internat. Conf. on The New Role of Higher Edn. in the Context of an Ind. Palestinian State, An-Najah Nat. U., Nablus, Palestine, 1996. Tv/radio appearances on: Black Women in Edn, Channel 23, WKAR, East Lansing, 1973, Black Women and Equality, Channel 2, Detroit, 1974, Women and Careers, Channel 7, Detroit, 1974, Black Women and Work: Integration in Schools, WITL Radio, Lansing, 1974, others; editor: Universities and Their Role in World Peace, 2003; contbr. articles to profl. jours. Mem. Commn. U. Peace, Costa Rica; bd. dirs. U. Pretoria (South Africa) Found., Nat. Peace Garden Found. Recipient Diana award Lansing YWCA, 1977, Outstanding Profl. Achievement award, 1987, award L.I. Ctr. for Bus. and Profl. Women, 1988, Educator of Yr. 100 Black Men of L.I., 1988, Black Women's Agenda award, 1988, Woman of Yr. Nassau/Suffolk Coun. of Adminstrv. Women in Edn., 1989, Disting. Ednl. Leadership award L.I. Women's Coun. for Equal Edn. Tng. and Employment, 1989, L.I. Disting. Leadership award L.I. Bus. News, 1990, Disting. Black Women in Edn. award Nat. Coun. Negro Women, 1991; named Outstanding Black Educator, NAACP, 1968, Outstanding Woman Educator, Mich. Women's Lawyers Assn. and Mich. Trial Lawyers Assn., 1975, Disting. Alumna, Nat. Assn. for Equal Opportunity in Higher Edn., 1990, Woman of Yr., Nassau County League of Women Voters, 1991, Disting. Alumna So. Ill. U., 1997, N.Y. State Senate resolution of commendation, 1998; Elected to Achievers Hall of Fame: Long Island Bus. and Profl. Women's Orgn., 2001 Mem. AASS, Nat. Assn. Acad. Affairs Adminstrs., Internat. Assn. Univ. Pres. (exec. com., v.p.), Phi Delta Kappa.

PETTIGREW, PIERRE S. Canadian government official; b. Quebec City, Can., Apr. 18, 1951; BA in Philosophy, U. Que., Trois-Rivières, 1972; M in Philosophy in Internat. Rels., Balliol Coll., Oxford, 1976. Dir. polit. com. NATO Assembly, Brussels, 1976-78; exec. asst. to the leader Que. Liberal Party, 1978-81; fgn. policy advisor Prime Min. Can., 1981-84; v.p. Samson Bélair Deloitte & Touche Internat., Montreal, 1985-95; co-chair First Nat. Forum on Can. Internat. Rels., 1994; min. internat. coop., min. responsible for La Francophonie Can. Ho. of Commons, 1996, min. human resources devel. Can., 1996-99, min. for internat. trade, 1999—2003; min. health, 2003—04; min. intergovernmental affairs, 2003—04; min. ofcl. languages, 2003—04; min. foreign affairs Canada, 2004—. Author: The New Politics of Confidence, 1999; contbr. articles to profl. jours. Office: House of Commons Rm 507 Confederation Bldg Ottawa ON Canada K1A 0A6 also: Foreign Affairs Canada 125 Sussex Dr Tower A Ottawa ON Canada KIA OG2

PETTIGREW, RODERIC I. federal agency administrator, radiologist, researcher; BS in Physics cum alude, Morehouse Coll.; MS in Nuc. Medicine and Engring., Rensselaer Poly. Inst.; PhD in Applied Radiation Physics, MIT; MD, U. Miami. Intern and resident internal medicine Emory U.; resident nuc. medicine U. Calif., San Diego; clin. rsch. scientist Picker Internat.; Robert Wood Johnson Found. fellow Emory, 1985; prof. radiology, medicine (cardiology) and bioengineering Emory U. Sch. Medicine, Atlanta, dir. Ctr. for MR RSch.; dir. Nat. Inst. Biomedical Imaging and Bioengineering NIH, Bethesda, Md., 2002—. Chmn. diagnostic radiology study sect. Ctr. for Sci. Rev. NIH; lectr. in field. Named Most Disting. Alumnus, U. Miami, 1990; recipient Bennie award, 1989; Merrill scholar, Morehouse Coll., Whitaker Harvard-MIT Health Sci. scholar, MIT. Fellow: Am. Coll. Cardiology, Am. Heart Assn.; mem.: Phi Beta Kappa. Achievements include research in dynamic three-dimensional imaging of the heart using magnetic resonance; co-developer first computer software package specifically designed for cardiac imaging using MRI. Office: Nat Inst Biomedical Imaging and Bioengineering 6707 Democracy Blvd Bethesda MD 20892

PETTIGREW, THOMAS FRASER, social psychologist, educator; b. Richmond, Va., Mar. 14, 1931; s. Joseph Crane and Janet (Gibb) Pettigrew; m. Ann Hallman, Feb. 25, 1956; 1 child, Mark Fraser. AB in Psychology, U. Va., 1952; MA in Social Psychology, Harvard U., 1955, PhD, 1956; DHL (hon.), Governor's State U., 1979. Rsch. assoc. Inst. Social Rsch., U. Natal, Republic South Africa, 1956; asst. prof. psychology U. N.C., 1956-57; asst. prof. social psychology Harvard U., Cambridge, Mass., 1957-62, lectr., 1962-64, assoc. prof., 1964-68, prof., 1968-74, prof. social psychology and sociology, 1974-80; prof. social psychology U. Calif., Santa Cruz, 1980-94, rsch. prof. social psychology, 1994—; prof. social psychology U. Amsterdam, 1986-91. Adj. fellow Joint Ctr. Polit. and Econ. Studies, Washington, 1982—; adv. bd. women's studies program Princeton (N.J.) U., 1985-2001; vis. prof. Westfaelishe Wilhelms-U., Germany, 1993, Philipps U., Germany, 2000, Schiller U., Germany, 2002; disting. vis. prof. Flinders U., Australia, 1997; sr. fellow Rsch. Inst. for the Comparative Study of Race and Ethnicity, Stanford U., 2001-02, mem. German govt. adv. com. Intercultural Conflicts and Social Integration, 2003-. Author: (with E.Q. Campbell) Christians in Racial Crisis: A Study of the Little Rock Ministry, 1959, A Profile of the Negro American, 1964, Racially Separate or Together?, 1971; (with Frederickson, Knobol, Glazer and Veda) Prejudice, 1982; (with Alston) Tom Bradley's Campaigns for Governor: The Dilemma of Race and Political Strategies, 1988, How to Think Like a Social Scientist, 1996; editor: Racial Discrimination in the United States, 1975, The Sociology of Race Relations: Reflection and Reform, 1980; (with C. Stephan & W. Stephan) The Future of Social Psychology: Defining the Relationship Between Sociology and Psychology, 1991; mem. editorial bd. Jour. Social Issues, 1959-64, Social Psychology Quarterly, 1977-80; assoc. editor Am. Sociol. Rev, 1963-65; adv. bd. Integrated Edn, 1963-84, Phylon, 1965-93, Edn. and Urban Society, 1968-90, Race, 1972-74, Ethnic and Racial Studies, 1978-95, Rev. of Personality and Social Psychology, 1980-85, Cmty. and Applied Social Psychology, 1989—, Individual and Politics, 1989-93, Jour. Ethnic and Migration Studies, 1994—, 21st Century Afro Rev., 1994—; contbr. articles to profl. jours. Chmn. Episcopal presiding Bishop's Adv. Com. on Race Relations, 1961-63; v.p. Episcopal Soc. Cultural and Racial Unity, 1962-63; mem. Mass. Gov.'s Adv. Com. on Civil Rights, 1962-64; social sci. cons. U.S. Commn. Civil Rights, 1966-71; mem. White House Task Force on Edn., 1967; mem. nat. task force on desegregation policies Edn. Commn. of States, 1977-79; trustee Ella Lyman Cabot Trust, Boston, 1977-79; Emerson Book Award com. United Chpts. Phi Beta Kappa, 1971-73; com. status black Ams. NRC, 1985-88. Guggenheim fellow, 1967-68, Sr. Scientist fellow NATO, 1974, Ctr. Advanced Study in Behavioral Scis. fellow, 1975-76, Sydney Spivack fellow Am. Sociol. Assn., 1978, Netherlands Inst. Advanced Study fellow, 1984-85, Bellagio (Italy) Study Ctr. resident fellow, Rockefeller Found., 1991; Fulbright New Century scholar, 2003-04; recipient Kurt Lewin Meml. award Soc. for Psychol. Study Social Issues, 1987, (with Martin) Gordon Allport Intergroup Rels. Rsch. prize, 1988, Faculty Rsch. award U. Calif., Santa Cruz, 1988, (with Tropp) Gordon Allport Intergroup Rels. Rsch. prize, 2003. Fellow APA (Weiss meml. lectr., 2003), Am. Sociol. Assn. (coun. 1979-82); mem. Soc. Psychol. Study Social Issues (coun. 1962-66, pres. 1967-68, Disting. Svc. award 1998), Soc. Exptl. Social Psychology (Disting. Scientist award 2002), European Assn. Social Psychology. Home: 524 Van Ness Ave Santa Cruz CA 95060-3556

PETTIJOHN, FRED PHILLIPS, retired newspaper executive, consultant; b. Balt., May 11, 1917; s. Fred and Adelaide Josephine (Phillips) P.; m. Elaine Wilson, Dec. 7, 1946; children: Fred Phillips, Mark Clay. BAE., U. Fla., 1941. Sports editor Tallahassee Democrat, 1946-53; with Fort Lauderdale (Fla.) News, 1953-82, exec. editor, 1960-68, gen. mgr., 1968-77, editorial dir., from 1977; 1st v.p. Gore Newspapers Co., from 1960; now cons. Bd. dirs. Salvation Army, 1975-79, v.p., 1979; bd. dirs. Fla. Council 100, 1976-78. Served with AUS, 1943-45. Recipient Disting. Service award Fla. Press Assn., 1976, Disting. Alumnus award U. Fla., 1977; inducted into Fla. Newspaper Hall of Fame, 1990. Mem. Fla. Press Assn. (pres. 1963-64, 69-70), AP Mng. Editors (bd. dirs. 1964-66), So. Newspaper Pubs. Assn., Lauderdale Yacht Club, Tower Club, Sigma Delta Chi, Theta Chi. Democrat. Presbyterian. Home: 1564 Marion Ave Tallahassee FL 32303-5831

PETTINELLA, EDWARD, real estate company executive; Degree, State U., Geneseo; MBA, Syracuse (N.Y.) U. With Rochester (N.Y.) Cmty. Savings Bank, 1980—97; pres. N.Y. Divsn. Charter One Bank, 1997—2001; exec. v.p. Charter One Fin., Inc., 1997—2001, Home Properties, Rochester, 2001—04, CEO, 2004—. Bd. dir. Home Properties, State U. Geneseo, Geneseo Found.; bd. dir. Sch. Bus. Syracuse U. Bd. dir. United Way, Rochester, YMCA, Rochester. Office: Home Properties 850 Clinton Square Rochester NY 14604*

PETTINELLA, NICHOLAS ANTHONY, financial executive; b. Little Falls, N.Y., Sept. 9, 1942; s. Nicholas and Rose (Zuccaro) P.; m. Nancy C. Whitehouse, Oct. 28, 1978; children: Albert J., Michael A. BS, Bentley Coll., 1968; MBA, Babson Coll., 1975; postgrad., Harvard U., 1979, Stanford U., 1983. CPA. Mass. auditor Coopers & Lybrand, Boston, 1970-76; treas. Courier Corp., Lowell, Mass., 1976-80; controller corp. ops. Digital Equipment Corp., Maynard, Mass., 1980-81; dir. fin. Intermetrics, Inc., Burlington, Mass., 1981-83, sr. v.p. fin., chief fin. officer, treas., 1983-98; sr. v.p. fin., treas. Averstar, Inc., Burlington, 1999-2000; v.p., CFO Iron Bridge Networks, Inc., Lexington, Mass., 2000—01; CFO ideaLogix, Inc., Framingham, Mass., 2001—02, Accordare, Arlington, Mass., 2002—. Bd. dirs. The Computer Mus., Boston, treas. 1988-98, bd. overseers 1997-99, Mus. Scis., Boston, 1999-2003. Chmn. fin. com. Town of Ashland, Mass., 1980-82. Served with U.S. Army, 1964-66. Mem. Fin. Execs. Inst., AICPA, Inst. Mgmt. Accts., Mass. Soc. CPAs, Treas. Club Boston, Pacioli Soc. Roman Catholic. Home: 141 South St Ashland MA 01721-2263

PETTIS-ROBERSON, SHIRLEY MCCUMBER, retired congresswoman; b. Mountain View, Calif. d. Harold Oliver and Dorothy Susan (O'Neil) McCumber; m. John J. McNulty (dec.); m. Jerry L. Pettis (dec. Feb. 1975); m. Ben Roberson, Feb. 6, 1988; children: Peter Dwight Pettis, Deborah Neil Pettis Moyer. Student, Andrews U., U. Calif., Berkeley; PhD (hon.), Loma Linda U., 2002. Mgr. Audio-Digest Found., LA, Glendale; sec.-treas. Pettis, Inc., Hollywood, 1958-68; mem. 94th-95th Congresses from 37th Calif. Dist.; mem. coms. interior, internat. rels., edn. labor 94th-95th Congresses 37th Calif. Dist. Pres. Women's Rsch. Edn. Inst., 1979-80; bd. dirs. Kemper Nat. Ins. Cos., 1979-97, Lumbermens Mut. Ins. Co.; bd. dir. Kemper Corp. Mem. Pres.'s Commn. Arms Control Disarmament, 1980-83, Commn. Presdl. Scholars, 1990-93; trustee U. Redlands, Calif., 1980-83, Loma Linda (Calif.) U. Med. Ctr., 1990-95; chair Loma Linda U. Children's Hosp. Found.; mem. Former Mems. Congress, 1988—. Mem.: Morningside Country Club (Rancho Mirage, Calif.).

PETTIT, CLAUD MARTIN, religious organization administrator; b. Okemah, Okla., Sept. 19, 1926; s. Frank Martin and Ruby May (Thompson) P.; m. Margaret Esta Cain, July 30, 1948; children: Ruth Elaine Maenpaa, Paul Martin. Degree, Denver Bible Inst., 1948; BS, Rockmont Coll., 1952; postgrad., Bill Ogden Engring./Radio Sch., 1961; DD, Pioneer Sem., 1954. Ordained pastor Conservative Bapt. Assn., 1952. Pastor First Bapt. Ch., Arvada, Colo., 1952-60, Coal Creek Canyon, Colo., 1960; ceo, owner Radio Sta. KEOS, Flagstaff, Ariz., 1960-61; pastor Elmwood Bapt. Ch., Brighton, Colo., 1962-65; ceo, owner Radio Sta. KWIV, Douglas, Wyo., 1965-74; pastor Bethany Bapt. Ch., North Fed. Bapt. Ch., Denver, 1973-95; ceo, owner Radio Sta. KCMP, Brush, Colo., 1976-87; gen. dir. Better Life Ministries, Arvada, 1992—; pastor Berkeley Bapt. Ch., Denver, 2001—. Trustee Colo. Christian U., Lakewood, 1967-2001, advisor radio network, 1971-2001; chmn. bd. Am. Indian Crusade, Oklahoma City, 1987-2001; dir. Compa Food Ministries, Denver, 1981-91. Mem. Radio Hist. Soc., Broadcast Pioneers of Colo., Broadcasters Found., Model T Ford Club Am. (Mile High chpt. 1969—). Avocations: collecting and restoring antique automobiles, collecting big band music. Home: 8320 W 66th Ave Arvada CO 80004-3327 Office Phone: 303-431-0103.

PETTIT, FREDERICK SIDNEY, metallurgical engineering educator, researcher; b. Wilkes Barre, Pa., Mar. 10, 1930; s. Edwin Humes and Edith Mae (Barnecut) P.; m. Lou-Jean Mary Corso, Aug. 30, 1958; children: Frederick N., Theodore E., John C., Charles A. B in Engring., Yale U., 1952, M in Engring., 1960, D in Engring., 1962. Jr. engr. Westinghouse Electric Corp., Pitts., 1952-54; engr. Avco-Lycoming, Stratford, Conn., 1957-58; postdoctoral student Max Planck Inst. Phys. Chemistry, Gottingen, Fed. Republic Germany, 1962-63; sr. staff scientist Pratt & Whitney Aircraft Co., East Hartford, Conn., 1963-79; prof. metall.-material engring. dept., chmn. U. Pitts., Pa., 1979-88, prof., 1988—, Harry S. Tack prof. materials engring., 1992—; mem. adv. bd. Jour. Oxidation of Metals, Plenum Press, N.Y., 1975—. 1st lt USMC, 1954-57. NSF fellow, 1962-63 Mem. Metall. Soc. (program dir. 1982-83), Electrochem. Soc. (sec.-treas. high temperature materials div. 1979-83), Am. Soc. Metals, Materials Rsch. Soc. Roman Catholic. Home: 201 Ennerdale Dr Pittsburgh PA 15237-4026 Office: U Pitts 848 Benedum Hall Pittsburgh PA 15261-2208 E-mail: pettit@engr.pitt.edu.

PETTIT, GEORGE ROBERT, chemist, educator, cancer researcher; b. Long Branch, N.J., June 8, 1929; s. George Robert and Florence Elizabeth (Seymour) P.; m. Margaret Jean Benger, June 20, 1953; children: William Edward, Margaret Sharon, Robin Kathleen, Lynn Benger, George Robert III. BS, Wash. State U., 1952; MS, Wayne State U., 1954, PhD, 1956. Tchg. asst. Wash. State U., 1950-52, lecture demonstrator, 1952; rsch. chemist E.I. duPont de Nemours and Co., 1953; grad. tchg. asst. Wayne State U., 1952-53, rsch. fellow, 1954-56; sr. rsch. chemist Norwich Eaton Pharms., Inc., 1956-57; asst. prof. chemistry U. Maine, 1957-61, assoc. prof. chemistry, 1961-65, prof. chemistry, 1965; vis. prof. chemistry Stanford U., 1965; prof. chemistry Ariz. State U., 1965—, chmn. organic chemistry divsn., 1966-68, disting. rsch. prof., 1978-79, Dalton prof. medicinal chemistry and rsch., 1986—, Regent's prof. chemistry, 1990—. Vis. prof. So. African, Univs., 1978; dir. Cancer Rsch. Lab., 1974-75, Cancer Rsch. Inst., 1975—; co-dir. Ariz. Prostate Cancer Task Force, 2000—; lectr. various colls. and univs.; cons. in field. Contbr. articles to profl. jours. Mem. adv. bd. Wash. State U. Found., 1981—85. With Res. USAF, 1949—53. Recipient Alumni Achievement award, Wash. State U., 1984. Fellow: Am. Inst. Chemists (Pioneer award 1989, Ariz. Gov.'s Excellence award 1993); mem.: Am. Soc. Oncology, Am. Assn. Cancer Rsch., Am. Soc. Pharmacognosy (Rsch. Achievement award 1995), Chem. Soc. London, Am. Chem. Soc. (mem. awards com. 1968—71, Guenther award in chemistry of natural products 1998), Phi Lambda Upsilon, Sigma Xi. Office: Ariz State U Cancer Rsch Inst Tempe AZ 85287

PETTIT, GHERY DEWITT, retired veterinary medicine educator; b. Oakland, Calif., Sept. 6, 1926; s. Hermon DeWitt Pettit and Marion Esther (St. John) Menzies; m. Frances Marie Seitz, July 5, 1948; children: Ghery St. John, Paul Michael. BS in Animal Sci., U. Calif., Davis, 1948, BS in Vet. Sci., 1951, DVM, 1953. Charter diplomate Am. Coll. Vet. Surgeons. Asst. prof. vet. surgery U. Calif., Davis, 1953-61; prof. vet. surgery Wash. State U., Pullman, 1961-91, prof. emeritus, 1991—. Mem. Wash. State Vet. Bd. Govs., 1981—88, chmn., 1987; vis. fellow Sydney U., Australia, 1977. Author/editor: Intervertebral Disc Protrusion in the Dog, 1966; co-author: Centennial History of the Washington State University College of Veterinary Medicine, 1999; cons. editoral bd. Jour. Small Animal Practice, Eng., 1970-88; mem. editoral bd. Compendium on C.E., Lawrenceville, N.J., 1983-86, editoral rev. bd. Jour. Vet. Surgery, Phila., 1984-86, editor 1987-92; contbr. articles to profl. jours., chpts. to books. Elder Presbyn. Ch., Pullman, 1967—. With USN, 1944—46. Recipient Norden Disting. Tchr. award Wash. State U. Class 1971, Faculty of Yr. award Wash. State U. Student Com., 1985. Mem.: AVMA, Am. Coll. Vet. Surgeons (recorder 1970—77, pres., chmn. bd. dirs. 1978—80), Kiwanis Internat., Am. Legion, Phi Kappa Sigma (chpt. advisor 1981—, 2d v.p. 1993—98, internat. pres. 1998—2000), Phi Zeta, Sigma Xi. Republican. Avocations: camping, small boat sailing.

PETTIT, GHERY ST. JOHN, electronics engineer; b. Woodland, Calif., Apr. 6, 1952; s. Ghery DeWitt and Frances Marie (Seitz) P.; m. Marilyn Jo Van Hoose, July 28, 1973; children: Ghery Christopher, Heather Kathleen. BS in Electrical Engring., Wash. State U., 1975. Nuclear engr. Mare Island Naval Shipyard, Vallejo, Calif., 1975-76; electronics engr. Naval Electronic Systems Engring. Ctr., Vallejo, 1976-79; sr. engr. Martin Marietta Denver Aerospace, 1979-83; staff engr. Tandem Computers Inc., Santa Clara, Calif., 1983-90, mgr. electromagnetic capability Cupertino, Calif., 1990-91, electromagnetic compatibility lead engr., 1991-95; electromagnetic compatibility engr. Intel Corp., Hillsboro, Oreg., 1995-96, Dupont, Wash., 1996—. Mem. U.S. tech. adv. group subcom. I, Spl. Com. on Radio Frequency Interferences subcom. Internat. Electrotechnical Commn.; mem. CISPR SC I, WG2, WG3 and WG4.

Asst. cubmaster Boy Scouts Am., San Jose, Calif., 1985-86, cubmaster, 1986-88, ast. scoutmaster, 1988-90, scoutmaster, 1990-93. Mem. IEEE (sr.), Nat. Rsch. Coun. (bd. assessment of NIST programs 1999—), EMC Soc. (bd. dirs. 1999—, v.p. commn. svcs. 2003—), Electromagnetic Capability Soc. (sec.-treas. Littleton, Colo. chpt. 1983, sec. Santa Clara Valley chpt. 1985-87, vice chmn. 1987-89, chmn. 1989-91, sec. Santa Clara Valley sect. 1991-92, treas. 1992-93, vice chmn. 1993-94, chmn. 1994-95), IEEE Electromagetic Capability Soc. (chmn. Seattle chpt. 1997-2000). Republican. Presbyterian. Avocations: flying, amateur radio, sailing. Office: Intel Corp 2800 Center Dr Dupont WA 98327-9773 Office Phone: 253-371-5515. Business E-Mail: ghery.pettit@intel.com.

PETTIT, JOHN DOUGLAS, JR., management educator; b. Alice, Tex, Aug. 19, 1940; s. John Douglas and Vivian Iola (Beaman) P.; m. Suzanne McLeod, Aug. 23, 1964; children: Melanie Ann Wilson, David Bryant. BBA, U. North Tex., 1962, MBA, 1964; PhD, La. State U., 1969. Instr. mgmt. Miss. State U., Starkville, Miss., 1964-65; grad. asst. La. State U., Baton Rouge, 1965-67, instr. mgmt., 1967-68; asst. prof. bus. Tex. Tech. U., Lubbock, Tex., 1968-69; assoc. prof. mgmt. U. North Tex., Denton, Tex., 1969-78, prof. mgmt., 1978-95; chair excellence in free enterprise Austin Peay State U., Clarksville, Tenn., 1995-96; interim chair and prof. dept. info. and decision scis. U. Tex., El Paso, Tex., 2000-2001. Bd. dirs. Capital Instnl. Svcs., Dallas and N.Y.C., mem. audit com., 2003—; cons. various orgns., 1969-98; mgr., co-owner Pettit's Cleaners/Hatters, Alice, 1992-96; vis. prof. mgmt. Wichita State U., Kans., 1994-95; vis. prof. Ecole Superieure de Commerce et de Management, Poitier and Tours, France, 2002-03, U. Kuopio, Finalnd, 2003-04. Kuopio, Finland, 2002, Co-author: Business Communication: Theory and Application, 7th edit. 1993, Report Writing for Business, 10th edit. 1998, Lesikar's Basic Business Communication, 8th edit. 1999; mem. editl. bd. Organl. Comm. Abstracts, 1980-85; mem. editl. bd. Jour. Bus. Comm., 1987-90, mng. editor, 1990-94. Mem. choir Trinity Presbyn. Ch., Denton, 1985-1996, 2002—; actor, singer Denton Cmty. Theater Summer Prodn., 1988-95. Recipient Master's Degree award Chgo. Bd. Trade, 1963. Fellow Assn. Bus. Comm. (pres., 1st v.p., exec. dir., 1990-94); mem. Southwestern Fedn. Adminstrv. Disciplines (pres., v.p.), Acad. Mgmt., Denton Country Club (bd. dirs.), Blue Key Nat. Hon. Fraternity, Beta Gamma Sigma (hon.), Phi Kappa Phi (hon.), Delta Sigma Pi. Presbyterian. Avocations: music, tennis. Home: 9122 David Fort Rd Argyle TX 76226-2953 Business E-Mail: jpettit@ujep.edu.

PETTIT, JOHN W. administrator; b. Detroit, Mar. 6, 1942; s. John W. and Clara (Schartz) P.; m. Kathleen Endres, Aug. 8, 1970; children: Julie, Andrew, Michael. BBA, U. Notre Dame, 1964; MBA, Mich. State U., 1974. CPA, Mich.; CFP, 2001. Acct. Ernst & Ernst, Detroit, 1964-67; chief acct. Detroit Inst. Tech., Detroit, 1967-69; controller, dir. adminstrn. & fin. Mich. Cancer Found., Detroit, 1969-80; chief adminstrv. officer Dana-Farber Cancer Inst., Boston, 1980-94; exec. v.p., chief oper. officer John Wayne Cancer Inst., Santa Monica, Calif., 1995-97; fin. cons. L.A., 1998—. Grant reviewer Nat. Cancer Inst., Bethesda, Md., 1979-94. Pres. advanced mgmt. program Mich. State U., 1978-79; mem. adv. bd. Arthritis Found. So. Calif. chpt., 1999—; mem. Town Meeting, Wellesley, Mass., 1991-94. Mem.: AICPA, Fin. Planning Assn. Avocations: sailing, woodworking, photography, music. Office: 21031 Ventura Blvd Ste 705 Woodland Hills CA 91364 E-mail: jwpettit@yahoo.com.

PETTIT, LAWRENCE KAY, university president; b. Lewistown, Mont., May 2, 1937; s. George Edwin and Dorothy Bertha (Brown) P.; m. Sharon Lee Anderson, June 21, 1961 (div. Oct. 1976); children: Jennifer Anna, Matthew Anderson, Allison Carol, Edward McLean; m. Elizabeth DuBois Medley, July 11, 1980 (div. Dec. 1998). BA cum laude, U. Mont., 1959; AM, Washington U., St. Louis, 1962; PhD, U. Wis., 1965. Legis. asst. U.S. Senate, 1959-60, 62; asst. & assoc. prof. dept. polit. sci. Pa. State U., 1964-67; assoc. dir. fed. rels. Am. Council Edn., Washington, 1967-69; chmn. dept. polit. sci. Mont. State U., 1969-72; adminstrv. asst. to gov. State of Mont., 1973; chancellor Mont. Univ. System, Helena, 1973-79; pvt. practice ednl. cons. Mont., 1979-81; dep. commr. for acad. affairs Tex. Coordinating Bd. for Higher Edn., 1981-83; chancellor Univ. System of South Tex., 1983-86; chancellor (now pres.) So. Ill. U., Carbondale, Edwardsville, 1986-91, Disting. svc. prof., 1991-92; pres. Indiana U. Pa., 1992—2003, ret., 2003. Mem. adv. bd. S & T Bancorp., 1997-2003; mem. regional adv. bd. Nat. City Bank, 1997-99; bd. dirs. Ind. Healthcare Corp. Author: (with H. Albinski) European Political Processes, 2d edit., 1974, (with E. Keynes) Legislative Process in the U.S. Senate, 1969, (with S. Kirkpatrick) Social Psychology of Political Life, 1972, (with J. Goetz and S. Thomas) Legislative Process in Montana, 1975; mem. editl. bd. Ednl. Record, 1985-98. Mem. adv. bd. Leadership Ctr. Ams., 1988-90, Ill. Coalition, 1989-92; candidate for 2d dist. U.S. Ho. of Reps., Mont., 1980; mem. Ill. Gov.'s Com. on Sci. and Tech., 1986-90; bd. dirs. Tex. Guaranteed Student Loan Corp., 1985-86, Reschini Found., 2003—; chmn. Ill.-Niigata Commn. on Edn. and Econ. Devel., 1990-92; chair bd. dirs. Nat. Environ. Edn. and Tng. Ctr., 1994—; mem. adv. bd. Princeton Review, 2003—. U. Wis. fellow 1962-63, Vilas fellow U. Wis., 1963-64. Mem. AAUP (pres. Mont. conf. 1971-72), Nat. Assn. Sys. Heads (pres. 1989), Am. Coun. on Edn. (chmn. leadership commn. 1989-90, sr. fellow 1991-92), Am. Assn. Higher Edn., Am. Assn. State Colls. and Univs. (Disting. Svc. award 1991), Newcomen Soc., Duquesne Club Pitts., Allegheny Club Pitts., World Affairs Coun. Pitts., Univ. Club Pitts., Pa. Soc. (life), Ind. Country Club, Rotary (Paul Harris fellow), Ind. C. of C. (bd. dirs. 1992—2003), Sigma Chi (Significant Sig award 1988), Phi Kappa Phi. Episcopalian. Home: 209 Saddlebrook Dr Indiana PA 15701 Office: NEETC Inc 1179 Grant St Indiana PA 15701 Office Phone: 724-465-9114 x16. Business E-Mail: lpettit@iup.edu.

PETTITT, JAY S. architect, consultant; b. Redford, Mich., Jan. 6, 1926; s. Jay S. and Florence Marian (Newman) P.; m. Ruth Elizabeth Voigt, June 21, 1947; children— J. Stuart, Laura Ellen, Patricia Lynn, Carol Ann B.Arch., U. Mich., 1951. Registered architect, Mich. Draftsman Frank J. Stepnoski and Son, Fond du Lac, Wis., 1951; project architect Albert Kahn Assocs., Inc., Detroit, 1951-62, chief archtl. devel., 1962-67, v.p., 1967-88, dir. architecture, 1975-88; archtl. cons. Beulah, Mich., 1988—. Active Jr. Athletic Assn., Redford, Mich., 1959-63; com. chmn. Boy Scouts Am., 1960-65; supr. Benzonia Twp. Served with U.S. Army. 1943-46, ETO. Fellow AIA; mem. Mich. Soc. Architects (pres. 1967), Am. Arbitration Assn., Am. Assn. Hosp. Planning, Engring. Soc. Detroit, U. Mich. Pres.' Club Avocations: sailing, skiing. Personal E-mail: jaypettit@bignetnorth.net.

PETTITTE, ANDREW EUGENE (ANDY PETTITTE), professional baseball player; b. Baton Rouge, June 15, 1972; m. Laura Pettitte, Jan. 9, 1993; children: Joshua Blake, Jared, Lexy Grace. Student, San Jacinto Coll., Tex. Pitcher N.Y. Yankees, Bronx, 1995—2003, Houston Astros, 2004—. Mem. World Series championship team, 1996, 1998, 1999, 2000; named lefthanded pitcher on The Sporting News Am. League All Star team, 1996, 2001. Office: Houston Astros PO Box 288 Houston TX 77001-0288*

PETTUS, E. LAMAR, lawyer; b. 1945; m. Donna C.; children: Evan Lamar, Carrie Anne, Samuel Chase. BSME, U. Ark., 1968, JD with honors, 1973. Bar: U.S. Dist. Ct. 1974 Ark., U.S. Ct. Appeals (8th cir.) 1974, Ark. Supreme Ct. 1974, U.S. Supreme Ct. 1979. Canton works plant engr. trainee Internat. Harvester, 1971; assoc. Pearson & Woodruff Law Firm, 1973; pvt. practice Pettus Law Firm, Fayetteville, Ark., 1974—. City atty. Farmington, 1981; mem. com. bar examiners Ark. Supreme Ct., 1986, chmn., 1988-89. Bus. mgr. Ark. Law Rev.; participant: televised "Ask Your Lawyer Program", 1981-83. Fin. chair Ctrl. United Meth. Ch., 1994-96, chair adminstrv. bd., 1997-2000; mem. Fayette Sch. Bd., 1991-97; active Assn. Voluntary Lawyers for Elderly, 1990—, Washington County Rep. Party. Comdr. USN, 1968-71, Vietnam, res. 1971-86. Recipient Navy Achievement medal, Navy Commendation medal. Mem. Ark. Bar Assn (pres. 1993-94, various positions and coms.), Ark. Trial Lawyers Assn., Washington County Bar Assn. (pres. 1989-90, v.p. 1989-90, sec.-treas. 1978-79), Fayetteville C. of C. (legis. com. 1994—), Rotary Internat. (various coms.). Office: PO Box 1665 151 W Dickson St Fayetteville AR 72702 E-mail: lpettus@pettuslaw.com.

PETTUS, WILLIAM G. retired nuclear scientist, research scientist; b. Lynchburg, Va., Aug. 6, 1925; s. Joseph Benjamin and Ruth Earle (Coleman) Pettus; m. Arline Cash Pettus, Mar. 22, 1947; 1 child, William Gower Jr. BS, Lynchburg Coll., Lynchburg, Va., 1949; MS, Univ. Va., Charlottesville, Va., 1953, PhD, 1956. Instr. physics/math Lynchburg Coll., Lynchburg, Va., 1950—52, asst. prof. physics, 1953—54; instr. physics Univ. Va., Charlottesville, Va., 1954—56; sr. nuc. physicist Babcock & Wilcox, Lynchburg, Va., 1956—91; vis. rsch. scientist Princeton Univ., Princeton, NJ, 1978—79; vis. prof. of nuc. engring. Va. Polytechnic and State Univ., Blacksburg, Va., 1981. Cons. radiology Univ. Va. Health and Sci. Ctr., Charlottesville, Va., 1998—99. CM3C USN, 1943—46. Mem.: Vet. of Foreign Wars, Am. Physics Soc., Am. Legion, Phi Beta Kappa, Sigma Xi. Republican. Meth. Achievements include patents for 8 U.S; design of thermonuclear weapons and delivery systems; yttrium-90 radiation treatment device for brain tumors; lithium deuteride first wall coating for tokamak fusion reactors. Avocations: swimming, hiking, sailing, number theory, cosmology. Home: 194 Crane Dr Monroe VA 24574

PETTY, DAVID, newspaper editor; b. Paris, Ark., Nov. 14, 1945; BA in History, U. Ark. Exec. editor The Clarion Ledger, Jackson, Miss., 1996—. Office: The Clarion Ledger Editorial Dept 201 S Congress St Jackson MS 39201-4202

PETTY, DONNA MATTHEWS, middle school educator; b. Charleston, South Carolina, Nov. 15, 1957; d. Duncan Newton Matthews Jr. and Calista Doris (Chapman) Matthews; m. Michael George Petty, May 31, 1980 (div. Mar. 1988); one child, Adrian Michael. BA, U. S.C., 1990, Interdisciplinary MA in Natural Sci., 2000. Cert. tchr. sci. nat. bd. cert. tchr. in early adolescence sci., 2002. Tchr. 7th grade math. and health Monetta Mid. Sch., Ridge Springs, SC, 1990-92; tchr. multi grade levels New Directions / S.C. Dept. Juvenile Justice, Columbia, SC, 1992-96; tchr. 8th grade earth sci. Dent Mid. Sch., Columbia, SC, 1996—. Facilitator PBS Mathline, Alexandria, Va., 1995-96; mem. Curriculum Leadership Inst., Columbia, S.C. 1995—. Den leader Boy Scouts Am., West Columbia, S.C., 1992-95; asst. cubmaster, 1995-96; Chinquapin Dist. webmaster, 1995-98; pack com. chair, 1996-98. Named Tchr. of the Yr., 1996, S.C. Dept. Juvenile Justice; Who's Who Among Am. Teachers, 2002. Baha'i faith. Avocations: computers, camping, environmental efforts. Office: Dent Mid Sch 6950 N Trenholm Rd Columbia SC 29206-1708 E-mail: dpetty@teacher.com.

PETTY, ELIZABETH MARIE, geneticist; b. Chgo., July 13, 1959; d. Ralph David and Joyce Elizabeth (Carlson) P.; life ptnr. Karen Kay Milner, Dec. 15, 1985. BA, Clarke Coll., 1981; MD, U. Wis., 1986. Diplomate Nat. Bd. Med. Examiners, Am. Bd. Pediats., Am. Bd. Med. Genetics, Molecular Genetics and Clin. Genetics. Pediat. intern and resident U. Wis., Madison, 1986-89; genetics fellow Yale U., New Haven, Conn., 1989-93; assoc. prof. U. Mich., Ann Arbor, 1994—, med. dir. genetic counseling program, 1996—, dir. med. genetics outpatient clinic, 1996—. Expert witness DNA testing in State of Ohio and Mich., 1995—; presenter regional, nat. and internat. confs. on genetics, 1991—. Contbr. chpt. to books, articles, editls. to profl. jours.; peer reviewer various jours., 1994—. Participant Gay and Lesbian Health Group, Ann Arbor, 1994—; apptd. to State of Mich.'s Gov.'s Commn. on Genetic Privacy and Progress, 1997-98. Recipient Clin. Investigator award NIH-NCI, 1995-2000, RO1 award, 1997—, Am. Cancer Rsch. Fund award, 1997-98, U. Mich. award for Disting. Pub. Svc., 2000, Breast Cancer award Dept. Def., 2001. Fellow Am. Soc. Human Genetics, Am. Coll. Med. Genetics; mem. AMA, Am. Acad. Scis., European Soc. Human Genetics, Human Genome Orgn., Alpha Omega Alpha. Democrat. Roman Catholic. Avocations: flutist, photographer. Office: U Mich 4301 MSRB III Ann Arbor MI 48109-0638

PETTY, GEORGE OLIVER, lawyer; b. L.A., Mar. 31, 1939; s. Hugh Morton and May (Johnson) P.; m. Sandra Diane Kilpatrick, July 14, 1962; children: Ross Morton, Alison Lee, Christopher Henry. AB, U. Calif., Berkeley, 1961; LLB, U. Calif., 1964. Bar: Calif. 1965, Eng. and Wales 1986, U.S. Supreme Ct. 1976. Atty. Huovinen & White, Oakland, Calif., 1967-69; counsel Bechtel Power Corp., San Francisco, 1969-83; prin. counsel Bechtel Ltd., London, 1983-86; gen. counsel Sun-Diamond Growers of Calif., Pleasanton, Calif., 1987-95; pvt. practice, 1995—96; gen. counsel Tone Bros. Inc., 1997—. Capt. U.S. Army, 1965-67. Mem. Calif. State Bar Assn., Alameda County Bar Assn., Eng. and Wales Bar Assn., Bar Assn. for Commerce, Fin. & Industry (Eng.), Middle Temple Inn. Office: Burns Philp Food Inc 8 California St 600 San Francisco CA 94111 Office Phone: 415-477-2800. E-mail: gopetty@aol.com.

PETTY, JAMES ALAN, mathematics educator, consultant; b. Dublin, Ind., Dec. 27, 1954; s. Orris Delmar and Blanche Irene Petty; m. Soranee Holasuit, May 17, 1980; 1 child, Krissada Holasuit Petty; m. Christy Foley, Feb. 18, 2001. BS in Math. and Econs., Ball State U., 1977, MS in Math., 1978; PhD, Purdue U., 1996. Instr. math. U. Guam, Mangilao, 1989-92, asst. prof., 1992-94; instr. math./statistics U. Md.-Asia, Andersen AFB, Guam, 1990-94; tchr. educator Western Ky. U., Bowling Green, 1994-95; asst. prof. math. Ind.-Purdue U., Ft. Wayne, 1995-97; asst. prof. edn. U. Tenn., Martin, 1997-00. V.p. mktg. FPA Ednl. Consulting, Martin, 1995-00. Contbg. author: Epistecybernetics, 1997; contbr. articles to profl. jours. Mem. Math. Assn. Am., Nat. Coun. Tchrs. Math., Navy League U.S., Psychology Math. Edn.-N.Am., Tenn. Assn. Math. Educators, Phi Delta Kappa (program coord. N.W. Tenn. chpt. 1998-00). Republican. Office: U Tenn 240 J Gooch Hl Martin TN 38238-0001 E-mail: jpetty@utm.edu.

PETTY, JOHN ROBERT, financier; b. Chgo., Apr. 16, 1930; s. Dewitt Talmage and Beatrice (Worthington) P.; children: L. Talmage, Robert D., George M., Victoria Lee. AB, Brown U., 1951; postgrad., NYU, 1953-54. With Chase Manhattan Bank, N.Y.C. and Paris, 1953-66, v.p., 1964-66; dep. asst. sec. Dept. Treasury, Washington, 1966-68, asst. sec. for internat. affairs, 1968-72; partner Lehman Bros., N.Y.C., 1972-76; pres., dir., chmn. exec. com. Marine Midland Banks, Inc., from 1976, chmn., chief exec. officer, 1976-88; mng. gen. ptnr. Petty-FBW Assocs., Washington, 1989-91; chmn. Fed. Nat. Payables Inc. Fed. Nat. Svcs. Inc., 1992—; chmn. Nippon Credit Trust Co., N.Y.C., 1990-98. Chmn. Hydro-Icona, Inc., chmn. TECSEC Inc., Czech & Slovak Am. Enterprise Fund, 1991-95; bd. dirs. Antec Corp., Magnetic Analysis Corp., Anixter Internat. Corp.; trustee Am. Univ. With USNR, 1951-53. Mem. Council Fgn. Relations, Fgn. Bondholders Protective Council (pres.). Office: Fed Nat Svcs Inc 7315 Wisconsin Ave Ste 820W Bethesda MD 20814-3225

PETTY, M. S. MARTY, publisher; b. St. Louis, Mo., Dec. 17, 1952; Publisher Hartford Courant, 1997—. Office: Hartford Courant 285 Broad St Hartford CT 06115-2510

PETTY, MARGE D. state senator; b. Ft. Wayne, Ind., Feb. 26, 1946; m. Tyrus C. Petty, 1968; children: Brandon, Megan. BS, Tex. Christian U., 1968; MEd, Kans. U., 1978; JD, Washburn U. Sch. Law, 1990. Tchr., 1968-69; mgmnt. consultant, 1981—; health educator, 1978-81; mem. City Council of Topeka, 1985-89; dep. mayor Topeka, Kans., 1986; mem. Kans. Senate, 1988—. Mem. Topeka Metro. Ballet, Chamber of Commerce, Mulvane Art Ctr. Episcopalian. Home: 106 SW Woodlawn Ave Topeka KS 66606-1241 Address: Kansas Senate State Capitol Rm 422-S Topeka KS 66612

PETTY, MARTY, publishing executive; m. Mark Petty; 2 children. BJ, U. Mo., 1975; MS in Mgmt., Harvard Grad. Ctr., 1989. Asst. mng. editor Kansas City Star and Times; mng. editor The Hartford Courant, 1983-86, v.p., dep. exec. editor, 1986-89, assoc. pub. for projects and planning, 1989, sr. v.p., gen. mgr., pub., CEO, 1997—2000; exec. v.p. St. Petersburgh Times, 2000—. Editor The Electronic Times, 1991-92. Mem. journalism bd. Wm. Randolph Hearst Found., 1987-89; mem. CEO adv. bd. Greater Hartford Arts Coun.; pres. bd. Camp Courant; bd. dirs. Hartford Courant Found., Hartford Hosp. Holding Co.; mem. The MetroHartford Growth Couns. millennium mgmt. com. Mem. Newspaper Assn. of Am. (Ptnrs. 2000 com., Copyright Clearance Ctr. adv. bd.), Soc. Newspaper Design (pres. 1985, active cons.), Am. Soc. Newspaper Editors, Am. Press Inst., AP Mng. Editors, Poynter Inst. Office: St Petersburg Times 490 1st Ave S Saint Petersburg FL 33701-1121

PETTY, PRISCILLA HAYES, writer, columnist, producer; b. Nashville, Aug. 22, 1940; d. Anderson Boyd and Margaret Louise Hayes; m. Gene Paul Petty, Jan. 10, 1961; children: Eric, Damon, Boyd. BA in English, Vanderbilt U., 1962; postgrad., Lang. Inst., Dartmouth Coll., 1965. Cert. tchr. Ohio. Tchr. English Cin. Suburban Pub. Schs., 1962-65, head dept. English, tchr., 1971-79; newspaper columnist Cin. Enquirer, 1978-89; also syndicated newspaper columnist Gannett News Svc., Washington, 1982-89. Cons. Arthur Andersen & Co., 1981-82; writer United Western Corp., 1982; exec. producer, on camera interviewer national TV documentary, 1992; commentator nat. bus. TV show, 1992; pres., owner, Petty Cons. Prodns., producer Total Quality Tng. Tapes. speaker W. Edwards Deming Seminars; cons. in field. Author: History of a Boardsman (oral history), 1979, Under a Lucky Star: The Story of Frederick A. Hauck, 1986, What's in It for You and the Firm: CEOs and Presidents Look at Community Involvement. Mem. Cin. Coun. World Affairs; chmn. Cin. Media-Bus. Exch., 1983; founder, pres., bd. trustees Cin. Oral History Found., 1984—. Named Outstanding Tchr., Project Teach, Ohio Edn. Assn., 1978; recipient WICI Great Lakes Regional Communicators' award; Pulitzer Prize nominee for Harvard U. Bus. Rev. article. Mem. Women in Comms. (Outstanding Communicator of Yr. 1985), Oral History Assn., Soc. Profl. Journalist, Wyo. Woman's Club. Home: 229 Oliver Rd Cincinnati OH 45215-2638

PETTY, RACHEL, academic administrator; BS in Psychology, MS, Howard U.; postgrad., George Washington U.; PhD in Human Devel., U. Md. Former mem. faculty dept. edn. Howard U., Washington; instr. dept. psychology Fed. City Coll. (now U. D.C.); from asst. prof. to prof. dept. psychology U. D.C., from asst. dean to dean Coll. Arts and Scis., v.p. acad. affairs, 2001—. Sch. psychologist D.C. Pub. Schs. Title I program, Prince George's County Pub. Schs.; staff psychologist, cons., clin. program dir. St. Ann's Infant and Maternity Home; consulting psychologist Bd. of Child Care, United Meth. Ch., Balt.-Washington Dist.; cons. child and family svcs. divsn. D.C. Dept. Human Svcs.; cons. Ednl. Testing Svc.; cons., evaluator Everyday Theater Youth Ensemble; cons. D.C. Ednl. Licensure Commn. Contbr. articles to profl. jours. Active Md. State Foster Care Rev. Bd., Conf. on Developing World Class Ednl. Stds. for D.C., Luth. Social Svcs. of Nat. Capital Area, D.C. Child Welfare Consortium. Named one of Outstanding Young Women of the Carolinas; recipient award, Nat. Assn. Equal Opportunity in Higher Edn.; fellow Minority Dissertation, State of Md. Mem.: AAUW, APA, D.C. Psychol. Assn. (bd. dirs.), Am. Psychol. Soc., Psi Chi. Office: U DC 4200 Connecticut Ave NW Washington DC 20008

PETTY, SCOTT, JR., rancher; b. San Antonio, Apr. 10, 1937; s. Olive Scott and Edwina (Harris) P.; m. Marie Louise James, June 10, 1959 (dec. Dec. 1981); children: Joan Louise Petty, Susan Harris Arnim, Scott James; m. Eleanor Oliver, Apr. 30, 1983; children: Tim A. Weed, Richard Oliver Weed. BS in Petroleum Engring., U. Tex., 1960, MS in Petroleum Engring., 1961. Profl. engr. Tex., La. Asst. to pres. Petty Geophys. Engring., 1961-63, v.p., 1963-65; pres., exec. officer Petty Labs., 1965-67; pres., dir. Petty Geophys. Engring., 1967-73; exec. v.p. Petty-Ray Geophys., 1973-74; cons. Geosource Internat., 1974-76; chmn. bd. C.H Guenther & Son, Inc., San Antonio, 1982—, White Lily Foods Co., Knoxville, Tenn. Mem. chancellor's coun. U. Tex., Austin, devel. bd., San Antonio; bd. dirs. Tex. and Southwestern Cattle Raisers, Ft. Worth, Nat. Cattleman's Beef Assn., N.Am. Deer Farmers Assn. Mem. Am. Assn. Petroleum Geologists, Am. Inst. Mining, Metall. & Petroleum Engrs., Assn. Profl. Engrs., Geologists & Geophysicists of Alberta, Geophys. Soc. Houston, Internat. Assn. Geophys. Contractors, Internat. Oceanographic Found., Soc. Exploration Geophysicists, Soc. Petroleum Engrs., South Tex. Geol. Soc., Tex. Soc. Profl. Engrs., Explorers Club. Republican. Episcopalian. Home: 202 La Jara Blvd San Antonio TX 78209-4444 Office: Petty Ranch Co 711 Navarro St Ste 235 San Antonio TX 78205-1710

PETTY, THOMAS LEE, physician, educator; b. Boulder, Colo., Dec. 24, 1932; s. Roy Stone and Eleanor Marie (Kudrna) P.; m. Carol Lee Piepho, Aug. 7, 1954; children: Caryn, Thomas, John. BA, U. Colo., 1955, MD, 1958. Intern Phila. Gen. Hosp., 1958-59; resident U. Mich., 1959-60, U. Colo., Denver, 1960-62, pulmonary fellow, 1962-63, chief resident medicine, 1963-64, instr. medicine, 1962-64, asst. prof., 1964-68, assoc. prof., 1968-74, prof. medicine, 1974—; pres. Presbyn./St. Luke's Ctr. for Health Scis. Edn., 1989-95; practice medicine, specializing in internal medicine, pulmonary medicine Denver, 1962—; prof. medicine Rush Univ., 1992—. Cons. Kindred Hosp., 1991-. Author: For Those Who Live and Breathe, 1967, 2d edit., 1972, Intensive and Rehabilitative Respiratory Care, 1971, 3d edit., 1982, Chronic Obstructive Pulmonary Disease, 1978, 2d edit., 1985, Principles and Practice of Pulmonary Rehabilitation, 1993, Enjoying Life With COPD, 1995, 3d edit., others; contbr. articles to profl. jours. NIH and Found. grantee, 1966-88. Master ACP, Am. Coll. Chest Physicians (master, pres. 1982); mem. Assn. Am. Physicians, Assn. of Pulmonary Program Dirs. (founding pres. 1983-84, chmn. nat. lung health edn. program 1995—, co-chmn. 2000-04), Am. Bd. Internal Medicine (bd. govs. 1986-92), Am. Thoracic Soc. (Disting. Achievement award 1995), Phi Beta Kappa, Phi Delta Theta, Alpha Omega Alpha, Phi Rho Sigma (pres. 1976-78). Home: 1940 Grape St Denver CO 80220-1353 Office: 899 Logan St Ste 203 Denver CO 80203 E-mail: tlpdoc@aol.com.

PETTY, TOM (THOMAS EARL PETTY), rock guitarist, band leader, composer; b. Gainesville, Fla., Oct. 20, 1950; s. Earl and Katherine Petty; m. Jane Benyo, 1974-96; children: Adria, Kim; m. Dana York, June 3, 2001. With band the Sundowners (1964) which later was called the Epics (1965-69) and Mudcrutch (1970-74), Gainesville, Fla.; songwriter, musician for Leon Russell, 1974—75; leader Tom Petty and the Heartbreakers, 1975—; toured the world with Bob Dylan, 1986; toured Am. with Georgia Satellites and Del Fuegos (Rock 'n' Roll Caravan tour), 1987. Albums: (with the Heartbreakers) Tom Petty and the Heartbreakers, 1976, You're Gonna Get It, 1978, Damn the Torpedoes, 1979, Hard Promises, 1981, Long After Dark, 1982, Southern Accents, 1985, Pack Up the Plantation, 1986, Let Me Up (I've Had Enough), 1987, Into the Great Wide Open, 1991 (Grammy nomination for Best Rock Performance by a Duo or Group with Vocal, 1992), Tom Petty and the Heartbreakers' Greatest Hits, 1993, She's The One (soundtrack), 1996, Echo, 1999 (Grammy nomination for Best Rock Album, 2000), The Last DJ, 2002; (solo) Full Moon Fever, 1989 (Grammy nomination for Album of Yr., 1990), Wildflowers, 1994 (Grammy nomination for Best Rock Album, 1996); (with the Traveling Wilburys) Traveling Wilburys Vol. 1, 1989 (Grammy Award for Best Rock Performance by a Duo or Group with Vocal, 1990, Grammy nomination for Album of Yr., 1990), Traveling Wilburys Vol. 3, 1990; hit singles include Breakdown, 1978, Here Comes My Girl, 1979, Refugee, 1979, The Waiting, 1981, You Got Lucky, 1982, Don't Come Around Here No More, 1985, Jammin' Me, 1987, Free Fallin', 1989, Playback, 1994, Wildflowers, 1994; Songs appear in films: Fast Times at Ridgemont High, 1982, Streets of Fire, 1984, The Silence of the Lambs, 1991, She's the One, 1996, Jerry Maguire, 1996; Actor: (films) Made in Heaven, 1987, The Postman, 1997. Grammy nomination for Best Rock Performance by a Duo or Group with Vocal (with Stevie Nicks for Stop Draggin' My Heart Around), 1982, Grammy nomination for Best Rock Song (Learning to Fly), 1992, Grammy nomination for Best Rock Performance by a Duo or Group with Vocal (with Bob Dylan, Roger McGuinn, Neil Young, Eric Clapton, and George Harrison for My Back Pages), 1994, Grammy nomination for Best Rock Song (with the Heartbreakers for Room At The Top), 2000, Grammy Award for Best Male Rock Vocal Performance (for You Don't Know How It Feels), 1996, MTV Video Music Award for Best Male Video (with the Heartbreakers for Mary Jane's Last Dance), 1994, Video Vanguard Award, MTV Video Music Awards, 1994, MTV Video Music Award for Best Male Video (for You Don't Know How It Feels), 1995, Songwriter Award, ASCAP, 1990, Golden Note Award, ASCAP, 1996, Nat. Veteran's Foundation Special Award of Recognition, 1995, UCLA George & Ira Gershwin Award, 1996, Bill Graham Lifetime Achievement Award, CA Music Awards, 1998, Hollywood Walk of Fame Star (with the Heartbreakers), 1999, inducted, Rock & Roll Hall of Fame (with the Heartbreakers), 2002, Legend Award, Radio Music Awards, 2003. Office: Warner Bros Records 3300 Warner Blvd Burbank CA 91505-4694*

PETTYJOHN, EMMA KENNEDY, fine arts educator; b. Claxton, Ga., Apr. 24, 1965; d. Jimmy Hinton and Reba Wilson Kennedy; m. Marvin Eugene Pettyjohn, June 23, 1990; children: Calvin James, Conner Wayne. BA, Shorter

Coll., Rome, Ga., 1987; MusM, U. of Ga., 1990, D of Mus. Arts, 1997. Cert. nat. coll. faculty Music Tchrs. Nat. Certification. Assoc. prof. of music Piedmont Coll., Demorest, Ga., 1996—2002; asst. prof. of fine arts Emmanuel Coll., Franklin Springs, Ga., 2003—. Organist Commerce (Ga.) Presbyn. Ch., 1994—; lectr. in field. Musician: (recital) Music by Women Composers. Christmas party pianist Hope Haven, Athens, Ga., 1993—2001. Mem.: Ga. Music Tchrs. Assn., Am. Guild Organists (assoc.), Music Tchrs. Nat. Assn. (assoc.; sec. of GMTA 2000—02). Conservative. Presbyterian Usa. Avocation: music. Home: 210 Beaverdam Dr Winterville GA 30683 Office: Emmanuel Coll PO Box 129 181 Springs St Franklin Springs GA 30639 Personal E-mail: emmakpj@yahoo.com. E-mail: epettyjohn@eclions.net.

PETTYJOHN, FRANK SCHMERMUND, cardiology and emergency medicine educator; b. Milford, Del., Sept. 28, 1934; s. James K. and Eloise K. (Kelley) P.; m. Jean A. Rovey, July 1, 1961; children: Elise K. Pettyjohn, Ellen E. Pettyjohn. BCE, U. Del., 1956; MD, Hahnemann U., 1963. Diplomate Am. Bd. Internal Medicine, Cardiovasc. Disease, Am. Bd. Preventive Medicine-Aerospace Medicine, Am. Bd. Emergency Medicine. Commd. 2d lt. U.S. Army, 1957, advanced through grades to col., 1977, intern, resident Madigan Gen. Hosp. Tacoma, 1963-69, chief med. staff aeromed. ctr., Lyster Army Community Hosp. Ft. Rucker, Ala., 1977-80, dir. applied aeromed. rsch. program Aerospace Med. Rsch. Lab., Fla., 1980-82; commdg. officer Winn Army Comty. Hosp. U.S. Army, Ft. Stewart, Ga., 1982-85; retired U.S. Army, 1986; clin. prof. medicine U. So. Ala. Coll. Medicine, Mobile, 1986-89, prof. medicine, 1989—, chmn. dept. emergency medicine, 1992—, dir. divsn. cardiology, 2001—. Med. dir. Southflite, Aeromed. Helicopter Svc., U. So. Ala. Med. Ctr., Mobile, 1990-2004; med. staff cardiology and emergency medicine U. South Ala. Med. Ctr., U. South Ala. Children's and Women's Hosp., U. South Ala. Knollwood Park Hosp., Mobile, 1991—; med. staff cardiology and internal medicine West Fla. Regional Med. Ctr., Pensacola, 1982—, Gulf Breeze (Fla.) Hosp., 1985—. Contbr. articles to profl. jours. Decorated Bronze Star, Legion of Merit, Air medal with two oak leaf clusters. Fellow ACP, Am. Coll. Cardiology, Am. Coll. Chest Physicians, Am. Coll. Preventive Medicine, Coun. Clin. Cardiology (Am. Heart Assn.), Aerospace Med. Assn. (exec. coun. 1979-82), Am. Coll. Emergency Physicians; mem. Soc. Acad. Emergency Medicine, Assn. Acad. Chmn. Emergency Medicine, Am. Coll. Physician Execs., Internat. Acad. Aviation and Space Medicine. Methodist. Avocations: jogging, fishing, sailing. Home and Office: 607 Silverthorn Rd Gulf Breeze FL 32561-4625 Office Phone: 850-932-6016. Business E-Mail: fpettyjo@usouthal.edu.

PETZ, EDWIN V. real estate executive, lawyer; b. Beatrice, Nebr., May 14, 1935; s. Virgil Leonard and Ruth Elenor (Thomsen) P.; m. Daphne Cross, May 17, 1958 (div. June 1964); 1 dau., Katherine J.; m. Anne Higgins, Dec. 3, 1964 (div. Sept. 1993); 1 son, W. Christopher; m. Louise Loosli, Jan. 9, 1997. BA, Principia Coll., Elsah, Ill., 1955; JD, Harvard U., 1958. Bar: N.Y. 1959, Mass. 1976. Assoc. Chadbourne, Parke, Whiteside & Wolff, N.Y.C., 1958-62; asst. gen. counsel Martin Marietta Corp., Bethesda, Md., 1963-64, 1965-75; gen. atty. sec. Bunker-Ramo Corp., Oakbrook, Ill., 1964-65; asst. gen. counsel United Brands Co., N.Y.C., 1975-82, v.p., gen. counsel, sec., 1982-84; sr. v.p., gen. counsel Milstein Properties Corp., 1985—2003; sr. v.p., gen counsel The Milstein Group Inc., 1992—; sr. v.p., gen. counsel Ogden CAP Properties, LLC, 2003—. Mem. ABA, Assn. of Bar of City N.Y. Clubs: University (N.Y.C.). Republican. Episcopalian. Office: Ogden CAP Properities LLC 390 Park Ave New York NY 10022

PETZ, THOMAS JOSEPH, internist; b. Detroit, Feb. 10, 1930; s. Arthur J. and Marie (McCarthy) P.; m. Catherine Crowe, June 13, 1959; children: Thomas Jr., William, David, John, Catherine. BS, U. Detroit, 1951; MD, Wayne State U., 1955. Diplomate Am. Bd. Internal Medicine and Pulmonary Disease. Intern Harper Hosp., Detroit, 1955-56, resident, 1958-59, 60-62, U. Calif., San Francisco, 1959-60; clin. instr. Wayne State U., Detroit, 1962-72, assoc. prof., 1972-76, clin. assoc. prof., 1976-95, clin. prof., 1996-97, prof. emeritus, 1997—; pvt. practice pulmonary disease and internal medicine Detroit, 1962-72, St. Clair Shores, Mich., 1977-96; med.-legal cons. Grosse Pointe, Mich., 1996—. Chief pulmonary Wayne State U., Detroit, 1974-76, Harper Hosp., Detroit, 1972-79; dir. med. intensive care unit Harper Hosp., Detroit, 1977-83; chmn. dept. medicine Bon Secours Hosp., Grosse Pointe, Mich., 1984-86; chmn. Gen. Motors human rsch. com., 1995. Bd. govs. Wayne State Sch. of Medicine Alumni Assn., Detroit, 1981-85. Fellow Detroit Acad. Medicine (pres. 1982-83), Am. Coll. Chest Physicians; mem. Am. Coll. Physicians, Detroit Med. Club. Republican. Roman Catholic. Avocations: golf, skiing.

PETZAL, DAVID ELIAS, editor, writer; b. N.Y.C., Oct. 21, 1941; s. Henry and Aline Born (Bixer) P.; m. Arlene Anne Taylor, May 29, 1974. BA, Colgate U., 1963. Editor Maco Publs., N.Y.C., 1964—69; mng. editor Davis Publs., N.Y.C., 1969—70; features editor Hearst Publs., N.Y.C., 1970—72; mng. editor CBS Publs., N.Y.C., 1972—79, editor, 1979—83, exec. editor, 1983—2001, Field & Stream Mag., N.Y.C., 1983—2001, mng. editor, 2001—03, dep. editor, 2002—. Author: The .22 Rifle, 1972; editor: The Experts Book of the Shooting Sports, 1972, The Experts Book of Upland Game and Waterfowl Hunting, 1975, The Experts Book of Big-Game Hunting in North America, 1976, The Ency. of Sporting Firearms, 1991. Office: Time 4 Mags 10th Fl 2 Park Ave New York NY 10016-5602 Office Phone: 212-779-5287. Business E-Mail: david.petzal@time4.com.

PETZEL, FLORENCE ELOISE, textiles educator; b. Crosbyton, Tex., Apr. 1, 1911; d. William D. and Eloise Petzel. PhB, U. Chgo., 1931, AM, 1934; PhD, U. Minn., 1954. Instr. Judson Coll., 1936-38; asst. prof. textiles Ohio State U., 1938-48; assoc. prof. U. Ala., 1950-54; prof. Oreg. State U., Corvallis, 1954-61, 67-75, 77, 77, prof. emeritus, 1975—, dept. head, 1954-61, 67-75; prof., divsn. head U. Tex., 1961-63; prof. Tex. Tech. U., 1963-67. Vis. instr. Tex. State Coll. for Women, 1937; vis. prof. Wash. State U., 1967. Author: Textiles of Ancient Mesopotamia, Persia and Egypt, 1987; contbr. articles to profl. jours. Effie I. Raitt fellow, 1949-50. Mem. Met. Opera Guild, Sigma Xi, Phi Kappa Phi, Omicron Nu, Iota Sigma Pi, Sigma Delta Epsilon. Home: 150 Downs Blvd Apt A206 Clemson SC 29631-2043

PETZOLD, CAROL STOKER, state legislator; b. St. Louis, July 28; d. Harold William and Mabel Lucille (Wilson) Stoker; m. Walter John Petzold, June 27, 1959; children: Ann, Ruth, David. BS, Valparaiso U., 1959. Tchr. Parkwood Elem. Sch., Kensington, Md., 1960-62; legis. aide Md. Gen. Assembly, Annapolis, 1975-79; legis. asst. Montgomery County Bd. Edn., Rockville, Md., 1980; cmty. sch. coord. Parkland Jr. H.S., Rockville, 1981-87; mem. Md. Ho. of Dels., Annapolis, 1987—, mem. constl. and adminstrv. law com., 1987-93, mem. judiciary com., 1994—, chair subcom. on criminal justice, 2003—, vice chair Montgomery County del., 1995—, dep. majority whip, 1999—2002. Vice chair spl. com. drug and alcohol abuse Md. Ho. Dels., 1999—; mem. transp. planning bd. Nat. Capitol Region, 1989—; vice chmn. assembly on fed. issues Nat. Conf. State Legislatures, 1996-97, chair adv. com. on energy, 1997-99, chair energy and transp. com., 1998-99, pres. women's legis. network, 2004—, mem. trans. com., 2004—. Editor Child Care Sampler, 1974, Stoker Family Cookbook, 1976. Pres. Montgomery Child Care Assn., 1976-78; mem. Md. State Scholarship Bd., 1978-87, chmn. 1985-87; chmn. Legis. Com. Montgomery County Commn. for Children and Youth, 1979-84; mem., v.p. Luth. Social Services Nat. Capitol Area, Washington, 1980-86; mem. exec. com. coun. Montgomery United Way, 1981-2000. Named Mother of Yr., March of Dimes, 2000; named one of Top 100 Md. Women, Daily Record, 2002, 2004; recipient Statewide award, Gov.'s Adv. Bd. on Homelessness, 1994, recognized for outstanding commitment to children, U.S. Dept. HEW, 1980, Award of Excellence, MADD, 2002, Disting. Legislator award, 2003, Impaired Driving Coalition, 2003, Legis. award, Md. Coalition Against Domestic Violence, 2003. Mem.: AAUW (honoree Kensington br. 1971, 2002, honoree Md. divsn. 1981), Women Legislators of Md., Md. Women Legislators Caucus, Women's Polit. Caucus (chmn. Montgomery County 1981—83, exec. com. 2003—04). Democrat. Lutheran. Home: 14113 Chadwick Ln Rockville MD 20853-2103 Office Phone: 410-841-3001.

PETZOLD, JOHN PAUL, judge; b. 1938; BA, U. Maine, 1961; LLB, Washington & Lee U., 1962. Bar: Ohio 1962, Va. 1962. Pvt. practice law, Ohio, 1962-91; asst. atty. gen. State of Ohio, 1964-71; law dir. City of Miamisburg, Ohio, 1979-91; judge Montgomery County Common Pleas Ct., Dayton, Ohio, 1991—. Bd. tax appeals City of Kettering, Ohio, 1971-91. Mem. ABA, Ohio State Bar Assn. (bd. govs., former chairperson young lawyers sect., chairperson pub. rels. com., vice chairperson lawyers assistance com., eminent domain com., banking, comml., and bankruptcy law com., pres. 1998-99), Dayton Bar Assn. (pres. 1989-90), Common Pleas Judge Assn. (mem. bd. commrs. on grievances and discipline 1995-97). Avocations: golf, swimming, writing, teaching, reading, genealogy. Office: Montgomery County Common Pleas Ct 41 N Perry St Dayton OH 45402-1431

PEUGEOT, PATRICK, insurance executive; b. Paris, Aug. 3, 1937; s. Jacques Louis and Edith (Genoyer) P.; m. Catherine Dupont, 1963; children: Hubert, Thomas, Camille. Degree, Ecole Poly., Paris, 1959, Ecole Nat. D'Adminstrn., 1965. Ins. auditor Ministry of Fin., Paris, 1962-65; auditor Cour des Comptes, Paris, 1965-83; spl. asst. Bur. Planning, Paris, 1966-70; sr. v.p. EMC, Toulouse, France, 1970-72, Hachette Inc., Paris, 1972-74; exec. v.p. ops. AGF Life, Paris, 1974-78; exec. v.p. AGF Reims, Paris, 1979-82; pres. Caisse Cen. de Reassurance, Paris, 1983-85; chmn., CEO Scor S.A., Paris, 1983-94, hon. chmn., 1994, 1994—; dir. SCOR U.S., 1994—; vice-chmn., CEO La Mondiale, Paris, chmn., CEO, 1996—. Home: 99 rue du Faubarg du Temple 75010 Paris France Office: La Mondiale 22 Blvd Malesherbes 75008 Paris France

PEVEAR, ROBERTA CHARLOTTE, retired state legislator; b. Bethel, Maine, July 4, 1930; d. Frank Albert Sr. and Thirza Estella (Hickford) Gibson; m. Edward Gordon Pevear, Aug. 21, 1971. Diploma in Comml. Art, Gould Acad., 1947. Sec. Wilner Wood Products, South Paris, Maine, 1947-50; sec. export dept. Whitaker Cable, North Kansas City, Mo., 1951-56; sec. br. and dist. Anheuser-Busch, Inc., Kansas City, Mo., 1957-59; legal sec. Johnson & Johnson, New Brunswick, N.J., 1960-65, St. John, Ronder & Bell, Kingston, N.Y., 1966; sec., adminstrv. asst. Sears-Roebuck & Co., Overland Park, Kans., 1967-70, Exeter, N.H., 1971-77; salesman Avon Products, Hampton Falls, N.H., 1978-86; mem. ho. reps. State of N.H., 1979-88, ret., 1988. Commr. Rockingham Planning Commn., N.H., 1979-88, N.H. Planning Com., 1985-88; clk. Environment and Agrl. Com. N.H. Ho. Reps., 1983-88; del. mem. Rockingham County, 1979-88, exec. bd., 1984-88; chmn. Rockingham County Home, 1987-88. Civil Def. dir., Hampton Falls, NH, 1980—88. Recipient Community Citizen award Hampton Falls Grange, 1982, Seacoast Retired Sr. Service award, 1985. Mem. Nat. Order Women Legislators, N.H. Order of Women Legislators, DAR. Avocations: writing, genealogy, travel.

PEVEC, ANTHONY EDWARD, bishop; b. Cleve., Apr. 16, 1925; s. Anton and Frances Darovec P. MA, John Carroll U., Cleve., 1956; PhD, Western Res. U., Cleve., 1964. Ordained priest Roman Cath. Ch., 1950. Assoc. pastor St. Mary Church, Elyria, Ohio, 1950—52, St. Lawrence Ch., Cleve., 1952—53; rector-prin. Borromeo Sem. H.S., Wickliffe, Ohio, 1953—75; adminstrv. bd. Nat. Cath. Edn. Assn., 1972—75; pastor St. Vitus Ch., Cleve., 1975—79; rector-pres. Borromeo Coll., Wickliffe, 1979—82; aux. bishop Diocese of Cleve., 1982—. Mem. v.p. Slovenian-Am. Heritage Found., Cleve., 1975—. Named Man of Yr., Fedn. Slovenian Nat. Homes, Cleve., 1985, Cath. Man of Yr., KC, 1998, Man of Yr., Pioneer Assn., 2001, Cathedral Latin Alumni Assn., 2003; named to Hall of Fame, St. Vitus Alumni Assn., 1989, Wickliffe Hall of Fame, 2000; recipient honoree, Heritage Found., Cleve., 1982, Alumni medal, John Carroll U., 2004. Mem.: KC (state chaplain 2003—), Cath. Order Foresters (state chaplain 2000—), U.S. Cath. Conf. (nat. adv. coun. 1996—97), Nat. Conf. Cath. Bishops (com. on vocations 1984—86, com. on pro-life activities 1990—92, com. on priestly formation 1993—95, com. on sci. and human values 1993—96). Democrat. Roman Catholic. Avocations: reading, music. Home and Office: Diocese of Cleve 28700 Euclid Ave Wickliffe OH 44092-2527 Office Phone: 440-944-1400. Business E-Mail: bpaepevec@dioceseofcleveland.org. *Ultimately I must always remember that the Lord is totally in control of my life, no matter how complicated it may seem to be. I am here to do the Lord's will, and wherever I go I come to do His will.*

PEW, JOHN GLENN, JR., lawyer; b. Dallas, Apr. 18, 1932; s. John Glenn Sr. and Roberta (Haughton) P. BA, U. Tex., 1954, LLB, 1955. Bar: Tex. 1955, U.S. Dist. Ct. (no. dist.) Tex. 1959, U.S. Supreme Ct. 1959, U.S. Ct. Appeals (5th cir.) 1961, U.S. Ct. Appeals (10th cir.) 1982. Ptnr. Jackson Walker LLP, Dallas, 1964—. With USNR, 1955-58. Mem.: Order of Coif, Phi Beta Kappa. Republican. Presbyterian. Office: Jackson Walker LLP 901 Main St Ste 6000 Dallas TX 75202-3797 E-mail: jpew@jw.com.

PEW, ROBERT ANDERSON, retired real estate and equipment leasing corporation officer; b. Phila., Aug. 22, 1936; s. Arthur Edmund and Mary Elizabeth (Elliott) P.; children from previous marriage: Robert Anderson (dec.), James Cunningham, Glenn Edgar, Joan Elliott; m. Daria S. Decerio, June 19, 1993; 1 child, Richard Westerman. Student, Princeton U., 1954-56; BS, Temple U., 1959; MS in Mgmt. (Alfred P. Sloan fellow), MIT, 1970; LLD (hon.), Widener U., 1982; DPS (hon.), Temple U., 1983; LHD (hon.), Gettysburg Coll., 1984. Ops. asst. prodn. div. Sun Oil Co., Premont, Tex., 1959-60, ops. asst. prodn. div. Morgan City, La., auditor internal audit dept. Phila., 1960-65, staff asst. treasury dept., 1965-69, asst. to exec. v.p. corp. projects group, 1970-71, sec.-treas., mgr. financial control of products group, 1971-74, corp. sec., 1974-77; pres. Helios Capital Corp., 1977-96; CEO Radnor Corp., 1995-96; bd. dirs. Glenmede Corp., Phila., chmn., 1997—2004. Bd. dirs. Sun Co., Inc., Phila., Pew Charitable Trusts, Phila., Glenmede Trust Co. N.A., Phila. Trustee Children's Hosp., Phila., vice chmn., 1991—. Served Pa. Air N.G., 1956—59. Recipient R. Kelso Carter award Widener U., 1971 Mem. Aircraft Owners and Pilots Assn. (trustee, chmn. 1974-77, 85-2002, vice-chmn. 1979-85), Am. Hosp. Assn. (hon.), Coll. Physicians Phila., Union League Club, Harbor Club (pres. 1992-96), Phila. Aviation Country Club, Merion Cricket Club, N.E. Harbor Fleet. Republican. Presbyterian. Home: 916 Muirfield Rd Bryn Mawr PA 19010-1921 Office: Sun Co Ten Penn Ctr 17th Flr 1801 Market St Philadelphia PA 19103-1699 E-mail: dungarnem@aol.com.

PEW, ROBERT CUNNINGHAM, II, office equipment manufacturing company executive; b. Syracuse, N.Y., June 4, 1923; s. Robert Carroll and Bernice (Evans) P.; m. Mary Bonnell Idema, Aug. 23, 1947; children: Robert Cunningham, John Evans, Kate Bonnell. BA, Wesleyan U., Middletown Conn.; HHD (hon.), LLD (hon.), Aquinas Coll. Labor relations exec. Doehler-Jarvis Corp., Grand Rapids, Mich., 1948-51; with Steelcase Inc., Grand Rapids, 1952—, exec. v.p., 1964-66, pres., 1966-79, chmn. bd., pres., 1974-99. Dir. Old Kent Financial Corp., Foremost Corp. Am. Bd. control Grand Valley State Coll.; bd. dirs. Econ. Devel. Corp. Grand Rapids, Mich. Strategic Fund, Nat. Orgn. on Disability; mem. Gov.'s Commn. on Jobs and Econ. Devel. Served to 1st lt. USAAF, 1942-45; to capt. USAAF, 1951-52. Decorated Purple Heart, Air medal with 2 oak leaf clusters. Mem. Grand Rapids C. of C. (dir.), Grand Rapids Employers Assn. (dir.), Chi Psi. Clubs: Lost Tree (North Palm Beach Fla.); Peninsular; University, Kent Country (Grand Rapids). Episcopalian. Home: 11307 Old Harbour Rd North Palm Beach FL 33408-3406 Office: PO Box 1967 Grand Rapids MI 49501-1967 also: Steelcase Inc 901 44th St SE Grand Rapids MI 49508-7575

PEYROT GONZALEZ, MARCO A. secretary of the navy of Mexico; b. Mexico City, June 10, 1940; B in Geograph. Engring., Heroic Mil. Naval Sch., 1957; M in Mil. Adminstrn. in Nat. Security and Def., Nat. Def. Coll.; grad., Naval Superior Studies Ctr., Mex. Navy, 1977. Lt. of corvette Mexican Navy, advanced through grades to adm., cargo officer, 1st officer, comdr. several ships and naval fleets, comdr. Pacific Naval Forces, chief of staff and comdr. different naval regions, naval zones and naval sectors; high-command activities relatied to planning and decision-making for naval ops. and applied logistics Navy Gen. Staff, Commn. on Spl. Studies, Commn. on Laws and Regulations, Social Security Inst. Mexican Armed Forces; naval attaché Mexican Embassy, Italy and France, France; tchr. maths., physics, ballistics, hygrographgy, artillery, electronics Heroic Mil. Naval Coll.; sec. of navy Govt. of Mex., 2000—. Instr. physics and math. and port engring. U. Veracruz; leader various confs.; spkr. in field. Contbr. articles on mil. adminstrn. in nat. security and def. Decorated Condecoracion al Merito Docente Naval. Office: Eje 2 Ote Tramo Heroica Escuela Naval # 861 04830 Mexico City Mexico

PEYSER, JOSEPH LEONARD, history professor, writer, translator; b. NYC, Oct. 19, 1925; s. Samuel and Sadye (Quinto) P.; m. Julia Boxer, May 30, 1948; children: Jay Randall, Jan Ellen. BA, Duke U., 1947, MA, 1949; profl. diploma, Columbia U., 1955; postgrad., U. Nancy, France, 1949-50; Ed.D., NYU, 1965. Prof., chmn. fgn. langs., adminstr. Nancy (France) École Normale, 1949-50; Tchr., chmn. fgn. langs. Monroe (N.Y.) Pub. Schs., 1951-54, Uniondale (N.Y.) Pub. Schs., 1954-61; asst. high sch. prin. Plainview, N.Y., 1961-63; mem. faculty Hofstra U., Hempstead, N.Y., 1963-68, assoc. prof. edn., 1966-68; asst. dean, then asso. dean Hofstra U. (Sch. Edn.), 1964-66; interim dean Sch. Edn. Hofstra U., 1966-68; dean acad. affairs, prof. French and edn. Dowling Coll., Oakdale, N.Y., 1968-70, v.p. acad. affairs, dean faculty, 1970-73; prof. French and edn. Ind. U., South Bend, 1973-94, prof. emeritus French, 1994—, dean faculties, 1973-75, chmn. fgn. lang. dept., 1987-89. Vis. asst. prof. NYU, 1964-66; adj. asst. prof. L.I. U., 1961-63; prin. researcher, translator French Michilimackinac Rsch. Project, Mich., 1991—; rsch. reviewer NEH, 1994-98. Author: Letters from New France, 1981, Letters from New France: The Upper Country, 1686-1783, rev. edit., 1992, Jacques Legardeur de Saint-Pierre: Officer, Gentleman, Entrepreneur, 1996, On the Eve of the Conquest: The Chevalier de Raymond's Critique of New France in 1754, 1997, Ambush and Revenge: George Washington's Adversaries in 1754, 1999; co-author, Fort St. Joseph, 1691-1781, 1991, The Fox Wars: The Mesquakie Challenge to New France, 1993; translator Fort St. Joseph Manuscripts, 1978, William Henry Harrison's French Correspondence, 1994; contbr. profl. publs. Bd. dirs. South Bend Symphony, 1979-86. Served with USNR, 1943-46. Recipient Founders Day award NYU, 1966, State Hist. Soc. of Wis. Hesseltine award, 1991, French Colonial Hist. Soc. Heggoy Book prize, 1994; tchg. fellow French Ministry Edn., 1949-50, Lilly Endowment faculty fellow, 1985-86, NEH fellow, 1988, 94-95, Lundquist faculty fellow, 1989-90; Newberry Libr. rsch. assoc., 1985-86. Mem. Ind. Hist. Soc. (Thornbrough award 1996), French Colonial Hist. Soc. (v.p. 1988-91, exec. com. 1988-94), Ctr. for French Colonial Studies.

PEYTON, DONALD LEON, retired standards association executive; b. Portland, Oreg., May 5, 1925; s. Bernard Thomas and Nelle (Moses) P.; m. Jane Frances Kirkman, Aug. 26, 1950; children: Patrick Philip, James Allen. Student, Mont. State U., 1946-47; BA, No. Colo. U., 1950. Civilian edn. specialist USAF, 1951-56; engaged in real estate Cheyenne, Wyo., 1956-57; adminstrv. asst. to congressman, 1957-60; with U.S. C. of C., 1960-66, gen. mgr. govt. relations, 1965-66; pres. Am. Nat. Standards Inst., Inc., 1966-89, ret., 1989, Peyton Assocs., Standards Cons., White Plains, N.Y., 1989—. Lectr. govt. bus. relations Am. U., 1965-66, Amos Tuck Sch., Dartmouth, 1965—. Author: Standards and Trade in the 1990's; author monographs. Pres., Cheyenne Jr. C. of C., 1955-56. Mem. Am. Soc. Assn. Execs., Old Guard of White Plains. Home and Office: 2 Beverly Rd White Plains NY 10605-3306 *My personal philosophy of life parallels that of my philosophy regarding voluntary organizations. In personal and professional life there is no hope for the self-satisfied individual or the self-satisfied organization.*

PEYTON, JOHN, mayor; m. Kathryn Pearson. Grad. Exec. Edn. Program, Harvard Bus. Sch.; BA, Mercer U., 1986. V.p. Gate Petroleum Co., Fla.; mayor City of Jacksonville, Fla., 2003—. Past pres. Greenscape of Jacksonville, 1998—99; chmn. Jacksonville Symphony Assn.; mem. St. John's Episcopal Ch.; bd. mem. Jacksonville Transp. Authority, 1996—99, chmn., 1999—2003. Republican.

PEZESHKI, S. REZA, education educator; m. Fataneh Farmani. BS, U. Tehran, Iran, 1971; MS, U. Wash, 1977, PhD, 1982. Cert. profl. wetland scientist 1997. Rsch. faculty La. State U., Baton Rouge, 1983—90, assoc. prof., 1990—94, U. Memphis, 1994—98, prof. biology, 1998—. Editor-in-chief: Americas & Australia, Environmental and Experimental Botany, 1998—2003. Mem.: Soc. Wetland Scientists (mem. exec. bd., pres.-elect, pres. Southcentral chpt. 1995—2000), Am. Soc. Plant Biologists, Sigma Xi. Office: U Memphis Dept Biology 3706 Alumni St Memphis TN 38152 Office Phone: 901-678-4187. Personal E-mail: pezeshki@memphis.edu.

PEZZELLA, JERRY JAMES, JR., investment and real estate executive; b. Chesapeake, Va., Sept. 30, 1937; s. Jerry James Sr. and Mabel (Aydlett) P.; m. Carolyn Blades; children: James M., Stanley J., Julie Pezzella Scanlon. BS, U. Richmond, 1963; MBA, U. Pa., 1964. Asst. v.p. Va. Nat. Bank (now Bank of Am.), Norfolk, 1964-68; chmn. bd., pres. First Am. Investment Corp., First Ga. Investment Corp., Atlanta, 1968-74; v.p. Great Am. Investment Corp., Atlanta, 1974-78; sr. exec. v.p., 1984-85; exec. v.p. Equity Fin. & Mgmt. Co., Chgo., 1978-99; pres., chmn. bd. First Capital Fin. Corp., Chgo., 1983-85; pres. GAFGI Holdings Inc., Chgo., 1983-98; chmn. bd. 1st Property Mgmt. Corp., 1990-92; dir., fin. officer, treas. Bear Paw Svc. Dist., 2002—. Bd. dirs. Great Am. Mgmt. and Investment, Inc., Chgo., Nat. Multi Housing Coun., 1992-94, mem. exec. com.; real estate cons., 1997—. Bd. dirs., exec. com. Nat. Multi-Housing Coun., 1991-93. Mem. Met. Club (Chgo.), Mountain Harbor Golf and Country Club (Hayesville, N.C.). Home: 1240 Village Rd Murphy NC 28906-1763

PEZZULLO, RALPH MICHAEL, writer, playwright; b. N.Y.C., Dec. 27, 1951; s. Lawrence Anthony Pezzullo and Josephine DiMattia; m. Alice Palmisano, Aug. 8, 1980 (div. Jan. 1994); children: John Lawrence, Michael Richard; m. Jessica Rae Pezzullo, May 19, 1994; children: Francesca Sophia, Alessandra Sabina. M in Pub. and Internat. Affairs, George Washington U., 1975. Grants specialist Nat. Endowment Arts, Washington, 1975-79. Author: At the Fall of Somoza, 1994, Eve Missing, 2003, (plays) From Behind the Moon, 1984, The Tail of the Tiger, 1985, Eating the Shadow, 1990, Wilderness of Mirrors, 1994, Hide Mother in My Heart, 1996, Gauquin's Parrot, 1997, Spain, 1998, Stakes, 1999, Okeechobee Split, 2000, Murder Sketched Gently, 2000, (radio drama/series) The Life and Times of Swamp Fox, 1985. Recipient Spl. citation Kesselring award, 1986, award, Ctr. Theater, 1994, Screenwriting award, Writer's Guild Am. E. Found., 1987; Playwriting fellow, Jerome Found., 1997, 1998, 1999, 2001. Mem.: PEN USA, Pvt. Eye Writers Am., Mystery Writers Am., Author's League Am., Art Student's League, Dramatists Guild. Avocations: painting, sports. Home: 918 Ninth St # A Santa Monica CA 90403 E-mail: pezzullo@mindspring.com., ralph@ralphpezzullo.com.

PFAELZER, MARIANA R. federal judge; b. L.A., Feb. 4, 1926; AB, U. Calif., 1947; LLB, UCLA, 1957. Bar: Calif. 1958. Assoc. Wyman, Bautzer, Rothman & Kuchel, 1957-69, ptnr., 1969-78; judge U.S. Dist. Ct. (ctrl. dist.) Calif., 1978—. Mem. Jud. Conf. Adv. Com. on Fed. Rules of Civil Procedure. Pres., v.p., dir. Bd. Police Commrs. City of L.A., 1974-78. UCLA Alumnus award for Profl. Achievement, 1979, named Alumna of Yr., UCLA Law Sch., 1980, U. Calif. Santa Barbara Disting. Alumnus award, 1983. Mem. ABA, Calif. Bar Assn. (local adminstrv. com., spl. com. study rules procedure 1972, joint subcom. profl. ethics and computers and the law coms. 1972, profl. ethics com. 1972-74, spl. com. juvenile justice, women's rights subcom. human rights sect.), L.A. County Bar Assn. (spl. com. study rules procedure state bar 1974), Ninth Cir. Dist. Judges Assn. (pres.). Office: US Dist Ct 312 N Spring St Ste 152 Los Angeles CA 90012-4703

PFAFF, JUDY, artist; b. London, 1946. Student Wayne State U., 1965-66, So. Ill. U., 1968-69; B.F.A., Washington U.-St. Louis, 1971; postgrad. Yale U., 1970, M.F.A., 1973. One-woman exhbns. include: Webb and Parsons Gallery, New Canaan, Conn., 1974, Artists Space N.Y., 1975, Theatre Gallery, U. So. Fla., Tampa, 1977, Los Angeles Contemporary Exhbn., 1978, Holly Solomon Gallery, N.Y., 1980, Daniel Weinberg Gallery, Los Angeles, 1984, Wacoal, Japan, 1985, Holly Solomon Gallery, 1986, Nat. Mus. Women in the Arts, Washington, 1989, Cleve. Ctr. for Contemporary Art., Cleve., 1990, Fabric Workshop, N.Y., 1991, Rotunda Gallery, N.Y., 1993; group exhbns. include: Whitney Mus. Am. Art, 1975, Hallwalls Gallery, Buffalo, 1976, Art Mus., U. Calif.-Santa Barbara, 1979, Neuberger Mus., SUNY-Purchase, 1979, Contemporary Arts Mus., Houston, 1980, Contemporary Arts Ctr., Cin., 1980, Mus. Modern Art, N.Y.C., 1984, Venice Biennale, 1984, Rotunda Gallery, Bklyn.,

1984, Bklyn. Mus., 1985, WHitney Mus. Am. Art., N.Y., 1988, Internat. Art Projects, Asia, 1990, Mis. Modern Art., 1989, Inst. Contemporary Art, Phila., 1991, Cultural Space, N.Y., 1992, Henie-Onstad Art Ctr., Norway, 1992, Whitney Mus. Am. Art at Champion, Stamford, Conn., 1993, Drawing Ctr., N.Y., 1993; commd. work Spokane City Hall, 1984. Nat. Endowment Arts grantee, 1979; Guggenheim fellow, 1983.

PFAFF, LAURA KING, auction house executive; b. San Francisco; m. Rick Pfaff. Sr. v.p., regional dir. Christie's, San Francisco, 1994—2001; chmn. Bonhams & Butterfields, San Francisco, 2001—. Bd. mem. San Francisco Symphony, No. Calif. Cancer Ctr., Calif. Pacific Med. Ctr., Fort Mason Found.; former bd. mem. San Francisco C. of C. Office: Bonhams & Butterfields 220 San Bruno Ave San Francisco CA 94103*

PFAFF, RICHARD WILLIAM, historian, educator; b. Oklahoma City, Aug. 6, 1936; s. Frederick Erwin Pfaff and Flora Kathryn Soergel; m. Margaret Campbell Pfaff, Dec. 27, 1962; 1 child, David Anthony. AB, Harvard U., 1957; BA, Oxford U., 1959, MA, 1963, DPhil, 1965, DD, 1995. English master Pembroke-Country Day Sch., Kansas City, 1959—60; asst. to pres Swarthmore Coll., Swarthmore, Pa., 1960—62, asst. rector Christ Ch., Suffern, NY, 1966—67; asst. prof. history U. N.C., Chapel Hill, NC, 1967—70, assoc. prof. history, 1970—75, prof. history, 1975—. Mem. state sel. com. Rhodes Scholarships, NC, 1967—72, 1993, instl. rep., 1975—89. Author: New Liturgical Feasts in Later Medieval England, 1970, Montague Rhodes James, 1980, Liturgical Calendars, Saints and Services in Medieval England, 1998. Priest assoc. Chapel of the Cross, Chapel Hill, 1967—. Fellow, Nat. Humanities, 1996—97; Rhodes scholar, 1957—59, 1962—63, Vis. fellow, Madgalen Coll., 1989. Fellow: Medieval Acad. Am., Soc. Antiquaries London, Royal Hist. Soc.; mem.: Henry Bradshaw Soc. (hon. v.p. 1996—). Democrat. Episcopalian. Avocations: music, English literature, architecture. Office: U NC Dept History CB #3195 Chapel Hill NC 27599

PFAFF, WILLIAM WALLACE, medical educator; b. Rochester, N.Y., Aug. 14, 1930; s. Norman Joseph and Eleanor Blakesley (Wells) P.; m. Patricia Ann Clark; children: Nancy, Karen, Margaret, Mary Catherine. AB, Harvard U., 1952; MD, SUNY, 1956. Intern U. Chgo., 1956-58; sr. asst. surgeon NIH, Bethesda, Md., 1958-60; resident Stanford U. Med. Ctr., Palo Alto, Calif., 1960-65; asst. prof. U. Fla., Gainesville, 1965-68, assoc. prof., 1968-71, prof. surgery, 1971-95, prof. emeritus, adj. prof., 1993—, dir. organ transplant programs, 1971-95. Bd. dirs. United Network for Organ Sharing, Richmond, Va., pres. elect, 1997-98, pres., 1998-99; pres., com. chmn. Southeastern Organ Procurement Found., Richmond, 1973-95. Fellow Am. Coll. Surgeons; mem. Am. Surg. Assn., Am. Soc. Transplant Surgeons, So. Surg. Assn., Transplantation Soc., Alachua County Med. Soc. (pres. 1977-78). Home: 2445 NW 15th Pl Gainesville FL 32605-5148 Office: U Fla Dept Surgery PO Box 100286 Gainesville FL 32610-0286 Office Phone: 352-265-0606. Business E-Mail: pfaff@surgery.ufl.edu.

PFAFFENROTH, PETER ALBERT, lawyer; b. Mineola, NY, Mar. 29, 1941; s. Albert and Genevieve Astrid (Anderson) P.; m. Sara Ann Beekey, June 26, 1966; children: Elizabeth Cartwright, Peter Cyrus, Catherine Genevieve. BS in Engring., Diploma in European Civilization, Princeton U., 1963; JD, U. Mich., 1966; LLM in Taxation, NYU, 1972, LLM in Corp., 1976, LLM in Internat. Law, 1998. Bar: N.J. 1966, U.S. Dist. Ct. (N.J. dist.) 1966. With Daimler-Benz, Stuttgart, Fed. Republic Germany, 1961, B.P. Benzin & Petroleum, Hamburg, Fed. Republic Germany, 1962, Office of Internat. Affairs, U.S. Treasury Dept., Washington, 1963, Office of Export Control, U.S. Commerce Dept., Washington, 1964, Commrs. Office, U.S. Patent Office, Washington, 1965; atty. McCarter & English, Newark, 1966-68, Kentz & Gilson, Esqs., Summit, NJ, 1968-69; corp. counsel Tex. Plastics, Maine Sugar Industries, Robbinsville, NJ, 1969-70; atty. c/o Lewis Stein, Esq., Netcong, NJ, 1970-71; pvt. practice Chester, NJ, 1971—. Avocations: antiques, foreign languages, travel, wine. Home: Twin Brooks Trail Chester NJ 07930

PFALTZ, HUGO MENZEL, JR., lawyer; b. Newark, Sept. 23, 1931; s. Hugo M. and Mary E. (Horr) Pfaltz; m. Marilyn M. Muir, Sept. 29, 1956; children: Elizabeth W., William M., Robert L. BA, Hamilton Coll., 1953; JD, Harvard U., 1960; LLM, NYU, 1965. Bar: N.J. 1960, U.S. Dist. Ct. N.J. 1960, U.S. Supreme Ct. 1977. Assoc. McCarter & English, Newark, 1960—61, Bourne & Noll, Summit, NJ, 1961—74; sole practice Summit, 1974—82; ptnr. Pfaltz & Woller, 1983—. Mem. Battleship N.J. Commn., 1985—, NJ Law Revision Commn., 1986—2003. Assoc. editor N.J. Law Jour., 1966—2002, editor, 1984—86. Chmn. Summit Rep. City Com., 1966; mem. N.J. Constl. Conv., 1966, N.J. Assembly, 1968—72. Served to lt. USNR, 1953—62. Mem.: ABA, Summit Bar Assn., Union County Bar Assn., N.J. Bar Assn., Summit Tennis Club, Beacon Hill Club (Summit), Baltusrol Club (Springfield, N.J.), Univ. Club (Washington), Univ Club (N.Y.C.). Home: 118 Prospect St Summit NJ 07901-2472 Office: 382 Springfield Ave Summit NJ 07901-2707 Office Phone: 908-273-1974. E-mail: hugopf@aol.com.

PFALTZ, KATHARINE, small business owner, writer; b. Syracuse, NY, Dec. 17, 1961; d. John Lucas and Susan (Ordway) Pfaltz. BA, U. of Va., 1979—83; MA, King's Coll., U. of London, 1989—90, PhD, 1993—99. Restaurant owner & chef Basic Necessities, Nellysford, Va., 1997—2003; asst. dir., prof. So. Meth. U., Paris, 1988—93; prof., cultural coord. James Madison U., Paris Program, 1988—88. Mem. U. Va. Riding Team, Charlottesville, 1979—83; winetasting instr., 1986—2003. Author: (book) Lauren's Story, (guide book) A Walk Through Paris, (jour.) Etudes britanniques contemporaines, (cookbook) The Basic Necessities Soup Cookbook; editor: (memoir) Choices. Mem., vol. Nelson County Humane Soc., Arrington, Va., 1998—2003; vol. Lovingston Sr. Ctr., Va., 2002—03. Mem.: Neighborhood Mcht. Assn. (assoc.), Oak Ridge Hunt Club (hon.; whipper-in 1998—2003, colours granted 1999). Avocations: foxhunting, running, hiking, travel writing. Home: 85 Hager Ln Roseland VA 22967 Office: Basic Necessities PO Box 40 Nellysford VA 22958

PFALTZGRAFF, ROBERT LOUIS, JR., political scientist, educator; b. Phila., June 1, 1934; s. Robert L. and Mary (Warriner) P.; m. Diane A. Kressler, May 20, 1967; children: Suzanne Diane, Robert Louis III. BA with honors, Swarthmore Coll., 1956; MBA, U. Pa., 1958, PhD in Polit. Sci. (Penfield fellow), 1964; MA in Internat. Relations, 1959. Research assoc. Fgn. Policy Research Inst., 1964-71; asst. prof. polit. sci. U. Pa., Phila., 1964-70; dep. dir. Fgn. Policy Research Inst., 1971-73; assoc. prof. internat. politics Fletcher Sch. Law and Diplomacy, Tufts U., Medford, Mass., 1971-78; pres. Inst. for Fgn. Policy Analysis, Cambridge, Mass., 1976—; prof. internat. politics Fletcher Sch. Law and Diplomacy, Tufts U., Medford, Mass., 1978-83, Shelby Cullom Davis prof. internat. security studies, 1983—. Vis. lectr. Fgn. Service Inst. Dept. State, 1970-71; George C. Marshall prof. Coll. of Europe, Bruges, Belgium, 1970-71; short term acad. guest prof. Nat. Defense Coll., Tokyo, Japan, 1981; pres. U.S. Strategic Inst., Washington, 1977-79; pres. Inst. Fgn. Policy Analysis, Cambridge, Mass. Author: Britain Faces Europe, 1957-1967, 1969, Politics and the International System, 1969, The Atlantic Community: A Complex Balance, 1969, The Study of International Relations, 1977, Power Projection and the Long Range Combat Aircraft: Missions, Capabilities and Alternative Designs, 1981, Contending Theories of International Relations: A Comprehensive Survey, 1981; co-editor: Contrasting Approaches to Strategic Arms Control, 1974, SALT: Implications for Arms Control in the 1970s, 1973, The Other Arms Race: New Technologies and Non Nuclear Conflict, 1975, Arms Transfers to the Third World: The Military Build-up in Less Industrial Countries, 1978, Intelligence Policy and National Security, 1981, Projection of Power: Perspectives, Perceptions and Problems, 1982, The U.S. Defense Mobilization Infrastructure: Problems and Priorities, 1983, International Dimensions of Space, 1984, National Security Policy: The Decision-Making Process, 1984, The Peace Movements in Europe and the United States, 1985, American Foreign Policy: FDR to Reagan, 1986, co-editor: Selling the Rope to Hang Capitalism? The Debate on West-East Trade and Technology Transfer, 1987, Emerging Doctrines and Technologies: Implications for Global and Regional Political-Military Balance, 1987, Protracted Warfare--The Third World Arena: A Dimension of U.S.-Soviet Conflict, 1988, Guerrilla Warfare and Counter-Insurgency: U.S.-Soviet Policy in the third World, 1988, U.S. Defense Policy in an Era of Constrained Resources, 1989, Contending Theories of International Relations: A Comprehensive Study, 1990, 4th edit., 1998, National Security Decisions: The Participants Speak, 1990, The United States Army: Challenges and Missions for the 1990s, 1991, The Future of Air Power in the Aftermath of the Gulf War, 1992, Naval Forward Presence and the National Military Strategy, 1993, Ethnic Conflict and Regional Instability: Implications for U.S. Policy and Army Roles and Missions, 1994, Naval Expeditionary Forces and Power Projection: Into the 21st Century, 1994, Roles and Missions of Special Operations Forces in the Aftermath of the Cold War, 1995, War in the Information Age: New Challenges for U.S. Security, 1997, NATO and Southeastern Europe: Security Issues for the Early 21st Century, 2000, The Role of Naval Forces in 21st Century Operations, 2000, Strategy and International Politics, 2000, Contending Theories of International Relations, 5th edit., 2001, others; contbr. articles to scholarly jours. Guggenheim fellow, 1968-69; Relm Found. grantee, 1969 Mem. Internat. Studies Assn., Coun. Fgn. Rels., Internat. Inst. Strategic Studies, Capitol Hill Club, Army and Navy Club (Washington). Home: 663 Wallace Dr Wayne PA 19087-1911 Office: Inst Fgn Policy Analysis 675 Massachusetts Ave Ste 10 Cambridge MA 02139-3309 E-mail: rlp@ifpa.org.

PFANNER, HELMUT FRANZ, German language educator; b. Hohenweiler, Vorarlberg, Austria, Nov. 8, 1933; came to U.S., 1957; s. Georg Franz and Luise (Huber) P.; m. Rosemary Griffin, Mar. 16, 1959 (div. 1964); 1 child, Renate; m. Beverly Louise Radcliffe, Sept. 16, 1966 (div. 1988); children: Heidi, Eric, Marta; m. Nasy Inthisone, Dec. 27, 1995; children: Franz, Maximilian. Grad., Tchr. Tng. Coll., Feldkirch, Austria, 1952; student, Kans. U., 1957—58, Stanford U., 1959—64. Cert. elem. and secondary sch. tchr. Tchr. Volksschule Seewald, Fontanella, Vorarlberg, 1952-53, Volksschule Hohenweiler, 1953-57; English tchr. Hauptschule Belruptstrasse, Bregenz, Austria, 1958-59; German instr. U. Wash., Seattle, 1964-67; asst. prof. U. Va., Charlottesville, 1967-69; assoc. prof. U. N.H., Durham, 1969-79; vis. prof. Purdue U., West Lafayette, Ind., 1979-82; prof. German U. N.H., Durham, 1982-86; prof. German, dept. chmn. U. Nebr., Lincoln, 1986-90; prof. German Vanderbilt U., Nashville, 1990—, dept. chmn., 1990-93. Dir. Summer Inst. German Lang. and Culture, U. Calif., Santa Barbara, 1992-99. Author: Hanns Johst, Vom Expr. z. Nationalsozial, 1970, Oskar Maria Graf. eine kritische Bibliogr., 1976, Exile in New York: German and Austrian Writers after 1933, 1983; co-editor: O.M. Graf: Beschreibung eines Volksschriftstellers, 1974, O.M. Graf in seinen Briefen, 1984; editor: Exile across Cultures, 1986, Oskar Maria Graf: Reden und Aufsätze aus dem Exil, 1989, Karl Jakob Hirsch: Quintessenz meines Lebens, 1990, World War II and the Exiles: A Literary Response, 1991, Karl Jakob Hirsch: Manhattan Serenade, 2001, Alfred Döblin, Briefe II, 2001. Fulbright scholar Kans. U., 1957-58, German Acad. Exch. scholar, 1963-64; Am. Philos. Soc. grantee, 1969, 73, Alexander von Humboldt fellow, 1972-73, 77-78, Am. Coun. Learned Socs. fellow, 1976-77, NEH fellow, 1996-97. Mem. MLA, PEN German Writers Abroad (Am. sec.-treas. 1979-2002), Internat. Assn. Germanic Studies, Am. Assn. Tchrs. German, German Studies Assn., Internat. Soc. for Exile Studies. Avocations: reading, skiing, tennis, music, travel. Office: Vanderbilt U Dept Germanic Slavic Langs PO Box 1567 Sta B Nashville TN 37235-1567

PFANSTIEL PARR, DOROTHEA ANN, interior designer; b. San Antonio, Nov. 10, 1931; d. Herbert Andraes and Ethel Missouri (Turner) Pfanstiel; m. Thurmond Charles Parr, Jr., Sept. 15, 1951; children: Thurmond Charles, III, Richard Marshall. AA, Coll. San Antonio, 1951. Asst. dean evening divsn. Alamo C.C., San Antonio, 1951; tchr., cons., dir. Humpty Dumpty Early Childhood Devel. Ctr., San Antonio, 1951-58; exec. sec., cons. Thurmond C. Parr, Jr. & Co., San Antonio, 1960-61; founder, pres. Creative Designs, Ltd., San Antonio, 1962—. Liaison, coord. Internat. Students Lang. Sch., Lackland AFB, San Antonio, 1959-65. Adv., cons. Urban Renewal Inner City San Antonio, 1959-61. Named Notable Woman of Tex., Awards and Hons. Soc. Am., 1984-85. Republican. Presbyterian. Avocations: travel, swimming, reading, studying, walking.

PFAU, RICHARD ANTHONY, university president; b. N.Y.C., Feb. 19, 1942; s. Hugo and Irene Beatrice P.; m. Nancy Ann DiPace, Sept. 12, 1964; children: Bradley Madison, Aleksandra Nicole. AB, Hamilton Coll., 1964; MA, U. Va., 1973, PhD, 1975. Systems analyst Equitable Life Ins. Co., N.Y.C., 1964-66; asst. prof. history Dickinson Coll., Carlisle, Pa., 1975-80; assoc. prof., assoc. dean U. Miami, Coral Gables, Fla., 1980-85; dean of faculty, provost Emory (Va.) and Henry Coll., 1985-93; pres. Ill. Coll., Jacksonville, Ill., 1993—2002, Averett U., Danville, Va., 2002—. Author: No Sacrifice Too Great: The Life of Lewis L. Strauss, 1985. Contbr. articles, book revs. to profl. publs. Vestryman St. Thomas Episc. Ch., Abingdon, Va., Epis. Ch. Epiphany, Denville, Va.; chmn., sec.-treas., exec. com., bd. dirs. Va. Found. for Humanities and Pub. Policy; mem. bd. trustees Carlisle Sch., Martinsville, Va.; mem. adv. bd. Salvation Army, Jacksonville, Ill. Capt. USAF, 1966-71. DuPont fellow, 1974-75; Hoover fellow, 1982. Mem. Danville Golf Club, Omicron Delta Kappa, Alpha Psi Omega, Pi Delta Epsilon. Home: 500 Hawthorne Drive Danville VA 24541 Office: Averett Univ Pres Office 420 West Main Street Danville VA 24541

PFEFFER, CYNTHIA ROBERTA, psychiatrist, educator; b. Newark, May 22, 1943; d. Edward I. and Ann Pfeffer. BA, Douglas Coll., 1964; MD, NYU, 1968. Assoc. dir. child psychiatry inpatient unit Albert Einstein Coll. Medicine, Bronx, N.Y., 1973-79; chief child psychiatry inpatient unit N.Y. Hosp. Cornell Med. Ctr., White Plains, N.Y., 1979-95; assoc. prof. clin. psychiatry Weill Med. Coll. Cornell U., N.Y.C., 1984—. Prof. psychiatry Cornell U. Med. Coll., 1989—; pres. N.Y. Coun. on Child and Adolescent Psychiatry, N.Y.C., 1989—; dir. childhood bereavement program Weill Med. Coll. Cornell U., 1999—. Author: The Suicidal Child, 1986, Difficult Moments in Child Psychotherapy, 1988; editor: Youth Suicide: Perspectives on Risk and Prevention, 1989, Intense Stress and Mental Disturbance in Children, 1996; co-editor: Neurologic Disorders: Developmental and Behavioral Sequelae for Child and Adolescent Psychiatric Clinics of North America, 1999. Recipient Erwin Stengel award Internat. Assn. Suicide Prevention, 1987, Wilford Hulse award N.Y. Coun. on Child & Adolescent Psychiatry, 1989, Sigmund Freud award Am. Soc. Psychoanalytic Physicians, 1994. Fellow Am. Psychiat. Assn., Am. Acad. Child and Adolescent Psychiatry (councillor-at-large 1989—, Norbert Rieger award 1988), Am. Psychopathological Assn.; mem. Am. Assn. Suicidology (pres. 1987, Young Contbrs. award 1981, 82). Office: NY Hosp Westchester Div 21 Bloomingdale Rd White Plains NY 10605-1504 also: 1100 Madison Ave New York NY 10028-0327 Office Phone: 212-717-2334. Business E-Mail: cpfeffer@med.cornell.edu.

PFEFFER, JEFFREY, business educator; b. St. Louis, July 23, 1946; s. Newton Stuart and Shirlee (Krisman) P.; m. Kathleen Frances Fowler, July 23, 1986. BS, MS, Carnegie Mellon U., 1968; PhD, Stanford U., 1972. Tech. staff Rsch. Analysis Corp., McLean, Va., 1968-69; asst. prof. U. Ill., Champaign, 1971-73; from asst. prof. to assoc. prof. U. Calif., Berkeley, 1973-79; prof. Grad. Sch. Bus., Stanford (Calif.) U., 1979—. Vis. prof. Harvard U. Sch. Bus., Boston, 1981-82; dir. SonoSite, Inc., Audible Magic, Inc., Actify, Inc., Unicru, Inc. Author: The External Control of Organizations, 1978, Organizational Design, 1978, Power in Organizations, 1981, Organizations and Organization Theory, 1982 (Terry Book award 1984), Managing with Power, 1992, Competitive Advantage Through People, 1994, New Directions for Organization Theory, 1997, The Human Equation, 1998, The Knowing-Doing Gap, 1999, Hidden Value, 2000. Fellow Acad. Mgmt. (bd. govs. 1984-86, New Concept award 1979, Richard D. Irwin award for scholarly contbns. to mgmt. 1989); mem. Indsl. Rels. Rsch. Assn. Jewish. Avocations: cooking, music. Home: 425 Moseley Rd Hillsborough CA 94010-6715 Office: Stanford U Grad Sch Bus Stanford CA 94305 Office Phone: 650-723-2915. E-mail: pfeffer_jeffrey@gsb.stanford.edu.

PFEFFER, PHILIP ELLIOT, biophysicist; b. N.Y.C., Apr. 8, 1941; s. Charles and Della (Smith) P.; m. Judith Stadlen, Dec. 22, 1962; children: Charles, Ari, Shira. AB, Hunter Coll., 1962; MS, Rutgers U., 1964, PhD, 1966. Rsch. asst. dept. chemistry Rutgers U., New Brunswick, N.J., 1964-66; rsch. fellow dept. chemistry U. Chgo., 1966-68; rsch. scientist Ea. Regional Rsch. Ctr. USDA, Phila., 1968-88, rsch. leader Ea. Regional Rsch. Ctr., 1976-88, lead scientist Ea. Regional Rsch. Ctr., 1988—. Editor-at-large Marcel Dekker, N.Y.C., 1990—; adj. prof. dept. biosci. and biotech. Drexel U., Phila., 1996—; vis. prof. U. Bordeaux, France, 1998. Editor: Nuclear Magnetic Resonance in Agriculture, 1989, Nuclear Magnetic Resonance in Plant Biology, 1996; mem. editl. bd. Jour. Carbohydrate Chemistry, 1985—, Jour. Magnetic Resonance Analysis; contbr. articles to profl. jours. including Plant Physiology, Carbohydrate Rsch., Biochemica Acta, Biophysica, Jour. Magnetic Resonance. Recipient Bond award Am. Oil Chemists Soc., 1976, Fed. Svcs. award Phila. Fed. Assn., 1979, Science and Edn. award USDA, 1982; fellow Orgn. for Econ. Cooperation and Devel., 1989; Agrl. Rsch. Svc. rsch. fellow, 1989; vis. scientist grantee Centre d'Etudes Nucleaires de Grenoble, 1986, Oxford U., 1989; Nat. Rsch. Initiative grantee, 1997, 2002. Mem. AAAS, Internat. Soc. for Magnetic Resonance, Am. Chem. Soc. (Phila. sect. Scientist of Yr. 1982), Soc. for Applied Spectroscopy. Achievements include patents and publs. concerning use of alpha-anions; discovery of deuterium isotope shift NMR method for determining carbohydrate structures; development of P-31 NMR in vivo methodology for studying metal ion transport and C-13 NMR for studying plant/microbe interactions in nitrogen fixing plant nodules and symbiotic mycorrhizae. Office: USDA 600 E Mermaid Ln Wyndmoor PA 19038-8598

PFEFFER, RICHARD LAWRENCE, meteorology and geophysics educator; b. Bklyn., Nov. 26, 1930; s. Lester Robert and Anna (Newman) P.; m. Roslyn Ziegler, Aug. 30, 1953; children— Bruce, Lloyd, Scott, Glenn. BS cum laude, CCNY, 1952; MS, MIT, 1954, PhD, 1957. Research asst. MIT, 1952-55, guest lectr., 1956; atmospheric physicist Air Force Cambridge Research Center, Boston, 1955-59; sr. scientist Columbia U., 1959-61, lectr., 1961-62, asst. prof. geophysics, 1962-64; assoc. prof. meteorology Fla. State U., Tallahassee, 1964-67, prof. meteorology, 1967 96, disting. rsch. prof., 1997—, Carl-Gustav Rossby prof. meteorology, 1999—; dir. Geophys. Fluid Dynamics Inst., 1967-93. Cons. NASA, 1961-64, N.W. Ayer & Son, Inc., 1962, Edml. Testing Service, Princeton, N.J., 1963, Voice of Am., 1963, Grolier, Inc., 1963, Naval Research Labs., 1971-76; Mem. Internat. Commn. for Dynamical Meteorology, 1972-76 Editor: Dynamics of Climate, 1960; Contbr. articles to profl. jours. Bd. dirs. B'nai B'rith Anti-Defamation League; chmn. religious concern and social action com. Temple Israel, Tallahassee, 1971-72. Fellow Am. Meterol. Soc. (program chmn. ann. meeting 1963); mem. Am. Geophys. Union, N.Y. Acad. Scis. (chmn. planetary scis. sect. 1961-63), Sigma Xi, Chi Epsilon Pi, Sigma Alpha. Home: 9042 Shoal Creek Dr Tallahassee FL 32312 Office Phone: 850-644-5594. Business E-Mail: pfeffer@gfdi.fsu.edu.

PFEFFER, ROBERT, chemical engineer, academic administrator, educator; b. Vienna, Nov. 26, 1935; arrived in U.S., 1938, naturalized, 1944; s. Joseph and Gisela (Aberbach) P.; m. Marcia Borenstein, Dec. 24, 1960; children: Michael, Jacqueline. B in Chem. Engring., NYU, 1956, M in Chem. Engring., 1958, D in Engring. Sci., 1962. Mem. faculty CCNY, 1957-92, asst. prof. chem. engring., 1962-66, assoc. prof., 1966-71, prof., 1971-92, chmn. dept. chem. engring., 1973-87, Herbert Kayser prof., 1980-92, dean grad. studies and rsch., dep. provost, 1987-88, provost, v.p. acad. affairs, 1988-92; v.p. rsch. and grad. studies, prof. chem. engring. N.J. Inst. Tech., Newark, 1992-97, Disting. prof. chem. engring., 1997—. Vis. prof. Imperial Coll., London, 1969; Fulbright scholar Technion-Israel Inst. Tech., 1976-77; cons. in field. Contbr. articles to tech. publs. Fulbright Hays scholar, 1976-77; DuPont faculty fellow, 1962; NASA faculty fellow, 1964-65 Mem. AIChE (Particle Tech. Forum Nat. award 1995, Thomas Baron Nat. award 2000), Am. Soc. Engring. Edn., Sigma Xi, Tau Beta Pi, Phi Lambda Upsilon. Jewish. Office: PO Box 37 Teaneck NJ 07666 Office Phone: 973-642-7496. E-mail: pfeffer@njit.edu.

PFEFFERBAUM, BETTY JANE, psychiatrist, educator; b. Seattle, Sept. 7, 1946; d. Lois (Yager) P.; m. Richard L. Van Horn, May 29, 1988. BA, Pomona Coll., 1968; MD, U. Calif., San Francisco, 1972; JD, U. Okla., Norman, 1993. Bar: Okla. 1993; diplomate Am. Bd. Psychiatry and Neurology with subspecialty in child psychiatry. Intern pediatrics Martin Luther King Jr. Gen. Hosp., Compton, Calif., 1972-73; resident in psychiatry Neuro Psychiat. Inst., UCLA, 1973-76, fellow in child psychiatry, 1975-77; pvt. practice psychiatry, L.A., 1977-78; prof. U. Tex. Med. Sch., Houston, 1978-89; v.p. for edn. U. Tex. Health Sci. Ctr., Houston, 1987-89; prof., chief child sect. dept. psychiatry U. Okla. Health Scis. Ctr., Oklahoma City, 1989-96, chair dept. psychiatry, 1996—; adj. prof. Oklahoma City U. Sch. Law, 1994-95. Mem. Okla. Indigent Def. Sys. Bd., 1992-93, Okla. Bd. Mental Health and Substance Abuse Svcs., 1993-99. Contbr. over 100 articles to med. jours. Grad. Leadership Tex., 1988, Leadership Okla., 1995. Fellow Am. Psychiat. Assn., Am. Acad. Child and Adolescent Psychiatry, Group for Advancement Psychiatry; mem. ABA, Order of Coif, Phi Beta Kappa, Pi Mu Epsilon. Jewish. Home: 3900 N Harvey PKWY Oklahoma City OK 73118 Office: U Okla Health Scis Ctr 920 S L Young Blvd Oklahoma City OK 73104-5020 Office Phone: 405-271-5121.

PFEIFER, HOWARD MELFORD, mechanical engineer; b. St. Louis, Aug. 23, 1959; s. Howard William and Ruth Joyce P. BS in Applied Sci. and Tech., Charter Oak State Coll., 1990; BSME, U. Hartford, 1991; MBA, Rensselaer Poly. Inst., 1997. Engr. in tng., Conn. Engr. asst. Pratt & Whitney, East Hartford, Conn., 1984-89; devel. engr. Chromalloy Rsch. and Tech. Divsn., Orangeburg, N.Y., 1991-93; process devel. engr. Howmet Corp., North Haven, Conn., 1993-95; process engr. Windsor Airmotive, The Barnes Group, East Granby, Conn., 1995-98; sr. engr. Pratt & Whitney, 1998—. Mem. U. Hartford Engring. Alumni Adv. Bd., Bloomfield, Conn., 1992-98, chmn., 1996-98; founder, prin., treas. WEMBA5 Investments LLC, Conn. Mem. NSPE, Sigma Xi (assoc.). Republican. Achievements include research, design and construction of a human powered helicopter, and research to map acoustical soundboard characteristics in a Steinway Grand Piano. Home: 83 Buckley Hill Rd Colchester CT 06415-1712 Office: Pratt & Whitney 400 Main St East Hartford CT 06108-0968

PFEIFER, LARRY ALAN, public health service coordinator; b. Rock Springs, Wyo., July 20, 1958; s. Jack Albert and Betty Lee (Ethington) P.; m. Sandra Lynn, June 20, 1986. BS cum laude, So. Oreg. State Coll., 1983, MS in Health Edn., 1989; paramedic diploma, Rogue Community Coll., 1984; postgrad., Columbia Pacific U. Cert. paramedic, Oreg. Cpt., paramedic Tualatin Valley Fire and Rescue, Portland, Oreg., 1991—. Adj. faculty Oreg. Health Scis. U. Sch. of Medicine, Dept. of Emergency Medicine, 1995; lectr. in field. Author (text) Non-Verbal Pre-Hospital Assessment of the Trauma Patient. Mem. Oreg. Paramedic Assn., Phi Kappa Phi, Kappa Delta Pi. Home: 10026 NW Priscilla Ct Portland OR 97229-5273

PFEIFER, PAUL E. state supreme court justice; b. Bucyrus, Ohio, Oct. 15, 1942; m. Julia Pfeifer; 3 children. BA, Ohio State U., 1963, JD, 1966. Asst. atty. gen. State of Ohio, 1967-70; mem. Ohio Ho. of Reps., 1971-72; asst. prosecuting atty. Crawford County, 1973-76; mem. Ohio Senate, 1976-92, minority floor leader, 1983-84, asst. pres. pro-tempore, 1985-86; ptnr. Cory, Brown & Pfeifer, 1973-92; justice Ohio Supreme Ct., 1992—. Chmn. jud. com. Ohio Senate, 10 yrs. Mem. Grace United Meth. Ch., Bucyrus. Office: Supreme Court of Ohio 65 S Front St Columbus OH 43215-3431

PFEIFER, WILLIAM LEE, JR., lawyer; b. Brunswick, Ga., Mar. 30, 1967; s. William L. and Peggy S. Pfeifer. BA, Samford U., 1989; JD, U. Ala., 1993. Atty. Walter Henley, Tuscaloosa, Ala., 1993—94, Kolb & Pfeifer, Foley, 1994—96; staff atty. Ala. Ct. Criminal Appeals, Montgomery, 1996—97; atty. pvt. practice, Foley, 1997—. Mem. adv. bd. Mitigation Svcs. Ala., Birmingham, 2003—; bd. dirs. La Clinica de Baldwin, Foley; mem. indigent def. task force Ala. State Bar, Montgomery, 2000—02. Chmn. Baldwin County Dem. Exec. Com., Ala., 2000—; pres. South Baldwin Jaycees, 1998; worshipful master Foley Lodge F & AM, 2000—02. Recipient William M. Lunceford award, Samford U., Birmingham, 1989. Avocations: writing, exercise. Office: Pfeifer Law Offices 623 W Laurel Ave Foley AL 36535 Office Phone: 251-943-6951.

PFEIFFER, GARY M. chemical company executive; b. Richmond, Va., Oct. 24, 1949; m. Lear Strange; 2 children. BA in Polit. Sci., MBA, Coll. William and Mary. From mem. staff to sr. v.p., CFO DuPont, Wilmington, Del., 1974-97, sr. v.p., CFO, 1997—. Office: DuPont 1007 Market St 8th Fl Wilmington DE 19898

PFEIFFER, JANE CAHILL, former broadcasting company executive, consultant; b. Sept. 29, 1932; d. John Joseph and Helen (Reilly) Cahill; m. Ralph A. Pfeiffer, Jr., June 3, 1975. BA, U. Md., 1954; postgrad., Cath. U. Am., 1956-57; LHD (hon.), Pace Coll., 1978, U. Md., 1979, Manhattanville Coll., 1979, Amherst U., 1980, Babson Coll., 1981, U. Notre Dame, 1991, Bryant Coll., 1995. With IBM Corp., Armonk, N.Y., 1955-76, sec. mgmt. rev. com., 1970, dir. comm., 1971, v.p. comm. and govt. rels., 1972-76, bus. cons., 1976-78; chmn. NBC, Inc., N.Y.C., 1978-80; bus. cons., 1980—. Dir. Ashland Oil Co., Mony Fin. Svcs., Internat. Paper Co., J.C. Penney Co.; trustee The Conf. Bd., 1991. Mem. pres.'s adv. com. White House Fellows, 1966, Pres.'s Gen. Adv. Commn. on Arms Control and Disarmament, 1977-80, Pres.'s Commn. Mil. Compensation; trustee Rockefeller Found., U. Md., Carnegie Hall, 1981-1986, U. Notre Dame; bd. mem., Catholic Univ. of Am., 1973-1978, Rockefeller Found., 1973-1985, White House Fellows, 1976-1981, Kettering Found., 1975-1979. Recipient Achievement award Kappa Kappa Gamma, 1974-80, Eleanor Roosevelt Humanitarian award N.Y. League for Hard of Hearing, 1980, Disting. Alumna award U. Md., 1975, Humanitarian award NOW, 1980, Centennial Alumna medallion U. Md., 1988; White House fellow, Washington, 1966, Making Waves award, Greatest 50 Women in Radio and Television-AWRT, 2002. Mem. Coun. Fgn. Rels., Overseas Devel. Coun., Econ. of N.Y. Club. Office: C/O Jonathan L Smith Chesapeake Asset Mgmt LLC 1 Rockefeller Plz Rm 1210 New York NY 10020-2002 Home: Johns Island 1050 Beach Rd Apt 1G Vero Beach FL 32963-3413 Office Phone: 212-218-4044.

PFEIFFER, LEONARD, IV, executive recruiter, consultant; s. Leonard Jr. and Felicia Pfeiffer; m. Anna Gunnarsson. BA, MBA, Harvard U. Mktg. mgr. Am. Express, N.Y.C., 1970-72; project dir. S.T.I., N.Y.C. and San Francisco, 1972-74; v.p. R. Olivier & Assocs., N.Y.C., 1974-76, A. Kane & Assoc., N.Y.C., 1976-78; v.p., mng. dir. Korn/Ferry Internat., Washington and N.Y.C., 1978-98; sr. ptnr., group leader Heidrick & Struggles, Washington, 1998—2001; pres. Leonard Pfeiffer & Co., Washington, 2001—. Bd. dirs. Cmty. Found., Washington, 1982-84, Nat. Ctr. for Missing Children, 1989—, Nat. Blood Found., 1995-97, Nat. Bldg. Mus., 1998-2001; founding mem. jr. bd. dirs. Washington Opera, 1983-93; men's com. Project Hope; devel. com. Nat. Head Injury Found., Choral Arts Soc., Nat. Symphony Orch. Lt. U.S. Army, 1968-70. Schepp Found. scholar, 1968-70. Mem. Am. Soc. Assn. Execs., Greater Washington Soc. Assn. Execs., Congl. Country Club, Harvard Club (activities com., admissions com. N.Y.C. chpt. 1975-81, 1st v.p. bd. dirs. Washington chpt. 1985-87). Avocations: water and snow skiing, power and sail boating, tennis. Office: Leonard Pfeiffer & Co 1319 F St NW Ste 800 Washington DC 20004-1140

PFEIFFER, MARGARET KOLODNY, lawyer; b. Elkin, N.C., Oct. 7, 1944; d. Isadore Harold and Mary Elizabeth (Brody) K.; m. Carl Frederick Pfeiffer II, Sept. 2, 1968. BA, Duke U., 1967; JD, Rutgers U., 1974. Bar: N.J. 1974, N.Y. 1976, D.C. 1981, U.S. Supreme Ct. 1979. Law clk. to Hon. F.L. Van Dusen U.S. Ct. Appeals 3d cir., Phila., 1974-75; assoc. Sullivan & Cromwell, N.Y.C. and Washington, 1975-82, ptnr., 1982—. Contbr. articles to profl. jours. Trustee Am. Found. for Blind, Nat. Law Ctr. on Homelessness and Poverty; mem. bd. visitors Trinity Coll. of Duke U. Mem. ABA, Internat. Bar Assn., D.C. Bar Assn., N.Y. State Bar Assn., Assn. of Bar of City of N.Y., Am. Soc. of Intl. Law. Avocations: gardening, reading, music. Office: Sullivan & Cromwell 1701 Pennsylvania Ave NW Washington DC 20006-5866 Office Phone: 202-956-7540. Business E-Mail: pfeifferm@sullcrom.com.

PFEIFFER, MICHELLE, actress; b. Santa Ana, Calif., Apr. 29, 1957; d. Dick and Donna P.; m. Peter Horton (div.); 1 adopted child, Claudia Rose; m. David Kelley, Nov. 13, 1993. Student, Golden West Coll., Whitley Coll. Actress: (feature films) Falling in Love Again, 1980, Hollywood Knights, 1980, Charlie Chan and the Curse of the Dragon Queen, 1981, Grease II, 1982, Scarface, 1983, Ladyhawke, 1985, Into the Night, 1985, Sweet Liberty, 1986, Amazon Women on the Moon, 1987, Witches of Eastwick, 1987, Married to the Mob, 1988, Tequila Sunrise, 1988, Dangerous Liaisons, 1988 (Acad. award nominee for best supporting actress, 1989, BAFTA award, 1990), The Fabulous Baker Boys, 1989 (L.A. Film Critics Assn. award for best actress, 1989, D.W. Griffith award Nat. Bd. Rev., 1989, N.Y. Film Critics award, 1989, Nat. Soc. Film Critics award for best actress, 1990, Golden Globe award for best actress drama, 1990, Acad. award nominee for best actress, 1990), The Russia House, 1990, Frankie & Johnny, 1991, Love Field, 1992 (Acad. award nominee for best actress, 1993), Batman Returns, 1992, The Age of Innocence, 1993, Wolf, 1994, Dangerous Minds, 1995, Up Close and Personal, 1996, To Gillian on her 37th Birthday, 1996, One Fine Day, 1996, A Thousand Acres, 1997, The Prince of Egypt (voice), 1998, The Story of Us, 1998, A Midsummer Night's Dream, 1999, Deep End of the Ocean, 1999, What Lies Beneath, 2000, I Am Sam, 2001, White Oleander, 2002, Sinbad: Legend of the Seven Seas (voice), 2003; (TV movies) The Solitary Man, 1979, Callie and Son, 1981, The Children Nobody Wanted, 1981, Splendor in the Grass, 1981, One Too Many, 1983, Tales from the Hollywood Hills: Natica Jackson, 1987, Power, Passion and Murder, 1987; (TV series) Delta House, 1979, B.A.D. Cats, 1980; prodr. (films) A Thousand Acres, 1997; exec. prodr.: (films) One Fine Day, 1996. Named Woman of the Yr., Harvard's Hasty Pudding Theater Club, 1995; recipient Crystal award, Women in Film, 1993. Office: care ICM 9830 Wilshire Blvd Beverly Hills CA 90211-1934*

PFEIFFER, NORMAN, architectural firm executive; b. Kirkland, Wash., 1940; married. Grad., U. Wash. Co-founder, ptnr. Hardy, Holzman, Pfeiffer Assocs. LLP, L.A., 1968—. Mem. Archtl. Commn. U. Wash., 1989—. Fellow: AIA. Office: HHPA Ste 430 811 W 7th St Los Angeles CA 90017*

PFEIFFER, PATRICIA RUTH, writer, consultant; b. Brainerd, Minn., Oct. 12, 1925; d. Francis Charles DeMars and Effie Shirley Usher-DeMars; m. Clyde Wayne Pfeiffer, July 22, 1945; children: David Eugene, Gerald Allan, Susan Eileen Pfeiffer-Davis, Barbara Dea Pfeiffer-Asbury, Joy Elaine Pfeiffer-Schell, Karen Louise Pfeiffer-Grassl, Diane Elizabeth Pfeiffer-Estep. Student, St. Cloud U. (formerly St. Cloud Tchrs. Coll.), St. Cloud, Minnesota, 1943—44. Writing cons. Clypat Svcs., Otis Orchards, Wash., 1987—; workshop leader. Author: (novel) The Sheriff's Wife, 2001, Keeping Her Head, 2002, Roughin' It In Montana, 2001, Bury Him Deeper, 2002, Above All Women, 1997; research consultant (documentary video) Hangin' The Sheriff; dir.: Spokane Christian Writers Conf. Precinct and election vol. Rep. Party, Otis Orchards, Wash., 1980—2004; supt., tchr. Sunday sch. N/A N/A. Recipient Cmty. Svc. award, PTA. Master: Spokane Novelists (assoc.; leader 2002—04). Republican. Baptist. Avocations: gem and mineral collecting, astronomy, geology, reading. Office: Clypat Svcs PO Box 104 Otis Orchards WA 99027

PFEIFFER, PHILIP J. lawyer; b. Houston, Aug. 16, 1947; BS, Sam Houston State U., 1969; JD, So. Meth. U., 1972. Bar: Tex. 1972. Mem. Fulbright & Jaworski L.L.P., San Antonio. Mem. ABA, State Bar Tex., San Antonio Bar Assn., Order of Coif, Phi Alpha Delta. Office: Fulbright & Jaworski 300 Convent St Ste 2200 San Antonio TX 78205-3792 E-mail: ppfeiffer@fulbright.com.

PFEIFFER, PHYLLIS KRAMER, publishing executive; b. N.Y.C., Feb. 11, 1949; d. Jacob N. and Estelle G. Rosenbaum-Pfeiffer; m. Stephen M. Pfeiffer, Dec. 21, 1969; children: Andrew Kramer, Elise Kramer. BS, Cornell U., 1970; postgrad., U. San Diego, 1976-78. Instr. Miss Porter's Sch., Farmington, Conn., 1970; tchr. Dewey Jr. H.S. N.Y.C. Bd. Edn., 1970-73; rschr. Hunter Coll., N.Y.C., 1971-72; account exec. La Jolla (Calif.) Light, 1973-75, advt. dir., 1975-77, gen. mgr., 1977-78, pub., 1978-87; exec. v.p. Harte Hanks So. Calif. Newspapers, 1985-87; gen. mgr. San Diego edit. L.A. Times, 1987-93; pres., pub. Marin Ind. Jour., Novato, Calif., 1993-2000; v.p. advt. and mktg. Contra Costa Times, 2000—. Dir. comm. ctr. San Diego State U., 1980-93. Bd. dirs. La Jolla Cancer Rsch. Found., 1979-82, YMCA, San Diego Ballet, 1980, Dominican Coll., San Rafael, Calif, 1994—, Marin Theater Co., Alvarado Hosp., 1981-88, chmn. fin. com., 1986, sec. bd., 1986; co-chmn. Operation USS La Jolla, USN, 1980—; mem. mktg. com. United Way, 1979-81, chmn., 1983; trustee La Jollan's Inc., 1975-78, Nat. Pk. Trust, 2000-02, Dogs for the Blind, 2001-; mem. Conv. and Visitors Bur. Blue Ribbon Com. on Future, 1983; mem. resource panel Child Abuse Prevention Found., 1983—; bd. overseers U. Calif., San Diego; mem. violent crimes task force San Diego Police Dept.; dir. Guide Dogs for the Blind, Oveland Mus. Grantee N.Y. Bd. Edn., 1971-72; named Pub. of Yr., Gannet Co., Inc., 1995. Mem. Newspaper Assn. Am., Calif. Newspaper Pubs. Assn. (bd. dirs., exec. com.), Chancellor's Assn. U. Calif.-San Diego, Clairemont Club. Office: Contra Costa Times 2640 Shadelands Dr Walnut Creek CA 94598 E-mail: ppfeiffer@cctimes.com.

PFEIFFER, SOPHIA DOUGLASS, state legislator, lawyer; b. N.Y.C., Aug. 10, 1918; d. Franklin Chamberlin and Sophie Douglass (White) Wells; m. Timothy Adams Pfeiffer, June 7, 1941; children: Timothy Franklin, Penelope Mesereau Keenan, Sophie Douglass. AB, Vassar Coll., 1939; JD, Northeastern U., 1975. Bar: R.I. 1975, U.S. Ct. Appeals (1st cir.) 1980, U.S. Supreme Ct. 1979. Editl. rschr. Time, Inc., N.Y.C., 1940-41; writer Office War Info., Washington, 1941-43, N.Y.C., 1943-45; editl. staff Nat. Geog. Mag., Washington, 1958-59, 68-70; editor Turkish Jour. Pediatrics, Ankara, 1961-63; staff atty. R.I. Supreme Ct., Providence, 1975-76, chief staff atty., 1977-86; mem. Maine Ho. Reps., 1990-94; lectr. U. So. Maine, 1995. Bd. dirs. Death and Dying project. Contbr. in field. Chair bioethics study League Women Voters; pres. Karachi (Pakistan) Am. Sch., 1955-56; chair Brunswick Village Rev. Bd., 1986-89; trustee Brunswick Sewer Dist., 2000—, vice chmn., 2003; bd. dirs. Coll. Guild, 2003—. Home: 15 Franklin St Brunswick ME 04011-2101

PFEIFFER, STEVEN BERNARD, lawyer; b. Orange, N.J., Jan. 19, 1947; s. Bernard Victor and Elizabeth Sophia (Bissell) P.; m. Kristin Reagan, June 27, 1970; children: Victoria Elizabeth Metz, Rachel Catherine, Emily Dorothea, Stephanie Kristin Bissell, Andrew Steven Bernard. BA in Govt., Wesleyan U., 1969; BA in Jurisprudence, Oxford U., 1971, MA, 1983; MA in African Studies, U. London, 1973; JD, Yale U., 1976. Bar: N.J. 1976, D.C. 1978. Assoc. Fulbright & Jaworski, Houston, London, 1976—83, ptnr. London, Washington, 1983—, ptnr.-in-charge London, 1983—86, 1989—2002, head internat. dept., 1989—2003, ptnr.-in-charge Washington office, 1998—2002, chmn. exec. com., 2003—. Bd. dirs. The Africa Am. Inst., N.Y.C., Project HOPE, Washington, Barloworld Ltd., Johannesburg, Sasol Ltd, Johannesburg. Contbr. articles to profl. jours. Alumni-elected trustee Wesleyan U., Middletown, Conn., 1976-79, charter trustee, 1980-92, vice chmn. bd. trustees, 1986-87, chmn. bd. trustees, 1987-92, chmn. emeritus, 1992—; trustee St. Andrews Sch., Middletown, Del., 1995—. With USN, 1969, 72-74; asst. cinceur plans officer, Office of CNO, Washington, 1972-73; spl. asst. to Sec. of Navy, Washington, 1973-74. Rhodes scholar, 1969-72; Thomas Watson Travel fellow, The Watson Found., 1969. Mem. ABA, N.J. State Bar Assn., Am. Soc. Internat. Law, Internat. Bar Assn. (past chmn. sect. energy and natural resources law 1992-94), Naval Res. Assn., Internat. Inst. Strategic Studies (London), Coun. Fgn. Rels. Avocations: tennis, history, fishing, books. Home: 301 N View Ter Alexandria VA 22301-2609 Office: Fulbright & Jaworski LLP 801 Pennsylvania Ave NW Washington DC 20004-2623

PFEIFFER, WERNER BERNHARD, artist, educator; b. Stuttgart, Germany, Oct. 1, 1937; came to U.S., 1961; s. Jakob and Emilie (Nufer) P.; children: Jan-Stephen, Michaela Veronica. Diploma, Grafische Fachschule, Stuttgart, Akademie Fine Arts. Instr. Pratt Inst., Bklyn., 1961-64, prof., 1968-75, adj. prof., 1976—; asst. prof. N.Y. Inst. Tech., Westbury, 1965-67. Dir. Pratt Adlib Press, Bklyn., 1968-75 Exhibited in over 60 one-man shows. Mem. Soc. Am. Graphic Artists Avocations: skiing, travel, music. Address: PO Box 147 Red Hook NY 12571

PFEISTER, RAYMOND LYNN, diversified financial services company executive; b. Cape Girardeau, Mo., May 31, 1946; s. Herman Joe and Imogene Elsie (Groseclose) P.; m. Susan Jane Selby, July 1, 1969; children: Joseph Robert, John Charles. BS, U. Ill., 1969, MBA, 1971; PhD, CUNY, 1978. Sales analyst Koppers Co., Magnolia, Ark., 1969-70; instr. bus. U. Ill., Urbana, 1971; spl. agt. Prudential Ins. Co. Am., Champaign, Ill., 1971, divsn. mgr. Balt., 1971-74, mktg. specialist, mgr. group pension Newark and NYC, 1974; account exec. Alexander & Alexander Inc., NYC, 1974-76, asst. v.p., 1976-78, v.p., 1978-80, Johnson & Higgins, NYC, 1980-83; founder, chmn. bd., CEO Pfeister Barter Inc., NY Reciprocal Trade Exch., 1979-87; founder, chmn., pres. Pfeister Corp., Wilmington, Del., 1977—; co-founder, pres., treas. Chattan Group, Ltd., NYC, 1983—; co-founder, pres., CEO Sheffield Assocs., Ltd., NYC, 1985—; co-owner Ceramic Design Ltd., Greenwich, Conn., 1987—; vice chmn. Fred Alger Mgmt., NYC. Bd. dirs. U.S. Ceramic Tile Corp., Canton, Ohio, London Pacific Life Ins. Co., Calif.; lectr., cons. in field. Author: The Strategic Planning Process for Alexander & Alexander Services, Inc. and Subsidiaries, 1980; contbg. author: The Practice of Planning—Strategic, Administrative and Operational, 1981. Pres. Jr. Achievement, Denver, 1963-64; active boy Scouts Am., 1964—, United Fund, 1973. Mem. APA, Acad. Mgmt., Nat. Eagle Scout Assn., Soc. Am. Foresters, Forest Products Rsch. Soc., Nat. Life Underwriters Assn., Nat. MBA Assn., U. Ill. Alumni Assn. (life, v.p. 1974—), Siwanoy Country Club, Campfire Club Am., Union League Club, Sigma Iota Epsilon. Office Phone: 212-806-2954. E-mail: rpfeister@alger-ny.com., raypfiester@yahoo.com.

PFENDER, EMIL, mechanical engineering educator; b. Stuttgart, Germany, May 25, 1925; came to U.S., 1964, naturalized, 1969; s. Vinzenz and Anna Maria (Dreher) P.; m. Maria Katharina Staiger, Oct. 22, 1954; children: Roland, Norbert, Corinne. Student, U. Tuebingen, Germany, 1947-49; diploma in physics, U. Stuttgart, Germany, 1953, D Ing. in Elec. Engring., 1959. Assoc. prof. mech. engring. U. Minn., Mpls., 1964-67, prof., 1967—2000, prof. emeritus, 2000—. Contbr. articles to profl. jours.; patentee in field. Fellow: ASME; mem.: NAE, IEEE (assoc.). Home: 1947 Bidwell St Saint Paul MN 55118-4417 Office: U Minn Dept of Mech Engrg 111 Church St SE Minneapolis MN 55455-0150 Office Phone: 612-625-6012. E-mail: pfender@tc.umn.edu.

PFENDT, HENRY GEORGE, retired information systems executive, management consultant; b. Frankfurt, Germany, Sept. 19, 1934; s. Georg and Elisabeth K. P.; m. Jane Ann Gossard, July 15, 1961; children: Katherine Ann, Henry G. Jr., Karen Jane. BS, postgrad., U. Rochester, N.Y., 1972, U. Mich., 1986. Dir. No. info. ctr. Eastman Kodak Internat., Göteborg, Sweden, 1972-73, sr. project mgr. Stuttgart, Fed. Republic of Germany, 1973-75; dir. adminstrv. svcs. Kodak Australasia Party Ltd., Coburg, Australia, 1975-77, dir. customer svcs. div., 1977-81; dir. mktg. Eastman Kodak Co. for Asia, Africa and Australia, 1981-84; dir. architecture devel. Eastman Kodak Info. Systems, Rochester, 1984-86, dir. corp. info. systems, 1986-93; ret., 1993; bus. and info. mgmt. cons., 1993—. Bd. dirs. client adv. coun. Compu Ware, Detroit. Creator concepts and mgmt. processes in field. Mem. indsl. devel. agy. adv. bd. Zoning Bd. Appeals, 2001; chmn. Yates County Fair Taxation Com.; elected town councilman Town Bd. of Barrington, 1999; charter mem. adv. bd. Rochester Inst. Tech. Sch. Computer Sci. and Tech., 1987; bd. dirs. YMCA of Maplewood, Rochester, 1989—; mem. Rep. Nat. Com. With USAF, 1955-59. Recipient Industry Visionary award of 25 Most Influential Communications Execs., 1991, Lectr. of Yr. award Australian Computer Soc., Editor's Choice award Nat. Libr. Poetry. Mem. Soc. for Info. Mgmt., Coun. of Logistics Mgmt., Ctr. for Info. Systems Rsch., Strategic Mgmt. Soc., Internat. Platform Assn., Interact Network (assoc.), C. of C., Am. Legion. Lutheran. Avocations: reading, golf, gardening, jogging, travel. Home: 968 E Lake Rd Dundee NY 14837-9749 E-mail: pfendt@linkny.com.

PFENNINGER, KARL H. cell biology and neuroscience educator; b. Stafa, Switzerland, Dec. 17, 1944; came to U.S., 1971, naturalized, 1993; s. Hans Rudolf and Delie Maria (Zahn) P.; m. Marie-France Maylié, July 12, 1974; children: Jan Patrick, Alexandra Christina MD, U. Zurich, 1971. Rsch. instr. dept. anatomy Washington U., St. Louis, 1971-73; rsch. assoc. sect. cell biology Yale U., New Haven, 1973-76; assoc. prof. dept. anatomy and cell biology Columbia U., N.Y.C., 1976-81, prof., 1981-86; prof., chmn. dept. cellular and structural biology U. Colo. Sch. Medicine, Denver, 1986—. Dir. interdeptmental program in cell and molecular biology Columbia U. Coll. Physicians and Surgeons, N.Y.C., 1980-85; chmn. Given Biomed. Inst., Aspen, Colo., 1992-93. Author: Essential Cell Biology, 1990, The Origins of Creativity, 2001; contbr. articles to profl. jours. Recipient C.J. Herrick award Am. Assn. Anatomists, 1977; I.T. Hirschl Career Scientist award, 1977; Javits neurosci. investigator awards NIH, 1984, 91. Mem. AAAS, Am. Soc. for Cell Biology, Am. Soc. for Biochemistry and Molecular Biology, Toxicology Forum (bd. dirs. 1995—), Assn. Anatomy, Cell Biology and Neurosci. Chairpersons (pres. 1998), Harvey Soc., Soc. for Neurosci., Internat. Brain Rsch. Orgn., Internat. Soc. for Neurochemistry. Office: U Colo Health Scis Ctr Dept Cellular & Structural Biology B 111 4200 E 9th Ave Denver CO 80262-0001 E-mail: Karl.pfenninger@uchsc.edu.

PFEUFFER, ROBERT JOHN, musician; b. Cleve., Dec. 25, 1925; s. Henry Vincent and Elmo Alice (Burger) P.; m. Betty June Weller, Sept. 21, 1946; children— Barbara (Mrs. Steven Mosley), Jeanne, Susan, Catherine. B.Mus. in Edn, U. Mich., 1950, M.Mus. in Edn, 1951. Contrabassoonist, bassoonist Detroit Symphony Orch., 1951-61, Phila. Orch., 1962-91; instr. bassoon Wayne State U., 1957-61, New Sch. Music, Phila., 1969—; prin. bassoon Lynchburg Symphony, 1994—, Roanoke Opera, 1996—. Served with AUS, 1942-44. Mem. U.S. Power Squadron, Kappa Kappa Psi, Pi Mu Alpha. Roman Catholic. Home: 6 Sharp Ln Camden Wyoming DE 19934-4526

PFIFFNER, JAMES PRICE, political science educator; b. Stevens Point, Wis., June 24, 1946; s. James Sturtevant and Alice Price Pfiffner; m. Debra Ann Jones, Aug. 11, 1979; children: Megan Cyr, Katherine Courtney, Morgan Meehan. BA in Polit. Sci., U. Wis., 1968, MA in Polit. Sci., 1972, PhD in Polit. Sci., 1975. Tchg. asst. U. Wis., Madison, 1971-74; rsch. fellow Brookings Inst., Washington, 1974-75; asst. prof. U. Calif., Riverside, 1975-78, Calif. State U., Fullerton, 1978-80, assoc. prof. polit. sci., 1980-84, John Brown Mason prof., 1983-84; spl. asst. to dir. Office Pers. Mgmt., Washington, 1980-81; assoc. prof. govt. and pub. policy George Mason U., Fairfax, Va., 1984-87, prof., 1987—, univ. prof., 2003—. Author: The President, the Budget, and Congress: Impoundment and the 1974 Budget Act, 1979, The Strategic Presidency: Hitting the Ground Running, 1988, 2d edit., 1996, The Modern Presidency, 1998, 4th edit., 2004, The Character Factor: How We Judge America's Presidents, 2004; editor: The President and Economic Policy, 1986, The Managerial Presidency, 1991, 2d edit., 1999, Governance and American Politics: Classic and Current Perspectives, 1995; co-editor: The Presidency in Transition, 1989, The Presidency and the Gulf War, 1993, Understanding the Presidency, 1997, 2d edit., 2000, The Future of Merit, 2000. With U.S. Army, 1969-70, Vietnam. Decorated Army Commendation medal for Valor, Vietnam/Cambodia, 1970; Brookings Instn. fellow, 1974-75, vis. scholar, 1983, 97; Nat. Assn. Sch. Pub. Affairs and Adminstrn. faculty fellow, 1980-81. Mem. Nat. Acad. Pub. Adminstrn., Cosmos Club. Office: George Mason U Sch Pub Policy 3C6 Fairfax VA 22030-4444 Office Phone: 703-993-1417. Business E-Mail: pfiffner@gmu.edu.

PFIFFNER, PATRICK MEEHAN, musician, educator; b. Stevens Point, Wis., Mar. 19, 1948; s. James Sturtevant and Alice Mary (Price) Pfiffner; m. Linda Sue Ridenour, Aug. 6, 1972; children: James Stanley, Jeffrey Allen. MusB, San Diego State U., 1976, MusM, 1977. Extra percussionist/timpanist San Diego Symphony, 1972—; percussionist Nederlander Orgn., San Diego, 1976—; resident drummer/percussionist/contractor Starlight Light Opera, San Diego, 1981—; extra percussionist/timpanist San Diego Opera, 1982—; prin. percussionist/timpanist San Diego Chamber Orch., 1985—; prof. music Point Loma Nazarene U., San Diego. Percussionist Sammy Davis, Bob Hope, George Burns, Mickey Rooney, Robert Goulet, Andre Bocelli, Johnny Mathis, Milton Berle, 1981—; dir. Grand Pacific Band, 1986—, Grossmont Coll. concert and jazz bands, 1979—86, Heartland Youth Orch., 1983—84. Author: The Ancestors of Patrick Meehan Pfiffner, 2002; contbr. articles to profl. jours.; performer: (CD) Those Hollywood Marches, with Lalo Shifrin, 1990, Russian CD, San Diego Chamber Orch., 1989, French CD, 1991, Malcolm Arnold CD, 1992, Magnification CD, Rock Group Yes, 2001, nat. tours Broadway shows, including Beauty and the Beast, Hello Dolly, King and I, Ragtime, The Producers, Hairspray, others. Musician 2d class USN, 1967—71, USS Little Rock, Mediterranean Sea. Mem.: ASCAP, Percussive Arts Soc., Am. Fedn. Musicians Local 325. Avocations: long distance running, genealogy. Home: 13138 Beechtree St Lakeside CA 92040-3307 Office: Pt Loma Nazarene U 3900 Lomaland Dr San Diego CA 92106 E-mail: patpfiffner@cox.net.

PFINSGRAFF, MARTIN, investment company executive; m. Joan Marsh Lange; 4 children. BA in Psychology, Allegheny Coll.; MBA, Harvard U., 1981. CFA. Witn portfolio and funds mgmt. dept. Mellon Bank, 1977, with treasury and capital markes divsn., 1981; mng. dir. corp. fin. group Prudential Ins. Co. Am., v.p., treas., 1991; exec. v.p., CFO, bd. dirs. Prudential Securities, N.Y.C.; pres. Capital Markets, N.Y.C., 1997-2000. Chmn. designate Prudential Bache Internat. Bank; mem. operating com. Prudential Securities Group, Inc. Trustee Allegheny Coll. Office: Capital Markets 1 New York Plz Fl 15 New York NY 10004-1901

PFISTER, ALFRED KARL, internist, educator; b. Wheeling, W.Va. s. Alfred and Anna Seeger Pfister; m. Nancy Ann Taylor, June 24, 1989; children: Alfred, Constance, Philip. BA, Washington & Jefferson U., 1958; MD, George Washington U., 1962. Diplomate Am. Bd. Internal Medicine. With Charleston (W.Va.) Med. Group, 1969—96, Integrated Healthcare, 1997—2002; prof. Sch. Medicine W.Va. U., 2003—. Contbr. articles to profl. jours. Lt. comdr. USPHS, 1966—68. Recipient Laureate award, W.Va. ACP, 1992. Republican. Unitarian. Avocations: running, plant biology. Home: 1 Beta Lane Charleston WV 25304 Office: Univ Health Assocs 3200 MacCorkle Ave SE Charleston WV 25304

PFISTER, CLOYD HARRY, consultant, former career officer; b. State College, Pa., Dec. 20, 1936; s. Rudolf John Pfister and June Ruth (Braun) Pfister Gray; m. Rita Askerc Kracht, Aug. 17, 1962 (div. Mar. 1982); m. Gail Williams, Apr. 24, 1982; children, Gabriele, Catherine, Michael, Romi, Eric Williams, Lori Williams. BA in Philosophy, Oberlin Coll., 1957; MA in Internat. Rels., Am. U., 1964, postgrad., 1964-67. Enlisted U.S. Army, 1957, advanced through grades to maj. gen., 1989; staff officer Nat. Security Agy., Fort Meade, Md., 1965-68; S3 (Ops.) 303d Radio Rsch. Bn., Plantation, Vietnam, 1968-69; instr. JFK Ctr. and Sch., Fort Bragg, N.C., 1969-72; politico-mil. officer, Office Dep. Chief of Staff for Ops. Hdqrs. Dept. Army, Washington, 1972-75; comdr. 307th U.S. Army Security Agy. Bn., VII U.S. Corps, Ludwigsburg, Fed. Republic Germany, 1975-77; asst. chief of staff intelligence 8th Mech. Inf. Div., Bad Kreuznach, Fed. Republic Germany, 1977-79; Mid. East staff officer Office Sec. Def., The Pentagon, 1979-82; comdr. U.S. Army Field Sta., Berlin, 1982-84; chief of staff U.S. Army Intelligence Ctr. and Sch., Fort Huachuca, Ariz., 1984-85, dep. comdt., 1985-86; dir. intelligence (J2), Hdqrs., U.S. Cen. Command, MacDill AFB, Fla., 1986-88; dep. chief of staff intelligence Hdqrs., U.S. Army Europe and 7th Army, Heidelberg, Fed. Republic Germany, 1988-91; asst. dep. chief of staff Intelligence Hdqrs., Dept. Army, Pentagon, 1991-93. Cons. Def. Sci. Bd., 1994, Def. Airborne Reccon Office, 1994-97, Nat. Imagery and Mapping Agy., 1999-2001; chmn. Cmty. Adv. Coun. on Cancer, Inova, 2000—. Decorated Def. D.S.M., D.S.M. Def. Superior Svc. medal, Legion of Merit with two oak leaf clusters, Nat. Intelligence D.S.M.; Ehrenkreutz der Bundeswehr (gold) (Fed. Republic Germany); other awards. Mem. Internat. Inst. for Strategic Studies, Middle East Inst., Security Affairs Support Assn., Assn. U.S. Army, Armed Forces Coomms. Electronics Assn.(intelligence com.), Nat. Correlation Working Group (bd. dirs.). Avocations: tennis, photography, gardening. Office: Tech Strategies & Alliances 5242 Lyngate Ct Burke VA 22015-1631 E-mail: pfister@tsanda.com.

PFISTER, DONALD HENRY, biology professor; b. Kenton, Ohio, Feb. 17, 1945; s. William A. and Dorothy C. (Kurtz) P.; m. Cathleen C. Kennedy, July 1, 1971; children: Meghan, Brigid, Edith. AB, Miami U., Oxford, Ohio, 1967; PhD, Cornell U., 1971; AM (hon.), Harvard U., 1980. Asst. prof. biology U. P.R., Mayaguez, 1971-74; asst. prof. biology, asst. curator Farlow Herbarium Harvard U., Cambridge, Mass., 1974-77, assoc. prof. biology, assoc. curator Farlow Herbarium, 1977-80, prof. biology, curator Farlow Herbarium, 1980—, dir. univ. herbaria, 1983-95, Asa Gray prof. botany, 1984—, dir. univ. herbaria, 1999—. Vis. mycologist U. Copenhagen, 1978; vis. prof. field station U. Minn., Itasca, 1979; master Kirkland House Harvard U., 1982-00. Contbr. over 80 articles to profl. jours. Grantee NSF, 1973-75, 81-85, 85—, Am. Philos. Soc., 1975-76, Whiting Found., 1986. Fellow AAAS, Linnean Soc.

London; mem. Mycol. Soc. Am. (sec. 1988-91, v.p. 1993-94, pres.-elect 1994-95, pres. 1995-96), Am. Phytopath. Soc., Am. Microbiol. Soc., New Eng. Bot. Club, Sigma Xi. Office: Harvard U Herbarium 22 Divinity Ave Cambridge MA 02138

PFISTER, HOWARD FREDERICK CARL, retired surgeon; b. Newport, Ky., 1917; BS, U. Cin., 1939, MD, 1943. Diplomate Am. Bd. Surgery. Intern Cin. Gen. Hosp., 1943-44, resident in surgery, 1944-45, 47-52; pvt. practice, Cin., 1951-95; ret., 1995. Former asst. clin. prof. surgery U. Cin. Mem. AMA.

PFISTER, KARL ANTON, industrial company executive; b. Ernetschwil St. Gallen, Switzerland, Oct. 17, 1941; came to U.S., 1966; s. Josef Anton and Paula Pfister; m. Karen Antonie Sievers; children: Kirsten, Marc, Theodore, Alexandra. Student trade sch., Rapperswil, Switzerland, 1957-61; student bus. sch., Zuerich, Switzerland, 1964-65. Tool and die maker H. Schmid, Rapperswil, Switzerland, 1957-61, Neher AG, Ebnat-Kappel, Switzerland, 1962-63; process engr. NCR, Buelach, Switzerland, 1964-66, Gretag, Regensdorf, Switzerland, 1966; tool and die maker Stoffel Fineflow Corp., White Plains, N.Y., 1966-67; mgr. mfg. Finetool Corp., Detroit, 1968; pres. Mich. Precision Ind., Inc., Detroit, 1969—, MPI Internat. Inc., Rochester Hills, Mich., 1990—; chmn. bd., pres. Kautex N.Am., Inc., Rochester Hills, Mich., 1994; pres. Kloeckner Automotive, Inc., Rochester Hills, Mich., 1996, MPI Internat. Inc., Rochester Hills, 1998—. Dir. Kloeckner Capital Corp., Gordonsville, Va., MPI Internat., Inc. Consul, consulate Switzerland, Detroit, 1984—. Republican. Roman Catholic. Office: MPI Internat Inc 2129 Austin Ave Rochester Hills MI 48309-3668

PFLANZE, OTTO PAUL, history professor; b. Maryville, Tenn., Apr. 2, 1918; s. Otto Paul and Katrine (Mills) P.; m. Hertha Maria Haberlander, Feb. 20, 1951; children: Stephen, Charles, Katrine. BA, Maryville Coll., 1940; MA, Yale U., 1942, PhD, 1950. Historian Dept. State, 1948-49; instr. N.Y. U., 1950-51; asst. prof. U. Mass., 1952-58, U. Ill., 1958-61; prof. history U. Minn., 1961-76, Ind. U., 1977-86, emeritus, 1986; Stevenson Prof. of History Bard Coll., Annandale On Hudson, N.Y., 1987-92, emeritus, 1992. Chmn. Conf. Group Central European History, 1978; mem. exam. bd., grad. record exam Ednl. Testing Service, 1972-76; mem. Inst. Advanced Study, 1970-71, mem. Historisches Kolleg, Munich, 1980-81. Author: Bismarck and the Development of Germany: Vol. 1.-The Period of Unification, 1815-1871, 1963 (Biennal Book award Phi Alpha Theta), rev. edit., 1990, Vol. 2-The Period of Consolidation, 1871-1880, 1990, Vol. 3-The Period of Fortification, 1880-1898, 1990 (3 vols. collectively named Most Outstanding Book in History, Govt. & Polit. Sci. by Assn. Am. Pubs., 1991); translated as Bd. I-Bismarck, Der Reichsgründer, 1997, Bd II-Bismarck, Der Reichskanzler, 1998 (Einhard prize 1999); co-author: A History of the Western World: Modern Times, 3d edit, 1975; editor: Innenpolitische Probleme des Bismarck-Reiches, 1983; co-editor: Documents on German Foreign Policy, 1918-1945, Vols. I-III, 1949-50; editor Am. Hist. Rev., 1976-85; mem. editl. bd. Jour. Modern History, 1971-73, Central European History, 1972-74. Served to 1st lt. U.S. Army, 1942-46. Fulbright research fellow, 1955-57; fellow Am. Council Learned Socs., 1951-52; fellow Guggenheim Found., 1966-67; fellow Nat. Endowment Humanities, 1975-76; fellow Internat. Research and Exchanges Bd., 1976; fellow Thyssen Stiftung, Essen, 1986; recipient Humanities award McKnight Found., 1962. Mem. Am. Hist. Assn., German Studies Assn.

PFLAUMER, KATRINA C. lawyer; BA in English Lit. cum laude, Smith Coll.; MA in Tchg. English, Columbia U.; JD, NYU. Tchr. English and Am. Lit. Westtown Sch., Pa., 1970-72; staff atty. Seattle King County Defender Assn., 1975-77, Fed. Pub. Defender's Office, Seattle, 1977-80; pvt. practice, 1980-93; U.S. atty. Dept. Justice (we. dist.) Washington, 1993-01. Pro tem judge King County Superior Ct.; adj. prof. U. Puget Sound Sch. Law; guest lectr. U. Washington, Hastings, Cardozo, Nat. Inst. Trial Advocacy programs; lawyer rep. 9th Cir. Jud. Conf.; named to Atty. Gen. Adv. Com., 1994-95. Mem. Fire Brigade Emergency Response Team. Mem. FBA (pres. we. dist. Washington 1991, chair implementation of gender task force report com.), Nat. Assn. Criminal Def. Lawyers (mem. nominating com.), U.S. Sentencing Commn. (practitioners adv. group), Am. Civil Liberties Union (mem. legal com.), Seattle-King County Bar Assn. (mem. jud. conf. com.), Washington Assn. Criminal Def. Lawyers (pres. 1988-89), State Bench Bar (mem. press com.), Phi Beta Kappa. Office: US Dept Justice 601 Union St Ste 5100 Seattle WA 98101

PFLUM, BARBARA ANN, pediatrician, allergist; b. Cin., Jan. 10, 1943; d. James Frederick and Betty Mae (Doherty) P.; m. Makram I. Gobrail, Oct. 20, 1973; children: Christina, James. BS, Coll. Mt. St. Vincent, 1967; MD, Georgetown U., 1971; MS, Coll. Mt. St. Joseph, 1993. Cons. Children's Med. Ctr., Dayton, Ohio, 1975—, dir. allergy clinic, 1983-89; dir. allergy divsn. Hopeland Splty. Clinic, Dayton, 1998-2000. Fellow Am. Acad. Pediatrics, Am. Acad. Allergy and Immunology, Am. Coll. Allergy and Immunology; mem. Ohio Soc. Allergy and Immunology, Western Ohio Pediatric Soc. (pres. 1985-86). Roman Catholic. Office: 207 E Stroop Rd Dayton OH 45429-2825 Office Phone: 937-293-8263. E-mail: bapflum@hotmail.com.

PFLUM, WILLIAM JOHN, physician; b. NYC, July 30, 1924; s. Peter Arthur and Caroline (Schmidt) P.; m. Roseann Sarah Stubing, Oct. 13, 1956; children: Carol Jean, Jeanine, Suzanne, Denise, Peter. BS, Georgetown U., 1947; MD, Loyola U., Chgo., 1951. Diplomate Am. Bd. Allergy & Immunology. Intern St. Vincent's Hosp, N.Y.C., 1951-52; resident in internal medicine NYU div. Goldwater Meml. Hosp., N.Y.C., 1952-53; resident in allergy Inst. Allergy Roosevelt Hosp., N.Y.C., 1956; attending internist allergy & immunology Overlook Hosp., Summit, N.J., 1958—. Assoc. attending Inst. Allergy, Immunology and Infectious Diseases, Roosevelt Hosp., N.Y.C., 1957-92; pvt. practice medicine, specializing in allergy and immunology, Summit, 1957-92; ret.; cons. in field. With USAAF, 1943—45, ETO. Decorated Purple Heart, air medal with two clusters, POW medal. Fellow Am. Acad. Allergy, Am. Coll. Allergists, Am. Assn. Clin. Immunology and Allergy; mem. Summit Med. Soc., Am. Assn. Clin. Immunology and Allergy (pres. Mid-Atlantic region 1975-76), Disabled Am. Vets., Mil. Order Purple Heart, Am. Ex-Prisoners of War, 8th Air Force Hist. Soc., World Marathon Runners Assn., Robert A. Cooke Allergy Alumni Assn. Achievements include completion of 26 consecutive Boston Marathons, 1971-1996 with Am. Med. Athletic Assn. Home: 922 North Shore Dr NE Saint Petersburg FL 33701

PFNISTER, ALLAN OREL, humanities educator; b. Mason, Ill., July 23, 1925; s. Ardon Orel and Rose Margaret (Sandtner) P.; m. Helen Edith Klobes, Dec. 18, 1948; children: Alicia Ann, Jonathan Karl, Susan Elaine. AB summa cum laude, Augustana Coll., 1945; MDiv summa cum laude, Augustana Theol. Sem., 1949; AM, U. Chgo., 1951, PhD, 1955; LLD (hon.), U. Denver, 1978. Instr. in religion Augustana Coll., 1946-47; instr. in philosophy and German Luther Coll., Wahoo, Nebr., 1949-52, dean, 1953-54; research asst., univ. fellow U. Chgo., 1952-53, instr., 1954-57, asst. prof., 1957-58; dir. research joint bds. parish edn. Lutheran Ch. Am., 1958-59; vis. asso. prof. U. Mich., 1959-62, asso. prof., 1962-63; dean Coll. Liberal Arts, prof. philosophy Wittenberg (Ohio) U., 1963-67, provost, prof., 1967-69, acting pres., 1968-69; prof. higher edn. U. Denver, 1969-77, 78-90, exec. vice chancellor and acting chancellor, 1977-78, vice chancellor acad. affairs, 1984-87, assoc. provost, 1988-89, prof. emeritus, 1990—. Dir. study fgn. study programs Fedn. Regional Accrediting Commns. Higher Edn., 1970-72; cons. in field; bd. dirs. Nat. Ctr. for Higher Edn. Mgmt. Systems Mgmt. Svcs.; trustee Capital U., Columbus, Ohio, 1983, vice chmn. bd., 1987-89, 91-94. Author: Teaching Adults, 1967, Trends in Higher Education, 1975, Planning for Higher Education, 1976; contbr. numerous articles on higher edn. to profl. jours. Bd. visitors Air Force Inst. Tech., 1978-83, chmn. bd. visitors, 1981-83. Recipient Outstanding Achievement Alumni award Augustana Coll., 1963, Outstanding Contributions to the Univ. award Univ. Denver, 1995. Mem. Am. Assn. Higher Edn., Assn. for Study Higher Edn., Comparative and Internat. Edn. Soc., Blue Key, Phi Beta Kappa. Democrat. Home: 7231 W Linvale Pl Denver CO 80227-3556 E-mail: apfnister@cs.com.

PFOUTS, RALPH WILLIAM, economist, consultant; b. Atchison, Kans., Sept. 9, 1920; s. Ralph Ulysses and Alice (Oldham) P.; m. Jane Hoyer, Jan. 31, 1945 (dec. Nov. 1982); children: James William, Susan Jane Pfouts Portman, Thomas Robert (dec.), Elizabeth Ann Pfouts Klenowski; m. Lois Bateson, Dec. 21, 1984 (div.); m. Felicia Sprincenatu, 1993 (div.); m. June St. James, July 14, 2001. BA, U. Kans., 1942, MA, 1947; PhD, U. N.C., 1952. Rsch. asst., instr. econs. U. Kans., Lawrence, 1946-47; instr. U. N.C., Chapel Hill, 1947-50, lectr. econs., 1950-52, assoc. prof. econs., 1952-58, prof. econs., 1958-87, chmn. grad. studies dept. econs. Sch. Bus. Adminstrn., 1957-62, chmn. dept. econs. Sch. Bus. Adminstrn., 1962-68; cons. econs. Chapel Hill, 1987—. Vis. prof. U. Leeds, 1983; vis. rsch. scholar Internat. Inst. for Applied Systems Analysis, Laxenberg, Austria, 1983; prof. Cen. European U., Prague, 1991. Author: Elementary Economics-A Mathematical Approach, 1972; editor: So. Econ. Jour, 1955-75; editor, contbr.: Techniques of Urban Economic Analysis, 1960, Essays in Economics and Econometrics, 1960; editorial bd.: Metroeconomica, 1961-80, Atlantic Econ. Jour, 1973—; contbr. articles to profl. jours. Served as deck officer USNR, 1943-46. Social Sci. Research Council fellow U. Cambridge, 1953-54; Ford Found. Faculty Research fellow, 1962-63. Mem. AAAS, Am. Statis. Assn., N.C. Statis. Assn. (past pres.), Am. Econ. Assn., So. Econ. Assn. (past pres.), Atlantic Econ. Soc. (v.p. 1973-76, pres. 1977-78), Population Assn. Am., Econometric Soc., Math. Assn. Am., Phi Beta Kappa, Pi Sigma Alpha, Alpha Kappa Psi, Omicron Delta Epsilon. Home and Office: 127 Summerlin Dr Chapel Hill NC 27514-1925 E-mail: rwpfouts@earthlink.net.

PFUND, EDWARD THEODORE, JR., electronics company executive; b. Methuen, Mass., Dec. 10, 1923; s. Edward Theodore and Mary Elizabeth (Banning) P.; BS magna cum laude, Tufts Coll., 1950; postgrad U. So. Calif., 1950, Columbia U., 1953, U. Calif., L.A., 1956, 58; m. Marga Emmi Andre, Nov. 10, 1954 (div. 1978); children: Angela M., Gloria I., Edward Theodore III; m. Ann Lorenne Dille, Jan. 10, 1988 (div. 1990). Radio engr., WLAW, Lawrence-Boston, 1942-50; fgn. svc. staff officer Voice of Am., Tangier, Munich, 1950 54; project. engr. Crusade for Freedom, Munich, Ger., 1955; project mgr., materials specialist United Electrodynamics Inc., Pasadena, Calif., 1956-59; cons. H.I. Thompson Fiber Glass Co., L.A., Andrew Corp., Chgo., 1959, Satellite Broadcast Assocs., Encino, Calif., 1982, TRW Inc., Redondo Beach, Calif., 1994; teaching staff Pasadena City Coll. (Calif.), 1959; dir. engring., chief engr. Electronics Specialty Co., L.A. and Thomaston, Conn., 1959-61; with Hughes Aircraft Co., various locations, 1955, 61-89, mgr. Middle East programs, also Far East, Latin Am. and African market devel., L.A., 1971-89, dir. internat. programs devel., Hughes Comm. Internat., 1985-89; mng. dir. E.T. Satellite Assocs. Internat., Rolling Hills Estates, Calif., 1989; dir. programs devel. Asia-Pacific TRW Space and Tech. Group, Redondo Beach, Calif., 1990-93, Pacific Telecom. Coun., Honolulu, 1993—. With AUS, 1942-46. Mem. AIAA, Phi Beta Kappa, Sigma Pi Sigma. Contbr. articles to profl. jours. Home: 25 Silver Saddle Ln Palos Verdes Peninsula CA 90274-2437

PHAIR, JOSEPH BASCHON, lawyer; b. N.Y.C., Apr. 29, 1947; s. James Francis and Mary Elizabeth Phair; m. Bonnie Jean Hobbs, Sept. 04, 1971; children: Kelly I., Joseph B., Sean P. BA, U. San Francisco, 1970, JD, 1973. Bar: Calif., U.S. Dist. Ct. (no. dist.) Calif., U.S. Ct. Appeals (9th cir.). Assoc. Berry, Davis & McInerney, Oakland, Calif., 1974-76, Bronson, Bronson & McKinnon, San Francisco, 1976-79; staff atty. Varian Assocs., Inc., Palo Alto, Calif., 1979-83, corp. counsel, 1983-86, sr. corp. counsel, 1986-87, assoc. gen. counsel, 1987-90, v.p., gen. counsel, 1990-91, v.p., gen. counsel, sec., 1991-99; v.p. adminstrn., gen. counsel, sec. Varian Med. Sys., Inc., Palo Alto, 1999—. Mem. devel. bd. St. Vincent de Paul Devel. Coun., San Francisco, 1992—. Mem. Bay Area Gen. Counsel, Silicon Valley Assn. Gen. Counsel, The Olympic Culb. Roman Catholic. Office: Varian Med Sys Inc M S V 250 3100 Hansen Way Palo Alto CA 94304-1030 Office Phone: 650-424-5918.

PHAIR, LIZ, recording artist, pop vocalist; b. Cin., Apr. 17, 1967; d. John and Nancy Phair. Diploma, Oberlin Coll., 1990. Freelance artist, 1990; singer, songwriter, 1992—. Albums include: Exile in Guyville (name Album of Yr. Village Voice), 1993, Whip-Smart, 1994, Whitechocolatespaceegg, 1998. Named Best New Female Vocalist Rolling Stone Critic's Poll. Office: Matador Records 625 Broadway New York NY 10012-2611

PHALEN, ROBERT FRANKLYNN, environmental scientist; b. Fairview, Okla., Oct. 18, 1940; married, 1966; 2 children. B in Physics, San Diego State U., 1964, M in Physics, 1966; PhD in Biophysics, U. Rochester, 1971. Engring. aide advanced space systems dept. Gen. Dynamics/Astronautics, San Diego, 1962-63; asst. to radiation safety officer, lab. teaching asst. San Diego State U., 1964-66, instr. physics dept., 1966; mem. summer faculty biology dept. Rochester (N.Y.) Inst. Tech., 1970-72; rsch. assoc. aerosol physics dept. Lovelace Found. for Med. Edn. and Rsch., Albuquerque, 1972-74; from adj. asst. prof. to assoc. prof. in residence dept. community and environ. medicine U. Calif., Irvine, 1974-84, prof., dir. Air Pollution Health Effects Lab., 1985—, faculty Ctr. for Occupl. Environ. Health, 1985—. Editor Aerosol Sci. and Tech.; reviewer Am. Rev. Respiratory Disease, Applied Indsl. Hygiene, Bull. Math. Biology, Exptl. Lung Rsch., Jour. Toxicology and Environ. Health, Jour. Toxicology and Applied Pharmacology, Jour. Aerosol Sci., Sci.; reviewer, mem. editl. bd. Fundamental and Applied Toxicology, 1986-92, Inhalation Toxicology, 1988-2004, Jour. Aerosol Medicine, 1988-98, Aerosol Sci. and Tech., 2002—; mem. safety and occupl. health study sect. NIH, 1988-01, mem. spl. study sects., 1980, 81, chmn. spl. study sects., 1982-84, 87, 88, 92, mem. site visit teams, 1980-2001; mem. expert panel on sulfur oxides EPA, mem. inhalation toxicology divsn. peer rev. panel, 1982, session chmn., 1983, participant workshop on non-oncogenic lung disease, 1984, mem. grants rsch. sci. rev. panel on health rsch., EPA advisor, 1985-88, 93-98, 2003; mem. task group on respiratory tract kinetic model Nat. Coun. Radiation Protection, 1978-97; mem. adv. panel on asbestos APHA, 1978; chmn. atmospheric sampling com. Am. Coun. Govtl. Indsl. Hygienists, 1982-92; chmn. NIOSH spl. study sect., 1983; panelist workshop Nat. Heart, Lung and Blood Inst., 1982; sci. advisor Prentice Day Sch., 1986-2002. Author: Inhalation Studies: Foundations and Techniques, 1984, The Particulate Air Pollution Controversy, 2002, (with others) Advances in Air Sampling, 1988, Concepts in Inhalation Toxicology, 1989, Deposition, Retention and Dosimetry of Inhaled Radioactive Substances, 1997; editor: Methods in Inhalation Toxicology, 1997; contbr. numerous articles to profl. jours. Am. Legion scholar. Fellow Acad. Toxicol. Scis.; mem. AAAS, Am. Assn. Aerosol Rsch. (charter, chmn. ann. meeting 1985), Am. Conf. Govtl. Indsl. Hygienists, Am. Indsl. Hygiene Assn. (jour. reviewer, chmn. ann. conf. 1981, 85, 86), Brit. Occupl. Hygiene Soc., Internat. Soc. Aerosols in Medicine, So. Calif. Acad. Scis., Soc. for Aerosol Rsch., Health Physics Soc., Soc. Toxicology (dir. 4 internat. confs. on health effects of particulate air pollution, Career Achievement award 2000). Achievements include research in nasal, tracheobronchial and pulmonary transport of inhaled deposited particles and effects of pollutant exposure on transport kinetcs, laboratory simulation and characterization of airborne environmental pollutants, respiratory tract deposition and clearance models for inhaled particles, including species comparisons and body size effects, behavior of highly-concentrated aerosols with respect to deposition in the respiratory tract. Office: U Calif Air Pollution Health Effects Lab Cmty & Environ Medicine Irvine CA 92697-1825 Business E-Mail: rfphalen@uci.edu.

PHAM, ANDREA HOA, educator, writer; b. Danang, Vietnam, Aug. 25, 1958; d. Pham Van Ngat and Dang Thi Nhiem; m. Thanh Nguyen, May 30, 1982 (dec. Jan. 6, 1985); 1 child, Andrew Nguyen. BA, U. Hue, 1977—81; MA in linguistics, U. Toronto, 1994—97, PhD in linguistics, 1997—2001. Lectr. Danang Coll. Edn., Vietnam, 1981—89; vis. scholar Saigon U., Vietnam, 1988—89; program prodr., editor, reporter Toronto Vietnamese Radio AM1430, 1997; instr. U. Toronto, 1999—2002; postdoctoral rsch. assoc. York U., Toronto, 2001—02; asst. prof. U. Fla., 2002—. Author: (collection of poems) Tieng Me (Mother's Voice); contbr. articles; author: Vietnamese Tone; A New Analysis, 2003. Recipient U. of Toronto Found. Grad. award, U. of Toronto, 2000—01; fellowship, Social Sciences and Humanities Rsch. Coun. of Can., 2000—03, Postdoctoral fellowships in the Humanities/Social Sciences, U. of Toronto, 2001—02, Ont. Grad. scholarship, Ministry of Tng., Colleges and Universities, 1999—2001. Mem.: Internat. Phonetic Assn. Avocations: argentine tango, music, travel. Office: U Fla 445 Grinter Hall PO Box 115565 Gainesville FL 32611-5565 Office Phone: 352-392-7084. Personal E-mail: apham@aall.ufl.edu.

PHAM, DAVID LAN, secondary school educator, writer; b. Binh Chuan, Thudaumot, Vietnam, Feb. 1, 1940; s. Khoai Van Pham and Chuc Thi Le; m. Tam Thi Nguyen, Nov. 22, 1965; children: Albert, Elizabeth, Wellington, An, Victoria. BEd, Faculty of Pedagogy, Saigon Vietnam, 1963; BA in History, Faculty of Letters, Saigon Vietnam, 1965; M in Libr. Sci, Faculty of Pedagogy, Saigon Vietnam, 1973. Tchr., chief libr. Ly Thuong Kiet Comprehensive H.S., Hoc Mon, Vietnam, 1963—75; social svcs. coord. Cath. Social Svcs. Refugee Resettlement Program, Bayou La Batre, Ala., 1987—96. Advisor Binh Duong Bo De Sch., 1968—75; advisor Binh Duong Confedn, Vietnamienne du Travail, 1968—75; vis. Thailand for Libr. Sci. Observation, 1973; advisor, founder Mutual Assistance Assn., Bayou La Batre, Ala., 1988—89. Columnist Thoi Bao Daily, Saigon, Vietnam, 1963—64, columnist Point South, Mobile, Ala., 1991—94; columnist: Binh Duong News, 2000— (award of appercia-tion, 2003); editor: (Bulletin) Bulletin Tin Viet, Dac San Que Huong, 1987—96; author: Two Hamlets in Nam Bo, 1999, Earthy Life, 2001, Vietnam History Dictionary, 2002, International Politico - Cultural Influences on Vietnam in the 20th Century, 2004. Gen. sec. Assn. Vietnamese Tchrs. of History and Geography, 1967—69, Viet. Libr. Assn, 1973—74; founder Tutorial Program, Bayou La Batre, Ala., 1992—96. Buddhist. Avocations: reading, travel, walking, writing, zen. Home: 1341 Leith Dr Toledo OH 43614 E-mail: davidlanpham@hotmail.com.

PHAM, DUC, engineering executive; b. Hoi An, Quang Nam Da Nang, Vietnam, Nov. 17, 1970; s. De Ba Pham and Tu Thi Cam Nguyen; m. Hong Hieu Nguyen, May 26, 1998. BS, Calif. Poly. State U., San Luis Obispo, 1998; MS, San Jose State U., Calif., 1999; DEng, Santa Clara U., Calif., 2002. Project engr. Remec Inc., San Jose, 1999—2000; product mgr. Micro Lambda Wireless, Inc., Fremont, Calif., 2000—02; pres., CEO Advanced Rsch. Labs, Inc, San Jose, 2002—. Cons. Gerson Lehrman Group, N.Y.C., 2001—, Avista Cons. Group, N.Y.C., 2002—. Mem.: N.Y. Acad. Sci. (hon.), Sigma Xi (hon.). Achievements include research in Electronic systems, nanotechnology. Avocations: golf, reading, travel. Office Phone: 408-691-7415. E-mail: dpham19@yahoo.com.

PHAM, LARA BACH-VIEN, small business owner; b. Ba-Xuyen, Vietnam, Jan. 11, 1962; d. Thi Van and Huong Thi Nguyen; m. Thien Van Pham, Apr. 17, 1982; children: Minh-Thu, Sheena, Lisa, Jimmy. Diploma, Brand's Beauty Coll., Charlotte, NC, 1990. Lic. securities NASD, life and health ins., in property and liability, in real estate sales. Hair stylist, owner Hair Studio, Charlotte, 1990—; beauty cons. Beauti Control, Charlotte, 1990—93, 2001—; flower arranger weddings, Charlotte, 1995—.

PHAM, QUANG XUAN, statistics educator; b. Mytho, Vietnam, Apr. 30, 1938; came to U.S., 1985; BS, U. Saigon, Vietnam, 1961; MS, Western Wash. U., Bellingham, 1971; PhD, U. Calif., Berkeley, 1974. Math tchr. Chu Van An High Sch., Saigon, Vietnam, 1961—70; info. analyst Henkel France, Gentilly, France, 1979—85; prof. stats. emeritus U. Alaska, Fairbanks, 1985—2001; adj. prof. stats. U. Calif., Berkeley, 2001—. Mem. Am. Statis. Assn., Biometrics Soc. Office: U Calif Berkeley Dept Stats Berkeley CA 94720

PHAM, SI MAI, cardiothoracic surgeon, medical educator; b. Ninh Hoa, Khanh Hoa, Vietnam, Oct. 6, 1955; came to U.S. 1975; s. Tro Pham and Nhung Thi Mai; m. Marie Christine Pham, Sept. 9, 1987; children: Benjamin Bartley, Anthony Ninh, Vivienne Elisabeth, Victoria B.H. Student, U. Saigon, Sch. Pharmacy, Vietnam, 1973-75; BS in Chem. magna cum laude, Lebanon Valley Coll., Annville, Pa., 1979; MD, U. Pitts., 1983; D (hon.), U. Morón, 2002. Diplomate Am. Bd. Surgery, Am. Bd. Thoracic Surgery. Intern, resident gen. surgery U. Pitts., 1983-86, rsch. fellow, cardiothoracic surgery, 1986-87, sr. and chief resident, gen. surgery, 1987-89, resident cardiothoracic surgery, 1989-92, asst. prof. surgery, Sch. of Medicine, 1992-97, dir. adult cardiac transplant program, Sch. of Medicine, 1993-97, assoc. dir. heart transplant and artificial heart program, 1997-98, dir. cardiothoracic transplant rsch., 1997-98; dir. extracorporeal membrane oxygenation svc. Presbyn. U. Hosp., Pitts., 1993-98; dir. cardiopulmonary transplantation and artifical heart program, divsn. cardiothoracic surgery U. Miami Sch. Medicine, 1998—; assoc. prof. surgery U. Miami Sch. Medicine, 1998—2002, prof., 2002—. Prof. surgery U. Miami Sch. Medicine, 2002—. Contbr. chpts. to books, articles to profl. jours. Recipient Am. Chem. award, 1979, Radiology award U. Pitts., 1983, Dalsemer rsch. scholar award Am. Lung Assn., 1997-99; ACS Faculty fellowship award, 1994-96; grantee Children's Hosp. Pitts., 1987, Am. Heart Assn., 1987-89, 94-96, 96-99, Thoracic Surgery Found., 1996-97, 97-98, Am. Lung Assn., 1997—, Presbyn. U. Hosp., 1987-89, NIH, 1999—. Fellow Am. Coll. Surgeons; mem. Am. Soc. Artificial Internal Organs, Internat. Soc. Heart and Lung Transplantation, Soc. Critical Care Medicine, Am. Assn. Advancement of Sci., Am. Soc. Transplant Surgeons, Soc. Thoracic Surgeons, Am. Assn. Thoracic Surgery, Extracorporeal Life Support Organization, Assn. for Acad. Surgery, Phi Alpha Epsilon. Home: 13250 SW 67th Ave Miami FL 33156-6929 Office: U Miami Sch Medicine Divsn Cardiothoracic Surgery PO Box 016960 (R-114) Miami FL 33101 Office Phone: 305-355-5070. Business E-Mail: spham@med.miami.edu.

PHAMBU, NSOKI, physical chemist, researcher; s. Cyrile Niati Phambu and Esther Khebani; m. Rose Lusangi Diala, Feb. 28, 1991; children: David Tsimba, Esther Nzuzi. PhD, Universite Henri Poincare, Nancy, France, 1996. Asst. prof. Johnson C. Smith U., Charlotte, NC, 1999—. Program dir. Johnson C.Smith U., Charlotte, NC, 2003—. Contbr. articles to profl. jour.; dir.: (program) Minority Biomedical Research Support (Program Dir., 2003). Youth ministry (leader) Fulllife Ch., Concord, NC, 1999—2003. Grantee Program Dir., Nat. Inst. of Health, 4. Mem.: Am. Chem. Soc. Achievements include research in Aluminum chemistry in water; effect of processing modes on the residual cyanogens in cassava roots; synthesis of aluminum hydroxide nanoparticles by precipitation method; interaction between toxic metals and polymers in water; design of preparation and characterization of aluminum hydroxide polymorphs. Home: 7407 E Quail Wood Dr Charlotte NC 28226 Office: Johnson C Smith Univ 100 Beatties Ford Rd Charlotte NC 28216 Office Phone: 704-378-1298. Business E-Mail: pnsoki2@jcsu.edu.

PHAN, ANH-VU, adult education educator, researcher; b. Saigon (Ho Chi Minh City), Vietnam, Aug. 16, 1959; s. Tinh Van Phan and Hao Thi Ly; m. Tran-Nam Phan, Jan. 4, 1995; 1 child, Johann Anh-Huy. B in Mech. Engring., Ho Chi Minh City U. of Tech., Vietnam, 1977—82; DEA (MS equivalent), Institut Nat. Polytechnique de Grenoble, France, 1992—93; PhD, Ecole Polytechnique, U. of Montreal, Can., 1994—97. Asst. lectr., dept. mech. engring. Ho Chi Minh City U. of Tech., Vietnam, 1982—84, lectr., dept. mech. engring., 1984—92; consulting engr. RENAULT, Ho Chi Minh City, 1993—93; lectr., assoc. chair, dept. mech. engring. Ho Chi Minh City U. of Tech., Vietnam, 1993—94; post-doctoral rschr., dept. mech. engring. Ecole Polytechnique de Montreal, 1998—99; post-doctoral rsch. assoc. Computer Sci. and Math. Divsn., Oak Ridge Nat. Lab., Tenn., 1999—2001; rsch. staff mem. Computational Scis. and Engring. Divsn., Oak Ridge Nat. Lab., 2002; asst. prof., dept. mech. engring. U. of South Ala., 2002—. Contbr. numerous articles in profl. jours. Grantee Bourse d'Excellence, Govt. of Que., 1994-1997, post-doctoral fellowship, Ecole Polytechnique de Montreal, 1998—99, Bourse de Stage, French Govt., 1992—93, post-doctoral rsch. assocs. fellowship, Oak Ridge Associated Universities, 1999—2001. Mem.: Am. Soc. for Engring. Edn., Internat. Assn. for Computational Mechanics, US Assn. for Computational Mechanics, Internat. Soc. of Structural and Multidisciplinary Optimization (assoc.). Achievements include research in Further development of the Boundary Contour Method for applications in Stress Analysis, Shape Optimization and Linear Fracture Mechanics; modeling the growth of nanostructures and the simulation of machining processes; invention of Development of a new crack tip element for Fracture Mechanics using the Boundary Element Methods. Office: U of South Alabama EGCB 212 307 University Blvd Mobile AL 36688-0002 E-mail: vphan@usouthal.edu.

PHAN, LONG THANH, structural engineer, researcher; b. Saigon, Vietnam, July 1, 1958; arrived in U.S., 1981; s. Tru Thanh Phan and Thanh Thi Dang; m. Trinh Thi Nguyen, Jan. 14, 1984; 1 child, Dexter Duy Viet Phan. BS in Civil Engring., PhuTho Poly. U., Saigon, 1980; MS in Civil Engring., Wash. U., 1984, PhD in Civil Engring., 1988. Registered profl. engr., Va., 1993. Rsch. structural engr. Nat. Inst. Stds. and Tech., Gaithersburg, Md., 1984—. Sr. mem. modelling and applications of mech. concrete properties at high temperatures com. Internat. Union Labs. and Experts in Constrn. Materials, Systems and Structures (RILEM), Paris, 1998—; chmn. fire protection structures com. Am. Concrete Inst., Ann Harbor, Mich., 1999—. Co-author: (spl. 9-11 report) The Pentagon Building Performance Report. Basketball coach St. Ambrose Cath. Sch., Arlington, Va. Mem.: ASCE. Achievements include research in punching shear resistance of Arctic offshore structures; effect of fire on high-strength concrete structures; serving as expert team member evaluating performance of Pentagon structures following the September 11 attacks. Avocations: travel, reading, soccer, building/carpentry, coaching basketball.

PHAN, RICHARD MAN, chemist; b. Saigon, Vietnam, July 30, 1970; came to U.S., 1993; s. Hong Van Phan and Tan Thi Nguyen; m. Ha Ngan Phung. BS, U. Utah, 1998, PhD, 2003. Project scientist Battelle, Dugway, Utah, 2003—04; sr. scientist Geomet Techs., Dugway, 2004—. NIH fellow, 2000. Mem. Golden Key Nat. Honor Soc. Office: Dugway Proving Ground PO Box 247 Dugway UT 84022 Home: 716 Deer Hollow Rd Tooele UT 84074 Office Phone: 435-831-7332. E-mail: phanmr@yahoo.com.

PHANSTIEL, HOWARD G. managed health care company executive; BA in Political Sci., M in Pub. Adminstrn., Syracuse U. Exec./mgmt. Prudential Bache Internat. Bank/Securities, Marine Midland Banks, Sallie Mae; exec. v.p. fin./info. svcs. WellPoint Health Networks, Inc., Woodland Hills, Calif.; chmn., CEO ARV Assisted Living, Inc., Costa Mesa, Calif.; exec. v.p., CFO PacifiCare Health Sys., Inc., Calif., 2000, pres., CEO, 2000—04, pres., CEO, chmn., 2004—. Office: PacifiCare Health Sys 3120 W Lake Ctr Dr Santa Ana CA 92704*

PHARES, ALAIN JOSEPH, physicist, researcher; b. Beirut, Apr. 20, 1942; came to U.S., 1975, naturalized, 1982; s. Joseph Michel and Renee Cecile (Doummar) P.; m. Claude Tawa, July 27, 1968; children— Caroline, Denis, Pascal. BS in Engring., St. Joseph U., 1964; Docteur-es-Sciences, U. Paris, 1971; PhD, Harvard U., 1973. Research fellow Nat. Council Sci. Research, Lebanon, 1973-75; assoc. prof. Lebanese U., 1973-75; research fellow Internat. Centre Theoretical Physics, Trieste, Italy, 1974, Harvard U., 1975-76; vis. asst. prof. U. Mont., 1976-77; asst. prof. physics Villanova U., Pa., 1977-79, assoc. prof., 1979-82, prof., 1982—, chmn. dept., 1981-91, dir. secondary sch. sci., 1981-94. Contbr. articles to profl. jours. Fellow, IAEA, 1974; grantee, NSF, 1991—98, PSC, 1991—, SDSC, 2002—03; French Govt. fellow, 1964—66. Mem. Am. Phys. Soc., Internat. Assn. Math. and Computers in Simulation, Sigma Xi Office: Villanova U Dept Physics Villanova PA 19085 Office Phone: 610-519-4889. Business E-Mail: alain.phares@villanova.edu.

PHARES, LYNN LEVISAY, public relations communications executive; b. Brownwood, Tex., Aug. 6, 1947; m. C. Kirk Phares, Aug. 22, 1971; children: Laura, Margaret, Adele, Jessica. BA, La. State U., 1970; MA, U. Nebr., 1987. Asst. to advt. mgr. La. Nat. Bank, 1970-71; writer, producer, asst. v.p., account exec. Smith, Kaplan, Allen & Reynolds, Inc., Omaha, 1971-80; assoc. dir. pub. affairs U. Nebr. Med. Ctr., 1980-83; dir. pub. rels. ConAgra Inc., Omaha, 1985-87, v.p. pub. rels., 1987-90, v.p. pub. rels. and cmty. affairs, 1990-97, v.p., corp. rels., 1997-2000. Pres. ConAgra Found., Feeding Children Better Found. Office: ConAgra Inc 1 ConAgra Dr Omaha NE 68102-5001

PHEFFER, AUDREY IRIS, state legislator; b. Aug. 14, 1941; d. Alex and Ruth Fagin; children: Mitchell, Stacey. Grad. cum laude, Queens Coll./CUNY, 1982. Advisor spl. edn. Occupational Tng. Ctr., 1973-77; mem. Neighborhood Stblzn. program N.Y.C. Commn. Human Rights, 1977, acting dir. Far Rockaway office, organizer Rockaway Interracial Coun.; exec. asst. N.Y. State Senator, 1980; spl. asst. to Pres. of City Coun., N.Y.C., 1986; mem. N.Y. State Assembly, 1987—. Mem. aging com., alcoholism and substance abuse com., govt. employees com., higher edn. com., social svc. com., vet. affairs com. Mem. 1st Police Precinct Cmty. and Youth Coun. Home: 108-14 Cross Bay Blvd Ozone Park NY 11417 Office: NY State Assembly 941 Legislative Ofc Bldg Albany NY 12248

PHELAN, ARTHUR JOSEPH, financial executive; b. N.Y.C., Oct. 26, 1915; s. Arthur Joseph and Josephine Adelaide (Barrett) P.; m. Mary Frances Ryan, Feb. 11, 1939; children— Jane Carolee, Leslie Diane, Sandra Christine. Student, Am. Inst. Banking, 1934-35, NYU, 1935-36. With Guaranty Trust Co. of N.Y., 1933-37; accountant N.Y. Post, 1937-38, Webb & Knapp, Inc., N.Y.C., 1938-41, asst. sec., 1941, comptroller, 1942-44, treas., 1944-53, v.p., treas., 1953-55, sr. v.p., dir., 1955-65; also trustee employees profit sharing plan, exec. v.p. David Greenewald Assocs., Inc., 1965-66; sr. v.p. Lefrak Orgn., Inc., Forest Hills, N.Y., 1966-92. Exec. v.p., dir. LOGO Inc., Tulsa, Okla., 1976-92. Mem.: North Hempstead Country. Roman Catholic. Home: 88 Summit Rd Port Washington NY 11050-3341

PHELAN, CHARLES SCOTT, retired lawyer; b. Saranac Lake, N.Y., Mar. 21, 1926; m. Ruth Rene Kuntzleman, Sept. 4, 1948; children: Susan P. Moser, Donna K. Merrick, Barbara K. Glumac. BSEE, Pa. State U., 1949; LLB, George Washington U., 1954. Bar: N.Y. 1955, U.S. Patent Office, 1956, U.S. Ct. Appeals (fed. cir.) 1982. Elec. engr. GE, Schenectady, N.Y., 1949-52, patent asst., 1950-54; sr. atty. AT&T Bell Labs., Whippany, N.J. and other cities, 1954-86; pvt. practice Millington, N.J., 1987-95; ret., 1995. Active Passaic Twp. (N.J.) Bd. Edn., 1962-64; vol. IRS, 1986-, Telecom Pioneers, 198-. 2d lt. U.S. Army, 1944-47. Mem. ABA, Am. Intellectual Property Law Assn., N.J. Patent Law Assn. (pres. 1964-65), Tau Beta Pi, Eta Kappa Nu. Avocations: fishing, hiking, sketching.

PHELAN, ELLEN, artist; b. Detroit, Nov. 3, 1943; d. Thomas Edward and Katherine Louise (Gojlewicz) P; m. Joel Elias Shapiro, Nov. 22, 1978. BFA, Wayne State U., 1969, MFA, 1971. Instr. Wayne State U., Detroit, 1969-72, Fairleigh Dickinson U., 1974, Mich. State U., East Lansing, 1974-75, Calif. Inst. Arts, 1978-79, Bard Coll., 1980, NYU, 1981, Sch. of Visual Arts, 1981-83, Calif. Inst. Arts, 1983; prof. of practice of studio art Harvard U., Cambridge, Mass., 1995—. Milton Avery vis. lectr. Bard Coll., 1994. One-woman exhbns. include Willis Gallery, Detroit, 1972, 74, Artist's Space, N.Y.C., 1975, Susanne Hilberry Gallery, Birmingham, Mich., 1977, 79, 81, 82, 84, 86, 88, 90, 92, 94, Wadsworth Athenaeum, Hartford, Conn., 1979, Ruth Schaffner Gallery, L.A., 1979, The Clocktower, N.Y.C., 1980, Hansen-Fuller-Goldeen Gallery, San Francisco, 1980, 82, Dart Gallery, Chgo., 1981, Barbara Toll Fine Arts, N.Y.C., 1982, 85, 86, 87-88, 89, 90, 92, 93, Asher/Faure, L.A., 1989, 92, 94, Balt. Mus. Art, 1989, Albright-Knox Art Gallery, Buffalo, 1991, U. Mass. Amherst Fine Arts Ctr., 1992, Saidye Bronfman Ctr., Montreal, Que., 1993, Contemporary Mus., Honolulu, 1993, John Stoller, Inc., Mpls., 1993, Cin. Art Mus., 1994; exhibited in group shows at Detroit Inst. Arts, 1970, 80, Willis Gallery, Detroit, 1971, 79, J.L. Hudson Gallery, Detroit, 1972, Cranbrook Acad. Art, Bloomfield Hills, Mich., 1972, 79, 84, Grand Rapids (Mich.) Art Mus., 1974, Paula Cooper Gallery, N.Y.C., 1975, 76, 77, 78, 79, 90, Fine Arts Bldg., N.Y.C., 1976, Acad. der Kunste, Berlin, 1976, Susanne Hilberry Gallery, Birmingham, 1976-77, 83, 85, 91, Willard Gallery, N.Y.C., 1977, Kansas City (Mo.) Art Inst., 1977, N.A.M.E. Gallery, Chgo., 1977, Hallwalls, Buffalo, 1977, Mus. Modern Art, N.Y.C., 1978, 89, 92, Weatherspoon Art Gallery U. N.C., Greensboro, 1979, 92, Albright-Knox Gallery, Buffalo, 1979, Brown U., Providence, 1980, XIII Olympic Winter Games, Lake Placid, N.Y., 1980, Jeffrey Fuller Fine Art, Phila., 1980, Portland (Oreg.) Ctr. for Visual Arts, 1980, The Drawing Ctr., N.Y.C., 1980, 82, Brooke Alexander Gallery, N.Y.C., 1980, Mus. Contemporary Art, Chgo., 1980, 81, P.S. 1 Mus., N.Y.C., 1981, 92, Art Latitude Gallery, N.Y.C., 1981, Leo Castelli Gallery, N.Y.C., 1981, Sutton Place, Guildford, Eng., 1982, Gallerie d'Arte Moderna di Ca'Pesaro, Venice, Italy, 1982, Inst. Contemporary Art of Virgini Mus., Richmond, Va., 1982, Galerie Biedermann, Munich, 1982, Thomas Segal Gallery, Boston, 1983, Fuller-Goldeen Gallery, San Francisco, 1983, 86, William Paterson Coll., Wayne, N.J., 1983, 89, Artist's Space, N.Y.C., 1983, 84, Harborside Indsl. Ctr., Bklyn., 1983, Orgn. Ind. Artists, N.Y.C., 1984, Bernice Steinbaum Gallery, N.Y.C., 1984, Brentwood Gallery, St. Louis, 1984, U. Calif., Irvine, 1984, U. No. Iowa Gallery Art, Cedar Falls, 1984, Hudson River Mus., N.Y.C., 1984, Barbara Toll Fine Arts, N.Y.C., 1984, 85, 86, 87, Detroit Focus Gallery, 1984, Cable Gallery, N.Y.C., 1984, Wayne State U., Detroit, 1984, Matthews Hamilton Gallery, Phila., 1984, Barbara Krakow Gallery, Boston, 1984, BlumHelman Warehouse, N.Y.C., 1984, Pam Adler Gallery, N.Y.C., 1985, Daniel Weinberg Gallery, L.A., 1985, 89, Knight Gallery, Charlotte, N.C., 1985, Bank of Boston, 1986, Whitney Mus. Am. Art, Stamford, Conn., 1987, 89, Scott Hansen Gallery, N.Y.C., 1987, Saxon-Lee Gallery, L.A., 1987, Parrish Art Mus., East Hampton, N.Y., 1987, Curt Marcus Gallery, N.Y., 1988, Loughelton Gallery, N.Y.C., 1988, 90, Whitney Mus. Am. Art, N.Y.C., 1988, 91, Hillwood Art Gallery C.W. Post Campus, Brookville, N.Y., 1989, USIA traveling exbhn., 1989, Edward Thorp Gallery, N.Y.C., 1989, Pine Street Lobby Gallery, San Francisco, 1989, Fuller Gross Gallery, San Francisco, 1989, Solo Press/Soho Gallery, N.Y.C., 1989, Maxwell Davidson Gallery, N.Y.C., 1989, Blum Helman Gallery, N.Y.C., 1989, R.I.S.D., Providence, 1989, Graham Modern, N.Y.C., 1990, Hood Mus. Art Dartmouth Coll., Hanover, N.H., 1990, 92, New Britain Mus. Am. Art, Hartford, Conn., 1991, Asher-Faure, L.A., 1991, Annina Nosei Gallery, N.Y.C., 1991, Lintas Worldwide, N.Y.C., 1991, Nina Fredenheim Gallery, Buffalo, 1991, Molica Guidarte Gallery, N.Y.C., 1991, Squibb Gallery, Princeton, N.J., 1991, Cleve. State U. Gallery, 1992, Ind. Curators Inc., N.Y.C., 1992, Wexner Ctr. for the Arts, Columbus, Ohio, 1992, Transamerica Corp., San Francisco, 1992, The Gallery Three Zero, N.Y.C., 1992, Haggerty Mus. Art, Milw., Barbara Methes Gallery, N.Y.C., Asher Fauve Gallery, L.A., Hillwood Art Mus., Brookville, N.Y., Pamela Auchincloss Gallery, N.Y.C., Leo Castelli Gallery, N.Y.C.; represented in permanent collections Mus. Modern Art, N.Y.C., Whitney Mus. Am. Art, N.Y.C., Bklyn. Mus., Walker Art Ctr., Mpls., Balt. Mus., Toledo Mus. Art, Hood Mus. Dartmouth Coll., High Mus. Art, Albright-Knox Art Gallery, Moderna Museet, Stockholm, Mus. Contemporary Art, Mexico City, Detroit Inst. Arts, MIT, Whitehead Inst., Philip Morris, Inc., Volvo Corp., Chase Manhattan Bank, Chem. Bank, BankAm., Bank of Am., Prudential Ins. Co., U.S. Trust & Co., Inter Metro Industries, Lannan Found., numerous pvt. collections. Nat. Endowment for Arts grantee, 1978-79; recipient Am. Acad. Arts and Letters award, 1995, Arts Achievement award Wayne State U., 1989.

PHELAN, JOHN DENSMORE, insurance executive, consultant; b. Kalamazoo, Aug. 31, 1914; s. John and Ida (Densmore) P.; m. Isabel McLaughln, July 31, 1937; children: John Walter, William Paul, Daniel Joseph. BA magna cum laude, Carleton Coll., 1935. Reporter New Bedford (Mass.) Std.-Times, 1935-36; with Hardware Mut. Ins. Co., Stevens Point, Wis., 1936-45, Am. States Ins. Co. (name now Safeco Ins.), Indpls., 1945-90, pres., 1963-76, chmn., 1976-79, also bd. dirs. numerous subs. Bd. govs. Internat. Ins. Soc. Author: Business Interruption Primer, 1949, also later edits; contbr. articles to profl. jours. Past pres. Marion County Assn. Mental Health; chmn. emeritus CPCU-Harry J. Loman Found. Named to Hon. Order Ky. Cols., Sagamore of Wabash. Mem. CPCU Soc. (past nat. pres.), CLU Soc., Woodland Country Club (Indpls.), El Conquistador Country Club, Phi Beta Kappa. Presbyterian. Home: 315 Park Side Pl Indian Harbor Beach FL 32937-4803

PHELAN, JOHN M. lawyer; b. Phila., Jan. 12, 1939; s. James J. and Gertrude (Murphy) P.; m. Joanne D'Arcy, Sept. 10, 1966; children: D'Arcy, John Jr., Sean. BS in Econs., U. Pa., 1960; LLB, Temple U., 1963. Bar: Pa. 1964, U.S. Dist. Ct. (ea. dist.) Pa. 1964, U.S. Ct. Appeals (3d cir.) 1972. Law clerk to chief justice Supreme Ct. of Pa., Phila., 1964-65; asst. dist. atty., Phila., 1966-69; assoc. Morgan, Lewis & Bockius, Phila., 1965-66, 1969-81; ptnr. Phelan, Pettit & Biedrzycki, Phila., 1981—. Mem. Phila. Country Club (Gladwyne chpt. tennis chmn. 1981-83), Union League (Phila.). Republican. Roman Catholic. Office: Phelan Pettit & Biedrzycki 121 S Broad St Ste 1600 Philadelphia PA 19107-4533

PHELAN, MARTHA ARMSTRONG, realtor; b. Shelby, Ohio, July 26, 1927; d. George Woodburn and Anna Louise (Wood) A.; m. Vincent Roche Phelan, Aug. 9, 1952 (dec. July 2000); children: Elizabeth Ann Riley, David Woodburn, Anne Louise. BA, Oberlin Coll., 1949. Sec. U.S. Govt., Washington, 1950-52; adminstrv. officer Com. for Free Asia, N.Y.C., 1952-53; legal sec. Atty. V.R. Phelan, Shelby, Ohio, 1975-79; realtor Mattox Realtors, Mansfield, Ohio, 1976-93, Hancock Agy., Shelby, Ohio, 1993—. Precinct committeeman Rep. Orgn., Shelby, 1965—; poll worker Richland County Bd. Elections, Shelby, 1960—; mem. exec. com. Richland County Reps., Mansfield, 1965—; mem. Kingwood Ctr. Gardens; elder Presbyn. Ch., mem. choir, pres. Presbyn. Women, 2002—. Mem. Nat. Assn. Realtors, Mansfield Bd. Realtors, Rotary, Shelby Garden Club (pres. 1997-99), Shelby Women's Club (sec. 1990-01), Presyn. Choir 45 yrs., ch. session 7 yrs., Pres. Presbyn. Women 20 yrs. Republican. Presbyterian. Avocations: gardening, reading, creative arts and crafts, swimming, music. Home: 26 Woodland Rd Shelby OH 44875

PHELAN, RICHARD MAGRUDER, mechanical engineer; b. Moberly, Mo., Sept. 20, 1921; s. Frederick William and Ethel Ray (Magruder) P.; m. Olive Bernice McIntosh, May 25, 1951; children— William James, Susan Ray. Student, Moberly Jr. Coll., 1939-41; BS in Mech. Engring, U. Mo., Columbia, 1943; M.M.E., Cornell U., 1950; postgrad., U. Mich., 1956-57. Instr. Cornell U., 1947-50, asst. prof. mech. engring., 1950-56, assoc. prof., 1956-62, prof., 1962-87, prof. emeritus, 1988—. Author: Fundamentals of Mechanical Design, 1957, 3d rev. edit., 1970, Dynamics of Machinery, 1967, Automatic Control Systems, 1977. Served with USNR, 1943-46. Mem. ASME, Am. Soc. Engring. Edn., Soc. Exptl. Stress Analysis, Am. Gear Mfrs. Assn., AAUP, AAAS, N.Y. Acad. Scis., Soc. Exptl. Mechanics, Sigma Xi, Phi Kappa Phi, Pi Tau Sigma, Tau Beta Pi. Home: 4 Cornell Walk Ithaca NY 14850-6145 Office: Cornell U Upson Hall Ithaca NY 14853

PHELAN, ROBIN ERIC, lawyer; b. Steubenville, Ohio, Dec. 28, 1945; s. Edward John and Dorothy (Borkowski) P.; m. JoAnn Keach, June 27, 1970 (dec. May 18, 1994); children: Travis McCoy, Tiffany Marie, Trevor Monroe; m. Melinda Jo Ricketts, May 27, 1995; 1 child, Taezja Monet. BSBA, Ohio State U., 1967, JD, 1970. Bar: Tex. 1971, U.S. Ct. Appeals (5th cir.) 1981, U.S. Ct. Appeals (11th cir.) 1981, U.S. Ct. Appeals (6th cir.) 1986, U.S. Ct. Appeals (10th cir.) 1988, U.S. Supreme Ct. Ptnr. Haynes and Boone, Dallas, 1970—. Co-author: Bankruptcy Practice and Strategy, 1987, Cowans Bankruptcy Law and Practice, 1987, Annual Survey of Bankruptcy Law, 1988, Bankruptcy Litigation Manual; contbr. articles to profl. jours. Mem. ABA (chmn. insolvency and secured transactions com. internat. law sect.), Internat. Bar Assn., Internat. Insolvency Inst. (bd. dirs.), Am. Bankruptcy Inst. (dir., past pres.), Am. Coll. Bankruptcy, State Bar Tex. (chmn. bankruptcy law com. sect. bus. law 1989-91), Dallas Bar Assn. Roman Catholic. Avocation: athletics. Home: 4214 Woodfin St Dallas TX 75220-6416 E-mail: phelanr@haynesboone.com.

PHELAN, THOMAS, clergyman, academic administrator, educator; b. Albany, N.Y., Apr. 11, 1925; s. Thomas William and Helen (Rausch) P. AB (N.Y. State Regents scholar 1942, President's medal 1945), Coll. Holy Cross, Worcester, Mass., 1945; S.T.L., Catholic U. Am., 1951; postgrad., Oxford (Eng.) U., 1958-59, 69-70. Ordained priest Roman Cath. Ch., 1951; pastor, tchr., adminstr. Diocese of Albany, 1951-58; resident Cath. chaplain Rensselaer Poly. Inst., Troy, N.Y., 1959-72, prof. history, 1972—, dean Sch. Humanities and Social Scis., 1972-95, inst. historian, inst. dean, sr. adviser to pres., 1995—. Chmn. architecture and bldg. commn. Diocese Albany, 1968-2003; cons. in field. Author: Hudson Mohawk Gateway, 1985, 2001, Achieving the Impossible, 1995; author monographs, articles, revs. in field. Treas. The Rensselaer Newman Found., 1962-2002; pres. Hudson-Mohawk Indsl. Gateway, 1971-84, bd. dirs. exec. com. 1984—; mem. WMHT Ednl. Telecomm. Bd., 1966-77, 84-90, chmn. 1973-77; chmn. Troy Hist. Dist. and Landmarks Rev. Commn., 1975-86, chmn. hist. adv. com., 1987-2003; v.p. Preservation League N.Y. State, 1979-82, mem. trustees coun., 1982-87, 89—, pres. 1987-89; sec. and bd. dirs. Ptnrs. for Sacred Places, 1989—; bd. dirs. Hall of History Found., 1983-87; trustee Troy Pub. Libr., 1992—. With USN, 1943-46. Recipient Paul J. Hallinan award Nat. Newman Chaplains Assn., 1967, Ann. award Albany Arts League, 1977, Disting. Cmty. Svc. award Rensselaer Poly. Inst., 1979, Edward Fox Demers medal Alumni Assn. Rensselaer Poly. Inst., 1986, Disting. Svc. award Hudson-Mohawk Consortium of Colls. and Univs., 1988; named Acad. Laureate of the SUNY Found. at Albany, 1988; Danforth Found. fellow, 1969-70; grantee Homeland Found., 1958-59, Dorothy Thomas Found., 1969-70. Fellow Soc. Arts, Religion and Contemporary Culture; mem. Ch. Soc. Coll. Work (dir., exec. com. 1970—), Am. Conf. Acad. Deans, Liturgical Conf., Soc. Indsl. Archaeology, Assn. Internat. pour l'Etudes des Religions Prehistoriques et Ethnologiques, Cath. Campus Ministry Assn., Cath. Art Assn., Assn. for Religion and the Intellectual Life (bd. dirs. 1987—), Soc. History of Tech. Clubs: Ft. Orange, Troy Country; Squadron A (N.Y.C.). Home: 5 Whitman Ct Troy NY 12180-4732 Office: Rensselaer Poly Inst Troy NY 12180 Business E-Mail: phelan@rpi.edu. *Service and community building have motivated most of my business and personal actions. I received these values from my parents and from the church. I work to make positive contributions towards a world in which there is more justice and consequent hope of peace.*

PHELIZON, JEAN FRANCOIS, business executive; b. Paris, Apr. 28, 1946; s. Christian and Anne (Camuset) P.; m. Isabelle Delatour, July 3, 1971; children: Camille, Constance, Charlotte. MBA and MS, Paris U., 1970, PhD in Econ. Sci., 1975. Contr. Flat Glass div. St. Gobain, Paris, 1979; CFO St. Gobain Spain, Madrid, 1983-85; CFO paper wood div. St. Gobain, Paris, 1985-89; CEO, Lembacel, Lyon, France, 1988-89; CFO, Compagnie St. Gobain, Paris, 1989-2000, sr. v.p., 1998—; pres., CEO, Saint-Gobain Corp., 2000—; CEO, Certain Teed, 2000—04. Editor: Economica, 1970, 2d edit. 1977, 3d edit. 1985, 4th edit. 1998, also 1998, 99, 2001, 02, 03, Masson, 1981, 2d edit. 1984, Citil (China), 2004. Decorated chevalier Order of Merit, Legion of Honor. Home: 1315 Wrenfield Way Villanova PA 19085 Office: SG Corp PO Box 860 750 E Swedesford Rd Valley Forge PA 19482 E-mail: jfp@sgcna.com.

PHELPS, AARON K(AY), lawyer; b. Aransas Pass, Tex., Mar. 13, 1918; s. Robert Noble and Lela Mae (Main) P.; m. Nancy Lee Worley, May 1, 1940; children— Hilarie, Hayden; m. Helen Patricia Moore, Sept. 19, 1981. A.B., Transylvania U., Lexington, Ky., 1941; LL.B., U. Okla., 1942. Bar: Okla. 1942, Calif. 1945. Practice, Los Angeles, 1948-50, Corona del Mar, Calif., 1950 65; referee in bankruptcy U.S. Bankruptcy Ct. (cen. dist.) Calif., 1965, judge, 1965-84; with Speers Dana Teal & Balfour, Costa Mesa, Calif., 1984—; adj. prof. Western State U. Law. Office: Speers Dana et al Cen Bank Bldg 611 Anton Blvd Costa Mesa CA 92626-7005

PHELPS, ASHTON, JR., newspaper publisher; b. New Orleans, Nov. 4, 1945; s. Ashton Sr. and Jane Cary (George) Phelps; m. Suzanne Dupuy Phelps; children: Cary Clifton, Mary Louise, Sanders. BA, Yale U., 1967; JD, Tulane U., 1970. Trainee Times-Picayune Pub. Corp., New Orleans, 1970—71, asst. to pub., 1971—79, pres., pub., 1979—97, pub., 1997—. Chmn. Audit Com. of Associated Press, 1986—90, mem. nominating com., 1996—2002; bd. dirs. Bur. Govtl. Rsch., New Orleans, 1973—89, Xavier U. La., New Orleans, 1974—82, Internat. House, New Orleans, 1981—83, Coun. for Better La., 1982—85, Ochsner Found. Hosp., New Orleans, 1982—, Pub. Affairs Rsch. Coun., New Orleans, 1982—85, 2000—, La. Children's Mus., New Orleans, 1983—90, Yale Alumni Assn. La., 1985, Newspaper Advt. Bur. Future of Advt. Com., 1986—89, Met. Area Com., New Orleans, UNCF, 2004—. Mem.: La. Press Assn. (bd. dirs. 1984—93, v.p. 1989—90, pres. 1991—92), So. Newspaper Pubs. Assn. (bd. dirs. 1982—85, found. bd. dirs. 1982—83, pres. 1990—91). Avocation: tennis. Office: The Times-Picayune 3800 Howard Ave New Orleans LA 70125-1429

PHELPS, BARTON CHASE, architect, educator; b. Bklyn., June 27, 1946; s. Julian Orville and Elizabeth Willis (Faulk) P.; m. Karen Joy Simonson; 1 child, Charlotte Simonson Phelps. BA in Art with honors, Williams Coll., 1968; MArch, Yale U., 1973. Registered architect, Calif. With Colin St. John Wilson & Ptnrs., London, 1972-73, Frank O. Gehry and Assocs., Inc., Santa Monica, Calif., 1973-76, Charles Moore/Urban Innovations Group, L.A., 1976-78; dir. architecture Urban Innovations Group, L.A., 1980-84; prin. Barton Phelps & Assocs., L.A., 1984—; asst. prof. architecture Rice U. Sch. of Architecture, Houston, 1977-79; asst. dean Grad. Sch. Architecture and Urban Planning, UCLA, 1980-83; former prof. architecture Sch. Arts and Architecture UCLA. Faculty mem. Nat. Endowment Arts, Mayors Inst. for City Design, 1990, 92. Author, editor Architecture California, 1988-92, mem. editl. bd., 1998; editor: Views From the River, 1998; mem. editl. bd. Archtl. Record, 1998—. Fellow Graham Found. for Advanced Studies in the Fine Arts, 1989, 96, Nat. Endowment for the Arts, 1990, 98. Mem. AIA (Coll. of Fellows, chair nat. com. on design, design excellence program USGSA, recipient design awards for L.A. Pub. Libr., Los Feliz and Woodland Hills, Cabrillo Marine Aquarium, Royce Hall at UCLA, Arroyo House, Kranz House, North Range Clark Libr. UCLA, L.A. Dept. Water and Power Ctrl. Dist. Hdqrs., No. Hollywood Pump Sta., East Bldg. Seeds U. Elem. Sch., UCLA, Inst. Honor for Collaborative Design, Games XXIII Olympiad L.A. 1984), L.A. Conservancy (bd. dirs.). Democrat. Home: 10256 Lelia Ln Los Angeles CA 90077-3144 Office: Barton Phelps & Assocs 5514 Wilshire Blvd Los Angeles CA 90036-3829

PHELPS, BONNIE NOREEN, language educator, secondary school educator; d. Norton Robert and Joyce Madelaine Phelps. B, U. Colo., 1966; M, Rivier Coll., 1974. Cert. tchr. State of NH., 1974. Sr. english tchr. Nashua H.S. North, NH, 1966—. Running start faculty mem. NH. Cmty. Tech. Coll., Claremont, NH, 2000—. Author: (poetry) The 14th (Illiand Lit. Presdl. Lit. award and hon. award, 1994), Hurricane Bonnie in POETRY'S ELITE Poetry.com, (poem) Sibilance (semifinalist N.Am. Open Poetry contest, 1993). Judge Yankee Pen Poetry Contest. Mem.: AFT, NCTE (assoc.), Poetry Soc. N.H. (corr.; sec. of round robins 1987—88). Independent. Avocations: reading, writing, research on alternative health. Office: Nashua High School North 10 Chuck Druding Drive Nashua NH 03063

PHELPS, CHARLES ELLIOTT, economics professor, director; b. N.Y.C., Apr. 20, 1943; s. McKinnie L. and Carolyn (McCleery) P.; m. Dale L. King, Sept. 2, 1967; children: Darin, Teresa. BA in Math., Pomona Coll., 1965; MBA, U. Chgo., 1968, PhD, 1973. Economist RAND Corp., Santa Monica, Calif., 1973-84; prof. econs. U. Rochester, N.Y., 1984—, provost, 1994—. Cons. JUREcon, Inc., L.A., 1977-86; pvt. cons., Rochester, N.Y., 1986—. Author: Health Economics, 3d edit., 2002; also over 70 articles. Fellow Nat. Bur. for Econ. Rsch.; mem. Inst. Medicine, Am. Econ. Assn., Nat. Acad. Social Ins., Soc. for Med. Decision Making (trustee 1991-93), Assn. for Pub. Policy Analysis (sec. 1982-91). Avocations: photography, archery, astronomy, canoeing, woodworking. Office: Office of the Provost U Rochester 200 Wallis Hall Rochester NY 14627-0001

PHELPS, CHARLOTTE DEMONTE, retired economics educator; b. East Orange, NJ, Jan. 26, 1933; d. Robert William and Marian Ethel (Page) DeMonte; m. Edmund Strother Phelps, 1957 (div. 1969). BA magna cum laude, Radcliffe Coll., 1955; MA, Yale U., 1956, PhD, 1961. Instr. Conn. Coll., New London, 1961; rsch. staff economist Cowles Found. and Econ. Growth Ctr., Yale U., 1963-65; postdoctoral rsch. fellow com. on econ. stblzn. Social Sci. Rsch. Coun., 1965-68; asst. prof. dept. econs. Temple U., Phila., 1967-68, assoc. prof., 1969-97, prof., 1998-2000; ret., 2000. Cons. Hay/McBer, 1999—2000. Author: Unconscious Motivation and Economic Choice, 1981; mem. editl. bd.: Jour. Econ. Behavior and Orgn., 1998—, Jour. Socio-Econs., 2001—; contbr. articles to profl. publs. Active Phila. Cmty. Coordinated Child Care Coun., 1970-72; schs. and scholarships com. Harvard-Radcliffe Clubs Phila., 1977-82. Named to Fulbright Sr. Specialist Roster, 2002—; grantee Murray Rsch. Ctr., Radcliffe Coll., 1998—2000, Smith Richardson Found., 1998—2000, Fulbright Sr. Specialists grant in Econs., Max Planck Inst. Rsch. in Econ. Sys., 2003; vis. fellow, Yale U., 1998—99, pre-doctoral grantee, Comm. on Money and Credit, 1959—60. Mem. Am. Econ. Assn., Soc. Advancement Behavioral Econs. (bd. dirs. 2003—), Assn. Yale Alumni (del. 1994-97), Yale Club Phila., Cosmopolitan Club Phila., Harvard Club Phila., Phi Beta Kappa. Home: 604 S Washington Sq Apt 2505 Philadelphia PA 19106-4129 Office: Temple U Dept Econs 879 Ritter Annex Philadelphia PA 19122 Office Phone: 215-204-1677. Business E-Mail: charlotte.phelps@temple.edu.

PHELPS, DAVID DWAIN, state agency administrator, former congressman; b. Eldorado, Ill., Oct. 26, 1947; m. Leslie Phelps; 4 children. BS, So. Ill. U. Mem. Ill. Ho. of Reps. from 118th dist., 1985-98; mem., 106th Congress from 19th Ill. dist., 1999—2003; mem. agr. com.; mem. small bus.; asst. sec. Ill. Dept. Transp., Springfield, Ill., 2003—. Mem. Transp. and Motor Vehicles, Appropriations I, Energy, Environ. and Natural Resources, Edn. Appropriations, Human Svcs., Elem. and Secondary Edn., Counties and Twp., Econ. Devel. Coms. Ill. Ho. of Reps., vice chmn. Coal Devel. and Mktg., Econ. and Urban Devel. Coms., chmn. Health Care Com. Democrat. Office: Ill Dept Transp 2300 S Dirksen Pkwy Rm 300 Springfield IL 62764

PHELPS, DENNIS LANE, minister, educator, author; b. Monroe, La., July 23, 1955; s. Vaughn Lavelle and Vestal (Humphreys) P.; m. Robbin Jean Loewer, May 27, 1979; children: Kristen Lane, David Loewer. BA, La. Coll., 1978; MDiv, New Orleans Bapt. Theol. Sem., 1981; PhD, Southwestern Bapt. Theol. Sem., 1990. Ordained to ministry Bapt. Ch., 1978; cert. intern supr. Coord. ch. ministries La. Moral and Civic Found., Baton Rouge, 1973-79; staff evangelist Dennis Phelps Evangelistic Ministries, 1979—; pastor Brownfields Bapt. Ch., Baton Rouge, 1981-82; grader/teaching fellow Southwestern Bapt. Theol. Sem., Ft. Worth, 1982-87; pastor St. Francis Village Protestant Fellowship, Crowley, Tex., 1986-88; assoc. prof. of preaching Bethel Theol. Sem., St. Paul, 1988-99; assoc. tchg. pastor, exec. adminstr. Severns Valley Ch., Elizabethtown, Ky., 1998—. V.p. Global Horizons, Inc., 1994—. Editor Jour. of Am. Acad. Ministry, 1995-98. Mem. strategy coun. AD2000: Mission Twin Cities, 1994-98; chmn. resolutions com. Ky. Bapt. Conv., 2000-2001; bd. dirs. Youth Connection, Inc., 1997-1999; v.p. Hardin County Ministerial Assn., 2002, pres. 2002-2003; bd. dirs., Helping Hand of the Heartland, 2002 . Named Southwesterner of Yr., Minn.-Wis. S.W. Bapt. Theol. Sem. Alumni, 1994. Mem. Inst. Bibl. Rsch., Religious Speech Comm. Assn., Acad. Homiletics, Am. Assn. Religion, Soc. Bibl. Lit., Assn. Practical Theology, Am. Acad. Ministry (charter), Nat. Storytelling Assn., Evang. Homiletics Soc. (charter), Southwestern Bapt. Theol. Sem. Alumni Assn. (pres. Ky. chpt. 1999-2000). Office: Severns Valley Ch PO Box 130 Elizabethtown KY 42702-0130

PHELPS, GEORGE GRAHAM, computer systems engineer, consultant; b. Radford, Va., Aug. 13, 1963; s. Eugene Graham and Flora Doris (Baird) P.; m. Vickie St. Claire, Feb. 19, 1994 (div. Feb. 1997); 1 stepchild, Chase Kevin Irby. BA in Polit. Sci., U. Tenn., 1986. Cert. Novell Netware engr.; cert. product specialist Microsoft Windows 3.1 and Windows 95, Microsoft Corp. Pers. clk. U.S. Army Total Army Pers. Agy., Washington, 1987-88, U.S. Army Corps Engrs., Washington, 1988; network sys. engr. U.S. Army RDAISA, Radford, Va., 1988—; computer cons. Acculan Consulting, Pulaski, Va., 1992—; prof. computer sci. New River C.C., Dublin, Va., 1996—. Vol. Habitat for Humanity, Christiansburg, Va., 1994, Montgomery County Xmas Store, Christiansburg, 1994—, Red Cross, Radford, Va., 1995. Methodist. Avocation: home improvement. Office: US Army RDAISA PO Box 4 Radford VA 24143-0004

PHELPS, GERRY CHARLOTTE, economist, minister; b. Norman, Okla., Oct. 15, 1931; d. George and Charlotte LeNoir (Yowell) P.; 1 child, Scott. BA, U. Tex., 1963, MA, 1984; MDiv, San Francisco Theol. Seminary, 1981. Cert. tchr., Calif. Lectr. in econs. U. Houston, 1966-69; pastor United Meth. Ch., Kelseyville, Calif., 1980-82; sr. pastor Bethany United Methodist Ch., Bakersfield, Calif., 1982-84; founding exec. dir. Bethany Svc. Ctr., Bakersfield, 1982-84; pres., founding exec. dir. Concern for the Poor, Inc., San Jose, Calif., 1985-92; pastor United Meth. Ch., Flatonia, Tex., 1993-97; founding exec. dir. CRISES, Austin, 1994-98, v.p. devel., 1998-99; pvt. practice cons. poverty issues, 1999—. Cons. in ch. growth, 2001—. Co-author: Nutrition for Better Living, 1999, Budgeting for Better Living, 1999; author: Out of the Iron Furnace, 2000, Up and Out: A Guide to True Compassion for the Poor, 2001. Mem. Task Force on the Homeless, San Jose, 1987, Santa Clara County, 1991. Recipient commendation Mayor of Bakersfield, 1984, Santa Clara County Bd. Suprs., 1992. Avocations: latin american studies, refugee assistance, homeless assistance, study of connections between economic and social problems. E-mail: gphelps@austin.rr.com.

PHELPS, JAMES FRANKLIN, retired county official; b. Mobile, Ala., May 29, 1940; s. James Carlton and Ela Kate (Hendrix) P.; m. Florence Annette Coley, June 30, 1972; children: Brant Michael, Kenneth Coley. Student, U. Ala., Mobile, 1962-63. Auditor Tax Collector's Office, Mobile, 1971-82, chief clk., 1983-86, chief adminstr., 1987-89; adminstr. collection divsn. Mobile County Revenue Commrs. Office, Mobile, 1989-96, adminstr., 1997—2002; ret., 2002. Republican. Baptist. Avocations: golf, woodworking, collecting and building die-cast model cars. Home: 9121 Howells Ferry Rd Semmes AL 36575-7207 E-mail: car57man@aol.com.

PHELPS, JAYCIE, gymnast, Olympic athlete; b. Indpls., Sept. 26, 1979; Mem. U.S. Women's World Gymnastics Team, 1994-95, U.S. Olympic Team, Atlanta, 1996. Recipient Sagamore of the Wabash award State of Ind., 1995, Gold medal team competition Olympic Games, Atlanta, 1996; placed 3rd in all around U.S. Olympic Festival, St. Louis, 1994, 2d for team Team World Championships, Dortmund, Germany, 1994, 3rd in all around Coca-Cola Nat. Championships, New Orleans, 1995, 3rd for team World Championships, Sabae, Japan, 1995. Avocations: coaching, swimming, shopping. Office: care USA Gymnastics Pan Am Plz 201 S Capitol Ave Ste 300 Indianapolis IN 46225-1058

PHELPS, JUDSON HEWETT, health facility administrator, marketing professional; b. Evanston, Ill., Oct. 18, 1942; s. Sidney Norman and Mary Schuyler (Coons) Phelps; m. Barbara Ann Ray, Dec. 21, 1963; children: Wyatt Hewett, Christopher Ashley, Whitney Magee. BA, Williams Coll., 1964; MS, Springfield Coll., 1993. Cert. nat. addictions counselor. Asst. brand mgr. Procter & Gamble Co., Cin., 1968—70; brand mgr. Memorex, Santa Clara, Calif., 1970—72; product mgr. Chesebrough Ponds Inc., Greenwich, Conn., 1972—76; v.p. mktg. L'Oreal subs. Cosmair Inc., NYC, 1976—77; v.p. sales Bio Products, Inc., Norwalk, Conn., 1978, exec. v.p., 1979, pres., 1980—86; corp. v.p. Ketchum & Co. parent co. Bio Products, Norwalk, 1982—86; mng. dir. Dameon Ptnrs. Inc., Wilton, Conn., 1987—88; pres. Theracom Corp., Rye, NY, 1988—89; v.p. Promotion Info. Bur., Norwalk, 1990; prin. Daniel Adams Co., Danbury, Conn., 1991—92; clin. coord., addictions therapist, counselor Ctr., Bridgeport, Conn., 1993—97; program dir. Gosnold-Thorne Counseling, Hyannis, 1998—2002, Gosnold Drug Ct. Treatment Program, Hyannis, 2003—. Adj. faculty Housatonic Cmty. Tech. Coll., Bridgeport, 1995—97. Family counselor Caregivers, Assn. Religious Communities, Danbury, Conn., 1975—79; leader, treas. Ridgefield Emmaus Teenage Christian Retreats, Conn., 1983—92; pres. Camp Dudley (YMCA) Alumni Assn., Westport, NY, 1974—79; chmn. Ridgefield Alcohol and Drug Use Commn., 1992—97. Lt. USNR, 1964—68. Home: 53 Gingerbread Ln Yarmouth Port MA 02675-1110

PHELPS, MICHAEL, Olympic athlete; b. Balt., June 30, 1985; Mem. U.S. Men's Olympic Swim Team, Sydney, 2000, Athens, 2004, Team Speedo, 2001—. Hon. bd. mem. Pathfinders for Autism. Named Swimmer of the Yr., 2001, 2003, Am. Internat. Athlete of Yr., 2004. Achievements include holds World Record in 200m fly, 200m IM, 400m IM; holds American Records in 200m fly, free, 200m IM, 400m IM, 400m free, 800m free; only swimmer in history to set 5 world records in one international meet; became the youngest world record holder in modern history at age 15, Sydney Olympic games, 2000; first male swimmer to break two world records in separate events in the same day; 5 time world champion, 21 national titles; Gold medal, 200m IM, 400m IM, 100m butterfly, 200m butterfly, 4x200m free relay, 400m MR, Bronze medal, 200m free, 4x100m free, Athens Olympic games, 2004; Tied World Record with 8 medals in single Olympic games, Athens, 2004. Office: USA Swimming 1 Olympic Plaza Colorado Springs CO 80909*

PHELPS, MICHAEL EDWARD, biophysics educator; b. Cleve., Aug. 24, 1939; s. Earl E. and Regina Bridget (Hines) P.; m. Patricia Emory, May 15, 1969; children: Patrick, Kaitlin. BA in Chemistry and Math., Western Wash. State U., 1965; PhD in Chemistry, Washington U., St. Louis, 1970. Asst. prof. Washington U. Sch. Medicine and Engring., 1970-73, assoc. prof., 1973-75; assoc. prof. dept. radiology U. Pa., Phila., 1975-76; prof. radiological sciences UCLA, 1976—92, prof. biomathematics, 1980—, chief divsn. biophysics, 1981—84, Jennifer Jones Simon prof., 1983—86, Norton Simon prof., 1996—, chief div. nuclear medicine, 1984—92, dir. Crump Inst. for Biol. Imaging, 1989—, chmn., dept. molecular and med. pharmacology, 1992—, chief, divsn. nuclear medicine, dept. molecular and med. pharmacology, 1992—; assoc. dir. UCLA/DOE Lab. Structural Biology and Molecular Medicine, 1984—, chief, divsn. nuclear medicine, 1984—; dir. UCLA/DOE Inst. Molecular Medicine, 1989—2002. Mem. study sect. NIH, Bethesda, Md., 1974-78. Author: Reconstruction Tomography in Diagnostic Radiology and Nuclear Medicine, 1977, Physics in Nuclear Medicine, 1980, 1987, 2002, Principles of Tracer Kinetics, 1983; contbr. articles to profl. jours. Recipient Von Hevesy Found. award, 1975,George Von Hevesy prize Von Hevesy Found., Zurich, 1978, 82, Oldendorf award, Soc. for Computerized Tomography and Neurologicval Imaging, 1981, S. Weir Mitchell award, Am. Acad. of Neuology, 1981, Ernest O. Lawrence award US Dept. Energy, 1984, Spec. award for Individual Distinction, Am. Nuclear Soc., 1984, Landauer Mem. award, Am. Assn. for Physicists in Medicine, 1988, Robert J. and Claire Pasarow Found. award, 1992, Disting. Scientists award, Inst. for Clin. PET, 1995, Enrico Fermi Presdl. award, 1999, Charles F. Kettering prize, GM Cancer Rsch. Found., 2001; holder Norton Simon endowed chair, 1983-; named Disting. Alumnus Western Wash. State U., 1980 Fellow Am. Heart Assn.; mem. ACP (Richard and Hinda Rosenthal award 1987), Inst. Medicine NAS (elected), Nat. Acad. Scis. (elected 1999), Soc. Nuclear Medicine (Paul Aebersold award 1983, Ted Block Mem. award, 1989), Internat. Soc. Cerebral Blood Flow and Metabolism (Cert. Excellence award 1979), NY Acad. Scis. (Sarah L. Poiley award 1984), Soc. Neuroscis. Roman Catholic. Home: 16720 Huerta Rd Encino CA 91436-3544*

PHELPS, ORME WHEELOCK, economics educator emeritus; b. Hobart, Okla., July 5, 1906; s. William Andrews and Kate Mae (Forman) P.; m. Jean Wright, Aug. 18, 1940; children— John Jackson, Sarah Hamilton; m. Barbara C. Green, July 25, 1981. AB, U. Chgo., 1937, MBA, 1939, PhD, 1945. Asst. prof. bus. adminstrn. U. Chgo., 1942-47; prof. econs. Claremont (Calif.) Men's Coll. and Grad. Sch., 1947-63, sr. prof., 1963-76, emeritus, 1976—, dean faculty, 1970-74. Vis. prof. UCLA, 1950, State U. N.Y. at Brockport, 1968-69; Fulbright research prof. Univ. Coll. of W.I., Kingston, Jamaica, 1957-58; Brookings research prof., Washington, 1962-63 Author: Introduction to Labor Economics, 4th edit, 1967, Discipline and Discharge in the Unionized Firm, 1959, Union Security, 1954, Legislative Background of the Fair Labor Standards Act, 1939; Contbr. articles, book revs. to profl. jours. Pub. mem., regional vice-chmn. Wage Stblzn. Bd., 1951-53; labor arbitrator, mem. various govt. bds. Ford found. fellow, 1953-54. Mem. Indsl. Relations Research Assn., Am., Western econ. assns., Am. Assn. U. Profs. Democrat. Episcopalian. Home: 509 Zitta Ct Danville CA 94526-5344

PHELPS, ROBERT J. lawyer; b. Davenport, Iowa, Apr. 20, 1946; s. Lowell Dean and Helen Berniece (Hall) P.; m. Cheryl Ann O'Brien, Sept. 3, 1966 (div. Nov. 1983); children: Kristin Marie, Randall L.; m. Lauren Gail McNaughton, June 16, 1984 (div. Dec. 2000). BA in History, U. Iowa, 1971; MA in Internat. Relations, U. Ark., 1972; JD, U. Tulsa, 1974. Bar: Okla. 1975, U.S. Dist. Ct. (no. dist.) Okla. 1975, Iowa 1987. Assoc. Drummond and Raymond, Pawhuska, Okla., 1975; from assoc. to ptnr. Byers and Phelps, Cleve., 1975-83; sole practice Cleve., 1983-87, Davenport, Iowa, 1987—. Mem. Pawnee County Rep. Cen. Com., Cleve., 1986; bd. dirs. Cleve. Area Health Care Found., 1977-87; mem. Davenport City Rep. Party Cen. Com., 1987-89. Served as sgt. USAF, 1968-72. Mem. Iowa Bar Assn., Scott County Bar Assn., Davenport C. of C., Cleve. C. of C. (chmn. indsl. devel. com. 1986-87). Avocations: reading, swimming. Office: 1622 E Lombard St Davenport IA 52803-2448 E-mail: rjp5555@aol.com.

PHEMISTER, ROBERT DAVID, veterinary medical educator; b. Framingham, Mass., July 15, 1936; s. Robert Irving and Georgia Nora (Savignac) P.; m. Ann Christine Lyon, June 14, 1960; children: Katherine, David, Susan. D.V.M., Cornell U., 1960; PhD, Colo. State U., Ft. Collins, 1967. Diplomate: Am. Coll. Vet. Pathologists. Research assoc. U. Calif., Davis, 1960-61, vis. rsch. pathologist, 1974-75; staff scientist Armed Forces Inst. Pathology, Washington, 1962-64; sect. leader to dir. collaborative radiol. health lab. Colo. State U., 1964-77; mem. faculty Coll. Vet. Medicine and Biomed. Scis., 1968-85, prof. vet. pathology, 1973-85, assoc. dean, 1976-77, assoc. dir. expt. sta., 1977-85, dean, 1977-85, interim acad. v.p. Univ., 1982, interim pres. Univ., 1983-84, spl. counselor to pres., 1984-85; vis. prof. Colo. State U., 1995-96; prof. vet. pathology Cornell U., 1985-99, dean and prof. emeritus, 1999—, dean Coll. Vet. Medicine, 1985-95. Cons. Miss. State U., 1977-81; commr. Colo. Advanced Tech. Inst., 1983-84; mem. governing bd. N.Y. Sea Grant Inst., 1985-95, vice chmn., 1990-92; mem. vet. medicine adv. com. FDA, 1984-88; mem. joint coun. on food and agrl. scis. USDA, 1988-92, mem. exec. com., 1989-92; chmn. Zweig Meml. Fund for Equine Rsch., 1985-95; mem. adv. panel for vet. medicine Pew Health Professions Commn., 1991-93. Author papers in field. Served to comdr. USPHS, 1960-68. Recipient Charles A. Lory award and Disting. Univ. Leadership award Colo. State U., 1984, Disting. Practitioner award Nat. Acad. Practice, 1985, Regional Health Adminstr.'s award, 1985; named Honor Alumnus, Colo. State U., 1989. Mem. AVMA (coun. on edn. 1985-91, adv. bd. vet. specialities 1985-89), Assn. Am. Vet. Med. Colls. (pres. 1982-83), Colo. Vet. Med. Assn. (Disting. Svc. award 1985), N.Y. State Vet. Med. Soc. (Centennial award 1990), Sigma Xi, Phi Zeta, Phi Kappa Phi, Gamma Sigma Delta (Merit award for Adminstrn. 1995). Home: 3136 Rock Park Dr Fort Collins CO 80528

PHENIS-BOURKE, NANCY SUE, educational administrator; b. Anderson, Ind., Oct. 29, 1943; d. Wilma (Anderson) Baker; m. Richard W. Phenis, June 11, 1966; 1 child, Heidi L. BA, Ind. State U., 1965; MA, Ball State U., 1974, postgrad., 1985. Elem. tchr. Highland Park (N.J.) Schs., 1966-68, Anderson City Schs., 1969-71; elem. tchr., tchr. gifted and talented South Madison Schs., Pendleton, Ind., 1974-85, elem. prin., 1985—. K-12 curriculum dir. South Madison Schs., 1984; mem. CAPE grant com. Eli Lilly Found., 2000. Bd. dirs. South Madison Community Found., Pendleton, 1991, First Am. Bank First-Grant; devel. bd. St. John's Health Care Systems; mem. Prin.'s Leadership Summit, U.S. Dept. Edn., 2000. Recipient Outstanding Contbn. award Internat. Reading Assn., 1991; grantee Eli Lilly Found., 1993. Mem. NAESP (Ind. state rep. 1998—, membership adv. com. 1999), AAUW (pres. 1985-87), Ind. Assn. Sch. Prins. (bd. dirs. 1994—), First Am. (bd. dirs. 1992-95), Phi Delta Kappa (historian 1987, Leadership award 1994), Delta Kappa Gamma (sec. 1990-92, pres. 1992-94, Leadership/Adminstr. award 1993). Office: East Elem Sch 893 E Us Highway 36 Pendleton IN 46064-9580

PHIBBS, CLIFFORD MATTHEW, surgeon, educator; b. Bemidji, Minn., Feb. 20, 1930; s. Clifford Matthew and Dorothy Jean (Wright) P.; m. Patricia Jean Palmer, June 27, 1953; children— Wayne Robert, Marc Stuart, Nancy Louise BS, Wash. State U., 1952; MD, U. Wash., 1955; MS, U. Minn., 1960; PhD (hon.), Iowa State, 2003. Diplomate Am. Bd. Surgery. Intern Ancker Hosp., St. Paul, 1955-56; resident in surgery U. Minn. Hosps., 1956-60; practice medicine specializing in surgery Oxboro Clinic, Mpls., 1962—, pres., 1985—; cons. to health risk mgmt. corps., 1994—. Mem. Children's Hosp. Ctr., Northwestern-Abbott Hosp., Fairview-Southdale Hosp., Fairview Ridges Hosp.; clin. asst. prof. U. Minn., Mpls., 1975-78, clin. assoc. prof. surgery, 1978—; med. dir. Minn. Protective Life Ins. Co. Contbr. articles to med. jours. Bd. dirs. Bloomington Bd. Edn., Minn., 1974—, treas., 1976, sec., 1977-78, chmn., 1981-83; mem. adv. com. jr. coll. study City of Bloomington, 1964-66, mem. community facilities com., 1966-67, advisor youth study commn., 1966-68; vice chmn. bd. Hillcrest Meth. Ch., 1970-71; mem. Bloomington Adv. and Rsch. Coun., 1969-71; bd. dirs. Bloomington Symphony Orch., 1976—, Wash. State U. Found., trustee, 1990—; dir. bd. mgmt. Minnesota Valley YMCA, 1970-75; bd. govs. Mpls. Met. YMCA, 1970—; bd. dirs. Bloomington Heart-Health Found., 1989—, Martin Luther Manor, 1989; pres. Oxboro Clinics, 1985—; bd. dirs. Bloomington History Clock Tower Assn., 1990—; bd. dirs. Fairview Hosp. Clinic, 1994—, Bloomington Sister city Orgn., 1999-, Bloomington Cmty. Found., 1997-, Bloomington Health Adv. Bd., 2000-, MMA Minority and Cross-Cult. Affairs Com., 2000-, Com. on Cult. Competence Minnesota Med. Assn., 1986. Capt. M.C., U.S. Army, 1960-62. Mem. ACS, AMA (Physician Recognition awards 1969, 73, 76, 79, 82, 85, 88, 91, 94), Assn. Surg. Edn., Royal Soc. Medicine, Am. Coll. Sports Medicine, Minn. Med. Assn. (del. 1991-94), Minn. Surg. Soc., Mpls. Surg. Soc., Hennepin County Med. Soc., Pan-Pacific Surg. Assn., Jaycees, Bloomington C. of C. (chmn. bd. 1984, chmn. 1985-86), Bloomington Adv. Bd. health, Bloomington Sister City Bd., Bloomington Cmty. Found. (bd. dirs. 1996-). Home: 9613 Upton Rd Minneapolis MN 55431-2454 Office: 600 W 98th St Minneapolis MN 55420-4773 E-mail: kphiibs@aol.com.

PHILBIN, ANN M. art facility director; b. Boston, Mar. 21, 1952; d. Richard Moore and Ann Theresa (Muller) P. BA, BFA, U. N.H.; MA, NYU, 1982. Rschr. Frick Art Reference Libr., N.Y.C., 1977-79; asst. to dir., program coord. Artists Space, N.Y.C., 1979-80; asst. curatorial coord. The New Mus., N.Y.C., 1980-81; curator Ian Woodner Family Collection, N.Y.C., 1981-83; asst. dir. Grace Borgenicht Gallery, N.Y.C., 1983-85; dir. Curt Marcus Gallery, N.Y.C., 1985-88; account dir., dir. Art Against AIDS Livet Reichard Inc., N.Y.C., 1988-90; dir. The Drawing Ctr., N.Y.C., 1990, UCLA Hammer Museum, Los Angeles. Bd. dirs. Elizabeth Streb, Ringside, N.Y., 1990, HIV Law Project, N.Y.C., 1993; founding mem. Women's Action Coalition, N.Y.C., 1991. Address: UCLA Hammer Museum 10899 Wilshire Blvd Los Angeles CA 90024

PHILBIN, REGIS, television personality; b. N.Y.C., Aug. 25, 1931; s. Frank and Florence P.; m. Kay Faylan, 1957 (div.); children: Amy, Danny; m. Joy Senese, Mar. 1, 1970; children: Joanna, Jennifer. Student, U. Notre Dame. Hollywood stagehand, NBC page The Tonight Show; truck driver, newswriter, sportscaster. Co-host The Joey Bishop Show, 1967-69, host Sta. KABC Am. L.A., Sta. WABC TV Morning Show, 1983-88 (with Kathy Lee Gifford in 1985); co-host (syndicated show) Live! With Regis and Kathie Lee, 1988-2000, Live! With Regis and Kelly, 2001 , exec. prodr., 2001—, Miss Am Pageant, 1991, 92, 95; host, Who Wants to be a Millionaire, 1999-2002; co-author: Cooking with Regis and Kathie Lee, 1993, Entertaining with Regis and Kathie Lee, 1994; author: I'm Only One Man, 1995, Who Wants to Be Me?, 2003. Office: Regis & Kelly 7 Lincoln Sq New York NY 10023-5900*

PHILBRICK, RODMAN, writer; b. Boston, Jan. 22, 1951; s. William Rodman Philbrick and Jane Elizabeth Merriman; m. Lynn M. Harnett, Aug. 30, 1980. Author: Freak The Mighty (Calif. Young Readers award, 1995), The Fire Pony (Capital Choice award, 1996), The Last Book In The Universe (Maine Lupine award, 2001). Mem.: Writers Guild Am. Achievements include The movie The Mighty by Miramax based on novel Freak The Mighty.

PHILIP, A. G. DAVIS, astronomer, editor, educator; b. N.Y.C., Jan. 9, 1929; s. Van Ness and Lillian (Davis) P.; m. Kristina Drobavicius, Apr. 25, 1964; 1 dau., Kristina Elizabeth Elanor. BS, Union Coll., 1951; MS, N.Mex. State U., 1959; PhD, Case Inst. Tech., 1964. Tchr. physics, math. and chemistry Brooks Sch., 1954-59; instr. Case Inst. Tech., 1962-64; asst. prof. astronomy U. N.Mex., 1964-66, SUNY-Albany, 1966-67, assoc. prof., 1967-76, mem. exec. com. Arts and Scis. Coun., 1975-76; rsch. prof. astronomy Union Coll., Schenectady, NY, 1976—, astronomer Dudley Obs., 1967-81, Frank L. Fullam chair astronomy, 1980-81, editor Dudley Obs. Reports, 1977-81; astronomer Van Vleck Obs. Wesleyan U., 1982-94; editor contbns. VVObs., 1982-94; pres. Inst. for Space Observation, 1986—. Guest, Acad. Scis. Lithuania, 1973, 76, 79, 86, Stellar Data Ctr., Strasbourg, France, 1978, 79, 80, 82, 85, 86; vis. astronomer Moletai Obs., 1988, 94, 99, 2000, Vatican Advanced Tech. Telescope, 1996—, CASLEO, Argentina, 2000—; bd. dirs., sec.-treas. N.Y. Astron. Corp., 1969-2001; pres., treas. L. Davis Press, Inc., 1982—; trustee, mem. Grants award com. Fund Astrophys. Rsch., 1985—; dir. Shapley Vis. Lectureships Program, 1994—; rsch. bd. advisors Am. Biog. Inst., 1996-. Exhibited: 2d Ann. Photography Regional, Albany, 1980; author: (with M. Cullen and R.E. White) UBV Color - Magnitude Diagrams of Galactic Globular Clusters, 1976; (with A. Robucci, M. Frame, K.W. Philip) Mm, Fractal Series, Vol. 1, Midgets on the Spike, 1991; editor: The Evolution of Population II Stars, 1972, (with D.S. Hayes) Multicolor Photometry and the Theoretical HR Diagram, 1975, (with M.F. Mc Carthy) Galactic Structure in the Direction of the Galactic Polar Caps, 1977, (with D. H. DeVorkin In Memory of Henry Norris Russell, 1977, (with Hayes) The HR Diagram, 1978, Problems in Calibration of Multicolor Systems, 1979, (with M.F. McCarthy and G.V. Coyne) Spectral Classification of the Future, 1979, X-Ray Symposium, 1981, (with Hayes) Astrophysical Parameters for Globular Clusters, 1981, (with A.R. Upgren) The Nearby Stars and the Stellar Luminosity Function, 1983, (with Hayes and L. Pasinetti) Calibration of Fundamental Stellar Quantities, 1985, (with D.W. Latham) Stellar Radial Velocities, Horizontal-Branch and UV-Bright Stars, 1985, Spectroscopic and Photometric Classification of Population II Stars, 1986, (with J. Grindley) IAU Symposium No. 126, Globular Cluster Systems in Galaxies, 1987, (with Hayes and Liebert) IAU Colloquium No. 95, The Second Conference on Faint Blue Stars, (with Hayes and Adelman) New Directions in Spectrophotometry, 1988, Calibration of Stellar Ages, 1988, (with A.R. Upgren) Star Catalogues; A Centennial Tribute to A.N. Vyssotsky, 1989, (with P. Lu) The Gravitational Force Perpendicular to the Galactic Plane, 1989, (with D.S. Hayes and S.J. Adelman) CCDs in Astronomy. II. Precision Photometry: Astrophysics of the Galaxy, 1991, (with Robucci, Frame and Philip K.) Midgets on the Spike, vol. I, 1991, (with A.R. Upgren) Objective-Prism and Other Surveys, 1991, N.Y. State Astronomy, 1992, (with B. Hauck and A.R. Upgren) Workshop on Databases for Galactic Structure, 1993, (with K.A. Janes and A.R. Upgren) IAU Symposium No. 167, New Developments in Array Technology and Applications, 1995, (with V. Straizys) Photometric Systems and Standard Stars, 1996, 30 Years of Astronomy at Van Vleck Observatory, 1997, (with Peter Boyce) Electronic Publishing: Now and the Future, 1997, (with J. Liebert and R. Saffer) The Third Conference on Faint Blue Stars, 1997, (with W. van Alterna and A. Upgren) Anni Mirabiles: A Symposium Celebrating the 90th Birthday of Dorrit Hottleit, 1999, The Kth Reunion, 2000, (with R.A. Koopmann) The Starry Universe: The Cecilia Payne-Gaposchkin Centenary, 2001, (with R.O. Gray and C. Corbally) The Garrison Festschrift, 2003; mem. editl. bd., 1994—, co-editor, 1998—, Baltic Astronomy, Astrometric and Photometric Group, Wesleyan U., 1997—; lectr. tours (with K.W. Philip) An Introduction to the Mandelbrot Set, 1988-91; contbr. chpts. to books, articles to profl. jours.; worked with Dr. Irving Langmuir on "The Pathology of Science", 1950—. Served with AUS, 1951-53. Yale U. vis. fellow, 1976; rsch. grantee Rsch. Corp., NSF, NASA, Nat. Rsch. Lab., NAS, Am. Astron. Soc. Fellow AAAS, Royal Astron. Soc., Am. Phys. Soc.; mem. Am. Astron. Soc. (Harlow Shapley lectr. 1973—, auditor 1977, 79-85), Am. Math. Soc., Can. Astron. Soc., Internat. Astron. Union (chmn., sec. various coms. and commns., pres. commn. 30 1982-85, chmn. working group on spectroscopic and photometric data 1985-94, chmn. sci. organizing com. symposium # 167, mem. working group on pub. 2000-), N.Y. Acad. Scis., Astron. Soc. Pacific, Astron. Soc. N.Y. (sec.-treas. 1969-2001, editor newsletter 1974-2001), Capital Computer Club (bd. dirs. 1990—, v.p. 1993—), H. Rider Haggard Soc., Sigma Xi. Achievements include being 1st U.S. observer Soviet 6M telescope, 1980. Home: 1125 Oxford Pl Schenectady NY 12308-2913 Office: Union Coll Physics Dept Schenectady NY 12308 E-mail: agdp@union.edu.

PHILIP, JAMES (PATE PHILIP), retired state legislator; b. Elmhurst, Ill., May 26, 1930; married; 4 children. Student, Kansas City Jr. Coll., Kans. State Coll. Ret. dist. sales mgr. Pepperidge Farm, Inc.; rep. State of Ill., 1967-74, senator, 1975—2002. Asst. senate minority leader, 1979, senate minority leader, 1981-93, senate pres., 1993-2002; chmn. DuPage County Rep. Ctrl. Com.; committeeman Addison Twp. Precinct 52; past Jr. Nat. Rep. Committeeman. Past dir. Nat. Found. March of Dimes; past gen. chmn. Elmhurst March of Dimes; spl. events chmn. DuPage Heart Assn.; mem. DuPage Meml. Hosp. Century Club; dir. Ray Graham Assn. Handicapped Children; mem. bd. sponsors Easter Seal Treatment Ctr.; active Lombard YMCA; bd. dirs. Danada Sculpture Garden. With USMC, 1950-53. Recipient Ill. Coun. on Aging award, 1989, Leaders of 90's award Downers Grove Twp., 1989, Man of Yr. award United Hellenic Voters Am., 1989, Legis. of Yr. award Ill. County Treas.'s Assn., 1990, Tax$avers award Ill. Assn. County Auditors, 1990, Statesman of Yr. award Internat. Union of Operating Engrs. Local 150, 1991, Friend of Youth award Assn. Ill. Twp. Com. on Youth, 1991, Spl. Svc. award Serenity House, 1991, Recognition award DuPage Ctr. Independent Living, 1991. Mem. Am. Legion, Ill. Young Reps. (past pres.), DuPage County Young Rep. Fedn. (past chmn.), DuPage County Marine Corps League (life), DuPage

Indsl. and Mfg. Assn. (past dir.), Suburban Bus. Mgmt. Coun. (past v.p.), Mil. Order Devil Dogs, Gocery Mgmt. and Sales Exec. Club Chgo., Exec. Club DuPage County, Shriners, Elks, Masons, Order of DeMolay (life), Moose. Republican.

PHILIP, PETER VAN NESS, former trust company executive; b. N.Y.C., Feb. 23, 1925; s. Van Ness and Lilian (Davis) P.; m. Sabina FitzGibbon, May 3, 1952; children: William Van Ness, Thomas Winslow, Peter Sandys. AB, Yale U., 1945W; MBA, NYU, 1950. With Price, Waterhouse & Co., N.Y.C., 1947-52; W.H. Morton & Co., Inc., N.Y.C., 1952-73; pres., CEO Equitable Securities, Morton & Co., Inc., 1970-73; sr. v.p., dir. White Weld & Co., Inc., N.Y.C., 1974-76; v.p. Morgan Guaranty Trust Co., N.Y.C., 1977-88, ret. With 86th inf. div. AUS, 1943-45. Decorated Purple Heart, Bronze Star. Mem.: Racquet and Tennis (N.Y.C.); Links; Yale (N.Y.C.), Downtown Assn. (N.Y.C.), Bond (N.Y.C.); Bedford ((N.Y.); Golf and Tennis; Ekwanok (Manchester, Vt.). Home: Box 395 740 Guard Hill Rd Bedford NY 10506-1042

PHILIP, ALICIA, community foundation executive; BA, Emory U.; MBA, Ga. State U. Exec. dir. Met. Atlanta Cmty. Found. Inc., Atlanta, 1977-99, pres., 1999—. Bd. dirs. Ctrl. Atlanta Progress, Ind. Sector, Funders Concerned About Aids, Investment Fund for Founds, Policy Bd. of Atlanta Project. Mem. Jr. League, Internat. Women's Forum, Acad. of Women. Recipient Roz Cohen Cmty. Action award YWCA; named as One of Top Women Mgrs. in U.S. Working Woman mag. Office: Met Atlanta Cmty Found The Hurt Bldg Ste 449 Atlanta GA 30303

PHILIPP, WALTER VIKTOR, mathematician, educator; b. Vienna, Dec. 14, 1936; came to U.S., 1963, naturalized, 1974; s. Oskar and Anna Julie P.; m. Ariane Randell, Dec. 10, 1984; children: Petra, Robert, Anthony, Andre. MS in Math. and Physics, PhD in Math., U. Vienna, 1960. Asst. U. Vienna, 1960-63, 65-67, dozent, 1967; asst. prof. U. Mont., 1963-64; vis. asst. prof. U. Ill., Urbana, 1964-65, mem. faculty, 1967—2004, prof. math., 1973—2000, prof. stats., 1988—2000, chmn. dept. stats., 1990-95, prf. emeritus, 2000—. Vis. prof. U. N.C., Chapel Hill, 1972, 88, MIT, 1980, Tufts U., 1981, U. Göttingen, 1982, 85, Imperial Coll., London, 1985; vis. rsch. prof. Beckman Inst., U. Ill., 2000—; mem. adv. bd. Monatshefte für Mathematik, 1994-2001. Assoc. editor Annals of Probability, 1976-81. Fellow Inst. Math. Stats.; mem. Am. Math. Soc., Austrian Math. Soc., Austrian Acad. Scis. (corr. mem.). Avocation: mountain climbing. Home: 1922 Maynard Dr Champaign IL 61822-5265 Office: U Ill Dept Stats Champaign IL 61820

PHILIPPON, MARC JOSEPH, orthopaedic surgeon; b. Quebec City, Can., May 9, 1965; arrived in U.S., 1990; s. Pontien Aderville and Micheline (Lortie) P.; m. Senenne Catalina Reid, Mar. 25, 1995; children: Michèle, Marc-Christophe, Mia-Véronique. BA with honors, Fla. Atlantic U., 1987; MD, McMaster U., Hamilton, Ont., Can., 1990. Lic. physician, Fla., Pa.; diplomate Am. Bd. Orthopaedic Surgery. Orthopaedic surgeon Holy Cross Hosp., Ft. Lauderdale, Fla., 1995—, chief orthopaedic surgery, 2000-01; chief orthopaedic surgeon humanitarian mission to Ukraine Kiev Orthopaedic Inst., 1997; orthopaedic surgeon Broward Gen. Hosp., Ft. Lauderdale, 1998—2002; dir. sports medicine/hip disorders dept. orthopaedic surgery U. Pitts. Med. Ctr.; dir. fellowship program U. Pitts. Med. Ctr. for Sports Medicine, dir. hip arthroscopy fellowship, dir. golf medicine program, dir. Fla. site. Cons. Howmedica Inc., Rutherford, N.J., 1996-97, Smith & Nephew Inc., Memphis, 1998-99; clin. adv. bd. Oratec Interventions, Inc., Menlo Park, Calif., 1998-2002; cons. Zimmer (Bristol-Myers Squibb); lectr. in field. Contbr. chapters to books, articles to profl. jours. Bd. dirs. Svc. Agy. for Sr. Citizens, Ft. Lauderdale, 1996-2000. Farquharson scholar Can. Med. Rsch. Coun., 1989. Fellow Internat. Coll. Surgeons, Am. Acad. Orthopaedic Surgeons; mem. AMA, Fla. Med. Assn., Phi Kappa Phi. Roman Catholic. Achievements include invention of orthopaedic surgery instrument and devices. Avocations: skiing, tennis, sailing, hockey, soccer.

PHILIPPS, EDWARD WILLIAM, banker, real estate appraiser; b. N.Y.C., Dec. 19, 1938; s. Edward Charles and Eleanor Elizabeth (Eisenger) P.; m. Diane Rose DiCuffa, June 12, 1960; children: James Michael, Robert Christopher. Appraiser Dry Dock Savs., N.Y.C., 1956-70, Nat. Bank of West, White Plains, N.Y., 1970-72, Aires Real Estate, Yonkers, N.Y., 1972-74; sr. v.p. Am. Savs. Bank (merger Empire Savs. Bank), N.Y.C., 1974-92; self employed real estate appraiser Yonkers, 1992-93; sr. v.p., chief lending officer LaJolla (Conn.) Bank, 1993-99; cons., 1999—. Mem. mortgage com. Cmty. Preservation Corp., N.Y.C., 1990-92. Mem. Am. Inst. Real Estate Appraisers, Homebuilders Assn. Fairfield County (bd. dirs.). Avocations: wood working, fishing. Home and Office: 261 Kimball Ave Yonkers NY 10704-3030 E-mail: ephilipp@optonline.net.

PHILIPPUS, AL A. protective services official; b. San Antonio, Mar. 18, 1951; m. Jeanne Theresa Philippus; children: Dawn Michelle, Jason Allen, Mary Lamm. A. in Law Enforcement, San Antonio Coll., 1977; BS in Criminal Justice magna cum laude, S.W. Tex. State U., 1979; MS in Criminal Justice Mgmt./Adminstrn., Sam Houston State U., 1992, PhD in Criminal Justice Mgmt./Adminstrn., 1994. Patrol officer City of San Antonio Police Dept., 1975-81, detective homicide unit, 1981-84, sgt. patrol divsn., 1984-86, sgt. internal affairs, 1986-88, lt., dir. rsch. and planning, 1988-89, capt., comdr. fiscal mgmt. and rsch. divs., 1989-94, dep. police chief, comdr. uniform divsn., 1994-95, chief of police, 1995—2001. Adj. prof. St. Mary's U., San Antonio, 1993—. Adv. bd. Police Found. Law Enforcement; law enforcement adv. bd. Alamo Area Coun. Govts.; mem. law enforcement coord. com. U.S. Western Dist. Tex.; bd. dirs. Tex. Ctr. for Legal Ethics and Professionalism. Sgt. USAF, 1969-73. Named Officer of the Yr., Greater San Antonio Builder's Assn., 1979, Optimist Club, 1993. Mem. Internat. City Mgmt. Assn., Nat. Assn. Rschrs. and Planners, Internat. Assn. Law Enforcement Planners, Internat. Assn. Chiefs of Police, Police Exec. Rsch. Found., Am. Pub. Welfare Assn., Assn. of Police Planning and Rsch. Officers, Combined Law Enforcement Assn. of Tex., San Antonio Police Officers Assn.

PHILIPS, CHUCK, journalist; Journalist L.A. Times, 1990—. Recipient Pulitzer prize for Beat Reporting, 1999. Office: c/o LA Times Bus Sect Times Mirror Sq Los Angeles CA 90053 E-mail: chuck.philips@latimes.com.

PHILIPS, JEREMY, media company executive; b. London, Eng. Grad., U. NSW, Harvard U. Various media and telecom. positions McKinsey & Co.; bus. devel. mgr. PBL Online Pub. and Broadcasting Ltd., Australia, 1997; dep. chmn. ecorp Ltd., Australia, 1999—2001; dir. strategic investments Citigroup; sr. v.p. office of the chmn. News Corp., N.Y.C., 2004—. Office: The News Corp Ltd 1211 Avenue of the Americas New York NY 10036*

PHILIPS, JOHN CHASE, retired process engineer; b. Washington, D.C., Apr. 1, 1930; s. Harold Kames and Dorothey Anderson Philips; m. Nancy Carolyn Sturgis, Nov. 25, 1956 (dic. July 1974); children: Netta Philips Dudley, James Anderson, Harry Victor; m. Harriette Chesley Chapin. BA, Catawba Coll., Salisbury, N.C., 1952; BS, U. S.C., Columbia, 1956. Organic unit supt. Va.-Carolina Chem. Corp., Charleston, SC, 1956—65; tech. dir. Westvaco Corp., Tyrone, Pa., 1965—68; process engr. The Mead Corp., Lynchburg, Va., 1968—74; project mgr. Chas T. Main Inc., Portland, Oreg., 1974—81; sr. staff specialist Rust Internat. Corp., Portland, Oreg., 1981—91, Harris Group Inc., Portland, Oreg., 1991—93; pres. J. Chase Philips, Inc., Scappoose, Oreg., 1993—95. Program dir. Tech. Assn. of Pulp & Paper, 1966—2002. Author: (book) Anderson's Bottom, 2002. Tech. advisor Va. Pollution Control Bd., Richmond, 1972—73; bd. dirs. Little Theater Inc., Lynchburg, Va., 1973—74. Cpl. U.S. Army, 1952—54, Korea. Conservative. Presbyterian. Avocations: boating, writing, travel, genealogy, photography. Home: 1111 N Lamb Blvd Las Vegas NV 89110 E-mail: h3034@webtv.net.

PHILIPS, SUZANNE MARGUERITE See CASEY, SUE

PHILIPSBORN, JOHN TIMOTHY, lawyer, writer; b. Paris, Oct. 19, 1949; s. John David and Helen (Worth) P. AB, Bowdoin Coll., 1971; MEd, Antioch Coll., 1975; JD, U. Calif., Davis, 1978. Bar: Calif. 1978, U.S. Dist. Ct. (no., ctrl. and ea. dists.) Calif. 1978, U.S. Ct. Appeals (9th cir.) 1985, U.S. Supreme Ct. 1985; cert-specialist in criminal law State of Calif. VISTA vol. Office of Gov. State of Mont., Helena, 1972-73; cons. U.S. Govt., Denver, 1974; lectr. Antioch New Eng. Grad. Sch., Keene, N.H., 1973-75, U. N.H., Durham, 1973-75; ptnr. Philipsborn & Cohn, San Jose, Calif., 1978-80; atty., supr. Defenders Inc., San Diego, 1980-83; assoc. Garry, Dreyfus & McTernan, San Francisco, 1983-87; pvt. practice, San Francisco, 1987—. Cons. Nicaraguan ct. evaluation projects, 1987-88, UN Internat. Tribunal, 1995—; coord. Internat. Conf. Adversarial Sys., Lisbon, Portugal, 1990; mem. adj. faculty New Coll. Law, San Francisco, 1991—; legal asst. project refugee camps S.E. Asia, 1992, legal edn. projects, Cambodia, 1995, Pakistan, 2001; cons. on continuing edn. of bar, 1995—. Bd. editors Champion, Forum; contbr. articles to profl. jours., chpts. to book. Founder trial program San Francisco Schs., 1986; bd. dirs. Calif. Indian Legal Svcs., 1990-96. Fulbright scholar, Portugal, 1989, Pakistan, 2001—. Mem. Nat. Assn. Criminal Def. Lawyers (assoc., co-chmn. death penalty impact litigation group 1989, co-chmn. govtl. misconduct com. 1990-92, vice chmn. task force on emerging democracies 1990-91), Calif. State Bar (evaluation panel criminal law specialists 1986—, com. on continuing edn. of bar 1991-94, criminal law subcom. state bd. legal specialists 1995-96), Calif. Attys. for Criminal Justice (bd. govs. 1989-94, 2003—, assoc. editor jour. 1987—, chmn. Amicus Curiae com. 1992—, co-chmn. govtl. misconduct com. 1989-92). Office: 507 Polk St Ste 250 Civic Ctr Bldg San Francisco CA 94102-3375

PHILIPSON, HERMAN LOUIS, JR., investment banker; b. Dallas, May 14, 1924; s. Herman and Lillian (Adler) P.; m. Sonia Topletz, July 20, 1955; children: Cynthia Ann, Leslie, Nancy, Julie. BS, Tex. A&M U., 1946; postgrad., Harvard Sch. Bus. Adminstrn., 1947-48. Pres. Philipson's, Inc., 1946-56; pres. Nat. Data Processing Corp., 1957-60, chmn. bd., 1960-61, Techno-Growth Capital Corp., 1962-72; pres. Recognition Internat. Inc., Dallas, 1961-73, chmn. exec. com., 1973-76; vice chmn. Recognition Equipment Inc., 1976-83; pres. Internat. Bus. Devel. Ltd., Dallas, 1973—, IBDL, Inc., Dallas, 1979—. Patentee in field. Former mem. Dallas Citizens Coun., also v.p., mem. exec. com.; bd. dirs. Dallas County Camp Fire Girls; trustee So. Meth. U. Found. for Sci. and Engring.; mem. engring. adv. coun. Tex. A&M U. 1st Lt. AUS, 1943-46. Decorated Bronze Star, Purple Heart with cluster; recipient Dallas Exporter of Yr. award, 1970, Ernest Thompson Seton award, 1975; named to Tex. A&M U. Acad. Disting. Mech. Engring. Grads. Mem. Dallas C. of C. (world trade com.), Japan-Tex. Assn. Lodges: Masons, Shriners. Home: 9100 Rockbrook Dr Dallas TX 75220-3907

PHILIPSON, MORRIS, university press director; b. New Haven, June 23, 1926; s. Samuel and Edith (Alderman) P.; m. Susan Antonia Sacher, Apr. 26, 1961; children: Nicholas, Jenny, Alex. Diploma, U. Paris, 1947; BA, U. Chgo., 1949, MA, 1952; PhD in Philosophy, Columbia U., 1959; L.H.D. (hon.), Coe Coll., 1985. Instr. English lit. Hofstra Coll., 1954—55; instr. philosophy Juilliard Sch. Music, 1955—58; lectr. Hunter Coll., 1957—60; editor Vintage Books, Alfred A. Knopf, Inc., N.Y.C., 1959—61, Modern Library, also trade books Random House, Inc., Pantheon Books, 1961—65; sr. editor Basic Books, N.Y.C., 1965—66; exec. editor U. Chgo. Press, 1966—67, dir., 1967—2000, dir. emeritus, 2000—. Author: Outline of Jungian Aesthetics, 1963, Bourgeois Anonymous, 1964, The Count Who Wished He Were a Peasant: A Life of Leo Tolstoy, 1967, Paradoxes, 1969, Everything Changes, 1972, The Wallpaper Fox, 1976, A Man in Charge, 1979, Secret Understandings, 1983, Somebody Else's Life, 1987; also short stories, articles; editor: Aldous Huxley on Arts and Artists, 1960, Aesthetics Today, 1961, Automation: Implications for the Future, 1962, (with Clapp, Rosenthal) Foundations of Western Thought, 1962. Served with AUS, 1944-46. Decorated comdr. Order Arts and Letters (France). Mem.: Arts (Chgo.), Caxton (Chgo.), Tavern (Chgo.), Quadrangle (Chgo.).

PHILLABAUM, LESLIE ERVIN, publisher; b. Cortland, N.Y., June 1, 1936; s. Vern Arthur and Beatrice Elizabeth (Butterfield) Phillabaum; m. Roberta Kimbrough Swarr, Mar. 17, 1962; children: Diane Melissa, Scott Christopher. BS, Pa. State U., 1958, MA, 1963. Editor Pa. State U. Press, 1961-63; editor-in-chief U. N.C. Press, 1963-70; assoc. dir., editor La. State U. Press, Baton Rouge, 1970-75, dir., 1975—2003, emeritus dir., 2003—. Served to 1st lt. U.S. Army, 1959—61. Mem.: Assn. Am. Univ. Presses (dir. 1978—80, 1983—86, pres. 1984—85), Acacia, Alpha Kappa Psi, Omicron Delta Kappa. Democrat. Home: 769 Castle Kirk Dr Baton Rouge LA 70808-6018

PHILLIPE, CHESTER TOLLESON, alcohol/drug abuse services professional, educator, substance abuse facility administrator; b. Long Beach, Calif., Oct. 15, 1929; s. Chester Marion Phillipe and Ethyle Kent Theinhaus; m. Florence Marie Phillipe (dec. July 1998); children: Jeffrey, Patrick, Melissa, Andrew, Aimee. BA in Religion and Bus. Adminstrn., Calif. Bapt. Coll., 1972; MDiv, Golden Gate Bapt. Theol. Sem., 1975. Cert. alcohol and drug abuse counselor; coll. instr. Calif. Alcohol and drug abuse counselor Calif. Assn. Alcohol and Drug Abuse Counselors, Sacramento, 1981—; CEO Family Addictions Ctr. Treatment. Mem. faculty in human svcs. Porterville Coll. Author: (book) Church Under Fire, 1998; editor: (addiction manuals) Substance Abuse, A Physical Disease, 1998. Bd. dirs. Calif. Alcohol and Drug Commn. Edn. Programs, Sacramento. Sgt. Army Security Agy. U.S. Army, 1947—50. Grantee, Idaho Mental Health, 1981. Mem.: Calif. Assn. Alcohol and Drug Abuse Counselors (bd. dirs. 1980—, Excellent Svc. award 1991), Nat. Assn. Alcohol and Drug Abuse Counselors, Internat. Consortium Reciprocity Commn. Republican. Avocations: reading, fishing, travel. Home: 3149 W Beech Ave Visalia CA 93277-6028 E-mail: chetp@psnw.com.

PHILLIPOFF, MARK JAMES, lawyer; b. Kansas City, Mo., Dec. 28, 1951; s. James George Phillipoff and Dorothy L. (Bartley) Probst; m. Sigrid M. Henn, July 6, 1974; children: Lyndsey Ann, James Alexander. AB, U. Notre Dame, 1974; JD, Ind. U., 1980. Bar: Ind. 1980, U.S. Dist. Ct. (so. dist.) Ind. 1980, U.S. Dist. Ct. (no. dist.) Ind. 1983, U.S. Ct. Appeals (7th cir.) 1983, Mich. 1983, U.S. Supreme Ct. 1983, U.S. Dist. Ct. (we. dist.) Mich. 1985. Dep. prosecuting atty. Greene County, Bloomfield, Ind., 1980-81; assoc. Mellen, Mellen & Wood, Bedford, Ind., 1981-83; ptnr. Jones, Obenchain LLC, South Bend, Ind., 1983—. Bd. dirs. Hospice St. Joseph County, Inc., South Bend, 1986-92. Mem. ABA, Ind. State Bar Assn., Mich. State Bar Assn., Notre Dame Club of St. Joseph County. Independent. Roman Catholic. Avocations: boating, computers, photography. Home: 17927 Augusta Ct Granger IN 46530-8417 Office: Jones Obenchain LLC PO Box 4577 South Bend IN 46634-4577

PHILLIPPE, RYAN, actor; b. Sept. 10, 1974; m. Reese Witherspoon; children: Ava Elizabeth, Deacon. Student, New Castle Bapt. Acad., 1992. Co-founder prodn. co. Actor: (TV series) One Life to Live, 1992, The Secrets of Lake Success, 1993; (films) Crimson Tide, 1995, White Squall, 1996, Nowhere, 1996, Little Boy Blue, 1997, I Saw What You Did Last Summer, 1997, 54, 1998, Playing by Heart, 1998, Cruel Intentions, 1999, The Way of the Gun, 2000, Antitrust, 2001, Gosford Park, 2001, Igby Goes Down, 2002, The I Inside, 2003. Office: c/o William Morris Agy Attn: John Fogelman 151 El Camino Dr Beverly Hills CA 90212*

PHILLIPPI, ELMER JOSEPH, JR., data communications consultant; b. Canton, Ohio, May 31, 1944; s. Elmer Joseph and Rita M. (Tillitski) P.; m. Susan Mary Schrader, July 10, 1971; 1 child, Nathan Audie. AB, Cornell U., 1966; MA, Rice U., 1970. Cert. energy auditor. Tchr. Brackenridge H.S., San Antonio, 1970-71; asst. prof. engring. tech. Muskingum Tech. Coll., Zanesville, Ohio, 1971-80, sec., treas. AAUP chpt.; data comm. analyst Chem. Abstracts Svcs., Columbus, Ohio, 1980-87; sr. software engr. Control Data Corp., Dayton, Ohio, 1987-89; analyst computing Boeing Computer Svcs., Huntsville, Ala., 1989; software engr. specxialist Ford Aerospace, Houston, 1989-92; computer sys. analyst Lockheed Engring. and Sci. Co., Houston, 1992-93; computer cons. CIBER, Houston, 1993-94; comm. cons. Genesis Data Sys., Houston, 1994; cons., lead cons. Deloitte & Touche Cons., Houston, 1994-98; sr. cons. KPMG, Houston, 1998-2000; ebus. arch. IBM, Washington, 2000—. Comm. cons. Ala. Supercomputer Network; designer, devel. Tech. Order Tracking System USAF; part-time instr. physics Ohio U.; editl. referee Am. Jour. Physics, 1975-85; network design cons. Aero. Systems div. USAF; subsystem mgr. for mission control ctr. upgrade, Johnson Space Ctr.; cons. U.S. Senate, 1998; adj. instr. physics San Jacinto Coll., 1992—; cons. Enterprise IT Architecture for U.S. Patent and Trademark Office, 2001, NASA Enterprise IT Architecture, 2002, cons. IT sys., Homeland Security, 2003. Grantee NSF, 1979. Mem. Assn. Computing Machinery (past treas. Ctrl. Ohio chpt., mem. symposium com.), N.Y. Acad. Scis., Rice Bus. Network. Avocations: amateur radio, music, bicycling, swimming, volunteer church work. Home: 1854 Yeoman Ct Crofton MD 21114 Office: IBM Global Svcs 11107 Sunset Hills Rd Reston VA 20190 E-mail: elmerp@us.ibm.com.

PHILLIPS, ALMARIN, economics educator, consultant; b. Port Jervis, NY, Mar. 13, 1925; s. Wendell Edgar and Hazel (Billett) P.; m. Dorothy Kathryn Burns, June 14, 1947 (div. 1976); children: Almarin Paul, Frederick Peter, Thomas Rock, David John, Elizabeth Linett, Charles Samuel; m. Carole Cherry Greenberg, Dec. 19, 1976. BS, U. Pa., 1948, MA, 1949; PhD, Harvard, 1953. Instr. econs. U. Pa., 1948-50, 51-53, asst. prof. econs., 1953-56, prof. econs. and law, 1963-91; Hower prof. pub. policy U. Pa, 1983-91; chmn. dept. econs. U. Pa., 1968-71, 72-73, assoc. dean Wharton Sch., 1973-74, dean Sch. Pub. and Urban Policy, 1974-77, chair faculty senate, 1990-91. Teaching fellow Harvard, 1950-51; assoc. prof. U. Va, 1956-61, prof., 1961-63; vis. prof. U. Hawaii, summer 1968, U. Warwick, London Grad. Sch. Bus. Studies, 1972, Ohio State U., McGill U., 1978, Calif. Inst. Tech, Northwestern U., 1980, Ariz. Coll. Law, 1987, Inst. Europeén d'Adminstrn. des Affairs (INSEAD), France, spring 1990; co-dir. Pres.'s Commn. Fin. Structure and Regulation, 1970-71; mem. Nat. Commn. Electronic Fund Transfers, 1976-77; chmn. bd. Econsult Corp., 1990-96. Author: (with R.W. Cabell) Problems in Basic Operations Research Methods for Management, 1961, Market Structure, Organization and Performance, 1962, Technology and Market Structure: A Study of the Aircraft Industry, 1971, (with P. Phillips and T.R. Phillips) Biz Jets: Technology and Market Structure in the Corporate Jet Aircraft Industry, 1994; Editor: Perspectives on Antitrust Policy, 1965, (with O.E. Williamson) Prices: Issues in Theory, Practice and Policy, 1968, Promoting Competition in Regulated Markets, 1975; editor Jour. Indsl. Econs., 1974-90; Contbr. articles to profl. jours. Served with AUS, 1943-45. Decorated Purple Heart, Bronze Star. Fellow: AAAS, Am. Statis. Assn.; mem.: Internat. Telecomms. Soc. (bd. dirs. 1990—2002), European Econ. Assn., Econometric Soc., Am. Econ. Assn. Home: 1115 Remington Rd Wynnewood PA 19096-4021 Office Phone: 610-896-5017.

PHILLIPS, ANNE LINNEA, writer; d. Carl Oscar and Hanna Tecla Grant; m. Francis Bradbury Phillips, June 8, 1946; children: Katherine, Thomas, Robert. Grad. high sch., Green Bay, Wis.

PHILLIPS, ANTHONY FRANCIS, lawyer; b. Hartford, Conn., May 18, 1937; s. Frank and Lena Phillips; m. Rosemary Karran McGowan, Jan. 28, 1967; children: Karran, Antonia, Justin. BA, U. Conn., 1959; JD, Cornell U., 1962. Bar: N.Y. 1964, U.S. Dist. Ct. (so. dist., ea. dist.) N.Y. 1965, (ctrl. dist.) Calif. 1980, U.S. Tax Ct. 1981, U.S. Ct. Appeals (2nd cir.) 1967, (3d cir.) 1985, (4th cir.) 1983, (5th cir.) 1972, (7th cir.) 1987, (9th cir.) 1983, (10th cir.) 1983, U.S. Supreme Ct. 1971. Assoc. Willkie, Farr & Gallagher, N.Y.C., 1963-69, ptnr., 1969—. Mem. adv. com. Cornell U. Law Sch., 1994—. Fellow Am. Bar Found.; mem. ABA, N.Y. State Bar Assn., N.Y. County Bar Assn. (bd. dirs. 1989-95), Assn. of Bar of City of N.Y. Home: 3 Elm Rock Rd Bronxville NY 10708-4202 Office: Willkie Farr & Gallagher 787 7th Ave Lbby 2 New York NY 10019-6018 E-mail: aphillips@willkie.com.

PHILLIPS, ANTHONY GEORGE, neurobiology researcher; b. Barrow, Cumbria, Eng., Jan. 30, 1943; came to Can., 1953; s. George William and Mabel Lilian (Wood) P. BA, U. Western Ont., London, Can., 1966, MA, 1967, PhD, 1970. Asst. prof. psychobiology U. B.C., Vancouver, Canada, 1970-75, assoc. prof., 1975-80, prof., 1980—, head dept. psychology, 1994-99, prof. dept. psychiatry, 1999—. Founder Quadra Logic Tech., Inc., Vancouver. Contbr. numerous papers to sci. jours. Chair inst. adv. bd. CIHR Inst. for Neurosci. Mental Health & Addiction; chmn. Can.-India Village Aid, Vancouver, 1981—86; bd. dirs. Tibetian Refuge Aid Soc., 1980—. Recipient Killam Rsch. prize Can. Coun., 1977, D.O. Hebb award Can. Psychol. Assn.; Steacie fellow Nat. Scis. and Engring. Rsch. Coun. Can., 1980. Fellow Royal Soc. Can.; mem. Soc. Neurosci., Can. Soc. for Neurosci., Can. Coll. Neuropsychopharmacology. Office: U BC Dept Psych 2255 Wesbrook Mall Vancouver BC Canada V6T 1Z4

PHILLIPS, BARNET, IV, lawyer; b. New York, N.Y., July 5, 1948; s. Barnet III and Isabelle (Auriema) P.; m. Sharon Walsted Packey, Jan. 2, 1981; children: Victoria Ilonka, Caroline Walsted. BA, Yale U., 1970; JD, Fordham U., 1973; LLM, NYU, 1977. Bar: N.Y. 1974. Assoc. Hughes Hubbard & Reed, N.Y.C., 1973-76, Skadden, Arps, Slate, Meagher & Flom, N.Y.C., 1977-81, ptnr., 1981—. Adj. assoc. prof. Fordham U., N.Y.C., 1987-88; articles editor The Tax Lawyer, 1989-91. Co-author: Structuring Corporate Acquisitions--Tax Aspects. Bd. dirs Student/Sponsor Partnership, N.Y.C., 1990-95; bd. cons. Portsmouth (R.I.) Abbey Sch., 1991-96, chmn.,1997-2002. Republican. Avocations: skiing, opera, triathlons. Home: 6 Hycliff Rd Greenwich CT 06831-3223 Office: Skadden Arps Slate Meagher & Flom Four Times Square 42nd Flr New York NY 10036-6522 Office Phone: 212-735-2220. Business E-Mail: bphillip@skadden.com.

PHILLIPS, BARRY, lawyer; b. Valdosta, Ga., Feb. 16, 1929; s. W. Otis and Gypsy (Mercer) P.; m. Grace Greer, Aug. 3, 1957; children: Mary Grace, Barry Jr., Greer, Quinton. AB, U. Ga., 1949, LLB, 1954. Bar: Ga. 1951, D.C. 1977. Assoc. Kilpatrick Stockton, Atlanta, 1954-60, ptnr., 1960-97, of counsel, 1997—. Bd. dirs., mem. exec. com., credit com. Bank South Corp., 1978-96. Mem. bd. regents Univ. Sys. Ga., 1988-94, vice chmn., 1991-93, chmn., 1993-94; trustee U. Ga. Found., Atlanta, 1983-87, treas., 1985-87; mem. bd. visitors U. Ga. Law Sch., 1983-87, chmn., 1985; dir. Ctrl. Atlanta Progress, 1985-86; dir. USA-ROC Econ. Coun., 1985-91; bd. dirs. Ga. Coun. Internat. Visitors, Atlanta, 1986-93, sec., 1986-87, pres., 1987-88; bd. dirs. Atlanta Conv. and Visitors Bur., 1986-91, sec., 1986-87, v.p., 1987-88; bd. dirs. Ga. Region NCCJ, 1980-98, co-chair, 1982-83; chmn. Met. Atlanta Olympic Games Authority, 1990-91; bd. dirs. Ga. Sports Hall of Fame, 1990—, vice chmn., 1993-95, chmn., 1995-96; attache Can. Olympic Team for 1996 Olympics, 1995-96. 1st lt. U.S. Army, 1951-53, Korea. Decorated Air medal; recipient Brotherhood-Sisterhood award Ga. Regional NCCJ, 1993. Fellow Am. Coll. Investment Counsel (bd. dirs. 1986-88), Ga. Bar Found., Soc. Internat. Bus. Fellows; mem. Ga. Bar Assn. (chmn. corp. and banking law sect. 1977-78), Atlanta Bar Assn., D.C. Bar Assn., Lawyers Club Atlanta, U. Ga. Law Sch. Alumni Assn. (trustee 1979-84, pres. 1982-83), Can. Am. Soc. (bd. dirs. 1981-90, pres. 1981-83), Brit. Am. Bus. Group (bd. dirs. 1985-95), Sphinx, Gridiron, Phi Beta Kappa, Phi Kappa Phi, Omicron Delta Kappa. Democrat. Methodist. Avocations: reading, travel. Home: 4850 Tanglewood Ct NW Atlanta GA 30327-4558 Office: Kilpatrick Stockton 1100 Peachtree St NE Ste 2800 Atlanta GA 30309-4530 Office Phone: 404-815-6380. E-mail: bphillips@kilstock.com., bphilatl@aol.com.

PHILLIPS, BARRY, artist, educator; b. Odessa, Tex., Mar. 9, 1960; s. Barry and Sharon (Shaw) P.; m. Glenda Means, May 4, 1984; children: Shanae, Kelsey. BA, Tex. Tech. U., 1983; MFA, East Tex. State U., 1987. Faculty, chmn. dept. art Odessa (Tex.) Coll., 1994—. Artist drawings/prints Sophisto series, 1984-87, mixed media Man Overboard, 1990-97; one-man shows include Cameron U., Lawton, Okla., 1993, St. Edward's U., Austin, 1994, Mus. of Abilene, Tex., 1995; exhibited in group shows Zaner Gallery, Rochester, N.Y., 1986, Fla. State U., Tallahassee, 1987, Clemson (S.C.) U., 1987, Nelson-Atkins Mus., Kansas City, Mo., 1989, Hoyt Inst. Fine Art, New Castle, Pa., 1990, San Diego Art Inst., 1991, Cullen Ctr., Houston, 1993. Recipient Kimbrough award Dallas Mus. Art, 1989; Nat. Endowment for the Arts Visual Artists fellow, 1987. Mem. Coll. Art Assn., Tex. Assn. Schs. of Art, Big Red's Art Groupies. Office: Odessa Coll 201 W University Blvd Odessa TX 79764-7105 E-mail: barryphillips3@grandecom.net.

PHILLIPS, BERNICE CECILE GOLDEN, retired vocational education educator; b. Galveston, Tex., June 30, 1920; d. Walter Lee and Minnie (Rothsprack) Golden; m. O. Phillips, Mar. 1950 (dec.); children: Dorian Lee, Loren Francis. BBA cum laude, U. Tex., 1945; MEd, U. Houston, 1968. cert.

tchr., tchr. coord., vocat. tchr., Tex. Dir. Delphian Soc., Houston, 1955-60; bus. tchr. various private schs., Houston area, 1960-65; vocat. tchr. coord. office edn. program Pasadena (Tex.) Ind. Sch. Dist., 1965-68, Houston Ind. Sch. Dist., John H. Reagan High Sch., 1968-85, ret., 1985. Bd. dirs. Regency House Condominium Assn., 1991-93. Recipient numerous awards and recognitions for vocat. bus. work at local and state levels. Mem. AAUW (life, 50 yr. mem., Houston Br. v.p. ednl. found. 1987-90, pres. 1992-94, bd. dirs. 1987-96, 50-Yr. mem. cert.), NEA, Nat. Bus. Edn. Assn., Am. Vocat. Assn. (life), Tex. State Tchrs. Assn. (life), Tex. Classroom Tchrs. Assn. (life), Tex. Bus. Edn. Assn. (emeritus, Life Mem. award, numerous other awards), Vocat. Office Edn. Tchrs. Assn. Tex. (past bd. dirs.), Greater Houston Bus. Edn. Assn. (reporter), Houston Assn. Ret. Tchrs., Tex. Assn. Ret. Tchrs., Delta Pi Epsilon (emeritus), Beta Gamma Sigma. Avocations: bridge, reading, arts, crafts, travel. Home: 1909 Emmorton Rd Bel Air MD 21015

PHILLIPS, BETTY LOU (ELIZABETH LOUISE PHILLIPS), writer, interior designer; b. Cleve. d. Michael N. and Elizabeth D. (Materna) Suvak; m. John S. Phillips, Jan. 27, 1963 (div. Jan. 1981); children: Bruce, Bryce, Brian; m. John D.C. Roach, Aug. 28, 1982. BS, Syracuse U., 1960; postgrad. in English, Case Western Res. U., 1963-64. Cert. elem. and spl. edn. tchr., N.Y.; cert. interior designer, Calif. Tchr. pub. schs., Shaker Heights, Ohio, 1960-66. Sportswriter Cleve. Press, 1976-77; spl. features editor Pro Quarterback Mag., N.Y.C., 1976-79; bd. dirs. Cast Specialties Inc., Cleve. Author: Chris Evert: First Lady of Tennis, 1977, Picture Story of Dorothy Hamill, 1978 (ALA Booklist selection), American Quarter Horse, 1979, Earl Campbell: Houston Oiler Superstar, 1979, Picture Story of Nancy Lopez, 1980 (ALA Notable book), Go! Fight! Win! The NCA Guide for Cheerleaders, 1981 (ALA Booklist), Something for Nothing, 1981, Brush Up on Your Hair, 1981 (ALA Booklist), Texas...The Lone Star State, 1989, Provençal Interiors-French Country Style in America, 1998, French by Design, 2000, French Influences, 2001, Villa Décor: Decidedly French and Italian Style, 2002 (Foreword Mag. Best Non-Fiction Book, 2003), Unmistakably French, 2003, Emily Goes Wild, 2004 (Tex. Inst. Letters Best Children's Book, 2004), Secrets of French Design, 2004; contbr. articles popular mags. Mem.: Am. Soc. Interior Designers (profl. mem., cert.), Soc. Children's Book Writers, Delta Delta Delta. Republican. Roman Catholic. Home: 4278 Bordeaux Ave Dallas TX 75205-3718

PHILLIPS, CARLY, writer; b. Mount Vernon, NY, July 7, 1965; d. Leonard Robert and Arlene Weinberg; m. Phillip Drogin, Mar. 23, 1965; children: Jaclyn Lindsay, Jennifer Ashley. BA, Brandeis U., Waltham, MA, 1987; JD, Boston U. Bar: N.Y. 1991, Conn. 1991. Author: (novels) The Bachelor, 2002 (NY Times Bestseller List, Reading with Ripa Nationally Televised Bookclub, 2002), The Playboy, 2003 (NY Times Bestseller List, 2003), The Heartbreaker (N.Y. Times extended Betsseller List). Mem.: Novelists, Inc., Romance Writers of Am. Office: Carly Phillips PO Box 483 Purchase NY 10577 E-mail: carlyphillips@optonline.net.

PHILLIPS, CARTER GLASGOW, lawyer; b. Canton, Ohio, Sept. 11, 1952; s. Max Dean and Virginia Scott (Carter) P.; m. Sue Jane Henry, June 5, 1976; children: Jessica, Ryan. BA, Ohio State U., 1973; MA, Northwestern U., 1975, JD, 1977. Bar: Ill. 1977, D.C. 1979, U.S. Dist. Ct. (no. dist.) Ill., U.S. Dist. Ct. (D.C. dist.), U.S. Ct. Appeals (1st, 2d, 3d, 4th, 5th, 6th, 7th, 8th, 9th, 10th, 11th, D.C. and Fed. cirs.). Law clk. U.S. Ct. Appeals (7th cir.), Chgo., 1977—78; law clk. to chief Justice Warren E. Burger U.S. Supreme Ct., Washington, 1978—79; asst. prof. law U. Ill., Champaign, 1979—81; asst. solicitor gen. U.S. Dept. Justice, Washington, 1981—84; ptnr. Sidley & Austin, Washington, 1984—; mng. ptnr. Sidley Austin Brown & Wood LLP, Washington, 1995—. Chmn. Fed. Cir. Adv. Coun., U.S. Ct. Appeals, 2003—; chmn. dean's adv. bd. Northwestern U. Law Sch., 2002—; chmn. adv. com. U.S. Ct. Appeals for Fed. Cir.; pres., master Edward Coke Appellate Inn of Ct. Contbr. articles to profl. jours. Bd. trustees Supreme Ct. Hist. Soc.; chmn. Northwestern Univ. Law Bd.; bd. advs. Georgetown Univ. Law Ctr.'s Supreme Ct. Inst. Mem.: Am. Coll. Trial Lawyers, Am. Acad. Appellate Lawyers, Am. Law Inst. Republican. Episcopalian. Office: Sidley Austin Brown & Wood LLP 1501 K St NW Fl 10 Washington DC 20005-3705 Office Phone: 202-736-8270. E-mail: cphillips@sidley.com.

PHILLIPS, CARYL, writer; b. St. Kitts, West Indies, Mar. 13, 1958; BA with honors, The Queen's Coll., Oxford, Eng., 1979; AM (hon.), Amherst (Mass.) Coll., 1995; DUniv (hon.), Leeds Metro. U., 1997; D (hon.), U. York, 2003; DLitt (hon.), U. Leeds, 2003. Writer in residence Factory Arts Ctr. Arts Coun. Great Britain, London, 1980-82; writer in residence U. Mysore, India, 1987, U. Stockholm, 1989; vis. writer Amherst Coll., 1990-92, writer in residence, 1992—98, co-dir. creative writing ctr., 1994-97, prof. English, writer-in-residence, 1994-98; prof. English, Henry R. Luce prof. migration and social order Barnard Coll., Columbia U., N.Y.C., 1998—, dir. Initiatives in the Humanities, 2003—. Vis. lectr. U. Ghana, 1990, U. Poznan, 1991; vis. writer Humber Coll., 1992, 93; writer-in-residence Nat. Inst. Edn., Singapore, 1994; vis. prof. English NYU, 1993; vis. prof. humanities U. W.I., 1999—2000; mem. arts coun. Gt. Britain Drama Panel, 1982—85; mem. prodn. bd. Brit. Film Inst., 1985—88, Bush Theatre, 1985—89; mem. Caribbean Writer bd. U.S. V.I., 1989—; hon. sr. mem. U. Kent, 1988—; cons. editor Faber & Faber, Inc., 1992—94, Caribbean series editor, 1996—2000; participant, keynote spkr 12 ann. confs. German-speaking countries New Lits. in English, Giessen, Germany, 1989; resident writer Hull (Engl.) Internat. Lit. Festival, 1992; instr. writing Arvon Found., summers, 1983—; reader, lectr. in field. Author: The Final Passage, 1985 (Malcolm X prize for lit., 1985), A State of Independence, 1986, Higher Ground, 1989, Cambridge, 1991, Crossing the River, 1993 (James Tait Black meml. prize), The European Tribe, 1987 (Martin Luther King Meml. prize, 1987), The Nature of Blood, 1997, The Atlantic Sound, 2000, A New World Order: Selected Essays, 2001, A Distant Shore, 2003 (PEN/Faulkner Award for Fiction nominee, 2004, Commonwealth Writers prize, 2004); editor: Extravagant Strangers: A Literature of Belonging, 1997, The Right Set: A Tennis Anthology, 1999; author: (plays) Strange Fruit, 1980, Where There Is Darkness, 1982, The Shelter, 1983, (TV documentary screenplays) Welcome to Birmingham, 1983, The Hope and Glory, 1984, Lost in Music, 1984, The Record, 1985, Darker Than Blue: Curtis Mayfield, 1995, BBC Profile Spl. Caryl Phillips Interviews Chinua Achebe, 2003, South Bank Show: Caryl Phillips, ITV, 2003, (films) Playing Away, 1986, The Final Passage, 1996, The Mystic Masseur, 2001 (Mar Del Plata Film Festival Silver Omby for Best Screenplay), (radio plays) The Wasted Years, 1984 (Best Radio Play of Yr. award BBC, 1984), Crossing the River, 1985, The Prince of Africa, 1987, Writing Fiction, 1991, A Kind of Home: James Baldwin in Paris, BBC Radio 4, 2004, (radio documentaries) St. Kitts (Pride of Place), 1983, Sport and the Black Community, 1984, No Complaints: James Baldwin at Sixty, 1985; contbr. (documentary programs) Bookmark, 1984, Black on Black, London Weekend TV, 1983, others; contbr. articles to periodicals. Recipient Young Writer of Yr. award, London Sunday Times, 1992, award, Lannan Lit., 1994; fellow, Guggenheim, 1992, 50th Anniversary, Brit. Coun., 1984, Royal Soc. Lit., 2000; Mel and Lois Tukman fellow, N.Y. Pub. Libr. Ctr. for Scholars and Writers, 2003. Office: care G Garrett AP Watt Ltd 20 John St London WC1N 2DR England also: Barnard Coll English Dept 3009 Broadway New York NY 10027-6501 E-mail: Ggarrett@apwatt.co.uk.

PHILLIPS, CHANDLER ALLEN, biomedical/human factors engineer; b. L.A., Dec. 21, 1942; s. Chandler A. and Ann P.; m. Jane Draper, Feb. 14, 1980. AB in Biol. Scis., Stanford U., 1965; MD, U. So. Calif., 1969; AB in Classical Langs., Wright State U., 1982; PhD (hon.), U. Human Studies, Las Vegas, 1985. Registered profl. engr., Ohio, Calif. Rsch. physician U. Dayton (Ohio), 1972-74; asst. prof. Wright State U., Dayton, 1975-79, assoc. prof. biomed. engring., 1979-84, prof. biomed. engring., 1984-91, prof. biomed. and human factors engring., 1991—99, prof. biomed. indsl. and human factors engring., 1999—. Author: Functional Electrical Rehabilitation, 1991, Human Factors Engineering, 2000; sr. editor: Mechanics of Skeletal and Cardiac Muscle, 1983, Effective Extremity Prostheses, 1989; regional editor Auto Medica, 1997—; mem. editl. bd. Jour. Biomechanics, 1984-87, Jour. Clin. Engring., 1984-98, Prosthetics-Orthotics Engring., 1995-98, Frontiers in Bioscience, 2003—. Capt. USAF, 1970-72. Fellow IEEE (Harry Rowe Mimno award 1984), Am. Inst. for Med. and Biol. Engring., Aerospace Med. Assn. (John Paul Stapp award 2002), Am. Acad. Neurologic Orthopedic Surgeons (hon.). Avocations: amateur radio, commercial-instrument pilot, fishing, classical philology. Office: Dept Biomed Indsl Human Factors Engring Wright State U Dayton OH 45435

PHILLIPS, CHARLES, computer company executive; BS in Computer Sci., USAF Acad.; MBA in Fin., Hampton U.; JD, N.Y. Law Sch. CFA; bar: Ga., D.C. Prin. Morgan Stanley & Co., Inc., 1994—95, mng. dir., 1995—2003; co-pres. Oracle Corp., Redwood City, Calif., 2004—, also bd. dirs. Trustee N.Y. Law Sch., Joing Ctr. for Polit. and Econ. Studies, Washington. Named one of 50 Black Profls. on Wall Street, Black Enterprise Mag. Office: Oracle Corp 500 Oracle Pkwy Redwood City CA 94065

PHILLIPS, CHARLES ALAN, accounting firm executive; b. Cin., Aug. 12, 1939; s. Charles Stanley and Mary Lucile (Kirkpatrick) P. BS in Bus. Adminstrn., Northwestern U., 1960, MBA, 1961. Cert. systems profl. Investment adviser Continental Ill. Bank, Chgo., 1960-65; asst. to pres. A.S. Hansen, Chgo., 1965-67; investment adviser Francis I. du Pont, N.Y.C., 1967-70; prof. North Central Coll., Mansfield, Ohio, 1970-73; prin. Peat, Marwick, Mitchell (now KPMG Peat Marwick), Cleve., Tulsa, Houston, 1973-88. Presbyterian. Avocations: classical music, natural history, gardening.

PHILLIPS, CHARLES FRANKLIN, JR., retired economist; b. Geneva, NY, Nov. 5, 1934; s. Charles Franklin and Evelyn (Minard) P.; m. Marjorie Hancock, June 22, 1957; children: Charles Franklin, Susan Hancock, Anne Davis. BA, U. N.H., 1956; PhD, Harvard U., 1960. Asst. prof. econs. Washington and Lee U., Lexington, Va., 1959-63, assoc. prof., 1963-66, prof., 1966—2003, Robert G. Brown prof., 1979—2003; ret., 2003. Mem. adv. bd. Shenandoah Valley area, First Union, 1971—; econ. cons. pub. utilities. Author: Competition in the Synthetic Rubber Industry, 1963, The Economics of Regulation, 1965, rev. edit., 1969, The Regulation of Public Utilities, 1984, 3d edit., 1993; editor: Competition and Monopoly in the Domestic Telecommunications Industry, 1974, Competition and Regulation-Some Economic Concepts, 1976, Expanding Economic Concepts of Regulation in Health, Postal and Telecommunications Services, 1977, Regulation, Competition and Deregulation-An Economic Grab Bag, 1978, Regulation and the Future Economic Environment-Air to Ground, 1980. Mem. city coun. Lexington, 1969-71, mayor, 1971-88; mem. Va. Rep. Ctrl. Com., 1974-76, 77-96; trustee Hebron Acad., Maine, 1971-82; mem. Presbyn. Ch., 1959—, elder, 1993-98, trustee, 1994—; mem. Commn. on Rev. of Nat. Policy Toward Gambling, 1972-76; chmn. Valley Program for Aging Svcs., 1993-95, treas., 1996-99; bd. dirs. Rockbridge Area Presbyn. Home, 1973—, Nat. Regulatory Rsch. Inst., 1992-95, Stonewall Jackson Found., 1997-2000, 2001—, treas., 2003—; pres. United Way of Lexington-Rockbridge County, 1996-98, crusade chmn., 1999; pres. Hist. Lexington Found., 1997-2000. Recipient award McKinsey Found., 1962, J. Rhoads Foster award, 1995. Mem. Am. Econ. Assn. (Disting. Mem. award transp. and pub. utility group 1997),, So. Econ. Assn., Am. Mktg. Assn., Kiwanis, Phi Beta Kappa, Omicron Delta Epsilon (pres. 1976-77, 78-79, 96-97, Outstanding Regional Dir. award 1971). Home: 414 Morningside Dr Lexington VA 24450-2739 Business E-Mail: phillipscf@wlu.edu.

PHILLIPS, CHARLES W. state agency administrator; BS in Indsl. Mgmt., U. Ky., 1950. Asst. examiner St. Louis dist. FDIC, 1950-54, examiner St. Louis dist., 1954-57; exec. v.p. Floyd County Bank, New Albany, Ind., 1958-62, pres., 1962-85; ret.; dir. Ind. Dept. Fin. Instns., 1989—. Mem. Ind. Bank Law Study Commn., 1963-64; mem. state banking law steering com. Am. Bankers Assn., 1965-66, mem. leadership coun., 1980-82; chmn. mems. Ind. Dept. Fin. Instns., 1965-68; chmn. sr. mgmt. com. Ind. Bankers Assn., 1972, chmn. legis. com., 1973. Mem. bd. advisors Ind. U. S.E., 1973-78, chmn. bd. escot, 1976-82; charter dir. Leadership Louisville, 1978-81; dir. WKPC Ch. 15 PBS, Louisville, 1980-85, mem. bd. overseers, 1985-88; active Metro United Way. Recipient Chancellor's medallion for disting. svc. Ind. U. S.E., 1994. Mem.: Conf. State Bank Suprs. (vice chmn. dist. 2 1992—99, bd. dirs., chmn. dist. 2 1999—). Office: Fin Instn Dept 30 S Meridian St Ste 300 Indianapolis IN 46204*

PHILLIPS, DANIEL ANTHONY, trust company executive; b. Boston, Feb. 24, 1938; s. Lyman Waldo and Harriet Anthony (Carlow) P.; m. Diana Walcott, Aug. 18, 1962; children: Lisa Walcott Phillips Harrington, Bradford Lyman, Phillips. AB cum laude, Harvard U., 1960, MBA, 1963. From v.p. to dir. to mem. exec. com. Fiduciary Trust Co., Boston, 1963-92, exec. v.p., dir., trust com. sec., trust officer, 1992—, exec. v.p., dir., trust com., trust officer, 1993-94, pres., CEO, 1993—2002, chmn., 2002—. Dir., sec., treas. Ways To Work, 1998—. Bd. dirs. Family Svc. Am., chair fin. comn., 1993-95, treas., chair bd. dirs., 1995-97; bd. dirs., mem. exec. com. Am. Meml. Hosp., Reims, France, pres., 1988-98, treas., 2002—; bd. dirs. Family Found., N.Am., 1993-99, Lend A Hand Soc.; bd. dirs., treas. Grimes-King Found. for the Elderly, Inc.; v.p., treas. Frederick E. Weber Charities Corp.; chair bd. dirs. Families Internat., Inc., 1997-99; founds. chair United Way Mass. Bay, 1996—, dir., 1998—, chair cmty. investments, 2000, vice chmn., bd. dirs., mem. exec. com.; trustee, French Libr. and Cultural Ctr., 2003—; overseer Cambridge Cmty. Found.; trustee Cambridge Homes. Staff sgt. USAR, 1960—66. Decorated chevalier Legion of Honor (France), 2002; recipient Grand medal of Reims Am. Meml. Hosp., 1998, Champagne Ardenne medal Am. Meml. Hosp., 1998. Mem. Boston Soc. Security Analysts, Harvard U. Alumni Assn. (1st v.p. 1996-97, pres. 1997-98, Harvard Alumni Assn. award 1995), Boston Econ. Club, Comml. Club. Office: Fiduciary Trust Co 175 Federal St Boston MA 02110-2210 Home: Po Box 381082 Cambridge MA 02238-1082 E-mail: DAPharvard@aol.com.

PHILLIPS, DAVID P. grocery company executive; CFO Publix Super Markets, Lakeland, Fla., 1999—. Office: PO Box 32018 Lakeland FL 33802-2018

PHILLIPS, DEBRA HELEN, soil scientist, researcher; b. Augusta, Ga., Jan. 23, 1962; d. Helen and Howard Weeks Phillips. BS, U. of Ga., 1984; MS, U. of Tenn., 1988; PhD, U. of Aberdeen, Scotland, 1994. Post-doctoral rsch. assoc. Dept. Plant and Soil Sci., Univ. of Tenn., Knoxville, 1995—98; rsch. assoc. Environ. Sci. Div., Oak Ridge Nat. Lab., Tenn., 1998—2004; faculty Geology Pellissippi State Tech. Cmty. Coll., Tenn. Fellow Internat. Rotary Found. Fellowship, Rotary Found., 1988—89, Vice-Chancellor's Overseas Rsch. Studentship award, 1989—91. Mem.: Soil Sci. Soc. of Am. Home: 811 Luttrell St Apt#1 Knoxville TN 37917 Office: Environ Sci Divsn Oak Ridge Nat Lab PO Box 2008 Bldg 1505 Oak Ridge TN 37831 Personal E-mail: dhphillips2003@yahoo.com. E-mail: phillipsdh@ornl.gov.

PHILLIPS, DON, investment research company executive; b. 1963; BA in engring., U. Tex., 1984; MA in lit., U. Chgo., 1986. Mutual fund analyst Morningstar Inc., 1986—95, pres., 1995—97, pres., CEO, 1997—2000, mng. dir., 2000—, editor Morningstar Mutual Funds. Named one of Most Influential People in Fin. Planning, Fin. Planning mag. and Investment Advisor mag., 2003, 10 Key Players in Industries, Registered Rep mag., 2002. Achievements include Morningstar's first mutual fund analyst; development of Morningstar Style Box and Morningstar Rating. Office: Morningstar Inc 225 W Wacker Dr Chicago IL 60606 Office Phone: 312-696-6000. Office Fax: 312-696-6001.

PHILLIPS, DOROTHY KAY, lawyer; b. Nov. 2, 1945; d. Benjamin L. and Sadye (Levinsky) Phillips; children: Bethann P., David M. Schaffzin. BS in English Lit. magna cum laude, U. Pa., 1964; MA in Family Life & Marriage Counseling, NYU, 1975; JD, Villanova U., 1978. Bar: Pa. 1978, N.J. 1978, U.S. Dist. Ct. (ea. dist.) Pa. 1978, U.S. Dist. Ct. N.J., 1978, U.S. Ct. Appeals (3d cir.), 1984, U.S. Supreme Ct. 1984. Tchr. Haddon (N.J.) Twp. H.S., Haddon Heights H.S., 1964-70; lectr., counselor Marriage Coun. of Phila., U. Pa., Hahnemann Med. Schs., Phila., 1970-75; atty. Adler, Barish, Daniels, Levin & Creskoff, Phila., 1978-79, Astor, Weiss & Newman, Phila., 1979-80; ptnr. Romisher & Phillips. P.C., Phila., 1981-86; prin. Dorothy K. Phillips & Assocs., LLC, 1986—. Faculty Sch,. of Law Temple U.; guest spkr. on domestic rels. issues on radio and TV shows; featured in newspaper and mag. articles; bd. mem. Anti-Defamation League of B'nai B'rith, Nat. Mus. Jewish History; mem. friend's circle, Athenaeum, Phila., shareholder. Contbr. articles to profl. jours. Mem.: ATLA (membership com. 1990—91, co-chair 1989—90), ABA, Lawyers Club, Montgomery County Bar Assn., Phila. Trial Lawyers Assn., Nat. Bus. Inst. (lectr. 1997—, Custody and Visitation in Pa. 1998, Planning, Taxation and Divorce 2002, Custody Modification 2003, Critical Fin. Mistakes Made in Divorce in Pa. 2004), Phila. Bar Assn. (chmn early settlement program 1983—84, custody rules drafting com. for Supreme Ct. Pa., spl. events spkr. on pensions, counsel fees, written fee agreements 1989—91, co-chair and moderator of panel mandatory continuing legal edn. 1994), N.J. Bar Assn., Pa. Bar Assn. (continuing legal edn. com. 1990—92, faculty, lectr. Pa. Bar Inst. Continuing Legal Edn. 1990, panel mem. summer meeting 1991), Pa. Trial Lawyers Assn. (chair membership com. family sect. 1989—90, presenter ann. update civil litigators-family law, author procedures practice of family law, Phila. County Family Law Litig. Sect. County praticed database 1991). E-mail: dkp@dkphillipslaw.com.

PHILLIPS, DOROTHY LOWE, nursing educator; b. Jacksonville, Fla., June 3, 1939; d. Clifford E. and Dorothy (MacFeeley) Lowe; m. Dale Bernard Phillips, Feb. 14, 1973; children: Francis D., Sean E., Dorothy F. AA in Nursing, Ventura Coll., 1969; BSN, Calif. State U. Consortium, San Diego, 1984; M. Nursing, UCLA, 1987; EdD, Nova Southeastern U., 1995. Cert. community colls. tchr., Calif.; RN, Calif., pub. health nurse, Calif., clin. nurse specialist maternal/child. Staff nurse Cmty. Meml. Hosp., Ventura, Calif., 1969-70; charge nurse women and children's clinic Ventura County Regional Med. Ctr., Ventura, 1974-76; staff nurse, RN II Pleasant Valley Hosp., Camarillo, Calif., 1978-85; lead instr. cert. nursing asst. program div. adult edn. Oxnard (Calif.) Union H.S. Dist., 1984-89; staff rsch. assoc. UCLA, 1988; clin. instr. Ventura C.C. Sch. Nursing, 1988; college nurse Ventura Community Coll., 1989; lectr. Sch. of Nursing UCLA, 1989, lectr., coord. maternity nursing Sch. of Nursing, 1989-90, 90-91; vocat. nursing dir., health scis. coord. Oxnard Union H.S. Dist., 1990-99; assoc. dean health occupations Allan Hancock Coll., 1999—. Vis. educator health careers unit Calif. Dept. Edn., 1992-94; cons. Oxnard Adult Sch.; mem. adv. com. nursing asst./home health aide program Ventura County Regional Occupational Program; presenter in field. Competitive events judge !st Annual Leadership Conf., Health Occupations Students of Am., Anaheim, Calif.; active St. John's Regional Med. Ctr. Health Fair, 1991, Pleasant Valley Hosp. Health Fair, 1991; seminar leader "Babies and You", March of Dimes, 1988. Grad. Div. Rsch. grantee UCLA, 1986; Calif. State PTA scholar UCLA, 1986, Ventura County Med. Soc. scholar, 1967, Audrienne H. Mosley Grad. scholar, 1987. Mem. Nat. League for Nursing, Calif. Assn. Health Career Educators (pres. 1994), So. Calif. Dirs. Vocat. Nursing Programs (rec. sec. 1996—), So. Calif. Vocat. Nurse Educators (exec. bd.), Assn. Calif. C.C. Adminstrs., Nat. Coun. Instrnl. Adminstrs., Calif. C.C. Assn. Occupl. Edn., No. Calif. ADN Dirs., Santa Maria Valley Leadership Class, Sigma Theta Tau. Republican. Lutheran. Avocations: skiing, reading, exercise, travel, backpacking. Home: 1448 Oakridge Park Rd Santa Maria CA 93455-4560 Office: Allan Hancock Coll 800 S College Dr Santa Maria CA 93454-6399

PHILLIPS, EARL NORFLEET, JR., diplomat, financial services executive; b. High Point, N.C., 1940; s. Earl Norfleet Phillips and Lillian Jordan; m. Sarah Boyle, Oct. 19, 1971; children: Courtney Dorsett, Jordan Norfleet. BSBA, U. N.C., 1962; MBA, Harvard U., 1965. Security analyst Wertheim & Co., N.Y.C., 1965-67; exec. v.p. Factors Inc., High Point, 1967-71, First Factors Corp., High Point, 1972-81, pres., 1982-98; chmn. GE Capital First Factors, High Point, 1998-2000; pres. Phillips Interests, 2000—; U.S. amb. to Eastern Caribbean, 2002—. Bd. dirs. Oakdale Cotton Mills, N.C. Enterprise Corp., Culp Inc. Mem. nat. adv. coun. SBA, 1988—91; trustee High Point Regional Hosp., Asian Inst. Tech., Bangkok; former mem. Piedmont Triad Airport Authority; trustee U. N.C., Chapel Hill, 1983—91, chmn. bd., 1989—91, mem. endowment bd., 1985—2001; mem. U. N.C. Found., 1987—91; bd. govs. U. N.C. Sys., 1995—99; mem. N.C. Econ. Devel. Bd., Raleigh, 1984—91; bd. dirs. N.C. Citizens for Bus. and Industry, chmn., 1999—2000. Named Young Man of Yr., High Point Jaycees, 1971, High Point Citizen of Yr., 2000; named one of Five Outstanding Young Men, N.C. Jaycees, 1971; recipient Global Leadership award, Kenan-Flagler Bus. Sch., U. N.C., 2001, Disting. Alumnus award, U. N.C. Alumni Assn., 2002. Mem. Nat. Comml. Fin. Assn. (bd. dirs.), The Brook (N.Y.C.), Country Club of N.C. (Pinehurst), High Point C.C. Club, String and Splinter Club (High Point), Linville (N.C.) Golf Club, Gorgons Head Lodge. Office: Phillips Interests Box 830 101 S Main St High Point NC 27261

PHILLIPS, EDWARD JOHN, consulting firm executive; b. Phila., Sept. 8, 1940; s. Harold E. and Mary C. P.; m. Kathleen A. Everett, July 23, 1960; children: Elizabeth J., Edward J. B of Mech. Engring., Villanova U., 1973; MBA, Widener U., 1975. Registered profl. engr., Ill., Pa., Ohio; chartered engr., U.K. Tech. ops. mgr. Motorola, Inc., Franklin Park, Ill., 1976-81; v.p. engring. Rival Mfg. Co., Kansas City, Mo., 1981-82; prin., sr. cons. Richard Muther & Assocs., Kansas City, 1982-85; chmn. KANDE, Inc., Overland Park, Kans., 1983-86; pres., CEO Sims Cons. Group Inc., Lancaster, Ohio, 1986—; chmn. bd. dirs., pres. Sims Consulting Group, Lancaster, Ohio. Bd. dirs. KANDE, Inc., Wilmington, Del. Author: Manufacturing Plant Layout, 1997; contbr. articles to profl. jours. Mem. NSPE, ASME (chmn. material handling divsn. 1989-91, mem. internat. mgmt. com. 1977), MIMechE, Soc. Mfg. Engrs., Tau Beta Pi, Pi Tau Sigma. Office: Sims Cons Group Inc PO Box 968 314 N Columbus St Lancaster OH 43130-3009

PHILLIPS, ELIZABETH JASON, lawyer, state agency administrator; b. Boston, Sept. 3, 1936; d. Richard Eliot and Elizabeth Harding (McClure) Jason; m. William Morris Phillips, Jr., Mar. 2, 1991; children: Meredith Rowe, william Morris III, Eleanor Anne, Robert J., Lee B. Stewart. BA in History, U. Mass., 1958; MEd, U. Hartford, 1969; JD, Western New Eng. Coll., Springfield, Mass., 1977. Bar: Mass. 1977, U.S. Dist. Ct. Mass. 1978, Va. 1981, U.S. Dist. Ct. (ea. dist.) Va. 1981, U.S. Dist. Ct. DC 1981, U.S. Dist. Ct. (we. dist.) Va. 1982, U.S. Ct. Appeals (4th cir.) 1982, U.S. Supreme Ct. 1984. Ptnr. Thompson & Stewart, Ludlow, Mass., 1977-80; adminstr. Office Atty. Gen., Commonwealth of Va., Richmond, 1980-82, asst. atty. gen., 1982-84; dep. Commr. Indsl. Commn. Va., 1984-91; dep. commr., mgr. dispute resolution divsn. Va. Workers' Compensation Commn., Richmond, 1991—2001. Trustee Gloucester County Libr., 2002, sec.; Trustee Ludlow Hosp., 1979—80. Mem.: ABA, Va. Exec. Inst., Va. Assn. Adminstrv. Law Judges and Hearing Officers (pres-elect 1999), Va. Bar Assn., Richmond Bar Assn., Ludlow C. of C. (pres. 1980). Episcopalian. Home: Cedar Shade 3859 Raymond Walker Rd Hayes VA 23072-4620 Personal E-mail: ephil75441@aol.com.

PHILLIPS, ELIZABETH JOAN, marketing professional; b. Cleve., July 8, 1938; d. Joseph Tinl and Helen Walter; m. Erwin Phillips, June 1956 (div. 1960); 1 child, Michael A. BA, Fordham U., 1980. Acct. exec. David Cogan Mgmt., NYC, 1969—77, N.F.L. Films, NYC, 1977—78; mgr. sports programs Avon Products, NYC, 1978—83; v.p. Needham, Harper & Steers (now D.D.B. Needham), NYC, 1983—86, Ted Bates Event Mktg., NYC, 1986—87; pres. Custom Event Mktg., 1987—. Adj. prof. NYU, NYC, 1987—. Exec. com. Vanderbilt YMCA, NYC, 1976—84; ofcl. Olympic Games, LA, 1984; referee Women's Olympic Marathon, LA, 1984; pres. Met. Athletics Congress, NYC, 1980—83. Mem.: Women's Sports Found. (bd. adv. 1983—94), Road Runners Club Am. (bd. dirs. 1992—98), NY Road Runners Club (v.p., exec. com. 1976—, pres. 1970—98, bd. dirs. 1992—98). Office: Custom Event Mktg Inc 444 E 75th St Apt 10D New York NY 10021-3448

PHILLIPS, EUAN HYWEL, publishing executive; b. Chipstead, Surrey, Eng., Mar. 31, 1928; s. Edgar Aneurin and Elsie Llewella (Davies) P.; m. Margaret June Savage, June 12, 1954; children: David John, Janet Margaret. BA, Emmanuel Coll., Cambridge, Eng., 1949, MA, 1965. Cost acct. J. Lyons & Co. Ltd., London, 1950-53; dispatch mgr. Pickerings Produce Canners Ltd., Manchester, Eng., 1953-56; mgmt. cons. P.A. Mgmt. Cons. Ltd., London, 1956-65; mng. dir. Unwin Bros. Ltd., Old Woking, Eng., 1965-73; univ. printer designate Cambridge (Eng.) U. Press, 1973-74, univ. printer, 1974-76; dir. Cambridge (Eng.) U. Press (Am. br.), N.Y.C., 1977-82; owner New Canaan Bibles and Manx Knitwear, Stamford, Conn., 1982-87; exec. dir. Assn. Am. Univ. Presses, 1987-90. Gov. Guildford Sch. Art, 1966-69, Cambridge Coll. Arts and Tech., 1974-76; dir. East Asian History of Sci., Inc., 1978-81 Contbr. to scholarly pub. With Royal Navy, 1946-48. Mem. Brit. Printing

Industries Fedn. (coun. 1966-73, pres. Home Counties Alliance 1970-71), Troupers Light Opera Co., Connestee Falls Golf Assn. (pres. 1996-97), Connestee Falls Property Owners Assn. (bd. dirs. 2001—04). Home: 140 Connestee Trl Brevard NC 28712

PHILLIPS, FREDERICK FALLEY, architect; b. Evanston, Ill., June 18, 1946; s. David Cook and Katharine Edith (Falley) P.; m. Gay Fraker, 1983 (div. 1993); m. Linda Gardner, 2002; 1 child, Daniel Gardner. BA, Lake Forest Coll., 1969; MArch, U. Pa., 1973. Registered architect, Ill., Wis. Intern Harry Weese & Assocs., 1974, 75; architect pvt. practice, Chgo., 1976-81; pres. Frederick Phillips and Assocs., Chgo., 1981—. Bd. dirs. Landmarks Preservation Coun., 1981-85, Chgo. Acad. Sci., 1988-97, Friends of Ceuros de Escazu, Costa Rica, 1992-95, Project Rush Chgo., 2001--; mem. aux. bd. Chgo. Architecture Found., 1975-89. Recipient award Townhouse for Logan Sq. Competition, AIA and Econ. Redevel. Corp. Logan Sq., 1980, Gold medal award Willow St. Houses, Ill. Ind. Masonry Coun., 1981, Silver award for pvt. residence, 1989, Gold medal award pvt. residence, 1994, Three Record Houses awards Archtl. Record, 1990, 95, award 2d Compact House Design Competition, 1990, award of exellence for pvt. residence AIA/Nat. Concrete Masonry Assn., 1992, 98, award pvt. residence Am. Wood Coun., 1993, Honorable mention-Best in Am. Living award Profl. Builders Mag., 1995, Builder's Choice award pvt. residence, Builder Mag., 1996, Jury's Choice award pvt. residence Chgo. Athenaeum, 1996, 2001, Am. Architecture award Chgo. Athenaeum, 2001, Grand award Residential Architecture Mag., 2003, award Custom Builder Mag., 2003, award Am. Inst. Steel Construction, 2004. Fellow AIA (Disting. Bldg. award for Willow St. Houses, Chgo. chpt. 1982, for Pinewood Farm 1983, for Pvt. Residences 1990, 92, 98, for Tower House, 2001, chmn. task group mfg. housing Nat. Com. Design 1994-96, mem. awards task group 1998-2001, chmn. 2000-01); mem. Chgo. Archtl. Club, Racquet Club (bd. govs. 1983-89), Arts Club, Cliff Dwellers Club (bd. govs. 1985-88). Office: Frederick F Phillips & Assocs 1456 N Dayton St Ste 200 Chicago IL 60622-2636

PHILLIPS, GAIL, state legislator; b. Juneau, Alaska; m. Walt Phillips; children: Robin, Kim. BA in Bus. Edn., U. Alaska. Mem. Homer (Alaska) City Coun., 1981-84, Kenai Peninsula Borough Assembly, 1986-87; chmn. legis. com. Alaska Mcpl. League; mem. Alaska Ho. of Reps., 1991-2000, house majority leader, 1993-94, spkr., 1995-98. Former owner, mgr. Quiet Sports; ptnr. Lindphil Mining Co.; pub. rels. cons. Active Homer United Meth. Ch., Rep. Ctrl. Com. Alaska, Kenai Peninsula Coll. Coun.; past mem. com. bd. and race coord. Iditarod Trail Dog Sled Race. Mem. Western States Legis. Coun. (exec. com.), Am. Legis Exch. Coun. (former state chmn.), Resource Devel. Coun. Alaska, Western Legis. Conf. (exec. bd.), Western States Coalition (exec. bd.), The Energy Coun. (exec. bd.). Home: PO Box 3304 Homer AK 99603-3304 also: Alaska Ho Reps State Capitol Juneau AK 99801-1182

PHILLIPS, GENEVA FICKER, academic editor; b. Staunton, Ill., Aug. 1, 1920; d. Arthur Edwin and Lillian Agnes (Woods) Ficker; m. James Emerson Phillips, Jr., June 6, 1955 (dec. 1979). BS in Journalism, U. Ill., 1942; MA in English Lit., UCLA, 1953. Copy desk Chgo. Jour. Commerce, 1942-43; editl. asst. patents Radio Rsch. Lab. Harvard U., Cambridge, Mass., 1943-45; asst. editor adminstrv. publs. U. Ill., Urbana, 1946-47; editl. asst. Quar. of Film, Radio and TV UCLA, 1952-53; mng. editor The Works of John Dryden, Dept. English UCLA, 1964—2002. Bd. dirs. Univ. Religious Conf., L.A., 1979— . UCLA teaching fellow, 1950-53, grad. fellow 1954-55. Mem. Assn. Acad. Women UCLA, Friends of Huntington Libr., Friends of UCLA Libr., Friends of Ctr. for Medieval and Renaissance Studies, Samuel Johnson Soc. So. Calif., Assocs. U. Calif. Press, Conf. Christianity and Lit., Soc. Mayflower Descendants. Lutheran. Home: 213 First Anita Dr Los Angeles CA 90049-3815 Office: UCLA Dept English 2225 Rolfe Hall Los Angeles CA 90024

PHILLIPS, GERALD BAER, internal medicine scientist, educator; b. Bethlehem, Pa., Mar. 20, 1925; s. Abel H. and Cecilia (Blum) P.; m. Maria Bonzi Lewis, July 15, 1970; children: Abigail, Elizabeth. AB, Princeton U., 1948; MD, Harvard U., 1948. Diplomate Am. Bd. Internal Medicine. Intern Presbyn. Hosp., N.Y.C., 1948-50; rsch. fellow Thorndike Meml. Lab., Med. Sch. Harvard U., Boston, 1950-53; vis. fellow biochemistry Columbia U. Coll. Physicians and Surgeons, N.Y.C., 1954-56, from assoc. in medicine to assoc. prof., 1956-73, prof., 1973—. Sr. attending physician Roosevelt Hosp.; attending physician N.Y.-Presbyn. Hosp. Sr. asst. surgeon USPHS, 1952-54. Mem.: Am. Soc. for Biochemistry and Molecular Biology, Am. Soc. for Clin. Investigation, Alpha Omega Alpha. Home: 196 E 75th St New York NY 10021-3257 Office: 1000 10th Ave New York NY 10019-1147 E-mail: gbp1@columbia.edu. *I attribute any success I may have had to heredity and luck.*

PHILLIPS, GRAHAM HOLMES, retired advertising executive; b. London, Jan. 30, 1939; emigrated to U.S., 1965, naturalized, 1974; s. Leonard George and Mary Marjorie (Holmes) P.; m. Laurel Gilbert; 1 child, Debra Ann. Student, RAF Coll. Cranwell, 1957-58; MBA, London U., 1962. Mgmt. trainee Shell Internat. Petroleum, Ltd., London, 1957-59; aviation sales rep., 1960-63; aviation sales mgr. Shell Philippines, 1964; with Ogilvy & Mather (U.S.), N.Y.C., 1965—, account mgr., 1965-73, dep. mgr., account supr. Houston, 1970, v.p., 1971-72, sr. v.p., mgmt. supr., 1972-73; mng. dir. Ogilvy & Mather Inc., Amsterdam, 1973-75; former pres., then chief exec. officer Ogilvy & Mather (Can.) Ltd., Toronto, from 1975, former chmn., from 1979; dir. Ogilvy & Mather, 1978-92; former chief fin. officer Ogilvy & Mather Internat., from 1983; former exec. v.p. Ogilvy & Mather (U.S.), N.Y.C., from 1979, former gen. mgr., from 1980, former mng. dir., chief fin. officer, from 1981; former chmn., CEO Ogilvy & Mather Worldwide, 92; chmn. Burson-Marsteller, New York, 1997—. Episcopalian. Office: Young and Rubican 285 Madison Ave New York NY 10017-6486

PHILLIPS, GRETCHEN, social worker; b. Erie, Pa., July 14, 1941; life ptnr. Beverly Campbell, June 10, 1989. BA, Mercyhurst Coll., 1966; MSW, Yeshiva U., 1972; postgrad., Advanced Ctr. Psychotherapy, 1972-73, Washington Sq. Inst., 1973-77. Diplomate clin. social work, cert. social worker N.Y. Psychiat. social worker, forensic social worker Creedmoor Psychiat. Ctr., Queens Village, NY, 1972-80; med. social worker Bellevue Hosp. Ctr., N.Y.C., 1980-83; intake probation officer N.Y.C. Probation, Family Ct., Bklyn., 1983—. Mem.: NASW. Home: 125 Radford St Apt 3C Yonkers NY 10705-3014 Office: Probation Intake Kings Family Ct 283 Adams St Brooklyn NY 11201-2804 Office Phone: 718-643-5677.

PHILLIPS, HARVEY G. musician, soloist, music educator, arts consultant; b. Aurora, Mo., Dec. 2, 1929; s. Jesse E. and Lottie A. (Chapman) P.; m. Carol A. Dorvel, Feb. 22, 1954; children: Jesse E., Harvey G., Thomas A. Student, U. Mo., 1947-48, Juilliard Sch. Music, 1950-54, Manhattan Sch. Music, 1956-58; MusD (hon.), New England Conservatory of Mu, 1971; HHD (hon.), U. Mo., Columbia, 1987. Founder, v.p. Mentor Music, Inc., N.Y.C., 1958—79; v.p. Wilder Music, Inc., N.Y.C., 1964-77, Magellan Music, Inc., N.Y.C., 1971—, Peaslee Music Inc., 1971—; established faculty position Aspen Sch. Music, summer 1962, U. Wis., summer 1963, Hartt Sch. Music, Hartford, Conn., 1962-64, Mannes Sch. Music, N.Y.C., 1964-65; exec. v.p. Orch. USA, N.Y.C., 1962-65; exec. v.p., pers. mgr., tubist Symphony of the Air N.Y.C., 1957-66; v.p. Brass Artists, Inc., N.Y.C., 1964—; adminstrv. asst. to Julius Bloom, Rutgers U., New Brunswick, N.J., 1966-67; v.p. fin. affairs New Eng. Conservatory of Music, Boston, 1967-71; mem. faculty Sch. Music, Ind. U., Bloomington, 1971-94, disting. prof. music, trustee, 1979, disting. prof. emeritus, 1994. Adv. bd. Am. Brass Chamber Music, Inc., 1971—; chmn. bd. Summit Brass/Keystone Brass Inst., 1985—92, Rafael Mendez Brass Inst., 1993—; cons. Margun Music, Inc., 1977—; bd. dirs. Summit Brass. Brass coach Festival at Sandpoint, Idaho, 1986-94; mem. faculty Joven Orch., Spain, 1987-94, Festival Casal Orch., San Juan, P.R., 1964-76; dir. 1st Internat. Tuba Symposium Workshop, 1973, Brass-Wind Music Studios, Carnegie Hall, N.Y.C., 1961-67; tubist, King Bros. Circus Band, 1947, Ringling Bros. & Barnum & Bailey Circus Band, 1948-50, N.Y.C. Ballet Orch., 1951-71, N.Y.C. Opera Orch., 1951-62, Voice of Firestone Orch., 1951-53, Sauter-Finegan Orch., 1952-53, Band of Am., 1952-54, NBC Opera Orch., 1956-65, Bell Tel. Hour Orch., 1956-66, Goldman Band, 1957-62; founding mem., tubist N.Y. Brass Quintet, 1954-67; condr., co-prodr. Burke-Phillips All Star Concert Band, 1960-62; co-founder, tubist Matteson-Phillips Tubajazz Consort, 1976—; founding mem. TubaShop Quartet, 1996—; rec. artist Crest Records, 1958-78—; originator Octubafest, TubaChristmas, Tubasantas, Tubajazz, TubaEaster, Tubacompany, Summertubafest; exec. editor Instrumentalist mag., 1986-96, bd. advisors, 1996—. Founder, pres. Harvey Phillips Found., Inc., N.Y.C., 1977—; bd. dirs. Mid-Am. Festival of the Arts, 1982-90, Bloomington Area Arts Coun., 1983-90; judge 1st Internt. tuba competition of CIEM Internat. Competition for Musical Performers, Geneva, 1991. Served with U.S. Army Field Band, 1955-56. Recipient Disting. Svc. to Music award Kappa Kappa Psi, 1978, Cmty. Svc. award City of Bloomington, 1978, Nat. Assn. Jazz Educators award, 1977, 78, Nat. Music Conf. award, 1977, T.U.B.A. award, 1978, MI Hummel The Tuba Player award, 1990, Disting. Achievement award Ednl. Press Assn. Am., 1991, Mentor Ideal award Assn. Concert Bands, 1994, Lifetime Achievement award United Music Instruments, 1995, Sudler award medal of the Order of Merit Sousa Found., 1995, Summit Brass Outstanding Svc. and Support Internat. Brassfest, 1995, Orpheus award Phi Mu Alpha Sinfonia, 1997; elected to Acad. Wind and Percussion Arts Nat. Band Assn., 1995; recipient Edwin Franko Goldman citation Am. Bandmasters Assn., 1996, Devel. of Mus. Artistry and Opportunities for Future Generations award Colonial Euphonium Tuba Inst., 1998, Lifetime Achievement award Rafael Mendez Brass Inst., 1998, Platinum Piston Lifetime Achievement award, U. Ga., 1999; Legion of Hon., Goldman Meml. Band, 2002; Harvey Phillips Day proclaimed New England Conservatory Music, 1971, Harvey Phillips Day proclaimed Marionville, Mo. Bicentennial, 1976, Harvey Phillips Weekend Gov. of Mo., 1982; named hon. mem. U.S. Army Band Pershings Own, 1984. Mem. Am. Fedn. Musicians, Tubists Universal Brotherhood Assn. (bd. advs. 1973—, pres. 1984-87, hon.), Hoagy Carmichael Jazz Soc. (founder, acting pres. 1983—), Tau Beta Sigma, Phi Mu Alpha Sinfonia (Orpheus award 1997), Kappa Gamma Psi. Home and Office: Tubaranch 4769 S Harrell Rd Bloomington IN 47401-9028 Office: Sch of Music Ind U Bloomington IN 47405 E-mail: philliph@indiana.edu. *The role of a performer and teacher is to give, to share skills and knowledge. My primary goal in life is to create new opportunities in the music profession, to develop, expand, and preserve the music arts.*

PHILLIPS, HOWARD WILLIAM, investment banker; b. N.Y.C., May 16, 1930; s. Louis and Helen (Klein) P.; children: Jan Davis, Richard Louis; m. Carol Napack, June 9, 1985. BA, Dartmouth Coll., 1951, MBA, 1952; JD, Harvard U., 1957. Bar: NY 1957. Assoc. Cahill, Gordon, Reindel & Ohl, N.Y.C., 1957-64; v.p., gen. counsel McCall Corp., N.Y.C., 1964-68, sr. v.p., 1968-69; ptnr. Oppenheimer & Co., N.Y.C., 1969-81; chmn. Holmes, Phillips & Co., N.Y.C., 1981-83; dir. corp. fin. D.H. Blair Investment Banking Corp., 1983-95. Bd. dirs. Pioneer Behavioral Health, Boston; pres. Asolo Theatre Co., Sarasota, Fla., 2004-. Served to lt. (j.g.) USNR, 1952-54. Mem. Easthampton (N.Y.) Tennis Club, Longboat Key Club (Sarasota), Sara Bay Country Club (Sarasota). Home: Box 2047 3 Cove Hollow Farm Rd East Hampton NY 11937 Office: 500 S Palm Ave Sarasota FL 34236 Office Phone: 941-365-1995.

PHILLIPS, J. DOUGLAS, financial company executive; Vice chmn., Ernst & Young LLP, N.Y.C. Office: Ernst & Young LLP 787 7th Ave Fl 14 New York NY 10019-6085

PHILLIPS, JAMES CHARLES, physicist, researcher; b. New Orleans, Mar. 9, 1933; s. William D. and Juanita (Hahn) P.; m. Joanna Vandenberg, Mar. 1, 1996. BA, U. Chgo., 1952, BS, 1953, MS, 1955, PhD, 1956. Mem. tech. staff Bell Labs., 1956-58; NSF fellow U. Calif. at Berkeley, 1958-59, Cambridge (Eng.) U., 1959-60; faculty U. Chgo., 1960-68, prof. physics, 1965-68; mem. tech. staff Bell Labs., 1968-96; cons. Bell Labs., Lucent Tech., 1996—. Sloan fellow, 1962-66; Guggenheim fellow, 1967. Fellow Am. Phys. Soc. (Buckley prize 1972), Minerals, Metals and Materials Soc. (William Hume-Rothery award 1992); mem. NAS. Home: 204 Springfield Ave Summit NJ 07901-3909

PHILLIPS, JAMES D. retired diplomat; b. Peoria, Ill., Feb. 23, 1933; s. James D. and Ehila (Hardy) P.; m. Rosemary Leeds, Mar. 30, 1957 (div. Dec. 1981); children: Michael, Madolyn, Catherine; m. Lucie Gallistel, Jan. 7, 1984; stepchildren: Charles, David BA, Wichita State U., 1956, MA, 1957; cert., U. Vienna, Austria, 1956; postgrad., Cornell U., 1958-61. Joined fgn. svc. Dept. State, 1961; served at Am. embassy Paris, before 1975; Am. Consulate Zaire, before 1975; Dept. State Washington, before 1975; dep. chief of mission Am. Embassy, Luxembourg, 1975-78, charge d'affaires, 1978—80; student Nat. War Coll., Washington, 1980-81; office dir. Dept. State, Washington, 1981-84; consul gen. Am. Consulate, Casablanca, Morocco, 1984-86; US Amb. to Burundi, 1986-90; US Amb. Republic of the Congo, 1990-93; diplomat in residence The Carter Ctr., Atlanta, 1993-94; ret., 1994; pres. Dan Phillips & Assoc., Arlington, Va., 1994—. Bd. dir. Gulf Resources, H.M. Salaam Found. Contbr. articles to profl. jours. Bd. dir. Jane Goodall Inst., 1994-2000. Mem.: Chevy Chase Club. Avocations: golf, tennis, skiing. Home: 3607 Military Rd Arlington VA 22207-4829 Office: 1101 30th St NW Ste 200 Washington DC 20007-3769

PHILLIPS, JAMES EDGAR, lawyer; b. N.Y.C., Aug. 30, 1947; s. Jack Louis Phillips and Jacqueline (Kasper) Ehrman; children: Zachary J., Mark H. BA, Boston U., 1971; JD, Case Western Reserve U., 1975. Bar: Ohio 1975, U.S. Supreme Ct. 1977, U.S. Dist. Ct. (so. dist.) 1978, U.S. Ct. Appeals (6th cir.) 1981, U.S. Dist. Ct. (no. dist.) 1982. Asst. prosecutor Franklin County Prosecutor Office, Columbus, Ohio, 1975-77, sr. asst. prosecutor, 1977-79; assoc. Vorys, Sater, Seymour & Pease, Columbus, 1979-84, ptnr., 1984—; spl. prosecutor State of Ohio, 1993—. Gen. counsel Nat. Fraternal Order of Police, Washington, 1987—, Conrail Police #1, U.S. Postal Police #2; mem. Bd. Profl. Law Enforcement Certification; pres. Ohio Ctr. for Law-Related Edn., 1985-95; mem. Wong Sun Soc., 1997—. Author: Civil Recovery in Ohio, 1986, Collective Bargaining in the Pub. Sector, 1988; editor Bar Briefs; contbr. articles Jours., 1987-89. Fellow Ohio Bar Found., Columbus Bar Found., Ohio Bar Assn. (chmn. com. law-related edn. 1982-86), Columbus Bar Assn., Am. Judicature Soc., Sixth Cir. Jud. Conf. (life); bd. dirs. Ohio Assn. Criminal Defense Lawyers. Office: Vorys Sater Seymour & Pease PO Box 1008 52 E Gay St Columbus OH 43215-3161 E-mail: phillips@vssp.com.

PHILLIPS, JAMES HAROLD, lawyer; b. Dec. 18, 1934; s. Frank Carroll and Mabel Lorraine (James) Phillips; m. Jean Kier Woodruff, Oct. 2, 1959 (dec.); children: Susan, John(dec.), Sara, Jamie. BSEE, Rose-Hulman Inst. Tech., 1960; JD, George Washington U., 1967. Bar: Ariz. 68, U.S. Dist. Ct. Ariz. 68, U.S. Patent Office 68, U.S. Supreme Ct. 72, U.S. Ct. Customs & Patent Appeals 74, Tex. 80, U.S. Ct. Appeals (fed. cir.) 82. Patent atty. GE, 1967—68; ptnr. Drummond, Cahill & Phillips, Phoenix, 1968—73; asst. patent counsel NCR Corp., Dayton, Ohio, 1973—76; sr. profl. atty. Sun Co. Inc., Dallas, 1976—84; ptnr. Cates & Phillips, Phoenix, 1984—88; asst. patent counsel Bull HN Info. Sys., Phoenix, 1988—95; patent cons. Bull NH Info. Sys., Phoenix, 2000—; counsel Squire, Sanders and Dempsey, Phoenix, 1995—2000. Contbr. articles to profl. jours. Charter mem. Phoenix Symphony Coun.; pres. AMICA-Tex. chpt. With USN, 1952—55. Mem.: Tex. Bar Assn., Ariz. Bar Assn. (chmn. patent, trademark and copyright sect. 1985—86). Home: 8519 W Coyote Dr Peoria AZ 85383 Office: Bull HN Info Sys Inc 13430 N Black Canyon Hwy Phoenix AZ 85029-1361

PHILLIPS, JANET COLLEEN, retired educational association executive, editor; b. Pittsfield, Ill., Apr. 29, 1933; d. Roy Lynn and Catherine Amelia (Wills) Barker; m. David Lee Phillips, Feb 7, 1954; children— Clay Cullen, Sean Vincent. BS, U Ill, 1954. Reporter Quincy (Ill.) Herald Whig, 1951, 52, soc. editor, 1953; editorial asst. Pub. Info. Office U. Ill.-Urbana, 1953-54, asst. editor libr., 1954-61; asst. editor Assn. for Libr. and Info. Sci. Edn., State College, Pa., 1960-61, mng. editor, 1961-89, exec. sec., 1970-89; adminstrv. dir. Interlibr. Delivery Svc. of Pa., 1990-99; ret. Mem. Palmer Mus. Arts, State Coll. Cmty. Theatre, Mt. Nittany Med. Ctr. Mem. Assn. for Libr. and Info. Sci. Edn., Embroiderer's Guild Am., Pa. State Blue Golf Course Club, Faculty Women's Club, Ctr. Hills Country Club, C.A.L.L., Delta Zeta. Presbyterian. Avocations: travel, golf, sewing, needlecraft. Address: 471 Park Ln State College PA 16803-3208 E-mail: janph2@aol.com.

PHILLIPS, JEANNE L. ambassador; b. Ark., Sept. 1939; Grad., So. Meth. U. Pres., CEO Jeanne Johnson & Co., Dallas; mng. dir. Pub. Strategies, Inc., Dallas; U.S. rep. to Orgn. for Econ. Cooperation and Devel., 2001—. Mem. M.D. Anderson Bd. Visitors; assoc. bd. mem. Cox Sch. Bus., So. Meth. U.; bd. dirs. John G. Tower Ctr. for Polit. Studies, So. Med. U.; exec. dir. 54th Presdl. Inaugural Com.; dep. chmn. ops. Rep. Nat. Com., Washington; bd. mem. Dallas Jr. League, Inc., Charter 100, Dallas Assembly. Office: DOS Amb Orgn for Econ Cooperation and Devel Washington DC 20521

PHILLIPS, JOHN, communications executive; Pres., COO Advanced Telecoms. Corp., 1985-88; CEO Resurgens Comms. Group, Inc., 1989-93; pres., CEO Actava, 1994-95; pres., CEO, dir. Metromedia Internat. Group Inc. (formerly Actava), 1995-96; chmn., CEO Resurgens Comms., 1997-99; pres., CEO World Access, Atlanta, 1999—. Office: World Access Inc 945 E Paces Ferry Rd NE Atlanta GA 30326-1376

PHILLIPS, JOHN A(TLAS), III, geneticist, educator; b. Sanford, N.C., Jan. 24, 1944; s. John A. and Rachael (Sloan) P.; m. Gretchen Lynch, Aug. 1, 1965; children: Jennifer Allene, John Atlas IV, Charles Andrew, James William. Student, U. N.C., 1962-65; MD, Wake Forest U., 1969. Diplomate Am. Bd. Pediatrics, Am. Bd. Med. Genetics. Intern Children's Hosp. Med. Ctr., Boston, 1969-70, jr. resident, 1970-71, sr. resident, 1973-74, chief resident, 1974-75; asst. prof. Johns Hopkins U., Balt., 1978-82, assoc. prof., 1982-84; prof. pediatrics Vanderbilt U., Nashville, 1984—, prof. biochemistry, 1986—, David T. Karzon chair genetics, 1992—. Bd. sci. counselors Nat. Inst. Child Health, Washington, 1984-88; counsilor Ctr. Study Polymorphisme Humain, Paris, 1988—; mem. adv. com. Ctr. Reproductive Biology, Nashville, 1990-94; bd. dirs. March of Dimes Birth Defects Found., Nashville, 1986—; mem. adv. bd. Nat. Neurofibromatosis Found., Tenn., 1990—; mem. Tenn. Genetics Adv. Com., Nashville, 1984—. Contbr. to profl. publs. Lt. comdr. USNR, 1971-73. Recipient Sidney Farber award Children's Hosp., Boston, 1975, E Mead Johnson award Mead Johnson Co., 1984; Pediatric Postdoctoral fellow Johns Hopkins U. Sch. Medicine, 1975-77. Mem. Am. Soc. Clin. Investigation, Soc. Pediatric Rsch., Am. Coll. Med. Genetics (founding, bd. dirs. 1995—), Phi Beta Kappa, Alpha Omega Alpha. Achievements include discovery of cause of hemoglobin H disease in Black Americans; chromosomal location of multiple genes in humans; improved diagnoses of cystic fibrosis, hemophilia, inborn metabolic errors, familial neurodegenerative diseases, familial pulmonary hypertension, familial pulmonary fibrosis. Office: Vanderbilt U Sch Medicine Divsn Med Genetics DD 2205 Nashville TN 37232-0001

PHILLIPS, JOHN BOMAR, lawyer; b. Murfreesboro, Tenn., Jan. 28, 1947; s. John Bomar Sr. and Betty Blanche (Primm) P.; m. Ellen Elizabeth Ellis, Aug. 9, 1969; children: John Bomar III, Anna Carroll, Ellis Elizabeth. BS, David Lipscomb Coll., 1969; JD, U. Tenn., 1974. Bar: Tenn. 1974, U.S. Dist. Ct. (ea. dist.) Tenn. 1975, U.S. Ct. Appeals (6th cir.) 1980. Assoc. Stophel, Caldwell & Heggie, Chattanooga, 1974-79; ptnr. Caldwell, Heggie & Helton, Chattanooga, 1979-91, Miller & Martin, Chattanooga, 1991—, mng. ptnr., 1997—2002; deputy gen. counsel labor and employment Coca-Cola Enterprises Inc., 2002—. Author: Tennessee Employment Law, 1989, 3d edit., 2000, Employment Law Desk Book for Tennessee Employers, 1989; editor: Tennessee Employment Law Letter, 1986—; host Danger Zones Video Tng. Series for Suprs., 1998—; mem. nat. moot ct. team U. Tenn. Law Rev. Pres. Chattanooga State coll. Found., 1992-94, Boys Club of Chattanooga, 1983-84; sec. Tenn. Aquarium, 1989—; chmn. Chattanooga Conv. and Visitors Bur., 1996-97; bd. dirs. Vol. Comty. Sch., Chattanooga, 1980-85, Coun. for Alcohol and Drug Abuse, Chattanooga, 1981-83, Creative Discovery Mus., 1994-99, Girls Prep. Sch., 1997-2002, Allied Arts of Gtr. Chattanooga, 1997-2002; mem. Hamilton County Juvenile Ct. Commn., 1995-99. Fellow Tenn. Bar Found., Chattanooga Bar Found.; mem. ABA (labor law sect.), Tenn. Bar Assn. (chair labor law sect. 1992-93, Justice Joseph W. Henry award 1986-87), Chattanooga Bar Assn. (bd. govs. 1978-79), Chattanooga C. of C. (bd. dirs. 1998-2001), Order of Coif, Fairyland Country Club (Lookout Mountain, Tenn.), Walden Club (bd. govs. 1992-95), Mountain City Club, Kiwanis (pres. Chattanooga 1986-87). Episcopal. Avocations: reading, writing. Home: 1107 E Brow Rd Lookout Mountain TN 37350-1015 Office: Miller & Martin 832 Georgia Ave Ste 1000 Chattanooga TN 37402-2289 E-mail: jphillips@millermartin.com.

PHILLIPS, JOHN C. lawyer; b. SI, NY, June 6, 1948; s. John D. G. and Eleanor (Stier) P.; m. Karen Francis McKenna, June 5, 1971; children: James, Thomas, Robert. AB in Govt., Cornell U., 1970; MA in Polit. Sci., Rutgers U., 1972, JD, 1975. Bar: NJ 1975, US Dist. Ct. NJ 1975, NY 1982, US Supreme Ct. 1985, US Ct. Appeals (3d cir.) 1985, Fla. 1988. Assoc. Carpenter, Bennett & Morrisey, Newark, 1975-79, Buttermore, Mullen & Jeremiah, Westfield, NJ, 1979-80; mng. ptnr. Buttermore, Mullen, Jeremiah & Phillips, Westfield, 1981-85, 87-2001; with DeVos, Phillips & Co. PC, 1986-87; of counsel Price, Meese, Shulman & D'Arminio, 2001—. Trustee, dir. Animal Care Fund Inc., East Smithfield, Pa., 1983-98. Author: (with others) New Jersey Transactions, Zoning and Planning, 1993. Dir., coach Police Athletic League, Berkeley Heights, NJ, 1967-99; mem. Kappa Alpha Literary Soc., 1967—, trustee Kappa Alpha Assn., 1974-90, v.p. Kappa Alpha Assn. Found., 1978-87, vice-chmn., 1983, chmn., 1984; dir. Youth Soccer Club, Berkeley Heights, 1983-94; mem. Berkeley Heights Twp. Com., 1985-87, dep. mayor, 1986, 87; Twp. atty., Berkeley Heights, 1989, 91, 94-2002; planning bd. atty. Twp. Warren, 1987-2001; mem. NJ Hotel and Multiple Dwelling Safety Bd., 1988—, vice chmn., 1998—; mem. Rep. Mcpl. Com., 1985-2000, vice chmn., 1990-92, 98-2000, mem. dist. XII ethics com., 1993-97, dist. XII fee arbitration com., 1998-2002. Recipient award for Assistance and Dedication to youth, Police Athletic League, Berkeley Heights, 1975, Dedicated Svc. award Berkeley Heights Twp. Com., 1983. Mem.: ABA, Inst. of Mcpl. Attys., Fedn. of Planning Ofcls., Urban Land Inst., Union County Bar Assn., N.J. State Bar Assn., Canoe Brook Country Club, Jaycees (sec. New Providence-Berkeley Heights chpt. 1982, Jaycee of Yr. 1982). Republican. Methodist. Home: 56 Emerson Ln Berkeley Heights NJ 07922-2414 Office: Price Meese Shulman & D'Arminio 50 Tice Blvd Woodcliff Lake NJ 07677 Office Phone: 201-391-3737. E-mail: jphillips@pricemeese.com.

PHILLIPS, JOHN EDWARD, zoologist, educator; b. Montréal, Que., Can., Dec. 20, 1934; s. William Charles and Violet Mildred (Lewis) P.; m. Eleanor Mae Richardson, Sept. 8, 1956; children: Heather Anne, Jayne Elizabeth, Jonathan David, Catherine Melinda, Wendy Susannah. BSc with honors, Dalhousie U., Halifax, N.S., 1956, MSc, 1957; PhD, Cambridge U., Eng., 1961. Asst. prof. Dalhousie U., Halifax, N.S., 1960-64; assoc. prof. U. B.C., Vancouver, Can., 1964-71, prof., 1971—, head dept. zoology, 1991-96. Vis. rschr. Cambridge (Eng.) U., 1972, 76, 81; chair grant selection com. Nat. Rsch. Coun. Can., Ottawa, Ont., 1969-71; mem. coun. Nat. Sci. and Engring. Rsch. Coun., Ottawa, 1983-87. Mem. editorial bd.: Can. Jour. Zoology, 1971-75, Am. Jour. Physiology, 1978-93, Jour. Experimental Biology, 1981-85, Am. Zool., 1996-01; contbr. articles to profl. jours. Mem. grant selection com. Can. Cystic Fibrosis Found., Toronto, 1989-91; active Vancouver Bach Choir. Named to James chair St. Francis Xavier U., Antigonish, N.S., 1993; recipient Killam Rsch. prize U. B.C. Fellow Royal Soc. Can.; mem. Can. Soc. Zoologists (sec. 1972-76, v.p. 1976-78, pres. 1979, Fry medal 2000), Am. Soc. Zoologists (exec. 1983-85, chair divsn. comp. physiol. biochemistry 1983-85). Avocations: music, choir. Home: 12908 22 B Ave White Rock BC Canada V4A 6Z3 Office: U BC Dept Zoology Vancouver BC Canada V6T 1Z4 E-mail: jephillips@telus.net.

PHILLIPS, JOHN GRANT (JACK PHILLIPS), theatre director; b. Chgo., May 17, 1941; s. Edward Grant and Mary Kathryn Phillips; m. Sharon Ferguson, June 29, 1964 (div. June 1976); 1 child, Brendan Grant; m. Deborah King Anderson, Apr. 22, 1978; 1 child, Kathryn Sarah. BA, Beloit Coll., 1963; MFA, Yale U., 1974. Actor, tech. dir. Ct. Theatre, Beloit, Wis., 1960-70; assoc. prodr. Westwood Playhouse, L.A., 1976-77; v.p. Garrett Co., L.A., 1977-81; prodn. stage mgr. Getting My Act Together..., L.A., Phila., 1980-81, Am. Repertory Theatre, Cambridge, Mass., 1982-88; co-chmn. Harvard Advanced Theatre Tng. Inst., Cambridge, 1988-89; exec. dir. Spokane (Wash.) Civic Theatre, 1991—. Guest artist Ithaca Coll., 1990; adj. faculty Gonzaga U., 1996, Eastern Wash. U., 2002, Lesley U. Grad. Sch. of Edn., Cambridge,

1988—. Dir over 250 live stage plays; actor various roles. Mem. Leadership Spokane, 1992; citizen's adv. com. Spokesman-Rev., 1993-2000. John Shubert Meml. scholar Yale Drama Sch., 1973-74; recipient Local Emmy, 1993. Mem. Am. Assn. Cmty. Theatre (pres. 1999-2001), Actors' Equity Assn., Screen Actors' Guild, Rotary Internat. Avocations: reading, hiking, camping. Office: Spokane Civic Theatre 1020 N Howard St Spokane WA 99201-2204 E-mail: civictheatre@mindspring.com.

PHILLIPS, JOHN P(AUL), retired neurosurgeon; b. Danville, Ark., Oct. 14, 1932; s. Brewer William Ashley and Wave Audrey (Page) P.; m. June Helen Dunbar, Dec. 14, 1963; children: Todd Eustace, Timothy John Colin, Tyler William Ashley. AB cum laude, Hendrix Coll., 1953; MD, U. Tenn., 1956. Diplomate Am. Bd. Neurol. Surgeons. Intern Charity Hosp. La., New Orleans, 1957; resident surgery U. Tenn. Hosps., 1958; resident neurol. surgery U. Tenn. Med. Units, 1958-62; practice medicine, specializing in neurol. surgery Salinas, Calif., 1962-93; ret., 1993. Chief of staff, chief of surgery Salinas Valley Meml. Hosp.; mem. staffs Community Hosp. Monterey Peninsula, U. Calif. Hosp., San Francisco; asst. clin. prof. U. Calif., 1962—. Commd. Ky. col. Mem. AMA, ACS, Internat. Coll. Surgery, Harvey Cushing Soc., Congress Neurol. Surgery, Western Neurosurg. Assn., San Francisco Neurol. Soc., Pan Pacific Surg. Assn., Stanford U. Faculty Club (emeritus), Alpha Omega Alpha, Phi Chi, Alpha Chi. Home: 6 Mesa Del Sol Salinas CA 93908-9324

PHILLIPS, JOHN ROBERT, political scientist, educator; b. Henderson, Ky., Dec. 16, 1942; s. Leander Armstead and Ann Reid (Brown) P. Diploma, Lang. Inst., Chateauroux, France, 1966, BA, Centre Coll., Danville, Ky., 1969; MA, Western Ky. U., Bowling Green, 1973. Instr. Drury Coll., Springfield, Mo., 1971-73, Western Ky. U., Bowling Green, 1975-79; asst. prof. Thiel Coll., Greenville, Pa., 1979-83, scholar-in-residence, 1983-85; pvt. cons., 1985—; adj. prof. Lockyear Coll., Evansville, Ind., 1987-88, prof. adminstrv. and social scis., 1988-91, acad. dean, 1988-90, v.p. acad. affairs, dean coll., 1990-91, Helen Hoffman disting. svc. prof., 1990-91; exec. dir. Henderson County Human Rels. Commn., 1991-93; dean acad. affairs, prof. political studies/govt. Springfield (Ill.) Coll., 1993-97, acting pres., 1996-97, provost, dean coll., 1997-98, prof. polit. and social scis., 1998—, Rose and H. Paul LaFata Endowed Chair for Disting. Tchg., 2003. Adj. prof. pub. adminstrn. Ind. State U., Terre Haute, 1991-92; field investigator on religion and culture in ancient city of Taxila, Pakistan, 1968, on indsl. pollution of hist. bldgs. and monuments, France, Italy, Austria, 1969; rschr. on nationalism, Scotland, 1972, 2002, on local Scottish govt. and urban deves., 1993; participant in internat. confs. on The Future of a United Germany, 1991; mem. adv. coun. St. John's Hosp. Sch. Respiratory Therapy, 1993-97, Ursuline Acad Sch. Bd., v.p., 1995-97, pres., 1997-99, Cen. Ill. Fgn. Lang. and Internat. Studies Consortium, 1993—, chmn., 1994-96; cons.-evaluator Higher Learning Commn., North Ctrl. Assn. Colls. and Schs., 1999—. Mem. editl. bd.: Jour. Urban Affairs, 1985—89, book rev. editor: Pub. Voices, 2003, manuscript referee: Pub. Adminstrn. Rev., 1985—87, contbr.: chpts. to multi-vol. reference series The Small City and Regional Cmty., contbr.: songs, contbr.: chpts. to multi-vol. reference series The Small City and Regional Cmty., contbr.: chpts. to multi-vol. reference series The Small City and Regional Cmty., contbr.: chpts. to multi-vol. reference series The Small City and Regional Cmty., asst. editor: Pub. Voices, 2001—03; contbr. scientific papers articles on urban affairs, ednl. policy and practice, the Am. Presidency, policy planning, and federalism/intergovtl. rels. to profl. jours. Policy advisor Lt. Gov.'s Office, Frankfort, Ky., 1985-86; cons. Commn. on Ky.'s Future, Frankfort, 1985-87; mem. Bd. Cath. Edn., Diocese of Springfield, 1994-97; trustee Springfield Coll., 1996-97, commn. on human sexuality Episcopal Diocese of Springfield, 1997-98; bd. dirs. Liturgical Arts Festival of Springfield, 1998-2001. With USAF, 1963-68. Recipient Outstanding Tchg. in Polit. Sci. award, Am. Polit. Sci. Assn. and Pi Sigma Alpha, 2003. Mem. Am. Polit. Sci. Assn. (Leon Weaver Award com. 1990-93), Am. Soc. Pub. Adminstrn. (publs. com. 1984-88, 92-95), Urban Affairs Assn. (publs. com. 1985-89, nominating com. 1984-85, 88-89), Pi Sigma Alpha, Alpha Sigma Lambda. Democrat. Episcopalian. Home: 2605 Delaware Dr Springfield IL 62702-1213 Office: Springfield College L-106 Becker Libr 1500 N 5th St Springfield IL 62702-2643 E-mail: phillips@sci.edu.

PHILLIPS, J(OHN) TAYLOR, judge; b. Greenville, S.C., Aug. 20, 1921; s. Walter Dixon and Mattie Sue (Taylor) P.; m. Mary Elizabeth Parrish, Dec. 18, 1954; children: John Allen, Susan, Linda-Lea, Julia. AA, Glenville State Coll., 1952; JD, Mercer U., 1955; LLD, Asbury Coll., 1992. Bar: Ga. 1954, U.S. Supreme Ct. 1969. Mem. Ho. of Reps. State of Ga., Atlanta, 1959-62, Senate, 1962-64. With USMC, 1942-51. Methodist. Home: 1735 Winston Dr Macon GA 31206-3241 Office: State Ct Bibb County PO Box 6242 Macon GA 31208

PHILLIPS, JOSEPH BRANTLEY, JR., lawyer; b. Greenville, S.C., Dec. 5, 1931; BS in Bus. Adminstrn., U. S.C., 1954, JD, 1955. Bar: S.C. 1955. Assoc. Leatherwood, Walker, Todd & Mann, Greenville, 1958-63, ptnr., 1963—. Chmn. bd. deacons Presbyterian Ch., 1970-71, pres. Men of Ch., 1968-69, chmn. Christian Service Ctr., 1972-73; bd. dirs. Greenville Urban Ministry, 1978. Mem. ABA, S.C. Bar Assn., Greenville Bar Assn., Greenville Young Lawyers Club (pres. 1961-62), Lawyers Pilots Bar Assn., Kiwanis (pres. 1973). Clubs: Greenville Country (pres. 1977). Home: 207 Butler Springs Rd Greenville SC 29615-2261 Office: PO Box 87 Greenville SC 29602-0087 E-mail: jbphillipsjr@aol.com.

PHILLIPS, JOSEPH DANIEL, geophysicist, oceanographer; b. Woodbury, NJ, Sept. 11, 1938; s. Joseph Francis and Katherine Cecelia (Browne) P.; m. Gwendolyn Williams, 1961; children: Julia Kear, Stephanie Morgan, Joseph Williams. BA, Rutgers U., 1961; MS in Engring., Princeton U., 1963, MA, 1964, PhD, 1966. Engr. trainee Mobil Oil Co., N.Y.C., 1957, N.Y. Shipbuilding Corp., Camden, N.J., 1958-60; engr. mgmt. trainee N.J. Bell Tel. Co., Newark/Camden, N.J., 1961; rsch. asst. Princeton (N.J.) U., 1962-65; asst. scientist Woods Hole (Mass.) Oceanographic Inst., 1965-68, assoc. scientist, 1968-77; staff rsch. scientist MIT, Cambridge, 1977-79; sr. rsch. scientist U. Tex., Austin, 1978-96; chief scientist World Geoscience Corp., Houston, 1996-1999; chief scientist, dir. tech. svcs. Fugro Airborne Surveys, Houston, 1999-2000; chief scientist, dir. tech. svs. Integrated Geophysics Corp., Houston, 2000. Cons. Mobil Oil Corp., Dallas, 1969, Exxon Corp., Houston, 1977, Bell Tel. Labs., Whippany/Murray Hill, N.J., 1976-78; vis. scholar U. Cambridge, Eng., 1974-75; adj. prof./instr. marine geophysics, seismics and geomagnetism, oceanography, acoustics and potential fields, faculty advisor MIT, Woods Hole Oceanographic Inst., U. Tex., 1968-96; cons. airborne/marine archeology Nat. Underwater and Marine Archeologic Agy., 1997, 98, 2003-. Contbr. articles to Jour. Geophys. Rsch. Sci., Geol. Soc. Am., Am. Petroleum Geologist, Ency. Brittanica. Fellow Explorers Club; mem. Am. Soc. Naval Engrs., Am. Geophys. Union, Soc. Exploration Geophysicists, AAAS, Marine Lodge, Phi Beta Kappa, Sigma Xi. Achievements include design of phase lock-in amplifiers for rock magnetometers; USN multi-beam sonar for seafloor geology; acoustically navigated vehicles for seafloor studies; vertical seismic profiling aboard deep ocean drilling project ships; aeromagnetic/electromagnetic detection of archeologic and groundwater salinity contamination sites; pipeline and wellhead surveying; multichannel acoustic reflection profile imaging of ocean watermasses. Home: 3805 Gaines Ranch Austin TX 78735 Personal E-mail: joephillipsD@sbcglobal.net.

PHILLIPS, KAREN A. urban planner; b. Ocilla, Ga. BA landscape architecture, Sch. Environ. Design U. Ga.; MA landscape architecture, Harvard U. Grad. Sch. Design, 1982. Urban planner, Atlanta, N.Y.C.; project mgr. econ. devel. dept. N.Y. State Urban Devel. Corp.; co-founder, pres., CEO Abyssinian Devel. Corp., N.Y.C., 1989—2002; mem. N.Y.C. Planning Commn., 2002—. Adj. prof. Sch. Architecture and Environ. Studies, City Coll, N.Y., 1992; cmty. devel. fellow Milano Grad Sch., New Sch. U., 2002—03. Mem. Parks Coun., Urban Design Inst., Preservation League of NY, Hamilton Heights Homeowners Assn., Manhattan Coun. Boy Scouts Am.; apptd. design com. Martin Luther King., Jr. Nat. Monument Project. Fellow: Am. Soc. Landscape Arch.; mem.: Assn. Real Estate Women. Office: NYC Dept City Planning 22 Reade St New York NY 10007-1216

PHILLIPS, KAREN BORLAUG, economist, railroad industry executive; b. Long Beach, Calif., Oct. 1, 1956; d. Paul Vincent and Wilma (Tish) Borlaug. Student, Cath. U. P.R., 1973-74; BA, BS, U. N.D., 1977; postgrad., George Washington U., 1978-80. Rsch. asst. rsch. and spl. programs adminstrn. U.S. Dept. Transp., Washington, 1977—78, economist, office of sec., 1978—82; profl. staff mem. (majority) Com. Commerce Sci., Transp. U.S. Senate, Washington, 1982—85, tax economist (minority) com. on fin., 1985—87, chief economist (majority) senate com. on fin., 1987—88; commr. Interstate Commerce Commn., Washington, 1988—94; v.p. legis. Assn. Am. Railroads, Washington, 1994—95, sr. v.p. policy, legis. and comm., 1995—98; pres. Policy & Advocacy Assocs., Alexandria, Va., 1998—2000; v.p. U.S. pub. and govt. affairs Can. Nat. Ry. Co., Washington, 2000—. Contbr. articles to profl. jours. Recipient award for Meritorious Achievement, Sec. Transp., 1980, Spl. Achievement awards, 1978, 80, Outstanding Performance awards, 1978, 80, 81. Mem. Am. Econ. Assn., Women's Transp. Seminar (Woman of Yr. award 1994), Transp. Rsch. Forum, Assn. Transp. Law, Logistics and Policy, Tax Coalition, Can.-Am. Bus. Coun. (bd. dirs.), Blue Key, Phi Beta Kappa, Omicron Delta Epsilon. Republican. Lutheran. Office: Can Nat Rlwy Co Ste 500 601 Pennsylvania Ave NW Washington DC 20004 Office Phone: 202-347-7816. E-mail: karen.phillips@cn.ca.

PHILLIPS, KEITH WENDALL, minister; b. Portland, Oreg., Oct. 21, 1946; s. Frank Clark and Velma Georgina (Black) P.; m. Mary Katherine Garland, July 16, 1973; children: Joshua, Paul, David. BA, UCLA, 1968; MDiv, Fuller Theology Sem., 1971, D. of Ministries, 1972; LHD (hon.), John Brown U., 1990; LHD (hon.), Sterling Coll., 2002. Dir. Youth For Christ Clubs, L.A., 1965-71; pres. World Impact, L.A., 1971—. Commencement speaker Tabor Coll., 1969, 91, John Brown U., 1990, Sterling Coll., 2002. Author: Everybody's Afraid in the Ghetto, 1973, They Dare to Love the Ghetto, 1975, The Making of a Disciple, 1981, No Quick Fix, 1985, Out of Ashes, 1996. Chmn. L.A. Mayor's Prayer Breakfast Com., 1985—; bd. dirs. Christian Cmty. Devel. Assn., 1992—; founder/coord. Crowns of Beauty Confs.; spkr. Promise Keeper. Named Disting. Staley lectr., 1969. Mem. Evangelistic Com. of Newark (pres. 1976—), World Impact of Can. (pres. 1978—), The Oaks (pres. 1985—), Faith Works (pres. 1987—) Baptist. Office: World Impact 2001 S Vermont Ave Los Angeles CA 90007-1279 *Our knowledge of God's Word outruns our obedience. The challenge for Christians is to live what we know.*

PHILLIPS, KENNETH WAYNE, music educator; b. Pensacola, Fla., Feb. 16, 1963; s. James F. and Jane K. Phillips; m. Elizabeth Gonzalez Phillips, June 22, 2003. AA, Pensacola (Fla.) Jr. Coll., 1984; BA in Ch. Music, U. of Mobile, 1987; M in Music Edn., U. So. Miss., 1992; PhD in Music Edn., Temple U., 1997. Cert. tchr. Fla. Dept. of Edn., 2002. Music tchr. Escambia County Sch. Dist., Pensacola, Fla., 1990—92; tchg. asst. Temple U., Phila., 1993—97; vis. prof. of music edn. Western Ill. U., Macomb, Ill., 1997—98; assoc. prof. music edn. Palm Beach (Fla.) Atlantic U., 1998—. Singer: (DVD) Sarah Brightman, La Luna, 2001. Scholar, Temple U., 1993—96. Mem.: Soc. for Rsch. in Music Edn., Fla. Collegiate Music Educators Assn., Fla. Music Educators Assn., Music Educators Nat. Conf. Home: 333 Palmetto Street West Palm Beach FL 33405 Office: Palm Beach Atlantic University PO Box 24708 West Palm Beach FL 33416-4708 Office Phone: 561-803-2411. Business E-Mail: ken_phillips@pba.edu. E-mail: ken_phillips@pba.edu.

PHILLIPS, LARRY ARTHUR, artist; b. Syracuse, N.Y., Mar. 6, 1951; s. Arthur Foster and Vivian Phillips. Cork Gallery, Lincoln Ctr., N.Y.C., 1990. Mem.: Ward-Nasse Gallery, Intuit the Ctr. for Intuitive and Outsider Art, Christians in Visual Arts. Home: 709 S West St Apt 4 Syracuse NY 13202

PHILLIPS, LARRY EDWARD, lawyer; b. Pitts., July 5, 1942; s. Jack F. and Jean H. (Houghtelin) P.; m. Karla Ann Hennings, June 5, 1976; 1 son, Andrew H.; 1 stepson, John W. Dean IV. BA, Hamilton Coll., 1964; JD, U. Mich., 1967. Bar: Pa. 1967, Fla. 2004, US Dist. Ct. (we. dist.) Pa. 1967, US Tax Ct. 1969. Assoc. Buchanan, Ingersoll PC, Pitts., 1967—73, shareholder, 1973. Mem. ABA (sect. taxation, com. on corp. tax and sect. real property, probate and trust law), Am. Coll. Tax Counsel, Pa. Bar Assn., Tax Mgmt. Inc. (adv. bd.), Pitts. Tax Club, Allegheny County Bar Assn., Duquesne Club. Republican. Presbyterian. Office: Buchanan Ingersoll PC One Oxford Ctr 301 Grant St Fl 20 Pittsburgh PA 15219-1410 Office Phone: 412-562-8846. E-mail: phillipsle@bipc.com.

PHILLIPS, LAUGHLIN, art museum chairman emeritus, former magazine editor; b. Washington, Oct. 20, 1924; s. Duncan and Marjorie Grant (Acker) P.; m. Elizabeth Hood, 1956 (div. 1975); children: Duncan Vance, Elizabeth Laughlin; m. Jennifer Stats Cafritz, 1975. Student, Yale U., 1942-43; MA, U. Chgo., 1949. Fgn. svc. officer, 1949—64, Hanoi, Vietnam, 1950—53, Tehran, Iran, 1957—59; co-founder Washingtonian mag., 1965, editor, 1965-74, editor-in-chief, 1974-79; pres. Washington Mag., Inc., 1965-79; dir. Phillips Collection, 1972-92, chmn. of bd., 1967—2002. Chmn. bd. dirs. Nat. Coun., UN Assn. Am. Trustee MacDowell Colony, 1977-79, Nat. Com. for an Effective Congress, 1966—. With AUS, 1943-46, PTO. Decorated Bronze Star; comendador Orden de Mayo al Mérito (Argentina); chevalier de l'Ordre de la Couronne (Belgium), knight's cross 1st class Order of Danebrog (Denmark); officier Arts et Lettres (France). Mem.: Rolling Rock Club (Ligonier, Pa.), Met. Club (Washington), Cosmos Club (Washington). Office: c o Dubois 3031 Federal Hill Dr Falls Church VA 22044

PHILLIPS, LAWRENCE H., II, neurologist, educator; b. Clarksburg, W.Va., Dec. 30, 1947; m. Elayne K. Phillips, 1985; children: Joshua, Melanie. AB, Princeton U., 1970; MD, U. W.Va., 1974. Diplomate Am. Bd. Psychiatry and Neurology. Intern U. Wis. Hosps., Madison, 1974-75; resident in neurology Mayo Clinic, Rochester, Minn., 1975-78, rsch. fellow neurophysiology, 1978-79; instr. neurology Mayo Med. Sch./U. Minn., 1979-80; asst. prof. U. Va. Med. Ctr., Charlottesville, 1981-87, dir. electromyography lab., 1981—, assoc. prof., 1987-95; dir. neuromuscular ctr. Muscular Dystrophy Assn. Clinic, Charlottesville, 1983—; prof. U. Va. Med. Ctr., Charlottesville, 1995—, vice chair dept. neurology and T.R. Johns prof., 1995—. Mem. med. adv. com. Diabetes Rsch. and Tng. Ctr., U. Va., 1981-88; cons. neurologist Mayo Clinic, 1979-80, VA Hosp., Salem, 1983—; cons. panel AMA Diagnostic and Therapeutic Tech. Assessment, 1989—, arbitrator panel, 1990—; expert panel mem. NIH, 1991. Recipient Young Investigator Travel award Internat. Congress Electromyography, 1979. Mem. Am. Neurol. Assn., Am. Acad. Neurology, Am. Assn. Electrodiagnostic Medicine, Assn. Univ. Profs. Neurology, Sigma Xi. Office: U VA Neuromuscular Ctr Med Health Sys PO Box 800394 Charlottesville VA 22908-0001

PHILLIPS, LAYN R. lawyer; b. Oklahoma City, Jan. 2, 1952; s. James Arthur Cole and Eloise (Gulick) P.; m. Kathryn Hale, Aug. 17, 1986; children: Amanda, Parker, Graham. BS, U. Tulsa, 1974, JD, 1977; postgrad., Georgetown U., 1978-79. Bar: Okla. 1977, D.C. 1978, Calif. 1981, Tex. 1991. Asst. U.S. atty., Miami, 1980-81, L.A., 1980-83; trial atty. Bur. of Competition, Washington, 1977-80; U.S. atty. U.S. Dist. Ct. (no. dist.) Okla., Tulsa, 1983-87; judge U.S. Dist. Ct. (we. dist.) Okla., Oklahoma City, 1987-91; litigation ptnr. Irell & Manella, Newport Beach, Calif., 1991—. Tchr. trial practice U. Tulsa Coll. Law, Okla. City U. Law Sch.; lectr. Attys. Gen's. Adv. Inst., Washington. Pres. Am. Inn of Ct. XXIII, Sch. Law, Okla. U., 1989-90; pres. Am. Inn. of Ct. CVIII, Sch. Law., Okla. City U. 1990-91. Named one of Outstanding Young Ams., U.S. Jaycees, 1989. Fellow: ACTL; mem.: Fed. Bar Assn. (pres. Orange County chpt.). Office: Irell & Manella 840 Newport Center Dr Ste 400 Newport Beach CA 92660-6323

PHILLIPS, LEO HAROLD, JR., lawyer; b. Jan. 10, 1945; s. Leo Harold and Martha C. (Oberg) P.; m. Patricia Margaret Halcomb, Sept. 3, 1983. BA summa cum laude, Hillsdale Coll., 1967; MA, U. Mich., 1968, JD cum laude, 1973; LLM magna cum laude, Free U. of Brussels, 1974. Bar: Mich. 1974, N.Y. 1975, U.S. Supreme Ct. 1977, D.C. 1979. Fgn. lectr. Pusan Nat. U., Korea, 1969-70; assoc. Alexander & Green, N.Y.C., 1974-77; counsel Overseas Pvt. Investment Corp., Washington, 1977-80, sr. counsel, 1980-82, asst. gen. counsel, 1982-85, Manor Care, Inc., Gaithersburg, Md., 1985-91, asst. sec., 1988-99, assoc. gen. counsel, 1991-99, v.p., 1996-99. Vol. Peace Corps, Pusan, 1968-71; mem. program for sr. mgrs. in govt. Harvard U., Cambridge, Mass., 1982. Contbr. articles to legal jours. Chmn. legal affairs com. Essex Condominium Assn., Washington, 1979-81; mem. fin. com., cmty. leadership bd. Miami City Ballet, 2001—; deacon Chevy Chase Presbyn. Ch., Washington, 1984-87, moderator, 1985-87, supt. ch. sch., elder, trustee, 1987-90, pres., 1988-90, mem. nominating com., 1995-96. Recipient Alumni Achievement award Hillsdale Coll., 1980; Meritorious Honor award Overseas Pvt. Investment Corp., 1981, Superior Achievement award, 1984. Mem. ABA (internat. fin. transactions com., vice-chmn. com. internat. ins. Law), Am. Soc. Internat. Law (Jessup Internat. Law moot ct. judge semi-final rounds 1978-83, chair corp. counsel com. 1993-97), Internat. Law Assn. (Am. br.; com. sec. 1982), D.C. Bar, N.Y. State Bar Assn., Royal Asiatic Soc. (Korea br.), State Bar Mich., Washington Fgn. Law Soc. (sec.-treas. 1980-81, bd. dirs., program coord. 1981-82, v.p. 1982-83, pres.-elect 1983-84, pres. 1984-85, chmn. nominating com. 1986, 88), Washington Internat. Trade Assn. (bd. dirs. 1984-87), Assn. Bar City N.Y., Hillsdale Coll. Alumni Assn. (co-chmn. Washington area 1977-90), Univ. Club (N.Y.C.), Rotary (Delray Beach treas. 2003-2004, pres.-elect 2004—).

PHILLIPS, LINDA GOLUCH, plastic surgeon, educator, researcher; b. Chgo., Nov. 11, 1951; d. Edward Walter and Rosemarie (Tomasek) Goluch; m. William Anthony Phillips, July 12, 1975; children: Cooper William, Nolan Edward, Spencer Geoffrey, Corinna Lee. BA, U. Chgo., 1974, MD, 1978. Diplomate Am. Bd. Surgery, Am. Bd. Plastic Surgery (mem. qualifying examination team 1993—). Intern U. Chgo., 1978-80; resident in gen. surgery Northwestern U., Chgo., 1980-83, instr., surgeon, 1982-83; asst. prof. Wayne State U., Detroit, 1985-88; asst. prof. plastic surgery U. Tex. Med. Br., Galveston, 1988-91, assoc. prof. plastic surgery, 1991-95; prof. plastic surgery, 1995—, Truman G. Blocker Jr., MD, Disting. chairperson U. Tex. Med. Br., Galveston, chief divsn. plastic surgery, 1994—; mem. consulting med. staff Shriners Burns Inst., Galveston, Tex., 1988—. Chmn. basic rsch. grants com. Plastic Surgery Edn. Found., Chgo., 1992-95, bd. dirs., 1995-98, 2000-03, mem. ednl. assessment com., mem. scholarship com., 1987-92, mem. plastic surgery-in-svc. exam. com., 1987-88, 89-93, mem. instrnl. course com., 1991-92, mem. rsch. fellowship com., mem. rsch. fund proposals com., 1993, 94; parliamentarian Plastic Surgery Rsch. Coun., 1991-93, pres., 1996-97; program chmn., 1996, pres., 1997, Morestin lectr. Nat. Med. Assn., 1991; guest spkr. Royal Coll. Surgeons, Eng., 1993; spkr. in field. Co-author book chpts.; contbr. articles, abstracts to profl. jours. Pres. Blue Marlin Swim Team, Houston, 1993; active Clear Creek Ind. Sch. Dist., Houston, 1992. Grantee in field. Fellow ACS; mem. AMA, Am. Assn. Plastic Surgeons, Am. Burn Assn. (orgn. and delivery of burn care com. 1988-91, ednl. com., 1991-94), Am. Soc. Plastic and Reconstructive Surgeons (program com. 1991-92, exhibits com. 1992, 93, chair, 1993-94, sci. program com. 1994), Am. Soc. Maxillofacial Surgeons (news com. 1992, membership com. 1992-93), Am. Assn. Surgery of Trauma (search com. editor of Jour. Trauma 1992), Am. Soc. Aesthetic Plastic Surgery, Fedn. Assn. Women Surgeons (chair, bd. trustees), Am. Assn. Hand Surgery, Am. Geriat. Soc., Am. Diabetes Assn., Surg. Infection Soc., Assn. Women Surgeons (pres. 1992-94, v.p.-pres.-elect 1990-92, chair program com. 1990-92, chair membership com. 1988-89, nominating com. 1989-92), Blocker-Lewis Surgery Soc. (exec. sec. 1988-92), Assn. Acad. Chairmen of Plastic Surgery (prerequisite com. 1990, 91), Wound Healing Soc. (honors and awards com. 1993, chmn. 1996—), Singleton Surg. Soc. (chmn. 1997), Soc. Head and Neck Surgeons, Tex. Soc. Plastic Surgeons, Assn. Acad. Surgery, N.Y. Acad. Scis., Tex. Med. Assn., Galveston Med. Soc., Plastic Surgery Rev. Com. (chmn. 2002-2003, vice-chair 2000-2001), Am. Bd. Plastic Surgery (chmn. written exam. com. 2003-, dir. 2000-, qualifying exam. team 1993-, certifying (oral) exam. team, comprehensive adv. coun. 1999-), Sigma Xi. Roman Catholic. Avocations: salt water tropical fish, gardening, gourmet cooking. Home: 15823 Sylvan Lake Dr Houston TX 77062-4795 Office: U Tex Med Br 6 124 Mccullough Bldg Galveston TX 77555-0001

PHILLIPS, LINDA LOU, pharmacist; b. Sept. 3, 1952; d. Reece Webster and Bettye Frances (Martin) P. BS in Pharmacy, U. Ark., 1976; MS in Pharmacy, U. Houston, 1980. Registered pharmacist, Tex. Intern Palace Drug Store, Forrest City, Ark., 1976-77; resident in pharmacy Hermann Hosp., Houston, 1978-79; dir. pharmacy Alvin Comty. Hosp., Tex., 1979-80; relief pharmacist Twelve Oaks Hosp., Houston, 1980; cons. pharmacist Health Facilities, Inc., Houston, 1980-81; pharmacy supr. Meth. Hosp., Houston, 1981-99; pharmacist Walmart, Fayetteville, Ark., 1999—2001; ind. relief pharmacist, 2001—. Sec. spl. interest group, IBAX Pharmacy, 1990-93; chmn. HBO and Co., Series 4000, materials mgmt. spl. interest group, 1994-98. Mem. Am. Soc. Hosp. Pharmacists, So. Meth. U. Alumni Assn., Ark. Alumni Assn., Girls' Cotillion Club (bd. dirs. 1983-85), Rho Chi, Pi Sigma Alpha. Republican. Methodist. Home and Office: 1732 Lancaster Dr Springdale AR 72762-8298

PHILLIPS, LOUIS J. humanities educator, writer; b. Lowell, Mass., June 15, 1942; s. Louis James Phillips and Dorothy Margaret Perkins; m. Patricia Louise Ranard, Aug. 26, 1972; children: Ian Donald, Matthew Louis. BA, Stetson U., 1964; MA, U. NC, 1965, CUNY, 1967. Prof. humanities Sch. Visual Arts, N.Y.C., 1977—. Author: (play) The Envoi Messages, 1976, (short story collections) A Dream of Countries Where No One Dare Live, 1992, (short story collection) The Bus to the Moon, 2002, more than 40 books for children and adults, plays produced in regional theaters and off-Broadway. Playwrighting fellow, NEA, 1975. Mem.: Dramatists Guild, Soc. Am. Magicians, Am. Philatelic Soc. Home: 375 Riverside Dr Apt 14-C New York NY 10025 Office: Sch Visual Arts 209 E 23d St New York NY 10010-3994

PHILLIPS, MARGARET A. pharmacology educator; BS in Biochemistry, U. Calif., Davis, 1981; PhD in Pharm. Chemistry, U. Calif., San Francisco, 1988. Prof. dept. pharmacology U. Tex. Southwestern Med. Ctr., Dallas. Office: U Tex Southwestern Med Ctr Dept Pharmacology 5323 Harry Hines Blvd Dallas TX 75390-9041

PHILLIPS, MARION GRUMMAN, writer, civic worker; b. N.Y.C., Feb. 11, 1922; d. Leroy Randle and Rose Marion (Werther) Grumman; m. Ellis Laurimore Phillips, Jr., June 13, 1942; children: Valerie Rose (Mrs. Adrian Parsegian), Elise Marion (Mrs. Edward E. Watts III), Ellis Laurimore III, Kathryn Noel Phillips, Cynthia Louise (Mrs. Charles Prosser). Student, Mt. Holyoke Coll., 1940-42; BA, Adelphi U., 1981. Civic vol. Mary C. Wheeler Sch., 1964-68, Historic Ithaca, Inc., 1972-76, Ellis L. Phillips Found., 1960-91. Bd. dirs. North Shore Jr. League, 19660-61, 64-65, 68-69, Family Svc. Assn. Nassau County, 1963-69, Homemaker Svc. Assn. Nassau County, 1959, 61. Author: (light verse) A Foot in the Door, 1965, The Whale-Going, Going, Gone, 1977, Doctors Make Me Sick (So I Cured Myself of Arthritis), 1979; editor: (with Valerie Phillips Parsegian) Richard and Rhoda, Letters from the Civil War, 1982, Wooden Shoes the story of my Grandfather's Grandfather (F.M. Sisson), 1990, Irish Eyes, family hist. of McTarsneys and Sissons, 1990, The Log Chapel, A History of the Congregational Community Church, Rockwood, Maine, 1999; editor Jr. League Shore Lines, 1960-61, The Werthers in America-Four Generations and their Descendants, 1987; A B-Tour of Britain, 1986; contbr. articles on fund raising to mags. Mem. New Eng. Hist. Geneal. Soc., N.Y. Geneal. Biographical Soc., Creek Club, Hannah Adams Womens Club, PEO Sisterhood. Congregationalist. Address: 279 North St Medfield MA 02052-1211

PHILLIPS, MARK, editor, writer, publishing executive, musician; b. Balt., Sept. 16, 1947; s. Aaron and Dorothy Podolnick; m. Debra M. Fishman, July 2, 1998; children: Tara, Jake, Rachel. MusB, Case Western Reserve U., Cleve., 1969; MusM, Northwestern U., Ill., 1970. Music dir. Warner Bros. Publs., N.Y.C., 1973—84; dir. publ. Cherry Lane Music, N.Y.C., 1985—. Author: (book) Metallica Riff by Riff, 1994, Guitar for Dummies, 1998, Sight-Read Any Rhythm Instantly, 2002, Sight-Sing Any Melody Instantly, 2002, Honeymooners Trivia, 2002; author: (publ.) The Wizard of Oz Vocabulary Builder, 2003, The Pinocchio Intermediate Vocabulary Builder, 2004. E-mail: mark@vocabularybuilders.com.

PHILLIPS, MICHAEL M. gastroenterologist; b. Bklyn., Aug. 20, 1940; s. Jacob and Ruth (Gordon) P.; m. Barbara Mary Posner, Dec. 25, 1966; children: Bradley Morse, Julie Anne. BA, Bklyn. Coll., 1962; MD, SUNY, Buffalo, 1967. Diplomate Am. Bd. Internal Medicine, Am. Bd. Gastroenterology. Intern San Francisco Gen. Hosp., 1967-68; resident in internal medicine

Montefiore Hosp. & Med. Ctr., Bronx, N.Y., 1968-70; fellow in gastroenterology Johns Hopkins U., Balt., 1970-71; fellow in liver disease Yale U., New Haven, 1971-72; gastroenterologist Malcolm Grow Hosp. USAF, Washington, 1972-74; chief divsn. gastroenterology Malcolm Grow Hosp., 1973-74; pvt. practice Washington, 1974—; assoc. clin. prof. medicine George Washington U. Sch. Medicine, 1978-2001; clin. prof. of medicine George Washington U. Sch. of Medicine, 2001—. Cons. gastroenterologist Social Security Adminstrn., Washington, 1976—. Contbg. editor Oakstone Publs. Educational Reviews in Gastroenterology, 1989—. Maj. USAF, 1970-72. Fellow ACP; mem. Am. Gastroenterology Assn., Am. Assn. for Study of Liver Disease, Am. Soc. Internal Medicine. Avocations: oenology, travel. Office: Michael M Phillips MD PC 2021 K St NW # 412 Washington DC 20006-1003 E-mail: barmike@bellatlantic.net.

PHILLIPS, MICHELLE GILLIAM, actress, writer; b. Long Beach, Calif., June 4, 1944; d. Gardner Burnett and Joyce Leon (Poole) Gilliam; m. John Phillips, Dec. 31, 1962 (div. 1970); children: Gilliam Chynna Phillips, Austin D. Hines, Aron S. Wilson. Grad. high sch., Ft. Jones, Calif. Model Francis Gill Agy., N.Y.C., 1962-64; singer Mamas and Papas, 1965-69. Guest appearances in TV shows include Vega$, 1980, The Fall Guy, 1983, Santa Barbara, 1984, Murder, She Wrote, 1984, Scene of the Crime, 1985, Alfred Hitchcock Presents, 1985, T.J. Hooker, 1985, Star Trek: The Next Generation, 1988, Herman's Head, 1994, Diagnsos Murder, 1994, 99, Burke's Law, 1994, Lois & Clark: The New Adventures of Superman, 1995, Too Something, 1996, Beverly Hills, 90210, 1997, 98, Pauly, 1997, The Magnificent Seven, 1998, 99, 2000, The Love Boat: The Next Wave, 1998, Rude Awakening, 1999, Providence, 1999, Twice in a Lifetime, 2000; appeared in tv movies The Death Squad, 1974, The California Kid, 1974, The Useres, 1978, Moonlight, 1982, Murder Me, Murder You, 1983, Secrets of a Married Man, 1984, Covenant, 1985, Paint Me a Murder, 1985, Stark: Mirror Image, 1986, Assault and Matrimony, 1987, Mike Hammer: Murder Takes All, 1989, Trenchcoat in Paradise, 1989, Appearances, 1990, Rubdown, 1993, Rock 'n' Roll Revolution: The British Invade America, 1995, 919 Fifth Avenue, 1995, No One Would Tell, 1996, Pretty Poison, 1996, Sweetwater, 1999; appeared in feature films Monterey Pop, 1969, The Last Movie, 1971, Dillinger, 1973, Valentino, 1977, Bloodline, 1979, The Man with Bogart's Face, 1980, Savage Harvest, 1981, American Anthem, 1986, Let It Ride, 1989, Flashing on the Sixties: A Tribal Document, 1990, Scissors, 1991, Army of One, 1993, Anna Petrovic, You Rock!, 1998, Lost in the Pershing Point Hotel, 2000, TV series Aspen, 1977, The French Atlantic Affair, 1979, Hotel, 1983, Knots Landing, 1979, Second Chances, 1993, Malibu Shores, 1996, Knots Landing: Back to the Cul-de-Sac, 1997; author: California Dreamin', 1986, Monday Monday (Grammy award). Recipient medal of Honor for Stop War Toys Campaign Alliance for Survival, 1987, Soap Opera Awards for Best Villainess, 1990.

PHILLIPS, NORMAN EDGAR, chemistry professor; b. Detroit, Dec. 20, 1928; s. Norman Christopher and Margaret Elma (Watson) P.; m. Paula Mae McCreery, July 3, 1951; children: Norman Christopher, Susan Margaret. BA, U. B.C., Vancouver, Can., 1949; MS, U. B.C., 1950; Phd, U. Chgo., 1954. Postdoct. fellow Nat. Rsch. Coun. U. Calif., Berkeley, 1954-55, instr. dept. chemistry, 1955-56, asst. prof. dept. chemistry, 1956-60, assoc. prof. dept. chemistry, 1960-66, prof. dept. chemistry, 1966—, assoc. dean grad. divsn., 1966-70, dean Coll. Chemistry, 1975-81; prin. investigator, sr. scientist Lawrence Berkeley Lab, Berkeley, 1960—, assoc. dir., 1984-91, head materials and molecular rsch. divsn., materials and chems. scis. divsn., 1984-91. Invited prof. U. Joseph Fourier, Grenoble, 1985; invited lectr. in physics Nat. Sci. Coun. Rep. of China, 1992. Alfred B. Sloan rsch. fellow, 1961-64; Guggenheim fellow Clarendon Lab. Oxford U., 1963-64; sr. fellow NSF Technical U. Helsinki, 1970-71; recipient Alexander von Humboldt Rsch. award for sr. U.S. scientists Technische Hochschule, Darmstadt, Germany, 1991-92. Fellow APS, AAAS; mem. ACS, Materials Rsch. Soc., Sigma Xi. Achievements include research in specific heat measurements, under high pressures and in high magnetic fields at temperatures from 5mK to 300K; superfluids, superconductors, normal metals, spin glasses, heavy-fermion compounds, other magnetic materials; development of techniques and temperature scales. Office: U Calif Dept Chemistry Berkeley CA 94720-1460

PHILLIPS, OLIVER, tropical forest ecologist; NERC Rsch. fellow U. Leeds, Eng., 1996-99, lectr., 1999—2003, reader in tropical biology, 2003—; rsch. assoc. Mo. Bot. Garden, 1997—. Recipient Edmund H. Fulling award Soc. Econ. Botany, 1992. Mem. Soc. for Econ. Botany (mem. coun. 1996-99), Assn. Trop. Biology, Brit. Ecol. Soc. (Founder's Prize, 2004). Office: U Leeds Geography Sch Earth & Biosphere Inst Leeds LS2 9JT England E-mail: oliverp@geog.leeds.ac.uk.

PHILLIPS, PATRICIA DOMINIS, lawyer; b. Los Angeles, July 21, 1934; d. Anthony P. and Louise Dominis (Brown) Phillips; m. John T. Phillips, Jan. 1, 1964; children: Toni, Lisa, Paul, Samantha, John. BA psychology, U. Calif., Santa Barbara, 1956; JD, Loyola U., Los Angeles, 1967. Bar: Calif. 1968, US Supreme Ct., US Dist. Ct. (cen. dist.)/Calif., US Dist. Ct. (so. dist.)/Calif. Law clk. Los Angeles County Superior Ct., Los Angeles, 1968; assoc. Beardsley, Hufstedler, Los Angeles, 1969—72; ptnr. Hufstedler, Miller, Carlson & Beardsley, Los Angeles, 1972, predecessor firm Beardsley, Hufstedler & Kemble, Los Angeles, 1972; lectr. continuing edn. of the bar Rutter Group. Contbr. articles profl. jour. Mem.: Loyola U. Law Sch. (bd. vistors 1985—), Los Angeles County Bar Assn. (pres. 1984—85, bd. gov. 1986—), State Bar Calif., Am. Acad. Matrimonial Lawyers, ABA, U. So. Calif. (bd. councillors 1983), Chancery. Office: Hufstedler Miller Carlson & Beardsley 700 S Flower St Ste 1600 Los Angeles CA 90017

PHILLIPS, PATRICIA JEANNE, retired school system administrator; b. Amarillo, Tex., Jan. 13, 1935; d. William Macon and Mary Ann (Cawthon) Patrick; m. William Henry Phillips, June 22, 1962; 1 child, Mary Jeanne. BA, Millsaps Coll., 1954; MA, Vanderbilt/Peabody U., 1957; EdD, U. So. Miss., 1978. Tchr. Jackson (Miss.) Pub. Schs., 1954-73, prin., 1973-75, asst. prin., 1975-77; dir. ednl. program Eden Prairie (Minn.) # 272, 1977-80; dir. elem. edn. Meridian (Miss.) Pub. Schs., 1980-91, asst. supt. curriculum, 1991; ret., 1991. Prof. Miss. Coll., Clinton, 1977, Miss. State U., Meridian, 1981-2000; cons. in field. Co-author: (testing practice) Test Taking Tactics, 1987; contbr. articles to profl. jours. Pres. Meridian Symphony Orch., 1987, 2000—; v.p. Meridian Coun. Arts, 1986; bd. dirs. Meridian Art Mus. Named Boss of Yr., Meridian Secretarial Assn., 1985, Arts Educator of Yr., Meridian Coun. Arts, 1991; recipient Excellence award Pub. Edn. Form, 1993. Mem. ASCD, Miss. ASCD, Miss. Assn. Women (pres.), Rotary, Phi Kappa Alpha, Phi Delta Kappa (pres. 1986-87), Alpha Delta Kappa Gamma (pres. 1962), Kappa Delta Phi. Republican. Methodist. Achievements include development of tng. materials Best Practices, Brain Growth: Applications for the Classroom. Avocations: grant writing, computers, golf. Home: 8450 SE 168th Kittredge Loop The Villages FL 32162-2851 E-mail: bjphill@thevillages.net.

PHILLIPS, PAUL EVERARD, physician, medical educator; b. London, Feb. 2, 1937; came to U.S., 1940; s. Ralph Francis and Barbara Alison (Reeves) P.; m. Charlotte Wood, 1962 (div. 1981); children: Christopher, Diane, Hugh; m. Sharon Patricia Sullivan, Mar. 10, 1984; 1 child, Margaret Helen. AB, Princeton U., 1958; MD, Albany Med. Coll., 1962. Diplomate Am. Bd. Internal Medicine, Am. Bd. Rheumatology. Resident in Medicine Roosevelt Hosp., N.Y.C., 1962-63; assoc. in Virology NIH, Bethesda, Md., 1963-65; resident in Medicine Bellevue Hosp., N.Y.C., 1965-67; fellow in rheumatology Columbia-Presbyn. Hosp., N.Y.C., 1967-69, assoc. in medicine, 1969-70; from asst. to assoc. prof. medicine Cornell U. Med. Coll., N.Y.C., 1970-81; prof. medicine SUNY Upstate Med. U., Syracuse, 1981—; also prof. pediatrics assoc. prof. rehab. medicine SUNY, Syracuse, 1981—, chief divsn. rheumatology, 1981-2001. Attending physician Univ. Hosp., Crouse-Irving Meml. Hosp., Syracuse, 1981—; cons. VA Med. Ctr., Syracuse, 1981—. Editor Clin. and Exptl. Rheumatology, 1982-2000; contbr. 70 articles to profl. jours. Trustee Everson Mus., 1998—. Recipient 40 rsch. grants various sources, N.Y.C., Syracuse, 1967—. Fellow Am. Coll. Physicians, Am. Coll. Rheumatology, Dewitt Fish and Game Club (pres. 1993-95). Avocation: shooting sports. Office: SUNY Upstate Med U 750 E Adams St Syracuse NY 13210-2306 Office Phone: 315-464-4194. Business E-mail: phillipp@upstate.edu.

PHILLIPS, PETER CHARLES BONEST, economist, educator, researcher; b. Weymouth, Dorset, Eng., Mar. 23, 1948; came to U.S., 1980; s. Charles Bonest and Gladys Eileen (Lade) P.; m. Emily Dowdell Birdling, Feb. 10, 1971 (div. 1980); 1 child, Daniel Lade; m. Deborah Jane Blood, June 13, 1981; children: Justin Bonest, Lara Kimberley. BA, Auckland (New Zealand) U., 1969, MA, 1971; PhD, London U., 1974; MA (hon.), Yale U., 1979. Teaching fellow U. Auckland, 1969-70, jr. lectr., 1970-71; lectr. in econs. U. Essex, Colchester, Eng., 1972-76; prof. econs. U. Birmingham, Eng., 1976-79, Yale U., New Haven, Conn., 1979-85, Stanley Resor prof. econs., 1985-89, Sterling prof. econs., 1989—; Alumni disting. prof. econs. U. Auckland, 1991—; pres. Predicta Software Inc., Madison, Conn., 1994—. Vis. scholar Ecole Polytechnique, Paris, 1977; univ. vis. prof. Monash U., Melbourne, Australia, 1986; vis. prof. Inst. Advanced Studes, Vienna, Austria, 1989; disting. visitor London Sch. Econs., 1989. Editor Econometric Theory jour., 1985; joint editor Asia Pacific Economic Review, 1995—; contbr. over 180 articles, book revs., notes to profl. jours. Recipient award for promotion of sci. Japan Soc., 1983, New Zealand medal Sci. and Tech., 1998, Plura Scripsit, 1997, Plurima Scripsit Econometric Theory award, 2000, Nzier Qantas Economist of Yr., 2000; Commonwealth Grants Com. scholar, Eng., 1971, Guggenheim fellow, N.Y., 1984-85. Fellow Am. Acad. Arts & Scis., Royal Soc. New Zealand (hon.), Econometric Soc., Jour. Econometrics, Am. Statis. Soc.; mem. Inst. Math. Stats., Modsim Soc. (Biennial Medal, 2003). Avocations: running, building, poetry, reading, native plant restoration. Home: 133 Concord Dr Madison CT 06443-1814 Office: Cowles Found PO Box 208281 New Haven CT 06520-8281 E-mail: peter.phillips@yale.edu.

PHILLIPS, PETER LAWRENCE, communications executive; b. Lynn, Mass., June 22, 1942; s. Raymond A. and Edna M. (Peterson) P.; m. Sybil Jean Lewis, Aug. 21, 1971; children: Benjamin James, Rebecca Lewis. BFA, U. Conn., 1964; MA, UCLA, 1966. Prof. Centenary Coll., Hackettstown, N.J., 1966-70; TV prodr./dir. Group W, Westinghouse Broadcasting Co., Boston, 1970-73; dir. promotional program devel. Stanmar, Inc., Sudbury, Mass., 1973-75; mgr. creative svcs. Gillette Co., Boston, 1975-79; pres., owner Creative Svcs. Group Ltd., Marblehead, Mass., 1979-80; cons. Newsome & Co., Inc., Boston, 1980-81; corp. creative dir. corp. comm. Digital Equipment Corp., 1982-87, mgr. corp. identity and design, 1987-89, dir. corp. identity, 1989-94; prin. Phillips Corp. Identity & Design Strategy, 1994—. Sec. bd. dirs. Design Mgmt. Inst., 1990—; mem. design mgmt. adv. coun. U. Westminster, London, 2000—. Author: An Iconography of American Scenic Design, 1966, Creating the Perfect Design Brief, 2004. Bd. dirs. Marblehead Cmty. Counseling Ctr.; chmn. bd. dirs. Salem Mission at Crombie St., 1998—. Mem. NATAS, Am. Inst. Graphic Arts, Corinthian Yacht Club, Masons. Episcopalian. Home and Office: 9 Upland Rd Marblehead MA 01945-1341

PHILLIPS, RANDY, state legislator, marketing professional; b. Seattle, Aug. 30, 1950; m. Norma Banta; children: Christopher, Matthew. BA in Polit. Sci. and History, Alaska Meth. U., 1973. Contract adminstrv. asst.; mktg. rschr. Gamel Homes, 1982-84; pres., mng. ptnr. No. Family Home Video, 1985-87; pvt. practice mktg. and rsch., 1988—; mem. Alaska Ho. of Reps., 1976-92, Alaska Senate, Dist. L, Juneau, 1992—. Chmn. senate labor & commerce com., senate state affairs com., senate rules com., senate cmty. & regional affairs com., legis. budget & audit com., Alaska Senate., Anchorage. Named Outstanding Freshman Legislator, Tenth Legislature, 1977-78, Outstanding Rep., Standing Together Against Rape, 1987. Mem. Eagle River Fine Arts Acad., Elks. Republican. Avocations: family cabin, hockey, classic cars, coin collecting/numismatics. Office: State Capitol 120 4th St Rm 103 Juneau AK 99801-1182 also: PO Box 142 Eagle River AK 99577 Fax: 907-465-4979. E-mail: senator_randy_phillips@legis.state.ak.us.

PHILLIPS, RENEÉ, editor-in-chief, writer, educator; b. Freeport, N.Y. Student, Art Students League, 1979, Am. Art Sch., 1979, Fashion Inst. Tech., 1980, New Sch. for Social Rsch., 1980. Dir., founder Artopia, not-for-profit art orgn., N.Y.C., 1980-84; pub., editor-in-chief Manhattan Arts Internat., N.Y.C., 1983—2000; editor-in-chief www.Manhattan Arts.com. Juror Excellence in Arts Awards, 1988, N.Y. Lung Assn. Ann. Exhbn., 1990, Manhattan Arts Internat. Ann. Internat. Art Competition, 1992—; juror, co-curator Redefining Visionary Art, Doma Gallery, N.Y.C., 1989; curator Synthesis of Painting and Sculpture exhbn., 1st Women's Bank, N.Y.C., 1984, Salute to Liberty internat. art exhbn., N.Y.C., 1986, HerStory exhbns., 1999-2004, Small Works, 2004, The Healing Power of Art, 2002, 03, 04; organizer over 40 art and cultural events; editor-in-chief www.ManhattanArts.com; curator I Love Manhattan, N.Y.C., 2003, The Healing Power of Art, N.Y.C., 2003, 04; bd. dirs., v.p. Women's Studio Ctr., L.I., N.Y., 2003—; spkr. in field; lectr. in field. Author: New York Contemporary Art Galleries Annual Guide, 1995-02, The Complete Guide to New York Art Galleries, 2004, Presentation Power Tools for Fine Artists, 1998, 2d edit., 2000, 3d edit., 2002, Success Now! for Artists: A Motivational Guide, 1998, 2d edit., 2003, The Complete Guide to New York Art Galleries, 2004; editor-in-chief Success Now!, 1991—. Recipient award of merit Muscular Dystrophy Assn., 1986, award for outstanding contbns. to arts Mayor of N.Y.C., 1987. Mem. Internat. Assn. Art Critics, N.Y. Artists Equity (former bd. dirs.). Office: Manhattan Arts Internat 200 E 72nd St New York NY 10021-4537 E-mail: info@ManhattanArts.com.

PHILLIPS, RICHARD B. paper company executive; b. Raleigh, 1942; BS in sci., NC State U., 1964, M in sci., PhD in chem. engring., NC State U., 1970. With Internat. Paper Co., Stamford, Conn., 1971—, v.p., tech., sr. v.p., tech., 1996—. Office: Internat Paper Co 400 Atlantic St Stamford CT 06921

PHILLIPS, RICHARD CAREY, real estate executive; b. Oklahoma City, Oct. 22, 1964; s. Carey R. and Margaret R. (Anderson) P.; m. Chalynn Lee Claunch. BBA in Fin., U. Okla., 1988. V.p. Womack Property Mgmt., Inc., Oklahoma City, 1988-93; owner, pres. Thomas Drayton & Co., Oklahoma City, 1993—; mem. Okla. Ho. of Reps., 1992—. Area coord. Inst. Real Estate Mgmt., Oklahoma City, 1992. Councilman, City of Warr Acres, Okla., 1989-92; vol. ARC, 1990. Mem. Warr Acres Putnam City C. of C., Putnam City Jaycees (dir. 1992—), Nat. Assn. Realtors, Met. Bd. Realtors. Republican. Baptist. Home: 5817 NW 40th St Warr Acres OK 73122-3101

PHILLIPS, RICHARD MYRON, lawyer, educator; b. N.Y.C., Sept. 8, 1931; s. Morris and Henrietta (Schatz) Phillips; m. Elda Marie Phillips, June 11, 1955; children: Laurie, David, Stephen. BA, Columbia U., 1951; LLB, Yale U., 1956. Bar: D.C. 1957. Atty. Office Gen. Counsel Bur. Aero., 1956—57; with SEC, Washington, 1960—68; spl. counsel Office Gen. Counsel, 1964—66, asst. gen. counsel, 1966—68; mem. Surrey, Karasik, Greene & Hill, Washington, 1968—71, Kirkpatrick & Lockhart, and predecessor firms, Washington, 1971—. Contbr. articles to profl. jours. Trustee SEC Hist. Soc. Served with USN. Mem.: ABA, Fed. Bar Assn. Office: Kirkpatrick & Lockhart Four Embarcadero Ctr San Francisco CA 94111 Office Phone: 415-249-1010. E-mail: rphillips@kl.com.

PHILLIPS, ROBERT DERRICK, psychiatrist; b. Laurinburg, N.C., Dec. 2, 1925; s. James Dickson and Helen Shepherd Phillips; m. Frances Dana Fulcher Olson, July 28, 1951 (div. Dec. 1974); children: Robert, Stuart, Helen, Jane, Anna, Betsy, Frances; m. Dorothy Jean Andersen, Oct. 17, 1997. BS, Davidson Coll., 1948; MD, U. Pa., 1952. Diplomate Am. Bd. Psychiatry, Am. Bd. Surgery. Surg. resident Med. Coll. S.C., Charleston, 1952-56, chief surg. resident, 1956-57; staff surgeon Presbyn. Med. Ctr., Chonju, Korea, 1957-59; psychiat. resident U. N.C. Meml. Hosps., Chapel Hill, 1960-63; pvt. practice psychiatry Chapel Hill, 1963-95; clin. asst. prof. psychiatry Duke U., Durham, N.C., 1972-95; clin. prof. psychiatry U. N.C. Sch. Medicine, Chapel Hill, 1974-95; ret., 1995. Exec. com. Com. of Responsibility to War-Injured and Burned Vietnamese Children, Boston, 1964-67. Author: The Recovery of the True Self, 1995, (monograph) Structural Symbiotic Systems, 1975. Trustee Union Theol. Sem., Richmond, Va., 1965-67; chmn. Human Rels. Commn., Chapel Hill, 1962-63; founder All Races Coalition with Native Am. People, Chapel Hill, 1991X. Ens. USNR, 1943-46, ATO. Recipient Martin Luther King award Orange County Black Caucus, 1987, Founders' Cir., Buffalo Trust, 1999. Mem. Am. Psychiat. Assn., Am. Coll. Surg.; mem. N.C. Psychiat. Soc. Democrat. Avocations: native american network support, golf, hiking, workshop leading.

PHILLIPS, ROBERT L., JR., application developer, consultant; s. Bettye Phillips and Robert L. Phillips, Sr.; m. Sarah E. Bohler, June 21, 2003; 1 child, Brandon. BS in computer sci., Miss. Valley State U., 1988—92. Java cert. Ga., 2000. Exec. dir., invoice presentation and enhancement H.O. Sys., Savannah, Ga., 2000—02; mgr., product devel. H.O. Software, Savannah, 1998—2000. Adv. cons. Savannah Tech, 2000—. Designer, developer (computer software) X-Solutions. Mem.: Alpha Phi Alpha (life). Avocations: travel, reading, sports. Office: VeriSign - VTS 222 W Oglethorpe Ave Savannah GA 31401 Office Phone: 912-527-4249. Personal E-mail: rphillipsjr1@comcast.net. E-mail: rphillips@verisign.com.

PHILLIPS, ROGER, retired steel company executive; b. Ottawa, Ont., Can., Dec. 17, 1939; s. Norman William Frederick and Elizabeth (Marshall) P.; m. Katherine Ann Wilson, June 9, 1962; 1 child, Andrée Claire. BSc, McGill U., Montreal, Can., 1960. V.p. mill products Alcan Can. Products Ltd., Toronto, 1969-70, exec. v.p., 1971-75; pres. Alcan Smelters and Chems. Ltd., Montreal, 1976-79; v.p. tech. Alcan Aluminium Ltd., Montreal, 1980-81; pres. Alcan Internat. Ltd., Montreal, 1980-81; pres., CEO IPSCO Inc., Regina, Canada, 1982—2001. Sr. mem. Conf. Bd., Inc., NY, 1987—2002; bd. dirs. Toronto Dominion Bank, Can. Pacific Rlwy., Imperial Oil Ltd.; hon. dir. IPSCO Inc.; dir. Inco Ltd., Cleveland-Cliffs Inc. Bd. dirs. Conf. Bd. of Can., 1984-87; chmn. Coun. for Can. Unity, 1987-88. Fellow Inst. of Physics U.K. (chartered physicist); mem. Can. Assn. Physicists, Am. Iron and Steel Inst. (bd. dirs. 1984—), Sask. C. of C. (bd. dirs. 1984-2001), Que. C. of C. (pres. 1981), Order of Can. (officer 1999), Assiniboia Club (Regina), St. Denis Club, Univ. Club (Montreal). Home: 3220 Albert St Regina SK Canada S4S 3N9 Office: IPSCO Inc Armour Rd Regina SK Canada S4P 3C7 E-mail: rphillips@ipsco.com.

PHILLIPS, RONALD EDWARD, artist, sales executive; b. Clovis, N.Mex., Apr. 10, 1937; s. Rodney Vernon and Ethel Edna (Huff) Phillips; m. May Frances Willingham, Aug. 27, 1957 (div.); children: Rhonda Louise, Russell Kent, Teresa Gail; m. Janet Irene Johnsonbaugh Smith, July 4, 1972 (dec. Nov. 29, 1999); stepchildren: Steven, Gregg, Laura. Student, Ea. N.Mex. U., 1955-56, U. N.Mex., 1957, Famous Artist Schs., 1963-64, North Light Art Sch., 1989-90. Group merchandiser women's fashions J.C. Penney Inc., Albuquerque, 1957-64; chem. salesman Take Over Products, Clovis, 1964-65; with International Auto Leasing, Albuquerque, 1965; salesman Pennsalt Chems., N.Mex. div., Albuquerque, 1965-67; N.Mex. sales rep. W.W. Grainger Inc., Chgo., 1967-72; nfounder Pueblo Arts, Inc., Albuquerque, 1972—; mgr. Dairy Queen, Santa Rosa and Lovington, N.Mex., 1982-85; owner, mgr. Western Pit n Grill & Food Gallery, Lovington, 1985-88; owner Pueblo Arts Inc./Trailwest Gallery, Albuquerque, 1988—. Tchr. quick draw, continuous line drawing, 1990; artist, guide Pueblo Arts Inc. Trailwest Paintouts, Guide for Artists, 1990—; ind. sales cons. SWEPCO Bldg. Projects, 1993—96. Sketchbooks, Traveling Man's Old Town Sketchbook, 1990, The Shooting of Wyatt Earp, 1994, 75th Anniversary Sketchbook of Route 66, 2001; movie extra: (films) Whitesands, 1991; Next Fire on Earth, 1992; Wyatt Earp, 1993; Desparate Trails, 1993; Buffalo Girls, 1995; East Meets West, 1995; Lazarus Man Premier, 1995—96. Pres. Albuquerque Wildlife and Conservation, 1963—64; active Albuquerque Conf. & Vis. Bur., 1988—, Albuquerque Arts Alliance, 1994—95, Tourism Assoc. N.Mex., Albuquerque Film Commn. Mem.: Guild Albuquerque Artist Models (advisor, bd. dirs. 1994—98), Albuquerque Arts Alliance, Indian Arts and Crafts Assn. (ethics com. 1973—74), N.Mex. Art League (hon.; pres. 1964—65, instr., bd. arts after sch. project 1995—96). Republican. Avocations: sales and marketing, art and art tours. E-mail: ronpuebloarts@juno.com.

PHILLIPS, RONALD FRANK, university administrator; b. Houston, Nov. 25, 1934; s. Franklin Jackson and Maudie Ethel (Merrill) P.; m. Jamie Jo Bottoms, Apr. 5, 1957 (dec. Sept. 1996); children: Barbara Celeste Phillips Oliveira, Joel Jackson, Phil Edward. BS, Abilene Christian U., 1955; JD, U. Tex., 1965. Bar: Tex. 1965, Calif. 1972. Bldg. contractor Phillips Homes, Abilene, Tex., 1955-56; br. mgr. Phillips Weatherstripping Co., Midland and Austin, Tex., 1957-65; corp. staff atty. McWood Corp., Abilene, 1965-67; sole practice law Abilene, 1967-70; mem. adj. faculty Abilene Christian U., 1967-70; prof. law Pepperdine U., Malibu, Calif., 1970—, dean Sch. Law, 1970-97, dean emeritus, 1997—, vice chancellor, 1995—. Mem. Nat. Conf. Commrs. on Uniform State Laws, 1988—2003. Deacon North A and Tenn. Ch. of Christ, Midland, 1959-62; deacon Highland Ch. of Christ, Abilene, 1965-70; elder Malibu Ch. of Christ, 1978-95; mgr., coach Little League Baseball, Abilene, Huntington Beach and Malibu, 1968-78, 90-95; coach Youth Soccer, Huntington Beach, Westlake Village and Malibu, 1972-80, 85-86, 91. Recipient Alumni citation Abilene Christian U., 1974 Fellow Am. Bar Found. (life); mem. ABA, State Bar Tex., State Bar Calif., Christian Legal Soc., L.A. Bar Assn., Assn. Am. Law Schs. (chmn. sect. on adminstrn. law schs. 1982, com. on cts. 1985-87), Am. Law Inst. Republican. Office: Pepperdine U 24255 Pacific Coast Hwy Malibu CA 90263-4951 E-mail: ronald.phillips@pepperdine.edu.

PHILLIPS, RONALD LEWIS, plant geneticist, educator; b. Huntington County, Ind., Jan. 1, 1940; s. Philemon Lewis and Louise Alpha (Walker) P.; m. Judith Lee Lind, Aug. 19, 1962; children: Brett, Angela. BS in Crop Sci., Purdue U., 1961, MS in Plant Breeding and Genetics, 1963, Doctorate (hon.), 2000; PhD in Genetics, U. Minn., 1966; postgrad., Cornell U., 1966-67. Rsch. and tchg. asst. Purdue U., 1961—62; rsch. asst. U. Minn., St. Paul, 1962—66, rsch. assoc., 1967—68, asst. prof., 1968—72, assoc. prof., 1972—76, prof. genetics and plant breeding, 1976—93, Regents prof., 1993—, McKnight presdl. chair in genomics, 2000—. Vis. prof., Italy, 1981, Canada, 83, China, 86, Japan, 90, Morocco, 96; program dir. Competetive Rsch. Grants Office USDA, Washington, 1979, chief scientist, 1996—98, mem. adv. grant panels, NSF, DOE; chmn. Gordon Conf. on Plant Cell and Tissue Culture, 1985; mem. sci. adv. coun. U. Calif. Plant Gene Expression Ctr., Berkeley, 1986—93, chair, 1992—93; program adv. com. Palm Oil Rsch. Inst. Malaysia, 1992—2001; non-resident fellow Noble Found., 2001—; sci. adv. bd. Donald Danforth Plant Sci. Ctr., St. Louis, 2000—; sci. liaison officer Internat. Rice Rsch. Inst. USAID, 2000—03, bd. trustees, 2004—, mem. adv. grant panels; dir. Plant Molecular Genetics Inst., 1991—94; trustee Biol. Stain Commn.; mem. Nat. Plant Genetic Resources Bd.; dir. Ctr. Microbial and Plant Genomics U. Minn., 2000—. Co-editor: Cytogenetics, 1977, Molecular Genetic Modification of Eucaryotes, 1977, Molecular Biology of Plants, 1979, The Plant Seed: Development, Preservation and Germination, 1979, Genetic Improvement of Crops: Emergent Techniques, 1980, DNA-Based Markers in Plants, 1994, 2d edit., 2001; assoc. editor Genetics, 1978—81, Can. Jour. Genetics and Cytology and Genome, 1985—90, mem. editl. bd. Maydica, 1978—. In Vitro Cellular and Devel. Biology, 1988—92, Cell Culture and Somatic Cell Genetics of Plants, 1983—91, Jour. of the Oil Palm, 1994—, Proc. NAS, 1996—98; contbr. chpts. to Maize Beeding and Genetics, 1978, Staining Procedures, 1981, Chromosome Structure and Function, 1987, Corn and Corn Improvement, 1988, Plant Transposable Elements, 1988, Chromosome Engring. in Plants, 1991, Maize Handbook, 1994, sci. articles to profl. jours. Mem. chmn. coun. on ministries, lay leader United Meth. Ch., 1968, dir. Project AgGrad, 1983—; Cub Scout Pack co-chmn. Boy Scouts Am., 1976-77; judge Minn. Regional and State Sci. Fair, 1970-80. Recipient Purdue Agrl. Alumni Achievement award, 1961, Purdue Disting. Agrl. Alumni award, 1993; NSF fellow, 1961; NIH fellow, 1966-67; recipient Northrup King Oustanding Faculty Performance award, 1985, DeKalb Genetics Crop Sci. Disting. Career award, 1997. Fellow: AAAS (chair sect. O, program com. 2003—), Crop Sci. Soc. Am. (awards com., divsn. chmn., bd. rep. 1988—91, pres.-elect 1998—99, pres. 1999—2000, past pres. 2000—01, Rsch. award 1988), Am. Soc. Agronomy (Caleb-Dorr award); mem.: NAS (chair sect. 62 1999—2002, nominating com. 2002), Am. Soc. Agronomy (award student sect.), Genetics Soc. Am., Sigma Xi, Alpha Zeta, Gamma Sigma Delta (award of merit 1994), Gamma Alpha (nat. treas.). Office: U Minn Dpt Agronomy-Plant Genetics Saint Paul MN 55108 E-mail: phill005@umn.edu.

PHILLIPS, RUSSELL ALEXANDER, JR., retired foundation executive; b. Charlotte, N.C., Sept. 19, 1937; s. Russell Alexander and Robmae (Black) P. AB, Duke U., 1959; LLB (Edward John Noble fellow), Yale U., 1962. Bar: N.C. 1962, D.C. 1966. Clk. to Sr. Judge, U.S. Ct. Appeals, 4th Circuit, 1962-63; legal adv. Ministry of Fin., Govt. No. Nigeria, 1963-65; asst. commr.

income tax (legal) East African Common Svcs. Orgn., Nairobi, Kenya, 1965-66; assoc. firm Wilmer, Cutler & Pickering, Washington, 1966-68; program officer Rockefeller Bros. Fund, N.Y.C., 1968-73, corp. sec., 1973-81, v.p., 1979-81, exec. v.p., 1982-98, acting pres., 1987-88. Trustee Asian Cultural Coun. Mem. N.C. Bar Assn., D.C. Bar, Phi Beta Kappa. Democrat. Presbyterian. Home: 40 E 88th St Apt 7D New York NY 10128-1176

PHILLIPS, SHIRLEY FLOWERS, food service executive; Co-chair Phillips Seafood Restaurants, Ocean City, Md., 1956—. Bd. vis. U. Md.; bd. trustees Balt. Internat. Coll., 1999; aux. bd. Washington Coll. Chestertown Md. Office: Phillips Seafood Restaurants 2004 N Philadelphia Ave Ocean City MD 21842-3560 Fax: 410-289-2053.

PHILLIPS, SIDNEY FREDERICK, gastroenterologist, educator; b. Melbourne, Australia, Sept. 4, 1933; s. Clifford and Eileen Frances (Fitch) P.; m. Decima Honora Jones, Mar. 29, 1957; children: Penelope Jane, Nichola Margaret, David Sidney. M.B.BS, U. Melbourne, 1956, MD, 1961. Resident med. officer Royal Melbourne Hosp., 1957-61, asst. sub-dean clin. sch., 1961-62; research asso. Central Middlesex Hosp., London, 1962-63; rsch. assoc. Mayo Clinic, Rochester, Minn., 1963-66, cons. in gastroenterology, 1966-2000; prof. medicine Mayo Med. Sch., 1976-2000, prof. medicine emeritus, 2000—, dir. gastroenterology rsch. unit, 1977-94; program dir. Mayo Gen. Clin. Rsch. Ctr., 1974-87; dir. Mayo Digestive Diseases Core Ctr., 1984-90; Karl F. and Marjory Hasselman prof. rsch., 1994-2000. Editor: Digestive Diseases and Sciences, 1977-82, Gastroenterology International, 1990-95; sr. assoc. editor: Gastroenterology, 1991-96; contbr. chpts. to books, articles to profl. jours. Fellow ACP, Royal Coll. Physicians, Royal Australian Coll. Physicians; mem. Am. Motility Soc. (pres. 1994-96), Am. Soc. Clin. Investigation (emeritus), Gastroenterology Soc. Australia (hon.), Am. Gastroenterology Assn. Assn. Am. Physicians, Brit. Soc. Gastroenterology (hon.). Home: 1207 19th Ave NE Rochester MN 55906-4317 Office: St Mary's Hosp Gastroenterology Unit 200 1st St SW Rochester MN 55905-0001 Personal E-mail: DecimaSidney@aol.com.

PHILLIPS, STEPHEN S. lawyer; b. Phila., 1946; BA, Wesleyan U., 1968; JD, Dickinson U., 1971. Bar: Pa. 1971, U.S. Ct. Appeals (3d cir.) 1971, U.S. Supreme Ct. 1980, Tenn. 1998. Sr. ptnr. Pepper Hamilton LLP, Phila., 1979-97; assoc. v.p., gen. counsel, sec. Sofamor Danek Group, Inc., Memphis, 1998-99; spl. counsel Medtronic, Inc., 1999—. Bd. dirs. Schindler Enterprises, Inc., Franke Holding USA, Inc., Rsch. Tech., Inc. Mem. ABA, Internat. Bar Assn., Pa. Bar Assn., Order of Barristers (pres. 1971-72), Phila. Country Club. Address: 976 Derring Ln Bryn Mawr PA 19010-1749

PHILLIPS, STEVE, computer company executive; arrived in U.S., 2001; BSEE with hons., Essex U. With Thorn EMI, 1984—96, Diageo, 1996—99; from v.p. info. tech. to sr. v.p., chief info. officer Gateway, Dublin, 1999—2003, sr. v.p. Poway, Calif., 2003—, chief info. officer, 2003—. Fellow: IEEE. Office: Gateway 14303 Gateway Place Poway CA 92064

PHILLIPS, STONE, television journalist; b. Texas City, Tex. married; 1 child. BA in Philosophy with honors, Yale Univ. Past prodr., reporter WXIA-TV, Atlanta; formerly with documentary unit Close-Up ABC News, assignment editor, 1979—81, gen. assignment corr., 1982—86, corr. 20/20, 1986—92; prin. anchor Dateline NBC-TV, N.Y.C., 1992—; contbg. corr. MSNBC. Past remedial-reading tchr. Fulton County Juvenile Ct., Atlanta; substitute host Good Morning America, 1986; guest sports anchor World News Sunday, 1986; past substitute anchor NBC Nightly News, Today, Meet the Press. Named to Scholar Athlete Hall of Fame, Nat. Football Found.; recipient F. Gordon Brown award, Yale U., 1976, 3 Nat. Headliner awards for Outstanding Journalism, Overseas Press Club award, Nat. Assn. Black Journalists award, AMA award, Am. Psychol. Assn. award, B'nai B'rith award; NCAA Post-Grad. scholar. Office: NBC News-Dateline Rm 408 30 Rockefeller Plz New York NY 10112-0002

PHILLIPS, SUSAN MEREDITH, financial economist, university administrator; b. Richmond, Va., Dec. 23, 1944; d. William G. and Nancy (Meredith) Phillips. BA in Math., Agnes Scott Coll., 1967; MS in Fin. and Ins., La. State U., 1971, PhD in Fin. and Economics, 1973. Asst. prof. La. State U., 1973—74, U. Iowa, 1974—78; econ. fellow Directorate of Econ. and Policy Rsch., SEC, 1976—78; assoc. prof. fin. dept. U. Iowa, 1978—83, assoc. v.p. fin. and univ. svcs., 1979—81; commr. Commodity Futures Trading Commn., 1981—83, chmn., 1983—87; prof. fin. dept., v.p. fin. and univ. svcs. U. Iowa, Iowa City, 1987—91; bd. govs. Fed. Res. Bd., Washington, 1991—98; dean Sch. of Bus., prof. fin. dept. George Washington U., Washington, 1998—. Bd. dirs. Chgo. Bd. Options Exchange, 2000—, Nat. Futures Assn., 2000—, Assn. to Advance Collegiate Schs. Bus., 1999—2004, Kroger Co., 2003—; trustee State St. Mut. Rsch. Funds, 1998—. Co-author (with J. Richard Zecher): The SEC and the Public Interest; contbr. articles to profl. jours. Fellow Brookings Econ. Policy fellow, 1976—77. Office: George Washington U Sch Bus and Pub Mgmt 710 21st St NW Ste 206 Washington DC 20052-0001

PHILLIPS, T. DANNY, insurance company executive; CPA Condley and Co.; various fin. mgmt. positions Harken Energy Corp.; CFO Aloha Petroleum, Ltd., AdvancePCS, Irving, Tex., 1992—2002, sr. exec. v.p., 2003—, also bd. dirs. Office: Advance PCS Inc Ste 1200 750 W John Carpenter Fwy Irving TX 75039

PHILLIPS, TARI, professional basketball player; b. Mar. 6, 1969; Student, U. Ga.; grad., Ctrl. Fla. U., 1991. With Orlando Miracle Women's Basketball Team, Fla., 1999, N.Y. Liberty, N.Y.C., NY, 2000—; player USA Basketball Women's Nat. Team, 2002, 2004. Named Most Improved Player, WNBA, 2000; named to All-WNBA Second Team, 2002; recipient Gold Medal, World Championships, 2002. Office: New York Liberty 2 Penn Plz 14th Fl New York NY 10121*

PHILLIPS, TAURENCE LAMAR, music educator; b. Miami, Fla., May 21, 1973; s. Carroll Phillips and Bobby Ann Melvin; m. Kasey Yolanda Dailey Flucas Phillips, Aug. 2, 1997; children: Alonza, Ashleigh, Ah'leesa. MusB, Valdosta State, Ga., 1996. Music tchr. Ware County Sch., Waycross, Ga., 1998—99; choral dir. Valdosta Mid. Sch., 1999—2003, Valdosta H.S., 2003—. Min. of music Joyful Praise Ch., Valdosta, Ga., 1994—. V.p. exec. bd. Joyful Praise Ch., Valdosta, 2003—. Recipient Vol. Tchr. of Yr., Waresboro Elem. Sch., 1999. Mem.: Ga. Music Educators Assn., Ga. Educators Assn. Avocations: singing, playing music, gardening, motivational speaking. Home: 3790 Robin Ln Valdosta GA 31605 Office: Valdosta HS 3101 N Forrest St Valdosta GA 31602 Office Phone: 229-333-8555. Office Fax: 229-333-8584. E-mail: tphillips@tomcat.gocats.org.

PHILLIPS, TEDDY STEVE, SR., conductor, saxophone player, production company executive; b. Chgo., June 15, 1917; s. Steve and Kaliope Phillips; children: Jody, Teddy. Saxophone player with big bands, across country, 1940-45; staff musician Radio Sta. CBS, Chgo., 1944-45; condr. Teddy Phillips Orch., across country, 1945-55, 57-62; prin. Teddy Phillips Show, Sta WBKB-TV-ABC, Chgo., 1956-57; condr. Tedd Phillips and Orch. Ambassador Hotel, L.A., 1962-80, Flamingo Hotel, Las Vegas, 1962-80, Statler Hotels, Aragon Ballroom, Hilton Hotels, Chgo.; dir. Guy Lombardo Orch. and Royal Conadians, 1980—. Pres. P&M Prodns., Woodland Hills, Calif., 1976—, Heads Hallmark Ltd.; pres. Encore Records, Encore Mgmt. Ltd.; sec./treas. Internat. Country Music Fanfest '94, L.A. TV prodr. Great Concert in the Sky; record prodr.; writer Do the Camel Hump?, Wishin; writer, arranger, condr. on tour Great Concert in the Sky, 1986—; prodr., condr., writer Lion and the Turtle; pres. Nostalgic Records. With U.S. Army, 1940-41. Recipient Gould Tech. Achievement award, Spl. award Rotary, Medal of Honor Heart Found., cert. Optimists Club, Musicians Union, Masons. Greek Orthodox. Home and Office: PO Box 8328 Calabasas CA 91372-8328

PHILLIPS, TERRY LEMOINE, investment advisor; b. Washington, July 27, 1938; s. Clifford LeMoin and Dorothy Louise (Schuman) P.; m. Lynne Ann Bruce, Aug. 12, 1962; children: Susan Rae, Stephen Kirk. BS, Purdue U., 1964, MS, 1966. CPA Ind., pers. fin. specialist, Ind. Assoc. program leader, data processing Purdue U. Lab. Applications of Remote Sensing, West Lafayette, Ind., 1966-71, program leader, 1971-74, dep. dir., 1974-85; mgr. personal computer svcs. Purdue U. Computing Ctr., West Lafayette, 1986-92; adminstr. Continuing Edn. Ctr., West Lafayette, 1992-2000; investment advisor rep. Diesslin & Assocs., West Lafayette, 2000—. Cons. AID, Computer Scis. Corp. Scoutmaster, explorer advisor Boy Scouts Am., bd. dirs. Sagamore Coun.; sports coord. youth sports Battleground, Ind.; elder, deacon, trustee, treas. Presbyn. Ch.; bd. dirs. Tippecanoe chpt. Am. Diabetes Assn. With USN, 1956-59. Recipient Most Innovative Idea award Am. Diabetes Assn., 1987. Mem. IEEE (sr.), AICPA, Assn. Inst. for Certification of Computer Profls. (cert. in date processing), Assn. Computing Machinery, Data Processing Mgmt. Assn. (internat. dir., co-founder, v.p., pres., treas. Sagamore chpt., Individual Performance award 1983, 85, 88), Rotary (bd. dirs., treas.), Tau Beta Pi, Eta Kappa Nu. Home: 1522 E 600 N West Lafayette IN 47906-8625 Office: Diesslin & Assocs 2639 Yeager Rd West Lafayette IN 47906 E-mail: terry@diesslin.com., tl.phillips@insightbb.com.

PHILLIPS, THEODORE LOCKE, radiation oncologist, educator; b. Phila., June 4, 1933; s. Harry Webster and Margaret Amy (Locke) Phillips; m. Joan Cappello, June 23, 1956; children: Margaret, John, Sally. BSc, Dickinson Coll., 1955; MD, U. Pa., 1959. Intern Western Res. U., Cleve., 1960; resident in therapeutic radiology U. Calif., San Francisco, 1963, clin. instr., 1963—65, asst. prof. radiation oncology, 1965—68, assoc. prof., 1968—70, prof., 1970—, chmn. dept. radiation oncology, 1973—98. Rsch. radiobiologist U.S. Naval Radiologic Def. Lab., San Francisco, 1963—65; rsch. physician Lawrence Berkeley Lab. Contbr. numerous articles to profl. publs. With USNR, 1963—65. Grantee, Nat. Cancer Inst., 1970—99. Mem.: Inst. Medicine, No. Calif. Radiation Oncology Assn., Radium Soc., Radiation Rsch. Soc. (pres. 1977), Am. Coll. Radiology, Calif. Med. Assn., Am. Assn. Cancer Rsch., N.Am. Hyperthermia Soc. (pres. 1994), Radiol. Soc. N.Am., Am. Soc. Clin. Oncology, Am. Soc. Therapeutic Radiology and Oncology (pres. 1984), Alpha Omega Alpha, Phi Beta Kappa. Republican. Office: U Calif San Francisco Dept Radiation Oncology 1600 Divisidero St ste H1031 San Francisco CA 94143-1708

PHILLIPS, THOMAS EDWORTH, JR., financial advisor, investment mangement consultant; b. Danville, Va., July 7, 1944; s. Thomas Edworth Sr. and Jean (Worley) P.; m. Claudia Mitchell, July 23, 1966; children: Kelly Marie, Melissa Joyce. BS in Econs., Va. Tech., 1966; cert. in investments, N.Y. Inst. Fin., 1969; MS in Bus., Va. Commonwealth U., 1973; postgrad., U. Pa., 1989. Cert. investment mgmt. analyst; registered investment adviser. Edn. coord. Prince William County Schs., Manassas, Va., 1966-67; investment broker Conrad and Co., Richmond, Va., 1967-68; investment exec. UBS Paine Webber, Inc., Richmond, 1968—, divisional v.p., 1980-99, sr. v.p. and PRIME cons., 2000—; registered prin. NYSE, NASD, 1987—. Access program nat. com. UBS Paine Webber, N.Y.C., Inc., 1989-90, mem. dir.'s coun., 1987-88, managed accounts nat. adv. bd., 1991-93; mem. mut. fund Nat. Adv. Coun., 1996—, pres.' council, 1997—; bd. dirs. Madison Group, Inc., Richmond, Meadowbrook Assocs., Inc., Richmond; speaker in field. Bd. dirs. Va. Non-Profit Housing Coalition, pres., 1992—; chmn. bd. deacons. Mt. Olivet Ch., Hanover, Va., 1984-85; trustee Hanover Acad., Ashland, Va., 1980-84; mem. alumni bd. Va. Commonwealth U., Richmond. Rotary Found. fellow, 1989. Mem. Investment Mgmt. Cons. Assn., Capital Soc., Melody Hills Property Owners Assn. (bd. dirs. 1980—), Va. Tech. Alumni Assn., Va. Commonwealth U. Alumni Assn., Rotary, Bull and Bear Club, Omicron Delta Epsilon. Baptist. Avocations: horses, tennis, golf. Home: 15058 Melody Hills Dr Doswell VA 23047-2075 Office: UBS Prime Consulting Group 1021 E Cary St Ste 1800 Richmond VA 23219-4000 Office Phone: 804-644-4111. E-mail: tom.phillips@ubs.com.

PHILLIPS, THOMAS JOHN, lawyer; b. Mpls., Nov. 24, 1948; BA, U. Minn., 1970; JD, U. Utah, 1973; LLM in Taxation, NYU, 1974. Bar: Wis. 1974. Ptnr. Quarles & Brady, Milw., 1991—. Co-author: Wisconsin Limited Liability Company Forms and Practice Manual, 1999. Mem. ABA (corp. tax com. tax sect.), Wis. Bar Assn., Profl. Inst. Taxation, Mil. Tax Club, North Shore Country Club, Order of Coif. Avocations: gardening, golf, hockey, jogging, racquetball. Office: 411 E Wisconsin Ave Ste 2550 Milwaukee WI 53202-4409 Office Phone: 414-277-5831.

PHILLIPS, THOMAS ROYAL, law educator; b. Dallas, Oct. 23, 1949; s. George S. and Marguerite (Andrews) P.; m. Lyn Bracewell, June 26, 1982; 1 son, Daniel Austin Phillips; 1 stepson, Thomas R. Kirkham. BA, Baylor U., 1971; JD, Harvard U., 1974; LLD (hon.), Tex. Tech. U., 1997; DHL (hon.), St. Edwards U., 1998. Bar: Tex. 1974; cert. in civil trial law Tex. Bd. Legal Specialization. Briefing atty. Supreme Ct. Tex., Austin, 1974-75; assoc. Baker & Botts, Houston, 1975-81; judge 280th Dist. Ct., Houston, 1981-88; chief justice Supreme Ct. Tex., Austin, 1988—2004; Spuregon E. Bell disting. vis. prof. South Tex. Coll. Law, Houston, 2004—. Mem. com. on fed.-state rels. Jud. Conf. U.S., 1990-96, Annenberg Found.; chair Tex. Jud. Dists. Bd., 1988-2004; mem. Tex. Jud. Coun., 1988-2004, chair, 1998-2004; mem. State Judges Mass Tort Litig. Com., 1991-96; bd. dirs. Elmo B. Hunter Citizens Ctr. for Jud. Selection, 1992-94, Ctr. Am. Internat. Law.; life mem. Nat. Conf. Chief Justices, pres., 1997-98; adv. dir. Rev. of Litig., U. Tex. Law Sch., 1990—; chair Nat. Mass Tort Conf. Planning Com., 1993-94; jud. bd. commn. Instns. of Democracy, 2003-04. Bd. advisors Ctr. for Pub. Policy Dispute Resolution, U. Tex. Law Sch., 1993—; mem. planning com. South Tex. Coll. of Law Ctr. for Creative Legal Solutions, 1993—; adv. dir. Austin Habitat for Humanity, 1993-96. Recipient Outstanding Young Lawyer award Houston Young Lawyers Assn., 1986, Outstanding Tex. Leader award John Ben Shepperd Pub. Leadership Forum, 1989, award of excellence in govt. Tex. C. of C., 1992, Disting. Svc. award Nat. Ctr. for State Cts., 1999, Rosewood Gavel award St. Mary's U. Sch. Law, 2002, Price Daniel award for disting. pub. svc. Baylor U., 2004; named Appellate Judge of Yr., Tex. Assn. Civil Trial and Appellate Specialists, 1992-93, Disting. Alumnus, Baylor U., 1998. Mem. ABA (task force lawyers polit. contbns. 1997-98, com. on 21st Century judiciary, 2002-03), Am. Law Inst. (advisor Fed. Jud. Code Project 1996-2001), Nat. Ctr. for State Ctrs. (chair, bd. dirs. 1997-98), State Bar Tex. (chmn. pattern jury charges IV com. 1985-87, vice chmn. adminstrn. justice com. 1986-87), Am. Judicature Soc. (bd. dirs. 1989-95, 99—, exec. bd. 1995-96), Tex. Philol. Soc., Houston Philol. Soc., Houston Bar Assn., Travis County Bar Assn., Bastrop County Bar Assn., Order of Coif. Republican. Episcopalian. Office Phone: 512-463-1316. E-mail: cj@tomphillips.com.

PHILLIPS, THOMAS WADE, judge, lawyer; b. Oneida, Tenn., July 6, 1943; s. W.T. and Lucille (Lewallen) P.; m. Dorothy Mills, Jan. 2, 1971; children: Lori Ann, Wade Thomas. BA, Berea (Ky.) Coll., 1965; JD, Vanderbilt U., 1969; LLM in Labor Law, George Washington U., 1973. Bar: Tenn. 1969, U.S. Supreme Ct. 1972, U.S. Ct. Appeals (6th cir.) 1980. Assoc., ptnr. Baker, Worthington, Crosley, Stansberry & Wolfe, Huntsville, Tenn., 1973—77; ptnr. Phillips & Williams, P.C., Oneida, Tenn., 1977—91; U.S. magistrate judge ea. dist., Tenn., 1991—2002, U.S. dist. judge, 2002—. County atty. Scott County, Huntsville, 1976-91; city atty. Town of Oneida, 1978-91. Capt. JAGC, U.S. Army, 1969-73. Mem. ABA, Tenn. Bar Assn. (ho. of dels. 1989-91), Scott County Bar Assn. Office: US District Court Howard H Baker Jr Courtho 800 Market St Knoxville TN 37902-2327

PHILLIPS, VICKI L. school system administrator; b. Marion, Ind., Jan. 15, 1958; d. Denver Phillips and Vivian (Burnette) Fuqua. BS in Edn., Western Ky. U., 1980, MA in Psychology, 1987; doctoral student, U. Ky., 1988—; EdD in instrnl. leadership, U. of Lincoln, Eng., 2002. Dir. devel. tng. dept. Panorama, Bowling Green, Ky., 1978—80; tchr. learning and behavior disorders Simpson County Bd. Edn., 1981—85; exceptional child cons. Ky. Dept. Edn. Office Edn. for Exceptional Children, 1986—90; chief exec. asst. to edn. commr. Ky. Dept. of Edn., 1986—93; dep. dir./chief of staff Nat. Alliance for Restructuring Edn., Wash., DC, 1993—95; dir. Greater Phila. First Partnership for Reform; exec. dir. Children Achieving Challenge, 1995—98; supt. Sch. Dist. of Lancaster, 1998—2003; sec. of edn. Pa. Dept. Edn., Harrisburg, 2003—04; supt. Portland Pub. Schools, Oreg., 2004—. Mem. ASCD, Nat. Coun. for Exceptional Children, Coun. for Behavior Disorders, Nat. Assn. for Sch. Psychologists, Ky. Assn. Sch. Adminstrs., Ky. Assn. for Psychology in the Schs., Ky. Assn. for Family-Based Svcs., Ky. Families for Family-Based Svcs., Ky. Families as Allies. Office: 501 N Dixon St Portland OR 97227-1804*

PHILLIPS, VIRGINIA A. judge; BA magna cum laude, U. Calif., Riverside, 1979; JD, Boalt Hall, 1982. Ct. commr. Calif. Superior Ct., Riverside, 1991-95; magistrate judge U.S. Dist. Ct., L.A., 1995-99, dist. judge, 1999—. Office: US Courthouse 3470 Twelfth St Riverside CA 92501

PHILLIPS, WADE, professional football team coach; b. Orange, Tex., June 21, 1947; s. Bum Phillips; m. Laurie Phillips; children: Tracey, Wesley. Student, U. Houston. Asst. football coach U. Houston, 1969; football coach Orange (Tex.) High Sch., 1970-72, Okla. State U., 1973-74, U. Kans., 1975; linebacker coach Houston Oilers, 1976, defensive line coach, 1977-80; defensive coord. New Orleans Saints, 1981-85, Phila. Eagles, 1986-88, Denver Broncos, 1989-93, head coach, 1993-94, Buffalo Bills, 1998—2000; def. coord. Atlanta Falcons, 2001—04, interim head coach, 2003—04; def. coord. San Diego Chargers, 2004—. Office: c/o San Diego Chargers PO Box 609609 San Diego CA 92160-9609

PHILLIPS, WALTER MILLS, III, psychologist, educator; b. N.Y.C., Sept. 29, 1947; s. Walter Mills and Grace Mary (Mullen) P.; m. Anne Marie Boyle, July 3, 1971; children: Jonathan, Elizabeth. BS, Fordham U., 1970; MA, U. S.D., 1973, PhD, 1975. Lic. clin. psychologist, Conn.; diplomate Am. Coll. Forensic Examiners, Am. Bd. Disability Evaluators, Am. Bd. Disability Analysts; cert. sr. disability analyst. Adolescent resident counselor Hawthorne (N.Y.) Cedar Knolls Sch., 1970—71; NIMH tng. fellow, 1971—75; clin. psychology intern Inst. of Living, Hartford, Conn., 1974—75, clin. staff psychologist, 1975—79, sr. staff psychologist, 1979—82, asst. dir. dept. clin. psychology, 1980—82, dir. clin. psychology tng., 1980—82; co-dir. outpatient psychiatry U. Conn., Farmington, 1982—88; asst. prof. psychiatry, dir. psychiatry evaluation svc. U. Conn. Health Ctr., 1982—88, dir. Anxiety Rsch. and Treatment Ctr., 1985—88; pvt. practice psychotherapy Hartford, 1976—; dir. adolescent/young adult svc. Grandview Psychiat. Resource Ctr., Waterbury, Conn., 1988—90; dir. psychology Waterbury Hosp., 1990—98; pvt. practice clin. psychology Waterbury and Middlebury, Conn., 1990—. Asst. clin. prof. psychiatry Sch. Medicine Yale U., New Haven, Conn., 1988—; mem. psychology exec. com. Sch. Medicine Yale U., New Haven, 1990-98. Contbr. articles to profl. jours. Bd. dirs. Mem. APA, Am. Psychotherapy Assn. (diplomate), Conn. Psychol. Assn., Soc. Psychotherapy Rsch., Soc. Personality Assessment, Conn. Hosp. Assn. (chmn., dir. psychology conf. 1992-96), N.Y. Acad. Scis., Sigma Xi. Office: 415 Middlebury Rd Middlebury CT 06762 E-mail: phillips.walter@comcast.net.

PHILLIPS, WALTER RAY, lawyer, educator; b. Democrat, N.C., Mar. 19, 1932; s. Walter Yancey and Bonnie (Wilson) P.; m. Patricia Ann Jones, Aug. 28, 1954; children: Bonnie Ann, Rebecca Lee. AB, U. N.C., 1954; LL.B., Emory U., 1957, LL.M., 1962, JD, 1970; postgrad., Yale U., 1965-66. Bar: Ga. 1957, Fla. 1958, Tex. 1969, Mo. 2001, U.S. Supreme Ct. 1962. With firm Jones, Adams, Paine & Foster, West Palm Beach, Fla., 1957-58; law clk. to chief judge U.S. Dist. Ct., Atlanta, 1958-59; with firm Powell, Goldstein, Frazer & Murphy, Atlanta, 1959-60; bankruptcy judge U.S. Cts., Atlanta, 1960-64; prof. law U. N.D., 1964-65; teaching fellow Yale U., 1965-66; prof. law Fla. State U., 1966-68, Tex. Tech. U., Lubbock, 1968-71; Disting. vis. prof. law Baylor U., 1971; atty. Commn. on Bankruptcy Laws of U.S., Washington, 1971-72; dep. dir., adminstrv. officer, 1972-73; prof. Sch. Law, U. Ga., 1973-2000, assoc. dean, 1975-83, acting dean, 1976, Joseph Henry Lumpkin prof., 1977-94, also dir. univ's self. study, 1978, Herman E. Talmadge prof., 1994-2000. Chapman disting. vis. prof. law U. Okla., 1985-86; vis. prof. law U. Okla., 1990, U. Mo., Columbia, 1993, 94, 2001—; reporter Gov.'s Legislation for Ga., 1973; v.p., dir. Killearn Estates, Inc.; mem. Conf. on Consumer Fin. Law; prof. London Law Consortium, 1999. Author: Florida Law and Practice, 1960, Encyclopedia of Georgia Law, 1962, Seminar for Newly Appointed Referees in Bankruptcy, 1964, Damages: Cases and Materials, 1967, (with James William Moore) Debtors' and Creditors' Rights, Cases and Material, 1966, 5th edit., 1979, The Law of Debtor Relief, 1969, 2d edit., 1972, supplement, 1975, (with James William Moore) Rule 6, Moore's Federal Practice, 1969, Adjustment of Debts for Individuals, 1979, 2d edit., 1981, supplement, 1982, 84, 85, Liquidation Under the Bankruptcy Code, 3d edit., 1988, supplement, 1989, 90, 91, 92, 93, 94, Cases and Materials on Corporate Reorganization, 1983, 3d edit., 1986, 4th edit., 1988, 5th edit., 1990, 7th edit., 1996, 8th edit., 1998, Family Farmer and Adjustment of Individual Debts, 1987, supplement, 1988, 89, 90, 91, 92, 93, 94, A Primer of Chapters 12 and 13 of the Bankruptcy Code, 1995. Bd. dirs. Lubbock Day Nurseries, 1969, pres., 1970-71. Served with USAF, 1950. Mem. ATLA, ABA (consumer bankruptcy com. 1973—, chmn. 1986-90), Fed. Bar Assn., Fla. Bar Assn., Tex. Bar Assn., Western Circuit Bar Assn., Ga. Bar Assn. (vice chmn. publs. com. 1977-89, com. on profl. responsibility 1983—2002), Mo. Bar Assn., Am. Judicature Soc., Phi Alpha Delta (chief tribune) Baptist. Home: 3800 Wakefield Dr Columbia MO 65203-5630 Office Phone: 573-882-0270. Personal E-mail: wrppjp033209321@aol.com. Business E-Mail: phillipswr@missouri.edu.

PHILLIPS, WARREN HENRY, publishing executive; b. June 28, 1926; s. Abraham and Juliette (Rosenberg) P.; m. Barbara Anne Thomas, June 16, 1951; children: Lisa, Leslie, Nina. AB, Queens Coll., 1947, LHD (hon.), 1987; JD (hon.), U. Portland, 1973; LHD (hon.), Pace U., 1982, L.I. U., 1987. Copyreader Wall St. Jour., 1947-48, fgn. corr., 1949-50, chief London bur., 1950-51, fgn. editor, 1951-53, news editor, 1953-54, mng. editor Midwest edit., 1954-57, mng. editor, 1957-65, pub., 1975-88; exec. editor Dow Jones & Co., 1965-70, v.p., gen. mgr., 1970-71, exec. v.p., 1972, editl. dir., 1971-88, pres., 1972-79, CEO, 1975-90, also bd. dirs., past chmn., 1972-97; co-pub. Bridge Works Pub. Co., 1992—. Copyreader European edit. Stars and Stripes, 1949; pres. Am. Coun. Edn. for Journalism, 1971-73; mem. Pulitzer Prize Bd., 1977-87; adj. faculty Grad. Sch. Journalism, Columbia U., 1992, John F. Kennedy Sch. Govt., Harvard Univ., 1992. Author: (with Robert Keatley) China: Behind the Mask, 1973. Trustee Columbia U., 1980-93, trustee emeritus, 1993—; mem. vis. com. John F. Kennedy Sch. Govt., Harvard U., 1984-90, 92-97; corp. adv. bd. Queens Coll., 1986-90, found. bd. trustees, 1990-97, trustee emeritus, 1997—. Named one of 10 Outstanding Young Men in U.S., U.S. Jaycees, 1958; inductee Info. Industry Assn.'s Hall of Fame, 1984. Mem. Am. Newspaper Pubs. Assn. (bd. dirs. 1976-84), Am. Soc. Newspaper Editors (pres. 1975-76), Bridgehampton Club, River Club. Office: Bridge Works Publ PO Box 1798 Bridgehampton NY 11932-1798

PHILLIPS, WILLIAM CHARLES, T'ai Chi instructor; b. N.Y.C., Jan. 28, 1947; s. Ned Richardson and Ruth Phillips. AA, S.I. C.C., 1966; BA, Bklyn. Coll., 1968; MS in Edn. Adminstrn., Supervision, St. Johns U., 1979; studied T'ai Chi under Grand Master, Ch'eng Man Ching, 1970-75. Chief instr., pres. Patience T'ai Chi Assn., Bklyn., 1982—. Instr. T'ai Chi and self def. Sheepshead Bay H.S. Adult Edn., 1975-77, Kingsborough C.C. divsn. continuing edn., 1977-80; adj. instr. T'ai Chi Kingsborough C.C. CUNY, 1987-92; lectr. Whole Life Expo, N.Y.C., 1983, 84, T'ai Chi Ch'uan Soc., Rutgers, N.J., 1983, Mind Devel. Assn., St. Louis, 1980, Festival of Yoga and Sci., Columbus, Ohio, 1980; demonstrator Oriental World of Martial Arts in Felt Forum, N.Y.C., 1977; designer T'ai Chi program for blind in conjunction with Kings Bay YMHA, Bklyn.; coord. ann. Holistic Weekends, Ellenville, N.Y., 1987—; presenter Chang San Feng Festival, Warwick, N.Y., 1989-99; judge T'ai Chi Nat. Tournament, Winchester, Va., 1991-93, U.S. Nat. Chinese Martial Arts Competitions, Houston, 1991; coach of competitors, 1997—. Author/narrator tape, video demonstrator T'ai Chi Meditative Exercise, 1984; columnist Natural Physique Mag., 1989. Mem. Manhattan Beach Cmty. Group, Bklyn., 1974-88; spl. advisor to pres. Am. Karate Coun., 1970-82, pres. coun., 1984-86; karate cons. 61st Precinct Youth Coun., 1984-86, Glenwood Houses recreation program, 1986; mem. N.Y. State Senator Donald Halperins Com. on Youth; mem. N.Y. Martial Arts Theater Group, 1985-87, Nat. T'ai Chi Referral Svc., 1990—; bd. dirs. Singles for Charities, 1991-95; organizer 100th Anniversary of birth of Prof. Cheng Man Ch'ing nat. event, 2000. Office: Patience T'ai Chi Assocs PO Box 350532 Brooklyn NY 11235-0532

PHILLIPS, WILLIAM DANIEL, physicist; b. Wilkes-Barre, Pa., Nov. 5, 1948; s. William Cornelius and Mary Catherine (Savine) Phillips; m. Jane Van Wynen, June 20, 1970; children: Catherine, Christine. BS, Juniata Coll., Huntingdon, Pa., 1970; PhD, MIT, 1976. Rsch. asst. MIT, Cambridge, 1970—76, Chaim Weizmann fellow, 1976—78; physicist Nat. Inst. Stds. and Tech., Gaithersburg, Md., 1978—90, group leader, 1990—95, fellow, 1995—. Vis. prof. Ecole Normale Sup+248rieure, Paris, 1989—90; disting. prof. physics U. Md., College Park, 1991—. Editor (author): Laser Manipulation of Atoms and Ions, 1992; contbr. articles to profl. jours. Co-recipient Nobel Prize for physics, 1997, Schawlow prize in laser sci., APS, 1998; named Outstanding Young Scientist, Md. Acad. Sci., 1982; recipient Gold medal, U.S. Dept. Commerce, 1993, Albert A. Michelson medal, Franklin Inst., 1996, Gold medal, Pa. Soc., 1999. Fellow: Am. Acad. Arts and Scis., Optical Soc. Am., Am. Phys. Soc.; mem.: NAS. Achievements include demonstrated laser cooling of atomic beams; electromagnetic trapping of neutral atoms; discovery of sub-doppler laser cooling; produced sub-microkelvin 3D kinetic temperatures. Office: Nat Inst Stds & Tech PHY A167 100 Bureau Dr Stop 8424 Gaithersburg MD 20899-0003

PHILLIPS, WILLIAM DAVID, history educator; b. Dallas, June 26, 1943; s. William David and Virginia (Mahan) P.; m. Carla Rahn, July 4, 1970. BA, U. Miss., 1964; MA, U. Tenn., 1966; PhD, NYU, 1971. Instr. R.I. Coll., Providence, 1969-70; asst. prof. history San Diego State U., 1970-75, assoc. prof., 1975-78, prof., 1978-88; prof. history U. Minn., Mpls., 1988—. Co-author: Spain's Golden Fleece, 1997 (Leo Gershoy award 1998), The Worlds of Christopher Columbus, 1992 (Spain in Am. second prize 1993); author: Slavery From Roman Times to the Early Transatlantic Trade, 1985, Enrique IV and the Crisis of Fifteenth-Century Castile, 1978; editor: Testimonies from the Columbian Lawsuits, 2000; sect. reviewer Archiv fur Reformationsgeschichte-Literaturbericht, Tübingen, Germany, 1985-94. Recipient Founders' Day award NYU, N.Y.C., 1972, grants U. Minn. and San Diego State U., grant-in-aid Am. Philos. Soc., Phila., 1980, fellowship NEH, Washington, 1988-89. Mem.: Forum on European Expansion and Global Interactions (founding mem.), Cnf. Latin Am. History (mem. Columbus quincentennial com. 1988—90), Soc. Spanish and Portuguese Hist. Studies (pres. 1994—96), Am. Hist. Assn. (sect. editor Recently Pub. Articles 1987—90, mem. Premio del Rey com. 1998—, chair 2000—01), Medieval Acad. Am. (life). Office: U Minn Dept History 267 19th Ave S Minneapolis MN 55455-0499 E-mail: phill004@tc.umn.edu.

PHILLIPS, WILLIAM E. advertising agency executive; b. Chgo., Jan. 7, 1930; s. William E. and Alice N. Phillips; children: Michael, Tom, Sarah; m. Barbara Smith, November 27, 1997. BS, Cornell U., 1951; MBA, Northwestern U., 1955. Brand mgr. Procter & Gamble, Cin., 1955-59; with Ogilvy & Mather, N.Y.C., 1959-90; CEO Ogilvy Group, 1981-88; exec. in residence, prof. Johnson Grad. Sch. Mgmt. Cornell U., 1989-90. Bd. dirs. Gen. Housewares, Sun Glass Hut, Inc., Alliance Nat. Office Ctrs. Chmn. emeritus Outward Bound Internat.; chair Outdoor Edn., Cornell U., 1990—; co-chair Cayuga Soc. for Planned Giving at Cornell U.; trustee emeritus Cornell U.; trustee Internat. Tennis Hall of Fame, Newport, R.I., Florence Griswold Mus., Old Lyme, Conn., 1991—. Lt. (j.g.) USN, 1951-54, Korea/Pacific/Mediterranean. Recipient Disting. Svc. award, Singapore Outward Bound, 1997, Kurt Hahn award, Outward Bound, 1998, Rhodes Exemplary Alumni Svc. award, Cornell U., 2001. Mem. Old Lyme Country Club, Am. Alpine Club, Explorers Club, Cornell Club, Univ. Club, Naval Mil. Club (London), Achilles Club N.Y.C. (bd. dirs.). Home: 200 N Cove Rd Old Saybrook CT 06475-2537

PHILLIPS, WILLIAM ROBERT, physician; b. Wash., Apr. 26, 1950; BA, U. Wash., 1971, MD, MPH, U. Wash., 1975. Diplomate Nat. Bd. Med. Examiners, Am. Bd. Family Practice, Am. Bd. Preventive Medicine; lic. physician and surgeon, Wash. Resident family practice Providence Med. Ctr., Seattle, 1975-78; resident preventive medicine U. Wash. Sch. Pub. Health & Cmty. Medicine, Seattle, 1976-79; vis. prof. U. Auckland, New Zealand, 1979, U. Tasmania, Hobart, Australia, 1979, U. Zimbabwe, Harare, 1993; clin. prof. family medicine U. Wash., Seattle, 1994—. Chief staff Ballard Cmty. Hosp., Seattle, 1985, chief family practice, 1984. Contbr. articles to profl. jours. Bd. trustees Ballard Cmty. Hosp., Seattle, 1985. Recipient USPHS primary care policy fellowship, 1995; named Family Physician of the Yr. Wash. Acad. Family Physicians, 1999. Fellow Am. Acad. Family Physicians (Mead Johnson award 1976, Warner-Chilcott award 1979), Wash. Acad. Family Physicians (Family Physician of Yr. 1999), Am. Coll. Preventive Medicine; mem. N.Am. Primary Care Rsch. Group (pres., rsch. awards), Soc. Tchrs. of Family Medicine. Office: Univ Washington Dept Family Medicine Box 356390 Seattle WA 98195-6390

PHILLIPS, WILLIAM THOMAS, nuclear medicine physician, researcher; b. Ulysses, Kans., June 29, 1952; s. Harold Wesley and Sheila (McGinnis) P.; m. Lauren Dorley, Sept. 20, 1981; children: Alison, Trevor, Caden. MD, U. Tex., Galveston, 1980. Diplomate Am. Bd. Nuclear Medicine, Am. Bd. Family Practice. Asst. prof. U. Tex. Health Sci. Ctr., San Antonio, 1987—92, assoc. prof., 1993—2001, prof., 2001—. Contbr. articles to sci. jours. NIH grantee, 1994-1997, Office of Naval Rsch. grantee, 2000—04. Mem.: Soc. Nuc. Medicine. Quaker. Achievements include patents for new method of labeling liposomes with 99m Technetium, new method of labeling liposomes with rhenium-186 for medical therapy, new method of treating diabetes by delaying gastric emptying; discovery that many diabetics have rapid gastric emptying. Office: UU Tex Health Sci Ctr 7703 Floyd Curl Dr San Antonio TX 78229 Business E-Mail: phillips@uthscsa.edu.

PHILLIPS, WILLIAM WATSON, gastroenterologist; b. Pitts., Pa., Nov. 23, 1949; s. James MacIlduff Phillips and Marjorie Watson Games; m. Constance Ann Connolly, June 19, 1976; children: Heather Frances, Michael Watson. BS, Allegheny Coll., 1968—72; MD, Hahnemann Med. Coll., 1972—76. Bd. cert. in internal medicine Am. Bd. Internal Medicine, bd. cert. in gastroenterology Am. Bd. Internal Medicine. Internship and residency in internal medicine Akron City Hosp., Ohio, 1976—79; fellowship in gastroent. Allegheny Gen. Hosp., Pitts., 1979—81; group practice Assoc. in Gastroent., Pitts., 1981—. Tchg. attending staff Allegheny Gen. Hosp., Pitts., 1981—86; tchg. fellow Presbyn. U. Hosp., Pitts., 1981; vis. physician Profl. Travel Abroad, 2001. Mem. Physicians for Social Responsibility, Cambridge, Mass., 1984—89; benefactor Carnegie Sci. Ctr., Pitts., 1989—94; contbr. Pitts. Aviary, 1984—. Recipient Solon Summerfield scholar award, Phi Kappa Psi, Allegheny Coll., 1972. Fellow: Am. Coll. Gastroent.; mem.: Allegheny County Med. Soc., Pa. Med. Soc., Pa. Soc. Gastroent., Pitts. Gut Club, Alpha Omega Alpha. Avocations: photography, travel, scuba diving, writing, history. Office: Assoc in Gastroenterology 9000 Perry Hwy Ste 216 Pittsburgh PA 15237

PHILLIPS, WINFRED MARSHALL, university administrator, biomedical research executive, mechanical engineer, educator; b. Richmond, Va., Oct. 7, 1940; s. Claude Marshall and Gladys Marian (Barden) P.; children: Stephen, Sean. BSME, Va. Poly. Inst., 1963; MA in Engring., U. Va., 1966, DSc, 1968. Mech. engr. U.S. Naval Weapons Lab., Dahlgren, Va., 1963; NSF trainee, tchg., rsch. asst. dept. aerospace engring. U. Va., Charlottesville, 1963-67, rsch. scientist, 1966-67; asst. prof. dept. aerospace engring. Pa. State U., University Park, 1968-74, from assoc. prof. to prof., 1974-80, assoc. dean rsch. Coll. Engring., 1979-80; head Sch. Mech. Engring. Purdue U., West Lafayette, Ind., 1980-88; dean Coll. Engring. U. Fla., Gainesville, 1988-99, assoc. v.p. engring., 1989-99, v.p. rsch., dean Grad. Sch., Don & Ruth Eckis prof., 1999—2002. Bd. dirs. 1st Union Bank, Gainesville, Enterprise North Fla. Corp., Gainesville, Wachovia, Gainesville; vis. prof. U. Paris, 1976—77; chmn. Fla. Tech. Devel. Bd., Southeastern Coalition for Minorities in Engring., vice-chmn., 1995—2000, chmn., 2001—; adv. com. Nimbus Corp., 1985—90, Hong Kong U. Sci. and Tech., 1990—93; co-founder, v.p. CEO Inc., 1990—; acad. adv. coun. Indsl. Rsch. Inst., 1990—93; sci. adv. com. Electric Power Rsch. Inst., 1994—99; adv. com. AvMed Inc.; exec. com. Accreditation Bd. on Engring. and Tech., 1991—96, internat. revs. for univs. in Saudi Arabia, Russia, Netherlands, Kuwait, pres., 1995—96; mem. U.S. Pres.'s Commn. on Nat. Medal of Sci., 2003—; chair coun., bd. dirs., mem. exec. com. Oak Ridge Associated Univs., 2002—. Sect. editor Am. Soc. Artificial Internal Organs Jour., 1985-99; contbr. over 175 articles to profl. jours., chpts. to books. Mem. Ind. Boiler and Pressure Vessel Code Bd., 1981—88; bd. dirs. Ctrl. Pa. Heart Assn., 1974—80, U. Fla. Found., 1989—91, 1995—2001. Named Disting. Hoosier Ind., 1987, Sagamore of the Wabash, 1988; recipient Career Rsch. award, NIH, 1974—78, NIH Surgery and Bioengring. Study sect., 1988—91, Fla. High Tech. and Industry Coun., 1990—94, Nat. Engring. award, Am. Assn. Engr. Socs., 2000, Linton Grinter award, 2000, Global Messenger award, Southeastern Consortium for Minorities in Engring., 2003. Fellow AAAS, AIAA, ASEE (vice chair 2001-02, chmn. bd. 2002—, Lamme award 2003), ASME (sr. v.p. edn. 1986-88, bd. dirs. 1995-2000, pres. 1998-99, Dedicated Svc. award 2001), ORAU (chair coun., bd. and exec. com. 2002—), NY Acad. Scis., Am. Astron. Soc., Am. Inst. Med. and Biol. Engring. (founding fellow, chair coll. fellows 1994-95, pres. 1996-97), Am. Soc. Engring. Edn. (past chmn. long range planning soc. awards 1990-92, vice chmn. engring. deans coun. 1991-93, chair 1993—, bd. dirs. 1994-98, 1st v.p. 1994-95, pres. 1996-97), Royal Soc. Arts; mem. Am. Soc. Artificial Internal Organs (trustee 1982-90, sec.-treas. 1986-87, pres. 1988-89, adv. bd. 1998—), Nat. Assn. State Univs. and Land-Grant Colls. (com. quality of engring. edn.), Univ. Programs in Computer-Aided Engring., Design and Mfg. (bd. dirs. 1985-91), Am. Phys. Soc., Biomed. Engring. Soc., Internat. Soc. Biotheology, Fla. Engring. Soc., Cosmos Club, Fla. Blue Key, Rotary (pres. Lafayette 1987-88), Sigma Xi, Phi Kappa Phi, Phi Tau Sigma, Sigma Gamma Tau, Tau Beta Pi (eminent engr.). Achievements include research and development of artificial heart pumps; research in reentry aerodynamics, on blood rheology, on modelling blood flow, on fluid dynamics of artificial hearts, on the use of smooth blood contacting surfaces, on prosthetic valve fluid dynamics and on laser Doppler studies of unsteady biofluid dynamics. Home: 4140 NW 44th Ave Gainesville FL 32606-4518 Office: U Fla Rsch and Grad Programs 223 Grinter Hall Gainesville FL 32611 Office Phone: 352-392-9271. Business E-Mail: wphil@ufl.edu.

PHILLIPS, WINIFRED PATRICIA, radio producer, composer; b. Mobile, Ala., Apr. 13, 1972; d. Winifred Waldron Phillips. BA summa cum laude in Comms., Kean U., 1994. Composer, prodr., actress, writer Nat. Pub. Radio, Washington, 1992—2002; composer, prodr., actress, writer Radio Tales XM Satellite Radio Dramas, Washington, 2002—; owner music and audio prodn. co. Gens. Prodns. Composer Sony Computer Entertainment Am., Santa Monica, Calif., 2004—. Composer, prodr., actress, writer (National Public Radio dramas) Generations Radio Theater Presents: Radio Tales, 1996—2002, (radio dramas) Radio Tales, XM Satellite Radio, 2002—, composer, prodr., actress (radio drama) The Odyssey Trilogy, 2003, Arabian Nights Trilogy, 2003, The Gift of the Magi, 1996, The Yellow Wallpaper, 1996, The Fall of the House of Usher, 1998, Sleepy Hollow, 1998, The Time Machine, 1999, Gulliver's Travels, 1999, The Mummy, 1999, The Island of Doctor Moreau, 2000, Dr. Jekyll and Mr. Hyde, 2000, Journey to the Center of the Earth, 2000, The Pit and the Pendulum, 2000, The Hunchback of Notre-Dame, 2001, Jason and The Argonauts, 2001, War of the Worlds, 2001, Phantom of the Opera, 2001, Beowulf, 2001, Twenty Thousand Leagues Under the Sea, 2001, The Invisible Man, 2001, The Lost World, 2002, composer, actress, author (radio musicals) Celtic Hero, 2000; composer, actress, author: radio musicals Lord of the Celts, 1998; author: (short stories) Breaking Point, 1991, Celtic Beauty for Sword and Sorceress 20 book anthology, 2003, (radio drama script) Light of Truth, 1985; composer: (video game) God of War, 2004. Recipient GRACIE award for best nat./network drama series, Am. Women in Radio and TV, 2001, 2003, 2004, N.Y. Festivals award, Internat. Radio Festivals, 1997, AUDIE Honors award, Audio Pubs. Assn., 1999, GOLDEN REEL Merit award, Nat. Fedn. Cmty. Broadcasters, 2001, GRACIE award for outstanding achievement by an actress, Am. Women in Radio and TV, 1998, N.Y. Festivals award, Internat. Radio Festivals, 2001, N.Y. Festivals World medal, 2004; grantee Endowment grantee, Wallace - Reader's Digest Funds, 1996—2002, NEA, 1996—2002, Durkin Hayes Publ., 1998. Mem.: SAG, BMI, NARAS. Avocations: reading, Web design, computer art, travel. Business E-Mail: phillips@radiotales.com.

PHILLIPS, ZAIGA ALKSNIS, pediatrician; b. Riga, Latvia, Sept. 13, 1934; came to U.S., 1949; d. Adolfs and Alma (Ozols) Alksnis; (div. 1972); children: Albert L., Lisa K., Sintija. BS, U. Wash., 1956, MD, 1959. Fellow Colo. Med. Ctr., Denver, 1961-62; sch. physician Bellevue and Issaquah (Wash.) Sch. Dists., 1970-77; pvt. practice Bellevue, 1977—; staff pediatrician Overlake Med. Ctr., 1977—, Childrens Hosp. and Med. Ctr., Seattle, 1977—, Evergreen Med. Ctr., 1977—. Attending physician Allergy Clinic, Childrens Hosp., Seattle, 1988—; cons. and contact to pediatricians in Latvia, 1988—; team mem. to Latvia, Healing the Children Contact with Latvia, 1993-97; bd. mem. Bellevue's Stay in Sch. Program, 1994-97. Mem. Am. Latvian Assn., 1972—, Wash. Latvian Assn., Seattle, 1972—; pres. Latvian Sorority Gundega, Seattle, 1990-93; bd. dirs. Sister Cities Assn., Bellevue, 1992-98, Wash. Asthma Allergy Found. Am., 1992-99. Recipient Recognition award, City of Liepaja, 1995, Latvian Assn. Am., 2003. Fellow Am. Acad. Pediat.; mem. Am. Latvian Physicians Assn. (bd. dirs. 1998—), Wash. State and Puget Sound Pediatric Assn. Office: Pediatric Assn 2700 Northup Way Bellevue WA 98004-1463 Office Phone: 206-827-4600. E-mail: zap@u.washington.edu.

PHILLIPSON, DONALD E. lawyer; b. Denver, July 22, 1942; BS, Stanford U., 1964, JD, 1968; MS, U. Calif., Berkeley, 1965. Former mem. Davis, Graham & Stubbs, Denver; now cons., writer. Mem. Nat. Soccer Hall of Fame (adminstr.). Office: 14325 Braun Rd Golden CO 80401-1431

PHILLIS, JOHN WHITFIELD, physiologist, educator; b. Port of Spain, Trinidad, Apr. 1, 1936; came to U.S., 1981; s. Ernest and Sarah Anne (Glover) P.; m. Pamela Julie Popple, 1958 (div. 1968); children: David, Simon, Susan; m. Shane Beverly Wright, Jan. 24, 1969. B in Vet. Sci., Sydney (Australia) U., 1958, D in Vet. Sci., 1976; PhD, Australian Nat. U., Canberra, 1961; DSc, Monash U., Melbourne, Australia, 1970. Sr. lectr. Monash U., 1963-69; vis. prof. Ind. U., Indpls., 1969; prof. physiology, assoc. dean rsch. U. Man., Winnipeg, Canada, 1970-73; prof., chmn. dept. physiology U. Sask., Saskatoon, Canada, 1973-81, asst. dean rsch., 1973-75; prof. physiology Wayne State U., Detroit, 1981—2004, prof. emeritus, 2004—, chmn. dept. physiology, 1981-97; affiliate prof. U. Fla., Gainsville, 2004—. Mem. scholarship and grants com. Can. Med. Rsch. Coun., Ottawa, Ont., 1973-79, rsch. prof., 1980; mem. sci. adv. bd. Dystonia Med. Rsch. Found., Beverly Hills, Calif., 1980-85, Curtis Rsch. Inst., Risingsun, Ohio, 1998-2000; mem. sci. adv. panel World Soc. for Protection of Animals, 1982-98; Wellcome vis. prof. Tulane U., 1986; mem. acad. scholars Wayne State U., 1995. Author: Pharmacology of Synapses, 1970; editor: Veterinary Physiology, 1976, Physiology and Pharmacology of Adenosine Derivatives, 1983, Adenosine and Adenine Nucleotides as Regulators of Cellular Function, 1991, The Regulation of Cerebral Blood Flow, 1993, Novel Therapies for CNS Injuries: Rationales and Results, 1996; editor Can. Jour. Physiology and Pharmacology, 1978-81, Progress in Neurobiology, 1973-97. Mem. grants com. Am. Heart Assn. of Mich., 1985-90, mem. rsch. coun., 1991-92, mem. rsch. forum com., 1991-96, chair, 1992-93; mem. Brain/Stroke Consortium Study Group, Am. Heart Assn., 1998. Wellcome fellow London, 1961-62; Can. Med. Rsch. Coun. grantee, 1970-81; NIH grantee, 1983-2000. Mem. Brit. Pharmacol. Soc., Am. Physiol. Soc., Soc. Neurosci., Internat. Brain Rsch. Orgn. Personal E-mail: jwphillis@bellsouth.net.

PHILLIS, MARILYN HUGHEY, artist; b. Kent, Ohio; d. Paul Jones and Helen Margaret (Miller) Hughey; m. Richard Waring Phillis, Mar. 19, 1949; children: Diane E., Hugh R., Randall W. Student, Kent State U., 1945; BS, Ohio State U., 1949. Chemist Battelle Meml. Inst., Columbus, Ohio, 1949-53; illustrator periodical Western Res. Hist. Mag., Garrettsville, Ohio, 1974-78; illustrator book AAUW, Piqua, Ohio, 1976; art instr. Edison State C.C., Piqua, Ohio, 1976; watermedia instr. Springfield (Ohio) Mus. Art, 1976-84. Juror art exhbns. state and nat. art groups, 1980—; painting instr. state and nat. orgns., 1980—; lectr. art healing Wheeling (W.Va.) Jesuit Coll., 1994—96; founder, coord. Nat. Creativity Seminar, Stretching Boundaries for Creative People, 1993, 1995, 1997, 1999, 2002. Author: Watermedia Techniques for Releasing the Creative Spirit, 1992, (chpt.) Bridging Space and Time, 1998; contbr. The Art of Layering: Making Connections, 2004, articles and illustrations to profl. jours.; one-woman shows include Stifel Fine Art Ctr., Wheeling, Va., Springfield Art Mus., Zanesville (Ohio) Art Ctr., Ohio U., Lancaster, Ohio U. East. St. Clairsville, Cleve. Inst. Music, Columbus Mus. Art, Cheekwood Mus. of Art, Bot. Hall, Nashville, Idaho Falls Art Ctr., Monroe (Mich.) C.C., exhibitions include, N.Y.C., Wheeling, W.Va, Butler Mus. Am. Art, Youngstown, Ohio, Taiwan Art Edn. Inst., Taipei, 1994, Represented in permanent collections Ohio U., Lancaster and St. Clairsville, Springfield (Ohio) Mus. Art, Heritage Hall mus., Talladega, Ala., Ohio Watercolor Soc., also corp. collections. Co-chmn. Cmty. Health and Humor Program, Wheeling, 1992. Recipient First awards Watercolor West, Riverside, Calif., 1990, Hudson Soc. award Nat. Collage Soc., 1995, Art Masters award Am. Artist Mag., 1996; elected to Hall of Fame, Kent, Ohio, 2000, Hall of Fame, Wheeling, Va., 2000. Mem. Internat. Soc. Study of Subtle Energies and Energy Medicine (art cons. sci. jour. 1992—, art and healing workshop 1995), Am. Watercolor Soc. (dir. 1991-93, newsletter editor 1992—,chmn. Jury of Awards, 2003, Osborne award 1975), Soc. Layerists in Multi-Media (nat. v.p. 1988-93), Ohio Watercolor Soc. (sec. 1979-82, v.p. 1982-89, pres. 1990-96, dir. biennial creativity seminars 1993-95, 97, 99, 2002, Gold medal, Best of Show 1993), Nat. Watercolor Soc. (chmn. selection jury 2001), Int. Noetic Sci., West Ohio Watercolor Soc. (pres. 1979-80, 2nd award 1982), Allied Artists N.Y., W.Va. Watercolor Soc. (1st award 1993), Ky. Watercolor Soc., Ga. Watercolor Soc., So. Watercolor Soc. (pres. 1997-98, Silver award 1999). Avocations: hiking, reading, genealogy, music, travel. Home and Office: Phillis Studio 72 Stamm Cir Wheeling WV 26003-5549

PHILOGENE, BERNARD J. R. academic administrator, science educator; b. Beau-Bassin, Mauritius, May 4, 1940; came to Can., 1961; s. Raymond Pierre and Simone Marie (Ruffier) P.; m. Hélène Marie Lebreux, July 7, 1964; children: Simone, Catherine. BS, U. Montreal, 1964; MS, McGill U., 1966; PhD, U. Wis., 1970; DSc (hon.), Compiègne, 1995. Research officer Can. Forestry Service, Que., 1966-70, research scientist, 1970-71; asst. prof. U. B.C., Vancouver, 1971-74; asst. prof., assoc. prof., then prof. entomology U. Ottawa, Can., 1974—, vice dean sci. and engring., 1982-85, acting dean, 1985-86, dean faculty of sci., 1986-90, acad. vice rector, 1990-97; pres. Can. Consortium of Sci. Socs., 1992-94. Cons. OAS, Washington, 1979-80, Agence de Coop. Culture & Tech., Paris, 1982-83, Can. Internat. Devel. Agy., Ottawa, 1983-85, UN Environ. Program, Geneva, Switzerland, 1985-86, Internat. Devel. Research Ctr., Ottawa, 1985—. Mem. Ont. Pesticide Adv. Com., 1987-91. Decorated commandeur de l'Ordre des Palmes Académiques (France); knight of merit Order of St. John of Jerusalem. Fellow Entomol. Soc. Can. (bd. dirs. 1977-80); mem. Am. Inst. Biol. Scis., Entomol. Soc. Am., Can. Pest Mgmt. Soc., Assn. Can.-Française Advancement Sci. (bd. dirs. 1984-86), Internat. Soc. Chem. Ecology, Entomol. Soc. of Can. (Gold Medal 2000). Office: U Ottawa PO Box 450 30 Marie Curie St Ottawa ON Canada K1N 6N5 E-mail: bphilog@science.uottawa.ca.

PHILPOTT, HARRY MELVIN, former university president; b. Bassett, Va., May 6, 1917; s. Benjamin Cabell and Daisy (Hundley) P.; m. Pauline Breck Moran, Sept. 15, 1943; children: Harry Melvin, Jean Todd, Benjamin Cabell II, Virginia Lee. AB, Washington and Lee U., 1938, LL.D., 1966; PhD, Yale U., 1947; D.D., Stetson U., 1960; LL.D., U. Fla., 1969, U. Ala., 1970; H.H.D., Samford U., 1978, Montevallo U., 1980, Auburn U., 1981. Ordained to ministry Bapt. Ch., 1942; dir. religious activities Washington and Lee U., 1938-40; prof. religion U. Fla., 1947-52, v.p., 1957-65; dean, head dept. religion and philosophy Stephens Coll., 1952-57; pres. Auburn U., 1965-80. Mem. Regional Edn. Bd., 1966-82, vice chmn., 1973-75; chmn. Ala. Edn. Study Commn., 1967-69; pres. Southeastern Conf., 1972-74. Served to 1st lt. Chaplains Corps., USNR, 1943-46. Mem. Nat. Assn. State Univs. and Land-Grant Colls. (chmn. council presidents 1972-73, exec. com. 1973-78, pres. 1976-77), Fla. Blue Key, Kappa Alpha, Omicron Delta Kappa, Kappa Delta Pi, Phi Kappa Phi, Phi Beta Kappa. Home: PO Box 3037 Auburn AL 36831-3037

PHILPOTT, LARRY LA FAYETTE, horn player; b. Alma, Ark., Apr. 5, 1937; s. Lester and Rena (Owens) P.; m. Elise Robichaud, Nov. 24, 1962 (div. June 1975); children: Daniel, Stacy; m. Anne Sokol, Feb. 14, 1984. BS, Ga. So. Coll., 1962; MusM, Butler U., 1972. Instr. in horn Butler U., De Pauw U.; dir. music Cedarcrest Sch., Marysville, Wash., 1991—; instr. horn Western Wash. U., Dept Music, Bellingham, 1995-98. Mem., N.C. Symphony, 1960, Savannah (Ga.) Symphony, L'Orchestre Symphonique de Quebec, Que., Can., 1962-64, prin. horn player, Indpls. Symphony Orch., 1964-89, Flagstaff Summer Festival, 1968-; artist in-residence Ind.-Purdue Indpls.; appeared with, Am. Shakespeare Theatre, summer 1965, Charlottetown Festival, summers 1967-68, Flagstaff Summer Festival, 1968-85, Marrowstone Music Festival, 1985—. Served with USN, 1956-60. Mem. Music Educators Nat. Conf., Am. Fedn. Musicians, Internat. Conf. Symphony and Opera Musicians, Internat. Horn Soc., Coll. Music Soc., Phi Mu Alpha Sinfonia. Home: 14925 63d Ave SE Snohomish WA 98296-5277

PHINIZY, ROBERT BURCHALL, electronics company executive; b. Ben Hill, Ga., June 30, 1926; children: Robert B., William, David. BS, U. Ariz., 1951; postgrad., U. So. Calif., 1952-55, UCLA, 1956-62. Pres. LB Products, Santa Monica, Calif., 1954—58, IMC Magnetics Western, South Gate, Calif., 1958—69, Am. Electronics, Fullerton, Calif., 1969-71; gen. mgr. electronics div. Eaton Co., Anaheim, Calif., 1971—72; pres., CEO Genisco Tech. Corp., Compton, Calif., 1972-83; chmn. bd., CEO Genisco Computers Corp., Costa Mesa, Calif., 1976—83. Bd. dirs. Microsemi Corp., 1992-2003, Santa Ana, Calif., 1990-03, Logisticsware, Inc., 1997-; bd. dirs., sec. Biosonics Inc., Seattle, 1989—. Contbr. articles to tech. jours.; patentee in field. Mem. Port Ludlow Yacht Club (commodore 1998). Office Phone: 360-437-9200.

PHINNEY, BERNARD O. research scientist, educator; b. July 29, 1917; s. Bernard Orrin and Franc Maude (Lawrence) P.; m. Sally Ball Bush; children: Scott, Katcha; m. Isabelle Jean Swift, Dec. 11, 1965; children: Peter, David. BA cum laude, U. Minn., 1940, PhD, 1946; DSc (hon.), U. Bristol, 1991. Teaching and rsch. asst. Dept. Botany U. Minn., Mpls., 1940-46; postdoctoral scholar Calif. Inst. Tech., Pasadena, 1946-48; from instr. to prof. U. Calif., L.A., 1947-88, prof. emeritus, 1988—. NSF sr. postdoctoral fellow Copenhagen U., 1959-60; NSF-U.S.-Japan rsch. sci. Internat. Christian U., Mitaka, Tokyo, 1966-67; vis. prof. Dept. Chem. U. Bristol, U.K., 1973, 83. Elected mem. Nat. Acad. Scis., Washington, 1985. Rsch. grantee NSF, Dept. Energy, 1956—. Fellow AAAS; mem. Am. Soc. Plant Physiologists (pres. 1989-90), Am. Inst. Biol. Scis., Am. Chem. Soc., Bot. Soc. Am., Genetics Soc. Am., Japanese Soc. Plant Physiologists, Internat. Soc. Plant Molecular Biologists, Phytochem. Soc. Am. Democrat. Avocations: skiing, hiking, fishing, classical music. Home: 257 Beloit Ave Los Angeles CA 90049-3009 Office Phone: 310-825-3177. Personal E-mail: bop@ucla.edu.

PHINNEY, JEAN SWIFT, psychology educator; b. Princeton, N.J., Mar. 12, 1933; d. Emerson H. and Anne (Davis) Swift; m. Bernard O. Phinney, Dec. 11, 1965; children: Peter, David. BA, Wellesley Coll., 1955; MA, UCLA, 1969, PhD, 1973. Asst. prof. psychology Calif. State U., L.A., 1977-81, assoc. prof. psychology, 1981-86, prof. psychology, 1986—. Editor: Children's Ethnic Socialization, 1987; asst. editor Jour. Adolescence; mem. editl. bd. Jour. Adolescent Rsch., Identity: An Internat. Jour.; contbr. articles to profl. jours. NIH and NSF grantee. Fellow APA; mem. Soc. for Rsch. in Child Devel., Soc. for Rsch. in Adolescence, Internat. Assn. Cross-Cultural Psychology. Avocations: skiing, hiking, travel. Office: Calif State U Dept Psychology 5151 State University Dr Los Angeles CA 90032-4226

PHINNEY, WILLIAM CHARLES, retired geologist; b. South Portland, Maine, Nov. 16, 1930; s. Clement Woodbridge and Margaret Florence (Foster) P.; m. Colleen Dorothy Murphy, May 31, 1953; children— Glenn, Duane, John, Marla. BS, MIT, 1953, MS, 1956, PhD, 1959. Faculty geology U. Minn., 1959-70; chief geology br. NASA Lyndon B. Johnson Space Center, Houston, 1970-82, chief planetology br., 1982-89, ret., 1994. NASA prin. investigator lunar samples. Contbr. articles to profl. jours. Served with C.E. AUS, 1953-55. Recipient NASA Exceptional Sci. Achievement medal, 1972, NASA Cert. of Commendation, 1987; NASA rsch. grantee, 1972-94, NSF rsch. grantee, 1960-70. Mem. Am. Geophys. Union, AAAS, Mineral. Soc. Am., Geol. Soc. Am., Minn. Acad. Sci. (dir.), Sigma Xi. Home: 18063 Judicial Way S Lakeville MN 55044-8895

PHIPARD, NANCY MIDWOOD, retired special education educator, poet; b. Boston, Jan. 31, 1929; d. William Henry and Jean Estelle (Dubbs) McAdams; m. Kenneth E. Brown, June 17, 1949 (div.); children: Christopher M. Brown, Jennifer Progodich, Michael H. Brown, Jeffrey D. Brown; m. Arnold J. Midwood, Jr., July 2, 1980 (dec.); m. Harvey F. Phipard, Jan. 14, 1998. Student, Mt. Holyoke Coll., 1946-48; BA, Wellesley Coll., 1973; MEd, Boston Coll., 1975. Dir. confs. and insvc. tng., chmn. bd. Mass. Assn. for Children with Learning Disabilities, Waltham and Framingham, 1969-75; chmn. core edn. teams, cons. to spl. programs, grant writer Needham (Mass.) Pub. Schs., 1974-79; ret., 1979; pres., feature writer S.D. Assocs., Inc., Wellesley, Mass., 1980-81; dir. pub. rels., women's career conf. Babson Coll., Wellesley, 1982. Mem. program evaluation team Mass. Dept. Edn., Quincy, 1978. Author (as Nancy Brown, with Louis Dickstein): Psychological Reports, 1974; author: (poems) Portraits of a Life, 1996, Fields of Gold, 1996, Ever-Flowing Stream, 1997, Best Poems of 1998, 1998, Colors of the Past, 2000, Echoes of Yesteryear, 2000, America at the Millennium, The Best Poems and Poets of the 20th Century, 2000, Memories of Tomorrow, 2000, Journey to Infinity, 2000, The Best Poems of 2002. Bd. dirs., fundraiser Hospice Palm Beach (Fla.) County S., 1993—97; bd. dirs. La Coqueille Villas, Inc., Manalapan, Fla., 1994—98; bd. dirs., chair cmty. rels. Lincoln Child Ctr., Oakland, Calif., 1983—85; docent Calif. Hist. Soc., San Francisco, 1982—87. Recipient Editor's Choice award, Internat. Libr. Poetry, 1996, 1998, 2000, 2003. Mem.: Internat. Soc. Poets (disting. mem.), Phi Beta Kappa. Avocations: tennis, travel, duplicate bridge. Home: 1630 Lands End Rd Manalapan FL 33462-4762

PHIPATANAKUL, WANDA, pediatrician, allergist, immunologist; b. St. Louis, Mar. 26, 1969; d. Supete and Chintana Phipatanakul. BS summa cum laude, Union Coll., Lincoln, Nebr., 1990; MD, Loma Linda U., Calif., 1994. Diplomate Am. Bd. Pediats., Am. Bd. Allergy and Immunology, lic. physician Calif., Md., cert. Mass. Intern in pediats. Loma Linda U., 1994—95; resident in pediats. Children's Hosp. of L.A., 1995—97; fellow in pediat. allergy and immunology Johns Hopkins U., Balt., 1997—2000; attending physician Children's Hosp., Boston, 2000—; asst. prof. pediats. Harvard Med. Sch., Boston, 2000—. Mem. com. of clin. investigation Instnl. Rev. Bd. for Clin. Rsch., 2000—; lectr. in field. Reviewer (pediats. supplement) Best Articles in Allergy/Immunology, 1999—, editl. bd. Pediat. Asthma, Allergy and Immunology, 2000; contbr. numerous articles, abstracts to profl. jours., chpts. to books. Vol. asthma physician Asthma Camp for Inner-City Children, Boston Pub. Health Commn., 2001. Recipient Nat. Med. Aux. award, 1989, Career Devel. award, NIH; grantee Children's Hosp. Cmty. Health Benefits grantee, 2001—, Deborah Munroe Noonan Meml. Fund grantee, 2001—; scholar Dalrymple Merit scholar for acad. excellence, Union Coll., 1988; Merck & Co. Inc. grantee, 2000—01. Fellow: Am. Acad. Pediats. (mem. allergy and immunology sect.); mem.: New Eng. Soc. Allergy, Am. Acad. Allergy, Asthma and Immunology (environmental and occupl. disorders interest sect. 2000, young allergist/immunologists com. 2000, women's involvement com. 2000), Am. Coll. Allergy, Asthma and Immunology. Achievements include research in environmental indoor allergens, animal allergens, Inner-city asthma. Office: Children's Hosp Boston 300 Longwood Ave Boston MA 02115

PHIPPS, ALLEN MAYHEW, management consultant; b. Seattle, Oct. 3, 1938; s. Donald Mayhew and Virginia (McGinn) P.; m. Joyce Elisabeth Alberti, Aug. 21, 1971; children: Ramsey Mayhew, Justin Beckwith. BA in Econs., U. Calif., Berkeley, 1961; MBA with honors, Stanford U., 1969. Security analyst Morgan Guaranty Trust Co., 1968; with Boston Cons. Group, Inc., 1969—, mgr., 1971-74; mem. sr. team Calif., 1974-77; corp. v.p., dir., 1975—. Mgr. Boston Cons. Group, G.mb.H, Munich. W. Ger., 1978-82, partner-in-charge West Coast client devel., Menlo Park, Calif., 1982-84; pres. Techno Digital Systems, Inc., 1984-86; pres., chief exec. officer, Techno Digital System (Sellectek, Inc.), 1984-85; exec. v.p., Regis McKenna Inc., Palo Alto, Calif., 1985-87; pvt. practice mgmt. cons., Menlo Pk., 1987-95; chief exec. officer Bio Electro Systems, Palo Alto, 1989-92; mng. dir., Bus. Engring. Inc., Menlo Park, Calif., 1992-95; sr. v.p. bus. and policy group SRI Internat., Menlo Park, Calif., 1995-96; pres., CEO SRI Consulting, Menlo Park, 1996-2000, ret., 2000; cons. Allen M. Phipps Mgmt. Consulting, Atherton, Calif., 2000—. Served to capt. U.S. Army, 1961-67. Decorated Bronze Star, Army Commendation medal with 2 oak leaf clusters. Mem.: Menlo Country Club (Woodside), Bohemian Club (San Francisco), Alpha Delta Phi. Republican. Presbyterian. Home: 33 Prado Secoya St Atherton CA 94027-4126 Office: Allen M Phipps Mgmt Consulting 33 Prado Secoya Atherton CA 94027 E-mail: allen@allenmphipps.com.

PHIPPS, BENJAMIN KIMBALL, II, lawyer; b. Boston, Jan. 16, 1933; s. Benjamin Kimball and Bertha Elizabeth (Forsyth) P.; m. Phyllis Jarrett Anderson, Jan. 10, 1962; children: Lisa Jarrett, Christina Caroline. BS in Commerce, U. Va., 1955, LLB, 1958. Bar: Fla. 1964, U.S. Dist. Ct. (no. dist.) Fla., U.S. Claims Ct., U.S. Ct. Appeals (5th and 11th cirs.), U.S. Tax Ct. Editor Mcpl. Code Corp., Tallahassee, 1964-65; pvt. practice Tallahassee, 1965—. Counsel tax com. Fla. Ho. of Reps., 1966-72, counsel to speaker, 1973-74, mem. adv. com. fin. & tax com., 1983-84; mem. Legis. Task Force Taxpayers' Bill Rights, 1989-91; elected dir. Fla. Coun. Property Tax Lawyers, 2003; cons. in field. Contbr. articles to profl. jours.; columnist Tallahassee Democrat. Chmn. Hist. Tallahassee Preservation Bd., 1970-91; trustee Maclay Sch.; mem. adv. coun., Sta. WFSU-TV, chmn., 1970-72; mem. Fla. Mus. History, 1990-2002, v.p., 1997-99; mem. Tallahassee Trust for Hist. Preservation, 1997—, treas., 1998—. Served to capt., U.S. Army, 1958-64. Mem. ABA (tax sect. state and local tax com.), Tallahassee Bar Assn., Fla. Bar (treas., vice chmn., chmn. tax sect. 1985-86, editl. bd. Fla. Bar News, chmn. 1975-76), Gov.'s Club, Univ. Ctr. Club, Cosmos Club, Exchange Club, Tiger Bay Club (dir.), Fla. Econ. Club, St. Andrews Soc. (pres. 1978-79), Sigma Alpha Epsilon, Phi Alpha Delta, Pi Delta Epsilon. Republican. Episcopalian. Office: PO Box 1351 Tallahassee FL 32302-1351

PHIPPS, JOHN RANDOLPH, retired army officer; b. Kansas, Ill, May 16, 1919; s. Charles Winslow and Kelsey Ethel (Torrence) P.; m. Pauline M. Prunty, Feb. 8, 1946; children: Charles W., Kelsey J. Phipps-Selander. BS in Econs. with honors, U. Ill., 1941; M.P.A., Sangamon State U., 1976; assoc. course, Command and Gen. Staff Coll., 1959, nuclear weapons employment course, 1962; course, U.S. Army War Coll., 1973, U.S. Nat. Def. U., 1978. Owner, operator chain shoe stores in, Eastern Ill., 1946-70; commd. 2d lt. F.A. U.S. Army, 1941, advanced through grades to capt., 1943; service in Philippines and Japan; discharged as maj., 1946; organizer, comdr. Co. E, 130th Inf., Ill.; N.G., Mattoon, 1947, comdg. officer 2d Bn., 130th Inf., 1951, lt. col. 2d Bn., 130th Inf., 1951; called to fed. service, 1952, adv. (29th Regt., 9th Republic of Korea Div.), 1952-53; comdr. officer 1st Bn., 130th Inf., Ill. N.G., 1954, col., 1959; comdg. officer 2d Brigade, 33d Div., 1963-67; asst. div. comdr. 33d Inf. Div., 1967, brig. gen., 1967; comdr. 33d Inf. Brigade, Chgo., 1967-70, Ill. Emergency Ops. Hdqrs., 1970, asst. adj. gen. Ill., 1970-77, acting adj. gen., 1977-78, adj. gen., 1978, promoted to maj. gen., 1978, now maj. gen. ret. Decorated Silver Star, Bronze Star, Disting. Service medal, Combat Infantry Badge, Army Disting. Service medal Ill., various Philippine and Korean decorations; State of Ill. Long and Honorable Service medal. Mem. VFW, Adj. Gens. Assn. U.S., N.G. Assn. U.S., N.G. Assn. Ill., Am. Legion, Amvets. Home: 100 Wabash Ave Mattoon IL 61938-4524 Office: Phipps 100 Wabash Ave Mattoon IL 61938-4524

PHIPPS, PATRICK MICHAEL, plant pathology educator; b. New Martinsville, W. Va., Oct. 19, 1945; m. Janet Phipps, 1967; 1 child, James. BS, Fairmont State Coll., 1970; MS, Va. Polytech. Inst. & State U., 1972; PhD in Plant pathology, W. Va. U., 1974. Asst. prof. plant pathology N.C. State U., 1974-78; prof. plant pathology Tidewater Agrl. Rsch. and Ext. Ctr. Va. Polytech. Inst. and State U., 1989—. Recipient Excellent in Ext. award Am. Phytopathol. Soc., 1994, Dow AgroScis. award for excellence in edn., 1999, award for contbns. to peanut industry Am. Peanut Coun., 2000. Fellow: Am Peanut Rsch. and Edn. Soc. Office: Tidewater Agrl Rsch & Ext Ctr 6321 Holland Rd Suffolk VA 23437-9588 E-mail: pmphipps@vt.edu.

PHO, LONG AMBROSE BA, business educator, consultant; b. Hanoi, Vietnam, Apr. 25, 1922; arrived in U.S., 1975; s. Thuan Ba Pho and Ninh Thi Nguyen; m. Claire Trung-Nghia Dang, Oct. 15, 1940; children: Cyril Hong-Phong, Anne Le-Thu, Pacific Hong-Tam, Michael Hong-Quang, Helen Long-Chau, Edward Hong-Minh. Bachelor's degree 2e Partie, Lycee Albert Sarraut, Hanoi, 1944; Pharmacien d'Etat, U. Indochina, Hanoi, 1950; MBA, Harvard U., 1956. Advanced profl.c ert. Program dir. Georgetown U., Washington, 1983-95; seminar escort interpreter U.S. Dept. State, Washington, 1978—. Bus. edn. cons. Vietnam Found., McLean, Va., also in Laos, Cambodia, 1995—. Min. labor Govt. of Republic of Vietnam, Saigon, 1987-88. Capt., mil. pharmacist North Vietnamese mil., 1946-50. Recipient Congl. citation U.S. Senate, 1986. Mem. Vietnam Found. (hon. mem., founder, past pres. 1978-89). Office: Vietnam Foundation 6713 Lumsden St Mc Lean VA 22101

PHOCAS, GEORGE JOHN, international lawyer, business executive; b. N.Y.C., Dec. 1, 1927; m. Katrin Gorny, Feb. 26, 1966; 1 child, George Alexander. AB, U. Chgo., 1950, JD, 1953. Bar: N.Y. 1955, U.S. Supreme Ct. 1962. Assoc. Sullivan & Cromwell, N.Y.C., 1953-56; counsel Creole Petroleum Corp., Caracas, Venezuela, 1956-60; internat. negotiator Standard Oil Co. N.J. (Exxon), 1960-63; sr. ptnr. Casey, Lane & Mittendorf, London, 1963-72, counsel, 1972-76. Exec. v.p. Occidental Petroleum Corp., Los Angeles, 1972-74; adv., U.S. del. UN, ECAFE, Teheran, 1963 Trustee Assn. Naval Aviation, Washington, Owl's Head Aviation Mus., Maine; mem. vis. bd. U. Chgo. Law Sch.; bd. visitors U. Chgo. Law Sch. Capt. U.S. Army Mem. ABA, Law Soc. London, Brit. Inst. Comparative Law, Am. Soc. Internat. Law, Assn. Bar City N.Y.; Clubs: Boodles (London), Met. (N.Y.C.). Home: 29 Duchess of Bedford Walk London W87 QH England also: 1605 Middle Gulf Dr 102 Sanibel FL 33957-7601

PHOENIX, G. KEITH, lawyer; b. Centralia, Ill., Aug. 13, 1946; BA in Liberal Arts, So. Ill. U., 1968; JD, St. Louis U., 1973. Bar: Mo. 74, U.S. Dist. Ct. (so. dist.) Ill. 75, U.S. Ct. Appeals (7th and 8th cirs.) 82. Assoc. Coburn, Croft & Shepherd & Putzell, St. Louis, 1974—79; ptnr., pres. Sandberg, Phoenix & von Gontard, St. Louis, 1979—. Legal cons. Am. Acad. Pedist. Contbr. articles on med./legal topics to profl. jours. 1st lt. U.S. Army, 1968—71, Vietnam. Decorated Bronze Star with cluster, Air medal with cluster, Vietnam medal. Mem.: Product Liability Adv. Coun., Am. Bd. Trial Advocacy (past pres.), Lawyer's Assn. (past pres.), St. Louis Bar Assn., Mo. Bar Assn., Ill. Bar Assn. (Named One of the Top Trial Lawyers in Am. 2002, 2003). Office: Sandberg Phoenix & von Gontard 1 City Ctr Ste 1500 Saint Louis MO 63101-1880 Office Phone: 314-231-3332. E-mail: kphoenix@spvg.com.

PHOENIX, JOAQUIN RAPHAEL, actor; b. San Juan, PR, Oct. 28, 1974; s. John Bottom Amram and Arlyn Dunitz Jochebed. Actor: (TV films) Backwards: The Riddle of Dyslexia, 1984, Kids Don't Tell, 1985, Secret Witness, 1988; (TV series) Morningstar/Eveningstar, 1986; (films) SpaceCamp, 1986, Russkies, 1987, Parenthood, 1989, Walking the Dog, 1991, To Die For, 1995, Inventing the Abbotts, 1997, U Turn, 1997, Return to Paradise, 1998, Clay Pigeons, 1998, 8MM, 1999, The Yards, 2000, Gladiator, 2000, Quills, 2000, Buffalo Soldiers, 2001, Signs, 2002, It's All About Love, 2003, (voice) Brother Bear, 2003, The Village, 2004. Office: 2603 NW 13th St Gainesville FL 32609 also: Iris Burton Agy 1450 Belfast Dr Los Angeles CA 90069*

PHUNG, NGUYEN DINH, medical educator; b. Ninh Binh, Vietnam, Sept. 25, 1950; came to U.S., 1975; s. Thu Dinh Nguyen and Minh Tuyet Le; m. Thuy Thanh Tran, Sept. 25, 1974; children: The-Ngoc, Khoi-Nguyen, Thien Huong. MD, Saigon Med. Sch., 1973. Diplomate Am. Bd. Internal Medicine, Am. Bd. Allergy and Immunology. Clin. instr. medicine, staff physician U. Okla. Health Scis. Ctr. & Vets. Hosp., Oklahoma City, 1982-84; clin. asst. prof. medicine U. Tex. Med. Sch., Houston, 1989—. Co-author: Practical Allergy & Immunology, 1983; contbr. articles to profl. jours. Mem. ACP, Am. Acad. Allergy and Immunology. Avocations: writing, music. Office: Allergy and Asthma Clinic 2905 Milam St Houston TX 77006-3609

PIA, PAMELA CARMEL, editor, director; d. Nunzie Peter and Theresa V. Pia; 1 child, Christopher M. BA, NYU, 1978; MBA, U. Bridgeport, 1987. Asst. program mgr. Easton Press, Norwalk, Conn., 1978—93; sr. editor Longmeadow Press, Stamford, Conn., 1993—95; editl. dir. Reader's Digest Young Families, Pleasantville, NY, 1995—. Editor: The Country Mouse and the City Mouse, 2003 (Silver award Soc. Illustrators, 2003), Pinocchio - A Tale of Honesty, 2004 (iParenting Media award, 2004). Mem.: LWV. Democrat. Avocations: travel, photography, reading, music. Office: Readers Digest Young Families One Readers Digest Road Pleasantville NY 10570 Office Phone: 914-244-4872. Business E-Mail: pam_pia@rd.com.

PIACENTINI, NICHOLAS A., JR., military officer; b. Sacramento, Calif. AA, Sacramento City Coll.; BS, Sacramento State Coll. Commd. USAR, 1970, advanced through grades to sgt. maj.; from drill sgt. to 1st sgt. for cos. B and D 3d Bn., 360th Regiment, 1st Brigade, 91st Divsn., Sacramento, 1970; command sgt. mjr. hq. 5th Bn., Lathrop, Calif.; command sgt. maj./commandant 91st Divsn. Leadership Drill Sgt. Sch., Dublin, Calif.; command sgt. maj. hq. 1st Brigade, Sacramento; command sgt. maj. 351st Civil Affairs Command, Mountain View, Calif., Army Res. Pers. Ctr., St. Louis, 1994—98, 3d Med. Command, Atlanta, 1998—2000, USAR Command, Ft. McPherson, Ga., 2000—. Decorated Meritorious Svc. medal with 4 oak leaf clusters, Army Commendation medal, Army Res. Components Achievement medal with 4 oak leaf clusters, Armed Forces Res. medal with silver hourglass device, many others; recipient Mil. Outstanding Vol. Svc. medal. Office: Army Reserve Command Hq Fort McPherson Fort Mcpherson GA 30330-1069

PIAGET, GERALD WARREN, psychologist, educator; b. Paterson, N.J., Nov. 10, 1942; s. Warren Edward Piaget and Mary Grace Fitzgerald; m. Joan Emerson Gianatasio, Mar. 7, 1981; children: Ryan, Craig. BS with honors, Lehigh U., 1964; PhD with honors, U. Mass., 1968. Rsch. profl. Behavior Change, Inc., Los Altos, Calif., 1969-72; clin. assoc. prof. dept. behavioral scis. Stanford U. Sch. Medicine, Palo Alto, Calif., 1975—; pres., CEO IAHB, Inc., Portola Valley, Calif., 1977—. Author: Overcoming Your Barriers, 1985, Control Freaks, 1991. Tng. fellow NIMH, 1967-68. Mem. APA. Office: IAHB Inc 4370 Alpine Rd Ste 209 Portola Valley CA 94028 Office Fax: (650) 851-0406. E-mail: gpiaget@aol.com.

PIAKER, PHILIP MARTIN, accountant, educator; b. N.Y.C., Oct. 26, 1921; s. Jacob and Sarah (Schloss) P.; m. Pauline Strum, Sept. 22, 1946; children: Susan, Alan, Matthew. BA, CCNY, 1943, MBA, 1949. Lectr. CCNY, 1949-52; asst. prof. acctg. SUNY, Binghamton, 1952-57, assoc. prof., 1957-62, prof., 1962—, Disting. Svc. prof. acctg., 1980—, chmn. dept. acctg., 1970-76, 77-89; chmn. bd. Endicott Rsch. Group, Inc., Johnson City, N.Y., 1983—. Adv. dir. Endicott Bank N.Y.; mem. N.Y. State Bd. for Pub. Accountancy, 1973-83, chmn., 1982-83; v.p. Piaker, Lyons, P.C., CPA's; mem. Nat. Bd. to Evaluate CPA Exams., 1979-83; Danforth Seminar on Bus. Morality fellow Harvard U., 1959; Summer Study on Ethics in Bus. fellow U. So. Calif., 1982. Mem. editorial bd. Binghamton Reporter, 1975—. Bd. dirs. Broome chpt. Am. Cancer Soc., 1974-79, Tri-Cities Opera; trustee Temple Israel Binghamton, 1978—. With U.S. Army, 1943-46. SUNY SWANA fellow Jerusalem, 1966, Am. Profs. for Peace in Middle East fellow Jerusalem, 1974; recipient Chancellors award for teaching excellence, 1975, David Ben Gurion award State of Israel, 1979, Outstanding Contbn. to Acctg. award Found. for Acctg., 1979, Outstanding Educator award Found. for Acctg. Rsch., 1986 . Mem. AICPA, N.Y. State Soc. CPA's (pres. Binghamton chpt. 1963-65), Am. Acctg. Assn., Acctg. Rsch. Assn., Nat. Assn. Accts., Bus. Ethics Soc., SUNY Alumni Assn. (Disting. Svc. award 1989), CHABAD (pres. 1989-92). Home: 301 Manchester Rd Vestal NY 13850-3604 also: 7421 Hearth Stone Ave Boynton Beach FL 33437-2924

PIAN, RULAN CHAO, musicologist, scholar; b. Cambridge, Mass., Apr. 20, 1922; d. Yuen Ren and Buwei (Yang) Chao; m. Theodore Hsueh-huang Pian, Oct. 3, 1945; 1 child, Canta Chao-po. BA, Radcliffe Coll., 1944, MA, 1946, PhD, 1960. Teaching asst., instr. in modern Chinese Harvard U., 1947-60, lectr. Chinese and Chinese music, 1961-74, prof. Ea. Asian langs. and civilizations, prof. music, 1974-92; prof. emerita, 1992—; coordinator modern Chinese lang. instrn. Harvard U., 1962-68, mem. council E. Asian studies, 1975-92, faculty mem. Com. on Degrees in Folklore and Mythology, 1976-92, master of South House, 1975-78. Vis. prof. dept. music The Chinese U. Hong Kong, 1975, 78-79, 82, 94, inst. humanities Nat. Tsing Hua U., Taiwan, 1990, Sch. Humanities, Nat. Cen. U., Taiwan, 1992; hon. prof. Ctrl. China U. of Sci. and Tech., Wuhan, 1990, Ctrl. S. U. Tech., Changsha, China, 1991, S.W. Jiaoting U., Chengdu, 1994, Shah-shih U., Hupei, 1996; hon. rsch. fellow Shanghai Conservatory Music, China, 1991, Inst. Music Rsch., China Acad. of Arts, Beijing, 1997; academician Academia Sinica, Taiwan, 1990. Author: A Syllabus for the Mandarin Primer, 1961, Sonq Dynasty Musical Sources and Their Interpretation, 1967; compiler: Complete Musical Works of Yuen Ren Chao, 1987; contbr. articles to scholarly jours. Recipient Caroline Wilby dissertation prize Radcliffe Coll., 1960, Radcliffe Grad. Soc. medal, 1980; NDEA Fulbright-Hayes research grantee Chinese Music Taiwan, 1964; NEH grantee Hong Kong, 1978-79 Mem. Am. Musicological Soc. (coun. 1993-96, Otto Kinkeldey book award 1968), Internat. Musicological Soc., Soc. Ethnomusicology (coun. 1968-75, 87-90), Conf. Chinese Oral and Performing Lit. (co-founder, pres. 1983-90, permanent hon. pres. 1995—), Assn. for Chinese Mus. Rsch. (co-founder), Internat. Coun. for Traditional Music. Home: 14 Brattle Cir Cambridge MA 02138-4625 Office: 2 Divinity Ave Cambridge MA 02138-2020 E-mail: thhpian@aol.com.

PIAN, THEODORE HSUEH-HUANG, engineering educator, consultant; b. Shanghai, Jan. 18, 1919; came to U.S., 1943; s. Chao-Hsin Shu-Cheng and Chih-Chuan (Yen) P.; m. Rulan Chao, Oct. 3, 1945; 1 child, Canta Chao-Po. B in Engring., Tsing Hua U., Kunming, China, 1940; MS, MIT, 1944, DSc, 1948; DSc (hon.), Beijing U. Aeros. and Astronautics, 1990; PhD (hon.), Shanghai U., 1991. Engr. Cen. Aircraft Mfg. Co., Loiwing, China, 1940-42, Chengtu Glider Mfg. Factory, 1942-43; tchg. asst. MIT, Cambridge, 1946-47, rsch. assoc., 1947-52, asst. prof., 1952-59, assoc. prof., 1959-66, prof., 1966-89, prof. emeritus, 1989—. Vis. assoc. Calif. Inst. Tech., Pasadena, 1965-66; vis. prof. U. Tokyo, 1974, Tech. U., Berlin, 1975; vis. chair prof. Nat. Tsing Hua U., Hsin Chu, Taiwan, 1990, Nat. Ctrl. U., ChungLi, Taiwan, 1992; hon. prof. Beijing U. Aero. and Astronautics, Beijing Inst. Tech., Southwestern Jaiotong U., Dalian U. Tech., Huazhong U. Sci. and Tech., Changsha Rwy. U., Ctrl.-South U. Tech., Hohai U., Nanjing U. of Aero. and Astronautics, Dalian Rwy. U., Shashi U. of Sci. and Tech. of China. Recipient von Karman Meml. prize TRE Corp., Beverly Hills, Calif., 1974. Fellow AAAS, AIAA (assoc. editor jour. 1973-75, Structures, Structural Dynamics and Materials award 1975), U.S. Assn. Computational Mechanics (founding mem.); mem. ASME (hon.), NAE, Am. Soc. Engring. Edn., Internat. Assn. for Computational Mechanics (hon. mem. gen. coun.). Home: 14 Brattle Cir Cambridge MA 02138-4625 Office: MIT Dept Aeronautics and Astronautics 77 Massachusetts Ave Dept And Cambridge MA 02139-4307 E-mail: thhpian@aol.com., thhpian@mit.edu.

PIANKO, THEODORE A. lawyer; b. Dennville, N.J., Sept. 5, 1955; s. Theodore and Pasqualina (Liguori) Pianko; m. Beatriz Maria Olivera (div. Dec. 1985); m. Kathryn Anne Lindley, Feb. 18, 1990; children: Matthew James, Samuel Wahoo, Zoe Wahoo. BA, SUNY, 1975; JD, U. Mich., 1978. Bar: Mich. 1978, Ill. 1979, Calif. 1980. Atty. Ford Motor Co., Dearborn, Mich., 1978-80; assoc. Lillick McHose & Charles, L.A., 1980-83; ptnr. Sidley & Austin, L.A., 1983-94, Christie, Parker & Hale, Newport Beach, Calif., 1994—. Office Phone: 949-476-0757. Personal E-mail: ted@pianko.com.

PIANO, PHYLLIS J. communications executive; b. Milw., Feb. 1956; BA, U. Wis., 1977. Pub. rels. staff GE Co., 1978—95; v.p. pub. affairs Cooper Industries, Inc., Houston, 1995—99; v.p., v.p. corp. affairs and comm. Raytheon Co., Lexington, Mass., 1999—. Office: Raytheon Co 141 Spring St Lexington MA 02421

PIANTADOSI, STEVEN, medical researcher, statistical consultant; b. Jersey City, July 19, 1951; s. Claude and Lucille (DiPoto) P.; m. Bonnie Roach, June 4, 1977; children: Anne Lauren, Steven Thomas. BA, U. N.C., 1973, MD, 1977; PhD, U. Ala., Birmingham, 1982. Med. staff fellow NIH, Bethesda, Md., 1982-88; dir. biostats. Johns Hopkins Oncology Ctr., Balt., 1988—; assoc. prof. oncology and biostats. Johns Hopkins U. Sch. Medicine, Balt., 1988—. Mem. oncologic drugs adv. com. FDA, Rockville, Md., neurologic devices adv. com.; lectr. Johns Hopkins Sch. Pub. Health, Balt., 1989—. Contbr. articles to profl. jours. Mem. Soc. for Clin. Trials, Am. Statis. Assn., Am. Soc. Clin. Oncology, Am. Assn. Cancer Rsch. Avocations: music, woodworking, sailing. Office: Johns Hopkins Oncology Ctr 550 N Broadway Ste 1103 Baltimore MD 21205-2013

PIAO, DAQING, biomedical researcher; m. Jiajun Luo, July 23, 1969; children: Aaron Park, Alexander Park. BS with honors, Tsinghua U., Beijing, China, 1990; MS, U. Conn., 2001, PhD (hon.), 2003. Engr. Guangdong Weida Med. Apparatus Corp., Jiexi, China, 1990—94; engr., dept. mgr. Shanghai Kanglian Med. Engring. Co. Ltd., 1994—99; rsch. asst. U. Conn., Storrs, 1999—2003, post-doctoral fellow, 2003—. Contbr. articles to sci. jours. Recipient Outstanding PhD Thesis award, U. Conn., 2003; Predoctoral Traineeship awardee, Dept. of Def., 2002—, PhD Dissertation fellow, U. Conn., 2003. Mem.: IEEE, Optical Soc. Am., Internat. Soc. Optical Engring. Achievements include invention of quantifying blood flow velocity in Doppler optical coherence tomography; first to Hybrid optical coherence tomogrpahy and radiation imaging for imaging and diagonosis of coronary artery diseases; research in Cancellation of coherent artifacts in optical coherence tomography; invention of Sliding-window filtering technique for Doppler shift and Doppler bandwidth measurements in Doppler optical coherence tomgraphy; Direct bi-directional angle-insensitive flow imaging in Doppler optical coherence tomography. Office: U Conn Unit 1157 371 Fairfield Rd Storrs CT 06269-1157 Office Phone: 860-486-6726. Business E-Mail: piao@engr.uconn.edu.

PIASECKI, FRANK NICHOLAS, aircraft corporation executive, aeronautics engineer; b. Phila., Oct. 24, 1919; s. Nikodem and Emilia (Lotocki) P.; m. Vivian O'Gara Weyerhaeuser, Dec. 1958; children: Lynn, Nicole, Frederick, Frank, John, Michael, Gregory. Student, U. Pa., 1936-39; BS in Aero. Engring, NYU, 1940, D Aero. Engring. (hon.), 1955; D Aero. Sci., Pa. Mil. Coll., 1953; DSc, Alliance Coll., 1970. Registered profl. engr., Pa. Aircraft designer Platt-LePage Aircraft Corp., Eddystone, Pa., 1940-41; aerodynamicist Edward G. Budd Mfg. Co., Phila., 1941-43; founded an engring. research group, 1940, (inc. as P-V Engring. Forum), 1943, later became Piasecki Helicopter Corp., 1946; later chmn. bd.; founded Piasecki Aircraft Corp., 1955; pres.; dir. Crown Cork Internat. Corp. Mem. NSF Commn. on Innovation Mem. Citizens' Adv. Com. Transp. Quality Dept. Transp.; mem. adv. com. indsl. innovation presentation, subcom. sci., tech. and space Senate Com. on Commerce, Sci. and Transp.; Trustee Kosciuszko Found., N.Y.C. Named hon. Coast Guard pilot, 1945, Elder Statesman of Aviation, 1987; recipient Lawrence Sperry award Inst. Aero. Scis., 1951; Mendel award Villanova U., 1954; Philip H. Ward, Jr. medal Franklin Inst., 1979; Penjerdel's Aviation award, 1983; Spirit of St. Louis award ASME, 1983; Explorers award Phila. chpt. Explorers Club, 1984; Disting. Citizen award Valley Forge council Boy Scouts Am., 1985; Presdl. Nat. Medal of Tech., 1986; Contemporary Pioneer award Colonial Soc. Pa., 1987; named to Army Aviation Hall of Fame, 1974; chosen one of nation's ten outstanding young men of year U.S. Jr. C. of C., 1952 Fellow Inst. Aero. Scis., Soc. Automotive Engrs.; hon. fellow Am. Helicopter Soc. (past pres.); mem. Am. Soc. Profl. Engrs., Soc. Exptl. Test Pilots, Nat. Air Carriers Assn.(indsl. cons. comn.). Clubs: Wings (N.Y.C.); Merion Golf, Merion Cricket (Haverford, Pa.); Engineers (Phila.), Union League, Corinthian Yacht (Phila.); Twirly Birds (founder mem.). Home: 26 Tunbridge Rd Haverford PA 19041-1038 Office: Piasecki Aircraft Corp 2nd St W Essington PA 19029

PIASSICK, JOEL BERNARD, lawyer; b. Atlanta, June 2, 1940; s. Louis S. and Sarah (Freeman) P.; m. Karen Pevow, Aug. 11, 1963; children: Joan, Louis. BA in Polit. Sci., Tulane U., 1962; LLB, U. Va., 1965. Bar: Va. 1965, Ga. 1966, Colo. 1999. Ptnr. Smith, Gambrell & Russell, Atlanta, 1967-90, Kilpatrick Stockton LLP, Atlanta, 1990—. Fellow Am. Coll. Bankruptcy. Office: Kilpatrick Stockton LLP 1100 Peachtree St NE Ste 2800 Atlanta GA 30309-4530 E-mail: jpiassick@kilstock.com.

PIAZZA, JO ANN CHRISTINE, sculptor; b. Pitts., Sept. 18, 1954; d. John Louis Piazza and Lois Jean Verba; m. James Roberston Jennings, June 18, 1979 (div. Mar. 2000). Grad. high sch., Putney, Vt. Exhibitions include New Mus., N.Y.C., 1985, U. Bklyn. Arts & Cultural Assn., 1986, Alan Stone Gallery, Foxworth Coll., N.Y.C., 1986, Carrie Haddad Gallery, Hudson, N.Y., 1996, Save Venize Benefit, N.Y.C., 2001, Sailors Vol. Gallery, Nantucket, Mass., 2002, Selby Gallery, Ringling Mus. Sch. ARt & Design, Sarasota, Fla., 2003. Avocation: gardening.

PIAZZA, KRIS A. writer, editor; b. Buffalo, Nov. 8, 1967; d. Andrew Nicholas Piazza and Jean Ann Reeves. BA in Media Comm., Medaille Coll., 1992. Dir., thinkfirst injury prevention program Kaleida Health, Buffalo, 1996—2001, project mgr., 2001—03, sr. writer/editor, 2003—. Cons. The We Care Group, Buffalo, 2002—. Author: IMPACT; contbr. articles to profl. jours. Bd. mem. United Way Buffalo & Erie County, 2003—, Child Care Coalition Niagara Frontier, 2002—; adv. bd. for consumer directed personal asst. program People, Inc., 1999—2004; insprirational speaker life after spinal cord injury. Recipient Chair Yr. award, United Way Buffalo & Erie County, 2001, Vol. of Yr., YWCA, N.Y., 2002, 2002 Salt Lake City Torch Relay, 2002, Alumni Yr., Medaille Coll., 2002, Lifesavers award, Nat. Hwy. Traffic Safety Adminstrn., 2001, Ms. Wheelchair N.Y., 2001. Office: Kaleida Health 901 Washington Street Buffalo NY 14203 Office Phone: 716-843-7456. Home Fax: NA. Personal E-mail: kp28f@aol.com. Business E-Mail: kpiazza@kaleidahealth.org.

PIAZZA, MARGUERITE, opera singer, actress, entertainer; b. New Orleans, May 6, 1926; d. Albert William and Michaela (Piazza) Luft; m. William J. Condon, July 15, 1953 (dec. Mar. 1968); children: Gregory, James (dec.), Shirley, William J., Marguerite P., Anna Becky; m. Francis Harrison Berghholdt, Nov. 8, 1970. MusB, Loyola U., New Orleans; MusM, La. State U.; MusD (hon.), Christian Bros. Coll., 1973; LHD (hon.), Loyola U., Chgo., 1975. Singer N.Y.C. Ctr. Opera, 1948, Met. Opera Co., 1950; TV artist, regular singing star Your Show of Shows NBC, 1950-54; entertainer various supper clubs Cotillion Room, Hotel Pierre, N.Y.C., 1954, Las Vegas, Los Angeles, New Orleans, San Francisco, 1956—; ptnr. Sound Express Music Pub. Co., Memphis, 1987—. Bd. dirs. Cemrel, Inc. Appeared as guest performer on numerous mus. TV shows. Nat. crusade chmn. Am. Cancer Soc., 1971; founder, bd. dirs. Marguerite Piazza Gala for the Benefit of St. Jude's Hosp., 1976; bd. dirs. Memphis Opera Co., World Literacy Found., NCCJ; v.p., life bd. dirs. Memphis Symphony Orch.; nat. chmn. Soc. for Cure Epilepsy. Decorated Mil. and Hospittaler Order of St. Lazarus of Jerusalem; recipient svc. award Chgo. Heart Assn., 1956, svc. award Fedn. Jewish Philanthropies of N.Y., 1956, Sesquicentennial medal Carnegie Hall, St. Martin De Porres award So. Dominicans, 1994, Lifetime Achievement award Germantown Arts Alliance, 1998; named Queen of Memphis, Memphis Cotton Carnival, 1973, Person of Yr., La. Coun. for Performing Arts, 1975, Woman of Yr., Nat. Am. Legion, Woman of Yr., Italian-Am. Soc. Mem. Nat. Speakers Assn., Woman's Exchange, Memphis Country Club, Memphis Hunt and Polo Club, New Orleans Country Club, Summit Club, Beta Sigma Omicron, Phi Beta. Roman Catholic. Home: 247 Baronne Pl Memphis TN 38117

PIAZZA, MIKE (MICHAEL JOSEPH PIAZZA), professional baseball player; b. Norristown, Pa., Sept. 4, 1968; Student, Miami-Dade C.C. Catcher L.A. Dodgers, 1992—97, N.Y. Mets, 1998—. Named Nat. League Rookie Player of Yr., Sporting News, 1993, Nat. League Rookie of Yr., Baseball Writers' Assn., 1993; named to Nat. League All-Star Team, 1993—2002, 2004, Slugger Team, Nat. League, 1993. Achievements include setting the Major League record for home runs by a catcher, 2004. Office: New York Mets Shea Stadium 123-10 Roosevelt Ave Flushing NY 11368*

PIBULSONGGRAM, NITYA, diplomat; b. Bangkok, June 30, 1941; s. Field Marshal P. and Lady La-iad (Bhandhukravi) P.; m. Patricia Osmond, July 3, 1965. AB in Govt., Dartmouth Coll., 1964; AM in Polit. Sci., Brown U., 1967. With fgn. news div. of info. dept. Ministry Fgn. Affairs Govt. of Thailand, Bangkok, 1968, with SEATO div. of internat. orgns. dept., 1969-72, with policy and planning div. Office of Permanent Sec. and Office of Minister of Fgn. Affairs, 1973-75, head polit. dept. S.E. Asia div., 1975-76, dep. dir. gen. info. dept., 1980, dep. dir. gen. polit. dept., 1981, amb.-at-large Fgn. Ministry, 1982, dir. gen. internat. orgns. dept., 1983-87, 1st sec. permanent Thai mission to UN N.Y.C., 1976-78, dep. permanent rep. Thai mission to UN, 1978-80, amb., permanent rep. to UN, 1988-96; amb. to U.S., 1996—. Decorated Knight Grand Cross (1st class) of Most Exalted Order of White Elephant, 1984, Spl. Grand Cordon of Most Noble Order of Crown of Thailand, 1988. Mem. Royal Bangkok Sports Club, Dartmouth Club (pres. Bangkok chpt. 1986-88). Buddhist. Avocations: skiing, golf, tennis. Home: 2145 Decatur Pl NW Washington DC 20008-1923 Office: Royal Thai Embassy 1024 Wisconsin Ave NW Washington DC 20007-3668

PICACHE, JOSEFINA REYES, travel service company executive, marriage counselor; b. Bulacan, Philippines, June 19, 1945; came to U.S., 1970; d. Cesar Garcia and Leona (Pilao) Delos Reyes; m. Danilo Sabal Picache, Oct. 20, 1968; children: Beverly Reyes, Abigail Reyes. BS in Edn.-Guidance and Counseling, U. Philippines/East, 1967; MS in Edn. Adminstrn./Supervision, Old Dominion U., 1980. Guidance counselor Torres High Sch., Manila, 1967; asst. dir. Philippine Soc. for Prevention of Cruelty to Animals, Manila, 1968; adminstrv. asst. to alumni dir. Old Dominion U., Norfolk, Va., 1976-83; pres./owner Picache Internat. Travel, Virginia Beach, Va., 1983—; pres., CEO, owner Freedom Travel, Inc., Va. Beach, Va.; owner JRP Travel, Missouri City, Tex., 1990—. Recipient Achievement award Atlantic Filipino News, Norfolk, 1980, Recognition award Old Dominion U. Alumni Assn., Norfolk, 1984. Fellow Nat. Assn. Female Execs.; mem. Better Bus. Bur., Hampton Road C. of C., Womens' Network. Avocations: tennis, basketball, reading, traveling. Home: 2655 Browning Dr Virginia Beach VA 23456-2534

PICADIO, ANTHONY PETER, lawyer; b. Latrobe, Pa., Dec. 7, 1941; s. Peter J. and Elsie M. (Caldarelli) P.; m. Lynette Norton. BA, U. Pitts., 1965, JD, 1970. Bar: Pa. 1970, U.S. Dist. Ct. (we. dist.) Pa. 1970, U.S. Ct. Appeals (3d cir.) 1971, U.S. Supreme Ct. 1998. Asst. atty. gen. Dept. Environ Protection Commonwealth Pa., 1970-72; ptnr. Reding, Blackstone, Rea & Sell, Pitts., 1972-75, Tucker, Arensberg, P.C., Pitts., 1975-85; founder, sr. ptnr. practice in bus. litigation and environ. law Picadio, Sneath, Miller & Norton, Pitts., 1985—. Mem.: Order of Coif. Office: Picadio Sneath Miller & Norton PC US Steel Tower 600 Grant St Ste 4710 Pittsburgh PA 15219-2703 Office Phone: 412-288-4000. E-mail: picadio@psmn.com.

PICARD, DENNIS J. retired electronics company executive; b. Providence, R.I., Aug. 25, 1932; m. Dolores Picard; 5 children. BBA, Northeastern U., 1962; doctorate (hon.), Merrimack Coll., Bentley Coll. With RCA, 1954—55; from elec. engr. to pres. Raytheon Co., 1955—91, CEO, 1989—99, Rayth of dirs., 1989—2001, chmn. emeritus, 1989—. Dir. State St. Boston Corp.; trustee Northeastern U.; trustee emeritus Bentley Coll.; dir. Discovery Mus., Acton, Mass. Active Def. Policy Adv. Com. on Trade, Pres.'s Export Coun., Pres.'s Nat. Security Telecomms. Adv. Coun. With USAF, 1951—53. Decorated Environ. Achievement award Nat. Security Indsl. Assn., Fleet Admiral Cheser W. Nimitz award Navy League of U.S., Intrepid Salute award Intrepid Mus. Found., John R. Allison award USAF Assn., John W. Dixon medal Assn. U.S. Army; recipient New Englander of Yr., New England Coun., 1997, Indsl. Leadership award, Nat. Def. Indsl. Assn., 1998, Rear Admiral John J. Bergen Leadership medal, Navy League, 1998. Mem.: IEEE, AIAA (pres.-elect, adv. bd.), NAE, Armed Forces Commns. and Electronics Assn., Bus. Coun., Mass. Bus. Roundtables, Algonquin Club of Boston. Office: AIAA Ste 500 1801 Alexander Bell Dr Reston VA 20191-4344

PICARD, LAURENT A(UGUSTIN), retired management educator, administrator, consultant; b. Quebec, Que., Can., Oct. 27, 1927; s. Edouard and Alice (Gingras) P.; m. Therese Picard; children: Andre, Marc, Robert (dec.), Denys, Jean-Louis, François (dec.). BA, Laval U., Quebec, 1947, BS, 1954; DBA, Harvard U., 1964. Prof. U. Montreal, Que., Can., 1962-68, dir. bus. adminstrn. dept., 1964-68; exec. v.p. Can. Broadcasting Corp., Ottawa, Ont., 1968-72, pres., CEO, 1972-75; joint prof. McGill U. and U. Montreal, 1977-78; dean faculty mgmt. McGill U., Montreal, 1978-86, prof., 1986-97; ret., 1997. Mem. Royal Commn. on Newspapers, Royal Commn. on Econ. Union and Devel. Prospects for Can.; conciliation commr. Maritime Employers Assn., Port of Montreal; bd. dirs. Lombard-Odier Trust Co., Jean Coutu Group, Dorel Ind. Inc.; cons. to industry; guest speaker at internat. meetings. Contbr. articles to profl. jours. Chmn. Nat. Book Festival, 1978-79; chmn. jury Prix Gerin Lajoie, Ministry Cultural Affairs, 1982. Recipient 125th Anniversary medal Can., 1992; decorated companion Order of Can., 1977. Mem. Commonwealth Broadcasting Assn. (1st pres.). Home: 5602 Wilderton Ave Montreal QC Canada H3T 1R9

PICARDI, GERARD A. publisher; b. Boston, Apr. 24, 1949; s. Antonio Sabine and Jane Elizabeth Picardi. BA in English Lit., St. Michael's Coll., 1970. Office mgr. Love's Furniture Co., Stoneham, Mass., 1970-75; sec. Little, Brown & Co., Boston, 1975-76, prodn. asst., 1976-79, asst. prodn. mgr., 1979-84; prodn. coord. Harvard U. Press, Cambridge, Mass., 1984-92, prodn. supr., 1992-97, asst. prodn. mgr., 1997-2000, frontlist mgr., 2000—. Named Harvard U. Hero, 1999. Mem. Bookbuilders Boston (mem. fall roundtable com. 1988-90, co-chair 1990-91, mem. publicity com. 1990-91, chair 1991-93, mem. advanced seminar com. 1992-95, bd. dirs. 1991-94, sec. 1993-94, mem. nominations com. 1993-95, mem. edn. com. 1994-95, chair endowment fund com. 1994-95, 1st v.p. 1994-95, pres. 1995-96, chair Dwiggins award com. 1996-97, judge New Eng. book show 1998-99), Am. Assn. Univ. Presses, Am. Inst. Graphic Arts. Roman Catholic. Home: 350 Sumner St East Boston MA 02128-2218 Office: Harvard U Press 79 Garden St Cambridge MA 02138-1423

PICCIANO, R.J. renal technician; b. Bronx, N.Y., Sept. 18, 1956; s. Robert and Josette LeBron. BA, Notre Dame Coll., 1978. Cert. nephrology technician, Ohio, hemodialysis technician, Ohio dialysis technician. Tech. patient care Ctr. Dialysis Care, Cleve., 1984—. Pres. Bd. Nephrology Examiners, Shawnee, Kans., 1999—. Office: Bd Nephrology Examiners PO Box 15945282 Shawnee Mission KS 66285 E-mail: rjpcht@aol.com.

PICCININI, ROBERT M. grocery store chain executive; CEO, chmn., pres. Save Mart Supermarkets, Modesto, Calif., 1952—. Office: Save Mart Supermarkets PO Box 4278 Modesto CA 95352-4278

PICCININNO, ANTHONY RAY, government administrative executive; b. Orange, N.J., Aug. 19, 1972; s. Michael Angelo and Dona Lee (Martin) Piccininno; m. Karen Veintimilla, July 25, 2003. AS, County Coll. of Morris, Randolph, N.J., 1994; BA, Rutgers U., 1997; grad. cert., U. of Oxford, Eng., 2000; postgrad., Georgetown U., 2001. Vol. income tax assistance, IRS; incident command sys. USCG, direct mktg. Montclair State U., cert. Leadership and Mgmt. Sch., USCG. Sales adminstr. Prestige Volvo, East Hanover, NJ, 1988—99; tech. materials analyst Volvo Cars of N.Am., Rockleigh, NJ, 1994—96; office adminstr. Harvard Coop. Soc., Cambridge, Mass., 1998—99; acctg. Bridgewater Volvo, Somerville, NJ, 1999—2000; svc. advisor Morristown (N.J.) BMW, 2000—01; adminstrv. exec. Exec. Office of the Pres., Washington, 2001—. Auxiliarist USCG Aux., 1999—. Decorated Nat. Def. Svc. medal USCG; recipient acad. scholarship, Harvard U., 2000, 1999. Conservative. Roman Catholic. Avocations: travel, reading. Home: 12367 Wadsworth Way Woodbridge VA 22192 Office: Exec Office of the Pres NEOB 7002 725 17th St NW Washington DC 20503

PICCININO, ROCCO MICHAEL, librarian; b. Phila., Aug. 21, 1949; s. Rocco Anthony and Ida Marie (Minicozzi) P. BA in History magna cum laude, LaSalle Coll., 1971; postgrad., U. N.C., 1971—73; MSLS, Drexel U., 1981. Ednl. resources specialist C.C. of Phila., 1973-74; asst./assoc. libr. United Engrs. & Constructors Inc. (A Raytheon Co.) Libr., Phila., 1974-81, head libr. Boston, 1981-84; asst./assoc. dir. Wentworth Inst. of Tech. Libr., Boston, 1984-89; sci. libr. Smith Coll. Librs., Northampton, Mass., 1989-91, coord. br. libr. svcs., sci. libr., 1991—. Mem. ALA (Assn. Coll. Rsch. Librs. divsn. instruction sect. policy com. 2002-04, sci. and tech. sect. coun., co-chair coll. libr. discussion group 1998-2002, forum for sci. and tech. libr. rsch. 2000-02, comparison of sci. and tech. com. 2002-04, conf. program planning com. 2003-); Libr. Adminstrn. and Mgmt. Assn.(bldg. and equipment sect., bldgs. for coll. and univ. librs. com., 2000-02), Libr. and Info. Tech. Assn., Spl. Librs. Assn. (sci.-tech. divsn., Boston chpt. adv. coun. 1996-, chair We. Outreach 1996-2004), IEEE (libr. adv. coun. 2002-03), Beta Phi Mu. Democrat. Roman Catholic. Avocations: travel, biking, reading, films. Home: 104 Woods Rd Northampton MA 01062-3507 Office: Smith Coll Young Sci Libr Northampton MA 01063-0001 Office Phone: 413-585-2951. Business E-Mail: rpiccini@smith.edu.

PICCIONE, TAL P. insurance company executive; b. N.Y.C., Feb. 9, 1948; s. Patric Francis and Maria Rose (Scandariato) P.; m. Lena Marie Tamburello, Feb. 22, 1970; children: Michael John, Marc Patric. AAS, Pace Coll., 1971; BBA, Pace U., 1973. V.p. Guy Carpenter & Co., Inc., N.Y.C., 1972-87; chmn., CEO U.S. RE Cos., Inc., N.Y.C., 1987—. Bd. dirs., mem. bus. adv. coun. Internat. Ins. Coun., Washington; chmn. CNSR Found., N.Y.C., Legatus; dir. Coun. Reins. Brokers. Mem. NRA, Columbus Citizens Found., India House, Nippon Club, Safari Club Internat., Sloane Club (London). Avocations: fishing, hunting, boating, opera. Office: 745 5th Ave #19 New York NY 10151-2003

PICCIOTTO, ROBERT, bank executive; b. Italy; Degree in civil engring., Ecole Nat. Superieure l'Aero., Paris; MPA, Princeton U. With industry divsn. The World Bank Group, summer 1961, devel. fin. co. analyst internat. fin. corp., 1962, various positions, including agr. economist, 1967-69, head agr. industries divsn., 1969-70, head spl. projects divsn., 1970, asst. dir. agr. and rural devel. Asia region, 1972, dir. South Asia projects dept., 1976, head Europe, Mid. East and North Africa projects dept., 1980, head Latin Am. and Caribbean projects dept., 1986, dir. planning and budgeting, 1987, v.p. corp. planning and budgeting, 1990, dir.-gen. ops. evaluation, 1992—. Office: Internat Bank for Reconstruction Devel Ops Evaluation 1818 H St NW Washington DC 20433-0001

PICCIRILLO, LINDA ANN, literature educator; d. Pete and Albina Piccirillo; children: David, Adam. BS in Secondary Edn., Kent State U., 1976, MA in English/French, 1980. Cert. tchr. Ohio. English tchr. Stow (Ohio) City Schs., 1976—77; French/English tchr. St. Vincent-St. Mary H.S., Akron, Ohio, 1980—82; French instr. Kent (Ohio) State U., 1982—87, English instr., 1987—, dir. Oscar Ritchie Help Ctr., 2001—. Exec. bd. mem. Summit Family Children First Coun., Akron, 1998—. Instrnl. grantee, U. Tchg. Coun., 1999. Office: Kent State Univ Pan African Studies Dept Oscar Ritchie Hall Kent OH 44242

PICCOLO, JOSEPH ANTHONY, hospital administrator; b. Phila., Aug. 1, 1953; s. Rudolph and Mary C. (Mellela) P.; m. Elizabeth J. Mullarkey, Mar. 24, 1984; children: Mary E., Sarah C., Theresa N. BA, U. Pa., 1975; MBA, LaSalle U., 1992. Cert. in healthcare compliance, Healthcare Compliance Bd. Mgr. health sci. store U. Pa., Phila., 1973-76; mgr. univ. store Hahnemann U., Phila., 1976-86, adminstr., clin. sr. instr. dept. pathology lab. medicine, 1986-94; assoc. adminstr., compliance officer, chief privacy officer, v.p. health svcs. Fox Chase Cancer Ctr., Phila., 1994—. V.p. Hahnemann Found. Pathology, Phila., 1986-94. Author: (with others): Health Science Store Manual, 1985; mem. editl. bd. Assn. Cancer Execs., 1999—. Mem. Med. Group Mgmt. Assn., Healthcare Compliance Assn., Healthcare Fin. Mgmt. Assn., Hahnemann Pathology Assocs., Inc. (v.p., treas. 1986-94), Big Sisters of Phila. Inc. (bd. dirs., 1996-98); Pa. Med. Group Memo Assn. (bd. mem., 2004-). Office: Fox Chase Cancer Ctr 333 Cottman Avenue Philadelphia PA 19111-2497 Business E-Mail: J_Piccolo@fccc.edu.

PICHETTE, CLAUDE, former banking executive, university rector, research executive; b. Sherbrooke, Que., Can., June 13, 1936; s. Donat and Juliette (Morin) P.; m. Renée Provencher, Sept. 5, 1959 (dec. 1994); children: Anne-Marie, Martin, Philippe; m. Denyse Gauthier, July 25, 1997. BA, U. Sherbrooke, 1956; MScSoc (Econ.), U. Laval, 1960; Doct. d'Etat es Sc. Econ, U. D'Aix-Marseille, France, 1970. Prof. U. Sherbrooke, 1960-70; civil servant Govt. Que., 1970-75; vice rector adminstrn. and fins. U. Que., Montreal, 1975-77, rector, 1977-86; pres., chief exec. officer La Financière prêts-épargne, 1986-90, La Financière Entraide-Cooperants (holding co.), 1987-90; pres. Que. Found. Econ. Edn., 1979-81; CEO Institut Armand-Frappier Rsch. Inst., 1991-97; dir. gen. Fondation Armand-Frappier. Chmn. bd. La Financière Entraide-Coopérants (holding co.), 1987-90, Shermag, Hema-Quebec, Hydra-Fab Indsl. Inc.; pres. Que. Found. Econ. Edn., 1979-81; CEO Institut Armand-Frappier Rsch. Inst., 1991-97; chmn. bd. La Financière Credit-Bail, 1989-90. Author: Analyse micro-economique et cooperative, 1972. Can. Council grantee, 1958; Federation nationale des cooperatives de consommation de France grantee, 1973 Mem. Que. Assn. Econs. (pres. 1977-78). Home: 5123A Jeanne-Mance Montreal QC Canada H2V 4K2 Office: Fondation Armand-Frappier 531 Blvd des Prairies Laval QC Canada H7V 1B7 E-mail: fondation.armand-frappier@inrs-iaf.uquebec.ca.

PICHLER, JOSEPH ANTON, food products executive; b. St. Louis, Oct. 3, 1939; s. Anton Dominick and Anita Marie (Hughes) Pichler; m. Susan Ellen Eyerly, Dec. 27, 1962; children: Gretchen, Christopher, Rebecca, Josh. BBA, U. Notre Dame, 1961; MBA, U. Chgo., 1963, PhD, 1966. Asst. prof. bus. U. Kans., 1964—68, assoc. prof., 1968—73, prof., 1973—80; dean U. Kans. Sch. Bus., 1974—80; exec. v.p. Dillon Cos. Inc., 1980—82, pres., 1982—86; exec. v.p. Kroger Co., Cin., 1985—86, pres., COO, 1986—90, pres., CEO, 1990, chmn., CEO, 1990—2003, chmn., 2003—, also bd. dirs. Spl. asst. to asst. sec. for manpower U.S. Dept. Labor, 1968—70; chmn. Kans. Manpower Svcs. Coun., 1974—78; bd. dirs. Cin. Milacron Inc., Federated Dept. Stores, Inc., Catalyst. Author (with Joseph McGuire): The Poor and the Rich in America, 1969; co-author: Creativity and Innovation in Manpower Research and Action Programs, 1970, Contemporary Management: Issues and Viewpoints, 1973, Institutional Issues in Public Accounting, 1974, Co-Creation and Capitalism: John Paul II's Laborem Exercens, 1983; co-editor (contbg. author): Ethics, Free Enterprise, and Public Policy, 1978; contbr. articles to profl. jours. Nat. bd. dirs. Boys Hope, 1983—96; mem. Nat. Alliance of Bus. Bd., 1988—95, chmn., 1991—93; mem. fellow adv. com. Woodrow Wilson Found., 1990—93; mem. adv. bd. Salvation Army Sch. for Officers Tng., 1994—2000; bd. dirs. Cin. Opera, 1987—96, adv. mem., 1996—; bd. dirs. Tougaloo Coll., 1986—; mem. Cin. Bus. Com., 1991—, chmn., 1997—98. Named Disting. Alumnus U. Chgo., 1994; recipient Disting. Svc. award, Nat. Conf. Cmty. Justice, 2000, William Booth award, Salvation Army, 1998, Horatio Alger award, 1999, Hall of Fame, Greater Cin. and No. Ky. Bus., 2001; Woodrow Wilson fellow, Ford Found. fellow, Standard Oil Indsl. Rels. fellow, 1966. Mem.: Greater Cin. C. of C. (trustee), Catalyst Bd., Bus. Roundtable, Comml. Club of Cin., Queen City Club. Office: Kroger Co 1014 Vine St Cincinnati OH 45202-1100

PICK, JAMES BLOCK, business educator, demographer; b. Chgo., July 29, 1943; s. Grant Julius and Helen (Block) Pick. BA, Northwestern U., 1966; MS in Edn., No. Ill. U., 1969; PhD, U. Calif., Irvine, 1974. Cert. computer profl. Asst. rsch. statistician, lectr. Grad. Sch. Mgmt., U. Calif., Riverside, 1975-91, dir. computing, 1984-91; co-dir. U.S.-Mex. Database Project, 1988-91; assoc. prof. mgmt. and bus., dir. info. mgmt. program U. Redlands, Calif., 1991-95, 99-01, prof. bus., 1995—, chair dept. mgmt. and bus., 1995-97, 98-99, chair faculty assembly Sch. Bus., 2001—04. Vis. prof. U. Iberoam., Mexico City, 1997, Mexico City, 2001; cons. internat. divsn. U.S. Census Bur., 1978; mem. Univ. Commons. Bd., 1982—86; mem. nat. curriculum task force IS, 1997; mem. U. Commn. Future Bus. Programs, 1998—2000; pres. Orange County chpt. Assn. Sys. Mgmt., 1978—79; mem. bd. govs. PCCLAS, Assn. Borderlands Studies, 1989—92, v.p., 2000—01, pres., 2002—; bd. profls. advisors demographic analysis U. Calif, Irvine, 2002—03; mem. exec. coun. Info. Resources Mgmt. Assn., 2003—. Author: (book) Geothermal Energy Development, 1982, Computer Systems in Business, 1986, Atlas of Mexico, 1989, The Mexico Handbook, 1994, Mexico Megacity, 1997, Mexico and Mexico City in the World Economy, 2001, Geographic Systems in Business, 2004; mem. editl. bd. Jour. Borderlands Studies, 1999—, Jour. Info. Tech. Cases and Applications, 2002—, condr. rsch. info. sys., population, environ. studies; contbr. articles to profl. jours. Trustee Newport Harbor Art Mus., 1981—87, 1988—96, Berkeley Art Mus. and Pacific Film Archives, 2003—; chmn. permanent collection com. Newport Harbor Art Mus., 1987—91, v.p., 1991—96; trustee, chmn. collection com. Orange County Mus. Art, 1996—; mem. com. Block Mus., 1999—2001. Recipient Thunderbird award, Bus. Assn. L.Am. Studies, 1993, Outstanding Alumnus award, No. Ill. U., 2004; Ford Found. grantee, 1998—99, Sr. Fulbright scholar, 2001. Mem.: AAAS, Am. Assn. Geographers, Sociedad de Demografia Mexicana, Internat. Union Sci. Study Population, Population Assn. Am., Am. Statis. Assn., Am. Sociol. Assn., Assn. Info. Sys., Assn. Computing Machinery, Standard Club (Chgo.). Office: U Redlands Sch Bus 1200 E Colton Ave Redlands CA 92374-3755

PICK, ROBERT S. communications executive; CPA. Mem. fin. staff KPMG Peat Marwick, Bell Atlantic; from mem. stafff to sr. v.p. corp. devel. Comcast Corp., Phila., 1989—2000, sr. v.p. corp. devel., 2000—. Office: Comcast Corp 1500 Market St Philadelphia PA 19102

PICKARD, JOHN BENEDICT, English language educator; b. Newton, Mass., Oct. 4, 1928; s. Greenleaf Whittier and Helen (Liston) P.; m. Margaret Suzanne Dederich, Nov. 24, 1956; children: Stephen, Ellen, Nathaniel, Thaddeus, John Samuel; m. Carol Jones Hutcheson, Nov. 22, 2003. BA, Holy Cross Coll., 1950; postgrad., Boston Coll., 1950-51; PhD, U. Wis., 1954. Instr. U. Calif. (Far East Extension), 1956; asst. prof. English Rice U., 1956-63; assoc. prof. U. Fla., Gainesville, 1963-68, prof., 1968—96; ret., 1996. Pres. Alachua Press, Inc., 1999—2003. Author: J.G. Whittier: an Introduction and Interpretation, 1961, Legends of New England by J.G. Whittier, 1965, Emily Dickinson, 1967, Memorabilia of J.G W., 1968, The Letters of John Greenleaf Whittier, 3 vols, 1975, Whittier and Whittierland, 1976, The Parkman Dexter Howe Library: Part IV, The John Greenleaf Whittier Collection, 1987; editor: Samuel Kipnis Film Collection, 1982, Historic Gainesville: A Tour Guide to the Past, 1990, rev., reprinted 1992, Florida's Eden: An Illustrated History of Alachua County, 1994, Historic Alachua County and Old Gainesville, 2002, Dudley Farm: A History of Florida Farm Life, 2003, A Partnership withthe Past: The Alachua County Historic Trust Story, 2004. Vp. Nat. Newman Orgn., 1962-63; bd. dirs. Hist. Gainesville, Inc., 1971-72, 86-90, v.p., 1987-88, editor newsletter, 1987-89, pres., 1988-89; bd. dirs. Matheson Hist. Ctr., 1989—, editor newsletter, 1991-98; bd. dirs. St. Augustine Sch. Religion, 1971-72; bd. dirs. Fla. Trail Assn., 1977-80, adv. bd., 1980-86; bd. dirs. Alachua County Hist. Soc., 1995-97, pres., 1997-99; pres. The Alachua Press, 1999-2003. Served with U.S. Army, 1954-56. Named Outstanding Tchr. Rice U., 1958; Am. Philos. Soc. grantee, 1962, 67, 69 Mem. MLA, South Cen. MLA, Fla. Coll. Tchrs., English, Am. Film Inst., Fla. Trail Assn., Fla. Trust for Hist. Preservation. Democrat. Roman Catholic. Home: 35 George Cir Maggie Valley NC 28751-7667

PICKARD, MYRNA RAE, dean; b. Sulphur Springs, Tex., Oct. 10, 1935; d. George Wallace and Ellie (Williams) Swindell; m. Bobby Ray Pickard, May 17, 1957; 1 child, Bobby Dale BS summa cum laude, Tex. Wesleyan Coll., 1957, MEd, 1964; MS, Tex. Women's U., 1974; EdD, Nova U., 1976. Instr. John Peter Smith Hosp., Fort Worth, 1956-58; pub. health nurse Forest County Health Dept., Hattiesburg, Miss., 1958-60; asst. nurse adminstrn. John Peter Smith Hosp. Sch. Nursing, Fort Worth, 1960-70, nurse adminstr., 1970-73; assoc. dean, dean U. Tex. System Sch. Nursing, Fort Worth, 1971-76; dean U. Tex. Sch. Nursing, Arlington, 1976-95; prof. nursing, 1976-98; dir. Rural Health Outreach U. Tex., Arlington, 1998—. Cons. in field; adv. com. Rural Health Rsch. Ctr., U. N.D., 1990. Mem. editorial bd. Jour. Rural Health, 1985-92, 94; contbr. articles to profl. jours., chpt. in book. Pres. Tex. League for Nursing, 1986-89; bd. mgrs. Tarrant County Hosp. Dist., 1995—; trustee Columbia Pla. Med. Bd., 1992—. Fellow Am. Acad. Nursing; mem. ANA, Nat. League Nursing, Nat. Rural Health Assn. (bd. dirs., treas. 1990-92), Sigma Theta Tau, sec. Ctr. Rural Health Initiatives, Austin TX, 1997—. Methodist. Avocations: jogging; gardening. Office: U Tex PO Box 19407 Arlington TX 76019-0001

PICKARD, WILLIAM FRANK, plastics company executive; b. LaGrange, Ga., Jan. 28, 1941; s. William H. and Victoria (Woodward) P. AS, Mott Community Coll., 1962; BS, Western Mich. U., 1964; MSW, U. Mich., 1965;

PhD, Ohio State U., 1971; PhD in Bus. Adminstrn. (hon.), Cleary Coll., 1980. Dir. employment and edn. Urban League Cleve., 1965-67; exec. dir. NAACP, Cleve., 1967-69; assoc. dir. dept. urban studies Cleve. State U., 1971-72; assoc. prof. Wayne State U., Detroit, 1972-74; owner, operator McDonald's Restaurants, Detroit, 1971—; chmn., chief exec. officer Regal Plastics, Roseville, Mich., 1985—. Vis. lectr. Cleve. State U., U. Chgo., Hiram Coll., U. Toledo, U. Mich., Case Western Res. U., Ohio State U., Wayne County Community Coll., McDonald's Hamburger U.; participant mgmt. seminar Case Western Res. U., Greater Cleve. Associated Found. and Rockefeller Found., 1968; chmn. Gov.'s adv. com. on minority bus., pres. 1976; bd. dirs. First Ind. Nat. Bank, Mich. Nat. Bank Corp., Farmington Hills. Mem. Pres.-elect Ronald Regan's transition team to SBA; chmn. econ. devel. com. Nat. Black Rep. Council, 1978, bd. dirs. com. to elect Gov. Ronald Reagan Pres., 1980, chmn. congl. liaison com., 1982; chmn. Mich. Reps. Urban Campaign to elect Gov. Reagan Pres., 1980; vice chmn. Mich. Rep. State Com., 1981; bd. control Grand Valley State Coll., Allendale, Mich.; bd. dirs. Oakwood Hosp., Kirkwood Gen. Hosp., Detroit, Detroit Black Causes, Detroit Econ. Devel. Corp., 1977, Nat. Minority Purchasing Council, Washington, Detroit Urban League, vice chmn.; appointed by Pres. Ronald Regan, and confirmed by U.S. Senate Chmn. of African Devel. Found., 1983. Named one of Ten Outstanding Young Men Cleve., Jaycees, 1969; Alice W. Gault schlor, 1962-63; Nat. Urban League fellow, 1964. Mem. Booker T. Washington Bus. Assn., NAACP, Jaycees, Alpha Phi Alpha. Home: 335 Pine Ridge Dr Bloomfield Hills MI 48304-2140 Office: 2990 W Grand Blvd Ste 15M Detroit MI 48202-3041

PICKEN, HARRY BELFRAGE, aerospace engineer; b. Grimsby, Ont., Can., Jan. 8, 1916; s. John Belfrage and Leila Lucinda (Jarvis) P.; m. Florence Elizabeth Runciman, July 7, 1945 (dec. 1994); m. Marylyn Joan Beattie, 1997; children: Roger Belfrage, Donald William, Wendy Elizabeth, Brian John, Karen Evelyn. BSc in Aero. Engring., U. Mich., 1940. Lic. profl. engr., Ont., Can. Chief engr. White Can. Aircraft Ltd., Hamilton, Ont., 1940-45, Weston Aircraft Ltd., Oshawa, Ont., 1946-47, Field Aviation Ltd., Oshawa, 1947-51; pres., chief engr. Genaire Ltd. (Aerospace), St. Catharines, 1951-81; v.p., tech. dir. Ardrox Ltd. (Chems.), Niagara on the Lake, 1968-75, Avionics Ltd. (Electronics), Niagara on the Lake, 1953-67; v.p. Rotaire Ltd. (Helicopters), St. Catharines, Ont., 1958-63. Design approval rep. acting on behalf of Dept. of Transport Can., Ottawa, 1948-78; mem. bd. govs. Niagara Coll., Welland, Ont., 1974-80 Editor, pub.: Early Architecture Town and Township of Niagara, 1968, architecture student edit., 1991, Map of the Colonial Town of Niagara-on-the-Lake, 1981; composer (music book) Calgary Song Suite, 1983, Chacun a son Goût, 1991 Chmn. Planning Bd. of Niagara-on-the Lake, 1963-65; pres. Niagara-on-the-Lake C. of C., 1961-62; bd. dirs., v.p. Niagara Found., Niagara-on-the-Lake, 1963-80; mem. tech. adv. bd. Niagara Coll., 1966-74; vice chmn. bd. govs. Niagara Coll. Applied Arts and Tech., 1979-81; mem. Ont. Coun. of Regents, 1987-93. Named Citizen of Yr. Niagara-on-the-Lake C. of C., 1968; recipient Award of Merit, Mohawk Community Coll., Hamilton, Ont., 1990, Medal-Community Svc., Profl. Engrs. Ont., 1981, Citation for Outstanding and Meritorious Work, Transport Can. Civil Aviation Ont. Region, 1978, Caring and Sharing award Niagara Regional Govt., 1992, Citation from Premier Ont., 1993. Fellow: Can. Aero and Space Inst. (assoc.); mem.: Am. Fedn. Musicians (local 298 Niagara Falls, Ont.) (v.p.), Assn. Profl. Engrs. Ont. (lic. profl. engr.), Am. Helicopter Soc., AIAA, Composers, Authors and Music Pubs. of Can. (assoc.). Achievements include patent for developing an entirely new type of honeycomb primary structure and beams fabricated using staples and acrylic adhesives; research in thermal electric modules independently used in cooling and refrigeration techniques; also applied rsch. leading to the development of cold vulcanization techniques relative to rubber. Home: 68 Bertram Dr Dundas ON Canada L9H 4T3 Office: Genaire Ltd Niagara Dist Airport Box 84 Saint Catharines ON Canada L2R 6R4

PICKENPAUGH, THOMAS EDWARD, archaeologist, anthropologist; b. St. Clairsville, Ohio, Feb. 8, 1945; s. Douglas Giffin and Betty June (Brown) P. BA, Kent State U., 1970, MA, 1971; ABD, Cath. U., 1980. Anthropologist, instr. sociology and anthropology Wheeling Coll., W.Va., 1972-73; anthropologist, instr., asst. prof. anthropology Ohio U.-Ea., 1972-74, 78, archaeologist, asst. prof. anthropology, 1986-95; mus. technician US Dept. Interior, Nat. Pk. Svc., Washington, 1983; mus. technican Nat. Mus. Natural History, Smithsonian Instn., Washington, 1984-87; mus. specialist, loan officer USN, Naval Hist. Ctr., Washington, 1987—. Dir. archaeol. excavations Brokaw Village Site, St. Clairsville, Ohio, 1972-74, 76-78, 82, 86-96, 98, mem. archaeol. staff Thunderbird Site, Front Royal, Va., Savannah River, Ga., SC, Richard B. Russell Dam Project, 1980, El Mirador Site, Guatemala, 1980, Louis Berger Internat. Project, Trenton, NJ, 1983-84, Sully Plantation, Loudon County, Va., 1984, Fells Point Project, Balt., 1984, exhibited rsch. on Symbols of Rank and Power, Ohio U. Eastern Art Gall., 1998, others. Author: Portraits of Leadership: Symbols of Rank and Power in Tradional Cultures, 2002; rsch. exhibition: Martin Luther King Meml. Libr., 2003—04; rsch. exhbn. Bead Mus., Washington, 2004—; contbr. articles to profl. jours. Rsch. grantee US Dept. Interior, Nat. Pk. Svc., 1978-79, Nat. Geog. Soc., 1992-93. Mem. AAAS, Am. Anthropol. Assn., Washington Assn. Profl. Anthropologists, Anthropol. Soc. Washington, Am. Assn. Museums, Internat. Platform Assn. Achievements include rsch. on prehistoric Am. Indians and the symbols of rank and power in traditional cultures; Nat. Geographic Soc. is currently considering my manuscript "Portraits of Leadership: Symbols of Rank and Power in Traditional Cultures" for publ. Home: # 201 12512 Village Square Ter Rockville MD 20852-1954 Office: Naval Hist Ctr Washington Navy Yard 805 Kidder Breeze SE Washington DC 20374-5060 Business E-Mail: thomas.pickenpaugh@navy.mil.

PICKENS, ALEXANDER LEGRAND, retired education educator; b. Waco, Tex., Aug. 30, 1921; s. Alex LeGrand and Elma L. (Johnson) P.; m. Frances M. Jenkins, Aug. 20, 1955. BA, So. Meth. U., 1950; MA, North Tex. U., Denton, 1952; EdD, Columbia U., 1959. Tchr. art public schs., Dallas, 1950-53, Elizabeth, N.J., 1953-54; instr. Coll. Architecture and Design U. Mich., 1954-59; assoc. prof. dept. art U. Ga., Athens, 1959-62; assoc. prof. Coll. Edn. U. Hawaii, Honolulu, 1962-68, prof. edn., 1969—2001, chmn. doctoral studies curriculum instrn. Coll. Edn., 1984-89, asst. to dean for coll. devel., 1989-01, ret., 2001, emeritus prof., 2002—. Dir. children's classes Ft. Worth Children's Mus., 1951-53; head art Nat. Music Camp, Interlochen, Mich., summers, 1957-58, U. Oreg., Portland, summers 1959-60, 62; cons. youth art activities Foremost Dairies, 1964-74; cons. art films United World Films, 1970-75; art edn. cons. Honolulu Paper Co., 1970-76, Kamehameha Sch., Bishop Estate, 1978-95. Exhibited ceramics, Wichita Internat. Exhbn., Syracuse (N.Y.) Nat. Exhbn., St. Louis Mus., Dallas Mus., San Antonio Mus., Detroit Art Inst., Hawaii Craftsmen, also others; editorial bd.: Arts and Activities mag, 1955-82; editor: U. Hawaii Ednl. Perspectives, 1964-99; contbr. articles to profl. jours. Mem. adult com. Dallas County chpt. Jr. ARC, 1951-53; mem. exec. com. Dallas Crafts Guild, 1950-53; v.p., publicity chmn. U. Ga. Cmty. Concert Assn., 1960-62, program chmn. Gov.'s Commn. Observing 150 Yrs. Pub. Edn. in Hawaii, 1990-91; bd. dirs. Honolulu Theatre for Youth, 1998-2003; bd. dirs., mem. exec. com. Honolulu Symphony, 1998—; bd. dirs. Chamber Music Hawaii, 2003 Served with USAAF. Recipient award merit Tex. State Fair, 1957, All-Am. award Ednl. Press Assn. Am., 1968, 70, 72, 75, 79, Regents' medal for tchg. U. Hawaii, 1989, Gov.'s Commn. Observance of 150 Yrs. Pub. Edn., 1990-91. Mem. AAUP, NEA, Internat. Soc. Edn., Nat. Art Edn. Assn., Coun. for Advancement and Support of Edn., Assn. Fundraising Profls., Nat. Planned Giving Coun., Hawaii Planned Giving Coun., Phi Delta Kappa, Kappa Delta Pi. Address: 1471 Kalaepohaku St Honolulu HI 96816-1804

PICKENS, FRANCES JENKINS, artist, educator; b. Dodd's, Tex., Feb. 26, 1927; d. John Morgan and Mary (Burton) Jenkins; m. Alexander Pickens, Aug. 20, 1955. BA, North Tex. U., 1947, MA, 1954; MEd, U. Hawaii, 1976. Tchr. art pub. schs., Dallas, 1948-55, Dearborn, Mich., 1955-58, White Plains, N.Y., 1958-59, Athens, Ga., 1960-62; gallery lectr. Honolulu Acad. Arts, 1962—63; tchr. art Punahou Sch., Honolulu, 1963-65, The Kamehameha Schs., Honolulu, 1965-85; jewelry and metal artist Honolulu, 1963—. Instr. jewelry U. Hawaii, Honolulu, 1967, 75, 77. Exhibited works in shows at Mus. of Contemporary Crafts, N.Y., Schmuckmuseum, Germany, Renwick Gallery, Washington, Wichita Nat., Women in Design Internat., Mich. Influence, 1981, Materials Hard and Soft, United States Metal, Hawaii Craftsmen Ann., Artists of Hawaii, 1965— (Disting. Artist 1991), East-West Ctr. Gallery, 2003, retrospective Honolulu Acad. Arts, 2001; represented in permanent collection at Acad. of Arts, The Contemporary Mus., Honolulu, Hawaii State Art Mus., Renwick Gallery, Washington, Wichita Art Assn., Kans.; photographs of work included in Goldsmith's Jour., Jewelry, Contemporary Design and Technique, Jewelry/Metalwork Survey, The Metalsmith's Book of Boxes and Lockets; contbr. articles to Arts and Activities mag., Sch. Arts, Ornament mag. Chmn. state crafts State Fair Tex., Dallas, 1954; Crafts Symposium planning com. Hawaii State Found. Culture and Arts, Honolulu, 1968-69; workshop for instrs. U.S. Army Arts and Crafts, Ft. Shafter, 1975. Named Distinguished Artist of Hawaii, Honolulu Acad. Arts, 1991. Mem. Soc. N.Am. Goldsmiths, Dallas Craft Guild, Hawai Craftsmen (charter, v.p., pres.), Renwick Alliance. Avocations: travel, jewelry, metalwork. Home: 1471 Kalaepohaku St Honolulu HI 96816-1804

PICKERELL, JAMES HOWARD, photojournalist; b. Dayton, Ohio, June 9, 1936; s. Howard and Frances (Harrison) P.; m. Mary Louise Fisher, June 26, 1965; children: Cheryl Elizabeth, Stacy Rae. Student, Ohio U., 1954-56; BA, UCLA, 1963. Comml. photographer, 1963—; ind. photographer, 1963-67. Author: Vietnam in the Mud, 1966, Marketing Photography in the Digital Environment, 1994, Negotiating Stock Photo Prices, 5th edit., 2001; writer, pub.: newsletter Selling Stock. With USN, 1956-60. Mem. Nat. Press Photographers Assn. (1st Pl. Spot News award 1965), Am. Soc. Mag. Photographers (nat. bd. 1987-89), Profl. Photographers Assn., Beta Theta Pi. Address: 8104 Cindy Ln Bethesda MD 20817-6913 Personal E-mail: jim@chd.com.

PICKERING, CHARLES W., SR., federal judge; b. Jones County, Miss., May 29, 1937; AA, Jones County Jr. Coll, 1957; BA, U. Miss., 1959, JD, 1968; Hon. Doctorate, William Carey Coll. Ptnr. Gartin, Hester and Pickering, Laurel, Miss., 1961-71; judge Laurel Mcpl. Ct., 1969; pvt. practice Laurel, 1971-72, 80; ptnr. Pickering and McKenzie, Laurel, 1973-80, Pickering and Williamson, Laurel, 1981—86, Pickering, Williamson and Walters, 1986—90; judge U.S. Dist. Ct. (so. dist.) Miss., Hattiesburg, 1990—2004, U.S. Ct. Appeals, (5th cir.), 2004—. Contbr. articles to Mississippi Law Journal. Chmn., Miss. Repub. Party, 1976-78, Mem. ABA, Miss. Bar Assn., Jones County Bar. Assn., State 4-H Adv. Coun., Assn. Trial Lawyers in Am., Miss. Trial Lawyers Assn., U. Miss. Alumni Assn., Jones County Jr. Coll., Jones County Farm Bur., Kiwanis Club. Office: US Ct Appeals 600 Camp St New Orleans LA 70130*

PICKERING, CHARLES W., JR., congressman; b. Laurel, Ms., Aug. 10, 1963; m. Leisha Jane Prather; children: Will, Ross, Jackson, Asher. BA in Bus. Adminstrn., U. Miss., 1986; MBA, Baylor U. Legis. asst. to U.S. Senator Trent Lott; apptd. to USDA; mem. U.S. Congress from 3rd Ms. dist., 1997; co-chmn. congl. wireless com., congl. sportsmen's caucus. Mem. energy and commerce com., agriculture com., livestock, dairy and poultry subcom., forestry, resource conservation, rsch. subcom., Transp. and Infrastructure com., vice chair surface transp. subcom., aviation subcom., Sci. com., vice chair basic rsch. subcom., space subcom.; asst. minority whip; mem. House Rep. Policy com.; mem. exec. com. Nat. Rep. Congrl. com. Republican. Office: US House of Reps 229 Cannon House Office Bldg Washington DC 20515-0001

PICKERING, JAMES HENRY, III, academic administrator, educator; b. N.Y.C., July 11, 1937; s. James H. and Anita (Felber) P.; m. Patricia Paterson, Aug. 18, 1962; children: David Scott, Susan Elizabeth. BA, Williams Coll., 1959; MA, Northwestern U., 1960, PhD, 1964. Instr. English Northwestern U., 1963-65; mem. faculty Mich. State U., East Lansing, 1965-81, prof. English, 1972-81, grad. and assoc. chmn. dept., 1968-75, dir. Honors Coll., 1975-81; dean Coll. Humanities and Fine Arts U. Houston, 1981-90, sr. v.p., provost, 1990-92, pres., 1992-95. Author: The Spy, 1971, The Harper Reader, 1971, Fiction 100, 1974, 78, 82, 85, 88, 92, 95, 98, 2001, 04, The World Turned Upside Down: Prose and Poetry of the American Revolution, 1975, The Spy Unmasked, 1975, The City in American Literature, 1977, Concise Companion to Literature, 1981, Literature, 1982, 86, 90, 94, 97, Mountaineering in Colorado, 1987, Wild Life on the Rockies, 1988, A Mountain Boyhood, 1988, The Spell of the Rockies, 1989, Purpose and Process, 1989, Poetry, 1990, In Beaver World, 1990, Rocky Mountain Wonderland, 1991, A Summer Vacation in the Parks and Mountains of Colorado, 1992, Fiction 50, 1993, Knocking Round the Rockies, 1994, Drama, 1994, Frederick Chapin's Colorado, 1995; This Blue Hollow: Estes Park, The Early Years, 1859-1915, 1999, Mr. Stanley of Estes Park, 2000, In The Vale of Elkanah, 2003, The Ways of the Mountains, 2003, Early Estes Park Historical Narratives, 2004. Mem. Coll. English Assn. (pres. 1980-81), Phi Beta Kappa, Phi Kappa Phi, Omicron Delta Kappa. Office: U Houston Dept English Houston TX 77204-0001

PICKERING, JOHN HAROLD, lawyer; b. Harrisburg, Ill., Feb. 27, 1916; s. John Leslie and Virginia Lee (Morris) P.; m. Elsa Victoria Mueller, Aug. 23, 1941 (dec. Nov., 1988); children: Leslie Ann, Victoria Lee; m. Helen Patton Wright, Feb. 3, 1990. AB, U. Mich., 1938, JD, 1940, LLD, 1996, D.C. Sch. Law, 1995. Bar: N.Y. 1941, D.C. 1947. Practiced in N.Y.C., 1941; practiced in Washington, 1946—; assoc. Cravath, de Gersdorff, Swaine & Wood, 1941; law clk. to Justice Murphy, Supreme Ct. U.S., 1941-43; assoc. Wilmer & Broun, 1946-48, ptnr., 1949-62, Wilmer, Cutler & Pickering, 1962-79, Wilmer & Pickering, 1979-81, Wilmer, Cutler & Pickering, 1981-88, sr. counsel, 1989—2004, Wilmer, Cutler, Pickering, Hale and Dorr, 2004—. Vis. lectr. U. Va. Law Sch., 1958; mem. com. visitors U. Mich. Law Sch., 1962-68, chmn. devel. com., 1973-81; mem. com. on adminstrn. of justice U.S. Ct. Appeals (D.C. cir.), 1966-72, chmn. adv. com. on procedures, 1976-82, chmn. mediation project, 1988—; bd. govs. D.C. Bar, 1975-78, pres., 1979-80; dir. Nat. Ctr. for State Cts., 1987-93. Lt. comdr. USNR, 1943-46. Recipient Outstanding Achievement award U. Mich., 1978, Disting. Svc. award Nat. Ctr. for State Cts., 1985, 50 Yr. award from Fellows Am. Bar Found., 1993, Paul. C. Reardon award Nat. Ctr. for State Cts., 1994, Pro Bono award NAACP Legal Def. Fund, 1990, Am. Bar Assn. medal, 1999, Justice William J. Brennan Jr. award, D.C. Bar, 1998, Justice Potter Stewart award, Coun. for Court Excellence, 1999, Lifetime Acheivement award, Am. Lawyer, 2004, numerous other awards. Mem. ABA (state del. 1984-93, chmn. commn. on legal problems of elderly 1985-93, sr. advisor 1993-95, chmn. 1995-96, commr. emeritus 1996—, chmn. sr. lawyers divsn. 1996-97), D.C. Bar Assn. (Lawyer of the Yr. 1996), Am. Law Inst., Barristers Washington, Lawyers Club, Met. Club, Chevy Chase Club, Wianno Club, Order of Coif, Phi Beta Kappa, Phi Kappa Phi. Democrat. Mem. United Ch. Christ. Home: 8100 Connecticut Ave Chevy Chase MD 20815 Office: Wilmer Cutler Pickering Hale and Dorr 2445 M St NW Ste 8 Washington DC 20037-1435 Office Phone: 202-663-6200. E-mail: john.pickering@wilmer.com.

PICKERING, THOMAS REEVE, diplomat; b. Orange, N.J., Nov. 5, 1931; s. Hamilton R. and Sarah C. (Chasteney) P.; m. Alice J. Stover, Nov. 24, 1955; children: Timothy R., Margaret S. AB, Bowdoin Coll., 1953; MA, Fletcher Sch. Law and Diplomacy, 1954, U. Melbourne, Australia, 1956. Joined U.S. Fgn. Svc., 1959; fgn. affairs officer ACDA, 1961; polit. adviser U.S. del. 18 Nation Disarmament Conf., Geneva, 1962-64; consul Zanzibar, 1965-67; counselor of embassy, dep. chief mission Am. Embassy, Dar es Salaam, Tanzania, 1967-69; dep. dir. Bur. Politico-Mil. Affairs, State Dept., 1969-73; spl. asst. to Sec. of State, 1973-74; exec. sec. Dept. State, 1973-74; U.S. amb. to Jordan, 1974-78; asst. sec. for Bur. Oceans, Internat. Environ. and Sci. Affairs, Washington, 1978-81; U.S. amb. to Nigeria, 1981-83; U.S. amb. to El Salvador, 1983-85; U.S. amb. to Israel, 1985-88; U.S. permanent rep. to UN, 1989-92; U.S. amb. to India, 1992-93; U.S. amb. to Russia, 1993-96; pres. Eurasia Found., 1996-97; undersec. of state for polit. affairs Dept. of State, Washington, 1997—2000; sr. v.p. internat. relations The Boeing Comp., 2001—. Served to lt. comdr. USNR, 1956-59. Mem. Council Fgn. Relations, Internat. Inst. Strategic Studies, Phi Beta Kappa. Address: 2318 Kimbro St Alexandria VA 22307-1822 Office: 1200 Wilson Blvd Arlington VA 22209

PICKETT, CALDER MARCUS, retired journalism educator; b. Providence, Utah, July 26, 1921; s. Leland M. and Julia (Gessel) P.; m. Nola Agricola, Mar. 20, 1947; children: Carolyn Zeligman, Kathleen Jenson. BS, Utah State U., 1944; MS in Journalism, Northwestern U., 1948; PhD, U. Minn., 1959. Copy editor Salt Lake (City) Tribune, 1946, Deseret News, Salt Lake City, 1948-49; instr. Utah State U., Logan, 1946-48, U. Denver, 1949-51; prof. U. Kans., Lawrence, 1951—, Oscar Stauffer prof. Journalism, 1973-77, Clyde M. Reed prof. Journalism, 1985-88, ret., 1988. Author: Ed Howe: Country Town Philosopher, 1968; author, editor: Voices of the Past, 1977; writer, producer, narrator radio program The Am. Past; contbr. articles to profl. jours. Recipient Disting. Teaching award Standard Oil Found., 1967, Frank Luther Mott award, 1969, George Foster Peabody award, 1974, HOPE award U. Kans., 1975, Mortar Bd. award U. Kans., 1983, Armstrong Broadcasting award, 1983, Chancellor's Club Career Teaching award, 1987. Avocations: history, music. Home: 712 Lawrence Ave Lawrence KS 66049-4521

PICKETT, CECIL, pharmaceutical executive; BS in Biology, Calif. State U., Hayward; PhD in Cell Biology, UCLA. Former sr. v.p. basic rsch. Merck Rsch. Labs.; joined advancing to exec. v.p. discovery rsch. Schering-Plough Rsch. Inst., 1993, pres. Spkr. in field; mem. sci. bd. FDA; adv. com. to dir. NIH; nat. cancer policy bd. Inst. Medicine; elected to Inst. Medicine Nat. Acad. Sci., 1993. Contbr. articles to profl. jours.; various editl bds.: med. jours. and rsch. orgns. Recipient Scholarly Achievement and Acad. Dist., UCLA Alumni Assn., 1976, Robert A. Scala award, Rugers U., 1993; scholar Macy scholar, Marine Biol. Labs, 1978. Mem.: AAAS, Am. Assn. Cancer Rsch., Am. Soc. Biochemistry and Molecular Biology, Am. Soc. Cell Biology. Office: Schering Plough Rsch Inst 2000 Galloping Hill Rd Kenilworth NJ 07033

PICKETT, CECIL BRUCE, cell biologist; b. Canton, Ill., Oct. 5, 1945; married; two children. BS, Calif. State U., 1971; PhD, UCLA, 1976. Fellow in cell biology UCLA, 1976-78; with Merck Sharp & Dohme Rsch. Labs., 1978—93; exec. v.p. discovery rsch. Schering-Plough Rsch. Inst., Kenilworth, NJ, 1993—2002, pres., 2002—; sr. v.p. Schering Corp., 2004—; pres. SPRI, 2004—. Macy scholar Marine Biol. Lab, Woods Hole, Mass., 1978; vis. asst. prof. Coll. Medicine Howard U., Washington, 1978-83; adj. assoc. prof. N.J. Sch. Medicine & Dentistry, 1985-88; assoc. prof. U. Montreal, 1989; adj. prof. McGill U., 1990; disting. lecturer, Jonsson Comprehensive Cancer Ctr., UCLA, 1995; mem. sci. adv. bd. FDA; member, mem. GM Adv. Council, Cancer Rsch. Found., 2004. Recipient Robert A. Scala Award and Lectureship in Toxicology, Rutgers U. & U. Medicine & Dentistry of NJ, 1993, Founders award, CIIT Centers for Health Research, 2001. Mem. AAAS, IOM, NAS, Am. Soc. Biochemistry & Molecular Biology, Am. Assn. Cancer Rsch., Am. Soc. Cell Biology, Am. Assn. Advancement Sci.; mem. adv. com. to dir. NIH. Office: Schering-Plough Rsch Inst 2015 Galloping Hill Rd Kenilworth NJ 07033-1300

PICKETT, CHRISTA LANGFORD, elementary school counselor; b. Hoschton, Ga., Aug. 2, 1943; d. Grady and Ruth Geraldine Langford; children: Mark, Paige Pastor. BA Elem. Edn., Emory and Henry Coll., 1974; MEd Spl. Edn., U. Tenn., Chattanooga, 1981. Cert. sch. counselor (P-12), interrelated spl. edn., elem. edn. Teacher (grades 4/5 &1) Oak Hill Elem., Morganton, NC, 1975—79; tchr. spl. edn. Red Bank Jr. HS, Red Bank, Tenn., 1980—81; teacher (grade 4) Thrasher Elem. Sch., Signal Mountain, Tenn., 1984; tchr. spl. edn. (gifted & handicapped) Lone Oak Elem., Signal Mountain, Tenn., 1985—88; tchr. spl. edn. Berkeley Lake Elem., Duluth, Ga., 1989—99, counselor elem. sch., 1999—. Mem. curriculum and instrn. counsel Berkeley Lake Elem. Sch., Duluth, 1998—, mem. Berkeley Lake team planning com., 1999—, coord. Berkeley Lake Care team, 1999—; facilitator student support team i Berkeley Lake Elem. Sch., Duluth, 1999—, member student support team ii, 2002—. Dir. mediation program Berkeley Lake; mem. Peachtree Presbyn. Ch., Atlanta, 1991—; mem., co-facilitator, facilitator Stephen's Ministry of Peachtree Presbyn. Ch., Atlanta, 1992—; relay for life team mem. of bles Am. Cancer Soc., Duluth, 1999—. Mem.: Am. Sch. Counselor Assn., Am. Counseling Assn., Pi Lambda Theta, Kappa Delta Pi. Protestant. Avocations: painting, reading, exercise. Office: Berkeley Lake Elem 4300 South Berkeley Lake Rd Duluth GA 30096 Business E-Mail: christa_pickett@gwinnett.k12.ga.us.

PICKETT, DAVID FRANKLIN, JR., technology company executive; b. Littlefield, Tex., May 3, 1936; s. David Franklin and Dottie Ardell (Britton) P.; m. B. Christine Klop, Aug. 21, 1971. AA, Del Mar Coll., Corpus Christi, 1960; BS in Chem., U. Tex., 1962, MA, 1965, PhD, 1970. Rsch. chemist Am. Magnesium Co., Snyder, Tex., 1969-70; chemist, chem. engr. Air Force Aero Propulsion Lab., Dayton, Ohio, 1970-78; sect. head Hughes Aircraft Co., El Segundo, Calif., 1978-84, asst. dept. mgr., 1984-86, dept. mgr., 1986-89, product line mgr., 1990-91, program mgr., 1991-95; retired, 1995; sr. scientist Eagle-Richer Techs., Colorado Springs, Colo.; pres. AAAA Energy Enterprises, Inc., Colorado Springs, Colo. ECS coordinator ann. battery conf. Calif. State U., Long Beach, 1987-89; sr. scientist Eagle-Picher Techs., LLC. Author: Nickel Electrode and NiCd Cell Technology, 1984-88; inventor in field. With USN, 1955-57. Mem. AIAA, Southern Calif./Nev. Electrochem. Soc. (sec. 1980-81, vice chmn. 1981-82, chmn. 1982-83), Am. Chem. Soc., Phi Lambda Upsilon. Baptist. Avocations: travel, fishing. Home: PO Box 16146 Colorado Springs CO 80935-6146 Office: Eagle-Picher Techs LLC 3820 Hancock Expy Colorado Springs CO 80911-1263 also: AAAA Energy Enterprises Inc PO Box 16146 Colorado Springs CO 80935-6146

PICKETT, OWEN B. lawyer, former congressman; b. Richmond, Va, Aug. 31, 1930; BS, Va. Poly. Inst., 1952; LLB, U. Richmond, 1955. CPA Va.; bar: Va. 1955, D.C. 1962. Lawyer practice, Va. Beach, Va., 1955—72; mem. Va. Ho. of Dels., Richmond, 1972—86, US Congress from 2d Va. dist., Washington, 1987—2001; of counsel Troutman, Sanders, LLP, Va. Beach, Va., 2001—. Mem. resources com. Armed Svcs. Com.; chmn. Va. Dem. State Ctrl. Com., 1980—82. Mem.: D.C. Bar Assn., Va. Bar Assn. Office: Troutman Sanders LLP Ste 2000 222 Ctrl Pk Dr Virginia Beach VA 23462 Office Phone: 757-687-7525. Business E-Mail: owen.pickett@troutmanssanders.com.

PICKETT, SANDRA, information scientist; BS, U. Tex.; MA, U. Houston. Councilwoman City of Liberty, Tex., 1974—98, mayor pro tem, 1976—98; commr., chair Tex. State Libr. and Archives Commn., Austin, 1995—. Past chmn. Liberty County Hist. Commn.; past dir., pres. Preservation Tex.; mem. Nat. Mus. and Libr. Svcs. Bd., Washington, 2004—. Named Citizen of Yr., C. of C., 1981; recipient John Ben Shepperd Leadership award, Tex. Hist. Commn., 1993; Paul Harris fellow, Rotary Internat., 1998. Mem.: Atascosito Hist. Soc. (pres.). Mailing: PO Box 19191 Liberty TX 77575 Office: Tex State Libr and Archives Commn PO Box 12927 Austin TX 78711*

PICKETT, STEPHEN ALAN, hospital executive; b. Ft. Wayne, Ala., Dec. 22, 1953; s. James Benjamin Pickett and Dorothy Jane (Howell) Pickett Fancher; m. Neil Annette Horsley, Mar. 5, 1977; children: Stefanie Leigh, Allison Marie. BBA, U. Montevallo, 1976; MPH, Tulane U., 1995. CPA, Ala. Sr. acct. Ernst & Whinney, Birmingham, Ala., 1976-78; contr. East End Meml. Hosp., Birmingham, 1978, v.p. fin., 1979-84, W. Va. U. Hosps., Morgantown, 1985-87, exec. v.p., adminstr., 1987-91; adminstr., COO Tulane U. Hosp. and Clinic, New Orleans, 1991-95, CEO, 1995—2004; CFO, UAB Health System, Birmingham, Ala., 2004—. Bd. dirs. Met. Hosp. Coun., 1991—, Associated Hosp. Svcs., 1991—. Active sustaining mem. campaign BSA, 1978; mem. Jefferson County Rep. Exec. Com., Birmingham, 1982, First Bapt. Ch. New Orlean (fin. com. 1993—). Fellow Healthcare Fin. Mgmt. Assn.; mem. AICPA, Ala. Soc. CPAs, U. Montevallo Alumni Assn. (life), Alpha Tau Omega Alumni Assn., Rotary. Baptist. Office: Chief Fin Officer UAG Health System 500 22d St S Ste 408 Birmingham AL 35233 Office Phone: 205-975-5412. Business E-Mail: spickett@uabmc.edu.

PICKETT, STEPHEN WESLEY, academic administrator, consultant; b. Billings, Mont., May 27, 1956; s. Wesley William and Carol Ann (Bollum) P. BA, Houston Bapt. U., 1980; MS, U. North Tex., 1988. Cert. elem. tchr., rehab. counselor, Tex. Hosp. tchr. Houston Ind. Sch. Dist., 1981-85; asst. to assoc. dean of students U. North Tex., Denton, 1988-90, asst. coord. disabled student svcs., Office Student Devel., 1990-91, dir. Office Disability Accom-

modation, 1991—2001, univ. mentor/advisor, 1992—2001; dir. disability svcs. U. Oreg., Eugene, 2002—, assoc. dir. office of acd. advising, 2002—. Co-author: curriculum guide The Newspaper as a Student Communicator, 1982 (winner Exxon Found.'s Impact Two award for creative teaching). Chair Mayor's Com. on Employment of Persons with Disabilities, Denton, 1990; mem. coun.-at-large Sam Houston Area Coun. Boy Scouts Am., Houston, 1975—; grad. Denton C. of C. Leadership Program, 1992; pub. rels. chair leadership Denton Steering Com., 1993-94; mem. ad. bd. city of Denton Transit, 1990-2001; exec. bd. Svc. provision for Aging Needs, a United Way Agy., 1997-2001; mem. U. of North Tex. Adv. Bd. for ADA Access, 1992-2001, co-chair UNT ADA adv. com., 2000-01; mem. budget com. Denton County United Way, 1998-2001. Recipient Cmty. Svc. award U. North Tex., 1992, award for svcs. to persons with disabilities North Tex. Rehab. Assn., 1993, Disting. Alumnus award Houston Bapt. U., 1994, Outstanding Alumnus award Ctr. for Rehab. Studies, U. North Tex., 1995. Mem. Assn. Higher Edn. and Disability, Nat. Assn. Student Pers. Adminstrs., Tex. Assn. Coll. and Univ. Student Pers. Adminstrs. (chair multicultural com. 1994-95, v.p. 1995-96, co-chair endowment found. com. 1996-97), Tex. Assn. Higher Edn. and Disabilities (sec. 1998-99, conf. co-chair 1999). Presbyterian. Avocations: reading, travel, stamp collecting/philately. Office: U Oreg Disability Svc 164 Oregon Hall 5278 U Oreg Eugene OR 97403-5278 E-mail: stevewp@att.net.

PICKETT, TINA L. state representative; b. Kingston, Pa., May 28, 1943; 1 child, Lynne. Pres. Ctrl. Bradford C. of C., 1992—94; commr. Bradford County, 1996—; state rep. Pa., 2001—. Owner Pickett's Dairy, 1964—68, The Fireplace Restaurant, 1968—85, The Williamston Inn, 1977—. Mem. CCAP Tax Reform Com., 2000—; bd. mem. Endless Mts. Vacation Bur., 1975—; v.p. Ptnrs. in Family and Cmty. Devel., 1998—; pres. Wysox Mcpl. Sewer Authority, 1994—. Mem.: Young Men's Christian Assn., Towands Lions Club (pres.). Republican. Office: 155A E Wing Harrisburg PA 17120-2020 E-mail: tpickett@pahousegop.com.

PICKETT, WILLIAM BEATTY, history educator; b. Crawfordsville, Ind., Mar. 12, 1940; s. Walter Nathan and Amy Beatty P.; m. Janet Elizabeth Hollingsworth, Aug. 29, 1963; children: Robert Matthew, Jeffrey Michael. BA, Carleton Coll., 1962; MA, Ind. U., 1968, PhD, 1974. Assoc. instr. Ind. U., Bloomington, 1968-69; asst. prof. Rose-Hulman Inst. Tech., Terre Haute, Ind., 1972-76, assoc. prof., 1976-82, prof. history, 1982—. Fulbright lectr. Nanzan U. and Nagoya U., Japan, 1989; vis. lectr. U. Md., Seoul, Republic of Korea, 1990; vis. prof. Am. U. in Kyrgyzstan, Bishkek, 2002. Author: Homer E. Capehart: A Senator's Life, 1990, Dwight David Eisenhower and American Power, 1995, To Be the Best: Rose-Hulman Institute of Technology, 1974-99, 1999, Eisenhower Decides to Run: Presidential Politics and Cold War Strategy, 2000; editor: Technology at the Turning Point, 1977, George F. Kennan and the Origins of Eisenhower's New Look: An Oral History of Project Solarium, 2004. Mem. Am. Hist. Assn., Orgn. Am. Historians, Ind. Assn. Historians, Soc. Historians of Am. Fgn. Rels., Soc. Mil. History, Internat. House Japan, Indian Coun. for History Edn. Methodist. Avocations: travel, photography, sailing. Home: 3224 Oak St Terre Haute IN 47803-2651 Office: Rose Hulman Inst Tech 5500 Wabash Ave Terre Haute IN 47803-3999

PICKETT, WILSON, vocalist, composer; b. Prattville, Ala., Mar. 18, 1941; Albums include If You Want Me, 1974, I Want You, 1979, The Right Track, 1981, Best of Wilson Pickett, 1985; singles include In the Midnight Hour, 1965, Land of 1000 Dances, 1966, Funky Broadway, 1967, She's lookin' Good, 1968, Engine Number 9, 1970, Don't Let the Green Grass Fool You, 1971; songwriter I Found A Love, 1962, (with others) If You Need Me, 1963, It's Too Late, 1963, (with others) In the Midnight Hour, 1966, I'm a Midnight Mover, 1968, Don't Knock My Love, 1971. Inducted into Rock and Roll Hall of Fame, 1991, The Alabama Music Hall of Fame, 1999. Office: Motown Record Corp 6255 W Sunset Blvd Los Angeles CA 90028-7403

PICKHARDT, CARL EMILE, JR., artist; b. Westwood, Mass., May 28, 1908; s. Carl Emile and Louise (Fowler) P.; m. Marjorie Sachs, June 15, 1935 (div. 1952); children: Nancy Louise Arnold, Carl Emile III, Sally Anne Duncan; m. Rosamond Forbes Wyman, Mar. 28, 1953. BA, Harvard U., 1931; studied with Harold Zimmerman, 1931-37. Tchr. Fitchburg Art Mus., 1951-62, Worcester Mus. Sch., 1949-50, Sturbridge Art Sch., 1952-60. Author: Portfolio of Etchings, 1942; one-man shows, Berkshire Art Mus., 1941, Doris Meltzer Gallery, N.Y.C., 1961, 68, 70, 71, 72, Jacques Seligmann Gallery, N.Y.C., 1935, 51, 52, 54, Stuart Gallery, Boston, 1946, Margaret Brown Gallery, Boston, 1951, Fitchburg Art Mus., 1951, 91, 98, 99, 2000, 01, 02, 03, 04, Lawrence Gallery, Kansas City, Mo., 1955, Artek Gallery, Helsinki, Finland, 1959, Laguna Gloria Art Mus., Austin, Tex., 1966, Radcliffe Coll., 1983, Providence Art Club, 1986, Sherborn Libr., 2002-03; exhibited in group shows at Carnegie Internat., 1951, Mus. Modern Art, N.Y.C., 1940, 63, 64, Whitney Mus., 1936, Nat. Acad., 1942, 49, Boston Inst. Contemporary Art, 1941, Internat. Exhbn., Japan., 1952, Exhbn. Am. Drawings, France, 1955, Art Inst. Chgo., Calif. Palace of Legion of Honor, 1953, Boston Arts Festival, 1950, Am. Drawing Biennial, Norfolk, 1964, Pa. Acad. Fine Arts, 1968, Laguna Gloria Art Mus., 1973, Fitchburg Art Mus., 1974, 91, 2000, 01, 02; represented in permanent collections, Mus. Modern Art, N.Y.C., Boston Mus. Fine Arts, Bklyn. Art Mus., Worcester Art Mus., Library of Congress, N.Y. Pub. Library, Newark Art Mus., Fogg Art Mus., Addison Gallery, Finch Coll. Art Mus., Pa. Acad. Fine Atrs, Boston Pub. Library, Fitchburg Art Mus., Wadsworth Athenaeum, De Cordova Mus. Served with USNR, 1942-45. Ford Found. and Am. Fedn. Arts artist-in-residence Laguna Gloria Art Mus. 1966; recipient Shope prize Nat. Acad. 1942. Address: 66 Forest St Sherborn MA 01770-1618 *My life-long purpose has been to create in visual images a new language and to express order in asymetrical terms.*

PICKHOLTZ, RAYMOND LEE, electrical engineering educator, consultant; b. N.Y.C., Apr. 12, 1932; s. Isidore and Rose (Turkish) P.; m. Eda Rebecca Mittler, June 30, 1957; children: Robin, Andrew, Julie. BEE, CUNY, 1954, MEE, 1958; PhD, Poly. U. N.Y., 1966. Research engr. RCA Labs., Princeton, N.J., 1954-57, ITT Labs., Nutley, N.J., 1957-61; assoc. prof. Poly. Inst. Bklyn., 1962-71; prof. elec. engring., chmn. dept. George Washington U., Washington, 1977-80, prof., 1971—; pres. Telecommunication Assocs., Fairfax, Va., 1963—; cons. Inst. Def. Analyses, 1971-90, IBM Research, Yorktown Heights, N.Y., 1968-72; del. Union Radio Scientifique, Geneva, 1979—, vice chmn., 1987; del. NRC, Washington, 1980-83; cons. Motorola, CBC, NAB, USADR, Lucent, Verizon, 1996—. Vis. prof. U. Que., 1977; vis. scholar U. Calif., 1983; chmn. U.S. Nat. Commn. C, Union Radio Sci. Internat., 1990-92; mem. sci. and indsl. adv. bd. Telecom. Inst. Ont., Can. and Inst. Nacionale de la Recherches Scientique; vice chair, wireless panel World Tech. Evaluation Ctr. Editor: book series Computer Science Press, 1979—; IEEE Trans., 1975-80; co-editor-in-chief Jour. of Comms. and Networks, 2003—; author: Local Area and Multiple Access Networks, 1986; contbr. articles to profl. jours.; patentee in field. Recipient rsch. award RCA Labs., 1955; rsch. grantee Office of Naval Research, Washington, 1982, E-Systems, Falls Church, Va., 1983-96, MCI, Falls Church, Va., Instelsat, Washington, Nortel Networks, 1996—, DARPA, NSF, 1999—. Fellow IEEE (bd. govs. 1979-82, digital comm. com., Centennial medal 1984), AAAS, Washington Acad. Scis.; mem. IEEE Comm. Soc. (v.p. 1986-88, pres. 1990-92, Donald W. McLellan award, 1994, Erskine fellow New Zealand 1997, Third Millennium medal 2000, ACM MSWIN prize paper award, 1999, Best paper of 1999 in Jour. of Comms. and Networks, 2000, gen. chair, Infocom, Kobe, Japan 1997, gen. chair, ACM Mobicom Y2K, Boston, 2000), Math. Assn. Am., Cosmos Club, Sigma Xi, Eta Kappa Nu. Home: 3613 Glenbrook Rd Fairfax VA 22031-3210 Office: George Washington U Dept Elec Computer Engring Washington DC 20052-0001

PICKLE, GEORGE EDWARD, lawyer; b. New Orleans, Nov. 22, 1950; s. George E. Sr. and Virginia (Crowe) P.; m. Karen Lyle, Sept. 18, 1976; children: George E. III, Lauren M. Student, Rhodes Coll., 1968-70; BA, Millsaps Coll., 1972; JD, Georgetown U., 1975. Bar: Miss. 1975, U.S. Ct. Claims 1979, U.S. Tax Ct. 1979, U.S. Ct. Mil. Appeals 1976, U.S. Ct. Appeals (D.C. cir.) 1979, U.S. Supreme Ct. 1979, U.S. Dist. Ct. (so. dist.) Miss. 1980, U.S. Ct. Appeals (5th cir.) 1980, La. 1982, U.S. Dist. Ct. (ea. dist.) La. 1982, U.S. Dist. Ct. (mid. dist.) La. 1985, Tex. 1986., U.S. Dist. Ct. (so. dist.) Tex. 1986, U.S. Dist. Ct. (we. dist.) La. 1988. Law clk.to presiding justice U.S. Ct. Appeals (5th cir.), Askerman, Miss., 1975-76; assoc. Upshaw & Ladner, Jackson, Miss., 1980-82, Barham & Churchill, New Orleans, 1982-85; sr. atty. litigation, energy, environ., admiralty and products Shell Oil Co., Houston, 1985-96, assoc. general counsel, 1997—. Contbr. law rev., 1975; co-author, editor: Syllabus on Environmental Law, 1986. Bd. dirs. Tex. Civil Justice League, 1996—, Product Liability Advisory Coun., 1997—, chair operating Com. Civil Justice Reform Group, 1994—, Lawyers for Civil Justice Class Action Task Force, 2001-; sr. warden Episcopal Ch. of the Good Shepherd, Kingwood, Tex., 1991, dir. capital fund corp., 1988, lay eucharistic min., 1986-99; del. Tex. Senatorial and State Rep. convs., 1988-92; mem. exec. and vacancy coms. Rep. Party Harris County, 1990-96, chmn. precinct, 1990-96; mem. Georgetown U. Barristers Coun., 1973-75; referee N.W. Aquatic League, 1990-97; pres. Bear Br. Swim Team, 1991-93. Lt. cmdr. (head environ. litigation) USNR, 1976-79. Southwestern Scholar Rhodes Coll., Memphis, 1968. Mem. ABA (chmn. legis. jud. and govt. com. 2002-, vice chmn. young lawyers div. com. on environ. law, exec. editor Am. Criminal Law Rev. 1973-75, award for Profl. Merit 1976), Def. Rsch. Inst., Miss. Bar Assn. (elections com. 1982), La. Bar Assn., Tex. Bar Assn., Internat. Assn. Defence Coun. (vice chmn., sec. corp coun. 1991—), Alpha Tau Omega, Phi Alpha Theta, Omicron Delta Kappa, Pi Kappa Delta. Republican. Avocations: golf, water-skiing. Home: 3507 Tree Ln Humble TX 77339-2639 E-mail: ed.pickle@shell.com.

PICKLE, JERRY RICHARD, lawyer; b. Paris, Tex., Feb. 2, 1947; s. Joseph Rambert and Martha Marie (Biggers) P.; m. Helen Leigh Russell, May 3, 1975; children: Jonathan Russell, Stephen Richard (dec.), Sarah Elizabeth. BA in History, U. Houston, 1969, JD, 1971. Bar: Tex. 1972, U.S. Dist. Ct. (no. dist.) Tex. 1974. Mem. Luna, Ballard & Pickle, Garland, Tex., 1972-74; assoc. Hightower & Alexander, Dallas, 1974-76, Cuba & Johnson, Temple, Tex., 1976-77; sr. corp. counsel Scott & White Clinic, Temple, 1977—. Asst. prof. Tex. A&M U. Coll. of Medicine, Temple, 1986—. Contbr. articles to profl. jours. V.p. The Caring House, Temple, 1989, Tex. divsn. Am. Cancer Soc., Temple, 1976-77; adv. bd. R.R. & Pioneer Mus., Temple, 1982-84; hist. preservation bd. City of Temple, 1979-90; chmn. Bell County Hist. Commn., 1980-82; bd. dirs. Bell County Mus., 1992-96, Temple Coord. Child Care Coun., 1991-93, Sr. Citizens Activites Ctr., Temple, 1993-94, pres., 1994-95; bd. dirs. Temple Cultural Activities Ctr., 1992-98, 2001—, pres., 1994-95; chair Heart o'Tex. Coun., Chisholm Trail Dist., Boy Scouts Am., 1987-88; mem. parent's coun. U. N.C., Chapel Hill, N.C., 2001—. Mem.: ABA, Temple C. of C. (bd. dirs. 1983—85, 1988—90), Coun. Med. Group Practice Attys. (chair 2001—02), Am. Health Lawyers Assn. (chair tchg. hosp. and acad. med. ctrs. 1997—99), Bell-Lampasas-Mills Counties Young Lawyers Assn. (pres. 1980—81), Bell-Lampasas-Mills Counties Bar Assn. (bd. dirs. 1985—90, pres. 1988—89), State Bar Coll., Tex. Bar Found., Tex. Young Lawyers Assn., State Bar Tex. (health law sect. councilman 1980—84, chmn. 1983—84, health law sect. councilman 1985—87), Univ. NC Chapel Hill Parents Coun. (mem. 2001—), Jaycees (chpt. dir. 1977—78), Rotary (chpt. dir. 1981—85, 1986—87). Democrat. Episcopalian. Avocations: reading, golf, music. Office: Scott & White Clinic 2401 S 31st St Temple TX 76508-0001 Office Phone: 254-724-3001. Office Fax: 254-724-4501. Business E-Mail: jpickle@swmail.sw.org.

PICKLE, JOSEPH WESLEY, JR., religious studies educator; b. Denver, Apr. 8, 1935; s. Joseph Wesley and Wilhelmina (Blacketor) P.; m. Judith Ann Siebert, June 28, 1958; children: David E., Kathryn E., Steven J. BA, Carleton Coll., 1957; B.D., Chgo. Theol. Sem., 1961; MA, U. Chgo., 1962, PhD, 1969. Ordained to ministry Am. Bapt. Conv., 1962. Asst. pastor Judson Meml. Ch., N.Y.C., 1959-60; acting dean summer session Colo. Coll., Colorado Springs, 1969-70, from asst. prof. to prof. religion, 1964—2002, faculty dir. internat. studies, 1994-98; prof. emeritus, 2002. Vis. prof. theology Iliff Sch. Theology, Denver, 1984, 2003; vis. prof. religious studies U. Zimbabwe, Harare, 1989; cons. Colo. Humanities Program, Denver, 1975-89; coord. Sheffer Meml. Fund, Colo. Coll., Colorado Springs, 1983—. Co-editor Papers of the 19th Century Theology Group, 1978, 88, 93. Pres. bd. dirs. Pikes Peak Mental Health Ctr., Colorado Springs, 1975; chmn. Colo. Health Facilities Rev. Coun., Denver, 1979-84; mem. Colo. Health Facilities Rev. Coun., Denver, 1976-84, Colo. Bd. Health, Denver, 1986-91; bd. dirs. Marson Found., Colorado Springs, 1994—. Am. Bapt. Conv. scholar, 1953-59; Fulbright Hays Grad. fellow U. Tübingen, Fed. Republic Germany, 1963-64, Danforth fellow, 1957-63, Joseph Malone fellow, 1987. Fellow Soc. for Values in Higher Edn.; mem. Am. Theol. Soc. (pres. 1996-97), Am. Acad. Religion (regional pres. 1983-84, 92-93), Cath. Theol. Soc. Am., Fulbright Assn., Phi Beta Kappa. Democrat. Home: 20 W Caramillo St Colorado Springs CO 80907-7314 Office: Colo Coll 14 E Cache La Poudre St Colorado Springs CO 80903-3298 E-mail: jpickle@ColoradoCollege.edu.

PICKLE, ROBERT DOUGLAS, lawyer, apparel executive; b. Knoxville, Tenn., May 22, 1937; s. Robert Lee and Beatrice Jewel (Douglas) P.; m. Rosemary Elaine Noser, May 9, 1964. AA summa cum laude, Schreiner Mil. Coll., Kerrville, Tex., 1957; BSBA magna cum laude, U. Tenn., 1959, JD, 1961; honor grad. seminar, Nat. Def. U., 1979; hon. grad., U.S. Army JAG Sch., U.S. Army Logistics Mgmt. Sch.; grad., U.S. Army Inf. Sch., Army Command-Gen. Staff Coll. Bar: Tenn. 1961, Mo. 1964, U.S. Ct. Mil. Appeals 1962, U.S. Supreme Ct. 1970. Atty. Brown Shoe Co., Inc., St. Louis, 1963-69, asst. sec., atty., 1969-74, sec., gen. counsel, 1974-85; v.p., gen. counsel, corp. sec. Brown Shoe Co., Inc. (formerly Brown Group, Inc.), St. Louis, 1985—. Indiv. mobilization augmentee, asst. army judge adv. gen. civil law The Pentagon, Washington, 1984-89. Provisional judge Municipal Ct., Clayton, Mo., summer 1972; chmn. Clayton Region attys. sect., profl. div. United Fund Greater St. Louis Campaign, 1972-73, team capt., 1974-78; chmn. City of Clayton Parks and Recreation Commn., 1985-87; liaison admissions officer, regional and state coordinator U.S. Mil. Acad., 1980—. Col. JAGC, U.S. Army, 1961-63. Decorated Meritorious Svc. medal; 1st U. Tenn. Law Coll. John W Green law scholar; recipient Cold War Recognition cert. Sec. Def. Fellow Harry S. Truman Meml. Library; mem. ABA, Tenn. Bar Assn., Mo. Bar Assn., St. Louis County Bar Assn., Bar Assn. Met. St. Louis, St. Louis Bar Found. (bd. dirs. 1979-81), Am. Corp. Counsel Assn., Am. Soc. Corp. Secs. (treas. St. Louis regional group 1976-77, sec. 1977-78, v.p. 1978-79, pres., mem. Quarter-Century Club 1979-80), U. Tenn. Gen. Alumni Assn. (pres., bd. dirs. St. Louis chpt. 1974-76, 80-84, bd. govs. 1982-89), U.S. Trademark Assn. (bd. dirs. 1978-82), Tenn. Soc. St. Louis (bd. dirs. 1980-88, treas., sec., v.p. 1984-87, pres. 1987-88), Smithsonian Nat. Assocs., World Affairs Coun. St. Louis, Inc., Am. Legion, University Club (v.p., sec. St. Louis chpt. 1976-81, bd. dirs. 1976-81), Stadium Club, West Point Soc. St. Louis (hon. mem., bd. dirs. 1992—), Conf. Bd. (coun. chief legal officers), Fontbonne Coll. Pres.'s Assocs. (O'Hara and Tower Socs), St. Louis U. Billiken Club, St. Louis U. DuBourg Soc. (hon. v.p.). Republican. Presbyterian. Avocations: reading, spectator sports. Home: 214 Topton Way Saint Louis MO 63105-3638 Office: Brown Shoe Co Inc 8300 Maryland Ave Saint Louis MO 63105-3645 E-mail: rpickle@brownshoe.com.

PICKLEMAN, JACK R. surgeon; MD, McGill U., Montreal, Que., Can., 1964. Intern Royal Victoria Hosp., Montreal, Que., Can., 1964-65; resident in surgery U. Chgo. Med. Ctr., 1967-73; asst. prof. surgery Loyola U., Chgo., 1973-77, assoc. prof. surgery, 1977-81, prof., chief gen. surgery, 1981—. Attending physician Loyola Med. Ctr., Maywood, Ill. Mem. ACS. Office: Loyola U Med Ctr 2160 S 1st Ave Maywood IL 60153-3304

PICKREL, PAUL, English educator; b. Gilson, Ill., Feb. 2, 1917; s. Clayton and Inez (Murphy) P. AB, Knox Coll., 1938; MA, Yale U., 1942, PhD, 1944. Instr. English Lafayette Coll., 1941-42; instr. Yale U., 1943-45, asst. prof., 1945-50, lectr. English, 1954-66, chmn. Scholar of House Program, 1959-60, 61-66; fellow Morse Coll., 1962-66; adviser John Hay fellows, 1959-66; vis. prof. English Smith Coll., Northampton, Mass., 1966-67, prof., 1967-87, prof. emeritus, 1987—, chmn. dept., 1972-75, 81-82. Author: (novel) The Moving Stairs, 1948; also essays on fiction, numerous book revs.; mng. editor: Yale Rev., 1949-66; chief book critic: Harper's mag., 1954-65. Mem. Aurelian Honor Soc., Elizabethan Club (New Haven), Faculty Club (Northampton), Phi Beta Kappa. Clubs: Elizabethan (New Haven), Faculty (Northampton); Yale (N.Y.C.).

PICKRELL, THOMAS RICHARD, retired oil company executive; b. Jermyn, Tex., Dec. 30, 1926; s. Mont Bolt and Martha Alice (Dodson) P.; m. M. Earline Bowen, Sept. 9, 1950; children: Thomas Wayne, Michael Bowen, Kent Richard, Paul Keith BS, North Tex. State U., 1951, MBA, 1952; postgrad., Ohio State U., 1954-55; advanced mgmt. program, Harvard U., 1979. CPA, Tex. Auditor, acct. Conoco, Inc., Ponca City, Okla., 1955-62, mgr. acctg. Houston, 1965-67, asst. controller Ponca City, 1967-81, v.p., controller Stamford, Conn., 1982-83, Wilmington, Del., 1983-85; asst. prof. Okla. State U., Stillwater, Okla., 1962-63; controller Douglas Oil Co., Los Angeles, 1963-65. Mem. adv. bd. dept. acctg. North Tex. State U., Denton, 1978-85; mem. adv. bd. Coll. Bus., Kansas State U., Manhattan, 1979-81 Bd. dirs. YMCA, Ponca City, 1976-78, Kay Guidance Clinic, Ponca City, 1971-74, United Way, Ponca City, 1979-81; chmn. Charter Rev. Com., Ponca City, 1971-72. Served to sgt. U.S. Army, 1944-46; ETO Mem. AICPA, Fin. Execs. Inst. (pres. Okla. chpt. 1972), Am. Petroleum Inst. (acctg. com., gen. com.), Ponca City Country Club (pres. 1980-81), Rotary (pres. Ponca City club 1973-74), Beta Gamma Sigma, Beta Alpha Psi Republican. Presbyterian. Home: 10 San Juan Ranch Rd Santa Fe NM 87506-7539

PICO, FERNANDO, historian, educator; b. San Juan, Aug. 15, 1941; s. Florencio Picó and Matilde Bauermeister. BA, Fordham U., 1965, MA in hist., 1966; PhD in hist., Johns Hopkins U., 1970; MDiv in theology, Woodstock Coll., 1971; PhD (hon.), U. Carlos Ablizu, 1996, U. Metropolitan, 1999. Prof., hist. U. de PR, Rio Piedras, PR, 1972—. Author: Libertad y Servidumbre, 1979, Historia General de Puerto Rico, 1986, El Dia Menos Pensado, 1997. Chaplain Anexo 292, Bayamor, 1988—. Named Educator of Yr., Assn. of U. Admin. of PR, 2002. Mem.: Assn. Puertorriqueña de Historiadores, Medieval Acad. of Am., Caribbean Historians Assn. (pres. 1990—92). Home: 1940 Savco Urb Santa Maria San Juan PR 00921 Office: U PR Hist Dept PO Box 23350 San Juan PR 00931 Office Phone: 787-764-0000 2076.

PICOTTE, LEONARD FRANCIS, naval officer; b. Calumet, Mich., Dec. 8, 1939; s. Irving René and Maria (Tamborino) P.; m. Sandra Lees Whiteley, July 14, 1984; children from previous marriage: Mary Elizabeth, Lance, Michael. BS in Econs. cum laude, U. No. Mich., 1963; MA in Polit. Sci., San Diego State U., 1975; grad. with distinction, Armed Forces Staff Coll., Norfolk, Va., 1976; M in Strategic Studies, Naval War Coll., Newport, R.I., 1985. Commd. ensign USN, 1963, advanced through grades to rear adm., 1991; comdg. officer USS Marathon, Vietnam, 1971-73; exec. officer USS Point Defiance, San Diego, 1976-78; exec. officer, officer in charge Surface Warfare Officers' Sch., Coronado, Calif., 1978-80; exec. officer Naval Sta., San Diego, 1980; comdg. officer USS Alamo, San Diego, 1980-82; surface warfare detailer Bur. Naval Pers., Washington, 1982-84; comdg. officer USS Duluth, San Diego, 1986-88; 1st comdg. officer USS Wasp, 1988-90; insp. gen. Comdr. in Chief, U.S. Atlantic Command, Comdr. in Chief, U.S. Atlantic Fleet, Norfolk, 1990-92; comdr. Amphibious Group Two, Norfolk, 1992-95; ret., 1995; v.p. expeditionary warfare programs Am. Systems Corp., Chesapeake, Va., 1995—. Decorated Legion of Merit (2); recipient Disting. Svc. medal. Mem. Surface Navy Assn., USS Wasp Assn. (hon.), Army and Navy Club, Town Point Club, Hampton Roads Coun. Navy League, Nat. Security Indsl. Assn. (exec. com. Naval Expeditionary Warfare). Republican. Roman Catholic. Avocations: jogging, hunting, reading, gardening, chess. Home: 119 Northgate Ln Suffolk VA 23434-4300 also: 213 Madawaska Rd Palmyra ME 04965-4064 Office: Am Sys Corp Greenbriar Circle Chesapeake VA 23320

PICOWER, WARREN MICHAEL, editor; b. N.Y.C., Aug. 21, 1934; s. Abraham and Nell (Bloom) P.; divorced; children: Jenny Emelia, Eve Julie. BA, Queens Coll., 1956; MA, New Sch. for Social Rsch., 1978; PsyD in Psychology, Heed U., L.A., 1982. Editorial asst. Newsweek mag., N.Y.C., 1956-59; assoc. editor Zimmerman Pub. Co., N.Y.C., 1961-63; assoc., mng. editor Fawcett Pubs., N.Y.C., 1963, 64-65; mng. editor Tuesday Publs., N.Y.C., 1965-67, exec. editor, v.p., 1967-73; sr. editor King Features Syndicate, N.Y.C., 1974-78; mng. editor Food & Wine Mag., N.Y.C., 1978-93; consulting editor Travel Holiday Mag., N.Y., 1993-94; mng. editor Zagat Survey restaurant and hotel guides, N.Y.C., 1994-97; sr. project editor Money Mag., N.Y.C., 1997-98. Cons. in field; awards judge James Beard Found. Contbr. articles to profl. jours. Mem. Am. Soc. Mag. Editors.

PICRAUX, SAMUEL THOMAS, applied science and physics researcher; b. St. Charles, Mo., Mar. 3, 1943; s. Samuel F. and Jeannette D. Picraux; m. Danice R. Kent, July 12, 1970; children: Jeanine, Laura, Samantha. BS in Elec. Engring., U. Mo., 1965; postgrad., Cambridge (Eng.) U., 1965-66; MS in Engring. Sci., Calif. Inst. Tech., 1967, PhD in Engring. Sci. and Physics, 1969. Mem. tech. staff Sandia Nat. Labs., Albuquerque, 1969-72, div. supr., 1972-86, dept. mgr., 1986-96, dir., 1996-2001; prof. materials engring., exec. dir. materials rsch. Ariz. State U., 2001—. Mem. solid state scis. com. NRC, 1996-98; vis. scientist dept. physics Aarhus U., Denmark, 1975; NATO lectr., 1979, 81, 83, 86.; NSF lectr. 1976, 81. Author: Materials Analysis by Ion Channeling, 1982; editor: Applications of Ion Beams to Metals, 1974, Metastable Materials Formation by Ion Implantation, 1982, Surface Alloying by Ion Electron and Laser Beams, 1986, Beam-Solid Interactions and Transient Processes, 1987; editor Nuclear Instruments and Methods International Jour., 1983-91; contbr. numerous articles to profl. jours. Recipient Ernest Orlando Lawrence Meml. award U.S. Dept. Energy, 1990, 3 Basic Energy Scis. Outstanding Rsch. awards U.S. Dept. Energy, 1985, 92, 94; Fulbright fellow, 1965-66. Fellow AAAS, Am. Phys. Soc. (chmn. materials physics divsn. 1990); mem. IEEE (sr.), Am. Vacuum Soc., Materials Rsch. Soc. (pres. 1993). Office: Ariz State U PO Box 876006 Tempe AZ 85287-6006 Business E-Mail: picraux@asu.edu.

PIDERIT, JOHN J. university educator; b. N.Y.C., Feb. 26, 1944; BA in Math. and Philosophy magna cum laude, Fordham U., 1967; Lic. in Sacred Theology cum laude, Philosophische und Theologische Hochschule Sankt Georgen, Frankfurt, West Germany, 1971; MPhil, Oxford U., 1974; MA, PhD in Econ., Princeton U., 1979. Ordained Jesuit priest Roman Cath. Ch., 1971. Tchr. math. Regis H.S., N.Y.C., 1967-68; asst. campus minister Fordham U., 1971-72, Princeton U., 1975-78, preceptor, 1976-77; asst. chairperson grad. studies Fordham U., 1984-88, dir. program internat. polit. econ. and devel., 1981-83, 87-88, asst. chairperson dept. econs., 1979-82, 88-89, asst. prof. econs., 1978-89, assoc. prof. econs., 1989-90; corp. v.p. Marquette U., 1990-93; pres. Loyola U. Chgo., 1993—. Vis. fellow Woodstock Theol. Ctr., Washington, summer 1982; sabbatical Santa Clara U., 1989-90; master Queen's Ct. Residential Coll., 1987-90; chmn. responsible investment com. N.Y. province SJ, 1986-88, mem. fin. com., 1986-88; mem. joint commn. govtl. rels. of Am. Coun. Edn., 1994—; mem. exec. com. Nat. Planning Com. Jesuit Assembly '89, 1988-90. Contbr. articles to profl. jours. Founder, moderator Friends of Loyola, 1987-90; pres. Univ. Neighborhood Housing Corp., 1986-90, Maroon Enterprises, Inc., 1986-90; trustee Canisius Coll., Buffalo, 1983-88, 89-94, Loyola Marymount U., L.A., 1996—, John Carroll U., University Heights, Ohio, 1996—; bd. dirs. Corp. Cmty. Schs. of Am., 1993—; promoter PIVOT H.S. and Middle Sch. with Milw. Pub. Schs., 1990-93; mem. Greater Milw. Edn. Trust, 1990-93; mem. steering com., chair edn. task force Milw. Cmty. Traffic Safety Com., 1991-93; mem. steering com. Libr. Literacy Soc. Milw., 1991-93; mem. scholarship com. Knitworkers Union Local 155, N.Y.C., 1982-90; mem. Princeton Schs. Com. N.Y. Region, 1985-88, chmn. Federation of Indp. Colls. and Univs., 1999—. Mellon grantee Fordham U., summer 1983, summer grantee Fordham U., 1979, Princeton U. fellow, 1974-78. Office: Loyola U Chgo 820 N Michigan Ave Chicago IL 60611-2147

PIDGEON, JOHN ANDERSON, headmaster; b. Lawrence, Mass., Dec. 20, 1924; s. Alfred H. and Nora (Regan) P.; children: John Anderson, Regan S., Kelly; m. Barbara Hafer, May 1986. Grad., Phillips Acad., 1943; BA, Bowdoin Coll., 1949; Ed.D., Bethany Coll., 1973; D.Litt., Washington and Jefferson Coll., 1979. Instr. Latin, adminstrv. asst. to headmaster Deerfield Acad., 1949-57; headmaster Kiskiminetas Springs Sch., Saltsburg, Pa., 1957—. Dir. Saltburg Savs. & Trust. Trustee Winchester-Thurston Sch. Served as ensign USNR, 1943-46. Mem. New Eng. Swimming Coaches Assn. (pres. 1956-57), Cum Laude Soc., Delta Upsilon. Home and Office: Kiski Sch 1888 Brett Ln Saltsburg PA 15681-8951

PIDGEON, LESLEA SHARON, artist, writer; b. Dayton, Ohio, Jan. 5, 1940; d. Charles Henry and Lettie Kathleen (Myers) P. Student, Brenau Coll., 1958-59, Dayton Art Inst., 1959-63, George Washington U., 1970's, Wright State U., Dayton, 1977. Office worker, Dayton, 1958-69; clk.-typist U.S. Army, 1969-77; trainee signal U.S. Army Res., Wright-Patterson AFB, Ohio, 1977-78; clk.-typist VA, Dayton, 1977, Def. Electronics Supply Ctr., Kettering, Ohio, 1977-79; illustrator Aero. Sys. Ctr., Wright-Patterson AFB, 1979-84; clk.-typist Smithsonian Instn., Washington, 1984-88. Exhibited in group show Nat. Capitol Ceramic Assn., 1998 (3d pl. award); contbr. poetry to books, jours. Democrat. Avocations: videos, tapes, jewelry, photography.

PIDOT, WHITNEY DEAN, lawyer; b. N.Y.C., Mar. 2, 1944; s. George B. and Virginia (Ulrich) P.; m. Jeanne Stoddard, April 23, 1973; children: Whitney Dean Jr., Philip Martin, Seth Thayer. AB magna cum laude, Harvard U., 1966; JD, MBA, Columbia U., 1970. Bar: N.Y. 1971. Ptnr. Shearman & Sterling, N.Y.C., 1970, global mng. ptnr., 1998—2002, mem. exec. goup, 1998—2003, Asia mng. ptnr., 2001—03; chair Goelet Co. LLC, 2004—. Mem. adv. bd. Barclays Bank N.Y., 1989-92, Molecular Tool, Inc. (biotech.) Balt., 1991-96, Equine Genetic Rsch. Ptnrs., Balt., 1991-95; trustee, vice chair Winthrop Univ. Hosp., Mineola, N.Y.; bd. dirs. Oneida Ltd., NORIC Corp., North Ctrl. Oil Corp., Houston, Cold Spring Harbor Labs., N.Y. Mayor, Village of Matinecock, Locust Valley, N.Y., 1977-92; vice chmn. North Shore Mayors Com., Long Island, N.Y., 1980-92; bd. dirs. Nassau County (N.Y.) Village Officials Assn., 1978-80; commr. Locust Valley Fire Dist., 1979-93. Mem. N.Y. Bar Assn., Piping Rock Club (pres. 1988-94), Union Club N.Y.C., Phi Delta Phi. Republican. Home: Matinecock Farms PO Box 653 Locust Valley NY 11560 Office: Shearman & Sterling 599 Lexington Ave Ste C-2 New York NY 10022-6030

PIECH, MARGARET ANN, mathematics professor; b. Bridgewater, N.S., Can., Apr. 6, 1942; d. Frederick Cecil and Margaret Florence (Laschinger) Garrett; m. Kenneth Robert Piech, June 19, 1965; children: Garrett Andrew, Marjorie Ann. BA, Mt. Allison U., Sackville, N.B., Can., 1962; PhD, Cornell U., 1967. Asst. prof. SUNY, Buffalo, 1967-72, assoc. prof., 1972-78, prof. math., 1978—. Cons. NSF, Washington, 1980-81, Aspen Analytics, Buffalo, 1986—; v.p. Seventy Niagara Svcs., 1990—. Contbr. articles to profl. jours. Woodrow Wilson fellow, 1962-63; grantee NSF, 1976-85, U.S. Army Rsch. Office, 1985-89. Mem. IEEE, Am. Math. Soc., Assn. Computing Machinery, Henry's Fork Found. Avocation: fly fishing. Office: U Buffalo Dept Math 244 Mathematics Bldg Buffalo NY 14260-0001

PIEDMONT, RICHARD STUART, lawyer; b. Niskayuna, N.Y., Mar. 28, 1948; s. Henry Stuart and Lucille (Gagnon) P.; m. Marcia J. Quick, Apr. 11, 1981; children: Denise Nicole Rochette, Michael Norman Rochette, Alexandria Q. BA, U. Notre Dame, 1971. Bar: N.Y. 1977, U.S. Dist. Ct. (no. dist.) N.Y. 1977. Pres. Phoenix Abstract Corp., Albany, N.Y., 1979-84, v.p., 1984-89; ptnr. Piedmont & Rutnik, Albany, 1980-85, Devine, Piedmont & Rutnik, Albany, 1985-89; 58482 Phoenix Abstract Corp., Albany, N.Y., 1979-84; pvt. practice Piedmont Law Firm, 1990-95; ptnr. Harris Beach, LLP (formerly Harris Beach & Wilcox LLP), Albany, 1995—2001, Piedmont Law Firm, Latham, NY, 2001—. Founding bd. dirs. Make-a-Wish Found. of Northeastern N.Y. Mem. N.Y. State Bar Assn., N.Y. State Land Title Assn., Ea. N.Y. Land Surveyors Assn., Aircraft Owners and Pilots Assn., Notre Dame Club Northeastern N.Y. Democrat. Roman Catholic. Home: 1016 N Country Club Dr Niskayuna NY 12309-5405 Office: Piedmont Law Firm 4 British American Blvd Latham NY 12110 E-mail: rich@piedmontlawfirm.com.

PIEHLER, WENDELL HOWARD, organist, choir director, fund raiser; b. Lyons, Kans., Sept. 21, 1936; s. Oscar Harold and Bessie Matilda (Colberg) P.; m. Nancy J. Nyren, Nov. 2, 1974. BM summa cum laude, Southwestern Coll., 1958; MusM, Yale U., 1961, MMA, 1970; PhD, U. Conn., 1985. Organist, asst. Yale U., New Haven, 1969-71; organist, choir dir. Whitneyville Congl. Ch., Hamden, Conn., 1969-72; music dir. United Ch. of Green, New Haven, 1973; choir dir. Salem Luth. Ch., Bridgeport, Conn., 1974; organist, choir dir. St. Peter's Episcopal Ch., Cheshire, Conn., 1976-86, Temple Mishkan Israel, Hamden, Conn., 1971—. Mem. vestry Trinity Episcopal Ch. on the Green, New Haven, 1994-97, 2003—; sr. adminstrv. asst. Med. Devel. Yale U., 1980-90, office mgr., 1990-94, bus. mgr., 1994-2000, (retired); mem. faculty Colby Sawyer Coll., 1961-70, Conn. Coll., 1976; adminstrv. asst. Gordon Sci. Confs., 1961-72. Rec. artist Lyrichord Disc.; patentee in field. Lectr. Neighborhood Music Sch., New Haven, 1975-85; chmn. Lyons H.S. Scholarship Fund, 1983—; asst. registrar New Haven Dem. Com., 1984-89, moderator, 1989-92; mem. pres.'s coun. Southwestern Coll., 1987—. Recipient Service award Congregation Mishkan Israel, 1985; grantee Conn. Commn. Arts, 1976, U. Conn., 1984. Mem. Shubert Theatre Gold Club, Long Wharf Theatre, Mory's Assn., Nat. Cathedral Assn., Order of Mound, Am. Legion, Nat. Cathedral Assn., Met. Opera Guild, Yale Club N.Y.C. Avocations: swimming, skiing, travel, cultural events. Home: Crown Towers 123 York St Apt 18G New Haven CT 06511-5640 E-mail: wndllpiehler@aol.com.

PIEKNIK, REBECCA ANNE, technologist, educator; b. Detroit, Sept. 30, 1960; AA in Allied Health, Baker Coll. Flint, 1998, BS in Health Svc. Adminstrn., postgrad., Baker Coll. Flint, 2002—. Cert. surg. technologist. Clin. instr. Baker Coll. Flint, 1999—; cert. surg. technologist Pontiac Osteopathic Hosp., Mich., 2001—02; program dir. surg. tech. Oakland C.C./William Beaumont Hosp., 2002—. Home: 5190 Timber Ridge Trl Clarkston MI 48346 Office Phone: 248-898-7685.

PIEL, EMIL J. retired science and engineering educator; b. Fairview, NJ, Apr. 17, 1918; s. Harry and Anna (Decker) P.; m. Elizabeth Mayer Lautenschlager, Apr. 7, 1945 (dec. July 1995); two children; m. Maybelle Rodgeres Buck, Sept. 15, 2001. BA, Montclair State U., 1940, MA, 1947; EdD, Rutgers U., 1960. Physics tchr. Ft. Lee (N.J.) H.S., 1940-41, 45-48; airway traffic controller FAA, Jacksonville, Fla., 1941-42; combat pilot USMC, South Pacific, 1942-45; physics tchr. Caldwell (N.J.) H.S., 1948-52; sci. dept. chair East Orange (N.J.) H.S., 1952-60; prin. West Essex H.S., North Caldwell, N.J., 1960-66; chair dept. sci. & technology SUNY, Stony Brook, 1966-87, prof. emeritus, 1987—. Co-author: The Man Made World, 1972, Technology: Handle with Care, 1978. Fellow AAAS; mem. Ret. Officers Assn. Home and Office: 459 Passaic Ave C300 West Caldwell NJ 07006 E-mail: jpiel8402@aol.com.

PIELE, PHILIP KERN, education infosystems educator; b. Portland, Oreg., May 14, 1935; s. Theodore R. and Helen D. (Hanson) P.; m. Sandra Jean Wright, Aug. 10, 1963; children: Melissa, Kathryn. BA, Wash. State U., 1957; student, U. Wash., 1960, San Jose State U., 1964; MS, U. Oreg., 1963, PhD, 1968. From asst. prof. to prof. ednl. policy and mgmt. U. Oreg., Eugene, 1968—, mem. faculty applied info. mgmt. program, 1989-99, dir. numerous ednl. orgns. and coms. Coll. Edn., 1968—; dir. clearinghouse on ednl. mgmt. U. Oreg., Edn. Resources Info. Ctr. (ERIC), Eugene, 1969—2003; assoc. dir. U. Oreg., Ctr. for Ednl. Policy and Mgmt., Eugene, 1973-76; head dept. ednl. leadership, tech. and adminstrn. U. Oreg., Eugene, 1997-99, dir. clearing house on ednl. policy, mgmt., 2004—. Vis. lectr. U. Western Australia, Monashe U., U. New S. Wales, other Australian Univs., 1973; vis. prof. Ontario Inst. for Studies in Edn., U. Toronto, 1974; vis. scholar Stanford U., 1984; exec. sec. Oreg. Sch. Study Coun., 1980-97; dir. Networks and Comms. Ctr. for Advanced Tech. in Edn., 1984-92. Author numerous books, chpts.; editor numerous books; contbr. articles to profl. jours. Bd. dirs. Oreg. Bach Festival, Eugene, 1980-83, Oreg. Mozart Players, Eugene, 1995-97, Eugene Opera, 2001—, mem. The Round Table of Eugene, 2000—. Mem.: Am. Ednl. Rsch. Assn. (sec. adminstrn. divsn. 1991—93), Nat. Sch. Devel. Coun. (pres. 1985—86), Ednl. Law Assn. (pres. 1977—78). Office: Clearinghouse on Ednl Policy and Mgmt 5207 U Oreg Eugene OR 97403-5207 E-mail: ppiele@uoregon.edu.

PIELET, BRUCE WILLIAM, obstetrician; b. Chgo., 1957; MD, Loyola U., 1981. Bd. cert. ob-gyn., bd. cert. maternal and fetal medicine. Resident ob-gyn. U. Chgo., 1981—85; fellow maternal fetal medicine Northwestern U., Chgo., 1985—87; physician Advocate Luth. Gen. Hosp., Park Ridge, Ill. Office: Luth Gen Hosp Ste 325 1875 Dempster St Park Ridge IL 60068-1127

PIEMME, THOMAS EUEGENE, medical educator; BS with high honors, U. Pitts., 1954, MD, 1958; postgrad., Ohio State U., 1964-65. Diplomate Nat. Bd. Med. Examiners; cert. Am. Bd. Family Practice. Intern Health Ctr. Hosps., Pitts., 1958-59, asst. resident in medicine, 1959-60; jr. asst. resident in medicine Peter Bent Brigham Hosp., Boston, 1960-61, fellow/AHA, asst. in medicine, 1961-63; rsch. cardiologist, chief bioanalysis br. Envrion. Med. Div. USAF, Wright-Patterson AFB, Ohio, 1964-66; asst. prof. medicine U. Pitts. Sch. of Medicine, 1966-69; asst. chief of medicine Presbyn. U. Hosp., Pitts., 1966-69; prof. medicine, dir. Divsn. Gen. Medicine George Washington U. Sch. of Medicine, Washington, 1969-74; various to prof. health care scis. and medicine, assoc. dean George Washington U. Sch. Medicine, Washington, 1977-98, prof. emeritus, 1998—. Contbr. articles to profl. jours. and publs. Maj. USAF. Scholar of John and Mary Markle Found., 1966-71; recipient Disting. Svc. award Nat. Bd. Med. Examiners, 1984, others. Mem. AAAS, AMA, AAUP, Am. Fedn. Clin. Rsch., Aerospace Med. Assn., Assn. Am. Med. Colls., Am. Soc. Internal Medicine, Am. Heart Assn., Soc. Tchrs. of Family Medicine, Assn. Phys. Asst. Programs, Am. Acad. Family Physicians, Alliance for Continuing Med. Edn., Soc. for Med. Decision Making (adminstrv. dir.), Phi Beta Kappa, Alpha Omega Alpha, others. Office: George Washington U Office Continuing Edn 2300 K St NW Washington DC 20037-1700

PIEN, HOWARD, pharmaceutical executive; b. 1958; BS, MIT; MBA, Carnegie Mellon U. V.p. & dir. product mktg.-US SmithKline Beecham, 1992—93, v.p. & dir. new product devel.-US, 1991—92, v.p. & dir. mktg.-US, 1993—95, mng. dir. & sr. v.p.-UK, 1995—97, sr. v.p. & dir.-North Asia, 1997; pres. pharm. internat. GlaxoSmithKline, 2000—03; pres., CEO & dir. Chiron Corp., Emeryville, Calif., 2003—, chmn., 2004—. Office: Chiron Corp 1560 Horton St Emeryville CA 94608-2916

PIEPER, DAROLD D. lawyer; b. Vallejo, Calif., Dec. 30, 1944; s. Walter A. H. and Vera Mae (Ellis) P.; m. Barbara Gillis, Dec. 20, 1969; 1 child, Christopher Radcliffe. AB, UCLA, 1967; JD, USC, 1970. Bar: Calif. 1971. Ops. rsch. analyst Naval Weapons Ctr., China Lake, Calif., 1966-69; assoc. Richards, Watson & Gershon, L.A., 1970-76, ptnr., 1976—; gen. counsel Foothill Transit, 2000—, Greater L.A. County Vector Control Dist., 2001—, Tri-City Mental Health Ctr., 2003—; spl. counsel L.A. Unified Sch. Dist., 2000—04. Spl. counsel L.A. County Transp. Commn., 1984-93, L.A. County Met. Transp. Authority, 1993-94; commr. L.A. County Delinquency and Crime Commn., 1983-94, pres., 1987-91; chmn. L.A. County Delinquency Prevention Planning Coun., 1987-90. Contbr. articles to profl. jours. Peace officer Pasadena (Calif.) Police Res. Unit, 1972-87, dep. comdr., 1979-81, comdr., 1982-84; chmn. pub. safety commn. City of La Canada Flintridge, Calif., 1977-82, commr. 1977-88; bd. dirs. La Canada Flintridge Coordinating Council, 1975-82, pres. 1977-78; exec. dir. Cityhood Action Com., 1975-76; chmn. Youth Opportunities United, Inc., 1990-96, vice-chmn. 1988-89, bd. dirs. 1988-96; mem. L.A. County Justice Systems Adv. Group, 1987-92; trustee Lanterman Hist. Mus. Found., 1989-94, Calif. City Mgmt. Found., 1992—. Recipient commendation for Community Service, L.A. County Bd. Suprs., 1978, Commendation for Svc. to Youth, 1996. Mem. La Canada Flintridge C. of C. and Cmty. Assn. (pres. 1981, bd. dirs. 1976-83), Peace Officers Assn., L.A. County, UCLA Alumni Assn. (life), L.A. County Bar Assn., Calif. Bar Assn., ABA, U. So. Calif. Law Alumni Assn. Office: Richards Watson & Gershon 40th Fl 355 S Grand Ave Los Angeles CA 90071-3101 Office Phone: 213-626-8484. Business E-Mail: dpieper@rwglaw.com.

PIEPER, MICHAEL JOSEPH, freelance/self-employed television producer; b. Detroit, July 12, 1958; s. Frank John Pieper and Marie Yolanda Dansereau. Actor Quixote Video, Calif., 1981—92, interview host, 1983—85, owner and prodr., 1981—. Mem.: Internat. Platform Assn. (life). Office: Quixote Video #502 16787 Beach Blvd Huntington Beach CA 92647-4848 E-mail: angelfeather2001@hotmail.com.

PIEPER, PATRICIA RITA, artist; b. Paterson, N.J., Jan. 28, 1923; d. Francis William and Barbara Margaret (Ludwig) Farabaugh; m. George F. Pieper, July 1, 1941 (dec. May 3, 1981); 1 child, Patricia Lynn; m. Russell W. Watson, Dec. 9, 1989. Student, Baron von Palm, 1937-39, Deal (N.J.) Conservatory, 1939, 40, Utah State U., 1950-52; student Baron von Palm, 1937—39, student Deal (N.J.) Conservatory, 1939—40, student Utah State U., 1950—52. One-woman shows include Charles Russell Mus., Great Falls, Mont., 1955, Fisher Gallery, Washington, 1966, Tampa City Libr., 1977-81, 83, 84, Ctr. Pl. Art Ctr., Brandon, Fla., 1985; exhibited in group shows Davidson Art Gallery, Middletown, Conn., 1968, Helena (Mont.) Hist. Mus., 1955, Dept. Commerce Alaska Statehood Show, 1959, Joslyn Mus., Omaha, 1961, Denver Mus. Natural History, 1955, St. Joseph's Hosp. Gallery, 1980, 82, 84-86; represented in pvt. collections. Pres. Bell Lake Assn., 1976-78, 79; mem. Pasco County (Fla.) Water Adv. Coun., 1978—, chmn., 1979-82, 83-84, 86-88, 92—; gov.'s appointee to S.W. Fla. Water Mgmt. Dist., Hillsborough River Basin Bd., 1981-82, 84-87, sec., 1988-91, vice chmn., 1992; active Save Our Rivers program, 1982-84, 85-86, 92—; ad hoc chmn., 1991-92; mem. adv. bd. Fla. Suncoast Expwy., 1988-90; pres. Bell Lake Assn., 1986, 87; mem. adv. bd. Tampa YMCA, 1979-80. Winner photog. competition Gen. Tel. Co. of Fla., 1979; recipient Outstanding Svc. award Bell Lake Assn., 1987, Meml. award Land O'Lake Bd. of Realtors, 1989, Appreciation award Southwest Fla. Water Mgmt. Dist., 1993, finalist, Awds. of Excellence, Photographers winner in top 100 out of 8,000 Nat. Wildlife Fedn. competition, 1986, 1st place photography MacDill AFB, 1991. Mem. VFW (life), Nat. League Am. Pen Women (v.p. Tampa 1976-78, Woman of Yr. award 1977-78), Tampa Art Mus., Ret. Officer's Wives Assn., Land O'Lakes C. of C. (bd. dirs. 1981-82, Outstanding Svc. award 1980), Fla. Geneal. Soc., West State Archaeol. Soc. (distaff mem.), Ret. Officer's Assn., Lutz Club, Land O'Lakes Women's Club, Moose. Home: 3304 E Derry Dr Sebastian FL 32958-8577 *I believe that those of us born with the gift of creativity are truly blessed. It is our duty to make the most of, and be worthy of that gift. And if we work hard and sincerely apply ourselves a chosen few will become immortal through the beauty we leave behind for others to enjoy. As an artist and photographer I am truly blessed.*

PIEPGRAS, DAVID G. neurosurgeon, educator; b. Luverne, Minn., 1940; MD, U. Minn., 1965. Diplomate Am. Bd. Neurol. Surgery. Intern Mary Hitchcock Hosp., Hanover, Minn., 1965—66; resident in surgery Hennepin County Gen. Hosp., Mpls., 1969—70; resident in neurol. surgery Mayo Grad. Sch. Medicine, Rochester, 1970—74; staff St. Mary's Hosp., Rochester, 1974—, Rochester Meth. Hosp., 1974—; staff cons. dept. neurosurgery Mayo Clinic, Rochester, 1974—, prof. neurol. surgery. Bd. dirs. Am. Bd. Neurol. Surgery, 2002—. Fellow: ACS; mem.: AMA, Congress of Neurol. Surgeons, Am. Acad. Neurol. Surgeons. Office: Mayo Clinic Dept Neurol Surgery Rochester MN 55905-0001

PIEPHO, LEE (EDWARD LEE PIEPHO), humanities educator; b. Detroit, Jan. 10, 1942; s. Edward Ernest and Dolores Faye (Dowis) P.; m. Susan Brand, June 13, 1964. AB, Kenyon Coll., 1964; MA, Columbia U., 1966; PhD, U. Va., 1972. Instr. Sweet Briar Coll., Va., 1969—72, asst. prof., 1972—78, assoc. prof., 1978—83, prof., 1983—94, Shallenberger Brown prof., 1994—, dept. chmn., 2000—01, coord. European civilization program, 1986—89. Author: Holofernes' Mantuan, 2001; translator, editor: Adulescentia: The Eclogues of Mantuan, 1989; contbr. articles to profl. jours. SIMRS fellow, 1979, Dulin fellow Folger Shakespeare Libr., 1989-90, Mednick fellow, 1996. Mem. Internat. Assn. for Neo-Latin Studies, Modern Lang. Assn. Am., Renaissance Soc. Am. Avocations: tennis, scuba diving. Home: 137 Woodland Rd Sweet Briar VA 24595-9999 Office: Sweet Briar Coll Dept English Sweet Briar VA 24595 E-mail: lpiepho@sbc.edu.

PIEPHO, ROBERT WALTER, pharmacy educator, researcher; b. Chgo., July 31, 1942; s. Walter August and Irene Elizabeth (Huybrecht) Apfel; m. Mary Lee Wilson, Dec. 10, 1981. BS in Pharmacy, U. Ill.-Chgo., 1965; PhD in Pharmacology, Loyola U., Maywood, Ill., 1972. Registered pharmacist, Ill., Colo. Assoc. prof. U. Nebr. Med. Ctr., Omaha, 1970-78; prof. pharmacy, assoc. dean Sch. Pharmacy U. Colo., Denver, 1978-86; prof. pharmacol., dean U. Mo. Sch. Pharmacy, Kansas City, 1987—. Contbr. articles to profl. jours., chpts. to books. Pres. Club Monaco Homeowners Assn., Denver, 1980-82. Named Outstanding Tchr. U. Nebr. Coll. Pharmacy, 1975; recipient Arthur Hassan Colo. Pharmacal Assn., 1983, Excellence in Teaching U. Colo. Med. Sch., 1983 Fellow Am. Coll. Clin. Pharmacology (regent 1983-88, 91-96, pres. 1998-2000); mem. Am. Soc. Hosp. Pharmacists, Am. Soc. Pharmacology and Exptl. Therapeutics, Rho Chi Roman Catholic. Office: U Mo Sch Pharmacy 5005 Rockhill Rd Kansas City MO 64110-2239

PIERARD, RICHARD VICTOR, history educator; b. Chgo., May 29, 1934; s. John Perkins and Diana Florence (Russell) P.; m. Charlene Burdett, June 15, 1957; children: David, Cynthia. BA, Calif. State U., L.A., 1958, MA, 1959; PhD, U. Iowa, 1964. Prof. history Ind. State U., Terre Haute, 1964-2000, emeritus, 2000—. Vis. prof. Greenville (Ill.) Coll., 1972-73, Free Theol. Acad., Seeheim, Fed. Republic Germany, 1971, 78, Regent Coll., Vancouver, B.C., Can., 1975, Trinity Evang. Div. Sch., Deerfield, Ill., 1982, No. Bapt. Theol. Sem., Lombard, Ill., 1987, Fuller Theol. Sem., Pasadena, Calif., 1988, 91, Moscow Theol. Sem., 1997, 99, 2001, Gordon Coll., Wenham, Mass., 2000-2001; scholar-in-residence Gordon Coll., 2000—; Fulbright prof. U. Frankfurt, Fed. Republic Germany, 1984-85; Fulbright prof. U. Halle, German Dem. Republic, 1989-90, Gordon Coll., Wenham, Mass., 2000—; mem. nat. adv. coun. Ams. United for Separation of Ch. and State, 1985—; pres. Greater Terre Haute Ch. Fedn., 1987-88; del. Lausanne II Congress on World Evang., Manila, Philippines, 1989; mem. Bapt. Heritage Study Commn., Bapt. World Alliance, 1990—. Author: The Unequal Yoke: Evangelical Christianity and Political Conservatism, 1970, Bibliography on the Religious Right in America, 1986; co-author: Twilight of the Saints: Biblical Christianity and Civil Religion, 1978, Civil Religion and the Presidency, 1988, Two Kingdoms: The Church and Culture through the Ages, 1993, The Revolution of the Candles: Christians in the Revolution of the German Democratic Republic, 1996, The New Millennium Manual, 1999; contbr. articles to religious and hist. publs. Del. White House Conf. on Librs., Washington, 1979, Ind. Dem. Party Convention, Indpls., 1980, 88; precinct committeeman Dem. Party, Terre Haute, 1978-80, 90—; mem. Ind. Gov.'s Adv. Com. on Librs., 1980-81. With U.S. Army, 1954-56. Recipient Terre award for cmty. svc., Terre Haute, Ind., 1991; Fulbright scholar U. Hamburg (Fed. Republic Germany), 1962-63; rsch. fellow U. Aberdeen (Scotland), 1978; Chavanne scholar Baylor U., 1988. Mem. Conf. on Faith and History (sec.-treas. 1967—), Evang. Theol. Soc. (pres. 1985), Am. Hist. Assn., Am. Soc. Ch. History, Ind. Assn. Historians, Am. Soc. Missiology, Internat. Assn. Mission Studies, Soc. for Encouragement and Preservation of Barbershop Quartet Singing in Am., Am. Bapt. Hist. Soc. (bd. mgrs. 1993—). Democrat. Home: 11 Pine Rd Beverly MA 01915

PIERCE, ALLAN DALE, engineering educator, researcher, editor; b. Clarinda, Iowa, Dec. 18, 1936; s. Franklin Dale and Ruth Pauline (Wright) P.; m. Penelope Claffey, Oct. 27, 1961; children: Jennifer Irene, Bradford Loren. BS, N.Mex. Coll. Agrl. and Mechanic Arts, 1957; PhD, MIT, 1962. Registered profl. engr., Mass. Staff rschr. Rand Corp., Santa Monica, Calif., 1961-63; sr. staff scientist Avco Corp., Wilmington, Mass., 1963-66; asst. prof. MIT, Cambridge, 1966-68, assoc. prof., 1968-73; prof. mech. engring. Ga. Inst. Tech., Atlanta, 1973-76, Regent's prof., 1976-88; Leonhard chair in engring. Pa. State U., University Park, 1988-93; chmn. dept aerospace and mech. engring. Boston U., 1993-99, prof., 1993—. Vis. prof. Max Planck Inst., Goettingen, Fed. Republic Germany, 1976-77; vis. scientist Woods Hole Oceanographic Inst., 2002-03, adj. scientist, 2003-; cons. in field. Author: Acoustics: An Introduction to Its Physical Principles and Applications, 1981, editor phys. acoustics monograph series, 1988-97; editor Jour. Computation Acoustics, 1992-99; contbr. articles to profl. jours. Recipient Sr. U.S. Scientist award Alexander von Humboldt Found., 1976, Cert. of Recognition Nat. Aeronautics and Space Adminstrn., 1984, Per Bruel Gold medal for noise control and acoustics ASME, 1995; NSF fellow, 1957-60, Shell Oil fellow, 1960-61, Faculty fellow U.S. Dept. Transp., 1979-80. Fellow Acoustical Soc. Am. (editor-in-chief 1999—, Silver medal 1991, Rossing prize in acoustics edn. 2004), ASME (Rayleigh lectr. 1992, Per Bruel Gold medal 1995, chair Noise Control and Acoustics Divsn. 1999-2000); mem. IEEE, AIAA. Home: PO Box 339 East Sandwich MA 02537-0339 Office: Boston U Dept Aerospace & Mech Engring 110 Cummington St Boston MA 02215-2407 E-mail: adp@bu.edu.

PIERCE, BYRON JAMES, research scientist; b. Berwyn, Ill., Apr. 8, 1953; s. Byron Philip and Jean Pierce; m. Joanna Patricia Remes, Sept. 4, 1982; children: Byron Joseph, Natalie Anne. PhD, Ariz. State U., 1989. Visual systems team lead Air Force Rsch. Lab., Mesa, Ariz., 1978—. Sr. scientist Air Force Rsch. Lab., Mesa, Ariz., 1989—. Mem.: Assn. for Rsch. in Vision and Ophthalmology, Soc. for Info. Display, Human Factors and Ergonomics Soc. Achievements include human centered research and design of flight simulation visual systems. Office: Air Force Rsch Lab 6030 S Kent St Mesa AZ 85212

PIERCE, CALISA A. director; d. Les and Wilma L Avis; m. Jim Pierce, June 21, 1986; children: Kimberly, Kelsey, Kevin. BA, Marshall U., 1983, MA, 1996, EdS, 2003. Adj. faculty So. W.Va. Comm. & Tech. Coll., Logan, 1992—98, dir. divsn. chair transitional studies, 1998—. Mem.: Nat. Assn. Devel. Edn. (mem. com. 2003—), W.Va. Assn. Devel. Edn. (pres. 2002—03). Office: So WVa Comm & Tech Coll PO Box 2900 Mount Gay WV 25637

PIERCE, CAROLE JEAN, artist; b. Dallas, Sept. 7, 1950; d. Bertrum Robert and Dorothy Lillian (Meyer) Brownie; m. Lee Pierce, Mar. 13, 1970; 1 child, Brandon. BFA in Painting and Printmaking, So. Meth. U., 1972; MFA in Printmaking, Calif. Coll. Arts & Crafts, 1994. Advt. prodn. Zale Corp., Dallas, 1972; mgr. direct mail Halle Bros., Cleve., 1973-75; advt. art dir. Sanger Harris, Dallas, 1975-79; photography coord. Neiman Marcus, Horchow Collection, Dallas, 1979-81; freelance art & photography coord. San Francisco, 1982-83; writer, researcher Culinary Historians Boston, 1983-85; researcher for curator N.Y. Pub. Libr., N.Y.C., 1985-87; tchr., artist Kala Inst., Berkeley, Calif., 1987—. Guest instr. art history San Francisco State U., 2001; instr. independent studies Calif. Coll. of Arts and Crafts, Oakland, 1999; pvt. printmaking instr. for Mrs. Ann Getty, San Francisco, 98. Solo exhbns. include Joan Roebuck Gallery, Lafayette, Calif., 1994, Calif. Coll. Arts and Crafts, 1994, Shidoni Contemporary Gallery, Tesuque, N. Mex., 1995, Carole Pierce-Bill Weaver Painting and Sculpture, 1995, Draighead Green Gallery, Dallas, 1996, numerous others to Diane Nelson Fine Art, Laguna Beach, Calif., 2002; group exhbns. include Kala Inst., Berkeley, Calif., 1989, 92, Accurate Art Gallery, Sacramento, 1989, Matrix Gallery, Sacramento, 1989, Gallery House, Palo Alto, Calif., 1989, Orange County Ctr. Contemporary Art, Santa Ana, 1989, Coll. San Mateo, Calif., 1990, Pacific Art League, Palo Alto, 1990, Ford Aerospace Corp., San Jose, Calif., 1990, San Diego Art Inst., 1992, Shidoni Contemporary Gallery, 1993, U. Oreg., Eugene, 1994, Berkeley (Calif.) Art Ctr. Assn., 1994, Osaka (Japan) Found. Culture, 1994, Columbia (Mo.) Coll., 1995, Southwest Tex. State U., San Marcos, 1995, Amador County Arts Coun., Sutter Creek, Calif., 1995, Triton Mus. Arts Biennial Print and Drawing Competition and Exhbn., 1995, Gallery Route One, Point Reyes Calif., 1995, Mus. Moderna Art, N.Y.C., 1995, Barrett House Galleries, Dutchess County Art Assn., Poughkeepsie, N.Y., 1995, Pro Arts, Oakland, Calif., 1996, The Haggin Mus., Stockton, Calif., 1996, U. Hawaii, Hilo, 1996, The Munson Gallery, Santa Fe, N.Mex., 1998, numerous others to Craighead Green Gallery, Dallas, Tex., 2002, Michael Martin Galleries, San Francisco, 2003, and others; represented in permanent collections U.S. Embassy Nairobe, Kenya, Havana, Cuba, Harvard U., Sandoz Pharm., Fidelity Securities, Goldman Sachs Internat. Collection, Indsl. Light and Magic, Morgan Libr., N.Y.C., numerous pvt. collections. Vol. Mus. Modern Art, San Francisco; art coord. children's program, 1988-90. Recipient Monoprint award Pacific Art League, Palo Alto, Calif., 1990; juror award Hill Country Arts Found., Austin, Tex., 1991, 1st pl. award Calif. Coll. Arts & Crafts, Oakland, 1993, Berkeley Art Ctr. Assn. 10th Ann. Nat. Juried Exhbn., 1994, Monoprint award Nat. Acad. Design, N.Y.C. Mem. Am. Inst. Wine & Food, Internat. Wine & Food Soc., L.A. Printmakers Soc. (Monoprint award 1990). Avocations: reading, swimming, yoga, travel. Home: PO Box 1032 Ross CA 94957-1032 Studio: #2 Bridge Ave San Anselmo CA 94960

PIERCE, CHARLES EARL, software engineer, entrepreneur; s. Charles William and Carrie (Rankins) P.; m. Jan Saunders, Nov. 16, 1991. BS in Math., L.I. U., 1977. Cert. project mgmt. expert 2000, tech. mgmt. prof. Rsch. analyst Equitable Life, N.Y.C., 1977—80; systems analyst CTEK Software, N.Y.C., 1980—83; sr. v.p. CEP Hatteras, Ridgefield, NJ, 2001—; pres. CP Hatteras

Group, Inc. Cons. Nibor Assocs., N.Y.C., Vital Cons.; asst. v.p. Bank N.Y., 1987, Chase Mellon Fin. Group, 1997-2001, sr. v.p. 2001-2002; sr. exec. v.p. CePHatteras, N.Y.C., 2002-. Mem. IEEE, Prof. Tech. Mgrs., Hudson Valley Bus. Continuity Group, N.Y. Acad. Scis., Data Processing Mgmt. Assn., Assn. for Computing Machinery, Math. Assn. Am. Mem. Pentecostal Ch. Mem. Pentecostal Ch. Mem. Pentecostal Ch. Achievements include development of of English test interpreter/command processing for mainframe at CTEK Software; automated phased conversion of DMS system; intelligent training systems and customer systems.

PIERCE, CHARLES ELIOT, JR., library director, educator; b. Springfield, Mass., Dec. 25, 1941; s. C. Eliot and Dora Mason (Redway) P.; m. Barbara G. Hanson, Oct. 18, 1969; children: Sheila H., Charles Eliot III BA, Harvard U., 1964, MAT., 1966, PhD, 1970. Prof. English Vassar Coll., Poughkeepsie, N.Y., 1970-87; dir. Pierpont Morgan Library, N.Y.C., 1987—. Mem. vis. com. Harvard U., Harvard U. Art Mus., Vassar Coll. Art Gallery. Author: (literary criticism) The Religious Life of Samuel Johnson, 1983 Mem. Art Mus. Dirs., Johnsonians, Century Assn., Grolier Club, Walpole Soc., Knickerbocker Club. Episcopalian. Home: 11 Clinton Corners Rd Salt Point NY 12578-2502 Office: Pierpont Morgan Libr 29 E 36th St New York NY 10016-3490 Office Phone: 212-590-0305. E-mail: cpierce@morganlibrary.org.

PIERCE, CHESTER MIDDLEBROOK, retired psychiatrist, educator; b. Glen Cove, N.Y., Mar. 4, 1927; s. Samuel Riley and Hettie Elenor (Armstrong) P.; m. Jocelyn Patricia Blanchet, June 15, 1949; children: Diane Blanchet, Deirdre Anona. AB, Harvard U., 1948, MD, 1952; ScD (hon.), Westfield Coll., 1977, Tufts U., 1984; D in Engring. Tech. (hon.), Wentworth Inst. Tech., 1997. Instr. psychiatry U. Cin., 1957-60; asst. prof. psychiatry U. Okla., 1960-62, prof., 1965-69; prof. edn. and psychiatry Harvard U., 1969—; pres. Am. Bd. Psychiatry and Neurology, 1977-78; ret. Mem. Polar Rsch. Bd.; cons. USAF. Author publs. on sleep disturbances, media, polar medicine, sports medicine, racism; mem. editl. bds. Advisor Children's TV Workshop; chmn. Child Devel. Assn. Consortium; bd. dirs. Action Children's TV. With M.C. USNR, 1953-55. Fellow: Brit. Royal Coll. Psychiatrists (hon.), Royal Australian and New Zealand Coll. Psyschiatrists (hon.); mem.: Am. Acad. Arts and Scis., Am. Orthopsychiat. Assn. (pres. 1983—84), Black Psychiatrists Am. (chmn.), Inst. Medicine of NAS. Democrat. Home: 17 Prince St Jamaica Plain MA 02130-2725

PIERCE, DANIEL THORNTON, physicist; b. L.A., July 16, 1940; s. Daniel Gordon Pierce and Celia Francis Thornton Thayer; m. Barbara Harrison, Nov. 19, 1988; children: Jed, Maia, Stephen. BS, Stanford U., 1962, PhD in Applied Physics, 1970; MA, Wesleyan U., Middletown, Conn., 1966. NSF rsch. asst. materials sci. dept. Stanford U., 1961; lectr in physics U.S. Peace Corps, Kathmandu, Nepal, 1962-64; rsch. asst. Wesleyan U., 1964-66, Stanford Electronics Lab., 1966-70, rsch. assoc., 1970-71; rsch. staff Solid State Physics Lab., Swiss Fed. Inst. Tech., 1971-75; physicist Nat. Inst. Standards and Tech. (formerly Nat. Bur Standards), Gaithersburg, Md., 1975—, fellow, 1994—. Contbr. chpts. to books, numerous articles to profl. jours. Trustee Unitarian Ch. of Rockville, Md., 1994-96 Recipient IR-100 award R&D Mag., 1980, 85, Gold medal Dept. Commerce, 1987, William P. Schlichter award Nat. Inst. Standards and Tech., 1992. Fellow Am. Phys. Soc. (exec. com. Materials Physics Divsn. 1998-2001), Am. Vacuum Soc. (surface sci. exec. com. 1984-88, Gaede-Langmuir prize 1994). Achievements include patents for source of spin polarized electrons, absorbed current and low energy spin polarization detectors; development of scanning electron microscopy with polarization analysis. Office: Nat Inst Standards and Tech Mail Stop 8412 Bldg 216 Rm A223 Gaithersburg MD 20899-8412 Business E-Mail: daniel.pierce@nist.gov.

PIERCE, DANNY PARCEL, artist, educator; b. Woodlake, Calif., Sept. 10, 1920; s. Frank Lester and Letitia Frances (Parcel) P.; m. Julia Ann Rasmussen, July 19, 1943; children: Julia Ann, Mary L., Danny L., Duane Nels. Student, Art Ctr. Sch., L.A., 1939, Chouinards Art Inst., 1940-41, 46-47, Am. Art Sch., N.Y.C., 1947-48, Bklyn. Mus. Art Sch., 1950-53; BFA, U. Alaska, 1963. Instr. Hunter Coll., N.Y.C., 1952-53, Burnley Sch. Art, Seattle, 1954-58, Seattle U., 1956-59; publ. Red Door Studio Press, Kent, Wash., 1959—; artist-in-res. U. Alaska, College, 1959-63; asst. prof. U. Wisc., Milw., 1964; head art dept. Cornish Sch. Allied Arts, Seattle, 1964-65; prof. art U. Wisc., Milw., 1965-84, prof. emeritus, 1984—. One-man shows include Contemporaries Gallery, N.Y.C., 1953, Handforth Gallery, Tacoma, Washington, 1958, U. Alaska, College, 1959, 63, 73, 74, Gonzaga U., Bradley Galleries, Milw., 1966, 68, 70, 72, 74, 76, 78-80, 82, Martin-Zambito Gallery, Seattle, 1997, 2002, Apple Blossom Time, 2000; father/son exhbn. 2002 Desert Images, Martin-Zambito Gallery, 1999; represented in permanent collections Bibliothèque Nationale, Paris, Mus. Modern Art, N.Y.C., Libr. Congress, Washington, Smithsonian Instn., Washington, Seattle Art Mus., U. Washington Henry Art Gallery, Bklyn. Mus., Princeton U., U. Alaska, U. So. Calif., William and Mary Coll., Oostduinkerke (Belgium) Nat. Fishing Mus., Nat. Mus. Sweden, Stockholm, Johnson Wax Found., Racine, Wisc., Gen. Mills Collection Art, Mpls., Huntington Libr., San Marino, Calif., various pvt. collections; pub. 26 ltd. edit. books, 1959-98. Recipient Best Oil Landscape award Conn. Acad. Fine Arts, Hartford, 1st Prize oil Kohler Gallery, Seattle, 1974, others; chosen one of twelve artists to represent State Wash. Expo 70, Osaka, Japan, rep. U.S. Internat. São Paulo Biannual Art Exhbn.; established archives at Golda Meier Libr., U. Wis.-Mils. Mem. Artist Equity Assn. (charter, pres. Seattle chpt. 1958), Am. Colorprint Soc., Internat. Arts and Letters (life). Office: Red Door Studio 404 Summit Ave N Kent WA 98030-4712

PIERCE, DAVID HYDE, actor; b. Albany, N.Y., Apr. 3, 1959; BA, Yale U., 1981. Appeared in plays Beyond Therapy, 1982, Holiday, 1982, Summer, 1983, That's It, Folks! 1983, Candida, 1984, The Seagull, 1984, The Grand Hysteric, 1984, The Three Zeks, 1984, Tartuffe, 1984, Donuts, 1985, Hamlet, 1986, The Author's Voice, 1987, The Maderati, 1987, Camille, 1987, The Cherry Orchard, 1988, Zero Positive, 1988, Much Ado About Nothing, 1988, The Heidi Chronicles, 1989, Elliot Loves, 1990, It's Only a Play, 1991; films include The Terminator, 1984, Moving Violations, 1985, Bright Lights, Big City, 1988, Crossing Delancey, 1988, Rocket Gibraltar, 1988, The Fisher King, 1991, Little Man Tate, 1991, Sleepless in Seattle, 1993, Addams Family Values, 1993, Wolf, 1994, Nixon, 1995, Hercules, 1998, A Bug's Life, 1998, Jackie's Back!, 1999, Mating Habits of the Earthbound Human, 1999, Isn't She Great, 2000, Chain of Fools, 2000, Osmosis Jones, 2001; TV series include The Powers That Be, 1993, Frasier, 1993— (seven Am. Comedy awards), Laud Weiner, 2001, Full Frontal, 2002, Treasure Planet (voice), 2002, Down with Love, 2003, wards 1994-2000, Emmy award, 1995, 98, 99, Golden Globe award, SAG Award, 1996, 2000, Q Award 1994, 95, 96, 98, TV Guide award, 2000.); prodr. Wet, Hot, American Summer, 2001. Recipient Emmy award, 1995, 98, 99, SAG award, 1996, 2000, Q award, 1994, 95, 96, 98, TV Guide award, 2000

PIERCE, DAVID R. educational administrator; AA in Math., Fullerton Coll., 1958; BA in Math., Long Beach State U., 1960, MA in Edn., 1961; MS in Math., Purdue U., 1965, PhD in Math. Edn., 1969. Math. instr. Orange Coast Coll., Costa Mesa, Calif., 1962-65; supr. math. student teaching Purdue U., Lafayette, Ind., 1965-66; chmn. natural scis. & math. divsn. Golden West Coll., Huntington Beach, Calif., 1966-67; dean instrn. Waubonsee C.C., Sugar Grove, Ill., 1967-70; supt., pres. North Iowa Area C.C., Mason City, 1970-80; exec. dir. Ill. C.C. Bd., Springfield, 1980-90; chancellor Va. C. C. Sys., Richmond, 1990-91; pres., chief exec. officer Am. Assn. C.C., Washington, 1991—; also joint Am. Assn. C.C./ACCT Commn. Fed. Rels. mem., 1984-86, 88-91; also bd. mem. Am. Assn. C.C., 1988-91, vice-chmn., 1990-91, chmn. task force on allied health, 1989-91, chmn. com. on fed. rels., 1990-91. Mem. Nat. Coun. State Dirs. Cmty. and Jr. Colls., 1981-91 (chmn. 1984-85), Ill. Employment & Edn. Subcabinet, 1980-90; cons., evaluator North Ctrl. Assn. Commn. Insts. Higher Edn. (commr.-at-large 1977-83). Mem. Ill. Econ. Devel. Subcabinet, 1980-90. Named Person of Yr. Nat. Coun. Cmty. Svcs. & Continuing Edn. Region 5, 1982, Nat. Person of Yr. Nat. Coun. Cmty. Svcs. & Continuing Edn., 1990; recipient Meritorious Svc. award Ill. C.C. Trustee Assn., 1988, Outstanding Ill. Citizen award Coll. Lake County, 1989, Outstanding Alumnus award Calif. C.C. League, 1991, Outstanding Alumnus award Fullerton Coll., 1992, B. Lamar Johnson Leadership award League for Innovation in the C.C., 1993. Mem. Nat. Policy Bd. Higher Edn. Instl. Accreditation, Washington Higher Edn. Secretariat, Nat. Alliance of Bus. Coun. on Workforce Excellence. Office: Am Assn Cmty Colls 1 Dupont Cir NW Ste 410 Washington DC 20036-1136

PIERCE, DIANE JEAN, artist; b. Evanston, Ill., Apr. 9, 1952; d. Kenneth William and Marjorie J. (Hansen) P.; m. William Carry Reuling, Sept. 8, 1991 (div. July 1992). BFA in Drawing and Painting, U. Utah, 1976. Illustrator Ensign Mag., Salt Lake City, 1977-79, Scott Foresman & Co. Pubs., Glenview, Ill., 1980, Children's Press, Chgo., 1981-82; mansion artist Adnan-Khoshagi's Devereaux Mansion, Salt Lake City, 1984-87; illustrator Friend Mag./Era Mag., Salt Lake City, 1978-80; artist-painter Lido Gallery, Park City, Utah, 1990-93, Thomas Charles Gallery, Las Vegas, Nev., 1994, Art Dimensions Gallery, Hollywood, Calif., 1994-96, Meyer Gallery, Park City, Utah, 1996-98; with Don Huntsman Gallery, Aspen, Colo., 1999—2001; artist Winter Olympics, Park City, Utah, 2002. Apprentice photographer Reynel Salgado Mirando, 1980 Elections, Acapulco, Mexico, 1980; juror exhbn. com. Alliance Gallery, Salt Lake Art Ctr., 1984, 85, invitational artist, fundraiser for Town and Country magazine: Women in Need, N.Y., 1998. Exhibited in group shows at New Genre, 1985, 5 Star Auction Invitational, 1985, Springville Nat. Salon, 1985, Utah Women Artists, 1985, Chase Mansion Guthrie Artists Show, 1986, Guthrie Artists, 1986, NAD, 1986, Eccles Art Ctr., 1986, 1987, Women's Show, 1987, 1989, 1991, 1993, Park City Open Painting Competition, 1989—90, 1993, Mus. Art, Alliance Gallery, Chase Mansion, Salt Lake Art Ctr., Tivoli Gallery, Cliff Lodge Gallery, U. Utah Mus. Art, Devereaux Mansion, 1984—87, Utah divsn. Assn. Women Artists traveling show, 1989—90, 100 Yrs.-100 Women traveling show, N.Y.C., 1989—91, Springville Mus. Art, 1992, Nat. Assn. Women ann. nat. competition, 1993, Janet Dumbar Interiors, Sun Valley, Idaho, 1991—93, Lido Gallery, 1990—93, Elouises' Interiors, Park City, Utah, 1993—98, Thomas Charles Gallery, 1994, Art Dimensions Gallery, 1994—96, Springville Mus. Art nat. competition, Art Space, 1995, Gallery Stroll, 1995, Nat. Assn. Women Artists ann., Soho, N.Y., 1995, Nat. Assn. Women Artists, Athens, Greece, 1996, NAWA NY Soho Show, 1999, Springville Mus. Natl. 75th April Salon, 1999—2000, Soho Nat. Assn. Women Artists, 1999, Represented in permanent collections Girl Scouts Hdqs., Salt Lake City, Profl. Figure Skaters Hdqs., Sun Valley, Springville Mus. Art, Moonie & O'Conner, Cin., Van Cott, Bagley, Cornwall & McCarthy, Salt Lake City, also pvt. collections; contbr. color plates Painting and Sculptors by Serdirect, Olphin, 1985, color plates in Visual Selling and Design by Mary Irish, 1990, articles to profl. jours. Recipient Art Dirs. award, Era Mag., 1979, Dirs. award, U. Utah Statewide Competition, Springville Mus. Fine Art, 1987, Best of Show, Eccles Statewide Competition, Ogden Utah, 1987, Best Traditional Painting, Nat. Assn. U. Women, Utah divsn., Ogden, 1989, Best of Show, Open Painting Exhbn., Kimball Art Ctr., Park City, Utah, 1989, 3rd pl. open painting competition, Kimball Art Ctr, 1990, Visual Merchandising & Design Mag. award, Designer Excellence, 1990, Best of Show open painting exhbn, Kimball Art Ctr., Park City, 1993, award of merit, Springville Mus. Fine Art, 1995; grantee, Artists Fellowship, Inc., N.Y.C., 1993. Mem. Nat. Assn. Women Artists (N.Y. chpt., Susan Kahn award 1987), Nat. Mus. Women in Arts.

PIERCE, DONALD FAY, lawyer; b. Bexley, Miss., Aug. 28, 1930; s. Percy O. and Lavada S. (Stringfellow) Pierce; m. Norma Faye Scribner, June 5, 1954; children: Kathryn Pierce Peake, D. F. Jr., John S., Jeff G. BS, U. Ala., 1956, JD, 1958. Bar: Ala. 1958, U.S. Ct. Appeals (5th cir.) 1958, U.S. Dist. Ct. (no., mid. and so. dists.) Ala. 1958, U.S. Ct. Appeals (11th cir.) 1982. Law clk. to presiding judge U.S. Dist. Ct. (so. dist.) Ala., 1958—59; ptnr. Hand, Arendall, Bedsole, Greaves & Johnston, Mobile, Ala., 1964—91, Pierce, Carr, Alford, Ledyard & Latta, P.C., 1991—; pvt. practice; of counsel Butlar Parras. Mem. Products Liability Adv. Coun., 1990—; bd. overseers Vanderbilt Cancer Ctr., 1994—. Contbr. articles to profl. jours. Trustee UMS Prep Sch., 1980—87. 1st lt. U.S. Army, 1951—53. Mem.: Def. Research Inst. (pres. 1987, chmn. 1988), Def. Counsel Trial Acad. (bd. dir. 1983—84), Internat. Assn. Def. Counsel, Am. Acad. Hosp. Attys., Fedn. Ins. and Corp. Counsel, Ala. Def. Lawyers Assn. (past pres.). Baptist. Home: 4452 Winnie Way Mobile AL 36608-2221 Office: Pierce Ledyard PC of counsel Butler Pappas LLP PO Box 161389 3801 Airport Blvd Mobile AL 36616 Office Phone: 251-338-3801.

PIERCE, DONALD SHELTON, retired orthopedic surgeon, educator; b. Castine, Maine, May 21, 1930; s. Frederick Ernest and Jeannie (Emmet) P.; m. Janet Ten Broeck, Dec. 29, 1956; children: Donald Shelton, Stanton ten Broeck, Frederick Ernest, Jennifer Emmet. AB cum laude, Harvard U., 1953, MD, 1957. Diplomate Am. Bd. Spine Surgery, Am. Bd. Orthop. Surgery. Intern U. Hosp., Cleve., 1957-58, resident, 1958-62; rsch. assoc. biomechanics lab. U. Calif., San Francisco, 1962-64; practice medicine specializing in orthopedic surgery San Francisco, 1962-64; instr. orthopedic surgery U. Calif. Med. Sch., San Francisco, 1962-64, Harvard Med. Sch., 1964-66; clin. and rsch. assoc. J.P. Kennedy Jr. Meml. Hosp., Brighton, Mass., 1964-66; clin. assoc. in orthopedics Harvard Med. Sch., 1966-67, clin. asst. prof. orthopaedic surgery, 1979-87, clin. assoc. prof., 1987-2000; ret., 2000; sr. orthopedic surgeon Mass. Gen. Hosp., Boston. Chief dept. rehab. medicine Mass. Gen. Hosp., Boston, 1965-72, assoc. orthopedic surgeon, 1969—, vis. orthopedic surgeon, 1969—; lectr. dept. mech. engring. MIT, 1970-72. Co-author: Amputees and Their Porstheses, 1971; author: The Total Care of Spinal Cord Injuries, 1977; contbr. articles in field to profl. jours. Pres. Wellesley (Mass.) Friendly Aid Assn., 1965-67, dir., 1967-70; dir. Family Svc. Counseling Region West, Wellesley, 1965-67; exec. com., task force chmn., adv. bd. Mass. State Rehab. Planning Commn., 1966-68. With USAF, 1951-52. Fellow ACS, Am. Acad. Orthopedic Surgeons, Royal Soc. Health, Pan Am. Med. Assn., Soc. Internat. Chirurgerie, Ortopaedie et Traumatologie; mem. Othopedic Rsch. Soc., Am. Orthopaedic Assn., NRC (musculosbeletal com.), Cervical Spine Rsch. Soc. (pres. 1986), Fedn. Spine Assns. (pres. 1987), N.E. Med. Assn. (pres.). Home: 22 Lathrop Rd Wellesley MA 02482 Personal E-mail: treetops-1@comcast.net.

PIERCE, DOROTHY KOHINKE, retired elementary school educator; b. Cooperstown, N.Y., Mar. 18, 1947; d. Theodore and Marion Bertha (Howard) Kohinke; m. James Andrew Pierce, Sept. 28, 1991. BA in Elementary Edn., SUNY, Oneonta, 1965—69, MS in Counselor Edn., 1979—81. French tchr. Margaretville Sch., NY, 1969—70; 2d grade tchr. Northville Ctr. Sch., NY, 1970—72, New Lebanon Ctrl. Sch., West Lebanon, NY, 1972—73; corrective reading tchr. Del. Acad., Delhi, NY, 1983; social work asst. Del. County Infirmary, Delhi, NY, 1981—83, Broome Devel. Ctr., Binghamton, NY, 1982—83; 3d grade & gifted tchr. Chenango Forks Schs., Binghamton, NY, 1984—86; 6th grade tchr. Chenango Valley Schs., Binghamton, NY, 1980—2002. Poetry tchr. Broome County Jail, Binghamton, NY, 2002—; mentor, edn. for ministry Trinity Episcopal Ch., Binghamton, NY, 2002—. Vol. Am. Red Cross, Endicott, NY, 2002—. Mem.: German Club of Binghamton. Avocations: yoga, poetry, singing.

PIERCE, ELIZABETH GAY, civic worker; b. N.Y.C., Mar. 26, 1907; d. Martin and Julia (Stone) Gay; AB, Barnard Coll., 1929; m. William Curtis Pierce, June 19, 1929; children: Martin Gay, Elizabeth Gay Pierce Fuchs, Josiah. Vol. worker Boston City Hosp., 1929-30, Community Service Soc., N.Y.C., 1931-32; mem. dependent children's sect. Welfare Council, N.Y.C., 1939-40; chmn. house com. North Shore Holiday House, Huntington, L.I., 1944, pres., 1945; co-chmn. thrift shop com. Knickerbocker Hosp., N.Y.C., 1957-64; mem. exec. com. of women's com. Legal Aid Soc., N.Y.C., 1958-59; mem. Women's Aux. Knickerbocker Hosp. (exec. com. 1960-64); adv. trustee Maine Citizens for Hist. Preservation, 1983-87; trustee Jones Mus. Ceramics and Glass, 1985-89. Mem. Soc. Colonial Dames in State N.Y. (bd. mgrs., 1962-67, corr. sec. N.Y. 1965-67, pres. 1967-70), Nat. Soc. Colonial Dames Am. (pres. 1972-76, nat. pres.), Soc. for Preservation New Eng. Antiquities (Maine council, former chmn. Marrett House, exec. com.), Mayflower Soc. N.Y. (sec. 1985-88), Daus. Founders and Patriots, Nat. Grange (mem. exec. com.). Episcopalian. Club: Colony, Ch. (N.Y.C.), Cumberland Club (Portland, Maine). Home: 9 Pierce Pl West Baldwin ME 04091-9736

PIERCE, FRANCIS CASIMIR, civil engineer; b. Warren, R.I., May 19, 1924; s. Frank J. and Eva (Soltys) Pierce; m. Helen Lynette Steinouer, Apr. 24, 1954; children: Paul F., Kenneth J., Nancy L., Karen H., Charles E. Student, U. Conn., 1943-44; BS, U. R.I., 1948; MS, Harvard U., 1950; postgrad., Northeastern U., 1951-52. Registered profl. engr. Conn., N.H., Mass., R.I., Vt.; registered profl. land surveyor R.I. Instr. civil engring. U. R.I., Kingston, 1948-49, U. Conn., Storrs, 1950-51; design engr. Praeger-Maguire & Ole Singstad, Boston, 1951-52; chief found. engr. C.A. Maguire & Assocs., Providence, 1952-59, assoc., 1959-69, v.p., 1969-72; sr. v.p. C.E. Maguire, Inc., 1972-76, officer-in-charge Honolulu office, 1976-78, exec. v.p., corp. dir. ops., 1975-87; dir. The Maguire Group, Inc., 1979—; gen. mgr. East Atlantic Casualty Co. Ltd., 1987-88; also dir. Pres. Magma, Inc., tech. ops. svc. co., 1986—88; lectr. found. engring. U. R.I., 1968—69, trustee, 1987—2002; 19mem. Coll. Engring. adv. coun., 1986—98; mem. U.S. com. Internat. Commn. on Large Dams; mem. register of expert witnesses in the constrn. industry ABA. Contbr. articles to profl. jours. Vice chmn. Planning Bd. East Providence, R.I., 1960-73; bd. dirs. R.I. Civic Chorale and Orch., 1986-90. With AUS, 1942-46. Decorated Bronze star, Combat Infantry badge, Presdl. Unit citation; named Acad. of Fellows, Am. Mil. Engr., 1996, Coll. Engring. Hall of Fame, U. R.I., 2000; recipient Commendation, Min. Pub. Works Rep. Venezuela, 1970, Geotech. award, ASCE sect. Boston Soc. Civil Engrs., 1979, USCG Meritorious Pub. Svc. award, 1987, Chester H. Kirk Disting. Engr. award, U. R.I. Coll. Engring., 1987. Fellow Soc. Am. Mil. Engrs., ASCE (life, chpt. past pres., dir.), NSPE (life); mem. Am. Arbitration Assn., R.I. Soc. Profl. Engrs. (nat. dir., engr. of yr. award 1973), ASTM, Am. Soc. Engring. Edn., Soc. Marine Engrs. and Naval Architects, Am. Soc. Planning Ofcls., Harvard Soc. Engrs., Scientists, Providence Engrs. Soc., R.I. Soc. Planning Agys (past pres.), U. R.I. Alumni Assn. (pres. and dir., S.W. Fla. Gators chpt. 2000-2002, Outstanding Svc. award 2002). Home: 64 Parkview Dr Apt 11 Pawtucket RI 02861 Office: 225 Foxborough Blvd Foxboro MA 02035-2854

PIERCE, HARVEY R. insurance company executive; m. Delor3es Pierce. Agt. Am. Family Ins. Group, 1963, exec. v.p. field ops., regional v.p., state dir., dist. sales mgr., pres., COO, 1990—99, chmn., CEO, 1999—. Mem. adv. bd. U. Wis. Children's Hosp.; mem. Founders' Club S.W. Mo. State U. Ins. Chair; trustee Am. Inst. Charter Property Casualty Underwriters-Ins. Inst. Am., Gov. Jim Doyle, Wis. Mem.: Ins. Inst. Hwy. Safety (chmn. 2004—), Property Casualty Insurers Assn. Am. (vice chmn. 2003—). Office: Am Family Ins Group 6000 American Pky Madison WI 53783-0001 Office Phone: 608-249-2111.

PIERCE, HILDA (HILDA HERTA HARMEL), painter; b. Vienna; arrived in U.S., 1940; m. Herman J. Slutzky; 1 child, Diana Rubin Daly (dec.). Student, Art Inst. Chgo.; studied with Oskar Kokoschka, Salzburg, Austria. Art tchr. Highland Park (Ill.) Art Ctr., Sandburg Village Art Workshop, Chgo., Old Town Art Ctr., Chgo.; owner, operator Hilda Pierce Art Gallery, Laguna Beach, Calif., 1981-85. Guest lectr. maj. art mus. and art tours, Carribean cruises, France, Switzerland, Austria, Italy, Mex., San Diego, China, India, 1998—2002, Russian river cruise and major art mus., St. Petersburg, Moscow, 1994; lectr., Mexico, 2002—04, U. Calif. Geisel Libr., San Diego, 2003; founder, chmn. Art Encounters, San Diego. One-woman shows include Fairweather Hardin Gallery, Chgo., Sherman Art Gallery, Marshall Field Gallery, exhibited in group shows at Old Orchard Art Festival, Skokie, Ill., Union League Club, North Shore Art League, ARS Gallery, Art Inst. Chgo., Represented in permanent collections U. Calif. San Diego Art Libr., La Jolla, numerous pvt. and corp. collections, 1200 large monoprints, oils, 17 murals for Carnival Cruise Lines megaliner M.S. Fantasy, 17 murals consisting of 49 paintings for megaliner M.S. Imagination, U. Calif. San Diego Geisel Libr., portrait, Melvin J. Voigt; featured (video) Survivors of the Shoa, Stephen Spielberg Found., 1996; contbr. articles to profl. jours. and newspapers. Founding libr. Geisel Libr. U. Calif., San Diego. Recipient Outstanding Achievement award, Chgo. Immigrants Svc. League. Office Phone: 858-558-7556. *An artist's most precious quality is curiosity. It has kept me young for many years, kept me searching, experimenting and never being complacent, in my life and my work.*

PIERCE, JAMES CLARENCE, surgeon, educator; b. Huron, S.D., Aug. 5, 1929; s. Henry Montraville and Carrie Bernice (Matson) P.; m. Carol Sue Wilson, 1967; children: Henry MacDonald, Richard Matson, Elizabeth Gail. BA, Carleton Coll., 1951; MD, Harvard U., 1955; MS, U. Minn., 1963, PhD in Surgery, 1966. Diplomate: Am. Bd. Surgery. Surg. intern Peter Bent Brigham Hosp., Boston, 1955-56; surg. fellow U. Minn., 1959-66; instr. surgery Med. Coll. Va., Richmond, 1966, prof. surgery and microbiology, 1972-75; dir. Tissue Typing Lab., 1969-75; attending surgeon, dir. surg. research, dir. transplantation service St. Luke's Hosp. Center, N.Y.C., 1975-78; prof. surgery Columbia U., 1976, Ailsa Mellon Bruce prof. surgery, 1977-78; clin. prof. surgery Pa. State U. and, 1979-88; chmn. dept. surgery Geisinger Med. Center, Danville, Pa., 1979-90, chmn. emeritus, 1990—. Clin. prof. surgery Jefferson U., 1990—. Contbr. articles to profl. jours. Elder Presbyn. Ch. With M.C., USAF, 1957-59. NIH fellow, 1963-65; Royal Soc. Medicine Found. travelling fellow, 1971; James IV Assn. Surg. traveller, 1978 Mem. ACS (pres. Ctrl. Pa. chpt. 1981-82), Transplant Soc., Am. Soc. Transplant Surgeons, Ea. Surg. Soc., N.Y. Clin. Soc., Soc. Univ. Surgeons, Sigma Xi. Republican. Home: 1906 Red Ln Danville PA 17821-8415

PIERCE, JERRY EARL, business executive; b. Hindsdale, Ill., Aug. 3, 1941; s. Earl and Adeline A. (Zaranski) P.; m. Carol Louise Martin, Aug. 15, 1964; children: Patricia, Barbara, Linda. Bradley. BS, U. Ill., 1964. With R.R. Donnelley & Sons, Chgo., 1964-70, Western Pub. Co., Racine, Wis., 1970—, nat. pubs. acct. exec., 1975—. Pres. Pierce Sale Co., Inc., Restaurant Equipment World, Inc., Heat Transfer Engring. Inc.; chmn. bd. Tech Industries & Millwork, Inc., 1989-93; pres. B.J. Installation Co., Inc., 1989-91, ROI World Equipment, 1993—; v.p., sec. Savers Clubs Am., Inc.; v.p. Pierce Aviation, 2000—; bd. dirs. Goldenrod Br., Bankfirst Bank, Winter Park, Fla. Vice chair Leadership Trust of Nat. Fedn. Ind. Bus. 1st lt. U.S. Army, 1968—70. Mem. East Orange County C. or C., Ctrl. Fla. Vets. Assn., Fla. Restaurant Assn., Food Svc. Cons. Soc., Food Equipment Distbrs. Assn. (bd. dirs. 1997-98), Nat. Bus. Aviation Assn., Interlachen Country Club (Winter Park, Fla.), Cleve. Advt. Club, Tiger Bay Club of Orlando. Republican. Episcopalian. Achievements include patents for refrigeration-to-water utility cost control system; invention of E-Commerce business model. Home: 2639 Ultra Vista Dr Maitland FL 32751 Office: 2413 N Forsyth Rd Orlando FL 32807-6455 Office Phone: 407-679-9004.

PIERCE, JOHN GERALD (JERRY PIERCE), lawyer; b. Winter Haven, Fla., Jan. 12, 1937; s. Francis E. and Margaret (Butler) P.; m. Kathleen E., Dec. 1, 1989; children: Kathleen M. Cooke, Nancy A., John Gerald Jr., Michael J. B in Chem. Engring., U. Fla., 1959, JD with honors, 1965. Bar: Fla. 1966, U.S. Dist. Ct. (mid. dist.) Fla. 1966, U.S. Ct. Appeals (11th cir.). Assoc. Anderson & Rush, Dean & Lowndes, Orlando, Fla., 1966-68, Arnold, Matheny & Eagen, Orlando, 1968-70; ptnr. Pierce, Lewis & Dolan, Orlando, 1970-74; sole practice Orlando, 1974—2002; ptnr. Pierce & Klein, PLC, Orlando, 2003—. Served to 1st lt. U.S. Army, 1959-62. Mem. ABA, Fla. Bar Assn., Orange County Bar Assn. Republican. Roman Catholic. Avocations: golf, boating, skiing. Home: 605 Fox Valley Dr Longwood FL 32779-2417 Office: 800 N Ferncreek Ave Orlando FL 32803-4127 E-mail: jerry@johnpierce.com.

PIERCE, LAWRENCE WARREN, retired federal judge; b. Phila., Dec. 31, 1924; s. Harold Ernest and Leora (Bellinger) Pierce; m. Wilma Taylor, 1948 (dec. May 1978); m. Cynthia Straker, July 8, 1979; children: Warren Wood, Michael Lawrence, Mark Taylor. BS, St. Joseph's U., Phila., 1948, DHL, 1967; JD, Fordham U., 1951, LLD, 1982, Fairfield U., 1972, Hamilton Coll., 1987, St. John's U., 1990. Bar: N.Y. 1951, U.S. Supreme Ct. 1968. Civil law practice, N.Y.C., 1951—61; asst. dist. atty. Kings County, N.Y., 1954—61; dep. police commr. N.Y.C., 1961—63; dir. N.Y. State Divsn. for Youth, Albany, 1963—66; chmn. N.Y. State Narcotic Addiction Control Commn., 1966—70; vis. prof. criminal justice SUNY, Albany, 1970—71; dist. judge U.S. Dist. Ct., So. Dist. N.Y., 1971—81; judge U.S. Fgn. Intelligence Surveillance Ct., Washington, 1979—81; cir. judge U.S. Ct. Appeals 2d Cir., 1981—95; ret., 1995. Dir. Cambodian ct. tng. project Internat. Human Rights Law Group, 1995. Past bd. dirs. CARE, Havens Fund Soc., Lincoln Hall for

Boys, S-R and S.A.R., N.Y. chpts., Cath. Interracial Coun., Practising Law Inst. Mem.: ABA (com. on corr. svc. and facilities 1970—71, alt. observer U.S. Mission to UN 1988—90, site evaluation com., sec. legal edn. 1996—98), Spl. Com. Army Confinement Faciltics (Office of Sec. of Army 1970), Urban League, Nat. Bar Assn., Am. Law Inst., Coun. Fgn. Rels. Home: PO Box 2234 Sag Harbor NY 11963-0111

PIERCE, LISA MARGARET, telecommunications executive, product and market development manager, lecturer; b. Nyack, NY, June 2, 1957; d. William and Elizabeth Pierce. BA with honors, Gordon Coll., Wenham, Mass., 1978; MBA, Atkinson Sch., Salem, Oreg., 1982. Campaign mgr. Carter/Mondale, Manchester, Mass., 1976; investigator Dept. Social Svcs., Nyack, 1977-78; paralegal Beverly, Mass., 1978-79; campaign mgr. Reagan Presdl. Primary, Rockland County, NY, 1980; cons. Sidereal, Portland, Oreg., 1981-82; performance analyst Dept. Social Svcs., Pomona, NY, 1982; market analyst Momentum Techs., Parsippany, NJ, 1983; cons. Booz Allen & Hamilton, Florham Park, NJ, 1984, Deloitte-Touche, Morristown, NJ, 1985; market rschr., forecaster AT&T, Bedminster, NJ, 1985-87, asst. pvt. line product mgr., 1987-89, Integrated Svcs. Digital Network product mgr., 1989-93; dir. Telecom. Rsch. Assocs., St. Marys, Kans., 1994-98; v.p., rsch. fellow Giga Info. Group/Forrester Rsch., Cambridge, Mass., 1998—. Panelist, contbr. TeleCom. Assn., San Diego, Internat. Comm. Assn., Atlanta, Ea. Comm. Forum, NY, Nat. Engring. Consortium, Chgo., Super Comm., Soc. Telecom. Consultants, MPLS Forum, Mid Atlantic Venture Assn., GSA Fed. Telecom. Svc. Forums, others; contbr. NY State ISDN/Internat User's Group; feature commentator Nat. Pub. Radio (All Things Considered), Pub. Broadcasting Svc. (Nightly Bus. Report), MSNBC, CNN and CNBC, Radio Wall Street, CBS Evening News. Columnist Network World, 2001—02, Bus. Comm. Rev., 2002—. Named one of Top 10 Most Influential IT Analysts, Tech. Mktg. Mag., 2002, 2003; grantee in field. Mem.: IEEE. Business E-Mail: lpierce@forrester.com.

PIERCE, MARGARET HUNTER, government official; b. Weedsport, NY, June 30, 1910; d. Thomas Murray and Ruby (Sanders) Hunter; m. John R. Pierce, Nov. 4, 1950 (div. May 1959); 1 dau., Barbara Hunter Churchill. BA, Mt. Holyoke Coll., 1932; JD, N.Y. U., 1939. Bar: NY 1941, DC 1958. Atty. Office Allen Property Custodian, Washington, 1942-43, 45, Office Solicitor, Dept. Labor, 1943-45, NLRB, 1946, 47-48; atty.-adviser U.S. Ct. Claims, 1947-48, 48-59, reporter decisions, 1959-68; commr. U.S. Indian Claims Commn., 1968-78; pvt. practice Washington, 1978—. V.p. Monday Night Musicales, Inc., 1995—. Mem. D.C. Bar Assn. (ct. claims com. 1958—, mil. law com. 1967), Fed. Bar Assn. (Indian law com. 1955—), ABA (sec. adminstrv. law-vets. com., mil. law com., immigration and nationality com.), Women's Bar Assn., Nat. Assn. Women Lawyers, Exec. Women in Govt., Bus. and Profl. Women (Cosmopolitan br.), Am. Women Composers, Zonta (Washington pres. 1977-78), Harvard Club (D.C.), Nat. Press Club Washington. Home: 3829 Garfield St NW Washington DC 20007-1319

PIERCE, MICHAEL NORMAN, internist; b. N.Y.C., May 1, 1955; s. Samuel and Ingeborg Pierce. BA in Biology, SUNY, Binghamton, 1977; MD, U. Vt., 1982. Diplomate Am. Bd. Internal Medicine. Intern, gen. surg. resident L.A. County/U. So. Calif. Med. Ctr., L.A., 1982—84; intern, resident in internal medicine Calif.-Pacific Med. Ctr., San Francisco, 1985—88; attending physician St. Francis Meml. Hosp., San Francisco, 1989—96, Montefiore Med. Ctr., East Elmhurst, NY, 1997—98, St. Barnabas Hosp./CHS/HHC, East Elmhurst, 1998—2000, PHS/CHS/HHC, East Elmhurst, 2001, St. Luke's Roosevelt Hosp. Ctr., N.Y.C., 2001—. Chair Spring conf. St. Luke's Roosevelt Hosp. Ctr., 2003; judge, mem. abstract rev. bd. for resident's poster competition N.Y. Downstate ACP-ASIM sci. meetings; asst. attending physician St. Luke's Roosevelt Hosp. Ctr., N.Y.C., 2002—, mem. CME med. bd. com., 2002—, key faculty, internal medicine residency program; asst. clin. prof. medicine Columbia U. Coll. Physicians and Surgeons, N.Y.C., 2002—; mem. HIV mgmt. preceptorship program Johns Hopkins U. Sch. Medicine, Balt., 2001; mem. Infectious Disease Soc. Am., Infectious Disease Soc. Am. HIV Med. Assn.; HIV med. specialist State of N.Y. Mem. editl. bd. Johns Hopkins U. Sch. Medicine Advanced Studies in Medicine, 2002—. Recipient Physician's Recognition award, AMA, 1991—; Pharm. Mfrs. Assn. grantee, 1979. Fellow: ACP (com. on med. students 2001—), Am. Soc. Gen. Internal Medicine; mem.: AMA, N.Y. County Med. Soc., Med. Soc. State N.Y. (surveyor-reviewer hosp. CME programs 1998—, mem. com. on edn.). Office: Roosevelt Hosp divsn St Luke's-Roosevelt Hosp Ctr 1000 Tenth Ave #2T New York NY 10019 Office Phone: 212-523-6500.

PIERCE, MILDRED LOUISE, librarian; b. Fulton County, Ga., Nov. 30, 1928; d. John Oliver Pierce and Florence Idella (Carr) Sansted; m. Harry Eugene Springer, Oct. 17, 1967; 1 child, Jesse Ladd. BS in Edn., SUNY, Geneseo, 1951; MA in Librarianship, U. Denver, 1955. Lic. Episcopalian lay reader, lay preacher. Libr. asst. SUNY, New Paltz, 1951; elem. libr. Hastings Pub. Schs., Hastings-on-the-Hudson, NY, 1951; libr. grad. student aide Denver Pub. Libr., 1954—55; children's bookmobile libr. Alexander Mitchell Pub. Libr., Aberdeen, SD, 1955—56; libr. Mineral County Sch. Dist., Hawthorne, Nev., 1956—64; adult edn. tchr. Clark County Sch. Dist., Las Vegas, 1964—65; tech. libr. RADSAFE, Reynolds Elec. and Engring. Co., Mercury, Nev., 1965—67; reference cons. Mother Lode Libr. Sys., Auburn, Calif., 1967—68; dir. Tech. Info. Svc., Hawthorne, 1976—; dep. gen. conv., commn. liturgy and music Domestic and Fgn. Missionary Soc. of Protestant in the Episcopal Ch. of U.S.A., 2003. Author: Nevada Rockfinder, 1970; columnist An Ounce of Prevention, 1973—75; editor: Wordwebs, 1979—81. Founder, trustee Walker-Wassuk Arts Alliance, Hawthorne, 1977; founder trustee Preservation Mineral County Courthouse and Flag Chowder and Marching Soc., 1982; pres. Desert Dance Arts Theater, 1989—; candidate Nev. Senate, 1976, Nev. Assembly, 1978, 1980. Mem.: NEA, ALA, States Assn., Am. Assn. Sch. Libr., Mineral County Tchrs. Assn., Nev. State Tchrs. Assn., Nev. Alliance for the Arts, Mineral County Coun. on Alcohol and Drug Abuse, Kappa Delta Pi. Republican. Episcopalian. Home: 674 I St PO Box 1721 Hawthorne NV 89415-1721 Office: Tech Info Svc PO Box 1721 Hawthorne NV 89415-1721 Office Phone: 775-945-3030. E-mail: derdlim674@yahoo.com.

PIERCE, MORTON ALLEN, lawyer; b. Liberec, Czechoslovakia, June 25, 1948; m. Nancy Washor, Dec. 14, 1975; children: Matthew J., Nicholas L. BA, Yale Coll., 1970; JD, U. Pa., 1974; postgrad., Oxford U., 1974-75. Bar: N.Y. 1975. Assoc. Reid & Priest, N.Y.C., 1975-83, ptnr., 1983-86, Dewey Ballantine, N.Y.C., 1986—, co-chmn., 2003—, vice-chmn., 2002—03, chmn., 2003—. Mem. mgmt. com. 1988—, chmn. corp. dept., 1999—, chmn., mergers and acquisitions group, 1990—, mem. exec. com., 2001—. Contbr. articles to profl. jours. Mem. ABA (chmn. subcom. on internat. securities matters 1985-91, adv. com. to fed. regulation of securities com. 1991-2000, task force on rev. of the fed. securities law 1991-2000), Assn. of the Bar of the City of N.Y. (securities law com. 1988-91, chmn. subcom. on securities and exch. commn. enforcement matters 1990-91), Internat. Bar Assn. (com. on securities transactions), Legal Aid Soc. (bd. dirs.), Gordon A. Rich Found. (bd. dirs.). Home: 188 E 76th St New York NY 10021-2826 Office: Dewey Ballantine LLP 1301 Ave Of The Americas New York NY 10019-6022 Office Phone: 212-259-6640. E-mail: mpierce@dbllp.com.

PIERCE, NAOMI ELLEN, biology professor, researcher; b. Denver, Oct. 19, 1954; d. Arthur Preble and Ruiko (Ishizaka) P; m. Andrew James Berry, Mar. 9, 1996; children: Kate Clark Berry, Megan Elizabeth Berry. BS, Yale U., 1976; PhD, Harvard U., k1983. Fulbright postdoctoral fellow Griffith U., Brisbane, Australia, 1983-84; rsch. lectr. Christ Ch., U. Oxford, Eng., 1984-86; asst. prof. Princeton U., N.J., 1986-91; Sydney A. and John H. Hessel prof. biology, curator lepidoptera Harvard U. and Harvard Mus. Comparative Zoology, Cambridge, Mass., 1991—. Contbr. articles to profl. jours. MacArthur Found. fellow, Chgo., 1988-93. Fellow Harvard Soc. of Fellows (sr.). Office: Harvard U 26 Oxford St Cambridge MA 02138-2902

PIERCE, PAUL, professional basketball player; b. Oct. 13, 1977; s. Lorraine Hosey. Degree in crime and deliquency studies, Kans. State U., 1999. Profl. basketball player Boston Celtics, 1998—. Avocation: music. Office: Boston Celtics 151 Merrimac St # 1 Boston MA 02114-4714

PIERCE, PHILIP SARGENT, clinical psychologist; b. Medford, Mass., Aug. 25, 1941; s. Elmer Grandville and Pauline Dudley Pierce; m. Rae Foster, Oct. 10, 1967; children: Jennifer, Jessica, John, Jill. BA, U. Maine, 1963; MA, U. N.H., 1965; PhD, U. S.C., 1971. Lic. psychologist, Maine. Clin. psychologist Pineland Ctr., Pownal, Maine, 1965-77, Togus (Maine) Vets. Med. and Regional Office Ctr., 1977-83, sr. psychologist, 1983—, acting chief mental health svc., 2003. Vis. prof. psychology U. So. Maine, Portland, 1971-72; asst. prof. psychology St. Joseph's Coll., North Windham, Maine, 1972-78, U. Maine, Augusta, 1977-78; clin. assoc. psychology U. Maine, Orono, 1981—; lectr. on psychology grad. program in sch. and health psychology U. New Eng., Biddeford Pool, Maine; adj. clin. faculty mem. Antioch New Eng. Grad. Sch., 1996-2000; cons., spkr., presenter in field; northeastern regional exam. coord. Am. Bd. Clin. Psychology, 1993-95, nat. credential rev. officer, 1995-97; mem. Am. Bd. Profl. Psychology, Inc. Contbr. numerous articles to profl. jours. Trustee Falmouth Congl. Ch., 1981-84, chmn. bd. trustees, 1983-84, sec. mem. giving and investments subcom., 1982-84, mem. Christian enlistment com., 1985-88, chmn., 1987-88, mem. nominations com., 1989-92, chmn. ch. coun., 1990-93, mem. bylaws com., 1994-97; bd. dirs. Falmouth Little League, 1984-90, coach, 1983-85, treas., 1984-90, umpire, 1983-93; bd. dirs. Maine Running Hall of Fame, 1994—, vice chmn., 1995-96, chmn., 1996-2002; bd. dirs. Maine Sports Hall of Fame, 1994—, 1st v.p., 1995-2001, chmn. honors and selection com., 1996-2002, pres. 2001-2002. With U.S. Army, 1966. Fellow APA (divsn. newsletter editor 1981-84, exec. bd. 1981-82, pres. 1985-86, chmn. fellow com. 1990-96, coun. of reps. 1977-79, coun. liaison to Maine psychol. Assn. 1995-97, coun. reps. for Maine and Vt., 1998-2001, chmn. rural caucus), Maine Psychol. Assn. (newsletter editor 1971-74, mem. exec. bd. 1971-88, pres. 1975-77, chmn. ethics com. 1992-98, policy coun. 1992-2002), Am. Psychol. Soc., Acad. Clin. Psychology (bd. dirs. 1993-2002, v.p. 1998-2002); mem. AAAS, N.Y. Acad. Sci., Assn. VA Lead Psychologists (chmn. gero-psychology task force 1983-84, chmn. APA-VA interaction task force 1984-85), Soc. Maine Psychologists (chmn. continuing edn. com. 1990-92, 98-2000, pres. 1992-94, treas. 1994-98), Maine Soc. Forensic Psychologists, Maine Track Club (sec. 1985-86, v.p. 1986-87, pres. 1987-88, race dir. 1984—). Democrat. Avocation: long distance running. Home: 79 Waites Landing Rd Falmouth ME 04105 E-mail: philip.pierce@med.va.gov.

PIERCE, PONCHITTA ANN, TV host, producer, journalist, writer, consultant; b. Chgo., Aug. 5, 1942; d. Alfred Leonard and Nora (Vincent) P. Student, Cambridge (Eng.) U., summer 1962; BA in Journalism cum laude, U. So. Calif., 1964; DHL, Franklin Pierce Coll., 1986. Asst. editor Ebony mag., 1964-65, assoc. editor, 1965-67; editor Ebony mag. (N.Y.C. office), 1967-68; chief N.Y.C. editl. bur. Johnson Pub. Co., 1967-68; corr. news divsn. CBS, N.Y.C., 1968-71; contbg. editor McCall's mag., 1971-77; editl. cons. Philps Stokes Fund, 1971-78; staff writer Reader's Digest, 1976-77, roving editor, 1977-80; co-prodr., host Today in New York, Sta. WNBC-TV, N.Y.C., 1982-87; freelance writer, TV broadcaster, media cons. Co-host Sunday WNBC-TV, 1973—77, The Prime of Your Life, 1977—80; author: Status of American Women Journalists on Magazines, 1968, History of the Phelps Stokes Fund 1911-1972; contbg. editor: Parade mag., 1993, Earth Times Monthly, 2002. Del. to WHO Conf., Geneva, 1973; bd. dirs. Morris-Jumel Mansion, Hirshhorn Mus. and Sculpture Garden, Xavier U. of La., Housing Enterprise for the Less Privileged, Third St. Music Sch. Settlement, Inner-City Scholarship Fund, Josephson Inst. Ethics, Marina del Rey, Sta. WNET-TV; mem. women's bd. Madison Sq. Boys and Girls Club; mem. Columbia Presbyn. Health Scis. Adv. Coun. Recipient Penney-Mo. mag. award excellence women's journalism, 1967; John Russwurm award N.Y.C. Urban League, 1968; AMITA Nat. Achievement award in communications, 1974 Mem. NATAS, Women in Comm. (Woman Behind the News award 1969, Nat. Headliner award 1970), Fgn. Policy Assn. (mem. bd. govs., bd. dirs.), Coun. on Fgn. Rels., Calif. Scholarship Fedn. (life), Econs. Club N.Y., Lotos Club, Nat. Honor Soc., Mortar Bd.

PIERCE, RICHARD HARRY, oceanographer; PhD in Chem. Oceanography, U. R.I., 1973. Sr. scientist, dir. Ctr. for Eco-Toxicology, Mote Marine Lab., Sarasota, Fla. Office: Mote Marine Lab 1600 Ken Thompson Pkwy Sarasota FL 34236-1096

PIERCE, RICKLIN RAY, lawyer; b. Waukegan, Ill., Sept. 16, 1953; s. Forest Ellsworth and Mildred Colleen (Cole) P. BBA in Acctg., Washburn U., 1975; BA in Econs., 1978, JD, 1978. Bar: Kans. 1978, U.S. Dist. Ct. Kans. 1978, U.S. Ct. Appeals (10th cir.) 1981, U.S. Supreme Ct. 1986. Assoc. Law Firm of C. C. Whittaker, Jr., Eureka, Kans., 1978-79; trust officer Smith County State Bank & Trust Co., Smith Center, Kans., 1979-80; staff atty. Northwest Kans. Legal Aid Soc., Goodland, 1980-81; assoc. Jochems, Sargent & Blaes, Wichita, Kans., 1981-82, Garden City, Kans., 1982-83; pvt. practice, Garden City, 1983-88; atty. County of Finney, 1988-93; pvt. practice, Garden City, 1993—. Pres., chmn. bd. dirs. Volunteers, Inc. of Finney County. Mem. Western Kans. Coun. Estate Planning & Giving. Mem. ABA, Assn. Trial Lawyers Am., Kans. Bar Assn., Southwest Kans. Bar Assn., Kans. Trial Lawyer Assn., Finney County Bar Assn. (treas.). Republican. Methodist. Home: 2015 Campus Dr Garden City KS 67846-3706 Office: 206 W Pine St Garden City KS 67846-5347

PIERCE, SHAHEEDA LAURA, midwife, consultant; b. Jersey City, Apr. 13, 1959; d. Lawrence Everett Pierce and Mary Dean Applegate Swing; m. James Shuffield, May 28, 1994; children: Juniper, Rama, Jasmine, Elijah, Jamila, Tara. AAS, Pima Coll., 1984. Cert. paralegal, cmty. meditation svcs., dance leader Dances Universal Peace; cert. profl. midwife. Pvt. practice mediation and paralegal svcs., Tucson, 1991—95, Maui, Hawaii, 1995-96, Tucson, 1996—98, Silver City, N.Mex., 1998-99, Vashon Island, Wash., 1999—. Nat. coord. group Movement For A New Soc., Phila., 1982-83; bd. dirs. Food Conspiracy Cooperative, Tucson, 1993-95; steering com. S.W. Sufi Cmty., Silver City, 1994-95, bd. dirs., 1995-97; mem. faculty adv. bd. Nat. Coll. Midwifery, 2002—; midwife, holistic health cons. Author: Recipes for the New Children, 1978; contbr. articles to profl. jours.; creator (bd. game) The Healing Game of Life, 1993; composer (musical album on cassette) Full Moon Woman, 1994; co-coord., disc jockey weekly women's radio program KXCI Cmty. Radio, Tucson, 1983. Active Georgians Against Nuc. Energy, Atlanta, 1980-81; organizer Nuc. Free State, Tucson, 1981-82; draft counselor Daring Disarmers, Phila., 1982; vice-chair heavy metals remediation com. Vashon Maury Island Cmty. Coun., 2003. Recipient Ordinary Extraordinary Women's award, 1982. Mem. N.Mex. Midwives Assn., Ariz. Assn. Midwives (co-coord. AHCCCS reimbursement task force 1997-98), Midwives' Alliance Hawaii, Washington Alliance Rural Midwives. Avocations: art, music, dance, nature.

PIERCE, SHELBY CRAWFORD, management and oil industry consultant; b. May 26, 1932; s. William Shelby and Iris Mae (Smith) Pierce; m. Marguerite Ann Grado, Apr. 2, 1954; children: Cynthia Dawn, Melissa Carol. BSEE, Lamar U., Beaumont, Tex., 1956; grad. program for sr. execs., MIT, 1980. With Amoco Oil Co., Texas City Refinery, 1956—, elec. engr., elec. foreman, area foreman, 1956—60, zone supr., gen. foreman, maintenance, 1961—67, oper. supt., 1967—69, coord. results mgmt., 1969—72; dir. results mgmt. Amoco Oil Co. Corp. Hdqs., Chgo., 1972-75; mgr. ops. Amoco Oil Co., Whiting (Ind.) Refinery, 1975—76, asst. refinery mgr., 1977-79; dir. crude replacement program Amoco Oil Co. Corp. Hdqs., Chgo., 1979-81, mgr. corp. refining and transp. engring., 1981-92, gen. mgr. engring. and constrn., 1992, v.p. internat. bus. devel., 1993-94, ret., 1994. Pres., dir. Amoco Eurasia Oil Co., Amoco Mex. Oil Co., Amoco India, Inc., Amoco Tech. Assistance Co., Trinidad; chmn., dir. Amoco Orient Oil Co.; v.p. Amoco Corp. Devel. Co., Latin Am., 1994; pres. Pierce Cons. Svc., 1995—; CEO, pres. Environ. Constrn. Co., 1996—98; mem. steering com. contractor safety U.S. Dept. Labor, 1989. Trustee Lamar U. Found., 1994—. Mem.: AIChE (mem. exec. bd. 1985—89, chmn. engring. constrn. contracting divsn. 1988, Divsn. Man of Yr. award 1995), N.W. Ind. Bus. Roundtable (organizer and user coun. chmn. 1986, chmn. exec. bd. 1986—87), The Bus. Roundtable (constrn. com., adv. bd., chmn. constrn. cost effectiveness task force 1992—94), Constrn. Industry Inst. (chmn. Bus. Roundtable coun., mem. strategic planning com. 1991—93), Flossmoor Country Club, Sigma Tau. Republican. Methodist. Home and Office: 1715 Brookwood Dr Flossmoor IL 60422-1823 Office Phone: 708-798-4498. Office Fax: 708-957-4995. Business E-Mail: ShelbyPierce@msn.com.

PIERCE, SUSAN RESNECK, academic administrator, literature educator; b. Janesville, Wis., Feb. 6, 1943; d. Elliott Jack and Dory (Block) Resneck; m. Kenneth H. Pierce; 1 child, Alexandra Siegel. AB, Wellesley Coll., 1965; MA, U. Chgo., 1966; PhD, U. Wis., 1972. Lectr. U. Wis., Rock County, 1970-71; from asst. prof. to prof. English Ithaca (N.Y.) Coll., 1973-82, chmn. dept., 1976-79; program officer Nat. Endowment for Humanities, 1982-83, asst. dir., 1983-84; dean Henry Kendall Coll. Arts and Scis. U. Tulsa, 1984-90; v.p. acad. affairs, prof. English Lewis and Clark Coll., Portland, Oreg., 1990-92; pres. U. Puget Sound, Tacoma, 1992—2003. Vis. assoc. prof. Princeton (N.J.) U., 1979; bd. dirs. Janet Elson Scholarship Fund, 1984-1990, Tulsa Edn. Fund, Phillips Petroleum Scholarship Fund, 1985-90, Okla. Math. & Sci. High Sch., 1984-90, Hillcrest Med. Ctr., 1988-90, Portland Opera, 1990-92, St. Joseph's Hosp., 1992—, Seattle Symphony, 1993—; cons. U. Oreg., 1985, Drury Coll., Springfield, Mo., 1986; mem. Middle States and N. Cen. Accreditation Bds.; mem. adv. com. Fed. Women's Program, NEH, 1982-83; participant Summit Meeting on Higher Edn., Dept. Edn., Washington, 1985; speaker, participant numerous ednl. meetings, sems., commencements; chair Frederick Ness Book Award Com. Assn. Am. Colls., 1986; mem. award selection com. Dana Found., 1986, 87; mem. Acad. Affairs Council, Univ. Senate, dir. tchr. edn., chmn. adv. group for tchr. preparation, ex-officio mem. all Coll. Arts and Scis. coms. and Faculty Council on Internat. Studies, all U. Tulsa; bd. dirs. Am. Conf. Acad. Deans; bd. trustees Hillcrest Med. Ctr.; participant Aspen Inst. Md. 1999, Annapolis Group Media Roundtable, 1996, Harvard Seminar, 1992; former bd. dirs. Assn. Am. Colls. and Univs., 1989-92, Am. Conf. of Academic Deans, 1988-91, Am. Assn. Colls., 1989-92. Author: The Moral of the Story, 1982, also numerous essays, jour. articles, book sects., book revs.; co-editor: Approaches to Teaching "Invisible Man"; reader profl. jours. Bd. dirs. Arts and Humanities Coun., Tulsa, 1984-90; trustee Hillcrest Hosp., Tulsa, 1986-90; mem. cultural series com., community rels. com. Jewish Fedn., Tulsa, 1986-90; bd. dirs. Tulsa chpt. NCCJ, 1986-90, Kemper Mus. 1996—, Seattle Symphony, 1993-96, St. Joseph Hosp., 1992-93, Portland Opera, 1990-92. Recipient Best Essay award Arix. Quar., 1979, Excellence in Teaching award N.Y. State Edn. Council, 1982, Superior Group Service award NEH, 1984, other teaching awards; Dana scholar, Ithaca Coll., 1980-81; Dana Research fellow, Ithaca Coll., 82-83; grantee Inst. for Ednl. Affairs, 1980, Ford Found., 1987, NEH, 1989. Mem. MLA (adv. com. on job market 1973-74), South Ctrl. MLA, NIH (subcom. on college drinking), Assn. Governing Bds. (coun. of pres.), Nat. Inst. on Alcohol Abuse (presl. advisory group), Soc. for Values in Higher Edn., Assn. Am. Colls. (bd. dirs.), Am. Conf. Acad. Deans (bd. dirs. 1988-91), Coun. of Presidents, Assn. Governing Bds., Phi Beta Kappa, Phi Kappa Phi, Phi Gamma Kappa.

PIERCE, TAMORA, writer; b. South Connellsville, Pa., Dec. 13, 1954; d. Wayne Franklin Pierce and Jacqueline Sparks; m. Timothy Erving Liebe, Dec. 14, 1985. BA, U. Pa., 1977. Data collector Office Assessment, Kingston, NY, 1976—77; sec. Office Town Assessor, Hardenburgh and Demming, 1977—78; housemother McAuley Home for Girls, Buhl, Idaho, 1978—79; lit. agt. asst. Harold Ober Assocs., N.Y.C., 1979—83; sec. Chase Manhattan Bank, 1983—89, Joseph Conklin, 1990—92; freelance writer, 1992—. Author: Alanna: The First Adventure, 1983, In the Hand of the Goddess, 1984, The Woman Who Rides Like A Man, 1986, Lioness Rampant, 1988, Wild Magic, 1992, Wolf Speaker, 1994, The Emperor Mage, 1995, The Realms of the Gods, 1996, Sandry's Book, 1997, Tris's Book, 1998, Daja's Book, 1998, Briar's Book, 1999, First Test, 1999, Plain Magic in Flights of Fantasy, 1999, Magic Steps, 2000, Page, 2000, Testing in Lost and Found, 2000, Street Magic, 2001, Squire, 2001, Folquin's Folly in Disney Adventures, 2001, Elder Brother in Half Human, 2001, Cold Fire, 2002, Lady Knight, 2002, Shatterglass, 2003, Trickster's Choice, 2003, Trickster's Queen, 2004; contbr. articles to profl. jours. and the Ultimate Book Guide. Mem. Greenpeace, 2001, World Wildlife Fedn., 1998—, Internat. Wolf Ctr., Ely, Minn., 1998—, N.Y. Ctr. Wildlife Conservation, N.Y.C., 1997—. Mem.: ACLU, Soc. Childrens Book Writers and Illustrators, Sci. Fiction and Fantasy Writers Am., The Authors Guild, Amnesty Internat. Avocations: radio theatre, recording books, military history. Office: 949 Columbus Ave NB New York NY 10025

PIERCE, THRESIA KORTE (TISH PIERCE), primary school educator; b. Maize, Kans. d. Herman and Marie Adeline (Lubbers) Korte; children: Judith, John, Mark. BS, Friends U., 1955; MS, U. Nev., Las Vegas, 1978. Cert. tchr., Nev., Nev. Life Ins. lic. Office worker Internat. Trust Co., Denver, Colo., 1951, Motor Equipment Co., Wichita, Kans., 1952-53; tchr. Wichita Pub. Schs., 1960-69, Clark County Sch. Dist., Las Vegas, Nev., 1970-2000. Author numerous short stories; contbr. acticles to profl. jours. Senator Clark County Edn. Assn., Clark County Classroom Tchrs. Mem. NEA, Epsilon Sigma Delta (v.p. 1962). bd. dirs. Kansas Newman U., Wichita, 1966-68. Home: 3105 Cardinal Dr Las Vegas NV 89121-2204

PIERCE, WALTER J. publishing executive; b. Champaign, Mar. 11, 1955; s. Walter Morton and Pauline Elizabeth Pierce; m. Linda G. Hageman, July 12, 1980; children: Riley Heath, Creighton August. Attended, Mahomet-Seymour, 1973. Sales Stripe 3 Inc., Champaign, 1976—83, Applause, Woodland Hills, Calif., 1983—2000; v.p. sales Sports Pub. LLC, Champaign, 2000—03; pres. Sport Book Promotion, Champaign, 2003—. Author: Citizen Pain, 2001. Mem. Lib. Bd., Pk. Bd., Sidney, Ill., 1998—2001; exec. bd. mem. Immanuel Mens Club, Broadland, Ill., 1996—; vol. Baseball Coach, 1990—2000, Football Coach, 1994—, Basketball Coach, 1994—. Office: Sport Book Promotions 804 N Neil Champaign IL 61820 Office Phone: 217-649-5215. Office Fax: 217-363-2073. E-mail: sportbookspromo19@yahoo.com.

PIERCE, WILLIAM SCHULER, cardiac surgeon; b. Wilkes-Barre, Pa., Jan. 12, 1937; s. William Harold and Doris Louis (Schuler) P.; m. Peggy Jayne Stone, June 12, 1965; children: William Stone, Jonathan Drew. BS, Lehigh U., 1958; MD, U. Pa., 1962. Intern U. Pa., 1962—63; resident in surgery Hosp. U. Pa., 1963—70; asst. prof. M.S. Hershey Med. Ctr., Pa. State U. Coll. Medicine, Hershey, 1970—73, assoc. prof., 1973—77, prof. surgery, 1977—, chief divsn. cardiothoracic surgery, 1991—95; assoc. chmn. dept. surgery, dir. rsch., dept. surgery, 1995—97. Contbr. over 300 articles to profl. jours. With USPHS, 1965—67. Fellow: ACS; mem.: AAAS, AMA, Soc. Clin. Surgery., Am. Surg. Assn., Soc. Univ. Surgeons, So. Pa. Assn. Thoracic Surgery, Inst. Medicine, Assn. Acad. Surgery, Am. Heart Assn., Soc. Vascular Surgery, Am. Soc. Artificial Internal Organs, Internat. Cardiovascular Soc. Achievements include invention of inventor cardiac valve, blood pump. Office: Milton S Hershey Med Ctr PO Box 850 Hershey PA 17033-0850 Business E-Mail: wpierce@psu.edu.

PIERCY, GORDON CLAYTON, bank executive; b. Takoma Park, Md., Nov. 23, 1944; s. Gordon Clayton and Dorothy Florence (Brummer) Piercy; m. Roberta Margaret Walton, 1985; children: Elizabeth Anne, Kenneth Charles, Virginia Walton, Zachary Taylor Walton. BS, Syracuse U., 1966; MBA, Pace U., 1973. Mgmt. trainee Suburban Bank, Bethesda, Md., 1962-66; mktg. planning assoc. Chemical Bank, N.Y.C., 1966-70; sr. market devel. officer Seattle-First Nat. Bank, 1970-74; product expansion adminstr., mktg. planning mgr. VISA, Inc., San Francisco, 1974-76; v.p., dir. mktg. Wash. Mutual Bank, Seattle, 1976-82; v.p., mktg. dir. First Interstate Bank Wash. N.A., Seattle, 1983-86; sr. v.p. mktg., dir. Puget Sound Nat. Bank, Tacoma, 1986-92; sr. v.p., dir. mktg. and sales Key Bank, Tacoma, 1993-94; dir. corp. sales Station KIRO-TV, Seattle, 1994; sr. v.p., dir. mktg. and sales Pacific N.W. Bancorp, 1994—2004; pres. Whidbey Western R.R., 1995—; prin. Whidbey Mktg., 2004—. Mem.: Motorcar Operators West, S.W. Railcar Ltd. (mem. exec. com.), Island County Econ. Devel. Assn. (bd. dirs.), Pacific Railcar Operators, Mktg. Comm. Exec. Internat. (bd. dirs.), Comm. Coun., Lions, Delta Mu Delta, Alpha Kappa Psi, Sigma Nu. Episcopalian. Home and Office: 750 N Snowberry Ln Coupeville WA 98239-3110

PIERCY, MARGE, poet, writer; b. Detroit, Mar. 31, 1936; d. Robert Douglas and Bert Bernice (Bunnin) P.; m. Ira Wood, 1982. AB, U. Mich., 1957; MA, Northwestern U., 1958; DHL (hon.), Hebrew Union Coll., 2004, Union Coll.,

2004. Instr. Gary extension Ind. U., 1960-62; poet-in-residence U. Kans., 1971; disting. vis. lectr. Thomas Jefferson Coll., Grand Valley State Colls., fall 1975, 76, 78, 80; vis. faculty Women's Writers Conf., Cazenovia (N.Y.) Coll.; Elliston poetry fellow U. Cin., 1986. DeRoy Disting. vis. prof. U. Mich., 1992; editor Leapfrog Press, 1997—; poetry editor Lillith, 1999—; fiction editor Seattle Rev., 2003—. Author: Breaking Camp, 1968, Hard Loving, 1969, Going Down Fast, 1969, Dance the Eagle to Sleep, 1970, Small Changes, 1973, To Be of Use, 1973, Living in the Open, 1976, Woman on the Edge of Time, 1976, The High Cost of Living, 1978, Vida, 1980, The Moon is Always Female, 1980, Braided Lives, 1982, Circles on the Water, 1982, Stone, Paper, Knife, 1983, My Mother's Body, 1985, Gone to Soldiers, 1988, Available Light, 1988 (May Sarton award 1991), Summer People, 1989, He, She and It, 1991, Body of Glass, 1991 (Arthur C. Clarke award 1993), Mars and Her Children, 1992, The Longings of Women, 1994, Eight Chambers of the Heart, 1995, City of Darkness, City of Light, 1996, What Are Big Girls Made Of?, 1997 (Notable Book award ALA 1997), Storm Tide, 1998, The Art of Blessing the Day, 1999, Early Grrrl, 1999, Three Women, 1999, (with Ira Wood) So You Want to Write: How to Master the Craft of Writing Fiction and the Personal Narrative, 2001, Sleeping With Cats, A Memoir, 2002, Colors Passing Through Us, 2003, Third Child, 2003; (CD) Louder: We Can't Here You Yet, 2004; author of poetry. Cons. N.Y. State Coun. on Arts, 1971, Mass. Found. for Humanities and Coun. on Arts, 1974; mem. Writer Bd., 1985-86; bd. dirs. Transition House, Mass. Found. Humanities and Pub. Policy, 1978-85, Am. ha-Yam, 1988-98, v.p., 1995-96; gov.'s appointee to Mass. Cultural Coun., 1990-91, Mass. Coun. on Arts and Humanities, 1986-89; artistic adv. bd. ALEPH Alliance for Jewish Renewal, Am. Poetry Ctr., 1988—; lit. adv. panel poetry NEA, 1989. Recipient Borenstone Mountain Poetry award, 1968, 74, Lit. award Gov. Mass. Commn. on Status of Women, 1974, Nat. Endowment of Arts award, 1978, Carolyn Kizer Poetry prize, 1986, 90, Shaeffer-Eaton-PEN New Eng. award, 1989, Golden Rose Poetry prize, 1990, Brit ha-Dorot award The Shalom Ctr., 1992, Notable Book award, 1997, Paterson poetry prize, 2000. Mem.: NOW, PEN, Am. Poetry Soc., Nat. Writers Union, Authors League, Authors Guild, Citizens for the Preservation of Wellfleet, Mass. Audubon Soc., New Eng. Poetry Club. Address: PO Box 1473 Wellfleet MA 02667-1473

PIERETTI, MICHAEL, product designer; b. Framingham, Mass. BS in Urban Planning and Design, Cornell U. Designer Nike, 1997—98; joined Gensler Studio 585, 1998; sr. designer Imagination USA, 2001—03; prin. Pieretti Design, N.Y.C., 2003—. Named to, Crain's N.Y. Bus. "40 under 40", 2004; recipient award, Japan Design Found., 2003.*

PIERLUISI, PEDRO R. lawyer; b. San Juan, P.R., Apr. 26, 1959; s. Jorge A. and Doris (Urrutia) Pierluisi; children: Anthony, Michael, Jacqueline, Rafael. BA, Tulane U., 1981; JD, George Washington U., 1984. Bar: D.C. 1984, U.S. Dist. Ct. D.C. 1985, U.S. Ct. Appeals (D.C. cir.) 1985, P.R. 1990, U.S. Dist. Ct. P.R. 1990, U.S. Supreme Ct. 1990, U.S. Ct. Appeals (1st cir.) 1993. Assoc. Verner, Liipfert, Bernhard, McPherson & Hand, Washington, 1984—85, Cole, Corette & Abrutyn, Washington, 1985—90; ptnr. Pierluisi Pierluisi & Mayol-Bianchi, San Juan, 1990—93; atty. gen. Govt. of P.R., 1993—96; ptnr. O'Neill & Borges, San Juan, 1997—. Mem.: ABA (ho. of dels. 1995—96, standing com. on substance abuse 1995—98, coordinating com. on gun violence 1998—2001, state membership chmn. 2000—03), Am. Arbitration Assn. (arbitrator), Nat. Assn. Securities Dealers (arbitrator), George Washington U. Internat. Law Soc. (pres. 1982—83), Nat. Assn. Attys. Gen. (chair ea. region 1996), Puerto Rico Homebuilders Assn. (bd. dirs. 1999—2003), N.Y. Stock Exch. (arbitrator), Phi Alpha Delta (hon.; Munoz chpt.). Avocation: jogging. Office: O'Neill & Borges 250 Ave Munoz Rivera Am Internat Plz San Juan PR 00918-1808 Office Phone: 787-282-5706.

PIERMATTI, JACK, dentist; b. Paterson, N.J., Sept. 25, 1953; s. Matthew and Viola Piermatti; m. Carol Ann Nakashian, July 30, 1978; children: Laura Ann, Valerie Jacqueline, John Michael. BS, DMD, Fairleigh Dickinson U., 1979. Cert. Doctor of Dental Medicine N.J. State Bd. Dentistry, 1979, diplomate Am. Bd. Oral Implantology, Internat. Congress Oral Implantologists. Gen. practice resident St. Joseph's Hosp., Paterson, NJ, 1970—80; prosthodontics resident N.J. Dental Sch., Newark, 2001—04; pvt. practice Dental Arts of South Jersey, PC, Voorhees, NJ, 1980—. Fellow: Am. Acad. Implant Dentistry. Office: Dental Arts South Jersey PC 709 Haddonfield-Berlin Rd Voorhees NJ 08043 E-mail: jpiermatti@yahoo.com.

PIERNO, ANTHONY ROBERT, lawyer; s. Anthony M. and Mary Jane (Saporita) P.; m. Beverly Jean Kohn; children: Kathryn Ann, Robert Lawrence, Linda Jean Derengowski, Diane Marie Leonard. BA with highest honors, Whittier Coll., 1954; JD, Stanford U., 1959; LLD (hon.), Whittier Coll., 2000. Bar: Calif. 1960, D.C. 1979, Tex. 1994. Assoc. Adams, Duque & Hazeltine, L.A.; ptnr. Poindexter & Barger, L.A.; chief dep. commr. State of Calif., 1967-69, commr. of corps., 1969-71; ptnr. Wyman, Bautzer, Rothman & Kuchel, Beverly Hills, Calif.; sr. ptnr. Memel, Jacobs, Pierno & Gersh, L.A., 1976-86; ptnr. Pillsbury, Madison & Sutro, L.A., 1986-89; sr. v.p., gen. counsel MAXXAM, Inc., L.A. and Houston, 1989-97. Author: Corporate Disaggregation, 1982; editor Stanford U. Law Rev. Trustee Whittier Coll., 1977-2000, chmn. bd. trustees, 1994-2000, chmn. presdl. selection com., 1989-90; chmn. Marymount Coll., Palos Verdes, Calif., 1989-92, trustee, 1976-93; past mem. Los Angeles County Children's Svcs. Commn. With U.S. Army, 1954-56. Recipient Emcalian award Marymount Palos Verdes Coll., 1983. Mem. ABA, Los Angeles County Bar Assn., State Bar Calif. (chmn. com. on corps. 1971-75, advisor to com. on corps. 1975-76, mem. exec. com. bus. law sect. 1976-80, chmn. spl. com. on franchise law), Calif. Club (L.A.). Republican. Roman Catholic. Office: 73255 El Paseo Ste 11 Palm Desert CA 92260-4125 Office Phone: 760-341-7595.

PIERONI, ROBERT EDWARD, internist, educator, military officer; b. Portland, Maine, June 20, 1937; s. Ansel Kirby and Agnes Mary (Dumais) P.; m. Dorothy Louise McDonnell, Oct. 3, 1970; children: Michelle Kirby, Robert Francis. BS, Boston Coll., 1959; MD, Pa. State U., 1971. Diplomate Am. Bd. Internal Medicine, Am. Bd. Family Practice, Am. Bd. Allergy and Immunology, Am. Bd. Quality Assurance, Am. Bd. Geriatric Medicine. Chemist Mass. Dept. Pub. Health, Boston, 1962-71, sr. bacteriologist, 1971-74; asst. prof. internal medicine U. Ala., Tuscaloosa, 1974-76, assoc. prof. dept. internal medicine and family practice, 1976-81, prof. internal medicine and family practice, 1981—; enlisted U.S. Army, 1961, advanced through grades to col., 1981. Prior cons. VA Hosp., Tuscaloosa, T. Hardin Med. Facility and Partlow State Hosp., Tuscaloosa, 1974—; cons. FDA, Dept. Def. Contbr. more than 250 textbooks, articles, chpts. and abstracts; mem. editl. bd. various jours. Decorated Bronze Star, 1991, Commendation for Valor; recipient Golden Stethoscope award, 1982, Faculty Recognition award, 1986, Ala. Golden Eagle Humanitarian award Ala. Sr. Citizens Hall of Fame, 1988 and Physicians award, 1998, Wright A. Garner scientist award Ala. Acad. Sci., 1997, Designator A Proficiency award Army Surgeon Gen., 2001. Mem. AMA, ACP, Am. Coll. Allergy, Asthma and Immunology, Am. Geriatric Soc., Gerontol. Soc. Am., Am. Acad. Family Physicians, Physicians for Human Rights, VFW, Am. Legion. Democrat. Roman Catholic. Avocations: mountain trekking, scuba diving, studying medical and military history, reading. Home: 398 Riverdale Dr Tuscaloosa AL 35406-1814 Office: U Ala Dept Internal Medicine PO Box 870326 Tuscaloosa AL 35487-0001

PIERPONT, ROSS Z. retired surgeon; b. Woodlawn, Md., Sept. 7, 1917; s. Edwin Lowell and Ethel Celeste (Zimmerman) P.; m. Grace Schmidt, Feb. 5, 1942; 1 child, Christine Pierpont von Klencke. BS in Pharmacy, U. Md., 1937, MD, 1940. Diplomate Am. Bd. Surgery. Intern Md. Gen. Hosp., Balt., 1940-41; resident in surgery Balt. City Hosps., 1941-44, U. Iowa, Iowa City, 1944-45; asst. clin. prof. emeritus U. Md.; pres., CEO Pierpont Sys. Cons. Internat. Pres. PSCI Internat. Healthcare; cons. pres. Gempro Internat. Mfg. of Healthcare Supplements; with Pierpont Health Ctr. Author: Indicted, 1982, Towson & The Tax Cap, 1991, Health Care System for USA "Its Not the Health Care it's the Health Care System Stupid", 1999, (autobiography) Never Never Ever Give Up, 2001. Bd. dirs. Pres. Club Heritage Found., Washington, 1995; mem. Empower Am., Washington, 1996; Rep. nominee U.S. Senate (Md.), 1998; chmn. adv. bd. Rep. Nat. Com.; active Rep. Senatorial Inner Cir.; candidate for Gov. of Md., 2002. Fellow ACS; mem. AMA, Soc. Am. Gastrointestinal and Endoscopic Surgeons, Kiwanis Internat. Republican. Methodist. Home: 215 Belmont Forest Ct Unit 408 Lutherville Timonium MD 21093-7792 Personal E-mail: russzpierpont@aol.com.

PIERRE, DWIGHT ANTHONY, mathematician, educator; b. Queens, N.Y., Mar. 24, 1969; s. Anthony Michael and Mary Alice (Wyckoff) Pierre. BSc in Applied Math., Union Coll., 1992; MA in Math., SUNY, 1994; postgrad., Columbia U., 2003—. Instr. math. Borough of Manhattan (N.Y.) C.C., N.Y.C., 1994—. GMAT Math Intructor Dyson Coll. Arts and Scis. Pace U., N.Y.C., NY, adj. prof. math., Globe Inst. Tech., N.Y.C., Coll. New Rochelle, Bklyn., Schenectady (N.Y.) County C.C.; math tchr. Mesifta Tifereth Jerusalem, N.Y.C., Fulton County Schs., Atlanta; adj. prof. academic opportunity program Union Coll., Schenectady, NY; math instr. summer bridge program SUNY, Albany, math instr. S.T.E.P.; cons. in field. Math instr. Upward Bound Program Atlanta (Ga.) Metro. Coll. Mem.: Math. Assn. Am. Office: Borough of Manhattan Community Coll Math Dept 199 Chambers St New York NY 10007 Home: 870 St Nicholas Ave B4 New York NY 10032 E-mail: dapierre@hotmail.com., dpierre@bmcc.cuny.edu., dap2112@columbia.edu.

PIERRE, JOSEPH HORACE, JR., commercial artist; b. Salem, Oreg., Oct. 3, 1929; s. Joseph Horace and Miriam Elisabeth (Holder) Pierre; m. June Anne Rice, Dec. 20, 1952 (dec. June 2001); children: Joseph Horace III, Thomas E., Laurie E., Mark R., Ruth A.; m. Luverne Melba Starnes, Jan. 9, 2002. Grad., Advt. Art Sch., Portland, Oreg., 1954, Inst. Comml. Art, 1951-52. Lithographic printer Your Town Press, Inc., Salem, Oreg., 1955-58; correctional officer Oreg. State Correctional Instn., 1958-60; owner Illustrators Workshop, Inc., Salem, 1960-61; advt. mgr. North Pacific Lumber Co., Portland, 1961-63; vocat. instr. graphic arts Oreg. Correctional Instn., 1963-70; lithographic printer Lloyd's Printing, Monterey, Calif., 1971-72; illustrator McGraw Hill, 1972-73; owner Publishers Art Svc., Monterey, 1972-81; correctional officer Oreg. State Penitentiary, 1982-90; ret. Owner Northwest Syndicate, 1993—. Editor/publisher: The Pro Cartoonist & Gagwriter; author: The Road to Damascus, 1981, The Descendants of Thomas Pier, 1992, The Origin and History of the Callaway and Holder Families, 1992, Firearms and Freedom, Their Care and Maintenance, 2002; author numerous OpEd cols. in Salem, Oreg. Statesman Jour., others; pub. cartoons nat. mags.; mural Mardi Gras Restaurant, Salem; cartoon strip Fabu, Oreg. Agr. mo. Mem. Rep. Nat. Com., Citizens Com. for Right to Keep and Bear Arms. Served with USN, 1946-51. Decorated victory medal WWII, China svc. medal, Korea medal, Navy occupation medal. Mem. U.S. Power Squadron, Nat. Rifle Assn., Acad. of Model Aeronautics, Oreg. Correctional Officers Assn. (co-founder, hon. mem.), Four Corners Rod and Gun Club. Republican. Avocations: sailing, flying, scuba, model aircraft building and flying. Home: 4822 Oak Park Dr NE Salem OR 97305-2931 E-mail: joe@joepierre.com.

PIERRE, NATASHA UNADA, accountant; b. San Fernando, Trinidad, June 14, 1973; d. Cleto Salazar Jamie and Leonora Shirley Pierre. BS, Jersey City State U., 1994; MBA, Seton Hall U., 1998. Acctg. specialist Prudential Ins. Co. Am., Newark, 1994—; sr. assoc. Ernst & Young LLP, Iselin, NJ, 2002. Roman Catholic. Avocations: travel, track and field.

PIERRE, PERCY ANTHONY, engineering educator; b. Donaldsville, La., Jan. 3, 1939; s. Percy John and Rosa (Villavaso) P.; m. Olga A. Markham, Aug. 8, 1965; children: Kristin Clare, Allison Celeste. BSEE, U. Notre Dame, 1961, MSEE, 1963, D of Engring. (hon.), 1977; PhD in Elec. Engring, Johns Hopkins U., 1967; postgrad., U. Mich., 1968; DSc (hon.), Rensselear Poly. Inst. Asst. prof. elec. engring. So. U., 1963; instr. Johns Hopkins U., Balt., 1963-64; instr. physics Morgan State Coll., 1964-66; instr. info. and control engring. U. Mich., Ann Arbor, 1967-68; instr. systems engring. UCLA, 1968-69; research engr. in communications RAND Corp., 1968-71; White House fellow, spl. asst. Office of Pres., 1969-70; dean Sch. Engring., Howard U., Washington, 1971-77; program officer for engring. edn. Alfred P. Sloan Found., 1973-75; asst. sec. for research, devel. and acquisition U.S. Dept. Army, 1977-81; engring. mgmt. cons., 1981-83; pres. Prairie View (Tex.) Agrl. and Mech. U. System, 1983-89, Honeywell prof. elec. engring., 1989-90; v.p. rsch. and grad. studies Mich. State U., East Lansing, 1990-95, prof. elec. engring., 1995—. Dir. engring. coll. council Am. Soc. for Engring. Edn., 1973-75; mem. sci. adv. group Def. Communications Agy., 1974-75; mem. adv. panel Office Exptl. Research and Devel. Incentives, NSF, 1973-74; mem. Commn. Scholars To Rev. Grad. Programs, Ill. Bd. Higher Edn., 1972-74; mem. panel on role U.S. engring. sch. in fgn. tech. assistance, 1972, co-chmn. symposium on minorities in engring., 1973; mem. rev. panel for Inst. for Applied Tech., Nat. Bur. Standards, 1973-77; chmn. com. on minorities Nat. Acad. Engring., 1976-77; cons. to dir. Energy Rsch. and Devel. Adminstrn., 1976-77; mem. Army Sci. Bd., 1984; mem. adv. bd. Sch. Engring., Johns Hopkins U., 1981-84; cons. Office Sec. Def., 1981-84; mem. adv. bd. Lincoln Labs., MIT. Contbr. articles on communications theory to profl. publs. Trustee U. Notre Dame, 1974-77, 81—; trustee, mem. exec. com. Nat. Fund for Minority Engring. Students, 1976-77; bd. dirs. The Hitachi Found., 1987, Ctr. for Naval Analysis, 1986, Assn. Tex. Colls. and Univs.; pres. Southwest Athletic Conf., 1985-87, bd. dirs. CMS Corp., 1990—, Defense Sci., 1992-94, Old Kent Fin. Corp., 1993—, bd. trustee Aerospace Corp., 1991—. Recipient Disting. Civilian Service award Dept. Army, 1981; award of merit from Senator Proxmire, 1979. Mem. IEEE (sr. mem.; Edison award com. 1978-80), Sigma Xi, Tau Beta Pi. Home: 2445 Emerald Lake Dr East Lansing MI 48823-7256 Office: Mich State U 357 Engineering East Lansing MI 48824-1226

PIERRE-LOUIS, ROSAIRE, elementary school educator, educator; b. North Miami, Fla., U.S., Jan. 10, 1972; d. Brenord and Genevieve (Cantave) Duclona; m. Pierre-Louis, Jan. 28, 1999; children: Brittany, Kasidy. AA, Miami Dade CC; BA, St. Thomas U., Miami; MA, Novasoutheastern Univ. Tchr. Miami Skill Ctr., Fla., substitute tchr. Mailing: 14899 NE 18th Ave #4A North Miami FL 33181 E-mail: Rosairerоro@aol.com.

PIERRI, MARY KATHRYN MADELINE, cardiologist, educator, emergency physician, educator; b. N.Y.C., Aug. 12, 1948; d. Charles Daniel and Margaret Loyola (Pesce) P. BA, Manhattanville Coll., 1969; MD, Med. Coll. Pa., 1974. Diplomate Am. Bd. Cardiology. Med. resident Med. Coll. Pa., Phila., 1974-77; fellow in cardiology N.Y. Hosp., N.Y.C., 1977-79; asst. physician Meml. Hosp., N.Y.C., 1980-89, assoc. physician, 1989-97, chief cardiology svc., 1991—2002, attending physician, 1997—. Assoc. prof. medicine Cornell Med. Coll., 1989—97, prof. clin. medicine, 1997—. Fellow Am. Coll. Cardiology, N.Y. Cardiological Soc.; mem. ACP, Soc. Critical Care Medicine, Alpha Omega Alpha. Office: Meml Hosp Sloan Kettering Cancer Ctr 1275 York Ave New York NY 10021-6094

PIERSKALLA, WILLIAM PETER, university dean, management-engineering educator; b. St. Cloud, Minn., Oct. 22, 1934; s. Aloys R. and Hilda A. Pierskalla; m. Carol Spargo, Children: Nicholas, William, Michael. AB in Econs., Harvard U., 1956, MBA, 1958; MS in Math., U. Pitts., 1962; PhD in Ops. Rsch., Stanford U., 1965; MA, U. Pa., 1978. Assoc. prof. Case Western Res. U., Cleve., 1965-68, So. Meth. U., Dallas, 1968-70; prof. dept. indsl. engring. and mgmt. scis. Northwestern U., Evanston, Ill., 1970-78; exec. dir. Leonard Davis Inst., U. Pa., Phila., 1978-83; prof., chmn. health care sys. dept. U. Pa., Phila., 1982-90, prof. decision sci. and systems engring., dep. dean acad. affairs Wharton Sch., 1983-89, Ronald A. Rosenfield prof., 1986-93; dir. Huntsman Ctr. Global Competition and Leadership U. Pa. Wharton Sch., 1989-91; John E. Anderson prof. UCLA, 1993—99, dean John E. Anderson Grad. Sch. Mgmt., 1993-97. Cons. HHS, Bethesda, Md., 1974-87, MDAX, Chgo., 1985-91, MEDICUS, Evanston, 1970-75, Sisters of Charity, Dayton, Ohio, 1982-83, Project Hope, 1990—; bd. dirs., chmn. The Bush Found.; bd. dirs. No. Wilderness Adventures, Informs. Contbr. articles to various publs. Mem. adv. bd. Lehigh U., 1986-93, U. So. Calif. Bus. Sch., 1987-93; regent St. Mary's Coll., 1998-2001, Hong Kong U. Sci. and Tech., 1992—. Recipient Harold Larnder Meml. prize Can. Oper. Rsch. Soc., 1993; grantee NSF, 1970-83, HHS, Washington, 1973-82, Office Naval Rsch., Arlington, Va., 1974-77. Mem. Ops. Rsch. Soc. Am. (pres. 1982-83, editor 1979-82, Kimball Disting. Svc. medal 1989), Inst. Mgmt. Scis. (assoc. editor 1970-77), Internat. Fedn. Operational Rsch. Socs. (pres. 1989-91), Inst. for Ops. Rsch. and Mgmt. Scis. (v.p. for publs. 2000—03), Omega Rho. Office: UCLA Anderson Grad Sch Mgmt 110 Westwood Plz Box 951481 Los Angeles CA 90095-1481

PIERSOL, ALLAN GERALD, mechanical engineer; b. Pitts., June 2, 1930; s. Robert James and Irene Laticia (Dematty) Piersol; m. Gertrud Teresia Moller, June 8, 1958; children: Allan Gerald Jr., Marie Theresa, John Robert. BS in Engring. Physics, U. Ill., 1952; MS in Engring., U. Calif., 1961. Lic. profl. engr., Calif. Rsch. engr. Douglas Aircraft Co., Santa Monica, Calif., 1952-59; mem. tech. staff Ramo Wooldridge Corp., Canoga Park, Calif., 1959-63; v.p. Measurement Analysis Corp., Santa Monica, Calif., 1963-71; prin. scientist Bolt Beranek and Newman, Inc., Conoga Park, 1971-85; sr. scientist Astron Corp., Santa Monica, 1985-88; owner Piersol Engring., Woodland Hills, Calif., 1988--. Lectr. U. So. Calif., L.A., 1965—95. Co-author: (book) Measurement and Analysis of Random Data, 1966, Random Data: Analysis and Measurement Procedures, 1971, 2000, Engineering Applications of Correletion and Spectral Analysis, 1980, 1993, Shock and Vibration Handbook, 2002. Mem.: ASME, Acoustical Soc. Am., Inst. Environ. Scis. and Tech. (Irwin Vigness Meml. award 1991). Achievements include patents for method and apparatus for determining terrain surface profiles. Home: 23021 Brenford St Woodland Hills CA 91364-4830 Office: Piersol Engring Co 23021 Brenford St Woodland Hills CA 91364-4830 Personal E-mail: apiersol@pacbell.net.

PIERSOL, LAWRENCE L. federal judge; b. Spirit Mound Township, S.D., Oct. 21, 1940; s. Ralph Nelson and Mildred Alice (Millette) P.; m. Catherine Anne Vogt, June 30, 1962; children: Leah C., William M., Elizabeth J. BA, U. S.D., 1962, JD summa cum laude, 1965. Bar: S.D. 1965, U.S. Ct. Mil. Appeals, 1965, U.S. Dist. Ct. S.D. 1968, U.S. Supreme Ct. 1972, U.S. Dist. Ct. Wyo. 1980, U.S. Dist. Ct. Nebr. 1986, U.S. Dist. Ct. Mont. 1988. Ptnr. Davenport, Evans, Hurwitz & Smith, Sioux Falls, S.D., 1968-93; judge U.S. Dist. Ct., Sioux Falls, 1993—; chief judge Dist. of S.D., 1999—. Mem. budget com. Jud. Conf. U.S., 1996-2003, chair economy subcom., 2001-03; chmn. tribal ct. com., security com. 8th Cir. Jud. Coun.; editor-in-chief Law Rev. Majority leader S.D. Ho. of Reps., Pierre, 1973-74, minority whip, 1971-72; del. Dem. Nat. Conv., 1972, 76, 80; S.D. mem. del. select comm. Dem. Nat. Com., 1971-75. Mem. ABA, State Bar S.D., Fed. Judges Assn. (bd. dirs., pres.). Roman Catholic. Avocations: reading, running, painting, sailing. Office: US Dist Ct 400 S Phillips Ave Sioux Falls SD 57104-6824

PIERSON, AERYK ALLEN, web site designer; b. Orange, Tex., Feb. 1, 1973; s. William Thomas Pierson; m. Kimberley Marie Thurston. B.A. in english and philosophy, U. of Houston, 1997—2002. Preprimary Paraprofessional Houston Montessori Ctr./TX, 1997. Systems adminstr. Sch. of the Woods, Houston, 1996—; webmaster self-employed, 2001—. Mem.: Sigma Tau Delta (life). Athiest. Avocations: writing, cartooning, movies. Office: School of the Woods 1321 Wirt Rd Houston TX 77055

PIERSON, AL See PIZZAMIGLIO, ALBERT THEODORE

PIERSON, ALBERT CHADWICK, business management educator; b. Pierson, Ill., Jan. 3, 1914; s. Charles Clevel and Gertrude Fannie (Gale) P.; 1 stepchild, Jay F. Lynch. BA in Liberal Arts and Scis, U. Ill., 1935; MBA with distinction, Harvard U., 1947; PhD, Columbia U., 1963. Merchandiser Montgomery Ward & Co., Chgo., 1935-41; mgmt. cons. N.Y.C., 1947-53; prof. mgmt. San Diego State U., San Diego State U., 1954—. Cons. in field; pub. accountant, Calif.; research editor Jour. Travel Research, 1967— Author: Trends in Lodging Enterprises, 1939-1963, 1963. Chmn. bd. Nat. Arts Found., N.Y.C.; mem. accreditation vis. teams Am. Assembly Collegiate Schs. Bus., 1977— . Served to col. AUS, 1941-46. Decorated Bronze Star. Fellow Soc. Applied Anthropology; mem. Acad. Mgmt. (pres. Western div. 1974-75), Western Council Travel Research (dir. 1965-67), Acad. Internat. Mgmt., Mil. Logistics Soc., James Joyce Soc., Beta Gamma Sigma, Sigma Iota Epsilon, Tau Sigma. Clubs: Harvard (Chgo.); Columbia (N.Y.C.); Marine Corps Officers (San Diego). Democrat. Methodist. Home: 1245 Park Row La Jolla CA 92037-3706 Office: San Diego State U Coll Bus San Diego CA 92182-0096

PIERSON, ANNE BINGHAM, physician; b. N.Y.C., June 9, 1929; d. Woodbridge and Ursula Wolcott (Griswold) Bingham; m. Richard N. Pierson Jr., July 10, 1954 (div. Aug. 1974); children: Richard N. III, Olivia Tiffany Jacobs, Alexandra deForest Griffin, Cordelia Stewart Comfort Smela; m. Richard Taliaferro Wright, Nov. 25, 1978 (div. Sept. 1997); m. Paul H. Altrocchi, May 9, 1998. Student, Katharine Branson Sch., Ross, Calif., 1943-47; BA, Vassar Coll., 1951; MD, Columbia U., 1955, MPH, 1972. Intern Lenox Hill Hosp., N.Y.C., 1955-56; substitute internship AUH, Beruit, Lebanon, 1955; mem. staff 7th Day Adventist Hosp., Taipei, Taiwan, 1957; clinic physician, med. dir. Planned Parenthood of Bergen County, Hackensack, N.J., 1960-74, also bd. dirs., 1966-69; asst. clin. prof. dept. ob-gyn. Columbia U. Coll. Physicians and Surgeons, Internat. Inst. Study of Human Reproduction, 1972-74; med. dir. Memphis Assn. for Planned Parenthood, Inc., 1974-75; staff physician N.Y. Telephone Co., 1976-87; med. dir. Planned Parenthood Assn. Hudson County, 1976-79; physician Sonalysts, Waterford, Conn., 1988—. Mem. nat. med. adv. com. Planned Parenthood-World Population, 1966-69. Pres. Vassar Class 1951, 1986-91; artist mem. Clinton Art Soc., 1989—, East Lyme Art League, 1991—; active Jr. League, 1969-69, sustainer, 1969—. Mem. AMA (Physicians Recognition award 1973—), Nat. Soc. Colonial Dames (life, asst. sec. 1991-94, 2d v.p. 1994-97), Cosmopolitan Club, Lyme Art Assn. (treas. 1998-99, pres. 1999—), Mystic Art Assn., Essex Art Assn. Office: Sonalysts 215 Parkway N Waterford CT 06385-1209

PIERSON, EDWARD SAMUEL, engineering educator, consultant; b. Syracuse, NY, June 27, 1937; s. Theodore and Marjorie O. (Bronner) P.; m. Elaine M. Grauer, June 6, 1971; 1 child, Alan. BS in Elec. Engring., Syracuse U., 1958; SM, MIT, 1960, ScD, 1964. Asst. prof., fellow MIT, 1965-66; assoc. prof., assoc. dept. head U. Ill., Chgo., 1966-75; program mgr. Argonne Nat. Labs., Ill., 1975-82; head dept. engring. Purdue U. Calumet, Hammond, Ind., 1982-95, spl. asst. to chancellor for environ. programs, 1995—. Cons. Argonne Nat. Lab., 1972-75, 82-93, Solmecs Corp., 1982-88, HMJ Corp., Washington, 1983-88, LM Mfg., 1994—. Contbr. articles to profl. jours. NSF fellow, 1958-60 Mem. IEEE, ASME, Am. Soc. Engring. Edn. Office: Purdue Univ Calumet Hammond IN 46323 Office Phone: 219-989-2467. E-mail: pierson@calumet.purdue.edu.

PIERSON, GREY, lawyer; b. Abilene, Tex., Dec. 31, 1950; s. Don and Annette (Grubbs) P. Student in history Baylor U., 1971, JD, 1974; student in internat. law Coll. William and Mary, Exeter, Eng., summer 1973. Bar: Tex. 1974, U.S. Dist. Ct. (no. dist.) Tex. 1974, U.S. Ct. Appeals (5th cir.) 1983, U.S. Supreme Ct. 1984. Assoc. Law Office of Tom Sneed, Odessa, Tex., 1974-76, Duke, Duke, & Jelinek, Arlington, Tex., 1976-78; ptnr. Duke & Pierson, Arlington, 1978-79, Pierson & Galyen, Arlington, 1983-88, Pierson, Baker & Ray, 1988-95, Pierson & Behr, 1995—; sole practice, Arlington, 1979-83; gen. counsel Mercer Internat. Transp., Ft. Worth, 1979-84; sr. legal adviser Dominica Caribbean Freeport Authority, Roseau, W.I., 1979; ptnr. Sta. KVMX-FM, Eastland, Tex., 1981-86. Contbr. articles to City Digest mag., 1979-80. Pres. Eastland Youth Council, 1967, Arlington Community Theatre, 1979; mem. Tarrant 2000 Commn. on Civil Justice, 1988; chmn. Tarrant County Rep. Jud. Recruitment Com., 1988; del. Rep. Nat. Conv., New Orleans, 1988. Recipient Disting. Svc. award Nat. Assn. Disabled Ams., Washington, 1982. Home: 301 W Abram St Arlington TX 76010

PIERSON, JEFFREY LYNN, protective services officer; m. Sara A. Scorr, 1969; children: Christine, Jennifer, Jeffrey Jr. BS in Pub. Adminstrn., Roger Williams U., 1997; M in Adminstrv. Scis., Fairleigh Dickinson U., 2001; grad., Army War Coll., Command and Gen. Staff Coll., Field Artillery Basic and Advanced Officers Course. Staff, commd. U.S. Army Nat. Guard, 1961—2001; asst. dep. chief of staff tng. Hdqs. Fourth U.S. Army, 1985—88; exec. officer Hdqs. 50th Armored Divsn. Art., 1988—89, G3, 1989—91; mobilization readiness officer, 1991—93; dir. Mil. Personnel Office, 1993; chief of staff, asst. adj. gen. N.J. Dept. Mil. Vet. Affairs, 1993—99;

undersheriff correctional divsn. Cape May County (N.J.) Sheriff's Office, 1999—. Spkr. in field on leadership, mgmt. and weapons of mass destruction; adj. prof. Fairleigh Dickinson U. Dep. chief safety and tng. Marmora Vol. Fire Co.; past. pres. Marmora Vol. Fire Dept., v.p. Ret. brigadier gen. U.S. Army, NG, N.J. Mem. Am. Correctional Assn., Am. Jail Assn. (cert. jail mgr.), N.J. Jail Wardens Assn., Fairleigh Dickinson U. Alumni Assn., Army War Coll. Alumni, Roger Williams U. Alumni, Masons (Cannon Lodge # 104 F&AM, past master). Avocations: golf, basketball, softball. Office: Cape May County Correctional Ctr 4 Moore Rd Cape May Court House NJ 08210

PIERSON, MARILYN EHLE, financial planner; b. Cleve., Feb. 27, 1931; d. Ernest John and Helen Irene (Steudel) Ehle; m. Edward G. Pierson, July 17, 1954; children: Melanie K., Edward G. III. BSBA, Miami U., 1953; grad., Coll. Fin. Planning, 1990, Inst. Cert. Divorce Planners, 1997. CFP. Sr. fin. advisor, advanced planner group Am. Express Fin. Advisors, Cleve., 1987—. Corp. presenter, fin. educator East Ohio Gas, AT&T, Cleve., Master Builders, Cleve., Preformed Line Products, Cleve., Parker Hannifin, Cleve.; guest lectr. Chagrin Valley C. of C., Chagrin Falls, Ohio; lectr. adult edn. Shaker Heights (Ohio). Fin. columnist Bainbridge Banter newspaper. Chair stewardship and resources Valley Presbyn. Ch., Bainbridge, Ohio, elder, 1991-93, planned giving chmn., 1991-95, 2000—. Mem. Fin. Planning Assn. (treas. exec. com. NE Ohio chpt. 1994-98), Exec. Women Internat. (advisor, bd. dirs. 1997, pres. 1996), Estate Planning Coun. Cleve. Avocation: travel. Home: 8178 Chagrin Mills Rd Chagrin Falls OH 44022-3807 Office: Am Express Fin Advisors 22901 Mill Creek Blvd #375 Cleveland OH 44122-4556 E-mail: marilyn.e.pierson@aefa.com.

PIERSON, RICHARD NORRIS, JR., medical educator; b. N.Y.C., Sept. 22, 1929; s. Richard Norris and Dorothy (Stewart) Pierson; m. Alice Roberts, Aug. 26, 1974; children from previous marriage: Richard N., Olivia Tiffany, Alexandra de Forest, Cordelia S.C. stepchildren: Alice W. Dunn, Eric C.W. Dunn. BA, Princeton U., 1951; MD, Columbia U., 1955. Diplomate Am. Bd. Internal Medicine, Am. Bd. Nuclear Medicine. Resident St. Luke's Roosevelt Hosp., N.Y.C., 1955—61, assoc. dir., 1961—65, dir. div. nuclear medicine, 1965—89, dir. body composition unit, 1965—2003, attending physician, 1975—; prof. clin. medicine Columbia U., 1980—; dir. medicine Hackensack Hosp., 1973—74; staff assoc. Brookhaven Nat. Lab., 1970—2002; rsch. scholar Lawrence Radiation Lab., Berkeley, Calif., 1970—71. Bioengring. inst. Columbia U., 1976—, chmn., 1989—94. Editor: Quantitative Radiocardiography, 1975; contbr. articles to profl. jours. Warden St. Paul's Ch., 1980—82; bd. dirs. Englewood Health Dept., NJ, 1966—74, Empire Blue Cross/Blue Shield, NY, 1978—91, v.p., 1990—91. NIH grantee, 1973—76, 1986—99, John A. Hartford grantee, 1967—70. Fellow: ACP, N.Y. Acad. Medicine; mem.: AAAS, N.Y. County Med. Soc. (pres. 1978—79), Soc. Nuclear Medicine (greater N.Y. area pres. 1982—83, del. to AMA 1991—2001, trustee 1991—, Berson-Yalow award 1995), Alliance for Continuing Med. Edn. (pres. 1987—89), Am. Med. Rev. Rsch. Ctr. (N.Y. State del. to AMA 1978—90, pres. 1985—89), Am. Bur. Med. Advancement in China (pres. 1979—87), N.Y. County Health Svc. Rev. Orgn. (chmn. 1980—82), Am. Inst. Nutrition, Am. Physiol. Soc., P&S Alumni Assn. (pres. 1989—91), Englewood Field Club, Century Club. Home: 60 Lincoln St Englewood NJ 07631-3117 Office: St Lukes Roosevelt Hosp Ctr 1111 Amsterdam Ave New York NY 10025-1716 Office Phone: 212-523-3385. Business E-Mail: RNP1@columbia.edu.

PIERSON, ROBERT DAVID, investor; b. Orange, N.J., Mar. 5, 1935; s. Carleton Wellington and Muriel Browning (Potter) Pierson; m. Virginia Duncan Knight, Apr. 30, 1960; children: Lisa Boles, Alexandra Mead, Robert Wellington. BA, Lehigh U., 1957. Exec. asst. 1st Nat. City Bank N.Y., N.Y.C., 1958-61; asst. to pres. Cooper Labs. Inc., N.Y.C., 1961-65; dir. mktg. svcs. Arbrook divsn. Johnson & Johnson, Somerville, NJ, 1965-69; v.p. Klemtner Advt. Inc., N.Y.C., 1969-71; sr. v.p. Bowery Savs. Bank, N.Y.C., 1972-80; vice chmn., dir. Carteret Bancorp, Inc., Wilmington, Del., 1980-90; pres. No. Divsn. Collective Bank, 1990-96, Collective Fin. Svcs., Inc., Harbor Mortgage Co. divsn. Collective Bank, Montclair, NJ, 1997-98; pvt. investor, 1998—. Mem. town coun. Twp. of Mendham, NJ, 1992—, mayor, 1995—96, 2003—04. With USCG, 1958—59. Mem.: Morristown Club, Morris County Golf Club. Republican. Presbyterian. Home: Green Hills Rd Mendham NJ 07945-3305

PIERSON, RODNEY, insurance company executive; CFO Safeco Corp., Seattle. Office: Safeco Corp Safeco Plaza Seattle WA 98185

PIERSON, W. DEVIER, lawyer; b. Pawhuska, Okla., Aug. 12, 1931; s. Welcome D. and Frances (Ratliff) P.; m. Shirley Frost, Feb. 1, 1957; children: Jeffrey, Elizabeth, Stephen. AB, U. Okla., 1953, LLB, 1957. Bar: Okla. 1957, US Dist. Ct. Okla. 1957, US Supreme Ct. 1966, US Ct. Appeals DC 1969, US Ct. Appeals (5th cir.) 1972, US Ct. Appeals (10th cir.) 1975, US Ct. Appeals (2d cir.) 1996. Assoc. Duval & Head, Oklahoma City, 1957-59; sole practice Oklahoma City, 1959-65; chief counsel Joint Com. on Orgn. of Congress, 1965-67; assoc. spl. counsel to Pres. and Counselor White House Office, 1967-68; spl. counsel to Pres. of US, 1968-69; ptnr. Pierson Semmes and Bemis and predecessor firms, Washington, 1969-2000; spl. counsel Verner, Liipfert, Bernhard, McPherson and Hand Chartered, Washington, 2000—02, Piper Rudnick LLP, Washington, 2002—04, Hunton & Williams LLP, Washington, 2004—. Trustee U. Okla. Found., 1996—; chmn. bd. visitors U. Okla. Coll. of Law; mem. bd. visitors U. Okla. Internat. Programs Ctr.; vice chmn., dir. Atlantic Coun. of US, 1995-. Served to 1st lt. US Army, 1953-54. Recipient Outstanding Alumnus award U. Okla., 1995; inducted into Okla. Hall of Fame, 2002. Mem. ABA, DC Bar Assn., Fed. Bar Assn., Okla. Bar Assn., Met. Club (Washington). Home: 5326 Chamberlin Ave Chevy Chase MD 20815-6661 Office Phone: 202-419-2098.

PIERSON, WAYNE GEORGE, trust company executive; b. L.A., Nov. 5, 1950; s. Norman Einar and Annabelle Florence (McLay) P.; m. Margaret Aileen Boyle, Mar. 18, 1972; children: Heather, Dawn, Mark, Michael. BS in Bus. Adminstrn. with honors, Calif. State U., Northridge, 1973. CPA, Oreg., Calif. Audit supr. Ernst & Whinney (now Ernst & Young), L.A. and Portland, Oreg., 1973-80; treas. Gregory Affiliates, Beaverton, Oreg., 1980-82; CFO, treas. Meyer Meml. Trust, Portland, 1982—. Mem. adv. com. Vega Ptnrs., Onset Ptnrs. Chair investment com. Columbia Cascade Scout Coun. Mem. AICPA, Chartered Fin. Analysts Inst., Oreg. Soc. CPAs, Portland Soc. Fin. Analysts, Found. Fin. Officers Group (bd. dirs.). Avocations: tennis, scouting, travel. Office: Meyer Memorial Trust STE 400 425 NW 10th Ave Portland OR 97209-3128

PIES, RONALD E. retired city official; b. Rochester, N.Y., Mar. 21, 1940; s. Herman S. and Sylvia Pies; m. Bernita Orloff, Aug. 27, 1964; children: Cara Jean Tracy, David Paul. BS, Ariz. State U., 1963. Recreation leader City of Phoenix, Ariz., 1962-64; head recreation divsn. City of Scottsdale (Ariz.) Parks and Recreation Dept., 1964-69; dir. parks and recreation City of Tempe, Ariz., 1969-84, cmty. svcs. dir., 1984-98, ret., 1998—. Guest lectr. Ariz. State U.; spl. projects coord. Ariz. Lottery, 1999—. Mem., pres. Kyrene Sch. Dist. Governing Bd., 1979-82; chmn., bd. regents Pacific Revenue Sources Mgmt. Sch. NRPA; gen. chmn. Fiesta Bowl Soccer Classic, 1982-98; founding mem. Tempe YMCA bd. mgrs.; apptd. mem. Ariz. State Parks Bd., 1987-93, chair, 1991. Named Outstanding Young Man, Jaycees; recipient Superior Svc. Mgmt. award ASPA, Ariz. chpt., 1988; named to Hall of Fame, Ariz. State U. Alumni for Coll. Pub. Programs, 1996, Hall of Fame, Tempe Elem. Sch. Dist., 1996. Mem. Tempe C. of C., Ariz. Parks and Recreation Assn. (bd. dirs. 1986-98, pres. adminstrs., Disting. Fellow award 1983, Life Mem. award 1998, L.E.G.E.N.D. award 2000), Nat. Recreation and Parks Assn. (Outstanding Profl. 1991), Cactus League Baseball Assn. (pres. 1993-94, apptd. mem. Ariz. baseball commn. by Gov. Symington 1994—, chair 1995-2000), Tempe Diablos Club, Sigma Alpha Epsilon. E-mail: eskimo1920@cox.net.

PIESTER, DAVID L(EE), magistrate judge; b. Lincoln City, Nebr., Nov. 18, 1947; s. George Piester; married; children. BS, U. Nebr., 1969, JD, 1972. Bar: Nebr. 1972, U.S. Dist. Ct. Nebr. 1972, U.S. Ct. Appeals (8th cir.) 1976, U.S. Supreme Ct. 1979. Staff atty. Legal Svcs. S.E. Nebr., Lincoln, 1972-73, exec. dir., 1973-79; asst. U.S. atty. Dept. Justice, Lincoln, 1979-81; magistrate judge U.S. Dist. Ct. Nebr., Lincoln, 1981—. Cons. Legal Services Corp., Nat. Legal Aid and Defender Assn., 1974-77. Mem. Lincoln Human rights commn., 1978-79. Mem. ABA (jud. adminstrn. divsn., Nat. Conf. Fed. Trial Judges), Nebr. State Bar Assn., Fed. Magistrate Judges Assn., Lincoln Bar Assn., Eighth Cir. Jud. Coun. (ex officio 1993-96). Office: US Dist Ct 100 Centennial Mall North 566 Fed Bldg Lincoln NE 68508

PIETERS, CARLE MCGETCHIN, geology educator, planetary scientist, researcher; widow. BA, Antioch Coll., 1966; BS, MIT, 1971, MS, 1972, PhD, 1977. Tchr. math. Somerville (Mass.) H.S., 1966-67; tchr. sci. Peace Corps, Sarawak, Malaysia, 1967-69; staff scientist rschr. Planetary Astron. Lab. MIT, 1972-75; space scientist Johnson Space Ctr. NASA, 1977-80; asst. prof. Brown U., Providence, R.I., 1980-83, assoc. prof. geology, 1983-94, prof. geoscis., 1994—. Asteroid named in honor, Pieters. Mem. AAAS, Am. Geophys. Union, Am. Astron. Soc., Meteoritical Soc. Office: Brown Univ PO Box 1846 Providence RI 02912-1846

PIETERS, RICHARD SAWYER, JR., radiation oncologist, educator; b. Lawrence, Mass., June 1, 1948; s. Richard Sawyer and Norma Kenfield Pieters; m. Edith M. Jolin, May 22, 1982; 1 child, Jennifer R. AB, Princeton U., 1970; MEd, Boston U., 1974; MD, Brown U., 1982. Diplomate Am. Bd. Radiology. Intern Wayne State Affiliated Hosp., Detroit, 1982-83; resident in therapeutic radiology Tufts-New Eng. Med. Ctr., Boston, 1983-86, co-chief resident, 1985-86; dir. radiation oncology Jordan Hosp., Plymouth, Mass., 1994—. Asst. prof. clin. radiology Ohio State U. Coll. Medicine, James Cancer Hosp. and Rsch. Inst., Columbus, 1987-94; lectr. Harvard U. Med. Sch., Boston, 1994—; clin. asst. prof. radiology Boston U. Sch. Medicine, 1994-98, clin. assoc. prof. radiology, 1998—. Trustee Mass. Med. South, 2001—. Mem. AMA, Am. Coll. Radiology, Am. Soc. for Therapeutic Radiology and Oncology, Am. Soc. Clin. Oncology, Radiation Rsch. Soc., Gilbert H. Fletcher Soc., S.W. Oncology Group, Children's Oncology Group, Plymouth Dist. Med. Soc. (treas. 2000, 02, pres. 2000-02 Office: Jordan Hosp Club Cancer Ctr 275 Sandwich St Plymouth MA 02360-2183 Business E-Mail: rpieters@jordanhospital.org.

PIETERSE, NATALIE L. writer, literature educator; b. N.Y.C., Jan. 30, 1932; d. Joseph A. Vasile and Lucy Adamo; m. Charles Ross (div. Dec. 1970); children: Pauline, Michael, Margaret. BSc, William Paterson U., 1960; MA summa cum laude, Fairleigh Dickinson U., 1974; MSc, Coll. New Rochelle, 1992. Elem. tchr. Pearl River (N.Y.) Schs., 1962—92, Internat. Sch. Aruba, 1994—96; adj. prof. Rockland C.C., Suffern, NY, 1997—2003; freelance writer Pearl River, 2003—. Tchr. Shakespear for Children Theater, 1984—92; tchr. Choral Reading Program Children, 1984—94. Interview and recording of war records of vets. Libr. Congress. Home: 3 Mercury Drive Pearl River NY 10965

PIETON, RICHARD, anesthesiologist; b. Krakow, Poland, Feb. 6, 1946; s. Roman and Balbina Pieton. M of Psychology, Jagiellonian U., 1968; MD, Med. Acad., Krakow, Poland, 1973; PhD, Med. Acad., 1979. Diplomate Am. Bd. Anesthesiology, Am. Bd. Internal Medicine. Staff physician Med. Acad. Krakow, Poland, 1974-80; resident in internal medicine Shadyside Hosp., Pitts., 1982-84; resident in anesthesiology U. Nebr. Med. Ctr., Omaha, 1985-86; fellow in neuroanesthesiology Hosp. U. Pa., Phila., 1987-88; staff anesthesiologist VA Hosp., West L.A., 1988—; asst. clin. prof. UCLA. Mem. ACP, Am. Soc. Anesthesiologists. Home: 1253 11th St Unit 1 Santa Monica CA 90401-2050

PIETRI, TODD T. venture capitalist; Grad. cum laude, Duke U., 1989; MBA, Ga. State U. Robinson Sch. Bus. Dir. IT consulting, direct sales divsns. CompuSys., 1992—97; with Callier Interests, Houston; v.p. Legacy Securities Corp., Atlanta; co-founder Legacy's Tech. and Comm. Investment Banking Group; co-founder, gen. ptnr. Milestone Venture Ptnrs., NY, 1999—. Dir. Bizbash.com, Inc., NavTrak, Inc.; bd. observer Derivatives Portfolio Mgmt., LLC, ExpertPlan, Inc., Octagon Rsch. Solutions, Inc. Office: Milestone Venture Ptnrs 551 Madison Ave 7th Fl New York NY 10022 Office Fax: 212-223-0315.

PIETRINI, ANDREW GABRIEL, automotive aftermarket executive; b. Bryn Mawr, Pa., Feb. 27, 1937; s. Bernard and Irene (Norcini) P.; m. Pam Mari, Sept. 29, 1962; children: Darrin, Wayne BS, Villanova U., 1958. C.P.A., Pa. Jr. acct. Fernald & Co., Phila., 1958-60; sr. acct. O & W Audit Co., Narberth, Pa., 1960-62; asst. sec. James Talcott, Inc., N.Y.C., 1962-68; pres. UIS, Inc., N.Y.C., 1968—, dir., 1972—, chmn., CEO, pres., 1986—. Bd. dirs. Lebensfeld Found., N.Y.C., 1979— Mem. Am. Inst. C.P.A.s, Fin. Execs. Inst. Republican. Roman Catholic. Avocations: sailing; golf. Office: UIS Inc 15 Exchange Pl Ste 1120 Jersey City NJ 07302-3912

PIETROCARLO, NICK, artist, consultant; b. Buffalo, May 11, 1971; s. Shirley and Nick Pietrocarlo. BS in Mgmt., Calif. Coast U. Project Mmgt. Profl. Project Mgmt. Inst., 2002. Graphic artist Arvin Calspan Corp., Buffalo, 1988—89; film intern Hallwalls Contemporary Arts Ctr., Buffalo, 1989—90, tech. asst., 1990—92; photo lab mgr. U. of Buffalo, 1991—91; treas. Topsy Turvy, Inc, Buffalo, 1992—94; video programmer Royal Caribbean Cruises, Ltd., Miami, 1994—97, interactive tv specialist, 1997—99, project mgr., 1999—2002, program mgr., 2002—. Freelance artist, Miami, 1990—; cons. Cruise Industry and Info. Tech., Miami, 2000—; mem. cmty. emergency response team, Miami Beach, Fla. *Career achievements and highlights include program managing the initiation, planning, and execution of Royal Caribbean's transformation initiative, inclusive of four portfolios with over 80 projects. Project managing the deployment of the cruise industry's largest interactive TV system onboard Royal Caribbean's Voyager of the Seas. Self starting own S-Corporation, at age 20, delivering video production and multimedia exhibitions in the Western New York area. Succeeding in developing two careers. The first, encompassing broadcast/analog technologies, and the current, encompassing digital and computer technologies. He continues to utilize his creative and artistic strengths to problem solve, manage risk, communicate, and lead teams.* Editor: (16mm film installation) Expanded Cinema; editor: (videographer) (video installation, video prodn.) Implosion; photographer (16mm film, 35mm slide installation) Snow; editor (videographer): (video exhbn., TV broadcast) Riding on the hair of a buffalo (Video Prodn. Grant - Owego Exptl. TV Ctr., 1991, Video Prodn. Grant Rochester Visual Arts Ctr., 1992, Video Prodn. Residency Oswego Exptl. TV Ctr., 1992, Video Prodn. Grant and Award, Niagara Coun. of the Arts, 1992), (video wallpaper) Topsy Turvy, (TV talk show) The Pink Flamingo Show; model (photography exhibit) Nick; editor: (TV pub. svc. announcements) AIDS Trilogy; creator (video installation) Eye; editor: (video installation) Opening Night; dir.: (segment for Jerry Lewis Telethon) Charo; associate producer (video prodn.) Casino Royale; editor: (video installation) Edge, Folk; photographer (35mm slide installation) Fruit; editor: (video installation) Industry; production manager (mixed media installation) First Night, curator (cocteau) Performance Art and Video Exhibitions. Mem.: Project Mgmt. Inst. Roman Catholic. Achievements include production of conceptual device. Avocations: target shooting, walking, bicycling. Office: Royal Caribbean Cruises Ltd 1050 Caribbean Way Miami FL 33132 Office Phone: 954-517-6041. Personal E-mail: nick@pietrocarlo.com. Business E-Mail: npietrocarlo@rccl.com.

PIETROFESA, JOHN JOSEPH, education educator; b. N.Y.C., Sept. 12, 1940; s. Louis John and Margaret P.; m. Cathy Marks, June 22, 1985; children: John, Paul, Maria, Dolores. EdB cum laude, U. Miami, 1961; MEd, 1963, Ed.D., 1967. Diplomate Am. Bd. Sexology; cert. cognitive behavior therapist, forensic counselor, sex therapist; lic. psychologist, social worker. Counselor Dade County (Fla.) pub. schs., 1965-67; prof. edn. Wayne State U., Detroit, 1967—; div. head theoret. and behavioral founds., 1977-83; dept. chair counselor edn., 1999—. Cons. to various schs., hosps. and univs. Author: The Authentic Counselor, 1971, 2nd edit., 1980, School Counselor as Professional, 1971, Counseling and Guidance in the Twentieth Century, 1971, Elementary School Guidance and Counseling, 1973, Career Development, 1975, Career Education, 1976, College Student Development, 1977, Counseling: Theory Research and Practice, 1978, Guidance: An Introduction, 1980, Counseling: An Introduction, 1984; mem. editl. bd. Counseling and Values, 1972-75. 1st lt. Mil. Police Corps, AUS, 1963-65. Mem. Am. Psychol. Assn., Am. Personnel and Guidance Assn., Mich. Personnel and Guidance Assn., Assn. Counselor Edn. and Supervision, Phi Delta Kappa. Home: PO Box 99 Bloomfield Hills MI 48303-0099 Office: Wayne State U 321 Education Detroit MI 48202

PIETROWSKI, JOHN A. performing company executive, educator; b. Trenton, N.J., Mar. 30, 1958; s. Eleanor A. and Frank A. Pietrowski. BS in Speech, Performance Studies, Northwestern U., 1980; MPA in Non-Profit Mgmt., Seton Hall U., 2001. Exec. prodr. Playwrights Theatre N.J., Madison, NJ, 1986—90; adj. prof. theatre Drew U., 1991—; artistic dir. Playwrights Theatre N.J., 1990—. Adj. prof. Fairleigh Dickinson U., Madison, 1997—. Dir.: (stage director) various prodns. Vice-president Nat. New Play Network, Kansas City, Mo., 2001. Scholar, Seton Hall U., 1993—94. Fellow: Leadership N.J.; mem.: N.J. Theatre Educators Coalition. Office: Playwrights Theatre of New Jersey PO Box 1295 33 Green Village Rd Madison NJ 07940-1295 E-mail: jpietrowski@ptnj.org.

PIETRUSKI, JOHN MICHAEL, JR., biotechnology company executive, pharmaceuticals executive; b. Sayreville, N.J., Mar. 12, 1933; m. Roberta Jeanne Talbot, July 3, 1954; children: Glenn David, Clifford John, Susan Jane. BS with honors, Rutgers U., 1954; LLD (hon.), Concordia Coll., 1993. With Proctor and Gamble Co., 1954-63; pres. med. products div. C.R. Bard, Inc., 1963-77; with Sterling Drug, Inc., N.Y.C., 1977-88; pres. Pharm. Group, 1977-81, corp. exec. v.p., 1981-83, pres., chief operating officer, 1983-85, chmn., chief exec. officer, 1985-88, ret., 1988; pres. Dansara Cons., 1988—; chmn. Encysive Pharms., Inc., 1990—. Bd. dirs. First Energy Corp., PDI, Inc., Xylos Corp., Trial Card, Inc. 1st lt. U.S. Army, 1955—57. Mem. Phi Beta Kappa Clubs: Union League (N.Y.C.). Home: 27 Paddock Ln Colts Neck NJ 07722-1266 Office: One Penn Plaza Ste 3408 New York NY 10119

PIETRUSZKA, MICHAEL F. judge; b. Buffalo, Oct. 20, 1956; s. Walter J. and Dorothy (Lutomski) P.; m. Patricia Ann Joyce, July 19, 1986. BA magna cum laude, Canisius Coll., 1978; JD cum laude, Syracuse U., 1981. Bar: N.Y. 1982, U.S. Dist. Ct. (we. dist.) N.Y. 1982, U.S. Ct. Internat. Trade 1985, U.S. Supreme Ct. 1986. Pvt. practice law, Buffalo, 1982-87; asst. corp. counsel City of Buffalo, 1983-86, dir. parking enforcement div., 1986-87; gen. counsel Buffalo Mcpl. Housing Authority, 1987; judge City Ct. of Buffalo, 1988-98, Erie County Ct., Buffalo, 1999—. Competition judge N.E. Regional Jessup Internat. Moot Ct., 1996; mem. faculty N.Y. State Ann. Jud. Seminar; mem. exec. com. Nat. Conf. Spl. Ct. Judges, ABA jud. sect., 1997—. Exec. editor Syracuse Jour. Internat. Law and Commerce, 1980-81; legal columnist Am-Pol Eagle, 1982-83, Metro Cmty. News, 1990, Polish Am. Jour., 1993—; author: Polonia Connections, 1997. Active Buffalo Urban League; dir. Floss Ave. Men's Choir, East Buffalo Civic Assn., 1984-87, N.W. Buffalo Cmty. Ctr.; pres. Forest Dist. Civic Assn., Monsignor Healy Found. Scholarship Com.; pres. Western N.Y. chpt. Kosciuszko Found., mem. nat. adv. com.; bd. dirs. Buffalo-Rzeszow Sister City Com.; dir. Gen. Pulaski Assn. of Niagara Frontier; nat. dir. Polish Am. Congress; mem. Polish Am./Jewish Am. Coun. Western N.Y.; hon. dir. Polish Cadets Buffalo, 1998. Recipient Jurist Citation of Honor award Nat. Columbus Day Com., 1988, Martin Luther King Human Rels. award Erie County So. Christian Leadership Conf., 1990, N.W. Buffalo Cmty. Svc. award, 1991, Pres.'s award Buffalo-Rzeszow Sister Cities Inc., 1993, Cert. of Spl. Congl. Recognition, 1996, Civic Recognition award Forest Dist. Civic Assn., 1996, others; named Man of Yr., Pulaski Police Assn., 1989, Am.-Pol Citizen of Yr., 1991. Mem. NAACP, N.Y. State Bar Assn. (cert. of honor 1992, 93, 94), Erie County Bar Assn., Am. Judges Assn., Polish Cadets, Profl. and Businessmen's Assn., K.C., Advocates Club (sec. 1990, v.p. 1991, pres. 1992, Pres.'s award 1993), YMCA Greater Buffalo Century Club, 100 Club Buffalo, Buffalo Canoe Club, Polish Union Am., St. Joseph's Guild, Chopin Singing Soc. Democrat. Roman Catholic. Avocations: travel, computers, website. Office: Erie County Ct 92 Franklin St Buffalo NY 14202-3902 E-mail: pietruszka@aol.com.

PIETRZAK, ALFRED ROBERT, lawyer; b. Glen Cove, N.Y., June 26, 1949; s. Alfred S. and Wanda M. (Wapniarski) P.; m. Sharon Esther Chizek, July 9, 1978; children: Eric A., Daniel J. BA, Fordham U., 1971; JD, Columbia U., 1974. Bar: N.Y. 1975, U.S. Dist. Ct. (so., ea., we. and no. dists.) N.Y. 1975, U.S. Dist. Ct. (no. dist.) Calif. 1983, U.S. Ct. Appeals (2d. cir.) 1975, U.S. Ct. Appeals (9th cir.) 1983, U.S. Ct. Appeals (11th cir.) 1985, U.S. Supreme Ct. 1985. Assoc. Brown & Wood (formerly Brown, Wood, Ivey, Mitchell & Petty), N.Y.C., 1974-82, ptnr., 1983—; also head litigation practice group. Mem. fin. products adv. com. Commodity Futures Trading Comm.; mem. CLE faculty Fordham U. Sch. Law.; mem. litig. adv. com. Bond Market Assn.; bd. advisors Rev. of Securities and Commodities Regulation; bd. editors Futures Internat. Law Letter; adv. bd. Fordham Internat. Law Jour. Contbr. articles to legal jours. Mem. ABA, Assn. Bar City N.Y. (securities regulation com., chmn. futures regulation com., retail fin. svcs. com.), Am. Law Inst. (lectr.), Securities Industry Assn., Futures Industry Assn. Democrat. Roman Catholic.

PIETZSCH, MICHAEL EDWARD, lawyer; b. Burlington, Iowa, Aug. 1, 1949; s. Walter E. and Leanna (Moore) P.; m. Ellen G. Hart; children: Christine E., Catherine M. AB, Stanford U., 1971; JD, U. Chgo., 1974. Bar: Ill. 1974, Ariz. 1976. Assoc. Schwartz & Freeman, Chgo., 1974-75; ptnr. McCabe & Pietzsch, Phoenix, 1975-90, Pietzsch & Williams, Phoenix, 1990-95, Polese, Pietzsch, Williams & Nolan, Phoenix, 1995—. Contbr. articles to profl. jours.; speaker at profl. confs. Del. White House Conf. Small Bus., Washington, 1986, White House Savs. Summit, 1998; chmn. bd. trustees Ariz. Sci. Ctr., 1994-98; pres. The Group, Inc., 1995-98. Fellow Am. Coll. Tax Counsel, Am. Coun. on Tax Policy, Am. Coll. Employee Benefits Counsel; mem. ABA (chmn. personal svc. orgns. com. tax sect. 1986-90), Stanford Phoenix Club (pres. 1982-84). Office: 2702 N Third St Ste 3000 Phoenix AZ 85004 Office Phone: 602-604-6250. E-mail: pietzsch@ppwn.com.

PIFER, ALAN (JAY PARRISH), former foundation executive; b. Boston, May 4, 1921; s. Claude Albert and Elizabeth (Parrish) P.; m. Erica Pringle, June 20, 1953 (div. 1994); children: Matthew, Nicholas, Daniel. AB, Harvard U., 1947; Lionel de Jersey Harvard student Emmanuel Coll., Cambridge (Eng.) U., 1947-48; LLD (hon.), Mich. State U., 1971, Hofstra U., 1974, Notre Dame U., 1975; DHL (hon.), Marymount Coll., 1983, Millsaps Coll., 1986; D of Univ. (hon.), Open U., Eng., 1974; JD (hon.), Atlanta U., 1980; DEd (hon.), U. Cape Town, South Africa, 1984. Exec. sec. U.S. Ednl. Commn. in U.K., London, 1948-53; program officer Carnegie Corp. N.Y., 1953-63, v.p., 1963-65, acting pres., 1965-67, pres., 1967-82, pres. emeritus, sr. cons., 1982-87; chmn., pres. Southport Inst. for Policy Analysis, 1987-91, chmn., 1991-94; v.p. Carnegie Found. for Advancement of Teaching, 1963-65, acting pres., 1965-67, pres., 1967-79, trustee, 1979-87. Bd. dirs. Technoserve, Inc. Author: (with others) Our Aging Society, 1986, (with others) Women on the Front Lines: Meeting the Challenge of an Aging America, 1993; Government for the People, 1987. Mem. mgmt. com. U.S.-South Africa Leader Exch. Program, 1957—, pub. policy com. Advt. Coun., 1987-91, adv. coun. Columbia U. Sch. Social Work, 1963-69, R & D ctr. panel U.S. Office Edn., 1963-65, adv. com. higher edn. U.S. Dept. Health Edn. and Welfare, 1967-68, bd. of overseers Harvard U., 1969-75, Charles Stark Draper Lab. bd. MIT, 1970-76, Commn. Pvt. Philanthropy and Pub. Needs, 1973-75; chmn. Consortium Advancement Pvt. Higher Edn., 1983-92, mayor's adv. com. Bd. Higher Edn. N.Y.C., 1966-69, Pres.'s Task Force on Edn., 1968, Aging Soc. Project, 1982-87, Nat. Conf. on Social Welfare Project, 1983-87; co-chmn. N.Y. State Nutrition Watch com., 1982; trustee U. Bridgeport, Conn., 1973—, Assn. Governing Bds. Colls. and Univs., 1985-91, African Am. Inst., 1957-71, Found. Libr. Ctr., 1967-71, Am. Ditchley Found., 1973-81; bd. dirs. Bus. Coun. Effective Literacy Inc., 1984-93, N.Y. Urban Coalition, 1967-71, Nat. Assembly for Social Policy and Devel., 1967-71, Coun. on Founds., Inc., 1970-76, Fed. Reserve Bank N.Y., 1970-76, Harry Frank Guggenheim Found., 1989—. Capt. U.S. Army, 1942-46, ETO. Recipient Barnard Coll. medal of distinction, 1980, Cleveland E. Dodge medal of distinction Tchrs. Coll., Columbia U., 1982. Fellow Am. Acad. of Arts and Scis., African Studies Assn. (founding), Royal Soc. Arts (London); mem. Am. Assn. for Higher Edn. (bd. dirs. 1982-90), Century Assn. Clubs: Harvard (N.Y.C.). Democrat. Avocation: gardening. Home: 3 Farm Rd New Canaan CT 06840-6626

PIGA, STEPHEN MULRY, retired lawyer; b. Bklyn., Apr. 9, 1929; s. Stephen Paul and Ella (Mulry) P.; married, Feb. 23, 1952 (div.); children: Maureen, Stephen, Susan, Elizabeth; m. Emilie Halliday, Aug. 1, 1975 (dec. Aug. 2003); 1 dau., Margaret. AB, Princeton U., 1950; LL.B., Columbia u., 1955. Bar: N.J. 1955, N.Y. 1956. Assoc. White & Case, N.Y.C., 1955-63, ptnr., 1964-92; ret., 1992. Lectr. Practicing Law Inst. N.Y. and various insts., bar assns. Served to capt. USMCR, 1951-53. Mem. ABA, N.Y. State Bar Assn. (exec. com. tax sect. 1981-89, chmn. employee benefits com.), Assn. of Bar of City N.Y., N.J. Bar Assn., Am. Contract Bridge League (life master), Profl. Bowlers' Assn. Am., High Mt. Golf Club. Republican. Avocations: fishing, golf, bowling.

PIGFORD, THOMAS HARRINGTON, nuclear engineering educator; b. Meridian, Miss., Apr. 21, 1922; s. Lamar and Zula Vivian (Harrington) P.; m. Catherine Kennedy Cathey, Dec. 31, 1948 (dec. 1992); children: Cynthia Pigford Naylor, Julie Pigford Brink; m. Elizabeth Hood Weekes, Nov. 12, 1994. BS in Chem. Engring., Ga. Inst. Tech., 1943; S.M. in Chem. Engring., M.I.T., 1948, Sc.D. in Chem. Engring., 1952. Asst. prof. chem. engring., dir. Sch. Engring. Practice, M.I.T., 1950-52, asst. prof. nuclear and chem. engring., 1952-55, assoc. prof., 1955-57; head engring., dir. nuclear reactor projects and asst. dir. research lab. Gen. Atomic Co., La Jolla, Calif., 1957-59; prof. nuclear engring., chmn. dept. nuclear engring. U. Calif., Berkeley, 1959—; sr. rsch. scientist Lawrence Berkeley Lab., 1959—. Mem. panel Nat. Atomic Safety Licensing Bd. AEC-Nuclear Regulatory Commn., 1963-77; mem. Pres.'s Commn. on accident at 3-Mile Island, 1979; mem. bd. radioactive waste mgmt. and energy engring. bd., NAS-NAE, chmn. waste isolation systems panel, waste isolation pilot plant panel, fusion hybrid panel, separations and transmutations panel, transmutation of military plutonium panel, panel on health standard for radioactive waste disposal, chmn. adv. coun. Inst. Nuclear Power Op.; mem. Sec. of Energy's expert cons. group on Chernobyl accident; chmn. nuclear oversight com. Sacramento Mcpl. Utility Dist.; chmn. nuclear safety com. Gulf States Utilities Co.; mem. expert cons. group Swedish Nuclear Power Inspectorate; mem. peer rev. group for waste isolation pilot plant; mem. corp. rev. com. Oak Ridge Nat. Lab; lectr. Taiwan Nat. Sci. Found., 1990; vis. prof. Kyoto U., 1975, Kuwait U., 1976; cons. in field. Author: (with Manson Benedict) Nuclear Chemical Engineering, 1958, 2d edit., 1981; contbr. numerous articles to profl. jours.; patentee in field. Served with USNR, 1944-46. Recipient John Wesley Powell award U.S. Geol. Survey, 1981; named Outstanding Young Man of Greater Boston, Boston Jaycees, 1955; E. I. DuPont DeNemours rsch. fellow, 1948-50; Berkeley citation U. Calif., 1987; Japan Soc. for Promotion Sci. fellow, 1974-75; grantee NSF, 1960-75, EPA, 1973-78, Dept. Energy, 1979-92, Ford Found., 1974-75, Electric Power Rsch. Inst., 1974-75, Mitsubishi Metals Corp., 1989-90; named to Ga. Tech. Hall of Fame, 1995. Fellow Am. Nuclear Soc. (bd. dirs., Arthur H. Compton award 1971); mem. AIME, NAE, Am. Chem. Soc., Am. Inst. Chem. Engrs. (Robert E. Wilson award 1980, Service to Society award 1985), Atomic Indsl. Forum (dir.), Sigma Xi, Phi Kappa Phi, Tau Beta Pi. Home: 166 Alpine Ter Oakland CA 94618-1823 Office: U Calif Dept Nuclear Engring Berkeley CA 94720-0001 E-mail: pigford@nuc.berkeley.edu.

PIGGREM, GARY WAYNE, science educator, writer; b. Proctor, Vt., Sept. 11, 1953; s. Lloyd A. Piggrem and Betty J. DuMouchel; m. Linda S. Hart, Oct. 17, 1981; children: Brian, Jeff. BA in psychology, St. John Fisher Coll., Rochester, NY, 1977; MA in psychology, Ohio State, 1980, PhD in psychology, 1983. Tchg. asst. Ohio State, 1978—81; prof. Columbus (Ohio) State Cmty. Coll., 1983—, DeVry U., Columbus, Ohio, 1983—. Author (with N. Holt, W. Walker and S. Woodworth): (textbook) The Best Test Preparation Grad. Record Exam., 1993; author: (with J. McDuffie and S. Woodworth) (textbooks) The Best Test Preparation Advanced Placement Exam, 1993; author: (with K. Huffman) (textbook) Psychology in Action: Active Learning edit., 2003, textbook supplements; contbr. chapters to books, articles to profl. jours. Coach boy's recreational baseball, 1999—2000. Mem.: Nat. Inst. on the Tchg. of Psychology, Coun. of Tchrs. of Undergraduate Psychology, Nat. Bus. Edn. Assn., Am. Assn. Advancement of Sci., Columbus N-Track Model R.R. Club, Rutland R.R. Hist. Soc., Bridge Line Hist. Soc., Columbus Garden R.R. Soc., Delta Epsilon Sigma, Pi Gamma Mu. Home: 166 Retreat Ln Westerville OH 43082 Office: DeVry University 1350 Alum Creek Dr Columbus OH 43209 Business E-Mail: gpiggrem@devrycols.edu.

PIGLIUCCI, RICCARDO, pharmaceutical executive; B.Indsl. Chemistry, Chem. Inst. of Milan, Italy. With Perkin-Elmer Corp., pres., COO, 1993—95; CEO Life Scis. Internat. PLC, 1996—97; pres., CEO Discovery Ptnrs. Internat., Inc., San Diego, 1998—, chmn. bd. dirs., 1999—. Dir. BioSphere Med., Inc., Dionex Corp., Epoch BioScis., Inc.; adv. bd. Chem. & Engring. News. Bd. trustees Worcester Found. for Biomed. Rsch. Office: Discovery Partners Internat Inc 9640 Towne Centre Dr San Diego CA 92121

PIGNATELLI, DEBORA BECKER, state legislator; b. Weehawken, N.J., Oct. 25, 1947; d. Edward and Frances (Fishman) Becker; m. Michael Albert Pignatelli, Aug. 22, 1971; children: Adam Becker, Benjamin Becker. AA, Vt. Coll., 1967; BA, U. Denver, 1969. Exec. dir. Girl's Club Greater Nashua, N.H., 1975-77; dir. tenant svcs. Nashua Housing Authority, 1979-80; vocat. counselor Comprehensive Rehab. Assocs., Bedford, N.H., 1982-85; specialist job placement Crawford & Co., Bedford, 1985-87; mem N.H. Ho. of Reps., Concord, 1986—91, mem. appropriations com., 1986-91, asst. minority leader, 1989—91; mem. N.H. Senate, Concord, 1992—2003, dep. Dem. whip, vice chair judiciary com., mem. capital budget com., chair enrolled bills com., long range capital budget overview com.; dir. Sky Meadow Condominium Assn., 2003—. Del. Am. Coun. Young Polit. Leaders, Germany, 1987. Mem. Nashua Peace Ctr., 1980—; asst. coach Little League Baseball, Nashua, 1987-90; steering com. Gephardt for Pres. Campaign, N.H., 1987-88; del. Dem. Nat. Conv., 1988; Gore del. Dem. Nat. Conv., 2000; bd. dirs. Sky Meadow Condominium Assn. Named One of 10 Most Powerful Women in N.H., N.H. Editions mag., 1995; recipient Meritorious Svc. award N.H. Women's Lobby, 1997, John F. Kennedy award Hillsborough County Dems., 2001, Anita and Norman Freedman award N.H. Dem. Party, 2004. Mem. N.H. Children's Lobby, Women's Lobby. Jewish. Avocations: skiing, swimming, boating. Home: 22 Appletree Grn Nashua NH 03062-2252

PI-GONZALEZ, AMAURY FRANCISCO, announcer, journalist; b. Havana, Cuba, Oct. 4, 1944; arrived in U.S., 1961; s. Joaquin Pi and Olga Isabel González; m. Gail Ann Clardy; children: Jonathan Amaury, Geoffrey Walter Armando. Diploma, U.S. Army Audio Visual, Ft. Lewis, Wash., 1967. Spanish play-by-play broadcaster CBS Hispanic Network, San Francisco, 1986—89, Oakland (Calif.) Athletics, 1977—94, Golden State Warriors (NBA), Oakland, 1991—97; sports anchor, prodr. Telemundo Network, San Jose, Calif., 1991—95; Spanish play-by-play broadcaster San Francisco Giants baseball, 1995—; Spanish play-by-play broadcaster World Series Caracol Radio Network, 2000; Spanish play-by-play broadcaster Nat. League playoffs Latino Broadcasting Co., 2001; English play-by-play broadcaster Fox Sports Internat., L.A., 2001; Spanis play-by-play announcer Seattle Mariners Spanish Radio Network, Wash. and Oreg., 2003—. Cons. APG Sports, Fremont, Calif., 1988—, Sports Byline USA, San Francisco, 1997—98; mem. adv. com. Oakland A's All Star Game, 1997. Author: (pamphlet) Candlestick Park Years, 1999; columnist: La Oferta News, columnist, feature writer: www.latinobaseball.com, writer: www.loveofthegame.com, writer, prodr., narrator: (audio cassette) Latin Baseball Legends, 1988. Bd. dirs., v.p. Hispanic Heritage Baseball Mus., San Francisco, 1999—. With U.S. Army, 1966—68. Named Announcer of Yr., Latin Am. Awards, 1987; recipient award of merit, San Francisco Mayor Dianne Feinstein, 1982. Mem.: CNP Profl. Assn. Cuban Journalists, Am. Sportscasters Assn. Republican. Roman Catholic. Achievements include being first Spanish play-by-play announcer in the USA to broadcast major league baseball and NBA games in concurrent seasons. Avocations: music, movies, collecting sports memorabilia. E-mail: scrmeagles@aol.com.

PIGOTT, CHARLES MCGEE, transportation equipment manufacturing executive; b. Seattle, Apr. 21, 1929; s. Paul and Theiline (McGee) P.; m. Yvonne Flood, Apr. 18, 1953. BS, Stanford U., 1951. With PACCAR Inc, Seattle, 1959—, exec. v.p., 1962-65, pres., 1965-86, chmn., pres., 1986-87, chmn., chief exec. officer, 1987-97, also bd. dirs., chmn. emeritus, 1997—. Dir. The Seattle Times, Chevron Corp., The Boeing Co. Pres. Nat. Boy Scouts Am., 1986-88, mem. exec. bd. Mem. Bus. Council. Office: Paccar Inc 777 106th Ave NE Bellevue WA 98004-5017

PIGOTT, JOHN DOWLING, geologist, geophysicist, geochemist, educator, consultant; b. Gorman, Tex., Feb. 2, 1951; s. Edwin Albert and Emma Jane (Poe) P.; m. Kulwadee Lawwongngam, May 28, 1994. BA in Zoology, BS in Geology, U. Tex., 1974, MA in Geology, 1977; PhD in Geology, Northwestern U., 1981. Ordained deacon Roman Cath. Ch., 2002, ordained Theravada Buddhist monk 2002. Geologist Amoco Internat., Chgo., 1978-80, sr. petroleum geologist Houston, 1980-81; asst., then assoc. prof. U. Okla., Norman, 1981—. Vis. prof. Mus. Natural History, Paris, 1988, Sun Yat Sen U., Kaohsiung, Taiwan, 1991; rsch. dir. 5 nation Red Sea-Gulf of Aden seismic stratigraphy and basis analysis industry consortium, 1992—; internat. energy cons., 1981—; instr. I.H.R.D.C., Boston, 1987-91, O.G.C.I., Tulsa, 1991—; energy advisor Ministry of Oil and Mineral Resources, Republic of Yemen, 1996—2000; advisor Prime Min. Rep. Yemen, 1998-2000; energy advisor Empresa Colombiana de Patroleos, Colombia, 2001, Petroleos de Venezuela, 2001-02. Mem. editl. bd. Geotectonica et Metallogenin Jour., 1992—2000. Mem. Am. Assn. Petroleum Geologists, Soc. Exploration Geophysicists, Soc. Petroleum Engrs., Geol. Soc. Am., Indonesian Petroleum Assn., Sigma Xi. Theravada Buddhist. Achievements include discovering relationship between global CO2 and natural tectonic cycles on the scale of millions of years showing previous greenhouse times during the Phanerozoic, processing first three-dimensional amplitude variation with offset seismic survey to quantify rocks, fluids, and pressures in rocks, processing and displaying first ground penetrating radar survey as a seismic section for ultrahigh resolution sequence stratigraphy, developing tectonic subsidence analysis as a practical tool for investigating the comparative anatomy of a sedimentary basins, their tectonic history, and evolving hydrocarbon potential, and constructing first paleo-heatflow maps of the Red Sea for the past 25 ma. Office: U Okla Sch Geology & Geophysics 100 E Boyd St Norman OK 73019-1000 Office Phone: 405-325-3253.

PIGOTT, MARK C. automotive executive; Chmn., CEO PACCAR, Bellevue, Wash., 1997—. Office: PACCAR PO Box 1518 777 106th Ave NE Bellevue WA 98004

PIHOS, SANDRA M, state representative; b. Pittsburgh, Pa., June 11, 1946; m. William Pihos; children: Andria, Peter, Deanna, Michael. BA, Mount Union Coll., 1968; MS, Northern Ill. Univ., 1971. State Rep. House of Rep., Dist. 42, Ill., 2002—; v.p. Pihos Enterprises, 1993—2000; Guidance Counselor Downers Grove N. HS, Dist. 99, 1970—74, 1988—93; tchr. Edison Jr. HS, Dist. 200, 1969—70. Mem.: Glenbard Enrollment Adv. Comm. (mem. 1991—92), Parternership for Ed. Progress Found. (trustee 1993—, sec. 1996—), Parkviewf Elem. Sch. Parent/Tchr. Assoc. (pres. 1985—86), Michael's Pl. Lit. Ctr. (Founder/Ex-Oficio, Dir./Vol. 2000—), Holy Apostles Ch. Women's Org. (sec. 1990—95), Glen Ellyn Lifelong Learning Partnership (Sec. 1992—94), Glen Ellyn Lib. Adv. Bd. (mem. 1990—92), Glen Crest Jr. High Student/Tchr./Parent Coun. (pres. 1989—90, 1992—94), DuPage County Workforce Develop. Bd. (Exec. sec. 2000—01), Citizens Adv. Coun., 1989-1997 (v.p. 1992—93), Local Gov., Glenbard Twp., Dist. 87 (v.p. 1997, pres. 2001—), Consumer Protection, Commerce & Bus. Develop., Appropriations - Human Svc., Appropriations - Elem. & Sec. Republican. Christian (Greek Orthodox). Office: Capitol 214-N Stratton Office Bldg Springfield IL 62706 also: District 799 E Roosevelt Rd Bldg 2 Suite 11 Glen Ellyn IL 60137

PIIRTO, DOUGLAS DONALD, forester, educator, academic administrator; b. Reno, Nev., Sept. 25, 1948; s. Rueben Arvid and Martha Hilma (Giebel) P.; m. Mary Louise Cruz, Oct. 28, 1978. BS, U. Nev., 1970; MS, Colo. State U., 1971; PhD, U. Calif., Berkeley, 1977. Registered profl. forester, Calif.; cert. silviculturist USDA Forest Svc. Rsch. asst. Colo. State U., 1970-71, U. Calif., Berkeley, 1972-77; forester, silviculturist USDA, Forest Svc., Sierra Nat. Forest, Trimmer and Shaver Lake, Calif., 1977-85; assoc. prof. natural resources mgmt. dept. Calif. Poly. State U., San Luis Obispo, 1985-90, prof., 1990—, dept. head, 2001—. Rschr. in field; instr. part-time Kings River C.C., Reedley, Calif.; forestry cons., expert witness. Contbr. articles to sci. and forestry jours. Mem. State Forest Adv. Com.; mem. sci. adv. com. Giant Sequoia Nat. Monument. Recipient Meritorious Performance and Profl. Promise awards CalPoly, 1989, 96-2001, CalPoly Coll. Agr. Outstanding Tchg. award Dole Food Co., 1995, Outstanding Contbn. to Coll. Agr. CalPoly award Plant Sci. Corp., 2000. Mem. Soc. Am. Foresters, Forest Products Rsch. Soc., Soc. Wood Sci. and Tech., Alpha Zeta, Xi Sigma Pi, Sigma Xi, Beta Beta Beta, Phi Sigma Kappa. Lutheran. Home: 115 Eagle Creek Ct Atascadero CA 93422-5957 Office: Calif Poly State U Dept Nat Resources Mgmt San Luis Obispo CA 93407 Business E-Mail: dpiirto@calpoly.edu.

PIKE, BURLYN, retired bank director, lawyer; b. Brodhead, Ky., May 28, 1921; s. John Daniel Pike and Jewel Francisco; m. Edith Nell Sanders, 1942 (div. 1971); children: Burnell True, David Alford; m. Joan Thomason, 1983. Student, U. Louisville, 1939-43. Bar: Ky. 1944. Free lance writer The Courier Jour., Louisville, 1941-43; pub. various, 1946-51; ptnr. Taylor & Pike-Pike & Schmidt, Shepherdsville, Ky., 1952—2003; ret., 2002. Author: Railroad Town, 2d edit., 1997. Sgt. U.S. Army, 1943-46. Mem.: Omicron Delta Kappa. Republican. Roman Cath. Avocation: historical research. Office: Pike & Schmidt Law Offices 148 E 2d St Shepherdsville KY 40165 Home: 609 Cressbrook Dr Louisville KY 40206-3054 E-mail: bpike01@aol.com.

PIKE, GEORGE HAROLD, JR., religious organization executive, clergyman; b. Summit, N.J., Jan. 14, 1933; s. George Harold and Ann Aurelia (Brewer) P.; m. Pauline Elizabeth Blair, Aug. 27, 1955; children: Elizabeth, George 3d, James. BA, Trinity Coll., Hartford, Conn., 1954; MDiv, Dubuque (Iowa) Theolog. Sch., 1957; DDiv (hon.), U. Dubuque, 1998. Ordained to ministry Presbyn. Ch. USA., 1957. Pastor 1st PResbyn. Ch., Kasson, Minn., 1956-59, 3d Presbyn. Ch., Dubuque, 1959-64; sr. pastor Presbyn. Ch., Bettendorf, Iowa, 1964-68, 1st Presbyn. Ch., Vancouver, Wash., 1968-78, Cranford, N.J., 1978-88; exec. chair Presbyn. Ch. USA, Louisville, 1988-93; interim pastor 2d Presbyn. Ch., Kansas City, Mo., 1993-95; dir. sem. devel. U. Dubuque, Iowa, 1995-98; retired, 1998; interim pastor Valley Presbyn. Ch., Green Valley, Ariz., 2000. Mem. exec. com. Consultation on Ch. Union, Princeton, 1980-89, pres., 1984-88. Dir. Bettendorf Bd. Edn., 1964-68, pres. 1967-68; bd. dirs. Southwest Wash. Hosps., Vancouver, 1969-78. Named Citizen of Yr., Jaycees, Bettendorf, 1967, Citizen of Yr., B'nai B'rith, Cranford, 1988; named to Honorable Order of Ky. Cols., 1989 Presbyterian. Avocations: golf, photography. Home: 928 W Union Bell Dr Green Valley AZ 85614-5928 E-mail: Ghpike@aol.com.

PIKE, JOHN NAZARIAN, optical engineering consultant; b. Boston, Feb. 13, 1929; s. Arthur Thorndike and Sarah Lucy (Nazarian) Pike; m. Margaretta May Horner, Dec. 28, 1957; 1 child, Susan Horner; 1 child, Sally Katharine. AB, Princeton U., 1951; PhD in Physics and Optics, U. Rochester, 1958. Staff scientist Parma (Ohio) Rsch. Ctr., Union Carbide Corp., 1956-63; mem. physics faculty Baldwin-Wallace Coll., Berea, Ohio, 1961-63; sr. scientist Tarrytown (N.Y.) Tech. Ctr., Union Carbide Corp., 1963-85; pres. J.J. Pike & Co., Pleasantville, NY, 1986—. Contbr. articles to profl. jours. Mem. nat. com. for planned giving United Way of Am., 1997—2001; bd. dir. United Way of Westchester and Putnam, NY, 1979—85, 1995—, chmn., 1996—98, 1999—2000, 2003; bd. dir. United Way of N.Y. State, 1999—. Recipient Harold J. Marshall citation Cmty. Svc, United Way No. Westchester, 1976, Cmty. Svc. award, Union Carbide Corp., 1982, Spirit of Westchester and Putnam Vol. Leadership award, United Way Westchester and Putnam, 2001. Mem.: Sigma Xi, Phi Beta Kappa. Achievements include patents for applied indsl. optics. Home and Office: 71 Cedar Ave Pleasantville NY 10570-1932

PIKE, JONATHAN HAMILTON, writer; b. Cambridge, Mass., Aug. 2, 1960; s. Galen Woodsum and Irene Rose (Mugar) Pike. BA in Econs. and Mgmt., Beloit Coll., 1983; MS in Print Journalism, Boston U., 1993. Freelance writer, Lowell, Mass., 1985—. Home and Office: Three River Pl Apt A2109 Lowell MA 01852-1065 E-mail: theroundtable@attbi.com.

PIKE, KERMIT JEROME, cultural organization administrator; b. East Cleveland, June 19, 1941; s. Frank James and Pauline Frances (Prijatel) P.; m. Joyce Rita Massillo, June 27, 1964; children: Christopher James, Laura Elizabeth. BA, Case Western Res. U., 1963, MA, 1965. Rsch. asst. Western Res. Hist. Soc., Cleve., 1965-66, curator manuscripts, 1966-72, chief libr., 1969-75, dir. libr., 1976—2002, COO, 1997—. Adj. prof. history, libr. sci. Case Western Res. U., 1975-84. Author: Guide to the Manuscripts and Archives, 1972, Guide to Shaker Manuscripts, 1974; editor: Guide to Jewish History Sources, 1983; Compiler: Guide to Major Manuscript Collections, 1987. Mem. Super Sesquicentennial Com., Cleve., 1971, Cleve. Bicentennial History Com., 1992—96, Ohio Preservation Coun., 1997—, Ohio Hist. Records Adv. Bd., 2002—; chmn. Family Heritage Adv. Bd., Numa Corp., 1995—99; chmn. vis. com. on humanities and arts Cleve. State U., 1980—82; trustee Nationalities Svc. Ctr., Cleve., 1978—86. Recipient Achievement award No. Ohio Live, Cleve., 1987; Spl. Recognition award Gov. Richard F. Celeste of Ohio, 1990. Mem. Soc. Ohio Archivists (co-founder 1968, pres. 1971-72), Black History Archives (founder 1970), Orgn. Am. Historians, Soc. Am. Archivists, Manuscripts Soc., Midwest Archives Conf., Ohio Geneal. Soc., Early Settlers Assn. of the Western Res., Rowfant Club, Lake County Farmers' Conservation Club, Lambda Chi Alpha. Roman Catholic. Home: 3985 Orchard Rd Cleveland OH 44121-2411 Office: Western Res Hist Soc 10825 East Blvd Cleveland OH 44106-1777 Office Phone: 216-721-5722. Business E-Mail: kermit@wrhs.org.

PIKE, LARRY SAMUEL, lawyer; b. Savannah, Ga., Feb. 23, 1939; s. Abram and Ida (Feinberg) P.; m. Bonnie Jo Haykin, June 21, 1959; children: Douglas, Stacey, Scott. BA, Emory U., 1960, LLB, 1963; postgrad., Leeds (Eng.) U., 1960-61. Assoc. L. Jack Swertfeger Jr. Atty., Decatur, Ga., 1963-65; ptnr. Swertfeger, Scott, Pike & Simmons, Decatur, 1966-75, Simmons, Pike & Warren, Decatur, 1975-76, Lefkoff, Pike & Sims, Atlanta, 1976-85, Branch, Pike & Ganz, Atlanta, 1985-95, Holland & Knight LLP, Atlanta, 1995—. Pres. Ansley Park Civic Assn., Atlanta, 1977-79, Northshore Homeowners Assn., Tybee Island, Ga., 1992-95, The Temple, Atlanta, 1979-81, trustee, 1977—, Am. Cancer Soc., DeKalb County, Ga. unit, 1970-71, crusade chmn., 1969-70; trustee Ansley Park Beautification Found., Inc., Atlanta, 1984—, treas., 2000—; trustee The Temple Endowment Fund, Atlanta, 1979-87, Atlanta Jewish Cmty. Ctr., 1973-76; bd. overseers Hebrew Union Coll., Cin., 1987-93; alumni coun. Emory U., Atlanta, 1966-72; bd. trustees Union of Am. Hebrew Congregations, 1991-99; mem. Rabbinical Placement Commn., 1994-2000; mem. St. Joseph's Hosp. Leadership Coun., 2003—. Editor-in-chief law jour. and newspaper; contbr. articles to profl. jours. Fulbright fellow, 1960-61; named Outstanding Young Man of Yr. North DeKalb Jaycees, 1968. Mem. ABA, State Bar Ga. (exec. coun. Young Lawyers sect. 1968-72), Atlanta Bar Assn., Decatur-DeKalb Bar Assn. (sec. 1965-66), Atlanta Legal Aid Soc. (pres. 1974-75, past bd. dirs.), Atlanta Tax Forum, Lawyers Club Atlanta, B'nai B'rith (pres. Atlanta lodge 1970-71, Ga. pres. 1974-75, dist. 5 bd. govs. 1973-76, chair Youth Orgn. Bd. 1971-73), Bryan Soc., Phi Beta Kappa, Omicron Delta Kappa. Office: Holland & Knight LLP 2000 One Atlantic Ctr Atlanta GA 30309 Business E-Mail: larry.pike@hklaw.com.

PIKE, MALCOLM CECIL, preventive medicine educator; b. Johannesburg, Republic of South Africa, May 2, 1935; m. Anne; 1 child. BS in Math. with honors, Witwatersrand U., Republic of South Africa, 1956; postgrad., London U., 1956; D Math. Stats., Cambridge (Eng.) U., 1958; PhD in Math. Stats., Aberdeen (Scotland) U., 1963. Asst. lectr., lectr. stats. U. Aberdeen, 1959-62; mem. sci. staff statis. rsch. unit Med. Rsch. Coun., London, 1963-69; 1st asst. Regius dept. medicine U. Oxford, Eng., 1969-73, dir. ICRF Cancer Epidemiology and Clin. Trials Units, 1983-87; prof. preventive medicine U. So. Calif. Sch. Medicine, L.A., 1973-83, 1987—, chair preventive medicine, 1989-99. Mem. coun. Royal Statis. Soc., 1972-73, chmn. med. sect., 1984-86; mem. devel. rsch. segment virus cancer program NCI, 1971-78; mem. pres.' biomed. rsch. panel Interdisciplinary Cluster in Epidemiology, Biostats. and Bioengring., 1976; mem. rev. group on analysis of case-control studies Internat. Agy. Cancer Rsch., 1977; mem. safe drinking water com. NAS, 1977-83, cons. to Radiation Effects Rsch. Found., Hiroshima, Japan, 1979, 81, mem. com. on Pyrenes, 1981-83, mem. commn. on life scis., 1992-95; mem. rev. com. Internat. Agy. Cancer Rsch., 1979; mem. adv. com. on breast cancer screening Internat. Union Against Cancer, 1982; mem. faculty Internat. Agy. for Cancer Rsch., 1985; mem. U.K. Coord. Com. on Cancer Rsch., 1985-86; mem. com. on immunology of leprosy WHO, 1986-87, mem. bd. sci. counselors tropical diseases rsch., 1989-93; mem. med. rsch. del. to USSR U.K. Dept. Health and Social Security, 1986; mem. adv. panel Nat. Cancer Inst., 1987; mem. coun. Nat. Inst. Environ. Health Scis., 1992-95; mem. sci. adv. com. Tobacco-Related Disease Rsch. program State of Calif., 1993-96; mem. adv. bd. GM Cancer Rsch, Found., 2004. Assoc. editlr Med. Stats. and Epidemiology of Biometrics, 1972-76; editl. bd. Brit. Jour. Haematology, 1972-73, Brit. Jour. Cancer, 1972-73; contbr. articles to profl. publs. Recipient Guy Bronze medal Royal Statis. Soc., 1968, Brinker Internat. award of the Susan G. Komen Breast Cancer Found., 1994, Am. Cancer Soc. award for rsch. excellence in cancer epidemiology & prevention, 2004. Mem. NAS (mem. inst. medicine). Office: Mail Stop 44 1441 Eastlake Ave Los Angeles CA 90089-0112 E-mail: mcpike@hsc.usc.edu.

PIKE, RALPH WEBSTER, chemical engineer, educator, university administrator; b. Tampa, Fla., Nov. 10, 1935; s. Ralph Webster and Macey (Adams) P.; m. Patricia Jennings, Aug. 23, 1958. B in Chem. Engring., Ga. Inst. Tech., 1957, PhD, 1962. Rsch. chem. engr. Exxon R & D Co., Baytown, Tex., 1962-64; Paul M. Horton prof. chem. engring. and sys. sci. La. State U., Baton Rouge, 1964—, assoc. vice chancellor for rsch., 1975-96, dir. La. Mineral Inst., 1979—, dean engring., 1999-2001. Cons. to chem. and petroleum refining industry, fed. govt. and State of La., 1964—. Author: Formulation and Optimization of Mathematical Models, 1970, Optimization for Engineering Systems, 1986, Optimizacion en Ingenieria, 1989. Active various civic, ch. and cmty. orgns., Baton Rouge, 1964—. 2d lt. U.S. Army, 1958-60. Recipient over 80 rsch. grants, including NASA, NSF, Dept. Interior, EPA, NOAA, state agys. and pvt. industry, 1964—. Fellow Am. Inst. Chem. Engrs. (chmn. nat. program com. 1984, local sect. 1985); mem. Am. Chem. Soc. (Charles E. Coates Mem. Award, 1994, univ. and profl.), Sigma Xi. Democrat. Methodist. Avocation: skiing. Home: 6063 Hibiscus Dr Baton Rouge LA 70808-8844 Office: La State U 1139 Energy Coast and Environment Bldg Baton Rouge LA 70803-0001 Office Phone: 225-578-3428. Business E-Mail: pike@lsu.edu.

PIKE, ROBERT WILLIAM, insurance company executive, lawyer; b. Lorain, Ohio, July 25, 1941; s. Edward and Catherine (Stack) P.; m. Linda L. Feitz, Dec. 26, 1964; children: Catherine, Robert, Richard. BA, Bowling Green State U., 1963; JD, U. Toledo, 1966. Bar: Ohio 1966, Ill. 1973. Ptnr. Cubbon & Rice Law Firm, Toledo, 1968-72; asst. counsel Allstate Ins. Co., Northbrook, Ill., 1972-74, assoc. counsel, 1974-76, asst. sec., asst. gen. counsel, 1976-77, asst. v.p., asst. gen. counsel, 1977-78, v.p., asst. gen. counsel, 1978-86, sr. v.p., sec., gen. counsel, bd. dirs., 1987-99, exec. v.p., 1999—. Bd. dirs. Allstate subs. Mem. bd. overseers Inst. for Civil Justice. Served to capt. inf. U.S. Army, 1966-68. Mem. ABA, Ill. Bar Assn., Ohio Bar Assn., Property Casualty Insurers Assn. Am. (bd. dirs., exec. com.), Ivanhoe (Ill.) Club. Roman Catholic. Home: 1795 W North Pond Ln Lake Forest IL 60045- Office: Allstate Ins Co 2775 Sanders Rd Ste F8 Northbrook IL 60062-6127

PIKE, WILLIAM EDWARD, business executive; b. Ft. Collins, Colo., Jan. 25, 1929; s. Harry H. and Alice Francis (Swinscoe) P.; m. Catherine Broward Crawford, June 26, 1965; children: Elizabeth Catherine, Robert Crawford, Daniel William. Student, U. Colo., 1947-48; BS, U.S. Naval Acad., 1952; MBA, Harvard, 1960. Commd. ensign USN, 1952, advanced through grades to lt., 1958; ret., 1958; asst. treas. Morgan Guaranty Trust Co., N.Y.C., 1962-64, asst. v.p., 1964-66, v.p., 1966-71, sr. v.p., 1971-74, chmn. credit policy com., 1974-86; exec. v.p. J.P. Morgan & Co. Inc., 1986-89; corp. dir., trustee, pvt. investor. Bd. dirs. Global Lift Techs., Inc. Mem. Harvard Club N.Y.C. Clubs: Country (New Canaan, Conn.). Episcopalian. Home: Indian Waters Dr New Canaan CT 06840 Office: 36 Grove St New Canaan CT 06840-5329

PILAND, NEILL FINNES, health services economist, researcher; b. Pomona, Calif., Nov. 6, 1943; s. Finnes Elmer and Sylvia Beatrice (Renick) PiL.; m. Diane Lynn Fiedor, Aug. 12, 1977; children: Evan Neill, Spencer Lowell, Arden Geneva. BA, UCLA, 1965, MPH, 1970, PhD, 1979; MA, U. Calif., Davis, 1966. Rsch. assoc. Sch. Pub. Health UCLA, 1971-73, sr. rsch. assoc., 1973; health economist Stanford Rsch. Inst., Menlo Park, Calif., 1973-77, asst. mgr. health svcs. rsch., 1974-77; dir. health ctr. study Jicarilla Apache Tribe, Dulce, N.Mex., 1978-82; dir. health systems evaluation program Lovelace Med. Found., Albuquerque, 1982-83, dir. health svcs. rsch. and edn., 1983-91; dir. Ctr. Health & Population Rsch., Albuquerque, 1991-94, Lovelace Inst. for Health and Population Rsch., Albuquerque, 1994-96; rsch. dir. Ctr. Rsch. Med. Group Mgmt. Assn., Englewood, Colo., 1996—2002; prof. and dir. Inst. Rural Health, Idaho State U., Pocatello, 2002—; clin. assoc. prof. U. Colo. Sch. Medicine; rsch. prof. U. Denver; dir. policy and rsch. Colo. Health Inst., Denver, 2004—. Clin. asst. prof. medicine U. N.Mex., Albuquerque, 1981, clin. assoc. prof., 1994—; vis. prof. U. N.H., Durham, 1989-90. Co-author: Strategic Nursing Management: Power and Responsibility in a New Era; mem. editorial bd. Jour. Managerial Issues, 1991—; co-editor: Physician Profiling: A Sourcebook for Adminstrators, Chart Accounts for Healthcare Organizations, Reinventing Medical Practice; contbr. over 90 articles to profl. jours. Mem. rsch. com. N.Mex. HealthNet, 1986-88; chair econ. issues N.Mex. Com. on Pub. Health Impact of Smoking, 1988; bd. dirs. Am. Geriat. and Gerontology, 1984-87, Healthcare for Homeless, 1988-92; mem. exec. coun. N.Mex. ASSIST Com., 1992—, sci. adv. com. N.Mex. ASSIST Project, 1992—; mem. steering com. Group Practice Improvement Network, 1996—; mem. workgroup smoking control Colo. Dept. Health and Environment, 1999-2002; scholarship interviewer NHSC, 2003—. Recipient traineeship, USPHS, 1968-70. Mem. APHA, Am. Econ. Assn., Soc. Rsch. Adminstrs., Assn. Health Svcs. Rsch. Avocations: tennis, hockey, hiking, biking. Office: CHI Ste 300 1576 Sherman St Denver CO 80203-1713 Home: 132 Fairway Dr Pocatello ID 83201 Office Phone: 303-831-4200 211. Business E-Mail: pilandn@coloradohealthinstitute.org.

PILAR, L. PRUDENCIO R. financial services executive; b. Bacarra, Philippines, Sept. 12, 1943; came to U.S., 1977; s. Francisco and Maria (Raralio) P.; m. Vivien Ruth Narciso, Aug. 20, 1967; children: Prudencio Rex Jr., Diogene Ruthard, Keith N., Xydia Vida Ruth N., Benedict. BS in Edn., No. Luzon Tchrs. Coll., Laoag City, Philippines, 1964; MA in Adminstrn. and Supervision, No. Luzon Tchrs. Coll., 1972. CLU, ChFC. Prin., tchr. Bur. of Pub. Schs., Solsona, Philippines, 1964-77; agt. The Equitable, Honolulu, 1978-95; pres. Pilar Fin. & Tax Strategies, Inc., Honolulu, 1995—. Pres. St. Anthony Sch. Parent-Tchrs. Guild, Honolulu, 1987, 88, 89, 94. Fellow Life Underwriter Tng. Coun.; mem. Internat. Assn. for Fin. Planning, Nat. Assn. Life Underwriters, Diocesan Congress of Filipino Cath. Clubs, Oahu Coun. Filipino Cath. Clubs, KC. Democrat. Roman Catholic. Avocation: giving seminars. Office: Pilar Fin Svcs 1580 Nobrega St Honolulu HI 96819-3747

PILARCZYK, DANIEL EDWARD, archbishop; b. Dayton, Ohio, Aug. 12, 1934; s. Daniel Joseph and Frieda S. (Hilgefort) Pilarczyk. Student, St. Gregory Sem., Cin., 1948—53; PhB, Pontifical Urban U., Rome, 1955, PhL, 1956, STB, 1958, STL, 1960, STD, 1961; MA, Xavier U., 1965; PhD, U. Cin., 1969; LLD (hon.), Xavier U., 1975, Calumet Coll., 1982, U. Dayton, 1990, Marquette U., 1990, Thomas More Coll., 1991, Coll. Mt. St. Joseph, 1994, Hebrew Union Coll., 1997. Ordained priest Roman Catholic Ch., 1959. Asst. chancellor Archdiocese of Cin., 1961—63; synodal judge Archdiocesan Tribunal, 1971—82; faculty Athenaeum of Ohio, St. Gregory Sem., 1963—74; v.p. Athenaeum of Ohio, 1968—74, trustee, 1974—; rector St. Gregory Sem., 1968—74; archdiocesan dir. ednl. services, 1974—82; aux. bishop of Cin., 1974—82; vicar gen., 1974—82; archbishop of Cin., 1982—. V.p. Nat. Conf. Cath. Bishops, 1986—89, pres., 1989—92, chmn. com. on doctrine, 1996—2000; U.S. rep. Episc. bd. Internat. Commn. on English in Liturgy, 1987—97, chmn., 1991—97; jt. com. Orthodox and Cath. Bishops, 2002. Author: Praepositini Cancellarii de Sacramentis et de Novissimis, 1964—65, Twelve Tough Issues, 1988, We Believe, 1989, Living in the Lord, 1990, The Parish: Where God's People Live, 1991, Forgiveness, 1992, What Must I Do?, 1993, Our Priests: Who They Are and What They Do, 1994, Sacraments, 1994, Bringing Forth Justice, 1996, 1999, Thinking Catholic, 1998, Practicing Catholic, 1999, Believing Catholic, 2000, Live Letters, 2001, Twelve Tough Issues and More, 2002. Trustee Cath. Health Assn., 1982—85, Cath. U. Am., 1983—91, 1997—2000, Pontifical Coll. Josephinum, 1983—92. Ohio Classical Conf. scholar, Athens, 1966. Mem.: Am. Philol. Assn. Roman Catholic. Home and Office: 100 E 8th St Cincinnati OH 45202-2129

PILCH, SAMUEL H. controller, corporate financial executive; B Acctg., Bryant Coll. COO Travelers Ins. Co., Hartford, Conn.; controller promoted to group v.p. Allstate Ins. Co., 1999; mem. sr. mgmt. team Allstate Corp., controller, acting CFO, 2001—. Served U.S. Army, 1968—70. Office: Allstate Plz 2775 Sanders Rd Northbrook IL 60062

PILCHEN, IRA A. editor; b. Chgo., Jan. 17, 1964; s. Bernard J. and Erna (Lee) P. BA in History, U. Ill., 1986. Assoc. editor Judicature jour., Chgo., 1991-98; dir. comms. Am. Judicature Soc., Chgo., 1991-98; editor Student Lawyer mag. ABA Publishing, Chgo., 1999—. Mem. adv. coun. Ill. State Justice Commn., 1995. Vol. interpretive guide Friends of the Chicago River, 1991—. Named Vol. of Yr., Friends of Chicago River, 1993. Avocations: swimming, bicycling, chicago history. Office: ABA Publishing 750 N Lake Shore Dr Fl 8 Chicago IL 60611-4403

PILCHER, GREGORY F. manufacturing executive; BS, MS in Bus. Adminstrn., Okla. State U.; JD with highest honors, U. Okla. CPA. Former pvt. practice in comml. litig.; with Kerr-McGee, Oklahoma City, 1992—, from assoc. to asst. gen. counsel litig. and civil procs., 1996—98, dep. gen. counsel bus. transactions, 1998—99, v.p., gen. counsel, corp. sec., 1999—2000, sr. v.p., gen. counsel, corp. sec., 2000—. Office: Kerr-McGee PO Box 25861 Oklahoma City OK 73125

PILCHER, JAMES BROWNIE, lawyer; b. Shreveport, La., May 19, 1929; s. James Reece and Martha Mae (Brown) P.; m. Lorene Pilcher; children: Lydia, Martha, Bradley. BA, La. State U., 1952; JD summa cum laude, John Marshall Law Sch., 1955; postgrad., Emory U., 1957. Bar: Ga. 1955. Legal aide to Spkr. of Ho. of Reps., Ga., 1961-64; assoc. city atty. City of Atlanta, 1964-69; pvt. practice law Atlanta, 1969—. Exec. com. Dem. Exec. Com. of Fulton County, Ga., 1974-86; bd. dirs. Whitehead Boys Club, 1961-89; trustee Ga. Inst. Continuing Legal Edn., 1988-89; pres. Atlanta Jaycees, 1961-62. Fellow Lawyers Found. Ga., 1996—. Mem. Ga. Assn. Criminal Def. Lawyers (pres. 1980-82), ABA, State Bar Ga. (chmn. 1988-89, gen. practice and trial sect., chmn. criminal law sect. 1986-87), Atlanta Bar Assn., Ga. Trial Lawyers Assn. (life), Ga. Claimants Attys. Assn. (pres. 1983-84), NACDL (bd. dirs. 1980-85), Ga. Inst. Trial Advocacy (bd. dirs. 1986-89), South Fulton Bar Assn. (pres. 1987-88), Am. Bankruptcy Inst., Nat. Assn. Consumer Bankruptcy Attys., Trial Lawyers for Pub. Justice, Atlanta Consumer Bankruptcy Attys. Group (pres. 2001-03), Kiwanis (Peachtree, Atlanta pres. 1983-84, gov. Ga. dist. 1992-93), Sierra Club Am. (life), Barristers Club of Emory U. Law Sch. Presbyterian. Home: 1195 W Wesley Rd NW Atlanta GA 30327-1407 Office: One Northside 75 Atlanta GA 30318-7715 E-mail: pilcherj@bellsouth.net.

PILE-SPELLMAN, JOHN MARTIN, radiology and neurosurgery educator; b. Sioux City, Iowa, Jan. 12, 1951; s. George Geneser and Mary Carol (Dwight) Spellman; m. Eliza R. Pile, June 2, 1973; children: Megan, Katherine, Julian. BS, U. S.D., 1976; MD, Tufts U., 1978. Diplomate Am. Bd. Radiology. Resident radiology Mass. Gen. Hosp., Boston, 1980-83, fellow neuroradiology, 1983-85; interventional fellow neuroradiology NYU Med., N.Y.C., 1986; prof. radiology and neurosurgery Med. Sch. Columbia U., N.Y.C.; attending radiologist, neurosurgeon Columbia U., N.Y.C.; radiologist Columbia Presbyn. Med. Ctr. Hosp., N.Y.C., 1992—. Adj. prof. radiology and neurosurgery Med. Sch. Cornell U.; vice chmn. radiology for rsch. Columbia U.; attending radiologist and neurosurgeon N.Y. Hosp., N.Y.C., 1997—; dir. Internat. MRI. Mem. Soc. Cardiovasc. Radiology, Alpha Omega Alpha. Avocations: sailing, drawing. Office: CPMC Milstein Hosp 8 South Knuckle 177 Fort Washington Ave New York NY 10032-3713 Office Phone: 212-305-6515. E-mail: jp59@columbia.edu.

PILGERAM, LAURENCE OSCAR, biochemist; b. Great Falls, Mont., June 23, 1924; s. John Rudolph and Bertha Roslyn (Phillips) P.; m. Cynthia Ann Moore, Apr. 16, 1971; children: Karl Erich, Kurt John. AA, U. Calif., Berkeley, 1948, BA, 1949, PhD, 1953. Instr. dept. physiology U. Ill. Profl. Coll., Chgo., 1954-55; asst. prof. dept. biochemistry Stanford (Calif.) U. Sch. Medicine, 1955-57; dir. arteriosclerosis rsch. lab. U. Minn. Sch. Medicine, Mpls., 1957-65, Santa Barbara, Calif., 1965-71; dir. coagulation lab., assoc. dir. Cerebrovascular Rsch. Ctr., Baylor Coll. Medicine, Tex. Med. Ctr., Houston, 1971-75; dir. Thrombosis Control Labs., Palo Alto, Calif., 1975-79, Santa Barbara, 1979—; prof. dept. molecular biology U. Calif., Santa Barbara, 2004—. Cons. NIH, Bio-Sci. Labs., FDA; del. Coun. on Thrombosis and Coun. on Strokes, Am. Heart Assn. Assembly. Co-editor: Nutrition and Thrombosis for the Nat. Dairy Coun., 1973; contbr. sci. articles to profl. jours. Recipient CIBA award, London, 1958, Karl Thomae award, Germany, 1973; NIH grantee, 1954-75; Life Ins. Med. Rsch. Fund fellow, 1952-54. Mem. Am. Soc. for Biochemistry and Molecular Biology. Office: PO Box 1583 Goleta PO Santa Barbara CA 93116 Office Phone: 805-967-5994.

PILGRIM, DIANNE HAUSERMAN, retired museum director; b. Cleve., July 8, 1941; d. John Martin and Norma Hauserman; divorced. BA, Pa. State U., 1963; MA, Inst. Fine Arts, NYU, 1965; postgrad., CUNY, 1971-74; LHD (hon.), Amherst Coll., 1991, Pratt Inst., 1994. Chester Dale fellow Am. wing. Met. Mus. Art, N.Y.C., 1966-68, rsch. cons. Am. paintings and sculpture, 1971-73; asst. to dirs. Pyramid Galleries, Ltd., Washington, 1969-71, Finch Coll. Mus. Art, Washington, 1971; curator dept. decorative arts Bklyn. Mus., 1973-88, chmn. dept., 1988; dir. Cooper-Hewitt Nat. Design Mus., N.Y.C., 1988-2000, dir. emeritus, 2000—. Mem. adv. com. Gracie Mansion, N.Y.C., 1980; mem. design adv. com. Art Inst. Chgo., 1988; mem. Hist. House Trust N.Y.C., Mayor's Office, 1989-94. Co-author, curator: (book and exhbn. catalogue) Mr. and Mrs. Raymond Horowitz Collection of American Impressionist and Realist Paintings, 1973, The American Renaissance 1876-1917, 1979; (book) The Machine Age in America 1918-1941, 1986 (Charles F. Montgomery prize Decorative Arts Soc.). Bd. dirs. Nat. Multiple Sclerosis Soc., 1989. Recipient Disting. Alumni award Pa. State U., 1991. Mem. Decorative Arts Soc. (pres. 1977-79), Art Deco Soc., Victorian Soc., Art Table.

PILGRIM, LONNIE (BO PILGRIM), poultry production company executive; b. 1928; married. Ptnr. Pilgrims Pride Corp., Pittsburg, Tex., 1953-68, chmn., CEO, 1968—. Chmn. First State Bank Pitts. Served with U.S. Armed Forces, 1951-53. Office: Pilgrim's Pride Corp 110 S Texas St Pittsburg TX 75686-1532

PILIGUIAN, TRO, advertising executive; b. Egypt;, naturalized, Canada; married; 2 children. Pres. Academie-Ogilvy, Montreal; chmn., CEO Ogilvy & Mather Canada, Toronto, 1990—; pres. Ogilvy & Mather NY, 1994—97; pres. CEO. Ogilvy & Mather N. Am., NYC, 1997—. fluent, 5 lang. Office: Ogilvy & Mather Worldwide Plz 309 W 49th St New York NY 10019-7316*

PILKERTON, ARTHUR RAYMOND, JR., surgeon, educator; b. Washington, Mar. 27, 1935; s. Arthur Raymond and Mary Rose (Ginechesi) P.; m. Sally Ann Madden, Aug. 6, 1966; children: A. Raymond III, Joseph A., Mary, Christopher, Jeanne Marie. BS in Biology, Georgetown U., 1952-56, MD, 1960. Diplomate Am. Bd. Opthalmology. Intern. U. Pitts., 1961; fellow retina surgery Wills Eye Hosp., Phila., 1964-65; resident ophthalmology Georgetown U. Med. Ctr., Washington, 1961-64, asst. prof., 1965-70, assoc. prof., 1971-78, clin. prof., 1978—; asst. clin. prof. George Washington U., Washington, 1985—; co-founder Retina Group Washington. Chief ophthalmology Veteran's Adminstrn. Hosp., Washington, 1965-82; chmn. ophthalmology cons., Veterans Adminstrn., Washington, 1978-82. Served with U.S. Army, 1961-70. Named Knight of Malta, Knight Comdr. Holy Sepulchre. Fellow Am. Acad. Ophthalmology (councilor), Am. Coll. Surgeons (councilor); mem. Retina Soc. U.S., Uitreous Soc., Retina Group of Washington (co-founder). Republican. Roman Catholic. Office: Retina Group Washington 5454 Wisconsin Ave Suite 1540 Chevy Chase MD 20815 E-mail: rpilkerton@retinagroup.org.

PILKINGTON, MARY ELLEN, stockbroker, trader; b. N.Y.C., Feb. 16, 1955; d. Charles Arthur Bertrand and Mary (Lynch) Perez; m. Scott Douglas Ballin (div. 1986); m. John J. Pilkington, Aug. 19, 1994. BA in Polit. Sci., Mt. Vernon Coll., Washington, 1976. Dir. materials ctr. Gen. Fedn. of Women's Clubs, Washington, 1978-80; broker, asst. to the chmn. Folger Nolan Fleming Douglas, Washington, 1980-85; broker, account exec. Rose & Co., N.Y.C., 1985-86; trader Bear Stearns, N.Y.C., 1986-88; trader, broker Robyns Capital, N.Y.C., 1988-89; trader, v.p. trading Jessop Capital Corp., N.Y.C., 1989-91, Kidder Peabody, 1992-94, Dean Witter, 1994-95, Gabelli & Co., 1996—. Trustee Mt. Vernon Coll., Washington, 1999. Roman Catholic. Avocations: golf, skiing, tennis, squash, photography.

PILL, CYNTHIA JOAN, social worker; b. N.Y.C., Mar. 30, 1939; d. Alfred and Edna (Strauss) Fruchtman; m. Robert Pill, July 29, 1961; children: Laura, Daniel, Karen. BS cum laude, Jackson Coll., Tufts U., 1961; MS in Social Work, Simmons Coll., 1963, PhD in Social Work, 1987. Lic. ind. clin. social worker. Clin. social worker Concord (Mass.) Family Sc., 1965-78; coord. family life edn. Family Counseling Svc., Newton, Mass., 1979-83; pvt. practice clin. social work Newton, 1979—; adj. asst. prof., rsch. advisor Smith Coll. Sch. for Social Work, 1988—99. Adj. asst. prof. Simmons Coll. Sch. Social Work, Boston, 1989-93. Contbr. articles to profl. jours. Vol. coord. Hospice at Home, Sudbury, Mass., 1986-88. Mem. NASW, Mass. Soc. Clin. Social Work, Register Clin. Social Workers (bd. cert. diplomate). Address: 435C Dedham St Newton MA 02459

PILLA, ANTHONY MICHAEL, bishop; b. Cleve., Nov. 12, 1932; s. George and Libera (Nista) P. Student, St. Gregory Coll. Sem., 1952—53, Borromeo Coll. Sem., 1955, St. Mary Sem., 1943, student, 1956—59; BA in Philosophy, John Carroll U., Cleve., 1961, MA in History, 1967. Ordained priest Roman Cath. Ch., 1959. Assoc. St. Bartholomew Parish, Middleburg Heights, Ohio, 1959—60; prof. Borromeo Sem., Wickliffe, Ohio, 1960—72, rector-pres., 1972—75; mem. Diocese Cleve. Liturgical Commn., 1964—69, asst. dir., 1969—72; sec. for svcs. to clergy and religious pers. Diocese Cleve., 1975—79; titular bishop Scardona; and aux. bishop of Cleve. and vicar Eastern region Diocese of Cleve., 1979—80, apostolic adminstr., 1980—; bishop Cleve., 1981—; pres. Nat. Conf. Cath. Bishops, 1995—98. Trustee Borromeo Sem., 1975—79, Cath. U., 1981—84; trustee, mem. bd. overseers St. Mary Sem., 1975—79; mem. adv. bd. permanent diaconate program Diocese of Cleve., 1975—79, hospitalization and ins. bd., 1979. Bd. dirs. NCCJ, 1986—. Mem.: Greater Cleve. Roundtable (trustee 1981—), Cath. Conf. Ohio, Nat. Conf. Cath. Bishops, U.S. Cath. Conf., Nat. Cath. Edn. Assn. (dir. 1972—75). Home and Office: Chancery Office Diocese of Cleveland 1027 Superior Ave E Ste 300 Cleveland OH 44114-2503

PILLAI, NARAYANA GOPALAKRISHNAN, internist, oncologist; b. Evoor, Kerala, India, 1951; s. Gopalakrishnan and Rajamma Nair; m. Priya Narayana Pillai, Nov. 30, 1975; cldren: Rathi, Rupa. MD, Trivandrum U., Kerala, 1974. Diplomate in internal medicine and oncology Am. Bd. Internal Medicine. Intern Med. Coll. Hosp., Trivandrum, 1973-74; resident in internal medicine Meml. U. St. Johns, 1979-80, Tex. Tech U., Amarillo, 1982-83; fellow in med. oncology M.D. Anderson Hosp., Houston, 1980-82; mem. staff N.W. Tex. Hosp., Amarillo, Bapt. St. Anthony's Hosp., Amarillo. Fellow ACP; mem. Am. Soc. Clin. Oncology, Royal Coll. Physicians (Ireland), Royal Coll. Physicians (U.K.). Office: 6611 W Amarillo Blvd Amarillo TX 79106-1755 Office Phone: 806-358-8011.

PILLALAMARRI, SESHASAYI, computer scientist and engineer, researcher; b. Masulipatam, India, Mar. 4, 1946; s. Ramadas and Umabala Pillalamarri; m. Indira Dantu, Feb. 5, 1977; children: Sandhya, Sirisha, Vamsee. BS, Osmania U., 1964; B in engring., Indian Inst. Sci., 1967; M in tech., Indian Inst. Tech., 1969; MS, SUNY Stonybrook, 1972; PhD, U. Linz, 2000. Sci. officer Indian Inst. Tech., Madras, 1974—76, asst. mgr., 1976—87, mgr., computer ctr., 1987—96; rsch. scientist Siemens AG, Munich, 1992—93, ICSI, U. Calif., Berkeley, 1993—94, Ariz. State U., Phoenix, 1996—2002; software engr. Computer Info. Tech. Corp., 1996—2002, City of Phoenix, 2002—02. Cons. Indian Inst. of Tech., Madras, Tamil nadu, India, 1976—96. Contbr. chapters to books, 2000. Mem.: Assn. for Computing Machinery (assoc.), IEEE (assoc.). Independent. Achievements include invention of the impact of source traffic distribution on quality of service (QOS) in ATM networks; stability of RYNSORD, a decentralized algorithm for railway networks; fundamental attributes of high speed networks. Avocations: music, poetry. Home: 3524 W Buckhorn Tr Phoenix AZ 85085 Office: City of Phoenix 300 W Washington St Phoenix AZ 85003 Business E-Mail: sesh.pilla@phoenix.gov.

PILLARI, VINCENT THOMAS, obstetrician-gynecologist, educator; b. N.Y.C., 1936; MD, Loyola U., 1962. Intern St. Vincents Hosp., N.Y.C., 1962-63; resident ob-gyn. Nassau Hosp., Mineola, N.Y., 1963-64, SUNY Upstate, Syracuse, 1964-66; chmn. dept. ob-gyn. St. Vincents Med. Ctr.-Richmond, S.I., N.Y. Prof. clin. ob-gyn. N.Y. Med. Coll., Valhalla. Fellow ACOG; mem. Bklyn. Gynecol. Soc., Martin L. Stone Ob-gyn Soc., N.Y. State Med. Soc. Office: 355 Bard Ave Staten Island NY 10310-1664 Office Phone: 718-818-4293.

PILLAY, ANAND, education educator, researcher; b. London, Eng., May 7, 1951; s. Vallaithan and Patricia O'Leary; m. Margit Messmer, July 9, 1993; children: Kalyan, Bhanu; m. Bronislava Jedrusik, July 26, 1978 (div. Mar. 1992); 1 child, Anusha. BA, U. Oxford, 1973; MSc, U. London, 1974, PhD, 1977. Rschr. CNRS, Paris, 1978—81; temp. lectr. U. Manchester, 1981—82; vis. lectr. U. McGill, 1982—83; assoc. prof. U. Notre Dame, 1983—86, 1986—88, full prof., 1988—96; prof. U. Ill., 1996—. Org. Math. Sci. Rsch. Inst., 1998. Contbr. scientific papers; author: (book) An Introduction to Stability Theory, 1983; author: (edited with Ali Nesin) The Model Theory of Groups, 1989; author: (with D. Marker and M. Messmer) Model Theory of Fields; author: Geometric Stability Theory, 1996; author: (edited with D. Haskell and C. Steinhorn) Model theory, Algebra and Geometry, 2000. Sitar player WEFT radio, 1997—2003. Recipient Humboldt prize, Humboldt Found., 2001; grant, NSF, 1983—2003, Rsch. grant, 2001—. Mem.: Assn. Symbolic Logic, Am. Math. Soc., Socialist Forum. Home: 2411 Branch Champaign IL 61822 Office: U Ill at Urbana-Champaign 1609 W Green St Champaign IL 61801 Office Phone: 217-333-6198.

PILLAY, GAUTAM, chemical engineer, chemist, academic administrator; b. Buffalo, Jan. 28, 1967; s. Sivasankara K. K. and Revathi (Krishnamurthy) Pillay; m. Amy Matthews, 2004. BS, N.Mex. State U., Las Cruces, 1988; PhD, Tex. A&M U., 1993. Grad. rschr., staff mem. Los Alamos Nat. Lab., 1984-87, mem. tech. staff, 1997—2001; grad. rschr. Tex. A&M U., College Station, 1988-92; rsch. engr. Pacific N.W. Lab., Richland, Wash., 1992-95, sr. rsch. engr., 1995-97; adj. faculty Wash. State U., Richland, 1993-97; exec. dir. Inland N.W. Rsch. Alliance, Idaho Falls, Idaho, 2001—04; v.p. rsch. S.D. Sch. Mines and Tech., Rapid City, 2004—. Contbr. articles to profl. jours. Recipient Fed. Lab. Consortium award for excellence in tech. transfer, 1997; NSF Grad. Rsch. fellow, 1988—91. Mem.: AIChE (symposium chair), N.Y. Acad. Scis., Am. Nuc. Soc., Am. Chem. Soc., Electrochemical Soc. (symposium chair 1993—, mem. exec. com. 1994—, pres. Pacific N.W. sect. 1996—97, v.p. IE & EE divsn. 2002—04, pres. 2004—), Phi Kappa Phi, Alpha Chi, Omega Chi Epsilon, Tau Beta Pi. Avocations: general aviation, musician. Office: SD Sch Mines and Tech 501 E Saint Joseph St Rapid City SD 57701 Office Phone: 208-524-4800.

PILLIOD, JAMES P. state legislator, physician; b. N.Y.C., Aug. 9, 1930; s. James J. and Mary Alice (Phillips) P.; m. Judith Bean. BA, Yale U., 1952; MD, Duke U., 1960. Diplomate Am. Bd. Pediatrics. Staff physician Lake Regional Gen. Hosp., 1964—; mem. N.H. Ho. of Reps., Concord, 1996—. Lt. (j.g.) USN. Diplomate Acad. of Pediatrics; mem. AMA (past del.), N.H. Med. Soc. (past pres.), N.H. Hosp. Assn. (Physician Staff Mem. of Yr. 1988), N.H. Pediat. Soc. (Pub. Servant of Yr. 1997). Office: NH State Legis State House Concord NH 03301

PILLOT, GENE MERRILL, retired school system administrator; b. Canton, Ohio, Apr. 13, 1930; s. John D. Pillot and Vera R. Granstaff; m. Beverly Ann Shaw, June 4, 1982; children: Vera Kathleen Martin, Michael Gene, Patrick Merrill. BS in Math., Ohio State U., 1952; MEd in Adminstrn. and Supervision, Kent State U., 1957; EdD in Adminstrn. and Supervision, U. Fla., 1970. Asst. prin. North Royalton (Ohio) High Sch., 1959-61, prin., 1961-63; asst. prin. Sarasota (Fla.) Sr. High Sch., 1963-64, prin., 1964-68; dir. staff development Sarasota Dist. Schs., 1968-70, asst. supt., 1970-71, supt., 1971-80; dir. human resources Sarasota Meml Hosp., 1980-83; owner, broker Pillot Realty, Sarasota, 1986-90; commr. Sarasota City, 1989-2001, vice mayor, 1992-93, 96-97, 99-2000, mayor, 1993-94, 97-98, 2000-2001. Prof. Am. Assn. Sch. Adminstrn., Nat. Acad. Sch. Execs., 1969-73; adj. prof. U. South Fla., Tampa, 1978-81; pvt. cons. edn. orgns., 1969-76. Author (chpt.) Differentiated Staffing, Strategies for D.S., 1971; contbr. articles to profl. jours. Trustee Fla. Sch. Deaf/Blind, St. Augustine, 1980—89, chmn. bd. trustees, 1986—89; active Civil Svc. Bd., Sarasota, 1984—89; mem. adv. bd. Cath. Social Svcs., 1987—89; bd. dirs. Riverview Found., 1985—94, Girls Club, Sarasota, 1985—89, Hospice Found., Sarasota Opera Assn., Hispanic Am. Alliance, Sarasota Mil. Acad., 2001—. Mem.: Phi Delta Kappa (Educator of Yr. 1980). Republican. Roman Catholic. Avocations: genealogy, ballroom dancing. Home: 10060 Cherry Hills Ave Cir Bradenton FL 34202 E-mail: gpillot@aol.com.

PILLSBURY, GEORGE STURGIS, investment adviser; b. Crystal Bay, Minn., July 17, 1921; s. John S. and Eleanor (Lawler) P.; m. Sally Whitney, Jan. 4, 1947; children: Charles Alfred, George Sturgis, Sarah Kimball, Katharine Whitney. BA, Yale U., 1943. Dir. emeritus Sargent Mgmt. Co. Mem. Seminole Golf Club (Juno Beach, Fla.), Lafayette Club, Woodhill Club, Minnetonka Yacht Club, Mpls. Club, River Club (N.Y.C.). Home: 1300 Bracketts Point Rd Wayzata MN 55391-9393 Office: 901 Marquette Ave Ste 2630 Minneapolis MN 55402-3230 E-mail: gspbury@aol.com.

PILLSBURY, HAROLD CROCKETT, III, otolaryngologist; b. Balt., Dec. 5, 1947; m. Sally Adrienne Pillsbury; children: Matthew, Benjamin, Thomas. BA, George Washington U., Washington, 1970, MD, 1972. Diplomate Nat. Bd. Med. Examiners, Am. Bd. Otolaryngology; lic. Conn., N.C. Resident gen. surgery U. N.C., Chapel Hill, 1972-73, resident otolaryngology, 1973-76; fellow Kantonsspital, Zurich, Switzerland, 1977; asst. prof. otolaryngology Yale U., New Haven, Conn., 1977-81, assoc. prof. otolayngology, 1981-82; assoc. prof. surgery, otolayngology, head and neck surgery U. N.C. Sch. Medicine, Chapel Hill, 1982-86, prof. surgery, otolaryngology, head and neck surgery, 1986—, Thomas J. Dark Disting. Prof., 1991—. Civilian cons. USAF Surgeon Gen. for Otolaryngology-Head and Neck Surgery, 1993; hon. guest lectr. Alpha Omega Alpha Induction Ceremonies, U. N.C., Chapel Hill, 1990, 91, Sch. of Medicine Commencement Ceremony, U. N.C., 1990. Alpha Omega Alpha Induction Ceremonies, U. W. Va., 1991; Boies lectr. and prof. U. Minn. Dept. Otolaryngology, 1992, Whitehead lectr. Whitehead Med. Soc., U. N.C., 1994. Countbr. numerous articles to profl. jours. Recipient John A Kirchner Tchg. award, 1980, Harris Mosher award Am. Laryngological, Rhinological and Otological Soc., 1986. Mem. Am. Acad. Otolaryngology-Head and Neck Surgery (pres. elect 1997, Honor award 1985, Disting. Svc. award 1994), Am. Bd. Otolaryngology (bd. dirs.), Alpha Omega Alpha. Office: U NC Dept Otolaryngology Head & Neck Surgery 1115 Bioinformatics Bldg 130 Mason Farm Rd CB # 7070 Chapel Hill NC 27599-7070

PILLSBURY, PENELOPE DELAIRE, library director; b. Bristol, Conn., Jan. 5, 1949; d. Edward William and Ellen Caroline (Jewett) DeLaire; m. Keith Anthony Pillsbury, Aug. 3, 1973; children: Ellen Kathleen Elizabeth, Caleb Edward Marshall. BA in History, U. Vt., 1971; MALS, U. Mich., 1973. Reference libr. U. Vt. Bailey/Howe Libr., Burlington, 1973-80, Fletcher Free Libr., Burlington, 1980-83; dir. N.W. Regional Libr. Dept. of Librs., Georgia, Vt., 1983-86; dir. Brownell Libr., Essex Junction, Vt., 1986—. Author: Essex, Vermont, An Annotated Bibliography to Sources, 1992; author essays and articles. Youth leader Cathedral Ch. St. Paul, Burlington, 1998—, chmn. parish life com., 2001—. Mem. Vt. Libr. Assn. (pres. coll./spl. libr. sect. 1978-79,

assn. pres.), New Eng. Libr. Assn. (bd. dirs.), Essex Rotary Club (pres. 1999-2000), Mortar Board, Phi Beta Kappa, Delta Delta Delta (scholar 1970). Democrat. Avocations: reading, bicycling, singing, cross country skiing, gardening. Home: 25 University Ter Burlington VT 05401-3527 Office: Brownell Libr/ Village of Essex Junction 6 Lincoln St Essex Junction VT 05452-3154 E-mail: jct@aol.state.vt.us.

PILNICK, GARY H. food products executive; b. Forest Hills, N.Y., 1964; Grad., Lafayette Coll., 1986; law degree, Duke U., 1989. Atty. Jenner and Block, 1989—95; v.p., chief corp. counsel Specialty Foods Corp., 1995—97; chief counsel corp. devel. and fin. Sara Lee Corp., 1997—99; v.p., chief counsel Sara Lee Branded Apparel, 1999—2000; v.p., dep. gen. counsel Kellogg Co., 2000—03, sr. v.p., gen. counsel corp. devel., sec., 2003—. Office: Kellogg Co Box 3599 1 Kellogg Sq Battle Creek MI 49016-3599 E-mail: gary.pilnick@kellogg.com.

PILSON, MICHAEL EDWARD QUINTON, oceanography educator; b. Ottawa, Ont., Can., Oct. 25, 1933; came to U.S., 1958; s. Edward Charles and Frances Amelia (Ferguson) P.; m. Joan Elaine Johnstone, July 6, 1957; children: Diana Jane, John Edward Quinton. BSc, Bishops U., Lennoxville, Que., Can.; MSc, McGill U., Montreal, Que., Can., 1958; PhD, U. Calif., San Diego, 1964. Chemist Windsor Mills (Can.) Paper Co., 1954-55; asst. chemist Macdonald Coll. of McGill U., 1955-58; biologist Zool. Soc. San Diego, 1963-66; asst. prof. U. R.I., Narragansett, 1966-71, assoc. prof., 1971-78, prof., 1978-2000, prof. emeritus, 2000—. Dir. Marine Ecosystems Rsch. Lab., Narragansett, 1976-97. Contbr. articles to profl. and popular jours.; author chpts. for 5 books, 1 textbook. Grantee NSF, NOAA, EPA, NIH. Mem. AAAS, AGU, ASLO, Oceanography Soc., Am. Soc. Mammalogists, Saunderstown Yacht Club (bd. govs. 1974-87, commodore 1985-87), Brome Cougar Spotters (pres. emeritus). Home: PO Box 27 Saunderstown RI 02874-0027 Office: U RI Grad Sch Oceanography Narragansett RI 02882 Office Phone: 401-874-6104. E-mail: pilson@gso.uri.edu.

PILZ, ALFRED NORMAN, manufacturing executive; b. Evergreen Park, Ill., Oct. 12, 1931; s. Alfred and Erma Louise (Deane) P.; m. Constance Ney, Nov. 1957; children: Kerry, Kurt, Stephen, Matthew. BS, Ill. Inst. Tech., 1953; MBA, Harvard U., 1960. Registered profl. engr., Mass. Indsl. engr. Harnischfeger Corp., Milw., 1956-58; cons. Arthur D. Little Co., Cambridge, Mass., 1959-60; asst. to exec. v.p., mgr. prodn. engring. Nat. Forge Co., Irvine, Pa., 1960-62; mgmt. cons. McKinsey & Co., N.Y.C. and Cleve., 1962-67; pres., gen. mgr. Ajax Iron Works div. Cooper Industries, Corry, Pa., 1967-72; pres., chief exec. officer WDP, Inc., 1972-79, Swank Refractories Co., Johnstown, Pa., 1972-77, Hyde Park (Pa.) Foundry & Machine Co., 1974-79, Shepard-Niles Corp., Montour Falls, N.Y., 1979-82, Acco Babcock Materials Handling, Frederick, Md., 1982-85; ptnr. Fagan and Co., Ligonier, Pa. Bd. dirs. Acco Babcock, Inc., Babcock Internat., Chemung Foundry, Parnell Precision Products Co., Carre-Orban and Partners, Liberty Mut. Ins. Co., Ind. Steel and Engring. Corp., Bedford Crane Co., Shepard Niles Corp., Marine Bank, WDP, Inc., Ligonier Valley (Pa.) R.R. Soc.; chmn. Parnell Precision Products, 1980-82, Ind. Steeland Engring., Bedford Crane Co., 1981-82, pres., chmn., CEO, Greenway Products. Served with USN, 1948—56, Korea. Mem.: Modern Railroad Industry Assn., Conveyor Equipment Mfg. Assn., Hoist Mfrs. Assn., Crane Mfrs. Assn., Ft. Ligonier Assn., Nat. Trust Soc., Tin Can Sailors Assn., Navy League, Auburn-Cord-Duesenberg Club, HYP (Pitts.). Home: 139 Ramsey Rd Ligonier PA 15658-2204 Office: 223 E Main St Ligonier PA 15658-1347 Personal E-mail: greenwayproducts@verizon.net.

PIMBLE, TONI, artistic director, choreographer, educator; b. Eng. Student, Elmhurst Sch. Ballet and Dramatic Arts, Royal Acad. Dancing, London. Resident choreographer Dance Aspen Co. Project; artistic dir., resident choreographer Eugene (Oreg.) Ballet Co., 1978—; artistic dir. Ballet Idaho, Boise. Past mem. faculty Dance Aspen Summer Dance Sch. Choreographer (festival) Carlisle Choreographer's Showcase, Pa. and Colo., (ballets) Two's Company, N.Y.C., Common Ground, Atlanta, 1994, Playing Field, Indlps., Borderline, Alice in Wonderland, Nebr., 1994, Wash., 1996, Quartet in Blue, Oreg., 1994, Petrushka, Nev., 1994, 95, Children of the Raven, India, Bangladesh, Sri Lanka, Syria, Jordan, Tunisia, 1995, 96, A Midsummer Night's Dream, Nev., 1997, numerous tours and sch. performances; choreographer, tchr. U. Iowa, Interlochen Sch. Arts; resident choreographer Dance On Tour Nat. Endowment Arts; artistic dir. Ballet Idaho. Active outreach programs Young Audiences Oreg., Wash. State Cultural Enrichment Program. Oreg. Arts Commn. artist fellow, Nat. Endowment Arts grantee; co-recipient Gov.'s Arts award, Oreg., 1996. Office: Ballet Idaho 501 S 8th St Ste A Boise ID 83702-7108

PIMENTAL, PATRICIA ANN, neuropsychologist, consulting company executive, author; b. Warwick, R.I., Feb. 2, 1956; d. Thomas Robert and Veronica Madeleine (Costa) P.; m. John V. O'Hara, Dec. 16, 1989; children: John Bernard, Padraic James. BS in Pre-Med, Speech Pathology, Northwestern U., 1978, MA in Speech Pathology with honors, 1980; PsyD in Clin. Psychology with honors, Chgo. Sch. Profl. Psychology, 1987. Lic. psychologist, speech pathologist, Ill.; diplomate Am. Bd. Vocat. Neuropsychology, Am. Acad. Pain Mgmt., Am. Bd. Prof. Disability Cons., Am. Bd. Profl. Neuropsychology (mem. exec. bd.). Clin. psychology extern child psychology clinic U. Ill., Chgo., 1984-85, dir. psychol. svcs. dept. phys. medicine and rehab., 1987-91, asst. prof. dept. phys. medicine and rehab., 1987-91; clin. psychology extern Filmore Mental Health Ctr., Berwyn-Cicero (Ill.) Sr. Svcs., 1985-86; clin. psychology intern St. Elizabeth's Hosp., Chgo., 1986-87; mem. faculty Chgo. Sch. Profl. Psychology, 1991—; pres. Neurobehavioral Medicine Cons., Ltd., Oak Brook, Ill., 1991—. Author (sr.): Neuropsychological Aspects of Right Brain Injury, 1989, Mini Inventory of Right Brain Injury, 1989, Mini Inventory of Right Brain Injury 2, 2000; book reviewer: Contemporary Psychology, 1991, Jour. Applied Neuropsychology, 2001, manuscript reviewer: Archives of Clinical Neurpsychology, 2001—, mem. editl. bd.: The Professional Neuropsychologist, 2002—. Vol. trainer ARC Disaster Stress Relief Program, 1991—; leader U. Ill. Stroke Club, 1988-91; bd. dirs. Older Adult Rehab. Svcs., Cicero, 1987-90; active Chgo. Anti-Cruelty Soc.; mem. music ministry-vocal soloist, choir Oak Brook Cmty. Ch. Named one of Outstanding Young Women Am., 1984, 92; Am. Cancer Soc. scholar, 1979, Outstanding Spkr. of 21st Century, 2001; recipient Outstanding Manuscript of Yr. award Am. Jour. of Pain Mgmt., 1993, Black Belt 1st Degree Sch. of Chung Moo Quan, 1998, Black Belt 2nd Degree Sch. of Chung Moo Quan, 2004. Fellow: Am. Acad. Learning Devel. Disabilities, Am. Coll. Profl. Neuropsychology, Nat. Acad. Neuropsychology, Ill. Psychol. Assn. (adv. bd. 1989—93, chair-elect, chair health and rehab. sect. 1991—92, 1992—93, chair prescription privilege task force 1992—95, continuing edn. chair/clin. practice sect. 1993—95, pres.-elect 1995—96, pres. 1996—97, immediate past pres. 1997—98, co-chair prescription privilege task force 1998—, Disting. Psychologist award 1997); mem.: APA, Am. Bd. Profl. Neuropsychology (mem.-at-large 2000—01, pres. elect 2001—03, pres. 2003—), Am. Speech and Hearing Assn., Midwest Neuropsychology Group, Soc. Clin. and Exptl. Hypnosis, Am. Congress Rehab. Medicine, Nat. Acad. Neuropsychology, Internat. Neuropsychol. Soc., Nat. Brain Injury Rsch. Found. (med. adv. coun. 1992—96), Am. Pain Soc. Avocations: gourmet cooking, piano, voice, martial arts. Office: Glen Oaks Hosp Med Ctr Neurobehavioral Medicine 701 Winthrop Ave Glendale Heights IL 60139-1405

PIMENTEL, BENJAMIN IMPELIDO, journalist; b. Manila, Philippines, June 20, 1964; s. Benjamin C. and Isabel (Impelido) P.; m. Maria Teresita Torres, Dec. 23, 1992. BA in Polit. Sci., U. The Philippines, 1985; M.Journalism, U. Calif., Berkeley, 1993. Staff writer Nat. Midweek mag., Manila, 1986-89; gen. assignment, Asian Am. affairs and transp. reporter San Francisco Chronicle, 1993—. Author: Rebolusyon: A Generation of Struggle in the Philippines, 1991; writer, prodr. Toxic Sunset: On the Trail of Hazardous Waste from Subic and Clark, Philippine Ctr. for Investigative Journalism, Manila, 1993. Mem. Asian Am. Journalists Assn. Office: San Francisco Chronicle 901 Mission St San Francisco CA 94103-2905

PIMENTEL, DAVID, entomologist, educator; b. Fresno, Calif., May 24, 1925; s. Frank and Marion V. (Sylva) P.; m. Marcia R. Hutchins, July, 16, 1949; children: Christina, Susan, Mark David. Student, St. John's U., Collegeville, Minn., 1943, Clark U., summer 1946; BS, U. Mass., 1948; PhD, Cornell U., 1951. Chief tropical rsch. lab. USPHS, San Juan, chief tropical research lab. P.R., 1951-54, project leader tech. devel. lab Savannah, Ga., 1954-55; postdoctoral investigator U. Chgo., winters 1954-55; postdoctoral investigator, OEEC rsch. fellow Oxford (Eng.) U., 1961; postdoctoral investigator, NSF computer scholar MIT, Cambridge, summer 1961; mem. faculty Cornell U., 1955—, prof. insect ecology, 1963-76, head dept. entomology and limnology, 1963-69, prof. entomology, ecology and systematics, 1969-76, prof. insect ecology and agrl. scis., 1976—; prof., core faculty Center Environ. Quality Mgmt., 1973-74. Cons. Office Sci. and Tech., Exec. Office Pres., 1964-67, 69-70, EPA, 1971; co-chmn. Commn. on Mosquito Control for Developing Countries, Nat. Acad. Scis., 1972-73; mem. commn. on pesticides and pest mgmt. in Inter-Am., 1973-77; mem. Nat. Adv. Coun. on Environ. Edn., 1973-74; chmn. panel on environ. impact of herbicides EPA, 1972-74, pesticide adv. coun., 1975-78; nat. adv. coun. environ. edn. Office Edn., HEW, 1975-78, chmn., 1975; chmn. study team on interdependence of food, population, health, energy, and environment World Food and Nutrition Study, Nat. Acad. Scis., 1976-77, chmn. environ. studies bd., 1980-83, mem. Opportunities in Agrl. Rsch. com., 2001—; mem. energy rsch. adv. bd. Dept. Energy, 1979-85; mem. rsch. adv. com. USAID, 1979-82, chmn. panel on land productivity; mem. Office of Tech. Assessment, U.S. Congress, 1979-80; hon. prof. Inst. Applied Ecology, Shengang, China, 1995—. Assoc. editor: Am. Midland Naturalist; contbr. articles to profl. jours. Trustee Village of Cayuga Heights, 1974—; pres. Rachel Carson Coun., 2001—. Served to 2d lt., pilot USAAF, 1943-45. Recipient Disting. Svc. award Rural Sociol. Coun., 1992, Rachel Carson award Soc. Environ. Toxicology and Chemistry, 2002. Mem. AAAS (climate com. 1979-82, population, resource and environ. com. 1985-91, chmn. subcom. on food, population, and resources 1986-87), NAS (chmn. panel on biology and renewable resources, exec. bd. com. on life scis. 1966-68, com. on world food, health and population 1974-75, chmn. panel on econ. and environ. aspects of pest mgmt. in Ctrl. Am. 1974-76, chmn. bd. on sci. and tech. for internat. devel. 1975-79, com. on food and food prodn. 1974-76, alt. agr. com. 1985-89, com. on role of alt. farming methods in modern productive agr. 1985-89), Entomol. Soc. Am. (gov. bd., chmn. editl. bd., pres. Eastern br. 1974-75), Ecol. Soc. Am., Am. Soc. Naturalists, Soc. Study of Evolution, Entomol. Soc. Can., Am. Soc. Zoologists, Nat. Geog. Soc. (com. on rsch. and explorations 1993-2000), Internat. Union for Conservation of Nature and Natural Resources (commn. on ecology 1981-90), Royal Swedish Acad. Scis. (bd. dirs. Beijer Inst. 1994-2000), Chinese Acad. Scis. (hon. prof., acad. com. Inst. Applied Ecology 1994—), Am. Inst. Biol. Scis. (bd. dirs. 1999—), Nat. Audubon Soc. (bd. dirs. 2000-02), Rachel Carson Coun. (pres. 2001—), Sigma Xi, Phi Kappa Phi, Gamma Alpha (nat. recorder 1960-62, AIBS bd. 1999—). Office: Cornell U Dept Ecology Comstock Hall Ithaca NY 14853

PIMENTEL, JULIO GUMERESINDO, lawyer, accountant; b. Chgo., Aug. 11, 1961; s. Julio Caesar and Jeannie Irene (Jakovac) P.; m. Margaret Mary O'Donnell, July 5, 1987 (div. Jan. 1995); children: Ashley Adel, Benjamin Maximillion. BS in Commerce, DePaul U., 1983, M of Accountancy, 1984; JD, John Marshall Law Sch., 1991. Bar: Ill. 1992; CPA, Ill.; cert. internal auditor. Deli clk. Jewel Food Stores, Chgo., 1978-84; field auditor Harris Bank, Chgo., 1984-85; asset-based lending field auditor Chase Comml. Corp., Chgo., 1985-86; acct. Allstate Ins., Northbrook, Ill., 1986-87; revenue agt. IRS, Chgo., 1987-91, estate tax atty., 1991—; pvt. practice, acct. Chgo., 1992—. Ill. State scholar, 1979. Mem. ATLA, Inst. Internal Auditors, Chgo. Bar Assn., IRS Bowling League (Most Polite award 1994-95), Freemen. Avocations: weightlifting, martial arts, gun collecting, old cars, archery. Home and Office: PO Box A3761 Chicago IL 60690-3761

PIMPER, ELIZABETH MARIE, naval officer; b. Flint, Mich., Aug. 28, 1973; d. Arthur Bowers Reid; m. Gregory David Pimper, July 8, 1997. BA summa cum laude, U. Md., 1999. Advanced through grades to lt. (j.g.) USN, 2004; naval flight officer. Vol. St. Vincent de Paul's Dining Rm., San Antonio, 2000-01. Mem. MLA, Women Officer's Profl. Assn., Assn. Naval Aviators, Chinese Lang. Tchrs. Assn., U.S. Naval Inst., Golden Key, Phi Beta Kappa. Avocations: swimming, cooking, running, weightlifting. Office: VP-9 Kaneohe HI 96601 E-mail: empimper@hotmail.com.

PINA, ILEANA, medical educator; arrived in U.S., 1954; d. Luis and Josefina Garcia; 1 child, Victoria. AA, Miami Dade Cmty. Coll., 1968—69; BS in Chemistry, magna cum laude, U. Miami, Coral Gables, 1970—72; MD, U. Miami, Sch. Medicine, 1972—76. Diplomate Nat. Bd. Med. Examiners, 1977, cert. Am. Bd. Internal Medicine, 1980, Cardiovascular Bd. (ABIM), 1985, Am. Bd. Clin. Pharmacology, 1991, lic. State Fla., Pa. Med. License, Ohio Med. License. Asst. prof., divsn. cardiology U. Miami Hosp. and Clinics, 1972—76, 1982—87, intern, straight surgery, 1976—77; staff physician Clearwater Cmty. Hosp., 1977—78; resident internal medicine U. South Fla., Tampa, 1978—80, chief resident, internal medicine, 1980; cardiology fellow U. Miami, Sch. Medicine, 1980—82; dir. exercise lab. U. Miami; attending physician, dir. exercise lab. Jackson Meml. Hosp., 1982—87; attending physician, dir. cardiac fitness ctr. Hahnemann U. Hosp., 1987—89; dir. heart failure and cardiac rehab. Hahnemann U., 1987—91, assoc. prof. medicine, 1987—91; mem. heart failue team, coord. cardiopulmonary exercise lab. Temple U., 1991, assoc. prof. medicine, 1991—98, dir. cardiomyopathy, 1993, attending physician, dir. cardiac rehab., 1994—99, prof. medicine, 1998—99; staff physician Temple U. Hosp., 1991—99, dir. heart failure, co-dir. heart failure/transplant, 1993—94; prof. medicine, dir. heart failure and cardiac transplantation, attending physician Dept. Medicine, Case Western Res. U., Cleve., 1999—; attending physician Vet. Affairs Med. Ctr., Cleveland, 2003—. Adviser devices sect. FDA, past mem. cardio-renal adv. com.; past chair coun. on cardiovasc. rehab. and secondary prevention World Heart Fedn.; mem. exec. coun. and care stds. com. Heart Failure Soc. Am.; founder, scholarship for med. student Miami Dade Cmty. Coll., 1987. Mem. editl. bd.: Am. Jour. Cardiology, Jour. Cardiac Rehab., Jour. Cardiac Failure; contbr. articles to profl. jours. Recipient Surgery award, Fomon, 1976, Cmty. Svc. award, Cuban Lions Club, 1982, Orden Martiana Liceo Cubano, 1982, Alumna award, MDCC, 1984, Floridana award, Cuban Women's Club, 1984, Trail Blazer award, Women's Com. of 100, 1984, award for funding a cardiology fellow for Cardiac Fitness Ctr., Kynett Meml. Found., 1988; grantee, Joseph Collins Found., 1976. Office: Univ Hosps Cleve 11100 Euclid Ave Cleveland OH 44106-1736

PINAC, ANDRÉ LOUIS, III, obstetrician, gynecologist; b. New Orleans, Dec. 8, 1955; s. André Louis Jr. and Patricia Elaine (Ledet) P.; 1 child, Amy Elizabeth. BS, U. Southwestern La., 1977; MD, La. State U., New Orleans, 1981. Diplomate Am. Bd. Ob-Gyn. Resident ob-gyn La. State U. Affiliated Hosps., New Orleans, Lafayette, Lake Charles and Baton Rouge, 1981-85; practice medicine specializing in ob-gyn Opelousas, La., 1985—; chief of staff Doctor's Hosp. Opelousas, 1993-94. Participant Cmty. Health Fair, Opelousas, 1987—; bd. dirs. Drs. Hosp. of Opelousas. Safety officer St. Landry Parish; bd. dirs. Little League, 1992-94. Named Duke at Mardi Gras Festival, Opelousas Garden Club, 1994, King Mardi Gras Ball Masque King Orme, 1999. Fellow Am. Coll. Ob-Gyn; mem. AMA, So. Med. Assn., La. State Med. Soc., St. Landry Parish Med. Soc., Opelousas Cath. Soccer Assn. (pres. 1991-93), Alpha Phi Alpha (life), Sigma Alpha Epsilon. Roman Catholic. Avocations: golf, jogging, swimming, basketball, trivia. Office: 816 Cresswell Ln Ste 1 Opelousas LA 70570-5881

PINALS, ROBERT STANTON, physician; b. Elizabeth, N.J., Aug. 23, 1931; s. Herman and Goldie (Kotler) P.; m. Emanuella DiAssisi, June 20, 1953; children: Deborah, David, Stephen. BA, Cornell U., 1952; MD, U. Rochester, 1956. Diplomate in internal medicine and rheumatology Am. Bd. Internal Medicine. Fellow in rheumatology Mass. Gen. Hosp., Boston, 1961-63; chief rheumatology Lemuel Shattuck Hosp., Boston, 1961-63; from instr. to asst. prof. medicine Tufts U. Sch. Medicine, Boston, 1963-69; from assoc. prof. to prof. medicine SUNY, Syracuse, 1969-78; prof. medicine U. Tenn., Memphis, 1978-84, UMDNJ-Robert Wood Johnson Med. Sch., Piscataway, 1984—, vice chmn. dept. medicine, 1997—; chmn. dept. medicine Med. Ctr. at Princeton, N.J., 1984-97. Mem., cons. arthritis adv. com. FDA, Wasington, 1985-93, chmn., 1986-89; mem. rheumatology subsplty. com. Am. Bd. Internal Medicine, 1988-95. Contbr. numerous chpts. to books, more than 100 articles to profl. jours. Bd. dirs. Ctrl. N.Y. chpt. Arthritis Found., 1969-78, pres., 1976-77. Capt. USAF, 1957-59. Master: Am. Coll. Rheumatology; fellow: ACP. Office: UMDNJ-Robert Wood Johnson Med Sch Dept Medicine PO Box 19 New Brunswick NJ 08903-0019

PINCH, TREVOR J. education educator; b. Lisnaskea, Northern Ireland, Jan. 1, 1952; arrived in US, 1992; s. Owain Fey Trevor and Joan Elizabeth Pinch; m. Christine Asako Leuenberger, Jan. 16, 1992; children: Benika, Annika. BS in Physics, London U., 1973; MSc, Manchester U., 1976; PhD, Bath U., 1982. Lectr. York U., England, 1983—90; prof. Cornell U., Ithaca, NY, 1990—. Author: The Golem, 1993 (Merton award, 1996), Analog Days, 2002 (Foreword prize, 2003). Mem.: Am. Sociol. Assn. Office: Cornell Univ Rockefeller Hall Ithaca NY 14853 Office Phone: 607-255-6048.

PINCHAK, ANN SIMCHA, lawyer; b. Waco, Tex., Sept. 6, 1957; d. Louis E. and Alice (Wright) P.; m. Richard Tomlinson, July 1, 1983; children: Will Tomlinson, David Tomlinson. BA, Rice U., Houston, 1979; student, U. Houston Coll. Law, 1982. Bar: Tex. 1982, U.S. Dist. Ct. (so. dist.) 1991, U.S. Ct. Appeals (5th cir.) 1988. Atty. East Tex. Legal Svcs., Tyler, 1982-84, Nelkin & Nelkin, Houston, 1984-85, Immigration Law, Houston, 1985-96, Pinchak and Assocs., Houston, 1996—. Lectr. Houston and Tex. chpt. Am. Immigration Law Assn., 1991—; pro bono asylum YMCA Internat. Svc. Houston, 1985-96; Coliason-Houston sect. Tex. Am. Immigration Law Assn., Houston, 1993-94. Contbr. articles to profl. jours. V.p. Hadassah, Houston, 1989-90; frequent spkr. bus. immigration, bus. immigration issues. Mem. Am. Immigration Law Assn., Nat. Access to Healthcare Coalition, State Bar Tex. Office: 1 E Greenway Plz Ste 325 Houston TX 77046-0198

PINCHIN, JANE, literature educator; BA, SUNY, Binghamton, 1964; MD, Columbia U., 1965, PhD, 1973. Instr. Bklyn. Coll., 1966—67; prof. English Colgate U., Hamilton, NY, 1969—, interim pres., 2001—02, v.p. academic advancement. Author: Alexandria Still: Forster, Durrell and Cavafy, 1977; contbr. articles to profl. jours., chpts. to books. Office: Colgate U 309 James B Colgate Hall 13 Oak Dr Hamilton NY 13346

PINCHUK, NICHOLAS THOMAS, manufacturing executive; b. Troy, N.Y., Oct. 11, 1946; s. Nicholas Thomas and Mildred Frances Pinchuk; m. Lee Joyce Pinchuk, Aug. 8, 1970; children: Madeline Pinchuk Boehning, Tanya, Thomas. BSEE, Rensselaer Poly. Inst., 1968, MEE, 1969; MBA, Harvard U., 1976. V.p., CFO Carrier Internat., Syracuse, N.Y., 1985-86; v.p. strategic planning Carrier Corp., Syracuse, 1986-87; pres. Carrier Asia Pacific Ops., Singapore, 1987-97. Mem. mgmt. adv. bd. Syracuse U., 1997—. Capt. U.S. Army, 1970-71, Vietnam. Mem. Am. Soc. Refrigeration and Air Conditioning Engrs. Office: Carrier Corp Carrier Pkwy PO Box 4805 Syracuse NY 13221-4805

PINCKERT, WARREN, II, pharmaceutical executive; CEO, pres. Cholestech Corp., Hayward, Calif. Office: Cholestech Corp 3347 Investment Blvd Hayward CA 94545-3808

PINCKNEY, CHARLES COTESWORTH, lawyer; b. Richmond, Va., Oct. 23, 1939; s. Thomas and Charlotte (Kent) P.; m. Helen Raney, Aug. 13, 1966; children: Sarah Whitley, Thomas. BA, Yale U., 1961; LLB, U. Va., 1967. Bar: Va. 1967. Assoc. Mays, Valentine, Davenport & Moore, Richmond, 1967-72; ptnr. Mays & Valentine, LLP, Richmond, 1972-2000, Troutman Sanders LLP, Richmond, 2001—. Bd. dirs. Sweet Briar Coll., 1996-2000; pres. Sheltering Arms Hosp., Richmond, 1986-87, bd. dirs., 1970-99, 2004-; trustee William H.-John G.-Emma Scott Found., 1974-, sec., 1994-99, v.p., 1999-; campaign chmn. United Way Svcs., 1998, bd. dirs., 1997-. Ensign lt. j.g. USNR, 1961-64. Mem. ABA, Va. Bar Assn., Phila. Quarry Club (pres. 1985-91), Country Club of Va., Commonwealth Club (bd. govs. 1986-92, pres. 1991-92), Richmond German (pres. 1996-98), Soc. of Cin. Republican. Episcopalian. Home: 2 Roslyn Rd Richmond VA 23226-1610 Office: Troutman Sanders LLP 1111 E Main St PO Box 1122 Richmond VA 23218-1122 Office Phone: 804-697-1383. Business E-Mail: cotes.pinckney@troutmansanders.com.

PINCUS, ANN TERRY, federal agency administrator, editor, writer; b. Little Rock, Sept. 12, 1937; d. Fred William and Cornelia (Witsell) Terry; m. Walter Haskell Pincus, May 1, 1965; children: Ward, Adam, Cornelia Battle. BA, Vassar Coll., 1959. Editorial asst., writer Glamour Mag., 1963; reporter Ridder Pubs., Washington, 1963-66; freelance writer Washington, 1966-76; dir. info. select com. on U.S. population U.S. Ho. Reps., Washington, 1977-79; nat. publicist Nat. Pub. Radio, Washington, 1979-83; press sec. U.S. Sen. Charles Mathias, Washington, 1983-87; profl. staff mem. Senate Com. on Rules, Washington, 1983-87; v.p. communications Stas. WETA-TV/Radio, Washington, 1987-93; dir. Office of Rsch., USIA, Washington, 1993-99, Office Rsch., Bur. Intelligence & Rsch., Dept. State, 1999-2001. Pres. bd. dirs. Woodley House. Editor: Kennedy Center Cookbook, 1977; contbr. articles to profl. jours. Avocations: politics, reading, walking, tennis. Home: 3202 Klingle Rd NW Washington DC 20008-3403 Office: US Dept of State SA-44 301 4th St SW Rm 352 Washington DC 20547-0009

PINCUS, HOWARD J. geologist, engineer, educator; b. N.Y.C., June 24, 1922; s. Otto Max and Gertrude (Jankowsky) P.; m. Maud Lydia Roback, Sept. 6, 1953; children: Glenn David, Philip E. BS, CCNY, 1942; PhD, Columbia U., 1949. Rsch. assoc. Lamont Geol. Obs., Columbia U., 1949-51; geologist Ohio Dept. Natural Resources, summers 1950-61; faculty Ohio State U., 1949-67, from instr. to assoc. prof., 1949-59, prof., 1959-67, chmn. dept. geology, 1960-65; rsch. geologist U.S. Bur. Mines, 1963—67, geologist, rsch. supr., 1967-68; prof. geol. sci. and civil engring. U. Wis., Milw., 1968-87, prof. emeritus, 1987—, dean Coll. Letters and Sci., 1969-72; cons. geology and rock mechanics, 1954-67, 68—. Sr. postdoctoral fellow NSF, 1962; U.S. nat. com. on tunnelling tech. NAE, 1972-74, U.S. nat. com. on rock mechanics NAS/NAE, 1975-78, 80-89, chmn., 1985-87; U.S. com. Internat. Assn. Engring. Geology/NAS, chmn., 1987-90. Tech. editor Geotech. Testing Jour., 1992-95, mem. editl. bd., 1996—. Served to 1st lt. C.E. AUS, 1942-46. Recipient award for tchg. excellence U. Wis.-Milw. Alumni Assn., 1978. Fellow ASTM (Reinhart award 1987, Award of Merit 1989), AAAS, Geol. Soc. Am.; mem. Am. Geophys. Union, Geol. Soc. Am. (chmn. engring. geology divsn. 1973-74), Soc. Mining Engrs., Internat. Assn. Engring. Geology, Internat. Soc. Rock Mechanics, Am. Rock Mechanics Assn., Assn. Engring. Geologists, Am. Inst. Profl. Geologists (pres. Ohio sect. 1965-66), Phi Beta Kappa (pres. Ohio State U. chpt. 1959-60, pres. U. Wis.-Milw. chpt. 1976-77), Sigma Xi. Home and Office: 17523 Plaza Marlena San Diego CA 92128-1807 Office Phone: 858-487-8466.

PINCUS, JONATHAN HENRY, neurologist, educator; b. Bklyn., May 4, 1935; s. Joseph Bernhard and Hannah Martha (Palestine) P.; m. Cynthia Sterling Deery, Jan., 1961 (div. 1983); children: Daniel, Jeremy, Adam; m. Fortuna Mizrahi Fries, Nov. 1983 (div. 1995). AB, Amherst Coll., Mass., 1956; MD, Columbia U., 1960; MA, Yale U., 1973. Asst. prof. neurology Yale U., New Haven, 1965-69, assoc. prof. neurology, 1969-73, prof. neurology, 1973-86; prof., chmn. neurology Sch. Medicine Georgetown U., Washington, 1987-95, prof. neurology, chmn. emeritus, 1995—; chief neurology VA Med. Ctr., Washington, 2001—. Author: Behavioral Neurology, 1974, 2002, Base Instincts - What Makes Killers Kill, 2001. Fellow Am. Acad. Neurology (v.p. 1991-93); mem. Am. Neurol. Assn. (counselor 1984-86). Achievements include linkage of anticonvulsant properties of phenytoin to reduction of Ca influx; introduction of protein redistribution diet to restore 1-dopa responsiveness in end stage Parkinsonism; correlation of neurologic deficits, the experience of abuse and paranoia with episodic violence in delinquents and criminals; proposition of defect in thiamine triphosphate as cause of Leigh's encephalomyelopathy. Office: VA Med Ctr Washington Dept Neurology 50 Irving St NW Washington DC 20422 E-mail: johnathan.pincus@med.va.gov.

PINCUS, LIONEL I. private equity investor; b. Phila., Mar. 2, 1931; s. Henry and Theresa Celia (Levit) P.; m. Suzanne Storrs Poulton (dec.). BA, U. Pa., 1953; MBA, Columbia U., 1956. Assoc. gen. ptnr. Ladenburg, Thalmann & Co., N.Y.C., 1955-63; pres. Lionel I. Pincus & Co., Inc., N.Y.C., 1964-66; pres., CEO E.M. Warburg & Co., Inc., N.Y.C., 1966-70; chmn., CEO E.M.

Warburg, Pincus & Co., LLC, N.Y.C., 1970—. Trustee N.Y. Presbyn. Hosp.; trustee, chmn. emeritus Columbia U.; trustee Sch. Am. Ballet, German Marshall Fund USA, 1982-88; mem. bd. overseers Columbia Grad. Sch. Bus.; bd. dirs. Am. Mus. Natural History, Nat. Park Found.; mem. Partnership for N.Y.C. Mem. Coun. Fgn. Rels., World Wildlife Fund (nat. coun.), Nat. Golf Links Am. Club, Meadow Club. Office: Warburg Pincus 466 Lexington Ave Fl 10 New York NY 10017-3147 E-mail: yoli2m@aol.com.

PINCUS, ROBERT LAWRENCE, art critic, cultural historian; b. Bridgeport, Conn., June 5, 1953; s. Jules Robert and Carol Sylvia (Rosen) P.; m. Georgianna Manly, June 20, 1981; 1 child, Matthew Manly. BA, U. Calif., Irvine, 1976; MA, U. So. Calif., 1980, PhD, 1987. Instr. U. So. Calif., L.A., 1978-83; art critic L.A. Times, 1981-85, San Diego Union, 1985-92, San Diego Union-Tribune, 1992—. Vis. prof. San Diego State U., 1985-86, 92, lectr. U. San Diego, 1998-, corr. editor, Art in America, 1988- Author: On A Scale That Competes with the World: The Art of Edward and Nancy Reddin Kienholz, 1990, (with others) West Coast Duchamp, 1991, But Is It Art: The Spirit of Art as Activism, 1994, Paradise, 1994, Anne Mudge: Traces, 1996; author introduction to W.D.'s Midnight Carnival, 1988, Kitchen: Liza Lou, 1996, Manuel Neri: Early Work, 1953-78, 97, Gordas: Paintings and Installations by Tania Candiani, 2002. Recipient Chem. Bank award, 1994, Best Critical Writing award, San Diego Press Club, 1994, Mo. Lifestyles Journalism award, 2001. Mem. Internat. Assn. Art Critics, Coll. Art Assn. Democrat. Office: San Diego Union Tribune PO Box 120191 350 Camino De La Reina San Diego CA 92108-3003 Office Phone: 619-293-1831.

PINCUS, STEPHANIE HOYER, dermatologist; b. Lakehurst, NJ, Feb. 28, 1944; d. Ernest Carl and Aviva (Silbert) Hoyer; m. David Frank Pincus, Aug. 22, 1965 (div. Dec. 1984); children: Matthew Jonah, Tamara Hope; m. Allan Roy Oseroff, Mar. 24, 1985; 1 child, Benjamin Henry Oseroff. BA, Reed Coll., 1964; MD cum laude, Harvard U., 1968; MBA, Northwestern U., 1998. Diplomate Am. Bd. Dermatology, Am. Bd. Internal Medicine. Intern Boston City Hosp., 1968-69; rsch. fellow U. Wash., Seattle, 1969-71, resident internal medicine, 1971-72; resident-fellow dermatology U. Washington, Seattle, 1972-74; fellow instr. dept. dermatology Harvard Med. Sch., Boston, 1974-75; asst. prof. medicine U. Wash., Seattle, 1975-77; lectr. Sch. Medicine Boston U., 1977-89; asst. prof. medicine Sch. Medicine Tufts U., Boston, 1977-82, mem. dept. immunology, 1977-89, asst. prof. dermatology, 1979-82, assoc. prof. dermatology and medicine, 1982-89; prof. medicine and dermatology, chairperson dermatology SUNY, Buffalo, 1989-2000; chief acad. affiliations officer Dept. Vets. Affairs, Washington, 2000—. Dermatology Found. fellow, Evanston, Ill., 1974-75, 77-78; Vets. Adminstrn. rsch. assoc., 1975-77; recipient Clin. Investigator award NIH, Bethesda, Md., 1979-81. Mem. Am. Contact Dermatitis Soc. (mem. liaison com. 1993—), Women's Dermatologic Soc. (bd. dirs. 1992—), Soc. Investigative Dermatology (chmn. com. on govt. and pub. rels. 1992-96), Profs. of Dermatology (mem. program com. 1993—), Harvard Med. Alumni (pres. 1995-96), Phi Beta Kappa, Alpha Omega Alpha. Office: Dept Vets Affairs Office Acad Affiliations 810 Vermont Ave Washington DC 20420

PINCUS, THEODORE, microbiologist, rheumatologist, educator; AB, Columbia U., 1961; MD, Harvard U., 1966. Assoc. Sloan-Kettering Inst., N.Y.C., 1973-75; asst. prof. medicine/immunology, dir. clin. immunology lab. Stanford (Calif.) U., 1975-76; prof. Wistar Inst., Phila., 1976-80; adj. assoc. prof. medicine-rheumatology U. Pa., Phila., 1976-80; prof. medicine and microbiology Vanderbilt U., Nashville, 1980—. Fellow ACP, Am. Rheumatism Assn., Am. Soc. Microbiology. Achievements include description of morbidity and mortility of rheumatoid arthritis; analyses of host genetic and psychosocial variables in chronic diseases; description of host genetic control of experimental retrovirus infection; description of psychological and economic consequences of chronic disease; analysis of "mind body" explanations of associations between socioeconomic status and chronic disease. Office: Vanderbilt U Divsn Rheumatology & Immunology 203 Oxford House Nashville TN 37232-0001

PINCUS, THEODORE HENRY, public relations executive; b. Chgo., Sept. 15, 1933; s. Jacob T. and J. (Engel) Pincus; m. Sharon Barr, Jan. 16, 1988; children: Laura, Mark, Susan, Anne, Jennifer. BS in Journalism, Ind. U., 1955. Free-lance bus. writer, 1955—58; sr. exec. Harshe Rotman & Druck, Chgo., 1958—62; owner Theodore Pincus & Assocs., Chgo., 1962—64; chmn., CEO Fin. Rels. Bd., Inc. subs. BSMG Worldwide, Chgo., 1965—98; vice chmn. BSMG Worldwide divsn. Interpub. Group, N.Y.C., 1998—2001; fin. columnist Chgo. Sun Times, 2002—. Pub. affairs advisor to Nelson Rockefeller, N.Y.C., 1960, N.Y.C., 68; advisor U.S. Info. Agy., 1993—; adj. prof. fin. MBA Sch., DePaul U., 2002—; former mem. adv. bd. NASDAQ; ind. comm. cons., 2003—. Author: Giveaway Day, 1977, On the Offensive, 2001; contbr. artcles to profl. jours. including Wall St. Jour., Fortune and N.Y. Times. Active presdl. nomination campaigns; vice-chmn. Midwest Region Am. Jewish Com.; mem. adv. bd. Ind. U. Bus. Sch., The Ill. Coalition. With USAF, 1955—57. Named Entrepreneur of Yr., Ernest and Young Merrill Lynch, 1998; recipient numerous nat. awards for profl. excellence in investor rels. and corp. pub. rels., including Silver Anvil award, Pub. Rels. Soc. Am., 1966, Civic Achievement award, Am. Jewish Com., 1993, Pub. Rels. Profl. of Yr., Pub. Rels. Soc. Am., 2002. Mem.: Nat. Investor Rels. Inst. (founding), Young Pres.'s Orgn., Union League, Standard Club. Office: Theodore Pincus & Assocs 400 E Ohio St Chicago IL 60611-3322

PINCUS, WALTER HASKELL, editor; b. Bklyn., Dec. 24, 1932; s. Jonas and Clare (Glassman) Pincus; m. Betty Meskin, Sept. 12, 1954; 1 child, Andrew John; m. Ann Witsell Terry, May 1, 1965; children: Ward Haskell, Adam Witsell, Cornelia Battle Terry. BA, Yale U., 1954; JD, Georgetown U., 2001. With Wall St. Jour., 1957—58; cons. Senate Fgn. Rels. Com., 1962-63; spl. writer Washington Evening Star, 1963-66; editor, reporter Washington Post, 1966-69; chief cons. Symington subcom. Senate Fgn. Relations Com., 1969-70; assoc. editor New Republic, 1972-74, exec. editor, 1974-75; spl. writer Washington Post, 1975—; cons. NBC News, 1971-79, CBS News, 1979-86, NBC News, 1987-88, Washington Post Co., 1989—. Vis. lectr. Yale U., 1988, 2002, Stanford U., 2003, 04. Trustee Shakespeare Theater, 1988—, co-chmn. edn. com., 1989—91, chmn. nominating com., 1992—96, chmn. exec. com., 1992—. With U.S. Army, 1957—58. Co-recipient Pulitzer prize, 2001; recipient Page One award, 1960, George Orwell award, 1977, George Polk award, 1978, Emmy award, 1981, Stewart Alsop award, 1999. Mem.: Coun. Fgn. Rels., Yale Club Washington. Home: 3202 Klingle Rd NW Washington DC 20008-3403 Office: Washington Post 1150 15th St NW Washington DC 20071-0001 E-mail: pincusw@washpost.com.

PINCZUK, ARON, physicist; b. San Martin, Argentina, Feb. 15, 1939; s. Faiwel and Ester (Wejeman) P.; m. Gladys Norma Teitelman, June 14, 1962; children: Ana Gabriela, Guillermo Fabian. Licenciado, U. Buenos Aires, Argentina, 1962; PhD, U. Pa., 1969; D (hon.), U Autonoma, Madrid, 1997. Staff mem. Nat. Rsch. Coun., Argentina, 1971-76; head physics dept. Faculty of Scis., U. Buenos Aires, Argentina, 1974; vis. scientist Max Planck Inst., Stuttgart, Germany, 1976, IBM Rsch., Yorktown Heights, N.Y., 1976-77; staff mem. Bell Labs., Murray Hill, N.J., 1978—; prof. Columbia U., N.Y.C., 1998—. Sec. Argentina Phys. Soc., Buenos Aires, 1972-75; editor Solid State Communications, 1989-92, assoc. editor in chief, 1992—. Contbr. over 200 articles to profl. jours. and numerous chpts. to books. Recipient Oliver E. Buckley Condensed-Matter Physics prize Am. Physical Soc., 1994. Fellow: AAAS, Am. Phys. Soc. Achievements include use and devel. novel optical methods in studies of structural phase transitions, semiconductor interfaces and interactions of free electrons in semiconductors; discovered novel phenomena in studies of quantum electron fluids. Office: Columbia U Dept Physics and Applied Physics New York NY 10027 also: Bell Labs Lucent Techs 600 Mountain Ave Rm 1d-433 New Providence NJ 07974-2008

PINDEL, DAVID LEE, biologist, educator; b. Milw., June 10, 1971; s. Kenneth Robert and Kathy Anne Kahn. BS with honors, U. of Wis., Stevens Point, 1994; MS, Western Ill. U., 1997. Zoology lab. asst. U. of Wis., Stevens Point, Wis., 1992—94; biology tchg. asst. Western Ill. U., Macomb, 1995—97; instr. of biology Spoon River C.C., Macomb, Ill., 1996—97, Corning C.C., Corning, NY, 1999—2001, asst. prof. of biology, 2002—. Bd. of dirs. Spencer Crest Nature Ctr., Corning, NY, 2000—. Co-author (book) Instructor's Resource Guide (for the textbook Biological Science by Scott Palmer; 1st edition, 2002. Bd. of dirs., sec. Spencer Crest Nature Ctr., Corning, NY, 2000—02. Recipient Brian Eagon Meml. award, U. of Wis. at Stevens Point, 1994; scholar Alumni scholar, 1990. Mem.: Phi Kappa Phi. Libertarian. None (Atheist). Avocations: philosophy, reading, playing basketball/watching football, travel, hiking. Office: Corning Community College 1 Academic Dr Corning NY 14830 Office Phone: 607-962-9536. Personal E-mail: pindel@corning-cc.edu. E-mail: pindel@corning-cc.edu.

PINDELL, HOWARDENA DOREEN, artist; b. Phila., Apr. 14, 1943; d. Howard Douglas and Mildred Edith (Lewis) P. BFA, Boston U., 1965; MFA, Yale U., 1967; DFA (hon.), Mass. Coll. Art, 1997, New Sch./Parsons Sch. Design, 1999. Curatorial asst. Mus. Modern Art, N.Y.C., 1969-71, asst. curator, 1971-77, asso. curator dept. prints and illus. books, 1977-79; asso. prof. art SUNY, Stony Brook, 1979-84, prof. art, 1984—. Contbr. articles to profl. jours.; exhbns. include, Mus. Modern Art, Stockholm and 5 European mus., 1973, Fogg Art Mus., Cambridge, Mass., 1973, Indpls. Mus., Taft Mus., Cin., 1974, Gerald Piltzer Gallery, Paris, 1975, Mus. Modern Art, Paris, 1975, Vassar Coll. Art Gallery, 1977; represented in permanent collections, Mus. Modern Art, N.Y.C., Fogg Art Mus., Met. Mus., N.Y.C., Whitney Mus. Am. Art; represented in travelling exhbns. Brandeis U., U. Calif. at Riverside, Cleve. Inst. Arts, SUNY, Potsdam, New Paltz, Wesleyan U., Davison Art Ctr., others. Recipient Artist award Studio Mus. of Harlem, 1994, Joan Mitchell Painting award Joan Mitchell Found., 1994/95, Women's Caucus for Art award for Disting. Contbns. and Achievement in Arts, 1996, Cmty. Svc. award N.Y. State United Tchrs., 1998, Juneteenth award Heckscher Mus., 1999, IAM Pioneer award, 2000; Japan/U.S. Friendship fellow, 1981-82, Guggenheim fellow, 1987-88; Ariana Found. grantee, 1984-85. Mem. Arts Coun. African Studies Assn., Coll. Art Assn. (Best Exhbn./Performance award 1990), Internat. Assn. Art Critics, Internat. House of Japan (acad.). Office: SUNY/Stonybrook Art Dept Stony Brook NY 11794-0001 Office Phone: 631-632-7266. Office Fax: 631-632-7261. Business E-mail: hpindell@notes.cc.sunysb.edu.

PINDER, GEORGE FRANCIS, engineering educator, scientist; b. Windsor, Ont., Can., Feb. 6, 1942; s. Percy Samuel and Stella Marie P.; m. Phyllis Marie Charlton, Sept. 14, 1963; children— Wendy Marie, Justin George. B.Sc., U. Western Ont., 1965, PhD, U. Ill., 1968. Research hydrologist U.S. Geol. Survey, 1968-72; mem. faculty dept. civil engring. Princeton U., 1972-89, prof., 1972-89, chmn. dept., from 1980, dir. water resources program, 1972-80; dean Coll. Engring. and Math. U. Vt., Burlington, 1989-96, dir. Rsch. Ctr. for Groundwater Remediation Design, 1993—. Recipient O.E. Meinzer award Geol. Soc. Am., 1975, WUC medal, 1992; U. Vt. Univ. scholar, 1993. Fellow Am. Geophys. Union (Robert E. Horton award 1969); mem. ASCE (Julian Hinds medal 2002), Am. Geophys. Union. Home: 188 Bishop Rd Shelburne VT 05482-6933 Office: U Vt Coll Engring And Math Burlington VT 05405-0001

PINDER, RENEE MONIQUE, diplomat; b. Nassau, Bahamas, Nov. 21, 1967; arrived in U.S., 1999; d. Harcourt Maxwell and Hazel Mae Pinder. BSc, Ga. Coll., 1994; MBA, U. Miami, 1996; cert. in Spanish, Coll. of the Bahamas, 1997; diplomatic tng. cert., Santiago, Chile, 1999. Clk. Min. Fgn. Affairs, Nassau, The Bahamas; exec. officer Passport Office, Nassau, The Bahamas, 1986—96, supr.; adminstrv. cadet Min. Fgn. Affairs, Nassau, The Bahamas, 1996—99, asst. sec., 1999—, vice consul Miami, 1999—, N.Y., 2002—. Mem. Fgn. Affairs Investigative, Nassau, 1996—99, Diplomatic Corps. Com., Miami, 1999—. Active Bahamas Red Cross Soc., 1994—. Mem.: Delta Sigma Theta (pres. 1993—94). Office: Bahamas Consulate Gen 25 SE 2nd Ave Ste 818 Miami FL 33131-1540 E-mail: bcg@bellsouth.net.

PINDERSKI, JEROME WILBERT, JR., lawyer; b. Jan. 12, 1957; s. Jerome W. Pinderski; m. Karen Marie Peterson, Oct. 1, 1983; children: Shaun, Heather, Victoria. BA magna cum laude, Marquette U., 1978; JD, JD, Loyola U., Chgo., 1981. Bar: Ill. 1981, U.S. Dist. Ct. (no. dist.) Ill. 1981, U.S. Ct. Appeals (7th cir.) 1983, U.S. Supreme Ct. 1988, U.S. Ct. Appeals (fed. cir.) 1989, U.S. Ct. Internat. Trade 1989, D.C. 1990. Mng. ptnr. Pinderski & Pinderski Ltd., Palatine, Ill., 1981—. Panel atty. Legal Assistance Found., Chgo., 1982—; bd. dirs. 1st Bank and Trust Co. Ill., Palatine, Performance Home Med. Equipment, Dallas; commr. Algonquin Econ. Devel. Commn., 1994—. Mem. planning com. United Way Crusade of Mercy, Chgo., 1991—93; sec. United Way of Palatine, Inverness, Rolling Meadows, Ill., 1986—88, 1st v.p., 1988—90, pres., 1990—92; active Palatine Twp. Human Needs Com., 1989—, Palatine-Inverness Healthier Comtys. Project, 1995—2002; trustee Palatine Libr. Dist. Found., 1993—95; chmn. candidate slating com. Palatine Twp. Rep. Orgn., 1990—92; bd. dirs. United Way Crusade of Mercy, Chgo., 1995—99, United Way of Palatine, Inverness, Rolling Meadows, Ill., 1985—2003; bd. dir. Bridge Youth & Family Svcs., 2004—; del. U.S. Japan bilateral session on law and econs., Tokyo, 1988, Moscow conf. on law and econ. coop., 1990; arbitrator Cook County Cir. Ct. Arbitration Program, 1990—95. Mem.: ATLA, ABA, Greater Palatine C. of C. and Industry (dir. 1982—89, v.p. 1985—86, 1st vice-chmn. 1987, chmn. 1988), Chgo. Coun. Fgn. Rels., Internat. Bar Assn. (London), D.C. Bar Assn., Ill. State Bar Assn., Palatine Jaycees (sec. 1984—85, legal counsel 1983—, John H. Ambruster Keyman award 1984—85, Dick Bayer Mr. Reliability award 1985—86), Ill. Jaycees (gen. coun. 1989), Terrace Hill Golf Club (Algonquin, Ill.), Rotary, Phi Beta Kappa, Alpha Sigma Nu. Republican. Roman Catholic. Home: 622 Greens View Dr Algonquin IL 60102-4408 Office: Pinderski & Pinderski Ltd 115 W Colfax St Palatine IL 60067-5086 Office Phone: 847-358-5220. E-mail: pinderlaw@aol.com.

PINDLE, ARTHUR JACKSON, JR., philosopher, researcher; b. Macon, Ga., May 26, 1942; s. Arthur Jackson Sr. and Beatrice Rosetta (Williams) P.; 1 child, Zhinga D. BS in Physics, Morehouse Coll., 1964; MA in Philosophy, Yale U., 1973, MPhil, 1974, PhD in Philosophy, 1978. Physicist IBM, Inc., Poughkeepsie, N.Y., 1964, Naval Ordinance Station, Indian Head, Md., 1966-69, Satellite Experiment Lab, Suitland, Md., 1970-71; philosophy prof. Fayetteville (N.C.) State U., 1976-83; pres. HRG, Inc., New Orleans, 1983—; dir. rsch. NITRT, Inc., New Orleans, 1993—; prof. philosophy So. U., New Orleans, 1997—; pres. Grael Electronics, Inc., 1998. Mem. bd. advs. Inst. Philosoph. Rsch., Boulder, Colo., 1980-83. Contbr. articles to profl. jours.; patentee personal computer console. Mem. Dem. Nat. Com., 1993-98. Avocations: yoga, chess. Home: 5000 Good Dr New Orleans LA 70127-3814 Office: Grael Electronics Inc 5000 Good Dr New Orleans LA 70127-3814 Personal E-mail: apindle@netscape.net.

PINDYCK, BRUCE EBEN, lawyer, corporate executive; b. N.Y.C., Sept. 21, 1945; s. Sylvester and Lillian (Breslow) P.; m. Mary Ellen Schwartz, Aug. 18, 1968; children: Ashley Beth, Eben Spencer, Blake Michael Lawrence. AB, Columbia U., 1967, JD, 1970, MBA, 1971. Bar: N.Y. 1971, Wis. 1987. Assoc. Olwine, Connelly, Chase, O'Donnell & Weyher, N.Y.C., 1971-80; asst. gen. counsel Peat, Marwick, Mitchell & Co., N.Y.C., 1980-82; ptnr. Hollyer, Jones, Pindyck, Brady & Chira, N.Y.C., 1983-87; pres., CEO Meridian Industries, Inc., Milw., 1985—, also chmn. bd. dirs.; CEO Majilite Corp., Dracut, Mass., 1987—, also chmn. bd. dirs. Mem. capital campaign com. Columbia U., 1984-87. Mem. bd. visitors Columbia Coll., 2001—; bd. dirs. Harambee Cmty. Sch., 1991—96, Milw. Ballet Co., 1993—97, Milw. Pub. Mus., 1994—98. Mem. Columbia Coll. Alumni Assn. (regional dir. 1988-94, v.p. 1994-98, exec. com., 1994-98), World Pres.'s Orgn. Address: 100 E Wisconsin Ave Milwaukee WI 53202-4107 E-mail: bpindyck@meridiancompanies.com.

PINE, BESSIE MIRIAM, social worker, editor, columnist; b. Toronto, Jan. 6, 1919; d. Moses and Annie (Rosenberg) Hadler; m. Kurt Pine, Mar 24, 1943 (dec. May 1962); children: Alfred Marc, Annie Laurie Reuveni. BA in Psychology, U. Toronto, 1939; M in Social Work, U. Pitts., 1944. Lic. social worker, N.Y. Br. dir. YM-YWHA, Toronto, 1940-42; case worker Family Svc. of Greater New Haven, Conn., 1944-47, Jewish Family Svc., Phila., 1947-49; divsn. unit supr. Ednl. Alliance, N.Y.C., 1949-51; older adult supr. Kings Bay YM-YWHA, Bklyn., 1955-59; editor pers. reporter Jewish Comty. Ctr. Program Aids, dir. part time pers. bur., N.Y.C., 1962-67; assoc. dir. pers. svcs. Jewish Comty. Ctrs. Assn., N.Y.C., 1967-93. Editor: (booklet) Viewpoints on Social and Social Work Issues, 1965; author: (rsch. study) Making Retirement Count: Options and Opportunities, 1989; author: (publ.) Looking Back and Looking Forward: A 75 Year Retrospective on the Assn. of Jewish Center Workers, 1993. Recipient Florence G. Heller award Jewish Comty. Ctrs. Assn., N.Y.C., 1994. Mem. Com. to Strengthen Group Work in Jewish Comty. Ctrs. (co-chair 1992-99), Assn. of Jewish Ctr. Profls. (columnist Ask Bessie 1994—, Profl. of Yr., Phila. 1990, Tikkun Olam award Balt. 1993), Nat. Assn. Social Workers (cert. social worker). Home: 150 Beaumont St Brooklyn NY 11235-4119

PINE, JEFFREY BARRY, lawyer, former state attorney general; b. N.Y.C., Jan. 10, 1955; s. Henry F. Pine and Irma (Goldberg) Nass; m. Faith Marcia Scavitti, May 20, 1984; children: Bethany Arielle, Jonathan Ian Lee, Jamie Ilysse. BA in Polit. Sci., Haverford Coll., 1976; JD, George Washington U., 1979. Bar: R.I. 1979, Mass. 1979, U.S. Dist. Ct. R.I. 1979, U.S. Supreme Ct. 1994. Asst. atty. gen. R.I. Dept. Atty. Gen., Providence, 1979—89; assoc. atty. Decof & Grimm, Providence, 1990—92; atty. gen. State of R.I., 1993—99; mng. ptnr. Jeffrey B. Pine Esq., Providence, 1999—. Trustee MADD, 1987—2000; mem. Bd. Bar Overseers Mass. Named Top Prosecutor, R.I. Monthly; recipient Beta Rho Sigma award. Mem.: R.I. Trial Lawyers Assn., Assn. Am. Trial Lawyers, R.I. Bar Assn. Home: 349 Wayland Ave Providence RI 02906-4531

PINE, PATRICIA PALMER, aging services administrator; b. Portland, Maine, Mar. 14, 1940; d. Maurice George and Elizabeth Wadsworth (Syphers) Palmer; m. James Erlon Hannaford, Oct. 1, 1960 (div. June 1970); children: Paula L., Brenda J.; m. Vanderlyn Russell Pine, Aug. 9, 1974; stepchildren: Gordon K., Brian T., Daniel R. AB, Vassar Coll., 1972; MA, Columbia U., 1975; PhD, SUNY, Albany, 1993. Dir. Dutchess County Office for the Aging, Poughkeepsie, N.Y., 1976-80; assoc. dir. Hudson Valley Health Systems Agy., Tuxedo, N.Y., 1980-83; exec. dir. Hospice Assn. of Ulster County, Kingston, N.Y., 1983-84; assoc. exec. dir. WellCare N.Y., Kingston and Newburgh, 1984-86; dir. Ulster County Office Aging, Kingston, 1986-95; exec. dep. dir. N.Y. State Office For The Aging, Albany, 1995-2001, dir., 2001—03; prof. pub. svc. SUNY Albany Sch. Social Welfare, 2003—. Adj. prof. SUNY, New Paltz, 1973-95, Marist Coll., Poughkeepsie, 1976-79, 95, Adelphi U., L.I. City, 1983; pres. CEO The Gerontol Inst., 1993—; mem. faculty Brookdale Ctr. of Hunter Coll., 2000-03. Pres. United Way of Ulster County, Kingston, 1989-90; mem. N.Y. State Adv. Commn. on Aging-In Initiative, 1991-2003; trustee The Kingston Hosp., 1993-96; co-chair Panel for Elderly Prescription Ins. Program, 2001-03; chair Gov.'s Osteoporosis Edn. and Prevention Com., 2001—. Gerontol. Soc. Am. fellow, 1987, Paul Harris fellow Rotary Internat., 1989; named Vol. of the Yr., United Way of Ulster County, 1990. Fellow Gerontol. Soc. of Am.; mem. NASW, Nat. Coun. on Aging, N.Y. State Assn. Area Agys. on Aging (rec. sec. 1978-80, chair statewide conf. 1980, chair tng. com. 1986-88, pres. 1995). Avocations: travel, family, reading. Home: 18 Plattekill Ave New Paltz NY 12561-1917

PINE, WILLIAM CHARLES, foundation executive; b. Canton, Ill., Nov. 4, 1912; s. William Charles and Katherine Pauline (Prichard) P.; m. Virginia Rae Keeley, June 14, 1945; children: William Charles, Barry Scott, Nancy Katherine Pine McMahon. BS, Monmouth Coll., Ill., 1939; DHL (hon.), Southwestern at Memphis, 1961; Dr.Laws (hon.), Mercy Coll. Detroit, 1966. Asst. dir. admissions Monmouth Coll., 1939-42; spl. agt. FBI, 1942-45; assoc. dir. Am. City Bur., N.Y.C. and Chgo., 1945-47; dir. pub. relations Lake Forest (Ill.) Coll., 1947-48, v.p., 1948-51; dir. scholarship prog. Ford Motor Co. Fund., Dearborn, Mich., 1951-72, asst. dir., 1972-75; prog. dir. The Collins Found., Portland, Oreg., 1976-79, exec. v.p., 1979-97; grant advisor Providence St. Vincent Med. Found., 1997—. Contbr. articles to profl. jours. Mem. Historic Records Adv. Bd., Salem, Oreg., 1984-87. Mem. Soc. Former Spl. Agts. of FBI. Avocations: reading, mail order bus. Office: Providence St Vincent Med Found 9205 SW Barnes Rd Portland OR 97225-6603

PINEDA, ALBERT ANTHONY, obstetrician, gynecologist, educator; b. N.Y.C., Feb. 15, 1937; MD, N.Y. Med. Coll., 1963. Diplomate Am. Bd. Ob-gyn. Intern St. Vincents Hosp., N.Y.C., 1963-64; resident in ob-gyn. Flower-Fifth Ave Hosp.-N.Y. Med. Coll., N.Y.C., 1964-68; fellow in gynecol. oncology Met. Hosp., N.Y.C., 1968-69; med. staff St. Joseph's Hosp. Med. Ctr., Paterson, N.J.; clin. assoc. prof. N.Y. Med. Coll., 1976, Seton Hall U. Grad. Sch. Med. Edn., 1991—; clin. prof. St. George's U. Sch. Medicine, 1995—; pvt. practice Clifton, N.J. Mem. ACOG, Soc. Gynecol. Oncology, N.J. Med. Soc., Passaic County Med. Soc. Office: 1035 Route 46 Clifton NJ 07013-2430

PINEDA, ANSELMO, neurosurgery educator; b. Lima, Peru, Apr. 3, 1923; s. Anselmo Vicente and Juana (Munayco)P.; m. Monique Yvonne Martin, Mar. 15, 1955; children: Patricia M., Richard A., Gilbert V., Katherine A. MD, San Marcos U., Lima, 1951; MS, Northwestern U., 1962. Diplomate Am. Bd. Neurol. Surgery. Rotating intern Loayza Hosp., Lima, 1950-51; head histology sect. Leprosy dept. Ministry Pub. Health, Lima, 1951; asst. pathologist Nat. Inst. Neoplastic Diseases, 1952; vol. asst. lab. normal and path. histology nervous system San Marcos U. Sch. Medicine, 1953; rotating intern Augustana Hosp., Chgo., 1954, resident in gen. surgery, 1955; jr. asst. resident in neurosurgery U. Chgo., 1955-56, sr. asst. resident in neurosurgery, 1956-57, chief resident in neurosurgery, 1957-58; assoc. instr. neurosurgery U. Tex., 1958-61; assoc. neurosurgeon John Sealy Hosp., Galveston, Tex., 1960-61, attending neurosurgeon, 1961; acting chief neurosurgery VA Hosp., Long Beach, Calif., 1962-63; asst. clin. prof. dept. neurobiology UCLA, 1963-82, assoc. clin. prof. divsn. neuro-biology/neurosurgery, 1982—. Cons. VA Hosp., Long Beach, 1966-67. NIH spl. fellow in Neuroanatomy Northwestern U., 1961-62. Fellow ACS, Am. Coll. Angiology, Royal Soc. Medicine; mem. AAUP, AAAS, AMA, Congress of Neurol. Surgeons, World Med. Assn., Am. Assn. Neurol. Surgeons, Calif. Med. Assn., Orange County Med. Assn., Am. Acad. Neurology, Am. Assn. Neuropathologists, Internat. Coll. Surgeons, Am. Assn. Anatomists, Am. Assn. Trauma, Am. Soc. Stereotaxic and Functional Neurosurgery, N.Y. Acad. Scis., Internat. Assn. Study Pain, U. Chgo. Surg. Soc., L.A. Surg. Soc., Sigma Xi. Home: 16571 Carousel Ln Huntington Beach CA 92649-2115 Office: 2880 Atlantic Ave Long Beach CA 90806-1714 E-mail: ap0423@aol.com.

PINELESS, HAL STEVEN, neurologist; b. Chgo., Oct. 19, 1954; s. William and Sophie (Lubnicka) P.; m. Edy Dianne Rudnick, Mar. 10, 1985; children: Adam, Emily. BS in Zoology, U. Ill., 1976; DO, Chgo. Coll. Osteo. Medicine, 1981. Diplomate Am. Osteo. Bd. Neurology and Psychiatry. Intern Chgo. Osteo. Hosp., 1981-82; resident Loyola U. Med. Ctr./Hines (Ill.) VA Ctr., 1982-85; asst. prof. neurology Chgo. Coll. Osteo. Medicine, 1985-86; pvt. practice Winter Park, Fla., 1986—. Pres. med. staff Fla. Hosp. East Orlando, 1990-93, bd. trustees, 1990-94. Contbr. articles to profl. jours and newspapers. Mem. Am. Osteo. Assn., Am. Acad. Neurology, Am. Coll. Neuropsychiatrists, Nat. Headache Found., Chgo. Coll. of Osteopathic Alumni Assn. (pres. 2000-03). Avocations: golf, swimming, computers, photography. Office: 1890 State Rd 436 Ste 255 Winter Park FL 32792-2285

PINEO, RONN, historian, educator; b. Seattle, Apr. 15, 1954; s. Ronn and Claudia Patricia Pineo; m. Ardis Ann O'Meara, June 25, 1978; 1 child, Tommy O'Meara. BA in History, Calif. State U., Fullerton, 1979; MA in History, U. Calif., Irvine, 1981, PhD in L. Am. History, 1987. Instr. Cypress (Calif.) Coll., 1985—86; vis. lectr. U. Nev., Las Vegas, 1986—87; vis. asst. prof. Emory U., Atlanta, 1987—88, Towson (Md.) U., 1988—95, asst. prof., 1995—96, assoc. prof., 1996—2001, prof. history, 2001—. Author: Social Economic Reform in Ecuador, 1996; contbg. author: Cities of Hope, 1998. Recipient rsch. award, NEH, 1992, Fulbright award in lecturing and rsch., Ecuador, 1997—98. Democrat. Avocations: fishing, baseball, tennis, basketball. Office: Towson U History Dept Towson MD 21252 Office Phone: 410-704-2918. Business E-mail: pineo@towson.edu.

PINES, ALEXANDER, chemistry educator, researcher, consultant; b. Tel Aviv, June 22, 1945; came to US, 1968. US citizen in 1981. s. Michael and Neima (Ratner) P.; m. Ayala Malach, Aug. 31, 1967 (div. 1983); children: Itai, Shani; m. Ditsa Kafry, May 5, 1983; children: Noami, Jonathan, Talia. BSc,

Hebrew U., Jerusalem, 1967; PhD in Chemical Physics, MIT, 1972; D (hon.), U. Paris "Pierre et Marie Curie", 1999, U. Rome "La Sapienza", 2001. Asst. prof. chemistry U. Calif., Berkeley, 1972-75, assoc. prof., 1975-80, prof., 1980—, Pres.'s chair, 1993-97, Chandellor's rsch. prof., 1997-99, Miller rsch. prof., 1998-99, Glenn T. Seaborg prof. chemistry, 1999—. Faculty sr. scientist materials scis. div. Lawrence Berkeley Nat. Lab., 1975—; cons. Mobil Oil Co., Princeton, N.J., 1980-84, Shell Oil Co., Houston, 1981—; chmn. Bytel Corp., Berkeley, Calif., 1981-85; vis. prof. Weizmann Inst. Sci., 1982; adv. prof. East China Normal U., Shanghai, People's Rep. of China, 1985; sci. dir. Naloarc, Martinez, Calif., 1986-92; Joliot-Curie prof. Ecole Superieure de Physique et Chemie, Paris, 1987; Walter J. Chute Disting. lectr. Dalhousie U., 1989, Charles A. McDowell lectr. U. B.C., 1989, E. Leon Watkins lectr. Wichita State U., 1990; Hinshelwood lectr., U. Oxford, 1990, A.R. Gordon Disting. lectr. U. Toronto, 1990, Venable lectr. U. N.C., 1990, Max Born lectr. Hebrew U. of Jerusalem, 1990; William Draper Harkins lectr. U. Chgo., 1991, Kolthoff lectr. U. Minn., 1991; Md.-Grace lectr. U. Md., 1992; mem. adv bd. Nat. High Magnetic Field Lab., Inst. Theoretical Physics, U. Calif. Santa Barbara, Ctr. Pure and Applied Math. U. Calif., Berkeley; mem. adv. panel chem. Nat. Sci. Found.; Randolph T. Major Disting. Lectr. U. Conn., 1992; mem. bd. sci. govs. Weizemann Inst. Sci., 1997—; Peter Smith lectr. Duke U., 1993, Arthur William Davidson lect. U. Kansas, 1992, Arthur Birch lect. Australian Nat. U., 1993, Richard C. Lord Meml. lectr. MIT, 1993, Steacie lectr. Nat. Rsch. Coun. Can., 1993, Morris Loeb lectr. Harvard U., 1994, Jesse Boot Found. lectr., U. Nottingham, 1994, Frontiers in Chemistry lectr. Tex. A&M U., 1995, Bergman lectr. Weizmann Inst. Sci., 1995, faculty rsch. lectr. U. Calif., Berkeley, 1996, Raymond & Beverly Sackler lectr. Tel Aviv U., 1996; Priestley lectr. Pa. State U., 1997; Amy Mellon lectr. Purdue U., 1997; Rsch. frontiers chemistry lectr. U. Iowa, 1998, Moses Gomberg lectr. U. Mich., 1998, J and N Max T. Rogers, Mich. State U., 1998, Frontiers in Chemistry lectr., Wayne State U., 1998, Lord Todd Prof., Cambridge U., 1999, Abbot lectr., U. N.D., 2000, John D. Roberts lectr., Calif. Tech. U., 2000, Willard lectr., U. Wis., 2000, Cliford lectr., U. Pitts., 2000, William Lloyd Evan lectr. Ohio State U., 2000, Jacob Bigeleisen lectr. Stony Brook U., 2001, Laird lectr. U. B.C., 2001; Alan S. Tetelman fellow Yale U., 2001, Regitze Vold Meml. lectr. U. Calif., San Diego, 2001, Sammet guest prof. Goëethe U., Frankfurt, 2001. Editor Molecular Physics, 1987-91; mem. bd. editors Chem. Physics, Chem. Physics Letters, Nmr: Basic Principles and Progress, Advances in Magnetic Resonance, Accounts Chemistry Research, Concepts in Magnetic Reson; adv. editor Oxford U. Press; contbr. articles to profl. jours.; patentee in field. Recipient Strait award North Calif. Spectroscopy Soc., Outstanding Achievement award U.S. Dept. of Energy, 1983, 87, 89, 97, 98, R & D 100 awards, 1987, 89, Disting. Teaching award U. Calif., Ernest O. Lawrence award, 1988, Pitts. Spectroscopy award, 1989, Wolf Prize for chemistry, 1991, Donald Noyce Undergrad. Teaching award U. Calif., 1992, Robert Foster Cherry award for Great Tchrs. Baylor U., 1995, F.A. Cotton Medal for Excellence in Chemical Rsch., 1998, Dickson prize Carnegie Mellon U., 2001; Guggenheim fellow, 1988, Christensen fellow St. Catherine's Coll., Oxford, 1990; named in honor of his 50th birthday, Ampere Advanced Inst., Varenna, Italy; named to Scientific American 50 List, 2002. Fellow Am. Phys. Soc. (chmn. divsn. chem. physics), Inst. Physics; foreign fellow Royal Soc.; mem. NAS, Am. Chem. Soc. (mem. exec. com. divsn. phys. chemistry, Nobel Signature award in Graduate Edu. 1982, Baekeland Medal for Pure Chemistry, 1985, Harrison Howe award 1991, Centennial Spkr., Jour. Physical Chemistry, 1997, Langmuir award in Chemical Physics, 1998, Remsen award (Md. sect.) 2000, Dickson prize 2001), Royal Soc. Chemistry (Bourke lectr., Bourke Medal, 1988, Centenary lectr. and medal 1994), Internat. Soc. Magnetic Resonance (v.p., pres. 1993-96), Lawrence Hall Sci. Outreach Com. Achievements include pioneering contributions to the development of nuclear magnetic resonance (NMR) spectroscopy; his techniques are widely used in chemistry and materials science. Office: U Calif Chemistry Dept D64A Hildebrand Hill Berkeley CA 94720-0001 Office Phone: 510-642-1220. Business E-Mail: pines@cchem.berkeley.edu.

PINES, BURTON YALE, media executive; b. Chgo., Apr. 6, 1940; s. Hyman and Mary Pines. BA, U. Wis., 1961, MA, 1963. Instr. U. Wis., Madison, 1962-65; corr., bur. chief Time mag., Bonn, Saigon and Vienna, 1966-73, editor N.Y.C., 1973-81; sr. v.p. Heritage Found., Washington, 1981-92; chmn. Nat. Ctr. for Pub. Policy Rsch., Washington, 1982-94; co-founder, exec. v.p. COO NET Polit. Newstalk Network (later known as America's Voice Cable TV Network), Washington, 1992-95; pres., CEO Booknet Cable TV Network, N.Y.C., 1995—; exec. editor Internet ops. GOP Nat. Conv., 2000—. Author: Back to Basics, 1982, Out of Focus, 1994; editor: Mandate for Leadership II, 1984, Mandate for Leadership III, 1988. Recipient Page One award N.Y. Newspaper Guild, 1976, 77, 78, Freedom's Found. award, 1983. Jewish. Office: BookNet 150 W 51st St Ste 1804 New York NY 10019-6848

PINES, WAYNE LLOYD, public relations executive; b. Washington, Dec. 31, 1943; s. Jerome Martin and Ethel (Schnall) Pines; m. Nancy Freitag, Apr. 16, 1966 (div. 2003); children: Noah Morris, Jesse Mireth. BA, Rutgers U., 1965; postgrad., George Washington U., 1969—71. Reporter, city editor Middletown (NY) Times Herald-Record, 1965-68; copy editor Reuters News, 1968-69; assoc. editor FDC Reports, Washington, 1969-72; chief consumer edn. and info. FDA, also editor, 1972-74, dep. asst. commr. for pub. affairs, chief press rels., 1975-78, assoc. commr. pub. affairs, 1978-82; exec. editor Product Safety Letter and Devices and Diagnostics Letter, Washington, 1974-75; spl. asst. to dir. NIMH, 1982-83; sr. v.p., sr. counselor Burson-Marsteller, 1983-87, exec. v.p., dir. med. issues, 1987-93; pres. regulatory svc. APCO Worldwide, Washington, 1993—; sr. counselor Grey Healthcare Group, 1993—; mng. dir. Comms. Ptnr. and Assoc., 1999—; exec. v.p. Garden City Group, 1996—; pres. Bio-pharm. Forum George Washington U., 2002—04. Adj. prof. Washington Pub. Affairs Ctr., U. So. Calif., 1980—81; instr. NYU Sch. Continuing Edn., NYC, 1982—84, Profl. Devel. Inst., 1983—85; columnist Med. Advt. News, 1985—90, WebMD, 1999—2001; chmn. Therametrix, Inc., 1999—2001; mem. ethics bd. Patient Channel, 2002—; mem. adv. bd. Nat. Orgn. Rare Disorders, Orphan Med.; bd. dirs. N.W. BioTherapeutics, Scolr Inc., Medstar Rsch. Inst., FDA Alumni Assn. Author: The Sermons of Jerome Martine Pines, 1978, FDA Advertising and Promotion Manual, 1992, When Lightning Strikes: A How-to Crisis Manual, 1994, A Practical Guide to Food and Drug Law and Regulation, 1999, How to Work with the FDA, 2000, Crisis Communication in Healthcare: A Delicate Balance, 2001, A Framework for Pharmaceutical Risk Management, 2003; contbr. articles to profl. jours. Home: 7406 Brookville Rd Chevy Chase MD 20815 Office: APCO Worldwide 1615 L St NW Washington DC 20036-5610 E-mail: wpines@apcoworldwide.com.

PING, CHARLES JACKSON, philosophy educator, retired university president; b. Phila., June 15, 1930; s. Cloudy J. and Mary M. (Marion) P.; m. Claire Oates, June 5, 1951; children: Andrew, Ann Shelton. BA, Rhodes Coll., 1951; B.D., Louisville Presbyn. Theol. Sem., 1954; PhD, Duke, 1961. Assoc. prof. philosophy Alma Coll., 1962-66; prof. philosophy Tusculum Coll., 1966-69, v.p., dean faculty, 1967-68, acting pres., 1968-69; provost Central Mich. U., Mt. Pleasant, 1969-75; pres. Ohio U., Athens, 1975-94, pres. emeritus, Trustee prof. philosophy and edn., 1994—, co.- dir. Manasseh Cutler Scholars Program, dir. Ping Inst. for Tchg. Humanities, 1994-99, dir. emeritus, 1999—. Bd. dirs. Wing Lung Bank Internat. Inst. for Bus. Devel., Hong Kong; trustee Louisville Presbyn. Theol. Sem., Muskingum Coll., Ohio; mem. adv. bd. Inst. Ednl. Mgmt. of Harvard U.; chair Commn. Planning for Future of Higher Edn., Kingdom of Swaziland; mem. Commn. on Higher Edn. Republic of Namibia. Author: Ohio University in Perspective, 1985, Meaningful Nonsense, 1966, also articles. Fulbright Sr. Rsch. scholar for So. Africa, 1995. Mem. Coun. on Internat. Ednl. Exch. (chair bd.), David C. Lam Inst. for East-West Studies (bd. dirs.), Coun. Internat. Exch. Scholars (bd. dirs., chair Africa com.). Office: Ohio U Office of Pres Emeritus Athens OH 45701 E-mail: ping@ohio.edu.

PINGREE, BRUCE DOUGLAS, lawyer; b. Salt Lake City, June 6, 1947; s. Howard W. and Lois (Ivie) P.; m. Lorraine Bertelli, Oct. 11, 1981; children: Christian James, Matthew David, Alexandra Elizabeth, Meredith Gillian, Lauren Ashley, Geoffrey Nicholas. BA in Philosophy, U. Utah, 1970, JD, 1973. Bar: Ariz. 1973, Tex. 1990. Ptnr. Snell & Wilmer, Phoenix, 1973-89; shareholder Johnson & Gibbs, Dallas, 1989-93; ptnr. Gardere & Wynne, Dallas, 1993-95, Baker Botts, L.L.P., Dallas, 1995—. Lectr. in field of taxation. Contbr. articles to profl. jours. Served to capt. USAR. Fellow Am. Coll. Employee Benefit Counsel, Inc. (charter); mem. ABA (tax sect., past chair employee benefits com., past vice chair, past chmn. various sub-coms., 1993-94, chair joint com. on employee benefits 1994-95), Tex. State Bar Assn. (chair, tax sect. benefits and compensation com. 2000), Dallas Bar Assn. (chair employee benefits sect. 2001-2002), S.W. Benefits Conf., Nat. Assn. Stock Plan Profls., Order of Coif. Episcopalian. Home: 4065 Bryn Mawr Dr Dallas TX 75225-7032 Office: Baker & Botts LLP 2001 Ross Ave Ste 600 Dallas TX 75201-2900 Office Phone: 214-953-6878.

PINGREE, DIANNE, sociologist, educator, psychotherapist; b. Dallas; BFA magna cum laude, So. Meth. U., 1976, MLA, 1989; PhD in Sociology, Tex. Woman's U., 1994. Diplomate Am. Psychotherapy Assn.; lic. Marriage and Family Therapy Assoc., cert. Family Life Educator. Found., editor, pub. Tex. Woman Mag., 1977-80; pres. Tex. Woman Inc., 1980-85; owner, pres. Dianne Pingree & Assoc., 1985-88; pub. cons. Tex. Elite Publications, Dallas, 1988-89; mediator Ctr. for Dispute Resolution Denton County, 1991; grad. tchng. assoc. Tex. Woman's U., 1990-92; postgrad. clin. intern SW Family Inst., Dallas, 1993-94; therapist J&L Human Sys. Devel., Dallas, 1994-95; psychotherapist Child and Family Svc. Inc., Austin, 1995-96; cons. Austin, 1996-98; dir. Liaison Assocs. Profl. Devel. Consultants, 1998—2001; psychotherapist, assoc. clin. staff mem. Austin Acad. for Individual and Relationship Therapy, 2001—03; psychotherapist Capital Area Mental Health Ctr., 2003; pvt. practice, 2004—. Spkr. in field. Vol., vice chmn. Mental Health and Wellness Com. United Way Capital Area, 1998—99; vol., legal adv. Safeplace; mem. Leadership Austin, 2000—01. Recipient Matrix award Women in Comms., Women Helping Women award, Women's Ctr. Dallas, Dallas Press Club award. Mem.: Tex. Coun. Family Rels. (bd. dirs. 2004—, chair com. for pub. policy), Nat. Coun. Family Rels., Am. Psychotherapy Assn. (diplomate), Tex. Assn. for Marriage and Family Therapy, Am. Assn. for Marriage and Family Therapy, Internat. Sociology Honor Soc., Alpha Kappa Delta (pres. TWU chpt. 1992). Office: 1000 MoPac Cir Austin TX 78746

PINGREE, ROCHELLE M. state legislator; b. Mpls., Apr. 2, 1955; m. Charles F. Pingree, 1975; chidlren: Hannah, Cecily, Asa. BA, Coll. of the Atlantic, 1976. Mem. Dist. 21 Maine Senate, 1993-95, mem. Dist. 12, 1995—, chmn. housing and devel. com., 1992-94, mem. maine resources and agrl. coms., 1992-96, majority leader, 1996—; co-chair Maine Econ. Growth Coun., 1997—. Mem. Eastern Maine Devel. Corp., Midcoast Devel. Corp., Econ. Devel. Incentive Commn. Mem. Inter-Island League, Grange, North Haven Devel. Corp. Office: PO Box 243 North Haven ME 04853-0243

PINGS, ANTHONY CLAUDE, architect; b. Fresno, Calif., Dec. 16, 1951; s. Clarence Hubert and Mary (Murray) P.; m. Carole Clements, June 25, 1983; children, Adam Reed, Rebecca Mary. AA, Fresno City Coll., 1972; BArch, Calif. Poly. State U., San Luis Obispo, 1976. Lic. architect, Calif.; cert. Nat. Council Archtl. Registration Bds. Architect Aubrey Moore Jr., Fresno, 1976-81; architect, prin. Pings & Assocs., Fresno, 1981-83, 86—, Pings-Taylor Assocs., Fresno, 1983-85. Prin. works include Gollaher Profl. Office (Masonry Merit award 1985, Best Office Bldg. award 1986), Fresno Imaging Ctr. (Best Instnl. Project award 1986, Nat. Healthcare award Modern Health Care mag. 1986), Orthopedic Facility (award of honor Masonry Inst. 1987, award of merit San Joaquin chpt. AIA 1987), Modesto Imaging Ctr. (award of merit San Joaquin chpt. AIA 1991), Peachwood Med. Ctr. (award of merit San Joaquin chpt. AIA). Mem. Calif. Indsl. Tech. Edn. Consortium Calif. State Dept. Edn., 1983, 84. Recipient Excellence in Bus. award Fresno, 1999. Mem. AIA (bd. dirs. Calif. chpt. 1983-84, v.p. San Joaquin chpt. 1982, pres. 1983, Calif. Coun. evaluation team 1983, team leader Coalinga Emergency Design Assistance team), Fresno Arts (bd. dirs., counsel 1989—, pres. 1990-93), Fig Gardens Home Owners Assn. (bd. dir. 1991—, pres. 1994—). Republican. Home: 4350 N Safford Ave Fresno CA 93704-3509 Office: Pings & Assocs 1640 W Shaw Ave Ste 107 Fresno CA 93711-3506

PINGS, CORNELIUS JOHN, educational consultant, director; b. Conrad, Mont., Mar. 15, 1929; s. Cornelius John and Marjorie (O'Loughlin) P.; m. Marjorie Anna Cheney, June 25, 1960; children: John, Anne, Mary. BS, Calif. Inst. Tech., 1951, MS, 1952, PhD, 1955. Inst. chem. engring. Stanford U., 1955-56, asst. prof., 1956-59; assoc. prof. chem. engring. Calif. Inst. Tech., 1959-64, prof., 1964-81, exec. officer chem. engring., 1969-73, vice-provost, dean grad. studies, 1970-81; provost, sr. v.p. acad. affairs U. So. Calif., 1981-93; pres. Assn. Am. Univs., Washington, 1993-98. Mem., dir. Nat. Commn. on Rsch., 1978—80; mem. bd. mgmt. Coun. on Govtl. Rels., 1980—83; bd. dirs. Nations Funds, Edelbrock, Inc., L.A.; pres. Assn. Grad. Schs., 1977—78, Western Coll. Assn., 1988—90; mem. sci. engring. and pub. policy com. NAS, 1987—92, chmn., 1988—92; bd. dirs. Amervest Inc. Contbr. articles to tech. jours. Mem., chmn. bd. trustees Mayfield Sr. Sch. Bd., 1979-85; mem. Pasadena Redevel. Agy., 1968-81, chmn., 1974-81; bd. dirs. Huntington Meml. Hosp., Pasadena, 1986-92; chmn. L.A. Ctrl. City Assn., 1992. Recipient Arthur Nobel medal, City of Pasadena, 1981, Disting. Alumni award Calif. Inst. Tech., 1989, Presdl. medallion U. So. Calif., 1993. Fellow AIChE, Am. Acad. Arts and Scis.; mem. NAE, Calif. Club, Twilight Club, Bohemian Club, Cosmos Club, Valley Hunt Club. Roman Catholic. Office: 480 S Orange Grove Blvd # 6 Pasadena CA 91105-1736 E-mail: cjpings@usc.edu.

PINIELLA, LOUIS VICTOR, professional baseball team manager; b. Tampa, Fla., Aug. 28, 1943; m. Anita Garcia, Apr. 12, 1967; children: Lou, Kristi, Derrick. Student, U. Tampa. Baseball player various minor-league teams, 1962-68, Cleve. Indians, 1968, Kansas City Royals, 1969-73, N.Y. Yankees, 1974-84, coach, 1984-85, mgr., 1985-87, 1988, gen. mgr., 1987-88, spl. advisor, TV announcer, 1989; mgr. Cin. Reds, 1990-92, Seattle Mariners, 1992—2002, Tampa Bay Devil Rays, 2002—. Named to Am. League All-Star Team, 1972; recipient Ellis Island Medal of Honor, 1990; Named A.L. Rookie of the Yr Baseball Writers Assoc of Amer, 1969, Named A.L. Manager of the Yr, 1995. Office: Tampa Bay Devil Rays Tropicana Field 1 Tropicana Dr Saint Petersburg FL 33705

PINK, MICHAEL, performing company executive; b. York, England; Trained as classical dancer, Royal Ballet Sch. Dancer English Nat. Ballet, 1975—85; founding dir. Ballet Ctrl., London, 1987—91; assoc. dir. Northern Ballet, 1988; artistic dir. Milwaukee Ballet. Internat. tchr. Norwegian Nat. Ballet, Aterballetto, Balleto di Toscanna Italy, The Hartford Ballet, Rozas Dance Co., London Contemporary Dance Co., Ballet Rambert, White Oaks Dance Project, English Nat. Ballet, Phoenix Dance Co., London City Ballet. Recipient First Pl. in inaugural, Ursula Moreton Choreographic Competition, First Pl., Royal Soc. of Arts Competition. Office: Milwaukee Ballet 504 W National Ave Milwaukee WI 53204

PINK, (ALECIA MOORE), singer; b. Doylestown, Pa., Sept. 8, 1979; With Arista Records, 2001—. Singer: (albums) Can't Take Me Home, 2000, M!ssundaztood, 2001, Try This, 2003 (Grammy for best female rock performance for single Trouble, 2004); singer: (with Mya, Lil' Kim, Christina Aguilera) (songs) Lady Marmalade, 2001 (Grammy award Song Yr., MTV Video Music award, Song Yr.). Office: Box #390 5701 E Circle Dr Cicero NY 13039

PINKARD, ANNE MERRICK, foundation administrator; b. Baltimore, Feb. 8, 1924; d. Robert Graff M.; m. Walter Devier Pinkard, Sept. 24, 1949 (dec. June, 1994); children: Walter D. Jr., Robert Merrick, Gregory Clyde, Peter McEvoy. BA, Goucher Coll., 1946; student, Cornell U., 1942—43; LLD (hon.), Johns Hopkins U., 1994. Bd. dirs. Citizens Planning and Housing, Balt., 1950-60; bd. dirs., sect. Soc. Md. Antiquities, Balt., 1955-63; pres. women's bd. Johns Hopkins Hosp., Balt., 1968-72, bd. dirs., 1976-92; pres. France Merrick Found., Balt., 1990—. Bd. dirs. Johns Hopkins U., Balt., 1972-94, trustee, 1972-94; trustee St. Mary's Sem. and U., 1974-80. Home: 613 Brightwood Club Dr Lutherville MD 21093-3632 Office: France Merrick Found 1122 Kenilworth Dr Baltimore MD 21204-2139

PINKAS, ROBERT PAUL, lawyer, venture capitalist; b. Cleve., Nov. 11, 1953; s. Ludvik and Esther (Safir) P.; m. Jane Elliott, July 14, 1979; children: Robert Paul Jr., Caroline L., Benjamin A., Elizabeth S., Katherine E. BA, Harvard U., 1975, MA cum laude, 1976; JD, U. Pa., 1978. Bar: N.Y. 1979. Corp. atty. Simpson Thacher & Bartlett, N.Y.C., 1978-80; sr. assoc. McKinsey & Co., Cleve., 1980—82; gen. ptnr. Brantley Ptnrs., Cleve., 1981-87, Brantley Venture Ptnrs., Cleve., 1987—; mng. gen. ptnr. Brantley Ptnrs., Cleve., 1980—. Bd. dirs. Brantley Capital Corp., Cleve., Pediatric Svcs. Am. Inc., Atlanta. Mem. Harvard Schs. and Scholarship Com., Cambridge, Mass., 1982—, Hotchkiss Sch. Regional Admissions Com., Lakeville, Conn., 1982—; mem. steering com. Hotchkiss Sch.; mem. centennial com. Hathaway Brown, Shaker Heights, Ohio, 1990—. Mem. Nat. Venture Capital Assn., N.Y. State Bar Assn., Ohio Venture Assn., Harvard Club of Cleve. (trustee 1982—), Union Club of Cleve., Power Ten. Avocations: running, reading, golf. Office: Brantley Partners 3201 Enterprise Pkwy Ste 350 Beachwood OH 44122 E-mail: rpinkas@brantleypartners.com.

PINKEL, DONALD PAUL, pediatrician; b. Buffalo, Sept. 7, 1926; s. Lawrence William and Ann (Richardson) P.; m. Marita Donovan, Dec. 26, 1949 (div. 1981); children: Rebecca, Nancy, Christopher, Mary, Thomas, Anne, Sara, John, Ruth; m. Cathryn Barbara Howarth, May 16, 1981; 1 child, Michael. BS, Canisius Coll., 1947; MD, U. Buffalo, 1951. Diplomate Am. Bd. Pediatrics, Pediatric Hematology and Oncology, Nat. Bd. Med. Examiners. From intern to resident to chief resident Children's Hosp., Buffalo, 1951-54; research fellow Children's Hosp. Med. Ctr., Boston, 1955-56; chief. of pediatrics Roswell Park Meml. Inst., Buffalo, 1956-61; founding dir. St. Jude Children's Rsch. Hosp., Memphis, 1961-73; chmn. pediatrics Med. Coll. Wis., Milw., 1974-78; pediatrician-in-chief Milw. Children's Hosp., 1974-78; founding dir. Midwest Children's Cancer Ctr., Milw., 1974; chief. of pediatrics City of Hope Med. Ctr., Duarte, Calif., 1978-82; chmn. pediatrics Temple U. Sch. Medicine, Phila., 1982-85; prof., Kana Rsch. chair, dir. pediatric leukemia program M.D. Anderson Cancer Ctr. U. Tex., Houston, 1985-93; prof. pediat. U. Tex. Med. Sch., Houston, 1985-99; prof. emeritus U. Tex.-M.D. Anderson Cancer Ctr., Houston, 1994—. Clin. prof. pediats. U. So. Calif., LA, 2002—; adj. prof. biol. scis. Calif. Polytechnic State U., San Luis Obispo, Calif., 2001—. Contbr. articles to profl. jours. Bd. dirs. Lee County Coop. Clinic, Mariana, Ark., 1972-74. Served with USN, 1944-45, served to 1st lt. U.S. Army, 1954-55. Recipient Albert Lasker award for Med. Rsch., Lasker Found., 1972, Windermere Lectureship Brit. Pediatric Assn., 1974, David Karnofsky award Am. Soc. Clin. Oncology, 1978, Zimmerman prize for Cancer Rsch. Zimmerman Found., 1979, Charles Kettering prize Gen. Motors Cancer Rsch., 1986, Clin. Rsch. award Am. Cancer Soc., 1988, Return of the Child award Leukemia Soc. Am., 1992, Pollin prize in pediat. rsch. N.Y. Presbyn. Hosp., 2003. Mem. Am. Soc. Clin. Oncology, Am. Pediat. Soc., Am. Assn. Cancer Rsch., Soc. Exptl. Biology and Medicine, Am. Soc. Hematology. Democrat. Roman Catholic. Avocations: swimming, sailing. Home: 275 Marlene Dr San Luis Obispo CA 93405 E-mail: donpinkel@yahoo.com.

PINKER, STEVEN A. cognitive scientist, educator; b. Montreal, Que., Can., Sept. 18, 1954; arrived in US, 1976; s. Harry and Roslyn (Wiesenfeld) P. BA in Exptl. Psychology, McGill U., Montreal, 1976; PhD, Harvard U., 1979; DSc (hon.), McGill U., 1999; DPhil (hon.), Tel Aviv. U., 2003; DUniv (hon.), U. Surrey, 2003. Postdoctoral fellow Center for Cognitive Sci., MIT; asst. prof., dept. of psychology Harvard U., Cambridge, Mass., 1980-81, Stanford U., Palo Alto, Calif., 1981-82, MIT, Cambridge, 1982—85, assoc. prof., dept. of brain and cognitive sci., 1985—89; co-dir. Center for Cognitive Sci., MIT, 1985—94; prof., dept. of brain and cogniive sci. MIT; dir. McDonnell-Pew Center for Cognitive Neuroscience, MIT, 1994—99; Peter de Florez prof. MIT, Cambridge, 2000—03; Johnstone Family prof. of psychol. Harvard U., 2003—. Cons. Cognitive and Instructional Scis. Group, Xerox Corp. Palo Alto Rsch. Centers, 1981—82; vis. scholar, dept. of psychology Brandeis Univ, 1987—88, Harvard Univ., 1987—88; vis. scholar, cognitive devel. unit Med. Rsch Coun., London, 1988; vis. scholar, dept. of psychology and linguistics Univ. Calif., Santa Barbara, 1995—96; hon. vis. prof., dept. of psychology Univ. of Auckland, New Zealand, 2001—04; spkr. in field. Author: Language Learnability and Language Development, 1984, Learnability and Cognition, 1989, The Language Instinct, 1994, How the Mind Works, 1997 (LA Times Science Book Prize, 1998, finalist for Pullitzer prize, 1998), Words and Rules, 1999, The Blank Slate, 2002 (finalist for Pullitzer prize, 2003); assoc. editor Cognition, 1984—; advisor, Am. Heritage Dictionary; serves on several advisory and editorial bds., contbr. articles to sci. jours. and chapters in books. Recipient Troland Rsch. award NAS, 1993, Internat. Acad. of Humanism and Ctr. of Inquiry, Golden Plate award, Am. Acad. of Achievement, 1999; named Humanist Laureate Internat. Acad. Humanism, 2001. Fellow AAAS, APA (Disting. Early Career award 1984, Boyd McCandless award 1986, William James Book prize 1995, 99, 2003, Eleanor Maccoby Book prize 2003), Am. Acad. Arts and Scis., Linguistics Soc. Am. (Linguistics, Lang. and Pub. Svcs. award 1997), Am. Psychol. Soc. Office: Dept of Psychology Harvard University William James Hall 970 33 Kirkland St Cambridge MA 02138 Office Phone: 617-495-0831. Office Fax: 617-495-3278. Business E-Mail: pinker@wjh.harvard.edu.*

PINKERTON, JOHN N. plant pathologist; b. Englewood, N.J., Apr. 27, 1945; PhD, Oreg. State U., Corvallis, 1983. Extension nematologist Oreg. State U., Corvallis, 1976—82; rsch. assoc. in nematology Wash. State U., 1983—86; plant pathologist Oreg. Dept. Agr., 1986—88; rsch. plant pathologist USDA-ARS Hort. Crops Rsch. Lab., Corvallis, 1988—. Contbr. articles to profl. publs. Recipient Lee M. Hutchins award Am. Phytopathol. Soc., 1998. Office: Hort Crops Rsch Lab 3420 NW Orchard Ave Corvallis OR 97330-5014

PINKERTON, RICHARD LADOYT, retired management educator; b. Huron, S.D., Mar. 5, 1933; s. Abner Pyle and Orral Claudine (Arneson) P.; m. Sandra Louise Lee, Aug. 28, 1965 (div. 1992); children: Elizabeth, Patricia. BA, U. Mich., 1955; MBA, Case Western Res. U., 1962; PhD, U. Wis., 1969. Sr. market rsch. analyst Harris-Intertype Corp., Cleve., 1957-61; mgr. sales devel. Triax Corp., Cleve., 1962-64; coord. mktg. program Mgmt. Inst., U. Wis., 1964-67; dir. exec. programs Mgmt. Inst., U. Wis. (Grad. Sch. Bus.), also asst. prof. mktg., 1969-74; prof. mgmt., dean Grad. Sch. Adminstrn., Capital U., Columbus, Ohio, 1974-86; prof. mgmt., dir. Univ. Bus. Ctr., Craig Sch. Bus. Calif. State U., Fresno, 1986-89, prof. mktg., 1989-2000, chmn. mktg. and logistics dept., 1996-2000, dir. London semester, prof. emeritus, mem. bd., 2000—. Adj. prof. Case Western Res. U., 2004-; trustee Ohio Coun. Econ. Edn., 1976-87; cons. to govt. and industry, 1960—. Co-author: The Purchasing Manager's Guide to Strategic Proactive Procurement, 1996; contbr. articles to profl. jours. Bd. govs. Hannah Neil Home for Children, Columbus, 1975—78; mem. indsl. and cmty. devel. commn. City of Strongsville, Ohio; bd. dirs. The Fresno Townhouse Assn., 1992—2001. Officer USAF, 1955—57, lt. col. USAF, 1957—78. La Verne Noyes scholar, 1952—55, Nat. Assn. Purchasing Mgmt. fellow, 1967—68. Mem.: Am. Mktg. Assn. (chpt. pres. 1972—73), Nat. Assn. Purchasing Mgmt. (chmn. acad. planning 1979—84, rsch. symposium 1992), Nat. Assn. Contract Mgmt. (chmn. validation cert. com. 1990), Navy League, Air Force Assn., Res. Officers Assn., City Club of Cleve., Marines Meml. Club, Columbia Hills Country Club, Phi Gamma Delta, Alpha Kappa Psi, Beta Gamma Sigma. Home: 18487 Woodside Crossing South Strongsville OH 44149-6891 Office Phone: 440-846-1430.

PINKERTON, ROBERT BRUCE, mechanical engineer; b. Detroit, Feb. 10, 1941; s. George Fulwell and Janet Lois (Hedke) P.; m. Barbara Ann Bandfield, Aug. 13, 1966; 1 child, Robert Brent. BSME, Detroit Inst. Tech., 1965; MA in Engring., Chrysler Inst. Engring., 1967; JD, Wayne State U., 1976. From mech. engr. to emissions and fuel economy planning specialist Chrysler Engring. Office Chrysler Corp., Highland Park, Mich., 1967-80; dir. engring. Replacement div. TRW, Inc., Cleve., 1980-83; v.p. engring. TRW Automotive Aftermarket Group, 1983-86; v.p. engring. and rsch. Blackstone Corp., Jamestown, N.Y., 1986-89, pres., CEO, 1989-90, Athena Corp., Beaufort, S.C., 1990—, Cedar Crest Corp., Beaufort, S.C., 1990—; chmn., CEO Beaufort Land Co., 1998—. Bd. dirs. VRI, LLC, Coastal Banking Co., Inc., Low Country Nat. Bank, Village Renaissance, Inc., Carpenters Hall, Coastal Banking Co., Inc.; chmn. redevelopment commn. City Beaufort, 2004—. Mem. exec. com. Beaufort Schs. Oversight Com., 1995-99, Pvt. Industry Coun., 1996-99. Mem.: Greater Beaufort C. of C. (bd. dirs. 1997—98),

Beaufort Roundtable (pres. 2000—02), Rotary (asst. dist. gov. 1997—98). Presbyterian. Home: PO Box 2417 Beaufort SC 29901-2417 Office: PO Box 2115 1203 Boundary St Beaufort SC 29902

PINKERTON, W. STEWART, JR., editor; b. Mpls., Nov. 30, 1942; s. William Stewart and Dorothy Naomi (Wilson) P.; m. Ann-Byrd Platt, Oct. 7, 1978 (div. Sept. 1994); children: Charlotte Lloyd, Margot Byrd; m. Meredith Hadley Nicholson, June 24, 1995. AB, Princeton U., 1964; JD, N.Y. Law Sch., 1982. News asst., copy reader, reporter Wall St. Jour., San Francisco, L.A., N.Y.C., 1964-70, mgr. N.Y. bur. N.Y.C., 1975-83, asst. mng. editor, 1983-85, dep. mng. editor, 1985-88; mng. editor Dow Jones Can., Montreal, 1971-75; mng. dir. Kidder Peabody & Co., N.Y.C., 1988-90; asst. mng. editor Forbes Mag., N.Y.C., 1990—. Mem. Coun. Fgn. Rels., Union League Club, Doubles Club. Republican. Episcopal. Avocations: tennis, squash, skiing. Home: 130 E 94th St Apt 5E New York NY 10128-1727 Office: Forbes Mag 60 5th Ave New York NY 10011-8802

PINKETT-SMITH, JADA, actress; b. Balt., Sept. 18, 1971; m. Will Smith, 1997; 2 children. Appeared in films Menace II Society, 1993, The Inkwell, 1994, Jason's Lyric, 1994, A Low Down Dirty Shame, 1994, Tales From The Crypt Presents Demon Knight, 1995, The Nutty Professor, 1996, Set It Off, 1996, Scream 2, 1997, Woo, 1998, Return to Paradise, 1998, Bamboozled, 2000, Ali, 2001, The Matrix Reloaded, 2003.

PINKHAM, DANIEL, composer; b. Lynn, Mass., June 5, 1923; s. Daniel R. and Olive C. (White) P. AB, MA, Harvard, 1944; Litt.D. (hon.), Nebr. Wesleyan U., 1976; Mus.D. (hon.), Adrian Coll., 1977, Westminster Choir Coll., 1979, New Eng. Conservatory, 1993, Ithaca Coll., 1994, Boston Conservatory, 1998. Mem. faculty New Eng. Conservatory Music, 1959—; music dir. King's Chapel, Boston, 1958-2000; co-founder Cambridge Festival Orch., 1948. Composer: Sonatas for Organ and Strings, 1943, 54, 86, Piano Concertino, 1950, Concerto for Celesta and Harpsichord, 1954, Wedding Cantata, 1956, Christmas Cantata, 1958, Easter Cantata, 1961, Symphonies, 1961, 64, 85, Signs of the Zodiac, 1964, St. Mark Passion, 1965, Jonah, 1966, In the Beginning of Creation, 1970, Ascension Cantata, 1970, Organ Concerto, 1970, When the Morning Stars Sang Together, 1971, the Other Voices of the Trumpet, 1971, Safe in Their Alabaster Chambers, 1972, To Troubled Friends, 1972, Daniel in the Lions' Den, 1973, The Seven Deadly Sins, 1974, Four Elegies, 1974, The Passion of Judas, 1975, Garden Party, 1976, Blessings, 1977, Company at the Creche, 1977, Miracles, 1978, Epiphanies, 1978, Serenades, 1979, Proverbs, 1979, Diversions for Organ and Harp, 1980, Descent Into Hell, 1980, Before the Dust Returns, 1981, The Death of the Witch of Endor, 1981, Prelude and Scherzo for Wind Quintet, 1981, The Dreadful Dining Car, 1982, Brass Quintet, 1983, In Heaven Soaring Up, 1985, The Left-Behind Beasts, 1985, A Biblical Book of Beasts, 1985, Versets, 1985, A Mast for the Unicorn, 1986, A Crimson Flourish, 1986, Winter Nights, 1986, De Profundis, 1986, In the Isles of the Sea, 1986, Antiphons, 1987, Getting To Heaven, 1987, Angels Are Everywhere, 1987, Heav'n Must Go Home, 1988, Four Marian Antiphons, 1988, Alleluias, 1988, Sonata da Chiesa, 1988, Sonata da Camera, 1988, Petitions, 1988, Pedals, 1988, The Seasons Pass, 1988, Reeds, 1988, Concerto Piccolo, 1989, The Small Passion, 1989, Requiem Collects, 1989, The Saints Preserve Us!, 1989, String Quartet, 1989, Stabat Mater, 1990, Symphony Number 4, 1990, The Book of Hours, 1990, Carols and Cries, 1990, The Dryden Te Deum, 1990, Pentecost Cantata, 1991, Three Canticles from Luke, 1991, For Solace in Solitude, 1991, Advent Cantata, 1991, Smart Set, 1991, First Organbook, 1991, The Small Requiem, 1991, Second Organbook, 1992, Christmas Symphonies, 1992, Overture Concertante, 1992, Nocturnes for Flute and Guitar, 1992, Vowels, 1993, Adagietto for Organ and Strings, 1993, Wondrous Love, 1993, When Love Was Gone, 1993, Missa Domestica, 1993, Miserere mei Deus, 1993, The Guiding Star, 1994, The Creation of the World, 1994, Reed Trio, 1994, Morning Music, 1994, Organ Concerto Number Two, 1995, Preludes for Piano, 1995, Passion Music, 1995, The Tenth Muse, 1995, The Inner Room of the Soul, 1995, Festive Processional, 1995, The White Raven, 1996, O Come, Emmanuel, 1996, Called Home, 1996, Organ Concerto Number Three, 1996, Tidings, 1996, Divertimento for Trumpet and Harp, 1997, Sagas, 1997, Music for an Indian Summer, 1997, The Four Winds, 1997, Celebrations, 1998, String Trio, 1998, Odes, 1998, Evening Music, 1998, Music for a Quiet Sunday, 1998, Saints' Days, 1999, Quarries, 1999, Weather Reports, 1999, Oration, 1999, The Green Wall, 1999, Shards, 2000, The Salutation of Gabriel, 2000, Picnic Music, 2000, The House of the Lord, 2000, January Music, 2000, Duo for Viola and Violoncello, 2000, Collects, 2000, Solemnities, 2001, September Music, 2001, Dragons and Deeps, 2001, Partita for Violoncello and Double bass, 2001, Triple Concerto, 2001, The Cask of Amontillado, 2001, Come, look quietly, 2001, Christmas Jubilations, 2002, Brass Trio Number Two, 2002, The Phoenix at Dawn, 2002, Forest Music, 2002, The Seven Days, 2002, Divertimento for Double Bass and Organ, 2002, A Spectacle of Glory, 2002, Make Way for Ducklings, 2002, Magnificat, 2003, Let the Word Go Forth, 2003, Conversing with Someone Invisible, 2003, Preludes for Piano: Book II, 2003, Irenicon, 2003, Dark Angels, 2004, Bright Angels, 2004, A Song for St. Cecilia's Day, 2004, Blue Blazes, 2004, Advent Canticles, 2004, Five Times Two, 2004, Streams, 2004, Woodwing Quartet, 2004, Oboe Quartet, 2004, Weather Reports for Orch., 2004, others. Fellow Am. Acad. Arts and Scis.; mem. Am. Guild Organists (past dean Boston chpt.) Home: 150 Chilton St Cambridge MA 02138-1227

PINKINS, TONYA, actress; b. Chicago, May 30, 1962; 4 children. Attended, Northwestern U., Summer Theater Inst., Chicago, 1978; student, Carnegie Mellon U., 1980—81; BA, Columbia Coll., Chicago, 1996; student, Calif. Western Law Sch., San Diego. Private acting instr. Montclair School of Dance, 1993; visual arts instr., 6th to 8th grades LAUSD, 2000—01; private coach voice, music performance, acting, 2002. Playwriting com. Playwrights' Preview Prodn., 1986—88; instr. cold reading Univ. Calif., San Diego, 2000. Actor: (Broadway plays) Merrily We Roll Along, 1981, Jelly's Last Jam, 1992 (Tony award best featured actress in a musical, 1992, Drama Desk award best featured actress in a musical, 1992, Clarence Derwent award, 1992, Outer Critics Circle award best featured actress in a musical, 1993), Chronicle of a Death Foretold, 1995, Play On!, 1997 (Tony nom. best actress in a musical, 1997), The Wild Party, 2000, Caroline, Or Change, 2004— (Tony nom. best actress in a musical, 2004, Obie award best perf., 2004), (Off Broadway plays) Little Shop of Horrors, 1983, A...My Name Alice, 1985, Just Say No, 1988, Believin'/Psychoneurotic Fantasies, 1990, The Caucasian Chalk Circle, 1990, The Merry Wives of Windsor, 1994, The Vagina Monologues, 2000, The House of Flowers, 2003; (plays) Stealin', Joe Turner's Come and Gone, 1989, The Piano Lesson, 1989, Approximating Mother, 1991, No Niggers, No Jews, No Dogs, 2000, Thoroughly Modern Millie, 2000; (TV series) As the World Turns, 1983—86, University Hospital, 1994, All My Children, 1991—95, 2003—; (TV films) American Dream, 1981, Rage of Angels: The Story Continues, 1986, Strapped, 1993, Against Their Will: Women in Prison, 1994, (TV Guest appearances) Crime Story, 1986, The Cosby Show, 1990, Law & Order, 1990, The Guardian, 2002; (films) Beat Street, 1984, See No Evil, Hear No Evil, 1989, Above the Rim, 1994, Love Hurts, 2002; voice (audio books) The Women of Brewster Place, 1992, The Book of Virtues I and II, 1993, The Moral Compass, 1995, Chocolate for a Woman's Soul, 1997, The Silent Cradle, 1998; singer: (albums) Live @ Joe's Pub. Achievements include co-founder of OPERATION Z: zero tolerance of violence against women and children. Office: Innovative Artist Talent and Lit Agy 1776 Broadway Ste 1810 New York NY 10019-2002

PINKNEY, D. TIMOTHY, investment company executive; b. Long Beach, Calif., June 6, 1948; s. Robert Patten and Mary (Chernus) P.; m. Nancy Dianne Fisher, Aug. 21, 1971; 1 child, Heather Anne. BA, Calif. Luth. U., 1970; MA, Pepperdine U., 1976. CFP. Membership mgr. Seattle C. of C., 1977—79; v.p. mktg. John L. Scott Investment, Bellevue, Wash., 1980—81, SRH Fin., Bellevue, 1981—82, Foster Investment Co., Bellevue, 1982—83; pres., CEO Footprint Fin. Planning, Bellevue, 1983—88, Sheppard & Assocs. Personal Fin. Advs., Bellevue, 1988—91; mgr. and v.p. asset mgmt. div. U.S. Bank, Tacoma, 1991—92; v.p., Calif. and Nev. mgr. trust and investment mgmt. U.S. Bank of Calif., Sacramento, 1992—96; prin. Savant/Russell, Inc., Citrus Heights, Calif., 1996—; founder, CEO Wealth Link Enterprises. Invited spkr. Russian Parliament, 1992. Author: book, video and cassete series Pathways to Wealth, Yes IRA's Still Make Cent$?, 1988. Co-chmn. Fin. Independence Week, Western Wash., 1987; bd. dirs. Traveler's Aid Soc., A United Way Agy., Seattle, 1988, pacesetter United Way, 1988-91; alumni class steward Calif. Luth. U., 1992-2003; chmn. Friends Scouting, 1994, chmn. bd. 1999, v.p. finance, 1997-98, Golden Empire Coun. Boy Scouts Am., 1999; chmn. investment com. Calif. State U. Sacramento Found., 1998-99; bd. dirs. McClellan Aviation Mus., 2000—, YMCA Found, 2002—; pres. Sacramento Rotary Found., 2000-2002. Lt. USN, 1970-77, comdr. USNR, ret., 1992. Selected as Jr. Officer of Yr., USNR, 1984, 85; Career Achievement award Calif. Luth. U., 2002; Recipient Silver Beaver award, Boy Scouts of Am., 2003, Rotary Fellow, Sacramento, 2004. Mem. Nat. Spkrs. Assn. (bd. dirs. N.W. chpt. 1992), Internat. Assn. Fin. Planning (chmn. West Region 1987-90, pres. Western Wash. chpt. 1986-87), Seattle Soc. Fin. Planners (bd. dirs. 1985-86), Inst. CFPs, Real Estate Securities and Syndication Inst. (v.p. 1980-83), East King County and Pierce County Estate Planning Coun., Seattle Res. Officer Assn. (pres., v.p. 1983-85), Puget Sound Naval Res. Assn. (v.p. 1985-90), Sacramento Rotary (chmn. edn. com. 1994), Sacramento Rotary Found. (pres. 2000-2002, bd. dirs. 1996-), Seattle Rotary (bd. dirs., chmn. membership devel. com.). Avocations: flying gliders, giant pumpkin growing and sculpting, photography. Office Phone: 916-721-1400. E-mail: tpinkney@starstream.net.

PINKWATER, JULIE, publishing executive; B, Boston U. With Sotheby's Internat. Realty, Network TV Assn; with advertising agency McCaffrey & McCall, Penchina Selkowitz, McCann Erickson; mgr. position Ladies Home Jour.; beauty dir. Allure; advertising dir. More, 1998—2000, pub., 2000—01, Fitness Mag., G&J USA, NY, 2001—04, v.p., pub. Ladies Home Jour., NY, 2004—. Office: Ladies Home Jour 125 Park Ave New York NY 10017-5529*

PINN, VIVIAN W. federal agency administrator, pathologist; b. Halifax, Va., 1941; BA, Wellesley Coll., 1963; MD, U. Va., 1967. Intern in pathology Mass. Gen. Hosp., Boston, 1967-68, rschr. in pathology, 1968-70; asst. pathologist Tufts U. New England Med. Ctr. Hosp., 1970-77, pathologist, 1977-82; from asst. to assoc. prof. pathology Tufts U., 1971-82, asst. dean student affairs, 1974-82; prof., dept. chair pathology Howard U., 1982-91; first dir. Office Rsch. on Women's Health, NIH, Bethesda, Md., 1991—, assoc. dir. rsch. women's health, 1994—, dir. Office Women's Health Rsch. Pres. Nat. Med. Assn., 1989—90. Office: NIH Office Rsch on Women's Health 9000 Rockville Pike Bldg 1 Rm 201 Bethesda MD 20892*

PINNELL, SHELDON RICHARD, dermatologist, researcher, retired educator; b. Dayton, Ohio, Feb. 3, 1937; s. Jacob and Nevella P.; m. Doren Madey, 1983; children: Kevin, Alden, Tyson. AB, Duke U., 1959; MD, Yale U., 1963. Intern in medicine U. Minn. Hosp., Mpls., 1963-65; resident in dermatology Harvard U., Boston, 1968-71; prof. medicine Duke U. Med. Ctr., Durham, N.C., 1978—, chief div. dermatology, 1982-97, asst. prof. biochemistry, 1988—, J. Lamar Callaway prof. dermatology, 1989—2002, prof. emeritus, 2002—. Founding scientist Fibrogen, 1994—. SkinCeuticals, 1997—. Skin-Research, 2002—04, Skin Sci. Inst., 2004—. Contbr. over 100 articles to profl. jours.; six patents in field. Office: Duke U Med Ctr PO Box 3135 Durham NC 27710-0001 E-mail: pinne002@mc.dukc.edu.

PINNEY, ALESIA L. lawyer; b. Seattle, 1963; m. Jack Brown; children: Keathley, Jon. BA, Seattle U.; MA, U. Denver, 1989; JD, U. Puget Sound, 1991. Acct. Deloitte & Touche, Denver, 1985—89; law clk. Chief Judge Lapsley W. Hamblen Jr. U.S. Tax Ct., 1991—93; employee Bogle & Gaes and Perkins Coie, 1993—98; sr. corp. counsel RealNetworks Inc., 1997; chief privacy officer, v.p., gen. counsel and sec. Drugstore.com, Inc., Bellevue, Wash., 1999—. Office: drugstorecom Inc Ste 300 13920 SE Eastgate Way Bellevue WA 98005*

PINNEY, SIDNEY DILLINGHAM, JR., lawyer; b. Hartford, Conn., Nov. 17, 1924; s. Sydney Dillingham and Louisa (Griswold) Wells P.; m. Judith Munch, Sept. 30, 1990; children from previous marriage: William Griswold, David Rees. Student, Amherst Coll., 1941—43, BA cum laude, 1947; student, Brown U., 1943, MIT, 1943—44; LLB, Harvard U., 1950. Bar: Conn. 1950. Pvt. practice, Hartford, 1950; assoc. Shepherd, Murtha and Merritt, Hartford, 1950-53; ptnr. Murtha, Cullina, Richter & Pinney (1967) (name changed to Murtha Cullina LLP 2000), 1953-92; of counsel Shepherd, Murtha and Merritt (name changed to Murtha Cullina LLP 2000), 1993—. Lectr. on estate planning. Contbr. Estate Planning mag. Bd. dirs. Greater Hartford Area TB and Respiratory Diseases Health Soc., 1956-69, pres., 1966-67; mem. Wethersfield (Conn.) Town Coun., 1958-62; trustee Hartford Conservatory Music, 1967-71, 75-81; trustee, pres. Hist. Wethersfield Found., 1961-81; bd. dirs. Hartford Hosp., 1971-80, adv. bd., 1980—; mem. adv. com. Jefferson House, 1978-82; mem. Mortensen Libr. Bd. Visitors U. Hartford, 1984—; corporator Hartford Pub. Libr., 1969—, Renbrook Sch., West Hartford, Conn., 1970-75. 1st lt. USAF, 1943-46. Fellow Am. Coll. Trust and Estate Counsel; mem. ABA, Nat. Acad. Elder Law Attys., Conn. Bar Assn. (com. elder law sect.), Hartford County Bar Assn. Republican. Congregationalist. Office: City Place 185 Asylum St Hartford CT 06103-3408

PINNEY, THOMAS CLIVE, retired English language educator; b. Ottawa, Kans., Apr. 23, 1932; s. John James and Lorene Maude (Owen) P.; m. Sherrill Marie Ohman, Sept. 1, 1956; children— Anne, Jane, Sarah. BA, Beloit Coll., Wis., 1954; PhD, Yale U., 1960. Instr. Hamilton Coll., Clinton, N.Y., 1957-61; instr. English Yale U., New Haven, 1961-62; asst. prof. to prof., chmn. dept. English Pomona Coll., Claremont, Calif., 1962-97; ret., 1997. Editor: Essays of George Eliot, 1963, Selected Writings of Thomas Babington Macaulay, 1972, Letters of Macaulay, 1974-81, Kipling's India, 1986, A History of Wine in America, 1989, Kipling's Something of Myself, 1990, Letters of Rudyard Kipling, 1990,-2004 The Vineyards and Wine Cellars of California, 1994, The Wine of Santa Cruz Island, 1994. Guggenheim fellow, 1966, 84,Recipient Disting. Svc. citation Beloit Coll., 1984; fellow NEH, 1980; grantee Am. Coun. Learned Socs., 1974, 84, Am. Philos. Soc., 1968, 82, 94. Mem. MLA, Elizabethan Club (New Haven), Zamorano Club (L.A.), Phi Beta Kappa. Home: 228 W Harrison Ave Claremont CA 91711-4323 Office: Pomona Coll Dept English Claremont CA 91711

PINNIX, JOHN LAWRENCE, lawyer; b. Reidsville, N.C., Oct. 8, 1947; s. John Lawrence and Esther (Cobb) P.; m. Sally Auman, June 15, 1985; children: Jennifer Elizabeth Haigwood, William C. Haigwood. BA, U. N.C., Greensboro, 1969; JD, Wake Forest U., 1973; MA, U. N.C., Greensboro, 1975. Bar: N.C. 1973, D.C. 1981; U.S. Dist. Ct. (ea. dist.) N.C. 1977, U.S Dist. Ct. (mid. and we. dists.) N.C. 1981; U.S. Ct. Appeals (4th cir.) 1981; U.S. Supreme Ct. 1981. Assoc. Fagg, Fagg & Nooe, Eden, N.C., 1973-74; spl. counsel Adminstrv. Office of the Cts., Morganton, N.C., 1975-76; ptnr. Allen and Pinnix (formerly Barringer, Allen & Pinnix), Raleigh, N.C., 1977—. Adj. N.C. Ctrl. U. Sch. Law, 1997; sr. lecturing fellow Duke U. Sch. Law, 1999. Contbr. articles to profl. jours. Alt. del. Dem. Nat. Conv., Miami, 1972, mem. rules com., Washington and Atlanta, 1988; bd. dirs. Farmworkers Legal Svcs., Raleigh, 1990-92. Mem. Am. Immigration Lawyers Assn. (founding mem. Carolinas chpt. 1980, chpt. chair 1984-85, 87-88, nat. bd. govs. 1993-2001, sec. nat. exec. com. 1997-99, 2d v.p. 1999-2000, 1st v.p. 2000-2001, pres.-elect 2001-02, nat. pres. 2002-03), Am. Immigration Law Found. (trustee 1992-97, vice chair 1994-97), N.C. Bar Assn. (chmn. immigration and nationality law com. 1989-91), N.C. State Bar (bd. cert. immigration specialist, immigration law specialty com. bd. legal specialization 1996—), U. N.C. Greensboro Alumni Assn. (bd. dirs. 1975-76, bd. dirs. Excellence Found. 1995-97), Internat. Focus Inc. (bd. dirs. 1998-99), N.C. Bar Assn. (internat. law sect. coun. 1999—). Baptist. Avocations: photography, film, reading. Home: 125 Ammons Dr Raleigh NC 27615-6501

PINO, JULIO CESAR, social studies educator, writer; b. Havana, Cuba, Dec. 30, 1960; arrived in U.S., 1968; s. Juliana Iraida Pino; m. Mia Kang, Aug. 16, 1992. PhD, UCLA, 1991. Asst. prof. History Dept., Kent State U., Kent, Ohio, 1992—97, assoc. prof., 1997—. Participating editor Latin Am. Perspectives, Irvine, Calif., 1996—. Trustee Islamic Soc. of Akron and Kent, Cuyahoga Falls, Ohio, 2004—04. Fellow Fulbright-Hays Dissertation Abroad Rsch. Fellow, US Dept. of Edn., 1989-1990. Mem.: Am. Hist. Assn. (assoc.). Muslim. Avocations: exercise, travel, performance poetry. Home: 1565 Morris Rd Kent OH 44240 Office: History Department Kent State University Kent OH 44242-0001 Office Phone: 330-672-8911. Business E-Mail: jpino@kent.edu.

PINO, NATHAN WILLETT, criminologist, educator, sociologist; b. Austin, Tex., Aug. 18, 1971; s. David James and Carol Lee Pino; m. Kyong Hee Chee, June 3, 1996. PhD, Iowa State U., 1999. Asst. prof. Ga. So. U., Statesboro, 1999—. Contbr. articles to profl. jours. Musician Ogeechee Area Symphonic Instrumental Soc., Statesboro, 2002. Mem.: So. Sociol. Soc., Am. Soc. of Criminology, Am. Sociol. Assn., Sigma Xi, Phi Kappa Phi. Green Party. Quaker. Avocations: travel, bicycling. Home: 1712 Sunnyview Ct Statesboro GA 30458 Office: Georgia Southern University PO Box 8051 Statesboro GA 30460-8051

PINOLA, RICHARD J. management consultant; CPA. Pres., COO Penn Mutual Life Ins. Co.; dir. Right Mgmt. Consultants, 1990—, chmn., CEO, 1992—. Bd. dirs. Reading is Fundamental, Inc., K-Tron Internat., Visiting Nurses' Assn.; past bd. dirs. Am. Lung Assn., Life Office Mgmt. Assn.; founder, bd. dirs. Mutual Assn. Prof. Svcs.; bd. dirs. King's Coll.; past bd. dirs. Janney Montgomery Scott, Horsham Clinic; founder, bd. dirs. Living Wills Archive Co. Office: 1818 Market St 33rd Fl Philadelphia PA 19103

PINSCHMIDT, ROBERT KRANTZ, JR., chemist, researcher; b. L.A., July 25, 1945; s. Robert K. and Louise M. Pinschmidt; m. Marilyn T. Pawlak, Aug. 24, 1968; children: Robert J., Alexandra M., Dustin M. BA, Wabash Coll., 1967; PhD, U. Oreg., 1971. Vis. asst. prof. Poly. U. of Wroclaw, Poland, 1971—73; rsch. assoc. U. Oreg., Eugene, 1973—74; sr. rsch. chemist Rohm & Haas Corp, Spring House, Pa., 1974—76; rsch. chemist, sr. rsch. assoc. Air Products & Chemicals, Inc., Allentown, Pa., 1976—. Contbr. numerous articles to profl. publs. Bd. dirs. Allentown Sch. Dist. Sch. Bd., 1999—2000. Fellow, U. of Ill., 1967—68, NIH, 1968—71; scholar, Wabash Coll., 1963—67. Mem.: Am. Chem. Soc., Phi Beta Kappa. Achievements include 45 patents in monomer and polymer chemistry; responsible for initiating and co-developing a large body of technology for amine functional polymers and copolymers based on N-vinylformamide; invention of new formaldehyde free and efficient water compatible crosslinking technology; created a series of new, low cost sulfonate terminated oligomeric and low polymeric vinyl acetates and vinyl alcohols as novel surfactants and paper additives; invention of new very high surface area styrene type adsorbent resins; discovery of three new techniques in ion chromatography; elucidated mechanisms orbital disallowed symmetry reactions. Home: 2549 Liberty St Allentown PA 18104 Office: Air Products & Chemicals Inc 7201 Hamilton Blvd Allentown PA 18195 E-mail: pinschrk@apci.com.

PINSDORF, MARION KATHRYN, business executive, educator, author; b. Teaneck, N.J., June 22, 1932; d. Charles W. and Katheryn S. (Green) P. BA cum laude, Drew U., 1954; MA, NYU, 1967, PhD, 1976; DSc in Bus. Adminstrn. (hon.), Nichols Coll., 1982. Polit. reporter, editor women's dept. The Record, Hackensack, NJ, 1954—61; assoc. copy editor Good Housekeeping mag., 1962-64; comms. specialist Borden, Inc., 1964-69; v.p. Hill and Knowlton, N.Y.C., 1970-77; v.p. corp. rels. Textron, Inc., Providence, 1977-80; v.p. corp. comms. INA Corp., Phila., 1980-82; ind. mgmt. cons. 1982—. Adj. asst. prof. Brazilian studies Brown U., 1979-89; assoc. prof. grad. sch. bus. Fordham U., 1987-94, sr. fellow in comms., 1994-2003; lectr. in field. Author: Communicating When Your Company Is Under Siege, Surviving Public Crisis, 1987, 3d edit., 1998, German Speaking Entrepreneurs: Builders of Business in Brazil South, 1990, All Crises are Global: Managing to Escape Chaos, 2004; mem. editl. adv. bd. Pub. Rels. Quar.; author book revs.; contbr. articles to profl. jours. Trustee, Drew U., Madison, N.J., 1977-81; pres. Leonia (N.J.) Pub. Libr., 1973-76. Mem. Arthur W. Page Soc. Home: 114 Leonia Ave Leonia NJ 07605-1916

PINSKER, PENNY COLLIAS (PANGEOTA PINSKER), television producer; b. Miami, Fla., Aug. 22, 1942; d. Theodore Peter and Agatha Madge (Bridgeman) Collias; m. Raymond Robert Elman, Feb. 19, 1962 (dec. 1967); 1 child, Alan; m. Lewis Harry Pinsker, Oct. 22, 1968. Grad. high sch., Miami, Fla. Operator So. Bell Telephone Co., Miami, 1960-67; asst. dir. pub. affairs Sta. WCKT-TV, Miami, 1968-70; dir. pub. affairs Sta. WOR-AM, N.Y.C., 1971-78; reporter documentary and consumer affairs Sta. WTFM, N.Y.C., 1978-81; dir. editorials and sta. svcs. Sta. WOR-TV, N.Y.C. and Secaucus, N.J., 1981-87; mgr. community affairs and spl. projects Sta. WWOR-TV, N.Y.C., Secaucus, N.J., 1987-91, dir. cmty. affairs and spl. projects Secaucus, 1991-2000, exec. prodr., pub. affairs programming and spl. projects, 1994—, dir. pub. affairs, 2000—02; cons. Penny Pinsker Comms., 2003—. Author, editor: (resource directory) Sta. WOR on Crime, 1982 (recipient George Washington Medal Honor Freedom Found., Emmy award for Outstanding Editorial, 1981), The Changing Family, 1982 (recipient Broadcast Media award San Francisco State U., Emmy nominated), A Child is Missing, 1983 (recipient Broadcast Media award San Francisco State U., Emmy nominated), Taking the High Out of High School, 1984 (recipient Broadcast Media award San Francisco State U, Angel award Religion Media, Bronze medal Internat. TV and Film Soc.); project mgr. A+ For Kids (Emmy award 1989, also Emmy nomination, named 12th nat. Point of Light, 1989), A+ For Kids: Project Director National, (Emmy nominations 1989-91; N.Y. Emmy award 1989, 1991; Nat. Edn. Assn. award 1991; Commr.'s award for child abuse prevention U.S. Dept. HHS 2003). Media advisor N.J. Crime Prevention Officers Assn.; mem. comm. com. N.J. affiliation Am. Heart Assn., Am. Cancer Soc.; bd. dirs. Queensboro Soc. Prevention Cruelty to Children, 1978-83, Hoboken Chamber Orch., 1989-90, N.J. Edn. Found., 1991-92; pub. mem. N.J. Gov.'s Task Force on Child Abuse and Neglect, 1988-97; mem. N.J. Task Force on Cild Abuse and Neglect, 1997—; trustee Assn. for Children of N.J., 1990—; mem. exec. coun. for comm. AARP-N.J., 2002--; mem. N.J. Coun. on Adult Edn. and Literacy, 1992-93; mem. exec. com. Partnership for a Drug Free N.J., 1997—; mem. N.J. Bus.-Edn. Summit, 1997-99, Am. Diabetes Assn. Nat. mktg. and Comm. Com., 2003-. Recipient Disting. Svc. award, N.J. Speech-Lang.-Hearing Assn., 1987, Cmty. Svc. award, Urban League Hudson County, 1986, Media award for achievement in preventing child abuse, N.J. Child Assault Prevention Project, 1993, Cmty. Svc. award, N.J. Gov.'s Conf. in Divesity, 1998, Seton Hall U., 2000, Triangle award for excellence in comms., March of Dimes, 2001, US Dept Health and Human Services Commissioner's award, NJ for Child Abuse Prevention, 2003. Mem.: AARP-N.J. (exec. coun. mem. comm. 2002—), NAFE, N.J. Broadcasters Assn. (bd. dirs. 1992—99, state legis. chair 1999—2001), Advt. Coun. N.J. (trustee 1986—2000), Nat. Broadcast Assn. Cmty. Affairs, Nat. Broadcast Editl. Assn. (bd. dirs. 1986—87), Meadowlands Regional C. of C. (bd. dirs. 1991—92), Leadership N.J. Grad. Orgn. Avocation: breeder thoroughbred horses. Home: Winterwood Farm 449 Kingwood-Locktown Rd Flemington NJ 08822 Office: 9 Broadcast Plz Secaucus NJ 07094-2913 Office Phone: 201-330-2148. E-mail: ppinsker@att.net.

PINSKER, WALTER, retired allergist, immunologist; b. Bay Shore, N.Y., Mar. 27, 1933; s. Albert and Irene (Kuchlick) P.; m. Tillene Giller, June 15, 1958; children: Neil, Andrew, Susann. BA, U. Rochester, 1954; MD, Chgo. Med. Sch. U. Health Sci., 1958. Diplomate Am. Bd. Allergy and Immunology. Intern L.I. Jewish Hosp., New Hyde Park, N.Y., 1958-59; resident internal medicine Bklyn. VA Hosp., 1959-60, Long Beach (Calif.) VA Hosp., 1960-61, resident allergy and immunology, 1961-62; chief of allergy Letterman Army Hosp., San Francisco, 1962-64; pres. Bay Shore Allergy Group, 1964-94. Attending physician Mather Hosp., Port Jefferson, N.Y., St. Charles Hosp., Port Jefferson, 1981-95, Southside Hosp., Bay Shore, 1964—, Good Samaritan Hosp., West Islip, N.Y., 1964-95, asst. clin. prof. medicine SUNY, Stony Brook, 1968—; mem. physicians adv. com. Group Health, 1997—. Contbr. articles to profl. jours.; patentee in treatment of migraine headaches and formulations. Bd. visitors Pilgrim State Hosp., Brentwood, N.Y., 1974-77; pres. Suffolk Assn. Children with Learning Difficulties, N.Y., 1972-74; trustee Leeway Sch., Stony Brook, 1974-75, Bay Shore Jewish Ctr., 1974-84; com. for handicapped West Islip Schs., 1971—. Capt. U.S. Army, 1962-64. Named Co-Humanitarian of Yr. L.I. Adults and Children with Learning and Developmental Disabilities, 1994; recipient Physician's Recognition award AMA, 1969—. Fellow Am. Acad. Allergy and Immunology, Am. Coll. Allergy and

Immunology, Am. Assn. Certified Allergists, Am. Coll. Chest Physicians, Am. Assn.- Study of Headaches, N.Y. Acad. Scis., Suffolk Acad. Medicine, Nassau-Suffolk Allergy Soc. (officer, bd. dirs. 1970-95, pres. 1980-82). Avocations: golf, boating, photography.

PINSKY, ROBERT NEAL, poet, educator; b. Long Branch, N.J., Oct. 20, 1940; s. Milford Simon and Sylvia (Eisenberg) P.; m. EllenJane Bailey, Dec. 30, 1961; children: Nicole, Caroline, Elizabeth. BA, Rutgers U., 1962; PhD, Stanford U., 1966. Mem. English faculty U. Chgo., 1967-68, Wellesley Coll., 1968-80; prof. English U. Calif., Berkeley, 1980-89; prof. Boston U., 1980-89, prof. creative writing, 1989—. Poetry editor New Republic mag., 1978; vis. lectr. Harvard U.; Hurst prof. Washington U., St. Louis Author: Landor's Poetry, 1968, Sadness and Happiness, 1975, The Situation of Poetry, 1977, An Explanation of America, 1980, History of My Heart, 1984, Poetry and the World, 1988, The Want Bone, 1990, The Inferno of Dante, 1994, The Figured Wheel: New and Collected Poems 1966-1996, 1996, The Sounds of Poetry, 1998, The Handbook of Heartbreak, 1998, Americans' Favorite Poems, 2000, Jersey Rain, 2000; editor poetry Slate mag., 1994-2000. Recipient Artists award Am. Acad. Arts and Letters, 1979; Saxifrage prize, 1980; William Carlos Williams prize, 1984; Shelley Meml. award, 1996, Harold Washington Lit. award, 1999; Guggenheim fellow, 1980; appointed U.S. poet laureate, 1997. Mem. AAAL, AAAS, PEN. Office: Boston U English Dept 236 Bay State Rd Boston MA 02215-1403

PINSKY, ROY DAVID, lawyer; b. Syracuse, NY, Feb. 1, 1948; s. Norman M. and Rose C. Pinsky; m. Stephanie V. Pinsky, June 9, 1968; children: Alissa Jill, Todd Justin. BS, Syracuse U., 1969, JD, 1971. Bar: N.Y. 1972, Fla. 1981. Ptnr. Pinsky, Canter and Pinsky, Syracuse, 1972, Pinsky and Pliskin, Syracuse, 1972-88, Pinsky & Skandalis, 1988—. Spl. cons. Syracuse Bd. Edn., 1972-74. Contbr. articles to profl. jours. Bd. dirs. Young Israel-Shaarei Torah of Syracuse; trustee Jewish Home of Ctrl. N.Y. Served with U.S. Army, 1969-75. Mem. N.Y. State Bar Assn., Fla. Bar Assn., Onondaga County Bar Assn., Transp. Lawyers Assn. (past trustee), Def. Rsch. Inst., Can. Transport Lawyers Assn. (freight control conf.), Syracuse U. Alumni Assn. (past. nat. pres.). Home: 4623 Glencliffe Rd Manlius NY 13104-2378 Office: PO Box 250 5790 Widewaters Pkwy Syracuse NY 13214-0250 Office Phone: 315-446-2384. E-mail: pinskyskan@aol.com.

PINSON, ARTIE FRANCES, retired elementary school educator; b. Rusk, Tex., June 20, 1933; d. Tom and Minerva (McDuff) Neeley; m. Robert H. Pinson, Dec. 14, 1963 (div. Nov. 1967); 1 child, Deidre R. BA magna cum laude, Tex. Coll., 1953; postgrad., U. Tex., 1956, North Tex. U., 1958, 63, New Eng. Conservatory, 1955, 57, 59, 62, Tex. So. U., 1971-72; MEd, U. Houston, 1970. Music tchr. Bullock High Sch., LaRue, Tex., 1953-59; music tchr., 9th grade English tchr. Story High Sch., Palestine, Tex., 1959-64; 6th grade tchr. Turner Elem. Sch., Houston, 1964-66; 3d, 5th and 6th grade tchr. Kay Elem. Sch., Houston, 1966-70; 6th grade tchr. Pilgrim Elem. Sch., Houston, 1970-75; 3d to 6th grade gifted and talented math. tchr. Pleasantville Elem. Sch., Houston, 1975-79; kindergarten to 5th grade computer/math. tchr. Betsy Ross Elem. Sch., Houston, 1979—2003; ret., 2003. Instnl. coord.; lead tchr. math./sci. program Shell/Houston Ind. Sch. Dist., 1986-87, Say "Yes" program, 1988-89; math. tchr. summer potpourri St. Francis Xavier Cath. Ch., 1991; math. tchr. sci. and engring. awareness and coll. prep. program Tex. So. U., 1993-2003; participant Project Sail math. curriculum devel., Prairie View U., 1997-98, 99; presenter confs. in field; condr. tchr. tng. workshops.= Author computer software in field; contbr. articles to mags. Musician New Hope Bapt. Ch., Houston, 1991—, Sunday sch. tchr.; pianist Buckner Bapt. Haven Nursing Home, Houston, 1990-91, inspirational spkr.; mem. N.E. Concerned Citizens Civic League. Recipient Excellence in Math. Teaching award Exxon Corp., 1990. Mem. Assn. African Am. Math. Educators (Salute to Math. Tchrs. award 1991, treas. 1991-93, sec. 1993-95), Nat. Coun. Tchrs. Math., Tex. Coun. Tchrs. Math. (Excellence in Math. Tchg. award 1988), Houston Coun. Tchrs. of Math. (Excellence in Math. Tchg. award 1993), Heoines of Jericho, Palestine Negro Bus. and Profl. Women (charter mem.). Avocations: needlecrafts, number puzzles, piano, photography, gardening. Office: Betsy Ross Elem Sch 2819 Bay St Houston TX 77026-3203 Home: 11341 Lamb DR Tyler TX 75709-5333 E-mail: artpin@msn.com.

PINSON, CHARLES WRIGHT, transplant surgeon, healthcare administrator, educator; b. Albuquerque, May 29, 1952; s. Ernest Alexander and Jean Elizabeth (Farnsworth) P. Student, Miami U., Oxford, Ohio, 1970-72; BA, U. Colo., Boulder, 1974, MBA, 1976; MD, Vanderbilt U., 1980. Diplomate Am. Bd. Surgery, Am. Bd. Surg. Critical Care, Nat. Bd. Med. Examiners, Tenn., Mass., Oreg. Resident in gen. surgery Oreg. Health Sci. U., Portland, 1980-86; fellow gastrointestinal surgery Lahey Clinic, Burlington, Mass., 1986-87; fellow transplant surgery Harvard U., Boston, 1987-88; dir. liver transplant program VA Western region, Portland, 1989-90, Oreg. Health Sci. U., Portland, 1988-90; interim chmn. dept. surgery Vanderbilt U., Nashville, 1993-95, chief divsn. hepatobiliary surgery and liver transplantation, 1990—2004, vice-chmn. dept. surgery, 1995-2001; dir. Vanderbilt Transplant Ctr., Nashville, 1993—; chmn. med. bd. Vanderbilt U. Med. Ctr., Nashville, 1997-99; chief of staff Vanderbilt U. Hosp., Nashville, 1997—2004; H. William Scott prof., chmn. dept. surgery Vanderbilt U., Nashville, 2001—04; chief med. officer, assoc. vice chancellor for clin. affairs Vanderbilt U. Med. Ctr., Nashville, 2004—. Adv. bd. Pacific N.W. Transplant Bank, Portland, 1989-90, Tenn. Donor Svcs., Nashville, 1991—, sec., 2003—. Mem. editl. bd. Annals of Surgery, Jour. Gastrointestinal Surgery, Liver Transplantation, HPB; contbr. articles to profl. jour., chpts. to books. Bd. dirs. ARC, Nashville, 1992-94, Am. Liver Found., 1992-96, Ronald McDonald House, 2002—; bd. dirs. United Network for Organ Sharing, 2000-02, chair liver and intestine allocation com., 2003—. Fellow, Am. Heart Assn., Oreg., 1983-84. Mem. Soc. Univ. Surgeons, Halsted Soc., Soc. Surg. Oncology, Am. Soc. Transplant Surgeons, Am. Soc. Study of Liver Diseases, Am. Gastroent. Assn., Am. Hepatopancreatobiliary Assn. (treas. 1999-2003, exec. com. 1997—, pres. elect 2001-03, pres. 2003-05), Am. Physiologic Soc., So. Med. Assn. (chmn. sect. surgery 1997-2001), Am. Surg. Assn., So. Surg. Assn., Western Surg. Assn., North Pacific Surg. Assn. (sci. program 1990-92), Assn. Acad. Surgery, Soc. Surgery of Alimentary Tract, Internat. Liver Transplantation Soc., Sigma Xi, Phi Beta Kappa, Alpha Omega Alpha. Office: Vanderbilt U Med Ctr Ste 3810 A Nashville TN 37232-5545

PINSON, JOSEPH, education educator, entertainer; s. Joseph Warren and Ida Mae Pinson; m. Saralyn Sue Judd; children: Joseph III, Martha Blair. MusB, So. Meth. Univ., Dallas, Tex., 1959; MA, Am. Univ., Washington, 1969. Cert. MT-BC Cert. Bd. for Music Therapists. Music dir. Denton State Sch., Denton, Tenn., 1974—97; lectr. Tex. Woman's Univ., Denton, Tenn., 1997—. Dir. Denton Bell Band, Denton, Tex., 1997—, Denton Cmty. Chorus, Denton, Tex., 1999—2003. Composer: (choir, quintet) Mathematical Zoo, 2000, (CD) Welcome to My May, 2003. Mem. Vol. Coun., Denton, Tex., 1999—. MU-2 USN, 1959—62, Washington. Mem.: Am. Soc. & Composers, Authors & Publ. (std. award 2000, 2001, 2002, 2003), Am. Music Therapy Assn. (regional pres. 2001—02). Home: PO Box 491 Denton TX 76202 Office Phone: 940-898-2515. E-mail: joseph.pinson@verizon.net.

PINSON, LARRY LEE, pharmacist; b. Van Nuys, Calif., Dec. 5, 1947; s. Leland J. and Audrey M. (Frett) P.; m. Margaret K. Pinson, Mar. 18, 1972; children: Scott C., Kelly E. Student, U. Calif., Davis, 1967-69; AA, Am. River Coll., Sacramento, 1969; PharmD, U. Calif., San Francisco, 1973. Staff pharmacist/asst. dir. pharm. svcs. St. Mary's Hosp., Reno, 1973-77; chief pharmacist May Ang Base USAF, 1973-77; owner/chief pharmacist Silverada Pharmacy, Reno, 1979-2001; mng. pharmacist Scolari's Food & Drug, Reno, 2001—04, Scolari's Food and Drug, Reno, 2004—. Cons. pharmacist Physicians Hosp., 1974-93, Reno Med. Plaza, 1973—, Rural Calif. Hosp. Assn., 1973-74, Ford Ctr. for Foot Surgery, 1980—; pharmacist coordinator Intensive Pharm. Svcs., 1986-87; cons. Calif. Dept. Health & Corrections, Susanville, 1975-76, Nev. Med. Care Adv. Bd., Carson City, 1984-87; provider and reviewer Nev. State Bd. Pharmacy, Reno, 1975-84; instr. we. Nev. Cmty. Coll., 1974-76; adj. prof. Idaho State U., Pocatello, 1989—. Co-author: Care of Hickman Catheter, 1984. Apptd. mem. Nev. State Bd. Pharmacy, 1995-2000, pres., 1996—, re-apptd. 2001—; apptd. mem. State of Nev. Pharmaceutics and Therapy Com., 2004—; mem. Nev. Arthritis Found.; bd. dirs. Am. Cancer Soc., 1986—90; softball coach Reno/Sparks Recreation Dept., 1973—92; cubmaster Pack 153, Verdi, Nev.; scoutmaster com. chmn. Reno troop 1, Boy Scouts Am., 1988-92. Recipient Bowl of Hygeia award (Pharmacist of the Year), Nev. Pharmacists Assn. and A.H. Robbins Co., 1984, named Pharmacist of the Year, Nevada Pharm. Alliance, 1999. Mem. Nat. Assn. Bds. of Pharmacy, Am. Pharm. Assn., Nev. Pharmacists Assn. (pres. 1981-82), Nev. Profl. Stds. Rev. Orgn., Greater Nev. Health Sys. Agy., Kappa Psi. Avocations: skiing, fishing, backpacking, softball, golf. Home: PO Box 478 Verdi NV 89439-0478 Office: Scolari's Pharmacy 6255 Sharlands Ave E Reno NV 89523 Office Phone: 775-746-7320. E-mail: Rx2005@aol.com.

PINSON, WILLIAM MEREDITH, JR., pastor, writer, administrator; b. Ft. Worth, Aug. 3, 1934; s. William Meredith and Ila Lee (Jones) P.; m. Bobbie Ruth Judd, June 4, 1955; children: Meredith Pinson Creasey, Allison Pinson Hopgood. BA, U. N. Tex., 1955; BD, Southwestern Bapt. Theol. Sem., Ft. Worth, 1959, ThD, 1963, MDiv, 1973; LittD (hon.), Calif. Bapt. Coll., Riverside, 1978; DD (hon.), U. Mary Hardin-Baylor, Belton, Tex., 1984; LHD (hon.), Howard Payne U., Brownwood, Tex., 1986; LittD (hon.), Dallas Bapt. U., 1990; LLD (hon.), Hardin Simmons U., 1999. Ordained to ministry Bapt. Ch., 1955. Assoc. sec. Christian Life Commn., Dallas, 1957-63; prof. Christian ethics Southwestern Bapt. Theol. Sem., Ft. Worth, 1963-75; pastor First Bapt. Ch., Wichita Falls, Tex., 1975-77; pres. Golden Gate Bapt. Theol. Sem., Mill Valley, Calif., 1977-82; vol. dir. Tex. Bapt. Heritage Ctr., 2000—; disting. prof. Dallas Bapt. U., 2001—; disting. vis. prof. Baylor U., 2001—. Exec. dir. Bapt. Gen. Conv. Tex., 1982—2000, exec. dir. emeritus, 2000—; chmn. program com. Christian Life Commn. So. Bapt. Conv., spl. rschr. for home mission bd., nat. task force planned growth in giving, 1984—94, stewardship commn., 1986—96; bd. dirs. T.B. Maston Found., 1991—98, Assn. So. Bapt. Schs., 1997—2002; adj. prof. Southwestern Bapt. Theol. Sem., 1976—77; chmn. study commn. freedom, justice and peace Bapt. World Alliance, 1975—80, study commn. on ethics, 1990—95, commn. on racism, 1992—, com. on polity and heritage, 2000—; v.p. Bapt. Gen. Conv. Tex., 1972—73, state missions commn., 1976—77, vice chmn. urban strategy com., chmn. order of bus. com., 1976, chmn. steering com. Good News Tex., 1976—77, chmn. resolutions com.; spkr. in field; bd. dirs., chair centennial com. Baylor U. Health Care Sys., 2002—. Contbr. articles and authored books for numerous theological publs. Adv. bd. Bapt. History and Heritage Soc., 2002—; mem. adv. com. Sch. Leadership Dallas Bapt. U., 2003—. Named Lilly Found. scholar Southwestern Bapt. Theol. Sem., 1960-62; recipient Disting. Alumni award Southwestern Bapt. Theol. Sem., 1979, U. North Tex., 1980, Mosaic Missions award Home Mission Bd., 1984, Parabolani award Tex. Bapt. Men, 1999, Spirit of Excellence award Houston Bapt. U., 2000, Tex. Bapt. Missions award State Missions Commn., 2000, Pioneer award Tex. Bapt. Missions Found., 2001, W. Winfred Moore award for lifetime achievement in ministry Baylor U., 2001, Officers' award Bapt. History and Heritage Soc., 2003. Mem. So. Bapt. Assn. Colls. and Schs., So. Bapt. Assn. of State Exec. Dirs. (pres. 1996-97). Baptist. Avocations: travel, reading. Office: Bapt Gen Conv Tex 333 N Washington Ave Dallas TX 75246-1782 Fax: 214-370-0228. Office Phone: 214-370-9471. Business E-Mail: pinson@bgct.org.

PINSTRUP-ANDERSEN, PER, economist, educator; b. Bislev, Denmark, Apr. 7, 1939; came to U.S., 1965; s. Marinus and Alma (Pinstrup) Andersen; m. Birgit Lund, June 19, 1965; 1 child: Tina. BS, Royal Vet. and Agrl. U., Copenhagen, 1965; MS, Okla. State U., 1967, PhD, 1969; Dr. Tech. Scis. (hon.), Swiss Fed. Inst. Tech., 1996; DSc (hon.), Tamil Nadu U., 1999, Animal Scis. U., 1999; LLD, U. Aberdeen, 1999; Dr. Agr. and Environment (hon.), Wageningen U., The Netherlands, 2000. Agrl. economist Centro Internacional de Agricultura Tropical, Cali, Colombia, 1969-72, head econ. unit, 1972-76; dir. agro.-econ. div. Internat. Fertilizer Devel. Ctr., Florence, Ala., 1976-77; sr. rsch. fellow, assoc. prof. Econ. Inst. Royal Vet. and Agrl. U., Copenhagen, 1977-80, prof. devel. econs., 2003—; rsch. fellow Internat. Food Policy Rsch. Inst., Washington, 1980, dir. food consumption and nutrition divsn., 1980-87, dir. gen., 1992—2002; dir. food and nutrition policy program, prof. food econs. Cornell U., Ithaca, NY, 1987-92, prof. applied econs. and mgmt., 2003—, H.E. Babcock prof. food, nutrition and pub. policy, 2003—; disting prof. Wageningen U., 2000—. Cons. The World Bank, Washington, 1978-92, Can. Internat. Devel. Agy., 1982-83, 86, UNICEF, N.Y.C.; cons. subcom. on nutrition UN, Rome, 1980-87; chmn. CGIAR Sci. Coun., 2004—. Author: more than 400 publs. including, The World Food and Agricultural Situation, 1978, Agricultural Research and Economic Development, 1979, The Role of Fertilizer in World Food Supply, 1980, Agricultural Research and Technology in Economic Development, 1982; editor: (with Magaret Biswas) Nutrition and Development, 1985, Food Subsidies in Developing Countries: Costs, Benefits, and Policy Options, 1988, Macroeconomic Policy Reforms, Poverty, and Nutrition: Analytical Methodologies, 1990, The Political Economy of Food and Nutrition Policies, 1993, (with David Pelletier and Harold Alderman) Child Growth and Nutrition in Developing Countries: Priorities for Action, 1995, Seed of Contention, 2001, The Unfinished Agenda, 2002; mem. editl. bd. coms. of several jours With Danish Army, 1958-59. Recipient cert. of appreciation People to People, 1967, competition prize Nordic Soc. agrl. Rschrs. and Norsk Hydro, 1979, cert. of merit Gamma Sigma Delta, 1991, Disting. Alumnus award U. Colo., 1993, Disting. Alumni award Okla. State U., 1998, World Food prize World Food Found., 2001; fellow Ford Found., 1965-66, Kellogg gravel fellow, 1979. Mem. Am. Assn. Agrl. Econs. (PhD Thesis award 1970, Outstanding Jour. Article award 1977, bd. dirs. 1996-99), Internat. Assn. Agrl. Econs., Columbian Nat. Orgn. Profls. in Agr. (hon., Charles Black award 1998, Agronomiprisen 2000, World Food prize 2001, Rosenhjaerprisen, 2002). Office: Cornell U Divsn of Nutrition 305 Savage Hall Ithaca NY 14853 Business E-Mail: pp94@cornell.edu.

PINTER, GABRIEL GEORGE, physiology educator; b. Bekes, Hungary, June 23, 1925; came to U.S., 1958; s. Lajos and Regina (Szilagyi-Farkas) Pinter; m. Berit Helgesen, Dec. 19, 1958 (dec. May 1980); children: Renee Astrid, Eva Ingelill; m. Vera Lederer Dallos, May 24, 1984. MD, U. Sch. Medicine, Budapest, Hungary, 1951. Asst. prof. U. Sch. Medicine, Budapest, Hungary, 1951-56; rsch. assoc. U. Inst. Med. Rsch., Oslo, Norway, 1957-58; asst. prof. U. Tenn., Memphis, 1958-61; from asst. prof. to prof. U. Md., Balt., 1961-92; retired. Vis. prof. King's Coll., London, 1990-94. Contbr. articles to profl. jours.; translator (with wife) philos. and lit. works into Hungarian. Recipient A.V. Humboldt prize, Germany, 1980; Swedish Royal Med. Soc. fellow, Uppsala, 1972. Mem. Am. Physiol. Soc., Physiol. Soc. Gt. Brit., Scandinavian Physiol. Soc., European Soc. Microcirculation. Personal E-mail: ggvp@comcast.net.

PINTO, EDWARD RALPH, internist, cardiologist; b. Mangalore, India, 1947; MD, Bangalore (India) U., 1970. Diplomate Am. Bd. Internal Medicine, Am. Bd. Cardiovascular Disease, Am. Bd. Geriatrics. Intern Bridgeport Hosp., 1971-72; resident internal medicine Bridgeport (Conn.) Hosp., 1972-75; fellow in cardiology Hosp. U. Pa., Phila., 1975-76; fellow cardiology Hershey Med. Ctr., 1976-77; sr. attending physician internal medicine and cardiology Bridgeport Hosp. Fellow Am. Coll. Cardiology. Office: 52 Beach Rd Fairfield CT 06430-6017

PINTO, JOSEPH GAMINI, manufacturing executive; b. Negombo, Sri Lanka, Oct. 27, 1948; arrived in U.S.A., 1973; s. Vincent M. and Margarita Francisca (Fernando) P.; m. Lilamany Mary Anne De Pinto, Jan. 20, 1973; children: Joseph Praveen, Nelangi Marie. BS in Engring. with honors, U. Ceylon, Sri Lanka, 1971; MS in Indsl. Engring., Purdue U., 1974. Materials mgr., plant mgr., dir. mfg. Sherwin Williams Co., Crisfied, Md., 1975-83; v.p. ops. Am. Brush Co., Claremont, 1983-85, Atworth Ltd., Seoul, South Korea, 1985-87; plant mgr., dir. bus. devel., mng. dir. PPG Industries Internat., Inc., Tokyo, 1987-95. Automotive refinish, mng. dir. PPG Industries, Inc., Hong Kong, 1996-99, mng. dir. Australia & New Zealand, 1999—; mng. dir. PPG Coating Co., Ltd., Hong Kong, 1995-98, Tianjin, China, 1995-98; asst. lectr. U. Ceylon, 1971-73. Inventor double cam lock, spray nozzle. Dir. Am. C. of C., Claremont, N.H., 1985. Grad. fellow Rotary Found., Sri Lanka, 1973. Mem. Inst. Indsl. Engrs., Soc. Mfg. Engrs., Inst. Mech. Engrs., Inst. Chem. Engrs., Am. Prodn. and Inventory Control Soc. Roman Catholic. Avocations: golf, travel. Home: 10 Sarah Crescent Templestowe Vic 3106 Australia Office: PPG Industries-Australia 1 Ppg Pl Pittsburgh PA 15272-0001

PINTO, MAXWELL SALUSTIANO, management consultant; b. Goa, India, Mar. 10, 1954; came to U.S., 1984; s. Maurice and Martha (Lopez) P.; m. Eusebia C. Fernandez, Jan. 25, 1987; children: Aaron Massimo, Esther Maxine. BA with honors, U. Leeds, Eng., 1978; PhD in Bus. Adminstrn., Pacific Southern U., 1987. Chartered acct., Eng. Auditor, acct. KPMG Peat Marwick Chartered Accts., London, 1978-82; dep. fin. and adminstrn. mgr. Elec. Bds. Mfg. Co., Kuwait, 1983-86; fin. cons. Tollafield & Assocs., Cyprus, 1986-87; dir. Brandon Planning & Corp. Analysis, Cyprus, 1987-88; mgmt. analyst The Citgo Group Inc., N.Y.C., 1989-93; bus. assoc. in ins. and investments N.Y. Life Ins. Co., N.Y.C., 1993-96; trust acct. CI Mutual Funds, Inc., Toronto, Canada, 1998—2001; bus. cons. Toronto, 2001—. Lectr. acctg. Plato Coll., 1987, Limassol, Cyprus, econs. Americanos Coll., Limassol, 1987, mgmt. and law, Intercollege, Limassol, 1988. Author: The Management Syndrome, 1998.; Mgmt...Flirting with Disaster!, 2004. Pacific Southern U. scholar, 1984. Mem. Inst. Profl. Mgrs. (life), Inst. Chartered Accts. (assoc.), Outdoor World, Coast to Coast. Avocations: tennis, swimming, pool, movies. Home and Office: 169 Morrison Ave Toronto ON Canada M6E 1M6 E-mail: crespin79@hotmail.com.

PINTO, ROSALIND, retired educator, civic volunteer; b. NYC; d. Barney and Jenny Abrams; m. Jesse E. Pinto (dec.); children: Francine, Jerry, Evelyn. BA in Polit. Sci. cum laude, Hunter Coll.; MA in Polit. Sci., History, Columbia U.; postgrad., Queens Coll., LaGuardia C.C. Lic. social studies tchr. jr. HS, NY, per diem substitute; cert. secondary sch. social studies grades 7-12, NY. Substitute tchr., 1966-69, 90, 91—; tchr. social studies I.S. 126Q, LI, NY, 1969-88, Jr. HS 217 Briarwood, NYC, 1988-89; ret., 1989; part-time cluster tchr. social studies and communication arts Pub. Sch. 140, Bronx, NY, 1990-92; substitute tchr. I.S. 227Q, 1992-93. Participant seminars and workshops. Author curriculum materials; contbr. study guide for regent's competency test, 1990; author numerous poems; contbr. articles to profl. jours. Enrollment asst. Insight Heart Team, 1989; vol. receptionist Whitney Mus., N.Y.C.; mem. com. on pub. transp. Cmty. Bd. 6, Queens, 1990—96, mem. com. on history, 1990—, chmn. beautification com., 1992—, mem. com. on planning and zoning, 1996—, mem. com. on environ. sanitation, 1999—; mem. Forest Hills Action League, 1999; advocate Census 2000 participation; active Gt. Smokies Song Chase Warren-Wilson Coll., NC, 1992; mem. Queens Hist. Soc., Forest Hills Van Ct. Homeowners Assn.; bd. dirs. Ctrl. Queens Hist. Soc.; past mem. Rego Park Coalition Against Crime; mem. Forest Hills Civic Assn., 1996—97; vol. local polit. campaigns. Recipient Cert. Appreciation for participation, Dept. Probate Cmty. Svc. Project, 1993, award for participation in Make a Difference Day, 1994—95, award for projects, Beautification Com., 1995, Rosemary Gunning award, Queens Borough Pres. for Women's History month, 2000, Editor's Choice award, Best Poems and Poets of 2001, 2002, Poet of Merit award, Poetry Conv., 2002, Cert. Appreciation for joining graffiti cleanup, 112th Precinct Cmty. Coun., 2002—03, Cert. of Appreciation for help in Night Out Against Crime, 2002—03, 2004, Poet of Merit award, Poetry Conv., 2003, Editor's Choice award, 2003, Cert. Appreciation for joining graffiti cleanup, 112th Precinct Cmty. Coun., 2004, 2004. Fellow Mcpl. Art Soc. (hon. mention design 2000 award); mem. NAFE, Internat. Soc. Poets (life mem. adv. panel, Internat. Poet of Merit award 1993, 2000, Editor's Choice award 2001), NY Insight Alumni Assn., Columbia U. Grad. Sch. Arts and Scis. Alumni Assn., Hunter Coll. Alumni Assn., Robert F. Kennedy Dem. Assn. (bd. dir.), Ctr. for Sci. in the Pub. Interest. Avocations: poetry, reading, long distance walking, art shows, plays. *Loving people and having faith in them and the possibility of happy outcomes is the greatest motivation toward achievement of goals.*

PIOMBINO, NICHOLAS, psychotherapist; b. N.Y.C., Oct. 5, 1942; s. Nicholas Bruce and Ruth Mary (Rothbart) P. BA with honors, CCNY, 1964; MSW, Fordham U., 1971; cert. in adult psychoanalysis and psychotherapy, Postgrad. Ctr. Mental Health, N.Y.C., 1982. Diplomate in clin. social work; cert. psychotherapist, social worker, N.Y. Social worker Manhattan State Hosp., N.Y.C., 1971-73; pvt. practice psychotherapy N.Y.C., 1976—; sch. social worker N.Y.C. Bd. Edn., 1974—2001; staff psychotherapist Postgrad. Ctr. Mental Health, 1978-86; supr., mem. faculty Psychoanalytic Inst. N.Y. Counseling and Guidance Svc., N.Y.C., 1987—. Author: Poems, 1988, Light Street, 1996, Theoretical Objects, 1999, (essays) The Boundary of Blur, 1993; contbr. articles and poems to numerous publs. Mem. Postgrad. Psychoanalytic Soc., Soc. Clin. Social Work Psychotherapists. Office: 680 W End Ave New York NY 10025-6815 Home: 44 Prospect Park W Apt F2 Brooklyn NY 11215-2344 Office Phone: 212-316-1871. E-mail: nickpoetique@earthlink.net.

PIONK, JEROME LEE, government official, association administrator; b. Watertown, S.D., Aug. 31, 1950; s. Jerome Ambrose and Helen Emeline Pionk; m. Song Yo Kim; children: Jerome, Angela Pionk Curtis. BS, SUNY, Albany, 1984; MA, Liberty U., 1991; grad., Command and Gen. Staff Coll., 1997. Cert. counselor. Enlisted man U.S. Army, 1970, advanced through grades to sgt. maj., 1989, recruiter, 1970—84; retention and recruiting staff specialist Army Enlistment Eligibility Activity, St. Louis, 1984—87; dir. theater army retention 8th Army, Seoul, 1987—92; sr. retention policy advisor Hdqs. Dept. Army, Washington, 1992—2000; ret., 2000; sr. def. analyst, rschr. Dept. Def. (Resource Cons. Inc.)_, Washington, 2000—03; rsch. analyst SAIC, 2003—. Prof. Am. Mil. U., 2000—; exec. dir. Nat. Assn. Recruiters and Career Counselors, Washington, 1983—; bd. dirs. Ctr. Mil. Sociol. Studies. Author: Prairie Vignettes, 1999 (MIdwest Lit. award 2000), History of Military Retention, 2001. Decorated Legion of Merit; recipient Olympic honor award Seoul Olympic Organizing Com., 1988, Order of Horatio Gates, Army Adj. Gen.'s Assn., 1992. Mem. VFW (life), DAV (life), Not Good Old Boys-Vets. Assn. (exec. dir. 1983—, Order of Merit 1994), Am. Vets. (life), Am. Legion. Republican. Avocations: skydiving, travel, writing, fencing, automobile racing. Office: Army Office Human Resource Mgmt 300 Army Pentagon Washington DC 20310 Home: 12241 Tilney Ct Woodbridge VA 22192-6611 E-mail: ngob1@aol.com.

PIONK, RICHARD CLETUS, artist, educator; b. Minn., Apr. 26, 1936; s. Franz E. Spielmann and Esther (Dufrane) Pionk. Cert. in fine arts painting, Art Students League, 1983. Tchr. Art Students League, N.Y.C., 1991—. Mem. bd. control Art Students League, 1983-90. Exhibited in one-man shows Moran Gallery, Tulsa, 1985, Connoisseur Gallery, Rhinebeck, N.Y., 1987, 88, 89, 90, Bklyn. Pub. Libr.; exhibited in group shows Queens Mus., N.Y.C., 1982, Hermitage Found., Norfolk, Va., 1985, Monmouth Mus., Lincroft, N.J., 1985, La Societe des Pastellistes de France, Lille, 1987, Canton (Ohio) Art Inst., 1987, Friends Art Mus., Naples, Fla., 1987, Mel Vin Gallery Southern Coll., Lakeland, Fla., 1987, Wind Borne Gallery, Southport, Conn., 1987, 89, Gregory Gallery, Darien, Conn., 1990, 91, 92, 93, 94, 95, 96, Geary Gallery, Darien, 1997, 98, 99, 2000, 01, 02, The Food Show at Grand Cen. Art Gallery, N.Y.C., 1989, Quincy (Ill.) Art Club, 1989, 90, Jordane Art Gallery, Ft. Myers, Fla., 1990, Pastel Soc., N.Y.C., 1991, Allied Artists, N.Y.C., 1991, Harman-Meek Gallery, Naples, 1992, Butler Inst. Art, 2000, 2003, Nat. Acad. Design, N.Y.C., 2004, others; represented in permanent collections Butler Inst. Art, Ohio, 1st Pastel Mus., China, SalmaGundi Club, N.Y.C., Kidder-Peabody, N.Y., others. Recipient Salzman award, 1999, 2001, Bernhardt Gold medal for pastel, 2002, numerous awards, including medal, Artist's Fellowship, 2002, medal, The Pastel Soc., 2002, 2003. Mem. Pastel Soc. Am. (1st v.p. 1978-91, exhbn. chmn. 1978—, master pastellist, Hall of Fame 1997), Allied Artists Am. (bd. dirs. 1986-91, asst. corr. sec. 1986—), Audubon Artists (juror 1989—), Artists Fellowship Inc. (bd. dirs. 1988—), Nat. Arts Club, Salmagundi Club (mem. curators com., chmn. art com. 1981—, pres. 1994—), Hudson River Club. Roman Catholic. Avocations: collecting 17th, 18th, and 19th century paintings and drawings. Home: 1349 Lexington Ave Apt 8B New York NY 10128-1511 Office: Studio 611 41 Union Sq W New York NY 10003-3208 Office Phone: 212-348-8991.

PIOVANI, NICOLA, composer; b. Rome, May 26, 1946; s. Alberico and Armanda Piovani; children: Duccio, Rocco. Maturitá classica, Liceo Terenzio Mamiani, Rome, 1966; degree in piano, Conservatorio G. Verdi, Italy, 1967; studied with Manos Hadjidakis, 1969. Composer: (film sound tracks) N.P. Il Segreto, 1969, Nel Nome Del Padre, 1970, Marcia Trionfale, Salto Nel Vuoto, Matti da Slegare, Speriamo Che Sia Femmina, il Male Oscuro, La Messa e'Finita, Palombella Rossa, Caro Diario, Il Camorrista, Segreti Segreti,

Domani Accadrà, La Notte di San Lorenzo, Kaos, Good Morning Babylon, Il Sole Anche di Notte, Fiorile, Ginger e Fred, L'Intervista, La Voce Della Luna, numerous others, (TV and theatrical scores) Un Treno per Istanbul, Il Generale, Lenin the Train, (musicals) I Sette Re Di Roma, La Cantata del Fiore, 1988, La Cantata del Buffo, 1990, also concert music, chamber music, trio and piece for 10 instruments, numerous other works. Office: Casa Editrice Alba Srl Case Editrice Alba Srl Via Lorenzo Valla 27 00152 Rome Italy also: Pacific Time Entertainment c/o Curtis Urbina PO Box 7320 New York NY 10150-7320

PIPCHICK, MARGARET HOPKINS, advance practice nurse, marriage and family therapist; m. Robert Pipchick; children: Christine, Kevin. BSN, Seton Hall U., 1968; MA, NYU, 1974; grad., Blanton Peale Grad. Inst., N.Y.C., 1981; PhD, The Union Inst., 2001. Various staff positions hosps., N.Y./N.J.; teaching asst. Seton Hall U., South Orange, N.J., 1971-72; staff therapist, faculty Blanton-Peale Counseling Ctr., Cranford, N.J., 1974-90; pvt. practice individual, couple and family therapy Cranford, 1981—. Adj. faculty Fairleigh Dickenson U., Teaneck, N.J., 1989-93, Kean Coll., 1994, 95. Drew U., 2003. Contbr. chpt. to Founds. Psychiat. Mental Health Nursing. Mem. ANA, N.J. State Nurses Assn., Am. Assn. Marriage and Family Therapists, Soc. Advanced Practice Psychiatric Nurses (pres.), Sigma Theta Tau. Office Phone: 908-272-9088.

PIPER, ADDISON LEWIS, securities executive; b. Mpls., Oct. 10, 1946; s. Harry Cushing and Virginia (Lewis) P.; m. Louise Wakefield (div.); children: Gretchen, Tad, William; m. Cynthia Schuneman, Nov. 14, 1979; children: Elisabeth LaBelle, Richard LaBelle. BA in Econs., Williams Coll., 1968; MBA, Stanford U., 1972. Mktg. cons. Earl Savage and Co., Mpls., 1968 69; mem. capital market dept. Piper and Jaffray, Mpls., 1969-70; asst. syndicate mgr. Piper, Jaffray and Hopwood, Mpls., 1972-73, v.p., 1973-79, dir. trading, 1973-77, dir. sales, 1977-79, exec. v.p., dir. mktg., 1979-83, chief exec. officer, chmn. mgmt. com., 1983—, chmn. bd. dirs., 1988—. Adv. com. N.Y. Stock Exch., 1966-90; bd. dirs. Allina Health Systems, Greenspring Corp., Mpls., Minn. Bus. Partnership, Mpls., Abbott Northwestern Hosp., Mpls.; trustee CARE Found., Mpls. Fin. chmn. Senator Durenberger Fin. Com., Mpls., 1980-88; chmn. Minn. Pub. Radio, 1985-95. Mem. Securities Industry Assn. (bd. govs. 1986-90, tax policy com.), Country Club of the Rockies (Colo.), Mpls. Club, Ventana Canyon (Tucson), Woodhill Country Club (Wayzata) Republican. Episcopalian. Avocations: skiing, golf, hunting, tennis, horses. Office: Piper Jaffray Cos J1012058 800 Nicollet Mall Ste 800 Minneapolis MN 55402-7020

PIPER, ADRIAN MARGARET SMITH, philosopher, artist, educator; b. N.Y.C., Sept. 20, 1948; d. Daniel Robert and Olive Xavier (Smith) P.; m. Jeffrey Ernest Evans, June 27, 1982 (div. 1987). AA, Sch. Visual Arts, 1969; BA in Philosophy, CCNY, 1974; MA, Harvard U., 1977, PhD, 1981; student, U. Heidelberg, Germany, 1977-78; LHD (hon.), Calif. Inst. Arts, 1992, Mass. Coll. Art, 1994. Asst. prof. U. Mich., Ann Arbor, 1979-86; Mellon rsch. fellow Stanford (Calif.) U., 1982-84; assoc. prof. Georgetown U., Washington, 1986-88, U. Calif., San Diego, 1988; prof. philosophy Wellesley (Mass.) Coll., 1990—. Disting. scholar Getty Rsch. Inst., 1998—; speaker, lectr. on both philosophy and art. Artist: one-woman exhbns. include N.Y. Cultural Ctr., N.Y.C., 1971, Montclair (N.J.) State Coll., 1976, Wadsworth Atheneum, Hartford, Conn., 1980, Nexus COntemporary Art Ctr., Atlanta, 1987, The Alternative Mus., N.Y.C., 1987, Goldie Paley Gallery, Phila., 1989, Power Plant Gallery, Toronto, 1990, Lowe Art Mus., Coral Gables, Fla., 1990-91, Santa Monica (Calif.) Mus. Contemporary Art, 1991, John Weber Gallery, N.Y.C., 1989, 90, 91, 92, Whitney Mus. Am. Art, N.Y.C., 1990, Hirschorn Mus., Washington, 1991, Ikon Gallery, Birmingham, Eng., 1991, Cornerhouse, Manchester, Eng., 1992, Cartwright Hall, Bradford, Eng., 1992, Kunstverein, Munich, Germany, 1992, Indpls. Ctr. Contemporary Art, 1992, Manasterio de Santa Clara, Moguer, Spain, 1992, Grey Art Gallery, N.Y.C., 1992, Paula Cooper Art Galler, 1992, 94; group exhbns. include Paula Cooper Gallery, 1969, Dwan Gallery, N.Y.C., 1969, 70, Seattle Art Mus., 1969, Stadtisches Mus., Leverkusen, Germany, 1969, Kunsthalle Berne, Berne, Switzerland, 1969, N.Y. Cultural Ctr., 1970, Allen Mus., Oberlin, Ohio, 1970, Mus. Modern Art, N.Y.C., 1970, 88, 91, Musee d'Art Moderne, Paris, 1971, 77, 89, Inhibodress Gallery, New South Wales, Australia, 1972, Calif. Inst. Arts, Valencia, 1973, Samuel S. Fleischer Art Meml., Phila., 1974, Mus. Contemporary Art, Chgo., 1975, Newberger Mus., Purchase, N.Y., 1978, Mass. Coll. Art, Boston, 1979, Artemesia Gallery, Chgo., 1979, A.I.R. Gallery, N.Y.C., 1980, Inst. Contemporary Arts, London, 1980, The New Mus., N.Y.C., 1981, 83, 85, Kenkeleba Gallery, N.Y.C., 1983, The Studio Mus. Harlem, N.Y.C., 1985, 89, Mus. Moderner Kunst, Vienna, Austria, 1985, Intar Gallery, N.Y.C., 1988, Whitney Mus. Downtown, N.Y.C., 1988, Art Gallery Ont., Toronto, 1988, Long Beach (Calif.) Art Mus., 1989, Simon Watson Gallery, N.Y.C., 1990, Feigen Gallery, Chgo., 1990, Barbara Krakow Gallery, Boston, 1990, Milw. Art Mus., 1990, Contemporary Arts Ctr., Houston, 1991, John Weber Gallery, 1991, Anne Plumb Gallery, N.Y.C., 1991, Hirschorn Mus., 1991, The Albuquerque Mus. Art, 1991, The Toledo Mus. Art, 1991, Denver Art Mus., Fukui Fine Arts Mus., Fukyui-ken, Japan, 1992-93, N.J. State Mus., Trenton, 1992-93, Philippe Staib Gallery, N.Y.C., 1992, New Loom House, London, 1992, Espace-Lyonnais D'Art Contemporain, Lyon, France, 1993, Am. Acad. Inst. Arts and Letters, N.Y.C., 1993; permanent collections include Met. Mus. Art, Whitney Mus., L.A. Mus. Contemporary Art, San Francisco Mus. Modern Art, The Bklyn. Mus., Denver Art Mus., Kunstmuseum Berne, Musee d'Art Moderne, The Mus. Contemporary Art, Chgo., The Wadsworth Atheneum, Met. Mus. Art; art performances include RISD, 1973, The Whitney Mus. Am. Art, 1975, Kurfurstendamm, Berlin, 1977, Hauptstrasse, Heidelburg, Germany, 1978, Allen Meml. Mus., Oberlin, Ohio, 1980, Contemporary Art Inst. Detroit, 1980, San Francisco Art Inst., 1985, Calif. Inst. Art, 1984, The Studio Mus. Harlem, 1988; performances on video, 1987—; contbr. articles to profl. jours. Recipient N.Y. State Coun. on Arts award, 1989, Visual Arts award, 1990, Skowhegan medal for sculptural installation, 1995, Dance Theatre Workshop award for New Genres, 2000; NEH Travel fellow, 1979, NEA Visual Artists' fellow, 1979, 82, Andrew Mellon Postdoctoral fellow, 1982-84, Woodrow Wilson Internat. Scholars fellow, 1988-89, Guggenheim Meml. fellow, 1989, non-resident fellow N.Y. Inst. for Humanities, NYU, 1996—; NEA Artists Forums grantee, 1987; rsch. fellowship NEH, 1998, Getty Rsch. Inst. Disting. scholarship, 1998—, Internat. Forschungszentrum Kulturwissenschaften fellow Vienna. Mem. AAUP, Am. Philos. Assn. (mem. ea. divsn.), Am. Soc. Polit. and Legal Philosophy, N.Am. Kant. Soc. Avocations: medieval and renaissance music, fiction, poetry, yoga, German. Office: Wellesley Coll 106 Central St Wellesley MA 02481-8268

PIPER, ANNETTE CLEONE, social services administrator, researcher; b. St. Paul, July 13, 1936; d. Frank Robert Zimmerman; m. Aaron Cleaves Piper, Apr. 17, 1958 (div. 1974); children: Michelle, Renee. BA, Wayne State U., 1960, MSW, 1965, postdoctoral, 1985—. Inst. rsch. Wayne State U., Detroit, 1965-69; program mgr. Ariz. Dept. Econ. Security, Bisbee, 1976-79; tng. and personnel coordinator Mich. Dept. Social Svcs., Detroit, 1971-73, mgr. svcs. sect., 1973-74, program mgr. Pontiac, 1974-76, dep. dir. Sta. WCCYS Detroit, 1979-88, dist. dir. Westland, 1988—; med. social worker Bariatric Treatment Ctrs., Ann Arbor, 1997-98. Instr., cons. Cochise Community Coll., Douglas, Ariz., 1979. Vol. Peace Corps, Dominican Republic, 1998. Mem. Nat. Assn. Child Welfare Adminstrs., Nat. Child Welfare Leadership Ctr., Am. Pub. Welfare Assn., Wayne State U. Alumni Assn. Psi Chi. Home: 23010 Webster Oak Park MI 48237-2119 E-mail: nettie7@comcast.net.

PIPER, DON COURTNEY, political scientist, educator; b. Washington, July 29, 1932; s. Don Carlos and Alice (Courtney) Piper; m. Rowena Inez Wise, July 6, 1956; children: Sharon, Valarie. BA, U. Md., 1954, MA, 1958; PhD (James B. Duke fellow), Duke U., 1961. Research assoc. Duke U., 1961-62; exec. sec. Commonwealth-Studies Center, 1962-64; asst. prof. dept. govt. and politics U. Md., College Park, 1964-67, assoc. prof., 1967-69, prof., 1969-97, prof. emeritus, 1997—, head dept. govt. and politics, 1968-74, dir. grad. studies dept., 1982-95, mem. coun. of system faculty, 1989-90; chmn. faculty council College Park Faculty Assembly, 1974-75, chmn. campus senate, 1975-77, 89-90, univ. marshal, 1981-97, mem. Athletic Council, 1986-93, mem. senate ad hoc com. on undergrad. edn., 1986-88, chmn. chancellor's ad hoc com. on campus ceremonies, 1986-87, chmn. acad. com. of Athletic Council, 1986-89; chmn. campaign for College Park, 1988-89; chmn. retention review com. U. Md., 1990-91, chmn. budget and facilities com. athletic coun., 1991-93, chmn. senate com. on programs courses and curriculi, 1991-93, co-chair Mid. States self-study exec. com., 1995-97; teaching fellow Lilly Ctr. for Teaching Excellence, 1994-95. Rsch. asst. Am. Coun. Edn., 1966—68; mem. faculty adv. com., mem. adv. com. Md. State Bd. Higher Edn., 1977—82. Author: International Law of Great Lakes, 1967; co-author: International Law Standard and Commonwealth Developments, 1966, De Lege Pactorum, 1970, Foreign Policy Analysis, 1975; editor (with R. Taylor Cole): Post-Primary Education and Political and Economic Development, 1964; editor, author (with Ronald Terchek): Interaction: Foreign Policy and Public Policy, 1983; bd. editors World Affairs, 1971—94, mem. editl. adv. com. Internat. Legal Materials, 1977—78. Served to 1st lt. USAF, 1955—58. Mem.: Phi Beta Kappa (pres. Gamma chpt. 1978—79), Pi Sigma Alpha, Omicron Delta Kappa (faculty advisor 1990—97), Phi Kappa Phi (chpt. pres. 1982—83). Methodist. Home: 4323 Woodberry St Hyattsville MD 20782-1174 Office: U Md Dept Govt & Politics College Park MD 20742-0001

PIPER, JAMI KATHLEEN, music educator, composer; b. Oakland, Calif., Dec. 31, 1955; d. Barry Eugene Piper and Margaret Letitia (Weis) Smythe; children: Stephanie June Hauck, Matthew Lewis Hook. MusB, U. of the Pacific, Stockton, Calif., 1976; MFA, Mills Coll., Oakland, Calif., 1989; tchg. cert., U. Colo., 1997. Cert. music specialist K thru 12, nat. cert. tchr. music. Piano accompanist, soloist contracted, Calif., 1962—; piano tchr. self employed, Calif., 1976—94; adj. educator Music Tchr. Assn. Calif., Calif., 1989—; vocal, instrumental music tchr Boulder Valley Sch., Boulder, Colo., 1995—2002; gen. music, theory, and history tchr Boulder Arts Acad., Boulder, Colo., 1995—98; piano accompanist, soloist contracted, Colo., 1995—2002; piano tchr. self employed, Colo., 1996—2002; adj. educator Music Tchr. Nat. Assn., Colo., 1994—2002. Pres. Music Tchr. Assn. of Calif., Alameda County, Calif., 1992—94; v.p. Boulder Area Music Tchr. Assn., Boulder, Colo., 1994—95; chair of auditions Colo. Music Tchr. Assn., Colo., 1996—98. Composer: (hymn) Benediction, 1986, Give Him the Praise, 1986, God Almighty, God of Love, 1987. V.p. and treas. Alameda County Br. of the Music Tchr. Assn. of Calif., Calif., 1990—92. Recipient U. of the Pacific Music Grant, U. of the Pacific, Stockton, Calif., 1973—76, Calif. State Scholarship, State of Calif., 1973—76, Mary M. Henry Prize, Mills Coll., Oakland, Calif., 1985—87. Mem.: NEA, Organization of Am. Kodaly Educators, Nat. Music Tchr. Assn., Music Tchr. Assn. Calif., Orff Schulwerk Assn., Pi Lambda Theta, Kappa Delta Pi. Democrat. Episcopalian. Achievements include arranger, performer, and asst. eng. for the album "Look into the Word" by Dean Ellenwood; world premier performance of "Awaken", by Ken McCaw; artist of the session, Festival Noord, Holland; doctoral work; ABT, U. Colo.in performance and pedagogy. Avocations: sewing, gardening, ballet, figure skating. Home and Office: 5643 Chris Ann Ct Sacramento CA 95841-2800 E-mail: jkpmuses@att.net.

PIPER, J.E. artist, photographer, historian; b. N.Y.C., Mar. 21, 1952; AA, John Jay Coll., 1973; AB, Herbert H. Lehman Coll., 1975; MA, U. Md., 1977. Editl. svc. Time Inc., N.Y.C., 1976—87; rschr. Cooper Union, N.Y.C., 1988—92; rschr./writer United Negro Coll. Fund, N.Y.C., 1992—94; rsch. analyst Am. Civil Liberties Union, N.Y.C., 1994—. Historian, ind. curator with numerous pubs. and exhbn., 1970—. Contbr./curator (art, photos, articles to Art/Life mag., 1983-90), contbr./editor (articles/photography, Bronx County Hist. Soc. Jour., 1970-73); exhibitions include work featured in art exhbn. in galleries and mus., U.S., Europe, and Japan, 1976—. Bd. dir. Bronx County His. Soc., NY, 1970—73, chmn. landmarks com., 1970—73; vice. pres. Bronx Soc. Sci. and Letters, 1974—77. Home: PO Box 601 New York NY 10268

PIPER, JOHN RICHARD, political science educator; b. Sewickley, Pa., Oct. 2, 1946; s. John Hubert and Carol Elizabeth (Coleman) P.; m. Hoa Thuy Pham, June 6, 1970; 1 child, Carolyn Hoa. BA, Pa. State U., 1968; MA, Cornell U., 1971, PhD, 1972. Prof. polit. sci. Blackburn Coll., Carlinville, Ill., 1972-76; asst. prof. polit. sci. U. Tampa (Fla.), 1976-80, assoc. prof. polit. sci., 1980-83; prof. polit. sci. U. Tampa, Fla., 1983—, chmn. dept. history, polit. sci. and sociology, 1990-96; dir. honors program, 1996—. Author: Ideologies and Institutions: American Conservative and Liberal Governance Prescriptions Since 1933, 97; contbr. articles to profl. jours. V.p. Fla. Collegiate Honors Coun., 1998—99, pres., 1999—2000; mem. Tampa Bay Com. Fgn. Rels., 1990—. Recipient Outstanding Educator award Blackburn Coll., 1974, Louise Loy Hunter award U. Tampa, 1981, award for teaching excellence Sears Roebuck Found., 1990; Fulbright-Hays grantee, 1988. Mem. Am. Polit. Sci. Assn., AAUP, Omicron Delta Kappa, Phi Beta Kappa, Pi Kappa Phi. Democrat. Avocations: travel, swimming, reading. Office: Univ of Tampa 401 W Kennedy Blvd Tampa FL 33606-1490 E-mail: rpiper@ut.edu.

PIPER, KATHLEEN, former political organization administrator; b. Ida County, Iowa; d. Pat and Rita Donahey McGuire; m. James Carl Piper, 1971; 2 children. Student, U. Iowa, Morningside Coll., Mt. Marty Coll. Co-owner Pied Piper Flower Shop, Yankton, S.D., 1986; vice chair Yankton County Dem. Com., 1980-95, state ctrl. committeewoman, 1995—; commr. Yankton County, 1986—, chair, 1996; state ctrl. com. S.D. Dem. Party, 1989-99, exec. bd., 1992-99, chairwoman, 1996-99. Mem. health care adv. com. Senator Tom Daschle, 1991—. Del. Nat. Dem. Conv., N.Y.C., 1992; mem. Gold adv. coun. appointed by Gov., 1993-95; participant Pres. Clinton and Hillary Rodham-Clinton's Health Care Inbitiative Rev., White House, 1993, Gt. Plains Rural Health Summit, 1994, Pres., Clinton and SBA Chief Roundtable Discussion Small Bus. and Health Care Reform, Washington, 1994; appointed del. White House Conf. Small Bus., 1994. Recipient Woman of Yr. award Ed Yankton Daily Press and Dakota, 1986, Emerging Leader for S.D. award Sioux Falls Argus Leader, 1990. Mem. S.D. County Commr. Assn. (exec. bd. 1992-94). Roman Catholic. Home: PO Box 737 Sioux Falls SD 57101-0737 Office: PO Box 43 Yankton SD 57078-0043

PIPER, LINDA AMMANN, staffing services executive; b. Nov. 29, 1949; d. Ernest D. and Marie (Liccese) Ammann; m. Stephen George Piper; 2 children. BA, W.Va. U., 1972. Cert. pers. cons. Mgr., asst. buyer Gilchrist Co., Boston, 1972—74; mgr. Harvard Coop. Soc., Cambridge, Mass., 1974—77; pers. cons. Wellesley Profl. Corp., Mass., 1977—82; pres. Career Connections, Inc., Nashua, NH, 1982—. Mem. regional adv. bd., mem. adv. bd. women's entrepreneur's connection BankBoston, 1998—2000. Mem.: Greater Nashua Human Resources Assn., N.H. Staffing Assn., No. New Eng. Assn. Pers. Svcs. (bd. dirs. 1982—, treas. 1983—84, v.p. 1984—85, sec. 1986—88, 1996—, dir. 2001—), Nat. Human Resource Assn. N.H. (ways and means chair 1994—97, membership chair 1997—98, bd. dirs.), Greater Nashua C. of C. (exec. bd.). Office: Career Connections Inc 74 Northeastern Blvd Ste 17 Nashua NH 03062-3192 E-mail: lpiper@careerconnectionsnh.com.

PIPER, LLOYD LLEWELLYN, II, engineer, government and service industry executive; b. Wareham, Mass., Apr. 28, 1944; s. Lloyd Llewellyn and Mary Elizabeth (Brown) P.; m. Jane Melonie Scruggs, Apr. 30, 1965; 1 child, Michael Wayne. BSEE, Tex. A&M U., 1966; MS in Indsl. Engring, U. Houston, 1973. Registered profl. engr., Tex.; diplomate hazardous waste mgmt. Am. Acad. Environ. Engrs. With Houston Lighting & Power Co., 1965-74; project mgr. Dow Chem. Engring. & Constrn Svcs., Houston, 1974-78, Ortloff Corp., Houston, 1978, mgr. engring., 1979-80, v.p., 1980-83; pres., chief exec. officer Plantech Engrs. & Constructors, Inc. subs. Dillingham Constrn. Corp., Houston, 1983-86; pres. The Delta Plantech Co., Houston, 1985-86; dir. on-site tech. devel. Chem. Waste Mgmt., Inc., Oak Brook, Ill., 1986-88, mgr. projects Houston, 1988-94, dir. facility devel., 1994-95; asst. mgr. Richland (Wash.) Ops. U.S. Dept. Energy, 1995-96, dep. mgr., 1996-99, adminstr., 1999—2002, asst. mgr., 2002—03; dep. mgr. Carlsbad Field Office, U.S. Dept. Energy, 2003—. Bd. dirs., pres. Harris County Water Control and Improvement Dist., 1973—83; bd. dirs. Environ. Sci. and Tech. Found., 1997—99, United Way, 1998—2003, exec. com., 1998—2001, treas., 2000—01; bd. dirs. United Way of Carlsbad, 2004—, Ponderosa Joint Powers Agy. Harris County, 1977—83, pres., 1977—83; pres. bus. and industry adv. coun. North Harris Montgomery C. C. Dist., 1991—92. Contbr. articles to profl. jours. Recipient Disting. Svc. award Engrs. Coun. Houston, 1970, Outstanding Svc. award Houston sect. IEEE, 1974; named Tex. Young Engr. of Yr., 1976, Nat. Young Engr. of Yr., 1976. Mem. IEEE, Nat. Soc. Profl. Engrs. (chpt. pres. 1978, nat. chmn. engrs. in industry div. 1977, nat. v.p. 1977, chmn. nat. polit. action com. 1979-82, vice chmn. nat. engrs. week 1988-92, nat. trustee edn. found. 1988-90), Audubon Soc., Project Mgmt. Inst., Phi Kappa Phi, Tau Beta Pi. Office: Dept Energy PO Box 3090 Carlsbad NM 88221 0550 Home: PO Box 5342 Carlsbad NM 88221

PIPER, MARK HARRY, retired banker; b. Flint, Mich., Apr. 17, 1931; s. James U. and Dorothy (Weed) P.; m. Wanda L. Hubbard, June 20, 1953; children: Mark T., Kathryn L. BS, St. John's Mil. Acad., 1949; AB with distinction and honors in Econs, U. Mich., 1953, JD cum laude, 1956. Bar: Mich. 1956. With Clark, Klein, Winter, Parsons & Prewitt, Detroit, 1956-57, Genesee Mchts. Bank & Trust Co., Flint, 1957-88, v.p., sr. trust officer, 1966-72, sr. v.p., 1972-88, NBD Genesee Bank (formerly United Mich. Corp.), 1985-88, cashier, sec. bd. dirs., 1985-88. Adj. instr. bus. adminstrn. U. Mich., Flint, 1976-80; interim co-pension officer Detroit Conf. United Meth. Ch, 1993-99; pres. Flint Estate Planning Coun., 1969-70; mem. Flint citizens adv. coun. U. Mich., 1974-82; vice chmn., 1975-82. Bd. dir. Retirement Homes of Detroit Ann. Conf. Meth. Ch., 1964-76, vice chmn. profl. ministry and support, 1975, mem. bd. support systems, 1975, coun. fin. and adminstrn., 1976-84, chmn. coun. fin. and adminstrn., 1980-84; bd. dirs. United Meth. Devel. Fund, 1986-90; gen. bd. pensions United Meth. Ch., 1988-96, mem. investment com., gen. bd. pensions, 1988-2000; mem. investment com. United Meth. Found. of Detroit. Conf. of United Meth. Ch., 1993-, interim exec. dir., 2004-; trustee Flint YMCA Boysfarm Found., 1964-78, chmn., 1976-78; bd. mgmt. Flint YMCA Boysfarm, 1968-74; mem. Detroit Conf. Bd. P. United Meth. Ch., 1968-76, chmn., 1972-75, 88-2002, mem., 1986-2002; bd. dirs. U. Mich. Devel. Coun., 1980-82; bd. dirs., asst. treas., sec.-treas. Flint Area Young Life Found., 1979, Mich. Area Young Life Com., 1980-88; bd. dirs., vice chmn. The Crim Road Race Inc., 1985-87, bd. mem. Stewardship Found. Mich., 2002-. Mem. Mich. Bar Assn., Genesee County Bar Assn., Inst. Continuing Legal Edn., U. Mich.-Flint Club (bd. dirs., pres. 1973-74), Rotary Club. also: PO Box 3121 Estes Park CO 80517-3121 Personal E-mail: MHPiper3@aol.com.

PIPER, ODESSA, chef; m. Terry Theise. Chef L'Etoile Restaurant, Madison, Wis., 1976—. Contbr. Wis. Pub. Radio, NPR; cons. Ctr. for Integrated Agrl. Sys., U. Wis., Madison. Contbr. Fine Cooking, Food & Wine, Bon Appetit, Eating Well, Wine Spectator, Sierra. Recipient award, James Beard Found., 2001. Mem.: Women Chefs and Restauranteurs (mem. scholarship com.), Chefs Collaborative 2000 (bd. dirs.). Office: L'Etoile Restaurant 25 N Pinckney Madison WI 53711

PIPER, ROBERT JOHNSTON, retired architect, urban planner; b. Byron, Ill., Feb. 2, 1926; s. Leo Edward and Helen Anna (Johnston) P.; m. Carol Jane White, June 23, 1951; children— Christopher White, Brian Douglas, Eric Johnston. BS in Archtl. Engring, U. Ill., 1951; M. City and Regional Planning, Cornell U., 1953. Architect, planner Orput & Assos., Rockford, Ill., 1953-61; dir. profl. services AIA, Washington, 1961-67; partner, v.p. Perkins & Will, Chgo., 1967-74; dep. dir. Northeastern Ill. Planning Commn., Chgo., 1974-76; asso. Metz, Train, Olson & Youngren, Inc., Chgo., 1976-79; dir. community devel. City of Highland Park, Ill., 1980-91; ret., 1991; coord. Chgo. '93 and Chgo. Design Consortium Chgo. Cultural Ctr., 1992—. Pres. Landmarks Preservation Council Ill., Chgo., 1976-80 Author: Careers in Architecture, vocat. guidance manuals, 1967, 71, 75, 80, 85, 93; author, editor: Architect's Handbook of Professional Practice, 7th edit., 1963; prin. works include Regional Open Space Plan, Northeastern Ill., Spring Valley Operations Breakthrough Housing Complex, Kalamazoo, CBD Streetscape and Skokie Corridor Master Plan, Highland Park. Trustee Village of Winnetka, Ill., 1978-83; mem. Potomac Planning Task Force Dept. Interior, 1967-68, Commn. on Fed. Procurement, Washington, 1970-71; mem. nat. advisory bd. cmty. characteristics HEW, 1970-78; mem. Burnham Plan 1909 Centennial Com., 1999—. Served with USNR, 1944-46, PTO. Fellow AIA (mem. Task Force Future of Inst. 1974-75, various coms., pres AIA Ill. coun. 1986, Disting. Achievement awards AIA Ill., AIA Chgo. 1993), Am. Inst. Cert. Planners; mem. Lambda Alpha (Chgo. Chpt. Mem. of Yr. award 1999, Daniel H. Burnham Disting. Svc. award, 2004). Episcopalian. Home: 1132 Oak St Winnetka IL 60093-2132 E-mail: bobcarolpiper@aol.com.

PIPER, STEVEN LEE, economist; b. Fort Morgan, Colo. BS in Econ., Colo. State U., 1983, MS in Agrl. and Natural Resource Econ., 1985; PhD in Econ., Colo. Sch. of Mines, 1996. Agrl. economist USDA Econ. Rsch. Svc., Washington, 1985—89; natural resource economist U.S. Dept. Interior, Bur. of Reclamation, Denver, 1989—. Adj. assoc. prof. Colo. Sch. Mines, Golden, 1998—; online tutor Smarthinking, Inc., Washington, 2000—. Contbr. articles to profl. jours. Coach Youth Sports, Colo., 1996—2003. Mem.: Western Regional Sci. Assn. Avocations: restoring automobiles, lacrosse, guitar, weight training, camping. Office: US Bur Reclamation Denver Federal Center 6th and Kipling Denver CO 80225 Office Phone: 303-445-2736. Business E-Mail: spiper@do.usbr.gov.

PIPER, THOMAS LAURENCE, III, banker; b. Washington, June 20, 1941; s. Thomas Laurence and Edna (Milewski) P.; m. Ann Runnette, Apr. 8, 1967; children: Thomas Laurence IV, Andrew Kerr. Student, U. Va., 1959—61. Assoc. Hodgdon & Co., Inc., Washington, 1962-65; sr. v.p., dir. Hayden Stone Inc., N.Y.C., 1966-73; mng. dir. New Court Securities Corp., N.Y.C., 1974-81, Dillon, Read & Co., Inc., N.Y.C., 1981—97, UBS Warburg LLC, 1997—2000, Citigroup Pvt. Bank, 2000—03; sr. advisor The Nassau Group, 2003—. Chmn. fund dir. New Canaan chpt. ARC, 1978; bd. dirs. Manhattan coun. Boy Scouts Am., Waveny Care Ctr., New Canaan, Our Lady Queen of Angels, Manhattan; vice-chmn. adv. bd. U. Va. Art Mus., Charlottesville. Mem.: Bond Club NY, Investment Assn. NY (pres. 1974), Quail Valley Club, Red Stick Golf Club, Blind Brook Club, Country Club of New Canaan, Brook Club (N.Y.C.), Racquet and Tennis Club (N.Y.C.). Home: 14 Westmere Ave Rowayton CT 06853 E-mail: tpiper3@optonline.net.

PIPES, DANIEL, writer; b. Boston, Sept. 9, 1949; s. Richard and Irene (Roth) P.; married; three children Student, U. Tunis, Institut Bourguiba des Langues Vivantes, 1970; BA in History Sci., Harvard U., 1971; postgrad., U. Cairo, 1971-72, U. Calif. (Berkeley) Ctr. for Arabic Studies Abroad, Cairo, 1971, 1972-73; reader, Orientalisches Sem., Freiburg U., 1976; PhD in Mid. Ea. History, Harvard U., 1978; hon. degree, Am. Coll. of Switzerland, 1988, Yeshiva U., 2003. Vis. fellow Princeton U., 1977-78; Harper instr., rsch. assoc. U. Chgo., 1978-82, mem. policy planning staff, Dept. of State, 1982-83; lectr. history Harvard U., 1983-84; prof. U.S. Naval War Coll., 1984-86; dir. Fgn. Policy Rsch. Inst., Phila., 1986-93, Mid. East Forum, 1994—. Author: Slave Soldiers and Islam, 1981, In the Path of God, 1983, An Arabist's Guide to Egyptian Colloquial, 1983, The Long Shadow, 1988, Greater Syria, 1990, The Rushdie Affair, 1990, Damascus Courts the West, 1991, Syria Beyond the Peace Process, 1996, The Hidden Hand, 1996, Conspiracy, 1997, Militant Islam Reaches America, 2002, Miniatures, 2004; co-editor: Friendly Tyrants, 1991; editor: Sandstorm, 1993, Orbis: Jour. World Affairs, 1986-90, Mid. East Quar., 1994-2001; columnist Jerusalem Post, 1999—. Vice chmn. J. William Fulbright Scholarship Bd., 1992-95; bd. dirs. U.S. Inst. Peace, 2003-. Woodrow Wilson nat. fellow, 1971-72, fellow NDEA Title VI, 1974-76, Am. Rsch. Ctr. in Egypt, 1979, vis. fellow Heritage Found., 1984, Japan Soc., Nat. Inst. for Rsch. Advancement, Tokyo, 1985, Washington Inst. for Near East Policy, 1986, 91, 94-95; rsch. grantee Israel Inter-Univ., 1979, Smith Richardson Found., 1980-82, 95-96, Schumann Found., 1990-91, U.S. Inst. Peace, 1990-91, Ford Found., 1992-93, Scaife Found., 1995-96, Bradley Found., 1996-98. Mem. Coun. on Fgn. Rels. (internat. affairs fellow 1982-83). Office: Middle East Forum 1500 Walnut Street, Suite 1050 Philadelphia PA 19102 E-mail: Pipes@meforum.org.

PIPES, DORIS PERRY, secondary school educator, consultant; b. Tyrone, N.Y., Dec. 21, 1923; d. Raymond James and Mildred (Wood) Perry; m. Vernon Thomas Pipes, 1951 (div. 1965); 1 child, Vernon Thomas, Jr. AA, Cerritos Coll., 1962; BA, U. Calif., Fullerton, 1964; MA, U. Calif., L.A., 1972. Cert. secondary sch. tchr. Coord. spl. programs, dept. chair program Pioneer High Sch., Whittier, Calif., 1964-65, dir. reading program, coord. tchr. tng., dept. head, 1966-67; instr. grad. sch. Whittier Coll., 1967-71; tchg. cons., classroom materials cons. Scholastic Mag., N.Y.C., 1969-73; resource splst. Calif. High

Sch., Whittier, 1973-90, cons. math dept., 1988-90; ret., 1990. Vis. guest lectr., dir. elem. reading clinic Loyola U., L.A., 1967-70; cons. Inglewood High Sch., 1971-72; adminstr. field testing parallel tests in Spanish and English, 1971, 77; reading tchr. Whittier Adult Sch., 1962-66. Contbr. article to jour. Mem. PTA Calif. High Sch., 1964-90 Recipient PTA award, 1989; named Outstanding Secondary Sch. Reading Program Nat. Assn. Secondary Sch. Prins., 1972, Outstanding Secondary Educator of Yr. Outstanding Secondary Educators, 1973. Mem. Internat. Reading Assn. (pres. Rio Hondo coun. 1967), Calif. Tchrs. Assn. (chair), Calif. High Sch. Tchrs. Assn., Alpah Gamma Sigma. Avocations: travel, reading, gardening. Home: 1005 Sugarloaf Blvd Big Bear City CA 92314-9350

PIPES, PAUL RAY, county commissioner; b. Truscott, Tex., Oct. 1, 1928; s. David and Maggie (Brown) Pipes; m. Linda Mullins, Dec. 17, 1961; children: Dana, Tricia. BBA, Sam Houston U., 1956, MEd, 1971. Acct. Pan Am. Petroleum Corp., Thibodaux, La., 1956-61; bus. tchr. Brenham (Tex.) H.S., 1962-90; county commr. Washington County, Brenham, 1991-98. With U.S. Army, 1951-53, Korea. Decorated Def. Disting. Svc. medal. Republican. Methodist. Avocations: gardening, nature study. Home: 2106 Jane Ln Brenham TX 77833-5331

PIPES, RICHARD, historian, educator; b. Cieszyn, Poland, July 11, 1923; came to U.S., 1940, naturalized, 1943; s. Mark and Sophia (Haskelberg) P.; m. Irene Eugenia Roth, Sept. 1, 1946; children— Daniel, Steven. Student, Muskingum (Ohio) Coll., 1940-43; AB, Cornell U., 1945; PhD, Harvard U., 1950; LLD (hon.), Muskingum Coll., 1988; LHD (hon.), Adelphi U., 1991; Doctor honoris causa, U. Silesia, Poland, 1994. Mem. faculty Harvard U., 1950—, prof. history, 1958-75, Frank B. Baird Jr. prof. history, 1975-96, Baird prof. emeritus, 1996-98, Baird Rsch. Prof., 1998-2001, Baird prof. emeritus, 2001—. Assoc. dir. Russian Rsch. Ctr., 1962-64, dir., 1968-73; sr. cons. Stanford Research Inst., 1973-78; expert Russian Constl. Ct., 1992; dir. East European and Soviet affairs NSC, 1981-82. Author: Formation of the Soviet Union, rev. edit., 1964, Karamzin's Memoir on Ancient and Modern Russia, 1959, Social Democracy and the St. Petersburg Labor Movement, 1963, Europe Since 1815, 1970, Struve: Liberal on the Left, 1870-1905, 1970, Russia Under the Old Regime, 1974, Struve: Liberal on the Right, 1905-1944, 1980, U.S.-Soviet Relations in the Era of Detente, 1981, Survival Is Not Enough, 1984, Russia Observed, 1989, The Russian Revolution, 1990, Communism: The Vanished Specter, 1993, Russia Under the Bolshevik Regime, 1994, A Concise History of the Russian Revolution, 1995, Three "Whys" of the Russian Revolution, 1996, Property and Freedom, 1999, Communism: A History, 2001, The Degaev Affair: Terror and Treason in Tsarist Russia, 2003, Vixi: The Memoir of a Non-Belonger, 2003; editor: Russian Intelligentsia, 1961; (with John Fine) Of the Russe Commonwealth (Giles Fletcher), 1966, Revolutionary Russia, 1968, Collected Works in Fifteen Volumes (P.B. Struve), 1970, Soviet Strategy in Europe, 1976, The Unknown Lenin, 1996; mem. editl. bd. Strategic Rev., Comparative Strategy, Jour. Strategic Studies, Internat. Jour. Intelligence and Counterintelligence, Nuova Storia Contemporanea. Mem. exec. com. Com. on Present Danger, 1977-92; chmn. Govt. Team B to Rev. Intelligence Estimates, 1976; mem. Reagan transition team Dept. State, 1980. Served with USAAF, 1943-46. Guggenheim fellow, 1956, 65, Walter Cabot Channing fellow Harvard U., 1990-91; fellow Am. Coun. Learned Socs., 1965; fellow Ctr. for Advanced Study in Behavioral Scis., Stanford, Calif., 1969-70; lectr. Spring lecture Norwegian Nobel Peace Inst., Oslo, 1993; recipient George Louis Beer prize Am. Historical Assn., 1955, Comdr.'s Cross of Merit, Republic of Poland, 1996; hon. consul Republic of Ga., 1997—, hon. citizen, 1997—. Fellow Am. Acad. Arts and Scis.; mem. Coun. Fgn. Rels., Polish Acad. (fgn. mem.). Home: 17 Berkeley St Cambridge MA 02138-3409 E-mail: rpipes23@aol.com.

PIPES, ROBERT BYRON, mechanical engineer, educator; b. Shreveport, La., Aug. 14, 1941; s. Walter H. and Mattye Mae (Wilson) P.; m. Ruth Ellen Franz, June 27, 1964; children: Christopher Franz, Mark Robert. BS, La. Poly. Inst., 1964, MS, 1965; MSE, MA, Princeton U., 1969; PhD, U. Tex., 1972. Sr. structures engr. Gen. Dynamics Corp., 1969-72; asst. prof. mech. engring. Drexel U., 1972-74; assoc. prof. mech. and aerospace engring. U. Del., 1974-80, prof., 1980-91, also dir. Center Composite Materials, 1978-85, dean Coll. Engring., 1985-91, provost, v.p. acad. affairs, 1991-93; pres. Rensselaer Polytech. Inst., N.Y., 1993-98; dir. Nat. Ctr. Composites Mfg. Sci. and Engring., 1985; Goodyear Prof. Polymer Engring. U. Akron, Ohio, 2001—. Disting. vis. scientist Coll. of William and Mary, 1998—2001; cons. in field; com. mem. NRC. Author: Experimental Mechanics of Fiber Reinforced Composite Materials, 1982, Characterization of Advanced Composite Materials, 1987, 3d edit., 2002; series editor 12 vols. Composite Materials; contbr. articles to profl. jours. Mem. ASME (Gustus Larson award 1983), Soc. Mfg. Engrs., Soc. Advancement of Material and Processing Engring., Nat. Acad. Engring. (elected 1987), Swedish Acad. Engring., Am. Soc. Composites, ASTM, Sigma Xi, Tau Beta Pi, Pi Tau Sigma, Omicron Delta Kappa. Methodist. Home: PO Box 1147 Hudson OH 44236-1147 Office: PEAC 22 Univ Akron Akron OH 44325-0301 E-mail: bpipes@uakron.edu.

PIPES, SALLY C. think-tank executive; Asst. dir. Fraser Inst., Vancouver, Canada, 1974—91; pres., CEO Pacific Rsch. Inst. for Pub. Policy, San Francisco, 1991—. Co-author (with Spencer Star): Income and Taxation in Canada, (with Michael Walker) 7 editions of Tax Facts; has appeared nationally on TV programs such as 20/20 and Politically Incorrect, Dateline, Inside Politics and PBS's Think Tank; regularly asked to comment on timely issues by radio and print journalists; opinion editls. have been published in various newspapers including San Francisco Chronicle, L.A. Times, Investor's Business Daily, L.A. Daily News, The Orange County Register; writes a bi-monthly column in Chief Executive mag. Bd. dirs. Fin. Instns. Commn. (B.C.), 1980-84 (vice chmn. 1982-84, chmn. 1989-); mem. Vancouver City Planning Commn., 1982-84; trustee St. Luke's Hosp. Found. in San Francisco; bd. dirs. Ind. Women's Forum; mem. bd. advisors Western Jour. Ctr. and Citizens for Term Limits, San Francisco Lawyers chpt. of the Federalist Soc.; commr. Calif. Commn. on Transp. Investment, 1996; bd. govs. Donner-Can. Found. Mem. Mont Pelerin Soc., Nat. Assn. Bus. Economists, Can. Assn. for Bus. Econs. (pres. 2 terms), Assn. Profl. Economists of B.C. Office: Pacific Rsch Inst Pub Policy 755 Sansome St Ste 450 San Francisco CA 94111-1709 Office Phone: 415-955-6100.

PIPITONE, PHYLLIS L. psychologist, educator, author; b. Chgo. m. Joseph Pipitone, Aug. 28, 1948 (dec.); children: Guy, Daniel, Paul; m. Thomas A. Cox, Jan. 3, 1980. Student, Chgo. Conservatory Music, 1941-44, Peabody Conservatory Music, Balt., 1945, Chgo. Tchrs. Coll., 1946-47, So. Meth. U., 1951-52; MA, U. Akron, 1967; PhD, Kent State U., 1974. With B.S. and H. Advt. Agy., Chgo., 1974; instr. piano and theory Music Acad. Chgo.; psychologist, instr. U. Akron and Kent State U., 1970-79; pvt. practice psychology Akron, 1967—. Lectr. in field in U.S and abroad. With WAC, AUS, 1944-46. NIMH grantee, 1974, HEW Child Devel. fellow, 1974. Mem. Am. Psychol. Assn., Nat. Assn. Sch. Psychologists, Mensa, Coun. Exceptional Children, Am. Hypnosis Soc., Study/Dreams, Am. Soc. Psychical Rsch., Akron Women's City Club, Wadsworth Women's Club, Phi Delta Kappa. Home: 224 Pheasant Run Wadsworth OH 44281-2344

PIPKIN, JAMES HAROLD, JR., lawyer; b. Houston, Jan. 3, 1939; s. James Harold and Zenda Marie (Lewis) P. BA, Princeton U., 1960; JD, Harvard U., 1963; Diploma in Law, Oxford (Eng.) U., 1965. Bar: D.C. 1964, U.S. Supreme Ct. 1969, D.C. Ct. Appeals, 1972. Law ck. to assoc. justice U.S. Supreme Ct., Washington, 1963-64; assoc. Steptoe and Johnson, Washington, 1965-70, ptnr., 1971-93; counselor to The Sec. of the Interior U.S. Dept. of the Interior, 1993-98; U.S. spl. negotiator for Pacific Salmon, Dept. of State, 1994-2001; rank of amb. Dept. of State, 1995-96; dir. office policy analysis U.S. Dept. Interior, 1998-2001; fgn. affairs officer U.S. State Dept., 2001—02. Counsel Friends of Music, Smithsonian Inst., Washington, 1984-88; mem. Nat. Arbitration Panel, 1983-94. Author or co-author: The English Country House: A Grand Tour, 1985, The Country House Garden: A Grand Tour, 1987, Places of Tranquility, 1990; contbr. photographs and articles to mags. including House & Garden, Smithsonian mag., The Mag. Antiques, Archtl. Digest. Grand officier Confrérie des Chevaliers du Tastevin, 1989—. Mem. ABA, D.C. Bar Assn., Met. Club. Home: 6109 Davenport Ter Bethesda MD 20817-5827

PIPKIN, MARVIN GRADY, lawyer; b. San Angelo, Tex., Nov. 15, 1949; s. Raymond Grady and Lillie Marie (Smith) P.; m. Dru Cheatham, July 24, 1971; children: Lacey Elizabeth, Matthew Todd. BBA, U. Tex., 1971, JD, 1974. Bar: Tex. 1974, U.S. Dist. Ct. (we. dist.) Tex. 1979, U.S. Ct. Appeals (5th cir.) 1983. Assoc. Green & Kaufman, San Antonio, 1974-79, ptnr., 1979-82, Kendrick & Pipkin, San Antonio, 1982-93, Drought & Pipkin L.L.P., San Antonio, 1993-98, Pipkin, Oliver & Bradley, LLP, San Antonio, 1998—. Mem. coms. on ethics and admissions Tex. Supreme Ct., admissions com.; adv. dir. Trinity Nat. Bank, San Antonio, 1983; bd. dirs. Allied Am. Bank, San Antonio, First Interstate Bank, San Antonio. Bd. dirs. Monte Vista Hist. Assn., San Antonio, 1975-78. Fellow Tex. Bar Found., San Antonio Bar Found.; mem. ABA, Tex. Assn. Def. Counsel, Tex. Bar Assn., Tex. Assn. Bank Counsel, San Antonio Bar Assn., Tex. Wildlife Assn. (dir. 1998-2004). Republican. Methodist. Avocations: sports, outdoor activities. Office: Pipkin Oliver & Bradley LLP 1020 NE 600 P 410 #810 San Antonio TX 78209 Office Phone: 210-820-0082. E-mail: mpipkin@pobllp.com.

PIPKIN, MARY MARGARET, artist; b. San Angelo, Tex., Mar. 17, 1951; d. Raymond G. and Lillie Marie S. (Billie) Pipkin; m. Robert A Boisture; children: Will, John, Jamie. BA U. Tex., MA U. Tex. One-woman shows include Addison Tate Gallery, Washington, Zigler Mus., Jennings, La., 2002, Louisburg (NC) Coll., 2003, Art Sta., Stone Mountain, Ga., 2003, Anderson (Ind.) Art Ctr., Ind., 2003, Mus. S.W., Midland, Tex., 2003, exhibitions include White House, Washington.

PIPPEN, SCOTTIE, professional basketball player; b. Hamburg, Ark., Sept. 25, 1965; Student, U. Ctrl. Ark., 1983—87. With Seattle Super Sonics, 1987; guard/forward Chgo. Bulls, 1987—98, Houston Rockets, 1998—99, Portland Trailblazers, Oreg., 1999—. Player NBA Championship Team, 1991, 92, U.S. Olympic Basketball Team, 1992, NBA Championship Team, 1993, 96. Named NBA All-Star Most Valuable Player, 1994; named to All-Star team, 1990, NBA All-Defensive 2d team, 1991, NBA All-Star team, 1992—94, All-Star team, 1992—93, NBA All-Defensive 1st team, 1992, 1993, 1994, All-NBA 1st team, 1994. Office: Portland Trailblazers One Ctr Ct Ste 200 Portland OR 97227

PIPPI, MIKEL EUGENE, cultural attache, television producer, arts administrator, television director; b. Portland, Oreg., Apr. 20, 1947; BA, Lewis and Clark Coll., 1969. Exec. dir. Frohman Acad./Am. Musical Theatre Festival, Inc., Carmel, Calif., 1983-91; dir. internat. rels., co-founder, dir. internat. rels. Acad. Russian TV, Moscow, 1992-95; dir. spl. projects Turner Internat. Broadcasting, Atlanta and, Russia, 1993-95; global dir., artist recruitment and tng. Walt Disney Feature Animation, Burbank, Calif., 1996-99; exec. dir. Regional Arts and Culture Coun., Portland, Oreg., 1999—2000; dir. creative industries studies Portland (Oreg.) State U., 2000—04. Mem. nat. policy bd. Americans for The Arts, Washington, 1999-2001; am. placement agent Russian Ministry of Culture, Moscow, 1987-92; vice chair cultural affairs com. St. Petersburg and LA Sister City Programs, 1991-95. Avocations: internat. rels., mktg. and promotions, global event mgmt. Home: PO Box 22962 Carmel CA 93922-0962

PIPPIN, JAMES ADRIAN, JR., middle school educator; b. Rockingham, N.C., Aug. 6, 1954; s. James A. Sr. and Essie Juanita (Rorie) P. BS, Appalachian State U., 1976; MEd, Columbus Coll., 1982. Tchr. Eddy Jr. H.S., Columbus, Ga., 1976-89; dir. N.C. Agrl. Extension Svc., Penn 4-H Ctr., Reidsville, 1980-89, Millstone 4-H Camp, Ellerbe, N.C., 1993; tchr. Arnold Mid. Sch., Columbus, Ga., 1989-99, Rockingham (N.C.) Jr. High Sch., 1999—. Mem. multicultural curriculum com., sick leave bank com., textbook adoption com. and tech. com. MCSD; tchg. program participant Found. Internat. Edn., Inverness, Scotland, 1986, Dunedin, New Zealand, 1989; curriculum devel. program participant Ga. Dept. Edn., Germany, 1989, 91; adv. com. Deutsche Welle Video, 1992, 95; internat. edn. adv. com. Ga. Dept. Edn., 1993—; tchr. cons. N.C. Geographic Alliance. Author: The Physiological and Psychological Effects of Space Flight Environments on Blood Glucose and Circadian Rhythms of the Human Body; contb. author: (curricuums) World Studies, Germany and Georgia: The Search for Unity, Education in Thailand, Germany Unity and Disunity: Ubersichten; Overview of the Federal Republic of Germany, Images of Germany: Past and Present, The Olympic Spirit; A Worldwide Connection, Vol. III. Mem. discovery gallery com. Columbus Mus. Arts & Scis., curriculum devel. com. Atlanta Com. for Olympic Games. Named Ga. State semi-finalist, NASA Tchr. Space Program, 1985, Richmond County Tchr. of Yr., 2003; named to USA Today All-U.S.A. 1st Tchr. Team, 1998; recipient Project award TV Worth Tchg., CBS, 1987; Fulbright scholar, Taiwan and Thailand, 1992. Mem. ASCD, NEA (congl. contact team), Columbus Social Sci. Alliance (bd. dirs.), Ga. Assn. Educators, Nat. Coun. Social Scis., Ga. Coun. Social Scis. (bd. dirs.), N.C. Assn. Educators, Musogee Assn. Edn. (v.p., 2d v.p., chmn. policies and grievences com., legis. com., chmn. officer nominating com.), Columbus Hist. Soc., Columbus Hist. Dist. Preservation Soc. (bd. dirs.), Chattahoochee Valley Archaeol. Soc., Phi Alpha Theta, Phi Delta Kappa.

PIPPIN, M. LENNY, food products executive; BA, Fla. Atlantic U. CEO Lykes Bros. Inc., Tampa, Fla., 1997-99; pres., CEO Schwan's Sales Enterprises, Marshall, Minn., 1999—. Bd. dirs.Lykes Bros.; former CEO Albert FIscher, Dallas. Office: Schwan's Sales Enterprises 115 W College Dr Marshall MN 56258

PIQUÉ, FERNANDO RAFAEL, international art dealer, artist; b. Havana, Cuba, Oct. 24, 1952; came to U.S., 1961; s. Arturo Raimundo and Arthemis (Serru) P.; m. Joan Dee Bennett, July 23, 1985 (div. Apr. 1996); 1 child, Nicole Erin. Grad. high sch., Miami, Fla. Dist. mgr. EHP, Inc., Pompano Beach, Fla., 1970-76; internat. account exec. to Africa, Europe, Mid. East, N.Am., South America Am. Beverage Machinery, Inc., Miami, 1976-78; salesman new car dealerships, Miami, 1978-81; account exec. Heath and Co., Dallas, 1981-83; founder, CEO Emporium Enterprises, Inc., Dallas, 1982-97, You Name It-We Frame It, Dallas, 1984—97, Emporium Art and Frames, Dallas, 1986-97, Club Emporium, Dallas, 1988-97, The Enchanted Galleries, Dallas, 1998-2000, Mission Gallery, Dallas, 2000, Piqué Fernando R., 1997—, theunknownartist-.com, Dallas, 2000—. Broker and cons. to collectors, galleries and frame shops. Mem. Profl. Picture Framers Assn. (adv. bd. North Tex. chpt. 1989), Profl. Assn. Divers Internat., Nat. Assn. Underwater Instrs. Republican. Roman Catholic. Avocations: movies, art, museums, collectables, painting. the. Office: theunkownartist dot com 610 Stone Canyon Dr Irving TX 75063 E-mail: pique_@hotmail.com, theunknownartist@hotmail.com.

PIRANI, CONRAD LEVI, pathologist, educator; b. Pisa, Italy, July 29, 1914; came to U.S., 1939, naturalized, 1945; s. Mario Giacomo Levi and Adriana P.; m. Luciana Nahmias, Mar. 12, 1955; children: Barbara, Sylvia, Robert. Diploma, Ginnasio-Liceo Beccaria, 1932; MD, U. Milano, Italy, 1938. Intern Columbus Meml. Hosp., Chgo., 1940-42; resident Michael Reese Hosp., Chgo., 1942-45; dir. exptl. pathology sect. U.S. Army Med. Nutrition Lab., Chgo., 1947—52; instr. pathology U. Ill., Chgo., 1945-48, asst. prof., 1948-52, asso. prof., 1952-55, prof., 1955-70; chmn. dept. pathology Michael Reese Hosp., Chgo., 1965-72; prof. pathology Coll. Physicians and Surgeons, Columbia U., N.Y.C., 1972-84, prof. emeritus, 1985—. Cons. Armed Forces Inst. Pathology; dir. Renal Pathology Lab., 1972-84; mem. sci. com. Kidney Found., N.Y., 1973-80; cons. and spl. lectr. Columbia U., 1985-95; mem. pathology study sect. NIH, 1973-78. Contbg. author various books.; assoc. editor Lab. Investigation, 1972-82, Nephron, 1975-92, Clin. Nephrology, 1989-92; contbr. numerous articles to profl. jours. USPHS, NIH grantee. Mem. Am. Assn. Pathologists, AAAS, Internat. Acad. Pathology (counselor 1966-69), Am. Soc. Nephrology (John P. Peters award 1987), Internat. Soc. Nephrology. Home and Office: 235 Walker St Apt 233 Lenox MA 01240-2748

PIRCHER, LEO JOSEPH, lawyer, director; b. Berkeley, Calif., Jan. 4, 1933; s. Leo Charles and Christine (Moore) P.; m. Phyllis McConnell, Aug. 4, 1956 (div. Apr. 1981); children: Christopher, David, Eric; m. Nina Silverman, June 14, 1987. BS, U. Calif., Berkeley, 1954, JD, 1957. Bar: Calif. 1958, (N.Y.) 1985, cert.: Calif. Bd. Legal Specialization (cert. specialist taxation law). Assoc. Lawler, Felix & Hall, L.A., 1957-62, ptnr., 1962-65, sr. ptnr., 1965-83, Pircher, Nichols & Meeks, L.A., 1983—. Adj. prof. Loyola U. Law Sch., L.A., 1959—61; corp. sec. Am. Metal Bearing Co., Gardena, Calif., 1975—; dir. Varco Internat., Inc., Orange, Calif.; spkr. various law schs. and bar assns. edn. programs. Author (with others): (novels) Definition and Utility of Leases, 1968. Chmn. pub. fin. and taxation sect. Calif. Town Hall, L.A., 1970—71. Mem.: ABA, Nat. Assn. Real Estate Investment Trusts Inc. (cert. specialist taxation law), L.A. County Bar Assn. (exec. com. comml. law sect.), N.Y. State Bar, Calif. State Bar, Regency (L.A.). Republican. Office: Pircher Nichols & Meeks Ste 1700 1925 Century Park E Los Angeles CA 90067-6022 Office Phone: 310-201-8901. Personal E-mail: lpircher@pircher.com.

PIRCHNER, HERMAN, JR., foreign policy specialist; b. Cleve., June 26, 1946; s. Herman Sr. and Constance Pirchner; m. Elizabeth Scull Wood. BBA, U. Toledo, 1970. Dir. fin. Chuck Grassley for U.S. Senate, Des Moines, 1979-80; dir. legislation U.S. Senator Roger Jepsen, Washington, 1981-82; pres. Am. Fgn. Policy Coun., Washington, 1982—, also bd. dirs. Bd. dirs. Geoinformatic, Inc., Front Royal, Va.; cons. to polit. campaigns Roger Jepsen for U.S. Senate, Iowa, 1982-84, Bob Kasten for U.S. Senate, Wis., 1982-86, George Voinovich for U.S. Senate, Ohio, 1988. Bd. dirs. Herbert Hoover Presdl. Libr. Assn., 1998—. Mem. Univ. Club. Republican. Avocations: pocket billiards, chess, squash. Office: Am Fgn Policy Coun 1521 16th St NW Washington DC 20036-1463 E-mail: herpirch@aol.com.

PIRIE, ROBERT BURNS, JR., defense analyst; b. San Diego, Sept. 10, 1933; s. Robert Burns and Gertrude May (Freeman) P.; m. Joan Adams, Dec. 23, 1960; children: John Winthrop, Carl Joseph Emil, Susan Gilman. Student, Princeton U., 1950-51; BS, U.S. Naval Acad., 1955; BA, Magdalen Coll., Oxford U., 1959, MA, 1963. Commd. ensign U.S. Navy, 1955, advanced through grades to comdr., 1969; comdg. officer (U.S.S. Skipjack), 1969-72; dep. asst. dir. Congl. Budget Office, 1975-77; prin. dep. asst. sec. for manpower, res. affairs and logistics Dept. Def., Washington, 1977-79, asst. sec., 1979-81; mgmt. cons., 1981—; def. analyst Ctr. for Naval Analyses, Alexandria, Va., 1981-83; asst. v.p. Inst. for Def. Analyses, Alexandria, 1983-86, v.p., 1986-87; exec. v.p. Essex Corp., Alexandria, 1987, pres., 1987-88; sr. economist Rand Corp., Washington, 1989; dir. strategic studies group U.S. Naval War Coll., 1989-92; v.p. Ctr. Naval Analyses, Alexandria, 1992-94; asst. sec. of Navy for Installations and Environ. USN, Washington, 1994-2000, undersec. of Navy, 2000—01; sr. fellow Ctr. for Naval Analysis, 2001—. Vestryman St. John's Episcopal Ch., Chevy Chase, Md., 1973-76, 81, jr. warden, 1982-84, sr. warden, 1984-87; trustee U.S. Naval Acad. Found., 1980-94. Rhodes scholar, 1956 Mem. U.S. Naval Inst., U.S. Naval Acad. Alumni Assn. (trustee 1967-70), Vincent's Club, Cosmos Club. E-mail: rpirie@aol.com.

PIRKEY, LOUIS THOMAS, lawyer; b. Ft. Worth, Dec. 6, 1937; s. Louis F. and Juanita (Copeland) P.; m. Jewell Katherine Buchanan, Oct. 19, 1940; children— Julia Hope, Jeffry Thomas. B.S.Ch.E., U. Tex., 1960; J.D. with honors, George Washington U., 1964. Bar: Tex. 1964, U.S. Supreme Ct. 1981, U.S. Ct. Appeals (5th and 11th cirs.), U.S. Dist. Ct. (we., so. and ea. dists.) Tex. Mem. Arnold, White & Durkee, Houston, 1964—, 1969—; chmn. intellectual property law sect. State Bar of Tex., 1982-83; mem. U.S. delegation Diplomatic Conf. on Rev. of Paris Conv., 1982. Fellow Tex. Bar Found.; mem. U.S. Trademark Assn. (dir.), ABA (chmn. Fed. trademark legislation com. 1972-74), Am. Patent Law Assn., Houston Bar Assn., Houston Patent Law Assn., Travis County Bar Assn., Licensing Execs. Soc., Interam. Assn. for Protection of Intellectual Property, Internat. Assn. Protection of Intellectual Property, Order of Coif, Phi Alpha Delta. Clubs: Headliners, Capital, Westwood Country (Austin); Univ. (Houston). Office: 600 Congress Ave Ste 2300 Austin TX 78701-2977

PIRKL, JAMES JOSEPH, industrial designer, educator, writer; b. Nyack, NY, Dec. 27, 1930; s. James and Ida Bertha (Gigrich) P.; m. Sarah B. W. Woolsey, June 8, 1974; children: Theo, James, Philip. Cert. advt. design, Pratt Inst., 1951, B of Indsl. Design cum laude, 1958. Design staff Gen. Motors Corp., Warren, Mich., 1958-65, sr. designer, 1961-64, asst. chief designer, 1964-65; instr. indsl. design Center for Creative Studies, Detroit, 1963-65; faculty dept. design Syracuse (N.Y.) U., 1965-92, assoc. prof., 1969-73, prof. indsl. design, 1974-92, prof. emeritus, 1992—, coord. indsl. design program, 1979-84, chmn. dept. design, 1985-91; exec. council chmn. Sch. Art, 1976-78, 80-81; sr. rsch. fellow All-U. Gerontology Ctr., 1990-92. Prin. James J. Pirkl/Design, 1965—; cons. Am. Soc. on Aging, 1995, Arthritis Found., 1993-96, GE Appliances, 1994, ProMatura Group, 1994—, Ford Motor Design Ctr., 1992, Loretto Geriatric Ctr., Pulos Design Assocs., 1972-80, Fed. Prison Industries, 1974, Gen. Electric Co., 1967-70, N.Y. State Coun. on Arts, 1968-69, Xerox Corp., 1975, Age Wave, Inc., 1993-96, universal kitchen product R.I. Sch. Design, 1996-98, The Boeing Co., 2004; chmn. accreditation council Design Found., 1982-84; interviewed on Nat. Pub. Radio, 1998; invited lectr. All Union Rsch. Inst., Moscow, 1974, The Bauhaus, Desseau, Germany, 1976, Royal Coll. Art, London, 1993, 95, Netherlands Design Inst., Amsterdam, 1993, 95, Inst. for Gerontech., Eindhoven, 1995, Nat. Coll. Art and Design, Dublin, Ireland, 1995, U. Art and Design, Helsinki, 1995, China Instnl. Design Assn., Taiwan, 1990, Korea Indsl. Design Soc., Taijon, 1992, Internat. Universal Design Symposium, Tokyo, 2001; project dir. The Transgenerational House, 2000—. Author: Transgenerational Design: Products for an Aging Population, 1994; co-author: Guidelines and Strategies for Designing Transgenerational Products, 1988; co-editor: State of Art and Science of Design, 1971; co-designer: Gen. Motors Futurama Exhbn., N.Y. World's Fair, 1964-65; contbr. articles to profl. jours. including Jour. Am. Soc. Aging, Design Mgmt. Jour., Jour. Indsl. Designers Soc. Am., Bus. Adminstrn. Jour., Design News, Design Perspectives, Indsl. Design. Mem. Everson Mus. Art, 1977-85; chmn. planning commn. Town of Cazenovia, N.Y., 1988-93; mem. senate Syracuse U., 1973-80; mem. adv. bd. SEARS Project, 1989-91; chmn. chancellor's citation com., 1988-92; mem. exhbns. com. Syracuse Cultural Resources Coun., 1992-93; coord. Tylenol/Arthritis Found. Student Design Awards Program, 1993-95. With SeaBees USN, 1951-55. Recipient Gold Indsl. Design Excellence award, Indsl. Designers Soc. Am. and Bus. Week Mag., 1994. Fellow: Indsl. Designers Soc. Am. (nat. bd. dirs. 1977—81, chmn. Ctrl. N.Y. chpt. 1977—81, v.p. Mid-East region 1978—81, chmn. NASAD liaison com. 1984—88, archives com. 1988—92, U.S. rep., del. Internat. Congress Socs. Indsl. Design 1989, chmn. universal design com. 1991—94, Edn. award 2001); mem.: Author's Guild, Am. Soc. Aging (contbr. articles to jour.), Nat. Ctr. for a Barrier Free Environment (adv. task force 1981), Human Factors Soc. (life), Nat. Assn. Schs. Art and Design (accreditation evaluator 1985—95), The Design Found. (chmn. accreditation coun. 1982). Achievements include patents for 4-way handle. Home: 3 Cloud View Ct Placitas NM 87043-5854 Personal E-mail: transgen@earthlink.net. Business E-mail: jjp@transgenerational.org.

PIRKLE, GEORGE EMORY, television and film actor, director; b. Sept. 3, 1947; s. George Washington and Glanna Adeline (Palmer) P.; m. Karen Leigh Horn, Oct. 20, 1973; 1 child, Charity Caroline. Student, North Ga. Coll., 1965-66; BA in Journalism, U. Ga., 1969, MA, 1971. Radio announcer, sportscaster various radio stations, North Ga. area, 1968-70; TV prodr., dir. Instructional Resources Ctr., Athens, Ga., 1969-70; info. officer Southeastern Signal Sch., U.S. Army, 1971; prodr., dir. DA MoPic Svc. Continental Army Command Network and Signal Corps TV Divsn., 1972-73; pub. info. officer Ga. Dept. Revenue, Atlanta, 1973-78; coord. TV prodn. svcs. So. Co. Svcs., Inc., Birmingham, Ala., 1978-88; exec. v.p. Mgmt. and Human Devel. Assocs., Inc., Birmingham, Ala., 1984-86; prodr. Prodn. Works, Birmingham, Ala., 1984-88. Actor for various radio and TV commercials, corp. TV programs, radio dramas, stage plays, 1968—; owner Talking Rock Prodns., Cumming, Ga., 1989—; instr. Cliff Osmond Acting Program, 1989-92 Editor monthly newsletter Ga. Revenews, 1973-78; editor, dir. Bankers TV Network, 1990-92; writer, prodr., dir., exec. prodr. more than 500 corp. and pub. svc. TV and film programs; exec. prodr. videotape for Birmingham Film Coun., 1985; prodr.,

dir. Highway in Crisis, 1986; writer, prodr., dir. campaign film Birmingham Area United Way, 1981, 86, 87; writer, prodr., narrator, 1987 campaign film; anchor This Week in Banking, 1990-92. Mem. Comms. com. Birmingham Area couns. Boy Scouts Am., 1983—85; master of ceremonies, gov.'s vet. awards presentation World Peace Luncheon, 1981, 82, 84, Birmingham; dir., campaign film United Way, Pensacola, 1989; bd. directors Birmingham Internat. Ednl. Film Festival, 1987—91; chmn. Sadie award com.; dir. student video competition; comml. acting instr. elan/Casablancas Modeling/Career Ctr., 1988—92; mem., tech. steering com. Forsyth Bd. Edn., 1995; mem. City Parks Recreation Bd., 1996—; bd. dirs. United Way of Forsyth County, 1995—2004, v.p. allocations, 2003, permanent mem., allocations com., 2000—; mem., vice chair Forsyth County Bd. Ethics, 2002—; vol. Am. Cancer Soc. Relay for Life, 1996—2002. 1st lt. U.S. Army, 1971—73. Recipient So. Superlative Outstanding employee award, So. Co. Svcs., 1986, Battles award 1988, various others. Mem.: So. Electric Sys. Visual Comms. Subcom. (founding), Internat. TV Assn. (charter pres. Birmingham chapter 1984—85, pres. pro tem 1984, editor newsletter Freeze Frame), Hist. Soc. Forsyth County (pres. 1996), Ga. Hist. Soc., Rotary Club (Paul Harris fellow 2001), Cumming/Forsyth C. of C. (Bus. Mem. of the Yr. 2002). Avocations: photography, astronomy, genealogy, hist. rsch., archaeology. E-mail: trvideo@bellsouth.net.

PIRMOT, THOMAS L. mathematician, educator; b. Scranton, Pa., Sept. 3, 1943; s. Victor D. and Julia M. Pirmot; m. Ann Wawrzak Pirmot, Dec. 28, 1968; children: Matthew, Anthony, Joanna, Michael. BA in Music, Wilkes Coll., 1965; PhD in Math., Pa. State U., 1970. Prof. math. Kutztown U., Pa., 1970—. Author: Mathematics: Tools & Models, 1977, Mathematics All Around, 2001, 2d edit., 2004. Named Disting. Tchg. Chair, State of Pa., 1979. Mem.: Nat. Coun. Tchrs. Math., Am. Math. Assn. Two Yr. Colls., Math. Assn. Am. Roman Catholic. Avocation: tennis. Home: 201 Fairview Dr Kutztown PA 19530 Office: Kutztown U Kutztown PA 19530 Office Phone: 610-683-4424. E-mail: pirnot@kutztown.edu.

PIRODSKY, DONALD MAX, psychiatrist, educator; b. Freeport, N.Y., Feb. 2, 1945; s. Max and Doris Geilhard (Biedermann) P.; m. Gail Giufre Pallotta, Jan. 4, 1997; children: Laura Anne, Jason Donald. BA, Hofstra U., 1966; MD, SUNY, Syracuse, 1970. Diplomate Am. Bd. Psychiatry and Neurology, Nat. Bd. Med. Examiners. Intern Northwestern U. Med. Ctr., Chgo., 1970-71; resident in psychiatry Strong Meml. Hosp., Rochester, N.Y., 1973-74, U. Ariz. Med. Ctr., Tucson, 1974-76; instr. psychiatry SUNY Health Sci. Ctr., Syracuse, 1976-78, attending psychiatrist, 1976-91, asst. prof. psychiatry, 1978-85, mem. exec. com. of med. coll. assembly, 1979-82, clin. assoc. prof., 1985—, adj. attending psychiatrist, 1991—; pvt. practice Syracuse and Fayetteville, N.Y., 1976—; staff psychiatrist, dir. consultation/liaison svc. Syracuse VA Med. Ctr., 1976-87, chmn. pharmacy rev. and therapeutic agts. com., 1980-86. Psychiat. cons. Ariz. Sch. for Deaf and Blind, Tucson, 1975-76, Syracuse Devel. Ctr., 1977—, Rochester Sch. for Deaf, 1978-81; ex-officio mem. Family Counseling Agy., Tucson, 1975-76; adj. attending psychiatrist SUNY Health Sci. Ctr., Syracuse, 1991—. Author: Primer of Clinical Psychopharmacology: A Practical Guide, 1981, (with Jerry S. Cohn) Clinical Primer of Psychopharmacology: A Practical Guide, 2d edit., 1992; contbr. articles to profl. jours., chpts. to med. books. Lt. comdr. USPHS, 1971 73. Fellow Am. Psychiat. Assn. (Disting., mem. cen. N.Y. dist. br.); mem. Am. Psychosomatic Soc., Am. Assn. Mental Retardation, Med. Soc. State of N.Y., N.Y. State Psychiat. Assn., Onondaga County Med. Soc. Episcopalian. Avocations: sports, collecting baseball cards and other sports memorabilia. Office: 7000 E Genesee St Fayetteville NY 13066-1131 Office Phone: 315-446-3001.

PIROLLI, JOHN PAUL, poet, writer, building materials company executive; b. Cambridge, Mass., Feb. 14, 1950; s. Michael John and Yolanda F. Pirolli; 1 child, John Michael. Student, U. Ky., 1969—75, Harvard U., 1975—76, student, 1993—94, U. Mass., 1994. V.p. M.J. Pirolli and Sons Inc., 1970—. Author: (Poetry Book) Madmen on the Merrimac, 1997, Humbug to Hallalaya, 2001; co-prodr.(and reader): (at numerous poetry readings), 1984—; featured in documentary video: Who Owns Jack Kerouac, 2003. Nominee for awards in Mixed Medi and Group Performance Categories, Cambridge Poetry awards, 2003; recipient Short Poem award, 2001, Poet That Makes You Think award, 2001, Mixed Media (Barnum and Buddha Poetry Circus), 2001, Radio Show award, 2001, Editor's Choice award, Poetry.Com and Internat. Libr. of Poetry, 2001, Special event award, Cambidge Poetry awards, 2002. Mem.: Internat. Soc. Poetry (internat. poet of merit 2002), Stone Soup Poetry Soc. (pres. bd. dirs. 1998—), Poetry Soc. Am. Home: PO Box 705 Watertown MA 02471-0705

PIROZZI, MILDRED JEAN, nursing administrator; b. Syracuse, N.Y., Jan. 22, 1943; d. Alfred George and Mildred Erma (Tripp) Farmer; m. Robert T. Pirozzi, Jan. 25, 1969; children: Matthew Robert, Michael Thomas. Diploma, Gen. Hosp. Syracuse, 1963; BS, SUNY, Utica, 1983. RN, N.Y. Med., surg. staff nurse Gen. Hosp. Syracuse, 1963-64; staff nurse ICU U. Rochester Strong Meml. Hosp., N.Y., 1964-65; nurse ICU Upstate Med. Ctr. U. Hosp., Syracuse, 1965-69, rschr. anesthesia Upstate Med. Ctr., 1969-70; nurse recovery room Highland Hosp., Rochester, 1970-71; nurse orthopedic unit Auburn (N.Y.) Meml. Hosp., 1978-80; home dialysis tng. unit nurse SUNY Health Sci. Ctr., Syracuse, 1980-88; with home dialysis tng. unit U. Dialysis Ctr., Syracuse, 1988-91, home program coord., 1991—. Chmn. com. profl. edn. Ctrl. N.Y. chpt. Nat. Kidney Found., Syracuse, 1986-91. Co-author: Hemodialysis Training Manual for Patients and Partners, 1981, CAPD Training Manual for Patients, 1982. Mem. folk ensemble St. Joseph's Ch., 1984—. Recipient Above and Beyond award Nat. Kidney Found., 1991. Mem. Am. Nephrology Nurses Assn. (pub. rels. com. 1988-91, sec., treas., pres. ctrl. N.Y. chpt. 1984-93, 96—, N.E. regional sec. 1987-89, legis. rep. 1991-95). Roman Catholic. Avocations: sewing, crafts, gardening, sports, music. Home: 4699 Howlett Hill Rd Marcellus NY 13108-9762 Office: U Dialysis Ctr/DCI 1127 E Genesee St Syracuse NY 13210-1911

PIRRERA, AARON CHARLES, priest, headmaster; b. Chgo., Aug. 7, 1944; s. Carl A. and Mary C. (Midiri) Pirrera. BA, St. Ambrose U., Davenport, Iowa, 1966; MSLS, U. Iowa, 1973; ESL Cert., U. Calif.-San Diego, 1999; postgrad., Pontifical Beda Coll., Rome, 1981—85. Vol. U.S. Peace Corps, Eritrea, 1966—68; tchr. Delwood Schs., Elwood, Iowa, 1968—69; tchr., libr. Davenport Pub. Schs., 1969—78; novice master Subiaco Abbey, Subiaco, Ark., 1985—90, dir. guest house, 1988—96, dir. devel., 1996—99; tchr. Subiaco Acad., 1985—88, 1999—2001, headmaster, 2001—. Bd. dirs. Subiaco Acad., 1996—99, Regional Aids Interfaith, Little Rock, 1989—91, Gateway House, Ft. Smith, Ark., Ark. Humanities Coun. Bd.; bd. dirs. Tchr. Edn. Adv. Coun. Union of Ozarks. Mem.: K.C. (4th deg.), Kiwanis. Roman Catholic. Avocations: reading, travel. Home and Office: Subiaco Abbey/Academy 405 N Sobiaco Ave Subiaco AR 72865

PIRRO, ALFRED ANTHONY, JR., physician; b. Stamford, Conn., May 17, 1961; s. Alfred Anthony Sr. and Frances (Battaglia) P. BA in Natural Scis., The Johns Hopkins U., 1983; MD, U. Conn., 1987. Diplomate in anesthesia and critical care medicine Am. Bd. Anesthesiology. Resident in surgery Hosp. of St. Raphael, New Haven, 1987-90; fellow in neurosurgery Hartford (Conn.) Hosp., 1991-92, resident in anesthesiology, 1992-95, critical care fellow, 1995-97, staff anesthesiologist, 1997-99; emergency medicine physician Windham Hosp., Willamantic, Conn., 1991—; instr. anesthesiology John Dempsey Hosp.-U. Conn. Sch. Medicine, Hartford, 1997-99; sr. hospitalist/intensivist Union Hosp.; founding ptnr. Hosp. Physician Specialists LLC, Elkton, Md.; med. dir. hospitalist program Union Hosp. of Cecil County, Elkton, 2004—. Physician monitor Md. Physician Rehab. Program, Cecil County, 2002—; med. dir. Union Hosp. of Cecil Cty. Hospitalist Program, Elkton, Md. Advisor Lally for Congress campaign, Mineola, N.Y., 1994. Beneficial-Hodson scholarship Johns Hopkins U., 1979, Pitney Bowes scholarship, 1979. Mem.: AMA, Soc. Critical Care Medicine, Cecil County Med. Soc., Md. State Med. Soc. Republican. Office Phone: 443-350-4544.

PIRSCH, CAROL MCBRIDE, county official, former state senator, community relations manager; b. Omaha, Dec. 27, 1936; d. Lyle Erwin and Hilfrie Louise (Lebeck) McBride; m. Allen I. Pirsch, Mar. 28, 1954 (dec.); children: Pennie Elizabeth, Pamela Elaine, Patrice Eileen, Phyllis Erika, Peter Allen, Perry Andrew. Student, U. Miami, Oxford, Ohio, U. Nebr., Omaha. Former mem. data processing staff Omaha Pub. Schs.; former mem. wage practices dept. Western Electric Co., Omaha; former legal sec. Omaha; former office mgr. Pirsch Food Brokerage Co., Inc., Omaha; former employment supr., mgr. pub. policy U.S. West Comm., Omaha; mem. Nebr. Senate, 1979-97; commr. Douglas County, 1997—, chair, 1999, 2004, vice chair, 2001, 2003. Founder, 1st pres., bd. dirs. Nebr. Coalition for Victims of Crime (Lifetime award 2002); bd. dirs. Centris Fed. Credit Union, 1st v.p., 2003—. Mem. Omaha Douglas County Bldg. Commn., 1997-2003, sec., 2000-03; cmty. advisor Omaha Jr. League. Recipient Golden Elephant award, Kuhle award, 1986, Nebr. Coalition for Victims of Crime, Outstanding Legis. Efforts award YWCA, 1989, Breaking the Rule of Thumb award Nebr. Domestic Violence Sexual Assault Coalition, 1989, Cert. of Appreciation award U.S. Dept. Justice, 1988, Partnership award N.E. Credit Union League, 1995, Wings award LWV Greater Omaha, 1995, N.E. VFW Spl. Recognition award for Exceptional Svc., 1995, Victim Rights Week Recognition award, 1995, Victim Adv. Lifetime Achievement award, 2002; Crime Victims Adv. award Nebr. Atty. Gen., 1995. Mem. VASA, Nat. Orgn. Victim Assistance (Outstanding Legis. Leadership award 1981), Freedom Found., Tangier Women's Aux., Footprinters Internat. (bd. dirs., sec.), Douglas County Hist. Soc., Nebr. Taxpayers Assn., Keystone Citizen Patrol (Comm. Network of Citizen Patrols award, 1995), Audubon Soc., N.W. Cmty. Club, Keystone Task Force (Keystoner of the month, 1987, Queen Keystone, 2002), Benson Rep. Women's Club. Office: Legis Chambers 2 Douglas County Civic Ctr Omaha NE 68102 E-mail: cpirsch@aol.com.

PIRSIG, ROBERT MAYNARD, author; b. Mpls., Sept. 6, 1928; s. Maynard Ernest and Harriet Marie (Sjobeck) P.; m. Nancy Ann James, May 10, 1954 (div. Aug. 1978); children— Christopher (dec. Nov. 17, 1979), Theodore; m. Wendy L. Kimball, Dec. 28, 1978; 1 dau., Nell. BA, U. Minn., 1950, MA, 1958. Author: Zen And The Art of Motorcycle Maintenance, 1974, Lila, 1991. Served with AUS, 1946-48. Recipient Award AAAL, 1979; Guggenheim fellow, 1974— Mem. Soc. Tech. Communicators (sec. Minn. chpt. 1970-71, treas. 1971-72) Office: care Harper Collins Pub 10 E 53d St New York NY 10022

PIRTLE, LAURIE LEE, women's college basketball coach; b. Columbus, Ohio, Jan. 1, 1958; BS in Phys. Edn., Ohio State U., 1980. Asst. coach girl's basketball William Fisher H.S., Lancaster, Ohio, 1981-82; coach women's basketball Capital U., Columbus, Ohio, 1982-86, U. Cin., 1986—. Named Coach of Yr. Dist.III Ohio Athletic Commn. and Converse III, 1985-86, Ohio Intercoll. Coaches Assn., 1985, Metro Conf., 1989, Conf. USA, 1999, Leading Woman in Cin., 2000. Mem. Women's Basketball Coaches Assn., Greater Cin. and No. Ky., Women's Sports Assn. (mem. com.). Office: U Cin Athletics Dept PO Box 210021 Cincinnati OH 45221-0021

PIRTLE, RONALD M. automotive executive; b. Jackson, Tenn. B in Indsl. Adminstrn., Kettering U., 1977; MBA, Harvard U., 1980. Indsl. engr. Chevrolet Motor Divsn., Flint, Mich., 1977—80; corp. fin. staff Gen. Motors, 1980—84, dir. overseas ops. analysis, 1984—87; mgr. fin. and planning Buick-Oldsmobile-Cadillac Group, Flint, 1987—88, comptr., Pontiac div., 1988—90; exec.-in-charge Gen. Motors Corp. Strategic Planning Group, 1990—92; fin. dir. AC Delco Sys., 1992—94; dir. north am. ops. Delphi Packard Electric Sys., 1994—96; gen. mgr., GM VP Delphi Harrison Thermal Sys., 1996—98; v.p, pres. Delphi harrison thermal sys. Delphi Corp., Lockport, NY, 1998—. Mem. NAACP, Urban Leagues. Named one of Ams. Best and Brightest Young Bus. and Profl. Men, Dollar and Sense Mag., 1990. Mem.: Buffalo Niagara Enterprise and Bus. Coun. of NY State, Buffalo Health Care Task Team (bd. mem.), Buffalo Niagara Partnership (bd. mem.), Univ. Pitts. Sch. Engring. (bd. mem.), Kettering Univ. Alumni Assoc. (bd. mem.), Kappa Alpha Psi. Office: Delphi Harrison Thermal Systems 200 Upper Mountain Rd Lockport NY 14094 also: Delphi Corp World Headquarters 5725 Delphi Dr Troy MI 48098-2815

PISANKO, HENRY JONATHAN, command and control communications company executive; b. Trenton, N.J., Mar. 14, 1925; s. Isadore Stephen and Victoria (Gula) P.; m. Sophia Emily Zudnak, May 29, 1949 (dec. 1998); children: Barbara, Henry Jonathan, Jr., Michael. B in Naval Sci., U. Notre Dame, 1945, BA, 1947; cert. in Japanese, U. Colo. and Okla. State U., 1945; postgrad. Woodrow Wilson Sch., Princeton U., Columbia U., 1948-50. Constrn. reporter ea. div. F.W. Dodge div. McGraw-Hill, N.Y.C. and Phila., 1950-52; internat. affairs analyst Dept. Def., Washington, 1953-59, ops. officer Pacific Rim, Japan and Hong Kong, 1960-63; sr. intelligence officer Internat. Security Affairs, Dept. Def., Washington, 1964-70; overseas adminstr. diplomatic telecommunications Dept. State, Asia, Africa, 1971-73; spl. advisor Def. Intelligence Coll., Washington, 1974-75; ctr. dep. chief, adminstrn. dir. Intelligence Community, Washington, 1976-82; exec. officer USA-EIGO Svcs. Co., Rockville, Md., 1983-87, Princeton, N.J., 1983-87, now bd. dirs.; pres. P.K. Co. Ltd., Bethesda, 1987—, chmn. bd. dirs. emeritus Hong Kong; assoc. Dawson Sci. Corp., Hong Kong, 1996—. Bd. dirs. Asia Mgmt. Internat., Princeton; assoc. Bi-Lingual U.S.A. Corp., Bethesda, Md., 1984, Mgmt. Logistics Internat., Arlington, Va., 1983-86; hon. dir. Pacific Rim Enterprises, Hong Kong, 1996. Editor, translator: Yoshio Kodama, 1952; author: (monographs) Items of Inquiry Far East, 1983, Japanese Technology-Ancient Culture, 1985, Augur, 1994 (pamphlet) Fiber Optics Across the Pacific, 1989; editor (handbook) Japanese-English Proprietary Business Lexicon for Command Control Communications Intelligence, 1990-93; author, producer handbook: Telecommunications Operations for Pacific Rim Enterprises, 1996. Sponsor, contbr. Pisanko-Kikan, 1982, Hotel Okura, Japan, 1983, Bungei Shunju, Japan, 1988. Lt. J.G., USN, 1942-46. Trenton Times scholar, 1942; recipient Moe Berg award Pub. Security Investigation Agy.-Japan, Tokyo, 1961, Order of Cariboe, Philippines, 1960-63, Telecommunications award Thai Gen. Staff, Bangkok, 1972, Shimoda Diplomatic award, Japan. Mem. Asian Rsch. Svc., Bus. Devel. Africa, Internat. Inst. Japan, Bus. Execs. for Internat. Security, Internat. Platform Assn., Info. Processing Soc. Japan, Naval Res. Officers Tng. Corps, Unit Alumni Club, Boulder (Colo.) Boys-Japanese Club, Shek-O Club (Hong Kong). Avocations: rare book collecting, cryptology, desert safaris. Office: PK Co Ltd Far East Hdqs Peninsula New Business Ctr Hong Kong Hong Kong *"I seek no other man's shoes. If I've misdirected my priorities, and I'm confident this is not so, I've had a fair time in lost country. There are no regrets."Moe Berg Pr #23.*

PISANO, VINCENT JAMES, lawyer; b. Englewood, N.J., Sept. 12, 1953; s. Vincent Paul and Georgette (Cernek) P.; m. Lissa Roth, May 4, 1996; children: Catherine Callahan Steele, Elisabeth Lynden Steele. BA, Vassar Coll., 1975; JD, St. Johns U., 1978. Bar: N.Y. 1979. With Skadden, Arps, Slate, Meagher and Flom, N.Y.C., 1978—2003; ptnr. Skadden, Arps, Slate and Meagher, N.Y.C., 1986—2003, Kirkland & Ellis, N.Y.C., 2003—. Bd. dirs. Make a Wish Found. Met. N.Y., 1988-90. Mem. N.Y. Bar Assn., N.Y.C. Bar Assn., Vassar Coll. Alumni Assn. Office: Kirkland & Ellis 153 W 53d St New York NY 10022 E-mail: vpisano@kirkland.com.

PISANSKY, THOMAS MICHAEL, physician; MD, U. of Minn. Diplomate Nat. Bd. of Med. Examiners. Prof. Mayo Grad. Sch. of Medicine, Rochester, Minn., 1987—2002. Grantee, Nat. Cancer Inst., 1996—. Mem.: Am. Soc. for Therapeutic Radiology and Oncology. Office: Mayo Clinc 200 First St SW Rochester MN 55905

PISCHINGER, FRANZ FELIX, engineer, researcher; b. Waidhofen, Austria, July 18, 1930; s. Franz and Karoline (Bentz) P.; m. Elfriede Pischinger-Goessler, 1957 (2001); children: Gerhard, Martin, Stefan, Thomas, Alice; m. Elisabeth Pischinger-Froehlich, 2003. Diploma in Engring., Tech. U., Graz, Austria, 1952, DR in Internal Combustion Engines, 1954, Habilitation degree, 1958, Dr (hon.), 1994. Asst. Tech. U., Graz, 1953-58; head rsch. dept. Inst. Internal Combustion Engines (AVL), Graz, 1958-62; leading positions in rsch., devel. Kloeckner-Humboldt-Deutz AG, Cologne, Germany, 1962-70; dir. Inst. Applied Thermodynamics RWTH, Aachen, Germany, 1970-97; pres., CEO FEV Motorentechnik, Aachen, 1978—; v.p. Deutsche Forschungsgemeinschaft, Bonn-Bad Godesberg, Germany, 1984-90. Contbr. articles to profl. jours. Decorated Ehrenring Sub auspiciis praesidentis republicae (Austria), 1954, Bundesverdienstkreuz 1st class (Germany), 1978; recipient Herbert Akroyd Stuard award Inst. Mech. Engrs., 1962, Carl-Engler-Medaille DGMK, Deutsche Wissenschaftliche Gesellschaft Erdöl, Erdgas Kohle, Hamburg, 1990, Austrian cross of Honor for Sci. and Art First Class, 1998. Fellow Soc. Automotive Engrs. U.S.A.; mem. ASME Internat. (Soichiro Honda medal 2000), NAE (USA) (fgn. assoc.), Verein Deutscher Ingenieure (medal of honor 1993, decoration of honor 1997), Deutsche Gesellschaft Mineralölwissenschaft U. Kohlechemie, Rheinisch-Westfälische Akademie Wissenschaften, Aachen-Frankenburg Club, Rotary. Office: FEV Motorentechnik Neuenhofstrasse 181 52078 Aachen Germany E-mail: pischinger_f@fev.de.

PISCHKE, VAIL W. lawyer, Judge; AB, LLB, JD, U. Notre Dame. Pres., chmn. bd., gen. counsel Met. Bank, Washington; developer, owner Nationally franchised hotels and motels, Shopping Ctr.; judge State of Va.; pvt. practice Falls Church, Va. Commr. chancery Cir. County Fairfax County, vol. judge pro tem; mem. Alcohol Safety Action Project Adv. Com. Va.; presenter, moderator state-wide Va. Jud. Seminars; legal advisor various ch. denominations in No. Va. and Washington; counsel, legal advisor Prison Fellowship; gen. counsel Christian Fellowship Ch. Past pres., v.p., chmn. bd. elders, gen. counsel, chmn. bd. trustees Our Savior Luth. Ch., Arlington, Va.; past pres., v.p., chmn. bd. elders, gen. counsel, trustee St. Paul's Luth. Ch., Falls Church; pres. Luth. Ch., Arlington, Va.; past pres. Fairfax chpt. Am. Cancer Soc., Va. Soc. Crippled Children and Adults; past dir. Salvation Army; past pres. Longfellow H.S. PTA, Fairfax County, Va.; past pres., v.p. McLean Sr. H.S. PTA, Fairfax County; past bd. dirs. Juvenile Detention Commn. No. Va., No. Va. Family Bd., No. Va. YMCA; bd. dirs. Washington United Givers Fund. Recipient Cert. Outstanding Svc., Va. Supreme Ct. Appeals. Mem. Assn. Dist. Ct. Judges in Va. (hon. life), Falls Church Bar Assn. (past pres., v.p., sec.), No. Va. Trial Lawyers Assn. (past parliamentarian, bd. dirs.), Va. Judges Assn. (life), Falls Church Rotary (past pres., v.p.), Nat. PTA (life). Home: 507 Roosevelt Blvd Apt C415 Falls Church VA 22044-3125

PISCHL, ADOLPH JOHN, school administrator; b. East Orange, NJ, Mar. 28, 1920; s. Adolph and Anna (Ellerman) P.; m. Tennessee Wild, Sept. 9, 1947; 1 child, Sallyann. Certificate, Drake Coll., 1940 With Juilliard Sch. Music, NYC, 1962-86, asst. concert mgr., 1962-66; dir. pub. relations Juilliard Sch. Music, NYC, 1966-68; concert mgr. Juilliard Sch. Music, NYC, 1966-86; adminstr. Sch. Strings, NYC, 1987-88. With The Dance Mart, NYC, 1950—, pub. dir. Am. Dance Festival, Conn. Coll., 1964-68; mgr. Betty Jones Dances I Dance, 1966-68, Ruth Currier Dance Co., 1966-68, Anna Sokolow Dance Co., 1966-68, Julliard Sch. Bookstore, 1971-86. Founder, editor: Dance Perspectives, 1958-64, Dance Data, 1977; editor: Juilliard News Bull. and Rev. Ann, 1964-85; pub.: Dance Horizons, 1965-86 (Dance mag. award 1999); Contbr. articles to dance mags. Bd. dirs. Dance Notation Bur.; sec. bd. dirs. Walter W. Naumburg Found., Inc. Served AUS, 1940-46. Home: 878 Warren Pkwy Teaneck NJ 07666-5640

PISCOPO, JOSEPH CHARLES, actor; b. Passaic, N.J., June 17, 1951; s. Joseph P. and Edith I. (LaMagna) P.; m. Nancy, 1973 (div.); m. Kimberly Driscoll, 1997; children: Joseph, Alexandra. BS, Jones Coll., 1973. Repertory player Saturday Night Live, NBC-TV, 1980-84; founder Piscopo Prodns. Inc.; appeared numerous regional theater prodns., dinner theater circuit, South and N.E.; stand-up comedian improvisation and comic strip clubs, N.Y.C., 1976-80, NBC-TV, 1981-83, Joe Piscopo HBO Spl. 1985, Joe Piscopo N.J. Spl., 1986; radio personality Joe Piscopo at Large, 1983—; appeared in films Johnny Dangerously, 1984, Wise Guys, 1986, Dead Heat, 1988, Sidekicks, 1992, Huck and the King of Hearts, 1993, Two Bits & Pepper, 1995, Multimedia Celebrity Poker, 1995, Captain Nuke and the Bomber Boys, 1995, Open Season, 1996, Weird Al' Yankovic: The Videos, 1996, Baby Bedlam, 2000, Bartleby, 2001; (tv series) (voice) 100 Deeds for Eddie McDowd, 1999; author: The Piscopo Tapes, 1984; TV guest appearances Law & Order, 1999, 2001, Arli$$, 2000. Recipient 2 Ace awards, Miller Lite Beer commls., 1986; named Father of Yr., Nat. Father's Day Com., 1983 Office: William Morris Agy 151 El Camino Dr Beverly Hills CA 90212*

PISCOPO, PHIL, wholesale distribution executive; CFO Neuman Distributors, Ridgefield, NJ. Office: Neuman Distributors Ste 2800 354 Eisenhower Pkwy Livingston NJ 07039-1023

PISTER, KARL STARK, engineering educator; b. Stockton, Calif., June 27, 1925; s. Edwin LeRoy and Mary Kimball (Smith) P.; m. Rita Olsen, Nov. 18, 1950; children: Francis, Therese, Anita, Jacinta, Claire, Kristofer. BS with honors, U. Calif., Berkeley, 1945, MS, 1948; PhD, U. Ill., 1952; D of Pub. Svc. (hon.), U. Fla., 2004. Instr. theoretical and applied mechanics U. Ill., 1949-52; faculty U. Calif., Berkeley, 1952-62, prof. engring. scis., 1962-96, Roy W. Carlson prof. engring., 1985-90, dean Coll. Engring., 1980-90, Roy W. Carlson prof. emeritus, chancellor Santa Cruz, 1991-96, pres., chancellor emeritus, 1996—, sr. assoc. to pres. Oakland, 1996-99, v.p. ednl. outreach, 1999-2000. Richard Merton guest prof. U. Stuttgart, Germany, 1978; cons. to govt. and industry; bd. dirs. Monterey Bay Aquarium Rsch. Inst.; trustee Am. U. Armenia; chmn. bd. Calif. Coun. Sci. and Tech.; regent Franciscan Sch. Theology, Berkeley. Contbr. articles to profl. jours.; mem. editl. bd. Jour. Optimization Theory and Applications, 1982, Ency. Phys. Sci. and Tech. Regent Franciscan Sch. Theology, Grad. Theol. Union, Berkeley, Calif. With USNR, WWII. Fulbright scholar, Ireland, 1965, West Germany, 1973; recipient Wason Rsch. medal Am. Concrete Inst., 1960, Vincent Bendix Minorities in Engring. award Am. Soc. for Engring. Edn., 1988, Lamme medal, 1993, Alumni Honor award U. Ill. Coll. Engring., 1982, Disting. Engring. Alumnus award U. Calif. Berkeley Coll. Engring., 1992, Berkeley medal, 1996, U. Calif. Presdl. medal, 2000, World Tech. Network award for policy, World Tech. Coun., London, 2002. Fellow: AAAS, ASME (Applied Mechanics award 1999, Internat. Pres.'s award 2000), Am. Acad. Arts and Scis., Am. Acad. Mechanics, Calif. Acad. Sci. (hon.); mem.: ASCE, NAE, Soc. Engring. Sci. Office: U Calif Dept Civil & Environ Engr Berkeley CA 94720 E-mail: pister@ce.berkeley.edu.

PISTOLE, THOMAS GORDON, microbiology educator, researcher; b. Detroit, Sept. 17, 1942; s. Leotis Merton Pistole and Lillian Nell (Bosley) Besser; m. Donna Dulcie Straw, Sept. 11, 1965; children: James Alexander, Jennifer Katharine. PhB, Wayne State U., 1964, MS, 1966; PhD, U. Utah, 1969. Postdoctoral fellow U.S. Army, Frederick, Md., 1969-70; research assoc. U. Minn., Mpls., 1970-71; asst. prof. U. N.H., Durham, 1971-77, assoc. prof., 1977-83, prof., 1983—, chmn., 1983-92. Vis. scientist Weizmann Inst., Rehovot, Israel, 1979; vis. prof. U. Edinburgh, Scotland, 1986; faculty fellow Office of V.P. for Acad. Affairs U. N.H., 1996-99; mem. ad hoc study sect. U.S. Dept. Agr., 2002. Co-editor: Biomedical Application of the Horseshoe Crab, 1979; mem. editl bd.: Jour. Invertebrate Pathology, 1988—90. NRC fellow, 1969-70, NIH sr. internat. fellow, 1986; grantee NIH, 1975-77, 89-93, 96—, NSF, 1981-84. Mem.: Soc. for Leukocyte Biology, Am. Assn. Immunologists, Am. Soc. for Microbiology. Avocations: singing, collecting old sheet music, walking, cooking. Office: U NH Rudman Hall Dept Microbiology Durham NH 03824-2617 Office Phone: 603-862-0111. Business E-Mail: thomas.pistole@unh.edu.

PISTON, WILLIAM GARRETT, historian, educator; b. Johnson City, Tenn., Feb. 14, 1953; s. Robert Ervin Piston and Laura Mays Caldwell; m. Nancy Claire Wall, May 30, 1982. BA, Vanderbilt U., 1975, MA, 1977; PhD, U. S.C., 1982. Chmn. Social Studies Dept. Louise S. McGehee Sch., New Orleans, 1982—85; prof. S.W. Mo. State U., Springfield, Mo., 1988—. Co-author: Kansans at Wilson's Creek: Soldiers' Letters from the Campaign for Southwest Missouri, 1993; editor: North and South Mag.; contbr. monographs (Mo. History Book award, 2001). Elder Westminster Presbyn. Ch., Springfield, Mo., 1991—2003. Presbyn. Home: 828 South Delaware Avenue Springfield MO 65802 Office: Southwest Missouri State University 901 South National Avenue Springfield MO 65804 Business E-Mail: wgp936f@smsu.edu.

PI-SUNYER, F. XAVIER, medical educator, medical investigator; b. Barcelona, Catalonia, Spain, Dec. 3, 1933; came to U.S., 1942; s. James and Mercedes (Diaz) Pi-S.; m. Penelope Wheeler; children: Andrea, Olivia, Joanna. BA, Oberlin (Ohio) Coll., 1955; MD, Columbia U., 1959; MPH,

Harvard U., 1963; D honoris causa, U. Barcelona, 2004. From instr. to asst. prof. Coll. of Physicians & Surgeons, Columbia U., N.Y.C., 1965-76, assoc. prof., 1976-85, prof. clin. medicine, 1985-91; prof. St. Luke's-Roosevelt Hosp. Ctr., N.Y.C., 1991—; from asst. to assoc. attending physician St. Luke's Hosp., N.Y.C., 1965-75; attending physician St. Luke's-Roosevelt Hosp. Ctr., N.Y.C., 1975—, chief divsn. endocrinology, diabetes and nutrition, 1988—, dir. Obesity Rsch. Ctr., 1988—; dir. Joslin Diabetes Ctr. at St. Luke's Hosp., 1994—, Van Itallie Ctr. for Nutrition and Weight Mgmt., 1994—. Mem. adj. faculty Rockefeller U., 1984—; vis. physician Rockefeller U. Hosp., 1984—; attending physician Presbyn. Hosp., 1985—; sr. investigator N.Y. Heart Assn., 1968-73; Hsien Wu investigator St. Luke's-Roosevelt Hosp., 1982-90; Sigma Xi lectr. Pa. State U., 1989; Howard Heinz vis. prof. Med. Coll. Pa., 1987; Pfizer vis. prof. in diabetes Boston U./Tufts U./Harvard U., 1995, U. Md., 1997; mem. C study sect. NIDDKD, 1988-92, mem. task force on obesity, 1990—, mem. nutrition study sect., 1983-87; v.p. Am. Bd. Nutrition, 1987-88; chmn. task force obesity treatment and prevention Nat. Heart, Lung and Blood Inst., 1995—mem. sci. bd. FDA, 2004-. Editor-in-chief Obesity Rsch. Jour., 1997-2002; assoc. editor: Internat. Jour. Obesity, 1994-; contbr. numerous articles to profl. jours. Fogarty Internat. fellow NIH, 1979-80. Mem. USDA/HHS (mem. U.S. dietary guidelines adv. com. 2004-), Am. Soc. for Clin. Nutrition (coun. 1987-90, pres. 1989-90), Am. Diabetes Assn. (exec. com. 1990-93, pres. 1992-93), N.Am. Assn. Study Obesity (v.p. 1992-93, pres. 1994-95, Stunkard award 2003), N.Y. State Health Rsch. Coun., N.Y. Acad. Medicine (com. on pub. health 1983-96), Inst. of Medicine (food and nutrition bd., task force on dietary reference intakes 1999-2002), NAS (mem. task force on opportunities in nutrition and food sci. 1992-93, task force on dietary reference intakes 1999-2002). Avocations: tennis, skiing, hiking, theater. Home: 305 Riverside Dr New York NY 10025-5286 Office: St Luke's-Roosevelt Hosp Ctr Dept Medicine 1111 Amsterdam Ave New York NY 10025-1716

PITCAVAGE, MARK THOMAS, political scientist, writer, historian; b. Kingston, Pa., Oct. 26, 1966; s. Thomas Robert and Elizabeth Ann Pitcavage. PhD, Ohio State U., 1995, MA, 1992; BA, Trinity U., San Antonio Tex., 1988. Tchg. asst. The Ohio State U., Columbus, Ohio, 1989—95; cons. Ohio Bd. of Regents, Columbus, Ohio, 1995—96; rsch. dir. State and Local Anti-Terrorism Tng. Program, Columbus, Ohio, 1996—2000; dir. of fact finding Anti-Defamation League, New York, NY, 2000—. Editor (contributor): (report) The Ku Klux Klan: 19th Century Terrorists in the 21st Century; author: (encyclopedia entry) Encyclopedia of Terrorism, Dictionary of American History, The Mexican War Encyclopedia, The James Madison Encyclopedia, The War of 1812 Encyclopedia, Reference Guide to U.S. Military History, (monograph) The Investigator and Prosecutor's Guide to Common Terms Used by Anti-Government Extremists, (report) Beyond Anthrax: Extremism and Bioterrorism; contbr. report; editor: (report) Extremism in Connecticut: A State Study, Border Disputes, Unraveling Anti-Semitic 9-11 Conspiracy Theories; contbr. articles to profl. jours. Fellow U.S. Army Ctr. for Mil. History Fellowship, U.S. Army Ctr. for Mil. History, 1994—95, U. Fellowship, Ohio State U., 1998. Mem.: Nat. White Collar Crime Rsch. Consortium, Am. Hist. Assn. Office: Anti-Defamation League 823 United Nations Plaza New York NY 10017 E-mail: mpitcavage@adl.org.

PITCHER, GRIFFITH FONTAINE, lawyer; b. Balt., Nov. 1, 1937; s. William Henry and Virginia Griffith (Stein) P.; m. Sandra E. Barnett, Dec. 16, 1994; children: Virginia T. Pitcher Ballinger, L. Brooke Pitcher Fick, William T.B., Margaret W. Pitcher Saylors. BA, Johns Hopkins U., 1960; JD, U. Va., 1963. Bar: Ala. 1963, Fla. 1971, Ga. 1996. Assoc. Bradley, Arant, Rose & White, Birmingham, Ala., 1963-71; mem. Van den Berg, Gay & Burke, Orlando, Fla., 1971-76, Mahoney, Hadlow & Adams, Jacksonville, Fla., 1976-82; ptnr. Squire, Sanders & Dempsey, Miami, Fla., 1982-93; of counsel Mershon, Sawyer, Johnston, Dunwoody & Cole, Miami, Fla., 1994-95, Chamberlain, Hrdlicka, White, Williams & Martin, Atlanta, 1996—2002, Seyfarth Shaw LLP, Atlanta, 1996—. Contbr. articles to profl. jours. Vice chmn. Winter Park (Fla.) Planning & Zoning Bd., 1974-75. With Army N.G., 1961-64. Fellow: Am. Coll. Bond Counsel (founding fellow, past treas.); mem.: Ala. State Bar Assn., Ga. State Bar, Fla. Bar, Nat. Assn. Bond Lawyers, Order of Coif, Delta Phi. Republican. Office Phone: 404-888-1884.

PITCHER, JONATHAN MICHAEL, language educator, researcher; b. Wokingham, Berkshire, Eng., Mar. 28, 1970; arrived in U.S., 1994; s. Michael Alexander and Veronica Joyce (Watts) Pitcher; m. Samantha Hamilton Yarry, Dec. 28, 1994; 1 child, Olivia E.H. BA in Hispanic Studies, U. Bristol, Eng., 1992; MA in Hispanic Studies, U. London, 1994; PhD in Spanish and Latin Am. studies, U. Coll., London, 2004. Asst. lectr. Spanish U. So. Calif., L.A., 1994—98; lectr. Spanish U. Coll. London, 1999—2000; vis. lectr. Spanish Fla. Atlantic U., Boca Raton, 2001—02; vis. coord. Spanish U. Miami, Coral Gables, Fla., 2002—. Contbr. articles to profl. jours. Grad. scholar, U. So. Calif., L.A., 1994—99, U. Coll., London, 1999—2004. Mem.: MLA, Smithsonian Instn., Brit. Libr. London. Avocations: travel, theater. Office: Univ Miami Dept Fgn Langs and Lit ASHE 527-A Coral Gables FL 33124-8093

PITCHER, THOMAS B. lawyer; b. Nov. 28, 1938; BS, U. Fla., 1960; JD, Duke U., 1966. Bar: Calif. 1967. Ptnr. Gibson, Dunn & Crutcher, Irvine, Calif. Note editor: Duke Law Jour., 1965-66. Mem. ABA, L.A. County Bar Assn., Orange County Bar Assn. Office: Gibson Dunn & Crutcher 4 Park Plz Ste 1400 Irvine CA 92614-8557

PITCHUMONI, CAPECOMORIN SANKAR, gastroenterologist, educator; b. Madura, India, Jan. 20, 1938; came to U.S., 1967; s. Sankara and Jaya (Lekshmi) Iyer; m. Prema Iyer, Nov. 11, 1964; children: Sheila, Shoba, Suresh. Student, St. Xavier Coll., India, 1953-55; MB BS, Trivandrum Med. Coll., India, 1959, MD, 1965. Intern Med. Coll., Trivandurm, India, 1961-63; resident in gastroenterology Yale U., 1967-69; N.Y. Med. Coll., 1969-72; practice medicine specializing in gastroenterology N.Y.C., 1972—; asst. prof. medicine Kottayam Med. Coll., India, 1967, N.Y. Med. Coll., 1972-75, assoc. prof., 1975-80, prof. clin. medicine, 1980-85, prof. medicine, 1985—, assoc. prof. preventive and social medicine, 1975-86, prof. community and preventive medicine, 1986—; chief sect. gastroenterology Our Lady of Mercy Med. Ctr., N.Y.C., 1980—, assoc. dir. medicine, 1985—, program dir. internal medicine, 1987—, dir. medicine, 1992, chmn. emeritus dept. medicine, 2002—; chief divsn. gastroenterology St. Peters U. Hosp., New Brunswick, NJ, 2002—. Contbg. author med. textbooks; contbr. articles to profl. jours. Recipient Om Prakash award Indian Soc. Gastroenterology, 1976, Outstanding Scientist of Yr. award MV Spltys., Madras, 1994, Oration award Thangavelu Endowment, 1994. Master Am. Coll. Gastroenterology (gov. 1996-2000); fellow Royal Coll. Physicians and Surgeons Can., Am. Coll. Nutrition; mem. Assn. Physicians India, Am. Coll. Nuitrition, Am. Gastroent. Assn., India Soc. Gastroenterology (life), Am. Inst. Nutrition, Gastrointestinal Endoscopy, Am. Soc. for Clin. Nutrition. Hindu. Home: 1 Nevius PL Somerset NJ 08873 Office: St Peters U Hosp New Brunswick NJ

PITCOCK, JAMES KENT, head and neck surgical oncologist; b. Tachikawa AFB, Japan, Nov. 18, 1951; s. James Kenneth and Helen (Robertson) P.; m. Cynthia H. Zipperly. Student, U. Houston, 1974; MD, Baylor U., 1979. Diplomate Am. Bd. Otolaryngology. Resident in gen. surgery Baylor Coll. Medicine, Houston, 1979-81, resident in otolaryngology, head and neck surgery, 1981-84; clinician Kelsey-Seybold Clinic, P.A., Houston, 1984-85; lectr. head and neck surgery Inst. Laryngology and Otology, U. London, 1985-86; instr., fellow head and neck surgery U. Chgo., 1986-88; asst. prof. dept. otolaryngology, head and neck surgery, chief div. head and neck surgical oncology U. Calif.-Irvine Med. Ctr., Orange, 1988-92. Dir. head and neck oncology clin. & rsch. program Clin. Cancer Ctr. U. Calif., Irvine. Author: Oral and Maxillofacial Trauma, 1989, Musculocutaneous Flap Reconstruction of the Head and Neck, 1989, Surgery of the Skull Base, 1989. Fellow Am. Acad. Otolaryngology, Head and Neck Surgery; mem. ACS. Office: Premier Med Grp 3701 Dauphin St Mobile AL 36608-1756

PITEGOFF, THOMAS MICHAEL, lawyer; b. Queens, N.Y., Aug. 12, 1949; s. Joseph and Libbie (Shapiro) Pitegoff. BA, Sarah Lawrence Coll., 1971; postgrad., U. Heidelberg, 1971—72; maitrise, Sorbonne U., 1973; JD, Syracuse U., 1976. Bar: N.Y. 1977. Counsel Hunton & Williams, N.Y.C., 1986—89; panelist numerous confs. and seminars. Contbr. articles to profl. jours. Westchester regional coord. Export Legal Assistance Network, 1995—; bd. govs. World Trade Coun. Westchester, 1995—; trustee Katonah Mus. Art, 2002—. Mem.: ABA (editor Franchise Law Jour. 1990—93, gov. com. forum on franchising 1993—96, co-chair internat. subcom. bus. sect. cyberspace law com. 1998—2002, former chair franchising subcom. bus. sect. small bus. com.), Computer Law Assn., Assn. of Bar of City of N.Y. (computer law com. 1988—91), N.Y. State Bar Assn. (mem. exec. com. bus. law sect. 2003—), Internat. Bar Assn. Office: Pitegoff Law Office 10 Bank St Ste 540 White Plains NY 10606 Office Phone: 914-681-0100. Business E-Mail: www.pitlaw-.com. E-mail: pitegoff@pitlaw.com.

PITERNICK, ANNE BREARLEY, librarian, educator; b. Blackburn, Eng., Oct. 13, 1926; emigrated to Can., 1956, naturalized, 1965; d. Walter and Ellen (Harris) Clayton; m. Neil Brearley, 1956 (div. 1971); m. George Piternick, May 6, 1971. BA, U. Manchester (Eng.), 1948, F.L.A., 1983. Mem. library staff U. B.C., Vancouver, Can., 1956-66, head sci. div., 1960-61, head social scis. div., 1965-66, prof. Sch. Library, Archival and Info. Studies, 1966-91, prof. emerita, 1991—, assoc. dean Faculty of Arts, 1985-90. Mem. Nat. Com. Bibliog. Svcs. Can., 1975-80, chmn. com. on bibliography and info. services for social scis. and humanities, 1981-84; mem. adv. acad. panel Social Scis. and Humanities Research Council, 1981-84; mem. adv. bd. Nat. Libr. Can., 1978-84; mem. Nat. Adv. Com. Culture Stats., 1985-90; organizer Confs. on Can. Bibliography, 1974, 81; pres. Can. Assn. Spl. Librs. Info. Svcs., 1969-70, Can. Libr. Assn., 1976-77. Author articles on electronic info. svcs. and scholarly communication. Bd. dirs. Vancouver Friends of Chamber Music, 2001—. Recipient Queen's Silver Jubilee medal, 1977, award for Spl. Librarianship Can. Assn. Spl. Librs. and Info. Svcs., 1987, 75th Anniversary medal U.B.C., 1990, Can. 125 medal, 1993; fellow Coun. on Libr. Resources, 1980. Mem. Assn. Profs. Emeriti U.B.C. (pres. 2003-04). Home: 1849 W 63rd Ave Vancouver BC Canada V6P 2H9 E-mail: annebp@interchange.ubc.ca.

PITINO, RICHARD, collegiate basketball coach, former professional basketball coach; b. N.Y.C., Sept. 18, 1952; Student, U. Mass. Asst. coach U. Hawaii, 1975-76, Syracuse U., 1976-78; coach Boston U., 1978-83; asst. coach N.Y. Knicks, 1983-85, coach, 1987-89, Providence U., 1986-87; basketball coach U. Ky., Lexington, 1989-97; head coach Boston Celtics, 1997—2001, Univ. of Louisville, 2001—. Author: (with Dick Weiss) Full Court Pressure: A Year in Kentucky Basketball, 1992. Named Coll. Coach of Yr., Sporting News, 1987. Office: Univ of Louisville Louisville KY 40292

PITKIN, EDWARD THADDEUS, aerospace engineer, consultant; b. Putnam, Conn., Dec. 14, 1930; s. Thaddeus Eugene and Florence Mabel (Brown) P.; m. Clara Lucy Modliszewski, June 13, 1953; children— Gayle Linda, Dale Edward. BS, U. Conn., 1952; MS (Guggenheim fellow), Princeton, 1953; PhD (NASA fellow), UCLA, 1964. Project engr. Astro Div. Marquardt Co., Los Angeles, 1956-59, mgr. space propulsion, 1959-61; engrng. cons. Los Angeles, 1961-64; asso. prof. aerospace engrng. U. Conn., Storrs, 1964-70, prof. mech. and aerospace engrng., 1970-90, prof. emeritus, 1990—; cons. engr., 1990—; asst. dean U. Conn., Storrs, 1977-87. Contbr. articles to tech. publs. Served as lt. USAF, 1953-55. Asso. fellow AIAA Mem. Solar Energy Soc. Home: 115 Brookside Ln Mansfield Center CT 06250-1001 Office: U Conn Dept Mech Engrng U-139 191 Auditorium Rd Storrs Mansfield CT 06269-3139

PITKIN, ROY MACBETH, retired obstetrician, educator; b. Anthon, Iowa, May 24, 1934; s. Roy and Pauline Allie (McBeath) Pitkin; m. Marcia Alice Jenkins, Aug. 17, 1957; children: Barbara, Robert Macbeth, Kathryn, William Charles. BA with highest distinction, U. Iowa, 1956, MD, 1959. Diplomate Am. Bd. Ob-Gyn. Intern King County Hosp., Seattle, 1959—60; resident in ob-gyn U. Iowa Hosps. and Clinics, Iowa City, 1960—63; asst. prof. ob-gyn U. Ill., 1965—68; assoc. prof. ob-gyn U. Iowa, Iowa City, 1968—72, prof., 1972—87, head dept. ob-gyn, 1977—87; prof. UCLA, 1987—97, head dept. ob-gyn., 1987—95, prof. emeritus, 1997—. Mem. residency rev. com. ob-gyn., 1981—87; chmn., 1985—87. Author: The Green Journal 50 Years On, 2003; co-editor: The Best of After Office Hours, 2003; editor: Obstetrics and Gynecology, 1985—2001; contbr. articles to med. jours. Served to lt. comdr. M.C. USNR, 1963—65. Recipient NIH career awardee, 1972—77, Disting. Alumni Achievement award, U. Iowa, 2002. Fellow: Royal Ob-Gyn. (ad eundem); mem.: Coun. Sci. Editors (Dist. Svc. award 2002), Inst. Medicine, NAS, Soc. Perinatal Obstetricians (pres. 1978—79), Soc. Gynecol. Investigation (pres. 1985—86), German Soc. Gyn-Ob. (hon.), Ctrl. Assn. Ob-Gyn., Am. Gyn-Ob. Soc. (pres. 1994—95), Am. Coll. Ob-Gyns., AMA (Goldberger award in clin. nutrition 1982). Presbyterian. Home: 78900 Rancho La Quinta Dr La Quinta CA 92253-6252 E-mail: r.pitkin@earthlink.net.

PITMAN, GERALD H. plastic surgeon; b. Newark; AB, Williams Coll., Williamstown, Mass.; MD, U. Pa. Diplomate Am. Bd. Plastic Surgery, lic. Pa., N.Y., Mass. Resident in gen. surgery Presbyn. Hosp., N.Y.C.; resident in plastic surgery NYU Med. Ctr., fellow in microsurgery; pvt. practice plastic surgery N.Y.C. Attending physician Manhattan Eye, Ear and Throat Hosp.; assoc. attending physician Tisch Hosp., NYU Med. Ctr., Bellevue Hosp. Ctr.; asst. attending physician N.Y. Eye and Ear Infirmary; attending physician Lenox Hill Hosp. Contbr. numerous articles to profl. jours. Fellow: ACS; mem.: N.Y. County Med. Soc., N.Y. State Med. Soc., Am. Assn. for Accreditation of Amb. Surgery Facilities, N.Y. Regional Soc. Plastic and Reconstructive Surgeons, N.E. Soc. Plastic Surgeons, Am. Soc. for Aesthetic Plastic Surgery, Am. Soc. Plastic Surgeons. Office: 170 E 73d St New York NY 10021 Office Phone: 212-517-2600.

PITMAN, LAVERN FRANK, librarian; b. Poynette, Wis., June 8, 1943; s. George and Carolyn (Hutchinson) P.; m. Rosa Papist, Sept. 8, 1973 (dec. Oct. 1996); 1 child, Christina. BA, Wis. State U., 1965; MSLS, Catholic U. Am., 1973; MA, Frostburg State U., 1985. Cataloger copyright office Libr. Congress, Washington, 1966-71, Spanish/Italian cataloger shared divsn., 1971-79; libr. Frostburg (Md.) State U., 1980-98. Author: The Family of John and Deborah Flick Meyers, 1989, The Robertsons: A Norwegian Family in America, 1993; co-author: A Century of Commitment: Frostburg State University, 1997; editor: Civil War Diary of Jesse Meyers, Co. I, 23d Regiment, Wisconsin Volunteer Infantry, 2002. Historic Interpreter, Mt. Vernon, 1999—; curator Wayside Found., 1999-2000; libr. Md. Bur. Mines, 2000—. Mem. Geneal. Soc. Allegany County, Geneal. Soc. Wis., State Hist. Soc. Wis., Frostburg Mus. Assn., Sons of Norway, Vesterheim Norwegian-Am. Mus., Clan Rose Soc. Am.

PITMAN, ROBERT L. judge; JD, U. Tex., 1988. Atty. advisor Executive Office for US Atty., Office of Legal Council, Washington, DC, 1996; cheif Austin Div., Western Dist., Tex.; asst US atty.; US atty. Western Dist., Tex., 2001—02; U.S. magistrate judge Tex., 2003—. Recipient commendations from Exec. Office for US Atty, Fed. Bureau of Investigation, US Dept. of State, US Drug Enforcement Adminstrn., US Secret Service. Office: US Magistrate Judge 200 W 8th St Austin TX 78701

PITMAN, SHARON GAIL, middle school counselor; b. Dayton, Ohio, June 13, 1946; d. Finley Andrew and Lena Kay (Wells) Jennings; m. Benjamin Pitman III, Jan. 19, 1980; children: Elizabeth Ann (dec.), Emily; stepchildren: Scott, Todd. BS in Edn., Miami U., Oxford, Ohio, 1968, MEd in Edn., 1970; sch. counseling cert., Ga. State U., 1979, MEd in Counseling, 1981, EdS in Guidance and Counseling, 1989. Tchr. pub. schs., Hamilton, Ohio, 1968-73, Gwinnett County, Ga., 1973-80; sch. counselor Buford (Ga.) Mid. Sch., 1981-89, Duluth (Ga.) Mid. Sch., 1989-96, Lanier (Ga.) Mid. Sch., 1998—. Conductor workshops in field. Mem. Am. Sch. Counseling Assn. (Nat. Mid. Sch. Counselor of Yr. 1989), Ga. Sch. Counselors Assn. (Mid. Sch. Counselor of Yr. 1988).

PITOFSKY, ROBERT, federal agency administrator, law educator; b. Paterson, N.J., Dec. 27, 1929; s. Morris and Sadye (Katz) P.; m. Sally Levy, June 4, 1961; children: Alexander, David, Elizabeth. BA, NYU, 1951; LLB, Columbia U., 1954; LLD (hon.), Georgetown U., 1989, Nyenrode U., Netherlands, 2002. Bar: N.Y. 1956, D.C. 1973, U.S. Supreme Ct. 1972. Atty. Dept. Justice, Washington, 1956-57; assoc. Dewey, Ballantine, Bushby, Palmer & Wood, N.Y.C., 1957-64; prof. law NYU, 1964-70; dir. Bur. Consumer Protection, FTC, 1970-73; prof. law Georgetown U. Law Ctr., Washington, 1973—83, 1989—, dean, exec. v.p. law ctr. affairs, 1983-89; commr. FTC, Washington, 1978-81, chmn., 1995-2001; of counsel Arnold & Porter, Washington, 1973-78, 81-95, 01—. Guest scholar Brookings Instn., Washington, 1989-90; vis. prof. law Harvard Law Sch., 1975-76; faculty mem. Salzburg (Austria) Seminar in Am. Studies, 1975; chmn. Def. Sci. Bd. task force on antitrust aspects of def. industry downsizing, 1994. Co-author: Cases on Antitrust Law, 1967, Cases on Trade Regulation, 5th edit. 2003; co-editor: Revitalizing Antitrust in Its Second Century, 1991; contbr. articles on consumer protection and antitrust to profl. publs. Served with U.S. Army, 1954-56. Recipient Disting. Service award FTC, 1972, Hart Pub. Svc. award Cons. Fedn. Am., 2001, Kirkpatrick Lifetime Achievement award FTC, 2002; named One of Ten Outstanding Mid-Career Law Profs. Time Mag., 1977. Mem. ABA (coun. antitrust sect. 1986-89), Am. Acad. Arts and Scis., Am. Law Inst., Assn. Am. Law Schs., Columbia U. Ctr. for Law Econ. Studies (adv. bd. 1975-95). Democrat. Jewish. Home: 3809 Blackthorn St Chevy Chase MD 20815-4905 Office Phone: 202-662-9049., 202-942-5662. Business E-Mail: Robert_Pitofsky@APorter.com.

PITONIAK, SCOTT MICHAEL, sportswriter; b. Rome, N.Y., Apr. 10, 1955; s. Andrew Edward and Edna (Holloway) Pitoniak; children: Amy Leigh, Christopher Drew. BS in Pub. Comm. magna cum laude, Syracuse U., 1977. Baseball writer Evening Times, Little Falls, N.Y., 1977; sportswriter Daily Sentinel, Rome, N.Y., 1977; sportswriter, columnist Observer-Dispatch, Utica, N.Y., 1978-84; pro football writer Dem. & Chronicle, Rochester, N.Y., 1985-90, sports projects writer, 1990—. Voter Heisman Trophy Award, 1981—; corr. Gannett News Svc., 1982—, Sporting News, 1982—; journalism prof. St. John Fisher Coll., 1995—. Author: (book) The Buffalo Bills Official Trivia Book, 1989, 1991; co-author: Silver Seasons: The Story of the Rochester Red Wings, 1996, Playing Write Field, 1997, Baseball in Rochester, 2003, Syracuse University Football, 2003; contbr. articles to mags., newspapers, news svcs. including Sporting News, USA Today, Washington Post, Phila. Inquirer, AP, UPI, others; co-host (TV series) Time Warner Comm., 1994—96. Vol. Alzheimer's Assn., Rochester, 1991—. Named one of Am.'s Top 10 Sports Columnist, APSE, 2000, torchbearer, Winter Olympics, 2002; named to Rochester Sports Walk of Fame, 1999, Syracuse U. Journalism Hall of Fame, 2000; recipient Disting. Health Journalism award Gold medal 1st Pl. newspaper divsn., 1991, 1st Pl. sports, N.Y. State AP Writing Contest, 1995, 2d Pl. features, 1993, 2d Pl. sports, 1991, 1997, 2d Pl. columns, 2001, Best of Gannett award, 1996—98, others; scholar Regents. Mem.: Basketball Writers Am., Coll. Football Writers Assn. Am. (bd. dirs.), Profl. Football Writers Am. (2d Pl. columns, 1st Pl. enterprise reporting 1999, 1st Pl. columns 2000), Phi Kappa Phi, Kappa Tau Alpha. Roman Catholic. Avocations: reading, sports memorabilia collecting, volunteering, 19th century baseball, coaching youth sports. Office: Gannett Rochester Newspapers 55 Exchange Blvd Rochester NY 14614-2001 Home: 1063 Stowell Dr Apt 7 Rochester NY 14616-1858 E-mail: spitoniak@democratandchronicle.com.

PITOT, HENRY CLEMENT, III, pathologist, educator; b. N.Y.C., May 12, 1930; s. Henry Clement and Bertha (Lowe) Pitot; m. Julie S. Schutten, July 29, 1954; children: Bertha, Anita, Jeanne, Catherine, Henry, Michelle, Lisa, Patrice. BS in Chemistry, Va. Mil. Inst., 1951; MD, Tulane U., 1955, PhD in Biochemistry, 1959, DSc (hon.), 1995. Instr. pathology Med. Sch. Tulane U., New Orleans, 1955-59; postdoctoral fellow McArdle Lab. U. Wis., Madison, 1959-60, mem. faculty Med. Sch., 1960—, prof. pathology and oncology, 1966-99, prof. emeritus, 1999—, chmn. dept. pathology, 1968-71, acting dean Med. Sch., 1971-73, dir. McArdle Lab., 1973-91. Recipient Borden Undergrad. Rsch. award, 1955, Leaderle Faculty award, 1962, Career Devel. award, Nat. Cancer Inst., NIH, 1965, Parke-Davis award, 1968, Noble Found. Rsch. award, 1984, Esther Langer award, U. Chgo., 1984, Hilldale award, U. Wis., 1991, Founders award, Chem. Industry Inst. Toxicology, 1993, Midwest Regional chpt. Soc. Toxicology award, 1996, Emeritus Faculty award, U. Wis. Med. Sch., 2001, Disting. Lifetime Toxicology award, Soc. Toxicology, 2003. Fellow: AAAS, N.Y. Acad. Scis.; mem.: Soc. Toxicologic Pathologists, Soc. Toxicology, Soc. Surg. Oncology (Lucy J. Wortham award 1981), Soc. Exptl. Biology and Medicine (pres. 1991—93), Am. Soc. Investigative Pathology (pres. 1976—77), Am. Cancer Soc. (life), Japanese Cancer Soc. (hon.), Am. Chem. Soc., Am. Soc. Biochemistry and Molecular Biology, Am. Assn. Cancer Rsch., Am. Soc. Cell Biology. Roman Catholic. Home: 314 Robin Pkwy Madison WI 53705-4931 Office: U Wis McArdle Lab Cancer Rsch 1400 University Ave Madison WI 53706-1599 Office Phone: 608-262-3247. Business E-Mail: pitot@oncology.wisc.edu. *Where and who we are today is the result of those whom we have met and known and loved until now.*

PITOVSKI, DIMITRI ZIVKO, otolaryngologist, educator; b. Bitola, Macedonia, Aug. 6, 1959; s. Zivko Naum and Velika Pitovski; m. Mirjana Markovska, Sept. 19, 1987; children: Naum Dimitri, Stefan Dimitri. MD, Skopje U., Macedonia, 1986. Asst. prof. Northwestern U. Sch. Medicine, Chgo., 1995—2000; assoc. prof. otolaryngology Wake Forest U. Sch. Medicine, Winston-Salem, NC, 2000—. Dir., smell and taste ctr. Wake Forest U. Sch. Medicine, Winston-Salem, 2000—, dir., allergy reference lab., 2001—. Recipient Clin. Investigator Devel. award, NIH, Nat. Inst. Deafness and Other Comm. Disorders, 1990—94; fellow, 1988—90. Achievements include development of world pronounced comprehensive, multidisciplinary treatment and academic research smell and taste center; first smell and taste center in southeastern U.S. Office: Wake Forest Univ Sch Medicine Medical Ctr Blvd Winston Salem NC 27157 E-mail: dzpito@wfubmc.edu.

PITT, BERTRAM, cardiologist, educator, consultant; b. Kew Gardens, N.Y., Apr. 27, 1932; s. David and Shirley (Blum) P., m. Elaine Liberstein, Aug. 10, 1962; children: Geoffrey, Jessica, Jillian BA, Cornell U., 1953; MD, U. Basel, Switzerland, 1959. Diplomate Am. Bd. Internal Medicine, Am. Bd. Cardiology. Intern Beth Israel Hosp., N.Y.C., 1959-60, resident Boston, 1960-63; fellow in cardiology Johns Hopkins U., Balt., 1966-67, from instr. to assoc. prof., 1967-77; prof. medicine, dir. div. cardiology U. Mich., Ann Arbor, 1977-91, prof. medicine Sch. Medicine, 1991—. Author: Atlas of Cardiovascular Nuclear Medicine, 1977; editor: Cardiovascular Nuclear Medicine, 1974; co-editor: Clinical Trials in Cardiology, 1997, Current Controlled Trials in Cardiovascular Medicine, 1999—. Served to capt. U.S. Army, 1963-65 Mem. ACP, Am. Coll. Cardiology, Am. Soc. Clin. Investigation, Assn. Am. Physicians, Am. Physiol. Soc., Am. Heart Assn., Assn. Univ. Cardiologists, Am. Coll. Chest Physicians, Johns Hopkins U. Soc. Scholars. Home: 24 Ridgeway St Ann Arbor MI 48104-1739 Office: U Mich Divsn Cardiology 1500 E Medical Center Dr Ann Arbor MI 48109-0005 Office Phone: 734-936-5260. Business E-Mail: bpitt@umich.edu.

PITT, BRAD, actor; b. Shawnee, Okla., Dec. 18, 1963; s. Bill and Jane P. Pitt; m. Jennifer Aniston, 2001. Appearences include: (TV series) Dallas, Another World, Growing Pains, The Image (HBO), Glory Days, Two-Fisted Tales; (TV movie) Too Young To Die?, 1989; (films) Cutting Glass, 1989, Happy Together, 1990, Across the Tracks, 1991, Thelma and Louise, 1991, Johnny Suede, 1991, Contact, 1992, Cool World, 1992, A River Runs Through It, 1992, Kalifornia, 1993, True Romance, 1993, The Favor, 1994, Interview with the Vampire, 1994, Legends of the Fall, 1994, 12 Monkeys, 1995 (Golden Globe award for best supporting actor in film 1996, Acad. award nominee for best supporting actor 1996), Sleepers, 1996, Seven Years in Tibet, 1997, The Devil's Own, 1997, Dark Side of the Sun, 1997, Meet Joe Black, 1998, Fight Club, 1999, Snatch, 2000, The Mexican, 2001, Spy Game, 2001, Ocean's Eleven, 2001, Full Frontal, 2002, Confessions of a Dangerous Mind, 2002, Sinbad: Legend of the Seven Seas (voice), 2003, Troy, 2004. Office: Creative Artists Agy care Kevin Huvane 9830 Wilshire Blvd Beverly Hills CA 90212-1825

PITT, GEORGE, lawyer, investment banker; b. Chgo., July 21, 1938; s. Cornelius George and Anastasia (Geocaris) P.; m. Barbara Lynn Goodrich, Dec. 21, 1963 (div. Apr. 1990); children: Elizabeth Nanette, Margaret Leigh; m. Pamela Ann Pittsford, May 19, 1990. BA, Northwestern U., 1960, JD, 1963; hon. grad., U.S. Army Intelligence Sch., Ft. Holabird, Md., 1964;

Leading Strategic Change course, U. Va., 1999. Bar: Ill. 1963. Assoc. Chapman and Cutler, Chgo., 1963-67; ptnr. Borge and Pitt, and predecessor, 1968-87, Katten Muchin & Zavis, Chgo., 1987-97; sr. mng. dir. Banc One Capital Markets, Inc. (formerly First Chgo. Capital Markets, Inc.), 1998-2000; mng. dir. UBS Fin. Svcs. Inc. (formerly UBS PaineWebber Inc.), Chgo., 2000—. Conf. chmn. Bond Buyer's 3d Ann. Midwest Pub. Fin. Conf., 1994; conf. co-chmn. Bond Buyer's 8th Ann. Midwest Pub. Fin. Conf., 1999. Notes and comments editor Northwestern U. Law Rev., 1962-63. 1st lt. AUS, 1964. Fellow: Am. Coll. Bond Counsel; mem.: Ill. State Bar Assn., Univ. Club. Chgo., Phi Gamma Delta, Phi Delta Phi, Eta Sigma Phi. Home: 600 N McClurg Ct Chicago IL 60611-3044 Office: UBS Fin Svcs Inc One N Wacker Dr 38th Fl Chicago IL 60606-2807 Business E-Mail: george.pitt@ubs.com.

PITT, HARVEY LLOYD, federal agency administrator; b. Bklyn., Feb. 28, 1945; s. Morris Jacob and Sara (Sapir) P.; m. Saree Ruffin, Jan. 7, 1984; children: Robert Garrett, Sara Dillard; children from previous marriage: Emily Laura, Jonathan Bradley. BA, CUNY, 1965; JD with honors (Univ. scholar), St. John's U., N.Y.C., 1968; LLD (hon.), St. John's U., 2002. Bar: N.Y. 1969, U.S. Supreme Ct. 1972, D.C. 1979. With SEC, Washington, 1968-78, legal asst. to commr., 1969; editor Instl. Investor Study, 1970-71; spl. counsel Office Gen. Counsel, Washington, 1971-72, chief counsel div. market regulation, 1972-73, exec. asst. to chmn., 1973-75, gen. counsel, 1975-78; ptnr. Fried, Frank, Harris, Shriver & Jacobson, Washington, 1978—2001; chmn. SEC, Washington, 2001—03; CEO, Kalorama Ptnrs., LLC. Adj. prof. law George Washington U. Nat. Law Ctr., 1974-82, U. Pa. Law Sch., 1983-84, vis. practitioner, 1984, Georgetown U. Law Ctr., 1976-84; comml. arbitrator Am. Arbitration Assn. Contbr. articles to profl. jours. V.p. Glen Haven Civic Assn., Silver Spring, Md., 1972-73, pres., 1974. Recipient Learned Hand award Inst. for Human Rels., 1988, Presdl. medal, Bklyn. Coll., 2003. Mem. ABA (past chmn. subcom. SEC practice and enforcement, past co-chmn. subcom. state takeover laws), Fed. Bar Assn. (Outstanding Young Lawyer award 1975), Adminstrv. Conf. U.S., Am. Law Inst. (project advisor on restatement law on corp. governance), Delta Sigma Rho, Tau Kappa Alpha, Phi Delta Phi. Office Phone: 202-349-4170. Business E-Mail: harvey@kaloramapartners.com.

PITT, JANE, medical educator; b. Frankfurt, Fed. Republic Germany, Aug. 25, 1938; came to U.S., 1939. d. Ludwig Friederich and Vera (Aberle) Ries; m. Martin Irwin Pitt, Aug. 12, 1962 (dec. 1980); children: Jennifer, Eric Jonathan; m. Robert Harry Socolow, May 25, 1986; stepchildren: David, Seth. BA, Radcliffe Coll., 1960; MD, Harvard U., 1964. Diplomate Am. Bd. Pediatrics, Am. Bd. Pediat. Infectious Diseases. Resident Children's Hosp. Med. Ctr., Boston, 1964-66; fellow Tufts U. Med. Sch., Boston, 1966-67, Harvard U. Med. Sch., Boston, 1967-69; asst. prof. SUNY Downstate Sch. Medicine, N.Y.C., 1970-71; asst. prof. Coll. Physicians and Surgeons Columbia U., N.Y.C., 1971-75, assoc. prof. Coll. Physicians and Surgeons, 1975-2000; prof. Coll. Physicians and Surgeons, 2000—. Mem. instl. rev. bd. Columbia Health Scis. Campus, N.Y.C., 1982—; mem. NIH study sect. Reviewer Jour. of Infectious Diseases, New Eng. Jour. Medicine, 1976—; contbr. articles to profl. jours. NIH grantee, 1974—. Fellow Infectious Disease Soc., Pediat. Infectious Disease Soc., Soc. Pediat. Rsch., Am. Pediatric Soc. Democrat. Jewish. Office: Columbia U Coll Physicians Surgeons 630 W 168th St New York NY 10032-3702 Home: 2620 7TH St Boulder CO 80304-3206 E-mail: jp25@columbia.edu.

PITT, JUDSON HAMILTON, publisher, author; b. Glen Cove, N.Y., June 7, 1953; s. Gavin Alexander and Eleanore Gaehler (Whiting) P.; m. Elena U. Tokaeva, Dec. 16, 1995. BS in Communications, Ariz. State U., 1977. Resident advisor fraternity Ohio State U., Columbus, 1977-79; supr. student svcs. Loyola U., Chgo., 1979-81; asst. to CEO Flair Communications Agy., Inc., Chgo., 1981—2001; v.p. Gavin Pitt Assocs., Inc., Chgo., 1986—; pub. Water Tower Pub. House, Chgo., 1989—. Dir. ops. Chgo. Marathon, 1984-93. Author: The Official Hard Rock Cafe Pin Collector's Guide, 1997. Mem. Am. Mktg. Assn., Newcomen Soc. U.S., Chgo. Soc. Assn. Execs., Saddle & Cycle Club, Pi Kappa Alpha. Republican. Presbyterian. Home: 5510 N Sheridan Rd Chicago IL 60640-1633

PITT, WILLIAM ALEXANDER, cardiologist; b. July 17, 1942; came to U.S., 1970; s. Reginald William and Una Sylvia (Alexander) P.; m. Judith Mae Wilson, May 21, 1965; children: William Matthew, Joanne Katharine. MD, U. B.C., Vancouver, 1967. Diplomate Royal Coll. Physicians Can. Intern Mercy Hosp., San Diego, 1967-68, resident, 1970-71, assoc. dir. cardiology, 1972-92; resident Vancouver Gen. Hosp., 1968-70, U. Calif., San Diego, 1971-72; with So. Calif. Cardiology Med. Group, San Diego, 1984—; pvt. practice Clin. Cons. Cardiology. Bd. trustees San Diego Found. for Med. Care, 1983-89, 91—, pres., chmn. bd. trustees, 1986-88, med. dir., 1991-96; trustee Pacific Found. for Med. Care, 1996—, med. dir., 1996—; bd. dirs. Mut. Assn. for Profl. Services, Phila., 1984-92; pres. Alternet Med. Svcs., Inc., 1992-95; pres. and med. dir. San Diego IPA, 1995—. Fellow Royal Coll. Physicians Can., Am. Coll. Cardiology (assoc.); mem. AMA, Am. Heart Assn., Calif. Med. Assn., San Diego County Med. Soc., San Diego County Heart Assn. (bd. dirs. 1982-88). Episcopalian. Office: So Calif Cardiology Med Group 6386 Alvarado Ct Ste 101 San Diego CA 92120-4906 Office Phone: 619-265-1237. Personal E-mail: wmapitt@aol.com.

PITTAWAY, DONALD EDWARD, endocrinology educator, gynecologist; b. Carbondale, Pa., May 8, 1947; s. Clifford Charles and Eleanor Ruth (Schwartztrauber) P.; m. Carmel Celine Imbalzano, June 27, 1970; children: Jennifer, Donald E. Jr. AB, Franklin and Marshall Coll., 1969; PhD, Tenn. U., 1974; MD, La. State U., Shreveport, 1977. Diplomate Am. Bd. Ob-Gyn, Am. Bd. Bioanalysis (high complexity lab. dir.); cert. reproductive endocrinologist. Clin. instr. Sch. Medicine La. State U., 1974-77; instr. Sch. Medicine Vanderbilt U., Nashville, 1981-83; from asst. to assoc. prof. reproductive endocrinology Wake Forest U., Winston-Salem, N.C., 1983-90, prof. endocrinology, sect. head, 1990-98, clin. prof., 1998—. Med. adv. bd. Smith Kline Beecham, Pitts., 1993—. Summer fellow NSF, 1971, Rsch. fellow March of Dimes Nat. Found., 1975-76, Ob-Gyn Clin. Rsch. fellow Mead Johnson Am. Coll., 1984-85. Mem. Soc. Gynecol. Investigation, Endocrine Soc., Am. Soc. Reproductive Medicine. Office: Brookview Women's Ctr Ste 105 3333 Brookview Hills Blvd Winston Salem NC 27103-5661 Office Phone: 336-765-1464.

PITTELKO, ROGER DEAN, clergyman, religious educator; b. Elk Reno, Okla., Aug. 18, 1932; s. Elmer Henry and Lydia Caroline (Nieman) Pittelko. AA, Concordia Coll., 1952; BA, Concordia Sem., St. Louis, 1954, MDiv, 1957, STM, 1958; postgrad., Chgo. Luth. Theol. Sem., 1959-61; ThD, Am. Div. Sch., Pineland, Fla., 1968; DMin, Faith Evang. Luth. Sem., Tacoma, 1983. Ordained to ministry Luth. Ch., 1958. Vicar St. John Luth. Ch., S.I., NY, 1955—56, asst. pastor New Orleans, 1958-59; pastor Concordia Luth. Ch., Berwyn, Ill., 1959-63, Luth. Ch. of Holy Spirit, Elk Grove Village, Ill., 1963-67; chmn. Commn. on Worship, Luth. Ch.-Mo. Synod, 1982—92, chmn. Commn. on Worship, 1994—98, asst. bishop Midwest region English dist., 1983, pres. and bishop English dist., 1987-97, 3d v.p., 1997—2001; prof. pastoral theology Concordia Theol. Sem., Ft. Wayne, Ind., 1997—2003; mem. pastoral staff Trinity Luth. Ch., Villa Pk., Ill., 2003—. Author: Guide to Introducing Lutheran Worship; contbr. articles to jours. Mem.: Luth. Acad. for Scholarship, Concordia Hist. Inst., Itasca Country Club (Ill.), Maywood Sportsmans Club (Ill.). Republican. Lutheran. Office: Trinity Evang Luth Ch 300 S Ardmore Villa Park IL 60181 Office Phone: 630-834-3440.

PITTELKOW, MARK ROBERT, physician, dermatology educator, researcher; b. Milw., Dec. 16, 1952; s. Robert Bernard and Barbara Jean (Thomas) P.; m. Gail L. Gamble, Nov. 26, 1977; children: Thomas, Cameron, Robert. BA, Northwestern U., 1975; MD, Mayo Med. Sch., 1979. Intern then resident Mayo Grad. Sch., 1979-84, post-doctoral exptl. pathology, 1981-83; from asst. to assoc. prof. dermatology Mayo Med. Sch., Rochester, Minn., 1984-95, prof. dermatology, 1995—, assoc. prof. biochemistry and molecular biology, 1992—. Cons. Mayo Clinic/Found., Rochester, 1984— Fellow Am. Acad. Dermatology; mem. AAAS, Am. Dermatol. Assn., Soc. Investigative Dermatology, Am. Burn Assn., Am. Soc. Cell Biology, N.Y. Acad. Scis., Chi Psi. Home: 721 12th Ave SW Rochester MN 55902-2027 Office: Mayo Clinic 200 1st St SW Rochester MN 55905-0002 Office Phone: 507-284-2758. Business E-Mail: pittelkow.mark@mayo.edu.

PITTENDRIGH, BARRY ROBERT, entomology professor; b. Regina, Saskatchewan, Canada, Oct. 29, 1968; s. Robert Lewis and Irene Joyce Pittendrigh; m. Julia Bello-Bravo, June 16, 1997; children: Quintin Robert, Natalia Carmen. PhD, U. Wis., Madison, 1994—99. Max planck fellow Max Planck Inst. Chem. Ecology, Jena, Germany, 1999—2000; asst. prof. Purdue U., West Lafayette, Ind., 2000—. Office: Purdue U 901 W State St West Lafayette IN 47907 Business E-Mail: pittendr@purdue.edu.

PITTI, DONALD ROBERT, financial services consultant; b. N.Y.C., Sept. 15, 1929; s. August and Mary (Vitaglione) P.; m. Grace Allen Curtis, Aug. 14, 1954; children: Gail, Robert. BA, NYU, 1959; postgrad., Adelphi U., 1963-65. Asst. v.p. Standard & Poor's Corp., N.Y.C., 1959—65; v.p. Quotron, Inc., N.Y.C., 1965—67; pres. Wiesenberger & Co., N.Y.C., 1967—76; v.p. John Nuveen & Co., Inc., N.Y.C., 1976—87; pres. Monarch Resources, Inc., N.Y.C., 1987—88; chmn., CEO Monarch Fin. Svcs., Inc., N.Y.C., 1988—89; pres., CEO Seligman Fin. Svcs. Inc., N.Y.C., 1989—95; pres. Graydon Consulting Corp., Manhasset, NY, 1996—; dir. Fin. Svcs. Inst. St. John's U., NY, 1995—, adj. prof. fin., 1995—. Chmn. Found. Fin. Planning, Atlanta, 1994-2000 Editor: Handbook of Financial Planning, 1988; contbr. articles to profl. publs. With USN, 1948-49, 50-52. Mem. Internat. Assn. Fin. Planning (pres.), Union League, Manhasset Bay Yacht Club, Met. Opera Club. Avocations: gardening, reading, swimming. Home: 169 Kensett Rd Manhasset NY 11030-2140

PITTMAN, CATHERINE SYLVIA, secondary school educator; b. Brunswick, Ga., Apr. 24, 1962; m. David Pittman; children: Drew, Meghan. BS, Ga. So. Coll., 1984, MEd, 1989, EdS, 1993. Tchr. grade 7,8 Risley Middle Sch., Glynn County, 1985-89; tchr. grades 9-12 Brunswick High Sch., Glynn County, 1989—. Named Ga. Tchr. of Yr., 1995, 1996, Milken Family Found. Nat. Educator, 1995; recipient YMCA Tribute to Women's Leaders, 1999. Mem. Glynn County Assn. of Educators, Ga. Assn. of Educators, Nat. Edn. Assn., Ga. Council of Social Studies, So. Assn. of Student Councils, Nat. Assn. of Student Activity Advisors. Home: 103 Marsh Landing Dr Brunswick GA 31523-9387 Office: Brunswick High Sch 3920 Habersham St Brunswick GA 31520-2799

PITTMAN, CONSTANCE SHEN, endocrinologist, educator; b. Nanking, China, Jan. 2, 1929; came to U.S., 1946; d. Leo F.-Z. and Pao Kong (Yang) Shen; m. James Allen Pittman, Jr., Feb. 19, 1955; children: James Clinton, John Merrill. AB in Chemistry, Wellesley Coll., 1951; MD, Harvard U., 1955. Diplomate Am. Bd. Internal Medicine, sub-bd. Endocrinology. Intern Baltimore City Hosp., 1955-56; resident U. Ala., Birmingham, 1956-57; instr. in medicine U. Ala. Med. Ctr., Birmingham, 1957—59, fellow dept. pharmacology, 1957-59, from asst. prof. to assoc. prof., 1959-70, prof., 1970—. Prof. medicine Georgetown U., Washington, 1972—73; mem. diabetes and metabolism tng. com. NIH, Bethesda, Md., 1972—76, mem. nat. arthritis, metabolism and digestive disease coun., 1975—78, mem. gen. clin. rsch. ctrs. com., 1979—83, 1987—90; bd. dirs. Internat. Coun. for Control of Iodine Deficiency Diseases, 1994—; mem. Iodine Deficiency Disorders Elimination Steering Com. Kiwanis Internat., 2002—. Master ACP; mem. Assn. Am. Physicians, Am. Soc. for Clin. Investigation, Endocrine Soc. (coun., 1978-79, pres. women's caucus 1978-79), Am. Thyroid Assn. (pres. 1990-91), Kiwanis (mem. iodine deficiency disorders steering com.). Achievements include research in activation and metabolism of thyroid hormone; kinetics of thyroxine conversion to triiodothyrine in health and disease states; control of iodine deficiency disorders. Emails. Office: U Ala Div Endocrinology/Metab Lab Med Ctr Birmingham AL 35294-0001 E-mail: cpittman@uab.edu.

PITTMAN, EDWIN LLOYD, state supreme court chief justice; b. Hattiesburg, Miss., Jan. 2, 1935; s. Lloyd H. and Pauline P.; m. Virginia Lund, 1996; children: Melanie, Win, Jennifer. BS, U. So. Miss.; JD, U. Miss., 1960. Bar: Miss. Practiced law until, 1964; mem. Miss. Senate, 1964-72; treas. State of Miss., Jackson, 1976-80, sec. of state, 1980-84, atty. gen., 1984-88; justice Supreme Ct. Miss., Jackson, 1990—; chief justice Miss. Supreme Ct., Jackson, Miss., 2000—. Trustee William Carey Coll. 2nd lt., Inf. U.S. Army. Mem. U. Miss. Alumni Assn., U. So. Miss. Alumni Assn., Miss. Jaycees (past state dir.), ABA, South Central Miss. Bar Assn. Clubs: Lions, Masons. Democrat. Baptist. Office: Miss Supreme Ct Gartin Justice Bldg PO Box 249 Jackson MS 39205-0117

PITTMAN, HUNTER, architecture educator, department chairman; Asst. prof. arch. Va. Tech., Blacksburg, assoc. prof., chair profl. program Sch. Arch. and Design. Mem. Commn. on Grad. Studies Policies Va. Tech., Blacksburg, Va. Office: Va Tech 0205 Sch Arch and Design 201 Cowgill Hall Blacksburg VA 24061*

PITTMAN, JACQUELYN, retired mental health nurse, nursing educator; b. Pensacola, Fla., Dec. 22, 1932; d. Edward Corry Sr. and Hettie Oean (Wilson) P. BS in Nursing Edn., Fla. State U., 1958; MA, Columbia U., 1959, EdD, 1974. Physician asst. Med. Ctr. Clinic, Pensacola, 1953-55; clin. instr., asst. dir. nursing svc. Sacred Heart Hosp., Pensacola, 1955-56; instr. psychiat. nurse Fla. State Hosp., Chattahoochee, 1958; instr. psychiat. nursing Pensacola Jr. Coll., 1959-60, 62-63; chmn. div. nursing Gulf Coast C.C., Panama City, Fla., 1963-66; asst. prof. U. Tex., Austin, 1970-72, assoc. prof., 1972-80; prof. nursing, coord. curriculum and tchg. grad. program La. State U. Med. Ctr., New Orleans, 1980-99, rep. faculty senate, 1997-99; pres.-elect faculty assembly Sch. Nursing La. State U. Med. Ctr. Sch. Nursing, New Orleans, 1997-98, pres., 1998-99; ret., 1999. Curriculum cons. Nicholls State U., Thibodaux, La., 1982, Our Lady of Lake Sch. Nursing, Baton Rouge, 1983; rsch. liaison So. Bapt. Hosp., New Orleans, 1987-89, Med. Ctr. La., 1992-99; mem. adv. bd. Sister Henrietta Guyot Professorship; mem. planning com. Nichols State U./La. State U. Med. Ctr. Partnership, 1996-99. Mem. ethics com., trustee Hotel Dieu Hosp., New Orleans, 1987—91; judge Internat. Sci. and Engring. Fair Assn., 1990, 1992; del. La. State Nurses' Assn. State Conv., 1992, 1994; assoc. Libr. of Congress, Smithonian Instn.; mem. Dem. Nat. Comm., Presdl. Task Force, 1992, Ctr. for Study of Presidency; tchr. Christian edn. program for mentally retarded St. Ignatius Martyr Ch., 1979—80; tchr. initiation team Rite of Christian Initiation of Adults, Our Lady of the Lake Cath. Ch., Mandeville, La., 1983—86; v.p., bd. dirs. St. Tammany Guidance Ctr., Inc., Mandeville, 1987—91; mem. parish outreach meals-on-wheels program St. Tammany, Covington, La., 2001—02. Mem. ANA, LWV, Am. Assn. Adv. Sci. Directory, N.Y. Acad. Scis., Acad. Polit. Sci., Libr. of Congress Assocs., Nat. Trust for Hist. Preservation, La. Endowment for Humanities, La. Nurses Assn. (archivist 1987-99, state task force com. to preserve hist. documents 1987-99), So. Nursing Rsch. Soc., Nat. League Nursing, Boston U. Nursing Archives, Women's Inner Cir. Achievement N.Am. Cmtys., Internat. Order of Merit, World Found. Successful Women, Wilson Ctr. Assocs., Kappa Delta Pi, Sigma Theta Tau. Democrat. Roman Catholic. Avocations: swimming, golf, travel, reading, louisiana history. Address: 204 Woodridge Blvd Mandeville LA 70471-2604 Office Phone: 985-845-4631.

PITTMAN, JAMES ALLEN, JR., endocrinologist, educator; b. Orlando, Fla., Apr. 12, 1927; s. James Allen and Jean C. (Garretson) Pittman; m. Constance Ming-Chung Shen, Feb. 19, 1955; children: James Clinton, John Merrill. BS, Davidson Coll., 1948; MD, Harvard, 1952; DSc (hon.), Davidson Coll., 1980, U. Ala., Birmingham, 1984. Intern, asst. resident medicine Mass. Gen. Hosp., Boston, 1952—54; tchg. fellow medicine Harvard U., 1953—54; clin. assoc. NIH, Bethesda, Md., 1954—56; instr. medicine George Washington U., 1955—56; chief resident U. Ala. Med. Ctr., Birmingham, 1956—58, instr. medicine, 1956—59, asst. prof., 1959—62, assoc. prof., 1962—64, prof. medicine, 1964—92, dir. endocrinology and metabolism divsn., 1962—71, co-chmn. dept. medicine, 1969—71, also prof., physiology and biophysics, 1967—92, dean, 1973—92, U. Ala. Birmingham Disting. prof., 1992—. Mem. endocrinology study sect. NIH, 1963—67; mem. nat. adv. rsch. resources coun. NIH, 1991—95; asst. chief med. dir. rsch. and edn. in medicine U.S. VA, 1971—73; prof. medicine Georgetown U. Med. Sch., Washington, 1971—73; mem. grad. med. edn. nat. adv. com. HEW, 1976—78; mem. HHS Coun. on Grad. Med. Edn., 1986—90; hon. prof. Chung Shan Med. and Dental Coll., Taiwan, 1994; sr. advisor Internat. Coun. on Ctrl. of Iodine Deficiency Diseases, 1994—96. Author: Diagnosis and Treatment of Thyroid Diseases, 1963; contbr. articles in field to profl. jours. Master: Am. Coll. Endocrinology; fellow: AAAS; mem.: ACP, Hist. Sci. Soc., Am. Soc. for the History of Medicine, So. Soc. Clin. Investigation (Founder's medal 1993), Am. Fedn. Clin. Rsch. (pres. So. sect., nat. coun. 1962—66), Am. Chem. Soc., Am. Diabetes Assn., Endocrine Soc. Ecuador (hon.), N.Y. Acad. Scis. (life), Am. Ornithologists Union (life), Soc. Nuc. Medicine, Am. Thyroid Assn., Am. Assn. Clin. Endocrinologists, Endocrine Soc., Assn. Am. Physicians, Inst. Medicine of NAS, Harvard U. Med. Alumni Assn. (pres. 1986—88), Wilson Ornithol. Club (life), Alpha Omega Alpha, Phi Beta Kappa, Omicron Delta Kappa. Office: U Ala Sch Med Pittman CAMS 1924 7th Ave S Birmingham AL 35294-0007 Office Phone: 205-934-3414. *I hope that each time I meet a person, both of us leave the encounter the better for it.*

PITTMAN, KATHLEEN M. education educator, consultant; b. Roswell, N.Mex., Nov. 15, 1945; d. Andrew Jackson and Rebecca Moore; m. Walter Earl Pittman, Aug. 8, 1990. BS, Jacksonville State U., 1978; MA, U. Ala., 1980, EdS, 1984, PhD, 1992. Cert. Prin., Supr., Tchr. State Ala., 1978, State N.Mex., 2003. Tchr. of gifted Hale County Schs., Greensboro, Ala., 1979—81, Tuscaloosa City Schs., Ala., 1981—92; assoc. prof. U. West Ala., Livingston, 1992—2003. Tchr. evaluator sys. evaluator trainer Ala. Dept. of Edn., Montgomery, 1994—; instr. Ea. N.Mex. U., 2004—. Home: 141 Willie Horton Dr Ruidoso NM 88345-7709

PITTMAN, LISA, lawyer; b. Limestone, Maine, Jan. 4, 1959; d. William Franklin and Rowena Paradis (Umphrey) P.; 1 child, Graham Edward Paradis. BA, U. Fla., 1980, postgrad., 1981, JD, 1984; LLM, George Washington U., 1988. Bar: Fla. 1984, D.C. 1993, U.S Supreme Ct. 1993. Spl. asst. to gen. counsel Nat. Oceanic and Atmospheric Adminstrn., Washington, 1984-85, atty., advisor, 1985-87; minority counsel Com. on Mcht. Marine & Fisheries, Ho. of Reps., Washington, 1987-95; dep. chief counsel Com. on Resources U.S. Ho. of Reps., Washington, 1995-2001, chief counsel Com. on Resources, 2001—02, 2003—, chief counsel, dep. chief of staff, 2002—03. Home: 7325 Eldorado St Mc Lean VA 22102-2904 Office: US House of Reps 1324 Longworth HOB Washington DC 20515-0001

PITTMAN, ROBERT TURNER, retired newspaper editor; b. Gates, N.C., Sept. 24, 1929; s. Thomas Everett and Lillian (Turner) P.; m. Ruth Fike, Aug. 25, 1956; children— Laura Emily, Mary Ann, Lillian Elizabeth. BA, Washington and Lee U., 1951; MA, U. N.C., 1957. Reporter Times Dispatch, Richmond, Va., 1951; editor, pub. Daily Ranger, Glendive, Mont., 1957-58; writer editorials Times Union, Jacksonville, Fla., 1958-63; editorial editor Times, St. Petersburg, Fla., 1963-92; dir. Times Pub. Co., 1968-92. Trustee Poynter Inst. Media Studies, St. Petersburg, 1978-92. Editor: (jour.) Masthead, 1980—81. Active St. Petersburg Charter Revision Com., 1992-93; dir. Fla. Bar Found., 1994-96. Lt. (j.g.) USNR, 1951-55. Recipient Pinellas Civil Liberties award, 1993; U. N.C.-Chapel Hill scholarship established in honor, 1994, Liberty Bell award St. Petersburg Bar Assn., 1995. Mem. Am. Soc. Newspaper Editors, Nat. Conf. Editl. Writers (pres. 1978, life), Nat. Conf. Editl. Writers Found. Inc. (pres. 1984) Methodist. Home: 736 18th Ave NE Saint Petersburg FL 33704-4608

PITTMAN, ROBERT WARREN, investor; b. Jackson, Miss., Dec. 28, 1953; s. Warren E. and Lanita (Hurdle) P.; m. Sandra Hill, July 27, 1979; 1 child, Robert Thomas; m. Veronique Choa, Nov. 28, 1997; children: Andrew Forest, Lucy Li. Student, Millsaps Coll., 1971-72, Oakland U., 1972-73, U. Pitts., 1973-74; AMP, Harvard U., 1984-85. Disc jockey Sta. WJDX-FM, Jackson, Miss., 1970-72, Sta. WRIT, Milw., 1972; research dir. Sta. WDRQ, Detroit, 1972-73; program dir. Sta. WPEZ, Pitts., 1973-74, Stas. WMAQ-WKQX NBC, Chgo., 1974-77, Sta. WNBC, N.Y.C., 1977-79; exec. producer Album Tracks, NBC TV, N.Y.C., 1977-78; dir., v.p., then sr. v.p. MTV Networks, N.Y.C., 1979-82, exec. v.p., COO, 1983-85, pres., CEO, 1985-86, Quantum Media, Inc., N.Y.C., 1987-89; exec. advisor Warner Communications, Inc., N.Y.C., 1989-90; pres., chief exec. officer Time Warner Enterprises, N.Y.C., 1990-95; CEO, Six Flags Entertainment, 1991-95; mng. ptnr., CEO, Century 21 Real Estate, 1995-96; pres., CEO Am. On-Line Networks, 1996-97; pres., COO Am. On-Line, Inc., 1997-2001; CO-COO AOL Time Warner, 2001, COO, 2002—; ptnr. Pilot Group, 2003—. Bd. dirs. Cendant Corp., Elec. Arts, N.Y.C. Ballet, N.Y. Shakespeare Festival, chmn., 1987—94; bd. dir. Robin Hood Found., Alliance Lupus Rsch. Recipient Program Mgr. of Yr. Billboard, 1977, Program Dir. of Yr. Hall Radio Report, 1978, Entrepreneur award White House SB Conf., 1986, Golden Plate award Am. Acad. Achievement, 1990, medal of Excellence Miss. U. Women, 1992, Vision award Retinitis Pigmentosa International, 1992, Lifetime Achievement Internat. Monitor award Internat. Teleproduction Soc., 1993; named Innovator of Yr. Performance Mag., 1981, Humanitarian of Yr., AMC, 1984, Time Mag. Man of Yr. runner-up, 1984, Esquire Mag. Under 40 Leadership, 1985; named one of Pioneers of New Am. Start-Up, Success mag., one of five Original Thinkers of 80s, Life mag, 1990, 8 of 50 Most Influential Baby Boomers, Life mag., 1996. Methodist. Office: Pilot Group LLC 625 Madison Ave New York NY 10023

PITTMAN, ROY CLINTON, JR., neurosurgeon, lawyer, theologian, philosopher; b. Florence, S.C., Oct. 12, 1931; s. Roy Clinton and Edna Hester (Altman) P.; m. Therese Huguette Lamarche Pittman, Apr. 1958 (div. May 1976); 1 stepdaughter, Michele Lois Young; children: Charlotte Elisabeth, Clinton Christopher, Russell Roy; m. Jeanne Elmore Waters Pittman, Oct. 10, 1976. BS magna cum laude, Wofford Coll., Spartanburg, S.C., 1952; MD, Med. U. S.C., Charleston, 1956; JD, Washburn U. Coll. Law, Topeka, Kans., 1991; MDiv with honors, Emory U. Candler Sch. Theology, Atlanta, 1995; DSc (hon.), The London Inst., 1973. Diplomate Am. Bd. Neurol. and Orthopedic Surgery; ordained to ministry Ea. Orthodox Ch., 2000; bar: Fla. 1992, U.S. Dist. Ct. (mid. dist.) Fla. 1992. Intern U.S. Naval Hosp., Newport, RI, 1956-57; resident in neurology U.S. Naval Hosp.-Nat. Naval Med. Ctr., Bethesda, Md., 1957-58; neurologist East Coast Neuropsychiat. Ctr.-U.S. Naval Hosp., Phila., 1958-59, head neurology br., 1959; resident in neurosurgery Jefferson Med. Coll. Hosp., Phila., 1959-61, chief resident, 1961-62; resident in gen. surgery Hahnemann Med. Coll. Hosp., Phila., 1962-63; pvt. practice neurol. surgery Morton Plant and Mease Hosps., Clearwater-Dunedin, Fla., 1963-82, Cmty. Hosp. of New Port Richey, New Port Richey, Fla., 1978-88; pvt. practice legal medicine, med. jurisprudence & bioethics Pittman Profl. Assn., Clearwater, Fla., 1995-98, Tarpon Springs, Fla., 1995-98; pres., gen. counsel The Quintessential Corp., Tarpon Springs, 1998-2000; founder, prior Trinity House Retreat, Greek Orthodox Monastery of the Holy Trinity, 2001—. Protestant chaplain Morton Plant/Mease Countryside Hosp., Clearwater, Fla., 1997-98. Contbr. articles to profl. jours. Pres. St. Petersburg (Fla.) Coll. Alumni Assn., 1973-75. Lt. MC, USN, 1956-59, lt. comdr., 1962. Recipient Top Paper Bioethics & The Law award Washburn U. Coll. Law, Topeka, Kans., 1990, Top paper Comparative Civil Law award Cumberland Sch. Law & U. Heidelberg Germany Faculty of Law, 1990. Fellow Internat. Coll. Angiology, Royal Soc. Health, Internat. Coll. Surgeons, Am. Coll. Legal Medicine; mem. AMA, Congress Neurol. Surgeons, Fla. Med. Assn., Fla. Bar, Phi Beta Kappa, Phi Delta Phi. Jeffersonian Democrat. Avocations: stamp collecting/philately, anthropology, travel. Home: 90 S Highland Ave Apt 1201 Tarpon Springs FL 34689-5351

PITTMAN, STEUART LANSING, lawyer; b. Albany, N.Y., June 6, 1919; s. Ernest Wetmore and Estelle Young (Romeyn) P.; children by previous marriage— Andrew Pinchot, Nancy Steuart, Rosamond Pinchot, Tamara Pickering; m. Barbara Milburn White, Mar. 29, 1958; children— Patricia Milburn, Steuart Lansing, Anne Romeyn. Grad., St. Paul's Sch., Concord, N.H., 1937; BA, Yale U., 1941, LLB, 1948. Bar: N.Y. 1948, D.C. 1954. With Pan Am. Airways Africa Ltd., Cairo, 1941-42, China Nat. Aviation Co., Calcutta, India, 1942; with firm Cravath, Swaine & Moore, N.Y.C., 1948-50; with govt. agys. ECA, Mut. Security Agy. and FOA, 1950-54; founder Shaw Pittman (and predecessors), Washington, 1954-61, 64—; asst. sec. of def., 1961-64. Cons. 2d Hoover Commn., 1954-55, Dept. State, 1955, Devel. Loan Fund, 1958-59; sr. fellow Inst. Def. Analysis. Bd. dirs. Hudson Inst.,

Chesapeake Environ. Protection Assn.; mem. Atlantic Coun. 1st lt. USMCR, WWII, CBI. Decorated Silver Star. Mem. Met. Club (Washington). Office: Shaw Pittman 2300 N St NW Washington DC 20037-1172

PITTMAN, VIRGIL, federal judge; b. Enterprise, Ala., Mar. 28, 1916; s. Walter Oscar and Annie Lee (Logan) P.; m. Floy Lasseter, 1944 (dec.) 2000; children— Karen Pittman Gordy, Walter Lee. BS, U. Ala., 1939, LL.B., 1940. Bar: Ala. bar 1940. Spl. agt. FBI, 1940-44; practice law Gadsden, Ala., 1946-51; judge Ala. Circuit Ct., Circuit 16, 1951-66; U.S. dist. judge Middle and So. Dist. Ala., 1966-71; chief judge U.S. Dist. Ct. for Ala. So. Dist., 1971-81; sr. judge, 1981—; periodically sat as judge U.S. Ct. Appeals 11th Cir., 1981—96. Lectr. bus. law, econs. and polit. sci. U. Ala. Center, Gadsden, 1948-66 Author: Circuit Court Proceedings in Acquisition of a Tract of Right of Way, 1959, A Judge Looks at Right of Way Condemnation Proceedings, 1960, Technical Pitfalls in Right of Way Proceedings, 1961. Mem. Ala. Bd. Edn., 1951; bd. trustees, life trustee Samford U, 1975-. Lt. (j.g.) USN, 1944-46, USS Wharton, Pacific Supply Corp. Mem. Ala. State Bar, Etowah County Bar Assn. (pres. 1949), Baptist Oaks (bd. dirs. lower income housing), Omicron Delta Kappa. Democrat. Baptist. Office: US Dist Ct 113 Saint Joseph St Mobile AL 36602

PITTMAN, WILLIAM CLAUDE, electrical engineer; b. Pontotoc, Miss., Apr. 22, 1921; s. William Claude and Maude Ella (Bennett) P.; m. Eloise Savage, Apr. 20, 1952; children: Patricia A. Pittman Ready, William Claude III, Thomas Allen. BSEE, Miss. State Coll., 1951, MSEE, 1957. From electronic engr. to supr. elec. engring. dept. U.S. Army Labs., Redstone Arsenal, Ala., 1951-59; supr. electronic engr. to aero. engring. supr. NASA/Marshall Space Flight Ctr., 1960; electronic engr. Army Missile Labs., 1962-82; program mgr. Army Labs. and R&D Ctr., Redstone Arsenal, 1982-99; vol. cons. AMCOM, 1999—. Organizer numerous sci. and tech. confs. Author patents, reports, papers. Sgt. USMC, 1940-46, PTO. Recipient Medal of Honor, DAR, Meritorious Civilian Svc. award Dept. Army, 1993. Fellow AIAA (assoc.; chmn. Miss.-Ala. chpt. 1981-82, Martin Schilling award 1980); mem. IEEE (sr. life), First Marine Div. Assn., DAV, IRE (chmn. Huntsville sect. 1957-58), Madison Hist. Soc., SAR (pres. Tenn. Valley chpt. 1984-85, Ala. Soc. 1990-91, Cert. 1991, Patriot medal), Tau Beta Pi, Phi Kappa Phi, Kappa Mu Epsilon. Avocations: history, genealogy. Home: 704 Desoto Rd SE Huntsville AL 35801-2032 Office: US Army Aviation Missile Command Huntsville AL 35898-5000 Office Phone: 256-876-1778.

PITTS, ANGELA L. humanities educator, researcher; d. Marietta Beougher and Jerry Pitts, Roger Beougher (Stepfather). B Arts and Scis, Ohio U., Athens, Ohio, 1996; MA, U. Wis., 1998, PhD. Army specialist; ada Ohio N.G., McConnellsville, 1991—96; lectr.; instr.; tchg. asst. U. of Wis., Madison, 1997—2002; asst. prof. classics Mary Wash. Coll., Fredericksburg, Va., 2002—. Mem.; dir. of local group Amnesty Internat., Columbus & Athens, Ohio, 1990—96; dir. Women's Affairs Commn., OU Student Senate, Athens, Ohio, 1994—95. Recipient Dr. Brenda Pfaehler Award for Tchg. Excellence, U. of Wis., 1998; fellow Dissertation fellowship, U. Wis., 2001; grantee Faculty Devel. Grant, Mary Wash. Coll., 2003; scholar Paul J. Murphy Scholarship, Classics Dept., Ohio U. Mem.: MLA, Classical Assn. of Va., Classical Assn. of the Mid. West and South, Golden Key Honors Soc., Phi Beta Kappa. D-Liberal. Achievements include research in Ancient Biographical Tradition of Sappho. Office: Mary Washington College 1301 College Ave Fredericksburg VA 22401

PITTS, BARBARA TOWLE, accountant, painter; b. St. Paul, Minn., Nov. 8, 1944; d. James Francis and Helen (Gorman) Towle; m. E. R. Pitts, Oct. 19, 1965; 1 child, Paris Tucker. BSBA with honors, U. Ala., 1980. CPA Wash., Tenn. Prin. Barbara M. Pitts Assocs., Fayetteville, Tenn., 1982-90, Barbara M. Pitts CPA, Seattle, 1990-98; ptnr. Art Painters Internat. Organizer Three Paths to Expression: Print Makers Ctrl. China; lectr. in field. One-woman shows include Wallenstien Gallery, Moses Lake, Wash., 1998, Columbia Basin Allied Arts, 1998, Artstall Gallery, Seattle, 1998, Ballard Fetherston Gallery, 1998, 2000, Arabella Gallery, Cannon Beach, Oreg., 1998, 2000, exhibited in group shows at Frye Art Mus., Midwest Watercolor Soc. 20th Ann. Nat. Open Show, 1996, Red River Watercolor Soc. 3d Ann. Nat. Juried Art Exhbn., 1996, Eastern Wash. Watercolor Soc. Ann. Nat. Competition, 1996 (Allied Arts award), Niagara Frontier Watercolor Soc. Nat. Exhbn., 1996, Watercolor Art Soc., Houston, 1997, La. Watercolor Soc., 1997, 1998, Watercolor Soc. Ala., 1997, Ga. Watercolor Soc., 1997, 1998, Red River Watercolor Soc., 1997, Pacific Gallery Artists Ann. Open Show, 1997, Midwest Watercolor Soc., 1997, Aqueous '97, 1997, Nat. Watercolor Okla., 1997, Watercolor West, 1997, Eastern Wash. Watercolor Soc., 1997, N.W. Watercolor Soc., 1997, 1999, 2000, Pacific Artists Gallery, 1997, Women Painters Wash., Seattle, Asian Art Mus. Kado Tea Garden, 1997, Tubac (Ariz.) Ctr. Arts, 1997, Tex. Watercolor Soc. 48th Ann. Mus. S.W., 1997 (Best of Show award), Mercer Island (Wash.) Gallery, 1998, Janet Laurel: A Woman's Gallery, 1998, Pacific Artists Gallery, 1997 (Best in Show award, 1997), Nat. Watercolor Okla., 1997 (3d pl. award, 1997), Ga. Watercolor Soc. 18th Nat. Exhbn., 1997 (Traveling Show award, 1997), Midwest Watercolor Soc. 21st Nat. Exhbn., 1997, Women Painters Wash., 1997 (Dorothy Arnston award, Gold medal award, Nancy Moffet award, 1998), Millennium Images Internat. Juried Show, others, exhibitions include Everett (Wash.) Ctr. Arts, 1998, Brea (Calif.) Cultural Ctr., Tolles Gallery, Mercer Island, Wash., 1998, Western Colo. Ctr. Arts, Grand Junction, Colo., 1998, Journey Mus., Rapid City, S.D., 1998, Frye Art Mus., Seattle, 1999, Ahmed Al-Adwany Gallery, Kuwait City, Kuwait, 1999, N.W. Watercolor Soc. 59th Ann. Open Show, 60th Ann. Open Show, N.W. Watercolor Hist. Retrosepctive, Glaway Arts Festival, Ireland, Waterfront Hall, Belfast, Northern Ireland, Golden Thread Gallery, Belfast, others, commd., Pike Pl. Market Festival poster, 1998, Inn at the Market, Seattle, Sound Transit Rail Sta., Tukwila Pk. & Ride, Bellevue CC/Costco Early Lng. & Family Ctr., Pike Pl. Market Found., 2001, Lilac Lodge, S.E. Effective Devel., Seattle, 2002; contbr. articles to profl. jours. Bd. dirs. Lincoln County Bd. Edn., Fayetteville, 1988—90, United Way Lincoln County, Fayetteville, 1989; mem. planning com. Tenn. Hist. Soc., Nashville, 1989. Named Woman of the Yr., Fayetteville Bus. and Profl. Women, 1988; recipient cert. of Recognition, Tenn. Main St. Program, 1989, Best of Show award, Juried Arts Ocean Shores, Wash., 1996, Mid. Ga. Art Assn. award, Ga. Watercolor Soc., 1997, Traveling Show, 1997, Forstall award, La. Watercolor Soc., 1998, Winsor and Newton award, Watercolor West, 1996, ColorQ award, 1998. Mem.: AICPA, Watercolor West (signature mem.), Women Painters Wash., Group Health Coop. Puget Sound (ctrl. region coun.), Red River Watercolor Soc. (Gold medal of Honor 1997), N.W. Watercolor Soc. (signature mem., treas., Past Pres. award 1997, Best of Show), Wash. Soc. CPA, Am. Watercolor Soc., Midwest Watercolor Soc., Nat. Watercolor Soc. Home: 3515 E Marion St Seattle WA 98122-5258 Studio: 5628 Airport Way South Ste 1 Seattle WA 98108 Office Phone: 206-763-3135. E-mail: barbara@pitts.net.

PITTS, BRYAN, performing company executive; Artistic dir. Ballet Okla., Oklahoma City, 1986—. Office: Ballet Okla 7421 N Classen Blvd Oklahoma City OK 73116

PITTS, DEBORAH KRUEGER, healthcare consultant; b. Jamestown, N.D., Mar. 11, 1956; d. Lester James and Phyllis Jean (Koenig) K.; B.A. in Biology, U. Calif.-Santa Barbara, 1978; M.H.A., Duke U., 1980. Cardiopulmonary clk. Cottage Hosp., Santa Barbara, 1978; patient account rep. Durham (N.C.) County Hosp., 1979-80; health adminstrn. fellow Duke U. Hosp., Durham, 1980-81; v.p. Amherst Assocs., Atlanta, 1981-84, Tampa, 1984-88; dir. cost analysis Daus. of Charity Nat. Health System-West, Los Altos Hills, Calif., 1988-89; dir. outpatient svcs. Seton Med. Ctr., 1989-91; exec. dir. Home Tech. Health Care, 1992-94; bus. advisor, 1994—. Vol. Imola State Hosp., Napa, Calif., 1973-74; big sister St. Vincents Sch. for Mentally Handicapped, Santa Barbara, 1974-78; fund raiser Duke U. Health Adminstrn. Dept., 1980-84; assoc. coordinator Catholic Young Adults, Durham, 1980-81; bd. dirs., vice chmn., chmn. fin., chmn. planning coms. Hospice of Pinellas County, St. Petersburg, Fla., 1984-88; v.p., Partners for Tampa Theatre, 1987-88; bd. dirs. Hospice of Tenn., 1995—; leader Girl Scouts Am., 1994-97; pres. Overbrook Sch. Parent Club, 1994-96; active Jr. League, 1995-2000, sustainer Jr. League, 2000—; vol. Morris Brandon Elem. Sch., Atlanta, 1997-2000, J. Green Elem., Nashville, 2000-01; chair 2002 Heart Gala Auction; pres. St. Cecilia Parents' Assn., 2002-03, Coord. Scarab Store, 2003-. Calif. State Scholar, 1974; scholar. Am. Bus. Women's Assn., Loyal Order of Moose, Napa, Calif. Mem. Am. Coll. Healthcare Execs., Nat. Assn. Home Health Care, Tenn. Assn. Home Health Care, Healthcare Fin. Mgmt. Assn., Chaine des Rotisseurs, Am. Hosp. Soc. for Mktg. and Planning, Sun Coast Adminstrs. Group, Bay Area Healthcare Planners Assn., Alpha Delta Pi (v.p., pres. 1977; Violet award 1978), Phi Sigma Kappa (little sister). Roman Catholic. E-mail: dkpitts@aol.com.

PITTS, E. HAMPTON, business educator, dean; b. South Mont, N.C. s. Romaine W. and Winnie L. Pitts; m. Lawana Pitts, Mar. 21, 1970; 1 child, Katherine. BBA, Oglethorpe U., 1967; MA, West Ga. Coll., 1973; MBA, Pfeiffer Coll., 1988; PhD, U. Miss., 1975. Mgr. Lockheed Martin Aircraft, Atlanta, 1965-71; dean Palm Beach Atlantic U., West Palm Beach, Fla., 1975-79; CFO Chesterfield-Marlboro Coll., Cheraw, S.C., 1981-84; prof. mgmt., dean Bus. Sch. Wingate (N.C.) U., 1984—; CEO Walker County Health Dept., Lafayette, Ga., 1991-93. Trustee Union Regional Med. Ctr., Monroe, N.C., 2001; cons. HRM & Leadership; bus. sch. evaluator Assn. Collegiate Bus. Schs. and Programs Accrediting Agy. Contbr. articles to profl. jours. Vol. United Way, Monroe, 1996—; active County Econ. Devel. Task Force, 2000—, Wingate Bapt. Ch. Sgt. USMC, 1961. Mem. Rotary. Republican. Baptist. Office: Wingate Univ Wingate NC 28174 Home: 3268 Wayside Rd Kingston GA 30145-1222

PITTS, EDGAR THURLOW, writer, retired educator; b. Rockport, Maine, Sept. 5, 1919; s. George Edgar and Mildred Nettie (Thurlow) Pitts; m. Elizabeth Knowlton, Dec. 21, 1942 (dec. May 1993); 1 child, Nathan Thurlow. BA with hons. in Math., U. Maine, 1942; diploma, U.S. Naval Acad., 1943; MEd in Adminstrn., U. Maine, 1953. Cert. tchr., prin., supt. schs. Maine. Math. tchr./prin. Stonington (Maine) H.S., 1946—53; prin. Ellsworth (Maine) H.S., 1953—70; supervising prin. Five Towns Sch. Dist., Western Hancock County, Maine, 1970—73; pvt. math. tchr. Eastern Maine, 1974—82. Co-author: Deer Isle Remembered, 1989, Stonington Past and Present, 1997; author: Long Ago and Far Away, 1936-45, 2d edit., 2001. Founder, chmn. Acad. Recognition Commn., State of Maine, 1959—63; various ad hoc com. chairs state, regional and local edn., Maine, 1960—98; past pres., exec. com. Main Tchrs. Assn. Lt. USNR, 1942—46. Mem.: NEA, Maine Edn. Assn. (life), Am. Legion (post comdr. 1997—2000), Masons, Phi Beta Kappa. Republican. Avocations: stamp collecting/philately, local and regional history, e-mail. Home: PO Box 14 Thurlow's Hill Stonington ME 04681 Office: Polaris Press PO Box 14 Stonington ME 04681 Office Phone: 207-367-2483.

PITTS, FERRIS NEWCOMB, physician, psychiatry educator; b. St. Louis, Feb. 11, 1931; s. Ferris Newcomb and Florence A. (Morris) P.; m. Jocelyn Millner, May 14, 1955; children: Andrew Ferris, Jonathan Millner, Amy Pitts Buckner. BA, Washington U., St. Louis, 1952, MD, 1955. Diplomate Am. Bd. Pediats., Am. Bd. Psychology and Neurology. Intern Wash U. St Louis Children's Hosp, 1955-56; resident pediats. Washington U., St. Louis, 1955-56, resident psychiatry, 1959-62, assoc. prof. psychiatry, 1963-76; prof. psychiatry U. So. Calif., L.A., 1976—. Pres. med. staffs several hosps., 1970—, Am. Assn. Advancement Electrotherapy, 1986. Editor-in-chief Jour. Clin. Psychiatry, 1980-88; patentee in field of hyperimmunization therapy for AIDS and other viral disorders; contbr. over 100 articles to profl. jours. Lt. comdr. USN, 1957-62. Career Rsch. Devel. award, NIMH. Fellow Am. Psychiat. Assn. (life); mem. Psychiat. Rsch. Soc. (founding mem.), Internat. Soc. Neurochemistry (founding mem.), Am. Soc. Neurochemistry (founding mem.), West Coast Coll. Psychiat. Rsch. (founding mem.). Avocations: ice hockey, tennis. Home and Office: 3500 E California Blvd Pasadena CA 91107-5653

PITTS, JAMES ATWATER, financial executive; b. Greenwich, Conn., Apr. 8, 1940; s. Jeremiah Patrick and Mary Louise (McGregor) P.; m. Noreen Mary Kiggins, July 20, 1963; children: Paul, Andrew, Sarah. BBA with honors, Niagara U., 1962; MBA, U. Conn., 1971. CPA, N.Y. Staff acct. Price Waterhouse, Stamford, Conn., 1962; tax specialist Deloitte Haskins & Sells, Rochester, N.Y., 1965-68; div. contr. Xerox Corp., Stamford, 1968-76; asst. corp. contr. Digital Equipment Corp., Maynard, Mass., 1976-81; v.p., corp. contr. Data Gen. Corp., Westboro, Mass., 1981-86; exec. v.p. fin. adminstrn. and strategic planning Cullinet Software, Inc., Westwood, 1986-88; v.p., chief fin. officer Bain & Co. Inc., Boston, 1988-91; sr. v.p. fin. and adminstrn., treas., CFO Clean Harbors Inc., 1992-96; pres. The Pitts Group, Boston, 1996—; v.p. for fin. and adminstrn. The Boston Found., 1996—2004, chief investment officer, treas., 2004—. Chmn. Sudbury (Mass.) Town Fin. Com., 1984; v.p., mem. exec. com. Children's Mus. Boston, 1984-96; bd. dirs. Mus. Wharf Inc., 1988-96, Lake Winniepesaukee Assn., Wolfeboro, N.H.; chmn. Sudbury Long Range Capital Expenditures Com., 1981; trustee Lake Regional Conservation Trust, Meridith, N.H. With U.S. Army, 1963-64, USAR, 1965-90, Desert Storm, 1991. Decorated Meritorious Svc. medal, 1991; recipient Internat. Exec. Mgmt. award Internat. Mgmt. Inst. U. Geneva, 1980. Mem. AICPAs, Conn. CPA Soc., N.Y. Soc. CPAs, Fin. Execs. Inst., Harvard Bus. Sch. Assn. Boston (bd. govs. 1992, pres. 1992-96), Res. Officers Assn. (life), Soc. Mil. Compts., Bald Peak Colony Club, Officers Club. Office: The Boston Foundation 75 Arlington St Boston MA 02116-3936 Home: 8 West Hill Pl Boston MA 02114-3265 Office Phone: 617-338-1223.

PITTS, JOE W., III, (CHIP PITTS), lawyer, law educator; b. Baton Rouge, Nov. 24, 1960; s. Joe Wise Pitts Jr. and Bobbie (Chachere) Edwards. Cert., Cambridge (Eng.) U., 1980; spl. diploma, Oxford (Eng.) U., 1981; BA, Tulane U., 1982; JD, Stanford U., 1985. Bar: Tex. 1986. Assoc. Legal Resources Ctr., Johannesburg, Republic South Africa, 1984, Carrington Coleman Sloman & Blumenthal, Dallas, 1985-88; vis. asst. prof. law So. Meth. U., Dallas, 1988-89; ptnr. Baker and McKenzie, Dallas, 1989-96; v.p., chief legal officer Nokia, Inc., 1996—. Del. UN Commn. on Human Rights, Geneva, 1989, 92-96; U.S. del. to internat. conf. on European security NATO, Rome, 1990. Author numerous articles in field. Bd. dirs. Shakespeare Festival Dallas, 1987-94, pres., 1990-91, chmn., 1991-93; bd. dirs. Proyecto Adelante, 1988—; bd. dirs. Dallas Dem. Forum, 1989-93, sec., 1991-92; chmn. pub. awareness effort Dallas Young Lawyers Constl. Bicentennial Program, 1985-87, bd. dirs., 1987-91; vol. Cath. Charities Dallas, 1987—, North Ctrl. Tex. Legal Svcs., 1985—. Recipient cert. of appreciation Lawyers Against Domestic Violence, Dallas, 1985-87, cert. of recognition North Cen. Tex. Legal Svcs., 1985-87. Fellow Tex. Bar Found.; mem. ABA (vice chmn. sect. of bus. law, young lawyers div. 1986-88, exec. com., internat. law com. 1990—, vice-chair 1991-92, chair 1993—, editor-in-chief law practice notes Barrister Mag. 1988-91, commn. on pub. understanding about law 1989-91), Dallas Bar Assn. (Disting. Pro Bono Svc. award, 1986, 87, 88, 91, coord. immigration amnesty appeals com. 1987-88, chair, minority participation com. 1988-89, Pro Bono Vol. of Yr. 1989, spl. recognition 1990, 92), Tex. Assn. Young Lawyers (internat. law, editorial coms. 1985-91, chair refugee com. 1988-90, co-chmn. internat. law com. 1991-93), Dallas Assn. Young Lawyers (co-chair internat. law com. 1990-92, chair membership com. 1987-88, chair bill of rights com. 1988-89, treas. 1989, v.p. 1989-90), Tex. Accts. and Lawyers for Arts, Dallas Com. Fgn. Rels. (gen. counsel 1987-96), Council on Fgn. Relations N.Y. (term mem.), Dallas Council on World Affairs, Dallas Assembly, Crescent Spa Club, Phi Beta Kappa, Pi Sigma Alpha, Omicron Delta Kappa. Democrat. Roman Catholic. Avocations: tennis, piano. Office: Nokia Inc 6000 Connection Dr Irving TX 75039-2600

PITTS, JOSEPH R. congressman; b. Lexington, Ky., Oct. 10, 1939; s. Joseph S. and Pearl Jackson P.; m. Virginia Pratt, 1961; children: Karen R., Carol J., Daniel J. AB, Asbury Coll., 1961; MEd, West Chester State Coll., 1973. Tchr. Great Valley (Pa.) H.S., 1969-73; rep. dist. 158 State of Pa., 1972-96; mem. U.S. Congress from 16th Pa. dist., 1997—, mem. energy and commerce com., internat rels. com. Transp. com. State of Pa., 1977-80, appropriations com., 1979-82, rep. policy com., chmn. labor rels. com., transp. and joint legis. budget and fin. coms., chmn. rep. appropriations com., 1989. Decorated Air medal with five oak leaf clusters; recipient Pub. Servant award Chester-Del. Pomona Grange, 1980, Cmty. Leadership award Pa. for Biblical Morality, 1984, Disting. Govt. Svc. award Am. Mushroom Inst., 1985, Defender of Life award Pro Life Coalition S.E. Pa., 1985, William Penn award Pa. FACTS, 1985. Mem. VFW (post 5467), Brandywine Valley Assn., Rotary. Republican. Address: 905 Mitchell Farm Ln Kennett Square PA 19348-1319 Office: US Ho of Reps 204 Cannon Ho Office Bldg Washington DC 20515-3816

PITTS, LEONARD GARVEY, JR., columnist, writer; b. Orange, Calif., Oct. 11, 1957; s. Leonard Garvey and Agnes (Rowan) P.; m. Marilyn Vernice Pickens, June 27, 1981; children: Markise Pickens, Monique Pickens; (stepchildren) Marlon, Leonard, Onjél. BA English, U. So. Calif., 1977. Editor, writer Soul Mag., L.A., 1976-80; writer KFWB Radio, L.A., 1980-83; editor Radioscope, L.A., 1983-86; writer Westwood One Inc., Culver City, Calif., 1989-91; columnist, writer Miami (Fla.) Herald, 1991—. Writer, co-producer (broadcast) King: From Atlanta to the Mountaintop, 1986 (CEBA award 1987), (documentary) Young Black Men: A Lost Generation?, 1990 (Armstrong award 1991); writer, producer (documentary) Who We Are, 1988 (CEBA award 1989). Recipient Internat. Radio Festival award, 1991, Nat. Headliner award Arts criticism, 1991, Pulitzer Prize for commentary, 2004. Mem. Fla. Soc. Newspaper Editors (award arts criticism), Nat. Headliners, Am. Assn. Sunday and Feature Editors (award arts criticism 1991), Nat. Assn. of Black Journalists (Award of Execllence in commentary 1994, 95). Democrat. Baptist. Avocations: computer strategy games, reading. Office: Miami Herald One Herald Plaza Miami FL 33132

PITTS, NEAL CHASE, rheumatologist; b. Jackson, Miss., Dec. 6, 1933; s. Guy Moselely and Nancy Salina (Chase) P.; m. Nelia Annette Gnuse; children: Erin Chase Scott, Heather Anne Pitts. BA, Culver-Stockton Coll., 1956; MD, U. Mo., 1960. Intern U. Miss., 1960-61, resident medicine, 1961-63, fellow, 1963-65; fellow rheumatology Mayo Clin., 1965-66; bd. dirs. Caylor Nickel Clinic, Bluffton, Ind., 1990—, pres., 1991-93, 95-97, treas., 1994-95. Pres. Ind. Arthritis Assn., Indpls., 1978; bd. dirs. Lupus Found., Ft. Wayne, Ind., 1990—. Maj. M.C., U.S. Army, 1966-69. Fellow Am. Coll. Rheumatology; mem. Ind. SAR (trustee 1997, Ind. Patriot medal 1997), Nat. Soc. Mil. Order Stars and Bars (surgeon gen. 1995-99), Huguenot Soc. Ind. (registrar 1994-98, pres. 1999), Ind. Soc. Colonial Wars (gov. 1993-95), Sons of Confederate Vets. (comdr. Ind. divsn. 1991-93, surgeon-in-chief 1998—), Masons (sr. steward 1996-97, sr. warden 1999—). Republican. Presbyterian. Avocation: genealogy. Home: 1020 Highland Park Cir Bluffton IN 46714-2807

PITTS, ROBERT EUGENE, JR., marketing educator, consultant; b. Griffin, Ga., Feb. 12, 1948; s. Robert Eugene and Oree Francis (Brown) P.; m. Cheryl Ann Belew, May 31, 1968. BBA, Ga. State U., 1970, M in Bus. Info. Systems, 1972; PhD, U. S.C., 1977. Account sect. leader Gen. Electric Corp., Atlanta, 1970-72; instr. mktg. Jacksonville (Ala.) State U., 1972-74; assoc. dir. consumer panel U. S.C., Columbia, 1974-77; asst. prof. mktg. U. Notre Dame, South Bend, Ind., 1977-82; assoc. prof. mktg. U. Miss., Oxford, 1982-83, dir. bur. bus. and econ. research, 1983-85; prof., chmn. dept. mktg. DePaul U., Chgo., 1985-97, dir. Kellstadt Ctr. Mktg. Analysis and Planning; dean Coll. Bus. Adminstrn. Creighton U., Omaha, 1997—. Cons. in mktg. strategy; expert legal witness in mktg. Author books on bank mktg.; contbr. articles on personal values in mktg. and pub. policy issues to profl. jours. Fellow Am. Mktg. Assn. (pres. acad. counsel), Assn. Mktg. Sci.; mem. Decision Sci. Inst., So. Mktg. Assn. Avocations: running, akido. Office: Creighton U 2500 California Plz Omaha NE 68178-0001

PITTS, TYRONE S. reverend; Gen. sec. Progressive Nat. Bapt. Conv. Inc., Washington. Baptist. Office: Prog Nat Baptist Conv 601 50th St NE Washington DC 20019-5498

PITTS, VIRGINIA M. human resources executive; b. Boston, Nov. 22, 1953; d. Harold Francis and Connie (Caico) Cummings; m. Daniel J. Pitts, Mar. 12, 1977. Student, Northeastern U., 1982-85, Harvard U., 1997—. Adminstrv. asst. J. Baker Inc., Hyde Park, Mass., 1980-82, fin. adminstr., 1982-84; dir. human resources Casual Male Corp., Hyde Park, Mass., 1984—; 1st sr. v.p. J. Baker Inc., Hyde Park, Mass., 1991—. Trustee New Eng. Joint Bd. AFL-CIO, Quincy, Mass., 1984-89; guest lectr. Aquinas Jr. Coll.; mem. bd. dirs. Boston Crusaders, Drum & Bugle Corps. Instr. Boston Crusaders Drum and Bugle Corps, 1973-85; regional v.p. 210 Charitable Assn., Watertown, Mass., 1989-90; bd. dirs. Handi-Kids, Boston Crusaders Drum and Bugle Corps. Mem. Am. Mgmt. Assn., Am. Compensation Assn. (cert. profl.), Soc. Human Resource Mgrs. Avocations: dressage, gardening. Office: Casual Male Corp 555 Turnpike St Canton MA 02021-2791 E-mail: gpitts@cmal.com.

PITYNSKI, ANDRZEJ PIOTR, sculptor; b. Ulanow, Poland, Mar. 15, 1947; naturalized citizen, 1987; s. Aleksander and Stefania (Krupa) P.; m. Christina Teresa Gacek, Aug. 6, 1976; 1 child, Alexander Mark. MFA in Sculpture, Acad. Fine Arts, Cracow, Poland, 1974; postgrad., Art Students League, N.Y., 1975. Cert. tchr., N.J.; supr. modeling, mold, enlarging, resin crafts. Supr. and instr. sculpture Tech. Inst. of Sculpture - Johnson Atelier, Mercerville, NJ, 1979—; instr. sculpture Rider U., Lawrenceville, NJ, 1992—97, Rutgers U., NJ, 1998—2002. Asst. to sculptor Alexander Ettl, Sculpture House, N.Y., 1975-79 Bronze/granite monumental sculptures include Count J. Tarnowski, Tarnobrzeg, Poland, 2003, General Kosciuszko, St. Petersburg, Fla., 2002, Sarmatian - Spirit of Freedom, Hamilton, N.J., 2001, Flame of Freedom, Balt., 2000, Blue Army-1998, Warsaw, Poland, Katyn-1940, Jersey City, N.J., 1991-92, Pope John Paul II, Manhattan, N.Y., 1991, Ulanow, Poland, 1989, General Anders, Doylestown, Pa., 1995, Father J. Popieluszko, Trenton, N.J., 1987, Avenger, Doylestown, Pa., 1987, Portrait Bust M Curie, 1986, Bayonne, N.J.; aluminum sculpture Partisans II, Hamilton, N.J., 1999, Partisans, Boston, 1983, Ignacy Paderewski, Cracow, Poland, 1973; one-man show at Hamilton, N.J., 2000, N.Y., 2001; exhbn. Mus. of Polish Army, Warsaw, 1995, Contemporary Artists Guild, Lever House, N.Y., 1991—, Zacheta Nat. Art Gallery, Warsaw, 1991, Fedn. Internat. De La Medaille/Brit. Mus., London, 1992, Cast Iron Gallery, Soho, N.Y., 1992, Alt. Ext. Gallery, Phila., 1992, Audubon Exhibits-54th Ann. Exhbn., Fed. Hall, N.Y.C., others. Recipient Polonia Restituta Cross, R.P. London, 1989, Gold Order of Merit, Rep. of Poland, 1990, Cultural award Am. Inst. Polish Culture, Washington, 1992; named Comdr. Order Merit of Republic of Poland, 1996, The Monuments Conservancy's Perennial Wisdom award-medal, N.Y.C., 1999, Honorary Citizen of Balt., 2001. Fellow Nat. Sculpture Soc.; mem. Allied Artists of Am. (Silver medal of honor 1985, Elliot Liskin Meml. award 1989, Mems. and Assocs. award 1994), Audubon Artists (Gold Medal of Honor 1996, Silver Medal of Honor 1997, 98), Contemporary Artists Guild, Am. Medallic Sculpture Assn. Republican. Roman Catholic. Avocations: horse jumping, hunting, Judo. Office: PO Box 220380 Brooklyn NY 11222

PITZER, JACK TODD, purchasing agent, consultant, purchasing agent, educator; s. Walter William and Kathryn Arvilla Pitzer; m. Tanya Lou Driver, June 22, 1963; children: LaTisha Beth Dew, Leyton Todd. BA cum laude, Lincoln U., 1969; MA, U. Mo., 1971, PhD, 1982. Cert. pub. purchasing officer Universal Pub. Purchasing Certification Coun., 1984, bus. mgr. Assn. Profls. Mgmt., 2002. Asst. dir. purchasing Office Adminstrn. State of Mo., Jefferson City, 1973—75; chief purchasing officer dept. gen. svcs. State of Iowa, Des Moines, 1978—85; dean svcs. Lincoln U., Jefferson City, 1985—87; pub./mng. editor The Albany (Mo.) Ledger, 1987—96; dir. purchasing City of Alexandria (Va.) Purchasing Divsn., 1994—. Adj. assoc. prof. Drake U., Des Moines, 1981—85, Lincoln U., Jefferson City, 1985—87; adj. instr. Nat. Capital Region Grad. Ctr. - Fla. Inst. Tech., Alexandria, 2003; chmn. of the bd. Va. Assn. of Govtl. Purchasing Profl. Devel. Found., Richmond, 1997—2000; chmn. chief purchasing officers com. Met. Washington Coun. Govts., 1998—2000; mem. bd. examiners Universal Pub. Purchasing Certification Coun., Herndon, Va., 1999—2003. Co-author: (textbook) Leadership and Management in Public Procurement; mem. editl. bd.: Jour. Pub. Procurement, 1998—2003. Col. USAR, 1958—2001. Decorated Legion of Merit U.S. Army, Brevet Brig. Gen. (Ret) Iowa Army N.G.; named Honor Grad., U.S. Army Command and Gen. Staff Coll., 1975; fellow, Woodrow Wilson Found., 1972—73. Mem.: Nat. Assn. State Procurement Officers (life; pres. 1984—85). Avocations: reading, walking, golf, travel. Home: 5900 Kingham Ct Alexandria VA 22310-1733

PIVA, GARY, retail grocery executive; CFO WinCo Foods, Boise. Office: WinCo Foods PO Box 5756 Boise ID 83705-5756 Office Fax: (208) 377-0474.

PIVEN, FRANCES FOX, political scientist, educator; b. Calgary, Alta., Can., Oct. 10, 1932; arrived in U.S., 1933, naturalized, 1953; d. Albert and Rachel (Paperny) F.; 1 dau., Sarah. BA, U. Chgo., 1953, MA, 1956, PhD, 1962; L.H.D. (hon.), Adelphi U., 1985. Mem. faculty Columbia, 1966-72; prof. polit. sci. Boston U., 1972-82, Grad. Ctr., CUNY, 1982—. Co-author: Regulating the Poor: The Functions of Public Welfare, 1971, 2d edit., 1993, The Politics of Turmoil: Essays on Poverty, Race and the Urban Crisis, 1974, Poor People's Movements, 1977, New Class War, 1982, The Mean Season, 1987, Why Americans Don't Vote, 1988; editor: Labor Parties in Post Industrial Societies, 1992, The Breaking of the American Social Compact, 1997, Why Americans Still Don't Vote, 2000, Work, Welfare and Politics, 2002, The War at Home, 2004. Recipient C. Wright Mills award Soc. Study Social Problems, 1971, Fulbright Disting. Lectureship award U. Bologna, 1990, President's award APHA, 1993, Annual award Nat. Assn. Sec. of State, 1994, Lifetime Achievement award Pol. Sociology Am. Sociological Assn., 1995, Disting. Career award, 2000, Pub. Understanding of Sociology award, 2003; Guggenheim fellow, 1973-74; Am. Coun. Learned Socs. awardee, 1982. Mem. Am. Polit. Sci. Assn. (v.p. 1981-82), Soc. Study Social Problems (pres. 1980-81, Lee founders award 1992), ACLU (dir.). Home: PO Box N Millerton NY 12546-0651 Office: CUNY Grad Sch 365 5th Ave New York NY 10016-4309 E-mail: fpiven@hotmail.com.

PIVEN, PETER ANTHONY, architect, management consultant; b. Bklyn., Jan. 3, 1939; s. William Meyer and Sylvia Lee (Greenberg) P.; m. Caroline Cooper, July 9, 1961; children: Leslie Ann, Joshua Lawrence. AB, Colgate U., 1960; MArch, U. Pa., 1963; MS, Columbia U., 1964. Diplomate: cert. Nat. Coun. Archtl. Registration Bds.; registered arch., NY, Pa., NJ. Arch. Westermann-Miller Assocs., NYC, 1964-66, Bernard Rothzeid, A.I.A., NYC, 1967-68; v.p. Caudill Rowlett Scott, NYC, 1968-72; prin. Geddes Brecher Qualls Cunningham, Phila., 1972-87; pres. The Coxe Group, Inc., Phila., 1980-90, dir., prin. cons., 1980—. Adj. prof. U. Pa. Grad. Sch. Fine Arts, 1989—, Rensselaer Poly. Inst. Sch. Architecture, 1994—; vis. instr. Harvard U. Grad. Sch. Design. Author: Compensation Management: A Guideline for Small Firms, 1982, Architect's Essentials of Ownership Transition, 2002; co-author: Success Strategies for Design Professionals, 1987, Architect's Essentials of Starting a Design Firm, 2003; contbg. editor: Archtl. Record and Design Intelligence; author (contbg.): Architects Handbook of Professional Practice, 1994, 2001. Mem. NYC Cmty. Planning Bd., 1969-72. Fellow AIA (chmn. fin. mgmt. com. 1976-80, chmn. Fellows Jury 1998, mem. conv. task force 1998, mem. Nat. Ethics Coun. 1998-2004, chmn. 2004, pres. Phila. chpt. 1980); mem. Phila. C. of C. (dir. 1980-81), The Carpenters Co. of City and County of Phila. (mng. com. 1989-91). Home: Apt 10 201 Queen St Philadelphia PA 19147 Office: The Coxe Group Inc 1218 3rd Ave Seattle WA 98101-3097 Office Phone: 215-952-2781. E-mail: ppiven@coxegroup.com.

PIVER, M. STEVEN, gynecologic oncologist; b. Washington, Sept. 29, 1934; s. Harry Samuel and Sonia (Bard) P.; m. Susan Myers, June 25, 1958; children: Debra Ellen, Carolyn Jan, Kenneth Stuart. BS, Gettysburg Coll., 1957; MD, Temple U., 1961. Diplomate Am. Bd. Ob-Gyn, Am. Coll. Surgeons. Intern Nazareth Hosp., Phila., 1961—62; resident Johns Hopkins U. Hosp., Balt., 1962; resident ob-gyn. Pa. Hosp. U. Pa., Phila., 1965—68; fellow gynecologic oncology Hosp. Tumor Inst. U. Tex., Houston, 1968—70; asst. prof. gynecologic oncology UNC Sch. Medicine, 1970—71; assoc. chief gynecologic oncology Roswell Park Cancer Inst., Buffalo, 1972—83, founder, dir. Gilda Radner Familial Ovarian Cancer Registry, 1981—, chief gynecologic oncology, 1984—97; clin. prof., dir. divsn. gynecologic oncology SUNY, Buffalo, 1986—87, prof. gynecology, 1998—, chair emeritus gynecologic oncology, 1998—. Cons., editor Yearbook of Cancer, 1972-88; assoc. editor Nat. Cancer Inst., PDQ, 1984—; mem. editl. bd. The Female Patient, 1989—, Oncology Reports, 1993—; author: Ovarian Malignancies: Clinical Care of Adults and Adolescents, 1983, Gilda's Disease: Sharing Personal Experiences and a Medical Perspective on Ovarian Cancer, 1996, Myths and Facts About Ovarian Cancer, 1997; editor: Ovarian Malignancies: Diagnostic and Therapeutic Advances, 1987, Manual of Gynecologic Oncology/Gynecology, 1989, Conversations About Cancer, 1990, Handbook of Gynecologic Oncology, 1995; contbr. more than 300 articles to profl. jours. Bd. dirs. United Way Buffalo Erie County, 1986-91; chmn. bd. trustees D'Youville Coll., Buffalo, 1989—; pres. Friends Night People, Buffalo, 1988-97. Capt. USAF, 1962-64. Hon. fellow Phi Beta Kappa, Gettysburg Coll., 1956, Tex. Assn. Obstetricians Gynecologists, 1983, Alpha Omega Alpha, Temple U. Sch. Medicine, 1995; named Citizen Yr., Buffalo News, 1989; recipient YMCA Leadership award Buffalo YMCA, 1990, Brotherhood/Sisterhood Award Medicine (Western NY Region), NCCJ, 1991, St. Marguerite D'Youville Coll. Cmty. Svc. award, 1992. Fellow ACS, Am. Coll. Obstetricians and Gynecologists; mem. Am. Soc. Clin. Oncology, Soc. Gynecologic Oncologists, Soc. Surg. Oncology, Am. Radium Soc., Phi Beta Kappa, Alpha Omega Alpha. Achievements include documentation of hydroxyurea as a radiation sensitizer in cervix cancer that significantly improves cure rate and that ovarian cancer can be inherited; patent for method of enhancing the efficacy of anti-tumor agents. Home: 315 Lincoln Pky Buffalo NY 14216-3127 Office: Sisters Hosp 2157 Main St Buffalo NY 14214-2692 Office Phone: 716-862-1310. E-mail: mpiver@wnychs.org.

PIVIROTTO, RICHARD ROY, former retail executive; b. Youngstown, Ohio, May 26, 1930; s. Arthur M. and Ruth (Erhardt) P.; m. Mary Burchfield, June 27, 1953; children: Mary B., Richard Roy, Susan W., Nancy P., David H., Jennifer P. AB, Princeton U., 1952; MBA, Harvard U., 1954. Pres. Joseph Horne Co., Pitts., 1954-70; vice chmn. Associated Dry Goods Corp., N.Y.C., 1970-72, pres., 1972-76, chmn. bd., 1976-81, also dir.; pres. Richard Pivirotto, Inc., 1983—; non-exec. chmn. The Gillette Co., Boston, 2000—. Bd. dirs. CBS Corp., N.Y., Gen. Am. Investors Co., N.Y.C., N.Y. Life Ins. Co., Gillette Corp., Immunomedics Inc., Morris Plains, N.J.; dir. Greenwich Bank & Trust Co., Infinity Broadcasting Co., Yale New Haven Health Svc., Inc. Trustee Princeton U., 1977—; trustee Greenwich Hosp.; bd. dirs. Gen. Theol. Sem., N.Y.C. Served with AUS, 1955-56. Mem. Am. Retail Fedn. (dir. 1968-81) Clubs: Princeton (N.Y.C.); Duquesne, Rolling Rock, Fox Chapel Golf (Pitts.); Greenwich, Country, Field of Greenwich; Bald Peak Colony (Melvin Village, N.H.). Office: The Gillette Co Prudential Tower Bldg Boston MA 02199

PIXLEY, CARL PRESTON, mathematician; b. Omaha, Nov. 3, 1942; s. William Robert and Lillus Marie (Petty) P.; m. Cynthia Marie Nardone, Dec. 21, 1968; children: Laura Elizabeth, Margaret Marie. BS in Math., U. Omaha, 1966; MS in Math., Rutgers U., 1968; PhD in Math., SUNY, Binghamton, 1972. Instr. U. Tex., Austin, 1972-73, asst. prof., 1974-77; assoc. prof. S.W. Tex. State U., San Marcos, 1978-81; sr. rsch. scientist Burroughs Corp., Austin, 1981-82, mgr., 1986-88; sr. mem. tech. staff Microelectronics and Computer Tech. Corp., Austin, 1988-92; mgr. adv. design verification tech. Motorola Inc., Austin, Tex., 1992—2001; sr. dir. Synopsys Inc., 2001—. Lectr. in field; invited spkr. Schloss Dagstahl workshop on logic representations, Germany, 1996, DIMACS workshop, New Brunswick, N.J., 1996, Internat. Test Conf., Washington, 1996, Applied Math. Colloquium U. Ariz., 1996, formal verification in industry workshops, 1998, Concurrent Sys. Design Conf., Aizu, Japan, 1998, Internat. Test Conf. Roundtable on microprocessor verification, Washington, 1998; invited panelist Design Automation Conf., 2003; invited spkr. Internat. Symposium Quality Electronic Design, 2001, High Level Design Validation and Test, Memocode, 2004, others; bd. dirs. Accellera; organizer tutorial ASICON, 2003. Contbr. articles to profl. publs. Mem. IEEE, Am. Math. Soc., Math. Assn. Am. Methodist. Achievements include co-invention of Pixley-Roy Space; patents in field; research in infinite dimensional spaces, symbolic model checking, constraint-based verification. Office: Synopsys 2025 NW Cornelius Pass Rd Hillsboro OR 97124 Home: 16670 NW Mission Oaks Dr Beaverton OR 97006-8410

PIZER, HOWARD CHARLES, sports and entertainment executive; b. Chgo., Oct. 23, 1941; s. Edwin and Estyr (Seeder) P.; m. Sheila Graff, June 14, 1964; children: Jacqueline, Rachel. BBA, U. Wis., 1963; JD magna cum laude, Northwestern U., 1966. Assoc. McDermott, Will & Emery, Chgo., 1966-72; ptnr. Katten, Muchin, Zavis, Chgo., 1972-74; exec. v.p., gen. counsel Balcor Co., Skokie, Ill., 1975-80; exec. v.p. Chgo. White Sox, Chgo., 1981—. Exec. v.p. United Ctr. Joint Venture. Past pres. Chgo. Spl. Olympics; bd. dirs. Chgo. Conv. and Tourism Bur., Inc., 1983—, Spl. Children's Charities, 1984—, Chgo. Baseball Cancer Charities, 1983—, Near West Side Cmty. Devel. Corp. Mem. Chgo. Bar Assn., Standard Club Chgo., Briarwood County. Home: 300 Euclid Ave Winnetka IL 60093-3606 Office: Chgo White Sox 333 W 35th St Chicago IL 60616-3651

PIZITZ, RICHARD ALAN, retail and real estate group executive; b. Birmingham, Ala., Feb. 24, 1930; s. Isadore and Hortense (Hirsch) P.; m. Joan Black; children: Richard Alan Jr., Jill Carole, Susan Lyn. BA, Washington & Lee U., 1951; MBA, Harvard U., 1953. Mdse. mgr. Pizitz Dept. Stores, Birmingham, 1953-59, v.p., 1959-66, pres., 1966-86, chmn. bd., 1986-87; chmn. Pizitz Mgmt. Group, Birmingham, 1987—. Pres. United Way, Birmingham, 1988, Ala. Commn. on Higher Edn., 1987-95; pres. Better Bus. Bur., Birmingham, 1962; mem. Ala adv. commn. U.S. Commn. on Civil Rights, 1985. Recipient Erskine Ramsay award, 1974; named Mktg. Man of Yr., Am. Mktg. Assn., 1966, Man of Yr., Young Men's Bus. Club, 1970. Mem. Ala. Commn. on Higher Edn., Birmingham C. of C. (pres. 1970), Ala. Retail Assn. (pres. 1965). Avocations: flying, skiing, tennis, scuba diving. Office: Pizitz Mgmt Group 2140 11th Ave S Ste 318 Birmingham AL 35205-2850 Address: 2936 Redmont Park Ln Birmingham AL 35205-2136

PIZZAGALLI, ANGELO, construction company executive; b. Lugano, Switzerland, July 1, 1934; came to U.S., 1937; s. Angelo and Theresa Pizzagalli; m. Patricia Haron, Jan. 19, 1935; children: Lisa, Mia, Jon. BSBA, U. Vt., 1956. Pres. Pizzagalli Constrn. Co., South Burlington, Vt., 1958-91, vice-chmn., 1991—; chmn. banknorth Group Inc., Burlington, Vt., 1998—. Bd. dirs. The Howard Bank, Burlington, Vt., Cen. Vt. Ry., Detroit. Past chmn. bd. trustees U. Vt.; active Vt. Indsl. Devel. Authority; past gov. Med. Ctr. Hosp. Vt., past trustee. Served to capt. USAF. Mem. Chief Execs. Orgn. Home: PO Box 2009 South Burlington VT 05407-2009 Office: 300 Financial Plaza PO Box 5420 Burlington VT 05402-5420

PIZZAGALLI, JAMES, construction executive; b. Burlington, Vt., Nov. 23, 1944; s. Angelo and Theresa (Moalli) P.; m. Judy Rock, June 21, 1969; 1 child, Michael. BS, U. Vt., 1966; JD, Boston U., 1969. Treas. Pizzagalli Constrn. Co., Burlington, Vt., 1969-76, v.p., 1976-91, chmn., CEO, 1991-98, co-chmn., 1998—. Dir. Chittenden Corp., Burlington, 1982—, AGC Edn. Found., Washington, 1992-2004, Shelburne (Vt.) Mus., 1983-92, 2000—; life dir. Assn. Gen. Contractors, Washington, 1976—, atty.-at law. Trustee U. Vt., 2000—. Mem. TheMoles, Ethan Allen Club. Republican. Roman Catholic. Home: 3393 Harbor Rd Shelburne VT 05482-7611 Office: Pizzagalli Constrn Co PO Box 2009 South Burlington VT 05407 E-mail: jpizzagalli@pizzagalli.com.

PIZZAMIGLIO, ALBERT THEODORE (AL PIERSON), conductor; b. Ill. m. Nancy Alice Gilman, Mar. 27, 1978; five children. Studied music theory and composition; BA, MA, Ill. State U.; advanced music studies, U. Ill. Condr. Al Pierson Big Band U.S.A., 1975-89, Guy Lombardo's Royal Canadians, Aubrey, Tex., 1989—. Nat. youth music dir. Am. Inst. of Cooperation; co-host, owner TV show, Bloomington, Ill.; tchr. high sch. and coll. Musician, composer, arranger, vocalist, band leader; founder Al Pierson & Big Band U.S.A. (Best New Dance Band in the Country 1975, America's Number One Dance Band 1977), performed for fourteen yrs. at numerous famous ballrooms in the midwest and many prestigious pvt. parties, on twenty internat. dance tours including Europe, the Orient, the Middle East, the Caribbean, Mexico, Hawaii, Alaska and Tahiti; released 15 albums; recorded Guy Lombardo music album, 2000, now with Guy Lombardo's Royal Canadians performing throughout the continental U.S. and Can. and 44 other fgn. countries; condr. PBS TV series (past three yrs. and continuing), 1977, PBS TV spls., 1994, 95, 96, 97, 2000, Presdl. Inauguration Festivities, 1994. Recipient Superman award for helping save 32 lives in snowstorm, 1997, 98, 99; inducted into Ballroom Dancers' Hall of Fame, 1976; named amb. Music for World pres. Ill. State U., 1998. Office: Gilman Inc Artists Mgmt RR 1 Aubrey TX 76227-9801

PIZZELLA, PATRICK, federal agency administrator; b. New Rochelle, N.Y., May 19, 1954; BSBA, U. S.C., 1976. Dep. undersecretary mgmt. Dept. Edn., Washington, 1988—89; chief adminstrv. officer Fed. Housing Fin. Bd., 1990—95; govt. affairs counselor Preston Gates Ellis & Rouvelas Meeds LLP, 1996—2001; asst. sec. adminstrn. and mgmt. U.S. Dept. Labor, Washington, 2001—. Office: US Dept Labor 200 Constitution Ave NW Washington DC 20210

PIZZINGRILLI, KIM, state official; BBA Econ., U. Pitts., Johnstown, 1981; M Govtl. adminstrn., U. Pa., 1988. Auditor, acct., and asst. dir. bur. of audits Pa. Treasury Dept., 1981-87; sr. regulatory analyst Pa. Ind. Regulatory Rev. Commn., 1987-95; spl. asst. to sec. Dept. of State, Harrisburg, Pa., 1995-96, dep. sec. regulatory programs, 1996-98, acting sec., 1998-99, sec. of the commonwealth, 1999—2002; commr. Pa. Pub. Utility Comm., 2002—. Mem. Bd. of Property, Bd. of Fin. and Revenue, State of Pa.; mem. Pa. State Athletic Commn., Pa. State Nav. Commn. for the Delaware River and its Navigable Tributaries, mem. Pa. Mcpl. Retirement Bd.; keeper Great Seal of the Commonwealth. Mem. Nat. Assn. Sec. of State, Women Exec. in State Govt. Republican. Office: Pennsylvania Pub Utility Comm PO Box 3265 Harrisburg PA 17105-3265

PIZZO, PHILIP A. pediatrics educator, university administrator; b. NYC, Dec. 6, 1944; BA, Fordham U., 1966; MD, U. Rochester, 1970. Diplomate Am. Bd. Pediat., Am. Bd. Hematology/Oncology. Intern Children's Hosp. Med. Ctr., Boston, 1970-71, jr. asst. resident, 1971-72, sr. resident, 1972-73; tchg. fellow Harvard U. Sch. Medicine, Boston, 1972-73; clin. assoc. Pediatric Oncology Br. of Nat. Cancer Inst., 1973-75, investigator, 1975-76, sr. investigator, 1976-80; head infectious disease sect. Pediatric Br. of Nat. Cancer Inst., 1980-96, chief pediat., 1982-96; sci. dir. divsn. clin. scis. Nat. Cancer Inst., 1994-96; prof. pediat. Sch. Medicine, Uniformed Svcs. U. Health Sci., 1987-96; Thomas Morgan Rotch prof., chmn. dept. pediat. Harvard U. Sch. Medicine, Boston, 1996—2001; dean Stanford (Calif.) U. Sch. Medicine, 2001—. Mem. clin. rsch. subpanel of Nat. Cancer Inst., 1978-81, infectious disease clin. ctr., NIH, 1978-96, transfusion com., 1984-87, pediatric core com., pediatric AIDS clin. trials group, 1988-94, sec. HIV task force, 1988; mem. sci. adv. bd. Children's Hospice Internat., 1988-94, AIDS program Nat. Inst. Allergy and Infectious Diseases, 1988-89; mem. clin. rsch. subcom. AIDS Rsch. Adv. Com., 1990-94; physician-in-chief, chmn. dept. medicine Children's Hosp., Boston, 1996—, Myron Karon Meml. lectr., 1986, Melissa Anne Krinsky Meml. lectr., 1989. Mem. AAAS, Inst. Medicine of NAS, Am. Soc. Hematology, Am. Fedn. for Clin. Rsch., Am. Soc. for Clin. Investigation, Am. Soc. Clin. Oncology (bd. dirs. 1996—), Elizabeth Glaser Pediatric AIDS Found. (bd. dirs. 1996—), Infectious Disease Soc. Am., Infectious Disease Soc. Am., Internat. Immunocompromised Host Soc. (pres.-elect), IDSA (bd. dirs. 1996—). Office: Stanford U Sch Med 300 Pasteur Dr, Ste M121 Palo Alto CA 94305

PIZZO, PIA, artist, educator; arrived in U.S., 1982, permanent resident, 1985; d. Rosario Pizzo and Rosa Greco; m. Chin Hsiao, Apr. 28, 1962 (div. May 1979); 1 child, Samantha Hsiao (dec.); m. Delbert O. Thompson, June 18, 1985. Diploma, Coll. of Art Orsoline, Milano, Italy, 1956; student, Brera Acad. Art, Milano, Italy, 1957—60; BFA, Ministry Pub. Instrn., Roma, Italy, 1957. Founder, propr. Sama Press, Long Beach, Calif., 1995—. Instr. design and color theory Brooks Coll. Design, Long Beach, Calif., 1998—; instr. art and creativity Dept. Parks, Recreation, Marine, Long Beach, Calif., 1987—; lectr. Dept. Art and Tech. Calif. State U., Long Beach, Calif., 1995—96. Exhibitions include 32 solo exhbns., Europe and USA, 1962—2003, 89 group shows, Europe, USA, Brasil, Taiwan, 1957—; author: The World is Waiting for the Sunrise, 1985 (hon. mention, 1987); co-author (with blind students): 6'x 8' tactile sculptural book-perm. pub. art, 1988; contbr. articles to profl. publs.; author (designer): adult and children books, 1970, 1981. Named Artist of Yr., Disting. Visual Artist, PCA Pub. Corp. for Arts, 1989; recipient Cert. Recognition award, Accademia Tiberina, Roma, Italy, 1957, cert. of Appreciation in Recognition of Outstanding Svc., City of Long Beach, Calif., 2000, permanent pub. art sign project, City of Gardena, Calif., 2001; fellow, Pollock-Krasner Found., NYC, 1984, Calif. Arts Coun., Sacramento, 1987, Pub. Corp. for the Arts, Long Beach, Calif., 2000. Mem.: Long Beach Mus. Art Artist's Coun. (solo exhbn. 1998), The Smithsonian Inst., Internat. Campaign for Tibet, Children Internat., Amnesty Internat. Avocations: classical piano, reading, concerts, museums, languages. Home and Studio: Artist's Studio 1022 E 1st St # 7 Long Beach CA 90802

PIZZO, SALVATORE VINCENT, pathologist; b. Phila., June 22, 1944; s. George J. P. and Aida (Alcaro) Lepore; m. Carol Ann Kurkowski, Dec. 28, 1968 (div. 1987); children: Steven, David, Susan. PhD, Duke U., 1972; BS, St. Joseph's Coll., 1966; MD, Duke U., 1973. Asst. prof. Duke U. Med. Ctr., Durham, N.C., 1976-80, assoc. prof., 1980-85, prof., 1985—, dir. med. scientist tng. program, 1987—, chmn., 1991—. Mem., chmn. program rev. com. NIH, Bethesda, Md., 1986-90; vice chmn. Gordon Conf. Proteases, Holderness, N.H., 1990, chmn., 1992-96; cons. in field, 1980—; mem. Cellular and Molecular Basis of Disease Rev. Com., 1990-96. Contbr. articles to profl. jours. Grantee NIH, 1976—, Am. Cancer Soc., 1976—. Fellow AAAS; mem. Am. Heart Assn. (exec. com. Thrombosis coun. 1990, 92), Am. Chem. Soc., Am. Assn. Pathologists (program com. 1985-88, long range planning com. 1990-92), Am. Soc. Biological Chemists, Alpha Sigma Nu, Phi Beta Kappa, Alpha Omega Alpha, Sigma Xi. Achievements include patents in field; research in lipoproteins in coagulation and fibronolysis, a link to atherosclerosis, anticoagulation drug development; identification of ATP synthase as the target for Angiostatin action. Office: Duke U Med Ctr PO Box 3712 Durham NC 27710-0001 Office Phone: 919-684-3528. Business E-Mail: pizzo001@mc.duke.edu.

PIZZORNO, JOSEPH EGIDIO, JR., business executive; b. San Gabriel, Calif., Dec. 7, 1947; s. Joseph Egidio Sr. and Mary (Carmela) P.; 1 child, Raven Muir; m. Lara Elise Udell, Sept. 28, 1985; 1 child, Galen Udell. BS with Distinction, Harvey Mudd Coll., Claremont, Calif., 1969; Naturopathic Doctor with honors, Nat. Coll. Naturopathic Medicine, Portland, Oreg., 1975. Rsch. asst. Lockheed Aircraft, Ontario, Calif., 1968; rsch. technologist U. Wash., Seattle, 1970-75; practice naturopathic medicine Seattle, 1975-82; practice midwifery, 1978-82; pres. Bastyr U., Seattle, 1978-2000, pres. emeritus, 2000—; pres. Salugenecists, Inc., Seattle, 2001—. Pres. Coun. on Naturopathic Med. Edn., Portland, Oreg., 1985-87; apptd. adv. panel safety and efficacy of dietary supplements U.S. Office of Tech. Assessment, 1993-95; sr. med. advisor Alternative and Complementary Therapies, 1995-97; mem. White House Commn. Complementary and Alternative Medicine Policy, 2000-02; mem. Medicare Coverage Adv. Com., 2003—. Author: Total Wellness, 1996; co-author: Handbook of Natural Medicine, 1983, 3d edit., 2001, Encyclopedia of Natural Medicine, 1990, 2d edit., 1998, Textbook of Natural Medicine, 1999, How to Prevent and Treat Cancer with Natural Medicine, 2002; editor: Integrative Medicine: A Clinician's Jour.; contbg. editor: Let's Live mag., 1987—; contbr. articles to profl. jours. Mem. Seattle/King County Bd. Health, 1996-2002; vice chair bd. dirs. Inst. for Functional Medicine. Mem.: Seattle Midwifery Sch. (edn. com. 1978—91), Wash. Assn. Naturopathic Physicians (edn. dir. 1976), Am. Assn. Naturopathic Physicians (bd. dirs. 1984—91). Libertarian. Avocations: microcomputers, basketball, ultimate frisbie. Home: 4220 NE 135th St Seattle WA 98125-3836 E-mail: president_emeritus@bastyr.edu., drpizzorno@salugenecists.com.

PIZZURO, SALVATORE NICHOLAS, special education educator; b. Passaic, N.J., Jan. 25, 1945; s. John G. and Mary F. (Interdonato) P. BA, Jersey City State Coll., 1970, MA, 1973; profl. diploma, Fordham U., 1980; EdD, Columbia U., 1991. Tchr. spl. edn. Garfield (N.J.) Pub. Schs., 1970-71, Lodi (N.J.) Pub. Schs., 1971-75, 76-78; learning cons. Mt. Carmel Guild, Newark, 1976-76; instr. Columbia U., N.Y.C., 1988-91; asst. prof. spl. edn. Jersey City State Coll., 1990—; learning cons. Elmwood Park (N.J.) Dept. Special Svcs., 2000—02, Passaic County Ednl. Svcs. Commn., 2002—; cons. com. on edn. and workforce U.S. House of Reps., 2003; dir. Transition Adv. Svcs., 2003—; cons. Jersey city Pub. Schs., 2003—. Rsch. chmn. Transition Coords. Network NJ; cons. Congressmen Rush Holt and Pete Stark, 2002-03; post-doctoral fellow U. Ky., 1993-94; dir. Learning Consultation Svcs., N.Y.C., 1990—; coord. pre-svcs. program in mental retardation Tchrs. Coll., Columbia U., 1990-91; rsch. assoc. U. Ill., 1991-92; chmn. Early Childhood Inclusion Conf., Phila., 1993; dir. United Learning Consultants, 1994—; chmn. conf. "Assessment: Impact on Svc. Delivery", N.J., 1995; cons. Ind. Child Study Teams, Inc., 1995—; mem. task force com. on econ. and ednl. opportunities U.S. Ho. of Reps., 1994-96, chair, cons. Com. Edn. & Workforce, 1997—; chmn. the Future of Edn. in N.J. Conf., 1996; adj. faculty mem. Kean Coll. of N.J., 1997—; cons. Ednl. Resource Ctr., N.J., 1998; learning cons. Elmwood Park Dept. Spl. Svcs., 2000-02, Rutherford Dept. Spl. Svcs., 2002—; chmn. symposium on edn. funding Eagleton Inst. Politics Rutgers U., 1997; chmn. N.J. Com. on Pers. Stds. in Edn.; cons. U.S. Ho. of Reps. com. on edn. and workforce, 2002—; learning cons. Rutherford Pub. Schs., 2002-03, Jersey City Pub. Schs., 2003; chmn. symposium on sch. constrn. Kean U., 1998, chmn. symposium on urban edn., 1998, chmn. symposium on legis. initiatives in edn., 1998; chmn. congl. symposium on disability issues Capitol Hill, 2003; founder, dir. Transition Adv. Svcs., 2003—. Author: The Individuals with Disabilities Education Act and the Nature of American Politics, 1999, (textbook) The Individuals with Disabilities Education Act and the Nature of American Politics, 2001, 2d edit., 2003 (statewide technical report) Engagment in Education, Training, Living Arrangements and Community Activities among Recent Graduates of New Jersey's High Schools Special Education Program, 2004; editor: Learning Consultant Journal, 1995, 96, Policy Statement on Education in New Jersey, N.J. Coalition for the Study for School Reform, 1998; cons. editor Diagnostique, 1997—. Chmn. Walk for Hunger, 1979, NE Regional Legis. Coalition, 1984-86, Nat. AD HOC Comm. on the Reauthorization of the Individuals with Disabilities Edn. Act, chmn. Nat. Forum on Reauthorization, 1996, Conf. on Future of Edn. in N.J., 1996—, N.J. Coalition on Study of Sch. Reform, 1996—; staff mem. for U.S. Congressman Major Owens, 1997—; chmn. press conf. with U.S. Congressman Robert Menendez on sch. constrn., 1998, with U.S. Congressman Donald Payne on urban edn., 1998; polit. cons. Dem. election orgn., 1999-2000; cons. Legis. Initiatives in Edn., 2000. Recipient award for dedication to mentally retarded Mt. Carmel Guild, 1972. Mem. Coun. for Exceptional Children, N.J. Coun. for Exceptional Children (pres. 1984-85), N.J. Divsn. on Mental Retardation (pres. 1986-87), Jersey City State Coll. Alumni Assn. (pres. 1974-75), Tchrs. Coll. Christian Fellowship (pres. 1988-90), Rehab. Engring. Soc. N.Am., Correctional Edn. Assn., Internat. Ctr. for Study of Psychiatry and Psychology. Roman Catholic. Avocations: writing nonfiction, jogging. Office Phone: 201-896-1755.

PLACE, JANEY, banking consultant, former bank executive; b. Denver, Jan. 25, 1946; m. Michael Hiles. BA, MA, UCLA, PhD in semiology, 1975, attended Grad. Sch. Mgmt. Info tech. mgr. Hughes Aircraft Co.; corp. mgr. Strategic Tech. Planning Tosco Corp.; sr. v.p. internet strategy, R&D Wells Fargo Bank, 1990—94; exec. v.p. Strategic Tech. Group Bank of Am., 1994—99; pres. Mellon Lab and Online Svcs., N.Y.C., 1999—2003; exec. v.p. Mellon Fin. Corp., N.Y.C., 1999—2003; founder, pres., CEO digitalthinking-.com, 1999—. Past lectr. in sys. and comm. theory U. Calif., Santa Cruz, Calif.; bd. dirs. PortBlue; spkr. in field. Contbr. articles to profl. jours.; author: The Western Films of John Ford, 1974, The Non-Western Films of John Ford, 1979. Named One of 25 Women to Watch in Banking, U.S. Banker Mag., 2003.

PLACE, MICHAEL D. health association administrator; b. 1944; MA in Ecclesiastical History, D in Sacred Theology, Cath. U. Am.; MDiv, lic. in sacred theology, St. Mary of the Lake Sem. Ordained priest Roman Cath. Ch., 1970. Assoc. pastor Most Holy Redeemer Parish, Evergreen, Ill., 1970—74; mem. faculty, adminstr. St. Mary of the Lake Sem., Mundelein, Ill., 1977—81; dean Athenaeum of Ohio, 1981—84; acad. dean Mt. St. Mary's Sem. of the West, 1981—84; consul for policy devel. Archdiocese of Chgo., 1984—98; pres., CEO Cath. Health Assn., St. Louis, 1998—. Rsch. theologian to curia Archdiocese of Chgo., Archbishop's rep. to Archiocesan Pastoral Coun., Presbyteral Coun., Women's Commn.; advisor Cath. Conf. of Ill.; chair Archdiocesan Health Care Ethics Commn.; mem. Archdiocesan Policy Devel. Com., Cath. Conf. of Ill. Task Force on Welfare Reform; mem. adj. faculty Inst. Pastoral Studies, Loyola U., Chgo., Mundelein Sem. of U. St. Mary of the Lake; chair Theologian/Ethicist Resource Group, Joint Mem./Mission Svcs. adv. com. Cath. Health Assn.; active Ill. Cath. Health Assn.; mem. Shared

Corp. Ethics Com. Ea. Mercy Health Sys. and Mercy Health Care Sys., Greater Cin. Region; lectr., presenter in field. Named one of 100 Most Powerful People in Healthcare, Modern Healthcare mag., 2002, 2003. Office: Cath Health Assn of US 4455 Woodson Rd Saint Louis MO 63134-3797 also: 1875 Eye St NW Ste 1000 Washington Washington DC 20006-3993

PLAČEK, ROMAN, cellist, music educator; b. Jesenik, Czech Republic, June 26, 1972; came to U.S., 1995; s. Bohumir and Marcela Plaček; m. Edita Blaskova, Apr. 15, 1976. Grad., Ostrava Conservatory, Czech Republic, 1993; grad. performing cert., Boston Conservatory, 1998; MusM, U. Mass., 2001. Ind. artist and educator, 1990—; founder, artist dir., composer Golden Mountain Chamber Ensemble, Czech Republic, 1993—, Golden Mountain Chamber Ensemble Music Acad. Inc., Amherst, Mass., 2001—; pres. Golden Mountain Chamber Ensemble Music Acad.; co-owner, artistic dir., pres. bd. dirs. Golden Mountain Summer Internat. Inc., Chamber Music Summer Sch. and Festival, Zlaté Hory, Czech Republic, 2003; co-owner, co-dir. Hudba Bez Hranic, Music Without Borders, Inc., Czech Republic, 2002—. Mem. string trio in-residence U. Mass., Amherst, 1998-2001. Author project Art Instn. for Czech-Am. Cultural Exch., 1999—. Mem. Amateur Chamber Music Players (bd. advisors 1998-2000). Avocations: drawing, photography, home improvement. Home: Sokolska' 290 Zlaté Hory Czech Republic Office: PO Box 9645 North Amherst MA 01059-9645 Office Phone: 413-549-1191. E-mail: roman_placek@gmcema.com.

PLACEK-ZIMMERMAN, ELLYN CLARE, school system administrator, educator, consultant; b. Chgo., Sept. 3, 1951; d. Clarence Joseph and Jerrine LaMarr (Ruhlow) Placek; m. Allan John Zimmerman, Aug. 10, 1974; 1 child, Alissa Jan. BS, No. Ill. U., 1973, MS, 1977, cert. in advanced study, 1978, EdD, 1982. Tchr. Arlington Heights (Ill.) Pub. Schs., 1973-75, 75-76, dir. libr. and learning ctr., 1976-81, tchr. lang. arts and reading jr. high sch., 1981-84, tchr. kindergarten, 1984-86; prin. Orchard Street Sch., Fox River Grove, Ill., 1988-89, Pritchett Sch., Buffalo Grove, Ill., 1989-90, Round Lake (Ill.) Pub. Schs., 1992-93, asst. supt. curiculum and instrn., 1993-2001; asst. to supt. curriculum and instrn. Wood Dale (Ill.) Pub. Schs., 2001—03, prin., 2003—. Dir. Ill. State grant "At Risk Program" for pre-sch. children, Cary Pub. Schs., 1986-87; mem. part-time faculty Coll. Edn., Roosevelt U., Chgo., 1983-84, 88-89; tchr. jr. high social, reading and lang. arts studies, 1988; cons. in field; mem. steering com. Curriculum 2000 Conf., De Kalb, Ill., 1985; lectr. in field; supr. student tchrs. Ill. State U., Normal, 1986, Roosevelt U., Chgo., 1988-89, Elmhurst Coll., 1992; freelance writer Daily Herald newspaper. Contbg. author: Feeling Good About Food. Sec. Scarsdale Estates Homeowners Assn., Arlington Heights, 1983; bd. dirs. ABC/25 Found., 1991-92. Mem. Ill. ASCD (registration com. for fall conf. 1987, triple I arrangements com. 1988), Ill. Assn. Tchrs. English (cons., spkr. conf. 1984), Ill. Women Adminstrs. (publicty com. conf. 1985), PTA (hon. life). Avocations: playing guitar, calligraphy. Home: 402 E Orchard St Arlington Heights IL 60005-2660

PLACHE, KIMBERLY MARIE, state legislator; b. Racine, Wis., Jan. 4, 1961; Student, U. Wis., Whitewater, 1978-81; BS, U. Wis., Parkside-Kenosha, 1984. Legis. asst. to state rep. Jeff Neubauer, 1984-88; mem. Wis. Assembly from 21st dist., madison, 1988-96, Wis. Senate from 21st dist., Madison, 1996—. Mem. NOW, AAUW, Wis. Action Coalition. Address: 2614 17th St Racine WI 53405-3522 Office: Wis State Assembly State Capital Madison WI 53702-0001

PLACHNO, RONALD JOHN, electrical engineer; b. Chgo., June 1, 1945; s. Joseph John Plachno; m. Valerie Lynn Zahorak; children: Kenneth, Gregory. BSEE, Ill. Inst. of Tech., 1968. Electronics design engr. Magnavox Govt. Divsn., Urbana, Ill., 1968—71; ops. dir. Motorola Cellular Ops., Schaumburg, Ill., 1971—94; v.p. Motorola, Swindon, England, 1994—97, v.p. of mfg. Arlington Heights, Ill., 1997—2000; sr. v.p. of ops. Novatel Wireless Inc., San Diego, 2001—02. Treas., team mgr. Itasca Athletic Assn., Itasca, 1988—93. Scholar, State of Ill., 1963—67. Mem.: IEEE. Roman Catholic. Achievements include invention of 13 software copyrights. Avocations: software, music, travel. Home: 41451 Grand View Dr Murrieta CA 92562 Personal E-mail: plachnor@aol.com.

PLACKE, JAMES A(NTHONY), foreign service officer, international affairs consultant; b. Grand Island, Nebr., June 14, 1935; s. Gerhard F. and Florence E. (McCormick) P.; m. Mary Sabina Shea, July 25, 1959; children—Elizabeth, Stephen, Carolyn B.Sc., U. Nebr., 1957, MA, 1959. Commd. fgn. service officer Dept. State, 1958; econ. counselor Am. embassy, Tripoli, Libya, 1970-71; fgn. service insp. Dept. State, Washington, 1971-73, dir. office food policy, 1974-76; econ. counselor Am. Embassy, Ottawa, 1977-79, minister Jidda, Saudi Arabia, 1979-82; dep. asst. sec. Nr. Eastern and South Asian Affairs Bur., Dept. State, Washington, 1982-85, ret., 1986; internat. affairs cons., 1986-90; dir. Cambridge Energy Rsch. Assoc., 1991-2000, sr. assoc., 2001—; non-resident sr. fellow The Brookings Inst., 2002. Del. UN World Food Conf., 1974. Recipient Meritorious Honor award Dept. State, 1969, 71; Presdl. Meritorious Service award, 1985 Office: Ste 201 1150 Connecticut Ave NW Washington DC 20036-4104

PLADEL, JOHN GERALD, psychiatric nurse practitioner, psychologist, psychotherapist; b. Albany, N.Y., Nov. 7, 1959; s. John and Joan Margret (Peacock) P. ADN, Hudson Valley C.C., Troy, N.Y., 1979; BSN, Oreg. Health Scis. U., Portland, 1993, MS, 1995, postgrad., 1998—2002; PsyD, Calif. Coast U., 2002. Cert. specialist in adult mental health nursing, AACN. Staff nurse Park Royal Health Care, Portland, 1979-80, Good Samaritan Hosp., Portland, 1980-95, critical care credentialer, 1980-95, intern preceptor, 1980-95, assoc. charge Obstet. Post-Anesthesia Care Unit, 1987-89, charge nurse, 1989-91, staff nurse, 1991-95. Data mgr. Oreg. Hospice Assn., 1994-95; traineeship State of Oreg., 1993-94; presenter conf. in field, Australia, 1991. Author cross-tng. modules in-house teaching, 1990. Gen. mgr. Neighborhood Orgn., Portland, 1987, mem. exec. bd., 1987; organizer, coord. Local Crime Watch, Portland, 1986; cellist Columbia Symphony Orch., 1985-89, Marylhurst Symphony Orch., 1983-85, Sibelius String Quartet, 1985-88. Regent's scholar State of N.Y., 1977-79. Mem. ANA, Oreg. Nurses Assn., Sigma Theta Tau. Avocations: cello, piano, literature, comparative religions, languages. Office: 2207 NE Broadway Portland OR 97232 E-mail: pladelj@yahoo.com.

PLAEGER, FREDERICK JOSEPH, II, lawyer; b. New Orleans, Sept. 10, 1953; s. Edgar Leonard and Bernice Virginia (Schiwetz) P.; m. Kathleen Helen Dickson, Nov. 19, 1977; children: Douglas A., Catherine E. BS, La. State U., 1976, JD, 1977. Bar: La. 1978, Tex. 1999, U.S. Dist. Ct. (ea. dist.) La. 1978, U.S. Ct. Appeals (5th cir.) 1981, U.S. Supreme Ct. 1989. Law clk. U.S. Dist. Ct. (ea. dist.) La., New Orleans, 1977-79; assoc. Milling, Benson, Woodward, Hillyer, Pierson & Miller, New Orleans, 1979-85, ptnr., 1985-89; v.p., gen. counsel, corp. sec. La. Land and Exploration Co., New Orleans, 1989-97; v.p., gen. counsel Burlington Resources Inc., Houston, 1997—. Mem. Am. Petroleum Inst., 1990—, chmn. gen. com. law, 2003—; selected mem. Met. Area Com. Leadership Forum, 1986; bd. dirs. Soc. Environ. Edn., La. Nature and Sci. Ctr., 1992—94; trustee Houston Ballet, 2001—; mem. adv. bd. Inst. for Energy Law, 2001—, mem. exec. com., 2002—; bd. dirs. New Orleans Speech and Hearing Ctr., 1985—91, pres., 1988—90; bd. dirs. Children's Oncology Svcs. La. (Ronald McDonald Ho. of New Orleans), 1987—90. Recipient Service to Mankind award Sertoma, 1989. Mem. ABA, La. Bar Assn., Am. Corp. Counsel Assn. (bd. dirs. New Orleans chpt. 1995-98), Am. Petroleum Inst. (mem. gen. commn. law), Univ. Club, Lakeside Country Club. Republican. Avocations: computers, hunting, fishing. Home: 5105 Longmont Dr Houston TX 77056-2417 Office: Burlington Resources Inc Ste 2100 717 Texas St Houston TX 77002-2712 Office Phone: 713-624-9161.

PLAGEMANN, SUSAN, publishing executive; Dir. fashion and advt. Madamoiselle, 1992—95; advt. mgr. Esquire, 1995, advt. dir., 1995—96, assoc. pub., 1996—97, Cosmopolitan Mag., 1997—99; publisher Cosmopolitan Magazine, N.Y.C., 1999—2002; v.p., pub. Lifetime Mag., N.Y.C., 2002—. Office: Hearst Magazines 224 W 57th St New York NY 10019-3212

PLAGER, S. JAY, judge; b. Long Branch, N.J., May 16, 1931; s. A. L. and Clara L. Plager; children: Anna Katherine, David Alan, Daniel Tyler. AB, U. N.C., 1952; JD, U. Fla., 1958; LLM, Columbia U., 1961. Bar: Fla. 1958, Ill. 1964. Asst. prof. law U. Fla., 1958—62, assoc. prof., 1962—64; assoc. prof. law U. Ill., Champaign-Urbana, 1964—65, prof., 1965—77; dir. Office Environ. and Planning Studies, 1972—74, 1975—77; dean, prof. law Ind. U. Sch. Law, Bloomington, 1977—84, prof. law, 1984—90; counselor to undersec. U.S. Dept. Health and Human Svcs., 1986—87; assoc. dir. Office of Mgmt. and Budget Office of Mgmt. and Budget, 1987—88; adminstr. info. and regulatory affairs Exec. Office of the Pres., 1988—89; cir. judge U.S. Ct. Appeals (fed. cir.), 1989—2000, sr. judge, 2000—. Vis. rsch. prof. law U. Wis., 1967—68; vis. scholar Stanford U., 1984—85. Author (with others): Water Law and Administration, 1968; author: Social Justice Through Law-New Approaches in the Law of Property, 1970; author: (with others) Florida Water Law, 1980. Chmn. Gainesville (Fla.) Planning Commn., 1962—63; mem. Urbana Plan Commn., 1966—70; mem. nat. air pollution manpower devel. adv. com., 1971—75; cons. Ill. Inst. for Environ. Quality, U.S. EPA; chmn. Ill. Task Force on Noise, 1972—76; vice chmn. Nat. Commn. on Jud. Discipline and Removal, 1991—93. With USN, 1948—70. Office: US Ct Appeals for Fed Cir The National Courts Bldg 717 Madison Pl NW Washington DC 20439-0002

PLAINE, DANIEL J. lawyer; b. Washington, Aug. 23, 1943; s. Herzel H.E. and Norma (Stein) P.; m. Susan Ambrose, Oct. 5, 1985; children: Caroline, Meredith. BA magna cum laude, Williams Coll., 1965; LLB, Cambridge U., Eng., 1967; JD, Yale U., 1970. Bar: DC 1970, US Dist. Ct. DC 1970, US Ct. Appeals (DC cir.) 1970, US Ct. Appeals (fed. cir.), 1985, US Supreme Ct., 1974. Ptnr. Steptoe & Johnson, Washington, 1970-97, Gibson, Dunn & Crutcher, Washington, 1997—. Marshall scholar, 1967. Mem. ABA, Am. Soc. Internat. Law, Washington Inst. Internat. Law. Office: Gibson Dunn & Crutcher LLP 1050 Connecticut Ave NW Ste 200 Washington DC 20036-5306 Office Phone: 202-955-8286. E-mail: dplaine@gibsondunn.com.

PLAINE, LLOYD LEVA, lawyer; b. Washington, Nov. 3, 1947; d. Marx and Shirley P. Leva; m. James W. Hill. BA, U. Pa., 1969; postgrad., Harvard U.; JD, Georgetown U., 1975. Bar: DC 1975. Legis. asst. to US Rep. Sidney Yates, 1971-72; with Sutherland, Asbill & Brennan, Washington, 1975-82, ptnr., 1982—. Fellow Am. Bar Found., Am. Coll. Trust and Estate Counsel (past regent), Am. Coll. Tax Counsel; mem. ABA (past chmn. real property, probate and trust law sect., coun. sect. of taxation). Office: Sutherland Asbill & Brennan Ste 6 1275 Pennsylvania Ave NW Washington DC 20004-2415 Office Phone: 202-383-0155.

PLAISANCE, MELISSA C. consumer products company executive; b. Feb. 12, 1960; BSBA cum laude, Bucknell U., 1982; MBA, UCLA, 1990. With Bankers Trust Co. Corp. Fin., L.A., 1982—90; dir., investor rels. Safeway Inc., 1990—93, v.p., investor rels., 1993—94, v.p., investor rels. & pub. affairs, 1994—95, sr. v.p. fin., investor rels. & pub. affairs, 1995—2000, sr. v.p., fin. & investor rels., 2000—04; sr. v.p., fin. & corp. comm. Del Monte Foods Co., San Francisco, 2004—. Office: Del Monte Foods One Market at The Landmark San Francisco CA 94119-3575

PLAISTED, HARRIS MERRILL, III, real estate executive; b. Portland, Maine, June 3, 1935; s. Harris Merrill and Elizabeth Parsons Plaisted; m. Patricia Walker, Feb. 20, 1982; children: Frederick William II, Parker Bennett; stepchildren: William H. Nau Jr., Mary Beth Nau. BA in Econs., Washington and Lee U., 1957. With Morton G. Thalhimer, Inc., Richmond, Va., 1960-66, v.p., 1966-80, sr. v.p., 1980-86, pres., 1986-92, vice chmn., 1992—. Pres. Ridgetop Recreation Assn., 1967, Big Bros. of Richmond, Inc., 1970; bd. dirs. Robert E. Lee coun. Boy Scouts Am., 1981; state dir. Internat. Coun. Shopping Ctrs., 1974-77. Capt. U.S. Army, 1957-59. Mem. Va. Assn. Realtors (bd. dirs. 1973-82), Richmond Bd. Realtors (pres. 1975, Realtor of Yr. 1975), Richmond Real Estate Group (pres. 1987), Richmond Jaycees (life, Key Man Club), Soc. Indsl. and Office Realtors (dist. v.p. 1979-80, regional v.p. 1984-85, Howell H. Watson Disting. Svc. award 1995), Sons of the Revolution (pres. 1999), Ships Watch Assn. (bd. dirs. 1994, pres. 1995), Mooreland Comms. Assn. (pres. 2004), Kiwanis Club Richmond (bd. dirs. 1978-79). Episcopalian. Avocations: golf, sailing. Home: 9013 Wood Sorrel Ct Richmond VA 23229-7072 Office: Thalhimer PO Box 702 Richmond VA 23218-0702 Office Phone: 804-697-3403. E-mail: hmplaisted@aol.com.

PLAISTED, JOAN M. diplomat; b. St. Peter, Minn., Aug. 29, 1945; d. Gerald A. and Lola May (Peters) Plaisted. Student, U. Grenoble, France, 1965—66, U. Calif., Berkeley, 1966; BA in Internat. Rels., Am. U., 1967, MA in Asian Studies, 1969; grad., Nat. War Coll., 1988. Korea desk officer Commerce Dept., Washington, 1969-72, Japan desk officer, 1972-73; comml. officer Am. Embassy, Paris, 1973-78; internat. economist Orgn. Econ. Cooperation & Devel., Paris, 1978-80; econ. officer Am. Consulate Gen., Hong Kong, 1980-83; trade negotiator White House Office of Spl. Trade Rep., Geneva, 1983-85; deputy dir. China desk State Dept., Washington, 1985-87; acting dep. dir., chief econ./comml. sect. Am. Inst. in Taiwan, Taipei, 1988-91; chargé d'affaires, dep. chief of mission Am. Embassy, Rabat, Morocco, 1991-94; dir. Thai and Burma affairs Dept. of State, Washington, 1994-95; sr. advisor U.S. Mission to UN N.Y.C., 1995; amb. to Republic of Marshall Islands and Republic of Kiribati, 1996—2000; amb., sr. advisor U.S. Mission to the UN, N.Y.C., 2000—04. Recipient Lodestar award, Am. U., 1993, Disting. Civilian Svc. decoration, Sec. of the Army, 2000, Alumna of Yr. award, Am. U. Sch. Internat. Svc., 2001, Supr. award, State Dept., 2002. Mem.: Am. Fgn. Svc. Assn., Asia Soc., Washington Inst. Fgn. Affairs, Hong Kong Wine Soc. (founding), Phillips Collection. Avocations: wine tasting, gastronomy, history, skiing, scuba diving. Address: 1310 33rd St NW Washington DC 20007-2818

PLAKMEYER, STEVE, food service executive; CFO Gordon Food Svc Inc., Grand Rapids, Mich. Office: Gordon Food Svc Inc 333 50th St SW Grand Rapids MI 49548

PLAKS, ALBERT I. electrical engineer, educator; b. Minsk, Russia, Apr. 17, 1941; came to U.S., 1990; s. Israel and Genia P.; children: Elena, Victoria, Giller; m. Anna Toporovsky. MSEE, Polytech. U., Minsk, 1963, PhD in Electrical Engring., 1973. Profl. engr., Israel. Designer, rschr. Inst. Autom. Industry, Minsk, 1963-67; asst. prof. Polytech. U., Minsk, 1970-76; pres., owner Electromat, Inc., Tel-Aviv, Israel, 1977-81; sr. lectr. Singalovsky Tech. Coll., Tel-Aviv, Israel, 1980-90; sr. project engr. Dept. Pub. Works, Rishon-le-Zion, Israel, 1981-90; control specialist Murray Corp., Hunt Valley, Md., 1990—; prof. Balt. Hebrew U., 1992—2003. Adviser Inst. Standards, Tel-Aviv, 1985-87, Ministry of Edn., Tel-Aviv, 1983-90; inspector edn. divsn. Min. of Labor, Jerusalem, Israel, 1985-90. Author: Electric Machines for Servo Systems, 1989, Power Electronics Basics, 2000, Isreal and Espionje, 2001; patentee in field. Program dir., host (radio show) Star of David, Washington-Balt., 1991—. Mem. Internat. Acad. Ecology Man and Nature Protection Scis. Avocations: swimming, theater, cinema, paper writer. Office: Murray Corp 260 Schilling Cir AP 1 Hunt Valley MD 21031-1109

PLAKS, LIVIA BASCH, foundation executive; b. Baia Mare, Romania, Apr. 29, 1947; came to U.S., 1964; naturalized, 1969; d. Kalman and Cecilia (Freund) Basch; m. Andrew H. Plaks, June 9, 1968; children: Jason, Eric. AB, Rutgers U., 1969; AM, NYU, 1971. Exec. assoc. Internat. Rsch. and Exch. Bd., Princeton, N.J., 1986-92; assoc. dir. Project on Ethnic Rels., Princeton, 1992-94, exec. dir., 1994—. Rapporteur Orgn. Security Cooperation in Europe on Roma issues, Warsaw, Poland, 1994; mem. U.S. Task Force on Romania, 1990-92; mediation team between Romanian Govt. and Dem. Union of Hungarians in Romania, 1992—; mem. Coun. for Ethnic Accord, 1992—; mediation team between Slovak and ethnic Hungarian Parliamentary parties of Slovakia, 1995-2002; mediation team Serbs and Albanians of Kosovo, 1995—; testified to and for Commn. on Security and Cooperation in Europe on issues of Roma/Gypsies, 1994, 98, ethnic minorities, 2003. Recipient Certificate of Merit Pres. Romania, 1996, 2000, Govt. Hungary, 1996, Govt. Slovakia, 1998. Mem.: AAAS, Women in Internat. Security, Coun. Fgn. Rels. Avocations: music, reading, hiking. Office: Project on Ethnic Rels 15 Chambers St Princeton NJ 08542-3707 E-mail: livia.plaks@per-usa.org.

PLAMANN, ALFRED A. wholesale distribution executive; Pres., CEO Cert. Grocers Calif., Unified We. Grocers Inc., Commerce, Calif., 2000—. Office: Unified Western Grocers Inc 5200 Sheila St City Of Commerce CA 90040

PLANCHON, HARRY PETER, JR., research development manager; b. Aurora, Mo., Aug. 28, 1941; s. Harry P. and Ruth Arminta (Eden) P.; m. Virginia Grace Sapp, June 13, 1964; children: Benjamin John, Matthew Brian. BSME, U. Mo., 1964; MS in Nuclear Engring., U. Ill., 1971, PhD in Nuclear Engring., 1974; MBA, U. Chgo., 1990. Cert. profl. engr. Rsch. assoc., asst. prof. U. Ill. Nuclear Engring. Dept., Urbana, 1970-74; sr. engr., mgr. Clinch River Breeder Reactor Plant Systems Westinghouse Advanced Reaction Div., Madison, Pa., 1974-84; mgr. reactor analysis Exptl. Breeder Reacter Div., Argonne (Ill.) Nat. Lab., 1984-90; assoc. dir. Reactor Analysis Div., Argonne Nat. Lab., 1990-91; assoc. dir. ENG divsn. Argonne Nat. Lab., Idaho Falls, Idaho, 1991-2000, dir. nuclear tech. divsn., 2000—. Contbr. articles to profl. jours. Lt. USN, 1964-70. Fellow Am. Nuc. Soc. (Seaborg medal 1996); mem. Am. Soc. Mech. Engrs., Beta Gamma Sigma, Tau Beta Pi, Pi Mu Epsilon, Pi Tau Sigma. Presbyterian. Avocations: hiking, skiing, photography, golf, reading. Office: Argonne Nat Lab West PO Box 2528 Idaho Falls ID 83403-2528

PLANE, DONALD RAY, management science educator; b. Evansville, Ind., July 17, 1938; s. Edward L. and Margaret I. (Downen) P.; m. Rosemary Bieber, Sept. 4, 1961; children: Brian Russell, Dennis Lowell, Margaret Diane. ME, U. Cin., 1961; MBA (NDEA fellow), Ind. U., 1963, DBA (NDEA fellow), 1965. Instr. econs. U.S. Air Force Acad., 1965-67, asst. prof. econs., 1967-68; assoc. prof. mgmt. sci. U. Colo., Boulder, 1968-72, prof. mgmt. sci. and info. systems, 1972-84, head div. mgmt. sci., 1976-84; prof. mgmt. sci. Crummer Grad. Sch. Bus., Rollins Coll., Winter Park, Fla., 1984-2000, faculty pres. Crummer Grad. Sch. Bus., 1992-93, prof. emeritus, 2000—. Vis. Fulbright prof. mgmt. sci. U. Nairobi, 1978-79; cons. in field. Co-author: (with E.B. Oppermann) Business and Economic Statistics, 3d edit., 1986; (with J. Dinkel, G. Kochenberger) Management Science: Text and Applications, 1978, Quantitative Tools for Decision Support Using IFPS, 1986, Management Science: A Spreadsheet Approach for Windows, 1996. Served with USAF, 1965-68. Ford Found. fellow, 1965 Achievements include research, publs. in field. Home: 4493 S Atlantic Ave #603 New Smyrna Beach FL 32169

PLANELLES, VICENTE, molecular biologist; b. Sant Carles de la Rapita, Spain, Nov. 28, 1960; s. Vicente Planelles Beltran; m. Audrey Suzanne Dufel, Oct. 5, 1964; children: Tristan Mateu, Sabine Isabel. BS, U Complutense de Madrid, Spain, 1984; MS, U Complutense de Madrid, 1985; PhD, U. Calif. at Davis, 1991. Postdoctoral fellow UCLA, Los Angeles, Calif., 1991—95; asst. prof., medicine U. Rochester, NY, 1996—2002; assoc. prof. pathology U. UT, Sch. of Medicine, Salt Lake City, 2002—. Contbr. articles numerous profl. jours., chapters to books various profl. manuals. Recipient Achievement in Academic Rsch. award, F.O.C.U.S., Seville, Spain, 1985; grantee RO1 grant, 2000—05; Postdoctoral fellowship, NIH, 1991-1994, R29 grant, 1998—2002, R21 grant, 2002-2004. Mem.: Am. Soc. of Gene Therapy, Am. Assoc. for the Advancement of Sci., Am. Soc. for Microbiology, Frontiers in Bioscience (editl. bd. mem. 1998—2003), Apoptosis (assoc.; editl. bd. mem. 2000—03). Achievements include discovery of early studies on recombinant vaccines against the simian immunodeficiency virus in rhesus macaques; discovery of important mechanisms of induction of disease by the human immunodeficiency virus; development of development of novel vectors for gene therapy derived from HIV. Office: U UT Sch of Medicine 30 N 1900 E SOM 5C210 Salt Lake City UT 84132 E-mail: vicente.planelles@path.utah.edu.

PLANGERE, JULES LEON, JR., retired media company executive; b. Spring Lake, N.J., Dec. 30, 1920; s. Jules Leona nd Jesse Alene (Davidson) P.; m. Virginia Polhemus, 1942 (dec. 1977); 1 son, Jules L. III; m. Jane Wallhauser, Feb. 5, 1978; stepchildren: Mrs. John bickart, John C. Conover III, Jeffrey Conover. Student, Rutgers U., 1942. With Asbury Park (N.J.) Press, 1947-97, pub., 1977-91, CEO, 1980-91, chmn. bd., 1980-97. Former chmn. bd. trustees Monmouth U., West Long Branch, N.J.; past rpes. Welfare Coun. Monmouth County. Lt. U.S. Army, 1942-46. Mem. Asbury Park C. of C. (past pres.), N.J. Press Assn. (past pres.), Am. Newspaper Pubs. Assn., N.J. State C. of C. (bd. dirs.), Spring Lake Bath and Tennis Club, Nassau Club, Quail Ridge Country Club, Metedeconk Nat. Golf Club.

PLANITZER, RUSSELL E. computer company executive; b. 1944; Student, U.S. Naval Acad, 1966, Harvard U., 1974; MBA, Harvard Bus. Sch. Chmn. bd. dirs. Computervision Corp., Bedford, Mass., 1974—; gen. ptnr. J.H. Whitney & Co., N.Y.C., 1981—93; chmn. bd. dirs., CFO DR Holdings Inc. of Del., 1990—; CEO Computervision (formerly Prime Computer); mng. prin. Lazard Tech. Ptnrs. Bd. dirs. Kubi Software, GGN, Tazz Software, Interwise, NetByTel, New River, Pass Key.com and Quantum Bridge Named CEO of Year, D.H. Brown Assocs., 1995. Office: Lazard Tech Partners 48th Floor 30 Rockefeller Plz New York NY 10020 Office Phone: 212-632-6000. Office Fax: 212-332-8677.

PLANK, BETSY (MRS. SHERMAN V. ROSENFIELD), public relations counsel; b. Tuscaloosa, Ala., Apr. 3, 1924; d. Richard Jeremiah and Bettye (Hood) P.; m. Sherman V. Rosenfield, Apr. 10, 1954. Student, Bethany (W.Va.) Coll., 1940-43; AB, U. Ala., 1944. Continuity dir. radio sta. KQV, Pitts., 1944-47; account exec. Mitchell McKeown Orgn., Chgo., 1947-54; pub. rels. counsel Chgo. chpt. A.R.C., 1954-57; dir. pub. rels. Chgo. Coun. on Fgn. Rels., 1957-58; v.p. Ronald Goodman Pub. Rels. Counsel, Chgo., 1958-61; exec. v.p., treas., dir. Daniel J. Edelman, Inc., Chgo., 1961-73; dir. pub. rels. planning AT&T, N.Y.C., 1973-74; asst. v.p. corp. comm. Ill. Bell, Chgo., 1974-90; prin. Betsy Plank Pub. Rels., Chgo., 1990—. Dep. chmn. VII World Congress on Pub. Rels., 1976; co-chmn. nat. commn. on Pub. Rels. Edn., 1984-87; mem. adv. bd. Ill. Issues, 1975—. Bd. dirs. United Way Chgo., 1986-90; chmn. Citizenship Coun. Met. Chgo., 1990-96, Betsy Plank chpt. Pub. Rels. Student Soc. Am., No. Ill. U.; trustee Found. for Pub. Rels. Rsch. and Edn., 1975-80; nat. bd. dirs. Girl Scouts U.S., 1975-85. Recipient Millennium award Coll. Journalism, U. Fla., 2000, Alexander Hamilton award, Inst. Pub. Rels., 2000; named one of World's 40 Leading Pub. Rels. Profls., Pub. Rels. News, 1984. Fellow Pub. Rels. Soc. Am. (accredited, nat. pres. 1973, Outstanding Profl. award 1977, Outstanding Cmty. Svc. award 1989, Disting. Svc. award 2001); mem. Publicity Club Chgo. (pres. 1963-64, Outstanding Profl. award 1961), Ill. Coun. on Econ. Edn. (past chmn. bd. trustees, Extraordinary Leadership award 2001), Internat. Pub. Rels. Assn., Chgo. Network (chmn. 1980-81), Arthur W. Page Soc. (lifetime achievement award 2000), Union League Club of Chgo., Econ. Club Chgo., Zeta Tau Alpha. Presbyterian. Home and Office: 421 W Melrose St Chicago IL 60657-3848

PLANK, RAYMOND, investment corporation executive; b. Mpls., May 29, 1922; s. Raby and Maude (Howe) P.; children:Katherine, Michael, Pamela, Roger, Dana. BA, Yale U., 1944. Founder, partner Plank & Somekawa (accounting), Mpls., 1946-53; founder, chmn., chief exec. officer Apache Corp., Mpls., 1954—. Former dir. St. Paul Securities, Inc. Past pres. Mpls. Boys Club; trustee Carleton Coll.; former chmn. U. Minn. Found. Served to 1st lt., pilot USAAF, World War II. Mem. Beta Theta Pi. Clubs: Minneapolis, Woodhill Country. Republican. Home: 550 Long Lake Rd E Wayzata MN 55391-9670 Office: Apache Corp 1 Post Oak Central Houston TX 77056

PLANK, ROGER B. oil and gas production company executive; With Apache Corp., Houston, 1981—, v.p., CFO, 1997-2000, exec. v.p., CFO, 2000—. Office: Apache Corp 2000 Post Oak Blvd Ste 100 Houston TX 77056-4400

PLANK, TERRY, geochemistry educator; BA in Earth Scis. summa cum laude, Dartmouth Coll., 1985; PhD with distinction, Columbia U., 1993. NSF postdoctoral fellow Cornell U., 1993-94; asst. prof. U. Kans., 1995-99; assoc.

prof. Boston U., 1999—. Mem. com. for the study of the earth's deep interior AGU, 1994-95; mem. U.S. Sci. Adv. Com., Ocean Drilling Program, 1995-98; mem. rev. panel NSF GEO-Profl. Opportunities for Women in Rsch. and Edn., 1997, NSF OCE-Marine Geology and Geophysics, 1997-98; mem. steering com. NSF MARGINS Initiative, 1997—, MARGINs Theoretical and Exptl. Inst., Inside the Subduction Factory, 1999-2000; vis. prof. U. Rennes, France, 1998; presenter in field. Mem. editl. bd. Geology, 1997-99; mem. adv. editl. bd. Earth and Planetary Sci. Letters, 1997-2000; contbr. articles to profl. jours. Recipient Houtermans Young Scientist medal European Assn. Geochemistry, 1998, Donath medal Geol. Soc. Am., 1998; summer undergrad. rsch. fellow GSO, U. R.I., 1984, grad. fellow NSF, 1985-88, postdoctoral fellow NSF, 1993-94. Mem. Phi Beta Kappa. Achievements include research on the study of magmas associated with the plate tectonic cycle, at both divergent and convergent plate margins, experimental determination of trace element partition coefficients by laser ablation microprobe, the volatile content of arc magmas melt inclusions, volatile-tracers, effects on magma evolution, high quality, trace element analysis of volcanic rocks by inductively-coupled plasma mass spectrometry, global relationships. Office: Boston Univ Dept Earth Scis 685 Commonwealth Ave Boston MA 02215 Fax: 617-353-3290. E-mail: tplank@bu.edu.

PLANT, ALBIN MACDONOUGH, lawyer; b. Balt., July 30, 1937; s. Albin Joseph and Ruth E. (Frech) P.; m. Anne Warwick Brown, June 17, 1961; children: Katherine, Albin MacDonough Jr., Elizabeth Ashby. BA, Princeton U., 1959; LLB, U. Va., 1963; MLA, Johns Hopkins U., 1978. Bar: Md. 1963, U.S. Dist. Ct. Md. 1963, U.S. Ct. Appeals 1970. Assoc. Semmes, Bowen & Semmes, Balt., 1963-71, ptnr., 1971-91, Stewart, Plant & Blumenthal, Balt., 1991—. Bd. dirs. T. Rowe Price Savs. Bank; adj. prof. law U. Balt., 1979, U. Md., 1979—83, 1984—85. Bd. dirs. Am. Horticulture Soc., Md. Club, Balt. Choral Arts Soc. Mem.: Am. Coll. Trust and Estate Counsel, Am. Bar Found. (life), Wednesday Law Club, Md. Club, Lawyers Roundtable. Democrat. Office: 7 St Paul St Baltimore MD 21202-1626 Office Phone: 410-347-0506. Business E-Mail: amplant@spblaw.com.

PLANT, JOHN CHARLES, automotive equipment company executive; b. West Bromwich, West Midlands, Eng., Aug. 1, 1953; s. John and Florence (Harrison) P.; m. Christine Ann; children: Alexa Jayne, John Alexander. B Commerce, Econs., Acctg. and Law, Birmingham (Eng.) U., 1974. Auditor Touche Ross, Birmingham, 1974-77; financier Lucas Auto Ltd., Birmingham, 1977—, Burnley, Eng., 1983—; mng. dir. Lucas Varity Elec. and Electronics, 1991—97; pres. Lucas Varity Automotive, 1999; pres., CEO TRW Chassis; gen. mgr. TRW Automotive; exec. v.p. TRW, 1999—2001; co-CEO TRW Inc.; pres., CEO TRW Automotive, Livonia, Mich., 2001—. Bd. dirs. Martin Currie Portfolio Investment Trust PLC. Fellow Inst. Chartered Accts. in Eng. and Wales (mng. dir., FCA award 1981). Avocation: tennis. Office: TRW Automotive 12025 Tech Center Dr Livonia MI 48150*

PLANT, LINDA R. music educator; b. Eugene, Oreg., Mar. 25, 1949; d. Robert Ward and Ruth Adeline Johnston; m. Allan F. Plant, June 15, 1968; children: Glenn A., Jason R. Piano tchr. Linda Plant Piano Studio, Springfield, Oreg., 1973—; organist Emerald Baptist Ch., Eugene, Oreg., 1989—. Vol. ARC, Oreg., 1983—, adminstr., 2001—; mem. bd., sec. Oreg. Camp Cherith, 1977—, pres., 1984-87, 89-94. Mem. Nat. Guild Piano Tchrs. (pres. 1981-84, chmn. 1985-97), Oreg. Music Tchrs. Assn. (state cert., event chmn. 1990-2000, libr. 2001—, dist. pres. 1995-97, state sec. 1996-98). Republican. Baptist. Avocation: lifeguard/canoe instructor for youth camps.

PLANT, ROBERT ANTHONY, singer, composer; b. Bromwich, Staffordshire, Eng., Aug. 20, 1948; Previously sang with rock groups Band of Joy and Alexis Korner, singer, composer Led Zeppelin, 1968—80, world-wide concert tours, performed (films) The Song Remains the Same, 1976; composer: (songs) Black Dog, Stairway to Heaven, D'Yer Mak'Er; albums include (with Led Zeppelin) Led Zeppelin, Led Zeppelin II, 1969, Led Zeppelin III, 1970, Led Zeppelin IV, Houses of the Holy, 1973, Physical Graffiti, 1975, The Song Remains the Same, Presence, 1976, In Through the Out Door, 1979, albums include (with Led Zepplin) Coda, 1982, solo albums include Pictures at Eleven, 1982, The Principle of Moments, Shaken N' Stirred, 1985, Now and Zen, 1988, Manic Nirvana, 1990, Fate of Nations, 29 Palms/Whole Lotta Love, 1994, No Quarter: Jimmy Page & Robert Plant Unledded, 1994, Walking into Calrksdale, 1998, Dreamland, 2002, albums (with the Honeydrippers) The Honeydrippers, Vol. I, 1985, performed at LIVE AID in Phila., with Jimmy Page and John Paul Jones, 1985; contbr. soundtrack to movie Wayne's World 2. Named to Rock and Roll Hall of Fame, 1995; recipient Grammy nomination (Best Hard Rock Performance) for "Calling to You", 1994, Grammy, 1999. Office: care Atlantic Rec Corp 1290 Avenue Of The Americas New York NY 10104-0101

PLANTE, ROBERT DONALD, dean; b. Providence, Feb. 7, 1948; s. Robert Annaclet and Grace Joan Plante; m. Jean Karole Hostetler, May 29, 1982; children: Michael, Eric, Jason. BS in Physics, Worcester Poly. Inst., Mass., 1970; PhD, U. Ga., 1980. Asst. prof. Purdue U., West Lafayette, Ind., 1980—84, assoc. prof., 1985—90, prof., 1991—2001, sr. assoc. dean, 1999—, named prof., 2002—. Area editor Prodn. and Ops., 1990—; mem. editl. bd. Strategic Mgmt., 1995—; contbr. over 50 articles to profl. jours. Vol. United Way, Lafayette, 2002—04, Spl. Olympics, Tippecanoe County, Ind., 2002—04. 1st lt. U.S. Army, 1970—74. Mem. Elks. Roman Catholic. Avocations: golf, reading, skiing. Office: Purdue University Krannert Grad Sch Mgmt West Lafayette IN 47907 Office Phone: 765-494-4364. E-mail: bob@mgmt.purdue.edu.

PLANTS, WALTER DALE, retired elementary school educator, minister; b. Middlefield, Ohio, June 8, 1942; s. William E. and Hazel A. Plants; m. Sarah A. Gaddis, July 5, 1962; children: Dale Anthony, Jeanette Marie. BD, Azusa Pacific U., 1967; MEd, U. Nev., 1970. Cert. elem. tchr., ednl. adminstr. Elem. tchr. Churchill County Sch. Dist., Fallon, Nev., 1967—69, 1970—72, elem tchr., 1988—2001; grad. asst. U. Nev., Reno, 1969-70; tchr. Kingman (Ariz.) Elem. Sch. Dist. #4, 1972-77; head sci. program E. C. Best Elem. Sch., Fallon, 1988—2001; ret., 2001. Adj. instr. Ariz. State U., Tempe, 1973-77; cons. sci. Ariz. State Dept. Edn., 1975-77. Bd. dirs. Solar Energy Commn. Mohave County, Ariz., 1974; coord. County Sci. Fair, 1988-93; active Western Regional Sci. Fair Com.; sci. fair coord. Churchill County, 1989-94; mem. com. Regional Sci. Fair, 1992-94. HEW fellow, 1969; NSF grantee, 1973; AIMS Found. scholar, 1988; recipient Ariz. State PTA award, 1977, Ruth Neldon award Ariz. State Dept., 1977, Conservation award Big Sandy Natural Resources Conservation Dist. Ariz., 1976, Community Builder Svc. award Masons, Fallon, 1991, Disting. Leadership award, 1991-93; named State Tchr. of Yr. Nev. PTA, 1991, Conservation Tchr. of Yr., 1991; named to Congl. Select Edn. panel U.S. Congress, 1993. Mem. NEA, AAAS, Nat. Sci. Tchrs. Assn., Nat. Coun. Tchrs. Math., Internat. Reading Assn., Churchill County Edn. Assn. (Tchr. of Yr. 1989), Internat. Platform Assn., Nat. Arbor Day Found., World Wildlife Fund, Nat. Parks and Conservation Assn., Nat. Audubon Soc., Nev. State Tchrs. of Yr. Assn. (pres. 1994-96, pres. 1996-97), Phi Delta Kappa.

PLANTZ, JERRY ANTHONY, writer, consultant, consumer products company executive; b. Pitts., May 6, 1936; s. John Albert and Francis Plantz. BA, Duquesne U., Pitts., 1966. Prodr., news writer Hearst Broadcasting, Pitts., 1964—67; prodr., entertainment editor Cox Broadcasting, Pitts., 1967—69; exec. news prodr., reporter Metromedia, Kans. City, Mo., 1969—75, news prodr., 1977—83; pres. Jerry Plantz Prodns., Kans. City, Mo., 1975—77, 1983—96, Lees Summit, Mo., 1999—; dir. comms., mktg. Quick Silver, Merriam, Kans., 1996—99. Author: (book) I Held The Flag Today, 2003. Dir. comms. Flame Spirit Run, Kansas City, Mo., 1988, World Ecol. Soc., Kansas City, Mo., 1995. Sgt. U.S. Army, 1957—63. Recipient Humanitarian of Yr., Gladstone C. of C., 1989. Independent. Roman Catholic. Avocations: writing, public speaking, crossword puzzles, computers. Office: Jerry Plantz Prodns 419 SW Lakeview Blvd Lees Summit MO 64063 E-mail: poetusa@swbell.net.

PLAPP, BRYCE VERNON, biochemistry educator; b. DeKalb, Ill., Sept. 11, 1939; s. Vernon Edgar and Eleanor Barbara (Kautz) P.; m. Rosemary Kuhn, June 13, 1962; children— Brendan Bryce, Laurel Andrea BS, Mich. State U., East Lansing, 1961; PhD, U. Calif.-Berkeley, 1966. Research assoc. J.W. Goethe U., Frankfurt/Main, Germany, 1966-68; research assoc. Rockefeller U., N.Y.C., 1968-70; faculty U. Iowa, Iowa City, 1970—, prof. biochemistry, 1979—. Contbr. articles to profl. jours.; mem. editorial bd. Archives Biochemistry and Biophysics. Am. Cancer Soc. fellow, 1966-68 Mem. Am. Soc. for Biochemistry and Molecular Biology, Am. Chem. Soc., Sigma Xi Avocations: travel, sports. Office: U Iowa Dept Biochemistry 4-370 BSB Iowa City IA 52242 E-mail: bv-plapp@uiowa.edu.

PLASIL, FRANZ, physicist; b. Prague, Czechoslovakia, May 17, 1939; came to U.S., 1960; s. Frank and Eva (Wenger) P.; m. Catherine Logan, Feb. 15, 1964 (div. Sept. 1979); two children: Maia, David; m. Carol Baratz, Apr. 12, 1980. BS, Queen Mary Coll., U. London, 1960; PhD, U. Calif., Berkeley, 1964. Chemist Lawrence Berkeley (Calif.) Lab., 1964-65; rsch. assoc. Brookhaven Nat. Lab., Upton, N.Y., 1965-67; rsch. staff physics div. Oak Ridge (Tenn.) Nat. Lab., 1967-78, group leader physics div., 1978-86, sect. head physics div., 1986-99; fellow U. Tenn.-Battelle, 1999—2002; hon. rsch. prof. dept. physics and astronomy U. Tenn., Knoxville, 2002—. Contbr. articles to Annals of Physics, Phys. Rev., Phys. Rev. Letters, Nuc. Phys., Phys. Letters. Recipient Alexander von Humboldt award 1985, E. Mach medal of honor Acad. of Sci. of the Czech Republic, 1998. Fellow Am. Phys. Soc. Achievements include rsch. in fission-imposed limits on the stability of rotating nuclei and rsch. in nucleus-nucleus collisions at ultrarelativistic energies. Home: 964 W Outer Dr Oak Ridge TN 37830 8607 Personal E-mail: plasil@comcast.net.

PLASKACZ, EDWARD JOHN, computational scientist, engineer; b. Chgo., Jan. 21, 1959; s. John T. and Pauline H. Plaskacz; m. Elizabeth Ellen Prindiville, July 14, 1990. BS, Ill. Inst. Tech., Chgo., 1981, MS, 1982; PhD, Northwestern U., 1990. Engr. in tng. City of Chgo. Dept. of Water, 1979-81; engring. intern Sargent & Lundy Engrs., Chgo., 1981-82, engring. analyst, 1982-85; rsch. asst. Northwestern U., Evanston, Ill., 1985-90; computational scientist Argonne (Ill.) Nat. Lab., 1990—. Contbr. numerous articles to profl. jours. Recipient Letter of Commendation Chgo. Dept. Water, 1980, Clinton Strycker award Ill. Inst. Tech., 1981, Atanasoff award Second Symposium on Parallel Computational Methods for Large-Scale Structural Analysis and Design, 1993, Exceptional Performance award Argonne Nat. Lab., 1995, 97. Mem. AAAS, Nat Geographic Soc., Nat. Trust Historic Preservation, Colonial Williamsburg Found., U.S. Assn. for Computational Mechanics, Sigma Xi, Tau Beta Pi, Chi Epsilon. Office: Argonne Nat Lab 9700 Cass Ave Argonne IL 60439-4803 E-mail: ejplaskacz@anl.gov.

PLASKETT, THOMAS GEORGE, transportation company executive, corporate director; b. Raytown, Mo., Dec. 24, 1943; s. Warren E. and Frances S. P.; m. Linda Lee Maxey, June 8, 1968; children: Kimberly, Keith. B in Indsl. Engring., Kettering U.; MBA, Harvard U. Supr. indsl. engring. GM, Flint, Mich., 1968, supt. indsl. engring., 1969-73, sr. staff asst., treas. N.Y.C., 1973; asst. contr. Am. Airlines, N.Y.C., 1974, v.p. mktg. adminstrn., 1975-76, sr. v.p. fin., 1976-80, sr. v.p. mktg. Dallas, from 1980; pres., CEO Continental Airlines Inc., Houston, until 1988; chmn., CEO, pres. Pan Am Corp., N.Y.C., 1988-91; chmn. Fox Run Capital Assocs., 1991—; dir., interim pres., CEO, acting CFO Greyhound Lines, Inc., Dallas, 1994-95; vice-chmn., exec. v.p. Legend Airlines, Dallas, 1996-2001. Bd. dirs. Radioshack Corp., Ft. Worth, Smart & Final, Inc., L.A., Novell Corp., Cambridge, Mass., Provo, Utah, Alcon Inc., Ft. Worth, pvt. cos. Trustee Kettering U., Flint. Avocations: golf, skiing, squash. Office: 5215 N O Connor Blvd Ste 1070 Irving TX 75039-3738 E-mail: tom@foxruncapital.com.

PLASTINA, FRANK, communications executive; From pres. svc. provider and corp. networks to pres. metro and enterprise networks Nortel Networks, Brampton, Canada, 1987—. Bd. dirs. MicroElectronic Ctr. N.C., NC, S.E. Interactive, Research Triangle Park, NC. Bd. dirs. N.C. Govs. Bus. Coun., N.C. Symphony, Wake County Boys and Girls Clubs, NC. Mem.: N.C. Electronics and Info. Tech. Assn. (bd. dirs.). Office: Nortel Metro and Enterprise Networks 8200 Dixie Rd Ste 100 Brampton ON L6T 5P6 Canada

PLATE, THOMAS GORDON, columnist, educator; b. N.Y.C., May 17, 1944; s. John William and Irene (Henry) P.; m. Andrea I. Margolis, Sept. 22, 1979; 1 child, Ashley Alexandra. AB, Amherst Coll., 1966; MPA, Princeton U., 1968. Writer Newsweek, N.Y.C., 1968-70; editor Newsday, L.I., N.Y., 1970-72; sr. editor N.Y. Mag., N.Y.C., 1972-75; editor edit. page L.A. Herald Examiner, 1978-82; sr. editor Time Mag., N.Y.C., 1982-83; editor in chief Family Weekly, N.Y.C., 1984-85; editor edit. pages N.Y. Newsday, N.Y.C., 1986-89, L.A. Times, 1989-95, Times Op-Ed Page columnist, contbg. editor, 1995—. Adj. prof. UCLA Pub. Policy Sch. and Letters and Scis.; mem. founders bd. UCLA Sch. Pub. Policy; founder Asia Pacific Media Network; participant World Econ. Forum, Davos. Author: Understanding Doomsday, 1971, Crime Pays!, 1975, Secret Police, 1981; co-author: Commissioner, 1978. Recipient Best Deadline Writing award Am. Soc. Newspaper Editors, 1981, Best Edit. awards L.A. Press Club, 1979, 80, 81, Best Edit. award Calif. Newspaper Pubs. Assn., 1991, 92, 94; media fellow Stanford U. Mem. Pacific Coun. on Internat. Rels., Century Assn. (N.Y.C.), Phi Beta Kappa. Avocations: tennis, photography, travel to asia. Office: LA Times 405 Hilgard Ave Los Angeles CA 90095-9000

PLATER, WILLIAM MARMADUKE, English language educator, academic administrator; b. East St. Louis, Ill., July 26, 1945; s. Everett Marmaduke and Marguerite (McBride) P.; m. Gail Maxwell, Oct. 16, 1971; children: Elizabeth Rachel, David Matthew. BA, U. Ill., 1967, MA in English, 1969, PhD in English, 1973. Asst. dir. Unit One, asst. to dean Coll. Liberal Arts and Scis. U. Ill., Urbana, 1971-72, acting dir. Unit One, 1972-73, asst. dean Coll. Arts and Scis., 1973-74, asst. dir. Sch. Humanities, 1974-77, assoc. dir., 1977-83, assoc. coordinator interdisciplinary programs, 1977-83; prof. English, dean Sch. Liberal Arts Ind. U., Indpls., 1983-87; dean of faculties Ind. U.-Purdue U., Indpls., 1987—, exec. vice chancellor, 1988—, acting chancellor, 2003. Bd. dirs. Met. Indpls. Pub. Broadcasting, Inc.; cons. in field. Author: The Grim Phoenix: Reconstructing Thomas Pynchon, 1978, also articles, revs., poetry. Trustee Coun. for Adult and Experiential Learning, 1995—; bd. dirs. Ind. Com. for Humanities, 1986—92, Ind. Repertory Theatre, 1987—93, Children's Mus., 1992—2001, U. Ill. YMCA, Urbana, 1982—83, Herron Gallery Contemporary Art, 1987—93; bd. govs. Ind. U. Ctr. on Philanthropy, 1997—; bd. dirs. Midwest Univs. Consortium for Internat. Activities, Inc., 1996—98. Recipient Program Innovation prize Am. Acad. Ednl. Devel., 1982. Home: 6477 Oxbow Way Indianapolis IN 46220- Office: IUPUI Adminstrn Bldg A0108 Indianapolis IN 46202 E-mail: wplater@iupui.edu.

PLATER-ZYBERK, ELIZABETH MARIA, architectural educator; b. Bryn Mawr, Pa., Dec. 20, 1950; d. Josaphat and Maria (Meysztowicz) P.-Z.; m. Andres M. Duany, June 12, 1976. BA in Architecture, Princeton U., 1972; MArch, Yale U., 1974. Registered architect, Fla. Architect, prin. Andres Duany & Elizabeth Plater-Zyberk, Architects, Miami, Fla., 1979—; prof. U. Miami, 1979—; dean Sch. Architecture U. Miami, 1995—. Contbr. numerous articles to profl. jours. and popular publs. Mem. adv. coun. Princeton (N.J.) U. Sch. Architecture, 1982—, trustee 1987-91, 93-2003; mem. vis. com. MIT Sch. Architecture, 1990—. Mem. AIA, Archtl. Club Miami (pres. 1982-87). Office: Duany Plater-Zyberk & Co 1023 SW 25th Ave Miami FL 33135-4824

PLATIS, CHRIS STEVEN, educator; b. East Chicago, Ind., May 21, 1926; s. Sam and Myra (Theodore) P.; m. Jeanette Brown. BS in Phys. Edn., Ind. U., 1955, MS in Edn., 1964, postgrad., 1965-68. Gen. foreman Cast Armor, Inc., East Chicago, 1951-53; tchr. East Chgo. and Ind. Pub. Schs., 1955—. Asst. sports editor East Chgo. Calumet News, 1973-78; asst. dir. No. Ind. State Sports Mus., 1984-95, 96, 97, 98, 00. Appearances include (films) A Bridge Too Far, The Longest Day, Bridge at Remagan, D-Day, The Battle of the Bulge; author: Teaching Kids of Tomorrow, 1978, Are Teachers Adequate for Today's Students?, 1997. Master Boy Scouts Am., East Chicago, 1965-87; asst. recreational dir. North Twp., Northern Ind., 1993; All-Pacific Army, Football, Basketball, Track, 1946. With U.S. Army, 1944-46. Named to East Chgo. Hall of Fame All Am. Amateur Baseball Congress, 1955, 56, 57, Ind. Amateur Baseball Hall of Fame, 1962, U.S. Masters Track and Field All Am., 1995-98 (ranked 8 times # 1 and 2 in the country in masters track and field, 8 times ranked # 1 and 2 in the world in masters track and field, 1996-98, 10 nat. sr. Olympic medals), 25 (20 gold) individual Indiana Hooster State Games Regional Medals, 25 (20 gold) individual Indiana Hooster State Games Final Medals, 1996, 97, 98, 2000, 01, 2 Alltime State Records; Nat. Sr. Olympic track and field qualifier, 1997-99; 90 Yr. Greatest Athletes in East Chgo.'s History, Individual and Team Records Baseball Hall of Fame Archives, Cooperstown, NY, 2003; recipient 12 league batting titles, 11 MVP awards, 16 times Ind. All State in Baseball, 21 times League Mgr. of Yr., Nat./European Tchr. of Yr., 1984; mem. team won 53 league championships, 54 playoff championships, 41 Ind. State baseball championships, 7 world regional titles, 5 world finalists, 2 runner-up world championships, Nat. C.I.O. baseball championship, 1949 Big Ten Baseball Champions, Ind. U.; conf. baseball champions, 1942, 43, 44; all-conf. team, 1942, 43, 44, capt., 1942, 43, 44; Ind. State Jr. Legion champions, all-state, Midwest All-Star team, 1942, Ind.-Ill. Bi-State champions, 1950, Most Valuable, Batting Champion, Best Infielder award; nominated Ind. Northwest Intriging Family of Yr., Times Newspaper, 2001. Fellow VFW (charter mem. World War II Meml. 1998), Am. Legion, Normandy Invasion Club, Nat. Assn. of Basketball Coaches, Nat. Wildlife Assn. Republican. Avocations: reading, writing, baseball, tennis, golf. Home: 920 Troon Ct Schererville IN 46375

PLATIS, JAMES GEORGE, secondary school educator; b. Detroit, Mar. 23, 1927; s. Sam and Myra (Theodore) P.; m. Mary Lou Campbell, Aug. 16, 1974. BS in Physical Edn., Ind. U., 1955, MS in Edn., 1965; postgrad., Ind. State U., 1967. Cert. physical edn. tchr., Ind. Foreman Cast Armor, Inc., East Chicago, Ind., 1951-53, Youngstown Sheet & Tube, East Chicago, 1953-54; dir., tchr. East Chicago Pub. Schs., 1955—. Sports editor East Chicago Globe/Calumet News, 1973-78, Herald Newspapers, Merrillville, Ind., 1973-78; asst. dir. No. Ind. State Sports Mus., 1984-99. Contbr. articles to newspapers, jours. Founder East Chicago Hall of Fame, 1975, Little Olympics, East Chicago, 1956; pres. Ind. Am. Amateur Baseball Congress, 1954-57, commr., 1984-98, dir. No. Ind. State Sports Mus., 1988-00. With AUS, 1945-47, ETO. Named to Ind. Amateur Baseball Hall of Fame, 1962, East Chicago Hall of Fame, 1976, All-Am. Amateur Baseball Congress, 1955, 56, The Athletic Congress Masters All Am., 1986-98, 99, 2000, 2001-02; selected to 90 Yr. Greatest Athletes in East Chicago History, Nat. Athletic Congress, 1990; named Amateur Coach of Yr., U.S. Baseball Fedn. Ind., 1990, Amateur Runner-up Coach of Yr., 1988; recipient 53 World and 61 Nat. No. 1 track rankings, Athletic Congress Masters, 1989-98, 2000, 2001-02, 14 League Batting Titles, 12 MV League Players awards; Ind. Jr. Legion State Champions, All-State Batting Champions, MVP in tournament, Conf. Baseball Champions, 1943, 44, 45, All-Conf. Team, 1944-45, Conf. Batting Champion, 1944, Team Cptn., 1945, All-Midwest team, Best Outfielder, 1944; 18 times Ind. all-state team; Ind. Nat. Baseball State Champions; mem. team won 53 League Championships, 54 Playoff championships, 41 Ind. State Baseball Championships, 5 Ind. State Champions Runner Up, 7 World Regional Titles, 5 World Finalists, 2 runner-up World Champions, Big Ten baseball champions Ind. U., 1949, Best Outfielder Congress All-State team, Ill., Ind. Bi-State Champions, 1950; Nat. C.I.O. Baseball Championship, 1951, 12 Times League Mgr. Of The Year, 1982-96; Big Ten Baseball Champions, Ind. U., 1949; named Athlete of Yr. Ind. Masters Track and Field, 1992, World Sr. Olympic Masters Track & Field Champion, Spain, 6 gold medals, named Best Performer, 3 Masters Track & Field World Records, 1992, Fla. Masters Track and Field Athlete of Yr., 1994-98; recipient 74 State Ind. Track and Field Individual Gold medals, 1983-99, 2000-02, 84 Ind. state regional individual gold medals, 1983-98, 2000-02, 291 All Am. Masters Track and Field Certs., 1986-99, 2000-02, 39 Ill. Grand Prix individual titles, 1989-92, 45 Mid-West Track and Field individual titles, 1989-92, 5 gold medals, silver medal World Sr. Olympic Masters Track & Field, 1996, Ga., 5 Masters Track & Field World Records, 1997, 2 Masters Track & Field World Records, 1998, Nat. Senior Olympics Qualifer, 1991, 93, 95, 97, 99, 2001, 03, 4 Gold medals, 2 World Records Nat. Sr. Olympics, 1999-2001, 7 gold medals World Sr. Olympic Masters Track and Field, Sydney, Australia, 2000, 5 World Records, selected Best Performer; named Internat. Man of the Yr. in Edn., 1991-92, 93, Professional of the Yr. in Edn., 1991, Master Track and Field All-Am., 1986-2003, Northwest Ind. Intriguing Family of the Yr., 2002, 8 Decades of Baseball, Individual & Team Records in Baseball Hall of Fame, Cooperstown, N.Y., 2003. Fellow Nat. Assn. Basketball Coaches, Am. Assn. Health, Phys. Edn. and Recreation; mem. Athletic Dirs. Assn. Sportswriters Guild, VFW, Am. Legion, WWII Meml. (82nd Airborne Divsn., 1st Inf. Divsn. 1998), Mens Club Ind. U. Republican. Avocations: reading, running, baseball, writing.

PLATKIN, RICHARD M. lawyer; b. 1963; m. Laurie Conway. BS, Rensselaer Poly. Inst., 1985; JD, Union U., Albany, 1993. Bar: N.Y. 1994. Computer engr.; law clk. to Hon. Roger J. Miner U.S. Ct. Appeals (2d cir.); asst. counsel Office Gov. State of N.Y., Albany, 1995—97, sr. asst. counsel, 1997—98, dep. counsel to gov., 1998—2003, counsel to gov., 2003—. Exec. editor: Union U. Law Rev. Office: State Capitol Albany NY 12224-0341

PLATNER, WARREN, architect; b. Balt., June 18, 1919; s. Warren Kelly and Alice Darling (Chapman) P.; m. Joan Payne, 1945; children: Bronson, Joan, Sharon, Madeleine. B.Arch., Cornell U., 1941. Assoc. Eero Saarinen and Assocs. (architects), 1950-65; propr. Warren Platner Assocs. (architects), New Haven, 1965—. Vis. lectr. archtl. schs. Prin. works include Kent Meml. Library, Suffield, Conn., 1972, Princeton U. Prospect Center, 1970, MGIC Hdqrs, Milw., 1973, Am. Restaurant, Kansas City, Mo., 1974; malls at Water Tower Pl., Chgo., 1975, Windows on the World, N.Y.C., 1976, Standard Brands Research Center, Wilton, Conn., 1979, Providence Athenaeum, 1980; Sea Containers Hdqrs., London, 1983, Wildflower Restaurant Lodge, Vail, Colo., 1985, Porter, Wright, Morris & Arthur Headqrs., Columbus, Ohio, 1986, Pan Am Bldg. additions, N.Y.C., 1987, ships Fantasia and Fiesta, 1990, Carlyle Hotel additions, 1990, Fain Residence, 1990, Friedman Residence, 1993, The Upstairs at '21', 2002. Recipient Rome prize architecture, 1955; advanced research Fulbright award architecture, 1955; Graham Found. award advanced studies fine arts, 1962; 1st ann. award Designers Lighting Forum, 1975; Pres.'s fellow R.I. Sch. Design, 1980; Interior Design Hall of Fame award, 1985; also several internat. design awards. Fellow AIA, Am. Acad. in Rome. Address: 18 Mitchell Dr New Haven CT 06511-2516

PLATNICK, NORMAN I. curator, entomologist; b. Bluefield, W.Va., Dec. 30, 1951; s. Philip and Fannie (Kascenewsky) P.; m. Nancy Stewart Price, June 14, 1970; 1 child, William Durin. BS in Biology, Concord Coll., 1968; MS in Zoology, Mich. State U., 1970; PhD in Biology, Harvard U., 1973. Asst. curator Am. Mus. Natural History, N.Y.C., 1973-77, assoc. curator, 1977-82, curator, 1982-98, chmn. dept. entomology, 1987-94, Peter J. Solomon Family curator, 1998—; program dir. biotic surveys and inventories NSF, 2002—03. Sci. attaché Consulate of Gondwana, N.Y.C., 1976—. Author: Advances in Spider Taxonomy, 1989, 93, 98; co-author: Systematics and Biogeography, 1981; co-editor: Advances in Cladistics, 1983. V.p. Ctr. Internat. de Documentation Arachnologie, 1986-89 (pres. 1995-98). Fellow Willi Hennig Soc. (founder, pres. 1990-92); mem. Am. Arachnological Soc. (charter, membership sec. 1976—2002). Office: Am Mus Natural History Central Pk W At 79th St W New York NY 10024 Office Phone: 212-769-5612.

PLATSOUCAS, CHRIS DIMITRIOS, immunologist; b. Athens, Greece, Apr. 17, 1951; came to U.S., 1973; s. Dimitrios Evagelos and Maria (Tsonidis) P.; m. Emilia L. Oleszak, Oct. 18, 1985. BS, U. Patras (Greece), 1973; postgrad., Purdue U., 1974; PhD, MIT, 1978. Rsch. fellow/assoc. Meml. Sloan-Kettering Cancer Ctr., N.Y.C., 1978-80, asst. mem., 1980-85, asst. prof., 1981-85, head lab. biol. response modifiers, 1981-85; assoc. prof. dept. immunology M.D. Anderson Cancer Ctr., Houston, 1985-89, prof., dep. chmn., 1989-93, Ashbel Smith professorship, 1991-92, H.L. and O. Stringer professorship in cancer rsch., 1992-93; L.H. Carnell prof. and chmn. dept. microbiology, immunology Temple U. Sch. Medicine, Phila., 1993—; acting dean Coll. Sci. and Tech. Temple U., Phila., 1998-2000, dean Coll. Sci. and Tech., 2000—04. Biotech. cons., sci. reviewer study sects. NIH, Bethesda, Md., 1982—. Contbr. numerous articles to profl. jours. Nat. Rsch. Svc. award

NIH, 1978-79; grantee NIH, Am. Cancer Soc., State of Tex., many others. Mem. Am. Assn. Immunologists, Am. Soc. Hematology, Am. Assn. Biochem & Molecular Biology, Soc. Investigative Pathology, Am. Assn. Cancer Rsch. Greek Orthodox. Achievements include patents in field; research on human T cell immunology, on T-cell antigen receptors, on tumor-infiltrating lymphocytes in malignant melanoma and ovarian carcinoma, on organ transplantation, on chronic rejection, on AIDS, and on autoimmune diseases. Office: Temple U Sch Medicine Dept Microbiology and Immunology 3400 N Broad St Philadelphia PA 19140-5104 Office Phone: 215-707-7929. Business E-Mail: chris.platsoucas@temple.edu.

PLATT, DAVID DAY, journalist, editor; b. Columbus, Ohio, June 5, 1942; s. Joseph Swan and Margaret Day Platt; m. Priscilla G. Gray, June 14, 1969; children: Joshua Gray, William Andrews. AB, Yale U., 1966; MS, Columbia U., 1969. Prodr.-dir. Wvia TV, Scranton, Pa., 1969—71; pub. affairs prodr. Maine Pub. Broadcasting Network, Orono, 1971—76; reporter, columnist Bangor Daily News, Bangor, Maine, 1976—86; editor, writer Maine Times, Topsham, 1986—91; editor, publs. dir. Island Inst., Rockland, Maine, 1993—. Editor: Penobscot: Forest, River and Bay, 1995, Holding Ground, 2004. Episcopalian. Avocations: sailing, travel. Home: PO Box 772 Yarmouth ME 04096 Office: Island Inst PO Box 648 Rockland ME 04841 Personal E-mail: dplatt@islandinstitute.org.

PLATT, GEORGE MILO, university administrator; b. Rapid City, S.D., Jan. 1, 1931; s. George Lee and Josephine M. (Paulson) P.; B.S., S.D. State U., 1953; M.A., Syracuse U., 1955, Ph.D., 1962. Asst. prof. U. S.D., 1962-65, U. Iowa, 1965-69; dir. planning and instl. research Wichita (Kans.) State U., 1969-79, assoc. v.p., 2nd assoc. prof. pub. adminstrn., 1869—97; Ford Found. adv. to secs. of local govt., East and West Pakistan, 1963, 65-66, 68. Served with AUS, 1955-57. Mem. Am. Soc. for Public Adminstrn., Am. Polit. Sci. Assn., Midwest Polit. Sci. Assn., Western History Assn., Soc. for Coll. and Univ. Planning. Author: (with Richard O. Niehoff) Local Government in East Pakistan, 1964; (with Alan L. Clem) A Bibliography of South Dakota Government and Politics, 1965, (with others) Administrative Problems in Pakistan, 1966, (with others) Presdl. Ptnrs.: First Ladies of the University, 2001. Office: Wichita State Univ Campus Box 155 Wichita KS 67260-0155 E-mail: george.platt@wichita.edu.

PLATT, JAMES DAVID, academic administrator, educator; b. Boston, Oct. 16, 1951; s. Henry and Carolyn Platt; m. Hilary Christner, July 25, 1980. BA, U. South Fla., 1974, MA, 1976. Cert. employee assistance profl. Employees Assistance Professionals in Edn., lic. alcohol and drug abuse counselor NH, clinical mental health counselor NH. Vocat. rehab. counselor State of Fla., Sarasota, 1977—79; counselor and sr. clinician First Step Sarasota, Sarasota, 1979—86, counselor, sr. clinician, 1979—86; substance abuse therapist Dartmouth Med. Sch., Hanover, NH, 1986—90, 1986—91, instr. psychiatry, 1990—; dir., faculty and employee assistance program Dartmouth Coll., Hanover, NH, 2001—. Bd. dirs. cert. bd. NH Office Alcohol and Drug Abuse Counselor, Concord, NH, 1990—98; bd. dirs., founding mem. Dartmouth Coll. Ctr. Addiction Edn., Hanover, NH; bd. dirs. HEADREST, Lebanon, NH, 1994—96; presenter in field. Co-author: (chpt.) Engaging the Patient in Treatment. Mem.: Nat. Assn. Employee Assistance Profls. (licentiate), Internat. Assn. Employee Assistance Profls. Higher Edn. (licentiate), Nat. Assn. Alcohol Drug Abuse Counselors (assoc.), Nat. Amateur Radio Relay League. Avocations: photography, amateur radio. Office: Dartmouth College F/EAP 40 North College Street Hanover NH 03755 Personal E-mail: james.d.platt@dartmouth, edu. E-mail: james.d.platt@dartmouth.edu.

PLATT, JAN KAMINIS, county official; b. St. Petersburg, Fla., Sept. 27, 1936; d. Peter Clifton and Adele (Diamond) Kaminis; m. William R. Platt, Feb. 8, 1963; 1 child, Kevin Peter. BA, Fla. State U., 1958; postgrad., U. Fla. Law Sch., 1958-59, U. Va., 1962, Vanderbilt U., 1964. Pub. sch. tchr. Hillsborough County, Tampa, Fla., 1959-60; field dir. Girl Scouts Suncoast Coun., Tampa, 1960-62; city councilman Tampa City Coun., 1974-78; county commr. Hillsborough County, 1978-94, 96—; chmn. Hillsborough County Bd. County Commrs., 1980-81, 83-84, 98-99, ret., 1994, re-elected, 1996, chmn., 1998-99. Chmn. Tampa Bay Regional Planning Coun., 1982, West Coast Regional Water Supply Authority, Tampa, 1985, Hillsborough County Coun. Govts., 1976, 79, Agy. Bay Mgmt., Hills Environ. Protection Commn., Sunshine Amendment Drive 7th Congrl. Dist., Tampa, 1976, Cmty. Action Agy., Tampa, 1981, 83-84,chmn. pro tem Tampa Charter Revision Commn., 1975, chmn. Prison Sitting Task Force, Tampa, 1983, Tampa Housing Study Com., 1983, Met. Planning Orgn., Tampa, 1984, Bd. Tax Adjustment, Tampa, 1984, Hartline, 2002-03, Friendship Trailbridge Oversight Com., 2002-03, Tampa Bay Water, 2003-04; appointee Constn. Revision Commn., Fla., 1977, HRS Dist. IV Adv. Coun., Fla.; mem. Hillsborough County Expy. Authority, Taxicab Commn., Ch. Hills Cmty. Youth Coun.; vice chmn. steering com. Nat. Counties Environ. Task Force; pres. Suncoast Girl Scout Coun., 1973-74, Head Start Cmty. Found., 1996. Bd. dirs. March of Dimes, Tampa, The Fla. Orch., Tampa, Tampa Bay Sierra, Tampa Audubon; trustee Hillsborough County Hosp. Authority, Tampa, 1984-94; pres. Citizens Alert, Tampa, Bay View Garden Club; v.p. Hillsborough County Bar Aux.; mem. adv. bd. Northside Cmty. Mental Health Ctr.: Access House, Tampa; active Arts Coun. Tampa-Hillsborough County, 1983-85, 96-2001, Drug Abuse Coordinating Coun. Orgn., Tampa, Bd. Criminal Justice, Tampa, Fla. Coun. on Aging, Inebriate Task Force, Tampa, Tampa Downtown Devel. Authority Task Force, Tampa Sports Authority, Tampa Area Mental Health Bd., Children's Study Commn., Manahill Area Agy. on Aging, Tampa, Athena Soc., Tampa Area Com. Fgn. Affairs, LWV; pres. Hills Children's Coun., Headstart Found.; bd. dirs. Arts Coun.; exec. com. Tampa Performing Arts Ctr.; mem. Com. of 100. Recipient Athena award, Women in Comm., 1976, Spessard Holland Meml. award, Tampa Bay Com. for Good Govt., 1979, First Lady of Yr. award, Beta Sigma Phi, 1980, First Ann. Humanitarian award, Nat. Orgn. of Prevention of Animal Suffering, 1981, Women Helping Women award, Soroptimist Internat. Tampa, 1983, Good Govt. award, Tampa Jaycees, 1983, LWV, 1983, John Books Meml. award, Fla. Audubon Soc., 1989, Girl Scout Woman of Distinction award, 1996, Girl Scout Thanks award, 1996, Libery Bell award, Hillsborough County Bar Assn., 2000, Black Bear award, Suncoast and Tampa Bay Groups of the Sierra Club, 2001, Eliza Wolff award, Tampa United Meth. Ctrs., Outstanding Leadership in Local Environ. Protection, Fla. Local Environ. Resource Agys., 2002, Lifetime Achievement award for outstanding leadership in local environ. protection, 2004. Mem. Am. Judicature Soc., State Assn. County Commrs. Fla. (at-large dir.), AAUW (bd. dirs.), Mortar Board, Garnet Key, Phi Beta Kappa (pres. local alumni), Phi Kappa Phi. Democrat. Episcopalian. Home: 3531 Village Way Tampa FL 33629-8914 Office: PO Box 1110 Tampa FL 33601-1110 Office Phone: 813-272-5730.

PLATT, JEB BUCHANAN, health facility administrator; b. Rock Island, Ill., Aug. 31, 1953; s. John Bowman and Joe-Ann Elizabeth P.; m. Susan, Jan. 17, 1973 (div. Jan. 1989); 1 child, Justice John Wesley. BA, Marycrest Coll. Clin. dir., founder Living Recovery, Milw. Peer rev. Wis. Certification Bd., Milw. Office: PO Box 6295 Milwaukee WI 53206-0295

PLATT, JEFFREY LOUIS, surgeon, immunologist, educator, pediatric nephrologist; b. Mt. Vernon, N.Y., Mar. 21, 1949; s. Charles Alfred and Paula Platt; m. Agnes M. Schipper. BA in Politics with honors, NYU, 1971; postgrad., Columbia U., 1971-73; MD, U. So. Calif., 1977. Diplomate Am. Bd. Pediatrics, Nat. Bd. Med. Examiners. Intern in pediatrics Children's Hosp. L.A., 1977-78, resident, 1978-79, Della M. Mudd resident, 1979-80; med. fellow in pediatric nephrology U. Minn., Mpls., 1980-85, instr. dept. pediatrics, 1985-86, asst. prof., 1986-88, assoc. prof. pediatrics and cell biology and neuroanatomy, 1988-92; prof. surgery, pediatrics and immunology depts. Duke U., Durham, NC, 1992—98, Dorothy W. and Joseph W. Beard prof. exptl. surgery, 1994—98; prof. surgery immunology and pediatrics Mayo Clinic, Rochester, Minn. Mem. editl. bd.: Transplantation, Transplant Immunology, Xenotransplantation, Jour. Immunology, Cellular Immunology; contbr. over 400 articles to med. jours.; author: 4 books. Recipient Clinician-Scientist award Am. Heart Assn., 1983-88, Established Investigator award Am. Heart Assn., 1988-93, Inst. Medicine of NAS. Mem. AAAS, Assn. Am. Physicians, Am. Heart Assn (coun. kidney in cardiovasc. disease, coun. basic sci.), Internat. Soc. Nephrology, Am. Assn. Immunologists, Am. Fedn. Clin. Rsch., Am. Soc. Nephrology, Am. Assn. Pathologists, Soc. for Devel. Biology, Clin. Immunology Soc., Soc. Pediatric Rsch., Soc. Glycobiology, Soc. Exptl. Biology and Medicine, Alpha Omega Alpha. Office: Mayo Found Medical Scis Bldg Rm 2 Rochester MN 55905-0001

PLATT, JOSEPH BEAVEN, former college president; b. Portland, Oreg., Aug. 12, 1915; s. William Bradbury and Mary (Beaven) P.; m. Jean Ferguson Rusk, Feb. 9, 1946; children: Ann Ferguson Walker, Elizabeth Beaven Garrow. BA, U. Rochester, 1937; PhD, Cornell U., 1942; LLD, U. So. Calif., 1969, Claremont McKenna Coll., 1982; DSc, Harvey Mudd Coll., 1981. Instr. physics U. Rochester, N.Y., 1941-43, from asst. prof. to prof., 1946-56, assoc. chmn. dept. physics, 1954-56; staff mem. Radiation Lab. MIT, Cambridge, 1943-46; founding pres. Harvey Mudd Coll., Claremont, Calif., 1956-76, now part-time sr. prof. physics; pres. Claremont U. Ctr., 1976-81. Trustee Aerospace Corp., 1972-85, Consortium for Advancement of Pvt. Higher Edn., 1985-92; chief physics br. AEC, 1949-51; cons. U.S. Office Ordnance Rsch., NSF, 1953-56; mem. com. on sci. in UNESCO, NAS-NRC, 1960-62, mem. com. on internat. orgns. and programs, 1962-64, sci. advisor U.S. Del., UNESCO Gen. Conf., Paris, 1960, alt. del., 1962, chmn. Subcom. on Sino-Am. Sci. Cooperation, 1965-79; mem. panel on internat. sci. Pres.'s Sci. Adv. Com., 1961; trustee Analytic Svcs., Inc., 1958-89, chmn., 1961-89; mem. adv. com. on sci. edn. NSF, 1965-70, 72-76, chmn., 1969-70, 73-74, 74-75; bd. dirs. Lincoln Found., 1979-85, Bell & Howell Corp., 1978-88, Am. Mut. Fund, 1981-88, DeVry, Inc., 1984-87, Sigma Rsch., 1983-87, Jacobs Engring. Co., 1978-86. Author: Harvey Mudd College: The First Twenty Years, 1994. Trustee China Found. for Promotion of Edn. and Culture, 1966—, Carnegie Found. for Advancement Tchg., 1970-78, Ancient Bibl. Manuscript Ctr., 1980—; chmn. select com. Master Plan for Higher Edn. Calif., 1971-73; mem. Carnegie Coun. for Policy Studies in Higher Edn., 1975-80. Fellow Am. Phys. Soc.; mem. IEEE, Automobile Club So. Calif. (bd. dirs. 1973-90, chmn. bd. dirs. 1986-87), Calif. Club, Sunset Club, Twilight Club, Cosmos Club, Bohemian Club, Phi Beta Kappa, Sigma Xi, Phi Kappa Phi. Home: 452 W 11th St Claremont CA 91711-3833 Business E-Mail: joseph_platt@hmc.edu.

PLATT, LESLIE A. lawyer; b. Bronx, N.Y., Aug. 7, 1944; s. Harold and Ann (Bienstock) P.; m. Marcia Ellin Berman, Aug., 1969; 1 son, Bill Lawrence. BA, George Washington U., 1966; JD, NYU, 1969. Bar: N.Y. 1970, U.S. Dist. Ct. D.C. 1972. Atty. advisor Office Gen. Counsel HUD, Washington, 1971-72, legis. atty., 1972-75, asst. gen. counsel for legis. svcs., 1975-78, assoc. gen. counsel for legis., 1978-80; dep. gen. counsel-legal counsel HEW (HHS 1980) Office Gen. Counsel, Washington, 1980-81, legal counsel and staff dir. White House Agent Orange group, 1980-81; pvt. practice Washington, 1982-91; exec. asst. to dir. NIH, 1991-92; exec. v.p., COO, gen. counsel The Inst. for Genomic Rsch., Gaithersburg, Md., 1992-95; sr. v.p. strategic devel., gen. counsel Am. Type Culture Collection, Manassas, Va., 1996-98; prin. assurance and adv. bus. practice Ernst & Young LLP, McLean, Va., 1999—. Pres, dir. Found. for Genetic Medicine, Inc., 1997-2004. Patentee in field. Chmn. cmty. adv. bd. Fairfax Hosp. Assn. Cameron Glen Facility; chair steering com. Reston/Herndon Bus.-H.S. Partnership; mem. Loudoun County Sci. and Tech. Cabinet, 2002—; bd. dirs. No. Va. Tech. Coun., 2002—. Recipient Disting. Svc. award HUD, 1978. Mem. ABA, Fed. Bar Assn., Am. Jud. Soc., Fed. Sr. Exec. Svc. (charter), Internat. Bar Assn. Home: 11901 Triple Crown Rd Reston VA 20191-3015

PLATT, LEWIS EMMETT, aerospace transportation executive; b. Johnson City, Apr. 11, 1941; s. Norval Lewis and Margaret Dora (Williams) Platt; m. Joan Ellen Redmund, Jan. 15, 1983; children: Caryn, Laura, Amanda, Hillary. BME, Cornell U., 1964; MBA, U. Pa., 1966. With Hewlett Packard, Waltham, Mass., 1966—99, engring. mgr., various pos., 1971—83, v.p., 1983—87, exec v.p., 1987—93, pres., CEO, chmn., 1993—99; ret., 1999; CEO Kendall-Jackson Wine Estates, 1999—2001; non-exec. chmn. The Boeing Co., 2003—. Trustee Waltham Hosp., 1978—80, Wharton Sch. Bd. Overseers, 1993, SETI Inst., 2002—; active Mid-Peninsula YMCA, 1980—; bd. couns. YMCA-USA, 1993—, Cornell U. Coun., 1992—, Computer Sys. Policy Project, 1993—, Calif. Bus. Roundtable, 1993—95, Bus. Coun., 1993—, Bay Area Coun., 1993—, Bus. Roundtable, 1993—; vice-chmn. Y Coun., 1989; bd. dirs. Joint Venture, Silicon Valley, 1996. Named Outstanding Alumnus, Wharton Sch. Bus., Univ. Pa., 1994—95; named to Wharton Alumni Honor Roll; recipient Red Triangle award, Min-Peninsula YMCA, 1992, Internat. Citizens award, World Forum Silicon Valley, San Jose, Calif., 1994, award for bus. excellence, U. Calif. Sch. Bus. Adminstrn., 1996, Tree of Life award, Jewish Nat. Fund, 1996, Leadership and Vision award, French-Am. C. of C., San Francisco, 1997. Mem.: IEEE, Sci. Apparatus Mfg. Assn. (bd. dirs. 1978—80).

PLATT, NICHOLAS, Asia specialist, retired ambassador; b. N.Y.C., Mar. 10, 1936; s. Geoffrey and Helen (Choate) P.; m. Sheila Maynard, June 28, 1957; children: Adam, Oliver, Nicholas. BA cum laude, Harvard U., 1957; MA, Johns Hopkins U., 1959. Commd. fgn. svc. officer Dept. State, 1959; vice consul Windsor, Ont., Can., 1959-61; Chinese lang. trainee, 1962-63; polit. officer consulate gen., 1964-68; chief Asian Communist areas divsn. Bur. Intelligence and Rsch., Dept. State, Washington, 1969; chief North Asia div., 1970, dept. dir. Exec. Secretariat staff, 1971, dir. staff, 1972-73; chief polit. sect. U.S. Liaison Office, Peking, China, 1973-74; 1st sec. Am. embassy, Tokyo, 1974-77; dir. Office of Japanese Affairs, Dept. State, 1977-78; mem. staff Nat. Security Council, White House, 1978-79; dep. asst. sec. for internat. security affairs Dept. Def., 1980-81; dep. asst. sec. for internat. orgn. affairs Dept. State, 1981-82; amb. Lusaka, Zambia, 1982-84; exec. sec., spl. asst. to sec. state Dept. State, 1985-87; amb. to The Philippines Am. Embassy, Manila, 1987-91, amb. to Pakistan, 1991-92; pres. Asia Soc., N.Y.C., 1992—2004, pres. emeritus, 2004—. Bd. dirs. Fiduciary Trust Internat. Recipient Meritorious award exemplary achievement pub. adminstrn. William A. Jump Found., 1973, Disting. Civilian Svc. medal Dept. Def., 1981, Presdl. Merit award, 1985, 87, Disting. Honor award U.S. Dept. State, 1987, 91, Wilbur Carr award, 1992. Mem. N.Y. Coun. Fgn. Rels., Met. Club (Washington), Century Club, Union Club. Home: 131 E 69th St New York NY 10021-5158

PLATT, NINA, law librarian; d. Harlan and Ethel (Byron) Thorlacius; m. Vernon Platt, Dec. 21, 1984. BS, U. ND, Grand Forks, 1980; Masters of Libr. and Info. Sci., Dominican U., River Forest, Ill., 1997. Libr. dir. Carnegie Libr., Devils Lake, ND, 1982—85; tech. svcs. mgr. Dorsey & Whitney, Mpls., 1986—95; systems libr. Minn. Office of Atty. Gen., St. Paul, 1995—97; dir. of libr. services Faegre & Benson LLP, Mpls., 1998—. Cons. Nina Platt & Associates, Prior Lake, Minn., 1993—98. Contbr. textbook Knowledge Management for the Information Professional, articles to profl. jours. and web sites. Mem.: Minn. Law Libr. Assn. (Law Librarianship award 2003), Spl. Libraries Assn. (Innovations in Tech. award 2003), Minn. Assn. Law Libraries, Am. Assn. Law Libraries (exec. bd. mem. 2002—), Minn. Libr. Assn. (assoc.), Hekla Club (pres. 1996—97). Achievements include development of Minn. appellate ct. opinions archive. Avocations: motorcycling, gardening. Office: Faegre & Benson LLP 2200 Wells Fargo Ctr 90 S 7th St Minneapolis MN 55402 Business E-Mail: nplatt@faegre.com.

PLATT, RUTHERFORD HAYES, lawyer, educator, geographer, consultant; b. N.Y.C., Nov. 1, 1940; s. Rutherford and Jean (Noyes) P.; children: Anne, Stephen. BA, Yale U., 1962; JD, U. Chgo., 1967, PhD, 1971. Bar: Ill. 1968. Staff atty. Open Lands Project, Chgo., 1968-72; prof. U. Mass., Amherst, 1972—. Cons. FEMA, World Bank, Lincoln Inst., EPA, and others; mem. 8 NRC coms., 1979—. Author: Land Use and Society, 1996, Disasters and Democracy, 1999; contbr. articles to profl. jours. Mem. Assn. Am. Geographers, Faculty Club (Mass.), Cosmos Club (Washington). Home: 78 Hillcrest Dr Florence MA 01062-1362

PLATT, STEVEN IRVING, lawyer, judge; b. Woodstock, Va., Jan. 1, 1947; s. Nathan and Adele P. (Lober) Platt; children: Jason Benjamin, Sarah Edan. BA, U. Va., 1969; JD, Am. U., 1973; cert. of completion, Nat. Jud. Coll., 1980, Nat. Coll. of Probate Judges, 1983. Bar: Md. 1976, U.S. Dist. Ct. Md., 1976. Ptnr. Stern, Platt & Risner, Oxon Hill, Md., 1976-79; judge Orphans Ct., Prince Georges County, Md., 1978-85; ptnr. Platt & Risner, Clinton, Md., 1980-86; chief judge Orphans Ct., Prince Georges County, Md., 1985-86; assoc. judge Dist. Ct. Md., Upper Marlboro, Md., 1986-88, adminstrv. judge Prince Georges County, 1988-90; assoc. judge Cir. Ct., Prince Georges County, Md., 1990—. Instr. Paralegal Inst. U. Md.; chmn. Jud. Adminstrn. Com., Md. Jud. Conf., 1989-90. Bd. dirs. United Way, Prince Georges, 1980; bd. mgrs. YMCA, Prince Georges, 1980; chmn. Labor Law Revision Task Force, Prince Georges, 1981—; chmn. bd. trustees Henson Valley Montessori Sch., Temple Hills, Md., 1985-86. With Md. NG, 1970-76; v.p. Md. Bus. and Tech. Case Mgmt. Task Force; chmn. Cong. of Cir. Ct. Judges Bus. & Tech. Case Mgmt. Implementation Com. Mem. ABA, Md. Bar Assn., Prince Georges Bar Assn. (bd. dirs. 1978-85, treas. 1985-86, sec. 1986-87), Am. Trial Lawyers Assn., Nat. Coll. Probate Judges (state rep. 1985-86), Md. State Bar Assn. (bd. govs., sect. coun. jud. adminstrn.), Prince Georges County Bar Assn. (pres. 1988—), Delta Theta Phi. Jewish. Home: 8607 Grey Fox Trl Upper Marlboro MD 20772-9618 Office: Cir Ct Judges Chambers 2D Fl Courthouse Upper Marlboro MD 20772

PLATT, THOMAS COLLIER, JR., federal judge; b. N.Y.C., N.Y., May 29, 1925; s. Thomas Collier and Louise Platt; m. Ann Byrd Symington, June 25, 1948; children: Ann Byrd, Charles Collier, Thomas Collier, III, Elizabeth Louise. BA, Yale U., 1947, LL.B., 1950. Bar: N.Y. 1950. Assoc. Root, Ballantine, Harlan, Bushby & Palmer, N.Y.C., 1950-53; asst. U.S. atty. Bklyn., 1953-56; assoc. Bleakley, Platt, Schmidt, Hart & Fritz, N.Y.C., 1956-60, ptnr., 1960-74; judge U.S. Dist. Ct. (ea. dist.) N.Y., 1974—, chief judge, 1988-95. Former dir. Phoenix Mut. Life Ins. Co., RAC Corp., McIntyre Aviation, Inc.; atty. Village of Laurel Hollow, N.Y., 1958-74; acting police justice Village of Lloyd Harbor, N.Y., 1958-63 Alt. del. Republican Nat. Conv., 1964, 68, 72; del. N.Y. State Rep. Conv., 1966; trustee Brooks Sch., North Andover, Mass., 1968-82, pres., 1970-74. Served with USN, 1943-46 Mem. Fed. Judges Assn. (sec., bd. dirs. 1982-91). Clubs: Phelps Assn. (New Haven) (bd. govs. 1960-98); Cold Spring Harbor Beach (N.Y.) (bd. mgrs. 1964-70); Yale of N.Y.C. Episcopalian. Office: US Dist Ct PO Box 9014 Central Islip NY 11722-9014 Office Phone: 631-712-5600.

PLATT, WARREN E. lawyer; b. McNary, Ariz., Aug. 5, 1943; BA, Mich. State U., 1965; JD, U. Ariz., 1969. Bar: Ariz. 1969, Calif. 1991, Texas 1993. Atty. Snell & Wilmer, Phoenix. Mng. editor: Ariz. Law Rev., 1968-69. Fellow Am. Coll. Trial Lawyers; mem. Blue Key, Order of Coif, Phi Alpha Delta Office: Snell & Wilmer One Arizona Ctr Phoenix AZ 85004-0001

PLATT, WILLIAM HENRY, judge; b. Allentown, Pa., Jan. 25, 1940; s. Henry and Genevieve (McElroy) P.; m. Maureen Hart, Nov. 29, 1969; children: Meredith H., William H., James H. AB, Dickinson Coll., 1961; JD, U. Pa., 1964. Bar: Pa. 1967, U.S. Supreme Ct. 1971. Ptnr. Yarus and Platt, Allentown, 1967-77; asst. pub. defender Lehigh County (Pa.), 1972-75, chief pub. defender, 1975-76, dist. atty., 1976-91; ptnr. Eckert, Seamans, Cherin & Mellott, 1991-95; city solicitor City of Allentown, 1994-95; judge Ct. Common Pleas of Lehigh County, Allentown, 1996—, pres. judge, 2002—. Mem. criminal procedural rules com. Supreme Ct. Pa., 1982-92, chmn., 1986-92; mem. Gov.'s Trial Ct. Nominating Commn. Lehigh County, 1984-87; mem. Pa. Commn. on Crime and Delinquency Victim Services Adv. Com., 1983-91. Served with M.P., U.S. Army, 1964-66. Mem.: ABA, Pa. Conf. of State Trial Judges (edn. com. 1997—2002), Pa. Assn. Dist. Attys. (exec. com. 1980—86, pres. 1983—84, chmn. 1986—87, tng. inst. mem. 1986—91), Nat. Assn. Dist. Attys. (state dir. 1982—84), Lehigh County Bar Assn., Pa. Bar Assn., Pa. Bar Inst. (hon.) (life; bd. dirs. 1989—2000, exec. com. 1994—2000, pres. 1997—98). Office: Lehigh County Courthouse 455 W Hamilton St Allentown PA 18101-1614 Office Phone: 610-782-3393.

PLATTE, MARK, editor; BA in Journalism, U. S.C. Staff writer City and Features Desks Atlanta (Ga.) Jour. Constn., 1982—84; staff writer Broward County Edit. Miami (Fla.) Herald, 1984—88; staff writer Orange County Register, 1988—90; from mem. staff to dep. city editor LA (Calif.) Times, 1990—98, dep. city editor, 1998—2000; asst. mng. editor news Honolulu (Hawaii) Advertiser, 2000—04, exec. editor, 2004—. Office: Honolulu Advertiser PO Box 3110 Honolulu HI 96802*

PLATTS, HOWARD GREGORY, scientific, educational organization executive; b. Aug. 14, 1947; s. Thayer Horton and Anne Elizabeth (Gregory) P.; m. Elizabeth Hertzler Murray, June 7, 1969; children: James Thayer, Christopher Wilke. AB, Harvard U., 1969; M. Pub. and Pvt. Mgmt., Yale U., 1980. Tchr. Potomac Sch., McLean, Va., 1969-72; investment officer First Am. Bank, Washington, 1972-78; fin. analyst Yale U., New Haven, 1979; fin. asst. to pres. Nat. Geog. Soc., Washington, 1980-82, asst. treas., 1982-91, sr. v.p., treas., 1992—. Trustee Nat. Presbyn. Sch., Washington, 1988-91; chmn., trustee regional blood svcs. ARC, Balt., 1992-2000; treas., bd. dirs. Friends of Fort Dupont, Washington, 1995-2002; trustee Decatur House, Washington, 1994-2004; mem. governing bd. St. Albans Sch., Washington, 1997-2003. Trustee Westmoreland Congl. Ch., 1988-91. Mem. Washington Soc. Investment Analysts (pres., bd. dirs. 1985-91). Home: 5302 Portsmouth Rd Bethesda MD 20816-2929 Office: Nat Geog Soc 1145 17th St NW Washington DC 20036-4701 E-mail: platts@aya.yale.edu.

PLATTS, TODD RUSSELL, congressman, state legislator; b. Mar. 5, 1962; m. Leslie Platts. BS summa cum laude, Shippensburg U. Pa., 1984; JD cum laude, Pepperdine U., 1991. Atty. Barley, Snyder, Senft & Cohen; rep. dist. 196 State of Pa., 1993-2001; mem. U.S. Congress from 19th Pa. dist., 2001—; mem. transp. and infrastructure com., edn. and workforce com., govt. reform com. Aging & youth edn. com. State of Pa., 1993—. Republican. Office: 1032 Longworth Ho Office Bldg Washington DC 20515

PLATTS-MILLS, THOMAS ALEXANDER E. immunologist, educator, researcher; b. Colchester, Essex, Eng., Nov. 22, 1941; came to U.S., 1982; s. John Faithful F. and Janet Katherine (Cree) P.-M.; m. Roberta Rosenstock, Apr. 9, 1970; children: Eliza, Timothy, James, Oliver. BA, Balliol Coll., Oxford (Eng.) U., 1963; MB, BChir, Oxford U., 1967; PhD, London U., 1982. Registrar in medicine Bury St. Edmunds, and New Market, England, 1968-71; fellow in medicine Johns Hopkins U., Balt., 1971-74; staff mem. Med. Rsch. Coun., England, 1976-82; hon. cons. physician Northwick Park Hosp., London, 1978-82; prof. medicine, head divsn. allergy and clin. immunology U. Va., Charlottesville, 1982—, dir. Asthma and Allergic Diseases Ctr., 1994. Mem. immunological scis. study sect. NIH, 1988. Editl. bd. Am. Jour. Respiratory Critical Care Medicine, Clin. and Exptl. Immunology, Clin. Allergy, Jour. Immunological Methods; contbr. articles to profl. jours. Grantee NIH. Fellow Royal Coll. Physicians, Am. Acad. Allergy; mem. Assn. Am. Physicians, Am. Acad. Allergy, Asthma and Immunology (v.p. 2004—), Southeastern Allergy Assn. (Hal Davidson award 1986, pres. 1987-88), Brit. Soc. Allergy and Clin. Immunology. Office: U Va Dept Medicine PO Box 225 Charlottesville VA 22908-0001 E-mail: tap2z@virginia.edu.

PLATUS, LIBBY, artist, sculptor, speaker; b. L.A., Aug. 18, 1939; d. Benjamin Lyon and Gertrude Goldman; children: Julie Linda, Diana Lisa. BA, UCLA, 1961. Lectr., condr. workshops numerous internat., nat., regional meetings and meetings in all 50 states, including World Craft Conf., Kyoto, Japan, 1978, Vienna, Austria, 1980, Glasgow (Scotland) Sch. Art, 1980, 84, Loughborough Coll. Art, Eng., 1980, 84, R.I. Sch. Design, 1982, Parsons Sch. Design, N.Y.C., 1982, Arrowmont, Gatlinburg, Tenn., 1978, 83, 87, Konstfackskolan, Sweden, 1984, Goldsmith's Coll., Eng., 1984, Taideteo Llinen Korkeakoulo, Finland, 1984, Fairbanks (Alaska) Art Assn., 1985, 95, 97, 2000, 04, Savannah (Ga.) Coll. Art and Design, 1987, 89, 90, 92, 94, 99, East N.C. U., Greenville, 1989, 92, 97, 2000, 02, Navajo C.C., Shiprock Reservation, N.Mex., 1992, World Wildfowl Carving Exhbn., Ward Found., Md., 1990, Kansas City Art Inst., 1990, 92, So. Ute Tribal Hdqrs., Ignacio, Colo., 1993, U. Western Sydney Design dept., 1993, Sydney Coll. Art, 1993, Victorian Coll. Art, Melbourne, Australia, 1993, U. South Australia, Underdale, 1993, Australian Nat. U., Canberra, 1993, Waiariki Polytech. Coll. Rotorua, New Zealand, 1993, Aotearoa Inst., mgr. South Auckland, New Zealand, 1993, Te Taumata Art Gallery, Auckland, New Zealand, 1993, Aotearoa Inst. Tertiary Sch., Te Awamutu, New Zealand, 1993, Small Bus. Devel. Ctr. Northland Pioneer Coll., Hollbrook, Ariz., 1994, N.Y. State Coll. Ceramics, Alfred U., 1994, 96, Bus. Dept., 2000, Tlingit-Gold Belt Corp., Juneau, 1993, Seneca Nation Econ. Devel. Corp., Jamestown, N.Y., 1996,

Assiniboine/Sioux/Gros Ventre-Tribal Bus. Info. Ctr., Ft. Belknap Reservation, Harlam, Mont., 1996, Nat. Home Based Bus. Conf. U. Wis.-Whitewater, Milw., 1996, 10th nat. conf. U.S. Assn. Small Bus. Entrepreneurship, Atlanta, 1996, So. Meth. U., Dallas, 1996, 99, New Orleans Jazz and Heritage Festival, 1994, Small Bus. Devel. Ctr., Binghamton (N.Y.) U., 1996, Small Bus. Devel. Ctr. and N.Mex. Main St. Program, Carlsbad, 1997, So. Ill. U., Carbondale, 1999, Arts Coun. N.W. Fla., Pensacola, 1989, 95, 97, 99, 2001, 03, Fla. Craftsmen and Pinellas County Art Coun., St. Petersburg, 1997, Oreg. Coll. Art and Craft, Portland, 1982, 99, Birmingham Mus. Art, Ala., 1995, 97, Montgomery Mus. Art, Ala., 1997, Huntsville Mus. Art, Ala., 1998, 2000, Syracuse (N.Y.) U., 1997, Va. Commonwealth Univ., Richmond, 1999, Towson Univ., Towson, MD, 1988, 99, Atlantic County Office of Cultural and Heritage Affairs, NJ, 1988, 91, 95, 98, 00, Bear Paw Devel. Corp., Havre, Mont., Ga. Appalachian Devel. Ctr. North Ga. Coll., Dahlonega, 2001, Riverbend Art Ctr., Dayton, Ohio, 1988, 90, 98, 99, 2001, 02, 03, 04, Pride of Dakota, Dept. Agr., N.D., 1999, Keynote Utah Heritage Industry Conf. Utah Divsn. Bus. and Econ. Devel., Ephriam, 1999, Tenn. Comty. Econ. Devel., Nashville, 2000, Keynote Vt. Tech. Assistance Providers Assn., Montpelier, 1999, Small Bus. Ctr., Carbondale, Ill., 1999, Wyo. Dept. Employment Vocat. Rehab., Casper, Sheyenne, Sheridan, Rock Springs, 2000, Native Am. Shoshone/Northern Arapahoe, Wind River Reservation, Wyo., 2000, Hand Made in Am., Asheville, N.C., 2000, United Arts Ctrl. Fla., Orlando, 2003, 04, Fla. Keys Coun. of Arts, Cheela Lodge, Islamorada, 2003, Small Bus. Devel. Ctr., U. N.Mex., Alamogordo, 2003, U. N.Mex., Las Cruces, 2003, So. Ill. Entrepreneurship Ctr., Carbondale, 2004, Women's Bus. Assistance Ctr., Mobile, Ala., 2004, Small Bus. Devel. Ctr., Amarillo, Tex., 2004, Wichita Falls, Tex., 2004, Abilene, Tex., 2004, numerous others, cons. Millstream Arts Festival Coll. St. Benedict, St. Joseph, Minn., 1992, Mountain State Art and Crafts Festival, Cedar Lakes, W.Va., 1992, Grand Junction area C. of C., Home Based Bus. Trade Fair, Colo., 1992, Yavapai Coll. Creative Comm. Convergence, Sedona, Ariz., 1995; judge culinary competition Western Food Svc. and Hospitality Expo, L.A., 2001, Art Harvest Jr. League Clearwater-Dunedin, Fla., 2000, Mont. Food and Gift Show Made in Mont. Program Mont. Dept Commerce, Great Falls, Mont., 1999; juror regional exhbn. Fairbanks Art Assn., Alaska, 1984; juror, judge, Greater Gulf Coast Art Festival, Pensacola, Fla., 1999; judge Millstream Arts Festival, Coll. St. Benedict, St. Joseph, Minnesota, 1992; participant Charmin Care TV comml., 1989, Rotary Internat. Group Study Exchange, Bangalore, India, 1998; panelist Western Food Svc. and Hospitality Expo, L.A., 2004. Group shows include Richmond (Calif.) Designer Craftsmen, 1971, E.B. Crocker Gallery, Sacramento, 1973, Comsky Gallery, Beverly Hills, Calif., 1973, Galeria del Sol, Santa Barbara, Calif., 1973, Laguna Beach (Calif.) Mus. Art, 1973, Riverside (Calif.) Art Ctr., 1974, Calif. State U. Northridge, L.A., 1974, Calif. State U., Fullerton, 1974, Calif. Design '76, L.A., 1976, Cleve. Mus. Art, 1977; represented in collections: Tex. Christian U., Faberge Hdqrs., N.Y.C., numerous other pub. and pvt. collections; commd. works: Big Canyon Country Club, Newport Beach, Calif., Carolando Hyatt Hotel, Orlando, Fla., McCulloch's Silver Lakes Resort Hotel, Victorville, Calif., Blue Cross So. Calif., L.A. Mem. L.A. Olympics 1984 Cultural and Fine Arts Commn., 1980-84, citizens adv. commn., 1980-84; adv. bd. Crafts Report Edn. Fund, 1985-88. Recipient Graphic Achievement award Fox River Paper Corp., 1974; winner Tex. Christian U. Nat. Invitational Fiberwork Competition, 1977. Mem.: Artists Equity (adv. bd. L.A. chpt. 1981—87). Home and Office: PO Box 55026 Sherman Oaks CA 91413-0026 Office Phone: 818-906-3989. E-mail: libbyplatus@earthlink.net.

PLATZMAN, GEORGE WILLIAM, geophysicist, educator; b. Chgo., Apr. 19, 1920; s. Alfred and Rose I. K.; m. Harriet M. Herschberger, Feb. 19, 1945 (dec. 1985). BS, U. Chgo., 1940, PhD, 1948; MS, U. Ariz., 1941. Instr. U. Chgo., 1942-45, rsch. assoc., 1947-48, faculty, 1949—, head phys. scis. in coll., 1959-60, prof. geophys. scis., 1960-90, chmn. dept. geophys. scis., 1971-74, emeritus prof., 1990—. Cons. Inst. Advanced Study, Princeton, 1950-53. Author: A Descriptive Catalogue of Early Editions of the Works of Frédéric Chopin in the University of Chicago Library, 2003; contbr. articles to profl. jours. Hydrologic engr. C.E., U.S. Army, 1945-46. Guggenheim fellow, 1967-68. Office: U Chgo Dept Geophys Scis 5734 S Ellis Ave Chicago IL 60637-1434

PLATZNER, LINDA, publisher; Assoc. pub. Modern Bride PRIMEDIA, pub. Seventeen mag. Office: Seventeen 1440 Broadway #21 New York NY 10018-2301

PLAUT, ERIC ALFRED, retired psychiatrist, educator; b. NYC, Nov. 16, 1927; s. Alfred and Margaret (Blumenfeld) P.; m. Eloine Raab, Sept. 5, 1976. BS, Columbia U., 1949, MD, 1953. Diplomate: Am. Bd. Psychiatry and Neurology. Intern Montefiore Hosp., Bronx, N.Y., 1953-54; psychiat. resident State Hosp., Worcester, Mass., 1954-55, Mass. Meml. Hosp., Boston, 1956-57; cons. psychiatrist Mass. Dept. Corrections, 1957; fellow student health psychiatry U. Calif., Berkeley, 1957-58; practice medicine specializing in psychiatry Berkeley, 1958-74; staff psychiatrist Kaiser Hosp., Oakland, Calif., 1958-62, Cowell Meml. Hosp., U. Calif., Berkeley, 1958-62; cons. psychiatrist Bur. Indian Affairs, Dept. Interior, 1967-68; program chief Berkeley Mental Health Services, 1968-71; dep. commr. Ind. Dept. Mental Health, Indpls., 1974-76; commr. Conn. Dept. Mental Health, Hartford, 1976-81; prof. Northwestern U. Med. Sch., Chgo., 1981-93, prof. emeritus, 1994—; asst. clin. prof. psychiatry U. Calif. Med. Sch., San Francisco, 1958-74; asso. clin. prof. psychiatry U. Ind. Med. Sch., Indpls., 1975-76; clin. prof. psychiatry U. Conn. Med. Sch., Farmington, 1978-81, Yale U. Med. Sch., 1979-81. Cons. Assembly Sci. Adv. Coun., Calif. Legislature, 1970; chmn. Bay Area region Calif. Conf. Local Mental Health Dirs., 1970-71; gen. ptnr. Vanguard Investments, Berkeley, 1971-78. Author: Grand Opera: Mirror of the Western Mind, 1993; co-author (with K. Andersen) Marx on Suicide, 1999; mem. editl. bd. Yale Psychiat. Quar., 1976-81; sect. editor Northwestern Univ. Press, 1991-2000; contbr. articles to profl. jours. Bd. dirs. ACLU, Berkeley, 1960-65; mem. task force on access and barrier Pres.'s Commn. on Mental Health, 1977; mem. psychiatry panel Grad. Med. Edn. Nat. Adv. Com., 1979-81; bd. dirs. Nat. Assn. State Mental Health Program Dirs., 1978-81. With USN, 1944-46. Fellow Am. Psychiat. Assn. (disting. life; cons. task force on govt. rels. 1973-76, chmn. com. public info. 1975-76, mem. com. cert. in adminstrv. psychiatry 1979-82, chmn. task force on problems of Americans overseas 1984-88, chmn. task force on joint meeting with German Psychiat. Soc., 1989-90, chmn. com. on internat. abuse of psychiatry 1997-98); mem. No. Calif. Psychiat. Soc. (chmn. com. law and legis. 1968-72, fed. legis. rep. 1972-74, councillor 1972-73, pres.-elect 1973-74), Calif. Med. Assn. (alt. del. 1968-71), Alameda-Contra Costa Med. Assn. (chmn. mental health com. 1972), Chgo. Psychoanalytic Soc. Address: 9310 N Bennett Ave Evanston IL 60203-1401 E-mail: e-plaut@northwestern.edu.

PLAUT, JONATHAN VICTOR, rabbi; b. Chgo., Oct. 7, 1942; s. W. Gunther and Elizabeth (Strauss) P.; m. Carol Ann Fainstein, July 5, 1965; children: Daniel Abraham, Deborah Maxine. BA, Macalester Coll., 1964; postgrad., Hebrew Union Coll., Jerusalem, 1967-68; BHL, Hebrew Union Coll., Cin., 1968, MA, 1970, DHL, 1977; DD (hon.), 1995. Ordained rabbi, 1970. Rabbi Congregation Beth-El, Windsor, Ont., Can., 1970-84; sr. rabbi Temple Emanu-El, San Jose, Calif., 1985-93; dir. comty. outreach and involvement Jewish Fed. of Met. Detroit, 1993-95; pres. JVP Fund Raising Cons., Inc., Farmington Hills, Mich., 1994—. Lectr. Assumption Coll. Sch., 1972-84, St. Clair Coll., 1982-84, U. Windsor, Ont., Can., 1984; adj. asst. prof. Santa Clara U., 1985-93; adj. prof. U. Detroit Mercy, 2002—; vis. Rabbinic scholar Temple Beth El, 1993—; pres. JVP Fund Raising Cons., 1994—; rabbi Congregation Beth El, Traverse City, Mich., 1999—, Temple Beth Israel, Jackson, Mich., 2000—. Contbg. author: Reform Judaism in America: A Biographical Dictionary and Sourcebook, 1993; editor: Through the Sound of Many Voices, 1982, Jour. Can. Jewish Hist. Soc., 1976-83; also articles; host weekly program Religious Scope, Sta. CBET-TV, Religion in News, Sta. CKWW, 1971-84. Pres. Jewish Nat. Fund Windsor, 1978-81, chmn. bd. dirs., 1981-84; chmn. United Jewish Appeal Windsor, 1981-83, State of Israel Bonds, Windsor, 1980; nat. bd. dirs. Jewish Nat. Fund Can., 1972-84; pres. Reform Rabbis of Can., 1982-84; bd. dirs. Can. Jewish Congress, 1978-84, Jewish Family Svc. Santa Clara County, 1987-90, Jewish Fedn. Greater San Jose, 1986-93; chaplain San Jose Fire Dept., 1987-93; mem. exec. cabinet United Jewish Appeal, Windsor, 1971-84, mem. nat. rabbinic cabinet, 1993-95; mem. exec. com. Windsor Jewish Community Coun., 1970-84, chmn. 1975-84; mem. adv. coun. Riverview unit Windsor Hosp. Ctr., 1972-81; pres. Credit Counselling Svc. Met. Windsor, 1977-79. Honoree Jewish Nat. Fund, 1985. Mem. NCCJ, Can. Jewish Congress (nat. exec. bd. 1978-84), Can. Jewish Hist. Soc. (nat. v.p. 1974-84), Calif. Bd. Rabbis, Rabbinic Assn. Greater San Jose (chmn. 1986-87), Ctrl. Conf. Am. Rabbis, Nat. Assn. Temple Educators. Home and Office: 30208 Kingsway Dr Farmington Hills MI 48331-1648 Office Phone: 248-505-8888. Fax: (248) 788-4144. E-mail: jvplaut@earthlink.net.

PLAUT, WOLF GUNTHER, minister, author; b. Muenster, Germany, Nov. 1, 1912; emigrated to U.S., 1935, arrived in Canada, 1961; s. Jonas and Selma (Gumprich) P.; m. Elizabeth Strauss, Nov. 10, 1938; children: Jonathan, Judith. LLB, U. Berlin, 1933, JD, 1934; MHL, Hebrew Union Coll., Cin., 1939, DD (hon.), 1964; LLD (hon.), U. Toronto, 1978; DLitt (hon.), Cleve. Coll. Jewish Studies, 1979; LLD (hon.), York U., 1987, McMaster U., 1998, Law Soc. Ont., 2000. Ordained rabbi 1939. Rabbi B'nai Abraham Zion, Chgo., 1939-48, Mt. Zion Temple, St. Paul, 1948-61; sr. rabbi Holy Blossom Temple, Toronto, Ont., Can., 1961-77, sr. scholar, 1978—. Adj. prof. York U., 1991—. Author: Mount Zion, 1956, The Jews in Minnesota, 1959, The Book of Proverbs: A Commentary, 1961, Judaism and the Scientific Spirit, 1962, The Rise of Reform Judaism, 1963, The Growth of Reform Judaism, 1964, The Case for the Chosen People, 1965, Your Neighbour is a Jew, 1967; author: (U.S. title) The Man in the Blue Vest, 1980; author: Numbers: A Modern Commentary, 1979; chief author, editor The Torah: A Modern Commentary, 1981, 12th edit., 1997, (autobiography) Unfinished Business, vol. I, 1981, Refugee Determination in Canada, 1985, The Letter, 1986, (fiction) The Magen David: How the Six Pointed Star Became the Jewish Symbol, 1991, The Man Who Would Be Messiah, 1988, 2nd edit., 1990, Asylum-A Moral Dilemma, 1995, (autobiography) More Unfinished Business, Vol. II, 1997, The Pirce and Privilege of Growing Old, 1999; co-author: The Rabbi's Manual, 1988, The Reform Judaism Reader, 2000; editor: Affirmation, 1981—87; editl. contbr. Toronto Globe and Mail, 1962—92, Can. Jewish News, 1980—, contbr. encys., anthologies, books, articles to mags., newspapers, —. Chmn. Minn. Gov.'s Commn. on Ethics in Govt., 1958-61; pres. St. Paul Gallery and Sch. Art (name changed to Minn. Mus.), 1953-59, World Federalists Can., 1966-68; nat. pres. Can. Jewish Congress, 1977-80; vice chmn. Ont. Human Rights Commn., 1978-85; bd. govs. World Union for Progressive Judaism, 1970— pres. Central Conf. Am. Rabbis, 1983-85, bd. inquiry human rights cases, 1987-98. Capt. AUS, 1943-46. Decorated Bronze Star, comanion Order of Can., Order of Ont., Order of Merit Germany, Plaut Chair for Project Mgmt. established in his honor Ben Gurion U., Israel. Mem.: York Racquets, Oakdale Golf and Country. Office: 1950 Bathurst St Toronto ON Canada M5P 3K9

PLAVINSKAYA, ANNA DMITRIEVNA, artist; b. Moscow, Nov. 26, 1960; came to U.S., 1989, naturalized, 1995; d. Dmitri Petrovich and Nina Nicolaevna; m. Gennady Ioffe, Jan 9, 1988 (div. July 1993). Diploma in Costume Design, Theatrical Art Coll., Moscow, 1976-80. Costume designer Evgeny Vahtangov Theater, Moscow, 1980-82; artist freelance Moscow, 1983-89; art restorer pvt. studio, N.Y.C., 1990-93; artist freelance N.Y.C., 1993—. Exhibited in group shows at Moscow, Gallery Moscow Artists, 1983, Ctrl. Exhbn. Hall, Moscow, 1984, 88, Kuznetzky Most Gallery, Moscow, 1985, Tbilisi Acad. Art, Georgia, 1986, Tallinna Moepaevad '87, Tallinn, Estonia, 1987, Remizovo St. Gallery, Moscow, 1988, Pushkin Sq. Gallery, Moscow, 1988, Textile Art Ctr., Chgo., 1991, Russian Nobility Assn., NYC, 1991, 11th Cleve. Internat. Drawing Biennale, Middlesbrough, Eng., 1993 (2d prize), BWA Gallery, Wroclaw, Poland, 1994, BWA Gallery, Lublin, Poland, 1994, Elblag (Poland) Gallery, 1994, Tatraniska Gallery, Poprad, Tatry, Slovakia, 1994, State Gallery, Ostrova, Czech Republic, 1994, Port Royal Mus. Gallery, Naples, Fla., 1994, Art Addiction Gallery, Stockholm, 1996-98 (cert. merit 1997), Art Addiction Gallery, Venice, Italy, 1998, Internat. Platform Assn., 1998, (1st place, Best of Show), 1999 (1st place award), Le Salon, Paris, 2000, 02-03 (Bronze medal 2000), Salon Internat. Beziers, 2001-04 (Bronze medal 2001, Prix de La Societe Des Beaux Arts 2002); represented in permanent collections Cleve. Contemporary Art Collection, Middlesbrough, Eng., Zimmerli Art Mus., Norton and Nancy Dodge Collection, NJ. Mem. Nat. Fedn. French Culture. Russian Orthodox. Avocations: fashion design, antique textile restoration, tennis. Home: 815 W 181st St Apt 3E New York NY 10033-4530 Office Phone: 212-795-4258.

PLAVSIC, BRANKO MILENKO, radiology educator; b. Zagreb, Yugoslavia, Croatia, Feb. 14, 1947; came to U.S., 1989; s. Milenko and Nevenka P. MD, U. Zagreb, 1972, MS, 1974, PhD, 1975. Asst. prof. U. Zagreb, 1986, prof. radiology, chief abdominal radiology, 1988; prof. radiology, vice-chmn., dir. abdominal radiol./rsch. Tulane U., New Orleans, 1991—. Co-author: (with A.E. Robinson, R.B. Jeffrey) Gastrointestinal Radiology: A Concise Text, 1992; contbr. articles to profl. jours. Avocations: poetry, music. Home: 4460 Lennox Blvd New Orleans LA 70131-8348 Office: Tulane U Med Ctr Dept Radiology 1430 Tulane Ave New Orleans LA 70112-2699

PLAWECKI, JUDITH ANN, nursing educator; b. East Chicago, Ind., June 5, 1943; d. Joseph Lawrence and Anne Marilyn (Hamnik) Curosh; m. Henry Martin Plawecki, June 10, 1967; children: Martin H., Lawrence H. BS, St. Xavier Coll., Chgo., 1965; MA, U. Iowa, 1971; PhD, 1974. Asst. prof. Mt. Mercy Coll., Cedar Rapids, Iowa, 1971-73; asst. dept. chmn., assoc. prof., 1974-75; assoc. prof. U. Iowa, 1975-76; asst. dean, assoc. prof. U. Minn., 1976-81; acting dean, assoc. dean and prof. U. N.D., Grand Forks, 1981-82, dean and prof. nursing, 1982-83, Lewis U., Romeoville, Ill., 1983-87; dean U. South Fla., Tampa, 1987-95, prof. nursing, 1987—. Univ. Iowa Fellow, 1973. Mem. AHNA, Nat. League for Nursing, Older Women's League, Sigma Xi, Sigma Phi Omega, Sigma Theta Tau, Phi Lambda Theta. Office: U South Fla Coll Nursing MDC 22 12901 Bruce B Downs Blvd Tampa FL 33612-4742

PLAX, KAREN ANN, lawyer; b. St. Louis, June 29, 1946; d. George J. and Evelyn G. Zell; m. Stephen E. Plax, Dec. 19, 1968; 1 child, Jonathan. BA magna cum laude, U. Mo., St. Louis, 1969; JD with distinction, U. Mo., Kansas City, 1976. Bar: Mo. 1976, U.S. Supreme Ct. 1980. Atty. Thayer, Gum & Wickert, Grandview, Mo., 1976-84, Plax & Cochet, Kansas City, Mo., 1984-87; pvt. practice Kansas City, 1987—. Past chair divsn. 3, region IV Mo. Supreme Ct. Com. to review ethical conduct of attys., 1997-98. Author: Missouri Bar Practical Skills, 1998; asst. editor: Racial Integration in the Inner Suburb, 1970; contbr. articles to profl. jours. Recipient Pub. Svc. award U. Mo. Kansas City Law Found., 1998, Woman of Yr. award Assn. Women Lawyers of Greater Kansas City, 1999. Fellow: Am. Acad. Matrimonial Lawyers (pres. Mo. chpt. 1999—2001); mem.: ABA (family law sect. 1976—), Mo. Bar Family Law (legis. chair 1997—98, v.p. 1999—2000, Spl. Commendation for Legis. Role in Family Law 1998), Kansas City Met. Bar Assn. Office: Ste 300 1310 Carondelet Dr Kansas City MO 64114-4803 Personal E-mail: kaplax@swbell.net.

PLAYER, THELMA B. librarian; b. Owosso, Mich. d. Walter B. and Grace (Willoughby) Player. BA, Western Mich. U., 1954. Reference asst. USAF Aero Chart and Info. Ctr., Washington, 1954-57; reference libr. USN Hydrographic Office, Suitland, Md., 1957-58, asst. libr., 1958-59; tech. libr.br. head USN Spl. Project Office, Washington, 1959-68, Strategic Sys. Project Office, Washington, 1969-76. Mem. ALA, AAUW, English Speaking Union, Spl. Librs. Assn., Nat. Geneal. Socl, Internat. Soc. Brit. Genealogy and Family History, Ohio Geneal. Soc. Royal Oak Found., Daus of Union Vets. of Civil War, David Ackerman Descs. Episcopalian. Home: 730 24th St NW Washington DC 20037-2519

PLAYFORD, NANCY JEAN, medical staff administrator; b. Lansing, Mich., May 23, 1960; d. Jack Frederick and Doris Jean Lillrose; children: Kimberley, Kristen. Med. staff coord. Valley Luth. Hosp., Mesa, Ariz., 1984-93, Scottsdale (Ariz.) Health Sys., 1993-95, credentials supr., 1995-97; dir. med. staff svcs. Tempe (Ariz.) St. Luke's Hosp., 1997—. Mem. adv. bd. Greater Ariz. Cen. Credentialing, Phoenix, 1995—; expert witness in ct. for credentialing issues. Mem. Nat. Assn. Med. Staff Svcs. (cert. med. staff coord. 1993, cert. provider credentialing specialist 1996), Ariz. Assn. Med. Staff Svc. (pres.-elect Superstition Mountain chpt. 1995-96, pres. Superstition Mountain chpt. 1996-97). Avocations: photography, hiking, playing piano, horses. Office: Tempe St Luke's Hosp 1500 S Mill Ave Tempe AZ 85281-6699 E-mail: nplayford@iasishealthcare.com.

PLAZEK, DONALD JOHN, materials scientist, educator; b. Milw., Jan. 12, 1931; s. Stanley and Marian (Parker) Plazek; m. Patricia Lenore Filkins, Oct. 29, 1955; children: Mary, Joseph, Caroline, Daniel, John, David, Anne. BS in Chemistry, U. Wis., 1953, PhD in Phys. Chemistry, 1957. Postdoctoral rsch. fellow U. Wis., Madison, 1957-58; fellow Mellon Inst., Pitts., 1958-67; assoc. prof. materials engring. U. Pitts., 1967-74, prof., 1974-93, prof. emeritus, 1993—. Adj. prof. chemistry Carnegie-Mellon U., Pitts., 1987—. Mem. adv. bd. Jour. Polymer Sci., 1991—98; assoc. editor: Rubber Chemistry and Tech., 1993—97; contbr. scientific papers to profl. jours. Brit. Rsch. Coun. sr. vis. fellow, U. Glasgow, Scotland, 1976—77, Japan Soc. Promotion Sci. fellow, 1987—88. Fellow: Am. Phys. Soc.; mem.: Soc. Rheology (Bingham medal 1995), Am. Chem. Soc. (George Stafford Whitby award for disting. tchg. and rsch. Rubber divsn. 1993). Avocations: tennis, tropical fish, mushrooms. Office: U Pitts Materials Sci Engring Dept Pittsburgh PA 15261-0001 Office Phone: 412-624-7864

PLEASANT, JAMES SCOTT, lawyer; b. Anniston, Ala., July 14, 1943; s. James C. and Barbara (Scott) P.; m. Susan M. Pleasant, May 17, 1966; children: Deborah Kaye, Carol Ann, Julie Ruth. BS, Oreg. State U., 1965; JD summa cum laude, Williamette U., 1972. Bar: Tex. 1972, U.S. Dist. Ct. (no. dist.) Tex. 1973, U.S. Ct. Appeals (5th cir.) 1975, U.S. Supreme Ct. 1977. Ptnr. Gardere Wynne Sewell, LLP, Dallas, 1972—. Mem. Smithsonian Assn., Washington, 1985—, Dallas Mus. of Art, 1987—. Capt. U.S. Army, 1966-69, Vietnam. Mem. ABA (partnership law sect. 1969—), Tex. Bar Assn. (partnership law sect. 1989—), Vietnam Pilots Assn., Dustoff Assn. Office: Gardere Wynne Sewell LLP 1601 Elm St Ste 3000 Dallas TX 75201-4761 Office Phone: 214-999-4690. E-mail: pleja@gardere.com.

PLEASANT-JACKSON, TONYA, therapist, consultant; b. Washington, Oct. 27, 1960; d. Oscar and Carolyn Estelle Pleasant; m. Anthony L. Jackson Sr., July 15, 1989; children: Anthony L. Jr., Amara N. V. BS in Family Therapy, U Md., 1984; D in Ministry, Friends Internat. Christian U., 1994; M in Rehab. Counseling, U. Md., 1996. Lic. mariage and family therapist, Va.; cert. rehab. counselor, Md., nat. cert. counselor, rehab. provider, Va., rehab. svc. provider, Md.; ordained to ministry Integrity Ch. Internat., 1993. Dir. counseling ministry Integrity Ch. Internat., 1990—; rehab. coord., vocat. evaluator, rehab. cons. St. Luke's Ho., Bethesda, Md., 1997-98; rehab. coord. CHI Ctrs., Silver Spring, Md., 1998—; pvt. practice therapist Greenbelt, Md., 1998—; therapist, cons. Residential Care Inc., 1999—. Outstanding Svc. award Regional Inst. Children and Adolescents, Md., 1986. Mem. Assn. Mental Health Counselors, Am. Assn. Christian Counelors. Avocations: singing, physical fitness. Office: 9841 Greenbelt Rd Ste 208 Lanham Seabrook MD 20706-6270

PLEASANTS, JOHN, online services company executive; BA, Yale U.; MBA, Harvard U. With Frito-Lay divsn. PepsiCo; with Hygiene Industries; exec. v.p. new markets Ticketmaster Online-CitySearch, Pasadena, Calif., pres. ticketing and transactions, pres., 2000 —. Office: Ticketmaster Online 790 E Colorado Blvd Ste 200 Pasadena CA 91101-2181

PLEASURE, ROBERT JONATHAN, association director, lawyer; b. Bayshore, N.Y., Nov. 17, 1942; s. Hyman and Edith Beatrice (Schlank) P.; children: Jennifer, Abigail, Benjamin, Jacob; m. Patricia A. Greenfield. BA, U. Pa., 1964; MSc, London Sch. Econs. and Polit. Sci., 1967; JD, U. Mich., 1967. Bar: N.Y. 1970, D.C. 1971, U.S. Ct. Appeals (D.C. cir.) 1971, U.S. Ct. Appeals (5th and 10th cirs.) 1975, U.S. Supreme Ct. 1974. Asst. to chmn. N.Y.C. Office of Collective Bargaining, 1968-69; atty. advisor NLRB, Washington, 1969-70; asst. gen. counsel Am. Fedn. State, County and Mcpl. Employees (AFL-CIO), Washington, 1970-72, United Brotherhood Carpenters and Joiners Am. (AFL-CIO), Washington, 1972-78, 79-84; gen. counsel Fed. Mine Safety and Health Rev. Commn., Washington, 1978; exec. dir. George Meany Ctr. for Labor Studies, Silver Spring, Md., 1984-96; asst. to pres. AFL-CIO, 1996-98; exec. dir. Ctr. to Protect Workers Rights, 1998-2001; pres., exec. dir. AFL-CIO Ctr. for Working Capital, 2001—. Mem. core faculty The McGregor Sch., Antioch U., chair labor studies, to 1996; vis. faculty grad. sch. U. Mass., Amherst, to 1997. Co-author: Organizing in the Construction Industry, 1978-84, 93-94, 2000; editor-in-chief: Manual on Collective Bargaining in Federal Sector of Federal Bar Association and American Arbitration Association, 1970. Vice-chmn. Village of North Chevy Chase, Md., 1983, 84; past mem. commn. on non-coll. ednl. credit and credentials Am. Coun. on Edn.; past AFL-CIO advisor on labor edn. Internat. Labor Orgn.; mem. FDA adv. com. on radiol. devices; panel mem. on residential constrn. Nat. Rsch. Coun.; environ. mgmt. adv. bd. subcom. on worker safety Dept. of Energy. Mem. ABA (mem. governing coun. sect. on labor and employment law 1984-88), Indsl. Rels. Rsch. Assn. (nat. bd. 1996-99), Fed. Bar Assn. (chmn. coun. on labor law and labor rels. 1970, Robert Rosenthal award 1969), Am. Coun. on Edn. (commr. commn. on acad. credit 1987-94). Democrat. Jewish. Home: 9350 Harvey Rd Silver Spring MD 20910-1639 Office: Ctr for Working Capital 888 16th St NW Washington DC 20006 E-mail: rpleasur@aflcio.org.

PLEBUCH, TOBIAS, musicologist; arrived in U.S., 1997; s. Horst Plebuch and Gisela Mumme; m. Elisabeth Eisenhauer, July 11, 1997; children: Magdalena Sonja, Miriam Johanna Eisenhauer. EdB in Music, Musik Hochschule für Künste, Bremen, 1991; PhD, Humboldt U., Berlin, 1996. Lectr. Albert-Ludwigs-Universität, Freiburg, Germany, 1993, Humboldt-Universität, Berlin, 1993—96; lectr. musicology Technische U., Dresden, Germany, 1996—97; asst. prof. musicology Stanford (Calif.) U., 1997—. Musician: (recordings) Ludwig van Beethoven, 1981, piano and chamber music by Sergey Prokofiev, 1984, piano and chamber music by Harald Genzmer, 1990, piano and chamber music by Hans Erich Apostel, 1991; co-editor: (conference proceedings) Musik als Text. Bericht über den Internationalen Musikwissenschaftlichen Kongreß der Gesellschaft für Musikforschung, (book/catalogue) Hommage à Ravel, 1987, (book) Carl Dahlhaus, Gesammelte Schriften. Fellow, Stanford Humanities Ctr., 2002—03; grantee, Office Tech. Licensing, Stanford, 2000; scholar, Richard Wagner Soc., 1989. Mem.: MLA, Gesellschaft für Musikforschung, Am. Soc. for Eighteen-Century Studies, Am. Musicological Soc. (no. Calif. chpt. adminstr. 2001). Office: Stanford Univ Dept Music Stanford CA 94305-3076 E-mail: plebuch@stanford.edu.

PLEHATY, PHYLLIS JULIETTE, curator; b. N.Y.C., Nov. 28, 1920; d. Aaron Neumann and Lillian Caroline Nagel; m. Carl William Plehaty Jr., Oct. 28, 1942 (dec. Jan. 1995); children: Carl. W. III, Phyllis Gretchen(dec.). Student, Parsons Sch. Design. With design dept. Schumacher-Waverly, N.Y.C., 1940—43; mgr. boutique, antiques The Place, Darien, Conn., 1957—69; archivist, vol. Darien Hist. Soc., 1960—65; photographer, tour guide Swan Ho. Atlanta Hist. Soc., 1969—71; photographer Jamaica Tourism, 1972—74; mgr., buyer Landlords Daughter Vintage '87, Yountville, Calif., 1974—76; curator collections Boulder History Mus., Colo., 1978—79. Cons. costume, collection named in hon. Boulder History Mus., 1990—; cons. exhibit Talbots Stores, 2000—; mem. adv. bd. Wise Homestead Mus., Erie, 2000—. Vol. libr. Loraine Davis Children's Libr., Erie, 2003. Republican. Lutheran. Avocations: jewelry design, silversmithing, blacksmithing, antiques, painting, crafts. Home: 12675 Kenosha Rd Erie CO 80516

PLEICONES, COSTA M. state supreme court justice; b. Greenville, SC, Feb. 29, 1944; BA in English, Wofford Coll., 1965; JD, U. SC, 1968. Pub. defender Richland County, SC; pvt. practice law; resident cir. ct. judge 5th Judicial Cir., 1991—2000; assoc. justice SC Supreme Ct., 2000. With JAG U.S. Army, 1968—73, with USAR, 1973—99. Office: 1231 Gervais St Columbia SC 29201-3206 also: PO Box 11330 Columbia SC 29211

PLENDL, HANS S. retired physicist, editor; arrived in U.S., 1948; s. Hans N. and Anna Katherina Plendl; m. Marion Setsuko Ito, Aug. 3, 1957 (div. Dec. 8, 1990); children: Konrad Alexander, David Christopher, Kathrin Francesca, Leilani Ann. BA, Harvard U., 1952; PhD, Yale U., 1958. Tchg. asst. physics dept. Yale U., New Haven, 1952—53, rsch. asst. Cyclotron Lab., 1954—56;

from asst. to assoc. to prof. physics dept. Fla. State U., Tallahassee, 1956—95, prof. emeritus physics dept., 1995—. Vis. staff mem. Nuclear Rsch. Ctr. and Max Planck Inst. for Nuclear Physics, Heidelberg, Germany, 1960—62; vis. prof. physics dept. Tech. U., Munich, 1985—86; guest scientist Rsch. Ctr., Juelich, Germany, 1989—98; sr. rsch. fellow Inst. for Internat. Coop. Environ. Rsch., Tallahassee, 1995—2002; vis. scientist Oak Ridge Nat. Lab., 1957—87, Brookhaven Nat. Lab., 1985—87, Los Alamos Nat. Lab., 1985—87; mem. program adv. com. NASA Space Radiation Effects Lab., Newport News, Va.; mem. U.S. Senate Edn. Adv. Com., Washington, 1983—85; bd. trustees Nautilus Found., Tallahassee, 1991—99; mem. adv. com. Internat. Conf. on Mesons and Nuclei, Dubna, Russia, 1994; co-chair Internat. Workshop on Nuclear Methods for Transmutation of Nuclear Waste, Dubna, Russia, 1996; mem. adv. com. 4th and 5th Internat. Symposia on Environ. Contamination in Ea. and Cen. Europe, Warsaw and Prague, 1998, 2000, 03; co-chair Internat. Workshop on Techs. in Nuclear Separations, Prague, 2000; cons. Springer Verlag, Heidelberg, Germany, 1962—70; mem. Recon Inc., Tallahassee, 1965—69; cons. Air Force Rsch. Ctr., Burlington, Mass., 1969—78; writer, editor Ricordiarte and Lem Art Pubs., Milan, 2000—. Editor: (treatise) Philosophical Problems of Modern Physics; co-editor: (conf. procs.) Nuclear Methods for Transmutation of Nuclear Waste; co-author: (textbook) Hands-on Astronomy; editor: (spl. jour. issues) Nuclear Transmutation Methods for Disposition of Long-Lived Radioactive Materials and Accelerator Driven Systems; co-editor: (treatise) Chemical Separations in Nuclear Waste Management - The State of the Art and a Look to the Future; contbr. articles to sci. jours. Recipient Travel award, Fulbright Found., 1963, Award for Excellence in Tchg., Amoco Found., 1975, Rsch. stipend, Deutsche Forschungsgemeinschaft, 1985. Achievements include discovery of several isomeric states in scandium and titanium isotopes. Avocations: popularization of scientific concepts and discoveries, study of classical and modern languages. Home: #29 3007 Shamrock N Tallahassee FL 32309 Office: Fla State U Physics Dept Tallahassee FL 32309 Personal E-mail: plendl@phy.fsu.edu.

PLESCIA, GEORGE A. state official; BA, Calif. State U., San Diego. State assembly mem. Dist. 75 Calif. State Assembly, 2002—. Mem. health com.; vice chair edn. com.; mem. water, parks, and wildlife com. Republican. Mailing: Rm 4009 PO Box 942849 Sacramento CA 94249 Office: Ste 130 9909 Mira Mesa Blvd San Diego CA 92131

PLESS, LAURANCE DAVIDSON, lawyer; b. Jacksonville, Fla., Dec. 22, 1952; s. James William Pless III and Anne (Dodson) Martin; m. Dana Halberg, June 20, 1980; children: Anna Amesbury, William Davidson, Deane Ahlgren. AB cum laude with distinction, Duke U., 1975; JD, U. N.C., Chapel Hill, 1980. Bar: Georgia 1980, U.S. Supreme Ct. 2001. Assoc. Neely & Player, P.C., Atlanta, 1980-86, ptnr., 1986-92, Welch Spell Attys., Atlanta, 1992—. Contbr. articles to profl. jours.; mem. staff N.C. Law Rev. Vol. Saturday Vol. Lawyers Found., Atlanta, 1980-92; mem. bd. visitors U. N.C., Chapel Hill, 2001—; bd. dirs. Christian Coun. Met. Atlanta, 1999-2002; trustee Asheville Sch., 2002—. Mem. ABA, Lawyer's Club of Atlanta, Atlanta Bar Assn. (bd. dirs. bus. and fin. law sect. 1999—), Capital City Club, Lake Rabun Assn. Democrat. Episcopalian. Avocations: hiking, tennis, canoeing. Home: 25 Palisades Rd NE Atlanta GA 30309-1530 E-mail: larry.pless@welchspell.com.

PLESS, RODNEY S. food products executive; V.p., contr., chief acctg. officer TransMontaigne, Tyson Foods Inc., Springdale, Ark., 2000—01, sr. v.p., contr., chief acctg. officer, 2001—. Office: Tyson Foods Inc 2210 W Oaklawn Dr Springdale AR 72762-6999

PLESTED, WILLIAM G., III, surgeon; b. Wichita, Kans., June 1, 1936; m. Carolyn Plested. BS, U. Colo.; MD, U. Kans., 1962. Diplomate Am. Bd. Surgery, Am. Bd. Thoracic Surgery. Intern UCLA, 1962-63, resident, 1963-68, asst. clin. prof. surgery; resident Mayo Clinic, Rochester, 1964; pvt. practice, thoracic and cardiovascular surgeon Los Angeles, 1970—. Bd. dirs. Santa Monica-UCLA Hosp., IPA, Blue Shield of Calif., Unihealth, Auto Digest Found. Mem. ACP, AMA (chair AMA bd. of trustees, 2003-), Calif. Med. Assn. (pres.), L.A. County Med. Assn., Soc. of Thoracic Surgeons, Western Thoracic Surg. Assn.Soc. for Clin. Vascular Surgery, Pacific Coast Surg. Assn., Am. Soc. of Gen. Surgery, Am. Coll. of Surgeons. Office: AMA 515 N State St Chicago IL 60610-4325 also: 1260 15th St Ste 913 Santa Monica CA 90404-1144

PLĒSUMS, GUNTIS, architect, retired educator; b. Riga, Latvia, Dec. 17, 1933; came to U.S., 1950, naturalized 1954; s. Valdemārs and Velta Plēsums; m. Māra Mazutis, Aug. 28, 1965; children: Jāna, Kārla. BArch, U. Minn., 1961; MArch, MIT, 1964. Registered architect, N.Y., Oreg. Arch. Affleck, Desbarats, Dimakopoulos, Lebensold & Sise, Montreal, Que., Can., 1964-66; instr. RISD, Providence, 1967-69; prof. arch. U. Oreg., Eugene, 1969—95, prof. emeritus, 1995—; pvt. practice arch. Eugene, 1980—; arch. emeritus, 2003. Vis. assoc. prof. Kans. State U., Manhattan, 1976; adj. assoc. prof. Oreg. Sch. Design, Portland, 1983; vis. prof., dir. MArch program Chinese U. Hong Kong, 1993-99; lectr. U.S., Eng., Japan, China, Latvia, Denmark, Tunisia. Author: Townframe: Environments for Adaptive Housing, 1978, (with Heino Engel, others) Structure Systems; contbr. articles to profl. publs., including Ency. of Vernacular Arch. of the World; prin. works include: theme pavilion Man the Producer for Expo 67, Montreal, 1964-66. Served as sgt. U.S. Army, 1953-56. Fulbright fellow, 1966-67, NEA fellow, 1982, 90; Graham Found. for Advanced Studies in Fine Arts grantee, 1974. Home: PO Box 1009 Lorane OR 97451-1009 E-mail: gplesums@darkwing.uoregon.edu.

PLETCHER, BETH, medical geneticist; b. Aurora, Ill., Apr. 25, 1956; d. Harold Delbert and Faye Boyle Pletcher; m. Paul Robert Glassberg, July 2, 1989; children: Brett Cameron Glassberg, Brittany Kara Glassberg. BS in Biology, Stanford U., 1978; MD, Rush Med. Coll., 1982. Diplomate Am. Bd. Pediatrics, Am. Bd. Med. Genetics. Intern Children's Hosp. LA, LA, 1982—83; resident in pediats. Children's Hosp. of L.A., 1982—85; fellow in genetics Yale U. Sch. Medicine, New Haven, 1985—87; med. geneticist North Shore U. Hosp., Manhasset, NY, 1987—93, U. Med. and Dentistry NJ/NJ Med. Sch., Newark, 1993—, tchr. Med. Sch., 1993—, tchr. Dental Sch., 1997—, asst. prof. to assoc. prof. of pediatrics, 1993—. Office: Ctr for Human and Molecular Genetics 90 Bergen St Ste 5400 Newark NJ 07103

PLETCHER, ELDON, retired cartoonist; b. Goshen, Ind., Sept. 10, 1922; s. Arthur and Dora (Cripe) P.; m. Barbara Jeanne Jones, Jan. 29, 1948; children— Thomas Lee, Ellen Irene. Student, Chgo. Acad. Fine Arts, 1941-42, U. Aberdeen, Scotland, 1945, John Herron Art Sch., Indpls., 1946-47. Editorial cartoonist Sioux City (Iowa) Jour., 1949-66; editorial cartoonist The Times-Picayune, 1966-85; free-lance gag cartoonist Sat. Eve. Post, Rotarian, Nat. Enquirer, other publs. Rep. permanent exhbns., Syracuse U., U. South Miss., U. Cin., Boston Mus. Art, Harry S. Truman Library, Lyndon B. Johnson Library, Wichita State U., John F. Kennedy Libr., Richard M. Nixon Libr., U. Mo.; cartoons appeared in The Continental Edit. of Yank (Army Weekly). Served with AUS, 1943-46. Recipient Christopher award, 1955, Freedoms Found. award, 12 years Mem. VFW, Assn. Am. Editorial Cartoonists. Democrat. Presbyterian. Personal E-mail: epletch@aol.com.

PLETSCH, MARIE ELEANOR, plastic surgeon; b. Walkerton, Ont., Can., May 3, 1938; came to U.S. 1962; d. Ernest John and Olive Wilhemina (Hossfeld) P.; m. Ludwig Philip Breiling, Aug. 25, 1967; children: John, Michael, Anne. MD, U. Toronto, 1962. Diplomate Am. Bd. Plastic Surgery. Intern Cook County Hosp., Chgo., 1962-63, resident, gen. surgery, 1963-64, St. Mary's Hosp., San Francisco, 1964-66; resident in plastic surgery St. Francis Hosp., San Francisco, 1966-69; practice med. specializing in plastic surgery Santa Cruz, Calif., 1969—; Monterey, Calif., 1990—; adminstr. Plasticenter, Inc., Santa Cruz, 1976-88, med. dir., 1987-88. Mem. AMA, Am. Soc. Plastic and Reconstructive Surgeons, Calif. Soc. Plastic Surgeons (mem. coun. 1986-89, sec. 1989-93, v.p. 1994-95, pres. elect 1995-96, pres. 1996-97), Am. Soc. Aesthetic Plastic Surgeons, Calif. Med. Assn., Assn. Calif. Surgery Ctrs. (pres. 1988-92), Santa Cruz County Med. Soc. (bd. govs. 1983-88, 1992-94), Santa Cruz Surgery Ctr. (bd. dirs. 1988-93). Roman Catholic. Office: Santa Cruz Can Am Med Group 1669 Dominican Way Santa Cruz CA 95065-1523: 24571 Silver Cloud Ct Monterey CA 93940 Office Phone: 831-462-1000. E-mail: pletsch@pacbell.net.

PLETZ, THOMAS GREGORY, lawyer; b. Toledo, Oct. 3, 1943; s. Francis G. and Virginia (Connell) P.; m. Carol Elizabeth Connolly, June 27, 1969; children: Anne M., John F. BA, U. Notre Dame, 1965; JD, U. Toledo, 1971. Bar: Ohio 1971, U.S. Ct. Appeals (6th cir.) 1978, U.S. Supreme Ct. 1985. Ct. bailiff Lucas County Common Pleas Ct., Toledo, 1967-71; jud. clk. U.S. Dist. Ct. (no. dist.) Ohio, Toledo, 1971-72; assoc. Shumaker, Loop & Kendrick, Toledo, 1972-76, litigation ptnr., 1976—. Acting judge Sylvania (Ohio) Mcpl. Ct., 1990—; mem. Ohio Bar Bd. Examiners, 1993-2003, chmn., 1996-99. Active Toledo Parish Coun., 1987-2003; chmn., trustee Kiroff Trial Adv. Com., Toledo, 1982-91; mem. Nat. Conf. Bar Examiners Com., 1996-2001. With USNR, 1965-92; ret. CDR. Recipient Toledo Jr. Bar award, 1995. Mem. ABA, Ohio State Bar Assn., Toledo Bar Assn. (trustee 1981-93), Diocesan Attys. Bar Assn., 6th Cir. Jud. Conf. (life). Roman Catholic. Office: Shumaker Loop & Kendrick 1000 Jackson St Toledo OH 43624-1573 Office Phone: 419-321-1231. E-mail: tpletz@slk-law.com.

PLEVY, ARTHUR L. lawyer; b. N.Y.C., May 26, 1936; s. Louis and Sarah Plevy; children: Scott Eric, Robert Todd. Student, Bklyn. Coll., 1953-57; BEE, CCNY, 1959; LLB, JD, Bklyn. Law Sch., 1967. Bar: N.Y. 1965, N.J. 1970, Ct. Customs and Patent Appeals 1970, U.S. Supreme Ct. 1970. Design engr. IT&T Labs., Nutley, N.J., 1959-60; project engr. Westrex, N.Y.C., 1960-62; sr. mem. tech. staff RCA, N.Y.C., 1962-65; patent counsel RCA Rsch. Ctr., Princeton, N.J., 1965-70; pvt. practice patent law Edison, N.J., 1970-98; sr. ptnr. Plevy & Assocs., Edison, N.J., 1991—. Cons. electronic firms; pres. New Ventures, Edison, N.J., 1970—; arbitrator Am. Arbitration Assn. Contbr. numerous articles on electronics, patent and trademark law to profl. jours.; patentee in field of electronics. Mem. ABA, IEEE, CCPA, N.J. Patent Law Sch., Fed. Bar Assn., N.Y. Bar Assn., N.J. Bar Assn., Masons. Office: Buchanan Ingersoll 650 College Rd E Princeton NJ 08540-6603 Home: 15 McConkey Dr Washington Crossing PA 18977 E-mail: plevyal@bipc.com.

PLEVYAK, THOMAS JOSEPH, communications executive; b. Simpson, Pa., Feb. 11, 1938; s. Joseph Bernard and Anna Stasia (Klemak) P.; m. Maureen Naomi Hogan, June 25, 1960; children: Stephen, Laura, Sharon. BS in Nuclear Engring., U. Notre Dame, 1960; MS in Nuclear Engring., U. Conn., 1962; grad. Comm. Devel. Tng. Program, Bell Labs., 1964; MS in Advanced Mgmt., Pace U., 1978. MTS Bell Labs, 1962-70; mgr. gen. depts. AT&T, Holmdel, N.J., 1970-80; mgr. AT&T Network Sys., Holmdel, N.J., 1980-90; dir. internat. standards Verizon, Arlington, Va., 1990—. Vice chair Inter-Am. Telecomms. Commn., Washington, 1994-98. Co-author, co-editor: Telecommunications Network Management into the 21st Century, 1994, Telecommunications Network Management: Technologies and Implementations, 1997; contbr. articles to profl. jours.; holder patents in field. Fellow: IEEE Comms. Soc. (bd. govs. 1995—97, pres. 1998—99, past pres. 2000—, operations review com. mem., Donald W. McLellan award 1995, 3rd Millennium medal for outstanding achievements and contbns. 2000); mem.: U.S. ITU Assn. (bd. dirs. 2003—, treas. 2003—). Avocations: travel, reading. Office: Verizon 2980 Fairview Park Dr Fl 5 Falls Church VA 22042 E-mail: thomas.j.plevyak@verizon.net.

PLEWES, THOMAS JEFFREY, military officer; b. Zeeland, Mich., Dec. 15, 1940; s. Lloyd Angus and Joyce (Wicht) P.; m. Elizabeth Marie Hall Feb. 20, 1971; children: Jeffrey Charles, Melissa Joy. BA, Hope Coll., Holland, Mich., 1962; MA in Econs., George Washington U., 1972. Economist U.S. Dept. Labor, Washington, 1962-66, Bur. Labor Stats., Washington, 1969-81, assoc. commr., 1981—. Pres. Sr. Army Res. Commdrs. Assn. Served to U.S. Army, 1966-69, maj. gen. Res., 1993—. Decorated Legion of Merit. Fellow Am. Statis. Assn.; mem. Assn. U.S. Army, Res. Officers Assn. Office: Chief, Army Reserve 2400 Army Pentagon Washington DC 20310-2400 E-mail: plewes@ocar.army.pentagon.mil.

PLEWMAN, PATRICK, health products executive; BA in Chemistry, U. N.C.; MBA, Harvard U. With SmithKline Beecham, 1989—97; v.p. corp. devel. diaDexus, Inc., Santa Clara, Calif., 1997—99, COO, 1999—, pres., bd. dirs., CEO, 2000—. Office: diaDexus Inc 3303 Octavius Dr Santa Clara CA 95054

PLIEGO-STOUT, PATRICIA, travel company executive; b. Mex. City; Founder, pres., CEO Alamo Travel Group, 1982—. Bd. mem. San Antonio Hispanic C. of C., San Antonio Greater C. of C., Sports Found., Libr. Found., 2001—02; pres. San Antonio Chpt. Nat. Assn. Women Bus. Owners; apptd. to San Antonio's Blue Ribbon com. internat. affairs; vice-chair Tex. Assn. Mex.-Am. C. of C. (TAMACC); apptd. by Gov. George W. Bush to State Commr. Tex. Bd. Lic. and Regulation. Named Entrepreneur Yr., San Antonio Hist. C. of C., 1992, Small Bus. Woman Yr., Rep. Women's Leadership Forum, 2000; named to San Antonio Women's Hall Fame, 1997; recipient RNC Hispanic Spirit Enterprise award, Nat. Assn. Women Bus. Owners, San Antonio chpt., 1999, Latina Excellence award, Hispanic mag., 2001, Bus. Entrepreneurship award, 2002. Achievements include led Alamo Travel Group to second place rankings in travel in San Antonio; recognized by Continental Airlines and Delta Airlines as top prodr. in federal and military sales for 1999; award incentive nat. contracts by Dell, Lehman Bros., Lockheed Martin and Am. Inst. Rsch; featured in Latina mag., Reader's Digest, Hispanic Bus. mag., Federal Reserve Bank Report 1995, vanidades mag., Federal Times, Travel Weekly, Bus. Travel mag. Office: Alamo Travel Corp HQ 9000 Wurzbach Rd San Antonio TX 78240 Office Phone: 210-593-0084. Office Fax: 210-614-2448.

PLIMPTON, CALVIN HASTINGS, physician, university president; b. Boston, Oct. 7, 1918; s. George Arthur and Fanny (Hastings) P.; m. Ruth Talbot, Sept. 6, 1941; children: David, Thomas, George (dec.), Anne, Edward. BA cum laude, Amherst Coll., 1939; MD cum laude, Harvard, 1943, MA, 1947; Med. Sci.D., Columbia, 1951; LL.D., Williams Coll., 1960, Wesleyan U., 1961, Doshisha U., Kyoto, Japan, 1962, St. Lawrence U., 1963, Amherst U., 1971; L.H.D., U. Mass., 1962; D.Sc., Rockford Coll., 1962, St. Mary's, 1963, Trinity Coll., 1966, Grinnell (Iowa) Coll., 1967; Litt.D., Am. Internat. Coll., 1965, Mich. State Coll., 1969; DSc, N.Y. Med. Coll., 1986. Diplomate: Nat. Bd. Med. Examiners, Am. Bd. Internal Medicine. Intern, asst. resident, resident medicine Presbyn. Hosp., N.Y.C., 1947-50; asst. attending physician Columbia-Presbyn. Med. Center, 1950-60; asso. medicine (Coll. Phys. and Surg.), 1950-59, asst. prof. clin. medicine, 1959-60; prof. medicine, chmn. dept. Am. U. Beirut, Am. U. Hosp., Beirut, Lebanon, 1957-59; pres. Amherst Coll., 1960-71, Downstate Med. Center, SUNY, 1971-79, dean med. sch., 1971-74, 76-79, prof. medicine, 1971-82, prof. emeritus, 1982—; pres. Am. U., Beirut, 1984-87. Vis. prof. Columbia Presbyn. Med. Center, 1976-77. Trustee Am. U., Beirut, 1960-90, trustee emeritus, 1990—, chmn. bd., 1965-82; trustee World Peace Found., 1962-77, Phillips Exeter Acad., 1963-76, Commonwealth Fund, 1962-83, Hampshire Coll., 1963-71, U. Mass., 1962-70, L.I. U., 1972-82, N.Y. Law Sch., 1976-84; mem. Harvard Bd. Overseers, 1969-75. Capt. U.S. Army, 1944-46, ETO. Decorated comdr. Order of Cedars Lebanon; recipient award Nat. Geog. Soc., award New Eng. Soc., John Phillips award Phillip Exeter Acad., Battle Star Ctrl. Europe. Fellow ACP; mem. Am. Acad. Arts and Scis., Russian Fedn. Acad. Med. Tech. Scis., Coun. Fgn. Rels., Soc. Mayflower Descs., Harvey Soc., Alpha Omega Alpha, Sigma Xi. Clubs: Century, Univ. (N.Y.C.), Charaka (N.Y.C.), Riverdale Yacht (N.Y.C.), Pilgrims (N.Y.C.); Tavern Boston. also: 10 Longwood Dr Apt 411 Westwood MA 02090

PLIMPTON, PEGGY LUCAS, trustee; b. Nov. 3, 1931; d. David Nicholson and Margaret (MacMillan) Lucas; m. Hollis Winslow Plimpton, June 11, 1955; children: Victoria P. Babcock, Priscilla P. Morphy, Hollis Winslow Plimpton III. AB, Duke U., 1954. Trustee Cape Cod Conservatory of Music, 1989—. Bd. trustees Carleton Williard Retirement Home, Bedford, Mass., 1968—, Cape Cod Conservatory Music, 1990—; bd. dirs. Episcopal Ch. Women, 1968-78, Brigham & Women's Hosp., Boston, 1975—; pres. Boston Lying-In Hosp., 1970-72; chmn. Mass. Nat. Cathedral Assn., Boston, 1978-80, 1985-88; pres. bd. trustees Women's Ednl. and Indsl., Boston, 1980-83. Mem. New Eng. Farm and Garden Club (bd. dirs. 1965—, pres. 1995—), Chestnut Hill Garden Club (bd. dirs. 1970-74), Jr. League Garden Club (pres. 1981-83), Colonial Dames (bd. mgrs. 1983-89, v.p. 1993-98, pres. 1998—), Vincent Club, Chilton Club. Republican. Episcopalian. Avocations: gardening, golf, bridge, grandchildren.

PLINER, EDWARD S. corporate financial executive; b. Providence, Jan. 1958; BS, Tufts U., 1980; MA, Harvard U., 1990. CPA Mass. With PwC Tech. divsn. PricewaterhouseCoopers, LLP, 1990—95, ptnr., 1995—2000, v.p., corp. contr., 2000—02; sr. v.p., CFO Raytheon Co., Lexington, Mass., 2002—. Treas. Phoenix Sch., Salem, Mass.; fin. dir. presdl. campaign Michael Dukakis, 1987—88. Mem.: AICPAs. Office: Raytheon Co 141 Spring St Lexington MA 02421

PLISCHKE, ELMER, political science educator; b. Milw., July 15, 1914; s. Louis and Louise (Peterleus) P.; m. Audrey Alice Siehr, May 30, 1941; children: Lowell Robert, Julianne. Ph.B. cum laude, Marquette U., 1937; MA, Am. U., 1938; certificate Carnegie summer session internat. law, U. Mich., 1938; PhD (fellow), Clark U., 1943; certificate, Naval Sch. Mil. Govt. and Civil Affairs, Columbia, 1944. Instr. Springfield Coll., 1940; dist. supr., state dir. Wis. Hist. Records Survey, 1940-42; exec. sec. War Records Commn., Wis. Council Def., 1942; asst. prof. DePauw U., 1946-48, U. Md., College Park, 1948-49, assoc. prof., 1949-52, prof., 1952-79, prof. emeritus, 1979—, head dept. govt. and politics, 1954-68; adj. prof. Gettysburg (Pa.) Coll., 1979-85. Spl. historian Office U.S. High Commr. for Germany, 1950-52; cons. Dept. State, summer 1952; adj. scholar Am. Enterprise Inst. Pub. Policy Research, 1978-; lectr. Air War Coll., Armed Forces Staff Coll., Army War Coll., Def. Intelligence Sch., Indsl. Coll. Armed Forces, Inter-Am. Def. Coll., Nat. War Coll.; lectr. Sr. Officers Seminar Fgn. Service Inst. Dept. State; lectr. Instituto de Altos Estudios Nacionales, Quito, Ecuador.; mem. adv. com. fgn. relations of U.S. Dept. State, 1967-72, chmn., 1969-70; assoc. fellow Gettysburg Coll., 1993—. Author 30 books and monographs including: Conduct of American Diplomacy, 3d edit, 1967, reissued, 1974, (with Robert G. Dixon, Jr.) American Government: Basic Documents and Materials, 1950, reissued, 1971, Berlin: Development of Its Government and Administration, 1952, reissued, 1970, The Allied High Commission for Germany, 1953, International Relations: Basic Documents, rev, 1962, American Foreign Relations: A Bibliography of Official Sources, 1955, reissued, 1966, American Diplomacy: A Bibliography of Biographies, Autobiographies, and Commentaries, 1957, Summit Diplomacy: Personal Diplomacy of the President of the United States, 1958, reissued, 1974, Contemporary Governments of Germany, 1961, rev. edit., 1969, Government and Politics of Contemporary Berlin, 1963, Foreign Relations Decisionmaking: Options Analysis, 1973, United States Diplomats and Their Missions: A Profile of American Diplomatic Emissaries Since 1778, 1975, Microstates in World Affairs: Policy Problems and Options, 1977, Neutralization as an American Strategic Option, 1978, Modern Diplomacy: The Art and the Artisans, 1979, U.S. Foreign Relations: A Guide to Information Sources, 1980, Presidential Diplomacy: A Chronology of Summit Visits, Trips and Meetings, 1986, Diplomat in Chief: The President at the Summit, 1986, Foreign Relations: Analysis of Its Anatomy, 1988, Contemporary United States Foreign Policy: Documents and Commentary, 1991, U.S. Department of State: A Reference History, 1999, others; contbr. more than 80 articles to profl. and lit. jours., and encyclopaedias; Americana Ann., 1972-83; also editorials in newspapers; editor, contbr. Systems of Integrating the International Community, 1964; mem. bd. editors Jour. Politics, 1966-68. Served from ensign to lt. USNR, 1943-46; exec. asst., then exec. officer Civil Affairs div., comdr. U.S. Naval Forces for Europe, London, 1944-45; charge denazcification policy coordination Office Dir. Polit. Affairs, Office Mil. Govt. for Germany 1945. Recipient research awards U. Md. Gen. Research Bd., 1956, 58, 69, Eliza Dodd and Henry White Ford rsch. award Clark U., 1940; research grantee Earhart Found., 1982-83, 86-87; book Interaction: Foreign Policy and Public Policy (Piper and Terchek) dedicated in honor, 1983; elected Knight Mark Twain, Mark Twain Jour., 1970. Mem. AAUP, Am. Soc. Internat. Law, Am. Polit. Sci. Assn. (coun.), D.C. Polit. Sci. Assn. (coun. mem., pres. 1961), So. Polit. Sci. Assn. (coun.), Internat. Studies Assn., Com. Study Diplomacy, Inst. Study Diplomacy, Internat. Torch Club (sec. Gettysburg club 1985-91, archivist 1991-2004 mem. 1995-97), Eclectic Club, Phi Beta kappa, Phi Kappa Phi, Pi Sigma Alpha, Sigma Tau Delta. Home: 227 Ewell Ave Gettysburg PA 17325-3108

PLISCHKE, LE MOYNE WILFRED, research chemist; b. Greensburg, Pa., Dec. 11, 1922; s. Fred and Ruth Naomi (Rumbaugh) P.; m. Joan Harper, Mar. 11, 1966. BS, Waynesburg Coll., 1948; MS, W.Va. U., 1952. Rsch. chemist U.S. Naval Ordinance Test Sta., China Lake, Calif., 1952-53; asst. prof. chemistry Commonwealth U., Richmond, Va., 1953-54; rsch. chemist E.I. du Pont, Gibbstown, N.J., 1955-57, Monsanto Chem. Co., Pensacola, Fla., 1957—. Mem. Am. Chem. Soc. Achievements include 18 U.S. patents and 51 foreign patents in field. Home: 2100 Club House Dr Lillian AL 36549-5402 Office: Monsanto Co The Chem Group PO Box 97 Gonzalez FL 32560-0097 E-mail: plis123@gulftel.com.

PLISKIN, WILLIAM AARON, physicist; b. Akron, Ohio, Aug. 9, 1920; s. Max and Lena (Slavin) P.; m. Miriam Jaffee, Mar. 15, 1944; children: Karen, Michael, Bina. BS, Kent State U., 1941; MS, Ohio U., 1943; PhD, Ohio State U., 1949. Rsch. physicist Texaco Rsch. Ctr., Beacon, N.Y., 1949-59; staff physicist IBM, Poughkeepsie, N.Y., 1959-60, adv. physicist, 1960-63, sr. physicist, mgr., 1964-79, sr. staff mem., 1979-82, mgr., sr. tech. staff mem., 1982-87, sr. tech. staff mem., 1987-90; cons. characterization and measurement of dielectric films, 1990—. Contbr. numerous articles to profl. jours., chpts. in books; patentee in field. Served to 1st lt. U.S. Army, 1943-46, PTO. Fellow IEEE, Electrochem Soc. (ann. award electronics div. 1973); mem. Am. Phys. Soc., Am. Chem. Soc. (ann. award Mid Hudson sect. 1964), Sigma Xi, Pi Mu Epsilon, Sigma Pi Sigma. Jewish. Home: 31 Greenvale Farms Rd Poughkeepsie NY 12603-4201 E-mail: WAPlisk@aol.com.

PLISKOW, VITA SARI, anesthesiologist; b. Tel Aviv, Sept. 13, 1942; arrived in Can., 1951; came to U.S., 1967; d. Henry Norman and Renee (Mushkatel) Stahl; m. Raymond Joel Pliskow, June 30, 1968; children: Tia, Kami. MD, U. B.C., Vancouver, 1967. Diplomate Am. Bd. Anesthesiology. Ptnr. Olympic Anesthesia, Bremerton, Wash., 1971-84, pres., anesthesiologist, 1974-84; co-founder Olympic Ambulatory Surgery Ctr., Bremerton, 1977-83; ptnr., anesthesiologist Allenmore Anesthesia Assocs., Tacoma, 1983—. Staff anesthesiologist Harrison Meml. Hosp., Bremerton, 1971-95, Allenmore Hosp., Tacoma, 1983—. Trustee Tacoma Youth Symphony Assn., 1994—; active Nat. Coun. Jewish Women, 1972—. Fellow Am. Coll. Anesthesiologists, Am. Coll. Chest Physicians; mem. Am. Soc. Anesthesiologists (del. Wash. State 1987—), Wash. State Med. Assn. (del. Pierce County 1993-94), Wash. State Soc. Anesthesiologists (pres. 1985-87), Pierce County Med. Soc. (sec.-treas. 1992). Avocations: classical music, opera, singing (mezzo soprano). Office: PO Box 65274 University Place WA 98464-1274

PLOMP, TEUNIS (TONY PLOMP), minister; b. Rotterdam, Netherlands, Jan. 28, 1938; arrived in Can., 1951; s. Teunis and Cornelia (Pietersma) P.; m. Margaret Louise Bone, July 21, 1962; children: Jennifer Anne, Deborah Adele. BA, U. B.C., Vancouver, Can., 1960; BD, Knox Coll., Toronto, Ont., Can., 1963, DD (hon.), 1988. Ordained to ministry Presbyn. Ch., 1963. Min. Goforth Meml. Presbyn. Ch., Saskatoon, Canada, 1963-68, Richmond (B.C.) Presbyn. Ch., 1968—2004. Clerk Presbytery of Westminster, Vancouver, 1969-2003; moderator 113th Gen. Assembly Presbyn. Ch. Can., 1987-88, dep. clk., 1988—; chaplain New Haven Correctional Centre, Burnaby, B.C., 1973-99. Contbr. mag. column You Were Asking, 1982-2002. Presbyterian. Avocations: record collecting, audiophile, biking, swimming. E-mail: tony_plomp@telus.net.

PLONK, WILLIAM MCGUIRE, retired minister; b. Franklin, N.C., Aug. 19, 1925; s. Thomas Motley and Mary Louise (McGuire) P.; m. Nancy Marie Moore, June 29, 1957; children: Mary Evelyn Plonk Lucas, William McGuire Plonk, Jr. BS, Davidson Coll., 1949; BD, Union Theol. Seminary, Richmond, Va., 1954. Ordained to ministry Presbyn. Ch., 1954. Pastor Lawrenceville (Va.) Presbyn. Ch., 1954-56, Rivermont Presbyn. Ch., Chester, Va., 1956-58;

youth minister First Presbyn. Ch., Greensboro, N.C., 1958-61; pastor Westminster Presbyn. Ch., Columbia, S.C., 1961-66, Covenant Presbyn. Ch., Spartanburg, S.C., 1966-69, Bow Creek Presbyn. Ch., Virginia Beach, Va., 1969-72; spl. agt. Jefferson Standard Ins. Co., Norfolk, Va., 1972-73; exchange pastor St. Stevens and West Church of Scotland, Broughty Ferry, Scotland, 1972; pastor Makemie/Naomi Makemie Presbyn. Chs., Accomac, Onancock, Va., 1974-90; interim pastor Manokin Presbyn. Ch., Princess Anne, Md., 1991, 92; stated supply Clark Presbyn. Ch., Daugherty, Va., 1993—2001; interim pastor Chatham (Va.) Presbyn. Ch., 2003—. Dist. chmn. Boy Scouts Am. 1st lt. U.S. Army, 1944-46. Mem. Rotary (pres. Onancock Club, Paul Harris Fellow 1993), Drummondtown-Lee Ruritan Club (pres.). Avocations: singing, early Am. ch. history. Home: 107 Settlers Bend Martinsville VA 24112-6616

PLONSEY, ROBERT, electrical and biomedical engineer; b. N.Y.C., July 17, 1924; s. Louis B. and Betty (Vinograd) P.; m. Vivian V. Vucker, Oct. 1, 1948; 1 child, Daniel. BEE, Cooper Union, 1943; MSEE, NYU, 1948; PhD, U. Calif., Berkeley, 1955; postgrad. med. sch., Case Western Res. U., 1969-71; D of Technol. Scis., Slovak Acad. Scis., 1995. Registered profl. engr., Ohio. Asst. prof. elec. engring. U. Calif., Berkeley, 1955-57, Case Inst. Tech., Cleve., 1957-60, assoc. prof., 1960-66, prof., 1966-68, dir. bioengring. group, 1962-68; prof. biomed. engring. Sch. Engring. and Sch. Medicine Case Western Res. U., 1968-83, chmn. dept., 1976-80; vis. prof. biomed. engring. Duke U., Durham, N.C., 1980-81, prof., 1983-96, prof. biomed. engring., Hudson prof. engring., 1990-93, Pfizer-Inc.-Edmond T. Pratt Jr. Univ. prof. biomed. engring., 1993-96, Pfizer Inc. Edmond T. Pratt Jr. Univ. prof. emeritus, 1996—. Mem. biomed. fellowships rev. com. NIH, 1966-70; mem. tng. com. Engrs. in Medicine and Biology, 1972-73, cons., 1974-96; cons. NSF, 1973-93; mem. internat. sci. adv. com. Ragnar Granit Inst., Tampere (Finland) U. Tech., 1992—; ad hoc mem. sci. adv. com. Whitaker Found., 1989-91. Author: (with R. Collin) Principles and Applications of Electromagnetic Fields, 1961, Bioelectric Phenomena, 1969, (with J. Liebman and P. Gillette) Pediatric Electrocardiography, 1982, (with T. Pilkington) Engineering Contributions to Biophysical Electrocardiography, 1982, (with J. Liebman and Y. Rudy) Pediatric and Fundamental Electrocardiography, (with R.C. Barr) Bioelectricity: A Quantitative Approach, 1988, 2d edit., 2000, (with J. Malmivuo) Bioelectromagnetism, 1995; mem. editorial bd. Trans. IEEE, Biomed. Engring, 1965-70; assoc. editor, 1977-79, editorial bd. TIT Jour. 1971-81, Electrocardiology Jour., 1974—, Medical and Biological Engineering and Computing, 1987—; procs. editor Engring. in Medicine and Biology, 17th Ann., Conf., 1965. Mem. com. on electrocardiography Am. Heart Assn., 1976-82; v.p. Your Schs., Cleveland Heights, Ohio, 1968-69, 73-75; provisional trustee Am. Bd. Clin. Engrs., 1973-74, pres. 1975, trustee, 1976-85. With AUS, 1944-46. Recipient sr. postdoctoral award NIH, 1980-81, Merit award Internat. Union Phys. and Engring. Scis. in Medicine, 1997, Ragnit Granit prize, 2003. Fellow AAAS, IEEE (chmn. Cleve. chpt. group on biomed. electronics 1962-63, chmn. publs. com. group on engring. in medicine and biology 1968-70, v.p. adminstrv. com. 1970-72, pres. 1973-74, chmn. fellows com. Engring. in Medicine and Biology Soc. 1986-88, 2000, v.p. tech. and conf. activities 1991, William S. Morlock award 1979, Centennial medal 1984, co-program chair ann. conf., Paris 1992, chmn. awards com. 1996, Millennium medal 2000, Ragnar Granit prize 2004); mem. AAUP, NAE (bioengring. peer com. 1988-91, 2001-04, chair 1990-91, 2003-04, nominating com. 1991-92, mem. com. 1992-94, program adv. com. 1996-98, NRC postdoctoral rsch. associateships evaluation panel 1987-90, Russ prize com. 2000-03), Internat. Acad. Med. and Biol. Engring. (founding mem. 1997), Am. Inst. Med. and Biol. Engring. (founding fellow 1992—), Alliance for Engring. in Medicine and Biology (treas. 1976-78), Biomed. Engring. Soc. (bd. dirs. 1975-78, 79-83, pres. 1981-82, chmn. affiliations com. 1987-89, ALZA Disting. lectr. 1988), Am. Physiol. Soc., Am. Soc. Engring. Edn. (bd. dirs. biomed. engring. divsn. 1978-83, chmn. 1982-83, Pilkington Outstanding Educator award, 2002). Office: Duke U Box 90281 Dept Biomed Engring Durham NC 27708-0281 Office Phone: 919-660-5131. Business E-Mail: robert.plonsey@duke.edu. *External recognition of success is not nearly so important as the inner awareness of coming to full grips with life, to be fully involved, bending all strengths to fulfill one's goals and philosophies. And of all involvements, those with people are most meaningful (to be aware of and share the feelings of colleagues, students, friends, and family—and to enrich these relationships)—and for me most difficult.*

PLONSKI, HALINA MARIA, retired pharmacist; b. Sejny, Poland, Aug. 1, 1923; arrived in US, 1962; d. Jozef and Wanda (Dlugoborska) Tarkowska; children: Olgierd-Piotr, Ewa Maria Hyjek, Anne-Marie Kern. M in Pharmacy Sci., Sch. of Pharmacy, Warsaw, 1950; PhD in History of Pharmacy, Med. Sch., Lublin, Poland, 1991. Lic. clin. lab. supr., registered pharmacist Poland. Sr. rsch. asst. Coll. Agr. Rutgers U., New Brunswick, NJ, 1962—63; rsch. assoc. dept. biochemistry Flower and Fifth Ave. Med. Sch., N.Y.C., 1963—66; staff dept. rehab. medicine Columbia U., N.Y.C., 1966—70; supr. clin. chemistry lab. N.Y. Infirmary, N.Y.C., 1970—71, Bronx-Lebanon Hosp., 1971—72; rsch. assoc., lab. supr. dept. exptl. medicine NYU, N.Y.C., 1972—76; ret., 1976. Assoc. prof. exptl. medicine and surgery in primates LEMSIP dept. biochemistry Coll. Agr., Warsaw, 1961—62; rsch. project supr. Inst. Meat Industry, Warsaw, 1958—61; with rsch. lab bromatology dept. Inst. Hygiene, Warsaw, 1951—53. Mem.: AAUW, Oerg. Hist. Soc., Polish-Am. Hist. Assn., Polish-Am. Med. Assn. (exec. sec., pres. charitable and ednl. fund 1976—91, Golden medal 1989), Am. Inst. History Pharmacy, Polish Nat. Alliance N.Am. Roman Catholic. Avocations: cultivation and use of medical plants and spices, travel, swimming. Home: 16525 SW Monterey Ln Portland OR 97224-2109

PLORDE, JAMES JOSEPH, physician, educator; b. Brewster, Minn., Feb. 16, 1934; s. James Arthur and Mary Jeanette (Lutz) P.; m. Diane Sylvia Koenigs, Aug. 28, 1964 (div. July 1974); children: Lisa Marie, Michele Louise, James Joshua; m. Jo Ann Gates, Dec. 22, 1986. BA, U. Minn., 1956, BS, 1957, MD, 1959. Diplomate Am. Bd. Internal Medicine, Am. Bd. Pathology. Vol. leader Peace Corps, Gondar, Ethiopia, 1964-66; intern King County Hosp., Seattle, 1959-60; resident U. Wash., Seattle, 1960-62, fellow infectious diseases, 1962-64; chief med. resident King County Hosp., Seattle, 1966-67; asst. prof. medicine U. Wash., Seattle, 1967-71, assoc. prof., 1971-78; fellow clin. microbiology, 1972-73; prof. medicine, lab. medicine U. Wash. Sch. Medicine, Seattle, 1978-98 (ret.), prof. emeritus medicine, lab. medicine, 1998—; head clin. investigation U.S. Naval Med. Research, Addis Ababa, Ethiopia, 1968-71; chief infectious diseases VA Hosp., Seattle, 1973-89, chief clin. microbiology, 1973-98; ret., 1998. Instr. U. Wash., 1966-67; cons. WHO, 1975, Suez Canal U. Faculty of Medicine, Ismailia, Arab Republic of Egypt, 1981-85. Contbr. numerous articles to profl. jours., chpts. to books. Fellow Infectious Disease Soc., ACP; mem. AAAS, Am. Soc. Microbiology, Acad. Clin. Lab. Physicians and Scientists. Home: 3164 W Laurelhurst Dr NE Seattle WA 98105-5346 Fax: 206-523-3541. E-mail: jjplorde@u.washington.edu.

PLOSCOWE, STEPHEN ALLEN, lawyer; b. N.Y.C., Jan. 30, 1941; s. Samuel Stuart and Molly Florence (Slutsky) P.; m. Wendie Sue Malkin, Sept. 5, 1964; children— Jon, Lauren. B.S., Cornell U., 1962, LL.B., 1965. Bar: N.J. 1965, U.S. Dist. Ct. N.J. 1965, U.S. Ct. Appeals (3d cir.) 1979. Assoc. Cole, Berman & Belsky (and predecessor firm) Paterson, N.J. also Rochelle Park, N.J. 1965-69, ptnr., 1970-78; ptnr. Grotta, Glassman & Hoffman, Newark also Roseland, N.Y., 1979—; borough atty. North Caldwell, N.J., 1973-79. Mem. Passaic County Bar Assn., Bergen County Bar Assn., N.J. State Bar Assn., Indsl. Relations Research Assn., ABA. Republican. Jewish. Club: Green Brook Country. Home: 76 Brookside Ter Caldwell NJ 07006-4413 Office: Grotta Glassman & Hoffman PA 75 Livingston Ave Ste 13 Roseland NJ 07068-3701 Business E-Mail: ploscowes@gghlaw.com.

PLOSSER, CHARLES IRVING, economist, educator; b. Birmingham, Ala., Sept. 19, 1948; s. George Gray and Dorothy (Irving) P.; m. Janet Schwert, June 26, 1976; children: Matthew, Kevin, Allison. B.E. cum laude, Vanderbilt U., 1970; MBA, U. Chgo., 1972, PhD, 1976. Cons. Citicorp Realty Cons., N.Y.C., 1972-73; lectr. Grad. Sch. Bus., U. Chgo., 1975-76; asst. prof. Grad. Sch. Bus. Stanford (Calif.) U., 1976-78; asst. prof. econs. W.E. Simon Grad. Sch. Bus., U. Rochester (N.Y.), 1978-82, assoc. prof., 1982-86, prof., 1986-89; Fred H. Gowen prof. econs. U. Rochester, N.Y., 1989-92, John M. Olin Disting. prof. econs. and pub. policy, 1992—, acting dean W.E. Simon Grad. Sch. Bus., 1990-91, 92-93, dean, 1993—2003. Chmn. bd. Consortium for Grad. Study in Mgmt., 1995-97; bd. dirs. ViaHealth, Inc., 1995-2000, Rochester Gas & Electric Corp, RGS Energy Group, 1996-2002, dir. adv. bd., 2002-; bd. dirs. Grad. Mgmt. Admission Coun., 1997-2003, chmn. bd., 2002-03. Editor, Jour. Monetary Econs., 1983—, Carnegie-Rochester Conference Series on Public Policy, 1989—; contbr. articles to profl. jours. 1st lt., U.S. Army, 1972-73. NSF research grantee, 1982, 84. Mem. Am. Econs. Assn., Econometrics Soc., Am. Fin. Assn., Tau Beta Pi, Beta Gamma Sigma. Home: 95 Ambassador Dr Rochester NY 14610-3402 Office: U Rochester Simon Grad Sch Rochester NY 14627 Office Phone: 585-275-3754.

PLOTCH, WALTER, management consultant, fund raising counselor; b. N.Y.C., July 19, 1932; s. Harry and Belle (Lebowsky) P.; m. Yvette Gabrielle Lambert, Mar. 20, 1957; children: Allison, Jennifer, Adrienne. AB, Queens Coll., 1957; MA, Harvard U., 1959; postgrad., 1959-62. Analyst L.F. Rothschild & Co., N.Y.C. and Boston, 1962-64; cmty. cons., 1964-65; edn. dir. New Eng. Anti-Defamation League B'nai B'rith, 1965-68; nat. edn. dir., 1968-76; v.p. Brakeley, John Price Jones Inc., N.Y.C., 1976-79; sr. v.p., dir., 1979-89; sr. v.p. The Oram Group, Inc., N.Y.C., 1989-92; exec. v.p.; pres., CEO Walter Plotch Assocs., Inc., Croton-On-Hudson, N.Y., 1992—. Mem. faculty Grad. Sch. Mgmt. and Urban Affairs, New Sch. U.; lectr. Harvard U. Grad. Sch. Edn.; cons. Harcourt, Brace, Plenum Pubs. Co-editor: Pluralism in a Democratic Society, 1977; gen. editor: The Job Corps Intergroup RElations Series, 1974; contbr. articles to profl. jours.; contbg. editor mag., Jour. Sponsored Rsch. Bd. dirs. Schizophrenia Found., 1975-90; nat. bd. dirs. NCCJ, 1980-81, Nat. Charitable Info Bur.,mem. exec. com. 1986-94. Served with USCGR, 1953-55, Korea. Grantee U.S. Office Edn., Dept. Labor, N.Y. Coun. Humanities; tchg. fellow Harvard U., 1959-61. Mem. Princeton Club, Univ. Club, Washington, Phi Alpha Theta. Democrat. Jewish. Office: 39 Furnace Dock Rd Croton On Hudson NY 10520-1406

PLOTKIN, IRVING H(ERMAN), economist, consultant; b. Bklyn., July 19, 1941; s. Samuel H. and Dorothy (Falick) P.; m. Janet V. Bufe, July 26, 1969; children: Aaron Jacob, Joshua Benjamin. BS in Econs., U. Pa., 1963; PhD in Math. Econs., MIT, 1968. Corp. planning analyst Mobil Oil Co., N.Y.C., 1962-63, Mobil Oil Italiana, Genoa, Italy, 1965; ind. cons. econs. and ops. rsch. to banks, mut. funds, ins. cos., govt. agys. Cambridge, Mass., 1965-68; sr. economist Arthur D. Little, Inc., Cambridge, 1968—2002. Dir. regulation and econs., 1974-2002, v.p., 1979-2002; bd. dirs. Arthur D. Little Valuation, Inc.; trustee Arthur D. Little, Inc., ESOP, 1988-2002; mgr. dir. tax svc. PricewaterhouseCoopers LLP, Boston, 2002—; instr. fin. and computer scis. MIT, 1965-68; lectr. maj. univs. U.S. and abroad; expert witness U.S. Ho. of Reps. and Senate coms., U.S. Ct. Claims, U.S. Tax Ct. I.C.C., FTC, Fed. Martime Commn., Fed. Dist. Cts., Fed. Res. Bd., other fed. and state govt. agys., 1967—. NASA fellow, 1963-66, NSF fellow, 1967, Am. Bankers Assn. fellow, 1968. Mem. Am. Econ. Assn., Econometric Soc., Am. Fin. Assn., Beta Gamma Sigma, Pi Gamma Mu, Tau Delta Phi (chpt. pres. 1962-63). Home: 975 Memorial Dr Apt 910 Cambridge MA 02138-5754 Office: One Post Office Square Boston MA 02109-2301 Office Phone: 617-530-5332. E-mail: irving.h.plotkin@us.pwc.com.

PLOTKIN, LOREN H. lawyer; b. Bklyn., Feb. 8, 1943; s. Arthur and Betty Ann (Strugatz); m. Carol Baxter, Aug. 25, 1990; children: Lily, Kate. BA, Harpur Coll., SUNY, Binghamton, 1963; JD, St. John's U., N.Y.C., 1966. Bar: N.Y. 1966, U.S. Dist. Ct. (so. and ea. dists.) N.Y. 1972, U.S. Tax Ct. 1976. Law asst. appellate divsn., first dept. N.Y. State Supreme Ct.; ptnr. Lans Feinberg & Cohen, N.Y.C., 1969-81; mem. Levine & Thall, P.C., N.Y.C., 1981-84, Levine Thall and Plotkin, N.Y.C., 1984-96, Levine Thall, Plotkin & Menin, L.L.P., N.Y.C., 1996-99, Levine, Plotkin & Menin, L.L.P., N.Y.C., 2000—. Lectr. on entertainment law. Notes and comments editor St. John's U. Law Rev., 1965-66. Home: 34 Lawrence Ln Palisades NY 10964-1604 Office: Levine Plotkin & Menin LLP 1740 Broadway Fl 22 New York NY 10019-4315

PLOTKIN, MANUEL D. management consultant, educator, former corporate executive and government official; s. Jacob and Bella (Katz) P.; m. Diane Fern Weiss, Dec. 17, 1967; 1 child, Lori Ann. BS with honors, Northwestern U., 1948; MBA, U. Chgo., 1949. Price economist, survey coordinator U.S. Bur. Labor Statistics, Washington, 1949-51, Chgo., 1951-53; sr. economist Sears Roebuck & Co., Chgo., 1953-61, mgr. market research, 1961-66, chief economist, mgr. mktg. rsch., 1966-73, dir. corp. planning and research, 1973-77, exec. corp. planner, 1979-80; dir. U.S. Bur. Census, Washington, 1977-79; v.p., dir. group practice Divsn. Mgmt. Cons. Austin Co., Evanston, Ill., 1981-85; pres. M.D. Plotkin Research & Planning Co., Chgo., 1985—. Tchr. statistics Ind. U., 1953-54; tchr. econs. Wilson Jr. Coll., Chgo., 1954-55; tchr. quantitative methods and managerial econs. Northwestern U., 1955-63; tchr. mktg. rsch. and mktg. mgmt. DePaul U., Chgo., 1992-95; mem. Conf. Bd. Mktg. Rsch. Adv. Coun., 1968-77, chmn.-elect, 1977; chmn. adv. com. U.S. Census Bur., 1974-75; trustee Mktg. Sci. Inst., 1968-77; mem. Nat. Commn. Employment and Unemployment Stats., 1978-79, Adv. Coun. Edn. Stats., 1977-79, Interagy. Com. Population Rsch., 1977-79; mem. adv. coun. Kellstadt Ctr., DePaul U., 1987-92; trustee U.S. Travel Data Ctr., 1977-79. Contbr. articles to profl. jours. Served with AUS, 1943-46, ETO. Decorated Bronze Star medal with oak leaf cluster. Mem. Am. Mktg. Assn. (pres. Chgo. 1968-69, nat. dir. 1969-70, nat. v.p. mktg. rsch. 1970-72, nat. v.p. mktg. mgmt. 1981-83, pres., CEO 1985-86), Am. Statis. Assn. (pres. Chgo. 1966-67, Forecasting award 1963), Am. Econ. Assn., Nat. Assn. Bus. Economists, Planning Execs. Inst., World Future Soc., Midwest Planning Assn., U. Ill. Businessmen Rsch. Adv. Group, Chgo. Assn. Commerce and Industry, Beta Gamma Sigma, Alpha Sigma Lambda, Delta Mu Delta. Home and Office: 2650 N Lakeview Ste 3910 Chicago IL 60614-1831

PLOTKIN, STANLEY ALAN, virologist; b. N.Y.C., May 12, 1932; s. Joseph and Lee (Fishbein) P.; m. Susan Lannon, Nov. 24, 1979; children: Michael, Alec. BA, NYU, 1952; MD, SUNY, N.Y.C., 1956; MA (hon.), U. Pa., 1974. Diplomate Am. Bd. Pediat., Am. Acad. Pediat. Intern Cleve. Met. Gen. Hosp., 1956-57; resident pediat. Phila. Children's Hosp., 1961—62, dir. divsn. infectious diseases, sr. physician, 1969—90; registrar Hosp. for Sick Children, London, 1962-63; assoc. mem. Wistar Inst., Phila., 1963-74, prof. virology, 1974—; asst. prof. pediat. U. Pa., Phila., 1966-71, assoc. prof., 1971-74, prof., 1974-91; prof. emeritus, 1991—; assoc. chmn. dept. pediat. U. Pa., Phila., 1986-88; med. and sci. dir. Pasteur-Mérieux-Connaught Labs. (now Aventis-Pasteur), Marnes-la-Coquette, France, 1991-97; advisor to pres. Aventis Pasteur, Lyon, France, 1997—. Adj. prof. internat. health Johns Hopkins U., Balt., 2000—. Assoc. editor: Am. Jour. Epidemiology, 1967-87, Proc. Soc. Exptl. Biology and Medicine, 1968-85, Pediatric Infectious Disease jour., 1982-87, Vaccine jour., 1983—, Molecular and Cellular Probes jour., 1987—, Clin. Diagnostic Lab. Immunology, 1996—. Served as med. officer USPHS, 1957-60. Decorated Legion of Honor (France); Joseph P. Kennedy Found. grantee, 1964-66, Hartford Found. grantee, 1971-73, NIH grantee, 1973—; recipient Bruce medal ACP, 1987, Clin. Virology award Pan Am. Group Rapid Viral Diagnosis, 1995, Gold medal Sabin Found., 2002, Bristol award, 2004; named Disting. Physician Pediatric Infectious Diseases Soc., 1993, Disting. Alumnus, Children's Hosp. of Phila., 2001. Fellow AAAS; mem. Soc. Pediatric Rsch., Am. Pediatric Soc., Infectious Diseases Soc. Am., Am. Epidemiology Soc., Am. Soc. Microbiology, Am. Acad. Pediatrics (chmn. infectious diseases com. 1987-90), World Soc. Pediatric Infectious Diseases (pres. 2003—). Achievements include pioneering work on vaccine strains for protection against polio, rabies, rubella and cytomegalovirus. Office Phone: 215-297-9321. Business E-Mail: stanley.plotkin@aventis.com.

PLOTNICK, HARVEY BARRY, publishing executive; b. Detroit, Aug. 5, 1941; s. Isadore and Esther (Sher) P.; m. Susan Regnery, Aug. 16, 1964 (div. Apr. 1977); children: Andrew, Alice; m. Elizabeth Allen, May 2, 1982; children: Teresa, Samuel. BA, U. Chgo., 1963. Editor Contemporary Books, Inc., Chgo., 1964-66, pres., 1966-94; CEO Molecular Electronics Corp., Chgo., 2000—01, Paradigm Holdings, Inc., Chgo., 1994—. CEO Molecular Electronics Corp., 2000—. Trustee U. Chgo., 1994—, Chgo. Acad. Scis., Argonne Nat. Lab. Office: Paradigm Holdings Inc 2 Prudential Plz Ste 3150 Chicago IL 60601-6790 E-mail: harvey1844@aol.com.

PLOTNICK, ROBERT DAVID, educator, economic consultant; b. Washington, Aug. 3, 1949; s. Theodore and Jean (Hirshfeld) P.; m. Gay Lee (Jensen), Dec. 22, 1972. BA, Princeton U., 1971; MA, U. Calif., Berkeley, 1973, PhD, 1976. Rsch. assoc. Inst. Rsch. on Poverty, Madison, Wis., 1973—75; asst. prof. Bates Coll., Lewiston, Maine, 1975—77, Dartmouth Coll., Hanover, NH, 1977—84; assoc. prof. U. Wash., Seattle, 1984—90, prof., 1990, assoc. dean, 1990—95, acting dean, 1994—95. Vis. scholar Russell Sage Found., 1990, U. New South Wales, 1997;London Sch. of Econ., 2004; rsch. affiliate Inst. Rsch. Poverty, 1989—, Nat. Poverty Ctr., 2004; chmn. Population Leadership Program, 1999—, dir. Ctr. for Studies in Demography and Ecology, 1997-2002; adj. fellow Pub. Policy Inst. Calif., 1998-2000; cons. Wash. Dept. Social and Health Svcs., Olympia, 1984-86, 90-96, 2000; cons. in field. Author: Progress Against Poverty, 1975; contbr. articles to profl. journals. Recipient Teaching Excellence Award U. Wash., 1985, 89. Mem. Am. Econ. Assn., Assn. Policy Analysis and Mgmt., Population Assn. Am. Avocations: tennis, hiking, birdwatching, scuba diving. Office: U Wash Evans Sch Pub Affairs PO Box 353055 Seattle WA 98195-3055 Business E-Mail: plotnick@u.washington.edu.

PLOTNICK, STANLEY D. recreational fee-based club executive; V.p. Encore Mktg. Internat., Inc., Lanham, Md., CEO, pres., sec., 1994—. Office: 4501 Forbes Blvd Lanham Seabrook MD 20706

PLOTNIK, ARTHUR, author, columnist; b. White Plains, NY, Oct. 1, 1937; s. Michael and Annabelle P.; m. Meta Von Borstel, Sept. 6, 1960 (div. 1979); children: Julia Nicole, Katya Michelle.; m. Mary Phelan, Dec. 2, 1983. BA, State U. N.Y., Binghamton, 1960; MA, U. Iowa, 1961; MS in L.S, Columbia U., 1966. Gen. reporter, reviewer Albany (N.Y.) Times Union, 1963-64; freelance writer, 1964-66; editor Librarians Office, Library of Congress, 1966-69; assoc. editor Wilson Library Bull., Bronx, N.Y., 1969-74; editor-in-chief Am. Libraries, Chgo., 1975-89; assoc. pub. ALA, 1989-97; editl. dir. ALA Editions, 1993-97; writer, 1997—. Adj. instr. journalism Columbia Coll., Chgo., 1988-89; speaker in field. Author: The Elements of Editing: A Modern Guide for Editors and Journalists, 1982, Jacob Shallus, Calligrapher of the Constitution, 1987, The Elements of Expression, 1996, The Urban Tree Book, 2000, Honk If You're a Writer, 1992, The Elements of Authorship (reprint of Honk if You're a Writer), 2000; contbg. editor: The Writer, 2000—; columnist: Editorial Eye, 1995—2001; exec. prodr.: Libr. Video mag., 1986—91; contbr. articles to profl. jours.; author: fiction and poetry. Bd. dirs. Am. Book Awards, 1979-82; bd. advs. Univ. Press of Am., 1982—1997. Served with USAR, 1962-67. Fellow Iowa Writers Workshop Creative Writing, 1961; recipient award Ednl. Press Assn. Am., 1973 (3), 77, 82, 83; cert. of excellence Internat. Reading Assn., 1970, First Pl. award Verbatim essay competition, 1986, award Am. Soc. Bus. Press Editors, 1987. Mem. ALA, ACLU, Morton Arboretum, Treekeepers (Openlands Project). Home and Office: 2120 W Pensacola Ave Chicago IL 60618-1718 also: N E Pub Assocs Literary Agents PO Box 5 Chester CT 06412-0005

PLOTTEL, GLORIA SUSANNE STONE, marketing professional; b. N.Y.C., Feb. 16, 1966; d. Leroy Saul and Karen Lila Stone; m. Philip Benjamin Plottel, June 9, 1996. BA cum laude Univ. Profs. Program, Boston U., 1988; MS in Forest Resources Mgmt, SUNY, Syracuse, 1992; MBA, NYU, 2002. Mgr. dept. geography Boston U., 1989-90; tchg. asst. coll. environ. sci. and forestry SUNY, Syracuse, 1990-92; asst. acct. exec. Lowe and Ptnrs./SMS, N.Y.C., 1993-95; asst. mgr. Champion Internat. Corp., Stamford, Conn., 1995-97; mktg. mgr. Bus. New Haven, 1997-98. Cons. Mass. Dept. Environ. Mgmt., Boston, 1993, No. Forest Lands Coun., Concord, N.H., 1993. Screenwriter: Seasoned Trails, 1989. Mem. exec. bd. U. Profs. Program, Boston U., 1997—; coun. mem. YMCA-YWCA Camping Svcs. of Greater N.Y., 1998—. SUNY internat. conf. grantee, 1991. Avocations: hiking, camping, swimming, ballroom dancing.

PLOTTEL, JEANINE PARISIER, foreign language educator; b. Paris, Sept. 21, 1934; came to U.S., 1943; m. Roland Plottel, 1956; children: Claudia S., Michael E., Philip B. Baccalauréat lettres, Lycée Français de N.Y., 1952; BA with honors, Barnard Coll., 1954; MA, Columbia U., 1955, PhD with distinction, 1959. Lectr. dept. French and Romance philology Columbia U., N.Y.C., 1955-59; rsch. assoc. fgn. lang. program MLA of Am., N.Y.C., 1959-60; lectr. dept. romance langs. CUNY, N.Y.C., 1960; asst. prof. div. humanities Julliard Sch. Music, N.Y.C., 1960-65; dir. lang. labs. Hunter Coll. CUNY, N.Y.C., 1965-69; asst. prof. dept. romance langs. Hunter Coll. CUNY, N.Y.C., 1965-69, assoc. prof. dept. romance langs., 1969-81, prof. dept. romance langs., 1981—2000, assoc. prof. French doctoral program grad. sch., univ. ctr., 1980-81, prof. French doctoral program grad. sch., univ. ctr., 1981—2000, prof. emeritus, 2000—. Exec. dir. AAVP NY state conf., 2002-. Extensive adminstrv. experience in CUNY including chair dept. Romance langs. Author: Les Dialogues de Paul Valéry, 1960; pub., editor N.Y. Literary Forum, 1978-88; contbr. articles to profl. jours., chpts. to books. Pres. Maurice I. Parisier Found., Inc. Named Officer des Palmes Acad., 1999; recipient NEH fellowship, 1979; grantee N.Y. Coun. for the Humanities, 1986, Helena Rubenstein Found., 1986, Florence J. Gould Found., 1986, 88, N.Y. Times Found., 1986. Mem. AAUP (exec. dir. N.Y. State Conf. 2002—), Maison Française (bd. dirs. Columbia U.), Peyre Inst., CUNY, Soc. French Am. Cultural Svcs. & Ednl. Aid, Hunter Coll. Art Galleries. Home: 50 E 77th St Apt 14A New York NY 10021-1836 Office: Hunter Coll-CUNY 695 Park Ave New York NY 10021-5024 Office Phone: 212-535-6668. E-mail: plottel@worldnett.att.net.

PLOTTEL, ROLAND, lawyer; b. N.Y.C., Oct. 1, 1934; s. Charles and Frances (Banner) P.; m. Jeanine Parisier, June 3, 1956; children— Claudia, Michael, Philip. B.A., Columbia U., 1955, LL.B., 1958, M.S. in E.E., 1964. Bar: N.Y. 1958, U.S. Patent Office 1962, U.S. Ct. Appeals 1964, U.S. Supreme Ct. 1964. House counsel Radiotronix Communications Labs., N.Y.C., 1958-61; patent atty. Bendix Corp., Teterboro, N.J., 1961-64; internat. patent atty. Western Electric Co., N.Y.C., 1964-70; sole practice, N.Y.C., 1970—; of counsel Frishauf, Holtz, Goodman & Woodward, N.Y.C.; lectr. patent law Practising Law Inst.; arbitrator Civil Ct., 1964—. Harlan Fiske Stone fellow. Mem. ABA, N.Y. County Lawyers Assn., Am. Intellectual Property Law Assn., N.Y. Patent Trademark and Copyright Law Assn., IEEE, Internat. Soc. Hybrid Microelectronics, Am. Arbitration Assn. Club: City N.Y. Home: 50 E 77th St New York NY 10021-1842 Office: 45 Rockefeller Plz New York NY 10111-0100

PLOUGH, ALONZO L. city health department administrator; BA in Biology, San Diego State U., 1973; MA in Sociology, Cornell U., 1975; MPH, Yale U. Sch. Medicine, 1977; PhD in Anthropology, Cornell U., 1978. Lectr., health policy and mgmt. Harvard U. Sch. Pub. Health, Cambridge, Mass., 1985—95; dep. commr., dir., pub. health Boston Dept. Health and Hosps., 1989—95; assoc. prof., health svcs. U. Wash. Sch. Pub. Health and Cmty. Medicine, 1995—; dir., health officer Seattle-King Co. Health Dept., 1995—. Mem., scientific adv. com. Nat. Ctr. for Health Statistics. Bd. dirs. Am. Lung Assn. of Wash., United Way of King Co., Wash. Dental Found.; chair, bd. Edn. Devel. Ctr., Inc.; chair, adv. com. King Co. Health Action Plan. Mem.: Nat. Assn. of City and County Health Officials. Office: Seattle-King Co Health Dept 999 Third Ave Ste 1200 Seattle WA 98104*

PLOURD, DAVID M. medical educator; b. New Haven, Conn., Oct. 18, 1956; s. Medrick Claude and Leatice Arpaia Plourd. BA in Natural Scis., Pepperdine U., 1978; MD, UCLA, 1982. Diplomate Am. Bd. Ob-Gyn. Intern, resident in ob-gyn. U. Calif. Irvine Med. Ctr., 1981; asst. prof. ob-gyn. Santa Clara Valley Med. Ctr./Stanford U., San Jose, Calif., 1987—95, Naval Med. Ctr. San Diego, 1995—. Examiner Am. Bd. Ob-Gyn., 2002—; expert reviewer Calif. State Med. Bd., 2003—; cons. various mags. Fellow: Am. Coll. Ob-gyn. Avocations: motoryachts, oceanography, marine biology.

PLOURDE, GERARD, company executive; b. Joliette, Que., Can., Feb. 12, 1916; s. Louis-George and Rose de Lima (Jolicoeur) P.; m. Jeannine Martineau, Dec. 4, 1943; children: Monique, Pierre, Marc-André. BA, Brébeuf Coll., 1936; M in Commerce, U. Montreal, Que., 1939, D. Honoris Causa, 1971. Accountant UAP Inc., Montreal, from 1941, pres., gen. mgr., 1951-70, chmn. bd., chief exec. officer, 1970-80, chmn. bd., 1980-86, hon. dir., 1986—, Molson Cos., Northern Telecom. Decorated Officer of Can. Mem. Soc. Automotive Engrs., Saint Denis Club, Mt. Bruno Country Club. Office: 1010 Sherbrooke W #1800 Montreal QC Canada H3A 2R7

PLOVNICK, MARK STEPHEN, business educator; b. N.Y.C., June 8, 1946; s. Jacob and Dorothy Edith (Berger) Plovnick; m. Daisy Shulan Chan, Mar. 13, 1982. BSME, Union Coll., 1968; BA in Econs., Union Coll., 1968; MS in Mgmt., MIT, 1970, PhD in Mgmt., 1975. Instr., rschr. MIT, Cambridge, 1970—76; asst. prof. Clark Univ., Worcester, Mass., 1976—79, assoc. prof., 1979—89, chmn. dept. mgmt., 1979—82, assoc. dean Grad. Sch. Mgmt., 1982—89; prof., dean Sch. Eberhardt Sch. Bus. U. Pacific, Stockton, Calif., 1989—. Cons. to various orgns., 1970—; dir. Devel. Rsch. Assocs., Reston, Va., 1979—82; adj. assoc. prof. U. Mass. Med. Sch., Worcester, Mass., 1982—89; adj. asst. prof. Boston Univ. Sch. Medicine, 1974—75; clin. instr. Harvard Med. Sch., Boston, 1977—78. Author: 5 books; contbr. numerous articles to profl. jours. Mem. Civil Svc. Commn., San Joaquin County, 1989—94; mem. gen. plan action team City of Stockton, 2004—; bd. dirs. United Way, 1991—94, Goodwill Industries, 1992—, Stockton Symphony, 1995—2001. Mem.: Greater Stockton C. of C. (bd. dirs. 1990—94), Yosemite Club (bd. dirs. 2004—). Office: U Pacific Eberhardt Sch Bus Stockton CA 95211-0001 Office Phone: 209-946-2466. E-mail: mplovnic@pacific.edu.

PLOWDEN, DAVID, photographer; b. Boston, Oct. 9, 1932; s. Roger and Mary Russell (Butler) P.; m. Pleasance Coggeshall, June 20, 1962 (div. 1976); children: John, Daniel; m. Sandra Oakes Schoellkopf, July 8th, 1977; children: Philip, Karen. BA Econs., Yale U., 1955; pvt. study with Minor White, Rochester, N.Y., 1959-60. Asst. O. Winston Link Studio, N.Y.C., 1958-59, George Meluso Studio, N.Y.C., 1960-62; photographer, writer, 1962—. Assoc. prof. Inst. Design, Ill. Inst. Tech., Chgo., 1978-86; lectr. U. Iowa Sch. Journalism, 1985-88; vis. prof. Grand Valley State Univ., 1988-90, 91—; artist-in-residence U. Balt., 1990-91. Author and photographer: Farewell to Steam, 1968, Lincoln and His America, 1970 (Benjamin Barondess award 1971), The Hand of Man on America, 1971, 2d edit, 1974, The Floor of the Sky: the Great Plains, 1972, Bridges: the Spans of North America, 1974, 2d edit. 1984, 3d edit., 2002, Commonplace, 1974, Tugboat, 1976 (notable Children's books ALA 1976, Children's Book Showcase 1976), Steel, 1981, An American Chronology, 1982 (Notable Books ALA 1982, Booklist's Best of the 80s 1989), Industrial Landscape, 1985, A Time of Trains, 1987, A Sense of Place, 1988, End of an Era: The Last of the Great Lakes Steamboats, 1992, Small Town America, 1994, Imprints: The Photographs of David Plowden, 1997, David Plowden: The American Barn, 2003; co-author, photographer, Nantucket, 1970, Cape May to Montauk, 1973, Desert and Plains, the Mountains and the River, 1975, The Iron Road, 1978 (notable children's books 1978, Honor list Horn Books 1979), Wayne County: the Aesthetic Heritage of a Rural Area, 1979; introduction The Gallery of World Photography/the Country, 1983; commd. illustrator Gems, 1967, The Freeway in the City, 1968, America the Vanishing, 1969, New Jersey, 1977, North Dakota, 1977, Vermont, 1979, New York, 1981, A Place of Sense, 1988; contbr. articles to numerous jours. including Time, Newsweek, Life, Audubon, Fortune, Smithsonian, Camera Arts, Lenswork; one-man shows include Columbia U., 1965, Smithsonian Instn., 1970, 71, 75, 76, 81, 89, Internat. Ctr. Photography, N.Y., 1976, Witkin Gallery, N.Y.C., 1979, Cin. Art Acad., 1979, The Gilbert Gallery, Chgo., 1980, 81, Chgo. Ctr. Contemporary Photography, 1982, Fed. Hall Mus., N.Y.C., 1982, Calif. Mus. Photography, Riverside, 1982-83, Chgo. Hist. Soc., 1985, Martin Gallery, Washington, 1987, Kunstmuseum, Luzern, Switzerland, 1987, Burchfield Ctr., Buffalo, 1987-88, Iowa State Mus., Des Moines, 1988-89, Catherine Edelman Gallery, Chgo., 1990, Grand Valley State U., 1993, Ewing Gallery, Washington, 1994, Beinecke Rare Book and Manuscript Lib. Yale U., 1997, Albright-Knox Art Gallery, 1997, Mus. Contemporary Photography, Chgo., 1998, Albin O. Kuhn Libr. & Gallery, U. Md., Balt., 1998, Tatar/Alexander Photogallery, Toronto, Ont., 1999, Lawrence Miller Gallery, N.Y.C., 2000, Peter Fetterman Gallery Photographic Works of Art, Santa Monica, Calif., 2004, The Chgo. Cultural Ctr., 2002, Copia, Napa, Calif., 2004; exhibited in group shows at Met. Mus. Art, N.Y.C., 1967, Kodak Gallery, N.Y.C., 1976, Currier Gallery Art, Manchester, N.H., 1978, Whitney Mus., 1979, Art Inst. Chgo., 1983-86, 87, Witkin Gallery, N.Y.C., 1988, Davenport (Iowa) Mus. Art, 1992, Mus. Contemporary Photography, Chgo., Ill., 1996, 98, 99, City, 2000, Fay Gold Gallery, Atlanta, 2003-04; represented in permanent collections Albright-Knox Gallery, Art Inst. Chgo., Calif. Mus. Photography, Ctr. Creative Photography, Chgo. Hist. Soc., Libr. Congress, Smithsonian Instn., U. Md., J.B. Speed Mus., Iowa Humanities Bd., Iowa State Hist. Dept., Burchfield Art Ctr., Buffalo and Erie County Hist. Soc., Internat. Mus. Photography George Eastman House, Internat. Ctr. Photography, Ekstrom Libr. U. Louisville, Beinecke Rare Book and Mauscript Libr., Yale U., 1995—, Mus. Contemporary Photography, Chicy, Bayly Mus. U. Va., Charlottesville. John Simon Guggenheim fellow, 1968; grantee N.Y. State Coun. Arts, 1966, 87, Smithsonian Inst., 1970-71, Dept. Transp. and Smithsonian Inst., 1975-76, H. E. Butt Found., 1977, United Bd. Homeland Ministries, 1976, Chgo. Hist. Soc., 1980-84, Seymour H. Knox Found., 1987, Baird Found., 1987, State Hist. Soc. Iowa, 1987-88, Iowa Humanities Bd., 1987-88; recipient R.R. History award, 1989, Honored Imagemaker, Soc. for Photographic Edn., 2002; subjectof PBS documentary: David Plowden: Light, Shadow & Form, 2000. Mem. Am. Soc. Media Photographers. Home and Office: 609 Cherry St Winnetka IL 60093-2614 Fax: 847-446-2795. E-mail: david@davidplowden.com.

PLOWMAN, BOYD R. automotive executive; BS in Acctg., Utah State U. With Fleetwood Enterprises, Inc., Riverside, Calif., 1969—87; pres., CEO Lee & Assocs. Comml. Real Estate Svcs., 1990—97; v.p. Retail Housing Fleetwood Enterprises, Inc., 1997—2000, CFO, 2000—, exec. v.p., 2001—. Office: Fleetwood Enterprises Inc 3125 Myers St Riverside CA 92513-7638*

PLOWMAN, JACK WESLEY, lawyer; b. Blairsville, Pa., Sept. 12, 1929; s. Ralph Waldo, Sr., and Ethel Beatrice (Nicely) P.; m. Barbara Ellen Brown, Apr. 5, 1952; children: Linda Ellen, Judith Lynn AB, U. Pitts., 1951, LL.B. with honors, 1956. Bar: Pa. 1956, U.S. Dist. Ct. (we. dist.) Pa. 1956, U.S. Ct. Appeals 1960, U.S. Supreme Ct. 1978. Assoc. Campbell, Houck & Thomas, Pitts., 1956-57; ptnr. Rose, Houston, Cooper & Schmidt, Pitts., 1957-63, Plowman & Spiegel, Pitts., 1963-2000; of counsel Bentz Law Firm, P.C., Pitts., 2000—. Adj. prof. emeritus Duquesne U. Sch. Law, 1963—80, 1983—2002. Editor-in-chief Pitts. Legal Jour., 1971-81, U. Pitts. Law Rev., 1955-56 Bd. dirs. United Meth. Pub. House, 1984-96, Ward Home for Children, United Meth. Ch. Union, 1977-83, Wesley Inst., 1977-81, Neighborhood Legal Svcs. Assn., 1969-74; chancellor emeritus Western Pa. Ann. Conf., United Meth. Ch. Capt. JAG, USAFR, 1979-2000. Fellow Am. Bar Found. (life mem.), Am. Coll. Trial Lawyers, Allegheny County Bar Found. (trustee, sec.); mem. ABA, Pa. Bar Assn., Allegheny County Bar Assn. (pres. 1982), Pa. Bar Inst. (bd. dirs. 1988-92), Am. Law Inst., Supreme Ct. Pa. Hist. Soc. (trustee, pres.). Republican. Home: 1025 Lakemont Dr Pittsburgh PA 15243-1817 Office: The Washington Ctr Bldg 680 Washington Rd Pittsburgh PA 15228 Office Phone: 412-563-4500. E-mail: jplowman@bentzlaw.com.

PLOWRIGHT, JOAN ANNE, actress; b. Brigg, Lincolnshire, Eng., Oct. 28, 1929; d. William and Daisy (Burton) P.; m. Roger Gage, 1953 (div.); m. Sir Laurence Olivier, 1961 (dec.); 3 children. Student, Old Vic Theatre Sch. Mem. Old Vic Co., toured S. Africa, 1952-53; 1st leading role in the Country Wife London, 1956; mem. English Stage Co., 1956, Nat. Theatre, 1963-74. Appearances include (plays) The Chairs, 1957, The Entertainer, 1958, Major Barbara and Roots, 1959, A Taste of Honey, 1960 (Tony Best Actress award 1960), Uncle Vanya, 1962-64, St. Joan, 1963 (London Evening Standard Best Actress award 1964), Hobson's Choice, 1964, The Master Builder, 1965, Much Ado About Nothing, 1967, Tartuffe, 1967, Three Sisters, 1967, 68, 69, The Advertisement, 1968, 69, Love's Labour's Lost, 1968, 69, The Merchant of Venice, 1970, 71-72, Rules of the Game, 1971-72, Woman Killed with Kindness, 1971-72, Taming of the Shrew, 1972, Doctor's Dilemma, 1972, Rosmersholm, 1973, Saturday Sunday Monday, 1973, Eden's End, 1974, The Sea Gull, 1975, The Bed Before Yesterday, 1975 (Variety award 1976), Filumena, 1977 (Soc. West End Theatres Best Actress award 1978), Enjoy, 1980, Who's Afraid of Virginia Woolf?, 1981, Cavell, 1982, The Cherry Orchard, 1983, The Way of the World, 1985, The House of Bernada Alba, 1986-87, Uncle Vanya, 1988, Time and The Conways, 1991, If We Are Women, 1995, Absolutely! (Perhaps)!, 2003, (films) Much Ado About Nothing, 1969, Equus, 1976, Richard Wagner, 1982, Brimstone and Treacle, 1982, Brittania Hosp., 1983, Revolution, 1985, The Dressmaker, 1987, Drowning By Numbers, 1987, I Love You To Death, 1990, Avalon, 1990, Enchanted April, 1992 (Acad. award nominee Best Supporting Actress, Golden Globe award 1992), Dennis the Menace, 1993, A Pin for the Butterfly, 1993, Last Action Hero, 1993, The Summer House, 1993, Widows' Peak, 1994, The Scarlet Letter, 1994, Pyromaniacs: A Love Story, 1995, The Grass Harp, 1995, Hotel Sorrento, 1995, Jane Eyre, 1995, Surviving Picasso, 1996, 101 Dalmations, 1996, Mr. Wrong, 1996, The Assistant, 1997, Tea with Mussolini, 1998, The Last Spy, 1998, Bailey's Mistake, 2000, Global Heresy, 2000, Callas Forever, 2001, George and the Dragon, 2002, Bringing Down the House, 2002, I Am David, 2003-; (tv films) Merchant of Venice, 1973, Daphne, Laureola, 1977, Saturday Sunday Monday, 1977, The Importance of Being Earnest, 1988, The Birthday Party, 1987, House of Bernarda Alba, A Nightingale Sang, 1989, Stalin, 1992 (Golden Globe Awd. 1992, Emmy nomination, supporting actress - miniseries, 1993), A Place for Annie, 1994, On Promised Land, 1994, Return of the Natives, This Could Be the Last Time, 1998, Encore, Encore, 1998, Back to the Secret Garden, 1999, Frankie and Hazel, 1999. Office: ICM care Harriet Robinson 76 Oxford St London WIN 0AX England

PLUCIENNIK, THOMAS CASIMIR, lawyer, former assistant county prosecutor; b. Irvington, N.J., Apr. 8, 1947; s. Casimir Stanley and Helen Victoria (Sienicki) P.; m. Maria Anna Soriano, June 16, 1974. BS in Acctg., Seton Hall U., 1969, JD, 1983; MA in Criminal Justice, CUNY, 1976. Bar: N.J. 1983, U.S. Ct. Mil. Appeals 1986, U.S. Dist. Ct. N.J. 1983, D.C. 1994, U.S. Supreme Ct. 1995, N.Y. 1996, U.S. Ct. Appeals (3rd cir.), U.S. Dist. Ct. (so., ea., fed. dists.) N.Y. 1998; cert. criminal trial atty., mil. trial atty.; lic. pvt. investigator. Mng. ptnr. Joe Bell's Tavern & Restaurant, Newark, 1979; police officer City of Newark, 1972-79; criminal investigator Essex County Prosecutor, Newark, 1980-84, asst. prosecutor, 1984-88; sr. asst. prosecutor Warren County, N.J., 1988-89; atty. Voorhees & Acciavatti Esq., Morristown, N.J., 1989-94; defense atty. Picillo Caruso, 1994-96; assoc. Netchert, Dineen & Hillman, 1996-97; litigator Francis J. Dooley, 1998-99; sole practitioner, 1999—. Cert. instr. N.J. State Police Tng. Commn., Trenton, 1984; asst. dir. instruction Officers Candidate Sch. N.J. Mil. Acad., Sea Girt. Committeeman South Orange Republican Club, N.J., 1978-83; treas., founder Tuxedo Park Neighborhood Assn., South Orange, 1977; fin. sec. J. T. Kosciusko Assn., Irvington, N.J., 1979. Served to 1st lt. U.S. Army, 1969-71, maj. (ret.) JAGC, USAR, 1985-90. Recipient Class C. Commendations, Newark Police Dept., 1973, 74, 75, Command Citations, 1973, 74, 75, 77, 78. Master: Worrall F. Mountain Inn of Ct.; mem.: ABA, ATLA, D.C. Bar Assn., N.Y. State Bar Assn., Morris County Bar Assn., N.J. Def. Assn., N.J. State Bar Assn., Trial Attys. N.J. (trustee), Polish Univ. Club, South Orange Lions Club (charter mem.), Picatinny Officers Club, Mil. Officers Club (pres. Sea Girt, N.J. 1979—81), Congdon-Overlook Lodge #163 (master), Ret. Officers Assn., Am. Legion. Republican. Roman Catholic. Home: 11 Laurel Ln Morris Plains NJ 07950-3216 Office Phone: 973-267-0067.

PLUGGE, SCOTT DOUGLAS, music educator, saxophonist; b. Shreveport, La., Oct. 23, 1962; s. George Edward and Margaret Plugge; m. Sandra Rochelle Palacios, Aug. 20; children: Christopher, Eric, Lauren. MusB in Performance, Baylor U., 1984; MusM in Performance, Northwestern U., Evanston, Ill., 1985; Mus D in Performance, Northwestern U., 2004. Lectr. saxophone So. Meth. U., Dallas, 1988—91, U. Tex., Arlington, 1988—91, Baylor U., Waco, Tex., 1989—90, DePaul U., Chgo., 1992—94; asst. prof. saxophone Ctrl. Conn. State U., New Britain, 1994—97; assoc. prof. saxophone, dir. Jazz studies Sam Houston State U., Huntsville, Tex., 1997—, grad. music supr., 2000—. Extra saxophone performer Dallas Symphony Orch., 1990—; host, conf. coord. N.Am. Saxophone Alliance, Dallas, 1991; guest artist Concertante d' Chicago, 1993, New Britain Symphony. Co-author: (textbook) American Popular Music, 1997; musician: (recording) Shall We Gather, 2001. Recipient Award for Outstanding Musicianship, Nat. Assn. Jazz Educators, 1984, State Concerto winner, Music Tchrs. Nat. Assn., 1983, Spl. Recognition award, Coll. of Arts and Scis., Sam Houston State U., 2001—02. Mem.: Coll. Music Soc., Tex. Bandmaster Assn., N.Am. Saxophone Alliance, Pi Kappa Lambda. Avocations: tennis, music, soccer, fishing. Office: Sam Houston State Univ Sch of Music PO Box 2208 Huntsville TX 77341-2208 Office Phone: 936-294-1393. Business E-Mail: mus_sdp@shsu.edu.

PLUIMER, EDWARD J. lawyer; b. Rapid City, S.D., 1949; BA cum laude, U. S.D., 1971; JD cum laude, NYU, 1974. Bar: Minn. 1975. Law clk. to Hon. Robert A. Ainsworth, Jr. U.S. Ct. Appeals (5th cir.), 1974-75; ptnr. Dorsey & Whitney, Mpls., 1975—. Mem. Minn. Supreme Ct. ADR Task Force, 1988-92. Editor N.Y. U. Law Rev. Mem. Order of the Coif. Office: Dorsey & Whitney LLP Ste 1500 50 S 6th St Minneapolis MN 55402-1498 E-mail: pluimer.ed@dorseylaw.com.

PLUKE, RICHARD WILLIAM HAY, entomologist, researcher; b. Gweru, Midlands, Zimbabwe, Aug. 15, 1970; s. Christopher Hay and Kay Pluke. BS in Biol. Sci., U. Durham, Eng., 1992; MS in Tropical Entomology, Nottingham U., Sutton, Eng., 1994; PhD in Entomology, U. Fla., Gainesville, 2004. Sci. officer Matopos Rsch. Sta., Bulawayo, Zimbabwe, 1992—93; R & D officer Ciba Bunting, Colchester, England, 1994—95; plant entomologist IICA VSO, Georgetown, Guyana, 1995—98; rsch. entomologist USDA-ARS, Gainesville, Fla., 1999—2000; post-doctoral rschr. U. of Fla., Gainesville, Fla., 2004—. Dir.: (plays) Black Comedy. Grantee, NSF, 2004. Mem.: Soc. Puertorriqueña de Ciencias Agrícolas (assoc.), Entomol. Soc. of Am. (assoc. Travel award 2004), Grupo Unido para Acción Ecológico (assoc.). Achievements include research in botanical pesticide, Guyana; systems in crop protection, Puerto Rico. Avocations: sports, international travel, reading, music. Home: Urb College Park Calle Alcala San Juan PR 00921 Office: Univ Puerto Rico Eea Rio Piedras Botanical Gardens 1193 Calle Guayacan San Juan PR 00926-1118 Personal E-mail: rpluke@hotmail.com. E-mail: rpluke@ufl.edu.

PLUM, FRED, neurologist; b. Atlantic City, Jan. 10, 1924; s. Fred and Frances (Alexander) Plum; m. Susan Butler, Apr. 23, 1990; children from previous marriage: Michael, Christopher, Carol. BA, Dartmouth Coll., 1944, postgrad., 1944—45; MD, Cornell U., 1947, Karolinska Inst., Stockholm, 1982; DSc (hon.), L.I. U., 1990. Resident N.Y. Hosp., 1947—50, fellow, 1950—53. Instr. neurology Sch. Medicine Cornell U., 1950—53, Anne Parrish Titzell prof. neurology, 1963—98, univ. prof., 1998—, chmn. dept. neurology, 1963—98; head neurology sect. U.S. Naval Hosp., St. Albans, NY, 1951—53; from asst. prof. to prof. neurology Sch. Medicine U. Wash., 1953—63; vis. scientist U. Lund, Sweden, 1970—71; vis. physician Rockefeller U. Hosp., 1975—85; assoc. neurosci. rsch. program MIT and Rockefeller U., 1977—87; mem. neurology study sect. NIH, 1964—68; nat. adv. coun. Nat. Inst. Neurol., Communicative Disorders and Stroke, 1984—86; founding mem. McKnight Endowment Fund for Neurosci., 1986, pres., 1986—90. Author (with J.B. Posner): Diagnosis of Stupor and Coma, 1966; author: 3d edit., 1982, Clinical Management of Seizures, 1976, 2d edit., 1983; author: (with others) Cecil Essentials of Medicine, 1986, 3d edit., 1995; editor, contbg. author: Cecil's Textbook of Medicine, 1968, chief editor neurology sect.: Contemporary Neurology series, 1980—96, founding editor: Vols. 1-40, 1966—93, Brain Dysfunction in Metabolic Disorders, 1974, mem. editl. bd.: Archives Neurology, 1958—68, chief editor:, 1972—76; editor: Annals of Neurology, 1977—85; founding editor:, 1986—; editor: Neurology Alert, 1981—; contbr. articles to sci. and profl. jours. Mem.: NAS, Assn. Am. Physicians, Assn. Rsch. Nervous Mental Diseases (pres. 1973, 1987), Am. Soc. Clin. Investigation, Soc. Neurosci., Am. Acad. Neurology (past mem. coun.), Am. Neurol. Assn. (v.p. 1974—75, pres. 1976—77, Jacoby award 1984), Inst. of Medicine, Am. Acad. Arts and Scis., Can., Brit., French, Itatlian, Swiss neurol. socs. (hon.), Alpha Omega Alpha. Achievements include research in conciousness, coma and stroke. Office: Weill-Cornell U Med Coll 525 E 68th St # A565 New York NY 10021-4870 E-mail: frp2005@mail.cornell.edu.

PLUM, KENNETH RAY, state legislator; b. Shenandoah, Va., Nov. 3, 1941; m. Jane M. Meacham, Aug. 9, 1990; children: Timothy R., David W., Helen, Augusta Meacham. BA, Old Dominion U., 1965; MEd, U. Va., 1967. Mem. Va. Ho. of Dels., Richmond, 1978-80, 82—. Mem. Sci. and Tech. Com., Higher Edn. Subcom., Transp. Subcom., Natural Resources Subcom. Appropriations, Corps., Ins. and Banking Com. (co-chair), Conservation and Natural Resources Com., Joint Subcom. Study Restructuring and Potential Changes in the Electirc Utility Industry, Joint Subcom. Studying Needs of Certain Underserved Gifted Student, Joint Subcom. Studying Early Intervention Svcs. for Infants and Toddlers with Disabilities, Joint Subcom. to Study the Future of Va.'s Environment,; chmn. Joint Commn. on Tech. and Sci. Mem. United Christian Parish of Reston (Va.); charter bd. dirs. Va. Literacy Found.; bd. dirs. Arts Coun. Fairfax County, Dem. Party Va., nat. capital area Coun. Boy Scouts Am. Recipient Human Rights award Fairfax County, 1982, Warren G. Stambaugh award forsupport of mental health programs, 1992, Good Guy award Nat. Women's Polit. Caucus, 1992, Outstanding Svc. award Va. Network for Victims and Witnesses of Crime, Inc., 1994, Outstanding Svc. to Children award No. Va. Assn. Edn. Young Children, 1995, Legislator of Yr. Chesapeake Bay Found., 1993, 95, Va. Assn. Soil and Water Conservation Dists., 1996, Pub. Citizen of Yr. award Va. chpt. Nat. Assn. Social Workers, 1995-96, Eco-Hero award Sierra Club, 1996, Legis. Leadership award Va. Ctr. Aging, 1996, Legis. award Va. Literacy Coun., 1996, Tech. Ten Legis. No. Va. Tech. Coun., 1996, 97, 98; named Adult Educator of Yr. Va., 1972, Drug Abuse Prevention Warrior of the Year, 1990, Champion of Children's Health Va. Coalition Children's Health, 1998; chosen to represent Gen. Assembly at Nat. Leadership Inst., 1997. Mem. NEA, Va. Edn. Assn., Fairfax Edn. Assns. Democrat. Office: 2073 Cobblestone Ln Reston VA 20191-4039 E-mail: Kenplum@aol.com.

PLUM, WILLIAM J. lawyer; s. W. and M. Plum. JD, Calif. Western Sch. Law, San Diego, 1982—85. Bar: Hawaii 1988. Atty. Hawaii Law Group LLP, Honolulu, 2003—; ptnr. Law Office Of William J. Plum, A Law Corp., Honolulu, 1992—. Bd. dirs. Consumer Credit Counseling of Hawaii, Honolulu, 1995—2003. Mem.: Hawaii State Bar Assn. (dir., collection law sect.). Avocation: water-skiing. Office: Hawaii Law Group LLP Pauahi Tower 1001 Bishop St Ste 1360 Honolulu HI 96813

PLUMB, RUSSELL H. business company executive; Mng. dir. Tunstall Cons., 1987-90; sr. mgr. corp. fin. group Ernst & Young, 1990-94; v.p. fin. and adminstrn., CFO, treas. Serologicals Corp., Atlanta, 1994—. Office: Serologicals Corp 5655 Spalding Dr Norcross GA 30092-2504

PLUMER, ALVIN H. (BUD), realtor; b. Phila., Sept. 10, 1925; s. Louis J. and Mary B. Plumer; m. Pearl Plumer, Dec. 24, 1950; 1 child, Mona Ann. BS, Temple U., 1947. Pres. Plumer & Assocs., Inc., Phila., 1947—. Pres. South Phila. Bd. Realtors, 1969-70; Hollywood Savs. Assn., Phila., 1980-90; v.p. Phila. Bd. Realtors, 1969-70. Vice-chmn. South St. Headhouse Dist., Phila., 1998, treas., 1999-2002; pres. Center City Coun. Realtors, 1985-87. Named to South St. Hall of Fame, South St. Headhouse Dist., 2000. Mem. Phila. Assn. Realtors (chmn. profl. stds. 1992-2002, Hall of Fame award 1999). Republican. Office: Plumer & Assocs 226 South St Philadelphia PA 19147-2310

PLUMERI, JOSEPH JAMES, II, financial executive; b. Trenton, N.J., July 7, 1943; s. Samuel J. and Josephine (Vaccaro) P.; m. Nancy Plumeri, June 18, 1966; children: Christian, Jay Michael, Leslie BA in History, Coll. of William and Mary, 1966; postgrad., N.Y. Law Sch., 1967-69. Trainee Carter Berlind & Weill, N.Y.C., 1968-69; stockbroker CBWL-Hayden Stone, N.Y.C., 1968-73; br. mgr. Shearson Hayden Stone, Fort Lauderdale, Fla., 1973-74, exec. v.p. western region San Francisco, 1974-81; sr. exec. v.p. Shearson Lehman Hutton, N.Y.C., 1981—, dir. mktg. and nat. sales, 1981-89, dir. domestic br. div., 1990-94; vice chmn., group CEO Travelers Group, Inc., N.Y.C., 1994-2000; chmn., CEO Willis Group, Ltd., Jacksonville, Fla., 2000—. Bd. dirs., trustee endowment assn. Coll. William and Mary Mem.: Columbus (N.Y.C.). Avocations: golf, reading. Home: 1461 Martine Ave Scotch Plains NJ 07076-2501

PLUMEZ, JEAN PAUL, advertising agency executive, consultant; b. N.Y.C., Oct. 31, 1939; s. Jean Paul and Marie Antoinette (Compagne) P.; m. Jacqueline Hornor, Feb. 20, 1965; children: Jean Paul, Nicole. BS in Chem. Engring., BA in Chemistry, Bucknell U., 1962; MBA, U. Pa., 1968. Product engr. Mobil Oil Co., Paulsboro, N.J., 1965-66; account mgr. Dancer Fitzgerald, Sample, Inc., N.Y.C., 1968-86, exec. v.p., 1979-86; pres. Leadership on Paper, Larchmont, N.Y., 1986—; founding ptnr. The Right Direction, 1987—. Served to capt. Signal Corps U.S. Army, 1962-64. Mem. Alpha Chi Sigma, Beta Gamma Sigma, Kappa Delta Rho Clubs: Larchmont Yacht, Wharton of N.Y., Princeton of N.Y. Home and Office: 90 Beechtree Dr Larchmont NY 10538-1202 Office Phone: 914-833-0332.

PLUMMER, AMANDA, actress; b. N.Y.C., Mar. 23, 1957; d. Christopher and Tammy (Grimes) Plummer. Student, Middlebury Coll. Has appeared in theatre roles: A Taste of Honey, 1981; A Month in the Country, 1980; N.Y.C. debut: Artichoke, 1979; The Glass Menagarie, 1983-84; motion picture debut: Cattle Annie and Little Britches, 1981, The World According to Garp, 1982, Daniel, 1983, Hotel New Hampshire, 1984, Static, 1985, Made in Heaven, 1987, Prisoners of Inertia, 1989, Joe Versus the Volcano, 1990, The Fisher King, 1991, Freejack, 1992, The Lounge People, 1992, So I Married an Axe Murderer, 1993, Needful Things, 1993 (Saturn award, 1994), Pax, 1994, Nostradamus, 1994, Pulp Fiction, 1994, The Final Cut, 1995, The Prophecy, 1995, Search and Destroy, 1995, Butterfly Kiss, 1995, Hysteria, 1996, Freeway, 1996, Dead Girl, 1996, American Perfect, 1997, Drunks, 1997, A Simple Wish, 1997, You Can Thank Me Later, 1998, October 22, 1998, L.A. Without a Map, 1998, Elizabeth Jane, 1998, Great Sex, 1999, Eight and a Half Women, 1999, The Million Dollar Hotel, 2000, Seven Days to Live, 2000, Triggermen, 2002, Ken Park, 2002, TMA, 2002, Pulp Fiction: The Facts, 2002, My Life Without Me, 2002, The Last Angel, 2002; (TV movies) The Dollmaker, 1984, True Blue, 1989, Kojak: None So Blind, 1990, Sidney Sheldon's The Sands of Time, 1992, Last Light, 1993, Whose Child Is This? The War for Baby Jessica, 1993, Under the Piano, 1995, Don't Look Back, 1996, The Right to Remain Silent, 1996, (voice) Hercules, 1997, Shadow Realm, 2002, Get a Clue, 2002, Broadway: The Golden Age, by the Legends Who Were There, 2002; other theatre roles include: Agnes of God (Tony, Drama Desk award, Outer Circle Critics award), 1982; A Lie of the Mind, 1985; TV appearances include Hallmark Hall of Fame: Miss Rose White (Emmy award supporting actress, 1992), TV series L.A. Law, Moonlighting, The Equalizer, The Outer Limits, (Emmy award best guest actress, 1996). Office: Innovative Artists Ste 2850 1999 Avenue Of The Stars Los Angeles CA 90067-4612

PLUMMER, CHRISTOPHER (ORME) (ARTHUR PLUMMER), actor; b. Toronto, Ont., Can., Dec. 13, 1929; s. John and Isabella Mary (Abbott) P.; m. Tammy Grimes (div.); 1 child, Amanda; m. Particia Andrew Lewis, May 4, 1962 (div.); m. Elaine Taylor. Ed. pub. and pvt. schs., Can.; pupil, Iris Warren, C. Herbertcasari. Stage debut in The Rivals with Can. Repertory Theatre, 1950; Broadway debut in Starcross Story, 1954; London debut in Becket, 1961; leading actor Am. Shakespeare Theatre, Stratford, Conn., 1955, Royal Shakespeare Co., London and Stratford, Avon, Eng., 1961-62, Stratford (Ont.) Shakespeare Festival, 1956, 57, 58, 60, 62, 67, Nat. Theatre Co., London; radio roles include Shakespeare, Canada; plays include Home is the Hero, 1954, Twelfth Night, 1954, 70-71, Dark is Light Enough, The Lark, Julius Caesar, The Tempest, 1955, Henry VI, 1956, Hamlet, 1957, Winter's Tale, 1958, Much Ado About Nothing, 1958, J.B., 1958, King John, 1960, Romeo and Juliet, 1960, Richard III, 1961, Arturo Ui, 1963, The Royal Hunt of the Sun, 1965, Antony and Cleopatra, 1967, Danton's Death, 1971, Amphitryon 38, 1971; (musicals) Cyrano, 1973, The Good Doctor, 1973, Love and Master Will, 1975; Othello, 1982, Macbeth, 1988, No Man's Land, 1993, Barrymore, 1996 (Tony award for best actor in a play, 1997), King Lear, 2004 (Tony nom.

best actor in a play, 2004); made TV debut 1953; TV prodns. include Little Moon of Alban, Johnny Belinda, 1958, Cyrano de Bergerac, 1962, Oedipus Rex, After the Fall, 1974, The Doll's House, The Prince and the Pauper, Prisoner of Zenda, Hamlet at Elsinore, BBC, 1964, Time Remembered, Capt. Brassbound's Conversion, The Shadow Box, 1981, The Thorn Birds, 1983, Little Gloria-Happy at Last, A Hazard of Hearts, 1987, Crossings, 1986, Danielle Steele's Secrets, 1992, Liar's Edge, 1992; star TV series The Moneychangers, 1977, Harrison Bergeron, 1995, We the Jury, 1996, The Conspiracy of Fear, 1996; made film debut in 1957; films include Stage Struck, 1957, Wind Across the Everglades, 1958, The Fall of the Roman Empire, 1963, Inside Daisy Clover, 1965, Sound of Music, 1965, Triple Cross, 1967, Nobody Runs Forever, 1969, The Battle of Britain, 1969, The Royal Hunt of the Sun, 1969, Lock up your Daughters, 1969, The Phyx, 1970, Waterloo, 1971, The Man Who Would Be King, 1975, The Return of the Pink Panther, 1975, Conduct Unbecoming, 1975, International Velvet, 1978, Murder By Decree, 1979, Starcrash, 1979, The Silent Partner, 1979, Hanover Street, 1979, Somewhere in Time, 1980, Eye witness, 1981, The Disappearance, 1981, The Amateur, 1982, Dreamscape, 1984, Ordeal by Innocence, 1984, Lily in Love, 1985, The Boss' Wife, 1986, The Boy In Blue, 1986, An American Tail, 1986 (voice), Souvenir, 1987, Dragnet, 1987, Light Years (voice), 1988, Where the Heart Is, 1989, Fire Head, 1991, Star Trek: VI: The Undiscovered Country, 1991, Rock a Doodle, 1992 (voice), Malcolm X, 1992, Wolf, 1994, Dolores Claiborne, 1994, Twelve Monkeys, 1995, Skeletons, 1996, The Arrow, 1997, Hidden Agenda, 1998, The Clown at Midnight, 1998, Winchell (TV), 1998, Blackheart, The Insider, 1999, All the Fine Lines, 1999, Celebrate the Century (TV mini-series), 1999, The Dinosaur Hunter, 2000, Dracula 2000, 2000, Nuremberg (TV mini-series), 2000, American Tragedy (TV mini-series), 2000, A Beautiful Mind, 2001, Nicholas Nickleby, 2002, Ararat, 2002. Decorated companion Order of Can., 1968; recipient Theatre World award, 1955, Evening Standard award, 1961, Delia Austrian medal, 1973, 2 Drama Desk awards, 1973, 82, Antoinette Perry award, 1974, Emmy award Nat. Acad. TV Arts and Scis., 1977, Genie award, Can., 1980, Golden Badge of Honor, Austria, 1982, Maple Leaf award Nat. Acad. Arts and Letters Mem. Theatre's Hall of Fame. Office: c/o Lou Pitt The Pitt Group 9465 Wilshire Blvd Ste 480 Beverly Hills CA 90212-2612*

PLUMMER, GAYTHER L(YNN), ecologist, climatologist, researcher; b. Indpls., Jan. 27, 1925; s. Conley L. and Rowena H. (Huber) P.; m. H. Eileen Barr, June 3, 1950. BS, Butler U., 1948; MS, Kans. State U., 1950; PhD, Purdue U., 1954. Instr. biology Knox Coll., Galesburg, Ill., 1950-51; naturalist Ind. Dept. Conservation, various locations, 1947-52; asst. prof. biology Antioch Coll., Yellow Springs, Ohio, 1954-55; prof. botany U. Ga., Athens, 1955-95, state climatologist, 1978-95. Rsch. fellow Oak Ridge (Tenn.) Inst. Nuclear Studies, 1958-62. Author: Georgia Weather Watchers, 1991, Georgia Temperatures, 1993, Georgia's Climate During 20th Century, 2001, U.S. National Climate During 20th Century, 2001; cartographer 160 vegetation maps of Ga., 1972-74; editor Ga. Jour. Sci., 1977-84; contbr. articles to profl. jours. 2d lt. USAAF, 1943-46. Fellow AAAS; mem. Ecol. Soc. Am., Ind. Acad. Sci., Ga. Acad. Sci., Soil Sci. Soc. Am., Crop Sci. Soc., Agron. Soc. Am., Sigma Xi, Phi Kappa Phi. Achievements include research in droughts in S.E. U.S. relating to astrogeophysical processes via geomagnetics; lightning history in Piedmont for over 70 million years etched in Stone Mountain granite. Office: Ga Climatology Assoc Inc 995 Timothy Rd Athens GA 30606-3838

PLUMMER, JACK MOORE, psychologist; b. Galveston, Tex., Apr. 19, 1940; s. Jack Moore and Sarah Carroll (Cochran) P.; m. Rose Marie Taylor, July 22, 1960; children: Cynthia Marie, Edward Moore, Elizabeth Anne, Sarah Lorraine, Jack Moore. BA, St. Mary's U., 1962; MS, Trinity U., 1968; PhD, Tex. Tech. U., 1969; AAS in Criminal Justice, Garland County Community Coll., 1978. Psychologist Okla. rehab. div. Okla. State Reformatory, Granite, 1968-69; dir. tng. Ark. Rehab. Rsch. and Tng. Ctr., Hot Springs, 1970-71; pvt. practice psychology, Hot Springs, 1971—; exec. dir. Plummer Assocs. for Consultation and Tng., 1982—; dir. Ark. Behavioral Svcs. Clinic, 1983—; exec. officer Tng. Inst. for Edn. in Security, 1983—; clin. dir. Transpersonal Psychology Inst., Pine Bluff, Ark., 1989-91, behavioral medicine, 1995—, hosp. affliate allied health, diabetes mgmt. and edn., diabetes rsch.; psychol. cons. to Rehab. Svcs., Dept. Correction, Probation and Parole Div., 1971-98, also to physicians, attys., cts., law enforcement agys.; instr. Garland County C.C., Hot Springs, 1973—; continuing edn. instr. nursing degree program Coll. St. Francis, Joliet, Ill., 1979-86; cons. Parents Without Ptnrs. Mem. bd. L.P.N. nurse program Ouachita Vocat.-Tech. Sch., Hot Springs, 1979-85. Fellow Ark. Psychol. Assn.; mem. Ark. Psychol. Assn. (chmn. fellow status rev. com. 1980, 81, chmn. profl. standards rev. com. 1982, 83), Hot Springs Psychol. Assn. (pres. 1979, 80), Internat. Soc. for Study Symbols, Elks, Lions. Democrat. Roman Catholic. Contbr. articles to profl. jours., chpt. in Handbook of Measurement and Evaluation in Rehabilitation. Address: 614 Ridgeview Dr Hot Springs National Park AR 71901-7901

PLUMMER, JASON STEVEN (JAKE PLUMMER), professional football player; b. Boise, Idaho, Dec. 19, 1974; Student, Ariz. State U. Quarterback Ariz. Cardinals, Phoenix, 1997—2003, Denver Broncos, 2003—. Named to NFL Pro-Bowl, 1997—2003. Office: Denver Broncos 13655 Broncos Pkwy Englewood CO 80112

PLUMMER, LAURA A. music educator; b. Alton, Ill., Dec. 24, 1966; d. David and JoAnn I Wilkinson; m. Todd A. Plummer, July 24, 1993; 1 child, Alyssa. MusB, Eastern Ill. U., 1989; M in music edn., instrumental conducting, U. Okla., 1991. Cert. tching. Ill. Orch. dir. Moline Sch. Dist., Ill., 1991—95, Alton Sch. Dist., Ill., 1995—. Conductor St. Louis Suburban 7th and 8th Honor Orch., Mo., 2004, Ala. All State String, 2003; coach, strings ISYM Univ. of Ill., 1994, 96, 2002. Bd. mem. and Family Selection Chair Habitat for Humanity, Alton, Ill., 1998—99; bd. mem. and section coach Alton Youth Symphony, 1997—2002. Mem.: Music Educators Nat. Conf., Nat. Sch. Orch, Assn., Am. String Tchr. Assn. Methodist. Office: Alton High Sch 2200 College Ave Alton IL 62002

PLUMMER, LEONE POINDEXTER, marriage and family therapist, nursing educator, nurse practitioner; b. Amarillo, Tex., Jan. 25, 1953; d. Hershel Clayton and Ellen Gertrude (Hadba) Poindexter; m. Dennis Patrick Plummer, May 20, 1978; 1 child, Cassandra Lanelle. RN diploma, NW Tex. Hosp. Sch. Nursing, Amarillo, 1975; BSN, West Tex. State U., 1978, M in Nursing, 1980; PhD, Tex. Tech U., 1985. Lic. profl. counselor; cert. respiratory therapist. From nurse critical care to nursing supr. NW Tex. Hosp., Amarillo, 1975-80; pvt. practice Amarillo, 1985—; dir. grad. nursing, assoc. prof. West Tex. State U., Canyon, 1986-92; statis. cons. Amarillo Cardiovascular Surgeons, 1992-95; geriatric and family nurse practitioner Bapt. St. Anthony Health Sys., Amarillo, 1996—. Cons. Vets. Affairs Med. Ctr., Big Springs, Tex., 1988-92, Harrington Cancer Ctr., Amarillo, 1989-92. Contbr. articles to profl. jours. Mem. Assn. Marriage and Family Therapy (workshop presenter), Nat. Coun. Family Rels. (workshop presenter), Tex. Nursing Assn. (nominating com. 1987-89), Sigma Theta Tau (pres. elect 1990-92, treas. 1989-90, rec. sec. 1987-88). Avocations: restoring antiques, needlecrafts, piano, reading, decorating.

PLUMMER, MICHAEL KENNETH, financial consultant; b. Jacksonville, Fla., Apr. 24, 1954; s. Kenneth Albert and Edith Lorraine (O'Brien) P.; m. Amy Forté, 1992; children: Brian Michael, Daniel James. BBA in Econs., U. North Fla., 1976; MS in Real Estate, Ga. State U., 1993, postgrad., 1993—. Econ. analyst Barnett Banks of Fla., Jacksonville, 1976-78; exec. v.p. Home Owners Warranty Corp., Jacksonville, 1978-80; market analyst Plantec Corp., Jacksonville, 1980-81; assoc. Laventhol & Horwath, Miami and Denver, 1981-84; sr. mgr., nat. coord. corp. real estate consulting svcs. KPMG Peat Marwick (formerly Peat, Marwick, Main & Co.), Atlanta, 1984-91; sr. mng. dir. Instnl. Real Estate Advisors, Inc., Atlanta, 1991—. Mem. Gov.'s Econ. ADv. Com., Fla., 1982-84; econ. cons. Atlanta com. for 1996 Olympic Games; mem. steering com. Mt. Pisgah Charter Sch. Fla. Bankers Assn. scholar; named Eagle Scout Boy Scouts Am., 1972. Mem. Urban Land Inst., Country Club of the south (mem. fin. com.). Republican. Methodist. Avocations: sailing, skiing. Office: Ire Advisors Inc Ste 170 33 Technology Pkwy S Norcross GA 32097 also: 8030 Pebble Creek Ln Ponte Vedra Beach FL 32082

PLUMMER, ORA BEATRICE, nursing educator, trainer; b. Mexia, Tex., May 25, 1940; d. Macie Idella (Echols); childeren: Kimberly, Kevin, Cheryl. BSN, U. N.Mex., 1961; MS in Nursing Edn., UCLA, 1966. Nurse's aide Bataan Meml. Meth. Hosp., Albuquerque, 1958-60, staff nurse, 1961-62, 67-68; staff nurse, charge nurse, relief supr. Hollywood (Calif.) Cmty. Hosp., 1962-64; instr. U. N.Mex. Coll. Nursing, Albuquerque, 1968-69; sr. instr. U. Colo. Sch. Nursing, Denver, 1971-74, asst. prof., 1974-76; staff assoc. III Western Interstate Commn. for Higher Edn., Boulder, Colo., 1976-78; DON Garden Manor Nursing Home, Lakewood, Colo., 1978-79, nurse surveyor, cons., 1979-87; ednl. coord. Colo. Dept. Health, Denver, 1987—96. Active in faculty devel. Colo. Cluster of Schs.; bd. dirs. Domestic Violence Initiative, 2000—. Contbr. articles to profl. jours. Mem. adv. bd. Affiliated Children's and Family Svcs., 1977; mem. Colo. Instnl. Child Abuse and Neglect Adv. Com., 1984-92; trustee Colo. Acad., 1990-96; mem. planning com. State Wide Conf. on Black Health Concerns, 1977; mem. staff devel. com. Western Interstate Commn. for Higher Edn., 1978, mem. minority affairs com., 1978, mem. coordinating com. for baccalaureate program, 1971-76; active in minority affairs, U. Colo. Med. Ctr., 1971-72; mem. ednl. resources com., pub. rels. com., rev. com. for reappointment, promotion and tenure U. Colo. Sch. Nursing, 1971-76, mem. regulatory tng. com., 1989-93; mem. gerontol. adv. com. Met. State Coll., 1989-94; mem. expert panel long term care tng. manual Health Care Financing Adminstrn., Balt., 1989; mem. employee diversity com. Colo. Dept. Health, 1989-96; mem. Nurse Del. to Cuba, 2000. Nominee Nightingale award, Colo., 2003. Avocations: public speaking, training. Office: 4300 Cherry Creek South Dr Denver CO 80246-1523

PLUMMER, PATRICIA LYNNE MOORE, chemistry and physics educator; b. Tyler, Tex., Feb. 26; d. Robert Lee and Jewell Ovelia (Jones) Moore; m. Otho Raymond Plummer, Apr. 10, 1965; children: Patrick William Otho, Christina Elisa Lynne. BA, Tex. Christian U., Ft. Worth, Tex., 1960; postgrad., U. N.C., 1960-61; PhD, U. Tex., Austin, 1964; grad., Bryn Mawr Summer Inst., 1992. Instr., Welch postdoctoral fellow U. Tex., Austin, 1964-66; postdoctoral fellow Dept. Chemistry, U. Ark., Fayetteville, 1966-68; rsch. assoc. Grad. Ctr., Cloud Phys. Rsch., Rolla, Mo., 1968-73; asst. prof. physics U. Mo., Rolla, 1973-77; assoc. dir. Grad. Ctr. Cloud Phys. Rsch., 1977-79, sr. investigator, 1980-85; assoc. prof. physics U. Mo., 1977-85, prof. dept. chemistry and physics, 1986—. Mem. internat. sci. com. Symposium on Chemistry and Physics of Ice, 1982—, vice chair, 1996—; nat. judge Siemens-Westinghouse Sci. Projects, 1999—. Assoc. editor Jour. of Colloid and Interface Sci., 1980-83; contbr. articles to profl. jours., chpts. to books. Rsch. grantee IBM, 1990-92, Air Force Office Rsch., 1989-91, NSF, 1976-86, NASA, 1973-78; Air Force Office Rsch. summer fellow, 1988, Bryn Mawr Summer Inst., 1992, Faculty fellow Cherry Emerson Ctr. for Sci. Computation, Emory U., 1998-99. Mem. Am. Chem. Soc., Am. Phys. Soc., Am. Geophys. Union, Sigma Xi (past pres., UM-Rolla chptr.). Democrat. Baptist. Avocations: sailing, gardening, tennis, photography. Office: U Mo 201 Physics Bldg Columbia MO 65211-0001 Fax: (573) 882-4195. E-mail: plummerp@missouri.edu.

PLUMMER, PAUL JAMES, energy executive; b. Scottsbluff, Nebr., Aug. 3, 1946; s. Virgil Frank and Helen Louise (Hultberg) Plummer; m. Pamela Lee Purdom, June 26, 1976; 1 child, Brittany Lane. BA, U. Nebr., 1968; postgrad., Platte Coll., 1974-75; MBA, U. Iowa, 1982. With Gen. Tel. Co. of the Midwest, 1968-82, divsn. traffic supr., 1969-75, divsn. traffic mgr. Columbia, Mo., 1975-78, labor rels. adminstr. Grinnell, Iowa, 1978-79, labor rels. mgr., 1979-82, compensation and svcs. mgr., 1982; staff specialist customer svc. GTE Svc. Corp., Stamford, Conn., 1982-83, group specialist cusotmer svc., 1983-84, customer svcs. mgr., 1984-87, ops. support planning mgr., 1987-90, mgr. strategic planning telephone ops. Irving, Tex., 1989-95; mgr. bus. devel. GTE Intelligent Network Svcs., Inc., 1995-96, group product devel. mgr. Vertical Markets, 1996-97; pres., dir., CEO Cytware Corp., Bedford, Tex., 1997-99; v.p. A-Net Consulting, Inc., 1998-2000; pres., CEO I-Mgmt. Svcs. Ltd., Colleyville, Tex., 2000—01; group product delivery exec. TXU Energy, Dallas, 2001—04; cons. Capgemini Energy, Dallas, 2004—. Vol. Nat. Marrow Donor Program; active Boy Scouts Am.; membership com. mem. North Tex. Tech. Coun.; vol. Tex. Scholar's Program; chmn. citizen's adv. com. Grapevine-Colleyville Ind. Sch. Dist., 1989—93; pres. parent-tchr. club St. Vincent Episcopal Sch., 1993—95. Mem.: Pers. Mgmt. Assn. Columbia (exec. bd. dirs., 1st v.p. 1975—78), Ind. Telephone Pioneer Assn., Am. Assn. Pers. Adminstrn., Brookmeadows Homeowner's Assn. (pres.), Elks, Optimists Club (past pres. Columbus, Nebr., lt. gov. Nebr. 1973—74). Episcopalian. Home: 2808 Meadowview Dr Colleyville TX 76034-4753 Office: Capgemini Energy 1601 Bryan St Dallas TX 75201 E-mail: pplummer@bigplanet.com.

PLUMMER, RISQUE WILSON, retired lawyer; b. Mobile, Ala., Oct. 13, 1910; s. Frederick Harvey and Caroline (Wilson) P.; m. Constance M. Burch, Feb. 21, 1939; children: Risque Wilson Jr., Richard Randolph. JD, U. Va., 1933. Bar: Va. 1932, Md. 1938. Atty. in charge of litigation Balt. Regional Office HOLC, 1933-38; pvt. practice law, 1938—; counsel U.S. Maritime Commn., 1942; partner firm Griffin & Plummer, 1951-73; counsel O'Connor, Preston, Glenn & Smith, Balt., 1979—; ret. Prof. law Am. Inst. Banking, 1948—52; chmn. spkrs. com. ARC Blood Bank for Md. Contbr. articles to profl. jours. Exec. sec. Md. Commn. on Anti-Subversive Activities, 1949-50; co-founder, pres. Roland Park Baseball Leagues, Inc., 1956-57; co-founder, pres. Wyndhurst Improvement Assn., Inc., 1957-59; mem. Selective Service Adv. Bd., 1940-42. Served to lt. USNR, 1943-46, ATO, PTO, Philippines Area Ops.; gunnery officer, WWII. Fellow Internat. Acad. Law and Sci.; mem. ABA (council sect. of family law 1966-70), Md. Bar Assn. (council sect. of family and juvenile law 1966-70), Md. Assn. Trial Lawyers (gov. 1966-67), Bar Assn. Baltimore City (com. on grievances 1966-69, chmn. com. on profl. ethics 1969-70, exec. com. 1969-70), Am. Judicature Soc., Md. Health Claims Arbitration Commn. (chair arbitration panels), Am. Contract Bridge League (Silver life master, cert. dir., author The Small Club), Soc. Colonial Wars, Sons of the Revolution, Delta Tau Delta (pres. U. Va. chpt.), Phi Delta Phi, Hon. Law Soc., Baltimore Country Club. Episcopalian. Home: Highfield House Unit 512 4000 N Charles St Baltimore MD 21218-1760

PLUMMER, VAL J. education educator, chaplain; b. Worcester, Mass., Oct. 7, 1939; d. William Nelson and Mary Mildred (Foley) Plummer. BA in Psychology, Columbia Coll. Mo., 1977; BA, U. N. Colo.; MA in Orgnl. Mgmt., U. Phoenix, 1997; grad., Humanist Inst., N.Y.C., 2001. Substitute tchr., Tex., 1993—94, 1994—95; prof. Cochise Coll., Sierra Vista, Ariz., 1997—. Chaplain Hospice Family Care, Sierra Vista, Ariz., 1997—98; EO advisor US Army Intelligence Ctr., Fort Huachuca, Ariz., 1983—85; substitute tchr., Ariz., 1994—95; bd. dirs. Humanist Inst., N.Y.C. Contbr. articles publ. to profl. jour. Sfc U.S. Army, 1973—93. Mem.: Humanist Soc. of Friends, Am. Humanist Assn., Hemlock Soc. Cochise County (chair). Am. Humanist Assn. Avocations: piano, writing. Home: 4685 Paseo Arruza Sierra Vista AZ 85635 Office: Cochise Coll Sierra Vista AZ 85635

PLUMMER, WILLIAM TORSCH, optical physicist; b. Balt. s. William Edwin and Margaret Fairchild (Torsch) P.; m. Susan Bowman White, Sept. 9, 1961; children: Kathryn, Hilleary. BA, Johns Hopkins U., 1960, PhD, 1965. Lens designer Muffoletto Optical Co., Towson, Md., 1963-69; sr. dir. optical engrng. Polaroid Corp., Cambridge, Mass., 1969—2001; pres. WTP Optics, Inc., Concord, Mass., 2002—. Asst. prof. astronomy U. Mass., Amherst, 1967-69; vis. prof. Tufts U., Medford, Mass., 1984-88; sr. lectr. MIT, 1991-2004. Capt. USAR, 1965-67. Recipient David Richardson medal, 1980, Joseph Fraunhofer award, 1997, Robert M. Burley prize, 1997. Fellow Soc. Photo-Optical Instrumentation Engrs., Nat. Speleological Soc., Optical Soc. Am.; mem. Nat. Acad. Engring., Phi Beta Kappa. Achievements include central optical and opto-mechanical developments in Polaroid SX-70 folding SLR camera, model 600 LMS camera, spectra camera, captiva camera, and in laser-based printing devices; implemented new concepts for precision in high-volume manufacture. Home: 129 Arena Ter Concord MA 01742-4413 E-mail: plummew@yahoo.com.

PLUMPTRE, TIM, think-tank executive; Founding pres. Inst. On Governance, Ottawa, Canada, 1990—, mng. dir. Adj. prof. Sch. Pub. Policy and Adminstrn. Carleton U.; spkr. in field; cons. in field. Author: Beyond the Bottom Line: Management in Government, 1988. Office: Inst Governance 122 Clarence St Ottawa ON Canada K1N 5P6*

PLUNKET, DANIEL CLARK, pediatrician, department chairman; b. Birmingham, Ala., May 7, 1929; s. Henry Clark and Carolyn Clark (Langford) P.; m. Lillian C. Barrington, Dec. 31, 1971; children: Dennis, Beth, Ann, Brenda, Scott. BS, Emory U., 1949, MD, 1952. Diplomate Am. Bd. Pediatrics. Intern Med. Coll. Va. Hosp., Richmond, 1952-53, resident in pediatrics, 1953-54, Tripler Army Med. Center, Honolulu, 1958-59, Walter Reed Army Inst., 1962-64; pediatrician, pediatric hematologist/oncologist acad. medicine, chief pediatric service William Beaumont Gen. Hosp., El Paso, Tex., 1959-62; commd. 1st lt. U.S. Army, 1955, advanced through grades to col., 1967; asst. chief dept. pediatrics Letterman Army Med. Center, San Francisco, 1964-65; chmn. dept. pediatrics Fitzsimons Army Med. Center, Denver, 1965-75; prof. pediat. U. Okla. Coll. Medicine, Tulsa, 1975-2000; sr. assoc. dean for clin. affairs U. Okla. Health Scis. Ctr., Tulsa, 1993-2000; chmn. dept. pediat. U. Okla. Coll. Medicine, Tulsa, 1975-96. Clin. prof. pediatrics U. Colo., Denver, 1974-75. Mem. adv. chmn. March of Dimes, Tulsa chpt., 1975-92; bd. dirs. ARC, Tulsa chpt., 1981—. Decorated Legion of Merit; Walter Reed Inst. Research fellow hematology and research, 1962-64 Mem. AMA, cad. Pediatrics, Am. Pediatric Soc., Am. Soc. Hematology. Episcopalian. Home: 2436 E 33rd St Tulsa OK 74105-2316 Fax: 918-742-2046. E-mail: dan5729@aol.com.

PLUNKET, DOLORES, art and archaeology educator; b. Chgo., Sept. 2, 1916; d. John Nagoda and Evangeline Kompare; m. John T. Plunket, July 15, 1944; children: Lucy Silver, Robert, John T. Jr., Patricia. BS, U. Ill., 1937; MA in Pre-Colombian Art, Nat. U. Mexico, Mexico City, 1975. V.p. Mexican-N.Am. Cultural Inst., Mexico City, 1985-88; dir. lecture series Selby Libr., Sarasota, Fla., 1992-96; lectr. in field. Co-author: (with A.R. L'huillier) Vision del Mundo Maya, 1978; editor Gardening in the Federal District, 1986; contbr. articles to profl. jours. V.p. Friends Selby Libr., 1992-95; pres. Mexico City Garden Club, 1985; bd. dirs. Am. Soc. Mexico, 1986-88. Home: 1301 N Tamiami Trail apt 406 Sarasota FL 34236-2423 E-mail: jplunket@aol.com.

PLUNKETT, JACK WILLIAM, writer, publisher; b. Dallas, May 17, 1950; s. Ivan Wayne and Waltina Lee (Roark) P.; m. Lynn Ann Richards (div.); 1 child, Jack W. Plunkett Jr.; m. Mary Lee Hartfelder, Dec. 8, 1972 (div.); children: Altus W., Robert L.; m. Martha Menefee Burgher, Oct. 7, 2000. Pres. Plunkett Properties Corp., Dallas, 1968-74; ind. mktg. cons. Dallas, 1974-83; mgr. ptnr. Brown-Plunkett, Waxahachie, Tex., 1983—; CEO, pub. Plunkett Rsch. Ltd., Houston, Tex., 1986—. Cons. Houston Symphony, 1996-97, The Odyssey House, Houston, 1997—. Author: The Almanac of American Employers, 1985, 8th edit., 2004, Plunkett's Health Care Industry Almanac, 1995, 7th edit., 2004, Plunkett's InfoTech Industry Almanac, 1995, 5th edit., 2004, Plunkett's Financial Services Industry Almanac, 1996, 4th edit., 2004, Plunkett's Retail Industry Almanac, 1996, 5th edit., 2004, Plunkett's Entertainment and Media Industry Almanac, 1998, 3d edit., 2002, Plunkett's Energy Industry Almanac, 1999, 3d edit., 2003, Plunkett's Telecommunications Industry Almanac, 2000, 3d edit., 2003, Plunkett's E-Commerce and Internet Business Almanac, 2000, 3d edit., 2003, Plunkett's Engineering and Research Industry Almanac, 2000, 2d edit., 2003, Plunkett's Biotech and Genetics Industry Almanac, 2001, 3d edit., 2003, Plunckett's Consulting Industry Almanac, 2003, Plunckett's Real Estate & Construction Industry Alamanac, 2003. Chmn. Mayor's Libr. Fundraising Com., Boerne, Tex., 1988-89; founding pres. Greater Boerne Area Econ. Devel. Corp., 1986-87; dir. Boerne Area Cmty. Ctr., 1983-86; area chmn. Lamar Smith for Congress, Boerne, 1986; bd. dirs. Boerne Econ. Devel. Coun., 1992-94, Galveston Hist. Found., 1996--, Sch. of Nursing, U. Tex. Med. Br., 1996—, Sch. of Bus., U. of Houston Downtown Campus, 2001—, Strand Theater, 1996—; trustee Galveston County United Way, 1996-97; bd. dirs. Houston Symphony Orch., 1999-2000; mem. Dickens on the Strand 25th Ann. Com., 1997-98; v.p. Houston Symphony Ptnrs., 1997-98, pres.-elect, 1998-99, pres., 1999-2000; founding pres. Tex. Entrepreneurs Exch., 2000—. Recipient Houston's Singular Best award Cystic Fibrosis Found., 1997, Outstanding Acad. Book of the Yr. award Choice Mag. Editors, 1996; named outstanding chmn. Boy Scouts Am., l983, Cmty. Vol. of Yr., Boerne Area C. of C., 1989; elected to Knights of Momus, 1998. Mem. Rotary (pres. Boerne chpt. 1988-89), The Centurions, Knights of Maximillian. Republican. Office: Plunkett Rsch Ltd PO Box 541737 Houston TX 77254-1737

PLUNKETT, JOSEPH CHARLES, electrical engineer, consultant; b. Dec. 3, 1933; s. Harold D. and Lorraine (Lewis) Plunkett. BSEE, U. Tenn., 1966; MSEE, Ga. Inst. Tech., 1973; PhD, Tex. A&M U., 1978. Registered profl. engr., Mass. Devel. engr. Martin Marietta Co., Orlando, Fla., 1966—69; rsch. engr. Raytheon Co., Wayland, Mass., 1969—71, IIT Rsch. Inst., Annapolis, Md., 1971—72, Tex. A&M U., College Station, 1974—77; assoc. prof. elec. engring. Calif. State U., Fresno, 1977—80, prof., 1980—93, prof. emeritus, 1993—, chmn. dept., 1980—84, 1989—92. Cons. in field. Contbr. articles to profl. jours. Capt. Ordnance Corps USAR, 1958—66. Mem.: Tau Beta Pi, Eta Kappa Nu. Republican. Mem. Ch. Of Christ. Home: 390 2d St Black Rock AR 72415

PLUNKETT, MELBA KATHLEEN, manufacturing company executive; b. Marietta, Ill., Mar. 20, 1929; d. Lester George and Florence Marie (Hutchins) Bonnett; m. James P. Plunkett, Aug. 18, 1951; children: Julie Marie Plunkett Hayden, Gregory James. Educated pub. schs. Co-founder, 1961, since sec.-treas., dir. Coils, Inc., Huntley, Ill. Mem. U.S. C. of C., U.S. Mfg. Assn., Ill. C. of C., Ill. Notary Assn. Roman Catholic. Home: 15n170 Sleepy Hollow Rd West Dundee IL 60118-9113 Office: 11716 Algonquin Rd Huntley IL 60142-7176

PLUNKETT, SARA L. communications company executive; BA in Acctg., U. Ala. CPA, Ala., Ga. Acct. Price Waterhouse, Atlanta, 1978-88; with ITC/DeltaCom, Huntsville, Ala., 1989—, v.p. fin., treas. Office: ITC/DeltaCom 700 Boulevard South SW Huntsville AL 35802-2115

PLUSK, RONALD FRANK, manufacturing executive; b. Chgo., Mar. 30, 1933; s. Frank and Ann (Petrauskas) P.; m. Rose Marie Pawlikowski, May 25, 1957; children— Frank A., Ronald S., Cynthia Marie. BSC., Loyola U., Chgo., 1954; postgrad., Northwestern U., 1957-59. Mgmt. cons. Peat, Marwick, Mitchell & Co., Chgo., 1963-66; corp. controller Varo, Inc., Garland, Tex., 1966-69; dir. planning and mgmt. systems Rucker Co., Oakland, Calif., 1969-72, dir. ops., audit and systems, 1972-76, v.p. ops., audit and systems, 1976-77; v.p. fin. adminstrn. Rucker Co. (merged with NL Petroleum Svcs. Co.), Houston, 1977-79; v.p. fin., treas. Cobe Labs., Inc., Lakewood, Colo., 1979-92; dir. Ctr. for Hearing Speech and Language, Denver, 1996—2003; pres. Ctr. for Hearing, Speech and Language, 2003—. Contbr. articles to profl. jours. Served to 1st lt. AUS, 1954-56, ETO. Mem. Am. Mgmt. Assn., Planning Execs. Inst., Fin. Execs. Inst. Roman Catholic. Home: 9 Middlefield Rd Columbine Valley CO 80123-6620

PLUSQUELLEC, HERVE LOUIS, irrigation and agricultural engineering consultant; b. France, Oct. 23, 1935; s. Andre Jules and Annick Germaine Plusquellec; m. Kyung-Hee Kim, Oct. 1997. Degree in hydraulics engring., Ecole Nat. Sup. d'Hydraulique, Grenoble, France, 1960; MS, U. Grenoble, 1960. Engr. Office Nat. des Irrigations, Rabat, Morocco, 1963-71; project mgr. ELC Electroconsult, Milan, 1971-76; adviser World Bank, Washington, 1976-97, cons., 1997—. Author: Water Control in Irrigation, 1990; Performance of Irrigation: Design Mgmt. and Policy, FAO book, 2002; contbr. articles to sci. and profl. jours. With French Navy, 1960-62. Recipient Best Response award ASCE, 2001. Mem. Assn. Française de l'Irrigation et du Drainage, Internat. Commn. on Irrigation and Drainage (observer). Avocations: overseas travel, hiking. Home: 3257 A Sutton Pl Washington DC 20016 E-mail: plusquel@earthlink.net.

PLUSQUELLIC, DONALD L. mayor; b. Akron, Ohio, July 3, 1949; m. Mary Plusquellic; children: Dave, Michelle. BS, Bowling Green State U., 1972; JD, U. Akron, 1981. Councilman Akron City Council, 1973-81, councilman-at-large, 1982-86, council pres., 1984-86; mayor City of Akron, 1987—. Trustee U.S. Conf. of Mayors. Home: 2785 Nesmith Lake Blvd Akron OH 44314-3427 Office: Office of the Mayor 200 Municipal Bldg 166 S High St Akron OH 44308-1626

PLUTA, RYSZARD, neuropathologist, educator; b. Biała Podlaska, Poland, Apr. 16, 1952; s. Marian and Antonina (Szarubko) P. Student, Humboldt U., Berlin, 1975, U. Cologne, Germany, 1976; MD, scientist, Med. Acad., Lublin, Poland, 1977; PhD, Polish Acad. Scis., Warsaw, 1983. Intern gynaecology unit State Hosp., Biała Podlaska, 1977; intern dept. pediatry Med. Acad., Warsaw, 1978; intern internal medicine and surgery units Czerniakowski Hosp., Warsaw, 1978; sci. visitor lab. of CNS Resuscitation Pathology, Inst. Gen. Reanimatology, USSR Acad. Med. Scis., Moscow, 1979; sr. rsch. asst. Polish Acad. Sci., Warsaw, 1981-87, asst. prof., 1987-94, assoc. prof., 1994—; postdoctoral fellow NIH, Bethesda, Md., 1986-88; prof. Acad. Phys. Edn., Warsaw, 1995—2002; resident neurology Med. Acad., Warsaw, 1997. Post-doctoral rsch. fellow, vis. prof. N.Y. State Inst. Basic Rsch., Staten Island, 1988—89, 1990—91, 1993—94, 1997; vice-chmn., bd. dirs. State Hosp., Biala Podlaska, 1999—2000; mem. sci. coun. Acad. Phys. Edn., Warsaw, 1995—2002, mem. senate, 1996—99; mem. sci. coun. Inst. Phys. Edn. and Sport, Biala Podlaska, 1996—2002; mem. Polish com. sci. rsch. SPUB, Warsaw, 2001—. Contbr. articles to profl. jours. Mem. Polish com. sci. rsch. SPUB, Warsaw, 2001—; chief Trade Union Solidarnosc Med. Rsch. Ctr., Warsaw, 1980—90, Dem. Union, Dist. Biala Podlaska, 1990—94; candidate Polish Parliament, 1991, 1993. 2nd lt. Polish mil., 1977. Mem.: U. Sports Assn. of Acad. Phys. Edn., Polish Acad. Sci., Polish Assn. Neuropathologists, N.Y. Acad. Sci., Internat. Soc. Neuropathology, Internat. Soc. Cerebral Blood Flow and Metabolism, Internat. Soc. Brain Edema Rsch., Polish Neurosci. Soc., European Soc. Clin. Respiratory Physiology. Roman Catholic. Avocations: politics, sports, good food, cooking. Office: Med Rsch Ctr Dept Neuropath Pawińskiego Str 5 02-106 Warsaw Poland

PLUTCHAK, NOEL BERNARD, meteorologist, management consultant; b. Green Bay, Wis., Dec. 14, 1932; s. Bernard Edward and Violet Marie P.; m. Sandra Kolvig (div.); 1 child, Channin. BS in Geology, U. Wis., 1960; MS in Meteorology, Fla. State U., 1964; postgrad., Oreg. State U. Research asst. Columbia U., Lamont Geol. Inst., Nyack, N.Y., 1960-64; dir. theoretical studies Bendix Marine Advisors, La Jolla, Calif., 1965-69; research assoc. U. So. Calif., Los Angeles, 1972-75; chief scientist Interstate Electronics, Ocean Engrng. Div., Anaheim, Calif., 1975-83, Raytheon Svcs., Ocean Engrng. Div., Ventura, Calif., 1984-87; chief exec. officer, chief scientist Active Leak Testing, Inc., San Pedro, Calif., 1987—. Contbr. articles to profl. jours.; patentee in field. With USAF, 1952-56. Mem. Am. Geophys. Union, Marine Tech. Soc., Exptl. Aircraft Assn., Am. Chem. Soc. Republican. Avocations: soaring, wind surfing, tennis. Office: Active Leak Testing Inc 2500 via Cabrillo Marina Ste 200 San Pedro CA 90731-7224 E-mail: noel90007@yahoo.com.

PLYLER, AARON W. state legislator, farmer, contractor; b. Union County, N.C., Oct. 1, 1926; m. Dorothy Plyler. Grad. mil. acad., Fla. Farmer, Monroe, N.C.; owner, mgr. grading and paving com., real estate co., restaurant, motel, Monroe; mem N.C. Ho. of Reps., Raleigh, 1975-82, N.C. Senate, Raleigh, 1983—. Chmn. appropriations and base budget com., mem. pensions and retirement and aging com., rules and ops. of senate, com., transp. com., ways and means com. Democrat. Presbyterian. Office: NC Senate 627 Legis Office Bldg 300 N Salisbury St Raleigh NC 27603-5925 also: 2170 Concord Ave Monroe NC 28110-8765

PLYLER, JOHN LANEY, JR., retired healthcare management professional; b. Greenville, S.C., Jan. 31, 1934; s. John Laney and Beatrice Elizabeth (Dennis) P.; m. Caroline Raysor Williams, June 26, 1959; children: Sharon, John III, James (dec.). Student, U.S. Naval Acad., 1953-54; BA, Furman U., 1956; MHA, Duke U., 1970. Prodn. planner J. P. Stevens & Co., Greenville, 1958-65; mgmt. engr., outpatient mgr. Greenville Hosp. Sys., 1967-68; assoc. dir. Cleveland Meml. Hosp., Shelby, N.C., 1970-79; exec. v.p., COO Bapt. Med. Ctr., Oklahoma City, 1979-85; group v.p. SunHealth Alliance, Charlotte, N.C., 1985-86, sr. v.p., 1986-96, ret., 1996. 2d lt. U.S. Army, 1957, capt. USAR, 1957-65. Fellow Am. Coll. Healthcare Execs. (life fellow, ethics com. 1990-93, chmn. 1992-93), Okla. Hosp. Assn. (coun. on edn.), N.C. Hosp. Assn. (coun. on pers.). Avocations: travel, photography. Home: PO Box 909 Davidson NC 28036-0909 E-mail: plylerj@bellsouth.net.

PLYMALE, ROBERT H. state legislator, lumber company executive; b. Huntington, W.Va., Feb. 21, 1955; s. Jennifer Thompson; 3 children. Student, Marshall U. Mem. W.Va. Senate, Charleston, 1993—. Mem. edn. com., fin. com., govt. orgn. com., health and human resources, pensions com., transp. com. Chmn. sch. improvement coun. C-K Mid. Sch.; mem. adv. bd. W.Va. Vets. Home. Mem. W.Va. Forestry Assn. (exec. bd.), Huntington Regional C. of C. Democrat. Methodist. Office: WVa Senate 1900 Kanawha Blvd E Rm 415M Charleston WV 25305-0009 also: PO Box 543 Ceredo WV 25507-0543

PNIAKOWSKI, ANDREW FRANK, structural engineer; b. Grodno, Poland, Aug. 18, 1930; s. Josef Leon and Janina (Kodzynski) Pniakowski; m. Margaret M. Czajkowski, Aug. 15, 1957; 1 child, Mary. Diploma Engr., Politechnika Warszawska, 1952. Registered profl. engr., Ont., Mass., Maine, N.H. Bridge design and field engr. Govt. of Poland, Ministry of R.R., Warsaw, 1952—57; bridge design engr. Dept. Hwys. of Ont., Toronto, Canada, 1958—66; sr. structural engr. Sverdrup & Parcel Assocs., Inc., Boston, 1967—71; chief structural engr. Louis Berger & Assocs., Inc., Needham, Mass., 1972—96; cons. engr. in transp., bridges, hwys., railroads, pub. bldgs., others. Mem.: Assn. Profl. Engrs. of Province of Ont., Prestressed Concrete Inst., Am. Concrete Inst., Am. Inst. Steel Constrn. Roman Catholic.

POAD, FLORA VIRGINIA, retired librarian and educator, retired elementary school educator; b. Roanoke, Va., Oct. 8, 1921; d. Thomas Franklin and Ethlind (Wertz) Huff; m. Stanley Theodore Benton, Dec. 24, 1942 (div. Oct. 1983); children: Peggy, Betty, Mary Jo, Lucy; m. James Joseph Poad, June 6, 1986. Student, Radford Coll., 1939-41, Ohio U., 1956-57; BS in Edn., Ohio No. U., 1960; MA in LS, U. Toledo, 1964; postgrad., Kent State U., 1964-66, 71. Reference asst. Roanoke Pub. Libr., 1939-42; catalog asst. Univ. Libr., Emory U., Atlanta, 1942; sec. ARC, Atlanta, 1943; catalog asst. Pickerington (Ohio) Pub. Libr., 1950-51; tchr. Celina (Ohio) Pub. Schs., 1957-62; tchr., libr. Toledo Pub. Schs., 1962-64; libr. supr. Oregon (Ohio) Pub. Schs., 1964-85; instr. U. Toledo, 1970, reference libr., 1971-86; tchr. Sylvan Learning Ctr., Toledo, 1985-92, ret., 1992. Mem. evaluation team Ohio Dept. Edn., Columbus, 1973; rep. Ohio Gov.'s Conf. on Librs., Columbus, 1974; chmn., mem. adv. bd. libr. sci. dept. Cmty.-Tech. Coll., 1965-69. Editor Ohio Assn. Sch. Librs. Bull., 1968-71. Vol. Am. Cancer Soc., Toledo, 1946—48, 1986—87, Mobile Meals, Toledo, 1986—93, Helping Hands, Toledo, 1994—2001. Mem. Am. Assn. Ret. Persons, Delta Kappa Gamma, Pi Lambda Theta, Kappa Delta Pi, Phi Kappa Phi. Avocations: reading, walking, crafts. Home: 3544 Bayberry Pl Oregon OH 43616-2475

POATS, LILLIAN BROWN, education educator; b. Gary, Ind., Dec. 4, 1951; d. Joe Freeman and Jimmye Marie (Jones) Brown; m. Greyling Byron Poats, June 30, 1973; 1 child, Greyling Byron II. BA, Purdue U., 1972; MEd, Tex. So. U., 1975, EdD, 1984. Tchr. Gary (Ind.) Cmty. Sch. Corp., 1972-74; univ. psychometrist Tex. So. U., Houston, 1974-77, 81-84; coord. acad. advising Purdue U., Hammond, Ind., 1977-79; educator, counselor Planned Parenthood-Northwest Ind., Merrillville, 1979-81; dir. student support U. Tex. Health Sci. Ctr., Houston, 1984-89; prof. edn. Tex. So. U., 1989—. Chair black caucus exec. bd. Am. Assn. Higher Edn., Washington, 1995-97; faculty fellow U.S. Dept. Def., Pentagon, Washington, 1993. Contbr. articles to profl. jours., chpts. to books. Mem. Ft. Bend Edn. Found., Ft. Bend County CPS Bd. Named Woman of Excellence Suburban Sugarland (Tex.) Women's Assn., 1994. Mem. Purdue U. Alumni Assn., Phi Delta Kappa, Delta Sigma Theta (pres. suburban Houston-Ft. Bond chpt. 1991-92). Avocations: reading, sewing. Home: 3702 Pin Oak Ct Missouri City TX 77459-7017 Office: Tex Southern U 3100 Cleburne St Houston TX 77004-4501 Office Phone: 713-313-7978. E-mail: Poats_lb@tsu.edu., Poats2@houston.rr.com.

POBEREZNY, TOM, federal agency administrator; m. Sharon Poberezny; 1 child, Lesley. B in Indsl. Engring., Northwestern U. Pres., CEO Exptl. Aircraft Assn., Oshkosh, Wis., 1989—. Mem. Eagles Aerobatic Team; chmn. ann. AirVenture Fly-In Conv. Exptl. Aircraft Assn., 1972—; founder Project SchoolFlight, EAA Air Acad., Air Adventure Days, Vision of Eagles; mem. Centennial of Flight Commn.; bd. dirs. Competitive Wis.; founding mem. U.S. Aerobatic Found. Achievements include U.S. Nat. Aerobatic champion, 1972; mem. team World Aerobatic Championship, France, 1972. Office: EAA Aviation Ctr PO Box 3086 Oshkosh WI 54903-3086

POCH, HERBERT EDWARD, retired pediatrician, educator; b. Elizabeth, N.J., Sept. 4, 1927; s. William and Min (Herman) P.; m. Leila Kosberg, Aug. 27, 1952; children: Bruce Jeffrey, Andrea Susan, Lesley Grace. AB, Columbia U., 1949, MD, 1953. Diplomate Am. Bd. Pediatrics. Intern Kings County Hosp. Ctr., Bklyn., 1953-54; resident Babies Hosp., Columbia-Presbyn. Med. Ctr., N.Y.C., 1954-56; pvt. practice medicine specializing in pediatrics Elizabeth, 1956-92. Pres. med. staff, 1989, attending pediatrician Elizabeth Gen. Med. Ctr., 1973, sr. attending pediatrician, 1990, hon. staff, 1993—; attending pediatrician St. Elizabeth Hosp., 1968, chmn. dept. pediatrics, 1971-81, attending pediatrician Monmouth Med. Ctr., 1991-99, emeritus, 1999—, assoc. program dir. pediatrics; instr. pediatrics Columbia U., 1956-72, asst. clin. prof. pediatrics, 1972-91; clin. assoc. prof. pediatrics MCP Hahnemann Sch. Medicine, 1997-99; clin. assoc. prof. pediat. Drexel U.; ret. With AUS, 1945-46. Fellow Am. Acad. Pediatrics; mem. N.J. Med. Soc., Ambulatory Pediatric Assn. Address: 1175 Ocean Ave Long Branch NJ 07740-4518 Personal E-mail: hpoch@comcast.net.

POCHES, CHARLES, JR., lawyer, magistrate; b. Sioux City, Iowa, Feb. 14, 1932; s. Charles and Lillian Mae (Phelps) P.; m. Barbara Jo Poches, Oct. 15, 1966; children— Charles III, Warren D., Jennifer K. B.S., U. S.D., 1957, J.D., 1959. Bar: S.D. 1959, Minn. 1959, U.S. Dist. Ct. S.D. 1959, U.S. Dist. Ct. Minn. 1962, U.S. Ct. Appeals (8th cir.) 1966. Asst. atty. gen. State of S.D., 1959-60; sole practice, Pierre, S.D., 1960-61; assoc. Johnson, Winter & Lundquist, Wheaton, Minn., 1961-62; ptnr. Roubideaux, Poches & Reade, Ft. Pierre, S.D., 1962-68; asst. states atty. Stanley County (S.D.), 1962-68; sole practice, Ft. Pierre, 1968-80; ptnr. Poches & Lee, Ft. Pierre, 1980—; magistrate U.S. Dist. S.D., Pierre, 1977—; city atty. City of Ft. Pierre, 1963-84. Mem. Stanley County (S.D.) Sch. Bd., 1981-84. Served with USAF, 1950-54. Mem. S.D. Bar Assn., Assn. Trial Lawyers Am., S.D. Trial Lawyers, Sixth Cir. Bar Assn., S.D. Mcpl. Atty. Assn., S.D. Trappers Assn. (Trapper of Yr. 1982), Nat. Trappers Assn., VFW, Prairie Antique Auto Club. Republican. Roman Catholic. Office: PO Box 617 Fort Pierre SD 57532-0617

POCHICK, FRANCIS EDWARD, financial consultant; b. Metuchen, NJ, May 28, 1931; s. Frank Stephen and Bertha Barbara Pochick; m. Shirley Ann Elliott, Feb. 16, 1957; children: Bonnie Lynn, Keith Francis. Student, Rutgers U., 1949-50, 54-55. Agt. New Eng. Mut. Life. Ins. Co., Newark and New Brunswick, N.J., 1958-61, Lambert M. Huppeler Co., Inc., N.Y.C., 1962-64, cons., 1964, sr. cons. employee benefits, 1967-87; fin. cons. Francis E. Pochick Assocs., N.Y.C., 1987—. Mem. adv. bd. Mercer Fund, Cmty. Found. N.J., 1986—, Rec. for the Blind, Princeton, 1989, charitable devel. officer Nat. Found., Inc., 1992, Nat. Coun. on The Aging, Planned Giving Coun. 1994; mem. com. bd. dirs. health Princeton Coun. Planned Giving, 1993; v.p. The Benefits Planning Co., Ltd., Charlottesville, Va., 1995. With USMC, 1951-54. Mem. Am. Soc. Pension Actuaries, Nat. Assn. Life Underwriters, Fin. Planning Assn., Estate Planning Coun., Nat. Assn. Philanthropic Planners, Lions, Glenmore Country Club. Home: 1451 Bremerton Ln Keswick VA 22947-9147 Office: PO Box 518 Keswick VA 22947-0518 also: No Jersey Br 30 Two Bridges Rd Fairfield NJ 07004-1550 Office Phone: 434-295-7173.

POCHINI, JUDY HAY, interior designer, writer, editor; b. Phoenix, Mar. 16, 1932; d. Cecil Clifford and Nadine Mary (Larimer) Cook; m. Gordon Eugene Hay, June 5, 1971 (dec. 1974); m. Robert Frank Pochini, Sept. 18, 1983 (dec. 1995). BA, U. Calif., Santa Barbara, 1953; MA in Journalism, U. Calif., Berkeley, 1965. Exec. sec. Mobil Oil Corp., Mpls., 1958-60, Kaiser Aluminum & Chem. Corp., Oakland, Calif., 1960-64; asst. trade publ. editor Sunset mag., Menlo Park, Calif., 1966-68, trade publ. editor, 1968-73; owner, home furnishings editor Lifestyle West, Walnut Creek, Calif., 1974-79; interior designer Berman's Drexel-Heritage, Oakland, 1979-85, Suburban House Drexel-Heritage, Concord, Calif., 1986-87; ptnr., interior designer Judy Hay Interiors, Lafayette and Santa Barbara, Calif., 1987-95, owner, 1995—. Mem. nat. consumer action panel Carpet & Rug Industry, Dalton, Ga., 1973-75; cons. in field. Contbr. articles to profl. jours. Mem. AAUW (pres. 2002-04), Internat. Furnishings and Design Assn., Women in Comms. Inc., U. Calif. Santa Barbara Alumni Assn. (music affiliates bd.), Chi Omega. Democrat. Mem. Unity Ch. Office: 1026 Coast Village Rd 140 Santa Barbara CA 93108

POCHIRAJU, KISHORE, mechanical engineer, educator; m. Seetha Ayyala; children: Saahith, Kavya. B in Engring., Nat. Inst. Tech., Warangal, India, 1986; MS in Tech., Indian Inst.Tech., Kanpur, India, 1988; PhD, Drexel U., Phila., 1993. Asst. prof. Stevens Inst. Tech., Hoboken, NJ, 1997—2003, assoc. prof., 2003—; dir. Design and Mfg. Inst., 2004—. Mem.: ASME (student sect. advisor 1999). Office: Stevens Inst Tech EAS 307 Castle Point on Hudson Hoboken NJ 07030 Office Phone: 201-216-8053. E-mail: kpochira@stevens.edu.

POCHYLY, DONALD FREDERICK, physician, hospital administrator; b. Chgo., June 3, 1934; s. Frank J. and Vlasta (Bezdek) P.; m. Diane Dilelio, May 11, 1957; children: Christopher, Jonathan, David. MD, Loyola U., 1959; M.Ed., U. Ill., 1971. Diplomate Am. Bd. Internal Medicine, Am. Bd. Geriatrics. Fellow ACP, 1966-67; asst. prof. med. edn. U. Ill., 1967-72, asso. prof., 1972-74; chmn. dept. health scis. edn. U. of Health Scis., Chgo. Med. Sch., 1975-77, provost, acting pres., 1977-79; prof. clin. medicine Loyola U., Chgo., 1980—; v.p. med. affairs N.W. Community Hosp., Arlington Heights, Ill. Chmn. com. rev. and recognition Am. Coun. Continuing Med. Edn., 1993; cons. Nat. Libr. Medicine, WHO. Contbr. articles to med. jours. Mem. AMA, Ill. Geriatrics Soc. (pres. Chgo. chpt. 1988-89), Ill. Med. Soc., Chgo. Med. Soc., Alpha Omega Alpha. Roman Catholic. Office: Northwest Community Hosp 800 W Central Rd Arlington Heights IL 60005-2392

POCOCK, J. MICHAEL, consumer products company executive; B in Telecomm., U. Ky., Lexington. Various sr. mgmt. pos., consumer products divsn. GE Co., Fairfield, Conn.; variuos sr. mgmt. pos. Xerox Corp., Rochester, NY, Murata Bus. Systems, Dallas; mem. mgmt. team Epson Am., Torrance, Calif.; v.p., gen. mgr. Digital Equipment Corp., Acton, Mass.; v.p., gen. mgr. N.Am. sales Compaq Computer Corp., Houston, 1996—99, gen. mgr. comml. products computer group, v.p. corp. strategy; pres., CEO Polaroid Corp., Waltham, Mass., 2003—. Office: Polaroid Corp Corporate HQ 1265 Main St Bldg W3 Waltham MA 02451

POCOSKI, DAVID JOHN, cardiologist; b. Waterbury, Conn., July 15, 1945; s. Edward J. and Stella E. (Kolpa) P.; m. Madelyn M. Pocoski, Sept. 25, 1971; 1 child, Sarah C. BS, U. Conn., 1967; MD magna cum laude, Upstate Med. Ctr., Syracuse, NY, 1971. From intern to fellow in cardiology U. Rochester, NY; founder, pres. Osler Clinic of Medicine, Melbourne, Fla.; pres., chief of staff, dir. cardiac rehab. Sea Pines Rehab. Hosp. Commr. Holy Name Jesus Cath. Ch. Maj. USAF, 1974-76. Recipient Outstanding Scientist of the 20th Century award. Fellow Am. Coll. Cardiology; mem. AMA. Republican. Roman Catholic. Avocations: music, art, running, community service. Office: 930 S Harbor City Blvd Melbourne FL 32901-1963

POCRASS, RICHARD DALE, management consultant; b. Meadville, Pa., Mar. 7, 1940; s. Irving F. and Roslyn (Sperber) P.; m. Rena Levy, Feb. 3, 1968; children: Michael B., S. Douglas. BS in Math., U. Pitts., 1962, MBA in Fin., 1964. EDP sales mgr. NCR Corp., Pitts., 1962-67, retail mktg. mgr. L.A., 1972-74; v.p., dir. Nanoseconds Sys., Fairfield, Conn., 1967-69, dir., 1968-72; v.p. gen. mgr. Hart Jewelry Co., Warren, Ohio, 1969-71, dir., 1981-84; mktg. mgr. Data Source Corps subs. Hercules, Inc., El Segundo, 1974-75; pres. Webster-Pocrass & O'Neil (name changed to Pocrass Assocs. 1981), L.A., 1976—, Health Tech. Inc. Pub. CEO, chmn. bd. dirs. Chocolates a la Carte, Valencia, Calif. Author: The Recruitment Letter; author (with Maronde) Drug Abuse Study for Hoffman LaRoche, 1980. Bd. dirs. West Valley Little League, U.S. Pastry Alliance, Providence Holly Cross Med. Ctr. Found., L.A. Mission Coll. Found., Western Overseas, Inc., Long Beach, Calif. Mem. Am. Mktg. Assn. L.A. Spkrs. Bur., Soc. for Human Resource Mgmt., L.A. Area C. of C., Bank Mktg. Assn., Retail Controllers Assn., Calif. Exec. Recruiters Assn., Pers. and Indsl. Rels. Assn., Internat. Platform Assn., Rotary. Republican. Jewish. Home: 18815 Paseo Nuevo Dr Tarzana CA 91356-5136 Office: 28455 Livingston Ave Valencia CA 91355-4173 Office Phone: 661-257-3700. Personal E-mail: rick@candymaker.com.

PODBERESKY, SAMUEL, lawyer; b. Cremona, Italy, Mar. 16, 1946; came to U.S., 1947; s. Noah and Mina (Milikowsky) P.; m. Rosita Rubinstein, March 8, 1970; children: Daniel J., Michael J. BS in Aeronautical Engring., U. Md., 1967; JD, U. Md., Balt., 1971. Bar: Md. 1972. Flight test engr. Vertol div. Boeing Co., Phila., 1967-68; regulatory atty. FAA, Washington, 1971-78; dep. asst. gen. counsel U.S. Dept. Transp., Washington, 1978-86, asst. gen. counsel aviation enforcement and proceedings, 1986—. Author: Never the Last Road, 2003. Office: US Dept Transp 400 7th St SW Washington DC 20590-0001

PODBOY, ALVIN MICHAEL, JR., law library director, lawyer; b. Cleve., Feb. 10, 1947; s. Alvin Michael and Josephine Esther (Nagode) P.; m. Mary Ann Gloria Esposito, Aug. 21, 1971; children: Allison Marie, Melissa Ann. AB cum laude, Ohio U., 1969; JD, Case Western Res. U., 1972, MLS, 1977. Bar: Ohio 1972, U.S. Dist. Ct. (no. dist.) Ohio 1973, U.S. Supreme Ct. 1992. Assoc. Joseph T. Svete Co. LPA, Chardon, Ohio, 1972-76; dir. pub. svcs. Case Western Res. Sch. Law Libr., Cleve., 1974-77, assoc. law libr., 1977-78; libr. Baker & Hostetler, LLP, Cleve., 1978-88, dir. librs., 1988—. Instr. Notre Dame Coll. of Ohio, Cleve., 1991-2002, Ursuline Coll., Cleve., 2003—, Am. Inst. Paralegal Studies, Cleve., 1991-96. Bd. overseers Case Western Res. U., 1981-87, vis. com. sch. libr. sci., 1980-86, Westlaw adv. bd., 1987-92, bd. govs. law sch. alumni assn., 1992-95, West's Legal Directory Ohio Adv. Panel, 1990-91; adv. com. West's Info. Innovators Inst., 1995-97; chmn. Case Western Res. Libr. Sch. Alumni Fund, 1979-80; Rep. precinct committeeman Cuyahoga County, Cleve., 1981-95, exec. com., 1984-87; Rep. precinct committeeman Portage County, Aurora, 2004—. 1st lt. USAF, 1972. Mem.: ABA, Arnold Air Soc., Case Western Res. U. Libr. Sch. Alumni Assn. (pres. 1981), Ohio Regional Assn. Law Librs. (pres. 1985), Am. Assn. Law Librs. (chmn. pvt. law librs. spl. interest sect. 1994—95, exec. bd. 2001—04, cert.), Cleve. Bar Assn., Ohio State Bar Assn. (chmn. librs. com. 1989—91), Phi Alpha Theta, Pi Gamma Mu. Roman Catholic. Avocation: alpine skiing. Home: 417 East Parkway Blvd Aurora OH 44202 Office: Baker & Hostetler LLP 3200 National City Ctr Cleveland OH 44114-3485 Office Phone: 216-861-7101. Business E-Mail: apodboy@bakerlaw.com.

PODBOY, JOHN WATTS, clinical, forensic psychologist; b. York, Pa., Sept. 27, 1943; s. August John and Harriett Virginia (Watts) P.; 1 son, Matthew John. B.A., Dickinson Coll., 1966; M.S., San Diego State Coll., 1971; Ph.D., U. Ariz., 1973. Dir., Vets. Counseling Center, U. Ariz., Tucson, 1972-73; project dir. San Mateo County (Calif.) Human Relations Dept., Redwood City, 1974; staff psychologist Sonoma State Hosp., Eldridge, Calif., 1975-81; cons. clin. psychologist Comprehensive Care Corp., Newport Beach, Calif., 1974-75, Sonoma County (Calif.) Probation Dept., 1976-88; pvt. practice, Kenwood, Calif., 1982—; cons. to Calif. Superior Cts., 1983-85; asst. prof. Sonoma State U., 1977-81; dir. Sonoma Diagnostic and Remedial Center, 1979-82. Chmn. San Mateo County Diabetes Assn., 1975. Served to lt. USNR, 1966-69. Fellow Am. Coll. Forensic Psychology, Am. Bd. Med. Psychotherapists (fellow); mem. APA, Western Psychol. Assn., Redwood Psychol. Assn. (pres. 1983), Nat. Council Alcoholism, Nat. Rehab. Assn. Home: PO Box 488 Kenwood CA 95452-0488 Office Phone: 707-833-6023.

PODD, ANN, newspaper editor; b. Buffalo, Jan. 15, 1954; d. Edward and Florence (Bojan) P.; m. Timothy Murray, 1980; children: Laura, Gregory. AB, Syracuse U., 1976; MBA, SUNY, Buffalo, 1981. Reporter AP, 1977, Buffalo Courier-Express, 1977-80, bus. editor, 1980-82, Bergen (N.J.) Record, 1982-88, N.Y. Daily News, 1988-90, assoc. editor, 1990-92, assoc. editor, dir. human resources, 1992-93; dep. spot news editor Wall St. Jour., N.Y.C., 1994, spot news editor, 1994—2000, nat. TV editor, 2000—03, day editor, 2003—. Office: Wall St Jour 200 Liberty St New York NY 10281-1003

PODELL, ROBERT MANN, obstetrician-gynecologist; b. Elizabeth, N.J., Jan. 17, 1941; s. William S. and Ceil (Silverman) P.; m. Judy Rothenberg, Aug. 27, 1967; 1 child, Deborah P. Fishkind. BA, Columbia U., 1963; MD, Georgetown U., 1967. Diplomate Am. Bd. Ob-Gyn. Intern Jewish Hosp. Med. Ctr., Bklyn., 1967-68; resident in ob-gyn. Bellevue Hosp. Ctr.-NYU, N.Y.C., 1968-72; staff Beth Israel Hosp., N.Y.C. Clin. asst. prof. NYU. Fellow ACOG. E-mail: robertpodell@msn.com.

PODESTA, ROBERT EDWARD, artist; b. Sept. 7, 1921; BCS, U. Santa Clara, 1943. Prin. R. Podesta & Assocs., San Jose, Calif., 1946-66; owner/mgr. Sta. KREP-FM, Santa Clara-San Jose, 1965-72; cartoonist Honolulu Advertiser, 1991—. Lectr. Coll. Bus. Adminstrn., U. Santa Clara, 1948-57. Cartoonist San Jose Bus. Jour., Denver Bus. Jour., Ft. Worth Bus. Jour., Pacific Bus. Rev. Home: # 3 Deer Path Rd Santa Cruz CA 95060 E-mail: topfish@cruzio.com.

PODESTO, GARY A. mayor; b. Stockton, Calif., 1941; Student, Marquette U., Milw.; BS in Econs., BS in Corp. Fin., Santa Clara U. Mayor City of Stockton, Calif., 1997—. Founding dir. Crime Stoppers & New Directions; mem. Intergovernmental Liaison Com. City Coun.; bd. regents U. Pacific; dir. Su Salud Health Fair; mem. CSU Stockton Ctr. Site Authority, Urban Area Water User's Com., City of Stockton/Stockton Unified Sch. Dist., Joint Com. and City-County Transit Dist. Liaison Com., League of Calif. Cities Legis. Liaison; bd. dir. San Joaquin County Coun. of Govts., San Joaquin Partnership, Regional Rail Commn., Auburn Dam Coalition. Named to Hall of Fame, St. Mary's HS. Office: Office Mayor & City Coun 425 N El Dorado St Stockton CA 95202-1951

PODGOR, ELLEN SUE, law educator; b. Bklyn., Jan. 30, 1952; d. Benjamin and Yetta (Shilensky) Podgor. BS magna cum laude, Syracuse U., 1973; JD, Ind. U., Indpls., 1976; MBA, U. Chgo., 1987; LLM, Temple U., 1989. Bar: Ind. 1976, N.Y. 1984, Pa. 1987. Dep. prosecutor Lake County Prosecutor's Office, Crown Point, Ind., 1976-78; ptnr. Nicholls & Podgor, Crown Point, 1978-87; instr. Temple U. Sch. Law, 1987-89; assoc. prof. law St. Thomas U., Miami, Fla., 1989-91, Ga. State U., Atlanta, 1991—. Vis. scholar Yale Law Sch., 1998; vis. prof. U. Ga., 2000; John S. Stone vis. endowed chair U. Ala., 2001; vis. prof. George Washington U., 2003. Author: (with Israel) White Collar Crime in a Nutshell, (with Israel, Borman, Henning) White Collar Crime: Law and Practice, (with Wise) International Criminal Law: Cases and Materials; assoc. editor Ind. Law Rev., 1975-76; contbr. articles to legal jours. Del. Ind. Dem. Conv., 1982. Mem. ABA, NACDL (bd. dirs.), Am. Law Inst., Ind. Bar Assn. Democrat. Jewish. Office: Ga State U Coll Law PO Box 4037 Atlanta GA 30302-4037

PODGORNY, GEORGE, emergency physician; b. Tehran, Iran, Mar. 17, 1934; s. Emanuel and Helen (Parsian) P.; came to U.S., 1954, naturalized, 1973. B.S., Maryville Coll., 1958; postgrad. Bowman Gray Sch. Medicine, 1958; M.D., Wake Forest U., 1962; m. Ernestine Koury, Oct. 20, 1962; children: Adele, Emanuel II, George, Gregory. Intern in surgery N.C. Bapt. Hosp., Winston-Salem, 1962-63, chief resident in gen. surgery, 1966-67, in cardiothoracic surgery, 1967-69; sr. med. examiner Forsyth County, N.C., 1972—; dir. dept. emergency medicine Forsyth Meml. Hosp., Winston-Salem, 1974-80; sec.-treas. Forsyth Emergency Services, Winston-Salem, 1970-80; clin. prof. emergency medicine East Carolina U. Sch. Medicine, Greenville, 1984—, chmn. residency rev. com. on emergency medicine, 1980-88; mem. Accreditation Coun. for Grad. Med. Edn. Dir. Emergency Med. Svcs. Project

Region II of N.C., 1975—; chmn. bd. trustees Emergency Medicine Found.; chmn. residency rev. com. emergency medicine Accreditation Coun. Grad. Med. Edn.; founder Western Piedmont Emergency Med. Svcs. Coun., 1973; mem. N.C. Emergency Med. Svcs. Adv. Coun., 1976-81, assoc. prof. clin. surgery Bowman Gray Sch. Medicine, Wake Forest U., Winston-Salem, 1979—. Bd. dirs. Piedmont Health Systems Agy., 1975-84; trustee Forsyth County Hosp., Authority, 1974-75; bd. dirs. N.C. Health Coordinating Coun., 1975-82, Medic Alert Found. Internat. Fellow Internat. Coll. Surgeons, Internat. Coll. Angiology, Royal Soc. Health (Great Britain), Royal Soc. Medicine, Southeastern Surg. Congress; mem. Am. Coll. Emergency Physicians (charter, pres. 1978-79), AMA, (chmn. coun. of sect. emergency medicine 1978-90, alt. del. for Am. Coll. Emergency Physicians, 1990—), Am. Bd. Emergency Medicine (pres. 1976-81). Contbr. articles to profl. publs. on trauma, snake bite and history of medicine; editorial bd. Annals of Emergency Medicine, Med. Meetings. Home and Office: 2115 Georgia Ave Winston Salem NC 27104-1917

PODGORSAK, ERVIN B. medical physicist, educator, administrator; b. Vienna, Sept. 28, 1943; arrived in Slovenia, 1946, came to U.S., 1968, Can., 1973; s. Franc and Gabriella (Cukale) P.; m. Mariana Ambrozic, Oct. 23, 1965; children: Matthew, Gregor. Dipl.Ing. in Physics, U. Ljubljana, Slovenia, 1968; MSc in Physics, U. Wis., 1970, PhD in Physics, 1973. Diplomate Am. Bd. Med. Physics. Rsch. asst. U. Ljubljana, 1965-68, U. Wis., Madison, 1968-73; postdoctoral fellow U. Toronto, Ont., Can., 1973-74; asst. prof. McGill U., Montreal, Que., Can., 1975-79, assoc. prof., 1980-84, prof. med. physics, 1985—, dir. med. physics unit, 1991—; dir. dept. med. physics Montreal Gen. Hosp., 1979—. Hon. vis. prof. U. Ljubljana, 1993—, presenter in field. Contbr. numerous articles to sci. jours., chpts. to books. Recipient (with C. Zankowski) of Sylvia Fedoruk prize in Med. Physics, 1997, Farrington Daniels award in Med. Physics, 1997. Fellow Can. Coll. Physicists in Medicine (bd. dirs. 1981-89, v.p. 1984-87, pres. 1987-89), Am. Assn. Physicists in Medicine (bd. dirs. 1990-93, assoc. editor Med. Physics Jour. 1989—, radiother. com. 1994-96); mem. Am. Coll. Med. Physics (bd. chancellors 1997-99), Am. Soc. Ther. Radiology and Oncology, Can. Assn. Physicists, Can. Orgn. Med. Physics, Can. Assn. Radiation Oncologists, Can. Radiation Protection Assn., Internat. Stereotactic Radiosurgery Soc. (bd. dirs. 1991-95). Home: 1540 croissant Seville Brossard QC Canada J4X 1J4 Office: Montreal Gen Hosp Dept Med Physics 1650 Cedar Ave Montreal QC Canada H3G 1A4 E-mail: epodgorsak@medphys.mcgill.ca.

PODHAJSKI, BLANCHE RITA, language foundation administrator; b. New Britain, Conn., Sept. 4, 1945; d. Charles Anthony and Blanche Margaret (Poplawski) P.; m. Kenneth R. Kreiling, June 22, 1990. BS in Speech and Hearing, Boston U., 1967; MS in Speech Pathology, U. Vt., 1969; PhD in Learning Disabilities, Northwestern U., 1980. Speech/lang. pathologist Ctr. Disorders of Comm. Med. Ctr. Hosp. of Vt., Burlington, 1968-70, acting dir. Ctr. Disorders of Comm., 1970-71, dir. Ctr. Disorders of Comm., 1971-78; asst. prof. learning disabilities Northwestern U., Evanston, Ill., 1980-81; pvt. practice as lang. and learning disabilities specialist Aesculapius Med. Ctr., South Burlington, Vt., 1981-83; founder, pres. Stern Ctr. for Lang. and Learning, Williston, Vt., 1983—; clin. assoc. prof. neurology dept. neurology U. Vt. Med. Sch., Burlington, 1971—. Field faculty Goddard Coll., Plainfield, Vt., 1973-76, summer vis. prof., 1980; adj. faculty Johnson (Vt.) State Coll., 1975-79; adj. faculty dept. comm. sci. and disorders, 1983—; mem. Vt. State Dept. Edn. Task Force, Vt. Spl. Edn. Evaluation Project, 1985; exec. bd. dirs. Vt. New Eng. br. Orton Dyslexia Soc., 1986; presenter in field. Co-author: Sounds Abound; contbr. articles to profl. jours. Commencement speaker Pine Ridge Sch., Williston, 1991, bd. dirs., edn. com. chair, 1989; steering com. Vt. State Colls. Am. Reads, 1997; adult edn. consortium Md. State Dept., 1997; mem. collaborative program com. Vt. Lab. Sch. Collaborative, 1998. Grantee Found. for Children with Learning Disabilities, 1985, Vt. Dept. Spl. Edn., 1986, Vt. Dept. Vocat. Rehab., 1992, Kresge Found., 1994, Freeman Found., 1994-00, Alma Gibbs Donchian Found., 1995-99; Turrell scholar, 1994-98. Mem. Am. Speech Lang. and Hearing Assn. (cert. clin. competence), Coun. for Exceptional Children (divsn. for children with learning disabilities), Vt. Speech and Hearing Assn. (pres.-elect 1977-78, clin. achievement award 1989), Vt. Assn. for Learning Disabilities (lifetime hon., outstanding leadership award for contbns. to learning disabled 1976, lamp of knowledge award 1983), Orton Soc. Office: 135 Allen Brook Ln Williston VT 05495-9209

PODHORETZ, NORMAN, magazine editor, writer; b. Bklyn., Jan. 16, 1930; s. Julius and Helen (Woliner) P.; m. Midge Rosenthal Decter, Oct. 21, 1956; children: Rachel, Naomi, Ruth, John. AB, Columbia, 1950; BHL, Jewish Theol. Sem., 1950, LLD (hon.), 1980; BA (Kellett fellow), Cambridge (Eng.) U., 1952, MA, 1957; LHD (hon.), Hamilton Coll., 1969, Yeshiva U., 1991, Boston U., 1995, Adelphi U., 1996. Assoc. editor Commentary, 1956-58, editor in chief, 1960-95, editor-at-large, 1995—; editor in chief Looking Glass Library, 1959-60; sr. fellow Hudson Inst., 1995—. Mem. U. Seminar Am. Civilization, Columbia, 1958. Author: Doings and Undoings, The Fifties and After in American Writing, 1964, Making It, 1968, Breaking Ranks, 1979, The Present Danger, 1980, Why We Were in Vietnam, 1982, The Bloody Crossroads, 1986, Ex-Friends, 1999, My Love Affair With America, 2000, The Prophets, 2002; editor: The Commentary Reader, 1966. Chmn. new directions adv. com. USIA, 1981-87. With AUS, 1953-55. Fulbright fellow, 1950-51. Mem. Coun. on Fgn. Rels. E-mail: NHP30@hotmail.com.

PODOS, STEVEN MAURICE, ophthalmologist; b. N.Y.C., Nov. 7, 1937; s. Mark A. and Sophia L. (Landress) P.; m. Salle Garber, June 20, 1959; children: Richard Lance, Lisa Beth. AB, Princeton U., 1958; MD, Harvard U., 1962. Diplomate Am. Bd. Ophthalmology. Intern U. Utah Affiliated Hosp., Salt Lake City, 1962-63; resident in ophthalmology Washington U. Med. Ctr., St. Louis, 1963-67, from asst. prof. to prof., 1969-75; practice medicine specializing in ophthalmology N.Y.C., 1975—; clin. assoc. NIH, 1967-69; prof. ophthalmology, chmn. dept. Mt. Sinai Med. Sch., N.Y.C.; also ophthalmologist in chief Mt. Sinai Hosp., N.Y.C., 1975—. Mem. editorial bds. various profl. jours.; contbr. articles to med. jours. Mem. sci. adv. bd. Fight for Sight, 1975—; bd. dirs. Nat. Soc. Prevention Blindness, 1977—. Grantee USPHS, 1975—. Mem. Am. Acad. Ophthalmology and Otolaryngology (award of merit), ACS, Am. Ophthalmol. Soc., AAAS, N.Y. Acad. Medicine, Assn. Research Vision and Ophthalmology (trustee 1977-81) Clubs: Princeton. Jewish. Office: Mt Sinai Med Ctr 1 Gustave L Levy Pl New York NY 10029-6500

PODOSHEVA, OLGA, lab administrator, researcher; b. Selidovo, Ukraine, Oct. 30, 1976; arrived in U.S., 1998; d. Anatoliy and Nina Zavgorodniy. MA, Kharkiv Univ., Ukraine, 1998. Histologists N.Y. Eye and Ear Infirmary, 1999—2000, histology lab mgr., 2000—01; surg. pathology mgr. Clin. Diagnostic Svc., Englewood, NJ, 2001—02, Raritan Med. Ctr., Perth Amboy, NJ, 2001—03, Meml. Sloan Kettering Cancer Ctr., N.Y., 2003—. Vol. sch. for kids with spl. needs. Grantee Grant for young scientists, Soros, 1998. Mem.: Nat. Soc. HIstotechnolgy. Avocations: knitting, photography, poetry. Home: 105 River Road Unit E1 Nutley NJ 07110

PODRATZ, KARL C. gynecologic surgeon, oncologist, educator; b. New Ulm, Minn., Feb. 7, 1943; s. Clarence F. and Elsa (Sievert) P.; m. Roxann Rochford; 1 child, Scott Karl. BA, U. Minn., 1966; MD in Medicine, PhD in Biochemistry, St. Louis U., 1974. Resident in ob-gyn. U. Chgo., 1974-77; gynecologic oncology fellow Mayo Clinic, Rochester, Minn., 1977-79, gynecologic surgeon/oncologist, 1979—, chmn. dept. ob-gyn., 1986-2000, Joseph and Barbara Ashkins prof. surgery, 1990—. Dir. gynecologic oncology tng. program Mayo Clinic, Rochester, 1985—. Assoc. editor Gynecologic Oncology; contbr. numerous articles to profl. jours. Fellow ACOG, ACS; mem. Soc. Gynecologic Oncology (pres. 1998-99), Cen. Assn. Ob-Gyn. (pres. 1997, past sec.-treas. 1987-95), Western Assn. Gynecologic Oncologists (past pres. 1991). Avocations: downhill skiing, golf, gardening, cooking, travel. Office: Mayo Clinic 200 1st St SW Rochester MN 55905-0002 E-mail: podratz.karl@mayo.edu.

PODWALL, KATHRYN STANLEY, biology professor; b. Chgo., Oct. 14; d. Frank and Marie C. Stanley. BS, U. Ill.; MA, NYU. Prof. biology Nassau C.C., Garden City, NY. Developmental reviewer West Ednl. Pub., Amesbury, Mass. and Highland Park, Ill., 1989, 91-92; reviewer AAAS, Washington, 1970—; exec. bd., advisor Women's Faculty Assn., Nassau C.C., 1990—, pres, 2000-2002; lectr. in field. Author: Tested Studies for Laboratory Teaching, vol. 5, 1993; editor: (books and cassettes) Rhyming Simon Books and Cassettes, 1990, Sight Reading Syncopation, 1998, Today's Way To Play the Standards, 2000, Today's Way To Play the Classics, 2000, (book and CD) Cartoons & Car Tunes, 2001, Cartoons & Kid Tunes, 2002, Cartoons and Christmas Tunes, 2003. Recipient L.I. Alzheimer's Found. Svc. award, 2002, Excellence award, Nat. Inst. for Staff and Orgnl. Devel., 2003, Chancellor's award excellence in tchg., SUNY, 2004. Mem. AAUW, Nat. Assn. Biology Tchrs. (life), Nat. Sci. Tchrs. Assn. (life), Soc. for Coll. Sci. Tchrs., Am. Women in Sci., Met. Assn. Coll. and Univ. Biologists, Nat. Cathedral Assn., N.Y. Acad. of Scis., Friends of Archives (charter), Xerces Soc., Southampton Colonial Soc., LaSalle County Hist. Soc. (life), Garden City Hist. Soc. (life), Soroptimists (bd. dirs. dist. 1 1994-96, club pres. 1992-94, Nassau County Pres. award 2001), U. Ill. Alumni Assn. (life). Avocations: travel, gardening, zoological pursuits. Office: Nassau Community College One Education Dr Garden City NY 11530 Office Phone: 516-572-7575. Business E-Mail: podwalk@ncc.edu.

POE, BOB, political organization worker, communications company executive; Exec. v.p., dir. mktg. Magnetix Corp., Orlando, Fla. Chmn. Fla. Dem. Party, 2000.

POE, FRANK, convention center administrator; Dir. event facilities, cultural affairs, WRR Dallas Conv. Ctr., 1972-97; exec. dir., ceo Birmingham-Jefferson Conv. Complex, 1997—. Vice chmn. IAAF; bd. trustees Internat. Assn. Assembly Mgrs. Found., 1996. Mem. Interant. Assn. Assembly Mgrs. (bd. dirs. 1993-95, mem., chair conv./exhibit halls com.), Internat. Assn. Exposition Mgrs. (bd. dirs. 1995-97), Profl. Conv. Mgmt. Assn. Office: Birmingham-Jefferson Conv Complex 2100 Richard Arrington Jr Blvd N Birmingham AL 35203-1117

POE, JUDITH A. JOYCE, writer; b. East St. Louis, Ill., July 1941; d. John V. Joyce and Virginia R. Jordan; m. Charles C. Joyce, July 2, 1971; children: Pamela M Schroeder, Debra W. Wade, Bryan Clifton, Regina R. Cert. profl. sec. Mo., 1986. Sec. McDonnell Douglas Corp, St. Louis, 1965—92. Author: (novel) But I Have Known You. Youth leader Dardenne Presbyn. Ch., Mo., 1978—81. Mem.. Wentzville Writers, Saturday Writer. R-Consevative, Presbyterian. Avocations: writing, reading, swimming, travel, golf. Home: 311 N Pt Prairie Wentzville MO 63385 Personal E-mail: poe_judy@hotmail.com.

POE, LAURA, nursing educator, administrator; b. Salt Lake City, July 20, 1962; d. William D. and Laree Jardine (Birch) P. Grad., Utah Tech. Coll., 1980; assoc. degree, Brigham Young U., 1984, B., 1986, MS, 1988. Asst. dir. Divsn. Occupl. and Profl. Licensing Utah Bd. Nursing, exec. dir. Author: (with others) Geri-Assistant Care Manual; contbr. articles to profl. jours. Mem. Utah Nurses Assn. (del., chair govt. rels. com.), Nightingale Soc., Phi Kappa Phi, Sigma Theta Tau.

POE, LUKE HARVEY, JR., lawyer; b. Richmond, Va., Jan. 29, 1916; s. Luke Harvey and Alice Morris (Reddy) Poe; m. Josephine Jaster, Mar. 20, 1998. BS in Math, U. Va., 1938, JD, 1941; postgrad. (Rhodes scholar), Oxford (Eng.) U., 1939; D.Phil., Christ Ch., 1957. Bar: Va. bar 1940, D.C. bar and D.C. Ct. Appeals bar 1967, U.S. Supreme Ct. bar 1969, Md. bar 1974. Assoc. Cravath, Swaine & Moore, N.Y.C., 1941—42; tutor St. John's Coll., Annapolis, Md., 1946—50, asst. dean, 1947—49, tenure tutor, 1953—60, dir. physics and chemistry lab., 1959—60; asst. chmn. Nat. Citizens Com. for Kennedy and Johnson and chmn. Citizens Com., Pres.'s Inaugural Com., 1960—61; asst. to chmn. bd. Aerojet-Gen. Corp., El Monte, Calif., 1961—63; divsn. pres. Internat. Tech. Assistance and Devel. Co., Washington, 1963—66; ptnr. Howard, Poe & Bastian, Washington, 1966—83; pvt. practice law, 1983—. Bd. dirs. First Am. Bank of Md.; cons. Dept. Transp., Dept. State, NEH; lectr. War Coll. of USAF, Gen. Studies program U. Va.; seminar leader Aspen Inst. Humanistic Studies; guest panelist Panel on Sci. and Tech. of Com. on Sci. and Astronautics, U.S. Ho. of Reps., 1970; pres. bd. dirs. Watergate East, Inc., 1976-79, 90-92; organizer U. Va. Unified Liberal Arts Program, 1988—. Author: The Combat History of the Battleship U.S.S. Mississippi, 1947, The Transition From Natural Law to Natural Rights, 1957; (with others) lab. manuals Einstein's Theory of Relativity, 1957, Electro-Magnetic Theory, 1959; editor: (with others) Va. Mag., 1936-38, U. Va. Law Rev., 1940-41. Dean's adv. coun. Lehigh U., 1962-65, mem. Seminar on Sci., Tech. and Pub. Policy, Brookings Instn., 1964-66; coun. on trends and perspectives U.S. C. of C., 1966-69; chmn. bd. Bristol Property Mgmt. and Svcs., Inc., 1967-88; chmn. Annapolis Bd. Zoning Appeals, 1966-75; mem. Annapolis Mayor's Task Force, 1967-74, Md. Gov.'s Commn. on Capital City, 1970-76. Lt. comdr. USNR, 1942-46. Decorated Jhalavada Order of Durbargadh, Dhrangadhara. Mem. Am. Law Inst., AAUP, Raven Soc. (pres.), Soc. of Cincinnati, Sr. Common Room and High Table (Christ Church), Met. Club (Washington), Travellers Club (London), Brook Club (N.Y.C.), New Providence Club (Annapolis), Vincent's Club (Oxford), Phi Beta Kappa, Phi Delta Phi. Episcopalian. Home: 139 Market St Annapolis MD 21401-2628 also: 2500 Virginia Ave NW Washington DC 20037-1901 Office: 2600 Virginia Ave NW Washington DC 20037-1905

POE, ROBERT ALAN, lawyer; b. Bracken County, Ky., Apr. 25, 1951; Student, U. Ky.; BA, Centre Coll., 1973; JD, U. Va., 1976. Bar: Colo. 1976. Mem. Holland & Hart, Denver, 1976—. Adj. prof. taxation U. Denver, 1986-88. Articles editor Va. Law Rev., 1974-76. Mem. ABA, Order of Coif, Phi Beta Kappa. Office: Holland & Hart 8390 E Crescent Pkwy Ste 400 Greenwood Village CO 80111-2822 Office Phone: 303-290-1616. E-mail: apoe@hollandhart.com.

POE, WILLIAM FREDERICK, insurance agency executive, former mayor; b. Tampa, Fla., July 22, 1931; s. Fred Holland and Zula Blanche (Willoughby) P.; m. Elizabeth Ann Blackburn, June 21, 1954; children— William, Keren, Janice, Marilyn, Charles. Student, Duke U., 1950; BS, U. Fla., 1953. Founder, pres. Poe & Assocs. (Ins. Agency), Tampa, 1956-74, chmn., 1979-87, chmn. bd., 1987-93; bd. Poe and Brown Inc. (formerly Poe & Assocs.), Tampa, 1993—; mayor City of Tampa, 1974-79. Mem. Hillsborough County Port Authority, 1961, chmn., 1963; pres. chpt. ARC, United Way of Greater Tampa. Served with USAF, 1955-56. Mem. Tampa Assn. Ins. Agents, Chief Execs. Orgn. Clubs: Yacht. Democrat. Baptist. Office: Poe Investments 302 Knights Run Ave Ste 700 Tampa FL 33602-5969

POEHLEIN, GARY WAYNE, retired chemical engineering educator; b. Tell City, Ind., Oct. 17, 1936; s. Oscar Raymond and Eva Lee (Dickman) P.; m. Sharon Eileen Wood., Jan. 1, 1958; children: Steven Ray, Timothy Wayne, Valorie Ann, Sandra Lee. BSChemE, Purdue U., 1958, MSChemE, 1961, PhD, 1966. Design engr. Proctor & Gamble, Cin., 1958-61; from asst. prof. to assoc. prof. Lehigh U., Bethlehem, Pa., 1965-75, prof. chem. engring., 1975-78, co-dir. emulsion polymers inst., 1973-78; dir. sch. chem. engring. Ga. Inst. Tech., Atlanta, 1978-86, assoc. v.p. rsch., dean grad. studies, 1986-91, v.p. interdisciplinary programs, prof. chem. engring., 1991-95; prof. chem. engring., 1978-96; dir. Chem. and Transport Systems Divsn. NSF, 1996-2000; ret., 2000. Bd. dirs. Flexible Products Co., Marietta, Ga.; interim chair chem. engring. dept., vis. prof. Lehigh U., 2001—02. Contbr. over 100 articles to tech. publs. Mem. sch. bd. Bethlehem Area Sch. Dist., 1969-75. Recipient Honor Scroll award Phila. br. Am. Inst. Chemists, 1977, Mac Pruitt award Coun. for Chem. Rsch., 1989. Fellow AIChE; mem. Am. Chem. Soc., Am. Soc. Engring. Edn., Sigma Xi. Avocations: woodworking, sailing. Home: 407 S Henry St Alexandria VA 22314-5901 E-mail: gspoehlein@aol.com.

POEHLMANN, CARL JOHN, agronomist, researcher; b. Jamestown, Mo., Jan. 29, 1950; s. Edwin William and Lucille Albina (Neu) P.; m. Linda Kay Garner, Dec. 29, 1973; children: Anthony, Kimberly. BS, U. Mo., 1972, MS, 1978. Farmer, Jamestown, Mo., 1972-73; vocat. agrl. tchr. Linn (Mo.) Pub. Schs., 1973-75, Columbia (Mo.) Pub. Schs., 1975-78; dir., mgr. agronomy rsch. ctr. U. Mo., Columbia, 1978-2000; dir. MOAES Field Ops., 2000—. Mem. Am. Soc. Agronomy (div. A-7 chair 1985-86, bd. mem. 1991-94, cert. crop advisor 1993—), Crop Sci. Soc. Am., Soil Sci. Soc. Am., Internat. Assn. Mechanization Field Experiments. Mem. Christian Ch. (Disciples Of Christ). Office: MU Field Ops 3600 New Haven Rd Columbia MO 65201 E-mail: poehlmannc@missouri.edu.

POEHNER, RAYMOND GLENN, retired bank executive; b. Cleve., Oct. 2, 1923; s. Raymond Frank and Winifred (Kirchbaum) P.; m. Frances E. Dunaway Gillespie, Jan. 4, 1958 (dec. 1993); children: R. David, Jacqueline Diane, Leslie Marie, Jon Anthony, Rebecca Glen; stepchildren: Bruce Gillespie, Tony Gillespie. Student, pub. schs., Chgo. and Cleve. Enlisted USN, 1941, advanced through grades to chief petty officer, 1957, ret., 1965; with Security Pacific Nat. Bank, San Diego, 1966-80, loan officer, 1971-74, credit card officer, 1975-80, asst. br. mgr., 1974-80, asst. mgr.; ret., 1980. Mem. VFW, U.S. Naval Inst. (assoc.), Fla. Sheriff's Assn., Am. Biog. Soc. (nat. bd. advisors), R.I. Rsch. (cert. assoc.), Fleet Res. Assn., Rep. Legion of Merit, Nat. Geographic Soc., Am. Legion, Nat. Assn. Civilian Conservation Corps Alumni, Optimist Club (dir. 1978), Fraternal Order Police (booster Fla. chpt.). Republican.

POEL, ROBERT WALTER, air force officer, physician; b. Muskegon, Mich., July 24, 1934; s. Abel John and Fannie M. (Vanderwall) P.; m. Carol Anne Noordeloos, June 24, 1960; children: Kathryn Anne Poel Engle, James Robert, Sharon Kay Poel Thompson. BS, Calvin Coll., 1957; MD, U. Mich., 1959. Diplomate Am. Bd. Surgery. Commd. capt. USAF, 1962, advanced through grades to brig. gen., 1988, ret., 1993; comdr. Hosp. Malmstrom AFB, Great Falls, Mont., 1971-73; dir. profl. svcs. Hdqrs. Tactical Air Command Command Surgeon's Office, Langley AFB, Va., 1973-74; div. chief, med. plans Office of Air Force Surgeon Gen., Wash., 1974-78; comdr. regional hosp. Sheppard AFB, Wichita Falls, Tex., 1978-83, dir. profl. svcs. Office of Air Force Logistics Command Surgeon, Wright-Patterson AFB, Ohio, 1983-85; vice-comdr. Wilford Hall USAF Med. Ctr., San Antonio, 1985-87; chief, quality assurance, dir. plans and resources Air Force Surgeon Gen., Bolling AFB, Washington, 1987-89; hosp. comdr. Malcolm Grow Med. Ctr., Andrews AFB, Washington, 1989-93; med. dir. near south office Meth. Occupational Healthctrs. Inc., Indpls., 1995—. Dir. Andrews Fed. Credit Union, 1991-95, vice chmn. bd. dirs., 1992-95. Advisor, bd. regents Uniformed Svcs. U. the Health Scis., Bethesda, Md., 1989-93; mem. pres. coun. Calvin Coll., 1990. Named Disting. alumnus, Calvin Coll., 1990; Paul Harris fellow Rotary Club of Wichita Falls, 1982. Mem. AMA, Am. Coll. Occupl. and Environ. Medicine, Assn. Mil. Surgeons of U.S. (life), Ret. Officers Assn. (life). Republican. Home: 12085 Waterford Ln Carmel IN 46033-5501 Office: 1101 Southeastern Ave Indianapolis IN 46202-3946 Office Phone: 317-955-2020. Personal E-mail: poelrc@indy.rr.com.

POELSTRA, EDWARD M. management consultant; b. Owosso, Mich. s. Ted and Harriet Poelstra. DD(hon.), World Christanship Ministries, 1992. Cert. safety/security mgmt. Internat. Assoc Hosp. Safety Security, 1995. Pub. info. officer U. Med. Ctr., Tucson, 1988—94; command staff Tucson Escort & Security, Tucson, 1988—95; security supr. Carondelet Health Care, Tucson, 1995—96; CEO EMP Cons. Group, Tucson, 1996—; rep. Ho. of Rep., Ariz., 2000—03. Vol. Ariz. Dept. Pub. Safety, Tucson, 1986—91; command staff Tucson Escort and Security, Tucson, 1988—95; advisor explorer post South Tucson Police Dept., 1991—92; rep. Pima County Rural Health Com., Tucson, 1994—95; co-chair mobile home water svc. comm Mobile Home Water Svc., Ariz.; housing commr. State of Ariz., Phoenix, 2000—03, co-chair rural physcian study com., 2000—03, co-chair corrections study com., mem. com. sr. programs, 2000—03; vol. coord., pub. info. Palo Verde Fire Dist., Tucson, 1994—95. Vol. Tucson Interfaith HIV Network, Balboa Pk. Neighborhood Assn., Tucson; advisor Students Against Drunk Driving, Tucson, 1988—89; rep. Tucson Clean & Beautiful, 1989; counslor Anytown Youth Camps, Ariz.; vol. So. Ariz.AIDS Found.; counslor AMPHI (Sch. Dist) Youth Camps, Ariz.; mem. fin. com. Boy Scouts of Am. Catalina Coun., Tucson, 2003; advisor Ch. of Divine Spirits, Tucson, 1992—94. Named State Legislator of Yr., Ariz. Cops; named one of Top Ten Legislators, Ariz. Software and Tech. Assn., 2001; recipient State Legislator of Yr., Ariz. Propane Assn. Independent-Republican. Avocations: hiking, art. Office: EMP Consulting Group PO Box 50142 Tucson AZ 85703 E-mail: ed poelstra@aol.com.

POESCH, JESSIE JEAN, art historian; b. Postville, Iowa, May 19, 1922; parents: Edward H. and Vina (Meier) P. BA, Antioch Coll., 1944; MA, U. Del., 1956; PhD, U. Pa., 1966. Relief worker Am. Friends Svc. Com., Phila., also, France, Germany, 1946-54; curatorial asst. H.F. DuPont Winterthur (Del.) Mus., 1956-58; from asst. prof. to prof. art history Tulane U., New Orleans, 1963-92, Maxine and Ford Graham chair in fine arts, 1988-92. Guest curator "Painting in the South", Va. Mus. Fine Arts, Richmond, 1980-84, "Jefferson's America and Napoleon's France", New Orleans Mus. Art, 2003; curator "Newcomb Pottery: An Enterprise for So. Women, 1895-1940", Newcomb Coll. Tulane U. and Smithsonian Instn. traveling exhbn. svc., 1980-87. Author: Titian Ramsay Peale, 1799-1885, and His Journals of the Wilkes Expedition, 1961, The Art of the Old South: Painting, Sculpture, Architecture and the Products of Craftsmen, 1560-1860, 1983, (with John Cuthbert) David Hunter Strother: "One of the Best Draughtsmen the Country Possesses", 1997; (book/exhbn. catalogue) The Early Furniture of Louisiana, 1972, Newcomb Pottery: An Enterprise for Southern Women 1895-1940, 1984, Will Henry Stevens, 1987; editor: (with Barbara Bacot) Louisiana Buildings 1720-1948, 1997, (with Nancy E. Green) Arthur Wesley Dow and American Arts and Crafts, 1999, Newcomb Pottery and Crafts, 2003; also numerous articles and book revs. Fellow U. Del., 1954-56; Fulbright scholar U. London, 1960-62; NEH grantee, London, 1969-70. Mem. Soc. Archtl. Historians (bd. dirs. 1986-89), Coll. Art Assn., Am. Antiquarian Soc., La. Endowment for the Humanities (bd. dirs. 1984-90, La. Humanist of Yr. 1992), Victorian Soc. Am. (bd. dirs. 1988-92). Office: Tulane U Dept Newcomb Art New Orleans LA 70118 Office Phone: 504-314-2225. Business E-Mail: jpoesch@tulane.edu.

POETHIG, EUNICE BLANCHARD, clergywoman; b. Hempstead, N.Y., Jan. 16, 1930; d. Werner J. and Juliet (Stroh) Blanchard; m. Richard Paul Poethig, June 7, 1952; children: Richard Scott, Kathryn Aileen, Johanna Klare, Margaret Juliet, Erika Christy. BA, De Pauw U., 1951; MA, Union Theol. Sem., 1952; MDiv, McCormick Theol. Sem., N.Y.C., 1975, STM, 1977; PhD, Union Theol. Sem., 1985. Ordained to ministry Presbyn. Ch., 1979. Missionary United Presbyn. Ch. USA to United Ch. of Christ, The Philippines, 1956-72; mem. faculty Ellinwood Coll. Christian Edn., Manila, 1957-61; mem. faculty, campus ministry Philippine Women's U., Manila, 1962-68. Bd. dirs. Jane Addams Conf., Journey's End Refugee Resettlement Agy., Coun. of Bishops and Execs. of Buffalo Area Met. Ministries; trustee Presbyn. Found., 1991-94, Gen. Bd. Nat. Coun. Chs. Christ, 1995-97; editor New Day Pubs., Manila, 1969-72; curriculum editor Nat. Coun. Chs., Manila, 1962-72; assoc. exec. Presbytery Chgo., 1979-85; exec. Presbytery of Western N.Y., 1986-93; dir. congl. ministries divsn. gen. assembly Gen. Assembly Coun., Presbyn. Ch. (U.S.A.), 1994-98; mem. Coun. Execs., Ill. Coun. Chs., 1980-85. Author: Bible Studies in Concern Response, A.D., 1975, (book) Good News Women, 1987, Sing, Shout and Clap for Joy: Psalms in Worship, 1989, Friendship Press Study on Philippines, 1989, Liturgy 9:1, 1990, Hunger Program Workbook, 1991; editor: (hym book series) Everybody, I Love You, 1971—72, 150 Plus Tomorrow: Churches Plan for the Future, 1982, 1985, Our Living Tradition, 1994, Women of Faith: 1986-1996, 1997, From Slavery to Promised Land, 1999, The Struggle for Equality: Women in Mission, 1999. Mem. Environ. Def. Fund; mem. planning com. Celebrate Adult Curriculum, 1987—93; mem. Erie County (N.Y.) Environ. Mgmt. Coun., 1990—93, NGO Forum UN Fourth World Conf. Women, Beijing, 1995; chmn. governing bd. Stony Point Ctr., 2003—, PC USA; mem. planning com. Transatlantic Dialogue, 2003—04; chmn. PC USA Celebrating the Ordination of Women; mem. Women's Ordination Conf. Nat. Presbyn. Ch. Com., Presbyn. Gen. Assembly Challenge to the Ch. Fund., 1989; mem. design team Covenant People Curriculum, 1997; mem. futures com. Highland Presbyn. Ch., chair, 1997—99; mem. organizing bd. Asian Ctr. Theology and Strategy, Chgo., 1974; bd. dirs. Ch. Women United, Chgo., 1974—79; trustee McCormick Theol. Sem., Chgo., 1974—75; bd. dirs., mem. exec. com. Presbyn. Cmty. Ctr., Louisville, 1999—2001; bd. dirs. More Light Presbyns., 2000—03. Recipient Walker Cup, DePauw U., 1951; Nettie F. McCormick fellow in Old

Testament Hebrew, McCormick Sem., Chgo., 1975; recipient Disting. Alumni award DePauw U., 2003. Mem. Internat. Platform Assn., Soc. Bibl. Lit., Soc. Ethnomusicology, Assn. Exec. Presbyters (bd. dirs., chairperson 1991-93), Am. Schs. Oriental Rsch., Witherspoon Soc., Nat. Assn. Religious Women, Internat. Assn. Women Mins., Nat. Assn. Presbyn. Clergywomen. Home: 1000 E 53rd St #613 Chicago IL 60615

POETTCKER, HENRY, retired academic administrator; b. Rudnerweide, Russia, Mar. 27, 1925; s. John and Margaretha (Voth) P.; m. Aganetha Baergen, July 4, 1946; children: Victoria, Ronald, Martin. AB, Bethel Coll., North Newton, Kans., 1950; B.D., Mennonite Bibl. Sem., Chgo., 1953; Th.D., Princeton Theol. Sem., 1961, converted PhD, 1973. Ordained to ministry Mennonite Ch., 1948; instr. Can. Mennonite Bible Coll., Winnipeg, Man., 1954-59, pres., 1959-78, Mennonite Bibl. Sem., Elkhart, Ind., 1978-90, assoc. for devel., 1991-93;, 1993. Interim dean Bluffton (Ohio) Coll., 1965-66; vis. lectr. Taiwan Theol. Coll. and Tainan Theol. Coll., Taiwan, 1973-74 Editor: (with Rudy A. Regehr) Call to Faithfulness, 1972, Alumni Bull. Can. Mennonite Bible Coll, 1960-73. Pres. Gen. Conf. Mennonite Ch., Newton, Kans., 1968-74. Mem. Soc. Bibl. Lit. and Exegesis. Home: 301-475 Lindenwood Dr E Winnipeg MB Canada R3P2P3 E-mail: henr2502@mts.net. *The secret of happiness lies not in doing what one likes, but in liking what one does.*

POFF, RICHARD HARDING, retired state supreme court justice; b. Radford, Va., Oct. 19, 1923; s. Beecher David and Irene Louise (Nunley) P.; m. Jo Ann R. Topper, June 24, 1945 (dec. Jan. 1978); children: Rebecca, Thomas, Richard Harding; m. Jean Murphy, Oct. 26, 1980. Student, Roanoke Coll., 1941-43; LL.B., U. Va., 1948, LL.D., 1969. Bar: Va. 1947. Partner law firm Dalton, Poff, Turk & Stone, Radford, 1949-70; mem. 83d-92d congresses, 6th Dist. Va.; justice Supreme Ct. Va., 1972-89, sr. justice, 1989—2002. Vice chmn. Nat. Commn. on Reform Fed. Crime Laws; chmn. Republican Task Force on Crime; sec. Rep. Conf., House Rep. Leadership. Named Va.'s Outstanding Young Man of Year Jr. C. of C., 1954; recipient Nat. Collegiate Athletic Assn. award, 1966, Roanoke Coll. medal, 1967, Distinguished Virginian award Va. Dist. Exchange Clubs, 1970, Presdl. certificate of appreciation for legislative contbn., 1971, legislative citation Assn. Fed. Investigators, 1969, Thomas Jefferson Pub. Sesquicentennial award U. Va., 1969, Japanese Am. Citizens League award, 1972, Carrio Professionalism award Va. State Bar Assn. Criminal Law Sect., 1998; named to Hall of Fame, Am. Legion Boys State, 1985; fellow Va. Law Found., 1997. Mem. Bar Assn., VFW, Am. Legion, Pi Kappa Phi, Sigma Nu Phi. Clubs: Mason, Moose, Lion. Office: Va Supreme Ct 100 N 9th St Richmond VA 23219-2335 *When you know you are right, fight. When you are in doubt, wait. When you know you are wrong, admit your mistake and correct it.*

POGEDE, ALEXANDER, consulting company executive; b. Berlin, Mar. 18, 1974; arrived in U.S., 1991; s. Viktor and Inge Pogede; m. Tiana Naoko Maeda, June 14, 2001. Pres. Aridis Corp., L.A., 1996—98, Aridis AG, Berlin, 1998—2000, Aridis KK, Tokyo, 2000—02; chmn. Aridis Corp., Miami, Fla., 2002—. Founder Alexander Pogede Found. Office: Aridis Corp 8345 NW 66th St #2708 Miami FL 33166-2626 Office Phone: 800-741-3054. Office Fax: 800-515-8216. E-mail: alexander_pogede@aridis.com.

POGNONEC, YVES MAURICE, steel products executive; b. Rennes, Bretagne, France, Jan. 21, 1948; came to U.S., 1983; s. Jean P. and Simone J. (Boudot) P. M in Engring., Centrale Paris, 1970; MA in Bus., CPA, Paris, 1982. Cons. Office of Graham Parker, Paris, 1972-75; sales mgr. fittings dept. Vallourec S.A., Paris, 1975-79, mgr. engring. dept., 1980-82; v.p. mktg. and sales Vallourec Inc., Houston, 1983-88, exec. v.p., 1989-97, pres., 1998—; v.p. Vallourec & Mannesmann Tubes Corp., 1997—. Advisor French Fgn. Trade Counselors, Houston, 1987—. Bd. trustees, v.p. Awty Internat. Sch., Houston, 1997—. Lt. French Air Force, 1970-71. Mem. Assn. Ecole Centrale, Nat. Assn. Steel Pipe Distbrs. (bd. dirs.). Avocations: pilot, scuba diving, tennis. Office: Vallourec Inc 1990 Post Oak Blvd Ste 1400 Houston TX 77056-3813

POGO, GUSTAVE JAVIER, cardiothoracic surgeon; b. Buenos Aires, Feb. 7, 1957; came to U.S., 1964; s. Angel Oscar and Beatriz (Garcia-Tuñon) P.; m. Janis Teitler, Feb. 17, 1983; children: Michael Tyler, Katherine Elizabeth. BA, NYU, 1979, MD, 1983. Gen. surgery resident North Shore Univ. Hosp., Manhasset, N.Y., 1983-88; cardiothoracic surgery resident Mt. Sinai Sch. Medicine, N.Y.C., 1988-91; attending, cardiothoracic surgery North Shore Univ. Hosp., Manhasset, 1991—. Contbr. articles to profl. jours. Fellow ACS, Am. Coll. Chest Physicians, Am. Coll. Cardiology; mem. Soc. Thoracic Surgery. Office: North Shore Univ Hosp 300 Community Dr Manhasset NY 11030-3801

POGREBIN, BERTRAND B. lawyer; b. Bklyn., Apr. 10, 1934; s. Abraham and Esther Pogrebin; m. Letty Cottin; children: Abigail, Robin, David. AB, Rutgers U., 1955; LLB, Harvard U., 1958. Bar: N.Y. 1959, U.S. Dist. Ct. (ea. and so. dists.) N.Y. 1963, U.S. Ct. Appeals (2d cir.) 1965, U.S. Ct. Appeals (4th cir.) 1965, U.S. Ct. Appeals (6th cir.) 1970, U.S. Ct. Appeals (9th cir.) 1987, U.S. Supreme Ct. 1991. Pres. Rains & Pogrebin, PC, NYC, 1959—2004; ptnr. Grotlar, Glassman and Hoffman PA, NYC, 2004—. Adj. prof. law NYU, 1975-90, Hofstra Law Sch., 1980-82, 86-91, 97-98; vis. lectr. Yale Law Sch., 1983. Co-author: Labor Relations: The Basic Process, Law and Practice, 1988, 2d edit., 1999; mem. editl. bd. NY Law Jour. Active Am. Jewish Congress; bd. dirs. Appleseed Found. Mem. ABA, N.Y.C. Bar Assn., Nassau County Bar Assn., Suffolk County Bar Assn., Indsl. Rels. Rsch. Assn. Home: 33 W 67th St New York NY 10023-6224 Office: 650 Fifth Ave New York NY 10019 Business E-Mail: pogrebinb@gghlaw.com.

POGREBIN, LETTY COTTIN, writer, lecturer; b. N.Y.C., June 9, 1939; d. Jacob and Cyral (Halpern) Cottin; m. Bertrand B. Pogrebin, Dec. 8, 1963; children: Abigail and Robin (twins), David. AB cum laude with spl. distinction in English and Am. Lit, Brandeis U., 1959. V.p. Bernard Geis Assocs. (book pubs.), N.Y.C., 1960-70; columnist The Working Woman column Ladies Home Jour., 1971-81; contbg. editor Tikkun mag., 1988—, Family Circle, 1989—; founding editor Ms mag., N.Y.C., 1971-87, columnist, editor at large, 1987-89, contbg. editor, 1990—; columnist The N.Y. Times, Newsday, Washington Post, Moment Mag., Washington, 1990—, Moment Mag., Washington, 1990—. Cons. Free to Be, You and Me projects, 1972—; lectr. women's issues and family politics, changing roles of men and women, friendship in Am., non-sexist child rearing and edn., Judaism and feminism, Mid-East politics. Author: How to Make It in a Man's World, 1970, Getting Yours: How to Make the System Work for the Working Woman, 1975, Growing Up Free, 1980, Stories for Free Children, 1982, Family Politics, 1983, Among Friends, 1986, Deborah, Golda, and Me: Being Female and Jewish in America, 1991, Getting Over Getting Older: An Intimate Journey, 1996, Three Daughters: A Novel, 2002; mem. editl. bd. Tikkun Mag., Commonquest mag.; contbr. articles to N.Y. Times, Washington Post, Boston Globe, The Nation, TV Guide, Family Circle, Elle, Travel & Leisure, also other mags., newspapers. Pres. Author's Guild, 1998-2002; bd. dirs. Ms. Found. for Edn. and Comm., New Israel Fund, Jewish Fund for Justice, Commn. on Women's Equality, Am. Jewish Congress, PEN Am.; mem. Task Force on Women Fedn. Jewish Philanthropies, Women's Forum. Pointer fellow Yale U., 1982, MacDowell Colony fellow, 1979, 89, 94, 2000, Cummington Colony Arts fellow 1985, Edna St. Vincent Millay Colony fellow, 1985; recipient Matrix award Women in Comm., 1981, Gloria Steinem Women of Vision award Ms. Found. for Women, 1990, Abram L. Sachar medal Brandeis U., 1994, Woman of Valor award Jewish Fund for Justice, 1997, Woman of Achievement award N. Shore Child and Family Assn., 1997, Hannah G. Solomon award Nat. Coun. Jewish Women, 1997, Woman of Distinction award Kingsborough Coll., 1998, U.S./Israel Women-to-Women award, 1999, N.Y.C. Contr.'s Jewish Heritage award, 1999; named Woman of Yr. Fifty-Plus Expo, 1997, Outstanding Scholars 21st Century, 2000, Vet. Feminists of Am. Hon. Roll, 2002. Address: care Rosenstone/Wender 3 E 48th St New York NY 10017-1027 Office: Rosenstone Wender 38 E 29th St New York NY 10016-7911*

POGSON, STEPHEN WALTER, lawyer; b. N.Y.C., May 11, 1937; s. Percy Walter and Catherine (Hawbaker) P.; m. Linda Hammond, Aug. 20, 1966; children: Clyde Hammond, Catherine Anne. BA, U. Ariz., 1958, LLB, 1961. Bar: Ariz. 1961, U.S. Ct. Appeals (9th cir.) 1968, U.S. Supreme Ct. 1970. Assoc. Evans, Kitchel & Jenckes, Phoenix, 1962-67, ptnr., 1967-90; adminstrv. law judge Indrl. Commn. Ariz., 1990—, vice chief ALJ, 1997—. Served with U.S. Army, 1961-62. Mem. ABA. Democrat. Presbyterian. Office: 800 W Washington St Ste 400 Phoenix AZ 85007-2934

POGUE, A MACK, real estate company executive; b. 1934; Real estate salesman Majors & Majors, Dallas, 1956-65; with Lincoln Property Co. (partnership with Trammell Crow), Dallas, 1965—, chmn. bd. dirs., pres., CEO, 1968—. Office: Lincoln Property Co 500 N Akard St Ste 3300 Dallas TX 75201-3347*

POGUE, DONALD CARL, federal judge; b. 1947; BA magna cum laude, Dartmouth Coll., 1969; student, U. Essex, 1969-70; MA, JD, Yale U., 1974. Bar: Conn. 1974. Pvt. practice, 1974-75; ptnr. Kestell, Pogue & Gould, 1976-89; commr. Conn. Commn. Hosps. and Health Care, 1989-94; judge Conn. Superior Ct., 1994-95, U.S. Ct. Internat. Trade, N.Y.C., 1995—. Mem. Phi Beta Kappa. Office: US Ct Internat Trade One Federal Plz New York NY 10278-0001

POGUE, JOHN MARSHALL, physician; b. Washington, Sept. 21, 1945; s. L(loyd) Welch and Mary Ellen (Edgerton) P. *His father and mother are his guiding lights. Ancestor William Bradford "was the first American citizen of the English race who bore rule by the free choice of his brethren" the first American historian, and thus the Father of American History. Ancestor Hannah (Bradford) Ripley (Governor William Bradford's granddaughter) was America's first Physician of her gender. His uncle, Massachusetts Institute of Technology Institute Professor Harold Eugene Edgerton, enhanced his interest in Science. He worked with Harold on ultra-high-speed photography in Harold's Stroboscopic Light Laboratory and on sonar probes. The difficult Harold did at once; the impossible took a little longer.* AB with honors, Princeton U.; MD, Georgetown U. Diplomate Nat. Bd. Med. Examiners. Intern, resident Georgetown U. Hosp., Washington; editor, author Bradford Jour., 1983—; historian Gov. Bradford Compact, 1996—, surgeon, 1999—. Spkr. and lectr. in field of cardiology. *He is a Fellow of five Scientific and Learned Societies, and he is active in numerous Cardiology Societies. He received Honors in various Medical School courses, having ranked within the top 5% of the entire Medical School class in those courses. As a premedical student at Princeton University, he achieved high academic distinction climaxed by his ranking within the top 2%of his class of 789 students in the junior year—the year that is particularly important for premedical students. He also received a Letter of Individual Commendation for his scholarship from the Dean of the College at Princeton.* Designer ofcl. Gov. William Bradford Flag, 1987 (New Constellation award Nat. Flag Found., 1996); editor, contbr.: Pogue/Pollock/Polk Genealogy as Mirrored in History, From Scotland to Northern Ireland/Ulster, Ohio, and Westward, 1990 (recipient 7 awards, 5 first pl. in genealogy and 2 meritorious in history), assoc. editor: Hereditary Soc. Blue Book, 1997—; author: Herbert Martin Giffin, M.D., A Role Model Physician and a Doctor's Doctor: From Princeton to Johns Hopkins, Mayo Clinic, USN, and Yater Clinic, 2000, Sir William Osler, M.D., The Preeminent Physician: From McGill to the University of Pennsylvania, Johns Hopkins, and Oxford, 2004; contbr. articles on cardiology to med. jours. Fellow: Royal Soc. Arts, Royal Geog. Soc., Royal Statis. Soc., Royal Soc. Medicine (cardiothoracic sect.), Royal Microscopical Soc. Oxford; mem.: AMA, World Heart Fedn. (Switzerland), Cardiac Muscle Soc., Internat. Soc. Heart Rsch. (Can.), Internat. Soc. Cardiovasc. Pharmacotherapy (Switzerland), Heart Failure Soc. Am., Capital Area Heart Failure Soc. (founding mem. 2002), Soc. Cardiovasc. Magnetic Resonance, Internat. Soc. Holter and Noninvasive Electrocardiology, Internat. Soc. Electrocardiology (Glasgow U.), Internat. Cardiac Doppler Soc., Internat. Soc. Cardiovasc. Ultrasound, Am. Soc. Echocardiography (coun. on cardiac sonography, coun. on intraoperative echocardiography), European Soc. Cardiology, Laennec Cardiovasc. Sound Soc., Am. Heart Assn. (coun. clin. cardiology), Oxford Bibliog. Soc. Oxford U. Bodleian Libr., The Princeton U. Club (Washington), RSM Music Soc./Royal Soc. Medicine Music Club, Royal Soc. Medicine Book Club, Kenwood Citizens Assn., Provincial Families Md., Nat. Gavel Soc., Order Descs. Colonial Physicians and Chirurgiens (surgeon gen. 1994—2000, chmn. hon. membership com. 1994—, v.p. gen. 2000—03, pres. gen. 2003—), Soc. Mayflower Descs. DC (surgeon 1998—), Princeton Tigertones Alumni, Princeton U. Alumni Assn., Internat. Shakespeare Assn. Stratford-upon-Avon, Oxford Hist. Soc., Ashmolean Natural History Soc. Oxford, Friends Oxford U. Mus. History of Sci., Friends McGill U. Osler Med. Libr., Friends Nat. Libr. Medicine (founding mem.). Avocations: reading Shakespeare, classical music. Home and Office: 5204 Kenwood Ave Chevy Chase MD 20815-6604

POGUE, RICHARD WELCH, lawyer; b. Cambridge, Mass., Apr. 26, 1928; s. Lloyd Welch and Mary Ellen (Edgarton) P.; m. Patricia Ruth Raney, July 10, 1954; children: Mark, Tracy, David. BA, Cornell U., 1950; JD, Mich. Law Sch., 1953. Bar: Mich. 1953, Ohio 1957, U.S. Dist. Ct. (no. dist.) Ohio 1960, U.S. Ct. Appeals (6th cir.) 1972, U.S. Ct. Appeals (D.C. and 9th cirs.) 1979. Assoc. Jones, Day, Reavis & Pogue, Cleve., 1957-60, ptnr., 1961—, mng. ptnr., 1984-92, sr. ptnr., 1993-94; sr. advisor Dix & Eaton, Cleve., 1994—. Vis. prof. Mich. Law Sch., 1993-95; bd. dirs.Continental Airlines, Inc., Houston, Roten Inc., Aurora, Ohio, Viztek Inc., Twinsburg, Ohio. Chmn. Cleve. Found., 1985-89, Greater Cleve. Roundtable, 1986-89, Greater Cleve. Growth Assn., 1991-93, Univ. Hosps., 1994—, trustee 1975—, Cleve. Ballet, 1983-85, United Negro Coll. Fund., Cleve., 1979, United Way Cleve., 1989, Kulas Found., 1998-, Bus. Vol. United, 1998-2001, Nat. Inventors Hall of Fame, 1996-, Newcomen Soc. U.S., Phila., 2000-; mem. Adminstrv. Conf. U.S., 1974-80; vice chmn. Cleve. Tomorrow, 1988-93; trustee Case Western Res. U.; active Coun. Fgn. Rels., 1989—, Am./EC Assn. Bus. Adv. Coun., 1988-93; trustee Rock and Roll Hall of Fame and Mus., 1986—; co-chmn. 1996 Cleve. Bicentennial Commn., interim chmn. Cleve. Inst. Music, 1994. Capt. U.S. Army, 1954-57. Recipient Outstanding Alumnus award U. Mich. Club, Cleve., 1983, Torch of Liberty award Anti-Defamation League, 1989, Leadership Cleve. Vol. of Yr. award, 1990, 1st Econ. Devel. Workshop award Nat. Coun. on Urban Econ. Devel., 1992, Humanitarian award Nat. Conf. Christians and Jews, 1992; named Cleve. Bus. Exec. of Yr., 2000, Cleve. United Way Vol. of Yr., 2002. Mem. ABA (chmn. antitrust sect. 1983-84), Ohio State Bar Assn. (chmn. antitrust sect. 1969-73). Clubs: Bohemian (San Francisco), Soc., Union (Cleve.). Republican. Mem. United Ch. of Christ.

POGUE, VELVIE ANNE, nephrologist, educator; d. Henry Robinson and Maggie Mandigo; m. Alfred Robert Ashford; children: Alfred C. Ashford III, Adrienne Ashford. BS, So. U., Baton Rouge, 1970; MD, Harvard U., 1974. Diplomate Am. Bd. Internal Medicine, 1978, nephrology Am. Bd. Internal Medicine, 1980. Intern in internal medicine Harlem Hosp. Ctr., N.Y.C., 1974—75, resident in internal medicine, 1975—77, fellow in clin. nephrology, 1977—79, attending physician, 1979—, chief divsn. nephrology, 1990—; assoc. prof. clin. medicine Coll. Physicians and Surgeons, Columbia U., N.Y.C., 2002—. Rschr. African Am. Study of Kidney Disease and Hypertension, N.Y.C. Named to America's Leading Black Doctors, Black Enterprise Mag., 2001. Mem.: Am. Heart Assn., Nat. Kidney Found., Internat. Soc. Hypertension in Blacks, Nat. Med. Assn., Am. Soc. Nephrology. Achievements include research in complications of hypertension, including hypertensive renal disease in blacks; impact of changes in blood pressure staging on recognized severity of hypertension. Office: Harlem Hospital Center 506 Lenox Ave New York NY 10037 Personal E-mail: vap1@columbia.edu. E-mail: vap1@columbia.edu.

POGUE, WILLIAM REID, former astronaut, foundation executive, business and aerospace consultant; b. Okemah, Okla., Jan. 23, 1930; s. Alex W. and Margaret (McDow) P.; m. Jean Ann Pogue; children: William Richard, Layna Sue, Thomas Reid. BS in Secondary Edn., Okla. Bapt. U., 1951, D.Sc. (hon.), 1974; MS in Math., Okla. State U., 1960. Commd. 2d lt. USAF, 1952, advanced through grades to col., 1973; combat fighter pilot Korea, 1953; gunnery instr., 1954; mem. acrobatic team USAF Thunderbirds, Luke AFB and Nellis AFB, Nev., 1955-57; asst. prof. math. USAF Acad., 1960-63; exchange test pilot Brit. Royal Aircraft Establishment, Ministry Aviation, Farnborough, Eng., 1964-65; instr. USAF Aerospace Research Pilots Sch., Edwards AFB, Calif., 1965-66; astronaut NASA Manned Spacecraft Center, Houston, 1966-75; pilot 3d manned visit to Skylab space sta.; ret. Decorated Air medal with oak leaf cluster, D.S.M.; named to Five Civilized Tribes Hall of Fame, Choctaw descent; recipient Distinguished Service medal NASA, Collier trophy Nat. Aero. Assn.; Robert H. Goddard medal Nat. Space Club; Gen. Thomas D. White USAF Space Trophy Nat. Geog. Soc.; Halley Astronautics award, 1975; de la Vaalx medal Fedn. Aeronautique Internat., 1974; V.M. Komarov diploma, 1974; inducted into Okla. Aviation and Space Hall of Fame, 1980, U.S. Astronaut Hall of Fame, 1997. Fellow Acad. Arts and Scis. of Okla. State U., Am. Astron. Soc.; mem. Soc. Exptl. Test Pilots, Explorers Club, Sigma Xi, Pi Mu Epsilon. Baptist (deacon). Home: 4 Cromer Dr Bella Vista AR 72715-5318

POHAN, ARMAND, transportation executive, professional hockey club executive, lawyer; b. Langley Field, Va., Apr. 28, 1944; s. Armen and Helen (Turner) P.; m. Margaret A. Neigel, Dec. 18, 1976; children: Andrew Stephen, Alicia Margaret, Amanda Turner AB, Harvard U., 1964, JD, 1967. Bar: N.J. 1967. Assoc. McCarter & English, Newark, 1968-70; asst. prosecutor Hudson County, N.J., 1970-72; assoc. McCarter & English, 1973-76, ptnr., 1976-77; v.p. A-P-A Transport Corp., North Bergen, N.J., 1977-83, pres., 1983—, Colo. Rockies Hockey Club, Denver, 1978-81; chmn. bd. dirs. NY Waterway, 2001—. Mem. Fort Lee Bd. Adjustment, N.J., 1977-78; mem. Fort Lee Planning Bd., 1979, 2002—, borough atty., Fort Lee, 1973-76, councilman, 2003—; bd. govs. Nat. Hockey League, 1978-81; trustee Bede Sch., Englewood, N.J., 1984-90; trustee Dwight-Englewood Sch., 1984-92, pres., 1985-92. Mem. N.J. Bar Assn. Office: A-P-A Transport Corp 2100 88th St North Bergen NJ 07047-4721 E-mail: apohan@aol.com.

POHAN, CATHY ANN, education educator, consultant; d. Aram and Seroy (Sue) (Hachadourian) Pohan. BA, Calif. State U., Fresno, 1975—80, MA, 1989—90; PhD, U. Nebr., Lincoln, 1991—94. Cert. Tchr. Calif. Tchg. Commn., 1980. Elem. sch. tchr. Fresno Unified, Calif., 1981—82, LA Christian Sch., 1982—89; prof. U. No. Colo., Greeley, Calif., 1994—96, San Diego State U., 1996—. Dir., coord. SDSU/CVESD Partnership Tchr. Preparation program, Chula Vista, Calif., 1998—. Contbr. articles pub. to profl. jour. Bd. mem. Asters Collection Home Owners Assn., Chula Vista, Calif., 2001—03. Recipient Outstanding Tchr. Yr., Delta Kappa Gamma, Colo., 1995. Mem.: ASCD, Am. Ednl. Rsch. Assn. (mem. and proposal reviewer 1995—2003). Office: San Diego State U 5500 Campanile Dr San Diego CA 92182-1153 Business E-Mail: pohan@mail.sdsu.edu.

POHL, ADOLF LEOPOLD, clinical chemist, quality assurance consultant; b. St. Poelten, Austria, Dec. 14, 1936; s. Adolf Theodor and Cornelia Maria Anna (Moerth) P.; m. Ingrid Maria Antonia Payer, Feb. 24, 1962 (div. Dec. 11, 1975); children: Martin, Ulrike; m. Nanako Tanaka, Mar. 14, 1989; 1 child, Anna Yumi. Grad. in classical studies, Stiftsgymnasium Melk, 1954; BSc, U. Vienna, 1957, MSc, 1965, DPhil, 1968. Rsch. asst. med. dept. I U. Vienna Med. Sch., 1967-69, asst. prof., 1969-85, head erythrocyte enzyme lab. med. dept. I, 1969-85, founder tumor marker lab., 1978, head tumor marker lab., 1984-85, assoc. prof. med. dept. I, dept. chemotherapy, 1985-87, assoc. prof. dept. clin. labs., 1987-97. Quality assurance cons. Med. Pharm. Rsch. Ctr., Vienna, 1993—. Mem. editl. bd. Cancer Molecular Biology Jour., 1994—; contbr. articles to profl. jours., chpts. to books. Recipient Austrian Med. Assn. award, 1969. Mem. Am. Assn. for Clin. Chemistry, N.Y. Acad. Scis., IEEE Computer Soc., Drug Info. Assn. Achievements include discovery in human blood serum of a new ADP-ribosyltransferase, implementation of advanced data analysis in clinical chemistry, detection by new micromethods of phospholipid metabolism in red blood cell membranes and study of its abnormalities in hemolytic anemia; research on serum glycosyltransferases as possible cancer markers and critical analysis of galactosyltransferase heterogeneity; leading of 1st foldboat expedition on Tenojoki, 1st behavioral studies of Thai ferret badger. Home: Lambrechtgasse 3/10 A-1040 Vienna Austria E-mail: adolf.pohl@chello.at.

POHL, ELIZABETH, contracting company executive; b. Dec. 15, 1957; CEO TC Enterprises, Inc., Albuquerque, 1986—. Mem.: Albuquerque Hispano C. of C. Office: TC Enterprises Inc 6000 Indian School Rd NE Albuquerque NM 87110-4178 Fax: 505-883-6275.

POHL, FREDERIK, freelance/self-employed writer; b. N.Y.C., Nov. 26, 1919; s. Fred George and Anna Jane (Mason) P.; m. Carol Ulf, Sept. 15, 1953 (div. 1981); children— Ann, Karen, Frederik, Kathy; m. Elizabeth Anne Hull, July 27, 1984 Editor Popular Pubs., N.Y.C., 1939-43; editor Popular Sci., N.Y.C., 1946-49; freelance writer N.Y.C., 1950-60, 80—; editor Galaxy Pubs., N.Y.C., 1961-69, Bantam Books, N.Y.C., 1973-80. Author: Man Plus, 1977 (Nebula award), Gateway, 1978 (Nebula, Hugo, Campbell awards, Prix Apollo award), Jem, 1979 (Am. Book award), The Years of the City (Campbell award 1985), Chasing Science, 2000, The Boy Who Would Live Forever, 2004. Served to sgt. USAAF, 1943-45; Italy Recipient Popular Culture Assn. award, 1982 Fellow AAAS; mem. Sci. Fiction Writers of Am. (pres. 1974-76, Grand Master award 1993), World Sci. Fiction (pres. 1980-82), Authors Guild, Astron. Soc. Pacific. Democrat. Unitarian Universalist. Home: 855 Harvard Dr Palatine IL 60067-7026

POHL, GUNTHER ERICH, retired library administrator; b. Berlin, July 22, 1925; came to U.S., 1927; s. Erich Ernst and Martha (Seidel) P.; m. Dorothy Edna Beck, Aug. 21, 1949; children: Christine, Louise, Elizabeth, Ronald BA, NYU, 1947, MA, 1950; MLS., Columbia U., 1951. Librarian local history and genealogy divsn. N.Y. Pub. Libr., N.Y.C., 1948-69, chief local history and genealogy divsn., 1969-85, ret., 1985. Compiler: N.Y. State Biography and Portrait Index. Fellow N.Y. Geneal. and Biog. Soc.; mem. ALA (chmn. genealogy com. 1971-73, 76-78, History sect. award 1996), N.Y. Geneal. and Biog. Soc. (libr., trustee 1982-92), Sigma Phi Epsilon (trustee local chpt. 1978—). Republican. Avocations: stamps, opera, collecting new yorkiana. Home: 134 Lowry Ln Wilmore KY 40390

POHL, KATHLEEN SHARON, editor; b. Sandusky, Mich., Apr. 7, 1951; d. Gerald Arthur and Elizabeth Louise (Neukamm) P.; m. Bruce Mark Allen Reynolds, June 11, 1982. BA in Spanish, Valparaiso U., 1973; MA in English, No. Mich. U., 1975. Producer, dir. fine arts Sta. WNMU-FM, Marquette, Mich., 1981-82; instr. communications Waukesha County (Wis.) Tech. Inst., 1983; editor Ideals mag., Milw., 1983-85; editor, mng. editor Raintree Pubs., Milw., 1985-87; mng. editor, now exec. editor Country Woman mag., Greendale, Wis., 1987—; exec. editor Country Handcrafts mag., Greendale, 1990-93, Taste of Home Mag., Greendale, Wis., 1993—; editor Talk About Pets, Greendale, 1994-95. Author nature book series, 1985-87; sr. editor: Country Woman Christmas Book, 1996—; mng. editor: Irwin the Sock (Chgo. Book Clinic award 1988); exec. editor Taste of Home's Quick Cooking Mag., 1998—, Down the Aisle Countr Style, 2000, Taste of Home's Light & Tasty Mag., 2000—. Mem. Nat. Mus. of Women in Arts, Alpha Lambda Delta (hon.). Home: N54 W26326 Lisbon Rd Sussex WI 53089-4249 Office: Country Woman Mag 5400 S 60th St Greendale WI 53129-1404

POHL, ROBERT OTTO, physics educator; b. Gottingen, Germany, Dec. 17, 1929; came to U.S., 1958; s. Robert Wichard and Auguste Eleonore (Madelung) P.; m. Karin Ursula Koehler, May 6, 1961; children: Helen M., Robert S., Otto C. Vordiplom, U. Freiburg, Fed. Rep. Germany, 1951; diploma, U. Erlangen, Fed. Rep. Germany, 1955, Dr. rer. nat., 1957. Asst. U. Erlangen, 1957-58; rsch. assoc. Cornell U., Ithaca, NY, 1958-60, asst. prof., 1960-63, assoc. prof., 1963-68, prof., 1968-2000, Goldwin Smith prof. physics emeritus, 2000—. Vis. prof. Tech. Hochschule Stuttgart, 1966-67, Tech. U. Munchen, 1973-74, Konstanz U., Regensburg U., 1987-88, all Fed. Republic Germany; vis. scientist Nuc. Research Ctr., Juelich, Fed. Rep. Germany, 1980-81, Hahn-Meitner Inst., Berlin, 1995. Contbr. articles on solid state physics to profl. jours. Recipient Sr. Scientist award Alexander von Humboldt Found., 1980; Guggenheim Found. fellow, 1973, Erskine fellow U. Canterbury, New Zealand, 1988. Fellow AAAS, Am. Inst. Physics (O.E. Buckley

award 1985); mem. NAS, Internat. Thermal Conductivity Confs. Office: Cornell U Physics Dept Ithaca NY 14853-2501 Office Phone: 607-255-3303. Business E-Mail: pohl@ccmr.cornell.edu.

POHLAD, CARL R. professional baseball team executive, bottling company executive; b. West Des Moines, Iowa; Ed., Gonzaga U. With MEI Diversified, Inc., Mpls., 1959—, chmn. bd., 1976—94; pres. Marquette Bank Mpls., N.A., pres., dir., Bank Shares, Inc.; owner Minn. Twins, 1985—. Bd. dirs. Meth. Hosp. Adminstrv. Group, T.G.I. Friday's, Tex. Air Corp., Ea. Airlines, Continental Airlines, Inc., Carlson Cos. Inc. Address: MN Twins Hubert H Humphrey Metrodome 34 Kirby Puckett Pl Minneapolis MN 55415-1523

POHLAD, ROBERT C. consumer products company executive; Dir. Mesaba Holdings Inc.; v.p. N.W. area Pepsi-Cola Bottling Group; pres. Pohlad Cos., 1987—; CEO PepsiAmericas, 2000—01, vice chmn., 2001—02, chmn., 2002—. Office: PepsiAmericas 4000 Dain Rauscher Plaza 60 S Sixth St Minneapolis MN 55402

POHLMAN, RANDOLPH A. business administration educator, dean; b. Topeka, Jan. 25, 1944; s. Clarence Alvin and Martha Melissa (McElheny) P.; m. Jeanne Lucille Gebhart, Aug. 22, 1965; children— Kristina, Lisa BS, Kans. State U., 1967, MS, 1969; PhD, Okla. State U., 1976. Asst. prof., assoc. prof. fin. Kans. State U., Manhattan, 1976-82, assoc. prof., head dept. fin., 1982-84, prof., dean Coll. Bus. Administrn., 1984-90; dir. employee devel. Koch Industries, 1990-91, dir. human resources, 1991-95; dean sch. bus. and entrepreneurship Nova Southeastern Univ., Ft. Laud, Fla., 1995—. Vis. rsch. scholar UCLA, 1983; holder L.L. McAninch Chair of Entrepreneuship, 1988-90; bd. dirs. Union Nat. Bank, Manhattan, mem. investment com., 1986-87, mem. trust mgmt. com., 1988. Author: International Investment, 1977, Financial Statement Analysis and Forecasting for the Non-Financial Executive, 1990, Understanding the Bottom Line: Finance for Non-financial Managers and Supervisors. Chmn. Kans. State U., United Way, 1982; trustee Meml. Hosp., Manhattan, 1984-90; treas. Kans. State U. Found., 1980-90, mem. investments com., 1988; mem. steering com. Ctr. for Workforce Mgmt.; mem. cost containment roundtable Sedgwick County med. Soc.; mem. bd. dirs. Wichita/Sedgwick County Partnership for Growth Employment and Tng.; mem. Broward Econ. Devel. Coun., 1995; mem. exec. edn. adv. bd. Wharton Sch. Univ. Pa., 1995. With USAF, 1971-73. Recipient Outstanding Tchr. award Coll. of Bus., Kans. State U., 1977, All-Univ. Disting. Tchg. award Kans. State U., 1977, Cutting Edge award selection com. Miami C. of C., 1995-96; investments rsch. grantee Kans. State U., 1978. Mem. Fin. Execs. Inst., Am. Fin. Assn., Am. Econ. Assn., Fin. Mgmt. Assn., Midwest Fin. Assn., Kans. State U. Alumni Assn. (treas. 1980-90, trustee 1983-90, bd. dirs.), Manhattan C. of C. (bd. dirs. 1987-90). Clubs: Manhattan Country (bd. dirs. 1983-85). Lodges: Rotary (bd. dirs. Manhattan club, 1986—, pres.-elect Manhattan chpt.). Republican. Avocations: golf, guitar playing, reading. Office: Nova Southeastern Univ Wayne Huizenga Grad Sch 3100 College Ave Fort Lauderdale FL 33314 E-mail: pohlman@nsunova.edu.

POHLMANN, MARCUS D. political science educator; b. Davenport, Iowa, Sept. 18, 1950; s. Clement A. and Lois L. (Smith) P.; m. Barbara A. Heimann, May 27, 1972; 1 child, Justin. BA, Cornell Coll., 1972; MA, Columbia U., 1974, MPhil, 1975, PhD, 1976. Rsch. assoc. Met. Applied Rsch. Ctr., N.Y.C., 1975-76; instr. The Spence Sch., N.Y.C., 1975-76; cons. Media and Soc., N.Y.C., 1982; Fulbright sr. lectr. Yerevan St. U., Armenia, USSR, 1982; asst. prof. Coll. of Wooster, Ohio, 1977-83; assoc. prof. Ark. State U., Jonesboro, 1983-86; prof. Rhodes Coll., Memphis, 1986—. Vis. asst. prof. Bates Coll., Lewiston, Maine, 1976-77. Author: Political Power in the Postindustrial City, 1986, Black Politics in Conservative America, 1990, 2d edit., 1999, Governing the Postindustrial City, 1993, Racial Politics at the Crossroads, 1996, Landmark Congressional Laws on Civil Rights, 2002, African American Political Thought, 2003. Recipient Lydia C. Roberts fellowship Columbia U., N.Y.C., 1972-76. Mem. Am. Polit. Sci. Assn., Acad. Polit. Sci., Am. Mock Trial Assn. (bd. dirs.), Authors Guild. Democrat. Avocations: basketball, bridge, golf, hiking, canoeing. Home: 367 Forest Hill Irene Cordova TN 38018-4628 Office: Rhodes Coll 2000 North Pky Memphis TN 38112-1624 E-mail: pohlmann@rhodes.edu.

POHORECKY-DOLINSKY, LARISSA ALEXANDRA, pharmacologist; b. Cholm, Ukraine, Jan. 16, 1942; came to U.S., 1959; d. Roman and Maria Pohorecky; m. Adrian A. Dolinsky. BS in Pharmacy, U. Ill., 1963; PhD in Pharmacology, U. Chgo., 1967. Postdoctoral fellow MIT, Cambridge, Mass., 1967-70, rsch. assoc., 1970-71; asst. prof. Rockefeller U., N.Y.C., 1971-79; assoc. prof. Rutgers U., Piscataway, N.J., 1979-86, prof., 1986—. Cons. Nat. Inst. Alcoholism and Alcohol Abuse, Bethesda, Md., 1976-81, VA, Washington, 1992-95. E-mail: larissa@rci.rutgers.edu.

POHOST, GERALD MICHAEL, cardiologist, medical educator; b. Washington, Oct. 27, 1941; married; 3 children. BS, George Washington U., 1963; MD, U. Md., 1967. Diplomate Am. Bd. Internal Medicine, Am. Bd. Cardiovascular Disease, Am. Bd. Nuclear Medicine. Intern Montefiore Hosp. & Med. Ctr., Bronx, N.Y., 1967-68, asst. resident, 1968-69; sr. resident Jacobi Hosp. Albert Einstein Coll. Medicine, Bronx, 1969-70; cardiology resident Montefiore Hosp. & Med. Ctr.; clin. & rsch. fellow in medicine Mass. Gen. Hosp., Boston, 1971-73; rsch. fellow in medicine Harvard Med. Sch., Boston, 1971-73, instr. medicine, 1974-77, asst. prof., assoc. prof. medicine, 1977-83; with dept. radiology Mass. Gen. Hosp., Boston, 1977-83, asst. gen. med. svcs., 1978-82; prof. medicine, radiology U. Ala., Birmingham, 1983—, Mary Gertrude Waters chair cardiovascular medicine divsn. cardiovascular disease, 1991—, prof. cardiovascular medicine, 1991—, dir. Ctr. for NMR R&D. Cons. nuclear medicine radiology dept. Mass. Gen. Hosp., 1977-83; dir. ctr. NMR R&D U. Ala. Hosp., Birmingham, 1986—. Sr. editor: Noninvasive Cardiac Imaging, 1983, New Concepts in Cardiac Imaging, 1985, 86, 87, 88, 89, The Principles and Practice of Cardiovascular Imaging, 1991; contbr. more than 400 articles, reviews, book chpts., editls. to profl. jours.; nat. and internat. spkr. in field; mem. editl. bd. Circulation, Jour. Magnetic Resonance in Medicine, Am. Jour. Cardiology, Internat. Jour. Cardiology, NMR in BioMedicine, Coronary Artery Disease, others; editor Jour. Cardiovasc. Magnetic Resonance, 1998—; editor-in-chief Jour. Cardiovascular Magnetic Resonance, 1999—; rsch. interests in radionuclide and nuclear magnetic resonance studies of the heart, myocardial metabolism, cardiac pathophysiology. SCOR grant NIH, 1990—, tng. grant, 1992—, Dept. Energy grant, 1992—, Nat. Ctr. Rsch. Resources, 1992—. Fellow Am. Coll. Cardiology (editl. bd. jour., chmn. cardiac imaging com. 1982-88, current procedural terminology com. 1988-94, gov. rels. com. 1989-95, trustee 1994-99), mem. AMA (chmn. panel nuclear magnetic resonance imaging 1985-88), Am. Fedn. Clin. Rsch., Am. Soc. Clin. Investigations, Am. Assn. Profs., Am. Heart Assn. (fellow coun. clin. cardiology 1975—, Mass. affiliate 1975-83, established investigator 1979-84, Richard and Hinda Rosenthal award for excellence in clin. investigation 1985, chmn. advanced cardiac tech. com. of coun. on clin. cardiology 1981-86, exec. com. 1981-95, 98—, Ala. affiliate 1983—, long range planning com. 1986-89, chmn. 1989-91, vice chmn. exec. com. coun. clin. cardiology 1989-91, nominating com. 1989-91, chmn. 1993-95, budget com. 1989-91, chmn. exec. com. 1991-93, immediate past chmn. 1994—, rsch. com. fellow subgroup A 1988-91), Soc. Nuclear Medicine (coun. nuclear Cardiology 1990-92), Soc. for Cardiovasc. Magnetic Resonance (pres. 1995-98, founder 1995, exec. com. 1995-99, trustees, 1995—), Soc. Magnetic Resonance in Medicine (exec. com. 1987—, sci. program com. 1988-89, pres. 1986-87), Nat. Heart, Lung and Blood Inst. (program project rev. com. A 1984-88, cardiovascular and renal study sect. 1991-94, radiol. study sect. 1994-99), So. Med. Assn., NIH Reviewers Res., U.S. Nuclear Regulatory Commn. (adv. com. 1984-93), Assn. Univ. Cardiologists, Assn. Profs. Cardiology (sec. treas. 1995-96), Sigma Xi. Office: U Ala Birmingham BDB 101 1808 7th Ave S Birmingham AL 35294-0001 Home: 638 Wilcox Ave Los Angeles CA 90004-1113 Fax: 205-975-1952.

POIAN, EDWARD LICIO, historian; b. Trieste, Friuli, Italy, June 10, 1946; came to U.S., 1954; s. Angelo Del Picollo and Zaira (de Bourbon-Comelli) P.; m. Maria Del Carmen Lopez Cintron, Nov. 22, 1969 (div. Mar. 1980); children: Jeanne Marie, Nicole Anna; m. Nancy FLynn, Sept. 18, 1982. AS, U.S. Govt. Inst., 1965; BS, Mercy Coll., 1988; MS, L.I. U., 1989; PhD, U. Ariz., 1992. Chief exec. Budget Fin. Inc., Pittsfield, Mass., 1968-70; acting postmaster U.S. Postal Svc., Chappaqua, 1971-80; v.p. Lehman Bros Khun Loeb, N.Y.C., 1980-83; chief exec. officer Cosmopolitan Armaments, N.Y.C., 1983-90; intern The UN Univ., 1989-90; prof. history Mercy Coll., Dobbs Ferry, N.Y., 1991—, prof. history and pollt. sci., 1991—. Cons. in field; trustee archaeology dept. U. Trieste, 1986—; rector, CEO The Internat. Ednl. Rsch. Found. Inc., Yonkers, N.Y., 1991—; intern UN Univ., 1990; dir. history and govt. assn. Mercy Coll., 1988. Author: On the Outside Looking In, 1972, Peace and Regional Security Through Education in Africa, 1992, Problems in Coordination Among Western Donor Governments in Relations to Multilateral and Social Programmes of the United Nations System, 1990; contbr. articles to profl. jours. With USCG, 1963-67, USCG Res., 1968-98, ret. capt., 2003. Decorated Knight of Malta Cross of Gregory the Great Vatican City. Recipient UN award, 1988. Fellow World Assn. of Former United Nations Interns and Fellows, U.S. Naval Inst. (life); mem. VFW, Yonker Hist. Soc., Am. Soc. Polit. Sci., Am. Legion, Navy League (life N.Y. chpt.), Military Officers Assn. of Am., Phi Alpha Theta, Phi Gamma Mu. Republican. Roman Catholic. Avocations: archeology, historical research, art collector, philanthropy. Home: 1930 Hone Ave Bronx NY 10461-1304 Office: Mercy Coll Dept History and Polit Sci 555 Broadway Dobbs Ferry NY 10522-1134 Office Phone: 914-693-4500.

POIANI, EILEEN LOUISE, mathematics educator, college administrator, higher education planner; b. Newark, Dec. 17, 1943; d. Hugo Francis and Eileen Louise (Crecca) P. BA in Math., Douglass Coll., 1965; MS in Math., Rutgers U., 1967, PhD in Math., 1971. Tchg. asst., grad. preceptor Rutgers U., New Brunswick, N.J., 1966-67, asst. counselor Douglass Coll., New Brunswick, 1967, 69-70, instr. math. St. Peter's Coll., Jersey City, 1967-70, asst. prof., 1970-74, dir. of self-study, 1974-76, assoc. prof., 1974-80, prof., 1980—, asst. to pres., 1976-80, asst. to pres. for planning, 1980-96, exec. asst. to pres., 1996-98, v.p. for student affairs, 1999—. Chair U.S. Commn. on Math. Instrn., NRC of NAS, Washington, 1983-90; founding nat. dir. Women and Math. Lectureship Program, Washington, 1975-81, adv. bd., 1981—; project dir. Consortium for Advancement of Pvt. Higher Edn., Washington, 1986-88; mem. N.J. Math. Coalition, 1991—, Nat. Seminar on Jesuit Higher Edn., 1990-94, strategic planning com. N.J. Assn. Ind. Colls. and Univs., 1990-92; charter trustee Rutgers U., 1992-2004; Nutley panelist Centennial Celebration, 2002; advisor NSF Funded Project of Bank St. Coll. and EDC/Ctr. for Children and Tech., 2003—. Author: (with others) Mathematics Tomorrow, 1981, Encyclopedia of Mathmatics Education; contbr. articles to profl. jours. Mem. Newark Mus., Nutley (N.J.) Hist. Soc., Friends of Newark Libr.; trustee Nutley Free Pub. Libr., 1974-77, St. Peter's Prep. Sch., Jersey City, 1986-92; active fee arbitration commn. N.J. Supreme Ct., 1983-86, ct. ethics com., 1986-90; U.S. nat. rep. Internat. Congress Math. Edn., Budapest, Hungary, 1988; statewide planning com. NCCJ, 1988-92, youth leadership coun., 1992—; chair evaluation teams Mid. States Assn. Coll. and Schs.; U.S. del. Internat. Congress on Math; trustee The Cath. Advocate, 1993-2003; adv. NSF Funded Project Bank St. Coll. & Ed. Ctr. for Children & Tech., 2003-. Recipient George F. Johnson, S.J. Alumni Faculty award, 1976, Douglass Soc. award Douglass Coll., 1982, Outstanding Cmty. Svc. award Christopher Columbus Found., N.J., 1994, Outstanding Svc. award Middle States Assn. Colls. and Schs., 1994, Cert. of Appreciation for outstanding contbns. as nat. dir. women and math. program, 1993, Varsity Letter plaque for leadership and svc. St. Peter's Prep, 1997; named Danforth Assoc., Danforth Found., 1972-86, SPC Legend, Students of St. Peters Coll., 2002, Humanitarian award NCCJ, 2003, N.J. Women of Achievement award N.J. State Fedn. Women's Clubs, 2003, Alumnae Recognition award Douglass Coll., 2003; named to Nutley Hall of Fame, 2003. Mem. AAUP, Math. Assn. Am. (bd. dirs. lectureship program, gov. NJ chpt. 1972-79, chair human resources coun. 1991-96, Outstanding Coll. Tchg. award 1993), Nat. Coun. Tchrs. Math. (spkr. 1974—), Soc. Coll. and Univ. Planning (program com. 1989—, spkr. nat. conf. 1986, 88-90, judge grad. paper competition), Com. on Math. with Disabilities, Com on Devel. of Man, Pi Mu Epsilon (pres. 1987-90, C.C. MacDuffee award for disting. svc. to math. 1995), Phi Beta Kappa, Alpha Sigma Nu, Beta Beta Beta. Roman Catholic. Avocations: gourmet cooking, travel, golf. Office: St Peter's Coll 2641 Kennedy Blvd Jersey City NJ 07306-5997

POINAR, GEORGE ORLO, JR., insect pathologist and paleontologist, educator; b. Spokane, Wash., Apr. 25, 1936; s. George O. and Helen Louise (Ladd) P.; m. Eva I. Hecht; children: Hendrik, Maya; m. 2d, Roberta Theresa Heil; 1 child, Gregory. BS, Cornell U., 1958, MS, 1960, PhD, 1962. Prof. dept. entomology U. Calif., Berkeley, 1964—95; courtesy prof. dept. zoology Oreg. State U., Corvallis, 1995—. Author: Entonmogenous Nematodes, 1975, Nematodes for Biological Control of Insects, 1979, The Natural History of Nematodes, 1983, co-author (with Roberta Polinar) The Quest for Life in Amber, (with Roberta Polinar) The Amber Forest, (with R. Milki) Lebanese Amber, 2001, (with Gerard M. Thomas) Diagnostic Manual for the Identification of Insect Pathogens, 1978, (with G.M. Thomas) Laboratory Guide to Insect Pathogens and Parasites, 1984, (with Hans-Börje Jansson) Diseases of Nematodes, Vols. 1, 2, 1988. Grantee NATO, NSF, NIH, 1962-72. Avocations: photography, classical piano, tennis. Office: Oreg State Univ Dept Zoology Corvallis OR 97331 Office Phone: 541-737-5366. Business E-Mail: poinarg@science.oregonstate.edu.

POINDEXTER, ALAN, astronaut; b. Pasadena, Calif., Nov. 5, 1961; s. John M. and Linda A. Poindexter; m. Lisa A. Pfeiffer; 2 children. B of Aerospace Engring., Ga. Inst. Tech., 1986; MS in Aeronautical Engring., Naval Postgrad. Sch., 1995. Commd. 2d lt. USN, 1986, advanced through grades to comdr.; with Hypervelocity Wind Tunnel Facility, Naval Surface Weapons Ctr., White Oak, Md.; naval aviator Naval Air Sta., Miramar, Calif.; wing qualified landing signal officer Fighter Squadron 211, Miramar, Calif., Arabian Gulf, Operation Desert Storm, Operation So. Watch; test pilot, project officer Naval Strike Aircraft Test Squadron, Naval Air Sta., Patuxent River, Md., lead test pilot; dept. head Astronaut Tng. Fighter Squadron 32, Naval Air Sta.; astronaut NASA, Houston, 1998—, tech. advisor Astronaut Office Shuttle Ops. Br. Mem.: Soc. Exptl. Test Pilots, Tau Beta Pi. Achievements include logged over 2,000 hours in 30 different aircraft; logged over 450 carrier landings. Office: Astronaut Office/CB NASA Johnson Space Ctr Houston TX 77058

POINDEXTER, CHRISTIAN HERNDON, utility company executive; b. Evansville, Ind., Sept. 20, 1938; s. Marlan Glenn and Ellen Mabelle (Sommers) P.; m. Marilyn Ann Mills, June 12, 1960; children: Scott H., Todd S. BS in Engring., U.S. Naval Acad., 1960; MBA in Fin., Loyola Coll., Balt., 1976. With Balt. Gas & Electric Co., 1967—, gen. supr. fin. dept., 1976-78, treas., asst. sec., 1978-79, v.p. engring. and constrn., 1980-85; pres., chief exec. officer, dir. Constellation Holdings, Inc. subs. Balt. Gas & Electric Co., 1985-89; vice chmn. bd. Balt. Gas & Electric Co., 1989-93, chmn., CEO, pres., 1993—. Chmn. bd., chief exec. officer Constellation Biogas Inc., Constellation Investments Inc., Constellation Properties Inc.; bd. dirs. The KMS Group, Inc., 1986—. Trustee Md. Acad. Scis., 1984—, Villa Julie Coll., 1986—; bd. dirs./sec. YMCA of Anne Arundel County, Md., 1985—; bd. dirs., pres. Scholarships for Scholars, Inc.; exec. bd. Balt. Area council Boy Scouts Am.; Served to lt. USN, 1960—67. Mem.: IEEE, Mem. Engring. Soc. Balt. Republican. Office: Balt Gas & Electric Co PO Box 1475 Baltimore MD 21203-1475

POINDEXTER, WILLIAM MERSEREAU, lawyer; b. Los Angeles, June 16, 1925; s. Robert Wade and Irene M. Poindexter; m. Jani Jennifer Wohlgemuth, Feb. 14, 2000; children: James Wade, David Graham, Honour Hélène, Timothy John, Cory Todd Christensen, E.W. Greg Christensen. BA, Yale U., 1946; postgrad., U. Chgo., 1946-47; LL.B., U. Calif., Berkeley, 1949. Bar: Calif. 1952. Practiced in, San Francisco, 1952-54, Los Angeles, 1954—; mem. firm Poindexter & Doutre, Inc., 1964—. Pres. Consol. Brazing & Mfg. Co., Riverside, Calif., 1949-52. Pres. South Pasadena-San Marino (Calif.) YMCA, 1963; Mem. San Marino Sch. Bd., 1965-69, pres., 1967; pres. Conf. of Ins. Counsel, 1975. Served with USMCR, 1943. Fellow Am. Coll. Trust and Probate Counsel; mem. ABA, L.A. County Bar Assn., State Bar Calif., Yale Club (pres. So. Calif. chpt. 1961), Calif. Lincoln Clubs (L.A. downtown chpt. chmn. 1997-2003). Republican. Presbyterian. Office: 1 Wilshire Bldg Ste 2420 Los Angeles CA 90017

POINSETTE, DONALD EUGENE, business executive, value management consultant; b. Ft. Wayne, Ind., Aug. 17, 1914; s. Eugene Joseph and Julia Anna (Wyss) P.; m. Anne Katherine Farrell, Apr. 15, 1939 (dec.); m. Carla Murphy, July 10, 2003; children: Donald J., Eugene J., Leo J., Sharon Poinsette Smith, Irene Poinsette Snyder, Cynthia Poinsette West, Maryanne Poinsette Stohler, Philip J. Student, Purdue U., 1934, Ind. U., 1935-37, 64. With GE Corp., RCA, Stewart Warner Corp., 1937-39; metall. rsch. and field sales cons. P.R. Mallory Corp., 1939-49; dist. sales mgr. Derringer Metall. Corp., Chgo., 1949-50; plant engr. Cornell-Dubilier Electric Corp., Indpls., 1950-53; with Jenn-Air Corp., Indpls., 1953-74, purchasing dir., 1953-71, mgr. value engring. and quality control, 1969-74; bus. mgmt. cons. Mays and Assocs., Indpls., 1974-76. Pres. Marian Coll. Parents Club, Indpls., 1969-70; com. mem. Boy Scouts Am.; nat. trustee Xavier U., 1972-73, Dad's Club, Cin.; mem. Triad choral groups. Recipient Testimonial Golden Anniversary award Purdue U., 1987; named to U.S. Finder's List, Nat. Engrs. Register, 1956, Army Navy E award for excellence in engring. and prodn., 1944. Mem. Nat. Assn. Purchasing Mgmt., Indpls. Purchasing Mgmt. Assn., Soc. Am. Value Engrs. (cert. value specialist, sec.-treas. Ctrl. Ind. chpt. 1972-73), Soc. Ret. Execs. Indpls., Ind. U. Alumni Assn., Purdue U. Alumni Assn., Columbian (pres. 1972-73), Internat. Platform Assn., Tau Kappa Epsilon, K.C. (4 deg.). Home: 5760 Susan Dr E Indianapolis IN 46250-1760

POINTER, MARSHA G. principal; b. St. Louis, Oct. 24, 1950; d. Robert Lee Gentry and Clarice Anita McClure; m. James Earl Pointer, Apr. 15, 1989; children: Tiffany, James Jr. BA, Albion Coll., 1973; MA, Mich. State U., 1977; prin. lic., U. Colo., Denver, 1995. Spl. edn. endorsement EBD (emotional and behavior disorder). Dean, tchr., coach Denver Pub. Schs., 1979—95, asst. prin., 1995—2001, H.S. prin., 2001—. Pres. Manual Leadership High Adv. Bd., Denver, 2001—03. Grantee, U.S. Dept. Edn., 1974, Bill and Melinda Gates Found., 2002. Mem.: Nat. Assn. Secondary Sch. Prins., Nat. Wildlife Assn. Jehovah'S Witness. Avocations: dance, gardening, reading. Home: 12410 E 55th Ave Denver CO 80239 Office: Denver Pub Schs Manual HS 1700 E 28th Ave Denver CO 80205

POINTER, MICHELLE PHILLIPS, counselor, educator, consultant; d. George and Ruth Phillips; m. L.P. Pointer, Jr.; 1 child, Lyle P. B Psychology, Fisk U., 1971; M Guidance and Counseling, Bowie State U., 1977; D Counseling, George Washington U., 2001. Cert. rehab. counselor, nat. cert. counselor, lic. clin. profl. counselor. H.S. psychology tchr. Anne Arundel County Pub. Schs., Annapolis, Md., 1972—73, mental health and gen. counselor Divsn. Rehab. Svcs., Rockville, Md., 1974—84, dist. supr., regional dir. Prince Georges and Montgomery Counties, Md., 1984—91, spl. asst. to asst. supt. Balt., 1991—93, dir. comms. and cmty. rels., 1991—93; state dir. divsn. vocat. rehab. State of Del., Wilmington, 1993—94; regional cons. George Washington U., Washington, 1996—99; adj. prof., instr. Coppin State Coll., Balt., 1995—2001, assoc. prof., 2001—; dir. counseling ministries Round Oak Missionary Bapt. Ch., Silver Spring, Md. Mem. nat. adv. coun. U. Okla., Norman, 1994—96, Howard U., Washington, 1994—, Very Spl. Arts, Washington, 1994—95; mem. regional adv. coun. U. Md., College Park, 2002—; nat. chmn. client svcs. Coun. State Adminstrn. Vocat. Rehab., Washington, 1994—95, regional rep., 1993—96; presenter in field. Dir.: (video) Del. Divsn. Vocat. Rehab., 1994. Mem. Del. Alcohol, Drug Abuse and Mental Health Adv. Coun., Wilmington, 1994—96, Del. Gov.'s Com. on Employment of Individuals with Disabilities, Wilmington, 1993—96, Md. Gov.'s Com. on Employment of Individuals with Disabilities, Balt., 1991—93, Del. Gov.'s Coun. on Equal Employment Opportunities, 1994—95, Del. State Coordinating Coun. for People with Disabilities. Recipient Second Genesis award, 1984, First State Projects with Industry award, 1994, 3d annual award, Nat. Head Injury Coun., Dover, Del., 1996, numerous others. Mem.: ACA, Nat. Assn. Multuval Rehab. Counseling, Nat. Rehab. Counseling Assn., Nat. Rehab. Adminstr. Assn., Internat. Assn. Marriage and Family Counselors, Md. Rehab. Assn. (pres.-elect), Nat. Rehab. Assn., Chi Sigma Iota, Phi Delta Kappa. Office: Coppin State Coll 2500 W North Ave Baltimore MD 21215

POINTER, SAM CLYDE, JR., retired federal judge, lawyer; b. Birmingham, Ala., Nov. 15, 1934; s. Sam Clyde and Elizabeth Inzer (Brown) P.; m. Paula Purse, Oct. 18, 1958; children: Minge, Sam Clyde III. AB, Vanderbilt U., 1955; JD, U. Ala., 1957; LL.M., NYU, 1958. Bar: Ala. 1957. Ptnr. Brown, Pointer & Pointer, 1958-70; judge U.S. Dist. Ct. (no. dist.) Ala., Birmingham, 1970-2000, chief judge, 1982-99; judge Temp. Emergency Ct. Appeals, 1980-87; mem. Jud. Panel Multi-dist. Litigation, 1980-87; ptnr. Lightfoot, Franklin & White, 2000—. Mem. Jud. Conf. U.S., 1987-90; mem. Jud. Coun. 11th Cir., 1987-90, mem. standing com. on rules, 1988-90, chmn. adv. com. on civil rules, 1990-93. Bd. editors: Manual for Complex Litigation, 1979-91. Mem. ABA, Ala. Bar Assn., Birmingham Bar Assn., Am. Law Inst., Am. Judicature Soc., Farrah Order of Jurisprudence, Phi Beta Kappa. Episcopalian. Office: Lightfoot Franklin & White The Clark Bldg 400 N 20th St Birmingham AL 35203 E-mail: spointer@lfwlaw.com.

POINTS, ROY WILSON, municipal official; b. Quincy, Ill., Oct. 21, 1940; s. Jess C. and Gladys (Wilson) P.; m. Karen Lee Olsen, July 23, 1966; children: Eric, Holly. BBA, Culver Stockton Coll., 1968. Tchr., coach Lewis County C-1, Ewing, Mo., 1968-69, Community Unit 3, Camp Point, Ill., 1969-78; real estate salesman Landmark, Quincy, 1978-80; supr. of assessment County of Adams, Quincy, 1980-90; assessor City Twp. of Quincy, 1990—. Chmn. Adams County Bd. Rev., 1977—80. Bd. dirs., 1st v.p., sec. Quincy Jaycees, 1970-76, Quincy Rotary East, 1980. Mem. Cert. Ill. Assessing Officers, Internat. Assn. Assessing Officers (cert. ednl. recognition 1988), Ill. Assessors Assn. (bd. dirs. 1992—), Twp. Ofcls. Ill. (bd. dirs. 1995-2001), North Ctrl. Regional Assn. Assessing Officers (bd. dirs. 1997—). Democrat. Avocations: fishing, hunting, jogging, raising cattle. Office: Quincy Twp Assessor City Hall Annex 706 Maine St Quincy IL 62301-4013 Office Phone: 217-228-4505.

POIRIER, ELIZABETH A. state representative, state legislator; Degree, Johnson & Wales Univ. State rep. legis., Mass., 1999—. Republican. Office: State Ho Rm 541 Boston MA 02133 also: Dist Office 117 Grove St North Attleboro MA

POIRIER, LOUIS JOSEPH, neurology educator; b. Montreal, Que., Can., Dec. 30, 1918; s. Gustave Joseph and Calixta (Brault) P.; m. Liliane Archambault, June 11, 1947; children: Guy, Michel, Louise, Esther. BSc, U. Montreal, 1942, MD, 1947; PhD, U. Mich., 1950; D (hon.), U. Rennes, France, 1973. Asst. prof. U. Montreal, 1950-55, assoc. prof., 1955-58, prof. faculty of medicine, 1958-65; chmn. dept. anatomy Faculty of Medicine, Laval U., Cité Universitaire, Que., 1970-78, prof. exptl. neurology, 1970-83; dir. Centre de Research in Neurobiology, Laval U. and Hosp. de l'Enfant-Jesus, 1977-85, prof. emeritus, 1985—. Contbr. articles to profl. jours.; editor the extrapyramidal system and its disorders in: Advances in Neurology, vol. 24, 1979. Pres. Que. Health Scis. Research Council, 1978-81, Decorated officer Order of Can.; recipient Que. sci. award, 1975; Killam commemorative scholar, 1977, 78 Mem. AAAS, Royal Soc. Belgium (hon.), Neurol. Soc. France (hon.), Am. Assn. Anatomists, Am. Physiol. Soc., Soc. for Neuroscis., Internat. Brain Research Orgn., Can. Med. Assn. (emeritus). Address: 603 Chemin Caron Lac Simon Montpellier QC Canada J0V 1M0

POIRIER, RICHARD, literary critic, educator, editor; b. Gloucester, Mass., Sept. 9, 1925; s. Philip and Annie (Kiley) P. AB, Amherst Coll., 1949; MA, Yale U., 1951; PhD, Harvard U., 1959; student, U. Paris, France, 1944-45; H.H.D., Amherst Coll., 1978. Mem. faculty Williams Coll., 1950-52, Harvard U., 1953-63; Disting. prof. English Rutgers U., 1963—. Bd. dirs., co-founder, chmn. bd. Libr. of Am.; Beckman prof. U. Calif., Berkeley, 1973; chmn. adv. English com. Harvard U., 1988-91; delivered Gauss Seminars, Princeton U., 1990, T.S. Eliot lectures, U. Kent, 1991, Henry James lectures, NYU, 1992. Editor: Partisan Rev, 1963-73, O Henry Prize Stories, 1961-65; editor/founder Raritan Quar., 1981—; author: The Comic Sense of Henry James, 1960, In Defense of Reading, 1962, A World Elsewhere, 1966, The Performing Self, 1971, Norman Mailer, 1973, Robert Frost: The Work of Knowing, 1977, The Renewal of Literature, 1987, Poetry and Pragmatism, 1992, Trying It Out In America, 1999; founder, editor: Raritan Quar., 1981-2001; contbr. author numerous articles, revs. to profl. jours. Served with AUS, 1943-46. Recipient achievement award AAAL, 1978, Jay B. Hubbell award, 1988, Lit. Lion award

N.Y. Pub. Libr., 1992; Fulbright scholar, Cambridge, Eng., 1952-53; Bollinger fellow, 1962-63, Guggenheim fellow, 1974-75, fellow NEH, 1978-79. Mem. Am. Acad. Arts and Scis., Am. Acad. Arts and Letters, P.E.N. (exec. bd. 1986), PMLA (editorial bd. 1977-79), nominating com. Nat. Medal for Lit., 1986, 87, Nat. Book Critics Cir., 1977-85, Century Club. Clubs: Century. Home: 104 W 70th St Apt 9B New York NY 10023-4457 Office: Libr of Am 14 E 60th St New York NY 10022-1006 Office Phone: 212-308-3360.

POIRIER, ROBERT J. floral company executive; BA In Polit. Sci. and Econs., Hamline U.; postgrad., Stanford U. With Florists' Transworld Delivery Assn., 1975, dir. electronic comm. sys., group dir.; pres., CEO Conroy's Flowers; v.p. 1-800-FLOWERS, N.Y.C., 1993-97; co-founder, chmn., CEO, pres. U.S.A. Floral Products, Inc., Washington, 1997—. Chmn. internat. tech. com. Florists' Transworld Delivery Assn. Office: USA Floral Products Inc Ste 300E PO Box 848246 Hollywood FL 33084-0246

POIROT, JAMES WESLEY, engineering company executive; b. Douglas, Wyo., 1931; m. Raeda Poirot. BCE, Oreg. State U., 1953. With various constrn. firms, Alaska and Oreg., CH2M Hill Inc., 1955, v.p., Seattle and Atlanta, from 1967; chmn. bd. CH2M Hill Ltd., Englewood, Colo., 1983-93. Former chmn. Western Regional Coun., Design Profls. Coalition, Accreditation Bd. Engring. and Tech., Indsl. Adv. Coun.; former mem. Oreg. Joint Grad. Schs. Engring., Engring. Coun.; mem. U.S. delegation UN Gen. Assembly, 1997; mem. internat. adv. bd. NRC, 1998—, chmn. com. truck size and weight, 1998—. Founding dir. World Partnership for Sustainable Devel.; mem. U.S. Earth Charter Commn.; trustee Oreg. State U. Fedn., 1992—. Named ENR Constrn. Man of Yr., 1988. Fellow: ASCE (pres. 1993—94), Am. Assn. Engring. Socs. (vice chmn. 1995), Am. Acad. Environ. Engrs. (diplomate), Am. Cons. Engrs. Coun. (life; pres. 1989—90); mem.: World Fedn. Engring. Orgns. (v.p. 1997—2001, com. on tech. transfer, pres. 1995—2001, Disting. Achievement in the Svc. of Humanity medal 2001), Japan Soc. Civil Engrs. (hon.), Nat. Acad. Engring. (nat. chmn. engrs. week 1994). Office: CH2M Hill Inc PO Box 22508 Denver CO 80222-0508

POITEVENT, EDWARD BUTTS, II, lawyer; b. New Orleans, Oct. 19, 1949; s. Eads and Elizabeth (Schramm) P.; m. Julia Dunbar Baños, Dec. 29, 1972; children: Sarah Dunbar,Elizabeth Grehan, Edward Scott, Mary McCutchen. BA, Tulane U., 1971, JD, 1974. Assoc. Jones, Walker, Waechter, Poitevent, Carrere & Denegre, New Orleans, 1974-79, ptnr., 1979-91, Phelps Dunbar, New Orleans, 1991—2001; of counsel King & Spalding, Houston, 2002—04; sr. counsel Akin, Gump, Strauss Hower & Feld, Houston, 2004—. Mem. ad hoc com. Pipeline div. La. Office of Conservation; mem. adv. coun. La. Mineral Law Inst. Mem. editorial bd. Oil and Gas Law and Taxation Rev.; contbr. articles to profl. jours.; presenter in field. Pres. La. chpt. Leukemia Soc. Am., Inc., New Orleans, 1991; trustee Ea. Mineral Law Found., 1988-93; co-chmn. oil and gas sect. Rocky Mountain Mineral Law Found. 36th Ann. Inst., Santa Fe; trustee-at-large Rocky Mountain Mineral Law Found., 1995-97. Mem. ABA (sect. on natural resources, energy and environ. law natural gas and oil coms., litigation sect. energy litigation com., chair program com., editor energy litigation com. newsletter, chair energy litigation com. natural gas mktg. and trans. com., mem. coun. 1994-98, mem. nominating com. 1995-96, CLE officer 1995-96, mem. exec. com. 1996-97), La. State Bar Assn., Fed. Energy Bar Assn., Am. Assn. Petroleum Landmen (chair ad hoc com. on model form gas Balancing Agreement). Republican. Roman Catholic. Office: Akin Gump Strauss Hower & Feld Ste 4400 1111 Louisiana Houston TX 77002 Office Phone: 713-220-8115.

POITIER, SIDNEY, actor, director; b. Miami, Fla., Feb. 20, 1927; s. Reginald and Evelyn (Outten) P.; m. Juanita Hardy (div.); children: Beverly, Pamela, Sherri, Gina; m. Joanna Shimkus; children: Anika, Sydney. Ed. pub. schs., The Bahamas. Ind. stage, screen, TV actor, 1948—. Bd. dirs. Walt Disney Co.; amb. to Japan from the Commonwealth of the Bahamas. Appeared at Am. Negro Theater in numerous prodns. including: Days of Our Youth, Strivers Road, You Can't Take It With You; various roles in Broadway prodns. including: Anna Lucasta, 1948, A Raisin in the Sun, 1959; films include: No Way Out, 1950, Cry, the Beloved Country, 1951, Red Ball Express, 1952, Blackboard Jungle, 1955, Something of Value, 1957, Edge of the City, Band of Angels, 1958, The Defiant Ones, 1958; film adaptation of Porgy and Bess, 1959, A Raisin in Sun, 1960, Paris Blues, 1960, Pressure Point, 1962, The Long Ships, 1964, Lilies of the Field, 1963 (Acad. award Best Actor), The Greatest Story Ever Told, 1965, Slender Thread, 1965, Duel of Diablo, To Sir With Love, 1967, In the Heat of the Night, 1967, Guess Who's Coming to Dinner, 1967, The Lost Man, 1968, For the Love of Ivy, 1968, They Call Me Mr. Tibbs, 1969, The Organization, 1971, Brother John, 1971, The Wilby Conspiracy, 1975, Little Nikita, 1987, Shoot to Kill, 1988, Sneakers, 1992, The Jackal, 1997; star, dir.: Buck and the Preacher, 1972, A Warm December, 1973, Uptown Saturday Night, 1974, Let's Do It Again, 1975, A Piece of the Action, 1977; dir.: Stir Crazy, 1980, Hanky Panky, 1982, Fast Forward 1984, Ghost Dad, 1990; TV mini series Separate But Equal, 1991, Children of the Dust, 1995; (tv movie) To Sir With Love II, 1996; (cable movie) Mandela and de Klerk, 1997; author: This Life, 1981. Served with 1267th Med. Detachment AUS, 1944-45. Decorated knight comdr. Order Brit. Empire; recipient Silver Bear award Berlin Film Festival, 1958, N.Y. Film Critics award and Acad. award nomination for The Defiant Ones, 1958, Best Actor award For Love of Ivy, San Sebastian Film Festival, 1968, Am. Film Inst. Lifetime Achievement award, 1992, Kennedy Ctr. Honors, 1995, Screen Actors Guild award for Lifetime Achievement, 1999, NAACP Hall of Fame Image Award, 2001, Honorary Oscar, 2002.

POJETA, JOHN, JR., geologist, researcher; b. N.Y.C., Sept. 9, 1935; s. John and Emilie (Pilat) P.; m. Mary Louise Eberz, June 23, 1957; children: Kim Louise, John Martin. BS, Capital U., Columbus, Ohio, 1957; MS, U. Cin., 1961, PhD, 1963. Teaching fellow U. Cin., 1957-63; geologist U.S. Geol. Survey, 1963—, chief lower paleozoic studies unit, 1969-74, chief br. paleontology and stratigraphy, 1989-94. Assoc. prof., lectr. George Washington U., 1965-74; research assoc. Smithsonian Instn., 1969—; U.S. Geol. Survey-Australian Bur. Mineral Resources exchange scientist, 1974-75 Author papers in field. Pres. Potomac Woods Citizens Assn.; mem. area 4 coun. Montgomery County (Md.) Bd. Edn.; mem. bd. Citizens for Good Govt.; trustee Paleontol. Rsch. Instn., 1976—85, 1999—, v.p., 1978—79, pres., 1980—82. Fellow: AAAS (coun.), Geol. Soc. Am.; mem.: Australasian Paleontologists, Paleontol. Soc. (sec. 1982—88, pres. 1989—, bus. mgr. spl. studies). Home: 1492 Dunster Ln Rockville MD 20854-6119 Office: US Geol Survey Smithsonian Instn Rm E-308 MRC137 Mus Natural History Washington DC 20560-0137 Office Phone: 202-343-5097. Business E-Mail: pojeta.john@nmnh.si.edu.

POKELWALDT, ROBERT N. former manufacturing company executive; b. North Tonawanda, N.Y. BS, SUNY, Buffalo, 1960. With York Internat. Corp., 1983—, pres., CEO, 1991-2000, now also chmn., dir.; ret., 2000; bd. dirs. GPU, Inc., Morristown, N.J., 2000—. Office: 300 Madison Ave Morristown NJ 07960-6116

POKEMPNER, JOSEPH KRES, lawyer; b. Monessen, Pa., June 11, 1936; s. Leonard and Ethel Lee (Kres) P.; m. Judith Montague Stephens, Aug. 23, 1970; children: Elizabeth, Jennifer, Amy. AB, Johns Hopkins U., 1957; LLB, U. Md., 1962. Bar: Md. 1962. Law clk. to judge Supreme Bench Balt., 1960-62; field atty. 5th region NLRB, 1962-64; pvt. practice labor law Balt., 1964—; ptnr. Wolf, Pokempner & Hillman, Balt., 1972-86, Whiteford, Taylor & Preston, Balt., 1986—. Contbr. articles to legal jours. Capt. AUS, 1969-74. Mem. ABA, Fed. Bar Assn. (pres. Balt. chpt. 1979-80), Md. Bar Assn., Balt. Bar Assn. (pres. 1984-85), Serjeant's Inn Law Club. Jewish. Home: 1500 Willow Ave Baltimore MD 21204-3611 E-mail: jpokempner@wtplaw.com.

POKER, NATHAN, retired radiologist; b. N.Y.C., Sept. 13, 1921; MD, Columbia P&S, 1950. Diplomate Am. Bd. Radiology. Intern Bellevue Hosp. Ctr., N.Y.C., 1950-51; resident in radiology N.Y. Hosp., 1951-54; prof. emeritus Cornell U. Med. Coll., 1992—. Lt. USNR, 1942-46. Mem. Am. Coll. Radiology.

POKORNY, ALEX DANIEL, psychiatrist; b. Taylor, Tex., Oct. 18, 1918; s. John Robert and Olga Frances (Susen) P.; m. Jeanice Brooke Allen, Mar. 13, 1948; children: Martha, Ross, Ellen, Sally. BA, U. Tex., 1939; MD, U. Tex., Galveston, 1942. Diplomate Am. Bd. Psychiatry and Neurology. Psychiatrist VA Hosp., Houston, 1949-55, chief psychiatry and neurology svc., 1955-73; from instr. to prof. psychiatry Baylor Coll. Medicine, Houston, 1949-89, acting chmn. dept. psychiatry, 1968-72, vice chmn. dept. psychiatry, 1972-89; ret. Editor (with others) 7 books, including Phenomenology and Treatment of Anxiety, 1979, Phenomenology and Treatment of Alcoholism, 1980, Phenomenology and Treatment of Psychosexual Disorders, 1983, Phenomenology and Treatment of Psychiatric Emergencies, 1984; editor numerous publs.; contbr. 100 articles to profl. jours. Capt. U.S. Army, 1943-46. Recipient Amersa award for Excellence in Med. Edu. Assn. Med. Edn. & Rsch. Substance Abuse, 1989, Dublin award Am. Assn. Suicidology, 1992. Fellow AAAS, Am. Psychiat. Assn. (life), Am. Coll. Psychiatrists (life); mem. Soc. Psychophysiological Rsch. Home and Office: 813 Atwell St Bellaire TX 77401-4718

POKOTILOV, ANDRIY, physicist; b. Kharkov, Ukraine; s. Anatoliy and Lyubov Pokotilov. MS(hon.), Kharkov Nat. U., Ukraine, 1998; MPhil, CUNY, 2001, PhD, 2004. Rsch. physicist Kharkov Nat. U., Ukraine, 1998—99; physics lectr., rsch. physicist, adj. asst. prof. CUNY, 1999—. Recipient Ukrainian Nat. Physics Competitions prize, Ministry of Edn., 1992—93, 1995—96; grantee in physics, George Soros Found., 1997; Sci. scholar, CUNY, 1999—2001, Univ. fellow, 2001—04. Mem.: AAAS, N.Y. Acad. Sci., Am. Phys. Soc., Sigma Xi (hon. The Cert. of Recognition 2002—04). Achievements include discovery of Interdependence between string theory and cosmology; technological applications of nuclear physics and physics of polymers. Office: CUNY 17 Lexington Ave A-0506 New York NY 10010 E-mail: apokotilov@gc.cuny.edu.

POKOTILOW, MANNY DAVID, lawyer, educator; b. Patterson, N.J., June 26, 1938; s. Samuel Morris and Ruth (Fuchs) P.; children: Mali, Charyse, Mona, Andrew. BEE, Newark Coll. Engring., 1960; LLB, Am. U., 1964. Bar: Pa. 1964, U.S. Supreme Ct. 1969. Examiner Patent Office, Washington, 1960-64; ptnr. Caesar, Rivise, Bernstein, Cohen & Pokotilow Ltd., Phila., 1965—. Lectr. Pa. Bar Inst., various trade assns., expert witness on protection of computer software, patents, trademarks, trade secrets and copyrights; faculty Temple U. Sch. Law, 1985-94. Vol. Support Ctr. for Child Advs., Phila., 1979—; bd. dirs., organizer Phila. Bar Assn. 10k Race, Phila., 1980-, Packard Press Road Run Grand Prix, 1986; bd. dirs. Hist. Soc. U.S. Dist. Ct. (ea. dist.) Pa., 1989-, v.p. 1998-2002, pres. 2002-03. Recipient Chair award for vol. excellence Am. Diabetes Assn., 1991; honored by Support Ctr. for Child Advocates, 1992 and Am. Diabetes Assn., 1997; named to Million Dollar Club, Am. Diabetes Assn., 2002; named one of Best Lawyers in Greater Phil. area Phil. Mag., 1999; named to Top Tier of Am. Leading Lawyers for Bus., 2003-04. Mem. ABA (chmn. proprietary rights in software com., coun. sci. and tech. sect. 1989—), IEEE, Assn. Trial Lawyers Am., Phila. Bar Assn. (bd. govs. 1982-84, chmn. sports and recreation com. 1977—, hon. trustee campaign for qualified judges 1993), Phila. Patent Law Assn. (bd. govs. 1982-84, chmn. fed. practice and procedure com. 1983-88), Phila. Trial Lawyers (chmn. fed. cts. com. 1986-90), Lawyers Club Phila. (bd. govs. 1984-94, chmn. publicity 1994-98), Pa. Trial Lawyers, Tau Epsilon Rho (vice chancellor Phila. grad. chpt. 1986-88, chancellor 1988-90). Office: Caesar Rivise Bernstein Cohen & Pokotilow Ltd 1635 Market St Fl 12 Philadelphia PA 19103-2212 Office Phone: 215-567-2010. E-mail: mpokotilow@crbcp.com.

POKRAS, SHEILA FRANCES, retired judge; b. Newark, Aug. 5, 1935; m. Norman M. Pokras, 1954; children: Allison, Andrea, Larry. Student, Beaver Coll., 1953-54; BS in Edn., Temple U., 1957; JD cum laude, Pepperdine U., 1969. Bar: Calif. 1970, U.S. Dist. Ct. D.C. 1970, U.S. Dist. Ct. Calif. 1970, U.S. Supreme Ct. 1975. Tchr. elem. and secondary schs., Phila. and Newark, 1957-59; pvt. practice law Long Beach, Calif., 1970-78; city councilwoman Lakewood, Calif., 1972-76; judge Long Beach Mcpl. Ct., 1978-80, L.A. Superior Ct., 1980-98; ret., 1998. Supervising judge, 1986; del. Calif. State Dem. Cen. Com., 1975, Calif. State Conv., 1975; mem. Com. on Gender Bias in Calif. Courts, 1986-89 Advisor Jr. League, 1980-85; mem. early childhood adv. bd. Long Beach City Coll.; bd. dirs. Long Beach Alcoholism Coun., 1979-80, Boys and Girls Club Am., 1981-89, Long Beach Symphony, 1985, Jewish Community Fedn., 1982-86, past mem. community rels. com.; active Nat. Women's Polit. Caucus, LWV. Named Woman of Yr. NOW, Long Beach, 1984; recipient Torch of Liberty award B'nai B'rith Anti-Defamation League, 1974; honoree Nat. Conf. Christians and Jews, 1986. Mem. ABA, AAUW, Nat. Assn. Women Judges (dist. supr. 1986), Calif. Bar Assn. (judges div.), Calif. Judges Assn. (mem. ann. seminar com. 1981-89), Mcpl. Cts. Judges Assn. (mem. Marshall com. 1979-80), L.A. County Bar Assn. (judges div., mem. arbitration com.), Women Lawyers Assn., L.A. (judges sect.), Women Lawyers Assn. Long Beach, Long Beach Legal Aid Found. (v.p. 1976-78), Long Beach Bar Assn. (active various coms., bd. govs. 1977-78, Judge of Yr. 1987), Long Beach C. of C. (bd. dirs.). Avocations: swimming, golf, jogging, classical music, movies.

POLACHEK, SOLOMON WILLIAM, economics educator, consultant; b. Washington, Aug. 27, 1945; s. Harry and Blanche (Katz) P.; m. Dora Eisenberg, July 23, 1972; 1 child, Nathaniel. AB, George Washington U., 1967; PhD, Columbia U., 1973. Postdoctoral fellow U. Chgo., 1972-73; from asst. prof. to assoc. prof. U. N.C., Chapel Hill, 1973-83; prof. econs. SUNY-Binghamton, 1983-96; disting. prof. econs., 1996—, acting chair econs., 1987, chair econs., 1994-96, dean Harpur Coll. Arts and Scis., 1996-2000; referee numerous acad. jours., pubs., govt. orgns., 1973—; cons. to govt. agys., law firms, 1975—; expert witness U.S. Civil Rights Commn., Washington, 1984, U.S. Senate Subcom. Hearings, Washington, 1985; vis. research prof. Erasmus U., Netherlands, 1984; vis. prof. Cath. U., Leuven, 1987, Bar Ilan U., 1992, Tel Aviv U., 1992; speaker, presenter in field. Editor Rsch. in Labor Econs., 1994—; mem. editorial bd. Internat. Studies Quar., 1989-94, Conflict Mgmt. and Peace Sci., 1989—, SUNY Press, 1998-2004, Jour. Economic Inequality, 2002-2004, Rev. of Econs. of the Household, 2002--. Co-author The Economics of Earnings, 1993, co-editor Peace Economics, Peace Science and Public Policy, 1994; contbr. articles to profl. publs. Presdl. fellow Columbia U., N.Y.C., 1968-72; Ford Found. faculty fellow, 1974-75; nat. fellow Hoover Instn., Stanford U., Palo Alto, Calif., 1979-80; fellow Inst. for Labor Rsch., Bonn, Germany, 2000—; vis. fellow Princeton U., 2002-03; grantee various govt. agys., 1975-85. Mem. Am. Econ. Assn., Econometric Soc., Internat. Peace Sci. Soc. (exec. com. 1983, pres. 1999-2000), Ea. Econ. Assn. (program com. 1985), N.Am. Econ. and Fin. Assn. (program com. 1989), Avocations: travel, swimming, cross-country skiing. Office: SUNY Dept Econs Binghamton NY 13902 Office Phone: 607-777-2572.

POLAD, FARHANG, company director; b. Bombay, Feb. 23, 1954; s. Polad Behram Irani and Banoo (Roshni) I.; m. Shahnaz Ruhbux, Oct. 11, 1978; children: Freyana, Khushnam. Degree in Hotel Mgmt and Catering Tech. Officer Shipping Corp. of India, Bombay, 1977-81; gen. mgr., dir., CEO Radhakrishna Offshore, Bombay, 1981-91; dir., CEO Eurest Consolidated Svcs., Singapore, 1991-94, Consolidated Svcs., Toronto, Canada, 1994-98; ind. entrepreuner, 1998—; stocks and equities investment trader, 2000—. Worldwide mktg. assoc. Britt & Assocs., Toronto, 1994—; ind. bus. owner Quixtar.com., e-commerce with Virtual Cyber-Mall. Sec., dir. Lions Intl., Singapore, 1992-94; dir., founder, mem. Team Alliance Network Mktg. Orgn., 1996-97. Melvin Jones fellow for dedicated humanitarian svcs. Lions Club Internat. Found. Mem. Singapore Parsi Zoarashtrian Assn. (v.p.), Singapore Inter-Religious Assn. (rep.), Inst. Hotel Mgmt. and Catering Tech., St. Mary's Sch. Alumni (Bombay), St. Xavier's Coll. Alumni (Bombay). Zoarashtrian. Avocation: investing. Home and Office: 13-3-8 Miguel de Cervantes 07181 Costa Den Blanes Mallorca Spain

POLAK, ELIJAH, engineering educator, computer scientist; b. Bialystok, Poland, Aug. 11, 1931; came to U.S., 1957, naturalized, 1977; s. Isaac and Fruma (Friedman) P.; m. Virginia Ann Gray, June 11, 1961; children: Oren, Sharon. BSE.E., U. Melbourne, Australia, 1957; MSE.E., U. Calif., Berkeley, 1959, PhD, 1961. Instrument engr. ICIANZ, Melbourne, Australia, 1956-57; summer student IBM Research Labs., San Jose, Calif., 1959-60; vis. asst. prof. M.I.T., fall 1964; asso. dept elec. engring. and computer scis. U. Calif., Berkeley, 1958-61, asst. prof. elec. engring. and computer scis., 1961-66, asso. prof., 1966-69, prof., 1969-94, prof. Grad. Sch., 1994—. Author: (with L.A. Zadeh) System Theory, 1969, (with E. Wong) Notes for a First Course on Linear Systems, 1970, (with others) Theory of Optimal Control and Mathematical Programming, 1970, Computational Methods in Optimization, 1971, Optimization: Algorithms and Consistent Approximations, 1997. Guggenheim fellow, 1968; U.K. Sci. Research Council sr. fellow, 1972, 76, 79, 82 Fellow IEEE; mem. Soc. Indsl. and Applied Math. (asso. editor Jour. Theory and Applications Optimization 1972—), Soc. Math. Programming. Home: 38 Fairlawn Dr Berkeley CA 94708-2106 Office: U Calif Dept Elec Engring Cp S Berkeley CA 94720-0001 Office Phone: 510-642-2644. Business E-Mail: polak@eecs.berkeley.edu.

POLAKIEWICZ, LEONARD ANTHONY, foreign language and literature educator; b. Kiev, Ukraine, Mar. 30, 1938; came to the U.S., 1950; s. Wladyslaw and Aniela (Ossowska) P.; m. Marianne Helen Swanson, Sept. 7, 1963; children: Barbara, Kathryn, Janet. BS in Russian with distinction, BA in Internat. Rels., U. Minn., 1964; MA in Russian, U. Wis., 1968; cert. Russian area studies, 1969; PhD in Slavic Langs./Lit., U. Wis., 1978; diploma in Polish Curriculum and Instrn., Curie-Sklodowska U., Lublin, Poland, 1981. Instr. U. Minn., Mpls., 1970-78, asst. prof., 1978-90, assoc. prof., 1990—, Morse Alumni disting. teaching assoc. prof. Slavic langs. and literatures, dir. Inst. Langs., 1991-93, chair Slavic dept., 1993-97, 99-2000. Vis. asst. prof. U. London, Eng., fall 1984; dir. U. Minn. Polish Lang. Program, Curie-Sklodowska U., Lublin, Poland, summers 1984-89, dir. Russian Faculty Exch., Herzen Pedagogical U., St. Petersburg, Russia, 1993—; mem. selection com. Fulbright Tchr. Exch. Program, USIA, 1989, Title VI Dept. Edn., 1990, NEH Tchr.- Scholar Program, 1994; reviewer divn. ednl. programs NEH, 1990, translation program, 1993, 94; mem. rev. bd. Ctr. Applied Linguistics Polish Proficiency Test, 1990; mem. exec. com. Coun. on Internat. Edn., N.Y.C., 1991-94; mem. Russian Lang. Program Acad. Policy Com. CIEE, N.Y.C., 1994—; mem. nat. task force Polish Studies in Am., Ind. U., 1995-96; project dir. Nat. Coun. Orgns. of Less Commonly Taught Langs. Polish Lang. Learning Framework, 1995-2001; dir. U. Minn. Curie Sklodowska U. Faculty Exch., 1988—, U. Minn. Cath. U. of Lublin Faculty Exch., 1995-2001; coord. Def. Lang. Inst. Polish Proficiency Testing, 1998. Author: Supplemental Materials for First Year Polish, 1991, Supplemental Materials for Fifteen Modern Polish Short Stories, 1994, Directory of US Institutions of Higher Education and Faculty Offering Instruction in Polish Language, Literature and Culture, 1996-97, Intermediate Polish: A Cultural Reader with Exercises, 1999, (with Joanna Radwanska Williams and Waldemar Walczynski) Polish Language Learning Framework, 2002; assoc. editor Slavic and East European Jour., 1988-94; mem. editl. bd. The Learning and Tchg. of Slavic Langs. and Cultures: Toward the 21st Century, 1996-2000; reviewer Choice Mag., Modern Lang. Jour., Canadian Slavonic Papers, Slavic and East European Jour., Soviet and Post-Soviet Rev. Bd. dirs. Immigration Hist. Rsch. Ctr., Mpls., 1984-89; co-founder Polish-Am. Cultural Inst., Mpls., 1986; vice-chair Polish Am. Congress' Commn. Edn., 1987; mem. gov.'s Commn. on Ea. Europe, St. Paul, 1991. With U.S. Army, 1961-63. Ford Found. fellow, 1964-65, Nat. Def. Edn. Act fellow, Title IV, 1966-68; grantee Kościuszko Found., 1981, Coun. for European Studies grantee Columbia U., 1981, 84, 86, Rsch. Assoc. grantee Russian and East European Ctr., U. Ill., 1982, 83, 84, Wasie Found. grantee, 1983, IREX Collaborative Activities and New Exchs. grantee, 1984, Ireland Travel grantee Trinity Coll., Dublin, 1984, Bush Found. Rsch. grantee, 1986-87, grantee U.S. Dept. Edn., 1988-91; Fulbright-Hays Group Projects Abroad grantee for Poland, 1989, USIA U. Linkage grantee for Poland, 1989-93, IREX Short Term Travel grantee, 1995, USIA Coll. & U. Affiliations grantee for Poland, 1995-2000; recipient Polanie Club of the Twin Cities Merit award, 1982, Curie-Sklodowska U. medal for acad. linkage devel., 1992, Cavalier's Cross of Order of Merit of Republic of Poland, 1999, Disting Svc. award Herzen Pedagogical U., St. Petersburg, Russia, 2002, Pres.'s Outstanding Svc. award, 2003. Mem. AAUP, Am. Assn. for the Advancement Slavic Studies, Am. Assn. Tchrs. Slavic and East European Langs. and Lits. (com. on testing and profl. devel. 1997—, Excellence in Tchg. in U.S. award 1994), Internat. Czeslaw Milosz Soc. (pres. 1984-85), N.Am. Chekhov Soc., Am. Coun. Tchrs. of Russian, Polish Inst. Arts & Scis. Am. (N.Y.C., Waclaw Lednicki Humanities award com. 1996), Assn. Literary Scholars & Critics, Soc. of Lovers of the Russian Book, Irish Assn. of Russian and East European Studies, Polish Tchrs. Assn. of Am., Polish Studies Assn. (mem. biannual prize jury 1998), Bristol Group Internat. Assn. Tchrs. Polish, U. Minn. Acad. Disting. Tchrs., The Australia and New Zealand Slavists' Assn. Roman Catholic. Avocations: reading, philatelics, genealogy, touring, gardening. Home: 466 Oak Creek Dr S Vadnais Heights MN 55127-7008 Office Phone: 612-625-1384. Business E-Mail: polak001@tc.umn.edu.

POLAKOFF, ABE, baritone; b. Bucharest, Rumania; s. Sam and Mary P. Ousherenkova; children: David Fred, Mark Evan, Robert Ira; m. Judyth Kanner, Dec. 5, 1992. Civil engring. student, CCNY; profl. tng. program, Am. Theater Wing, 1952-54; student, N.Y. Coll. Music, 1955-57. Dir. Island Opera Players; opera lectr. Arts Couns. (municipalities and schs.); cantor Progressive Shaari Zedek synagogue, Bklyn., 1972-77, Temple Emanuel, Denver, 1984-94. Debuts include Marcello in La Boheme, Milan, Florence, 1960; leading baritone Zurich Opera, 1961-63, numerous appearances with N.Y. Met. Opera, City Opera N.Y., Phila. Lyric Opera, Pitts. Opera, Seattle Opera, Berlin Deutsche Opera, Frankfurt Opera, Cinn. Opera, Hamburg, Munich Staatsoper, Stuttgart Staatsoper, The Netherlands Opera, Cin. Opera, Kansas City Lyric Opera, Canadian Opera Co., others; soloist with Mex. State Symphony Orch., Kalamazoo Symphony Orch., Winston-Salem (N.C.) Symphony, numerous concert and recital appearances Sgt. U.S. Army, 1943-46. 1st prize winner Am. Theatre Wing Vocal Profl. Scholarship award, 1954, 1st prize winner Am. Opera Auditions, 1960, Silver medal Vercelli (Italy) Internat. singing contest, 1960; Rockefeller Found. grantee, 1961-62; Bayreuth Festival Masterclass scholar. Mem. Cen. Opera Service, Am. Guild Musical Artists, Actors Equity Assn. Address: 11132 76th Ave Apt 7H Forest Hills NY 11375-6409

POLAKOFF, MURRAY EMANUEL, university dean, economics and finance educator; b. N.Y.C., Dec. 18, 1922; s. Joseph and Elizabeth (Zimmerman) P.; m. Sheila Doreen Brazil, Dec. 23, 1951; children: Michael Anton, Toni. BA summa cum laude, NYU, 1946; MA, Columbia U., 1951, PhD, 1955. Asst. prof. econs. U. Tex., Austin, 1951-57, assoc. prof. econs., 1957-61; prof. econs. and fin. U. Rochester, NY, 1961-63; prof., chmn., vice dean Grad. Sch. Bus. Adminstrn. NYU, 1968-71; leading prof., dean Sch. Mgmt. SUNY, Binghamton, 1971-77; prof. econs. and fin., provost U. Md., College Park, 1977-86, dean, 1986-91, dir. internat. devel. and conflict mgmt., 1991-92, prof. emeritus, 1993—. Cons. U.S. House Com. on Banking and Currency, Washington, 1964; lectr. and cons. Brazilian Ctrl. Banking, Dept. State, São Paulo, 1966-68; chmn. bd. advisors of joint ventures Ctrl. Inst. Math. and Econ. Modelling of Soviet Acad. Scis., USSR and U. Md., College Park, 1989. Editor, sr. author: Financial Institutions and Markets, 2d edit., 1981; contbr. articles to profl. jours. Scholar Sch. Law Columbia U., N.Y.C., 1946; Fund for Advancement Edn. faculty grantee, 1955-56; Found. Econ. Edn. fellow, summer 1956; Social Sci. Rsch. Coun. fellow, 1957; Ford Found. faculty rsch. grantee, 1961-62. Mem. Fin. Mgmt. Assn., Phi Beta Kappa. Jewish. Avocations: squash, theater. E-mail: murf121822@aol.com.

POLAN, MARY LAKE, obstetrics and gynecology educator; b. Las Vegas, N.Mex., July 17, 1943; Student, Smith Coll., Paris, 1963—64; BA cum laude, Conn. Coll., 1965; PhD in Biophysics and Biochemistry, Yale U., 1970, MD, 1975. Diplomate Am. Bd. Ob-Gyn., Am. Bd. Reproductive Endocrinology, Nat. Bd. Med. Examiners. Postdoctoral fellow dept. biology, NIH postdoctoral fellow Yale U., New Haven, 1970—72, resident dept. ob-gyn. Sch. Medicine, 1975—78, fellow in oncology, then fellow in endocrinology-infertility, 1978—80, asst. instr., then lectr. molecular biophysics-biochemistry, 1970—72, instr., then asst. prof. ob-gyn., 1978—79, 1980—85, assoc. prof., 1985—90; clin. clk. in ob-gyn. and pediat. Radcliffe Infirmary, Oxford (Eng.) U. Med. Sch., 1974; instr. Pahlavi U., Shiraz, Iran, 1978; Katharine Dexter McCormick and Stanley McCormick Meml. prof. Stanford (Calif.) Sch. Medicine, 1990—, chmn. dept. gynecology and obstetrics, 1990—. Vis. prof. Hunan Med. Coll., Changsha, China, 1986; mem. med. bd. Yale-China Assn.,

1987—90; liaison com. on ethics in modern world Conn. Coll., New London, 1988—90; mem. med. adv. bd. Ova-Med Corp., Palo Alto, Calif., 1992—95, Vivus, Menlo Park, Calif., 1993—; bd. dirs. Metra Biosys., Mountain View, Quidel, San Diego, Am. Home Products, Madison, NJ, 1994—; mem. reproductive endocrinology study sect. NIH, 1989—90, co-chmn. task force on opportunities for rsch. on woman's health, 1991. Author: Second Seed, 1987; guest editor: Seminars in Reproductive Endocrinology, 1984, Infertility and Reproductive Medicine Clinics of North America: GnRH Analogues, Vol. 4, 1993; editor, with DeCherney: Surgery in Reproductive Endocrinology, 1987;; editor: (with DeCherney, S. Boyers and R. Lee) Decision Making in Infertility; ad hoc reviewer: Jour. Clin. Endocrinology and Metabolism, Fertility and Sterility, Ob-Gyn., others; contbr. chapters to books, articles to med. jours. Fellow, NSRA, 1981—82; grantee, NIRA, 1982—85, HD, 1985—90, NRSA, 1987—88, Johnson & Johnson, 1993—96; scholar, Assn. Acad. Health Ctrs., 1993—96. Fellow: ACOG (PROLOG task force for reproductive endocrinology and infertility 1988—89, rep. to CREOG coun. 1994—97); mem.: Bay Area Reproductive Endocrine Soc., San Francisco Gynecologic Soc., Inst. Medicine (com. on rsch. capabilities of acad. depts. ob-gyn 1990—91, bd. on health scis. policy 1992—96), Am. Gynecologic and Obstetric Soc., Soc. for Reproductive Endocrinologists, Soc. for Gynecologic Investigation, Am. Fertility Soc., Phi Beta Kappa. Home: 4251 Manuela Ct Palo Alto CA 94306-3731 Office: Stanford U Sch Medicine Dept Gyn OB 300 Pasteur Dr Stanford CA 94305-5317*

POLAND, ALAN PAUL, oncology educator; Prof. oncology McArdle Lab. for Cancer Rsch. U. Wis., Madison; sci. advisor, team leader Ctr. for Disease Control and Prevention, Morgantown, W.Va., 1998—. Recipient Founders award Chem. Industry Inst. Toxicology Bristol-Myers Squibb Found., 1996. Office: Nat Inst Occupl Safety and Health/HELD Ctr Disease Control 1095 Willowdale Rd Morgantown WV 26505-2845

POLAND, SYDNEY WADE, software designer; b. Heflin, La., June 18, 1933; s. Howard Brazil and Helen Lucille (Ryan) P.; m. Evelyn Lucille Miller, Nov. 30, 1956; children: Susan Elizabeth Poland Finch, Stanley Eugene. BS in Physics, La. Tech. U., Ruston, 1955; MS in Math., Tex. Christian U., 1962; MS in Computer Sci., So. Meth. U., 1972. Sci. programmer Temco Aircraft co., Dallas, 1955-58, Chance Vought Aircraft, Dallas, 1958-60; sys. programmer Tex. Instruments Geophys. Svcs., Dallas, 1960-72; sys. designer Tex. Instruments Calculator Divsn., Dallas, 1972-77, Tex. Instruments Equipment Group, Dallas, 1977-80, Tex. Instruments Corp. Engring. Ctr., Dallas, 1980-82; sr. cons. BP Exploration, Dallas and Houston, 1982-90; sys. designer Tex. Instruments DSP R&D, Stafford, Tex., 1990-95; sr. sys. software designer Tex. Instruments Tech. Tng., Stafford, 1995-98. Author manual and applications notes. Mem. Am. Bonanza Soc., Aircraft Owners and Pilots Assn. Achievements include 29 patents for calculators, digital signal processors, others. Home: 22307 Prince George Ln Katy TX 77449-2811

POLANIS, JULIE, accountant; b. West Allis, Wis., Dec. 10, 1974; d. Mark Florian and Gloria Jean (Grebe) P. BS in Acctg., Wingate (N.C.) U., 1997. Store contr. Harris Teeter, Charlotte, N.C., 1990-98; fin. analyst The Hearst Corp., Charlotte, 1997—2003; treas. analyst Coca-Cola Bottling Co. Consolidated, Charlotte, NC, 2003—. Roman Catholic. Avocations: working out, racquetball, kickboxing. Home: 3305 Fortis Ln Matthews NC 28105-3754

POLANSKI, ROMAN, film director, writer, actor; b. Paris, Aug. 18, 1933; s. Ryszard and Bule (Katz-Przedborska) P.; m. Barbara Lass (div.); m. Sharon Tate (dec.); m. Emmanuelle Seigner. Student, Art Sch., Cracow, State Film Coll., Lodz. Appeared in (children's radio show) The Merry Gang, (stage prodn.) Son of the Regiment; dir.: (films) Two Men and a Wardrobe, 1958, When Angels Fall, 1958, Le Gros et le Maigre, 1960, Knife in the Water, 1962 (Venice Film Festival award), The Mammals, 1963 (Tours Film Festival award), Repulsion, 1965 (Berlin Film Festival award), Cul-de-Sac, 1966 (Berlin Film Festival award), The Vampire Killers, 1967, Rosemary's Baby, 1968, Macbeth, 1971, What?, 1972, Chinatown, 1974 (Best Dir. award Soc. Film and TV Arts, Priz Raoul-Levy, 1975), The Tenant, 1976, Tess, 1980 (Cesar award), Pirates, 1986; dir., co-writer (films) Frantic, 1988; dir.: (films) Bitter Moon, 1994, Death and the Maiden, 1994, The Ninth Gate, 1999, The Pianist, 2002 (Best Dir. Acad. award, 2003, Best Film, British Acad. Film Award (BAFTA), 2003, The David Lean Award for Achievement in Direction, 2003, 2003); actor: (on stage) The Metamorphosis, 1988; (films) A Generation, The End of the Night, See You Tomorrow, The Innocent Sorcerers, Two Men and a Wardrobe, The Vampire Killers, What?, The Magic Christian and Andy Warhol's Death, Back in the U.S.S.R., A Pure Formality, Chinatown, The Tennant; actor, dir.: (plays) Amadeus; Warsaw, 1981; Paris, 1982; Amadeus/Italy, 1999; dir.: (Operas) Lulu, 1974, Rigoletto, 1976; (Operas, (musical comedy) Tales of Hoffman, Master Class, 1996—97; (Operas) Tanz der Vampire, 1997, 2000; author: (autobiography) Roman, 1984. Office: ICM 8942 Wilshire Blvd Beverly Hills CA 90211-1934

POLANSKY, ANDY, electronics executive; Chmn. global areas Weber Shandwick Worldwide, pres., COO, ea. & ctrl. regions; reporter Bucks County Courier Times, Levittown, Pa.; writer Princeton Packet, Princeton, NJ; sports writer The Trentonian, Trenton, NJ. Serves exec. com. Weber Shandwick Worldwide Bd. Dirs. Office: Weber PR Worldwide 640 Fifth Ave New York NY 10019

POLANSKY, LARRY PAUL, court administrator, consultant; b. Blkyn., July 24, 1932; s. Harry and Ida (Gershgom) P.; m. Eunice Kathryn Neun; children: Steven, Harriet, Bruce. BS in Acctg., Temple U., 1958, JD, 1973. Bar: Pa. 1973, U.S. Dist. Ct. (ea. dist.) Pa. 1973, U.S. Ct. Appeals (3d cir.) 1973, D.C. 1978, U.S. Supreme Ct. 1980. Acct., systems analyst City of Phila., 1956-63; data processing mgr. Jefferson Med. Coll. and Hosp., Phila., 1963-65; systems engr. IBM Corp., Phila., 1965-67; dep. ct. adminstr. Common Pleas Cts. of Phila., 1967-76; dep. state ct. adminstr. Pa. Supreme Ct., Phila., 1976-78; exec. officer D.C. Cts., Washington, 1979-90. Presdl. appt. to bd. dirs. State Justice Inst., 1985-89; bd. dirs. Search Group, Inc. Author: A Primer for the Technologically Challenged Judge, 1995; contbr. articles to profl. jours. Served as cpl. U.S. Army, 1951-53, Korea. Fellow Inst. for Ct. Mgmt., Denver, 1984; recipient Reardon award Nat. Ctr. for State Cts., 1982, Disting. Svc. award Nat. Ctr. for State Cts., 1986, Justice Tom C. Clark award Nat. Conf. of Metro. Cts., 1991, award of merit Nat. Assn. Ct. Mgmt., 1996. Mem. ABA (jud. adminstrn. divsn., chmn. tech. com. 1991-93, 95, exec. com. lawyers conf. 1985-98, chmn. 1991-92, JAD coun. 1994-97), Conf. State Ct. Adminstrn. (bd. dirs. 1980-86, pres. 1984-85). Republican. Jewish. Avocations: tennis, skiing, computers, golf. Home and Office: PO Box 752 Lake Harmony PA 18624-0752 Office Phone: 570-722-9288. E-mail: polanskyl@aol.com.

POLANYI, JOHN CHARLES, chemist, educator; b. Berlin, Jan. 23, 1929; m. Anne Ferrar Davidson, 1958; 2 children. BSc, Manchester (Eng.) U., 1949, MSc, 1950, PhD, 1952, DSc, 1964; DSc (hon.), U. Waterloo, 1970, Meml. U., 1976, McMaster U., 1977, Carleton U., 1981, Harvard U., 1982, Rensselaer U., Brock U., 1984, Lethbridge U., Sherbrooke U., Laval U., Victoria U., Ottawa U., 1987, Manchester U. and York U., Eng., 1988, U. Montreal, Acadia U., 1989, Weizmann Inst., Israel, 1989, U. Bari, Italy, 1990, U. B.C., 1990, McGill U., 1990, Queen's U., 1992, Free U. Berlin, 1993, Laurentian U., 1995, U. Toronto, 1995, U. Liverpool, 1995; LLD (hon.), Trent U., 1977, Dalhousie U., 1983, St. Francis-Xavier U., 1984, Concordia U., 1990, Calgary U., 1994. Mem. faculty dept. chemistry U. Toronto, Ont., Canada, 1956—, prof., 1962—. William D. Harkins lectr. U. Chgo., 1970; Reilly lectr. U. Notre Dame, 1970; Purve lectr. McGill U., 1971; F.J. Toole lectr. U. N.B., 1974; Philips lectr. Haverford Coll., 1974; Kistiakowsky lectr. Harvard U., 1975; Camille and Henry Dreyfus lectr. U. Kans., 1975; J.W.T. Spinks lectr. U. Sask., Canada, 1976; Laird lectr. U. We. Ont., 1976; CIL Disting. lectr. Simon Fraser U., 1977; Gucker lectr. Ind. U., 1977; Jacob Bronowski Meml. lectr. U. Toronto, 1978; Hutchinson lectr. Rochester (N.Y.) U., 1979; Priestley lectr. Pa. State U., 1980; Barré lectr. U. Montreal, 1982; Sherman Fairchild disting. scholar Calif. Inst. Tech., 1982; Chute lectr. Dalhousie U., 1983; Redman lectr. McMaster U., 1983; Wiegand lectr. U. Toronto, 1984; Edward U. Condon lectr. U. Colo., 1984; John A. Allan lectr. U. Alta., 1984; John E. Willard lectr. U. Wis., 1984; Owen Holmes lectr. U. Lethbridge, 1985; Walker-Ames prof. U. Wash., 1986; John W. Cowper disting. vis. lectr. SUNY, Buffalo, 1986; vis. prof. chemistry Tex. A&M U., 1986; Disting. vis. spkr. U. Calgary, 1987; Morino lectr. U. Japan, 1987; J.T. Wilson lectr. Ont. Scil. Ctr., 1987; Welsh lectr. U. toronto, 1987; Spiers Meml. lectr. Faraday divsn. Royal Soc. Chemistry, 1987; Polanyi lectr. Internat. Union Pure and Applied Chemistry, 1988; W.B. Lewis lectr. Atomic Energy of Can. Ltd., 1988; Consol. Bathurst vis. lectr. Concordia U., 1988; Priestman lectr. U. N.B., 1988; Killam lectr. U. Windsor, 1988; Herzberg lectr. Carleton U., 1988; Falconbridge lectr. Laurentian U., 1988; DuPont lectr. Ind. U., 1989; Luther lectr. U. Regina, 1989; Franklin lectr. Rice U., 1990; Laurier lectr. Wilfred Laurier U., 1990; Pratt lectr. U. Va., 1990; Goodrich lectr. Case Western Reserve U., 1990; Phillips lectr. U. Pitts., 1991; Albert Noyes lectr. U. Tex., 1992; John and Lois Dove Meml. lectr. U. Toronto, 1992; Fritz London lectr. Duke U., 1993; Castle lectr. U. South Fla., 1993; Linus Pauling lectr. Calif. Inst. Tech., 1994; Hagey lectr. U. Waterloo, 1995; Larkin Stuart lectr. U. Toronto, 1995; Hungerford lectr. York Club, 1995; disting. lectr. ser. Meml. U., 1995; John C. Polanyi Nobel Laureate lectr. U. Toronto, 1995; Floyd E. Bartell Meml. lectr. U. Mich., 1996; Christian Culture award lectr. Assumption U., 1996; Liversidge lectr. U. Sydney, 1996; disting. scientist lectr. Apotex, Inc., 1996; mem. sci. adv. bd. Max Planck Inst. Quantum Optics, Germany, 1982—92; mem. nat. adv. bd. on Sci. and Tech., 1987—89; hon. cons. Inst. Molecular Sci., Okazaki, Japan, 1989—94; bd. dirs. Steacie Inst. Molecular Scis., Ottawa, Ont.; founding mem., pres. Can. Com. of Sci. and Scholars; Beam Disting. vis. prof. U. Iowa, 1992; Charles M. and Martha Hitchcock prof. U. Calif., Berkeley, 1994; Young Meml. visitor Royal Mil. Coll., 1994. Editor (with F.G. Griffiths): The Dangers of Nuclear War, 1979; contbr. articles to jours., mags., newspapers; prodr. (film) Concepts in Reaction Dynamics, 1970. Mem. Queen's Privy Coun. for Can., 1992; founding mem. Can. Pugwash Com., 1960; Can. Ctr. for Arms Control and Disarmament. Decorated Officer Order of Can., Companion, knight Grand Cross Order St. John of Jerusalem; co-recipient (with N. Bartlett) Steacie prize, 1965, Wolf prize in Chemistry, 1982; recipient Marlow medal, Faraday Soc., 1962, Centenary medal, Chem. Soc. Gt. Brit., 1965, Norandaaward, Chem. Inst. Can., 1967, award, Brit. Chem. Soc., 1971, Mack award and lectureship, Ohio State U., 1969, medal, Chem. Inst. Can., 1976, Remsen award and lectureship, Am. Chem. Soc., 1978, Nobel prize in Chemistry, 1986, Izaak Walton Killam Meml. prize, 1988, C. Polanyi award, Can. Soc. Chemistry, 1992, Floyd E. Bartell Meml. lectureship, U. Mich., 1996, Liversidge lectureship, U. Sydney, 1996, Christian Culture award and lectureship, Assumption U., 1996; fellow Sloan Found., 1959—63, Guggenheim, 1979—80, Geoffrey Frew, 1996, Disting. Anniversary, Australian Nat. U., 1996. Fellow: Royal Soc. Chemisry (Michael Polanyi medal 1989), Royal Soc. Edinburgh, Royal Soc. London (Royal medal 1989, Bakerian lectureship and award 1994), Royal Soc. Can. (founding mem., pres., com. on scholarly freedom, Marshall Tory medal 1977), Chem. Inst. Can. (hon.); mem.: NAS (fgn. mem.), Pontifical Acad. Scis. (Rome), Am. Acad. Arts and Scis. (mem. com. on internat. security studies, hon. fgn.). Office: U Toronto Dept Chemistry Rm 262 80 St George St Toronto ON Canada M5S 3H6

POLASCIK, MARY ANN, ophthalmologist; b. Elkhorn, W.Va., Dec. 28, 1940; d. Michael and Elizabeth (Halko) Polascik; m. Joseph Ellie, Oct. 2, 1971; 1 dau., Laura Elizabeth Polascik Jr. BA, Rutgers U., 1967; MD, Pritzker Sch. Medicine, 1971. Jr. pharmacologist Ciba Pharm Co., Summit, N.J., 1961-67; intern Billings Hosp., Chgo., 1971-72; resident in ophthalmology U. Chgo. Hosp., 1972-75; practice medicine specializing in ophthalmology Dixon, Ill., 1975—. Pres. McNichols Clinic, Ltd.; cons. ophthalmology, Jack Mabley Devel. Ctr., 1976-93; mem. staff Katherine Shaw Bethea Hosp. Bd. dirs. Sinnissippi Mental Health Ctr., 1977-82, Dixon Cmty. Trust Mental Health Ctr., 1989—. Mem. Am. Acad. Ophthalmology, Alpha Sigma Lambda, Galena Territory Club. Roman Catholic. Office: 1700 S Galena Ave Dixon IL 61021-9695

POLASEK, EDWARD JOHN, retired electrical engineer, consultant; b. Cudahy, Wis., Oct. 12, 1927; s. John Vincent and Mary Ann (Totka) P.; m. Alice S. Nee (Harnecki), Aug. 18, 1948. BSEE, Marquette U., 1948. Registered profl. engr., Wis., Fla. Cons. engr. Eau Claire, Wis., Gainesville, Fla., 1955-60, various countries, Korea, Vietnam, Nicaragua, 1960-72; v.p., dir. Finley Engring. Co., Eau Claire, 1972-78; pres. Chippewa Devel. Co., Eau Claire, 1978-82; planning engr. Harza Engring. Co. in Cairo, Egypt and Dominican Rep., 1982-86; cons. engr. Gainesville, 1986-99; ret. Cons. Lake Altoona Rehab. Dist., Eau Claire, 1974. Author: Planning Methods, 1982, Feasibility Study, 1984; editor: Field Engineer's Handbook, 1982. Chmn. Eau Claire chpt. Am. Cancer Soc.; master gardner U. Fla. Ext. Svc., Gainesville, 1990. With USN, 1944-46, PTO. Mem. Nat. Soc. Profl. Engrs. (pres. 1956), IEEE, Audobon Soc., Tau Beta Pi, Eta Kappa Nu. Avocations: mycology, fishing, arts. Home: 8620 NW 13th St Lot 350 Gainesville FL 32653-7971 Address: 3532 Hwy 51 N Woodruff WI 54568 Office Phone: 715-385-2402.

POLAY, BRUCE, music educator, conductor; b. Bklyn., Mar. 22, 1949; s. Benjamin and Joan Polay; m. Louise Phillips, Dec. 17, 1983; children: Elizabeth Louise, Bruce Adam, Rachel Joanne, Jacob Benjamin, Julia Christine. MusB, U. So. Calif., 1971; MA, Calif. State U., 1977; DMA, Ariz. State U., 1989. Music dir. So. Calif. Philharm., Long Beach, 1971-81; grad. asst. in theory and orch., asst. condr. univ. symphony Ariz. State U., Tempe, 1981-83; condr. Phoenix Symphony Guild Youth Orch., 1981-83; music dir. Knox-Galesburg (Ill.) Symphony, 1983—; prof. music Knox Coll., Galesburg, 1983—, chair music dept., 2001—. Guest condr. in Belarus, Eng., Romania, Russia, Ukraine, Spain; bd. dirs. Ill. Coun. of Orchs., 1992—; mem. adv. bd. Found. for New Music, 1996—; bd. advisors Barlow Endowment for Music Composition; mem. music program adv. panel Ill. Arts Coun., 2004—. Orchestral compositions include Enconium, 1986, Perspectives, 1989, Concerto for Tenor Trombone, 1990, Tranquil Cycle for Tenor and Orch., 1992, Cathedral Images, 1993, Bondi's Journey: An Orchestral Rhapsody on Jewish Themes, 1994, Golden Oldie, 2001, Elegy For Violin and Orch., 2002; orchestrator Poulenc Oboe Sonata, 1985, Sound Images for Piano, 1995, Anniversary Mourning for a cappella choir, 1996, Sandburg Cycle for Soprano, Tenor and Piano, 2000, Semi-suite for Vin, Cello and Piano, 2001, Elegy for Violin and Small Orchestra, 2002, Suite of Preludes for Organ, 2002, Illumination for Orchestra, 2003. Recipient Ill. Condr. of Yr. award Ill. Coun. Orchs., 1997, 2004. Mem. ASCAP, Am. Music Ctr., Phi Kappa Phi. Avocations: body surfing, reading, American history, 1985 Corvette. Home: 1577 N Cherry St Galesburg IL 61401-1820 Office: Knox Coll Campus Box 5 Galesburg IL 61401-4999 Office Phone: 309-341-7208. E-mail: bpolay@knox.edu.

POLEDOURIS, BASIL K. composer; b. Kansas City, Mo., Aug. 21, 1945; s. Konstantine John and Helen Poledouris; m. Barbara Renée Godfrey, Aug. 15, 1969; children: Zoë Renée, Alexis Elene. BA in Music and Cinema, U. So. Calif., 1967, postgrad., 1967-69. Intern Am. Film Inst., L.A., 1969; freelance composer Hollywood, Calif., 1970—; pres. Basil Poledouris, Inc., Encino, Calif., 1987—. Bd. dirs. Blowtorch Flats, Venice, Calif.; mem. adv. bd. Soc. for Preservation Film Music, L.A., 1985—. Composer (film music) 90028, 1971, Extreme Close-Up, 1973, Tintorerra, 1977, Big Wednesday, 1979, Defiance, 1979, The Blue Lagoon, 1988, The House of God, 1988, Conan the Barbarian, 1981, Summer Lovers, 1982, Making the Grade, 1984, Conan the Destroyer, 1984, Red Dawn, 1984, Protocol, 1984, Flesh and Blood, 1985, Cherry 2000, 1986, Iron Eagle, 1986, Robocop, 1987 (BMI award 1988), No Man's Land, 1987, Split Decisions, 1988, Spellbinder, 1988, Farewell to the King, 1989, Wired, 1989, Hunt for Red October, 1990 (BMI award 1991), Quigley Down Under, 1990, Flight of the Intruder, 1991, White Fang, 1992, Return to the Blue Lagoon, 1991, Harley Davidson and the Marlboro Man, 1991, Robocop III, 1992, Free Willy, 1992 (BMI award 1994, gold record 1994), Hot Shots! Part Deux, 1993, Serial Mom, 1993, On Deadly Ground, 1994, Lassie, 1994, Jungle Book, 1994, Free Willy II, 1995, Under Seige II, 1995, It's My Party, 1995, Celtic Pride, 1996, Amanda, 1996, The War at Home, 1996, Switchback, 1996, Breakdown, 1997, Starship Troopers, 1997, Les Miserables, 1998, Mickey Blue Eyes, 1999, Amanda, 1999, For Love of the Game, 1999, Cecil B DeMented, 2000, Crocodile Dundee in L.A., 2001, The Touch, 2002, (TV film music) Congratulations It's A Boy, 1973, A Whale for the Killing, 1981, Fire on the Mountain, 1981, Amazons, 1984, Single Women, Single Bars, 1984, Amerika, 1987, Intrigue, 1988, Lonesome Dove, 1989 (Emmy award 1988, BMI award 1989), Nasty Boys, 1989, Lone Justice, 1990, Return to Lonesome Dove, 1993, TV pilots Alfred Hitchcock Presents, 1985, Misfits of Science, 1986, Island Sons, 1987, Murphy's Law, L.A. Takedown, 1989, Life and Times of Ned Blessing, 1991, Zoya, 1995, Tradition of Games Opening Ceremonies, 1996 Olympics, If These Walls Could Talk II, 2000, Dark Targets, 2001. Recipient resolution Calif. Legislature, 1990, Orange County Bd. Suprs., 1990, Key to City, Garden Grove City Coun., 1990, Disting. Artist award Calif. State U., Long Beach, 1992. Mem. NARAS, BMI, Am. Fedn. Musicians, Acad. Motion Picture Arts and Scis., Soc. Lyricists and Composers. Avocations: sailing, surfing.

POLEFKA, THOMAS GREGORY, biochemist; b. Passaic, N.J., Mar. 12, 1952; s. Emil Stanley and Stephanie (Kroczynski) P.; m. Maryann Brigida, Aug. 29, 1981; 1 child, Sara Jane. BS, Upsala Coll., 1974; PhD, U. Medicine/Dentistry N.J., 1979. Postdoctoral rsch. fellow Boston Biomed. Rsch. Inst./Harvard U. Med. Sch., 1979-80; rsch. assoc. Colgate-Palmolive Tech. Ctr., Piscataway, 1980—, dir. skin rsch., 2000—. Patentee in field; contbr. chpts. to books, articles to profl. jours. Mem. AAAS, Soc. Investigative Dermatology, Am. Chem. Soc., U. Medicine/Dentistry N.J. Sch. Biomed. Scis. Alumni Assn. (exec. coun. 1990-95). Avocations: bicycling, fishing, gardening, outdoor activities. Home: 79 Ellison Rd Somerset NJ 08873-2257 Office: Colgate-Palmolive Tech Ctr 909 River Rd Piscataway NJ 08854-5596 E-mail: thomas_polefka@colpal.com.

POLEMITOU, OLGA ANDREA, accountant; b. Nicosia, Cyprus, June 28, 1950; d. Takis and Georgia (Nicolaou) Chrysanthou. BA with honors, U. London, 1971; PhD, Ind. U., Bloomington, 1981. CPA Ind. Asst. productivity officer Internat. Labor Office/Cyprus Productivity Ctr., Nicosia, 1971-74; cons. Arthur Young & Co., N.Y.C., 1981; mgr. Coopers & Lybrand, Newark, 1981-83; dir. Bell Atlantic, Reston, Va., 1983-97; v.p. corp. auditing Columbia Energy Group, Herndon, 1997—2000; pres., CEO Aristion, Inc., Reston, Va., 2000—. Chairperson adv. coun. Extended Day Care Cmty. Edn., West Windsor Plainsboro, NJ, 1987—88. Contbr. articles to profl. jours. Bus. cons. project bus. Jr. Achievement, Indpls., 1984—85. Mem.: AICPAs, NAFE, Princeton Network Profl. Women, Va. Soc. CPAs, N.J. Soc. CPAs (sec. mem. in industry com.), Ind. CPA Soc., Nat. Trust Hist. Preservation. Avocations: water-skiing, tennis. Home: PO Box 2744 Reston VA 20195-0744 Office: 11921 Freedom Dr Ste 550 Reston VA 20190

POLENZ, JOANNA MAGDA, psychiatrist; b. Cracow, Poland, Oct. 20, 1936; came to U.S., 1961; d. Mieczyslaw and Nusia (Goldberger) Uberall; m. Daryl Louis Polenz, July 8, 1962 (div. 1991); children: Teresa Ann, Daryl Philip, Elizabeth Sophia. MD, U. Sydney, Australia, 1960; MPH, Columbia U., 1992. Diplomate Am. Bd. Psychiatry and Neurology. Intern Bklyn. Hosp., 1961-62; resident in psychiatry Mt. Sinai Med. Ctr., N.Y.C., 1962-65, ednl. fellow, 1965-66, rsch. assoc., 1966-67; med. dir. Tappan Zee clin. Phelps Meml. Hosp., Tarrytown, NY, 1968-71, dir. dept. psychiatry, 1972-77; sr. attending psychiatrist Meml. Hosp. Ctr., 1972-93; pvt. practice Briarcliff Manor, NY, 1971-91; physician Joint Commn. Accreditation of Healthcare Orgns., Oakbrook Terrace, Ill., 1993—; pres. Sch. of Health.com, N.Y.C., 1998—. Lectr. in field. Author: In Defense of Marriage, 1981; (with other) Test Your Marriage IQ, 1984, Test Your Success IQ, 1985, The Last Sick Generation, 2000; contbr. articles to profl. jours.; numerous TV appearances including Phil Donahue, 1988, Oprah Winfrey 1984. Grant Found. grant, 1970. Fellow Am. Psychiat. Assn. (disting. life); mem. AMA, Westchester Psychiat. Assn. (sec. 1982-85, chmn. fellowship com. 1989-98). Avocations: travel, international affairs. Home and Office: SchoolofHealth.com 123 E 75th St Ste 10B New York NY 10021 Office Phone: 212-426-5605. Office Fax: 212-828-2507. Business E-Mail: jpolenz@nyc.rr.com.

POLESE, KIM, software company executive; BS, U. Calif., Berkeley, 1984; student, U. Wash. Product mgr. Sun Microsys., 1988—95; co-founder, pres., CEO Marimba, Inc., 1996—2000, chmn., 1996—2003, bd. dirs., 1996—. Bd. dirs. TechNet. Bd. dirs. Do Something, Global Security Inst., U. Calif. President's Bd. Sci. and Innovation, Carnegie Mellon Computer Sci. Advisory Coun. Named one of Time Mags. Most Influential Ams. Mem.: Silicon Valley Mfg. Group. Achievements include a pivotal role in launching Java. Office: Marimba Inc 440 Clyde Ave Mountain View CA 94043-2232

POLESKIE, STEPHEN FRANCIS, artist, retired educator, writer; b. Pringle, Pa., June 3, 1938; s. Stephen Francis and Antoinette Elizabeth (Chludzinski) P.; m. Jeanne Mackin, 1979. BS, Wilkes Coll., 1959; postgrad., New Sch. for Social Research, 1961. Owner Chiron Press, N.Y.C., 1961-68; instr. Sch. Visual Arts, N.Y.C., 1968; prof. art Cornell U., Ithaca, N.Y., 1969-2001, prof. emeritus, 2001—. Vis. critic Pratt Graphic Arts Center, N.Y.C., 1965-68; vis. artist Colgate U., Hamilton, N.Y., 1973, USSR, 1979, Escuela de Bellas Artes, Honduras, 1980, Loughborough Coll. Art and Design, Eng., 1989; vis. prof. U. Calif., Berkeley, 1976; reviewer in field. Contbr. short stories to mags. and book; one-man shows include Louis K. Meisel Gallery, N.Y.C., 1978-80, Galerie Kupinski, Stuttgart, Germany, 1979, Palace of Culture and Sci., Warsaw, Poland, 1979, Sky Art Presentation, MIT, 1981, Am. Ctr., Belgrade, 1981, William and Mary Coll., 1983, McPherson Art Gallery, Victoria, B.C., Can., 1984, Studio D'Ars, Milan, 1985, Gallery Flaviana, Locarno, Switzerland, 1985, Il Salatto Gallery, Como, Italy, 1985, Galleria Schneider, Rome, 1987, Mus. Sztuki Lodz, Poland, 1987, Alternative Mus., Lido di Spina, Italy, 1987, Galerie Klaus Lea, Munich, 1987, Patricia Carega Gallery, Washington, 1988, Nine Columns Gallery, Palermo, Italy, 1988, John Hansard Gallery, Southampton, Eng., 1989, Quai Art Gallery, Isle of Wight, Eng., 1989, Lee Art Gallery, Clemson (S.C.) U., 1990, Apogeeairway, N.Y.C., 1991, Nine Columns Gallery, Brescia, Italy, 1991, Glenn Curtiss Mus., Hammondsport, N.Y., 1993, Caproni Mus., Trento, Italy, 1995, Temple U., Rome, 1995, Gallery Modern Art, Maribor, Slovenia, 1995, Palazzo Communale, Todi, Italy, 1995, Palazzo Della Pretura, Piacenza, Italy, Internat. Art Ctr., Kyoto, Japan; represented in collections at Met. Mus., N.Y.C., Mus. Modern Art, N.Y.C., Victoria and Albert Mus., London, Whitney Mus., N.Y.C., Walker Art Center, Mpls., Tate Gallery, London, Fort Worth Art Center, Nat. Collection, Washington, others; pub. Onager Edits., 2004. Am. Fedn. of Arts grantee, 1965; Carnegie Found. grantee, 1967; Nat. Endowment for Arts grantee, 1973; N.Y. State Council on Arts grantee, 1973; Creative Artists Public Service Program grantee, 1978; Best Found. grantee, 1985 Home: PO Box 849 Ithaca NY 14851-0849 Office Phone: 877-275-6388. Personal E-mail: onageredition@aol.com.

POLEVOY, NANCY TALLY, lawyer, social worker, genealogist; b. N.Y.C., May 27, 1944; d. Charles H. and Bernice M. (Gang) Tally; m. Martin D. Polevoy, Mar. 19, 1967; children: Jason Tally, John Gerald. Student, Mt. Holyoke Coll., 1962—64; BA, Barnard Coll., 1966; MSW, Columbia U., 1968, JD, 1986. Bar: N.Y. 1987. Caseworker unmarried mothers' svc. Louise Wise Svcs., N.Y.C., 1967, caseworker adoption dept., 1969-71; caseworker Youth Consultation Svc., N.Y.C., 1968-69; asst. rsch. scientist, psychiat. social worker NYU Med. ctr., N.Y.C., 1973-81; adv. ct. apptd. spl. advs. Manhattan Family Ct., N.Y.C., 1981-82; cons. social work, 1981-86; matrimonial assoc. Ballon, Stoll & Itzler, 1987, Herzfeld & Rubin, P.C., 1987-88; pvt. practice N.Y.C. Contbr. articles to profl. jours. Mem. parents' adv. bd. Riverdale Country Sch., 1988—93; mem. outreach bd. Manhattan divsn. United Jewish Appeal Fedn., 1990—94, exec. bd. Manhattan divsn., 1992—94, mem. met. campaign cabinet, 1994—95, mem. task force aging, 2004—; trustee Am. Jewish Hist. Soc., 1992—, asst. treas., 1995—98, v.p., 1998—2003; trustee Jewish Assn. Svcs. to Aged, 1996—, v.p., 1999—2003; bd. dirs. Ctr. Jewish History, 1996—; mem. archives com. Ctrl. Synagogue, 1991—, chmn., 1994—. Recipient French Govt. prize, 1963, honor for lifetime cmty. svc., United Jewish Appeal Fedn. N.Y., 2003. Mem.: NASW, Acad. Cert. Social Workers, N.Y. State Bar Assn., Assn. Bar City of N.Y., Barnard Coll. Alumni Assn. (v.p. 1966, class pres. 1966 1996—). Home and Office: 1155 Park Ave New York NY 10128-1209

POLEWAY, CHRISTOPER J. publishing executive; b. Brooklyn, NY, 1958; m. Poleway; 2 children. BA, St. Bonaventure Univ., Olean, NY; MBA, Fordham Univ. Mgr. fin. sys. HBO, 1982—88; gen. mgr. Corp. Fin. Reporting, 1988—91; Circulation Planning Mgr. Fortune, 1991—92, asst. bus. mgr., 1992—94, advertising bus. mgr., 1994—97, dir. of fin. and op., 1997—99, v.p. and gen. mgr., 1999—2000, chief op. officer, 2000—01, pres., 2001. Office: Time and Life Bldg Rockefeller Ctr New York NY 10020-1393

POLHAMUS, BARBARA, nutritionist, educator; d. Helen and Leslie Polhamus. PhD, MPH, U. N.C., Chapel Hill, 1991—97. Registered dietitian Am. Dietetic Assn., 1982. Nutrition dir. Dorchester Ho. Multi-Svc. Ctr., Mass., 1982—84; nutrition dir., maternal and child health Mass. Dept. Pub. Health, Boston, 1984—91; rsch. assoc. U. N.C., Chapel Hill, 1998—2000; nutritionist CDC, Nat. Ctr. for Chronic Disease Prevention and Health Promotion, Divsn. Nutrition and Phys. Activity, Atlanta, 2000—. Tech. cons., Ukraine micronutrient survey CDC, Atlanta, 2002. Contbr. chapters to books, articles to profl. jours. Fellow, Dannon Inst., 1998; grantee, Inst. Nutrition, 1994. Mem.: APHA (elected sect. mem. 2002—04). Liberal. Avocations: yoga, hiking, travel. Office: CDC 4770 Buford Hwy NE MS K-25 Atlanta GA 30341 Business E-Mail: bfp9@cdc.gov.

POLHEMUS, ROBERT M. language educator; b. San Francisco, Dec. 12, 1935; m. Carol Shloss; m. Elizabeth Polhemus (div.); children: Camilla, Robert, Josiah, Andromeda. AB, U. Calif., Berkeley, 1957; MA, U. Calif., 1959, PhD, 1963. Asst. prof. English dept. Stanford U., Calif., 1963—68, assoc. prof. English dept., 1968—79, prof. English dept., 1979—. Chair English dept. Stanford U., 1981—84, 2000—, dir. grad. studies English dept., 1973—75. Author: Comic Faith, 1980, Erotic Faith, 1990. Fellow, Stanford Humanities Ctr., 1997—98; Guggenheim fellow, 1980—81. Mem.: Modern Lang. Assn. Office: Stanford U English Dept Stanford CA 94305 E-mail: polhemus@stanford.edu.

POLI, KENNETH JOSEPH, editor, writer, photographer; b. Bklyn., June 8, 1921; s. Joseph H. and Irene (Seeman) P.; m. Virginia Osk, Dec. 14, 1946; 1 child, Bruce. Student, Goddard Coll., 1938-40. Writer, photographer North Atlantic Area Office ARC, N.Y.C., 1946-49. Editorial cons., 1965— Author Critical Focus Column, 1972-83; editor: External House Mags., Internat. Nickel Co., N.Y.C., 1949-53, Leica Photography mag., E. Leitz, Inc., N.Y.C., 1953-65; assoc. editor Popular Photography mag., Ziff-Davis Pub. Co., N.Y.C., 1965-69, sr. editor, 1969-70, editor, 1970-83, cons. editor, 1983-87; cons. editor Photography Ann., 35-mm Photography, Photography Directory and Buying Guide, 1970-83; contbr. articles to photog. jours. and encys. With inf. U.S. Army, 1942-45, PTO. Decorated Purple Heart medal. Mem. Am. Photog. Hist. Soc., Photographic Adminstrs., Circle of Confusion, Mensa. Home and Office: Apt 6167 1 Jefferson Ferry Dr South Setauket NY 11720-4727 E-mail: heremi_2000@yahoo.com.

POLIAKOFF, GARY A. lawyer, educator; b. Greenville, SC, Nov. 25, 1944; s. Herman and Dorothy (Ravitz) P.; m. Sherri D. Dublin, June 24, 1967; children: Ryan, Keith. BS, U. S.C., 1966; JD, U. Miami, 1969. Bar: Fla. 1969, DC 1971, Colo. 1999. Founding prin., pres. Becker & Poliakoff, P.A., Hollywood, Miami, Naples, Sarasota, West Palm Beach, Largo, Jacksonville, Orlando, Ft. Walton Beach, Fla., Prague and Beijing, 1973—. Adj. prof. condominium law and practice Nova Southeastern U.; panelist Nat. Confs. Cmty. Assn.; testified before coms. of the US Senate on Condominiums; lectr. ann. condominium seminars Fla. Bar; participant Fla. Law Revision Council; cons. to State Legis. and the White House in drafting Condominium and Coop. Abuse Relief Act, 1980; mem. condominium study commn. State of Fla., 1990; chmn. State of Fla. Advisory Coun. on Condominiums, 1992, 93.; atty. Town of Southwest Ranches. Author: The Law of Condominium Operations, 1988; co-author: Florida Condominium Law and Practice, 1982, The Florida Bar Continuing Legal Education, 1982; contbr. articles to legal jour. Mem. pres. adv. group U. SC, U.S.C. Ednl. Found., 1999—. Recipient Judge Learned Hand award Am. Jewish Com. for devel. of co-ownership housing law, 1999. Mem. Fla. Bar, Coll. Cmty. Assn. Lawyers (bd. gov.), Scribes.

POLICANO, ANDREW J. dean, finance educator; b. July 4, 1949; m. Susanne Policano; children: Emily, Keith. BS in Math., SUNY, Stony Brook, 1971; MA in Econs., Brown U., 1973, PhD in Econs., 1976. Asst. prof. U. Iowa, Iowa City, 1975-79, assoc. prof. dept. econs., 1979-81, prof., chair dept. econs., 1984-87, sr. assoc. dean academic affairs, 1987-88; prof. dept. econs. Fordham U., N.Y.C., 1981-84, asst. chair, dir. grad. studies, 1982-83; rsch. assoc. Ctr. for Study of Futures Markets Columbia U., N.Y.C., 1982-86; dean divsn. social & behavioral sci. SUNY, Stony Brook, 1988-91; dean Sch. Bus., U. Wis., Madison, 1991—2001, Kuechenmeister Prof. Bus., 2001—04; dean Grad. Sch. Mgmt., U. Calif, Irvine, 2004—. Guest prof. Inst. Advanced Studies, Vienna, Austria, 1985; dir. Nat. Guardian Life, Madison, 1991-, PIC Wis., 1995-, Badger Meter, 1997-; mem. Wis. Glass Ceiling Commn., 1995-2000. Contbr. articles profl. jours. Recipient Disting. Alumnus award SUNY, Stony Brook, 1994. Mem. Assn. to Advance Collegiate Schs. of Bus. (bd. dirs., 1997-98). Office: U Wis Sch Bus Grainger Hall 975 University Ave Rm 5110 Madison WI 53706-1324

POLICINSKI, EUGENE FRANCIS, foundation executive, newspaper editor, radio and television host, producer; b. South Bend, Ind., Aug. 31, 1950; s. E.T. and Margaret C. (O'Neill) P.; m. Kathleen Beta O'Donnell Powell, Aug. 19, 1972; children: Ryan, David. Degree in journalism and polit. sci., Ball State U., 1972. Corr. Gannett News Svc., Washington, 1979-82; Washington editor USA Today, Arlington, Va., 1982-83, page one editor, 1983-85, mng. editor sports, 1989—96; spl. asst. to chmn./CEO The Freedom Forum, Arlington, Va., 1996-98; wash. editor Freedom Forum Website, 1998-99; dep. dir. First Amendment Ctr., Nashville, 1999—2004, acting dir., 2004—. Host, commentator USA Today Sky Radio, Arlington, 1992—95; host Newseum Radio, 1998—2001; adj. faculty Winthrop U., 1999—; exec. prodr. Speaking Freely (PBS), 2001—. Founding editor USA Today Baseball Weekly, 1991. Bd. advisors Ctr. Study Sport in Soc., 1995—; trustee U.S. Sports Acad., 1997—, Watkins Coll. Art and Design, 2001—04; dir. J-IDEAS program Ball State U., 2003—. Named one of 100 Most Important People in Sports Sporting News, 1992-93, 95, Sports Person of Yr., U.S. Sports Acad., 1996; named to Journalism Hall of Fame, Ball State U., 1989, Alumni of Yr., 1996. Mem. NATAS (gov. 2004), Am. Soc. Newspaper Editors, Soc. Profl. Journalists, Assn. Educators in Journalism and Mass Comms. Avocations: sailing, bicycling, golf. Office: First Amendment Center Acting Director 1207 18th Ave S Nashville TN 37212-2807 Office Phone: 615-727-1303. Business E-Mail: gpolicinski@fac.org.

POLICOFF, STEPHEN PHILLIP, writer, educator; b. Richmond, Va., Apr. 27, 1948; s. Leonard David and Naomi Lewis Policoff; m. Kate Beck, Apr. 29, 1989; children: Anna Helena Hui Beck-Policoff, Jane Quianshu Beck-Policoff. BA, Wesleyan U., Middletown, Conn., 1970. Adj. assoc. prof. of writing NYU, 1990—94, master tchr. of writing, 1994—. Dir. of creative writing program Ctr. for Creative Youth, Middletown, Conn., 1978—95. Author: (novel) Beautiful Somewhere Else (James Jones 1st Novel Fellowship, 2000), (nonfiction book) The Dreamer's Companion; author: (co-author) Real Toads in Imaginary Gardens (NY Pub. Libr. Best YA Books, 1991); author: (children's book) Cesar's Amazing Journey. Grantee Commn. to write libretto for children's opera, Lincoln Ctr. Inst., 1990. Home: 3 Washington Sq Village Apt 9 I New York NY 10012 Office: NYU GSP 726 Broadway 6th Fl New York NY 10003 E-mail: sp1@nyu.edu.

POLICY, CARMEN A. professional sports team executive; b. Youngstown, Ohio, Jan. 26, 1943; s. Albert and Ruby (Tisone) P.; m. Aug. 8, 1964 (div. Mar. 1989); children: James, Daniel, Edward, Kerry, Kathy; m. Gail Marie Moretti, June 27, 1991. Grad., Youngstown State U., 1963; JD, Georgetown U., 1966. Bar: Ohio 1966, Va. 1966, D.C. 1966. Assoc. Nadler & Nadler, Youngstown, 1966-68; asst. prosecutor City of Youngstown, 1968-69; ptnr. Flask & Policy, Weimer & White, Youngstown, 1969-90; spl. counsel to atty. gen. State of Ohio, 1970-91; v.p., gen. counsel San Francisco 49ers, NFL, 1983-90, pres., 1990-99; pres., CEO & co-owner Cleve. Browns, 1998—2004, consultant, 2004—. Mem. various coms. NFL, 1990—; bd. dirs. World League Am. Football, N.Y.C., 1991—. Com. mem. various charities, Youngstown, 1969-90, San Francisco, 1990—. Mem. Va. Bar Assn., Ohio Bar Assn., D.C. Bar Assn. Roman Catholic. Avocations: scuba diving, hiking. Office: Cleve Browns 76 Lou Groza Blvd Berea OH 44017

POLIN, COLLEEN MARIE, special education educator; b. Detroit, Feb. 3, 1954; d. Henry George and Lorraine Cynthia (Spisz) Geppert. BA in Spl. Edn., Ea. Mich. U., 1975, M.Early Childhood Edn., 1981. Tchr. austically impaired Wayne County Intermediate Schs., 1976-78, Garden City (Mich.) pub. schs., 1978—. Internat. speaker in field. Active Boy Scouts Am., Garden City, 1986-87; host children's program "Alphabet Soup", MacLean Hunter Cable TV, Garden City, 1988—; bd. dirs. Mich. Partnership for New Edn. Named Tchr. of the Yr., Wayne County Soc. Autistic Citizens, 1988, Golden Apple Teaching award, Wayne County Intermediate Sch. Dist., 1989, Disting. Alumni award, Schoolcraft Coll., Livonia, 1990, Flag of Lng. and Liberty, 1992. Mem. Autism Sch. Soc., Autism Soc. Am., Coun. for Exceptional Children. Avocations: calligraphy, antique restoration, gardening. Home: 1028 Church St Plymouth MI 48170-1149 Office: Burger School 30922 Beechwood St Garden City MI 48135-1993

POLIN, JANE L. foundation official; b. N.Y.C., Sept. 30, 1958; BA, Wesleyan U., Middletown, Conn., 1980; MBA, Columbia U., 1988. Asst. dir. ann. giving Wesleyan U., 1980-82; centennial fund assoc. Met. Opera Assn., N.Y.C., 1982-84; devel. officer Columbia U., N.Y.C., 1984-88; program mgr., comptr. GE Fund, Fairfield, Conn., 1988-99; v.p. cmty. devel. and corp. affairs Sperry & Hutchinson, Inc., 1999—2000, philanthropic advisor, 2001—. *Jane L. Polin brings more than twenty years of innovative leadership experience within the nonprofit and private sectors in developing and investing philanthropic resources. Now serving as a philanthropic advisor, principally in the areas of the arts, education, and public policy, her current and recent clients include: The American Music Center / Andrew W. Mellon Foundation; The Atlantic Philanthropies/ National Dance Institute; Bennington College/ The J. Paul Getty Trust; The Dana Foundation; The Thomas S. Kenan Institute for the Arts; WNYC; and Young Audiences.* Panelist arts-in-edn. Nat. Endowment for Arts, Washington, 1989—90, 1994—95, NEH, 1997; adv. bd. mem. ARC, 1991—99, United Way Am., 1991—99, Inst. for Internat. Econs., 1995—99, Young Audiences, N.Y.C., 1991—2000, mem. Advt. Coun., 1998—2003; judge Frances Hesselbein Cmty. Innovation Fellows Program, 2001—02, Peter F. Drucker Award for Nonprofit Innovation, 1996—2000. Mem.: Alpha Delta Phi. Home and Office: 67 Riverside Dr Apt 7D New York NY 10024-6136 Fax: 212-873-1568. E-mail: janepolin@aol.com.

POLING, KERMIT WILLIAM, minister; b. Elkins, W.Va., Oct. 1, 1941; s. Durward Willis and Della Mae (Boyles) P.; m. Patricia Ann Groves, June 12, 1965; children: David Edward Elson, Mikael Erik. Diploma in Bible, Am. Bible Sch., 1966; BA in Bible, Reed Coll. Religion, 1968; AA, W.Va. U., 1970; ThD, Zion Theol. Sem., 1971; postgrad., Wesley Theol. Sem., 1974; LLD, Geneva Theol. Coll., 1980; DSL (hon.), Berean Christian Coll., 1981; postgrad., Mansfield Coll., U. Oxford, Eng., 1986, Mansfield Coll., U. Oxford, 1990, postgrad., 1991; D Ecumenical Rsch., St. Ephrem's Inst. for Oriental Studies, 1989; BRE, Am. Bible Coll., 1991; M of Herbology, Emerison Coll., 1994. Ordained to ministry United Meth. Ch., 1967. Pastor Parkersburg-Crossroads (W.Va.) Cir., 1967-70; asst. sec. W.Va. Ann. Conf., 1967-69; pastor Hope-Halleck Morgantown Cir., 1970-76, Trinity-Warren Grafton (W.Va.) Charge, 1976-83, 1st Trinity Pennsboro (W.Va.) Charge, 1983-97, South Parkersburg United Meth. Ch., 1997—2004. Editor local ch. news; instr. Bible Bodkin Bible Inst., 1975-75, United Meth. Lay Acad., 1992—2004; mem. staff Taylor County Coop. Parish, 1976-83; coord. Hughes River Coop. Parish, 1983-86; mem. chaplains com. Grafton City Hosp., 1976-82; mem. coun. Ctr. d'Etudes et d'Action Oecumeniques, 1972-74; bishop in Partibus of Tayma. Author: A Crown of Thorns, 1963, A Silver Message, 1964, History of the Halleck Church, 1970, Eastern Rite Catholicism, 1971, From Brahmin to Bishop, 1976, Cult and Occult: Data and Doctrine, 1978, The Value of Religious Education in Ancient Traditional Churches, 1993, Anniversary History of Trinity Church, Pennsboro, 1997; editor: Jane's Heirs; contbr. articles and poems to religious jours. Decorated Royal Afghanistan Order of Crown of Amanullah, Byzantine Order of Leo the Armenian, Order of Polonia Resitutia, Mystical Order of St. Peter, knight Grand Cross of the Order of St. Dennis of Zante, 1990; recipient Good Citizenship award Doddridge County, 1954, Silver medal Ordre Universel du Merit Humain, Geneva, 1973, Commendation for Outstanding Achievement in Ministry, Ohio Ho. of Reps., 1988; recipient U.S. Heritage award, 2002; named Chief of Dynastic Ho. of Polanie-Patrikios, 1988. Mem. SAR, Assn. Bible Tchrs. (founder), Internat. Platform Assn., Naval Order U.S., Sovereign Order St. John Jerusalem, Ritchie County Ministerial Assn. (pres. 1984-97), Order Sacred Cup, Knights of Malta, Order of the Crown of Lauriers. Home: 101 E Myles Ave Pennsboro WV 26415

POLINGER, IRIS SANDRA, dermatologist; b. N.Y.C., Feb. 10, 1943; m. Harvey I. Hyman, Feb. 6, 1972. AB, Barnard Coll., 1964; PhD, Johns Hopkins U., 1969; MD, SUNY Downstate, Bklyn., 1975. Diplomate Am. Bd. Dermatology. Teaching positions various schs. including NYU Coll. Dentistry and Harvard Med. Sch., 1969-73; med. intern Baylor Coll. Medicine, 1975-76, resident in dermatology, 1976-79; pvt. practice dermatology Houston, 1979—. Bd. dirs. Ft. Bend County Women's Ctr., Richmond, Tex., 1993—. Mem. Am. Bus. Women's Assn. (chair scholarship com. 1992, 96, chair scholarship event com. 1993—). Office: 4915 S Main St Ste 104 Stafford TX 77477-4601

POLINSKY, JANET NABOICHECK, retired state official, former state legislator; b. Hartford, Conn., Dec. 6, 1930; d. Louis H. and Lillian S. Naboicheck; m. Hubert N. Polinsky, Sept. 21, 1958 (div.); children: Gerald, David, Beth. BA, U. Conn., 1953; postgrad., Harvard Bus. Sch., 1954. Mem. Waterford 2d Charter Commn. (Conn.), 1967-68, Waterford Conservation Commn., 1968-69; Waterford rep. Town Meeting, 1969-71, S.E. Conn. Regional Planning Agy., 1971-73; mem. Waterford Planning and Zoning Commn., 1970-76, chmn., 1973-76; mem. Waterford Dem. Town Com., 1976-92. Del. State Dem. Conv., 1976, 78, 80, 82, 84, 86, 90, 92; mem. Conn. Ho. of Reps. from 38th Dist., 1977-82, asst. majority leader, 1981-83, chmn. appropriations com., 1983-85, 87-89, ranking mem., 1985-87, minority whip, 1985-86, dep. spkr., 1989-92; dep. commr. dept. adminstrv. svcs. State of Conn., 1993-94, chmn., 1994-95, asst. sec. of state, 1995, commr. utilities ctrl. auth., 1995-97. Trustee Eugene O'Neill Meml. Theatre Ctr., 1973-76, 81-92; corporator Lawrence and Meml. Hosps., 1987-88; mem. New Eng. Bd. Higher Edn., 1981-83; mem. fiscal affairs com. Eastern Conf. Coun. State Govts., 1983-88; mem. Limoge Village Bd., 2000-02; sec. Cascades, 2000—, sec., 2002—. Named Woman of Yr., Waterford Jr. Women's Club, 1977, Nehantic Women's Bus. and Profl. Club, 1979, Legislator of Yr., Conn. Libr. Assn., 1980. Mem. Order of Women Legislators, Delta Kappa Gamma (hon.). Home: 7141 Haviland Cir Boynton Beach FL 33437-6463 Personal E-mail: naboi1@aol.com.

POLINSKY, JOSEPH THOMAS, recruiting and training consultant; b. Kingston, Pa., Mar. 10, 1947; s. Joseph Patrick and Margaret Ceclia Polinsky; m. Donna Lee Miles, Dec. 28, 1968 (div. Nov. 1990); children: Jon Douglas, Jennifer Susan, Jeffrey David; m. Diane Walsh, Apr. 19, 1997. BSBA, King's Coll., 1968; MBA in Mgmt., Fairleigh Dickinson U., 1977. Fin. svcs. specialist Bell Labs., Murray Hill, N.J., 1968-74, adminstrv. asst. Whippany, N.J., 1974-76, supr. adminstrn. svcs., 1977, tech. employment rep. Holmdel, N.J., 1977-80, sr. systems analyst Short Hills, N.J., 1981-82; mgr. tech. employment Bellcore, Piscataway, N.J., 1983-85, mgr. logistics, 1986-92, mgr. purchasing, 1992-96; dir., tech. recruiting Youngtech, Inc., Edison, N.J., 1996; employment rep. Lucent Tech., Holmdel, 1996-97, coll. recruiting and tng. cons., 1997-98, mem. faculty, 1999-2000; dir. recruiting and talent devel. Cybertel, Inc., Middletown, N.J., 2000; cons., owner JTP Cons., Holmdel, N.J., 2000—; adj. prof. Sch. Bus. Adminstrn., Monmouth U., Long Branch, NJ, 2001—02. Mem. indsl. com. United Way, Morris County, N.J., 1977, allocation com., Monmouth County, N.J., 1985; cub master Boy Scouts Am., Raritan, N.J., 1983-86; mem. Bd. Adjustment, Raritan, 1988-89. With U.S. Army, 1969-70. Roman Catholic. Avocations: fishing, stamp collecting/philately, cooking, baseball cards. Home and Office: 185 Escondido Ct Holmdel NJ 07733-2531 E-mail: joesonline@aol.com.

POLISAR, JOSEPH MICHAEL, protective services official; b. Bklyn., June 25, 1952; s. Ira Allen and Rose (Gimpelman) P.; m. Shirley Elizabeth Chavez, Nov. 1, 1986; children: Brooklyn Joseph, Savannah Janelle. BA in Mgmt., U. Phoenix, 1993; grad., FBI Acad., 1993; postgrad., FBI Nat. Exec. Inst., 1995; grad., JFK Sch. Govt., 1996. Officer, detective Albuquerque Police Dept., 1977-81, sgt., 1981-85, lt., 1985-92, capt., 1992-94, chief of police, 1994-97, Garden Grove (Calif.) Police Dept., 1998—. Staff instr. Northwestern U., Evanston, Ill., 1989—. Fund raiser Am. Cancer Soc., Muscular Dystrophy, Juvenile Diabetes, Crimestoppers, Cystic Fibrosis. Recipient 1995 Albuquerque Human Rights award, Martin Luther King "Keep the Dream Alive" award NAACP, Albuquerque, 1996. Mem. Internat. Police Assn., FOP, Internat. Assn. Chiefs of Police (pres. 2003-04), FBI Nat. Acad. Assn., Kiwanis (v.p.). Avocations: bowhunting, motorcycle touring, jogging.

POLISAR, LEONARD MYERS, lawyer; b. Bklyn., Oct. 25, 1929; s. Aaron and Anna (Myers) P.; m. Judith Sarah Weisstein, Aug. 16, 1959; children: Mark Joseph, Daniel Aaron. BA, Bklyn. Coll., 1950; LLB, Yale U., 1953; LLM in Taxation, NYU, 1959. Bar: N.Y. 1954. Assoc. Hays, Podell, Algase, Crum & Feuer, N.Y.C., 1955-63; asst. to gen. counsel CIT Fin. Corp., N.Y.C., 1963-65; v.p. law and pub. affairs Mgmt. Assistance Inc., N.Y.C., 1966-72; v.p., gen. counsel Internat. Controls Corp., Fairfield, N.J., 1972-73; v.p., sec., gen. counsel Baker Industries Inc., Parsippany, N.J., 1973-80; ptnr. Herzfeld & Rubin, P.C., N.Y.C., 1980—, co-chmn. corp. and securities law dept., 1988—, also bd. dirs. Arbitrator N.Y. Stock Exch., 1987—; speaker at computer, securities and corp. seminars. Editor Yale Law Jour., 1953. Bd. dirs. Mental Health Assn. of N.Y.C., 1960—, chmn., 1985—; trustee Union Temple Bklyn., 1988—, v.p. 1990-99; bd. dirs. Routes to Roots Found. Mem. ABA, Assn. of Bar of City of N.Y., Am. Soc. Corp. Secs. (chmn. audit com. 1989-92), Bus. Coun. for UNA (bus. adv. com.), Bus. Execs. for Nat. Security, Computer Law Assn., Citizens Union, Yale Club of N.Y., Yale Club of Montclair, Phi Beta Kappa. Jewish. Avocations: skiing, sailing, spectator sports, music, drama. Home: 63 Briarcliff Rd Mountain Lakes NJ 07046-1304 Office: Herzfeld & Rubin PC 40 Wall St Fl 54 New York NY 10005-2301

POLISAR, LISA, writer; b. Taunton, Mass., Oct. 10, 1966; d. Richard Ralph and Constance Cecile Striano; m. Stephen Matthew Polisar, Sept. 6, 1996. MusB, Martt Sch. Music, 1988. Cert. artorist Internat. Soc. Agr. Freelance writer, 1992—; profl. tech. writer B&B Tech., Albuquerque, 2003—. Cons. writing instr., 2002—. Author: Blackwater Tango, 2001, Knee Deep, 2003. Recipient comm. award, N.Mex. Press Women, 2004. Mem.: Myster Writers Am., Sisters in Crime, SW Writers (bd. dirs. 2004, chmn. confs. 2004, chmn. critique svc. 2003). Avocations: reading, hiking, movies, tai chi. E-mail: Polisar2@msn.com.

POLISI, JOSEPH W(ILLIAM), academic administrator; b. N.Y.C., Dec. 30, 1947; married Elizabeth; 2 children. BA in Polit. Sci., U. Conn., 1969; MA in Internat. Relations, Tufts U., 1970, MusM, 1973, M of Mus. Arts, 1975; DMA, Yale U., 1980; DHL (hon.), Ursinus Coll., Collegetown, Pa., 1986; MusD (hon.), Curtis Inst. Music, 1990; DMA, New England Conservatory Music, 2001. Exec. officer Yale Sch. of Music, New Haven, 1976-80; dean of faculty Manhattan Sch. of Music, N.Y.C., 1980-83; dean Coll. Conservatory of Music U. Cin., 1983-84; pres. The Juilliard Sch., N.Y.C., 1984—. Performances as bassoonist throughout the U.S.; contbr. articles to various publs. in U.S. and France; author The Artist as Citizen, 2004. Dir. Edward John Noble Foundation, Irene Diamond Fund. Mem.: Royal Acad. Music London (hon.). Office: Juilliard Sch Office of the Pres 60 Lincoln Center Plz New York NY 10023-6588*

POLISTENA, JOYCE CAROL, art historian, educator; d. Fred and Frances Polistena. BA, St. John's U., 1970; MA, Hunter Coll., 1980; MPhil, The Grad. Sch. and U. Ctr. of The City U. of NY, 1995; PhD, The Grad. Sch. and U. Ctr., 1997. Cert. tchr. The U. of the State of NY, State Edn. Dept., 1990. Asst. prof. Pratt Inst., Bklyn, NY, 1997—2003, assoc. prof., 2003—. Symposia participant Am. Bible Soc., NYC, 2002; conf. participant Coll. Art Assn., NYC, 2000, NYC, 03; lectr. 92nd St. YMYWHA, NYC, 2002, Graymoor Spiritual Life Ctr., Garrison, NY, 2002. Contbr. articles to profl. jours. Exec. bd. Harlem Valley Churches, NY, 1988—94. Mem.: Assn. of Art Historians of Am. Art, Assn. of Historians of Nineteenth Century Art, Coll. Art Assn. Roman Cath.

POLISTUK, EUGENE V. electronics manafacturing services executive; B Applied Sci. in Elec. Engring., U. Toronto; D Engring. (hon.), Ryerson U., 2001. Founder, chmn., CEO Celestica Inc., Toronto, Canada, 1994—, pres., 1994—2001; with IBM Can. Recipient Meritorious Svc. medal, U. Toronto Engring. Alumni Assn., Outstanding CEO award, Electronic Bus. Office: Celestica Inc 12 Concorde Pl Toronto ON Canada M3C 3R8

POLITE, CARLENE HATCHER, writer, educator; b. Detroit; d. John and Lillian Hatcher; m. James S. Patrick, July 21, 2003; children from previous marriage: Glynda Morton, Lila Ashaki. Student, Martha Graham Sch. Dance, N.Y.C., 1952-56; diploma, Acad. Leonardo da Vinci, Rome, 1980. Dancer, student Martha Graham Sch., N.Y.C., 1952-56; dancer Alvin Ailey Dance Co., N.Y.C., 1957-58, Edith Stephen Co., N.Y.C., 1958; dancer, actress Vanguard Playhouse, Detroit, 1960-62; prof. English SUNY, Buffalo, 1971—2000, chair dept. Am. Studies, 1981, prof. emerita, 2000. Tchr. Golden Dragon Kung Fu Acad., 1974-75, Himalayan Inst. Yoga, 1980-82; panelist NEA, Washington, 1981, N.Y. State Coun. Arts, N.Y.C., 1982, N.Y. Found. Arts, 1983, Seattle Arts in Pub. Places, 1989. Author: The Flagellants, 1966, Paris edit., 1967, N.Y. edit., 1968, also other European edits. (Pulitzer prize nominee, 1967, NEA grant, 1967, Rockefeller grant, 1968), Sister X and The Victims of Foul Play, 1975. Coord. Walk to Freedom with Martin Luther King, Detroit, 1963; del., participant UN-Non-Govtl.Orgns. 4th World Conf. on Women, Beijing, 1995. Recipient numerous nat. and internat. awards as artist and educator; invited 1st Ann. Conf. African Presence, Paris, 1991, Internat. Educators and Writers Oxford U., 1997. Avocation: yoga.

POLITE, EVELYN C. retired middle school educator, counselor, evangelist; b. Pineland, S.C., Dec. 25, 1937; d. Martin and Mary Brantley Coger; m. Horace Polite, Jan. 1, 1958 (dec. Jan. 1987); children: Horace Lenton, Tracy Polite Floyd. BS, Allen U., 1960; M in Elem. Edn., Armstrong-Savannah (Ga.) State U., 1976; cert. specialist of arts in theology, Zoe U., Jacksonville, Fla., 2000; PhD in Christian Counseling, Zoe U., 2001. Tchr. math. Beaufort County Bd. Edn., Bluffton, SC, 1960—61, Florence County Bd. Edn., Florence, SC, 1961—63, Jasper County Bd. Edn., Ridgeland, SC, 1963—64, 1991—92, Savannah Pub. Schs., 1964—90; math. tutor Dept. Family and Children, Savannah, 1992—94. Mem. curriculum devel. com. Savannah Pub. Schs., 1983—84, mem. staff devel. coun., 1983—84; test-item writer Ednl. Testing Svc., Princeton, NJ, 1990. Pres. 42d St Civic Club, Savannah, 2000—; exec. v.p. Cuyler-Brownsville Neighborhood Orgn., Savannah, 2001—. Recipient Outstanding Tchr. award, Math.-Sci. Roundtable, Atlanta, 1990. Mem. Ch. Of God. Avocations: world missions, travel, physical fitness, reading Christian literature. Office: Coastal Cathedral Ch of God 2208 E DeRenne Ave Savannah GA 31406 Home: 33 Wild Heron Villas Rd Savannah GA 31419-8981

POLITES, MICHAEL EDWARD, aerospace engineer, educator; b. Belleville, Ill., Mar. 19, 1944; s. Matthew Charles and Edith Louise (Schwarz) P. BS in Sys. and Automatic Controls, Washington U., St. Louis, 1967; MSEE, U. Ala., 1971; PhD in Elec. Engring., Vanderbilt U., 1986. Aerospace rsch. engr., guidance, navigation and control sys. NASA/Marshall Space Flt. Ctr. Structures & Dynamics Lab, Huntsville, Ala., 1967-95; supervisory chief, instrumentation and control divsn. Astrionics Lab. NASA/Marshall Space Flight Ctr., Huntsville, Ala., 1995-98, dep. dir. astronics lab., 1998-99, dep. mgr. avionics dept., 1999-2001—; assoc. prof. aerospace engring. and mechanics U. Ala., 2001—. 4 patents in field; contbr. numerous articles to profl. jours.; referee various jours. and confs. Mem. adv. bd. Coll. Engring. leadership bd. U. Ala., 1999-2001. Recipient 71 NASA awards in the field including NASA-Marshall Co-Inventor of Yr., 1995; U. Ala. Coll. Engring. Disting. fellow, elec. engring. dept. outstanding fellow; named Outstanding Engr., Engrs. Coun., 2000. Fellow AIAA (assoc., guidance navigation and control tech. com. 1990-2002, digital avionics tech. com. 1996-2002, U. Ala. AIAA faculty advisor 2001-2002); mem. IEEE (sr. Outstanding Engr. Huntsville sect. 1995), ASME, Am. Astronautical Soc. (session co-chmn. 1995, 97, 98, 99, 2000, 01, Guidance and Control Conf.), Mensa, Tau Beta Pi, Eta Kappa Nu, Pi Tau Sigma. Office: U Ala Dept Aerospace Engring and Mechanics Box 870280 Tuscaloosa AL 35847

POLITI, BETH KUKKONEN, publishing services company executive; b. Englewood, N.J., Sept. 18, 1949; d. Andrew and Beatrice G. (Druskin) Kukkonen; m. Joseph Politi, Oct. 21, 1982; children: Andrew, Joseph. BS in Mktg., Miami U., Oxford, Ohio, 1971. Media buyer Schwab, Beatty & Porter, Inc., 1971-72; media planner Adler, Schwartz & Connes, 1972-73; media buyer/planner Schwab Beatty divsn. Marstellar, 1973-74; dir. insert advt. Benjamin Co., Inc., Elmsford, N.Y., 1975-78, prodn. mgr., 1978-80, v.p. client svcs., 1980-83, editor supr., 1979-83; v.p. Bergen County Profl. Svcs., Ft. Lee, N.J., 1983—. Assoc. pub. various books Benjamin Co., Inc., 1981-83; freelance proofreader Montge Media, Montvale, N.J., 1999—. Trustee bd. edn. Pascack Valley Regional H.S. Dist., 1999—; mem. dist. fee com. Office of Atty. Ethics of Supreme Ct. of NJ, 2001—; del. exec. com. Bergen County Sch. Bd. Assn., 2003—; tax assessor Borough Bogota, 2004—. Home: 4 Smoke Rise Ct Montvale NJ 07645-1139

POLITI, JOHN J. association administrator; b. Sedalia, Mo. m. Terri Hatch; children: Pam, Eileen, Jay, Stephanie, Chip. BA in Polit. Sci., U. Colo.; MS in Econs., S.D. State U. Commd. 2d lt. USAF, 1966, advanced through grades to col.; comdr. Air Divsn.; with Joint Staff and Air Staff; ret. USAF, 1992; nat. dir. Air Force Assn., Arlington, Va., nat. v.p. Midwest Region, Mo. state pres., chmn. audit com., membership com., ad hoc fin. com., nat. pres., 2001—. Pres. Excellence in Mo. Found. Decorated Legion of Merit. Office: c/o AFA Nat Hqrs 1501 Lee Hwy Arlington VA 22209-1198

POLITO, ROBERT J. federal agency administrator; m. Michele Polito; 3 children. B in Health Edn., Pa. State U. Creator, leader Bowery Mission Transitional Ctr., N.Y.C., 1994—99; founder FaithWorks, Milw., 1999; founder, past pres. FaithWorks Internat., N.Y.C.; dir. Ctrs. for Faith-Based and Cmty. Initiatives U.S. Dept. Health and Human Svcs., Washington, 2002—. Office: US Dept HHS Ctr for Faith-Based and Cmty Initiatives 200 Independence Ave SW Rm 118F Washington DC 20201

POLITZER, HUGH DAVID, physicist, educator; b. N.Y.C., Aug. 31, 1949; s. Alan A. and Valerie T. (Diamant) P. BS, U. Mich., 1969; PhD, Harvard U., 1974. Jr. fellow Harvard U. Soc. Fellows, 1974-77; mem. faculty Calif. Inst. Tech., 1977—, prof. theoretical physics, 1979—, exec. officer for physics, 1986-88. Recipient J.J. Sakurai prize, 1986, High Energy and Particle Physics prize European Phys. Soc., 2003; fellow NSF, 1969-74, Sloan Found., 1977-81, Woodrow Wilson grad. fellow, 1969-74, Guggenheim fellow, 1997-98. Mem. Phi Beta Kappa. Address: 452-48 Calif Inst Tech Pasadena CA 91125-0001 E-mail: politzer@theory.caltech.edu.

POLIZZOTTI, MARK, writer, translator, publishing executive; b. NYC, July 22, 1957; s. Mario and Grace Polizzotti; m. Sarah Ranson-Polizzotti; 1 child, Alex. BA, Yale U., 1979; MA, Columbia U., 1983. Editl. dir. David R. Godine, Inc., Boston, 1993—99; dir. of intellectual property and pub. Mus. Fine Arts, Boston, 1999—. Author: (novel) S: a novel (collaborative), (poetry) The New Life, (biography) Revolution of the Mind: The Life of Andre Breton (Finalist, PEN/Martha Albrand Award, 1995). Fellow Tchg. Fellowship, Fulbright-Hayes Found., 1979-80, Creative Writing Fellowship, Atlantic Ctr. for Arts, 1990; grantee Rsch. Grant, Nat. Endowment for Humanities, 1989-90, French Ministry of Culture, 1991, Transl. Grant, Nat. Endowment for Arts, 1994-95. Office: Mus Fine Arts Boston 465 Huntington Avenue Boston MA 02115 E-mail: mp@mfa.org.

POLJAK, ROBERTO J(UAN), research director, biotechnology educator; b. Buenos Aires, Sept. 17, 1932; s. Giovanni P. and Josephine (Zorzut) P.; m. Mabel Amelia Iglesias, Dec. 28, 1956; children: Leonora, Gustavo. BSc, Coll. Nat. Quilmes, Argentina, 1949; PhD, U. de la Plata, Argentina, 1956. Teaching assoc. Instituto de Fisica, Bariloche, Argentina, 1957; fellow Sch. for Advanced Studies MIT, Boston, 1958-60; postdoctoral fellow Davy Faraday Rsch. Lab., Royal Instn., London, 1960-62; postdoctoral fellow MRC Unit for Molecular Biology, Cambridge, Eng., 1962; asst. prof. biophysics Johns Hopkins Sch. Medicine, Balt., 1962, assoc. prof. biophysics, 1966, prof. biophysics, 1972-81; prof. Institut Pasteur, Paris, 1981-92; dir. rsch. CNRS, Paris, 1981-92; prof., dir. Ctr. Advanced Rsch. in Biotech. U. Md./Nat. Inst. Stds. and Tech., Balt., 1992—; W.H. Elkins prof. U. Md., 1994—. Contbr. about 150 rsch. papers to sci. jours. Recipient Rsch. Career Devel. award USPHS, 1972-77, gold medal Soc. d'Encouragement au Progres, Paris, 1986, Jacques Monod prize Fondation de France, 1986, Disting. Scientist award S.W. Found. for Biomed. Rsch., 1987, Louis Jeantet Found. Medicine prize, Geneva, 1989, Gold medal Jimenez Diaz Found., 1991; Macy Faculty scholar, 1977-78. Mem. European Molecular Biology Orgn., Am. Assn. Immunologists. Office: Ctr for Advanced Rsch Biotech 9600 Gudelsky Dr Rockville MD 20850-3479

POLK, HIRAM CAREY, JR., surgeon, educator; b. Jackson, Miss., Mar. 23, 1936; s. Hiram Carey and Dorris (Hemby) P.; m. Susan Galandiuk; children: Susan Elizabeth, Hiram Cary. BS, Millsaps Coll., 1956; MD, Harvard U., 1960. Intern Barnes Hosp., St. Louis, 1960-61, resident, 1961-65; instr. in surgery Washington U., St. Louis, 1964-65; asst. prof. surgery U. Miami, Fla., 1965-69, assoc. prof., 1969-71; prof. chmn. dept. surgery U. Louisville, 1971—; pres., chmn. bd. Univ. Surg. Assocs., P.S.C., 1971—; chmn. bd. Clin. Services Assn., Inc. Mem. merit rev. bd. for surgery VA, 1983-85. Author: (with H.H. Stone) Contemporary Burn Management, 1971, Hospital-Acquired Infections in Surgery, 1977; (with B. Gardner, H.H. Stone and W.L. Sugg) Basic Surgery, 1978, (with H.H. Stone and B. Gardner) 2d edit., 1983, 3d edit., 1987, 4th edit., 1992, 5th edit., 1995; (with D.C. Carter) Trauma, 1982; (with J.E. Conte Jr. and L.S. Jacob) Antibiotic Prophylaxis in Surgery: A Comprehensive Review, 1984; (with J.D. Richardson and L.M. Flint Jr.) Trauma: Clinical Care and Pathophysiology, 1987; contbr. numerous articles to profl. publs.; mem. editl. bd. So. Med. Jour., 1970-72, Jour. Surg. Rsch., 1970-72, 75-77, 78-80, Current Problems in Surgery, 1973—, Surgery, 1975-85, Current Surgery, 1977—, Current Surg. Techniques, 1977—, Emergency Surgery: A Weekly Update, 1977—, Collected Letters in Surgery, 1978—, Brit. Jour. Surgery, 1981-94; chief editor Am. Jour. Surgery, 1986—. Bd. govs. Trover Clinic Found., Madisonville, Ky. Fellow Royal Coll. Surgeons Edinburgh (hon.); mem. ACS (gov. 1972-80, commn. on cancer 1975-80), AMA, Allen O. Whipple Soc. (exec. coun. 1977-80), Am. Assn. Cancer Edn. (exec. coun. 1986-72), Am. Assn. Surgery of Trauma, Am. Burn Assn., Am. Cancer Soc. (pres. Ky. div. 1989-90, nat. del. dir. 1989-92, 93-95), Am. Surg. Assn. (sec. 1984-89, pres. 2004—), Acad. Surgery (pres. 1975-76), Cen. Surg. Assn., Assn. Am. Med. Colls. (chmn. ad hoc com. on Medicare and Medicaid 1978-79), Collegium Internationale Chirurgiae Digestivae (sec.-treas. 1981-86, pres. 1986-87), Council on Public Higher Edn. (task group on health scis.), Halsted Soc., Jefferson County Med. Soc., Ky. Med. Assn., Ky. Surg. Soc. (pres. 1982-83), Louisville Surg. Soc. (pres. 1989-90), Residency Rev. Com. for Surgery (vice chmn. 1981-83, chmn. 1983-85), Société Internationale de Chirurgie, Soc. Surgery Alimentary Tract (treas. 1975-78, pres. 1985-86), Soc. Clin. Surgery, Soc. Surg. Chairmen, Soc. Surg. Oncology (pres. 1984-85), Soc. Univ. Surgeons (treas. 1971-74, pres. 1979-80), James IV Assn. Surgeons (v.p. 2002—), Southeastern Surg. Congress (exec. coun. for Ky. 1985-86, pres. 1994-95), So. Med. Assn. (vice chmn. sect. on surgery 1969-70, chmn. sect. 1972-73, sec. 1970-72, exec. coun. for Ky. 1971-77, 89-90), So. Surg. Assn. (pres. 1988-89), Alpha Omega Alpha. Home: 5609 River Knoll Dr Louisville KY 40222-5846 Office: U Louisville Dept Surgery Louisville KY 40292-0001 Office Phone: 502-852-5442. Business E-Mail: hcpolk01@gwise.louisville.edu.

POLK, JAMES RAY, journalist; b. Oaktown, Ind., Sept. 12, 1937; s. Raymond S. and Oeta (Fleener) P.; m. Bonnie Becker, Nov. 4, 1962; children: Geoffrey, Amy; m. Cara Bryn Saylor, June 21, 1980; 1 child, Abigail. BA, Ind. U., 1962. With A.P., Indpls., 1962-65, Milw., 1965, Madison, Wis., 1966-67, Washington, 1967-71; investigative reporter Washington Star, 1971-75; correspondent NBC News, Washington, 1975-92; sr. producer CNN Spl. Assignment, 1992—. Pres. Investigative Reporters and Editors, Inc., 1978-80, chmn. bd., 1980-82, nat. coll. chmn., 1983-90. With U.S. Navy, 1955-58. Recipient Pub. Affairs Reporting award Am. Polit. Sci. Assn., 1961, Raymond Clapper Meml. award, 1972, 74, Pulitzer prize for nat. reporting on Watergate, 1974, Sigma Delta Chi award, 1974, Nat. Headliner awards for investigative reporting, 1994, 96, 2003, Emmy award for coverage of Oklahoma City bombing, 1996, Ind. U. Disting. Alumni award; named to Ind. Journalism Hall of Fame, 1994. Mem. Phi Kappa Psi. Office: CNN Center Atlanta GA 30348

POLK, STEVEN R. military officer; BS in Aero. Engring., USAF Acad., 1968; MS in Engring., Ariz. State U., 1974; MA in Nat. Security & Strategic Studies, Naval War Coll., 1988. Commd. 2d lt. USAF, 1968, advanced through grades to lt. gen., 2002; aircraft comdr., instr. pilot, flight comdr. 55th Tactical Fighter Squadron, RAF, Upper Heyford, Eng., 1978-81; F-16 pilot 613th Tactical Fighter Squadron, chief tng. 401st Tactical Fighter Wing, Torrejon Air Base, Spain, 1983-84; ops. officer, comdr. 612th Tactical Fighter Squadron Torrejon Air Base, 1984-87; chief war and mobilization planning divsn. Hdqs. USAF, Washington, 1988-89, exec. officer to vice chief of staff, 1989-90; vice comdr., comdr. 58th Tactical Tng. Wing, Luke AFB, Ariz., 1990-91; comdr. 58th Ops. Group, Luke AFB, 1991-92, 8th Fighter Wing, Kunsan Air Base, South Korea, 1992-93; chief quality divsn. Directorate of Programs and Evaluation Hdqs. USAF, Washington, 1993-94; asst. chief of staff for ops. Hdqs. Allied Air Forces Northwestern Europe, 1994-95; comdr. 51st Fighter Wing, Osan Air Base, South Korea, 1995-97; dir. of ops. Hdqs. Pacific Air Forces, Hickam AFB, Hawaii, 1997-98, dir. air and space ops., 1998-99; comdr. 19th Air Force, Randolph AFB, Tex., 1999—2002; vice comdr. Pacific Air Forces, Hickam AFB, 2002—. Decorated Def. Superior Svc. medal, Legion of Merit with oak leaf cluster, Meritorious Svc. medal with 4 oak leaf clusters; recipient Disting. Svc. medal. Office: 25 E St Hickam AFB HI 96853

POLK, WILLIAM ROE, historian; b. Ft. Worth, Tex., Mar. 7, 1929; m. Joan Alison Cooledge, Dec. 1950, children: Milbry Catherine Polk, Alison Elizabeth Polk, m. Ann Borders Cross, June 9, 1962 (div. Oct. 1979); children: George Washington Polk, Eliza Polk; m. Baroness Elisabeth von Oppenheimer, Dec. 29, 1981. BA with honors, Harvard U., 1951, PhD, 1958; BA with honors, Oxford, Eng., 1955, MA, 1959; LLD (hon.), Lake Forest Coll., 1967. Asst. prof. Harvard Univ., 1956-62; fgn. svc. res. officer class 1, mem. policy planning coun. U.S. State Dept., 1961-65; prof. U. Chgo., 1965-73; pres. Adlai Stevenson Inst., Chgo., 1967-72; sr. dir. W.P. Carey Found.; chmn. EP Systems, N.Y.C., 1990-93, Chaika Oil Co., London and Moscow, 1993-95. Bd. dirs. Hyde Park Bank, Chgo., Microform Data Systems, Arlington Books, Cambridge, Naftex Ltd., Harris & Harris, Chaika Corp., Morrison Internat. Ltd., The Salzburg Seminar; cons. Aetna Life and Casualty, Time Inc., TWA, Crocker Nat. Bank, Wheelabrator Frye Inc., Fuller Petroleum, GTE, Teledyne, J. Henry Schroder, U.K., Power Corp., Can., Allianz Versicherungs A.G., Germany, Volkswagen A.G., Germany, Flughafen Frankfurt Main A.G., Germany, Louis Féraud & Cie, France, UN Stockholm and Vancouver Confs. on the Environment; sr. dir. W.P. Carey Found., 2001—; lectr. in field. Author: What the Arabs Think, 1952, Backdrop to Tragedy, 1957, The Opening of South Lebanon, 1963, The United States and the Arab World, 1965, The United States and the Arab World, 3rd edit., 1975, Passing Brave, 1973, 1974, The Golden Ode, 1974, 1977, 1993, The Elusive Peace, 1979, The Arab World, 1980, The Arab World Today, 1991, The Vence Partitas, 1992, Neighbors and Strangers: The Fundamentals of Foreign Affairs, 1997, Polk's Folly: An American Family History, 2000, 2001; editor: The Civilization of Islam, 1962, 1975, The Developmental Revolution, 1963, The Beginnings of Modernization in the Middle East, 1968; contbr. articles to books and profl. jours. including Fgn. Affairs, N.Y. Rev. Books, The Atlantic, etc. Bd. dirs. The Salzburg Seminar, YMCA C.C., The Middle East Inst., The Adlai Stevenson Inst., W.P. Carey Found., 2001—. Recipient Medal of Honor, Kingdom of Afghanistan, 1967; fellow Rockefeller Found., 1951-55, Ford Found., 1954, Guggenheim Found., 1961. Mem. The Century Assn., Coun. on Fgn. Rels., Middle East Studies Assn. (bd. dirs.), Soc. of the Cin. Democrat. Avocations: exploration, tennis, sailing, gardening. Home: 669 Chemin de la Sine F-06140 Vence France E-mail: williamrpolk@post.harvard.edu.

POLKING, PAUL J. lawyer; BS, U. Notre Dame, 1959, JD, 1966. Bar: Iowa 1966, N.C. 1978. Atty. office of comp. of currency Dept. of Treasury, 1966-70; asst. v.p. Bank of Am., Charlotte, NC, 1970—88, gen. coun., 1988; chmn. The Fin. Svc. Roundtable Lawyers Coun., 2000. Office: Bank of Am Corp Ctr NC1-007-56-11 Charlotte NC 28255

POLL, HEINZ, choreographer, artistic director; b. Oberhausen, Germany, Mar. 18, 1926; arrived in U.S., 1964, naturalized, 1975; s. Heinrich and Anna Margarete (Winkels) Poll. Co-founder, dir. The Dance Inst., U. Akron, 1967-77; founder, artistic dir., choreographer Ohio Ballet, Akron, 1968-99. Tchr. Chilean Instituto de Extension Musical, 1951—61, N.Y. Nat. Acad., 1965—66. Dancer Göttingen Mcpl. Theatre, 1947—49, Deutsches Theatre Konstanz, 1949—50, East Berlin State Opera, 1950—51, Nat. Ballet Chile, 1964, Ballet de la Jeunesse Musicales de France, 1963—64, choreographer Nat. Ballet Chile, Paris Festival Ballet, Ballet de la Jeunnesses Musicales de France, Nat. Ballet Can., Pa. Ballet, Ohio Ballet, Limon Dance Co., dancer Ellen Kogan. Recipient Ohio Dance award, 1983, 1988—89, Achievement Dance award, No. Ohio Live Mag., 1985—86, 1988—89, 1993—94, 1994—95, 1996—97, Cleve. Arts prize, 1995, Irma Lazarus Govs. award, 1999; grantee, Endowment for Arts, 1974—75. Mem.: NEA (dance panelist 1987—89, 1992—93).

POLL, MARTIN HARVEY, film producer; b. N.Y.C. s. David and Fay (Tamber) P.; m. Lee Lindenberg, May 21, 1954 (div. Oct. 10, 1967); children: Mark, Jonathan; m. Gladys Peltz Jaffe, Oct. 31, 1976; 1 son, Anthony. BS, Wharton Sch. Bus. U. Pa., 1943. Pres. Inter-Continental TV Films Inc., N.Y.C., 1952; exec. producer Theatre Network TV Inc., N.Y.C., 1953; pres. Gold Medal Studios, Bronx, N.Y., 1954-62; ind. producer, 1962—. (Named Hon. Commr. Motion Picture Arts N.Y.C. 1958, recipient David Di Donatello Best Film Producer award Pres. Italy 1968, N.Y. Film Critics award 1968, Hollywood Fgn. Press Assn. Golden Globe award 1968, Brit. Acad. award 1968); films include Love is a Ball, 1962, Sylvia, 1964, The Appointment, 1968, The Lion in Winter, 1968 (Best Picture award), The Magic Garden of Stanley Sweetheart, 1970, Night Watch, 1972, The Man Who Loved Cat Dancing, 1973, Love and Death, 1975, The Sailor Who Fell From Grace with The Sea, 1976, The Dain Curse, Somebody Killed Her Husband, 1978, Nighthawks, 1981, Arthur the King, 1984, Gimme An F, 1984, Haunted Summer, 1987, My Heroes Have Always Been Cowboys, 1991, (TV miniseries) Diana—Her True Story, 1993. Served with AUS, 1944-47. Mem. Producers Guild of Am., Acad. Motion Picture Arts and Scis., Cinema Circulus, Friends of Library U. So. Calif.

POLL, ROBERT EUGENE, JR., bank executive; b. Urbana, Ill., Apr. 16, 1948; s. Robert E. Sr. and Dorothy (Baker) P.; m. Leslie Tompkins, Aug. 8, 1970 (div. Mar. 1980); m. Virginia O'Donnell, July 17, 1982 (div. Sept. 2002); children: Alexandra, Bianca, Paulo Felipe Kos. BA, Kenyon Coll., 1970; MBA, Ind. U., 1972. V.p. Chase Manhattan Bank, N.Y.C., 1972-78; assoc. Lazard Freres & Co., N.Y.C., 1978-82, mng. dir., mgr. mcpl. divsn., 1985-98; gen. ptnr. William Blair & Co., Chgo., 1982-84; sr. mng. dir. Poll Financial, LLC, 1998—; co-chmn. Chief Consol. Mining Co.; pres., CEO Bernard Techs., Inc. Adv. bd. Pub. Fin. Inst., N.Y.C., 1976, Worldvest. Trustee Citizens Budget Commn. Mem. N.Y. Acad. Sci., Tavern Club (Chgo.), N.Y. Athletic Club. Office: Poll Fin LLC 350 Central Park West New York NY 10025 Home: Apt 13A 350 Central Park W New York NY 10025-6503 E-mail: rppollfin@att.net.

POLLACE, PAMELA L. public relations executive; b. San Jose, Calif., May 1953; BA, U. Santa Clara, 1975. Acct. mgr. mktg. comm. Oxbridge, Inc.; acct. supr. Burson Marsteller; spokesperson, mgr., dir. Intel Corp, Santa Clara, Calif., 1987-96, v.p., dir. worldwide press rels., 1996—2000; v.p. dir. corp. comms. Intel Corp., Santa Clara, Calif., 2000—. Office: Intel Corp Worldwide Press Rels PO Box 58119 Santa Clara CA 95052-8119

POLLACK, BARBARA GRACE, writer; b. N.Y.C., May 17, 1927; m. Merrill S. Pollack, Nov. 27, 1947; children: Elise, Diana, Steven, Anne. Student, Am. Acad. Dramatic Art, 1946, Fordham U., 1978-79, Georgetown U., 1980-81. Rsch. asst. art and archaeology dept. Princeton (N.J.) U., 1964-67; with Social Security Adminstrn. Office Hearings and Appeals U.S. Govt., N.Y.C., 1987—. Vol. coord. employee art hobby shows Social Security, NYC, 2003—04. Co-author: (with Doris Humphrey) The Art of Making Dances, 1959, The Collectors, 1962, (with Charles H. Woodford) Dance is a Moment, 1993; contbr. articles to mags. Vol. Smithsonian Instn., The White House, Cooper-Hewitt Mus., N.Y.C., ARC; vol. mentor in English lang., Am. history and music and art. Home: 30 E 30th St New York NY 10016-7902

POLLACK, DANIEL, concert pianist; b. Los Angeles, Jan. 23, 1935; MS in Music, Juilliard Sch., 1957, Acad. Musik, Vienna, Austria, 1958. Asst. prof. U. Hartford, Conn., 1966-70; prof. piano U. So. Calif., Los Angeles, 1971—. Mem. vis. faculty Juilliard Sch., Yale Sch. Music. Concert debut N.Y. Philharm.; solo recitals at Royal Festival Hall, London, Musikverein, Vienna, Austria, Concertgebouw, Amsterdam, Teatro Colon, Buenos Aires, Arts Ctr., Seoul, Korea, Bolshoi Zaal, Moscow, Carnegie Hall, N.Y.C., Orch. Hall, Chgo., Music Ctr., L.A.; concert performances in U.S., USSR, Europe, Far East, South Am. including N.Y. Philharm., L.A. Philharm., Balt. Symphony, Minn. Orch., San Francisco Symphony, Moscow State Philharm., Royal Philharm., London, Bergen (Norway) Symphony, Seoul Philharm., Hong Kong Philharm., Nat. Symphony Orch. of Bogota, Colombia, Montevideo (Uruguay) Symphony, others; numerous recs. Recipient prize Internat. Tschaikowsky Piano Competition, Moscow, USSR, 1958; Fulbright grantee, 1957-58; Martha Baird Rockefeller Found. grantee, 1963. Mem. Am. Fedn. Musicians, Kosciuszko Found., Chopin Found., Music Tchrs. Nat. Assn. (nat. exec. bd.). Office: U So Calif Dept Music RHM 100 University Park Mc 0851 Los Angeles CA 90089-0001

POLLACK, GERALD ALEXANDER, economist, government official; b. Vienna, Jan. 14, 1929; came to U.S. 1938; s. Stephen J. and Tini (Herschel) P.; m. Patricia E. Sisterson; children: Nora S., Carol A. BA, Swarthmore (Pa.) Coll., 1951; MA, MPA, Princeton U., 1953, PhD, 1958. Corp. economist Leeds & Northrup Co., Phila., 1958-62; officer in charge internat. payments U.S. Dept. State, Washington, 1962-63; internat. economist Joint Econ. Com. of Congress, Washington, 1963-65; chief economist Office Spl. Rep. for Trade Negotiations, 1964; dep. asst. sec. U.S. Dept. Commerce, Washington, 1965-68; v.p. Loeb, Rhoades & Co., N.Y.C., 1968-69, Bendix Corp., Southfield, Mich., 1969-70, Citibank, N.Y.C., 1970-71; internat. economist Exxon Corp., N.Y.C., 1971-86; v.p., chief economist Overseas Shipholding Group, N.Y.C., 1986-89; assoc. prof. fin. Pace U., N.Y.C., 1990-94; assoc. dir. for internat. econs. Bur. Econ. Analysis, U.S. Dept. Commerce, 1994-99. Contbr. articles to profl. jours. Bd. dirs. Jamaica Estates Assn., 1976-80, Oakwood Sch., Poughkeepsie, N.Y., 1979-89; trustee Lindley Murray Fund, 1990-94; mem. Greenwich Dem. Town Com., 1992-94, 2001—; clk. Flushing Monthly Meeting Soc. of Friends, 1990-94; mem. Greenwich Rep. Town Meeting, 1999-2003. With U.S. Army, 1953-55. Mem.: Violoncello Soc., Coun. on Fgn. Rels., Phi Beta Kappa. Mem. Soc. Of Friends. Avocations: cello, classical music, photography, hiking, bicycling. E-mail: gapollack@hotmail.com.

POLLACK, GERALD LESLIE, physicist, researcher; b. Bklyn., July 8, 1933; s. Herman and Jennie (Tenenbaum) P.; m. Antoinette Amparo Velasquez, Dec. 22, 1958; children: Harvey Anton, Samuela Juliet, Margolita Mia, Violet Amata. BS, Bklyn. Coll., 1954; Fulbright scholar, U. Gottingen, 1954-55; MS, Calif. Inst. Tech., 1957, PhD, 1962. Physics student trainee Nat. Bur. Standards, Washington, 1954-58, solid state physicist, 1961-65, cons. Boulder, Colo., 1965-70; assoc. prof. dept. physics Mich. State U., East Lansing, 1965-69, prof., 1969—; cons. NRC, Ill. Dept. Nuclear Safety; physicist Naval Med. Rsch. Inst., Bethesda, Md., summer 1979. Physicist USAF Sch. Aerospace Medicine, San Antonio, Tex., summer 1987. Co-author (with D.R. Stump): Electromagnetism, 2002; contbr. articles to profl. jours. Fellow Am. Phys. Soc.; mem. AAAS, Am. Assn. Physics Tchrs. Office: Mich State U Dept Physics and Astronomy East Lansing MI 48824-1116

POLLACK, HENRY NATHAN, geophysics educator; b. Omaha, July 13, 1936; s. Harold Myron and Sylvia (Chait) P.; m. Lana Beth Schoenberger, Jan. 29, 1963; children: Sara Beth (dec.), John David. AB, Cornell U., 1958; MS, U. Nebr., 1960; PhD, U. Mich., 1963. Lectr. U. Mich., 1962, asst. prof., asso. prof., prof. geophysics, 1964—, assoc. dean for research, 1982-85, chmn. dept. geol. scis., 1988-91. Rsch. fellow Harvard U., 1963-64; sr. lectr. U. Zambia, 1970-71; vis. scientist U. Durham, U. Newcastle-on-Tyne, Eng., 1977-78, U. Western Ont., 1985-86; chmn. Internat. Heat Flow Commn., 1991-95. Author: Uncertain Science...Uncertain World, 2003. Fellow: AAAS, Geol. Soc. Am.; mem.: Am. Geophys. Union. Achievements include research on thermal evolution of the earth, recent climate change. Office: U Mich Dept Geol Scis Ann Arbor MI 48109

POLLACK, IRWIN WILLIAM, psychiatrist, educator; b. Phila., Aug. 14, 1927; s. Nathan and Rose (Bergman) P.; m. Barbara Jean Callaway, Oct. 9, 1988; children from previous marriage: Nathaniel Edward, Joshua Frank, Jonathan Daniel. AB, Temple U., 1950; MA, Columbia, 1951; student, U. Pa., 1951-52; MD, U. Vt., 1956. Diplomate: Am. Bd. Psychiatry and Neurology. Intern Grad. Hosp. U. Pa., 1956-57; asst. resident psychiatry Henry Phipps Psychiat. Clinic (John Hopkins Hosp.), 1957-60; chief resident psychiatry Johns Hopkins Hosp., 1960-61, adminstr. psychosomatic clinic, psychiat. liaison service, 1961-64; psychiatrist-in-chief Sinai Hosp., Balt., 1964-68; mem. faculty psychiatry Coll. Medicine and Dentistry N.J. (Rutgers Med. Sch.), 1968-87, 1987—, clin. prof. psychiatry, 1998, prof. emeritus, 1999—. Assoc. prof. psychiatry, 1968-70, prof. psychiatry, 1979-99, emeritus prof. psychiatry 1999-, chmn. dept. Univ. Medicine and Dentistry, prof. neurology, dir. Ctr. for Cognitive Rehab.; exec. dir. Coll. Medicine and Dentistry (Community Mental Health Ctr.), 1970-77. Served with USNR, 1945-46. Fellow Am. Psychiat. Assn. (life); mem. N.J. Psychiat. Assn., Am. Psychosomatic Soc., Am. Congress Rehab. Medicine, Alpha Omega Alpha. Achievements include spl. research or problems of time and space perception, psychology of phys. disability, doctor-patient relationships, cognitive retraining of brain-injured persons. Home: 36959 S Ridgeview Blvd Tucson AZ 85739 Office: 36959 S Ridgeview Blvd Tucson AZ 85739 E-mail: iwpollack@aol.com.

POLLACK, JEFFREY LEE, restaurateur; b. San Francisco, May 1, 1945; s. Albert and Loretta (Popper) P.; m. Patricia Bowdle Connell, Feb. 20, 1983; children: Lizabeth Ann, Hilary Margaret, Nicholas Albert. BA, San Jose State U. Owner, surety underwriter North Beach Bonding Co., San Francisco, 1968-75; proprietor Old Waldorf, San Francisco, 1974-80, Punchline, 1978-80, Julius' Castle, San Francisco, 1980—, New Joe's, San Francisco, 1984-99, Shadows, San Francisco, 1985-95, Iron Horse, 1986-92, Pollack Group, San Francisco, 1985—, Nick's Lighthouse Restaurant, San Francisco, 1991—, Original Joe's # 2, 1992-95, O'Connell's, 1994-96, Dalla Torre, 1996—. Mem. Downtown Assn. (bd. dirs. 1987—, v.p. 1992), Union Sq. Assn., North Beach C. of C. (bd. dirs. 1989, v.p. 1992), Port Tenants Assn., Fisherman Wharf Assn., Commonwealth Club. Democrat. Avocations: classic car collecting, movies. Home: 302 Greenwich St San Francisco CA 94133-3210 Office: Pollack Group Ltd 1541 Montgomery St San Francisco CA 94133-3232

POLLACK, JOE, retired newspaper critic and columnist, writer; b. Bklyn., Feb. 3, 1931; s. Samuel H. and Anna (Weisman) P.; m. Joan S., Mar. 6, 1952 (div. 1964); children: Wendy, Dara, Sharon; m. Carol Atchison, Dec. 1, 1964 (dec. 1993); m. Ann Lemons, Nov. 20, 1994. BJ, U. Mo., 1952. Sports writer St. Louis Globe-Democrat, 1955-61; dir. pub. rels. St. Louis Football Cardinals, 1961-72; critic, columnist St. Louis Post-Dispatch, 1972-95. Critic Sta. KSDK-TV, St. Louis, 1973-88, Sta. KMOV-TV, St. Louis, 1988-92; commentator Sta. KMOX, St. Louis, 1960-85, Sta. KWMU, St. Louis, 1994—. Author: Joe Pollack's Guide to St. Louis Restaurants, 1988, updated, 1992, (with Ann Lemons Pollack) Beyond Toasted Ravioli, 1998, Beyond Gooey Butter Cake, 2001; contbr. numerous articles to mags. Mem. Am. Theatre Critics Assn., Profl. Football Writers Assn., Am. Soc. Profl. Journalists. Home: 7417 Oxford Dr Saint Louis MO 63105-2915 Office Phone: 314-862-3321. Personal E-mail: jpalfood@aol.com.

POLLACK, MICHAEL, lawyer; b. N.Y.C., July 14, 1946; s. Irving and Bertha (Horowitz) P.; m. Barbara Linda Shore, Aug. 23, 1970; children: Matthew, Ilana. BEng, Cooper Union, 1967; MS, U. Pa., 1970; JD, Temple U.,

1974. Bar: Pa. 1974, U.S. Dist. Ct. (ea. dist.) Pa. 1974, N.Y. 2000. Rsch. scientist Pa. Rsch. Assocs., Phila., 1968-69; engr. GE Co., Valley Forge, Pa., 1969-70, Burroughs Corp., Great Valley, Pa., 1970-71; assoc. Blank, Rome, Comisky & McCauley, Phila., 1974-82, ptnr., mgr. dept. real estate, 1982—. Lectr., course planner Pa. Bar Inst., Phila. Mem. ABA, Pa. Bar Assn., Phila. Bar Assn., Internat. Assn. Attys. and Execs. in Corp. Real Estate (vice chmn., bd. dirs.), Eta Kappa Nu, Tau Beta Pi. Republican. Avocations: music, tennis. Office: Blank Rome LLP 1 Logan Sq Fl 3 Philadelphia PA 19103-6998 Office Phone: 215-569-5670. E-mail: pollack@blankrome.com.

POLLACK, PAUL ROBERT, airline service company executive; b. N.Y.C., Nov. 17, 1941; s. Harry and Hilda (Tepper) P.; m. Linda Weinstein, Aug. 14, 1965; children: Mark, Melissa. BBA, CCNY, 1962; MBA, L.I. U., Greenvale, N.Y., 1993. CPA, N.Y. Staff acct. Seidman & Seidman, N.Y.C., 1962-68; with GlobeGround N.Am., Great Neck, NY, 1968—, exec. v.p., COO, 1990—, pres., 1996—, sr. adviser, 2001—. With U.S. Army, 1962. Mem. N.Y. State Soc. CPAs (Haskins award 1966). Office: GlobeGround NAm 111 Great Neck Rd Ste 600 Great Neck NY 11021-5401

POLLACK, ROBERT ELLIOT, biologist, educator, author; b. Bklyn., Sept. 2, 1940; s. Hyman Ephraim and Molly (Pollack) P.; m. Amy Louise Steinberg, Dec. 23, 1961; 1 child, Marya BA in Physics, Columbia U., 1961; PhD in Biology, Brandeis U., 1966. Asst. prof. pathology Med. Sch. NYU, N.Y.C., 1969-70; sr. scientist Cold Spring Harbor Lab., N.Y., 1971-75; prof. microbiology Med. Sch., SUNY-Stony Brook, 1975-78; prof. biol. sci. Columbia U., N.Y.C., 1978—; dean Columbia Coll., N.Y.C., 1982-89. Bd. dirs., chmn. sci. adv. bd. AMBI, 1994—; instr. Pratt Archtl. Sch., Bklyn., 1970; lectr. psychiatry Ctr. for Psychoanalytic Tng., Columbia U., 1999—, dir. Ctr. for the Study of Sci. and Religion, 1999—; vis. prof. pharmacology Albert Einstein Coll. Medicine, Bronx, N.Y., 1977-92; dean's disting. lectr. in Humanities, Columbia Med. Sch., 2000; lectr. Rosenthal Colloquium, March of Dimes, 1989; McGregory lectr. Colgate U., 1979; du Vigneaud lectr. Med. Sch., Cornell U., 1983. Co-editor: Readings in Mammalian Cell Culture, 1973, 3d rev. edit., 1981, Signs of Life, 1984 (translations in 7 langs., Lionel Trilling award 1995), The Missing Moment, 1999, The Faith of Biology and the Biology of Faith, 2000; mng. editor BBA Revs. on Cancer, 1980-86; contbr. numerous rsch. articles on molecular cell biology to profl. jours. Trustee N.Y. Found., 1988-96, Brandeis U., 1989-94, Solomon Schechter Sch. of N.Y.C., 1996-98; fellow World Econ. Forum, 1995—; bd. overseers List Coll. of the Jewish theol. Sem. of Am., 1996-99; pres. Jewish Campus Life Fund, Columbia U., 1997-2001. Recipient Rsch. Career Devel. award NIH, 1974, Alexander Hamilton medal, 1989, Lionel Trilling award Columbia U., 1995; NIH spl. fellow Weizmann Inst., Rehovot, Israel, 1970-71; grantee Nat. Cancer Inst., NIH, 1968-92, Am. Cancer Soc., 1985-94; John Simon Guggenheim fellow, 1993. Fellow AAAS; mem. N.Y. Acad. Scis., Am. Soc. Microbiology. Office: Columbia U Fairchild Hall 1212 Amsterdam Ave # Mc2419 New York NY 10027-7003 Office Phone: 212-854-2409. Business E-Mail: pollack@columbia.edu.

POLLACK, ROBERT HARVEY, psychology educator; b. N.Y.C., June 26, 1927; s. Solomon and Bertha (Levy) P.; m. Martha Dee Katz, Aug. 20, 1948; children: Jonathan Keith, Lance Michael, Scott Evan. BS, CCNY, 1948; MS, Clark U., Worcester, Mass., 1950, PhD, 1953. Lectr. U. Sydney, Australia, 1953-61; spl. rsch. fellow Columbia U., N.Y.C., 1960-61; chief div. cognitive devel. Inst. Juvenile Rsch., Chgo., 1961-63, dep. dir. rsch., 1963-69; from clin. asst. prof. to clin. assoc. prof. rsch. U. Ill. Coll. Medicine, Chgo., 1962-67; prof. psychology U. Ga., Athens, 1969-96, chair grad. program. exptl. psychology, 1970-78, chair grad. study com., 1978-86; prof. emeritus, 1996—; chair grad. program in life-span psychology U. Ga., Athens, 1988-96. Editor: The Experimental Psychology of Alfred Binet, 1969; contbr. over 100 articles and chpts. to profl. publs. Cpl. U.S. Army, 1945-46. Grantee Nat. Inst. Child Health and Human Devel., 1965, 67, 72, 78. Fellow AAAS, Am. Psychol. Assn.; mem. Am. Assn. Sex Edn., Counsellors and Therapists, Gerontol. Soc. Am., Australian Psychol. Soc., Soc. for Researching Child Devel., Soc. for Sci. Study Sex, Sigma Xi. Democrat. Avocations: travel, stamp collecting/philately, opera, military history. Office: U Ga Dept Psychology Athens GA 30602 Office Phone: 706-542-3084.

POLLACK, ROBERT WILLIAM, psychiatrist; b. N.Y.C., May 22, 1947; s. George and Esther P.; m. Pam Gregory, Sept. 15, 1984; 1 child, Jessie. BS in Biology, Yale U., 1969; MD, SUNY Downstate Med. Ctr., Bklyn., 1973. Diplomate Am. Bd. Psychiatry and Neurology. Tng. resident U. Fla., 1973-76, chief resident dept. psychiatry, 1975-76, asst. prof. dept. psychiatry, 1976-77; clin. asst. prof. dept. psychiatry Shands Hosp., Gainesville, 1977—; chief dept. psychiatry Fla. Hosp., Orlando, 1983, 84; clin. dir. assessment and evaluation team West Lake Hosp., Longwood, Fla., 1984-87, clin. dir. intensive evaluation unit, 1987-89; med. dir. Fla. Psychiat. Assocs., Winter Park, 1989-92, Fla. Psychiat. Mgmt., Winter Park, 1990-97; corp. med. dir. FPM Behavioral Health, 1993-97; co-founder Profl. Quality Analysts, Inc., Casselberry, Fla., 1997—2001; CEO VShift, Orlando, Fla., 2002—03; pres. Matrix Network Tech. Group, Orlando, Fla., 2003—; CMIO Ctrl. Fla. Healthcare Coalition, 2003—; pres. Quantum Delta Enterprises, Orlando, 2004—. Med. dir. consultation, liaison svc. and spl. med. unit Winter Park Meml. Hosp., 1992; integrated surveyor Jt. Commn. for Accreditation of Healthcare Orgns., 1998—2000, sentinel event, 1999—2000; pres., CEO The Rondo Group, Longwood, Fla., 2000—; CEO, Cory Marvin Erving Found, 2001—; chief med. info. officer Ctrl. Fla. Healthcare Coalition, 2003—; bd. dirs. Analytic Data Systems, Inc.; chmn. Bd. Living Hope Ministries, 2004—. Contbr. 4 articles to profl. jours.; author sci. reports. Chmn. Retinitis Pigmentosa Casino Night, Orlando, 1988-92; vice-chmn. nat. championship com. U.S. Blind Golfers Assn., 1991-92, chair 48th ann. championship com., 1992-93; bd. dirs. Tennis with a Different Swing, Orlando, 1988-92; mem. Seminole County Assn. on Domestic Violence, 1998—. Recipient Quality Achievement award, Ctrl. Fla. Healthcare Coalition, 2003. Mem. U.S. Blind Golfers Assn. (chairperson, nat. championships 1998, 99, 2000), Alaqua Country Club (bd. dirs.). Achievements include introduction of use of computerized topographical brain mapping as a diagnostic tool in central Florida; development of DAta Portals, wireless/web-based data acquisition system. Office: Quantum Delta Enterprises 20 N Orange Ave Ste 1400 Orlando FL 32801 Office Phone: 321-229-9750. E-mail: Bob@QDEFL.com., rwpollack@earthlink.net.

POLLACK, RONALD F(RANK), healthcare organization executive, lawyer; b. N.Y.C., Feb. 21, 1944; s. Max Louis and Hanna Esther (Borchardt) Pollack Baruch; m. Rebecca Lucy Bolling, Jan. 8, 1972; children: Sarah Shoshana, Abraham Max, Martin Landrum. BA, Queens Coll., 1965; JD, NYU, 1968. Bar: N.Y. 1968, D.C. 1978, U.S. Ct. Appeals (D.C. cir) 1970, U.S. Ct. Appeals (5th cir.) 1971, U.S. Ct. Appeals (6th cir.) 1974, U.S. Supreme Ct. 1973. Atty. Ctr. on Social Welfare Policy and Law, N.Y.C., 1968-73; founder, exec. dir. Food Research and Action Ctr., N.Y.C., 1970-80; dean Antioch Sch. Law, Washington, 1980-83; exec. dir. Families U.S.A., Washington, 1983—. Sec. treas., bd. dirs. Food Research and Action Ctr., Washington, 1980—; mem. civil legal services D.C. Jud. Conf. Com., 1980-83; appointee Pres.'s Adv. Commn. on Consumer Protection and Quality in the Health Care Industry, 1997-98. Author: If We Had Ham, We Could Have Ham and Eggs...If We Had Eggs: A Study of the National School Breakfast Program, 1972, Out to Lunch: A Study of USDA's Child Care Feeding and Summer Feeding Programs, 1974; co-author: On the Other Side of Easy Street: Myths and Facts About the Economics of Old Age, 1987. Treas. Jewish Fund for Justice, 1985-88, bd. dirs., 1985-93; bd. dirs. Am. Jewish World Service, Self-Help Community Services, 1974-77; mem. domestic adv. bd., project rev. bd. U.S.A. for Africa/Hands Across Am., 1986-88; v.p. of bd. dirs. Burgundy Farm Country Day Sch., 1988-90, pres. 1990-91; bd. dirs. Americans for Health, 1986-81. Arthur Garfield Hays Civil Liberties fellow, 1967; research fellow Legal Services Corp., Washington, 1978-80 Office: Families USA 1334 G St NW Washington DC 20005-3117

POLLACK, SEYMOUR VICTOR, computer science educator; b. Bklyn., Aug. 3, 1933; s. Max and Sylvia (Harrison) P.; m. Sydell Altman, Jan. 23, 1955; children: Mark, Sherie. BChemE, Pratt Inst., 1954; MChemE, Bklyn. Poly. Inst., 1960. Lic. chem. engr., Ohio. Engr. Schwarz Labs., Mt. Vernon, N.Y., 1954-55; design engr. Curtiss-Wright, Wood-Ridge, N.J., 1955-57, Fairchild Engines, Deer Park, N.Y., 1957-59, GE, Evendale, Ohio, 1959-62; rsch. assoc. U. Cin., 1962-66; prof. computer sci. Washington U., St. Louis, 1966-95, prof. emeritus, 1995—. Cons. Mo. Auto Club, St. Louis, 1969-82, United Van Lines, Fenton, Mo., 1984-86, Computer Sci. Accreditation Bd., N.Y.C., 1985-93. Author: Structured Fortran, 1982, UCSD Pascal, 1984, Studies in Computer Science, 1983, The DOS Book, 1985, Turbo Pascal Programming, 1991; cons. editor Holt Rinehart & Winston, N.Y.C., 1979-86. Bd. dirs. Hillel orgn., Washington U., 1983-84. Recipient Alumni Achievement award Pratt Inst., 1966, Outstanding Teaching award Burlington Northern Found., 1987. Mem. Assn. for Computing Machinery, Am. Assn. for Engring. Edn. Jewish. Avocations: trombone, walking, classical and jazz piano, jogging. Office: Washington U PO Box 1045 Saint Louis MO 63188-1045 Business E-Mail: sup@sce.wustl.edu.

POLLACK, STANLEY P. lawyer; b. N.Y.C., Apr. 23, 1928; s. Isidor and Anna (Shulman) P.; m. Susan Aronowitz, June 16, 1974; 1 child, Jane. BA, NYU, 1948; JD, Harvard U., 1951; LLM in Taxation, NYU, 1959. Bar: N.Y. 1951, U.S. Dist. Ct. (so. dist.) N.Y. 1955. Sole practice, N.Y.C., 1955-61; v.p., gen. counsel James Talcott, Inc., N.Y.C., 1961-73; sr. exec. v.p. Rosenthal & Rosenthal Inc., N.Y.C., 1973—. Served to j.g. lt. USNR, 1951-54. Mem. Bklyn. Bar Assn. (banking com., bankruptcy com.), Fed. Bar Council, Assn. Comml. Fin. Atty.'s (pres. 1968), Factors Chain Internat. Clubs: Harvard (N.Y.C.). Home: 6 Peter Cooper Rd New York NY 10010-6701 Office: Rosenthal & Rosenthal Inc 1370 Broadway # 2 New York NY 10018-7302

POLLACK, STEPHEN J. stockbroker; b. NYC, Aug. 25, 1937; s. Harold S. and Gladys H. P. BS in Econs., U. Pa., 1960. V.p. retail sales Drexel Burnham Lambert, N.Y.C., 1960-77; 1st v.p. investments Dean Witter Reynolds Inc., N.Y.C., 1978-98; 1st v.p., fin. advisor Morgan Stanley, N.Y.C., 1998—, v.p., fin. advisor, 2001—03; ret.; with Pollack Asset Management, 2004—. Pres. B'nai B'rith Gothem, N.Y.C.; exec. v.p. Cosmopolitan League of City of HOpe, v.p. circle mem. Whitney Mus., N.Y.C.; treas. Sutton Pl. Synagogue, pres. Havurah Group. With USAR, 1966. Recipient Double Chai Citation, State of Israel Bonds, 1984, Appreciation award City of Hope, 1984, Kiter Key Club award Franklin Funds, Million Dollar Club Svc. award, B'nai B'rith Internat. award. Mem. Internat. Assn. Fin. Planners, Assn. Investment Brokers (bd. dirs.), Youngmen's Philanthropic League (bd. dirs.), Internat. Study Rsch. Inst., Exec. Forum, Fin. Analysts Money Mgrs. Soc., Town Club, Atrium Club, Schuylkill Country Club, Wharton Sch. Club, U. Pa. Club, Yale Club, East River Tennis Club, Fresh Meadow Country Club, Matterhorn Sports Club, East Side Rep. Club, Knickerbokker Rep. Club, Berks County Tennis Club, Penn. Club (charter). Home: 245 E 40th St Apt 14E New York NY 10016-1714 Office: Pollack Asset Mgmnt 40th Fl 245 E 40th St New York NY 10016 Personal E-mail: stephenpollack12@yahoo.com. E-mail: stephen.pollack@morganstanley.com.

POLLACK, SYDNEY, film director; b. Lafayette, Ind., July 1, 1934; s. David and Rebecca (Miller) P.; m. Claire Griswold, Sept. 22, 1958; children: Steven, Rebecca, Rachel. Grad., Neighborhood Playhouse Theatre Sch., N.Y.C., 1954. Asst. to Sanford Meisner, Neighborhood Playhouse Theatre, 1954, instr. acting, 1954-60. Exec. dir. West Coast br. The Actors Studio. Appeared in Broadway prodns.: The Dark Is Light Enough, 1954, A Stone For Danny Fisher, 1955; appeared on live TV programs: Alcoa Presents, others; toured in Stalag 17; dir. TV programs: The Chrysler Theatre, Ben Casey, 1962-63, Something About Lee Wiley, 1963-64; dir: (films) The Slender Thread, 1965, This Property is Condemned, 1966, The Scalphunters, 1968, Castle Keep, 1969, Jeremiah Johnson, 1972, Three Days of the Condor, 1975, The Electric Horseman, 1979, The Firm, 1993; dir., prodr. They Shoot Horses, Don't They?, 1969, The Way We Were, 1973, The Yakuza, 1975, Bobby Deerfield, 1977, Absence of Malice, 1981, Out of Africa, 1985 (Academy Award for Best Picture and Dir.), Havana, 1990, The Firm, 1993, Sabrina, 1995; prodr. Songwriter, 1984, Bright Lights, Big City, 1988, The Fabulous Baker Boys, 1989, Presumed Innocent, 1990, Sliding Doors, 1998, The Talented Mr. Ripley, 1999; exec. prodr.: Honeysuckle Rose, 1980, White Palace, 1990, King Ralph, 1991, Dead Again, 1991, Leaving Normal, 1992, Searching for Bobby Fischer, 1993, Flesh and Bone, 1992, Sense and Sensibility, 1995, Sliding Doors, 1997, Up At the Villa, 1998, The Talented Mr. Ripley, 1998, For Love of the Game, 1998, Blow Dry, 2001, Birthday Girl, 2001, Iris, 2001, Heaven, 2002, The Quiet American, 2002; (actor) The Player, 1992, Death Becomes Her, 1992, Husbands and Wives, 1992, The Firm, 1993, Eyes Wide Shut, 1997, Civil Action, 1998, (voice) The Majestic, 2001, Changing Lanes, 2002, (TV) Mad About You, 1998, Eyes Wide Shut, 1999; dir., prodr., actor: Tootsie, 1982, Random Hearts, 1999. Served with U.S. Army, 1957-59. Recipient Acad. award for best dir. and best picture, 1986. also: Deloitte & Touche 350 S Grand Ave Los Angeles CA 90071-3406 Office: Artists Mgmt Group 9465 Wilshire Blvd Ste 519 Beverly Hills CA 90212-2604

POLLAK, BARTH, mathematics professor; b. Chgo., Aug. 14, 1928; s. Samuel and Esther (Hirschberg) P.; m. Helen Charlotte Schiller, Aug. 22, 1954; children: Martin Russell, Eleanor Susan. BS, Ill. Inst. Tech., 1950, MS, 1951; PhD, Princeton U., 1957. Instr. math. Ill. Inst. Tech., Chgo., 1956-58; asst. prof. Syracuse (N.Y.) U., 1958-63; assoc. prof. U. Notre Dame, Ind., 1963-67, prof., 1967-2000, prof. emeritus, 2000—. Office: U Notre Dame Dept Math Notre Dame IN 46556 E-mail: pollak.1@nd.edu.

POLLAK, JOANNE E. lawyer; b. Cleve., July 16, 1944; m. Mark Pollak, Dec. 26, 1976; children: Elizabeth, Joshua, Rebecca, Benjamin, Jonathan. BA magna cum laude, Dickinson Coll., 1965; JD with honors, U. Md., 1976. Bar: Md. 1976. V.p., gen. counsel The Johns Hopkins Health System Corp./Johns Hopkins Medicine, Balt.; assoc., ptnr. and head of health care practice group Piper & Marbury Law Offices, 1976-93. Instr. bus. of medicine Sch. Medicine, Johns Hopkins U., Internat. Bus. Sch.; mem. bd. advisors U. Md. Law Sch., 2002-. Bd. dirs. Charlestown Cmty., Inc., 1992—, Mid-Atlantic affiliate Am. Heart Assn., 1991—2004, chair bd. dirs., 2002—03, chair rsch. for life campaign, 1999; mem. bd. advisors U. Md. Law Sch., 2002—. Named One of Md.'s Top Women, Daily Record, 1996, 98, 2000. Office: Johns Hopkins Health Sys Corp 600 N Wolfe St Baltimore MD 21287-1974

POLLAK, KEVIN, actor; b. Oct. 30, 1957; m. Lucy Webb, 1995. Appeared in films Avalon, 1990, L.A. Story, 1992, Another You, 1991, Ricochet, 1991, A Few Good Men, 1992, Indian Summer, 1993, The Opposite Sex (And How to Live With Them), 1993, Grumpy Old Men, 1993, Clean Slate, 1994, Miami Rhapsody, 1995, The Usual Suspects, 1995, Canadian Bacon, 1995, Casino, 1995, Grumpier Old Men, 1995, House Arrest, 1996, Apt Pupil, 1997, Cannes Man, 1996, Truth or Consequences N.M., 1997, The Sex Monster, 1998, She's All That, 1999, End of Days, 1999, Deterrence, 1999, Deal of a Lifetime, 1999, The Whole Nine Yards, 2000, Steal This Movie!, 2000, The Wedding Planner, 2001, 3000 Miles to Graceland, 2001, Dr. Dolittle 2, 2001, Stolen Summer, 2002, Juwanna Mann, 2002, Mother Ghost, 2002, The Santa Clause 2, 2002, Rolling Kansas, 2003, Blizzard, 2003, Seven Times Lucky, 2004, The Whole Ten Yards, 2004; appeared on TV in The Don's Analyst, 1997, Salute to Martin Scorsese, 1997, Ruby Bridges, 1998, From the Earth to the Moon, 1998, others, (tv series) Work with Me, 1999, Movie Lover's Road Trip, 2003, Celebrity Poker Showdown, 2003. Office: ICM 8942 Wilshire Blvd Beverly Hills CA 90211-1934*

POLLAK, LISA, columnist; Grad., U. Mich., 1990. Columinist Balt. Sun. Recipient Pulitzer prize for feature writing, 1997. Office: Balt Sun 501 N Calvat St Baltimore MD 21278-0001

POLLAK, LOUIS HEILPRIN, judge, educator; b. N.Y.C., Dec. 7, 1922; s. Walter and Marion (Heilprin) P.; m. Katherine Weiss, July 25, 1952; children: Nancy, Elizabeth, Susan, Sarah, Deborah. AB, Harvard U., 1943; LLB, Yale U., 1948; LLD (hon.), Wilkes U., 2002, Columbia U., 2004. Bar: N.Y. 1949, Conn. 1956, Pa. 1976. Law clk. to Justice Rutledge U.S. Supreme Ct., 1948-49; with Paul, Weiss, Rifkind, Wharton & Garrison, N.Y.C., 1949-51; spl. asst. to Amb. Philip C. Jessup State Dept., 1951-53; asst. counsel Amalgmated Clothing Workers Am., 1954-55; mem. faculty Yale Law Sch., 1955-74, dean, 1965-70; Greenfield prof. U. Pa., 1974-78, dean Law Sch., 1975-78, lectr., 1980—; judge U.S. Dist Ct. (ea. dist.) Pa., Phila., 1978—, now sr. judge. Vis. lectr. Howard U. Sch. Law, 1953; vis. prof. U. Mich. Law Sch., 1961, Columbia Law Sch., 1962. Author: The Constitution and the Supreme Court: A Documentary History, 1966. Mem. New Haven Bd. Edn., 1962-68; chmn. Conn. adv. com. U.S. Civil Rights Commn., 1962-63; mem. bd. NAACP Legal Def. Fund, 1960-78, v.p., 1971-78. Served with AUS, 1943-46. Mem.: ABA (chmn. sect. individual rights 1970—71, Spirit of Excellence award 2003), Am. Law Inst. (coun. 1978—), Am. Acad. Polit. and Social Sci. (bd. dirs. 2001—), Am. Philos. Soc., Am. Acad. Arts and Scis., Assn. Bar City N.Y., Phila. Bar Assn., Fed. Bar Assn. Office: US Dist Ct 16613 US Courthouse 601 Market St Philadelphia PA 19106-1713 Office Phone: 215-597-9590.

POLLAK, MARK, lawyer; b. Paris, July 16, 1947; came to U.S., 1955; s. Joseph and Zofia (Berkowitz) P.; m. Joanne Elizabeth Harris, Dec. 26, 1976; children: Joshua David, Jonathan Stephen, Benjamin Eric, Rebecca Lynn. BA, Bklyn. Coll., 1968; MA in City Planning, JD, U. Pa., 1972. Bar: Md. 1972. Assoc. Piper & Marbury, Balt., 1972-81, ptnr., 1981-99, Wilmer, Cutler & Pickering, Washington, 1999—2004, Wilmer Cutler Pickering Hale & Dorr, LLP, Washington, 2004—. Bd. dirs. Jack Kent Cook Found. Author: Sports Leagues and Teams--An Encyclopedia 1871 to 1996, 1997. Bd. dirs. Balt. Children's Mus., Downtown Partnership of Balt., Inc. Mem. ABA, Md. Bar Assn., Am. Coll. Real Estate Lawyers, Am. Planning Assn., Nat. Assn. Bond Lawyers. Office: Wilmer, Cutler & Pickering 100 Light St Baltimore MD 21202-1036 Office Phone: 410-986-2860. E-mail: mark.pollak@wilmerhale.com.

POLLAK, MARTIN MARSHALL, lawyer, training company executive; b. N.Y.C., July 31, 1927; s. Edward and Jennie (Horowitz) P.; m. Ellen R. Spiegel, Sept. 16, 1929; children: David W., Richard M., Barbara S. AB, Syracuse U., 1950; LLB, St. John's U., Bklyn., 1953. Bar: N.Y. 1953, U.S. Dist. Ct. (ea. and so. dists.) N.Y. 1957, U.S. Supreme Ct. 1959. Ptnr. Feldman & Pollak, Attys., N.Y.C., 1953-59; atty. N.Y. State, 1953—; founder, exec. v.p., treas. G.P. Strategies Corp. (formerly Nat. Patent Devel. Corp.), N.Y.C., 1959-99. Trustee Worcester Found. for Exptl. Rsch., Shrewsbury, Mass., 1977—; cons. Allergan Optical Corp., Irvine, Calif., 1988-89; chmn. bd. Czechoslovak-U.S. Econ. Coun., Washington, 1987-96, vice-chmn., 1996—; pres. Internat. Hydron Corp., Woodbury, N.Y., 1981-88, NPO Trading USA, Inc., N.Y.C., Washington, Prague, Czechoslovakia, 1990-98, Am. Drug Co., Washington, N.Y.C., Moscow, 1993-98, Millennium Cell Corp., 1998-2000; bd. dirs. GSE Sys., Inc. Vice chmn. bd. Worcester Found., 2000—. With USN, 1945-47. Recipient gold medal Czechoslovakian Rep. C. of C., 1984. also: Gen Physics Corp 6700 Alexander Bell Dr Ste 300 Columbia MD 21046-2185 Office: GP Strategies Corp 777 Westchester Ave Fl 4 White Plains NY 10604-3520

POLLAK, NORMAN LEE, accountant; b. Chgo., Aug. 16, 1931; s. Emery and Helen P.; m. Barbara Zeff, Aug. 21, 1955 (div. 1980); children: Martin Joel, Elise Susan McNeal, Rhonda Louise Wilder. BS, Northwestern U., 1955. CPA, Calif.; lic. real estate agt. Calif. Sr. acct., staff acct., 1952-58; pvt. practice, 1958-88; fin. and mgmt. adv. svcs. Expert witness on domestic dissolution, 1984-87; lectr. profl. orgns.; bus. mgr. for Steven Martin, Nitty Gritty Dirt Band, 1967-77. Former pres. Ventura County Estate Planning Coun., 1975-78, 78-79); founder San Fernando Valley Estate Planning Coun., 1962, chpt. pres., 1964-65; founder Ventura Co. Estate Planning Coun.; chmn. Comm. Contest for Hearing Impaired Optimist Club, emergency com. Disaster Preparedness, Oak Forest Mobile Estates Assn.; vol. disaster preparedness plan; coach Braille Olympics for Blind; mem. Conejo Future Found.; bd. dirs. Oak Forest Homeowners Assn., Honokowai Palms Homeowners Assn.; bd. trustees Westlake Cultural Found.; sponsor Code 3 for Homeless Children, 1993. Mem. AICPA (apptd. CPA key person for legis.- polit. program Washington), Calif. Soc. CPAs (former chmn. San Fernando tech. discussion group 1960-61, former mem. com. on cooperation with credit grantors), Nat. Assn. Accts., Westlake Village C. of C., Northwestern U. Alumni Club, Kellogg Sch. Mgmt. Alumni Club, UCLA Alumni Club, Delta Mu Delta. Address: 1930 Village Center Cir #3-428 Las Vegas NV 89134

POLLAK, RAYMOND, general and transplant surgeon; b. Johannesburg, Nov. 12, 1950; came to U.S., 1977; MB BCh, U. Witwatersrand, Johannesburg, 1973. Diplomate Am. Bd. Surgery. Rotating intern Gen. Hosp., Johannesburg, 1974; intern in surgery U. Ill. Hosps. and Clinics, Chgo., 1977-78, resident in surgery; immunology and transplant fellow U. Ill., Chgo., 1982-84, assoc. prof. surgery, chief divsn. transplant dept. surgery, 1988-98, prof. surgery dept., surgeon, 1995—, chief divsn. transplant Peoria, 2000—. Fellow ACS, Royal Coll. Surgeons Edinburgh. Office: U Ill Dept Surgery 624 NE Glen Oak Ave North Bldg 2d Floor Peoria IL 61603-3135 Office Phone: 309-655-2383. Business E-Mail: rpollak@uic.edu.

POLLAN, CAROLYN JOAN, state legislator, job research administrator; b. Houston, July 12, 1937; d. Rex and Faith (Basye) Clark; m. George A. Pollan, Jan. 6, 1962; children: Cee Cee, Todd (dec.), Robert. BS in Radio and TV, John Brown U., 1959; postgrad, NYU, 1959; PhD in Edn., Walden U., 1993. Mem. Ark. House of Reps., 1974-98, asst. to gov., legis. dir., 1999—. Sr. Rep. mem., asst. speaker pro-tempore, 1993; apptd. by Gov. numerous coms., commns.; ex-officio mem. Workplace Literacy Project Adv. Bd. U.S. Dept. Labor & Ednl. Testing Svc., 1990-93, Nat. Adult Literacy Survey, 1990-93; del. Am. Soviet Seminar, Am. Council Young Polit. Leaders, Exeter, N.H., 1976; co-developer Total Touch Test; owner Patent Model Mus.; v. chmn. Ark. Rep. Com., 1972-76; del. Rep. Nat. Conv., 1976; bd. dirs. Ark. Cancer Soc., Ark., Easter Seals Soc.; bd. dirs. Greg Kistler Treatment Ctr. for Physically Handicapped, Ark. Found. Assoc. Colls., 4-H Found. for Sebastian County; trustee John Brown U.; mem. legis. adv. com. So. Regional Edn. Bd., chmn. edn. com. So. Legis. Conf., 1994-96. Recipient Conservation Legislator of Yr. award Ark. Wildlife Fedn., Nat. Wildlife Fedn., Sears Roebuck & Co., 1976, Outstanding State Legislator of Yr. award Ark. Pub. Employees Assn., 1979, Lifetime Mem. award Ark. PTA, 1994, Ark. Kids Count award, 1997, many others; named 1 of 10 Outstanding Legislators, Assembly of Govtl. Employees, 1980, Legislator of Yr., Ark. Human Svc. Providers Assn., 1982, Citizen of Yr. by Ark. Social Workers, 1993, Outstanding Women in Ark. Politics by Ark. Dem., 1990, One of 10 Top Legislators in 1993 Ark. Dem. Gazette, 1993, onf of Top 100 Women in Ark., Ark. Bus. Publ., 1995, 96, 97, Woman of Yr., Fort Smith Bus. and Profl. Women, 1997; voted 1 of Ft. Smith's 10 Most Influential Citizens, S.W. Times Record Readers, 1979. Mem. Ark. Internat. Woman's Forum (founding mem.), Ft. Smith Car Restoration Assn. (bd. dirs.). Baptist. Office: Gov's Office State Capitol Little Rock AR 72201-1088

POLLARA, BERNARD, pediatrician, educator; b. Chgo. s. Joseph and Mamie P. PhB, Northwestern U., 1951, MS, 1954; MD, U. Minn., 1960, PhD, 1963. Intern USPHS Hosp., Seattle, 1960; resident in pediatrics U. Minn. Hosps., 1968-69; rsch. assoc. pediatrics U. Minn., 1960-63, assoc. prof. biochemistry and pediatrics, 1969; prof. pediatrics Albany (N.Y.) Med. Coll., 1969-94, chmn. dept., 1979-93; pediatrician in chief Albany Med. Ctr. Hosp., 1979-93; sabbatical leave, pediatrician Yukon Kuskokwim Regional Hosp., 1992-93; John and Aliese Price prof. pediatrics & adolescent medicine U. South Fla., Tampa, 1994—, head divsn. gen. pediatrics, dept. pediatrics, 1994—, interim chmn. pediats., 1999-2001. V.p. for rsch. affairs Albany Med. Ctr., 1986-89. Dir. N.Y. State Kidney Disease Inst., 1969-79. With USN, 1945-46. Recipient Acad. Laureate award SUNY, Albany, 1991; Arthritis and Rheumatism Found. fellow, 1961-64. Fellow Am. Acad. Pediats.; mem. AAAS, Am. Assn. Immunologists, Am. Pediat. Soc., Am. Soc. Cell Biology, Clin. Immunology Soc., Ambulatory Pediat. Assn., Sigma Xi, Phi Lambda Upsilon, Alpha Omega Alpha. Office: U South Fla Sch Medicine Dept Pediatrics 17 Davis Blvd Ste 308 Tampa FL 33606-3475 Office Phone: 813-259-8752. E-mail: bpollara@hsc.usf.edu.

POLLARA, JOANNE, learning disabilities educator consultant; b. Hoboken, N.J., Apr. 18, 1954; d. Ralph Frank and Katharine Stark (Cunningham) Pollara; children: Angela, Joshua. BA, St. Joseph Coll., 1976; MA, Montclair State U., 1994. Cert. tchr. elem., spl. edn., L.D.T.C., N.J.; professionally recognized spl. educator in ednl. diagnosis; cert. supr. 4th grade tchr. Holy Trinity Sch., Hackensack, N.J., 1976-77; tchr. of handicapped Kessler Inst., West Orange, N.J., 1978-86; bedside instructor West Orange Bd. of Edn.,

1976-86, spl. edn. inst. aide, 1986-88; tchr. of handicapped Redwood Sch., West Orange, N.J., 1988-97; learning disabled tchr. cons. West Orange Pub. Schs., 1997—. Mem. spl. edn. curriculum com., W. Orange, N.J., 1989, bldg. mgmt. com., 1991-92; spl. edn. rep. reading curriculum com., W. Orange, 1990; PTA faculty rep. Redwood Sch., W. Orange, 1994-95. Religious educator Our Lady of Lourdes Ch., West Orange, N.J., 1984-85, Notre Dame Ch., North Caldwell, N.J., 1991-92; girl scout leader Girl Scouts of U.S., W. Orange, N.J., 1983-84, 86-87. Mem. Coun. for Exceptional Children (learning disabilities divsn.), Coun. for Ednl. Diagnostic Svcs., Assn. Learning Consultants, Phi Kappa Phi. Avocations: reading, music (piano, guitar), swimming. Home: 23 Espy Rd Apt B5 Caldwell NJ 07006-4855 Office: Dept Student Support Svcs 179 Eagle Rock Ave West Orange NJ 07052

POLLARD, C. WILLIAM, environmental services administrator; m. Judy Pollard; four children. Grad., Wheaton Coll.; JD, Northwestern U. of Law. Lawyer, 1963-72; v.p., faculty Wheaton (Ill.) Coll., 1972-77; CEO The ServiceMaster Co., Downers Grove, Ill., 1983-93, chmn., 1993-99, chmn., CEO, 1999—. Bd. dirs. Herman Miller, Inc., Coro, Inc., UnumProvident Corp., Inst. for Diversity in Health Mgmt.; chmn. bd. trustees Wheaton Coll.; chmn. bd. dirs. Hosp. Rsch. and Ednl. Trust; mem. adv. bd. Drucker Found. for Nonprofit Mgmt.; bd. visitors Drucker Grad. Mgmt. Ctr. at Claremont. Author: The Soul of the Firm; contbr. author books and mags. Office: ServiceMaster Co 1 ServiceMaster Way Downers Grove IL 60515-1700 Office Phone: 800-333-6678., 630-271-1300. Office Fax: 630-271-5750. Business E-Mail: billpollard@svm.com.

POLLARD, C(HARLES) WILLIAM, diversified services company executive; b. Chgo., June 8, 1938; s. Charles W. and Ruth Ann (Humphrey) P.; m. Judith Ann, June 8, 1959; children: Julie Ann, Charles W., Brian, Amy. AB, Wheaton Coll., 1960; JD, Northwestern U., 1963. Bar: Ill. 1963. Mem. firm Wilson and McIlvaine, 1963-67, Vescelus, Perry & Pollard, Wheaton, Ill., 1968-72; prof., v.p. fin. Wheaton Coll., 1972-77; sr. v.p. ServiceMaster Industries, Downers Grove, Ill., 1977-80, exec. v.p., 1980-81, pres., 1981-83, pres., COO, 1981-83; pres., CEO ServiceMaster Co., Downers Grove, Ill., 1983-93, chmn. bd. dirs., mem. exec. com., 1994—, now chmn., CEO. Bd. dirs. Wheaton Coll., Herman Miller, Inc., Provident Life and Accident Ins. Co. Office: The ServiceMaster 1 Servicemaster Way Downers Grove IL 60515-1700

POLLARD, FRED DON, finance company executive, director; b. Proctorsville, Vt., Sept. 15, 1931; s. Bryant Frank and Millie Viola (Brobst) P.; m. Sandra Jean Norton, Oct. 19, 1957; children: Fred Don, Bruce Gardiner, Mark Bryant. BA, Dartmouth Coll., 1953, MBA, 1954. CPA, N.Y. Staff auditor Touche, Niven, Bailey & Smart, Chgo., 1954-55, 57-58; with Hertz Corp., Chgo., 1958-60, London, 1960-62, Paris, 1962-64, N.Y.C., 1964-65; European controller Avis Rent A Car, London, 1965-69, internat. treas., 1969-71, asst. v.p., dir. fin., 1971-72, asst. treas., 1972-75; treas. Garcia Corp., Teaneck, N.J., 1975-78; v.p. fin., treas. Augsbury Orgn., Inc., Ogdensburg, N.Y., 1978-79, sr. v.p. fin., treas., 1979-83, also dir.; pres. Corp. Fin. Assocs. No. N.Y., Canton, 1983—, Agrl. Processing Corp., Canton, 1983-98; pres. and treas. AG Pro Ltd., Massena, NY, 1998—. Mem. adv. bd. Clarkson Sch. Mgmt., Potsdam, N.Y., 1979-83; vis. lectr. sch. of mgmt. Clarkson U., Potsdam, 1986-87; vis. lectr. dept. econs. St. Lawrence U., Canton, N.Y., 1987-88. Exec. bd. Seaway Valley coun. Boy Scouts Am., 1980-86, adv. bd., 1986-95. Served with U.S. Army, 1955-57. Mem. N.Y. State Soc. CPAs, Am. Inst. CPAs., St. Lawrence county C. of C. (bd. dirs. 1997—). Lodges: Masons; Shriners. Presbyterian. Home: Old Stone House 1129 County Route 25 Canton NY 13617-6539 Office: 1129 County Rte 25 Canton NY 13617 E-mail: stonhous@northnet.org.

POLLARD, HARVEY B. medical educator, neuroscientist; b. San Antonio, May 26, 1943; BA in Biology, Rice U., 1964; MS in Biochemistry, MD, U. Chgo., 1969, PhD, 1973. Rsch. assoc. NIH-Nat. Inst. Arthritis and Metabolic Diseases, Bethesda, Md., 1969-71, sr. investigator, 1972-74, 1977-79, sect. chief, 1979-81; lab. chief Nat. Inst. Diabetes, Digestive and Kidney Diseases, Bethesda, 1981-96; prof., chair dept. anatomy, physiology and genetics Uniformed Svcs. U. Sch. Medicine, Bethesda, 1997—. Contbr. over 250 articles to profl. jours. With USPHS, 1969-96. Recipient Commendation medal USPHS, 1982, Alumni award for Disting. Svc., U. Chigo. Alumni Assn., 1989, NIH Inventor's award, 1991. Mem. Biophys. Soc., Soc. for Neurosci., Am. Soc. for Pharmacology and Exptl. Therapeutics, Soc. for Cell Biology, Endocrine Soc., Am. Coll. Psychoneuropharmacology, Am. Soc. for Biochemistry and Molecular Biology, Am. Assn. Anatomists., Am. Physiol. Soc., Institute of Medicine of Washington, D.C. Office: USU Sch Med Dept Anatomy Physiology and Genetics Bethesda MD 20814-4712 E-mail: hpollard@usuhs.mil.

POLLARD, HENRY, mediator, arbitrator; b. N.Y.C., Jan. 10, 1931; s. Charles and Sarah (Lanster) P.; m. Adele Ruth Brodie, June 16, 1954; children: Paul A., Lydia S. AB, CCNY, 1953; JD, Columbia U., 1954. Bar: N.Y. 1954, Calif. 1962. Assoc. Sullivan & Cromwell, N.Y.C., 1954, 56-61; ptnr. Kaplan, LIvingston, Goodwin, Berkowitz & Selvin, Beverly Hills, Calif., 1962-81, Pollard, Bauman, Slome & McIntosh, Beverly Hills, 1981-87, Seyfarth, Shaw, L.A., 1987-95; of counsel Oberstein, Kibre & Horwitz, L.A., 1995-99. Judge pro tem L.A. County Mcpl. Ct.; arbitrator/mediator, mem. large complex case program Am. Arbitration Assn.; arbitrator/mediator Nat. Assn. Securities Dealers, N.Y. Stock Exch., Am. Stock Exch., Pacific Stock Exch., L.A. County Dispute Resolution Svcs.; settlement officer Beverly Hills Mcpl. Ct., L.A. County Superior Ct. Editor Columbia U. Law Rev., 1953-54. Served with U.S. Army, 1954-56. Harlan Fiske Stone scholar, 1953-54. Mem. ABA, Calif. Bar Assn., Beverly Hills Bar Assn. Office Phone: 310-457-1713. Home Fax: 310-457-1713. Personal E-mail: adrpollard@aol.com.

POLLARD, JEFFREY WALLACE, college counseling, health services director; b. Bethesda, Md., July 8, 1946; s. Eric George Frederick and Eldred (Wallace) P. BS, Old Dominion U., 1970, MS, 1994; PhD, U. Va., 1978. Lic. psychologist, Ohio; diplomate Am. bd. Profl. Psychology, Internat. Acad. Behavioral Medicine, Counseling, Psychotherapy. Probation officer Juvenile, Domestic Rels. Court, Norfolk, Va., 1970-74; counselor Comprehensive Addictive Svcs. Program, Norfolk, Va., 1974-75; practicum counselor U. Va. Counseling Ctr., Charlottesville, Va., 1976-77; intern in clinical psychology Eastern Va. Graduate Sch. Med., Norfolk, Va., 1977-78; psychologist Villanova (Pa.) U. Counseling Ctr., 1978-82; dir. counseling svcs. Denison U., Granville, Ohio, 1982-89, dir. health and counseling svcs., 1989—. Author: Treatment of Violence Perpetrators, 1991, Treatment for Perpetrators of Rape and Other Violence, 1994; co-editor: Campus Violence: Kinds Causes and Cures, 1994; mem. editl. bd. Jour. of Counseling and Devel., 1996-99, Jour. of Coll. Student Psychotherapy, 1994—; contbr. articles to profl. jours. Grantee U.S. Dept. Edn. Fund, 1989. Fellow Acad. Counseling Psychology (treas. 1997—, pres.-elect). Home: 5025 Blendon Ravine Ct Columbus OH 43230-4214 Office: Denison Univ Whisler Hall Granville OH 43023-1368 E-mail: pollard@denison.edu.

POLLARD, JOSEPH AUGUSTINE, advertising and public relations consultant; b. N.Y.C., June 22, 1924; s. Joseph Michael and Mary Theresa (Sheerin) P.; m. Helen Frances O'Neill, Jan. 18, 1947 (dec.); children: Christopher (dec.), Kenneth, Eugene, Daniel (dec.), Theresa, Michael; m. Lee Sharon Rivkins, Jan. 1, 1981. Student, Pratt Inst., 1946-50. Advt. mgr. Boston Store, Utica, N.Y., 1951-53; sales promotion dir. Interstate Stores, N.Y., 1954-60, 67-70; v.p. sales Cmty. Discount Stores, Chgo., 1960-63; dir. sales S. Klein, N.Y.C., 1964-66; v.p. advt. and pub. rels. Peoples Drug Stores, Alexandria, Va., 1970-89; ret. Trustee D.C. divsn. Am. Cancer Soc., 1978-95, pres., 1985-86, nat. del., 1991-94; pres. Modern Retailers Ill., 1962; bd. dirs. Brunswick County Literacy Coun., 2001—. With USAF, 1943-46, 50-51. Recipient Am. ADvt. Fedn. Silver medal award, 1982, St. Georges medal Am. Cancer Soc., 1984. Mem. Advt. Club Washington (pres. 1975-76), Country Club Fairfax (pres. 1994, bd. dirs. 1992-95), Lockwood Folly Country Club (Holden Beach, N.C., bd. dirs. 1997). Home and Office: 173 Clubhouse Dr SW Supply NC 28462-2108

POLLARD, MICHAEL ROSS, lawyer, health policy researcher and consultant; b. Flint, Mich., Apr. 14, 1947; s. Gail Winton Pollard and Evelyn Georgeanna (LeMire) Goplen; m. Penelope Brigham, Aug. 22, 1970. AB in Polit. Sci., U. Mich., 1969; JD, Harvard U., 1972, MPH, 1974. Bar: Mass. 1972, D.C. 1975. Profl. assoc. for program devel. Nat. Acad. Scis. Inst. Medicine, Washington, 1974-77, dir. law and ethics div., 1977-78; atty. advisor Office of Policy Planning, FTC, Washington, 1978-81, asst. dir. Bur. Consumer Protection, 1981-83; dir. Office of Policy Analysis, Pharm. Mfrs. Assn., Washington, 1983-88; exec. dir. Am. Pharm. Inst., Washington, 1988-89; counsel Michaels, Wishner & Bonner, P.C. (now Michaels & Bonner PC), Washington, 1988-89, ptnr., 1989—. Cons. Nat. Ctr. for Health Svcs. Rsch., Rockville, Md., 1975-80, Office Tech. Assessment U.S. Congress, 1984-95; dir. Inst. for Health Policy Solutions, 1992—. Contbr. articles to profl. jours. Treas. Nat. Leadership Coalition on AIDS, 1988-93; treas. and dir.-at-large Nat. Commn. on Cert. of Physician Assts., 1991-97, James B. Angell scholar U. Mich., 1967, 68, 69. Mem. ABA, Phi Beta Kappa, Pi Sigma Alpha. Democrat. Avocations: running, bicycling, gardening, architectural drawing. Home: 7300 Maple Ave Chevy Chase MD 20815-5108 also: 29 Paradise Lane West Southport ME 04576 Office: Michaels & Bonner 1140 Connecticut Ave NW Ste 900 Washington DC 20036-4009

POLLARD, MORRIS, microbiologist, educator; b. Hartford, Conn., May 24, 1916; s. Harry and Sarah (Hoffman) P.; m. Mildred Klein, Dec. 29, 1938 (dec. 2001); children: Harvey, Carol, Jonathan. D.V.M., Ohio State U., 1938; MS, Va. Poly. Inst., 1939; PhD (Nat. Found. Infantile Paralysis fellow), U. Calif.-Berkeley, 1950; D.Sc. (hon.) Miami U., Ohio, 1981. Mem. staff Animal Disease Sta., Nat. Agrl. Research Center, Beltsville, Md., 1939-42; asst. prof. preventive medicine Med. br. U. Tex., Galveston, 1946-48, assoc. prof., 1948-50, prof., 1950-61; prof. biology U. Notre Dame, Ind., 1961-66, prof., chmn. microbiology, 1966-81, prof. emeritus, 1981—, dir. Lobund Lab., 1961-85, Coleman dir. Lobund Lab., 1985—. Vis. prof. Fed. U. Rio de Janeiro, Brazil, 1977; vis. prof. Katholieke U., Leuven, Belgium, 1981; mem. tng. grant com. NIH, 1965-70; mem. adv. bd. Inst. Lab. Animal Resources NRC, 1965-68; mem. adv. com. microbiology Office Naval Research, 1966-68, chmn., 1968-70; mem. sci. adv. com. United Health Found., 1966-70; cons. U. Tex., M.D. Anderson Hosp. and Tumor Inst., 1958-66; mem. colon cancer com. Nat. Cancer Inst., 1972-76, chmn. tumor immunology com., 1976-79; mem. com. cancer cause and prevention NIH, 1979-81; program rev. com. Argonne Nat. Lab, 1979-85, chmn., 1983-85; lectr. Found. Microbiology, 1978 Editor: Perspectives in Virology Vol. I to XI, 1959-80; contbr. articles to profl. jours. Served from 1st lt. to lt. col. Vet. Corps, AUS, 1942-46. Recipient Disting. Alumnus award Ohio State U., 1979, Army Commendation medal, Presdl. citation, Hope award Am. Cancer Soc., 2000; named Hon. Alumnus U. Notre Dame, 1989; McLaughlin Faculty fellow Cambridge U., 1956; Raine Found. prof. U. Western Australia, 1975; vis. scientist Chinese Acad. Med. Scis., 1979, 81; hon. prof. Chinese Acad. Med. Scis., 1982. Mem. Am. Acad. Microbiology (charter), Brazilian Acad. Scis., Soc. Exptl. Biology and Medicine, Am. Soc. Microbiology (Acad. Sci. Achievement award 1990), Am. Soc. Investigative Pathology, Am. Assn. Cancer Rsch., Am. Soc. Lab. Animal Sci., Assn. Gnotobiotics (pres.), Internat. Commn. Lab. Animal Sci., AAAS, Internat. Assn. Gnotobiology (pres.), Internat. Assn. Gnotobiotics (hon. pres. 1987), Sigma Xi, Phi Delta Epsilon (hon.), Phi Zeta (hon.). Office: Lobund Lab U Notre Dame Notre Dame IN 46556 Home: 1025 Park Pl Apt 137 Mishawaka IN 46545-3537

POLLARD, OVERTON PRICE, retired state agency executive, lawyer; b. Ashland, Va., Mar. 26, 1933; s. James Madison and Annie Elizabeth (Hutchinson) P.; m. Anne Aloysia Meyer, Oct. 1, 1960; children: Mary O., Price, John, Anne, Charles, Andrew, David AB in Econs., Washington and Lee U., 1954, JD, 1957. Bar: Va. Claims supr. Travelers Ins. Co., Richmond, Va., 1964-67; asst. atty. gen. State of Va., Richmond, 1967, 70-72; spl. asst. Va. Supreme Ct., Richmond, 1968-70; exec. dir. Pub. Defender Commn., Richmond, 1972—2003; ptnr. Pollard & Boice and predecessor firms, Richmond, 1972-87. Bd. govs. Va. Criminal Law Sect., Richmond, 1970-72; chmn. prepaid legal svcs. com. Va. State Bar, Richmond, 1982-85, chair sr. lawyers sect., 1999; pres. Met. Legal Aid, Richmond, 1978. Del. to State Dem. Cong., Richmond, 1985; mem. Va. Commn. on Family Violence Prevention, 1995; bd. dirs. Henrico Cmty. Housing Corp., 1999. With USN, 1957-59. Recipient Svc. award, Criminal Law Bd. of Govs. for Pub. Defender Study, 1971, Outstanding Svc. award, Pub. Defender Commn., 1998. Fellow Va. Law Found.; mem. ABA, Va. Bar Assn. (chmn. criminal law sect. 1991-93), Richmond Bar Assn., Nat. Legal Aid and Defender Assn. (Reginald Heber Smith award 1991), Va. Bar Assn. (Pro Bono Publico award 1995). Democrat. Baptist. Avocation: fishing. Home: 7726 Sweetbriar Rd Richmond VA 23229-6622

POLLARD, SHIRLEY, employment training director, community services administrator, consultant; b. Brunswick City, Va., July 8, 1939; 1 child, Darryl. Degree in bus. adminstrn., Upper Iowa U., 1978. Adminstr. East. Balt. Cmty. Corp.; tng. coord. Balt. County Concentrated Employment Tng. Program; exec. dir. Park Heights Cmty. Corp., Balt.; dir. Linkages, Inc., Balt. Contbr. articles to Afro Am. newspaper. Pres. Park Hts. Cmty. Devel. Corp., United Black Fund, Balt., 1989—, Presdl. Task Force, 1992; active Balt. Urban League, Balt. Welfare Rights Orgn.; founder, pres. Balt. County Polit. Action Coalition, 1982—; founder, dir. Linkages, Inc., 1980; founder, dir. Tng. and Placement Svcs., 1989; active United Svc. Orgn., Md. Minority Contractors Assn., U.S. Civil Rights Mus. and Hall of Fame, Smithsonian Instn.; founder African Am. Culture Ctr.; co-founder Project Lou, Inc.; founder The Afro Fund, Inc.; active Fund for a Free South Africa's Founding Assocs. Leadership Coun., Nat. Women's Hall of Fame, Nat. Abortion Rights Action League, Srs. Coalition, Md. Edn. Coalition, CORE, So. Christian Leadership Conf., Nat. Trust for Hist. Preservation; presdl. appointment Md. Selective Svc. Bd., 1993, Exec. Com. of Am. Friends Svc. Com.; mem. women's adv. coun. Sinai Hosp., 1994—. Recipient Outstanding Achievement award Md. Minority Contractors Assn., Mayor's Citation, Martin Luther King Civil Rights award, 1987, Md. State Dept. Edn. award, 1987, congl. Achievement award, Kool Achiever awards, 1990, Nat. Black Caucus Spl. award, 1990, Congressional Achievement award, 1988, Svc. award The Writers Club, 1991, USO Meritorious Svc. award, 1991, Gov.'s Vol. award, 1992, Acad. of Excellence award, 1992, Signs of Hope award, 1995, Mayor's citation, 1984, Gov.'s citation, 1995, Senatorial award, 1995; recipient Bud Achiever award 1996. Mem. Am. Soc. Pers. Adminstrn., Am. Soc. Health/Manpower/Edn./Tng., Assn. for Providers Employment and Tng., NAACP (founder, pres. Randallstown chpt. 1988-95, Signs of Hope award), Balt. Coun. on Fgn. Affairs, Transafrica, USO, Md. Minority Contractors Assn. (Achievement award 1986, bd. dirs. 1984-89), Smithsonian Assoc., Md. C. of C. (greater Balt. com. 1985). Office: PO Box 32051 Baltimore MD 21282-2051

POLLARD, THOMAS DEAN, cell biologist, educator; b. Pasadena, Calif., July 7, 1942; s. Dean Randall and Florence Alma (Dierker) Pollard; m. Patricia Elizabeth Snowden, Feb. 7, 1964; children: Katherine, Daniel. BA, Pomona Coll., Claremont, Calif., 1964; MD, Harvard U., 1968. Intern Mass. Gen. Hosp., Boston, 1968—69; staff assoc. NIH, Bethesda, Md., 1969—72; from asst. prof. to assoc. prof. Harvard Med. Sch., Boston, 1972—78; prof., dir. dept. cell biology and anatomy Johns Hopkins Sch. Medicine, Balt., 1977—96; pres. Salk Inst. for Biological Studies, LaJolla, Calif., 1996—2000, prof., 1996—2001, U. Calif., San Diego, 1996—2001; Eugene Higgins prof. molecular, cellular and devel. biology Yale U., 2001—. Mem. Commn. on Life Sci. NRC, 1990—97; chair Commn. on Life Sci., NRC, 1993—97; mem. coun. Nat. Inst. Gen. Med. Sci., NIH. Recipient Lewis S. Rosentiel Disting. Work in Basic Med. Rsch. award, Brandeis U., 1966; fellow, Guggenheim Found., 1984. Fellow: Am. Acad. Arts and Scis.; mem.: Marine Biol. Lab. (trustee 1991—97), Biophys. Soc. (pres. 1992—93), Am. Soc. Cell Biology (pres. 1987—88, K.R. Porter lectr., 1989, pres. 1987-88), Inst. Medicine, NAS. Office: Dept Molecular, Cellular and Developmental Biology Yale U PO Box 208103 New Haven CT 06520-8103 E-mail: thomas.pollard@yale.edu.

POLLARD, VERONICA, automotive executive; m. Joel Dreyfuss; 1 child, Justin. Student, U. Wis.; Bachelor's Degree, Boston U.; Master's Degree, Columbia U. First grade tchr., NY; mgr. internat. affairs Cosmo Pub. Rels. Corp., Tokyo; staff writer San Francisco Chronicle; asst. dir. pub. affairs Newsweek Mag.; publicist ABC TV Network, mgr. bus. info.; dir. corp. comm. Capital Cities/ABC, Inc.; v.p. corp. pub. rels. ABC; v.p., external affairs Toyota Motor Corp. Services N.Am., 1998—2002; group v.p. corp. comm. Toyota Motor N.Am., Inc., 2002—. Bd. dirs. Granite Broadcasting Corp.; mem. individual investor adv. com. N.Y. Stock Exch. Former dir. Nat. YMCA of the U.S.A., YMCA Greater N.Y.; trustee Mus. for African Art, NY, active YMCA; hon. bd. mem. West Side YMCA, NY, 1990—98, bd. chair; dir. The Doe Fund, NY. Mem.: Women's Forum. Office: Toyota Motor NAm Ste 4900 Nine West 57th St New York NY 10019

POLLARD, WILLIAM ALBERT, lawyer; b. Nashville, July 7, 1946; s. Thomas Brown and Hilda Alexine (Jolly) Pollard; m. Sharon Corbett Pollard; children: William A. Jr., Thomas Barnes. BS, U. SC, 1968; JD, 1974. Bar: SC 1974, US Dist. Ct./SC 1974, US Ct. Appeals (4th cir.) 1974, US Tax Ct. 1977. Clin. prof. SC Sch. Medicine; assoc. Nexsen, Pruet, Jacobs & Pollard, Columbia, SC, 1974—78; ptnr., 1978—; chmn., mng. ptnr., 1993—; mem. adv. bd. Midlands Tech. Coll., Columbia, 1978—84. Founder, chmn. Healthy Learners, 1990—2002, chmn. emeritus, 2003—; endowment chmn., exec. coun. Indian Rivers Coun. Boy Scouts Am., 1986—; mem. AC Moore Edn. Found.; chmn. Heart Walk Am. Heart Assn., 1999; chmn. profl. divsn. United Way of the Midlands, 2003; chmn. Cystic Fibrosis Fund, 1998; mem. Windsor Edn. Found.; bd. dirs. Richland Sch. Dist. One Found. Lt. USN, 1968—71. Mem.: SC Bar Assn. (med., legal affairs com. 1986—88, chmn. 1992—93), ABA (forum com. on health law), SC Soc. Hosp. Atty. (bd. gov. 1985—, pres. 1988—94), SC Hosp. Assn., Nat. Health Lawyers Assn., Am. Soc. Law and Medicine, Am. Soc. Hosp. Atty., Bank of Am., Columbia C. of C. (health care task force), Capitol City, Sertoma (pres. 1981—82). Methodist. Home: 321 Trentwood Dr Columbia SC 29223 8417 Office: Nexsen Pruet Jacobs & Pollard PO Box 2426 Columbia SC 29202-2426 Office Phone: 802-253 8246.

POLLARD, WILLIAM BARLOW, III, university educator; b. Greenville, S.C., Nov. 24, 1946; s. William Barlow and Nellie Griffin (Martin) P.; m. Betty Kathryn Henley, Nov. 21, 1970; children: William Joseph, Jeremiah Martin. BA in English, Mars Hill Coll., 1969; MA, Appalachian State U., 1974; M in Accountancy, U. S.C., 1980, PhD, 1981. Pub. sch. tchr. Hendersonville (N.C.) City Sch., 1970-72; tchg. asst. Appalachian State U., Boone, N.C., 1973-75, instr. acctg., 1976-77, prof. of acctg., 1981—; tchg. asst. U. S.C., 1978-80. Contbr. articles to profl. jours. With USAR, 1968-75. Mem. Am. Acctg. Assn., Inst. of Mgmt. Accts. Office: Appalachian State U Dept Acctg Boone NC 28608-0001

POLLARO, PAUL PHILIP, artist; b. NYC, Aug. 2, 1921; s. Charles and Maria (Aprile) P.; m. Jo Ann Stover, July 16, 1962 (div. Nov. 1979); children: Lauren, Paul Jr.; m. Laura Clayton, Apr. 2, 1985. Student, Art Students League, 1945-48, Pratt Graphic Ctr., 1972. Instr. painting The New Sch. of Social Rsch., N.Y.C., 1964-69; vis. artist Notre Dame U., South Bend, Ind., 1965-67; asst. prof. art, chmn. art dept. Wagner Coll., Staten Island, N.Y., 1970-73; asst. dir. The MacDowell Colony, Peterborough, N.H., 1973-76; pvt. practice Hancock, N.H., 1976—. One-man shows include Jersey City Mus., NJ, 1966 (2d prize), S.I. Mus. Art, NY, 1973, Manchester Inst. Arts and Scis., Manchester, NH, 1970-85, Chryser Mus., Norfolk, Va., 1991, others. Sgt. U.S. Army, 1942-45, PTO. Tiffany Found. grantee, NYC, 1967, N. State Coun. Arts grantee, 1985; MacDowell Colony fellow, 1965-69. Roman Catholic. Home: Norway Hill Hancock NH 03449

POLLAZZI, ROGER G. transportation executive; b. 1937; BS, Lawrence Inst. Tech.; MBA, Mich. Rackum Meml. Campus, 1972. With ExCello Corp., Houston, 1964-70, Joy Mfg. Co., Pitts., 1970-83, pres., 1983-88; founder Atlantic Products and Fa-Presto, Pitts., 1988-91; pres., CEO Pullman Co., Lebanon, N.J., 1990—. Office: Harvard Industries Inc 3 Werner Way Ste 210 Lebanon NJ 08833

POLLEN, RAYMOND JAMES, lawyer; b. Manitowoc, Wis., June 10, 1956; s. Frank R. and Clara R. (Aulik) P.; m. Kay A. Wifler, Dec. 31, 1983; 1 child, Joseph. BS, U. Wis., 1978; JD, Marquette U., 1983. Bar: Wis. 1983, U.S. Dist. Ct. Wis. 1983, U.S. Ct. Claims, U.S. Ct. Appeals (7th cir.) 1985, U.S. Supreme Ct. 1986, U.S. Dist. Ct. Ill. 1994. Shareholder Crivello Carlson & Mentkowski, Milw., 1983—. Village atty. Shorewood, Wis., 1995—. Assessor Alverno Coll., Milw., 1981-2002; bd. dirs. Marian Ctr., 1989-95, 97-2001. Mem. ABA, Wis. Bar Assn., Internat. Mcpl. Lawyers Assn. Office: Crivello Carlson Mentkowski 710 N Plankinton Ave Milwaukee WI 53203-2404 E-mail: ray@milwlaw.com.

POLLEY, RICHARD DONALD, microbiologist, inorganics and polymer chemist; b. Bklyn., Feb. 23, 1937; s. George Weston and Evelyn (Tuttle) P.; m. Linda R. Radford, Sept. 21, 1991; children from previous marriage: Gordon MacHeath, Jennifer Elizabeth, Tabitha Isabelle, Sean Sullivan. Student, Trinity Coll., 1954-57; BS, Hofstra U., 1960. Lic. nuclear radiation tech. U.S. Govt., 2003. Asst. advt. mgr. tech. Permatex Chem. Corp., Huntington, N.Y., 1960-61, Sun Chem. Corp., 1961-63; advt. mgr. Celanese Plastics Co., Newark, 1963-67; account dir. McCann Indsl. Tech. Sci. Mktg., N.Y.C., 1967-68, v.p., gen. mgr. Miami, 1968-70; pres. Intercapital Belgium S.A., Brussels, Nassau, Bahamas, Panama City, Panama, 1970-72; cons. Nuclear Regulatory Commn., Atomic City, Idaho, 1975—76; founder, pres., tech. dir. Iodinamics Corp., Lancaster, Pa., El Paso, Tex., El Paso, Tex., 1973-76; founder, CEO, COO, tech. dir. Hydrodine Corp., Miami, 1976—2002, chmn., CEO, tech. dir., 1986—2002, also bd. dirs. Founder, chmn. CEO, COO, tech. dir. Polymorphic Polymers Corp., Miami, 1978—90; founder, COO, tech. dir. Omnidine Corp., Miami, 1980—98, bd. dirs.; pres. and tech. dir. Skin Care Labs. Inc., Miami, 1979—90; bd. dirs., tech. dir. Hydrodine Biotech (Far East) Ltd., Bangkok, Thailand, Hong Kong, Singapore and Kuala Lumpur, 1989—98; CEO, tech. dir. Polllabs., Sao Paulo, Brazil, 1990—2000; tech. dir. Ecology Tech. do Brasil, Sao Paulo, 1993—2000; tech. dir., environ. and agrl. mgr. Environ. Tech. do Brasil, Sao Paulo, 1995—; chief internat. tech. dir. environ. microbiology Gen. Environ. Sci. Corp., Solon, Ohio, 1993—2000; chmn., co-founder Peer Group Influencers Ltd., London, Miami, 1988—98; bd. dirs., v.p. Internat. Airlines, Long Beach, Calif., 1984—2000; CEO, tech. dir. Swiver Corp., Miami, 1994—2002; tech. dir. Aquaterra s.a., Panama City, Panama, 1998—99; tech. dir. chief scientist Snowplace Corp., Panama, 1996—98, Infinity Techs., Ltd., Panama City, 1996—98; COO, CEO, pres., tech. dir. Aegis Protective Coating Corp., Miami, 1996—98; founder, bd. dirs., CEO, pres., tech. dir. PolleyTech Corp. (Estradero Environ. Corp.), Pembroke Pines, Fla., 1998—; overseas dir. field iodine goiter med. demonstration projects Beth Israel Hosp., Harvard U. Med. Sch., 1977—88; lectr. Harvard Bus. Sch., 1980; cons. water microbiology and disinfection control, water environments Pan Am. Health Orgn., others; med. and tech. dir. Enzymes Brasil, Ltd., Sao Paulo, 2001—, med. mgr., tech. dir., Guayaquil, Ecuador, 2001—; chmn. med./sci. adv. bd., found. tech. dir. RAH Found., Napa Valley, Calif., 2001—; med. mktg. dir., cons. Spina Med. Corp., Hallandale, Fla., 2002—03; cons. IGFA Wetlands Project, 2001—; tech. dir. Rapid Rds. Inc., Seattle, 2004—; chief scientist Rapid Rds. Ltd., Beijing, 2004—. Mem. editl. adv. bd. Chem. Week, 1988; contbr. articles to profl. jours.; patentee. Recipient Buckminster Fuller Home of the Future award, 1976. Mem. AAAS, NRA, Am. Concrete Inst., N.Y. Acad. Scis., Internat. Iodine Inst. (chmn. bd. and tech. dir. 1976—), Associaçao de Ciencia e Tecnologia Ambiental (bd. dirs. Sao Paulo 1993—), Amnesty Internat., The Nature Conservancy, World Wildlife Fund, Sierra Club, Audubon Soc., Wilderness Soc., Defenders of Wildlife, Environ. Defense Org., Fla. Wildlife Fedn., Internat. Game Fish Assn., others. Achievements include patents for farm and household water treatment devices, nuclear industry; fields of medicine, environmental protection, agriculture and enzymes soil road building, asphalt and soil enzymes roads, lagoons, aquaculture, ponds, hazardous waste areas soil reservoirs. Office Phone: 954-434-5062. E-mail: estradero@bellsouth.net.

POLLIACK, ADRIAN A. biomedical engineer, researcher; arrived in U.S., 1987; s. Joe and Dinah Polliack; m. Kristin F. Bell, Feb. 5, 2000; 1 child, Samuel Ford. DPhil, Oxford (Eng.) U., 1994. V.p. R & D The Seaberg Co., Inc., Newport, Oreg., 2001—. Recipient Mary E. Switzer Merit Rsch. fellowship, Nat. Inst. on Disability and Rehab. Rsch., U.S. Dept. of Edn., 1998—99.

POLLIN, ABE, professional basketball team executive, builder; b. Phila., Dec. 3, 1923; s. Morris and Jennie (Sack) P.; m. Irene S. Kerchek, May 27, 1945; children: Robert Norman, James Edward. BA, George Washington U., 1945; student, U. Md., 1941-44. Engaged in home bldg. bus., 1945—; pres. Abe Pollin Inc., Balt., 1962—; chmn. Balt. Bullets Basketball Club, Inc. (now Washington Bullets), 1964-97, Washington Wizards, 1997—; chmn. bd., CEO Washington Sports & Entertainment, Washington. Dir. County Fed. Savs. & Loan Assn., Rockville, Md. Bd. dirs. United Jewish Appeal, Nat. Jewish Hosp., Jewish Community Center; bd. dirs., adv. com. John F. Kennedy Cultural Center. Mem. Nat. Assn. Home Builders, Asso. Builders and Contractors Md., Washington Bd. Trade. Jewish. Office: Washington Wizards 718 7th St NW Washington DC 20001-3716 also: Washington Capitals US Air Arena Landover MD 20785 also: Washington Sports & Entertainment MCI Ctr 601 F St NW Washington DC 20004-1605

POLLIN, BURTON RALPH, English educator; b. Worcester, Mass. s. Louis and Rae (Cohen) P.; m. Alice Pollin, Jan. 30, 1944; children: Diana Claire, Myles Clement. BA, CCNY, 1936; PhD, Columbia U., 1962. Tchr. English NYC Bd. Edn., 1936-62, chmn. dept. English, 1956-62; lectr. English CUNY, 1957-62, assoc. prof. to full prof., 1962-73, prof. emeritus, 1973—. Lectr. on Poe NY State Coun. Humanities, 1996—99, 2003—. Author: Education and Enlightenment in the Works of William Godwin, 1962, Godwin Criticism: A Synoptic Bibliography, 1967, Dictionary of Names and Titles in Poe's Collected Works, 1968, Discoveries in Poe, 1970, Benjamin Constant's Translation of Godwin's Political Justice, 1972, The Music for Shelley's Poems: An Annotated Bibliography of 1309 Compositions, 1974, Poe, Creator of Words, 1974, The Imaginary Voyages, vol. 1 of Collected Writings of...Poe, 1994, Word Index to Poe's Fiction, 1982, The Brevities of Poe, vol. 2 of Collected Writings of Poe, 1985, Poe's Writings in the Broadway Jour., 1986, Insights and Outlooks: Essays on Great Writers, 1986, Images of Poe's Works: A Comprehensive Descriptive Catalogue of Illustrations, 1989, The German Face of Poe (with Thomas Hansen), 1995, Poe's Writings in the Southern Literary Messenger, vol. 5 of Collected Writings of Poe, 1986, Poe's Seductive Influence on Great Writers, 2004; adv. bd. editors Poe Studies, 1980—, Poe Rev., 2000—; contbr. over 180 articles to profl. jours. Founder, continuing bd. dirs. Bronxville Beautification Coun., 1980—; active Friends of NY Pub. Libr., Carnegie Hall, Libr. of Bronxville, Eastchester Arts Coun., Columbia U. Libr. Friends, Supporters of Guggenheim Found.; bd. trustees Poe Mus., Richmond, Va. Recipient Poe award, Bronx County Hist. Soc., 2001, Rotary Club award, 2002, Alice and Burton Pollin for effective beautification of Bronxville, 2002; fellow John Hay Whitney, 1947; grantee Am. Philos. Soc., U.S., 1964—65, Am. Philos. Soc., London, 1965, 1968, NY State U. Rsch. Found., 1966, Carl and Lily Pforzheimer, 1966, 1969, SUNY, 1967—73, Am. Coun. Learned Socs., 1968, 1975, 1984, Guggenheim Found., 1973—74, CUNY, 1973, 1980, 1986, NEH, 1983—84, Lectureship on Poe, NY State Humanities Coun., 1996—99, 2003—05. Mem. MLA (life), Poe Studies Assn. (hon., life), Am. Lit. Assn. Avocations: literary research, piano playing, travel, environmentalism. Home: 3 Stoneleigh Plz Apt 4D Bronxville NY 10708

POLLINGER, WILLIAM JOSHUA, lawyer; b. Passaic, N.J., Dec. 14, 1944; s. Irving R. and Ethel (Groudan) P.; m. Helen Rizzo, May 30, 1977; children: Samantha, Zachary. BA, Rutgers U., 1966; JD, Am. U., 1969. Bar: N.J. 1969, U.S. Dist. Ct. N.J. 1969, N.Y. 1981, U.S. Supreme Ct. 1982, U.S. Ct. Appeals (3d cir.) 1986; cert. Civil Trial Atty. N.J. Supreme Ct., 1983; masters level cert. U.S.A. Track and Field Ofcl. Assoc. Krieger & Klein, Passaic, 1969-75; ptnr. Delorenzo & Pollinger, Hackensack, N.J., 1975-84; pres. William J. Pollinger, P.A., Hackensack, 1984-88, Pollinger, Fearns & Kemezis, P.A., 1988-90, Pollinger & Fearns, P.A., Hackensack, 1990-92, William J. Pollinger P.A., Hackensack, N.J., 1992—. Mem. Bergen County Ethics Com., NJ, 1984—88; lectr. ins. N.J.-ICLE. Arbitrator Better Bus. Bur. of Bergen and Rockland Counties, Paramus, N.J., 1983-89, Am. Arbitration Assn., 1983—. Assoc. of Yr. award Builders Assn. No. N.J., Paramus, 1981. Master: Justice Robert L. Clifford Am. Inn of Ct.; mem.: ATLA, Def. Rsch. Inst., Am. Arbitration Assn., Trial Attys. N.J., Bergen County Bar Assn., N.J. State Bar Assn. (ins. law com.), Masons (past master), Phi Delta Phi. Avocation: track and field officiating. Office: 302 Union St Hackensack NJ 07601-4303

POLLIO, RALPH THOMAS, managing editor, writer, magazine publishing consultant; b. Bronx, N.Y., Nov. 1, 1948; s. Thomas and Dolores (Miccioli) P.; m. Rita Lucia Napolitano, Sept. 29, 1974 (div. 1991); 1 child, Christopher. BCE, Manhattan Coll., 1978; postgrad., Columbia U., 1988—. Founding pub., editor, owner Ea. Basketball Publs., Franklin Square, N.Y., 1975-88; cons., ptnr., founder Ea. Basketball Mag., Rochester, Mich., 1988—; founding pub., owner, editor High School News, 1984, EB News, 1981; mng. editor Harman Consumer Group, Woodbury, N.Y. Contbr. articles to mags. and profl. jours., 1985—. Sgt. U.S. Army N.G., 1969-74. Mem. U.S. Basketball Writers Assn. (1st Place award for best mag. feature 1984), ASCE, Soc. Profl. Journalists, Sigma Delta Chi, Internat. Soc. Philos. Enquiry, World Lit. Acad., Mag. Pubs. Assn., Am. Soc. Mag. Editors, Mensa, and numerous other high IQ socs. Roman Catholic. Clubs: N.Y. Road Runners (N.Y.C.), Dix Hills Runners. Avocations: working out, listening to jazz, gourmet cooking, reading, film. Home: 1201 Hempstead Ave Malverne NY 11565-1213

POLLITT, BYRON H. retail executive; BS in Bus. Econs., U. Calif.; MBA, Harvard U. Mgmt. cons. McKinsey & Co.; v.p. corp. ops. planning Walt Disney Co., 1990—92, v.p. bus. planning, 1992—94, CFO, 1994—95, sr. v.p., CFO Disneyland Resorts, 1995—99, exec. v.p., CFO Walt Disney Parks and Resorts, 1999—2003; exec. v.p., CFO Gap, Inc., San Francisco, 2003—. Office: Gap Inc 2 Folsom St San Francisco CA 94105

POLLITT, JEROME JORDAN, art history educator; b. Fair Lawn, N.J., Nov. 26, 1934; s. John Kendall and Doris B. (Jordan) P.; m. Susan Baker Matheson, Feb. 10, 1977. BA, Yale U., 1957; PhD, Columbia U., 1963. Instr. history of art Yale U., New Haven, 1962-64, asst. prof., 1964-68, assoc. prof., 1969-73, prof., 1973-98, prof. emeritus, 1998—, chmn. dept. classics, 1975-77, chmn. dept. history of art, 1981-84, dean, 1986-91. Author: Art and Experience in Classical Greece, 1972, The Ancient View of Greek Art, 1975, Art in the Hellenistic Age, 1986, The Art of Greece: Sources and Documents, 1990, Personal Styles in Greek Sculpture, 1996; editor-in-chief: Am. Jour. Archaeology, 1973-77; contbr. articles to profl. jours. Mem. Archaeol. Inst. Am., Coll. Art Assn. Home: 48 Dillon Rd Woodbridge CT 06525-1219 Office: Dept History of Art Yale U PO Box 208272 New Haven CT 06520-8272 E-mail: Jerome.Pollitt@yale.edu.

POLLNER, JULIA A. financial executive; BBA, Miami U., Oxford, Ohio. CPA, Ohio. With Red Roof Inns Inc., Columbus, Ohio, 1987; v.p., contr., asst. treas. Metatec Internat. Inc., Columbus, v.p. fin., sec., treas., 1997—. Mem. AICPA, Ohio Soc. CPAs, Fin. Execs. Inst. Office: Metatec Internat Inc 7001 Metatec Blvd Dublin OH 43017-3219

POLLNOW, C. lumber company executive; CFO Simpson Investment Co., Seattle. Office: Simpson Investment Co 1201 3d Ave Ste 4900 Seattle WA 98101-3045

POLLOCK, ALEXANDER JOHN, retired banker; b. Indpls., Jan. 28, 1943; s. Alex S. and Doris L. (VanHorn) P.; m. Anne M. Fryfogle, Jan. 27, 1968; children: Elizabeth, Alexander, Evelyn, James. BA, Williams Coll., 1965; MA, U. Chgo., 1966; M.P.A., Princeton U., 1969. Instr. philosophy Lake Forest Coll., (Ill.), 1967; with internat. banking dept. Continental Ill. Nat. Bank, Chgo., 1969-77, v.p., 1977-82, sr. v.p., 1982-85; prin. Nolan Norton & Co., Chgo., 1985-86; chief fin. officer Marine Corp., Milw., 1986; pres. Marine Bank N.A., Milw., 1987; pres., CEO Cmty. Fed. Savs., St. Louis, 1988-90; vis. scholar Fed. Res. Bank of St. Louis, 1991; pres., CEO Fed. Home Loan Bank Chgo., 1991—2004; fellow Am. Enterprise Inst. Pub. Policy Rsch., Washington, 2004—. Bd. dirs. Gt. Lakes Higher Edn. Corp., Allied Capital Corp., Chgo. Mercantile Exch.; past pres. Internat. Union for Housing Fin. Trustee Ill. Coun. on Econ. Edn.; Bd. dirs. Great Books Found. Mem.: Union League Club (Chgo.), Univ. Club (Washington) (past pres.), Phi Beta Kappa. Office: Am Enterprise Inst 1150 Seventeenth St NW Washington DC 20036 Office Phone: 202-862-7190. Business E-Mail: APollock@aei.org. *Omnia superans vi rationis et arte loquendi.*

POLLOCK, BRUCE GERALD, lawyer; b. Providence, Feb. 18, 1947; s. Reuben and Stella (Reitman) P.; m. Sheri Barbara Tepper, Dec. 21, 1969; children: Dawn, Meah. BA, U. R.I., 1968; JD, Suffolk U., 1974. Bar: R.I. 1974, U.S. Supreme Ct. 1978, U.S. Dist. Ct. R.I. 1980. Law clk. R.I. Superior Ct., Providence, 1974, adminstrv. asst. to chief justice, 1975; asst. pub. defender R.I. Dept. Pub. Defender, Providence, 1975-80; pvt. practice Warwick and West Warwick, R.I., 1980—. Adj. instr. So. N.E. Law Sch., New Bedford, Mass., 1990. Dist. chmn. Narragansett Coun. Shawomet Dist. Boy Scouts Am., 1996-98. Fellow R.I. Bar Found. (bd. dirs. 1990-2000; v.p. 2000—); mem. ABA, Nat. Conf. Bar Pres., New Eng. Bar Assn. (del. 1991-93), R.I. Bar Assn. (pres. 1992-93, ho. of dels. 1986—, award of merit 1995). Democrat. Avocations: golf, skiing, stained glass craftsman, bicycling, tai chi. Office: 45 Providence St West Warwick RI 02893-3714 E-mail: brucepollock@juno.com., bgpollock@yahoo.com.

POLLOCK, BRUCE GODFREY, psychiatrist, educator; b. Toronto, Ont., Can., Aug. 18, 1952; s. Ira Justus and Sheila Joy (Godfrey) P.; m. Judith Arluk, May 18, 1982; children: Debra, Ariel. BS, U. Toronto, 1975, MD, 1979; PhD, U. Pitts., 1987. Chief resident Clarke Inst. Psychiatry, Toronto, 1982-83; fellow U. Pitts., 1983-84, asst. prof. dept. psychiatry, 1984-90, assoc. dir. clin. pharmacology dept. psychiatry, 1987-95, assoc. prof. dept. psychiatry and pharmacology, 1990-96, dir. geriat. psychopharm. dept. psychiatry and pharmacology, 1995—, prof. depts. psychiatry, pharmacology and pharm. scis., 1997—, chief acad. divsn. geriatrics and neuropsychiatry, 2001. Contbr. over 250 articles to profl. jours.; contbg. author books in field. Centennial fellow Med. Rsch. Coun. of Can., Ottawa, 1983, Merck fellow geriatric clin. pharmacology, Am. Fedn. for Aging Rsch., N.Y.C., 1988; recipient Geriat. Mental Health award NIMH, Bethesda, Md., 1992, Ind. Scientist award, 1997, Sr. Investigation Award, Am. Assoc. for Geniatric Psychiatry, Bethesda, Md., 2003. Fellow Royal Coll. Physicians Can., Am. Psychiat. Assn. (disting.). Home: 7032 Meade St Pittsburgh PA 15208-2429 Office: Western Psychiat Inst/Clin 3811 Ohara St Pittsburgh PA 15213-2593 Office Phone: 412-246-6274. Business E-Mail: pollockbg@upmc.edu.

POLLOCK, DAVID DANIEL, biologist, educator, research scientist; b. Calif. s. Alan Pollock and Urashan; m. Anabel E. Adler; children: Heather E. Adler-Pollock, Liam D. Adler-Pollock, Gabriel Adler-Pollock. BA in Biochemistry, U. Calif., Berkeley, 1986; PhD, Stanford U., 1995. Burroughs-Wellcome Fund fellow Nat. Inst. for Med. Rsch./Cambridge (England) U., 1997—99, U. Calif., Berkeley, 1999—2000; dir.'s fellow Los Alamos (N.Mex.) Nat. Lab.; asst. prof., adj. La. State U., Baton Rouge, 2000—01, asst. prof., 2001—. Grantee Rsch. Competitiveness Subprogram, State of La. Bd. of Regents, 2001—04; Hitchings-Elion fellow, Burroughs-Wellcome Fund, 1997—2000, R24 Glue grantee, NIH, 2002—, R22/R33 Innovation/Devel. grantee, 2002—. Mem.: AAAS, Internat. Soc. Computational Biologists, Protein Soc., Soc. Systematic Biology. Avocations: guitar, hiking. Office: La State U 202 Life Scis Bldg Baton Rouge LA 70803 E-mail: dpollock@lsu.edu.

POLLOCK, EARL EDWARD, lawyer; b. Decatur, Nebr., Feb. 24, 1928; s. Herman and Della (Rosenthal) P.; m. Betty Sokol, Sept. 8, 1951; children: Stephen, Della, Naomi. BA, U. Minn., 1948; JD, Northwestern U., 1953; LLD (hon.), Morningside Coll., 1995. Bar: D.C. 1955, Va. 1955, Ill. 1959, U.S. Supreme Ct. 1960. Law clk., chief justices Vinson and Warren, U.S. Supreme Ct. Washington, 1953-55; atty. antitrust div. Dept. Justice, Washington, 1955-56, asst. to solicitor gen., 1956-59; ptnr. Sonnenschein Nath & Rosenthal, Chgo., 1959—. Trustee Loyola U., Chgo., 1983-92; life trustee Northwestern Meml. Hosp.; pres. Fla. West Coast Symphony. Mem. Chgo. Bar Assn. (chmn. antitrust law com. 1967-68), ABA (chmn. antitrust law sect. 1979-80), Alumni Assn. Northwestern U. Sch. Law (pres. 1974-75, svc. award 1976). Office: Sonnenschein Nath 233 S Wacker Dr Ste 8000 Chicago IL 60606-6491

POLLOCK, JOHN PHLEGER, lawyer; b. Sacramento, Apr. 28, 1920; s. George Gordon and Irma (Phleger) P.; m. Juanita Irene Gossman, Oct. 26, 1945; children: Linda Pollock Harrison, Madeline Pollock Chiotti, John, Gordon. AB, Stanford U., 1942; JD, Harvard U., 1948. Bar: Calif. 1949, U.S. Supreme Ct. 1954. Ptnr. Musick, Peeler & Garrett, L.A., 1953-60, Pollock, Williams & Berwanger, L.A., 1960-80, Rodi, Pollock, Pettker, Galbraith & Cahill, L.A., 1980-89, of counsel, 1989—. Contbr. articles to profl. publs. Active Boy Scouts Am.; trustee Pitzer Coll., Claremont, Calif., 1968-76, Pacific Legal Found., 1981-91, Fletcher Jones Found., 1969—, Good Hope Med. Found., 1980—. Fellow Am. Coll. Trial Lawyers; mem. ABA, Los Angeles County Bar Assn. (trustee 1964-66). Home: 30602 Paseo Del Valle Laguna Niguel CA 92677-2317 Office: 444 S Flower St Ste 1700 Los Angeles CA 90071-2918 Office Phone: 213-895-4900. E-mail: Phleger1@msn.com.

POLLOCK, KAREN ANNE, computer analyst; b. Elmhurst, Ill., Sept. 6, 1961; d. Michael Paul and Dorothy Rosella (Foskett) P. BS, Elmhurst Coll., 1984; MS, North Cen. Coll., 1993. Formatter Nat. Data Corp., Lombard, Ill., 1985; computer specialist Dept. VA, Hines, Ill., 1985—. Lutheran. Avocations: cross-stitch, mystery books, bowling, bicycling, softball.

POLLOCK, M. DUNCAN, advertising executive; m. Christen Houlahan, 1983; children: Michael, John. BA in Art History, Yale U.; MBA, NYU. Journalist Rock Mountain News, Denver; asst. account exec. Young & Rubican, v.p., mgmt. supr.; with Hal Riney & Ptnrs., San Francisco; sr. v.p. Ammirati & Puris, N.Y.C., 1985-94; mem. merger transition team Ammirati Puris Lintas (merger Ammirati & Puris, Lintas N.Y.), N.Y.C., 1994-95, chmn., CEO, 1995-98, pres. N.Am., 1997-98; pres. Focus Vision Worldwide Inc., Stamford, Conn., 1998—. Bd. dirs. Upward, Inc., The Advt. Coun.; trustee Kent Sch. Ford Found. fellow Ctr. for Internat. Studies, NYU. Mem. Am. Assn. Advt. Agys. (mem. bd. govs. Ea. region, mem. large agy. mgmt. com.). Office: Focus Vision Worldwide Inc 1266 E Main St Stamford CT 06902-3546

POLLOCK, MARGARET LANDAU PEGGY, elementary school educator; b. Jefferson City, Mo., Oct. 18, 1936; d. William Wold and Grace Elizabeth (Creamer) Anderson; children by previous marriage: Elizabeth, Charles, Christopher, Jeffrey; m. William Whalen Pollock, Jan. 30, 1993. AA, Stephens Coll., 1956; BS in Elem. Edn., U. Mo., Columbia, 1958; MA in Reading Edn., U. Mo., Kansas City, 1987. Cert. elem. tchr., Mo. Kindergarten tchr. Columbia Schs., 1958-59, Moberly (Mo.) Schs., 1960-62; 1st grade tchr. Kansas City Schs., 1962-63; kindergarten tchr. Independence (Mo.) Schs., 1966-75; chpt. I reading specialist Thomas Hart Benton Elem. Sch., Independence, 1975-93; book reviewer Corpus Christi (Tex.) Caller Times, 1994—; children's libr. Corpus Christi Pub. Libr., 1995-97; dir. Johnson City (Tex.) Libr., 1997—. Cons., presenter in field. Bd. dirs. Boys and Girls Club, Independence, 1990-93; coord. Independence Reading Fair, 1989-93; coord. books and tutoring Salvation Army, Kansas City, 1990-92. Mem. AAUW, Internat. Reading Assn. (People to People del. to USSR 1991, local v.p. 1990-91, pres. 1991-92), Internat. Platform Assn., Austin Writer's League, Archeol. Inst. Am., Tex. Libr. Assn., Earthwatch, Nature Conservancy, Sierra Club, Phi Kappa Phi, Pi Lambda Theta (pres. Beta Upsilon chpt. 1992-93). Avocations: native american history, rights and education, archeology, reading, travel, conservation. Home: PO Box 482 Johnson City TX 78636-0482

POLLOCK, R. JEFFREY, lawyer; b. San Francisco, Jan. 5, 1946; BA, DePauw U., 1968; MT, Harvard U., 1971; JD, Northeastern U., 1976. Bar: Ohio 1976. Asst. sec. dept. community devel. Commonwealth of Mass., 1972—73; atty. McDonald, Hopkins, Cleve.; gen. counsel Metaltyar Corp., 2001—. Gen. counsel Metaldyne Corp. Mem. ABA, Ohio State Bar Assn., Cleve. Bar Assn. Office: McDonald Hopkins 2100 Bank One Ctr 600 Superior Ave E Ste 2100 Cleveland OH 44114-2653 Office Phone: 216-348-5400. E-mail: jpollck@mcdonaldhopkins.com.

POLLOCK, RACHEL REBECCA, publishing executive, educator; d. John Andrew and Rosemarie Millin; m. Timothy Paul Pollock, Sept. 26, 1998; 1 child, Samuel Ayden. BA in German and Comm., Heidelberg Coll., 1995; MA in Speech Comm., Miami U., 1996. Pres. Floating Table Co. Pub., North Canton, Ohio, 2001—. Cons. Drawing Rm., Hartville, Ohio, 2003—. Author: Closing Pandora's Box: Unlocking the Woman-Hero; editor: (e-zine) Table's Edge; dir.: (plays) The Laramie Project. Dir. forensics Heidelberg Coll., Tiffin, Ohio, 1999—2002. Named Educator of Yr., Ohio Forensics Assn., 2002—03. Mem.: Nat. Communication Assn. (corr.), Internat. Forensics Assn. (corr.; exec. liasons officer 2000—01), Ohio Forensics Assn. (hon.; mem. at large 2001—02), Poetry Soc. Am., Ohio Poetry Assn. (hon.; judge 2003). Office: Floating Table Company Publishing 8362 La Donna Circle NW North Canton OH 44720 E-mail: ftco@earthlink.net.

POLLOCK, ROBERT ELWOOD, nuclear scientist; b. Regina, Sask., Can., Mar. 2, 1936; s. Elwood Thomas and Harriet Lillian (Rooney) Pollock; m. Jean Elizabeth Virtue, Sept. 12, 1959; children: Bryan Thomas, Heather Lynn, Jeffrey Parker, Jennifer Lee. BSc hon., U. Man., Can., 1957; MA, Princeton U., 1959, PhD, 1963. Instr. Princeton (N.J.) U., 1961—63, asst. prof., 1964—69, rsch. physicist, 1969—70; Nat. Rsch. Coun. Can. postdoctoral fellow Harwell, England, 1963—64; assoc. prof. Ind. U., Bloomington, 1970—73, prof., 1973—84, disting. prof., 1984—2001, prof. emeritus, 2001—, dir. Cyclotron Facility, 1973—79, mem. nuc. sci. adv. com., 1977—80. Recipient Alexander von Humboldt Sr. U.S. Scientist award, 1985—88. Fellow: Am. Phys. Soc. (Bonner prize 1992). Home: 2811 Dale Ct Bloomington IN 47401-2414 Office: Ind U Swain Hall Dept Physics Bloomington IN 47405

POLLOCK, SAMUEL, diversified financial services company executive; b. Montreal, Que., Can., Dec. 15, 1925; m. Mary Mimi Kinsella, Dec. 27, 1962; children: Mary, Sam, Rachel. Grad., Westmount H.S. Chmn. John Labatt Ltd., Carena Bancorp Equities Ltd.; chief exec. ofcr., gov. Toronto Blue Jays, Toronto, 1994—. Bd. dirs. Carena Devels. Ltd., John Labatt Ltd., Trizen Corp., Toronto Blue Jays Club, Hockey Can. Chmn. Internat. and Olympic Com. Hockey Can., 1982-88; corporate chmn. Can. Cerebral Palsy, 1989; co-chmn. Miss Edgars and Miss Cramps Bldg. Campaign, 1987-89. Decorated officer Order of Can.; named to Can. Sports Hall of Fame, Hockey Hall of Fame. Mem. Gt. Montrealers. Office: John Labatt Ltd, PO Box 811 BCE Place, 181 Bay St Ste 200 Toronto ON Canada M5J 2T3

POLLOCK, STEPHEN MICHAEL, operations research engineer, educator, consultant; b. N.Y.C., Feb. 15, 1936; s. Meyer and Frances R. Pollock; m. Bettina Dorn, Nov. 22, 1962; children: Joshua, Aaron, Ethan. B in Engring. Physics, Cornell U., 1958; SM, MIT, 1960, PhD in Physics and Ops. Research, 1964. Mem. tech. staff Arthur D. Little Inc., Cambridge, Mass., 1964-65; asst. prof. Naval Postgrad. Sch., Monterey, Calif., 1965-68, assoc. prof., 1968-69, U. Mich., Ann Arbor, 1969-73, prof., dept. indsl. and ops. engring., 1974—, chmn. dept., 1980-90. Cons. to over 40 orgns. Area editor Ops. Rsch. Jour., 1977-82; sr. editor Inst. Indsl. Engrs. Trans., 1985-89, Army Sci. Bd., 1994-99; contbr. more than 60 tech. papers to profl. jours. Fellow, Space Tech. Labs., 1960, Inst. Ops. Rsch. Mgmt. Sci.; sr. fellow NSF, 1975. Fellow: AAAS; mem.: Nat. Acad. Engring., Ops. Rsch. Soc. Am. (pres. 1986—87), Inst. Mgmt. Sci. Office: U of Mich Dept Indsl Ops Engring Ann Arbor MI 48109-2117

POLLOCK, STEWART GLASSON, lawyer, former state supreme court justice; b. East Orange, N.J., Dec. 21, 1932; BA, Hamilton Coll., 1954, LLD (hon.), 1995; LLB, NYU, 1957; LLM, U. Va., 1988. Bar: N.J. 1958. Asst. U.S. atty., Newark, 1958-60; ptnr. Schenck, Price, Smith & King, Morristown, N.J., 1960-74, 76-78; commr. N.J. Dept. Pub. Utilities; counsel to gov. State of N.J., Trenton, 1978-79; assoc. justice N.J. Supreme Ct., Morristown, 1979-99; of counsel Riker Danzig Hyland & Perretti, Morristown, 1999—. Mem. N.J. Commn. on Investigation, 1976-78; chmn. coordinating coun. on life-sustaining med. treatment decision making Nat. Ctr. for State Cts., 1994-96; bd. dirs. NYU Law Ctr. Found., Inst. Jud. Adminstrn., N.J. Conservation Found., 1999-2003; chmn. commn. on the rules of profl. conduct N.J. Supreme Ct., 2000—. Assoc. editor N.J. Law Jour.; contbr. articles to legal jours. Trustee Coll. Medicine and Dentistry, N.J., 1976. Fellow Am. Coll. Comml. Arbitrators; mem. ABA (chmn. appellate judges conf. 1991-92), N.J. Bar Assn. (trustee 1973-78), Am. Judicature Soc. (dir. 1984-88), Morris County Bar Assn. (pres. 1973). Office: Riker Danzig Scherer Hyland & Perretti LLP Hdqs Plz 1 Speedwell Ave Morristown NJ 07962-1981

POLLOCK, WILSON F. architectural firm executive; BArch, Pa. State U.; MS in Architecture, Columbia U. Cert. Nat. Coun. Archtl. Registration Bds.; registered architect, 15 states. Formerly with Sert, Jackson Assocs., Cambridge, Mass., Cambridge Seven Assocs., Eshback Pullinger, Phila., Emo Goldfinger, London; founder, pres. ADD Inc., Cambridge, 1971—. Lectr. in field. Prin. works include One Federal Street Renovation, Boston, Hewlett Packard's Med. Products Group Expansion, Andover, Mass., 404 Wyman Street, Waltham, Mass. Bd. trustees Boston Found. for Architects; bd. dirs. Newton Community Devel. Found., Jackson Homestead Mus.; frequent sem. leader Build Boston. Recipient Alumni Achievement award Pa. State U., 1991. Fellow AIA; mem. I.D.R.C., Nat. Assn. Indsl. and Office Parks (assoc.), Boston Soc. Architects (past pres.), Urban Land Inst. Office: ADD Inc 210 Broadway Cambridge MA 02139-1944

POLLOCK-O'BRIEN, LOUISE MARY, public relations executive; b. Tarentum, Pa., Mar. 14, 1948; d. Louis P. and Amelia M. (Ballay) Pollock; m. Vincent Miles O'Brien. BS, Ind. U. of Pa., 1970. Tchr. Archbishop Wood H.S., Warminster, Pa., 1970-75; spokesperson, publicist Calif. Olive Industry, Fresno, 1976-78; account exec. Ketchum Pub. Rels., N.Y.C., 1979-81, account supr., 1982-83, v.p., 1984, v.p., group mgr., 1985-88, sr. v.p., group mgr., 1988-89, assoc. dir., dir. food mktg., sr. v.p., 1990-91; chmn. Aronow & Pollock Comm., Inc., N.Y.C., 1991—. Mem. pub. rels. adv. com. Mayor's Vol. Action Com., N.Y.C., 1986; mem. food svc. adv. bd. L.I. City Coll., Bklyn., 1987-88. Y.p., fundraiser West 76th St. Block Assn., N.Y.C., 1982. Mem. Internat. Foodservice Editl. Coun. (v.p., bd. dirs. 1984-85). Avocations: watercolor painting, skiing. Office: Aronow & Pollock Comm Inc 665 Broadway New York NY 10012-4408 Office Phone: 212-941-1414. E-mail: LPollock@apc-pr.com.

POLOIAN, LYNDA GAMANS, retailing educator; b. Manchester, N.H., Nov. 7, 1943; d. Herbert V. and Rose A. (Hammarbeck) Rauding; children: Kristen Soterion, Erik. BA in Psychology, U. N.H., 1976; MEd, Notre Dame Coll., Manchester, N.H., 1979. Sales promotion dir. A. Machinist, Inc., Manchester, 1966-78; prin. R.G. Cons., Manchester, 1977-89; prof. retailing So. N.H. U. (formerly N.H. Coll.), Manchester, 1975—; pres. Silk Accent, Inc., Manchester, 1991-97. Ptnr. Sylyn Enterprise Senderian Berhad, Alor Setar, Kedah, Malaysia, 1991-93; asst. prof. Lansdown Coll., London, 1985-86; presenter in field. Author: Retailing Principles: A Global Outlook, 2003; Co-author: (textbooks) Fashion: A Marketing Approach, 1983, Retailing: New Perspectives, 1992; (jour.) Nat. Bus. Edn. Assn. Yearbook, 1994. Mem. Miss N.H. Scholarship Program State Com., 1982-89; chair edn. com. Retail Merchants Assn. of N.H. Mem. Am. Collegiate Retailing Assn. (pres. 2000-2002, mem. exec. bd.). Avocations: art, watercolor and oil painting, designing silk scarves. Office: So NH Univ 2500 N River Rd Manchester NH 03106-1045 Office Phone: 603-644-3181. E-mail: l.poloian@snhu.edu.

POLON, IRA H. lawyer; b. N.Y.C., Mar. 9, 1943; BA, Lehigh U., 1965; LLB, Columbia U., 1968. Bar: N.Y. 1968, D.C. 1971, U.S. Ct. Appeals (D.C. cir.) 1972. Ptnr. Dickstein Shapiro Morin & Oshinsky LLP, Washington. Mem. ABA (mem. corporation, banking and bus. law sect.), D.C. Bar, N.Y. State Bar Assn., Bar Assn. D.C. Office: Dickstein Shapiro Morin & Oshinsky LLP 2101 L St NW Washington DC 20037-1526 E-mail: poloni@dsmo.com.

POLONCHAK, RICHARD, music educator; s. Andrew and Julia (Giglio) Polonchak; m. Cathy Fulkrod, July 29, 1972; children: Michael, Matthew. MusB Music ed., Duquesne U., Pitts., PA, 1966—70, MusM ed., 1970—72. Licensed Professional Counselor DC Bd. of Profl. Counseling, 1996, Bioen-

ergetic Therapist Phila. Inst. for Bioenergetic Analysis, 1996. Bioenergetic therapist Polonchak Ednl. Associates, Silver Spring, Md., 1983—; prin. bassoonist US Marine Band & White Ho. Orch., Washington, 1972—79. Bassoon instr. U. of the DC (formerly Fed. City Coll.), Washington, 1974—77; bassoon clinician Custom Music Co., Ferndale, Mich., 1978—; bassoon instr. Cath. U. of Am., Washington, 1984—85, U. of Va., Charlottesville, Va., 1984—85, Am. Band Coll., Ashland, Oreg., 1985—, James Madison U., Harrisonburg, Va., 1990—91. Author: (textbook) Primary Handbook for Bassoon, (articles) The Double Reed, Bandworld Mag., The Sch. Musician, The Instrumentalist; contbr. redesigned musical instrument the Kroner Bassoon. GY Sgt. USMC, 1972—79, Washington, DC. Mem.: Internat. Double Reed Soc., Am. Fedn. of Musicians, DC Guild for Body Psychotherapy, US Assn. for Body Psychotherapy, Phila. Inst. for Bioenergetic Analysis, Internat. Inst. for Bioenergetic Analysis, Am. Psychotherapy Assn., Am. Counseling Assn.

POLONSKY, ARTHUR, artist, educator; b. Lynn, Mass., June 6, 1925; s. Benjamin and Celia (Hurwitz) P.; children: Eli, D.L., Gabriel. Diploma with highest honors, Sch. Mus. Fine Arts, Boston, 1948. Instr. painting dept. Sch. Mus. Fine Arts, Boston, 1950-60; asst. prof. dept. fine arts Brandeis U., 1954-65; assoc. prof. Boston U., 1965-90, prof. emeritus, 1990—. Exhibited in group shows at Met. Mus., NYC, 1950, The Salon Des Jeunes Peintres, Paris, 1950, Stedelijk Mus., Amsterdam, The Netherlands, 1950, one-man shows include Boris Mirski Gallery, Boston, 1950, exhibited in group shows at Carnegie Internat. Expn., 1951, Boston Arts Festival, 1954, one-man shows include Boris Mirski Gallery, 1954, exhibited in group shows at Boston Arts Festival, 1955, one-man shows include Boris Mirski Gallery, 1956, exhibited in group shows at Inst. Contemporary Art, Boston, 1960, one-man shows include Boris Mirski Gallery, 1964, Durlacher Gallery, NYC, 1965, Mickelson Gallery, Washington, 1966, Boston Pub. Libr., 1969, Mickelson Gallery, 1974, exhibited in group shows at Mus. Fine Arts, Boston, 1976, one-man shows include Boston Ctr. for Arts, 1983, Exhibited in group shows at Boston Arts Festival, 1985, Expressionism in Boston, Decordova Mus., Lincoln, Mass., 1986, one-man shows include Starr Gallery, Boston, 1987, Boston Pub. Libr., 1990, Fitchburg Art Mus., 1990, exhibited in group shows at Palais Univ. de Strasbourg, France, 1992, one-man shows include Boston Pub. Libr., 1993, exhibited in group shows at Boston's Honored Artists, Danforth Mus., Framingham, Mass., 1995, one-man shows include Boston Pub. Libr., 1996, 1999, exhibited in group shows at Decordova Mus., Lincoln, Mass., 2002, one-man shows include Kantar Fine Arts, Newton, Mass., 2002, exhibited in group shows at Sagendorph Gallery, Keene State Coll., Keene, NH, 2003, Francesca Anderson Gallery, Lexington, Mass., 2004, Represented in permanent collections Mus. Fine Arts, Boston, Fogg Mus., Harvard U., Addison Gallery of Am. Art, Andover, Mass., Stedelijk Mus., Amsterdam, Walker Art Ctr., Mpls., Zimmerli Art Mus., Rutgers U., New Brunswick, NJ, Honolulu Acad. Arts, Decordova Mus., Lincoln, Mass., High Mus. Art, Atlanta. Recipient Louis Comfort Tiffany award for painting, 1951, 1st prize Boston Arts Festival, 1954; European travelling fellow Sch. Mus. Fine Art, Boston, 1948-50 Mem. Artists Equity Assn., Inc. (founding, former dir. New Eng. chpt.). Address: 364 Cabot St Newtonville MA 02460-2252

POLOVITZ, MICHAEL, state legislator; m. Barbara Polovitz; 4 children. MusM, U. Mich. Mem. N.D. Senate from 42d dist., Bismark, 2001—. With USN, 1944-46. Democrat. Office: 2529 9th Ave N Grand Forks ND 58203 E-mail: mpolovit@state.nd.us.

POLOZOLA, FRANK JOSEPH, federal judge; b. Baton Rouge, Jan. 15, 1942; s. Steve A. Sr. and Caroline C. (Lucito) P.; m. Linda Kay White, June 9, 1962; children: Gregory Dean, Sheri Elizabeth, Gordon Damian. Student bus. adminstrn., La. State U., 1959-62, JD, 1965. Bar: La. 1965. Law clk. to U.S. Dist. Ct. Judge E. Gordon West, 1965-66; assoc. Seale, Smith & Phelps, Baton Rouge, 1966-68, ptnr., 1968-73; part-time magistrate U.S. Dist. Ct. (mid. dist.) La., Baton Rouge, 1972-73, magistrate, 1973-80, judge, 1980—, chief judge, 1998—. Adj. prof. Law Ctr., La. State U., 1977-95. Bd. dirs. Cath. High Sch. Mem. La. Bar Assn., Baton Rouge Bar Assn., Fed. Judges Assn., 5th Cir. Dist. Judges Assn., La. State U. L Club, KC, Wex Malone Inns of Ct., Omicron Delta Kappa. Roman Catholic. Office: US Dist Ct Russell B Long Fed Bldg & US Courthouse 777 Florida St Ste 313 Baton Rouge LA 70801-1717

POLSBY, GAIL K. psychotherapist; b. Washington, Jan. 13, 1939; d. Thomas Edward and Elise Wildman (Hammer) Kissling; m. Allen I. Polsby, Aug. 30, 1963; children: Daniel, Abigail. BA, U. Md., 1960; MSW, Cath. U., 1963. Mem. faculty Washington Sch. Psychiatry, 1967—2001, chmn. bd. dirs., 2001—; pvt. practice psychotherapy, Chevy Chase, Md., 1969—; cons. doctoral program Clin. Social Work Inst., Washington, 1999—. Sec., bd. dirs. Washington Sch. Psychiatry, 1995—2001, chair faculty coun. Editor quar. newspaper Washington Sch. Psychiatry News, 1997. Mem. Am. Group Psychotherapy Assn., Nat. Fedn. Clin. Social Workers. Avocations: hiking, biking. Home: 5651 Bent Branch Rd Bethesda MD 20816-1049

POLSKY, CYNTHIA HAZEN, artist, art collector, art dealer; b. N.Y.C., Feb. 28, 1939; m. Leon B. Polsky; 2 children. BA, Marymount Coll., 1978; MBA, Fordham U., 1981. Art collector arts of Southeast Asia and India, 20th century American and European paintings, sculpture, 19th and 20th century decorative arts; one-woman shows include U.S. galleries and mus., Represented in permanent collections Corcoran Mus., Washington, D.C., Fogg Mus., Cambridge, Mass., Johnson Mus., Cornell U., Ithaca, N.Y., N.Y. Acad. Scis. and Rockefeller U., N.Y.C. Mem. collector's com. Nat. Gallery Art; trustee Met. Mus. Art, N.Y.C., mem. acquisitions com., mem. exec. com., chmn. membership com.; hon. life trustee Asia Soc., Storm King Art Ctr., Mountainville, NY; trustee, vice chair, mem. exec. com. Am. Acad. in Rome; trustee Pierpont Morgan Libr, N.Y.C.; mem. Bryant Park Art Commn.; mem. exec. com. Rockefeller U. Coun. Office: 667 Madison Ave New York NY 10021

POLSKY, DONALD PERRY, architect; b. Milw., Sept. 30, 1928; s. Lew and Dorothy (Geisenfeld) P.; m. Corinne Shirley Neer, Aug. 25, 1957; children: Jeffrey David, Debra Lynn. BArch, U. Nebr., Lincoln, 1951; postgrad., U. So. Calif., 1956, U. Calif., Los Angeles, 1957, U. Nebr., Omaha, 1964, U. Ill., 1965. Project architect Richard Neutra, Architect, Los Angeles, 1953-56, Daniel Dworsky, Architect, Los Angeles, 1956; prin. Polsky, AIA & Assocs., Los Angeles, 1956-62, Omaha, 1964—; dir. dept. architecture MCA, Inc., Universal City, Calif., 1962-64. Founder Arch. Sch. U. Nebr. Prin. works include Mills residence, 1958, apt. bldgs., 1960, Polsky residence, 1961, Milder residence, 1965. Chmn. Design Control I480 Study Mayor's Riverfront Devel., Omaha, 1969, 71; pres. Swanson Sch. Community Club, Omaha, 1972; mem. Mayor's Adv. Panel Design Services, Omaha, 1974; vice chmn. Omaha Zoning Bd. Appeals, 1976; dir. Siena/Francis House. Recipient archtl. awards Canyon Crier Newspaper, Los Angeles, 1960, House and Home Mag., Life Mag., AIA, Santa Barbara, Calif., 1962, Gold medal AIA Nebr., 2002. Mem. AIA (pres. Omaha chpt. 1968, fellow 2003, Harry F. Cunningham Gold medal 2002), Nebr. Soc. Archs. (pres. 1975, awards 1964, 68, 87, 91, 93, 94, 95, 97, 01, Firm of Yr. 1997, Harry F. Cunningham Gold medal 2002). Achievements include completed the drawings of our state capitol, saw it through the 10 years of construction to completion. Home: 10010 Frederick St Omaha NE 68124-2651 Office Phone: 402-391-7176 15.

POLSTER, LEONARD H. investment company executive; b. Columbus, Ohio, June 24, 1921; s. Max and Henrietta Polster; m. Constance L. Buderus, Mar. 20, 1948 (dec. Aug. 1967); children: Leonard M., Lance E., Lewis E.; m. Edith Motridge, Nov. 19, 1968. BA, Ohio State U., 1942. Pres. Polster, Inc., 1952-68, pres. real estate and investments co., 1968—; sr. v.p. PaineWebber Inc., L.A. and Rancho Santa Fe, Calif., 1971-91. Author: Pearls Before Swine, 1994. Pres. Polster Found., Rancho Santa Fe, 1988—; fin. officer, bd. dirs. San Dieguito Boys Club, Solana Beach, Calif., 1991—; bd. dirs. Fairbanks Ranch Cmty. Svcs. Dist., Rancho Santa Fe, 1987-92; pres. Fairbanks Ranch Assn., Rancho Santa Fe, 1985-86, bd. dirs., 1984-86. With USAF, 1942-46. Recipient Commitment to Youth award San Dieguito Boys and Girls Club, 1989, Chancellor's Philanthropy award Found. for Edn. Achievement, 2002, Outstanding Philanthropist award Assn. Fund Raising Profls., San Diego, 2003; Olympic torch bearer, 1996, 2002, Outstanding Philanthropist award Assn. Fundraising Profls. San Diego Chpt., 2003; Boys Club br. named in his honor, Carmel Valley, Calif., 2000, Scripps breast care bldg. named in his honor, 2001. Mem.: Scripps Heritage Circle, Fairbanks Ranch Country Club, Phi Alpha Theta. Republican. Presbyterian. Avocations: tennis, reading, music. Home and Office: PO Box 8291 Rancho Santa Fe CA 92067-8291

POLUMBO, JOHN, communications executive; Grad., U. Pitts.; MS in Mgmt., Stanford U. Founder, pres. Nat. Tel. Sys., 1983; dir. mktg. ISA-COMM; sr. exec. Sprint Comm.; v.p. Synbase, Inc.; pres. consumer markets group Pacific Bell, 1995; pres., CEO Pacific Bell Mobile Svcs. (now Cingular Wireless), 1997; pres., COO Excite; pres. Concert's Global Svcs.; sr. v.p. AT&T Bus. Global Ventures, Global Mktg. and Global Wholesale Orgns. AT&T Corp., 1999—2002, pres., CEO AT&T Consumer, 2002—. Office: AT&T Corp One AT&T Way Bedminster NJ 07921

POLVERINI, PETER J. dean, dental educator; m. Carol Polverini. B in biology, Marquette U., 1969, DDS Dental-Oral Pathology, 1973; DMS, Harvard U. Cert. in oral and maxillofacial pathology Harvard U. Asst. prof. dept. diagnostic and surgical sciences U. Pittsburgh Sch. Dental Medicine, 1977—81; various positions Northwestern U. Med. and Dental Sch., 1981—92; prof. dentistry and chief oral and maxillofacial pathology U. Mich. Sch. Dentistry, 1992—95, chair dept. oral medicine, pathology, and surgery, 1995—96, chair dept. oral medicine, pathology, and oncology, 1996—2000, Donald A. Kerr Endowed Collegiate Prof., 1996—2000, dean, 2003—, U. Minn. Sch. Dentistry, 2000—03. Mem. editl. bd. Lab. Investigation, Jour. Oral Pathology and Medicine; assoc. editor Angiogenesis. Address: U Mich Sch Dentistry 1011 N Univ Ave Ann Arbor MI 48109-1078*

POMBO, RICHARD, congressman, rancher, farmer; b. Tracy, Calif., 1961, m. Annette, 1983; children: Richard Jr., Rena, Rachael. Student, Calif. State U., Pomona, 1981-83. Councilman City of Tracy, 1991-92; mayor pro-tem Tracy City Coun., 1992; mem. U.S. Congress from 11th Calif. dist., 1993—; mem. agrl. com., chmn. subcom. on livestock and horticulture; mem. resources com., transp. and infrastructure com. Chmn. Pvt. Property Rights Task Force, 1993-94, Endangered Species Act Task Force, 1995-96; co-chmn. Spkr.'s Environ. Task Force, 1996. Co-founder San Joaquin County Citizen's Land Alliance, Calif., 1986—; active San Joaquin County Econ. Devel. Assn., Tracy Bus. Improvement Dist., City Coun. (vice chmn. Cmty. Devel. Agy., Cmty. Parks Com., and Waste Mgmt. Com.), San Joaquin County Rep. Ctrl. Com. Mem. Rotary Club. Republican. Roman Catholic. Office: US Ho Reps 2411 Rayburn HOB Washington DC 20515

POMERANCE, HERBERT HART, pediatrician; b. N.Y.C., Mar. 28, 1918; s. Nathaniel and Ida (Warfman) P.; m. Ruth Elizabeth Segal, Dec. 25, 1940 (dec.); children: Glenn N., Roger M. BS, NYU, 1937; MD, Columbia U., 1941. Licentiate Am. Bd. Pediatrics. Intern Meml. Hosp., Wilmington, Del., 1941-42; resident Gouverneur Hosp., N.Y.C., 1946-47, Willard Parker Hosp., N.Y.C., 1947; chief resident Lincoln Hosp., N.Y.C., 1948; pvt. practice pediatrics N.Y.C., 1949-70; chmn. pediatrics Charleston (W.Va.) Area Med. Ctr., 1970-73; prof., chmn. dept. pediatrics W.Va. U. Sch. Medicine, Charleston, 1973-84; prof. pediatrics U. South Fla., Tampa, 1984—, prof., chmn. pediatrics, 1990-91. Author: Growth Standards in Children, 1979; co-editor: Topics in Pediatrics, 1990. Maj., M.C., U.S. Army, 1942-46. Fellow Am. Acad. Pediatrics (chpt. chmn. W.Va. chpt. 1976-82, mem. com. on practice 1974-84, chmn. com. on comm. Fla. chpt. 1990—2001). Avocations: computers, stained glass. Home: Apt 807 2611 Bayshore Blvd Tampa FL 33629-7362 Office: Ste 200 17 Davis Blvd Tampa FL 33606-3438 Office Phone: 813-259-8802. Business E-Mail: hpomeran@hcs.usf.edu.

POMERANTZ, CHARLOTTE, writer; b. Bklyn., July 24, 1930; d. Abraham L. and Phyllis (Cohen) P.; m. Carl Marzani, Nov. 12, 1966; children: Gabrielle Rose, Daniel Avram. BA, Sarah Lawrence Coll., 1953. Children's books include The Bear Who Couldn't Sleep, 1965, The Moon Pony, 1967, Ask the Windy Sea, 1968, Why You Look Like You Whereas I Look Like Me, 1968, The Day They Parachuted Cats on Borneo, 1971 (chosen for Internat. Year of the Child 1977-78), The Princess and the Admiral, 1974 (Jane Addams Children's Book award), The Piggy in the Puddle, 1974 (Featured on Reading Rainbow in Claymation, 1992, NYT Outstanding Picture Book of the Year award 1974), The Ballad of the Long Tailed Rat, 1975, Detective Poufy's First Case, 1976, The Mango Tooth, 1977 (Jr. Literary Guild Selection), The Downtown Fairy Godmother, 1978, The Tamarindo Puppy and Other Poems, 1980 (an ALA Notable Book), Noah's and Namah's Ark, 1980, If I Had a Paka, 1982 (Jane Addams Honor award 1983), Buffy and Albert, 1982, Posy, 1983 (1984 Christopher award), Whiff, Sniff, Nibble and Chew, 1984, Where's the Bear?, 1984, The Half-Birthday Party (Jr. Literary Guild Selection), 1984, All Asleep, 1984, One Duck, Another Duck, 1984, How Many Trucks Can a Tow Truck Tow? (Children's Book of the Year Libr. of Congress 1991) 1987, Timothy Tall Feather, 1987, The Chalk Doll (Top 10 Picture Books of 1989 Boston Globe, Parents Choice award, 1990) 1989, Flap Your Wings and Try, 1989, Serena Katz, 1992, The Outside Dog (One of 100 Books Recommended by the N.Y. Pub. Libr., 1993, ALA Notable) 1993, Halfway to Your House, 1993, Here Comes Henny, 1994, Mangaboom, 1997, You're Not My Best Friend Anymore, 1998 (Jr. Libr. Guild Selection 1998), Poncho's Older Brother, 1998, The Birthday Letters, 2000, The Mousery, 2000; co-author, lyricist play Eureka!, 1997; author radio play Whiff Sniff Nibble and Chew, 1997; contbr. stories to mags.; spl. editorial asst.: Einstein on Peace, 1960; editor: A Quarter Century of Un-Americana, 1963. Address: 260 W 21st St New York NY 10011-3447

POMERANTZ, JAMES ROBERT, psychology educator, academic administrator; b. N.Y.C., Aug. 21, 1946; s. Mihiel Charles and Elizabeth (Solheim) P.; divorced; children: Andrew Emil, William James; m. Mary B. McIntire, May 23, 1998. BA, U. Mich., 1968; PhD, Yale U., 1974. Prize teaching fellow Yale U., New Haven, 1973-74; asst. prof. psychology Johns Hopkins U., Balt., 1974-77; assoc. prof. SUNY, Buffalo, 1977-83, prof., 1983-88, chmn. dept. psychology, 1986-88, assoc. dean, 1983-86; dean social scis., Elma W. Schneider prof. psychology Rice U., Houston, 1988-95; provost, prof. cognitive and linguistic scis. Brown U., Providence, 1995-98, acting pres., 1997; adj. prof. psychology, dir. neuroscis. Rice U., Houston, 1998-99, prof. psychology, 2000—. Adj. prof. Baylor Coll. Medicine, 1992—. Editor: Perceptual Organization, 1981, The Perception of Structure, 1991. Fellow APA, Am. Psychol. Soc.; mem. Psychonomic Soc., Soc. Exptl. Psychologists. Office Phone: 713-348-3419. E-mail: pomeran@rice.edu.

POMERANTZ, MARTIN, chemistry educator, researcher; b. N.Y.C., May 3, 1939; s. Harry and Pauline (Sietz) P.; m. Maxine Miller, June 4, 1961; children: Lee Allan, Wendy Jane, Heidi Lauren. BS, CCNY, 1959; MS, Yale U., 1961, PhD, 1964. NSF postdoctoral fellow U. Wis.-Madison, 1963-64; asst. prof. Case Western Res. U., Cleve., 1964-69; assoc. prof. chemistry Yeshiva U., N.Y.C., 1969-74, prof., 1974-76, chmn. dept., 1971-72, 73-76; prof. chemistry U. Tex.-Arlington, 1976—; co-dir. Ctr. for Advanced Polymer Rsch., 1988-91; dir. Ctr. for Advanced Polymer Rsch., 1991—; vis. assoc. prof. U. Wis.-Madison, 1972; vis. prof. Columbia U., N.Y.C., 1970-75, Ben Gurion U. of the Negev, Beer Sheva, Israel, summers 1981, 85. Contbr. articles to sci. jours. Fellow Alfred P. Sloan Found., 1971-76, NSF and Sterling, 1962-63, Leeds and Northrup Found., 1960-62, Woodrow Wilson fellow, 1959-60; grantee NSF, Robert A. Welch Found., Def. Adv. Rsch. Projects Agy., Air Force Office Sci. Rsch., Dept. Energy, Petroleum Rsch. Fund, Tex. Advanced Tech. program, Tex. Advanced Rsch. program, Disting. Record of Rsch. award U. Tex., Arlington, 1997, also others. Mem. Am. Chem. Soc. (Wilfred T. Doherty award Dallas-Fort Worth sect. 1997), Phi Beta Kappa, Sigma Xi. Achievements include research in synthesis, reactions and properties of organo lambda-5-phosphazenes, reactions of carbenes with other molecules, with themselves and with diazo precursors; design, synthesis and study of electronically conducting polymers with enhanced properties, synthesis and study of electroluminescent (light emitting) polymers, preparation and study of polymeric ionic self-assembled monolayers (ISAMs), non-linear optical materials. Home: 5521 Williamstown Rd Dallas TX 75230-2127 Office: U Tex Dept Chemistry-Biochemistry PO Box 19065 Arlington TX 76019-0065 Office Phone: 817-272-3811. Business E-Mail: pomerantz@uta.edu.

POMERANTZ, MARTIN ARTHUR, astronomer, educator; b. Bklyn., Dec. 17, 1916; AB, Syracuse U., 1937; MS, U. Pa., 1939; PhD, Temple U., 1951; Fil. Dr. (hon.), U. Uppsala, Sweden, 1967; ScD (hon.), Swarthmore Coll., 1973; DSc (hon.), U. Del., 2001. Rsch. asst. Bartol Rsch. Found., 1938—41, rsch. fellow, 1941—43, physicist, 1943—59, dir., 1959—85, pres., 1985—87; v.p. The Franklin Inst., 1967—85, exec. v.p., 1985—87, Bartol prof., 1968—89; prof. emeritus Bartol Rsch. Inst. U. Del., 1990—. Fulbright scholar, vis. prof. Muslim U., Aligarh, India, 1952—53; leader Nat. Geog. Soc. expeditions, 1948—59; chmn. U.S. Com. for Internat. Yrs. of the Quiet Sun Nat. Acad. Scis., 1962—66, mem. Com. on Polar Rsch., 1959—71, mem. Space Sci. Bd., 1963—70, mem. Geophysics Rsch. Bd., 1959—73; v.p. Com for Internat. Yrs. of the Quiet Sun Internat. Coun. Sci. Unions, v.p. Com. Internat. Geophysique, 1962—66; mem. Com. on Solar-Terrestrial Rsch. Nat. Acad. Scis., 1981—86; vis. prof. astronomy Swarthmore Coll., 1961, 64, 67; vis. prof. U. Tokyo, 1983, Potchefstroom U., South Africa, 1987; Sigma Xi nat. lectr., 68; OAS vis. prof., 73. Editor: Jour. of the Franklin Inst.; mem. editl. bd.: Space Sci. Revs.,: Antarctic Rsch. Series. Recipient Centennial Gold medal, Syracuse U., 1970, Prix de la Belgica, Acad. Royal des Scis., des Lettres et des Beaux Arts de Belgique, 1985, Disting. Pub. Svc. award, NSF, 1987, medal for disting. sci. achievement, NASA, 1990. Fellow: AAAS, Am. Geophys. Union, Am. Phys. Soc.; mem.: Am. Polar Soc. (hon.), Rotary Internat., Cosmos Club, Explorers Club, Sigma Pi Sigma (hon.). Home: 100 Deer Valley Rd Apt GE San Rafael CA 94903

POMERANTZ, MARVIN, thoracic surgeon; b. Suffern, N.Y., June 16, 1934; s. Julius and Sophie (Luksin) Pomerantz; m. Margaret Twigg, Feb. 26, 1966; children: Ben, Julie. AB, Colgate U., 1955; MD, U. Rochester, 1959. Diplomate Nat. Bd. Med. Examiners, Am. Bd. Surgery, Am. Bd. Thoracic Surgery (bd. dirs. 1989-95). Intern Duke U. Med. Ctr., Durham, NC, 1959—60, resident, 1960—61, instr. surgery, 1966—67, asst. prof. surgery U. Colo. Med. Sch., Denver, 1967—71, assoc. prof. surgery, 1971—74, assoc. clin. prof. surgery, 1974—93, prof. surgery, chief gen. thoracic surgery, 1992—; chief thoracic and cardiovascular surgery Denver Gen. Hosp., 1967—73, asst. dir. surgery, 1967—70, assoc.dir. surgery, 1970—73; pvt. practice Arapahoe CV Assocs., Denver, 1974—92; prof., chief gen. thoracic surgery sect. U. Colo. Health Sci. Ctr., 1992—; resident Duke U. Med. Ctr., Durham, NC, 1963—67. Clin. assoc. surgery br. NCI, 1961—63; mem. staff Univ. Hosp., Denver, Denver Gen. Hosp., Rose Med. Ctr., Denver, Denver VA Med. Ctr., Children's Hosp., Denver, U. Coll. Health Sci. Ctr., 1992—, bd. dirs., 1990—96; vice chmn. Am. Bd. Thoracic Surgery, 1995—97, chmn., 1997—99. Guest editor Chest Surgery Clinics N.Am., 1993; contbr. numerous articles to profl. publs., chapters to books. Master: AMA; fellow: ACS, Am. Coll. Chest Surgeons; mem.: Soc. Vascular Surgeons, Soc. Thoracic Surgeons (nomenclature/coding com. 1991—95, standards and ethics com., govt. rels. com., chmn. program com. 1994—95), Rocky Mtgn. Traumatologic Soc., rgery Soc., Internat. Cardiovascular Soc., Denver Acad. Surgery (pres. 1980), Colo. Med. Soc., Am. Heart Assn. (bd. dirs. Colo. chpt. 1993), Am. Assn. Thoracic Surgeons (program com. 1991), Western Thoracic Surg. Assn. (v.p. 1992, pres. 1993—94, counselor-at-large 1988—90). Office: UCHSC Divsn CTS 4200 E 9th Ave # C310 Denver CO 80262-0001

POMERANTZ, MARVIN ALVIN, manufacturing executive; b. Des Moines, Aug. 6, 1930; s. Alex and Minnie (Landy) P.; m. Rose Lee Lipsey, Nov. 12, 1950; children: Sandy Pomerantz, Marcie Morrison, Vickie Ginsberg, Lori Long. BS in Commerce, U. Iowa, 1952. Exec. v.p. Midwest Bag Co., Des Moines, 1952-60; founder, pres., gen. mgr. Gt. Plains Bag Corp., Des Moines, 1961-75; v.p. Continental Can Co. Inc., Greenwich, Conn., 1971-75; v.p., gen. mgr. Forest Products Brown Systems Operation (div. Continental Can Co. Inc.), Greenwich, Conn., 1975-77; pres. Diversified Group Internat. Harvester, Chgo., 1980-81, ex. v.p., 1981-82; pres., chmn., chief exec. officer The Mid-Am. Group, Des Moines, 1981—; chmn., chief exec. officer Gaylord Container Corp., Deerfield, Ill., 1986—2002. Mem. Greater Des Moines Commn.; trustee Drake U., 1978—; pres. Iowa State Bd. Regents, 1987-93, 95-96; mem. U.S. Olympic Budget and Audit Commn., Colorado Springs., Colo., 1989-92. Republican. Office: The Mid-Am Group 4700 Westown Pkwy Ste 303 West Des Moines IA 50266-6718

POMERANZ, FELIX, accounting educator; b. Vienna, Mar. 28, 1926; s. Joseph and Irene (Meninger) P.; m. Rita Lewin, June 14, 1953; children: Jeffrey Arthur, Andrew Joseph. BBA, CCNY, 1948; MS, Columbia U., 1949; PhD, U. Birmingham, Eng., 1992. Diplomate Am. Bd. Forensic Acctg.; CPA, N.Y., Va., La., N.C.; cert. computer profl., fraud examiner, govt. fin. mgr. Audit staff Coopers & Lybrand, CPAs, N.Y.C., 1949-56; mgr. Marks, Grey & Shron (now Ernst & Young, CPA's), N.Y.C., 1956-58; asst. chief auditor Am.-Standard, N.Y.C., 1958-62; mgr. systems Westvaco Corp., N.Y.C., 1962-66; dir. operational auditing Coopers & Lybrand, CPAs, N.Y.C., 1966-68, ptnr., 1968-85; disting. lectr./dir. Ctr. for Acctg., Auditing, Tax Studies Fla. Internat. U., Miami, 1985-93, prof. acctg., 1993—2002, assoc. dir. sch. acctg., 1993—99, affil. faculty dept. religious studies, 1996—2002, prof. emeritus, 2003—. Author: Managing Capital Budget Projects, 1984; The Successful Audit: New Ways to Reduce Risk Exposure and Increase Efficiency, 1992; co-author: Pensions-An Accounting and Management Guide, 1976; Auditing in the Public Sector: Efficiency, Economy, and Program Results, 1976; Comparative International Auditing Standards, 1985; contbr. articles to profl. jours. Emeritus trustee Nat. Ctr. for Automated Info. Rsch.; founding mem. Ctr. for Study of Islam and Democracy; chair bus. sch. adv. bd. Carlos Albizu U.; founder Afghan Inst. Accts. 1st lt. AUS, 1944-46, 51-52. Recipient Spear Safer Harmon faculty fellow Coll. Bus. Administrn., 1987, Outstanding Svc. award, 1998, Matriculation Merit award, 2000. Mem. AICPA, N.Y. State Soc. CPA, Assn. Sys. Mgmt., Acad: Acctg. Historians, Assn. Govt. Accts., N.Y. Acad. Scis., Am. Acctg. Assn., Inter-Am. Acctg. Assn., Assn. Cert. Fraud Examiners, Beta Gamma Sigma, Beta Alpha Psi (Most Disting. and Most Outstanding Profl. awards 1993, Most Supportive Profl. award 2002), Alpha Kappa Psi (Dr. Felix Pomeranz Faculty of Yr. award, Endless Work award). Home: 250 Jacaranda Dr Apt 406 Fort Lauderdale FL 33324-2532 Office: Fla Internat U Sch Acctg University Park Miami FL 33199-0001 E-mail: pomeranf@fiu.edu.

POMERENE, JAMES HERBERT, retired computer engineer; b. Yonkers, N.Y., June 22, 1920; s. Joel Pomerene and Elsie Bower; m. Edythe R. Schwenn, Dec. 1, 1944; children: James Bennett, Katherine Ellen, Andrew Thomas Stewart. BSEE, Northwestern U., 1942; postgrad., Princeton U., 1950. Elec. engr. Hazeltine Corp., Little Neck, N.Y., 1942-46; mem. staff electronic computer project Inst. for Advanced Study, Princeton, N.J., 1946-51, chief engr., 1951-56; sr. engr. IBM Corp., Poughkeepsie, N.Y., 1956-67, sr. staff mem. Armonk, N.Y., 1967-76. Cons. in field. Patentee in field. IBM fellow T.J. Watson Rsch. Ctr., 1976—. Fellow IEEE (Computer Pioneer award Computer Soc. 1986, Edison medal 1993); mem. NAE, Sigma Xi, Tau Beta Pi. Episcopalian. Home: 403 Bedford Rd N Chappaqua NY 10514-2207 E-mail: jhpomerene@aol.com.

POMEROY, EARL R. congressman, former state insurance commissioner; b. Valley City, N.D., Sept. 2, 1952; s. Ralph and Myrtle Pomeroy; m. Laurie Kirby, Dec. 26, 1986. BA, U. N.D., 1974, JD, 1979. Atty. Sproul, Lenaburg, Fitzner and Walker, Valley City, 1979-84; commr. of ins. State of N.D., Valley City, 1984-92; mem. U.S. Ho. Reps. from N.D. (at large), Washington, 1993—; mem. ways and means com. State rep. N.D. Legis. Assembly, 1980-84. Recipient Found. award Rotary, 1975; named Outstanding Young North Dakotan N.D. Jaycees, 1982. Mem. Nat. Assn. of Ins. Commrs. (chmn. midwest zone 1987-88, exec. com. 1987-88), Phi Beta Kappa. Democrat. Presbyterian. Office: US Ho Rep 1110 Longworth Bldg Washington DC 20515-3401

POMEROY, LEE HARRIS, architect; b. N.Y.C., Nov. 19, 1932; s. Alfred and Florence Pomeroy; m. Sarah Pomeroy; children: Jordana, Jeremy, Alexandra. BArch, Rensselaer Poly. Inst., 1955; MArch, Yale U., 1961. Registered arch., N.Y., Conn., Mass., Vt., N.J., Fla., Pa., Maine, Nat. Coun. of Registrators Bd. Arch. William Tabler, N.Y.C., 1958-59, The Archs. Collaborative, Cambridge, Mass., 1959-60; pres. Lee Harris Pomeroy Archs., N.Y.C., 1965-87. Prof. Sch. Architecture, CUNY, 1962-87; prin. solar rsch. group ECOSOL, Conn., Eng., Spain, 1965-84; dir. Project for Pub. Spaces, Inc.,

N.Y.C., 1982-88; dean's adv. coun. Sch. Architecture, Resselaer Poly. Inst., 1991—, adv. to pres., 1994-98. Prin. works include Swiss Bank Tower and Saks Fifth Ave. ext., N.Y.C. (Arthur Ross award 1991), Teda Conv. Ctr., Tanjuin, China; restoration of Plaza Hotel, N.Y., Sch. Art and Dance City Coll., N.Y.C., 1989, New Rochelle Pub. Libr., 1980 (AIA-ALA design award 1980, N.Y. State AIA and Urban Design awards 1980), Dutchess County Jail, Poughkeepsie, N.Y. (AIA-ACA design award 1981), HBO Satellite Comm. Ctr., 1983 (N.Y. State AIA design award 1984), Manitou Sta. planned cmty., 1973 (AIA and Progressive Architecture awards 1973), Henry St. studios artists housing (Progressive Architecture mag. design award 1963, AIA design award 1975), Bedford Mews housing (AIA, Owens Corning energy conservation and Record Homes design awards 1980), Fulton Mall, Bklyn., 1985 (City Club N.Y.C. Bard award for design 1985), Trinity Ch. Bridge (AIA design award 1991), Hotel Usixtu, Prague, Czech Republic, Lally Sch. of Mgmt. and Tech., Rensselaer Poly. Inst., Troy, N.Y., Reconstrn. of Union Square Subway, 2001, M.O.M.A., Bleeker St.and Dekalb Ave. Stas., Fulton St. Transit Ctr., Lower Manhattan, N.Y.C.; renovated Cosco Housing and Comml. Ctr., Shanghai, Jin Ling Hotel on Hynan Island, Parish House and St. James Ch., N.Y.C., N.Y. Mem. Cmty. Bd. 5, Midtown Manhattan, N.Y.C., 1980-91; bd. dirs. Bellview Assn., with Bellview Med. Ctr., N.Y.C., 1992—; trustee, v.p. Putnam County Hist. Soc. and Foundry Mus. 1st lt. USA Signal Corp., 1955-57. Recipient Mcpl. Arts Soc. award, N.Y.C., 1982; Nat. Endowment for Arts grantee, N.Y.C., 1983. Fellow AIA (bd. dirs. 1979-81), Inst. of Urban Design; mem. Royal Inst. of British Archs., Mcpl. Arts Soc., Regional Plan Assn., Yale Club, Century Club, City Club N.Y. (co-chmn. Bard award program for excellence in urban design 1988-90, 94). Avocations: tennis, photography, travel. Home: 285 Central Park W New York NY 10024-3006 Office: 462 Broadway Fl 3 New York NY 10013-2696 Office Phone: 212-334-2600. Business E-Mail: leepom@lhparch.com.

POMEROY, ROBERT CORTTIS, lawyer; b. Syracuse, N.Y., Sept. 17, 1943; s. Stuart E. and Elizabeth (Corttis) Pomeroy; m. Sandra Campbell; children: Lisa, Robert Jr., Heather. AB, Hamilton Coll., 1965; LLB, Harvard U., 1968. Bar: Mass. 1968, Fla. 1981. Assoc. Goodwin Procter LLP (formerly Goodwin, Procter & Hoar LLP), Boston, 1968-76, ptnr., 1977—. Mem.: Am. Coll. Trust and Estate Counsel. Avocations: skiing, golf, sailing. Home: 3 Pier 7 Charlestown MA 02129-4225 Office: Goodwin Procter LLP Exchange Pl Boston MA 02109-2881 Office Phone: 617-570-1150. Business E-Mail: rpomeroy@goodwinprocter.com.

POMFRET, DAVID B. medical educator, internist; b. Somerset, Mass., Nov. 22, 1937; s. David B. Pomfret and Rhea Chouinard; m. Anna Rafferty, Mar. 31, 1964; children: Mark, Bruce, Scott, Heidi. BS, Stonehill Coll., 1959; MD, Univ. Coll., Dublin, Ireland, 1964. Diplomate Am. Bd. Internal Medicine. Chief of medicine Leonard Morse Hosp., Natick, Mass., 1968—71, chief of staff, 1976—80; clin. prof. Tufts U., Boston, 1976—; prof. medicine Tumaini U., Moshi, Tanzania, 1996—2000. Author: Computer Science, 1998, Dispatches From Kilimanjaro, 2001. Fellow: ACP. Avocations: skiing, sailing, offshore racing. Home: 20 Grey Gull Rd Jamestown RI 02835-2808 Office: Kilimanjaro Christian Med Ctr Box 3010 Moshi Tanzania E-mail: pomfret1@cox.net.

POMMERENING, EDWIN CARLTON, lawyer, manufacturing company executive; b. Milw., Oct. 7, 1938; s. Edwin Carl and Emily P.; m. Sandra Bloom, Sept. 13, 1969; children— Bradford, William, Douglas Edwin. B.S., U. Wis., 1961, J.D., 1964. Bar: Wis. Asst. gen. counsel Ansul Co., Marinette, Wis., 1968, mgr. subs. ops., 1969, gen. mgr. chmn. div., 1970-72, gen. mgr. internat. div., 1972, sec., 1973-76, gen. counsel, 1976, v.p., gen. counsel, sec., 1977-85, v.p. adminstrn. and law, 1985—. Served to capt. U.S. Army, 1964-66. Mem. Am. Soc. Corp. Secs., ABA, Wis. Bar Assn., Marinette Bar Assn., Internat. Bar assn., InterAm. Bar Assn., C. of C. Republican. Lutheran. Clubs: Twi Cees (Marinette), Elks. Office: 15806 Midway Rd Addison TX 75001-4259

POMORSKI, STANISLAW, lawyer, educator; b. Lwow, Poland, Nov. 23, 1934; arrived in U.S., 1972, naturalized, 1983; s. Juliusz and Maria (Ziemba) Pomorski; m. Patricia Smith; children: Lukasz, Christopher, Maria. M.Law, U. Warsaw, 1956, D.Law, 1968. Law clk., 1958-61; pvt. practice law, 1961-64; vis. scholar Harvard U. Law Sch., Cambridge, Mass., 1964-66; rsch. assoc. Polish Acad. Scis., 1966-72; mem. faculty Rutgers U. Law Sch., Camden, N.J., 1973—, prof. law, 1977-81, disting. prof. law, 1981—. Fellow Soviet law U. Leyden, Netherlands, 1980—81; trustee Nat. Coun. Soviet and East European Rsch., Washington, 1988—94. Author: (book) American Common Law and the Principle Nullum Crimen Sine Lege, 2d edit., 1975, Restructuring the System of Ownership in the USSR, 1991, On Multiculturalism, Concepts of Crime and the De Minimis Defense, 1997, Justice in Siberia, 2001. Fellow, Ford Found., 1972—73. Office: Rutgers U Law Sch 5th And Penn St Camden NJ 08102 Office Phone: 856-225-6395. Business E-Mail: pomorski@crab.rutgers.edu.

POMPADUR, I. MARTIN, communications executive; b. Bklyn, June 25, 1935; s. Jack and Florence (Raitbord) P.; m. Joan Lynn Krassner, Dec. 18, 1960 (div. 1986); children: F. Douglas (dec.), Jana Sue; m. Marian Hackett, Dec. 23, 1987 (div. 2003); 1 child, Chelsea Rae. BA, Williams Coll., 1955; LLB, U. Mich., 1958. Bar: Conn. 1958, NY 1961. Atty. ABC-TV Network, NYC, 1960-61, 61-66, chief adminstrv. officer, 1966-68, gen. mgr., 1968-70, v.p. broadcast div., 1970-72, corp. v.p., 1972; pres. ABC Leisure Group I, 1973-75, asst. to pres. parent co., 1975-76; also dir. parent co.; sr. v.p. Ziff Corp., 1977-78, pres., 1978-82; chmn., chief exec. officer GP Sta. Ptnr., 1982-96; mng. gen. ptnr. TV Sta. Ptnr., 1982-96; chmn., CEO PBTV, Inc., 1984-96; mng. gen. ptnr Northeastern TV Investors Ltd. Partnership, 1984-96; prin. owner, sec. Caribbean Internat. News Corp., 1985—, also bd. dir.; CEO, COO RP Media Mgmt., Inc., 1986; CEO ML Media Ptnr., L.P., 1986—; CEO, COO RP Opportunity Mgmt., 1988—2002; CEO ML Media Opportunity Ptnr., L.P., 1988—2002; exec. v.p. News Corp.; pres. News Corp. Ea. Ctrl. Europe; chmn. News Corp. Europe, 2000—. Prin. shareholder Hispanic Media Inc., 1986-90; prin. shareholder, vice-chmn. Hunter Pub. L.P., 1986-94; co-trustee Lidan Trust, 1983—; atty. Young & Rubicam, Inc., advt. agy., NYC, summer 1961. Mem. Stamford bd. reps., chmn. legis. and rules com., 1959-60. Office: News Corp 4th Fl 1211 Ave of the Americas New York NY 10036 also: News Corp Europe 1 Virginia St 6th Fl London England

POMPER, PHILIP, history educator; b. Chgo., Apr. 18, 1936; s. Solomon and Rebecca (Fenigstein) P.; m. Alice N. Epstein, Aug. 27, 1961 (div.); children: Erica, Stephen, Karen; m. Emily Meyer, June 26, 1994 (dec. July)2003. BA, U. Chgo., 1959, MA, 1961, PhD, 1965. Instr. history Wesleyan U., Middletown, Conn., 1964-65, asst. prof., 1965-71, assoc. prof., 1971-76, prof., 1976—, chmn. dept. history, 1981-84; William F. Armstrong prof. history, 1992—. Author: The Russian Revolutionary Intelligentsia, 1970, 2nd edit., 1993, Peter Lavrov and the Russian Revolutionary Movement, 1972, Sergei Nechaev, 1979 (Choice award 1979), The Structure of Mind in History: Five Major Figures in Psychohistory, 1985, Trotsky's Notebooks, 1933-35: Writings on Lenin, Dialectics and Evolutionism, 1986, Lenin, Trotsky, and Stalin: The Intelligentsia and Power, 1990; assoc. editor History and Theory, 1991—; editor: World History: Ideologies, Structures, and Identities, 1998; co-editor: History and Theory, Contemporary Readings, 1998; co-editor: The Return of Science: Evolution, History and Theory, 2002; contbr. articles on Russian history and theory of history to profl. jours. Fellow, Ford Found., 1963-64, Social Scis. Rsch. Coun., 1968, Hoover Instn., 1987, Wilson Ctr., 1988; Russian Rsch. Ctr. scholar, 1987—. Mem.: Am. Assn. for Advancement of Slavic Studies, Conn. Acad. Arts and Scis. Home: 13 Red Orange Rd Middletown CT 06457-4916 Office: History Dept Wesleyan U Middletown CT 06459-0001 Office Phone: 860-685-2398. E-mail: ppomper@wesleyan.edu.

PONCE, ARNOLDO A. financial analyst, poet; b. San Salvador, El Salvador, Ctrl. Am., Dec. 2, 1945; s. Francisco A. and Julia Ponce; m. Thelma D. Ponce, May 25, 1975; children: Julia M., Jorge A. Acct., Escuela Nacional De Comercio, 1964. Mgr. fire ins. dept. Seguros E Inversiones S.a., San Salvador, El Salvador, 1965—74; purchase agt. Mkay Teer Constructors, San Salvador, El Salvador, 1975—78; mgr. claim dept. Aseguradora Popular S. A., San Salvador, El Salvador, 1979—86; pres. Patria S.a. De C.v. Asesores De Seguros, San Salvador, El Salvador, 1986—88; fin. advisor Provident Mut. Life Ins., Terrytown, 1989—93; rsch. analyst Thomson Fin., Northport, NY, 1993—. Claim pres. Asociacion Salvadorena De Aseguradores, San Salvador, 1982—83. Author: (poetry book) Pedazos De Cristal. Vol. Cath. Charities, Huntington, NY, 1992—94. Mem.: Asociacion De Contadores Publicos De El Salvador (assoc.). Democrat-Npl. Roman Catholic. Achievements include design of Forms And Operative Manuals For Claims Insurance. Avocations: travel, camping, poetry. Personal E-mail: arnoldoponce@hotmail.com.

POND, DALE C. company executive; Sr. v.p. mktg. and merchandising Payless Cashway; sr. v.p. mktg. Montgomery Ward & Co., Chgo., 1989—92, Lowe's Cos. Inc., 1993—, exec. v.p. merchandising and mktg., 1998—99, sr. exec. v.p. merchandising and mktg., 1999—. Office: Lowe's Companies 1000 Lowe's Blvd Mooresville NC 28117*

POND, KIRK, electronics and computer parts company executive; BSEE, U. Ark.; MBA, U. Pa. Various mgmt. level positions Tex. Instruments, Timex Corp.; joined Fairchild Semiconductor, South Portland, Maine, 1984, v.p. Logic, 1984, exec. v.p. Logic, Memory, Discrete and Analog groups, v.p. Logic, 1987-91, pres. Standard Products Group, 1991-94, exec. v.p., COO, 1994, pres., CEO, chmn. bd. dirs. Mem. Maine Sci. and Tech. Found., Nat. Assn. Mfts. (past bd. dirs.).

POND, PATRICIA BROWN, library science educator, university administrator; b. Mankato, Minn., Jan. 17, 1930; d. Patrick H. and Florence M. (Ruehle) Brown; m. Judson S. Pond, Aug. 24, 1959. BA, Coll. St. Catherine, St. Paul, 1952; MA, U. Minn., 1955; PhD, U. Chgo., 1982. Sch. libr., Minn., N.Y., 1952-62; asst. prof. libr. sci. U. Minn., 1962-63; reference libr. U. Mont., 1963-65; asst. prof. U. Oreg., 1967-72, assoc. prof., 1972-77; prof., dept. chair, assoc. dean Sch. Libr. and Info. Sci. U. Pitts., 1977-85. Mem. ALA (life), Phi Beta Kappa, Beta Phi Mu, Delta Phi Lambda, Kappa Gamma Pi. Home: 15829 SW Village Cir Beaverton OR 97007-3532

POND, THOMAS ALEXANDER, physics educator, university official; b. L.A., Dec. 4, 1924; s. Arthur Francis and Florence (Alexander) P.; m. Barbara Eileen Newman, Sept. 6, 1958; children: Arthur Phillip Ward, Florence Alexandra. AB, Princeton U., 1947, AM, 1949, PhD, 1953; DSc, SUNY, Stony Brook, 1998. Instr. physics Princeton U., 1951-53; asst. prof., then assoc. prof. physics Washington U., St. Louis, 1953-62; prof. physics SUNY, Stony Brook, 1962-81, prof. emeritus, 1982—, chmn. dept., 1962-68, exec. v.p., 1967-79, acting pres., 1970, 75, 78; prof. physics Rutgers U., New Brunswick, N.J., exec. v.p., chief acad. officer, 1982-91, exec. v.p., chief acad. officer emeritus, 1991—, acting pres., 1990, prof., 1991-97, prof. emeritus, 1997—; acting sr. v.p. for acad. affairs U. Medicine and Dentistry N.J., New Brunswick, 1998. Bd. dirs. Action Com. for L.I., 1978-80, Tri-State Regional Planning Commn., 1979-82; trustee Univs. Research Assn., 1985-87; bd. dirs. Fermilab, 1987-89. Served to ensign USNR, 1943-46. Fellow AAAS; mem. Am. Phys. Soc., Phi Beta Kappa, Sigma Xi. Home: 2569 Heathrow Ln Manasquan NJ 08736-2229 E-mail: aandbpond@aol.com.

PONDEL, ROGER S. public relations executive; BA in Pub. Rels., Calif. State U., San Jose. Pub. rels. dir. Cordon Internat. Corp., Cordura Corp., Bekins Co.; pres. Pondel/Wilkinson, Inc., LA, 1977—. Adj. faculty Pepperdine U., Malibu, Calif.; spkr. Reporter San Jose Mercury News. Mem. Nat. Investor Rels. Inst., Pub. Rels. Soc. Am., L.A. Soc. Fin. Analysts. Office: Pondel Wilkinson Inc Ste 700 1880 Century Park E Los Angeles CA 90067 Office Phone: 310-279-5980. Business E-Mail: rpondel@pondel.com.

PONDER, ANNE, dean; b. Asheville, N.C., Apr. 26, 1950; d. Herschel Doyle and Mary Eleanor (Israel) Ponder; m. John Christopher Brookhouse, Mar. 3, 1973; stepchildren: Stephen Christopher, Nathaniel. AB, U. N.C., 1971, MA, 1973, PhD, 1979. Dir. honors Elon Coll., N.C., 1977-85; assoc. acad. dean Guilford Coll., Greensboro, N.C., 1985-89; acad. dean, prof. Kenyon Coll., Gambier, Ohio, 1989—. Mem. Nat. Collegiate Honors Coun. (pres. 1988-89), N.C. Honors Assn. (pres. 1983), Order of Valkyries. Episcopalian. Office: Kenyon Coll 105 Park St Gambier OH 43022

PONDER, CATHERINE, clergywoman, author; b. Hartsville, S.C., Feb. 14, 1927; d. Roy Charles and Kathleen (Parrish) Cook; 1 child, Richard. Student, Worth Bus. Coll., 1948; BS in Edn., Unity Ministerial Sch., 1956; doctorate (hon.), Unity Sch., 1976. Ordained to ministry Unity Sch. Christianity, 1958. Min. Unity Ch., Birmingham, Ala., 1958-61, founder, min. Austin, Tex., 1961-69, San Antonio, 1969-73, Palm Desert, Calif., 1973—. Author: (books) The Dynamic Laws of Prosperity, 1962, The Prosperity Secret of the Ages, 1964, The Dynamic Laws of Healing, 1966, The Healing Secret of the Ages, 1967, Pray and Grow Rich, 1968, The Millionaires of Genesis, 1976, The Millionaire Moses, 1977, The Millionaire Joshua, 1978, The Millionaire from Nazareth, 1979, The Secret of Unlimited Prosperity, 1981, Open Your Mind to Receive, 1983, Dare To Prosper!: The Prospering Power of Prayer, 1983, The Prospering Power of Love, 1984, Open Your Mind to Prosperity, 1984, The Dynamic Laws of Prayer, 1987, (memoir) Prosperity Love Story, From Rags to Enrichment, 2003. Office: 73-669 US Hwy 111 Palm Desert CA 92260-4033

PONDER, DAN, public relations executive; MBA, BA, Mich. State U.; grad., Leadership Detroit X. Mem. pvt. co. adv. svc. Deloitte & Touche, Detroit; CFO Franco Pub. Rels. Group, 1985, CEO, 1985—93. Mem.: Henry Ford Estate Adv. Bd., Mich. Coun. Econ. Edn. (bd. trustees), Alliance for a Safer, Greater Detroit (mem. bd. dirs.), Mich. State Chamber (mem. bd. dirs.), Detroit Regional Chamber (mem. bd. dirs., past chmn. small bus. exec. com., Svc. award 1996—97). Office: Franco Pub Rels Group 400 Renaissance Ctr Ste 1050 Detroit MI 48243 Business E-Mail: ponder@franco.com.

PONDER, HENRY, educational association administrator; m. Eunice Wilson; children: Cheryl, Anna. BS, Langston U.; MS, Okla. State U.; PhD, Ohio State U. Asst. prof. Va. State Coll., Petersburg, chmn. dept. agri-bus.; chmn. dept. bus. and econs. Ft. Valley (Ga.) State Coll.; v.p. acad. affairs Ala. A&M U., Normal, dean; pres. Benedict Coll., Columbia, S.C., Fisk U., Nashville, Talladega Coll., Ala., Nat. Assn. for Equal Opportunity in Higher Edn., Silver Spring, Md. Cons. Fed. Res. Bank, N.Y., Phila. Nat. Bank, Chase Manhattan Bank, Irving Trust Co., Omaha Nat. Bank; bd. dirs. Fed. Res. Bank of Richmond, Va., chmn. bd. dirs.; bd. dirs. J.P. Stevens & Co., Inc., Sunstrust Bank of Nashville, Tenn., SCANA Corp. S.C., C.C. of the Air Force, ETV Endowment S.C. Mem. scholarship fund com. Bishop Desmond Tutu So. African Refugee Assn.; chmn. United Negro College Fund, Inc., Nat. Assn. for Equal Opportunity in Higher Edn.; mem. exec. coun. Commn. on Colls. Mem.: Tenn. Coll. Assn. (pres. 1992), Alpha Phi Alpha (gen. pres.). Home: 3 Covington Ct Hilton Head Island SC 29928

PONDER, HERMAN, geologist; b. Light, Ark., Jan. 31, 1928; s. Herman Cook and Sylvia Adell (Cameron) P.; m. Barbara Elaine Sando, May 10, 1947; children: Teresa Elaine, David Mark. BA, U. Mo., 1955, PhD, 1959. Rsch. engr. A.P. Green Refractories Co., Mexico, Mo., 1959-61, lab mgr., 1961-63; project engr., then mgr. mining div. Colo. Sch. Mines Rsch. Inst., Golden, 1963-67, dir. rsch., 1967-70, pres., 1970-85, ATI Exploration, Golden, Colo., 1985-90; chmn. bd. dirs. Analytica, Inc. V.p. Copper Range Co., White Pine, Mich., 1985-89. Served with USN, 1946-47. Recipient Disting. Alumnus award U. Mo., 1993. Home: 2725 E Papago Trl Sierra Vista AZ 85650-8112

PONDER, MARIAN RUTH, retired mathematics educator; b. Waterloo, Iowa, July 12, 1932; d. Lee Roland and Leone Hyacinth (Holdiman) Ridgon; m. Joseph Glen Ponder, June 28, 1953; children: Dwight Lee, David Glen, Dean Joseph. BA (Purple and Gold math. scholar), U. No. Iowa, 1952; MSE, Drake U., 1960; postgrad., U. Wis., 1961—62, San Diego State U., 1980—81, Carleton Coll., 1980—81, U. No. Iowa, 1961—66, Drake U., 1971—75, Chico State U., 1985—86, U. Iowa, 1988, U. Tex., 1990, Des Moines Area C.C., 2003. Tchr. math., sci., Anamosa, Iowa, 1952-53, Monroe, Iowa, 1953-56, Newton, Iowa, 1956-64, 66-92; head dept. math. Newton Schs., 1978-92. Ch. treas. Cmty. Heights Alliance Ch., 1980-82, 83-87, Sunday sch. secretariat, 1966-82, fin. sec., 1993-94, 97-98, women's ministries treas., 1997-2001. Maytag scholar, 1960; Maytag Corp. grantee; Delta Kappa Gamma scholar, 1960, 81, 95, 2002. Mem. NEA, Nat. Coun. Tchrs. Math., Iowa Ret. Sch. Pers. Assn., Iowa Edn. Assn., Newton Cmty. Edn. Assn. (chief negotiator 1985-87, pres. 1985-87), Iowa Coun. Tchrs. Math., Jasper County Hist. Soc., Jasper County Geneaol. Soc., Delta Kappa Gamma (state treas. 1978—2004, internat. fin. chmn. 1990-92, trustee ednl. found. 1992-98), Jasper County Ret. Sch. Pers. Assn. (treas. 1992-96, v.p. 1996-98, pres. 1998-2000), Kappa Mu Epsilon, Kappa Delta Pi, Lambda Delta Lambda, Delta Kappa Gamma. Republican. Mem. Christian and Missionary Alliance Ch. Home: 3791 Highway F36 W Newton IA 50208-8061

PONDER, RON J. insurance company executive; MBA in Mgmt. Sci., La. Poly. U.; PhD in Info. Sys. and Opers. Rsch., Miss. State U. Chief info. officer Fed. Express, Sprint, AT&T; pres., CEO BDSI, Inc., Cap Gemini Ernst & Young; exec. v.p., chief info. officer WellPoint Health Networks, Inc., 2002—. Office: WellPoint Health Networks Inc One WellPoint Way Thousand Oaks CA 91362

PONEMAN, DANIEL BRUCE, lawyer; b. Toledo, Mar. 12, 1956; s. Meyer and Delores Suzanne (Shapiro) P.; m. Susan Anne Danoff, Aug. 12, 1984; children: Claire Gillian, Michael Bruder, William Meyer. AB in Govt. and Econs. magna cum laude, Harvard Coll., 1978; MLitt in Politics, Lincoln Coll., Oxford, Eng., 1981; JD cum laude, Harvard U., 1984. Bar: D.C. 1985, N.Y., 1985. Vis. fellow Internat. Inst. Strategic Studies, London, 1980-81; rsch. fellow ctr. sci. and internat. affairs Kennedy sch. govt. Harvard U., 1981-84; assoc. Covington & Burling, 1985-89; White House fellow U.S. Dept. of Energy, 1989-90; dir. def. policy and arms control NSC, Washington, 1990-93, spl. asst. to the Pres., sr. dir. nonproliferation and export controls, 1993-96; counsel Hogan & Hartson L.L.P., 1996-97, ptnr., 1999—2002; prin. The Scowcroft Group, 2001—. Author: Nuclear Power in the Developing World, 1982, Argentina: Democracy on Trial, 1987, Going Critical, 2003; contbr. articles to profl. jours. and newspapers including N.Y. Times, Washington Post, Wall Street Jour., L.A. Times, Boston Globe. Mem. Commn. to Asses the Orgn. of Govt. to Combat the Proliferation of Weapons of Mass Distruction, 1997-99; mem. Pres.' Export Coun. Subcom. on Export Adminstrn. Grantee Corp. Pub. Broadcasting; Lord Crewe scholar. Mem. D.C. Bar, N.Y. Bar, Coun. Fgn. Rels., Phi Beta Kappa. Home: 1541 Forest Ln Mc Lean VA 22101 Office: The Scowcroft Group 900 17th St NW Ste 500 Washington DC 20006 Business E-Mail: poneman@scowcroft.com.

PONITZ, DAVID H. former academic administrator; b. Royal Oak, Mich., Jan. 21, 1931; s. Henry John and Jeanette (Bouwman) P.; m. Doris Jean Humes, Aug. 5, 1956; children: Catherine Anne, David Robinson. BA, U. Mich., 1952, MA, 1954; EdD, Harvard U., 1964; degree (hon.), U. Dayton, 1996. Prin. Waldron (Mich.) Area Schs., 1956-58, supt., 1958-60; cons. Harvard U., Boston Sch. Survey, 1961-63; supt. Freeport (Ill.) Pub. Schs., 1962-65; pres. Freeport C.C., 1962-65, Washtenaw C.C., 1965-75, Sinclair C.C., 1975-97, pres. emeritus, 1997—. Cons. to community colls.; chmn., pres. Ohi Advanced Tech. Ctr. Mem. editorial adv. bd. Nations Schs, 1963-70; chmn. adv. bd. Community Coll. Rev, 1978-89. Past chmn. Dayton Mayor's Coun. on Econ. Devel., 1977-85; mem. Nat. Adv. Coun. on Nursing; former co-chair Performing Arts Edn. Task Force; bd. dirs. Alliance for Edn.; former campaign chmn. Ann Arbor and Dayton United Way; past vice chmn. Dayton Citizens Adv. Coun. for Desegregation Implementation; v.p. Miami Valley Rsch. Park; mem., past chmn. Area Progress Coun., Dayton; bd. dirs. Dayton Devel. Coun.; mem. F.S.B. bd. Citizens Fed. Banks, Universal Energy Systems Bd.; past chmn. Miami Valley Joint Labor/Mgmt. Profls., Area Progress Coun.; chmn. bd. dirs Ctr. Occupational R & D; bd. chair Wright Tech. Network; bd. dirs. Dean Family Funds; trustee Thomas B. Fordham Found.; mem. Midwestern Higher Edn. Commn.; vice chair Miami Valley Rsch. Found.; past chmn. bd. dirs. League Innovation C.C.; bd. dirs. Miami Valley Regional Planning Commn. Served with U.S. Army, 1954-56. Named Outstanding Alumnus, U. Mich., One of Top 100 Pres. in U.S. Coun. for Advancement and Support of Edn., Exec. of Yr., Bd. Realtors; named to Hall of Fame, Nat. Mgmt. Assn., 2001; recipient Presdl. medallion, Patron emeritus Horry-Georgetown Tech. Coll., Bogie Buster Red Jacket award, 1987, Thomas J. Peters award for Excellence, Assn. Cmty. and Jr. Colls., 1988, Marie N. Martin Chief Exec. Officer award, ACCT, 1989, The Living Legend award, Martin Luther King Jr. Holiday Celebration Com., 1991, Hon. Alumnus award, Sinclair, 1991, honor, India Found., 1992, Disting. Eagle Scout award, Nat. Eagle Scout Assn., 1993, Smitty award, Anti-Defamation award, Anti-Defamation League, 1996, Citizen Legion of Honor award, 1997, hon. award, Citizen Legion, 1997, Edn. award, Gov., 1999. Mem. Am. Assn. Community and Jr. Colls. (nat. future commn., bd. dirs., chmn. 1988-89, Nat. Leadership award 2002), Ohio Tech. and Community Coll. Assn. (pres. 1979-80), Nat. Mgmt. Assn. (Hall of Fame award 2001), Rotary. Methodist. Office: Sinclair Community Coll Office of Pres Emeritus 444 W 3rd St Dayton OH 45402-1421 Fax: 937-512-2865. E-mail: dponitz@sinclair.edu.

PONKA, LAWRENCE JOHN, automotive executive; b. Detroit, Sept. 1, 1949; s. Maximillian John and Leona May (Knobloch) P.; m. Nancy Kathleen McNamara, Feb. 20, 1988; 1 child, Chloe M. AA, Macomb County C. C., Mich., 1974; BS in Indsl. Mgmt., Lawrence Tech. U., 1978; MA in Indsl. Mgmt., Ctrl. Mich. U., 1983, postgrad. in Bus. Mgmt. Cert. internat. cons. Engr.'s asst. Army Tank Automotive Command, 1967-68; with Sperry and Hutchinson Co., Southfield, Mich., 1973, Chrysler Corp., Detroit, 1973, GM Corp., Warren, Mich., 1973-82, coord. engring. staff engring. systems, 1976-82; mfg. engr. Buick-Oldsmobile, Cadillac Group GM Assembly Divsn., Orion Pontiac, Mich, 1982-84; sr. anayst advanced vehicle engring. Chevrolet-Pontiac-Can. group Engring. Ctr., Warren, 1985-86; mfg. planning adminstr. Allanté Detroit Hamtramck Assembly Ctr. Cadillac Luxury Car Divsn., 1986-92, mgr. Cadillac Alante Assembly Ops., 1992—. Plant planning adminstr. Cadillac luxury car divsn. Detroit/Hamtramck Assembly Ctr., Cadillac El Dorado, Seville, Deville, Concours, 1993—, sr. mfg. project engr. N. Am. Ops., 1994, Flint, Mich., 96; advanced mfg. engr. N.Am. ops. mfg. process liaison Cadillac luxury car divsn., 1996—97; total mfg. integration engr. Advanced Product Devel. Ctr., 1997—2001, mfg. integration mgr., 2001; full size trucks Global Portfolio Devel. Ctr., 1997—2002; mem. people strategy team on environ. Cadillac Motor Car till 1992; mem. adj. faculty U. Phoenix Grad. Sch. Bus., Mich. campus; mfg. program mgr. concurrent build, full size trucks Pontiac Product Ctr., mfg. program mgr.-concurrent build full size truck, 2002—. Elected del Dem. County Conv. With USAF, 1968—72. Decorated Air Force Commendation medal. Mem. DAV (life), VFW, Vietnam Vets Assn. (life), Am. Diabetes Assn. Roman Catholic. Home: 35537 Oakdale St Livonia MI 48154-2237 Office: U Phoenix Mich Campus 26999 Central Park Blvd Southfield MI 48076-4174 also: GM Full Size Truck Pontiac Ctr Campus N 585 E South Blvd Pontiac MI 48341

PONKO, ANNE MARIE, adult nurse practitioner; d. William and Mary Barbara (Moxin) Ponko. ADN in Nursing, Union U., Jackson, Tenn., 1977; BS, Saint Joseph's Coll., Windham, Maine, 2001. RN Calif. Charge nurse, surgery U. Utah, Salt Lake City, 1977—78, St. Thomas Hosp., Nashville, 1978—85; traveling nurse Overlook Hosp., Summit, NJ, 1985—86, Am. Hosp., Miami, Fla., 1986—87; staff nurse, post anesthesia care unit St. Joseph's Med. Ctr., Ft. Wayne, Ind., 1987—90, Sunrise Hosp. Med. Ctr., Las Vegas, Nev., 1990—94; pub. health nurse II Clark County Health Dist., Las Vegas, Nev., 1994—2000; pre/post-op cardiovascular nurse Valley Hosp. Med. Ctr., Las Vegas, Nev., 2000—01; home health-bound specialist Vis. Nurse Assn., Modesto, Calif., 2001—04; staff nurse post-anesthesia care unit Meml. Med. Ctr., Modesto, Calif., 2004—. 2d lt. Women's Army Nurse Corp., 1978—90. Mem.: ASPCA, USO, LWV, Am. U. Women Assn., Calif. Nurses Assn., Spl. Olympics, So. Poverty Law Ctr., Nat. Audubon Soc., Earth Justice, Blinded VA, ALS Found., Women for Women, Girls, Inc., Global Fund for Women, Oceanic Alaska Wilderness League, Nat. Holocaust Mus., Smithsonian Am. Indian Mus., Nat. Women's History Mus. Democrat. Avocations: woodworking, writing, bowling, reading. Home: 1320 Lakewood Ave #14 Modesto CA 95355 Office: Meml Med Ctr 1700 Coffee Rd Modesto CA 95355 Office Phone: 209-572-7036. E-mail: potenn1@fishgrin.net.

PONKO, WILLIAM REUBEN, architect; b. Wausau, Wis., Apr. 4, 1948; s. Reuben Harrison and Ora Marie (Ranke) P.; m. Kathleen Ann Hilt, May 5, 1973; children: William Benjamin, Sarah Elizabeth. BArch magna cum laude, U. Notre Dame, 1971. Cert. Nat. Coun. Archtl. Registration Bds. V.p., arch., dir. ednl., instl. specialty Le Roy Troyer & Assocs. (now the Troyer Group), Mishawaka, Ind., 1971—; design instr. dept. arch. U. Notre Dame, 1976. Mem. Ind. State Bd. Registration for Architects, 1990—; mem. registration exam com. Nat. Coun. Archtl. Registration Bds., 1992—, vice chair 1996, chair 1997. Prin. archtl. works include: St. Peter Luth. Ch., Mishawaka, Ind., 1979, 4 brs. for South Bend Pub. Libr., 1983, Edward J. Funk & Sons office bldg. Taylor U., Upland, Ind., 1982, Taylor U. Lbir., carillon tower, 1985, Early Childhood Devel. Ctr. U. Notre Dame, 1994, Convents for Sisters of Holy Cross St. Mary's, Notre Dame, Ind., 1995. Mem. AIA (gold medal for exellence in archtl. edn. 1971), Ind. Soc. Archs. (Design Excellence award 1978, chpt. pres. 1985, Juliet Peddle award 2000). Office: The Troyer Group Inc 550 Union St Mishawaka IN 46544-2346

PONNAMBALAM, ANANTHASEKAR, pediatrician, gastroenterologist; arrived in U.S., 1997; s. Arumugam Ponnambalam and Lalitha Krishnaswamy; m. Kalpana Ananthasekar, July 1, 1993; children: Shivani Ananthasekar, Skandan Ananthasekar. MB, BChir, Stanley Med. Coll., Madras, 1985; Diploma in Child Health, Madras Med. Coll., 1987, MD, 1990, DM, 1993. Diplomate Am. Bd. Pediat., 2000. Attending physician Primary Health Care, Tamilnadu, India, 1990—91; attending physician in pediat. and gastroenterology India, 1993—94; attending physician in pediat. Ministry of Health, Oman, 1994—97; resident in pediat. SUNY Downstate Med. Ctr., Bklyn., 1997—2000, fellow pediat. gastroenterology, 2000—03, rschr. Question writer Am. Bd. Pediats. Contbr. chapters to books. Fellow: Am. Acad. Pediat.; mem.: AMA, Am. Coll. Gastroenterology, Am. Gastroenterology Assn., Naspghan (hepatology com.). Achievements include research in mast cells. Home: Apt C3 1123 Avenue K Brooklyn NY 11230 Office: SUNY Downstate Med Ctr 450 Clarkson Ave Box 49 Brooklyn NY 11203

PONNÉ, NANCI TERESA, entertainment promoter, writer; b. Chgo., May 10, 1958; d. Joseph Anthony and Irene Theresa (Nasadowski) P.; m. Lee Darrow, Oct. 26, 1996. BA, DePaul U., 1980. Performer, 1961—; dancer, choreographer, 1974—; actress, model, 1978—; pub. Chgo. Talent Directory, 1985—, Spotlight, 1989; pres./owner Chgo. Talent Enterprises Inc., 1991—; freelance writer, 1992—; graphic designer, 1993—; clairvoyant, 1996—, website designer, 1998—. Prodr. VIP Forums on Progress in Chgo. Talent Industry, 1990; speaker in field; mem. Loretta Rozek Dance Co., 1975-79. Prodr.: (radio talk show) The Strange World of Lee Darrow, Sta. WONX-AM, 1993. Dem. vol. to Re-elect Mayor Washington, 1987; Dem. vol. for Clinton/Gore, 1992; Dem. vol. to elect Patrick Quinn to Sec. State, Ill., 1990. Named Miss Chgo., recipient Spl. Judges award Miss America Scholarship Pageant, 1981-82; Goodman Sch. of Drama scholar, 1978. Mem. NATAS, HEREIU, Nat. Assn. Photoshop Profls., Chgo. Conv. and Tourism Bur., Ice Skating Inst. (3 Gold medals World Championships, 1994), Ind. Writers of Chgo., Goldfish Soc. Am. Celtic Catholic. Avocations: competitive figure skating, star trek, raising exotic goldfish, metaphysics. Address: 5250 N Broadway St Ste 204 Chicago IL 60640-2304

PONSOR, MICHAEL ADRIAN, federal judge; b. Chgo., Aug. 13, 1946; s. Frederick Ward and Helen Yvonne (Richardson) P.; children from previous marriage, Anne, Joseph; 1 stepchild, Christian Walker; m. Nancy L. Coiner, June 30, 1996. BA magna cum laude, Harvard Coll., 1969; BA, Oxford U., 1971, MA, 1979; JD, Yale U., 1975. Bar: Mass., U.S. Dist. Ct. Mass., U.S. Ct. Appeals (1st cir.), U.S. Supreme Ct. Tchr. Kenya Inst. Administrn., Nairobi, 1967-68; law clk. U.S. Dist. Ct., Boston, 1975-76; assoc. Homans, Hamilton, Dahmen & Lamson, Boston, 1976-78; ptnr. Brown, Hart & Ponsor, Amherst, Mass., 1978-83; U.S. magistrate judge U.S. Dist. Ct., Springfield, Mass., 1984-94, U.S. dist. judge, 1994—. Adj. prof. Western N.E. Coll. Sch. Law, Springfield, 1988—, U. Mass., 1999-2001, Yale Law Sch., New Haven, 1989-91; presenter in field. Rhodes scholar Oxford U., 1969. Mem. Mass. Bar Assn., Hampshire County Bar Assn., Boston Bar Assn. Office: US Dist Ct Rm 539 1550 Main St Springfield MA 01103-1422

PONT, JOHN, football coach, educator; b. Canton, Ohio, Nov. 13, 1927; s. Bautista and Susie (Sikurinec) P.; m. H. Sandra Stoutt, June 23, 1956; children: John W., Jennifer Ann, Jeffrey David. BS, Miami U., Oxford, Ohio, 1952, MS, 1956. Profl. football player, Can., 1952-53; instr., freshman football and basketball coach Miami U., 1953-55, asst. prof., head football coach, 1955-62; head football coach Yale U., 1963-65; prof., head football coach Ind. U., Bloomington, 1965-73; head coach Northwestern U., Evanston, Ill., 1973-77, athletic dir., 1974-79; head football coach, athletic dir. Hamilton, Ohio; head football coach, tennis coach, asst. athletic dir. Coll. Mt. St. Joseph, Cin.; now head football coach Gakusei-Engo-Kai Inc., Tokyo; dir. football ops. Ohio Dominican U., Columbus, 2003—. Agt. Equitable Assurance Soc., U.S., 1981-82; v.p. Fin. Leasing Corp., 1983-85, Splty. Brush, Inc.; athletic dir. Jewish Community Center, Canton, 1953; v.p. NCAA Coun., 1979-80; mem. bd. dirs. Cin. chpt. Nat. Football Found. Hall Of Fame. Mem. Pres.'s Coun. on Phys. Fitness; chmn. Ind. Easter Seal, 1968-69, Ind. div. Cancer Crusade, 1969; bd. dirs. Multiple Sclerosis, N.E. Ill. counc. Boy Scouts Am., Boys Hope. Served with USN, 1945-47. Named Coach of Year Coaches Assn., 1967, Coach of Year Football Writers, 1967, Coach of Yr. Washington Touchdown Club, 1968, Coach of Yr. Walter Camp Found.; recipient Significant Sig award, 1968, Disting. Am. award Nat. Football Found., 1987, Lifetime Achievement award All Am. Football Found., 1997; charter mem. Miami U. Hall of Fame, 1968; elected Ind. Football Hall of Fame, 1984, Butler County Hall of Fame, 1986, Mid-Am. Conf. Hall of Fame, 1992, Ind. U. Sports Hall of Fame, 1992. Mem. Am. Football Coaches Assn. (chmn. ethics com.), Kusatsu City Football Assn. Japan (hon. chmn.), Am. Legion, Blue Key, Sigma Chi, Phi Epsilon Kappa, Omicron Delta Kappa. Republican. Home: 482 White Oak Dr Oxford OH 45056-9272

PONTES, MARCOS C. astronaut; b. Bauru, Sao Paulo, Brazil, Mar. 11, 1963; s. Vergilio and Zuleika Pontes; m. Francisca de Fatima Cavalcanti; 2 children. BS in Aeronautical Tech., Brazil Air Force Acad., Pirassununga, Sao Paulo, 1984; BS in Aeronautical Engring., Instituto Tecnologico de Aeronautica, Sao Jose dos Campos, Sao Paulo, 1993; MS in Systems Engring., Naval Postgrad. Sch., Monterey, Calif., 1998. Commd. 2d lt. Brazil Air Force, 1984, advanced through grades to maj.; jet pilot 2/5 Instrn. Aviation Group, Natal; pilot 3/10 Strike Aviation Advanced Air Controlling; flight safety officer; astronaut NASA, Houston, with Astronaut Office Space Sta. Ops. Br. Achievements include logged over 1,700 flight hours in over 20 different aircraft. Avocations: weightlifting, soccer, guitar, piano, sketching. Office: Astronaut Office/CB NASA Johnson Space Ctr Houston TX 77058

PONTIFF, PAUL E. lawyer; b. Bklyn., June 6, 1930; s. Louis J. and Catherine A. (Menig) P.; m. Judy A. Dufour, June 13, 1998; children: Paul L., Thomas M., Matthew J., Kathy Braley, Shawna Braley, Lynn Lafond. BBA in Acctg., St. Johns U., N.Y.C., 1954, JD, 1959. Bar: N.Y. 1959, U.S. Tax Ct. 1962, U.S. Dist. Ct. (no. dist.) N.Y. 1974. Acctg. tax mgr. Ball George & Co. CPAs, Glens Falls, N.Y., 1960-62; lawyer Bartlett, Pontiff Stewart & Rhodes PC, Glens Falls, 1962—. Bd. dirs. World Awareness Children's Mus., 1986—, past pres.; bd. dirs., treas. Adirondack Vets House, Inc. With U.S. Army, 1954—56. Mem. Warren County Bar Assn. (pres. 1977-78), Estate Planning Coun. Eastern N.Y. (pres. 2000-01), Glens Falls Elks, Glens Falls Rotary Club (past pres.). Avocations: mountain climbing, tennis, golf. Office: Bartlett Pontiff et al PO Box 2168 One Washington St Glens Falls NY 12801 E-mail: pep@bpsrlaw.com.

PÖNTINEN, PEKKA JUHANI, anesthesiologist, consultant; b. Tampere, Finland, Apr. 5, 1932; s. Otto Edvard and Ellen Margareta (Heiniö) P.; m. Anja Anita Kuukankorpi; children: Anna-Katriina, Juha-Pekka, Riikka-Leena, Hanna-Maaria; m. Irja Tuulikki Ketovuori, Jan. 8, 1976; 1 child, Mika Juhani. B in med., Helsinki U., Finland, 1953; MD, Turku U., Finland, 1957; PhD, Kuopio U., Finland, 1977. Diplomate Finnish Bd. Health Legitimation, Finnish Bd. Anesthesiology. Chief dept. anesthesiology Savonlinna Cen. Hosp., Finland, 1965-69, Kainuu Cen. Hosp., Finland, 1969-75; asst. prof. neurophysiology Kuopio U., Finland, 1974-75; med. dir. Kankaanpää Rehabilitation Ctr., Finland, 1989-92; assoc. prof. anesthesiology Kuopio U., 1978—, Tampere U., Finland, 1980—. Chief acupuncture rsch. project Kuopio U., 1976—; cons. dept. neurology Tampere U. Hosp., 1976-93, adv. Ministry of Health & Social Affairs, Helsinki, 1975—, WHO Com. Standardisation Acupuncture Nomenclature, Geneva, Switzerland, 1989 95, European Coun. Subcom. Higher Edn., Strassbourg, France, 1990-95. Author: Acupuncture as a Medical Treatment Modality (in Finnish), 1983, Laser as a Medical Treatment Modality (in Finnish), 1988, Low Level Laser as a Medical Treatment Modality (in Swedish), 1991, Low Level Laser Therapy as a Medical Treatment Modality, 1992, Laseracupuncture (in German), 1993, 2d edit., 1998; co-author: TENS Transcutaneous Electrical Nerve Stimulation in Pain Treatment (in German), 1992, 2d edit., 1996, 3d edit., 2003, Triggerpoints and Triggermechanisms, 1997, 2d edit. (in German), 2001, Alternative and Complementary Therapies in Veterinary Medicine, 1997, Lasers in Medicine and Dentistry, 2000; editor-in-chief Scandinavian Jour. Acupuncture and Electrotherapy, 1987-92; editor Acupuncture & Electrotherapeutics Rsch. Internat. Jour., 1981—, AKU, Akupunktur, Theorie und Praxis, 1991-99, Nordisk Tidskrift for Biologisk Medisin, 2000—; mem. sci. com. Internat. Jour. Pain Therapy, 1991-95. Recipient German Promotion award Pain Rsch. and Therapy, 1988. Fellow: Am. Soc. Laser Medicine and Surgery, European Med. Laser Assn. (2d v.p. 2001—), Am. Coll. Acupuncture (charter), Internat. Coll. Acupuncture and Electro-Therapeutics Rsch. (vice chmn. coun. 1987—), Acupuncture Found. of India (hon.), Am. Acad. Acupuncture (hon.); mem.: Finnish Soc. Anesthesiologists (v.p. 1970—71, pres. 1972—73), Finnish Med. Acupuncture Soc. (hon.), German Med. Acupuncture Soc. (hon.), Brit. Med. Acupuncture Soc. (hon.), Can. Acupuncture Assn. (hon.), Soc. Internat. de Laserterapia Medico Chirugica (v.p. for Finland 1989—), Internat. Assn. Study of Pain (founding), Nordic Acupuncture Soc. (pres. 1980—07, 1909—), Am. Pain Soc. Avocations: classical music, fishing, gardening, skiing, ice hockey. Home: Pikkusaarenkuja 4B 77 33410 Tampere Finland

PONTIUS, STANLEY N. bank holding company executive; b. Auburn, Ind., Aug. 26, 1946; s. Clayton and Frances (Beuret) P.; m. Cheryl Ann Dawson, Aug. 3, 1968; children: Jarrod B., Dorian K. BS, Ind. U., 1968; grad., Stonier Grad. Sch. of Banking, 1979. Bank One, 1968-91; dir., pres., COO 1st Fin. Bancorp, Hamilton, Ohio, 1991, dir., pres., CEO, 1992—2003, 1st Nat. Bank of Southwestern Ohio, Hamilton, 1991-97, chmn., CEO, 1997-98, chmn., 1998—2003. Bd. dirs. Health Alliance Greater Cin., Ohio Casualty Corp., Fort Hamilton Health Network (chmn.), Hamilton Cmty. Found. With U.S. Army, 1968-70. Mem. Am. Bankers Coun., Hamilton-Fairfield Arts Assn. Leadership Hamilton, Metropolitan Growth Alliance, "The Community Banker" magazine (adv. bd.).

PONTON, MICHAEL KAMANO, engineer, educator; s. William Fordyce and Kikue Kamano Ponton; m. Janet Renee Ponton, Jan. 2, 1981; children: Michael Lee, Kathryn Marie. EdD, George Wash. U., Washington, DC, 1996—99, MS, 1986—91; BS, Old Dominion U., Norfolk, VA, 1979—83. Mech. engr./mech. engr. trainee Applied Tech. Lab., Ft. Eustis, Va., 1981—82; acoustics engr., sr. acoustics engr. PRC-Kentron, Inc., Hampton, Va., 1983—87; adj. lectr. Thomas Nelson C.C., Hampton, Va., 1994—95; adj. prof. George Wash. U., Washington, 1998—99; aerospace engr. NASA Langley Rsch. Ctr., Hampton, Va., 1987—99; sr. rsch. & devel. engr., asst. prof. of higher edn. U. Miss., University, Miss., 1999—2001; assoc. prof. higher edn., sr. r & d engr. U. of Miss., University, Miss., 2001—. Sr. assoc. Human Resource Devel. Enterprises, Arlington, Va., 1999—. Fellow NASA Administrator's Fellowship, NASA, 1997-1998; scholar Randolph-Macon Coll. Award Scholarship, 1978—79. Mem.: AIAA, Am. Assn. for Adult and Continuing Edn., Assn. for the Study of Higher Edn., Am. Soc. of Engring. Edn. Achievements include research in NASA Langley Research Center Superior Accomplishment Award for the identification of nonlinear interactions in supersonic free jet flows; NASA Langley Research Center Group Achievement Award for performance as a member of the supersonic twin-jet resonance research team; NASA Group Achievement Award for performance as a member of the B-1B engine nozzle sonic fatigue team; NASA Group Achievement Award for performance as a member of the supersonic jet noise reduction team; development of NASA Langley Research Center Performance Award for contributions resulting in the enhancement of the research capability of the Jet Noise Laboratory; NASA Langley Research Center Superior Accomplishment Award for contributions resulting in the successful modification of the Low Speed Aeroacoustic Wind Tunnel; research in NASA Langley Research Center Turning Goals into Reality Award for performance as a member of the advanced subsonic technology engine systems noise reduction team; NASA Langley Research Center Certificate of Appreciation for efforts leading to the successful demonstration of advanced noise reduction technologies for aircraft applications.

PONTY, JEAN-LUC, violinist, composer, producer; b. Avranches, Normandy, France, Sept. 29, 1942; arrived in U.S., 1973; Grad., Conservatoire National Superieur de Musique, Paris, 1960. Classical violinist to 1964, played with Concerts Lamoureux Symphony Orch, jazz violinist Europe, 1964—69, night club and music festivals with George Duke Trio, U.S., 1969, toured with own group, Europe, 1970—72, recorded with Elton John, Honky Chateau, 1972, with Frank Zappa and the Mothers of Invention, 1973, Mahavishnu Orch., 1974—75, pioneer of electric violin Jazz innovator, headlining internat. concerts with own group since, 1975, appearances (music festivals) in the U.S. including Meadowbrook, Artpark, Wolf Trap, and in Europe Montreux, North Sea Festival, Paris Jazz Festival, spl. appearance as guest soloist with Montreal Symphony Orch., 1984, Toronto Symphony Orch., 1986, New Japan Philharm., 1987, Radio City Orch. N.Y., 1990, Oklahoma City, 1995, world tour with Stanley Clarke and Al DiMeola The Rite of Strings, 1994, 1995, own-produced (albums) Upon the Wings of Music, Aurora, Imaginary Voyage, Enigmatic Ocean, Cosmic Messenger, Jean-Luc Ponty: Live, Civilized Evil, A Taste for Passion, Mystical Adventures, Individual Choice, Open Mind, Fables, The Gift of Time, Storytelling, Tchokola (with African musicians), No Absolute Time, Live at Chene Park, The Very Best of Jean-Luc Ponty, 2000, appearances (with Doug Kershaw and Itzhak Perlman TV series) Fiddlers Three, Soundstage, Rock Concert, The Tonight Show, The Merv Griffin Show, Solid Gold, Pat Sajak Show CNN Entertainment, (TV series) throughout Europe, Brazil, Chile and Venezuela. Recipient internat. awards. Office: c/o Gary S Kleinman 10340 Santa Monica Blvd Los Angeles CA 90025

PONZI, JAMES DOUGHLAS, police officer, computer specialist; b. Denver, May 7, 1947; s. Andrew Joseph and Susie Marie Ponzi; m. Dixie Jean Ponzi, Oct. 17, 1993; children: James, Joseph, Matthew; stepchild: Shelly. BA in English, U. Colo., 1972, BA in Psychology, 1990; MA in Comm., U. Denver, 1999. Produce clk. Del Farm Foods, Denver, 1962-68, 70-73; patrolman Denver Police Dept., 1973-81, sgt., 1981-92, lt., 1992—. Instr. project Prince Denver Police Dept., 1996-98. Author: (manual) Building the Pentium II, 1999. Vol. restoration closed recreation ctr. Denver Police Brotherhood, 1996, fundraiser 1990—; youth fitness instr. Denver Police Dept., 1974. Sgt. U.S. Army, 1968-70. Decorated Bronze star. Mem. U.S. Powerlifting Fedn., Footprinters. Republican. Roman Catholic. Avocations: powerlifting, computers, reading, writing. Office: Denver Police Dept 1331 Cherokee St Denver CO 80204-2720

PONZI KAY, MARYLOU, human resources specialist; b. NYC, Oct. 14, 1950; d. Bruno and Constance Louise (DeLuca) P.; m. William J. Kay, Jr., Oct. 24, 1993. BA, SUNY, Geneseo, 1972; MA, U. Iowa, 1974, SUNY, Buffalo, 1979; cert. in advanced study in labor rels., N.Y. Inst. Tech., 1995. Cert. sr. profl. in human resources Soc. for Human Resources Mgmt. Cert. Inst., 2002. Pers. adminstr. Michelin Tire Corp., Lake Success, N.Y., 1978-83; tech. recruiter 1st Data Resources, Lake Success, N.Y., 1983-84; mgr. human resources Chem. Bank, Jericho, N.Y., 1984-87; pers. officer J.P. Morgan Inc., N.Y.C., 1987-89; mgr. employment Am. Express Inc., N.Y.C., 1989-92; dir. human resources RockBottom Stores, Inc., 1992-95; asst. dir. human resources Canon U.S.A., Lake Success, N.Y., 1995-97, dir. human resources, 1997-2000, dir. corp. human resources and devel., 2000; dir. human resources Esselte Ams., Melville, NY, 2000—02; v.p. global compensation benefits and svcs. Esselte Corp., 2002—. Adj. prof. human resources N.Y. Inst. Tech., 2000—; instr. French and Spanish, Amityville H.S. Adult Edn., 1986-96. Editor: New England Guide, 1982, Canada Guide, 1982. Pres. LeBourget Alliance, Amityville, N.Y., 1995-97; pres. bus. adv. coun. Adults and Children with Learning Disabilities, 1994-97, trustee, 1997—. Mem. ASTD, N.Y. Compensation Assn., Soc. Human Resources Mgmt., Human Resources Strategic Issues Coun., World at Work. Roman Catholic. Avocations: languages, travel, cooking, sports. Office: 48 S Service Rd Melville NY 11747 Office Phone: 631-675-3236. Personal E-mail: mwk93@aol.com. Business E-Mail: mponzi@esselte.com.

POOL, DAVID, software executive; BA, Wash. State U. Product mgr. Clouston LTD; prin. SPRY Inc. (acquired by CompuServe 1995), 1989-95; v.p. Compuserve, 1995-96; prin. DataChannel, 1996-99; founder XML Fund, Bellevue, Wash., 1999—. Office: XML Fund 777 108th Ave NE Ste 1870B Bellevue WA 98004-5142

POOL, MARY JANE, writer, lecturer; d. Earl Lee and Dorothy (Matthews) P. Grad., St. de Chantal Acad., 1942; BA in Art with honors, Drury Coll., 1946; LHD (hon.), Drury U., 2002. Mem. staff Vogue mag., N.Y.C., 1946-68, assoc. merchandising editor, 1948-57, promotion dir., 1958-66, exec. editor, 1966-68; editor House and Garden mag., 1969, editor-in-chief, 1970-80. Cons. Baker Furniture Co., 1981-94, Aves Advt., Inc., 1981-94, bd. dirs.; mem. bd. govs. Decorative Arts Trust; past mem. bd. govs. Fashion Group, Inc., N.Y.C. Author: The Gardens of Venice, 1989, The Gardens of Florence, 1992, Gardens in the City-New York in Bloom, 1999; co-author: The Angel Tree, 1984, The Angel Tree—A Christmas Celebration, 1993, The Christmas Story, 2001; editor: 20th Century Decorating, Architecture, Gardens, Billy Baldwin Decorates, 26 Easy Little Gardens. Mem. bus. com. N.Y. Zool. Soc., 1979-86; trustee Drury Coll., 1971—; bd. dirs. Isabel O'Neil Found., 1978—. Recipient award Nat. Soc. Interior Designers, Disting. Alumni award Drury Coll., 1961, Edith Wharton Women of Achievement award, 1999. Address: 1 E 66th St New York NY 10021-5854

POOL, PHILIP BEMIS, JR., investment banker; b. N.Y.C., Apr. 11, 1954; s. Philip B. and Virginia Middleton (French) P.; m. Joan H. Barnes, May 19, 1978; children: Elliott Livingston, Victoria Middleton. BS in Commerce, U. Va., 1976; MBA, Columbia U., 1980. Asst. treas. The Bank of N.Y., N.Y.C., 1976-78; v.p. Kidder Peabody & Co., Inc., N.Y.C., 1980-85; mng. dir. Merrill Lynch & Co., N.Y.C., 1985-94, Donaldson, Lufkin & Jenrette, N.Y.C., 1994—. Mem. Piping Rock Club (gov. 1989—), Meadow Brook Club, Lyford Cay Club, Racquet and Tennis Club, The Links, U. Va. Alumni Assn. (bd. mgrs.). Republican. Episcopalian. Avocations: golf, squash.

POOLE, EDWARD G. attorney; b. Palo Alto, Calif., May 26, 1960; s. Gordon Leicester and Lois (Teasdale) P.; m. Lynn Anderson, Oct. 17, 1992; children: Sara Elizabeth, William Michael. BA in History cum laude, Bowdoin Coll., Brunswick, Maine, 1982; JD, U. of the Pacific, 1985. Assoc. Ropers, Majeski, Kohn & Bentley, Redwood City, Calif., 1985-87, Anderson & Poole, San Francisco, 1987-90, ptnr., 1990—. Legis. editor McGeorge Law Jour., 1984-85. Bd. dirs., pres., sec. San Francisco Boys Chorus, 1989-96; chair Citizens for a Better San Francisco, 1995—; active alumni coun. Bowdoin Coll., Brunswick, 1998—. Mem. Pacific Union Club. Republican. Presbyterian. Avocations: gardening, bird watching, swimming. Office: Anderson & Poole 601 California St 1300 San Francisco CA 94108

POOLE, EVA DURAINE, librarian; b. Farrell, Pa., Dec. 20, 1952; d. Leonard Milton and Polly Mae (Flint) Harris; m. Tommy Lynn Cole, May 15, 1970 (div. Sept. 1984); 1 child, Tommy Lynn Cole; m. Earnest Theodore Poole, Sept. 22, 1990; 1 child, Aleece Remelle Poole. BA in LS, Tex. Woman's U., 1974, MLS, 1976; postgrad., U. Houston, 1989. Libr. asst. Emily Fowler Pub. Libr., Denton, Tex., 1970-74; children's libr. Houston Pub. Libr., 1974-75, 1st asst. libr., 1976-77; children's libr. Ector County Libr., Odessa, Tex., 1977-80; head pub. svcs. Lee Davis Libr. San Jacinto Coll., Pasadena, Tex., 1980-84; libr. dir. San Jacinto Coll. South, Houston, 1984-90; libr. svcs. mgr. Emily Fowler Pub. Libr., Denton, 1990-93, interim dir., 1993; dir. librs. Denton Pub. Librs., 1993—. Mem. Libr. Svcs. Constrn. Act Adv. Coun., 1994-97, Libr. Svcs. Tech. Act Adv. Coun., 1997-2000; mem. TEXSHARE adv. bd. Tex. State Libr. and Archives Commn., 1999—, chmn., 2003—; bd. dirs. Denton Area Tchrs. Credit Union, 2003—; mem. adv. bd. U. North Tex. Sch. Libr. and Info. Sci., 2000—. Bd. dirs. Amigos Libr. Svcs., 2000-03, Girl Scouts Cross Timbers Coun., 2002-04, United Way of Denton County, 2002—, exec. com., Friends of Librs. U.S.A., 2003—, . Named to Outstanding Young Women of Am., 1991. Mem. ALA (chair Loleta Fyan jury com. 1999-2000), Pub. Libr. Assn. (mem. budget and fin. com. 1999-2002, chair budget and fin. com. 2001-2002, 2004—, nat. conf. com. 2002-04, chair bylaws and orgn. 2002-03), Libr. Adminstrn. and Mgmt. Assn. (program com. 1994-97, mem.-at-large bd. dirs. 2000-02, chair cultural diversity com. 2000-01, com. on orgn. 2002—, rep. to Freedom to Read Found. 2002-03), Tex. Libr. Assn. (pub. libr. divsn. sec. 1995-96, chair 1997-98, leadership devel. com. 1995-97, leadership devel. com. chair 1996-97, alumnae 1st class Tex. Accelerated Libr. Leaders 1994, legis. com. 1997-99, Dist. 7 coun. 1996-99, exec. bd. 1998-2000, 2002-, ad hoc comn. on pub. lib. stds. com. chair 1998-2000, 2002 conf. local arrangements com. 2001-02, chair 2000 conf. program com. 1998-2000, chair awards com. 2001-02, pres.-elect 2002-03, pres. 2003-04), Pub. Libr. Adminstrs. North Tex. (vice chair 1994-95, chair 1995-96), Tex. Mcpl. Libr. Dirs. Assn. (pres. 1995-96, grantee 1993, Libr. of Yr. 1998), Denton Rotary Club, Tex. Mcpl. League (bd. dirs. 1997-2000). Office Phone: 940-349-8750. Business E-Mail: eva.poole@cityofdenton.com.

POOLE, GALEN VINCENT, surgeon, educator, researcher; b. Pewee Valley, Ky., Apr. 13, 1951; s. Galen Vincent and Audrey (Taylor) P.; m. Carol Ruth Shepherd, Aug. 11, 1974; children: Erin Ruth, Matthew Shepherd. AB, Hanover Coll., 1973; MD, U. Ky., 1978. Diplomate Am. Bd. Surgery; added qualifications in surg. critical care. Intern, resident in surgery Bowman Gray-Wake Forest U., Winston-Salem, N.C., 1978-85; asst. clin. prof. Sch. Medicine U. Ill., Urbana, 1986-89; assoc. prof. Med. Ctr. U. Miss., Jackson, 1989-93, prof. surgery, 1993—. Author: Abdominal Wound Dehiscence, 1987; contbr. articles various profl. jours. Chmn. Miss. State Com. on Trauma, Jackson, 1993-2003; dir. Trauma, Surg., and Critical Care, Jackson, 1989-2001; mem. adv. coun. Emergency Med. Svcs. Trauma Care Task Force, Jackson, 1993-2001; mem. Miss. Trauma Adv. Coun., 1998-2002. Lt. col. USAFR, 1985—. Fellow ACS (com. on trauma), Southeastern Surg. Congress; mem. Southern Surgical Assn., Am. Assn. for Surgery of Trauma, Soc. of Univ. Surgeons, Soc. for Surgery of the Alimentary Tract, Soc. for Critical Care Medicine, Alpha Omega Alpha. Home: 145 Summerwood Dr Jackson MS 39208-9075 Office: U Miss Med Ctr Dept Surgery 2500 N State St Jackson MS 39216-4500 Office Phone: 601-984-5115.

POOLE, GORDON LEICESTER, lawyer; b. Mpls., Dec. 25, 1926; s. Arthur Bensell and Mildred Loyal (Wood) P.; m. Lois Claire Teasdale, Oct. 30, 1954; children— David Wilson, Edward Gray, Elisabeth Claire AB, Harvard U., 1949, LL.B., 1952. Assoc. Treadwell & Laughlin, San Francisco, 1953-54, Lillick, McHose & Charles, San Francisco, 1955-63, ptnr., 1963-97, mem. exec. com., 1977-81, chmn. mgmt. com., 1981-84, chmn., 1984-86; of counsel Lillick & Charles LLP, 1997-2001, Nixon Peabody LLP, 2001—. Contbr. articles to profl. jours. Pres. Young Republicans, San Mateo County, Calif., 1958-59; vestryman Trinity Episcopal Parish, Menlo Park, Calif., 1968, 70, 76-78, sr. warden, 1970. Served as sgt. U.S. Army, 1945-47, Korea Mem. Calif. Bar Assn., San Francisco Bar Assn., Maritime Law Assn. (com. on marine financing), Maritime Adminstrv. Bar Assn., ABA, Mng. Ptnrs. Assn. Clubs: Bohemian, World Trade (San Francisco); Ladera Oaks (Menlo Park). Avocations: stamp collecting/philately, marine paintings, prints and memorabilia. Home: 2280 Stockbridge Ave Woodside CA 94062-1130 Office: Nixon Peabody LLP 2 Embarcadero Ctr Ste 2700 San Francisco CA 94111-3996

POOLE, NANCY GEDDES, art gallery curator; b. London, Ont., Can., May 10, 1930; d. John Hardy and Kathleen Edwards (Robinson) G.; m. William Robert Poole, Aug. 15, 1952; 1 child, Andrea Mary. BA, U. Western Ont., 1956, LLD, 1990. Owner, dir. Nancy Poole's Studio, Toronto, Ont., Can., 1969-78; acting dir. London Regional Art Gallery, Ont., Can., 1981—, exec. dir., 1985-89; dir. London Regional Art and Hist. Museums, Ont., Can., 1989-95. Chair governing coun. Ont. Coll. Art, 1972-73; bd. dirs. Robarts

Rsch. Inst., 1995. Author: The Art of London 1939-1980, 1984; editor Jack Chambers, 1978, The Collection, 1990. Bd. govs. U. Western Ont., 1974-85; bd. dirs. Western Area Youth Svcs., 1996. Fellow Ont. Coll. Art. Mem.: Order of Can. Office: 420 Fanshawe Park Rd London ON Canada N5X 2S9

POOLE, RHONDA ANN, editor, reporter; b. Lewisburg, Tenn., Sept. 16, 1958; d. Jimmie Thomas Pruitt, Nannie Ruth Pruitt; m. Russell Dean Poole. Grad., Marshall County H.S., Lewisburg, Tenn., 1976. Graphic artist, reporter Lewisburg (Tenn.) Tribune, 1987—91, reporter, 1991—93, mng. editor, reporter, 1993—2001, editor, reporter, 2001—. Recipient Vol. of Yr., March of Dimes, 2001, Svc. award, Am. Heart Assn., 2000, Good Citizenship award, Cornersville Lions Club, 1999, Cmty. Svc. award, Ladies Aux., Vets. of Foreign Wars, 1999, Svc. award, United Givers Fund, 1996, 1998, Cmty. Svc. award, Marshall County Edn. Assn., 1993, 1995, 1996, 1997, Dedication award, Berlin Vol. Fire Dept., 1996, Ptnrs. In Edn., Spot Lowe Tech. Ctr., 1995, Outstanding Coverage award, Tenn. Gen. Assembly. Mem.: Rotary (hon.; Lewisburg chpt., Paul Harris fellow 2000). Avocations: gardening, travel, writing, counted cross stitch. Office: Lewisburg Tribune 121 First Ave S Lewisburg TN 37091 Office Phone: 931-359-1188. Business E-Mail: rpoole@ltrib-gaz.com.

POOLE, RICHARD WILLIAM, economics professor; b. Oklahoma City, Dec. 4, 1927; s. William Robert and Lois (Spicer) Poole; m. Bertha Lynn Mehr, July 28, 1950; children: Richard William, Laura Lynne, Mark Stephen. BS, U. Okla., 1951, MBA, 1952; postgrad., George Washington U., 1957-58; PhD, Okla. State U., 1960. Rsch. analyst Okla. Gas & Electric Co., Oklahoma City, 1952- 54; mgr. sci. and mfg. devel. dept. Oklahoma City C. of C., 1954-57; mgr. Office of J.E. Webb, Washington, 1957-58; from instr. to prof. econs. Okla. State U., Stillwater, 1960-65, prof. econs., dean Coll. Bus. Adminstrn., 1965-72, v.p., prof. econs., 1972-88, Regents Disting. Svc. prof., prof. econs., 1988-93, emeritus v.p., dean, Regents Disting. Svc. prof./prof. econ., 1993—. Cons. to adminstr. NASA, Washington, 1961—69; adviser subcom. govt. rsch. U.S. Senate, 1966—69; lectr. Intermediate Sch. Banking, Ops. Mgmt. Sch., Okla. Bankers Assn., 1969—88; lectr. internat. off-campus programs Oklahoma City U., 1994—96. Author (with others): The Oklahoma Economy, 1963, County Building Block Data for Regional Analysis, 1965. Mem. Gov.'s Com. Devel. Ark.-Verdigris Waterway, 1970—71, Gov.'s Five-Yr. Econ. Devel. Plan, 1993; past v.p., bd. dirs., past chmn. Mid-Continent R & D Coun. 2d lt. arty. U.S. Army, 1946—48. Named to Coll. Bus. Adminstrn. Hall of Fame, Okla. State U., 1993, Stillwater Hall of Fame, Payne county Hist. Soc. and Stillwater C. of C., 1996, Okla. Higher Edn. Hall of Fame, 1998; recipient Delta Sigma Pi Gold Key award, Coll. Bus. Adminstrn. U. Okla., 1951, Tchg. award on Am. free enterprise sys., Merrick Found., 1992, Disting. Alumni award, Okla. State U., 1995, Henry G. Bennett Disting. Svc. award, 1999. Mem.: Southwestern Bus. Adminstrn. Assn. (past pres.), Nat. Assn. State Univs. and Land Grant Colls. (past chmn. commn. edn. for bus. professions), Am. Assembly Collegiate Schs. Bus. (past bd. dirs.), Southwestern Econ. Assn. (past pres.), Stillwater C. of C. (past bd. dirs., pres.), Santa Fe Trail Assn. (bd. dirs. 2001—02), Okla. C. of C. (past bd. dirs.), Okla. Heritage Assn. (bd. dirs. 2000—), Omicron Delta Kappa, Phi Eta Sigma, Phi Kappa Phi, Beta Gamma Sigma (past bd. dirs.). Home: 815 S Shumard St Stillwater OK 74074-1136

POOLE, ROBERT STEVEN, lawyer, writer; b. San Diego, Calif., June 21, 1952; s. Robert and Billie Poole; m. Anne Rutter, Mar. 1983 (div. Aug. 1984); m. Jennifer Sandra Krauss, May 1990 (div. Oct. 1991). BA, Duke U., 1973; MA in philosophy, U. Fla., 1977; MA in English, U. NH, 1984; JD, U. Mich., Ann Arbor, 1994. Bar: NC 1995. Atty. Harriss & Marion, PLLC, Durham, NC, 1995—2002, private practice, 2003—. Contbr. academic journal articles. Mem.: NC Bar Assn., Am. Assn. of Poets and Writers. Office: Lighthouse Law PO Box 27702 Durham NC 27702 Office Phone: 919-680-8818.

POOLE, ROBERT WILLIAM, JR., foundation executive; b. Englewood, N.J., July 4, 1944; s. Robert William and Frances Ann (Giese) P.; m. Lou Villadsen, May 28, 1983; m. Marilyn V. Kinsky, June 1968 (div. 1974). BS, MIT, 1966, MS, 1967. Systems analyst Sikorsky Aircraft, Stratford, Conn., 1967-70; criminal justice analyst Gen. Rsch. Co., Santa Barbara, Calif., 1970-74; cons. local govt. mgmt. Santa Barbara, 1974-76; pres. Local Govt. Ctr., Santa Barbara, 1976-78, Reason Found., Santa Monica, Calif., 1978—. Author: Cutting Back City Hall, 1980; editor: Instead of Regulation, 1982, Defending a Free Society, 1984, Unnatural Monopolies, 1985; editor, pub. mag. Reason, 1971-89. Bd. dirs. Mission Canyon Assn., Santa Barbara, 1984-85, Santa Barbara Futures Found., 1982-83, Reason Found., 1978—, State Policy Network, 1999—. Fellow NSF, 1966-67. Mem. AAAS, Sigma Xi. Libertarian. Office: Reason Found 3415 S Sepulveda Blvd Ste 400 Los Angeles CA 90034-6014

POOLE, SCOTT, architecture educator; MArch, U. Tex. Registered arch., Va. Instr. Va. Tech., Blacksburg, 1986—, prof. arch., dir. Sch. Arch. and Design, 2003—. Lectr. Yale U., U. Va., Sch. arch., Aarhus, Denmark; Gilmore vis. lectr. U. Calgary, 2000; workshop presenter Royal Danish Acad. Art, Copenhagen, Royal Inst. Tech., Stockholm. Recipient Tchg. Excellence award, Vt. Coll. Arch. and Urban Studies, 2002; Fulbright scholar, Finland. Office: Va Tech Sch Arch and Design 201 Cowgill Hall Blacksburg VA 24061*

POOLE, THOMAS RICHARD, endowment capital campaign director, fund raising counsel; b. Newark, July 15, 1947; s. Frank Baldwin and Edna Laura (Harper) Poole. BA, Ohio Wesleyan U., 1969; MEd, Wright State U., 1975. Cert. fund-raising exec., 1985. Assoc. program dir. Brakeley, John Price Jones Inc., Stamford, Conn., Newport Beach, Calif., 1976-79, program dir., 1979-81, v.p., 1981-91, sr. v.p., 1991—. Assoc. campaign dir. Columbia-Presbyn. Med. Ctr., N.Y.C., 1976-79; campaign dir. Manhattan Eye, Ear and Throat Hosp., N.Y.C., 1979-82; endowment/capital campaign dir., cons. Albany (N.Y.) Med. Ctr., 1984-89; endowment/capital campaign dir. Long Beach (Calif.) Meml. Med. Ctr., 1989-95; campaign dir. Samaritan Health Sys., Phoenix, 1995-2000; cons., 2001—. Author various corporate reports and feasibility studies. Mem. Nat. Soc. Fund-Raising Execs., Assocs. Ohio Wesleyan U. Avocations: reading, sailing, hiking, swimming. Office: Brakeley John Price Jones Inc 2503 Eastbluff Dr Ste 203 Newport Beach CA 92660-3550 Fax: 949-721-1502. E-mail: brakeleynb@aol.com.

POOLE, WILL, information technology executive; BS in Computer Sci., Brown U. Sr. mktg. & engring. mgmt. Sun Microsystems Inc., 1985—90; co-founder eShop Inc., 1991—96; corp. v.p. Microsoft, Redmond, Wash., 1996—. Avocations: bicycling, sailing, building furniture. Office: One Microsoft Way Redmond WA 98052-6399

POOLE, WILLIAM, bank executive; b. Wilmington, Del., June 19, 1937; s. William and Louise (Hiller) P.; m. Mary Lynne Ahroon, June 26, 1960 (div. May 1997); children: William, Lester Allen, Jonathan Carl; m. Geraldine S. Stroud, July 12, 1997. AB, Swarthmore Coll., 1959, LLD (hon.), 1989; MBA, U. Chgo., 1963, PhD, 1966. Asst. prof. polit. economy Johns Hopkins U., Balt., 1963-69; professorial lectr. Am. U., Washington, 1970-71; assoc. professorial lectr. George Washington U., Washington, 1971-73; professorial lectr. Georgetown U., Washington, 1972; vis. lectr. Harvard U., Cambridge, Mass., 1973, MIT, Cambridge, 1974, 77; Bank Mees and Hope vis. prof. econs. Erasmus U. Rotterdam, 1991; prof. econs. Brown U., Providence, 1974-98, dir. ctr. for study fin. markets and insts., 1987-92, chmn. econs. dept., 1981-82, 85-86; economist Bd. Govs. of FRS, Washington, 1964, 69-70, sr. economist, 1970-74; pres., CEO Fed. Res. Bank, St. Louis, 1998—. Adviser Fed. Res. Bank, Boston, 1973-74, cons., 1974-81; vis. economist Res. Bank of Australia, 1980-81; mem. Coun. Econ. Advisers, 1982-85; adj. scholar Cato Inst., 1985-98. Mem. Am. Econ. Assn., Am. Fin. assn. (mem. nominating com. 1979), Western Econ. Assn. (mem. internat. exec. com. 1986-89, mem. nominating com. 1995). Office: Fed Res Bank St Louis 411 Locust St Saint Louis MO 63102-2005 Office Phone: 314-444-8301.

POOLE, WILLIAM DANIEL, writer, editor; b. Statesville, N.C., Nov. 3, 1932; s. William Oscar and Edna (Brewer) P.; m. Sandra Ball, June 14, 1980. BA, Wake Forest U., 1955. Reporter Norfolk (Va.) Virginian-Pilot, 1955-57, Washington Star, 1957-61, real estate editor, 1961-71, features editor, asst. mng. editor, 1971-81; v.p. Ins. Info. Inst., N.Y.C., 1981-91; pub. Insurance Rev. mag., N.Y.C., 1986-91. Contbr. articles to profl. jours. Mem. White House Corr. Assn., Nat. Assn. Real Estate Editors (pres. 1970-71), Newspaper Comics Coun. (chmn. 1975-77), Soc. Am. Travel Writers, Mystery Writers of Am., Ins. Mktg. Comms. Assn., Am. Assn. Sunday and Feature Editors, Amateur Comedy Club, Dutch Treat Club, The Players Club (1st v.p.), Nat. Press Club (D.C.), Omicron Delta Kappa, Sigma Phi Epsilon. Republican. Baptist. Home: 139 E 63rd St New York NY 10021-7408

POOLER, ROSEMARY S. federal judge; b. 1938; BA, Brooklyn Coll., 1959; MA, Univ. of Conn., 1961; JD, Univ. of Mich. Law Sch., 1965. With Crystal, Manes & Rifken, Syracuse, 1966—69, Michaels and Michaels, Syracuse, 1969—72; asst. corp. counsel Dir. of Consumer Affairs Unit, Syracuse, 1972—73; common counsel City of Syracuse Pub. Interest Rsch. Group, 1974—75; chmn., exec. dir. Consumer Protection Bd., 1975—80; commr. N.Y. State Pub. Services Commn., 1981—86; staff dir. N.Y. State Assembly, Com. on Corps., Authorities and Commns., 1987—94; judge Supreme Ct., 5th Jud. Dist., 1991—94; dist. judge U.S. Dist. Ct. (no. dist.) N.Y., Syracuse, 1994—98; cir. judge U.S. Ct. Appeals, 2nd cir., 1998—. Vis. prof. Syracuse Univ. Coll. of Law, 1987—88; v.p. legal affairs Atlantic States Legal Found., 1989—90. Mem.: Assn. of Supreme Ct. Justices of the State of N.Y., Women's Bar Assn. of the State of N.Y., N.Y. State Bar Assn., Onondaga County Bar Assn. Office: 40 Foley Square New York NY 10007

POON, CHRISTINE A. pharmaceutical executive; BS in Biology, Northwestern U.; M in Biology and Biochemistry, St. Louis U.; MBA in Fin., Boston U. Various mgmt. positions Bristol-Myers Squibb, 1985—2000, v.p., sr. v.p. for Can. and L.Am. pharm. ops., pres., gen. mgr. Squibb Diagnostics' Can. operation, 1994, pres. Med. Devices, 1997—98, pres. internat. medicines, 1998—2000; co. group chmn. pharm. group Johnson & Johnson, New Brunswick, NJ, 2000—01, worldwide chmn. pharms. group, 2001—. Bd. dirs. Fox Chase Cancer Ctr., Phila. Named Woman of Yr., Healthcare Businesswomen's Assn., 2004. Office: Johnson & Johnson 1 Johnson and Johnson Plaza New Brunswick NJ 08901

POON, PETER TIN-YAU, engineer, physicist; b. Hengyang, Hunan, China, May 31, 1944; came to U.S., 1967; s. Sam. Chak-Kwong and Lai (Yiu) P.; m. Mable Tsang, Apr. 13, 1974; children: Amy Wei-Ling, Brian Wing-Yan. BS, U. Hong Kong, 1965; MA, Calif. State U., Long Beach, 1969; PhD, U. So. Calif., L.A., 1974. Tech. mgr., sr. engr. Jet Propulsion Lab./Calif. Inst. Tech., Pasadena, 1974—83; advisor Space Sta. Ada Task, task leader software mgmt. and assurance program NASA, 1984—85, software mgmt. stds., element mgr. software info. sys., 1986—88; from multimission sys. mgr. to telecomm. and mission sys. mgr. Jet Propulsion Lab., Pasadena, 1988—2001, telecomm. and mission sys. mgr. Mars Odyssey, Mars Global Surveyor, Mars Exploration Rovers relay and Mars Telecom Orbiter, 2001—. U.S. chmn., program mgmt. com., panel chair Internat. Software Engring. Stds. Symposium, Eng., 1992-93, Can., 1994-95, U.S., 1995-97, 2000—, Brazil, 1998-99; session chair, mem. program com. IEEE Internat. Conf. on Engring. of Complex Computer Systems, Montreal, 1995-96, Como, Italy, 1996-97, Monterey, 1997-98, Tokyo, 1999-2000, Skövde, Sweden, 2000-01, Greenbelt, Md., 2001-02; mem. Internat. Orgn. for Standardization in Info. Tech. Subcom. and U.S. Tech. Adv. Group, 1995—; del. various confs.; mgr. organizing com. European Very Long Baseline Interferometry Network Project mtg., Madrid, 2003, 3rd World Congress on Software Quality, Munich, 2004—. Mem. editl. bd.: Software Quality Profl., Am. Soc. for Quality, 1998—; contbr. articles to profl. jours. Active steering com. United Way, Jet Propulsion Laboratory, 1998-2003. Recipient Group awards NASA, 1977-2002, Recognition cert., Inventions and Contbns. Bd., award from Mars Global Surveyor and Mars Odyssey, 2002. Mem. IEEE (exec. com. software engring. stds. 1993-2000), Arcadia Music Club (pres. 1994-95), Sigma Xi, Eta Kappa Nu, Phi Kappa Phi, Athenaeum. Avocations: music appreciation, hiking, theatre arts. Office: Jet Propulsion Lab Calif Inst Tech 4800 Oak Grove Dr Pasadena CA 91109-8001 Personal E-mail: Petertpoon@yahoo.com.

POONS, LARRY, artist; b. Tokyo, Oct. 1, 1937; came to U.S., 1938; Student, New Eng. Conservatory Music, 1955-57, Boston Mus. Fine Arts Sch., 1958. Mem. vis. faculty N.Y. Studio Sch., 1967. Lectr. in field. Author: The Structure of Color, 1971; exhibitions include include Green Gallery, N.Y.C., 1963—65, exhibitions include Art Inst. Chgo., 1966, Corcoran Gallery Art, Carnegie Inst., 1967, Leo Castelli Gallery, 1967—68, Documenta IV, Kassel, W. Germany, 1968, Whitney Mus. Am. Art Ann., 1968, 1972, Lawrence Rubin Gallery, 1970—73, Whitney Biennial, 1973, Knoedler & Co., 1973—78, Knoedler Contemporary Art, N.Y.C., 1974—78, Andre Emmerlich Gallery, 1979—87, Albright-Knox Art Gallery, Buffalo, 1968, 1970, Pasadena Art Mus., 1969, Gallery 99, Bar Harbor Islands, Fla., 1981, Mus. Fine Arts, Boston, 1981—82, Galerie Montaigne, Paris, 1990, Helander Gallery, Palm Beach, Fla., 1990, Salander-O'Reilly Galleries, N.Y.C., 1991—96, 1998, solo and group shows, Beverly Hills, Calif., 1990, Berlin, 1990, Gallery Afinsa, Madrid, 1991, Frederick Spratt Gallery, San Jose, 1996, 1997, Ruth Bachofner Gallery, Santa Monica, 1996, Art Pub., Geneva, Switzerland, 1997, Claudia Carr Gallery, 1997, Larry Evan/James Willis and Frederick Spratt Gallery, San Francisco, 1997, exhibited in group shows at Matthew Mark, Pat Hearn, 1998, Sideshow 195, Bklyn., 1998, Art and the Am. Experience, Kalamazoo Inst. of the Arts, 1998, Staatliche Kunsthalle, Baden-Baden, Germany, 1999, Ameringe Howard Fine Art, N.Y.C., 2000, Bernard Jacobson, 2002, Side Show Gallery, Bklyn., 2003, Studio 18 Gallery, N.Y.C., 2004, Represented in permanent collections Mus. Modern Art, Allen Meml. Art Mus., Oberlin Coll., Cleve. Mus. Art, Hirschhorn Mus. and Sculpture Garden, Washington, Milw. Art Ctr., Solomon R. Guggenheim Mus., N.Y.C., Tate Gallery, London, Whitney Mus. Am. Art, Met. Mus. Art, Chgo. Art Inst., Denver Mus., Boston Mus. Fine Arts, Albright-Knox Art Gallery, Stedelijk Mus., Amsterdam, Woodward Found., Washington, David Mirvish Gallery, Toronto, Bernard Jacobson Gallery, London, one-man shows include Salander-O'Reilly Gallery, N.Y.C., 2001, Theo Waddington, Boca Raton, Fla., 2000, Galleria Metta, Madrid, 2000, Perrella Gallery, Johnstown, N.Y., 2000, Bernard Jacobson, 2002, Jacobson Howard Gallery, 2004, exhibited in group shows at Studio 18, N.Y., N.Y., 2004, Jacobson Howard, 2003, 2004. Address: 831 Broadway New York NY 10003-4706

POOR, ANDREW FORD, music educator; b. Tucson, Ariz., Oct. 20, 1965; s. William Brown and Shirley Yvonne Poor; m. Marilyn Claire King; children: Kathryne, Addison. BA Music Edn., U. Fla., 1988; MMus Trumpet Performance, U. Cin., 1993, D Music Edn., 1999. Lic. tchr. Ga., 1999, cert. Clin. Educator Fla., 1996. Dir. bands Beaumont Mid. Sch., Kissimmee, Fla., 1988—91; instr. trumpet Cin. Conservatory Prep. Dept., 1992—95; dir. bands Haines City H.S., Fla., 1995—99; brass caption head Drum Corps Internat., Addison, Ill., 2000—02; dir. bands Osborne H.S., Marietta, Ga., 1999—2002. Music adjudicator Bands of Am., Schaumburg, Ill., 1996—2002; music cons. Bibb County Sch. Bd., Macon, Ga., 2002—02; music adjudicator Drum Corps Internat., 1994—2002. Composer: (musical work for band) United We Stand, 2002, (musical work for brass choir) Declarations, 2001, (musical work for band) To Challenge the Spartans, 2001, Faith!, 1999; author: (book) Middle School Music Education, 1999. Festival chmn. Fla. Bandmasters Assn., Tallahassee, 1995—98. Recipient Jim Ott Meml. Scholarship, Sponsors of Musical Enrichment, 1988; fellow, U. Cin., 1993—95. Mem.: Internat. Assn. of Jazz Educators, ASCD, Ga. Music Edn. Assn., Phi Mu Alpha Sinfonia (life; edn. leader for local chpt. 1984—87). Conservative-R. Methodist. Avocation: composing, golf, reading, drawing. Home: 4557 Darrowby Drive Powder Springs GA 30127 Office: Robert L Osborne HS 2451 Favor Rd Marietta GA 30060 Personal E-mail: andrewfpoor@cobbk12.org. Business E-Mail: andrewfpoor@cobbk12.org.

POOR, CLARENCE ALEXANDER, retired physician; b. Ashland, Oreg., Oct. 29, 1911; s. Lester Clarence and Matilda Ellen (Doty) P. AB, Willamette U., 1932; MD, U. Oreg., 1936. Diplomate Am. Bd. Internal Med. Intern U. Wis., Madison, 1936-37, resident in internal med., 1937-40, instr. dept. pathology Med. Sch., 1940-41, clin. instr., clin. asst. dept. internal med., 1942-44; pvt. practice med. specializing in internal med. Oakland, Calif., 1944-97; mem. emeritus staff Highland Alameda County Hosp., Oakland, 1949—; mem. staff Providence Hosp., Oakland, 1947-97, pres. staff, 1968-69; staff mem. Samuel Merritt Hosp., Oakland, 1947-97, Summit Med. Ctr. (merger Providence Hosp. and Samuel Merritt Hosp.), 1991-97; ret., 1997. Mem. Nat. Coun. on Alcoholism, 1974—, bd. dirs. Bay Area, 1977—. Mem. Am., Calif., Alameda-Contra Costa med. assns., Alameda County Heart Assn. (trustee 1955-62, 72-82, pres. 1960-61), Calif. Heart Assn. (dir. 1962-72), Soc. for Clin. and Exptl. Hypnosis, Am. Soc. Clin. Hypnosis, San Francisco Acad. Hypnosis (dir. 1966—, pres. 1973), The Commonwealth Club Calif. Home: 1241 West View Dr Berkeley CA 94705-1650 *Personal philosophy: No matter how easy or how hard the task, the goal is that it be an enjoyment on final review.*

POOR, HAROLD VINCENT, electrical engineering educator; b. Columbus, Ga., Oct. 2, 1951; s. Harold Edgar and Virginia (Hardin) P.; m. Connie Irene Hazelwood, Sept. 1, 1973; children: Kristin Elizabeth, Lauren Alissa. BEE with highest honors, Auburn U., 1972; PhD, Princeton U., 1977. From asst. prof. to prof. U. Ill., Urbana, 1977—90; prof. dept. elec. engring. Princeton (NJ) U., 1990—2003, George Van Ness Lothrop prof. engring., 2003—. Acad. visitor Imperial Coll. London U., 1985, 2003; vis. prof. Newcastle (Australia) U., 1987, Stanford U., 2004; vis. scholar Harvard U., 2004; sr. vis. fellow Imperial Coll., London U., 1993; cons. in field. Author: An Introduction to Signal Detection and Estimation, 1988, 2d edit., 1994, Wireless Communication Systems: Advanced Techniques for Signal Reception, 2004; co-editor: Wireless Communications: Signal Processing Perspectives, 1998; contbr. articles to profl. jours. Grantee NSF, Office of Naval Rsch., Army Rsch. Office, 1978—; recipient NSF Dir.'s award Disting. Teaching scholars; fellow John Simon Guggenheim Meml. Found., 2002—. Fellow IEEE (bd. dirs. 1991-92, Third Millennium medal 2000, grad. tch. award 2001, EAB Major Ednl. Innovation award, 2004), AAAS, Acoustical Soc. Am., Am. Soc. Engring. Edn. (Terman award 1992, Centennial cert. 1993), Inst. Math. Stats., Optical Soc. Am.; mem. NAE, Info. Theory Soc. IEEE (pres. 1990, joint paper award with IEEE Comm. Soc., 2001), IEEE Control Sys. Soc. (editor-in-chief IEEE Transaction Info. Theory, 2004-, Disting. Mem. award 1994), Cosmos Club (Washington). Office: Princeton Univ Dept Elec Engring Princeton NJ 08544-0001 Office Phone: 609-258-1816.

POOR, PETER VARNUM, producer, director; b. N.Y.C., May 17, 1926; s. Henry Varnum and Bessie Breuer (Freedman) P.; m. Eloise Marcovicci Miller, Sept. 27, 1950; children: Candida Eustacia, Anna Maria, Graham Varnum. BA, Harvard U., 1947; postgrad., Centro Sperimentale di Cinematografia, Rome, 1951-52. Prodn. asst. New World Films, N.Y.C., 1948; editor, dir. Willard Pictures, N.Y.C., 1948-51; film editor, dir. and producer CBS News-Airpower, 1954-57, 7 Lively Arts, 1957-58, Twentieth Century, 1958-66, 21st Century, 1966-69, 60 Minutes, 1970-71, CBS Reports, 1971-75; sr. producer NBC News, Monitor, First Camera, White Paper, 1977-87; freelance producer and dir. Crow House Prodns., N.Y.C., 1988—. Instr. in TV journalism Fordham U., 1976-78; mem. Screening Com. for Fulbright Grants in Film, TV and Radio, 1965-67, chmn., 1967, 70; adj. assoc. history of documentary Columbia U. Grad. Sch. Journalism, 1987; adj. asst. prof. visual arts NYU, 1991-92. Producer-dir.: (TV documentary films) What's New at School, 1972, The IQ Myth, 1975, The Biggest Lump of Money in the World, 1985, The Japan They Don't Talk About, 1986, Nuclear Power in France, 1987, The Cronkite Report, 1993. Served with USAF, 1944-45. Recipient Emmy award Acad. TV Arts and Sci., 1961, 62, 67, Lasker TV award Lasker Found., 1968, 69, U.S. CEA Forum award, 1967, 87; hon. mention Robert Kennedy Journalism Award in TV, 1976; Fulbright scholar, 1951-52. Mem. Dirs. Guild Am. (coun. 1980-90), Film Editors Union, Writers Guild Am. East. Clubs: Phoenix S-K (Cambridge, Mass.). Avocations: bicycling, reading, photography, gardening. Home and Office: 1150 5th Ave New York NY 10128-0724 Office Phone: 212-722-3836.

POORMAN, ROBERT LEWIS, education consultant, former college president; b. Germantown, Ohio, Dec. 9, 1926; s. Dale Lowell and Bernice Velma (Krick) P.; m. Lois May Romer, Dec. 26, 1949; children: Paula Beth, Janice Marie, Mark Leon, John Alex, Lisa Ann, Daniel Romer. Student, Ohio Wesleyan U., 1944-45, U. Va., 1945-46; BSEd., Ohio State U., 1948, MA, 1950; postgrad., U. So. Calif., 1951-53; Ed.D. (Kellogg fellow 1960-62, Disting. Scholar Tuition grantee 1960-62), UCLA, 1964. Tchr., counselor, adminstr., secondary schs., Colo., Mo., Ariz., 1948-57; registrar Phoenix Coll., 1957-60; intern Bakersfield Coll., 1960-63, asst. to pres., 1963-64, asso. dean instrn., 1964-65, dean students, 1965-67; founding pres. Lincoln Land C.C., 1967-88, pres. emeritus; edn. cons. MARA of Malaysia, 1983; higher edn. cons. Springfield, Ill., 1988—; interim pres. Parkland Coll., Champaign, Ill., 1989-90. Vis. assoc. prof. Fla. Internat. U., 1994-95; lectr. in field; cons. in field. Contbr. articles to profl. jours. Bd. dirs. (past) United Way of Springfield, bd. dirs. Urban League of Springfield, Good Will Industries of Springfield, Springfield (Ill.) Symphony, Catholic Youth Orgn., Springfield, Gov.'s Prayer Breakfast, Springfield Mental Health, Griffin H.S. Bd., Diocesan Sem.; mem. adv. bd. Sacred Heart Acad., Springfield Commn. on Internat. Visitors, Sister Cities Assn. Served with USNR, 1944-46. Recipient Midwest region CEO of Yr. Assn. C.C. Trustees, 1988, recognition Ill. C.C. Trustees Assn., 1988; named an Outstanding CEO for Ill. Cmty. Colls. U. Tex. Leadership Program, 1987; named a leader in shaping the century State Jour. Register, 1999; Phi Theta Kappa fellow, 1981; Fulbright Sr. scholar, Lithuania, 1993, Ukraine, 1996, China, 2000; Fulbright sr. specialist, Tanzania, 2003-04. Mem. Am. Assn. Cmty. and Jr. Colls., Ill. Coun. Pub. C.C. Pres. (sec. 1973-74, vice chmn. 1974-75, chmn. 1975-76), Coun. North Ctrl. Cmty. and Jr. Colls. (exec. bd. 1979-81), North Ctrl. Assn. (cons., evaluator 1984-88) Republican. Roman Catholic. Home and Office: 2324 Willemoore Ave Springfield IL 62704-4362 Fax: 217-793-6939. E-mail: robert.poorman@llcc.edu.

POORMAN, RONALD JAMES, music educator; b. Hershey, Pa., Sept. 27, 1941; s. Ernest and Mary E. Poorman; m. Karen M. Mellinger, Dec. 19, 1964; children: Melinda Sweeney, Jennifer Hodgson. BS in Music Edn., Lebanon Valley Coll., Annville, Pa., 1963; MS in Music Edn., Ithaca Coll., 1965. Woodwind instr. Middletown (Pa.) Sch. Sys., 1963—66; dir. bands Pleasantville (NJ) Pub. Schools, 1966—73, So. Regional HS Dist., Manahawkin, NJ, 1973—2000; asst. prof. music, dir. bands Richard Stockton Coll. NJ, Pomona, 2000—. Assoc. condr. South Jersey Area Wind Ensemble, Linwood, NJ, 1997—; pvt. woodwind instr., Egg Harbor Twp., NJ, 1963—. Author: Everyone's Guide to Instrumental Music Lessons, 1990. Staff sgt. USAF, 1960—69. Mem.: Music Educator Nat. Conf. Home: 214 Blackman Rd Egg Harbor Township NJ 08234 Office: Richard Stockton Coll NJ PO Box 195 Pomona NJ 08240 Personal E-mail: ronald.poorman@comcast.net.

POP, EMIL, research chemist; b. Tirgu Mures, Romania, Aug. 12, 1939; came to U.S., 1983; s. Victor and Rosalia (Graf) P.; m. Elena Petrina Petri, Apr. 28, 1964; 1 child, Andreea Cristina. BS, Babes- Bolyai U., Cluj., Romania, 1961; PhD, Inst. Chemistry, Cluj., and Supreme Coun. for Sci. Titles, Dept. of Edn. B, 1973. Chemist Chem.-Pharm. Rsch. Inst., Cluj, 1962-65, rsch. sci., group leader, 1965-78, prin. rsch. sci., group and compartment leader, 1978-83; rsch. assoc. Dept. Medicinal Chemistry Coll. Pharmacy, U. Fla., Gainesville, 1983-86; rsch. sci. Pharmatec, Inc., Alachua, Fla., 1986-87, group leader, 1987-89, assoc. dir. chem. devel., 1989-92, dir. chemistry, 1992, Pharmos Corp., Alachua, 1992-95, sr. dir. chemistry, 1995-98; founder, pres., CEO Alchem Labs Corp., Alachua, Fla., 1998—. Courtesy prof. Health Sci. Ctr., Ctr. for Drug Discovery, U. Fla., 1998. Contbr. articles to profl. jours.; inventor in field. Inaugural mem. adv. bd. Fla. Ctr. for Heterocyclic Compounds, U. Fla., 1999—. Recipient N. Teclu award Romanian Acad. Sci., 1980. Fellow Am. Inst. Chemists, Am. Assn. Pharm. Sci.; mem. AAAS, Am. Chem. Soc., Internat. Union Pure and Applied Chemistry, N.Y. Acad. Scis., Internat. Soc. Quantum Biology and Pharmacology, Assn. de Pharmacie Galenique Industrielle. Greek Catholic. Achievements include design and synthesis of pharmaceutical compounds in particular prodrugs, brain specific chemical drug delivery systems and synthetic cannabinoids; M.O. calculations. Home: 1113 NW 58th Ter Gainesville FL 32605-4477

POP, IGGY (JAMES NEWELL OSTERBERG), composer, singer, musician; b. Muskegon, Mich., Apr. 21, 1947; s. James Newell and Louella Kristine (Christensen) Osterberg. Student, U. Mich., 1963-64. Drummer, lead singer, composer The Iguanas, 1966-67; lead singer, composer The Stooges, 1967-74; solo artist, 1975—; toured extensively with David Bowie and others.

Composer music and lyrics for over 90 songs including China Girl (recorded by David Bowie); rec. artist, albums include The Stooges, 1970, Funhouse, 1972, Raw Power, 1973, Kill City, 1976, The Idiot, 1977, Lust for Life, 1977, TV Eye, 1977, New Values, 1979, Soldier, 1980, Party, 1982, Zombie Birdhouse, 1983, Blah, Blah, Blah, 1986, Instinct (Grammy nomination 1988), 1988, Brick by Brick, 1990, ArizonaDream, 1992, American Caesar, 1993, We Are Not Talking About Commercial Shit, 1995, Wake Up Suckers, 1995, Naughty Little Doggie, 1996, Nued & Rude: The Best of Iggy Pop, 1997, Avenue B, 1999; has recorded for Elektra, Columbia; RCA, solo albums for Arista, Chrysallis, A&M; guest appearances on television and prodns.; known as Godfather of Punk; appeared in films including Sid & Nancy, 1986, The Color of Money, 1986, Cry-Baby, 1990, Coffee and Cigarettes (Palme d'Or 1993), Tank Girl, 1995, Howard Stern's Private Parts, 1997, The Rugrats Movie (voice), 1998, Snow Day, 1999. Named Punk of the Yr. Creem Mag.

POPE, ALEXANDER H. former lawyer, county assessor and non-profit administrator; b. NYC, June 4, 1929; s. Clifford H. and Sarah H. (Davis) P.; m. Katherine Mackinlay, Sept. 14, 1985; children by previous marriage: Stephen C., Virginia L., Daniel M. AB with honors, U. Chgo., 1948, JD, 1952. Bar: Ill. 1952, Republic of Korea 1953, Calif. 1955, U.S. Supreme Ct. 1970. Pvt. practice, L.A., 1955-77, 87-96; assoc. David Ziskind, L.A., 1955; ptnr. Shadle, Kennedy & Pope, L.A., 1956, Fine & Pope, L.A., 1957-59, 61-77; legis. sec. to gov. State of Calif., 1959-61; county assessor Los Angeles County, L.A., 1978-86; ptnr. Mayer, Brown & Platt, L.A., 1987-88, Barash & Hill, L.A., 1989-92; of counsel Seyforth, Shaw, Fairweather & Geraldson, L.A., 1993-96; exec. dir. Calif. citizens budget commn. Ctr. Govtl. Studies, Los Angeles, 1997-2000. Nat. bd. mem. Vols. for Stevenson, 1952; vice-chmn. L.A. County Dem. Cen. Com., 1958-59; pres. Westchester Mental Health Clinic, 1963; mem. Calif. Hwy. Commn., 1966-70; mem. L.A. Bd. Airport Commrs., 1973-77, v.p., 1973-75, pres., 1975-76; trustee, sec. L.A. Theatre Ctr., 1984-89; trustee Spring St. Found., 1990-2004. With U.S. Army, 1952-54, Korea. Mem. ACLU, U. Chgo. Alumni Clubs Greater L.A. and San Francisco Bay area (pres. 1970-71), Population Connection, Ams. United, Sierra Club, Common Cause, Order of Coif, Phi Beta Kappa. Democrat. Unitarian. Home: 1155 Euclid Ave Berkeley CA 94708-1602

POPE, ANDREW, health science association administrator; Acting dir., sr. program officer Bd. on Neuroscience and Behavioral Health, Inst. of Med., 1998-99; dir. Bd. on Health Sciences Policy, Inst. of Medicine, 1999—; acting dir. Bd. on Neuroscience and Behavioral Health, Inst. of Med., 2003—. Office: Inst Medicine 500 5th St, NW Washington DC 20418-0007*

POPE, ANDREW JACKSON, JR., (JACK POPE), retired judge; b. Abilene, Tex., Apr. 18, 1913; s. Andrew Jackson and Ruth Adelia (Taylor) P.; m. Allene Esther Nichols, June 11, 1938; children: Andrew Jackson III, Walter Allen. BA, Abilene Christian U., 1934, LLD (hon.), 1980; LLB, U. Tex., 1937; LLD (hon.), Pepperdine U., 1981, St. Mary's U., San Antonio, 1982, Okla. Christian U., 1983. Bar: Tex. 1937. Practice law Corpus Christi, Corpus Christi, 1937-46; judge 94th Dist. Ct., Corpus Christi, 1946-50; justice Ct. Civil Appeals, San Antonio, 1950-65, Supreme Ct. of Tex., Austin, 1965-82, chief justice, 1982-85. Author: John Berry & His Children, 1988; chmn. bd. editors Appellate Procedure in Tex., 1974; author numerous articles in law revs. and profl. jours. Pres. Met. YMCA, San Antonio, 1956-57; chmn. Tex. State Law Libr. Bd., 1973-80; trustee Abilene Christian U., 1954—. Seaman USNR, 1944-46. Recipient Silver Beaver award Alamo council Boy Scouts Am., 1961, Distinguished Eagle award, 1983; Rosewood Gavel award, 1962, St. Thomas More award, St. Mary's U., San Antonio, 1982; Outstanding Alumnus award Abilene Christian U., 1965; Greenhill Jud. award Mcpl. Judges Assn., 1980; Houston Bar Found. citation, 1985; San Antonio Bar Found. award, 1985; Disting. Jurist award Jefferson County Bar, 1985; Outstanding Alumnus award U. Tex. Law Alumni Assn., 1988; George Washington Honor medal Freedom Found., 1988; Disting. Lawyer award Travis County, 1992. Fellow Tex. Bar Found. (Law Rev. award 1979, 80, 81); mem. ABA, State Bar Tex. (pres. jud. sect. 1962, Outstanding Alumnus U. Tex. Sch. of Law 1994, Outstanding Fifty Years Lawyer award 1994), Tex. Bar Found., Order of Coif, Nueces County Bar Assn. (pres. 1946), Travis County Bar Assn., Bexar County Bar Assn., Tex. Philos. Soc., Austin Knife and Fork (pres. 1980), Am. Judicature Soc., Tex. State Hist. Assn., Tex. Supreme Ct. Hist. Soc. (v.p.), Sons of Republic of Tex., Statesmanship award State Bar Tex., 1998, Christian Chronicle Coun. (chmn.), Masons, K.P. (grand chancellor 1946), Alpha Chi, Phi Delta Phi, Pi Sigma Alpha. Mem. Ch. of Christ. Home: 2803 Stratford Dr Austin TX 78746-4626

POPE, ANDY, musician, educator; b. Moscow, Idaho, Mar. 27, 1953; s. David Kenneth and Mary Elizabeth Pope; m. Janet Elizabeth Sanborn, Sept. 3, 1984 (div. Sept. 3, 1991); 1 child, Angela Mary. Cert. Calif. Basic Edn. Skills Test. Rock musician The Flock, Naples, Italy, 1966—69, Rhubarb, Stockton, Calif., 1969—71; asst. mus. dir. Lincoln Summer Theatre, Stockton, 1971—73, mus. dir., 1974—77, ASUCD Mus. Theatre, Davis, Calif., 1977—79; asst. mus. dir. Pacific Conservatory of the Performing Arts, Santa Maria, Calif., 1980—82; singer-songwriter Blackwater Cafe, Stockton, 1982—85; mus. dir. Gt. Am. Melodrama and Vaudeville, Bakersfield, Calif., 1986; accompanist, condr. Stockton Civic Theatre, 1987—88; piano tchr. Music Masters Studio, Calif., 1987—88; accompanist Mason St. Wine Bar, San Francisco, 1988—90; singer-songwriter Simple Pleasures Cafe, San Francisco, 1988—90; house pianist Gulliver's of San Francisco, Burlingame, Calif., 1990—99; owner, pvt. piano and voice instr. Andy Pope, San Mateo, Calif., 1992—; ch. organist Good Shepherd Luth. Ch., Burlingame, 1997—99; instrnl. aide in spl. edn. Burlingame Sch. Dist., 1997—99, accompanist, 1997—2003; mus. dir. San Carlos Children's Theater, Calif., 2000—03, 2000—03; accompanist Pensinsula Voice Studio, Redwood City, Calif., 2001—03; piano tchr. Spindrift Sch. of Performing Arts, Pacifica, Calif., 2001—02; accompanist Broadway By the Bay, Calif., 2001; min. of music Holy Cross Luth. Ch., Pacifica, 2001—03; musical dir. Hillbarn Theatre Summer Youth Conservatory, Foster City, 2002; mus. dir. St. Mark's Sch. Mus. Theatre Program, Terra Linda, Calif., 2002, Yes Theatre, San Anselmo, Calif., 2002; music tchr. Kids Connection Elem. Sch., Foster City, Calif., 2002—04; music dir. Kids Connection Children's Choir, Foster City, 2003—04; singing tchr. Broadway By the Bay Youth Theatre Conservatory, Hillsborough, Calif., 2003. Cons. Andy Pope, San Mateo, 1983—; dir. Turnbull Children's Acad. Children's Theatre Program, San Mateo, 1992—93; dir., choreographer, music. dir., piano-condr. for Popesongs Lincoln Summer Theatre After Hours, Stockton, 1977, dir., choreographer, music. dir., piano-condr. for A Tribute to the Beatles, 75, dir., choreographer, music. dir., piano-condr. for Andy Pope Is Alive and Well, 74; actor ASUCD Mus. Theatre, Davis, Calif., 1974; actor dramatic arts dept. U. Calif., Davis, 1974; actor Lincoln Summer Theatre, Stockton, 1972—73; pres. Burden Project LLC, 2004. Author: (book) Reflections of a Growing Christian; librettist, lyricist: mus. play The Burden of Eden, lyricist: mus. revue Popesongs, Andy Pope is Alive and Well, librettist, lyricist: mus. comedy Over My Dead Body (1st Pl. award in Playwrighting Competition, 1974), lyricist: rock opera Euphoria, Evil. Supporter Police Activities League, San Mateo, 2003—04. Recipient Best Letter to the Editor award, The Bakersfield Californian, 1986, H.S. Math award, Bank of Am., 1971, First Pl. award in Jr. Advanced Category in Piano Performance, Music Tchrs. Assn. of Solano, Sonoma and Napa Counties, 1966, Calif. State scholarship, State of Calif., 1971—74, Class C Rating, Internet Chess Club, 2002. Libertarian. Avocations: long distance running, long distance walking, long distance bicycling, chess, yoga. Mailing: 6333 Pacific Ave Box 312 Stockton CA 95207 Home: 7512 Lordsburg Dr Bakersfield CA 93309 Office Phone: 209-430-9559. Personal E-mail: minstrelite@yahoo.com. E-mail: minstrelite@earthlink.net.

POPE, ANNE B. agency head, business executive, lawyer; Degree, Vanderbilt U.; degree Cumberland Sch. of Law, Samford U. Bar: Tenn., DC. Commr. State of Tenn. Dept Commerce and Ins., 1999—2003; fed. co-chair Appalachian Regional Commn., 2003—; assoc. atty. Webster, Chamberlain and Bean, Washington, 1988—92; pres., CEO, v.p., CFO, Parks-Belk Co., 1992—95; pres. Proffitts of the Tri-Cities, 1995—97; exec. dir. Tenn. Film Entertainment, and Music Commn., 1997—99; clk. US Dist. Judge James D. Todd, Jackson, Tenn. Mem. Gov. Sundquist's Coun. of Excellence in Higher Edn., 1997, Gov. Sundquist's Commn. on Practical Govt., 1999. Mem.: Johnson City C. of C. Office: 1666 Connecticut Ave NW Washington DC 20009-1068

POPE, CARL, professional society administrator; BA summa cum laude, Harvard U., 1967. Vol. Peace Corps, Barhi Barhi, India, 1967-69; with Sierra Club, San Francisco, assoc. conservation dir., polit. dir., conservation dir., exec. dir., 1992—. Bd. dirs. Calif. League of Conservation Voters, 1986-87, exec. dir., 1973-83; bd. dirs. Pub. Voice, 1989 92, Nat. Clean Air Coalition, Calif. Common Cause, 1976-78, Pub. Interest Econs., Inc., 1973-76; bd. dirs. Zero Population Growth, 1972-90, also polit. dir., 1970-73. Address: Sierra Club 85 2nd St Fl 2 San Francisco CA 94105-3456

POPE, CHARLES C. data processing executive; BS in Acctg., U. Utah; MBA, Brigham Young U. With Hewlett Packard Co., Diasonics Corp.; dir. budgets and analysis Seagate Technology, Scotts Valley, Calif., 1985, dir. fin. for Thailand ops., v.p. fin. Far East ops., v.p. fin., treas.; v.p., gen. mgr. Seagate Magnetics; sr. v.p. storage products Seagate Technologies, sr. v.p. fin., CFO, 1998—. Office: Seagate Technology Inc PO Box 66360 Scotts Valley CA 95067-0360

POPE, FRANCES ELAINE, music educator; b. Connellsville, Pa., Apr. 6, 1947; d. George Coldren and Margaret C. (Martin) Pratt; m. Daniel Ferree Pope; children: Natalie Pope VanCleave, Richard Martin Ferree, Julia Therasse. BA, Ohio State U., 1969; MLS, U. Mich., 1970. Reference libr. Marion (Ohio) Pub. Libr., 1970—73; founder, CEO, dean St. Michael's Music Acad., Issaquah, 1994—99; founder, dean Winn Acad. Music, Preston, Wash., 2000—. Part-time libr., receptionist Boeing Co., Bellevue, Wash., 1990—92; part-time reporter Issaquah (Wash.) Press, 1976—80; freelance writer. Pres., bd. dirs. Issaquah Libr., 1974—89; pres. Greater Issaquah Coalition, 1986; vestry mem. St. Michael & All Angels Episcopal Ch., Issaquah, 1991—93; mem. Microsoft Orch., 1999—, Sammamish Symphony, 2002—. Mem.: Alpha Gamma Delta. Episcopalian. Avocations: reading, writing, violin, horseback riding. Home: 624 Mt Fury Cir SW Issaquah WA 98027 Office: Winn Acad Music 43233 176th St North Bend WA 98045 E-mail: winnmusicdean@aol.com.

POPE, FRED WALLACE, JR., lawyer; b. Sanford, Fla., Feb. 9, 1941; s. Fred Wallace and Dorothy (Marshall) P.; m. Jane Laird Miller, Dec. 27, 1962 (div. Oct. 1986); children: Catherine W., Gregory W.; m. Christine R. Fredrick, Jan. 4, 1991. BA in Polit. Sci., U. Fla., 1962, JD with honors, 1969; AM in Internat. Rels., Boston U., 1965. Bar: Fla. 1970, U.S. Dist. Ct. (so., mid. and no. dists.) Fla., U.S. Supreme Ct. 1975, U.S. Ct. Appeals (11th cir.) 1983. Rsch. aide 2d Dist. Ct. Appeal, Lakeland, Fla., 1970; assoc. Trenam, Simmons, Kemker, Scharf & Barkin, Tampa, Fla., 1970-74; ptnr. Johnson, Pope, Bokor, Ruppel & Burns, P.A., Clearwater, Fla., 1974—. Dir. Citizens Bank Clearwater, 1986-98, First Nat. Bank of Fla., 1998-01. Trustee The Fla. Orch., Tampa, 1984—, chmn. bd. trustees, 1991-93; bd. dirs. Pinellas County Arts Coun., Clearwater, 1988-93. Capt. U.S. Army, 1962-67. Mem. ABA (coun. mem. sect. litigation 1983-86, editor, chief Litigation 1979-80), The Fla. Bar (gov. 1982-86), Clearwater Bar Assn. (pres. 1980-81). Office: Johnson Blakely Pope Bokor Ruppel & Burns PA 911 Chestnut St Clearwater FL 33756-5643 E-mail: wallyp@jpfirm.com.

POPE, HARRISON GRAHAM, JR., psychiatrist, educator; b. Lynn, Mass., Dec. 26, 1947; s. H. Graham and Alice (Rider) P.; m. Mary M. Quinn, June 7, 1974; children: Kimberly, Hilary, Courtney. AB summa cum laude, Harvard U., 1969, MPH, 1972, MD, 1974. Diplomate Am. Bd. Psychiatry and Neurology. Resident in psychiatry McLean Hosp., Belmont, Mass., 1974-77, clin. rsch. fellow Mailman Rsch. Ctr., 1977-79, asst. psychiatrist, 1979-84, assoc. psychiatrist, 1984-92, psychiatrist, 1992—, chief biol. psychiatry lab., 1984—; Dupont-Warren rsch. fellow Harvard Med. Sch., Boston, 1976-77. Instr. psychiatry Harvard Med. Sch., Boston, 1977-82, asst. prof., 1982-85, assoc. prof., 1985-99, prof. 1999—; staff psychiatrist Hampstead (N.H.) Hosp., 1976-80; vis. fellow The Maudsley Hosp., London, 1977, Hôpital. Ste. Anne, Paris, 1977; mem. Am. Psychiat. Assn., 1976-80, adv. com. on schizophrenic, paranoid and affective disorders, 1979, adv. com. on preparation of DSM-III-R, 1984, task force on nomenclature and stats., 1979, 84. Author: Voices from the Drug Culture, 1971, The Road East, 1974, (with J.I. Hudson) New Hope for Binge Eaters: Advances in the Understanding and Treatment of Bulimia, 1984; co-editor: The Psychobiology of Bulimia, 1987, Use of Anticonvulsants in Psychiatry: Recent Advances, 1988, Psychology Astray: Fallacies in Studies of "Repressed Memory" and Childhood Trauma, 1997; The Adonis Complex: The Secret Crisis of Male Body Obsession, 2000; mem. editl. bd. European Psychiatry, Paris, 1984—, Internat. Jour. of Eating Disorders, 1984—, Jour. Clin. Psychiatry, 1993-; contbr. numerous articles to profl. jours. Named one of Outstanding Americans under 40 Esquire mag., 1984; fellow Scottish Rite Schizophrenia Program, No. Masonic Jurisdiction, 1977-81, Charles A. King Trust, Boston, 1977-79. Avocation: weightlifting. Office: McLean Hosp 115 Mill St Belmont MA 02478-1048

POPE, INGRID BLOOMQUIST, sculptor, poet, painter; b. Arvika, Sweden; became U.S. citizen. d. Oscar Emanuel and Gerda (Henningson) Brostrom; m. Howard Richard Bloomquist, Feb. 14, 1941 (dec. Nov. 1982); children: Dennis Howard, Diane Cecile Connelly, Laurel Ann Shields; m. Marvin Hoyle Pope, Mar. 9, 1985 (dec. June 1997). BA cum laude, Manhattanville Coll., 1979, MA in Humanities, 1981; MA in Religion, Yale U., 1984. Exhbns. include Manhattanville Coll., Purchase, N.Y., Yale Div. Sch., Ch. of Sweden in N.Y.C., First Ch. of Round Hill; author: (books) Musings, 1994, Hosannah, Help Please, 1999, Blessings, 2003. Past bd. dirs. N.Y.C. Mission Soc., Greenwich YWCA, Greenwich Chaplaincy, Greenwich Acad. Parents' Assn., past pres; past trustee First Ch. Round Hill, Greenwich; pres. Ch. Women United, Greenwich, 1989-91. Mem. AAUW, Nat. Assn. Pen Women, English Speaking Union, Nat. Wildflower Assn., Yale Club N.Y.C., Lakeview Club (Austin, Tex.), Acad. Am. Poets, Nat. Mus. of Women in Arts, Yale Alumnae Club (Austin and Greenwich, Conn.). Home: 538 Round Hill Rd Greenwich CT 06831-2641 *I need to share my feelings deep inside be it in verse or prose or form or line. I need to say it, do it, show, or write and so creatively I try to do my best. I lift up brush and paint a scene, I struggle with a stone or mold in clay or write my verse just as I do today.*

POPE, JOHN EDWIN, III, newspaper sports editor, columnist; b. Athens, Ga., Apr. 11, 1928; s. Henry Louis and Rose (McAfee) P.; m. Eileen Pope. BA in Journalism, U. Ga., 1948. Sports editor Banner-Herald, Athens, Ga., 1943-48; So. sports editor UPI, Atlanta, 1948-50; sports writer Atlanta Constn., 1950-54; exec. sports editor Atlanta Jour., 1954-56; asst. sports editor Miami (Fla.) Herald, 1956-67, sports editor, 1967—2001. Author: Football's Greatest Coaches, 1956, Baseball's Greatest Managers, 1960, Encyclopedia of American Greyhound Racing, 1963, Ted Williams: The Golden Year, 1970, (with Norm Evans) On the Line, 1976, The Edwin Pope Collection, 1988; contbr. articles to popular mags. and Ency. Brittanica, World Book. Recipient Bill Corum Meml. award Thoroughbred Racing Assn., 1962, top sports column award Nat. Headliners Club, 1962, 79, 82, 86, Eclipse award Thoroughbred Racing Assn., 1976, 82, 86, Red Smith award AP Sports Editors, 1989; named to Internat. Churchmen's Sports Hall of Fame, 1976; recipient Knight-Ridder editl. excellence award, 1996, Nat. Sportswriters and Sportscasters Assn. Hall of Fame, 1995, Fla. Sports Hall of Fame, 1996, Bert McGrane award Coll. Football Hall of Fame, 2000, Dick McCann award NFL Pro Football Hall of Fame, 2002; named Orange Bowl Hall of Fame, 2003. Mem. Profl. Football Writers Am. (pres. 1968-69), Football Writers Assn. Am., Golf Writers Am., Nat. Turf Writers, U.S. Tennis Writers. Presbyterian. Office: Miami Herald 235 Harbor Dr Key Biscayne FL 33149 E-mail: epope@herald.com.

POPE, JOHN M. journalist; b. Hattiesburg, Miss., Nov. 5, 1948; s. Paul M. Jr. and Mary Lee (Scott) P.; m. Diana Pinckley, May 19, 1984. BA cum laude, U. Tex., 1970, MA, 1972. Copy editor The States-Item, New Orleans, 1972-73, reporter, 1973-80, The Times-Picayune, New Orleans, 1980-86, med.-health reporter, 1986—. Co-author: American First Ladies: Their Lives and Their Legacy, 1996. Recipient Frank Allen award, La.-Miss. AP, 1989, Med. Writing award, La. State Med. Soc., 1990, 1998, Louise McFarland award for excellence in pub. health comm., La. Pub. Health Assn., 2003; fellow, CDC, 2001; Knight Ctr. for Specialized Journalism fellow, 1999, Phi Beta Kappa Soc. fellow. Mem. Soc. Profl. Journalists, Nat. Assn. Sci. Writers, Investigative Reporters and Editors, Press Club New Orleans (4 1st pl. awards 1978-87, Alex Waller award 1987), Phi Beta Kappa. Avocations: running, travel, aerobics. Office: The Times-Picayune 3800 Howard Ave New Orleans LA 70125-1429 Office Phone: 504-826-3317. E-mail: jpope@timespicayune.com.

POPE, KERIG RODGERS, magazine executive; b. Waukesha, Wis., Sept. 30, 1935; s. Kerig James Pope and Mildred (Offerman) Troemel; m. Claudia T. Koralewski, Nov. 1961 (div. 1975); children— Kerig William, Giles Thomas; m. Beth Leslie Kasik, May 24, 1980; children: Kolin Jared, Zoe Alissa. Grad., Art Inst. Chgo., 1958. Designer Jack Denst Wallpaper Designs, Chgo., 1958-60; designer Continental Casualty Ins. Co., Chgo., 1960-62, Leo Burnett Advt. Agy., Chgo., 1962-63; art dir. Mercury Records Corp., Chgo., 1963-66; mng. art dir. Playboy mag., Chgo., 1966—. Exhibited in group shows Whitney Mus. Am. Art, N.Y.C., 1969, Mus. Contemporary Art, Chgo., 1972, Bienal de Sao Paulo, Brazil, 1973, Museo de Arte Moderno, Mexico City, 1974, Nat. Collection Fine Arts, Washington, 1979, Moderno, Mexico City, 1974, Mus. Contemporary Art, Chgo., 1996; represented in permanent collections Nat. Collection Fine Arts, Washington, Mus. Contemporary Art, Chgo., Smart Mus., U. Chgo. Recipient silver medal Communigraphics, N.Y.C., 1971, gold medal, 1971, 72; award of excellence Soc. Publ. Designers, 1979, 4 awards of excellence Design Ann., 1984, Silver medal Illustrators 29, 1986, Silver medal Soc. of Illustrators, 1988. Mem.: Soc. Publ. Arts (3 Silver awards 1987), Soc. Typog. Arts (Silver medal 1998, Gold medal 1999, 2001), Art Dirs. Club N.Y., Soc. Illustrators (Gold medal 1981, 1984, Silver medal 1988, Gold medal 1991, Silver medal 1998, Gold medal 1999), Arts (Chgo.), Arts Club (Chgo.). Office: Playboy Enterprises Inc 680 N Lake Shore Dr Fl 15 Chicago IL 60611-4455 E-mail: kengp@playboy.com.

POPE, LEAVITT JOSEPH, broadcast company executive; b. Boston, Apr. 2, 1924; s. Joseph and Charlotte (Leavitt) P.; m. Martha Pascale, Nov. 20, 1948; children— Joseph, Daniel, Patricia, Elizabeth, Nancy, Maria, Joan, Christopher, Virginia, Matthew, Charles. BS, Mass. Inst. Tech., 1947. Adminstrv. asst. N.Y. Daily News, N.Y.C., 1947-51; asst. to gen. mgr. Sta. WPIX-TV, N.Y.C., 1951-56, v.p. ops., 1956-72, Sta. WPIX-FM, N.Y.C., 1956-72; sec. WPIX, Inc., N.Y.C., 1958-75, exec. v.p., 1972-75, pres., chief exec. officer, 1975-92, also dir. Sec., exec. v.p. Conn. Broadcasting Co., Bridgeport, 1967-75, pres., chief exec. officer, dir., 1975-87; dir. N.Y. Daily News, 1975-78, Tribune Co., 1978-81; founder Ind. Network News, 1978-89; chair N.Y.C. TV all industry com., advanced TV sys. com. HDTV; chair copyright com. NAB, 1985—. Mem. N.Y. State Regents Ednl. TV Adv. Council, 1958; bd. govs. Daytop Village, 1972—; trustee Catholic Communications Found., St. Thomas Aquinas Coll., 1968-75, Cardinal Cooke Hosp., 1979—, vice chair, 1998—; dir. Archdiocese N.Y. Instructional TV com. 1976—; trustee St. Patrick's Cathedral, N.Y.C., 1992—. Served with Signal Corps U.S. Army, 1942-46. Mem. Assn. Ind. TV Stats. (pres. 1976-78, bd. dirs.), ASME, Internat. Radio and TV Soc., Nat. Assn. Broadcasters (dir. 1982-86), N.Y. State Broadcasters (pres. 1976-78), Sigma Nu, Knight of Malta. Clubs: Univ. (N.Y.C.); Riverbend (Tequesta, Fla.). Home: 173 Dorchester Rd Scarsdale NY 10583-6052

POPE, LENA ELIZABETH, human resources specialist; b. Brookhaven, Miss., Jan. 25, 1935; d. James S. and Elease (Edwards) Smith; m. Roland Van Pope, Dec. 22, 1955 (dec. 1967); children: Nikki D., Ronald V., Ouida. BS, Alcorn A&M Coll., 1955; student, Northwestern U., 1961, DePaul U., 1975-78; MA, Nat. Coll., 1987. Asst. to registrar Alcorn A&M Coll., Lorman, Miss., 1955-57; tchr. Alexander High Sch., Brookhaven, 1957-60, Magnolia High Sch., Moss Point, Miss., 1960-62; asst. student pers. Jackson (Miss.) State Coll., 1962-64; tchr. Chgo. Pub. schs., 1964-65, 78-80; adminstrv. asst. aide U.S. Senator Charles H. Percy, Chgo., 1965-78; tchr. Citywide Colls., Chgo., 1976-79; v.p. human resources Human Resources Devel. Inst., Chgo., 1982—. Cons. Foundatin I, Harvey, Ill., 1989—, Safer Found., Chgo., 1990—, Foster Park Community Orgn., Chgo., 1991—. Office mgr. Percy for Senator, Chgo., 1966, 70, 74, 78; transp. dir. Rep. Nat. Conv., Kansas City, Kans., 1976; vol. Thompson For Gov., Chgo.; sec. Oakdale Covenant Ch., 1985-89. Mem. Alcorn State Alumni (sec., con. 1990—), Eta Phi Beta (Soror of Yr. 1987; pres. Alpha Lambda chpt. 1999—). Republican. Avocations: desk top publishing, travel, reading. Office: Human Resources Devel Inst 222 S Jefferson St Chicago IL 60661-5603

POPE, LISTON, JR., writer, journalist; b. New Haven, Dec. 26, 1943; s. Liston and Bennie (Purvis) P. BA in English, Duke U., 1965; postgrad., Sorbonne, Paris, 1965-70, U. Vienna, 1966-67. Probation officer Bronx (N.Y.) Supreme Ct., 1972-73; freelance journalist N.Y.C., 1972—; war correspondent World Coun. of Chs., Beirut, 1978-79, Nat. Cath. News Svc., Managua, Nicaragua, 1983-84; radio prodr. Pacifica Radio, N.Y.C., 1983-90; critic art/lit. Pacifica News, N.Y.C., 1984-89; sr. editor N.A. Gilbert & Sons Publs., N.Y.C., 1993—; pub. Mantis Press, N.Y.C., 1995—. Press agent Liston Pope & Assocs., N.Y.C., 1983-90; media dir. Casa Nicaragua, N.Y.C., 1983-90. Author: Redemption: A Novel of War in Lebanon, 1994, Living Like the Saints: A Novel of Nicaragua, 1996, Floriane: Stages of Love, 1998, (plays) Somoza's Niece, 1987, Oratorio, 1987, Canto Epico, 1989. Vis., supporting vol. Meml. Sloan-Kettering, 1972-78; recreation dir., tutor Cath. Guardian Group Home, 1975-90; life skills tchr. Harlem I Men's Shelter, N.Y.C., 1991-93; AIDS support worker St. Vincent's Supportive Care, Bellevue Visitation Program, Bellevue Pediatrics. Recipient Narrative Poetry award, NY Poetry Soc., 1972, Grand prize, Am. Poetry Assn., 1986. Home and Office: 126 W 73rd St Apt 11A New York NY 10023-3031

POPE, MARK ANDREW, lawyer, university administrator; b. Munster, Ind., May 22, 1952; s. Thomas A. and Eleanor E. (Miklos) P.; m. Julia Risk Pope, June 15, 1974; children: Brent Andrew, Bradley James. BA, Purdue U., 1974; JD cum laude, Ind. U., 1977. Bar: Ind. 1977, U.S. Dist. Ct. (so. dist.) Ind. 1977, U.S. Ct. Appeals (7th cir.) 1984. Assoc. Johnson & Weaver, Indpls., 1977-79, Rocap, Rocap, Reese & Young, Indpls., 1980-82, Dutton & Overman, Indpls., 1982-88, ptnr., 1988-89; asst. gen. counsel Lincoln Nat. Corp., Fort Wayne, Ind., 1989-91, sr. counsel, 1991-95, v.p. govt. rels., 1995-2001; dir. athletics Ind. U.-Purdue U., Ft. Wayne, 2001—. Bd. dirs. Ft. Wayne Bicentennial Coun.; pres., bd. dirs. ARCH, Inc., 1994-97. Bd. editors, devel. editor Ind. U. Law Rev., 1976-77 Mem. pres.'s coun. Purdue U., 1977—; applied econs. cons. Jr. Achievement, 1989—95; bd. dirs. Jr. Achievement of No. Ind., 1992—94; grad. Leadership Ft. Wayne, 1992; adv. coun. Ind. U. Bus. Sch., Purdue U., Ft. Wayne, 2000—02; trustee Allen County War Meml. Coliseum, 2002—; mem. parish coun. St. Elizabeth Ann Seton Ch., 1993—96, pres., 1993—95; bd. edn. mem. Bishop Luers H.S., 2000—03, pres., 2002—03. Named Disting. Hoosier, Gov. of Ind., 1974. Fellow Ind. Bar Found., Indpls. Bar Found. (disting.); mem. ABA (dist. rep. young lawyers divsn. 1981-83, dir. 1983-84, liaison coord. 1985-86, 87-88, exec. coun. 1981-88; cabinet 1982-88, gen. practice sect. coun. mem. 1986—, membership chmn. 1987-89, chmn. career and family com. 1990-92, dir. 1991-93), Indpls. Bar Assn. (v.p. 1983, chmn. young lawyers divsn. 1981), 500 Festival Assocs. (vice-chmn. of 500 festival parade 1985-89), Orchard Ridge Country Club (bd. dirs. 1995-2001, sec. 1996-97, pres. 1999-2001). Avocations: tennis, golf, running. Office: Ind U-Purdue U at Fort Wayne Gates Sports Ctr 2101 E Coliseum Blvd Fort Wayne IN 46805-1499 Office Phone: 219-481-5443. E-mail: popem@ipfw.edu.

POPE, MICHAEL THOR, chemistry professor; b. Exeter, Devon, Eng., Apr. 14, 1933; came to U.S. 1962; naturalized, 1992; s. Hector Maurice and Edith Mary (Hewett) P.; m. Ann Mavis Potter, July 12, 1957; children: Gregory (dec.), Lucy. BA, Oxford U., 1954, DPhil, 1957; postdoctoral, Boston U., 1957-59. Rsch. chemist Laporte Chems., Luton, Eng., 1959-62; asst. prof. Georgetown U., Washington, 1962-67, assoc. prof., 1967-73, prof., 1973—, dept. chair, 1990-96. Vis. prof. Tech. U., Vienna, Austria, 1970-71, Free U. of Berlin, 1979, Northeast Normal U., Changchun, China, 1985, U. Umeå, U. Bielefeld, Germany, 1989; prof. associé U. Pierre et Marie Curie, Paris, 1979, U. de Versailles, 1997. Author: Heteropoly and Isopoly Oxometalates, 1983, Polyoxometalates: From Platonic Solids to Anti-Retroviral Activity, 1994, Polyoxometalate Chemistry: From Topology vis Self-Assembly to Applications, 2001, Polyoxometalate Chemistry for Nano-Composite Design, 2002; contbr. articles to profl. publs. Recipient Sr. U.S. Scientist award Alexander von Humboldt Found., 1989-90, Hillebrand prize Chem. Soc. Washington, 1999; Petroleum Rsch. Fund Internat. award fellow, 1970-71; Rsch. grantee

Dept. Energy, NSF, NIH, Petroleum Rsch. Fund, Office Naval Rsch., Army Rsch. Office, Air Force Office of Sci. Rsch. Mem. Royal Soc. Chemistry (London), Am. Chem. Soc., Sigma Xi (chpt. pres. 1969-70). Episcopalian. Avocations: music, art. Office: Georgetown Univ Chemistry Dept Washington DC 20057-1227

POPE, NANCY, historian, curator; b. Pendleton, Oreg., Jan. 28, 1957; d. Joseph W. Pope and Paula Marie Conlee. BA in History, BA in French, U. of Oreg., 1979; MA, The George Wash. U., 1985. Mus. specialist Nat. Mus. of Am. History, Washington, 1984—91; mus. program specialist Nat. Postal Mus., Washington, 1991—. Curator Nat. Postal Mus., Wash., DC, 1994—2002. Author: (mus. catalog) Illustrated Guide to the National Postal Museum; contbr. articles to profl. pubs. Vol. Whitman Walker Clinic, Washington, 1990—2001. Recipient Outstanding Team Achievement award, Smithsonian Instn., 1993, Unsung Hero award, 1996. Mem.: Am. Studies Assn., Am. Hist. Assn., Orgn. of Am. Historians, Material Culture Forum, Smithsonian Instn. (steering com. mem. 1998—). Democrat. Methodist. Achievements include Curated opening exhibits of the Smithsonian's National Postal Museum. Avocations: swimming, research, travel. Office: National Postal Museum Smithsonian Inst 2 Massachusetts Ave NE Washington DC 20002 E-mail: popena@npm.si.edu.

POPE, NORRIS, publishing executive; BA, Stanford U., 1968; PhD, Oxford U., 1976. Asst. editor Stanford (Calif.) U. Press, 1978-80, assoc. editor, 1980-83, CFO, 1983-85, editor-in-chief, 1985-96, dir., 1993—. Author: Dickens and Charity, 1978. Office: Stanford U Press 521 Lomita Dr Stanford CA 94305-2208

POPE, ROBERT DEAN, lawyer; b. Memphis, Mar. 10, 1945; s. Ben Duncan and Phyllis (Drenner) P.; m. Elizabeth Dante Cohen, June 26, 1971; 1 child, Justin Nicholas Nathanson. AB, Princeton U., 1967; Diploma in Hist. Studies, Cambridge U., 1971; JD, Yale U., 1972, PhD, 1976. Bar: Va. 1974, D.C. 1980. Assoc. Hunton & Williams, Richmond, Va., 1974-80, ptnr., 1980—. Mem. steering com. Bond Attys. Workshop, 1994—98; lectr. in law U. Va. Law Sch., 2000—02; advisor, com. on govtl. debt and fiscal policy Govt. Fin. Officers Assn., 1993—99. Author: Disclosure Rules of Counsel in State and Local Government Securities Offerings, 2d edit., 1994, Making Good Disclosure: The Role and Responsibilities of State and Local Officials Under the Federal Securities Laws, 2001. Mem. adv. com. Va. Sec. of Health and Human Svcs. on Continuing Care Legislation, 1992-94; mem. Anthony Commn. on Pub. Fin.; adv. coun. dept. history Princeton U., 1987-91; mem. Mcpl. Securities Rulemaking Bd., 1996-99, vice chmn. 1998-99. Mem.: Nat. Council Cmty. Justice, Nat. Conf. Cmty. Justice (bd. dirs. Richmond), Yale Law Sch. Assn. (exec. com. 1985—88), Va. Bar Assn. (chmn. legal problems of elderly 1982—88), Am. Coll. Bond Counsel (bd. dir. 2003—), Am. Acad. Hosp. Attys., Nat. Assn. Bond Lawyers (bd. dirs. 1982—89, treas. 1984—85, sec. 1985—86, pres. 1987—88, Bernard P. Friel medal for contbns. to pub.fin. 1994), Bond Club Va. (bd. dirs. 1990—98, v.p. 1993—94, pres. 1994—95), Phi Beta Kappa. Republican. Episcopalian. Avocations: history, golf, music, book reviews. Home: 8707 Ruggles Rd Richmond VA 23229-7918 Office: Hunton & Williams 951 E Byrd Richmond VA 23219-4074 Office Phone: 804-788-8438. E-mail: dpope@hunton.com.

POPE, ROBERT E(UGENE), fraternal organization administrator; b. Wellington, Kans., Sept. 10, 1931; s. Samuel E. and Opal Irene (Davis) P. BSChemE with honors, U. Kans., 1952, MS, 1958. Registered profl. engr., Kans. Asst. instr. U. Kans., Lawrence, 1952-56; lab. technician Monsanto Co., St. Louis, 1952; project engr. Mallinckrodt, Inc., St. Louis, 1953-59; traveling sec. Theta Tau, St. Louis, 1959-62, exec. sec., 1963-84, exec. dir., 1984-96, exec. dir. emeritus, 1996—. Carillonneur, Grace United Meth. Ch., St. Louis, 1985—, chmn. adminstrv. coun., 1991-95, trustee, 1997-99, comms. chmn. 2000—; trustee Theta Tau Ednl. Found., 1997—. Mem. Am. Soc. Assn. Execs. (life), Am. Soc. Engring. Edn., Profl. Fraternity Execs. Assn. (charter), Profl. Fraternity Assn. (exec. sec. 1977-86, Disting. Svc. award 1995), Creve Coeur Country Club, Theta Tau (Alumni Hall of Fame 1988, mem. bd. editors The Gear of Theta Tau 1993—, editor-in-chief 1996—), Tau Beta Pi, Phi Lambda Upsilon, Omicron Delta Kappa. Democrat. United Methodist. Avocations: physical fitness, sports, photography, stamp collecting/philately, writing. Home: 13 Sona Ln Saint Louis MO 63141-7742 Office: Theta Tau 655 Craig Rd Ste 128 Saint Louis MO 63141-7168

POPE, SUSAN W. state legislator; Grad., Centenary Coll. Mem. Mass. Ho. of Reps., Boston, 1997—, mem. health care com., mem. local affairs, mem. ethics com. Mem. subcoms. Redistricting for 2001, SBAB funding, zoning issues, cardiac task study. Mem. Wayland Rep. Town Com., Wayland Sch. Com., Bd. Selectman. Mem. Mass. Mcpl. Assn. Republican. Office: Mass State Legis Rm 237 State House Boston MA 02133-2305

POPE, WILEY JACKSON, lawyer, small business owner; b. Dunn, N.C., Mar. 2, 1976; s. Patrick Harris Pope and Tilghman Pope Mary; m. Jodi Nicole May, Nov. 3, 2001. BBA with cert. in Trust Mgmt., Campbell U., 1998; JD, 2001. Ptnr. Pope & Tart Attys.-at-Law, Dunn, NC, 2001—; mgr. Sassy Tree, LLC, Dunn, 2002—. Chmn. Harnett County Planning Bd., Lillington, NC, 2004—. Fundraising chmn. Averasboro Battlefield Commn., Inc., Dunn, 2002. Gilbert Trust scholar, Campbell U. Mem.: N.C. Bar Assn. R-Conservative. Presbyterian. Office: Pope & Tart Attys at Law 403 West Broad St Dunn NC 28334 Office Phone: 910-892-4029. Office Fax: 910-892-7275.

POPE, WILLIAM L. lawyer, judge; b. Brownsville, Tex., 1960; s. William E. and Maria Antonieta P.; m. Sandra Solis, May 16, 1992; children: Ana Lauren, William E.H. AA, Tex. Southmost Coll., 1980; postgrad., U. Tex., 1980-81, Tex. Christian U., 1982, Tex. Coll. Osteo. Medicine, 1982-83; JD, Baylor U., 1986; MD (hon.), Cosmopolitan U. & Rsch. Inst., Vina del Mar, Chile, 1998. Bar: Tex. 1986, U.S. Dist. Ct. (so. dist.) Tex. 1988, U.S. Supreme Ct. 1990. Assoc. Adams & Graham, Harlingen, Tex., 1986-91, ptnr., 1991—; mcpl. ct. judge City of La Feria, Tex., 1987—. Bd. trustees Episcopal Day Sch., Brownsville, Tex., 1999—2000. Mem.: Cameron County Bar Assn., Am. Coll. Legal Medicine, Tex. State Bar Assn. (mem. judiciary rels. com. 1999—). Ch. Of Christ. Office: Adams & Graham LLP PO Drawer 1429 Harlingen TX 78551-1429

POPEJOY, JAMES RICHARD, music educator; b. Independence, Mo., Feb. 17, 1959; s. Ronald Dean and Shirley Ann Popejoy; m. Melanie Ann Popejoy, Aug. 2, 1980. B in Music Edn., Ctrl. Mo. State U., 1981; MA, U. Iowa, 1987; D in Musical Arts, U. North Tex., 2000. Dir. bands Moniteau Co. R-I Schs., California, Mo., 1981-85; grad. tchg. asst. U. Iowa, Iowa City, 1985-87; dir. bands, music dept. chair Raytown (Mo.) H.S., 1987-92; dir. bands and percussion McLennan C.C., Waco, Tex., 1992-97; tchg. fellow U. North Tex., Denton, 1997-2000; dir. bands U. N.D., Grand Forks, 2000—. Music dir., condr. Calif. Cmty. Band, 1982—84, Raytown (Mo.) Cmty. Band, 1990—92, Waco (Tex.) Cmty. Band, 1992—97, Waco Area Youth Wind Ensemble, 1993—97. Mem. Nat. Band Assn., World Assn. for Symphonic Bands and Ensembles, Music Educators Nat. Conf., Internat. Assn. Jazz Educators, College Band Dirs. Nat. Assn., Percussive Arts Soc. Avocation: playing jazz. Office: U. N.D. PO Box 7125 Grand Forks ND 58201 Office Phone: 701-777-2815. Business E-Mail: james.popejoy@und.edu.

POPEK, GERALD JOHN, computer software company executive, educator; b. Passaic, N.J., Sept. 22, 1946; s. Joseph John Popek; m. Paulene Bunker; children: Sarah, Darren. BS, NYU, 1968; SM, Harvard U., 1970, PhD, 1972. V.p. Palyn Assocs., San Jose, Calif., 1978-83; dir. Ctr. for Exptl. Computer Sci., UCLA, 1981-84; prof. computer sci. UCLA, from 1973; chief exec. officer Locus Computing Corp., Santa Monica, Calif., 1982-87, chmn., 1982-95; chief tech. officer Platinum Tech. Inc., 1995-99, CarsDirect.com, 1999-2000, NetZero, 2000—. Bd. dirs. Palyn Assocs., San Jose. Author, editor: The Locus Distributed System Architecture, 1985. Served to capt. USAF, 1972-78. Republican. Roman Catholic. Home: 1716 Roscomare Rd Los Angeles CA 90077-2213

POPENOE, HUGH LLYWELYN, soils educator; b. Tela, Honduras, Aug. 28, 1929; s. Frederick Wilson and Dorothy (Hughes) P. BS, U. Calif., Davis, 1951; PhD, U. Fla., 1960. Mem. faculty U. Fla., Gainesville, 1960—, dir. ctr. tropical agr., 1965—2002, dir. internat. programs, 1966—92, dir. Fla. Sea Grant Coll., 1971—81. Bd. dirs. Escuela Agricola Panamericana, Zamorano, Honduras, Orgn. Tropical Studies. Contbr. numerous articles to profl. jours. Chari Assn. U.S. Univ. Dirs. Internat. Agrl. Programs, 1969-70, Joint Rsch. Com. Bd. Internat. Food and Agrl. Devel., 1977-82, Joint Com. Agrl. Rsch. and Devel., 1982-86; chair numerous reports Bd. Sci. and Tech. in Devel., 1979-84; trustee Internat. Found. for Sci., Stockholm, 1984-87; mem. sci. liaison officer Internat. Inst. for Tropical Agr., Nigeria, 1983-88; mem. adv. com. internat. programs NSF, 1985-87; bd. dirs. League for Internat. Food Edn., 1976-87. With U.S. Army, 1952-54. Recipient Sci. Pioneer prize Egyptian Vet. Assn. for Buffalo Devel., 1985. Fellow AAAS, Am. Soc. Agronomy, Am. Geog. Soc., Internat. Soil Sci. Soc., Am. Water Buffalo Assn. (pres. 1988—), Cosmos Club. Office: U Fla PO Box 110286 Gainesville FL 32611-0286 Office Phone: 352-392-2643. Business E-Mail: hlp@ufl.edu.

POPEO, R. ROBERT, lawyer; b. Boston, Apr. 9, 1938; AB, Northeastern U., 1958; JD, boston Coll., 1961. Bar: Mass. 1961, D.C. 1972. Law clerk U.S. Dist. Ct. Mass., 1961-63; instr. Sch. Law Boston U., 1964-67; U.S. Commr., 1967-71; asst. atty. gen. Commonwealth of Mass., 1970-74; chmn. Mintz, Levin, Cohn, Ferris, Glovsky and Popeo, P.C., Boston, 1974—. Editor Boston Coll. Indsl. and Comml. Law Rev., 1960-61; student editor Ann. Survey Mass. Law, 1960-61. Fellow Am. Coll. Trial Laywers; mem. ABA, Practising Law Inst., Mass. Bar Assn., Boston Bar Assn. (chmn. com. on state ct. study 1991—). Office: Mintz Levin Cohn Ferris Glovsky & Popeo PC One Financial Center Boston MA 02111

POPE-ROBERTS, SONDY, state legislator; b. Apr. 27, 1950; Student, Edgewood Coll. Mem. Wis. State Assembly, Madison, 2002—, mem. aging and long-term care com., mem. edn. com., mem. rural affairs com., mem. small bus. com. Democrat. Office: State Capitol Bldg Rm 420 W PO Box 8953 Madison WI 53708 Address: 3426 Valley Woods Dr Verona WI 53593

POPESCU, DANIEL, interior designer; b. Bucharest, Romania, July 22, 1943; arrived in U.S., 98; s. Eugen and Lucia Popescu; m. Luminita Serbanescu, May 7, 1975 (div. Aug. 1995); 1 child, Dinu; m. Nina Bouzanis, July 22, 2000; 1 child, Jason Bouzanis. Diploma, Archtl. Coll., Bucharest, 1972. Rsch. and design team leader R.D.I.A.D., Bucharest, 1970—82; pres. Jetset Design Interior Inc., Toronto, Canada, 1984—; chief designer, cons. Madison Design Group, Troy, Mich., 1998—; sr. design cons. Richard M. Tumis Inc., Chevy Chase, Md., 1998—. Cons., chief designer Poggempohl, Toronto, 1996—98; cons. Artcraft Kitchen, Niagara Falls, Ont., 1994—, Mazar Keer Arch., Detroit, 1998—. Over 200 comml. and residential projects in Romania, Can. and U.S. Cpl. Romanian armed forces, 1966—68. Orthodox. Avocations: art, classical music, travel, skiing, dancing. Home: 1501 Crystal Dr Apt 1029 Arlington VA 22202 Office: Richard M Tunis Inc 7032 Wisconsin Ave Bethesda MD 20815 E-mail: ninapopescu@aol.com.

POPIK, WILLIAM C, insurance company executive; BA in psychology, Yale U.; MD, Columbia U. Coll. of Physicians and Surgeons. Bd. cert. family physician. Physician, family and emergency medicine Calif.; various positions CIGNA Healthcare, 1996; sr. v.p., chief med. officer Health Net HMO Calif.; v.p., med. affairs QualMed Plan for Health, 1990—94; sr. v.p., chief med. officer Aetna Inc. Mem.: Am. Coll. Physician Executives. Office: Aetna Inc 151 Farmington Ave Hartford CT 06156

POPKIN, ALICE BRANDEIS, lawyer; b. N.Y.C. d. Jacob H. and Susan Brandeis Gilbert; m. Jordan J. Popkin; children: Susan Cahn, Anne, Louisa. AB magna cum laude, Radcliffe Coll., 1949; JD, Yale U., 1953. Bar: N.Y. 1953, U.S. Dist. Ct. (so. dist.) N.Y. 1956, U.S. Ct. Appeals (2nd cir.) 1959, U.S. Supreme Ct. 1962, D.C. 1972, Mass. 1987. Assoc. Cahill Gordon & Reindel, 1953—61; dir. internat. programs Peace Corps, 1961—63; project co-dir. Georgetown Inst. Criminal Law and Procedure, 1967—72; spl. counsel Senate Sub-Com. to Investigate Juvenile Delinquincy, 1972—74; atty., prof. Antioch Sch. Law, 1974—77; assoc. adminstr. EPA, 1977—79; pvt. practice cons. on internat. environ. issues, 1979—81; practicing atty., 1981—87; of counsel Toabe and Riley, Chatham, Mass., 1987—. Fellow Brandeis U.; bd. trustees Radcliffe Coll.; mem. Chatham Harbor Mgmt. Com.; trustee Eldredge Pub. Libr., 1994—. Mem. ABA, Mass. Bar Assn., Barnstable County Bar Assn., Estate Planning Coun. Cape Cod, Planned Giving Coun. Cape Cod. Office: Toabe & Riley Box 707 154 Crowell Rd Chatham MA 02633-2800 Office Phone: 508-945-5400.

POPKIN, DAVID RICHARD, obstetrician, health science administrator; m. Linda Popkin, 1964; 4 children BSc in Agr., McGill, 1962, MD, CM, 1966. Head divsn. gynecology and gynecologic oncology Royal Victoria Hosp., Montreal, 1976—82; head dept. ob-gyn. Royal Univ. Hosp. U. Saskatchewan, Saskatoon, Canada, 1982—91, assoc. dean postgrad. med. edn. and clin. affairs, 1991—93, dean Coll. Medicine, 1993—2002; prof., dept. ob-gyn and reproductive scis. Coll. Medicine and Health Scis., Saskatoon, Canada, 1993—; exec. dir. Saskatoon Cancer Ctr., 2002—. Office: Saskatoon Cancer Ctr 20 Campus Dr Saskatoon SK Canada S7N 4144 E-mail: dpopkin@scf.sk.ca.

POPKIN, JOEL, economist, consultant; b. Trenton, NJ, July 6, 1932; s. Nathaniel Robert and Betty (Finkle) Popkin; m. Elizabeth Rose Alk, Oct. 17, 1968; children: Neil Robert, Sara Rachel. BS in Econs., U. Pa., 1954, PhD, 1965. Asst. economist Allied Chem. Co., NYC, 1957—59; lectr., rschr. U. Pa., Phila., Northwestern U., Evanston, Ill., George Washington U., Washington, 1960—64; econometrician Dept. Commerce, Washington, 1964—66; divsn. chief, asst. commr. US Bur. Labor Stats., Washington, 1966—73; sr. staff economist Pres.'s Coun. Econ. Advisors, Washington, 1973—74; dir., mem. rsch. staff Nat. Bur. Econ. Rsch., Washington, 1974—78; pres. Joel Popkin and Co., Washington, 1978—. Mem. visitors econs. dept. U. Pa., 1987—2001. Lt. USAR, 1955—57. Recipient Julius Shiskin award for contbns. to econ. stats., 1994. Fellow: Am. Statis. Assn.; mem.: Internat. Assn. Rsch. on Income and Wealth, Nat. Assn. Bus. Economists, Conf. Bus. Economists (chmn. 1989), Am. Econ. Assn., Cosmos Club, Nat. Economists Club (chmn. bd., pres. 1978—80). Home: 6706 Loring Ct Bethesda MD 20817-3148 Office: 2030 M St NW Washington DC 20036-3379 Office Phone: 202-466-9063.

POPLACK, DAVID G. pediatric oncologist; BA, Tufts U., 1964; MD cum laude, Boston U., 1970. Pediat. intern Stanford (Calif.) U. Hosp.; resident Children's Hosp. Med. Ctr., Boston; clin. assoc. pediat. oncology br. Nat. Cancer Inst., Nat. Inst. Health, Bethesda, Md., 1973-93; dir. Tex. Children's Ctr., Houston, 1993—. Elise C. Young chair pediat. oncology, chief hematology/oncology svc. dept. pediat. Baylor Coll. Medicine. Co-editor: Principles and Practice of Pediatric Oncology; contbr. chpts. to books and articles to profl. jours. Office: CC 1410 00 6621 Fannin St Houston TX 77030-2303 E-mail: dpoplack@txccc.org.

POPLER, KENNETH, behavioral health services administrator, psychologist; BA in Psychology, CUNY, 1967; MA in Psychology, New Sch. Social Rsch., N.Y.C., 1969, PhD in Psychology, 1974; MBA, Wagner Coll., 1994. Diplomate Am. Bd. Profl. Psychology. Case worker N.Y.C. Dept. Social Svcs., 1967-70; intern Bklyn. Psychiat. Ctrs., 1970-72; sch. psychologist N.Y.C. Bd. Edn., 1972-73; psychologist Mid Nassau Cmty. Guidance Ctr., Hicksville, NY, 1973-77; dir. St. Mary Cmty. Mental Health Ctr., Hoboken, NJ, 1978-81; pres., CEO S.I. Mental Health Soc., Inc., 1981—. Asst. rsch. scientist N.Y. State Psychiat. Inst., N.Y.C., 1971; psychometrician L.I. Hillside Jewish Med. Ctr., Queens, NY, 1972—73; vol. rsch. Manhattan Sch. Seriously Disturbed Children, N.Y.C., 1972—73; instr. CUNY, Bklyn., 1972—73; sr. psychologist dir. psychol. svcs. HHC Gouverneur Hosp., N.Y.C., 1973—78; pvt. practice, N.Y.C., 1976—85; asst. clin. prof. psychiatry Mt. Sinai Med. Sch., N.Y.C., 1978—95; apptg. by mayor N.Y.C. Bd. Health, 2003—. Apptd. by mayor N.Y.C. Cmty. Svcs. Bd., 1984—, chmn., 2003—; pres. Coalition Voluntary Mental Health Agys., Inc., 1991—94; sec. Head Start Sponsoring Bd. Coun., N.Y.C., 1985—92; chmn. S.I. United Way Execs. Com., 1985, Mental Health Coun., S.I., 1987—89. Mem.: Rotary. Office: SI Mental Health Soc Inc 669 Castleton Ave Staten Island NY 10301-2099

POPOFSKY, MELVIN LAURENCE, lawyer; b. Oskaloosa, Iowa, Feb. 16, 1936; s. Samuel and Fannye Charlotte (Rosenthal) P.; m. Linda Jane Seltzer, Nov. 25, 1962; children: Mark Samuel, Kaye Sylvia. BA in History summa cum laude, U. Iowa, 1958; BA in Jurisprudence (first class honors), Oxford U., Eng., 1960; LLB cum laude, Harvard U., 1962. Bar: Calif. 1962. Assoc. Heller, Ehrman, White & McAuliffe, San Francisco, 1962-69, ptnr., 1969—, mem. exec. com., 1980-93, co-chair, 1988-93. Contbr. articles to law jours. Bd. dirs. Mt. Zion Hosp., San Francisco, 1982-88, U.S. Dist. Ct. (no. dist.) Calif. Hist. Soc., 1988—. Jewish Home for Aged, San Francisco, 1989-96, Golden Gate U., 1997-2000, Jewish Cmty. Fedn., 1997-2001. Recipient Anti-Defamation League's Disting. Jurisprudence award, 2000; named State Bar of Calif. Antitrust Lawyer of the Yr., 2000; Rhodes scholar, 1958. Fellow Am. Bar Found., Am. Coll. Trial Lawyers; mem. ABA, Calif. Bar Assn., San Francisco Bar Assn., Bur. Nat. Affairs (adv. bd. antitrust sect.), Calif. Acad. Appellate Lawyers. Democrat. Jewish. Home: 1940 Broadway Apt 10 San Francisco CA 94109-2216 Office: Heller Ehrman 333 Bush St Ste 3000 San Francisco CA 94104-2834 Office Phone: 415-772-6310. Business E-Mail: lpopofsky@hewm.com.

POPOVA, NINA, dancer, choreographer, director; b. Novorossisk, USSR, 1922; ed. in Paris, studied ballet with Olga Preobrajenska, Lubov Egorova, Anatole Vilzak, Anatole Oboukhov, Igor Schwezoff. Ballet debut with Ballet de la Jeunesse, Paris, London, 1937-39; soloist Original Ballet Russe, 1939-41, Ballet Theatre (now Am. Ballet), 1941-42, Ballet Russe de Monte Carlo, 1943, 47, Ballet Alicia Alonso, Cuba; mem. faculty Sch. Performing Arts, N.Y.C., from 1954; later artistic dir. Houston Ballet, 1975; tchr. Nat. Acad. Arts, Champaign, Ill., also N.Y.C., 1975—, now Eglevsky Ballet Sch., L.I.; tchr. ballet Mexico City, Mex.; asst. choreographer mus. comedy Birmingham So. Coll., Ala., 1960; numerous appearances on Broadway stage, TV; former mem. regular cast Your Show of Shows; currently tchg. N.Y.C. Address: 33 Adams St Sea Cliff NY 11579-1614

POPOVA, OLGA K, geologist, researcher; b. Novosibirks, Russia, Dec. 25, 1960; d. Khurshed R Isokhodjavye and Elvira S Popova; m. Boris S Yaroslavtsev, July 20, 1994; 1 child, Alla Golovina. MSc in geology, Novosibirsk State, Russia, 1984. Registered geologist State of Wash., Geologist Lic. Bd., 2003. Geologist Exploration Expedition, Kular, Russia, 1984—86; geoscientist Siberian Scientific Rsch. Inst. of Geology, Geophysics and Minerals, Novosibirsk, Russia, 1986—92; engr. Ctr. of Sic. and Tech., Novosibirsk, Russia, 1993—97; well-site geologist Calif. and Alaska Epoch Well Services, Inc., Bakersfield, Calif., 2000—02; geologist Delta Environ. Cons., Inc., Seattle, 2002—. Contbr. articles. Bd. mem. sch. coun. Tyee H.S., Seattle, 1998—99. Recipient Cert. of Appreciation, Ministry of Geology of Russia, 1986, 1987, 1990, cert. of award for the reports on the conferences, Ministry of Geology of Russia, Acad. of Sci. of Russia, 1984, 1985, 1987, 1990. Mem.: Friends of Infinity Soc., Wash. Hydrologic Soc., Northwest Geol. Soc., Am. Assn. of Petroleum Geologist. Avocations: music, reading, camping. Home: 22244 35th Pl S #F-306 Kent WA 98032 Office Phone: 425-558-0134.

POPOVICH, GREGG, professional basketball coach; b. Jan. 28, 1949; m. Erin; 2 children. Grad. in Soviet studies, Air Force Acad., 1970; MA, Univ. of Denver. Asst. coach Air Force Acad., 1975-81; head coach Pomona-Pitzer Coll., Claremont, Calif., asso. prof.; asst. coach San Antonio Spurs, 1988-92, Golden State Warriors, 1992—94; gen. mgr. San Antonio Spurs, 1994—2002, head coach, exec. v.p. basketball ops., 1996—. Head coach USA Senior National Team, 2003; asst. coach U.S. Olympic Team, Athens, 2004. 2nd lt. USAF, 1970-75. Recipient Daily Point of Light award President George Bush, 1992. Achievements include coach NBA Champion San Antonio Spurs, 1999, 2003. Office: 100 Montana St San Antonio TX 78203-1033*

POPOVICI, ADRIAN, law educator; b. Bucharest, Rumania, Sept. 6, 1942; came to Can., 1951; s. Adrian and Alice (Moruzi) P.; children— Adrian, Alexandra. BA, Stanislas Coll., Montreal, 1959; B.C.L., McGill U., 1962; D.E.S., U. Paris, 1965. Bar: Que. 1963. Prof. law U. Montreal, Que., Can., 1968—. Author: L'Outrage au Tribunal, 1977, La Couleur du Mandat, 1995; editor: Problèmes de Droit Contemporain, 1974 Roman Catholic. Home: 5589 Canterbury Montreal QC Canada H3T 1S8 Office: U Montreal Faculte de Droit CP 6128 Succursale A Montreal QC Canada H3C 3J7 E-mail: adrian.popovici@umontreal.ca.

POPOVICS, SANDOR, civil engineer, educator, researcher; b. Budapest, Hungary, Dec. 24, 1921; came to U.S., 1957; s. Milan and Erzsebet (Droppa) P.; m. Lea M. Virtanen, Aug. 29, 1960; children: John, Lisa. 1st Degree in Civil Engring., Poly. U., Budapest, Hungary, 1944; Advanced Degree in Civil Engring., Poly. U., 1956; PhD, Purdue U., 1961. Registered profl. engr. Ariz., Pa. Rsch. engr. Met. Lab., Budapest, 1944-48; adj. prof. Tech. Coll., Budapest, 1949-52; rsch. engr., mgr. Inst. for Bldg. Scis., Budapest, 1949-56; grad. asst. Purdue U., Lafayette, Ind., 1957-59; prof. engring. Auburn (Ala.) U., 1959-69; prof. civil engring. No. Ariz. U., Flagstaff, 1968-76; prof. engring. King Abdulazziz U., Jeddah, Saudi Arabia, 1977-78; Samuel S. Baxter prof. civil engring. Drexel U., Phila., 1979-92, rsch. prof., 1992—. Pres. Optimum Engring. Rsch. Author: Fundamentals of Pc Concrete, 1982, Concrete Materials, 1992, Strength and Related Properties of Concrete, 1998, others; author more than 200 tech. papers in various langs. Recipient numerous grants and awards. Fellow ASCE (life), Am. Concrete Inst.; mem. ASTM, Ala. Acad. Scis., Ariz. Acad. Scis., Sigma Xi, Chi Epsilon. Avocations: jogging, music, fine art. Home and Office: 283 Congress Ave Lansdowne PA 19050-1206 Office: Drexel U Dept Civil & Archtl Engring 32nd and Chestnut Philadelphia PA 19104 Office Phone: 215-895-2345. Business E-Mail: popovics@coe.drexel.edu.

POPP, DAVID A. editor, educator; b. Elgin, Ill., July 10, 1964; s. Alvin D. and Linda R. Popp; m. Ingrid S. Hanson-Popp, July 9, 1994. BA in English, No. Ill. U., DeKalb, 1994. Tchr. English, speech, and drama Sycamore H.S., Ill., 1995—2001; assoc. editor Model Railroader mag. Kalmbach Pub. Co., Waukesha, Wis., 2001—. Author: (column) Step-by-Step, Model Railroad News, (series) Wow! The Mus. of Sci. and Industry's Gt. Train Story. Mem.: Nat. Model R.R. Assn. (assoc.). Republican. Lutheran. Avocations: writing, photography, history, woodworking, gardening. Office: Kalmbach Publishing Co PO Box 1612 21027 Crossroads Cir Waukesha WI 53187-1612 E-mail: dpopp@mrmag.com.

POPP, JOSEPH BRUCE, manufacturing executive; b. Chgo., July 9, 1919; s. Peter Leon and Anna (Chomyz) P.; m. Mabel Lydia Szymanski, Oct. 23, 1941 (dec. Mar. 1993); m. Elinor A. Maves, Jan. 27, 1996; children: Dianne, Lydia, Bruce, Anita, Gregory. Founder, owner Poultry Farm, Westville, Ind., 1941-48, Gary (Ind.) Undercoating Co., 1948-51; survey analyst George S. May Co., Chgo., 1952-54; gen. sales mgr. Maurey Instrument Corp., Chgo., 1958-64; founder, owner Joe Popp Sales Co., North Riverside, Ill., 1964-89, Chart Pool USA Inc., Portage, Ind., 1966—. Bd. dirs. YMCA Camp Tecumseh, Brookston, Ind., 1973—. Sgt. U.S. Army, 1942-46. Mem. Nat. Fedn. of Ind. Bus., Greater Portage C. of C., Ind. C. of C., Better Bus. Bur., The Gideons Internat. Republican. Achievements include patents in field. Home: 1133 Lincoln St Hobart IN 46342-6039 Office: Chart Pool USA Inc 5695 Old Porter Rd Portage IN 46368-1194 Office Phone: 219-763-1541.

POPP, LILIAN MUSTAKI, writer, educator; b. N.Y.C. d. Peter and Mae Claire (Cary) Mustaki; m. Robert J. Popp. BA, Notre Dame Coll.; postgrad., Columbia U.; MS in Edn., Hunter Coll. Tchr. English McKee Vocat. and Tech. H.S., S.I., N.Y., 1946-63, chmn. acad. studies, 1963-71; prin. William Howard Taft H.S., Bronx, N.Y., 1971-79; adj. prof. Wagner Coll., S.I., 1960-85; instr. Richmond Coll., CUNY, 1968-70; prof. St. John's U., 1991-93. Mem. Cmty. Sch. Bd., 1980—93, chmn., 1989—90, chmn. legis. com., chmn. substance abuse and adolescent issues com., chmn. pupil pers. svcs. com.; chmn. curriculum com.; asst. examiner N.Y.C. Bd. Edn., 1960—85. Author, editor: Journeys in Science Fiction, 1961, Four Complete World Novels, 1961,

Gertrude Lawrence as Mrs. A., 1961, Four Complete Modern Novels, 1962, Four Complete Heritage Novels, 1963, Four Complete Novels of Character and Courage, 1964; contbr. articles to profl. jours. Chmn. vols. N.Y.C. Child Abuse Prevention Program, 1984—86; regional dir., mem. exec. bd. March of Dimes; book discussion leader Snug Harbor Cultural Ctr., 1981—; pres. Com. for a Nuclear-Free Island, 1986—91; v.p. Staten Islanders Against Nuclear Weapons, 1991—95; pres. S.I. chpt. Brandeis U. Nat. Women's Com., 1996—99, leader News and Shmews; founder, pres. Coalition of S.I. Women's Orgns., 1996—; mem. edn. com. Staten Island Cmty. TV; mem. Libr. com. Staten Island Hist. Richmond Town; pres. Staten Island Youth Coun.; mem. libr. com. Coll. Staten Island; cmty. outreach chair Women for Women of Sierra Leone, 2001; bd. dirs. Staten Island Mental Health Soc. Recipient Women Helping Women award Soroptimists, 1985, Thomas Wilson award for Substance Abuse Prevention, 1990, S.I. Advance Woman of Achievement award, 1994, Cmty. Hero award S.I. Register, 1996, Woman of Distinction award World of Women, 1998, Paul O'Dwyer Humanitarian award Staten Is. Dem. Assn., 1999, Distinction award Bus. and Profl. Women's Club, Staten Island, N.Y., 2004; named Outstanding Woman by N.Y. State Sen. Vincent J. Gentile, 1998, Women's History Month award N.Y. City Coun. Spkr. Peter Vallone and Councilmen Jeremiah O'Donovan, Oddo and Fiala, 2001, Bus. and Profl. Women's CLub S.I. award of distinction, 2004. Mem. AAUW, Belles Lettres Lit. Soc. (pres.), S.I. Hist. soc., N.Y.C. Assn. Tchrs. English (pres. 1967-71), Nat. Coun. Tchrs. English (bd. dirs. 1968-69), Acad. Pub. Edn., McKee Tchrs. Assn. (pres. 1969), H.S. Prins. Assn. (exec. bd.), Arista Hon. Soc. (hon.), Delta Kappa Gamma (pres. Alpha Beta chpt.), Phi Delta Kappa (v.p. 1990-92). Avocations: travel, reading, photography, jewelry making. Home: 40 Flagg Pl Staten Island NY 10304-1119

POPP, NATHANIEL, archbishop; b. Aurora, Ill., June 12, 1940; s. Joseph and Vera (Boytor) P. BA, St. Propcopius Coll., 1962; MDiv, Pontifical Gregorian U., Rome, 1966; PhD, U. Oradea, Romania, 2003. Ordained priest Romanian Greek Cath. Ch., 1966; consecrated bishop Romanian Orthodox Episcopate of Am., 1980; elevated to archbishop, 1999. Asst. pastor St. Michael Byz Ch., Aurora, 1967; parish priest Holy Cross Romanian Orthodox Ch., Hermitage, Pa., 1975-80; aux. bishop Romanian Orthodox Episcopate of Am., Orthodox Ch. in Am., Jackson, Mich., 1980-84, ruling bishop Detroit, 1984—; mem. Holy Snyod Orthodox Ch. in Am., Syosset, N.Y., 1980—; Episcopal moderator Pastoral Life Ministries, O.C.A., 1991—. Bd. dirs. Moldovita Romanian Orthodox Ch., Hayward, Calif, 1982; tchr. summer youth programs Romanian Diocese; confessor to sisterhood Holy Transfiguration Monastery; rep. Conf. on Monasticism, Cairo, 1978; participant Monastic Consultation, Cairo, 1979, Seventh Assembly, Vancouver, Can., 1983; active mem. diocesan liturgical commn.; spkr., lectr. in field. Author: Holy Icons, 1969; editor newspaper Solia; contbr. numerous articles to profl. jours. Chmn. Romanian-Am. Heritage Ctr., Grass Lake, Mich.; organizer, chmn. Help for Romania Nat. Relief Fund and Help the Children of Romania Relief Fund; chmn. Congress of Romanian Ams., 1991—; mem. adv. bd. Orthodox Christian Laity, 1999—; pres. Ctr. for Orthodox Christian Studies, St. Andrew, Detroit, 2000; Dr. Honoris Causa, U. Oradea, Romania, 2003; chmn. bd Orthodox Witness, 2003-. Romanian Orthodox. Home and Office: Romanian Orthodox Episcopate Am 2535 Grey Tower Rd Jackson MI 49201-9120 also: PO Box 185 Grass Lake MI 49240-0185 Office Phone: 517-522-4800. E-mail: hgbnpopp@aol.com.

POPP, SHAUN RAYMOND, secondary school educator, music educator; b. Sassafras, Ky., Sept. 15, 1978; s. Raymond and Sharon Popp. B of Music Edn. magna cum laude, Morehead State U., 2000; MusM in Performance/Instrumental Conducting, U. Louisville, 2004. Band dir. Perry County Ctrl. High Sch., Hazard, Ky., 2000—01, JEefersontown High Sch., Louisville, 2001—. Choir dir. Met. Cmty. Ch., Louisville, 2002—. Mem.: Ky. Educators Assn., Ky. Music Educators Assn., Music Educators Nat. Conf. Democrat. Avocations: singing, saxophone, travel. Office: Jeffersontown High Sch 9600 Old Six Mile Ln Louisville KY 40299 Office Phone: 502-485-8130. E-mail: spopp1@jefferson.k12.ky.us.

POPPEL, SETH RAPHAEL, entrepreneur; b. Bklyn., Mar. 17, 1944; s. Frank M. and Fritzi R. (Axenzow) P.; m. Danine Voki, June 30, 1974; children: Clarysa, Jared, Stacy. BS magna cum laude, L.I. U., 1965; MBA, Columbia U., 1967. Asst. prof. L.I. U., Greenvale, N.Y., 1967-68; v.p. Synergistic Sys. Corp., N.Y.C., 1968-77; v.p., dir. corp. planning Chase Manhattan Corp., N.Y.C., 1977-90; owner, pres. Yearbook Libr., N.Y.C., 1980—; chmn., pres. Am. Vision Ctrs., N.Y.C., 1990-96. Owner harness horses Seth Poppel Stables, 1983—; founder, owner, operator Seth Poppel Yearbook Archives, 1986-2000. Recipient Claire F. Adler award in math., 1964-65, Mepham H.S. Hall of Fame award, 1993; E.I. DuPont fellow, 1965-67, Downie Muir fellow, 1965-66. Mem. U.S. Trotting Assn., Beta Gamma Sigma, Psi Chi, Omega Epsilon. Home and Office: 38 Range Dr Merrick NY 11566-3233 Personal E-mail: sethpoppel@aol.com.

POPPENGA, ROBERT H. veterinary toxicology educator; DVM, PhD, U. Ill. Assoc. prof. vet. clin. toxicology Sch. Vet. Medicine U. Pa., chief Diagnostic Toxicology Lab. dept. pathobiology. Contbr. articles to profl. pubIs. Mem.: Am. Bd. Vet. Toxicology (pres.), Soc. Toxicologic Pathologists, Soc. Environ. Toxicology and Chemistry, Am. Assn. Vet. Lab. Diagnosticians. Office: U Pa Sch Vet Medicine 382 W Street Rd Kennett Square PA 19348

POPPENSIEK, GEORGE CHARLES, veterinary scientist, educator; b. N.Y.C., June 18, 1918; s. George Frederick and Emily Amelia (Miller) P.; m. Edith M. Wallace, July 3, 1943; children: Neil Allen, Leslie Marion. Student, Cornell U., 1936-37, MS, 1951; student, U. Pa., 1937-42, V.MD, 1942. Diplomate Am. Bd. Microbiology, Am. Coll. Vet. Microbiology (charter), Am. Coll. Vet. Preventive Medicine (hon.). Asst. instr. medicine U. Pa. Sch. Vet. Medicine, 1943; asst. prof. vet. sci. U. Md., 1943-44; head dept. vet. virus vaccine prodn. Lederle Labs. div. Am. Cyanamid Co., 1944-49; dir. diagnostic lab. N.Y. State Coll. Vet. Medicine Cornell U., 1949-51, research assoc. Vet. Virus Research Inst., 1951-55; veterinarian Plum Island Animal Disease Ctr., animal disease and parasite research div. Agrl. Research Service, U.S. Dept. Agr., 1955-56, acting-in-charge diagnostic investigations, 1956-58, charge immunological investigations, 1958-59; dean and prof. microbiology N.Y. State Coll. Vet. Medicine, Cornell U., 1959-74, James Law prof. comparative medicine, 1974-88, dean emeritus, James Law prof. comparative medicine emeritus, 1988—; guest prof. U. Bern, Switzerland, 1975. Mem. exam. com. Nat. Bd. Vet. Med. Examiners, 1976-79; bd. dirs. Cornell Research Found., 1963-74; chmn. bd. dirs. Cornell Veterinarian, Inc., 1976-86 Recipient Certificate of Merit award U.S. Dept. Agr., 1958; citation Sch. Vet. Med., U. Pa., 1978, Centennial medals U. Pa., 1984, Ohio State U., 1985; others. Charter fellow Am. Acad. Microbiology; fellow AAAS; charter mem. Am. Soc. Virology; mem. AVMA, N.Y. State Vet. Med. Soc. (disting. life), Am. Bd. Microbiology, U.S. Animal Health Assn., Assn. Am. Vet. Med. Colls. (pres. 1970-71), So. Tier Vet. Med. Assn., Am. Vet. Radiology Soc., Am. Soc. for Microbiology, N.Y. Agrl. Soc. (life), Argentine Nat. Acad. Agronomy and Vet. Medicine (hon.), Societas Polona Medicinae Veterinariae (hon.), Sigma Xi, Phi Kappa Phi, Alpha Psi, Omega Tau Sigma, Phi Zeta. Congregationalist. Home: 32 Horizon Dr Ithaca NY 14850-9769 E-mail: poppensiek@clarityconnect.com.

POPPER, ARTHUR N. biology professor; b. NYC, May 9, 1943; s. Martin and Evelyn (Levine) P.; m. Helen Apfel, Nov. 30, 1968; children: Michelle, Melissa. BA, NYU, 1964; PhD, CUNY, 1969. Asst. prof. zoology U. Hawaii, Honolulu, 1969-72, assoc. prof. zoology, 1972-78; assoc. prof. dept. anatomy & cell biology Georgetown U., Washington, 1978-83, prof. dept. anatomy & cell biology, 1983-87; prof. dept. biology U. Md., College Park, 1987—, chmn. dept. zoology, 1987-97, dir. neurosci. and cognitive sci. program, 1998—2004. Editor: Comparative Studies of Hearing in Vertebrates, 1980, Hearing and Sound Communication in Fishes, 1981, Sensory Biology of Aquatic Animals, 1988, Evolutionary Biology of Hearing, 1992, Springer Handbook of Auditory Research, 1992—. Recipient Rsch. Career Devel. award, NIH, 1978—83. Fellow AAAS, Acoustical Soc.; mem. Soc. for Neurosci., Am. Assn. for Rsch. in Otolaryngology, Internat. Soc. Neuroethology (sec. 1998—), Sigma Xi. Office: U Md Dept Biology College Park MD 20742-0001 Business E-Mail: apopper@umd.edu.

POPPER, ROBERT, law educator, former dean; b. N.Y.C., May 22, 1932; s. Walter G. and Dorothy B. (Kluger) P.; m. Mary Ann Schaefer, July 12, 1963; children: Julianne, Robert Gregory. BS, U. Wis., 1953; LLB, Harvard U., 1956; LLM, NYU, 1963. Bar: N.Y. 1957, U.S. Dist. Ct. (so. dist.) N.Y. 1962, U.S. Ct. Appeals (2d cir.) 1962, U.S. Supreme Ct. 1962, U.S. Dist. Ct. (ca. dist.) N.Y. 1969, U.S. Ct. Appeals (7th cir.) 1970, U.S. Ct. Appeals (8th cir.) 1971, Mo. 1971, U.S. Dist. Ct. (we. dist.) Mo. 1973. Trial atty. criminal br. N.Y.C. Legal Aid Soc., 1960-61; asst. dist. atty. N.Y. County, 1961-64; assoc. Seligson & Morris, N.Y.C., 1964-69; mem. faculty School of Law U. Mo, Kansas City, 1969-96, prof., 1973-96, acting dean, 1983-84, dean, 1984-93, dean and prof. emeritus, 1996—. Cons. and lectr. in field. Author: Post Conviction Remedies in a Nutshell, 1978, De-Nationalizing the Bill of Rights, 1979; contbr. articles to profl. jours. Bd. trustees Rsch. Psychiat. Ctr. (HCA Midwest). Fellow ABA; mem. Mo. Bar, Kansas City Met. Bar Assn., Mo. Inst. of Justice. Home: 6229 Summit St Kansas City MO 64113-1556 Office: U Mo Kansas City Sch Law 1500 Rockhill Rd Kansas City MO 64110-2467 Fax: (816) 235-5276. Office Phone: 816-235-1006. E-mail: popperr@umkc.edu.

POPPERS, PAUL JULES, anesthesiologist, educator; b. Enschede, Netherlands, June 30, 1929; came to U.S., 1958; naturalized, 1963; s. Meyer and Minca (Ginsburg) P.; m. Ann Feinberg, June 3, 1969; children: David Matthew, Jeremy Samuel. MD, U. Amsterdam, 1955. Diplomate Am. Bd. Anesthesiology. Instr. anesthesiology Columbia U., N.Y.C., 1962-63, assoc., 1963-65, asst. prof. anesthesiology, 1965-71, assoc. prof. anesthesiology, 1971-74; prof., vice chmn. dept. anesthesiology NYU, 1974-79; prof., chmn. dept. anesthesiology Stony Brook U., NY, 1979—97, disting. prof., chmn. dept anesthesiology, 1997—2000, disting. prof. emeritus, 2000—. Cons. Brookdale Med. Ctr., Bklyn., 1973-2000, VA Med. Ctr., Northport, N.Y., 1979-2000, The N.Y. Hosp. Med. Ctr. of Queens (formerly Booth Meml Hosp.), Flushing, N.Y., 1979-98, L.I. Jewish Med. Ctr., New Hyde Park, N.Y., 1980-98, Ea. L.I. Hosp., Greenport, N.Y., 1995-99, Am. Hosp. Paris, 1989-93; cons., lectr. USN, 1968-85 Author: Regional Anesthesia, 1977; editor: Beta Blockade and Anaesthesia, 1979; sect. editor Jour. Clin. Anesthesia, 1990-2000; mem. editl. bd. Internat. Jour. Clin. Monitoring and Computing, 1990-2000, Anaesthesiology Digest, 1991-94, Gynecologic and Obstetric Investigation, 1996-2001; contbr. over 200 articles to profl. jours. Rsch. fellow NIH, 1961; recipient medal Polish Acad. Scis., Poland, 1987, Univ. medal Jagiellonian U., Krakow, Poland, 1987, 1st Sci. award Post-grad. Assembly in Anesthesiology; named Hon. Prof. Anesthesiology, U. Leiden, The Netherlands, 1977. Fellow Am. Coll. Anesthesiology, Am. Coll. Ob-gyns., Royal Soc. Medicine, Post-grad. Assembly in Anesthesiology (hon. chmn. 1989—); mem. Am. Soc. Anesthesiologists, Assn. Univ. Anesthesiologists, Internat. Anesthesia Rsch. Soc.; Soc. Obstetric Anesthesia and Perinatology, Am. Soc. Regional Anesthesia, Jerusalem Acad. Medicine, Am. Soc. Pharmacology and Exptl. Therapeutics, Fedn. Am. Soc. Exptl. Biology, Sigma Xi. E-mail: paulpoppers@hotmail.com.

POPPLER, DORIS SWORDS, lawyer; b. Billings, Mont., Nov. 10, 1924; d. Lloyd William and Edna (Mowre) Swords; m. Louis E. Poppler, June 11, 1949; children: Louis William, Kristine, Mark J., Blaine, Claire, Arminda. Student, U. Minn., 1942-44; JD, Mont. State U., 1948. Bar: Mont. 1948, U.S. Dist. Ct. Mont. 1948, U.S. Ct. Appeals (9th cir.) 1990. Pvt. practice law, Billings, 1948-49; sec., treas. Wonderpark Corp., Billings, 1959-62; atty. Yellowstone County Attys. Office, Billings, 1972-75; ptnr. Poppler and Barz, Billings, 1972-79, Davidson, Veeder, Baugh, Broeder and Poppler, Billings, 1979-84, Davidson and Poppler, P.C., Billings, 1984-90; U.S. atty. Dist. of Mont., Billings, 1990-93; field rep. Nat. Indian Gaming Commn., Washington, 1993-2000. Pres. Jr. League, 1964-65; bd. dirs., pres. Yellowstone County Metre Bd., 1982; trustee Rocky Mt. Coll., 1984-90, mem. nat. adv. bd., 1993—; mem. Mont. Human Rights Commn., 1988-90; bd. dirs. Miss Mont. Pageant, 1995—; elected to Billings City Coun., Billings, Mont., 2002; elected dep. mayor coun. woman Ward4, 2002—. Recipient Mont. Salute to Women award, Mont. Woman of Achievent award, 1975, Disting. Svc. award Rocky Mt. Coll., 1990, Disting. Female Alumna award U. Montana Law Sch., 1996, 2004, Status Women award Zonta Club, 2004. Mem. AAUW, Mont. Bar Assn., Nat. Assn. Former U.S. Attys., Nat. Rep. Lawyers Assn., Internat. Women's Forum, Yellowstone County Bar Assn. (pres. 1990, Lifetime Achievement award 2004), Alpha Chi Omega. Republican.

POPPLETON, JANET WATERS, legislative staff member; b. Camden, Ark., Dec. 5, 1950; d. William J. and Sybil (Butcher) Waters; m. Glenn A. Perry, May 20, 1972 (div. Jan. 1993); 1 child, Marcus Perry; m. Miller John Poppleton Jr., Mar. 20, 1999; stepchildren: Ashley, Aubrey. BA with highest honors, So. State Coll., Magnolia, Ark., 1972; MA, Stephen F. Austin State U., 1976. Press sec. Rep. Ralph Hall, Washington, 1993-96, chief staff, 1996—. Bd. dirs., fundraiser Habitat for Humanity, Am. Cancer Soc., Longview, 1985-91; bd. dirs. Jr. League, Longview, 1988-91; pres., bd. dirs. Gregg County Early Childhood Devel. Ctr., Longview, 1990-92; precinct chmn. Gregg County Dems., Longview, 1990-92; trustee Trinity Sch. Tex., Longview, 1991-92. Mem. U.S. Ho. Rep. Adminstrv. Asst. Assn. Lutheran. Avocations: travel, performing arts, skiing, writing. Office: Rep Ralph Hall 2221 Rayburn Washington DC 20515-0001

POPRADY, GÉZA, librarian; b. Tök, Hungary, Mar. 19, 1940; s. Géza and Ilona (Lugmayer) P.; m. Maria Wéber, July 13, 1963; children: Géza, Judit, Peter. Student, Eötvös Lorand U., Budapest, Hungary, 1958-63. Cert. librarian, tchr. Librarian Architectural Info. Ctr., Budapest, 1963-64, Ctrl. Rsch. and Design Inst. for Silicate Industry, Budapest, 1964—83; head dept. Nat. Széchényi Library, Budapest, 1984-90, dep. dir.-gen., 1990-93, acting dir.-gen., 1993-94, dir.-gen., 1994-99, counsellor, 1999—. Author: (book) The Application of Technical Information, 1977, The Systematic Catalogue, 1981, Preservation of Library Materials, 2000, Trends of Librarianship (Handbook of Librarians), 2003; contbr. articles to profl. jours. Recipient Szabó Ervin medal Min. of Culture, 1989. Mem. Assn. Hungarian Librarians (sec.-gen. 1987-90, v.p. 1990-98, award 1988). Avocations: reading, gardening. Home: Buza u 16 H-1033 Budapest Hungary Office: Nat Széchényi Library Budavári Palota F-épület 1827 Budapest Hungary E-mail: geza.poprady@oszk.hu.

POPRAWA, ANDREW, financial services executive, accountant; b. Toronto, Ont., Can., Nov. 13, 1952; s. Mieczyslaw and Wanda P.; m. Rita Poprawa, Oct. 10, 1981; children: Alexandra, Jason. B.Commerce, U. Toronto, 1975. Chartered acct., Can. CEO St. Stanislaus Credit Union, Toronto, 1980-82; dir. Office of Supt. of Fin. Instns. (Can.), Toronto, 1982-92, Ministry of Fin., Province of Ont., Toronto, 1992-93; pres., CEO Deposit Ins. Corp. of Ont., Toronto, 1993—. Mem. Inst. Chartered Accts. Ont. (cert. govt. fin. mgr.), Lakeshore Yacht Club, Toronto Bd. of Trade. Roman Catholic. Avocations: sailing, tennis, skiing, hockey. Office: Deposit Insurance Corp of Ontario 4711 Yonge St #700 Toronto ON Canada M2N 6K8 Office Phone: 416-325-9580. E-mail: apoprawa@dico.com.

PORACKY, BERNARD FRANCIS, radiologist; b. Whiting, Ind., Jan. 29, 1924; MD, Ind. U., 1946. Diplomate Am. Bd. Radiology, 1950. Intern St. Margaret Hosp., Hammond, Ind., 1946-47, resident, 1947-48, U. Pa., Phila., 1948—49; fellow Cook County Hosp., Chgo., 1949-51; staff radiologist Porter Meml. Hosp., Valparaiso, Ind., 1951—. Fellow Am. Coll. Radiology; mem. AMA, Am. Coll. Radiologists (bd. cert.), Radiol. Soc. N.Am. Home: 148 Shore Dr Portage IN 46368-1015 Office: Porter Meml Hosp Valparaiso IN 46383

PORCARO, MICHAEL FRANCIS, advertising agency executive; b. N.Y.C., Apr. 3, 1948; s. Girolamo M. and Marianna (DePasquale) P.; m. Bonnie Kerr, Apr. 7, 1972; children: Sabrina, Jon. BA in English, Rockford (Ill.) Coll., 1969. Broadcaster Sta. KFQD-AM; KENI-AM/TV, Anchorage, 1970-71, Sta. KENI-AM/TV, Anchorage, 1972-73; v.p. ops. Cook Inlet Broadcasters, Anchorage, 1973-74; owner Audio Enterprises, Anchorage, 1974-75; asst. Alaska Pub. Broadcasting Commn., Anchorage, 1975-76, exec. dir., 1976-81; CEO, ptnr. Porcaro Blankenship Advt. Corp., Anchorage, 1981-97; CEO Porcaro Comms., Anchorage, 1997—; chmn. bd. Bernholz & Graham, Pub. Rels., 2001—; ptnr. Porcaro Vancouver Ad and Pub. Rels., 2003. Cons. Arco Alaska TV sta., Anchorage, 1981; expert witness U.S. Senate Subcom. on Telecom., Washington, 1978; chmn. citizens adv. com. dept. journalism U. Alaska, 1995-96. Afternoon talk show host KENI, 2000—. Chmn. Municipality of Anchorage Urban Design Commn., 1990-93; mem. mayor's transition team Municipality of Anchorage, 1987-88; bd. dirs. Anchorage Glacier Pilots Baseball Club, 1987-88, Anchorage Mus. History and Art, Alaska Ctr. Internat. Bus., 1996, Commonwealth North, 1996-2000, Friends of Alaska Children's Trust, 1996-97, Anchorage Symphony Orch.; chmn. bd. dirs. Brother Francis Shelter for the Homeless, Anchorage, 1993-96; mem. mktg. com. gov.'s transition team, 1995; mem. United Way Anchorage Cabinet, 1996; bd. dirs. Alaska Spl. Olmpics, 2001, Anchorage Econ. Devel. Corp., 2001, Alaska Moving Image Preservation Assn., 2001. Recipient Silver Mike award Billboard mag., 1974, Bronze award N.Y. Film Critics, 1981, Best of North award Ad. Fedn. Alaska, 1982—, Addy award, 1985, 91, Grand Addy award 1990, Cable TV Mktg. award 1986; Paul Harris fellow. Mem. Advt. Fedn. Alaska, Anchorage C. of C. (bd. dirs.), Alaska Moving Image Preservation Assn. (bd. dirs. 2001). Republican. Roman Catholic. Avocations: softball, hockey, travel, exercise. Office: Porcaro Comm 433 W 9th Ave Anchorage AK 99501-3519 Office Phone: 907-276-4262. Personal E-mail: mike.porcaro@porcaro.ca.

PORCELLO, LEONARD JOSEPH, engineering research and development executive; b. N.Y.C., Mar. 1, 1934; s. Savior James and Mary Josephine (Bacchi) P.; m. Patricia Lucille Berger, July 7, 1962 (dec. Sept. 1991); children: John Joseph, Thomas Gregory; m. Victoria Roberta Smith, June 21, 1996. BA in Physics, Cornell U., 1955; MS in Physics, U. Mich., 1957, MS in Elec. Engring, 1959, PhD in Elec. Engring, 1963. Research asst. U. Mich., Ann Arbor, 1955-58, instr. elec. engring., 1958-61; research engr. Radar & Optics Lab., 1968-72; asso. dir. Willow Run Labs., 1970-72, asso. prof., 1969-72, prof., 1972-73, adj. prof., 1973-75. Dir. radar and optics divsn. Environ. Rsch. Inst. of Mich., Ann Arbor, 1973-76, v.p., 1973-76, trustee, 1975; asst. v.p., mgr. sensor sys. operation Sci. Applications Internat. Corp., Tucson, 1976-79, v.p., 1979-85, corp. v.p., 1985-87, mgr. def. sys. group, 1986-95, sr. v.p., 1987—, dep. mgr. tech. and advanced sys. sector, 1993-97, mgr. applied sys. group, 1995-2000, dep. mgr. space and tech. solutions sector, 1997-99; CFO, bd. dirs. TIAS ARMS, 2004—. Bd. dirs. Tucson Jr. Strings, 1977-79, chmn., 1978-79 Fellow IEEE; mem. Optical Soc. Am., AAAS, Sigma Xi, Eta Kappa Nu. Roman Catholic. Achievements include research on imaging radar, synthetic aperture radar systems and radar remote sensing. Home: 5072 Grandview Ave Yorba Linda CA 92886-4216 Office: Sci Applications Internat Corp Attn LJ Porcello PO Box 820 Yorba Linda CA 92885-0820 Office Phone: 714-695-1465. Business E-Mail: Leonard.J.Porcello@saic.com.

PORDUM, FRANCIS J. former state legislator, educator, marketing professional; b. Lackawanna, N.Y. 1 child, Carolyn. BA, Colgate U., 1968; MEd, SUNY, Buffalo. Formerly tchr. and coach; mem. N.Y. State Assembly, 1983-96, mem. majority steering com., chmn. local govts. com., chmn. com. on state and local rels., chmn. ethics com.; v.p. mktg. and profl. svcs. Capitol Hill Mgmt. Svcs., Inc., Albany, N.Y., 1997—. Former mem. banking com., corrections com., ins. com., racing and wagering com., transp. com., commn. on critical transp. choices and hazardous wastes and toxic substances N.Y. County. Legislator, Erie County. Recipient Pub. Servant of Yr. award Erie County Fedn. Sportsmen, 1983, Citizen of Yr. award Am.-Polish Eagle, 1984, Legislator Citation of Merit award Nat. Columbus Day Com., 1985, Friend of Edn. award Hamburg Tchrs. Assn., 1986, others. Mem. Hamburg C. of C. (N.Y. retirement bd. del.), Profl. and Businessmen's Assn. Western N.Y., Chopin Singing Soc., Polish Am. Congress, Lackawanna Tchrs. Fedn. Address: 7476 Derby Rd Derby NY 14047-9687

PORFILIO, JOHN CARBONE, federal judge; b. Denver, Oct. 14, 1934; s. Edward Alphonso Porfilio and Caroline (Carbone) Moore; m. Joan West, Aug. 1, 1959 (div. 1983); children: Edward Miles, Joseph Arthur, Jeanne Kathrine; m. Theresa Louise Berger, Dec. 28, 1983; 1 stepchild, Katrina Ann Smith. Student, Stanford U., 1952—54; BA, U. Denver, 1956, LLB, 1959, LLD (hon.), 2000. Bar: Colo. 1959, U.S. Supreme Ct. 1965. Asst. atty. gen. State of Colo., Denver, 1962—68, dep. atty. gen., 1968—72, atty. gen., 1972—74; U.S. bankruptcy judge Dist. of Colo., Denver, 1975—82; judge U.S. Dist. Ct. Colo., Denver, 1982—85, U.S. Ct. Appeals (10th cir.), Denver, 1985—99, sr. judge, 1999—. Instr. Colo. Law Enforcement Acad., Denver, 1965—70, State Patrol Acad., Denver, 1968—70; guest lectr. U. Denver Coll. Law, 1978. Committeeman Arapahoe County Rep. Com., Aurora, Colo., 1968; mgr. Dunbar for Atty. Gen., Denver, 1970. Mem.: ABA. Roman Catholic. Office: US Ct Appeals Byron White US Courthouse 1823 Stout St Denver CO 80257-1823

PORGES, DAVID L. utilities, gas, oil executive; b. 1958; BS in indsl. engring., Northwestern U.; MBA, Stanford Grad. Sch. Bus. Sales mgmt. Exxon Corp.; mgmt. Bankers Trust, 1987-98; sr. v.p., CFO Equitable Resources, Inc., Pittsburgh, 1998—. Mem. United Way, Alley Theatre (exec. com.), Houston. Mem. Independent Producers Assn. Am. Office: Equitable Resources Inc One Oxford Ctr Ste 3300 301 Grant St Pittsburgh PA 15219

PORIES, WALTER JULIUS, surgeon, educator; b. Munich, Jan. 18, 1930; s. Theodore Francis and Frances (Lowin) P.; m. Muriel Helen Aronson, Aug. 18, 1951; children: Susan E., Mary Jane, Carolyn A., Kathy G.; m. Mary Ann Rose McCarthy, June 4, 1977; children: Mary Lisa, Michael McCarthy. BA, Wesleyan U., Middletown, Conn., 1952; MD with honors, U. Rochester, 1955. Diplomate Am. Bd. Surgery, Am. Bd. Thoracic Surgery. Intern Strong Meml. Hosp., Rochester, NY, 1955-56, resident, 1958-62; chmn. dept. surgery Wright-Patterson AFB, Ohio, 1952-67; asst. prof. surgery and oncology U. Rochester, 1967-69; prof. surgery and assoc. chmn. dept. surgery Case Western Res. U., 1969-77; prof. surgery and biochemistry East Carolina U., Greenville, NC, 1977—, chmn. dept. surgery, 1977-96; chief surgery Pitt County Meml. Hosp., 1977-96, prof. surgery U. Health Scis. of Uniformed Svcs., 1982—; founder, assoc. dir. Rochester Cancer Ctr., 1967-69; founder, dir. Cleve. Cancer Ctr., 1972-77, Hospice of Cleve., 1975; founder, chmn. bd. Hospice of Greenville, 1981; med. dir. Home Health Care of Greenville, 1978-83. Founder, chmn. bd. Ctr. for Creative Living, 1985-91; pres., chmn. Echo Mgmt. Orgn., 1994—; vis. scholar NIH, 1996; sec. treas., pres. N.C. Med. Bd., 1997-2003. Author: Clinical Applications of Zinc Metabolism, 1974; editor: Operative Surgery series, vols. 1-4, 1979-83, Office Surgery for Family Physicians, 1985; editor in chief Current Surgery, 1990—; editor Nat. Curriculum for Residency in Surgery, 4th edit., 1988—. Bd. dirs. Boy Scouts Am., Cleve., 1974-77, Greenville Arts Mus., 1980-82; pres. Sequoiah, Inc., 1999—; bd. dirs. East Carolina U. Found., United Meth. Homes, 2003-. Maj. USAF, 1955-67; col. USAR, 1979-91, comdr. USAF Hosp., Durham, N.C.; activated Desert Shield, 1990. Decorated Legion of Merit; Thorndyke scholar, 1948-51; recipient McLester award USAF, 1966, Miss. Magnolia Cross, 1989, Presdl. citation for Desert Shield, 1994; named to Hon. Order of Ky. Cols., 1965. Fellow ACS, Am. Coll. Cardiology, Am. Coll. Chest Physicians; mem. Soc. for Vascular Surgery, Soc. Surg. Oncology, Soc. Univ. Surgeons, Am. Surg. Assn., Soc. Environ. Geochemistry (past pres.), Residency Rev. Com. for Surgery (vice-chair 1992-98), So. Surg. Assn., Soc. for Thoracic Surgery, Ea. Carolina Health Orgn. (pres., chmn. bd. 1994-99), Assn. Programs Dirs. in Surgery (pres. 1995-96), N.C. Surg. Assn. (pres. 1995-96), Am. Soc. Bariatic Surgery (pres. 2002), Sigma Xi (O. Max Gardner prize), Phi Kappa Phi. Home: Deep Sun Farm 7464 NC 43 N Macclesfield NC 27852 Office: East Carolina U Dept Surgery Greenville NC 27858 E-mail: pories@aol.com.

PORILE, NORBERT THOMAS, chemistry professor; BA, U. Chgo., 1952, MS, 1954, PhD, 1957. Rsch. assoc. Brookhaven Nat. Lab., Upton, N.Y., 1957-59, assoc. chemist, 1959-63, chemist, 1963-64; vis. prof. chemistry McGill U., 1963-65; assoc. prof. chemistry Purdue U., West Lafayette, Ind., 1965-69, prof. chemistry, 1969—. Rsch. collaborator Brookhaven Nat. Lab., Argonne Nat. Lab., Los Alamos Sci. Lab., Lawrence Berkeley Lab.; vis. prof. Facultes des Scis., Orsay, France; fellow Soc. Promotion of Sci. in Japan, Inst. Nuclear Study, U. Kyoto, 1961. Editor: Radiochemistry of the Elements and Radiochemical Techniques, 1986-90. John Simon Guggenheim meml. fellow Institut de Physique Nucleaire Orsay, 1971-72; recipient F.D. Martin Undergrad. Teaching award, 1977; Von Humboldt Sr. U.S. Scientist award Philipps U., Marburg, W. Ger., 1982 Mem. Am. Chem. Soc., Am. Phys. Soc. Office: Purdue U Dept Chemistry Brown Lab Lafayette IN 47907

PORITZ, DEBORAH T. state supreme court chief justice, former attorney general; b. Bkln., Oct. 26, 1936; married; 2 children. BA, Brooklyn Coll., City U. NY, 1958; JD, U. Penn., 1977. Dep. atty. gen. NJ Dept. Law and Pub. Safety, 1977—81, asst. chief environ. protection section, 1981—84, dep. atty. gen. in charge of appeals, chief banking, ins. and pub. securities section, 1984—86, asst. atty. gen., dir. divsn. law, 1986—89; chief counsel to Gov. Thomas Kean, 1989—90; ptnr. Jamieson, Moore, Peskin and Spicer law firm, Princeton, 1990—94; atty. gen. State of N.J., 1994—96; chief justice Supreme Ct. N.J., Trenton, 1996—. Office: Supreme Ct NJ Hughes Justice Complex PO Box 23 Trenton NJ 08625-0023*

POROSOFF, HAROLD, chemist, research and development director; b. Bklyn., Apr. 3, 1946; s. Solomon and Ruth (Goldberg) P.; m. Leslie Pamela Freiman, May 19, 1948; children: Lauren, Stephen, Marc. BS, MIT, 1966; PhD, Brown U., 1970. Various rsch. and mgmt. positions fibers div. Am. Cyanamid Co., Stamford, Conn. and Milton, Fla., 1970-78, various mgmt. positions Shulton Rsch. div. Clifton, N.J., 1978-83, dir., 1983-88, v.p. R & D chem. rsch. divsn. Stamford, 1989-93; v.p. R & D Cytec Industries Inc., Stamford, 1993-95; v.p., chief tech. officer Cytec Industries, Inc., Stamford, 1995-98, cons., 1998—. Patentee in field. Mem. AAAS. Office: 22 Olmsted Rd Scarsdale NY 10583-2324 E-mail: hpphd@optonline.net.

PORPER, MARY, comptroller; V.p., comptroller Suissa Miller, L.A. Office: 8687 Melrose Ave Los Angeles CA 90069-5701 Fax: 310-392-2625.

PORRATA, SAMUEL M. education director, foreign language educator; b. San Juan, P.R., May 11, 1968; arrived in U.S., 1987; s. Samuel Luis and Angeles Josefina Porrata; m. Sandra Porrata, Dec. 8, 2000. BA, Hofstra U., 1991; MA, Villanova U., 1993; PhD, Temple U., 1997. Part-time instr. Villanova (Pa.) U., 1991-93; lectr. Ursinus Coll., Collegeville, Pa., spring 1993; tchg. asst. Temple U., Phila., 1993-95; adj. instr. St. Joseph's U., Phila., 1995-96; instr. Temple U. Center City, Phila., 1996-97; lectr. U. Pa., Phila., 1996-98; instr. West Chester (Pa.) U., 1997-99; asst. prof. Spanish, dir. internat. edn. Fairmont (W.Va.) State Coll., 1999-2001; asst. prof. Spanish Shenandoah U., Winchester, Va., 2001—. Presenter in field. Author: The Creationism of Gerardo Diego and Vicente Huidobro, 2001; editor: TPR Storytelling, 2000, author poems. Mem. Ednl. Testing Svc., MLA, N.E. MLA, Am. Assn. Tchrs. Spanish and Portuguese, Faculty and Course Devel. in Internat. Studies, Nat. Assn. Fgn. Students Advisors, Internat. Soc. for Luso-Hispanic Humor, Sigma Delta Pi. Roman Catholic.

PORRAZ, MAURICIO JIMENEZ LABORA, civil engineer, researcher; b. Mexico City, Mar. 24, 1938; s. Manuel Guillen Porraz and Dolores Jimenez Labora; m. Margarita Lando Coindreau, Oct. 1, 1966; children: Margarita, Mauricio, Miguel. BA, La Salle U., Mexico City, 1954; degree in civil engrng. with honors, Autonomous Nat. U. Mex., Mexico City, 1961; degree in ocean engrng., Assn. Orgn. des Stages France, Paris, 1964; degree in petroleum offshore engrng., Assn. Coop. Technique Internat. Maritime, Marseille, France, 1968; postgrad., Nat. Engrng. Acad., Mex., 1977, Corpus Christi, Toledo, Spain, 1988. Pres. Orgn. Submarina Mexicana, Mexico City, 1965-2001, Equipos y Tecnicas, Mexico City, 1967-2001, Control de Erosion, Mexico City, 1971-2001, Conersa, Mexico City, 1973-91, Estructuras Marinas Concreto, Mexico City, 1979-91, Constrn., Cons. y Comercializadora, Mexico City, 1991-2001, Soluciones Ecoambientales, 2000—. Engr. in geosyntetics, interlocked interconnected concrete blocks for breakwaters; patentee in field. Bd. dirs. Panam. Fedn. on Oceanic Coastal Engrng., Stevens Inst. Tech., 1989; corr. mem. Royal Acad. Nice Arts and Hist. Scis., Toledo, 1989; mem. Royal Inst. Geography, Madrid, 1970-91. Lt. Mexican Infantry, 1956-57. Recipient Best Thesis in Yr. award Engrng. Found. (Mex.), 1963, rsch. and invention medal Soc. for Rsch. and Invention (Paris), 1977, Internat. Coastal Engrng. award ASCE, 1977, 91; named Man of Yr., Group Expansion Economy and Fins. Bus. (Mex.), 1983-84, Hon. Armed Knight Toledo, Spain, Knight Marshal D. Mexico Mil. and Hospitaller Order of St. Lazarus of Jerusalem, 1998. Fellow Mexican Assn. Architects and Engrs. (centenary 1968); mem. Venezuela's Engrs. Soc. (dir. A, goco award 1972), Panam. Fedn. Engrng. Assn. (oceanic engrng. com. 1981), Ctr. Profl. Actualization (prof. 1981), Mex. Acad. Engrs. Roman Catholic. Office: Acad Scis Gen Sec Pla Villa de Madrid # 3 06700 Mexico City Roma Mexico E-mail: mauricio@porraz.com., mporrazjl@hotmail.com.

PORT, ARTHUR TYLER, retired government administrator, lawyer; b. Chgo., Oct. 4, 1916; s. Arthur Christopher and Helen Elizabeth (Brown) P.; m. Aline Helen Gooding, Oct. 21, 1950; children: Cynthia Helen, Christopher Tyler. BA cum laude, Davidson Coll., 1937; JD, Yale U., 1940; LLD, Coll. Advanced Sci., 1962. Bar: N.C. 1940. Law practice, Winston-Salem, N.C., 1940-41; radio announcer Sta. WMRF, Lewistown, Pa., 1941-43; civil atty. Judge Adv. div. Hdqrs. European Command, U.S. Army, Frankfurt, Germany, 1946-47; chief policy sect. Mil. Justice Div., 1947-48; legal asst. to spl. advisor to comdr.-in-chief ETO and mil. govt. Germany, 1949; spl. counsel Sec. of Army, 1949-50, spl. asst., 1950-55; dep. dir. office NSC Affairs Office Sec. Def., 1955-56; exec. asst. to asst. sec. def. ISA, 1956-57; dir. office of security policy and dir. indsl. pers. access authorization Office Asst. Sec. Defense, 1957-61; dep. asst. sec. logistics/installatons and logistics Dept. of Army, 1961-67; fgn. ser. res. officer Dept. of State, 1967-73; asst. sec. gen. def. support NATO, Brussels, 1967-73; spl. asst. Asst. Sec. of Army for Energy Policy, 1973-74; dep. for supply, maintenance and transp. Office Asst. Sec. Army, 1974. Cons. NATO affairs Stanford Rsch. Inst., Gen. Rsch. Corp., Logistics Mgmt. Inst., 1975-81. With USAAC, 1942-45, USASIGC, 1945-46, ETO, lt. col. USAR, 1946-68. Recipient Meritorious Civilian Svc. award Dept. Army, 1953, decoration for exceptional civilian svc., 1967; Disting. Civilian Svc. award Dept. Def., 1961. Mem. Kenwood Golf and Country Club (Bethesda, Md.), Scabbard and Blade, Omicron Delta Kappa, Phi Gamma Delta. E-mail: atport@att.net.

PORT, SIDNEY CHARLES, mathematician, educator; b. Chgo., Nov. 27, 1935; s. Isadore and Sarah (Landy) P.; m. Idelle Jackson, Mar. 24, 1957; children— Ethan, Jonathan, Daniel. AB, Northwestern U., 1957, MS, 1958, PhD, 1962. Staff mathematician Rand Corp., 1962-66; asso. prof. math. U. Calif. at Los Angeles, 1966-69, prof., 1969—. Author: (with P. Hoel and C. Stone) Probability, Statistics and Stochastic Processes, 1971, (with C. Stone) Brownian Motion and Classical Potential Theory, 1978, Theoretical Probability for Applications, 1993; contbr. articles to profl. jours. Fellow Inst. Math. Statistics; mem. Am. Math. Soc. Home: 680 Kingman Ave Santa Monica CA 90402-1334 Office: UCLA Dept Math Los Angeles CA 90024 E-mail: sport@ucla.edu.

PORT, STEVEN CHARLES, cardiologist, educator; b. N.Y.C., Nov. 23, 1947; m. Karen Port; children: Jesse, Michelle. MD, Mt. Sinai Sch. Medicine, 1972. Diplomate Am. Bd. Internal Medicine, Am. Bd. Cardiovascular Disease, Am. Bd. Nuclear Cardiology. Intern, resident Mt. Sinai Hosp., N.Y.C., 1973-75; fellow in cardiology Duke U. Med. Ctr., 1975-79, rsch. assoc. medicine, 1979-80; asst. prof. medicine U. N.C., Chapel Hill, 1980-82, Sinai Samaritan Med. Ctr.-U. Wis. Med. Sch., Milw., 1982-86, assoc. prof., 1986-92, prof., 1992-95, clin. prof., 1995—; pvt. practice cardiology Milw., 1995—. Active staff St. Luke's Med. Ctr., Sinai Samaritan Med. Ctr.; courtesy staff St. Francis Hosp., Waukesha (Wis.) Meml. Hosp., St. Agnes Hosp., West Allis (Wis.) Meml. Hosp., St. Mary's Hosp., St. Michael Hosp.; mem. cardiovascular task force Prime Care, Inc., 1993—. Contbr. articles to profl. jours. and chpts. to books; spkr. in field. Grantee Mt. Sinai Med. Ctr. Found., 1985-86. Fellow Am. Coll. Cardiology; mem. Am. Heart Assn., Am. Soc. Nuc. Cardiology (bd. dirs., treas. 1996—). Avocation: aviation. Office: Cardiovascular Assoc Ltd 2801 W KK River Pkwy Ste 840 Milwaukee WI 53215-3660 E-mail: sport@cva-ltd.com.

PORTA, SIENA GILLANN, sculptor, educator; b. N.Y.C., Nov. 5, 1951; d. Vincent Anthony Porta and Barbara Ann Gill Porta Hutchinson; m. Robert Christopher Dell, May 30, 1986; 1 child, Malcolm Vincent Dell. BS in Studio Arts, Bklyn. Coll., CUNY, 1977; MFA in Sculpture, Pa. State U., 1979. Sci. illustrator Columbia U./Lamont-Doherty Geol. Obs., Palisades, NY, 1980—87; scenic artist Saturday Night Live, N.Y.C., 1986—89, Met. Opera, N.Y.C., 1987—92; master scenic artist numerous Broadway prod., including Frankie and Johnny, Boiler Rm., Sorrows and Rejoicings, 1992—; adj. prof. contemporary arts Ramapo Coll., 2000—; adj. prof. art St. Thomas Aquinas, Sparkill, NY, 2000—; represented by Noho Gallery, N.Y.C., 14 Sculptors Inc., N.Y.C. Adj. prof. Bergen CC, Paramus, NJ, 1984—85; artist-in-residence Brisons Veor, Cornwall, England, 2003. One-woman shows include 14 Sculptors Gallery, NYC, 1984-85, 88, 90, Mid-Hudson Arts and Sci. Ctr., Poughkeepsie, NY, 1992-93, Dominican Coll., Blauvelt, NY, 1980, Noho Gallery, NYC, 2003; group shows at A.B. Condon Gallery, NYC, 1982-83, Terrain Gallery, NYC, 1984, Am. Cultural Ctr., Reykiavik, Iceland, 1988, Notre Dame U., South Bend, Ind., 1990, Lehigh U., Phila., Blue Hill Cult. Ctr., Pearl River, NY, 1995, Eighth Floor Gallery, NYC, 1996, NJ City U., Jersey City, Nassau C.C., Garden City, NY, The Interchurch Ctr., Riverside Dr., NY, 1998, Adelphi U., NY, 2000, St. Thomas Aquinas Coll., Sparkhill, NY, 2000, Galleri Ofeigur, 2001, Noho Gallery, 2001-02, Snaefelsness Regl. Museum, 2002, Hafnarborg Ctr. for Culture, Mus, 2002-03, Regional Mus. of Hornafjorduv, 2003, Rutgers U., 2003, others; represented in collections at Fulbright Commn., Reykjavik, Bergen C.C., Paramus, NJ, 1988, St. Philip R.C. Ch., Norwalk, Conn., Jacob Riis Nat. Park US Embassy, Iceland, Brisons Veor Trust, Cornwall, England, Brisons Veor Trust, Cornwall, Eng.; subject of video Me and The Mirror, 1990; contbr. articles to popular mag. Pa. State Arts Coun./Hershey Med. Coll. grantee, 1978-79; NY State Coun. on the Arts grantee, 1986; USIA-Ptnrs. of Ams. travel grant to St. Lucia, W.I., 1992, NY Fdn. for the Arts grantee, 2002.; artist resident Brisons Veor, Cornwall, Eng., 2003. Mem. Zen Ctr. of San Diego. Home: PO Box 46 Palisades NY 10964-0046 Personal E-mail: sportaedu@aol.com.

PORTAL, GILBERT MARCEL ADRIEN, oil company executive; b. Paris, Aug. 2, 1930; came to U.S., 1982; s. Emmanuel Jules and Henriette Josephine (Bonnard) P.; m. Monique Janine Adam, July 12, 1951; children: Dominique, Veronique, Marc-Emmanuel. Baccalaureate, Lycee Charlemagne U., Paris, 1949; Ingenieur Civil des Mines, Sch. of Mines, St. Etienne, 1955; diplome du C.P.A., Ctr. Advanced Bus., Paris, 1969; auditeur 30 eme session IHEDN, Higher Studies Nat. Defense, Paris, 1978. Geophysicist Societe Nationale Elf Aquitaine, Sahara, Algeria, 1957-63, exploration mgr. north sea, 1963-65, dep. exec. v.p. Europe, 1965-68, dep. exec. v.p. North and South Am., 1968-70, chief exec. officer, 1970-72, dir., chief exec. officer, 1972-76, dep. exec. v.p. hydrocarbons, 1976-78, exec. v.p. North Africa, Mid. East, Far East, 1978-82; pres. Elf Aquitaine Petroleum, Houston, 1982-89; chmn., chief exec. officer Elf Exploration, Inc., Houston, 1989-90; sec.-gen. European Petroleum Industry Assn., 1990-95; ptnr. G.M.H. Internat. Oil and Gas Consulting, Paris, 1995—; pres. internat. devel. Howard Energy Internat. LLC, 1999—2002. Served to lt. French Army, 1955-57. Decorated Legion of Honor (France), Nat. Merit Order (France); Equatorial Star (Gabon). Mem. Cercle Royal Gaulois Artistique et Littéraire. Roman Catholic. Business E-Mail: gmh@portal-consult.com.

PORTALE, ALFRED, chef, restaurant owner; Grad., Culinary Inst. Am., 1981. Chef, co-owner Gotham Bar and Grill, N.Y.C. Author: Gotham Bar and Grill Cookbook, 1998 (Julia Child Cookbook award, 1998), 12 Seasons Cookbook, 2001. Named Best Chef in N.Y., 1993. Office: Gotham Bar & Grill 12 E 12th St New York NY 10003-4498

PORTANOVA, CAROLYN AMICK, religious organization administrator; b. Bedford, Pa., July 30, 1945; d. James T. and Elizabeth D. (DiLbert) Amick; m. Andrew J. Portanova, Apr. 17, 1982. BS, Pa. State U., 1967; MEd, U. Rochester, 1974. Supr. Cath. Family Ctr. Substance Abuse Svcs., Rochester, N.Y., 1974-83, dir., 1983-89; pres., CEO Cath. Family Ctr., Rochester, N.Y., 1989—. Chairperson monitoring com. N.Y. State Bd. Regents, Rochester, 1989—; bd. trustees Coun. Accrediation, Rochester, 1996—; adv. bd. Blue Cross/Blue Shield, Rochester, 1996—; com. mem. Family Svcs. Am., Rochester, 1996. Bd. dirs. United Neighborhood Ctrs., Rochester, 1995—, Monroe County Bar, 1996—; mem. corp. body United Way, Rochester, 1992—. Recipient Outstanding Contbn. award N.Y. State Div. Substance Abuse Svc, 1986, Leadership, Faith and Courage award Interfaith Action Cmty., 1997; named Exec. Yr. United Way Greater Rochester, 1992. Mem. Rotary. Avocations: photography, travel. Office: Catholic Family Ctr 25 Franklin St Fl 7 Rochester NY 14604-1002

PORTE, DANIEL, JR., physician, educator, health facility administrator; b. N.Y.C., Aug. 13, 1931; s. Daniel and Majorie Veronica (Clark) P.; m. Eunice Claire Ungerleider, Mar. 21, 1951; children— Jeffrey, Michael, Kenneth BA, Brown U., 1953; MD, U. Chgo., 1957. Assoc. prof. medicine U. Wash., Seattle, 1969-73, prof. medicine, 1973—; dir. U. Wash. Diabetes-Endocrinology Rsch. Ctr., 1977—; ACOS for rsch. and devel. VA Med. Ctr., Seattle, 1971—, chief div. endocrinology and metabolism, 1975—. Chmn. med. sci. adv. bd. Juvenile Diabetes Found., N.Y.C., 1977-78; cons. Scripps Clinic and Research Found., San Diego, 1978-81; Connaught lectr. Can. Diabetes Assn., Toronto, Ont., 1984 Assoc. editor Am. Jour. Physiology, 1976-78, Jour. Diabetes, 1984—; contbr. numerous articles, chpts. to profl. publs., 1965— Served to lt. comdr. USN, 1959-61 Recipient Career Devel. award NIH, 1968-70, David Rumbaugh award Juvenile Diabetes Found., 1984; Guggenheim fellow, 1985 Fellow ACP; mem. Assn. Am. Physicians, Am. Soc. Clin. Investigation, Am. Diabetes Assn. (pres. 1986-87, Eli Lilly award 1970), Am. Diabetes Assn. (Wash. affiliate) (pres. 1984-85), Western Assn. Physicians (councillor 1982-85) Avocation: skiing. Home: 1660 Via Corona La Jolla CA 92037-7837 Office: U Wash Diabetes-Endocrinology Rsch Ctr-VA Med Ctr 2B-21 1660 S Columbian Way Seattle WA 98108-1532

PORTE, JOEL MILES, English educator; b. Bklyn., Nov. 13, 1933; s. Jacob I. and Frances (Derison) P.; m. Ilana D'Ancona, June 17, 1962 (div. 1977); 1 child, Susanna Maria; m. Helene Sophrin, Oct. 18, 1985. AB magna cum laude, CCNY, 1957; A.M., Harvard U., 1958, PhD, 1962. Instr. English Harvard U., Cambridge, Mass., 1962-64, asst. prof., 1964-68, assoc. prof., 1968-69, prof., 1969-82, Bernbaum prof. lit., 1982-87, chmn. dept. English and Am. Lit., 1985-87; Frederic J. Whiton prof. English Cornell U., Ithaca, NY, 1987-89, Ernest I. White prof. Am. Studies and Humane Letters, 1989—. Vis. lectr. Am. Studies Rsch. Ctr., Hyderabad, India, spring 1976. Author: Emerson and Thoreau: Transcendentalists in Conflict, 1966, The Romance in America: Studies in Cooper, Poe, Hawthorne, Melville and James, 1969, Representative Man: Ralph Waldo Emerson in His Time, 1979, In Respect to Egotism: Studies in American Romantic Writing, 1991; editor: Emerson in His Journals, 1982, Emerson: Prospect and Retrospect, 1982, Emerson: Essays and Lectures, 1983, New Essays on Portrait of a Lady, 1990, A Cambridge Companion to Ralph Waldo Emerson (with Saundra Morris), 1999, Emerson's Prose and Poetry: A Norton Critical Edit. (with Saundra Morris), 2001, Consciousness and Culture: Emerson and Thoreau Reviewed, 2004. Scholar in Residence, Rockefeller Found., Bellagio, Italy, 1979; fellow John Simon Guggenheim Found., 1981-82. Mem. Am. Lit. Assn., Phi Beta Kappa. Home: 700 Warren Rd 23 1A Ithaca NY 14850-1237 Office Phone: 607-255-8349. E-mail: jp26@cornell.edu.

PORTE, MICHAEL SHELDON, communication educator, consultant; b. Chgo., Jan. 20, 1932; s. Robert Harold and Rose (Ellman) P.; m. Barbara Alice Beers, Dec. 20, 1959; children: Stephen, Eric, Alice. BS in Journalism, MS in Journalism, Northwestern U., 1953, PhD, 1960. Instr. Wilson Jr. Coll., Chgo., 1954-55, Northwestern U., Evanston, Ill., 1956-60; from asst. prof. to prof. U. Cin., 1960—2003, prof. emeritus, 2003—. Vis. prof. U. So. Calif., L.A., 1966, No. Jiaotong U., Beijing, People's Republic of China, 1986; cons. Monsanto Rsch. Corp., Miamisburg, Ohio, 1963, U.S. Dept. Labor, Washington, 1973, Procter & Gamble, Cin., 1970-74, 80, GE, Cin., 1990, Loews, 1991. Author: (manual) Technical Writers, 1963, Media Coverage of Events Relating to the Swine Flu Program, 1981; co-editor: Mei Guo Jing Ji, 1988, Cinema Now. Tour guide NY Arts tour, NYC, 1969-2003; reviewer Choice, Middletown, Conn., 1982-91; judge Assn. for Cmty. Theatres, Cin., 1970-96; film adv. Ohio Arts Coun., Columbus, 1972-76. Mem. Assn. Bus. Communication (life, pres. 1968). Avocation: tap dancing. Office: U Cin PO Box 210184 Cincinnati OH 45221-0184 Office Phone: 513-556-4456. Business E-Mail: michael.porte@uc.edu.

PORTELLI, VINCENT GEORGE, business executive, consultant; b. Detroit, Jan. 6, 1932; s. Camillo and Mary (Borg) P.; B.S., U. Detroit, 1953, tchr. cert., 1961; M.A., U. Mich., 1965; postgrad. Harvard Grad. Sch. Bus. Adminstrn., summer 1971; m. Eugenia A. Naruc, Feb. 7, 1959; children: Debra, Mark, David, Anne, James. Mgmt. trainee, cost acct., cost analyst, sr. internal auditor, sr. cost acct. Ford Motor Co., Dearborn, Mich., 1953-60; tchr. Bedford Sch., Dearborn Heights, Mich., 1960-62; bus. mgr., adminstrv. asst. to dir. Wayne State U. Center For Adult Edn., 1962-64; controller, dir. bus. affairs Mercy Coll. of Detroit, 1964-73; sec.-treas. Am. Sunroof Corp., v.p., corp. sec., 1977-81; sec.-treas. Automobile Splty. Corp., Southgate, Mich., 1973-81; pres., dir. Servia, Inc., cons. to mgmt., Livonia, Mich., 1980-81; corp. v.p. ops. Crown Group, Inc., 1981-83; v.p., gen. mgr. Mktg. Displays, Inc., 1983-85; chief exec. officer Physicians Health Plan (United Health Care), Lansing, Mich., 1985-86, Physicians Choice Northwest, Ind. (Unted Healthcare), Merrillville, 1986-87; exec. dir. Capital Dist. Physician's Health Plan, Albany, N.Y., 1987-92; exec. v.p. Emerald Health Network, Inc., Cleve., 1992-94; pres., CEO Emerald HMO, Inc., 1994-95; gen. mgr. Genesis Health Plans of Ohio, Inc., 1996-97; cons. Managed Health Care, 1995—. Rep. adv. council Livonia Bd. Edn., 1968-71; v.p. Country Homes Estates Civic Assn., 1971-73; commr. Econ. Devel. Corp.; mem. U. Albany Found. Mem. Employers Assn. Detroit, Am. Soc. Tng. Dirs., Am. Arbitration Assn. (mem. nat. panel), Am. Managed Care and Rev. Assn. (founder exec. leadership program), Nat. Found. for Iletitis and Colitis (bd. dir. capital dist. chpt.), Albany Execs. Assn., Group Health Assn. Am., Delta Sigma Pi, Beta Gamma Sigma. Republican. Roman Catholic. Home: 4286 Sabal Pointe Dr SE Grand Rapids MI 49546-8251

PORTEOUS, G. THOMAS, JR., judge; b. 1946; BA, La. State U., 1968, JD, 1971. Spl. counsel, atty. gen., 1971-73; asst. dist. atty. Dist. Atty. Office Parrish of Jefferson, 1973-75; ptnr. Edward, Porteous & Amato, Grenta, La., 1973-74, Edwards, Porteous & Lee, Grenta, 1974-76, Porteous, Lee & Mustakas, 1976-80, Porteous & Mustakas, Metairie, La., 1980-84; city atty. City of Harahan, La., 1982-84; dist. ct. judge divsn. A State of La., 1984-94; dist. judge U.S. Dist. Ct. (ea. dist.), La., 1994—. Mem. ABA, Fed. Bar Assn., La. State Bar Assn., 4th and 5th Cir. Judges Assn., Jefferson Bar Assn., Am. Judges Assn., La. Dist. Atty. Assn. Office: US Dist Ct E Dist 500 Camp St Rm C-206 New Orleans LA 70130-3313

PORTEOUS, SKIPP, private investigator, writer; b. Hartford, Conn., Feb. 7, 1944; s. Charles Robert and Marian Berle (Guy) P.; m. Linda Marie Silvernail, Mar. 25, 1965 (div. Feb. 1977) children: Angela Monique, Charles Mark, Marylisa; m. Barbara Ann Simon, May 1, 1983 (div. June 2002). Student, Life Bible Coll., LA, 1966-67, East LA C.C., 1969, Columbia Green C.C., Greenport, NY, 1978. Ordained ministry Elim Fellowship, 1968; cert. radio mktg. cons. Licensed private investigator, Mass., NY. Evangelist Chapel on the Strip, Hollywood, Calif., 1967-68; pastor Pasadena (Calif.) Christian Fellowship, 1968-74, West Copake (NY) Reformed Ch., 1974-76, Agape House Christian Ctr., Hillsdale, NY, 1976-77; sales exec., promoter various radio stas. newspapers, NY, Mass., 1977-84; pres. Inst. First Amendment Studies, Inc., Gt. Barrington, Mass., 1984—; pvt. investigator, owner Sherlock Investigations, NY, Mass., 1998—. Radio TV talk show guest, nationwide, 1986—; rschr. TV news networks, mags. Author: Jesus Doesn't Live Here Anymore-From Fundamentalist to Freedom Writer, 1991; co-author: Challenging, The Christian Right - The Activist's Handbook; author mag. articles, columns. Elim fellow. Democrat. Jewish. Avocations: photography, painting. Office Phone: 212-579-4302. E-mail: skipp@sherlockinvestigations.com.

PORTER, ADAM LOWRY, religious studies educator; b. Pitts., July 4, 1966; s. Warren Keifer and Sarah Katherine Porter; m. Clare Lynd (div.); children: Jonah, Isaiah. BA, Oberlin Coll., Ohio, 1984—88; MTS, Harvard Divinity Sch., 1990—93; PhD, Duke U., Durham, N.C., 1993—99. Vis. prof. Duke U., Durham, NC, 1999—2000; asst. prof. Ill. Coll., Jacksonville, 2000—. Author: (textbook) Introducing the Bible, 2004. Avocation: Aikido. Office: Illinois Coll 1101 W College Ave Jacksonville IL 62650

PORTER, ALAN LESLIE, industrial and systems engineering educator; b. Jersey City, June 22, 1945; s. Leslie Frank and Alice Mae (Kaufman) P.; m. Claudia Loy Ferrey, June 14, 1968; children: Brett, Doug, Lynn. BSChemE, Calif. Inst. Tech., 1967; MS, UCLA, 1968, PhD in Psychology, 1972. Rsch. assoc., asst. prof. program social mgmt. tech. U. Wash., Seattle, 1972-74; asst. prof. indsl. sys. engrng. Ga. Inst. Tech., Atlanta, 1975-78, assoc. prof., 1979-85, prof., 1986—, dir. tech. policy assessment ctr., 1989—2001, prof. pub. policy, 1990—2001, prof. emeritus, 2001—, co-dir. tech policy assessment ctr., 2002—; dir. rsch. devel. Search Tech., Inc., Norcross, Ga., 2002—. Cons. Search Tech., IBM, Coca Cola, Rexam, SAIC, SRI. Author, editor: (with others) A Guidebook for Technology Assessment and Impact Analysis, 1980, Interdisciplinarity, 1986, Impact of Office Automation on Clerical Employment, 1985, Forecasting and Management of Technology, 1991, (with Wm. Read) Information Revolution: Present and Future Consequences, 1998, Environmental Methods Review, 1998. NSF grantee, 1974-75, 78-86, 89—, Dept. Transp. grantee, 1977-79. Mem. Internat. Assn. Impact Assessment (co-founder, sec. 1981-87, exec. dir. 1987-90, pres. 1995-96), IEEE Sys. Man and Cybernetics Soc. (chmn. tech. forecasting com., Bellcore adv. coun.). Home: 110 Lake Top Ct Roswell GA 30076-3017 Office: School Industrial and Systems Engineering Georgia Tech Atlanta GA 30332-0001 Office Phone: 770-441-1457. Business E-Mail: alan.porter@isge.gatech.edu.

PORTER, ANDREW CALVIN, academic administrator, psychologist, educator; b. Huntington, Pa., July 10, 1942; s. Rutherford and Grace (Johnson) P.; children: Matthew, Anna, John, Joe, Kate. BS, Ind. State U., 1963; MS, U. Wis., 1965, PhD, 1967. Vis. asst. prof. Ind. State U., 1967; asst. prof. ednl. psychology Mich. State U., East Lansing, 1967—70, dir. office rsch. consultation, 1967—73, assoc. prof. ednl. psychology, 1970—74; vis. scholar Nat. Inst. Edn., Washington, 1973—74, chief measurement and methodology divsn., 1974—75; prof. ednl. psychology Mich. State U., East Lansing, 1974—88; assoc. dir. basic skills group Nat. Inst. Edn., Washington, 1975-76; dir. Sch. Advanced Studies Coll. Edn. Mich. State U., East Lansing, 1979—81, assoc. dean rsch. and grad. study Coll. Edn., 1981—85; Anderson-Bascom prof. edn., prof. ednl. psychology U. Wis., Madison, 1988—2003, dir. Wis. Ctr. Edn. Rsch., 1988—2003; Patricia and Rodes Hart prof. ednl. leadership and policy Vanderbilt U., Nashville, 2003—, dir. Learning Scis. Inst., 2003—. Mem. adv. bd. Am. Jour. Edn., 1988—, editl. bd. Tchrs. Coll. Record, 1995-, adv. com. What Works Clearinghouse Inst. Edn. Scis., 2002-, steering com. math./sci. partnerships, Nat. Acad. Sci., 2003-; chmn. adv. coun. on edn. stats., U.S. Dept. Edn., 1994-2001; chair bd. Internat. Studies, Nat. Acad. Sci., Nat. Rsch. Coun., 1998-2001 Editor: (with A. Gamoran) Methodological Advances in Cross-National Surveys of Educational Achievement, 2002. Bd. dirs. Madison Urban League, 1992-96. Recipient Disting. Alumni award, Ind. State U., 1994, Crystal Apple Award, Mich. State U., 1996, Sch. Edn. Dean's Club Faculty Disting. Achievement Award, U. Wis.-Madison, 2001. Mem. Am. Ednl. Rsch. Assn. (pres. 2001), Nat. Coun. Edn. Measurement, Nat. Coun. Tchrs. Math., Nat. Acad. Edn., Phi Delta Kappa (life). Office: Vanderbilt U Learning Scis Inst Box 59 Peabody Sta Nashville TN 37203 E-mail: andy.porter@vanderbilt.edu.

PORTER, ARTHUR T. oncologist, educator, medical administrator; b. Freetown, Sierra Leone, June 11, 1956; m. Pamela Porter; 4 children. Student, U. Sierra Leone, 1974-75; BA in Anatomy, Cambridge U., 1978, MB, BChir, MD, 1980, MA, 1984; DMRT, Royal Coll. Radiologists, Eng., 1985; postgrad., U. Alta., 1984-86; FRCPC, Royal Coll. Physicians and Surgeons, Can., 1986; cert. for physicians mgr. program, U. Toronto, 1990; MBA, U. Tenn., 1998. Lic., bd. cert., Mich., Can., Eng.; diplomate Health Care Adminstrn. House physician gen. medicine Norfolk and Norwich Hosp., Eng., 1981; house sugeon gen. surgery New Addenbrookes Hosp., Cambridge, Eng., 1981-82; sr. house officer clin. hematology No. Gen. Hosp., Sheffield, Eng., 1982; sr. house officer gen. medicine Huntington County Hosp., Hinchingbrooke Hosp., Eng., 1982-83; sr. house officer radiotherapy and oncology Norfolk and Norwich Hosp., Norwich, 1983-84; chief resident radiation oncology Cross Cancer Inst., Edmonton, Alta., Can., 1984-86, from radiation oncologist to sr. radiation oncologist, 1986-87, sr. radiation oncologist, 1987; asst. prof. medicine U. Alta., Edmonton, 1987, assoc. clin. prof. dept. surgery

faculty medicine, 1988; head divsn. radiation oncology U. Western Ont., London, Can., 1988; cons. radiation oncologist, chief dept. radiation oncology London Regional Cancer Ctr., 1988, program dir. radiation oncology, 1989-91; chmn. dept. oncology Victoria Hosp. Corp., London, 1990; assoc. prof. dept. oncology U. Western Ont., 1990; program dir. radiation oncology Wayne State U., Detroit, 1991-92; prof., chmn. dept. radiation oncology Wayne State U. Sch. Medicine, Detroit, 1991-99; chief Gershenson Radiation Oncology Ctr. Harper Hosp., Detroit, 1991-99; radiation oncologist-in-chief Detroit Med. Ctr., 1991-99; pres., CEO Radiation Oncology R & D Ctr., Detroit, 1991-99; dir. multidisciplinary svcs. Meyer L. Prentice Comprehensive Cancer Ctr., Detroit, 1992-99; chmn. radiation oncology Grace Hosp., Detroit, 1993-99; assoc. dean Wayne State U. Sch. Medicine, Detroit, 1998—; pres., CEO Detroit Med. Ctr., 1999—2003. Author: (with others) Fundamental Problems in Breast Cancer, 1985, Therapeutic Progress in Urological Cancers, 1988, Proceedings of the Consensus Meeting of the Treatment of Bladder Cancer-1987, 1988, Brachytherapy, 1989, High and Low Dose Rate Brachytherapy, 1989, Brachytherapy of Prostate Cancer, 1991; co-editor Treatment of Cancer, 1991—; assoc. editor Can. Jour. Oncology, 1990—, Antibody and Radiopharmaceuticals, 1992—; contbr. articles to profl. jours. Recipient Nat. award Sierra Leone, 1975-80, Commonwealth Found. scholarship, 1980, Best Doctor in Am. award, 1992, 93, 94, 95, 96, 97, 98, Testimonial Resolution, City of Detroit, 1993, Wayne County, 1993, Mich., 1997. Fellow Am. Coll. Angiology, Detroit Acad. Medicine, Royal Soc. Medicine, Royal Coll. Radiology, Am. Coll. Radiation Oncology (chancellor 1994-97); mem. AMA (Physicians Recognition award 1986), Am. Soc. Therapeutic Radiation Oncology, Am. Radium Soc., Am. Soc. Clin. Oncology, Am. Coll. Oncol. Adminstrs. (pres. 1994-96), Am. Acad. Med Adminstrs., Am. Endocurietherapy Soc. (pres. 1994-95), Mich. State Med. Soc., Mich. Soc. Therapeutic Radiation Oncology, Mich. Radiol. Soc. Detroit Med. Soc. (Ann. award for Excellence 1993), Wayne County Med. Soc., European Soc. Therapeutic Radiation Oncology, Brit. Inst. Radiology, Can. Oncology Soc., Can. Assn. Radiation Oncology, Royal Coll. Radiologists, Sierra Leone Med. and Dental Assn., Greater Detroit C. of C., Sigma Xi. Achievements include patent in a perineal applicator; research in novel methods in delivery dose, brachytherapy, intraoperative therapy, unsealed source therapy, verification and dosimetry, real time portal imaging, three-dimensional and planning, unsealed source dosimetry, the design of perineal applicators. Office: Detroit Med Ctr Dept Oncology 3663 Woodward Ave Ste 200 Detroit MI 48201-2400*

PORTER, BARBARA, anchorwoman, writer, educator; m. Henry Stroud Elms III; children: Tommy, Dorian. Anchorwoman NBC Radio; dir. pub. affairs George Washington U., Washington. Tchr. in dramatics and journalism; writer cable TV children's programming. Office: George Washington Univ Ste 1200 2121 I St NW Rm 512 Washington DC 20052-0001

PORTER, BERNARD HARDEN, consulting physicist, author, publisher; b. Porter Settlement, Maine, Feb. 14, 1911; s. Lewis Harden and Etta Flora (Rogers) P.; m. Helen Elaine Hendron, July 15, 1946 (div. Aug. 1947); m. Margaret Eudine Preston, Aug. 27, 1955 (dec. April 1975); m. Lula Mae Blom, Sept. 9, 1976 (div. Nov. 1986). BS, Colby Coll., 1932; MS, Brown U., 1933; DSc (hon.), Inst. Advanced Thinking, Calais, Maine, 1959. Physicist Acheson Colloids Corp., Port Huron, Mich., 1935-40; rsch. physicist Manhattan Dist. Engrs., Princeton, N.J., Berkeley, Calif. and Oak Ridge, 1940-45; cons. physicist San Francisco and Pasadena, Calif., Waldwick, N.J., Rockland, Belfast, Maine, 1945—; chmn. bd. Bern Porter Inc., Pasadena, Rockland, Belfast, 1945—; pres. Bern Porter Books, Pasadena, Rockland, Belfast, 1929—, Bern Porter Internat., Belfast, 1974—. Cons. Internat. Exec. Service Corps, 1968, SBA, 1968-88. Author: The 14th of February, 1971, I've Left, 1971, Founds, 1972, Hand Coated Chocolates, 1972, Contemporary Italian Painters, 1973, Trattoria Due Forni, 1973, The Book of Do's, 1974, The Manhattan Telephone Book, 1975, Run-On, 1975, Where, 1975, Selected Founds, 1975, Gee-Whizzles, 1976, Don't Book, 1981, Last Acts, 1985, My, My, 1985, Left Leg, 1988, Neverends, 1988, Numbers, 1989, Sweetend, 1989, Bern Porter and Fa Gaga, 1990, Sounds That Arouse Me, 1992, Less Than Overweight, 1992, Mothering Time, 1993; contbr. numerous articles to profl. jours. Rep. candidate for gov. Maine, 1969; bd. dirs. Inst. Advanced Thinking, Belfast, chmn. bd., 1959—. Recipient awards PEN, 1975, 76, 77, Authors League, 1977; Carnegie author, 1975; diploma merit Centro Studi E Scambi Internazionale, Rome, 1976; Nat. Endowment for Arts lit. award, 1979. Fellow Am. Astronautical Soc., Tech. Pub. Soc., Am. Rocket Soc. (assoc.), Soc. Tech. Writers and Pubs. (assoc.), Internat. Acad. Poets (London, founding); mem. Am. Phys. Soc., Soc. Internat. Devel., Nat. Soc. Programmed Instrn., Fenway Club (Boston), Algonquin Club, St. Andrews Club (N.B., Can.), Phi Beta Kappa, Sigma Xi, Kappa Phi Kappa, Chi Gamma Sigma. Roman Catholic. Address: 50 Salmond St Belfast ME 04915-6111

PORTER, BLAINE ROBERT MILTON, sociology and psychology educator; b. Morgan, Utah, Feb. 24, 1922; s. Brigham Ernest and Edna (Brough) P.; m. Elizabeth Taylor, Sept 27, 1943 (dec.); children: Claudia Black, Roger B., David T., Patricia A. Hintze, Corinna; m. Myrna Katherine Kennedy, Feb. 26, 1988. Student, Utah State U., 1940-41; BS, Brigham Young U., 1947, MA, 1949; PhD (Grant Found. fellow family life edn. 1951-52), Cornell U., 1952. Instr. sociology Iowa State Coll., 1949-51; asst. prof. sociology and child devel. Iowa State U., 1952-55; prof., chmn. dept. human devel. and family relationships Brigham Young U., 1955-65, dean Coll. Family Living, 1966-80, Univ. prof., 1980-87. Vis. prof. Fulbright rsch. scholar U. London, 1965-66; vis. prof. U. Wurzberg, 1980, 81, 83; facilitator human rels. workshops for the Human Devel. Inst., Denver, 1988-90, pres./CEO Families for Children Internat., Inc., 2001—. Editor: The Latter-day Saint Family, 1963, rev. edit., 1966; editor quar. jour.: Family Perspective, 1966-82; contbr. articles to profl. jours. Pres. elect Iowa Coun. Family Rels., 1954-55; pres. Utah Coun. Family Rels., 1957-58; chmn. sect. marriage counseling Nat. Coun. Family Rels., 1958-59, bd. dirs., 1957-60, exec. com., 1958-72, pres., 1963-64; bd. dirs. Am. Family Soc., 1975-85. Pilot USAAF, 1942-45. Recipient Prof. of Yr. award Brigham Young U., 1964. Mem. Am. Home Econs. Assn. (vice chmn. sect. family relations and child devel. 1955-56), Am. Sociol. Assn. (sec. sect. on family 1964-67), Am. Assn. Marriage and Family Therapy, Am. Psychol. Assn., Soc. Research in Child Devel., Sigma Xi, Phi Kappa Phi (chpt. pres. 1969-71) Home: 1675 Pine Ln Provo UT 84604-2163 Office: 4505 HBLL Brigham Young U Provo UT 84602

PORTER, BRUCE JACKMAN, military engineer, computer software engineer, application developer, investment broker, civil engineer; b. El Paso, Tex., Aug. 7, 1954; s. Covington Baskin and Carolyn Fee (Bruce) P.; m. Janette Anne Brown, Oct. 19, 1985; children: Laura, Holly, Travis. BS, US Mil. Acad., 1976; MS in Computer Sci., MS in Civil Engring., Stanford U., 1985; grad., U.S. Army War Coll., 1997. Engr. in tng., Pa. Commd. 1st lt. U.S. Army, 1979-80, advanced through grades to lt. col., 1993, co-commdr. 17th armored engr. bn., 1977-80, constrn. engr. Misawa, Japan, 1981-83, orgnl. evaluator Ft. Leavenworth, Kans., 1989-90, ops. officer 5th engr. combat bn., 1990-91; assoc. prof. mathematics U.S. Mil. Acad., West Point, N.Y., 1985-88; chief concepts officer USA Engr. Sch., Ft. Leonard Wood, Mo., 1991-93; logistics assistance officer 1st Cavalry Divsn., Ft. Hood, Tex., 1993-94; comdg. officer 20th Engr. Bn., 1st Cavalry Divsn., Ft. Hood, Tex., 1994-96; sr. engr. trainer Nat. Tng. Ctr., Ft. Irwin, Calif., 1997-98; cmdr., engr. brigade 4th Infantry Divn., Ft. Hood, Tex., 1998—99; exec. officer Army chief of staff for ops. Pentagon, Washington, 1999—2001; investment rep. Edward Jones & Co., Buellton, Calif., 2001—. Pioneer new courses in computer theory and discrete math. U.S. Mil. Acad., 1987-88; proponent Army Engr. Restructive Initiative, 1991-92; panel mem. Army Study Team for Battle Dynamics, 1992; mem. Summer Study for Chief of Staff of Army, 1992. Co-author: Army Keystone Operations Field Manual, 1993; pub. papers on combat engr. reorgn., 1991-92, 98. Decorated DSM, Bronze Star, Legion of Merit. Home: 345 Meadowlark Rd Santa Ynez CA 93460 Office: 175 H McMurray Rd Buellton CA 93427

PORTER, CHARLES KING, advertising executive; b. Mpls., Oct. 10, 1945; s. King E. and Bernetta Porter Andrews; m. Margit Gammeltoft, Feb. 26, 1972; children: Kristin, Catherine, James. BS in Journalism, U. Minn., 1967. Ptnr. Breen & Porter Co., Miami, Fla., 1974-85; pres. Porter Creative Svcs., Miami, 1985-88, Crispin, Porter & Bogusky Advt., Miami, 1988-97, chmn., ptnr., 1997—. Dir. Miami Ad Sch. Trustee Beacon Coun., Miami, 1988—. Recipient Nat. Addy award Am. Advt. Fedn., 1991, 92, Andy award Advt. Club N.Y., 1993, 94. Mem. Am. Assn. Advt Agys. (forum, Nat. A Plus award 1991, 94, 95, 96). Presbyterian. Avocations: skiing, travel, history. Office: Crispin Porter & Bogusky Advt 2699 S Bayshore Dr Miami FL 33133-5408

PORTER, CHARLES MICHAEL (MIKE PORTER), diversified financial services company executive; b. Danville, Ill., Jan. 11, 1957; s. Charles K. Jr. and Constance K. (Kinnaman) P.; m. Kathryn S. Klein, July 15, 1990; children: Eric J., Jerry D. AA, Danville Area C.C., 1986; BS in Accountancy, U. Ill., 1988, MS in Taxation, 1989. Owner C.M. Porter Realty, Danville, Ill., 1980-85; staff acct. Clifton Gunderson & Co., Danville, Ill., 1989; staff tax acct. McGladrey & Pullen, Peoria, Ill., 1989-91, Galesburg, Ill., 1991-95; dir. tax Dollar Gen. Corp., Goodlettsville, Tenn., 1995—2002; v.p., CFO Clear Check, Inc., Greenville, SC, 2002—; pres., chmn. Rodeo Stockyard, Inc. Co-owner Thunder Run Ranch. Former bd. dirs., treas. Dollar Gen. Literacy Found. Mem. Tax Execs. Inst., Internat. Mass Retailers Assn. (former chmn. tax adv. com.), Am. Paint Horse Assn., Profl. Rodeo Cowboys Assn. (assoc.), N.Am. Bucking Bull Assn., U. Ill. Alumni Assn., Am. Bucking Bull Assn. Avocations: rodeo, stock and ranch horses, rodeo bull breeding. Office: Clear Check Inc 135 Interstate Blvd Ste 6 Greenville SC 29615 Office Phone: 864-527-9125. Business E-Mail: mikep@clearcheck.com.

PORTER, CHARLES RALEIGH, JR., retired lawyer; b. Waco, Tex., Sept. 22, 1922; s. Charles Raleigh and Virginia Louise (Bowen) P.; m. Alice Mungall, Sept. 16, 1946; children: Charles Raleigh III, Melissa Ann, Alice Marguerite, Daniel Bowen. BBA, U. Tex., 1943, JD, 1949. Bar: Tex. 1948, U.S. Dist. Ct. (so. dist.) Tex. 1949, U.S. Ct. Appeals (5th cir.) 1955, U.S. Dist. Ct. (we. dist.) Tex. 1972, U.S. Dist. Ct. (no. dist.) Tex. 1977. Asst. Nueces County Attys. Office, Corpus Christi, Tex., 1949-50, Asst. Dist. Attys. Office, Corpus Christi, 1950-53; ptnr. Anderson & Porter, Corpus Christi, 1953-63, Sorrell, Anderson & Porter, 1964-68, Porter, Rogers, Dahlman & Gordon, 1969-92; ret., 1992. Mem. adv. bd. dirs. Frost Nat. Bank, San Antonio. Past mem. exec. bd. Perkins Sch. Theology, So. Meth. U.; past chairperson adminstrv. bd. First United Meth. Ch.; mem. chancellor's com. U. Tex.; past mem. adv. bd. U. Tex. Marine Sci. Inst.; active Dean's Roundtable, U. Tex. Sch. Law, 2001; Past mem. bd. dirs. Meth. Home, Waco. Lt. USNR, 1944—46. Mem.: Spanish Oaks Golf Club, Spanish Oaks Golf Club (Austin, Tex.), Rockport Country Club, Scottish Rite, Masons. Home: 33 Blue Heron Dr Rockport TX 78382-3771 Personal E-mail: crockport@sbcglobal.net.

PORTER, CHRISTY LEE, music educator; b. Pasay City, Ritzal, Philippines, Aug. 18, 1969; d. Wilmer Ted and Fern Porter. BFA, Ariz. State U., 1995; MA, No. Ariz. U., 1999—99. Tchrs. Cert. Ariz. Dept. of Edn., 1994. Music tchr. Mesa Pub. Schs., Ariz., 1995—. Coord., young people's orch., jr. high festival orch. Mesa Pub. Schools, Mesa, Ariz., 1997—, curriculumn steering com. elem. and jr. HS music edn. Edn. bd. Mesa Symphony Orch., 1997—2001. Mem.: Ariz. Educator's Assn., Nat. Educator's Assn., Ariz. Music Educator's Assn., Ariz. Band and Orch. Assn., Ariz. String Tchrs. Assn. R-Consevative. Latter Day Saint. Avocations: horseback riding, reading, travel. Home: 639 N Date Mesa AZ 85201 Office: Fremont Jr High 1001 N Power Rd Mesa AZ 85205

PORTER, DANIEL REED, III, museum director; b. Northampton, Mass., July 2, 1930; s. Daniel Reed and Eleanor (Parsons) P.; m. Joan Joyce Dornfeld, Nov. 22, 1958; children: Leslie Marie, Andrew Gregory. BA, U. Mass., 1952; MA, U. Mich., 1956. Asst. to dir. State Hist. Soc. Wis., Madison, 1956-58; dir. Hist. Soc. York County, Pa., 1958-61; asst. dir., dir. Ohio Hist. Soc., Columbus, 1961-74; exec. dir. Preservation Soc. Newport County, R.I., 1974-78; dir., prof. Cooperstown (N.Y.) Grad. Programs, 1978-82; dir. N.Y. State Hist. Assn. Farmer's Mus. Cooperstown, 1982-92. Hist. preservation officer State of Ohio, Columbus, 1967-74. Editor: N.Y. Heritage, 1984-92; contbr. articles to publs. in field. With U.S. Army, 1952-54, Korea. Recipient Spl. award of Merit Ohio Assn. Hist. Socs., 1970. Mem. Am. Assn. Mus. (accreditation commn. 1982-88, councillor-at-large 1981-84), Am. Assn. State and Local History (coun., Nashville 1971-73, councillor 1985-87). Congregationalist.

PORTER, DARWIN FRED, writer; b. Greensboro, NC, Sept. 13, 1937; s. Numie Rowan and Hazel Lee (Phillips) P. BA, U. Miami, 1959. Bur. chief Miami Herald, 1959-60; v.p. Haggart Assoc., NYC, 1961-64; editor, author Arthur Frommer Inc., NYC, 1964-67, Frommer/Pasmantier Pub. Corp., NYC, 1967-86, Prentice Hall Press, NYC, 1987-90, Simon & Schuster, NYC, 1991—. Author: Frommer Travel Guides to: England, 1964, Spain, 1966, Scandinavia, 1967, Los Angeles, 1969, London, 1970, Lisbon/Madrid, 1972, Paris, 1972, Morocco, 1974, Rome, 1974, Portugal, 1968, England, 1969, Italy, 1969, Germany, 1970, France, 1970, Caribbean, Bermuda, the Bahamas, 1980, Switzerland, 1984, Austria and Hungary, 1984, Bermuda and the Bahamas, 1985, Scotland and Wales, 1985, the Virgin Islands, 1991, Scotland, 1992, Jamaica/Barbados, 1992, Puerto Rico, 1992, the Caribbean, 1993, Bermuda, 1993, the Bahamas, 1993, Austria, 1993, Madrid & the Costa del Sol, 1993, San Francisco, 1996, California, 1996, Caribbean Cruises, 1996, Caribbean Ports of Call, 1996, Georgia and the Carolinas, 1996, Charleston and Savannah, 1996, Munich and The Bavarian Alps, 1996, Vienna & the Danube, 1996, Guide to Caribbean Cruises, 1997, Frommer's Europe, 1997, Frommer's Venice, 1997, Barcelona, Madrid & Seville, 1997, Frommer's Portable London, 1998, Frommer's Portable Bahamas, 1998, Frommer's Portable Paris, 1998, Frommer's Portable Berlin, 1999; author: Butterflies in Heat, 1976, Marika, 1977, Venus, 1982, Razzle-Dazzle, 1998, Blood Moon, 1998, Frommer's Sweden, 1999, Frommer's Denmark, 1999, Midnight in Savannah, 2000, Hollywood's Silent Closet, 2000, Frommer's Frankfurt, 2001, Frommer's Great Britain, 2001, Bahamas for Dummies, 2002, Caribbean for Dummies, 2002, Rhinestone Country, 2002, Frommer's Charleston, 2003, Frommer's Savannah, 2003, Frommer's Sicily, 2003, Frommer's Norway, 2003, France for Dummies, 2003, Frommer's Cayman Islands, 2003, Frommer's Dominican Republic, 2003, The Secret Life of Humphrey Bogart, 2003, Katharine the Great, 2004, Fommer's Europe By Rail, 2004. Recipient Silver award Internat. Film and TV Festival NY, 1977. Mem. Soc. Am. Travel Writers, Smithsonian Assoc., Nat. Trust for Hist. Preservation, Sigma Delta Chi. Home: 75 Saint Marks Pl Staten Island NY 10301-1606

PORTER, DAVID HUGH, pianist, classicist, academic administrator, liberal arts educator; b. N.Y.C., Oct. 29, 1935; s. Hugh B. and Ethel K. (Flentye) P.; m. Laudie Ernestine Dimmette, June 21, 1958 (dec. Nov., 1986); children: Hugh, Everett, Helen, David; m. Helen Louise Nelson, Aug. 24, 1987. BA with highest honors, Swarthmore Coll., 1958; PhD (Danforth Grad. fellow, Woodrow Wilson Grad. fellow), Princeton U., 1962; student, Phila. Conservatory Music, 1955-61. Instr. in classics and music Carleton Coll., Northfield, Minn., 1962-63, asst. prof., 1963-68, assoc. prof., 1968-73, prof., 1973-87, William H. Laird prof. liberal arts, 1974-87, pres. faculty, 1980-82, coll. pres., 1986-87; pres. Skidmore Coll., Saratoga Springs, NY, 1987—99, prof. classics, 1987—99. Phi Beta Kappa vis. lectr., 1979-92, vis. scholar, 1994-95; vis. prof. classics Princeton U., 1986; vis. prof. classics Williams Coll., Williamstown, Mass., 1999—; Harry C. Payne vis. prof. liberal arts Williams Coll., 2000—; recitalist, lectr., especially on contemporary music, at colls., univs. throughout U.S., U.K., on radio and TV; chmn. Hudson-Mohawk Assn., 1990-92, Inst. for Internat. Edn. of Students, 2004—. Author: Only Connect: Three Studies in Greek Tragedy, 1987, Horace's Poetic Journey: A Reading of Odes I-III, 1987, Virginia Woolf and Logan Pearsall Smith, 2002, Virginia Woolf and the Hogarth Press, 2004; editor: Carleton Remembered, 1909-86, 1987, The Not Quite Innocent Bystander: Writings of Edward Steuermann, 1989; contbr. articles on classics, music, twentieth-century lit. and edn. to profl. jours. NEH rsch. fellow, 1969-70, 83-84; Am. Coun. Learned Socs. rsch. fellow, 1976-77. Mem. Am. Philological Assn., Classical Assn. Atlantic States. Democrat. Mem. United Ch. Of Christ. Avocations: hiking, reading, collecting rugs and books. Home: 5 Birch Run Dr Saratoga Springs NY 12866-1023 E-mail: ddodger@skidmore.edu.

PORTER, DAVID LINDSEY, history and political science educator, author; b. Holyoke, Mass., Feb. 18, 1941; s. Willis Hubert and Lora Frances (Bowen) P.; m. Marilyn Esther Platt, Nov. 28, 1970; children: Kevin, Andrea. BA magna cum laude, Franklin Coll., 1963; MA, Ohio U., 1965; PhD, Pa. State U., 1970. Asst. prof. history Rensselaer Poly. Inst., Troy, N.Y., 1970-75, co-dir. Am. studies program, 1972-74; ednl. adminstrv. asst. Civil Svc. Office State of N.Y., Troy, 1975-76; asst. prof. history William Penn U., Oskaloosa, Iowa, 1976-77, assoc. prof. history, 1977-82, prof. history and polit. sci., 1982-86, Louis Tuttle Shangle prof. history and polit. sci., 1986—, chmn. Sperry & Hutchinson Found. lectureship series, 1980-82, acting chair social and behavioral scis. divsn., 2000—01. Supr. legis. internship program Iowa Gen. Assembly, 1978—, records inventory project Mahaska County, 1978-79, internship program Washington Ctr., 1985—; active Franklin D. Roosevelt Meml. Commn.; chpt. adviser Phi Alpha Theta, 1977—. Author: The Seventy-sixth Congress and World War II, 1939-40, 1979, Congress and the Waning of the New Deal, 1980; co-author: The San Diego Padres Encyclopedia, 2002; contbr. to Dictionary of American Biography, 1981, 88, 94, 95, Directory of Teaching Innovations in History, 1981, The Book of Lists #3, 1983, Biographical Dictionary of Internationalists, 1983, The Hero in Transition, 1983, Herbert Hoover and the Republican Era: A Reconsideration, 1984, The History of Mahaska County, Iowa, 1984, Franklin D. Roosevelt, His Life and Times: An Encyclopedic View, 1985, The Rating Game in American Politics: An Interdisciplinary Approach, 1987, Sport History, 1987, Book of Days, 1988, Sports Encyclopedia North America, 1988, The Harry S. Truman Encyclopedia, 1989, Encyclopedia of Major League Baseball Team Histories: The National League, 1991, Twentieth Century Sports Champions, 1992, Statesmen Who Changed the World, 1993, Ency. Modern Social Issues, 1996, Advanced Placement U.S. History 2, 1996, Encyclopedia of United States Popular Culture, 1997, Encyclopedia of Civil Rights, 1997, Encyclopedia of Propaganda, 1997, Total Padres, 1997, The Scribner Encyclopedia of American Lives, 1998, 99, 2001, 02, American National Biography, 1999, The Sixties in America, 1999, Racial and Ethnic Relations in America, 1999, History of Mahaska County, Iowa, 2000, Great Athletes, rev. edit., 2001, The Scribner Encyclopedia of American Lives, Sports Figures, 2002, Great Events: 1900-2001, rev. edit., 2002, The Scribner Encyclopedia of American Lives, The 1960's, 2003, Encyclopedia of U.S. History, 2003, Dictionary of American History, 3rd. edit., 2003, Encyclopedia of the Great Depression, 2003, Native Americans in Sports, 2004; editor, contbr.: Biographical Dictionary of American Sports: vols. Baseball, 1987, Football, 1987, Outdoor Sports, 1988, Basketball and Other Indoor Sports, 1989, 1989-92 Supplement for Baseball, Football, Basketball and Other Sports, 1992, 1992-95, Supplement for Baseball, Football, Basketball and Other Sports, 1995, African-American Sports Greats, 1995, Baseball, revised and expanded edit., 3 vols., 2000, Latino and African American Athletes Today, 2004; compiler, A Cumulative Index to the Biographical Dictionary of American Sports, 1993; assoc. editor: (with others) American National Biography, 24 vols., 1999; contbr. weekly column to Oskaloosa Herald, 1994—, numerous articles to various dictionaries, directories, encys., jours., revs., newspapers, commentary to Nat. Pub. Radio. Mem. Franklin D. Roosevelt Meml. Commn.; participant Green Bay Packers Project, 1992; historian United Meth. Ch.; official scorer Babe Ruth State Tournament, 2000, 03. Grantee NSF, 1967, NEH, 1974, Rensselaer Poly. Inst., 1974, Eleanor Roosevelt Inst., 1981, William Penn Univ., 1986, 89, 92; recipient Choice Outstanding Acad. Book awards, 1989. Mem. AAUP, Am. Hist. Assn., Orgn. Am. Historians, N.Am. Soc. for Sport History, Soc. History Am. Fgn. Rels., Ctr. for Study of the Presidency, Soc. Am. Baseball Rsch., Friends of the Nat. Baseball Hall of Fame, Popular Culture Assn., Profl. Football Rschrs. Assn., Coll. Football Rschrs. Assn., Coll. Football Hist. Soc., State Hist. Soc. Iowa, Mahaska County Hist. Soc. (v.p.), Iowa State UN Assn. (chmn. ann. assembly 1982, nat. soc. Disting. Svc. award 1981), Mahaska County UN Assn. (v.p.), Oskaloosa Babe Ruth League (bd. dirs.), Oskaloosa Cmty. Choir, Friends of Oskaloosa Pub. Libr. (mem. nominating com.), Friends of the Nat. Baseball Hall of Fame, Phi Alpha Theta, Kappa Delta Pi. Home: 2314 Ridgeway Ave Oskaloosa IA 52577-9109 Office: William Penn Univ Dept Social and Behavioral Scis Divsn Oskaloosa IA 52577-1757

PORTER, DIXIE LEE, insurance company executive, consultant; b. Bountiful, Utah, June 7, 1931; d. John Lloyd and Ida May (Robinson) Mathis. BS, U. Calif., Berkeley, 1956; MBA, U. Calif., 1957. CLU. Personnel aide City of Berkeley, 1957-59; employment supr. Kaiser Health Found., L.A., 1959-60; personnel analyst UCLA, 1961-63; personnel mgr. Reuben H. Donnelley, Santa Monica, Calif., 1963-64; personnel officer Good Samaritan Hosp., San Jose, Calif., 1965-67; fgn. svc. officer AID, Saigon, Vietnam, 1967-71; gen. agt. Charter Life Ins. Co., L.A., 1972-77, Kennesaw Life Ins. Co., Atlanta, 1978—, Phila. Life Ins. Co., San Francisco, 1978—; pres. Womens Ins. Enterprises, Ltd., 1976—. Cons. in field. Co-chair Comprehensive Health Planning Commn. Santa Clara County, Calif., 1973-76; bd. dirs. Family Care, 1978-80, Aegis Health Corp., 1977-92, U. Calif. Sch. Bus. Adminstrn., Berkeley, 1974-76; task force on equal access to econ. power U.S. Nat. Womens Agenda, 1977—, Lake County Transp. Coun., 2000—. With USMC, 1950-52. Mem. AAUW, CLU Soc., U. Calif. Alumni Assn., U. Calif. Sch. Bus. Adminstrn. Alumni Assn., Bus. and Profl. Women, Prytanean Alumni, The Animal Soc. Los Gatos/Saratoga (pres. 1987-90), Beta Gamma Sigma, Phi Chi Theta. Republican. Episcopalian.

PORTER, DUNCAN MACNAIR, editor, educator; b. Kelseyville, Calif., Apr. 20, 1937; s. James Duncan and Dorothy May P.; m. Sarah Holyoke, Sept. 10, 1966; children: Charles P. Holyoke, Dorothy P. Carr, Christina P. Margaret, Susannah P. Reaves. AB, Stanford U., 1959, AM, 1961; PhD, Harvard U., 1967. Asst. Calif. Acad. Scis., San Francisco, 1966-67; asst. prof. biology U. San Francisco, 1967-68; curator flora Panama Mo. Bot. Garden, St. Louis, 1968-72; editor-in-chief flora N.Am. project Smithsonian Inst., Washington, 1972-73; assoc. program dir. systematic biology NSF, Washington, 1973-75; assoc. prof. bot. Va. Polytech. Inst. & State U., Blacksburg, 1975-84, prof. bot., 1984—; sr. editor Darwin Corr. Project, Cambridge, England, 1991—, dir., 1997—. Rsch. assoc. biology Stanford U., 1966-68; asst. prof. bot. Washington U., 1968-70, adj. asst. prof. biology, 1970-73; sec., program chmn. Am. Soc. Plant Taxonomists, 1972-73. Author: Rare and Endangered Vascular Plant Species of Virginia, 1980; co-author: Flora of the Calapagos Islands, 1971, The Portable Darwin, 1993, Categorical Glossery for the Flora of North America Program, 2000; editor: The Correspondence of Charles Darwin, vol. 8, 1993, vol. 9, 1994, vol. 10, 1997, vol. 11, 1999, vol. 12, 2001, vol. 13, 2002, vol. 14, 2004. Vis. fellow U. Cambridge, 1980-81, U. Canterbury, New Zealand, 1986, Thomas Jefferson medal for outstanding contbn. to natural sci., Virginia Mus. Natural History Found., 2004, Albert L. Sturm award for excellence in faculty rsch. Fellow AAAS, Linnean Soc. London; mem. Calif. Bot. Soc. (bd. editors 1970-76, 78-83), History Sci. Soc., Soc. History Natural Hist., Sigma Xi, Phi Beta Kappa Democrat. Episcopalian. Avocations: reading, travel, walking, gardening. Home: 1002 E Roanoke St Blacksburg VA 24060 Office: Va Tech Dept Biology Blacksburg VA 24061 Fax: 540-231-9307. E-mail: duporter@vt.edu.

PORTER, ELSA ALLGOOD, writer, lecturer; b. Amoy, China, Dec. 19, 1928; d. Roy and Petra (Johnsen) Allgood; m. Raeford B. Liles, Mar. 19, 1949 (div. 1959); children: Barbara, Janet; m. G. Hinckley Porter, Nov. 22, 1962; children: David, Brian, Wendy. BA, Birmingham-So. Coll., 1949; MA, U. Ala., 1959; M in Pub. Adminstrn., Harvard U., 1971; LHD (hon.), U. Ala., 1986. With HEW, Washington, 1960-73; with U.S. CSC, Washington, 1973-77; asst. sec. Dept. Commerce, Washington, 1977-81; disting. practitioner in residence Washington Pub. Affairs Ctr., U. So. Calif., Washington, 1982-84; v.p. R & D The Maccoby Group, Washington, 1990-96; sr. fellow Meridian Internat. Inst., 1990—. Chair comml. adv. subcom. NASA, 1997—2003. Fellow World Acad. Art & Scis., Nat. Acad. Pub. Adminstrs.; mem. Women's Nat. Dem. Club. Home: 2309 SW 1st Ave Apt 742 Portland OR 97201-5008

PORTER, GERALD JOSEPH, mathematician, educator; b. Elizabeth, N.J., Feb. 27, 1937; s. Fred and Tillie Florence (Friedman) P.; m. Judith Deborah Revitch, June 26, 1960; children: Daniel, Rebecca, Michael. AB, Princeton U., 1958; PhD, Cornell U., 1963; MA (hon.), U. Pa., 1971. Instr. MIT, Cambridge, 1963-65; asst. prof. math. U. Pa., Phila., 1965-69, assoc. prof., 1969-75, prof., 1975—, chmn. undergrad. affairs dept. math., 1971-73, assoc. dean computing Sch. Arts and Scis., 1981-91, dir. Interactive Math. Text Project, 1991-96. Chair-elect faculty senate U. Pa., 1992-93, chair, 1993-94, past chair, 1994-95, 2001-02; prin. investigator NSF MACMATC Grant, 1997-2001. Author: (with D.R. Hill) Interactive Linear Algebra, 1996. Mem. Dem. Com., Haverford

Twp., Pa., 1976-82, ward leader, 1980-84, treas., 1984-87. Postdoctoral fellow Office Naval Rsch., 1965-66. Mem. AAUP, AAAS, Am. Math. Soc., Math. Assn. Am. (chmn. com. computers in math. edn. 1983-86, chmn. investment com. 1986-2003, bd. govs. 1980-83, 86-2002, mem. fin. com. 1986-2000, exec. com. 1992-2002, chmn. audit and budget com. 1988-90, 92, treas. 1992-2002, chair com. on profl. devel. 1995-2001, chair membership com. 2004), Nat. Assn. Mathematicians. Democrat. Jewish. Home: 161 Whitemarsh Rd Ardmore PA 19003-1698 Office: U Pa 4N69 DRL 209 S 33rd St Philadelphia PA 19104-6395 E-mail: gjporter@math.upenn.edu.

PORTER, HAYDEN SAMUEL, computer science educator; b. Cin., June 2, 1945; s. Hayden Samuel and Thelma (Wulfeck) P.; m. Patricia Maloney, Sept. 28, 1967; children: Hayden, Emily. BS, U. Cin., 1967, PhD, 1973. Postdoctoral fellow U. Fla., Gainesville, 1973-76; sr. mem. tech. staff Computer Sci. Corp., Silver Springs, Md., 1976-79; pres. A2D, Co., Inc., Greenville, S.C., 1981—; Daniel disting. prof. computer sci. Furman U., Greenville, 1979—, chmn., 1986-92. Author: Exploring Macintosh, 1989, Exploring Macintosh Applications, 1989, Exploring Microsoft Works, 1991, Essentials of Lotus 1-2-3 for Macintosh, 1992; contbr. articles to profl. jours. Grantee in field. Mem. Am. Geophys. Union, Am. Phys. Soc., IEEE, Assn. for Computing Machinery (activity monitor 1983-93), Sigma Xi. Avocations: sailing, boating, fishing.

PORTER, HENRY HOMES, JR., investor; b. Chgo., Nov. 13, 1934; s. Henry H. and Mary (Kinney) P.; m. Louisa Catherine Perkins, June 10, 1961; children: Mary Porter Johnson, Catherine. AB, Yale U., 1956; MBA, Harvard U., 1962. With Gen. Mills, Inc., Mpls., 1962-76, asst. treas., 1964-67, treas., 1967-76, v.p. fin., treas., 1969-76; sr. v.p., chief fin. officer, dir. Brown & Williamson Industries, Inc., 1977-79, Batus, Inc., 1980; now ret. Chmn. bd. Active Ankle Systems, Inc.; bd. dirs. SEI Investment Co., Caldwell & Orkin Funds, Inc. Lt. (j.g.) USNR, 1957-60. Home and Office: 5806 River Knoll Dr Louisville KY 40222-5863

PORTER, HOWARD LEONARD, III, health and education policy consultant; b. July 12, 1945; s. Howard Leonard and Margaret (Johnson) P.; m. Mary Ellen Biciste, June 22, 1968; 1 child, Andrew James. BA, Monmouth (Ill.) Coll., 1967; MS, U. Ill., 1968; MBA, U. Fla., 1995; PhD, U. South Fla., 2001. Pres. The Porter Co., 1968—. Sr. v.p. HCI Preferred Car, Inc., Auburndale, Fla., 1992—2002; v.p. Roswell E. Johnson Inst. Comm. Rsch., 1992—. Contbr. articles to profl. publs. With Med. Svc. Corps, USAF, 1969-72. Mem. Phi Kappa Phi (hon.). Republican. Presbyterian. Home: 2068 Katie Ct SE Winter Haven FL 33884-3113 Office: 509 Avenue B NW Winter Haven FL 33881-4607 Office Phone: 941-293-2550. E-mail: roswell@msn.com.

PORTER, J. REID, engineering executive; BA, Colgate U., 1971; MBA in Fin., U. Chgo., 1975. With fin. analysis staff Rockwell Internat., Chgo., 1975—78; with McGraw-Edison Co., Rolling Meadows, Ill., 1978—82; various sr. exec. positions Onan Corp., Mpls., 1982—95; v.p., gen. mgr. Renewal by Anderson, Minn., 1996—98; v.p., ptnr. Hidden Creek Industries, Mpls., 1998—2001; CFO Heavy Duty Holdings, Mpls., 1998—2001; exec. v.p. IMC Global Inc., Lake Forest, Ill., 2001—, CFO, 2001—. Office: IMC Global Inc 3600 S Yosemite St Ste 900 Denver CO 80237*

PORTER, J. RIDGELY, III, lawyer; b. Va., Apr. 28, 1948; s. John R and Mary Manning (Barclay) P.; m. DeLane Williams, 1978; 1 child, Eleanor M. BA, U. Va., 1970; JD, Washington & Lee U., 1973. Law clerk to U.S. judge, 1973-74; ptnr. Carr & Porter, 1974—; pres. Va. Internat. Terminals, 1985-92; chmn. bd. Chesapeake Gen. Hosp., 1986-96; owner Cattle Farms. Mem.: ABA, Va. Bar Assn., Met. Club (DC). Episcopalian. Office: 355 Crawford Pkwy Portsmouth VA 23704 Office Phone: 757-393-6018. Personal E-mail: carrporter.law@verizon.net.

PORTER, JACK NUSAN, writer, sociologist, educator, political activist; b. Rovno, Ukraine, USSR, Dec. 2, 1944; came to U.S., 1946; s. Irving Puchtik and Faye (Merin) P.; m. Miriam Almuly, Sept. 18, 1977 (div. 2000); children: Gabriel, Danielle. Cert., Machon Inst., Jerusalem, 1963; BAS cum laude, U. Wis., Milw., 1967; MA, Northwestern U., 1969; PhD in Sociology, Northwestern U., 1971; Rabbinical tng., Acad. for Jewish Religion, 1998-99. Ordained rabbi Vaad HaRabbainim, N.Y., 2000. Rsch. assoc. Harvard U. Ukrainian Rsch. Inst., Cambridge, Mass., 1982-84; pres. The Spencer Group, Newton, Mass., 1984—; exec. dir. The Spencer Sch. Real Estate, Newton, 1986—; dir. The Spencer Inst. for Bus. and Soc., Newton, 1984—; asst. prof. Coll. of Basic Studies Boston U., 1989-90. Vis. lectr. Boston U. Met. Coll., 1987, 88, Bryant Coll., Smithfield, R.I., 1991; adj. prof. sociology U. Mass., Lowell, 1976-79, 1994-2004; adj. prof. sociology Stonehill Coll., Easton, Mass., 1996-97; presenter White House Conf. on Family, 1980; mem. Gov. Dukakis' Adv. Coun., 1982-84; panelist on Comparative Genocide, The Oxford (Eng.) Conf., 1988; panelist Mackon Reision, Jerusalem, Israel, 2003; Boston area coord. Seminars on Zionist Thought, World Zionist Orgn., 1996—; cons. in non-fiction Nat. Book Critics Circle Awards, 1997-98. Author or editor 30 books and anthologies including Confronting History and Holocaust, 1983, Sexual Politics in Nazi Germany, 1991, Kids in Cults, 1977, 85, 94, Jews and the Cults, 1981, Genocide and Human Rights, 1982, (with Ruth Taplin) Conflict and Conflict Resolution: A Sociological Introduction, 1987, (with Peter Dreier) Jewish Radicalism, 1973, Jewish Partisans (2 vols.), 1982, Conflict and Conflict Resolution: A Historical Bibliography, 1982, The Jew as Outsider, 1981, The Sociology of Jewry: A Curriculum Guide, 1992, 99, The Sociology of American Jews: A Critical Anthology, 1980, 98, The Sociology of Jewry: Collected Essays, 1998, Forclosed Property (with Gerry Glazer), 1990, (with Steve Hoffman) The Sociology of Genocide and the Holocaust: A Curriculum Guide, 1992, 99, The Sociology of Business: A Curriculum Guide, 1992, Women in Chains: Sourcebook on the Agunah, 1996, A Life of Mitzvah: Rabbi Joseph Mayer Jacobson of Boston; The Genodical Mind: Toward a Sociology of the Holocaust, (collected essays) Anti-Semitism: From Deicide to Genocide, The Speeches and Writings of Jack Nusan Porter, 2004, The Soc. Imagination of American Jewry: Collected Essays, 2004, The Radical Writings of J.N. Porter, 2004; co-author: Sexual Politics in the Third Reich, 1997; contbr. chpts. in books, more than 600 articles and revs. to jours. in field; founder, pub. Jour. of the History of Sociology, 1977-85, The Sociology of Bus. Newsletter, 1977-79; mem. editl. bd. Contemporary Jewry, 1995-97; dep. editor, dep. pub. Jewish Family and Life, 1997-98; author (films) Key West Rabbi, Partisans, Dressed to Kill. Founder Holocaust Survival Video Project, Newton, Mass., 1992—; judge Nat. Jewish Book Awards, 1993-95; mem. Jewish Radical Edn. Project, 1994-99; spiritual leader Temple Emmanuel, Chelsea, Mass., 1999-2001; rabbi Cong. B'nai Zion, Key West, Fla., 2001; candidate alderman at large, Newton, 2003. John Atherton fellow Breadloaf Writers Conf., Middlebury, Vt., 1976; recipient Spl. award Boston Police Dept., 1986. Mem. PEN (newsletter com. 1992-95), Am. Sociol. Assn. (mem. coun. 2004, recipient Disting. Contbn. award 2004), Ea. Sociol. Soc., New Eng. Soc., Internat. Assn. of Genocide Scholars (v.p. 1996-98), Tikkun, Workman's Circle, PEN New Eng., Cong. Kehillat Israel, Brookline, Mass. Avocations: collecting Jewish baseball cards, reading, spiritual thinking. Home and Office: 12 Dunstan St 1 West Newton MA 02465-2115 Office Phone: 617-965-8388. Personal E-mail: jacknusan@earthlink.net. *The older I get, the important things in life are my children, good health, a few good friends, my brother and sister and Mom, a good meal, and lastly - some money and a little fame. That's all I need. Oh, yes - love. One needs lots of love.*

PORTER, JAMES KENNETH, retired judge; b. Newport, Tenn., Apr. 6, 1934; s. John Calhoun and Bessie Betis (Crouch) P.; m. Evelyn Janet Rhodes, Sept. 17, 1955; children: Jane Caroline, James Kenneth Jr. BS, U. Tenn., 1955, JD, 1957. Bar: Tenn. 1957, U.S. Dist. Ct. (ea. dist.) Tenn. 1958, U.S. Ct. Appeals (6th cir.) 1971. Ptnr. Porter, Porter & Dunn, Porter & Porter, Newport, 1957-74; state rep. Tenn. Gen. Assembly, Nashville, 1961-65, minority fl. leader, 1963-65; county atty. Cocke County, Tenn., 1961-63, commr. County Election Commn., 1966-72, chmn., 1968-70; mem. Tenn. Senate, Nashville, 1972-74; state cir. judge 4th Jud. Cir., Newport, 1974-93; ret., 1993; state presiding judge 4th Jud. Cir., Newport, 1984-86, 88-90, 1992-93; judgeship nominee U.S. Dist. Ct. (ea. dist.), Tenn., 1986; Tenn. Ct. Appeals nominee, 1990. Del. S.E. Law Rev. Conf., Durham, N.C., 1957, Nat. Conf. State Legislator Leaders, Boston, 1963; discussion leader Nat. Jud. Coll., Reno, 1981, faculty adviser, 1982; mem. Gov.'s Correction Overcrowding Commn., Nashville, 1985-86. Contbr. articles to U. Tenn. Law Rev., 1956-57, editor in chief, 1957. Active Farm Bur., 1962-82; mem. adv. coun., trustee Walters State Community Coll., Morristown, Tenn., 1975-86. Mem. ABA (Tenn. jud. del. 1984), Tenn. Jud. Conf. (v.p. 1980-81), Tenn. Trial Judges Assn. (bd. dirs. 1976-86, pres. 1982-85), Tenn. Bar Assn. (spl. trial counsel 1973-76), Cocke County Bar Assn., Smoky Mountain Country Club (bd. dirs. 1964-67, v.p. 1966-67), Order of Coif, Sigma Alpha Epsilon (Highest Effort Law award 1986), Phi Delta Phi. Republican. Baptist. Avocations: golf, gardening, guitar. Home: 306 North St Newport TN 37821-2413 Office: 106 S Mims Ave Newport TN 37821-3125 E-mail: porterk@planetc.com.

PORTER, JAMES MORRIS, retired judge; b. Cleve., Sept. 14, 1931; s. Emmett Thomas and Mary (Connell) P.; m. Helen Marie Adams, May 31, 1952; children: James E., Thomas W., William M., Daniel J. AB, John Carroll U., 1953; JD, U. Mich., 1957. Bar: Ohio 1957. Assoc. firm M.B. & H.H. Johnson, Cleve., 1957-62, McAfee, Hanning, Newcomer, Hazlett & Wheeler, Cleve., 1962-67; ptnr. firm Squire, Sanders & Dempsey, Cleve., 1967-92; judge Ohio Ct. Appeals, 8th Dist., Cleve., 1993-2000, Cuyahoga County Common Pleas Ct., Cleve., 2001. 1st lt. U.S. Army, 1953-55. Fellow Am. Coll. Trial Lawyers; mem. The Country Club (Cleve.). Republican. Roman Catholic.

PORTER, JAMES T. computer company executive; BS in Indsl. Health/Safety, N.W. Mo. State U.; grad. advanced mgmt. program, Harvard U. With Honeywell Inc., 1980—, various mgmt. postions, corp. v.p. of human resources, 1993-98, v.p., chief adminstrv. office, 1998—. Bd. dirs. Nat. Com. for Econ. Devel. Office: Honeywell Internat Inc 101 Columbia Rd PO Box 2245 Morristown NJ 07962-2245

PORTER, JENNY LIND, writer; b. Fort Worth, Tex., Sept. 3, 1927; d. Drue J. and Josephine Trammell Porter; m. Lawrence E. Scott. BA summa cum laude, Tex. Christian U., 1948; MA, Tex. Christian U., Ft. Worth, 1949; PhD, U. of Tex., Austin, 1955; Hon. Doctorate (hon.), Pepperdine U., 1980. Asst. prof. The U. Tenn., Knoxville, Tenn., 1958—59, West Tex. A&M U., Canyon, Tex., 1959—61; assoc. prof. Southwest Tex. State U., San Marcos, Tex., 1961—64, Tex. Luth. U., Sequin, Tex., 1964—68; prof. Huston-Tillotson Coll., Austin, Tex., 1968—96; guest prof. Pepperdine U., Malibu, Calif., 1981. Vis. prof. Pepperdine U., Malibu, Calif., 1981. Author: (numerous works including) Three Dramatic Monologues, 1980, Verses on Death, Les Vers de la Mort, 1999 (Tex. Inst. Letters Translation award, 2000), El Sol Colorado, 2001, O. Henry, Witter Bynner, and A Fog in Santone, 2002. Named Jenny Lind Porter Day in Austin, Tex. named in her honor for contbns. to lit. and the O. Henry Mus., City Coun., Austin, 1996; named to Tex. Women's Hall of Fame, Austin, 1985; recipient Piper Prof. award, Piper Found., San Antonio, Tex., 1976. Home: 51 Summit View Place Austin TX 78703

PORTER, JILL, journalist; b. Phila., Aug. 5, 1946; d. Sidney and Mae (Merion) Chalfin; m. Eric Porter, Mar. 7, 1970 (div. 1975); m. Fred Hamilton, Oct. 28, 1983; 1 child, Zachary. BA, Temple U., 1968. Pub. rels. Manning Smith P.R., Phila., 1968-69; reporter Norristown Times Herald, Norristown, Pa., 1969-72, The Trentonian, Trenton, N.J., 1972-75, The Phila. Daily News, Phila., 1975-79, columnist, 1979—. Instr. Temple U., 1976-80. Contbr. articles to numerous mags. Vol. Phila. Futures, 1994, 95, 96, Phila. Cares, 1997. Recipient numerous journalism awards. Avocations: dance, biking, reading. Home: 134 Rolling Rd Bala Cynwyd PA 19004-2615 Office: Phila Newspapers Inc Phila Daily News 400 N Broad St Philadelphia PA 19130-4015

PORTER, JOHN EDWARD, former congressman; b. Evanston, Ill., June 1, 1935; s. Harry H. and Beatrice V. P.; 5 children. Attended, MIT; BSBA, Northwestern U., 1958; JD with distinction, U. Mich., 1961; degree (hon.), Northwestern U., Tufts U., Mt. Sinai Sch. Medicine, Oreg. Health Scis. U., Howard U., Rush U. Bar: Ill. 1961, U.S. Supreme Ct. 1968. Former honor law grad. atty., appellate div. Dept. Justice, Washington; mem. Ill. Ho. of Reps., 1973—79, 96-106th Congresses from 10th Ill. Dist., Ill., 1980-2001; ptnr. Hogan & Hartson, Washington, 2001—. Founder, co-chmn. Congl. Human Rights Caucus; legis. sponsor Radio Free Asia; founder Congl. Coalition on Population and Devel.; chmn. Global Legislators Organized for a Balanced Environment; mem. Commn. on Security and Cooperation in Europe; mem. com. future roles acad. health ctrs. Inst. Medicine, NAS. Past editor: Mich. Law Rev. Bd. dirs. PBS, Rand Corp., Rsch.! Am., Found. for NIH, Am. Heart Assn., Brookings Instn., Chgo. Botanic Gardens, Population Resource Ctr., Princeton, NJ; trustee emeritus John F. Kennedy Ctr. for Performing Arts. Recipient Best Legislator award League of Conservation Voters, 1973, Ind. Voters Ill., 1974, Chgo. Crime Commn., 1976, Lorax award Global Tomorrow Coalition, 1989, Spirit of Enterprise award U.S. C. of C., 1988, 89, 90, Golden Bulldog award Watchdogs of the Treasury, 12 times, Taxpayer's Friend award Nat. Taxpayers Union, Taxpayer Superhero award Grace Commn.'s Citizens Against Government Waste, Mary Wood Lasker award for pub. svc., Edwin C. Whitehead award Rsch! Am., Carter award Nat. Found. Infectious Diseases, Pub. Svc. award Fedn. Am. Socs. for Exptl. Biology, Svc award Am. Soc. Cell Biology, Disting. Pub. Svc. award Am. Soc. Microbiology, Pub. Svc. Excellence award Assn. Am. Med. Colls., Lifetime Achievement award Juvenile Diabetes Found., Decade of Brain award Nat. Found. Brain Rsch., Lifetime Achievement award Am. Psychiat. Assn. and Acad. Consortium, Dr. Nathan Davis award AMA, Morris K. Udall Pub. Svc. award Michael J. Fox Found., Pub. Health Continuum award Coalition for Health Funding, Beacon award Am. Soc. Assn. Execs., Henry M. Jackson Leadership award Union Couns. for Soviet Jewry, Anatoly Scharansky Freedom award Chgo. Action for Soviet Jewry, others. Mem.: Inter-Am. Dialogue, Coun. Fgn. Rels. Republican. Office: Hogan & Hartson 555 13th St NW Washington DC 20004

PORTER, JOHN PAUL, artist, educator; b. Alturas, Calif., Nov. 26, 1935; s. Carlton Lewis and Bernice (Smith-Schulz) P.; m. Carol Lynn Jones, Apr. 20, 1957 (div. Apr. 1978); children: Sean Michal, Sheryl Lynn. BA in Art, Calif. State U., Chico, 1958; MA in Art, UCLA, 1962; postgrad., Calif. State U., Chico, 1958, Calif. State U., Sacramento, 1959-67, Calif. State U., Northridge, 1958-63, Calif. State U., San Jose, 1978, Stanford U., 1986. Cert. secondary tchr., Calif. Prof. art, chair dept., coord. dist. Antelope County Unified Sch. Dist. & Jr. Coll., Lancaster, Calif., 1958-67; prof. art Gavilan Coll., 1967-2000, chair fine arts and humanities, 1969-75. Vis. prof. U. London, 1988; consortium prof. Calif. CC; judge various local, regional and national shows; rschr. in field. Exhbns. and one-man shows include Chico State Libr., 1958, Benny Barrio Gallery, Carmichael, Calif., 1959, Allied Arts Gallery, Lancaster, 1961, Aldous Huxley Show, Porter Show Allied Arts, 1962, Charles Parker Estates, Quartz Hill, Calif., 1963, Chic Sale Art Competition, Lancaster, 1964, Tumbleweed Gallery, Pearblossom, Calif., 1964-66, Edwards AFB, 1965, Oldfield Studio, Lancaster, 1967, Hollister Art League, 1967, 70, Gilroy Mus., 1972, 78, 80, UC Davis Student Union Gallery, 1978, Faye Dixon's Mariposa House, 1973, El Cerrito Open Studio Show, Gilroy, Calif., 1975, De Saisset Gallery, 1978, Oaktree Allied Arts Gallery, 1978-80, Spring Art-Music Fesitval, 1970-78, San Jose Art League, 1980, Children's Home Soc. Benefit, 1981, Friendly Inn Art and Flower Show, Morgan Hill, 1979-80, 82, Vacaville State Art Competition, 1982, Am. Greeting Card Print Nat. Convention, San Francisco, 1983, Union Street Gallery, 1984, Russian River State Festival, Forestville, Calif., 1984-85, Bay Area Fine Arts Exhbn., San Francisco, 1985, Steinbeck Gallery, 1986, Glen Loma Estates, 1987, Thackery House, London, 1988, Santa Clara County Fair, 1989, Avina Gallery, Sao Paolo, Brazil, 1991, Carlton House, London, 1992, Skyline Coll, 1993, San Jose Art League, 1994, Beaux Artes Show, Reno, Nev., 1995, Willows Mansion, 1996, So. Valley Symphony Benefit, 1997, Growth and Opportunity Exec. Offices, Morgan Hill, Calif., 1997, 98; mem. editl. bd. Collegiate Press, 1990-94; contbr. articles to profl. jours., chpts. to books; represented in over 1200 pvt. collections. Co-founder Mushroom Festival, Morgan Hill, 1990—; commr. City of Gilroy, 1970—76; com. mem. Santa Clara County Fair, Tapestry in Talent, 1987; active Gilroy Garlic Festival Art, 1980—99; neighborhood com. San Jose Solari Ctr.; geneology and staff cons. LDS Family History Ctr. Danforth fellow Stanford U., 1975-76; recipient Jay Stott award, 1957, Crown Zellerbach award, 1958, Nat. AVIP Tchr. of Yr. award, 1964, award Nat. Neighborhood Youth Corp., 1967, Mayoral Citation Svc. City of Gilroy, 1978, 96; named Man of Yr. Lancaster C. of C., 1967. Mem. Commonwealth Club, South Bay Scottish Soc. (acting chief, bd. govs.), San Francisco World Coun., Hearaldry Soc. Great Britain, Clan Cian Soc., Clan Boyd, Clan McNaughten, Clan McAlpin, Clan O'Neal, Nat. Thespians (award 1965). Democrat. Congregationalist. Avocations: dance, swimming, tennis, crafts. Home: 4002 San Ysidro Way San Jose CA 95111 E-mail: art-e-facts@webtv.net.

PORTER, JOHN STEPHEN, retired television executive; b. Avoca, NY, Sept. 2, 1932; s. Frank R. and Margaret H. (McGreel) P.; m. Marie C. Eiffert, Sept. 6, 1958; children: Stephen, David, Mark, Kevin, Matthew. BA in English, St. John Fisher U., 1958; MS in Radio/TV, Syracuse U., 1959; postgrad. in Edn, U. Rochester, 1960-61. Producer, broadcaster weekly news analysis N.Y. State Empire State FM Sch. of Air, 1962-64; producer, narrator weekly series sta. WROC-FM, Rochester, N.Y., 1964-65; pres., gen. mgr. sta. WXXI-TV, Rochester, 1966-69; trustee Eastern Ednl. TV Network, Boston, 1966-68, mem. exec. com., 1967-68, exec. dir., 1969-89, pres., mem. exec. com., 1989-92, Am. Program Svc. (formerly Ea. Ednl. TV Network), Boston, 1992—. Served to 1st lt. AUS, 1952-56. Mem. N.Y. State Ednl. Radio/TV Assn. (treas. 1962-64), Pub. TV Sta. Mgrs. New York State (chmn. 1968-69), Nat. Assn. Ednl. Broadcasters (adv. com.) Home: 28 Main St # 115 Mashpee MA 02649 Personal E-mail: jport@comcast.net.

PORTER, JOHN WESTON, counselor, consultant, hospital administrator; b. Fostoria, Ohio, Dec. 26, 1939; s. William Thomas and Ida Elizabeth (Carter) Porter. Student, U. Cin., 1958; BA, Heidelberg Coll., 1961; MA in Cmty. Psychology, U. D.C., 1973, MA in Counseling, 1975; postgrad., Antioch Coll., 1974, Frostburg (Md.) U., 1970, George Washington U., 1968. Cert. Nat. Bd. Cert. Counselors, DC. Claims rep. Social Security Adminstrn., Cleve. and Akron, Ohio, 1961-62; office mgr. Phoenix Cos., Washington and L.A., 1966-70; rschr. Frostburg U., U.D.C., 1970-73; edn. and career devel. specialist D.C. Pub. Schs., 1973-79, career edn. unit, 1979-83, Career Assessment Ctr., 1983-85, asst. dir. guidance and counseling, 1985-95; mem. cmty. adv. coun. Washington Hosp. Ctr., 1987—. Counseling mentor DC Pub. Schs., 1998—2003; dir. Westport Consulting, 2001—; cons. DC Pub. Sch. HiScip program, New Couns. Mentor, 2001—02. Contbr. articles to profl. jours. Vice chmn. adv. coun. Group Health Assn., Washington, 1977—79, 1981—83; sec. Md.-DC Am. Coll. Testing Coun., 1987—88, vice chair, 1988—90, chair, 1990—91, mem. exec. com., 1991—; mem. adv. com. Children's Edn. Found., 1989—93, mem. fund raising com., 1989—, exec. bd., 1992—, asst. treas., 1992—93, treas., 1993—95; pres. N.E. Hill Found., 1990—92; mem. com. DC Career and Tech. Edn. Task Force, 2000; team chmn. Wilson HS, 2002, mem. student mgmt. task force, 2002—03, grant rev. panelist, 1998, 2002—03. Lt. (j.g.) USN, 1962—66, lt. USNR. Recipient award, Ohio Acad. Sci., 1954—57, Cleve. Plain Dealer Operation Demonstrate, 1956, Svc. award, Heidelberg Coll. Publs., 1961, Recognition cert., DC Assn. Career Devel., 1975, 1976, DC City Coun., 1982, Children's Edn. Found., 1990, Recognition award Outstanding Contbn. to Guidance and Counseling, 1987. Mem.: ACA (counselor adv.-legis.), Coun. Accreditation Counseling and Related Ednl. Programs (site visit team 2000—), Assn. Counselor Edn. and Supervision, DC Career Devel. Assn. (exec. bd. 0983—1990, treas. 1983—86), DC Sch. Counselors Assn. (Outstanding Leadership award 1994), Nat. Career Devel. Assn. (assembly del. 1984, master career coun. 2003), Am. Sch. Counselors Assn. (chair rsch. com. 1990—91, career guidance com., leadership recognition cert. 1987), Am. Counseling Assn. (chmn. govt. rels. N. Atlantic region 1980—81, cert. Outstanding Contbn. in Govt. Rels. 1982, Recognition award 1987), DC Counseling Assn. (treas. 1975—77, exec. bd. 1975—80, sec. 1977—78, pres. 1979—80, trustee 1989—92, treas. 1991—92, trustee 2003—04, counselor adv.-legis., Mem. of the Yr. 1980, Outstanding Leadership award 1980), Phi Delta Kappa (edn. found. rep. 1993—95, v.p. membership 1995—96, pres. 1996—97, MACI project adv. coun. Hosp. Sick Children 1997—98, rev. panel DC vocat. edn. grants 1998, lic. profl. counselor, DC). Home: 821 Taylor St NE Washington DC 20017-2009 Personal E-mail: jw.wb.porter@erols.com.

PORTER, JOHN WILSON, education executive; b. Ft. Wayne, Ind., Aug. 13, 1931; BA, Albion Coll., 1953; MA, Mich. State U., 1957, PhD, 1962; D in Pub. Adminstrn. (hon.), Albion Coll., 1973; LLD (hon.), Mich. State U., 1977, Cleary Coll., 1987; LHD, Adrian Coll., 1970, U. Detroit, 1979; LLD, Western Mich. U., 1971, Eastern Mich. U., 1975; HHD, Kalamazoo Coll., 1973, Detroit Coll. Bus., 1975, Madonna Coll., Livonia, Mich., 1977; DEd, Detroit Inst. Tech., 1978; AA, Schoolcraft Coll., Livonia, Mich., 1979; DBA, Lawrence Inst. Tech., 1988; LLD, Cleary Coll., 1989. Counselor Lansing (Mich.) Pub. Schs., 1953-58; cons. Mich. Dept. Pub. Instrn., 1958-61; dir. Mich. Higher Edn. Assistance Authority, 1961-65; assoc. supt. for higher edn. Mich. Dept. Edn., 1966-69, state supt. schs., 1969-79; pres. Ea. Mich. U., Ypsilanti, 1979-89; v.p. Nat. Bd. for Profl. Teaching Standards, 1989; gen. supt. Detroit Pub. Schs., 1989-91; CEO Urban Edn. Alliance, Inc., Ypsilanti, Mich., 1991—. Mem. numerous profl. commns. and bds., 1959—, including Commn. on Financing Postsecondary Edn., 1972-74, Commn. for Reform Secondary Edn., Kettering Found., 1972-75, Edn. Commn. of States, 1973-79, Nat. Commn. on Performance-Based Edn., 1974-76, Nat. Commn. on Manpower Policy, 1974-79, Mich. Employment and Tng. Svcs. Coun., 1976-79, Nat. Adv. Coun. on Social Security, 1977-79, Commn. on Ednl. Credit, Am. Coun. on Edn., 1977-80; task panel on mental health of family Commn. on Mental Health, 1977-80; mem. Nat. Coun. for Career Edn. (HEW), 1974-76; pres. bd. dirs. Chief State Sch. Officers, 1974-79; pres. Coun. Chief State Sch. Officers, 1977-78; bd. dirs. Comerica Bank; former chmn. bd. Coll. Entrance Exam. Bd., 1984-86. Trustee Nat. Urban League, 1973-79, Charles Stewart Mott Found., 1981—, Albion Coll., 1989—; bd. dirs. Mich. Internat. Council, 1977—, Mich. Congress Parents and Tchrs.; mem. bd. overseers com. for Grad. Sch., Harvard U., 1980-88; mem. edn. com. NAACP; convener goal 6 Nat. Edn. Goals Panel, 1990—; mem. East Lansing Human Relations Commn.; chmn. Am. Assn. State Colls. and U.'s Task Force on Excellence in Edn.; mem. Mich. Martin Luther King, Jr. Holiday Commn., Gov.'s Blue Ribbon Commn. on Welfare Reform; trustee East Lansing Edgewood United Ch.; mem. Catherine McAuley Health Systems Bd., 1990—. Recipient numerous awards including Disting. Svc. award Mich. Congress Parents and Tchrs., 1963, Disting. Svc. award NAACP, Lansing, 1968; cert. of outstanding achievement Delta Kappa chpt. Phi Beta Sigma, 1970; award for disting. svc. Assn. Ind. Colls. and Univs. Mich., 1974; Disting. Alumni award Coll. Edn., Mich. State U., 1974; award for disting. svc. to edn Mich. State U., 1974; Disting. Alumni award, 1979; award for disting. svc. to edn. in Mich. Mich. Assn. Secondary Sch. Prins., 1974; Pres.'s award as disting. educator Nat. Alliance Black Sch. Educators, 1977; Marcus Foster Disting. Educator award, 1979; recognition award Mich. Ednl. Rsch. Assn., 1978; recognition award Mich. Assn. Secondary Sch. Prins., 1978; recognition award Mich. Assn. Intermediate Sch. Adminstrs., 1979; recognition award Mich. Assn. Sch. Adminstrs., 1979; Mich. Sch. Bus. Ofcls., 1979; resolution Mich. State Legislature, 1978; Anthony Wayne award Coll. Edn., Wayne State U., 1979; Educator of Decade award Mich. Assn. State and Fed. Program Specialists, 1979; Spirit of Detroit award Detroit City Coun., 1981; Disting. Svc. award Ypsilanti Area C. of C., 1988; Philip A. Hart award Mich. Women's Hall of Fame, 1988; Summit award Greater Detroit C. of C., 1991; Mich. State C. of C. award 1991; Olivet Coll. award for Leadership and Social Responsibility, 2001; Lifetime Achievement award Albion Coll., 2003; inducted Mich. Edn. Hall of Fame, 1992; John W. Porter Disting. Chair endowed at Eastern Mich. U., 1999; Coll. of Edn. bldg. at Eastern Mich. U. named for him, 1999. Mem. Am. Assn. Sch. Adminstrs., Am. Assn. State Colls. and Univs. (president's council, chmn. task force on excellence in edn.), Nat. Measurement Council, NAACP (life), Greater Detroit C. of C. (Summit award 1991), Mich. State C. of C. (Disting. Svc. and Leadership award 1991), Tuskeegee Airmen (Disting. Svc. award 1991), Mich. PTA (hon. life), Ea. Mich. U. Alumni Assn. (Disting. Svc. award 1997), Econ. Club (dir. 1979), Sigma Pi Phi, Phi Delta Kappa.

PORTER, JON CHRISTOPHER, congressman; b. Fort Dodge, Iowa, May 16, 1955; m. Laurie Porter; children: J. Christopher, Nicole. Student, Briar Cliff Coll. Formerly dist. mgr. ins. co.; mem. Nev. Senate, Dist. 1, 1994—2002, U.S. Ho. Reps. from 3rd Nev. dist., 2003—. Mem. Western Ins. Info. Svc./Nev. Ins. Coun.; mem. Inst. for Ins. and Risk Mgmt., U. Nev., Las Vegas. Mem. City Coun., City of Boulder City, 1983-93, mayor, 1987-91; chair bd. dirs. Las Vegas Events, pres., 1993-95; charter bd. dirs. So. Nev.

Water Authority; bd. dirs. Las Vegas Conv. and Visitors Authority; bd. dirs. Nev. League of Cities; mem. civilian mil. coun. Nellis AFB. Republican. Office: 218 Cannon Ho Office Bldg Washington DC 20515-2803

PORTER, JUDITH DEBORAH REVITCH, sociologist; b. Phila., Mar. 26, 1940; d. Eugene and Esther (Tulchinsky) Revitch; m. Gerald Joseph Porter, June 26, 1960; children: Daniel, Rebecca, Michael. Student, Vassar Coll., 1958-60; BA, Cornell U., 1962, MA, 1963; PhD, Harvard U., 1967. Lectr. Bryn Mawr (Pa.) Coll., 1966-67, asst. prof., 1967-73, assoc. prof., 1973-79, prof. sociology, 1979—, chair dept. sociology, 1987-93. Author: Black Child, White Child: The Development of Racial Attitudes, 1971; contbr. articles to profl. jours. Committeeperson Haverford Twp. Dem. Party, 1976-96; bd. dirs. Phila. AIDS Fund, 1992-98; Congreso de Latinos Unidos, Inc.; vice-chair Mayor's Commn. on Drugs and Alcohol, City of Phila. Recipient Shannon award NIMH, 1992-94; Ford Found. fellow, 1973-74; NSF fellow, 1967; NIDA grant Co-PI, 1998-2001. Mem. APHA, Am. Sociol. Assn., Phi Beta Kappa, Phi Kappa Phi. Jewish. Address: 161 Whitemarsh Rd Ardmore PA 19003-1634 Office: Bryn Mawr Coll Dept Sociology Bryn Mawr PA 19010 E-mail: jporter@brynmawr.edu.

PORTER, KAREN ANN, anthropologist, educator; b. Seattle, Wash., July 14, 1960; d. George Arnold Porter and Carole Diane Mattson. BA cum laude with distinction, U. of Wash., 1986; MA, U. of Rochester, 1988, PhD, 1997. Program dir. & folklorist Arts and Cultural Coun. of Greater Rochester, Rochester, NY, 1997—98; asst. prof. U. of Puget Sound, Tacoma, 1998—. Cons. in field; mem. various adv. com. U. of Puget Sound, 1999—. Editor: Demele: Making It - Migration and Adapation Among Haitian Boat People in the U.S.A., 1988; author: (manual) Folk Music, Dance, and Choreographed Dance, 1998; contbr. articles to profl. jours. Vol. Food Connections, Tacoma, 2000—02, Habitat for Humanity, Rochester, 1996—97, St. Joseph's Ho. of Hospitality, Rochester, 1994—98; vol. St. Paul's Episcopal Ch., Rochester, 1994—98, chmn. refugee resettlement task force, 1997—98. Recipient Faith In Action award, Greater Rochester Cmty. of Ch., 1997; fellow Lewis Henry Morgan fellowship in Anthropology, U. of Rochester, 1986—89, Lang. Fellowship, Cornell U. Africana Studies and Rsch. Ctr., 1988—89, Fulbright Hays fellow, 1989, Rsch. in Africa fellow, Joint Com. on African Studies of the Social Sci. Rsch. Coun. & Am. Coun. of Learned Societies, 1990, Coun. of Ind. Coll. Tchg. fellowship, U.S. Dept. of Edn., 1994—95, U. of Rochester, 1996—97; grantee Geneseo Found. Rsch. Travel grant, SUNY-Geneseo, 1997, Oct. Event grant, N.Y. Coun. for the Humanities, 1998, W.M. Keck Found. & Project Kaleidoscope, 2002. Mem.: Soc. for the Anthropology of Work (gen. editor 1997—2001), Fedn. of Small Anthropology Programs, Am. Ethnol. Soc., Am. Anthrop. Assn., African Studies Assn., Inst. for Devel. Anthropology (rsch. assoc. 2001), Soc. for Applied Anthropology, YMCA, City Club, Phi Beta Kappa Soc. Avocations: gardening, travel, calligraphy. Office: University of Puget Sound 1500 North Warner Tacoma WA 98416

PORTER, KARL HAMPTON, orchestra musical director, conductor; b. Pitts., Apr. 25, 1939; s. Reginald and Naomi Arzetta (Mitchell) P. Student, Carnegie-Mellon U., 1957-60, Peabody Conservatory, 1960-62, Juilliard Sch. Music, 1962-63, Domaine Sch. Condrs., 1961-63, Am. Symphony Orch. League, Tanglewood, 1962-72; student Polit. Sci., Fordham U., 1978; student Bus. Computer Tng., SUNY, 1986; BA, John Hopkins U., 1987. Judge for Congress of Strings, BMI Composers Competition, 1970-74; instr. theory Mt. Morris Park, 1969-73; instr. woodwind L.I. Inst. Music, 1969-75, U. Denver, 1963-64, Coll. New Rochelle, 1980; tchr. bassoon Newark Community Arts Center, 1969-71; instr. music N.Y.C. Tech. Coll., 1972-90; pres. Finale Prodns. Mem. Denver Symphony Orch., 1963-64, Met. Opera Nat. Co., 1965-67, Gil Evans Band, 1967-69, formed, Harlem Youth Symphony, 1968, Harlem Philharmonic Orch., 1969—, New Breed Brass Ensemble, Harlem String Quartet, Harlem Woodwind Quintet, 1970, condr., Balt, Symphony, 1970, mus. dir., condr., Harlem Philharmonic Orch., 1970—, N.Y.C. Housing Authority Orch., 1972-86, Massapequa (N.Y.) Symphony Soc., 1974-80, condr., Park West Symphony, Northeastern Philharmonic of Pa., Scranton Philharmonic, Ridgefield Symphonette, 1971, mus. dir. for Josephine Baker, 1972-75, free lance bassoonist, Am. Symphony, Bklyn. Philharmonic, N.J. Symphony, 1967—; min. of music St. Thomas the Apostle, 1989—; dir. Independence Community Ctr., 1993—; dir. counselor Elmcor Youth Ctr., 1991-93. Mem. nat. adv. bd. Dance Theatre of Harlem, Air Force Assn., Mental Health Assn.; bd. dirs. Empire Trust; hon. bd. dirs. Sickle Cell, Baton Rouge, La.; performing arts coord. Afro-Acad. Cultural Tech. Sci. Olympics; cons. N.Y. State Coun. Arts; dir. Ind. Cmty. Ctr., 1993—; field ops. supr.; U.S. Bur. Census. Recipient Martha Baird Rockefeller Found. grant, 1969, Nat. Endowment grant, 1970 Mem. NAACP, Nat. Soc. Lit. and Arts, N.Y. State Assn. Jr. Colls., Am. Symphony Orch. League, Performing Arts Assn. N.Y., Soc. Black Composers, Nat. Soc. Symphony Condrs. Clubs: The Bohemians. Home: 425 Central Park W New York NY 10025-4381 Office: PO Box 445 New York NY 10025-0008 also: 114 Taylor St Brooklyn NY 11211-6806

PORTER, KIMBERLY K. education educator, consultant; b. Oskaloosa, Iowa, Apr. 3, 1962; d. Joseph Warren and Shirley Mae Porter; life ptnr. Linda Marie Baeza. BA, Ctrl. Coll., Pella, Iowa, 1984; MA, U. Iowa, Iowa City, 1987, PhD, 1995. Asst. prof. U. N.D., Grand Forks, ND, 1996—2001, assoc. prof., 2001—. Author: (monograph) Uncommon Heroes: The City of Grand Forks Flood Fight, 1997, Legacy in the Sand: The United States Armament, Munitions and Chemical Command in Operations Desert Shield and Desert Storm. Regional dir. Consortium of Oral History Educators, Balt., 2003. Mem.: Agrl. History Soc. Democrat. Avocations: reading, golf, gardening. Home: 1885 22nd St NE Emerado ND 58228 Office: Univ N D Box 8096 Grand Forks ND 58202 Office Phone: 701-777-6230. Business E-Mail: kimberly_porter@und.nodak.edu.

PORTER, LAURINDA WRIGHT, communications educator, consultant; b. N.Y.C., June 10, 1946; d. Thomas Archibald Jr. and Christine (Allen) W.; m. Charles A. Porter Jr., June 14, 1969 (div. Mar. 1986); children: Elizabeth, Sarah. BS, Northwestern U., 1968; MA, U. Minn., 1971, PhD, 1981. From instr. to asst. prof. Concordia Coll., St. Paul, 1976-80; asst. prof. St. Olaf Coll., Northfield, Minn., 1984; comm. cons. State Ct. Judges, Minn., 2001—03; prof. of comm. studies St. Cloud U., 1984—. Asst. prof., assoc. prof. St. Mary's Grad. Ctr., Mpls., 1984-87; bd. dirs. Ctrl. Minn. Ch., Minn. Land Trust and Quantum Connections, Inc., mem. Citizen Energy Resource Taskforce of Ctrl. Minn., 2003-. Contbr. articles to profl. jours. Active Colonial Ch. of Edina, Minn., 1976-92. Grantee St. Cloud State U., 1988, 92-96, 99, 2000, 01, Nat. Endowment for the Humanities, Washington, 1991. Mem. Minn. Hist. Soc., S.D. Hist. Soc., Nebr. Hist. Soc., Buffalo Bill Hist. Ctr., Inter Faculty Orgn., Sierra Club. Democrat. Avocation: American Indian history. Office: St Cloud State Univ 720 4th Ave S Saint Cloud MN 56301-4442

PORTER, LILIANA ALICIA, artist, photographer, painter, printmaker, filmmaker; b. Buenos Aires, Oct. 6, 1941; came to U.S., 1964, naturalized, 1982; d. Julio and Margarita (Galetar) P.; m. Luis Camnitzer, 1965 (div. 1978); m. Alan B. Wiener, May 28, 1980 (div. 1991). Grad., Nat. Sch. Fine Arts, Argentina, 1963. Co-dir., instr. Studio Camnitzer-Porter summer workshops, Lucca, Italy, 1974, 75, 76, 77; prof. art Queens Coll., CUNY, N.Y.C., 1991—. Adj. lectr. SUNY Coll., Old Westbury, N.Y., 1974-76, Purchase br., 1987; co-dir. Studio Porter-Wiener, N.Y.C., 1979-87. One-woman shows of prints/paintings/photographs include Galeria Artemultiple, Buenos Aires, Argentina, 1977, 78, Galleria Arte Comunale, Adro, Brescia, Italy, 1977, Hundred Acres Gallery, N.Y.C., 1977, Mus. Modern Art, Cali, Colombia, 1978, Center for Interamerican Relations, N.Y.C., 1980, Galeria Arte Nuevo, Buenos Aires, 1980, Barbara Toll Fine Arts, N.Y.C., 1979, 81, 82, 84, Galerie Jolliet, Montreal, 1983, Museo de Arte Contemporaneo, Panama City, Panama, 1984, Dolan/Maxwell Gallery, Phila., 1985, U. Alta., Edmonton, 1985, Dolan/Maxwell Gallery, Phila., 1985, Galeria Luigi Marrozzini, San Juan, P.R., 1986, Galería-Taller, Museo de Arte Moderno, Cali, Colombia, 1987, The Space, Boston, 1988, Syracuse U., N.Y., 1990, Steinbaum-Krauss Gallery, N.Y.C., 1993, Galeria Ruth Benzacar, Buenos Aires, 1994, U. Art Gallery, N.Mex. State U., Las Cruces, 1995, Monique Knowlton Gallery, 1996, Ruth Benzacar Gallery, N.Y., 1997, Mus. de Bellas Artes Juan Manuel Blanes, Montevideo, Uruguay, 1997, Espacio Minimo, Murcia, Espana, 1998, Annina Nosei Gallery, N.Y., 1999, Artcore Gallery, Toronto, Can., 1999, Espacio Minimo, Murcia, Spain, 2000, Ruth Benzacar Gallery, Buenos Aires, 2000, Sicardi Gallery, Houston, 2000, Annina Nosei, N.Y., 2000, Ctr. Photography, Woodstock, N.Y., 2000, Phoenix Mus., 2000, Galeria Espacio/Mimimo, Madrid, 2000, Brito-Cimino, Sao Paulo, Brazil, 2001, Annina Nosei Gallery, N.Y., 2002, Sicardi Gallery, Houston, 2002, Casas Riegner Gallery, Miami, Fla., 2003, Hosfelt Gallery, San Francisco, 2003, Galeria Espacio Minimo, Madrid, Spain, 2003, Centro Cultural Recolete, Buenos Aires, 2003; retrospective exhibits 1968-90 Fundacion San Telmo, Buenos Aires, 1990, Museo Nacional de Artes Plasticas, Montevideo, Uruguay, 1991, Centro de Recepciones del Gobierno, San Juan, P.R., 1991, Bronx Mus. Art, N.Y.C., 1992, retrospective exhibit Archer Huntington Art Gallery U. Tex. Austin, 1993, Staller Ctr. for the Art SUNY at Stony Brook, N.Y., 1998, Centro Cultural Recoleta, Sla Cronopios, Buenos Aires, Argentina, 2003; exhibited in numerous group shows including most recently El Mus. del Barrio, N.Y.C., 2000,Casa de America, Madrid, 2000, Contemporary Mus., Balt., 2000, N.Y., others, Mass. Coll. Art, Huntington Gallery, Boston, 2001, ARCO, Madrid, 2001, Centro Cultural Borges, Buenos Aires, 2001, Peter Lewis Theater, Guggenheim Mus., N.Y., 2001, Hosfelt Gallery, San Francisco, 2001, Fundacion Telefonica, Madrid, 2001, Fundacion Joan Miro, Barcelona, 2001, Carrie Secrist Gallery, Chgo., 2001, Contemporary Art Ctr., N.Y., 2001, The Mahady Contemporary Gallery at Marywood U., Scranton, Pa., 2002, Kunst Werke, Berlin, 2003; represented in permanent collections Mus.Phila., Mus. Modern Art, N.Y.C., RCA Corp., N.Y.C., N.Y. Public Library, N.Y.C., La Biblioteque Nationale, Paris, France, Museo del Grabado, Buenos Aires, Museo Universitario, Mexico City, Mexico, Museo de Art Moderno, Cali, Colombia, Museo de Bellas Artes, Caracas, Venezuela, Met. Mus. Art, N.Y.C. Recipient 1st prize Argentinian Art 78 Mus. Fine Arts, Buenos Aires, 1978, Grand Prix XI, Internat. Print Biennial, Cracow, Poland, 1986, 1st prize VII Latin Am. Print Biennial, San Juan, Puerto Rico, 1986; fellow Guggenheim Found., 1980-81, N.Y. Found. for the Arts, 1985, grantee, 1999. Address: 720 Greenwich St 10G New York NY 10014 Office Phone: 718-997-4800. Personal E-mail: lilianaporter@earthlink.net.

PORTER, LOUISA S. federal judge; Apptd. presiding magistrate judge so. dist. U.S. Dist. Ct. Calif., 1997—2002. Mem.: Fed. Magistrate Judges Assn. (pres. 2003—04). Office: 1140 US Courthouse 940 Front St San Diego CA 92101 Office Fax: 619-702-9925.

PORTER, MARC BENNETT, auction house executive; b. July 30, 1960; Various positions including assoc. in bus. devel. and mgr. estates and appraisals Christie's Fine Art Auctioneers, N.Y.C., 1990—96, internat. bus. dir. 19th and 20th century art, 2000—03, internat. mng. dir., 2003—; pres. Christie's Am., 2004—. Office: Christies Fine Art Auctioneers 20 Rockefeller Plaza New York NY 10020*

PORTER, MICHAEL E. competitive strategy educator; b. Ann Arbor, Mich., May 23, 1947; s. Howard Eugene and Stana (Vernerova) P. BS, Princeton U., 1969; MBA, Harvard U., 1971, PhD, 1973. Asst. prof. Grad. Sch. Bus., Harvard U., 1973-77, assoc. prof., 1977-82, prof., 1982—, C. Roland Christensen Prof. Bus. Admin., Bishop William Lawrence U. Prof., 2000—. Bd. dirs. Alpha-Beta Techs., Hyatt Mgmt. Co., Inforte, Corp.; bd. advisers, WebEx Communications Inc.; adviser to several fgn. govts., including Canada, India, Ireland, New Zealand, Portugal, the U.K. Author: Interbrand, Choice, Strategy and Bilateral Market Power, 1976, Competitive Strategy: Techniques for Analyzing Industries and Competitors, 1980 (Outstanding Acad. Book selection Choice mag. 1980-81), (with R.E. Caves and A.M. Spence) Competition in the Open Economy, 1980, Competitive Advantage: Techniques for Achieving and Sustaining Superior Performance, 1985, Competition in Global Industries, 1986, The Competitive Advantage of Nations, 1990; mem. editorial adv. bd. Long Range Planning, Antitrust Law and Econs. Rev. Mem. Presdl. Commn. on Indsl. Competitiveness, 1983, Gov's Council on Econ. Growth and Technology, Mass., 1991; . Served to capt. AUS, 1969-76. Recipient David A. Wells Prize in Econs. Harvard U., 1973-74, McKinsey award for best article Harvard Bus. Rev., 1979, 87, Charles Coolidge Parlin award Am. Mktg. Assn., 1991, Adam Smith award, Nat. Assoc. Bus. Economists, 1997. Fellow Acad. Mgmt. (George R. Terry award 1985), Fin. analysts Fedn. (Graham and Dodd award 1980), Internat. Acad. Mgmt.; mem. Am. Mktg. Assn., Strategic Mgmt. Soc. Clubs: Cap and Gown. Republican. Office: Harvard Bus Sch Soldiers Field Rd Boston MA 02163-1317 *My work has sought to make a positive impact on the ability of companies to compete effectively and on the ability of government to play a constructive role in that process. I have tried to bring a new level of sophistication to the understanding of competition by combining the tools of an economist with a strong awareness of and interest in the problems of the practicing manager. I have also sought to influence public policy by bringing to its formulation a closer awareness of the realities of competition than is embodied in contemporary economic theory.**

PORTER, MICHAEL PELL, lawyer; b. Indpls., Ind., Mar. 31, 1940; s. Harold Troxel and Mildred Maxine (Pell) P.; m. Alliene Laura Jenkins, Sept. 23, 1967 (div.); 1 child, Genevieve Natalie Porter Eason; m. Janet Kay Smith Hayes, Feb. 13, 1983 (div.). Student, DePauw U., 1957-58; BA, Tulane U., 1961, LLB, 1963. Bar: La. 1963, U.S. Ct. Mil. Appeals 1964, N.Y. 1969, Hawaii 1971. Clk. U.S. Ct. Appeals (5th cir.), New Orleans, 1963; assoc. Sullivan & Cromwell, N.Y.C., 1968-71, Cades Schutte Fleming & Wright, Honolulu, 1971-74, ptnr., 1975-94; mem. faculty Addis Ababa (Ethiopia) U. Sch. Law, 1995-99; sr. regulatory advisor Egyptian Capital Market Authority, Cairo, 1999—2002; advisor capital market Palestinian Nat. Authority, 2002—03; lectr. Arab Acad. Banking and Fin. Scis., 2003. Legal advisor St. Matthews Anglican Ch., Addis Ababa, Ethiopia, 1995—99; cons, Rep. of Yemen, 1997; mem. deans coun. Law Sch. Tulane U., 1981—88; dep. vice chancellor Episcopal Diocese Hawaii, 1980—88, chancellor, 1988—94, Episcopal Ch., Micronesia, 1988—95; legal cons. Bangladesh SEC, 2004—. Author: Hawaii Corporation Law & Practice, 1989; Hawaii reporter State Limited Partnership Laws, 1992-94. Bd. dirs. Jr. Achievement Hawaii, Inc., 1974-84; Inst. Human Svcs., Inc., 1980-88; donor Michael P. Porter Dean's Scholastic Award, U. Hawaii Law Sch., 1977—. With JAGC, U.S. Army, 1963-66, Vietnam. Fulbright scholar, 1997-99; Tulane U. fellow, 1981; lectorship named in his honor, Addis Abba, 1994-97; established Michael P. Porter Prizes on Ethnic Harmony and Religious Tolerance in a Dem. Soc. at Addis Ababa, 1995. Mem.: ABA, Hawaii Bar Assn. Republican. E-mail: porterconsultant@yahoo.com.

PORTER, PHILIP THOMAS, retired electrical engineer; b. Clinton, Ky., Mar. 18, 1930; s. Philip Henry and Ruth Frances (Pennebaker) P.; m. Louise Monroe Jett, July 3, 1957; children: Philip C., Sara Shelby Porter Taylor. BA in Physics, Vanderbilt U., 1952, MA in Physics, 1953. Mem. tech. staff Bell Telephone Labs., Murray Hill, N.J., 1953-62, Holmdel, N.J., 1962-70, supr., 1971-78, West Long Branch, N.J., 1979-83; dir. wireless and wireline network compatiblity studies Telcordia Tech., Red Bank, N.J., 1984-94; ret., 1994. U.S. del. Consultative Com. for Internat. Radio, Geneva, 1984-93. Contbg. author: Electronics Engineers' Handbook, 1982, History of Science and Technology in the Bell System, 1985, Digital Communications, 1986; patentee in field. Fellow IEEE. Unitarian Universalist. Avocations: group singing, bridge.

PORTER, PHILIP WAYLAND, geography educator; b. Hanover, N.H., July 9, 1928; s. Wayland Robinson and Bertha Maria (LaPlante) P.; m. Patricia Elizabeth Garrigus, Sept. 5, 1950; children: Janet Elizabeth, Sara Louise, Alice Catherine. AB, Middlebury Coll., 1950; MA, Syracuse U., 1955; PhD, U. London, 1957. Instr. geography U. Minn., Mpls., 1957-58, asst. prof., 1958-64, assoc. prof., 1964-66, prof., 1966-2000, prof. emeritus, 2000—; assoc. to v.p. acad. affairs, also dir. Office Internat. Programs, 1979-83. Geography panel Com. on Space Programs for Earth Observations Nat. Acad. Scis., 1967-71; liaison officer Midwest Univs. Consortium for Internat. Activities, 1979-83 Author: (with Eric S. Sheppard) A World of Difference: Society, Nature, Development, 1998; contbr. articles to profl. jours. With AUS, 1952-54. Grantee Ctrl. Rsch. Fund, 1955-56, NSF, 1961-62, 78-80, 92-93, Social Sci. Rsch. Coun., 1966-67, Rockfeller Found., 1969, 71-73, Gen. Svc. Found., 1981-83, Exxon Edn. Found., 1983-84, Fulbright, 1992-93; Bush Sabbatical fellow, 1985-86. Mem. Assn. Am. Geographers (Lifetime Achievement award 2004). Home: 10 Burkehaven Terr Sunapee NH 03782-2402 Office: U Minn Dept Geography Minneapolis MN 55455 E-mail: pwporter@tds.net., porter@atlas.socsci.umn.edu.

PORTER, RHONDA CATINA, mathematician, educator; d. Harrison III and Linda (Slaughter) Porter. BS in Math. Edn., Fla. A&M U., 1995; MEd in Secondary Math., Columbus State U., 1996; M Applied Math., Auburn U., 1999, PhD, 2000. Math. tchr. Randolph-Clay Mid. H.S., Cuthbert, Ga., 1995—97; asst. prof. math. edn. Fla. A&M U., Tallahassee, 2000—. Office: Florida A&M U GEC-A 315/South Adams St Tallahassee FL 32307 E-mail: rhonda.porter@famu.edu.

PORTER, ROBERT CARL, JR., lawyer; b. Cin., Sept. 21, 1927; s. Robert Carl and Lavinia (Otte) P.; m. Joanne Patterson, July 5, 1952; children: Robert Carl III, David M., John E. BA with distinction, U. Mich., 1949; JD, Harvard U., 1952. Bar: Ohio 1952, U.S. Dist. Ct. (so. dist.) Ohio 1954, U.S. Ct. Appeals (6th cir.) 1954, U.S. Ct. Mil. Appeals 1956, U.S. Tax Ct. 1980, U.S. Supreme Ct. 1956. Ptnr. Porter & Porter, Cin., 1953-54; sole practice Cin., 1954-63; sr. ptnr. Porter & McKinney, Cin., 1963-88, Porter & Porter, Cin., 1989—. Dir. and officer numerous cos. Served with JAGC, USAF, 1952-53. Mem. ABA, Ohio State Bar Assn., Cin. Bar Assn., Cin. Country Club, Univ. Club, U. Mich. Club, Harvard Law Sch. Assn., Masons, Scottish Rite, Shriners, Phi Beta Kappa. Presbyterian. Home: 2365 Bedford Ave Cincinnati OH 45208-2656 Office: Porter & Porter 2100 4th and Vine Tower Cincinnati OH 45202 Office Phone: 513-621-3993.

PORTER, ROGER BLAINE, government official, educator; b. Provo, Utah, June 19, 1946; s. Blaine Robert and Elizabeth M. (Taylor) P.; m. Ann Robinson, Jan. 6, 1972; children: Robert Roger, Stacy Ann, David R., Rachel Elizabeth. BA in History and Polit. Sci., Brigham Young U., 1969; PhB, Oxford U., 1971; MA, PhD, Harvard U., 1978, Weber State U., 2003. Asst. dean, tutor in politics Queen's Coll., Oxford U., 1971-72; spl. asst. to pres. The White House, 1974-77; rsch. assoc. Kennedy Sch. Govt. and Grad. Sch. Bus., Harvard U., Cambridge, Mass., 1977-79, asst. prof. pub. policy, 1979-81, assoc. prof., 1981, prof. govt. and bus., 1985—; spl. asst. to Pres. of U.S., 1981-82; dep. asst. to Pres. of U.S., 1982-85; dir. White Ho. Office of Policy Devel., Washington, 1982-85; counselor to sec. U.S. Treasury, 1981-85; exec. sec. Nat. Productivity Adv. Com., 1981-85, Cabinet Coun. on Econ. Affairs, 1981-85, Econ. Policy Coun., 1985, asst. to U.S. Pres. for econ. and domestic policy, 1989-93. Exec. sec. Pres.'s Econ. Policy Bd., 1974—77; sr. scholar Woodrow Wilson Internat. Ctr. for Scholars, 1993—; dir. Ctr. for Bus. and Govt. Harvard U., 1995—2000, master Dunster House, 2001—; mem. Pres.'s Commn. on White House Fellowships, 1976—2001; bd. dirs. Zions Bancorp., Pactiv Corp., Nat. Life Ins. Co., Tenneco Automotive, Inc., Mutual of Am. Author: Presidential Decision Making, 1980, U.S.-USSR Grain Agreement, 1984, Efficiency, Equity, Legitimacy: The Multilateral Trading System at the Millenium, 2001; asst. editor: Public Policy, 1979—81. Mem. Utahns for Effective Govt., Salt Lake City, 1971-72; mem. Rep. Nat. Com. Econ. Adv. Com., 1977-81. Rhodes scholar, 1969; Woodrow Wilson fellow, 1969; White House fellow, 1974; recipient spl. citation U.S. Sec. Treasury, 1977, Rolex Intercollegiate Tennis Achievement award, 1996; named One of 10 Outstanding Young Men in Am., 1981 Fellow Nat. Acad. Pub. Adminstrn.; mem. White House Hist. Assn. (bd. dirs. 1995—), Phi Kappa Phi, Pi Sigma Alpha, Phi Eta Sigma, Phi Alpha Theta. Republican. Mem. Lds Ch. Avocations: classical music, basketball, tennis, travel. Home: 12 Clifton St Belmont MA 02478-3363 Office: Harvard U Kennedy Sch Govt 79 JFK St Cambridge MA 02138-5801

PORTER, ROGER JOHN, medical research executive, educator, neurologist, pharmacologist; b. Pitts., Apr. 4, 1942; s. John Keaggy and Margaret (Parker) P.; m. Candace Marie Leland, Feb. 17, 1968; children: David, Stacey. BS, Eckerd Coll., 1964; MD, Duke U., 1968. Diplomate Nat. Bd. Med. Examiners, Am. Bd. Neurology, Am. Bd. Electroencephalography. Intern U. Calif., San Diego, 1968-69, resident in neurology San Francisco, 1971-74; fellow rsch. tng. program Duke U., Durham, N.C., 1966-67; staff assoc. sect. epilepsy Nat. Inst. Neurol. Diseases and Stroke, NIH, Bethesda, Md., 1969-71; investigator U. Calif., San Francisco, 1972-73; sr. rsch. assoc. epilepsy br. neurol. disorders program Nat. Inst. Neurol. and Communicative Disorders and Stroke, NIH, Bethesda, 1974-78, asst. chief epilepsy br., 1977-79, acting chief, 1979-80, acting chief clin. epilepsy sect., IRP, 1979-84, chief epilepsy br. neurol. disorders program, 1980-84, chief med. neurology br. and clin. epilepsy sect. IRP, 1984-87; dep. dir. Nat. Inst. Neurol. Disorders and Stroke, NIH, Bethesda, 1987-92; v.p., clin. pharmacology Wyeth-Ayerst Rsch., Radnor, Pa., 1992-97, v.p. clin. rsch., 1997—99, v.p., dep. head clin. rsch., 1999—2002; cons., 2002—. Adj. prof. neurology U. Pa., 1993—; prof. neurology Uniformed Svcs. U. Health Scis., Bethesda, 1980-93, adj. prof. pharmacology, 1982—; cons.-lectr. neurology Nat. Naval Med. Ctr., Bethesda, 1978-93; chmn. White House Subcom. on Brain and Behavioral Scis., 1990-92; scholar-in-residence Assn. Am. Med. Colls., Washington, 1989-90; mem. NIMH/Nat. Inst. Neurol. Disorders and Stroke Coun. of Assembly of Scientists, 1983-86, pres., 1985-86; mem. pharmacy and therapeutics com. NIH, 1977-86, chmn., 1978; mem. instnl. rev. bd. human subjects Nat. Inst. Neurol. Disorders and Stroke, 1984-87, chmn., 1986-87. Author/editor 13 books; mem. editl. bd. Acta Neurologica Scandanavica, 1991-97, Annals of Neurology, 1987-92, Epilepsia, 1982-86, Clin. Neuropharmacology, 1999-2001; contbr. articles to profl. jours.; writer, contbr. 5 motion pictures, 1 exhibit. Bd. trustees Eckerd Coll., 1994-97. With USPHS, 1969-92. Recipient MacArthur Outstanding Alumnus award Eckerd Coll., 1977, Fulbright Disting. Prof. award, 1985, Disting. Alumnus award Duke Duke U. Med. Ctr., 1989, USPHS Dist. Svc. Medal, 1991, USUHS Commendable Svc. Award, 2001. Fellow Coll. Physicians Phila., Am. Acad. Neurology, Am. Neurol. Assn.; mem. Am. Electroencephalographic Soc., Am. Epilepsy Soc. (pres. 1989-90), Soc. Neurosci., Am. Soc. Clin. Pharmacology and Therapeutics, Am. Soc. Experimental Neurol. Therapeutics, Internat. League Against Epilepsy (sec.-gen. 1989-93), Am. Soc. Pharmacology and Exptl. Therapeutics. Home and Office: 461 Timber Ln Devon PA 19333-1232 Office Phone: 610-989-3767.

PORTER, STEPHEN CUMMINGS, geologist, educator; b. Santa Barbara, Calif., Apr. 18, 1934; s. Lawrence Johnson Porter Jr. and Frances (Cummings) Seger; m. Anne Mary Higgins, Apr. 2, 1959; children: John, Maria, Susannah. BS, Yale U., 1955, MS, 1958, PhD, 1962. Asst. prof. geology U. Wash., Seattle, 1962-66, assoc. prof., 1966-71, prof., 1971—2002, dir. Quaternary Research Ctr., 1982-98, prof. emeritus, 2002—. Mem. bd. earth scis. Nat. Acad. Sci., Washington, 1983-85; mem. adv. com. divsn. polar programs NSF, Washington, 1983-84; vis. fellow Clare Hall Cambridge (Eng.) U., 1980-81; guest prof. Chinese Acad. Scis., People's Republic of China, 1987—; v.p. Internat. Union Quaternary Rsch., 1992-95, pres., 1995-99. Co-author: Physical Geology, 1987, The Dynamic Earth, 1989, 92, 95, 99, 2004, The Blue Planet, 1995, 99, Environmental Geology, 1996, Dangerous Earth, 1997; editor: Late Quaternary Environments of the United States, 1983; editor Quaternary Rsch., 1976-2000; co-editor The Quaternary Period in the U.S.; assoc. editor Radiocarbon, 1982-89, Am. Jour. Sci., 1997—; mem. editl. bd. Quaternary Sci. Revs., 1988—, Quaternary Internat., 1989—. Served to lt. USNR, 1955-57. Recipient Benjamin Silliman prize Yale U., 1962; Willis M. Tale lectr. So. Meth. U., 1984, S.F. Emmons lectr. Colo. Sci. Soc., 1996; Fulbright Hays sr. rsch. fellow, New Zealand, 1973-74. Fellow Geol. Soc. Am. (Kirk Bryan award 2004), Arctic Inst. N.Am. (bd. govs.), AAAS; mem. Am. Quaternary Assn. (coun., pres. 1992-94, Disting. Career award 2004). Avocations: photography, mountain climbing. Home: 18034 15th Ave NW Shoreline WA 98177-3305 Office: U Wash Dept Earth and Space Scis PO Box 351360 Seattle WA 98195-1310

PORTER, STEPHEN WINTHROP, stage director; b. Ogdensburg, N.Y., July 24, 1925; s. Charles T. and Anna (Newton) P. BA, Yale U., 1945, M.F.A., 1948. Asst. prof. English in charge of drama McGill U., Montreal, 1949-56. Stage dir. plays on Broadway Right You Are, Wild Duck, 1966, The Show Off, 1967, The Misanthrope, 1968, 83, The Wrong Way Light Bulb, Private Lives, 1969, Harvey, 1970, The School for Wives, 1971, Captain Brassbound's Conversion, 1972, Don Juan, 1973, Chemin de Fer, 1974, Rules of the Game, 1975, They Knew What They Wanted, 1976, Days in the Trees, 1976, The

Importance of Being Earnest, 1977, Tartuffe, 1977, Man and Superman, 1978, Major Barbara, The Man Who Came to Dinner, 1980, You Never Can Tell, 1986, The Devil's Disciple, 1988, The Miser, 1990, Getting Married, 1991. Address: 25 W 54th St New York NY 10019-5404

PORTER, TERRY, professional basketball coach; b. Milw., Apr. 8, 1963; Student, U. Wis., Stevens Point, 1981-85. Guard Portland Trail Blazers, 1985-97, Minn. Timberwolves, Mpls., 1997-98, Miami Heat, 1998-99, San Antonio Spurs, 1999—2002; head coach Milw. Bucks, 2003—. Recipient Citizenship award, 1993; named to NBA All-Star team, 1991, 93. Achievements include holding single game record for most three point field goals without a miss-7, 1992. Office: 1001 N 4th St Milwaukee WI 53203

PORTER, THOMAS WILLIAM, III, lawyer; b. Dallas, Aug. 23, 1941; s. Thomas William and Ruth Mae (Campbell) P.; m. Sally Ann Shell, May 10, 1963 (div. July 1983); children: Elizabeth Elisse, Laura Christina; m. Patty Ann Sanders, Nov. 2, 1985. BBA in Fin., So. Meth. U., 1963; LLB, Duke U., 1966. Bar: Tex. 1966, U.S. Dist. Ct. (no. dist.) Tex. 1967, U.S. Dist. Ct. (so. dist.) Tex. 1975, U.S. Dist. Ct. (we. dist.) Tex. 1977, U.S. Ct. Appeals (5th cir.) 1977. Assoc. Jackson & Walker, Dallas, 1966-72; ptnr. Bracewell & Patterson, Houston, 1972-74, Foreman & Dyess, Houston, 1974-81; sr. ptnr. Porter & Hedges LLP, Houston, 1981—, chmn., 2000—. Bd. dirs. US Concrete, Cal Dive Internat. Life mem. bd. visitors Duke U. Law Sch.; trustee Tex. Heart Inst.; dir. Alley Theatre. Fellow: Tex. Bar Found.; mem.: ABA (fed. regulation of securities com. 1979—, com. on law firms 1981—), State Bar Tex. Assn. (coun. mem. sect. bus. law 1984—86, securities and investment banking com. 1976—), Coronado Club, River Oaks Country Club, Lochinvar Golf Club, Phi Delta Phi. Republican. Methodist. Office: Porter & Hedges LLP Bank of Am Ctr 35th Fl 700 Louisiana St Houston TX 77002-2700 Business E-Mail: bporter@porterhedges.com.

PORTER, VERNA LOUISE, lawyer; b. May 31, 1941; BA, Calif. State U., 1963; JD, Southwestern U., 1977. Bar: Calif. 1977, U.S. Dist. Ct. (ctrl. dist.) Calif. 1978, U.S. Ct. Appeals (9th cir.) 1978. Ptnr. Eisler & Porter, LA, 1978-79, mng. ptnr., 1979-86; pvt. practice, 1986—. Judge pro-tempore LA Mcpl. Ct., 1983—, LA Superior Ct., 1989—, Beverly HIlls Mcpl. Ct., 1992—; mem. subcom. landlord tenant law, State Calif., panelist conv.; mem. real property law sect. Calif. State Bar, 1983; mem. client rels. panel, vol. LA County Bar Dispute Resolution; ct. appointed arbitrator civil cases, fee arbitrator LA Superior Ct.; mem. BBB Abitrator Automobile Lemon Laws, 2000—. Editl. asst., contbr. Apt. Bus. Outlook, Real Property News, Apt. Age. Mem. adv. coun. Freddie Mac Vendor, 1995—; mem. World Affairs Coun. Mem. ABA, LA County Bar Assn. (client-rels. vol. dispute resolution fee arbitration 1981—; arbitrator lemon law claims), LA Trial Lawyers Assn., Wilshire Bar Assn. Women Lawyers' Assn., Landlord Trial Lawyers Assn. (founding, pres.), Da Camera Soc. Republican. Office: 2500 Wilshire Blvd Ste 1226 Los Angeles CA 90057-4365 Office Phone: 213-385-1568.

PORTER, VICTORIA JEAN, editor, writer; b. Flushing, N.Y., Mar. 14, 1962; d. Ottar Kristian and Gerd Bjerring Sandvik; m. Dennis Patrick Porter, Aug. 1, 1999. BA in English, CUNY, 1984. Editl. asst. Macmillan Publ., N.Y.C., 1984—86; assoc. editor Travel Age, Cahners Publ., N.Y.C., 1986—89; freelance editor, writer, 1989—92; copy editor, writer SCP Comms., N.Y.C., 1992—98, Medscape/WebMD, N.Y.C., 1999—. Author: Single in New York, 1992. Libertarian. Avocations: flute, cat rescue, jewelry making, ice skating, bowling. E-mail: veepjean@msn.com.

PORTER, WALTER ARTHUR, retired judge; b. Dayton, Ohio, June 6, 1924; s. Claude and Estella (Raymond) P.; m. Patricia Reeves Higdon, Dec. 3, 1947; children— Scott Paul, David Bryant. BS in Engring, U. Cin., 1948, LL.B., 1949. Bar: Ohio 1949. Legal dep. Montgomery County Probate Ct., 1949-51; asst. pros. atty. Montgomery County, 1951-56; with Albert H. Scharrer (atty.), Dayton, 1956-61; mem. firm Smith & Schnacke, Dayton, 1962-85, pres., 1980-85; judge Montgomery County Common Pleas Ct., 1985-95; of counsel Thompson Hine & Flory, Dayton, 1996-2001. Served with inf. U.S. Army, 1943-45, ETO. Mem. ABA, Ohio Bar Assn. (pres. 1973-74), Dayton Bar Assn., Am. Coll. Trial Lawyers, Am. Coll. Probate Counsel, Phi Alpha Delta, Omicron Delta Kappa. Clubs: Mason. Democrat. Presbyterian. Home: 872 Timberlake Ct Kettering OH 45429-3494 E-mail: wapphp@aol.com.

PORTER, WALTER THOMAS, JR., retired bank executive; b. Jan. 8, 1934; s. Walter Thomas and Mary Rebecca (Brookes) P.; m. Dixie Jo Thompson, Apr. 3, 1959; children: Kimberlee Paige, Douglas Thompson, Jane-Amy Elizabeth. BS, Rutgers U., 1954; MBA, U. Wash., 1959; PhD, Columbia U., 1964. CPA, Wash., N.Y. Staff cons. Touche Ross & Co., N.Y.C., 1959-61, dir. edn., 1964-66; NDEA fellow Columbia ., 1961-64; assoc. prof. U. Wash., 1966-70, prof., 1970-74; vis. prof. N. European Mgmt. Inst., Oslo, 1974-75; nat. dir. planning Touche Ross & Co., Seattle, 1975-78, dir. exec. fin. counseling, 1978-84; exec. v.p., mgr. pvt. banking Rainier Nat. Bank, 1984-87, exec. v.p., mgr. capital mgmt. and pvt. banking, 1987-88, vice-chmn., 1988—92, Security Pacific Bank Washington, 1989-92; exec. v.p., mgr. capital mgmt. group Bank of Am., Seattle, 1992-99; chmn. Porter Investments LLC, 1999—. Vis. lectr. taxation U. Wash., 1978—85; vis. lectr. strategic planning Nat. U. Ireland, 2003; bd. dirs. Shugard Self-Storage, Coldstream Capital Mgmt., Flexcar. Author: 11 books, the most recent being The Bank of America Guide to Personal Financial Solutions, 2d edit., 1998, The Glory of Washington: The People and Events That Shaped the Husky Athletic Tradition, 2001, Husky Stadium: Great Games and Golden Moments, 2004. Mem. Seattle adv. bd. Salvation Army, 1975-83, 89-97, pres., 1993-95; trustee Ryther Child Ctr., 1975-85, pres., 1979-81; trustee Lakeside Sch., 1977-87, pres., 1984-86; trustee Va. Mason Med. Ctr., 1986-97, chair bd. govs., 1994-96; chair Nat. Campaign for Student Athlete U. of Wash., 1995-2000, Mus. History and Industry, 1982-83, Olympic Park Inst., 1996-2001. With U.S. Army, 1955-57. Mem. Sand Point Country Club. Congregationalist. E-mail: djoporter@msn.com.

PORTER, WAYNE RANDOLPH, dermatologist; b. Washington, Jan. 10, 1948; s. James Randolph and Betty Rose (Burgess) P. BS, MIT, 1970; MD, Duke U., 1973. Diplomate Am. Bd. Internal Medicine, Am. Bd. Dermatology. Intern U. Miami (Fla.) Affiliated Hosps., 1973-74; resident in internal medicine U. Miami Sch. Medicine, 1973-76, resident in dermatology, 1976-78, clin. instr., then asst. prof. dermatology (vol.), 1978-85, assoc. prof. (vol.), 1985—. Adj. prof. Barry U. Sch. Grad. Medicine, 2000—; practice medicine specializing in dermatology, North Miami Beach, 1978—; mem. staff U. Miami-Jackson Meml. Hosp. Mem. med. adv. bd. Dade-Broward chpt. Lupus Found. Am. Fellow Internat. Soc. for Dermatologic Surgery, Am. Acad. Dermatology, Am. Assn. Dermatologic Surgeons; mem. AMA, ACP, Internat. Soc. Pediat. Dermatology, Fla. Med. Assn., Fla. Dermatology Soc., Miami Dermatol. Soc. (pres.), Dade County Med. Assn., So. Med. Assn., Bath Club (Miami Beach), Coral Reef Yacht Club. Office: 909 N Miami Beach Blvd Miami FL 33162-3712 Office Phone: 305-949-4223. E-mail: wrpmd@bellsouth.net.

PORTER, WILLIAM LYMAN, architect, educator; b. Poughkeepsie, N.Y., Feb. 19, 1934; s. William Quincy and Lois (Brown) P.; m. Lynn Rogers Porter; children: Quayny Lyman, Zoe Lynn, Eve Lyman. BA, Yale U., 1955, M.Arch., 1957; PhD, MIT, 1969. Designer, job capt. Louis I. Kahn (architect), Phila., 1960-62; urban designer, asst. chief of design Ciudad Guayana project Joint Center for Urban Studies of Harvard and MIT, Caracas, Venezuela, 1962-64; Mellon fellow dept. urban studies and planning MIT, 1964-65; Samuel Stouffer fellow Joint Center for Urban Studies, Harvard and MIT, 1966-67; asst. prof. urban design, depts. architecture and urban studies and planning MIT, 1968-70, assoc. prof. urban design, 1970-71, prof. architecture and planning, 1971—2004, Norman B. and Muriel Leventhal prof. architecture and planning, 1988—2004, prof. emeritus, 2004—, head. dept. architecture, 1987-91, dean Sch. Architecture and Planning, 1971-81; co-dir. Aga Khan Program for Islamic Architecture Harvard U.-MIT, 1979-85. Cons. in field; mem. Nat. Archtl. Accrediting Bd., 1978-80, pres., 1979; mem. Mass. Designer Selection Bd., 1978-79, chmn., 1979; mem. steering com. Aga Khan Award for Architecture, 1977-86, mem. master jury, 1989; prin. Four Architecture Inc., Boston, 1994—. Co-author: Excellence by Design: Transforming Workplace and Work Practice, 1999; co-founder, co-editor Places: A Quarterly Jour. Environ. Design, 1982-88, Facilities Engineering and Management Handbook: Commercial, Industrial and Institutional Buildings, 2000, Design Representation, 2003. Trustee Milton (Mass.) Acad., 1989-2001; mem. bd. overseers Coll. Fine Arts, U. Pa., 1984-90, Mus. Fine Arts, Boston, 1992-94. Fellow AIA; mem. Boston Soc. Architects (dir. 1969-73, 77-81) Clubs: Harvard Musical Assn. (Boston). Home: 17 Concord Ave Cambridge MA 02138-2321 Office: MIT Sch Architecture & Planning 77 Massachusetts Ave Cambridge MA 02139-4307 E-mail: wlporter@mit.edu.

PORTER, WILMA JEAN, educational consultant; b. Sylacauga, Ala., May 30, 1931; d. Harrison Samuel and Blanche Leonard Butcher; m. Douglas Taylor Porter, Apr. 18, 1953; children: Daria Cecile, Blanche Evette, Douglas Vincent. BS, Tuskegee U., 1951; MS, Mich. State U., 1966; PhD, Iowa State U., 1980. Asst. dietitian Miss. State Tb Sanatorium, 1951-52; therapeutic dietitian dept. of hosp. City of N.Y., S.I., 1952-53; libr. asst. Mississippi Valley State Coll., Itta Bena, Miss., 1963-65; asst. prof. Grambling (La.) State U., 1966-75, Howard U., Washington, 1976-80; country dir. U.S. Peace Corps, Tonga, 1980-82; asst. dir. internat. programs Ft. Valley (Ga.) Coll., 1983-84, dir. Inst. Advancement, 1984-88; dir. Sch. Home Econs., Tenn. Technol. U., Cookeville, 1989-96; pvt. ednl. cons. Cookeville, 1996-98. Project dir. Capitol Hill Health and Homemaker, Washington, 1982-83; interim dir. Inst. Advancement Alcorn State U., Lorman, Miss., 1988-89. Author lab. manual for quantity foods, 1977; editor: (cookbook) Some Christmas Foods and Their Origins from Around the World, 1983. Convenor Nat. Issues Forums, Ga. and Tenn., 1985-90; citizen participant Nat. Issues Forums Soviet Dialogue, Newport Beach, Calif., 1988; bd. dirs. Leadership Putnam, Cookeville, 1990-94; chmn. Tenn. Technol. U. campaign United Way, 1989; mem. devel. and planning com. Peach County Ft. Valley, 1985-87; mem. Peach County Heart Fund Dr., 1986-88; participant People to People Citizens Amb. program U.S./China Women's Issues Program, 1995. Title III grantee U.S. Dept. Edn., 1986, 87; Tenn. Dept. Human Svcs. grantee, 1993, 94. Mem. AAUW (program chair 1991-92, pres. Cookeville br. 1993-94), Am. Family and Consumer Scis. Assn., Am. Dietetic Assn., Nat. Coun. Adminstrs. Home Econs., La. Assn. Family and Consumer Scis., La. Dietetic Assn. Democrat. Roman Catholic. Avocations: writing, vegetable and flower gardening. Home: 1415 ML King Jr Ave Grambling LA 71245

PORTERFIELD, CHRISTOPHER, magazine editor, writer; b. Weston, W.Va., Apr. 3, 1937; s. James Herman and Irene (Smith) P.; m. Stephanie Brown, Jan. 20, 1962; children: Christopher Brown, Tessa Louise, Kevin Stephenson. BA, Yale U., 1958; MA, Columbia U., 1965. Music critic Time mag., N.Y.C., 1967-69, cultural correspondent London, 1969-72; exec. producer Daphne Prodns., N.Y.C., 1974-79; sr. editor Time mag., N.Y.C., 1980-93, asst. mng. editor, 1993-96; exec. editor, 1996—2003; contbr., 2003—. Co-Author: (with Dick Cavett) (books) Cavett, 1973, Eye on Cavett, 1983; contbr. articles to popular mags. and periodicals, 1975—. Mem. Writer's Guild of Am. Avocations: reading, music, tennis. Home: 315 Central Park W New York NY 10025-7664 Office: Time Mag 1271 Avenue Of The Americas New York NY 10020-1300

PORTERFIELD, JAMES TEMPLE STARKE, business administration educator; b. Annapolis, Md., July 7, 1920; s. Lewis Broughton and Maud Paxton (Starke) P.; m. Betty Gold, Apr. 23, 1949 (dec. 1985); m. Janet Patricia Gardiner Roggeveen, Oct. 5, 1986. AB, U. Calif., Berkeley, 1942; MBA, Stanford U., 1948, PhD, 1955. From asst. to assoc. prof. Harvard U. Bus. Sch., Boston, 1955—59; prof. fin. Stanford (Calif.) U. Grad. Sch. Bus., 1959-79, James Irvin Miller Prof. fin., 1979-90, prof. emeritus, 1990—; prof. IMEDE Mgmt. Devel. Inst., Lausanne, Switzerland, 1962-63. Author: Life Insurance Stocks as Investments, 1955, Investment Decisions and Capital Costs, 1965; co-author: Case Problems in Finance, 1959. Served as lt. USNR, 1941-46. Recipient Salgo Noren award Stanford U., 1966, Richard W. Lyman award Stanford U. Alumni Assn., 1995. Home: 295 Golden Oak Dr Portola Valley CA 94028-7730 Office: Stanford U Grad Sch Bus Stanford CA 94305

PORTERFIELD, WILLIAM WENDELL, chemist, educator; b. Winchester, Va., Aug. 24, 1936; s. Donald Kennedy and Adelyn (Miller) P.; m. Dorothy Elizabeth Dail, Aug. 24, 1957; children: Allan Kennedy, Douglas Hunter. BS, U. N.C., 1957, PhD, 1962; MS, Calif. Inst. Tech., 1960. Sr. research chemist Hercules, Inc., Cumberland, Md., 1962-64; asst. prof. chemistry Hampden-Sydney (Va.) Coll., 1964-65, assoc. prof., 1965-68, prof. chemistry, 1968—, Charles Scott Venable prof. chemistry, 1989—, chmn. natural sci. div., 1973-77, chmn. dept. chemistry, 1982-85, 93-96, 2002—. Vis. fellow U. Durham (U.K.), 1984 Author: Concepts of Chemistry, 1972, Inorganic Chemistry, 1984, 2d edit., 1993; contbr. articles to profl. jours. Mem. Am. Chem. Soc., Royal Chem. Soc. (London, Eng.), Phi Beta Kappa Home: PO Box 697 Hampden Sydney VA 23943 Office Phone: 434-223-6179. E-mail: wporterfield@hsc.edu.

PORTES, RICHARD DAVID, economics professor; b. Chgo., Dec. 10, 1941; s. Herbert and Abra (Halperin) P.; m. Barbara Diana Frank, 1963; children: Jonathan, Alison. BA summa cum laude, Yale U., 1962; MA, Balliol and Nuffield Colls., Oxford, 1965, DPhil, 1969; DSc honoris causa, U. Libre de Bruxelles, 2000, London Guildhall U., 2000. Asst. prof. econs. and internat. affairs Princeton U., 1969-72; prof. econs. U. London, 1972-94; head dept. econs. Birkbeck Coll., 1975-77, 80-83; pres. Ctr. for Econ. Policy Rsch., 1983—; dir. Ecole des Hautes Etudes, Paris, 1978—; prof. econs. London Bus. Sch., 1995—. Disting. Global vis. prof. U. Calif., Berkeley, 1999—2000; assoc. Nat. Bur. Econ. Rsch., Cambridge, Mass., 1980—; vis. prof. Harvard U., Cambridge, 1977—78; dir. European Corp. Governance Inst.; Joel Stern disting. vis. prof. internat. fin. Columbia Bus. Sch., 2003—. Editor, author: Planning and Market Relations, 1971, The Polish Crisis, 1981, Deficits and Detente, 1983, Threats to International Financial Stability, 1987, Global Macroeconomics, 1987, Blueprints for Exchange Rate Stability, 1989, Macroeconomic Policies in an Interdependent World, 1989, External Constraints on Macroeconomic Policy, 1991, The Path of Reform in Central and Eastern Europe, 1991, Economic Transformation in Central Europe, 1993, European Union Trade with Eastern Europe, 1995, Crisis? What Crisis? Orderly Workouts for Sovereign Debtors, 1995; contbr. numerous articles to profl. jours. Decorated comdr. Brit. Empire; Rhodes scholar; fellow Balliol Coll., 1965-69; Guggenheim fellow, 1977-78. Fellow Econometric Soc.; mem. Coun. Royal Econ. Soc. (exec. com. 1987-92, sec.-gen. 1992—), Econ. Policy (bd. govs., sr. editor 1985—), Coun. on Fgn. Rels., Royal Inst. Internat. Affairs, Commn. Econ. de la Nation (France). Avocation: living beyond my means. Office: London Bus Sch Regents Park London NW1 4SA England E-mail: rportes@london.edu.

PORTIS, ALAN MARK, physicist, researcher; b. Chgo., July 17, 1926; s. Lyon and Ruth (Libman) P.; m. Beverly Portis, Sept. 5, 1948; children: Jonathan, Stephen, Sara, Eliyahu. Ph.B., U. Chgo., 1948; AB, U. Calif., Berkeley, 1949, PhD, 1953. Mem. faculty U. Pitts., 1953-56, U. Calif.-Berkeley, 1956—, prof. physics, 1964-95, prof. emeritus, 1995—, asst. to chancellor for research, 1966-67, asso. dean grad. div., 1967-68, dir. Lawrence Hall Sci., 1969-72, univ. ombudsman, 1981-83, 92-94, assoc. dean Coll. Engring., 1983-87, 94-95. Author: Electromagnetic Fields/Sources and Media, 1978, Electrodynamics of High-Temperature Superconductors, 1993; contbg. author: Berkeley Physics Laboratory, 1964, 65, 66, 71. Fulbright fellow, 1961, 67, Guggenheim fellow, 1965, SERC sr. fellow, U.K., 1991-92. Fellow Am. Phys. Soc.; mem. Am. Assn. Physics Tchrs. (Robert Andrews Millikan award 1966). E-mail: portis@socrates.berkeley.edu.

PORTIS, ARCHIE RAY, JR., plant physiologist, agronomy educator; b. Winston-Salem, N.C., Aug. 17, 1949; s. Archie Ray and Louise (Nichols) P.; m. Diane Marie Hurley, June 20, 1975; children: Eric T., Lisa M. BS in Organic Chemistry, Duke U., 1971; PhD in Biochemistry, Cornell U., 1976. Postdoctoral research fellow U. Munich, 1975-77, Roswell Park Meml. Inst., Buffalo, 1977-78, U. Calif. Sch. Medicine, San Francisco, 1978; USDA plant physiologist U. Ill., Urbana, 1978—, from affiliate asst. prof. to affiliate assoc. prof. agronomy, 1978-87, prof., 1988—. Contbr. articles to profl. jours. R.J. Reynolds Tobacco Co. scholar, 1967. Fellow AAAS; mem. Am. Soc. Plant Biologists, Phi Beta Kappa. Office: U Ill Dept Crop Sci 1201 W Gregory Ave Urbana IL 61801-3838

PORTIS, CHARLES MCCOLL, reporter, writer; b. El Dorado, Ark., Dec. 28, 1933; s. Samuel Palmer and Alice (Waddell) P. BA, U. Ark., 1958. Reporter The Comml. Appeal, Memphis, 1958, Ark. Gazette, Little Rock, 1959-60, N.Y. Herald Tribune, N.Y.C., 1960-64. Author: Norwood, 1966, True Grit, 1968, The Dog of the South, 1979, Masters of Atlantis, 1985, Gringos, 1991. Sgt. USMC, 1952-55, Korea. Presbyterian. Home: 7417 Kingwood Rd Little Rock AR 72207-1734

PORTIS, CLINTON, professional football player; b. Laurel, MS, Sept. 1, 1981; Degree, U. Miami. Running back Denver (Colo.) Broncos, 2002—03, Washington Redskins, 2004—. Named NFL Offensive Rookie of the Yr., AP, 2002; named to NFL Pro-Bowl, 2003. Achievements include mem. NCAA Champion Miami Hurricane's, 2001. Office: 21300 Redskins Park Dr Ashburn VA 20147*

PORTLAND, CHARLES DENIS, publishing executive; b. N.Y.C., July 11, 1952; s. William and Berta Portela. AAS, CUNY, N.Y.C., 1974; AA, U. Md., 1978, BS, 1979; M in Accounting, U. Okla., 1982; postgrad., Nova U. CPA, Fla. Sr. auditor Arthur Anderson & Co., Oklahoma City, 1982-86; sr. fin. analyst Knight Ridder, Inc., Miami, Fla., 1986-88; special project Miami Herald, Miami, Fla., 1988-89; prin. Denis Portela, CPA, Miami Beach, Fla., 1989-93; founder, pres. Grove Mktg. (dba Charlden Consulting), 1990-95; pub. Portland Pub., Miami, FL, 1997—. Cons. Carlson Travel Network, MGM Grand Hotel & Casino, City of Miami, Fla., Microsoft; owner, operator Miami Cruise, 1999—. Author: Portland's Computer Guide, 1996, Personal Computer Reference and Training, 1997, Mighty Good Stuff, 2001, The Crucial Concordance, 2001, The Sanctuary, 2002. With U.S. Army, 1974-80, Germany, Korea. Mem. AICPA's, Fla. Inst. CPA's, Am. Mgmt. Assn., Governor's Indsl. Dev. Bds. Subcomm. on Computing and Data Communications. Lutheran. Office: 2020 NW 1st Ave Miami FL 33127-4902 Fax: 305-519-5789.

PORTMAN, GLENN ARTHUR, lawyer; b. Cleve., Dec. 26, 1949; s. Alvin B. and Lenore (Marsh) P.; m. Katherine Seaborn, Aug. 3, 1974 (div. 1984); m. Susan Newell, Jan. 3, 1987. BA in History, Case Western Res. U., 1968; JD, So. Meth. U., 1975. Bar: Tex. 1975, U.S. Dist. Ct. (no. dist.) Tex. 1975, U.S. Dist. Ct. (so. dist.) Tex. 1983, U.S. Dist. Ct. (we. and ea. dists.) Tex. 1988, Ct. of Appeals, Ffith Cir., 1998. Assoc. Johnson, Bromberg & Leeds, Dallas, 1975-80, ptnr., 1980-92, Arter, Hadden, Johnson & Bromberg, Dallas, 1992-95, Arter & Hadden LLP, Dallas, 1996—2003, Bennett, Weston & LaJone, PC, Dallas, 2003—. Chmn. bd. dirs. Physicians Regional Hosp., 1994-96; mem. exec. bd. So. Meth. U. Law, 1994—; lectr. bankruptcy topics South Tex. Coll. Law, State Bar Tex.; mem. vis. com. Coll. Arts and Scis., Case Western Res. U., 1999-2004. Asst. editor-in-chief Southwestern Law Jour., 1974-75; contbr. articles to profl. jours. Firm rep. United Way Met. Dallas, 1982-92; treas. Lake Highlands Square Homeowners Assn., 1990-93. Mem. ABA, Am. Bankruptcy Inst., State Bar Tex., Dallas Bar Assn., Turnaround Mgmt. Assn., So. Meth. U. Law Alumni Assn. (coun. bd. dirs., v.p. 1980-86, chmn. admissions com., chmn. class agt. program 1986-89, chmn. fund raising 1989-91), 500 Club Inc., Assemblage Club. Republican. Methodist. Office: 1750 Valley View Ln Ste 120 Dallas TX 75234 Home: 9503 Winding Ridge Dr Dallas TX 75238 Office Phone: 214-691-1776 207. E-mail: glennportman@comcast.net., gportman@bwlpc.com.

PORTMAN, JOHN C., JR., architect, developer; b. Walhalla, S.C., Dec. 4, 1924; s. John Calvin and Edna (Rochester) P.; m. Joan Newton, Dec. 23, 1944; children: Michael Wayne, John Calvin III, Jae Phillip, Jeffrey Lin, Jana Lee, Jarel Penn. Midshipman, U.S. Naval Acad., 1944; BS in Architecture, Ga. Inst. Tech., 1950, DFA, 1993, Emory U., 1993, Atlanta Coll. Art, 1993. Diplomate: Registered architect, Ga. With Ketchum, Gina and Sharp, H.M. Heatly, Asso. (Architects), N.Y.C. and Atlanta, 1945-49, Stevens & Wilkinson, Atlanta, 1950-53; individual practice Atlanta, 1953-56; partner Edwards and Portman (Architects), Atlanta, 1956-68; prin. John Portman and Assocs., 1968—; chmn., CEO The Portman Cos., Atlanta, 1971—. Bd. dirs. Nations Bank.; pres. Central Atlanta Progress, 1970-72. Prin. works include: The Regent Hotel, Marina Sq., both Singapore, Embarcadero Center, The Pan Pacific-San Francisco, San Francisco Fashion Ctr., Hyatt Regency O'Hare Hotel, Chgo., Peachtree Center, Atlanta; George W. Woodruff Phys. Edn. Ctr., R. Howard Dobbs Student Ctr., both Emory U., Atlanta, Atlanta Merchandise Mart, Atlanta Apparel Mart, Atlanta Decorative Arts Center, Atlanta Gift Mart, Inforum, One Peachtree Ctr., Kennedy Community Center and Middle Sch, Hyatt Regency Hotel, Westin Peachtree Plaza Hotel, Atlanta Marriott Marquis, Northpark Town Ctr., Riverwood, Greenbriar Shopping Ctr., Olympic Village Housing, all Atlanta, Blue Cross-Blue Shield Bldg, Chattanooga, Ft. Worth Nat. Bank Bldg. and Garage, Brussels Internat. Trade Mart, Dana Fine Arts Bldg. at Agnes Scott Coll, Decatur, Ga., Renaissance Center, Detroit, Bonaventure Hotel, Los Angeles, N.Y. Marriott Marquis, Rockefeller Ctr. renovation, N.Y.C., Shanghai Centre, Dream Lake Villas, Hangzhou Qiantang River City, Shandong Bldg., Guomai Bldg., BAODA Bldg., Senfuli Bldg., S Renzhill Complex, Peoples Republic of China, Capital Sq., Kuala Lumpur, Malaysia. Co-author: The Architect as Developer, 1990. Hon. counsul, Denmark; sponsor Atlanta Symphony; mem. nat. adv. bd. Ga. Inst. Tech. Found. Bd. Inc.; trustee Atlanta Arts Alliance, Nat. Jewish Hosp. and Research Center; Dean's adv. coun. Emory U. Sch. Bus.; dir. Atlanta C. of C. (named famous Georgian 1991). Served with USNR, 1942-44. Decorated knight Royal Order Knights of Dannebrog, Denmark; officer Royal Order of the Crown, Belgium; recipient Ivan Allen award N. Ga. chpt. AIA, 1964; award excellence Am. Inst. Steel Constrn., 1973; Design in Steel award Am. Iron and Steel Inst., 1975; medal for hotel design AIA, 1978; Silver medal for innovative design Ga. chpt. AIA, 1981, Community Devel. award Atlanta Bus. League, 1986, others; named Outstanding Young Man of Year, Ga. Jr. C. of C., 1959; Salesman of Year, Sales and Mktg. Execs., Atlanta, 1968; recipient Exceptional Achievement award Ga. Inst. Tech. Alumni Assn., 1985, Disting. Service award Empire Real Estate Bd., Atlanta, 1984, Martin Luther King Salute to Greatness, 1993, Disting. Community Svc. award Atlanta Urban League Inc., 1991, Disting Svc. award Atlanta Bus. League, 1991, Atlanta Downtown Partnership's Resurgens award Design of Peachtree Plz. Park, 1991, Altanta Downtown Partnership's Resurgens award Design of One Peachtree Ctr., 1993, Horatio Alger award Horatio Alger Assn., 1990, Nat. Home Furnishings Assn. Disting. Svc. award, 1990, Shaping the City award Atlanta Convention and Visitors Bureau, 1988, Trendsetter award Foodsvc. Cons. Soc. Internat., 1987, Torch of Liberty award Anti-Defamation League, 1994; named Man of Yr. Danish Am. Soc., 1986, Father of Yr. Southeast Father's Day Council, 1986; named to Bus. Hall of Fame Coll. Bus. Adminstrn. Ga. State U., 1987, Atlanta Bus. Chronicle, 1991, Atlanta Entrepreneurs Hall of Fame Atlanta Entrepreneurs Network, 1990; named Famous Georgian, Atlanta C. of C.; Paul Harris fellow Rotary Found. Rotary Internat., 1991. Fellow AIA (Atlanta Svc. to Profession award 1992); mem. Nat. Council Archtl. Registration Bds., Am. Inst. Interior Designers (hon.), Soc. Internat. Bus. Fellows (hon.), World Trade Club (founding), Ga. Archtl. and Engring. Soc., Atlanta Rotary Club, Atlanta Action Forum, Omicron Delta Kappa, Tau Sigma Delta Clubs: Commerce (bd. dirs.). Office: John Portman & Assocs 225 Peachtree St NE Ste 200 Atlanta GA 30303-1727

PORTMAN, NATALIE, actress; b. Jerusalem, June 9, 1981; BS in Psychology, Harvard U. Appeared in motion pictures including The Professional, 1994, Developing, 1995, Heat, 1995, Everyone Says I Love You, 1996, Beautiful Girls, 1996, Mars Attacks!, 1996, Star Wars: Episode I-The Phantom Menace, 1999, Anywhere But Here, 1999, Where the Heart Is, 1999, Zoolander, 2001, Star Wars Episode II-Attack of the Clones, 2002, Cold Mountain, 2003, Garden State, 2004, True, 2004; appeared in stage prodns. including Diary of Anne Frank, 1997, The Seagull, 2001. Office: Internat Creative Mgmt 8942 Wilshire Blvd Beverly Hills CA 90211-1934*

PORTMAN, ROB, congressman; b. Cin., Dec. 19, 1955; m. Jane Portman; children: Jed, Will. BA, Dartmouth Coll., 1979; JD, U. Mich., 1984. Ptnr. Head & Ritchey, Cin., 1986-89; assoc. counsel to President of U.S., then dep. asst. to President, dir. Office Legis. Affairs White House, Washington, 1989-92; mem. U.S. Del. to UN Subcom. on Human Rights, 1992, U.S. Congress from 2nd Ohio dist., 1993—, Ways & Means Com., Budget Com., Ethics Com.; mem. select com. Homeland Security; chmn. Rep. leadership. Bd. trustees Springer Sch., The United Way, Hyde Park Community United Meth. Ch.; founding trustee Cin.-China Sister City Com.; former bd. dirs. United Home Care; vice chmn. Hamilton County George Bush for Pres. Campaign, 1988, 92; chmn. Rep. Early Bird Campaign com., 1992; del. Rep. Nat. Conv., 1988, 92; active Hamilton County Rep. Party Exec. com., Hamilton County Rep. Party Fin. Com. Mem. Cin. World Trade Assn. Republican. Office: US Ho of Reps 238 Cannon Hob Washington DC 20515-3502 also: Dist Office 8044 Montgomery Rd Rm 540 Cincinnati OH 45236

PORTMAN, RONALD JAY, pediatric nephrologist, researcher; b. Portsmouth, N.H., June 8, 1950; s. Harry and Sylvia Rosa (Applebaum) P.; m. Joan Marie Welch, June 29, 1974; children: Wendi Alana, Shayna Matana, Solomon Zachary. BS, Northeastern U., 1973; MD, Dartmouth Coll., 1976. Diplomate Am. Bd. Pediat., Am. Bd. Pediat. Nephrology. Commd. 2d lt. U.S. Army, 1976, advanced through grades to maj., 1981; pediatric house officer Fitzsimons Army Med. Ctr., Denver, 1976-79, pediatric nephrologist, 1983-86; chief dept. pediat. Würzburg (Germany) Army Hosp., 1979-81; fellow in pediatric nephrology Washington U., St. Louis, 1981-83; resigned, Fitzsimmons Army Med. Ctr., U. Colo., 1986; pediatric nephrologist, assoc. prof. U. Tex. Med. Sch., Houston, 1986-92, dir. divsn. pediatric nephrology and hypertension, 1992—; dir. pediat. spl. care unit and Hermann Chronobiology Ctr., Hermann Hosp., Houston, 1992—; pediatric nephrologist Fitzsimmons AMC, Univ. Colo., Houston, 1983-86; prof. U. Tex. Med. Sch., 1997—. Mem. med. adv. bd. Nat. Kidney Found. S.E. Tex., Houston, 1986—; cons. M.D. Anderson Hosp., Houston, 1986—, Chronobiology Ctr. Tel Hashomer, Tel Aviv, 1995—; mem. med. rev. bd. End Stage Renal for Disease Network 14, Dallas, 1992-2000; mem. Kidney Disease Outcome Quality Initiative work group, 2000—; mem. cardiovasc. and pend drug adv. bd. FDA, 2003. Contbr. articles numerous pub. to med. jours., chapters to books; editor: Pediatric Neurology. Bd. dirs. Congregation Brith Shalom, Bellaire, Tex., 1990-94. Recipient svc. award Nat. Kidney Found., 1995; numerous rsch. grants. Mem. FDA (cardiovasc.-renal med. adv. panel), Nat. Heart Lung and Blood Inst. (working group on high blood pressure in children), Am. Soc. Transplant Physicians, Am. Soc. Pediatric Nephrology, Am. Soc. Nephrology, Am. Soc. Hpertension, Am. Assn. Medical Chronobiology and Chronotherapeutics (sec., treas.), N.Am. Pediatric Renal Transplant Study Group, S.W. Pediatric Nephrology Study Group, Internat. Pediatric Hypertension Assn. (chmn. exec. com.), Am. Bd. of Pediatrics (assoc., mem. pediat. nephrology sub-bd.). Jewish. Avocations: choir, baseball umpire, tennis, golf. Office: U Tex Med Sch 7431 Fannin St Houston TX 77054-1901

PORTNEY, JOSEPH NATHANIEL, retired aerospace executive, navigation consultant; b. L.A., Aug. 15, 1927; s. Marcus and Sarah (Pilson) P.; m. Ina Mae Leibson, June 20, 1959; children: Philip, Jeffrey. BS, U.S. Naval Acad., 1952. Commd. 2d lt. USAF, 1952, advanced through grades to maj., 1960; with Litton Systems, Inc., Woodland Hills, Calif., 1960—; project engr. Litton Aero Products, 1967-68; program mgr. Litton Aero Products Litton Systems, Inc., Woodland Hills, 1968-72, advanced program mgr. Guidance and Control Sys., 1972-85, mgr. advanced programs Guidance and Control Sys., 1985-98, ret., 1998; pres. NAVSENSE cons., 1998—. Navigator engr. on 3 historic inertial crossings of the North Pole. Author: Portney's Ponderables; creator: Earthshapes, solar compass, pilot and navigator's calendar. Mem. Inst. of Navigation (v.p. 1988-89, pres. 1989-90, Weems award 1994), U.S. Naval Acad. Alumni Assn. (trustee 1980-83). Jewish. Avocation: classical piano. Office: NAVSENSE 4981 Amigo Ave Tarzana CA 91356-4505 E-mail: navsense@earthlink.net.

PORTNEY, LESLIE GROSS, physical therapist; b. N.Y.C., Feb. 17, 1948; d. Harold and Ida (Stein) Gross; m. Merrill B. Portney, May 13, 1979; children: Devon, Lindsay. BA, Queens Coll., N.Y.C., 1968; Cert. in Phys. Therapy, U. Pa., 1969; MS, Med. Coll. Va., 1974; PhD, Lowy cert. in gerontol. studies, Boston U., 1993; DPT, MGH Inst. Health Professions, 2002. Lic. phys. therapist Mass., N.Y. Phys. therapist Rusk Inst. Rehab. Medicine, N.Y.C., 1969—72; lectr. NYU, N.Y.C., 1971—72; asst. prof. Sargent Coll., Boston U., 1974—88, assoc. dean ad interim, 1982—83; rsch. therapist New Eng. Med. Ctr., Boston, 1987—89; prof. MGH Inst. Health Professions, Boston, 1990—, assoc. dir. grad programs in phys. therapy, 1994—2002, dir., prof. program in phys. therapy, 1994—2002, dir. grad. programs in phys. therapy, 2002—. Rsch. cons. Spaulding Rehab. Hosp., Boston, 1993-95; statis. cons. New Eng. Med. Ctr., Boston, 1985-90. Author: Foundations of Clinical Research, 1993 (Hawkins award 1993), 2d edit., 2000; contbr. articles to profl. jours., chpts. to books. Recipient doctoral edn. award Found. Phys. Therapy, 1988. Mem. Am. Phys. Therapy Assn. (sect. on rsch., sect. on edn., sect. on ortho, sect. on geriatrics, Outstanding Rschr. award Mass. chpt. 1986, Catherine Worthingham fellow 2002), Am. Soc. on Aging, Gerontol. Soc. Am., Internat. Soc. Electrophysiol. Kinesiology. Jewish. Office: MGH Inst of Health Prof Charlestown Navy Yard 36 1st Ave Boston MA 02129 Office Phone: 617-726-3170. E-mail: lportney@mghihp.edu.

PORTNEY, PAUL ROGERS, research and educational organization executive; BA in Econs. and Math., Alma Coll., 1967; PhD in Econs., Northwestern U., 1973. Vis. prof. grad. sch. pub. policy U. Calif., Berkeley, 1977-79; chief economist Coun. on Environ. Quality, Exec. Office of Pres., Washington, 1979-80; with Resources for the Future, Washington, 1980—, v.p., dir. Ctr. for Risk Mgmt., Quality of Environment divsn, 1989-95, pres., 1995—. Mem. bd. environ. studies and toxicology NAS; mem. panel on contingent valuation NOAA; exec. com. EPA Sci. Adv. Bd., chmn. environ. econs. adv. com.; lectr. in field; vis. lectr. Woodrow Wilson Sch. Pub. and Internat. Affairs, Princeton (N.J.) U., 1992. Author: Footing the Bill for Superfund Cleanups: Who Pays and How?, others; contbr. articles to profl. jours. Office: Resources for the Future 1616 P St NW Washington DC 20036-1400

PORTNOY, DANIEL, microbiology educator; b. Sept. 3, 1956; married; 1 child. BA in Bacteriology, UCLA, 1978; PhD in Microbiology and Immunology, U. Washington, St. Louis, 1983; postgrad., Stanford U., 1981-83. Postdoctoral fellow Zanvil Cohn Lab. Rockefeller U., 1983-85; from instr. to asst. prof. dept. microbiology and immunology U. Washington Sch. Medicine, 1986-88; asst. prof. dept. microbiology U. Pa. Sch. Medicine, Phila., 1988-92, assoc. prof. dept. microbiology, 1992—. Lectr. in field. Author numerous chpts. to books, reviews and books; mem. editl. bd. Infection and Immunity, 1990—, Jour. Exptl. Medicine, 1992—; reviewer NIH, 1989, 90, 93; contbr. over 40 articles to profl. jours. Am. Soc. for Microbiology Found. lectr., 1990; recipient Nat. Rsch. Svc. award NIAID, 1985-86, Merit award NIAID, NIH, 1995, Rsch. award in microbiology and immunology Eli Lilly and Co., 1996, grants NIH-NIAID, 1993—. Office: U Calif Molecular Cell Biology 401 Barker Hall Spc 3202 Berkeley CA 94720-3202

PORTNOY, DARIN ARTHUR, medical association administrator; b. 1962; MD, PhD, Tulane U., 1989. Diplomate Am. Bd. Family Practice. Chief of staff Indian Health Svc., N.Mex., 1992—97; med. coord. tuberculosis project Doctors Without Borders, Uzbekistan, 1997—98; physician Conejos County Med. Clinic, LaJara, Colo., 1998—. Bd. dirs., v.p. Doctors Without Borders US. Office: Conejos County Med Clinic PO Box 639 19021 State Hwy 285 S La Jara CO 81140

PORTNOY, HAROLD DAVID, neurologist, surgeon; b. Detroit, May 19, 1932; s. Peter and Ethel Portnoy; m. Lynne Ann Laffrey, May 16, 1982; children: Bradley Peter, Lisa Gail Portnoy-Kreger, Steven Mark, Susan Beth. BS in Chemistry, Wayne State U., 1953, MD, 1956. Attending neurosurgeon St. Joseph Mercy Hosp., Pontiac, Mich., 1964—, chief divsn. neurol. surgery, 1987—90; attending neurosurgeon North Oakland Med. Ctr., Pontiac, Mich., 1964—, Crittenton Hosp. and Med. Ctr., Rochester, 1968—, chief dept. surgery, 1991—93. Clin. prof. med. physics dept. physics Oakland U., Rochester, 1983—; mem. adv. bd. Oakland U. Coll. Arts and Scis., Rochester, 1995—; chmn. med.-legal com. Coun. State Neurosurg. Socs., Chgo., 1993—99, chmn. AANS appointees com., 1995—2001; pres., editor Your-.Surgery.Com, West Bloomfield, Mich., 1998—; chief of staff St. Joseph Mercy Hosp., Pontiac, 2004— Cons. editor: Surg. Neurology, 1993—; contbr. articles to profl. jours. Recipient Excellence in Rsch. award, Oakland Health Edn. Program, Ctr. for Med. Edn., 1992, Humanitarian of the Yr. award, March of Dimes, 1992, Robert H. Pudenz Award for Excellence in CSF (Cerebrospinal Fluid) Physiology, Medtronic PS Med., 1998. Fellow: ACS; mem.: AMA, Mental Illness Rsch. Assn. (founding mem. 1993—, mem. exec. com. 1993—, Gold Key award 1998, Pat Elwell Above and Beyond award 1999), Congress Neurol. Surgeons, Am. Assn. Neurol. Surgeons, Soc. for Rsch. into Hydrocephalus and Spina Bifida, Internat. Soc. for Pediat. Neurosurgery, Am. Soc. for Pediat. Neurosurgery (hon.), Forest Lake Country Club. Achievements include research in Hydrocephalus; Intracranial Pressure; Cerebral spinal fluid wave form analysis; patents for Means for cutting nerve tissue; Plug valve for physiological shunt systems; Retractor for soft tissue for example brain tissue; Shunt system resistant to overdrainage and siphoning and valve therefor; Physiological draining system with differential pressure and compensating valves. Avocations: golf, scuba diving, computers. Business E-Mail: hportnoy@michheadspine.com.

PORTNOY, JEFFREY STEVEN, lawyer; b. Bklyn., July 5, 1947; s. Bernard and Edna (Fure) Portnoy; m. Sandi Edelstein, Mar. 29, 1970; 1 child, Carrie Paige. AB in Polit Sci. cum laude, Syracuse U., 1969; JD, Duke U., 1972. Bar: Hawaii 72, U.S. Dist. Ct. Hawaii 72, U.S. Ct. Appeals (9th cir.) 73, U.S. Supreme Ct. 78, U.S. Dist. Ct. No. Mariana Islands 84. With Cades, Schutte, Fleming and Wright, Honolulu, 1972—78; ptnr. Cades Schutte, Honolulu, 1979—. Adj prof media law dept. journalism U. Hawaii, Honolulu, 1986—92; chmn. biden com. U.S. Dist. Ct., 1991—94. Editor-in-chief: Hawaii Employment Law Letter. Pres., bd. dirs. Manoa Valley Theatre, Honolulu, 1980—97; mem. Honolulu Cmty. Media Coun., 1983—; chmn. Honolulu Neighborhood Commn., 1984—88, We The People; mem. Hawaii Bicentennial Commn.; pres., bd. dirs. Hawaii Internat. Film Festival. Recipient Freedom of Press award, Sigma Delta Chi, 1984. Mem.: Def. Rsch. Inst. (HSBA del. to ABA House Dels. 1994—96, DRI Amb. award 1988, Exceptional Performance award 1991—92), Hawaii Def. Lawyers Assn. (lawyer del. 9th cir. jud. conf. 1989—91, assoc. pres. 1991—95), Hawaii State Bar Assn. (bd. dirs. 1990—93, lawyer del. 9th cir. jud. conf. 2003—). Jewish. Home: 5111 Palaole Pl Honolulu HI 96821-1530 Office: Cades Schutte 1000 Bishop St Honolulu HI 96813 Office Phone: 808-521-9221. E-mail: jportnoy@cades.com.

PORTNOY, SARA S. lawyer; b. N.Y.C., Jan. 11, 1926; d. Marcus and Gussie (Raphael) Spiro; m. Alexander Portnoy, Dec. 13, 1959 (dec. 1976); children: William, Lawrence. BA, Radcliffe Coll., 1946; LLB, Columbia U., 1949. Bar: N.Y. 1949, U.S. Dist. Ct. (so. dist.) N.Y. 1952, U.S. Dist. Ct. (ea. dist.) N.Y. 1975, U.S. Ct. Appeals (2d cir.) 1975, U.S. Supreme Ct. 1975. Assoc. Seligsberg, Friedman & Berliner, N.Y.C., 1949-51; atty. AT&T, N.Y.C., 1951-61; vol. atty. Legal Aid Soc. of Westchester, NY, 1966-74; assoc. Proskauer Rose Goetz & Mendelsohn, N.Y.C., 1974-78, ptnr., 1978-94; ret., 1994 Mem. Commn. on Human Rights, White Plains, N.Y., 1973-78; mem. bd. visitors Columbia Law Sch., 1996-02; bd. dirs. Legal Aid Soc. of Westchester County, N.Y., 1975-83, Columbia Law Sch. Assn., 1990-94, Mosholu Montifiore Cmty. Ctr., 1998—; mem. Pres.'s Coun. Yaddo; dir. Muscular Dystrophy Assn., 2000-03. Mem. Assn. Bar City of N.Y. (chair com. legal support staff 1994, mem. Com. on Homeless, Sr. Lawyer's Com. and chair Pub. Svc. Network 2003—), South Fork Country Club (dir. 1997—), The Children's Storefront (dir. 1998—).

PORTOGHESE, PHILIP SALVATORE, medicinal chemist, educator; b. N.Y.C., June 4, 1931; s. Philip A. and Constance (Antonelli) P.; m. Christine L. Phillips, June 11, 1960; children— Stephen, Stuart, Philip. BS, Columbia U., 1953, MS, 1958; PhD, U. Wis., 1961; Dr. honoris causa, U. Catania, Italy, 1986, Royal Danish Sch. Pharmacy, Copenhagen, 1992. Asst. prof. Coll. Pharmacy, U. Minn., Mpls., 1961-64, assoc. prof., 1964-69, prof. medicinal chemistry, 1969—, prof. pharmacology, 1987—, dir. grad. study in medicinal chemistry, 1974-86, head dept., 1974-83; disting. prof. medicinal chemistry, 2000. Cons. NIMH., 1971-72; mem. med. chemistry B sect. NIH, 1972-76; mem. pharmacology, substance abuse and environ. toxicology interdisciplinary cluster President's Biomed. Research Panel, 1975; mem. expert panel of Flavor and Extract Mfrs. Assn. of U.S., 1984—. Mem. editorial adv. bd. Jour. Med. Chemistry, 1969-71; editor-in-chief, 1972—; mem. editorial adv. bd. Med. Chem. series, 1972-77. U.S. Army, 1954—56. Named Highly Cited Rschr., Inst. for Sci. Info., 2001; recipient Ernest H. Volwiler award (oustanding contbns. to pharm. scis., Am. Assn. Colls. Pharmacy, 1984, N.B. Eddy Meml. award, Coll. on Problems of Drug Dependency-NAS NRC, 1991, Recognition award, U. Wis., 1996, Merit award, NIH, 1997, Oak and the Tulip award, European Fedn. Medicinal Chemistry, 1999. Fellow AAAS, Acad. Pharm. Scis., Am. Assn. Pharm. Scientists (Rsch. Achievement award 1990); mem. Am. Chem. Soc. (Medicinal Chemistry award 1990, E.E. Smissman-Bristol-Meyers-Squibb award 1991, Alfred Burger award in medicinal chemistry 2000), Am. Soc. Pharm. Exptl. Therapeutics, Internat. Union Pure and Applied Chemistry (commn. on medicinal chemistry 1978-82, internat. com. med. chemistry 1982-85), Soc. Neurosci., Sigma Xi, Rho Chi (lecture award 1999), Phi Lambda Upsilon. Home: 17 Oriole Ln Saint Paul MN 55127-6334 Office: U Minn Coll of Pharmacy 308 Harvard St SE Minneapolis MN 55455-0353

PORTUONDO, JOSE FRANCISCO, management consultant; b. Havana, Cuba, Mar. 21, 1953; s. Jose Maria and Odette Maria (Diaz) P.; m. Maria Luisa Wilson, Sept. 4, 1977; children: Maria Cristina, Jose Francisco. B of Civil Engring., MIT, 1975, M of Civil Engring., 1976; MBA, Harvard U., 1980. Ops. rsch. analyst U.S. Dept. Transp., Washington, 1975-78; mgr. McKinsey & Co., Inc., N.Y.C., 1980-86; v.p. mktg. Glasrock Home Health Care, Atlanta, 1986-87; dir. Arthur D. Little, Inc., Cambridge, Mass., 1995-96; pres. Decision Analytics, Inc., Newton, Mass., 1987-94, 96—. Coach Newton Girls Soccer, 1987-93. Mem. Harvard Club Boston, MIT Club Boston. Roman Catholic. Avocations: marathon/long distance running, travel, stamp collecting/philately, reading. Office: Decision Analytics Inc PO Box 182 Waban MA 02468-0002

PORTWAY, PATRICK STEPHEN, telecommunications consulting company executive, telecommunications educator; b. June 18, 1939; s. Christopher Leo and Ceciala (King) P.; m. Malle M. Portway: children by previous marriage: Shawn, Pam, Vicki. BA, U. Cin., 1963; MA, U. Md., 1973; postgrad., Columbia U. Regional ADP coord. GSA, Washington, 1963-68; mgr. strategic mkt. planning Xerox Corp., 1969-74; mgr. plans and programs System Devel. Corp., 1974-78; fin. indsl. mktg. exec. Satellite Bus. Sys., 1978-80; western regional mgr. Am. Satellite Co., 1980-81; CEO Applied Bus. Telecomm., Livermore, Calif., 1981-98; prof., lectr. Golden Gate U. Grad. Sch., San Francisco, 1983—. Pub. mag. Teleconference, 1981-98; pub. (newspapers) Discovery Bay, Delta Clippers; prodr. Telecon & Ioccon Confs., 1981-98, CEO ET3 Internet Edn. Co., 1998—. Author: (with others) Teleconferncing and Distance Learning, 1992, 3rd edit., 1997. Presdl. elector Electoral Coll., Va., 1976; candidate Va. State Legislature from 19th Dist., 1971; mem. Discovery Bay Mcpl. Adv. Coun., 1992-96, chmn., 1992; mem. adv. com. Congl. Internet Caucus. 1st lt. U.S. Army, 1963-65. Recipient Internat. Rotary award for Higher Edn., Bombay, India, 1999. Mem. Internat. Teleconferencing Assn. (founder, bd. dirs. 1983-88), Nat. Univ. Teleconferencing Network (mem. adv. bd., bd. dirs. 1986-89), U.S. Distance Learning Assn. (founder, exec. dir. 1987-99), Electronic Funds Transfer Assn. (founder, bd. dirs. 1980), Satellite Profls., Internat. Internet Assn. (pres. 2001—), Internat. Higher Edn. Acad. of Sci., Global Distance Learning Assn. (founder, exec. dir., COO 1998-99), Jaycees (charter pres. Chantilly, Va., Disting. Svc. award Dale City, Va.), Commonwealth. E-mail: portwayinva@aol.com.

PORZAK, GLENN E. lawyer; b. Ill., Aug. 22, 1948; m. Judy Lea McGinnis, Dec. 19, 1970; children: Lindsay and Austin. BA with distinction, U. Colo., 1970, JD, 1973. Bar: Colo. 1973. Assoc. Holme Roberts & Owen, Denver, 1973-80, ptnr., 1980-85, mng. ptnr. Boulder office, 1985-95; mng. ptnr. Porzak Browning & Bushong LLP, Boulder, 1996—. Bd. dirs. Wells Fargo Bank Boulder, Ctr. of Am. West, U. Colo., U. Colo. Mus. Contbr. articles to profl. jours. Bd. dirs. Manor Vail Resorts Condominium Assn., 2001, pres., 2003—; bd. dirs. U. Colo. Found., 2002—. Named Disting. Alumnus U. Colo., 1991. Fellow Explorers Club (bd. dirs. 1995-96, Citation of Merit 1998); mem. Am. Alpine Club (pres. 1988-91), Colo. Mtn. Club (pres. 1983, hon. mem. 1983—), Colo. Outward Bound (trustee 1992-2002, vice chmn. 1997-99, chmn. 1999-2001), Phi Beta Kappa. Achievements include reaching summit of Mt. Everest, climbing highest peak on all seven continents. Home: 405 Baseline Rd Boulder CO 80302 Office: Porzak Browning & Bushong 929 Pearl St Ste 300 Boulder CO 80302-5108

PORZIG, ULLRICH E. retail executive; With May Co., 1982—93, sr. v.p. fin., CFO Foley's, 1988—93; sr. v.p., CFO, treas. Payless ShoeSource, Inc., Topeka, 1986—88, 1996—, Petro Stopping Ctrs. L.P., 1993—96. Office: Payless ShoeSource Inc 3231 SE 6th Ave Topeka KS 66607-2207

POSADA, JORGE RAFAEL, professional baseball player; b. Santurce, P.R., Aug. 17, 1971; s. Jorge Posada Sr. Assoc., Calhoon C.C., 1991. Profl. baseball player N.Y. Yankees, 1995—. Office: NY Yankees Yankee Stadium 161st St and River Ave Bronx NY 10451

POSAMENTIER, ALFRED STEVEN, mathematics educator, university administrator; b. NYC, Oct. 18, 1942; s. Ernest and Alice (Pisk) P.; children: Lisa Joan, David Richard. AB, Hunter Coll., 1964; MA, CCNY, 1966; postgrad., Yeshiva U., N.Y.C., 1967-69; PhD, Fordham U., 1973; Nostrifizierung of Doctorate, U. Vienna, Austria, 1992. Tchr. math Theodore Roosevelt H.S., Bronx, N.Y., 1964-70; asst. prof. math. edn. CCNY, N.Y.C., 1970-76, assoc. prof., 1977-80, prof., 1981—, dept. chmn. dept. secondary and continuing edn., 1974-80, chmn., 1980-86; assoc. dean Sch. Edn., CCNY, N.Y.C., 1986-95, dep. dean, 1995-99, dean, 1999—; dir. select program in sci. and engring. CCNY, N.Y.C., 1978—; dir. initiatives program City Coll. U.K., 1983—; dir. Germany/CCNY Exch. Program CCNY, 1985—, dir. Austria/CCNY Exch. Program, 1987—, dir. Czech Republic/CCNY Exch. Program, 1989—, dir. sci. lectr. program, 1981-94. Chmn. bd. dirs. Salvadori Ednl. Ctr. on Built Environ., 1988-99; supr. math. and sci. Mamaroneck H.S., N.Y., 1976-79; NSF math. devel. program for secondary sch. tchrs. math., N.Y.C., 1978-82; project dir. numerous NSF sponsored math./sci. tchr. devel. insts., 1976-99; cons. N.Y.C. Bd. Edn., 1973-75, N.Y.C. Bd. Edn. Office of Evaluation, 1974-80, N.Y.C. Bd. Edn. Examiners, 1979-92, Ossining Bd. Edn., 1975-83, numerous others; coord. NSF N.E. Resource Ctr. Sci. and Engring., 1980-90; lectr. various confs.; vis. prof. U. Vienna, Austria, 1985, 87, 88, 90, Tech. U., Berlin, 1989, 95, Tech. U., Vienna, 1993-98, Pedgogical Inst., Vienna, 1993—, Humboldt U., Berlin, 1996; dir. N.Y.C. Maths. Project, 1994—, Math for the New Millennium Project, 1995-2000. Author: A Study Guide for the Scholastic Aptitude Test in Math., 1969, Challenging Problems in Geometry, 1970, Challenging Problems in Algebra, 1970, Geometry, Its Elements and Structure, 1972, rev. edit., 1977, Geometric Constructions, 1973, Excursions in Advanced Euclidean Geometry, 1980, 2d edit., 1984, Teaching Secondary School Mathematics: Techniques and Enrichment Units, 1981, 6th edit., 2002, Uncommon Problems for Common Topics in Algebra, 1981, Unusual Problems for Usual Topics in Algebra, 1981, Math Motivators: Investigations in Pre-Algebra, 1982, Math Motivations: Investigations in Geometry, 1982, Using Computers in Mathematics, 1983, 2d edit., 1986, Math Motivators: Investigations in Algebra, 1983, Using Computers: Programming and Problem Solving, 1984, 2d edit., 1989, Advanced Geometric Constructions, 1988, Challenging Problems in Algebra, 1988, 2d edit., 1996, Arbeitsmaterialien: Mathematik, 1994, The Art of Problem Solving: A Resource for the Mathematics Teacher, 1996, Students! Get Ready for Mathematics for SAT-I: Problem Solving Strategies and Practice Tests, 1996, Teachers! Prepare Your Students for Mathematics for SAT-I: Methods and Problem-Solving Strategies, 1996, Deutsch-Englisch Mathematik Worterbuch, 1996, 2d edit., 2000, Tips for the Mathematics Teacher: Research-Based Strategies to help Students Learn, 1998, Problem-Solving Strategies for More Effective and Elegant Solutions: A Resource for the Mathematics Teacher, 1998, Making Pre-Algebra Come Alive, 2000, Making Algebra Come Alive, 2000, Making Geometry Come Alive, 2000, (with Dr. H.A. Hauptman Nobel Laureate) 101 Great Ideas for Introducing Key Concepts in Mathematics, 2001, Advanced Euclidean Geometry: Excursions for Secondary Teachers and Students, 2002, Math Wonders: To Inspire Teachers and Students, 2003, Math Charmers: Tantalizing Tidbits for the Mind, 2003, Pi: A Biography of the World's Most Mysterious Number, 2004; contbr. articles to profl. jours. and newspapers. Trustee Demarest Bd. Edn., 1977-80. Decorated Austrian Cross of Honor for Sci. and Art-First Class, Grand Medal of Honor, Austria, 1994; named Tchr. of Yr. CCNY Alumni Assn., 1993; hon. fellow U. South Bank, London, 1988, Vienna U. Tech., 2003; Fulbright scholar U. Vienna, 1990; recipient Medal of Distinction City of Vienna, 1996, Medal of Honor Technische Fachhochschule Berlin, 1996, 1000 Years Austria commemorative medal Govt. of Austria, 1997, Hon. Univ. Prof. of Austria, 1999. Mem. Math. Assn. Am., Sch. Sci. and Math. Assn., Nat. Coun. Tchrs. Math., (reviewer new publs., referee articles Math. Tchr. Jour.), Assn. Tchrs. Math. N.Y.C. (exec. bd. 1966-67), Assn. Tchrs. Math. N.Y. State, Assn. Tchrs. Math. N.J., Nat. Coun. Suprs. of Math. Home: 634 Caruso Ln Rivervale NJ 07675-6210 Office Phone: 212-650-5471. E-mail: asp2@juno.com.

POSCH, ROBERT JOHN, JR., lawyer; b. Levittown, NY, Feb. 24, 1950; s. Robert John and Maryrose (Finnegan) P.; m. Mary Lou Collins, July 28, 1974; children: Judith Ann, Robert III, Eric. BA, Manhattan Coll., 1972; JD, Hofstra U., 1975, MBA, 1981. Bar: N.Y. 1977, U.S. Ct. Appeals (2d cir.) 1977. From legal asst. to assoc. counsel Doubleday & Co., Inc., Garden City, NY, 1975—87; sec., counsel Doubleday Book & Music Clubs, Inc., Garden City, 1987-2000; v.p. legal postal and govt. affairs Doubleday Direct, Inc., Garden City, 2000—; sr. v.p. legal postal and govt. affairs BOOKSPAN, Garden City, 2000—, chief compliance officer, chief privacy officer, sec. Instr. Nassau C.C., Hempstead, N.Y., 1984—; mem. adv. bd. real estate symposium Hofstra U.; bd. dirs. Crossings, Inc.; v.p. Literary Express sect. Profl. Book Clubs Inc.; spkr. in field. Author: Direct Marketer's Legal Adviser, 1983, What Every Manager Needs to Know About Marketing and the Law, 1984, Marketing and the Law, 1988, Cumulative Supplement, 1989, 90; (with others) The Direct Marketing Handbook, 1984, 91; columnist: Direct Marketing, 1981—; contbr. articles to profl. jours. Mem. ABA, Am. Corp. Counsel Assn. (newsletter editor 1988-92, bd. dirs. Greater N.Y. chpt.), Postcom (bd. dirs., exec. com.), Direct Mktg. Assn. (privacy, use tax and legal lobbying groups, various coms. 1986—), Continuity Mailers Assn., Christian Legal Soc., Nassau Bar Assn. (com. mem. 1977—, AAP Postal Affairs), L.I. Assn., N.Y. State Bus. Coun., Alpha Mu Alpha, Beta Gamma Sigma. Republican. Home: 3151 Grand Blvd Baldwin NY 11510-4826 Office: BOOKSPAN 401 Franklin Ave Ste 100 Garden City NY 11530-5945 Office Phone: 516-490-4628. Business E-Mail: robert.pasch@bookspan.com.

POSCOVER, MAURY B. lawyer; b. St. Louis, Jan. 13, 1944; s. Edward and Ann (Chapnick) P.; m. Lorraine Wexler, Aug. 14, 1966; children: Michael, Daniel, Joanna. BA, Lehigh U., 1966; JD, Washington U., 1969. Bar: Mo. 1969. Assoc. Husch & Eppenberger LLC, St. Louis, 1969-75, ptnr., mem., 1975—. Lectr. Washington U., St. Louis, 1972—79. Editor-in-chief: The Business Lawyer, 1995-96; contbr. articles to profl. jours. Bd. dirs. Childhaven, St. Louis, 1978-92, pres. 1986; pres. Jewish Community Rels. Coun., 1990-92. Mem.: Am.-Israel C. of C. (pres. 2000—02, chair 2002—), Wash. U. Alumni Law Assn. (pres. 1980—81), Am. Judicature Soc. (dir. 1981—87), Mo. Bar Assn. (bd. govs. 1979—81), Bar Assn. Met. St. Louis (pres. 1983—84), ABA (chair bus. law sect. 1997—98, bd. govs. 1999—2002, mem. exec. com. bd. govs. 2001—02, chair ops. and comms. com. 2001—02, chmn. comml. fin. svcs. com. bus. law sect. coun., editor-in-chief jour.). Jewish. Office: Husch & Eppenberger LLC 190 Carondelet Plz Ste 600 Saint Louis MO 63105-3441 E-mail: maury.poscover@husch.com.

POSEN, RICHARD L. lawyer; b. N.Y.C., May 26, 1950; AB, Johns Hopkins U., 1972; JD, NYU, 1975. Bar: N.Y. 1976. Mem. Willkie Farr & Gallagher LLP, N.Y.C. Articles editor Annual Survey Am. Law, 1974-75. Mem. Assn. Bar City N.Y. Office: Willkie Farr & Gallagher LLP 787 7th Ave New York NY 10019-6018

POSEN, ZAC, apparel designer; b. N.Y.C., Oct. 24, 1980; s. Stephen and Susan. Student, Ctrl. St. Martins Coll. Art and Design, London, 1999—2001. Intern N.Y. Costume Inst., Met. Mus. Art, Nicole Miller, Tocca; founder, designer Outspoke LLC, N.Y.C., 2001—. Named to, Crain's N.Y. Bus. "40 under 40", 2004. Office: Outspoke LLC 13-17 Laight St New York NY 10013*

POSES, FREDERIC M. engineering company executive; b. 1942; BBA in Fin., NYU, 1965. Vol. Peace Corps, 1967-69; various positions Allied Corp., 1969-85; pres. plastics and engineered materials divsn. AlliedSignal Inc., Morristown, N.J., 1985-86, pres. fibers divsn., 1986-88, exec. v.p., pres. engineered materials, 1988-98, pres. and COO, 1998-99; chmn. and CEO Am. Standard Cos., Piscataway, NJ, 1999—. Office: 1 Centennial Ave Piscataway NJ 08854-3921

POSEY, ADA LOUISE, human resources specialist; BA, Carleton Coll. Expense mgmt. and pension operation staff Prudential Ins. Co., 1978—85, internal auditing staff, 1985—89; corp. budgeting staff Minn. Mut., 1989—93; assoc. dir. for gen. svcs. Office Adminstrn., The White House, Washington, 1993-96, dep. dir., 1996-97, dir., 1997-99; spl. advisor Office of Nat. Drug Control Policy, Washington, 1999—; sr. policy advisor Dept. of Energy, Washington, 1999-2001; pres. Posey Cons. Group, 2001—03; dir. diversity and compliance Raytheon Tech. Svcs., Reston, Va., 2003—. Trustee Carleton Coll.; mem. Capital City Links chpt., Washington. Office: Raytheon Tech Svcs 12160 Sunrise Valley Dr Reston VA 21910 E-mail: ada_l_posey@raytheon.com., noah0496@aol.com.

POSEY, ELDON EUGENE, mathematician, educator; b. Oneida, Tenn., Jan. 25, 1921; s. Daniel M. and Eva (Owens) P.; m. Christine K. Johnson, Dec. 25, 1943; children: Margaret Posey McQuain, Daniel Marion. BS, East Tenn. State U., 1947; MA, U. Tenn., 1949, PhD, 1954. Instr. U. Tenn., 1954-55; asst. prof. W.Va. U., 1955-59; assoc. prof. Va. Poly. Inst., 1959-61, prof., 1961-64; prof. math. U. NC, Greensboro, 1964-88, prof. emeritus, 1988—, head dept. math., 1964-80. Served to capt. USAAF, 1941-46. Decorated Air medal with 18 oak leaf clusters, DFC, Silver Star, Purple Heart, Bronze Star with 6 oak leaf clusters. Mem. Am. Math. Soc., Math. Assn. Am., Sigma Xi, Pi Mu Epsilon. Home: 4311 Dogwood Dr Greensboro NC 27410-5611 Personal E-mail: eeposey@bellsouth.net.

POSEY, PARKER, actress; b. Laurel, Miss., Nov. 8, 1968; d. Chris Posey. Student, SUNY, Purchase. Appearances include (films) The Wake, 1993, Confused, 1993, Coneheads, 1993, Mixed Nuts, 1994, Amateur, 1994, Sleep With Me, 1994, Frisk, 1995, Party Girl, 1995, Kicking and Screaming, 1995, Flirt, 1995, Waiting for Guffman, 1996, SubUrbia, 1997, The House of Yes, 1997, What Rats Won't Do, 1998, You've Got Mail, 1998, The Misadventures of Margaret, 1998, The Venice Project, 1999, Dinner at Fred's, 1999, Scream 3, 2000, Best in Show, 2000, Josie and the Pussycats, 2001, The Anniversay Party, 2001, The Sweetest Thing, 2002, The Event, 2003, A Mighty Wind, 2003, Laws of Attraction, 2004, (TV) As The World Turns, 1991-92, (TV miniseries) Armistead Maupin's Tales of the City, 1993, More Tales of the City, 1998; screenwriter (with Rory Kelly) Dumb in Love, 1995. Recipient Spl. Jury prize Sundance Film Festival, 1997. Office: William Morris Agy 151 S El Camino Dr Beverly Hills CA 90212-2775

POSEY, TERRY WAYNE, lawyer; b. Springfield, Ohio, Nov. 9, 1950; s. William Eugene and Nancy Lougene (Lakins) P.; children: Terry Wayne Jr., Ryan Christopher; m. Cheryl Ann Poskus, July 1, 2000. BS, U. Dayton, 1983; JD, Capital U. Sch. Law, 1988. Bar: Ohio 1988, U.S. Dist. Ct. (so. dist.) Ohio 1988, U.S. Supreme Ct. 1992. Police officer Dayton (Ohio) Police Dept., 1968-87; pvt. practice law Dayton, 1987—. Recipient Mem. of Yr. award Fraternal Order of Police of Ohio, 1987. Mem. ABA, Ohio State Bar Assn., Dayton Bar Assn., Scottish Rite (trustee), Masons (Dayton pres. bd. dirs., 33 degree, Grand Lodge officer 2002—), Shriners. Home: 7842 Winding Way N Tipp City OH 45371-9243 Office: 7460 Brandt Pike Dayton OH 45424-3240

POSGAY, BETTY MARIE, medical equipment company executive, artist; b. Frankenstein, Mo., Dec. 15, 1933; d. August Peter and Gertrude Johanna (Koenigsfeld) Stiefermann; m. John George Posgay, Jr., June 12, 1954; children: Elaine Marie, Laura Elizabeth, Martin John. Student, U. Mo., 1952-54. Receptionist St. Mary's Hosp., Jefferson City, Mo., 1951; sec. March of Dimes, St. Louis, 1954-57; demonstrator CDI, St. Louis, 1983-86; sec. Archway Med. Supply, Inc., Clayton, Mo., 1988-96; pres. Crown Med. Equipment, Inc. (Southtown), St. Louis, 1996—. Exhibited in group shows at St. Louis Artists Guild/Two Oak Knoll Park, Clayton, Mo., 1998, Am. Art Alliance, St. Louis, 1997. Chmn. Am. Cancer Soc., Affton, Mo., 1984-85; former crusader Heart Fund, and March of Dimes, Affton. Mem. Am. Art Alliance (sec. 1997), Mo. Bot. Garden, Friends of Art Mus. Roman Catholic. Avocations: playing piano, sketching, writing in diary, painting, walking. Office: Crown Med Equipment Inc 5639 S Kingshighway Blvd Saint Louis MO 63109-3508

POSHARD, GLENN W. former congressman; b. Herald, Ill., Oct. 31, 1945; BA, So. Ill. U., 1970, MS, 1974, PhD, 1984. Tchr. high sch.; asst. dir. then dir. Ill. State Regional Edn. Svc. Ctr.; mem. Ill. State Senate, 1984-88, 101st-105th Congresses from 22nd (now 19th) Ill. Dist., 1989-98; tchr., adminstr. John A. Logan Coll., Carterville, Ill.; vice chancellor for adminstrn. So. Ill. U., Carbondale, 1999—. Founder The Poshard Found. for Abused Children. With U.S. Army. Democrat. Office: So Ill U Mail Code 4314 Carbondale IL 62901

POSIN, KATHRYN OLIVE, choreographer; b. Butte, Mont, Mar. 23, 1943; d. Daniel Q. and Frances (Schweitzer) P. BA in Dance, Bennington Coll., 1965; MFA in Interdisciplinary and World Dance, NYU, 1994; studies in composition, 1965-78, studies in ballet, 1965-90, studies in modern dance, 1967-80. Mem. dance co. Am. Dance Theater at Lincoln Ctr., 1965; dancer Anna Sokolow Dance Co., 1965-73; artistic dir. Kathryn Posin Dance Co., NYC, 1972-91; choreographer Eliot Feld Ballet, NYC, 1978, Netherlands Dance Theater, Den Hague, Switzerland, 1980, Alvin Ailey Am. Dance Theater, NYC, 1980; mem. dance faculty U. Wis., Milw., 1984-86, choreographer, 1984-88; tchr., choreographer UCLA, 1988-90, Trinity Coll., Hartford, Conn., 1990-91. Mem. dance faculty, choreographer U. Calif., Santa Barbara, 1986; tchr. dance technique and performance Tchr.'s Coll. Columbia U., spring 1990; tchr. composition and technique Nat. Inst. of Arts, Taiwan, 1991; founding chair Joffrey Ballet Sch., New Sch. U. BFA in Dance, 1998. Choreographer (performing cos./orgns.) Cherry Orchard, Lincoln Ctr., NYC, 1978, Alvin Ailey Am. Dance Theater 1981, Netherlands Dans Theater 84182, Extemporary Dance Co. London, Balletmet, Columbus, Ohio, Milw. Ballet, 1991, 93, 95, 96, Cin. Ballet, 1997; (prin. works) Salvation, Off-Broadway, NYC, 1969, Waves, 1975 (Am. Dance Festival commn.), The Cherry Orchard, NY Shakespeare Festival, 1979, Mary Stuart, Acting Co., 1980, Shady Grove (grantee joint program of Ohio Arts and Humanities Couns. 1991), The Tempest, Am. Shakespeare Festival, Strratford, Conn., 1982, Midsummer Night's Dream, Arena Stage, Washington, 1982, Boys From Syracuse, Am. Repertory Theater, Harvard U., 1983, The Paper Gramophone, Hartford Stage, 1989, Of Rage and Remembrance, 1990 (Premiere of Yr. in Music and Dance, Milw. Jour.), Stepping Stones, 1993 (co-recipient Meet the Composer/Choreographer award Milw. Ballet 1993), many others; subject of documentary Kathy's Dance. Grantee Guggenheim Found., 1978, NY State Coun. on Arts, 1977, 79, 80, Jerome Robbins Found., 1972; grantee Nat. Endowment for Arts 1981, 82, 85-87, choreography fellow, 1995-96; Doris Humphrey fellow Am. Dance Festival, New London, Conn., 1968. Office: Kathryn Posin Dance Co 20 Bond St New York NY 10012-2406 Personal E-mail: Pozndance@aol.com.

POSITAN, WAYNE JOHN, lawyer; b. Newark, Sept. 11, 1948; BA in Govt. magna cum laude, Boston U., 1970; JD, NYU, 1974. Bar: N.J. 1974, U.S. Dist. Ct. N.J. 1974, U.S. Dist. Ct. (ea. dist.) N.Y. 1987, U.S. Dist. Ct. (so. dist.) N.Y. 1989, U.S. Ct. Appeals (3d cir.) 1981, U.S. Supreme Ct. 1989. Assoc. Lum, Biunno & Tompkins, Newark, 1974-82; ptnr. Lum, Danzis, Drasco & Positan, Roseland, NJ, 1982—; mng. ptnr. Lum Hoens Conant Danzis & Kleinberg, Roseland, N.J., 1990—. Author: (with others) Business Torts Desk Reference, 1992, Jury Instructions in Employment Litigation, 1994; assoc. editor Annual Survey of American Law, 1972-73; editor-in-chief N.J. Labor and Employment Law, 1998. Staff sgt. USAR, 1970-76. Mem. ABA (chmn. employment and labor law com. sect. litig. 1990-93, chmn. sect. litig. ann. meeting 1995-96, CLE and programs com. 1994-96, co-chair task force on merit selection of judges 1996-97, coun. mem., sec. litig., 1997-2000, house of del., 2003-, chair commn. MJP, 2000-2002, dir. divisn., 2001-2002), N.J. Bar Assn. (exec. com. labor and employment sect. 1987—, treas. 1992, vice chmn. 1993-95, chmn. 1995-97, co-chmn. EEO com. 1983-87, coord. NLRB 1989-92, gen. coun. 1989-92, 1st v.p., 2004-2005, treas., 2002-2004, sec., 2002, chair fin. ops. com., 2002-2004, chair long term planning com., 2002-2004), Am. Inns of Ct. (master Sidney Reitman Labor and Employment 1993-2004), Confrerie de la Chaine des Rotisseurs (vice conseiller gastronomique Saddle River Valley chpt. 1987—), Essex Fells Country Club, Phi Sigma Delta. Republican. Presbyterian. Avocations: golf, photography, fishing. Office: Lum Danzis Drasco Positan LLC 103 Eisenhower Pky Roseland NJ 07068-1049 Office Phone: 973-228-6730. E-mail: wpositan@lumlaw.com.

POSLER, GERRY LYNN, agronomist, educator; b. Cainsville, Mo., July 24, 1942; s. Glen L. and Helen R. Posler; m. O. Shirley Weeda, June 23, 1963; children: Mark L., Steven C., Brian D. BS, U. Mo., 1964, MS, 1966; PhD, Iowa State U., 1969. Asst. prof. Western (Macomb) Ill. U., 1969-74; assoc. prof. Kans. State U., Manhattan, 1974-80, prof., 1980—, asst. dept. head, 1982-90, dept. head, 1990-98. Contbr. articles to profl. jours. and popular publs., abstracts, book reviews. Fellow Am. Soc. Agronomy, Crop Sci. Soc. Am.; mem. Am. Forage Grassland Coun., Crop Science Soc. Am. (C-3 div. chmn. 1991), Coun. Agrl. Science Tech. (Cornerstone club), Nat. Assn. Colls. Tchrs. Agr. (tchr. fellow award 1978, ensminger interstate dist. teaching award, 1987, north cen. region dir. 1989, v.p. 1990, pres. 1991; life mem.), Kans. Assn. Colls. Tchrs. Agr. (pres. 1983-85), Kans. Forage Grassland Coun. (bd. dirs. 1989-92), Gamma Sigma Delta (Outstanding Faculty award 1991, pres. 1987). Home: 3001 Montana Ct Manhattan KS 66502-2300 Office: Kans State U Dept Agronomy Throckmorton Plant Sci Ctr Manhattan KS 66506 E-mail: gposler@oznet.ksu.edu.

POSNER, DAVID S. lawyer; b. Pitts., Dec. 27, 1945; s. Mortimer B. and Lillian P.; m. Marilyn Hope Ackerman, Aug. 14, 1966; children: Morton J., Jennifer L. BS, Carnegie Mellon U., 1969; JD, U. Pitts., 1972. Bar: Pa. 1972, U.S. Supreme Ct. 1981. Ct. adminstr. Washington County, Pa., 1972-76, asst. dist. atty., 1976-79; ptnr. Goldfarb & Posner, Washington, Pa., 1979-97, Goldfarb, Posner, Beck, DeHaven & Drewitz, Washington, 1997—. Pres. Pa. Council of Trial Ct. Adminstrs., 1972-76; solicitor Clk. of Cts., Washington, 1983—. Mem. sect. 85 YMCA, Washington, 1980—85; chmn. East Washington Zoning Hearing Bd., 1992—; bd. dirs. Washington County Redevel. Authority, 2002—03, chmn., 2003; bd. dirs. United Way, 1979—85; pres. Beth Israel Congregation, 1992—94. With USAR, 1966—72. Mem. ABA, Pa. Bar Assn. (ho. of dels. 1995-97), Washington County Bar Assn. (treas. 1982-83, pres. 1995), B'nai B'rith (past pres.). Home: 149 S Wade Ave Washington PA 15301-4926 Office: Goldfarb Posner Beck DeHaven & Drewitz 26 S Main St Ste 200 Washington PA 15301-6812 E-mail: dsp.gpbdd@verizon.net.

POSNER, DONALD, art historian, educator; b. N.Y.C., Aug. 30, 1931; s. Murray and Frances (Teitel) P.; 1 dau., Anne Tyre. AB, Queens Coll., 1956; MA, Harvard U., 1957; PhD, NYU, 1962. Lectr. Queens Coll., 1957; asst. prof. art history Columbia U., N.Y.C., 1961-62; mem. faculty Inst. Fine Arts, NYU, 1962—, Ailsa Mellon Bruce prof. fine arts, 1975—, acting dir. Inst. Fine Arts, 1978-79, dep. dir., 1980—2002; Robert Sterling Clark prof. Williams Coll., 1973; William R. Kenan, Jr. prof. U. Va., 1976-77. Vis. prof. U. Wash., 1991. Author: Annibale Carracci, 1971, Watteau: A Lady at Her Toilet, 1973, Seventeenth and Eighteenth Century Art, 1971, Antoine Watteau, 1984; editor-in-chief: The Art Bull, 1968-71. Served with USAF, 1951-55. Am. Acad. in Rome fellow, 1959-61; Inst. for Advanced Study fellow, 1976; recipient Charles Rufus Morey award, 1972. Mem. Coll. Art Assn. Am. (dir. 1970-74), Am. Soc. 18th Century Studies. Office: Inst Fine Arts 1 E 78th St New York NY 10021-0178 E-mail: donald.posner@nyu.edu.

POSNER, EDWARD MARTIN, lawyer; b. Phila., Oct. 20, 1946; BA, Amherst Coll., 1968; JD, Harvard U., 1974. Bar: Pa. 1974. Exec. asst. to sec. of pub. welfare Commonwealth of Pa., Harrisburg, 1971-72; assoc. Drinker Biddle & Reath, Phila., 1974-80, ptnr., 1980—. Democrat. Avocation: fly fishing. Office: Drinker Biddle & Reath LLP One Logan Sq 18th & Cherry Sts Philadelphia PA 19103-6996 E-mail: edward.posner@dbr.com.

POSNER, GARY HERBERT, chemist, educator; b. N.Y.C., June 2, 1943; s. Joseph M. and Rose (Klein) P.; children: Joseph, Michael. BA, Brandeis U., 1965; MA, Harvard U., 1965, PhD, 1968. Asst. prof. Johns Hopkins U., Balt., 1969-74, assoc. prof., 1974-79, prof. dept. chemistry, 1979—, Scowe prof. chemistry, 1989—, prof. dept. environ. chemistry, 1982—, chmn. dept. of chemistry, 1987-90. Mem. medicinal chemistry study sect. NIH, 1986-89; cons. Batelle Meml. Inst., Columbus, Ohio, 1983, S.W. Rsch. Inst., San Antonio, Nova Pharm. Co., Balt.; mem. Fulbright-Hays Adv. Screening Com. in Chemistry, 1978-81; Fulbright lectr. U. Paris, 1976; Michael vis. prof. Weizmann Inst. Sci., Rehovot, Israel, 1983; leader Round Table discussion Welch Found. Conf. Chem. Rsch., Houston, 1973, 83; Plenary lectr. Nobel Symposium on Asymmetric Synthesis, Sweden, 1984. Author: Introduction to Organic Synthesis Using Organocopper Reagents, 1980; mem. editl. bd. Organic Reactions, 1976-89; exec. editor Tetrahedron Reports, 1996—. Named Chemist of Yr., State of Md., 1987; fellow Japan Soc. for Promotion Sci., 1991; recipient Johns Hopkins U. Disting. Tchng. award, 1994. Mem. AAAS, AAUP, AAUP, Am. Chem. Soc. (A.C. Cope Sr. Scholar award 2004), Phi Beta Kappa Office: Johns Hopkins U Dept Chemistry 3300 N Charles St Baltimore MD 21218 E-mail: ghp@jhu.edu.

POSNER, JEROME BEEBE, neurologist, educator; b. Cin., Mar. 20, 1932; s. Philip and Rose (Goldberg) Posner; m. Gerta Grunen, Aug. 29, 1954; children: Roslyn, Joel, P.J. BS, U. Wash., 1951, MD, 1955. Intern King County Hosp., Seattle, 1955—56; asst. resident in neurology U. Wash. Affiliated Hosps., Seattle, 1956—59, fellow in neurology, 1958—59; spl. fellow NIH, U. Wash., 1961—63; instr. medicine U. Louisville Sch. Medicine, 1959—61; attending neurologist King County Hosp., 1962—63; asst. prof. neurology Cornell U. Med. Coll., N.Y.C., 1963—67, assoc. prof., 1967—70, prof., 1970—, vice chmn. dept. neurology, 1978—87; asst. attending neurologist N.Y. Hosp., 1963—67, assoc. attending neurologist, 1967—70, attending neurologist, 1970—; assoc. Cotzias Lab. of Neuro-Oncology, Sloan Kettering Inst. Cancer Research, N.Y.C., 1967—76, mem., 1976—; chief neuropsychiat. service, attending physician dept. medicine Meml. Hosp. for Cancer and Allied Diseases, 1967—75, attending physician, 1975—, chmn. dept. neurology, 1975—87, 1989—97, Cotzias chair neuro-oncology, 1986—; Evelyn Frew clin. rsch. prof. Am. Cancer Soc., 1996—. Mem. med. adv. bd. Burke Rehab. Ctr., White Plains, NY, 1973—; adj. prof., vis. physician Rockefeller U. and Hosp., N.Y.C., 1973—75; mem. neurology B study sect. NIH, 1972—76; coun. mem. NINDS, 1998—2001. Author (with F. Plum): Diagnosis of Stupor and Coma, 3d edit., 1980; author: (with H. Gilbert and L. Weiss) Brain Metastasis, 1980, Neurologic Complications of Cancer, 1995; mem. editl. bd.: Archives of Neurology, 1971—76, Annals of Neurology, 1976—80, Am. Jour. Medicine, 1978—93, Neurology, 1992—96; contbr. articles to med. jours.; author: Intracranial Tumor (with DeAngeles), 2002. Served with M.C. U.S. Army, 1959—61. Fellow: AAAS; mem.: AMA, Am. Acad. Arts and Scis., Soc. Neuroscis., Inst. Medicine N.Y. Acad. Scis., Harvey Soc., Assn. Am. Physicians, Am. Physiol. Soc., Am. Neurol. Assn. (pres. 1997—99), Am. Fedn. Clin. Rsch., Am. Assn. Cancer Rsch., Am. Acad. Neurology (Farber Brain Tumor award 1988), Can. Neurol. Soc. (hon.), Alpha Omega Alpha. Office: Meml Sloan-Kettering Cancer 1275 York Ave New York NY 10021-6094 Office Phone: 212-639-7047. Business E-Mail: posnerj@mskcc.org.

POSNER, KATHY ROBIN, communications executive; b. Oceanside, N.Y., Nov. 3, 1952; d. Melvyn and Davonne Hope (Hansen) P. BA in Journalism, Econs., Manhattanville Coll., 1974. Corp. liaison Gulf States Mortgage, Atlanta, 1980-82; dir. promotion Gammon's of Chgo., 1982-83; coordinator trade show mktg. Destron, Chgo., 1983-84; pres. Postronics, Chgo., 1984-87; v.p. Martin E. Janis & Co., Inc., Chgo., 1987-90; chmn. Comm 2 Inc., Chgo., 1990—. Editor: How to Maximize Your Profits, 1983; contbg. editor Internat. Backgammon Guide, 1974-84, Backgammon Times, 1981-84, Chgo. Advt. and Media; columnist Food Industry News. Bd. dirs. Chgo. Beautification Com., 1987, Concerned Citizens for Action, Chgo., 1987, Midwest Bd. Shaare Zedek, Med. Ctr. Jerusalem; mem. steering com. Better Boys Found.; campaign mgr. Brown for Alderman, Chgo., 1987; mem. bd. cons. Little City Found.; mem. benefit bd. C.A.U.S.E.S. Mem. NATAS, NOW, Women in Comm., Am. Soc. Profl. and Exec. Women, Women in Film-Chgo. (bd. dirs.), Mensa, Acad. Arts (v.p.), Ill. Restaurant Assn. (mem. adv. bd.), Chgo. Area Pub. Affairs Group, City Club Chgo. (bd. dirs.), Chgo. Legal Clinic (bd. dirs.). Republican. Jewish. Avocations: politics, reading. Home: 100 E Huron # 3505 Chicago IL 60611 E-mail: kathyposner@aol.com., krp01@aol.com.

POSNER, LOUIS JOSEPH, lawyer, accountant; b. NYC, May 29, 1956; s. Alex Pozner and Hilda G. (Gottlieb) Weinberg; m. Betty F. Osin, June 21, 1986; 1 child, Daniel. BS in Acctg., Drexel U., 1979; MS in Taxation, Pace U., 1985; JD, NY Law Sch., 1989. Bar: NY 1990, NJ 1990, US Dist. Ct. (so. and ea. dists.) NY, 1990, DC 1991, US Ct. Appeals (2d cir.) 1993, US Supreme Ct. 1994. Auditor Arthur Andersen & Co., CPAs, Phila., 1979-81; tax sr. Kenneth Leventhal & Co., CPAs, NYC, 1981-82; tax mgr. Mann Judd Landau, CPAs, NYC, 1983-86; tax dir. Integrated Resources, Inc., NYC, 1986-89; pvt. practice NYC, 1989—; instr. Nat. Bus. Inst., 2003—. Spkr. field. Prodr., dir. TV show Your Legal Rights. Founder, exec. dir. Voter March, 2000—. Mem.: AICPA, ABA, Nat. Lawyers Guild, NY State Bar Assn. (trusts estates sect.), Assn. Atty CPA's, NY County Lawyers Assn. (trusts estates sect.), NY State Soc. CPA's (tax. com. 1985—90, mem. faculty NYC chpt. Found. Acctg. Edn. 1989—90), Assn. Bar. City NY, Mensa (coord. spl. interest group NYC chpt. 1978—99). Home: 160 E 48th St Apt 12T New York NY 10017-1225 Office: 305 Madison Ave Ste 1740 New York NY 10165 Office Phone: 212-490-4500. E-mail: lawfind@verizon.net.

POSNER, PAUL LEONARD, government official; b. Washington, Nov. 16, 1946; s. Bernard and Bess Posner; m. Arlene S. Posner; 1 child, Jennifer M. BA, Miami U. Ohio, 1968; MA, Columbia U., 1972, MPhil, 1989, PhD, 1995. Dir. fed. program review N.Y.C. Office Mgmt. and Budget, 1973-76; evaluator intergovtl. rels. GAO, Washington, 1976-84, asst. dir. intergovtl. rels., 1984-89, assoc. dir. tax policy, 1989-92, mng. dir. budget issues, 1992—. Adj. prof. Georgetown U., Johns Hopkins U., George Uason U. Author: The Politics of Unfunded Federal Mandates, 1998; contbr. articles to profl. jours., chpt. in books. Fellow Nat. Acad. Pub. Adminstrn. (chmn. fed. sys.); mem. ASPA (chmn. intergovtl. mgmt. sect. 1985), Am. Polit. Sci. Assn. (chmn. federalism sect.), Assn. for Budgeting and Fin. Mgmt. (pres. 2000). Avocations: biking, photography. Office: GAO 441 G St NW Washington DC 20548-0001 E-mail: posnerp@gao.gov.

POSNER, RICHARD ALLEN, judge; b. NYC, Jan. 11, 1939; s. Max and Blanche Posner; m. Charlene Ruth Horn, Aug. 13, 1962; children: Kenneth A., Eric A. AB, Yale U., 1959, LLD (hon.), 1996; LLB, Harvard U., 1962; LLD (hon.), Syracuse U., 1986; LLD (hon.), Georgetown U., 1992, U. Pa., 1997; LLD (hon.), Northwestern, 2001, Aristotle Univ. Thessaloniki, 2002; PhD (hon.), U. Ghent, 1995, Univ. Athens, 2002. Bar: N.Y. 1963, U.S. Supreme Ct. 1966. Law clk. to Hon. William J. Brennan Jr. U.S. Supreme Ct., Washington, 1962—63; asst. to commr. FTC, Washington, 1963—65; asst. to solicitor gen. U.S. Dept. Justice, Washington, 1965—67; gen. counsel Pres.'s Task Force on Comm. Policy, Washington, 1967—68; assoc. prof. Stanford U. Law Sch., Calif., 1968—69; prof. U. Chgo. Law Sch., 1969—78, Lee and Brena Freeman prof., 1978—81, sr. lectr., 1981—; circuit judge U.S. Ct. Appeals (7th cir.), Chgo., 1981—, chief judge, 1993—2000. Rsch. assoc. Nat. Bur. Econ. Rsch., cambridge, Mass., 1971—81; pres. Lexecon Inc., Chgo., 1977—81. Author: Antitrust Law: An Economic Perspective, 1976, The Economics of Justice, 1981; author: (with William M. Landes) The Economic Structure of Tort Law, 1987; author: The Problems of Jurisprudence, 1990, Cardozo: A Study in Reputation, 1990, Sex and Reason, 1990, Sex and Reason, 1992, The Essential Holmes, 1992; author: (with Tomas J. Philipson) Private Choices and Public Health: The AIDS Epidemic in an Economic Perspective, 1993; author: Overcoming Law, 1995, Aging and Old Age, 1995, The Federal Courts: Challenge and Reform, 1996, Law and Legal Theory in England and America, 1996, Law and Literature, revised and enlarged edit., 1998, The Problematics of Moral and Legal Theory, 1999, An Affair of State: The Investigation, Impeachment, and Trial of President Clinton, 1999, Frontiers of Legal Theory, 2001, Breaking the Deadlock: The 2000 Election, The Constitution, and the Courts, 2001, Antitrust Law, 2d edit., 2001, Public Intellectuals, 2001, Law, Pragmatism and Democracy, 2003; author: (with William M. Landes) Economic Analysis of Law, 6th edit., 2003, The Economic Structure of Intellectual Property Law, 2003; pres. Harvard Law Rev., 1961—62, editor Jour. Legal Studies, 1972—81, Am. Law and Econs. Rev., 1999—. Fellow: AAAS, Brit. Acad., Am. Law Inst.; mem.: Am. Law and Econ. Assn. (pres. 1995—96), Am. Econ. Assn., Century Assn. Office: US Ct Appeals 7th Cir 219 S Dearborn St Chicago IL 60604-1702

POSNER, ROY EDWARD, retired finance executive; b. Chgo., Aug. 24, 1933; s. Lew and Julia (Cvetan) P.; m. Donna Lea Williams, June 9, 1956 (div. May 1991); children: Karen Lee, Sheryl Lynn. Student, U. Ill., 1951-53, Internat. Accountants Soc., 1956-59, Loyola U., Chgo., 1959; grad., Advanced Mgmt. Program, Harvard U., 1976. CPA, Ill. Pub. acct. Frank W. Dibble Co., Chgo., 1956-61; supr. Harris, Kerr, Forster & Co. (C.P.A.s), Chgo., 1961-66; with Loews Corp., N.Y.C., 1966-98, v.p. fin. svcs., chief fin. officer, 1973-86, sr. v.p., chief fin. officer, 1986-98, ret. Fin. cons. N.Y. Football Giants, Inc., Rutherford, N.J.; bd. dirs. Bulova Italy S.P.A., Milan, Bulova Systems and Instruments Corp., N.Y.C., Loews Hotels Monaco S.A.M., Monte Carlo, Monaco, Loews Internat. Svcs. S.A., Switzerland, G F Corp., Youngstown, Ohio, Taj Mahal Holding Corp., Atlantic City, CNA Surety Corp., Chgo. Mem. editorial com.: Uniform System of Accounting for Hotels, 7th edit. Pres. No. Regional Valley High Sch. Music Parents Assn., 1978-79; trustee Loews Found., N.Y.C. With U.S. Army, 1953-55. Mem. AICPA, Fin. Execs. Inst., Ins. Acctg. and Stats. Assn., Internat. Hospitality Accts. Assn., Am. Hotel and Motel Assn., Ill. Soc. CPAs, N.Y. State CPAs (chmn. com. on hotel restaurant and club acctg. 1980-82), Tri-County Golf Assn. (treas. 1985-88, v.p. 1988-89), Alpine Country Club (bd. govs. 1982-94, exec. com. 1982-90, pres. 1988-90), Delta Tau Delta. Home: 273 Whitman St Haworth NJ 07641-1315 E-mail: sherylroy@aol.com.

POSNER, SIDNEY, advertising executive; b. Syracuse, N.Y., Jan. 14, 1924; s. Harry and Fannie (Hoffman) P.; m. Miriam Frances Kaplowitz, June 8, 1952; children: Steven Charles, Peter Scott, Robert Keith. BS, Syracuse U., 1947. Asst. advt. mgr. Rudolph Bros., Syracuse, 1947-48; copy chief Kaletski Advt. Agy., Syracuse, 1948-50; promotion mgr. Photo Trade News, N.Y.C., 1950-53; asst. to pres. Dobin Advt. Agy., N.Y.C.; pres. S. Posner & Co. Advt. Agy., N.Y.C., 1955-59, Constellation Art Corp., 1959-76, Communicorp, N.Y.C., 1959-76, Bus. Counselors Corp., N.Y.C., 1959-76, Newmark, Posner & Mitchell Inc., N.Y.C., 1959-92, Posner Comm. Inc., Boca Raton, Fla., 1993-94. E-mail: sidandmimi@adelphia.net.

POSPICHAL, MARCIE W. neuroscientist, psychologist, educator; b. Great Lakes, Ill., Feb. 22, 1959; BS in Psychology, Fla. So. Coll., 1985; MA in Psychology, Neurosci., Vanderbilt U., Nashville, 1990, PhD in Psychology, 1991. Tchg. asst. Vanderbilt U., Nashville, 1988—91, faculty lectr. dept. psychology, 1991—95, rsch. assoc. dept. psychology, 1991—97, editl. asst. Jour. Comparative Neurology, 1992—97, asst. dir. programs Ctr. for Molecular Neurosci., 1996—2001, coord. grad. studies Vanderbilt Brain Inst., 1997—2001, asst. dir. programs in neurosci. edn. Vanderbilt Brain Inst., 1999—2001; adj. instr. dept. psychology Fla. So. Coll., Lakeland, 2001—. Neurosci. cons. Bd. of Nat. Health Mus., 1999; lectr. in field; condr. seminars in field; mem. neurosci. coun. com. Vanderbilt U., Nashville, 1999—2001; Assoc. Vice-Chancellor's planning com. for the 2001 Consortium on Neurogenetics Vanderbilt Med. Ctr., 1999—2001, Vice-Chancellor's Com. on Cmty. Outreach, 1998—2001; mem. neurosci. PhD curriculum com. Vanderbilt U., 1997—2001; adj. mem. Ctr. for Molecular Neurosci. Faculty Recruitment Com., 1997—2001. Contbr. articles and abstracts to profl. jours. Vol. WDCN, Nashville, 1999; mem. Safe and Drug-Free Nashville Metro Schs. Com., 1997; vol. reader for the blind WPLN Listening Libr., Nashville, 1992—93.

Co-recipient NSF grantee, 1999; recipient Rsch. Svc. award, Nat. ., 1995; fellow postdoctoral fellow, Vanderbilt U., 1996, 1993—94, 1991—92, grad. rsch. fellow, 1986—88, 1991; grantee Fight for Sight Postdoctoral Tng. grantee, 1992—93. Mem.: Internat. Brain Rsch. Orgn., Soc. for Neurosci. (com. on neurosci. liberacy 2001—), Assn. of Neurosci. Depts. and Programs. Achievements include research in in neuroanatomy; neurotoxic and electrolytic stereotaxic brain lesioning in rodents; also in pressure injectin and iontophoretic application of tract tracing substances such as HRP and its conjugates in non-human primates; also in tract tracing using live slice tissue preparation in non-human primates; other areas. Office: thern Coll Dept Psychology Lakeland FL

POSPISIL, GEORGE CURTIS, human research educator; b. Thomas, Okla., Aug. 8, 1945; s. George Frank and Zelpha Earline (Hensley) P.; children: Heather Elizabeth, Derek Curtis; m. Hoda Nasr, Aug. 24, 2002. Student, Wheaton Coll., 1963-64; BA, U. Okla., 1968; MA, 1971. Tchr. Peace Corps, Maseru, Lesotho, 1973-74; dir. health svcs. fin. project State of Wis., Madison, 1975-76; pub. health advisor USPHS, Rockville, Md., 1972-73, program/policy analyst, 1977—81, 1984—86, congl. liaison, 1989—99, clin. trials policy adv., 1998-2001, contract mgr., 1982-84; dir. Svcs. Crime Victims/Witnesses Project, Tioga County, N.Y., 1986—; pub. health educator Office of the Sec., OHRP, HHS, 2001—. Guest lectr. U. Wis., Summer Inst., Carthage Coll.; analyst biomed. rsch. program NIH, 1989—; sci. editor The Johns Hopkins U. Krieger Mind/Brain Inst., 1993—95; pub. health analyst U.S. Dept. Health and Human Svcs., Office of Sec. Editor: Decde of the Brain, 1990, Maximizing Human Potential: Decade of the Brain, 1991. Mem. Rockville Humanities Commn., 1981-83, spokesperson Neighborhood Planning Com., 1980-82; coordinator mental health svcs. Cuban Refugee Project, Ft. McCoy, Wis., 1980; sec. cmty. adv. com. mental health program Montgomery House, 1982-86; rsch. and tng. adminstr. Cornell U., Ithaca, N.Y., 1986-89; bd. dirs. Family Svc. Mongomery County, 1984-86; legis fellow U.S. Senate Labor and Human Resources Com./Health Office, 1991; mem. county Spl. Olympics Com., 1982-86; mem. Citizens' Planning Subcom. Carroll County Md.; insp. gen. Civil Air Patrol; mem. adv. com. troop 321 Boy Scouts Am.; bd. dirs. Shepherd's Staff Cmty. Svc. program. Mem. Soc. Rsch. Adminstrs. Office: OHRP US Dept Health and Human Svcs Office of Sec Tower Bldg Rockville MD 20852-3802 E-mail: gpospisil@os.osphs.dhhs.gov.

POSPISIL, LEOPOLD JAROSLAV, anthropology and law educator; b. Olomouc, Czechoslovakia, Apr. 26, 1923; came to U.S., 1949, naturalized, 1954; s. Leopold and Ludmila (Petrlak) P.; m. Zdenka Smyd, Jan. 31, 1945; children: Zdenka, Mira. Juris Universae Candidatus, Charles U., Prague, Czechoslovakia, 1947, JD, 1991; BA in Sociology, Willamette U., Salem, Oreg., 1950; MA in Anthropology, U. Oreg., 1952; PhD, Yale U., 1956; ScD (hon.), Willamette U., 1969; PhD (hon.), Charles U., Prague, Czech Rep., 1994. Instr. Yale U., New Haven, 1956-57, asst. prof., 1957-60; asst. curator Peabody Mus., 1956-65, assoc. prof., 1960-65, prof., curator, 1965-93, dir. divsn. anthropology, 1966-93; prof. anthropology, 1965-93; prof. and curator emeritus, 1993—. Dir. Peabody Mus. Anthropology divsn. Yale U., New Haven, 1966—93; Robert Merton Prof. Law U. Munich, Germany, 1978—79; vis. prof. Anthropology Charles U., Prague, Czech Republic, 1991—; vis. prof. Law Capetown U., South Africa, 1989; DFC prof. Law U. Munich, 1982. Author: Kapauku Papuans and Their Law, 1958, Kapauku Papuan Economy, 1963, Kapauku Papuans of West New Guinea, 1963, Anthropology of Law, 1971, Ethnology of Law, 1972, Anthropologie des Rechts, 1981, Sprache, Symbole und Symbolverwendungen in Ethnologie, Kulturanthropologie, Politik, Religion und Recht, 1993, Obernberg: Quantitative Analysis of a Tyrolean Economy, 1996, Etnologie Prava, 1997, Sociocultural Anthropology, 2004; contbr. articles to profl. jours. Guggenheim fellow, 1962, NSF fellow, 1962, 64-65, 67-71, NIMH fellow, 1973-79; Social Sci. Rsch. Coun. grantee, 1966. Fellow AAAS, N.Y. Acad. Scis., Am. Anthrop. Assn.; mem. NAS, Conn. Acad. Arts and Scis., Explorers Club, Czechoslovakian Acad. Arts and Scis. (past pres.), Coun. Free Czechoslovakia, Assn. for Polit. and Legal Anthropology (pres.-at-large), Assn. for Social Anthropology in Oceania, Soc. for Econ. Anthropology, Sigma Xi. Independent. Avocations: gardening, mountain climbing. Home: 554 Orange St New Haven CT 06511-3819 Office: 51 Hillhouse Ave New Haven CT 06520-3703 Office Phone: 203-432-3771. E-mail: anthropology@yale.edu.

POSS, JEFFERY SCOTT, architect, educator; b. Harvey, Ill., May 20, 1956; m. Barbara Young Cook, May 1, 1999. BAS, U. Ill., 1978, MArch, 1980. Intern architect Charles Kober Assocs., Chgo., 1980-81, Skidmore, Owings and Merrill, Chgo., 1981; designer Newman/Lustig and Assocs., Chgo., 1983-84; design assoc. Kevin Roche John Dinkeloo and Assocs., Hamden, Conn., 1985-87; project architect and designer Tai Soo Kim Assocs., Hartford, Conn., 1987-89; pvt. practice Urbana, Ill., 1989—; assoc. prof. U. Ill. Sch. Arch., Champaign-Urbana, Ill., 1989—. Vis. prof. Glasgow Sch. Art, 1999, 2001; design cons. Isaksen Glerum Archs., P.C., Urbana, 2001—; invited juror, lectr. in field. Contbr. articles to profl. jours. Recipient 1st Alt. Paris prize, Nat. Inst. for Archtl. Edn., 1981, 1st pl., Champaign Pk. Dist./AIA, 1989, Nat. Design award, Concrete Steel Reinforcing Inst./AIA, 1992, 2d pl. WWII Meml., State of Md., 1996, Merit award, Saluda Shoals Amphitheater, State of N.C., 2001. Mem. AIA (Excellence in Edn. Honors award 1993, Ctrl. Ill. award for design excellence, 1993, 97, 2000), Am. Soc. Archtl. Perspectives (Excellence in Graphic Representation Architecture award 1990, 93, 1st Pl. Francis J. Plym Travelling fellow 2004). Office Phone: 217-333-1992. Business E-Mail: poss@uiuc.edu.

POSS, STEPHEN DANIEL, lawyer; b. Buffalo, Jan. 13, 1955; s. Gilbert H. and Bernice L. (Lippman) Poss; m. Jane Fitz Simon, 1990. BA magna cum laude, Amherst Coll., 1978; JD, U. Chgo., 1981. Bar: N.Y. 1982, Mass. 1988; U.S. Dist. Ct. (so. dist.) N.Y. 1984, U.S. Dist. Ct. Mass. 1988; U.S. Tax Ct. 1983; U.S. Supreme Ct. 1986; U.S. Ct. Appeals (1st cir.) 1989, U.S. Ct. Appeals (fed. cir.) 1992. Assoc. Cravath, Swaine & Moore, N.Y.C., 1981-87, Goodwin Procter LLP, Boston, 1988-89, ptnr., 1989—. Teaching asst. to prof. Henry Steele Commager, 1977; lectr. Mass. Continuing Legal Edn., 1987—, Mass. Bar Assn. Ednl. Seminars, 1992-94; seminar chmn. SEC Inst. II, 1998; lectr. Nasdaq Exec. Forum, 1998, 2001; mem. civil litigation curriculum com. Mass. Continuing Legal Edn., 1997—; lectr. SEC Inst., 1999-2001, mem. nat. adv. bd., 2001--; mem. Nasdaq Investor Rels. Forum, 2000. Advisor campaign Bill Guy for U.S. Senate from N.D., 1974, Quentick Burdick for U.S. Senate, N.D., 1976, Bill Bradley for U.S. Senate, N.J., 1978, Gary Hart for U.S. Senate, Colo., 1980, Jeff Bingaman for U.S. Senate, N.Mex., 1982; pro bono counsel to Dem. Nat. Com., 1986-87; bd. dirs. Internat. Forum, N.Y.C., 1984; counsel of N.Y. Law Assocs., N.Y.C., 1985; assoc. dir., bd. dirs. Mass. Audubon Soc., 1997-2000, adv. counsel, 2001—. John Woodruff Simpson fellow, 1978. Mem.: ABA (vice chair securities litigation subcom. bus. law sect. 2000—), SEC Inst., Inc. (nat. adv. bd. 2001—), Boston Bar Assn., Mass. Bar Assn. (vice chair bus. litigation com. 1992—94), Internat. Churchill Soc. Office: Goodwin Procter LLP Exchange Pl Boston MA 02109-2803 E-mail: sposs@goodwinprocter.com.

POST, AUGUST ALAN, economist, artist; b. Alhambra, Calif., Sept. 17, 1914; s. Edwin R. and Edna (Stickney) P.; m. Helen E. Wills, Nov. 21, 1940; 1 child, David Wills. AB, Occidental Coll., 1938; student, Chouinard Inst. Art, 1938; MA, Princeton U., 1940; LLD, Golden Gate U., 1972, Occidental Coll., 1974, Claremont Grad. Sch., 1978. In banking bus., 1933-36; instr. econs. Occidental Coll., 1940-42; asst. prof. Am. U., 1943; economist Dept. State, 1944-45; rsch. dir. Utah Found., 1945-46; chief economist, adminstrv. analyst State of Calif., 1946-50, state legis. analyst, 1950-77. Cons. Com. Higher Edn. and State, 1964; mem. Nat. Com. Support of Pub. Schs., 1967; mem. nat. adv. panel Nat. Ctr. Higher Edn. Mgmt. Systems, 1971-72; chmn. Calif. Gov.'s Commn. on Govt. Reform, 1978; mem. faculty U. So. Calif. Grad. Sch. Pub. Adminstrn., 1978-80; Regents' prof. U. Calif., Davis, 1983, vis. prof., 1984-85; spl. cons. Touche Ross and Co., 1977-87; cons., interim exec. dir. Calif. Commn. for Rev. of Master Plan for Higher Edn., 1985; mem. adv. bd. Calif. Tomorrow nat. shows and one-man shows; dir. Crocker Art Gallery Assn., pres., 1966-67. Trustee U. Calif., Berkeley Art Mus., 1986-91; mem. adv. com. on future ops. Coun. State Govts., 1965; bd. mgrs., pres. YMCA; bd. dirs. Sacramento Civic Ballet Assn.; trustee Calif. Coll. Arts and Crafts, 1982-86; chmn. Calif. State Task Force on Water Future, 1981-82, Sacramento Regional Found., bd. dirs., 1983-91; bd. dirs. Calif. Mus. Assn., pres., 1976-77, Policy Analysis for Calif. Edn., 1985—, Senate Adv. Commn. on Control of Cost of State Govt., 1986—, Pub. Policy Inst. Calif., 1994-2004; co-chmn. Calif. Citizen's Budget Commn., 1992-99, chmn., 1999—; chmn. Citizen's Commn. on Ballot Initiatives, 1992—, Catalonia Sister State Task Force, 1988—, Commn. on Innovation, Calif. Cmty. Colls., 1992; chair Judicial Coun. Select Com. on Judicial Retirement, 1993—; mem. Supreme Ct. Select Com. Judicial Ethics, 1995-96; bd. dirs. Ctrl. Valley Found., 1994-99. With USNR, 1943-44. Mem. Nat. Acad. Pub. Adminstrn., Phi Beta Kappa, Kappa Sigma. Home: 1900 Rockwood Dr Sacramento CA 95864-1527 Personal E-mail: aphp@wnet.com.

POST, AVERY DENISON, retired church official; b. Norwich, Conn., July 29, 1924; s. John Palmer and Dorothy (Church) P.; m. Margaret Jane Rowland, June 8, 1946; children: Susan Post Ross, Jennifer C., Elizabeth Post Elliott, Anne Post Roy. BA, Ohio Wesleyan U., 1946; B.D., Yale U., 1949, S.T.M., 1952; L.H.D. (hon.), Lakeland Coll., Sheboygan, Wis., 1977; D.D. (hon.), Chgo. Theol. Sem., 1978, Middlebury Coll. (Vt.), 1978, Defiance Coll. (Ohio), 1979; LL.D. (hon.), Heidelberg Coll. (Ohio), 1982, Chapman Coll.; Litt.D. (hon.), Elmhurst Coll. Ordained to ministry, 1949; pastor chs. in, 1946-63; sr. minister Scarsdale (N.Y.) Congl. Ch., 1963-70; minister, pres. Mass. conf. United Ch. Christ, 1970-77; pres. United Ch. Christ, N.Y.C., 1977-89; mem. central com. World Council Chs., 1978-91; exec. com., bd. govs. Nat. Council Chs., 1977-89. Moderator, planning com. 7th Gen. Assembly World Coun. Chs.; lectr. Bible Adelphi Coll., Garden City, N.Y., 1958-59; Luccock lectr. Yale U. Div. Sch., 1961; lectr. homiletics Union Sem., N.Y.C., 1967-69, bd. dirs., 1967-77; trustee Andover Newton Theol. Sem., 1970-80, del. numerous internat. ch. meetings, sr. fellow Hartford Sem., 1989-93. Bd. dirs. Bridges for Peace, 1990-94; exec. dir. Bangor Theol. Sem., Hanover, N.H., 1991-93. With USNR, 1943-45. Decorated Comdr.'s Cross (Federal Republic Germany), 1990; recipient 1st Ecumenical award Mass. Coun. Chs., 1976; Disting. Achievement award Ohio Wesleyan U., 1983 Mem. PTA (life), Randolph Mountain Club (N.H.), Phi Beta Kappa, Omicron Delta Kappa. Democrat.

POST, DAVID ALAN, media executive; b. N.Y.C., Oct. 20, 1941; s. Emil R. and Ruth (Rosen) P.; m. Arline Goldbrum, June 10, 1962 (div. 1981); children: Randee, Lori, Jill; m. Katlean de Monchy, Dec. 13, 1984; 1 dau., Emily Hart. Student, CCNY, 1959-61; grad., Fleigenheimer Ins. Inst., 1961, N.Y. Inst. Fin., 1968. Sales rep. Aetna Life Ins. Casualty, Hartford, Conn., 1961-63; sales mgr. Globe Rubber Products, Phila., 1963-67; ptnr. Zuckerman Smith and Co., N.Y.C., 1968-71; dir. corp. fin. Andersen and Co., N.Y.C., 1971-72; exec. v.p., dir. R.K. Pace Post Investment Bankers, N.Y.C., 1973-76; chmn., chief exec. officer, founder Page Am. Group, Inc., Hackensack, N.J., 1976-86; co-founder, bd. dirs. Cellular Sys. Inc., 1991-92; chmn., founder Channel Am. TV Network, N.Y.C., 1987-96; chmn., co-founder Can Do Woman TV & Other Media, N.Y.C., 1996-2000; chmn., CEO UMagic Systems, Inc., an Internet Tech. Co., N.Y.C., 2000—; chmn., exec. prodr. Can do Woman div. of Nextpert News, N.Y.C., 2000—; exec. prodr. Nextpert News Network, 2002—. Contbr. articles to INC. mag.; creator several TV series. Mem. Nat. Assn. TV Programming Execs. Republican. Jewish. Avocation: writing. Office: Nextpert News Network 350 Fifth Ave Ste 5600 New York NY 10118 Home: 35 Sutton Pl #150 New York NY 10022-2464 E-mail: david@nextpert.com.

POST, DIANA CONSTANCE, retired librarian; b. Anoka, Minn., Oct. 17, 1929; d. Kenneth Fred and Emma Constance (Fredrickson) Davis; husband dec., June 1996; children: Leslie Post, Paul Post, Tom Post. BS, U. Minn., 1970, MLS, 1976. Cert. libr., media specialist, Minn. Libr., media specialist Lake City (Minn.) H.S., 1970-94. Bd. dirs. Zumbrota (Minn.) Pub. Libr.; mem. SELCO governing bd. regional libr. sys., Rochester, Minn., 1980-86; pres. SELCO exec. com., 1984-86; SELS adv. com., 1990-94. Editor Lake City Sch. Dist. News, 1988-89. Scholar LaVerne Noyes Found., 1947-48, Delta Delta Delta, 1949. Mem. Beta Phi Mu. Avocations: golf, swimming, volunteering. Home: 695 Jefferson Dr Zumbrota MN 55992-1103 E-mail: DPost3@aol.com.

POST, GERALD STEVEN, veterinarian; b. Lake Success, N.Y., June 16, 1961; s. Stanley and Sandra Mae (Newman) P. BS with distinction, Cornell U., 1983; DVM, U. Minn., 1988. Diplomate Am. Coll. Veterinary Internal Medicine. Intern Animal Med. Ctr., N.Y.C., 1988-89, resident in oncology, 1990-92; staff oncologist Darien (Conn.) Animal Hosp., 1992-94, Companion Animal Hosp., Belmont, Calif., 1995-97, Vet. Referral and Emergency Ctr., Norwalk, Conn., 1997—; founder and pres. Animal Cancer Found. Co-author: Tigers of the World, 1987. Recipient Excellence in Feline Medicine and Surgery award Assn. Feline Practioners, 1988. Mem. Am. Vet. Med. Assn., N.Y. Acad. Scis., Conn. Vet. Med. Assn., Phi Kappa Phi, Phi Zeta. Avocations: tennis, skiing, rollerblading. Office: Vet Referral Emer Ctr 123 W Cedar St Norwalk CT 06854*

POST, GERALD V. business educator; b. Chippewa Falls, Wis., Nov. 27, 1955; s. Vernon Otto and Doris Post; m. Sarah S. Post, Aug. 14, 1982. BA, U. Wis., Eau Claire, 1978; PhD, Iowa State U., 1983. Asst. prof. Oakland U., Rochester Hills, Mich., 1982-89; prof. Western Ky. U., Bowling Green, 1989-99; prof. dept. bus. U. of the Pacific, Stockton, Calif., 1999—. Cons. analyst/programmer The Wala Group, Arden Hills, Minn., 1985-99. Author: Management Information Systems, 2003; contbr. articles to profl. jours. Office: Univ of the Pacific 3601 Pacific Ave Stockton CA 95211-0197

POST, GLEN FLEMING, III, telecommunications executive; b. El Dorado, Ark., Oct. 4, 1952; s. Glen F. Jr. and Mary L. (Tubberville) P.; children: Brad, Luke, Matt. BS in Acctg., La. Tech. U., 1974, MBA, 1976. Pvt. practice tax acctg., 1974-76; dir. fin. reporting Century Telephone Enterprises, inc., Monroe, La., 1982-83; v.p., 1983-87; treas., 1984-86; CFO, 1986—; exec. v.p. & COO, 1987-90; pres. & COO CenturyTel, Inc. (formerly Century Telephone EnterprisesInc.), 1990—. Mem. Am. Mgmt. Assn., STICC (subcom. acctg.), Beta Alpha Psi. Home: RR 3 Box 225 Farmerville LA 71241-9803 Office: CenturyTel Inc 100 Century Park Monroe LA 71203

POST, JERRY T, retail executive; B in econ., Hartwick Coll. Gen. mdse. mgr., NY region Sears Roebuck and Co., 1976—80, territorial mdse. mgr., 1980—82, nat. mdse. mgr., sporting goods, 1984—87, nat. mgr. hardware stores, 1987—91, nat. mdse. mgr., automotive, 1991—92, nat. bus. mgr., home improvement, 1993—96, v.p. and gen. mgr., the gt. indoors, 1996—98, pres. hardware stores, 1998—99; sr. v.p. gen. mgr. home improvement category, 1999—2002; sr. v.p., gen. mgr. Sears off mall strategy, Sears retail for Sears Sears Roebuck and Co., 2002—. Office: Sears Roebuck and Co 3333 Beverly Rd Hoffman Estates IL 60179

POST, PETER DAVID, lawyer; b. Reading, Pa., Jan. 2, 1947; s. Carl B. and Frances (Gaughan) P.; children: Michael, Elizabeth. BS, Pa. State U., 1968; JD, Harvard U., 1971. Bar: Pa. 1971, La. 1974. Assoc. Reed, Smith, Shaw & McClay, Pitts., 1975-81, ptnr., 1982—, dept. head, 1992—2000. Commr. Upper St. Clair (Pa.) Twp., 1989-93. Lt. USN, 1971-75. Avocations: golf, skiing. Office: Reed Smith Shaw & McClay 435 6th Ave Pittsburgh PA 15219-1886

POST, RICHARD BENNETT, retired human resources executive; b. Clyde, Ohio, July 5, 1936; s. Robert Irving and Elinor May (Bennett) P.; m. Nancy Jane Wardlow, Aug. 31, 1956; children: David Bennett, Todd McKinley, Amy Ellen, Brett Richard, Brina Marie. BS in Psychology, Iowa State U., 1958; student, Ohio U., Athens, 1954-56; postgrad., George Washington U., 1959-60, So. Ill. U., Edwardsville, 1972-74. With U.S. Civil Svc. Commn., 1958-79, chief evaluation div., 1967-71, chief staffing div., 1971-74, dep. reg. dir., 1974-79; dep. assoc. dir. staffing U.S. Office Pers. Mgmt., Washington, 1979-81, assoc. dir. staffing, 1982-86, dir. Washington area svc. ctr., 1986-94; retired, 1994. Cert. lay spkr. United Meth. Ch., 1973—; treas. Meadows Homeowners Assn., 2000—. Recipient Dirs.' Disting. Svc. award U.S. Office Pers. Mgmt., 1986, Dirs.' citation for Exemplary Pub. Svc., 1994. Mem. AARP (pres. King George Area chpt. 2003-04), Sr. Execs. Assn. (life), Fed. Exec. Inst. Alumni Assn., Vienna Choral Soc. (pres. 1987-89), Masterworks Chorus, King George, Va. Avocations: woodworking, singing, gardening. E-mail: Postrn@Worldskyline.com.

POST, RICHARD HENRY, pharmaceuticals executive; b. Glendale, Calif., May 3, 1956; s. Henry A. and Doris J. P. BA, Simpson Coll., 1978; M in Edn., Rutgers U., 1989. Tchr. Matawan Regional H.S., Aberdeen, NJ, 1980—89; guidance counselor Plainfield (N.J.) H.S., 1990, Bound Brook (N.J.) H.S., 1990—92; regional dir. Solvay Pharm., Inc., Flemington, NJ, 1998—. Home and Office: Solvay Pharm 32 Windham Ct Flemington NJ 08822

POST, ROBERT CHARLES, law educator; b. Bklyn., Oct. 17, 1947; s. Ted and Thelma (Feifel) P.; m. Fran Layton, Jan. 22, 1981; children: Alexander, Amelia. AB, Harvard U., 1969, PhD, 1980; JD, Yale U., 1977. Bar: D.C. 1979, Calif. 1983. Law clk. to chief judge U.S. Ct. Appeals (D.C. cir.), 1977-78; law clk. to justice William Brennen Jr. U.S. Supreme Ct. D.C., 1978-79; assoc. Williams & Connelly, Washington, 1980-82; acting prof. law U. Calif., Berkeley, 1983-87, prof. law, 1987-94, Alexander F. and May T. Morrison prof. law, 1994—. Author: Constitutional Domains, 1995; editor: Law and the Order of Culture, 1991, Censorship and Silencing: Practices of Cultural Regulation, 1998; co-editor: Race and Representation: Affirmative Action, 1998, Human Rights in Political Transistions: Gettysburg to Bosnia, 1999, Civil Society and Government, 2001; co-author: Prejudicial Appearances: the Logic of America Antidisaimation Law, 2001. Gen. counsel AAUP, 1992-94. Fellow Guggenheim Found., 1990-91, Am. Coun. Gen. Socs., 1990-91. Mem. AAUP, Am. Acad. Arts and Scis. Office: U Calif Sch Law Boalt Hall Berkeley CA 94720

POST, RUTH-ELLEN, lawyer, educator; b. Audubon, N.J., Mar. 6, 1946; d. Theodore J. and Margaret E. Post; m. D.R. Karklin (div. 1981); 1 child, Kenneth D. Karklin; m. Dale H. Corliss, Mar. 23, 1984; 1 child, Rebecca Post Corliss. BA, Montclair State U., 1967; JD, Rutgers U., Camden, N.J., 1975. Bar: N.J. 1976, Mass. 1979, N.H. 1987. Gen. practice law William V. Eisenberg, Esq., Haddonfield, N.J., 1975-76; sole practitioner Medford, N.J., 1976-78, Pittsfield, Mass., 1983-84, Pelham, N.H., 1987-88; prof., chmn. dept. Rivier Coll., Nashua, NH, 1988—2001; prof. legal skills Franklin Pierce Law Ctr., Concord, NH, 2001—02; arbitrator Nat. Assn. Securities Dealers, 2001—. Mem. certifying bd. Nat. Assn. Legal Assts., Tulsa, 1994-98; bd. dirs. Am. Assn. for Paralegal Edn., Overland Park, Kans., 1996-98. Author: (textbook) Paralegal Internships: Finding, Managing, and Transitioning Your Career, 1999; co-author: (manual) Preventing Unauthorized Practice of Law: For the Paralegal in New Hampshire, 1998. Mem. Pelham Planning Bd., 1986-88. Named Atty. of Yr., Paralegal Assn. N.H., 1996. Mem. N.H. Bar Assn. (chair paralegal task force 1994, mem. com. on unauthorized practice of law 1996-98).

POST, STEPHEN GARRARD, theologian, philosopher, educator; b. Bayshore, N.Y., May 6, 1951; s. Henry Albertson Van Zo and Marguerite Magee Post. MA in Religious Studies, U. Chgo., 1979; PhD in Ethics and Soc., U. Chgo., 1983. Prof. dept. humanities Marymount Coll., Tarrytown, NY, 1985—88; prof. dept. bioethics Sch. Medicine, Case Western Res. U., Cleve., 1988—. Mem. nat. ethics adv. bd. Alzheimer's Assn., Chgo., 1997—; bd. advisors John Templeton Found., Radnor, Pa., 1998—2002; pres. Inst. for Rsch. on Unltd. Love, Altruism, Compassion, Svc., Cleve., 2001—. Author: (book) The Moral Challenge of Alzheimer Disease, 2000; editor-in-chief (ency.) Ency. of Bioethics, 2003. Episcopalian. Avocations: sailing, gardening, writing. Office Phone: 216-368-6205.

POST, STEPHEN LIGHTNER, psychiatrist, psychoanalyst, educator; b. St. Louis, May 4, 1927; s. Lawrence Tyler Post and Bernice Dorothy Clute Lightner; m. Ann Whelan, Aug. 31, 1953 (dec. Dec. 1958); m. Jane Conant, June 1960 (div. Oct. 1975); children: Nancy Whelan Post Hunter, Kenneth Conant, Louise Lightner, Eric Stephen; m. Ellen Eisendrath, Nov. 8, 1975; stepchildren: William C. Steinert, Sylvia C. Steinert, Eric C. Steinert. AB cum laude, Princeton U., 1950; MD, Columbia U., 1957; grad., Chgo. Inst. for Psychoanalysis, 1974. Diplomate Nat. Bd. Med. Examiners, Am. Psychoanalytic Assn. Intern Montefiore Hosp., NYC, 1957-58; resident in psychiatry Strong Meml. Hosp., Rochester, NY, 1958, Washington U., St. Louis, 1959-61, fellow in child psychiatry, 1960-62; faculty dept. psychiatry St. Louis U. Med. Sch., 1965—. Mem. adv. bd. Pastoral Counseling Inst., St. Louis, 1964-74; med. dir. St. Louis Clin. Assn. for Religious and Ednl. Counseling, 1979-81, bd. dirs., 2003-; mem. faculty St. Louis Psychoanalytic Inst., 1973—, chmn. cmty. edn. com., 1980-83, chmn. inst. edn. com., 1987-91, tng. and supervising analyst, 1982—, inst. assoc. dir., 2001—; clin. prof. psychiatry St. Louis U. Med. Sch., 1996—. Contbg. editor Psychoanalytic Inquiry, 1984-2001, issue co-editor, 1985; contbr. chpts. to books, articles to profl. jours. Fellow Am. Coll. Psychoanalysts; mem. AMA, Am. Psychoanalytic Assn. (del. to exec. coun. 1982-85, fellow bd. profl. stds. 1987-91, mem. com. on founds. 1993—), Mo. State Med. Assn., Ea. Mo. Psychiat. Soc. (sec.-treas. 1967-69), Greater St. Louis Med. Soc., St. Louis Psychoanalytic Soc. (membership com. chmn. 1977-78, 87-88, program chmn. 1977-79, pres. 1980-82), Sigma Xi. Avocations: tennis, sailing, music, bicycling, snorkeling. Home: 9 Southmoor Dr Clayton MO 63105-3016

POSTAER, LARRY, advertising executive; b. Chgo. Grad., U. Mo. Sch. Journalism, 1959. Catalog copywriter Sears; with Stern, Walters & Simmons, Chgo., 1962-64, creative dir., 1964-76; sr. v.p., group creative dir. Needham Harper & Steers, Chgo., 1976-81, exec. v.p., dir. creative svcs. L.A., 1981-86; co-founder, exec. v.p., dir. creative svcs. Rubin Postaer and Assoc., Santa Monica, 1986—. Named Co-leader of Yr. for 1990, Western States Advt. Agys. Assn., 1991. Office: 1333 2d St Santa Monica CA 90401-1100

POSTE, GEORGE HENRY, pharmaceutical company executive; b. Polegate, Sussex, Eng., Apr. 30, 1944; came to U.S., 1972; s. John H. and Kathleen B. (Brooke) P.; 1 child, Eleanor Kathy; m. Linda C. Suhler Lopez, Nov. 21, 1992; stepchildren: John Robert, Lisa Carolyn. DVM, U. Bristol, 1966, PhD, 1969, DSc, 1987, LLD (hon.), 1995. Lectr. U. London, 1969-72; assoc. prof. SUNY, Buffalo, 1972-76; prof. pathology Roswell Park Meml. Inst., Buffalo, 1976-80; v.p. rsch. SmithKline Beckman, Phila., 1980-82, v.p. R & D, 1982-86, v.p. worldwide rsch. and pre-clin. devel., 1987-88, pres. R & D, 1988-89; pres. R & D techs. SmithKline Beecham, King of Prussia, Pa., 1989-90, vice-chmn., exec. v.p. R & D, 1990-91, pres. and chmn. R & D, 1992-97; chief sci. and tech. officer SmithKline Beecham Corp. PLC, King of Prussia, Pa., 1997-99, bd. dirs.; chief exec. officer Health Tech. Networks, Gilbertsville, Pa., 2000—. Mem. pathology B study sect. NIH, Bethesda, Md., 1978-82; chmn. Gordon Conf., N.H., 1985-86, diaDeXus, 1997, Cerebrus, 1997; pres. coun. U. Tex. M.D. Anderson Cancer Ctr.; mem. adv. coun. Beckman Ctr. for Molecular and Genetic Medicine, Stanford U.; mem. coun. Oxford Internat. Biomedical Centre. Editor: Cell Surface Revs., New Horizons in Therapeutics, Cancer Metastasis Revs., Advanced Drug Delivery Revs., 15 books; contbr. articles to profl. jours. Mem. governing bd. UCLA Symposia, Life Sci. Rsch. Found.; mem. bd. Overseers Sch. Vet. Medicine, U. Penn., Gov.'s adv. com. Sci. and Tech., Pa.; mem. adv. bd. Natural Sci. Assn., U. Pa. Fleming fellow U. Oxford, Eng., 1995, Pitt fellow U. Cambridge, Eng., 1995; named Comdr. of British for svcs. in devel. of bioscis., 1999. Fellow Royal Soc., Royal Coll. Vet. Surgeons, Royal Coll. Pathologists, Ins. Biology (London), Acad. Med. Scis. (London); mem. AAAS, Am. Soc. Cell Biology, Pathol. Soc., Nat. Assn. Biomed. Rsch. (bd. govs. 1984), Univ. Assn. Space Rsch. (mem. coun. 1984), Pharm. Mfrs. Assn. (former chmn. rsch. and devel. section 1988). Avocations: military history, foreign affairs, photography, auto racing. Office: Health Tech Networks PO Box 647 Gilbertsville PA 19525-0647

POSTER, ELIZABETH C. dean; BSN, Boston U., 1968, MSN in Child Psychiatric Nursing, 1970; PhD in Ednl. Psychology, Boston Coll., 1981. Asst. prof., asst. dean student affairs Sch. Nursing UCLA, 1981-84, dir. nursing rsch. and edn. Neuropsychiatric Hosp., 1984-95; dean, prof. Sch. Nursing U. Tex., Arlington, 1995—. Bd. dirs. Tex. Bd. Nurse Examiners. Editor Jour.

Child, Adolescent Psychiatric Nursing, 1992—. Office: U Tex Arlington Sch Nursing Box 19407 411 S Nedderman Dr Arlington TX 76019-0407 Fax: 817-272-5006. E-mail: poster@uta.edu.

POSTER, MERYL, film company executive; With William Morris Agy.; exec. asst. to co-chmn Harvey Weinstein Miramax Film Corp., 1989—91, dir. devel., 1991—93, v.p. east coast prodn., 1993—94, sr. v.p. prodn., 1994—97, exec. v.p. prodn, 1997—98, co-pres. prodn., 1998—. Exec. prodr.: (films) Smoke, 1995, Marvin's Room, 1996, The Pallbearer, 1996, Cop Land, 1997, Wide Awake, 1998, Shakespeare in Love, 1998 (Acad. Award for Best Picture), Cider House Rules, 1999, Chocolat, 2000, Bounce, 2000, The Shipping News, 2001, Kate and Leopold, 2001, Blow Dry, 2001, Chicago, 2002 (Acad. Award for Best Picture), Duplex, 2003; co-prodr.: Music of the Heart, 1999. Office: Miramax Film Corp 375 Greenwich St Fl 3 New York NY 10013*

POSTHUMUS, RICHARD EARL, state offical, farmer; b. Hastings, Mich., July 19, 1950; s. Earl Martin and Lola Marie (Wieland) P.; m. Pamela Ann Bartz, June 23, 1972; children: Krista, Lisa, Heather, Bryan. BS in Agrl. Econs. and Pub. Affairs Mgmt., Mich. State U., 1972. Exec. v.p. Farmers and Mfrs. Beet Sugar Assn., Saginaw, Mich., 1972-74, Mich. Beef Commn., Lansing, 1974-78; dir. constituent rels. Rep. Caucus, Mich. Ho. of Reps., 1979-82, senator, Mich., 1983-98, senate majority leader, 1991-98, lt. gov., 1999-2002; self-employed farmer, 1974—. Third vice-chmn. Mich. Republican Com., 1971-73; mem. Hope Ch. of the Brethren. Mem. Alpha Gamma Rho. Republican. Office: Varnum Riddering Schmidt and Howlett Bridgewater Pl 333 Bridge St NW PO Box 352 Grand Rapids MI 49501-0352

POSTMA, HERMAN, physicist, consultant; b. Wilmington, NC, Mar. 29, 1933; s. Gilbert and Sophia Postma; m. Patricia Dunigan, Nov. 25, 1960; children: Peter, Pamela. BS summa cum laude, Duke U., 1955; MS, Harvard U., 1957, PhD, 1959. Registered profl. engr., Calif. Summer staff Oak Ridge Nat. Lab., 1954-57, physicist thermonuclear div., 1959-62, co-leader DCX-1 group, 1962-66, asst. dir. thermonuclear div., 1966, asso. dir. div., 1967, dir. div., 1967-73, dir. nat. lab., 1974-88; v.p. Martin Marietta, 1984-88, sr. v.p., 1988-91. Vis. scientist FOM-Inst. for Plasma Physics, The Netherlands, 1963; cons. Lab. Laser Energetics, U. Rochester; arbitrator AAA 2002, mem. energy rsch. adv. bd. spl. panel Dept. Energy; bd. dirs. Nashville br. Fed. Res. Bank Atlanta, ICS Corp., PAI Corp., ORAS, Inc., Allmeds, M4 Corp., ASIC Corp., Studio212.com Corp. Contbr. numerous articles to profl. jours. Bd. dirs. The Nucleus; chmn. bd. trustees Hosp. of Meth. Ch.; mem. adv. bd. Coll. Bus. Adminstrn., U. Tenn., 1976-2000, Energy Inst., State of N.C.; bd. dirs., exec. com. Tenn. Tech. Found., 1982-88, Venture Capital Fund; vice chmn., commr. Tenn. Higher Edn. Commn., 1984-92; trustee Duke U., 1987-99, Pellissippi State Coll., 1991-98; chmn. Meth. Hosp. Found., 1990; pres. East Tenn. Econ. Coun., 1998; mem. adv. bd. Inst. Pub. Policy Vanderbilt U., 1986-88, conf. chmn. 1987. Fellow Am. Phys. Soc. (exec. com. div. plasma physics), AAAS, Am. Nuclear Soc. (dir., chair East Tenn. econ. coun. 1997—); mem. C. of C. (v.p. 1981-83, chmn. 1987), Indsl. Rsch. Inst., Gas Rsch. Inst. (adv. bd. 1986-88), Oak Ridge Rotary (pres. 1996-97), Phi Beta Kappa, Beta Gamma Sigma, Sigma Pi Sigma, Omicron Delta Kappa, Sigma Xi, Pi Mu Epsilon, Phi Eta Sigma. Home and Office: 104 Berea Rd Oak Ridge TN 37830-7829

POSTOL, LAWRENCE PHILIP, lawyer; b. Bridgeport, Conn., Oct. 18, 1951; s. Sidney Samuel and Eunice Ruth (Schine) P.; m. Ellen Margaret Russell, Mar. 22, 1975; children: Raymond Russell, Stephan Russell, Carolyn Russell. BS, Cornell U., 1973, JD, 1976. Bar: Conn. 1976, D.C. 1977, U.S. Dist. Ct. D.C. 1977, U.S. Ct. Appeals (D.C. cir.) 1977, U.S. Supreme Ct. 1980, Va. 1982, U.S. Ct. Appeals (4th cir.) 1982, U.S. Dist. Ct. (ea. dist.) Va. 1985, U.S. Dist. Ct. Md. 1989, U.S. Dist. Ct. Conn. 1990. Assoc. Arent, Fox, Kintner & Plotkin, Washington, 1976-80, Seyfarth, Shaw, Washington, 1980-83, ptnr., 1985—; assoc. Jones, Day, Reavis and Pogue, Washington, 1983-85. Lectr. Loyola U., New Orleans, 1983—, U. Cin., 1987-93; bd. advisers The Environ. Counselor Jour.; spl. counsel Greater Washington Bd. Trade, 1991-93. Author: Legal Guide to Handling Toxic Substances in the Workplace, 1990, Americans with Disabilities Act - A Compliance Manual for Employers, 1993. Jewish. Avocation: sports. Home: 6340 Chowning Pl Mc Lean VA 22101-4129 Office: Seyfarth Shaw 815 Connecticut Ave NW Washington DC 20006-4004 Fax: 202-828-5393. Office Phone: 202-828-5385. E-mail: lpostol@seyfarth.com.

POSTON, ANITA OWINGS, lawyer; b. Sylacauga, Ala., Sept. 24, 1949; d. John T. and Margaret Owings; m. Charles E. Poston, June 9, 1973; children: Charles E. Jr., John W., Margaret Elizabeth. BA, U. Md., 1971; JD, Coll. William & Mary, 1974. Bar: Va. 1974. Atty. Vandeventer Black LLP, Norfolk, Va., 1974—. Substitute judge Norfolk (Va.) Gen. Dist. Cts., 1982-90; mem. Bar Examiners Bd.; mem. bd. vistors Coll. William and Mary Mem. State Bd. for Community Colls., Richmond, 1985-90, chmn. 1988-89; mem. Norfolk Sch. Bd., 1990-2002, chmn. 1998-2002; bd. dirs. WHRO Pub. Broadcasting, chair, 2002-04; bd. dirs. Learning Bridge Acad. Mem. ABA (law fellows), Va. Bar Assn. (pres. 2000), Norfolk-Portsmouth Bar Assn. (pres. 1998-99), Va. Law Fellows, Am. Inn of Ct. Office: Vandeventer Black LLP 500 World Trade Ctr Norfolk VA 23510-1679 Office Phone: 757-446-8600. Office Fax: 757-446-8670. Business E-Mail: aposton@vanblk.com.

POSTON, WALKER SEWARD, II, medical educator, researcher; BA in Biol. Scis., U. Calif., Davis, 1983; PhD in Psychology, U. Calif., Santa Barbara, 1990; MPH, U. Tex., Houston, Health Sci. Ctr. Clin. psychology resident USAF Med. Ctr., Wright-PAtterson AFB, Ohio, 1989-90; dir. psychology svcs., asst. chief mental health svcs. 9th Med. Group, Beale AFB, 1990-92; fellow in behavioral medicine Wilford Hall Med. Ctr., 1992-93; chief health and rehab. psychology svc. Malcolm Grow Med. Ctr., 1993-95, faculty, 1993-95; clin. asst. prof. dept. med. and clin. psychology F. Edward Herbert Sch. Medicine, Bethesda, Md., 1993-95; asst. prof. medicine Baylor Coll. Medicine, Houston, 1995-99; assoc. prof. U. Mo., Kansas City, 1999—. Rsch. exch. scientist Karolinska Inst., Stockholm, Sweden, 1997, 98. Contbr. articles to profl. jours. Recipient Minority Scientist Devel. award Am. Heart Assn., 1995; U. Calif. Doctoral scholars fellow, 1984-85, 85-86, 86-87, 88-89, Clin. fellow Wilford Hall Med. Ctr., Lackland AFB, 1992-93; Nat. Merit scholar, 1979-80. Fellow, Am. Heart Assn., North Am. Assoc. for the Study of Obesity. Office: Univ Mo 5319 Holmes St Kansas City MO 64110-2437

POSUNKO, BARBARA, retired elementary education educator; b. Newark, July 17, 1938; d. Joseph and Mary (Prystauk) P. BA, Rutgers U., Newark, 1960; MA, Kean U., Union, N.J., 1973; teaching cert., Seton Hall U., Newark, 1966. Cert. elem. tchr., reading specialist, N.J. Social case worker Newark City Hosp., 1960-65; elem. tchr. Plainfield (N.J.) Bd. Edn., 1966; elem., jr. and sr. high sch. tchr. minimum basic skills and reading Sayreville (N.J.) Bd. Edn., 1966-82, tchr. Chpt. I and minimum basic skills, 1982-95, cooperating tchr. to student tchrs., 1983-95, coord. testing, 1984-95; ret., 1995. Sch. coord. for congressionally mandated study of ednl. growth and opportunity, 1991-95; mem. numerous reading coms. Recipient Outstanding Tchr. award N.J. Gov.'s Tchr. Recognition Program, 1988. Mem. NEA, Internat. Reading Assn., N.J. Reading Assn., N.J. Edn. Assn. Home: 17 Drake Rd Mendham NJ 07945-1805

POSVAR, MILDRED MILLER, opera singer; b. Cleve. d. William and Elsa (Friedhofer) Mueller; m. Wesley W. Posvar, Apr. 30, 1950; children: Wesley, Margot Marina, Lisa Christina. MusB, Cleve. Inst. Music, 1946; hon. doctorate, Cleve. Ins. Music, 1983; artists' diploma, New England Conservatory Music, 1948, hon. doctorate, 1966; MusD (hon.), Bowling Green State U., 1960; hon. doctorate, Washington and Jefferson U., 1988. Founder Opera Theater of Pitts., 1978—; mem. music faculty Carnegie-Mellon U., 1996—. Operatic debut in Peter Grimes, Tanglewood, 1946; appeared N.E. Opera Theater, Stuttgart State Theater, Germany, 1949-50, Glyndebourne Opera, Edinburgh Festival; debut as Cherubino in Figaro, Met. Opera, 1951; 23 consecutive seasons Met. Opera; radio debut Bell Telephone Hour; TV debut Voice of Firestone, 1952; appeared in films including Merry Wives of Windsor (filmed in Vienna), 1964; Vienna State Opera debut, 1963, appearances with San Francisco, Chgo. Lyric, Cin. Zoo, San Antonio, Berlin, Munich, Frankfurt, Pasadena, Ft. Worth, Kansas City, Pitts., Tulsa and St. Paul operas. Bd. dirs. Gateway to Music. Recipient Frank Huntington Beebe award for study abroad, 1949, 50, Grand Prix du Disque, 1965, Outstanding Achievements in Music award Boston C. of C., 1959, Ohioana Career medal, 1985, Outstanding Achievement in Opera award, Slippery Rock U., 1985, YWCA Ann. Tribute to Women award, 1989, Keystone Salute award Pa. Fedn. Music Clubs, 1994; named one of outstanding women of Pitts., Pitts. Press-Pitts. Post-Gazette, 1968, Person of Yr. in Music, Pitts. Jaycees, 1980. Mem. Nat. Soc. Arts and Letters (pres. 1989-90, Gold medal 1984), Disting. Daus. Pa. (pres. 1991-93), Tuesday Mus. Club, Phi Beta Kappa, Phi Delta Gamma, Sigma Alpha Iota. Office: Opera Theater of Pittsburgh PO Box 110108 Pittsburgh PA 15232-0608

POTAMKIN, ALAN, automotive company executive; CEO, Potamkin Co., Miami, Fla.; co-chmn. Plant Auto Group, Inc., Coral Gables, Fla. Office: 1 Casuarina Concourse Coral Gables FL 33143-6501

POTAMKIN, ROBERT, automotive executive; b. Mar. 12, 1946; Grad., U. Pa., 1970, JD, 1972. CEO Potamkin Cos., Phila., 1972—; bd. of overseers U. Pa. Law Sch. Office: Potamkin Cos 130 Spruce St Apt 30B Philadelphia PA 19106-4325

POTASH, JEREMY WARNER, public relations executive; b. Monrovia, Calif., June 30, 1946; d. Fenwick Bryson and Joan Antony (Blair) Warner; m. Stephen Jon Potash; 1 son, Aaron Warner. AA, Citrus Coll., 1965; BA, Pomona Coll., 1967. With Forbes Mag., NYC, 1967-69, JETRO, San Francisco, 1970-75; v.p., co-founder, pres. Potash & Co. Pub. Rels., Oakland, Calif., 1980—. Founding exec. dir. Calif.-Asia Bus. Coun., Alameda, 1991—; editor Cal-Asia Member Alert, 1991—; exec. dir. Customs Brokers and Forwarders Assn., San Francisco, 1990—; adv. bd. Asia Pacific Econ. Rev., 1996—; mem. No. Calif. Dist. Export Coun., 2000—, Pacific Coun. Internat. Policy, 2000—. Editor: Southeast Asia Environmental Directory, 1994, Southeast Asia Infrastructure Directory, 1995-96. Co-founder J.L. Magnes docent program, 1980; pres. NorCal WAORT, 1985—86; bd. dirs. Temple Sinai, Oakland, 1984—86, Judah L. Magnes Mus., Berkeley, 1981—94. Named Export Citizen of Yr., U.S. Dept. Commerce, 1998. Mem. Oakland Women's Lit. Soc., Book Club Calif. Office: Potash & Co Pub Rels 1050 Marina Village Pkwy Alameda CA 94501

POTE, HAROLD WILLIAM, banker; b. Phila., Sept. 18, 1946; s. Frank Lafferty and Lucille (Bock) P.; m. Judy Elizabeth Constantine, Oct. 12, 1968. AB, Princeton U., 1968; MBA, Harvard U., 1972. Dir. investor relations Fidelcor/Fidelity Bank, Phila., 1974-76, v.p., head corp. devel. dept., 1976-78, sr. v.p., head corp. devel. dept., 1978-80, exec. v.p., treas. fin. and planning dept., 1980-83, vice chmn., treas. fin. and planning dept., 1983-84; chmn. bd., chief exec. officer Fidelity Bank, Phila., 1984-88; pres., chief exec. officer Fidelcor, Inc., 1986-88; pres. and chief exec. officer First Fidelity Bancorp., Phila., 1988; chief exec. officer Spl. Situation Fund, N.Y.C., 1988-93; ptnr. The Beacon Group (acquired by J.P. Morgan), N.Y.C., 1993—2000; head, regional banking J.P. Morgan Chase & Co., 2000—04, vice chmn. retail fin. services, 2004—. Asst. prof. La Salle Coll., Phila., 1972-79; bd. dirs. Norfolk So. Corp. Trustee Pa. Ballet Assn., Phila., 1976-92; mem. exec. coun. Harvard Bus. Sch. Assn., 1980—. Mem. AICPA, Merion Golf Club, Locust Club. Office: JP Morgan 270 Park Ave New York NY 10017

POTEAT, JAMES DONALD, retired diaconal minister, retired military officer; b. Spindale, N.C., Feb. 27, 1935; s. Albert Carl and Daliah Elizabeth (Freeman) P.; m. Clara Walker Yelton, Oct. 12, 1957; children: Deborah Poteat Emmons, Clara Poteat Frederick, James Donald Jr., Teresa Poteat Morris. BA disting. mil. graduate, The Citadel, Charleston, S.C., 1957; MA, Kans. State U., 1973; graduate, U.S. Army War Coll., 1980. Ordained to ministry United Meth. Ch. Commd. 2nd lt. U.S. Army, 1957, advanced through grades to col., 1979, master army aviator and parachutist, ret., 1983; mgmt. cons., 1983—88; pastor's adminstrv. asst. Prospect United Meth. Ch., Covington, Ga., 1988—95. Author: Long Range Planning, Prospect United Methodist Church, 1990, Presidential Decision-Making: Presidents Lincoln and Polk, 1973, others. Decorated Bronze Star medal, three Air medals, Vietnam Cross of Gallantry, three Army Commendation medals with v., Viet Nam Svc. Medal with 3 Campaign Battle Stars. Mem. Ret. Officers Assn., United Meth. Ch. Bus. Adminstrs. Assn. (cert.).

POTEET, WILLIAM MARK, education educator, writer; b. Norton, Va., July 24, 1958; s. William Gilbert and Helen Myers Poteet. BA, The U. of Va. at Wise, 1976—81; MA, Marshall U., 1995—97; postgrad., Ind. U. of Pa., 1997—. English prof. Ind. U. of Pa., 2000—. Author: (short story) Back Through the Delicious (Writers' workshop fiction writing award for best short story of the yr., 1989, John Fox Jr. writing award for best short story of the yr., 1988, 1992), The Southern Journal. Mem.: MLA, Phi Kappa Phi. Personal E-mail: mpoteet@iup.edu.

POTEMPA, KATHLEEN, dean; Diploma in nursing, Providence Hosp. Sch. Nursing, Southfield, Mich., 1970; BA in Psychology summa cum laude, U. Detroit, 1974; MS in Nursing, Rush U., 1978, D of Nursing Sci., 1986. Charge nurse coronary ICU Holy Cross Hosp., Ft. Lauderdale, Fla., 1970-71; staff nurse, charge nurse cardiovasc. ICU Henry Ford Hosp., Detroit, 1971-74; nurse practitioner Rush-Presbyn.-St. Luke's Med. Ctr., Chgo., 1974-75; nursing edn. coord. dept. nursing Michael Reese Hosp. and Med. Ctr., Chgo., 1975-77, nursing supr., 1977-78; asst. unit leader dept. gerontol. nursing Rush U. Coll. Nursing, Chgo., 1978-79, asst. chmn., 1979-80, assoc. chmn., asst. prof. gerontol. nursing, 1980-85, asst. prof. gerontol. nursing, 1985-86; asst. prof. nursing, dept. internal medicine, practitioner Rush Med. Coll., Rush U., 1987-88; asst. then assoc. prof. dept. med.-surg. nursing Coll. Nursing, U. Ill., Chgo., 1988—96, dir. tng., pre and postdoctoral fellowship instnl. rsch., 1992—94, exec. assoc. dean Coll. Nursing, 1994-95, interim dean Coll. Nursing, 1995-96; prof., dean Sch. Nursing Oreg. Health Scis. U., Portland, 1996—, v.p., 2002—. Rsch. assoc. Robert Wood Johnson Tchg. Nursing Home Project, VA Edward Hines Jr. Hosp., Hines, Ill., 1985-86, co-dir. Exercise Rsch. Lab., 1985-86; dir. nursing Johnston R. Bowman Health Ctr. for Elderly, Rush Presbyn. St. Luke's Med. Ctr., Chgo., 1980-85. Contbr. articles to profl. jours. Fellow Am. Acad. Nursing; mem. ANA (coun. nurse rschrs.), Am. Soc. Hypertension, Gerontol. Soc. Am., Midwest Nursing Rsch. Soc., Heart Assn. Met. Chgo., Am. Heart Assn. Oreg., Ill. Coun. Nurse Rschrs., Am. Heart Assn. (coun. cardiovasc. nursing, coun. hypertension, coun. on strokes), Sigma Theta Tau. Office: SN ADM Oreg Health Scis U Sch Nursing 3181 SW Sam Jackson Park Rd Portland OR 97201-3011*

POTEMPA, PHILIP MATTHEW, journalist, columnist, communications educator; b. San Pierre, Ind., Aug. 13, 1970; s. Chester John and Peggy Louise Potempa. BA, Valparaiso U., 1992. Arts and entertainment reporter Vidette-Messenger Newspaper, Valparaiso, Ind., 1991-95, Times Newspaper N.W. Ind., Munster, 1995—; adj. prof. comms. Valparaiso U., 1997—. Arts and entertainment corr. South Bend (Ind.) Tribune, 1993—; prof. comm. Purdue U., Westville, Ind., 1998—; radio commentator WLJE-FM, Ind., 2002—; corr. Indpls. Star Newspaper, 2003—. Co-author: It's a Wonderful Life: A Memory Book, 2003; author: From the Farm, 2004. Bd. dirs. Ind. Journalism Hall of Fame. Recipient Reporting award, Hoosier State Press Assn., 1995, AP Mng. Editors, 1997. Mem.: Ind. Hist. Soc., Soc. Profl. Journalists (award 1996), Chgo. Headline Club (bd. dirs.). Republican. Roman Catholic. Avocation: collecting historical autographs. Home: PO Box 68 San Pierre IN 46374-0068 Office: Times Newspaper 601 W 45th St Munster IN 46321 Office Phone: 800-837-3232 3247. E-mail: ppotempa@NWITimes.com.

POTENTE, EUGENE, JR., interior designer; b. Kenosha, Wis., July 24, 1921; s. Eugene and Suzanne Marie (Schmit) P.; m. Joan Cioffe, Jan. 29, 1946; children: Eugene J., Peter Michael, John Francis, Suzanne Marie. PhB, Marquette U., 1943; postgrad., Stanford U., 1943, N.Y. Sch. Interior Design, 1948; DFA, Carthage Coll., 1997; DLitt (hon.), Concordia U., 1997. Cert. lighting Nat. Coun. on Lighting Qualification. Founder, chmn. Studios of Potente, Inc., Kenosha, Wis., 1949—; pres., founder Archtl. Svcs. Assocs., Kenosha, 1978—, Bus. Leasing Svcs. of Wis. Inc., 1978—. Past nat. pres. Inter-Faith Forum on Religion, Art and Architecture; vice chm. Wis. State Capitol and Exec. Residence Bd., 1981—. Sec. Kenosha Symphony Assn., 1968-74; bd. dirs. Ctr. for Religion and the Arts, Wesley Theol. Sem., Washington, 1983-84. With U.S. Army, 1943—46, WWII, ETO. Recipient Disting. Alumni award Marquette U., 1999; named to St. Catherine's HS Hall of Fame, 2002. Mem. Am. Soc. Interior Designers (treas., pres. Wis. chpt. 1985-86, 94-95, chmn. nat. pub. svc. 1986, Gold medal Wis. chpt. 2003), Interior Design Coalition Wis (pres 2003-04), Illuminating Engring. Soc. N.Am. Internat. Interior Design Assn., Elks, Am. Legion (life), Sigma Delta Chi. Roman Catholic. Home: 8609 2nd Ave Pleasant Prairie WI 53158-4720 Office: 914 60th St Kenosha WI 53140-4041 Office Phone: 262-654-3535. Personal E-mail: gpotente@wi.rr.com.

POTENZA, JOSEPH MICHAEL, lawyer; b. Stamford, Conn., June 27, 1947; s. Michael Joseph Sr. and Rose Elizabeth (Coppola) P.; m. Karen Louise Yankee, Jan. 28, 1978; children: Wendy Lynn, Chiara Micol. BSEE cum laude, Rochester Inst. Tech., 1970; JD, Georgetown U., 1975. Bar: Va. 1975, D.C. 1976, U.S. Dist. Ct. D.C., U.S. Ct. Appeals (fed. cir.), U.S. Ct. Appeals (6th cir.), U.S. Supreme Ct. Patent examiner U.S. Patent and Trademark Office, Arlington, Va., 1970-74, law clk. bd. appeals, 1974-75, law clk. to presiding judge 6th cir. U.S. Ct. Appeals, 1975-76; assoc. Banner, Birch, McKie & Beckett, Washington, 1976-80, ptnr., 1980—, Banner & Witcoff, Washington, 1995. Adj. prof. Georgetown U. Law Ctr., Washington, 1985—; faculty Nat. Inst. Trial Advocacy--Patent Inst., 1996—. Editor (monographs) Sorting Out Ownership Rights in Intellectual Property, 1980, Recent Developments in Licensing, 1981. Bd. dirs. Found. for a Creative Am., 1991—. Recipient Patent and Trademark Office Superior Performance award Dept. Commerce, 1973-75. Fellow Am. Bar Found.; mem. ABA (young lawyers divsn. exec. coun. 1979—, chmn. legis. action com. 1980—, chmn. patent trademark and copyright com. 1977—, house of dels. 1984-86, sci. and tech. sect., coun. mem. 1985—, membership chmn. 1985—, budget co-chmn. 1987—, budget officer 1988—, vice chmn. 1991—, chmn.-elect 1992-93, chmn. 1993, chmn. standing com. on pub. oversight, 1996—, fed. practice and procedure com. intellectual property law sect. 1995-96, spring CLE program 1997-98, chmn. summer CLE 1999, 2001, chair fed. practice and procedure com. div. chmn., div. VI IP law sec. 1995-97, sec. sec. 2001—), IEEE, AAAS (nat. conf. lawyers and scientists), Am. Intellectual Property Law Assn. (chmn. unfair competition com. 1980-81), D.C. Bar Assn. (sec. patent, trademark, copyright sect.), Va. Bar Assn., Wash. Patent Lawyers Club (pres. 1988-89), Am. Inns of Ct. (founding mem. and exec. com. Giles S. Rich 1991—, v.p. 1997, pres. 1998-99), Phi Sigma Kappa, Alpha Sigma (pres. 1979-80), Tau Beta Pi. Home: 1238 Gilman Ct Herndon VA 20170-2418 Office: Banner & Witcoff 1001 G St NW Ste 1100 Washington DC 20001-4545 Office Phone: 202-824-3100. Business E-Mail: jpotenza@bannerwitcoff.com.

POTERBA, JAMES MICHAEL, economist, educator; b. Flushing, NY, July 13, 1958; s. William Samuel and Margaret Mary (Toale) P.; m. Nancy Lin Rose, June 23, 1984; children: Matthew Robert, Timothy James, Margaret Rose. AB, Harvard U., 1980; MPhil, Oxford U., Eng., 1982, DPhil, 1983. From asst. to assoc. prof. MIT, Cambridge, Mass., 1983-88, prof., 1988—, Mitsui prof., 1996—. Dir. pub. econs. rsch. program Nat. Bur. Econ. Rsch., Cambridge, 1990—; fellow Ctr. Advanced Study in Behavioral Scis., 1993-94, Hoover Instn. Stanford U., 2000-01. Editor: Economic Policy Responses to Global Warning, 1991, International Comparisons of Household Saving, 1994, Housing Markets in the United States and Japan, 1994, Empirical Foundations of Household Taxation, 1996, Fiscal Institutions and Fiscal Performance, 1999, Jour. Pub. Econs.; contbr. articles to profl. jours. Recipient award for Excellence in Sci. Reviewing NAS, 1999; Marshall scholar, 1980-83, Batterymarch fellow, 1986. Fellow: Ctr. Advanced Study in Behavioral Scis., Econometric Soc., Am. Acad. Arts and Scis.; mem.: Am. Econ. Assn. (exec. com. 2001—03), Phi Beta Kappa. Office: MIT 50 Memorial Dr Rm E52-350 Cambridge MA 02142-1347 Office Phone: 617-253-6673. E-mail: poterba@mit.edu.

POTH, STEFAN MICHAEL, retired sales financing company executive; b. Detroit, Dec. 9, 1933; s. Stefan and Anna (Mayer) P.; m. Eileen T. McClimon, May 28, 1966; 1 child, Stefan Michael Jr. Cert. in acctg., Walsh Inst., Detroit, 1954. CPA, Mich.; cert. consumer credit exec. Sr. acct. Lybrand, Ross Bros. & Montgomery, Detroit, 1953-56, 58-61; with Ford Motor Credit Co., Dearborn, Mich., 1961-91, v.p. leasing truck and recreational products and tractor financing, 1973-77; v.p. cen. and western U.S. ops. Ford Motor Credit CO., Dearborn, 1977-79; v.p. mktg. and ops. svcs. Ford Motor Credit Co., Dearborn, 1979-85, v.p. bus. planning, 1985-90, v.p. credit policy, 1990-91. Bd. dirs. GE Credit Auto Resale Svcs., Inc.; adv. coun. Credit Rsch. Ctr., Krannert Grad. Sch. Mgmt., Purdue U., 1984-91. Chmn. adv. coun. Credit Rsch. Ctr. Krannert Grad. Sch. Mgmt., Purdue U., 1989-90; mem. bd. dirs. Internat. Credit Assoc., 1989-91. With AUS, 1956-58. Roman Catholic. Home: 7230 Mohansic Dr Bloomfield Hills MI 48301-3550

POTLURI, VENKATESWARA RAO, medical facility administrator; b. Krishna Dist., India, Jan. 1, 1955; came to U.S., 1983; s. Venkata Krishnaiah and Bulli Ademma (Koduru) P.; m. Padma Sree Peddu, Dec. 4, 1986; children: Vani, Vamsee Krishna, Varun. BSc, ANR Coll., Gudivada, India, 1975; MSc, AU Coll. Sci. and Tech., Waltair, India, 1977; MPhil, Delhi (India) U., 1979, PhD, 1982. Diplomate Am. Bd. Med. Genetics, 1984. Postdoctoral fellow Mt. Sinai Med. Ctr., N.Y.C., 1983-85, vis. asst. prof., 1985-87; lab. dir., adj. mem. med. staff Norwalk (Conn.) Hosp., 1987-98; lab. dir. Lab. Diagnostics (divsn. Cytogenetics), Norwalk, 1998—2001; lab dir. Ctr. for Genetic Svcs. Inc. (divsn. Lab. Corp. of Am.), Corpus Christi, Tex., 2001—03, Dynagene divsn. Lab. Corp. Am., Houston, 2003—. Fellow: Am. Coll. Med. Genetics (founding); mem.: Am. Soc. Human Genetics. Avocations: classical music, Telugu literature, home improvement. Home: 4018 Blue Bonnet Blvd Apt D Houston TX 77025 Office: Dynagene 7400 Fannin Ste 1200 Houston TX 77054

POTOK, NANCY ANN FAGENSON, federal agency administrator; b. Detroit, May 20, 1955; d. William and Harriet Fagenson; m. Barry Potok, May 16, 1976; children: Benjamin, Leah. BA, Sonoma State U., 1978; MAS, U. Ala., 1980. Cert. govt. fin. mgr. Presdl. mgmt. intern U.S. Dept. Transp., Washington, 1980-82; budget examiner U.S. Office Mgmt. & Budget, Washington, 1982-89; deputy asst. adminstr. fin. and budget Adminstrv. Office U.S. Cts., Washington, 1989-95; controller U.S. Census Bur., Washington, 1995-97, prin. assoc. dir., CFO, 1997—2002; vis. exec. Nat. Opinion Research Ctr., U. Chgo., 2003—. Pres., treas. Women's Transp. Sem., Washington, 1983-84; advisor Presdl. Mgmt. Intern Career Devel. Group, Washington; co-chmn. Census Bur. Labor-Mgmt. Partnership coun., 1997-2002; assoc. mem. exec. orgn./mgmt. panel, Nat. Acad. Pub. Adminstrn., 2000—, bd. dirs. The Public Manager, 2002—. Contbr. articles to profl. jours. Chmn. Citizens Adv. Com., Crofton, Md., 1996-98; mem. exec. bd. PTA, Crofton, 1990-95; judge Odyssey of the Mind Creative Problem Solving Competition, Md., 1995; coach Destination Imagination, Creative Problem Solving 1st Pl. Team, 1999. Recipient Arthur S. Flemming award, 1991, Silver medal Sec. Commerce, 1998. Mem. Am. Assn. Budget & Program Analysts, Am. Soc. Pub. Adminstrn., Assn. Govt. Accts. Avocations: writing, music. Office: US Census Bur Fob 3 Washington DC 20233-0001 E-mail: Nancy.A.Potok@census.gov.

POTRA, FLORIAN ALEXANDER, mathematics professor; b. Cluj, Romania, Dec. 7, 1950; came to the U.S., 1982; s. Ioan and Ana (Popa) P.; m. ELena Lavric, Nov. 15, 1973; 1 child, Valentin. MS, Babes-Bolyai U., Cluj, 1973; PhD, U. Bucharest, 1980. Analyst IPGGH, Bucharest, Romania, 1974-78; researcher INCREST, Bucharest, 1978-82; postdoctoral researcher U. Pitts., 1982-83, asst. prof., 1983-84; assoc. prof. U. Iowa, Iowa City, 1984-90, prof., 1990-98, U. Md. Baltimore County, 1998—. Vis. rschr. Lawrence Livermore Nat. Lab., 1991, U. Catania, Italy, Konrad Zuse Zentrum, Berlin, U. Darmstadt, Germany, 1990, U. Karlsruhe, Germany, 1987-91, Argonne Nat. Lab., 1991, U. Geneva, 1993, U. NSW, Sydney, 1995, U. Rome, 1996, INRIA, France, 1996, City U. Hong Kong, 1999; program dir. NSF, 1997-98; prof. U. Md., 1998—; adv. Nat. Inst. Stds. and Tech., 2003-. Assoc. editor: SIAM Jour. on Optimization, 1991-99, Jour. Optimization Theory and Applications, 1991—, Jour. Optimization Methods and Software, 1997—, Numerical Functional Analysis and Optimization, 1999—, Optimization and Engineering, 1999—; co-author: Research Notes in Mathematics 103, 1984; contbr. articles to profl. jours. Andrew Mellon fellow, 1982, Old Gold fellow, 1984, James Van Allen fellow in natural scis., 1991; NSF grantee, 1985-87., 94-96, 97—. Mem.: Math. Programming Soc., Inst. Ops. Rsch. and Mgmt. Scis., Soc.

Indsl. and Applied Math., NY Acad. Scis. Home: 13 Brian Daniel Ct Reisterstown MD 21136 Office: U Md Baltimore County Dept Math 1000 Hilltop Cir Baltimore MD 21250-0001

POTSIC, WILLIAM PAUL, physician, educator; b. Berwyn, Ill., May 22, 1943; s. Andrew M. and Estella (Buschak) P.; m. Roberta I. Kite; children: Amie, Jordan. BS, U. Ill., 1965; MD cum laude, Emory U., 1969; postgrad., U. Pa.; M in Med. Mgmt., Tulane U., 1998. Intern, resident U. Chgo., 1969-74; practice medicine specializing in pediatric otolaryngology Phila., 1974—; staff Presbyn. Hosp., U. Pa. Hosp., Phila., Children's Seashore House, Phila.; prof. otorhinolaryngology and human comm. U. Pa., Phila., 1974-93, E. Mortimer Newlin prof., 1993—; dir. div. otorhinolaryngology and human comm. Children's Hosp., Phila., 1975—, pres. med. staff, 1982-84, vice-chmn. clin. affairs dept. surgery, 1995—, dir. ambulatory surg. svcs., 1997—, dir. ctr. for childhood comm., 1999. Author: Surgical Pediatric Otolaryngology, 1997; contbr. articles to profl. jours. Recipient 1st prize for clin. rsch. Am. Acad. Ophthalmology and Otolaryngology, 1977, Sylvan E. Stool award for outstanding lifetime contbns. in ear nose and throat advances in children, Presdl. award Soc. Otorhinolaryngology and Head and Neck Nurses, 2002; NIH grantee. Mem. AMA, Am. Acad. Otolaryngology Head and Neck Surgery, Am. Laryngology, Otolgy and Rhinology Soc., Am. Coll. Physician Execs., Internat. Acad. Cosmetic Surgery, Pa. Med. Soc., Phila. Coll. Physicians, Phila. County Med. Soc., Phila. Laryngol. Soc. (treas. 1983), Phila. Pediatric Soc., Phila Laryngol. Soc. (pres. 1984), Phila. Soc. Facial Plastic Surgeons, Politzer Soc., Soc. Ear, Nose and Throat Advances in Children (pres. 1983), Am. Soc. Pediatric Otolaryngology (pres. 1991), Soc. Univ. Otolaryngologists, Am. Acad. Pediat., Alpha Omega Alpha, Phi Chi. Home: 1057 Beaumont Rd Berwyn PA 19312-2007 Office: Children's Hosp Phila 34th And Civic Center Blvd Philadelphia PA 19104 Office Phone: 215-590-3450. E-mail: potsic@email.chop.edu.

POTT, JAMES THOMAS, civil engineer, consultant; b. Shanghai, Feb. 28, 1927; (father Am. citizen); s. James Hawks and Nancy (Yang) P.; m. Lois Jane Donaldson, July 16, 1955; children: Nancy, Catherine, Margaret. BSCE, Stanford U., 1949, MSCE, 1950. Registered profl. engr., Calif., Colo. Civil engr. Kennedy/Jenks/Chilton, San Francisco, 1950-60; county engr. County of Santa Clara, San Jose, Calif., 1960-77, dir. pub. works, 1963-73, dir. transp., 1973-77, asst. county exec., 1977-78; city engr., dir. pub. works City of Long Beach, Calif., 1978-84; v.p. O'Brien-Kreitzberg & Assocs., Encino, Calif., 1984-87; propr., engrng. cons. James Pott & Co., Long Beach, 1987—94; ret., 1994. Patentee transit wheelchair lift. Bd. dirs. Rail Constrn. Corp. of L.A. County Transp. Commn. 1990-92; 1st lt. U.S. Army, 1944-46, 52-53. Recipient S.I.R. award Assoc. Gen. Contractors Calif., 1976; Disting. Service award Calif. Council Civil Engrs. and Land Surveyors, 1967. Fellow: ASCE (life); mem.: Pub. Works Officers League Calif. Cities (v.p. 1983—84), Nat. Assn. County Engrs. (1st v.p. 1976—77, Urban County Engr. of Yr. 1973), County Engrs. Assn. Calif. (life; pres. 1971—72), Am. Pub. Works Assn. (life; rsch. found. 1982—84, Top Ten Pub. Works award 1976), Long Beach Area C. of C. (vice chmn. 1986—90, chmn. strategic plan task force 1988), Tau Beta Pi. Republican. Episcopalian.

POTTASH, A. CARTER, psychiatrist, hospital executive; b. Phila., Nov. 30, 1948; s. R. Robert and Elizabeth (Braunschweig) P. BS with high honors, Trinity Coll., Hartford, Conn., 1970; MD, Yale U., 1974. Intern Tufts U. Sch. Medicine, Springfield, Mass., 1974-75; clin. fellow Yale-New Haven Hosp., 1977-78; fellow Yale U., New Haven, 1975-78; med. dir. Psychiatric Diagnostic Labs. Am., Summit, N.J., 1979-83. Lectr., cons. in field; vis. prof. St. Elizabeth Med. Ctr., Northeastern Ohio U. Coll Medicine, 1979; clin. prof. NYU, 1989—; pres. Fla. Consultation Svcs., P.A., West Palm Beach, 1992—, Psychiatric Assocs. N.J., P.A., Summit, N.J., 1978-93, Met. Med. Group P.C., N.Y.C., 1981-92, So. Fla. Med. Group P.A., Delray Beach, 1984-93, Stony Lodge Hosp., Inc. and Stony Lodge Med. Group P.C., Briarcliff Manor, N.Y., 1985—, Hampton Med. Group, P.A., Rancocas and Summit, N.J., 1986—; exec. med. dir. Fair Oaks Hosp., Summit, 1978-92, The Regent Hosp., N.Y.C., 1981-92, Lake Hosp of the Palm Beaches, Lake Worth, Fla., 1984-92, Fair Oaks Hosp. at Boca/Delray, Fla., 1984-92, Hampton Hosp., Rancocas, N.J., 1986-95—; chmn. Stony Lodge Hosp., Briarcliff Manor, N.Y., 1985—. Editor Psychiatry Letter, 1980-91; mem. editl. bd. Internat. Jour. Psychiatry in Medicine, 1978-87, The Psychiatric Hosp., 1982—, Jour. Nat. Assn. Pvt. Psychiatric Hosps., 1980-81, Fla. Psychiatry Newsletter, 1992—; reviewer Jour. Nervous and Mental Disorders, Alcoholism, Clin. and Exptl. Rsch., JAMA, Hosp. and Cmty. Psychiatry; contbr. articles to profl. jours. Mem. adv. bd. Mothers for More Halfway Houses, N.Y.C., 1986—; cons. com. on women and alcoholism Jr. League of N.Y.C., 1987; bd. dirs. Met. Soc. Arts, N.Y.C., 1984-87. Fellow Am. Coll. Clin. Pharmacology, Assn. Clin. Scientists, Nat. Acad. Clin. Biochemistry, Am. Psychiat. Assn. (disting. fellow), The Acad. Medicine N.J.; mem. AMA, Soc. Neurosci., Nat. Acad. Clin. Biochemistry, Palm Beach County Med. Soc., Am. Acad. Clin. Psychiatrists, Brit. Brain Rsch. Assn. (hon.), European Brain and Behavioral Soc. (hon.), Am. Soc. Addiction Medicine, Am. Academy of Addiction Psychiatry (founding mem. 1987), Fla. Med. Soc., Palm Beach County Psychiat. Soc., Med. Soc. State N.Y., Med. Soc. N.J., Union County Med. Soc., N.Y. Athletic Club, Canoe Brook Country Club, Beacon Hill Club, Phi Beta Kappa, Delta Phi Alpha. Office: PO Box 511 West Palm Beach FL 33402-0511 Office Phone: 561-837-2215.

POTTER, ALICE CATHERINE, clinical laboratory scientist; b. Oil City, Pa., June 24, 1928; d. Howard Taylor and Hilda Marian (Lewis) P. BA, U. Findlay, 1949; postgrad., Springfield (Ohio) City Hosp., 1949-50. Registerd med. technologist Am. Soc. Clin. Pathologists; cert. clin. lab. scientist. Med. technologist Mercy Hosp., Springfield, 1950-54, Oil City Hosp., 1954-67; staff med. technologist Thomas Jefferson U. Hosp., Phila., 1968-83, sr. med. technologist, 1983—97, retired, 1997. Vol. Acad. Natural Scis., Phila., 1995—. Mem. Am. Soc. Clin. Lab. Scientists, Pa. Soc. Clin. Lab. Scientists (membership chmn. Delaware Valley chpt. 1977-78, chmn. pub. rels. 1982-94, 96-97, bd. dirs. 1989-91, 97-98, 98-99, 99—, pres.-elect 1991-92, pres. 1992-93, Scrimshaw award 1992). Republican. Avocations: travel, needlecrafts. Home: 1701 Wallace St Philadelphia PA 19130-3312

POTTER, ANDREW HAROLD, secondary school educator; b. Mpls., Dec. 11, 1972; s. Alan Ladd and Patricia Lee Potter; m. Sandy Lee Frazee, July 25, 1995; children: Emily Grace, Lauren Olivia. BA in History and Bibl. Studies, Pillsbury Coll., 1995; MA in History: Ancient Mediterranean Civilizations, Calif. State U., Northridge, 2000; MA in Ancient Near East and Hebrew Bible, Brandeis U., 2002. Prof. Ctr. for Profl. Studies The Master's Coll., Santa Clarita, Calif., 1998—2000, adj. prof., 1998—2000; upper sch. tchr. Christian Heritage Sch., Trumbull, Conn., 2002—; adj. prof. History dept. Sacred Heart U., 2004—. Team leader Rep. Nat. Com., Conn., 2003—. Named to, Nat. Christian H.S. Honor Soc., 1991; fellow, Acton Inst., 2004. Mem.: Acad. Polit. Sci. (assoc.). Avocations: fly fishing, linguistics. Home: 58 Patricia Rd Unit I Bridgeport CT 06606 Office: Christian Heritage Sch 575 White Plains Rd Trumbull CT 06611

POTTER, BLAIR BURNS, editor; b. Spartanburg, SC, Mar. 11, 1946; d. Leonard Hill and Nancy Milner (Vaughan) Burns; m. Robert Arthur Potter, May 24, 1974; children: Lillian Howard, Gordon Leonard. BA, Hollins Coll., Roanoke, Va., 1968; MA, U. N.C., Chapel Hill, 1971. Manuscript editor Science, Washington, 1970—74; freelance editor, 1974—85; assoc. editor Health Adminstrn. Press/U. Mich., Ann Arbor, 1985—87; freelance editor NAS, Inst. Medicine, Office Tech. Assessment, Washington, 1987—92; assoc. editor Science News, Washington, 1992, mng. editor, 1992—98; dir. Urban Inst. Press, Washington, 1998—2000, dir. acquisitions, 2000—01; freelance editor, 2000—. Editl. cons. Surgeon Gen.'s Report on Youth Violence, Washington, 2000-2001, White House Task Force on Infant Mortality, Washington, 1990, Nat. Commn. on Orphan Diseases, Washington, 1988-89, Nat. Comm. on Children, Washington, 1992-93, White House Commn. on Complementary & Alternative Medicine Policy, Washington, 2002; lay mem. protocol com. Nat. Heart, Lung and Blood Inst., Bethesda, Md., 1973. Whittaker fellow, 1969-70; Hollins Coll. scholar, 1964-68, English-Speaking Union scholar, 1967. Mem.: Am. Soc. Mag. Editors, Nat. Press Club. Avocations: gardening, historic preservation, antique american furniture, sailing. Address: 8607 North Bend Circle Easton MD 21601-7327 Home and Office: 8607 Northbend Cir Easton MD 21601-7327

POTTER, BRAD J. dean, researcher, educator; BS, Colo. State U., 1975; DDS, Northwestern U., 1979; MS, U. Tex., San Antonio, 1991. Prof. oral diagnosis and patient svcs. Med. Coll. Ga., prof. oral biology and maxillofacial pathology, prof. grad. studies, dean dentistry, 1997—. Office: 1459 Loney Walker Blvd Augusta GA 30912 Business E-Mail: bpotter@mail.mcg.edu.

POTTER, CALVIN J. retired library director; b. Sheboygan, Wis., Nov. 3, 1945; married. Student, U. Wis., Sheboygan; BA, Lakeland Coll., 1968; postgrad., U. Wis. Past Wis. state assemblyman dist. 26; with dist. 9 Wis. State Senate, 1990-98, chmn. edn. com.; asst. supt. Dept. Pub. Instrn., Madison, Wis., 1998—2003. Former tchr. Mem. Sheboygan County Hist. Soc. Mem. NEA, Wis. Edn. Assn., Izaak Walton League. Address: N6266 Rio Rd Sheboygan Falls WI 53085-2203

POTTER, CLEMENT DALE, district attorney general; b. McMinnville, Tenn., Dec. 22, 1955; s. Johnnie H. and Elnora (Harvey) P.; children: Cory, Sarah, John Warren. BS, Middle Tenn. State U., 1984; JD, U. Tenn., 1987; cert., Tenn. Law Enforcement Acad., 1980. Bar: Tenn. 1987, U.S. Dist. Ct. (ea. dist.) Tenn. 1989. Pvt. practice law, McMinnville, 1987-89; city judge City of McMinnville, Tenn., 1988-89; pub. defender 31st Dist. State Tenn., McMinnville, 1989-98, dist. atty. gen., 1999—. Asst. to gen. editor Tools for the Ultimate Trial, 1st edit., 1985. Mem. Leadership McMinnville, 1989, chmn., 1995, 96. Staff sgt. USAF, 1974-80. Named McMinnville Warren County C. of C. Vol. of Yr., 1995; recipient D. Potter Henegar & Fred L. Hoover Sr. Bell Ringer award, 1995, Upper Cumberland award of merit 2000. Mem. ABA, Cheer Mental Health Assn. (dir. 1988—, pres. 1991-96), Harmony House Inc. (dir. 1993-95), Noon Exch. Club McMinnville (dir. 1992-94, sec. 1994, pres.-elect 1995, pres. 1996-97), Kiwanis Club of Warren County (pres. 1986-87), Tenn. Secondary Schs. Athletic Assn. (h.s. football referee 1988—), Am. Legion. Avocations: computers, gardening, coaching youth softball. Office: Dist Atty Gen 31st Dist PO Box 510 455 N Chancery Mc Minnville TN 37111

POTTER, DAVID L. academic administrator; Degree, Amherst Coll.; MS, PhD, Syracuse U. Instr., asst. to dir. pub. affairs program Syracuse (N.Y.) U., 1968-70; mem. staff Denison U., Ohio, 1970-81, Silliman U., The Philippines, 1970-81, State Coun. Higher Edn. Va., 1981-86; exec. asst. to pres. George Mason U., Fairfax, Va., 1986, v.p. exec. affairs, 1987-91, dean Coll. Arts and Scis., 1991-96, provost, 1996—, prof. anthropol. theory and cultural anthropology. Office: Delta State U PO Box A1 Cleveland MS 38733-1300

POTTER, DAVID SAMUEL, former automotive company executive; b. Seattle, Jan. 16, 1925; children: Diana (Mrs. Paul Bankston), Janice (Mrs. Robert Meadows), Tom, Bill; m. Nancy Shaar, Dec. 1979. BS, Yale U., 1945; PhD, U. Wash., 1951. Mem. staff Applied Physics Lab., U. Wash., 1946-60, asst. dir., 1955-60; with Gen. Motors Corp., 1960-73; chief engr. Milw. ops. GM Delco Electronics div., 1970-73; dir. research and devel. Detroit Diesel Allison div., 1973; asst. sec. for research and devel. Dept. Navy, 1973-74, under sec., 1974-76; v.p. environ. activities staff Gen. Motors Corp., Detroit, 1976-78, v.p. and group exec. public affairs group, 1978-83, v.p. in charge power products and def. ops. group, 1983-85; ret., 1985. Mem. Gov. Calif. Adv. Commn. Ocean Resources, 1964-68; mem. adv. panel Nat. Sea Grant Program, 1966; adv. bd. Naval Postgrad. Sch., Dept. Energy; bd. dirs. Sanders Assocs. Inc., Sci. Applications Internat. Co., John Fluke Mfg. Co., Lockheed Martin Corp. Served to ensign USNR, 1943-46. Mem. Nat. Acad. Engrng., NSF, Marine Tech. Soc., Am. Phys. Soc., AIAA, Am. Acoustical Soc., Nat. Oceanographic Assn. (v.p. 1966), Soc. Automotive Engrs. (chmn. tech. bd. 1978-79, dir. 1981-83), Cosmos Club (Washington), Detroit Club, Birmingham Athletic Club (Mich.), Birnam Wood Country Club (Montecito, Calif.), Santa Barbara Club. Achievements include research on cosmic rays, magnetics, underwater acoustics. Home: 877 Lilac Dr Santa Barbara CA 93108-1449

POTTER, DEBORAH ANN, news correspondent, educator; b. Hagerstown, Md., June 10, 1951; d. Peter R. and H. Louise (McDevitt) P.; m. Robert H. Witten; children: Cameron, Evan. BA, U. N.C., 1972; MA, Am. U., 1977. Assignment editor Sta. WMAL-TV, Washington, 1972-73, prodr., 1973-74; reporter Voice of Am., Washington, 1974-77; anchor Sta. KYW, Phila., 1977-78, CBS Radio, N.Y.C., 1978-81; White House corr. CBS News, Washington, 1981-85, state dept. corr., 1985-87, congl. corr., 1987-89, environ. corr., 1989-91; contbg. corr. 48 Hours, 1989-90; host Nightwatch CBS News, Washington, 1991; Washington corr. Cable News Network, Washington, 1991-94; asst. prof. Sch. Comm. Am. U., Washington, 1994-95. Mem. faculty Poynter Inst. Media Studies, St. Petersburg, Fla., 1995-98; exec. dir. NewsLab, Washington, 1998—. Co-author: Poynter Election Handbook; host (video prodns.) Beyond the Spotted Owl, 1993, Health Beat, 1994, Risk Reporting, 1995, Kids at Risk, 1997, (PBS series) In the Prime, 1996-97. Mem. adv. coun. Environ. Journalism Ctr., Radio and TV News Dirs. Found., Washington, 1994—; lay reader St. Alban's Episc. Ch., Washington, 1988-89, vestry, 1998-01. Mem. Radio TV News Dirs. Assn., Investigative Reporters and Editors, Assn. for Edn. in Journalism and Mass Comm., Nat. Press Photographers Assn., U. N.C. Alumni Assn. (bd. dirs. 1990-93, Disting. Young Alumna award 1990). Office: NewsLab 1900 M St NW Ste 210 Washington DC 20036-3530 E-mail: potter@newslab.org.

POTTER, DOUGLAS R. pharmaceutical executive; BS, Purdue U.; MBA, Boston U. CPA. Acct. SofTech, Inc., PriceWaterhouseCoopers; v.p., CFO Dynamics Rsch. Corp.; CFO, v.p. fin. Anika Therapeutics, Inc., Woburn, Mass., 2000—01, CEO, 2001—. Mem.: Fin. Exec. Inst., Treasurers Club of Boston. Office: Anika Therapeutics 236 W Cummings Park Woburn MA 01801

POTTER, EMMA JOSEPHINE HILL, language educator; b. Hackensack, N.J., July 18, 1921; d. James Silas and Martha Loretta (Pyle) Hill; m. James H. Potter, Mar. 26, 1949. AB cum laude with honors in classics, Alfred U., 1943; AM, Johns Hopkins U., 1946. Tchr. Latin, Balt. County Pub. Schs., 1943-44; instr. French and Spanish, Balt. Poly. Inst., 1950-83, instr. Spanish adult edn. classes, 1946-48; treas. Bruno-Potter, Inc. Trustee James Harry Potter Gold Medal award of ASME. Donor commemorative plaque in honor of Martha Pyle Hill to Chenango County Coun. Arts, 1996. Mem. Internat. Platform Assn., Clan Hay Soc. Scotland (Am. br.), John Hopkins U. Faculty Club. Democrat. Home: 419 3d Ave Avon By The Sea NJ 07717-1244

POTTER, FRED LEON, lawyer, insurance company executive, consultant; b. Kansas City, Kans., Dec. 15, 1948; s. Donald Warren and Olive Lucile (Ater) P.; m. Mertie Lorraine Scribner, June 13, 1970; children: Mark, Amy, Joy. BA, Harvard U., 1970, MBA, 1972; JD, U. Mich., 1975. Bar: N.H. 1975, U.S. Dist. Ct. N.H. 1975. Atty. Sulloway, Hollis & Soden, Concord, NH, 1975-80, 96—; pres., gen. counsel Christian Mut. Life Ins. Co., Concord, NH, 1980-96; exec. dir. NH Health Plan, NH, 2002, NH Vaccine Assoc., NH, 2002. Ptnr., mgmt. cons. Potter-Brock Assn., Tucson, 1969-82; trustee Gordon-Conwell Theol. Seminar, South Hamilton, Mass., 1983—; bd. dirs. N.H. Savs. Bank Corp., Concord, 1987-90; exec. dir. N.H. Health Plan N.H. Vaccine Assn., 2002--. Clk. Concord Union Sch. Dist., 1978-84; deacon 1st Bapt. Ch., Concord, 1978-85; elder Grace Bible Fellowship, 1993—; coach Concord Little League, 1985-87, 90-93. Mem. ABA, N.H. Bar Assn. (treas. 1980-84, v.p. 1984-85, pres. 1986-87, Pres. Disting. Service award 1983), Merrimack County Bar Assn. (sec. 1976-80), Christian Legal Soc., Computer Law Assn., Order of Coif. Evangelical. Home: 4 Pond Place Ln Concord NH 03301-3033 Office: 9 Capitol St Concord NH 03301-6310 E-mail: FPotter@sulloway.com.

POTTER, GARY THOMAS, lawyer; b. Boulder, Colo., Nov. 12, 1941; s. Ralph Boyce Potter and Patricia Jamie O'Rourke; m. Pamela Closson, Aug. 3, 1963 (dec. Jan. 1992); children: Matthew, Michael, Andrew, Katie. BA, Regis Coll., 1963; JD, U. Colo., 1966. Atty. Kayne Watson Potter, Boulder, 1966-67, State of Colo. Dept. of Law, Denver, 1967-68; trust atty. First Nat. Bank of Denver, Denver, 1968—77; mktg. v.p. Integrated Resource, Denver, 1977-78; pvt. practice Denver, 1978—. Pres. Lakewood Jr. Basketball, 1977-78; athletic dir. St. Bernadettes, Lakewood, 1992-93; bd. dirs., pres. Tchrs. Award Found., Denver, 1974-75; bd. dirs. Craig Hosp., Denver, 1977-80. Mem. U.S. Golf Assn. (sectional affairs com. 1980-98), Colo. Golf Assn. (bd. govs. 1974-88), Trans-Miss. Golf Assn. (trustee 1980—), Pacific Coast Golf Assn. (past pres. 1977, 88), Denver. C. of C. (pres. 1994-95). Roman Catholic. Office: 1700 Broadway Ste 430 Denver CO 80290-1201 E-mail: gpotter@mho.com.

POTTER, GEORGE WILLIAM, JR., mining executive; b. St. Louis, Aug. 5, 1930; s. George William and Fay Marguerite (Finch) P.; m. Emily Louise Withers, Feb. 11, 1956; 1 child, Anne Finch Russ. BA, U. Mo., Kansas City, 1952. Pres. Oritz Mines, Inc., Joplin, Mo., 1962-64, chmn. bd. dirs., 1964-87, Nancy Oil & Royalty Co., Joplin, 1981-86; pres., chmn. bd. dirs. Potter Industries, Inc., Joplin, 1981-90; chmn. bd. dirs. Cresset Corp., Joplin, 1986. Art exhibited in one-man shows at Barn Gallery, Kansas City, Mo., 1974, Fountain Valley Sch., Colorado Springs, Colo., 1974, U. Leyden, The Netherlands, 1977, others; author books (under pseudonym E.L. Withers): The House on the Beach, 1957, The Salazar Grant, 1959, Diminishing Returns, 1960, Heir Apparent, 1961, The Birthday, 1962, Royal Blood, 1964; fgn. edits. include Brit., French, Italian, German, Scandinavian, Japanese. Founding bd. dirs. Winfred L. and Elizabeth C. Post Meml. Art Reference Libr., 1977-82, Kansas City Ballet, 1976-79; trustee Conservatory of Music, Kansas City, 1988-2001. Recipient Mo. Writers award, 1967. Mem. Authors Guild, Nat. Trust for Hist. Preservation, Soc. Fellows Nelson Gallery Found. (coun. 1988-91), Kansas City Country Club. Home: 1239 W 61st Terr Kansas City MO 64113-1327

POTTER, HOLLIS GROMISCH, radiologist; b. NYC, 1958; MD, NY Med. Coll., 1985. Nat. Bd. of Med. Examiners 1985, diplomate Am. Bd. Radiology, Diagnostic Radiology 1990. Intern Danbury Hosp., 1985 -86; resident No. Shore U. Hosp., Manhasset, NY, 1986—90; fellow, skeletal radiology NY Hosp., Cornell U. Med. Coll., NY, NY, 1990—91; fellow, muscular skeletal radiology Hosp. Spl. Surgery, NYC, 1990—91, attending radiologist, chief, divsn. of magnetic resonance imaging, co-dir. rsch., 1992—, assoc. scientist-rsch. divsn.; attending radiologist NY Presbyn. Hosp. Prof. radiology Weill Med. Coll., Cornell U.; spkr. in field. Contbr. scientific papers, chapters to books; reviewer: Jour. of Am. Acad. of Orthopaedic Surgeons, Jour. of Biomechanics, Radiology, Jour. of Orthopaedic Rsch., Jour. of Bone and Joint Surgery. Recipient Editor's Recognition award with Distinction, 1996, 1997. Mem.: Am. Orthopaedic Soc. for Sports Medicine, Soc. of Skeletal Radiology, Radiological Soc. of N.Am., Internat. Soc. for Magnetic Resonance in Medicine, AMA, Am. Coll. of Radiology, Am. Acad. of Orthopaedic Surgeons, ACL Study Group, NY Roentgen Soc., Am. Roentgen Ray Soc., Phi Beta Kappa, Alpha Omega Alpha. Office: Hosp for Spl Surgery 535 E 70th St New York NY 10021-4872 Office Phone: 212-606-1023. Business E-Mail: potterh@hss.edu.

POTTER, J. STEWART, property manager; b. Ft. Worth, July 8, 1943; s. Gerald Robert Potter and Marion June (Mustain) Tombler; m. Dianne Eileen Roberb, Dec. 31, 1970 (div. Aug. 1983); 1 child, Christopher Stewart; m. Deborah Ann Blevins, Oct. 20, 1991. AA, San Diego Mesa Coll., 1967. Cert. apt. mgr., apt. property supr., housing adminstr. Sales mgr. Sta. KJLM, La Jolla, Calif., 1964-67; mgr. inflight catering Host Internat., San Diego, 1967-69; lead aircraft refueler Lockheed Co., San Diego, 1969-70; property mgr. Internat. Devel. and Fin Corp., La Jolla, 1970-72; mgr. bus. property BWY Constn. Co., San Diego, 1972-73; mgr. residents Coldwell Banker, San Diego, 1973-74; mgr. Grove Investments, Carlsbad, Calif., 1974-76, Villa Granada, Villa Seville Properties Ltd., Don Cohn, Chula Vista, Calif., 1976-83; gen. mgr. AFL-CIO Bldg. Trades Corp., National City, Calif., 1983—2003; instr., Cert. Apt. Mgmt. San Diego Apt. Assn., 1995-98. Bd. dirs. San Diego County Apt. Assn., 1995-97, San Diego County Policy Panel Youth Access to Alcohol, 1994-2002, San Diego Crime Victims Fund, 1998-2003, Founding Families San Diego Hist. Soc. Mem. Am. Assn. Retired Persons, San Diego County Apt. Assn. (bd. dirs.), La Jolla Monday Night Club (treas. 1984-89), La Jolla Hist. Soc. Roman Catholic. Avocation: golf. Personal E-mail: jspotter@san.rr.com.

POTTER, JACQUELINE JEAN, writer; b. Carthage, Mo., Dec. 8, 1929; d. Perry and Lorraine Riley; m. E. Elliott Potter, Feb. 4, 1952; children: Jamey Neal, Lisa Gail. AA, U. Calif., Berkeley, 1947—49; BA in English, U. Ill., Champaign-Urbana, 1950—51. Jr. copywriter Speigel, Chgo., 1952—53; continuity editor Radio Sta. KSWM, Joplin, Mo., 1953—54; copywriter Carthage Marble Corp., Mo., 1954—61, advt. mgr., 1962—67; pres. Jacqueline Potter Advt., Carthage, Mo., 1967—78; freelance writer Carthage, Mo., 1978—. Author: Silver Enchantment, 1984, Love Notes, 1985, By Surf and By Stream, 2003, 2005. Recipient Architectural Record award for advertising excellance, 1965. Mem.: Carthage Shakespeare Soc., Ozark Writers League. Methodist. Avocations: gardening, travel, reading. Office: Living Water Press PO Box 567 Carthage MO 64836

POTTER, JAMES EARL, retired international hotel management company executive; b. Utica, N.Y., July 25, 1933; s. Earl Moses and Helen May Potter. BS in Hotel Mgmt. with distinction, Cornell U., 1954, postgrad., 1955-56. Owner, propr. Old Drovers Inn, Dover Plains, N.Y., 1956-89; various acctg. positions Inter-Continental Hotels Corp., N.Y.C., 1960-62, fin. dir. for Asia and Pacific, 1963-69; v.p. Overseas Nat. Airways Hotels, N.Y.C., 1969-71; sr. v.p. Inter-Continental Hotels Corp., N.Y.C., 1972-89, London, 1990-92. Instr. acctg. Cornell U., Ithaca, N.Y., 1957-59. Author: A Room with a World View, 1996. Trustee Opera Co. Boston, 1978-85; mem. Cornell U. Coun., 1988-91; mem. patron com. Met. Opera, N.Y.C.; bd. dirs., mem. investment com., treas. Santa Fe Opera. Mem. Culinary Inst. Am. (trustees com. on acad. policy 1980-90), Met. Opera Club (bd. dirs., treas.), Cornell Hotel Soc., Cornell Club (N.Y.C.), Santa Fe Opera Found. (trustee, mem. fin. com. 2002-03). Presbyterian. Avocation: opera.

POTTER, JAMES VINCENT, association executive; b. Walla Walla, Wash., July 17, 1936; s. James Floyd and Dorothy May (Turner) P.; m. Margaret Mae Fogerson, July 4, 1954 (div. Apr. 1970); children: Deborah Ann, David Allan, Rebecca Lynn, Mary Michelle, Randy J., Jonathan James; m. Paula Maureen Brutsman, Feb. 28, 1986; stepchildren: Carolyn June, Catherine Doreen, Paul Clayton, Connie Lynn. BA in Bibl. Studies, Logos Bible Coll., 1989; MA in Theology, Logos Grad. Sch., 1989; PhD, Vision Christian U., 1990, postgrad., 1991-95. Diplomate Nat. Bd. Addiction Examiners, Am. Coll. Profl. Mental Health Practitioners, Am. Coll. Forensic Counselors; lic. clin. pastoral counselor; cert. temperament therapist, doctoral addictions counselor, domestic violence counselor, diplomat clin. hypnotherapist; cert. clin. psychopathologist; cert. Christian marraige and family therapist. Lectr., nat. presenter on addiction tratment and comestic violence, lit. evang. Seventh-day Adventist Ch., Idaho, 1956-60; staff mem. U. of the Nations Family Ministries, Kailua-Kona, Hawaii, 1989; pastor Gospel of Salvation Ministries, 1989-93; dean Coll. Christian Counseling, Vision Christian U., Hilo, Hawaii, 1990-93; pres. Family Care Svcs. Internat., 1990-93; v.p., mem. faculty Vision Christian U., Ramona, Calif., 1991-92, 1998—; adminstr., clinician Hawaii Family Care Ctrs., Hilo, 1989—95; exec. dir. Agape Family Svcs., Inc., Alliance Recovery Svcs., 1995—2003, Agape Family Svcs. Family Skills Inst.; dir. Jubilee Enterprises, 2003—. Vice chmn. Teen Challenge of Hawaii, 1991-93, govtl. apptd. mem. Hawaii Area Commn. on Mental Health and Substance Abuse, 1991-94; pres. Profl. Assn. Christian Therapists, 1989-94, Internat. Christian Counselors Assn., 1988—, Calif. Bd. Addiction Examiners, 2000—; lectr. western states, 1989—; nat. presenter on addictions and domestic violence and addictions prevention and treatment. Author: Soul Care, 1989, Untwisting Twisted Temperaments, 1991, (book and curriculum), Save Our Families, Pulling Down Strongholds, 1998, Breaking Free, 1998, Discovering Our True Selves, 1999, Mastery Over Anger, 2000, Assertiveness & Self-Ownership, 2000, Codependency and Self-Identity, 2000, Healing the Jekyll-Hyde Schism, 2000, Healing Inner-Child Wounds, 2000, Toxic Shame and the Journey Out, 2002, Relapse Prevention and Rage, 2002, Adolescence and Beyond, 2003, Counseling Addicts & Offenders, 2003; co-author: Family Care Center Manual, 1991, Christian Character Alignment, 1991; editor newsletter Gem-State Surveyor, 1976. Dem. nominee Idaho State Legis., House Rep., Boise, 1976, 78; vice chmn. Idaho Tech. Adv. Coun., Boise, 1976-83; pres.

Idaho Assn. Land Surveyors, Boise, 1976-77; chmn. Western Fedn. Profl. Land Surveyors, 12 western states, 1979-80; nat. dir. Am. Congress Surveying Mapping, Washington, 1981-83; gov. Nat. Soc. Profl. Land Surveyors; state del. Mont./Hawaii State Rep. Conv., Turtle Bay, 1988. With USN, 1953. Am. Congress Surveying Mapping fellow, Washington, 1980. Fellow: Nat. Assn. Forensic Counselors (diplomate, cert. ednl. provider); mem.: Am. Assn . Family Counselors, Am. Coll. Cert. Forensic Counselors (bd. govs.), Am. Assn. Christian Therapists, Christian Assn. Psychol. Studies, Am. Assn. Christian Counselors, Nat. Christian Counselors Assn. (bd. dirs. 1988), Nat. Assn. Family Counselors, Nat. Bd. Cert. Hypnotherapists, Nat. Bd. Addiction Examiners. Office: PO Box 994114 Redding CA 96099 Business E-Mail: docpotter@jubileeenterprises.com. *Sin, which separated man from God, is the "distortion" from all that which God intended man to be. It is our "missing the mark" of being a fully realized child of God (Romans 8:18 27). Jesus Christ "became sin" (2 Corinthians 5:21), assuming in His flesh the distortion of humanity, that we might in Him have "the right to become children of God." (John 1:12). Christian ministries are called to minister this healing of personhood to a sin sick world. (Isaiah 61: 1,2). The "new-birth" experience enables an individual to reclaim his/her heritage as a child of God, and to begin to "grow-up" in the wisdom and stature thereof. A process that the entire universe-antimate and inantimate is waiting for with eager anticipation (Romans 8:18-27).*

POTTER, JANET L. university librarian, administrator; b. Oneonta, N.Y., Oct. 24, 1947; d. R. Waldo and Emily Potter; m. Peter Molinari, 1983; 1 child, Lindsay Molinari; m. John M. Reilly, 1995. BA, SUNY, Albany, 1969, MLS, 1973; MA in History, SUNY, Binghamton, 1979. Reference librarian SUNY, Oneonta, 1973—95, libr. dir., 1995—97, assoc. provost for libr. and info. svcs., 1997—. Union officer and legis. chair United Univ. Professions, 1987-93; trustee Four County Libr. Sys., 1998—, pres., 1999-2001; mem. SUNY Connect Adv. Coun., 2000—, chair, 2002-03. Bd. dirs. SUCO Children's Ctr., 1983-88, N.Y. State Childcare Adv. Com., 1986-93. Mem. ALA, N.Y. Librs. Assn., SUNY Librs. Assn. Office: Milne Library SUNY Oneonta NY 13820 Office Phone: 607-436-2723.

POTTER, JOHN E. postal service executive; m. Maureen Potter; 2 children. B in Econs., Fordham U.; M in Mgmt., MIT. With USPS, 1977—, mgr. of Capital Metro ops., 1998—2000, sr. v.p. ops., 2000—01, postmaster gen., CEO, 2001—. Office: USPS 475 L'Enfant Plz Rm 5021 Washington DC 20260-0004

POTTER, JOHN FRANCIS, surgical oncologist, educator; b. N.Y.C., July 26, 1925; s. John Albert and Isabelle Cecelia (Sullivan) P.; m. Tanya Agnes Kristof, Nov. 19, 1955; children: Tanya Jean, Miriam Isabelle, John Mark. Student, Holy Cross Coll., 1943-45; MD, Georgetown Med. Sch., 1949. Intern Grasslands Hosp., Valhalla, N.Y., 1949-50, resident in surgery, 1949-50, Georgetown U. Hosp., Washington, 1953-56; sr. investigator Nat. Cancer Inst., Bethesda, Md., 1957-60; chief divsn. surg. oncology Georgetown Med. Ctr., Washington, 1960-85; instr, asst.prof., then assoc. prof. surgery Georgetown U. Sch. Medicine, 1957-64, prof., 1969—2000; dir. Vincent T. Lombardi Cancer Rsch. Ctr., Washington, 1967-87, U.S. Mil. Cancer Inst., Bethesda, Md., 2000—. Mem. U.S. Mil. Health Adv. Com.; presdl. apptd. mem. bd. regents Uniformed Svcs. U. of the Health Scis., 1999. Hon. prof. Universidad Cayetano Heredia, Lima, Peru, 1980. Lt. (j.g.) USNR, 1951-53. Recipient Pres.'s medal Georgetown U., 1991. Mem. Soc. Surg. Oncology (rep. adv. bd.), ACS, Assn. Am. Cancer Insts. (v.p. 1985-86, pres. 1986-87, bd. dirs. 1982, chmn. bd. dirs. 1987-88), So. Surg. Assn., Peruvian Cancer Soc. (hon.), Knights of Malta. Office: US Mil Cancer Inst Walter Reed Army Med Ctr Bldg # A109 6900 Georgia Ave NW Washington DC 20307 Business E-Mail: john.potter.1@na.amedd.army.mil.

POTTER, JOHN LEITH, mechanical and aerospace engineer, educator, consultant; b. Metz, Mo., Feb. 5, 1923; s. Jay Francis Lee and Pearl Delores (Leeth) P.; m. Dorothy Jean Williams, Dec. 15, 1957; children: Stephen, Anne, Carol. BS in Aerospace Engring., U. Ala., Tuscaloosa, 1944, MS in Engring., 1949; MS in Engring. Mgmt., Vanderbilt U., 1976, PhD in Mech. Engring., 1974. Engr., educator various indsl., ednl. and govt. orgns., 1944-52; chief, flight and aerodyns. lab. Redstone Arsenal, Ala., 1952-56; mgr., div. chief, dep. tech. dir., sr. staff scientist Sverdrup Tech., Inc., Tullahoma, Tenn., 1956-83; research prof. Vanderbilt U., Nashville, 1983-92, prof. emeritus, 1992—; cons. engr. Nashville, 1983—. Convener NATO-AGARD, U.S. and Eng., 1980-82, mem. working group, 1984-88; mem. adv. com. Internat. Symposium on Rarefied Gasdynamics, 1970—; invited lectr. USSR Acad. Scis., 1967; mem. NRC com. on assessment nat. aeronautical wind tunnel facilities, 1987-88; mem. NASA working groups, 1987—; mem. Engring. Accreditation Commn., 1985-90. Editor: Rarefied Gas Dynamics, 1977. Contbr. articles to profl. publs., chpts. to books Chmn. bd. dirs. Coffee County Hist. Soc., Tenn., 1971-72; bd. dirs. Southeastern Amateur Athletic Union, 1972-73; pres. Tullahoma Swim Club, 1972-73. Recipient Outstanding Fellow award U. Ala. Aerospace Engring. Dept., 1987; elected 150th Anniversary Disting. Engring. Fellow U. Ala. Coll. Engring., 1988; USAF Arnold Engring. Devel. Ctr. fellow, 1993. Fellow AIAA (assoc. editor jour. 1970-73, publs. com. 1973-78, assoc. editor Progress in Astronautics and Aeronautics 1981-85, Gen. H.H. Arnold award Tenn. chpt. 1964); mem. Capstone Engring. Soc. (regional bd. dirs. 1972-77), Sigma Xi, Tau Beta Pi, Theta Tau, Pi Tau Sigma, Sigma Gamma Tau. Home: 400 University Park Dr Apt 394 Birmingham AL 35209

POTTER, JOHN WILLIAM, federal judge; b. Toledo, Ohio, Oct. 25, 1918; s. Charles and Mary Elizabeth (Baker) P.; m. Phyllis May Bihn, Apr. 14, 1944; children: John William, Carolyn Diane, Kathryn Susan. PhB cum laude, U. Toledo, 1940; JD, U. Mich., 1946. Bar: Ohio 1947. Assoc. Zachman, Boxell, Schroeder & Torbet, Toledo, 1946-51; ptnr. Boxell, Bebout, Torbet & Potter, Toledo, 1951-69; mayor City of Toledo, 1961-67; asst. atty. gen. State of Ohio, 1968-69; judge 6th Dist. Ct. Appeals, 1969-82, U.S. Dist. Ct., Toledo, 1982—, sr. judge, 1992—. Presenter in field. Sr. editor U. Mich. Law Rev., 1946. Pres. Ohio Mcpl. League, 1965; past assoc. pub. mem. Toledo Labor Mgmt. Commn.; past pres., bd. dirs. Commn. on Rels. with Toledo (Spain); past bd. dirs. Cummings Sch. Toledo Opera Assn., Conlon Ctr.; past trustee Epworth United Meth. Ch.; hon. chmn. Toledo Festival Arts, 1980. Capt. F.A., U.S. Army, 1942-46. Decorated Bronze Star; recipient Leadership award Toledo Bldg. Congress, 1965, Merit award Toledo Bd. Realtors, 1967, Resolution of Recognition award Ohio Ho. of Reps., 1982, Outstanding Alumnus award U. Toledo, 1966, conf. rm. named in his honor, U.S. Courthouse, Toledo, 1998; named to Field Arty. Officer Candidate Sch. Hall of Fame, 1999. Fellow Am. Bar Found., Am. Judicature Soc., 6th Jud. Cir. Dist. Judges Assn., Fed. Judges Assn.; mem. ABA, Ohio Bar Assn. (Found. Outstanding Rsch. award 1995), Toledo Bar Assn. (exec. com. 1962-64, award 1992), Lucas County Bar Assn., U. Toledo Alumni Assn. (past pres.), Toledo Zool. Soc. (past bd. dirs.), Old Newsboys Club, Toledo Club, Kiwanis (past pres.), Phi Kappa Phi. Home: 2418 Middlesex Dr Toledo OH 43606-3114 Office: US Dist Ct 307 US Courthouse 1716 Spielbusch Ave Toledo OH 43624-1363

POTTER, LORRAINE K. career military officer; m. Robert Saunders. BS, Keuka Coll.; MDiv, Colgate Rochester Div. Sch. Former pastor, N.Y.; clin. pastoral educator Yale-New Haven Med. Ctr.; commd. 2d lt. USAF, 1971, advanced through ranks to maj., 2001; various assignments to command chaplain Hdqtrs. Air Edn./Tng. Command, Randolph AFB, Tex., 1998-99; dep. chief of Chaplain Svc. Hdqtrs. USAF, Bolling AFB, D.C., 1999—. At-large mem. Am. Bapt. Chs. Gen. Bd.; active Ministers Coun. for Chaplains and Pastoral Counselors. Office: Chief Chaplain HQ USAF/Bolling AFB 112 Luke Ave SW Washington DC 20332-5113

POTTER, MICHAEL, genetics researcher, medical researcher; b. East Orange, N.J., Feb. 27, 1924; AB, Princeton U., 1945; MD, U. Va., 1949. Research asst. dept. microbiology U. Va. Med. Sch., 1952-54, biologist, 1954-70, head immunochemistry sect. Lab. Cell Biology, 1970-82; chief genetics lab., divsn. basic scis. Nat. Cancer Inst., Bethesda, Md., 1982—. Recipient Paul-Ehrlick & Ludwig-Darmstaedter prize, 1983, Lasker award in basic med. research, 1984. Mem. Nat. Acad. Sci., Am. Assn. Cancer Research, Am. Assn. Immunologists. Office: Nat Cancer Inst 9000 Rockville Pike Bldg 37 Bethesda MD 20892-0001

POTTER, MICHAEL J. retail stores executive; b. Oreg., 1960; BS, U. Oreg., 1983; MBA, Capital U., Ohio. CFO, sr. v.p. Consolidated Stores Corp. (now Big Lots), Columbus, Ohio, 1991—2000; pres., CEO Big Lots, Columbus, Ohio, 2000—. Office: Big Lots 300 Phillipi Rd Columbus OH 43228-5311

POTTER, MYRTLE S. research and development company executive; B, U. Chgo. Formerly with Merck and Co.; v.p. strategy and econ. Bristol-Myers Squibb, 1996, pres.; exec. v.p. Genetech, Inc., South San Francisco, 2000—01, exec. v.p. comml. ops., COO, 2001—. Bd. dirs. Calif. Healthcare Inst., 2001—. Office: Genetech Inc 1 DNA Way South San Francisco CA 94080

POTTER, NED, science journalist, writer; b. N.Y.C., Sept. 23, 1956; s. Gene and Marlies Potter; m. Beth Thomas; children: David, Katherine. AB, Princeton U., 1977. Corr. CBS News, Chgo., Boston, 1980-87; environ. corr. ABC News, N.Y.C., 1987-95, chief sci. corr., 1995—. Contbr. articles to mags. Recipient Edward R. Murrow award, Radio-TV news dirs. assn. (RTNDA), 2004, Emmy award, NATAS, 1985, 97, World medal, N.Y. Festivals, N.Y.C., 1999, 2000, Golden Eagle award, CINE, Washington, 1997, duPont-Columbia award, Columbia U. Grad. Sch. Journalism, 1996, 2003. Office: ABC News 47 W 66th St New York NY 10023

POTTER, RICHARD KEVIN, accountant, controller, consultant; b. Fayetteville, Tenn., Aug. 27, 1972; s. Larry Joe and Angela Fay (Thompson) Holtzhouser; m. Johnna Kaye Fourthman, May 28, 1994; children: Melissa Ellen, Richard Nolan. BS in Econs., Acctg. and Polit. Sci., S.E. Mo. State U., 1994. Sr. account mgr. Nat. Rent to Own, St. Louis, 1994; prodn. supr. Gates Rubber Co., Charleston, Mo., 1995-96, cost/budget acct., 1996—, interim contr., 1997-98; corp. acct. Delta Cos., Cape Girardeau, Mo., 1998-2000; with DeWitt Co., Inc., Sikeston, Mo. Cons. FayJoe Enterprises, Lilbourn, Mo., 1997—. Vol. fireman Lilbourn Vol. Fire Dept., 1993-99; EMT Mississippi County Ambulance Dist., Charleston, Mo., 1997-99. Mem. Inst. Mgmt. Accts. Avocations: golf, emergency public service work, professional journal reading, do it yourself work. Home: 404 Country Club Dr Scott City MO 63780-1441 Office: Delta Companies (DLH Svcs) PO Box 880 Cape Girardeau MO 63702-0880

POTTER, ROBERT DANIEL, federal judge; b. Wilmington, N.C., Apr. 4, 1923; s. Elisha Lindsey and Emma Louise (McLean) P.; m. Mary Catherine Neilson, Feb. 13, 1954; children: Robert Daniel Jr., Mary Louise, Catherine Ann. AB in Chemistry, Duke U., 1947, LLB, 1950; LLD (hon.), Sacred Heart Coll., Belmont, N.C., 1982. Bar: N.C. 1951. Pvt. practice law, Charlotte, NC, 1951-81; dist. judge U.S. Dist. Ct. (we. dist.) N.C., 1981-2000, chief judge, 1984-91, now sr. judge. Commr. Mecklenburg County, Charlotte, 1966-68. Served as 2d lt. U.S. Army, 1944-47, ETO. Mem. N.C. Bar Assn., Charlotte City Club. Republican. Roman Catholic. Office Phone: 704-552-7742.

POTTER, ROBERT JOSEPH, technical and business executive; b. N.Y.C., Oct. 29, 1932; s Mack and Ida (Bernstein) P.; married; children: Diane Gail, Suzanne Lee, David Craig. BS cum laude, Lafayette Coll., 1954; MA in Physics, U. Rochester, 1957, PhD in Optics, 1960. Cons. ANPA Research Inst., AEC Brookhaven Nat. Lab., RCA Labs., U.S. Naval Research Labs., 1952-60; mgr. optical physics and optical pattern recognition IBM Thomas J. Watson Research Center, Yorktown Heights, N.Y., 1960-65; assoc. dir. Applied Research Lab., Xerox Corp., Rochester, N.Y., 1965-67; v.p. advanced engring. Xerox Corp., 1967-68, v.p. devel. and engring., 1968-69, v.p., gen. mgr. Spl. Products and Systems divsn., 1969-71, v.p. info. tech. group Rochester, 1971-73, Dallas, 1973-75, pres. Office Sys. divsn., 1975-78; sr. v.p., chief tech. officer Internat. Harvester Co., Chgo., 1978-82; group v.p. integrated office sys. Nortel Networks, Richardson, Tex., 1985-87; pres., CEO Datapoint Corp., San Antonio, 1987—90, R.J. Potter Co., Dallas, 1990—. Zebra Techs. Corp., Cree Corp. Pres., CEO Molex, Inc., Bradshaw Group, Speed FC; bd. govs., vice chmn. IIT Rsch. Inst., 1999—2002; chmn. Tatum CIO Ptnrs., LLP, 2000—02; bd. dirs. Am. Nat. Bank; mem. adv. bd. U. Tex., Dallas. Contbr. articles to profl. jours. Trustee Ill. Inst. Tech., Alliance for Higher Edn. Recipient IBM Outstanding Tech. Contbn. award, 1964, Disting. Achievement award Soc. Mfg. Engrs., 1981; Kroner scholar Lafayette Coll., 1954; Disting. Rochester scholar U. Rochester, 1995. Fellow Optical Soc. Am., Am. Phys. Soc.; mem. Phi Beta Kappa, Sigma Xi. Office: R J Potter Co 5215 N O Connor Blvd Ste 1110 Irving TX 75039-3739 E-mail: RJPotter@RJPotter.com.

POTTER, RONALD NEAL, JR., newspaper distribution specialist; b. Orlando, Fla., Jan. 19, 1974; s. Ronald Neal Potter and Tania Juana Gonzalez; m. Lisa Ann Kinchen, Apr. 2, 1994; children: Ronald Neal III, Brianna Elise, Evan Reece. BA in Theology, Bapt. Coll. Fla., 1995. Phys. edn. instr. Day Spring Christian Acad., Marianna, Fla., 1995—97; min. of youth New Oak Grove Bapt. Ch., Alachua, Fla., 1996—97; min. of youth and music Downtown Bapt. Ch., Ocala, Fla., 1998—99; min. of youth Goldenrod Bapt. Ch., Winter Park, Fla., 2000—01; distbn. supr. Orlando Sentinel, 2001—03, 2003—; dist. mgr. Dothan (Ala.) Eagle, 2003. Author/performer: (CDs) Juniper, Unspoken, 2003. Recipient Total Release award, The Masters Acad., Orlando, 1991. Mem.: ASCAP, Woodmen of the World. Avocations: basketball, Corvette collecting, comic book collecting, writing, music. Office: Orlando Sentinel Publs Orange Ave Orlando FL

POTTER, ROSEMARY, state legislator; b. Apr. 15, 1952; m. Steve Nichols, 1994. BA, U. Wis., Milw., 1974, MA, 1983. Former dist. dir. Combined Health Appeal Wis. Ho. of Reps.; chairwoman Dem. Caucus; Wis. state assemblywoman Dist. 20, 1989-98; pub. polit. advocate Foley & Lardner, Milw., 1998—. Former tchr. Office: Doley & Lardner 1st Star Center 777 E Wisconsin Ave Ste 3800 Milwaukee WI 53202-5367 Home: W314n8709 Winchester Trl Hartland WI 53029-9525

POTTER, SCOTT MICHAEL, artist, writer; b. Grand Rapids, Mich., Feb. 18, 1966; s. James Nicholas Potter and January Friesner. Degree in Visual Arts Adminstrn., Aquinas Coll., 1995, MA in Mgmt., 2001; postgrad., Pacifica Grad. Inst., 2002—. V.p. Operation Feed, Inc., Grand Rapids, 1998—99, exec. dir., 1998—99; v.p. Telepoetic Network, Grand Rapids, 1999—2000, exec. dir., 1999—2000; founder Union of Faces, Grand Rapids, 2001—. Founder, dir. Konstruct U., Grand Rapids, 1996—98; tri-founder Get Off Yer Ass, Grand Rapids, 1997—98. Author, editor Voices From the Third Coast, 1997; This is it! The Power of Voices..., 1998. Vol. Frederick Meijer Gardens, Grand Rapids, 1995—2002; event organizer Wholistic Health Doesn't Just Happen Fest, Grand Rapids, 1995, Abuse Benefit for Children at Billy's, Grand Rapids, 1997. Hruby scholar, Aquinas Coll., 1999—2001. Avocations: poetry, piano, painting, photography, pottery, mythology, psychology. Home: 6615 Kings Valley Rd Crescent City CA 95531

POTTER, SUSAN KUNIHOLM, bank executive; BA, Cornell U., 1988; MBA, U. Pa. Sr. mgr. Sotheby's, 1992—94; bus. analyst McKinsey & Co., Cleve., 1994—98, engagement mgr., 1998—2002; exec. v.p. product mgmt. consumer banking group KeyCorp, Cleve., 2002—04, exec. v.p. retail bus. devel., 2004—. Named One of 25 Women to Watch, U.S. Banker Mag., 2003. Office: KeyCorp 127 Public Square Cleveland OH 44114-1306

POTTER, SYLVIA, education educator; b. Buchanan County, Va., Feb. 4, 1942; d. Kelly C. and Virgie E. (Osborn) Runyon; m. Hersel E. Potter, Apr. 23, 1961 (div. 1992); children: Barbara L., Timothy H., Jonathan, Amanda. AS summa cum laude, Southwest Va. Cmty. Coll., 1985; BS summa cum laude, Pikeville Coll., 1987; MA with honors, Va. Tech. Inst., 1994. Lic. reading specialist, early edn. educator, mid. edn. educator, spl. edn., Va. LPN Grundy (Va.) Hosp., 1962-72; tchr. Buch County Schs., Grundy, 1972-76, 89-92, Commonwealth of Va. Dept. of Corrections, Hanover, 1993—. Mem. curriculum com. Dept. Correctional Edn., 1997-99, mem. interview panel for hiring com., 1996-2001. Mem. com. Office on Youth, Grundy, 1991-93; scout leader Boy Scouts Am., 1986-93, com. mem. Matlapanai coun. 1996-99, Order of Arow Brotherhood, Sequoyah coun., 1990-94. Mem. Correctional Edn. Assn., Va. Assn. Correctional Edn., Internat. Reading Assn., VA Assn. for Gifted. Democrat. Mem. Ch. of Christ. Avocations: reading, physical work outs, scouting, camping, travel. Home: 8601 S Fork Ct Fredericksburg VA 22407-8723

POTTER, TREVOR ALEXANDER MCCLURG, lawyer; b. Chgo., Oct. 24, 1955; s. Charles Steele and Barbara (McClurg) P. AB, Harvard Coll., 1978; JD, U. Va., 1982. Bar: Ill. 1983, D.C. 1988, U.S. Supreme Ct. 1997. Counsel office of legal policy U.S. Dept. Justice, Washington, 1982-84; asst. gen. counsel FCC, Washington, 1984-85; atty. Wiley, Rein & Fielding, Washington, 1985-88, ptnr., 1988-91,96-2001; commr. Fed. Election Commn., Washington, 1991—, vice chmn., 1993, chmn., 1994-95; ptnr. Caplin & Drysdale, Washington, 2001—. Merrill lectr. Sch. Law U. Va., 1996-97. Republican. Episcopalian. Fellow Brookings Instn. (sr.); mem. ABA (chmn. com. on election law, adminstrv. law sect. 1993-95, 99—, mem. standing com. on election law 2000—). Office: Caplin & Drysdale One Thomas Cir NW Washington DC 20005 E-mail: tp.@capdale.com.

POTTER, WILLIAM BARTLETT, business executive; b. Washington, Jan. 4, 1938; s. George Holland and Virginia (Bartlett) P.; m. Simone Robert, June 6, 1964; children: Eva Simone, William Bartlett. AB, Princeton U., 1960; MBA, Emory U., 1962. With Merc.-Safe Deposit & Trust Co., Balt., 1962—, asst. sec., asst. treas., 1964-66, asst. v.p., 1966-68, v.p., 1968-69, sr. v.p., 1969-76, exec. v.p., 1976, Preston Trucking Co., 1976-77, pres., 1977-86; chmn., pres. Preston Trucking, 1986-92; Preston Corp., 1986-93, chmn., 1994—. Home: 3215 Owen Baldwin Pkwy Trinidad CO 81082-9004

POTTER, WILLIAM JAMES, investment banker; b. Toronto, Aug. 11, 1948; s. William Wakely and Ruby Loretta (Skidmore) P.; m. Linda Lee, Nov. 25, 1972; children: Lisa Michelle, Meredith Lee, Andrew David. AB, Colgate U., 1970; MBA, Harvard U., 1974. With White Weld & Co., Inc., N.Y.C., 1974-75, Toronto Dominion Bank, Toronto (Can.) and N.Y., 1975-78, group mgr. Toronto, 1979-82; 1st v.p. Barclays Bank PLC, N.Y.C., 1982-84; mng. dir. Prudential-Bache Securities, Inc., N.Y.C., 1984-89; pres. Ridgewood Capital Funding Inc., N.Y.C., 1989—, Ridgewood Group Internat. Ltd., N.Y.C., 1989—2004; chmn. R. Meredith & Co., Inc., 2004—. Advisor Ladenberg Thalman Internat., 1990—92, Laidlaw Holdings, Inc., 1992—93; bd. dirs. Aberdeen Australian Equity Fund Inc., Md., Aberdeen Asia Pacific Income Fund Inc., Md., Aberdeen Asia Pacific Income Fund Ltd., New Zealand, Alexandria Bancorp, Canada, Columbus Mills Ltd., Ghana, E.C. Power Inc., Aberdeen Commonwealth Fund Inc., Md., Voicenet Inc., Del.; advisor Centennial Fund LLP, Canada. Author: Finance for the Minerals Industry, 1985. Trustee Glen Ridge Ednl. Found, 1994—; bd. dirs. Glen Ridge (N.J.) Cmty. Fund, 1985—94. Mem.: Nat. Fgn. Trade Coun. (Washington, bd. dirs., chmn. fin. com., exec. com. 1983—), New England Club N.Y., Econ. Club N.Y., Buck Hill Country Club (Pa.), Glen Ridge Country Club (NJ), Nat. Club (Toronto), Williams Club (N.Y.C.), Harvard Club (N.Y.C.). Congregationalist. Avocations: golf, tennis. Office: Ridgewood Group Internat Inc 236 W 27th St Fl 3 New York NY 10001-5906

POTTHAST, DAVID RAYMOND, retired military officer, secondary school educator; b. Albuquerque, Aug. 24, 1954; s. Jerome Henry and Jean Marie Potthast; m. Susan Lee Hawkins, May 22, 1976; children: Seth, Jeanna. Student, Greenville (Ill.) Coll., 1972—73; BA in History, Ea. Ill. U., 1976; MA in History, We. Ill. U., 2001. Cert. secondary edn. Ill. Commd. ensign USN, 1972, advanced through ranks to lt. comdr.; divsn. officer USS Thomaston (LSD-28), San Diego, 1977—81; combat systems officer Fleet Tng. Group, San Diego, 1981—83; intelligence officer Fosif Westpac, Kami Seya, Japan, 1983—86, USS Belleau Wood (LHA-3), San Diego, 1986—88, Jt. Nat. Intel Devel. Staff, Suitland, Md., 1988—92, Office Naval Intelligence, Suitland, Md., 1992—94; ret. USN, 1994; tchr. history, social scis. Rockridge H.S., Taylor Ridge, Ill., 1994—. Mem.: Org. of Am. History, Am. Hist. Assn., Mil. Officers Assn., Am. Numismatic Assn. Republican. Baptist. Avocations: coin collecting/numismatics, antiques, nautical lore, reading, gardening. Office: Rockridge High Sch 14110 134th St W Taylor Ridge IL 61284

POTTIE, ROSWELL FRANCIS, Canadian federal science and technology consultant; b. St. Peter's, N.S., Can., Oct. 28, 1933; s. John Henry and Margaret Mary (Landry) P.; m. Huguette Lacoste, Aug. 18, 1989; children: Michael F., Gregory J., Lisa M., David S. BS in Chemistry summa cum laude, St. Francis Xavier Univ., 1954; PhD in Chemistry, Notre Dame U., 1958. Postdoctoral fellow Notre Dame (Ind.) U., 1957-58, E.I. Du Pont de Nemours, Inc., Wilmington, Del., 1960-64, NRC Can., Ottawa, 1958-60, research officer, 1964-74, asst. to sr. v.p., 1976-80, Atlantic regional dir. Halifax, N.S., 1980-83, v.p. regional labs. Ottawa, 1983-84, v.p. physical scis. and engring., 1984-86, sr. v.p. labs., 1986-87, exec. v.p., 1987-91; pvt. cons., 1991—; program officer Ministry of State for Sci. and Tech. (secondment), Ottawa, 1974-75; program analyst Treasury Bd. Can. (secondment), Ottawa, 1975-76. Bd. govs. Ctr. for Cold Regions Resources Engring., St. John's; mem. N.B. (Can.) Research and Productivity Council, Fredericton, 1981—. Contbr. articles to profl. jours. Coach, exec. baseball, swimming and soccer clubs, Gloucester, Ont., 1970-76; pres. Gloucester Swim Club, 1973-75; exec. North Gloucester Recreation Assn., 1971-74. Recipient Gov. Gen.'s medal, St. Francis Xavier U., 1954. Mem. Can. Research Mgmt. Assn., St. Francis Xavier Alumni Assn. (Ottawa pres. 1970-73), Sigma Xi. Roman Catholic. Avocations: swimming, badminton, carpentry, ancient history. Home: 28 Bellefontaine Ct Lawrencetown NS Canada B2Z 1L3

POTTLITZER, JOANNE, freelance/self-employed writer, theater producer, theater director; d. Joseph Klein Pottlitzer and Madonna Mae Mahoney. BS, Purdue U., 1955—59; MA, Middlebury Coll., 1963—64. Program officer Inst. of Internat. Edn., N.Y.C., 1964—68; founder, artistic dir. Theatre of L.Am., Inc., N.Y.C., 1966—80; freelance writer/dir. N.Y.C., 1983—. Vis. prof. Yale U. Sch. of Drama, New Haven, 1996; cons., transl. program Theatre Comm. Group, Inc., NYC, 1985—87; cons./on-site evaluator Nat. Endowment for the Arts, Washington, 1992—93; cons./panel Ariz. Commn. on the Arts, 1987; vis. faculty fellow Univ. of Notre Dame, Kellogg Inst., Notre Dame, Ind., 1995; sr. Fulbright prof. Cath. U. of Chile Theater Sch., Santiago, 1988; sr. Fulbright prof. dept. theater U. of Chile, Santiago, 1994—95; cons., internat. exch. program New Dramatists, N.Y.C., 1994; writer/cons., comm. program INTAR Hispanic Arts Theatre, New York, NY, 1993—93; vis. prof. Ohio U. Sch. of Theatre, 1993; vis. prof., undergrad. theater program NYU, Tisch Sch. of the Arts, NYC, 1991—92; cons., edn. and culture program The Ford Found., NYC, 1984—91; Rockefeller Fedn. writing resident, Bellagio, Italy, 2004. Prodr.: (theatre) Tres Marías y una Rosa, Arena Conta Zumbi, Vimazoluleka, La Remolienda; dir.: Frankie and Johnny in the Claire de Lune, An Open Window, Pim, Pam, Pum!, Ud. También Podrá Disfrutar de Ella, Kathie and the Hippopotamus, Burning Patience, The Young Lady from Tacna, Pol, Opposites; author: (theatre) Kate's Place, Paper Wings; prodr.: (concert) Inti-Illimani, Festival of Drums II, Angel and Isabel Parra, (performance/exhibition) Theatre in the Americas Festival (The Villager Award, 1979); author: (book) Hispanic Theatre in the United States and Puerto Rico, (theatre critic) Other Stages, (column) The Soho Weekly News; contbr.; translator: (play) Daedalus in the Belly of the Beast; prodr.: (concert) Quilapayún in Concert: Santa María de Iquique; prodr., prodr.: Chile, Chile!, (Obie Award, 1976); translator: (book of poetry) Book of the Ocean, (play) Saying Yes, Nelson 2 Rodrigues (NY State Coun. on the Arts Transl. Award, 1992), The Toothbrush, Kathie and the Hippopotamus (Nat. Endowment for the Arts Transl. Award, 1987), Mythweavers, (film) The Holy Mountain, (film/book) El Topo; prodr.: (concert) La Música Jíbara de Puerto Rico, (theatre/music/exhibition) Latin American Fair of Opinion (Obie Award, 1972), (concert) Gilberto Gil in Concert, (theatre) Ceremony for a Murdered Black, (presenter) (film/exhibition) Alexandro Jodorowsky Festival, (theatre) Arena Conta Bolivar; contbr. articles. Recipient Acknowledgement and Appreciation of Contributions toward Restoring Democracy in Chile, Permanent Rep. of Chile to the UN, 2001, Travel and Study award, The Ford. Found., 1970, Travel & Study award, The Ford Found., 1968, Travel and Study award, The Ford Foun., 1973, The Ford Found., 1981; scholar Hon. Scholarship, Purdue U., 1955—59; Sr. Fulbright fellowship, U.S. Dept. of State, 1994—95, 1988, Individual Artist award, NY State Coun. on the Arts, 1988, Fulbright-Hays Student fellowship, U.S. State Dept., 1963—64, Rotary

Internat. fellowship, Rotary Club, 1961. Mem.: League of Profl. Theatre Women (mem. of the bd. 1987—2004), The Women's Project & Productions, Soc. of Stage Directors and Choreographers (assoc.), The Dramatists Guild (assoc.), The Art Students League (life). Achievements include first to bring Latin American theatre to the United States; research in the artists' influence on the political process in Chile 1973-1990. Avocations: painting, travel. Home: 38 West 56th St New York NY 10019 Personal E-mail: jomaka56@msn.com.

POTTORFF, JO ANN, state legislator; b. Wichita, Kans., Mar. 7, 1936; d. John Edward McCluggage and Helen Elizabeth (Alexander) Ryan; m. Gary Nial Pottorff; children: Michael Lee, Gregory Nial. BA, Kansas State U., 1957; MA, St. Louis U., 1969. Elem. tchr. Pub. Sch., Keats and St. George, 1957-59; cons., elem. specialist Mid Continent Regional Edn. Lab., Kansas City, Mo., 1971-73; cons. Poindexter Assocs., Wichita, 1975; campaign mgr. Garner Shriver Congl. Camp, Wichita, 1976; interim dir. Wichita Area Rape Ctr., 1977; conf. coord. Biomedical Synergistics Inst., Wichita, 1977-79; real estate sales asst. Chester Kappelman Group, Wichita, 1979-98, J.P. Weigard & Sons, Wichita, 1998—; state rep. State of Kans., Topeka, 1985—. Mem. exec. com. Nat. Conf. State Legis. Com. Mem. sch. bd. Wichita Pub. Schs., 1977-85; bd. dirs. Edn. Consol. and Improvement Act Adv. com., Kans. Found. for the Handicapped; mem. Children and Youth Adv. com. (bd. dirs.); active Leadership Kans.; chairperson women's network Nat. Conf., State Legislators; mem. Wichita Children's Home Bd.; vice chmn. Nat. Assessment Governing Bd.; chair edn. com. assembly on state issues Nat. Conf. State legislators. Recipient Disting. Svc. award Kans. Assn. Sch. Bds., 1983, Outstanding Svc. to Sch. Children of Nation award Coun. Urban Bds., 1984, awards Gov.'s Conf. for Prevention of Child Abuse and Neglect, Kans. Assn. Reading. Mem. Leadership Am. Alumnae (bd. dirs., sec) Found. for Agr. in Classroom (bd. dirs.), Jr. League, Vet. Aux. (pres.), Bd. Nat. State Art Agys., Rotary, Ky. Assn. Rehab. Facilities (Ann. award), Nat. Order Women in Legislature (past bd. dirs.), Nat. Conf. State Legislatures (chmn. edn. assembly state issues, exec. com.), Rotary, Chi Omega (pres.). Avocations: politics, travel. Office: Weigard 6530 E 13th St N Wichita KS 67206-1247

POTTRUCK, DAVID STEVEN, brokerage house executive; b. 1948; m. Emily Pottruck; 2 children. BA, U. Pa., 1970, MBA with honors, 1972. Now pres., CEO U.S. Govt., 1972-74; with Arthur Young & Co., 1974-76, sr. cons.; with Citibank N.Am., 1976-81, v.p.; with Shearson/Am. Express, 1981-84, sr. v.p. consumer mktg. and advt.; with Charles Schwab & Co., San Francisco, 1984—; exec. v.p. mktg., br. adminstr. Charles Schwab and Co., Inc.; pres. Charles Schwab & Co., 1992—94; pres., COO The Charles Schwab Corp., 1994—98, pres., co-CEO, 1998—2003, pres., CEO, 2003—04. Apptd. commr. by Congress The Advisory Commn. on Internet Commerce; bd. dirs. Intel Corp., US Trust Co., N.A., DoveBid, Inc. Co-author: Clicks and Mortar: Passion Driven Growth in an Internet Driven World. Bd .dirs. US Ski and Snowboard Team Found.; trustee U. Penn. Named Exec. of the Year, San Francisco Bus. Times, CEO of the Year, Morningstar; named one of Top 15 CEOs, Worth mag.; recipient Torch of Liberty award, Anti-Defamation League, 2000.*

POTTS, ANTHONY VINCENT, optometrist, orthokeratologist; b. Detroit, Aug. 10, 1945; m. Susan Claire, July 1, 1967; 1 child, Anthony Christian. Student, Henry Ford Community Coll., 1964—65, Eastern Mich. U., 1965—66; OD, So. Coll. Optometry, 1970; MS in Health Svcs. Mgmt., LaSalle U., 1995. Practice orthokeratology and contact lenses, Troy, Mich., 1975—. Adj. prof. optometry So.Calif. Coll. Optometry, Pa. Coll. Optometry; lectr., author orthokeratology, contact lenses and astigmatism. Comdr. USNR, MSC USNR, 1992—. Fellow Internat. Orthokeratology Soc. (membership chmn. 1976-83, bd. dirs. local chpt. 1976-83, chmn. Internat. Eye Rsch. Found. sect. 1981-83, bd. dirs. nat. chpt. 1985—, adminstrv. dir. nat. chpt. 1985—, chmn. nat. chpt. 1987-1992), Fellow Am. Acad. Optometry, Am. Optometric Assn.; mem. Am. Assn. Healthcare Execs., Armed Forces Optometric Soc., Nat. Eye Rsch. Found., Naval Order Am., Assn. of Mil. Surgeons of U.S., Naval Hosp. Am. Care Ctr., Am. Coll. Healthcare Execs. Roman Catholic. Office: Med Sq Troy 1575 W Big Beaver Rd Ste 11C Troy MI 48084-3525

POTTS, BARBARA JOYCE, retired historical society executive; b. L.A., Feb. 18, 1932; d. Theodore Thomas and Helen Mae (Kelley) Elledge; m. Donald A. Potts, Dec. 27, 1953; children: Tedd, Douglas, Dwight, Laura. AA, Graceland Coll., 1951; grad., Radiol. Tech. Sch., 1953; grad. program for sr. execs. in state and local govt., Harvard U., 1989. Radiol. technician Independence (Mo.) Sanitarium and Hosp., 1953, 58-59, Mercy Hosp., Balt., 1954-55; city coun. mem.-at-large City of Independence, 1978-82, mayor, 1982-90; exec. dir. Jackson County Hist. Soc., 1991-97; ret., 1997. Chmn. Mid-Am. Regional Coun., Kansas City, Mo., 1984-85; bd. dirs. Mo. Mcpl. League, Jefferson City, 1982-90, v.p., 1986-87, pres., 1987, 88; chmn. Mo. Commn. on Local Govt. Cooperation, 1985-90; chair ind. adv. bd. Mercantile Bank, 1997-99; bd. dirs. Women's Found. of Greater Kansas City, 1997-2003; mem. chancellor's adv. bd. UMKC Women's Ctr., 1996-; mem. adv. bd. Comprehensive Mental Health Svcs., 1997-. Author: Independence, 1985. Mem. Mo. Gov.'s Conf. Edn., 1976, Independence Charter Rev. Bd., 1977; bd. dirs. Hope House Shelter Abused Women, Independence, 1982—, Vis. Nurses Assn., 1990-93, Truman Heartland Cmty. Found., 1990-2003, bd. chmn., 1997-99, Mid-Continent coun. U.S. Girl Scouts, 1991-95, Harry S. Truman Libr. Inst., 1995—, Truman Med. Ctr., 2001—, Coun. on Philanthropy, 2001-03, Leadership 20/20 Vision; adv. bd. Ewing M. Kauffman Fund, 2002—, Greater Kansas City Cmty. Found., 1999-02, Salvation Army, 1999—; pres. Child Placement Svcs., Independence, 1972-89, Greater Kansas City region NCCJ, 1990—; bd. vis. UMKC Sch. Medicine, 2002—; trustee Independence Regional Health Ctr., 1982-90, 94-2001, Park Coll., 1989-99, 2004—, chmn. bd. trustees, 1995-99. Eye Found. Kansas City, 1997-99; mem. Nat. Women's Polit. Caucus, 1978—; mem. adv. bd. Greater Mo. Focus on Leadership, mem. steering com., 1989—. Recipient George Lehr Meml. award for cmty. svc., 1989, Woman of Achievement award Mid-Continent coun. Girl Scouts U.S.A., 1983, 75th Anniversary Women of Achievement award Mid-Continent coun. Girl Scouts, 1987, Jane Adams award Hope House, 1984, Cmty. Leadership award Comprehensive Mental Health Svcs., Inc., 1984, 90, Graceland Coll. Alumni Disting. Svc. award 1991, Disting. Citizen award Independence C. of C., 1993, Outstanding Cmty. Svc. award Jackson County Inter-Agy. Coun., 1994, Outstanding Cmty. Svc. award Cmty. Svcs. League, 1996, Jackson County Humanitarian of Yr. award, 1997, Disting. Citizen award, 1997, Paul Harris award Ind. Rotary Club, 1997, Outstanding Svc. award City of Independence Human Rels. Commn., 1999, Greater Kans. City Coun. Philanthropy Vol. of Yr. award, 2000; named Friend of Edn. Indpendence NEA, 1990. Mem. LWV (Cmty. Svc. award 1990), Jackson County Hist. Soc., Nat. Trust for Hist. Preservation. Mem. Reorganized Lds Ch. Home: 18508 E 30th Ter S Independence MO 64057-1904

POTTS, CHARLES AARON, management executive, writer, publishing executive; b. Idaho Falls, Idaho, Aug. 28, 1943; s. Verl S. and Sarah (Gray) Potts; m. Judith Samimi, 1977 (div. 1986); children: Emily Karen, Natalie Larise; m. Ann Weatherill, June 19, 1988. BA in English, Idaho State U., 1965. Lic. real estate broker Wash. Owner Palouse Mgmt., Inc., Walla Walla, Wash., 1979—; pres. Walla Walla Rental Properties, 1984-86; dir. Washington Apt. Assocs., 1984-88. Founder, dir. Litmus Inc., 1967—77; founding editor COSMEP, Berkeley, Calif., 1968; host poetry radio program Oasis NPR-KUER, Salt Lake City, 1976—77; N.W. rep. Chinese Computer Comm., Inc., Lansing, Mich., 1988—94; pres. Tsunami Inc.; founder Temple Bookstore, 2002, Temple Sch. Poetry, 2002. Author: Blues from Thurston County, 1966, Burning Snake, 1967, The Litmus Papers, 1969, Little Lord Shiva, 1969, Blue Up the Nile, 1972, Waiting in Blood, 1973, The Trancermigracion of Menzu, 1973, The Golden Calf, 1975, Charlie Kiot, 1976, The Opium Must Go Thru, 1976, Valga Krusa, 1977, Rocky Mountain Man, 1978, A Rite to the Body, 1989, The Dictatorship of the Environment, 1991, Loading Las Vegas, 1991, How the South Finally Won the Civil War, 1995, 100 Years in Idaho, 1996, Lost River Mountain, 1999, Facist Haikus, 1999, Little Lord Shiva: The Berkeley Poems, 1968, 1999, Angio Gram, 2000, Nature Lovers, 2000, prophet/profit, 2001, Slash and Burn, 2001, Across the Pacific, 2002, Lucintite, 2002, Compostrella/Star Field, 2004, Kiot: the selected early poems of Charles Potts, 1963-1977, 2004; editor: Pacific Northwestern Spiritual Poetry, 1998, The Temple, 1997—2002, Wallawalla Poetry Party, 1990—2003; columnist (with Kyushu Gleaner): Japan's Polit. Choices, 1995—. Rep. to exec. com. 5th Congl. Dist., Wash. State Dems., 1993—95. Recipient Profl. Achievement award, Idaho State U., 1994. Mem.: Soc. Neurolinguistic Programming (master practitioner), Chinese Lang. Computer Soc., Pacific N.W. Booksellers Assn., Toastmasters, Fukuoka Internat. Forum, Italian Heritage Assn. (ice cream chair 1990, award 1993). Avocations: tennis, raspberries. Office: Palouse Mgmt Inc 129 E Alder St PO Box 1773 Walla Walla WA 99362-1962 Office Phone: 509-529-0766. Office Fax: 509-522-0766. Business E-Mail: tsunami@innw.net.

POTTS, GERALD NEAL, manufacturing executive; b. Franklin, N.C., Apr. 10, 1933; s. Joseph Thomas and Virgie (Bryant) Potts; m. Ann Eliza Underwood, Dec. 21, 1956 (div. 1991); children: Catherine, Thomas, Alice. BS, U. N.C., 1954; grad., Advanced Mgmt. Program, Harvard, 1973. With Vulcan Mold & Iron Co., Chgo., 1957-59, sales engr., 1959-62, gen. sales mgr. Latrobe, Pa., 1963-65, v.p. sales, 1965-68; v.p. Vulcan, Inc., Latrobe, 1968-72, exec. v.p., 1972-73, pres., 1973-85, CEO, 1977-85, chmn., 1981-85; group exec. Teledyne Inc., 1985-92; pres. Woodings Verona Tool Works Inc., 1993-97. Trustee Greater Latrobe Cmty. Chest, 1970—87, pres., 1978—79; bd. dirs. Latrobe Area Hosp., chmn., 1985—88; mem. adv. bd. U. Pitts., Greensburg, Pa., 1974—80; trustee Seton Hill Coll., Greensburg, 1974—80. With U.S. Army, 1954—56. Mem.: Duquesne Club (Pa.), Rolling Rock Club, Chi Phi.

POTTS, GLENDA RUE, music educator; b. Butler, Ala., Nov. 26; d. Jennings Herschel and Erma Rue (Holdridge) Moseley; m. Billy Wayne Blackwell, June 23, 1963 (div. Aug. 1977); children: William Stephen, Melton Jennings; m. Willis Jones Potts, Jr., July 13, 1985; 1 stepchild, Timothy Brendon. BM in Music, Auburn U., 1963. Organist Beverly Meth. Ch., Birmingham, 1964-65; music tchr. grades 3-8 Birmingham Pub. Schs., 1964-65; music tchr. grades 7-9 Chattanooga Pub. Schs., 1965-66; tchr., owner piano/pipe organ studio Kreative Keyboards, Prattville, Ala., 1967-93, Savannah, 1993-99, Rome, Ga., 1999—. Pipe organist 1st Bapt. Ch., Prattville, 1969-85, 87-93, music asst. dir., 1980-85; pianist, dir. children's choirs, asst. organist Bull St. Bapt. Ch., Savannah, 1995-99; sec., mem. chair Savannah Symphony Women's Guild, 1993-99; soprano Savannah Symphony Chorale, 1993-94; mem. chair Savannah Newcomer's, 1994-95; substitute organist and pianist First Baptist Ch., Rome, Ga., 2000-. Honored as one of Top 400 Women Grads. of Centennial of Admission of Women Students, Auburn U., 1992. Mem. Ga. Music Tchrs. Assn. (pres. Savannah chpt. 1997-99, pres. Rome chpt. 2001-03, treas. 2003—), Music Tchrs. Nat. Assn. (nat. and state cert. tchr. and adjudicator), Nat. Guild of Piano Tchrs. (nat. cert. tchr. and adjudicator, established audition ctrs., chmn. Prattville 1967-93, Rome area fall 2001—, Hall of Fame 1990), Am. Coll. Musicians. Republican. Baptist. Home: 2614 Horseleg Creek Rd SW Rome GA 30165-8583

POTTS, HAROLD FRANCIS, JR., elevator company executive; b. Pittsfield, Mass., July 25, 1955; s. Harold Francis and Dorothy (Anderson) P.; m. Annie Laura Towle, May 14, 1977; children: David Francis, Douglas Norman, Joseph Harold. AA, Holyoke (Mass.) Community Coll, 1975; BS in BA, We. New Eng. Coll., Springfield, (Mass.), 1977; MBA, We. New Eng. Coll., 1989. Sales rep. Bay State Elevator Co., Springfield, Mass., 1977-81, customer svc. mgr., 1981-84, v.p., treas., 1984-91; pres., 1991—; bd. dirs. Bay State Elevator Co., 1986—; treas., bd. dirs. Air Flyte, Inc., Westfield, Mass., 1989—. Bd. dirs. Nat. Elevator Industry, Inc. Sec. sch. bldg. com. Town of Granville, Mass., 1987-90, mem. fin. bd., 1988-89, moderator, 1990-91; mem. ops. com. Mt. Washington Obs., 1992-93, trustee, 1993-94; mem. devel. com. The Master's Sch., 1991-93, trustee, 1993-99, treas., 1994-99. Mem. Assn. Am. Weather Observers (v.p. 1988-89, 92-93, sec. 1991-92), Internat. Weather Watchers. Republican. Avocations: hiking, camping, computers, weather observation. Office: Bay State Elevator Co PO Box 910 Agawam MA 01001-0910 Home: PO Box 311 Suffield CT 06078-0311

POTTS, JOHN THOMAS, JR., physician, educator; b. Phila., Jan. 19, 1932; married; 3 children. BA, LaSalle Coll, Phila., 1953; MD, U. Pa., Phila., 1957. From intern to asst. resident in medicine Mass. Gen. Hosp., Boston, 1957—59; resident Nat. Heart Inst., 1959—60; rsch. fellow in medicine Mass. Gen. Hosp., Boston, 1960—63; sr. research staff Nat. Heart Inst., 1963—66, head sect. polypeptide hormones, 1968—81; from asst. to assoc. prof. medicine Harvard U. Med. Sch., Boston, 1968—75, prof., 1975—; chief endocrine unit Mass. Gen. Hosp., Boston, 1968—81, chief gen. medicine, physician-in-chief, 1981—96, Jackson prof. Clin. Medicine, 1981—96, disting. Jackson prof. clin. medicine, 1996—, dir. rsch., 1996—. Recipient Andre Lichwitz prize, Endocrine Soc., 1968, William F. Neumann award, Am. Soc. Bone and Mineral Rsch., 1987. Mem.: AAAS, A.m Soc. Clin. Investigation, Assn. Am. Physicians, Endocrine Soc. (pres. 1987, Ernest Oppenheimer award 1968, Fred Konrad Koch award 1991), Am. Soc. Biology and Chemistry, Inst. Medicine NAS. Office: Mass Gen Hosp Dir Rsch 149 13th St # 1494005 Charlestown MA 02129-2020

POTTS, MARJORIE, executive secretary, systems support specialist; b. Batesville, Miss., May 10, 1948; d. James Louis and Mary Elois Bankston; m. Charles William Potts, Dec. 22, 1967; children: Charles William Jr., Benjamin Louis. Grad., Oxford (Miss.) H.S., 1967. Office mgr. Judge T.H. McElroy, Oxford, 1964—67; ins. clk. Oxford Lafayette County Hosp., 1974—79, supr., 1980—84; sr. systems operator U. Miss., University, 1984—90, sr. sec., 1990—. Mgmt. asst. Oxford Shakespeare Festival, 2004; leader, asst. cubmaster Boy Scouts Am.; Sunday sch. tchr. Recipient Merit award, Boy Scouts Am. Home: 103 CR 469 Oxford MS 38655 Office: U Miss Isom Hall Rm 110 PO Box 1848 University MS 38677 Office Phone: 662-915-5816. Office Fax: 662-915-5968. Business E-Mail: stpotts@olemiss.edu.

POTTS, RAMSAY DOUGLAS, lawyer, aviator; b. Memphis, Oct. 24, 1916; s. Ramsay Douglas and Ann Clifton (VanDyke) P.; m. Veronica Hamilton Raynor, Dec. 22, 1945 (dec. May 1993); children: Ramsay Douglas, David Hamilton, Lesley Ann, Lindsay Veronica. BS, U. N.C., 1941; LL.B., Harvard U., 1948. Bar: Tenn. 1948, D.C. 1954, U.S. Supreme Ct. 1957. Commd. 2d lt. USAAF, 1941, advanced through grades to maj. gen. Res., 1961; various combat and operational assignments (8th Air Force and Air Force Res.), 1942-60; chmn. Air Force Res. Policy Com., 1967-68; practice law, Washington, 1955—; spl. asst. to chmn. Nat. Security Resources Bd., 1951; pres. Ind. Mil. Air Transport Assn., 1952-55; ptnr. Shaw, Pittman, Potts & Trowbridge, 1956-86, sr. counsel, 1986—. Publisher: Air Power History, 1989-93; contbr. articles to profl. jours. Mem. State Council Higher Edn. for Va., 1968-71; Trustee Air Force Hist. Found., pres., 1971-75; pres. Washington Area Tennis Patrons Found., 1984-87; trustee emeritus. Physicians for Peace, 199789—. Decorated D.S.C., other combat decorations Mem. ABA, D.C. Bar Assn., Met. Club (Washington), Army Navy Country Club (Arlington, Va.), Internat. Lawn Tennis Club (U.S., Gt. Brit., India), Phi Beta Kappa. Home: 2818 27th St N Arlington VA 22207-4921 Office: Shaw Pittman 2300 N St NW Washington DC 20037-1128 Office Phone: 202-663-8020.

POTTS, ROBERT LESLIE, academic administrator; b. Jan. 30, 1944; s. Frank Vines and Helen Ruth (Butler) Potts; m. Irene Elisabeth Johansson, Aug. 22, 1965; children: Julia Anna, Robert Leslie. BA, So. Coll., 1966; JD, U. Ala., 1969; LLM, Harvard U., 1971. Law clk. to chief judge U.S. Dist. Ct. (no. dist.) Ala., 1969—70; rschr. Herrick, Smith, Donald, Farley & Ketchum, Boston, 1970—71; lectr. Boston U., 1971, U. Ala., 1973—75, 1988; ptnr. Potts & Young, Florence, Ala., 1971—84; gen. counsel U. Ala. Sys., 1984—89; pres. U. North Ala., 1990—2004; chancellor ND Univ. Sys., 2004—. Mem. Nat. Adv. Com. on Instnl. Quality and Integrity, 1994—2001; com. on colls. So. Assn. Colls. and Schs., 2001—04; chmn. Nat. ROTC subcom. for Sec. of Army, 1999—2001; adv. com. rules of civil procedure Ala. Supreme Ct., 1973—88; chmn. Ala. Bd. Bar Examiners, 1983—86, Ala. Coun. Coll. and Univ. Pres., 2001—03, Nat. Conf. Bar Examiners, 1994—95. Contbr. numerous articles to profl. jours., edn. and schs. Trustee Ala. State U., 1976—79, Oakwood Coll., 1978—81; pres. Ala. Higher Edn. Loan Corp., 1988—93. Mem.: ABA (ho. of dels. 2001—03), Am. Assn. State Colls. and Univs. (bd. dirs. 2002—), Ala. Bar Assn. (pres. young lawyers sect. 1979—80). Office: ND Univ Sys 600 E Blvd Ave Dept 215 Bismarck ND 58505-0230 Office Phone: 701-328-2963. Business E-Mail: robert.potts@ndus.nodak.edu.

POTTS, STEPHEN DEADERICK, lawyer; b. Memphis, Nov. 20, 1930; s. Ramsay Douglas and Anne (Van Dyke) P.; m. Irene Potter, Mar. 14, 1953; children: Lori Potts-Dupre, Stephen Deaderick Jr., Stacy Potts Krogh. AB, Vanderbilt U., 1952, LLB, 1954. Bar: Tenn. 1954, D.C. 1961. Assoc. Farris, Evans & Evans, Nashville, 1957-61; ptnr. Shaw, Pittman, Potts & Trowbridge, Washington, 1961-90; dir. U.S. Office Gov. Ethics, Washington, 1990-2000; chmn. fellows program, sr. ethics counselor Ethics Resource Ctr., Washington, 2001—. Past mem. Pres.'s Coun. on Integrity and Efficiency, Pres.'s Commn. on the Fed. Appt. Process. Past pres. Washington Tennis Patrons Found., 1970—72; chmn. USTA Olympic com. 1st lt. U.S. Army, 1954—57. Mem. ABA, U.S. Supreme Ct. Bar Assn., D.C. Bar Assn., Chevy Chase Club (bd. govs. 1982-86), Met. Club (bd. govs. 2000), Alibi Club, U.S. Tennis Assn. (bd. dirs., won 5 nat., 1 internat. father/son championships, twice ranked 1st in U.S.). Methodist. Office: Ethics Resource Ctr Ste 400 1747 Pennsylvania Ave Washington DC 20006

POTTY, GOPU RAMACHANDRAN, marine engineer, researcher; b. Trivandrum, Kerala, India, Sept. 19, 1962; arrived in U.S., 1995; s. Ramachandran Potty and Padmavathy Ammal; m. Savita Gopu Potty, Jan. 29, 1990; children: Vishakh Ram Gopu, Chitanya Gopu. MTech, Indian Inst. Tech., Madras, 1987; PhD, U. RI, Kingston, 2000. Rsch. assoc. Indian Inst. Tech., Madras, 1987—88; sr. lectr. Cochin U. Sci. and Tech., India, 1988—95; grad. asst. U. R.I., Narragansett, 1995—2000, asst. marine scientist, 2000—. Cons. Pyrcon, LLC, Narragansett, RI, 2000—02, Associated Structural Cons., Cochin, India; presenter to internat. confs. Contbr. scientific papers to profl. jours. Grantee, Office of Naval Rsch. Mem.: Acoustical Soc. of Am. (mem. subcom. on integrated acoustic sys. ocean observatories 2001—, technical com. mem. 2001—04, acoustical oceanography sect., Best Student Paper 1996, 2000), Indian Soc. of Tech. Edn. (life). Office: Univ RI South Ferry Rd Narragansett RI 02882 Office Phone: 401-874-6591. E-mail: potty@oce.uri.edu.

POTUZNIK, CHARLES LADDY, lawyer; b. Chgo., Feb. 11, 1947; s. Charles William and Laverne Frances (Zdenek) P.; m. Mary Margaret Quady, Jan. 2, 1988; children: Kylie Brommell, Kathryn Mary. BA with high honors, U. Ill., 1969; JD cum laude, Harvard U., 1973. Bar: Minn. 1973. Assoc. Dorsey & Whitney LLP, Mpls., 1973-78, ptnr., 1979—. Co-head Broker-Dealer and Investment Markets Regulation Practice Group. Mem. Minn. State Bar Assn. (chmn. state securities law subcom. 1987-2000), Hennepin County Bar Assn., Minn. Securities Adv. Com., Phi Beta Kappa. Mem. Evang. Free Ch. Avocations: hunting, fishing, camping, canoeing, foreign travel. Office: Dorsey & Whitney LLP 50 South Sixth St Minneapolis MN 55402-1498 Office Phone: 612-340-2914. E-mail: potuznik.charles@dorsey.com.

POTVIN, ALFRED RAOUL, engineering executive; b. 1965; m. Janet Holm, Mar. 20, 1965 BEE, Worcester Poly. Inst., 1964; MSEE, Stanford U., 1965, Engr. in EE, 1967; MS in Bioengring., MS in Psychology, U. Mich., 1970, PhD in Bioengring., 1971. Registered profl. engr., Tex. Asst. prof. elec. engring. U. Tex., Arlington, 1966-68, assoc. prof. biomed. engring. and elec. engring., 1971-76, prof., 1976-84, chmn. biomed. engring., 1972-84; dir. med. instrumentation sys. rsch. divsn. Eli Lilly & Co., Indpls., 1984—90, dir. tech. assessment and project mgmt., 1990-92; dir. engring., med. devices and diagnostics divsn., 1992-93; prof. elec. engring. Purdue Sch. Engring. and Tech., Ind. U.-Purdue U., Indpls., 1993-96; dean engring. and tech. Ind. U.-Purdue U., Indpls., 1991—94; pres. MEECO, Melbourne, Fla., 1996—. Faculty fellow, life scientist, cons. NASA, Houston, 1972-76, NASA and Moffett Field, 1974-76; clin. prof. biophysics U. Tex. Health Sci. Ctr., Dallas, 1967-84; mem. phys. med. device panel FDA, Washington, 1978-84; mem. adv. bd., reviewer Biomed. Engring. NSF, Washington, 1983-89, 92-97; founding dir. Ctr. Advanced Rehab. Engring., 1983-84, mem. adv. bd., 1984-88; mem. adv. bd. Engring. Rsch. Ctrs. NSF, Washington, 1988-92, Biomed. Engr. Worcester Polytech. Inst., Mass., 1987—, Coll. Engrs. Duke U., Durham, N.C., 1987-94, U. Calif., Berkeley, 1989-92, Coll. Engrs. U. Denver, 1990-93, Sch. Engr. and Tech. Ind. U.-Purdue U., Indpls, 1992-93, med. engring. Jet Propulsion Lab., Pasadena, Calif., 1989; chmn. NIH Resource Ctr. Case Western Res. U., Cleve., 1988-96; bd. advisors Sch. of Health and Rehab. Sci., U. Pitts., 1993-97; mem. adv. com. NIH, 1993, 95; bd. dirs. Biomed. Engring. Alliance for Engring. in Medicine and Biology. Author: (with W.W. Tourtellotte) Quantitative Examination of Neurologic Functions, 1985; editl. bd. IEEE Spectrum, 1987-90, 92-95, Biomed. Sci. and Tech., 1990-93; co-editor spl. issue on biosensors IEEE Trans. on Biomed. Engring., 1986, spl. issue on status and future directions in biomed. engring. Medicine and Biol. Mag., 1989; mem. editl. bd. Biomed. Sci. and Tech., 1990-92; mem. adv. bd. The Biomed. Engring. Handbook, 1995, 2000. Mem. Masthead Property Owners Assn., Indpls., 1984-96, Manasota Key Property Owners Assn., Englewood, Fla., 1985-98. Recipient Life Scientist award NASA, 1974; spl. fellow NIH, 1968. Fellow IEEE (pres. Engring. in Medicine and Biology Soc. 1983, re-elected 1984, gen. chmn. annual conf. 1982, chmn. health care engring. com. 1986, mem. editorial bd. spectrum 1987-89, 92-94, founding mem. steering com. symposium on computer based med. systems 1988-94, Centennial award 1984, co-editor spl. issue Medicine and Biology, 1989, mem. internat. conf. com. 1993—), Am. Inst. Med. and Biol. Engring. (bd. dirs. 1991-94, v.p. pub. awareness 1993-94, elected founding fellow 1992, co-pres. world congress on med. biological engring. in Chgo in the yr. 2000, 1993-1999, devel. com. 1996-99), Houston Soc. Engrs. in Medicine and Biology (Career Achievement award 1993), Assn. Advancement of Med. Instrumentation; mem. Am. Soc. Engring. Edn. (chmn. biomed. engring. div. 1979-80), Biomed. Engring. Soc. (sr. mem. 1972-88, chmn. edn. and pub. affairs com. 1979-83), Alliance Engrs. in Medicine and Biology (v.p. nat. affairs 1987-89, pres. 1989-92), Assn. Advancement of Med. Instrumentation, Ind. Elec. Mfg. Assn. (bd. dirs. 1993-96, Svc. to Industry award 1996), Presdl. Founders Worcester Poly. Inst., Appalachian Trail Club, Freedom Boat Club, Ski Club Sarasota. Avocations: boating, travel, gourmet dining, skiing.

POTVIN, FELIX, professional hockey player; b. Anjou, Que., Canada, July 23, 1971; Goalie Chicoutimi, QMJHL, 1988-91, St. John's, AHL, 1991-92, Toronto Maple Leafs, 1991-99, N.Y. Islanders, 1999, Vancouver Canucks, 1999—2001, L.A. Kings, 2001—. Recipient Goaltender of the Year Award, Can. Hockey League, 1990-91, Hap Emms Mem. Trophy, 1990-91, Jacques Plante Trophy, 1990-91, Shell Cup, 1990-91, Guy Lafleur Trophy, 1990-91, Baz Bastien Trophy, 1991-92, Dudley Garrett Mem. Trophy, 1991-92. Achievements include All-Star first team goalie, QMJHL, 1990-91, All-Star first team goalie, AHL, 1991-92, All-Rookie Team, NHL, 1992-93. Office: LA Kings Staples Ctr 1111 S Figueroa St Los Angeles CA 90015

POTVIN, PIERRE, physiologist, educator; b. Quebec City, Que., Can., Jan. 5, 1932; s. Rosario and Eva (Montreuil) P.; m. Louise Dube, Aug. 31, 1963; children: Aline, Bernard. BA, Laval U., 1950, MD, 1955; PhD, U. Toronto, 1962. Asst. prof. Faculty of Medicine Laval U., Quebec City, 1956-63, assoc. prof., 1963-68, prof., 1968-98, prof. emeritus, 1998—, vice dean exec., 1977-86, dean, 1986-94. V.p. Internat. Conf. of Deans of French-Speaking Faculties of Medicine, 1990-96, pres. evaluation coun., 1994—; hon. prof. Norman Bethune U. Med. Sci., Changchun, China, 1992. Assoc. editor Modern Medicine Can., 1958-61, Laval Med., 1962-70. Fellow Royal Coll. Physicians and Surgeons Can. (hon.), Ordre Nat. du Lion (officer), Senegal, Sahamatrei Order, Cambodia, Order Can., Ordre Nat. des Palmes académiques, Légion dHonneur, France. Roman Catholic. Avocation: painting. Home: 1915 Bourbonniere Sillery PQ Canada G1S 1N3 Office: Laval U Faculty of Medicine Dept Anat & Physiology Quebec City PQ Canada G1K 7P4 Business E-Mail: pierre.potvin@phs.ulaval.ca.

POTVIN, WILLIAM TRACEY, management consultant; b. Milw., June 20, 1951; s. William John and Joan (Wach) P.; m. Louisa I. Vorosmarty, July 23, 1983. BS in Internat. Econs., Georgetown U., 1973; MBA, Am. U., 1975. Investment mgr. GEICO, Washington, 1973-78; mgmt. cons. Touche Ross & Co. (now Deloitte & Touche LLP), N.Y.C., 1978-85, ptnr., 1985-2000; nat. dir. Fin. Inst. Cons., N.Y.C., 1987-90; mng. ptnr., CEO Deloitte & Touche CIS,

Moscow, 1990-96; nat. dir. Deloitte & Touche Actuarial and Ins. Cons. Group, N.Y.C., 1996-99; ret. ptnr. Deloitte & Touche, 2000—; pres., CEO The ESP Group LLC, Arlington, Va., 1999—. Chmn. adv. group to Russian govt. on mass privatization World Bank, 1992-94, acting CFO Russian Privitization Ctr., 1996; speaker to ins. groups, N.Y.C., 1985—. Contbr. articles to profl. jours. Bd. dirs. Am. Russian Youth Orch., 1996—. Mem. Coll. of Ins. (mem. fin. industries task force 1985-90, lectr. 1985-90). Roman Catholic. Office: The ESP Group LLC Ste 1103 1225 Jeff Davis Hwy Arlington VA 22202 also: The ESP Group LLC 76 Chestnut Ridge Rd Armonk NY 10504-3001 E-mail: wpotvin@espgroup.net., potvin@msn.com.

POU, NELLIE, assemblywoman; Degree in mcpl. budget and fin., Rutgers U. Assemblywoman N.J. Gen. Assembly, 1997—; assembly asst. minority leader, 2000—01; dep. spkr., 2002—. Mem. N.J. Dept. Health, Profl. Adv. Com., 1991—92, Passaic County Human Svcs. Adv. Coun., 1991—95, Passaic County-Bergen County HIV Health Svcs. Adv. Coun., 1993—97; chair Mayor's Health Planning Task Force, 1988—97; mem. Passaic County Planning and Policy Partnership Com., 1996—. Commr. Paterson Pub. Libr. Bd. Trustees, 1983—84; mem. N.J. Task Force on Child Abuse and Neglect, 1997—. Democrat. Office: 100 Hamilton Plz Ste 1403-05 Paterson NJ 07505 E-mail: AswPou@njleg.org.

POUCHER, JOHN SCOTT, systems engineer, physicist; b. Evanston, Ill., Apr. 10, 1945; s. George Edward and Marcia Irene (Smith) P.; m. Lois Miriam Gross, Aug. 2, 1969; children: Gregory Evan, Brian Eric. BS, MIT, 1967, PhD, 1971. Instr. in physics MIT, Cambridge, Mass., 1971-74; asst. prof. physics Vanderbilt U., Nashville, 1974-80; mem. tech. staff AT&T Bell Labs., Holmdel, N.J., 1981-86, disting. mem. tech. staff, 1986-96, technology cons., 1996-98; network svcs. arch. Cisco Sys., Freehold, NJ, 1998—2002, team leader, 2002—. Vis. fellow Cornell U., Ithaca, N.Y., 1978-79. Contbr. articles to Phys. Rev. Letters, Phys. Letters, Phys. Rev., other jours. and confs. Mem. IEEE, AIAA, AAAS, Am. Phys. Soc., Union Concerned Scientists, Fedn. Am. Scientists, Common Cause, Sigma Xi. Achievements include architect for high speed data network services, strategic planning for high tech government projects, operations systems planning; research in electron-positron annihilation, deep-inelastic electron-nucleon scattering and nucleic acid structure. E-mail: poucher@alum.mit.edu.

POUILLON, NORA EMANUELA, food service executive; b. Vienna, Oct. 26, 1943; came to U.S., 1965; d. Leopold and Gertraude (Mayr) Aschenbrenner; m. Pierre Pouillon, Dec. 3, 1965 (separated 1978); children: Alexis, Olivier; m. Steven Damato; 1 child, Nina Fiona Emanuela. Baccalaureat, Neuland Schule, Vienna, 1961; Moderne Rechentechnic, Technische Hochschule, Vienna, 1962-63; Bus. Degree, Handelsakademie, Vienna, 1964; drawing cert., Corcoran Sch. Art, 1967; diploma, Internat. Sch. Interior Design, 1968. Tchr. and owner Guerilla Gourmet, Washington, 1973-76; owner Food for Friends, Washington, 1973-76; chef Tabard Inn Hotel, Washington, 1977-78; co-owner, chef Restaurant Nora, Washington, 1979—, City Cafe, Washington, 1986—. Food writer Washington Mag., 1975-76. Sponsor Pub. Voice, Washington, 1991—. Voters for Choice, Washington, 1991—, Share Our Strength, Washington, 1991—; active with food safety advocacy groups. Named Outstanding Chef Am. 2000, 1990, Best Restaurant Dossier Mag., 1987-89, Outstanding Restaurant Pub. Voice, 1990; recipient Excellence in Restaurant Industry award Dinesty, 1990, Achievement in Culinary Arts award Gault Millau, 1990. Avocations: synergy exercise, yoga, hiking, downhill and cross-country skiing. Home: 1910 Biltmore St NW Washington DC 20009-1510 Office: Restaurant Nora 2132 Florida Ave NW Washington DC 20008-1925

POUL, FRANKLIN, lawyer; b. Phila., Nov. 6, 1924; s. Boris and Anna P.; m. Shirley Weissman, June 26, 1949; children— Leslie Poul Melman, Alan M., Laurie Price. Student, U. Pa., 1942-43, Haverford Coll., 1943-44; LL.B. cum laude, U. Pa., 1946. Bar: Pa. 1949, U.S. Supreme Ct. 1955. Asso. firm Gray, Anderson, Schaffer & Rome, Phila., 1948-56, Wolf, Block, Schorr and Solis-Cohen, Phila., 1956-60, partner, 1960-93. Bd. dirs. ACLU, Phila., 1955-80, pres., 1975-76. Served with AUS, 1943-46. Mem. ABA, Am. Law Inst., Order of Coif. Office: Wolf Block Shorr & Solis-Cohen 1650 Arch St Philadelphia PA 19103-2097 Office Phone: 610-977-2200.

POULARD, JEAN VICTOR, political scientist, educator; b. Mareuil-Sur-Ay, France, Aug. 13, 1939; arrived in U.S., 1957; s. Victor Jules and Louise Poulard; m. Regina Anna Fehrens, Aug. 5, 1966; children: Johannes, Roger. BA with honors, Otterbein Coll., 1963; MA, U. Chgo., 1965, PhD, 1976. Vis. asst. prof. Valparaiso (Ind.) U., 1979—80, Ind. U. NW, Gary, 1983—85, asst. prof., 1985—91, assoc. prof., 1991—2001, prof. polit. sci., 2001—. Corr. mem. Ctr. d'Etudes Philosophiques and Politiques, U. Reims-Champagne-Ardenne, 1995—. Contbr. articles to profl. publs., chpts. to book. Scoutmaster Boy Scouts Am., Long Beach, Ind., 1982—94; pres. Michiana Shores (Ind.) Town Coun., 1996—2000, v.p., 2004—. With U.S. Army, 1958—61. Mem.: Ind. Acad. Socia. Sci. (editor jour. 1996—), Lions Club. Republican. Roman Catholic. Avocations: miniature trains, woodworking. Home: 205 Shadow Tr Michigan City IN 46360 Office: Ind U NW 3400 Broadway Gary IN 46408 Fax: 219-980-6737. Business E-Mail: jpoulard@iun.edu.

POULETTY, PHILIPPE, health products executive; MD, U. Paris VI; degrees in immunology and virology, Inst. Pasteur. Postdoctoral fellow dept. med. microbiology and immunology Stanford U.; intern Hopitaux de Paris, 1981—84; founder, dir. rsch. Clonatec, France, 1984—88; founder SangStat, 1988—, pres., CEO, bd. dirs., 1988—95, chmn. bd. dirs., CEO, 1995—98, chmn., 1998—; founder DrugAbuse Scis., Inc., Los Altos, Calif., 1994—; chmn. bd. dirs., pres. DrugAbuse Scis. SAS. Bd. dirs. Conjuchem. Office: DrugAbuse Scis Inc 25954 Eden Landing Rd 2nd Fl Hayward CA 94545-3899

POULEUR, HUBERT GUSTAVE, cardiologist, consultant; b. Bouffioulx, Belgium, June 6, 1948; m. Michelle Leonet, July 7, 1973; children: Anne-Catherine, Jean-Hubert. MD, U. Louvain, Belgium, 1973, PhD, 1980. Intern, resident, then fellow in internal medicine U. Louvain, Belgium, 1973-77; Pub. Health Service internat. research fellow U. Calif. San Diego, 1977-79; asst. prof. U. Louvain, Brussels, 1979-83, assoc. prof., 1983-91, prof., 1991-94; assoc. dir. clin. rsch. Pfizer Inc., Groton, Conn., 1993-95; v.p. cardiovascular clin. R&D Bristol-Myers Squibb, Princeton, N.J., 1996-2000; exec. dir. cardiovasc. and metabolic group Pfizer Inc., N.Y.C., 2001—. Disting. clin. scientist Syntex Clin. Rsch., Palo Alto, Calif., Maidenhead, U.K., 1988-93. Contbr. numerous sci. articles to profl. jours. Recipient Damman prize Damman Found., 1977, Bekales prize Bekales Found., 1986; Squibb Cardiovascular fellow Belgian Soc. Cardiology, 1982. Fellow Am. Coll. Cardiology; mem. Am. Heart Assn. (fellow Coun. of Circulation, fellow Coun. Clin. Cardiology), Atlantic Salmon Fedn., Trout Unltd. Avocation: fly fishing. Home: 43 Woodlane Rd Lawrenceville NJ 08648-5544 E-mail: hubert.pouleur@pfizer.com.

POULIN, MARIE, Canadian government official; b. Sudbury, Ont., Can., June 21, 1945; d. Alphonse-Emile and Lucille Charette; m. Bernard A. Poulin, May 21, 1977; children: Elaine, Valérie. BA magna cum laude, Laurentian U., Sudbury, 1966; M of Social Svcs., U. Montréal, Que., Can., 1969; PhD (hon.), Laurentian U., Sudbury, 1995. Lectr. U. Montreal, 1969-70, Coll. of Gen. and Profl. Instrn., Hull, Que., 1972-73; rschr. Ctr. Social Svcs., Hull, 1972-73; interviewer, rschr. French Radio and TV, Ottawa, Ont., 1973-74; prodr. Sta. CBOF-CBC, Ottawa, 1974-78; founder and dir. svcs. in N.E. and N.W. Ont. Sta. CBON (French Network-CBC), Sudbury, 1978-83; exec. dir. regional programming CBC, Ottawa, 1983-84, assoc. v.p. regional broadcasting, 1984-88, v.p., sec. gen., 1988-90, v.p. human resources, 1990-92; dep. sec. for comm. and consultation The Privy Coun. Govt. of Can., Ottawa, 1992-93; founding chmn., CEO Can. Artists and Prodrs. Profl. Rels. Tribunal, Ottawa, 1993-95; senator Can. Govt., Ottawa, 1995—. Mem. Senate Standing com. Internal Economy, Budgets and Adminstrn.; former chair Senate Standing Com. on Transport and Comms., Can.'s Competitive Position in Comms.; first woman to chair Senate Liberal Caucus; first sen. to chair No. Ontario Liberal Caucus; bd. dirs. Cité Collégiale, Ottawa, 1989-91. Commr. for French lang. svcs. Province of Ont., 1986-89; regent U. Sudbury, 1979-83; bd. dirs. Laurentian Hosp., Sudbury, 1980-83, Cambrian Coll.Found., Sudbury, 1983-88; v.p. Art Ctr., Ottawa, 1988-90; pres. Regroupement gens d'affaires, Ottawa, 1991-92, Bell Globemedia, 2001-03. Recipient medal for contbn. to Can. Culture, Coun. of French-Am. Life, 1987, Prix Marcel-Blouin for best morning program in Can., 1983, Profl. Woman of Yr. award Réseau des femmes d'affaires professionnelles, 1990; named Chevalier Ordre de la Pléiade, 1995, Officier de l'Ordre national de la Legion d'Honneur de la France, 2003; named CEO of Yr., ACTRA Fraternal Benefit Soc. Mem. various parliamentary assns. and friendship groups including Canadian-Japan Inter-Parliamentary Group (co-chmn.), Can.-France Fedn. (pres.), Can.-Japan Inter-Parliamentary Group (co-chair). Avocations: running, reading, swimming. Office: Senate Can Ottawa ON Canada K1A 0A4 E-mail: poulim@sen.parl.gc.ca.

POULIOT, ASSUNTA GALLUCCI, retired business school owner and director, consultant; b. West Warwick, R.I., Aug. 14, 1937; d. Michael and Angelina (DeCesare) Gallucci; m. Joseph F. Pouliot Jr., July 4, 1961; children: Brenda, Mark, Jill, Michele. BS, U. R.I., 1959; MS, U. R.I., 1971. Bus. tchr. Cranston High Sch., R.I., 1959-61; bus. dept. chmn. Chariho Regional High Sch., Wood River Junction, R.I., 1961-73; instr. U. R.I., Kingston, 1973-78; founder, dir. Ocean State Bus. Inst., Wakefield, R.I., 1977-95, fin. aid cons., 1995—, ednl. cons., 1996—. Dir. Fleet Nat. Bank, 1985-91; bd. mgrs. Bank of New Eng., 1984-85; commr. Accrediting Coun. Ind. Colls. and Schs., 1995-98, chair accreditation com. team visits, 1998-2001, intermediate rev. com., 2000-01, rev. bd., 2000—; spkr. in field including Glencoe/McGraw-Hill Pub. Co., 1995—. Ednl. author, Glencoe McGraw Hill Pub. Co., 1999-2002. Pres. St. Francis Women's Club, Wakefield, 1975; sec. St. Francis Parish Coun., Wakefield, 1980; mem. Econ. Devel. Commn., Wakefield, 1981-85; mem. South County Hosp. Corp., Wakefield, 1978-97; fin. dir. Bus. and Profl. Women's Club, Wakefield, 1982-84; chmn. Ladies Golf Charity, 1985-91; mem. Computer Info. Systems Com., Chariho Regional Career and Tech. Ctr. Mem. R.I. Bus. Edn. Assn. (newsletter editor 1979-81), New Eng. Bus. Coll. Assn. (sec. 1984-86, pres. 1985-87), R.I. Assn. Career and Tech. Schs. (treas., bd. dirs. 1979-95), Eastern Bus. Edn. Assn. (conf. leader), Nat. Bus. Edn. Assn. (conf. leader), Career Coll. Assn. (conv. speaker, pub. rels. com., govt. rels. com., membership com., key mem., nominating com., evaluator), Assn. Colls. and Schs. (commr. commn. on postsecondary schs. accreditation 1994-98), R.I. Women's Golf Assn., Am. Cancer Soc., U. R.I. Alumni Assn. (Excellence Bus. award 1992), Phi Kappa Phi, Delta Pi Epsilon (pres., newsletter editor). Clubs: Point Judith Country (past ladies golf chmn., R.I. Women's golf rep.). Roman Catholic. Avocations: golf, gardening. Home and Office: 137 Kenyon Ave Wakefield RI 02879-4242 Office: 15835 Sandy Point Dr Fort Myers FL 33917-5464 Personal E-mail: sjpouliot@aol.com.

POULIOT, GEORGE A. physical scientist, researcher; s. Raymond G. and Suzzanne M. Pouliot. BA, St. Vincent Coll., 1992; MS, N.C. State U., 1995, PhD, 2000. Lead sys. programmer Dyntel Corp., Research Triangle Park, NC, 2000—02; phys. scientist Atmospheric Sci. Modeling Divsn., Research Triangle Park, NC, 2002—. Contbr. articles to profl. jours. Mem.: Am. Meteorol. Soc. (fellow 1992—93). Achievements include research in global nonhydrostatic semi-implicit semi-lagrangian variable resolution dynamical core for an atmospheric model. Office: US EPA Mail Drop E243-04 Atmospheric Sci Modeling Divsn Research Triangle Park NC 27711 E-mail: pouliot.george@epa.gov.

POULOS, CYNTHIA JENKS, parochial school educator; b. Bklyn., Mar. 25, 1948; d. Harford Perry and Mable (Sawyer) Jenks; m. Thomas Poulos, Jr., June 13, 1970; children: Lynette Carolyn Rodi, Kristin Anne, Matthew Thomas. MEd in Reading Edn., MEd in Elem. Edn., Auburn U., 1988. Cert. tchr. La., Fla., Ala. Reading specialist Islamic Saudi Acad., Alexandria, Va., 1993—94; tchr. grade 1 Trinity Christian Sch., Fairfax, Va., 1994—95; tchr. grade 5 St. James Sch., Montgomery, Ala., 1995—96; tchr. grades 4-5 Dept. Def. Sch., Osan, Republic of Korea, 1996—99; tchr. grade 4 Iliahi Elem. Sch., Wahiawa, Hawaii, 1999—2001; tchr. grade 8 St. Thomas More Cath. Sch., Baton Rouge, 2002—04; tchr. Trinity Presbyn. Sch., Montgomery, 2004—. Adj. prof. Wayland Bapt. U., Aiea, Hawaii, 1999—2001. Editor: Write to Read, 1999. Chmn. Hickam AFB Officer's Wives Club Thrift Shop, Honolulu, 2000—02. Allie Harper Strickland scholar, 1987—88. Republican. Episcopalian. Avocations: golf, scuba diving.

POULOS, JAMES THOMAS, endocrinologist, educator; b. Lynn, Mass., Apr. 11, 1938; s. Thomas Dimitrios and Christine Julia (Zorzy) Poulos; m. Mary Margaret White, June 22, 1963; 1 child, Christopher Kreag. BS, Tufts U., 1959, MD, 1963. Diplomate Am. Bd. Internal Medicine, Am. Bd. Endocrinology and Metabolism. Intern New Eng. Med. Ctr., Boston, 1963-64, resident, 1964-65; resident and fellow in endocrinology U. Chgo., 1967-70; practice medicine specializing in endocrinology Arnett Clinic, Lafayette, Ind., 1970—2004, v.p., bd. dir., 1979-95. Adj. prof. clin. pharmacology Purdue U., West Lafayette, Ind., 1976—95; mem. therapeutics com. Ind. Dept. Medicaid, 2002—; clin. faculty Ind. U. Sch. Medicine, mem. dean's search com., 1998, mem. therapeutics com., 2002—04; bd. dirs. Lafayette Home Hosp., 1980—85, dir., pres. med. staff, 1978—79; pres. Arnett HMO, 1986—97; dir. North Ctrl. Health Svc., 1985—98; mem. therapeutics com. State of Ind. Family and Social Svc. Adminstrn., 2002—; dir. regional diabetes ctr. Sisters of St. Francis Health Systems Inc., 1985—, Greater Lafayette Health Svc., 1985—. Co-author: The Metabolic Influence of Progestins Advances in Metabolis Disorders, 1971; contbr. articles to profl. publ. Mem. Nat. Rep. Senatorial Com., Nat. Rep. Congrl. Com. With M.C., US Army, 1965-67. Fellow ACP, Am. Coll. Endocrinology, Am. Assn. Clin. Endocrinologists; mem. AMA, Am. Diabetes Assn. (dir. Ind. chpt. 1980—, pres. 1986-88, 96-98, bd. dirs., com. profl. practice 1987-88, pres. 1994—), Endocrine Soc., Internat. Diabetes Fedn., Am. Lung Assn. (pres. West Cen. Ind. 1982-83), Lafayette C. of C. Home and Office: 1000 Windwood Ln West Lafayette IN 47906-4737 Office Phone: 765-743-1741. Personal E-mail: jpoulos@insightbb.com.

POULOS, MICHAEL JAMES, insurance company executive; b. Glens Falls, N.Y., Feb. 13, 1931; s. James A. and Mary Poulos; m. Mary Kay Leslie; children: Denise, Peter. BA, Colgate U., 1953; MBA, NYU, 1963. CLU, 1970. With sales and mgmt. U.S. Life Ins. Co., N.Y.C., 1958-70, dir., 1968, mem. exec. com., 1970; with Calif.-Western States Life Ins. Co., Sacramento, 1970-79, pres., chief exec. officer, 1975-79, dir., 1975; with Am. Gen. Corp., Houston, 1979-93, pres., 1981-91, mem. exec. com., dir., 1981-93, vice chmn., 1991-93; chmn., CEO, pres. Western Nat. Corp., Houston, 1993-98, now bd. dirs., 1998; ret., 1998. Mem. Sam Houston Area coun. Boy Scouts Am. Mem. Am. Soc. CLU's, Nat. Assn. Life Underwriters, Houston Assn. Life Underwriters, Am. Mgmt. Assn., River Oaks Country Club, Univ. Club of N.Y.C. Greek Orthodox. Home: 2121 Kirby Dr Unit 73 Houston TX 77019-6066 Office: 2727 Allen Pky Ste 450 Houston TX 77019

POULSEN, JAMES VIGGO, III, music educator, composer; b. Burlington, Iowa, Dec. 12, 1958; s. James Viggo and Marilyn Elizabeth (Brubaker) Poulsen; m. Lori Lynn Zender, Aug. 3, 1985; children: Christopher, Elise. BA, Buena Vista Coll., 1984; MusM, U. SD, 1985. Comml. music composer SR Audio, Des Moines, 1990—. Lectr. music Simpson Coll., Indianola, Iowa, 1991—. Composer numerous works. Recipient Telly award, 1992—2003, Addy award, 1992—2003, First prize, Presbyn. Metro Ministries of Omaha Composition Contest, 1985. Mem.: Music Tchrs. Nat. Assn. United Methodist. Avocations: history, reading, travel. Office: Simpson Coll 701 N C St Indianola IA 50125 Office Fax: 515-961-1637. Personal E-mail: jlpoulsen@aol.com.

POULSON, RICHARD JASPER METCALFE, lawyer; b. Elizabeth City, N.C., Sept. 4, 1938; s. Richard Jasper and Dorothy (Morse) P.; m. Anne Keenan, Dec. 21, 1963 (div. 1976); m. Anne Dare Wrenn, Sept. 25, 1993; children: Richard Hugh Hundley, Anna Blair Masters. BA, U. Va., 1960; JD, Am. U., 1968; ML in Taxation, Georgetown U., 1970. Bar: Va. 1968, D.C. 1969, U.S. Supreme Ct. 1976. V.p. Am. Security & Trust Co., Washington, 1968-70; assoc. Hogan & Hartson, Washington, 1970-73, ptnr., 1973-94, sr. ptnr. London, 1990-93; chmn. Rapidan Capital Ptnrs., 1994—; CEO, sr. mng. dir. The Appian Group, Washington, 1995-98; chmn., CEO The Animex Group, Warsaw, 1998—; exec. v.p., sr. advisor to chmn. Smithfield Foods, Inc., N.Y.C., 1998—. Adj. prof. Georgetown U. Law Ctr., 1971-78; lectr. Law and Fgn. Svc. Schs. Georgetown U.; internat. advisor in field; active Euro-Arab Conciliation and Arbitration Sys. Trustee, bd. mgrs. U. Va., Charlottesville, 1992—98, v.p., 1994—95, pres., 1995—97; dir., chmn. exec. com. Mary & Daniel Loughran Found., Washington, 1976—, pres., 2002—; chmn., dir. Montpelier Steeplechase Found., Orange, Va., 1991—98; chmn., trustee U.S. Rugby Football Found., Boston, 1988—2001. 1st lt. USAR, 1961—63. Mem. Law Soc. of Eng. and Wales, Metro. Club, Norfolk Yacht Club, Keswick Country Club, Commonwealth Club. Republican. Episcopalian. Avocations: horseback riding, hunting, steeplechase racing, thoroughbred breeding. Home: Hare Forest Farm PO Box 287 Orange VA 22960 Office: Smithfield Foods 499 Park Ave 6th Fl New York NY 10022 Office Phone: 212-758-2100. Business E-Mail: dickpoulson@smithfieldfoods.com.

POULTER, CHARLES DALE, chemist, educator, consultant; b. Monroe, La., Aug. 29, 1942; s. Erwin and Mary Helen Poulter; m. Susan Raetzsch, Aug. 24, 1964; children: Mary Christa, Gregory Thomas. BS, La. State U., Baton Rouge, 1964; PhD, U. Calif., Berkeley, 1967. NIH postdoctoral fellow UCLA, 1967-68; asst. prof. chemistry U. Utah, Salt Lake City, 1969-75, assoc. prof., 1975-78, prof., 1978-94, John A. Widtsoe prof. chemistry, 1994—, chair dept. chemistry, 1995-2000; editor-in-chief Jour. Organic Chemistry, 2001—. Fellow AAAS; mem. Am. Chem. Soc. (organic exec. com. 1983-86, biol. divsn. councillor 1993-98, chair organic divsn. 1998, Ernest Guenther award 1991, Utah award 1992, Arthur C. Cope scholar 1998, Repligen award 2002, James Flack Norris award 2004). Office: U Utah Dept Chemistry 340 S 1500 E Rm 2020 Salt Lake City UT 84112

POULTON, BEVERLY ANN, medical/surgical nurse; b. Ganado, Tex., May 17, 1965; d. Jerry Don and Margaret Faye Bassham; m. Paul Eric Poulton, Nov. 12, 1983; children: Paul Eric II, Jacob Daniel, Caitlin Lauren. Diploma, Victoria Sch. Nursing, 1984. Registered massage therapist Tex., 1995. Vocat. nurse S.W. Plastic Surgery Ctr., SugarLand, Tex., 1992—93; vocat nurse, massage therapist Aesthetic Ctr. Plastic Surgery, Houston, 1993—. Author: (poetry) National Library of Poetry A Voyage To Remember (Editors Choice award, 1996). Mem.: Soc. Plastic Surgery Skin Care Specialists, Am. Soc. Plastic Surgery Nurses. Conservative. Southern Baptist. Office: Aesthetic Center for Plastic Surgery 12727 Kimberley Lane Ste 300 Houston TX 77024

POULTON, ROBERTA DORIS, nurse, consultant; b. Balt., Oct. 19, 1943; d. Charles Robert and Mary Doris (Guercio) P. Nursing diploma, Md. Gen. Hosp., 1964. Staff nurse Md. Gen. Hosp., 1964-67, Project Hope, Colombia, 1967, 1969-70, St. Agnes Hosp., Balt., 1968-69, team leader, 1972-83, staff nurse-preceptor, 1983-88, nurse mgr. pediatric emergency rm./ambulatory svcs., 1988-93, pediat. hemophilia coord., 1993—2003; cons., 2003—. Pediat. ambulatory specialty clin. nurse; hemophilia nurse Johns Hopkins Med. Instn., Balt., 1998-2003; cons. Girl Scouts U.S.A., Balt., 1972-2003, Bapt. Conv. Md., 1963-2004. Mem.: ANA, Md. Nurses Assn. Democrat. Baptist. Personal E-mail: rpoulton43@aol.com.

POUND, JOHN BENNETT, lawyer; b. Champaign, Ill., Nov. 17, 1946; s. William R. and Louise Catherine (Kelly) P.; m. Mary Ann Hanson, June 19, 1971; children: Meghan Elizabeth, Matthew Fitzgerald. BA, U. N.Mex., 1968; JD, Boston Coll., 1971. Bar: N. Mex. 1971, U.S. Dist. Ct. N. Mex. 1971, U.S. Ct. Appeals (10th cir.) 1972, U.S. Supreme Ct., 1993. Law clk. to Hon. Oliver Seth, U.S. Ct. Appeals, 10th Cir., Santa Fe, 1971-72. Asst. counsel Supreme Ct. Disciplinary Bd., 1977-83, dist. rev. officer, 1984—; mem. Supreme Ct. Com. on Jud. Performance Evaluation, 1983-85; bd. dirs. Archdiocese Santa Fe Cath. Social Svcs., 1995—. Contbr. articles to profl. jours. Pres. bd. dirs. N.Mex. Ind. Coll. Fund, Santa Fe; chmn. N.Mex. Dem. Leadership Coun., 1991—; bd. dirs. Santa Fe Boys Club, 1989-92; rules com. N.Mex. Dem. Party, 1982—; v.p. Los Alamos Nat. Lab. Comm. Coun., 1985-90; fin. chmn. N.Mex. Clinton for Pres. campaign, 1992; co-chmn. Clinton-Gore Re-election Campaign, N.Mex., 1996, 2000; co-chmn. Gore for Pres., N.Mex., 2000; co-chmn. Kerry for Pres., N.Mex., 2004. Fellow Am. Bar Found., Am. Coll. Trial Lawyers, N.Mex. Bar Found.; mem. ABA, Am. Bd. Trial Advocates, N.Mex. Bar Assn. (health law sect. 1987—), Santa Fe County Bar Assn. Democrat. Roman Catholic. Avocations: history, foreign language, literature, swimming, baseball. Office: Herrera Long Pound Komer PA PO Box 5098 2200 Brothers Rd Santa Fe NM 87505-6903 Office Phone: 505-982-8405. E-mail: HLPLaw@aol.com.

POUND, RICHARD WILLIAM DUNCAN, lawyer, accountant; b. St. Catharines, Ont., Can., Mar. 22, 1942; s. William Thomas and Jessie Edith Duncan (Thom) P.; m. Julie Houghton Keith, Nov. 4, 1977. B in Commerce, McGill U., Montreal, 1962, B in Civil Law, 1967; BA, Sir George Williams U. (now Concordia U.), Montreal, 1963; PhD (hon.), U.S. Sports Acad., 1989; LLD (hon.), U. Windsor, Can., 1997, U. We. Ont., 2004. Bar: called to Que. bar 1968, Ont. bar, 1980; chartered acct., 1964, F.C.A, 2001. Auditor Riddell, Stead, Graham & Hutchinson, Montreal, 1963-65; law clk., then atty. firm Laing, Weldon, Courtois, Clarkson, Parsons, Gonthier & Tétrault, Montreal, 1965-71; mem. firm Stikeman Elliott, Montreal, Toronto, Ottawa, Calgary, Vancouver, London, N.Y.C., Sydney, 1972—. Lectr. taxation McGill U. Faculty Law; lectr. Que. Real Estate Assn.; mem. Ct. of Arbitration of Sport, Lausanne, 1991—; officer Order of Can., officer Ordre nat. du Quebec, Order of St. John of Jerusalem, Queen's Counsel, 1992; comdr. Mil. and Hospitaler Order of St. Lazarus of Jerusalem. Author: Five Rings Over Korea, 1994, Chief Justice W.R. Jackett: By the Law of the Land, 1999, Stikeman Elliott The First Fifty Years, 2002, High Impact Quotations, 2004, Canadian Facts and Dates, 2004, Inside the Olympics, 2004; editor-in-chief: Doing Business in Canada, 1987—, Canada Tax Cases, 1993—, Stikeman Income Tax Act (annotated); author: Pound's Tax Case Notes, 1988—, Legal Notes, CGA mag., 1986-2003; mem. editl. bd. Can. Tax Svc., 1972-82. Pres. Can. Olympic Assn., 1977-82, sec., 1968-76, dir., 1968—; mem. Internat. Olympic Com., 1978—, exec. bd., 1983-87, 92-2000, v.p., 1987-91, 1996-2000; bd. govs. McGill U., 1986—, chmn., 1994-99, chancellor, 1999—; gov. Martlet Found.; former trustee Stanstead Wesleyan Coll.; chmn. McGill U. Athletic Bd.; chmn. McGill U. Fund Coun.; founding chmn., pres. World Anti-Doping Agy., 1999—. Named to Can. Swimming Hall of Fame, 1969, Sports Fedn. Can. Hall of Fame, 1976, Can. Olympic Order, 1995, Quebec Sports Hall of Fame, 2001, Gold Medallion award Internat. Swimming Hall of Fame, 2002. Fellow Order of Chartered Accts.; mem. Can. Bar Assn., Can. Tax Found., Internat. Fiscal Assn., Internat. Assn. Practicing Lawyers, Can. Squash Racquets Assn., Royal Life Savs. Soc., Alumni Assn. McGill U. (former pres.). Clubs: Montreal Amateur Athletic Assn. (pres. 1987-88), Badminton and Squash (Montreal); Jesters, Mt. Bruno Country. Home: 87 Arlington Ave Westmount QC Canada H3Y 2W5 Office: Ste 4000 1155 Rene Levesque Blvd W Montreal QC Canada H3B 3V2 Office Phone: 514-397-3037. Business E-Mail: rpound@stikeman.com.

POUND, ROBERT VIVIAN, physics educator; b. Ridgeway, Ont., Can., May 16, 1919; arrived in U.S., 1923, naturalized, 1932; s. Vivian Ellsworth and Gertrude C. (Prout) Pound; m. Betty Yde Andersen, June 20, 1941; 1 child, John Andrew. BA, U. Buffalo, 1941; AM (hon.), Harvard Coll., 1950; DSc (hon.), SUNY, Buffalo, 1994. Rsch. physicist Submarine Signal Co., 1941—42; staff mem. Radiation Lab. MIT, Cambridge, 1942—46; Soc. Fellows jr. fellow Harvard U., Cambridge, 1945—48; asst. prof. physics Harvard Coll., Cambridge, 1948—50, assoc. prof., 1950—56, prof., 1956—68; chmn. dept. physics, 1968—72; Mallinckrodt prof. physics, 1968—89; emeritus, 1989—; dir. Physics Lab. Harvard U., Cambridge, 1975—83. Fulbright rsch. scholar Oxford (Eng.) U., 1951; vis. rsch. fellow Merton Coll., 1980; Fulbright lectr., Paris, 58; vis. prof. Coll. de France, 1973; vis. fellow Joint Inst. Lab. Astrophysics, U. Colo., 1979—80; Zernike vis. prof. U. Groningen, The Netherlands, 1982; vis. sr. scientist Brookhaven Nat. Lab., 1986—87; vis. prof. U. Fla., 1987; W.G. Brickwedde lectr. Johns Hopkins U., Balt., 1992; Julian Mack lectr. U. Wis., 1992. Author, editor Mmicrowave Mixers, 1948; contbr. articles to profl. jours. Associated Univs., Inc., 1976—. Recipient B.J. Thompson Meml. award, Inst. Radio Engrs., 1948, Eddington medal, Royal Astron. Soc., 1965, Nat. medal Sci., Pres. U.S., 1990; fellow John Simon Guggenheim, 1957—58, 1972—73. Fellow: AAAS,

Am. Acad. Arts and Scis., Am. Phys. Soc.; mem.: NAS, French Phys. Soc. (mem. coun . 1958—61), French Acad. Scis. (assoc.; fgn.), Sigma Xi, Phi Beta Kappa. E-mail: pound@fas.harvard.edu.

POUNDS, WILLIAM FRANK, management educator; b. Fayette County, Pa., Apr. 9, 1928; s. Joseph Frank and Helen (Fry) P.; m. Helen Anne Means, Mar. 6, 1954; children: Thomas Mcclure, Julia Elizabeth. BSChemE, Carnegie Inst. Tech., 1950, MS in Math. Econs., 1959, PhD in Indsl. Adminstrn., 1964. Indsl. engr. Eastman Kodak Co., 1950-51, 55-57; cons. Pitts. Plate Glass Co., 1958-59, asst. to gen. mgr. Forbes finishes divsn., 1960—61; faculty Sloan Sch. Mgmt., MIT, 1966-98, prof. mgmt., 1966-98, dean, 1966-80; sr. adv. Rockefeller Family and Assocs., 1981-91. Bd. dirs. Idexx Labs., Inc., Mgmt. Scis. for Health, Inc.; bd. dir. Sunoco, Inc., 1973—2000, General Mills, Inc., 1979—91; trustee/vice chmn. Putnum Funds, 1974—2000. Chmn. bd. trustees Boston Mus. Fine Arts, 2000-03; trustee WGBH Ednl. Found., 2002—. Served as aviator lt. (j.g.) USNR, 1951-55. Fellow Am. Acad. Arts and Scis. Home: 83 Cambridge Pkwy # W1205 Cambridge MA 02142-1241

POUNDSTONE, SALLY HILL, library director; m. Robert Bruce Poundstone; children: Nancy Katrina, Holly Megan, Angus Bruce, Alice Heather. BA, U. Ky., 1954, MA in Libr. Sci., 1955. Asst. head ref. dept. Louisville Free Pub. Libr., 1955-59; libr. Folger Shakespeare Libr., Washington, 1959-60; chief acquisition dept. White Plains (N.Y.) Pub. Libr., 1960-62; libr. Bedford Hills (N.Y.) Pub. Elem. Sch., 1965-66; dir. Mamaroneck (N.Y.) Free Libr. and Emelin Theatre, 1966-87, Westport (Conn.) Pub. Libr., 1987-98; prin. SHP Libr. Consultants, 1998—. Instr. libr. sci. N.Y. U., 1968-69, Coll. of New Rochelle (N.Y.), 1970-71; adv. coun. mem. Pratt Inst. Grad Sch. of Libr. and Info. Sci., 1978-87; adminstrv. svcs. chmn. N.Y. Met. Ref. and Res. Libr. Agy., 1977-79, bd. trustees, 1979-88, 2d v.p. and chair, 1984-85, pres., 1985-88; planning and devel. com. mem. Bibliomation, Inc., 1988-90; chair Conn. State Adv. Coun. for Libr. Planning and Devel., 1988-90. Pres. Garden Club of Mamaroneck, 1969-70, Larchmont-Mamaroneck Film Coun., 1971-72, Mamaroneck Hist. soc., 1976-77, bd. mem., 1976-87; vice chmn. Village of Upper Nyack Planning Bd., 1988-89; leadership com. and task force mem. Westchester 2,000, 1984-87; com. mem. Rotary Club of Westport, 1987—; active Downtown Westport Adv. Com., 1989-90, Rep. Town. Com., Weston, Conn., 1990-93, Westport Bridge & Traffic Com., 1990-97, Honorable Order of Ky. Cols., 1995—, United Way Profl. Adv. Com., 1994-97, Westport Telecomm. Com., 1994-96, and others; v.p., dir. Woodcock Nature Ctr., 1998—, pres., 2001—; mem. Wilton Rep. Town Com., 2000—, Planning & Zoning Bd. Commns., 2000—. Mem. ALA, Conn. Libr. Assn., Fairfield Libr. Adminstrs. Group, Archons of Colophon, Pub. Libr. Dirs. Assn. Westchester County (various offices and chairs), N.Y. Libr. Assn. (sec. treas. adult librs. assn. 1970-72, pres. pub. librs. sect. 1981-82, chair planning com. 1984-85). Home and Office: 48 Sharp Hill Rd Wilton CT 06897-3531

POURBAIX, ALEXANDER, energy executive; BA with distinction, LLB, U. Alta. Pres., dir. TransCanada Power Power Svcs.; exec. v.p. power TransCanada Corp., 1997—; responsible for ops. Cancarb Ltd., Medicine Hat; chmn., dir. TransCanada Turbines Ltd. Mem. bd. mgmt. Alta. Econ. Devel. Authority; active Calgary Homeless Found.; bd. dirs. Jr. Achievement of So. Alta. Recipient Top 40 Under 40 award for leadership excellence, 2002—03. Office: TransCanada Power 450 1st St SW Calgary AB Canada T2P 5H1

POURCIAU, LESTER JOHN, JR., retired librarian; b. Baton Rouge, La., Sept. 6, 1936; s. Lester John and Pearlie M. (Hogan) P.; m. Rebecca Anne Thomas, 1975; 1 son, Lester John III. BA, La. State U., 1962, MS, 1964; PhD, Ind. U., 1975. Asst. ref. libr. U. S.C., Columbia, 1963-64; ref. libr. Florence (S.C.) County Pub. Libr., 1964-65; ref. svcs. coord. U. Fla., Gainesville, 1966-67; dir. librs. U. Memphis, 1970-99, assoc. v.p. for acad. affairs, dir. librs., 1987-91. Chmn. coun. of head librarians State Univ. and C.C. System Tenn., 1980, 87, 97; acad. assoc. Atlantic Coun. of U.S., U. Memphis; fgn. expert, vis. lectr. Beijing U. of Posts & Telecomms., Beijing Normal U., Peking U., Renmen U., Qinghua U., Chingqing Inst. Posts & Telcomms., Guizhou Normal U., Republic of China, 1993; fgn. expert/vis. lectr. Beijing U. Posts and Telecom, 1993; fgn. expert, vis. lectr. Nanjing U. Posts and Telecom., Anhui Normal U., Beijing U. Posts and Telecom., 1994, People's Republic of China, 1994; cons. prof. Beijing U. of Posts and Telecom., 1996—; participant 2d Internat. Conf. Crimea 95, Librs. and Assn. in the Transient World, Republic of Crimea; participant, dep. chair organizing com., 1996—; Peking U. Internat. Conf., Beijing, 1998. Contbr. articles to profl. jours. With USAF, 1955-59. Recipient Adminstrv. Staff award Memphis State U., 1981, Commendation Boy Scouts Am., 1985, Commendation Tenn. Sec. State, 1989, Honor award Tenn. Libr. Assn., 1990, Allen J. Hammond award for Disting. Svc. U. Memphis, 1999, SLIS Disting. Alumni award Ind. U., 1999, TRACES award U. Memphis Assn. Retirees, 2003; named Outstanding Alumnus, La. State U., 1988; named Libr. of Yr., Memphis Libr. Coun., 1989; fellow Higher Edn. Act Ind. U.; named to 30th Ann. Honor Roll. ALA Office Intellectual Freedom and Freedom to Read Found. U. Memphis, 1999. Mem.: ALA, Memphis Old Time Car Club (sec. 1981, pres. 1982, 1989), Mid-Am. Old Time Automobile Assn., Antique Automobile Club Am., Nat. Assn. Watch and Clock Collectors (chpt. pres. 1983, sec.-treas. 1988—89). Office: Memphis State U U Libr Memphis TN 38152-0001

POUSADA, LIDIA, physician; b. Mt. Kisco, N.Y., July 21, 1957; d. Manuel and Maria Nieves (Mejuto) P.; m. Andrew Kemper Goodman, June 26, 1983 (div. Sept. 1986); 1 child, Sara Pousada Goodman; m. Wayne William Maibaum, Apr. 11, 1987 (div. July 1993); 1 child, Anna Pousada Maibaum; m. James Paul Kreindler, Mar. 2, 1996; 1 child, Victoria Pousada Kreindler. BS, CUNY, N.Y.C., 1978; MD, N.Y. Med. Coll., 1980. Diplomate Am. Bd. Internal Medicine, Am. Bd. Geriatric Medicine. Student geriatric fellowship NYU Med. Sch., N.Y.C., 1978-80; resident in internal medicine Montefiore Med. Ctr., Bronx, N.Y., 1980-83, dir. geriatric unit, 1986-89; with nat. health svc. North Cent. Bronx Hosp., 1983-84, Morris Heights Health Ctr., Bronx, 1985; instr. City Coll. Med. Sch., N.Y.C., 1982-85, Albert Einstein Coll. Medicine, Bronx, 1983-84, 86-89, asst. prof. medicine, 1988-89; assoc. prof. clin. medicine N.Y. Med. Coll., 1993—; pvt. practice geriatric medicine, 2002—. Dir. geriatric cons. svc. Montefiore Med. Ctr., 1987—89, assoc. chief divsn. geriatrics, 1988—92; chief divsn. geriatrics and gerontology Sound Shore Med. Ctr., 1992—2002. Author: Geriatric Diagnostics, 1983, Emergency Medicine for the House Officer, 1986, 2d edit., 1995, Emergency Medicine for Nurses, 1989, Perioperative Medical Care of the Geriatric Patient, 1989, Case Studies in Emergency Medicine for the House Officer, 1993. Physician scholar Nat. Health Svc., 1978-80. Fellow ACP, Gerontol. Soc. Am., Am. Geriatric Soc.; mem. Physicians for Social Responsibility. Office: 141 North State Rd Briarcliff Manor NY 10510

POUSCHINE, JOHN LAURENCE, private equity investment executive; b. Glen Cove, N.Y., Jan. 28, 1957; s. Ivan and Helen (Carlson) P.; m. Catherine Dana, Nov. 16, 1991; children: Alexander, Anna. BA, Princeton U., 1979; MBA, Harvard U., 1983. Officer's asst. JP Morgan, N.Y.C., 1979-81; assoc. Prudential Securities, Inc., N.Y.C., 1983-85; v.p. Bradford Ventures Ltd., N.Y.C., 1985-88; sr. v.p. Electra Inc., N.Y.C., 1989-96; mng. dir. Pouschine Cook Capital Mgmt., LLC, 1997—. Bd. dirs. MasterCraft Boat Co., Inc., Vonore, Tenn., Ampac Packaging, LLC, Cin., Latex Foam Internat., Shelton, Conn., Spring Air Ptnrs. N.Am., N.Y.C., St. Clair Entertainment, Princeton, N.J. Bd. dirs. Russian Children's Welfare Soc., N.Y.C. Mem. Bridgehampton Club, Nassau Club, Princeton Club of N.Y., Union Club. Avocation: sports. Office: Pouschine Cook Capital Mgmt 410 Park Ave Ste 810 New York NY 10022-4407 E-mail: jpouschine@pouschinecook.com.

POUTSMA, MARVIN L. chemical research administrator; b. Grand Rapids, Mich., Aug. 7, 1937; m. Yolanda Arco, July 20, 1968; children: John C., Julie A. BS, Calvin Coll., 1958; PhD, U. Ill., 1962. Staff scientist corp. rsch. Union Carbide, Tarrytown, N.Y., 1961-65, group leader corp. rsch., 1965-68, sr. scientist corp. rsch., 1968-73, sr. group leader corp. rsch., 1972-78; group leader chemistry divsn. Oak Ridge (Tenn.) Nat. Lab., 1978-80, sect. head chemistry divsn., 1980-83, dir. chemistry divsn., 1984-93, dir. chem. & analytical scis. divsn., 1994-2000, ret., 2000. Contbr. chpts. to books and articles to profl. jours. Fellow AAAS; mem. Am. Chem. Soc. Office: Oak Ridge Nat Lab PO Box 2008 Oak Ridge TN 37831-6197 Office Phone: 865-576-8339. Business E-Mail: poutsmaml@ornl.gov.

POVICH, DAVID, lawyer; b. Washington, June 8, 1935; s. Shirley Lewis and Ethyl (Friedman) Povich; m. Constance Enid Tobriner, June 14, 1959; children: Douglas, Johanna, Judtih, Andrew. BA, Yale U., 1958; LLB, Columbia U., 1962. Bar: D.C. 1962, U.S. Ct. Appeals (4th cir.) 1980, U.S. Tax Ct. 1981, U.S. Ct. Appeals (5th and 11th cirs.) 1984, U.S. Dist. Ct. Md., U.S. Ct. Appeals (3d cir.) 1997. Law clk. to assoc. judge D.C. Ct. Appeals, Washington, 1962-63; ptnr. Williams & Connolly, Washington, 1963—, exec. com., 1986-87. Bd. dirs., officer Lisner Home for Aged. Mem.: ABA, Barristers (exec. com. 1992—93), Bar Assn. D.C., D.C. Bar Assn. Office: Williams & Connolly 725 12th St NW Washington DC 20005-5901 Office Phone: 202-434-5071. E-mail: dpovich@wc.com.

POVICH, LYNN, journalist, magazine editor, internet executive; b. Washington, June 4, 1943; d. Shirley and Ethyl P.; m. Stephen B. Shepard, Sept. 16, 1979; children: Sarah, Ned. AB, Vassar Coll., 1965. Rschr., reporter, writer, editor, sr. editor Newsweek mag., N.Y.C., 1965—91; editor-in-chief Working Woman mag., N.Y.C., 1991—96; mng. editor, sr. exec. prodr. East coast programming MSNBC Interactive, Secaucus, NJ, 1996—2001. Co-chair Internat. Women's Media Found., 2002—; adv. com. women's rights divsn. Human Rights Watch. Recipient Matrix award N.Y. Women in Comms., 1976; named to Acad. of Women Achievers YWCA, 1993.

POVMAN, MORTON, lawyer; b. Bklyn., Jan. 13, 1931; s. Morris and Dora (Lifschitz) M.; m. Sandra Arkow, June 8, 1958; children: Michael, Bruce. BBA, Bernard Baruch Coll., CCNY, 1952; LLB, Bklyn. Law Sch., 1955. Pvt. practice, N.Y.C., 1955—. Mem. N.Y. City Coun., 1971—; bd. dirs. First Rehab. Ins. Co., Manhasset, N.Y.; gen. counsel Physician Reciprocal Insurers, Manhasset, 1983—. Dist. leader Dem. Com. Queens, 1970—; bd. dirs. Jewish Ctr. Kew Gardens Hills, N.Y.C.-Queens, 1980—. Recipient Svc. award United Jewish Appeal, 1980, Svc. award State of Israel Bonds, 1980, Disting. Svc. award Yad Benjamin Edn. Ctr., 1987. Mem. N.Y. State Trial Lwyers Assn. Avocations: tennis, sailing, travel. Home: 14704 75th Ave Flushing NY 11367-2932 Office: 10818 Queens Blvd Forest Hills NY 11375-4748

POWDERLY, WILLIAM H., III, lawyer; b. Pitts., Feb. 23, 1930; BS, Georgetown U., 1953; LLB, U. Pitts., 1956. Bar: Pa. 1956. Of counsel Tucker Arensberg PC, Pitts. Office: Tucker Arensberg PC 1500 One PPG Pl Pittsburgh PA 15222 Business E-Mail: wpowderly@tuckerlaw.com.

POWDRELL-CULBERT, JANE E. state representative; b. Albuquerque; B, postgrad. in MPA program. Liaison between cmty. groups and Albuquerque Police Dept.; exec. dir. N.Mex. Commn. on Status of Women; tchr. rifle safety NRA, Va.; apptd. N.Mex. Parole Bd., 1999—2003; state rep. dist. 44 N.Mex. Ho. of Reps., Santa Fe, 2002—, mem. bus. and industry, transp. and enrolling and engrossing-A coms. Republican. Office: State Capitol Room 203GCN Santa Fe NM 87503

POWDRILL, GARY LEO, production operations manager; b. Butte, Mont., Nov. 26, 1945; s. Harold Holmes and Genevieve Marie (Tansey) P.; m. Marsha A. McKeon, Oct. 6, 1979 (div.); 1 child, Amy Marie. BS, Gonzaga U., 1969; MBA, U. Detroit, 1973; MPA in Environ. Policy, Ind. U., 1984. Lic. profl. engr., Ind.; cert. plant engr. Plant design engr. Ford Motor Co., Sterling Heights, Mich., 1969-73, divsn. plant engr. Chassis divsn., 1973-74, supr. plant engring. sect. Indpls. plant, 1974-78, mgr. plant engring., 1978-80, mgr. engring. and facilities, 1980-87, mgr. mfg., plant engring. dept., 1987-88, pres., mgr. prodn. ops. area A, 1988-95, mgr. plant engring. and tech. svcs., 1996-97, mgr. power steering pump product line, 1997-98, mgr. power steering gear product line, 1998-2000, mgr. facilities and indsl. engring., 2000-01, ret., 2001. Chmn. Ind. State Water Pollution Control Bd., 1986-91; mem. Indpls. Mayor's Tech. Adv. Com., 1975—; mem. labor and mgmt. del. to U.S.-USSR Emerging Leaders Summit Conf., USSR, 1990; bd. dirs., chmn. Ruth Lilly Health Edn. Ctr.,; chmn. environ. com. Ind. State C. of C. Mem. Ind. Soc. Profl. Engrs., Elks. Roman Catholic. Home: 6 Forest Ct Greenfield IN 46140-8739

POWE, NEIL RICHARD, physician, educator, epidemiologist, health services researcher; b. Phila., May 11, 1955; BA, Princeton U., 1976; MD, MPH, Harvard U., 1981; MBA, Wharton Grad. Sch., Phila., 1986. Intern, resident hosp. U. Pa., 1981-84, Robert Wood Johnson Clin. scholar; instr. Johns Hopkins U., Balt., 1986-88, asst. prof., 1988-94, assoc. prof., 1994-98, prof., 1998—. Dir. Welch Ctr. for Prevention, Epidemiology and Clin. Rsch., 1998—, Johns Hopkins Evidence Based Practice Ctr.; co-dir. Robert Wood Johnson Clin. Scholars Program. Contbr. articles to profl. jours. Assn. Health Svcs. Rsch. fellow, 1997. Fellow: ACP (tchg. and rsch. scholar); mem.: Inst. Medicine, 2004, Am. Soc. Clin. Investigation. Office: Johns Hopkins U 2-600 2024 E Monument St Baltimore MD 21287-0007 E-mail: npower@jhsph.edu.

POWELL, ALAN, scientist-engineer; b. Buxton, Derbyshire, Eng., Feb. 17, 1928; arrived in U.S., 1956; s. Frank and Gwendolen Marie (Walker) P.; m. June Sinclair, Mar. 28, 1956. Student, Buxton Coll., 1939-45; diploma in aeros., Loughborough Coll., 1948; BSc in Engring. with 1st class honors, London U., 1949; honours diploma 1st class, Loughborough Coll., 1949; D.Tech. (hon.), Loughborough U. Tech., 1980; PhD, U. Southampton, 1953. Chartered engr. Engr. Percival Aircraft Co., Luton, Eng., 1949-51; from rsch. asst. to lectr. U. Southampton, Eng., 1951-56; rsch. fellow Calif. Inst. Tech., Pasadena, 1956-57; engr. Douglas Aircraft Co., 1956; assoc. prof. UCLA, 1957-62, prof. engring., 1962-65, head Aerosonics lab., 1957-65; assoc. tech. dir., head acoustics and vibration lab. David Taylor Model Basin, Dept. Navy, Washington, 1965-66, tech. dir., 1966-67, David Taylor Naval Ship Research & Devel. Center, Bethesda, Md., 1967-85; mem. Undersea Warfare Research & Devel. Council, 1966-76, chmn., 1971-72; mem. council on Fed. Labs., 1972-85; prof. mech. engring. U. Houston, 1985-2000, chmn., 1985-87, prof. emeritus, 2000—. Com. on hearing bioacoustics and biomechs. NAS-NRC, 1961-85, exec. coun., 1963-65, chmn., 1965-66, advisor, 1985-95, mem. naval studies bd. 1990-95; mem. various coms. Naval Studies Bd. and Marine Bd., 1990-96; advisor Chinese U. Devel. Project, 1989-91; cons. Douglas Aircraft Co., 1956-65, others; adv. coun. Internat. Towing Tank Conf., 1981-85; mem. advisor U.S.-Japan Program Natural Resources, 1987-90, mem. Marine Facilities Panel; gen. chmn. 3d advanced vehicles conf. AIAA and Soc. Naval Archs. and Marine Engrs., 1976; chmn. internat. conf. Computer Aided Design, Manufacture and Ops. in Marine and Offshore Industries, 1987-88; cons. Sci. Applications Internat., Inc., 1987-90; governing bd. Am. Inst. Physics, 1995-97. Contbr. articles to profl. jours. Recipient Navy Meritorious Civilian Service award, 1970; Brit. Empire scholar, 1945; named Meritorious Exec. Pres. of U.S., 1982; Capt. Robert Dexter Conrad gold medal for sci. achievement Sec. Navy, 1984; dedication spl. issue Internat. J. Aeronautics role nos. 3/4, 2003. Fellow Royal Aero. Soc. London (Baden-Powell prize 1948, Wilbur Wright prize 1953), Acoustical Soc. Am. (biennial award 1962, assoc. editor Jour. 1962-67, chmn. edn. com. 1964-66, exec. coun. 1966-69, chmn. medals and awards com. 1978-81, v.p. elect 1981-82, v.p. 1982-83, pres. elect 1989-90, pres. 1990-91, past pres. 1991-92, Silver medal in engring. acoustics 1992, designated Nat. Spkr. in Engring. Acoustics 1994-98), Inst. Mech. Engrs., Inst. Acoustics (U.K.); mem. AIAA (assoc. fellow, Aeroacoustics award 1980), ASME (Rayleigh lectr. 1988, Per Brüel Gold medal 1991), Inst. Noise Control Engrs. (initial mem., dir. 1974-77, Disting. lectr. 1975, 83, v.p. 1981-84, bd. cert. 1993), Acoustics, Speech and Signal Processing Soc. (exec. com. 1969-72, awards com. 1971-73, bylaws com. chmn. 1973-75), Am. Soc. Naval Engrs. (life), Am. Acad. Mechanics, Tau Beta Pi (hon. life). Office: U Houston Dept Mech Engring Houston TX 77204-4006

POWELL, ALMA JOHNSON, writer, advocate, foundation administrator; b. Birmingham, Al., Oct. 27, 1937; d. Robert and Mildred Johnson; m. Colin L. Powell, Aug. 1962; children: Michael, Linda, Annemarie. BA, Fisk U., 1957; LHD (hon.), Emerson Coll., 1996. Audiologist Boston Guild Hard of Hearing, 1959—62; co-chair America's Promise: Alliance Youth, 1997—. Author: (children's books) America's Promise, 2003, My Little Wagon, 2003. Bd. trustees Kennedy Ctr., 1991—, vice chair, 1993; chair nat. coun. Best Friends Found., 1989—. Named one of 100 Most Powerful Women in Wash., Washingtonian mag., 2001.

POWELL, ANNE ELIZABETH, editor; b. Cheverly, Md., Nov. 11, 1951; d. Arthur Gorman and Barbara Anne (MacAran) P.; m. John Alan Ebeling Jr., 1972 (div. 1983). BS, U. Md., 1972. Reporter Fayetteville (N.C.) Times, 1973-75; home editor Columbus (Ga.) Ledger-Enquirer, 1976; assoc. editor Builder mag., Washington, 1977-78; architecture editor House Beautiful's Spl. Publs., N.Y.C., 1979-81; editor Traditional Home mag., Des Moines, 1982-87, Mid-Atlantic Country mag., Alexandria, Va., 1987-89; editor in chief publs. Nat. Trust for Hist. Preservation, Washington, 1989-95; editor-in-chief Landscape Architecture Mag., Washington, 1995-98, Civil Engring. Mag., Washington, 1998—. Author: The New England Colonial, 1988. Mem. Nat. Press Club, Am. Soc. Mag. Editors. Home: 1105 Park St NE Washington DC 20002-6317 Office: American Society of Civil Engrs Civil Engring Mag 1801 Alexander Bell Dr Reston VA 20191-4344 E-mail: apowell@asce.org.

POWELL, BARRY BRUCE, classicist, educator; b. Sacramento, Apr. 30, 1942; s. Barrett Robert and Anita Louise (Burns) Powell; m. Patricia Ann Cox, children: Elena Melissa, Adam Vincent. BA in Classics, U. Calif., Berkeley, 1963, PhD, 1971; MA, Harvard U., 1965. Asst. prof. Northern Ariz. U., Flagstaff, 1970-73; from asst. prof. to prof. U. Wis., Madison, 1973—, chmn. dept. classics, 1985-92, chmn. program integrated liberal studies. Author: Composition by Theme in the Odyssey, 1973, Homer and the Origin of the Greek Alphabet, 1991, Classical Myth, 1995, 1997, 2000, 2003, New Companion to Homer, 1997, A Short Introduction to Classical Myth, 2001, Writing and the Origins of Greek Literature, 2002, Homer, 2003; author: (with Ian Morris) The Greeks: Society, Culture, History, 2004; contbr. articles to profl. jours. Woodrow Wilson fellow, 1965. Mem.: Am. Acad. in Rome, Classical Assn. Midwest and South, Archeol. Inst. Am., Am. Sch. Classical Studies at Athens (mng. com.), Am. Philol. Assn., Phi Beta Kappa (former pres. Madison chpt.). Home: 1210 Sweetbriar Rd Madison WI 53705-2228 Office: Univ Wis Dept Classics Madison WI 53707 E-mail: bbpowell@wisc.edu.

POWELL, BOONE, JR., hospital executive; b. Knoxville, Tenn., Feb. 9, 1937; married. BA, Baylor U., 1959; MA, U. Calif., 1960. Adm. intern Marin Gen. Hosp., Greenbrae, Calif., 1959; adm. resident Baptist Meml. Hosp., Memphis, 1960-61; asst. adminstr. Hendrick Med. Ctr., Abilene, Tex., 1961-69, assoc. adminstr., 1969-70, adminstr., 1970-73, pres., 1973-80; pres., CEO Baylor Health Care System, Dallas, 1980-2000, chmn., 2000—. Contbr. articles to profl. jours. Mem. Am. Coll. Healthcare Execs., Tex. Hosp. Assn. (chair community svc., trustee). Office: Baylor Health Care System 3500 Gaston Ave Dallas TX 75246-2096

POWELL, BURNELE VENABLE, dean; b. Kansas City, Kans., Mar. 5, 1947; s. Lorenzo Roland and Teola (Sykes) P.; m. Brenda Joyce Venable, June 30, 1973; children: Bradley Venable, Berkeley Venable. BA, U. Mo., Kansas City, 1970; JD, U. Wis., 1973; LLM, Harvard U., 1979. Bar: Wis. 1973, Mass. 1977. Assoc. regional counsel HUD, Boston, 1973-77; grad. law teaching fellow Harvard U. Law Sch., Cambridge, Mass., 1977-79; asst. prof. U. N.C. Sch. Law, Chapel Hill, 1979-84, assoc. prof., 1984-88, prof., 1988—95, assoc. dean, acad. affairs, 1990-93; dean U. Mo. Sch. Law, Kansas City, 1995—2003, U. S.C. Sch. Law, Columbia, 2004—. Vis. assoc. prof. law U. Oreg. Sch. Law, Eugene, 1987; vis. prof. law Washington U., St. Louis, summer 1990; cons. Adminstrv. Conf. U.S., Washington, 1983-86; arbitrator Nat. Future Adminstrn., Chgo., 1990. Bd. dirs. Consumers Union, 1997—, Planned Parenthood of Orange and Durham Counties, 1992—, Am. Lung Assn. Mo., 1997—. Mem. ABA (coms. 1987—, chmn. standing com. on profl. discipline 1991—, N.C. ethics com. 1990-92, chmn. governing com. Profl. Responsibility Ctr. 1997—), AAUP (chpt. pres. 1990-91), Am. Law Inst., Am. Bar Found., Assn. Am. Law Schs. (coms. 1981—), Mo. Bar Assn. (chmn. venue com. 1997—, mem. foresight com. 1997—), Midwest Bioethics Assn. (bd. dirs. 1997—). Democrat. Unitarian Universalist. Office: USC Sch of Law Main & Greene Sts Columbia SC 29208*

POWELL, CAROLYN WILKERSON, retired music educator; b. Hamburg, Ark., Oct. 9, 1920; d. Claude Kelly and Mildred (Hall) Wilkerson; m. Charles Luke Powell, Dec. 12, 1923; children: Charles Luke Jr., James David, Mark Wilkerson, Robert Hall. AB, Ctrl. Meth. U., Fayette, Mo., 1942; MA in Tchg., U. N.C., 1970. Life tchg. cert. Mo., cert. tchr. N.C. Choral dir. Maplewood-Richmond Heights Sch., St. Louis, 1943-45; pvt. piano tchr. Greensboro, NC, 1951-63; organist Presbyn. and Meth. chs., Greensboro, 1950-61; dir. ch. youth choirs, Greensboro, 1958-61; choral and humanities tchr. Page HS, Greensboro, 1963-67; choral dir. Githens Jr. HS, Durham, NC, 1967-80; ret., 1980. Chmn. Choral Festival N.C. Dist., 1968—78; accompanist, music dir. Altavista (Va.) Little Theatre, 1981—83. Den mother Boy Scouts Am., Greensboro, 1951—57; mem. Chapel Hill (N.C.) Preservation Soc., 1985—; vol., chapel organist, pediat. tutor U. N.C. Hosps., Chapel Hill, 1984—89; mem. Chapel Hill Hist. Soc.; Sunday and vacation schs. tchr., organist Grace Meth. Ch., Greensboro; organist St. Peter's Episcopal Ch., Altavista, 1981—83; organist Episcopal ch. svc. Carol Woods Retirement Cmty., Chapel Hill, 1999—. Mem.: AAUW, NEA, Classroom Tchrs. Assn., Am. Organists Guild, Music Educators Nat. Conf., Ackland Art Mus. Assn., Carolina Club, Nat. Federated Music Club Euterpe, Chapel Hill Country Club, Univ. Woman's Club, Delta Kappa Gamma. Avocations: reading, golf, needlecrafts, gardening, travel. Home: 750 Weaver Dairy Rd Apt 142 Chapel Hill NC 27514-1440

POWELL, COLIN LUTHER, secretary of state, retired military officer, author, public speaker; b. N.Y.C., Apr. 5, 1937; s. Luther and Maud Ariel (McKoy) P.; m. Alma V. Johnson, Aug. 25, 1962; children: Michael, Linda, Annemarie. BS in Geology, CUNY, 1958; MBA, George Washington U., 1971. Commd. 2d lt. U.S. Army, 1958; advanced through grades to gen., 1989; comdr. 2d Brigade, 101st Airborne Div., 1976—77; exec. asst. to sec. Dept. Energy, 1979; sr. mil. asst. to Dep. Sec. Def. Dept. Def., 1979—81, asst. div. comdr. 4th Inf. Div., 1981—83, mil. asst. to Sec. of Def. Washington, 1983—86; assigned to U.S. V Corps, Europe, 1986—87; dep. asst. to the pres. for nat. security affairs The White House, Washington, 1987; asst. to Pres. for nat. security affairs Washington, 1987—89; comdr.-in-chief Forces Command, Ft. McPherson, Ga., 1989—94; chmn. Joint Chiefs of Staff The Pentagon, Washington, 1989—93; ret., 1993; sec. U.S. Dept. State, Washington, 2001—. Founding chair America's Promise.; pub. spkr. addressing audiences across the country and abroad. Author: My American Journey, 1995. Decorated Legion of Merit, Bronze Star, Air medal, Purple Heart; named hon. knight comdr. Most Honorable Order of the Bath Queen Elizabeth II, 1993; recipient Medal of Freedom (2), President's Citizens Medal, Congressional Gold Medal, Sec. of State Disting. Svc. Medal, Sec. of Energy Disting. Svc. Medal, several sch. and other inst. have been named in his honor; The White House fellow, 1972—73. Mem. Assn. U.S. Army. Republican. Episcopalian. Office: Dept State 2201 C St NW Washington DC 20520

POWELL, DAN CLAYTON, physician; b. Amarillo, Tex., July 23, 1965; s. Robert Luther and Merrilyn Kay (Gober) P.; m. Lisa Marie Gomez, June 10, 1989; children: Gabrielle Marie, Landon Wren. BS in Biology, Abilene Christin U., 1987; MD, U. Tex., 1991. Diplomate Am. Bd. Family Practice. Resident in family practice St. Joseph Hosp., Denver, 1991-94; family physician Family Medicine Ctr., Pampa, Tex., 1994-97. Chief dept. medicine Columbia Med. Ctr., Pampa, 1996, chmn. emergency com. 1997, med. dir. Columbia Home Health, Pampa, 1995-97; sec. staff Pampa Regional Med. Ctr., 2000; hon. co-chmn. Physician's Adv. Bd., Nat. Rep. Congl. Com. Author/co-editor: The Pickwicker, 1990, 91; author: (poetry) Of Time and Tide, 1998. Bd. dirs. ARC, Gray County, Tex., 1995-97; deacon and mem. Mary Ellen and Harvester Ch. of Christ, Pampa, 1997-2000; cmty. sponsor, spkr. Tar Wars, Pampa, 1996—; curriculum instr. Worth the Wait, 1997—, bd. dirs., 2001—; elder Body of Christ Ch., Pampa, 2001—. Recipient dean's scholarship U. Tex. Med. Sch., San Antonio, 1988, Tex. Businessman of Yr. award Nat. Rep. Congl. Com., 2001; named Outstanding Young Man of Am., 1998, Physician of Yr., Nat. Rep. Congl. Com. Physician Adv. Bd., 2003.

Mem. AMA, Tex. Med. Assn., Am. Acad. Family Practice, Tex. Acad. Family Practice, Internat. Soc. Poets. Avocations: reading, writing, music, church, running. Office: Family Medicine Ctr 3023 Perryton Pkwy Ste 101 Pampa TX 79065 E-mail: dpowmd@hotmail.com.

POWELL, DAVID CHARLES, music educator, meteorologist; b. Keokuk, Iowa, May 14, 1926; s. Othello Dotson and Miriam Estella (Trittschuh) Powell; m. Judith Ann Ahrens, Feb. 2, 1950; children: Walter David, Katharine Elise. MusB, Ind. U., 1949, MusM, postgrad., Ind. U., 1951; BS, U. Utah, 1964, MA, 1968, PhD, 1974. Cert. music tchr. Instr. piano Ea. Ky. State Coll., Richmond, 1951—52; tchr. math. and music Darby (Mont.) Pub. Schs., 1953—56; pvt. piano instr. Whitefish, Mont., 1956—62; rsch. scientist, sr. scientist meteorology Battelle, Pacific NW Nat. Lab., Richland, Wash., 1968—88; pvt. piano instr. Richland, 1989—. Contbr. articles and papers to profl. publs. Cmty. educator classical music history, 1981—. With U.S. Army, 1944—46, ETO. Grad. fellow, NASA, 1965—67. Mem.: Nat. Guild Piano Tchrs., Wash. State Music Tchrs. (treas., publicity com. 1989—91), Nat. Music Tchrs. Assn., Audubon Soc. (pres. lower Columbia Basin chpt. 1975—76). Episcopalian. Achievements include development of computer programs to model atmospheric conditions. Avocations: hiking, birdwatching, camping, travel, music. Home and Office: 2110 Hudson Ave Richland WA 99354

POWELL, DAVID W. manufacturing executive; V.p., stationary and office supplies 3M Co., sr. v.p., mktg., 1999—. Mem., bd. overseers Carlson Sch. Mgmt., U. Minn., 2003—04. Pres. 3M Found. Office: 3M Co 3M Ctr Saint Paul MN 55144

POWELL, DEBORAH ELIZABETH, pathologist, dean; b. Lynn, Mass., Nov. 28, 1939; MD, Tufts U., 1965. Diplomate Am. Bd. Pathology. Intern Georgetown Med. Ctr., Washington, 1965-66; resident in pathology NIH, Bethesda, Md., 1966-69; exec. dean, vice-chancellor clin. affairs U. Kans. Sch. Medicine, Kansas City, 1997—2002; dean, asst. v.p. for clin. affairs U. Minn. Med. Sch., Mpls., 2002—. Past pres. U.S. & Can. Acad. Pathology, Inc.; trustee Am. Bd. Pathology. Mem.: Inst. Medicine, Internat. Assn. Pathologists, Am. Assn. Pathologists. Office: U Minn Med Sch Dean's Office 420 Delaware St SE MMC 293 Minneapolis MN 55455 Business E-Mail: dpowell@umn.edu.

POWELL, DENNIS, computer systems network executive; BBA in Acctg., Oreg. State U. Former sr. ptnr. Coopers & Lybrand LLP; v.p., corp. contr. Cisco Systems, Inc., San Jose, Calif., 1997—2002, sr. v.p. corp. fin., 2002—03, sr. v.p., CFO, 2003—. Mem. FDIC Adv. Com. on Banking Policy; expert witness on fin. reporting Senate Banking Com. and Ho. Fin. Subcom. Mem.: AICPA (task force for in-process R&D 2000), Fin. Execs. Internat. Office: Cisco Systems Inc 170 W Tasman Dr San Jose CA 95134

POWELL, DONALD ASHMORE, clinical research psychologist; b. Spartanburg, S.C., Oct. 29, 1938; s. Russell Kermit Powell and Mignon Kathlene Cox; m. Palmyra Langston, 1961 (div. 1972); children: Donald Langston, Donetta Plamyra, Ashley Preston, Stephanie Anne; m. Shirley L. Buchanan, Aug. 17, 1992 (dec. June 1998); m. Trisha Pope, Apr. 18, 2002. BS, U. S.C., 1960, MA, 1962; PhD, Fla. State U., 1967. Rsch. pychologist Dorn VA Med. Ctr., Columbia, S.C., 1969—, acting dir. R&D, 1996-2000; prof. U. S.C. Sch. Medicine, Columbia, 1979—. Adj. prof. U. S.C., Columbia, 1969—; cons. U.S. Heart, Lung and Blood Inst., Bethesda, 1986—; program specialist VA Mental Health and Behavioral Scis., Washington, 1984-88. Author: (with others) Eyeblink Conditioning, 1999. Rsch. fellowship NIH, 1967-69; vis. scholar NIH, 1974; recipient Merit Rsch. award Dept. of Vet. Affairs, 1996—. Mem. Soc. for Neurosci., Am. Psychol. Soc., Pavlovian Soc. (Pavlovian Rsch. award 1991), Soc. for Neurosci. (pres. S.C. chpt. 1980-81, councilor 1982-85). Democrat. Avocations: running, reading. Home: 405 Hunt Cliff Dr Columbia SC 29229 Office: Dorn VA Med Ctr 6439 Garners Ferry Rd Columbia SC 29209-1638

POWELL, DONALD DAVID, religious studies educator; b. Brandon, Manitoba, Can., Mar. 24, 1928; s. Clifford Seymour and Harriet Ethel Powell; m. Ruby Lillian Kemp, Sept. 30, 1952; children: Dorothy Lorraine, Judi Marlene, Marjorie Donia, Darlene Joyce. B of Religious Edn., Prairie Bible Coll., Three Hills, Alta., Can., 1986; M of Religious Edn., Luth. Rice Sem., Jacksonville, 1988. Clergyman Bapt. Gen. Conf. Missionary Can. Sunday Sch. Mission, Blue Wing, Canada, 1952—53; pastor Mallaig Bapt. Ch., Mallaig, 1953—56, 1st Bapt. Ch., Swan River, 1952—62; faculty Prairie Bible Inst., Three Hills, 1964—93. Sec. Bapt. Gen. Conf., Canada. Author: (booklet) A Morgan Story, 2000. Avocation: walking.

POWELL, DONALD E. federal agency administrator; b. Tex. m. Twanna Powell; 2 children. BS Econs., West Tex. StateU.; grad., So. Meth. U. CEO First Nat. Bank Amarillo, Tex.; chmn. FDIC, Washington, 2001—. Active City of Amarillo Housing Bd., Lindsay Student Aid Fund, Cal Farley's Boys Ranch; past bd. dirs. High Plains Bapt. Hosp., Harrungton Regional Med. Ctr. Office: FDIC 550 17th St NW Washington DC 20429-0001*

POWELL, DURWOOD ROYCE, lawyer; b. Raleigh, N.C., Nov. 21, 1951; s. Albert Royce and Powell; m. Leej Ida Copperfield, Mar. 1, 1980. BS, U. N.C., 1974, JD, 1979; LLM in Taxation, Emory U., 1985. Bar: N.C. 1979, U.S. Dist. Ct. (ea., mid. and we. dists.) N.C. 1981, U.S. Tax Ct. 1981, U.S. Ct. Appeals (4th cir.) 1984, U.S. Ct. Claims 1984, U.S. Supreme Ct. 1984, D.C. 1988, U.S. Ct. Appeals (D.C. cir.) 1988, N.Y. 1989. Mgmt. analyst GAO, Norfolk, Va., 1974-76; tax staff Arthur Andersen & Co., Washington, 1979-80; assoc. Biggs, Meadows, Etheridge & Johnson, Rocky Mount, N.C., 1980-82, Biggs Law Firm, Rocky Mount, 1982-83; ptnr. Maupin, Taylor, Ellis & Adams, Raleigh, N.C., 1985—, also bd. dirs., 1985—. Adj. prof. corp. taxation Grad. Sch. Bus., U. N.C., Chapel Hill, 1989-92; faculty Duke U. Tax and Estate Planning Conf., 1991; mem. negotiation project Harvard U., Cambridge, Mass., 1992. Contbr. articles to profl. jours. Tax reform com. Duke U., Washington, 1988. Mem. ABA (tax, corp., banking and securities sects.), N.C. Bar Assn. (tax and corp. sects.), Phi Beta Kappa, Phi Eta Sigma. Home: 7616 Wingfoot Dr Raleigh NC 27615-5485 Office: Maupin Taylor Ellis & Adams 3200 Beech Leaf Ct Ste 500 Raleigh NC 27604-1064

POWELL, EARL ALEXANDER, III, art museum director; b. Spartanburg, S.C., Oct. 24, 1943; s. Earl Alexander and Elizabeth (Duckworth) P.; m. Nancy Landry Powell, July 17, 1971; children: Cortney, Channing, Sumner. AB with honors, Williams Coll., 1966; AM, Harvard U., 1970, PhD, 1974; DFA (hon.), Williams Coll., 1993. Tchg. fellow in fine arts Harvard U., 1970-74; curator Michener Collection U. Tex., Austin, 1974-76, asst. prof. art history, 1974-76; mus. curator, sr. staff asst. to asst. dir. and chief curator Nat. Gallery Art, Washington, 1976-78, exec. curator, 1979-80; dir. L.A. County Mus. Art, 1980-92, Nat. Gallery Art, Washington, 1992—. Trustee Am. Fedn. Arts, Morris and Gwendolyn Cafritz Found., White House Hist. Assn., Nat. Trust Hist. Preservation; Georgia O'Keeffe Found.; mem. fine arts com. Friends of Art and Preservation in Embassies; nat. adv. bd. O'Keeffe Mus.; mem. com. for preservation The White House; fed. coun. Arts and Humanities; fine arts adv. panel Fed. Res. Bd.; mem. overseer's com. Visit the Art Mus., Harvard; mem. Nat. Portrait Gallery Com., Commn. Fine Arts; mem. Pres.'s Com. on Arts and Humanities; mem. vis. com. Williams Coll. Mus. Art. Author: American Art at Harvard, 1973, Selections from the James Michener Collection, 1975, Abstract Expressionists and Imagists: A Retrospective View, 1976, Milton Avery, 1976, The James A. Michener Collection: Twentieth Century American Painting, catalogue raisonne, 1978, Thomas Cole monograph, 1990. Mem. Nat. Coun. on the Arts; mem. Pres.'s Com. on the Arts and Humanities. With U.S. Navy, 1966-69, comdr. Res., 1976-80. Decorated chevalier Arts and Letters,chevalier Legion of Honor; grand ofcl. Order of the Infante D. Henrique medal, 1995; recipient King Olav medal, 1978, Bicentennial medal Williams Coll., 1995; Harvard U. travelling fellow, 1973-74, Mexican Cultural award, 1996, commendatore dell'Ordine al Merito della Republica Italiana, 1998. Mem. Walpole Soc., Assn. Art Mus. Dirs., Am. Philos. Soc. Office Phone: 202-842-6001.

POWELL, GREGORY DAVID, secondary school educator, coach, musician; b. Seattle, Wash., May 5, 1954; s. David and Dorthella Powell; m. Margo Ellen Graham, Aug. 6, 1989; children: Evan Gregory, Mandy Rae, Martin Thomas Rodin, Heather Marie Rodin. AA, Yakima Valley Coll., Yakima, Wash., 1974; BA History, Wash. State U., Pullman, Wash., 1977; MA Ednl. Tech., City U., Bellevue, Wash., 1997, MA Ednl. Tech, 1999. Cert. Continuing Edn. Wash., 1986. Tchr., libr., basketball-volleyball coach Selkirk Sch. Dist., Metaline, Wash., 1982—87; history tchr., head volleyball coach Darrington Sch. Dist., Darrington, Wash., 1987—. Recipient 200 Wins Coaching Plaque, Wash. State Coaches Assn., 2004. Mem.: Assn. of Am. Historians, Nat. Coun. of Edn. Historians. Achievements include All-State Volleyball Coach. Home: PO Box 951 413 Trail St W Darrington WA 98241 Office: Darrington Schl Dist 1085 Fir St Darrington WA 98241 Personal E-mail: gpowell@dsd.k12.wa.us. Business E-Mail: gpowell@dsd.k12.wa.us.

POWELL, JAMES BOBBITT, biomedical laboratories executive, pathologist; b. Burlington, N.C., Aug. 28, 1938; s. Thomas Edward and Sophia (Sharpe) P.; m. Pamela Oughton, Sept. 12, 1969 (div. Sept. 1979); 1 child, Daphne P. Markcrow; m. Anne Ellington, Oct. 20, 1984; children: James Bobbitt (dec.), John Banks, James Rosser, Helen Bobbitt. BA, Va. Mil. Inst., 1960; MD, Duke U., 1964. Diplomate Am. Bd. Pathology. Intern Duke U. Med. Ctr., Durham, N.C., 1964-65; resident Cornell Med. Ctr., N.Y.C., 1965-67, Englewood (N.J.) Hosp., 1967-69; founder Biomed Labs, Burlington, N.C., 1969—; pres. Roche Biomed. Labs., 1982-95; pres., CEO Lab. Corp. Am. Holdings, 1995-97; CEO Tripath Imaging, Burlington, NC, 1997—2000. Bd. dirs. Mid-Carolina Bank, Lab. Corp., Inc., Warren Land Co., Mercury, Md. Contbr. articles to sci. publs. Vice chmn., trustee Elon (N.C.) U., 1979—; chmn. bd. dirs. Alamance Found.; vice chmn. bd. dirs. Alamance Regional Med. Ctr.; bd. dirs. Alamance Extended Care. Maj. Med. Corps U.S. Army, 1969—72. Mem. Alamance Country Club. Republican. Methodist. Avocations: tennis, U.S. military history. Home: 1573 York Pl Burlington NC 27215-3360 Office: 1573 York Pl Burlington NC 27215 E-mail: jpowellyorkplace@aol.com.

POWELL, JAMES HENRY, lawyer; b. N.Y.C., May 1, 1928; s. Milton Jerome and Doris (Unterberg) P.; m. Connie Lu Egger, Oct. 5, 1958; children: David E., Andrew J., Jeffrey K. AB, Harvard U., 1949; LLB, Yale U., 1952. Bar: N.Y. 1952. Assoc. McLaughlin and Stern, N.Y.C., 1955-69; atty. ABC, N.Y.C., 1969-72; assoc. Fried Frank Harris Shriver & Jacobson, N.Y.C., 1972-76, Patterson Belknap Webb & Tyler, N.Y.C., 1976-80, ptnr., 1980-95; pvt. practice N.Y.C., 1996—. Mem. exec. com. Lexington Dem. Club, 1961-63. With U.S. Army, 1953-55. Mem. Assn. of Bar of City of N.Y., City Athletic Club N.Y.C. (mem. bd. govs. 1973-81), Phi Beta Kappa. Office: 477 Madison Ave New York NY 10022-5802 Office Phone: 212-355-3111.

POWELL, JAMES LAWRENCE, museum director; b. Berea, Ky., July 17, 1936; s. Robert Lain and Lizena (Davis) P.; m. Joan Hartmann; children: Marla, Dirk, Joanna. AB, Berea Coll., 1958; PhD, MIT, 1962; DSc (hon.), Oberlin Coll., 1983; LHD (hon.), Tohoku Gakuin U., 1986; DSc (hon.), Beaver Coll., 1992. Mem. faculty Oberlin Coll., Ohio, 1962-83, also prof. geology, asso. dean, 1973-75, v.p., provost, 1976-83; pres. Franklin and Marshall Coll., Lancaster, Pa., 1983-88, Reed Coll., Portland, Oreg., 1988-91; pres., chief exec. officer The Franklin Inst., Phila., 1991-94; pres., dir. Los Angeles County Mus. Natural History, L.A., 1994—. Mem. Nat. Sci. Bd., 1986-98. Author: Strontium Isotope Geology, 1972, Pathways to Leadership: Achieving and Sustaining Success: A Guide for Nonprofit Executives, 1995, Night Comes to the Coctzcems; Dinosaur Extinction and the Transformation of Modern Geology, 1998. Fellow Geol. Soc. Am. Office: LA County Mus Nat Hist 900 Exposition Blvd Los Angeles CA 90007-4057

POWELL, JAMES MATTHEW, history professor; b. Cin., June 9, 1930; s. Matthew James and Mary Loretta (Weaver) P.; m. Judith Catherine Davidorf, May 29, 1954 (dec. 1992); children: James, Michael, Mark, Mary Helen, Miriam, John BA, Xavier U., Cin., 1953, MA, 1955; postgrad., U. Cin., 1955-57; PhD, Ind. U., 1960. Instr. Kent State U., Ohio, 1959-61; asst. prof. U. Ill., Urbana, 1961-65, Syracuse U., N.Y., 1965-67, assoc. prof., 1967-72, prof. history, 1972—, dir. Ranke Cataloging Project, 1977—. Disting. vis. prof. medieval history Rutgers U., New Brunswick, 1996—. Author: Medieval Monarchy and Trade, 1962, Civilization of the West, 1967, Anatomy of a Crusade, 1213-1221, 1986, 2d edit., 1990, Albertanus of Brescia: The Pursuit of Happiness in the Early Thirteenth Century, 1992; translator: Liber Augustalis, 1971, The Deeds of Pope Innocent III, 2004; editor: Innocent III: Vicar of Christ or Lord of the World, 1963, revised and enlarged 2d edit., 1994, Medieval Studies, 1976, 2d edit., 1992; (with George G. Iggers) Leopold von Ranke and the Shaping of the Historical Discipline, 1989, Muslims Under Latin Rule, 1100-1300, 1990, (with Michael Gervers) Tolerance and Intolerance: Social Conflict in the Age of the Crusades, 2001; contbg. editor: New Catholic Encyclopedia, 2000—; cons. Ency. of the Crusades, 2000-; contbr. articles to profl. jours. Grantee NEH, 1977-84, 84, Inst. for Advanced Study, Princeton, N.J., 1989-90, Progetto Radici, Brescia, Italy, 1994-95; Fritz Thyssen Stiftung, 1986, 89; recipient John Gilmary Shea prize Am. Cath. Hist. Assn., 1987, Fellow Royal Hist. Soc. (corr.); mem. Am. Hist. Assn., Am. Cath. Hist. Assn., Medieval Acad. Am., Soc. for Italian Hist. Studies (coun. 1976-79, v.p. 1991-92, pres. 1993-95), Midwest Medieval Conf. (pres. 1965-66), Soc. for Study of the Crusades and the Latin East (sec. 1989-95), Haskins Soc. Democrat. Roman Catholic. Office: Syracuse U Maxwell School Syracuse NY 13244-0001

POWELL, JAMES R. wholesale distribution executive; V.p. sales Daisytek Internat. Corp., Plano, Tex., 1992-96, sr. v.p. sales and mktg., 1996-2000, pres., CEO, dir., 2000—. Dir. PFSweb. Office: Daisytek Internat Corp 500 N Central Expy Plano TX 75074

POWELL, JOHN S., III, lawyer, writer; b. Houston, May 8, 1968; s. John Sanford Powell and Kenda Lee Spalding; m. Stacia Brayton, May 9, 1998; 1 child, Samantha. JD, U. Tulsa, 1997; LLM, U. Houston, 2001. Paramedic Am. Med. Transport, Pasadena, Tex., 1992—94, Cox Paramedics, Springfield, Mo., 1994—95; law clerk Wagner, Stuart & Cannon, Tulsa, 1996; attorney Sanford-Powell Law Firm, Houston, 1997—. Gen. counsel Access Tex. Mag., Austin, Tex., 2000—02. Author: Hunter and Hunted, 2004, It's Not Working, 2002. Mem. Health Law Orgn. U. Houston, 2001. Recipient First degree black belt, Am. Tae Kwon Do Assn. Mem.: ABA, Tomiki Aikido Assn. (gen. counsel 2002—, second degree black belt), U.S. Judo, Inc. (green belt), U.S. Assn. Blind Athletes. Republican. Avocations: Judo, writing, Aikido, reading, Tae Kwon Do. Home: 2601 Sun Stone Ln Pearland TX 77584

POWELL, JOUETT LYNN, college dean, philosophy and religious studies educator; b. Dallas, Dec. 2, 1941; s. Hiram Wheeler and Evelyn Ruth (Foster) P.; m. Mary Ellen Beall, Aug. 15, 1964; 1 child, Kristen Lynn. BA, Baylor U., 1964; BD, So. Bapt. Theol. Sem., 1967; MPhil, Yale U., 1970, PhD, 1972. Instr. relgion U. N.C., Chapel Hill, 1971-72, asst. prof. religion, 1972-78; asst. prof. philosophy and religious studies Christopher Newport U., Newport News, Va., 1978-80, assoc. prof., 1980-89, prof., 1989, dean Sch. Letters and Natural Sci., 1983-92, dean Coll. Arts and Humanities, 1992-95, dir. grad. studies, 1992-95, acting provost, 1995-96, dean Coll. Liberal Arts, 1996-2000. Vis. assoc. prof. religion Coll. William and Mary, 1984-85, 87-90. Contbr. articles to scholarly and profl. jours. Recipient summer seminar stipend NEH, 1981, summer rsch. stipend, 1982; Rockefeller doctoral fellow Yale U., 1969-70; Smith-Reynolds Found. grantee, 1974. Mem.: AAUP, Am. Acad. Religion. Democrat. Episcopalian. Avocations: classical music, carpentry. Home: 65 Rivermont Dr Newport News VA 23601-4232 Office: Christopher Newport U Newport News VA 23606-2998 Office Phone: 757-594-7425. E-mail: jouettpowell@netscape.net.

POWELL, LARRY, communications educator; b. Greenville, Ala., May 14, 1948; s. A. Harold Powell and Virginia Brown; m. Clarine Thrower, Dec. 19, 1970. BA, Auburn U., Ala., 1970; MA, Auburn U., 1971; PhD, U. Fla., 1975. From asst. prof. to prof. Miss. State U., Starkvill, 1975—86; vcons. Kitchens, Powell & Kitchens, Orlando, Fla., 1987—96; owner Powell Cons., Orlando, 1996—98; prof. U. Ala., Birmingham, 1998—. Vis. prof. Meisei U., Hino, Japan, 1984—85; prof. Ctrl. Fla. U., Orlando, 1996—98; media pollster Birmingham News/Huntsville Times, Birmingham, 2001—; editl. reviewer N.Am. Jour. Psychology, Winter Park, Fla., 2000—; cons. in field. Co-author: (book) Political Campaign Communication, 2003; contbr. articles to profl. jours. Polit. advisor Bus. Coun. of Ala., Montgomery, 1994—96, WVTM-TV/WBRC-TV, Birmingham, 2001—02. Named one of Top 100 Comm. Rschrs., Assn. of Comm. Adminstrs., 1998; recipient Miss. Jaycee Gov. award, 1986; Ala. Dept. Pub. Health grantee, 1999—2000. Master: So. States Comm. Assn. (life; chair polit. com. 1999—2000); mem.: Nat. Comm. Assn., Religious Comm. Assn. (life). Home: 328 Shadeswood Dr Hoover AL 35226 Office: Univ of Alabama Comm Studies Dept 901 S 15th St Birmingham AL 35294

POWELL, LEWIS FRANKLIN, III, lawyer; b. Richmond, Va., Sept. 14, 1952; s. Lewis F. Jr. and Josephine (Rucker) P.; m. Lisa T. LaFata; children: Emily, Hannah, Luke. BA, Washington & Lee U., 1974; JD, U. Va., 1978. Bar: Va. 1978, U.S. Dist. Ct. (ea. and we. dists.) Va. 1979, U.S. Ct. Appeals (4th cir.) 1979, U.S. Ct. Appeals (2d cir.) 1983, U.S. Ct. Appeals (11th cir.) 1992, U.S. Supreme Ct. 1985. Law clk. to judge U.S. Dist. Ct. (ea. dist.), Richmond, 1978-79; assoc. Hunton & Williams, Richmond, 1979—86, ptnr., 1986—. Pres. young lawyers conf. Va. State Bar, 1986-87. Bd. dirs. William Byrd Cmty. Ho., Richmond, 1982-87, Boys Club of Richmond, 1984-90, Maymont Found., Richmond, 1987-92, St. Christopher's Sch., Richmond, 1989-96. Mem. Richmond Bar Assn. (chmn. improvement justice com. 1982-83), 4th Cir. Jud. Conf., Am. Law Inst. Avocations: skiing, mountain climbing, backpacking, fishing, duck hunting. Office: Hunton & Williams Riverfront Plz East Tower 951 E Bird St Richmond VA 23219

POWELL, LILLIAN MARIE, retired music educator; b. DeLand, Fla., June 1, 1927; d. Francis Charles and Jessie Agnes (Niven) P.; m. James Armbruster, May 1950 (div. 1957); children: Jeffrey L. Armbruster, Leslie J. Armbruster; m. Dwight M. Liller, Dec. 8, 1957 (div. June 1972). B. Pub. Sch. Music, Capital U., 1950; MA, Ohio State U., 1957. Lic. tchr., N.Y., N.J., Va., Ohio. Vocal and instrumental music tchr. Community Sch., Stoutsville, Ohio, 1949-50, Roosevelt Jr. High Sch., Newark, 1950-51; elem. music tchr. at several schs. Norfolk, Va., 1951-53; music tchr. Naval Base Sch., Guantanomo Bay, Cuba, 1953-55; instr. voice Otterbein Coll., Ohio, 1955-56; music tchr. several elem. and jr. high schs. Lorain, Ohio, 1956-60; music cons. elem. schs. South Orange, N.J., 1960-61; music tchr. elem. schs. Livingston, N.J., 1963-66; music tchr. Roosevelt Jr. high Sch., West Orange, N.J., 1965-72; instr. music lit. County Coll. Morris County, Dover, N.J., 1970-72; elem. sch. tchr. music Pub. Sch. 86, Jamaica Heights, N.Y., 1973-75; tchr. Satellite East Jr. High Sch. for Gifted, Bklyn., 1977-89, Stephen Halsey Jr. High Sch., N.Y.C., 1989-96, ret., 1996. Music theater dir. Children's Theater, Guantanamo Bay, 1953-55; ch. choir dir. Naval Base Chapel, Guantanamo Bay, 1953-55; ch. choir dir., soloist Congregational Ch., Lorain, Ohio, 1956-60; ch. soloist, organist Religious Sci. Ch., Morristown, Ohio. CORO assoc. orgn. activities CORO Leadership Found., Manhattan, N.Y., 1985—; vol. vocal/drama coaching Vocal Students for Profl. Goals and Producing Major Musical Prodn., Bklyn., 1977-85. Named Outstanding Woman of State of N.Y., N.Y. State Senate, 1984. Eckankar. Avocations: equestrian activities, astrology, writing, musical composition. Home: 4551 College Ave Ellicott City MD 21043-6817 E-mail: LeeMPowell@aol.com.

POWELL, LURA J. science association administrator; b. Balt., Aug. 26, 1950; m. Arthur J. King, May 22, 1982; 2 children. BS in Chemistry, U. Md., 1972, PhD (hon.), 1978. Rsch. chemist inorganic analytical rsch. divsn. Nat. Inst. Stds. & Tech., 1987-88, acting deouty dir. nat. measurement lab., 1987-88, dir. program office nat. measurement lab., 1988-89, deputy dir. Ctr. Chem. Tech. nat. measurement lab., 1989-91, chief biotech. divsn. nat. measurement lab., 1991-95, chief biotech. divsn., 1995—. Recipient Disting. Pub. Svc. award Internat. Personnel Mgmt. Assn., 1991, Silver medal Dept. Commerce, 1992. Mem. Am. Chem. Soc., Exec. Women Govt., Sigma Xi. Methodist. Office: Nat Inst Stds & Tech Dept Commerce Rm A333 Adminstrn Bldg Gaithersburg MD 20899-0001

POWELL, MICHAEL KEVIN, federal agency administrator; b. Birmingham, AL, Mar. 23, 1963; s. Colin and Alma Powell; m. Jane Knott; children: Bryan, Jeffrey. BA, Coll. William and Mary, 1985; JD, Georgetown U., 1993. Policy advisor to sec. def. for internat. security affairs, Washington, 1988—90; jud. clk. to Hon. Harry T. Edwards U.S. Ct. Appeals D.C. cir., Washington, 1993—94; assoc. O'Melveny & Myers LLP, 1994—96; chief of staff divsn. antitrust U.S. Dept. Justice, 1996—97; commr. FCC, 1997—2001, chmn., 2001—. Bd. visitors Georgetown U. Law Ctr.; bd. dirs. U.S. Telecomm. Tng. Inst. Cavalry platoon leader, troop exec. U.S. Army, 1985—88, Amberg, Germany. Recipient Freedom of Speech medal, Media Inst., 1999; Henry Crown fellow, Aspen Inst., 1999. Office: FCC 445 12th St SW Washington DC 20554*

POWELL, NANCY J. ambassador; b. Cedar Falls, Iowa; Dep. chief of mission, Lome, Togo, 1990—92; polit. counselor New Delhi, 1993—95; consul gen. Calcutta, India, 1992—93; dep. chief of mission US Embassy, Khaka, Bangladesh, 1995—97; U.S. amb. to Uganda U.S. Dept. State, Kampala, 1997—99, prin. dep. asst. sec. African affairs, 1999—2001, acting asst. sec. African affairs, 2001, U.S. amb. to Ghana Accra, 2001—02, U.S. amb. to Pakistan Islamabad, Pakistan, 2002—. Office: Embassy of USA Diplomtic Enclave PO Box 1048 Ramna 5 Islamabad Pakistan Office Fax: +92 51 214222.

POWELL, ROBERT ELLIS, mathematics educator, college dean; b. Lansing, Mich., Mar. 16, 1936; s. James Ellis and Mary Frances (Deming) P.; children: Carl Robert, Glenn Arthur, Charles Addison; m. Lisbeth Nilsen, Nov. 21, 1992. BA, Mich. State U., 1958, MA, 1959; PhD, Lehigh U., 1966. Instr. math. Lehigh U., 1964-66; asst. prof. math. U. Kans., Lawrence, 1966-69; vis. asst. research prof. U. Ky., Lexington, 1967-68; vis. asst. prof. math. Ind. U., Bloomington, summer 1969; assoc. prof. math. Kent State U., Ohio, 1969-74, prof. math., 1974-95, dean grad. coll., 1980-92, prof. math emeritus, dean emeritus grad. coll., 1995—; prof. math., dean grad. sch., dir. rsch. U. Scranton, Pa., 1995-2000. Mem. Ohio Bd. Regents' Adv. Com. on Grad. Study, 1980-92, chmn., 1983-84. Co-author: Summability Theory, 1973, rev. edit., 1988, Intuitive Calculus, 1973; contbr. numerous articles to profl. jours. Bd. dirs. Kent State U. Found., 1981-91. NSF summer grantee, 1964, 65; recipient Fulbright award, 1988. Mem. Midwestern Assn. Grad. Schs. (bd. dirs. 1988-92, chmn. 1990-91), Coun. Grad. Schs. (bd. dirs. 1990-91), Northea. Assn. Grad. Schs. (bd. dirs. 1998-2000). Home: 3490 Wild Indigo Ln Bonita Springs FL 34134

POWELL, ROSEPHANYE DUNN, composer, music educator; d. Ross and Rosa L. Dunn; m. William Clayton Powell, June 25, 1988; children: Camille Elise, Kaitlyn Elizabeth. MusB in Edn., Ala. State U., 1980—84; MusM, Westminster Choir Coll., Princeton, N.J., 1984—87; Mus D, Fla. State U., 1990—93. Asst. prof. Ga. So. U., Statesboro, 1987—90; assoc. prof., music dept. chair Philander Smith Coll., Little Rock, Ark., 1993—2001; assoc. prof. Auburn U., Ala., 2001—. Composer: (choral music) Numerous Commissioned, Sacred, Secular, And Multicultural Choral Works For Satb, Ssa, Ttbb And Children's Voices. (Works performed by the Nat. Men's, Boy's and Women's Honor Choirs of the Am. Choral Directors Assn. Nat. Conv., 2003); editor: (vocal collection) The Art Songs of William Grant Still: A Collection; singer: (lecture-recitals) The Art Songs of William Grant Still. Mem.: ASCAP, Coll. Music Soc., Am. Choral Directors Assn. (Ark. state chair, ethnic and multicultural divsn. 1998—2001), Nat. Assn. Teachers of Singing, Alpha Kappa Mu, Pi Kappa Lambda. Independent. Mem. Christian Ch. Avocations: reading, exercise. Home: 1376 Lakeshore Ln Auburn AL 36830 Office: Auburn Univ 101 Goodwin Hall Auburn University AL 36849 Office Phone: 334-844-3163. Personal E-mail: rdpowell2@aol.com. E-mail: dunnprt@auburn.edu.

POWELL, RUSSELL A. lawyer; b. Mesquite, Tex., Dec. 13, 1954; s. Gerald L. and Charlotte A. Powell; m. Teresa J. Whaley, July 8, 1999. BS in Engring. Physics, U. Calif., 1977; LLM, U. Edinburgh, 1992; JD, U. Calif., 1982; PhD

(hon.), Northrup U., 1993. Bar: Tex. 1983, Calif. 1989, Tenn. 1993. Atty. L.A. County Pub. Defenders Office, 1987—89; county ct. judge L.A. County, 1989—93; constl. atty Powell & Associates, Gatlinburg, Tenn., 1993—99. Legal cons. immigration issues Grey's Ct., London, 1993—99; asst. dist. atty., Dallas, 1982—89; legal advisor Cherokee Nation, NC, 1985—. Author: Indian Law and Congressional Corruption. Cons. Constl. Party, Fla., 2000; rep. strategist Presdl. Electorial Party, Tenn., 1996. Staff sgt. Green Beret U.S. Army, 1970—74. Mem.: ABA, Am. Judges Assn., Fla. Bar Assn. Conservative. Avocations: hunting, fishing, golf, woodworking. Office: Russell Powell Attorney At Law 650 Buckhorn Rd Gatlinburg TN 37738 E-mail: uclavol@juno.com.

POWELL, SANDY, costume designer; b. London, Jan. 12, 1959; Costumer designer for films including Caravaggio, 1986; The Last of England, 1987; Stormy Monday, 1988; Venus Peter, 1989; Killing Dad, 1989; For Queen and Country, 1989; Shadow of China, 1991; The Pope Must Die, 1991; Edward II 1991; The Miracle, 1991; Orlando, 1992 (Nominated BAFTA Award, Academy Award; Best Costume Design, 1994); The Crying Game, 1992; Wittgenstein, 1993; Being Human, 1993; Interview with a Vampire, 1994 (Nominated BAFTA Award, Best Costume Design, 1995); Rob Roy, 1995; Michael Collins, 1996; The Wings of a Dove, 1997 (Nominated Golden Satellite Award, BAFTA Award; Best Costume Design, 1998); The Butcher Boy, 1997; Velvet Goldmine, 1998 (Nominated Academy Award, Best Costume Design; Won Best Costume Design, British Academy Awards, 1998); Hilary and Jackie, 1998; Shakespeare in Love, 1998 (Won Academy Award, Best Costume Design; Nominated BAFTA Award, Best Costume Design, 1998). Office: c/o Costume Designers Guild 13949 Ventura Blvd Ste 309 Sherman Oaks CA 91423-3570

POWELL, STEPHEN WALTER, judge; b. Hamilton, Ohio, Jan. 25, 1955; s. Walter E. and Bobbi M. (Powell) P.; m. Kathryn Powell; children: Eric R.W., S. Michael; stepchildren: Greggory A., Garrett A. BA, Heidelberg Coll., 1977; JD, U. Dayton, 1981. Bar: Ohio 1981, U.S. Dist. Ct. (so. dist.) Ohio 1982. Referee Common Pleas Ct., Juvenile, Domestic and Probate, Hamilton, 1984-88; ptnr. Powell, Napier, Carmella and Allen, Hamilton, 1986-91; judge Area II Ct., Butler County, Ohio, 1989-91; judge probate div. Butler County Common Pleas Ct., Hamilton, 1991-95; presiding judge Ohio Ct. Appeals, 12th Appellate Dist., Middletown, 1995-97, adminstrv. judge, 1997-98, presiding judge, 1999—. Agt. Commonwealth Land Title, Louisville, 1988-90; parliamentarian Judges Assn. Ohio Ct. Appeals, 1995—. Sec. Butler County Rep. Cen. Com., 1982-88; trustee Union Twp., Butler County, West Chester, 1979-88; bd. dirs. United Way Hamilton Area, 1986-90. Named Man of the Day Sta. WMOH, Hamilton, 1986; recipient Meritorious Svc. award Ohio Assn. Probate Judges, 1992, 93, 94. Mem. ABA, Ohio Bar Assn., Butler County Bar Assn. Presbyterian. Office: Ohio Ct Appeals 12th Appellate Dist 1 City Centre Plz # 1009 Middletown OH 45042-1901

POWELL, SUZANNE K. K. nurse, consultant; b. Chgo., Jan. 12, 1951; d. Harry and Leah Lillian (Reitman) Kotlicky; m. James Howard Powell, June 18, 1978. ADN, Phoenix Coll., 1987; BSN, U. Phoenix, 1991, MBA, 2002. Cardiovasc. ICU nurse St. Joseph's Hosp. and Med. Ctr., Phoenix, 1987—88; case mgr. utilization mgmt.-medicaid HMO plan Mercy Care Plan, Phoenix, 1988—92; primary care case mgr. St. Joseph's Hosp. and Med. Ctr., Phoenix, 1992—95; dir. case mgr., interventions mgr. Health Svcs. Adv. Group, Inc., Phoenix, 1995—. Spkr. Case Mgmt. Soc. Am., 1995—2000. Author: Nursing Case Management: A Practical Guide to Success in Managed Care, 1996, Case Management: A Practical Guide to Success in Managed Care, 2000, Advanced Case Management: Outcomes and Beyond, 2000; sr. editor Case Mgmt. Soc. Am.: Case Mgmt. Core Curriculum; editor-in-chief: Lippincott's Case Management: Managing the Process of Patient Care. Mem. Case Mgmt. Soc. Am. Avocations: composing music for harp, piano and keyboard, owning and breeding horses. Office: Health Svcs Adv Group Inc 1600 E Northern Ste 100 Phoenix AZ 85020

POWELL, THOMAS EDWARD, III, biological supply company executive, physician; b. Elon College, N.C., Aug. 1, 1936; s. Thomas Edward, Jr., and Sophia Maude (Sharpe) P.; m. Betty Durham Yeager, June 19, 1965; children: Frances Powell Barnes, Thomas Edward IV, Caroline Powell Rogers. AB in Biology, Va. Mil. Inst., 1957; MD, Duke U., 1961; MA, Harvard U., 1966. Surgeon USPHS, 1966-68; co-founder Biomed. Reference Labs., Inc., Burlington, N.C., 1969, exec. v.p., 1969-75, chmn. exec. com., 1979-82, also dir.; exec. v.p. Carolina Biol. Supply Co., Burlington, N.C., 1968-80, chmn., 1977-80, 94—, pres., 1980-94; pres. Wolfe Sales Corp., Burlington, 1980-84, Waubun Labs. Inc., Schriever, La., 1980—, Bobbitt Labs., Inc., Burlington, 1983-94; bd. mgrs. Wachovia Bank and Trust Co. N.A., Burlington. Contbr. articles to profl. jours. Bd. dirs. United Way Alamance County, Burlington, 1968—; bd. dirs. Elon Coll., N.C., 1968—, sec., 1975—; bd. dirs. Am. Cancer Soc., Burlington, 1971-81; bd. dirs. Burlington Day Sch., 1973—, pres., 1974-78, 80-84; bd. dirs. N.C. Citizens for Bus. and Industry, Raleigh, 1983-87, Nat. Found. for Study of Religion and Econs., Greensboro, 1984-88, Blue Ridge Sch., Dyke, Va., 1985-90. Served to capt. USAR, 1957-66. Recipient Citizens Service award Elon Coll. Alumni Assn., 1980. Mem. Assn. Biology Lab. Edn., N.C. Acad. Sci., Alamance-Caswell Med. Soc., N.C. Med. Soc., Assn. Venture Founders, Newcomen Soc. Democrat. Mem. United Ch. of Christ. Clubs: Alamance Country (Burlington); Capital City (Raleigh, N.C.); Congl. Country (Washington); N.C. Country (Pinehurst); Hope Valley Country (Durham, N.C.); Greensboro City.

POWELL, TIMOTHY WOOD, information executive, consultant; b. Phila., June 22, 1949; s. James Rennie and Elizabeth Clay (Thurman) P.; children: Michael Ross, David Alexander. BA, Yale U., 1971, MBA, 1979. Field psychologist LEAP, Inc., 1971-73; outreach mgr. State of Conn., 1973-74; contracts and systems analyst State of N.J., Trenton, 1975-76; sr. fin. analyst State of N.Y., N.Y.C., 1976-77; sr. cons. KPMG, N.Y.C., 1979-83; mgr. nat. mktg. PricewaterhouseCoopers, N.Y.C., 1983-89; rsch. dir. FIND/SVP, N.Y.C., 1989-95; mng. dir. TW Powell Co. The Knowledge Agy., 1995—. Author: The High Tech Marketing Machine, 1993, Analyzing Your Competition, 1993; contbr. numerous articles to profl. jours. Fellow Soc. Competitive Intelligence Profls. (bd. dirs. 1994-97, Catalyst award 1994); mem. ASCAP, Am. Mktg. Assn. Avocation: music. Office: 156 Fifth Ave New York NY 10010 E-mail: tim.powell@knowledgeagency.com.

POWELL, WALTER HECHT, retired labor arbitrator; b. N.Y.C., Apr. 13, 1915; s. Arthur Lee and Stella (Hecht) P.; m. Dorothy Meyer, Mar. 15, 1945; children: Lawrence L., Alan W., Lesley A., Steven H. BS, NYU, 1938, JD, 1940; MA, U. Pa., 1948. Bar: N.Y. 1940, Pa. 1956. Asst. prof. Temple U., Phila., 1946-51, v.p. for pers. resources, 1973-78; asst. dir. pers. Am. Safety Razor, Kingsbury, Ind., 1951-53; v.p., dir. ops. Internat. Resistance Co., Phila., 1953-69, v.p., dir. indsl. rels., 1956-69; sr. v.p. 1st Pa. Banking & Trust Co., Phila., 1969-73; v.p. human resources Temple U., 1973-77; ind. labor arbitrator Phila., 1978—. Mem. panel Am. Arbitration Assn., Fed. Mediation and Conciliation Svc., Pa., N.J. labor rels. bds.; lectr. U. Pitts., Temple U., U. Richmond, Vanderbilt U., Am. U., others.; bd. dirs. Auerbach Corp., Phila. Contbr. book chpts., articles to profl. jours. Commr. Phila. Commn. on Human Rels., 1969—; bd. dirs. Opportunities Industrialization Ctr. Capt. AUS, 1942-46. Recipient award Phila. C. of C., 1968, Distinguised Svc. award Am. Arbitration Assn., 1997, citation City of Phila., 1997. Mem. Am. Mgmt. Assn. (adv. coun. 1963—), Indsl. Rels. Assn., Indsl. Rels. Rsch. Assn. (pres. local chpt. 1966), Nat. Acad. Arbitrators. Home and Office: 2401 Pennsylvania Ave Ste 9a7 Philadelphia PA 19130-3002

POWELL, WILLIAM ARNOLD, JR., retired bank executive; b. Verbena, Ala., July 7, 1929; s. William Arnold and Sarah Frances (Baxter) Powell; m. Barbara Ann O'Donnell, June 16, 1956; children: William Arnold III, Barbara Calhoun, Susan Thomas, Patricia Crain. BSBA, U. Ala., 1953; grad., La. State U. Sch. Banking of South, 1966. With Am. South Bank, N.A., Birmingham, Ala., 1953—93, asst. v.p., 1966, v.p., 1967, v.p., br. supr., 1968-72, sr. v.p., br. supr., 1972-73, exec. v.p., 1973-79, pres., 1979-83, vice chmn. bd., 1983-93, also bd. dirs.; pres. AmSouth Bancorp., 1979—93; ret., 1993. Bd. dirs. AmSouth Bank, Fla. Bd. dirs. United Way Found.; past pres. United Way, campaign chmn., 1987; life mem. Birmingham Met. Devel. Bd.; bd. dirs. Warrior-Tombigbee Devel. Assn.; life trustee Ala. Ind. Colls.; trustee Ala. Hist. Soc., Birmingham Hist. Soc.; mem. pres.'s coun. U. Ala., Birmingham, life mem. bd. visitors. Lt. U.S. Army, 1954—56. Named William A. Powell, Jr. Endowed Professorship in his honor, U. Ala. Mem.: Met. Devel. Assn. (life; bd. dirs.), Birmingham Area C. of C. (life; bd. dirs.), Birmingham Country Club, The Club, Mountain Brook. Home: 2114 Hickory Ridge Cir Birmingham AL 35243-2925

POWELL, WILLIAM COUNCIL, SR., service company executive; b. Burlington, N.C., Nov. 5, 1948; s. Thomas Edward Jr. and Annabelle (Council) P.; m. Jacqueline Garrison, July 3, 1976; children: William C. Jr., Ashley C. Student, U. S.C., 1968-69; BS, Va. Mil. Inst., 1971; MBA, Wake Forest U., 1974; postgrad., Elon Coll., 1972. Lic. pilot. Lic. real estate broker, N.C. Adminstrv. assoc. Carolina Biol. Supply Co., Inc., Burlington, 1971-91; also bd. dirs.; v.p. Bobbitt Labs., Burlington, 1974-77; pres., 1977-82; owner HEADS, Inc., 1978—, pres., 1984—; owner Ashwil Acres Farm, Mebane, N.C., 1981—. Pres. Granite Diagnostics, Inc., Burlington, 1981-84, UST Specialists Inc., 1991-2000, Merrymount Property Owners Assn., Inc., 1996-2000, Merrymount Boat Slip Assn., Inc., 1996—, Stratonet Inc., 1996-2001, Forest Realm, Inc., 2001—, Goat Island Maritime Inc., 2001—, Powell Realm Inc., 2001—, Poignard Compact Inc., 2001-; owner Powell Real Estate, Burlington, 1979—; bd. dirs. Excalibur Lock Co., Inc., Waubun Labs, Inc., Schriever, La., 2002—, Burlington, Warren Land Co., 1990-94, pres., 1994—; v.p. fin., bd. dirs. Environ. Responsible Bus. Inc., 1992-97; mem. Babcock Sch. Alumni Coun. Wake Forest U., 1981-85; mgr. Macon Farm, 1992-95; chmn. bd. Ensci Corp., Inc., 1991-95, ptnr. Port Assocs., 1987-2002, Port Assocs. II, 1992-2002; chmn. bd. Netpath Inc., 1995-96, bd., 2001—; filed for election N.C. Senate, 2000, 02. Bd. advisors Elon Coll. (N.C.), 1984-86, bd. visitors, 1987-92; bd. advisors Duke U. Marine Lab., Beaufort, N.C., 1985-92; nat. adv. coun. Baruch Marine Inst., 1998—; mem. adv. panel Air Quality Compliance Panel State of N.C. Dept. Environ. Health and Natural Resources, 1994—; guardian mem. Boy Scouts Am., Burlington, 1985; trustee Dr. T.E. Powell Jr. Trust, 1989-95; v.p. fin. Cherokee Coun. Boy Scouts of Am., 1990-92, exec. bd., 1990-94, exec. bd. Old N. State Coun., 1994-95; mem. Front St. United Meth. Ch., Burlington, N.C. Capt. USAR, 1971-79. Recipient Bill Fish Cert. State of S.C., 1983, 2 Bill Fish Certs. State of N.C., 1990, Sower's award Duke U., 1985, N.C. Gov.'s Cup for Billfishing, 1991, 3rd Pl., Big Rock Blue Marlin Tourn. 1998. Mem. NRA (life), Newcomen Soc. N.Am. (life mem.), Billiard Congress Am., Am. Angus Assn., Billiard and Bowling Inst. Assn., N.C. Forestry Assn. (legis. affairs com. 1994—), N.C. Wildlife Habitat Found. (life), Ducks Unltd. (life sponsor, area chmn. 1985-87, 97—), N.C. Chpt. Safari Club Internat. (state pres. 1985-88, life mem.), Aircraft Owners and Pilots Assn., Cessna Owner Orgn., Atlantic Coast Conservation Assn. (life), Alamance Wildlife Club (bd. dirs. 1992-95, 2000-03, pres. 1999-2000), Rolls Royce Owners Club (life), N.Am. Hunting Club (life), Found. N.Am. Wild Sheep (life), Chaine des Rotisseurs (chevalier 1991), Brotherhood of the Knights of the Vine (master knight 1991), 10 Point Hunt Club, Am. Angus Assn., Nat. Wild Turkey Fedn., Quail Unltd. (life), N.C. Cattlemans Assn. (life), Nat. Cattlemans Assn., Inc., Internet Users Group Alamance, Debordieu Club, Nat. Soc. SAR, Sons Confederate Vets., Alamance County Cattleman's Assn., Citation Fishing Team (capt. 1979—), Alamance Country Club, Debordieu Beach Club, Litchfield Carriage House Club. Home: 1109 W Front St Burlington NC 27215-3610 Office: HEADS Inc 945 E Haggard Ave Elon NC 27244 also: Netpath Inc 2260 S Church St Ste 601 Burlington NC 27215-5380 Personal E-mail: wcp@netpath.net.

POWELL GEBHARD, JOY LEE (BOK SIN LEE), small business owner; b. Jan. 29, 1936; arrived in U.S., 1956, naturalized, 1962; d. Yong Joon and Chun Jal Lee; m. Jimmy Wayne Powell, Sept. 24, 1960; children: Chun Jal Lee, Miran Victoria, D. Gibbhard; m. Karl Ten Eyck Gebhard, Oct. 15, 1995. Student, Internat. Speech Coll., Pusan, Korea, 1952, Nat. U. Pusan, 1953—55, McMurry Coll., Abilene, Tex., 1956—58; BA, Wayland Bapt. U., Plainview, Tex., 1966; postgrad., Cen. State U., Okla., 1967—68. Cert. antique appraiser and cons. Nurse Rok Med. Sch., Pusan, 1950—53; news announcer Pusan Radio Sta., 1953; sec., ret. choir organizer chaplain's office U.N. Army divsn. 8069, Pusan, 1954—56, Meth. Mission, Pusan, 1955—56, U.S. A.S.C. Office, Ploydada, Tex., 1958, Am. U., Washington, 1958—60; with Washington Post, U.S. Acad. Sci., 1960; with spl. study of prejudice among children grades 1 to 12 Pub. Opinion and Propaganda, 1965—66; tchr. Oklahoma City Sch. Sys., 1968—70; head social studies dept. Dunjee H.S., 1968; tchr. Spanish Carl Albert H.S., 1969; owner Internat. Antiques, Upperville, Va., 1973—; founder, dir. Healing Inc., 1997—. Co-founder, charter mem. lit. mag. Mang Hiang. Contbr. articles to profl. jours., poetry New Voices in American Poetry, 1978, poems and essays to Korean periodicals. Mem.: World Affairs Coun. Washington, Nat. History Preservation, Smithsonian Assocs. Avocations: music, writing, swimming, collecting, travel. Home and Office: PO Box 221 Upperville VA 20185-0221

POWER, A. KATHRYN, social services administrator; m. Brian Power; children: Matthew, Brendan. BA, St. Joseph's Coll., Md.; MEd, Western Md. Coll.; postgrad. Harvard U. Tchr. various pub. schs.; computer systems analyst U.S. Dept. Def.; exec. dir. R.I. Coun. Cmty. Mental Health Ctrs., 1985—90; dir. R.I. Office Substance Abuse, Gov.'s Drug Program, R.I. Anti Drug Coalition, R.I. Dept. Mental Health, Retardation and Hosps., 1993—2003, Ctr. for Mental Health Svcs., Rockville, Md., 2003—. Capt. USNR. Fellow Toll fellow, Coun. State Legislators, 1991. Mem.: Nat. Assn. State Mental Health Program Dirs. (pres. 1997). Office: Substance Abuse/Mental Health Svcs Ctr for Mental Health Svc 5600 Fisher Ln Parklawn Bldg #12 Rockville MD 20857

POWER, DAVID M. advertising executive; BA, Univ. Louisville, 1993. Pres., COO Power Creative, Louisville. Office: 11701 Commonwealth Dr Louisville KY 40299-2358

POWER, FRANCIS WILLIAM, newspaper publisher; b. Webster, S.D., Aug. 12, 1925; s. Frank B. and Esther C. (Fowler) P.; m. Margaret Jean Atkinson, Mar. 24, 1951; children: Patricia Ann, John Michael, Kerry Jean. BBA, U. N.Mex., 1948. Display advt. sales rep. The Register, Santa Ana, Calif., 1948-51; advt. mgr. Valley Morning Star, Harlingen, Tex., 1951-62; gen. mgr. Pampa (Tex.) Daily News, 1962-69; bus. mgr. Brownsville (Tex.) Herald, 1969-75; pub. The Lima (Ohio) News, 1975-91; v.p. Freedom Comm., Inc., until 1991; ret., 1991. Served with USNR, 1943-46. Mem.: Shawnee Country Club, Elks, Rotary. Roman Catholic. Office: Freedom Comm Inc 17666 Fitch Irvine CA 92614-6022

POWER, JAMES TRACY, historian; b. Atlanta, July 3, 1958; s. James Charley, Jr. and Claudett Fagan Power; m. Carolyn Nell Thompson, June 27, 1987. BA, Emory U., Atlanta, 1976—80; MA, U. S.C., Columbia, 1981—84, PhD, 1986—93. Historian, state hist. preservation office S.C. Dept. Archives and History, Columbia, 1986—. Author: (book) I Will Not Be Silent And I Will Be Heard: Martin Luther King, Jr., the Southern Christian Leadership Conference, and Penn Center, 1964-1967, 1993, Lee's Miserables: Life in the Army of Northern Virginia from the Wilderness to Appomattox, 1998; co-editor (with F.W. Taylor & C.T. Matthews): The Leverett Letters: Correspondence of a South Carolina Family, 1851-1868, 2000. Andrew Mellon Rsch. Fellowship, Va. Hist. Soc., Richmond, 1999—2000. Mem.: S.C. Hist. Assn. (pres. 2003—). Office: SC Dept Archives and History 8301 Parklane Rd Columbia SC 29223 E-mail: power@scdah.state.sc.us.

POWER, JOHN BRUCE, lawyer; b. Glendale, Calif., Nov. 11, 1936; m. Sandra Garfield, Apr. 27, 1998; children by previous marriage: Grant, Mark, Boyd. AB magna cum laude, Occidental Coll., 1958; JD, NYU, 1961; postdoctoral, Columbia U., 1972. Bar: Calif. 1962. Assoc. O'Melveny & Myers, L.A., 1961-70, ptnr., 1970-97, resident ptnr. Paris, 1973-75; Sheffelman disting. lectr. Sch. Law, U. Wash., Seattle, 1997. Mem. Social Svcs. Commn. City of L.A., 1993, pres., 1993; pres. circle, exec. com. Occidental Coll., 1979-82, 91-94, chair, 1993-94; adj. prof. UCLA Sch. Law, 1999. Contbr. articles to jours. Bd. dirs. Met. L.A. YMCA, 1988—, treas., 1998-2001; mem. bd. mgrs. Stuart Ketchum Downtown YMCA, 1985-92, pres., 1989-90; mem. Los Angeles County Rep. Ctrl. Com., 1962-63; trustee Occidental Coll., 1992—, vice-chmn., 1998-2001, chmn., 2001-03. Recipient YMCA Golden Book of Disting. Svc. award, 2002, Alumni Seal award Occidental Coll., 2003; Root Tilden scholar. Fellow Am. Coll. Comml. Fin. Lawyers (bd. regents 1999-2003); mem. ABA (comml. fin. svcs. com., com. 3d party legal opinions, UCC com., bus. law sect.), Am. Bar Found. (life), Calif. Bar Assn. (chmn. partnerships and unincorporated assns. com. 1982-83, chmn. uniform commn. code com. 1984-85, chmn. opinions com. 2000-04, exec. com. 1987-91, chmn. bus. law sect. 1990-91, chmn. coun. sect. chairs 1992-93, liaison to state bar commn. on future of legal profession and state bar 1993-95), L.A. County Bar Assn. (exec. com. comml. law and bankruptcy sect. 1970-73, 86-89), Internat. Bar Assn., Fin. Lawyers Conf. (bd. govs. 1982—, pres. 1984-85), Exec. Svc. Corps (sec. 1985-2000, vice-chmn. 2000—, dir. 1994—), Occidental Coll. Alumni Assn. (pres. 1967-68), Phi Beta Kappa (councilor So. Calif. 1982—, pres. 1990-92). Office: O Melveny & Myers 400 S Hope St Los Angeles CA 90071-2899 Office Phone: 213-430-6610. E-mail: jpowerl1441@aol.com.

POWER, JOSEPH ALOYSIUS, JR., lawyer; b. Oct. 15, 1952; s. Joseph Aloysius and Mary Ellen (Cavenaugh) Power; m. Susan Vohs, Apr. 26, 1980; children: Joseph Aloysius III, Michael Anthony, Ryan Patrick, James Ian. BA, U. Notre Dame, 1974; JD, Loyola U., Chgo., Ill., 1977. Bar; Ill. 1977, U.S. Dist. Ct. (no. dist.) Ill. 1977, U.S. Ct. Appeals (7th cir.) 1994, U.S. Supreme Ct. 1992. Assoc. John D. Hayes & Assocs., Chgo., 1977—84; ptnr. Hayes & Power, Chgo., 1984—91, Power, Rogers & Lavin, Chgo., 1991—93, Power, Rogers & Smith, Chgo., 1993—. Chmn. bd. dirs. Assn. of Trial Lawyers Assurance a mutual risk retention group, 1988—2000; author, lectr. Ill. Inst. Contg. Legal Edn., Springfield, Ill., 1983—89; bd. mgrs. Trial Lawyers for Pub. Justice, 1994—, v.p., 1996—97, pres.-elect, 1997—98, pres., 1998—99. Bd. dir. Ill. Pub. Action, Chgo., 1987—93. Fellow: Inner Cir. of Advocates, Internat. Acad. Trial Lawyers, Am. Coll. Trial Lawyers; mem.: U.S. Sen. Judiciary Com. (chmn.'s adv. coun. 1994, Ill. Supreme Ct. rules com. 1995—2004, chmn. 1996—2001), ATLA, Ill. Bar Assn., Ill. Trial Lawyers Assn. (author, lectr. 1984—, bd. mgrs. 1984—, chmn. membership com. 1985—87, chmn. legis. com. 1987—89, 3d v.p. 1989—90, 2d v.p. 1990—91, pres. elect 1991—92, pres. 1992—93), Chgo. Bar Assn. (chmn. young lawyers sect. fed. trial bar advocacy program No. dist. Il 1984), ABA, Chgo. Athletic Assn. Democrat. Roman Catholic. Home: 344 W Wellington Ave Chicago IL 60657-5637 Office: Power Rogers & Smith Three First National Plaza 70 West Madison St Suite 5500 Chicago IL 60602 Office Phone: 312-236-9381. Business E-Mail: joepower@prslaw.com.

POWER, JOSEPH EDWARD, lawyer; b. Peoria, Ill., Dec. 2, 1938; s. Joseph Edward and Margaret Elizabeth (Birkett) P.; m. Camille June Repass, Aug. 1, 1964; children— Joseph Edward, David William, James Repass Student, Knox Coll., Galesburg, Ill., 1956-58; BA, U. Iowa, 1960, JD, 1964; CAP, The Am. Coll., Bryn Mawr, Pa., 2004. Bar: Iowa 1964. Law clk. to judge U.S. Dist. Ct., 1964-65; mem. Bradshaw, Fowler, Proctor & Fairgrave, P.C., Des Moines, 1965—. Trustee Am. Inst. Bus., 1987-2002, chmn., 1992-2002; bd. dirs. Iowa Law Sch. Found., 1992-2004, Plymouth Ch. Found., 1991-99; bd. dirs. Des Moines Cmty. Found., 1996—, sec.-treas., 2001-; bd. dirs. Iowa Natural Heritage Found., 1995—, chmn., 2003-; mem. Des Moines Civil War Roundtable. Fellow Am. Coll. Trust and Estate Counsel (state chair 1994-2000), Am. Coll. Real Estate Lawyers; mem. ABA, Iowa Bar Assn. (chmn. probate, property and trust law com. 1983-87), Polk County Bar Assn., Des Moines Estate Planners Forum (pres. 1982-83) Mem. United Ch. of Christ. Clubs: Des Moines, Rotary. Home: 1928 Elm Cr West Des Moines IA 50265 Office: Bradshaw Fowler Proctor & Fairgrave 801 Grand Ave Ste 3700 Des Moines IA 50309-8004 Office Phone: 515-243-4191. Business E-Mail: www.power.edward@bradshawlaw.com.

POWER, MARY SUSAN, political scientist, educator; b. Hazleton, Pa., July 5, 1935; d. Younger L. and Cleo (Brook) Power; 1 child, Catherine Laverne. BA, Wells Coll., 1957; postgrad., Exeter (Eng.) U., 1955-56, Yale U., 1958-59; MA, Stanford U., 1960; PhD, U. Ill., 1961. Asst. prof. Susquehanna (Pa.) U., 1961-64; assoc. prof. U. Ark., Fayetteville, 1965-68; assoc. prof. polit. sci. Ark. State U., State University, 1968-79, prof., 1979—2000, prof. emeritus, 2000—. Author: (book) Before the Convention, Religion and the Founding Fathers, 1984, Jacques Maritain and the Quest for a New Commonwealth, 1992, Political Philosophy & Cultural Renewal: Collected Essays of Francis Wilson, 2001; contbr.: Jonesboro Sun, 2003—; contbr. articles to profl. jours. Mem. Fed. Edn. Commn. States, 1982—84; N.E. chair Arkansans for Progress, 1990—96; alt. del. Rep. Nat. Conv., 1972, 1976, 1988, del., 1992; mem. State com. Ark. Rep. Com., 1968—96, sec., 1978—80; mem. Craighead County Election Commn., 1986—88; chmn. Craighead County GOP, 1986—88, vice chmn., 1990—96, N.E. regional chmn., 1988—96; chmn. Craighead County Sheffield for Gov., 1990; mem. exec. com. Ark. Rep. Party, 1990—96, N.E. regional chair, 1988—96; treas. women's soc. Blessed Sacrament Ch., Jonesboro, 1996—2000, chmn. jubilee 2000; chair Silver Caths., 2002—. Relm Found. fellow, 1960, NSF-Am. Polit. Sci. Assn. fellow, 1963, Nat. Def. Seminar fellow, Nat. War Coll., 1973, NEH fellow, 1978, Pres.'s fellow, Ark. State U., 1988—89. Mem.: AAUP (state sec. 1978—80, pres. 1983—90), So. Polit. Sci. Assn., Am. Polit. Sci. Assn., Ark. Polit. Sci. Assn. (bd. dirs., v.p. 1992—93, pres. 1993—94), Phi Kappa Phi (pres. 1991), Phi Gamma Mu (sec.-treas. 1990—2000), Phi Sigma Alpha. Republican. Roman Catholic. Personal E-mail: spower@fastdata.net.

POWER, MICHAEL L. advertising executive; BA, Univ. Louisville, 1965. CEO, founder Power Creative (formerly Power Graphics), Louisville, 1976—. Office: 11701 Commonwealth Dr Louisville KY 40299-2358

POWER, SAMANTHA, academic administrator, writer; b. Ireland, 1970; Grad., Yale U., Harvard U. Law Sch. Lectr. pub. policy, founding exec. dir. Carr Ctr. for Human Rights, Harvard U.; reporter covering wars in former Yugoslavia US News and World Report and Economist, 1993—96; polit. analyst Internat. Crisis Group. Author: (book) A Problem from Hell: America and the Age of Genocide (Pulitzer prize, 2003); co-editor (with Graham Allison): Realizing Human Rights, 2000. Office: Harvard U John F Kennedy Sch Govt 79 John F Kennedy St Eliot-217 Cambridge MA 02138

POWERS, BRUCE RAYMOND, writer, English language educator, consultant; b. Bklyn., Dec. 10, 1927; s. George Osborne and Gertrude Joan (Bangs) P.; m. Dolores Anne Dawson, July 25, 1969; children: Christopher, Patricia. Student. U. Conn., 1947-49; AB, Brown U., 1951, MA (tuition scholar 1961-62), 1965; postgrad., U. Pa., 1961. Announcer, engr. Sta. WNLC, New London, Conn., 1946—47; tng. officer CIA, Dept. Def., 1951—55; TV sales/svc. rep. NBC, 1955; TV news writer and reporter Movietone News UP Assns., Inc., 1955—56; asst. to pres. Gotham-Vladimir Advt., Inc., 1956—57; asst. account exec. D'Arcy Advt. Co., 1957—58; asst. campaign dir. Cmty. Counseling Svcs., Inc., 1958—59; fund-raising campaign dir. Tamblyn & Brown, Inc., 1959—60; instr. Brown U., Providence, 1963—65, Ryerson Poly. Inst., Toronto, 1966, Nazareth Coll., Rochester, NY, 1966—67; asst. prof. English and comm. studies Niagara U., Lewiston, NY, 1967—86, assoc. prof., 1986—92, prof., 1986—92, chmn. permanent curriculum com. English dept., 1970—71; dir. Film Repertory Ctr., 1971—92, dir. comm. studies program, 1973—87. Prodr., mng. dir. Exptl. Film Retrospective, N.Y. State Coun. of the Arts, Buffalo, 1972; narrator (documentary) Niagara: Fading in the Mist, 1996; panelist, judge Artists Com. 2d World Festival of Animated Films, Zagreb, Yugoslavia, 1974; lectr., vis. artist ARTPARK, Lewiston, N.Y., 1975; project dir. Bicentennial Symposium, N.Y. State Am. Revolution Bicentennial Commn., Buffalo, 1975-76; rsch. assoc. Ctr. Culture and Tech., U. Toronto, 1977-81; keynote spkr. Dupont de Nemours & Co. Health and Safety Conf., Buffalo, 1990; ptnr. Moon Island Documentary Group, 1997—. Co-author: (with Marshall McLuhan) The Global Village, Oxford, 1989; editor The Film and Study Guide, 1973-74. Served with Underwater Demolition Teams, USNR, PTO, 1945-46. Recipient Carpenter prize in elocution Brown U., 1951. Mem. MLA, Underwater Demolitions Teams/Seal Assn. Va. Beach, Broadcast Edn. Assn., Soc. Cinema Studies, Am. Soc. Journalism Sch. Adminstrs., Assn. Edn. Journalism and Mass Comm., Internat. Exptl. Film Soc. (founding pres. 1971-73), Ariz. Sr. Acad. U. Ariz., We. N.Y. Audio-Visual Assn., N.Y. Coll. English Assn., Phi Beta Kappa. Roman Catholic. Home: 915 Sun Valley St North Tonawanda NY 14120-1952

POWERS, CLAUDIA MCKENNA, state legislator; b. Key West, Fla., May 28, 1950; d. James Edward and Claudia (Antrim) McKenna; children: Gregory, Theodore, Matthew, Thurston. BA in Edn., U. Hawaii, 1972; MA, Columbia U., 1975. Cert. tchr., N.Y. Mem. Greenwich Rep. Town Meeting, Conn., 1979-93, sec. bldg. com., 1982-84, sec. legis. com., 1986—88, 1990—93; mem. Conn. Ho. of Reps., Hartford, 1993—, ranking mem. govt. adminstrn. and elections com., 1995-96, asst. minority leader, 1997-98, vice chmn. Rep. bill rev. com., 1997—, house minority whip, 1999—2003, dep. minority leader, 2003—, mem. spl. com. of inquiry into impeachment of the gov., 2004. Mem. editl. bd. Greenwich Mag., 1995-98. Conn. commr. Edn. Commn. of the States, 2000—, also mem. steering com.; campaign chmn. Greenwich Rep. Town Com., 1984, 85, chmn., 1986-90; sec. Rep. Round Table, Greenwich, 1988-90; bd. govs. Riverside Assn., Greenwich, 1987-91, sec., 1991-92; class mother Riverside Sch., Greenwich, 1984-90; mem. altar guild Christ Ch., Greenwich, 1990—. lay eucharistic min., 2004—; adminstrv. coord. Greenwich Teen Ctr., 1990-91; alt. del. Rep. Nat. Conv., New Orleans, 1984—, San Diego, 1996; v.p. LWV of Greenwich, 1990-91; bd. trustees Norwalk Maritime Ctr., 2001—; bd. dirs. Gov.'s Prevention Partnership, 2004—. Episcopalian. Home and Office: 15 Hendrie Ave Riverside CT 06878-1808

POWERS, EDWARD ALTON, minister, educator; b. Jamestown, N.Y., Oct. 26, 1927; s. Leslie Edgar and Mabelle Florence (Alton) P.; children: Randall Edward, Christopher Alan, Ann Lynn. BA, Coll. of Wooster, 1948; MDiv, Yale U., 1952; EdD, Columbia U., 1973. Ordained to ministry Congl. Ch., 1951. Pastor, Hamden, Conn., 1949-53, Pleasant Hill, Ohio, 1953-56; sec. dept. youth work Congl. Christian Ch. Bd. Home Missions, 1956-60; gen. sec. divsn. Christian edn., bd. home missions Congl. and Christian Chs., 1960-61; divsn. Christian edn., bd. homeland ministries United Ch. of Christ, 1962-73; gen. sec., divsn. evangelism, edn., ch. ext. United Ch. Bd. Homeland Ministries, 1973-79; mem. faculty Inst. Mgmt. Competency, Am. Mgmt. Assn., N.Y.C., 1980-87; affiliate faculty Milano Grad Sch., New Sch. U., 1981—. Mem. program bd. divsn. edn. and ministry Nat. Coun. Chs., 1963-80; mem. edn. working group World Coun. Chs.; chmn. Peace Priority Team, United Ch. of Christ, 1970-75, adminstr., editor sexuality study, 1977; ptnr. Cane Powers Cons., and Powers, Wayno & Assocs.; mem. faculty Milzno Grad. Sch., New Sch. U., 1981-. Author: Journey Into Faith, 1964, Signs of Shalom, 1973, (with Rey O'Day) Theatre of the Spirit, 1980, In Essentials Unity, 1982, Youth in the Global Village, 1982; also articles. Home: 7 Gramercy Park W Apt 5B New York NY 10003-1759 Office Phone: 212-229-5311 ext. 1520. E-mail: powerseaA@aol.com.

POWERS, ELDON NATHANIEL, computer mapping executive; b. Wichita, Kans., Feb. 14, 1932; s. Ernie Lee and Bessie Othella (Loomis) P.; m. Betty Jean Zeigler, Sept. 4, 1954; children: Rebekah Jean, Robert John, Samuel Tyler. Student, Friends U., 1950-51; BA in Missions, Central Bible Coll., 1954; BA in Modern Lang. Edn., Evangel Coll., 1963; MS in Math., Tulsa U., 1971. Pastor Assembly of God Ch., Hays, Kans., 1955-60; data processing technician Gospel Pub. House, Springfield, Mo., 1960-63; data processing analyst Amoco Prodn. Co., Oklahoma City, 1963-65, research scientist Tulsa, 1965-67, staff research scientist, 1968-81; sr. system analyst Electro Mech. Research, Bloomington, Minn., 1967-68; mgr. info. service Fox Drilling Co., Tulsa, 1981-82; pres. ENP Software, Inc., Sapulpa, Okla., 1982-92; computer mapping specialist PowersTech, Tulsa, 1992—. Cons. in field. Contbr. articles to profl. jours.; author various computer programs including automatic contouring and geol. subsurface structural analysis; co-author Jupiter Mapping System for the Oil and Gas Industry, and Tract Mapper for the Bur. of Indian Affairs. Adv. bd. Cen. Okla. Vocat. Tech. Sch., Sapulpa, 1986-89. Democrat. Methodist.

POWERS, ELIZABETH T. economist; PhD, U. of Pa., Phil. Asst. prof. U. of Ill., Urbana, 1996—2003, assoc. prof., 2003—. Economist Fed. Res. Bank of Cleve., 1993—96. Office: Inst of Govtl and Pub Affairs 1007 W Nevada St Urbana IL 61801 Business E-Mail: epowers@uiuc.edu.

POWERS, ELIZABETH WHITMEL, lawyer; b. Charleston, S.C., Dec. 16, 1949; d. Francis Persse and Jane Coleman Cotten (Wham) P.; m. John Campbell Henry, June 11, 1994 (dec. Jan. 1997); m. Henry C. B. Lindh, June 16, 2000. AB, Mt. Holyoke Coll., 1971; JD, U. S.C., 1978. Bar: S.C. 1978, N.Y. 1979. Law clk. to justice S.C. Cir. Ct., Columbia; assoc. Reid & Priest, N.Y.C., 1978—86, ptnr., 1986—97; of counsel LeBoeuf, Lamb, Greene & MacRae, N.Y.C., 1997—2004, ptnr., 2004—. Exec. editor S.C. Law Rev., Columbia, 1977-78. Vol. N.Y. Jr. League, N.Y.C., 1983—; bd. dirs. The Seamen's Ch. Inst., 1996—; sec. The Seamen's Ch. Inst., 1999—; trustee Ch. Club, 1991—94, 1997—2001, v.p., 1992—94. Mem.: Nat. Soc. Colonial Dames in State of N.Y. (pres. 1992—95), Nat. Soc. Colonial Dames of Am. (parliamentarian 1994—2000, regent Gunston Hall 2001—02), S.C. Bar Assn., ABA.

POWERS, FRANCIS J. physical therapist; b. Danville, Pa., Dec. 30, 1972; s. Gerald W. and Nancy M. Powers; m. Cara T. Powers, Sept. 25, 2003 (div. Nov. 2003). BS in Polit. Sci., Quinnipial Coll.; M of Instructional Tech., Bloomburg U. Lic. physical therapist Mass., 1995, Wash., 1998, Mont., 1998. Sr. phys. therapist Beth Israel Deaconess Med. Ctr., Boston, Yakima Med. Meml. Sports Phys. Therapy, Yakima, Wash.; dir. rehab. Mainline Nursing & Rehab., Phila.; lead instructional designer Click & Learn, Boston; dir. rehab. Spaulding Rehab. Hosp.; lead instructional designer Animation Tech., Inc. Coord. adv. com. Bloomsburg U., Pa. Mem.: Am. Phys. Therapy Assn., Sigma Chi. Democrat. Roman Catholic. Home: 9 Wampus Ave Unit #7 Acton MA 01720 Office: Animation Tech Inc 60 Canal St Boston MA 02114

POWERS, HELEN, columnist, writer; b. Alton, Ill., Jan. 13, 1925; d. Charles Lawrence Rayborn and Ethel Lowder Howard; m. Henry Powers (dec.); children: Lawrence Anthony, Timothy Joseph. Columnist Florissant Valley Reporter, Mo., 1959—61; theater critic Beloit Daily News, Wis., 1961—63, Johnson County Squire, Leawood, Kans., 1963—64, Johnson County Scout, 1964—65, News Times, Danbury, Conn., 1965—72; feature writer and columnist Sunday Post, Bridgeport, 1970—73; freelance pub. rels. Candlewood Theatre, New Fairfield, Conn., 1974—81, Conn. and N.Y., 1974—81; lectr. women's clubs, 1974—93; columnist Citizen News, New Fairfield, Conn., 1990—. Author: Signs of Silence, 1972 (First prize, Conn. Press Women, 1973, Second prize, Nat. Press Women, 1973); performer: How to Live Like a Super Star, 1974 (Spkr. of Yr., Conn. Fedn. of Women's Clubs, 1980); author: Biggest Little Cat Book, 1978 (First prize, Conn. Press Women, 1979, Second prize, Nat. Press Women, 1979), Parents' Guide to the Five U.S. Svc. Acads., 1985 (cert. of appreciation, U.S. Military Acad., 1987), Winding Roads - A New Eng. Notebook of Wisdom and Wit, 1999, Winding Roads - The Perfect Prince or Just Another Frog, 2000, Winding Roads - Star Struck, 2001, Winding Roads - Treasures from an Attic in New England, 2002, (plays) A Nice Jewish Affair, 1974, Save the Seeds, Darling, 1977, Of Hearts and Hoofers, 1978, (newspaper column) Winding Roads, 1991—. Vol. Meals -on-Wheels, Wethersfield Hist. Soc., Rocky Hill Hist. Soc., Fairfield Hills Hosp.; exec. bd. Old Forge Condominiums, Rocky Hill, Conn., 1989—, sec. and newsletter. Scholar, Godfrey Geneal. Libr. Mem.: Pyquag Writers, Wethersfield Hist. Soc., Rocky Hill Hist. Soc., DAR. Independent. Roman Catholic. Avocations: doll collecting, dollhouses, miniatures, genealogy. Home: 602 Briarwood Ct Rocky Hill CT 06067

POWERS, HENRY MARTIN, JR., oil industry executive; b. Bath, Maine, July 18, 1932; s. Henry Martin and Eva (Saunders) Powers; m. Hepzibah Hinchey Reed, June 20, 1959; children: Henry Martin III, Carlton Reed. BS, Maine Maritime Acad., 1954. Marine engr. Am. Export Lines, N.Y.C., 1954-58; staff engr. Bull & Roberts Inc., N.Y.C., 1958-59; gen. sales mgr. Williams Bros., Inc., Portland, Maine, 1959-61; v.p. C. H. Sprague & Son Co., Boston, 1961-72, pres., 1972—, also chmn. bd. dirs.; chmn. bd. dirs. Sprague, Inc., Portsmouth, NH, 1999—. Chmn. Pease Devel. Authority, 1990—93; bd. dirs. Shanley Corp., Strawbery Banke Inc., 1st N.H. Banks, Seaward Constrn. Co., Santa Holding Co., Intelligent Controls, Environ. Resource Return. V.p. Seacoast United Fund, 1967—69; chmn. fuels, energy com. New Eng. Coun., 1974—75; pres. Portsmouth Coun., 1966—67; bd. visitors Maine Maritime Acad. Served to lt. USNR, 1956—58. Mem.: Mechanic Fire Soc., Navy League, Cumberland Club (Portland), Algonquin Club (Boston), Masons. Home: 7 Boat Club Dr Stratham NH 03885-2356 Office: Sprague Inc 2 Intl Dr Ste 1 Portsmouth NH 03801-6810 Office Phone: 603-431-1000. Personal E-mail: hpowers5@comcast.net.

POWERS, HUGH WILLIAM, newspaper executive; b. Slaton, Tex., Dec. 20, 1926; s. James Jerome and Myrtle (Black) P.; m. Constance Margaret Cornwall, Aug. 30, 1952; children: Nan Margaret, Sarah Ann. Student, W.Va. U., 1943-47. Mng. editor AGC News Svc., Houston, 1949-56; city editor Houston Press, 1956-64; asst. city editor Houston Chronicle, 1964-65, bus. editor, 1965-67, feature editor, 1967-73, assoc. editor, 1973-95; dir. Taping for the Blind, 1995-98, v.p., 1997. Mem. Press Club of Houston (pres., dir. 1968-72), Ducks Unltd. (dir. Houston chpt. 1989—, chmn. 1995, Tex. State trustee Nat. Del., 1996—, zone chmn. 1997-2001), Phi Kappa Psi. Home: 1613 Marshall St Houston TX 77006 E-mail: hpowers1@email.msn.com.

POWERS, J. D., III, marketing executive; Pres. J.D. Powers & Assocs., Calif., chmn. Office: J D Powers & Assocs 30401 Agoura Rd Agoura Hills CA 91301-2084

POWERS, JAMES G. corporate financial executive; With Arthur Andersen & Co., 1983—91; controller Moog Automotive, Inc., 1991—93; v.p., controller Berg Elec. Corp., 1993—95; v.p. fin. Crain Industries, Inc.; exec. v.p. Viasystems, 1997—2001, sr. v.p., cheif fin. officer, 2001; chief fin. officer UniGroup, 2002—. Office: UniGroup 1 Premier Dr Fenton MO 63026

POWERS, JAMES MATTHEW, neuropathologist; b. Cleve., Sept. 15, 1943; s. Alfred Patrick and Margaret Anne (Gunther) P.; m. Karen P. Smith, 1983; children: Kristin, Scott, Conor. BS in Biology, Manhattan Coll., 1965; MD, Med. U. S.C., Charleston, 1969. Diplomate in anatomic pathology and neuropathology Am. Bd. Pathology. Asst. prof. pathology Med. U. S.C., Charleston, 1973-76; dir. electron micros. lab. VA Hosp., Charleston, 1973-76; assoc. prof. pathology Med. U. S.C., Charleston, 1976-80, prof. pathology, 1980-88; vice chmn. dept. pathology Columbia Coll. Physicians and Surgeons, N.Y.C., 1989-92; assoc. chair of edn. U. Rochester (N.Y.), 1994-97, dir. residency tng. program, 1994—2003, prof., dir. neuropathology, 1992—. Sec. Biol. Stain Commn., 1994—2001. Author: (practice guidelines) Archives Pathology and Laboratory Medicine, 1995, (book chpt.) Anderson's Pathology, 10th edit., 1996, Greenfield's Neuropathology, 2002; mem. editl. bd.: Human Pathology, 1991—, Brain Pathology, 1995—2000, Acta Neuropathologica, 1995—, Biotech. and Histochemistry, 1994—2001, Modern Pathology, 1996—2004, Neurology, 1999—2004, Am. Jour. Surg. Pathology, 1999—, Jour. Neuropath. Exptl. Neurology, 2000—. Mem. Internat. Soc. Neuropathology (v.p. 1994-97), Am. Assn. Neuropathologists (pres. 1993, Moore award 1975, 76, 77, 81), U.S.-Can. Acad. Pathology. Office: U Rochester Box 626 601 Elmwood Ave Rochester NY 14642-0001 Office Phone: 585-275-3202. Business E-Mail: james_powers@urmc.rochester.edu.

POWERS, JOHN KIERAN, lawyer; b. Schenectady, Aug. 2, 1947; s. Paul Joseph and Anne Marie (Leahy) P.; children: Erin Kelly, Megan Kerry. BS, U. Notre Dame, 1969; JD, Union U., 1972. Bar: N.Y. 1973, U.S. Dist. Ct. (no. dist.) N.Y. 1973, U.S. Dist. Ct. (so., ea. and we. dists.) N.Y. 1982, U.S. Ct. Appeals (2d cir.) 1984, U.S. Supreme Ct. 1985, U.S. Dist. Ct. Vt. 1988. Assoc. Medwin and McMahon, Albany, 1973-77; pvt. practice law Albany, 1973-80; pres. John K. Powers, P.C., Albany, 1980-87; ptnr. Powers and Santola, Albany, 1987—. Contbr. articles to profl. publs. Trustee N.Y. State Lawyers Polit. Action Com., 1983-88, treas., 1989-93, chair, 1993—; trustee ATLA Polit. Action Com., 1995-98. Fellow Roscoe Pound Found. Mem. ABA (sustaining vice-chair, legis. subcom., automobile law com., trial and ins. practice sect., state leader com. on state legis. sect.), Nat. Coll. Adv. (co-founder), ATLA (life, state del. 1990, bd. govs. 1990—, exec. com. 1995—), Am. Bd. Trial Advocates (advocate), N.Y. State Bar Assn. (sustaining, lectr., exec. com. and chmn. legis. com. trial lawyers sect.), N.Y. State Trial Lawyers Assn. (sustaining, bd. dirs. 1983-88, chmn. key person legis. com., chmn. pubs. com., chmn. atty. referral com., exec. com. 1986—, treas. 1988-89, v.p. 1989-91, 1st v.p. 1990-91, pres.-elect 1991-92, pres. 1992-93, award of merit 1990, 94, award of excellence 1991, Pres. award 1995, 96, 98, 99, 2000, dist. svc. award 1997), N.Y. Trial Lawyers Inst. (lectr. and program chmn. 1981—, treas. 1988-89, pres. 1992-93), (life) N.Y. State Head Injury Assn. (co-counsel 1983-85, bd. dirs. 1992-93, 1st v.p. 1993—), Capitol Dist. Trial Lawyers Assn. (bd. dirs. 1979-81, v.p. 1983-85, pres. 1985-86), Pa. Trial Lawyers Assn., Alban County Bar Assn. (lectr.), Chief Judge's Com. to Improve Availability of Legal Svcs., Chief Judge's Pro-Bono Monitoring Com., Civil Justice Found. (guest lectr. Law Sch. NYU, Albany Law Sch., U. Syracuse Law Sch., Albany Med. Coll.), Trial Lawyers for Pub. Justice, Lions (pres. Scotia, N.Y. chpt. 1979-80). Democrat. Roman Catholic. Home and Office: 39 N Pearl St Albany NY 12207-2785

POWERS, JOHN T., JR., former mayor; Mayor City of Spokane, Wash., 2001—03. Bd. dirs. Assn. Wash. Cities, Inland Northwest Tech. Edn. Ctr., Spokane Regional Econ. Devel. Coun.; co-chair Spokane Task Force on Race Rels., U.S. Conf. Mayors; mem. Gas & Elec. Utility Restruction Task Force, Wash. State Competitiveness Coun., Assn. Northeast Wash. Mayors.

POWERS, LARRY K. lighting fixtures manufacturing executive; BS in Econs. and Bus. Adminstrn., Brigham Young U. Pres., bd. dirs. The Genlyte Group, Inc., Louisville, 1993—, pres., CEO, 1994—, chmn. bd., 2000—; pres., CEO Genlyte Thomas Group, 1998—. Mem. Am. Lighting Assn. (pres., bd. dirs.). Office: The Genlyte Group Inc 4360 Brownsboro Rd Louisville KY 40207 E-mail: lpowers@genlyte.com.

POWERS, MALA, actress; b. San Francisco, Dec. 20, 1931; d. George Evart and M. Dell (Thelen) P.; 1 child, Toren Michael Vanton. Student, UCLA; studied with Michael Chekhov. V.p. Book Pubs. Enterprises Inc., 1985; internat. lectr. Chekhov Drama Method; entertainer troops USO, Korea, 1951-52; founder, bd. dirs. West Coast Michael Chekhov Drama Group, 1988—; presenter bus. and theater workshops and seminars. Writer, narrator: (sponsored by telephone cos. in various cities) Children's Story, Tele-Story and Dial-A-Story, 1979— (sponsored nationally 1988—); author: Follow the Year, 1985, French edit. 1986; editor: The Secret Seven and the Old Fort Adventure, 1972; rec.: Advent calendar and author book Follow the Star, 1980, Spanish edit., 1981, Italian edit., 1982; films: Cyrano de Bergerac, 1950, Outrage, Edge of Doom, Yellow Mountain, Bengazi, Tammy, Cheyenne, Daddy's Gone A'Hunting, Six Tickets to Hell, 1975;, Hitters, 2003; rec. artist, RCA, records for pre-Christmas, 1977, album Follow the Star; stage prodns. include Absence of a Cello (Broadway), 1964-65; Hogan's Goat, Night of the Iguana, Bus Stop, Far Country, The Rivalry, Mr. Shaw Goes to Hollywood, 2003; also starred in radio and TV prodns. including Medical Story, Ironside, Charlie's Angels; co-star with Anthony Quinn in The Man and the City, 1971-72, Murder She Wrote, 1990. Chmn. So. Calif. Mothers' com. March of Dimes, 1972—; bd. dirs. Layman's Nat. Bible Com., 1981—. Mem. NATAS, Acad. Motion Picture Arts and Scis. (fgn. film com.), ANTA (v.p., exec. com. 1974-75), PEN, Actors Equity Assn.,, Women in Film, Authors Club (London). Mem. Christian Community Ch. Home: 15455-61 Glenoaks Blvd Sylmar CA 91342-2852 Office Phone: 818-367-0022.

POWERS, MARIAN, accounting educator; PhD in Acctg., U. Ill. Acctg. faculty Kellogg Grad. Sch. Mgmt. Northwestern U., Evanston, Ill., 1980-88; dept. acctg. U. Ill., Chgo., 1989-92; prof. acctg. Allen Ctr. Exec. Edn., 1987; vis. assoc. prof. acctg. Kellogg Grad. Sch. Mgmt. Northwestern U., 1993—. Rschr. in field. Contbr. articles to profl. jours.; co-author software. Mem. Am. Acctg. Assn., Ill. CPA Assn., European Acctg. Assn., Internat. Assn. Acctg., Edn. and Rsch., Am. Soc. Women Accts. (past pres. Chgo. chpt.), Edn. Found. Women in Acctg. (trustee 1999). Office: The Allen Ctr Northwestern U 633 Clark St Evanston IL 60208-0001

POWERS, MICHAEL J. retired financial company executive; Vice chmn. Ernst & Young LLP, N.Y.C.; chmn., CEO Intellinex LLC, N.Y.C.

POWERS, MICHAEL ROLAND, educator, insurance consultant; b. Wilkinsburg, Pa., Nov. 19, 1959; s. John Nolan and Dorothy Ann (Hladio) P.; m. Imelda Wan-Har Yeung, June 9, 1984; children: Thomas Yang, Andrew Yang. BS, MA, Yale U., 1982; PhD, Harvard U., 1987. Ins. cons. Chang and Co., Boston, 1981-87; dep. ins. commr. Pa. Ins. Dept., Harrisburg, 1987-90; prof. risk mgmt. and ins. Temple U., Phila., 1990—. Author: Icons, 2003; contbr. articles to profl. jours. Active Pa. Health Care Cost Containment Coun., Harrisburg, 1989-90. Mem. Phi Beta Kappa. Office: Temple Univ 479 Ritter Anx Philadelphia PA 19122

POWERS, PAUL J. manufacturing executive; b. Boston, Feb. 5, 1935; s. Joseph W. and Mary T. Powers; m. Barbara Ross, June 3, 1961; children: Briana, Gregory, Jeffrey. BA in Econs., Merrimack Coll., 1956; MBA, George Washington U., 1962. Various mfg. and fin. positions with Chrysler Corp., Detroit and overseas, 1963-69; v.p., gen. mgr. Am. Standard, Dearborn, Mich., 1970-78; pres. Abex-Dennison, Columbus, Ohio, 1978-82; group v.p. Comml. Intertech Corp., Youngstown, Ohio, 1982-84, pres., chief ops. officer, 1984-87, chmn., pres., CEO, 1987-00, Chairman of the Compensation Committee Chairman of the Compensation Committee and member of the Executive Committee., Chairman of the Compensation Committee and member of the Executive Committee and Nominating and Governance Committee. Bd. dirs. 1st Energy Corp., Twin Disc, Inc., Global Marine Inc., CUNO, Inc., 19 96—. Bd. dirs. Youngstown Symphony, 1984-88. Lt. USNR, 1957-63. Mem. NAM (bd. dirs. 1986-93, 95—), Nat. Fluid Power Assn. (bd. dirs. 1984-87), Mfrs. Alliance (bd. dirs. 1995—), Youngstown Area C. of C. (bd. dirs. 1990—). Office: Commercial Intertech Corp PO Box 239 Youngstown OH 44501-0239

POWERS, PAULINE SMITH, psychiatrist, educator, researcher; b. Sept. 23, 1941; m. Henry P. Powers; children: Jessica, Samantha. AB in Math., Washington U., 1963; MD, U. Iowa, 1971. Med. intern Emanuel Hosp., Portland, Oreg., 1971-72; psychiatry resident U. Iowa, Iowa City, 1972-74, U. Calif., Santa Barbara, 1974-75; from asst. prof. to assoc. prof. psychiatry Coll. Medicine U. So. Fla., Tampa, 1975-85, prof., 1985—, dir. eating disorder program, 1979—, dir. psychosomatic medicine divsn., 1979—. Author: Obesity: The Regulation of Weight, 1980; editor: The Current Treatment of Anorexia Nervosa and Bulimia, 1984. Fellow: Am. Psychiat. Assn. (Rush Gold Outstanding Exhibit medal 1976, Dorfman Jour. Paper award 1987); mem.: Nat. Eating Disorders Assn. (pres.-elect 2003—), Acad. Eating Disorders ((founding pres.), Women Helping Women award 1995, Profl. Excellence award 1997, Outstanding Clinician award 2000). Office: U So Fla Coll Medicine Dept Psychiatry 3515 E Fletcher Ave Tampa FL 33613-4706 Office Phone: 813-974-2926. Business E-Mail: ppowers@hsc.usf.edu.

POWERS, RAY LLOYD, former state senator, dairy farmer, rancher; b. Colorado Springs, June 27, 1929; s. Guy and Cora (Hill) P.; m. Dorothy Parrish, Dec. 14, 1975; 1 child, Janet. Student, Pub. Schs. Dairy farmer, Colo. Springs, 1947—; v.p. bus. devel., dir. The Capitol Pulse Inc., Washington, 2000—. Mem. Colo. Ho. of Reps., 1978-80; mem. Colo. Senate, 1981-2000, senate pres., 1998-2000; bd. dirs. Mountain Empire Dairyments Coop., Denver, 1967-81. Mem. Colo. Cattlemen, Republican Men's Club, Lions. Republican.

POWERS, REBECCA ANN, psychiatrist, health facility administrator; b. Portland, Oreg., Sept. 28, 1955; m. Gary A. Gusewitch. B in Tech. and Med. Tech., Oreg. Inst. Tech., 1977; M in Pub. Health, Loma Linda U., 1983, MD, 1990. Cert. Am. Bd. Psychiatry and Neurology. Receptionist and vet. asst. Gresham (Oreg.) Vet. Clinic, 1969-77; micobiologist clin. lab. Portland Adventist Med. Ctr., 1977-86; rsch. asst. dept. microbiology Loma Linda (Calif.) U. Med. Ctr., 1987, residency gen. psychiatry, 1990-93; cons. psychiatrist arrowhead home Geriatric Psychiat. Home, San Bernardino, Calif., 1992-93; gen. psychiat. review instr. nat. med. bds. Arc Ventures, Pasadena, Calif., 1992-93; fellowship child and adolescent psychiatry Stanford (Calif.) U. Hosp., 1993-95; psychiat. disability evaluations state Calif. Sunnybrook, Amberstone and Stanford Med. Groups, 1994-95; cons. child and adolescent psychiatry Seneca Ctr. Day Treatment, Fremont, Calif., 1994—; attending staff physician comprehensive pediatric care unit, med. psychiat. unit Stanford U. Hosp., 1995-97, developer and med. dir. clin. faculty co. Terminus Adolescent Alcohol and Drug Treatment Program, 1995-96; pvt. practice physician Child, Adolescent, Adult and Family Psychiatry, Los Gatos, Calif., 1995—; attending for eating disorders clin., clin. faculty co. Terminus Lucile Salter Packard Children's Hosp. at Stanford, 1995—. Founder and pres. Art Soc., 1976-77; planning com. Portland Adventist Med. Ctr., 1982-83, team capt. fund raising program, 1984, cmty svc., 1983-86, instr. clin. lab, 1977-86; cons. pub. health Clackamas County Health Dept., 1983; pub. rels. officer Med. Sch. Class 1990, 1987-90; PULSE rep. Loma Linda U. Sch. Med., 1988-90; rsch. aid, schizophrenia dopamine receptor rsch. Jerry L. Pettis VA Meml. Hosp., Loma Linda, 1991; lecturer Am. Lupus Soc., 1991, Loma Linda U. Med. Ctr., 1992; mem. com. Treatment Improvement Group for anxiety and personality disorders Behavioral Medicine Ctr. Loma Linda U. Med. Ctr., 1991-92;psychiat. evaluations smoking cessation Wellburtin Study Jerry L. Pettis Va Meml. Hosp., Loma Linda, 1992-93; co-founder, pres. elect L.A. Preventive Psychiatry Tak Force So. Calif. Psychiat. Soc., 1992-93; del. Calif. Med. Assn. Calif. House Officer Med. Soc.; developer and coord. Pediatric Psychiatry Lecture Series for pediatricians and other primary care physicians Lucile Salter Packard Children's Hosp. at Stanford, 1994-95; com. Forensic Cmty. Project for Oakland Neighborhood Steering and Oakland Planning Commn., 1994; dir. Pediatric Psychiatry Screening Stanford U., 1994; appointment prevention com. Am. Acad. Child and Adolescent Psychiatry, 1994-97, com. Well Being Physicians Calif. Med. Assn., 1995—, adv. bd. Adult and Adolescent Alcohol and Drug Treatment Program, Stanford U. Hosp, 1995-96; assoc. mem. Consortium Med. Educators in Substance Abuse, 1994; program development adolescent alcohol and drug treatment Stanford U. Med. Ctr., 1995-96; vol. clin. instr. and supervisor Stanford U. Hosp., 1995—. Asst. editor newsletter Lab Lines, 1984-86; planned and presented symposium Everything you always wanted to know about Mediacl Practice, San Bernardino County Med. Soc., 1989; contbr. chpts. to books. Recipient Janssen Clin. Scholar award U.S. Psychiat. and Mental Health Congress, 1994, Presdl. Scholar award Am. Acad. Child and Adolescent Psychiatry, 1995. Mem. AMA, Am. Acad. Child and Adolescent Psychiatry, Am. Assn. Orthopsychiatry, Am. Lupus Soc., Am. Psychiatric Assn., Calif. Acad. Preventive Medicine, Calif. Med. Assn. (com. for Well Being of Physicians), Calif. Soc. Addiction Medicine, Healthy Young 2000, No. Calif. Psychiat. Soc., No. Calif. Region Child and Adolescent Psychiat. Home: 36275 Easterday Way Fremont CA 94536-1671 Office: Stanford U Child Psychiatry 401 Quarry Rd MC 5540 Stanford CA 94305-5540 also: 14651 S Bascom Ave Ste 225 Los Gatos CA 95032-2005

POWERS, RICHARD EDWARD, JR., lawyer; b. Evanston, Ill., July 20, 1952; s. Richard Edward and Helen Lufen Powers; m. Diane Wojda, Aug. 12, 1978. BS, Gonzaga U., 1974; JD, U. Notre Dame, 1977. Ptnr. Butler & Binion LLP, Washington, 1977-99, Dorsey & Whitney LLP, Washington, 1999—. Mem. ABA, Tex. Bar Assn., D.C. Bar, Energy Bar Assn. Home: 5233 Elliott Rd Bethesda MD 20816-2910 Office: Dorsey & Whitney 1001 Penn Ave NW Ste 300S Washington DC 20004-2505

POWERS, ROBERT DAVID, physician; b. Plainfield, N.J., Nov. 6, 1953; s. John B. and Marian E. (Kuhn) P.; m. Sally Ann Harmet, 1977; children: Alison, Elizabeth, Carolyn. BA, Amherst Coll., 1975; MD, U. Va., 1979; MPH, Yale U., 1999. Intern U. Minn., Mpls., 1979-81; resident U. Va., Charlottesville, 1981-83, from asst. to assoc. prof., 1983-94; assoc. prof. U. Conn. Sch. Medicine, Farmington, 1994—, chief emergency medicine, 1997—, vice chmn. dept. trauma and emergency medicine, 1997—, assoc. prof., 1994-99, prof., 1999—. Fellow ACP. Office: Hartford Hosp Dept Emergency Medicine Hartford CT 06115 Office Phone: 860-545-4187. Business E-Mail: RPowers@Harthosp.org.

POWERS, ROBERT LAWRENCE, civilian military employee; b. Bklyn., Apr. 3, 1942; s. Lawrence Robert and Audrey Buchanan Powers; m. Susan McCormick, June 13, 1964; children: Jennifer Powers Kane, Megan Powers Dosher. BS in Chemistry, Math., U.S. Naval Acad., 1964; MS in Ops. Rsch., Naval Postgrad. Sch., Monterey, Calif., 1972. Commd. officer USN, 1964,

officer, 1964-81; commdg. officer USS Fairfax County, Norfolk, Va., 1981-83; chief staff officer Amphibious Squadron 10, Norfolk, 1983-85; sr. analyst Sonalysts, Inc., Norfolk, 1985-92; tng. coord. Fleet Tactical Readings Group, Norfolk, 1992-98; sr. doctrine writer Fleet Info. Warfare Ctr., Norfolk, 1998—2000, with experimentation divsn., 2001—. Adj. prof. U.S. Naval War Coll., Norfolk, 1985—. Co-founder Children's Coun. S. Hampton Rds., Norfolk, 1998; mem. Naval War Coll. Found. Mem. U.S. Naval Inst., Ret. Officers Assn., Kiwanis (Hixson fellow 1993, webmaster capital dist. 1998—, editor Great Bridge Kiwanis Newsletter 1998—, gov. 1998-99, Circle K internat. circle of svc.), Assn. for Ednl. Comm. and Tech. (Crystal award for distance edn. 2002), Sigma Xi. Episcopalian. Avocations: computers, naval history, war games. Home: 1100 West Rd Chesapeake VA 23323 E-mail: bpowers100@aol.com.

POWERS, ROBERT P. electric power industry executive; B in Biology, Tufts U., 1975; M in Radiol. Hygiene, U. N.C., 1976. Cert. sr. reactor operator 1991. Radiation protection engr. Pacific Gas & Electric Co., San Francisco, 1982; sr. engr. radiation protection Diablo Canyon, 1984, radiation protection mgr., 1987, dir. mech. maintenance, 1991, mgr. site svcs., 1992, mgr. quality svcs., 1993, mgr. ops. svcs., 1996, v.p., 1996; sr. v.p. nuc. generation Am. Electric Power Co., 1998, exec. v.p. generation, 2001—. Office: Am Electric Power Co 1 Riverside Plaza Columbus OH 43215-2372

POWERS, RONALD GEORGE, management consultant; b. N.Y.C., July 9, 1934; s. Lee Whitney and R. Anne Powers; m. Elizabeth Braislin McClellan, July 24, 1980. Chmn. Boardroom Advisors, Inc., Winter Park and Tampa, Fla., The Strategic Mgmt. Adv. Group, Inc., Winter Park and Tampa, Fla. Adviser to chief execs. of banks, corps. and govts. on strategic mgmt. issues, 1971—. Trustee Trinity Sch., Fla. Symphony Orch. Mem. Interlachen C. of C. Republican. Episcopalian. Home: PO Box 2174 Winter Park FL 32790-2174 Office: PO Box 1922 Winter Park FL 32790-1922 E-mail: boardroomadvisor@mindspring.com.

POWERS, ROSS, Olympic athlete; b. Bennington, Vt., Feb. 10, 1979; Mem. U.S. Snowboard Team; olympic gold medalist in halfpipe, 2002; founder Ross Powers Found., 2001. Named Nat. Champion, 1993, 1994, 1997, Grand Prix Champion, FIS World and Overall Champion, 1998, US Open title, 1998; recipient 2nd pl., 1992, 3rd pl., 1993, 1st pl., World Cup, 1995, 1996, 2nd pl., 1995, 3rd pl., 1995, 2nd pl., 1996, 3rd pl., 1996, 1st pl., World Championship, 1996, 2nd pl., World Cup, 1997, Bronze medal in Snowboarding (Halfpipe), Nagano Olympics, Japan, 1998, 1st pl., World Championship, 2000, Gold medal, NBC Gravity Games, 2000, TNT Winter Goodwill Games, 2000, Silver medal, ESPN X Games, 2000, Bronze medal, 2001, Gold medal in Snowboarding (Halfpipe), Olympic games, 2002. Office: The Ross Powers Found c/o Pete Carlisle P O Box 17574 Portland ME 04112

POWERS, RUNA SKÖTTE, artist; b. Anderstorp, Sweden, Oct. 29, 1940; d. Gösta Nils Folke and Kristina Torborg (Andersson) S.; m. David Britton Powers, Mar. 13, 1965; children: Kristina, Davis. Student, Art Inst. So. Calif., 1976-83; BMA, U. So. Calif., 1986. Exhbns. include Newport Festival Arts, Newport Beach, 1980, Costa Mesa Art League, 1980, Orange County Fair, Costa Mesa, 1980, Art Inst. So. Calif., Laguna Beach, 1976-83, Studio Sem Ghelardini, Pietrasanta, Italy, 1983, Design House, Laguna, 1984, Vorpal Gallery, 1983-84, Laguna Beach Mus. Art, 1984, Gallery Sokolov, Laguna Beach, 1985-93, Margareta Sjödin Gallery, Malibu, 1988, Ana Izax Gallery, Beverly Hills, 1988, Envision Art, 1991, Gallery Slottet, Hörle, Sweden, 1990-92, J.F. Kennedy Performing Arts Ctr., Washington, 1991, Internat. Art Expn., L.A., 1985, N.Y., 1986-87, San Bernardino County Mus., 1993. Founder Found. Hörle Manor House, Värnamo, Sweden, 1987—. Avocations: music, reading, cooking, swimming. Home: 1831 Ocean Way Laguna Beach CA 92651-3235

POWERS, SCOTT, producer, actor; b. Chgo., Aug. 23, 1948; s. Raymond Alford and Ruby Marilyn (Ivacko) P. BS, Ithaca Coll., 1970; MBA, Fairleigh Dickinson U., 1971. Producer Young & Rubicam, Inc., NYC; account exec. Kelly, Nason, Inc., NYC; sr. account exec. Bozell & Jacobs, Inc., NYC; account supr. Foote, Cone & Belding, Inc., NYC; actor NYC, LA, 1982—; pres. Scott Powers Prodns., Inc., NYC, 1988—. Pres. CaribCom, Inc., NYC, 1996—. Author: Here's Looking At You!, 1997; contbr. articles to publs.; cartoonist Thankyounext, 1990—. Mem. Better Bus. Bur. NYC, 1991—, Knickerbocker Rep. Club, NYC, 1971—; bd. dirs. Profl. Comedians Assn., NYC, 1988-91, v.p., 1989-91; bd. dirs. One World Arts Found., 1992—; judge Internat. Film and TV Festivals, NYC, 1991—. Mem. AFTRA (bd. dirs. 1989-91), SAG, Actor's Equity Assn., NATAS (judge Emmys 1985—), NYC C.of C., Met. Club, NY Athletic Club, Players Club, Mensa, Intertel. Republican. Congregationalist. Avocations: skiing, sailing, tennis, squash, international river running. Home: 180 Central Park S New York NY 10019-1562 Office: Scott Powers Prodns Inc Ste 405 22 W 21st St New York NY 10010-6904

POWERS, THOMAS MOORE, writer; b. N.Y.C., Dec. 12, 1940; s. Joshua Bryant and Susan (Moore) P.; m. Candace Molloy, Aug. 21, 1965; children: Amanda, Susan, Cassandra. BA, Yale U., 1964. Reporter Rome (Italy) Daily American, 1965-67, U.P.I., N.Y.C., 1967-70; freelance writer, 1970—; contbg. editor The Atlantic mag.; editor, founding ptnr. Steerforth Press, So. Royalton, Vt., 1993—. Author: Diana: The Making of a Terrorist, 1971, The War at Home, 1973, The Man Who Kept the Secrets: Richard Helms and the CIA, 1979, Thinking About the Next War, 1982, Total War: What It Is, How It Got That Way, 1988, Heisenberg's War: The Secret History of the German Bomb, 1993, The Confirmation, 2000, Intelligence Wars: American Secret History from Hitler to Al Qaeda, 2002. Recipient Pulitzer prize for nat. reporting, 1971 Mem. PEN Am. Center, Council on Fgn. Relations. Address: 106 Chelsea St South Royalton VT 05068-9800 also: Lit Rep Lynn Nesbit 445 Park Ave New York NY 10022-2606 Office Phone: 802-763-8585. E-mail: tom@steerforth.com.

POWERS, WILLIAM CHARLES, JR., dean, law educator; b. 1946; AB, U. Calif., Berkeley, 1967; JD, Harvard U., 1973. Bar: Wash. 1974, Tex. 1980. Law clk. to Hon. E. A. Wright U.S. Ct. Appeals (9th cir.), Seattle, 1973-74; asst. prof. Wash. U., Seattle, 1974-77; assoc. prof. Wash. U., Seattle, 1977-78; prof. law U. Tex., Austin, 1978—, assoc. dean acad. affairs, 1984—87, 1994—95, univ. disting. prof. and Hines H. Baker and Thelma Kelly Baker chair in law, 1997—, John Jeffers Rsch. Chair in law, 2000—, dean Sch. Law, 2000—. Office: U Tex Sch Law 727 E Dean Keeton St Austin TX 78705-3224

POWERS, WILLIAM DOUGLAS, theater director, actor, educator; b. Poplar Bluff, Mo., Dec. 17, 1967; s. Chester Douglas Powers and Patsy Imogene Swallows; life ptnr. James F. Black, Oct. 28, 1994. BA, S.E. Mo. State U., 1990; MFA, Ohio U., 1994; MA, U. Mo., Kansas City, 1997; PhD, U. Mo., Columbia, 2001. Asst. prof. theatre Susquehanna U., Selinsgrove, Pa., 2000—. Dir. theatrical prodns. Susquehanna U., Pa.; artistic dir. Susquehanna U. Summer Theatre, Selinsgrove. Author: (monograph) An Eliadean Interpretation of Frank G. Speck's Account of the Cherokee Booger Dance. Mem. People for the Ethical Treatment of Animals, PA Pets, Congregation Beth El, Sunbury, Pa., 2003. Frank Loesser Musical Theatre scholar, Estate of Frank Loesser, 1987—90. Mem.: Shakespeare Oxford Soc., Am. Soc. Theatre Rsch., Assn. Theatre in Higher Edn., Wordcraft Cir. Native Writers and Storytellers, Actors' Equity Assn. D-Liberal. Avocation: genealogy. Office: Susquehanna Univ 133 Degenstein Selinsgrove PA 17870 E-mail: powers@susqu.edu.

POWERS, WILLIAM EDWARD, emergency physician, educator; b. Atlanta, Sept. 16, 1957; s. Richard Candler and Olive Carol Osburn Powers; m. Nancy Carolyn Freeman, May 17, 1986; children: Nicole, Will. MS in Biomed. Engring., U. Ill., Chgo., 1981; MS in Aerospace Medicine, Wright State U., 1991; MD, Rush U., 1985; postgrad., U. Houston, 2001—03. Diplomate Am. Bd. Emergency Medicine, Am. Bd. Preventive Medicine. Intern in gen. surgery Orlando (Fla.) Regional Med. Ctr., 1985-86, resident in emergency medicine, 1986-88; resident in aerospace medicine Wright State U., Dayton, Ohio, 1989-91; biomed. engr., rsch. asst. U. Ill., Chgo., 1980-81; chief resident emergency medicine Orlando (Fla.) Regional Med. Ctr., 1987; assoc. dir. emergency medicine Kissimmee (Fla.) Meml. Hosp., 1988-89; asst. med. dir. Martin-Marietta Aerospace, Orlando, Fla., 1988-89; emergency med. physician, clin. instr. Wright State U. Med. Sch., Dayton, Ohio, 1989-91; med. officer, flight surgeon NASA Johnson Space Ctr., Houston, 1991-92; asst. med. dir. Cape Canaveral Hosp., Cocoa Beach, Fla., 1991-93, Twin Cities Hosp., Niceville, Fla., 1991-93; asst. prof. emergency medicine, rsch. dir. U. Tex. Med. Sch., Houston, 1993-95; asst. prof. family medicine, dir. urgent care U. Tex. Med. Br., Galveston, 1995-96; asst. prof. medicine Baylor Coll. Medicine, Houston, 1996—2001; med. dir. emergency dept. Meml. Hermann Hosp. S.E., 2002—03; flight surgeon U. Tex. Med. Branch, 2003—. Contbr. articles to profl. publs. Med. missionary Missionary Ventures, Honduras, 1995, 98. Fulbright Found. grantee U. Vienna, Austria, 1996. Fellow Am. Coll. Emergency Physicians, Aerospace Med. Assn. (assoc. fellow); mem. AIAA, Am. Phys. Soc., Exptl. Aircraft Assn. Avocations: flying, soccer, basketball, photography, piano. Office: 2437 Bay Area Blvd #112 Houston TX 77058 E-mail: WEPowers@aol.com.

POWERS, WILLIAM JOHN, neurologist; b. Northampton, Mass., Apr. 28, 1949; s. John Bernard and Marian Erna (Kuhn) P.; m. Karen Diane McElvany, Mar. 9, 1983; children: Katherine Elizabeth, Brian Ward. AB, Dartmouth Coll., 1971; MD, Cornell U., 1975. Resident dept. internal medicine Duke U., Durham, N.C., 1975-77; resident dept. neurology U. Calif., San Francisco, 1977-80; instr. depts. neurology/radiology Washington U., St. Louis, 1980-82, asst. prof., 1982-87, assoc. prof., 1987—98, prof. neurology, neurol. surgery and radiology, 1998—; neurologist-in-chief Jewish Hosp., St. Louis, 1986-92, head cardiovasc. disease sect. Chmn. Neurol. Disorders Program Project Rev. A com. NIH, 1994-98. Office: Washington Univ Med Ctr East Bldg Imaging Ctr 4525 Scott Ave # Box 8225 Saint Louis MO 63110-1030

POWLEDGE, FRED ARLIUS, freelance writer; b. N.C., Feb. 23, 1935; s. Arlius Raymond and Pauline (Stearns) P.; m. Tabitha Morrison, Dec. 21, 1957; 1 child, Pauline Stearns. AB in English, U. N.C., 1957. Writer, editor AP, New Haven, 1958-60; reporter Atlanta Jour., 1960-63, N.Y. Times, N.Y.C., 1963-66; freelance journalist, 1966—. Lectr. New Sch., N.Y.C., 1967-69, 80-82; narrator, co-producer, writer WNET-TV/13, N.Y.C., 1972. Author: Black Power/White Resistance: Notes on the New Civil War, 1967, To Change a Child: A Report on the Institute for Developmental Studies, 1967, Model City: A Test of American Liberalism. One Town's Efforts to Rebuild Itself, 1970, Mud Show: A Circus Season, 1976, Born on the Circus, 1976, The Backpacker's Budget Food Book, 1977, Journeys Through the South, 1979, So You're Adopted: A Book About the Experience of Being Adopted, 1982, Water: The Nature, Uses and Future of Our Most Precious and Abused Resource, 1982, A Forgiving Wind: On Becoming a Sailor, 1983, Fat of the Land, 1984, The New Adoption Maze: And How to Get Through It, 1985, You'll Survive, 1986, Free at Last? The Civil Rights Movement and the People Who Made It, 1991, We Shall Overcome: The Heroes of the Civil Rights Movement, 1993, Working River, 1995, Pharmacy in the Forest, 1998; author, editor: About Biodiversity.org, 2001—. Mem. Bd. Library Trustees, St. Mary's County, Md. With USAR, 1957. Russell Sage fellow Russell Sage Found., 1966-67; travel and study grantee Ford Found., 1971, 93-94. Mem. Nat. Assn. Sci. Writers. Home and Office: 25040 Old Brick Way Hollywood MD 20636-2939 E-mail: fredpowledge@nasw.org.

POWLEN, DAVID MICHAEL, finance company executive, director; b. Logansport, Ind., May 28, 1953; s. Daniel Thomas and Bertha Frances (Cappa) P.; m. Karen Lamb Gentleman, Aug. 5, 1978 (div. Jan. 1984); 1 child, Brooks Ryan. AB, Harvard U., 1975, JD, 1978. Bar: Ind. 1978, U.S. Dist. Ct. (so. dist.) Ind. 1978, U.S. Ct. Appeals (7th cir.) 1985, Bus. Bankruptcy Law Am. Bd. Cert., 2001. Assoc. Barnes & Thornburg, Indpls., 1978-84, ptnr., 1985-01, chmn., adminstr. creditors rights dept.; mng. dir., mgr. restructuring group McDonald Investments Inc., Cleve., 2001—04; dir. KPMG Corp. Fin., NYC, 2004—. Contbr. articles to profl. jours. Mem. ABA (bus. bankruptcy com., secured creditors and chpt. 11 subcom., comml. fin. svcs. com., creditors rights subcom.), Am. Bankruptcy Inst., Assn. Insolvency and Restructuring Adv., Ind. Bar Assn. (chmn. bankruptcy and creditors rights sect. 1990-91), Indpls. Bar Assn. (chmn. edn. com. 1984, chmn. ct. liaison com. 1985, bankruptcy and comml. law sect.), Am. Bankruptcy Inst., Turnaround Mgmt. Assn. (bd. dirs. NE Ohio chpt. 2001-04), Comml. Law League Am. (bankruptcy and insolvency sect.), Harvard Club, Phi Beta Kappa. Home: Unit P108 2001 Hamilton St Philadelphia PA 19130 Office: KPMG Corp Fin 345 Park Ave 13th Fl New York NY 10154 Office Phone: 317-727-2211. Personal E-mail: dmpowlen@aol.com. Business E-Mail: dpowlen@kpmg.com.

POWLEY, EDWARD HARRISON, III, musicology educator; b. Orange, NJ, Jan. 10, 1943; s. Edward Harrison and Elizabeth Frances (Malinowski) P.; m. Ellen Mildred Lockwood, June 12, 1967; children: William, Barrett, Martha, Edward, Philip, Julianne, Sarah. MusB, Eastman Sch. Music, 1965; postgrad., U. Vienna (Austria), 1965-66, Acad. Music, Vienna, Austria, 1965-66; MA, Eastman Sch. Music, 1968, PhD, 1975. Percussionist Rochester (N.Y.) Philharm. Orch., 1964-68; instr. Eastman Sch. Music, Rochester, 1966-69; asst. prof. mus. Brigham Young U., Provo, 1969-74, assoc. prof., 1974-82, prof., 1982—, area head musicology, 1986—. Editor: Symphonies of Druschetzky, 1985, Il Trionfo di Dori, 1990; contbr. articles to profl. jours. Grantee NDEA, 1966, Fulbright, Vienna, Austria, 1965-66. Mem. Am. Musicol. Soc. (chmn. local chpt. 1986-87, 94-95, nat. coun. 1985-87), Percussive Arts Soc. (chmn. rsch. com. 1977-87), Internat. Musicol. Soc, Soc. Am. Music, Coll. Music Soc., Am. Musical Instrument Soc. (v.p. 1995-99, pres. 1999-2003). Mem. Lds Ch. Avocations: hiking, camping. Office: Brigham Young U Sch Music E-563 HFAC Provo UT 84602-1026

POWLICK, GEORGE, shoe and clothing manufacturing executive; b. 1944; Accountant Grant Thornton, 1975—87; CFO, v.p. fin., sec., and dir. K-Swiss, Inc., Westlake Village, Calif., 1988—. Recipient INC. 500 award, INC. Mag., 2001. Office: K-Swiss Inc 31248 Oak Crest Dr Westlake Village CA 91361-4643

POWLISON, DAVID A. writer; b. Honolulu, Hawaii, Dec. 14, 1949; s. Peter A. and Dora M. Powlison; m. Nancy H. Gardner, Aug. 20, 1977; children: Peter, Gwenyth, Hannah. AB, Harvard U., 1971; MDiv, Westminster Theol. Sem., 1980; MA, U. Pa., 1986, PhD, 1996. Worker Mental Health Dept. McLean Psychiatric Hosp., Belmont, Mass., 1973—76; writer, editor, counselor CCEF, Glenside, Pa., 1980—. Lectr. Westminster Theol. Sem., Phila., 1980—; bd. dirs. NANC, Indpls. Author: Power Encounters, 1995; contbr. articles to profl. jours. Presbyterian. Office: CCEF 1803 E Willow Grove Ave Glenside PA 19038

POWSNER, EDWARD RAPHAEL, physician; b. N.Y.C., Mar. 17, 1926; m. Rhoda Lee Moscovitz, June 8, 1950; children: Seth, Rachel, Ethan, David. SB in Elec. Engring., MIT, 1948, SM in Biology, 1949; MD, Yale U., 1953; MS in Internal Medicine, Wayne State U., 1957; MHSA, U. Mich. Diplomate Am. Bd. Nuclear Medicine, Am. Bd. Pathology in clin. pathology and anatomic pathology, Am. Bd. Internal Medicine; lic. physician, Mich. Intern Wayne County Gen. Hosp., Eloise, Mich., 1953-54, resident internal medicine, 1954-55, Detroit Receiving Hosp., 1955-56; fellow in hematology Wayne State U. and Detroit Receiving Hosp., 1957-58; clin. investigator VA Hosp., Allen Park, Mich., 1958-61, chief nuclear medicine svc., 1961-78; dir. clin. labs. Mich. State U., East Lansing, 1978-81; staff pathologist Ingham Med. Ctr., Lansing, Mich., 1978-81; dir. nuclear medicine St. John Hosp., Detroit, 1982-95. Rsch. asst. biology MIT, 1948-49, 50; asst. instr. medicine Wayne State U. Coll. Medicine, 1954-56, instr., 1959-61; assoc. prof. pathology Wayne State U. Sch. Medicine, 1961-68, assoc. medicine, 1961, prof. pathology, 1968-78; prof. pathology Mich. State U., 1978-81, assoc. chairperson, 1980-81, clin. prof., 1981-82; chief clin. labs. Detroit Gen. Hosp., 1969-73; chief lab. svcs. Health Care Inst., Wayne State U., 1976-78; mem. adv. coun. Nuclear Medicine Tech. Cert. Bd., 1990-91. Bd. editors Am. Jour. Clin. Pathology, 1963-76, 83-88; author 2 textbooks, 11 chpts., 50 peer reviewed papers, 17 abstracts and other publs. With U.S. Army, 1944-47. Mem. AMA (sect. coun. on pathology), Am. Soc. Clin. Pathologists (rep. 1978-89, 93-2000, govt. rels. com. 1993-95, mem. coun. nuclear medicine 1978-82, chmn. 1982-84), Am. Coll. Nuclear Physicians, Am. Soc. Nuclear Cardiology, Coll. Am. Pathologists, Detroit Acad. Medicine, Mich. Soc. Pathologists, Mich. State Med. Soc., Soc. Nuclear Medicine, Washtenaw County Med. Soc., Sigma Xi, Tau Beta Pi. Office: Eastside Nuclear Medicine 2370 E Stadium Blvd #315 Ann Arbor MI 48104-4810

POWSNER, SETH, psychiatry educator, medical computing researcher; BSEE, MIT, 1974; MD, Yale U., 1978. Cert. bd. cert. psychiatrist Amer Bd. of Psychiatry and Neurology, added qualifications in geriatric psychiatry Amer Bd. of Psychiatry and Neurology. Psychiatry resident Michael Reese Hosp., Chgo., 1978—82; pvt. practice as gen. psychiatrist Chgo., 1982—84; clin. computing Ill. State Psychiat. Inst., Chgo., 1984—85; engrng. cons. sect. cardiology U. of Chgo., 1985—86; asst. prof. of psychiatry Yale U. Sch. of Medicine, New Haven, 1986—92, assoc. prof. of psychiatry, 1992—2002, assoc. prof. of psychiatry and emergency medicine, 2002—. Recipient Biomed. Pilot Projects Initiative grant, Culpepper Found., 1998—99. Fellow: Acad. of Psychosomatic Medicine (chair membership com. 2001—02). Achievements include patents for graphical summary of patient status. Office: Yale Psychiatry Rm 2039cb 20 York St New Haven CT 06504-8900

POXON, STEPHANIE LYN, music specialist, accompanist; b. Columbus, Ohio, Sept. 10, 1971; m. Scott William Poxon, Aug. 16, 1996. AA, Brevard C.C., Melbourne, Fla., 1992; MusB Edn. summa cum laude, U. of Ctrl. Fla., Orlando, 1995; MusM in Musicology, U. of Fla., Gainesville, 1998. Adj. prof. of music U. Ctrl. Fla., Orlando, 1997—99, Va. Commonwealth U., Richmond, 1999—2001; adj. prof. of piano J. Sargeant Reynolds C.C., 2000—01; adj. prof. of piano and staff accompanist Randolph Macon Coll., Ashland, 1999—2002; music specialist Music Divsn. Libr. of Congress, Washington, 2001—. Com. for career-related issues Am. Musicological Soc., 2001—; local arrangements com. Music Libr. Assn., 2003—, program annotator Richmond Philharm. Orch., 2002—, Charlotte Civic Orch., NC, 2003—. Chorus mem. Libr. of Congress Chorale, 2003, Richmond Concert Chorale, 1999—2000. Recipient Outstanding Student Paper Award, Coll. Music Soc., So. Chpt., 1998; scholar Benjamin T. Rome Sch. of Music Scholarship, Cath. U. of Am., 1999-2004, Grad. Tchg. Assistantship, U. of Fla., 1995-1998. Mem.: Coll. Music Soc. (corr.), Music Libr. Assn. (corr.), Am. Musicological Soc. (corr.). Office: Library of Congress Music Division 101 Independence Ave SE Washington DC 20540 Office Phone: 202-707-2703. Personal E-mail: spox@loc.gov. E-mail: spox@loc.gov.

POYDASHEFF, ROBERT STEPHEN, lawyer; b. NYC, Feb. 13, 1930; s. Stephen Alexander Poydasheff and Pauline M. Miller; m. Anastasia Catherine Latto, Aug. 29, 1954; children: Catherine Alexandra, Robert Stephen Jr. BA in Polit. Sci., The Citadel, 1954; JD, Tulane U., 1957; MA, Boston U., 1966; diploma, Command and Gen. Staff Coll., 1969, Army War Coll., 1976. Bar: S.C. 1958, Ga. 1979, US Supreme Ct. 1964, US Ct. Mil. Appeals, US Ct. Mil. Rev., US Dist. Ct. (fed. dist.) S.C., US Dist. Ct. (fed. and mid. dists.) Ga. Commd. 2d lt. U.S. Army, 1955, advanced through grades to col., 1975, ret., 1979; sr. v.p. SunTrust Bank of West Ga., Columbus, 1979-95; pvt. practice Columbus, 1995—. Instr. bus. law Am. U. Ext. Divsn., Ft. Benning, 1961-63; adj. prof. internat. law, Am. govt., and bus. law U. Md. Ext. Divsn., Berlin, 1964-67, Vietnam, 1967-68; adj. prof. Troy State U., Ft. Benning, Ga., 1976—; cons., exec. v.p. ATI-Allied Tech. Internat. Inc., Columbus, 1995—; past legal advisor to Sec. of Army and Sec. of Def. on mil. dependent sch. and labor rels. Contbr. commentaries, papers, and analyses to profl. jours. City councilor City of Columbus, 1996-2002; mayor of Columbus, Ga., 2003; bd. dir. Springer Opera House Assn., 1998—; trustee Ga. Coun. of Humanities, exec. com., 1998—; bd. edn. Ft. Benning Sch., 1976-79, chmn. pers. actions com., 1976-79; trustee Dr. Hosp., Columbia; bd. dirs. Columbus United Way, River Ctr. Performing Arts; past pres. Chattahoochee coun. Boy Scouts Am., Columbus; past pres. Chattahoochee Valley, Assn. of US Army, Anne Elizabeth Shepherd Home, Columbus Symphony, ARC; chmn. bd. dir. Leadership Morality Inst.; chmn. Civilian Mil. Coun., Ga. Govs. Commn. on Transp. Decorated Legion of Merit with 2 oak leaf clusters, Bronze Star, commendation medal with oak leaf cluster, DFC, DSM with four bronze stars, Order of St. George, Episcopal Ch., Infantry Order of St. Maurice; parachutist badge; badge of The Army secretariet; recipient Ga. Govs. medal. Fellow Leadership Morality Inst.(chair of bd.); mem. Ga. Mcpl. Assn. (bd. dirs.), Columbus Bar Assn., C. of C. (mil. affairs com., bd. dirs.), Kiwanis, Masons (32 deg.), Phi Delta Phi, Pi Sigma Alpha. Republican. Episcopalian. Avocations: jogging, reading, gymnastics. Home: 6349 Mountainview Dr Columbus GA 31904-2213 Office: 3575 Macon Rd Ste 11 Columbus GA 31907-8229 Office Phone: 706-653-4712. E-mail: b.poydasheff@columbus.ga.org.

POYNTER, DAN, author, publisher, speaker; b. N.Y.C., Sept. 17, 1938; s. William Frank and Josephine E. (Thompson) P. BA, Calif. State U., Chico, 1960; postgrad., San Francisco Law Sch., 1961-63. federally lic. master parachute rigger; lic. pilot. Pub., prin. Para Pub., Santa Barbara, Calif., 1969—. Listed as expert witness Nat. Forensic Ctr., Tech. Adv. Service for Attys., Consultants and Consulting Organizations Directory, Lawyer's Guide to Legal Consultants, Expert Witnesses, Services, Books and Products. Author: The Parachute Manual, Parachuting, The Skydiver's Handbook, Parachuting Manual with Log, Hang Gliding, Manned Kiting, The Self-Publishing Manual, How to Write, Print & Sell Your Own Book, Publishing Short Run Books, Business Letters For Publishers, Computer Selection Guide, Word Processing and Information Processing, Publishing Forms, Parachuting Manual for Square/Piggyback Equipment, Frisbee Players' Handbook, Toobee Players' Handbook, Writing Nonfiction, Successful Nonfiction, 100 others, some translated in fgn. languages; past editor news mag. Spotter; monthly columnist Parachute mag., 1963—; contbr. over 500 tech. and popular articles and photographs to mags; patentee parachute pack, POP TOP. Recipient numerous certs. of appreciation for directing parachuting competitions. Mem. U.S. Parachute Assn. (life, chmn. bd., exec. com. 12 yrs., nat. and internat. del., achievement award, 1981, cert. 40 yr. mem., awarded Gold Parachute Wings, 1972), Parachute Industry Assn. (pres. 1985, 86), AIAA, Soc. Automotive Engrs., Nat. Aeronautic Assn., Aviation Space Writers Assn. (internat. conf. mem. 1978, 79, 82), Calistoga Skydivers (past sec.), No. Calif. Parachute Coun. (past sec.), U.S. Hang Gliding Assn. (life, past dir., del.), Internat. Assn. Ind. Pubs. (past bd. dirs., pres. Santa Barbara chpt. 1979-82), Assn. Am. Pubs., Pub. Mktg. Assn. (bd. dirs., v.p.), Book Pubs. So. Calif., Am. Booksellers Assn., Commn. Internat. de Vol Libre of Fedn. Aero. Internat. in Paris (U.S. del., past pres., lifetime Pres. d'Honneur award 1979, recipient Paul Tissander diploma, 1984), Nat. Spkrs. Assn. Home: RR 1 Santa Barbara CA 93117-1047 Office: Para Publishing PO Box 8206 Santa Barbara CA 93118-8206 E-mail: danpoynter@ParaPublishing.com.

POYTHRESS, VERN SHERIDAN, religion educator, minister; b. Madera, Calif., Mar. 29, 1946; s. Ransom Huron and Carola Eirene (Nasmyth) P.; m. Diane Marie Weisenborn, Aug. 6, 1983. BS, Calif. Inst. Tech., 1966; PhD, Harvard U., 1970; MDiv, ThM, Westminster Theol. Sem., 1974; MPhil, Cambridge (Eng.) U., 1977; ThD, U. Stellenbosch, Republic of South Africa, 1981. Ordained to ministry Presbyn. Ch. in Am., 1981. Asst. prof. N.T., Westminster Theol. Sem., Phila., 1976-81, assoc. prof., 1981-87, prof., 1987—. Author: Philosophy, Science and the Sovereignty of God, 1976, Understanding Dispensationalists, 1987, Symphonic Theology, 1987, Science and Hermeneutics, 1988, The Shadow of Christ in the Law of Moses, 1991, God-Centered Biblical Interpretation, 1999, The Returning King, 2000; assoc. editor Westminster Theol. Jour., 1981-2004. Fellow NSF, 1966-70, Ned B. Stonehouse fellow, 1974. Mem. Linguistic Assn. Can. and U.S. Home: 510 Twickenham Rd Glenside PA 19038-2033 Office: Westminster Theol Sem Chestnut Hill Philadelphia PA 19118-0009

POZA, ERNESTO, business consultant, educator; b. Havana, Cuba, Mar. 27, 1950; came to U.S., 1961; s. Hugo Ernesto and Carmen (Valle) P.; m. Karen Elizabeth Saum, Oct. 14, 1978; 1 child, Kali Jennette. BS in Adminstrv. Sci., Yale U., 1972; MS in Mgmt., MIT, 1974. Personnel mgr. rsch. Sherwin Williams Co., Chgo., 1974-75, orgn. specialist Cleve., 1975-77, dir. orgn. planning, 1977-79; pres., sr. mgmt. cons. E.J. Poza Assoc., Cleve., 1979—; prof. Weatherhead Sch. Mgmt. Case Western Res. U., Cleve., 1996—. Advisor Family Firm Inst., 1986; bd. dirs. several privately held firms; vis. lectr. Yale U., U. Chile, MIT, Sloan Sch. Mgmt. Author: A la Sombra del Roble: La Empresa Privada Familiar y Su Continuidad, 1995, Smart Growth: Critical Choices for Business Continuity and Prosperity, 1997, La Empresa Familiar

Por Dentro, 1998, Family Business, 2004; contbg. editor Family Bus. Mag.; mem. editl. bd. Family Bus. Rev., 1997—; contbr. articles to profl. jours. Bd. dirs. Neighborhood Health Care, 1980, Family Firm Inst., 1990; program com. United Way, Cleve., 1985, Hispanic Leadership, 1986; founding mem. Family Firm Inst., 1985. Fellow Family Firm Inst. (sr., Richard Beckhard Practice award 1996); mem. Acad. Mgmt. (entrepreneurship divsn. 1980—, orgn. devel. network, 1975—). Office: 37300 Jackson Rd Chagrin Falls OH 44022 Office Phone: 440-247-6300. E-mail: Ernesto.Poza@case.edu., poza@family-business.com.

POZA, HUGO BERNARDO, aerospace company executive; b. Havana, Mar. 12, 1945; s. Hugo Ernesto and Carmen (Valle) P.; m. Mary Karen Connors, Jan. 21, 1967; children: Hugh Thomas, Sean Christopher, Vanessa Kristi. BS in Elec. Engring., U. Dayton, 1966; MS in Elec. Engring., Purdue U., 1967, PhD, 1971. Mem. tech. staff TRW Systems Group, Redondo Beach, Calif., 1971-73, dept. staff engr., 1973-75, sr. staff engr., 1975-77, asst. program mgr., 1977-80; mgr. mil. systems ops. Mil. Electronics Div. TRW, San Diego, 1981-84, v.p., gen. mgr. Mil. Electronics and Avonics Div., 1985—86; sr. v.p. M/A-COM Government Systems, 1986—88; v.p., gen. mgr., Avionics div. Lockheed Martin-Sanders, 1988—95, exec. v.p., 1995; v.p., aerospace electronic Lockheed Martin; v.p., gen. mgr., Strategic Systems div. Raytheon Co., Falls Church, Va., v.p., Homeland Security, 2002—. Mem. tech. adv. bd. Quest Tech. mag. Contbr. articles to profl. jours; patentee in field. Bd. dirs. Am. Martyrs Youth Group, 1975-78; bd. dirs. Manhattan Beach Single Young Adults, 1979-81; mem. Christian Family Movement, 1979-81, St. Gabriel's Youth Ministry, 1981— . Mem. IEEE, AIAA, World Affairs Council Los Angeles, Old Crows, Tau Beta Pi Clubs: Escondido, Tennis. Roman Catholic. Office: Raytheon Co 7700 Arlington Blvd Falls Church VA 22042 *I have always believed in giving all I have to anything I dedicate myself. I have strived to be the very best in all my endeavors, but never by stepping on someone else's pride. I am a positive thinker with a winning attitude. My success in life has been greatly due to the support of my family and my strong belief in the Lord.*

POZDRO, JOHN WALTER, music educator, composer; b. Chgo., Aug. 14, 1923; s. John and Rose Anna (Mossman) P.; m. Shirley Allison Winans, June 12, 1954; children— John Winans, Nancy Allison Thellman. Student, Am. Conservatory Music, Chgo., 1941-42; B.M. in Music, Northwestern U.-Evanston, Ill., 1948, M.M. in Music, 1949; PhD in Music, Eastman Sch. Music, 1958. Instr. Iowa State Tchrs. Coll., Cedar Falls, 1949-50; instr. to assoc. prof. U. Kans., Lawrence, 1950-64, prof. music, 1964-93, dir. theory and composition, 1961-88; ret., 1993; teaching fellow Eastman Sch. Music, Rochester, NY, 1956-57. Chmn. symposium com. U. Kans., Lawrence, 1958-69. Representative works include Third Symphony, 1960, Piano Sonata No. 4, 1976, Malooley & Fear Monster, 1977, Impressions, Winds, Piano, 1984, Tryptich for Carillon, 1996, the Spirit of Mt. Oread, 1989. Winds of Autumn, 1996. Served with U.S. Army, 1943-46. Recipient U. Calif. Berkeley medal for Disting. Svc., 1993; grantee Ford Found., 1960, Nat. Endowment Arts, 1976; nominated for Pulitzer prize in Music, 1960. Mem. ASCAP, Pi Kappa Lambda. Presbyterian. Avocations: golf, photography, writing. Home: 4700 Muirfield Dr Lawrence KS 66047-1820

POZEN, ROBERT CHARLES, investment company executive; b. N.Y.C., Aug. 8, 1946; s. Morris and Miriam Pozen; m. Elizabeth Kelner, Apr. 11, 1976; children: Joanna, David. BA, Harvard U., 1968; JD, Yale U., 1972, JSD, 1973. Bar: N.Y. 1977, D.C. 1978, U.S. Supreme Ct., U.S. Ct. Appeals (4th, 5th, 7th and D.C. cirs.). Assoc. prof. law NYU, 1974-77; assoc. gen. counsel SEC, Washington, 1978-80; ptnr. Caplin & Drysdale, Washington, 1981-86; sr. v.p., gen. counsel, mng. dir. FMR Corp./Fidelity Investments, Boston, 1987—96; pres. Fidelity Mgmt. and Rsch. Co., Boston, 1997—2001; vice chmn. Fidelity Investments, Boston, 2001—02; secy. econ. affairs Commonwealth Mass., 2003; non-exec. chmn. Mass. Fin. Svcs. Investment Mgmt., Boston, 2004—. Mem. adv. bd. Securities Regulation Law Reporter Bur. Nat. Affairs, Washington, 1981; vis. lectr. Harvard Law Sch., Cambridge, Mass., 1986; mem. legal adv. com. N.Y. Stock Exchange, 1987; appt. mem., Commn. to Strengthen Social Security John Olin Visiting Prof., Harvard Law Sch, 2002-2003. Author: Financial Institutions: Investment Mgmt. Cases, Materials and Problems, 1977; contbr. articles to profl. jours. Mem. ABA (securities com. 1981—, employee retirement income security act 1985-86). Office: MFS 500 Boylston St Boston MA 02116-3470*

POZNANSKI, ANDREW KAROL, pediatric radiologist; b. Czestochowa, Poland, Oct. 11, 1931; came to U.S., 1957, naturalized, 1964; s. Edmund Maurycy and Hanna Maria (Ceranka) P.; children: Diana Jean, Suzanne Christine. BSc, McGill U., 1952, MD CM, 1956. Diplomate: Am. Bd. Radiology, Royal Coll. Physicians and Surgeons Can. Intern Montreal (Que., Can.) Hosp., 1956-57; resident Henry Ford Hosp., Detroit, 1957-60, staff radiologist, 1960-68, U. Mich. Med. Center, Ann Arbor, 1968-79; co.-dir. pediatric radiology C.S. Mott Children's Hosp., Ann Arbor, 1971-79; radiologist-in-chief Children's Meml. Hosp., Chgo., 1979-99; prof. radiology U. Mich., 1971-79, Northwestern U. Med. Sch., 1979—. Bd. dirs. Nat. Coun. on Radiation Protection, 1983-90; mem. Internat. Commn. on Radiologic Protection, 1981-89; mem. adv. panel on radiologic devices FDA, 1975-77, chmn., 1976-77; trustee Am. Bd. Radiology, 1993-2003. Author: The Hand in Radiologic Diagnosis, 1974, 2d edit., 1983, Practical Approaches to Pediatric Radiology, 1976; co-author: Bone Displasias, An Atlas of Genetic Disorders of Skeletal Development, 2002 bd. editors: Skeletal Radiology, 1975-95, Radiographics, 1980-84, Pediatric Radiology, 1986-91. Mem.: AMA, Internat. Skeletal Soc. (founder, pres. 1992—94), John Caffey Soc., Radiol. Soc. N.Am., Soc. Pediatric Radiology (pres. 1980—81), Am. Roentgen Ray Soc. (pres. 1993—94), Polish Radiol. Soc. (hon.), Can. Assn. Radiologists (hon.), European Soc. Radiology (hon.), Alpha Omega Alpha. Home: 2400 N Lakeview Ave Chicago IL 60614-2747 Office: Childrens Meml Hosp 2300 N Childrens Plz Chicago IL 60614-3394 E-mail: apoznanski@ameritech.net.

POZZATTI, RUDY OTTO, artist; b. Telluride, Colo., Jan. 14, 1925; s. Innocente and Mary L. (Mimiolla) P.; m. Dorothy I. Pozzatti, May 20, 1946; children— Valri Marie, Rudy Otto, Gina Maria, Mia Ines, Illica Lara. B.F.A., U. Colo., 1948, M.F.A., 1950, D.H.L., 1973. Mem. faculty dept. art U. Nebr., Lincoln, 1950-52, 53-56, Ind. U., Bloomington, 1956-91, prof. fine arts, 1964-91, disting. prof., 1975-91; ret., 1991; artist-in-residence Roswell Mus. and Art Ctr. One-man exhbns. include Cleve. Mus. Art, 1955, Whitney Mus. Am. Arts, N.Y.C., 1961, Tyler Sch. Art, Rome, 1969, Sheldon Meml. Art Gallery U. Nebr., 1969, Mitchell Mus. Art, Mt. Vernon, Ill., 4 other sites, 1992-93, Ind. U. Art Mus., Bloomington, 2002, Evansville Mus. ARt, 2002; represented in permanent collections, Mus. Modern Art, N.Y.C., Libr. Congress, Washington, Art Inst. Chgo., Cleve. Mus. Art. Served with AUS, 1943-46. Recipient George Norlin silver medal U. Colo., 1974; Fulbright grantee, 1952-53, 63-64, grantee U.S. Dept. State, USSR, 1961, Yugoslavia, 1965, Brazil, 1974, Hungary, 1986; grantee Rockefeller Found., Bellagio, Italy, 1995; Guggenheim fellow, 1963-64; Fellow Ford Found., 1963, grantee, Japan, 1981. Mem. Soc. Am. Graphic Artists, Am. Color Print Soc., Coll. Art Assn. (bd. dirs.), Artists Equity Assn., Ind. Acad. (elected). Roman Catholic. Business E-Mail: rpozzatt@indiana.edu.

POZZO, MARY LOU, retired librarian, writer; b. L.A., June 18, 1945; d. Clayton Oliver and Violet Elizabeth (Webb) Straub; m. Richard Louis Pozzo, Nov. 10, 1984; stepchildren: Heidi, Peter; m. Richard Lee Horttor, Apr. 15, 1968 (div. 1969). AA, Pasadena C.C., 1965. Asst. legal dept. L.A. City Attys. Office, L.A., 1968—72; sec. fgn. law dept. L.A. County Law Libr., L.A., 1972—78; libr. Musick, Peeler & Garret, L.A., 1979—84, Bronson, Bronson & McKinnon, L.A., 1984—90, Bolton Hall Mus., L.A., 1992—. Pres. Zinnia Press of Tujunga. Author: When Hollywood Came to Sunland-Tujunge-1920-1995, 1997, Founding Sisters: Life Stories of Tujunga's Early Women Pioneers 1886-1926. Trustee Verdogo Hills Cemetary, Tujunga, Calif., 1992—; regional v.p. Conf. of Calif. Hist. Socs., L.A.; docent Bolton Hall Mus., Tujunga, 1992—; co-founder Sunland-Tujunga Historic Home & Garden Tour. Mem.: Sunland-Tujunga Little Landers Hist. Soc. (pres. 1995—96), The Westerners L.A. Corral, Sunland-Tujunga Women's Club, Bus. & Profl. Womens Club (Cmty. Woman of Yr. award 1998). Avocations: travel, reading, gardening, cooking, animal rescue. Home and Office: 10966 Hillhaven Ave Tujunga CA 91042 Office Phone: 818-353-1718.

POZZO, RICCARDO, philosophy educator; b. Milan, June 7, 1959; s. Giancarlo and Carla (Rizzani) P.; m. Annette Popel, Sept. 4, 1992; 1 child, Carlo. Laurea in Philosophy, U. Milan, 1983; Promotion in Philosophy, U. Saarland, Saarbrücken, 1988; Habilitation in Philosophy, U. Trier, 1995. Rsch. assoc. U. Saarland, 1984-85; fellow Deutscher Akademischer Austauschdienst, 1985-97, Herzog August Bibliothek Wolfenbüttel, 1988-90, Alexander von Humboldt-Stiftung, 1990-98; h.s. tchr. Sch. Superintendency Lombardy, Milan, 1994-96; tchr. Cath. U. Am., Washington, 1996—2003, U. Verona, 2003—. Lectr. U. Trier, 1991-96. Author: Hegel: Introductio in Philosophiam, 1989, Kant und das Problem einer Einleitung, 1989, El giro kantiano, 1998, Georg Friedrich Meiers Vernunftlehre, 2000; editor: The Impact of Aristotelianism on Modern Philosophy, 2004; co-editor: (with Karl-Otto Apel) Zur Rekonstruktion der praktischen Philosophie, 1990; (with Michael Oberhausen) Vorlesungsverzeichnisse der Universität Königsberg 1720-1804, 1999; (with Michael Oberhausen and Heinrich P. Delfosse) Vernunftkritik und Aufklärung, 2001; cons. editor: Longanesi Editore, 1988-89, Feltrinelli Editore, 1989—. Recipient 6th Study Tour of Japan, Japanese Ministry of Fgn. Affairs, 1984. Mem.: Soc. Medieval and Renaissance Philosophy, Hegel Soc. N.Am., Italian Soc. Kant Studies, N.Am. Kant Soc., Alexander von Humboldt Assn. Italy (sec., bd. dirs. 2003—), Alexander von Humboldt Assn. Am. (bd. dirs. 2002—03), Am. Philos. Assn., Rotary Internat. (internat. dist. 2040 Milano Ovest). Roman Catholic. Avocation: contemporary literature. Office: via San Francesco 22 I-37129 Verona Italy Business E-Mail: riccardo.pozzo@univr.it.

PRABAKARAN, DANIEL, biochemist, researcher; b. Mel Siviri, Tamil Nadu, India, June 25, 1959; came to U.S., 1989; s. Daniel Chinathambi and Kamala Serkad (Mani) P.; m. Crenie Sarah Paul, Feb. 14, 1992; 1 child, Elizabeth Jane. BSc, U. Madras, India, 1979, MSc, 1982; PhD, All India Inst. Med. Scis., 1989. Asst. rsch. officer All India Inst. Med. Sci., New Delhi, 1984-85, rsch. officer, 1985-88, postdoctoral fellow, 1988-89, Beth Israel Deaconess Med. Ctr./Harvard Med. Sch., Boston, 1989-97, instr., 1998—. Contbr. numerous articles to profl. jours. Indian Coun. Med. Rsch. Jr. Rsch. fellow, 1983; Dept. Sci. and Tech. Travel grantee, 1988. Mem. AAAS, Am. Soc. Cell Biology, Endocrine Soc., N.Y. Acad. Scis. Home: 1 Trudeau Ter Wayland MA 01778-5122 E-mail: dprabakaran@rics.bwh.harvard.edu.

PRABHALA, RAO H. pharmaceutical executive; b. Guntur, AP, India, July 15, 1955; s. Sastry Pk and Sesha A. Prabhala; m. Nalini R. Reddy, May 15, 1982; children: Harsha K., Nithya S., Neelima D. MSc, Nagarjuna U., India, 1977; MS, Calif. State U., Los Angeles, 1985; PhD, U. Az., 1989; Post-doctorate, Darmouth Coll., 1991. Cert. coll. tchg. Calif., 1982. Rsch. assoc. King Drew med. Ctr., Los Angeles, 1982—85; asst. prof. Midwestern U., Downers Grove, Ill., 1991—93; sr. immunologist Zonagen, Woodlands, Tex., 1993; asst. prof. Darmouth Hitchcock Med. Ctr., Lebanon, NH, 1994—97; dir. NIMI Bio Tech, Guntur, India, 1997—2000; sr. staff scientist DFCI Harvard Med. Sch., Boston, 2000—02; mgr. of microbiology Nucryst Pharmaceuticals, Wakefield, Mass., 2002—. Reader Nagarjuna U., Guntur, India, 1997—2000; mentor DFCI Harvard med. Sch., Boston, 2002. Author: Handbook of Mucosal Immunology, 1994; contbr. articles various profl. jours. Recipient Meritorious Rsch. award, AMA, 1988, Coll. Tchr. award, AP Parents Club, 1999; Immunology Training grant, NIH, 1990. Mem.: Infectious Diseases Soc. of Am., Am. Assn. of Immunology, Am. Soc. of Microbiology. Democrat. Hindu. Achievements include research in how to turn off immune system to facilitate transplantation without rejection. Avocations: running, basketball, singing, cooking, drawing. Home: 96 Manning St Needham MA 02494 Office: Nucryst Pharmaceuticals 50 Audubon Rd Ste B Wakefield MA 01880 E-mail: rprabhala@nueryst.com.

PRABHU, KRISH ANANT, telecommunications company executive, educator; b. Ankola, India, Aug. 2, 1954; came to U.S., 1975; s. Anant K. and Indira (Mahale) P.; m. Shuba George, June 14, 1980; children: Sarita, Vinay, Sanjay. BSc with honors, Bangalore (India) U., 1973; MSc, Indian Inst. Tech., Bombay, 1975; MS, U. Pitts., 1977, PhD, 1980. Mem. tech. staff Bell Labs., Holmdel, N.J., 1980-84; mem. tech. staff, also mgmt. positions Rockwell Internat., Richardson, Tex., 1984-92; v.p. R & D, Alcatel Network Systems, Richardson, 1992—95; pres. Alcatel Broadband Products, 1995—97; CEO Alcatel USA, Inc., 1997—99; COO Alcatel S.A., 1999—2001; venture ptnr. Morgenthaler Ventures, 2001—04; pres., CEO Tellabs, Inc., Naperville, Ill., 2004—. Adj. prof. U. Tex. at Dallas, Richardson, 1988—; mem. adv. coun. U. Tex., Arlington, 1992—. Contbr. articles to tech. jours. Mem. IEEE (sr.), NMA. Avocations: tennis, chess, reading. Office: Tellabs Inc One Tellabs Ctr 1415 W Diehl Rd Naperville IL 60563*

PRABHU, VASANT, corporate financial executive; Grad., Indian Inst. Tech., Bombay, India; MBA, U. Chgo. V.p., ptnr. N.Y. office Booz, Allen & Hamilton; with Pepsico Inc., U.S., Europe, Latin Am.; sr. v.p., CFO Pepsico Internat.; pres. info. and media group McGraw-Hill Cos., Inc., 1998—2000; exec. v.p., CFO Safeway Inc., 2000—03; CFO Starwood Hotels & Resorts Worldwide Inc., 2003—. Office: Starwood Hotels & Resorts Worldwide Inc 1111 Westchester Ave White Plains NY 10604

PRABHUDESAI, MUKUND M. pathology educator, laboratory director, researcher, administrator; b. Lolyem, Goa, India, Mar. 17, 1942; came to U.S., 1967; s. Madhav R. and Kusum M. Prabhudesai; m. Sarita Mukund Usha, Feb. 1, 1972; 1 child, Nitin M. MB, BS (MD), G.S. Med., Bombay, 1967, postgrad., 1973-75. Diplomate Am. Bd. Pathology. Asst. pathologist Fordham Hosp., Bronx, N.Y., 1973-74, assoc. pathologist, 1974-76; assoc. dir. clin. pathology Lincoln Med., Bronx, 1976, dep. dir. pathology, 1977-79; chief pathology and lab. medicine svc., coord. R&D VA Med. Ctr., Danville, Ill., 1979—, dir. electron microscopy lab., 1987—. Senator U. Ill. Chgo.; co-investigator U. Ill. Coll. Medicine, Urbana-Champaign, clin. prof. pathology and internal medicine, 1982—. Contbr. articles to Am. Jour. Clin. Nutrition, Jour. AMA, Am. Jour. Clin. Pathology. Member Gifted Student Adv. Bd., Danville, 1984-86; v.p. Am. Cancer Soc. Vermilion County chpt., 1982, pres., 1986-88. VA rsch. grantee, 1980-82, 82-85, 83. Fellow Coll. Am. Pathology (inspector 1981-, Ill. state del. to C.A.P. Ho. Dels. 1992-, mem. reference com. 1993, chair, standard and integration com., 2000-); mem. AAAS, Am. Coll. Physician Execs., Ill. State Soc. Pathologists (bd. dirs. 1990-, chmn. membership com. 1990-). Achievements include development of cancer of bladder following portocarval shunting; research in adverse effects of alcohol on lung structure and metabolism; on effects of soy and bran on cholesterol, endocrine response to soy protein, in induction and reversibility of atherosclerosis in trout, effects of ethanol on Vitamin A, lymphatics in atherosclerosis, iron in atherosclerosis, development of dermofluorometer for detection of P.V.D. Office: VA Med Ctr Pathology and Lab Med Svcs 1900 E Main St Danville IL 61832-5100 Office Phone: 217-748-6272. E-mail: sarita@soltec.net., mpdesai1942@hotmail.com.

PRACHT, DRENDA KAY, psychologist; b. Carrollton, Missouri, Jan. 15, 1952; d. Ethan Lyle Pracht and Wilma Estelene (Henderson) Lucas; one child, Matthew Kent. BA in Psychology, William Jewell Coll., 1974; MS in Clinical Psychology, Cen. Mo. State U., 1976; postgrad. in clin. psychology, Fielding Inst., Santa Barbara, Calif., 1995. Therapist Briscoe Carr Cons., Kansas City, Mo., 1978—79; psychologist Crittenton Ctr., Kansas City, Mo., 1979—81, Cen. Minn. Mental Health Ctr., St. Cloud, 1981—85, St. Cloud Hosp., Minn., 1985—87; gen. practice psychology St. Cloud, 1985—92, Kansas City, Mo., 1992—96, CMQ Health, 1996—97, Am. Psychology Sys., 1998—2000, SR Clarke, Inc., 2000—02. Cons. St. Benedict Ctr., Country Manor, 1986-92. Mem. Cen. Minn. Child Abuse Team, St. Cloud, Minn. 1981-85; bd. dir. Cen. Minn. Child Care Assn., St. Cloud, 1982-83. Mem. Cen. Minn. Psychol. Assn. (pres. 1984-85), Alpha Delta Pi Alumni Assn. Baptist. Avocations: piano, needlecrafts, reading, arts and crafts.

PRADERE, SONIA, accounting administrator; b. Bklyn., Sept. 22, 1965; d. Miguel Mercado and Candita P.; m. Mario Pradere, July 18, 1986; children: Michael, Stephanie. BS in Human Resource Mgmt., Palm Beach Atlantic Coll., 1995; M Acctg., Nova Southeastern U., 1998. Asst. controller Diversified Comms., Inc., West Palm Beach, Fla., 1990-95; sr. acct. Oxbow Corp., West Palm Beach, 1995-99; acctg. mgr. Sara Lee Branded Apparel, West Palm Beach, 1999—. Office: Prado Medical Park Inc 485 NE 28th Rd Boca Raton FL 33431-6830

PRADHAN, SANDEEP, engineering educator; b. Madikeri, India, Aug. 14, 1971; s. Nirupama Madikeri; m. Sonali Shanbhag, Jan. 22, 1999. PhD, U. Calif., Berkeley, 2001. Asst. prof. U. Mich., Ann Arbor, 2002—. Mem.: IEEE. Office: Univ Mich 1301 Beal Ave Ann Arbor MI 48109

PRADO, EDWARD CHARLES, federal judge; b. San Antonio, June 7, 1947; s. Edward L. and Bertha (Cadena) P.; m. Maria Anita Jung, Nov. 10, 1973; 1 child, Edward C. AA, San Antonio Coll., 1967; BA, U. Tex., 1969, JD, 1972. Bar: Tex. 1972. Asst. dist. atty. Bexar County Dist. Atty.'s Office, San Antonio, 1972-76; asst. pub. defender U.S. Pub. Defender's Office, San Antonio, 1976-80; judge U.S. Dist. Ct. Tex., San Antonio, 1980; U.S. atty. Dept. Justice, San Antonio, 1981—84; judge U.S. Dist. Ct. (we. dist.) Tex., 1984—2003, U.S. court of Appeals (5th cir.), 2003—. Served to capt. U.S. Army. Named Outstanding Young Lawyer of Bexar County, 1980. Mem. ABA, Tex. Bar Assn., San Antonio Bar Assn., San Antonio Young Lawyers Assn., Fed. Bar Assn. Republican. Roman Catholic.

PRADO, GERALD M. investment banker; b. Langeloth, Pa., Jan. 19, 1946; s. Caesar S. and Anita A. P.; m. Judith A. Pompe, May 20, 1967; children— Dennis, Eric, Lynn, Christopher. BA, Washington and Jefferson Coll., 1963-67; MBA, U. Pitts., 1983. Sr. acct. Haskins and Sells, Pitts., 1967-72; auditor G.C. Murphy Co., McKeesport, Pa., 1972-76, asst. controller, 1976-78, treas., 1979-80, asst. v.p., treas., 1980-82, v.p., treas., 1982-85, Russell, Rea & Zappala, Pitts., 1986-87, sr. v.p., 1987-90; pres. Westinghouse Mcht. Banking, Inc., Pitts., 1990-94; prin., co-mgr. Main St. Capital Holdings L.L.C., Pitts., 1994—. Roman Catholic. Home: 205 Overlook Dr Mc Murray PA 15317-2657 Office: Main St Capital Holdings 1001Corporate Dr Ste 200 Canonsburg PA 15317 Office Phone: 724-743-5650. E-mail: prado@mainstcap.com.

PRADOS, JOHN WILLIAM, engineering educator; b. Spring Hill, Tenn., Oct. 12, 1929; s. Gustave Olivier and Elizabeth Branham Prados; m. Ruth Lynn Baird, Sept. 2, 1951; children: Elizabeth Pauline Bowman, Laura Lynn, Anne Caroline Lynch. BS in chem. engring., U. Miss., Oxford, Miss., 1947—51; PhD, U. Tenn., Knoxville, 1954—57, MS, 1953—54. Registered Profl. Engr., State Bd. of Archtl. and Engring. Examiners/Tenn., 1964. Asst. prof. of chem. engring. The U. of Tenn., Knoxville, Tenn., 1956—59, assoc. prof. of chem. engring., 1959—64, prof. of chem. engring., 1964—, assoc. dean of engring., 1969—71, dean of admissions and records, 1971—73, acting chancellor, knoxville campus, 1973—73, v.p. for academic affairs, statewide sys., 1973—81, v.p. for academic affairs and rsch., statewide sys., 1981—88, v.p. emeritus, 1989—, u. prof., 1989—, head, chem. engring. dept., 1990—93, acting chancellor, martin campus Martin, Tenn., 1979—79; cons. Nuc. Divsn., Union Carbide Corp., Oak Ridge, Tenn., 1957—84, Martin Marietta Energy Systems, Oak Ridge, Tenn., 1984—86; sr. edn. assoc. NSF, Arlington, Va., 1994—97. Editor, jour. of engring. edn. Am. Soc. for Engring. Edn., Washington, 1996—2001; sec. Accreditation Bd. for Engring. and Tech., Inc., Baltimore, Md., 1989—90, pres., 1991—92; commr. Commn. on Colleges, So. Assn. of Colleges and Schools, Decatur, Ga., 1986—92, exec. councillor, 1986—89; trustee So. Assn. of Colleges and Schools, Decatur, Ga., 1995—98, F. W. Olin Coll. of Engring., Needham, Mass., 2002—; vice chmn. Engring. Accreditation Commn., Accreditation Bd. for Engring. and Tech., Inc., Baltimore, Md., 1981—84, chmn., 1984—85; dir. Accrediation Bd. for Engring. and Tech., Baltimore, Md., 1988—93; cons. nuclear divsn. Union Carbide Corp., Oak Ridge, 1957—84; cons. Martin Marietta Energy Sys., Inc., 1984—86; sr. edn. assoc. NSF, Arlington, Va., 1994. First lt. U. S. Air Force, 1951—53, Biloxi, MS; Albuquerque, NM; Limestone, ME. Recipient L. E. Grinter Award for Contributions to Engring. Edn., Accreditation Bd. for Engring. and Tehcnology, Inc., 1993, Alumni Outstanding Tchr., U. Tenn., 1967, 1992, Outstanding Engring. Alumnus, 1975, Faculty Macebearer, 1997—98. Fellow: Am. Inst. Chem. Engrs. (Knoxville-Oak Ridge Chem. Engr. of Yr. 1977, treas. 1996—2001), Am. Inst. of Chemists (life), Am. Soc. for Engring. Edn. (life); mem.: Am. Chem. Soc., Tech. Soc. of Knoxville, Torch Club, Phi Kappa Phi (Disting. Mem. 1974), Tau Beta Pi (exec. coun. 1986—90), Sigma Xi, Sci. Rsch. Soc. (pres. 1983—84, treas. 1990—2002), Alpha Tau Omega. Roman Catholic. Home: 7021 Stagecoach Trail Knoxville TN 37909-1112 Office: 419 Dougherty Engineering Building 1512 Middle Drive Knoxville TN 37996-2200

PRADZYNSKI, ANDRZEJ HENRYK, chemist; b. Plock, Poland, Jan. 1, 1924; arrived in U.S., 1969; s. Maurycy and Frania (Goldkind) Nejman; m. Halina Romana Bromberger, Apr. 1, 1946; children: Richard E. Neuman, Zgibniew Jacek. BS, U. Wroclaw, Poland, 1949, MS, 1951. Asst. prof. crystallography, chmn. dept. U. Wroclaw, 1948-51; sect. mgr. materials testing Inst. Aviation, Warsaw, Poland, 1951-57; adj. prof. Polish Acad. Scis., Warsaw, 1957-68; dept. dir. Atomic Energy Commn. Poland, Warsaw, 1959-68; rsch. assoc. IV nuclear reactor U. Tex., Austin, 1969-80; exec. v.p. Halinco Skin Care Products, Inc., Austin, 1980-2000. Cons. IAEA, Vienna, Austria, 1968-69. Author: Industrial Radiography (in Polish), 1957; also more than 30 articles in IAEA Conf. Procs., Nukleonika, ISA Trans., others. Mem. Am. Chem. Soc., N.Y. Acad. Scis. Achievements include patent for method and apparatus for collection and analysis of mercury in the atmosphere; developer method of photo-nuclear activation analysis of copper in ores and concentrates, synthetic standards for EDX-ray analysis, method of collection and analysis of mercury in air, method of nondestructive X-ray analysis of heavy metals in toys. Developed pre-concentration methods of trace elements in water for EDX-ray analysis. Personal E-mail: apradzynski@austin.rr.com.

PRAEGER, SANDY, state legislator; b. Oct. 21, 1944; m. Mark A. Praeger. Student, U. Kans., 1966. V.p. Douglas County Bank; mem. Kans. Senate from 2nd dist., Topeka, 1992—. Vice chmn. Douglas County Rep. Cent. Com.; chmn. Leadership Kans.; pres. bd. dirs. United Way. Home: 3601 Quail Creek Ct Lawrence KS 66047-2134 Office: Kans State Senate State Capitol Rm 128S Topeka KS 66612

PRAGER, ALICE HEINECKE, music company executive; b. NYC, Aug. 2, 1930; d. Paul and Ruth (Collin) Heinecke; m. George L. Drescher, 1963 (dec. Dec. 2002). BA, Russell Sage Coll., 1951; postgrad., NYU, 1952-55. V.p. SESAC Inc., N.Y.C., 1956-73, pres., 1973-78, pres., chmn. bd., 1978-92. Chmn. bd. Personal Touch, Inc. Mem. Internat. Radio and TV Soc., Am. Inst. of Mgmt., NARAS, Country Music Assn. (bd. dirs., 1986, life), Gospel Music Assn. (life). Office: The Personal Touch Inc 68-34 Fleet St Forest Hills NY 11375-5051 E-mail: apd3700@aol.com.

PRAGER, DAVID, retired state supreme court chief justice; b. Ft. Scott, Kans., Oct. 30, 1918; s. Walter and Helen (Kishler) P.; m. Dorothy Schroeter, Sept. 8, 1945; children: Diane, David III. AB, U. Kans., 1939, JD, 1942. Bar: Kans. 1942. Practiced in, Topeka, 1946-59; dist. judge Shawnee County (Kans.) Dist. Ct., 1959-71; assoc. justice Kans. Supreme Ct., Topeka, 1971-87, chief justice, 1987-88; ret., 1988. Lectr. Washburn Law Sch., 1948-68. Served to lt. USNR, 1942-46, ETO, PTO. Mem. Kans. Dist. Judges Assn. (past pres.), Order of Coif, Phi Beta Kappa, Phi Delta Theta, Lions Lodge, Arab Shrine Lodge.

PRAGER, ELLIOT DAVID, surgeon, educator; b. N.Y.C., Sept. 10, 1941; s. Benjamin and Sadye Zelda (Newman) P.; m. Phyllis Damon Warner, July 1, 1967; children: Rebecca, Sarah, Katherine. AB, Dartmouth Coll., 1962; MD, Harvard U., 1966. Diplomate Am. Bd. Surgery, Am. Bd. Colon and Rectal Surgery. Surg. resident Roosevelt Hosp., N.Y.C., 1966-71; colon-rectal fellow Lahey Clinic, Boston, 1971-72; staff surgeon Sansum Clinic, Santa Barbara, Calif., 1974—, dir. colorectal fellowship, 1982-97, chief of surgery, 1986-94; dir. surg. edn. Cottage Hosp., Santa Barbara, 1994-96. Mem., vice chair

Residency Rev. Com., 1992—. Author: (with others) Operative Colorectal Surgery, 1994, Current Therapy in Colon and Rectal Surgery, 1990; contbr. articles to profl. jours. Lt. comdr. USN, 1972-74. Fellow Am. Coll. Surgeons (adv. coun. 1992—), Am. Soc. of Colon and Rectal Surgeons (v.p. 1992, sec. of program dirs., 1990—). Achievements include 5 patents for colostomy control devices. Office: Sansum Clinic 317 W Pueblo St Santa Barbara CA 93105-4365

PRAGER, KENNETH MICHAEL, pulmonologist, educator; b. Bklyn., Jan. 3, 1943; s. Max and Hilda Prager; m. Regene Eleanore Gronich, June 25, 1967; children: Karen Rachel Kramer, Joshua Harris, Tamar Anne, Benjamin Dov. BA, Columbia U., 1964; MD, Harvard U., 1968. Cert. ME in internal med. Am. Bd. Internal Med. Intern Columbia Presbyn. Med. Ctr., N.Y.C., 1968—69, resident, 1971—72; chief med. resident Billings Hosp. U. of Chgo., 1972—73; from assoc. in medicine to clin. prof. Columbia Coll. of Physicians and Surgeons, N.Y.C., 1973—99, clin. prof. of medicine, 1999—. Dir. of clin. ethics Columbia Presbyn. Med. Ctr., 1998—, chmn. of med. ethics com., 1994—. Co-author: Medical Ethics Issues in the Elderly, 2003; contbr. articles to profl. jours. and newspapers. Bd. dirs. Am. Coun. on Sci. and Health, N.Y.C., 2001—; mem. Bd. of Health, Englewood, NJ, 1989—92; chmn. bd. dirs. Moriah Sch., Englewood, NJ, 1983—85. Asst. surgeon, acting med. dir. USPHS Indian Health Svc., 1969—71. Named One of N.Y.C.'s Best Pulmonologists, N.Y. Mag., 1991, 1998, 1999, One of N.Y.C.'s Best Internists, Castle Connoly Guide, Best Doctors, 1994, 1997, 1999, 2001, 2002, 2003, 2004, One of N.Y.C.'s Best Internists/Pulmonologist, 2001, 2002, 2003, 2004. Fellow: ACP; mem.: AMA, Am. soc. for bioethics and Humanities, Med. Soc. of the State of N.Y., Am. Coll. of Chest Physicians. Jewish. Home: 231 South Dwight Place Englewood NJ 07631 Office: Columbia Presbyterian Medical Center 161 Fort Washington Avenue New York NY 10032 Personal E-mail: kmp43@aol.com. E-mail: kmp43@aol.com.

PRAGER, LESLIE BETH, career counselor; b. N.Y.C., May 9, 1953; d. Irving Prager and Ruth Rotenberg; m. Barry S. Bernstein, June 5, 1988; 1 child, Jared D. Bernstein. BA in Psychology, SUNY, Binghamton, 1974; MA in Art Therapy, U. Louisville, 1975. Cert. career mgmt. practitioner. Art therapist Houston Internat. Hosp., 1976-77; exec. trainee, asst. buyer Lord & Taylor, N.Y.C., 1977-80; corp. recruiter Chem. Bank, N.Y.C., 1980-82; employment mgr. R.H. Macy & Co., N.Y.C., 1982-84; asst. personnel mgr. Garan, Inc., N.Y.C., 1984-85; v.p., human resources dir. Std. Security Life Ins. Co., N.Y.C., 1986-90; sr. ptnr., career counselor The Prager Bernstein Group, N.Y.C., 1991—. Spkr. in field. Contbr. articles to profl. jours. Mem. Internat. Assn. Career Mgmt. Profls. (pres. NY Chptr.), Am. Counseling Assn., N.Y. Assn. Career Mgmt. Profls. (treas. 1993-98), Soc. Human Resource Mgmt. Human Resources Assocs. N.Y. (jour. editor, dir., exec. bd. mem.), Exec. Women Internat. (treas., bd. dirs.). Jewish. Avocations: travel, hiking, reading, photography, antiquing. Home: 2 Bay Club Dr # 14G Bayside NY 11360 Office: The Prager-Bernstein Group 441 Lexington Ave Ste 1404 New York NY 10017 E-mail: Leslie-PBG@msn.com.

PRAGER, STEPHEN, chemistry professor; b. Darmstadt, Germany, July 20, 1928; came to U.S., 1941, naturalized, 1950; s. William and Gertrude Ann (Heyer) P.; m. Julianne Heller, June 7, 1948. B.Sc., Brown, 1947; PhD, Cornell, 1951. Mem. faculty U. Minn., Mpls., 1952—, assoc. prof. chemistry, 1956-62, prof., 1962-90, prof. emeritus, 1990—. Cons. Union Carbide Corp., Oak Ridge, 1954-74 Asso. editor: Jour. Phys. Chemistry, 1970-79. Fulbright scholar and Guggenheim fellow, 1958, 59; Fulbright lectr. and Guggenheim fellow, 1966-67 Mem. Am. Chem. Soc., Am. Phys. Soc. Home: 3320 Dunlap St N Saint Paul MN 55112-3709 E-mail: pspragen@cs.com.

PRAGER, SUSAN WESTERBERG, law educator, provost; b. Sacramento, Dec. 14, 1942; d. Percy Foster Westerberg and Aileen M. (McKinley) P.; m. James Martin Prager, Dec. 14, 1973; children: McKinley Ann, Case Mahone. AB, Stanford U., 1964, MA, 1967; JD, UCLA, 1971. Bar: N.C. 1971, Calif. 1972. Atty. Powe, Porter & Alphin, Durham, N.C., 1971-72; acting prof. law UCLA, 1972-77, prof. Sch. Law, 1977—, Arjay and Frances Fearing Miller prof. of law, 1992-99, assoc. dean Sch. Law, 1979-82, dean, 1982-98; provost Dartmouth Coll., Hanover, N.H., 1999—. Bd. dirs. Pacific Mut. Life Holding Co., Newport Beach, Calif. Editor-in-chief, UCLA Law Rev., 1970-71. Trustee Stanford U., 1976-80, 87-97. Mem. ABA (council of sect. on legal edn. and admissions to the bar 1983-85), Assn. Am. Law Schs. (pres. 1986), Order of Coif. Address: Dartmouth College Office of the Provost 6004 Parkhurst Hall Rm 204 Hanover NH 03755-3529

PRAGER-KAMEL, NANCY ANN, investment banker, artist, business development firm executive; b. N.Y.C., Mar. 17, 1943; d. Sigmund Godfrey and Eleanor Pauline Prager; BA Cooper Union, MS, Maxwell Sch. Polit. Sci. Syracuse U., BFA, Accademia de Belle Arte, Florence, Italy, 1964-65; m. Barry Lawrence Benett, June 19, 1966 (div.); children: Lara Christina, Andrew Bernard, Ariane Alison; m. Ahmed Abdul Monein Kamel, Aug. 28, 1993. Founder, pres. Boskoff-Präger Group Ltd.; pres., founder ARK Devel. Group, 1992-, mng. dir., gen. ptnr. Wolff Investment Group, 1996-98, mng. dir. investment banking Bottom Line Fin. Group, 1998-99; sr. v.p. bus. devel. Resource Recovery Assocs. Inc., 1998-99; exec. v.p., head investment banking U.S. Securities and Futures, 1999—; pres. Lampert Bros. Internat.; pres. Lempert Bros. Internat. USA, 2003—. Dir. Bus. devel. Merchant Bank-Continental Capital; mng. dir. Selby; past dir. World's Children's Day NGO, U.N., 1984-91. Work exhibited in mus. and univ. one woman and group shows, U.S., Can., Turkey, Italy, France, Eng., also Am. Consulate, Istanbul, Turkey, Resim ve Hey Kel Mus., Dolmabahce Palace, Istanbul, UN; represented pvt. and corp. collections, U.S., Italy, Eng., Turkey, Can., France; tchr. Met. Mus. Art and Black Emergency Cultural Coalition, State of N.Y. Prison System; dir. aux. events Suliman the Magnificent Exhbn.; prodr. Dance exhbn. at Costume Inst. Met. Mus., 1986-87. Chmn. bd. Prep. Sch. Mannes Coll. Music, 1975-76. Author: Turkish Costumes in the Collection of Metropolitan Museum. Bd. dirs. Georgetown U. Sch. Lang. and Linguistic, Amalfi Coast Consortium, TV Acad. Arts and Sci., Acad. Arts and Sci., Am. Ballet Theatre II, Mid. East Ctr. Conservation and Preservation, Human Rights Watch, Fgn. Press Assn., Vital Voices for Women, Global Acad.; dir. for devel. and pub. rels. UN World Children's Day; bd. dirs. UNICEF (vice chmn. exec. bd. N.Y. Metro Area), 1991-2002; adv. Global Acad. Head U.N. Artists Group. Recipient Prix de Paris, 1975, Grand Prix Humanitaire de France, 1976. Bd. dirs. Immigration and Refugee Svc. Am. Mem. Am.-Scandinavian Found., Les Surindependants Societaire, Graphic Art Assn., Am. Italian Found. Cancer Research (bd. dirs., editor Research for Life), Smithsonian Assos., Met. Mus., Archaeology Inst. Am. Presbyterian. Club: Saltaire Yacht (bd.). Work noted in Artist USA Bicentennial, N.Y. Art Yearbook, Nouvelle Littaire, Art News Mag., Arts Mag., Fine Art Mag., 2002. Office: 667 Madison Ave New York NY 10021 E-mail: npk@lempertusa.com.

PRAGMAN, KURT DANIEL, media specialist; b. Highland Park, Mich., Jan. 12, 1964; s. Robert Wayne and Ruth Ann Pragman; m. M. Gabriela Diaz, July 20, 1991; children: Cynthia Gabriela, Anna Rosa. Owner Pragman Prodn. Svcs., Hyde Park, NY, 1980—. Engring. cons. Riverside Marine Svcs., Highland, NY, 1996—; tech. dir. Ctr. For Performing Arts at Rhinebeck, NY, 1998—; theatrical cons. The Millbrook Sch., Millbrook, NY, 2002—, Cocoon Theater, Rhinebeck, NY, 2001—. Designer (musical tour and video) None for the Road (Emmy Award, 1985). Recipient Sci. and Engring. Fair Medallion, US Army, 1981. Mem.: U.S. Inst. for Theater Tech. Office: Pragman Production Services 49 Spooky Hollow Rd Hyde Park NY 12538 Office Phone: 845-266-8415. Office Fax: 845-266-8414. E-mail: pragman@att.net.

PRAGUE, EDITH G. state legislator; b. Methuen, Mass., Nov. 23, 1925; m. Franklyn Prague, 1946; 4 children. BS, MA, Ea. Conn. State U.; MSW, U. Conn. Newspaper columnist, Columbia, Conn.; mem. Dist. 19 Conn. Senate, Hartford, 1995—. Mem. Columbia Bd. Edn., 1977-82, Conn. Ho. of Reps.; del. White House Conf. on Aging, 1980—; commr. State Dept. Aging, Mass., 1991-93. Mem. Beta Sigma Phi Internat. (First Lady of Yr. 1986). Democrat. Office: Conn Senate Rm 3800 Legislative Office Bldg Hartford CT 06106

PRAKAPAS, EUGENE JOSEPH, art gallery director; b. Lowell, Mass., July 29, 1932; s. Joseph S. Prakapas and Viola Schensnol; m. Dorothy A. Seitner, Dec. 1, 1971. BA, Yale U., 1953; MA, Oxford U., Balliol, 1959. Editor-in-chief, v.p. Trident Press and Pocket Books divsn. Simon & Schuster, Inc., N.Y.C., 1960-70; co-dir. Carus Gallery, N.Y.C., 1973-75; dir. Prakapas Gallery, N.Y.C., 1976—. Vis. curator San Francisco Mus. Modern Art, 1986. Author: Bauhaus Photography, 1985. Lt. (s.g.) USNR, 1953-57. Fulbright fellow, 1957-59; Yale U. scholar, 1949-53. Mem. Art Dealers Assn. Am., Assn. Internat. Photography Art Dealers. Office Phone: 914-961-5091. E-mail: eugeneprakapas@earthlink.net.

PRAKASH, UDAYA B.S. internist, educator; b. Bangalore, Mysore, India, July 22, 1945; s. Putta Honnappa, Lakshmidevamma Sanjivappa; m. Pushpa Iyengar; children: Apurva, Anna, Amita. MB BS, Bangalore Med. Coll., 1970. Diplomate Am. Bd. Internal Medicine, Pulmonary Disease Am. Bd. Internal Medicine. Edward W. and Betty Knight Scripps prof. medicine Mayo Med. Sch./Mayo Grad. Sch. Medicine, Rochester, Minn. Cons. pulmonary, critical care and internal medicine, dir. bronchoscopy Mayo Clinic/Mayo Med. Ctr., Rochester. Author: Bronchoscopy, 1994. Recipient Shigeto Ikeda award, World Assn. for Bronchology, 1998. Fellow: RCPC, Am. Coll. Chest Physicians (pres.-elect 2002—, chair nominations com., chair program com., editl. bd., dept. editor, regent at large, continuing edn. com.). Office: Mayo Clinic Rochester MN 55905-0001

PRAKASH, VIKRAMADITYA (VIKRAM), architecture educator; b. Chandigarh, India; BArch, Chandigarh Coll. Arch., 1986; MA, Cornell U., 1989, PhD, 1994. Co-dir. Re-Envisioning San Juan dept. arch. Poly. U. P.R., San Juan, 1995—96; chair, assoc. prof. dept. arch. U. Wash., Seattle. Co-chair Theatres of Decolonization: Arch. Agy. Urbanism Conf., Chandigarh, 1994—95; invited lectr., reviewer Cornell U., MIT, Ariz. State U., SCI-Arc, U. B.C., Urban Design Rsch. Inst., Bombay, 1993—. Author (with J. Biln): The Open Hand: Le Corbusier, Chanigarh, and the Re Making of a Cultural Artifact-A Working Demo, 1995; author: (with A. Prakash) Chandigarh: City of the Open Hand, 1998; author: Le Corbusier's Chandigarh: The Making of an Indian Modern Architecture, 2001; editor (author introduction): Proceedings of Theatres of Decolonization: Architecture, Urbanism and Agency, 1997. Office: U Wash Coll Arch and Urban Planning 208F Gould Hall Box 355720 Seattle WA 98195-5720*

PRAMANIK, BIRENDRA NATH, research executive; b. Santahar, Bogra, Bangladesh, Jan. 23, 1944; came to U.S., 1970; s. Kanai Lal and Charu Bala Pramanik; m. Nandita Pramanik, Aug. 16, 1964; children: Barnali, Bidyut. MSc, Rajshahi (Bangladesh) U., 1965; MS, Stevens Inst. of Tech., 1973, PhD, 1977. Sr. analytical chemist Richarson-Vicks, Inc., Mount Vernon, N.Y., 1978-80; sr. scientist Schering-Plough Corp., Bloomfield, N.J., 1980-83, prin. scientist, 1984-87; sr. prin. scientist Schering-Plough Rsch. Inst., Bloomfield, N.J., 1987-90, devel. fellow Kenilworth, N.J., 1990-95, sr. devel. fellow, 1996, sr. rsch. fellow, 1996-2000, sr. disting. fellow, 2000—. Course dir. Ea. Analytical Symposium, 1996—; vis. scientist Stevens Inst. Tech., N.J., 1996—; vis. spkr. mass spectrometry Columbia U., N.Y.C., 1990-2001; spkr in field. Editor Applied Electrospray Mass Spectrometry, 2002; contbr. chpts. to books and over 111 articles to profl. publs. Recipient N.J. regional award in mass spectrometry Am. Chem. Soc., 2000. Mem. N.J. Mass Spectrometry Assn., (chmn.-elect 1989, chmn. 1990), Am. Soc. Mass Spectrometry (oral co-chair 1999). Avocations: gardening, tennis. Home: 3 Tara Dr Parsippany NJ 07054-3312 Office: Schering-Plough Rsch Inst 2015 Galloping Hill Rd Kenilworth NJ 07033-1300 E-mail: birendra.pramanik@spcorp.com.

PRAMER, DAVID, microbiologist, educator, research administrator; b. Mt. Vernon, N.Y., Mar. 25, 1923; s. Coleman and Ethel (Toback) P.; m. Rhoda Lifschutz, Sept. 6, 1950; children— Andrew, Stacey Student, St. John's U., 1940, Tex. A&M Coll., 1941; BS cum laude, Rutgers U., 1948, PhD, 1952. Vis. investigator Butterwick Research Labs., Welwyn, Eng., 1952-54; from asst. to assoc. prof. microbiology Rutgers U., New Brunswick, N.J., 1954-60, prof., 1960-67, disting. prof., 1967—, dir. biological scis., 1969-73, dir. univ. research, 1973-75, assoc. v.p. research, 1973-80; dir. Waksman Inst. Microbiology, 1980-88, assoc. v.p. corp. liaison, 1988-93; exec. asst. and disting. prof. emeritus, exec. asst. Rutgers U., New Brunswick, N.J., 1993—. Cons. various fed. agys., 1965—; dir. New Brunswick Sci. Co., Edison, R&D Coun. of N.J., Nanodyne, Inc., New Brunswick, Organica, Inc., Great Neck, N.Y.; served on numerous chmn., com. and adv. posts. Author: Life in the Soil, 1964, Experimental Soil Microbiology, 1965, The Microbes, 1971, Engineered Organisms in the Environment, 1985; also over 250 articles in profl. jours.; regional editor World Jour. Soil and Biology and Biochemistry; mem. editl. bd. Soil Sci., BioSci., Applied Microbiology and Biotech. Bd. dirs. Library, Highland Park, N.J., 1966-75, chmn., 1976-78; committeeman Democratic Party, Highland Park, 1958-66. Served to cpl. USAF, 1943-46 Fulbright-Hays Sr. Research fellow, 1969; recipient Waksman award, Theobald Smith Soc., 2000. Fellow Am. Acad. Microbiology; mem. Am. Soc. Microbiology, Internat. Commn. Microbial Ecology (chmn.), Internat. Cell Rsch. Orgn., Nat. Acad. Scis. India (hon.), Am. Soc. Microbiology (hon., founders award, 2001), Phi Beta Kappa, Alpha Zeta, Sigma Xi Jewish. Avocations: jogging, travel. Home: 407 Rhoads Dr Belle Mead NJ 08502-4113 Office: Rutgers Univ Office Rsch & Sponsored Programs 3 Rutgers Plaza New Brunswick NJ 08901 E-mail: pramer@orsp.rutgers.edu.

PRANGE, ARTHUR JERGEN, JR., psychiatrist, neurobiologist, educator; b. Grand Rapids, Mich., Sept. 19, 1926; s. Arthur Jergen and Martha Frances (Elliott) P.; m. Sarah Elizabeth Bowen, Feb. 4, 1950; children— Christine Anne, Martha Louise, Laura Beth, David Elliott. BS, U. Mich., 1947, MD, 1950. Intern Wayne County Gen. Hosp., Eloise, Mich., 1950-51; resident in psychiatry U. N.C., Chapel Hill, 1954-57, instr., 1957-60, asst. prof., 1960-64, asso. prof., 1964-68, prof. psychiatry, 1968-83, Boshamer prof. psychiatry, 1983—, acting chmn. dept. psychiatry, 1983-85, dir. NIMH Clin. Rsch. Ctr., 1979—. Vis. scientist Med. Rsch. Coun. Unit, Epson, Surrey, Eng., 1968-69; chmn. clin. projects rsch. rev. com. HEW, NIMH, 1975-76, chmn. bd. sci. counselors, 1986-87; mem. psychopharmacologic drugs adv. com. HEW, FDA, 1979-82. Editor: The Thyroid Axis, Drugs and Behavior, 74; Contbr. articles to med. jours. Recipient NIMH Career Devel. award 1961-69, Career Scientist award, 1969-95, Gold Medal award Soc. of Biol. Psychiatry, 1992, Exemplary Psychiatrist award Nat. Alliance for the Mentally Ill, 1997, Selo prize Nat. Alliance for Rsch. in Schizophrenia and Affective Disorders, 1997. Fellow Am. Psychiat. Assn. (life, Rsch. in Psychiatry award 1996), Am. Coll. Neuropsychopharmacology (life, pres. 1987, Hoch award 1995); mem. Internat. Soc. Psychoneuroendocrinology (founding mem.), N.C. Neuropsychiat. Assn., Collegium Internationale Neuropsychopharmacologicum, Royal Coll. Psychiatrists (London). Home: 6503 Meadowview Rd Hillsborough NC 27278-8314 Office: Univ NC Sch Medicine Dept Psychiatry Chapel Hill NC 27599-0001

PRANGE, HILMAR WALTER, neurology educator; b. Reichenbach/Eule, Silesia, Germany, Aug. 4, 1944; s. Georg Friedrich Reinhold and Gertrud Wilhelmine (Mueller) P.; m. Carin Juliane Schroeter, Mar. 14, 1970; children: Klaus Richard, Juliane. MD, U. Rostock, Germany, 1969, lic. specialist neurology and psychiatry, 1974; Habilitation, Georg-August U., Goettingen, Germany, 1982. Medical diplomate. Med. resident Regional Hosp., Stralsund, Germany, 1969-71; med. asst. then psychiatrist Univ. Hosp., Rostock, 1971-75; asst. med. dir. Ev. Johannes Hosp., Bielefeld, Germany, 1975-76; head neurologic out-patient clinic Univ. Hosp., Goettingen, Germany, 1976-78, asst. med. dir. dept. neurology, 1979—87, dir. neurol. intensive care unit, 1987—. Author: Neurosyphilis, 1987, Infectious Diseases of the Central Nervous System, 1995; editor: CNS Barriers and Modern CSF Diagnostics, 1993, Systemic Infections Causing Bacterial CNS Diseases, 1997, Infectious Diseases of the Central Nervous System, 2001, Emergencies in Neurology, 2002, Neurological Intensive Medicine, 2004; contbr. articles to profl. jours. Grantee Deutsche Forschungsgemeinschaft, German Tech. Cooperation, German MS Soc. Mem. European Neurol. Soc., German Med. Assn. (mem. commn. drug security). Lutheran. Avocation: Cultural history, sports, jogging (marathons), swimming. Office Phone: 0049-551-392355. Business E-Mail: hprange@gwdg.de.

PRANGE, MICHAEL J. finance company executive; V.p., gen. merchandise mgr. Prange Dept. Stores, 1985—87, the id, 1987—89; pres., gen. merchandising mgr. Specialty Stores, 1989—94; v.p., gen. merchandising mgr. Christopher & Banks, 1994—95, sr. v.p., gen. merchandising mgr., 1995—97, pres., chief merchandising mgr., 1997—98, pres., CEO, 1998—99, chmn., CEO, 1999—. Office: 2400 Xenium Ln N Minneapolis MN 55441

PRANGE, ROY LEONARD, JR., lawyer; b. Chgo., Sept. 12, 1945; s. Roy Leonard and Marjorie Rose (Kauppi) P.; m. Carol Lynn Poels, June 5, 1971; children: David, Ellen, Susan. BA, U. Iowa, 1967; MA, Ohio State U., 1968; JD, U. Wis.-Madison, 1975. Bar: Wis. 1975, U.S. Dist. Ct. (we. and ea. dists.) Wis. 1975, U.S. Ct. Appeals (7th cir.) 1978, U.S. Supreme Ct. 1978. Assoc. Ross & Stevens, S.C., Madison, Wis., 1975—79, ptnr., 1979—90, Quarles & Brady, LLP, Madison, 1990—. Lectr. bankruptcy, debtor-creditor rights, U. Wis., Madison, 1982--. Contbr. Wis. Lawyer's Desk Reference Manual, 1987, Comml. Litigation in Wis. Practice Handbook, 1995, West's Bankruptcy Exemption Manual, 1997—. 1st lt. U.S. Army, 1969-72. Fellow Am. Coll. Bankruptcy; mem. ABA, Wis. State Bar (dir. bankruptcy, insolvency, creditors rights sect. 1985-91, chair 1990-92, mem. continuing legal edn. com. 1990-95), Am. Bankruptcy Inst., Dickens Fellowship (v.p 1980-84). Avocations: swimming, bicycling, scuba diving. Office: Quarles & Brady LLP PO Box 2113 1 S Pinckney St Madison WI 53701-2113

PRANSES, ANTHONY LOUIS, retired electric company executive, organization executive; b. Claracq, France, May 3, 1920; s. Anthony Kasimer and Georgette (Pilon) F.; m. Margaret Louise Hamill, July 24, 1943; children— Anthony Randolph, Terry Jay, Renee Louise. Student, Sorbonne, Paris, France, 1937-39; BS in Metall. Engring. Carnegie Inst. Tech., 1942, grad. student, 1946-48. With Westinghouse Electric Corp., 1945-86, mgr. mfg. planning, 1954-57, plant mgr., 1958-59, mgr. mfg. services, 1959-72, mgr. mfg., 1972-80, cons., 1980-86. Joined Am. Youth Hostels, 1935, founder Pitts. council, 1947, pres. council, 1947-50, mem. nat. bd. dirs., 1954-72, Midwest regional v.p., 1957-59, nat. pres., 1959-62, pres. Lima council, 1962-75, 87-91, chmn. nat. bd. dirs., 1963-67. Served to capt., C.E. AUS, 1942- 45. Home: 6005 Poling Rd Lima OH 45807-9492 E-mail: pranses@wcoil.com.

PRASAD, BIRENDRA (BRIAN), mechanical engineer; b. Patna, Bihar, India, June 30, 1949; came to U.S., 1973; s. Baidyanath Prasad Gupta and Ramrati Devi; m. Pushpa Gupta, May 13, 1973; children: Rosalie, Gunjan, Palak. BSME, Bihar Coll. Engring., Patna, 1969; MSME, Indian Inst. Tech., Kanpur, 1971; DEng, Stanford U., 1975; PhD in Mech. and Aerospace Engring., Ill. Inst. Tech., 1977. Rsch. asst. Ill. Inst. Tech., Chgo., 1976-77, lectr., 1978-79; prin. rsch. scientist Sci. Rsch. Lab., Ford Motor Co., Dearborn, Mich., 1982-85; sr. cons. engr. Electronic Data Sys. Corp., West Bloomfield, Mich., 1985-98; dir. Unigraphics Solutions, Inc. Knowledge based Engring. (KBE) B, Cypress, Calif., 1998—, U. Calif. Continuing Edn., Irvine, Calif., 2001—; mng. dir. Spec2market Solutions, Tustin, Calif.; chief knowledge officer Parker Hannifin, Irvine, Calif. Author: 12 books; contbr. more than 100 articles to profl. jours. Recipient award NASA, 1981. Fellow AIAA (chmn. structural dynamics and materials conf. organizing com., treas. Mich. chpt. 1986—), ASME, ASCE (chmn., mem. control group aerospace div. conf. com.); mem. Soc. Automotive Engring. Home: 2966 Penman Tustin CA 92782-3313 Office: Spec2 market Solutions Mng Dir Knowledge Based Engring PO Box 3882 Tustin CA 92781-3882 E-mail: prasadb1@cox.net.

PRASAD, NIRU, physician, television personality; b. Feb. 10, 1940; s. Sadashiv and Saraswati Prasad; m. Bala Prasad, Mar. 9, 1962; children: Abhilasha, Ashish, Anjali, Ashoke. Emergency rm. physician Henry Ford Hosp., Detroit, Mich., 2002; pediatric urgent care St. Joseph Mercy Hosp., Pontiac, Mich., 2002; occupl. physician Med. Plant Physician, Auburn Hills, Mich., 2002. Contbr. (book) How to Keep Your Child Safe and Healthy; contbr. articles to profl. jours.; host (television program) Health Talk. Recipient AMA Physician Recognition Award, 1992, Svc. of Justice and Mercy Recognition Award, 1993, America's Registry of Outstanding Professionals, 2001, Physician Recongnition award, 1995, Ams. Top Pediatricians, 2002—, Angel award, 2002, 2003. Home: 264 Pine Ridge Drive Bloomfield Hills MI 48304 Personal E-mail: niruprasad@aol.com.

PRASSE, KEITH W. dean; b. Freeport, Ill., Sept. 17, 1940; married; 2 children. BS in Farm Operation, Iowa State U., 1963, DVM, 1965, MS in Vet. Parasitology, 1968, PhD in Vet. Pathology, 1971; grad., Nat. Leadership Inst., Adult and Continuing Edn., U. Ga., 1991. NIH trainee in biomed. electronics and classical physiology Baylor U. Coll. Medicine, 1968; pvt. practice as vet. Oregon, Ill., 1965—66; instr., asst. prof., assoc. prof. vet. pathology Iowa State U., 1967—72; assoc. prof. vet. pathology U. Ga., Athens, 1972—78, prof. vet. pathology, 1978—, assoc. dean for svcs., 1990—96; dean U. Ga. Coll. Vet. Medicine, Athens, 1996—. Cytologist, cons. Atlanta Vet. Lab., 1982—87; examiner in clin. pathology Australian Coll. Vet. Surgeons, 1986; guest lectr. continuing edn. in clin. pathology for practitioners U. Sydney, Australia, 1986; grant reviewer Natural Scis. and Engring. Rsch. Coun. Can., 1989. Co-author: (book) Veterinary Laboratory Medicine, 1977, Veterinary Laboratory Medicine, 3d edit., 1994; assoc. editor: Veterinary Pathology, 1989—91, reviewer: jours., mem. editl. bd.: Am. Jour. Vet. Rsch., 1979—81, Vet. Clin. Pathology, 1982—. Mem.: AAVMC (pres.-elect 2001), Am. Coll. Vet. Pathologists (bd. cert. in vet. pathology, bd. cert. vet. clin. pathology, pres. 1985, counselor 1980—86, mem. various coms. 1972—89). Office: U Ga Coll Vet Medicine Athens GA 30602-7371

PRATER, ELNER W. elementary school educator; b. Balt. d. Eustice Darrow and Lucy James Watson; 1 child, Albert W. Prater Jr. BS in Edn., Towson State U., Md., 1967; MS in Reading, Johns Hopkins U., Balt., 1976; EdD in Leadership, Morgan State U., Balt., 1988—90. Cert. tchr. Md. Tchr. Balt. City Pub. Sch. System, 1970—. Writer, columnist Afro-Am. Newspaper, Balt., 1990—92; ESOL instr. Balt. City C.C., 1999—. Mem. Balt. County Commn. for, Md. Coun. of Children, Youth and Families, Balt.; sec. WIN of NAACP, Balt.; writer Bapt. Congress of Christian Edn., Balt. Recipient Plaque, Parents of Students, Balt. Mem.: Md. TESOL, Phi Delta Kappa, Sigma Gamma Rho. Baptist. Avocations: sewing, dance, chess, creative writing, singing.

PRATER, ROBERT STANLEY, JR., broker; b. Atlanta, Feb. 15, 1965; s. Robert Stanley and Linda Lynne (Haney) P.; m. Mary Jo Grippo, Oct. 5, 1996; children: Alison Christine, Robert III. BBA in Fin., U. Ga., 1987; MBA in Fin., Wake Forest U., 1990. Sr. analyst Pepsico, N.Y.C., 1990-92; 1st v.p. Interstate/Johnson Lane, Atlanta, 1992-97; investment ptnr. J.C. Bradford, Atlanta, 1997—. Baptist. Office: J C Bradford & Co 3060 Peachtree Rd NW Atlanta GA 30305-2234

PRATHER, GERALD LUTHER, management consultant, retired air force officer, judge; b. LaGrange, Ga., Apr. 7, 1935; s. Luther Pate and Hazel Belle (McCullough) P.; m. Carolyn Pearson, Nov. 22, 1956; children: Dean Allen, Bryan Pate, Jeri Lynn, Angela BSE.E., Auburn U., 1966; MS in Mgmt., Air Force Inst. Tech., 1972; postgrad. advanced mgmt., U. Houston, 1978; grad., SQ Officer Sch., Maxwell AFB, 1963, ICAF, Washington, 1974. Enlisted USAF, 1954-56, commd. 2d lt., 1956, advanced through grades to maj. gen., 1981, various assignments as pilot, 1956-68, served in Vietnam, 1967-68, commdr. 1963d Comm. Squadron, 1968-69, comdr. 1918th Comm. Squadron Scott AFB, Ill., 1969-70, dep. dir. comm.-electronics for 15th Air Force March AFB, Calif., 1970-72, chief comm. ops. div. hdqrs. Washington, 1972-75, comdr. strategic comm. div. Offutt AFB, Nebr., 1975-77, comdr. European Comm. Div. Ramstein AFB, W. Ger., 1977-80; dir. Command Control, Comm. & Computer Systems, Hdqrs. U.S. Readiness Command MacDill AFB, Fla., 1980-81; asst. chief of staff of Info. Systems Hdqrs. USAF, Washington, 1981-84, comdr. Air Force Comm. Command Scott AFB, Ill., 1984-86, ret., 1986; pvt. practice mgmt. cons. Del Rio, Tex., 1986-1997; Justice of the Peace Val Verde County, Tex., 1987-97. Lectr. in field; also air traffic controller, parachutist. Speech writer Team America 1983 (Freedom Found. nat. award 1984). Scoutmaster Boy Scouts Am., Sacramento, 1963, chmn. com., 1964, cub master Auburn, Ala.; sponsor Explorer Troop, Boy Scouts Am., Scott AFB, Ill., 1969; chmn. Amistad Dist. Boy Scouts Am., 1988, Eagle Scout advancement, 1994—2004, Val Verde County United Way campaign, 1989,

pres., bd. dirs., 1990; pastoral counselor St. James Ch., 2002, pastoral care specialist, 2002—; chaplain Val Verde Regional Hosp., 2002—, Juvenile Detention Ctr., 1998—. Decorated DSM with oak leaf cluster, Legion of Merit with one oak leaf cluster, DFC, Bronze Star with V device, Air medal with two oak leaf clusters, Republic of Vietnam Gallantry Cross with Palm; recipient Gen. Edwin W. Rawlings award Air Force Inst. Tech., 1972, Comdt.'s award, 1972, also numerous other decorations and awards; recipient Silver Beaver award Boy Scouts Am., 2003. Mem.: VFW (life), Army Airways Comm. Svc. Alumni Assn. (dir. 2000—), Del Rio C. of C. (v.p. 1989—90, bd. dirs. 1990—99, v.p. 1991—92, pres. 1995—96, v.p. 1995—96, 1995—96, bd. dirs. 1999—2000), Air Force Assn. (Jimmy Doolittle award 1984), Telephone Pioneers of Am., Soc. Logistics Engrs., Justice of the Peace and Constables Assn., Soc. Am. Mil. Engrs., Air Traffic Control Assn., Armed Forces Comm.-Electronics Assn. (mem. com. 1981—82, chmn. ethics com. 1982—83, internat. v.p. 1982—84, assoc. dir. 1984—96, Meritorious Gold medal 1976, 1983), Non-Commd. Officers Assn. (hon.), Air Force Sgts. Assn. (hon.), Disabled Am. Vets. (life), Ret. Officers Assn. (life), Vietnam Vets. Am. (life), Del Rio Club, Lions (dir. 1989—94, v.p. 1994, Svc. award 1992—93, 2002—03), Civitan, Am. Legion, Order of Daedalians (life). Avocations: singing, gardening, sketching, automotive mechanics, private pilot. Address: HC 1 Box 7 Del Rio TX 78840-9720 Office Phone: 830-774-4483. Personal E-mail: prather@delrio.com.

PRATHER, JOHN GIDEON, lawyer; b. Somerset, Ky., Dec. 12, 1919; s. James Frederick and Josephine Linnwood (Collier) Prather; m. Marie Jeanette Moore, Oct. 1945; children: John G., Jerome Moore. BA, U. Ky., 1940, JD, 1947. Bar: Ky. 1947, U.S. Dist. Ct. (ea. dist.) Ky. 1950. Pros. atty., Somerset, 1950—63; commonwealth atty. 28th Jud. Dist., 1963—64; sole practice Somerset; sr. ptnr. Law Offices of John G. Prather, Somerset. Bd. dirs. First & Farmers Bank, Somerset. Served to lt. USN, 1942—46. Mem.: ABA (probate sect.), Def. Rsch. Inst., Ky. Bar Assn. (ethics com., com. on fees), Pulaski County Bar Assn., Odd Fellows, Shriners, Kiwanis. Democrat. Mem. Christian Ch. (Disciples Of Christ). Office: PO Box 616 Somerset KY 42502-0616 Office Phone: 606-679-1626.

PRATHER, KENNETH EARL, lawyer; b. Detroit, May 9, 1933; s. Earl and Agnes (Mesanko) P.; m. Shirley Armstrong, Dec. 26, 1955; children: Eric, Kimberly, Jon, Laura, Lisa; m. Jeanette M. Elder, June 30, 1973; 1 child, Kenneth. PhB, U. Detroit, 1955, JD 1960. Bar: Mich. 1960. Assoc. Kenney, Radom, Rockwell & Kenney, Detroit, 1960-66; ptnr. Kenney, Kenney, Chapman & Prather, Detroit, 1966-76; pvt. practice, Detroit, 1976-82; ptnr. Prather, Hilborn & Harrington, P.C., Detroit, 1982, Prather & Assocs., P.C., Detroit, 1982—; adj. prof. law U. Detroit. Fellow Am. Acad. Matrimonial Lawyers (bd. govs. 1988-89), Internat. Acad. Matrimonial Lawyers (bd. mgrs. 1989); mem. Am. Coll. Family Law Trial Lawyers, State Bar Mich. (chairperson family law sect. 1983-84), Detroit Athletic. Contbr. articles to legal jours. Home: 5 Stratford Pl Grosse Pointe MI 48230-1907 Office: Kenneth E Prather Sr PC 19846 Mack Ave Grosse Pointe Woods MI 48236 E-mail: kprather@quixnet.net.

PRATHER, LENORE LOVING, former state supreme court chief justice; b. West Point, Miss., Sept. 17, 1931; d. Byron Herald and Hattie Hearn (Morris) Loving; m. Robert Brooks Prather, May 30, 1957; children: Pamela, Valerie Jo, Malinda Wayne. BS, Miss. Univ. Women, 1953; JD, U. Miss., 1955; D (hon.), Miss. Univ. Women, 2003. Bar: Miss. 1955. Practice with B. H. Loving, West Point, 1955-60; sole practice, 1960-62, 65-71; assoc. practice, 1962-65; mcpl. judge City of West Point, 1965-71; chancery ct. judge 14th dist. State of Miss., Columbus, 1971-82, supreme ct. justice Jackson, 1982-92, presiding justice, 1993-97, chief justice, 1998-2001; interim pres. Miss. U. for Women, Columbus, Miss., 2001—02. V.p. Conf. Local Bar Assn., 1956-58; sec. Clay County Bar Assn., 1956-71 1st woman in Miss. to become chancery judge, 1971, and supreme ct. justice, 1982, and chief justice, 1998-2000. Mem. Miss. State Bar Assn., DAR, Rotary, Pilot Club, Jr. Aux. Columbus Club. Episcopalian.

PRATHER, ROBERT CHARLES, SR., lawyer; b. Kansas City, Mo., Feb. 16, 1945; s. Charles William and Shirley Anne P.; m. Lana Jo Ball, Jan. 25, 1969; children: Robert Charles Jr., Lisa Michelle. BSc in Comm., U. Tex., 1967, JD, 1970; postgrad., U. Tasmania, Australia, 1968. Bar: Tex. 1971, U.S. Dist. Ct. (no. dist.) Tex. 1978, U.S. Ct. Appeals (5th and 11th cirs.) 1981, U.S. Supreme Ct. 1978. Staff atty., com. clk. Senator W.T. Moore State Affairs Com. Tex. State Senate, Austin, 1971; asst. dist. atty. Dallas, 1971-74; asst. atty. U.S. No. Dist. Tex., Dalls, 1974-80; econ. crime enforcement specialist U.S. Dept. Justice, Dallas, 1980-81; assoc. trial atty. Turner, Rodgers, Sailers, Jordan & Calloway, Dallas, 1981-83; ptnr., trial atty. Jordan, Dunlap, Prather & Harris LLP, Dallas, 1983—. Author: (with others) A Document Numbering System, 1981, Texas ADR Practice Guide West, 1995. Gen. counsel, bd. dirs. Childrens Cancer Fund Dallas, Inc., 1982-91; soccer coach YMCA, North Dallas C. of C., 1979-84. Recipient Spl. Achievement award U.S. Dept. Justice, Washington, 1976; Rotary Found. fellow, 1968. Mem. ABA, Dallas Bar Assn., Assn. Atty.-Mediators (pres. North Tex. chpt. 2003), Am. Arbitration Assn. (panel 1992—), Argyle Club (pres. Dallas), Park City Club (bd. dirs.), Rotary (parliamentarian, bd. dirs.), Phi Alpha Delta. Baptist. Office: Jordan Dunlap Prather & Harris LLP 8111 Preston Rd Ste 400 Dallas TX 75225-6373 Business E-Mail: prather@jdplegal.com.

PRATHER, ROBERT FRANKLIN, fund administrator; b. N.Y.C., Aug. 20, 1935; s. Theodore Roosevelt and Evelyn Trimarco P.; m. Jessie Holtby Prather, Nov. 14, 1959 (dec. Jan. 1989); children: Craig, Keith, Debra Jo, Todd, Adam, Jennifer; m. Monica Marshall Prather, Feb. 10, 1990; children: Kathy, Natalie. BS in Journalism, Ohio U., 1957; MA, Columbia U., 1964, EdD, 1981. Mng. editor Corning (N.Y.) Glass Works, 1964-66; dir. devel. The Coll. of Ins., N.Y.C., 1966-73; v.p. for devel. Mercyhurst Coll., Erie, Pa., 1973-80, Olivet (Mich.) Coll., 1980-82; v.p. univ. rels. Tiffin (Ohio) U., 1984-86; pres. W.Va. Found. for Ind. Colls., Charleston, 1986-93, Tex. Ind. Coll. Fund, Fort Worth, 1993—. Presiding officer Found. for Ind. Higher Edn., Washington, 1998-2001, southwestern regional rep., 1995-98, midwestern regional rep., 1990-93, dir., 1995—. Edn. com. State of W.Va., Charleston, 1990-93, advanced placement adv. com., 1990-93; pres. Erie (Pa.) Playhouse, 1973-80; co-pres. Coun. on Adoptable Children, Erie, 1973-80. Capt. U.S. Army, 1957-59, 61-62. Mem. Fort Worth Rotary, Found. for Ind. Higher Edn. (dir 1995—). Democrat. Avocations: reading, thinking. Office: Tex Ind Coll Fund 4200 S Hulen St Ste 314 Fort Worth TX 76109 E-mail: ticf@mindspring.com.

PRATHER, SUSAN LYNN, public relations executive; b. Melrose Park, Ill. d. Horace Charles and Ruth Anna Paula (Backus) P.; divorced. BS, Ind. U., 1973, MS, 1975. Arts administr. Lyric Opera Chgo., 1975; jr. account exec. Morton H. Kaplan Assocs., Chgo., 1976-78, sr. account exec., 1978-81; account supr. Ketchum Pub. Relations, Chgo., 1981-83, v.p., 1983-87, v.p., group mgr., 1985-87; v.p., dir. pub. relations Cramer-Krasselt, Chgo., 1987-95, sr. v.p., dir. pub. rels., 1996—. Cons. Velamints, Foster Wheeler, Kellogg Co., Battle Creek, Mich., 1985—, Village of Rosemont, Ill., PrincCo Personal Comm., Sr. Friendlys, Anti-Cruelty Soc. Chgo., Ill. State Toll Hwy. Authority. Singer various recitals; founder, dir. Chgo. Sports Hall of Fame, 1978-81. Mem. archives com. Chgo. Symphony Orch., 1986—, mem. long term planning com., 1987-89; mem. press advance team Papal Visit to Chgo., 1978; mem. White House Press Advance Team, Chgo., 1976-80. Mem. Pub. Rels. Soc. Am. (bd. dirs. Chgo. chpt. 1987—), Internat. Pub. Rels. Assn., Publicity Club (bd. dirs. 1986—, Merit award 1982, Golden Trumpet awards, Silver Trumpet awards), Bus. and Profl. Assn. Lutheran. Avocation: figure skating. Home: 155 N Harbor Dr Apt 2212 Chicago IL 60601-7321

PRATHER, WILLIAM C., III, lawyer, writer; b. Toledo, Ill., Feb. 20, 1921; s. Hollie Cartmill and Effie Fern (Deppen) P. BA, U. Ill., 1942, JD, 1947. Bar: Ill. 1947, U.S. Supreme Ct. 1978. Co-pres. student govt. U. Ill., 1942, asst. dean, 1942-43; atty. First Nat. Bank Chgo., 1947-51; asst. gen. counsel U.S. Savs. and Loan League, Chgo., 1951-59; gen. counsel U.S. League of Savs. Instns., Chgo., 1959-82, gen. counsel emeritus, 1982—; sole practice Cumberland County, Ill., 1981—. Sem. lectr. in law, banking. Editor: The Legal Bulletin, 1951-81, The Federal Guide, 1954-81; author: Savings Accounts, 8th edit., 1981; contbr. articles to publs. Lt. U.S. Armed Forces, 1943-45. Decorated Bronze Star. Mem. ABA, FBA, Internat. Bar Assn., Ill. Bar Assn., Chgo. Bar Assn., Union Internat. des Avocats, Nat. Lawyers Club Washington, Cosmos Club, Univ. Club Chgo., Kiwanis, Mattoon Golf and Country Club, Exeter and County Club (Eng.), Am. Club Riviera (France), Tennis Club de Beaulieu (France), Soc. Colonial Wars, St. Andrew's Soc., Am. Legion, Phi Delta Phi, Phi Gamma Delta, Phi Eta Sigma, Phi Alpha Chi. Home: Applewood Farm PO Box 157 Toledo IL 62468-0157 Office: 142 Courthouse Sq Toledo IL 62468 also: L'Orangeraie 42 Av General Leclerc Villefranche-sur-Mer 06230 France

PRATO, KIMBERLY, public affairs officer; b. Waterbury, Conn., June 13, 1967; d. Thomas Elia Dimo and Gayla Belle Owens; m. Anthony Wayne Prto, June 8, 1991; children: Anthony, Nicholas. BA, Cen. Conn. State U., 1990; MA, U. Okla., 1998; cert. in pub. affairs, Def. Info. Sch., Ft. George Meade, Md., 1998. Anchorperson, promotional dir. Sta. WTLV, Jacksonville, 1990-93; newsrier Sta. KUSI-TV, San Diego, 1995-96; pub. affairs officer U.S. Dept. Army, Torii Sta., Japan, 1996-99, U.S. Dept. of Navy, Camp Pendleton, Calif., 1999—. Editor (manual) for Am. Assn. for Critical Care Nurses, (story) for Am. Chiropractic Assn., 2000. Mem. Oceanside (Calif.) Editl. Adv. Com., 1999—. Mem. Am. Soc. for Pub. Adminstrn., Healthcare Consumer Coun. Republican. Roman Catholic. Avocations: scuba diving, horseback riding, golf, running. Home: 3785 Carnegie Dr Oceanside CA 92056 Office: US Dept Navy Box 555191 Camp Pendleton CA 92055

PRATS, MICHAEL, petroleum engineer, educator; b. Tampa, Fla., Dec. 18, 1925; s. Miguel and Maria (Carbó) P.; m. Mary Blanche Flaherty, Apr. 7, 1951; children: Delicia Anne, Barbara Eileen, Teresa Kaye, Steven Michael. BS in Physics, U. Tex., 1949, MA in Physics, 1951. With Shell Devel. Co., Houston, 1950—, cons. research engr., then sr. research assoc., 1972-89; pres. Michael Prats & Assocs., Houston, 1989—. Cons. prof. petroleum engring. dept. Stanford U., 1997—99; adj. prof. dept. geosystems petroleum engring. U. Tex., Austin, 1991—2001; participant scientist exch. Royal/Dutch Shell Lab., Amsterdam, Netherlands, 1954, 55, Shell Internat. Petroleum, The Hague, Netherlands, 1981, Maraven, S.A., Caracas, Venezuela, 1981-83. Author: Thermal Recovery, 1982, Spanish transl., 1987; contbr. articles to profl. jours.; 23 patents in field. Served to staff sgt. USAAF, 1944-46, PTO. Recipient Diploma of Honor Pi Epsilon Tau, 1986, Disting. Svc. award Rep. Honduras, 1989, Thermal Recovery Disting. Achievement award SPE Thermal Ops. Symposium, 1991, KAPITSA medal Acad. Natural Scis. (Moscow), 1995; named to Internat. Hall of Fame, 1989. Mem. AIME (hon.), NAE, Soc. Petroleum Engrs. (hon., bd. dirs. 1976-79, sr. tech. editor 1987-90, Enhanced Oil Recovery Pioneer 1986, Uren award 1974, Disting. Mem. award 1983, Anthony F. Lucas Gold medal 1993), Acad. Medicine, Engring. and Sci. of Tex., Can. Inst. Mining, Asociacion De Ingenieros Petroleros De Mexico, Mex. Nat. Acad. Engring. (corr.), Acad. Engring. Armenia (fgn. mem.), Russian Acad. Nat. Scis. (fgn.), Pi Epsilon Tau (hon.). Avocation: travel. Address: 2834 Bellefontaine St Houston TX 77025-1610 E-mail: mikep@mprats.com.

PRATSCH, LLOYD WILMER, government official; b. Green Bay, Wis., Dec. 28, 1941; s. Lloyd Anthony and Blanche (Goffard) P.; m. Rita Noel Wormley, Feb. 16, 1974; children: Candice, Laurie. BA, U. Wis., 1964, postgrad., 1964-66. With Dept. Army, 1966-71, Dept. Interior, 1971-86, Dept. Commerce, 1986-87; dir. procurement svcs. divsn. Dept. Treasury, Washington, 1987-92; procurement exec. Dept. State, Washington, 1992—. Pres. Fox Lake Property Owners Assn., Oakton, Va., 1990-92. With USMCR, 1966-72. Avocations: swimming, skiing. Home: 11217 Sweetwood Ln Oakton VA 22124-1327 E-mail: pratschlw@state.gov.

PRATS PALERM, ROBERT L. political party chairman; b. San Juan, P.R., 1966; m. Heddle Fernandez; 2 children. Degree, Cornell U., 1990; postgrad., Georgetown U., 1991—92; JD, Inter-Am. U. P.R., 1994. Notary pub. Aux. advisor Gov. Rafael Hernandez Columbus, 1990—91; mem. staff U.S. Congress, Washington, 1991—92; econ. advisor, minority spokesman P.R. Senate, 1993—94, senator, 2000—, pres. commn. govt. and pub. security; atty. Goldman, Antonetti & Córdova, 1995—97; advisor, coords. pub. rels. Municipality of San Juan, 1997—99; pvt. practice atty., 2000; Dem. Party chmn., 2003—. V.p. infrastructure, technol. devel., commerce and govtl. integrity, property, appointments, legal, internat. and fed. subjects, mcpl. govt. commns. P.R. Senate, also mem. pub. corps. and urban subjects commns. Fundraising participant Alzheimer's Assn., PR, 2002; mem. adv. bd. Cornell U., Ithaca, NY. Office: PR Dem Party Chmn PO Box 9023431 San Juan PR 00902 Business E-Mail: rprats@legislatura.gov.pr.*

PRATT, CARIN, television executive; b. Marshfield, Mass., Aug. 22, 1956; m. John Echeverria; children: Nicholas, Edward. BA, Harvard U., 1978. Staff mem. Nieman Found. Harvard U., Boston, 1977-79; staff mem. Tex. R.R. Commn. Campaign, 1979-80; asst. to Tex. bur. chief Washington Post, Austin, 1981-83, rschr., 1981-83, editor, 1981-83; asst. to assoc. prodr. Face the Nation CBS News, N.Y.C., 1984-87, sr. prodr. Face the Nation, 1987-93, exec. prodr., Face the Nation with Bob Schieffer, 1993—. Office: CBS News 2020 M St NW Washington DC 20036-3369

PRATT, DANA JOSEPH, publishing consultant; b. Cambridge, Mass., Dec. 9, 1926; s. Carroll Cornelius and Marjory (Bates) P.; m. Therese Louis, July 14, 1957; children: Joseph Caldwell, Michael Louis, Benjamin Lyon B.Naval Sci., Tufts U., 1946, BA, 1948. Mgmt. trainee N.J. Bell Telephone Co., Newark, 1948-50; sales asst. Princeton U. Press, N.J., 1950-53; sales mgr. U. Ill. Press, Urbana, 1953-55; field cons. Franklin Book Programs, N.Y.C., 1955-59; staff assoc. Am. Book Pubs. Council, N.Y.C., 1959-62; exec. sec. Assn. Am. Univ. Presses, N.Y.C., 1962-66; asst. dir. Yale U. Press, New Haven, 1966-78; dir. pub. Library of Congress, Washington, 1978-93. Contbr. articles to profl. jours. Served as ensign USNR, comdg. officer PC 566, 1946-47 Recipient Award for Superior Svc. Libr. of Congress, 1993. Mem. Washington Book Pubs. (pres. 1984-85), Soc. for Scholarly Pub. (bd. dirs. 1982-86), Washington Map Soc., Washington Rare Book Group. Home and Office: 7514 Old Chester Rd Bethesda MD 20817-6163 Office Phone: 301-320-2538. E-mail: danajpratt@aol.com.

PRATT, DIANE ADELE, talented and gifted education educator; b. Battle Creek, Mich., Oct. 24, 1951; d. John Robert and Kathleen Adele (Cooper) Dickert; m. Stephen Howard Pratt, Apr. 29, 1972; children: Eric Stephen, Elizabeth Adele. BS, Western Mich. U., 1972; MS in Edn., Buenta Vista U., 2000. Endorsement K-12 talented and gifted, Iowa. Elem. tchr. Berea (Ohio) Cmty. Schs., 1973-76; tchr. Lemon Tree Nursery Sch., Battle Creek, 1985-88; elem. tchr. Ft. Dodge (Iowa) Cmty. Schs., 1976-78, middle sch. tchr., 1990—, team leader, 1994-97, tchr. talented and gifted, 1997—, advisor talented and gifted for H.S., 2002—. Chearleading coach Ft. Dodge Sr. H.S., 1997-99, 2000-01, Pep Club advisor, 1997-99; advt. exec. Ft. Dodge Today mag., 1989-92; ednl. tutor, Battle Creek, Ft. Dodge, 1986-96; mem. adv. bd. Inst. for Instrn. Svcs., Battle Creek, 1984-88; dir., instr. Battle Creek Presch. Enrichment Program, 1984; chmn. Ft. Dodge Supr.'s Comty. Com. to Study K-8 Curriculum, 1988-89, facilitator K-3 human growth and devel. curriculum, 1989-92; mem. standing com. early childhood needs assessment com. Ft. Dodge Comty. Schs., 1989-95; mem. adv. bd., instr. Kids on Kampus Iowa Ctrl. C.C., Ft. Dodge, 1990-95; trustee Ft. Dodge Comty. Sch. Found. Bd., 1992-97, mem. talented and gifted selection com. Ft. Dodge Comty. Schs., 1993—, mem. promotion taskforce, 1998-99; mem. pub. rels. com. Ft. Dodge Comty. Sch. Dist., 1992-94, mem. ednl. outcomes standing com., 1993-94. Author, editor Headcase and various newsletters. Mem., past chmn. bd. Christian edn. 1st Bapt. Ch., Ft. Dodge, 1978-79, 89-96, music com., 1992-94, dir. children's choirs, 1988-90, mem. bell choir, 1990-91, ch. sch. supt. 1993-96, pastoral rels. com., 1997-99; neighborhood coord. mothers' march March of Dimes, Battle Creek, 1981-83, Ft. Dodge, 1999—; troop leader Lakota coun. Girl Scouts U.S., 1988-90; pres. La Mora Park PTA, 1985-87, Phillips Mid Sch. PTA, Ft. Dodge, 1990-91; bd. dirs. Main Stage Players, jr. theater, Ft. Dodge, 1990-91; sec., pres. Jr. Women's Club, Ft. Dodge, 1977-80; mem. kickoff com. United Way, 1991, Curriculum Instn. Adv. Coun., 2001-, Insvc. Adv. Com., 2000—; tchr. mentor, 2001-; bd. dirs. Nat. Coun. on Youth Leadership, Ft. Dodge, 2002—. Recipient Mem. of Yr. award La Mora Park PTA, 1987, Iowa Talented and Gifted Rsch. award, 2000, David Belin Excellence in Tchg. award, 2000. Mem. NEA, ASCD, AAUW (sec., pres. Battle Creek br. 1986-88), PEO (N.J. chpt., Ft. Dodge chpt. 1990-94), Iowa Edn. Assn., Ft. Dodge Edn. Assn., Iowa Assn. Middle Level Educators, Iowa Assn. for Talented and Gifted (bd. dirs. 2001—), Study Club (treas. 1999-2000, pres. 2000-02), Nat. Assn. Gifted Children, Delta Kappa Gamma, Kappa Delta Pi Hon. Soc. Presbyterian. Avocations: educational research, cross country skiing. Home: 1851 9th Ave N Fort Dodge IA 50501

PRATT, DONALD GEORGE, physician; b. Higgins, Tex., Oct. 19, 1946; s. George Horace and Esta Vici (Barker) P. BS in Biomed. Sci., West Tex. State U., 1970; MD, U. Tex., Galveston, 1974. Diplomate Am. Bd. Family Practice, Am. Bd. Radiology (Radiation Oncology). Intern Scott & White Meml. Hosp., Temple, Tex., 1974-75, resident in gen. surgery and pathology, 1975-77, physician, 1979-83; resident in family practice McLennan County Med. Edn. and Rsch. Found., Waco, Tex., 1977-79; physician Family Practice Assocs., El Paso, Tex., 1983; owner, pvt. contractor Minor Emergency Ctrs., Amarillo, Tex., 1983-85; resident in radiation therapy U. Tex., Galveston, 1985-88; ptnr. Cons. in Radiation Oncology, P.A., Amarillo, 1988—2003, pres., 1994—2003, Cons. in Radiation Oncology, 1994—2003; dir. dept. radiation oncology Harrington Cancer Ctr., Amarillo, 1994—2003, pres. staff, bd. dirs., 1995-99; prin. investigator Radiation Oncology Group, 1988-95; pres. of staff Harrington Cancer Ctr., 1995—99; ptnr. Cons. in Radiation Oncology, P.A., Amarillo, 1988—2003, pres., 1994—2003; cons. in radiation oncology, 1994—2003. Dir. Dept. Radiation Oncology Harrington Cancer Ctr., Amarillo, Tex., 1994—2003. Mem. AMA, Am. Soc. Therapeutic Radiology and Oncology, Tex. Med. Assn., Potter/Randall County Med. Soc., Tex. Radiol. Soc. Home: 261 S Timbercreek Dr Amarillo TX 79118-3751 Office: Cons Radiation Oncology PA 1600 Coulter Dr Ste 402 Amarillo TX 79106-1721

PRATT, GEORGE CHENEY, law educator, retired federal judge; b. Corning, N.Y., May 22, 1928; s. George Wollage and Muriel (Cheney) Pratt; m. Carol June Hoffman, Aug. 16, 1952; children: George W., Lise M., Marcia Pratt Burke, William T. BA, Yale U., 1950, JD, 1953. Bar: N.Y. 1953, U.S. Supreme Ct. 1964, U.S. Ct. Appeals 1974. Law clk. to Charles W. Froessel (Judge of N.Y. Ct. Appeals), 1953—55; assoc. then ptnr. Sprague & Stern, Mineola, NY, 1956—60; ptnr. Andromidas, Pratt & Pitcher, Mineola, 1960—65, Pratt, Caemmerer & Cleary, Mineola, 1965—75; partner Farrell, Fritz, Pratt, Caemmerer & Cleary, 1975—76; judge U.S. Dist. Ct. (Ea. Dist. of N.Y.), 1976—82, U.S. Cir. Ct. Appeals for 2d cir. (Uniondale), NY, 1982—93; sr. circ. judge U.S. Cir. of Appeals for 2d Cir., NY, 1993—95; counsel Parnon & Pratt L.L.P., N.Y.C., 1995—2000, Farrell Fritz PC, 2001—. Prof. Touro Law Sch., Huntington, NY, 1993—2003. Fellow: Coll. Comml. Arbitrators; mem.: ABA, Nassau County Bar Assn., N.Y. State Bar Assn. United Ch. Of Christ. Office: Farrell Fritz PC EAB Plaza West Tower 14th Fl Uniondale NY 11556-0120 Office Phone: 516-227-0604. E-mail: gpratt@farrellfritz.com.

PRATT, GEORGE JANES, JR., psychologist, author; b. Mpls., May 3, 1948; s. George Janes and Sally Elvina (Hanson) P.; m. Vonda Pratt; 1 child, Whitney Beth. BA cum laude, U. Minn., 1970, MA, 1973; PhD with spl. commendation, Calif. Sch. Profl. Psychology, San Diego, 1976. Diplomate Am. Bd. Med. Psychotherapists, Am. Acad. Pain Mgmt., Am. Coll. Forensic Examiners, Am. Assn. Integrative Medicine; lic. psychologist, Calif., 1976. Psychology trainee Ctr. for Behavior Modification, Mpls., 1971-72, U.Minn. Student Counseling Bur., 1972-73; predoctoral clin. psychology intern San Bernardino County (Calif.) Mental Health Svcs., 1973-74, San Diego County Mental Health Services, 1974-76; mem. staff San Louis Rey Hosp., 1977-78; postdoctoral clin. psychology intern Mesa Vista Hosp., San Diego, Calif., 1976; clin psychologist, dir. Psychology and Cons. Assocs. of San Diego, 1976-90; chmn. Psychology and Cons. Assocs. Press, 1977-94. Bd. dirs. Optimax, Inc., 1985-94; pres. George Pratt Ph.D., Psychol. Corp., 1979—; chmn. Pratt, Korn & Assocs., Inc., 1984-94; mem. staff Scripps Meml. Hosp., La Jolla, Calif., 1986—, chmn. psychology, 1993-95, 2000—; founder La Jolla Profl. Workshops, 1977-81; clin. psychologist El Camino Psychology Ctr., San Clemente, Calif., 1977-78; grad. teaching asst. U. Minn. Psychology and Family Studies divsn., 1971; teaching assoc. U. Minn. Psychology and Family Studies divsn., Mpls., 1972-73; instr. U. Minn. Extension divsn., Mpls., 1971-73; faculty Calif. Sch. Profl. Psychology, 1974-83, San Diego Evening Coll., 1975-77, Nat. U., 1978-79, Chapman Coll., 1978, San Diego State U., 1979-80; vis. prof. Pepperdine U., L.A., 1976-78; cons. U. Calif. at San Diego Med. Sch., 1976-78, also instr. univ., 1978—; psychology chmn. Workshops in Clin. Hypnosis, 1980-84; cons. Calif. Health Dept., 1974, Naval Regional Med. Ctr., 1978-82, ABC-TV; also speaker. Author: Sensory/Progressive Relaxation, 1979, Effective Stress Management, 1979, Clinical Hypnosis: Techniques and Applications, 1985, Rx for Stress, 1994; co-author: A Clinical Hypnosis Primer, 1984, 88, HyperPerformance, 1987, Release Your Business Potential, 1988, Instant Emotional Healing, 2000, Emotional Self-Management, 2000; contbr.: Hypnosis: Questions and Answers, 1986, Handbook for Hypnotic Suggestions and Metaphors, 1990, Imagery in Sports and Physical Performance, 1994. With USAR, 1970-76. Fellow Am. Soc. Clin. Hypnosis (cert., approved cons.); mem. APA, Nat. Register of Health Svc. Providers in Psychology, Internat. Soc. Hypnosis, Am. Assn. Sex Educators, Counselors and Therapists (cert.), San Diego Soc. Sex. Therapy and Edn. (past pres.), San Diego Soc. Clin. Hypnosis (past pres.), San Diego Psychol. Assn., Am. Assn. Integrative Medicine, U. Minn. Alumni Assn., Beta Theta Pi. Office: Scripps Meml Hosp Campus 9834 Genesee Ave Ste 321 La Jolla CA 92037-1216 Home: 1127 Muirlands Vista Way La Jolla CA 92037-6210 Office Phone: 858-457-3900.

PRATT, HARRY DAVIS, retired entomologist; b. North Adams, Mass., Apr. 13, 1915; s. Harry Edward and Ethel Mae (Davis) P.; m. Caroline Georgine Kreiss, Apr. 13, 1944 (dec. May 1951); children: Harry Davis Jr., Katherine Maria Pratt Garrison, George Kreiss; m. Dora Belle Ford, Nov. 29, 1952 (dec. July 1998). BS, Mass. State Coll., 1936, MS, 1938; PhD, U. Minn., St. Paul, 1941. Registered profl. entomologist. Asst. entomologist USPHS Malaria Control War Areas, San Juan, P.R., 1942-46; chief med. entomol. lab. USPHS Communicable Disease Ctr., Atlanta, 1946-53, chief insect rodent tr., 1953-63, chief Aedes aegypti control tng., 1964-68; chief insect rodent control tng. Environ. Control Agy., Atlanta, 1968-72; cons., tchr., writer Atlanta, 1972—. Spl. cons. Econ. Coop. Administrn., Saigon, Vietnam, 1950, WHO, Geneva, 1966, Kuala Lumpur, Malaysia, 1969. Fellow Entomol. Soc. Am. (life); mem. Am. Mosquito Control Assn. (pres. 1967), Entol. Soc. Washington, Ga. Entomol. Soc. Mem. Christian Ch. (Disciples Of Christ). Home: 104 So Almond Dr Simpsonville SC 29681 Office Phone: 864-228-4941. Personal E-mail: hdpsr@juno.com.

PRATT, HELEN DIANN, clinical psychologist, educator; b. Du Quoin, Ill., Dec. 14, 1947; d. Herbert and Nellie Delois (Sadberry) McCall; m. Robert Edward Pratt, Sept. 20, 1979; children: Kevin, Terry, Jeffery, Brandy, Robert Edward III. BA summa cum laude, Western Mich. U., 1980, MA, 1984, PhD in Clin. Psychology, 1988. Lic. clin. psychologist, Mich. Clin. psychologist Pratt and Assocs. Human Svcs. Consultants, Kalamazoo, 1986—; psychologist Kalamazoo Regional Psychiat. Hosp., 1986-91; clin. psychologist Mich. State U./Kalamzaoo Ctr. Med. Studies, 1991—. Asst. adj. prof. Western Mich. U.; asst. prof. pediatrics and human devel. Coll. Human Medicine, Mich. State U., 1991-94; clin. dir. adolescent behavioral medicine Kalamazoo Ctr. for Med. Studies, 1991—. Vol. Kalamazoo area Boy Scouts Am., 1972-85; vol. Big Bros.-Big Sisters, 1981-84, bd. dirs., 1984-85; bd. dirs. East Side Community Assn., Kalamazoo, 1981-84, Eastman Pre-Sch., Kalamazoo. Waldo Sangren scholar, 1978-80, Am. Bus. Women's Assn. scholar, 1978, Thurgood Marshall scholar, 1980-83. Merm. APA, Assn. Behavior Analysis, Mich. Psychol. Assn., Western Psychol. Assn., Assn. for Advancement of Behavior Therapists, Ministry with Cmty. (bd. dirs. 1992-95, pres. 1995), Altrusa (pres., bd. dirs. Kalamazoo chpt.). Methodist. Home: 2988 N 30th St Kalamazoo MI 49048-9211 Office: Spectrum Adolescent Behavioral Medicine Bldg B 4341 S Westnedge Ave Ste 2215 Kalamazoo MI 49008-3289

PRATT, IRENE AGNES, state legislator; b. Jaffrey, N.H., Mar. 30, 1924; m. Philip E. Pratt (dec.); 4 children. Student, U. N.H., Mass. Gen. Sch. Nursing, 1946. N.H. state rep.; mem. children and family law com. N.H. Ho. of Reps.; ret. pub. health nurse Dept. Health, N.H., 1988. Bd. dirs. Monadnock Family Svc., 1984-89, Big Bros. & Big Sisters of Monadnock Region, 1984-89; active

Home Health Care & Comty. Svc.; Keene Interdisciplinary Child Abuse Team, 1980-88. Mem. C&H Health Sys. Monadnock Region. Office: NH State Senate Legislative Office Bldg Concord NH 03301

PRATT, JACK E., SR., hotel executive; b. 1927; Commd. USAF, 1942, advanced through grades, resigned, 1951; ptnr. Wes-Tex Vending Co., 1951—; founder, ptnr. Dairy Queen, Mineral Wells, Tex., 1954-64, Bonanza Steakhouse Restaurants, Tex., 1964-68; chmn., CEO Pratt Hotel Corp., Dallas, 1968—. Office: Hollywood Casino Shreveport 5601 Bridge St Ste 300 Fort Worth TX 76112-2355

PRATT, JOAN M. comptroller; b. Balt., Jan. 15; BS, Hampton Univ., 1976; M, U. Balt., 1978. Comptroller Office of Mayor, Balt., 1995—. Office: Office of Comptroller City Hall 100 N Holliday St Ste 204 Baltimore MD 21202-3417

PRATT, JOHN JACKSON, property manager, retired telephone installer; b. Benton Harbor, Mich., July 25, 1946; s. Harry Adelbert Pratt and Edith Jane Monteverde; m. Binh-An Thi Pham; children: Joseph, Harold. AA, N.Mex. Mil. Inst., 1966. Lic. real estate salesperson, Calif. Assn. Realtors. Lineman, cable splicer installer, repairman Pacific Bell, Riverside, Calif., 1973-2000; property mgr. John J. Pratt Properties, Riverside, 1978—; mem. grower Sunkist Coop. Growers, 1984—. With USAF, 1967-71, res. ret., 1994. Mem. Apt. Assn. of Greater Inland Empire, Comms. Workers of Am. (local 9400), Am. Legion (post 289). Avocation: history studies especially world war ii and general world history. Home: PO Box 70122 Riverside CA 92513-0122 Office: JJP Properties 7929 Bolton Ave Riverside CA 92503-3125 Office Phone: 951-237-6390. Personal E-mail: johnj.pratt@yahoo.com.

PRATT, JOHN PATRICK, lawyer; b. Managua, Nicaragua, Nov. 19, 1967; s. Alfred Sidney Pratt and Thelma Reyes; 1 child, Patrick Alexander. BA in Philosophy, Fla. State U., 1994; JD, Tulane U., 1997. Bar: Fla. 1998, D.C. 1999, U.S. Dist. Ct. (so. dist.) Fla. 1998, U.S. Ct. Appeals (11th cir.) 1998, U.S. Supreme Ct. 2001, U.S. Ct. Appeals (9th cir.) 2002. Law clk. Office of Dist. Counsel IRS, St. Paul, 1995; law clk. Office of Asst. Chief Counsel U.S. Customs Svc., New Orleans, 1996-97, assoc. Zyne, Saleeby & Saleh, P.A., Miami, 1997-98, Montiel Davis & Woodward Kimber, P.A., Miami, 1998-2000, Leaf & Assocs., P.A., Miami, 2000-01, Kurzban, Kurzban, Weinger & Tetzeli, P.A., 2001—. Cons. Beacon Coun., Miami. Mem. ABA, Am. Immigration Lawyers Assn., Hispanic Nat. Bar Assn., Beacon Coun. Roman Catholic. Avocations: reading, tennis. Office: Kurzban Kurzban Weinger & Tetzel PA 2650 SW 27 Ave Ste 200 Miami FL 33133 Office Phone: 305-444-0060 Ext.203. E-mail: jpatrickpratt@aol.com.

PRATT, KATHERINE MERRICK, environmental consulting company executive; b. Alexandria, Egypt, July 4, 1951; d. Theodore and Bettie (Curland) R.; m. Harry Kenneth Todd (div.); 1 child, Kirsten Todd Pratt. BBA in Mgmt. Systems, U. Iowa, 1980; postgrad., U. Tex., 1985—87. Program data mgr. Rockwell Internat., Dallas, 1981-85; support coord. GTE Govt. Systems, Taunton, Mass., 1987-89, support engr., 1989-93; pres. Enviro-Logistics Inc., Harwood, Md., 1993—; sole propr. Internat. Soc. Logistics. Recipient Rear Admiral Bernard Eccles award, 1997, Cert. Commendation for Superior Performance as Dist. Dir., 1997. Mem. Soc. Logistics Engrs. (officer, mem. standing com. environ. applications, bd. dirs. New Eng. dist. 1996, dir. New Eng. dist., nat. chpt. newsletter judge), U.S. Pony Club (Ctrl. New Eng. championship chmn., nat. recognition for outstanding contbn. 1997). Avocations: sailing, reading, equitation. Office: Enviro-Logistics Inc PO Box 723 West River MD 20778-0723 Office Phone: 410-867-6220. E-mail: envirolog@earthlink.net.

PRATT, LEIGHTON CALVIN, state legislator; b. Hartford, Conn., Apr. 23, 1923; s. Calvin and Jessie (White) P.; m. Sally Burgess, Oct. 21, 1961; children: Randall Leighton, Bruce Charles. BS, U. Vt., 1951; MS, U. R.I., 1953. Plant pathologist Vt. Dept. Agr., Montpelier, 1952-62; tchr. sci. Cabot (Vt.) H.S. and J. H.S., 1962-65; tchr. biology, asst. prin. Newport (Vt.) H.S., 1965-67; tchr. biology North Country Union H.S., Newport, 1967-79; Coos agrl. ext. agt. U. N.H., Durham, 1969-88, prof. emeritus ext. edn., 1988—; mem. N.H. Ho. of Reps., Concord, 1991—. Named hon. state farmer Future Farmers Am., 1986. Mem. Rotary (dir. exch. to Brazil dist. 1986, pres. Lancaster, N.H.), Epsilon Sigma Phi. Republican. Congregationalist. Avocations: travel, gardening. Home: 63 Water St Lancaster NH 03584-3129

PRATT, MINNIE BRUCE, writer, educator; b. Selma, Ala., Sept. 12, 1946; d. William Luther Jr. and Virginia Earl (Brown) P.; m. Marvin Eugene Weaver II, Dec. 19, 1966 (div. Nov. 1976); children: Ransom Jones Weaver, Benjamin Carr Weaver; life ptnr.: Leslie Feinberg, July 31, 1992. BA with honors, U. Ala., 1968; PhD in English Lit., U. N.C., 1979. Lectr. Fayetteville (N.C.) State U., 1975-80; asst. prof. Shaw U., Raleigh, N.C., 1980-82; adj. lectr. Women's Studies Program, George Washington U., Washington, 1984-88; adj. lectr., vis. asst. prof. Women's Studies Program, U. Md., College Park, 1984-93; grad. faculty The Union Inst., Cin., 1990—; Jane Watson Irwin chair in women's studies Hamilton Coll., 2002—03. Writer-in-residence The Cmty. Writers' Project, Syracuse, N.Y., 1988, The Lit. Festival at St. Mary's Coll., St. Mary's City, Md., 1999, Nat. YMCA Writers Voice Program, N.Y.C., 2000. Author: The Sound of One Fork, 1981, Yours In Struggle: Three Feminist Perspectives on Anti-Semitism and Racism, 1984, We Say We Love Each Other, 1985, Crime Against Nature, 1990 (Lamont Poetry selection of Acad. Am. Poets 1990, ALA Gay and Lesbian Book award for lit. 1991), Rebellion: Essays 1980-1991, 1992 (Outstanding Book award Gustavus Myers Ctr. for Study of Human Rights in US 1992), S/HE, 1995, Walking Back Up Depot Street, 1999 (Best Gay and Lesbian Book of Yr., ForeWord: Mag. of Ind. Bookstores and Booksellers 1999), The Dirt She Ate: Selected and New Poems, 2003; mem. editl. collective Feminary: A Feminist Jour. for the South, Emphasizing Lesbian Visions, 1978-83. Fulbright fellow, 1968, Woodrow Wilson fellow, 1968, NDEA fellow, 1968; recipient Creative Writing fellowship in poetry Nat. Endowment for Arts, 1990, Lillian Hellman-Dashiell Hammett award The Fund for Free Expression, 1991 Ind. grant for lit. DC. Commn. on Arts, 1992, Ind. Artist grant Puffin Found., 1994, Larry Levis award for poetry Prairie Schooner mag., 1999, Ind. Artist award Ludwig Vogelstein Found., 2000, Lucille Medwick award Poetry Soc. Am., 2002; named one of Top 31 Alumnae, 1892-1992, XXXI Women's Leadership Hon., U. Ala., 1992. Mem. Poetry Soc. Am. (judge Celia B. Wagner Award 1992), Nat. Writers Union, Southerners on New Ground, Phi Beta Kappa. Office: PO Box 8212 Jersey City NJ 07308 Fax: 201-795-3208. E-mail: mbpratt@earthlink.net.

PRATT, MURRAY LESTER, collaborative commerce specialist; b. Mt. Holly, NJ, Mar. 11, 1956; 8. John N. and Mildred E. P.; m. Sharon Louise Busby, Aug. 13, 1988; children: Kevin Harrison, Brian Gavel, Melissa Anne, Heather Marie. BS in Indsl. Engring., Northwestern U., 1976; MS in Computer Sci., Ill. Inst. Tech., Chgo., 1983. Sys. analyst Gen. Foods USA, Chgo., 1981—84, sys. specialist, 1984—87, mgt. computer integrated mfg., 1987—91; mgr. KF logistics sys. Kraft Foods, Northfield, Ill., 1991—99, mgr. supply chain optimization, 1999—2001, program mgr. collaborative planning, forecasting and replenishment and vendor mng. inventory, 2001—, assoc. dir. customer supply chain integration. Presbyterian. Avocations: current affairs, tennis, volleyball, hiking. Home: 1241 Swainwood Dr Glenview IL 60025-2839 Office: Kraft Foods Three Lakes Dr NF168 Northfield IL 60093-2753 Office Phone: 847-646-6779. Business E-Mail: mpratt@kraft.com.

PRATT, RENEE GILL, state legislator; BA, Dillard U.; MEd, U. New Orleans. Teacher; mem. for dist. 91 La. Ho. of Reps., Baton Rouge, 1991—. Named Spl. Educator of Yr. Mem. Nat. Honor Soc. Alpha Kappa Mu. Democrat. Roman Catholic. Office: 1636 Toedano St Ste 304 New Orleans LA 70115 Address: 1636 Toledano St Ste 304 New Orleans LA 70115-4542

PRATT, ROBERT CRANFORD, political scientist, educator; b. Montreal, Que., Can., Oct. 8, 1926; s. Robert Goodwin and Henrietta (Freeman) P.; m. Renate Hecht, July 15, 1956; children: Gerhard, Marcus, Anna. BA, McGill U., Montreal, 1947; postgrad., Inst. Science Politique, Paris, 1948; MPhil, Oxford U., Eng., 1952. Lectr. McGill U., 1952-54, 56-58, Makerere U., Uganda, 1954-56; rsch. officer Oxford Inst. Commonwealth Studies, 1958-60; prin. Univ. Coll., Dar-es-Salaam, Tanzania, 1961-65; chmn. internat. studies program U. Toronto, Ont., Can., 1966-71, prof. polit. sci., 1966—. Spl. asst. to pres., Tanzania, 1965, 69; rsch. fellow Internat. Devel. Rsch. Ctr., 1978; commonwealth vis. prof. U. London, 1979-80; dir. Rsch. Project on Western Mid. Powers and Global Poverty, 1985-89; vis. fellow Devel. Ctr. Orgn. for Econ. Cooperation and Devel., Paris, 1986-87. Author: (with Anthony Low) Buganda and British Overrule, 1960, The Critical Phase in Tanzania, Nyerere and the Emergence of a Socialist Strategy, 1976, Towards Socialism in Tanzania, 1979, (with Robert Matthews) Human Rights in Canadian Foreign Policy, 1988, Internationalism Under Strain: The North-South Policies of Canada, The Netherlands, Norway and Sweden, 1989; (with Roger Hutchinson) Christian Faith and Economic Justice: A Canadian Perspective, 1989); Middle Power Internationalism: The North-South Dimension, 1990, Canadian International Development Assistance Policies: An Appraisal, 1994, 2nd edit., 1996. Decorated officer Order of Can.; recipient Killam award Can. Coun., 1968, Ludwik and Estelle Jus Meml. Human Rights award, 1995; Rhodes scholar Oxford U., 1950. Fellow Royal Soc. Can.; mem. Can. Polit. Sci. Assn., Can. African Studies Assn. (past pres.), Can. Assn. for Study of Internat. Devel. (mem. exec. coun.), Ecumenical Forum Can. (past chmn.). Mem. New Democratic Party. Home: 205 Cottingham St Toronto ON Canada M4V 1C4 Office: U Toronto Dept Polit Sci Toronto ON Canada M5S 1A1 E-mail: cranford.pratt@utoronto.ca.

PRATT, ROBERT WINDSOR, lawyer; b. Findlay, Ohio, Mar. 6, 1950; s. John Windsor and Isabelle (Vance) P.; m. Catherine Camak Baker, Sept. 3, 1977; children: Andrew Windsor, David Camak, James Robert. AB, Wittenberg U., Springfield, Ohio, 1972; JD, Yale U., 1975. Bar: Ill. 1975, U.S. Dist. Ct. (no. dist.) Ill. 1976, U.S. Dist. Ct. (we. dist.) Mich. 1995, U.S. Ct. Appeals (fed. cir.) 1984, U.S. Ct. Appeals (7th cir.) 1996. Assoc. Keck, Mahin & Cate, Chgo., 1975—81, ptnr., 1981—97; pvt. practice Wilmette, Ill., 1998—99; sr. asst. atty. gen. Office Ill. Atty. Gen., 1999—2001, chief antitrust bur., 2001—. Bd. dirs. Chgo. region ARC, 1985-96, vice chmn., 1988-92, chmn., 1992-96, bd. dirs. Mid-Am. chpt., 1992-96. Mem. ABA, Yale Club (Chgo.). Office Phone: 312-814-3722. Personal E-mail: rowpr50@msn.com. Business E-Mail: rpratt@atg.state.il.us.

PRATT, SCOTT OWEN, lawyer; b. Glendale, Calif., Oct. 18, 1955; s. Donald Hugh and Marlene Fay (Johnson) P.; m. Teresa Jean Browning, Sept. 6, 1996; 1 child, Avery J. BS, U. Wis., Eau Claire, 1978; JD, Willamette U., 1981. Bar: Oreg., Wash., U.S. Dist. Ct. (we. dist.) Wash., U.S. Dist. Ct. Oreg.; U.S. Ct. Appeals (9th cir.) Oreg. Assoc. Webb & Martinez, Salem, 1981-82; pvt. practice Portland, Oreg., 1983—. Pres. Laurelhurst Neighborhood Assn., Portland, 1994-96; chair Oreg. League of Conservation Voters, Portland, 1987-93, 2003-04; candidate for bd. of Portland Met. Area Regional Govt., 1998. Office: 806 SW Broadway Ste 1200 Portland OR 97205-3314 Office Phone: 503-241-5464. Business E-Mail: scopratt@netscape.net.

PRATT, SUZANNE, producer, reporter; BA in History, Tulane U.; MS in Journalism, Columbia U. Reporter Bucks County Courier Times, Pa.; reporter, editor McGraw-Hill News; with. N.Y. bur. Nightly Bus. Report, N.Y.C., 1990—, sr. prodr., reporter, 1997—; contbr. Morning Bus. Report, Miami. Office: NBR 74 Trinity Pl New York NY 10006-2003

PRATT, WILLIAM CROUCH, JR., English language educator, writer; b. Shawnee, Okla., Oct. 5, 1927; s. William Crouch and Irene (Johnston) P.; m. Anne Cullen Rich, Oct. 2, 1954; children: Catherine Cullen, William Stuart, Randall Johnston. BA, U. Okla., 1949; MA, Vanderbilt U., 1951, PhD, 1957. Rotary Internat. fellow U. Glasgow, Scotland, 1951-52; instr. English Vanderbilt U., 1955-57, Miami U., Oxford, Ohio, 1957-59, asst. prof., 1959-64, assoc. prof., dir. freshman English, 1964-68, prof., 1968—98; prof. emeritus Mami U., 1998—. Fulbright-Hays lectr. Am. lit., prof. Am. lit. Univ. Coll., Dublin, Eire, 1975-76; resident scholar Miami U. European Ctr., Luxembourg, fall 1976; lectr. Yeats Internat. Summer Sch., Sligo, Eire, 1979, 81, 82, 83, James Joyce Summer Sch., Dublin, Ireland, 1996; writer-in-residence Tyrone Guthrie Ctr., County Monaghan, Ireland, summer 1992, 96. Author: The Imagist Poem, 1963, rev. edit., 2001, The Fugitive Poets, 1965, rev. edit., 1991, The College Writer, 1969, College Days at Old Miami, 1984, The Influence of French Symbolism on Modern American Poetry, 1985, Miami Poets, 1988, Homage to Imagism, 1992, The Big Ballad Jamboree, 1996, Singing the Chaos: Madness and Wisdom in Modern Poetry, 1996, Miami University: A Personal History, 1998, Ezra Pound, Nature and Myth, 2002; contbr. essays, translations, poems, revs. to lit. jours., books. Served to lt. USNR, 1953-55. Mem.: Internat. Contemporary Lit. and Theatre Soc., Ezra Pound Internat. Conf. (sec. 1991—), Omicron Delta Kappa, Sigma Alpha Epsilon, Phi Beta Kappa. Republican. Home: 212 Oakhill Dr Oxford OH 45056-2710 *True happiness is to live in the understanding of what we love, the pursuit of what we believe in.*

PRATTE, GEOFFREY LYNN, lawyer, arbitrator; b. Bonne Terre, Mo., Sept. 14, 1940; s. Charles John and Ruth Jane (Thornton) P.; m. Gretchen Ann Westendorf, Mar. 15, 1969; children: Stephen Charles, Geoffrey Marc, Nicole Elizabeth, Gregory Lynn, Robert Wendell. BA in Philosophy, Kilroe Coll., 1963; MA in French, St. Louis U., 1967; JD, Wash. U., 1974. Bar: Mo. 1974, U.S. Dist. Ct. (ea. dist.) Mo. Tchr. Divine Heart Sem., Donaldson, Ind., 1963-65; analyst CIA, McLean, Va., 1967-71; assoc. Roberts & Roberts, Farmington, Mo., 1974-87; pvt. practice Farmington, Mo., 1987—; asst. pros. atty. St. Francois County, Farmington, Mo., 1987-93; city pros. atty. Bonne Terre, Mo., 1988—2003. Labor arbitrator Fed. Mediation and Conciliation Svc., Washington, 1988—. Bd. dirs. Terre du Lac Property Owners Assn., 1976-87. Mem. Order of the Coif, KC. Roman Catholic. Avocations: jogging, gardening. Office: 205 E Liberty St Farmington MO 63640-3129 Office Phone: 573-756-8082.

PRATTE, ROBERT JOHN, lawyer; b. Victoria, B.C., Can., Feb. 14, 1948; s. Arthur Louis Jr. and Marie Bertha (Latremouille) P.; children from previous marriage: Merie Elise, Jessica Louise, Allison Adele; m. Erica Catherine Street, Oct. 20, 1984; 1 child, Chelsea Nicole. BA, Northwestern U., 1970; JD, Tulane U., 1976. Bar: Minn. 1976, Ariz. 1997. Ptnr. Best & Flanagan, Mpls., 1976-84, Briggs & Morgan, Mpls., 1985—, head mortgage banking group. Editor: Mortgage Lending in Minnesota—A Desktop Reference Guide, 1990. Ex-officio mem. Wilderness Inquiry, Minn.; pres. Twin Cities Northwestern U. Alumni Assn., 1978; active Wayzata Cmty. Ch., Mpls. Fellow Am. Coll. Mortgage Attys. (regent) Home: 19900 Manor Rd Excelsior MN 55331-9256 Office: Briggs & Morgan 2200 IDS Ctr 80 S 8th St Ste 2400 Minneapolis MN 55402-2157 E-mail: rpratte@briggs.com. *Undertake with enthusiasm and pursue to completion the tasks that others are unwilling or unable to do. Never be satisfied with mediocrity. Surround yourself with those who are smarter than you; have the patience and judgement to let them succeed. Success can be measured by the hours you spend with your children--reading, fishing, and playing.*

PRAUSNITZ, FREDERIK WILLIAM, conductor; b. Cologne, Germany, Aug. 26, 1920; came to U.S., 1937; s. Friedrich Julius and Maja Eleanor (Moritz) P.; m. Margaret Violet Prausnitz; children: Sebastian, Maja. Grad. diploma in conducting, Juilliard Grad. Sch., 1946. Condr., adminstr. Juilliard, N.Y.C., 1946-61; condr. of recs. for Angel Argo Columbia, EMI, Philips, 1947—; condr. New Eng. Conservatory, Boston, 1961-69; music dir. Syracuse (N.Y.) Symphony Orch., 1971-74; music dir. to dir. of conducting programs Peabody Conservatory of Johns Hopkins U., Balt., 1976-97. Cons. The Lincoln Ctr., N.Y.C., 1963, Oakland U., Sussex (Eng.) U., 1969-71, Libr. of Congress, 2000. Author: Score and Podium, 1983, Roger Sessions, How a Difficult Composer Got That Way, 2002. Recipient 1st prize for young condrs. Detroit Symphony, 1944, Mahler Medal of Honor Am. Bruckner Soc., 1974; Hon. Fellow Sussex U., Eng., 1969; Condr. Laureate Peabody Orch., Balt., 1982; Rockefeller Found. writing grantee. Mem. Savage Club (London). E-mail: frederik@prausnitz.com.

PRAVEL, BERNARR ROE, lawyer; b. Feb. 10, 1924; BSChemE, Rice U., 1947; JD, George Washington U., 1951. Bar: D.C. 1951, Tex. 1951, U.S. Supreme Ct. 1951. Ptnr. Pravel, Hewitt firm, 1956—99; sr. counsel Akin, Gump, Houston, 1999—2002. Patent editor George Washington U. Law Rev., 1950. Precinct chmn. Houston Rep. Com., 1972-74. Served to lt. (j.g.) USNR. Fellow Am. Bar Found., Tex. Bar Found.; mem. ABA (chair intellectual property sect. 1991-92), Tex. Bar Assn. (chmn. patent, trademark sect. 1968-69, bd. dirs. 1976-79, Outstanding Contbn. 1982), Nat. Coun. Patent Law (chmn. 1970-71), Am. Intellectual Property Law Assn. (pres. 1983-84), Houston Intellectual Property Law Assn. (pres. 1983-84, Outstanding Svc. award 1986), Order of Coif, Kiwanis, Tau Beta Pi. Home: 10806 Oak Hollow St Houston TX 77024-3017 Personal E-mail: bpravel@sbcglobal.net.

PRAY, DONALD GEORGE, retired aerospace engineer; b. Troy, NY, Jan. 19, 1928; s. George Emerson and Jansje Cornelia (Ouwejan) P.; m. Betty Ann Williams, Oct. 1, 1950; children: Jennifer Loie, Jonathan Cornelius, Judy Karen, Jeffrey Donald. BA in Physics, Tex. Christian U., 1955; MSME, So. Meth. U., 1979. Sr. structures engr. Gen. Dynamics Corp., Ft. Worth, 1955-62, 67-84; engring. specialist LTV Astronautics Corp., Dallas, 1962-65, sr. engring. specialist, 1989-91; aero. group engr. space divsn. Chrysler Corp., New Orleans, 1965-67; V-22 group engr. Bell Helicopter Textron, Ft. Worth, 1984-89; structural integrity program mgr. E-3 sys. program mgmt. divsn. Okla. City Air Logistics Ctr., Tinker AFB, 1991—95; sr. stress engr. Northrop Grumman Corp., Dallas, 1997; ret., 1997. Prin. Donald G. Pray, Cons., Ft. Worth, 1959-61. Contbr. articles to profl. jours. Chmn. bd. trustees Cope Cemetery Assn., Johnson County, Tex., 1987—; corps comdr., v.p. bd. dirs. Masqueraders Drum and Bugle Corps, New Orleans, 1965-67; scoutmaster, cubmaster, explorer advisor, dist. com. chmn. Longhorn coun. Boy Scouts Am., Ft. Worth, 1967-75. With USAF, post WWII. Recipient Grand Championship Mardi Gras award, 1966. Mem.: SAR (pres. Van Zandt chpt. Ft. Worth 1996—97, treas. 1997—, N.W. Tex. dist. v.p. 1999—2004, Patriot medal 2001), NRA (marksman award 1980), ASME, Perrin AFB Pilots Assn., Acoustical Soc. Am. (emeritus 1997—), Internat. Pray Family Assn. (trustee 1996—), Ft. Worth Geneal. Soc. (bd. dirs. 1983—84), Train Collectors Assn., Soc. Mayflower Descendants Tex. (sec. 1983—85, 1988—91, chmn. Dallas colony scholarship com. 1988—2001, gen. soc. edn. com. 1990—99, gov. 1991—93, dep. gov. gen. 1993—98, gov. Dallas/Ft. Worth colony 1995—97, treas. 1999—2001), Shriners, Scottish Rite, Masons, Legion of Honor (adjutant/fin. officer 2000—01, comdr. 2002), Pi Mu Epsilon, Sigma Pi Sigma. Baptist. Achievements include analytical engineering contributions to numerous aircraft and spacecraft programs including B-36, B-58, NX-2, Robot, Dynasoar, Scout, Apollo, F/FB-111, F-16, V-22 Osprey, C-17, E-3 AWACS. Home and Office: 3628 Wedgway Dr Fort Worth TX 76133-2135 also: Lazy Acres Farm 5750 Lazy Bend Rd Millsap TX 76066-3732 Office Phone: 817-292-0256. E-mail: dgpray1@swbell.net. *Learn what talents you have been blessed with; then exercise them for the betterment of humanity.*

PRAY, LLOYD CHARLES, geologist, educator; b. Chgo., June 25, 1919; s. Allan Theron and Helen (Palmer) P.; m. Carrel Myers, Sept. 14, 1946; children: Lawrence Myers, John Allan, Kenneth Palmer, Douglas Carrel. BA magna cum laude, Carleton Coll., 1941; MS, Calif. Inst. Tech., 1943, PhD (NRC fellow 1946-49), 1952. Geologist Magnolia Petroleum Co., summer 1942, U.S. Geol. Survey, 1943-44; hydrographic officer USN, 1944-46; Geologist U.S. Geol. Survey, 1946-56 part time; instr. to assoc. prof. geology Calif. Inst. Tech., 1949-56; sr. research geologist Denver Research Ctr., Marathon Oil Co., 1956-62, research assoc., 1962-68; prof. geology U. Wis., Madison, 1968-88; emeritus prof. geology, 1989—. Short course vis. prof. U. Tex., Austin, 1964, U. Colo., 1967, U. Miami, 1971, U. Alta., 1969, Colo. Sch. Mines, 1985; vis. scientist Imperial Coll. Sci. and Tech., London, 1977, U. Calif. Santa Cruz, 1987, Nat. Park Svc. Geology panel, 1993. Author articles sedimentary carbonates, the Permian Reef complex, stratigraphy and structural geology So. N.M. and W. Tex., porosity of carbonate facies, Calif. rare earth mineral deposits. Pres. Colo. Diabetes Assn., 1963-67, v.p., 1968; mem. adv. panel earth scis. NSF, 1973-76. Served as hydrographic officer USNR, 1944-46. Named Layman of Year Am. Diabetes Assn., 1968; recipient Disting. Teaching award U. Wis. Madison, 1988, Disting. Achievement citation Carleton Coll., 1991, Wallace Pratt Resources Stewardship award Guadalupe Mountains Nat. Pk., 1998. Fellow Geol. Soc. Am. (rsch. grants com. 1965-67, com. on nominations 1973, com.Penrose medal 1979-81); mem. Am. Assn. Petroleum Geologists (rsch. com. 1958-61, lectr. continuing edn. program 1966-69, continuing edn. com. 1978-80, Levorsen award 1966, Matson trophy 1967, Disting. lectr. 1986-87, 87-88, Disting. Educator award 1998), Soc. Sedimentary Geologists (hon. life mem. Permian Basin sect. 1977, hon. mem. internat. soc. 1982, sec.-treas. 1961-63, v.p. 1966-67, pres. 1969-70, Twenhofel award 1999), Am. Geol. Inst. (edn. com. 1966-68, ho. bd. dels. 1970-72), Phi Beta Kappa. Office: Univ Wis Dept Geology Madison WI 53706

PRAY, RALPH EMERSON, metallurgical engineer; b. Troy, N.Y., May 12, 1926; s. George Emerson and Jansje Cornelius (Owejan) P.; m. Beverley Margaret Ramsey, May 10, 1959; children: Maxwell, Ross, Leslie, Marlene. Student, N.Mex. Inst. Mining & Tech., 1953-56, U. N.Mex., 1956; BS, U. Alaska, 1961; DSc, Colo. Sch. Mines, 1966. Electrician, miner, 1944-57; engr.-in-charge Dept. Mines and Minerals, Ketchikan, Alaska, 1957-61; asst. mgr. mfg. rsch. Universal Atlas Cement div. U.S. Steel Corp., Gary, Ind., 1965-66; rsch. metallurgist Inland Steel Co., Hammond, Ind., 1966-67; owner, dir. Mineral Rsch. Lab., Monrovia, Calif., 1968—. Pres., Keystone Canyon Mining Co., Inc., Pasadena, Calif., 1972-79, U.S. Western Mines, 1973—, Silveroil Rsch. Inc., 1980-85, v.p. Mineral Drill Inc., 1981-90; pres., CEO Copper de Mex. S.A. de C.V.; prime contractor def. logistics agy. U.S. Dept. def., 1989-92; designer Vanavara Electrolytic Gold Refinery, Krasnoyarsk, Russia, 1995; owner Precision Plastics, 1973-82; bd. dirs. Bagdad-Chase Inc., 1972-75; ptnr. Mineral R&D Co., 1981-86; lectr. Purdue U., Hammond, Ind., 1966-67, Nat. Mining Seminar, Barstow (Calif.) Coll., 1969-70; guest lectr. Calif. State Poly. U., 1977-81, Western Placer Mining Conf., Reno, Nev., 1983, Dredging and Miner Conf., Reno, 1985, others; v.p. dir. Wilbur Foote Plastics, Pasadena, 1968-72; strategic minerals del. People to People, Rep. South Africa, 1983; expert witness, cons. Bur. Land Mgmt., U.S. Dept. of Interior, 2000-2002; hist. cons. gold mining History TV Channel, 1999; guest spkr. Greater L.A. County Svc. Clubs, 1980-81; workshop condr. King Abdullaziz U., Jeddah, Saudi Arabia, 2002. Author: Jingu, The Hidden Princess, 2002; guest editor Calif. Mining Jour., 1978—; contbr. articles to profl. jours.; contbr. author Bre-x Gold Today, Gone Tomorrow, 1997. Vol. Monrovia Police Dept.; city coord. Neighborhood Watch., 1990-99, Citizen Patrol, 1997-99. With U.S. Army, 1950-52. Recipient Disting. Svc. medal Monrovia Police Dept., 1998. Fellow Geol. Mining and Metall. Soc. India (life), Am. Inst. Chemists, South African Inst. Mining and Metallurgy; mem. Soc. Mining Engrs., Am. Chem. Soc., Am. Inst. Mining, Metall. and Petroleum Engrs., NSPE, Can. Inst. Mining and Metallurgy, Geol. Soc. South Africa, Soc. Mineral Analysts, Sigma Xi, Sigma Mu. Achievements include research on recovery of metals from refractory ores, benefication plant design, construction and operation, underground and surface mine development and operation, mine and process plant management; syndication of natural resource assets with finance sources; freelance fiction and nonfiction writer; patents for chemical processing and steel manufacture; measurement of residual mercury in ancient and modern mine wastes of Chile. Office: 805 S Shamrock Ave Monrovia CA 91016-3651 Office Phone: 626-357-6511.

PRAYTOR, KENT DWAYNE, career planning administrator; b. Pitts., Aug. 9, 1963; s. Hubert Henry and Juanita Pecola Praytor. BA in Psychology, California U. of Pa., 1991; EdM, Bowie State U., 1996. Cert. guidance and counseling Harrisburg, Pa., 1996. Acad. counselor Pitts. Pub. Sch., 1990—. Author: Closer Than Skin. With USN, 1981—85. Recipient medal, DAR. Home: 3519 Centralia St Pittsburgh PA 15204 Office: Columbus Middle School 1805 Buena Vista St Pittsburgh PA 15212 E-mail: kdpraytor@yahoo.com.

PREBLE, LAURENCE GEORGE, lawyer; b. Denver, Apr. 24, 1939; s. George Enos and Ruth (Jewett) Preble; m. Deborah Joan Horton, Aug. 24, 1963; children: Robin Lee, Randall Laurence. B in Petroleum Refining Engring., Colo. Sch. Mines, 1961; JD cum laude, Loyola U., Los Angeles, 1968. Bar: Calif. 1969, D.C. 1983, N.Y. 1987, U.S. Dist. Ct. (cen. dist.) Calif.

1969. Assoc. firm O'Melveny & Myers, Los Angeles, 1968-76, ptnr. L.A., 1976—2000; dir. devel. KUD Internat. LLC, 2001—. Adj. prof. law Southwestern U., 1970-75, Loyola U. of L.A. Sch. Law, 1984-92, 99-2000, Fordham U. Sch. Law, 1992-98, Calif. Continuing Edn. of the Bar; lectr., author Practicing Law Inst. Trustee Harvey Mudd Coll., 1991-94, Citizens Bidget Commn. N.Y.C., 1994-98, Ho. Ear Inst., 1998—, vice-chmn., 2001—. Recipient Disting. Achievement medal, Colo. Sch. Mines, 1998. Mem. Los Angeles County Bar Assn. (chmn. real property sect. 1979-80, Outstanding Leadership award 1999), Assn. Bar City of N.Y. (real property sect. exec. com. 1993-96), N.Y. State Bar Assn. (exec. com. real property sect. 1996—), Calif. Bar Assn. (mem. exec. com. real property sect.), ABA, Am. Coll. Real Estate Lawyers (bd. govs. 1986—), Anglo-Am. Real Property Inst., La Canada-Flintridge C. of C. (pres. 1974-75), Loyola Law Sch. Alumni Assn. (pres. 1978). Office: KUD Internat LLC STE 950 100 Wilshire Blvd Santa Monica CA 90401-1145

PREBLE, ROBERT CURTIS, JR., insurance executive; b. Oak Park, Ill., Dec. 19, 1922; s. Robert Curtis and Dorothy (Seidel) P.; m. Lidia Blazik, May 29, 1963. BA, Amherst Coll., 1947; MBA, Harvard U., 1949, postgrad., 1971. CLU, Chartered Fin. Cons. Pvt. to 1st lt. U.S. Army, 1943—46; 33rd divsn. capt. Nat. Guard, Ill., 1950—53; asst. to gen. supt., asst. buyer Carson Pirie Scott & Co., Chgo., 1949-52; with sales dept. Northwestern Mut. Life Ins. Co., Chgo., 1952-53, Nat. Life Ins. Co., Chgo., 1953-59; prin. Preble Assocs., Chgo., 1959—; pres., treas. Savs. Plans Inc., Chgo., 1980—. Cons. Iowa Savs. & Loan League, 1959-82; consul of Colombia, 1981-86, Bolivia, 1965-70; bd. dirs., chmn. fin. com. Guardsman Life Ins. Co., 1962-74; chmn. exec. com. World Book Life Ins. Co., 1974-83; gov.'s adv. bd. Ill. Dept. Ins., 1965-70; dir. Scandia Savs. & Loan Assn., 1968-83, Chgo. Coun. on Fgn. Rels., 1971-77, Chgo. Estate Planning Coun., 1977-80. Dept. regional chmn. Dem. Nat. Fin. Com., 1952; bd. dirs. Sr. Ctrs. Met. Chgo., 1974—77, McCormick Theol. Sem., 1977—83; deacon 4th Presbyn. Ch. of Chgo., 1967—70. Recipient Svc. award Chgo. coun. Boy Scouts Am., 1962; record holder Ill. Masters Swimming, 2003. Mem. Soc. Fin. Svc. Profls. (past pres. Chgo. chpt., Huebner scholar 1991, Grauer award 1998), Million Dollar Roundtable (life), Nat. Assn. of Insurance and Fin. Advisors, Assn. for Advanced Life Underwriting (founding pres. 1957), Harvard Bus. Sch. Assn. (alumni coun. 1977-82), Harvard Alumni Assn. (dir. 1980-82), Inst. Internat. Edn. (midwest adv. bd., 1979-99), Found. Study Cycles (internat. adv. bd.), Soc. Colonial Wars (coun.), Mil. Order World Wars, Univ. Club (Lifetime Achievement award 2004), Chgo. Club, Harvard Bus. Sch. Club (past pres.), Amherst Club (past pres.), Oak Park Country Club, Spanish Wells Country Club, Econ. Club Chgo., Chi Psi (past chmn. ednl. trust, pres. 1992-95, Svc. award 1986). Home: 300 N State St Apt 5406 Chicago IL 60610-4870

PRECOURT, CHARLES J. astronaut, retired military officer; b. Waltham, Mass., June 29, 1955; s. Charles and Helen Precourt; m. Lynne Denise Mungle; 3 children. BS in Aeronautical Engring., USAF Acad., Colo. Springs, 0977; MS in Engring. Mgmt., Golden Gate U., 1988; MA in Nat. Security Affairs, Strategic Studies, US Naval War Coll., 1990. Commd. 2d lt. USAF, 1977; advanced through grades to Col. USAF (ret.); student pilot USAF, Reese AFB, Tex., 1977—78, instr. pilot T-37, 1979—82; pilot F-15 USAF Bitburg Air Base, Germany, 1982—84; student test pilot sch. USAF, Edwards AFB, Calif., 1985; test pilot USAF, Edwards AFB, 1985—89; postgrad. studies U.S. Naval War Coll., Newport, RI, 1989—90; astronaut NASA Johnson Space Ctr., Houston, 1990—. Decorated Disting. Flying Cross USAF, 4 Space Flight medals NASA; recipient David B. Barnes award, USAF Test Pilot Sch., 1989. Mem.: Soc. Exptl. Test Pilots, Exptl. Aircraft Assn., Assn. Space Explorers (v.p.). Achievements include 4 space flights; over 7000 flight hours in 60 types of civil and military aircraft; approximately 40 days spent in space. Office: Astronaut Office/CB Johnson Space Ctr Houston TX 77085*

PREDDY, RAYMOND RANDALL, retired newspaper publisher, educator; b. Texarkana, Ark., Feb. 1, 1940; s. Raymond Watson and Dorothy Belle (Long) P.; m. Sarah Elizabeth Mitchell, Nov. 20, 1965; children: Lewis, Tiffany. BS, Northwestern U., 1961, MS in Journalism, 1962. Copy editor Louisville Courier-Jour., 1965-69; with Dayton (Ohio) Daily News, 1969-74, asst. city editor, 1971, met. editor, 1971-74; systems mgr. Dayton Newspapers, Inc., 1974-76; bus. mgr. Waco (Tex.) Tribune-Herald, 1976-77, asst. pub., 1977-78; pub. Waco Tribune-Herald, 1978-96. Part time journalism instr. Baylor U., Waco. Pres. Waco United Way, 1986, Waco Found., 1984-86, Waco Symphony Assn., 1985-86; vice moderator Grace Presbyn., 2004. Served with USN, 1962-65; capt. Res. (ret.) Named Tex. Newspaper Leader of 1994; recipient Pat Taggart award from Tex. Daily Newspaper Assn. Mem.: Rotary. Presbyterian. Personal E-mail: rrpreddy@aol.com.

PREECE, LYNN SYLVIA, lawyer; b. Birmingham, Eng., June 13, 1955; d. Norman and Sylvia Florence (James) Preece. LLB, Leeds (Eng.) U., 1976; postgrad., Washington U., St. Louis, 1978-79; JD, Loyola U., 1981. Bar: Ill., 1981. Assoc. Barnes Richardson, Chgo., 1980-86; from assoc. to ptnr. Burditt & Radzius, Chgo., 1986-88; ptnr. Katten Muchin & Zavis, Chgo., 1988-96, Baker & McKenzie, Chgo., 1996—. Adj. prof. John Marshall Law Sch., 1998—. Contbr. articles to profl. jours. Chair customs com. Chgo. Bar Assn., 1986-87, Am. Bar Sect. Internat. Law, Washington, 1993-95, practitioners workshop bd., 1995-97; sec., dir. Women in Internat. Trade, Chgo., 1986-89, British Am. C. of C., Chgo., 1990; dir. Chgo. Internat. Sch., 1994-96. Recipient Gold medal Duke of Edinurghs award Scheme, London, 1973. Mem.: ABA (program officer, coun. mem., newsletter editor 1996—98), Internat. Bar Assn., Ct. Internat. Trade Bar Assn. Avocations: gardening, dogs. Office: Baker & McKenzie Ste 3500 130 E Randolph Dr Chicago IL 60601-6342 Office Phone: 312-861-8022. E-mail: Lynn.S.Preece@Bakernet.com.

PREECE, SCOTT, food products executive; From mem. staff to pres., COO WinCo Foods, Woodburn, Oreg., 1969—2001, pres., 2001—, COO, 2001—. Office: WinCo Foods Woodburn Distbn Ctr PO Box 400 Woodburn OR 97071

PREER, JAMES RANDOLPH, science educator; b. Monahans, Tex., May 22, 1944; s. John R. Jr. and Louise B. (Brandau) P.; m. Jean H. Lyon, June 24, 1967; children: Genevieve L., Stephen R. AB, Swarthmore (Pa.) Coll., 1965; PhD, Calif. Inst. Tech., 1970. Woodrow Wilson teaching intern, 1969-71; asst. prof. chemistry Fed. City Coll., Washington, 1969-73; asst. prof. interdisciplinary sci. U. D.C., 1973-76, assoc. prof. interdisciplinary sci., 1976-79, prof. interdisciplinary sci., 1979-80, acting chairperson, 1979-80, 86-89, prof. environ. sci., 1980—, asst. provost acad. programs and rsch., 1997-99, assoc. provost acad. programs & rsch., 1999-2000. Vis. scholar Inst. Environ. Studies, U. Wis., Madison, 2000-2001. Co-author: Integrated Science, 1976, 88; contbr. over 30 articles to profl. jours. Asst. scoutmaster Boy Scouts Am., Washington, 1990-93, chmn. troop com., 1993-95; bd. dirs. Beauvoir Sch., Washington, 1983-86. Woodrow Wilson Found. fellow Columbia U., 1965-66, NSF fellow Calif. Inst. Tech., 1966-69, MIT, 1976-77; U. D. C. grantee, 1978-98. Mem. Am. Chem. Soc., Phi Beta Kappa, Sigma Xi. Office: Dept Biol & Environ Scis 4200 Connecticut Ave NW Washington DC 20008-1122

PREER, JEAN LYON, information science educator; b. Rochester, N.Y., June 25, 1944; d. Henry Gould and Helen Corinne (McTarnaghan) Lyon; m. James Randolph Preer, June 24, 1967; children: Genevieve, Stephen. BA in History with honors, Swarthmore Coll., 1966; MLS, U. Calif., Berkeley, 1967; JD with highest honors, George Washington U., 1974, PhD, 1980. Bar: D.C. 1975. With Henry E. Huntington Libr., San Marino, Calif., 1967-69; Woodrow Wilson Found. teaching intrn Fed. City Coll., Washington, 1969-70; cons. Inst. for Svcs. to Edn., Silver Spring, Md., 1981-82; vol. edn. divsn. Nat. Archives, Washington, 1981-89; adj. prof. U. D.C., 1984-85, Cath. U. Am., Washington, 1985-87, asst. prof. sch. libr. and info. sci., 1987-92, assoc. prof., 1993—, assoc. dean., 1991-93, 94-98, acting dean, 1993-94, 99; adj. assoc. prof. George Washington U., 1985-87. Vis. scholar, U. Wis., Madison, Sch. Libr. and Info. Studies, 2000-01. Contbr. articles to profl. jours. Mem. governing bd. Nat. Cathedral Sch., Washington, 1987—91; bd. dirs. Westmoreland Vol. Corps, 1997—2000; mem. strategic planning com. D.C. Pub. Libr., Washington, 1998—99. Fellow Nat. Acad. Edn., 1984-85; grantee Nat. Endowment for Humanities. Mem. Order of Coif, Beta Phi Mu. Home: 2900 Rittenhouse St NW Washington DC 20015-1524 Office: Cath U Am Sch Libr And Info Sci Washington DC 20064-0001 E-mail: preer@cua.edu.

PREGERSON, HARRY, federal judge; b. L.A., Oct. 13, 1923; s. Abraham and Bessie (Rubin) P.; m. Bernardine Seyma Chapkis, June 28, 1947; children: Dean Douglas, Kathryn Ann. BA, UCLA, 1947; LL.B., U. Calif.-Berkeley, 1950. Bar: Calif. 1951. Pvt. practice, Los Angeles, 1951—53; Assoc. Morris D. Coppersmith, 1952; ptnr. Pregerson & Costley, Van Nuys, 1953—65; judge Los Angeles Mcpl. Ct., 1965—66, Los Angeles Superior Ct., 1966—67, U.S. Dist. Ct. Central Dist. Calif., 1967—79, U.S. Ct. Appeals for 9th Circuit, Woodland Hills, 1979—. Faculty mem., seminar for newly appointed distr. Judges Fed. Jud. Center, Washington, 1970—72; mem. faculty Am. Soc. Pub. Adminstrn., Inst. for Ct. Mgmt., Denver, 1973—; panelist L.A. chpt. FBA, 1989, Calif. Continuing Edn. of Bar, 9th Ann. Fed. Practice Inst., San Francisco, 1986, Internat. Acad. Trial Lawyers, L.A., 1983; lectr. seminars for newly-appointed Fed. judges, 1970—71. Author: over 450 published legal opinions. Mem. Community Rels. Com., Jewish Fedn. Coun., 1984—, Temple Judea, Encino, 1955—; bd. trustees Devil Pups Inc., 1988—; adv. bd. Internat. Orphans Inc., 1966—, Jewish Big Brothers Assn., 1970, Salvation Army, Los Angeles Met. area, 1988—; worked with U.S. Govt. Gen. Svcs. to establish the Bell Shelter for the homeless Child Day Care Ctr., the Food Partnership and Westwood Transitional Village; bd. dirs. Marine Corps Res. Toys for Tots Program, 1965—, Greater Los Angeles Partnership for the Homeless, 1988—. 1st lt. USMCR, 1944—46. Decorated Purple Heart, Medal of Valor Apache Tribe; recipient Promotion of Justice Civic award, City of San Fernando, 1965, award, San Fernando Valley Jewish Fedn. Coun., 1966, Profl. Achievement award, Los Angeles Athletic Club, 1980, Profl. Achievement award UCLA Alumni Assn., 1985, Louis D. Brandeis award, Am. Friends of Hebrew U., 1987, award of merit, Inner City Law Ctr., 1987, Appreciation award, Navajo Nation and USMC for Toys for Tots program, 1987, Humanitarian award, Los Angeles Fed. Exec. Bd., 1987—88, Grateful Acknowledgement award, Bet Tzedek Legal Svcs., 1988, Commendation award, Bd. Suprs. Los Angeles County, 1988, Others award, Salvation Army, 1988. Mem.: ABA, Marines Corps Res. Officers Assn., State Bar Calif., San Fernando Valley Bar Assn., L.A. County Bar Assn., Am. Legion (Van Nuys Post), DAV (Birmingham chpt.). Office: US Ct Appeals 9th Cir 21800 Oxnard St Ste 1140 Woodland Hills CA 91367-7919

PREIKSAITIS, RAYMOND V. food products executive; b. 1950; From officer to group v.p. Archer Daniels Midland Co., Decatur, Ill., 1988—97, group v.p., 1997—. Office: Archer Daniels Midland Co 4666 Faries Pkwy Decatur IL 62526

PREIS, CHRISTY CHARLENE, mathematics professor; b. Leslie, Ark., Dec. 8, 1963; d. Harvey Harold and Carolyn L. (House) Davis; m. Kelvin Preis, July 30, 1988; 1 child, Beau Hunter. BSE, U. Ctrl. Ark., Conway, 1982—86; MSE, U. Ctrl. Ark., 1986—88; EdD, U. Ark., Fayetteville, 1997—2000. Math. tchr. Vilonia Pub. Schs., Ark., 1986—88, Salem Pub. Schs., 1988—89, Mammoth Spring Pub. Schs., 1989—90, Cotter Pub. Schs., 1991—94; math. instr. Ark. State U., Mountain Home, 1994—2000, asst. prof. math., 2000—. Contbr. articles. Mem., com. chair Gen. Fedn. Women's Clubs Cameo Club of Mountain Home, Ark., 1998—2002. Mem.: Ark. Math. Assn. Two-Year Colls., Ark. Coun. Tchrs. of Math., Nat. Coun. Tchrs. of Math., N. Ark. Twin Lakes Chpt. Phi Delta Kappa Internat. (co-pres. 2002—04, PDK pres. 2004—). Home: 140 Marquis Dr Mountain Home AR 72653 Office: Ark State U Mountain Home 1600 S Coll St Mountain Home AR 72653 Business E-Mail: cpreis@asumh.edu.

PREIS, MARY LOUISE, commissioner, former state legislator; b. Jacksonville, Ill., Oct. 10, 1941; m. Frederick G. Preis; children: Elizabeth, John, Mary. BA, U. Strasbourg, France, 1963; MS, Georgetown U., 1967; JD, U. Md. Sch. Law, 1983. Bar: Md. 1983, U.S. Dist. Ct. Md. 1984, U.S. Ct. Appeals (4th cir.) 1986. Tchr. Notre Dame Prep., Balt., 1966—67, Rose Tree Sch., Media, Pa., 1967—69; reporter The Record, Havre de Grace, Md., 1975—79; dir. devel. Loyola H.S., 1979—80; dep. dir. cmty. and govt. rels. Md. Dept. Econ. and Employment Devel., 1983—84; counsel Office Atty. Gen., Balt., 1984—86, asst. atty. gen., 1986—90; lawyer Bel Air, Md., 1991; del. Md. Ho. Reps., Balt., 1991—99; commr. Divsn. Fin. Regulations, Balt., 1999—. Adv. bd. Harford County Econ. Devel., 1992—98; bd. mem. Md. Commn. on Future of Cts., 1995—97, Md. Commn. on Alternative Dispute Resolution, 1997—, Coll. Notre Dame Md., Women in Millennium Com., 1999. Adv. bd. Md. Bar Jour., 1990. Bd. mem. State Bank Suprs. Edn. Found., 1999, United Way of Ctrl. Md., 1995, Rockford Found. Bel Air, 1996, Harford C.C. Found., 1990—99. Recipient Disting. Svc. award, Rte. 40 Bus. Assn., 1998. Mem.: U. Md. Law Sch. Alumni Assn. (bd. mem. 1995), Chesapeake Heritage Conservancy (bd. dirs.), Harford County Bar Assn., Md. Bar Assn. (Exceptional Svc. award 1995).

PREISS, JACK, biochemistry educator; b. Bklyn, June 2, 1932; s. Erool and Gilda (Friedman) P.; m. Karen Sue; children: Jennifer Ellen, Jeremy Oscar, Jessica Michelle. BS in Chemistry, CCNY, 1953; PhD in Biochemistry, Duke U., 1957. Scientist NIH, Bethesda, Md., 1960-62; asst. prof. dept. biochemistry, biophysics U. Calif., Davis, 1962-65, assoc. prof., 1965-68, prof., 1968-85, chair dept. biochemistry, 1971-74, 77-81; prof. dept. biochemistry Mich. State U., East Lansing, 1985-2000, chair dept., 1985-89, Univ. Disting. Prof., 2001—. Mem. editl. bd. Jour. Bacteriology, 1969-74, Arch. Biochem. Biophysics, 1969—, Plant Physiology, 1969-74, 77-80, assoc. editor, 1980-92, editor, 1993-95; editor Jour. Biol. Chemistry, 1971-76, 78-83, 94-99, 2000-04, Plant Physiol. Biochemistry, 1997—; 16th loomis lectr. Iowa State U., 1997-98. Recipient Camille and Henry Dreyfus Disting. scholar award Calif. State U., 1983, Alexander von Humboldt Stiftung Sr. US Scientist award, 1984, Award of Merit, Japanese Soc. Starch Sci., 1992, Disting. Faculty Mem. award Mich. Assn. Governing Bds. of State Univ., 1997, Mich. Sci. of Yr. award Impressions 5 Mus., 1997, Pan-Am. Biochemistry and Molecular Biology award lectr. Spanish Biochem. Soc., 2000; Alsberg-Schoch Meml. lectr. Am. Assn. Cereal Chemists, 1990, Nat. Sci. Coun. lectr. Republic of China, 1988; Guggenheim Meml. fellow, 1969-70, Japan Soc. for Promotion of Sci. fellow, 1992-93; grantee NIH, 1963-97, NSF, 1978-89, Dept. of Energy, 1993—, USDA, 1988—. Mem. AAAS, Am. Chem. Soc. (Charles Pfizer award in enzyme chemistry 1971), Biochem. Soc., Am. Soc. Biol. Chemists and Molecular Biology, Am. Soc. Microbiologists, Am. Soc. Plant Physiologists, Soc. for Complex Carbohydrates, Protein Soc., Pan Am. Soc. Biochemistry and Molecular Biology (sec. gen., 1994-96, vice chmn. 1997-99, chmn. 2000-02, past chmn. 2003-). Office: Mich State Univ Dept Of Biochemistry & Molecular Biology East Lansing MI 48824 Office Phone: 517-353-3137. Business E-Mail: preiss@msu.edu.

PREISTER, DONALD GEORGE, state legislator, greeting card manufacturer; b. Columbus, Nebr., Dec. 23, 1946; s. Maurice J. Preister and Leona T. (Dusel) Chereck. BS in Edn., U. Nebr., 1977. Unit dir. Boys' Clubs of Omaha, 1973-83; dep. city clk. City of Omaha, 1984-85; tchr. The Great Peace March, U.S., 1986; founder, owner Joy Creations, Co., Omaha, 1988—; mem. Nebr. Legislature from 5th dist., Lincoln, 1992—. Instr. Metro C.C., Omaha, 1979-80. Author: (sect.) Drug Abuse Prevention, 1977. Troop leader Boy Scouts Am., Omaha, 1973-83. Served with U.S. Army, 1966-68, Vietnam. Decorated Bronze Star. Mem. Vets. for Peace, Nebr. Sustainable Agr. Soc., Optimist. Democrat. Roman Catholic. Avocations: gardening, running, horses. Home: 3937 W St Omaha NE 68107-3152 Office: State Capitol Dist # 5 Lincoln NE 68509

PREM, F. HERBERT, JR., lawyer; b. N.Y.C., Jan. 14, 1932; s. F. Herbert Prem Sr. and Sybil Gertrude (Nichols) Prem; m. Patricia Ryan, Nov. 18, 1978; children from previous marriage: Julia Nichols, F. Herbert III(dec.). AB, Yale U., 1953; JD, Harvard U., 1959. Bar: NY 1960. Assoc. Whitman and Ransom, N.Y.C., 1959-66, ptnr., 1967-93, co-chmn. exec. com., 1988-92, chmn., 1993, Whitman Breed Abbott & Morgan LLP, N.Y.C., 1993-99, of counsel, 2000. Bd. dirs. Fuji Photo Film U.S.A., Inc., Fuji Film Med. Sys. U.S.A., Inc., Seiko Instruments Am., Inc., 1974—2004, Noritake, Inc., 1974—2002. Vol. atty. The Legal Aid Soc., N.Y.C., 2000—03; vol. chaplain Sharon (Conn.) Hosp., 2003—; bd. dirs. Bagaduce Music Lending Libr., Inc., 1988—95, pres., 1989—93; bd. dirs. The Health Care Chaplaincy, Inc., 1998—2004, Inter Faith Neighbors, Inc., 2001—03, Legal Aid Soc., N.Y.C., 1969—73, Cmty. Action for Legal Svc., Inc., 1967—70, treas. Lt. j.g. USNR, 1953—56. Mem. ABA, Assn. of Bar of N.Y.C., (sec. 1967-69), N.Y. State Bar Assn., Am. Law Inst. (life), Union Club, Yale Club. Episcopalian.

PREMACK, ANN J. writer; b. Shanghai, Jan. 5, 1929; interned in Japanese detention ctr., 1943-45; came to the U.S., 1945; d. John Joseph James and Mae Victoria Parker; m. David Premack, Oct. 26, 1951; children: Ben, Lisa, Tim. BS with distinction, U. Minn., 1951. Author: Why Chimps Can Read, 1975; co-author (with D. Premack): The Mind of An Ape, 1983; co-editor: Causal Cognition: A Multidisciplinary Debate, 1995; co-author (with D. Premack): Original Intelligence: Unlocking the Mystery of Who We Are, 2003, French translation, 2003; contbr. chapters to books, articles to profl. jours. Avocation: owning and running an avocado grove. Home: 6163 Heatherton Dr Somis CA 93066-9716 E-mail: dpremack@aol.com.

PREMACK, DAVID, psychologist; b. Aberdeen, S.D., Oct. 26, 1925; s. Leonard B. and Sonja (Liese) P.; m. Ann M. James, Oct. 26, 1951; children: Ben, Lisa, Timothy. BA magna cum laude, U. Minn., 1949, PhD, 1955. Rsch. assoc. Yerkes Labs. Primate Biology, Orange Park, Fla., 1955; rsch. assoc., asst. prof. psychology U. Mo., Columbia, 1956-58, assoc. prof., 1959-62, prof., 1963-64, U. Calif., Santa Barbara, 1965-75; vis. prof. Harvard U., 1970-71; prof. U. Pa., 1975—. Artist-in-residence Yaddo, Saratoga Springs, N.Y., 1955; fellow Van Leer Jerusalem Inst., 1980, Inst. for Advanced Study, Berlin, 1985-86; vis. scientist Japan Soc. for Promotion Sci., 1980; univ. rsch. lectr. U. Calif., Santa Barbara, 1973; mem. sci. gov. bd. Fyssen Found., Paris, 1989—; assoc. neurosci. rsch. program, La. Jolla, Calif., 1991—. Author: Intelligence in Ape and Man, 1976, (with Ann James Premack) The Mind of an Ape, 1983, Gavagai! Or the Future History of the Animal Language Controversy, 1986 (with Dan Sperber and Ann James Premack) Causal Cognition: A Multidisciplinary Debate, 1995, (with Ann James Premack) Original Intelligence: Unlocking the Mystery of Who We Are, 2003; mem. editl. bd. Jour. Exptl. Psychology: Animal Processes, 1976—, Cognition, 1977—, Brain and Behavior Sci., 1978—, Jour. Cognitive Neurosci. Served with U.S. Army, 1943-46. Ford Found. tchg. intern, 1954; USPHS postdoctoral fellow, 1956-59; Social Sci. Rsch. Coun. fellow, summer 1963; Ctr. for Advanced Study in Behavioral Scis. fellow, 1972-73; Guggenheim fellow, 1979-80; grantee NSF, 1961—, USPHS, 1960-80; recipient Kenneth Craik Resch. award St. John's Coll.-Cambridge U., 1987, Internat. Sci. prize Fyssen Found., Paris, 1987. Fellow AAAS; mem. Soc. Exptl. Psychologists. Personal E-mail: dpremack@aol.com.

PREMCHAND, ARIGAPUDI, retired financial consultant; b. Kadavakollu, India, Aug. 22, 1933; arrived in U.S., 1970; s. Venkataramiah and Manikyamma Arigapudi; m. Rama Premchand, May 8, 1953; 2 children. Diploma in econ. adminstrn., Delhi Sch. Econs., 1954; MA, Andhra U., 1953; DLitt (hon.), Krishna Devaraya U., 2002. Lectr. Andhra U., India, 1954—57; rsch. officer Union Min. Fin., Delhi, 1957—68; cons. Ford Found., 1968—70; economist to asst. dir. Internat. Minority Fund, Washington, 1970—98; cons. Asian Devel. Bank, 1970—98, World Bank, 1970—98, Kennedy Sch., 1970—98; ret. Author (editor) 11 books; contbr. chapters to books. Fellow, Indian Inst. Econs., 1960, Oxford U., 1980. Hindu. Avocations: reading, writing. Home: 5 Sonrisa Irvine CA 92620-7915 Home Fax: 714-669-9374. E-mail: apremchand@cox.net.

PREMEAUX, SHANE RICHARD, marketing educator; b. Gueyden, La., Mar. 13, 1954; s. Percy Donat and Florence Mary Premeaux; m. Jennifer Lynn Brandlein; 1 child, Paige Elizabeth. BS in Acctg., McNeese State U., 1976, MBA, 1977; PhD in Mktg., U. Ark., 1982. Asst. prof. mktg. Northwestern La. U., Natchitoches, 1981-82, N.E. La. U., Monroe, 1982-84, Southeastern U., Hammond, La., 1984-85; prof. mktg. McNeese State U., Lake Charles, La., 1985—. Reviewer Bus. Jour., Jour. Bus. Strategies; cons. in field. Author: Personal Selling: Function, Theory, and Practice, 4th edit., 1998, Supervision, 3d edit., 1998, Human Resources Management, 8th edit., 2002, Management and Organizational Behavior, 1990, Management Concepts and Practices, 5th edit., 1990, Management Concepts and Practices, 8th edit., 2000, among others; contbr. over 65 articles to profl. and acad. jours. including Transp. Jour., Jour. Bus. Ethics. Recipient numerous grants. Mem. Assn. Grad. Bus. Dirs., McNeese U. MBA Assn., McNeese U. Alumni Assn., U. Ark. Alumni Assn., Southwestern Mktg. Assn., Soc. for Advancement of Mgmt., Sigma Iota Epsilon, Alpha Mu Alpha, Delta Nu Alpha, Tau Kappa Epsilon. Republican. Roman Catholic. Office: McNeese State U Coll Bus PO Box 92135 Lake Charles LA 70609-0001

PREMO, PAUL MARK, oil company executive; b. Syracuse, N.Y., Nov. 20, 1942; s. Matthias George and Kathryn (Whitbread) P.; m. Mary Catherine Hennessy, June 19, 1965; children: Deborah, Mark. BSChemE, Manhattan Coll., Riverdale, N.Y., 1964; MS in Chem. Engring., MIT, 1965. Chem. engr. Chevron Rsch., Richmond, Calif., 1965-69; fin. analyst Chevron Corp., San Francisco, 1969-72, coord., mgr. supply and distbn., 1972-79; mgr. petroleum regulations Chevron USA, San Francisco, 1979-81, sec.-treas., 1981-85, mgr. property tax adminstrn., 1985-86, mgr. natural gas regulatory affairs, 1986-92; exec. cons. Resource Mgmt. Internat., San Rafael, Calif., 1992-95; v.p. Foster Assoc., Inc., San Francisco, 1996—; prin. Energy Econs. Consulting, Mill Valley, Calif., 1998—. Dir. Ky. Agrl. Energy Corp., Franklin. Trustee Calif. Tax Found., 1985-. Mem. Calif. State C. of C. (tax com.), Western Oil and Gas Assn., Am. Petroleum Inst. (property tax com.), Natural Gas Supply Assn., Inst. Property Taxation, Calif. Taxpayers Assn. (bd. dirs. 1985-), MIT Alumni Assn., Commonwealth (San Francisco), Sigma Xi, Tau Beta Pi. Avocations: sailing, investments, carpentry. Home: 310 Hazel Ave Mill Valley CA 94941-5054 Office: 310 Hazel Ave Mill Valley CA 94941-5054 E-mail: paulpremo@msn.com.

PRENDERGAST, FRANKLYN G. health facility administrator, medical educator; b. Linstead, Jamaica, 1945; MD, U. West Indies, 1968; PhD in biochemistry, U. Minn., 1977; BA in physiology, Oxford U., 1971, MA in physiology, 1979; DSc (hon.), Purdue U., 1994. With Mayo Clinic, Rochester, Minn., 1975—; instr. Mayo Med. Sch., Rochester, Minn., 1975—77, asst. prof. in pharmacology, 1977—81, assoc. prof. pharmacology, 1981—86, prof. in pharmacology, biochemistry, and molecular biology, 1986—, Edmond and Marion Guggenheim Prof. of Biochemistry and Molecular Biology, 1987—; named Mayo Disting. Investigator, 1988; assoc. cons. pharmacology Mayo Found., Rochester, Minn., 1977—81, cons. pharmacology, 1981—85, named cons. and chair dept. biochemistry and molecular biology, 1985, bd. trustees; named dir. rsch. Mayo Clinic, Rochester, Minn., 1992; dir. Mayo Clinic Comprehensive Cancer Ctr, Rochester, Minn., 1995—. Bd. dirs. Eli Lilly & Co., 1995—; mem. Bd. on Radiation Effects Rsch. NAS. Contbr. articles to profl. jours. Named a Disting. Alumnus, U. West Indies, 1991; recipient E.E. Just Award, Am. Soc. Exptl. Biology, 1997, Musgrave Gold Medal, Inst. Jamaica, 2003; Rhodes Scholar, 1969, Minnesota Heart Postdoctoral Fellow, 1975—77, Searle Foundation Fellow, 1980—83. Mem.: Sigma Xi, Am. Soc. Biochemistry and Molecular Biology, Biophysical Soc., AAAS, Am. Soc. Photobiology, Am. Chem. Soc. Office: Mayo Cancer Ctr 200 1st St SW Rochester MN 55905-0001*

PRENDERGAST, GEORGE C. cancer biologist, researcher; b. Phila., Aug. 25, 1961; s. George A. and Mary C. P.; m. Kristine Kushmeider, Oct. 25, 1986. BA magna cum laude, U. Pa., 1983; MS, Yale U., 1984; PhD, Princeton U., 1989. Postdoctoral fellow NYU Med. Ctr. Am. Cancer Soc., 1989-91; sr. rsch. biochemist Am. Cancer Soc. Merck and Co., Inc., West Point, Pa., 1991-93; asst. prof. Wistar Inst., U. Pa., Phila., 1993-97, assoc. prof., 1997—2001; sr. dir. cancer rsch. DuPont Pharms. Co., Glenolden, Pa., 1999—2001; sr. investigator Lankenau Inst. Med. Rsch., 2002—; prof. Thomas Jefferson U., Phila., 2002—. Sr. editor jour. Cancer Rsch.; contbr. articles to profl. jours.; patentee in field. Recipient Jr. Faculty award Am. Cancer Soc., 1995—97, Biomed. Scholar award Pew Charitable Trusts, 1995-99, Rsch. award NIH, 1995—, CaPCURE Prostate Cancer award, 1996, 97; Pfizer traveling fellow, 1997. Mem. Am. Assn. Cancer Rsch. Office: Lankenau Inst for Med Rsch 100 Lancaster Ave Wynnewood PA 19096 Office Phone: 610-645-8475. Business E-Mail: prendergastg@mlhs.org.

PRENDERGAST, KENNETH LEE MICHAEL, JR., career officer; b. Macdill Air Force Base, Fla., Sept. 16, 1956; s. Kenneth Lee and Pauline Ann (Hall) P.; m. Naomi Sue Kincade, Aug. 6, 1976; children: Melissa Ann, Robert Anthony. BA, Jacksonville State U., 1986; BS, U. N.Y., 1986; MA, U. Fla., 1990; MPA, Troy State U., 1997; M of Strategic Studies, U.S. Army War Coll., 2003. Enlisted U.S. Army, 1978, commd. 2d lt. mil. police corps, 1982; advanced through ranks to lt. col., 1997; exec. officer Company D 1st Bn., Ft. McClellan, Ala., 1983; aide de camp to dep. comdg. gen., M.P. sch. commandant Ft. McClellan, Ala., 1984-85; ops. tng. officer Provost Marshal's Office U.S. Army WESTCOM, Ft. Shafter, Hawaii, 1987; co. commdr. mil. police U.S. Army Support Commd., Ft. Shafter, 1988-89; ops. officer Provost Marshal's Office U.S. Army Law Enforcement Command, Ft. Shafter, Hawaii, 1989; fgn. area officer U.S. Embassy, Kinshasa, Zaire, 1991, Yaounde, Cameroon, 1992-93; internat. officer instr. U.S. Army Command and Gen. Staff Coll., Ft. Leavenworth, Kans., 1993; joint task force 161 and ARFOR plans officer Guantanamo Bay, Cuba, 1994; MP long range plans officer 89th Mil. Police Brigade, Ft. Hood, Tex., 1994-95; exec. officer 720th Mil. Police Battalion, Ft. Hood, 1995-96; Am. Polit. Sci. Assn. congrl. fellow Senator Bob Graham, Washington, 1996-97; chief of plans and ops. office Chief of Legis. Liaison Office of Sec., U.S. Army, Washington, 1997-98; dir. legis. strategy Washington, 1998-99; bn. comdr. 19th Mil. Police Bn., Seoul, Republic of Korea, 1999—2001; provost marshal, joint task force patriot Ft. George G. Meade, Md., 2001—02. Vol. coach youth football, soccer, baseball, 1974—; leader Boy Scouts Am., Ft. Hood, 1989—, mem. com., 1994-96. Decorated Legion of Merit. Mem. VFW, Ret. Officers Assn., Korean-Am. Assn., Assn. U.S. Army, 720th Mil. Police Battalion Reunion Assn. (life), Mil. Police Regimental Assn., Mil. Officers Assn. Am., Fgn. Area Officer Assn. (founding), U. Fla. Nat. Alumni Assn. (life), Jacksonville State U. Alumni Assn. (life), Am. Polit. Sci. Assn., Am. C. of C. in Korea, Harley Owners Group, Alpha Kappa Delta. Roman Catholic. Avocations: sailing, scuba diving, water-skiing, skydiving, foreign travel. Home: 1359 Staff Row SW Atlanta GA 30310-5123 E-mail: kenneth.prendergast@us.army.mil.

PRENDERGAST, ROBERT ANTHONY, pathologist educator; b. Bklyn., Nov. 6, 1931; BA, Columbia U., 1953; MD, Boston U., 1957. Intern Bellevue Hosp., 1957-58; resident Boston City Hosp., 1958-59, Meml. Sloan-Kettering Hosp., 1959-61; vis. physician Rockefeller U., 1963-65, asst. prof., 1963-70, assoc. prof. opthamology, 1970-99; prof. ophthalmology and pathology Johns Hopkins U. Sch. Medicine, 1999—. Bd. dirs. Marine Biol. Lab. Mem. Am. Assn. Immunology, Am. Soc. Exp. Pathology, H.G. Kunkel Soc., Assn. Vision & Ophthal., Pluto Club. Achievements include research in cellular immunology, ontogeny of the immune response, transplantation immunology, viral immunopathology, immunopathology of ocular inflammatory diseases. Office: Marine Biol Lab Woods Hole MA 02543 E-mail: rprender@mbl.edu.

PRENDERGAST, TERRY NEILL, lawyer; b. Sioux Falls, S.D., May 25, 1953; s. Harry Neill and Dorothy Gretchen (Angerhofer) P.; m. Susan Jane Lucas, Aug. 2, 1980; children, Christopher Neill, Steven Robert. B.A. cum laude, Augustana Coll., 1975; M.B.A., U. S.D., 1978, J.D. magna cum laude, 1978. Bar: S.D. 1978, U.S. Dist. Ct. S.D. 1978, U.S. Tax Ct. 1981, U.S. Ct. Appeals (8th cir.) 1981. Law clk. U.S. Dist. Ct., Sioux Falls, 1978-79; ptnr. Boyce, Murphy, McDowell & Greenfield, Sioux Falls, 1979—2002; founding ptnr. Murphy, Goldammer & Prendergast, L.L.P., Sioux Falls, 2003–; chmn. continuing legal edn. com. State Bar S.D., Pierre, 1984-87, Bar Commr., 1987-90; city atty. Lennox, S.D., 1980-82. Mem. ABA (coms. on corp., banking and bus. law, sci. and tech.), Assn. Trial Lawyers Am., S.D. Trial Lawyers Assn., Comml. Law League Am., Am. Judicature Soc., Assn. Coll. and Univ. Attys. Republican. Methodist. Lodges: Kiwanis (bd. dirs. 1981-83, v.p. 1986-87, pres. 1987-88), Elks. Home: 2904 S 1st Ave Sioux Falls SD 57105-4915 Office: Murphy Goldammer & Prendergast LLP 402 Wells Fargo Bldg PO Box 1728 Sioux Falls SD 57101-1728 Office Phone: 605-331-2975.

PRENDERGAST, THOMAS A. investments and management consultant; b. Dec. 10, 1933; m. Mary Alice Peinado; children: Elizabeth Jane Mettler, Laura Ann Gordon. BS, Fordham U., 1955; postgrad., U. Tex., El Paso, 1960. CPA, Tex. Pvt. practice acctg., 1957-61; v.p. fin. Farah Mfg., Inc., 1961-71; chmn. bd. Billy the Kid, Inc., 1971-81, Jetco, 1972-74, Fashion Enterpreses, Inc., 1982-84, Air Cargo Equipment Corp., 1983-88, investments, mgmt. cons.; chmn. bd. El Paso Gibson's, Inc., 1988—92; chmn. Sunland Audio Ltd. Co., 1994—98, N.Am. Bender, Inc., 1995—2000. Chmn. bd. dirs. Baron Chem., Inc., Clinitech, Inc., 1986-91, Steel Corp. Tex., Texzona Industries, Inc., True Blue Sky, Inc.; bd. dirs. Market Guide Inc., Air Cargo Inc., Fischback and Moore Inc., Double Eagle Petroleum, Inc., Intellicheck, Inc.; chmn. Market Guide, 1997-2000. Composer; author poetry, film criticsm; contbr. articles to profl. jours. Founder, pres. bd. trustees El Paso Community Coll, 1969-82. Home: 725 Montoya Oak El Paso TX 79932

PRENDERGAST, WILLIAM JOHN, ophthalmologist; b. Portland, Oreg., June 12, 1942; s. William John and Marjorie (Scott) P.; m. Carolyn Grace Perkins, Aug. 17, 1963 (div. 1990); children: William John, Scott; m. Sherryl Irene Guenther, Aug. 25, 1991. BS, U. Oreg., Eugene, 1964; MD, U. Oreg., Portland, 1967. Diplomate Am. Bd. Ophthalmology. Resident in ophthalmology U. Oreg., Portland, 1970-73; pvt. practice specializing in ophthalmology Portland, 1973-82; physician, founder, ptnr. Eye Health NW (formerly Oreg. Med. Eye Clinic), Portland, 1983—; also bd. dirs.; founder, pres. (Focus Group) Inc. Focus Group Inc., Ophthalmic Clinic Networking Venture, Portland, 1992—. Clin. asst. prof. ophthalmology Oreg. Health Sci. U., 1985—; dir. Eye Health Ptnrs. Med. Optometric Managed Eye Care Venture, 1998. Vol. surgeon, Hosp. de la Familia, Nuevo Progreso, Guatamala, 2001-2003, vol. surgeon N.W. Med. Teams, Oaxaca, Mexico, 1989, 90. With USPHS, 1968-70. Fellow Am. Acad. Ophthalmology; mem. Met. Bus. Assn., Multnomah Athletic Club, Mazamas Mountaineering Club, Portland Yacht Club, Phi Beta Kappa, Alpha Omega Alpha. Avocations: yacht racing, mountain climbing. Office: Eye Health NW 1955 NW Northrup St Portland OR 97209-1614 Office Phone: 503-227-2020. Business E-Mail: prenderw@omec.ehnpc.com.

PRENG, DAVID EDWARD, management consultant; b. Chgo., Sept. 30, 1946; s. Edward M. and Frances (Maras) P.; m. Joanne Ferzoco, Dec. 6, 1969; children: Mark, Laura, Stephen, Michael. BS, Marquette U., 1969; MBA, DePaul U., 1973. Supr. Shell Oil Co., Houston, 1969—73, Chgo., 1969—73; contr. Litton Office Products, Houston, 1973—74; v.p. Addington & Assoc., 1976—77; sr. assoc. Energy divsn. Korn/Ferry Internat., 1977—78; v.p. Kors Marlar & Assoc., 1978—80; pres. Preng & Assoc., 1980—85, Preng Zant & Assoc., 1985—87, Preng & Assoc., 1987—. Bd. dir. Cmty. Nat. Bank Tex., 2002, Remington Oil & Gas Corp., 1997. Mem. Sugar Creek Country Club. Home: 607 Chevy Chase Cir Sugar Land TX 77478-3601

PRENGLE, HERMAN WILLIAM, JR., chemical engineer, educator; b. Pa., Nov. 6, 1919; s. Herman William and Irene (Smith) P.; m. Ruth Hamilton, Dec. 6, 1941; children: Pixie Bernice Irene, Karl William, Scott Hamilton. BS, Carnegie-Mellon U., 1941, MS, 1947, DSc, 1949. Registered profl. engr., Tex. Rsch. engr. Linde Air Products Co., Tonwanda, N.Y., 1941; sr. engr. Shell Oil Co., Houston, 1949-53; assoc. prof. U. Houston, 1953-59, prof., 1959-97, prof. emeritus, 1997—, chmn. chem. engring. dept., 1958-61, assoc. dean Cullen Coll. Engring., 1981-85, dir. MChE program chem. engring. dept., 1985-97. Vis. scholar chemistry dept. Cambridge (Eng.) U., 1971-72, Corpus Christi Coll., 1988, Darwin Coll., 1990; cons. chem. and petroleum industries U.S. Govt., 1958—; panel mem. peer rev. of rsch. U.S. EPA, Washington, 1975-97. Contbr. articles to profl. jours. Chmn. Charter Commn., Friendswood, Tex., 1970-71; mem. Nat. Rep. Com., Washington, 1980—; mem. Rep. Presdl. Task Force, Washington, 1983—; mem. U.S. Com. Battle Normandy Mus., Caen, France, 1988—. Lt. col. U.S. Army, 1941-46, ETO. Decorated Bronze Star with oak leaf cluster; recipient Kittinger Tchg. award U. Houston Cullen Coll. Engring., 1971, award of Merit, Pollution Engring. Mag., Chgo., 1976, Tchg. Excellence award Haliburton Found., 1989, 92, 94, 96. Fellow Am. Inst. Chemists; mem. AIChE, Am. Chem. Soc., Royal Chem. Soc. (London), Army-Navy Club, Brotherhood of St. Andrew, Sigma Xi, Tau Beta Pi, Phi Kappa Phi. Episcopalian. Achievements include 3 patents (with others) for ozone-UV advanced oxidation prodess for water borne toxic compounds; invention (with other) of ammonium hydrogen sulfate (AHS) and duplex AHS solar energy storage process; invention (with others) of infrared radiometry spectroscopy method (IRSM) for remote sensing of temperatures, gradients and pollutant concentrations from stationary emission sources; invention (with others) of the hydrogen peroxide-VisUV process (HP/VisUV) for treatment of hazardous water borne substances and gaseous emissions; invention and patent (with others) for improved apparatus for fractional distillation of multi-component hydrocarbon mixtures. Home: 642 Babcock Rd #10D San Antonio TX 78201

PRENSKY, ARTHUR LAWRENCE, pediatric neurologist, educator; b. N.Y.C., Aug. 31, 1930; s. Herman and Pearl (Newman) P.; m. Sheila Carr, Nov. 13, 1969. AB, Cornell U., 1951; MD, N.Y. U., 1955. Diplomate: Am. Bd. Psychiatry and Neurology. Intern Barnes Hosp., St. Louis, 1955-56; resident and research fellow in neurology Harvard U., Mass. Gen. Hosp., Boston, 1959-66; instr. neurology Harvard Med. Sch., 1966-67; mem. faculty Washington U. Sch. Medicine, St. Louis, 1967—, prof. pediatrics and neurology, to 1975, Allen P. and Josephine B. Green prof. pediatric neurology, 1975-2000, prof. emeritus of neurology, 2000—; pediatrician St. Louis Children's Hosp.; neurologist Barnes and Allied Hosps., Jewish Hosp., St. Louis. Author: (with others) Nutrition and the Developing Nervous System, 1975; editor: (with others) Neurological Pathophysiology, 2d edit, 1978, Advances in Neurology, 1976; mem. editorial bd. Pediatric Neurology, 1984-90, Jour. Child Neurology, 1985—. Served with USAF, 1957-59. Fellow Am. Acad. Neurology; mem. Am. Neurol. Assn., Am. Soc. Neurochemistry (mem. council 1973-77), Central Soc. Neurol. Rsch. (pres. 1977-78), Child Neurology Soc. (pres. 1979-80, Hower award 2000), Am. Pediatric Soc., Internat. Child Neurology Assn., Japanese Soc. Child Neurology, Profs. Child Neurology (pres. 1984-86) Home: 15 Monarch Hill Ct Chesterfield MO 63005-4004 Office: 400 S Kingshighway Blvd Saint Louis MO 63110-1014 Office Phone: 314-454-6120. Business E-Mail: prensky@neuro.wustl.edu.

PRENTICE, ANN ETHELYND, university dean; b. Grafton, Vt., July 19, 1933; d. Homer Orville and Helen (Cooke) Hurlbut; divorced; children: David, Melody, Holly, Wayne. AB, U. Rochester, 1954; MLS, SUNY, Albany, 1964; DLS, Columbia U., 1972; LittD (hon.), Keuka Coll., 1979. Lectr. sch. info. sci. and policy SUNY, Albany, 1971-72, asst. prof., 1972-78; prof., dir. grad. sch. library and info. sci. U. Tenn., Knoxville, 1978-88; assoc. v.p. info. resources U. South Fla., Tampa, 1988-93; dean Coll. Info. Studies, U. Md., College Park, 1993—, acting asst. v.p. for info. resources, 1994-98. Y2K compliance coord. U. Md., 1998—. Author: Strategies for Survival, Library Financial Management Today, 1979, The Library Trustee, 1973, Public Library Finance, 1977, Financial Planning for Libraries, 1983, 2d edit., 1996, Professional Ethics for Librarians, 1985; editor Pub. Libr. Quar., 1978-81; co-editor: Info. Sci. in its Disciplinary Context, 1990; assoc. editor Library and Info. Sci. Ann., 1987-90. Cons. long-range planning and pers. Knox County Libr. System, 1980, 85-86, Richland County S.C. Libr. System, 1981, Upper Hudson Libr. Fedn., N.Y., State Libr. Ohio, 1986, Am. U., 1996; trustee Hyde Park (N.Y.) Free Libr., treas., 1973-75, pres., 1976; trustee Mid-Hudson Libr. System, Poughkeepsie, N.Y., 1975-78; trustee adv. bd. Hillsborough County Libr., 1991-93. Recipient Disting. Alumni award SUNY, Albany, 1987, Columbia U., 1991. Mem. ALA, CAUSE, Am. Soc. Info. Sci. (exec. bd. 1986-89, conf. chmn. 1989, pres. 1992-93, chmn. info. policy com. 1994-96), Assn. for Libr. and Info. Sci. Edn. (pres. 1986). Office: Univ Md Coll Libr and Info Svcs 4105 Hornbake Bldg College Park MD 20742-0001

PRENTICE, MARGARITA, state legislator, nurse; Student, Phoenix Coll., Youngstown U.; RN, St. Joseph's Hosp. Sch.; student, U. Wash. RN, Wash. Nurse, Wash.; mem. Wash. Senate, Dist. 11, Olympia, 1988—; majority caucus vice chair Wash. Senate, Olympia, 1993-94; mem. agr. and rural econ. devel. com. Wash. Legislature, Olympia, mem. transp. com. Mem. Dem. Nat. Com. Recipient Legislator of Yr. Retail Assn. and Mortgage Bankers Assn., Wash. Health Care Assn., Wash. State Labor Coun., Wash. State Nurses Assn., Home Health Care Assn., King County Nurse of Yr., Champion of Health Care award Valley Med. Ctr., Disting. Svc. award Wash. Assn. Homes for Aging, Legislator of Yr. Wash. State Dental Hygienists Assn. Mem. ACLU, Amnesty Internat., Wash. State Nurses Assn. (1st v.p. 1968-72, labor officer 1974-78), Sierra Club, Renton Hist. Soc., Audubon Soc., Humane Soc. U.S. Democrat. Office: 419 John Cherberg Bldg Olympia WA 98504-0001

PRENTISS, C. J. state legislator; BA in Edn., Cleve. State U., 1969, MEd, 1975; cert., Kent State U., 1976; grad. Weatherhead Sch. Mgmt., Case Western Res. U., 1978. Mem. Ohio Ho. of Reps. from 8th dist., Columbus, 1990-98, Ohio Senate from 21st dist., Columbus, 1999—; mem. econ. devel., tech. and aerospace com., edn. com., fin. and financial instns. com., health, human svcs. and aging com. Chair edn. policy Ohio legislative Black Caucus and Black elected Democrats of Cleve., vice-chair edn. com. Nat. Conf. State Legislatures; past vice-chair HouseEdn. com., ways and means, ins.; mem. State Bd. Edn., 1984-90, chair lit. and youth-at-risk com., legis. stds. com., past chair joint select com. on infant health and family support. Past Vice-chair Black Leadership Cleve. Alumni; past mem. gov.'s com. Socially Disadvantaged Black Males. Office: Senate Bldg Rm 57 Columbus OH 43215

PRENTISS, MICHAEL VERNON, urban planner; b. Albuquerque, Oct. 16, 1943; s. Vernon and Florence May (Madden) P.; m. Betty Ann Bradbury, July 9, 1966 (div. 1976); m. Patricia Gayle Galt, Mar. 15, 1979; children— Paige Elizabeth, Kennedy Anne, Michael Brian BS in Civil Engring., BA in Bus. Adminstrn., Washington State U., 1966; M. BA, Harvard U., 1973. Registered profl. engr., Wash. Pres. Ackerman Devel. Co., Atlanta, 1973-79; pres. Cadillac Fairview Urban Devel., Dallas, 1979—. Dir. Cadillac Fairview Corp., Ltd., Toronto, Central Atlanta Progress. Bd. dirs. Taca, Dallas, 1980; mem. Dallas Citizens Council, 1981—; bd. dirs., mem. exec. com. Central Dallas Assn., 1980—; mem. Dallas Assembly, 1985— . Served to lt. USN, 1966-71 Mem. Urban Land Inst., Young Pres. Orgn. Republican. Avocations: tennis; golf; basketball.

PREOBRAZHENSKY, ALEXANDER ANATOLIYEVICH, biochemist; b. Chita, Russia, Sept. 29, 1946; s. Anatoliy Nikolayevich and Magdalina Sergeyevna (Knyaginicheva) P.; m. Ekaterina Sergeyevna Grigoriyan, Mar. 14, 1970 (div. Jan. 1981); 1 child, Elena; m. Olga Stefanovna Zakharova, Dec. 22, 1984; 1 child, Sergei. Student, Moscow State U., 1970, PhD in Biology, 1976, DSc, 1996. Rsch. asst. Inst. for Protein Rsch., Pouschino, Russia, 1970-72; rsch. assoc. A.N. Bach Inst. of Biochemistry, Moscow, 1975-86, sr. scientist, 1986—. Grantee Ministry of Sci. and Tech., 1989, Russian Found. for Fundamental Rsch., 1994, 97, Internat. Sci. Found. Mem. Russian Biochem. Soc., N.Y. Acad. Scis. Avocations: hiking, internet, orienteering, reading. Office: 2540 Olentangy River Rd Columbus OH 43202-1505

PRESANT, SANFORD CALVIN, lawyer, educator, writer, tax specialist; b. Buffalo, Nov. 15, 1952; s. Allen and Reeta Presant; children: Jarrett, Danny, Lauren; m. Nancy Loeb. BA, Cornell U., 1973; JD cum laude, SUNY, Buffalo, 1976; LLM in Taxation, Georgetown U., NYU, 1981. Bar: N.Y. 1977, D.C. 1977, U.S. Tax Ct. 1977, U.S. Ct. Claims 1978, Calif. 1992, U.S. Supreme Ct. 1982. Staff atty. SEC Options Task Force, Washington, 1976-78; assoc. Barrett Smith Schapiro, N.Y.C., 1978-80, Trubin Sillcocks, N.Y.C., 1980-81; ptnr. Carro, Spanbock, Fass, Geller, Kaster, N.Y.C., 1981-86, Finley, Kumble, Wagner, Heine, Underberg, Manley, Myerson & Casey, N.Y.C., 1987, Kaye, Scholer, Fierman, Hays & Handler, N.Y.C., 1987-95, Battle Fowler LLP, L.A., 1995-2000, Ernst & Young, L.A., 2000—; nat. dir. real estate tax strategies, opportunity funds Ernst & Young LLP, L.A., 2000—. Adj. assoc. prof. real estate NYU, 1984—; frequest lectr. in tax law; regular TV appearances on Nightly Bus. Report, PBS, 1986-88; co-chmn. NYU Conf. Fed. Taxation of Real Estate Transactions, 1987, PLI Advanced Tax Planning for Real Estate, 1987, PLI Ann. Real Estate Tax Forum, 1999—; program dir. Nareit Law and Acctg. Conf., 2003; conf. chmn. various confs. in field. Author: (with others) Tax Aspects of Real Investments, 2002, Understanding Partnership Tax Allocations, 1987, Realty Joint Ventures, 1980-86, Tax Sheltered Investments Handbook-Special Update on Tax Reform Act of 1984, Real Estate Syndication Handbook, 1986, Real Estate Syndication Tax Handbook, 1987, The Tax Reform Act of 1986, 1987, The Final Partnership Nonrecourse Debt Allocation Regulations, 1987, Taxation of Real Estate Investments, 1987, Understanding Partnership Tax Allocations, 1987, Tax Aspects of Environmental (Superfund) Settlements, 1994, The Proposed Publicly Traded Partnership Regulations, 1995, others. Kripke Securities Law fellow NYU, 1976. Mem. ABA (nat. chmn. audit subcom. of tax sect. partnership com. 1984-86, partnership tax allocation subcom. chmn. 1986-90, nat. chmn. partnership com. 1992-94, chmn. task force publicly traded partnerships 1995—, others), N.Y. State Bar Assn. (tax sect. partnership com. 1980—), Assn. Bar City of N.Y. Republican. Jewish. Office: Ernst & Young LLP Ste 1800 2049 Century Park E Los Angeles CA 90067-3119 Fax: 310-284-7970. Office Phone: 310-551-7805. E-mail: sanford.presant@ey.com.

PRESBY, J. THOMAS, financial advisor, director, arbitrator; b. Newark, Feb. 15, 1940; s. George and Shirley (Kandel) P.; m. Elaine Merle Smith, Aug. 19, 1961; children: Philip, Terry, Mona. BSEE, Rutgers U., 1961; MS in Indsl. Adminstrn., Carnegie-Mellon U., 1963. CPA, Ohio, N.Y. Ptnr. Touche Ross, N.Y.C., 1972-76; regional ptnr. Touche Ross Internat., Paris, 1976-79, nat. dir. client svcs., 1979-81, exec. dir. internat., 1981-82, ptnr.-in-charge fin. svcs. ctr., 1982-90, mng. ptnr. Ea. Europe, Brussels, 1990-94, chief exec. officer Europe, Paris, 1991-95; COO Deloitte Touche Tohmatsu Internat., N.Y.C., 1995—, dep. chmn., chief oper. officer, 1997, chief staff, mem. exec. group, 1999—2002. Mem. bus. adv. coun. Grad. Sch. Indsl. Adminstrn., Carnegie-Mellon U., Pitts., 1984-2001; trustee Rutgers U., New Brunswick, N.J., 1985-90; bd. dirs. Tiffany & Co., Greenpoint Financial, World Fuel Services, Turbochef Technologies, German Marshall Fund. Mem. AICPA, Ohio Soc. CPAs, N.Y. Soc. CPAs, Harmonie Club. Avocations: antique autos, racquet-ball, squash, motorcycling, fly fishing. Home: 6 Holton Ln Essex Fells NJ 07021-1709 Office: Deloitte Touche 1633 Broadway New York NY 10019-6708 E-mail: tpresby@deloitte.com.

PRESCHLACK, JOHN EDWARD, management consultant; b. N.Y.C., May 30, 1933; s. William and Anna M. (Hrubesch) P.; m. Lynn A. Stanley, Dec. 29, 1962; children: John Edward Jr., James S., David C. BSEE, MIT, 1954; MBA, Harvard U., 1958. Ptnr. McKinsey & Co., Inc., N.Y.C., London, Düsseldorf, Germany, 1958-73; pres. ITEK Graphic Products Co., Lexington, Mass., 1973-77; pres., CEO Gen. Binding Corp., Northbrook, Ill., 1977-83; pres. Roberts & Porter, Inc., Des Plaines, Ill., 1984-86; sr. dir. Spencer Stuart, Chgo., 1987-96; chmn., pres. Jepcor, Inc., Lake Bluff, Ill., 1996—. Bd. dirs. Blyth Inc., Greenwich, Conn., 1989—. Trustee Chgo. Hort. Soc., 1979—; chmn. Lake Forest (Ill.) Planning Commn., 1982-88; alderman City of Lake Forest, 1990-96, mayor, 2002—; mem. corp. devel. com. MIT, 1986-92. Lt. USAF, 1954-56. Recipient Corp. Leadership award MIT, 1978. Mem. Onwentsia Club, Chgo. Club, John's Island Club. Republican. Roman Catholic. Avocations: tennis, golf, boating, travel. E-mail: jepcor@aol.com. *Focus on what's right, not who's right; be honest and candid in dealing with others; don't get hung up on who gets credit for what you've done; select and reward outstanding people.*

PRESCOTT, BARBARA LODWICH, educational administrator; b. Chgo., Aug. 15, 1951; d. Edward and Eugenia Lodwich; m. Warren Paul Prescott, Dec. 2, 1979; children: Warren Paul Jr., Ashley Elizabeth. BA, U. Ill., Chgo., 1973, MEd, 1981; MA, U. Wis., 1978; postgrad., Stanford U., 1983-87. Cert. tchr., learning handicapped specialist, cmty. coll. instr., Calif. Grad. rschr. U. Ill., Chgo., 1979-81; learning handicapped specialist St. Paulus Luth. Sch., San Francisco, 1981-83; grad. rsch. asst. Sch. Edn. Stanford (Calif.) U., 1983-87, writing cons. for law students, 1985-86; learning handicapped specialist/lead therapist Gilroy Clinic Speech-Hearing-Learning Ctr., Crippled Children's Soc., Santa Clara, Calif., 1988-89; ednl. dir. Adolescent Intensive Resdl. Svc. Calif. Pacific Med. Ctr., San Francisco, 1989-95; exec. dir. Learning Profiles, South Lake Tahoe, Calif., 1995—. Instr. evening San Jose City Coll., 1988-92. Contbr. articles to profl. jours.; author: Proceedings of Internat. Congress of Linguistics, 1987; editor: Proceedings - Forum for Research on Language Issues, 1986; author videotape: Making a Difference in Language and Learning, 1989. Recipient Frederick Bork Teaching Trainee award San Francisco State U., 1983; Ill. State scholar, 1973. Mem. Calif. Assn. Pvt. Specialized Edn. and Svcs., Phi Delta Kappa (v.p. 1984-86), Pi Lambda Theta (sec. 1982-83), Phi Kappa Phi, Alpha Lambda Theta.

PRESCOTT, DANA E. lawyer; b. Aug. 1958; BA, Western New Eng. Coll.; JD, Vt. Law Sch. Bar: Maine 1983. Atty. Prescott Lemoine Jamieson & Nelson, PA, Saco, Maine. Mem.: Maine State Bar Assn. (pres.-elect). Office: Prescott Lemoine Jamieson and Nelson PO Box 1190 Saco ME 04072-1190

PRESCOTT, DAVID L. C., JR., music educator; s. David L. C. Prescott, Sr. and Lavina Hall Prescott. BS in Bus. Adminstrn., Old Dominion U., 1981, MusB in Music Edn., 1992, MS in Secondary Edn., Choral Conducting, 2002. Acct. W. E. Moulton, Jr. & Assocs., Portsmouth, Va., 1981—90; music specialist Tanners Creek Elem. Sch., Norfolk, Va., 1992—93; dir. choral activities Ocean Lakes H.S., Virginia Beach, Va., 1993—97, Kempsville H.S., Virginia Beach, Va., 1997—. Guest clinician, condr. Various Churches And Civic Choirs, Va., 1992—; dir. music Holland Rd. Bapt. Ch., Virginia Beach, 1983—97, Faith Wesleyan Ch., Norfolk, 1995—. King herod: (musical theatre) Jesus Christ Superstar; costumer (dramas and musical theatre works) A Man for All Seasons, Christ and St. Luke's Arts Guild, 2000, Our Town, Christ and St. Luke's Art Guild, 1999, Jesus Christ Superstar, Christ and St. Luke's Art Guild, 2001, Guys and Dolls, Wizard of Oz, Annie Get Your Gun, Mame, Cinderella, Kempsville H.S., 1999—2003. Mem. bd. dirs. Virginia Beach Ballet, 1990—93. Recipient Award of Distinction - Choral Conducting, Fest. Music Competitions, 1999. Mem.: Music Educators Nat. Conf., Va. Music Educators Assn., Am. Choral Dir.'s Assn., Phi Mu Alpha Sinfonia. Wesleyan. Avocations: antiques, flower arranging. Office: Kempsville High School 5194 Chief Trail Virginia Beach VA 23464 E-mail: dlpresco@vbcps.k12.va.us.

PRESCOTT, DAVID MARSHALL, biology educator; b. Clearwater, Fla., Aug. 3, 1926; s. Clifford Raymond and Lillian (Moore) P.; m. Gayle Edna Demery; children: Lavonne, Jason, Ryan. BA, Wesleyan U., 1950; PhD, U. Calif., Berkeley, 1954. Asst. prof. UCLA Med. Sch., 1955-59; biologist Oak Ridge (Tenn.) Nat. Lab., 1959-63; prof. U. Colo. Sch. Medicine, Denver, 1963-66; prof. molecular, cell and devel. biology U. Colo., Boulder, 1966-80, Disting. prof. molecular, cell and devel. biology, 1980—2002, Disting. prof. emeritus, 2002—. Pres. Am. Soc. Cell Biology, 1966. Author: Cell Reproduction, 1976, Cancer: The Misguided Cell, 1986, Cells, 1988; also numerous rsch. reports; editor: Methods in Cell Biology, 15 vols., 1963-78. Adv. com. March of Dimes, 1979-90. Recipient von Humboldt prize Fed. Republic Germany, 1979; grantee NIH, 1985-95, 97-2002, Nat. Found. Cancer Rsch., 1985-89, NSF, 1990-91, 95—; John Simon Guggenheim Meml. Found. fellow, 1990-91. Fellow Am. Acad. Arts and Scis.; mem. NAS, Soc. Protozoologists (pres. 1995-96). Avocations: coin collecting/numismatics, gardening. Home: 285 Brook Pl Boulder CO 80302-8031 Office: Univ Colo Campus Box 347 MCDB Biology Boulder CO 80309-0347

PRESCOTT, EDWARD C. economist, educator; Formerly regents prof. U. Minn.; now W.P. chair Ariz. State U., Tempe. Sr. monetary adviser Fed. Res. Bank, Mpls. Recipient Erwin Plein Nemmers prize in Econ. Office: Ariz State U Dept Econs Tempe AZ 85287-3806

PRESCOTT, JOHN MACK, biochemist, retired university administrator; b. San Marcos, Tex., Jan. 22, 1921; s. John Mack and Maude (Raborn) P.; m. Kathryn Ann Kelly, June 8, 1946; children: Stephen Michael, Donald Wyatt. BS in Chemistry, S.W. Tex. State Coll., 1941; MS in Biochemistry and Nutrition, Tex. A&M U., 1949; PhD in Biochemistry, U. Wis., 1952. Lab. asst. Dow Chem. Co., Freeport, Tex., 1942-43; faculty Tex. A&M U., College Station, 1946-49, 52-85, prof. biochemistry, 1959-85, dean Coll. Sci., 1970-77, v.p. for acad. affairs, 1977-81, dir. Inst. Occupational and Environ. Medicine, 1981-87, prof. med. biochemistry, 1981-85, prof. emeritus, 1985—, spl. asst. to dep. chancellor for biotech. devel., 1987-88; research asst. U. Wis.-Madison, 1949-51, U. Tex., Austin, 1951-52; vis. prof. Harvard Med. Sch., 1982. Contbr. articles profl. jours. Mem. Tex. Bd. Examiners in Basic Scis., 1974-79, mem. Tex. State Bd. Edn., 1984-88. Served to lt. USAAF,

1943-46; lt. col. USAF Res., 1946-68. Mem. Am. Soc. for Biochemistry and Molecular Biology, Soc. for Exptl. Biology and Medicine, Sigma Xi, Phi Lambda Upsilon. Home: 31 Forest Dr College Station TX 77840-2337

PRESCOTT, LAWRENCE MALCOLM, medical and health science writer; b. Boston, July 31, 1934; s. Benjamin and Lillian (Stein) P.; m. Ellen Gay Kober, Feb. 19, 1961 (dec. Sept. 1981); children: Jennifer Maya, Adam Barrett; m. Sharon Lynn Kirshen, May 16, 1982; children: Gary Leon Kirshen, Marc Paul Kirshen. BA, Harvard U., 1957; MSc, George Washington U., 1959, PhD, 1966. Nat. Acad. Scis. postdoctoral fellow U.A. Army Rsch., Ft. Detrick, Md., 1965-66; microbiologist/scientist WHO, India, 1967-70, 1970-72, 1972-78; with pub. rels. GCI, Hill & Knowlton, Aventis, Astra Zeneza, others, 1984—; cons. to internat. orgns. San Diego, 1978—. Author manuals; contbr. articles in diarrheal diseases and lab. scis. to profl. jours., numerous articles, stories, poems to mags., newspapers, including Living in Thailand, Jack and Jill, Strawberry, Bangkok Times, Spring, 1977-81; mng. editor Caduceus, 1981-82; pub., editor: Teenage Scene, 1982-83; pres. Prescott Pub. Co., 1982-83; med. writer numerous jours. including Modern Medicine, Dermatology Times, Drug and Market Devel., P&T, Clinical Cancer Letter, Anesthesiology News, Arzte Zeitung, Australian Doctor, Inpharma Weekly, Chronicle of Cardiovascular and Internal Medicine, Ophthalmology Times, Pharmacy Practice News, Body Positive, AIDS Update, Medical Allert, Infectious Diseases, Urology Times, Genetic Engineering News, Medical Week, Gastroenterology and Endoscopy News; author: Curry Every Sunday, 1984. Home and Office: 18264 Verano Dr San Diego CA 92128-1262 Office Phone: 858-487-3871. Personal E-mail: sprescott@aol.com.

PRESCOTT, PERRY DON, psychology educator, counselor; b. Jasper, Ala., Mar. 15, 1952; s. Howard J. and Mary Lou Prescott; m. Hazel Ann Prescott, June 12, 1975; children: Justin H., Nigel A., Trevor G. BS, U. Ala., 1974, MA, 1978, PhD, 1984. Asst. prof. psychology Miss. Coll., Clinton, 1988-89; asst. prof. counseling U. Ga., Athens, 1989-90, U. Guam, Mangilao, 1990-91; pvt. practice Tuscaloosa, Ala., 1991-92; asst. prof. psychology McNeese State U., Lake Charles, La., 1992-93; counselor, tchr. State of Ala. Schs., Jasper, Double Springs, 1993-97; PACE psychology prof. Navy program Ctrl. Tex. Coll., San Diego, 1997—2002; psychotherapist, consortium between Auburn U. and UJ. Ala. Montgomery State of Ala., 2002—. Cons. Profl. Counseling Svcs., Jasper, Ala., 1994, Walker Regional Hosp., Jasper, 1994. Contbr. articles to profl. jours. including Ala. Assn. Counselors Jour., Jour. Reading. With USAR, 1972-78. Named one of Outstanding Young Men in Am., Jaycees, 1982. Mem So. Assn. Coll. Student Adminstrs. (com. 1986-87), William Glasser Inst. (cert.), Phi Delta Kappa, Kappa Delta Pi. Avocations: travel, foreign languages, reading. Home and Office: 11531 Shalom Rd Duncanville AL 35456-2533

PRESCOTT, RICHARD CHAMBERS, writer; b. Houston, Apr. 1, 1952; s. Chambers Richard and Dorothy Mae (Bashara) P.; m. Sarah Elisabeth Grace, Oct. 13, 1981. Author: The Sage, 1975, Moonstar, 1975, Neuf Songes (Nine Dreams), 1976, 2nd edit., 1991, The Carouse of Soma, 1977, Lions and Kings, 1977, Allah Wake Up, 1978, 2nd edit., 1994, Night Reaper, 1979, Dragon Tales, 1983, Dragon Dreams, 1986, 2nd edit., 1990, Dragon Prayers, 1988, 2nd edit., 1990, Dragon Songs, 1988, 2nd edit., 1990, Dragon Maker, 1989, 2nd edit., 1990, Dragon Thoughts, 1990, Tales of Recognition, 1991, Kings and Sages, 1991, Dragon Sight: A Cremation Poem, 1992, Three Waves, 1992, Years of Wonder, 1992, Dream Appearances, 1992, Remembrance Recognition and Return, 1992, Spare Advice, 1992, The Imperishable, 1993, The Dark Deitess, 1993, Disturbing Delights: Waves of The Great Goddess, 1993, The Immortal: Racopa and the Rooms of Light, 1993, Hanging Baskets, 1993, Writer's Block and Other Gray Matters, 1993, The Resurrection of Quantum Joe, 1993, The Horse and the Carriage, 1993, Kalee Bhava: The Goddess and Her Moods, 1995, The Skills of Kalee, 1995, Because of Atma, 1995, Measuring Sky Without Ground, 1996, The Goddess And The God Man, 1996, Kalee: The Allayer of Sorrows, 1996, Living Sakti, 1997, The Mirage and the Mirror, 1998, Inherent Solutions to Spiritual Obscurations, 1999, The Ancient Method, 1999, Quantum Kamakala, 2000; contbr. articles and essays to profl. publs.

PRESCOTT, THOMAS W. bank executive; b. Oct. 24, 1954; BBA in Acctg., Columbus Coll., 1976. From v.p. fin. to exec. v.p., CFO Synovus Fin. Corp., Columbus, Ga., 1987—96, exec. v.p., 1996—, CFO, 1996—. Bd. dir. Family Counseling Ctr. Mem.: Ga. Soc. CPAs, Kiwanis Club N.Columbus. Office: Synovus Financial Corp 1 Arsenal Place 901 Front Ave Ste 301 Columbus GA 31901*

PRESECAN, NICHOLAS LEE, environmental and civil engineer, consultant; b. Indpls., Sept. 4, 1940; s. Nicholas Eli and Dorothy Lee (Moore) P.; m. Joan Westin, Nov. 11, 1940; children: Julie Marie, Mary Lee, Anne Westin. BSCE, Purdue U., 1963; MS in Engring., U. Calif., Berkeley, 1967. Registered profl. engr., 35 states; cert. value specialist. Project engr. San Bernardino County (Calif.) Flood Control, 1963, Engring. Sci. Inc., Arcadia, Calif., 1968-70, office mgr. Cleve., 1970-72, v.p., chief engr., 1972-81, v.p. internat. divsn. Arcadia, 1981-84, group v.p., 1984-87; sr. v.p. Parsons Engring. Sci. Inc., Pasadena, Calif., 1987—2002; cons. engr. pvt. practice, 2003—. Industry adv. bd. Sch. Engring. and Tech. Calif. State U., L.A., 1986-99. Contbr. articles to profl. jours. Commr. Archtl. Commn., Claremont, Calif., 1980-86; councilman Claremont City Coun., 1986-94; mayor City of Claremont, 1989-92; mem. Pasadena Tournament of Roses Assn., 1980-96, L.A. 2000 Environ. Com., 1987-88; dir. Claremont Cmty. Found., 1994-2000, Citrus Coll. Found., 1994-2000, Rec. for Blind and Dislexic Bd., 2003—; pres. Claremont Hills Conservation Corp., 1997—; mem. adv. com. San Gabriel Valley Water Quality Authority, 2002—. With USMC, 1963-67. Recipient Disting. Engring. Achievement award Inst. for Advancement of Engring., 1993. Fellow ASCE (mem. internat. adv. com. 1987-90); mem. NSPE, Am. Acad. Environ. Engrs., Am. Water Works Assn. (life), Water Environ. Fedn., Soc. Am. Value Engrs., Rotary. Republican. Avocations: skiing, hiking, fishing, boating, writing. Home: 727 E Alamosa Dr Claremont CA 91711-2008

PRESKA, LORETTA A. federal judge; b. 1949; BA, Coll. of St. Rose, 1970; JD, Fordham U., 1973; LLM, NYU, 1978; LHD (hon.), Coll. of St. Rose, 1995. Assoc. Cahill, Gordon & Reindel, N.Y.C., 1973-82; ptnr. Hertzog, Calamari & Gleason, N.Y.C., 1982-92; fed. judge U.S. Dist. Ct. (so. dist.) N.Y., N.Y.C., 1992—. Mem. N.Y. State Bar Assn., N.Y. County Lawyers Assn., Fed. Bar Coun., Fordham Law Alumni Assn. (v.p.). Office: US Courthouse 500 Pearl St Rm 1320 New York NY 10007-1316

PRESKA, MARGARET LOUISE ROBINSON, education historian, administrator; b. Parma, N.Y., Jan. 23, 1938; d. Ralph Craven and Ellen Elvira (Niemi) Robinson; m. Daniel C. Preska, Jan. 24, 1959; children: Robert, William, Ellen Preska Steck. BS summa cum laude, SUNY, 1957; MA, Pa. State U., 1961; PhD, Claremont Grad. Sch., 1969. Instr. LaVerne (Calif.) Coll., 1968-75, asst. prof., asso. prof., acad. dean, 1972-75; instr. Starr King Sch. for Ministry, Berkeley, Calif., summer, 1975; v.p. acad. affairs, equal opportunity officer Minn. State U., Mankato, 1975-79, pres., 1979-92; project dir. Kaliningrad (Russia) Mil. Re-Tng., 1992-96; disting. svc. prof. Minn. State U. Sys., 1993—; pres. Inst. for Effective Tchg. Minn. State U., Winona, 1993—98; owner BuildaBikeInc.com, 2000—. Bd. dirs. XCEL Energy Co., Milkweed Edits.; pres. emerita Minn. State U., Mankato, 1992—; provost, CEO AbuDhabi Campus, Zayed U., United Arab Emirates, 1997-99. Pres. Pomona Valley chpt. UN Assn., 1968-69, Unitarian Soc. Pomona Valley, 1968-69, PTA Lincoln Elem. Sch., Pomona, 1973-74; pres., chmn. bd. Nat. Camp Fire Boys and Girls, 1984-88; mem. Pomona City Charter Revision Commn., 1972; chmn. The Fielding Inst., Santa Barbara, 1983-86; bd. dirs. Elderhostel Internat., 1983-87, Minn. Agrl. Interpretive Ctr. (Farmam.), 1983-92, Am. Assn. State Colls. and Univs., Moscow on the Mississippi - Minn. Meets the Soviet Union; nat. pres. Campfire, Inc., 1985-87; chmn. Gov.'s Coun. on Youth, Minn., 1983-86, Minn. Edn. Forum, 1984; mem. Gov.'s Commn. on Econ. Future of Minn., 1985—, NCAA Pres. Commn., 1986-92, NCAA Cost Cutting Commn., Minn. Brainpower Compact, 1985; commr. Great Lakes Govs.' Econ. Devel. Coun., 1986, Minn Gov.'s Commn. on Forestry. Carnegie Found. grantee Am. Coun. Edn. Deans Inst., 1974; recipient Outstanding Alumni award Pa. State, Outstanding Alumni award Claremont Grad. Sch., YWCA Leader award 1982, Exch. Club Book of Golden Deeds award, 1987; named One of top 100 alumni, SUNY, 1895-1985, 1985, Hall of Heritage award, 1988, Wohelo Camp Fire award, 1989. Fellow Fielding Inst.; mem. AAUW (pres. Mankato 1990-92), LWV, Women's Econ. Roundtable, St. Paul/Mpls. Com. on Fgn. Rels., Am. Assn. Univ. Adminstrs., Rotary, Horizon 100. Unitarian Universalist. Home: 10 Sumner Hls Mankato MN 56001-3931 E-mail: mpreska@hickorytech.net.

PRESKILL, JOHN PHILLIP, physics educator; b. Highland Park, Ill., Jan. 19, 1953; m. Roberta M. Gross, June 22, 1975; children: Carina Lou, Micaela Marie. AB in Physics, Princeton U., 1975; AM in Physics, Harvard U., 1976, PhD in Physics, 1980. Jr. fellow Harvard Soc. Fellows, 1980-81; asst. prof. physics Harvard U., Cambridge, Mass., 1981-82, assoc. prof., 1982-83; assoc. prof. theoretical physics Calif. Inst. Tech., Pasadena, 1983-90, prof., 1990—. Recipient Presdl. Young Investigator award NSF, 1984-89; fellow NSF, 1975-78, Alfred P. Sloan Found., 1982-86. Fellow Am. Phys. Soc. Office: Calif Inst Tech 452-48 Div Physics Math & Astronomy Pasadena CA 91125-0001

PRESLAR, LEN BROUGHTON, JR., hospital administrator; b. Concord, N.C., Aug. 13, 1947; s. Len B. and Billie M. (James) P.; m. Joyce W. Whittington, July 11, 1971; children: Bradley E., Whitney A., Andrew C. BA, Wake Forest U., 1971; MBA, U. N.C., Greensboro, 1980. Admissions clk. N.C. Bapt. Hosp., Winston-Salem, 1969-71, systems analyst, 1971-72, budget mgr., 1973, contr., 1973-75, v.p. fin. mgmt., 1975-88, pres., chief exec. officer, 1988—. Bd. dirs. Univ. Healthsystem Consortium; bd. mgrs. Wachovia Bank; mem. owenrs and affiliate rels. com. Premier, Inc. Deacon local Bapt. ch. Fellow Hosp. Fin. Mgmt. Assn.; mem. N.C. Hosp. Assn. (bd. dirs.). Republican. Baptist. Avocations: gardening, golf. Office: NC Bapt Hosp Medical Center Blvd Winston Salem NC 27157-0001

PRESLEY, BRIAN, investment company executive; b. Evansville, Ind., Dec. 28, 1941; s. Harry and Ruth P.; m. Mary Nell Minyard, Aug. 17, 1972; children: Debra, Cynthia, David, Jeffrey, Clark, Gregory, Steven. BSBA, U. Evansville, 1963; MBA, Mich. State U., 1964; diploma, Wharton Sch., U. Pa., 1995. Market rsch. analyst Stanley Works, New Britain, Conn., 1964-68; tax shelter coord. F.I. Dupont, Memphis, 1968-73; v.p. Bullington Schas, Memphis, 1973-75; pres., mng. ptnr. Presley Assocs., Memphis, 1965-93; pres., CFO CSG, Inc., Memphis, 1975—. Gen. ptnr. various real estate and oil and gas partnerships, 1974-1986; pres. Cooper St. Group Securities, Inc., 1983-86; divsn. mgr. Advantage Capital Corp. (divsn. SunAmerica, Inc.), 1986-89, reg. v.p., 1989, CEO 1990-94, mng. dir., mktg. strategist, 1995; pres. Presley Adv. Inc., 1995—, pub. Presley Adv. Letter; instr. fin. divsn. continuing edn. Memphis U. Bd. dirs. Apt. Coun. Tenn., 1980-86, sec.-treas., 1982-83; pres. Memphis Apt. Coun., 1983; mem., U. Evansville Nat. Alumni Bd., 1988-91; prodr. 2 daily radio stock market commentary shows, 1988; fin. commentator Sta. WEVU-TV (ABC), Ft. Myers/Naples, 1988-89; host syndicated radio show for sr. citizens, 1979-81; mem. found. bd. Fla. Gulf Coast U., 2001—. Mem. Leadership Charlotte; chmn. Charlotte County Econ. Devel. Coun., 1999-2002; pres. Enterprise Charlotte Found., 2002—, Angels Found. Charlotte County Fla., Inc., 2002—; bd. dir., fin. com. Fla. Gulf Coast U., 2002—. Recipient Richard L. McLaughlin award, Econ. Devel. Coun., Fla., 2002. Mem. Internat. Assn. Fin. Planners (broker dealer adv. coun. 1993-97), Admirals Club (life, bd. dirs.), Naples Jazz Soc. (chmn. bd. dirs. 1993-96), Naples Sailing and Yacht Club (bd. dirs.1991-96), Pi Sigma Epsilon, Beta Gamma Sigma, Tau Kappa Epsilon Alumni Assn. (pres. Memphis area 1979-80), Isles Yacht Club (bd. dirs. 2001-04). Presbyterian. Home and Office: Acorn Ranch 35600 Bermont Rd Punta Gorda FL 33982-9511

PRESLEY, JAMES WRIGHT, writer, environmentalist; b. Nash, Tex., Jan. 13, 1930; s. James Alexander and Lola Opal (Wright) Presley; m. Fran Burton, Jan. 13, 1962; children: John Francis, Ann Burton. BA, East Tex. State Tchrs. Coll., 1950; MA, U. Tex., Austin, 1955, Mexico City Coll., 1955; PhD, U. Tex., Austin, 1991. Reporter Texarkana (Tex.-Ark.) Gazette, 1947—49; asst. news editor Amarillo (Tex.) Globe-Times, 1956; staff writer Shreveport (La.) Times, 1958—59; copy editor The Light, San Antonio, 1959—61, 1969; part-time news editor Texarkana Gazette, 1969—71; polit. cons. Texarkana, 1960—; freelance writer, 1961—. Contbg. editor, editl. adv. bd. Tex. Observer, Austin, 1960—80; mgmt. cons. Red River Regional Coun. Alcoholism, Texarkana, 1975; spkr. workshops, Tex. and Ark. Co-author: Center of the Storm, 1967, Please Doctor, Do Something!, 1972, Vitamin B6: The Doctor's Report, 1973, Public Defender, 1974, Human Life Styling, 1975, Food Power, 1978; author: A Saga of Wealth: Rise of the Texas Oilmen, 1978, Never in Doubt, 1981; featured interviewee PBS-TV Documentary series on Tex., 1986; featured interviewee: other documentaries. Co-founder, pres., etc. Texarkana Anti-Pollution Soc.; co-founder, bd. dirs., etc. Friends United for a Safe Environ., Tex.-Ark., 1988—; press aide Henry Gonzalez-for-Gov., San Antonio, 1958. Staff sgt. USAF, 1950—53. Recipient various news prizes, AP, various other news assns., 1969—71, Anson Jones award, Tex. Med. Assn., 1971, John H. McGinnis Meml. award, Southwest Rev., 1981. Mem.: Am. Med. Writers Assn., N.Y. Acad. Scis., Oral History Assn., Soc. Environ. Journalists, Internat. Soc. Fluoride Rsch., Am. Assn. History of Medicine. Democrat. Achievements include author history of diabetes mellitus in the U.S. (1880-1990), 1991, 2 vols; led numerous environmental campaigns. Avocations: book collecting, investigating unsolved cases, fencing, running. Home and Office: 417 W 27th St Texarkana TX 75503-4232

PRESLEY, JOHN WOODROW, academic administrator; b. Jonesboro, Ark., Mar. 24, 1948; s. Marvin Woodrow and Willa Louise (Taylor) P.; m. Katherine Bailey Harrison, Oct. 17, 1978. BSE, Ark. State U., 1970; MA, So. Ill. U., 1972, PhD, 1975; postgrad., Johns Hopkins U., 1976, U. Tex., 1980. Assoc. prof. Augusta State U., 1974—89, Lafayette Coll., 1989—92; dean Coll. of Arts, Scis. and Letters U. Mich., Dearborn, 1992-99; provost, v.p. acad. affairs SUNY at Oswego, 1999—2003; v.p. acad. affairs, provost Ill. State U., 2003—. Presenter in field. Author: The Robert Graves Letters and Manuscripts at Southern Illinois University, 1976. NDEA fellow, 1972. Office: Ill State Univ 410 Hovey Hall Normal IL 61790 E-mail: jwpresl@ilstu.edu.

PRESLEY, LISA MARIE, musician; b. Memphis, Tenn., Feb. 1, 1968; d. Elvis and Priscilla Presley; m. Danny Keough, 1988 (div. 1994); children: Danielle Riley Keough, Benjamin Storm Keough; m. Michael Jackson, 1994 (div. 1997); m. Nicholas Cage, 2002 (div. 2004). Mgmt. Elvis Presley Trust; owner, chmn. bd. Elvis Presley Enterprises, Inc.; co-owner with mother Priscilla Elvis Presley's Memphis nightclub, operated by Presley Estate, 1997—2003. Musician: (albums) To Whom It May Concern, 2003 (cert. Gold), (songs) Lights Out, 2003; actor: (music video) You Are Not Alone, Michael Jackson, (car commercial), 1989; appeared on (cover of Vogue mag.), 1996. Internat. spokesperson Citizens Commn. on Human Rights; co-founder (with Isaac Hayes) LEAP (Literacy, Edn., and Ability Program). Office: Elvis Presley Enterprises Inc PO Box 16508 3734 Elvis Presley Blvd Memphis TN 38186-0508

PRESLEY, PRISCILLA, actress; b. Bklyn., May 24, 1945; m. Elvis Presley, 1967 (div. 1973); 1 child, Lisa Marie. Studied with Milton Katselas; student, Steven Peck Theatre Art Sch., Chuck Norris Karate Sch. Co-owner Bis and Beau Boutique; co-executor, pres. Elvis Presley Enterprise, Memphis. Launched internat. fragnance line. Appearances include (films) The Naked Gun, 1988, The Adventures of Ford Fairlaine, 1990, The Naked Gun 2 1/2, 1991, The Naked Gun 33 1/3, 1994, (TV series) Those Amazing Animals, 1980-81, Dallas, 1983-88, (TV movies) Love Is Forever, 1983, Breakfast With Einstein, 1998, Hayley Wagner, Star, 1999, After Dallas, 2002; prodr. (TV movie) Elvis and Me, 1988; exec. prodr. The Road to Graceland, 1998; author: Elvis and Me, 1989. Office: Michelle Bega c/o Rogers & Cowan 1888 Century Park E Los Angeles CA 90067-1702

PRESLEY, VIVIAN MATHEWS, junior college administrator; b. West Point, Miss., Oct. 12, 1952; d. Beatrus and Lula (Butler) Mathews; m. Dwight Presley, Sept. 12, 1971; 1 child, Julian. BA, Miss. State U., 1973, MA, 1975, Cert. Edn. Specialist, 1978, EdD, 1983. Counselor Coahoma Jr. Coll. (named changed to Coahoma Community Coll.), Clarksdale, Miss., 1975-80; title III coordinator Coahoma Jr. Coll., Clarksdale, Miss., 1981-82, asst. to pres., 1982-83, v.p., 1983—. Vice chairperson Miss. State Council on Vocat. Edn., Jackson, Miss., 1984. Named One of Outstanding Young Woman of Am., 1981, 84, 85, 88. Mem. Nat. Assn. Female Execs., Assn. Univ. Women, Nat. Council for Resource Devel., Psi Kappa Psi, Delta Sigma Theta. Democrat. Methodist. Avocations: reading, biking. Home: 3240 Friars Point Rd Clarksdale MS 38614-9359 Office: Coahoma Community Coll RR 1 Box 616 Clarksdale MS 38614-9801

PRESNIAKOV, ALEXANDER, painter, sculptor, inventor, novelist, writer; b. San Francisco, June 28, 1963; s. Alexander Alexandervich and Nina (Hanova) P. Student, Acad. of Art Coll., San Francisco, 1979-82. Curator Gen. Svcs. Adminstrn., Washington, 1983; artist Washington, 1984-85, San Francisco, 1986—. Songwriter Hilltop Records, L.A., 1996—, Amerecord, L.A., 1996—, Premier Melodies, N.Y.C. Commd. to paint life-size portraits of Prince Charles, Princess Diana, Miss Dame Barbara Cartland, 1982, Amb. Gerald Posner Carmen, 1983, life-size portraits of presdl. candidates for 1985 Polit. Conservative Action Conf., Sheraton Hotel, Washington; series Women in Love Cycle, 1986—; inventor Manshield Deflector, 1983; commissioned to paint life-size portrait of Pres. Ronald Reagan, 1983; author 6 novels, including Eagle's Nest, 2001; screenwriter. Recipient Literary Excellence award Iliad Press, 1995; named Prof. and Corr. Academician Dept. Arts Accademia Internazionale, Italy. Mem. Internat. Soc. Poets (disting. mem., Hall of Fame 1997-98), Legion of Honor Mus., De Young Mus., Gallery Marabella (hon.). Republican. Russian Orthodox. Achievements include creation of artistic ideal. Ultrafictrification, utilized in all U.S. gov. Agys., 1983. Home: 3928 Cabrillo St San Francisco CA 94121 Office Phone: 415-221-2973.

PRESS, AIDA KABATZNICK, former editor, writer, poet; b. Boston, Nov. 18, 1926; m. Newton Press, June 5, 1947; children: David, Dina Press Weber, Benjamin Presskreischer. BA, Radcliffe Coll., 1948. Reporter Waltham (Mass.) News-Tribune, 1960-63; freelance writer, 1960-63; editl. cons. Mass. Dept. Mental Health, Boston, 1966-72; Waltham/Watertown reporter Boston Herald Traveler, 1963-70; dir. news and publs. Harvard Grad. Sch. Design, Cambridge, Mass., 1972-78; publs. editor Radcliffe Coll., Cambridge, 1978-81, dir., editor of publs., 1981-83, editor Radcliffe Quar., 1971-93, dir. pub. info., 1983-93; cons. editor Regis Coll. Alumnae Mag., Weston, Mass., 1994. Editor emerita Radcliffe Quar., 1993—; contbr. articles to newspapers and mags. Recipient Publs. Distinction award Am. Alumni Coun., 1974, Top 5 coll. Mag., Coun. for Advancement and Support of Edn., 1984, Top 10 Univ Mags., 1991, Gold medal Coll. Mags., 1991, Alumnae Achievement award Radcliffe Coll., 1994, Radcliffe Coll. Presdl. Commendation, 1992. Mem. Phi Beta Kappa. Avocations: hiking, playing recorder.

PRESS, BETH, publishing executive; Sr. account mgr. Conde Nast's GQ, 1998-99; dir. advt. Teen Magazine, 1999-2000, group pub., 2000—. Office: EMAP USA 6420 Wilshire Blvd Los Angeles CA 90048-5502

PRESS, CHARLES, retired political science educator; b. St. Louis, Sept. 12, 1922; s. Otto Ernst and Laura (Irion) P.; m. Nancy Miller, June 10, 1950; children: Edward Paul, William David, Thomas Leigh, Laura Mary. Student, Elmhurst (Ill.) Coll.; B of Journalism, U. Mo., 1948; MA, U. Minn., 1951, PhD, 1953. Faculty N.D. Agrl. Coll., 1954-56; dir. Grand Rapids Area Study, 1956-57; with Bur. Govt., U. Wis., 1957-58; faculty Mich. State U., East Lansing, 1958-91, prof. polit. sci., 1964-91; emeritus, 1991—; chmn. dept. Mich. State U., 1966-73. Cons. Mich. Constl. Conv., 1962-63; supr. Ingham County, 1966-72; tchr. summers, London; tchr. U. N.S.W., Sydney, Mich. State U. Author: Main Street Politics, 1962, (with Charles Adrian) The American Government Process, 1965, Governing Urban America, 1968, 5th edit., 1977, American Politics Reappraised, 1974, (with Kenneth VerBurg) States and Community Governments in a Federal System, 1979, 3d edit., 1991, American Policy Studies, 1981, The Political Cartoon, 1982, (with others) Michigan Political Atlas 1984, (with Kenneth VerBurg) American Politicians and Journalists, 1988, (with Kenneth VerBurg) Looking Over Sir ARthur's Shoulder, How Doyle Turned the Trick, 2004, (weekly newspaper column) The Pros and Cons of Politics. Sec. Ingham County Bd. Health, 1983-93; chmn., mem. East Lansing Bd. Rev., 1966-86; bd. dirs. Urban League, 1971-73; mem. East Lansing Housing and Urban Devel. Commn., 1988-93. Served with AUS, 1943-45. Recipient Disting. Prof. award Mich. State U., 1980, Alumni Merit award Elmhurst (Ill.) Coll., 1995. Mem. Am. Polit. Sci. Assn., Midwest Polit. Sci. Assn. (pres. 1974-75), So. Polit. Sci. Assn., Mich. Conf. Polit. Scientists (pres. 1972-73), Nat. Municipal League, B.S.I. Home: 987 Lantern Hill Dr East Lansing MI 48823-2831 Office: Mich State U 315 S Kedzie Hall East Lansing MI 48824-1032 Business E-Mail: pressc@pilot.msu.edu.

PRESS, EDWARD, consulting physician; b. N.Y.C., 1913; s. Louis and Anna Press; m. Ruth Scheffer, July 8, 1951; children: Stephen, Phyllis. BA, Ohio U., 1934; MD, NYU, 1937; M.P.H., Harvard U., 1947. Diplomate: Am. Bd. Pediatrics, Am. Bd. Preventive Medicine. Intern Beth Israel Hosp., N.Y.C., 1938-40; resident Lincoln Hosp., Bronx, N.Y., 1940; psychiatric resident E.P. Bradley Home, East Providence, R.I., 1940-41; asst. dir. maternal and child health div. W.Va. Health Dept., 1941-42; pediatric cons. Mich. Health Dept., 1946; regional med. dir. U.S. Children's Bur., Chgo., 1947-50; asso. dir. div. services crippled children U. Ill., 1950-55; field dir. Am. Public Health Assn., N.Y.C., 1955-59; dir. Dept. Public Health, Evanston, Ill., 1959-64; med. asst. to dir. Ill. Dept. Public Health, 1964-67; state health officer (Oreg. Health Div.), Portland, 1967-79; public health cons., 1979—; emeritus sec.-treas. Press Internat. Sales Corp., 1978—. Asst. prof. preventive medicine U. Ill., 1950-55; asst. prof. pediatrics Northwestern U., 1964-67; clin. prof. pub. health, preventive medicine and pediatrics Med. Sch., Oreg. Health Scis. U., 1967-79, emeritus clin. prof., 1979—; vice chmn. Tech. Adv. Group for Fire Safe Cigarette Act of 1990-93. Mem. editorial adv. com. The Nation's Health, 1989-91; contbr. articles to profl. jours. Organizer Poison Control Ctr., Chgo., 1953; trustee Underwriters' Labs., Inc., 1969-79. Served to maj. USAAF, 1942-46. Recipient Clifford G. Grulee award Am. Acad. Pediatrics, 1961; recognition award Am. Assn. Poison Control Centers, 1975 Mem. AMA, Am. Pub. Health Assn. (founder and pres. Conf. Emeritus Mems. 1986-89, Excellence in Health Admintrn. award 1992), Nat. Soc. Prevention of Blindness, Am. Assn. Public Health Physicians (pres. 1971-72, Bronze medal 1979, 50th Anniversary Benn Freedman award 2004), Conf. State and Provincial Health Authorities N.Am. (pres. 1971-72), Assn. State and Territorial Health Officers (mem. exec. com. 1972-75, Arthur G. McCormack award 1978), Am. Assn. Sr. Physicians (pres. 1984-86), Oreg. Pub. Health Assn. (Leadership award 1986), Oreg. Med. Assn. (presdl. citation 1980), Am. Acad. Pediatrics, Portland City Club, Multnomah Athletic Club, Rotary. Home: 2221 SW 1st Ave # 2322 Portland OR 97201-5023

PRESS, FRANK, geophysicist; b. Bklyn., Dec. 4, 1924; s. Solomon and Dora (Steinholz) Press; m. Billie Kallick, June 9, 1946; children: William Henry, Paula Evelyn. BS, CCNY, 1944, LLD (hon.), 1972; MA, Columbia U., 1946, PhD, 1949; DSc (hon.), 28 univs. Rsch. assoc. Columbia U., 1946—49, instr. geology, 1949—51, asst. prof. geology, 1951—52, assoc. prof., 1952—55; prof. geophysics Calif. Inst. Tech., 1955—65, dir. seismol. lab., 1957—65; prof. geophysics, chmn. dept. earth and planetary scis. MIT, Cambridge, 1965—77, inst. prof., 1981; sci. advisor to pres., dir. Office Sci. and Tech. Policy, Washington, 1977—81; pres. NAS, 1981—93, pres. emeritus, 2000—; Cecil & Ida Green sr. fellow Carnegie Inst. of Washington, 1993—97; ptnr. Washington Adv. Group, 1996—. Mem. Pres.'s Sci. Adv. Com., 1961—64, Com. on Anticipated Advances in Sci. and Tech., 1974—76, Nat. Sci. Bd., 1970—76; mem. lunar and planetary missions bd. NASA; participant bilateral scis. agreement with Peoples Republic of China and USSR; mem. U.S. delegation to Nuc. Test Ban Negotiations, Geneva and Moscow; prof. emeritus MIT, 2000—. Author (with M. Ewing, W.s. Jardetsky): Propagation of Elastic Waves in Layered Media, 1957; author: (with R. Siever) Earth, 1986; author: Understanding Earth, 2003; author: (contbr.) articles to over 160 publs. Decorated cross of Merit Germany, Legion of Honor France; named Sherman Fairchild Disting. scholar, Calif. Inst. Tech., 1994, A.D. White prof., Cornell U.; recipient Columbia medal for Excellence, 1960, Pub. Svc. award, U.S. Dept. Interior, 1972, Gold medal, Royal Astron. Soc., 1972, Pub. Svc. medal, NASA, 1973, Japan prize, Sci. and Tech. Found. Japan, 1993, Pupin medal,

Columbia U., 1993, Nat. medal of Sci., Pres. U.S., 1994, Philip Hauge Abelson prize, AAAS, 1995, Lomonosov Gold medal, Russian Acad. Sci., 1998. Mem.: NAS, Engring. Acad. Japan (fgn. assoc.), Acad.Scis. Russia (fgn. mem.), Royal Soc. U.K., French Acad. Scis., Am. Philos. Soc., Seismol. Soc. Am. (pres. 1963), Soc. Exploration Geophysicists, Am. Geophys. Union, Geol. Soc. Am. (councilor), Am. Acad. Arts and Scis. Office: Ste 616 South 2500 Virginia Ave Washington DC 20037-1901 Office Phone: 202-682-0164. Business E-Mail: fpress@nas.edu. E-mail: fpress@theadvisorygroup.com.

PRESS, FRED, artist; b. Boston, Oct. 14, 1919; s. Samuel and Rose Press; m. Alice Bernadette, Nov. 4, 1942; children: David, Peter, Christopher. Student, Vesper George Sch. Art, Boston, 1938-39. Founder, chief designer sculpture collection Contemporary Arts, Inc., Boston, 1937-62; tchr. Vesper George Sch. Art, Boston, 1945—50; chief designer, exec. v.p. sales agy. N.Y.C., 1951—70; freelance in design field, 1970—85. Mem. Mass. Art Commn. One-man shows include Stuart Art Gallery, Boston, 1947, Jaffrey Civic Ctr., 1989, Granary Gallery, Martha's Vineyard, Mass., 1990, exhibited in group shows at NAD, N.Y.C., Delgado Mus. Art, New Orleans, Springfield Art League, Mass., Pan Am. Soc., Boston, Conn. Acad. Fine Arts, Allied Artists, N.Y., Vose Galleries, Boston, Boston Mus. Fine Arts, Silvermine Guild Artists, Conn., Mus. Contemporary Art, Boston, Ky. Derby Mus., Nat. Art League, Olin Art Ctr., Hoyt Inst. Fine Arts, Sharon Arts Ctr., Represented in permanent collections Worcester (Mass.) Art Mus., prin. works include 2 Bronze Reliefs, U.S. Navy Meml., Washington, individual pvt. collections; featured in Am. Artist Mag., Christian Sci. Monitor, Dance Mag.; author: (book) Sculpture at Your Fingertips, 1961; mng. editor: Ofcl. 6th Air Force Mag., 1944—45. Tech. sgt. USAF, 1942—45. Recipient ann. awards for soap sculpture, Proctor and Gamble Co., 1936—39, 1st prize for Slave sculpture, Delgado Mus. Art, 1946; scholar, HS Commerce. Home: 262 Hadley Rd Jaffrey NH 03452

PRESS, JAMES E. transportation executive; b. Calif., Oct. 4, 1946; m. Linda Press; 4 children. BA in Bus. Adminstrn., Kans. State U., 1968. With Ford Motor Co., 1968—70; from mem. staff to exec. v.p., COO Toyota Motor Sales, U.S.A., Inc., Torrance, Calif., 1970—2003, exec. v.p., 1999—, COO, 1999—; mng. officer Toyota Motor Corp., 2003—. Avocations: boating, motorcycling, auto racing, skiing, scuba diving. Office: Toyota Motor Sales USA Corp 19001 South Western Ave Torrance CA 90509

PRESS, MARLYN ROTHMAN, special education and literacy educator; d. Arthur Abbot and Ruth Rothman; m. Morton Robert Press, Aug. 24, 1997. BA in Social Studies Edn., Syracuse U., 1968; MA in Remedial Reading, Columbia U., 1969; specialist cert. in spl. edn., Yeshiva U., 1977; EdD in Edn. Adminstrn. and Supervision, U. Houston, 1982. Reading tchr. Roosevelt (N.Y.) Pub. Schs., 1969—79; grad. asst. U. Houston, 1979—82; reading tchr. Hempstead (N.Y.) Pub. Schs., 1984—94, Massapequa (N.Y.) Pub. Schs., 1994—99; adj. prof. literacy and spl. edn. courses St. John's U., Jamaica, 1999—2002, Adelphi U., Garden City, 2001, C.W. Post Coll., Brookville, 2002—04, Touro Coll., Bklyn., 2002—04, ADD, asst. prof. grad. edn., 2004—. Pvt. tutor literacy and spl. edn., Lawrence, NY, 2000—. Contbr. articles to profl. jours. Recipient Pres. Recognition award for excellence in tchg., Medgar Evers Coll. CUNY, Queens, 1991. Mem.: Internat. Reading Assn., Omicron Delta Kappa, Phi Delta Kappa. Jewish. Avocations: travel, reading. Home and Office: 14 Hawthorne Ln Lawrence NY 11559

PRESS, WILLIAM HENRY, astrophysicist, computer scientist; b. N.Y.C., N.Y., May 23, 1948; s. Frank and Billie (Kallick) P.; m. Margaret Ann Lauritsen, 1969 (div. 1982); 1 dau., Sara Linda; m. Jeffrey Foden Howell, Apr. 19, 1991; 1 son, James Howell. AB, Harvard Coll., 1969; MS, Calif. Inst. Tech., 1971, PhD, 1972. Asst. prof. theoretical physics Calif. Inst. Tech., 1973-74; asst. prof. physics Princeton (N.J.) U., 1974-76; prof. astronomy and physics Harvard U., Cambridge, Mass., 1976-98, chmn. dept. astronomy, 1982-85; dep. lab. dir. Los Alamos Nat. Lab., 1998—2004, sr. fellow, 2004—. Mem. numerous adv. coms. and panels NSF, NASA, NAS, NRC; vis. mem. Inst. Advanced Study, 1983-94; mem. Def. Sci. Bd., 1985-89, sci. adv. com. Packard Found., 1988—, program com. Sloan Found., 1985-91; chmn. adv. bd. NSF Inst. Theoretical Physics, 1986-87; mem. Computer Sci. and Telecomm. Bd., 1991-96; U.S. del. IUPAP Gen. Assembly, 1996; cons. MITRE Corp., 1977—; trustee Inst. Def. Analysis, 1988—, exec. com., 1990—; chief naval ops. Exec. Panel, 1994-2000. Author: Numerical Recipes, 1986; contbr. articles to profl. jours. Sloan Found. research fellow, 1974-78 Fellow: Am. Phys. Soc., Am. Acad. Arts and Scis.; mem.: NAS, Coun. on Fgn. Rels., Assn. for Computing Machinery, Internat. Soc. Relativity and Gravitation, Internat. Astron. Union, Am. Astron. Soc. (Helen B. Warner prize 1981). Office: Los Alamos Nat Lab MS A 121 Los Alamos NM 87545-0001

PRESSEISEN, BARBARA ZEMBOCH, retired educational director, researcher; b. Dayton, Ohio, June 15, 1936; d. William and Ida (Wise) Zemboch; m. Ernst Leopold Presseisen, June 30, 1963; children: Joshua William, Benjamin David. BA, Brandeis U., 1958; MAT, Harvard U., 1959; EdD, Temple U., 1972. Tchr., counselor Sequoia Union High Sch. Dist., East Palo Alto, Calif., 1959-63; lectr. No. Ill. U., De Kalb, 1963-65; teaching assoc. Temple U., Phila., 1967-69; asst. prof. Swarthmore (Pa.) Coll., 1969-71; curriculum coord. Rsch. for Better Schs., Phila., 1971-75, project dir., 1975-80, asst. dir., 1980-85, dir. nat. networking, 1985-99; ret., 1999. V.p. edn. Nobel Learning Communities, Inc., Media, Pa., 1996-99. Author: Unlearned Lessons, 1985; editor and author: At-Risk Students and Thinking, 1988, Teaching for Intelligence, 1999; contbr. editor: (newsletter) Teaching Thinking and Problem Solving, Phila., 1981-96. Bd. trustees Friends Select Sch., Phila., 1987-95. Mem. ASCD (task force 1981—), Am. Ednl. Rsch. Assn., Pi Lambda Theta (editl. bd. 1983—), Nat. Ind. Pvt. Sch. Assn. (bd. dirs. 1998—), Phi Delta Kappa (Ralph D. Owen scholar 1958), Brandeis U. Alumni Assn. (Phila.). Democrat. Office: 1943 Pine St Philadelphia PA 19103-6616

PRESSER, CARY, research engineer; b. Bklyn., June 20, 1952; s. Harry and Regina Deborah (Lieberman) P.; m. Karen Leslie Antonoff, Feb. 27, 1977; children: Yona Ruth, Aliza Miriam. BSc in Aerospace Engring., Poly. U., 1974, MSc in Aero. Engring., 1976; DSc in Aero. Engring., Technion-Israel Inst. Tech., 1980. Tchg. fellow Poly. U., 1974-75; tchg. instr., rsch. asst. Technion-Israel Inst. Tech., Haifa, 1975-80; rsch. engr. Nat. Inst. Stds. and Tech., Gaithersburg, Md., 1980, group leader high temperature processes, 1994—99, group leader thermal and reactive processes, 1999—2004, rsch. engr., 2004—. Mem. N.Am. Rsch. Strategy for Tropospheric Ozone Exec. Assembly, 2004—. Contbr. articles to profl. jours. Recipient Silver medal, U.S. Dept. Commerce, 1991, SMART Bonus award, 1992, Sustained Superior Performance award, Nat. Inst. Stds. and Tech., 1983—89; fellow Lady Davis grad., Technion-Israel Inst. Tech., 1975—76. Fellow: ASME (com. heat transfer in energy sys. heat transfer divsn. 1986—, com. acad. and indsl. rsch. fuels and combustion techs. divsn. 1995—, energy sys. tech. com., computers and info. engring. divsn. 2000—), AIAA (assoc.; propellants and combustion tech. com. 1987—90, terrestrial energy sys. tech. com. 1992—, computational fluid dynamics com. on stds. 1997—, Best Paper award terrestrial energy sys. tech. com. 1994, Best Paper award propellants and combustion tech. com. 1987, 1989); mem.: ASTM (com. on particle size measurements 1991—, subcom. on liquid particle measurements 1991—, subcom. internat. coop. terminology, stds. and methods particle size 1991—, chmn. subcom. reference materials 1992—95), AIChE (sr.), AAAS, North Am. Rsch. Strategy for Tropospheric Ozone (exec. assembly 2004—), Com. for Environ. and Natural Resources (air quality rsch. subcom. 2004—), Interagency propulsion com. Joint Army-Navy-NASA-Air Force (subcom. modeling and simulation 1991—2003), Optical Soc. Am., Combustion Inst. (symposium program rev. subcom. 1989—), Assn. Orthodox Jewish Scientists, Inst. Liquid Atomization and Spray Sys. (diesel and automotive sprays tech. com. 1997—, computational and modeling tech. com. 1997—, measurement and instrumentation tech. com. 2003—), N.Y. Acad. Scis., Am. Assn. Aerosol Rsch. (combustion chmn. and materials synthesis working group 2004, climate change sci. program carbon cycle interagency working group 2003—, chmn. combustion and materials synthesis working group 2004), Am. Chem. Soc., Instrument Soc. Am. (sr.), Sigma Xi (admission com. NIST chpt. 1990—93, life mem.), Tau Epsilon Phi, Sigma Gamma Tau. Office: Nat Inst Stds and Tech 100 Bureau Dr Stop 8360 Gaithersburg MD 20899-8360 Office Phone: 301-975-2612. Business E-Mail: cpresser@nist.gov.

PRESSER, HARRIET BETTY, sociology educator; b. Bklyn., Aug. 29, 1936; d. Phillip Rubinoff and Rose (Gudowitz) Jabish; m. Neil Nathan Presser, Dec. 16, 1956 (div.); 1 child, Sheryl Lynn. BA, George Washington U., 1959; MA, U. N.C., 1962; PhD, U. Calif., Berkeley, 1969. Statistician Bur. Census, Washington, 1959; research assoc. Inst. Life Ins., N.Y.C., 1962-64, lectr. demography U. Sussex, Brighton, England, 1967-68; staff assoc. Population Council, N.Y.C., 1968-69; asst. prof. sociomed. scis. Columbia U., N.Y.C., 1969-73, assoc. prof. sociomed. scis., 1973-76; prof. sociology U. Md., College Park, 1976—99, dir. Ctr. on Population, Gender, and Social Inequality, 1988—2001, disting. faculty rsch. fellow, 1993-94, disting. univ. prof., 1999—; fellow in residence Netherlands Inst. for Advanced Study in Humanities & Social Sci., Wassenaar, The Netherlands, 1994-95. Fellow-in-residence Ctr. for Advanced Study in the Behavioral Scis., Stanford, Calif., 1986-87, 91-92, 2003-04; bd. dirs. Population Reference Bur., 1993-99; scholar-in-residence Russell Sage Found., N.Y.C., 1998-99,2000; resident scholar Bellagio Study and Conf. Ctr., Rockefeller Found., 2000; acad. visitor Gender Inst. London Sch. Econs and Polit. Scis., 2000. Editl. bd. Time and Soc., 1991-95, Social Forces, 1984-87, Signs, 1975-85, Applied Population and Policy, 2002—, Rose Monograph Series, 2003—, Jour. of Marriage and the Family, 2003; assoc. editor Jour. Health and Social Behavior, 1975-78; co-editor (with Gita Sen) Women's Empowerment and Demographic Processes: Moving Beyond Cairo, 2000; author: Working in a 24/7 Economy: Challenges for Am. Families, 2003 Nat. Inst. for Child Health and Devel. grantee, 1972-78, 83-88, Population Coun. grantee, 1976-79, NSF grantee, 1982-83, 90-94, 2000-03, Rockefeller Found. grantee, 1983-85, 88-94, William and Flora Hewlett Found. grantee, 1989—, Andrew W. Mellon Found. grantee, 1994-95, W. T. Grant Found., 1996-99, Russel Sage Found., 1976-79, 2003 ; recipient Rosabeth Moss Kanter award for excellence in work-family rsch., 2001, Lawrence R. Klein award, 2003. Fellow AAAS, Sociol. Rsch Assn.; mem. APHA (coun. mem. population sect. 1976-79), Population Assn. Am. (bd. dirs. 1972-75, 2nd v.p. 1983, 1st v.p. 1985, pres.-elect 1988, pres. 1989), Am. Sociol. Assn. (coun. mem. at large 1990-93, chmn., coun. mem. population sect. 1978-83). Office: U Maryland Dept Sociology College Park MD 20742-0001

PRESSER, JANICE, business executive; b. N.Y.C., Feb. 14, 1946; m. Barry S. Perlman; 2 children. BA, CCNY, 1967; BSN, Columbia U., 1978; MA, Hunter Coll., 1981; PhD, Union Inst., 1990. Pres., CEO The Gabriel Inst., Phila. Office: The Gabriel Inst Suite 804 1520 Locust St Philadelphia PA 19102 Office Phone: 215-825-2500. Business E-Mail: jpresser@thegabrielinstitute.com.

PRESSER, MICHAEL, performing company executive; b. Philadelphia, Pa., Oct. 15, 1947; s. Nathan and Theresa Presser. BS, Temple U., 1965—69. Exec. dir./pres. Inside Broadway, NYC, 1982—. Cons. Deutsche Oper Am Rhein, Dusseldorf, Germany, 1999—, Theater Des Westerns, Berlin, 2000—02, Theater Aachen, Aachen, Germany, 1997—99. Mem., former chmn. Manhattan Cmty. Bd. #5, NYC, 1982; mem. Mayor's Midtown Citizens Com., NYC, 1982, Town Hall Found., Inc., NYC, 1992. Recipient Heart to Heart award, Encore Cmty. Services, 1999. Mem.: Met. Opera Club, The U. Club. Office: Inside Broadway 630 Ninth Ave Ste 802 New York NY 10036 Office Phone: 212-245-0710. E-mail: mpresser@insidebroadway.org.

PRESSER, STANLEY, sociology educator; b. Bklyn., Feb. 18, 1950; s. Sidney and Sydonia (Cohen) P.; m. Yan Yu; 1 child, Solomon Zhi-Qian. AB, Brown U., 1971; PhD, U. Mich., 1977. Rsch. investigator Survey Rsch. Ctr., U. Mich., 1977-78, head field office, 1981-83; rsch. assoc. Inst. Rsch. Social Sci., U. N.C., 1978-81; dir. Detroit Area Study, U. Mich., 1983-85; assoc. dir. sociology program NSF, 1985-87, dir., 1987-88; prof. sociology U. Md., 1989—; dir. Survey Rsch. Ctr., 1989-2000. Vis. prof. sociology U. Md., 1988-89; dir. joint U. Md. and U. Mich. program in Survey Methodology, 1992-96; bd. overseers Nat. Opinion Rsch. Ctr. Gen. Social Survey, 1984-85, 93-97; spl. cons. Nat. Econ. Rsch. Assocs., 1986-89; cons. U.S. Dept. Justice, 1995, Dept. Commerce, 1991, GAO, 1988-89, EEO Commn., 1985, NOAA, 1991-94, State of Alaska Atty. Gen., 1989-92. Co-author: Questions and Answers in Attitude surveys, 1981, Survey Questions: Handcrafting the Standardized Questionaire, 1986; editor Pub. Opinion Quar., 1993-97; co-editor: Sourcebook of Harris National Surveys, 1981, Survey Rsch. Methods, 1989, Methods for Testing and Evaluating Survey Questions, 2004; mem. editl. bd. Pub. Opinion Quar., 1983-87, Sociol. Methods and Rsch., 1980-83, Social Psychology Quar., 1979-82; contbr. articles to profl. jours. Fellow: Am. Statis. Assn.; mem.: Am. Sociol. Assn. (chair profl. ethics com. 1999—2001), Am. Assn. Pub. Opinion Rsch. (pres. 1993—94). Office: U of Md Sociology Dept College Park MD 20742-1315

PRESSER, STEPHEN BRUCE, lawyer, educator; b. Chattanooga, Aug. 10, 1946; s. Sidney and Estelle (Shapiro) P.; m. Carole Smith, June 18, 1968 (div. 1987); children: David Carter, Elisabeth Catherine; m. ArLynn Leiber, Dec. 13, 1987; children: Joseph Leiber, Eastman Leiber. AB, Harvard U., 1968, JD, 1971. Bar: Mass. 1971, D.C. 1972. Law clk. to Judge Malcolm Richard Wilkey U.S. Ct. Appeals (D.C. cir.), 1971-72; assoc. Wilmer, Cutler & Pickering, Washington, 1972-74; asst. prof. law Rutgers U., Camden, N.J., 1974-76; vis. assoc. prof. U. Va., 1976-77; prof. Northwestern U., Chgo., 1977—, class 1940 rsch. prof., 1992-93, Raoul Berger prof. legal history, 1992—, assoc. dean acad. affairs Sch. Law, 1982-85. Prof. bus. law Kellogg Sch. Mgmt., Northwestern U., Chgo., 1992—. Author: (with Jamil S. Zainaldin) Law and Jurisprudence in American History, 1980, 5th edit., 2003, Studies in the History of the United States Courts of the Third Circuit, 1983, The Original Misunderstanding: The English, The Americans and the Dialectic of Federalist Jurisprudence, 1991, Piercing the Corporate Veil, 1991, revised ann., (with Ralph Ferrara and Meredith Brown) Takeovers: A Strategist's Manual, 2d edit., 1993, Recapturing the Constitution, 1994, (with Douglas W. Kmiec) The American Constitutional Order: History, Cases, and Philosophy, 1998, 2d edit., 2004; assoc. articles editor Guide to American Law, 1985. Trustee Village of Winnetka, Ill., 2000-04; mem. acad. adv. bd. Washington Legal Found. Recipient summer stipend NEH, 1975; Fulbright Sr. scholar Univ. Coll., London Sch. Econs. and Polit. Scis., 1983-84, Inst. Advanced Legal Studies, 1996; Adams fellow Inst. U.S. Studies, London, 1996; assoc. rsch. fellow Inst. U.S. Studies, 1999—. Mem. Am. Soc. Legal History (bd. dirs. 1979-82), Am. Law Inst., Univ. Club Chgo. (bd. dirs. 1997-99, sec. 1999), Legal Club Chgo., Reform Club (London). Office: Northwestern U Law Sch 357 E Chicago Ave Chicago IL 60611-3069 E-mail: s-presser@law.northwestern.edu.

PRESSLER, LARRY, former senator, lawyer; b. Humboldt, S.D., Mar. 29, 1942; s. Antoine Lewis and Loretta Genevieve (Claussen) P.; m. Harriet Dent, 1982; a child, Laura. BA, U. S.D., 1964; diploma (Rhodes scholar), Oxford U., Eng., 1965; MA in Govt., JD, Harvard U., 1971. Bar: N.Y., D.C. Mem. 94th-95th Congresses from 1st S.D. Dist., 1974-78, U.S. Senate from S.D., 1979-97; pres. Pressler and Assocs.; U.S. del. Inter-Parliamentary Union for 97th Congress; mem. bd. visitors all mil. svc. academies; chmn. commerce, sci. and transp. coms. U.S. Senate, 1995-96; founder telecomm. group Pressler & Assocs., Washington, 1997—. Prin. sponsor Telecomm. Act of 1996, Pressler Telecomm. Act; U.S. Senate subcoms. on aviation, oceans and fisheries, sci., tech. and space; fin. com. mem.; chmn. comms. subcom., 1995-96; ranking mem. small bus. com., 19959-96; mem. spl. com. on aging, 1981-96; mem. fgn. rels. com., 1980-95; congl. del. to UN Gen. Assembly, 1986, 92; mem. U.S. Commn. on Improving the Effectiveness of UN, 1993; former bus. cons. McKinsey & Co.; former atty. U.S. State Dept. Legal Advisor's Office; vis. prof. U. S.D., Lower Brule C.C.; sr. fellow U. Calif., L.A., 2000—. Author: U.S. Senators from the Prairie, 1982, Star Wars: The SDI Debates in Congress, 1986. All-Am. del. 4-H agrl. fair, Cairo, 1961. 1st lt. U.S . Army, 1966-68, Vietnam. Recipient Report to the Pres. 4-H award, 1962. Mem. Am Assn. Rhodes Scholars, VFW, ABA, Century Club (N.Y.), Met. Club (Washington), St. Albans Tennis Club, Bohemian Club Calif., Phi Beta Kappa. Avocations: golf, tennis, rowing.

PRESSLER, PAUL S. retail executive; BS in Bus. Econs., SUNY, Oneonta. V.p. mktg. and design Kenner-Parker Toys; sr. v.p. licensing Disney, 1987—94, sr. v.p. consumer products; pres. Disneyland, 1994—98; chmn. Walt Disney Parks and Resorts, 1998—2002; pres., CEO Gap, Inc., 2002—. Adv. bd. Children Affected by AIDS Found.; bd. dirs. Resources Children with Spl. Needs, Big Bros. Big Sisters Greater LA, Disney GOALS, Anaheim, Calif. Office: 2 Folsom St San Francisco CA 94105*

PRESSLEY, JAMES RAY, electrical engineer; b. Ft. Worth, July 14, 1946; s. Loy Dale and Dorothy Helen (Foust) P.; m. Barbara Kay McMillin, Oct. 9, 1968 (div. 1981); children: James Foust Pressley, Kreg Milam Pressley; m. Susan Marie Straw, Apr. 27, 1985 (div.); children: Shaye Eugene Straw, Rebecca Alycen Straw, Rachel Leilani Straw. BSEE, U. Tex., Arlington, 1970. Registered profl. engr., Alaska, Hawaii, Oreg., Wash., Guam. Designer, draftsman Romine & Slaughter, Ft. Worth, 1967-71; engr. Crews MacInnes & Hoffman, Anchorage, 1971-73, O'Kelly & Schoenlank, Anchorage, 1973-75, Theodore G. Creedon, Anchorage, 1975-77; v.p. Fryer, Pressley Elliott, Anchorage, 1977-80, Fryer/Pressley Engring., 1980-91, FPE Roen Engrs., Inc., 1991-98; also chmn. bd., 1991-95; v.p., bd. dirs., 1991—; v.p., bd. dirs., mgr., prin. in charge Anchorage ofc. PDC, Inc. Cons. Engrs., 1998—. Mem. elec. constrn. and maintenance industry evaluation panel, 1982-96. Mem.: NSPE, IEEE, Am. Soc. Quality, Nat. Fire Protection Assn., Internat. Assn. Elec. Insps., Illuminating Engring. Soc. (sustaining). Office: PDC Inc Cons Engrs 1231 Gambell St Anchorage AK 99501 Office Phone: 907-561-1666. E-mail: jimpressley@pdceng.com.

PRESSLY, THOMAS JAMES, history professor; b. Troy, Tenn., Jan. 18, 1919; s. James Wallace and Martha Belle (Bittick) P.; m. Lillian Cameron, Apr. 30, 1943; children: Thomas James II, Stephanie Suzuki. AB, Harvard U., 1940, AM, 1941, PhD, 1950; LLD (hon.), Whitman Coll., 1981. Instr. history Princeton (NJ) U., 1946-49; asst. prof. U. Wash., 1949-54, assoc. prof., 1954-60, prof., 1960-87, prof. emeritus, 1987—. Vis. assoc. prof. Princeton U., 1953-54, Johns Hopkins U., 1969 70. Author: Americans Interpret Their Civil War, 1954; editor: (with W. H. Scofield) Farm Real Estate Values in the United States, 1965, (with others) American Political Behavior, 1974, Diary of George Templeton Strong (abridged), 1988, (with Glenn M. Linden) Voices From the House Divided, 1995, (with Maclyn P. Burg) The Great War At Home and Abroad, 1999. Served with AUS, 1941-45. Ford Found. Faculty fellow, 1951-52; Ctr. for Advanced Study in Behavioral Scis. fellow, 1955-56. Mem. Am. Hist. Assn., So. Hist. Assn. (editl. bd. Jour. So. History 1973-77), Orgn. Am. Historians. Home: 4545 E Laurel Dr NE Seattle WA 98105-3838 Office: U Wash Dept History PO Box 353560 Seattle WA 98195-3560 Office Phone: 206-543-5790.

PRESSMAN, ANDY, architecture educator; BArch, Rensselaer Poly. Inst.; M in Design Studies, Harvard U. Registered arch., N.Y., 1983, Ill., 1987, N.J., 1989, N.Mex., 1996, Maine, 1997, Nat. Coun. Archtl. Registration Bds., 1983. With Norman Rosenfeld, FAIA, Archs., 1978—83; prin. Andrew Pressman, FAIA, Arch., 1983—. Adj. asst. prof. U. Wis.-Milw. Sch. Arch. and Urban Planning, 1987—91; asst.-in-instrn. Harvard U. Grad. Sch. Design, 1993—94; with U. N.Mex. Sch. Arch. and Planning, Albuquerque, 1995—, assoc. prof., 1998—2003, prof., 2003—, dir. arch. program, 2000—. Author: Architecture 101: A Guide to the Design Studio, 1993, 2000, 2003, The Fountainheadache: The Politics of Architect-Client Relations, 1995, Professional Practice 101: A Compendium of Business and Management Strategies in Architecture, 1997, Architectural Design Portable Handbook: A Guide to Excellent Practices, 2001, 2002. Nominee Outstanding Tchr. of Yr. award, U. N.Mex. Enhancement Com. on Awards and Fellowships, 1997; recipient First Pl. award Internat. Housing Design Competition, Bldg. Ctr. Japan and Misawa Homes, Tokyo, 1982, citation Evanston 2063 Design Competition, Evanston Art Ctr., 1983, Gen. Libr. Recognition award, U. N.Mex., 1997, Disting. Svc. award, N.Mex./AIA, 1997, Alumni Assn. Faculty award, U. N.Mex., 1998, Svc. award, Assn. Collegiate Schs. Arch., 1999, Dean's award for excellence in rsch. and creative work, U. N.Mex., 1997. Fellow: AIA (bd. dirs. Albuquerque chpt. 2000—, award for outstanding support and contbns. Albuquerque chpt. 1996). Office: Univ NMex Sch Arch and Planning 2414 Central Ave SE Albuquerque NM 87131*

PRESSMAN, GABE STANLEY, television reporter; b. NYC, Feb. 14, 1924; s. Benjamin and Lena (Rifkin) P.; m. Emma Mae Kracht, Nov. 8, 1953 (div. 1967); children: Mark, Elizabeth, Margaret; m. Vera Elisabeth Olsen, Apr. 1, 1972; 1 child, Michael. BA in History magna cum laude, NYU, 1946; MS in Journalism, Columbia U., 1947; degree (hon.), Marist Coll., 2002, Coll. S.I., 2003. Reporter Peekskill (NY) Star, 1941-42, Newark Evening News, 1947; corr. Overseas News Agy., NYC, 1948-49; reporter World-Telegram Sun, NYC, 1949-54, WRCA and WRCA-TV, NBC, NYC, 1954-72, WNEW-TV, NYC, 1972-80, WNBC-TV, NYC, 1980—; anchor News Forum, NYC. Served to lt. (j.g.) USN, 1943-46, PTO. Mem. N.Y. Press Club (1st v.p. 1988-97, pres. 1997-00), Inner Cir. (pres. 1990). Office: WNBC 30 Rockefeller Plz 7th Fl New York NY 10112-0036

PRESSMAN, JACOB, retired rabbi; b. Phila., Oct. 26, 1919; s. Solomon David and Dora (Levin) P.; m. Marjorie Steinberg, June 14, 1942; children: Daniel Joseph, Joel David, Judith Sharon. BA, U. Pa., 1940; MHL, Jewish Theol. Sem., 1944, Dr.Hebrew Letters, 1960, Dr. Humane Letters, 1979. Ordained rabbi, 1945. Rabbi Forest Hills Jewish Ctr., N.Y.C., 1944-46, Congregation Sinai, L.A., 1946-50, Temple Beth Am, L.A., 1950—85; ret. Dir. Bonds of Israel, L.A., 1988-90, city chmn., 1990-91; vice chmn. bd. govs. L.A. Jewish Fedn. Coun., 1988—; founder U. Judaism, L.A. Hebrew High Sch., Herzl Sch., Camp Ramah at Ojai, Akiba Acad., Rabbi Jacob Pressman Acad. Author: Dear Friends, 2001, This Wild and Crazy World, 2001. Recipient Simon Greenberg award for Outstanding Achievement in Rabbinate, Ziegler Sch. Rabbinic Studies, U. Judaism, L.A., 2004. Mem. Rabbinical Assembly Western Region (pres. 1954-56), Bd. Rabbis So. Calif. (pres. 1958-61). Office: Temple Beth Am 1039 S La Cienega Blvd Los Angeles CA 90035-2507 E-mail: jpress6511@aol.com. *God is. God is good. His creation is good, and so, mankind, being of His creation is good. As an act of grace, God gives man the power to choose between good and evil in his ways, and with even greater grace gives man the awareness that he has this choice. Man is perfectible. His perfect stage, the Messianic era, is coming; but it will always be coming, never at a moment in time to arrive, but always inviting us to progress to newer and higher goals personally and as a society. each new mountaintop of human progress toward that nobler future merely opens our eyes to visions of even greater and more God-like human life.*

PRESSMAN, RONALD R. utilities executive; b. New York, N.Y., Apr. 11, 1958; Grad., Hamilton College, NY, 1980. Gen. mgr. ctr. and ea. Europe GE, London, 1990—92; CEO GE Power Sys. Europe, 1992—95, CEO Power Sys. global mktg., 1995—96; pres., CEO GE Capital Real Estate, 1997; sr. v.p. GE Co., 2000—; Pres., CEO G.E. Employers Reinsurance Co., 2000—. Bd. dirs. A Better Chance, Kansas City Civic Coun.; mem. exec. bd. Nat. Realty Com., Wharton Real Estate Bus. Sch. Recipient Crown American Golden Crown award, 1998, Fin. Svcs. Exec. of Yr., Comml. Property News. Office: GE Employers Reinsurance Co PO Box 2991 Shawnee Mission KS 66201-1391

PRESSMAN, THANE A. consumer products executive; b. San Diego, June 6, 1945; s. Harold Andrew and Audre Ethelyn (Negus) P.; m. Caroline Hannah Hood Snyder, Nov. 23, 1966; children: Sean, Steven. BS, Springfield (Mass.) Coll., 1967; MS, Syracuse U., 1969. Various to brand mgr. Procter & Gamble Co., Cin., 1968-76, assoc. mgr. advt., 1976-79; v.p. Lamalie Assocs., Inc. Chgo., 1979-81; dir. new products Alberto Culver Co., Melrose Park, Ill., 1981-84; group staff, v.p. Sara Lee Corp., Northbrook, Ill., 1984-85; pres., COO Kitchens of Sara Lee Can., Bramalea, Ont., 1986-88; exec. v.p. Sara Lee Bakery Co., Bramalea and Deerfield, Ill., 1988-90; pres., CEO Crestar Food Products, Inc. (affiliate of H.J. Heinz Co.), Eugene, Oreg., 1991-92, Crestar Food Products Inc. & Crestar Food Products Can. Ltd., Nashville and Mississauga, Ont., Can., 1992-93; pres. Labatt Ont. Breweries, Etobicoke, 1993-95; pres., CEO Labatt U.S.A. LLC., Norwalk, Conn., 1995-98, Tone Bros. Inc., Ankeny, Iowa, 1998—. Guest lectr. U. Mich. Grad. Sch. Bus., Ann Arbor, 1977-79; bd. dirs. Brewers Retail Inc., Toronto, ENESCO Group Inc., 2000—; bd. dirs. Brewers of Ont., 1994-95, chmn., 1995. Bd. dirs. Am. Field Svc. U.S.A., N.Y.C., 1986-91, Greater Des Moines Partnership, 2000—; trustee AFS Intercultural Programs, N.Y.C., 1988-93; trustee Springfield Coll., 1988—. Mem. Assn. Governing Bds. Univs. and Colls., David Allen Reed Soc., Food and Consumer Products Mfrs. Can., Grocery Mfrs. Am., Glen Oaks

Country Club, Vintage Sports Car Club Am., Vintage Automobile Racing Assn. Can., Vintage Sports Car Drivers Assn., Vintage Drivers Club Am. Home: 21 Chestnut Hill Rd West Hartford CT 06107-3151

PREST, NERISSA, newscaster; married; 1 child. Grad., Calif. State U., Columbia Grad. Sch. Jouralism. News asst. CNN Bus. News, N.Y.C.; gen. assignment reporter, fill-in anchor Sarasota (Fla.) News Now; anchor, reporter, prodr. WFMZ-TV, Allentown, Pa.; anchor WFLA-TV, Tampa, Fla., 2000—. Office: WFLA-TV PO Box 1410 Tampa FL 33601

PRESTAGE, JAMES JORDAN, university chancellor; b. Deweyville, Tex., Apr. 29, 1926; s. James J. and Mona (Wilkins) P.; m. Jewel Limar, Aug. 12, 1953; children— Terri, James Grady, Eric, Karen, Jay BS cum laude, So. U., Baton Rouge, 1950; MS, U. Iowa, 1955, PhD, 1959. Instr. biology Prairie View Coll., Tex., 1955-56; asst. prof. So. U., Baton Rouge, 1959, assoc. prof. biology, 1959-61, prof. biology, 1961—, dir. computer sci. ctr., 1968-71, 72-73, dean acad. affairs, v.p. acad. affairs, 1973-81, exec. v.p., 1981-82, chancellor, 1982-85, univ. disting. prof. emeritus, 1985—; univ. disting. prof. biology Dillard U., New Orleans, 1987—. Chair divsn. natural scis. Dillard U., 1990-97; asst. dir. La. Coordinating Council for Higher Edn., Baton Rouge, 1971-72; mem. commn. on scholars Ill. Bd. Higher Edn., 1975-82; mem. com. on off-campus instrn. La. Bd. Regents, 1975—; mem. La. Data Processing Council, Baton Rouge, 1979-82; vis. prof. biology Dillard U., New Orleans; trustee Am. Coll. Testing Program, 1983—; faculty assoc. Danforth Found., 1966-70. Mem. exec. bd. Istrouma council Boy Scouts Am.; vice chmn. bd. trustees Greater Mt. Carmel Baptist Ch., Baton Rouge; bd. dirs. Capital Area United Way, Baton Rouge. Served with USN, 1944-46, 50-52; ETO, Korea Named Most Outstanding Faculty Mem., So. U., 1966-67; Nat. Med. Fellowships fellow U. Iowa, Iowa City, 1956-59; NIH grantee, 1960-65 Mem. Contl. Acad. Deans So. States. NAACP, Sigma Xi, Alpha Chi, Alpha Phi Alpha (chpt. pres.), Sigma Pi Phi Democrat. Avocations: fishing; reading; gardening. Home: 2145 77th Ave Baton Rouge LA 70807-5508 Office: So Br PO Box 9222 Baton Rouge LA 70813

PRESTAGE, JEWEL LIMAR, political science educator; b. Hutton, La., Aug. 12, 1931; d. Brudis L. and Sallie Bell (Johnson) Limar; m. James J. Prestage, Aug. 12, 1953; children— Terri, James, Eric, Karen, Jay. BA, So. U., Baton Rouge, 1951; MA, U. Iowa, 1952, PhD, 1954; LHD (hon.), U. D.C., 1994, Loyola U., Chgo., 1999; LLD (hon.), Spelman Coll., 1999. Assoc. prof. polit. sci. Prairie View (Tex.) Coll., 1954-55, 56; assoc. prof. polit. sci. So. U., 1956-57, 58-62, prof., 1962—, chairperson dept., 1965-83; disting. prof. emeritus Prairie View Coll., 1989—; dean pub. policy and urban affairs So. U., 1983-89; prof. polit. sci. Prairie View U., 1989-90; dean Benjamin Banneker Honors College, Prairie View (Tex.) Coll., 1990-98, prof. political sci., 1998—; disting. prof. emeritus polit. sci. Benjamin Banneker Honors Coll., 2000—. Chmn. La. adv. com. to U.S. Commn. on Civil Rights, 1975-85; mem., chmn. nat. adv. coun. on women's ednl. programs U.S. Dept. Edn., 1980-82; vis. prof. U. Iowa, 1987-88. Author: (with M. Githens) A Portrait of Marginality: Political Behavior of the American Woman, 1976; contbr. articles to profl. jours. Rockefeller fellow, 1951-52; NSF fellow, 1964; Ford Found. postdoctoral fellow, 1969-70 Mem. NAACP, Am. Polit. Sci. Assn. (v.p. 1974-75, Frank Goodnow award 1998), So. Polit. Sci. Assn. (pres. 1975-76, Manning Daver award 1998), Nat. Conf. Black Polit. Scientists (pres. 1976-77), Nat. Assn. African Am. Honors Programs (pres. 1993-94), Am. Soc. for Pub. Adminstrn. (pres. La. chpt. 1988-89, nat. exec. coun. 1989-90), Policy Studies Orgn. (exec. coun. 2000), Links Inc., Alpha Kappa Alpha. Home: 11114 Wortham Blvd Houston TX 77065 Office: So Univ PO Box 125 Prairie View TX 77446-0125 *Commitments which guide my life are: (1) maximum development of personal potential through pursuit of excellence in all endeavors; (2) fair play, respect, compassion and quest of community in relations with fellow human beings; (3) utilization of personal talents in the interest of removing impediments to the good life "for all persons"; (4) pursuit of truth as the pervasive concern in academia; and (5) transmission of the above as priority goals to all with whom I have contact.*

PRESTBO, JOHN ANDREW, newspaper editor, journalist, author; b. Northwood, N.D., Sept. 26, 1941; s. Oscar Bernt and Jeanne (Schol) P.; m. Darlene Parrish, Aug. 14, 1965; children: Bradford Jonathan, Laura Christine. BS, Northwestern U., 1963, MS, 1964. Reporter, writer Wall Street Jour., Chgo., 1964-74, staff editor, Page 1 N.Y.C., 1974-75, commodities editor, 1975-77, bur. chief Cleve., 1977-81, markets editor N.Y.C., 1984—, editor Dow Jones Indexes, 1993—; v.p. editorial Dow Jones Radio 2, Inc., Princeton, N.J., 1981-83. Author: Sleuthing, 1976; co-author: (with Frederick C. Klein) News and the Market, 1974, (with Douglas R. Sease) Barron's Guide to Making Investment Decisions, 1994, 2nd edit., 1998, The Wall Street Jour. Book of Internat. Investing, 1997; editor: This Abundant Land, 1975, Dow Jones Commodities Handbook, 1976-79, The Dow Jones Guide to the World Stock Market, 1994-98, The Market's Measure, 1999. Served with USAFR, 1966-73. Recipient Econ. Reporting award Ind. Natural Gas Assn., U. Mo., 1967; recipient Achievement-bur. writing award G.M. Loeb, 1968 Home: 14 Charleston Dr Skillman NJ 08558-1801 Office: 4300 Rte 1 Monmouth Junction NJ 08852 Office Phone: 609-520-7079. E-mail: john.prestbo@dowjones.com.

PRESTIA, MICHAEL ANTHONY, accounting executive; b. S.I., N.Y., Oct. 6, 1931; s. Anthony and Antoinette (Folino) Prestia; m. Nancy Ferrandino, July 4, 1959 (div. May 1970); 1 child, Anthony; m. Janet Swanson, July 22, 1987 (dec. May 2001). BA, NYU, 1953, MBA, 1956. CPA N.Y. Sr. acct. Gluckman & Schacht, CPAs, N.Y.C., 1953—60; CFO Franklin Broadcasting Co., N.Y.C., 1960—63; chief acct., asst. to bus. officer, sec. Cooper Union for Advancement of Sci. and Art, N.Y.C., 1963—66; bus. officer Inst. Pub. Adminstrn., N.Y.C., 1966—71, contr., 1971—78, treas., 1978—84; cons. taxation and tax planning, 1959—. With U.S. Army, 1953—55. Mem.: AICPAs, N.Y. State Soc. CPAs. Home: 53-06 Francis Lewis Blvd Bayside NY 11364-1633 Office: 445 5th Ave New York NY 10016-0109

PRESTIFILIPPO, JOHN, air transportation executive; m. Debra Prestifilippo; 3 children. Student, U. Md., U. Calif., Stockton State U. Airframe and powerplant license. V.p. tech. svcs. and ops. Continental Express Airlines, 1986—2001; sr. v.p. maintenance US Airways Inc., Arlington, Va., 2002—. With USAF. Office: US Airways 2345 Crystal Dr Arlington VA 22227*

PRESTLEY, MARK DOUGLAS, video director; b. Morrison, Ill., Sept. 2, 1963; s. Arnold and Mona Prestley; m. Deanna Jean Nichols, Feb. 28, 1999; children: Nicholas James, Grace Marie, Amanda Giese, Kiel Giese, Cody Giese. AS, Sauk Valley Coll., Dixon, Ill., 1983; BA, No. Ill. U., Dekalb, 1987. News photographer WHBF-TV/Coronet Comm., Rock Island, Ill., 1991—94; v.p. D&M Prodns./Cons., Platte City, Mo., 1994—; video svcs. mgr. Sta. Casino Kans. City, Kansas City, Mo., 1996—97; video prodr./sr. dvd author Garmin Internat., Inc., Olathe, Kans., 1997—. Advt. Main St. Program, Morrison, Ill., 1995—96. Fellow Comm. fellow, No. Ill. U., 1987. Mem.: Masons (assoc.), Dunlap Lodge #321 (life; sr. warden 1995—96), Golden Key (life), Alpha Epsilon Rho (assoc.; student advisor 1985—87). Methodist. Avocations: automotive restoration, furniture refinishing, motorcycles, swimming. Office: Garmin International Inc 1200 E 151st St Olathe KS 66062 E-mail: mark.prestley@garmin.com.

PRESTON, ALAN R. human resources specialist; b. Bay City, Mich., Oct. 1951; Student, Delta Coll., Mich. State U. With dept. engrng. Chevron Texaco Corp., San Ramon, Calif., 1973—81, compensation dept. corp. human resources San Francisco, 1981—89, mgr. mgmt. planning, 1989—90, mgr. compensation, 1990—93, mgr. strategy and policies, 1993—94, project coord. human resources, 1994—95; gen. mgr. human resources Chevron Products Co., San Francisco, 1995—99; gen. mgr. orgn./compensation Chevron Texaco Shared Svcs., San Francisco, 1999—2001; gen. mgr. global remuneration Chevron Texaco Corp., San Francisco, 2001—03, Chevron Texaco, San Ramon, Calif., 2003—. Mem. compensation coun. Conf. Bd., World at Work Orgn. Office: Chevron Texaco Corp 6001 Bollinger Canyon Rd San Ramon CA 94583-2324

PRESTON, ANDREW JOSEPH, pharmacist, drug company executive; b. Bklyn., Apr. 19, 1922; s. Charles A. and Josephine (Rizzutto) Pumo; m. Martha Jeanne Happ, Oct. 10, 1953; children: Andrew Joseph Jr., Charles Richard, Carolyn Louise, Frank Arthur, Joanne Marie, Barbara Jeanne. BSc, St. John's U., 1943. Cert. bus. intermediary Internat. Bus. Brokers Assn. Mgr. Press Club, Bklyn. Nat. League Baseball Club, 1941-42; purchasing agt. Drug and Pharm. divsn. Intrassind, Inc., 1947; chief pharmacist Hendershot Pharmacy, Newton, NJ, 1949; agt. Bur. of Narcotics, U.S. Treasury Dept., 1948-49; owner Preston Drug & Surg. Co., Boonton, NJ, 1949-86; CEO Preston Pharmaceutics, Inc., Butler, NJ, 1970-80, Preston Bus. Cons., Inc., Kinnelon, NJ, 1987—. Commr. NJ State Bd. Pharmacy, 1970—72, pres., 1973; organizer State of NJ Drug Abuse Spkrs. Program, 1970—76; chmn. Morris County Drug Abuse Coun., 1969—70; lectr. drug abuse and narcotic addition various cmty. orgns., 1968—78; mem. adv. bd. Nat. Cmty. Bank, Boonton, 1973. Contbr. editls. to profl. jours. Chmn. bldg. fund com. Riverside Hosp., Boonton, 1963; mem. exec. com. Gov. Tom Kean Ann. Ball, 1985—86; chmn. Pharmacists of NJ for election of Pres. Ford, 1976, Pharmacists for Gov. Tom Kean, 1981—84, NJ Pharmacists for Reagan/Bush, 1984; mem. exec. com. Morris County Overall Econ. Devel. Com., 1976—82; chmn. Pharmacists for Fenwick, 1982; v.p. Kinnelon (NJ) Rep. Club, 1980; Rep. com. Kinnelon, 1990; mem. adv. com. to Congressman Dean Gallo on Pres. Clinton's Health Security Plan, 1994; mem. Morris County (NJ) Rep. Fin. Com., 1972; pres. Ronald Reagan NJ Re-Election Adv. Bd., 1984. Lt. (j.g.) USNR, 1943—46. Recipient Bowl Hygeia award, Robbins Co., 1969, Pres.'s award, E.R. Squibb, 1968, Square Club award, NJ Pharm., 1969, Andrew J. Preston award for Polit. Action established in his honor, 1999, Spl. NJ Pharmacists award for loyal svc., NJ Pharm. Assn., NJ Polit. Action Com., 2002. Mem.: VFW, Morris-Sussex Pharmacists Soc., Morris County Pharm. Assn., NJ Pub. Health Assn., Pharmacists Guild NJ, Pharmacists Guild Am. (pres. NY divsn. 1946—47), Inst. Bus. Appraisers, Internat. Bus. Brokers Assn., NJ Narcotic Enforcement Officers Assn., Internat. Narcotic Enforcement Officers Assn., Nat. Cmty. Pharmacists Assn., NJ Pharm. Assn. (econs. com. 1960—65, pres. 1967—68, Oscar Singer Meml. award 1987, William H. McNeil award 1994, Presdl. Citation award 2000, Spl. NJ Pharmacists award 2002), Am. Pharm. Assn., St. John's Alumni Assn., NJ Assn. Realtors, Nat. Assn. Realtors, Morris County Bd. Realtors, Am. Legion, Smoke Rise Club, KC, Elks. Roman Catholic. Home and Office: 507 Pepperidge Tree Ln Kinnelon NJ 07405-2223

PRESTON, CHARLES GEORGE, lawyer; b. Nov. 11, 1940; s. Charles William and Gudveig Nicoline (Hoem) P.; m. Hilde Delphine van Stappen, Mar. 12, 1970; children: Charles William, Stephanie Delphine, Christina Nicoline. BA, U. Wash., 1963, MPA, 1968; JD, Columbia U., 1971. Bar: Wash. 1971, D.C. 1981, U.S. Dist. Ct. D.C. 1981, U.S. Dist. Ct. (we. dist.) Wash. 1971, U.S. Ct. Appeals (9th cir.) 1972, U.S. Ct. Appeals (4th cir.) 1979, U.S. Ct. Appeals (5th and D.C. cirs.) 1978, U.S. Ct. Appeals (2d cir.) 1980, U.S. Ct. Appeals (11th cir.) 1981, U.S. Supreme Ct. 1977, U.S. Ct. Claims 1982, U.S. Ct. Appeals (1st cir.) 1984, U.S. Ct. Appeals (3d, 6th and 7th cirs.) 1987, Va. 1987, U.S. Dist. Ct. (ea. dist.) Va. 1989, U.S. Dist. Ct. (we. dist.) Wash. 1971, U.S. Dist. Ct. (no. dist.) Calif. 1981, U.S. Bankruptcy Ct. Va. 1990. Assoc. Jones, Grey, Bayley & Olson, Seattle, 1971-72; atty., asst. counsel for litigation Officer of Solicitor U.S. Dept. Labor, Seattle, 1972-76, Washington, 1976-81; atty. Air Line Pilots Assn., Washington, 1981-82; mng. ptnr. MacNabb, Preston & Waxman, Washington, 1981-86, Preston & Preston, Great Falls, Va., 1986-95, Charles G. Preston, P.C., 1995—. Pres. Preston Group, Inc., 1989—98; lectr. in field. Mem. Wash. State Bar, D.C. Bar Assn., Va. Bar Assn., Tng. Law Inst. (pres. 1985-95), Gt. Falls Bus. and Profl. Assn. (pres. 1990), The Serbian Crown, Va. (pres. 1989-99). Office: Charles G Preston PC 774C Walker Rd Great Falls VA 22066-2639 Office Phone: 703-759-3300. E-mail: preston.law@verizon.net.

PRESTON, COLLEEN ANN, lawyer; b. Monterey, Calif., Oct. 11, 1955; d. Howard Houston and Catherine (Reid) Harrison; m. Raymond C. Preston Jr., June 12, 1982. BA, U. Fla., 1975, JD, 1978; LLM, Georgetown U., 1985. Bar: Fla. 1979, U.S. Ct. Claims 1979, U.S. Ct. Appeals (fed. cir.) 1979. Assoc. Akerman, Senterfitt & Eidson, Orlando, Fla., 1978-79; atty. advisor, office of gen. counsel Sec. USAF, 1979-83; counsel com. on armed svcs. U.S. Ho. Reps., Washington, 1983-89, gen. counsel, 1990-93; spl. asst. to Sec. Def. for legal matters Dept. Def., Washington, 1993, dep. under sec. of def. for acquisition reform, 1993-97. Cons. Preston & Assocs., 1997—. Capt. USAF, 1979-83. Avocations: golf, tennis, cross country and downhill skiing, waterskiing.

PRESTON, FORREST L. health care executive; Founder, chmn., CEO Life Care Ctrs. of Am., Cleveland, Tenn., 1970—, chmn. Cleve. Office: Life Care Ctrs of Am 3570 Keith St NW Cleveland TN 37312

PRESTON, FRANCES WILLIAMS, performing rights organization executive; children: Kirk, David, Donald. Hon. degree, Lincoln (Ill.) Coll.; degree (hon.), Berklee Sch. Music. With BMI (Broadcast Music Inc.), Nashville, 1958—, v.p., 1964-85; sr. v.p. performing rights BMI, N.Y.C., 1985, exec. v.p., chief exec. officer, 1986, pres., chief exec. officer, 1986—, also bd. dirs. Mem. Film, Entertainment and Music Commn. Adv. Council State of Tenn.; founding mem. bd. dirs. Leadership Nashville; past pres. bd. dirs. John Work Meml. Found.; chmn. bd. dirs. Country Music Found., Inc., 1983-85, trustee, past pres., chmn. bldg. com.; mem. Commn. on White House Record Library, Carter adminstrn., Pres.'s Panama Canal Study Com., Carter adminstrn.; bd. dirs. Rock & Roll Hall of Fame; mem. adminstrv. council Internat. Confedn. of Socs. of Authors and Composers; v.p. Nat. Music Council; past bd. dirs. Peabody Awards; hon. trustee Nat. Acad. Popular Music; pres. bd. dirs. T.J. Martell Fedn. for Leukemia, Cancer and AIDS Rsch.; established Frances Williams Preston Rsch. Labs. for T.J. Martell Fedn., 1993; bd. dirs. R&B Found. Recipient achievement award Women's Equity Action League, spl. citation award NATAS, Golden Baton award Young Musicians Found., Humanitarian award Internat. Achievement in Arts award, 1995, Creative Achievement award Elaine Kaufman Cultural Ctr., 1996, Lester Sill Humanitarian award, 1996, Nat. Trustees award Grammys, 1998; named one of Am.'s 50 Most Powerful Women Ladies' Home Jour.; named to Country Music Hall of Fame. Mem. Country Music Assn. (life mem. bd. dirs., Irving Waugh Award of Excellence), Nashville Symphony Assn. (past sec., bd. dirs.), NARAS Found. (bd. dirs., pres.'s adv. bd.), Nashville Songwriters Assn. (life mem., bd. dirs.), Gospel Music Assn. (life mem. bd., past chmn., past pres.), Am. Women in Radio and TV (past nat. dir.). Clubs: (Friars Found. Applause award). Lodges: Rotary (1st woman mem. Nashville club), Friars. Presbyterian. Office: BMI 320 W 57th St Fl 3 New York NY 10019-3790

PRESTON, HARRY, writer, scriptwriter; b. Howick, South Africa, Sept. 4, 1923; arrived in US, 1948; s. Richard Henry and Lilian Catherine Pimm. BA in English, Natal U., Durban, South Africa, 1942. News editor WFAA-TV, Dallas, 1957—59; rewrite man MGM Studio, Hollywood, Calif., 1959—62. Instr. screenwriting Richland Coll., Dallas, 1991—2003. Author: Faces of Angels, 2001, Thelma Who?, 2002, Shot in Dallas, 2003. Recipient Lifetime Achievement award, Corpus Christi Film Festival, 1989. Home: 4413 Clemson Dr Garland TX 75042 Personal E-mail: prestone@earthlink.net.

PRESTON, JAMES E. retired cosmetics company executive; b. 1933; BS, Northwestern U., 1955. With Avon Products, Inc., N.Y.C., 1964—, from mgmt. trainee to dir. sales promotion, 1964-70, dir. personnel, 1970-71, v.p. corp. personnel, 1971-72, from group v.p. mktg. to sr. v.p. field ops. worldwide, 1972-77, exec. v.p., 1977-81, exec. corp. v.p., pres., 1981-88, pres., chief operating officer, 1988-89, chief exec. officer, 1988-98, chmn. bd. dirs., 1989—; ret. Bd. dirs. ARAMARK Corp., Woolworth Corp. Mem.: Reader's Digest Assn. (bd. dirs. 1994). Office: Avon Products Inc 1345 Avenue Of The Americas New York NY 10105-0302

PRESTON, KELLY, actress; b. Oct. 13, 1962; m. John Travolta, 1991; 2 children. Student, U. So. Calif., UCLA. Represented by Internat. Creative Mgmt., Beverly Hills, Calif. Appeared in films, including Mischief, 1985, Space Camp, 1986, 52 Pick-Up, 1986, A Tiger's Tale, 1987, Spellbinder, 1988, Twins, 1988, The Experts, 1989, Run, 1991, Love is a Gun, 1994, Jerry Macguire, 1996, Citizen Ruth, 1997, Addicted to Love, 1997, Nothing to Lose, 1997, The Holy Man, 1998, Jack Frost, 1998, For Love of the Game, 1999, Battlefield Earth, 2000, Daddy and Them, 2001, View from the Top, 2003, What a Girl Wants, 2003, The Cat in the Hat, 2003.

PRESTON, RICHARD ARTHUR, historian; b. Middlesbrough, England, Oct. 4, 1910; s. Frank and Florence Rachel (Carter) P.; m. Marjorie Fishwick, Sept. 2, 1939; children— David Frank, Carol Jane, Peter Eric. BA, Leeds U., 1931, MA, 1932, Dip.Ed., 1933; PhD, Yale U., 1936; LL.D., Royal Mil. Coll. Can., 1977. Mem. faculty U. Toronto, 1936-38, U., Coll. South Wales, 1938-45, U. Toronto, 1945-48; mem. faculty Royal Mil. Coll. Can., Kingston, 1948-65, prof. history. to 1965, Duke U., Durham, N.C., 1965-80, 1st N.K. Boyd prof. history, 1980—, dir. Can. studies, 1973-79. Author: Gorges of Plymouth Fort, 1953, Men in Arms, 1956-91, Royal Fort Frontenac, 1958, Kingston Before the War of 1812, 1958, Canada in World Affairs, 1959-61, 1965, Canada and Imperial Defense, 1967, Canada's R.M.C, 1969, For Friends at Home, 1974, Defence of the Undefended Border, 1977, Perspectives in the History of Military Education and Professionalism, 1980, the Squat Pyramid: Canadian Studies in the U.S, 1980, To Serve Canada, 1991. Served with RAF, 1940-45. Commonwealth Fund fellow, 1933-36; Can. Coun. fellow, 1963-64; Social Sci. Rsch. Coun. fellow, 1963-64; Guggenheim fellow, 1972-73; recipient Achievement award City Kingston, 1959, Can. Confedn. medal, 1967, Queen's Jubilee medal, 1975, Donner medal, 1977, No. Telecom. Internat. Can. Studies award and Gold medal, 1983, Kingston Hist. Soc. Centennial award, 1994. Mem. Can. Hist. Assn. (pres. 1961-62), Assn. Can. Studies U.S. (founding pres. 1971-72), Am. Mil. Inst. Home: Olsen # 245 2701 Pickett Rd Durham NC 27705-5648

PRESTON, ROBERT BRUCE, retired lawyer; b. Cleve., Feb. 24, 1926; s. Robert Bruce and Erma May (Hunter) P.; m. Agnes Ellen Stanley, Jan. 29, 1949; children— Robert B., Patricia Ellen Preston Kiefer, Judith Helen Preston Yanover. AB, Western Res. U., 1950, JD, 1952. Bar: U.S. Dist. Ct. (no. dist.) Ohio 1953, U.S. Ct. Appeals (6th cir.) 1959, U.S. Supreme Ct. 1964. Assoc. Arter & Hadden, Cleve., 1952-63, ptnr., 1964-93; ret., 1994. Dir. Service Stampings Inc., Willoughby, Ohio. Vice pres. Citizens League Cleve., 1965; chmn. Charter Rev. Com., Cleveland Heights, Ohio, 1972; mem. Zoning Bd. Appeals, Cleveland Heights, 1974-76; trustee Women's Philanthropic Union, 1977—. Mem. Ohio Bar Assn., Greater Cleve. Bar Assn. Republican. Presbyterian. Avocations: tennis, fishing, travel. Home: 117 Manor Brook Dr South Russell OH 44022-4163

PRESTON, SAMUEL HULSE, demographer; b. Morrisville, Pa., Dec. 2, 1943; s. Samuel H. and Dora (Berrell) P.; m. Winnifred de Witt, June 19, 1965; children: Samuel, Andrew, Benjamin, Leah. BA in Econs., Amherst Coll., 1965; PhD in Econs., Princeton U., 1968. Asst. prof. demography U. Calif., Berkeley, 1968-72; dir. Ctr. for Demography U. Wash., Seattle, 1972-77; chief, population structure sect. UN, N.Y.C., 1977-79; prof. sociology U. Pa., Phila., 1979—, dir. Population Studies Ctr., 1982—89, Frederick J. Warren prof. demography, 1988—, dean Sch. Arts and Scis., 1998—. Author: Patterns of Urban and Rural Population Growth, 1980, (with M. Haines) Fatal Years, 1991, (with M. Guillot and P. Heuveline) Demography, 2000. Fellow AAAS, Am. Acad. Arts and Scis, Am. Statis. Assn.; mem. NAS, Inst. Medicine, Am. Philos. Soc., Population Assn. Am. (pres. 1984, Irene B. Tauber award for Excellence in Demographic Research 1983), Internat. Union for Sci. Study of Population (council 1981-88). Methodist. Home: 234 Walnut Ave Wayne PA 19087-3445 Office: Univ Pa Sch Arts and Scis Dean's Office Philadelphia PA 19104

PRESTON, SEYMOUR STOTLER, III, chemicals executive; b. Media, Pa., Sept. 11, 1933; s. Seymour Stotler and Mary Alicia (Harper) P.; m. Jean Ellen Holman, Sept. 8, 1956; children: Courtney J., Katherine E., Alicia D., Shelley S. BA, Williams Coll., 1956; MBA, Harvard Coll., 1958. With Pennwalt Corp., Phila., 1961-89, exec. v.p. in charge of chems. and equipment ops., worldwide, 1975-77, pres., COO, 1977-89; pres., CEO Elf Atochem N.Am., Inc. (formerly Atochem N.Am.), Phila., 1990-93. Chmn. AAC Engineered Sys. Inc., 1994-2003; bd. dirs. Scott Splty. Gases, Inc., Albermarle Corp., Tufco Techs., Inc., Ocean Power Tech. Inc., Ind. Publs., Inc. Trustee Shipley Sch., Bryn Mawr, Pa., 1976-88, Phila. Orch. Assn., 1992-95; trustee Acad. Natural Scis., 1980—, chmn., 1995-2000, pres., CEO, 2000-02; bd. mgrs. Franklin Inst., Phila., 1980-92; bd. dirs. Lawrenceville (NJ) Sch., 1982-99, Wistar Inst., 1997—, Barra Found., 1998—, chmn., 2004—. 1st lt. USAF, 1958-61. Mem. Soc. for Chem. Industry, Greater Phila. C. of C. (bd. dirs. 1979-94), Radnor Hunt Club (Malvern, Pa.). Personal E-mail: spmillrace@aol.com.

PRESTON, STEPHEN W. lawyer; BA summa cum laude, Yale U., 1979; diploma., Trinity Coll., U. Dublin, 1980; JD magna cum laude, Harvard U., 1983. Bar: D.C. Law clk. to Hon. Phyllis A. Kravitch U.S. Ct. Appeals (11th cir.), 1983-84; vis. fellow Ctr. for Law in Pub. Interest, Washington, 1984-85; ptnr. Wilmer, Cutler & Pickering, Washington, 1986-93; prin. dep. gen. counsel, acting gen. counsel Dept. of Def., 1993-95; dep. asst. atty. gen. Dept. of Justice, 1995-98; gen. counsel Dept. of Navy, 1998-2000; ptnr. Wilmer Cutler Pickering Hale and Dorr LLP, Washington, 2001—. Recipient Disting. Pub. Svc. medal Dept. of Def., 1995, 2000, Dept. of Navy, 2000. Office: Wilmer Cutler Pickering Hale & Dorr 2445 M St NW Washington DC 20037-1420 E-mail: stephen.preston@wilmerhale.com.

PRESTON, STEVEN C. investment company executive; BA with highest distinction, Northwestern U.; MBA, U. Chgo.; student, U. Munich, Germany. Investment banker Lehman Bros., 1985-93; sr. v.p., treas. 1st Data Corp.; v.p., CFO, ServiceMaster, Downers Grove, Ill., 1997—. Office: The ServiceMaster Company 1 ServiceMaster Way Downers Grove IL 60515

PRESTON, THOMAS RONALD, English language educator, researcher; b. Oct. 31, 1936; s. Thomas and Marie Katherine (Nettlow) P.; m. Mary Ruth Atkinson, June 4, 1960; children: Lorel, Mary, Thomas BA, U. Detroit, 1958; MA, Rice U., 1960, PhD, 1962. Asst. prof. English Duquesne U., Pitts., 1962-63; Asst. prof. English U. Fla., Gainseville, 1963-67; assoc. prof., chmn. dept. Loyola U., New Orleans, 1967-69; prof., chmn. dept. U. Tenn., Chattanooga, 1969-73, U. Wyo., Laramie, 1973-82; prof., dean arts and scis. U. North Tex., Denton, 1982-92, prof. English, 1992—. Chmn. Wyo. Council for Humanities, Laramie, 1976-77 Author: Not in Timon's Manner, 1975; editor U. Ga. edit. of Smollett's Humphry Clinker, 1990; contbr. articles on 18th century lit. to profl. jours. Recipient John W. Gardner award Rice U., 1962; George Duke Humphrey award U. Wyo., 1982; NEH grantee, 1979; Am. Council of Learned Socs. grantee, 1980 Mem. Am. Soc. for 18th Century Studies, South Ctrl. Soc. for 18th Century Studies (pres. 1986-87). Democrat. Anglican. Office: U North Tex Dept English Box 311307 Denton TX 76203 E-mail: trpatlake@cs.com.

PRESTON-MARTIN, SUSAN, epidemiologist, educator; b. N.Y.C., Jan. 18, 1942; d. George Davies and Elizabeth Carver Preston; m. David R. Williams; 3 children. BA in Exptl. Psychology, Swarthmore Coll., 1963; MPH in Health Svc., UCLA, 1972, PhD in Epidemiology, 1978. Instr. U. So. Calif. Sch. Medicine, 1972—78, asst. prof., 1978—82, assoc. prof., 1982—90, prof., 1990—; adj. assoc. prof. UCLA Sch. Pub. Health, 1985—. Advisor NIOSH, NCI, NAS, NRC, Ctrl. Brain Tumor Registry of the US, Wireless Tech. Group, IARC. Grantee, NIH, Internat. Agy. for Rsch. on Cancer, Am. Cancer Soc., Calif. State Dept. Health Svc., Cancer Rsch. Found. of Am., Children's Hosp. of Phil., Fogarty Internat. Ctr., Cancer Epidemiology in Adventists, NCH, 1991—94, NINDS, NEI, NIH, 1980—98, NIOSH, NIH/NIAID, NIH/NCI. Mem.: APHA, Soc. for Neuro-Oncology, Soc. for Epidemiol. Rsch., Internat. Epidemiol. Assn., Bioelectromagnetics Soc., Am. Soc. for Preventive Oncology. Achievements include research in Epidemiology of brain tumors and leukemia; effects in human of exposure to radiation, N-nitroso compounds,electric and magnetic fields and the effects to offspring from parental exposures; relationship of diet and supplement use to develop. of cancer and disease; Methodological issues in epidemiol. studies: questionnaire construction; control selection; comparability of data sources. Office: Keck Sch of Medicine Dept Preventive Med 1441 Eastlake Ave M/S #44 Stes 4411 &4415, PO Box33800 Los Angeles CA 90033-0800

PRESTOPNIK, RICHARD JOHN, electronics and computer educator; b. Little Falls, N.Y., Nov. 23, 1951; s. John William and Frances (Grabowski) P.; m. Jan Sponenberg, June 16, 1973; children: Nathan Richard, Emily Kate, Adam Christopher. AAS in Elec. Tech., Mohawk Valley C.C., 1971; B Engring. Tech. in Elec. Engring., Rochester Inst. Tech., 1974; MSEE in Computer Engring., Syracuse U., 1982. From jr. engr. to sr. assoc. engr. IBM, Endicott, NY, 1974-80; from asst. to assoc. prof. elec. tech. dept. Fulton-Montgomery C.C., Johnstown, NY, 1980-89, prof., 1989-95, acting dean career edn., 1995-96, dean bus. and tech., 1996-99, prof., 2001—; dir. NASA-Fulton-Montgomery C.C. Spatial Info. Tech. Ctr., 2000—01; advisor Spatial Info. Tech. Ctr., 2001—. Coll. rep. on bd. dirs. Fulton-Montgomery, Schoharie Pvt. Industry Coun.; participant long distance learning project Gloversville High Sch.; mem. tech. prep. steering com. Fulton County Econ. Devel. Corp.; v.p. CPT Assocs., Inc., computer and electronic cons., 1983-85; book reviewer Prentice-Hall, Inc. Revision author: The Encyclopedia of Integrated Circuits, 2d edit., 1987; author: The Microprocessor IC Reference Manual, 1989, Digital Electronics: Concepts and Applications for Digital Design, 1990, also lab. manual, 1990; also articles. Faculty grantee SUNY Rsch. Found., 1986, faculty excellence grantee Fulton-Montgomery C.C., 1992, numerous others; NASA/ASEE faculty fellow in aeronautics and space rsch., 1995, 96; recipient V.P. Gore's Nat. Performance Rev. Hammer award, 1997, Chancellor's award for excellence in scholarship and creative activities SUNY, 2003. Mem. IEEE, Am. Soc. Engring. Edn. (Outstanding Educator award St. Lawrence sect. 1990), N.Y. State Engring. Tech. Assn. Avocations: golf, hiking, travel. Office: Fulton-Montgomery CC 2805 State Highway 67 Johnstown NY 12095-3749 Office Phone: 518-762-4651. Business E-Mail: rprestop@fmcc.suny.edu.

PRESTOWITZ, CLYDE VINCENT, economist, researcher; b. Wilmington, Del., Sept. 6, 1941; s. Clyde Vincent and Lillian (Lang) Prestowitz; m. Carol Ann Jay, Mar. 29, 1964; children: Anne, Clyde, Brian. BA, Swarthmore Coll., 1963; MA, U. Hawaii, 1965; MBA, U. Pa., 1980. Mgr. market devel. Scott Paper Co., Phila., 1968—72, dir. planning Europe Brussels, 1972—76; v.p. Japan Egon Zehnder Internat., Tokyo, 1976—78; dir. mktg. Am. Can Co., Greenwich, Conn., 1978—79; pres. Prestowitz Assocs., New Canaan, Conn., 1979—81; dep. asst. sec. internat. econ. policy U.S. Dept. Commerce, Washington, 1981—82, acting asst. sec. internat. econ. policy, 1982—83, counselor to sec., 1983—86; Wilson fellow, 1986—87; sr. assoc. Carnegie Endowment for Internat. Peace, Washington, 1987—89; pres. Econ. Strategy Inst., Washington, 1989—. Vice-chmn. Pacific Basin Econ. Coun., 1989—; vice chmn., presdl. com. U.S./Pacific Trade and Investment Policy. Republican. Presbyterian. Home: 10420 Masters Ter Potomac MD 20854-3862 Office: Econ Strategy Inst 1401 H St NW Ste 560 Washington DC 20005-2110

PRESTRIDGE, PAMELA ADAIR, lawyer; b. Delhi, La., Dec. 25, 1945; d. Gerald Wallace Prestridge and Louis Baugh and Peggy Adair (Arender) Martin. BA, La. Poly. U., 1967; M in Edn., La. State u., 1968, JD, 1973. Bar: U.S. Dist. Ct. (mid. dist.) La. 1975, U.S. Dist. Ct. (so. dist.) Tex. 1982, U.S. Ct. Appeals (5th cir.) 1982, U.S. Supreme Ct. 1990. Law clk. to presiding justice La. State Dist. Ct., Baton Rouge, 1973-75; ptnr. Breazeale, Sachse & Wilson, Baton Rouge, 1975-82, Hirsch & Westheimer P.C., Houston, 1982-92; pvt. practice, Houston, 1992—. Counselor Big Bros./Big Sisters, Baton Rouge, 1968-70; legal cons., bd. dirs. Lupus Found. Am., Houston, 1984-93; bd. dirs. Quota Club, Baton Rouge, 1979-82, Speech and Hearing Found., Baton Rouge, 1981-82, The Actors Workshop, Houston, 1988-93, Tex. Satsang Soc., 2000—. Recipient Pres.'s award Lupus Found. Am., 1991, cert. of appreciation Assn. Atty. Mediators, 1992, Outstanding Profl. Woman of Houston award Fedn. Profl. Women, 1984. Mem. ABA, La. Bar Assn., Tex. Bar Assn., Houston Bar Assn., Houston Bar Found., Assn. Atty. Mediators (bd. dirs. 1994-96, Citation for Outstanding Mems. 1993), Profl. Atty.-Mediators Coop. (v.p. 1994, bd. dirs. 1994-96, pres. 1995), Phi Alpha Delta. Eckankar. Avocations: acting, ultralite flying. Home: 1701 Hermann Dr Unit 407 Houston TX 77004-7345 Office: 3200 Southwest Freeway Ste 3300 PO Box 130987 Houston TX 77219-0987

PRESTWOOD, ALVIN TENNYSON, lawyer; b. Roeton, Ala., June 18, 1929; s. Garret Felix and Jimmie (Payne) Prestwood; m. Sue Burleson Lee, Nov. 27, 1974; children: Ann Celeste Prestwood Campbell, Alison Bennett, Cynthia Joyce Lee Koplos, William Alvin Lee. BS, U. Ala., 1951, LLB, 1956, JD, 1970. Bar: Ala. 1956, U.S. Ct. Appeals (4thj, 6th and 11th cirs.) 1981, U.S. Supreme Ct. 1972. Law clk. Supreme Ct. Ala., 1956-57; asst. atty. gen. Ala., 1957-59; commr. Ala. Dept. Pensions and Security, 1959-63; pvt. practice Montgomery, Ala., 1963-65, 77-82; ptnr. Volz, Capouano, Wampold, Prestwood & Sansone, 1965-77, Prestwood & Rosser, 1982-85, Capouano, Wampold, Prestwood & Sansone, 1986-94, Volz, Prestwood & Hanan, Montgomery, 1995—2001, Prestwood & Assocs., 2002—. Mem. adv. com. Dept. Health, Edn. and Welfare, 1962; sec. Nat. Coun. State Pub. Welfare Adminstrs., 1962. Mem. editl. bd. Ala. Law Rev., 1955—56; contbr. articles to profl. jours. Chmn. Gov.'s Com. White House Conf. Aging, 1961; chmn. bd. mgmt. East Montgomery YMCA, 1969; pres. Morningview Sch. PTA, 1970; chmn. legal com. Am. Nursing Home Assn., 1972; chmn. deacons Cloverdale Bapt. Ch., 1994—95, 1998; bd. dirs. Montgomery Bapt. Hosp., 1958—65. 1st lt. inf. U.S. Army, 1951—53. Decorated Combat Inf. badge; recipient Sigma Delta Kappa Scholastic Achievement award, U. Ala. Sch. Law, 1956, Law Day Moot Ct. award, 1956. Mem.: ABA (chmn. com. jud. performance and conduct 1996, chmn. judiciary's image evaluation task force 1996—2000), Am. Judicature Soc., 11th Cir. Jud. Conf., Farrah Order Jurisprudence, Montgomery County Bar Assn. (chmn. exec. com. 1971), Ala. Bar Assn. (chmn. adminstrv. law sect. 1972, 1978, 1983, 1997), Kappa Sigma. Home: 1431 Magnolia Curv Montgomery AL 36106-2043 Office: Prestwood & Assocs 350 Adams Ave Montgomery AL 36104-4204 E-mail: attys@bellsouth.net.

PRETLOW, THOMAS GARRETT, physician, pathology educator, researcher; b. Warrenton, Va., Dec. 11, 1939; s. William Ribble and May (Tiffany) P.; m. Theresa Pace, June 29, 1963; children: James Michael, Joseph Peter, David Mark. AB, Oberlin Coll., 1960; MD, U. Rochester, 1965. Intern U. Hosps., Madison, Wis., 1965-66; fellow McArdle Lab., 1966-67; rsch. assoc. Nat. Cancer Inst., Bethesda, Md., 1967-69; asst. prof. pathology Rutgers Med. Sch., Piscataway, N.J., 1969-70; assoc. prof. pathology U. Ala., Birmingham, 1971-73, prof. pathology, 1974-83, prof. biochemistry, 1982-83; vis. prof. pathology Harvard Med. Sch., Boston, 1983-84; prof. pathology Case Western Res. U., Cleve., 1983—, prof. oncology, 1987—, prof. environ. health scis., 1991—, prof. urology, 1994—. Cons. NIH, Bethesda, 1976-2000, Am. Inst. Cancer Rsch., 1995-98; chmn. pathobiolog y 2 prostate cancer grant reviewer U.S. Army, 1998, 99. Mem. editl. bd. Cell Biophysics, Cambridge, Mass., 1978-82; editor: Cell Separation: Methods and Selected Applications, 5 vols., 1982, 83, 84, 87, Biochemical and Molecular Aspects of Selected Cancers, 2 vols., 1991, 94. Mem. exec. bd. Birmingham coun. Boy Scouts Am., 1979-83, Greater Cleve. coun. Boy Scouts Am., 1984-90. Served to lt. comdr. USPHS, 1967-69. Recipient Rsch. Career Devel. award Nat. Cancer Inst., 1973-78; grantee for cancer rsch. Mem. Am. Assn. Pathologists, Am. Assn. Immunologists, Internat. Acad. Pathology, Am. Soc. Clin. Oncology, Am. Assn. Cancer Rsch., Serra Club (pres. Birmingham chpt. 1982-83). Avocations: camping, fishing, boy scouts, classical music, biking. Home: 3061 Chadbourne Rd Cleveland OH 44120-2446 Office: Inst Pathology Case Western Reserve U Cleveland OH 44106 Business E-Mail: tgp3@cwru.edu.

PRETO-RODAS, RICHARD A. retired foreign language educator; b. N.Y.C., May 30, 1936; s. Manuel and Beatrice Alina (Carvalho) Preto-R. BA, Fairfield U., 1958; MA in Philosophy, Boston Coll., 1960; MA in Spanish, U. Mich., 1962, PhD in Romance Langs. (fellow Rackham Sch. Grad. Studies 1965), 1966. Instr. U. Mich., 1964-66; asst. prof. U. Fla., 1966-70; assoc. prof. U. Ill., Urbana-Champaign, 1970-74, prof., 1974-81, chmn. Spanish, Italian, 1978-81; dir. lang. U. South Fla., Tampa, 1981-89, prof. lang., 1989-98, prof. emeritus, 1998—. Cons. MLA; Fulbright vis. prof. comparative lit. U. Stendhal, Grenoble, France, 1994-95, U. Perpignan, France, 2000, 2001. Author: Negritude as A Theme in the Poetry of the Portuguese-Speaking World, 1971, Dialogue and Courtly Lore in Renaissance Portugal, 1971; co-author: Cronicas Brasileiras: A Portuguese Reader, 1980, rev. 1994 as Cronicas Brasileiras, Nova Fase, 40 Historinhas of C.D. de Andrade, 1983; co-editor, contbr: Empire in Transition: The Portuguese World in the Time of Camoes, 1985; contbg. editor: Handbook of Latin American Studies, 1983-95; contbg. reviewer World Lit. Today, 1986-99. NDEA fellow, 1965 Mem. MLA, Am. Council on Teaching Fgn. Langs., Am. Assn. Tchrs. of Spanish and Portuguese, Phi Beta Kappa. Democrat. Home: 4483 Vieux Carre Cir Tampa FL 33613-3057 Office: U South Fla CPR-107 Tampa FL 33620 E-mail: preto_ro@chumai.cas.usf.edu.

PRETTYMAN, ELIJAH BARRETT, JR., lawyer; b. Washington, June 1, 1925; s. Elijah Barrett and Lucy Courtney (Hill) P.; children by previous marriage: Elijah Barrett III, Jill Savage Lukoschek. BA, Yale U., 1949; LLB, U. Va., 1953. Bar: Wash., D.C. 1954, U.S. Supreme Ct. 1957. Pvt. practice, Washington, 1955—; law clk. to Hon. Justices Jackson, Frankfurter and Harlan U.S. Supreme Ct., 1953-55; assoc. Hogan & Hartson, Washington, 1955—63, ptnr., 1964—2001, of counsel, 2002—; inspector gen. Dist. of Colo., Washington, 1998—99. Spl. asst. to Atty. Gen. U.S., 1963, White House, 1963-64; also Pres. rep. to Interagy. Com. on Transport Mergers; spl. cons. subcom. to investigate problems connected with refugees and escapees, U.S. Senate Judiciary Com., Vietnam, 1967-68; outside cons. to subcom. on oversight and investigations, Ho. of Reps. com. on internal and fgn. commerce, 1978; spl. cons. for ABSCAM investigation to Com. on Standards of Ofcl. Conduct, U.S. Ho. of Reps., 1980-81; trustee emeritus, past exec com. Am. U., Washington; past trustee, mem. exec. com. Washington Journalism Ctr.; past adv. com., Media Law Reporter. Author: Death and the Supreme Court, 1961 (Edgar Allan Poe award); Editor: (with William E. Jackson) The Supreme Court in the American System of Government (Justice Robert H. Jackson), 1955; contbr. articles to profl. jours. Past corp. mem. Salvation Army; past mem. adv. com. Procedures of Jud. Coun., D.C., past mem. adv. bd. Inst. Comm. Law Studies, Cath. U.; bd. govs., St. Albans Sch., 1957-63, 65-72, chmn., 1965-67; past mem. nat. adv. com., Nat. Inst. for Citizen Edn. in Law; bd. dirs., past pres. PEN/Faulkner Found.; v.p., chmn. publ. com., exec. com. Supreme Ct. Hist. Soc.; past internat. adv. group Toshiba Corp.; past commr. Supreme Ct. Jud. Fellows Commn., chmn., 2003— With AUS, 1943-45. Chmn. recipient Pub. Achievement award Common Cause, 1999, Justice Potter Stewart award Coun. for Ct. Excellence, 2000, disting. pub. svc. award D.C. 1999. Fellow: ABA; mem.: D.C. Cir. Hist. Soc. (pres. 2000—02, chmn. 2003—), Am. Acad. Appellate Lawyers (past pres.), Am. Judicature Soc. (past vice chair exec. com.), Met. Washington Bd. Trade, DC Bar Assn. (bd. govs., Lawyer of Yr. award 1998), DC Bar (1st pres. 1972—73, bd. govs. 1973—74, jud. evaluation com.), DC Bar Found. (pres. 1983—84), Jud. Conf. DC Cir., Am. Coll. Trial Lawyers, Chevy Chase Club, Met. Club, Alfalfa Club, Barristers Club, Lawyers Club (past pres.). Methodist. Home: 2737 Devonshire Pl NW # 424 Washington DC 20008-5148 Office: Columbia Sq 555 13th St NW Washington DC 20004-1109 Office Phone: 202-637-5685.

PRETTYMAN, WENDY PETTIT, management company executive; b. Gary, Ind., Oct. 6, 1945; d. Wendell E. and Ethel Pettit; m. Ted Prettyman, Aug. 2, 2000. BA, MacMurray Coll., 1967; MSBA, Ind. U., 1978, Cert. in Acctg., 1992, MBA, 1993. Acctg. clk. J. Walter Thompson USA, Chgo., 1967-68, adminstrv. asst., 1968-72, pers. asst., 1973-74, fin. analyst, 1974-78, office svcs. asst., 1978-80, acctg. dept. mgr., 1980-90; pres. Pettit Acctg. & Mgmt. Svcs. LLC., Gary, Ind., 1990—; asst. contr. Inland Employees Fed. Credit Union, Schererville, Ind., 1993-99, contr., 1999-2000. Bd. dirs. Miller Citizens Corp., Gary, 1979-86, treas., 1979-82. Named Career Woman of the Yr., Bus. and Profl. Women, Gary, 1967. Mem. NAFE, LWV, AAUW, Am. Mgmt. Assn., BBB, Miller Bus. Assn. Methodist. Avocations: singing, piano, cooking. Home: 8000 Oak Ave Gary IN 46403-1369 Office: 650 Lake St Gary IN 46403-2927 Fax: 219-938-2649. Office Phone: 219-938-2644.

PRETZEL, MARK WILLIAM, musician; BM, MM, U. Cin., 1979—86; MM, Bowling Green State U., Ohio, 1986—88; DMA, U. Mo., Kansas City, 1988—95. Adj. prof. Avila U., Kansas City, Mo., 1990—2000, Johnson County C.C., Overland Park, Kans., 1997—. V.p. U. Mo. Conservatory Alumni Assn., Kansas City, 2002. Home: 16633 W 145th St Olathe KS 66062 Office: Johnson County Comty Coll 12345 College Blvd Overland Park KS 66062 Personal E-mail: mwpretzel@aol.com. E-mail: mpretzel@jccc.net.

PREUDHOMME, MARCIA DENRIQUE, finance company executive, writer; b. San Fernando, Trinidad, West Indies, Nov. 12, 1966; d. Ronald and Sarah Preudhomme. Diploma in gen. draftsmanship, San Fernando Tech. Inst., Trinidad, 1991; cert. in stage mgmt., U. West Indies, Trinidad, 1992; student, Montgomery Coll., 1995. Draftsman San Fernando City Hall, 1994; mgr., team developer Brinker Internat., Inc., Washington, 1997—99; referral coord. Washington Hosp. Ctr., 1999—2001; assoc. BDO Seidman, LLP, Bethesda, Md., 2001—04. Author: Reflections of Realism, 2003, Stranger Than Fiction, 2004. Recipient Editor's Choice, Internat. Libr. Poetry, 2003. Avocations: reading, board games, philosophy, exercise. Office Phone: 202-546-1708.

PREUS, DAVID WALTER, bishop, minister; b. Madison, Wis., May 28, 1922; s. Ove Jacob Hjort and Magdalene (Forde) P.; m. Ann Madsen, June 26, 1951; children: Martha, David, Stephen, Louise, Laura. BA, Luther Coll., Decorah, Iowa, 1943, DD (hon.), 1969; postgrad., U. Minn., 1946-47; BTh, Luther Sem., St. Paul, 1950; postgrad., Union Sem., 1951, Edinburgh U., 1951-52; LLD (hon.), Wagner Coll., 1973, Gettysburg Coll., 1976; DD (hon.), Pacific Luth. Coll., 1974, St. Olaf Coll., 1974, Dana Coll., 1979, Tex. Luth. Coll., 1994; LHD (hon.), Macalester Coll., 1976; DD (hon.), Luther Coll., 1969. Ordained to ministry Luth. Ch., 1950; asst. pastor First Luth. Ch., Brookings, S.D., 1950-51; pastor Trinity Luth. Ch., Vermillion, S.D., 1952-57; campus pastor U. Minn., Mpls., 1957-58; pastor Univ. Luth. Ch. of Hope, Mpls., 1958-73; v.p. Am. Luth. Ch., 1968-73, pres., presiding bishop, 1973-87; exec. dir. Global Mission Inst. Luther Northwestern Theol. Sem., St. Paul. Disting. vis. prof. Luther-Northwestern Sem., St. Paul, 1988-94; Luccock vis. pastor Yale Div. Sch., 1969; chmn. bd. youth activity Am. Luth. Ch., 1960-68; mem. exec. com. Luth. Council U.S.A.; v.p. Luth. World Fedn., 1977-90; mem. cen. com. World Council Chs., 1973-75, 80-90; Luth. del. White House Conf. on Equal Opportunity Chmn. Greater Mpls. Fair Housing Com., Mpls. Council Chs., 1960-64; Mem. Mpls. Planning Commn., 1965-67; mem. Mpls. Sch. Bd., 1965-74, chmn., 1967-69; mem. Mpls. Bd. Estimate and Taxation, 1968-73, Mpls. Urban Coalition; sr. public adv. U.S. del. Madrid Conf. of Conf. on Security and Cooperation in Europe, 1980-81; bd. dirs. Mpls. Inst. Art, Walker Art Center, Hennepin County United Fund, Ams. for Childrens Relief, Luth. Student Found., Research Council of Gt. City Schs., Urban League, NAACP; bd. regents Augsburg Coll., Mpls. Served with Signal Corps AUS, 1943-46, PTO. Decorated comdr.'s cross Royal Norwegian Order St. Olav, Order of St. George 1st deg. Orthodox Ch. of Georgia (USSR), 1989; recipient Regents medal Augustana Coll., Sioux Falls, S.D., 1973, Torch of Liberty award Anti-Defamation League, 1973, St. Thomas Aquinas award St. Thomas U., Pax Christi award St. John's Univ/. Collegeville, Minn., 1997. Lutheran.

PREUSS, ROGER E(MIL), artist; b. Waterville, Minn., Jan. 29, 1922; s. Emil W. and Edna (Rosenau) P.; m. MarDee Ann Germundson, Dec. 31, 1954 (dec. Mar. 1981). Student, Mankato Comml. Coll., Mpls. Sch. Art. Emeritus instr. Mpls. Coll. Art and Design; emeritus Mpls. Inst. Arts Speakers Bur.; former judge Goodyear Nat. Conservation Awards Program; founder U.S. Fed. Roger Preuss Waterfowl Prodn. Area, LeSueur County, Minn., 1997; former advisor Wildlife Forever Nat. Fish-Art Contest. One-man shows include St. Paul Fine Art Galleries, 1959, Albert Lea Art Ctr., 1963, Hist. Soc. Mont., Helena, 1964, Brotherhood Fine Arts Ctr., 1965, Le Sueur County Hist. Soc. Mus., Elysian, Minn., 1976, Merrill's Gallery Fine Art, Taos, N.Mex., 1980; exhbns. include Mpls. Inst. Art Msa exhibit, 1946, Midwest Wildlife Conf. Exhbn., Kerr's Beverly Hills Calif., 1947, Laguna Art Mus., Calif., 1947, Joslyn Meml. Mus., Omaha, 1948, Hollywood Fine Arts Center, 1948, Minn. Centennial, 1949, Federated Chaparral Authors, 1951, Nat. Wildlife Art, 1951-52, N.Am. Wildlife Art, dir. exposition, 1952, Ducks Unltd. Waterfowl exhibit, 1953-54, St. Paul Winter Carnival, 1954, St. Paul Gallery Art Mart, 1954, Harris Fine Arts Ctr., Provo, Utah, 1969, Galerie Internat., N.Y.C., 1972, Holy Land Conservation Fund, N.Y.C., 1976, Faribault Art Ctr., 1981, Wildlife Artists of the World Exhbn., Bend, Oreg., 1984, U. Art Mus., U. Minn., Mpls., 1990, Rochester Art Ctr., 1991, Minn. Hist. Soc.-Hill House, 1992, Bemidji Art Ctr., 1992, Jack London Ctr., Dawson City, Yukon Territory, Can., 1992, Weyerhaeuser Meml. Mus., Little Falls, Minn., 1995, Minn. Valley Nat. Wildlife Refuge Ctr., Bloomington, 1995, Sagebrush Artists Exhbn., Klamath Falls, Oreg., 1995; represented in permanent collections: Demarest Meml. Mus., Hackensack, N.J., Smithsonian Instn., N.Y. Jour. Commerce, Mont. Hist. Soc., Inland Bird Banding Assn., Minn. Capitol Bldg., Mont. State U., Wildlife Am. Collection, LeSueur Hist. Soc., Voyageurs Nat. Park Interpretive Ctr., Krause-Hartig VFW Post, Mpls., Nat. Wildlife Fedn. Collection, Minn. Ceremonial House, U.S. Wildlife Svc. Fed. Bldg., Fort Snelling, Minn., Crater Lake Nat. Park Visitors Ctr., VA Hosp., Mpls., Luxton Collection, Banff, Alta., Can., Internat. Inst. Arts, Geneva, Mont. Capitol Bldg., People of Century-Goldblatt Collection, Lyons, Ill., Harlem Savings Collection, N.Y.C., Weisman Art Mus., Mpls., Minn. Vets. Home, Mpls., Blauvelt Art Mus., Oradell, N.J., Roger Preuss Art Collection, Augustana Ctr. for Western Studies, Sioux Falls, S.D., Minn. Mus. Am. Art, St. Paul, U. Minn. Art Mus., C.M. Russell Mus., Great Falls, Mont., Le Sueur County Courthouse, Le Center, Minn., others, numerous galleries and pvt. collections; designer: Fed. Duck Stamp, U.S. Dept. Interior, 1949, Commemorative Centennial Pheasant Stamp, 1981, Gold Waterfowl medallion Franklin Mint, 1983, Gold Stamp medallion Wildlife Mint, 1983, 40th Anniversary Commemorative Fed. Duck Stamp etching, 1989; panelist: Sportsman's Roundtable, Sta. WTCN-TV, Mpls. (emeritus), from 1953; author: Is Wildlife Art Recognized Fine Art?, 1986; contbr.: Christmas Echos, 1955, Wing Shooting, Trap & Skeet, 1955, Along the Trout Stream, 1979; contbr. Art Impressions mag., Can., Wildlife Art, U.S.; contbr. illustrations and articles in Nat. Wildlife; assoc. editor emeritus: Out-of-Doors mag.; compiler and artist: Outdoor Horizons, 1957, Twilight over the Wilderness, 1972, 75 limited edition prints Wildlife of America, from 1950; contbr. paintings and text Minnesota Today; creator paintings and text Preuss Wildlife Calendar, inventor: paintings and text Wildlife Am. Calendar; featured artist Art West, 1980-84, Wildlife Art; featured in films Your BFA-Care and Maintenance, Black Ducks Along the Border. Former del. Nat. Wildlife Conf.; bd. dirs. emeritus Voyageurs Nat. Park Assn., Deep-Portage Conservation Found.; former bd. dirs. Wetlands for Wildlife U.S.A.; active Wildlife Am.; co-organizer, v.p., bd. dirs. Minn. Conservation Fedn., 1952-54; mem. U.S. Hospitalized Vets. Venison Program, 1957—; trustee Liberty Bell Edn. Found.; Waseca Arts Coun.; founder, dir. Roger Preuss Conservation Preserve for Study of Nature, 1990—; adv. Wildlife Forever. With USNR, WWII. Recipient Stamp Design award U.S. Fish and Wildlife Svc., 1994, Minn. Outdoor award, 1956, Patron of Conservation award, 1956, award for contbns. conservation Minn. Statehood Centennial Commn., 1958, 1st award Am. Indsl. Devel. Coun., citation of merit VFW, award of merit Mil. Order Cootie, 1963, merit award Minn. Waterfowl Assn., 1976, Silver medal Nat. SAR, 1978, Svcs. to Arts and Environ. award Faribault Art Ctr., 1981, Ptnrs. for Wildlife award U.S. Fish and Wildlife Svc., 1994; named Wildlife Conservationist of the Yr., Sears Found.-Nat. Wildlife Fedn. program, 1966, Am. Bicentennial Wildlife Artist, Am. Heritage Assn., 1976; hon. mem. Ont. Chippewa Nation of Can., 1957; named Knight of Mark Twain for contbns. to Am. art Mark Twain Soc., 1978; named to Water, Woods and Wildlife Hall of Fame, named Dean of Wildfowl Artists, 1981, Hon. Ky. Col.; recipient hon. degree U.S. Vets. Venison program, 1980, Western Am. award significant contbns. to preservation arts and history No. Prairie Plains, Augustana Coll. Ctr. for Western Studies, Sioux Falls, S.D., 1992, Pub. Svc. award U.S. Dept. Interior, 1996, Marshall award 2004; named creator first signed, numbered photolithographic modern print pub. in N.Am., 1959, documented Colorado Springs Fine Arts Ctr., 1993, colleague of Frederick R. Weisman Mus., Mpls., 1994; grantee NEH, 1995, Prairie Lakes Arts Coun., 1995. Fellow Internat. Inst. Arts (life), Nat. Wildlife Fedn. (past nat. wildlife week chmn. Minn.), Minn. Ducks Unltd. (bd. dirs. emeritus), Minn. Artists Assn. (v.p., bd. dirs. 1953-59), Minn. Mycol. Soc. (pres. emeritus, hon. life), Le Sueur County Hist. Soc. (hon. life), Minn. Conservation Fedn. (hon. life), Wildlife Artists World (charter, emeritus internat. v.p., chmn. fine arts bd.), Prairie Chicken Soc. (patron), Mission Oceanic Arctic, Minn. Press Club (emeritus), Silver Lake Sports (hon.), Wildlife Rehab. Ctr. Minn. Office: care Wildlife Am PO Box 580004-a Minneapolis MN 55458-0004 *With a modicum of natural skills in painting and writing, my basic goal throughout all my work has been to help people appreciate and understand nature. If I as a naturalist am a small voice for our world's waters, woods, and wildlife, if I have influenced many children and adults to become more environment conscious, if my art brings to others a measure of joy, then my best aspirations for my creations have been fulfilled.*

PREVE, ROBERTA JEAN, librarian, researcher; b. Wilmington, Del., Feb. 27, 1954; d. Burton Hugo Sanders and Betsy (Kan) Klein; m. Thomas Alan Preve, Sept. 23, 1978; children: Stephanie Jean, Melanie Marie. BA, U. N.H., 1975; MLS, Simmons Coll., 1985. Rschr. U. N.H., Durham, 1974-75; rsch. asst. Eikonix Corp., Burlington, Mass., 1976-79; asst. cashier, credit dept. mgr. Dania (Fla.) Bank, 1980-83; rsch. assoc. Ctr. for Strategy Rsch., Cambridge, Mass., 1984-86; info. svcs. Braxton Assocs., Boston, 1986-87; mktg. adminstr. Summit Tech., Waltham, Mass., 1987-91; mgr. market rsch. AT&T Capital Corp., Framingham, Mass., 1991-95; mgr. Bus. Info. Ctr. Raytheon Co., Lexington, Mass., 1995—. Co-owner T&R Pest Mgmt., Attleboro, Mass., 1988—95. Mem. Spl. Librs. Assn., New England Online (dir., logistics chair 1986-90), Beta Phi Mu. Avocations: hiking, reading, needlecrafts, sports. Office: Raytheon Co Bus Info Ctr 870 Winter St Waltham MA 02451 Office Phone: 781-522-5183. Business E-Mail: roberta-j-preve@raytheon.com.

PREVIN, ANDRE, composer, conductor; b. Berlin, Apr. 6, 1930; came to U.S., 1938, naturalized, 1943; s. Jack and Charlotte (Epstein) P.; m. Mia Farrow, Sept. 10, 1970 (div. 1979); children: Matthew and Sascha (twins), Fletcher, Lark, Daisy; m. Heather Hales, Jan. 1982; 1 child, Lukas. Student, Berlin Conservatory, Paris Conservatory; privately with, Pierre Monteux, Mario Castelnuovo-Tedesco. Mem. faculty Guildhall Sch., London, Curtis Inst., Phila., Berkshire Music Ctr. Rec. artist classical music for RCA, EMI, Phillips, Telarc, Deutsche Gramophone, 1946—; composer chamber music Cello Concerto, Guitar Concerto, piano music, serenades for violin, brass quintet, song cycle on poems by Philip Larkin Every Good Boy Deserves Favour, Principals, Reflections, Piano Concerto, Triolet for Brass Ensemble, Haydn variations for piano solo, 4 songs of Toni Morrison for soprano, Cello Sonata, Violin Sonata, Trio for Piano Oboe and Bassoon, Two Remembrances (soprano and piano), Sallie Chisum (soprano and orch.), Tango Song and Dance (violin and piano), The Magic Number (soprano and orch.), film scores, 1950-59; condr.-in-chief Houston Symphony, 1967-69; prin. condr. London Symphony Orch., 1968-79, Royal Philharm. Orch., Eng., 1985-91; music dir. L.A. Philharm., 1985-89; condr. laureate London Symphony Orch., 1992—; guest condr. maj. symphony orchs. and festivals in U.S. and Europe including: festivals in Salzburg, Edinburgh, Flanders, Vienna, Osaka, Prague, Berlin, Bergen; music dir. South Bank Music Festival, London, 1972-74, Pitts. Symphony, 1976-84, L.A. Philharmonic, 1984-89; author: Music Face to Face, 1971, Orchestra, 1979, No Minor Chords, 1992. Served with AUS, 1950-51. Knighted (KBE), Her Majesty Queen Elizabeth II, 1996; recipient awards Nat. Grammophone Soc., Acad. Motion Picture Arts and Scis. Mem. Acad. Motion Picture Arts and Scis., Dramatists Guild, Brit. Composers Guild, Nat. Composers and Condrs. League, Degrees Curtis Inst., Royal Acad., Guild Hall Sch./Duquesne U. Office: care Columbia Artists 165 W 57th St New York NY 10019-2201

PREVITS, GARY JOHN, accounting educator, consultant; b. Cleve., Oct. 23, 1942; s. J.A. and L.M. (Guta) P.; m. F.A. Porubsky, Oct. 3, 1964; children: Robert, Susan, Joanne, Matthew. BSBA, John Carroll U., 1963; M Acctg., Ohio State U., 1964; PhD, U. Fla., 1972. CPA, Ohio, Ala. Mem. staff Deloitte, Cleve., 1963-68; asst. prof. Augusta (Ga.) Coll., 1968-70; instr. U. Fla., Gainesville, 1970-72; prof. U. Ala., 1973—79; prof. acctg. Case Western Res U., Cleve., 1979—, assoc. dean undergrad. program, 1994—. Vis. assoc. prof., Northwestern U., 1977. Author: (with others) A History of Accounting in America, 1979, 98; editor Acctg. Historians Jour., 1977-80, 87-89; Ohio CPA Jour., 1982-85, Rsch. in Acctg. Reg., 1987-2004. Coach Rocky River (Ohio) Baseball Recreation, 1980-81; mem. nat. com. career exploring Boy Scouts Am., 1985-91; mem. Rocky River City Charter Rev. Com., 1990, 2002; chmn. Rocky River Mayor's Vision Com., 1995, 99. 1st lt. U.S. Army, 1965-67. Mem. AICPA (governing coun. 1986-87, 89—, bd. dirs. 1995-98, Outstanding Educator 1996), Internat. Assn. Fin Execs. Inst. (fin. ethics com. 1997-2000, comm. com. 2000-02, edn. policy commn. 2002-04), Acad. Acctg. Historians (pres. 1974-78, Hourglass award 1980), Am. Acctg. Assn. (v.p. Ohio region 1983-84, dir. edn., exec. com. 1987-89), Ohio Soc. CPAs (v.p. 1987-88, pers.

1993-94, Gold medal 2002), Playhouse Club, VFW, KC. Roman Catholic. Avocations: reading biography, handball, jobbing, jogging. Home: 3420 Bradfords Gate Cleveland OH 44116-3804 Office: Case Western Res U Weatherhead Sch Mgmt Dept Acctg Cleveland OH 44106-7235 Office Phone: 216-368-2074. Personal E-mail: gary_previts@email.com.

PREVITTI, JAMES P. real estate executive; Founder Forecast Group, Rancho Cucamonga, Calif., 1971—, pres., CEO, 1989—. Recipient Fair Housing award L.A. Times; named Builder of Yr., Real Estate Entrepreneur of Yr. Mem. Calif. Bldg. Industry Assn. (pres., Medal of Honor). Office: Forecast 3536 Concours Ste 320 Ontario CA 91764-5593

PREVOST, ROXANE LISE, music theory educator; d. Roger Andre and Lise Houle Prevost. BA, U. Guelph, Ont., 1992; MusB, U. Ottawa, 1997; MusM, U. Western Ont., 1999; PhD, SUNY at Buffalo, 2003. Tchg. asst. U. Western Ont., London, 1997—99, SUNY, Buffalo, 1999—2001, instr., 2001—02; asst. prof. dept. music U. Ottawa, 2003—. Chair music grad. symposium SUNY, Buffalo, 2002—03; presenter in field; publ. in field. Ont. Grad. scholar, Govt. Ont., 1997—99, Pres. scholar, U. Western Ont., 1997—99, Social Scis. and Humanities Rsch. Coun. of Can. Doctoral fellow, Govt. Can., 2002—03, Coll. of Arts and Scis. Dissertation fellow, SUNY at Buffalo, 2002—03. Mem.: Music Theory Soc. N.Y. State, Can. U. Music Soc., Soc. for Music Theory. Roman Catholic. Avocations: violin, piano. Office: U Ottawa Dept Music 50 University Ottawa ON K1N 6N5 Canada Personal E-mail: rprevost@uottawa.ca.

PREVOZNIK, MICHAEL E. health facility administrator; With Dechert Price & Rhodes; chief legal compliance officer SBCL, 1994—96; v.p., chief legal compliance officer SmithKline Beecham Healthcare Svcs., 1996—98, v.p. compliance, 1998—99; v.p. legal Quest Diagnostics, Teterboro, NJ, 1999—, gen. counsel compliance, 1999—. Office: Quest Diagnostics One Malcolm Ave Teterboro NJ 07608

PREWITT, ALAN JAY, playwright, performing company executive; b. St. Louis, Apr. 3, 1952; s. Ralph Wilburn and Gladys Maxine Prewitt; life ptnr. Todd Lee Witman, Aug. 31, 1986. BA, Park Coll., 1974. Cert. secondary edn. tchr. Mo., 1974. Artistic dir., playwright-in-residence Phoenix Theatre's Cookie Co., dir. of edn. devel. and resources Phoenix Theatre, 1981—. Tchr., roster artist, peer cons. Ariz. Commn. On Arts, 1995—. Family musical, The Quiltmaker's Gift (Arizoni Award, Best Overall Prodn., Best Original Script, Original Musical, 2003). Mem. com. Maricopa County Superior Ct. Selection, Phoenix, 2004. Recipient Career Achievement award, Nat. Soc. of Arts and Letters, 1994, Outstanding Contbn. award, Arizoni Theatre of Excellence Awards, 1996. Avocations: painting, hiking, travel. Office: Phoenix Theatre 100 E McDowell Rd Phoenix AZ 85004 Personal E-mail: bfranklinalive@aol.com. Business E-Mail: a.prewitt@phxtheatre.org.

PREWITT, CHARLES THOMPSON, geochemist; b. Lexington, Ky., Mar. 3, 1933; s. John Burton and Margaret (Thompson) P.; m. Gretchen B. Hansen, Jan. 31, 1958; children: Daniel Hansen. SB, MIT, 1955, SM, 1960, PhD, 1962. Rsch. scientist E.I. DuPont De Nemours & Co. Inc., Wilmington, Del., 1962-69; assoc. prof. SUNY, Stony Brook, 1969-71, prof., 1971-86, chmn. dept. earth and space scis., 1977-80; dir. Geophys. Lab., Carnegie Inst. of Washington, 1986-98, mem. rsch. staff, 1998—2003; adj. prof. Dept. Geoscis. U. Ariz., Tucson, 2003—. Sec.-treas. U.S. Nat. Com. for Crystallography, Washington, 1983-85, 99—; gen. chmn. 14th Meeting of Internat. Mineral Assn., Stanford, Calif., 1986; chmn. NRC/NAS com. on physics and chemistry of earth materials, 1985-87; mem. bd. govs. Consortium for Advanced Radiation Svcs.; co-dir. NSF Ctr. for High Pressure Rsch., 1991—; disting. vis. prof. chemistry Ariz. State U., 1983. Editor: (jour.) Physics and Chemistry of Minerals, 1976-85; contbr. more than 180 articles to profl. jours. Bd. dirs. Internat. Ctr. for Diffraction Data, 1998-2002. Capt. USAR, 1956-65. NATO sr. postdoctoral fellow, 1975, Churchill overseas fellow, 1975, Japan Soc. for Promotion of Sci. fellow, 1983, Ernst Cloos Meml. scholar Johns Hopkins U., 2002-. Fellow AAAS, Mineral. Soc. Am. (pres. 1983-84, Roebling medal 2003), Am. Geophys. Union, Internat. Centre Diffraction Data; mem. Geol. Soc. Am., Am. Crystallographic Assn., Materials Rsch. Soc., Mineral. Soc. Gt. Britain and Ireland, Cosmos Club. Office: Dept Geoscis Univ Arizona Tucson AZ 85721-0077

PREWITT, DEBRA A. state legislator; b. Livonia, Mich., Apr. 19, 1963; BA in Bus. Adminstrn., Eckerd Coll., 1998. Mem. New Port Richey (Fla.) City Coun., 1989-91; vice-mayor New Port Richey, 1991-92; mayor, 1992-94; mem. Fla. Ho. of Reps., Tallahassee, 1994—. Mem. cmty. colls. and career prep com., tourism com., juvenile justice com.; exec. dir. Deaf Svc. Ctr. of Pasco/Hernando County. Mem. Breast Cancer Awareness Task Force, 1996—; v.p. Deaf Svc. Ctr. Assn., 1992. Democrat. Office: State Capitol Rm 1402 Tallahassee FL 32399-1300

PREWITT, JEAN, not-for-profit organization executive; Degree, Harvard U.; degree in law, Georgetown U. Formerly lawyer Donovan Leisure Newton & Irvine; sr. v.p., gen. counsel United Internat. Pictures, 1982—89; with Nat. Telecomm. and Info. Adminstrn. U.S. Dept. Commerce, 1989—94; prin. Podesta Assocs., Washington, 1994—99; pres., CEO Ind. Film and TV Alliance, L.A., 2000—. Office: 10850 Wilshire Blvd 9th Fl Los Angeles CA 90024-4321

PREWITT, KENNETH, political science educator, foundation executive; b. Alton, Ill., Mar. 16, 1936; s. Carl Kenneth and Louise (Carpenter) P.; children: Jennifer Ann, Geoffrey Douglas. BA, So. Meth. U., 1958; MA, Washington U., St. Louis, 1959; PhD, Stanford U., 1963. Prof. polit. sci. U. Chgo., 1964-80, chmn. dept. polit. sci., 1975-76; dir. Nat. Opinion Rsch. Ctr., 1976-79; pres. Social Sci. Rsch. Coun., N.Y.C., 1979-85, 95-98; sr. v.p. Rockefeller Found., N.Y.C., 1985-95; dir. U.S. Census Bur., Washington, 1998-2001; dean grad. faculty New Sch. U., N.Y.C., 2001—02; Carnegie Prof. of Public Affairs School of International and Public Affairs, Columbia Univ., N.Y.C., 2002—. Vis. scholar U. Nairobi, Kenya, 1968-71; bd. dirs. Washington U., So. Meth. U., Energy Found., Ctr. Advanced Study Behavioral Scis. Author: Political Socialization, 1969, Ruling Elites, 1973, Labyrinths of Democracy, 1973, Introduction to American Government, 1983, 6th edit., 1991. Guggenheim fellow, 1983; fellow Center Advanced Study in Behavioral Scis., 1983; recipient Officer's Cross of Order of Merit, Rep. of Germany. Fellow AAAS, Am. Acad. Arts and Scis.; mem. Am. Polit. Sci. Assn., Coun. on Fgn. Rels.

PREWOZNIK, JEROME FRANK, lawyer; b. Detroit, July 15, 1934; s. Frank Joseph and Loretta Ann (Parzych) Prewoznik; m. Marilyn Ruth Johnson, 1970; 1 child, Frank Joseph II. AB cum laude, U. Detroit, 1955; JD with distinction, U. Mich., 1958. Bar: Calif. 1959. Pvt. practice, Calif., 1960-91. Served in U.S. Army, 1958—60. Mem.: State Bar Calif. Republican. Home: 431 Georgina Ave Santa Monica CA 90402-1909

PREY, BARBARA ERNST, artist; b. N.Y.C., Apr. 17, 1957; d. Herbert Henry and Margaret (Joubert) Ernst; m. Jeffrey Drew Prey, Jan. 11, 1986; children: Austin William Ernst Prey, Emily Elizabeth Prey. BA with honors, Williams Coll., 1979; MDiv, Harvard U., 1986. Sales staff Tiffany and Co., N.Y.C., summer 1977; intern Met. Mus. Art, N.Y.C., summer 1979; pers. asst. Prince Albrecht Castell, Castell, Germany, 1980-81; with modern painting dept. Sotheby's Auction House, N.Y.C., 1981-82; sales asst. Marlborough Gallery, N.Y.C., 1982; tchg. asst. Boston Coll., 1984, Harvard U., Cambridge, Mass., 1984-85; vis. lectr. Tainan (Taiwan) Coll. and Sem., 1986-87; artist Oyster Bay, N.Y., 1987—. Artist-in-residence Westminster Sch., Simsbury, Conn., 1998; art juror Washington and Jefferson Coll., Washington, Pa., 1990; presenter in field. Illustrator: Boys Harbor Cookbook, 1988, A Dream Became You, A City Grows Up, 1991, (cover) Am. Artist Mag., 1994, Barbara Ernst Prey: Watercolors, 1998, Internat. Art Newspaper, 2001, N.Y. Post, 2001, N.Y. Daily News, (PBS) True North, 2001, (PBS) Metro Section, 2001, Arts and Antiques Mag., 2001, 03, Barbara Ernst Prey: A Trace in the Mind, 2002, N.Y. Times, 2002, 04, Newsday, 2002, Artwork in the American Embassy Prague, 2002, Artwork in the American Embassy Oslo, 2003, The Robb Report, 2003, White House Christmas Card, 2003, The New Yorker, 2004, Larry King Live CNN, 2004; exhibited in group shows at Mus. Fine Arts, Nassau County, N.Y., 1988, Nat. Arts Club NYC, 1988, Gallery One, Rockland, Maine, 1992, Williams Coll., Williamstown, Mass., 1993, Johnstown (Pa.) Art Mus., 1993, Blair Art Mus., Holidaysburg, Pa., 1993, Phila. Mus. Art Gallery, 1995, Westmoreland Mus. Am. Art, Greensburg, Pa., (Best in Show award), 1996, Mus. the Southwest, Midland, Tex., Farnsworth Mus. Art, Rockland, Maine, 1997, Guild Hall Mus., East Hampton, N.Y., 1998, Portland (Maine) Mus. Art, 1998, U.S. Embassy, Prague, 2002, Heckscher Mus. Art, Huntington, N.Y., 2002, Guild Hall Mus., East Hampton, N.Y, 2002, 04, Gilcrease Mus., Tulsa, 2002, NASA Commn.: The Internat. Space Station, 2003, The White House, Collection of Pres. and Mrs. George Bush, 2003, Kennedy Space Ctr., 2003, 04, U.S. Embassy, Oslo, Prague, Liberia, Belarus, 2003, 04, NASA Commn.: Columbia Tribute, 2004; one-woman shows include Harvard-Yale-Princeton Club, Pitts., 1991, Jensen Fine Arts, NYC, 1999, 2001; represented in pvt. collections including Pres. and Mrs. George Bush Farnsworth Mus. Art; displayed 1997 Holiday Card on 80,000 screens worldwide Bloomberg Bus. News; featured on Fox TV News, 1999; contbr. to popular mags., local newspapers. Class agt. Williams Coll., Williamstown, Mass., 1981-91; bd. mem. Citizens Libr., Washington, 1992-93; active 1st Presby. Ch., Oyster Bay, N.Y. Fulbright scholarship Fulbright Assn., Germany, 1979-80; grantee Roothbert Fund, Chataugua, N.Y., 1982-84, Ch. History award Gordan-Conwell Sem., S. Hamilton, Mass., 1984, Henry Luce Found., Taiwan, 1986-87, Women of Distinction award, N.Y. State Senate, 2004. Mem. Pitts. Watercolor Soc. (Jean Thoburn award 1994), Nat. Mus. Women in the Arts. Avocations: tennis, skiing, birdwatching, reading, squash. Home and Office: 22 Pearl St Oyster Bay NY 11771-2305

PREYSZ, LOUIS ROBERT FONSS, III, management consultant, educator; b. Quantico, Va., Aug. 1, 1944; s. Louis Robert Fonss, Jr. and Lucille (Parks) P.; m. Patricia Dianne Yelland; children: Louis Robert Fonss IV, Christine Elizabeth, Michael Anthony, Daniel Timothy. BA, U. Wis., 1968; MBA, U. Utah, 1973; postgrad., Rutgers U., 1983; grad., Command and Gen. Staff Coll., Ft. Leavenworth, Kans., 1986. Tchg. and rsch. asst. U. Utah, Salt Lake City, 1972-73; mktg. and pers. officer Security 1st Nat. Bank of Sheboygan, Wis., 1973-76; mktg. dir. 1st Nat. Bank Rock Island, Ill., 1976-77; asst. v.p., mktg. sales mgr. 1st Nat. Bank Birmingham, Ala., 1977—78; v.p. mktg. mgr. Sun 1st Nat. Bank Orlando, Fla., 1978—80; pres. Preysz Assocs., Fla., 1980—. Assoc. prof. mgmt. and banking Flagler Coll., St. Augustine, Fla., 1982—; faculty U. Wis., Sheboygan, 1973-76, Fla. Inst. Tech., 1976-77, St. Ambrose Coll., Davenport, Iowa, 1976-77, U. Ctrl. Fla., 1979-81, Columbia (Mo.) Coll., 1981-82; mem. tng. and profl. devel. coun. Bank Mktg. Assn., 1976-78, chmn., 1978; mem. mktg. and pub. rels. com. Wis. Bankers Assn., 1975; v.p. Ala. Automated Clearing House Assn., 1977-78; spkr. in field; host to daily FM radio program Money Issues. Author: How to Introduce a New Service, 1976, Energy Efficiency Programs and Lending Practices for Florida's Financial Institutions, 1980, Credit Union Marketing, 1981, An Effective Management Structure for Multi-Bank Holding Companies, 1983, Credit Union Strategic Marketing, 1993; contbg. editor: Target Market, an Instructional Approach to Bank Cross Selling of Services, New Accounts Training Manual, 1977, Tested Techniques in Bank Marketing, 1977; contbg. author: Rapid Debt Reduction Strategies, 1990, The Debt Free Army, 1993; mem. editl rev. bd. SAM Advanced Mgmt. Jour.; contbr. articles to mags. Mem. Rep. Presdl. Task Force, 1982-86, Rep. Nat. Com., 1980-89, 2000—, Rep. Nat. Com. Victory, 2000; charter mem. George W. Bush for Pres.; mem. Nat. World War II Meml.; bd. dirs. Cath. Charities Bur. Inc., 1988-89, v.p., 1989; bd. dirs. United Way St. Johns County, 1989-95, chmn., 1991-95; bd. dirs., treas., deacon Grace Cmty. Ch., 1996-99; charter mem. U.S. Com. for Battle Normandy Mus., 1989, Reagan Presdl. Libr.; fin. chair for Billy Graham Crusade, Jacksonville Crusade. Capt. U.S. Army, 1968-72; officer Fla. Army N.G. Recipient Congrl. Order Merit, Rep. Congrl. Com., 2003. Fellow Soc. Advancement Mgmt. Honor Soc. (internat. v.p., bd. dir., cons., Mgmt. Excellence award 1990); mem. U. Wis. Alumni Assn., U. Utah Alumni Assn., N.G. Officers Assn. Fla., N.G. Assn. U.S., U.S. Holocaust Meml. Mus. (charter mem.), Nat. Trust Hist. Preservation, Civil War Soc., St. Augustine Officers Club, Rotary (Paul Harris fellow), Civil War Preservation Trust, Phi Gamma Delta. Republican. Mem. Assemblies Of God. Office: PO Box 1027 Saint Augustine FL 32085-1027 Office Phone: 904-829-6481 243. Personal E-mail: mosserrs@aol.com. Business E-Mail: preyszlr@flagler.edu.

PRIBANIC, GERALD J. manufacturing executive; BS in Acctg., Pa. State U.; MBA in Bus. Mgmt. magna cum laude, Fairleigh Dickinson U. Cert. mgmt. acct. With Am. Cyanamid; asst. contr. chems. group Borg-Warner, 1974—78, dir. fin. Borg-Warner Chems. Europe, 1978—82, contr. automotive-transmission and engine components group, 1982—84, v.p., contr. automotive-transmission and engine components group, 1984; v.p. fin., contr. Hover N.Am., 1990—96; CFO, exec. v.p. Maytag Corp., Newton, Iowa, 1996—99; CFO Milliken; ptnr. Tatum CFO Ptnrs. LLP, Greenville, SC. Spkr. in field. Office: Tatum Ptnrs PO Box 8568 Greenville SC 29604*

PRIBANIC, VICTOR HUNTER, lawyer; b. McKeesport, Pa., Apr. 7, 1954; s. John Edward and Marlene Cecilia (Hunter) P. BA, Bowling Green State U., 1976; JD, Duquesne U., 1979. Bar: Pa. 1979, U.S. Dist. Ct. (we. dist.) Pa. 1979, U.S. Ct. Appeals (3d cir.) 1979, U.S. Supreme Ct. 1989, U.S. Ct. Claims 1990. Asst. dist. atty. Office of Dist. Atty., Pitts., 1980-82; law clk. to presiding justice Pa. Ct. Common Pleas, Pitts., 1982-85; pvt. practice Pitts. and McKeesport, 1982—; pres. Pribanic & Pribanic, P.C., 1987—. Mem.: ATLA, Million Dollar Adv. Forum, Roscoe Pound Found., Acad. Trial Lawyers Allegheny County, Pa. Trial Lawyers Assn., Nat. Assn. Criminal Def. Lawyers. Democrat. Roman Catholic. Home: 100 Victoria Dr Mc Keesport PA 15131-1224 Office: 1735 Lincoln Way White Oak PA 15131-1715 Address: 513 Court Pl Pittsburgh PA 15219-2002

PRIBBENOW, PAUL C. higher education administrator, consultant; b. Decorah, Iowa, Jan. 18, 1957; s. Jerome Carroll and Elsie Mae (Zellmer) P.; m. Ann F. Raney, Sept. 4, 1982 (div. Sept. 1995); m. Abigail G. Crampton, Apr. 27, 1996. BA, Luther Coll., Decorah, 1978; AM in Divinity, U. Chgo., 1979, PhD in Ethics, 1993. Cert. fund raising exec. Dir. devel. Sch. Art Inst. Chgo., 1985-89; assoc. dean Sch. Social Svc. Adminstrn., U. Chgo., 1989-91, Div. Sch., U. Chgo., 1991-93; v.p. Sch. Art Inst. Chgo., 1993-96; dean for coll. advancement Wabash Coll., Crawfordsville, Ind., 1996-2001, rsch. fellow Ctr. Inquiry in Liberal Arts, 2001—02; pres. Rockford (Ill.) Coll., 2002—. Mem. faculty Sch. Art Inst. Chgo., 1993-96, Spertus Coll., Chgo., 1990-96, De Paul U., 2000-2003. Contbr. articles to profl. jours.; editor 2 books. Mem. vis. com. Div. Sch., U. Chgo., 1996—; sec. bd trustees Wabash Coll., 1998-2001. Recipient McCormick Tribune Presdl. Civic fellowship, 2003—04. Mem. Assn. Fundraising Profls. (Pres.'s award for profl. leadership 1994), Coun. for Advancement and Support of Edn. Democrat. Lutheran. Avocation: reading. Office: Rockford Coll 5050 E State St Rockford IL 61108 E-mail: president@rockford.edu.

PRICE, ALFRED LEE, lawyer, mining company executive; b. Little Rock, May 19, 1935; s. Dewey Ernest and Dorothy Ava (Cooper) P.; m. Magdalena Torres, June 20, 1958; children: Gregory L., Ana Maria. BA, Hendrix Coll., 1956; JD, Tulane U., 1967. Bar: La. 1967, Miss. 1974, D.C., U.S. Supreme Ct., 1980, U.S. Tax Ct., 1977, cert. arbitrator, mediator, Am. Arbitration Assn. and Better Bus. Bur., Nat. Arbitration Forum. Office mgr., dir. personnel Petroleum Helicopters Co., Lafayette, La. and New Orleans, 1956-67; atty. Offshore Navigation and Petroleum Helicopters Co., New Orleans, 1967-74; gen. counsel First Miss. Corp., Jackson, 1974-93, corp. sec., 1988-93; commr. Miss. Employment Commn., Jackson, 1994—2002. Arbitrator Am. Arbitration Assn., 1998—. Mem. Jackson C.of C., chmn. legislative com., 1991-94. Recipient Arbitrator of Yr., Better Bus. Bureau, 1998. Mem. ABA, La. Bar Assn., Miss. Bar Assn., Hinds County Bar Assn., Miss. Mfrs. Assn. (bd. dirs.), Miss. Econ. Coun. (chmn. tort reform com.), River Hills Club. Methodist.

PRICE, ALICE LINDSAY, writer; b. Augusta, Ga., Oct. 21, 1927; d. William Lloyd and Orlana Jerome (Gould) P. BA in English Lit., Okla. State U., 1949; MA in English, U. Tulsa, 1970. Mus. asst. Philbrook Art Mus., Tulsa, 1949-51; recreation supr. U.S. Army Europe, 1951-54; neighborhood ctr. dir. City of Monterey (Calif.) Parks and Recreation Dept., 1955-59; art gallery dir., co-owner Gallerie Quais de la Roquette, Arles, France, 1960-62; program dir. City of Tulsa (Okla.) Parks and Recreation Dept., 1963-69; instr. English lit. and creative writing Holland Hall Sch., Tulsa, 1970-86; artist-in residence Okla. State Arts Coun., Oklahoma City, 1986-91; scholar in residence Tulsa City-County Libr. of NEH, Tulsa/Washington, 1988, 90, 91; pub. HCE Publs./Riverrun Press, Tulsa, 1974—. Acquisitions editor Coun. Oak Books, Tulsa, 1986-89; lectr. Gilcrease Inst., Tulsa, 1984, 86, 90, 94, Trumpeter Swan Soc., Mpls., 1997, Kans. State U., Manhattan, 1997. Author: (poetry) Faces of the Waterworld, 1970, Our Dismembered Shadow, 1981 (Pegasus award 1981); author/illustrator Swans of the World: Nature, Hist., Myth, Art, 1994 (Feldman award 1993), Cranes: The Noblest Flyers in Natural History and Cultural Lore, 2001. Bd. edn. chair Swan Lake Waterfowl Soc., Tulsa, 1986—; mem. lit. arts com. Arts and Humanities Coun., 1990—; creative writing workshop dir. Tulsa Ctr. Phys. Ltd., Tulsa, 1990. First pl. Folger scholarship Kans. City Art Inst., 1945; grantee Arts and Humanities Coun., 1990, 92. Mem. Trumpeter Swan Soc., Author's Guild, Pen West, Internat. Wild Waterfowl Assn., Tulsa Artists Coalition (First Pl. 1997), Living Arts (poetry coord. 1978-85), Phi Beta Kappa. Avocations: travel, listening music, photography. Office: HCE Pubs/Riverrun Press 3113 S Florence Ave Tulsa OK 74105-2407

PRICE, AMELIA RUTH, not-for-profit foundation president, artist, small business owner; b. Bklyn., Sept. 4, 1942; d. Dr. Alphonse Frederick Pagano and Adele Marie Savarese; 1 child, Ean James. BA, Georgian Ct. Coll., Lakewood, NJ, 1964; MA in Art Hist., Cath. U. of Am., Washington, DC, 1968. Cert. Permanent Certificate, Art State of N.Y. Edn. Dept., 1971. Art tchr. Bd. Coop. Ednl. Svcs., Patchogue, NY, 1967—68; art director Roland Advt. Co., N.Y.C., 1968—69; art dept. chair Bd. Coop. Ednl. Svcs. II, Deer Park, NY, 1969—78; v.p. Delicious Selections Ltd, White Plains, NY, 1991—95; pres., owner Parker Commodities Ltd, Kings Park, NY, 1995—; owner Bubbling Oaks Samoyeds, Commack, NY, 1974—. Co-founder bubbling oaks samoyeds kennels Bubbling Oaks Samoyeds, Commack, NY, 1974—2002. Samoyed Newsletter and other publs.featuring Samoyeds, 1999—; contbr. articles on Samoyeds and their care to various publs. ., 1999. Pres. Samoyed Club of Am. Edn. and Rsch. Found., Inc., Madison, Wis., 2001—, v.p., 1997—2001. Recipient # 1 Samoyed Bitch, Kennel Rev., 1974, 1975, 1976, 1977, 1978, 1983, 1984, # 3 Samoyed, Dogs in Canada, 1976, Top Winning Team, Orgn. for the Working Samoyed Inc., 1986, 1988. Mem.: Habour Lights Painter, Decorative Artists LI, Soc. Decorative Painters, Nat. Assn. Woman Bus. Owners (pub. affairs com. 2003—), Suffolk County Kennel Club Inc. (chmn. hospitality 1989—99, bd. dirs. 1996—99), Westbury Kennel Association (chmn. of trophies 1985, chmn. judges' transport. 2000), Samoyed Club of America Inc. (pres. 1997—99, Top Winning Bitch 1975, 1976, 1985, Top Winning Team 1985, Top Winning Bitch 1986, Top Winning Team 1987). Home: 128 Cowie Rd Commack NY 11725 Personal E-mail: arprice@optonline.net.

PRICE, B. BYRON, historian; BS, U.S. Mil. Acad., 1970; MA in Mus. Sci., Tex. Tech. U., 1977; postgrad., Am. U., Washington, 1975. Tchg. asst. Tex. Tech. U., Lubbock, 1975, rsch. coord. Ranching Heritage Ctr./Mus., 1976-77; curator of history Panhandle-Plains Hist. Mus., Canyon, Tex., 1977-82, exec. dir., 1982-86, Nat. Cowboy Hall of Fame and Western Heritage Ctr., Oklahoma City, 1987-96, Buffalo Bill Hist. Ctr., Cody, Wyo., 1996—. Lectr. in field; condr. seminars in field; cons. in field. Advisory editor: The Handbook of Texas, 1986-96; editl. bd. N.Mex. Hist. Rev., 1990-93, Jour. Ariz. History, 1993-95; assoc. editor The Ency. of the West, 1996; author: Cowboys of the American West, 1996, Crafting a Southwestern Masterpiece, 1986, Imagining the Open Range: Erwin E. Smith, Cowboy Photographer, 1997, Longheed: A Painter's Painter, 1991, The National Cowboy Hall of Fame Chuck Wagon Cook Book, 1995, She Doesn't Write Like a Woman: Mari Sandoz and the Cattlemen, 1996; co-author: The Golden Spread: An Illustrated History of Amarillo and the Texas Panhandle, 1986; co-editor: Cowboy Justice, 1997, Adventuring with the Old-Timers: Trails Traveled and Tales Told, 1979; contbr. articles to profl. jours. Mem. tourism task force Okla. Dept. Commerce, 1987; mem. Okla. Film Adv. Commn., 1988-90; bd. dirs. Okla. Ctr. for the Book, 1990—; judge Arts for the Parks Ann. Exhbn., 1992-93; mem. cultural opportunities work group Okla. Futures, 1993; mem. Oklahoma City Conv. and Visitors Commn., 1996—. Recipient Gov.'s Arts award State of Okla., 1994. Mem. Tex. Assn. Mus. (exec. coun. 1985-86), Okla. Mus. Assn. (v.p. 1993-95), Mus. West Consortium (pres. 1996—), Western History Assn. (mem. program com. 1997), Am. Assn. Mus., Tex. State Hist. Assn., Western Writers of Am., Panhandle Plains Hist. Soc. Office: Buffalo Bill Hist Ctr 720 Sheridan Ave Cody WY 82414-3428

PRICE, BARBARA GILLETTE, college administrator, artist; b. Phila., June 26, 1938; d. Philip and Frances (Bressler) Gillette; 1 child, Michelle Cutler. BFA, U. Ala., Tuscaloosa, 1966, MA, 1968. Acting chair dept. art Judson Coll., Marion, Ala., 1969; faculty Corcoran Sch. of Art, Washington, 1970-78; acad. dean Cranbrook Acad. of Art, Bloomfield Hills, Mich., 1978-82; v.p. acad. affairs Md. Inst. Coll. of Art, Balt., 1982-93; pres. Moore Coll. of Art and Design, Phila., 1994-98; art edn. cons., 1998—. Bd. dirs. AICAD, Washington, Fleisher Art Meml., Phila. One person shows include Cranbrook Acad. Art Mus., Bloomfield Hills, 1980, Robert Kidd Gallery Assocs., Birmingham, Mich., 1980, Ferris State, Big Rapids, Mich., 1981, Schweyer Galdo Galleries, Birmingham, 1982, Md. Inst. Coll. of Art, Balt., 1982, 94, Coll. of Notre Dame of Md., Balt., 1985, Columbia (Md.) Assn. Ctr. for Arts, 1989, Loyola Coll., Balt., 1991, Artshowcase, Balt., 1993; group exhbns. include Gallery 641, Washington, 1975, Washington Women's Art Ctr., 1975, Foundry Gallery, Washington, 1975, 76, Rutgers U., New Brunswick, N.J., 1975, Olympia Internat. Art Ctr., Kingston, Jamaica, 1975, Robert Kidd Gallery Assocs., Birmingham, 1980, Grimaldis Gallery, Balt., 1983, Artscape, Balt., 1986, Md. Inst. Coll. of Art, Balt., 1983, 85, 91, 92, 93, Art in the Bell Tower, Balt., 1988, Morris Mechanic Theatre Gallery, Balt., 1989, Artshowcase, Balt., 1990, 91, 92, 93, Frostburg State U., 1991. Bd. dirs. Friends of Logan Square, Phila., 1994-95, Phila. Vol. Lawyers Arts, Phila., 1994-95. Mem. Nat. Assn. Schs. of Art and Design (bd. dirs., sec. exec. com.), Nat. Coun. Art Adminstrs., Coll. Art Assn. (assoc.), Am. Assn. Higher Edn., Soc. for Coll. and Univ. Planning.

PRICE, BETTY JEANNE, choirchime soloist, writer; b. Long Beach, Calif., June 12, 1942; d. Grant E. and Miriam A. (Francis) Sickles; m. Harvey H. Price, Aug. 6, 1975; children: Thomas Neil Gering, Timothy Ray (dec.), Pamela Kay (dec.). Degree in Acctg., Northland Pioneer Coll., Show Low, Ariz., 1977. Youth missionary Open Bible Standard Missions, Trinidad, 1958-59; typographer Joel H. Weldon & Assocs., Scottsdale, Ariz., 1980-89; exec. chief acct. Pubs. Devel. Corp., San Diego, 1991-93; coord. music and worship College Ave. Bapt. Ch., San Diego, 1994-95; ChoirChime soloist, 1986—; exec. acct. Advance Reprographics, San Diego, 1996—, 1996—. Author: 101 Ways to Fix Broccoli, 1994, ABC's of Abundant Living, 1995, Breaking Free from Financial Bondage: A Guide to Living Debt Free, 2004; co-author: God's Vitamin C for the Spirit, 1995, Bounce Back, 1997, You Can Bounce Back Too, 1998, Pathway of Love, One Man's Remarkable Journey, 2002, One Man's Remarkable Journey, 2002; dir.: (handbell/chimes) Classical Sounds, A Musical Tour Around the World, Music for Special Occasions, Sounds for Christmas, A Musical Christmas Story, Hymns of Faith. Personal E-mail: chimesoloist@aol.com.

PRICE, CELES E. retired music educator; b. San Diego, Apr. 27, 1949; d. Clyde Eugene and Beulah Jane Homan; m. Gary Wayne Price, May 1, 1951. BS in concentration, secondary edn. and music, Old Dominion U., 1975. Instrumental music educator, founder string orchestra program Va. Beach Pub. Schs., 1971—2004; ret., 2004. Guest spkr. Stds. of Learning and Lessons Plans, 2002. PTA Brandon Mid. Sch., Va. Beach, 2004; music dept. chmn., assoc. concert master Va. Beach Symphony; guest condr. Chesapeak, Nofolk, Va. Beach, Fairfax, James Madison Univ. Mem.: Music Educators Nat. Conf. Avocations: cooking, aerobics, reading, gardening, tennis. Home: 5576 Stonehaven Dr Virginia Beach VA 23464 Office: Brandon Mid Sch 1700 Pope St Virginia Beach VA 23464 Office Phone: 757-366-4545. E-mail: mmprice@whro.net.

PRICE, CHARLES H., II, former ambassador; b. Kansas City, Mo., Apr. 1, 1931; s. Charles Harry and Virginia (Ogden) P.; m. Carol Ann Swanson, Jan. 10, 1969; children: Caroline Lee, Melissa Marie, Charles H., C. B., Pickette. Student, U. Mo., 1951-53; LLD (hon.), Westminster Coll., 1984, U. Mo.,

1988; LHD (hon.), Baker U., 1991; DSc (hon.), U. Buckingham, Eng., 1993. Chmn. bd., dir. Price Candy Co., Kansas City, 1969-81, Am. Bancorp., Kansas City, 1973-81; chmn., chief exec. officer Am. Bank & Trust Co., Kansas City, 1973-81; Am. ambassador to Belgium Brussels, 1981-83; Am. ambassador to U.K. London, 1983-89. Chmn. bd. Americanc, Inc., St. Joseph, Mo., 1989—92, pres., CEO, 1990—92; chmn. bd. Merc. Bank Kansas City, Mo., 1992—96. Trustee Midwest Rsch. Inst., Kansas City, chmn., 1990-93. Hon. fellow Regent's Coll., London, 1986; recipient William Booth award Salvation Army, 1985, World Citizen of Yr. award Mayor of Kansas City, 1985, Trustee Citation award Midwest Rsch. Inst., 1987, Disting. Svc. award Internat. Rels. Coun., 1989, Mankind award Cystic Fibrosis Found., 1990, Gold Good Citizenship award SAR, 1991, Chancellor's medal U. Mo. Kansas City, 1992, William F. Yates medallion William Jewell Coll., 1996. Mem.: The Vintage Country Club, White's Club, Swinley Forest Club, Kansas City Country Club, Eldorado Country Club, Brook Club, Cypress Point Club, Los Angeles County Club, River Club, Sigma Alpha Epsilon. Republican. Episcopalian. Office: 1 W Armour Blvd Ste 300 Kansas City MO 64111-2087

PRICE, CHARLES LEE, science educator; b. Charleston, Ill., July 9, 1950; s. Thomas C. and Blanche H. Price; m. Megan S. Price, June 19, 1976. BS in Edn., Ea. Ill. U., 1972, MS in Edn., 1975; PhD, Ohio State U., 1978. H.S. tchr. Ill. schs., 1972—75; prof. edn. U. So. Ind., Evansville, 1979—, chmn. tchr. edn. dept., 1995—. Natural Beauty at USI, 1992—94 (grantee). Avocation: nature photography. Home: 2343 W Summit Dr Evansville IN 47712 Office: U So INd 8600 University Blvd Evansville IN 47712 Office Fax: 812-465-1029. Business E Mail: cprice@usi.edu.

PRICE, CHARLES R., JR., advertising executive; Chmn. Price/McNabb Inc., Charlotte, N.C. Office: Price/McNabb Inc Unit 500 1001 S Morehead Square Dr Charlotte NC 28203-4270

PRICE, CHARLES T. lawyer; b. Lansing, Mich., Feb. 11, 1944; BA, Ohio Wesleyan U., 1966; JD, Harvard U., 1969. Bar: Ohio 1969, U.S. Dist. Ct. (no. dist.) Ohio 1974, U.S. Ct. Appeals (6th cir) 1981, U.S. Supreme Ct. 1982, Ill. 1989. Former ptnr. Baker & Hostetler, Cleve.; pres., pub. Chgo. Sun-Times, 1987-88; exec. v.p. Sun-Times Co., 1989-92; ptnr. Foley & Lardner, Chgo., 2000—. Mem. bd. govs. Sch. of Art Inst. of Chgo., former chmn.; mem. bd. trustees LaRabida Children;s Hosp. Mem.: Econ. Club. Office: Foley & Lardner 321 N Clark St Chicago IL 60610

PRICE, CLARA SUE, state legislator; b. Sept. 10, 1953; m. Gary Price; 1 child. BA in Bus. Adminstrn., Minot State U., 1977. Mem. N.D. Ho. of Reps., 1991—, chmn. Rep. caucaus, 1993-94, vice chair human svcs. com., 1995, mem. transp. com., chmn. human svcs., 1997—. Employee benefit specialist BCBS of N.D., 1982-87; stockbroker INVEST, 1988-90; sec. Cal-Dak Cabinets, 1975—; owner, operator Dakota Gardens & Herbs, 1993—. Past mem. Minot Commn. Status of Women; bd. dirs. Trinity Health. Mem. Internat. Peace Garden, C. of C. Republican. Lutheran. Home: 3520 30th St NW Minot ND 58703-0312 Office: ND Ho of Reps State Capitol Bismarck ND 58505 E-mail: cprice@state.nd.us.

PRICE, CLIFFORD WARREN, retired metallurgist, researcher; b. Denver, Apr. 22, 1935; s. Warren Wilson and Vivian Fredricka (Cady) P.; m. Carole Joyce Watermon, June 14, 1969; children: Carla Beth, Krista Lynn Price. MetE, Colo. Sch. Mines, 1957; MS, Ohio State U., 1970, PhD, 1975. Design engr. Sundstrand Aviation-Denver, 1957-60; materials specialist Denver Rsch. Inst., 1960-63; sr. metallurgist Rocky Flats div. Dow Chem. Co., Golden, Colo., 1963-66; staff metallurgist Battelle Columbus (Ohio) Labs., 1966-75; sr. scientist Owens-Corning Fiberglas, Granville, Ohio, 1975-80; metallurgist Lawrence Livermore (Calif.) Nat. Lab., 1980-93; retired, 1993. Contbr. articles to profl. jours. Battelle Columbus Labs. fellow, 1974-75. Mem. Metall. Soc. AIME, Microscopy Soc. Am. (treas. Denver 1961-62), Am. Soc. Metals Internat. Achievements include research on electron, scanning probe and optical microscopy, secondary ion mass spectroscopy, deformation, fracture and recrystallization mechanisms in metals, recrystallization kinetics. Personal E-mail: clifford.price@comcast.net.

PRICE, DANIEL MARTIN, lawyer; b. St. Louis, Aug. 23, 1955; s. Albert and Edith S. (Werner) P.; m. Kim Ellen Heebner, July 15, 1984; children: Emma Rachel, Joseph Armin, Joshua Simon. BA, Haverford Coll., 1977; diploma in law, Cambridge U., 1979; JD, Harvard U., 1981. Bar: D.C. 1981, Pa. 1987. Assoc. Drinker, Biddle & Reath, Phila., 1981-82, 86-89; dep. gen. counsel Office of U.S. Trade Rep., Washington, 1989-92; ptnr. Powell, Goldstein, Frazer & Murphy, Washington, 1992—2002, Sidley Austin Brown & Wood, Washington, 2002—. Atty., adviser Dept. State, Washington, 1982-84; dep. agt. U.S. Iran-U.S. Claims Tribunal, Hague, The Netherlands, 1984-86; lectr. Haverford Coll., 1982; mem. adv. bd. Can.-U.S. Law Inst. Articles editor Harvard Law Rev., 1980-81; contbr. articles to profl. jours. including Am. Jour. Internat. Law, Internat. Lawyer, Internat. Fin. Law Rev., Harvard Internat. Law Jour., others. Mem. Bush-Cheney Transition Team, 1999—2000. Am. Keasbey scholar Cambridge U., 1977-78. Mem. ABA, Internat. Bus. Forum (legal adv. bd. 1987-89), Am. Arbitration Assn. (panel arbitrators), Internat. C. of C. (arbitrator), Orgn. for Internat. Investment (counsel), Coun. on Fgn. Rels., Phi Beta Kappa., Intl. Ctr. for Settlement of Investment Disputes (mem. panel of arbirators), Dept. of State Adv. Com. on Intl. Economic Policy, Georgetown U. Law Center Inst. of Intl. Economic Law (mem. adv. bd.). Office: 1501 K St NW Washington DC 20005

PRICE, DAVID, golf courses facilities executive; b. 1933; With Am. Golf Corp., Santa Monica, Calif., 1972—, now chmn.; chmn. Nat. Golf Properties, Santa Monica, Calif., 1993—. Office: Am Golf Corp 2951 28th St Santa Monica CA 90405-2961

PRICE, DAVID EUGENE, congressman, educator; b. Johnson City, Tenn., Aug. 17, 1940; s. Albert Lee and Elna (Harrell) P.; m. Lisa Beth Kanwit, July 27, 1968; children: Karen Elizabeth, Michael Edmond. BA, U. N.C., 1961; BD, Yale U., 1964, PhD, 1969. Legis. aide to U.S. senator from Alaska, 1963-67; prof. Duke U., Durham, N.C., 1973-86; mem. U.S. Congress from 4th N.C. dist., Washington, 1987—; mem. appropriations com., budget com. Exec. dir. N.C. Dem. Party, Raleigh, 1979-80, chmn., 1983-84, mem. 1983—; staff dir. nat. com. on presdl. nomination Dem. Party, 1981-82 Author: Bringing Back the Parties, The Commerce Committees, Who Makes the Laws, The Congressional Experience: A View From the Hill. Mem. Am. Polit. Sci. Assn., Soc. for Values in Higher Edn., Phi Beta Kappa. Lodges: Kiwanis. Democrat. Baptist. Avocations: jogging, music. Home: 2200 N Lakeshore Dr Chapel Hill NC 27514-1726 Office: US Ho of Reps 2162 Rayburn Ho Office Bldg Washington DC 20515-3304

PRICE, DAVID HAROLD, anthropologist, educator; b. Seattle, Apr. 15, 1960; s. William John and Jewel Fernell Price; m. Midge Danger Miller, Aug. 16, 1986; children: Milo, Nora. BA, Evergreen State Coll., 1983; AM, U. Chgo., 1985; PhD, U. Fla., 1993. Assoc. prof. anthropology St. Martin's Coll., Lacey, Wash., 1994—. Author: Atlas of World Cultures: A Geographical Guide to Ethnographic Literature, 1989, The Evolution of Irrigation in Egypt's Fayoum Oasis: State, Village and Conveyance Loss, 1993, Threatening Anthropology: McCarthyism and the FBI's Surveillance of Activist Anthropologists, 2004; contbr. articles to profl. pubs. Grantee, NSF, 1989—90, Boeing Corp., 2001; Malone Fellowship, Nat. Coun. U.S.-Arab Rels., 1995. Fellow: Soc. of Fellows; mem.: Nat. Writers Union, Am. Rsch. Ctr. in Egypt, Royal Anthrop. Inst., Am. Anthrop. Assn. Green Party. Achievements include research in the FBI and CIA's monitoring of anthropologists using the Freedom of Information Act, leading to the release of over 30,000 pages of documents (1992-2002). Avocations: mountain climbing, hiking. Home: 615 Governor Stevens Ave Olympia WA 98501 Office: St Martins Coll 5300 Pacific Ave Lacey WA 98503 E-mail: dprice@stmartin.edu., dprice@stmartin.edu.

PRICE, DONALD ALBERT, veterinarian, consultant; b. Bridgeport, Ohio, Dec. 25, 1919; s. Arthur David and Louise Ann (Knellinger) P.; m. June Loree Fleming, July 16, 1945; children: Karen Price Privett, Benita Price Esposito, Donna Price Rocap. Grad., Elliott Sch. Bus., 1938; DVM, Ohio State U., 1950. Lic. veterinarian, Ohio, Ill., Tex. Adminstrv. asst. Wheeling (W.Va.) Steel Corp., 1938-41; counselor psychol. dept. Ohio State U., Columbus, 1946-48, lab. asst. vet. parasitology dept., 1948-50; mem. tech. faculty Tex. A&M U., Sonora, 1950-55; ptnr. San Angelo (Tex.) Vet. Hosp., 1955-58; assoc. editor AVMA, Chgo., 1958-59, editor-in-chief, 1959-72, exec. v.p., 1972-85; cons., adj. prof. Tex. A&M U., College Station, 1985—. Capt. USAAF, 1941-46. Recipient Disting. Alumnus award Coll. Vet. Medicine, Ohio State U., 1966. Fellow Am. Med. Writers Assn.; mem. AVMA (Svc. Commendation award 1984, Appreciation award, 1984, CEO 1972-85), Ill. Vet. Med. Assn. (hon. life), Mich. Vet. Med. Assn. (hon. life), Tex. Vet. Med. Assn. (disting. life), Am. Equine Practitioners Assn. (hon.), Am. Assn. Sheep and Goat Practioners (hon.), Am. Animal Hosp. Assn. (hon., Merit award 1983), Bexar County Vet. Med. Assn. (hon.), Masons, Phi Eta Sigma, Phi Zeta, Alpha Psi. Republican. Presbyterian. Avocations: woodworking, ranching. Home and Office: 361 Rock Bottom Rd SW Hunt TX 78024-3050

PRICE, DONALD L. pathology educator; Prof. pathology, neurology and neurosci. Johns Hopkins U. Sch. Medicine, dir. Alzheimer's Disease Rsch. Ctr., dir. neuropathology lab. Mem. panel on Alzheimer's Disease, U.S. Congress. Mem. editl. bd. Jour. Neurosci., Current Opinioin in Neurobiology, Jour. Neuropathology and Exptl. Neurology, Neurobiology of Disease; contbr. articles to profl. jours. Mem. Soc. for Neurosci. (chair pub. info. com. 1989-91), Am. Assn. Neuropathologists (past pres.). Office: Johns Hopkins Med Dept Pathology Ross 558 720 Rutland Ave Baltimore MD 21205-2109 E-mail: adrc@welchlink.welch.jhu.edu.

PRICE, DONALD RAY, university official, agricultural engineer; b. Rockville, Ind., July 20, 1939; s. Ernest M. and Violet Noreen (Measel) P.; m. Joyce Ann Gerald, Sept. 14, 1963; children: John Allen, Karen Sue, Kimberly Ann, Daniel Lee BS in Agrl. Engring., Purdue U., 1961, PhD in Agrl. Engring., 1971; MS in Agrl. Engring., Cornell U., 1963. Registered profl. engr., Fla. From asst. prof. to prof. Cornell U., Ithaca, N.Y., 1962-80, dir. energy programs, 1975-77, 78-80; program mgr. Dept. Energy, Washington, 1977-78, cons.; assoc. dean research U. Fla., Gainesville, 1980-83, dean Grad. Sch., 1983-84, v.p. rsch., 1984—; pres. U. Fla. Rsch. Found., Inc.; program dir. NSF, 2003—. Chmn. bd. dirs. Progress Research, Inc., cons. to Pres. Carter, Washington, 1978; bd. dirs. Nat. Food and Engring. Council, Columbia, Mo., 1978-85, S.E. Healthcare Found., Gainesville, Fla., 1985 Contbr. numerous articles on engring. to profl. jours.; patentee mech. device Mem. Ithaca Sch. Bd., N.Y., 1979-80; elder Ch. of Christ, Gainesville, Fla., 1983—. Recipient citation Pres. Carter, 1979, Disting. Alumnus award Purdue U., 1990. Fellow Am. Soc. Agrl. Engrs. (dir. 1990, paper awards 1963, 77, 78, Young Engr. of Yr. award 1980); mem. Soc. Research Adminstrs., Nat. Assn. Univ. Research Adminstrs., S.E. Univ. Research Assn., Research Univs. Network Lodges: Rotary. Democrat. Avocations: tennis, jogging, woodworking. Office: NSF 4201 Wilson Blvd Arlington VA 22203 Home: 9299 Tower Side Dr Apt 239 Fairfax VA 22031-6033 E-mail: dprice@nsf.gov.

PRICE, DONNA B. special education services professional; b. San Antonio, Sept. 24, 1943; d. Herman David Zweiban; m. Harry Roger Price, Aug. 16, 1964; children: Martin, Brian, Eric. BS in Edn., Ind. U., 1964; EdM, U. Houston, 1977. Lic. profl. counselor Tex. Bd. Examiners Profl. Counselors, marriage and family therapist Tex. Bd. Examiners Marriage and Family Therapists, nat. cert. counselor Nat. Bd. Cert. Counselors, nat. cert. career counselor Nat. Bd. Cert. Counselors. Secondary English and Latin tchr. Speedway HS, Indpls., 1964—67; ednl. therapist St. Joseph Hosp., Houston, 1977—78; job placement program dir. Jewish Family Svc., Houston, 1978—83; therapist Greenway Psychotherapy Assn., Houston, 1983—92; ADA counselor Houston CC Sys., 1992—99, ADA coord., 1999—. Mem. Gov.'s Adv. Coun. Tech. and Vocat. Edn., Austin, 1990—2000. V.p. Women's Am. Ort, Houston, 2003, Hadassah, Houston, 2003, Nat. Coun. Jewish Women, Houston, 2003; bd. mem. Mental Health and Mental Retardation Assn., Houston, 1994—99. Mem.: Tex. Assn. for Higher Edn. and Disabilities (dir. 1990—93), Assn. for Higher Edn. and Adults with Disabilities (bd. mem. 1995—97). Avocations: walking, travel, swimming, raising standard poodles.

PRICE, DOUGLAS ARMSTRONG, chiropractor; b. Pitts., Feb. 17, 1950; s. Walter Coachman and Janet (Armstrong) P.; m. Ann Georgette Martino, Jan. 31, 1989; 4 children. BA, Brown U., l972; D Chiropractic, Life Chiropractic Coll., Atlanta, l983. Diplomate Am. Bd. Chiropractic Examiners; cert. rehab. doctor; life extension physician; ind. med. examiner, Fla. Owner, CEO Applied Biomech. and Musculoskeletal Rehab., Tampa, 1989—, All Am. Chiropractic Clinic; pvt. practice Tampa, 1984—, Manalapan, Fla., 1994-96; clin. dir. Camber Clinics, South Tampa, Haines City, Fla., 1999—2001, Fla. Pain, Trauma, and Injury Clinics, Tampa, 2001—. Dir. Myofascial Therapy Found. Author: Protocols for Practioners Utilizing Myofascial Trigger Point Treatment, 1998; prodr. therapeutic exercise video for cervical and lumbar rehab.; contbr. articles to profl. jours. Magnetic Resonance Imaging fellow; named to Brown U. Athletic Hall of Fame; Southeastern Masters Champion Shotput, Discus, 1990-91. Fellow: Am. Gerontology Assn., Chiropractic Rehab. Assn., Am. Coll. Sports Medicine; mem.: APHA, Hillsborough County Chiropractic Soc. (bd. dirs. 1990—93, pres. 1992—93), Fla. Chiropractic Assn., Am. Chiropractic Assn., KC (trustee). Democrat. Roman Catholic. Achievements include research in Russian stimulation applications in low back rehabilitation; application of micro and interferential currents with utilization of manual travel myofascial release techniques, use of micro and interferential currents with manual treatment of myofascial pain syndromes. Home: 90 W Davis Blvd Tampa FL 33606-3535 Office Phone: 813-849-2459. Personal E-mail: douglasmyodoc@aol.com.

PRICE, EDGAR HILLEARY, JR., business consultant; b. Jacksonville, Fla., Jan. 1, 1918; s. Edgar Hilleary and Mary Williams (Phillips) P.; m. Elise Ingram, June 24, 1947; 1 son, Jerald Steven. Student, U. Fla., 1937-38. Mgr. comml. flower farm, 1945-49, Fla. Gladiolus Growers Assn., 1949-55; exec. v.p. Tropicana Products, Inc., Bradenton, Fla., 1955-73, dir. div. govt. and industry regulations, to 1979; dir.; exec. v.p. Indsl. Glass Co., Inc., Bradenton, 1963-73; pres., chmn. bd. Price Co., Inc., Bradenton, cons., 1973—. Dir. emeritus F.P.L. Group, Inc.; past chmn. Fla. Citrus Commn., Fla. Gov.'s Freeze Damage Survey Team, Spl. Commn. for Study Abolition Death Penalty; bd. dirs. Fla. Power and Light Co., Fla. Fair Assn., Fla. Citrus Expn., Fla. Fruit and Vegetable Assn., G.T.E. Fla., Fla. Cyprus Gardens, Ellis Bank Co.; past chmn. Joint Citrus Legis. Com.; past mem. Fla. Plant Bd., Fla. Bd. Control, Fla. Legis. Coun.; exec. com. Growers and Shippers League Fla., Fla. Agrl. Council, Spl. Health Agrl. Research and Edn.; past pres., chmn. bd. Fla. Hort. Soc. Past chmn., commr. census 12th Jud. Circuit; mem. Gov. Fla. Com. Rehab. Handicapped, Fla. Commn. on Ethics, 1976-77, Pres. Carter Inaugural Fin. com., 1977, Ea. 5th Circuit U.S. Jud. Nominating Commn., 1977—, Fla. Senate from 36th Dist., 1958-66; past chmn. Manatee County Bd. Sch. Dist. Trustees, Local Housing Authority Bradenton, Bradenton Sub. Std. Housing Bd., Bradenton Charter Adv. Com.; del. Dem. Nat. Conv., 1960, dist. del., 1964; past trustee, mem. exec. com. Stetson U.; former trustee New Coll., Aurora Found. Served to 1st lt. USAAF, 1941-45. Named Boss of Yr., Nat. Secs. Assn., 1959, Man of Yr. for Fla. agr. Progressive Farmer mag., 1959; recipient merit award Am. Flag Assn., 1962, Gamma Sigma Delta, 1965, leadership award Fla. Agrl. Ext. Svc., 1963, Outstanding Senator award Fla. Radio Broadcasters, 1965, Allen Morris award s most valuable mem. Fla. Legislature, 1965, Most Valuable Mem. award Fla. Senate, St. Petersburg Times, 1965, Brotherhood award Sarasota chpt. NCCJ, 1966, Disting. Citizen award Manatee County, 1970, Disting. Alumnus award U. Fla., 1972, Svc. to Mankind award Sertoma Internat., 1976, Goodwill Disting. Citizen award, 1979, Crystal Shield award Salvation Army, 1996; inducted into Fla. Agrl. Hall of Fame, 1992, Tampa Bay Bus. Hall of Fame, 1992. Mem. Fla. C. of C. (bd. dirs. emeritus and past chmn.), Manatee C. of C. (past pres.), Fla. Hort. Soc. (past pres., chmn. bd.), Fla. Flower Assn., ARC Clara Barton Soc., Blue Key (hon.), Omicron Delta Kappa (hon.), Kiwanis (pres. 1955), Sigma Alpha Epsilon. Home: 3009 Riverview Blvd W Bradenton FL 34205-3420 Office: PO Box 9270 Bradenton FL 34206-9270 *The turning point in my life came at the age of 32 when I accepted Jesus Christ as my personal Lord and Saviour. I believe every person should live his life up to the fullest extent of his God-given talents and ability. I think we have a responsibility to "pay our dues" for the privilege of living in a free land by being actively involved in our government.*

PRICE, EDWARD WARREN, aerospace engineer, educator; b. Detroit, Dec. 6, 1920; s. Frank E. and Elizabeth Alleyne (Rattray) P.; m. Mary Kate Howard, June 21, 1952; children: Douglas Brian, Alison Tamara, Carolyn Louise. BA in Physics, Math, UCLA, 1948. Ballistician Calif. Inst. Tech., Pasadena, 1941-44; physicist U.S. Naval Weapons Ctr., China Lake, Calif., 1946-74; prof. aerospace engring. Ga. Inst. Tech., Atlanta, 1967—68, 1974—. V.p. tech. AIAA, mem. Am. Acad. Scis.-Nat. Rsch. Coun. Space Shuttle Booster Redesign Rev. Panel, 1986-89; cons. in field. Contbr. articles to profl. jours. With USNR, 1944—46. Recipient Pub. Svc. award, Astronauts award NASA, 1987. Fellow AIAA (Rsch., Pendrary, Goddard awards 1966, 71, 76); mem. AAAS, Nat. Acad. Engring., Combustion Inst., Sigma Xi. Achievements include numerous contributions to science in areas of rocket propulsion and combustion. Home: 5058 Highpoint Rd NE Atlanta GA 30342-2313 Office: Ga Inst Tech 225 North Ave Mail Code 0150 Atlanta GA 30332

PRICE, ELIZABETH ANNE, lawyer; b. Boston, Aug. 23, 1960; BA, George Washington U., 1983, JD with honors, 1986. Bar: Ga. 1986, U.S. Dist. Ct. (no. dist.) Ga. 1986, U.S. Ct. Appeals (11th cir.) 1986, U.S. Supreme Ct. 1995. Ptnr. Alston & Bird, Atlanta, 1986—. With U.S. Army, 1978-81. Mem. State Bar Ga. (access to justice com., ct. futures com.), Atlanta Bar Assn. (bd. dirs. 1996—, chmn. continuing legal edn. com. 1991-92, pres.-elect). Office: Alston & Bird 1 Atlantic Ctr Atlanta GA 30309-3400

PRICE, ELY, dermatologist; b. N.Y.C., Aug. 9, 1932; s. Jacob and Mary (Flattau) P.; m. Ilona Brodie, Apr. 30, 1989; children from previous marriage: Jeremy, Andrew. BS cum laude, CCNY, 1953; AM, Ind. U., 1956; MD, U. Lausanne, Switzerland, 1964. Diplomate Am. Bd. Dermatology. Intern Brookdale Hosp. Med. Ctr., Bklyn., 1964-65, resident internal medicine, 1965-66; fellow Mt. Sinai Hosp., N.Y.C., 1965-66; resident in dermatology Kings County Hosp., Bklyn., 1966-69; practice dermatology Bay Ridge Skin and Cancer Dermatology, P.C., Bklyn., 1969—; attending-in-charge, head dermatology Maimonides Med. Ctr., Bklyn., 1985—; clin. assoc. prof. dermatology SUNY Sci. Ctr., Bklyn., 1985—. Cons. in medicine Luth. Med. Ctr., Bklyn., 1988—; cons. in dermatology Victory Med. Hosp., Bklyn., 1989—. Fellow ACP, Am. Acad. Dermatology, Am. Soc. Dermatol. Surgery, N.Y. Acad. Medicine. Avocation: golf. Home: 674 W Fingerboard Rd Staten Island NY 10305-2631 Office: Bay Ridge Skin & Cancer Dermatology PC 9921 4th Ave Brooklyn NY 11209-8347 E-mail: elyilona@aol.com.

PRICE, FRANK, motion picture and television company executive; b. Decatur, Ill., May 17, 1930; s. William F. and Winifred A. (Moran) P.; m. Katherine Huggins, May 15, 1965; children: Stephen, David, Roy, William. Student, Mich. State U., 1949-51, HHD (hon.), 2003. Writer, story editor CBS-TV, N.Y.C., 1951-53, Columbia Pictures, Hollywood, Calif., 1953-57, NBC-TV, Hollywood, Calif., 1957-58; producer, writer ZIV-TV, Hollywood, Calif., 1958, Universal Television, Universal City, Calif., 1959-64, v.p., 1964-71, sr. v.p., 1971-73, exec. v.p. in charge of production, 1973-74, pres., 1974-78; v.p., dir. MCA, Inc., 1976-78; pres. Columbia Pictures Prodn., 1978-79; chmn., chief exec. officer Columbia Pictures, 1979-84, also bd. dirs.; chmn. MCA Motion Picture Group, 1984-86; chmn., chief exec. officer Price Entertainment Inc., 1987-90; chmn. Columbia Pictures, 1990-91; chmn., chief exec. officer Price Entertainment, 1991—; prodr. The Tuskegee Airmen, 1996. With USN, 1948-49. Recipient Peabody award, 1996, NAACP Image award, 1996. Mem. Writers Guild Am. West, N.Y. State Soc. Cin. Office: Price Entertainment Inc 527 Spoleto Dr Pacific Palisades CA 90272-4517

PRICE, FREDERIC D. pharmaceutical executive; BA, Dartmouth Coll.; MBA, U. Pa. With Pfizer Pharm.; strategy cons.; v.p. fin. & adminstrn., CFO Regeneron Pharm., Inc.; pres., CEO Applied Microbiology, Inc.; chmn., CEO BioMarin Pharm. Inc., Novato, Calif., 2000—. Adv. bd. Equity4Life AG, Zurich, Switzerland. Office: BioMarin Pharmaceutical Inc 371 Bel Marin Keys Blvd Ste 210 Novato CA 94949

PRICE, GLENDA DELORES, university dean; b. York, Pa., Oct. 10, 1939; d. William B. Price and Zelma E. Holmes McGeary. BS, Temple U., 1961, MEd, 1969, PhD, 1979. Clin. lab. specialist. Cytotechnologist Temple U. Hosp., Phila., 1961-67; faculty Coll. Allied Health Professions, Temple U., Phila., 1967-79, asst. dean allied health, 1979-86; dean allied health Sch. Allied Health Professions, U. Conn., Storrs, 1986—. Contbr. articles to profl. jours., chpts. to books. Bd. trustees U. New Eng., Biddeford, Maine, 1989—; bd. dirs. Windham Hosp., Willimantic, Conn., 1989—, E. Hartford VNA, 1989—; allied health adv. Pew Health Prof. Commn., Durham, N.C., 1991—. Recipient Leadership Award SUNY-Buffalo, 1982; named Mem. of the Yr., Pa. Soc. for Med. Tech., 1979; decorated Legion of Honor, Chapel of Four Chaplains, 1977. Mem. Am. Soc. Allied Health Professions (sec. 1985-87), Am. Soc. for Med. Tech. (pres. 1979-80), Alpha Kappa Alpha, Alpha Mu Tau, Alpha Eta, Phi Kappa Phi. Democrat. Baptist. Office: U Conn 358 Mansfield Rd Storrs Mansfield CT 06269-9000

PRICE, GRIFFITH BALEY, JR., lawyer; b. Lawrence, Kans., Aug. 15, 1942; s. Griffith Baley and Cora Lee (Beers) P.; m. Maria Helena Martin, June 29, 1968 (div.); children: Andrew Griffith, Alexandra Helena; m. Nancy Culver Rhodes, Aug. 17, 1997; children: Carolyn Rhodes, Sarah Culver. AB (cum laude), Harvard U., 1964; LLB, NYU, 1967. Bar: N.Y. 1967, D.C. 1991, U.S. Ct. Appeals (6th cir.) 1975, U.S. Ct. Appeals (2nd cir.) 1978, U.S. Ct. Appeals (3d, 5th and 11th cirs.) 1981, U.S. Ct. Appeals (1st cir.) 2002, U.S. Ct. Appeals (fed. cir.) 1984, U.S. Supreme Ct. 2001. Assoc. Dewey, Ballantine, Bushby, Palmer & Wood, N.Y.C., 1967-75; ptnr. Milgrim Thomajan & Lee, N.Y.C., 1976-86; of counsel, ptnr. Finnegan, Henderson, Farabow, Garrett & Dunner, LLP, Washington, 1987—. Adj. prof., lectr. George Washington U. Law Ctr., Washington, 1989—93; mem., chair pub. adv. com. U.S. Patent and Trademark Office, 1999—; lectr., spkr. in field. Author: (with others, treatise) Milgrim on Trade Secrets, 1986; contbr. articles to profl. jours. Root-Tilden scholar NYU Law Sch., 1964-67. Mem.: ABA (intellectual property sec., com. chmn.), Assn. Interamerican Indsl. Property, Fed. Cir. Bar Assn., Licensing Execs. Soc., Am. Intellectual Property Law Assn. (bd. dirs., com. chmn.), Internat. Trademark Assn. (bd. dirs., com. chmn.), Cosmos Club, Nat. Press Club, Harvard Club (Washington), N.Y. Athletic Club. Unitarian Universalist. Office: Finnegan Henderson Farabow Garrett & Dunner LLP 901 New York Ave Washington DC 20001-4413 E-mail: gbprice@finnegan.com.

PRICE, HENRY ESCOE, broadcast executive; b. Jackson, Miss., Oct. 13, 1947; s. Henry E. Price Sr. and Alma Kate (Merrill) Noto; m. Maria Diane Harper, Apr. 8, 1972; children: Henry E. III, Norman Harper. BS in Radio, TV, Film, Journalism, U. So. Miss., 1972. Announcer, news dir. Sta. WROA Radio, Gulfport, Miss., 1967-69; comml. producer Sta. WJTV-TV, Jackson, Miss., 1969-73; prodn. mgr. Sta. WAAY-TV, Huntsville, Ala., 1973-77, Sta. WPEC-TV, West Palm Beach, Fla., 1977-79; dir. promotion Sta. WPTV-TV, Palm Beach, Fla., 1979-81; TV cons. Frank Magid Assoc., Marion, Iowa, 1981-83; dir. advt. and promotion Sta. WJLA-TV, Washington, 1983-84; v.p., dir. programming Sta. WUSA-TV, Gannett TV, Washington, 1984-88; pres., gen. mgr. Sta. WFMY-TV, Gannett TV, Greensboro, N.C., 1988-91, Sta. KARE-TV, Mpls., 1991-96; v.p., gen. mgr. Sta. WBBM-TV, CBS TV Stas., Chgo., 1996—. Pres. Carolina News Network, 1988-91; adj. faculty media mgmt. Ctr. Northwestern U., 2000—. Vice chair, bd. dirs. The Courage Ctr., Mpls.; regional dir. Nat. Conf.; mem. exec. com., bd. dirs. The Minn. Orch.; Pacesetter program chair Mpls. United Way Campaign; active Twin Cities Dunkers, Twin Cities Comm. Coun., 11 Who Care. Mem. Chgo. C. of C. (bd. dirs.), Ill. Broadcasters Assn. (bd. dirs.). Avocations: furniture design and constrn., reading, walking, bicycle riding. Home: PO Box 11847 Winston Salem NC 27116-1847 Office: Sta WBBM-TV CBS Television 630 N Mcclurg Ct Chicago IL 60611-4495

PRICE, ILENE ROSENBERG, lawyer; b. Jersey City, July 2, 1951; d. Irwin Daniel and Mildred (Riesberg) Rosenberg; m. Jeffrey Paul Price, Feb. 18, 1973. AB, U. Mich., 1972; JD, U. Pa., 1977. Bar: Pa. 1977, D.C. 1978, U.S. Dist. Ct. D.C. 1979, U.S. Ct. Appeals (D.C. cir.) 1979. Assoc. Haley, Bader & Potts, Washington, 1977-80; staff atty. Mut. Broadcasting System Inc., Arlington, Va., 1980-82, asst. gen. counsel, 1982-85; gen. counsel MultiComm Telecommunications Corp., Arlington, 1985-88; east coast counsel Westwood One, Inc., Arlington, 1988-91; gen. counsel Resource Dynamics Corp., Vienna, Va., 1991—2001; legal search cons. The McCormick Group, Arlington, 2001—03; gen. counsel Bluewave Resources, LLC, McLean, Va., 2003—. Mem. Fed. Communications Bar Assn., Wash. Met. Area Corp. Counsel Assn., Women's Bar Assn. D.C. (bd. dirs. 1984-87). Office: Bluewave Resources LLC Ste 310 6830 Elm St Mc Lean VA 22101 E-mail: ileneprice@aol.com.

PRICE, JACK C. association administrator; Student, Weber State Coll. Various positions to dep. dir. distbn. Ogden Air Logistics Ctr., Hill AFB, Utah, 1953—88, ret., 1988; various positions to nat. pres., chmn. bd. Air Force Assn.; sustaining life mem., trustee Aerospace Edn. Foun., 1984—, v.p., 1994—96, pres., 1998—, chmn. bd., 2000—. Nat. dir., chmn. Air Force Assn. 50th Anniversary of Air Force Steering Com.; chmn. futures planning com. Aerospace Edn. Found.; aerospace industry cons. on solid rocket motor systems. With USAF, Korea. Office: c/o Aerospace Edn Found 1501 Lee Hwy Arlington VA 22209-1198

PRICE, JAMES GORDON, physician, educator; b. Brush, Colo., June 20, 1926; s. John Hoover and Rachel Laurette (Dodds) Price; m. Janet Alice McSween, June 19, 1949; children: James Gordon II, Richard Christian, Mary Laurette, Janet Lynn. BA, U. Colo., 1948, MD, 1951. Diplomate charter Am. Bd. Family Practice . Intern Denver Gen. Hosp., 1951—52; practice medicine specializing in family medicine Brush, 1952—78; prof. family practice U. Kans. Med. Ctr., 1978—93; chmn. dept. U. Kans. Med. Center, 1982—90, exec. dean, 1990—93, prof. emeritus in family practice, 1993—. Dir., pres. Am. Bd. Family Practice, 1979; mem. Inst. Medicine of NAS, 1973—. Med. editor: Gen. Learning Corp., 1973—92, mem. editl. bd.: Med. World News, 1969—79; editor: Am. Acad. Family Physician Home Study Self Assessment Program, 1978—83; columnist: Your Family Physician, 1973—90. Trustee Family Health Found. Am., 1970—82; vol. physician St. Jude's Hosp., St. Lucia, West Indies, 1998—99. With USNR, 1943—46. Fellow: Am. Acad. Family Physicians (charter, pres. 1973); mem.: Alpha Omega Alpha, Phi Beta Kappa. Home: 12205 Mohawk Rd Shawnee Mission KS 66209-2137

PRICE, JAMES MELFORD, retired physician, researcher; b. Onalaska, Wis., Apr. 3, 1921; s. Carl Robert and Hazel (Halderson) P.; m. Ethelyn Doreen Lee, Oct. 23, 1943 (div.); children: Alta Lee, Jean Marie, Veda Michele; m. Charlotte E. Schwenk, Sept. 27, 1986; children: Shirley S. Bunn, Cindy S. Davis, Irene S. McCumber. BS in Agr., U. Wis., 1943, MS in Biochemistry, 1944, PhD in Physiology, 1949, MD, 1951. Diplomate Am. Bd. Physician Nutrition Specialists. Intern Cin. Gen. Hosp., 1951-52; mem. faculty U. Wis. Med. Sch., 1952—, prof. clin. oncology, 1959—, Am. Cancer Soc.-Charles S. Hayden Found. prof. surgery, 1957—; on leave as dir. exptl. therapy Abbott Labs., 1967—, v.p. exptl. therapy, 1968, v.p. corp. rsch. and exptl. therapy, 1971—, v.p. corp. sci. devel., 1976-78; v.p. med. affairs Norwich-Eaton Pharms., 1978—. V.p. internat. R&D, 1980-82; pres. RADAC Group, Inc., 1982-90, Biogest Products, Inc., 1984-88; mem. metabolism study sect. NIH, 1959-62, pathology B study sect., 1964-68; sci. adv. com. PMA Found.; chmn. rsch. adv. com. Ill. Dept. Mental Health; sci. com. Nat. Bladder Cancer program; mem. Drug Rsch. Bd. Nat. Acad. Scis./NRC. Bd. dirs. Grandview Coll., Des Moines, 1977-78. With USNR, 1944-45. Fellow Am. Coll. Nutrition, Royal Soc. Medicine London; mem. Am. Soc. Pharmacology and Exptl. Therapeutics, Am. Assn. Cancer Rsch., Am. Cancer Soc. (com. etiology 1957-61), Pharm. Mfrs. Assn. (chmn. R&D sect. 1974-75), Am. Soc. Biol. Chemists, Am. Inst. Nutrition, Am. Soc. Clin. Nutrition, Rsch. Dirs. Assn. Chgo., Soc. Exptl. Biology and Medicine, Soc. Toxicology. Achievements include research on trytophan metabolism, metabolism vitamin B complex, chemical carcinogenesis; research and development pharmaceutical, diagnostic and consumer products, licensing and business development.

PRICE, JAMES TUCKER, lawyer; b. Springfield, Mo., June 22, 1955; s. Billy L. and Jeanne Adele Price; m. Francine Beth Warkow, June 8, 1980; children: Rachel Leah, Ashley Elizabeth. BJ, U. Mo., 1977; JD, Harvard U., 1980. Bar: Mo. 1980. Assoc. firm Spencer Fane Britt & Browne, Kansas City, 1980-86; ptnr. Spencer Fane Britt & Browne LLP, Kansas City, 1987—, chair environ. practice group, 1994—, mem. exec. com., 1997—. Mem. Brownfields Commn., Kansas City, 1999—; mem. steering com. Kansas City Bi-State Brownfields Initiative, 1997—. Contbr. to monographs, other legal publs. Mem. ABA (coun. sect. environ, energy and resources 1992-95, vice chmn. solid and hazardous waste com. 1985-90, chmn. 1990-92, chmn. brownfields task force 1995-97, vice chmn. environ. transactions and brownfield com. 1998-2000), Mo. Bar Assn., Kansas City Met. Bar Assn. (chmn. environ. law com. 1985-86), Greater Kansas City C. of C. (co-chair Brownfields Working Group, 1996-98, chmn. energy and environ. com. 1987-89). Office: Spencer Fane Britt & Browne LLP 1000 Walnut St Ste 1400 Kansas City MO 64106-2140 E-mail: jprice@spencerfane.com.

PRICE, JOE (JOE ALLEN), artist, former educator, actor; b. Ferriday, La., Feb. 6, 1935; s. Edward Neill and Margaret (Hester) P. BS, Northwestern U., 1957; post grad., Art Ctr. Coll., L.A., 1967-68; MA, Stanford U., 1970. Free-lance actor, artist, NYC, 1957-60. Freelance illustrator, actor, L.A., 1960-68; freelance comml. artist, San Carlos, Calif., 1968-69; package designer Container Corp. Am., Santa Clara, Calif., 1969; prof. studio art and filmmaking, chmn. dept. art Coll. San Mateo, Calif., 1970-94. One-man shows include Richard Sumner Gallery, Palo Alto, Calif., 1975, San Mateo County Cultural Ctr., 1976, 82, Tahir Galleries, New Orleans, 1977, 82, Kerwin Galleries, Burlingame, Calif., 1977, Edits. Gallery, Melbourne, Australia, 1977, Ankrum Gallery, L.A., 1978, 84, Edits. Ltd. West Gallery, San Francisco, 1981, Miriam Perlman Gallery, Chgo., 1982, San Mateo County Arts Coun. Gallery, 1982, Candy Stick Gallery, Ferndale, Calif., 1984, Assoc. Am. Artists, N.Y.C. and Phila., 1984, Gallery 30, Burlingame, 1991, San Mateo, 1984, Triton Mus. Art, Santa Clara, Calif., 1986, Huntsville (Ala.) Mus. Art, 1987, Gallery 30, San Mateo, 1988-97, Concept Art Gallery, Pitts., 1991, Eleonore Austerer Gallery, San Francisco, 1995, Vault Gallery, Sonora, 1995, Robert Wright Cmty. Gallery, Grayslake, Ill., 2003; exhibited in groups shows at Berkeley Art Ctr., Calif., 1976, Burlingame Civic Art Gallery, 1976, Syntex Gallery, Palo Alto, Calif., 1977, Gump's Gallery, San Francisco, 1976, 77, Nat. Gallery of Australia, 1978, Sonoma County Gallery, 1979, Gov. Dummer Acad. Art, Byfield, Mass., 1979, Miss. Mus. Art, 1982, C.A.A. Galleries, Chautauqua, NY, 1982, Huntsville Mus. Art, 1983, Tahir Gallery, New Orleans, 1983, Hunterdon Art Ctr., NJ, 1984, Editions Galleries, Melbourne, Australia, 1988, Van Stratten Gallery, Chgo., 1988, 6th Internat. Exhbn., Carnegie-Mellon U., Pa., 1988, Forum Gallery, Jamestown, NY, 1988, 5th Internat. Biennale Petite Format de Papier, Belgium, 1989, 4th Internat. Biennial Print Exhibit, Taipei Fine Arts Mus., People's Republic China, 1990, Interprint, Lviv '90, USSR, 1990, New Orleans Mus. Art, 1990, Internat. Print Triennale, Cracow, Poland, 1991, 15th Ann. Nat. Invitational Drawing Exhbn. Emporia State U., Kans., 1991, Haggar U. Gallery, U. Dallas, 1991, Directions in Bay Area Printmaking: Three Decades Palo Alto Cultural Ctr., 1992, Am. Prints: Last Half 20th Century, Jane Haslem Gallery, Washington, 1992, Wenniger Graphics, Boston, 1993, Eleonore Austerer Gallery, San Francisco, 1994, Triton Mus. Art, Santa Clara, 1994, Mobile Mus. Art, 1995, Huntsville (Ala.) Mus. Art, 1995, J.J. Brookings Gallery, San Francisco, 1996, 1997, Grisham Cornell Gallery, Decatur, Ala., 1996, St. Francis Festival of the Arts Invitational, San Francisco, 1996, The Vault Gallery, Sonora, 1997, 98, Heritage Bank Gallery, San Jose, 1998, Arches Paper "Printed on Paper" Competition (touring, 1st pl. winner), 1998, Kautz Internat. Vineyards Nat. Art Exhbn., Murphys Calif., 1998, Audubon Artists 56th Ann. Exhbn., NYC, 1998; represented in permanent collections San Francisco Mus. Modern Art, Achenbach Found. Graphic Arts, San Francisco, Phila. Mus. Art, New Orleans Mus. Art, Portland Mus. Art, Maine, The Libr. of Congress, Washington, Huntsville Mus. Art, Midwest Mus. Am. Art, Ind., Cracow Nat. Mus., Poland, Cabo Frio Mus., Brazil, Nat. Mus. Am. Art, Smithsonian Inst., Washington, actor: (movies) The Princess Diaries, 2000, Seven Swans, 2002, The Gentlman Don La Mancha, 2002, The Clinic, 2002, Raising Helen, 2003, Princess Diaries II, 2004; theatre: Wicked, Hudson Theatre Mainstage, LA, 2001, After life, Actors Forum, LA, 2002, Geography of a Horse Dreamer, Next Stage, LA, 2003, Rise Up, Hudson Mainstage Theatre, 2004, others; co-star: (TV series) Frasier, 2000—, George Lopez Show, 2002, Port Charles, 2003.; guest star (Chinese TV show) NY Blues, 2002. Recipient Kempshall Clark award Peoria Art Guild, 1981, Paul Lindsay Sample Meml. award 25th Chautauqua Nat. Exhbn. of Am. Art, 1982, 1st Ann. Creative Achievement award Calif. State Legislature/Arts Coun. San Mateo County, 1989. Mem. Am. Color Print Soc., Audubon Artists (Louis Lozowick Meml. award 1978, Silver medal of honor award 1991), Boston Printmakers (Ture Bengtz Meml. award 1987), Calif. Soc. Printmakers (mem. council 1979-81), Los Angeles Printmaking Soc., Phila. Print Club (Lessing J. Rosenwald prize 1979), Arts Council of San Mateo County, Ctrl. Sierra Arts Coun., Theta Chi. Democrat. Office: 6221 Cartwright Ave North Hollywood CA 91606-3801 E-mail: joeaprice@earthlink.net. *Personal philosophy: In being an artist, I do not wish to be just a "recorder" of my time, what I see, what I think. To me, the joy of art is in expressing the love of being an artist, for in loving without shame, without fear, and without doubt one transcends to the moment and speaks with integrity. For the rest of my life I wish to reflect on what life is, and to have the courage to create that which touches not only men's eyes, but their hearts and spirits. I seek the profound truth of what it is to be human and the universal truth of what is means to be creative in expressing the love of being.*

PRICE, JOHN ALEY, lawyer; b. Maryville, Mo., Oct. 7, 1947; s. Donald Leroy and Julia Catherine (Aley) P.; m. Deborah Diadra Gunter, Aug. 12, 1995; children: Theodore John, Joseph Andrew. BS, N.W. Mo. State U., 1969; JD, U. Kans., 1972. Bar: Kans. 1972, U.S. Dist. Ct. Kans. 1972, U.S. Ct. Appeals (10th cir.) 1972, Tex. 1984, U.S. Ct. Appeals (5th cir.) 1984, U.S. Supreme Ct. 1987; cert. civil trial law Tex. Bd. Legal Specialization, pro bono atty. Tex., 1992. Law clk. U.S. Dist. Ct. Kans., Wichita, 1972-74; from assoc. to ptnr. Weeks, Thomas and Lysaught, Kansas City, Kans., 1974-82; ptnr. Winstead, Sechrest & Minick, Dallas, 1982-96, litigation sect. coord., 1990-92, intellectual property sect. litigation coord., 1993-95; gen. counsel Travelhost Inc., Dallas, 1996—, Club Co., Inc., 1999-2001. Pres. Umansys, Inc., Dallas, 2000—; spl. prosecutor Leavenworth County Office Dist. Atty., 1970-71, Sedgwick County Office Dist. Atty., Wichita, Kans., 1971-72. Author: Our Boundless Self (A Call to Awake), 1992, A Gathering of Light: Eternal Wisdom for a Time of Transformation, 1993; co-author: Soular Reunion: Journey to the Beloved, 1998; editor (mag.) Academic Analyst, 1968-69; assoc. editor U. Kans. Law Rev., 1971-72, Dallas Bus. Jour.; contbr. articles to profl. jours. Co-dir. Douglas County Legal Aid Soc., Lawrence, Kans., 1971-72; co-pres. Northwood Hills PTA, Dallas, 1984, Westwood Jr. H.S. PTA, 1989-90; founder New Frontiers Found., 1993; co-founder Wings of Spirit Found., 1994, dir., v.p. 1994—. Recipient Tex. Super Lawyer, Law and Politics and Tex. Monthly Mag., 2003. Mem. ABA, Kans. Bar Assn. (mem. task force for penal reform; Pres.'s Outstanding Svc. award 1981), Tex. Bar Assn., Pro Bono Coll., State Bar Tex., World Bus. Acad., Inst. Noetic Scis., UN Assn. (human rights com. Dallas chpt. 1991-93, bd. dirs. 1991-93), Campaign for the Earth (chpt. coord. Global Report 1991-92, coord. govt. and polit. area 1991-92), Blue Key, Order of Coif, Phi Delta Phi, Sigma Tau Gamma (v.p. 1968-69). Mem. Unity Ch. Office: Travelhost Inc 10701 N Stemmons Fwy Dallas TX 75220-2419 Office Phone: 972-556-0541. Personal E-mail: japrice@travelhost.com. *We create our reality every moment of existence. Our only limitations are those we choose to accept.*

PRICE, JOHN EDWARD, religion educator; b. Chgo., Mar. 7, 1942; s. Edward Price and Carolyn Maxine Polachek; m. Julia Valeriyevna Shvartser; children: Larissa Marie, James Thomas, Elizabeth Suzanne, Victoria Ivana. BA, Univ. of St. Mary of the Lake, 1964, STB, 1966, STL, 1968. Lic. dir. religious edn. Tchr. Mother of God Sch., Waukegan, Ill., 1968-69; tchr., chmn. religion dept. Holy Trinity High Sch., Chgo., 1969-70; coord. religious edn. Transfiguration Ch., Wauconda, Ill., 1970-75; dir. religious edn. St. Athanasius Ch., Evanston, Ill., 1975-91, Ch. of St. Mary, Lake Forest, Ill., 1991—. Catechist resource person Archdiocese Office of Religious Edn., Chgo., 1977-80; field supr. Mundelein Coll. and Inst. Pastoral Studies, Chgo., 1979-80, 84; team mem. North Ctrl. Evaluation, Chgo., 1984; presenter, lectr. Archdiocese of Chgo., 1979, 80, 84, 85, mem. Dir. Religious Edn. Cert. Commn., 1997—. Author: (filmstrip) Learning Right and Wrong, 1978, (testing svc.) Religious Education Diagnostic Survey, 1983; contbr. articles to religious publs. Del. Ill. White House Conf. on Librs. and Info. Svcs., Springfield, 1978. Mem. Cath. Theol. Soc. Am., Religious Edn. Assn., Nat. Assn. Parish Coords. and Dirs., Chgo. Assn. Religious Educators (treas. 1979-82, Care award 1983). Avocations: religious art, fishing, scuba diving, bicycling, poetry. Home: 737 E Glendale Rd Libertyville IL 60048-3329 Office: St Mary's Religious Edn Ctr 185 E Illinois Rd Lake Forest IL 60045-1915 E-mail: dre@restmary.com.

PRICE, JOHN RANDOLPH, writer; b. Alice, Tex., Feb. 12, 1932; s. John Randolph and Eva Mae (Boney) P.; m. Janis Bryant Price, June 20, 1953; children: Susan Lynn, Leslie Anne. BS, U. Houston, 1957; PhD (hon.), Emerson Inst., 2001; DHL (hon.), Holmes Inst., 2003. Dir. advt. Gates Radio Corp., Quincy, Ill., 1957-62; v.p. Sander Rodkin, Ltd., Chgo., 1962-64; exec. v.p. Stewart, Price, Tomlin, Inc., Chgo., 1964-67; v.p. Goodwin, Dannenbaum, Littman & Wingfield, Inc., Houston, 1967-70; pres. O'Neill, Price, Anderson, Fouchard, Inc., Houston, 1970-74, John Price & Co., Houston, 1974-79, Arnan, Inc., Austin, 1979-81; chmn. bd. The Quartus Found. Inc., Boerne, Tex., 1981—. Author: The Superbeings, 1981, The Manifestation Process, 1983, The Planetary Commission, 1984, Practical Spirituality, 1985, With Wings as Eagles, 1987, The Abundance Book, 1987, Prayer, Principles & Power, 1987, A Spiritual Philosophy for the New World, 1990, Empowerment, 1992, The Angels Within Us, 1993, Angel Energy, 1995, Living a Life of Joy, 1997, The Success Book, 1998, The Wellness Book, 1998, The Meditation Book, 1998, The Love Book, 1998, The Jesus Code, 2000, The Alchemist's Handbook, 2000, Removing the Masks That Bind Us, 2001, Nothing Is Too Good to Be True, 2003. Staff sgt. USAF, 1952-56. Recipient Joseph S. Cullinan award U. Houston, 1956, Grand Prix Best Consumer Mag. Advt. award, 1970. Mem. Internat. New Thought Alliance (Humanitarian award 1992, Joseph Murphy award 1994). Achievements include organizer of first annual World Peace day on December 31, 1986. Office: The Quartus Found Inc PO Box 1768 Boerne TX 78006-6768 Office Phone: 830-249-3985.

PRICE, JOHN RICHARD, lawyer, law educator; b. Indpls., Nov. 28, 1934; s. Carl Lee and Agnes I. P.; m. Suzanne A. Leslie, June 22, 1963; children: John D., Steven V. BA with high honors, U. Fla., 1958; LL.B. with honors, NYU, 1961. Bar: Wash. 1977, U.S. Ct. Appeals (9th cir.), U.S. Dist. Ct. (we. dist.) Wash. Assoc. McCutchen, Doyle, Brown & Enersen, San Francisco, 1961-69; prof. law U. Wash., Seattle, 1969-97, dean, 1982-88; of counsel Perkins Coie, Seattle, 1976—. Author: Contemporary Estate Planning, 1983, Price on Contemporary Estate Planning, 1992, 2d edit., 2000, Conflicts, Confidentiality and Other Ethical Issues, 2000. Served with U.S. Army, 1953-55 Root-Tilden fellow NYU Sch. Law, 1958-61 Fellow Am. Coll. Trust and Estate Counsel (former regent); mem. ABA, Am. Law Inst., Order of Coif, Phi Beta Kappa. Congregationalist. Home: 3794 NE 97th St Seattle WA 98115-2564 Office: 1201 3rd Ave Ste 4800 Seattle WA 98101-3099 E-mail: jprice@perkinscole.com.

PRICE, JOHN ROY, JR., financial executive; b. N.Y.C., Dec. 20, 1938; s. John Roy and Pauline Bernice (Milnes) P.; m. Victoria Scott Pohle, Dec. 19, 1970 (div. 1982); 1 child, Matthew Roy; m. Marion Cobb Hardie, Oct. 1, 1988 (div. 1996); m. Svetlana Sergeyeva, July 11, 1999. BA, Grinnell Coll., 1960, Queens Coll., Oxford (Eng.) U., 1962, MA, 1965; JD, Harvard U., 1965. Assoc. Casey, Lane & Mittendorf, N.Y.C., 1965-67; v.p. Bedford-Stuyvesant D & S Corp., N.Y.C., 1967-68; spl. asst. to Pres. U.S., Washington, 1969-71; assoc. Donaldson, Lufkin & Jenrette, N.Y.C., 1971-72; v.p. Mfrs. Hanover Trust, N.Y.C., 1972-75, Mfrs. Hanover Corp., N.Y.C., 1975-80, sr. v.p. non-bank subs., 1980-83, sr. v.p., sec., 1983-87; mng. dir. Mfrs. Hanover Trust Co., 1987-88, Mfrs. Hanover Securities Corp., 1988-92; mng. dir. govt. affairs Chem. Bank, 1992-96, Chase Manhattan, 1996—. Bd. dirs. Am. Trust for Oxford, 1990-94; chmn. Bklyn. Acad. Music Cmty. Devel. Corp.; dir. Prin. Fin. Group (formerly Bankers Life Co.), Bankers Assn. for Fgn. Trade, 1990-97, pres., 1994-95, Nat. Fgn. Trade Coun., 1991—; pres. Am. for Oxford, 1987-99, chmn., 1999—. Nat. chmn. Ripon Soc., 1967-68; trustee Grinnell Coll., 1970—; bd. dirs. New Communities Corp., 1976-77; mem. exec. panel Chief of Naval Ops., 1972-79. Rhodes scholar; named Disting. Friend of Oxford, 2000. Mem. Council Fgn. Relations, Phi Beta Kappa. Clubs: Harvard (N.Y.C.). Home: 3144 Granite Rd Woodstock MD 21163-1004

PRICE, JOHNNIE ULMER, retired music educator; b. North, S.C., Jan. 8, 1929; d. John Shadrach and Mary Annie (Varn) Ulmer; m. Coker Nelson Price, Sr., June 21, 1951; children: Coker Nelson Jr., Joanne Price Glover, Donna Kay Price Peterson. BSc, Winthrop U., 1949; M in Music Edn., U. S.C., 1977. Cert. elem. and secondary music tchr. S.C. Music tchr. Whitmire (S.C.) Pub. Schs., 1949—51, Orangeburg (S.C.) Dist. 5 Schs., 1952—86; ret., 1986. Organist 1st Bapt. Ch., Orangeburg, 1955—57. Mem.: S.C. Music Educators Assn. (pres. choral divsn. 1980—82, v.p. 1982—84, mem. exec. bd. 1980—2004, editor state jour. 1986—97, ret. mems. chmn. 1997—2004, Hall of Fame 1998), Orangeburg Music Club (pres., state bd. dirs. 2000—04), Delta Kappa Gamma (pres. 1980—82, com. chmn. music 2000—04). Avocations: gardening, travel, genealogy, reading. Home: 6136 North Rd Orangeburg SC 29118

PRICE, JONATHAN G. geologist; b. Danville, Pa., Feb. 1, 1950; s. A. Barney and Flora (Best) P.; m. Elisabeth McKinley, June 3, 1972; children: Alexander D., Argenta M. BA in Geology and German, Lehigh U., 1972; MA, U. Calif., Berkeley, 1975, PhD, 1977. Cert. profl. geologist. Geologist Anaconda Copper Co., Yerington, Nev., 1974-75, U.S. Steel Corp., Salt Lake City, 1977, Corpus Christi, 1978-81; rsch. assoc. Bur. Econ. Geology, U. Tex., Austin, 1981-85, rsch. sci., 1984-88, program dir., 1987-88; dir. Tex. Mining & Mineral Resources Rsch. Inst., Austin, 1984-88; dir., state geologist Nev. Bur. Mines & Geology, U. Nev., Reno, 1988-92, 95—. Staff dir. Bd. on Earth Scis. & Resources Nat. Rsch. Coun., Washington, 1993-95; asst. prof. Bucknell U., Lewisburg, 1977-78; chair We. States Seismic Policy coun., 1998-2002. Author, editor: Igneous Geology of Trans-Pecos Texas, 1986. Vol. instr. CPR and first aid ARC, 1983-95, bd. dirs. Sierra Nev. chpt., 1991-92. German Acad. Exch. Svc. fellow U. Heidelberg, 1972-73; recipient Explorer award Am. Geol. Inst., 1995. Fellow Geol. Soc. Am., Soc. Econ. Geologists (nat. pres. 2003); mem. Am. Inst. Profl. Geologists (Nev. sect. pres. 1992, nat. pres. 1997, John T. Galey Sr. Meml. pub. Svc. award 1999), Assn. Am. State Geologists (pres. 2000-01), Mineral. Soc. Am., Phi Beta Kappa. Office: Nev Bur Mines & Geology UNR Ms 178 Reno NV 89557-0088 Office Phone: 775-784-6691 x126. Business E-Mail: jprice@unr.edu.

PRICE, JOSEPH HUBBARD, lawyer; b. Montgomery, Ala., Jan. 31, 1939; s. Aaron Joseph and Minnie Jule (Reynolds) P.; m. Cynthia Winant Ramsey, Sept. 14, 1963 (div. 1980); children: Victoria Reynolds, Ramsey Winant; m. Courtney McFadden, Apr. 25, 1980. AB, U. Ala., 1961; LLB, Harvard U., 1964; postgrad., London Sch. Econs., 1964-65. Bar: Ala. 1964, D.C. 1968. Law clk. to justice Hugo L. Black U.S. Supreme Ct., Washington, 1967-68; assoc. Leva, Hawes, Symington, Martin & Oppenheimer, Washington, 1968-71; v.p. Overseas Pvt. Investment Corp., Washington, 1971-73; ptnr. Leva, Hawes, et. al., Washington, 1973-83, Gibson, Dunn & Crutcher, Washington, 1983—. Mem. CARE Com. Washington; mem. adv. com. Hugo Black Meml. Libr., Ashland, Ala. Capt. U.S. Army, 1966-67, Vietnam. Decorated Bronze Star; Frank Knox Meml. fellow London Sch. Econs., 1964-65. Mem. ABA, Am. Soc. Internat. Law, Supreme Ct. Hist. Soc., Phi Beta Kappa, Met. Club. Home: 3104 Cathedral Ave NW Washington DC 20008-3419 Office: Gibson Dunn & Crutcher 1050 Connecticut Ave NW Ste 900 Washington DC 20036-5306

PRICE, JOSEPH MICHAEL, lawyer; b. St. Paul, Dec. 2, 1947; s. Leon and Rose (Kaufman) P.; m. Louise Rebecca Braunstein, Dec. 19, 1971; children: Lisa, Laurie, Julie. BA, U. Minn., 1969, JD, 1972. Bar: Minn. 1972, U.S. Dist. Ct. Minn. 1974. Ptnr. Faegre & Benson, Mpls., 1972—. Mem. Minn. Bar Assn., Hennepin County Bar Assn. Home: 4407 Country Club Rd Minneapolis MN 55424-1148 Office: Faegre & Benson 2200 Wells Fargo Ctr 90 S 7th St Ste 2200 Minneapolis MN 55402-3901 Office Phone: 612-766-8617. E-mail: Jprice@faegre.com.

PRICE, JOSEPH STERLING, retired air force officer; b. Rockville Centre, NY, June 2, 1954; s. Harold Lloyd and Lola Peele (Talton) P.; m. Karen Lee Peters, Oct. 14, 1978. BS in Indsl. Mgmt., Ga. Inst. Tech., 1976; MS in Logistics Mgmt., Air Force Inst. Tech., 1980. Quality control chemist Jesco Lubricants Co., Atlanta, 1976; commd. 2d lt. USAF, 1976, advanced through grades to lt. col., 1992—2002, ret., 2002; instr. Presdl. Classroom for Young Ams., 1998, cons., 2002—. Mem. Ga. Tech. Alumni Assn., Nat. Eagle Scout Assn. (life), Air Force Assn. (life), Nat. Def. Indsl. Assn. (life), Appalachian Trail Conf. (life). Avocations: hiking, history.

PRICE, KATHLEEN MCCORMICK, book editor, writer; b. Topeka, Kans., Dec. 25, 1932; d. Raymond Chesley and Kathleen (Shoffner) McCormick; m. William Faulkner Black, Aug. 25, 1956 (div. 1961); 1 child, Kathleen Serena; m. William Hillard Price, Aug. 13, 1976. BA, U. Colo., Denver, 1971. Book reviewer Denver Post, 1971-78; book editor San Diego Mag., 1978-92. Cons. editor St. John's Cathedral, Denver, 1985-95. Author: There's a Dactyl Under My Foot, 1986, The Lady and the Unicorn, 1994, From Vision to Vestment, 2001. Dir. Colo. Episcopal Vestment Guild. Fellow Phi Beta Kappa; mem. PEN, Denver County Club, La Garita Club. Episcopalian. Home: 27 Crestmoor Dr Denver CO 80220-5853

PRICE, LEONTYNE (MARY VIOLET LEONTYNE PRICE), retired concert and opera singer, soprano; b. Laurel, Miss., Feb. 10, 1927; d. James A. and Kate (Baker) Price; m. William Warfield, Aug. 31, 1952 (div. 1973). BA, Central State Coll., Wilberforce, Ohio, 1949, DMus, 1968; student, Juilliard Sch. Music, 1949-52; pupil, Florence Page Kimball; LHD, Dartmouth Coll., 1962, Fordham U., 1969, Yale U., 1979; MusD, Howard U., 1962; Dr. Humanities, Rust Coll., 1968. Singer: (Operas) (debut) in 4 Saints in 3 Acts, 1952, (appeared) Bess in Porgy and Bess, Vienna, Berlin, Paris, London, under auspices U.S. State Dept., N.Y.C. and U.S. tour, 1952—54; recitalist, soloist (symphonies) U.S., Can., Australia, Europe, 1954—, appeared concerts in India, 1956, 1964, soloist Hollywood Bowl, 1955—59, 1966, Berlin Festival, 1960, role as Mme. Lidoine in Dialogues des Carmelites, San Francisco Opera, 1957; singer: (Operas) NBC-TV, 1955—58, 1960, 1962, 1964, San Francisco Opera Co., 1957—59, 1960—61, 1963, 1965, 1967, 1968, 1971, as Aida at La Scala, 1957;: (Operas) Vienna Staatsoper, 1958, 1959—60, 1961, Berlin Opera, 1964, Rome Opera, 1966, 1968, (recital) Brussels Internat. Fair, auspices State Dept., 1958, Verona Opera Arena, 1958—59, Yugoslavia for, State Dept., 1958; rec. artist RCA-Victor, 1958—, appeared Covent Garden, London, 1958-59, 70, Chgo. Lyric Theatre, 1959, 60, 65, Oakland (Calif.) Symphony, 1980, soloist Salzburg Festival, 1959—63, appeared Tetro alla Scala, Milano, 1960-61, 63, 67, Met. Opera, N.Y.C., 1961-62, 64, 66, 75, 76, since resident mem., until 1985, soloist Salzburg Festival, 1950, 60, debut Teatre Dell'Opera, Rome, 1967, Teatro Colon, Buenos Aires, Argentina, 1969, Hamburg Opera, 1970, recordings A Christmas Offering with Karajani, God Bless America with Charles Gerhardt, Arias from Don Giovanni, Turandot, Aida, Emani, Messa di Requiem, Trovatore, Live at Ordway, The Prima Donna Collection, A Program of Song with D. Garvey, Right as the Rain with André Previn. Co-chmn. Rust Coll. Upward Thrust Campaign; trustee Internat. House.; hon. vice-chmn. U.S. com. UNESCO; Hon. bd. dirs. Campfire Girls. Decorated Order at Ment Italy; named Musician of Year, Mus. Am. mag., 1961; recipient Merit award for role of Tosca in NBC-TV Opera, Mademoiselle mag., 1955, 20 Grammy awards for classical vocal recs. Nat. Acad. Rec. Arts and Scis., citation YWCA, 1961. Spirit of Achievement award Albert Einstein Coll. Medicine, 1962, Presdl. medal of freedom, 1964, Springarn medal NAACP, 1965, Schwann Catalog award, 1968, Nat. Medal of Arts, 1985, Essence award, 1991, others. Fellow: Am. Acad. Arts and Sci.; mem.: AFTRA, Actors Equity Assn., Am. Guild Mus. Artists, Delta Sigma Theta, Sigma Alpha Iota. Inducted into Am. Classical Music Hall of Fame, 1998. Office: Price Enterprises 1133 Broadway Ste 920 New York NY 10010-7901*

PRICE, LEW PAXTON, writer, engineer, scientist; b. Takoma Park, Md., Dec. 19, 1938; s. Raymond Miller and Clarene Pearl (Morris) P.; m. Sherrie Darlene Sellers, June 25, 1960 (div. Apr. 1979); children: Terilyn Ann, Heather Rae, Crystal Alene. BS, U.S. Air Force Acad., Colorado Springs, Colo., 1960. Hon. Ho-O Ryu Bushido 6th Dan Master. Electronics engr. Pacific Telephone, Sacramento, Calif., 1965-66, engring. coord., bldgs., 1966-85; pres., design engr. Condor Aeroplane Works, Ltd., Sacramento, 1983-85; engring. coord. Tuttle Engring. and Constrn. Consultants, El Dorado Hills, Calif., 1989-92; scientist, flute design cons., writer, flutemaker Fair Oaks, Garden Valley, Calif., 1977—. Cons. flute design and physics. Author: The Cosmic Stradivarius, 1974, Aquarian Anastasis, 1975, The Music of Life, 1984, Dimensions in Astrology, 1986, Native North American Flutes, 1990, Secrets of the Flute (Math, Physics & Design), 1991, Creating & Using the Native American Love Flute, 1994, Creating & Using Grandfather's Flute, 1995, The Oldest Magic (Prehistory & Influence of Music), 1995, Creating & Using Older Native American Flutes, 1995, Creating & Using Smaller Native American Flutes, 1995, Creating & Using the Native American Concert Flute, 1996, More Secrets of the Flute, 1997, Creating and Using Larger Native American Flutes, 1998, Creating and Using the Largest Native American Flutes, 1998, Creating and Using Very Small Native American Flutes, 1998, Behind Light's Illusion (7-book series), 1999, 2000, 2001, Climbing on Course, 2003, (biography) When a Man is a Man, 2003; author, programmer: (computer program) Flute Design (Native American), 1996. Co-advisor Aviation Explorers, archery/space/sci. merit badge instr./examiner, Boy Scouts Am., North Highlands, Calif., 1968-70; panelist United Crusade, Sacramento, Calif., 1971; rifle/pistol/shotgun safety instr. NRA, Fair Oaks, Calif., 1970-72. Capt. USAF, 1960-65. Mem. No. Calif. Flute Circle (co-organizer 1996), Oreg. Native Am. Flute Circle (hon.). Avocations: flying, singing, flute playing, hiking, archery. Home and Office: PO Box 88 Garden Valley CA 95633-0088 Personal E-mail: lewprice@softcom.net.

PRICE, LIA SCOTT, writer; BA in Journalism, U. Calif., Santa Cruz, 1990. Writer Norris Theater, L.A., 2002—; prodr. Tritan-Northstar Entertainment, Hollywood, Calif., 2000—; screenwriter Act Full Time Hollywood, Hollywood, 2000—; author Pumpkin Pub., L.A., 1997—. Author: (novels) Ghostwriter, 2002, The Frog Asylum, 2001, (short stories) Without Wings, 2001, (novels) The Guardian, 2000; co-author: (book) Body and Blood, 1997, contbr. short story Without Wings The Spirit of Writing. Office: Pumpkin Pub PMB 335/POB 7000 Rolling Hills Estates CA 90274 Business E-Mail: princesslia@hotmail.com.

PRICE, MARIAN L. state legislator; b. Page, Nebr., Aug. 6, 1938; children: Mark Reed Price, Penni Lou Price Godemann, Randall Joseph Price, Ronald Noble Price. Student, Wesleyan U., 1955-56; grad., Bryan Meml. Hosp. Sch., 1959. RN, Nebr. With Bryan Meml. Hosp., 1959—63; co-owner family restaurants, Lincoln, Nebr., 1971—90; mem. Nebr. Legislature from 26th dist., Lincoln, 1998—. Bd. dirs. Home Health Svcs. for Independent Living, Inc., VITAL Inc. Mem. Lincoln Bd. Edn., 1985-98, pres., 1994-97, chair legis. subcom., 1997-98; chair Lancaster County Reorgn. Com., 1990-98; pres. Ednl. Svc. Unit No. 18, 1991-96; del. Nat. Sch. Bds. Assns. Fed. Rels. Network, 1989-98; mem. Bethany Christian Ch., Lincoln, past pres., mem. Christian women's fellowship, past ch. wedding coord.; past bd. dirs. Lincoln Cmty. Playhouse Guild. Mem. Bryan Meml. Sch. Nursing Alumnae Assn. (past bd. dirs.), Bethany Women's Club, Alpha Gamma Delta Alumnae Assn. (past bd. dirs.), Phi Sigma Alpha (past pres., bd. dirs.). Home: 6735 Lexington Cir Lincoln NE 68505-1338 Office: State Capitol Dist 26 PO Box 94604 Rm 1117 Lincoln NE 68509-4604

PRICE, MARILYN, lawyer; BS in Human Devel., Cornell U.; JD, Hofstra U. With Certilman Balin Adler & Hyman LLP, 1983, of counsel, 1993, ptnr., 1997—. Instr. Acad. Law, Nassau County Bar Assn.; vice chair adv. bd. Hofstra U. Named March of Dimes Woman of Distinction, 2001; named one of Top 50 Long Island Women, 2001. Mem.: Long Island Builders Inst., Cornell Alumni Ambs. Admissions Network (chairperson), Cornell Club Long Island (past pres., treas.). Office: Certilman Balin Adler & Hyman LLP 90 Merrick Ave East Meadow NY 11554

PRICE, MARY SUE SWEENEY, museum director; d. William Robert Sweeney; m. Clement A. Price, 1988. BA in English, Allegheny Coll., 1973; D.H.C. (hon.), Caldwell Coll. With textbook pub. co., N.Y.C.; supr. pub. rels. Newark Mus., 1975, dep. dir., 1990—93, dir., 1993—, with, 1995—. Past pres. ArtTable Inc.; v.p. ArtPrice NJ Inc.; bd. dirs. St. Vincent Acad., Newark Arts Coun. Mem.: Assn. Art Mus. Dirs., Am. Assn. Mus., NJ Assn. Mus. (bd. dirs.). Office: Newark Mus 49 Washington St Newark NJ 07102 Office Phone: 973-596-6550.

PRICE, MICHAEL F. money management executive; b. 1952; div., 3 sons. Graduate, U. Okla., 1975. Rsch. asst., mgr., to CEO Heine Securities, Short Hills, N.J., 1975-97; CEO Franklin Mutual Advs. Inc. (formerly Heine Securities), Short Hills, N.J., 1997—. Pres., chmn. bd. dirs. Franklin Mutual Series Fund Inc. Office: Franklin Mutual Advisers Inc 51 John F Kennedy Pkwy Short Hills NJ 07078-2702

PRICE, MICHAEL HOWARD, journalist, critic, composer, cartoonist, theatrical operator; b. Amarillo, Tex., Sept. 14, 1947; s. John Andrew and Thelma Adeline (Wilson) P.; m. Christina Renteria, Aug. 31, 1980. BA in Journalism, West Tex. State U., 1970. Edn. writer Amarillo Globe-News, 1968-74, fin. editor, 1974-76, city editor, 1976-77; adminstr. Amarillo Coll., 1977-80; bur. chief Ft. Worth Star-Telegram, 1980-83, features editor, 1983-85, film critic, 1985-98; dir. motion picture programming Sundance Sq. Entertainment Dist., Ft. Worth, 1998—2002; critic-at-large Ft. Worth Bus. Press, 2002—. Cons. journalism West Tex. State U., Canyon, 1977-90, Tex. Tech U., Lubbock, 1982-85; dirs. The Harvey Awards comic-book profls. awards, 1990—; syndicated columnist N.Y. Times News Svc., 1990-98; critic-in-residence Sta. KRLD Newsradio, Dallas-Ft. Worth, 1998—; columnist Fangoria mag., 2002—. Author: (CD-ROMs) A Century of Fantastic Cinema, 1995, Silver Screen Sensations, 1996; (albums) Cognitive Dissonance, 1994, The Last Temptation of Price, 1995, R. Crumb—The Musical, 1995, Swingmasters Revue, 1995, Claus & Effect, 1996, Diddy Wah Diddy, 1997, Big Hoedown Tonight!, 1999, From Hell to Texas, 1999, Arghlebargle, 2001; (books) Forgotten Horrors: The Definitive Edition, 1999, Forgotten Horrors II, 2001, Hollywood and the Piano, 2001, Spawn of Skull Island, 2002, Human Monsters in the Movies, 1994, Krime Duzzin't Pay, 1995, The Guitar in Jazz, 1996, Stitches, 1996, Frights Genuine & Fancied, 1996; (novels) The Prowler, 1989, Carnival of Souls, 1991, Holiday for Screams, 1992, Lon Chaney, Jr.: A Critical Biography, 1997; co-author: The Big Book of Biker Flicks, 2002; screen actor: Ramming Speed, 1997, Southern Fried Homicide, 1998, Beauty & the Beasts, 1998, Vincent Price: A Critical Biography, 1998, It's Christmastime at the Movies, 1998. Creative dir. Tex. Gridiron Show, Fort Worth, 1984-85, 92-93; pres. Ft. Worth Film Festival, Inc., 1997—. Grad. fellow in journalism U. Mo., 1975; inducted into Tex. Tornados Blues Hall of Fame, 1995. Mem. ASCAP, Soc. Profl. Journalists (bd. dirs. 1992-94), Soc. Film Critics. Office: Sundance Sq Management 420 Throckmorton St Ste 950 Fort Worth TX 76102-3726 E-mail: mprice@sundancesquare.com. *People who believe that writing is a glamour gig often ask, "How do you become a writer?" as if in search of some magical formula. The only answer is: "WRITE." For whatever purpose and however large or small a readership: WRITE.*

PRICE, MITCHELL R. pediatric surgeon; MD, U. Chgo., 1986. Intern in surgery NYU Sch. of Medicine, N.Y.C., 1986—87, resident in surgery, 1987—88, 1991—94; Extracorporeal Membrane Oxygenation fellow Columbia Babies Hosp., N.Y.C., 1988—91; fellow pediatric surgery U. Colo. Denver Children's Hosp., 1994—96; asst. prof. divsn. pediat. surgery UMDNJ-Robert Wood Johnson Med. Sch., Brunswick, NJ, 1996—. Office: Robert Wood Johnson Med Sch 1 Robert Wood Johnson Pl New Brunswick NJ 08903-0019 Office Phone: 732-235-7821.

PRICE, NANCY, education educator, writer; b. Sioux Falls, SD, Mar. 16, 1925; d. Malcolm Poyer and Mary Day Price; m. Howard John Thompson, May 2, 1945 (div. 1987); children: Catherine, John, David. BA, Cornell Coll., 1942—46; MA, U. No. Iowa, 1964; grad study, U. Iowa, 1964. Prof. English U. No. Iowa, 1979—. Resident Karolyi Found., France, 1975, Rockefeller Found., Italy, 1982, Tyrone Guthrie Ctr., Ireland, 1983. Author: (book) A Natural Death, 1973, An Accomplished Woman, 1978, Sleeping with the Enemy, 1987, Night Woman, 1992, No One Knows, 2004, 3 novels translated to French. Recipient Nat. Endowment for the Arts award, 1978, Nat. Endowment for the Arts/Pen Story Competitions, 1983—85. Mem.: Aus. Guild. Avocation: book illustration. Office: U No Iowa Dept English 117 Baker Hall Cedar Falls IA 50614

PRICE, NANCY D. retired banker, writer; b. Abington, Pa., Apr. 6, 1934; d. Harry S. Drum and Annette Grant Krewson; m. Robert A. Price, Aug. 27, 1955; children: Elizabeth Gorman, Robert K., William Daniel, Barbara Camusi, James M. BA, Mount Holyoke Coll., 1955. Svc. mgr. Core States Bank, Phila., 1975—98; ret. Author: Living with Robbie, 2003. Mem.: Nat. Family Assn. for Deaf/Blind, ARC Montgomery County, Parents' Group ALTEC. Republican. Roman Catholic. Avocations: reading, bridge, line dancing. Home: 2718 Hazel Ave North Hills PA 19038

PRICE, NELSON (JOHN NELSON PRICE), author, journalist; b. Augusta, Ga., May 7, 1957; s. John Paul and Joy Gertrude (Scheck) P. BA in Journalism and Psychology, Ind. U., 1978. City hall reporter Lawrence (Kans.) Journal-World, 1978-79; fed. cts. reporter, social issues writer Fort Wayne (Ind.) Journal-Gazette, 1979-80; edn. writer Indpls. News, 1981-85; columnist, feature writer Indpls. Star-News, 1985—2002. Bd. dirs. The Sagamore, Indpls. Author: Indiana Legends: Famous Hoosiers from Johnny Appleseed to David Letterman, 1997, Indianapolis: Leading the Way, 2000, Legendary Hoosiers: Famous Folks from the State of Indiana, 2001, Indianapolis Then and Now, 2004; contbr. articles to profl. jours., chapters to books. Recipient Sagamore of the Wabash award Gov. Ind., 1995, 2002, Martin Luther King Jr. award Indpls. Edn. Assn., 1986, Best Sports Writing award Hoosier State Press Assn., 1994, Best Column award, 1994, Best Feature Story award, 1994, Best Personality Profile award, 1994. Mem. Soc. Profl. Journalists (awards), Mental Health Assn. Marion County (awards). Avocations: swimming, theater, travel, olympic sports.

PRICE, NICK, professional golfer; b. Durban, South Africa, Jan. 28, 1957; m. Sue Price; children: Gregory, Robyn Frances, Kimberly. Profl. golfer PGA, 1977—. Winner Asseng Invitational, 1979, Canon European Masters, 1980, Italian Open, 1981, South African Masters, Vaals Reef Open, 1982, World Series of Golf, 1983, Trophee Lancome, 1985, ICL Internat. Open, West End South Australian Open, 1989, GTE Byron Nelson Golf Classic, 1991, Canadian Open, Air New Zealand/Shell Open, 1992, PGA Championship, 1992, 1994, H.E.B. Tex. Open, The Players Championship, 1993, Canon Greater Hartford Open, Sprint Western Open, Fed. Express St. Jude Classic, HondaClassic, 1994, Southwestern Bell Colonial, Motorola Western Open, Bell Canadian Open, Alfred Dunhill Challenge Hassan II Golf Trophy, Zimbabwe Open, British Open, 1994, MCI Classic, 1997, Dimension Data Pro-Am, 1997, 97, Suntory Open, 1999; 3rd PGA Tour Money Leader, 1992, PGA Tour Money Leader, 1993, 10 USPGA Tour Victories, 26 World Wide Victories; recipient Vardon Trophy, 1993; named Player of Yr., 1993; recipient, Payne Stewart award, 2002; ASAP/Jim Murray award, 2002; named to World Golf Hall of Fame, 2003. Achievements include holding PGA Tournament record for lowest score (269), 1994.

PRICE, PAUL BUFORD, physicist, researcher; b. Memphis, Nov. 8, 1932; s. Paul Buford and Eva (Dupuy) P.; m. JoAnn Margaret Baum, June 28, 1958; children— Paul Buford III, Heather Alynn, Pamela Margaret, Alison Gaynor. BS summa cum laude, Davidson Coll., 1954, DSc, 1973; MS, U. Va., 1956, PhD, 1958. Fulbright scholar U. (Eng.) Bristol, 1958-59; NSF postdoctoral fellow Cambridge (Eng.) U., 1959-60; physicist R&D Ctr., GE, Schenectady, 1960—69; prof. physics U. Calif., Berkeley, 1969—, Miller rsch. prof., 1972—73, chmn. dept. physics, 1987—91, McAdams prof. physics, 1990—92, dean phys. scis., 1992—2001, dir. Space Scis. Lab., 1979—85, prof., 2002—. Vis. com. Bartol Rsch. Inst., 1991-94; adv. bd. Indian Inst. Astrophysics, Bangalore, 1993-95; cons. to lunar sample analysis planning team NASA; space sci. bd. Nat. Acad. Scis.; adj. prof. physics Rensselaer Poly. Inst., 1967-68; vis. prof. Tata Inst. Fundamental Rsch., Bombay, 1965-66, U. Rome, 1983, 92; sci. assoc. Ctr. d'Etude Rsch. Nuclear, 1984; mem. polar rsch. bd. NAS; rschr. in space and astrophycs, nuclear physics; mem. U.S. Ice Core Working Group, 2002—. Author: (with others) Nuclear Tracks in Solids; Contbr. (with others) articles to profl. jours. Regional dir. Calif. Alliance for Minority Participation, 1993—. Recipient Disting. Svc. award Am. Nuclear Soc., 1964, Indsl. Rsch. awards, 1964, 65, E.O. Lawrence Meml. award AEC, 1971, medal for exceptional sci. achievement NASA, 1973; Sci. Symposium in honor of 65th birthday, Aug 23-24, 1997, Berkeley Leadership and Rsch. Distinction citation, 2002; John Simon Guggenheim fellow, 1976-77. Fellow: Am. Geophys. Union, Am. Phys. Soc., Indian Inst. Astrophysics (hon.); mem.: NAS (chmn. geophysics sect. 1981—84, sec. class phys.-math. scis. 1985—88, chmn. 1988—91), Bohemian Club. Office Phone: 510-642-4982. Business E-Mail: bprice@uclink4.berkeley.edu.

PRICE, PETER WILFRID, ecology educator, researcher; b. London, Apr. 17, 1938; arrived in U.S., 1966; BSc with honors, U. Wales, Bangor, 1958-62; MSc, U. New Brunswick, Fredericton, 1964; PhD, Cornell U., 1970. Asst. prof. U. Ill., Urbana, 1971-75, assoc. prof., 1975-79; research ecologist Mus. No. Ariz., Flagstaff, 1979-80; assoc. prof. No. Ariz. U., 1980-85, prof. ecology, 1985-94, Regents' prof., 1994—2002, Regents' prof. emeritus, 2002—. Author: Evolutionary Biology of Parasites, 1980, Biological Evolution, 1996, Insect Ecology, 3d edit., 1997, Macroevolutionary Theory on Macroecological Patterns, 2003; editor: Evolutionary Strategies of Parasitic Insects, 1975, A New Ecology, 1984, Plant-Animal Interactions, 1991, Effects of Resource Distribution on Plant-Animal Interactions, 1992, The Ecology and Evolution of Gall-Forming Insects, 1994, Population Dynamics, 1995, Population Dynamics: New Approaches and Synthesis, 1995. Guggenheim fellow, 1977—78, Fulbright Sr. scholar, 1993—94. Fellow: NSF (panel mem. 1978—81, 1991—93), Entomol. Soc. Am. (Founders award 1993), Brit. Ecol. Soc., Ecol. Soc. Am. (bd. editors 1973—76), Royal Entomol. Soc. (hon.). Office: No Ariz U PO Box 5640 Flagstaff AZ 86011-5640

PRICE, R. ARLEN, psychology and psychiatry educator; Student, Ga. State U., 1962-65, BS in Psychology, 1972, MA in Social Psychology, 1974; MA in Biol. Psychology, U. Colo., 1977, PhD in Psychology, 1980. Postdoctoral fellow genetics Stanford (Calif.) U., 1980-82, Yale U., 1982-83; prof. psychology and psychiatry U. Pa. Health Sys., Phila., dir. Behavioral Genetics Lab. Contbr. articles to profl. jours. Achievements include research on identifying and characterizing human genes for complex traits, particulary obesity and related traits. Office: Ctr for Neurobiology & Behavior 135B Clinical Rsch Bldg 415 Curie Blvd Philadelphia PA 19104-4218 Fax: 215-573-2041. E-mail: arlen@bgl.psycha.upenn.edu.

PRICE, REYNOLDS, novelist, poet, playwright, essayist, educator; b. Macon, N.C., Feb. 1, 1933; s. William Solomon and Elizabeth (Rodwell) P. AB summa cum laude (Angier Duke scholar), Duke, 1955; BLitt (Rhodes scholar), Merton Coll., Oxford U., Eng., 1958; LittD, St. Andrews Presbyn. Coll., 1978, Wake Forest U., 1979, Washington and Lee U., 1991, Davidson Coll., 1992; LittD, Elon Coll., U. N.C., 2003. Mem. faculty English Duke U., 1958—; asst. prof., 1961-68; assoc. prof., 1968-72; prof., 1972-77; James B. Duke prof., 1977—; acting chmn., 1983; writer in residence U. N.C., Chapel Hill, 1965, U. Kans., 1967, 69, 80, U.N.C., Greensboro, 1971; Glasgow prof. Washington and Lee U., 1971; faculty Salzburg Seminar, 1977. Author: A Long and Happy Life, 1962, The Names and Faces of Heroes, 1963, A Generous Man, 1966, Love and Work, 1968, Permanent Errors, 1970, Things Themselves, 1972, The Surface of Earth, 1975, Early Dark, 1977, A Palpable God, 1978, The Source of Light, 1981, Vital Provisions, 1982, Private Contentment, 1984, Kate Vaiden, 1986, The Laws of Ice, 1986, A Common Room, 1987, Good Hearts, 1988, Clear Pictures, 1989, The Tongues of Angels, 1990, The Use of Fire, 1990, New Music, 1990, The Foreseeable Future, 1991, Conversations with Reynolds Price, 1991, Blue Calhoun, 1992, Full Moon, 1993, The Collected Stories, 1993, A Whole New Life, 1994, The Promise of Rest, 1995, Three Gospels, 1996, The Collected Poems, 1997, Roxanna Slade, 1998, Learning a Trade, 1998, Letter to a Man in the Fire, 1999, A Perfect Friend, 2000, Feasting the Heart, 2000, Noble Norfleet, 2002. A Serious Way of Wondering, 2003, Recipient William Faulkner Found. award notable 1st novel, 1962, Sir Walter Raleigh award, 1962, 76, 81, 84, 86, award Nat. Assn. Ind. Schs., 1964, Roanoke-Chowan Poetry award, 1982; Guggenheim fellow, 1964-65; fellow Nat. Endowment for Arts, 1967-68, lit. adv. panel, 1973-76, chmn., 1976; recipient Nat. Inst. Arts and Letters award, 1971, Bellamann Found. award, 1972, Lillian Smith award, 1976, N.C. award, 1977, Nat. Book Critics Circle award, 1986, Elmer H. Bobst award, 1988, R. Hunt Parker award N.C. Lit. and Hist. Soc., 1991, Northcarolinana award, 1999. Mem. Am. Acad. Arts and Scis., Am. Acad. Arts and Letters, Phi Beta Kappa, Phi Delta Theta. Home: PO Box 99014 Durham NC 27708-9014 Office: care Harriet Wasserman Lit Agy Inc 137 E 36th St New York NY 10016-3528

PRICE, ROBERT, media and communications executive, investment banker, lawyer; b. NYC, Aug. 27, 1932; s. Solomon and Frances (Berger) P.; m. Margery Beth Wiener, Dec. 18, 1955 (div.); children: Eileen Marcia, Steven. AB, NYU, 1953; LLD, Columbia U., 1958. Bar: N.Y. 1958, U.S. Dist. Ct. 1958, U.S. Ct. Appeals 1958, U.S. Supreme Ct 1958, ICC 1958, FCC 1958, IRS 1958. With R.H. Macy & Co., Inc., 1955-58; practiced in N.Y.C., 1958—; law clk. to judge U.S. Dist. Ct. (so. dist.) N.Y., 1958-59; asst. U.S. atty. So. Dist. N.Y., 1959-60; ptnr. Kupferman & Price, 1960-65; dep. mayor N.Y.C., 1965-66; exec. v.p., dir. Dreyfus Corp., N.Y.C., 1966-69; v.p., investment officer Dreyfus Fund, until 1969; gen. ptnr. Lazard, Freres & Co., 1972-82; pres. N.Y. Law Jour., Nat. Law Jour.; pres., treas., dir. Price Comm. Corp., 1979—; chmn., pres., dir. PriCellular Corp., 1988-95, pres., dir. TLM Corp., 1989—2000. Mem. adv. com. Bankers Trust Co. N.Y.; dir. Holly Sugar Corp., Lane Bryant, Inc., Graphic Scanning Corp.; chmn. N.Y.C. Port Authority Negotiating Com. for World Trade Ctr., 1965-66; spl. counsel N.Y. State Joint Legis. Com. on Ct. Reorgn.; asst. counsel N.Y. State Joint Legis. Com. on N.Y. Banking Laws; mem. The N.Y. State Mcpl. Assistance Corp., 1996-2000; commr. N.Y. State Commn. of Investigations, N.Y.C., 2000—. Contbr. articles to profl. publs. Trustee CUNY, 1996-98; chmn. govt. and civil svc. divsn. United Jewish Appeal Greater N.Y., 1966; co-chmn. met. N.Y. blood drive ARC, 1966; campaign mgr. John V. Lindsay, Campaigns for Congressman, N.Y.C., 1958, 64, for Nelson A. Rockefeller Oreg. Rep. presdl. primary campaign, 1964, Lindsay campaign for mayor, N.Y.C., 1965; del. N.Y. Rep. State Conv., 1962, 66; del. Rep. Nat. Conv., 1988, 92, 96; lectr. Rep. Nat. Com., 1966; bd. dirs. Am. Friends Hebrew U.; past trustee Columbia U. Sch. Pharm. Scis. With U.S. Army, 1953-55. Recipient Yeshiva U. Heritage award, Pub. Svc. award Queens Catholic War Vets. Mem. ABA, FCC Bar Assn., Assn. Bar City N.Y., N.Y. State Dist. Attys. Assn., Coun. Fgn. Rels., Columbia Law Sch. Alumni Assn. (dir.), Scribes, Tau Kappa Alpha. Home: 25 E 86th St New York NY 10028-0553 Office: Price Communications Corp 45 Rockefeller Plz Ste 3200 New York NY 10111-0100 Office Phone: 212-757-5600.

PRICE, ROBERT DEMILLE, lawyer; b. N.Y.C., Oct. 11, 1915; s. Willard DeMille Price and Eugenia Reeve; m. Newell Potter, Aug. 15, 1940 (div. May 1946); 1 child, Jonathan; m. Ruth Bentley, July 5, 1946; children: Katharine, Susannah, Rebecca. AB in Econs. with honors, Cornell U., 1936; JD, Harvard U., 1940; MBA, Clark U., 1973. Bar: Mass. 1940, U.S. Dist. Ct. Mass. 1941, U.S. Ct. Appeals (1st cir.) 1976, U.S. Tax Ct. 1977, U.S. Supreme Ct. 1978. Assoc. Ropes & Gray, Boston, 1940-43, 1946-50; ptnr. Vaughan, Esty, Crotty & Mason, Worcester, Mass., 1950-53, Sibley, Blair & Mountain, Worcester, 1953-70, Corbin, Sarapas, Madaus & Arakelian, Worcester, 1970-73, Price & Madaus, Worcester, 1973-87; pres. Robert D. Price, PC, Holden, Mass., 1987—. Dir. Appian Way Pizza, Ltd., Worcester, 1951-61, Food Specialties, Inc., Worcester, 1951-61, James Monroe Wire and Cable Co., S. Lancaster, Mass., 1973—; mem. Fin. Com., Holden, 1989-95, conservation com., 1999-2003. Moderator (TV series) Am. Bar Assn. Jr. Bar Assn., 1947-50. Bd. dirs. Friends Gale Free Librs., Inc., Holden, 1988—; mem. adv. bd. Met. Dist. Commn., 1990—96; pres. Humanist Chaplaincy at Harvard, 1995—; bd. dirs., sec. Humanist Assn. Mass., 1979—, Am. Humanist Assn., 1991—94; trustee AHA Humanist Found., 1999—2003. Lt. USNR, 1943—50. Mem. Mass. Bar Assn., Worcester County Bar Assn., Worcester Club (dir. 1953-56), Boston Athenaeum (propr. 1949—). Avocations: museum and art shows, photography, alpine climbing, sailing. Office: 11 Malden St Holden MA 01520-1826

PRICE, ROBERT E. manufacturing executive; b. 1942; BA, Pomona Coll., 1964. V.p. Fed-Mart Corp., 1964-75; pres., chief exec. officer Price Corp., San Diego, 1976-89; pres., chmn. bd., chief exec. officer Price Enterprises, San Diego, 1989-91, chmn. bd., chief exec. officer, 1991—, also bd. dirs. Office: Excel Legacy Corp 17140 Bernardo Ctr Dr San Diego CA 92128

PRICE, ROBERT EBEN, judge; b. Waco, Tex., Jan. 13, 1931; s. Robert Eben and Mary Hamilton (Barnett) P.; m. Ann Hodges, June 4, 1954; children— Eben, Mary, Ann, Emily. BA, So. Methodist U., 1952, JD, 1954, LL.M., 1972; postgrad., Air War Coll., 1976. Bar: Tex. 1954, U.S. Supreme Ct., U.S. Ct. Mil. Appeals, U.S. Ct. Claims, U.S. Dist. Ct. (no. dist.) Tex. 1954. Mem. firm Taylor, Mizell, Price, Corrigan & Smith, Dallas, 1956-86; judge Dallas County Probate Ct. No. 2, 1986—. Lectr. continuing legal edn. program U. Houston Law Found., 1993—; lectr. law So. Meth. U. Law Sch., 1973-74, faculty paralegal cert. program Sch. Continuing Edn., 1987-89; lectr. practice skills program State Bar Tex., 1974-78. Editor-in-chief: Southwestern Law Jour., 1953-54. Trustee and sec. St. Michael and All Angels Found., 1984-88; bd. dirs. Downtown Ministry, Diocese of Dallas Episcopal, 1986-88; chmn. legis. and legal awareness subcom., vice chmn. Tex. Gov.'s Com. on Employment of Handicapped, 1978-82. Served as legal officer USAF, 1954-56; col. JAGC Res. ret. Fellow: Tex. Bar Found., Am. Coll. Trust and Estate Counsel; mem.: ABA (nat. conf. spl. ct. judges com. on probate and surrogates cts. 1992—), Tex. Coll. Probate Judges (mem. faculty), State Bar Tex. (lectr. profl. devel. program 1988—), Dallas Bar Assn., Coll. State Bar Tex., Nat. Coll. Probate Judges, Phi Delta Theta, Phi Eta Sigma, Phi Alpha Delta. Episcopalian. Home: 4300 Arcady Ave Dallas TX 75205-3704 Office: Probate Ct 2 ste 211 509 Main St Dallas TX 75202-3508

PRICE, ROBERT IRA, coast guard officer; b. N.Y.C., Sept. 22, 1921; s. Alfred and Mary Edna (Schweitzer) P.; m. Virginia Louise Miller, June 20, 1946; children: Andrea Jean, Keven Virginia. BBA, CCNY, 1942; BS, U.S. Coast Guard Acad., 1945; postgrad., M.I.T., 1950-53. Registered profl. engr., D.C. Commd. ensign U.S. Coast Guard, 1945, advanced through grades to vice adm., 1978; asst. chief Mcht. Marine Tech. Div., Washington, 1965-67; chief planning staff Office Mcht. Marine Safety, 1967-71; capt. Port of Phila., 1971-73; chief Office Marine Environ. Washington, 1974-76; comdr. 11th Coast Guard Dist. Long Beach, Calif., 1976-78; comdr. Atlantic Area and 3d Coast Guard Dist. N.Y.C., 1978-81; ret., 1981; sr. v.p. J.J. Henry Co. (marine engrs.), N.Y.C., 1981-86; maritime cons., 1986—. Prin. U.S . negotiator to tech. programs Intergovtl. Maritime Consultative Orgn., UN, 1962-71 Contbg. author: Ship Design and Construction, 1980; Contbr. articles to profl. jours. Decorated D.S.M. with gold star, Legion of Merit with gold star, Meritorious Service medal with gold star, Coast Guard Commendation medal. Fellow Royal Instn. Naval Architects, Soc. Naval Architects (Land medalist 1982); mem. Sigma Xi. Clubs: Propeller, Army Navy, N.Y. Yacht.

PRICE, ROBERT J, corporate financial executive; BS, Pa. State U. CPA. Former audit ptnr. Price Waterhouse; various positions Aetna Inc., 1989—2000, sr. v.p., CFO, 1998—2000; pres., CEO CitiInsurance, 2000—01; sr. v.p., controller The Hartford Fin. Svcs. Group, Inc., 2002—. Bd. mem. Greater Hartford Arts Coun.; Bushnell Park Carousel Soc. Mem.: Conn. Soc. of Cert. Pub. Accountants, Am. Inst. Office: Hartford Fin Svcs Group Hartford Plaza 690 Asylum Ave Hartford CT 06115

PRICE, ROBERT OTIS, former mayor; b. Abilene, Kans., Jan. 4, 1932; s. Iru Paul and Irene Isabel (Parrish) P.; m. Dorothy Faye Price, Jan. 26, 1951 (dec. 1996); m. Sondra Boyd, Mar. 28, 1997; children: Fred Dennis, Donald Eugene. BA, U. Redlands, 1978. Patrolman, sgt., lt., capt. Bakersfield Police Dept., 1956-73, chief police, 1973-88; cons., troubleshooter, various cities, 1988-92; mayor City of Bakersfield, 1993—2001. Pres. Secret Witness Bd.,

1980-83. Mem. Calif. Coun. on Criminal Justice, Sacramento, 1983-93; chmn. State Adv. Group on Juvenile Justice, Sacramento, 1988-93, Citizens Adv. Com., Fresno, Calif., 1993—, Youth Devel. Coalition, Bakersfield, 1993—, Econ. Devel. Discussion Group, Bakersfield, 1993—; chmn. western region Nat. Coalition Juvenile Justice and Delinquency Prevention, 1988-93; founder, cons. Youth Adv. Coun., Bakersfield, 1993—; founder Bakersfield Action Team, 1994. Sgt. U.S. Army, 1952-54. Recipient John W. Doubenmier award Am. Soc. Pub. Admins., 1978, Califf Morris award Calif. Probation, Parole and Corrections Officers Assn., 1982. Mem. Internat. Assn. Chiefs Police, Calif. Police Chiefs Assn., Calif. Peace Officers Assn., Calif. Council Criminal Justice, Kern County Police Chiefs Assn. (pres. 1979), Kern County Law Enforcement Admin. Assn. (pres. 1974). Republican. Avocations: photography, fishing, travel.

PRICE, ROBERT STANLEY, lawyer; b. Phila., Jan. 21, 1937; s. Benjamin and Estelle B. (Muchnick) P.; m. Emilie W. Kirschbaum, June 27, 1965 (dec. Mar. 1998); children: Louise P. Kelly, Marianna R. BA, Kenyon Coll., 1958; LLB, Yale U., 1961. Bar: Pa. 1963, U.S. Dist. Ct. (ea. dist.) Pa. 1963, U.S. Ct. Appeals (3d cir.) 1963, N.Y. 1993. Assoc. Dechert, Price & Rhoads, Phila., 1961-63; asst tax atty. Smith, Kline & French, Phila., 1963-67; tax atty. Pa. Ctrl. Transp. Co., Phila., 1967-70; tax counsel IU Internat., Phila., 1970-72; ptnr. Townsend, Elliott & Munson, Phila., 1972-76, Pepper, Hamilton & Scheetz, Phila., 1977-86, Saul, Ewing, Remick & Saul, Phila., 1986-93; spl. cons. Saul, Ewing, Remick & Saul (now Saul Ewing LLP), Phila., 1994—2001. Ind. tax cons. Fischbein-Badillo-Wagner-Harding, N.Y.C., 1998—2001, Mintz, Levin, Cohn, Ferris, Glovsky and Popeo, P.C., N.Y.C., 2001—. Author: ABCs of Industrial Development Bonds, 1981, 5th edit., 1990; contbr. articles to profl. jours. Pres. Samuel Eells Lit. and Ednl. Found., 1980—. Served with U.S. Army, 1961—62. Mem. ABA (tax exempt fin. com.), Pa. Bar, Phila. Bar Assn., N.Y. Bar, Racquet Club Phila. (v.p. 1987-88), Alpha Delta Phi (pres. 1975-78). Office: 3800 Centre Sq W Philadelphia PA 19102-2186 E-mail: rpricedj@earthlink.com.

PRICE, RUTHE GEIER, actress, writer, educator; b. New Brunswick, N.J., Dec. 16, 1922; d. Morris Payenson and Anne (Payenson) Dorfman; m. Arnold Geier, July 1, 1951 (div. Nov. 1976); children: Donald Lloyd, Michael Jay; m. Nathaniel Wolfred Price, Oct. 9, 1988 (dec. Nov. 2003). Student, State Tchrs. Coll., Trenton, N.J., 1941-43; BS in Edn., NYU, 1945, MA in Theater, 1946. Dir. Parker Playhouse, Plainfield, N.J., 1947, Newark Acad. Dramtic Art, 1948; asst. dir., theater chair Essex Conservatory, Newark, 1949-51; soc. editor Edison Jour., Miami, Fla., 1954; comptroller Nat. Ins. Cons., Miami, 1974-76; actress Miami, 1977—; mng.editor Starbooks Inc., 1999—. Drama coach, Fla., 1990—; media cons., Fla., 1983—. Appeared in films including Let It Ride, Making Mr. Right, Italian Taxi Driver, The Bellboy, Hardly Working, Last Plane Out; TV appearances include Miami Sands, Miami Vice, The Sunset Gang; plays include Save Me a Place at Forest Lawn, Pocket Watch, Ladies in Retirement, Hamlet, You Can't Take it With You, The Male Animal, Blithe Spirit, Lady Precious Stream, As You Like It, Guest in the House, Godperson, Forty Carats, Medea, Skin of Our Teeth, Romeo and Juliet, A Choice to Make; hostess TV talk show Ruthe Geier Presents; hostess radio show Spotlight on Stars; Author: (book) Acting in On-Camera Commercials, 2001; contbr. poetry to Harper's mag. Recipient CLIO award, 1982, Emmy award, 1982, Addy award, 1982. Mem. AFTRA (columnist 1985-93, v.p. 1985-93), Screen Actors Guild (bd. dirs. so. dist. 1990-93), Actors Equity Assn. Avocations: stamp collecting/philately, reading, music, theater, travel. E-mail: writegal@bellsouth.net.

PRICE, STEVEN, venture capitalist, communications executive, lawyer; b. NYC, Feb. 14, 1962; s. Robert and Margery Price; m. Tina Gitlin, Mar. 16, 1991. BS magna cum laude, Brown U., 1984; JD, Columbia U. Sch. Law, 1989. Spl. asst. to US Amb. to the START Talks in Geneva US Dept. State, 1989—90; assoc. Davis Polk & Wardell, 1991; with mergers and acquisitions group Goldman, Sachs & Co.; COO PriCellular Corp., 1994—97, bd. dirs., 1996, pres., CEO, 1997—2001; deputy asst. sec. def. spectrum and command, control and communications policy US Dept. Def., 2001—03; pres., CEO LiveWire Capital, 2003—04; gen. partner Spectrum Equity Investors, 2004—. Dir. Met. Coun. Poverty, 1999—, UJA Fedn. NY, 2000—, US Nat. Archives Bd., 2003—; advisory bd. for computing and IT Brown U., 2003—; cons. Office Sec. Def. and Def. Sci. Bd., 2003—. Co-founder Brown U. Ctr. for Combat Casualty Recovery. Mem.: ABA, Bar Assn. Wash., DC, Assn. Bar NY, Phi Beta Kappa. Office: Spectrum Equity Investors One International Place Boston MA 02110 Office Phone: 617-464-4600. Office Fax: 617-464-4601.*

PRICE, TERESA ANNETTE, elementary school educator; b. Riverdale, Md., Jan. 13, 1961; d. Carl William and Mary Helen Gohr; m. Darryl Scott Price, Nov. 20, 1982 (div. Oct. 2003); children: John, Mark. BS in Elem. Edn., U. Md., College Park, 1979—85; MS in Curriculum and Instrn., We. Md. Coll., 1992—98. Cert. natl. bd. early childhood generalist 2000. Elem. tchr. Prince George's County Pub. Sch., Upper Marlboro, Md., 1986—88, Charles County Pub. Sch. - Indian Head Elem., Indian Head, Md., 1988—; So. regional network 1 faciliator/ coord. Md. State Dept. Edn. - Nat. Bd. Profl. Tchg. Standards, Brandywine, 2002—; second grade team leader Indian Head Elem., Md., 2002—; curriculum design grad. course, instr. curriculum and instruction McDaniel Coll., Westminster, Md., 2003—. Curriculum developer/writer Charles County Pub. Sch., LaPlata, 1998—99; del. Nat. Edn. Assn./Edn. Assn. Charles County, LaPlata, 2000—01, Md. State Tchr. Assn., LaPlata, 2003—, "I Can Do It" classroom mgmt. trainer, Annapolis, 2000—; adv. bd. com. grad. curriculum and instrn. McDaniel Coll., 2001—; summer enrichment reading tchr. Charles County Pub. Sch., Waldorf, Md., 2002—. Avocations: camping, golf, reading, crafts, fishing. Home: 2805 Lohengrin Ct Waldorf MD 20601 Office: Charles County Pub Sch IHES 4200 Indian Head Hwy Indian Head MD 20640 Personal E-mail: turbotepee13@aol.com. Business E-Mail: tprice@ccboe.com.

PRICE, THEODORA HADZISTELIOU, individual, child and family therapist; b. Athens, Greece, Oct. 1, 1938; arrived in U.S., 1967; d. Ioannis and Evangelia (Emmanuel) Hadzisteliou; m. David C. Long Price, Dec. 26, 1966 (div. 1989); children: Morgan N., Alkes D. L. BA in History/Archaeology, U. Athens, 1961; DPhil, U. Oxford, Eng., 1966; MA in Clin. Social Work, U. Chgo., 1988; diploma in piano tchg., Nat. Conservatory, Athens, 1958. LCSW, bd. cert. diplomate in clin. social work. Mus. asst., resident tutor U. Sydney, Australia, 1966-67; instr. anthropology Adelphi U., N.Y.C., 1967-68; archaeologist Hebrew Union Coll., Gezer, Israel, 1968; asst. prof. classical archaeology/art U. Chgo., 1968-70; jr. rsch. fellow Harvard Ctr. Hellenic Studies, Washington, 1970-71; clin. social worker Harbor Light Ctr., Salvation Army, Chgo., 1988-89; therapist Inst. Motivational Devel., Lombard, Ill., 1989-90; caseworker Jewish Family & Cmty. Svc., Chgo., 1989-90; staff therapist Family Svc. Ctrs. of South Cook County, Chicago Heights, 1990-91; pvt. practice child, adolescent, family therapy Bolingbrook, Ill., 1991—; dir. counseling svcs., clin. supr., psychotherapist Family Link, Inc., Chgo., 1993; staff therapist Cen. Bapt. Family Svcs., Gracell Rehab., Chgo., 1991, 91-92; casework supr., counselor Epilepsy Found. Greater Chgo., Chgo., 1992-93; therapist children, adolescents and families dept. foster care Cath. Charities, Chgo., 1993-94; individual and family therapist South Ctrl. Cmty. Svcs. Individual-Family Counseling Svcs., Chgo., 1994-97. Bd. dirs., counselor Naperville Sch. Gifted and Talented, 1982—84; lectr. in field. Author: (monograph) Kourotrophos, Cults and Representations of the Greek Nursing Deities, 1978; contbr. articles to profl. jours. Eleutherios Venizelos scholar, 1962—65, Meyerstein Traveling grantee, Oxford, Eng., 1963, 1964. Mem.: NASW, Ill. Clin. Social Workers, Nat. Acad. Clin. Social Workers. Avocations: yoga, piano playing, Byzantine chanting, writing. Home and Office: 10 Pebble Ct Bolingbrook IL 60440-1557 Office Phone: 630-378-1187. *Nobody stands alone, for each of us partakes and contributes to universal energy and creation. Every thought or action has progressively timeless impact. Therefore, working in helping people is influencing the flow of creation.*

PRICE, THOMAS EMILE, investment company executive; b. Cin., Nov. 4, 1921; s. Edwin Charles and Lillian Elizabeth (Werk)P.; m. Lois Margaret Gahr Matthews, Dec. 21, 1970 (dec. Nov. 26 1988); 1 child by previous marriage, Dorothy Elizabeth Wood Price; stepchildren: Bruce Albert, Mark Frederic, Scott Herbert, Eric William Matthews. BBA, U. Tex., 1943; postgrad., Harvard U., 1944. Co-founder Pirce y Cia., Inc., Cin., 1946—; sec., 1946-75; treas., 1946—; pres., 1975—; also bd. dirs.; co-founder Price Paper Products Corp. (merger Price y Cia, Inc.), Cin., 1956; treas., 1956-75; pres., 1975-90; sec., 1956-75; bd. dirs., also bd. dirs. Mem. Cin. Regional Export Expansion Com., 1961-63; bd. dirs. Ctrl. Acceptance Corp., 1954-55; founding mem. and dir. Cin. Royals Basketball Club Co., 1959-73. History columinst Tennis Talk Greater Cin., 1978-80. Referee Tri-State Tennis Championships, 1969-70, Nat. FAther-Son Clay Ct. Championships, 1974—, Tennis Grand Masters Championships, 1975-77, 80; vol. coach Walnut Hills High Sch. Boys Team, Cin. Jr. Davis Cup, 1968-78; co-founder Tennis Patrons of Cin., Inc., 1951, trustee, 1951-79, pres., 1958-63, 68; co-founder Greater Cin. Tennis Assn., 1979; participant in fundraising drives in Cin. Boys Amateur Baseball Fund; chmn. greater Cin. YMCA World Svc. Fund Drive, 1962-64; trustee Cin. World Affairs Inst., 1957-60, gen. chmn., 1959. 1st lt. USAAF, 1943-46, ETO. Elected to Western Hills High Sch. Sport Hall of Honor; named hon. Almaden Grand Master, 1980; Cin. Met. Tennis Tournament renamed Thomas E. Price Cin. Met. Tennis Tournament, 1991; nationally ranked boys 15, 1936, jr. tennis player, 1939. Mem. Cin. World Trade Club (pres. 1959), U.S. Trotting Assn., Cin. Hist. Soc., U.S. Lawn Tennis Assn. (trustee 1959-60, 62-64, chmn. Jr. Davis Cup com. 1960-62, founder Col. HJames H. Bishop award 1962), Ohio Valley Tennis Assn. (trustee 1948—, Gillespie award 1957, Dredge award 1973, pres. 1952-53, Tom Pirce award named in his honr at Jr. Davis Cup), Western Tennis Assn. (trustee 1951—, mem. championships adv. com. 1969-78, pres. 1959-60, Hall of Fame 1994, Melvin R. Bergman Disting. Svc. award 1989), Greater Cin. Tennis Assn. (named after and recipient Tom Price award), Assn. Tennis Profl. (nat. championships adv. 1979—), Cin. Country Club, Univ. Club, Cin. Tennis Club (hon., life, pres. 1957-58, adv. com. 1959—, Founders and Guardians award 1983), Indoor Tennis Club, Ea. Hills Indoor Tennis Club, Phi Gamma Delta. Republican. Presbyterian. Home: 3249 Epworth Ave Cincinnati OH 45211-7037 Office: Dixie Terminal Bldg Ste 216 Cincinnati OH 45202-3812 *Personal philosophy: Follow the Ten Commandments and the Golden Rule.*

PRICE, THOMAS FREDERICK, theatre educator; b. Salt Lake City, June 19, 1937; s. Thomas William P. and Caryl Susan Brown; children: Devin, Jennifer. BA in Drama, Pomona Coll., 1960; MA in Theatre, San Francisco State U., 1962; PhD in Drama, Stanford U., 1968; student, Columbia U. Rare Book Sch., 1983. Asst. prof. English U. of the Pacific, Stockton, Calif., 1968-70; asst. prof. drama U.S. Internat. U., Sch. Performing Arts, San Diego, 1970-74; archivist, curator The Philibrick Theatre Libr., Los Altos Hills, Calif., 1975-85; vis. prof. English Tianjin (China) Normal U., 1985-87; adj. prof. theatre So. Oreg. State Coll., Ashland, 1991-92. Assoc. prof. English Tanmkang U., Taipei, Taiwan, 1993—2004; ednl. broadcaster (original staff) KPFA-FM, L.A., 1959—62, KSRO-FM, Ashland, Oreg., 1990—92; organizer Gordon Craig retrospective Stanford U. Dept Spl. Collections, 1985; drama Caligula, Old Globe Theatre, San Diego, 1973, Mother Courage & Her Children, Allen Theatre, Claremont Coll., 2004. Author: Edward Gordon Craig Revisited, 1984, Edward Gordon Craig and the Theatre of the Imagination, 1985, Dramatic Structure and Meaning, 1992, rev. edit., 1999; editor: Critical Edition of the Jealous Wife and Polly Honeycombe by George Colman the Elder, 1997; contbr. articles to profl. jours. Recipient Taiwan Nat. Sci. Found., 1998, Disting. Tchr. award Tamkang U., 1998, Emma May Shiel Fellow, Stanford U. Mem. Calif. Scholarship Fedn. (hon. life).

PRICE, TIMOTHY R. accountant; b. Reigate, Eng., Jan. 26, 1943; m. Frances Baird; 4 children. BA, U. Victoria, Can., 1964. Chartered acct. Touche Ross & Co., Montreal, 1965-69; pres., COO Mico Enterprises Ltd., 1970-80; pres., CEO Hees Internat. Bancorp Inc., Toronto, 1980-88, mng. ptnr., chmn., 1988—96; chmn. The Edper Group Ltd., Toronto, 1997, Trilon Fin. Corp., Toronto, 1997—2002, Brascan Fin. Corp., Toronto, 2002—. Bd. dirs. Astral Media Inc., Morguard Corp., Nexfor Inc.; chmn. Edper Brascan Found., 1997—. Bd. dirs. St. Michael's Hosp. Found.; bd. govs. York U., Can. Office: Brascon Fin Corp PO Box 771 BCE Pl 181 Bay St Ste 300 Toronto ON Canada M5J 2T3

PRICE, TINA S. administrative assistant; b. Selma, Ala., Dec. 31, 1963; d. William Hardy and Mary Belle (Price) Smiley; m. Kirk Price, Oct. 6, 1989 (div. June 2000); children: Timorra, Kirk II. Student, Auburn U., 1982—84, Columbia Sch. Broadcasting, 1985—88. Cert. family devel. trainer Corp. Found. for Children. Co-founder, dir. CANDO-Ctrl. Ala. Neighborhood Devel. Orgn., Selma, 1990—; state facilitator Corp. Found. for Children, Montgomery, Ala., 2000—03; field dir. Ala. Dept. Childrens' Affairs, Montgomery, 2000—01; ACATA coord. Coun. on Substance Abuse, Montgomery, 2001—02; office adminstr. Ctr. for Commerce, Selma, 2003—. Author: Seven Steps in Planning a Family Reunion, 2001, The Richness of Night, 2002. Exec. sec., mem. Selma to Montgomery Nat. Hist. Trail, 2000—; mem. Class VII Leadership Selma/Dallas County, 2001; bd. mem. Habitat Selma, Selma AIR (AIDS, Info., Referrals), treas., 2001—02. Avocations: racquetball, body sculpting. Office: Ctr for Commerce 912 Selma Ave Selma AL

PRICE, TOM, journalist; b. Pitts., May 26, 1946; s. H. Samuel and Anna Mae (Nicholson) P.; m. Susan Crites; 1 child, Julianna Margaret. BS in Journalism, Ohio U., 1968. Writer, editor Athens (Ohio) Messenger, 1968-73; freelance writer, 1973-75; politics writer Dayton (Ohio) Jour. Herald, 1975-82; corr. Washington bur. Cox Newspapers, Washington, 1982-96; freelance writer politics, govt., tech., bus. and edn., 1996—; Washington columnist Optics and Photonics News, 2002—; contbg. writer Congl. Quar. Rschr., 2004. Author: Frommer's Washington, DC, for Dummies, 2d edit., 2003; co-author: (with Susan Crites Price) The Working Parents Help Book, 1994 (Parent's Choice award, Scholastic Book Club selection), rev. edit., 1996, Working Solutions Internet Column; nat. newspaper columnist Working Parents Lifeline, 1996-98. Mem.: Washington Ind. Writers, Am. Soc. Journalists and Authors. Presbyterian. Avocations: photography, hiking, travel, reading.

PRICE, TOM, automotive sales executive; Founder Tom Price Dealership, Colma, Calif., 1976; mgr. corp. growth including franchising, other acquisitions FirstAm. Automotive Inc. (formerly Tom Price Dealership), San Francisco, 1997, CEO, pres. Office: 135 E Sir Francis Drake Blvd Larkspur CA 94939-1860

PRICE, TREVOR ROBERT PRYCE, psychiatrist, educator; b. Concord, N.H., Nov. 29, 1943; BA, Yale U., l965; MD, Columbia U., l969. Diplomate Am. Bd. Psychiatry and Neurology (examiner 1985—), with Geriatric Psychiatry, Am. Bd. Internal Medicine, Nat. Bd. Med. Examiners. Intern in medicine Med. Ctr. U. Calif., San Francisco, 1969-70; resident in internal medicine Med. Ctr. of U. Calif., San Francisco, 1972-74; resident in psychiatry Dartmouth Med. Sch., Hanover, N.H., 1974-77, asst. prof., assoc. prof. psychiatry and medicine, 1977-85; assoc. prof., prof. psychiatry U. Pa. Sch. Medicine, Phila., 1985—88; dir. psychiat. in-patient svcs. Hosp. of U. Pa., 1985-88; prof. psychiatry Med. Coll. Pa., Pitts., 1989-90, prof. psychiatry and medicine, 1991-95, 1993—2002; chmn. dept. psychiatry Med. Coll. Pa. and Hahnemann U., Pitts., 1989-95, sr. assoc. dean, 1993-95; pres. Allegheny Neuropsychiat. Inst. Allegheny Neuropsychiat. Inst., Pitts., 1992-94, exec. dir., 1994—; chmn. dept. psychiatry Med. Coll. Pa. Hahnemann Sch. Medicine, Phila., 1995—2002; prof. psychiatry and med. Drexel U. Coll. Med., Phila., 2002—03, chmn. dept. psychiatry, 2002; pvt. practice Bryn Mawr, Pa., 2002—. Bd. dirs. Coll. Health Consortium, Inc., Phila., Highland Dr. Rsch. and Edn. Found., Yale Club Pitts., Pitts. Psychoanalytic Found., Med. Coll. Pa. Hosp.; mem. blue ribbon bd. Alzheimer's Disease Alliance, Western Pa., 1989-97; mem. governing bd. Med. Coll. of Pa. Hosp., 1999-2002. Mem. editl. bd. Convulsive Therapy, 1984-94, Jour. Neuropsychiatry and Clin. Neurosci., 1992—, Allegheny Gen. Hosp. Jour. Neurosci., 1992-98, Seminars in Neuropsychiatry, 1995—; editl. reviewer 15 psychiat. and med. jours., 1978; contbr. chpts. to books and articles in profl. jours. Mem. N.H. Commn. on Laws Effecting Mental Health, 1974-75; bd. dirs. Advanced Studies Program, Friends of St. Paul's Sch., Concord, N.H., 1983-87. Recipient William C. Menninger award Ctrl. Neuropsychiat. Assn., 1977, Faculty Teaching award dept. psychiatry Dartmouth Med. Sch., 1984, Pres. award for Exceptional Achievement AHERF, 1994, numerous grants. Fellow: Am. Coll. Psychiatrists, Am. Neuropsychiat. Assn. (bd. dirs. 1993—95, exec. dir. 1995), Am. Psychiat. Assn. (disting. fellow); mem.: Assn. Medicine and Psychiatry, Assn. Convulsive Therapy, Assn. Acad. Psychiatry, Am. Assn. Dirs. Psychiat. Residency Tng., Assn. for Acad. Psychiatry, Soc. Biol. Psychiatry, Am. Assn. Chairmen of Depts. Psychiatry, Pa. Psychiat. Assn., H-Y-P Club Pitts., Yale Club Pitts. Avocations: fly fishing, tennis, reading, piano. Office: 950 Haverford Rd Ste 302 Bryn Mawr PA 19010 Office Phone: 610-527-5926. *Life at its best is being continually challenged and fully engaged, yet not self-absorbed.*

PRICE, WILLIAM ANTHONY, psychiatrist; b. Youngstown, Ohio, Aug. 15, 1959; s. Edward J. and Margaret (Krispli) P.; divorced; children: Matthew, Nicole; m. Pamela R. Gardner, Nov. 18, 1985; 1 child, Andrew A.; m. Sheryl A. Neider, Sept. 23, 1995. BS, Kent State U., 1983; MD, Northeastern Ohio U., 1983. Diplomate Am. Bd. Psychiatry and Neurology, Nat. Bd. Med. Examiners; lic. psychiatrist, Ohio, Pa. Intern U. Health Ctr., Pitts., 1983-85; resident in psychiatry Northeastern Ohio U., 1985-86, chief resident, clin. assoc. prof., 1986-87; psychiatrist Splty. Care Psychiat. Svcs., Boardman, Ohio, 1987—; med. dir. PsyCare, Boardman, Belmont Pines Hosp., Youngstown, 1990-91, adult program dir., 2000—, adult program med. dir., 2000—; med. dir., clin. dir. NEO-Therapeutic Mgmt. Svcs., Warren, Ohio, 1997—; cons. psychiatrist Pathways Ctr. for Geriatric Psychiatry, 1997—, med. dir., 1999—; co-med. dir. Ivy Woods Manor, 2000—; dir. psychiat. svcs. Middlebury Manor, Akron, Ohio, 2001—; clin. assoc. prof. psychiatry Ohio U. Coll. Osteo. Medicine, 1998—. Psychiat. clerkship dir. Youngstown Osteo. Hosp., 1998—; med. dir. Premenstrual Syndrome Program, Parkview Counseling Ctr., Youngstown, 1985-88, Child and Adolescent Diagnostic and Devel. Ctr., Youngstown, 1988-95, Psycare; assoc. med. dir. psychiatry Windsor Hosp., Chagrin Falls, 1989—; clin. asst. prof., Northeastern Ohio U., 1987—; clin. assoc. prof. Ohio U. Coll. Medicine, 1997—; adj. prof. psychiatry Coll. Osteo. Medicine and Sci., 1997—; chief clin. officer, Mahoning County Mental Health Bd, 1990—; clerkship dir. psychiatry, St. Elizabeth Hosp. Med. Ctr., Youngstown, 1987—, Western Res. Care Sys., Youngstown, 1988-90; regional clerkship dir. psychiatry Ohio U. Coll. Medicine, 1998—, clin. asst. prof. medicine, 1998—; reviewer Jour. Clin. Psychiatry, 1987—, Am. Jour. Psychiatry, 1987—, Psychosomatics, 1987—, lectr. various confs., forums, seminars, 1985—. Author: (with others) Opiate Addiction in the Biological Foundations of Clinical Psychiatry, 1986, Nootropics: Toward the Mind in the Biological Foundations of Clinical Psychiatry, 1986, (audiocassettes) Mitral Valve Prolapse and Bipolar Affective Disorder, 1985, Dealing with PCP, 1985; contbr. numerous articles to profl. publs., poems and 2 short stories to nat. mags. Recipient Founders Day award for Sci. Rsch., Ohio Psychiat. Assn. Edn. and Rsch. Found., 1986, hon. mention Lebenson award, Am. Assn. Gen. Hosp. Psychiatrists, 1987, Founder's award, Am. Assn. Psychiatrists in Alcoholism and Addictions, 1987, fellowship award, Assn. Acad. Psychiatrists, 1987; Laughlin fellow, Am. Coll. Psychiatrists. Mem. Am. Psychiat. Assn., Am. Acad. Clin. Psychiatry, Am. Soc. Clin. Pharmacology, Am. Assn. Psychiatrists in Alcoholism and Addiction, Am. Gen. Hosp. Psychiatrists, Am. Soc. Psychosomatic Ob-Gyn., Am. Coll. Psychiatrists, Am. Assn. Geriatric Psychiatry, Assn. for Acad. Psychiatry (regional coord. 2000-), Internat. Soc. Psychosomatic Ob-Gyn., Nat. Fedn. Ind. Bus., Assn. Acad. Psychiatrists, Ctrl. Neuropsychiat. Assn., Soc. Neurosci., Soc. Menstrual Cycle Rsch., Ohio State Med. Assn., Ohio Psychiat. Assn., Mahoning County Med. Assn., Mahoning County Mental Health Bd., Coun. Chiefs Psychiatry, Parents Supporting Parents (Youngstown, adv. bd. dirs.), Phi Delta Epsilon. Avocations: gourmet cooking, wine tasting, art collecting, skiing. Office: 4171 W Middletown Rd Canfield OH 44406

PRICE, WILLIAM RAY, JR., state supreme court judge; b. Fairfield, Iowa, Jan. 30, 1952; s. William Ray and Evelyn Jean (Darnell) P.; m. Susan Marie Trainor, Jan. 4, 1975; children: Emily Margret, William Joseph Dodds. BA with distinction, U. Iowa, 1974; postgrad., Yale U., 1974-75; JD cum laude, Washington and Lee U., 1978. Bar: Mo. 1978, U.S. Dist. Ct. (we. dist.) Mo. 1978, U.S. Ct. Claims 1978, U.S. Ct. Appeals (8th cir.) 1985. Assoc. Lathrop & Norquist, Kansas City, Mo., 1978-84, ptnr., 1984-92, chmn. bus. litigation sect., 1987-88, 90-92, exec. com., 1989-92; judge Supreme Ct. Mo., Jefferson City, 1992—, chief justice, 1999—2001. G.L.V. Zumwalt monitoring com. U.S. Dist. Ct. (we. dist.) Mo., Kansas City. Pres. Kansas City Bd. Police Commrs.; mem. Together Ctr. & Family Devel. Ctr., Kansas City; chmn. merit selection com. U.S. marshal Western Dist. of Mo., Kansas City; bd. dirs. Truman Med. Ctr., Kansas City. Rockefeller fellow, 1974-75; Burks scholar Washington & Lee U., 1976. Mem. Christian Ch. Office: Supreme Ct Mo PO Box 150 207 W High St Jefferson City MO 65102-0150

PRICE-SMITH, ANDREW THOMAS, social sciences educator, consultant; b. Toronto, Ontario, Canada, Oct. 11, 1968; s. Cynthia Thomas Smith-McLeod and Jack Tennyson McLeod. BA, Queen's U., Kingston, Can., 1992; PhD, U. Toronto, Can., 1999. Post-doctoral rschr. and adj. prof. Columbia U., N.Y.C., NY, 1999—2000; asst. prof. U. South Fla., St. Petersburg, 2001—. Cons. US Inst. of Peace, Washington, 2001—, World Bank, Washington, 2003—04. Author: The Health of Nations: Infectious Disease, Environ. Change and their Effects on Nat. Security and Devel. (finalist, Grawemeyer award, 2003), Plagues and Politics. Co-dir. dance com. Pavilion, Tampa, Fla., 2004. Mem.: Internat. Studies Assn. (assoc.). Achievements include design of emprical index to measure state capacity; development of new social sci. rsch. teams to slow the spread of epidemic diseases such as HIV/AIDS and SARS; research in population health as major driver of economic productivity and political stability. Avocations: music, archaeology, skiing, hiking. Office: Univ S Fla St Petersburg DAV 226 140 7th Ave S Saint Petersburg FL 33701-5016 Office Fax: 727-553-4526. E-mail: atp2@stpt.usf.edu.

PRICHARD, JOYCE S. music educator; d. Raymond Allen and Virginia Marie Sholl; m. Jeffrey William Prichard, July 9, 1977 (dec. July 2001); children: Gregory William, Scott Thomas. MusB, Ithaca Coll., 1975; MusM, West Chester U., 1982. Dir. secondary sch. orch. Haverford Twp. Sch. Dist., Havertown, Pa., 1975—84; dir. music, chair fine arts Villa Maria Acad., Malvern, Pa., 1989—. Guest condr. Berks County Honors Orch., Reading, Pa., 1984, Musical Coterie, Wayne, Pa., 1988; v.p. bd. dirs. Main Line Symphony Orch., Wayne, Pa., 1990—; clinician Archdiocese Phila. Orch., 1991; with Phila. All-Cath. Orch., 2004—. Contbr. articles to profl. jours. Co-founder life raft group Assn. Cancer Online Resources, NJ, 1999. Mem.: Nat. Cath. Educators Assn., Pa. Music Educators Assn., Music Educators Nat. Conf., Tri-M Music Honor Soc. (life). Avocations: art, architecture, antiques. Office: Villa Maria Acad 370 Old Lincoln Hwy Malvern PA 19355 Business E-Mail: jprichard@vmahs.org.

PRICHARD, PETER S. newspaper editor; b. Auburn, Calif., Dec. 18, 1944; s. Jarvis B. and Floris C. (Smith) P.; m. Ann O'Donnell, Nov. 13, 1971; children: Oliver W., Lindsay M. AB, Dartmouth Coll., 1966. Wire editor Greenwich (Conn.) Time, 1970-72; reporter Democrat and Chronicle, Rochester, N.Y., 1972-75; assoc. news dir. WOKR TV, Rochester, N.Y., 1975-76; reporter Times Union, Rochester, 1976-78; asst. to chmn. communications Gannett Co. Inc., Rochester, 1980-82, dir. communications, Office of Chief Exec., 1980-82; columns editor USA Today, Washington, 1982-83, dep. assoc. editorial dir., 1983-84, assoc. editorial dir., 1984-86, mng. editor spl. projects, 1986-87, sr. editor, 1988, editor, sr. v.p., news, 1988—; sr. v.p. News Gannett Co. Inc., Washington, 1988—, chief news exec., 1990—. Author: The Making of McPaper: The Inside Story of USA Today, 1987 (Frank Luther Moh Rsch. award Kappa Tau Alpha 1987). Vice chmn., bd. trustees Washington Journalism Ctr., 1989—. With U.S. Army, 1967-69, Vietnam. Decorated Bronze Star. Mem. Nat. Press Club, Am. Soc. Newspaper Editors (Reston, Va.) (various coms. 1985—). Office: USA Today 7950 Jones Branch Dr Mc Lean VA 22108-0001

PRICKETT, DAVID CLINTON, physician; b. Fairmont, W.Va., Nov. 26, 1918; s. Clinton Everett and Mary Anna (Gottschalk) Prickett; m. Mary Ellen Holt, June 29, 1940 (dec. Feb. 1987); children: David C., Rebecca Ellen, William Radcliffe, Mary Anne, James Thomas, Sara Elizabeth; m. Pamela S. Blackstone, Nov. 17, 1991 (dec. Mar. 2002). Student, Fairmont State Coll., 1940—42; AB, W.Va. U., 1944; MD, U. Louisville, 1946; MPH, U. Pitts., 1955. Pres. Prickett Chem. Co., 1938-43; acct. W.Va. Conservation Commn. and Fed. Works Agy., 1941, 42; lab. asst., instr. chemistry W.Va. U., 1943; intern Louisville Gen. Hosp., 1947; surg. resident St. Joseph's Hosp., Parkersburg, W.Va., 1948-49; gen. practice W.Va., 1948-50, 55-61; mem. staff

Fairmont (W.Va.) Gen. Hosp., 1955-60, Fairmont Emergency Hosp., 1955-60; physician USAF, N.Mex. and Calif., 1961-62, U.S. Army, Fort Ord, Calif., 1963-64; resident physician San Luis Obispo County Hosp., 1965-66; pvt. practice LA, 1967—; mem. staff St. Francis Hosp., LA, 1970-71; physician So. Calif. Edison Co., 1981-84. Physician Bethlehem Mines Corp., Idamay, W.Va., 1956; resident physician Sedgwick County Hosp., Wichita, Kans., 1964-65; med. dir. South Gate auto assembly plant GM, 1969-71; staff physician City of LA, 1971-76; relief med. practice Appalachia summer seasons, W.Va. & Ky., 1977, 86, 88-97. Author: The Newer Epidemiology, 1962, rev., 1990, Public Health, A Science Resolvable by Mathematics, 1965; contbr. articles to profl. jours. Med. officer USPHS, Navajo Indian Reservation, Tohatchi (N.Mex.) Health Ctr., 1953-55, surgeon, res. officer, 1957-59; pres. W.Va. Pub. Health Assn., 1951-52; sec. indsl. and pub. health sect. W.Va. Med. Assn., 1956; W.Va. dist. 4 health officer; health officer Marion County, W.Va., 1951-53; dist. health officer Allegheny County, Pa., 1957; officer Aux. Civil Def. Police, W.Va., 1942; med. advisor Boy Scouts Am., W.Va., N.Mex. 2d lt. AUS, 1943-46. Dr. Thomas Parran fellow U. Pitts. Sch. Pub. Health, 1955; named to Hon. Order Ky. Cols. Fellow APHA; mem. AMA, S.R., Am. Occupl. Med. Assn., Am. Acad. Family Physicians, Western Occupl. Med. Assn., Calif. Med. Assn., LA County Med. Assn., Am. Legion, Elks, Phi Chi, Rio Hondo Symphony Guild. Avocations: photography, auto repairs, amateur radio, square dancing. Address: PO Box 4032 Whittier CA 90607-4032 Office Phone: 626-330-4106.

PRIDE, BENJAMIN DAVID, sales executive; b. Staten Island, NY, Sept. 20, 1952; s. Benjamin David and Evelyn Marie (Dann) Pride; m. Jane Jeanette Adams, Oct. 12, 2002; stepchildren: Emily Adams, Phillip Adams. BA, St. Francis Coll., Bklyn., 1974. Office mgr., prodn. estimator Leber Katz Ptnrs., N.Y.C., 1975-76; prodn. estimator, media planner, out-of-home media buyer, sports buyer Dancer, Fitzgerald & Sample, N.Y.C., 1976-81; v.p. sports and promotion Backer, Spielvogel, Bates Worldwide, N.Y.C., 1981-95, Zenith Media, N.Y.C., 1995-96; ptnr. Schineller & Pride, N.Y.C., 1996-97; account exec. Newport Media, N.Y.C., 1997-99; asst. mgr., sr. membership dir. UCC Total Home, Eatontown, NJ, 2001—03; advt. cons. Rosnik Pub., Inc., NYC, 2003—04; bus. devel. mgr. Securitas Security Svcs. USA, Inc., 2004—. Divsn. capt. USCG Aux., 2000. Republican. Roman Catholic. Avocations: boating, fishing. Office Phone: 212-609-4307.

PRIDE, MIRIAM R. college president; b. Canton, China, June 6, 1948; d. Richard E. and Martha W. Pride; divorced. Grad., Berea College Found. Sch., 1966, Coll. of Wooster, 1970; MBA, U. Ky., 1989. Intern in administrn. in higher edn., head resident Coll. of Wooster, Ohio, 1970-72; accounts payable clk., dir. Boone Tavern Hotel, head resident, dir. student activities Berea Coll., 1972-88; eligibility worker dept. human resources State of Ky., 1975-76; asst. in undergrad. advising Coll. Bus., U. Ky., 1987-89; asst. to pres. for campus life, v.p. for administrn., pres. Blackburn Coll., Carlinville, Ill., 1989—. Chmn. United Way Berea, Carlinville, 1989—92; fin. chmn. Carlinville Hosp., 1995—97; mem. Ill. Commn. on Status of Women; bd. dirs. Land of Lincoln Girl Scouts, 1993—2000, fin. chmn., 1995—2000, mem. nominating com., 2000—; bd. dirs. Carlinville Area Hosp., 1993—97, Assn. Presbyn. Colls. and Univs., Fedn. Ill. Colls. and Univs., 1993—, Federated Ch. Bd., 1998—2001. Mem. Carlinville C. of C. (bd. dirs.), Rotary (bd. dirs. 1996—). Mem. Federated Ch. Avocations: reading, walking, knitting. Office: Blackburn Coll Office of the President Carlinville IL 62626

PRIDGEN, RUFUS ALLEN, retired literature educator; b. Portsmouth, Va., Oct. 16, 1943; s. Jessie Lois Pridgen-Barnes and Rufus Allen Pridgen; m. Linda Lucille Poland, May 28, 1973; 1 child, Nathaniel. PhD in English, Fla. State U., 1967—71. Prof. English Chowan Coll., Murfreesboro, NC, 1979—87; chair/prof. English Va. Intermont Coll., Bristol, 1987—2001. Author: (scholarly book, literary criticism) Walker Percy's Sacramental Landscapes: The Search in the Desert. Fellow Andrew W. Mellon Post-Doctoral Rsch. Fellowships, Appalachian Coll. Assn., 1996-98. Roman Catholic. Personal E-mail: apridgen@pinehurst.net.

PRIDHAM, THOMAS GRENVILLE, retired research microbiologist; b. Chgo., Oct. 10, 1920; s. Grenville and Gladys Etheral (Sloss) P.; m. Phyllis Sue Hokamp, July 1, 1943 (dec. Feb. 1994); children: Pamela Sue, Thomas Foster, Grenville Thomas, Rolf Thomas, Montgomery Thomas; m. Edna Lee Boudreaux, Mar. 6, 1995. BS in Chemistry, U. Ill., 1943, PhD in Bacteriology, 1949. Instr. bacteriology U. Ill., Champaign-Urbana, 1947; rsch. microbiologist No. Regional Rsch. Lab., USDA, Peoria, Ill., 1948-51, 53-65, U.S. Indsl. Chems., Balt., 1951-52; supr. tech. ops. Acme Vitamins, Inc., Joliet, Ill., 1952-53; sr. rsch. biologist U.S. Borax Rsch. Corp., Anaheim, Calif., 1965-67; supervisory rsch. microbiologist No. Regional Rsch. Ctr. USDA, Peoria, 1967-81, head agrl. rsch. culture collection No. Regional Rsch. Lab., 1967-81; ret., 1981. Cons. Mycogen Corp., San Diego, 1985-87; U.S. sr. scientist Fed. Republic Germany, Darmstadt, 1977. Contbg. author: Actinomycetales: The Boundary Microorganisms, 1974, Bergey's Manual of Determinative Bacteriology, 1974, Synopsis and Classification of Living Organisms, 1982; mem. editorial bd. Jour. Antibiotics, 1969-81; contbr. articles to Jour. Bacteriology, Applied Microbiology, Phytopathology, Actinomycetes, Mycologia, Devel. Indsl. Microbiology, Jour. Antibiotics, Internat. Bull. Bacteriological Nomenclature Taxonomy, Antibiotics Ann., Antimicrobial Agts., Chemotherapy, also others. With USNR, 1943-45, with Rsch. Res., 1945-54, lt. ret. Fulbright scholar, Italy, 1952; grantee Soc. Am. Bacteriologists, 1957. Fellow: Am. Acad. Microbiology; mem.: Alexander von Humboldt Assn. Episcopalian. Achievements include patents in fermentative production of riboflavin and of antibiotics; research in microbial culture collection technology and management, systematics of streptomycetes, industrial microbiology. Home: 38 Mayo Br/Brandy Keg Rd Prestonsburg KY 41653-8114

PRIDMORE, ROY DAVIS, government official; b. Gaffney, S.C., May 18, 1925; s. Davis Bailey and Ethel (Hughes) P.; m. Doris Hedy Glatzl, July 16, 1960 (dec. Aug. 5, 2000); children: Lisa Ann, David Michael. Cert., Columbus U., Washington, 1949, Am. Inst., 1953, U.S. Dept. Agr. Grad. Sch., 1957. Pers. asst. Dept. Army, Fort Myer, Va., 1955-58; staff asst. D.C. Hwy. Dept., Washington, 1962-67; adminstrv. asst. Dept. Transp., Washington, 1958-62, adminstrv. officer, 1967-94, ret., 1994. Vice pres. Springboard Swim Club, Springfield, Va., 1984-85. Served with U.S. Army, 1946-47; mem. Res. (ret.) Decorated Legion of Merit. Democrat. Roman Catholic. Avocations: swimming, gardening.

PRIEBE, CEDRIC JOSEPH, JR., pediatric surgeon; b. NYC, Feb. 7, 1930; s. Cedric Joseph and Mary Martha (O'Beirne) P.; m. Cynthia Amelia Cali, June 11, 1955; children: Diane Marie, Janice Marie, Cedric Joseph III, Catherine Marie, Michael Stephen, Gregory Paul, Marta Marcella. BS cum laude, Fordham U., 1951; MD, Cornell U., 1955. Surg. resident The Roosevelt Hosp., NYC, 1955-60; pediatric surg. resident Ohio State U., Children's Hosp., Columbus, 1965-67; pediatric surgeon, asst. and assoc. prof. The Roosevelt Hosp., Colombia U., NYC, 1967-79; chief pediatric surgery, prof. surgery La. State U., Charity Hosp., New Orleans, 1979-82; dir. surg. edn. Children's Hosp. of New Orleans, 1979-82; chief pediatric surgery, prof. surgery SUNY at Stony Brook, U. Hosp., 1982—; adminstrv. vice chmn. dept. surgery Stony Brook Sch. Medicine, 2002—, faculy senate, 1991—, apt. com., 2001—, exec.com., 1999—, pres., 2003—. Sr. clin. trainee in cancer control NIH, Washington, 1963—65. Editl. cons. Jour. of Pediatric Surgery, Phila., 1994—; author: (with others) Neoplasia in Childhood, 1966; contbr. articles to profl. jours. Maj. USAF, 1956—65. Mem.: ACS, NY Soc. for Pediat. Surgery (v.p. 1976—78, pres. 1978—79), Children's Oncology Group, Pediat. Oncology Group (cancer control com. 1992—2000), Am. Pediat. Surg. Assn. (membership com. 1990—93, by-laws com. 1993—95, cancer com. 1996—99), Am. Acad. Pediat. (surg. sect. publs. com. 1989—92, chair publs. com. 1992), Soc. for Surgery Alimentary Tract, Am. Burn Assn. Republican. Roman Catholic. Avocations: tennis, squash racquets, travel. Home: 9 Woodhull Cove Ln Setauket NY 11733-1643 Office: SUNY at Stony Brook HSC T 19 Stony Brook NY 11794-8191 Office Phone: 631-444-2045. Personal E-mail: priebe@optonline.net. Business E-Mail: cjpriebe@notes.cc.sunysb.edu.

PRIEM, RICHARD GREGORY, writer, information systems executive; b. Munich, Sept. 18, 1949; arrived in U.S., 1953; s. Richard Stanley and Elizabeth Teresa (Thompson) Priem; m. Janice Lynne Holland, July 27, 1976; children: Michael John, Matthew Warren(dec.), Kathryn Elizabeth Guthrie. BS in Radio-TV-Film, U. Tex., 1970; MEd in Ednl. Tech., U. Ga., 1979; postgrad., Coll. William and Mary, 1981-82. Cert. fraud examiner. Radio personality, sales exec. KOKE, Inc., Austin, Tex., 1968-73; numerous positions including asst. prof. dept. behavioral scis. and leadership U.S. Mil. Acad., staff officer anti terrorism and inspector gen. U.S. Army, 1973-94; exec. v.p. It's Your Party, Herndon, Va., 1992-97; dep. divsn. mgr. Sci. Applications Internat. Corp., Vienna, Va., 1994-97; pres., COO, Commerce Tech., Inc., Centreville, Va., 1997—; asst. v.p. SAIC, 2003—. Cons. Dallas Cowboys Football Club, 1981; scouting coord. Army Football, 1983-85; cons. in field of anti-terrorism. Contbr. articles to profl. jours. Mem. Assn. Cert. Fraud Examiners, Internat. Soc. for Performance Improvement, Phi Kappa Phi, Kappa Delta Pi, Internat. Assn. Bomb Technicians and Investigators. Office: Commerce Techs Inc PO Box 221254 Chantilly VA 20153-1254 Home: 13813 Jefferson Park Dr Apt 4104 Herndon VA 20171-4786 E-mail: rpriem@commerce-tech.com.

PRIEN, SAMUEL DAVID, medical educator, researcher; b. Amarillo, Tex., May 30, 1956; s. Lester Joseph and Joyce Ann Prien; m. Cynthia Kay Collier, Dec. 28, 1977; children: Angela Marie, Jennifer Nicole. BS in Botany, Tex. Tech U., 1978, MS in Botany, Plant Physiology, 1980, PhD in Animal Sci., Reproductive Physiology, 1991. Lic. high complexity clin. lab. dir. Am. Bd. of Bioanalysts. Electron microscopy tech. II Tex. Tech U. Health Scis. Ctr., Lubbock, 1980—82, coord. electron microscopy labs., 1982—84, mgr. Electron Microscopy Ctr., 1984—87, med. rsch. tech. IV, embryologist, 1987—88, med. rsch. asst., embryologist, 1988—91, faculty assoc., 1991—92, asst. prof., 1992—98, assoc. prof., 1998—. Co-dir. ob.-gyn clin. labs Tex. Tech U. Health Scis. Ctr., Lubbock, 2001—, dir. art lab., 1988—; cons. dir. mid-Mo. art program Boone Hosp., Columbia, 1998—2003; cons. Organ Transport Sys., Lubbock, 2001—; com. mem. biotech. initiative Market Lubbock Inc., 2002—03. Contbr. articles, bulls., and abstracts to profl. publs. Sunday sch. tchr. Southland (Tex.) Bapt. Ch., 1993—2003. Recipient 20 sci. rsch. grants, Tchr. Fellow award, No. Am. Coll. and Tchrs. of Agri., 2003. Mem.: Am. Assn. of Bioanalyst, Endocrine Soc., Soc. for Assisted Reproductive Tech., Am. Soc. for Reproductive Medicine (chair abstract com 1997—2002), Soc. for Gynecologic Investigation (assoc.). Achievements include patents for improvement of assisted reproductive technologies. Avocations: nature walks, gardening. Home: 16418 NCR 1400 Shallowater TX 79363 Office: Texas Tech U Health Sci Ctr 3601 4th Lubbock TX 79430 Office Phone: 806-743-2352. E-mail: samuel.prien@ttmc.ttuhsc.edu.

PRIESAND, SALLY JANE, rabbi; b. Cleve., June 27, 1946; d. Irving Theodore and Rosetta Elizabeth (Welch) P. BA in English, U. Cin., 1968; B.Hebrew Letters, Hebrew Union Coll.-Jewish Inst. Religion, 1971, MA in Hebrew Letters, 1972; D.H.L. (hon.), Fla. Internat. U., 1973; DD (hon.), Hebrew Union Coll., 1997. Ordained rabbi, 1972. Student rabbi Sinai Temple, Champaign, Ill., 1968, Congregation B'nai Israel, Hattiesburg, Miss., 1969-70, Congregation Shalom, Milw., 1970, Temple Beth Israel, Jackson, Mich., 1970-71; rabbinic intern Isaac M. Wise Temple, Cin., 1971-72; asst. rabbi Stephen Wise Free Synagogue, N.Y.C., 1972-77, assoc. rabbi, 1977-79; rabbi Temple Beth El, Elizabeth, N.J., 1979-81, Monmouth Reform Temple, Tinton Falls, N.J., 1981—; chaplain Lenox Hill Hosp., N.Y.C., 1979-81. Author: Judaism and the New Woman, 1975. Mem. commn. on synagogue rels. Fedn. Jewish Philanthropies N.Y., 1972-79, mem. com. on aged commn. synagogue rels., 1972-75; mem. task force on equality of women in Judaism pub. affairs com. N.Y. Fedn. Reform Synagogues, 1972-75; mem. com. on resolutions Ctrl. Conf. Am. Rabbis, 1975-77, com. on cults, 1976-78, admissions com., 1983-89; chmn. Task Force on Women in Rabbinate, 1977-83, chmn. 1977-79, mem. exec. bd., 1977-79, com. on resolutions, 1989-92, chmn. com. conv. program, 1993-96; mem. joint commn. on Jewish edn. Ctrl. Conf. Am. Rabbis-Union Am. Hebrew Congregations, 1974-77; mem. task force on Jewish singles Commn. Synagogue Rels., 1975-77; mem. N.Y. Bd. Rabbis, 1975—, Shore Area Bd. Rabbis, 1981—; mem. interim steering com. Clergy and Laity Concerned, 1979-81; bd. dirs. NCCJ, N.J., 1980-82, Jewish Fedn. Greater Monmouth County, trustee, 1988-2000, strategic planning commn., 1996—, hon. v.p., 2000—; trustee Planned Parenthood of Monmouth County, 1982-90; v.p. Interfaith Neighbors, 1988-96, pres., 1997—; mem. UAHC-CCAR Joint Commn. on Synagogue Affiliation, 1992—2002; bd. govs. Hebrew Union Coll.-Jewish Inst. Religion, 1993—; trustee Union Am. Hebrew Congregations, 1994-98. Cited by B'nai Brith Women, 1971; named Woman of Yr. Temple Israel, Columbus, Ohio, 1972, Woman of Yr. Ladies Aux. N.Y. chpt. Jewish War Vets., 1973, Woman for All Seasons N. L.I. region Women's Am. ORT, 1973, Extraordinary Women of Achievement NCCJ, 1978, Woman of Achievement Monmouth County Adv. Commn. on Status Women, 1988; recipient Quality of Life award Dist. One chpt. B'nai B'rith Women, 1973, Medallion Judaic Heritage Soc., 1978, Eleanor Roosevelt Humanities award Women's div. State of Israel Bonds, 1980, Rabbinical award Coun. Jewish Fedn., 1988, Woman of Leadership award Monmouth Coun. Girl Scouts U.S., 1991, The Woman Who Dares award Nat. Coun. Jewish Women, 1993, Women's Studies Disting. Alumnae award Friends of Women's Studies U. Cin., 1997; named to Alumni Hall of Fame, Fairview Park H.S., 2002. Mem. Hadassah (life), Ctrl. Conf. Am. Rabbis, NOW, Am. Jewish Congress, Am. Jewish Com., Assn. Reform Zionists Am., Jewish Women Internat. (life), Jewish Peace Fellowship, Women's Rabbinic Network, Nat. Breast Cancer Coalition, HUC-JIR Rabbinic Alumni Assn. (sec., treas. 1997-99, v.p. 1999-2001, pres. 2001-03). Home: 10 Wedgewood Cir Eatontown NJ 07724-1203 Office: 332 Hance Ave Eatontown NJ 07724-2730 Office Phone: 732-747-9365. E-mail: spriesand@monmouth.com.

PRIEST, ALEXIA Z. purchasing agent; b. Waterbury, Conn., Sept. 17, 1954; d. John Joseph and Vera (Mandzik) Zurlis; 1 child, Jason Farrell; m. Alan Priest, Apr. 30, 2004; stepchildren: Brandon, Tyson. BBA, U. Miami, Coral Gables, Fla.; MBA, U. New Haven. Buyer Hewlett Packard, Cupeztino, Calif., 1981-83; purchase mgr. ICI, Redmond, Wash., 1983-84; commodity mgr. No. Telecom, St. Mountain, Ga., 1985-88; mfg. rep. Montgomery Mktg., Norcross, Ga., 1988-90; internat. purchasing agt. Sci. Atlanta, Norcross, Ga., 1990-91; sr. buyer Amphenol, Danbury, Conn., 1992-94; purchasing mgr. Danaher-Gulton Graphic, East Greenwhich, R.I., 1994-96; materials control mgr. Amphenol Corp., Danbury, Conn., 1996-2000; materials mgmt. The Siemon Co., Watertown, Conn., 2000—; purchasing agt. Boehinger-Ingelheim Pharms., Inc., 2001—. Prof. econs., internat. bus., logistics and mgmt. Teikyo Post U. U. Miami scholar, 1974-75. Mem. Women in Electronics (v.p. sponsors 1989-90, guest speaker 1989), NAFE, Nat. Assn. Purchasing Mgrs. Republican. Roman Catholic. Avocations: golf, tennis, swimming, reading, jogging. Home: 18 Cynthia St Waterbury CT 06708-2702 Office: Boehringer Ingelheim Purchasing Agt Ridgefield CT 06877 Personal E-mail: aclaryhome@aol.com.

PRIEST, GEORGE L. law educator; b. 1947; BA, Yale U., 1969; JD, U. Chgo., 1973. Assoc. prof. U. Puget Sound, Tacoma, 1973-75; law and econ. fellow U. Chgo., 1975-77; prof. U. Buffalo, 1977-80, UCLA, 1980-81, Yale U., New Haven, 1981—. Dir. program in civil liability; John M. Olin prof. law and econs., 1986—. Mem. Pres.' Com. on Privatization, 1987-88. Office: PO Box 208215 New Haven CT 06520-8215

PRIEST, HARTWELL WYSE, artist; b. Brantford, Ont., Can., Jan. 1, 1901; d. John Frank Henry and Rachel Thayer (Gavet) Wyse; m. A.J. Gustin Priest, Aug. 4, 1927; children: Paul Lambert, Marianna Thayer. BA, Smith Coll. Former tchr. graphic art Va. Art Inst., Charlottesville. Former lectr. on prints and lithography; juror art exhbn. Unitarian Ch., 1993. One-woman shows include Argent Gallery, N.Y.C., 1955, 58, 60, 73, 77, 81, Va., 1969, 71, Nantucket, Mass., 1956, Ft. Lauderdale, Fla. Art Ctr., 1956, McGuffey Gallery, Charlotsville, Va., 1998; Pen & Brush, N.Y.C., 1973, 91, 97, invitational retrospective exhbn. McGuffey Art Ctr., Charlottesville, Va., 1984, Va., N.Y., 1984, 88; work represented in permanent collections Library of Congress Washington, Norton Gallery, Palm Beach, Fla., Soc. Am. Graphic Artists, Hunterdon County Art Ctr., Longwood Coll., Smith Coll., Va. Mus., Richmond, Carnegie Mellon U. and numerous others; solo exhbn. of prints McGuffey Art Ctr., Charlottesville, Va., 1988, 90, 93, Woodstock Artist Gallery, 1990, Soc. Am. Graphic Artists, 1988-89, 92, Bombay, 1989, U. Va. Hosp., 1989, Bergen Mus. Art and Sci., 1991; represented in group shows McGuffey Gallery, 1988, 94, Gallery Show, Richmond, Va., 1988, Nat. Assn. Women Artists, Florence, Italy, 1972, N.Y.C., 1989, 96, ann. show Ojibway Hotel Club, Pointe au Baril, Georgian Bay, Ont., Can., 1991, Soc. Am. Graphic Srts, N.Y.C., 1989, 92, Woodstock, N.Y. Art Assoc., 1990, McGuffey Art Ctr., Charlottesville, Va., 1990, 94, 98, Pen and Brush ann. Graphic Show, N.Y.C., 1991 (award for etching Spring, Ada Rosario Cecere Meml. award), Bergen Mus., N.J., 1991, Ojibway Club, Ont., Can., 1991; Pen and Brush Christmas exhbn., 1994-95, Showing of a Video, Harrisonburg, Va.; represented in traveling group shows Nat. Assn. Women Artists, Puerto Rico, 1987, India, 1989, N.Y.C., 1994; pvt. collection U. Va. Hosp., Charlottesville, 1989; subject of TV documentary Hartwell Priest: Printmaker, 1995. Recipient awards for lithograph Field Flowers, Longwood Coll., 1965, Nat. Assn. Woman Artists, 1965, lithograph West Wind, A Buell award, 1961, print Streets of Silence, T. Giorgi Meml. award, 1973, lithograph Blue Lichen, Pen & Brush, 1984, award for collage, 1985; 1st award for graphics Blue Ridge Art Show, 1985, Gene A. Walker award for print Glacial Rocks, 1986, award for print Blue Ridge Show, 1987, Philip Isenburg award for graphic PreCambrian Rock Pattern, 1988, Ada R. Cecere Meml. award Pen and Brush, 1991, Art award Piedmont Coun. Arts, 1993. Mem. Nat. Assn. Women Artists (Travelling Printmaking Exhbn. 1987-89), Pen and Brush, Soc. Am. Graphic Artists, Washington Print Club, 2d St. Gallery, Charlottesville, McGuffey Art Ctr. Avocations: walking, singing in choir, gardening, playing Bach and Mozart, playing recorder and piano. Home: 41 Old Farm Rd Charlottesville VA 22903-1725

PRIEST, MELVILLE STANTON, retired consulting hydraulic engineer; b. Cassville, Mo., Oct. 16, 1912; s. William Tolliver and Mildred Alice (Messer) P.; m. Vivian Willingham, Mar. 22, 1941 (dec.); m. Virginia Young, Dec. 16, 1983. BS, U. Mo., 1935; MS, U. Colo., 1943; PhD, U. Mich., 1954. Registered profl. engr., Ala., La., Miss. Jr. engr. U.S. Engrs. Office, 1937-39; from jr. to asst. engr. Bur. Reclamation, 1939-41; from instr. to assoc. prof. civil engring. Cornell U., 1941-55; prof. hydraulics Auburn (Ala.) U., 1955-58, prof. civil engring., head dept., 1958-65; dir. Water Resources Research Inst., Miss. State U., 1965-77. UN adviser on hydraulics, Egypt, 1956, 57, 60; Mem. Ala. Bd. Registration Profl. Engrs., 1962-65 Contbr. articles to profl. jours. Fellow ASCE (pres. Ala. 1962, exec. com., pipeline div. 1971-74), Am. Water Resources Assn. (dir. 1973-75), Sigma Xi, Tau Beta Pi, Chi Epsilon, Pi Mu Epsilon. Address: Sunny Brook Est Apt 135 248 Locust Ln Madison MS 39110

PRIEST, SHARON DEVLIN, association executive, former state secretary of state; b. Montreal; m. Bill Priest; one son Adam. Tax preparer, instr. H & R Block, Little Rock, 1976-78; owner, founder Devlin Co., Ark., 1983-86; account exec. Greater Little Rock C. of C., 1990-94; vice mayor Little Rock, 1989-90, mayor, 1991-92; Sec. of State State of Ark., 1994—2002; exec. dir. The Downtown Partnership, 2002—. Bd. dir. Invesco Inc., New Futures. Bd. dir., past pres. Metroplan (Environ. Svc. Award 1982), YMCA, Southwest Hosp.; mem. Advt. and Promotion commn., Ark. Internat. Visitors Coun., Pulaski Are Transp. Svc. Policy Com., St. Theresa's Parish Coun., Exec. com. for Ark. Mcpl. League, Nat. League of Cities Trans. and Comm. Steering Com. and Policy Com., adv. bd. M.M. Cohn., Little Rock City Beautiful Commn., 1980-86; former bd. dir. Downtown Partnership, S.W. YMCA, 1984, 86, sec.; former mem. Cmty. Housing Resource Bd., 1984-86, Pub. Facilities Bd. S.W. Hosp., 1985-86, S.W. Merchants' Assn., 1985—, 2d v.p., 1985; chmn. Little Rock Arts and Humanities Promotion Commn.; led petition dr. for appropriation for Fourche Creek Plan 7A. Recipient of the Fighting Back Freedom Fighter Award, 1995; Environ. Svc. Award from the Little Rock Metroplan Comm., 1982. Mem. Leadership Inst. Alumni Assn. (4 Bernard de la Harpe Awards). Achievements include being selected by Ark. Bus. as one of the Top 100 Women in Ark. Office: Downtown Partnership PO Box 1937 Little Rock AR 72203 Office Phone: 501-375-0121. E-mail: spriest@downtownlr.com.

PRIESTLEY, G. T. ERIC, manufacturing executive; b. Belfast, Northern Ireland, May 7, 1942; came to U.S., 1990; s. Thomas John McKee P.; m. Carol Elizabeth Gingles Nelson, June 8, 1966; children: Peter, Gaye, Simon. BS, Queens U., 1963; postgrad. Bus. Sch., Harvard U., 1989. Sales trainee Burroughs Machines Ltd., 1963-64; dealer, sales devel. Regent Oil Co., 1964-66; ops. mgr. RMC (Ulster) Ltd., 1967-70; distbn. mgr. Bass Charrington, Ireland, 1970-71; dir., gen. mgr. Farrans Ltd., 1971-80; dir., CEO Redland plc/British Fuels/Cawoods, 1980-88; dir. Bowater plc, London, 1988-90; pres., CEO Rexam Inc., Charlotte, N.C., 1990-96; exec. v.p., COO Jefferson Smurfit Corp., St. Louis, 1996-97. Non-exec. dir. Southwire Inc. Bd. advisors U. N.C., Charlotte. Mem. Moortown Golf Club, Aloha Golf Club, Royal Ulster Yacht Club, Quail Hollow Country Club. Home: 5639 Legacy Cir Charlotte NC 28277-8103

PRIESTLEY, JASON, actor; b. Vancouver, B.C., Can., Aug. 28, 1969; Actor: (TV series) Sister Kate, 1989-90, Beverly Hills 90210, 1990-1998 (Golden Globe award nominee for best actor in a drama series 1993), Tru Calling, 2003; (TV movies) Vanishing Point, 1997, Kiss Tomorrow Goodbye, 1999 (also exec. prodr., dir.), Common Ground, 2000, Homicide: The Movie, 2000, Warning: Parental Advisory, 2002, The True Meaning of Christmas Specials, 2002, Sleep Murder, 2004, I Want to Marry Ryan Banks, 2004; (films) Calendar Girl, 1993, Tombstone, 1993, Cold-Blooded, 1995, Love and Death on Long Island, 1997, Hacks, 1997, Eye of the Beholder, 1998, Dill Scallion, 1999, Zigs, 1999, Barenaked in America, 1999 (also prodr., dir.), The Highwayman, 1999, Cover Story, 2002, Darkness Falling, 2002, Die, Mommie Die, 2003, Chicks with Sticks, 2004; guest appearances include Spin City, 1996, 8 Simple Rules...for Dating My Teenage Daughter, 2002, Celebrities Uncensored, 2003, 04; prodr., dir. episodes TV series Beverly Hills 90210, 1995-96. Office: c/o Wolf Kasteler 132 S Rodeo Dr Ste 300 Beverly Hills CA 90212-2414*

PRIETO, CLAUDIO R. academic administrator, lawyer; b. Caguas, P.R., Aug. 17, 1933; s. Claudio Prieto and Carmen (Gutierrez) del Arroyo; m. Myrna Irizarry; children: Claudio, Carmen, Isabel, Rosa, Anna, Alfonso. BS, U. P.R., 1954, JD, 1971. Bar: P.R. Asst. prof. U. P.R., Rio Piedras, 1956-70, coord. student affairs, 1957-59, dir. extension div., 1959-61, assoc. prof. Sch. Law, 1970-71; dir. edn. press Commonwealth of Puerto Rico, Rio Piedras, 1961-65, asst. sec. edn., 1965-67, asst. to gov. San Juan, 1967-68; asst. to dep. commr. Dept. Edn. State of N.Y., Albany, 1977-78, asst. commr., 1978-88; chancellor Turabo U., Gurabo, P.R., 1989-93; exec. dir. office of equity and acccess policy studies N.Y. State Dept. Edn., Albany, 1993-94; dep. asst. sec. for higher edn. programs Dept. Edn., Washington, 1994—2001; chancellor InterAmerican U. of PR - Met. Campus, 2001—. Cons. to chancellor U. P.R., 1969, legal plannning and adminstrn. Tech. Svcs. P.R., 1973-76. Columnist San Juan Star, 1973-76, 1992— Trustee Ewald B. Nyquist Meml. Fund, Albany, 1990—; bd. overseers Regents Coll., 1989-93. Named Edn. Exec. of Yr. Sales and Mktg. Assn., P.R., 1989. Mem. Intercollegiate Athletic League (bd. govs.). Democrat. Roman Catholic.

PRIETO, MONIQUE N. artist; b. L.A., 1962; BFA, UCLA, 1987, Calif. Inst. Arts, 1992, MFA, 1994. One-woman shows include ACME, Santa Monica, Calif., 1994, 1995, 1996, 1997, Bravin Post Lee, N.Y.C., 1996, one-woman shows include Anderson Gallery, Va. Commonwealth U., Richmond, 1997, Pat Hearn Gallery, N.Y.C., 1998, Robert Prime, London, 1998, exhibited in group shows at Wight Gallery, UCLA, 1987, Bacilla Hernandez Gallery, Long Beach, Calif., 1989; actor: Lockheed Gallery, 1994; Exhibited in group shows at Pat Hearn Gallery, N.Y.C., 1996, 1997, Factory Place Gallery, L.A., 1996, Armand Hammer Sales and Rental Gallery, 1997, ACME, Santa Monica, 1997, Orange County Mus. Art, Newport Beach, Calif., 1997. Herb Alpert scholar, 1992—93, Philip Morris fellow, 1992—94, Skowbegan Sch. Painting and Sculpture fellow, 1994. Office: c/o Pat Hearn Gallery 530 W 22nd St New York NY 10011-1108

PRIEVE, E. ARTHUR, arts administration educator; BBA in Adminstrn. and Art History, U. of Wis., 1959, MBA in Mgmt. and Orgn. Behavior, 1961; DBA in Mgmt. and Psych., George Washington U., Washington, 1965. Asst. dean adminstrv. affairs Sch. Bus. U. Wis., Madison, 1966-69, prof. mgmt. Grad. Sch. Bus., 1969—, dir. exec. MBA program, 1993—; dir. Ctr. For Arts Adminstrn., Madison, 1969—. Curriculum cons. for arts adminstrn.; cons. visual, performing and arts svc. orgns.; workshops and presentations on planning, bd. dirs. Mem. Assn. of Arts Adminstrn. Educators (chmn. U.S., Can.). Office: U Wis Ctr Arts Adminstrn 4171 Grainger Hall 975 University Ave Madison WI 53706-1324

PRIMANZON, ANDREA JESSICA, special events coordinator; b. Washington, July 8, 1969; d. Carol Ann and Henry Alvin Cirbee(Stepfather); m. Michael Scott Primanzon, Sept. 13, 2003. MBA, Marymount U., Va., 1993. Cert. mgr. exhibits Ppogram Trade Show Exhibitors Assn. Adminstrv. asst. to dir. mktg. C & G Distbrs., Inc., Laurel, Md., 1994; asst. dir. mktg. DPI-C & G Distbrs., Inc, Laurel, 1994—2000; spl. events coord. Adventist HealthCare, Rockville, Md., 2000—02; publs. mgr., exhibit mgr. Pub. Health Found., Washington, 2002—. Bd. trustees devel. com. rep. St. Mary's Coll. of Md., 2003; bd. dirs. Cipriano Woods Homeowners Assn., Lanham, Md., 1997—99. Mem.: Am. Bus. Women's Assn. (assoc.; sec., exec. bd. mem. 2002—03), St. Mary's Coll. of Md. Alumni Assn. (bd. dirs. 2001—). Republican. Roman Catholic. Avocation: antiques.

PRIMAVERA, FRED JOSEPH, music educator; b. Euclid, Ohio, Feb. 23, 1966; s. Fred Angelo and Sandra Ann Primavera. MusB, Youngstown State U., 1992; MusM in Edn., VanderCook Coll. Music, 1996. Cert. music edn. grades K-12 Ohio. Band dir. Willoughby (Ohio) South HS, 1992—. Mem.: Nat. Band Assn., Music Educators Nat. Conf., Ohio Music Edn. Assn. Home: 5617 Seneca Place Willoughby OH 44094 Office: Willoughby South High School 5000 Shankland Bloulevard Willoughby OH 44094 Personal E-mail: fprimavera@prodigy.net.

PRIMEAU, KEITH, professional hockey player; b. Toronto, Nov. 24, 1971; Drafted Detroit Red Wings, 1990-97; right wing Carolina Hurricanes, 1997-99, Phila. Flyers, 1999—. Office: Phila Flyers First Union Ctr 1 Corse State Complex Philadelphia PA 19148

PRIMEAUX, HENRY, III, automotive executive, author, speaker; b. New Orleans, Nov. 16, 1941; s. Henry Jr. and Ethel (Ritter) P.; m. Jane Cathrine Velcich, July 23, 1960; children: Joann Primeaux Longa, Lisa Primeaux Lotz, Henry Joseph. Student, La. State U., New Orleans, 1959-63. Compt. Jimco, New Orleans, 1965-66; owner, mgr. Picone Seafood, New Orleans, 1966-67; v.p. NADW Inc., Metairie, La., 1967-78, Am. Warranty Corp., L.A., 1978-80; pres. F&I Warranty Corp., Arlington, Tex., 1980-87; exec. v.p. F&I Mgmt. Corp., Arlington, 1980-87; pres., CEO Primco Corp., Arlington, 1987-91; owner Flavors Restaurant, Tulsa, Okla., Primeaux Mktg. Mng. ptnr. Crown Auto World, Bristow; founder, Pimeaux Family Found., 1998; mgr., Primeaux Family Dealerships; mng. ptnr., Primeaux Family Realty; cons., corr. Wards Auto Dealer, Detroit, 1987-95, weekly TV program Automotive Satellite TV Network; cons. Nissan Motor Co., L.A., 1988-89, Convergent div. Unisys, Hunt Valley, Md., 1988-90; cons. Mercedes-Benz N.Am.; exec. com. Okla. Workforce Investment Bd.; chmn. Tulsa Workforce Investment Bd. Writer Auto Age mag.; author: F&I Handbook. Mem. Rep. Task Force Okla. Workforce Devel. Com.; bd. dirs. John Starks Found., Boy Scouts U.S.; mem. nat. adv. bd. Automotive Yes Sch. to Work Initiative; mem. Okla. Sch. to Work Commn.; bd. regents Okla. State U., Tulsa. With USN, 1959-61. Mem. Am. Internat. Automobile Dealers Assn., Assn. of F&I Profls. (bd. dirs. 1990—, pres. 1994), Nat. Auto Dealers Assn. (pres. Tulsa chpt. 1994, Time Quality Dealer of Yr. 1994), Okla. State C. of C. (bd. dirs.), Met. Tulsa C. of C. (bd. dirs. 1998-2000). Roman Catholic. Office: Crown Bristow 901 S Roland Bristow OK 74010 Home: 6201 E 108th St Tulsa OK 74137-8903 E-mail: primeaux1@aol.com., crownhen@aol.com.

PRIMI, DON ALEXIS, advertising executive, public relations executive, railroad transportation executive; b. N.Y.C., Jan. 14, 1947; s. John Prosper, Sr. and Eileen Mary P.; A. in Advt., State U. N.Y., 1967; B.S. in Mktg. and Advt., Hofstra U., 1971; advanced astron. studies degree, Vanderbilt Mus. and Planetarium, 1967. Gen. mgr., Recreational Pub. Corp.; pres., owner Fantasia Trains/REE R.R. Equipment Exchange, 1980, Don Primi Designs, 1984, Rail Industries, Rail Fin. Corp., 1987, Gold Coast Ltd./Royal Rail, 1987, Rail Enterprises, 1990, LPA North Am., 1992, Alexis Daniels, 1992, Salon Promotions, 1992, Trans Fla. Express, Inc., 2001; cons. in field, ry. industry, brick and clay products industry; designer corp. identity programs. Recipient awards Printing Industries Met. N.Y., Gold Boli advt. awards, Kimberly-Clark Graphic excellence awards, Astrophotoawards. Mem. Assn. Ry. Progress Inst., R.R. Pub. Relations Assn., Nat. R.R. Assn. Passengers, Sales and Mktg. Execs., Astron Soc. L.I. (pres., pub. rel dir.), Rail Mktg. Club N.Y. Designs published in periodicals. Home: 4065 Old Settlement Rd Merritt Island FL 32952-6211 Office: 160 5th Ave New York NY 10010-7003 E-mail: dprail21@brevard.net.

PRIMM, EARL RUSSELL, III, publishing executive; b. Rhinelander, Wis., Oct. 24, 1958; s. Earl Russell and Betty Joan (Dennis) P. AB in Classics (hon.), Loyola U. Chgo., 1980; MA in Libr. Sci., U. Chgo., 1990. Asst. to edn. dir. J.G. Ferguson Pub. Co., Chgo., 1981-84; prodn. mgr. Joint Commn. on Accreditation of Hosps., Chgo., 1984-85; sr. editor J.G. Ferguson Pub. Co., Chgo., 1985-87; asst. editor U. Chgo. Press, 1987-88; editorial dir. J.G. Ferguson Pub. Co., Chgo., 1988-89; project mgr. Children's Press, Chgo., 1989-92; exec. editor Franklin Watts, Inc., Chgo., N.Y.C., 1992-95; editl. dir. Grolier Children's Pub., Danbury, Conn., 1995-97; pres. Editl. Directions, Inc., Chgo., 1997—. Mem. adv. bd. U. Chgo. Pub. Program, 1990-2000; judge Lambda Lit. awards, Washington, 1994-2000; guest lectr. Sch. Edn. Harvard U., 2004. Editl. chief: Career Discovery Encyclopedia, 1990, Favorite Children's Authors and Illustrators, 2002; editor: Civil Rights Movement in America, 2nd edit., 1991, Extraordinary Hispanic Americans, 1991; editl. dir. The Child's World, 2002, Tradition Books, 2002. Mem. crisis counselor Nat. Runaway Switchboard, Chgo., 1985-88; Horizon's hotline counselor, Chgo., 1987-88; bd. dirs. Gerber/Hart Libr. and Archives, Chgo., 1992-94. Named Honors Sr. of Yr., Loyola U. Chgo., 1980; recipient Mertz Latin Scholarship key Loyola U. Chgo., 1980. Mem. Pub. Triangle, Chgo. Book Clinic, Am. Libr. Assn. Democrat. Home: 1000 W Washington Blvd #147 Chicago IL 60607-2148 Office: 1000 W Washington Blvd # 203 Chicago IL 60607 E-mail: russell@editorialdirections.com.

PRIMO, JOAN ERWINA, retail and real estate consulting business owner; b. Detroit, Aug. 28, 1959; d. Joseph Carmen and Marie Ann (Nash) P.; m. David James Yared, Sept. 20, 1997; 1 son, Benjamin Primo Yared. BA, Wellesley Coll., 1981; MBA, Harvard U., 1985. Acct. exec. Michigan Bell, Detroit, 1981-82, AT&T Info. Sys., Southfield, Mich., 1983; planning analyst Gen. Motors, Detroit, 1984; v.p. Howard L. Green & Assocs., Troy, Mich., 1985-89; prin., founder The Strategic Edge, Inc., Southfield, 1989—. Contbr. articles to profl. jours. Founders soc. mem. Detroit Inst. Arts, 1989—. Mem.: Internat. Coun. Shopping Ctrs. (faculty, seminar leader 1987—), Ivy Club Detroit (bd. dirs. 1994—, sec. 1995—99), Harvard Bus. Sch. Club Detroit (bd. dirs. 1994—98, v.p. 1995—96, exec. v.p. 1996—97), Wellesley Club Southeastern Mich. (pres. 1994—98). Republican. Avocations: antiques, travel, theater, gourmet cooking. Home: 224 Woodwind Dr Bloomfield Hills MI 48304-2172 Office: The Strategic Edge 24333 Southfield Rd Ste 211 Southfield MI 48075-2849 Office Phone: 248-557-1664. Personal E-mail: joanprimo@aol.com. E-mail: jprimo@thestrategicedge.com.

PRIMO, QUINTIN E., III, real estate company executive; BS in Fin. with honors, Ind. U.; MBA, Harvard U. Former mng. dir. Q. Primo & Co., Inc.; CEO, co-founder, co-chmn. Capri Capital L.P., Chgo., 1992—. Chmn. Urban Family and Cmty. Ctrs.; chmn. Com. of 100 Ill. Pub. Policy Caucus. Mem.: Urban Land Inst., Pension Real Estate Assn., Real Estate Roundtable (dir.). Office: Capri Capital LP Ste 3430 875 N Michigan Ave Chicago IL 60611*

PRIMOSCH, JAMES THOMAS, music educator, composer, musician; b. Cleve., Oct. 29, 1956; s. Edward Joseph and Rose Marie (Potochar) P.; m. Mary Marguerite Murphy, April 5, 1986. BA in Composition magna cum laude, Cleve. State U., 1978; MA in Composition, U. Pa., 1980; DMA in Composition awarded with distinction, Columbia U., 1988; studied piano privately with Lambert Orkis, Phila., 1978-80; studied composition with John Harbison, Tanglewood, 1984. Asst. prof. music U. Pa., 1988—94, assoc. prof. music, 1994—2001, prof. music, 2001—. Grad. assistantships Columbia-Princeton Electronic Music Ctr., 1982-84, 86-87, preceptorship Columbia U., 1984-85; residency Va. Ctr. Creative Arts, 1985, MacDowell Colony, 1988, Bellagio Conf. Ctr., 1992; regional vis. artist Am. Acad. in Rome, 1994; composer in residence Marlboro Music Festival, 1994. Composer over 40 compositions and 26 published works; compositions performed by Chgo. Symphony Orch., LA Philharm., St. Paul Chamber Orch., Cleve. Chamber Symphony, NY New Music Ensemble; compositions performed at Carnegie Hall, Dorothy Chandler Pavilion, Town Hall, Weill (Carnegie) Recital Hall, others; reviewer High Performance Rev. Mag., 1987-95. Recipient 3rd prize, People's prize Internat. Gaudeamus Competition, The Netherlands, 1977, Helen L. Weiss prize U. Pa., 1979, David Halstead prize U. Penn., 1980, 3rd prize Shreveport Symphony Composer's Competition, 1980-81, John H. Bearns prize, 1981, 1st. prize Holtkamp Organ Composition Contest, 1982, Eda and Boris Rappoport prize Columbia U., 1984, Tanglewood prize in Composition Berkshire Music Ctr., 1984, Cleve. Arts prize, 1992, Elise Stoeger prize Chamber Music Soc. Lincoln Ctr., 1999; recipient Recognition award Mader Meml. Fund, 1980, BMI Student Composers award, 1982; New Music Consort Composition Contest winner, 1987, League of Composers ISCM winner, 1988; Fine Arts scholar Cleve. State U., 1974-78, scholar Cleve. Fortnightly Music Club, 1976-78, Arthur Loesser Meml. scholar, 1977-78, Yale Composer's Workshop at Norfolk, 1981, Columbia U. scholar, 1981-82, Charles Ives scholar Am. Acad. Inst. Arts & Letters, 1985; U. fellow U. Penn., 1978-79, Composers Conf. Johnson Vt., 1979-80, CBS Found. fellow U. Penn., 1979-80, Margaret Lee Crofts fellow Berkshire Music Ctr. Tanglewood, 1984, Guggenheim fellow, 1985, NEA, 1991-92, Goddard Lieberson fellow Am. Acad. Arts and Letters, 1993, Pew fellow in arts, 1996; ASCAP Found. Young Composers grant, 1984, 82, Meet The Composer grant 1980, 82, 85, 87, 89-90, 94, 96-97, Am. Music Ctr. Copying Assistance grant, 1985, 90, Pa. Coun. on the Arts, 1990, 98, 2002, Presser Found. grantee U. Pa. Mem. BMI, Pi Kappa Lambda. Roman Catholic. Avocation: reading.

PRIMPS, WILLIAM GUTHRIE, lawyer; b. Ossining, NY, Sept. 8, 1949; s. Richard Byrd and Mary Elizabeth (Guthrie) P.; m. Sophia Elizabeth Beutel, Aug. 25, 1973; children: Emily Ann, Elizabeth Armstrong, William Andrew. BA, Yale U., 1971; JD, Harvard U., 1974. Bar: N.Y., 1975. Assoc. LeBoeuf, Lamb, Leiby & MacRae, N.Y.C., 1974-82; ptnr. LeBoeuf, Lamb, Greene & MacRae, N.Y.C., 1983—. Counsel to Bd. Zoning Appeals, Bronxville, 1988-89, chmn., 1989-91. Class coun. Yale U., New Haven, 1986-91; trustee Village of Bronxville, 1991-97, dep. mayor, 1995-97; deacon Reformed Ch. Bronxville, 1989-94, elder, 1998-2002; bd. dirs. Bronxville Sch. Fdn. 1998—, v.p., 2003—, Football Assn., 2003—, mem. adv. coun. Atlantic Legal Found. Inc., 2002-. Mem. ABA, N.Y. State Bar Assn., Assn. Yale Alumni (class rep. 1986-91), Yale Club, Bronxville Field Club. Republican. Home: 71 Summit Ave Bronxville NY 10708-1815 Office: LeBoeuf Lamb Greene & MacRae 125 W 55th St New York NY 10019-5369

PRINA, L(OUIS) EDGAR, journalist; b. West New York, N.J., Oct. 7, 1917; s. Louis Edgar and Marion (Duggan) P.; m. Frances Lee Lorick, Feb. 14, 1947; 1 dau., Lee Lorick II. AB, Syracuse U., 1938, MA, 1940. Copy editor, asst. night city editor N.Y. Sun, N.Y.C., 1946-48, Washington corr., 1948-50; nat. affairs writer Washington Star, 1950-66; mil. affairs writer/editor Copley News Svc., Washington, 1966-77, bur. chief, 1977-84, sr. corr., 1984-87; editor Navy mag., Washington, 1961-68; columnist Sea Power mag., 1968—. Author: The Political Virgin, 1958, Flew to South Pole for Overnight Visit, 1966. Served with USN, 1941-46, 51-53; capt. Res. (ret.). Recipient honorable mention-Heywood Broun award, 1956, Disting. Public Svc. award USN, 1965, Alfred Thayer Mahan award Navy League U.S., 1987, Copley Ring of Truth award, 1971, 74-76, 79, 80-81, Chancellor's Sr. Alumni award Syracuse U., 1998; nominated for Pulitzer Prize (twice). Mem. U.S. Naval Inst., Nat. Press Club (chmn. bd. govs.), White House Corrs. Assn., Explorers Club, Soc. Profl. Journalists (pres. Washington chpt., named to Hall of Fame 1999), Kappa Sigma, Phi Kappa Phi. Clubs: Gridiron, Chevy Chase, Met. of Washington. Roman Catholic. Home: 4813 Quebec St NW Washington DC 20016-3228 Office: The Metro Club Box 47 1700 H St NW Washington DC 20006-4689

PRINCE, ANDREW STEVEN, lawyer, former government official; b. Bklyn., Oct. 9, 1943; s. Milton S. and Beatrice M. (Ratkin) P.; m. Rochelle Moskowitz, July 4, 1973; children: Brett, Kenneth. BS, U.S. Naval Acad., 1965; MBA, JD, Harvard U., 1974. Bar: N.Y. 1975, U.S. Supreme Ct. 1980. Assoc. firm Shearman & Sterling, N.Y.C., 1974-81; dep. asst. sec. Navy Dept., Washington, 1981-86; exec. v.p., gen. counsel Urquhart and Co., Inc., McLean, Va., 1986-94; mng. dir. Nat. Capital Cos. LLC, Bethesda, Md., 1997-2000; mng. dir., COO HFS Capital LLC, McLean, Va., 2000—02; CEO, pres. Bretken Enterprises, 2002—03, Prince Strategic Group LC, McLean, Va., 2003. Sec. Potash Import & Chem. Corp., N.Y.C., 1979-81; mem. panel of arbitrators Am. Arbitration Assn., N.Y.C., 1979—. Bd. dirs. Harvard Coop. Soc., Cambridge, Mass., 1972-74; bd. dirs. USO, Washington, 1982-86, N.Y.C., 1979-81. Served with USN, 1965-70; capt. Res., ret. Mem. Harvard Bus. Sch. Club, Washington, DC (bd. dir., pres.), Mil Order World Wars (judge adv.), Naval Acad. Alumni Assn., Naval Acad. Found. (dir.). E-mail: aprince65@hotmail.com.

PRINCE, CHARLES O., III, (CHUCK PRINCE), bank executive; b. Lynwood, Calif., Jan. 13, 1950; BA, U. So. Calif., 1971, MA, JD, 1975; LLM, Georgetown U., 1983. Bar: Pa. 1975, Md. 1979, Minn. 1982. Atty. U.S. Steel Corp., 1975—79; gen. counsel Commercial Credit Co., 1979—86; exec. v.p., gen. counsel, sec. Traveler's Group, N.Y.C., 1986-98; co-gen. counsel, sec. Citigroup (merger of Traveler's Group and Citibank), N.Y.C., 1998—2000; chief admin. officer Citigroup Inc., 2000, COO, 2001—02; chmn. & CEO, global corp. & investment bank group Citigroup, 2002—03; CEO Citigroup Inc., 2003—. Mem. Coun. Foreign Relations. Bd. dirs. United Negro Coll. Fund, Teachers Coll. Columbia U. Office: Citigroup Inc 399 Park Ave New York NY 10022 also: Citigroup 153 E 53rd St New York NY 10043-0001*

PRINCE, DANFORTH, publishing executive, journalist; b. Toledo, June 14, 1953; s. Edward Mitchell Prince and Elizabeth Jane Danforth. BA, Hamilton Coll., Clinton, N.Y., 1975. Dir. rsch. and writer the Frommer Guides Porter & Prince Corp., N.Y.C., NY, 1983—; pres. and CEO Blood Moon Prodn., N.Y.C., NY, 1997—, The Ga. Lit. Assn., N.Y.C., 1997—. Co-author: The Frommer Guides, 1983—. Mem.: North Am. Travel Journalists Assn. Office: Blood Moon Productions Ltd 75 Saint Marks Pl Staten Island NY 10301 Office Phone: 718-556-9410. Office Fax: 718-816-4092. E-mail: danforthpr@aol.com.

PRINCE, GEORGE EDWARD, retired pediatrician; b. Erwin, N.C., Nov. 25, 1921; s. Hugh Williamson and Helen Herman (Hood) P.; m. Millie Elizabeth Mann, Nov. 26, 1944; children: Helen Elizabeth, Millie Mann, Susan Hood, Mary Lois. MD, Duke U., 1944. Diplomate Am. Bd. Pediatrics, Am. Bd. Med. Examiners. Intern Boston Children's Hosp. Harvard Svc., Boston, 1944-45; resident pediatrics Children's Hosp., Louisville, 1945-47; instr. pediatrics U. Louisville, 1947; founder Gastonia (N.C.) Children's Clinic, 1947, pediatrician, 1947-86; pub. health physician Gaston County Health Dept., Gastonia, N.C., 1986-98, med. dir., 1995-98, ret., 1998. Chmn. bd. dirs. Carolina State Bank; bd. dirs. So. Nat. Bank, Gastonia, 1979-95, Hospice, Gastonia, 1987-92; organizer, dir. AIDS Adv. Coun., Gaston County, N.C., 1988-94; coord. N.C. chpt. Pediatric Rsch. in Office Setting, 1986-92. Contbr. articles to profl. jours. Mem. Gaston County Human Rels. Com., Gastonia, 1966; mem. Sch. Health Adv. Coun., Gaston County, 1980-97. Maj. USAF, 1955-57. Recipient Balthis Heart Assn. award, Gaston County, 1981, 1998, Good Amb. award, Health Dept., 1986, Family Adv. award, Commn. on the Family, Gaston County, 1995, commendation, City of Gastonia, 2001, Gaston County Bd. Commrs., 2001. Fellow Am. Acad. Pediatrics (pres. N.C. chpt. 1984-86); mem. AMA, N.C. Pediatric Soc. (hon., pres. 1970), N.C. Med. Soc., Gaston County Med. Soc. (pres. 1966), Rotary (pres. 1984), County Club (bd. dirs. 1975-76). Democrat. Methodist. Avocations: golf, skiing, sailing, bridge. Home: 2208 Cross Creek Dr Gastonia NC 28056-8808 Office Phone: 704-864-3322.

PRINCE, GREGORY SMITH, JR., academic administrator; b. Washington, May 7, 1939; s. Gregory Smith and Margaret (Minor) P.; m. Toni Layton Brewer; children: Tara Wyndom, Gregory S. III. BA, Yale U., 1961, M in Philosophy, 1969, PhD, 1973; cert. in teaching English as a Second Language, Georgetown U., 1961; DHL (hon.), LLD (hon.), Amherst Coll., 1991. Instr. New Asia Coll., Kowloon, Hong Kong, 1961-62, Chinese U., Kowloon, 1962-63, Yale China Assn., Kowloon, 1961-63, Woodberry Forest (Va.) Sch., 1963-65; dean summer programs Dartmouth Coll., Hanover, N.H., 1970-72, asst. dean faculty, 1972-78, assoc. dean faculty, 1978-89; pres. Hampshire Coll., Amherst, Mass., 1989—. Vice chair coun. on racial and ethnic justice ABA; bd. dirs. Mass Ventures. Producer: (film) A Way of Learning, 1988. Trustee Montshire Mus. Sci., Hanover, 1973-89, Washington Campus, 1978—; trustee, chmn. Univ. Press New England, Hanover, 1983-84; trustee, pres. Yale-China Assn., New Haven, 1969-84; bd. dirs. Five Colls., Inc., Amherst, 1989—; bd. dirs. Mass. Internat. Festival for Arts, 1994-98; chmn. bd. dirs. Assn. Ind. Colls. and Univs. Mass., 1994-95; chair commn. on accreditation Am. Coun. Edn.; bd. dirs. Mass. Nature Conservancy, 1996—; bd. dirs. Nat. Assn. Ind. Colls. and Univs., 1999-2001, Friendship House, 2002—. Coe fellow Stanford U., 1965, Woodrow Wilson fellow Yale U., 1966, NDEA fellow, 1967-70. Mem. Internat. Assn. of Chiefs Police Found. (bd. dirs. 1991-95), Nat. Assn. of Ind. Colls. and Univs. Democrat. Episcopalian. Home: 15 Middle St Amherst MA 01002-3009 Office: Hampshire Coll 893 West St Amherst MA 01002-3372

PRINCE, HAROLD, theatrical director, producer; b. N.Y.C., Jan. 30, 1928; s. Milton A. and Blanche (Stern) P.; m. Judith Chaplin, Oct. 26, 1962; children: Charles, Daisy. AB, U. Pa., 1948, DFA (hon.), 1971; LittD, Emerson Coll., 1971. Chmn. Performing Arts Libr., N.Y.C. Co-prodr.: Pajama Game, 1954-56 (Antoinette Perry award), Damn Yankees, 1955-57 (Antoinette Perry award), New Girl in Town, 1957-58, West Side Story, 1957-59, A Swim in the Sea, 1958, Fiorello, 1959-61 (Antoinette Perry award, Pulitzer prize), Tenderloin, 1960-61, A Call on Kuprin, 1961, They Might Be Giants, London, 1961, Side by Side by Sondheim, 1977; prodr.: Take Her, She's Mine, 1961-62, A Funny Thing Happened on the Way to the Forum, 1962-64 (Antoinette Perry award), Fiddler on the Roof, 1964-72 (Antoinette Perry award), Poor Bitos, 1964, Flora the Red Menace, 1965; dir., prodr.: She Loves Me, 1963-64, London, 1964, Superman, 1966, Cabaret, 1966-69 (Antoinette Perry award 1968), Zorba, 1968-69, Company, 1970-72 (Antoinette Perry award 1972), A Little Night Music, 1973-74 (Antoinette Perry award 1975), Pacific Overtures, 1976, A Doll's Life, 1982; co-dir., prodr.: Follies, 1971-72 (Tony award for directing), Faust, 1990; co-prodr., dir.: Candide, 1974-75 (Tony award for directing), Merrily We Roll Along, 1981; dir.: A Family Affair, 1962, Baker Street, 1965, Great God Brown, 1972-73, The Visit, 1973-74, Love for Love, 1974-75, Ashmedai, 1976, Some of My Best Friends, 1977, On The Twentieth Century, 1978, La Fanciulla Del West, 1978, Evita, London, 1979, N.Y.C., 1980, L.A., 1982, Australia, 1980, Chgo., 1980, Detroit, 1982, Sweeney Todd, The Demon Barber of Fleet Street, Broadway, 1979, London, 1980, Silverlake, 1980, Willie Stark, 1981, Candide, 1982, 94, 97, Madama Butterfly, 1983, Turandot, 1983, Play Memory, 1984, End of the World, 1984, Grind, 1985, Cabaret Revival, 1987, Roza, 1987, Phantom of the Opera, London, 1986, N.Y.C., (Antoinette Perry award) 1988, Kiss of the Spider Woman, Toronto, 1992, London, 1992, N.Y.C., 1993, Show Boat, Toronto, 1993, N.Y.C., 1994 (Tony award for directing), La Fanciula del West, Don Giovanni, N.Y. City Opera, 1989, Faust, Met. Opera, 1990, The Petrified Prince, 1994, (off broadway) Diamonds, 1984; adapter, dir. (off broadway) Grandchild of Kings, 1992, Candide, Broadway, 1997, Parade, Broadway, 1998, Hollywood Arms, Broadway, 2002, Bounce, Chgo., Wash., 2003; co-prodr: (films) The Pajama Game, 1957, Damn Yankees, 1958; dir.: (films) Something for Everyone, 1970, A Little Night Music, 1978, 3Hree, Phila. & L.A. Mem. coun. Nat. Endowment Arts; pres. League N.Y. Theatres, 1964-66; chmn. Performing Arts Libr., N.Y.C. Recipient 20 Antoinette Perry (Tony) Meml. awards, Critics Circle awards, Pulitzer prize, 1961, Best Mus. awards London Evening Std., Kennedy Ctr. Honors, 1994. Office: 10 Rockefeller Plz Ste 1009 New York NY 10020-1972

PRINCE, JOHN LUTHER, III, engineering educator; b. Austin, Tex., Nov. 13, 1941; s. John Luther and Glynda (Chollett) P.; m. Martha Ann Hight, Mar. 4, 1960; children: Cynthia Kay, John Luther IV, Alan Douglas, David William. BSEE, So. Meth. U., 1965; MEE, N.C. State U., 1968, PhD, 1969. Research engr. RTI, Res. Tri. Park, N.C., 1968-70; mem. tech. staff Tex. Instruments, Dallas, 1970-75; from assoc. prof. to prof. Clemson (S.C.) U., 1975-80; dir. R.A. Intermedics, Inc., Freeport, Tex., 1980-83; prof. U. Ariz., Tucson, 1983—. Acting dir. packaging scis. Semiconductor Rsch. Corp., 1991-92; cons. numerous semi-conductor and electronics cos., 1983—; dir. Electronic Packaging Lab., 1984-91, Ctr. for Electronic Packaging Rsch., 1991—, SEMATECH Ctr. of Excellence for Contamination and Defect Control, 1988-90. Contbr. articles to profl. jours. Named Ariz. Innovator of the Yr., 1992; NSF fellow, 1965-68. Fellow IEEE; mem. Am. Philatelic Soc. Lutheran. Avocations: stamp collecting/philately, classic cars, motorcycles. Home: 7542 N San Lorenzo Dr Tucson AZ 85704-3141 Office: U Ariz Dept Engineering Tucson AZ 85721-0001 Office Phone: 520-621-6187. Business E-Mail: prince@ece.arizona.edu. E-mail: jlpmhp@aol.com.

PRINCE, JULIUS S. (BUD PRINCE), retired foreign service reserve officer; b. Yonkers, N.Y., July 21, 1911; s. Julius and Clara B. (Rich) P.; m. Eleanora Molloy, July 6, 1943; children: Thomas Marc, Tod Ainslee (dec.), Richard M. Johnson. BA, Yale U., 1932; MD, Columbia U., 1938, M.P.H., 1948; Dr.P.H., Harvard, 1957. Intern Sinai Hosp., Balt., 1939-40; asst. resident medicine N.Y. U. div. Goldwater Meml. Hosp., 1941-42; dist. state health officer N.Y. State Dept. Health, Jamestown, 1948-58; chief pub. health div. USAID, Ethiopia, 1958-67; prin. investigator demonstration and evaluation project AID, Ethiopia, 1959-67; chief Africa div. Population and Humanitarian Affairs, Population Office, AID, Washington, 1967-73; dir. Africa Regional Population Office, Accra, Ghana, 1973-74; chief health, population and nutrition projects AID, Ghana, 1974-76; cons. internat. health APHA, 1977-78, Pacific Cons., Inc., 1978-82, RONCO Inc., 1982; pub. health specialist/sr. health advisor One Am., Inc., 1982-87; sr. pub. health and nutrition specialist Internat. Sci. and Tech. Inst. Inc., 1985-94; cons. on internat. health, 1985—. Report on sustainability of AID supported health, population and nutrition programs, Ghana, 1963-85, Ctr. Devel. Info. and Evaluation AID, 1988, Annotated History of AID-Supported Health and Nutrition Rsch.: From Outset to Present, Introduction and Background, AID Office Health, 1991, Compendium of Abstracts, 1985-92, rsch. by historically black colls. and univs. under AID Univ. Ctr./Rsch. and Univ. Devel. Linkages, 1985-92. Contbr. chpt. to book. Served from lt. to maj. M.C. Royal Canadian Army, 1942-46. Recipient Letter of Commendation, Adj. Gen. Can. Army, 1946, Superior honor award AID, 1968, Letter of Commendation, 1977 Fellow APHA (Lifetime Achievement award 1996), Soc. Applied Anthropology, Washington Acad. Scis., Royal Soc. Health, Am. Coll. Preventive Medicine; mem. AMA, N.Y. State Pub. Health Assn. (pres. 1957), Pan Am. Med. Assn., Am. Assn. World Health (emeritus mem. bd. dirs.), Internat. Soc. Hypertension in Blacks, Internat. Union for Sci. Study of Population, Population Assn. Am., Soc. Internat. Devel., Nat. Coun. Internat. Health (award 1992), World Med. Assn., Soc. Prospective Medicine, Can. Soc. Internat. Health. Home and Office: 7103 Pinehurst Pky Chevy Chase MD 20815-3144

PRINCE, KENNETH STEPHEN, lawyer; b. Newton, Mass., Jan. 28, 1950; s. Samuel and Edna L. Prince; m. Patricia Denning, Jan. 15, 1977 (dec. Nov. 1985); 1 child, Kenneth Stephen Jr.; m. Jane M. McCabe, Sept. 5, 1987; 1 child, Allison Pamela. BA, U. Pa., 1972; JD, Boston Coll., 1975. Bar: N.Y. 1976, Mass. 1975, U.S. Dist. Ct. (so. and ea. dists.) N.Y. 1978. Assoc. Shearman & Sterling, N.Y.C., 1975-83, ptnr., 1984—, antitrust group practice leader, 1992—2003. Mem. N.Y. Law Inst. (exec. com. 1984-96), Order of Coif. Home: 15 Dellwood Rd Darien CT 06820-2915 E-mail: kprince@shearman.com.

PRINCE, LARRY L. automotive parts and supplies company executive; b. 1937; With Genuine Parts Co., Atlanta, 1958—, v.p., then group v.p., 1977-83, exec. v.p., 1983-86, pres., chief oper. officer, 1986-90, chief exec. officer, 1989—, chmn. bd. dirs., CEO, 1990—, also bd. dirs. Office: Genuine Parts Co 2999 Circle 75 Pky NW Atlanta GA 30339

PRINCE, LEAH FANCHON, art educator and research institute administrator; b. Hartford, Conn., Aug. 12, 1939; d. Meyer and Annie (Forman) Berman; m. Herbert N. Prince, Jan. 30, 1955; children: Daniel L., Richard N., Robert G. Student, U. Conn., 1957-59, Rutgers U., Newark, 1962; BFA, Fairleigh Dickinson U., 1970; postgrad., Caldwell Coll. for Women, 1973-75, Parsons Sch. of Design, N.Y.C., 1978. Cert. tchr. art, N.J. Tchr. art Caldwell-West Caldwell (N.J.) Pub. Schs., 1970-75; pres. Britannia Imports Ltd., Fairfield, N.J., 1979-89; tchr. religious studies Bohrer-Kaufman Hebrew Acad., Randolph, N.J., 1981-82; co-founder, corp. sec. Gibraltar Biol. Labs., Inc., Fairfield, 1970—; dir., co-founder Gibraltar Inst. for Rsch. and Tng., Fairfield, 1984—. Cons. Internat. Antiques and Fine Arts Industries, U.K., 1979-89; cons. in art exhibitry Passaic County Coll., Paterson, N.J., 1989-93; art curator Fairleigh Dickinson U., Rutherford, N.J., 1972-74; curator history of design Bloomfield (N.J.) Coll., 1990-91; lectr. Am. Soc. Microbiology, New Orleans, 1989; spkr. in field. Exhibited in group shows at Bloomfield (N.J.) Coll., 1990, Caldwell Women's Club, N.J., 1991, State Fedn. Women's Clubs Ann. Show, 1992 (1st pl. award 1992), Newark Art Mus., 1992, West (N.J.) Essex Art Assn., 1990, Somerset (N.J.) Art Assn., 1994, Mortimer Gallery, Gladstone, N.J., 1994 (1st pl. award 1998), Tewksbury His. Soc. (1st pl. award 1994), Tewksbury Hist. Soc., 2001, 02, 04, Nat. Meeting Am. Pen Women, Calif., 2002, Washington, D.C., 2004; one-woman shows include Passaic County Coll., N.J., 1990, Caldwell Coll., N.J., 1990; author children's stories. Chair ann. juried art awards Arts Coun. of Essex Bd. Trustees, Montclair, N.J., 1984-90; chair fundraising Arts Coun. Essex County, N.J., 1989. Recipient 1st place award, N.J. Tewksbury Hist. Soc., 1994, 1998, Juried Art award, 2001, 2002. Mem. AAUW, Soc. Childrens Book Writers and Illustrators, Somerset Art Assn., Nat. League Am. Pen Women (pres. N.J. br., Juried Art award 2001), Barnegat Light Yacht Club. Republican. Avocations: boating, tennis, opera, painting, travel. Home: 5 Standish Dr Mendham Twp Morristown NJ 07960-3224 E-mail: herbleah@aol.com.

PRINCE, MATTHEW SPERRY, religious organization executive; b. Jacksonville, Fla., Sept. 29, 1928; s. Thomas Chafer and Abby Gail Prince; m. Beverly Ross Stanton, June 7, 1952 (div. Nov. 1977); children: Matthew Sperry Jr., David, Peggy, Patricia, Penny, Beverly; m. Judithe Seidell Boensch, June 30, 1979. BA, U. Tenn., 1949, JD, 1958; ThM, Dallas Theol. Sem., 1954. Pastor McKinney Meml. Ch., Ft. Worth, 1953-55, Bethany Bible Ch., Knoxville, Tenn., 1956-58; assoc. Ambrose, Wilson, Saulpaw, Knoxville, 1958-61; asst. to pres. Young Life, Inc., Colorado Springs, Colo., 1961-64; pvt. practice Knoxville, 1964-65; ptnr. Privette, Mann, Prince & Smith, Knoxville, 1965-69; pres. New Life, Inc., Knoxville, 1969—, Lewis Speary Chafer Theol. Sem., Knoxville, 2000—. Pres. Chafer Inst. Biblical Studies, 2000—. Author: Winning Through Caring, 1980. Chmn. Rep. Primary Election Commn., Knoxville, 1959-61. Named Tenn. Clergyman of Yr., Tenn. Christian Coalition, 1994. Baptist. Avocations: physical conditioning workouts, golf, playing instrumental music, barbershop quartet singing, gardening. Home: 1012 Edenbridge Way Knoxville TN 37923-6612 Office: New Life Inc 9040 Executive Park Dr Ste 222 Knoxville TN 37923-4671 E-mail: mattprince@IOL24.com.

PRINCE, THOMAS RICHARD, accountant, educator; b. New Albany, Miss., Dec. 7, 1934; s. James Thompson and Callie Florence (Howell) P.; m. Eleanor Carol Polkoff, July 14, 1962; children: Thomas Andrew, John Michael, Adrienne Carol. BS, Miss. State U., 1956, MS, 1957; PhD in Accountancy, U. Ill., 1962. CPA, Ill. Instr. U. Ill., 1960-62; mem. faculty Northwestern U. Kellogg Grad. Sch. Mgmt., 1962—, prof. acctg. info. and mgmt., 1969—, chmn. dept. acctg. info. and mgmt., 1968-75; prof. health industry mgmt. Northwestern U., 1980—; cons. in field. Dir. Applied Research Systems, Inc. Author: Extension of the Boundaries of Accounting Theory, 1962, Information Systems for Management Planning and Control, 3d edit. 1975, Financial Reporting and Cost Control for Health Care Entities, 1992, Product Life-Cycle Costing and Management of Large-Scale Medical Systems Investments, 1997, Strategic Management for Health Care Entities: Creative Frameworks for Financial and Operational Analysis, 1998. Served to 1st lt. AUS, 1957-60. Mem. Am. Accounting Assn., Am. Inst. C.P.A.s, Am. Econ. Assn., INFORMS, AHA, HFMA, HIMMS, AUPHA, Fin. Execs. Inst., AAAS, Ill. Soc. C.P.A.s, Inst. Mgmt. Acct., Alpha Tau Omega, Phi Kappa Phi, Omicron Delta Kappa, Delta Sigma Pi, Beta Alpha Psi. Congregationalist. Home: 303 Richmond Rd Kenilworth IL 60043-1138 Office: Northwestern U Leverone Hl Evanston IL 60208-2002 Business E-Mail: t-prince@kellogg.northwestern.edu.

PRINCE, WILLIAM TALIAFERRO, retired federal judge; b. Norfolk, Va., Oct. 3, 1929; s. James Edward and Helen Marie (Taliaferro) P.; m. Anne Carroll Hannegan, Apr. 12, 1958; children: Sarah Carroll Prince Pishko, Emily Taliaferro, William Taliaferro, John Hannegan, Anne Martineau Thompson, Robert Harrison. Student, Coll. William and Mary, Norfolk, 1947-48, 49-50; AB, Williamsburg, 1955, BCL, 1957, MLT, 1959. Bar: Va. 1957. Lectr. acctg. Coll. William and Mary, 1955-57; lectr. law Marshall-Wythe Sch. Law, 1957-59; assoc. Williams, Kelly & Greer, Norfolk, 1959-63, ptnr., 1963-90; U.S. magistrate judge Eastern Dist. of Va., Norfolk, 1990-2000; ret., 2000; recalled Ct. Appeals 4th Cir., 2000—, Ct. Appeals 10th Cir., 2002, Ct. Appeals 3d Cir., 2002, Ct. Appeals 6th Cir., 2003, Ct. Appeals 5th Cir., 2003. Pres. Am. Inn of Ct. XXVII, 1987-89. Bd. editors: The Virginia Lawyer, A Basic Practice Handbook, 1966. Bd. dirs. Madonna Home, Inc., 1978-93, Soc. Alumni of Coll. William and Mary, 1985-88. Fellow Am. Coll. Trial Lawyers, Am. Bar Found., Va. Law found. (bd. dirs. 1976-90); mem. ABA (ho. of dels. 1984-90), Am. Judicature Soc. (bd. dirs. 1984-88), Va. State Bar (coun. 1973-77, exec. com. 1975-80, pres. 1978-79). Roman Catholic. Home: 1227 Graydon Ave Norfolk VA 23507-1006 Office: Walter E Hoffman US Courthouse 600 Granby St Ste 341 Norfolk VA 23510-1915 E-mail: WTPrince1@aol.com.

PRINCE, (PRINCE ROGERS NELSON), musician, actor; b. Mpls., June 7, 1958; s. John L. and Mattie D. (Shaw) Nelson; m. Mayte Garcia, 1996 (div., 2000); 1 son (dec.). Singer, songwriter, actor. Albums include For You, 1978, Dirty Mind, 1979, Controversy, 1981, 1999, 1983, film star and soundtrack Purple Rain, 1984 (Academy Award for best original score, 1984), Around the World in a Day, 1985 (Best Soul/Rhythm and Blues Album of the Yr., Downbeat readers poll, 1985), Parade, 1986, Chaos and Disorder, 1996, Sign O' the Times, 1987, Lovesexy, 1988, Batman: Motion Picture Soundtrack, 1989 (Soundtrack of Yr. award Playboy mag. readers' poll, Best Pop/Rock album Downbeat mag. readers' poll), (with the New Power Generation) Diamonds and Pearls, 1991, (symbol as title), 1992, Come, 1995, The Greatest Romance Ever Sold, 1999, 94 East, 2000, The Very Best of Prince, 2001, Beautiful Experience, 2001; films include Purple Rain, 1984, film star and soundtrack Under the Cherry Moon, 1986, film star and soundtrack Sign O' the Times, 1987; film appearance and soundtrack Graffiti Bridge, 1990 (ASCAP award for most performed songs from a motion picture, 1991); formerly mem. group Prince and the Revolution (Best Soul/Rhythm and Blues Group of Yr. Downbeat mag. readers poll 1985); composer Showgirls, 1995, Girl 6, 1996, The Gold Experience, 1995, Crystal Ball, 1998, Rave Un2 the Joy Fantastic, 1999, Bamboozled, 2000. Recipient 3 Grammy awards, 1985, Am. Music Achievement award for infuence on look and sound of the 80's, NAACP Spl. Achievement award, 1997; named Rhythm and Blues Musician of Yr. Down Beat mag. readers' poll, 1984, 1992; inducted Rock and Roll Hall of Fame, 2004. Office: Paisley Park Studios 7801 Audubon Rd Chanhassen MN 55317-8201

PRINCES, CAROLYN DIANE WILBON, educational director; b. Kansas City, Mo., Nov. 15, 1950; d. Will Lee (dec.) and Subemer Jean (Wiggins) Wilbon; m. Donald Louis Princes, July 15, 1972 (div.); children: Donald Jermaine, Aaron Jamelle Meade. BS in Psychology, U. Ill., 1973, MEd in Adminstrn. and Supervision, 1979; EdD in Curriculum and Instrn., U. Md., 1989; postdoc., U. Ghana, 1994, George Washington U., 1994. Cert. substitute tchr. K-12, Ill.; temporary cert. H.S. math., Ill. Asst. dir., acad. devel. specialist Frostburg (Md.) State U., 1980-86; admissions and records clk. Loyola U. Chgo., 1972-73; paralegal, asst. mgr. tng., instr. profl. tng. Chgo. Title and Trust Co., 1973-80; asst. dir. academic devel. spec., dir. student support svcs./disabled student svcs. Frostburg (Md.) State U., 1986-90; dir. African American Cultural Ctr., Indiana U. of Pa., 1990—. Mem. Act 101 Adv. Bd., Indiana, 1993—. Author: (book chpt.) ABCC Monograph, 1995; contbr. articles to profl. jours. and mags. Mem. Cmty. Rels. Adv. Bd., 1991-94; bd. dirs. Indiana County Day Care, 1993-96, Longstretch Youth Homes, Frostburg, 1983-86; bd. dirs., mem. edn. com. Human Resources Devel. Commn., Allegany County, Md., 1983-86; chair, instr. cultural arts program, NAACP, Cumberland, Md., 1983-86; chair United Negro Coll. Fund, Cumberland, 1983-85. Recipient Cert. of Appreciation, Mayor's Office of New Orleans, 1997, Dirs. Awd. for Instl. Membership, The Natl. Assn. of Black Culture, 1998, 99, Lifetime Achievement Awd., NAACP Indiana U. Pa. chpt., 1998, Trailblazer Awd., Black Stud. League, Indiana U. Pa., 98; co-recipient Excellence in Programming award Nat. Assn. Campus Activities, 1994, 95, 96, 97, 98, Multicultural Program award, 1993; Ebony and Ivory Outstanding Svc. Awd., SSDS grantee U.S. Dept. Edn., 1986, 90, Internat. Venture grantee Indiana U. of Pa., 1994, Social Equity grantee Pa. State Sys. of Higher Edn., 1992, 96, Edn. Svcs. Fee grantee Indiana U. of Pa., 1992-99. Fellow Nat. Coun. for Black Studies, 1994; WCBC Radio, Celebrity of the Day, Cumberland, 1988; mem. ASCD, Indiana County, Pa. NAACP, Indiana County PTA (gen. mem. 6th-grade dance com. 1997), Assn. for Black Culture Ctrs. (bd. dirs., chair of pub. rels. 1991—), Social Equity Com. Indiana U. of Pa., Pa. Black Conf. on Higher Edn. (editl. bd. jour. 1996-2001, chair program booklet com. 1999 ann. conf.). African Methodist Episcopalian. Avocations: dance, aerobics, travel, music. Office: Indiana U of Pa 1074 Washington St Indiana PA 15705-0001

PRINCIPE, MICHAEL LUIS, political science educator; b. Yakima, Wash., Dec. 22, 1952; s. Luis A. and Molly V. (Rider) P.; m. Lisa K. Principe (dec. Feb. 1982); children: Jacqueline, Crystal; m. Nancy L. Principe, Nov. 13, 1993; children: Michael Jr., Steven, Meghann, Camille. BA in Sociology, Whitman Coll., 1978; JD, U. Wash., 1983; PhD in Polit. Sci., U. Calif., Santa Barbara, 1992. Prof. polit. sci. William Paterson, Wayne, NJ, 1998—. Vis. prof. law Salmon P. Chase Coll. Law, Highland Heights, Ky., 1995-96; vis. scholar polit. sci. Santa Barbara City Coll., 1997-98; vis. fellow in constnl. law St. Edmund's Coll., Cambridge (Eng.) U., 1993—; assoc. mem. human rights sem. Columbia U., N.Y.C., 2003-05. Author: Bill of Rights: A Comparative Constitutional Analysis, 2000; editor: American Government, Policy and Law, 2000. Fulbright Commn. scholar Inst. Internat. Edn., (New Zealand), 1990-91. Mem. N.E. Assn. Prelaw Advisors. Avocations: jogging, golf, hiking. Office: William Paterson U Dept Polit Sci 300 Pompton Rd Wayne NJ 07470

PRINCIPI, ANTHONY JOSEPH, secretary of veterans affairs; b. N.Y.C., Apr. 16, 1944; s. Antonio Joseph and Theresa (Princiotta) P.; m. Elizabeth Ann Ahlering, June 26, 1971; children: Anthony, Ryan, John BS, U.S. Naval Acad., 1967; JD, Seton Hall U., 1975. Commd. 2d lt. U.S. Navy, 1967, advanced through grades to comdr., 1984, line officer, 1967-72; atty. JAGC, San Diego, 1975-80; counsel Com. on Armed Service U.S. Senate, Washington, 1980-83, staff dir. Com. on Vet.'s Affairs, 1984—88; dep. adminstr. congl. and pub. affairs VA, Washington, 1983-84; dep. sec. Dept. of Veterans Affairs, 1989-90; ptnr. Luce, Forward, Hamilton & Scripps, San Diego, 1990-95; sr. v.p., CEO Lockheed Martin IMS Integrated Solutions Co., Santa Clara, Calif., 1995-2001; pres. QTC Medical Services, 2001; sec. Dept. Veterans Affairs, Washington, 2001—. Decorated Bronze Star with combat "V", Vietnamese Cross of Gallantry, Navy Commendation medal with combat "V" (3); recipient Meritorious Service medal VA, 1983 Mem. ABA (chmn. subcom. gen. practice sect. 1985—) Republican. Roman Catholic. Avocations: gardening, skiing. Office: 810 Vermont Ave NW Washington DC 20420

PRINDLE, WILLIAM ROSCOE, retired glass company executive; b. San Francisco, Dec. 19, 1926; s. Vivian Arthur and Harriette Alnora (Nickerson) P.; m. June Laverne Anderson, June 20, 1947; children— Carol Susan, William Alastair. BS, U. Calif., Berkeley, 1948, MS, 1950; Sc.D., M.I.T., 1955. Asst. tech. dir. Hazel-Atlas Glass Co., 1954-56; mgr. research Hazel-Atlas Glass div. Continental Can Co., Wheeling, W.Va., 1956-58, gen. mgr. research and devel., 1959-62; mgr. materials research Am. Optical Co., Southbridge, Mass., 1962-65; v.p. research Southbridge and Framingham, Mass., 1971-76; dir; research Ferro Corp., Cleve., 1966-67, v.p. research, 1967-71; exec. dir. Nat. Materials Adv. Bd., NRC-NAS, Washington, 1976-80; dir. adminstrv. and tech. svcs. R & D div. Corning Glass Works, N.Y., 1980-85, dir. materials rsch., 1985-87; assoc. dir. R & D, Engring. div. Corning Glass Works (now Corning, Inc.), N.Y., 1987-90; div. v.p., assoc. dir. tech. group Corning Inc., N.Y., 1990-92; ret. Pres. XII Internat. Glass Congress, 1980, Internat. Commn. on Glass, 1985-88. Served with U.S. Navy, 1944-46. Named Disting. Ceramist of New Eng., New Eng. sect. Am. Ceramic Soc., 1974, Toledo Glass and Ceramic award NW Ohio sect., 1986, Albert Victor Bleininger Meml. award Pitts. sect., 1989, Phoenix award as Glass Industry Man of Yr., 1983; Friedberg Meml. lecture Nat. Inst. Ceramic Engrs., 1990, Greaves-Walker award, 2004. Fellow Am. Ceramic Soc. (disting. life, pres. 1980-81), Soc. Glass Tech., Am. Soc. for Metals Internat.; mem. NAE, AAAS, World Acad. of Ceramics, Cosmos Club (Washington), Sigma Xi, Phi Gamma Delta. Home: 1556 Crestline Dr Santa Barbara CA 93105-4611 Personal E-mail: wprindle@aol.com.

PRING, ROBERT BRADFORD, financial consultant; b. St. Louis, July 22, 1951; s. Charles Branscombe Pring and A Helen Crosson Reim; m. Bernice Rosalyn Crisp, Oct. 25, 1975 (div. Dec. 2001); children: Robert Bradford III, Jennifer Christiane; m. Linda Colleen Mueller, Aug. 10, 2002. BS in Agr., U. Mo., Columbia, 1973; postgrad., U. Mo., 1973. Lic. life, accident and health ins agt; cert. fin planner, stockbroker, registered investment advisor rep. Ptnr. Prings Nursery, St. Louis, 1973-74; dist. sales mgr. Curtis Circulation Co., Nashville, 1974-75, reg. mktg. mgr. Orlando, Fla., 1975-77, West Coast account exec. West Caldwell, N.J., 1977-79, div. mktg. supr. St. Louis, 1979-81; trust mktg. officer Commerce Bank, St. Louis, 1982-84; v.p. bus. devel./comml. lending Commerce Bank St. Charles County, N.A., St. Peters, Mo., 1984-91; v.p., comml. devel. officer Commerce Bank St. Louis, St. Peters, Mo., 1991-97; bus. mgr. program First State Bank St. Charles, St. Charles, Mo., 1997-2001; fin. advisor, investment mgr., personal fin. planning INVEST Fin. Corp., 2001—02; ins. cons. fin. advice, mortgage banking Robert B. Pring & Assocs., 2002—. Prodr., dir.: St. Charles County, A World of Opportunity, 1987. Pres, chmn United Serv Handicapped, St Charles, 1988—89; treas bd dirs YMCA St Charles County, 1989—99, chmn bd dirs, 1991—92; treas Citizens St Charles County CC, 1990, co-chmn, 1991; bd dirs YMCA Greater Metropolitan St Louis, 1991—92, Mid-Am Theatre Co, St Charles, St Charles YMCA, 1985—2000; bd. dirs. St. Charles C.C. Found., 1995—, past chmn., v.p. fin. Recipient Meritorious Serv Award, United Servs Handicapped, 1989, Bell Vol Award, St Charles County Community Coun and Southwestern Bell, 1990. Mem.: Fin. Planning Assn., Inst. Cert. Fin. Planners, Greater St. Louis Soc. Cert. Fin. Planners (bd dirs 1990—91), St. Peters C. of C. (past dir, pres, chmn 1988, Disting Leadership Award 1990), Rotary (bd dirs St Charles chpt 1992). Presbyterian. Avocations: flying, soaring, water sports. Home and Office: 2163 Roselake Cir Saint Peters MO 63376-7772 Office Phone: 636-928-3719. E-mail: rbpring@charter.net.

PRINGLE, BARBARA CARROLL, state legislator; b. N.Y.C., Apr. 4, 1939; d. Nicholas Robert and Anna Joan (Woloshinovich) Terlesky; m. Richard D. Pringle, Nov. 28, 1959; children: Christopher, Rhonda. Student, Cuyahoga C.C. With Dunn & Bradstreet, 1957-60; precinct committeewoman City of Cleve., 1976-77; elected mem. Cleve. City Coun., 1977-81; mem. Ohio Ho. of Reps., Columbus, 1982—. 20th dist. state ctrl. committeewoman, 1982-92; asst. minority leader econ. devel. & small bus. com., pub. utilities com.; mem. Children & Family Svcs. com.; mem. Ohio Legis. Svc. Commn.; mem. Ohio Children's Trust Fund, Midwestern Legis. Conf. Coun. State Govts.' Com. Status Children. Vol. Cleve. Lupus Steering Com., various community orgns.; charter mem. Statue of Liberty Ellis Island Found. Recipient cert. of appreciation Cleve. Mcpl. Ct., 1977, Exch. Club Bklyn., 1978, Cmty. Recreation Appreciation award City of Cleve., 1978, Key to City of Cleve., 1979, Cleve. Area Soapbox Derby cert., 1976, 77, 81, cert. of appreciation Ward 9 Youth League, 1979-82, No. Ohio Patrolman's Benevolent Assn. award, 1983, Cuyahoga County Firefighters award, 1983, Outstanding Pub. Servant award for Outstanding Svc. to Hispanic Cmty., 1985, Nat. Sr. Citizen Hall of Fame award, 1987, cert. of appreciation Cleve. Coun. Unemployed Workers, 1987, Ohio Farmers Union award, 1990, award of appreciation United Labor Agy., 1993, Susan B. Anthony award, 1995. Mem. Nat. Order Women Legislators, Fedn. Dem. Women of Ohio, Nat. Alliance Czech Catholics, St. Michael Ch. Altar and Rosary Soc., Ward 15 Dem. Club, Polish Falcons. Democrat. Home: 708 Timothy Ln Cleveland OH 44109-3733

PRINGLE, CURT, mayor; m. Alexis Pringle; children: Katie, Kyle. BBA, MPA, Calif. State U., Long Beach. Pres. Curt Pringle and Assocs., LLC, Irvine, Calif.; mayor Anaheim, Calif., 2003—. Vis. faculty mem. U. Calif., Irvine. Bd. mem. Leadership Traq; mem. Calif. Film Commn., 1996—99, Calif. State Assembly, 1988—90, 1992—98, Rep. leader, Rep. Caucus chair, chmn. appropriations com., chmn. rules com., vice chmn. budget com.; nominee Calif. State Treas., 1998; Calif. del. Nat. Rep. Conv., 1996; active Calif. Rep. Ctrl. Com. Office: Anaheim City Hall 200 S Anaheim Blvd Anaheim CA 92805 Office Phone: 714-765-5247.

PRINGLE, LAURENCE PATRICK, writer; b. Rochester, N.Y., Nov. 26, 1935; s. Laurence Erin and Marleah Elizabeth (Rosehill) P.; m. Judith Malanowicz, June 23, 1962 (div. 1970); children: Heidi Elizabeth, Jeffrey Laurence, Sean Edmund; m. Alison Newhouse, July 14, 1971 (div. 1975); m. Susan Deborah Klein, Mar. 13, 1983; children: Jesse Erin, Rebecca Anne. BS in Wildlife Biology, Cornell U., 1958; MS in Wildlife Biology, U. Mass., 1961. Tchr. sci. Lima (N.Y.) Cen. Sch., 1961-62; editor Nature and Sci. mag. Am. Mus. Natural History, N.Y.C., 1963-70; free-lance writer, 1970—. Writer-in-residence Kean College, Union, N.J., 1985-86. Author: (children's books) Dinosaurs and Their World, 1968, The Only Earth We Have, 1969, From Field to Forest, 1970, In a Beaver Valley, 1970, One Earth, Many People, 1971, Ecology: Science of Survival, 1971, Cockroaches: Here, There, Everywhere, 1971, From Pond to Prairie, 1972, This Is a River, 1972, Pests and People: The Search for Sensible Pest Control, 1972, Estuaries: Where Rivers Meet the Sea, 1973, Into the Woods: Exploring the Forest Ecosystem, 1973, Follow a Fisher, 1973, Twist, Wiggle and Squirm: A Book about Earthworms, 1973, Recycling Resources, 1974, Energy: Power for People, 1975, City and Suburb: Exploring an Ecosystem, 1975, Chains, Webs and Pyramids. The Flow of Energy in Nature, 1975, Water Plants, 1975, The Minnow Family: Chubs, Dace, Minnows and Shiners, 1976, Listen to the Crows, 1976, Our Hungry Earth: The World Food Crisis, 1976, Death is Natural, 1977, The Hidden World: Life Under a Rock, 1977, The Controversial Coyote: Predation, Politics and Ecology, 1977, The Gentle Desert: Exploring an Ecosystem, 1977, Animals and Their Niches: How Species Share Resources, 1977, The Economic Growth Debate: Are There Limits to Growth?, 1978, Dinosaurs and People: Fossils, Facts and Fantasies, 1978, Wild Foods, 1978, Nuclear Power: From Physics to Politics, 1979, Natural Fire: Its Ecology in Forests, 1979, Lives at Stake: The Science and Politics of Environmental Health, 1980, What Shall We Do with the Land?: Choices for America, 1981, Frost Hollows and Other Microclimates, 1981, Vampire Bats, 1982, Water: The Next Great Resource Battle, 1982, Radiation: Waves and Particles/Benefits and Risks, 1983, Wolfman: Exploring the World of Wolves, 1983, Feral: Tame Animals Gone Wild, 1983, The Earth Is Flat—and Other Great Mistakes, 1983, Being a Plant, 1983, Nuclear War: From Hiroshima to Nuclear Winter, 1985, Animals at Play, 1985, Here Come the Killer Bees, 1986, Throwing Things Away: From Middens to Resource Recovery, 1986, Restoring Our Earth, 1987, Home: How Animals Find Comfort and Safety, 1987, Rain of Troubles: The Science and Politics of Acid Rain, 1988, Living in a Risky World, 1989, Nuclear Energy: Troubled Past, Uncertain Future, 1989, Bearman: Exploring the World of Black Bears, 1989, The Animal Rights Controversy, 1989, Saving Our Wildlife, 1990, Global Warming: Assessing the Greenhouse Threat, 1990, The Golden Book of Insects and Spiders, 1990, Killer Bees (rev. edit.), 1991, Batman: Exploring the World of Bats, 1991, Living Treasure: Saving Earth's Threatened Biodiversity, 1991, Antarctica: The Last Unspoiled Continent, 1992, The Golden Book of Volcanoes, Earthquakes, and Powerful Storms, 1992, Chemical and Biological Warfare: The Cruelest Weapons, 1993, revised edit., 2000, Oil Spills: Damage, Recovery, and Prevention, 1993, Jackal Woman: Exploring the World of Jackals, 1993, Scorpion Man: Exploring the World of Scorpions, 1994, Dinosaurs! Strange and Wonderful, 1995, Vanishing Ozone: Protecting Earth from Ultraviolet Radiation, 1995, Coral Reefs: Earth's Undersea Treasures, 1995, Dolphin Man: Exploring the World of Dolphins, 1995, rev. edit., 2002, Fire in the Forest: A Cycle of Growth and Renewal, 1995, Taking Care of the Earth: Kids in Action, 1996, Smoking: A Risky Business, 1996, An Extraordinary Life: The Story of a Monarch Butterfly, 1997, Nature! Wild and Wonderful, 1997, Everybody Has a Bellybutton: Your Life Before You Were Born, 1997, Elephant Woman: Cynthia Moss Explores The World of Elephants, 1997, Drinking: A Risky Business, 1997, One Room School, 1998, Explore Your Senses: SIGHT, 1999, Explore Your Senses: HEARING, 1999, Explore Your Senses: TASTE, 1999, Explore Your Senses: TOUCH, 1999, Explore Your Senses: SMELL, 1999, BATS! Strange and Wonderful, 2000, The Environmental Movement: From Its Roots to the Challenges of a New Century, 2000, Sharks! Strange and Wonderful, 2001, Global Warming: The Threat of Earth's Changing Climate, 2001, A Dragon in the Sky: The Story of a Green Darner Dragonfly, 2001, Scholastic Encyclopedia of Animals, 2001, Strange Animals, New to Science, 2002, Crows! Strange and Wonderful, 2002, Dog of Discovery: A Newfoundland's Adventures with Lewis and Clark, 2002, Whales! Strange and Wonderful, 2003, Snakes! Strange and Wonderful, 2004, (fiction) Jesse Builds a Road, 1989, Octopus Hug, 1993, Naming the Cat, 1997, Bear Hug, 2003, (adult books) Wild River, 1972, Rivers and Lakes, 1985. Recipient Spl. Conservation award Nat. Wildlife Fedn., 1978, Eva L. Gordon award Am. Nature Study Soc., 1983, Orbis Pictus award Nat. Coun. Tchrs. English, 1998, Nonfiction award Washington Post/Childrens Book Guild, 1999. Mem.: The Authors Guild. Home and Office: PO Box 252 West Nyack NY 10994-0252

PRINGLE, LEWIS GORDON, marketing professional, educator; b. Lansing, Mich., Feb. 13, 1941; s. Gordon Henry and Lucile Roxana (Drake) P.; children: Lewis Gordon Jr., William Davis, Thomas Benjamin. BA, Harvard U., 1963; MS, M.I.T., 1965, PhD, 1969. Vice pres., dir. mktg. sci. BBDO, Inc., N.Y.C., 1968-73; asst. prof. mktg. Carnegie-Melon U., Pitts., 1973-74; exec. v.p., dir. rsch. svcs., corp. dir. BBDO, Inc., N.Y.C., 1978-91; exec. v.p. BBDO Worldwide, 1986-91; chmn., CEO BBDO Europe, 1986-91, LG Pringle and Assocs., 1992-95; Joseph C. Seibert prof. of mktg. Farmer Sch. Bus. Adminstrn., Miami U., Oxford, Ohio, 1995—2000. Bd. dirs. Yorktown U., prof.; mem. vis com. Sloan Sch. Mgmt., MIT. Assoc. editor Jour. Advt. Rsch.; mem. editl. bd. Jour. Mktg. Sci.; mem. editl. bd. Jour. Market Rsch.; contbr. numerous articles to Harvard Bus. Rev., Mktg. Scis., others. Active local Boy Scouts Am. Ford Found. fellow, 1967 Fellow Royal Statis. Soc.; mem. INFORMS (chmn. mktg. strategy com.), Market Rsch. Coun., Am. Psychol. Assn., European Soc. Mktg. and Opinion Rsch., Am. Mktg. Assn., Inst. Ops. Rsch. and Mgmt. Sci. Office: Silver Creek Farm 2858 N Stout Rd Liberty IN 47353

PRINGLE, MARY BETH, language educator, writer; b. July 20, 1943; BA, U. Denver, 1964, MA, 1967; PhD, U. Minn., 1977. Prof. Wright State U., Dayton, Ohio, 1975—. Vis. lectr. U. Pitts., 1997, 2002; instr. U. Minn., Iowa State U., S.W. Mo. State U., U. Denver. Home: 8497 N Lebanon Pike Waynesville OH 45068 Office: Wright State U Dept English Dayton OH 45435 Office Phone: 937-775-2265. Business E-Mail: marybeth.pringle@wright.edu.

PRINGLE, ORAN ALLAN, mechanical and aerospace engineering educator; b. Lawrence, Kan., Sept. 14, 1923; s. Oran Allan and Mae (McClell) P.; m. Billie Hansen, June 25, 1947; children— Allan, Billie, James, Rebecca. BS in Mech. Engring, U. Kan., 1947; MS, U. Wis., 1948, PhD, 1967. Registered profl. engr., Mo. Mech. engr. Black and Veatch (cons. engrs.), Kansas City, Mo., 1947-48; engr. Boeing Airplane Co., Wichita, 1952—; prof. U. Mo., Columbia, 1948—90, prof. emeritus, 1991—. Co-author: Engineering Metallurgy, 1957; contbr. articles to profl. lit. Bd. dirs. United Cerebral Palsy Boone County, Mo. Served with AUS, 1943-45. Ford Found. grantee. Mem. Am. Soc.

M.E. (chmn. fastening and joining com., design engring. div.), Sigma Xi. Home: 1820 University Ave Columbia MO 65201-6004 Office: Dept Mech and Aerospace Engring U Mo Columbia MO 65201

PRINGLE, REBECCA, elementary school educator; b. Phila. m. Nathan Pringle; children: Nathan III, Lauren. BS in Elem. Edn., U. Pitts., 1976; EdM, Pa. State U., 1989. Phys. sci. tchr. Susquehanna Twp. Middle Sch., Harrisburg, Pa. Mem. strategic planning com. on diversity Susquehanna Twp. Sch. Dist.; mem. Inst. for Ednl. Leadership Task Force. Named Cmty. Woman of the Yr., Harrisburg Br. AAUW, 2002; recipient award, Pa. Acad. for the Profession of Tchg. Mem.: NEA (mem. exec. com., bd. dirs., mem. women's issues com., dist. learning task force, chair reading task force 1999—2000), Pa. State Edn. Assn. (bd. dirs., chair human and civil rights award com., task force on minority representation, regional chair leadership devel. com.), Nat. Bd. for Profl. Tchg. Stds. (bd. mem.). Office: Susquehanna Twp Middle Sch 801 Wood St Harrisburg PA 17109

PRINGLE, ROBERT MAXWELL, diplomat; b. N.Y.C., Nov. 12, 1936; s. Henry Fowles and Helena Huntington (Smith) Pringle; m. Barbara Ann Cade, Sept. 26, 1964; children: James Maxwell, Anne Elizabeth. BA, Harvard U., 1958; PhD, Cornell U., 1967. Dir. econ. policy staff Bur. African Affairs Dept. State, 1981-83; dep. chief mission Ouagadougou, Burkina Faso, 1983-85, Port Moresby, Papua New Guinea, 1985-87; ambassador to Mali, 1987-90; dir. cen. African affairs U.S. Dept. State, 1990-93; dir. ecology and terrestrial conservation U.S. Dept. of State, 1993-95; dir. sr. seminar U.S. Dept. State, 1995-96; dep. chief of mission Dept. State, Pretoria, 1996-99; prof. nat. security policy Nat. War Coll., 1999—2001. Author: Rajahs and Rebels: The Ibans of Sarawak Under Brooke Rule, 1970, Indonesia and the Philippines: American Interests in Island Southwest Asia, 1980, A Short History of Bali, 2004. Mem.: African Studies Assn., Assn. Asian Studies. Avocations: photography, gardening, scuba diving. Home: 216 Wolfe St Alexandria VA 22314-3858 Office Phone: 703-519-8252. E-mail: pringler@post.harvard.edu.

PRINN, RONALD G. atmospheric science educator; b. Hamilton, New Zealand, June 11, 1945; BSc, U. Auckland, New Zealand, 1967, MSc with 1st honors, 1968; ScD, MIT, 1971. Asst. prof. MIT, Cambridge, Mass., 1971-76, assoc. prof., 1976-82, prof., 1982-93, Tepco prof., 1993—, head dept. earth, atmospheric and planetary scis., 1998—2003. Chair com. on earth sci. NAS, Washington, 1982-84; chair Internat. Global Atmospheric Chemistry Project, Stockholm, 1988-95. Recipient Vernadsky Meml. lectr. Russian Acad. Sci., Moscow, 1984. Fellow Am. Geophys. Union (Macelwane medal 1981), AAAS (chmn. atmospheric and hydrospheric scis. 1999). Office: MIT Bldg 54-1312 Cambridge MA 02139

PRINS, CAROL, not-for-profit developer, consultant; b. N.Y.C., Aug. 23, 1940; d. J. Warner and Gertrude (Buttenwieser) Prins; m. John H. Hart, June 26, 1994; children from previous marriage: Jessica Eve(dec.), Audrey, Joseph Stephen Patt. Student, Vassar Coll., 1958—59, Barnard Coll., 1962, Neighborhood Playhouse Sch., N.Y.C., 1962—64. Ptnr. Just Causes, Chgo., 1978-87; cons. in field, 1987—. Pres. The Jessica Fund, a pvt. family found., Chgo. Mem. nat. found. bd. NARAL; mem. nat. adv. bd. Santa Fe Opera; mem. women's bd. dirs. Am. Cancer Soc.; mem. costume com. Chgo. Hist. Soc.; mem. adv. bd. Aspen/Santa Fe Ballet; trustee SITE, Santa Fe; chair bd. trustees Goodman Theatre; pres. nat. bd. dirs., trustee Georgia O'Keeffe Mus., Santa Fe; nat. bd. dirs. Art Inst. Santa Fe; bd. dirs. Goodman Theatre, Chgo., pres., 1993—, trustee, mem. exec. com.; bd. dirs. Chgo. Found. Women; trustee Neighborhood Playhouse Sch. Theatre, N.Y.C. Mem. The Arts Club, Las Campanas (Santa Fe). Avocations: poetry, gardening, travel, poetry.

PRINS, JOHANNA, literature educator; PhD in Comparative Lit., Princeton U. Assoc. prof. English and comparative lit. U. Mich., Ann Arbor. Recipient Guggenheim fellowship, 2003. Office: U Mich Dept English and Comparative Lit 3184 Angell Hall Ann Arbor MI 48109

PRINS, ROBERT JACK, retired academic administrator; b. Grand Rapids, Mich., Oct. 12, 1932; s. Jacob and Marie (Vanden Brink) P.; m. Ruth Ellen John, Oct. 10, 1950; children: Linda, Douglas, Debra, Nancy, Eric, Sarah. BA, Hope Coll., 1954; DBA, Coll. Emporia, 1974; DHL, Iowa Wesleyan U., 1999. With Mich. Bell Tel. Co., Detroit area, 1954—64, Chesapeake and Potomac Tel. Co., 1964—66; dir. devel. Bethesda Hosp., Denver, 1966-68; v.p. planning and devel. Park Coll., Parkville, Mo., 1969-70; chief adminstrv. officer Coll. of Emporia, Kans., 1970-75; dir. fin. and devel. The Abbey Sch., Canon City, Colo., 1975-79; dir. devel. Kirksville Coll. Osteo. Medicine, Mo., 1979-84; v.p. devel. McKendree Coll., Lebanon, Ill., 1984-86; pres. Iowa Weslyan Coll., Mt. Pleasant, 1986-99, pres. emeritus, 1999—; exec. dir. Internat. Student Svcs., Canon City, Colo., 1999—. Bd. dirs. Iowa Coll. Found., Iowa Commn. on Vol. Svc.; mem. Iowa Assn. Ind. Colls. and Univs.; former chmn., mem. bd. Potomak Worldwide, Taipei, Taiwan. Mem. Nat. Assn. Ind. Colls. and Univs., Coun. for Advancement and Support Edn.

PRINZ, KRISTIE DAWN, lawyer; b. Columbus, Ga., July 26, 1973; d. Stephen Charles and Helen Ann (Dunlap) P. BA in Spanish and Polit. Sci. summa cum laude, Furman U., 1995; JD, Vanderbilt U., 1998. Bar: Ga. 1998, Calif. 2001. Summer assoc. Rose Immigration Law Firm, Nashville, Tenn., 1996; rsch. asst. Vanderbilt U., Nashville, 1996-97; summer assoc. Bruce, Weathers, Corley, Dughman & Lyle, Nashville, 1997; assoc. Mozley, Finlayson & Loggins, LLP, Atlanta, 1998, Schnader Harrison Segal & Lewis LLP, Atlanta, 1999-2000, Pennie & Edmonds LLP, Palo Alto, Calif., 2000—. Mem. adv. bd. Knoxville Jour., 1990-91. Vol. tchr. English Classes for Refugees, Knoxville, Tenn, 1993; mem. Collegiate Ednl. Svc. Corps. Furman U., Greenville, S.C., 1991-95. Mem.: ABA, Computer Law Assn., Licensing Execs. Soc., Calif. Lawyers for the Arts, Forum for Women Entrepreneurs, Calif. Women Lawyers, Nat. Assn. Women Lawyers, San Francisco Bar Assn., Atlanta Bar Assn. (mem. Therell H.S. Com.), Palo Alto Bar Assn., Churchill Club, Phi Sigma Iota, Sigma Delta Pi, Phi Beta Kappa, Sr. Order Furman U., Kappa Alpha Theta (Elizabeth Staley Leadership award 1995), Phi Sigma Alpha. Avocations: running, playing piano, watching Spanish language movies and programs, tennis.

PRINZ, RICHARD ALLEN, surgeon; MD, Loyola U., Chgo., 1972. Diplomate Am. Bd. Surgery, bd. dirs., 1994—. Intern Barnes Hosp., St. Louis, 1972-73, resident in surgery, 1973-74, Loyola U., Chgo., 1974-77, attending surgeon, 1980-93; staff Rush Presbyn.-St. Luke's Med. Ctr., Chgo., 1993—; Helen Shedd Keith prof., chmn. dept. gen. surgery Rush U., Chgo., 1993—. Mem. Am. Surg. Assn., Am. Assn. Endocrine Surgeons (pres. 1996), Midwest Surg. Assn. (pres. 1997), Western Surg. Assn. (treas. 1993-97, pres. 2002-), Chgo. Surg. Soc. (pres.-elect 2002-, pres. 2003). Office: Rush U 818 Professional Bldg 1725 W Harrison St Chicago IL 60612-3828 E-mail: rprinz@rush.edu.

PRINZO, O. VERONIKA, engineering research psychologist; d. Joseph and Teofila Cyc; m. Phillip N. Prinzo, May 9, 1970 (div. Aug. 1992); children: Caitlin, Jon, Cassandre, Zackery. PhD in Psychology with distinction, Kent State U., 1987. Asst. prof. of psychology Ft. Hays State U., Hays, Kans., 1991; engring. rsch. psychologist FAA/Civil Aerospace Med. Inst., Oklahoma City, 1991—. Jour. reviewer Aviation, Space, & Environ. Medicine, Washington, 1996—; vis. prof. psychology Wabash Coll., Ind., Oberlin Coll., Ohio, 1987—88, Coll. Wooster, Ohio, 1988—89. Contbr. articles to profl. jours. Mem. Parish Pastoral Coun., Mustang, Okla., 1997—2004. Named Parent of the Yr., YMCA; recipient Coss Faculty Devel. Grant, Wabash Coll., Grants-in-Aid of Rsch., Sigma Xi; grantee Hughs-Supported Faculty Rsch. in the Scis., Coll. of Wooster. Fellow: Aerospace Med. Assn. (assoc.); mem.: Aerospace Human Factors Assn. (mem.-at-large). Avocations: travel, hiking, reading. Office: FAA/Civil Aerospace Med Inst 6500 S MacArthur Blvd Oklahoma City OK 73169 E-mail: roni.prinzo@faa.gov.

PRIOLEAU, DARWIN E. dance educator, choreographer; b. N.Y.C., May 10, 1949; p. E. Louis and Marietta Camilla Prioleau; m. Carl Victor Conrad, Dec. 19, 1992. BA, Bennett Coll., 1971; MA, NYU, 1981; EdD, U. Mass., 1999. Dancer Ed Kresley Jazz Co., N.Y.C., 1974-76; soloist, dancer Nat. Horne Dance Co., N.Y.C., 1976-79; featured dancer, guest artist various dance cos. and off-Broadway prodns., N.Y.C., 1977-81; artistic dir. Young Peoples Dance Co., N.Y.C., 1978-81; assoc. prof. dance So. Meth. U., Dallas, 1981-88; head dance divsn. Kent (Ohio) State U., 1988-95, prof. dance, 1995—, asst. dean. Coll. Fine & Proff. Arts, 2001—02; chair dance divsn SUNY, Brockport, NY, 2004—. Dance coord. Internat. Ctr. for Integrative Studies, N.Y.C., 1975-81; artistic cons. Dallas Black Dance Theatre, 1983-88; trustee Am. Dance Guild, N.Y.C., 1993-95, Internat. 39th Bartholin Ballet Seminar, Copenhagen, 2001. Choreographer (commd. choreography) Dance Black Dance Theatre, 1983, 84, 88, 91, Dallas Theatre Ctr., 1985, 86, Dance Cleveland/Cain Pk., 1991, Opus II Dance Co., 1994, Ashland Regional Ballet, 2001; solo performer, Tex., N.Y.C., France, 1985-88; mem. editl. bd. Nat. Dance Edn. Jour.; contbr. articles to profl. jours. Mentor I Had A Dream Program, Dallas, 1986-88; guest tchr. Urban League, Akron, Ohio, 1994; adv. bd. Cleve. Sch. of the Arts, 1994-95; mem. Ohio Arts Coun., 2000, Arts Midwest, 2000, Columbus, 2000, Pitts. on Tour, 2000. Grantee NEA Arts Expansion Program, Washington, 1980, Vira I. Heinz Endowment, Pitts., 1994, Ohio Joint Programs in the Arts, Columbus, 1995. Mem. Nat. Assn. Schs. Dance, Internat. Black Dance Assn., Ams. for Arts. Nat. Dance Edn. Assn., Am. Assn. Higher Edn. Avocations: travel, hiking, jazz music. Home: 182 Gaylord Dr Munroe Falls OH 44262-1141 Office: SUNY at Brockport 300 New Campus Dr Brockport NY 14420 Fax: 330-672-4897. Office Phone: 585-395-2023. E-mail: dpriolea@brockport.edu.

PRIOLEAU, SARA NELLIENE, dentist; b. Hopkins, S.C., Apr. 10, 1940; d. Willie Oree and Wilhelmina Illorah (Neal) P.; m. William F. McKeever, Aug. 31, 1969 (div. Mar. 1982); children: Kara, William P.; m. William R. Montgomery, Dec. 18, 1984; stepchildren: Sharon, Myra, John. BS, S.C. State U., 1960, MS, 1966; DMD, U. Pa., 1970. Rotating gen. dentist intern Phila. Gen. Hosp., 1970-71; staff dentist Comprehensive Group Health Ctr., Phila., 1971-72; dental dir. Hamilton Health Ctr., 1972-97; CEO Cmty. Dental Assocs., P.C., Harrisburg, 1976—; dental dir. Selinsgrove Ctr., 1999—2002. Cons. Region III Head Start, Phila., 1972—; dental dir. Healthmate HMO-Hamilton Health Ctr., Harrisburg, 1988-96, Healthmate HMO/Health Am., Harrisburg, 1996-97; v. p. bd. dirs. Harrisburg Area C.C., 1990-99, v.p., 1997-99; adv. bd. Mellon Bank Commonwealth Region, Harrisburg, 1995-2001, Capital Area Math./Sci. Alliance, Harrisburg, 1995-99. Named one of 50 Best Women in Bus., Dept. of Commerce and Econ. Devel., Harrisburg, 1997; recipient Athena award C. of C., 1995. Fellow Internat. Coll. Dentists; mem. ADA, Am. Assn. Women Dentists, Nat. Dental Assn., Pa. Dental Assn., Harrisburg Area Dental Soc. (v.p. 2000-01, pres. 2001-02), Soroptimist Internat. (past pres. Harrisburg chpt.), The Links Inc (past pres. Herrisburg chpt.). Republican. Baptist. Avocations: travel, golf, shopping. Home: 1094 Cardinal Dr Harrisburg PA 17111-3730 Office: Cmty Dental Assocs PC 2451 N 3rd St Harrisburg PA 17110-1902 Office Phone: 717-238-8163.

PRIOR, CORNELIUS BERNARD, JR., utilities company executive, financial consultant; b. Hartford, Conn., Feb. 26, 1934; s. Cornelius B. Sr. and Katherine (Daly) P.; m. Trudie Yolleck, 1993; children: Elizabeth, Michael, Sarah. AB, Holy Cross Coll., 1956; LLB, Harvard U., 1962. Bar: NY 1963. Assoc. atty. Sullivan and Cromwell, N.Y.C., 1963-68; gen. counsel Private Investment Co. for Asia, Tokyo, 1969-71; v.p. Drexel Firestone, N.Y.C., 1971-75; sr. v.p. Blythe Eastman Dillon, N.Y.C., 1975—78; mng. dir. Paine Webber, N.Y.C., 1978—80, Kidder, Peabody and Co., N.Y.C., 1980-87; chmn. & CEO Atlantic Tele-Network, Inc., St. Thomas, V.I. Bd. dirs. Atlantic Telenetwork Co., St. Thomas. Bd. dirs. Holy Cross Coll., trustee; mem. vis. com. Harvard Law Sch., dean's adv. coun.; trustee, chair capital campaigns Antilles Sch.; chmn. Caribbean Assn. of Nat. Telephone Orgns.; mem. adv. bd. Peter Gruber Found. Served to lt (j.g.) USN, 1956-59. Fulbright scholar, 1962—63. Mem.: Bar Assn. of NY, Univ. Club (N.Y.C.). Roman Catholic. Office: Atlantic Tele-Network Inc PO Box 12030 Saint Thomas VI 00801 Office Phone: 340-774-2260.

PRIOR, DAVID B. academic administrator; m. Anny Prior; children: Kylie, Jonathan. BA, Queen's U. Belfast, No. Ireland, 1964, PhD in Geomorphology, 1968. Dir. Atlantic Geosci. Ctr. Bedford Inst. Oceanography, Halifax; prof. geology and geophysics Tex. A&M U., College Station, 1996—97, dean, 1997—2002, provost, 2002—. Fellow: Geol. Soc. London. Office: Office Exec VP and Provost Tex A&M Univ 1248 TAMU College Station TX 77843-1248*

PRIOR, GARY L. lawyer; b. Niagara Falls, N.Y., June 26, 1943; s. Harold D. and Adeline Thelma (Lee) Prior; m. Nancy O'Shaughnessy, Aug. 23, 1975; children: Joseph Lee, Julia Elizabeth. BS, Tulane U., 1965; JD, U. Chgo., 1968. Bar: Ill. 1968, U.S. Dist. Ct. (no. dist.), Ill. 1968, U.S. Ct. Appeals (7th cir.) 1973, U.S. Ct. Appeals (3d cir.) 1974, U.S. Trial Bar 1983, U.S. Supreme Ct. 1989, U.S. Dist. Ct. (we. dist.) Wis. 1992, U.S. Dist. Ct. (ea. dist.) Wis. 1993, U.S. Dist. Ct. Minn. 1994, U.S. Ct. Appeals (fed. cir.) 2002. Assoc. Rooks, Pitts, and Poust, Chgo., 1968-71, McDermott, Will, and Emery, Chgo., 1971-74, ptnr., 1974—2002, dir. trial dept. tng., 1980-85, mem. securities approval com., 1986—94, mem. nominating com., chmn., 1988-89, partnership com., 1989-92, mem mgmt. com., 1991-93; of counsel Tabet, DiVito, and Rothstein, LLC, Chgo., 2002—03, ptnr., 2004—. Trustee Prior Family Charitable Found., Furry Friends Found. Mem.: Ill. State Bar Assn., Ill. Appellate Lawyers Assn., Sports Law. Avocations: farming, scuba diving. Home: 2512 N Burling St Chicago IL 60614-2510 Office: Tabet DiVito & Rothstein 180 N La Salle Ste 1510 Chicago IL 60601 Business E-Mail: gprior@tdrlawfirm.com.

PRIOR, JOHN THOMPSON, pathology educator; b. St. Albans, Vt., Oct. 8, 1917; s. Thomas William and Pauline Thompson Prior; m. Elizabeth Titus Troy, July 24, 1948; children: Anne, Polly, John Jr., Thomas, Jeffrey, Timothy. BS, U. Vt., 1939, MD, 1943. Diplomate Am. bd. Pathology. Resident in pathology Binghamton (N.Y.) City Hosp., 1946-47; fellow in pathology Syracuse (N.Y.) U. Med. Coll., 1947-49; asst. prof. pathology SUNY, Syracuse, 1949-54, assoc. prof., 1954-63, prof., 1963-72, clin. prof. pathology, 1972—. Active ARC Blood Bank, Syracuse, 1966-70; pres. N.Y. State Assoc. Lab., Syracuse, 1959-60; med. dir. PSRO Ctrl. N.Y., Syracuse, 1983-84; mem. N.Y. Stat Hosp. Rev. & Planning Assn., Albany, 1980-82; bd. dirs. Am. Med. Peer Rev. Assn., 1985-90. Contbr. articles to profl. jours. Bd. dirs. Lung Assn. Ctrl. N.Y., Syracuse, 1994—. Col. M.C., U.S. Army, 1944-77. Decorated Bronze Star, Silver Star, Legion of Merit, Belgian Croix de Guerre; recipient William Hammond Citation, N.Y. State Jour. Medicine, N.Y.C., 1984, Disting. Alumnus award U. Vt., Burlington, 1994. Mem. Onondaga County Med. Soc. (pres. 1974, disting. svc. award 1981). Avocations: golf, tennis. Home: 4615 Pewter Ln Manlius NY 13104-9329

PRIOR, WILLIAM ALLEN, electronics company executive; b. Benton Harbor, Mich., Jan. 14, 1927; s. Allen Ames and Madeline Isabel (Taylor) P.; m. Nancy Norton Sayles, July 7, 1951 (div. Oct. 1971); children: Stephanie Sayles, Alexandra Taylor, Robert Eames, Eleanor Norton; m. Carol Luise Becker-Ehmck, Oct. 30, 1971; children: Michael Becker-Ehmck, Jeffrey Renner. AB in Physics, Harvard Coll., 1950, MBA, 1954. Salesman IBM, Mineola, L.I., N.Y., 1950-52; sales engr. Lincoln Electric Co., Cleve., 1954-57; ptnr. Hammond Kennedy & Co., N.Y.C., 1957-66; v.p. The Singer Co., N.Y.C., 1967-68; pres. Tansitor Electronics, Bennington, Vt., 1969-71, Aerotron Inc., Raleigh, N.C., 1971-82; v.p. J. Lee Peeler & Co., Durham, N.C., 1986-89; pres. Accudyne, Inc., Raleigh, 1990-99. Chmn. Royal Blue Capital, Inc., Raleigh; bd. dirs. NeoDyne, Inc., Raleigh. Cpl. USAAF, 1945-46, Germany. Mem. IEEE, North Ridge Country Club (Raleigh), Raleigh Racquet Club, Harvard Club of N.Y.C., 50 Group. Republican. Avocations: tennis, skiing, computer programming. Home: 329 Meeting House Cir Raleigh NC 27615-3133 Personal E-mail: wprior@mba1954.hbs.edu.

PRIORE, CHRISTOPHER ANSELMO, artist; b. Buffalo, N.Y., Apr. 28, 1959; s. Robert Michael and Annetta Anselmo Priore. Studied, Tyler Sch. Art/Temple U., Rome, 1979—80; BFA, Carnegie Mellon U., Pitts., 1981. One-man shows include E.M. Donahue/Sosinski Art, N.Y.C., 1997, Cardozo Gallery, 2000, Museo ItaloAmericano, San Francisco, 2004, Italian Am. Mus., N.Y.C., 2004, exhibited in group shows at Carnegie Mus. Art, Pitts., 1986, So. Alleghenies Mus. Art, Loretto, Pa., 1988, Albright-Knox Art Gallery, Buffalo, N.Y., 1990, Fukuya Art Gallery, Hiroshima, Japan, 1995, Kunstun Technik, Berlin, 1998, L Gallery, Moscow, 1998, Del. Ctr. for Contemp. Arts, Wilmington, 2003, prin. works include Sky, The Pitts. Children's Mus., 1988—98, Rise!, MTA N.Y.C. Transit, 1997—98. Represented in permanent collections Singer's Forum, N.Y.C., Westinghouse Energy Ctr., Monroeville, Pa. Grantee, Richard King Mellon Found., 1988, Eben Demarest Trust, 1988, 1991, N.Y. Found. Arts., 1997—98, 1999. Democrat. Roman Catholic. Avocations: weightlifting, swimming. Office Phone: 212-568-2836. E-mail: christopherpriore@earthlink.net.

PRIORE, ROGER L. biostatistics educator, consultant; b. Buffalo, Apr. 21, 1938; s. Anthony J. and Linda M. (DeMarchi) P.; m. Carol A. Cooper, Sept. 3, 1960; children— Howard W., Susan L., John D. BA, SUNY-Buffalo, 1960, MS, 1962; Sc.D., Johns Hopkins U., 1965. Jr. cancer research scientist Roswell Park Meml. Inst., Buffalo, 1960-65, sr. cancer research scientist, 1965-67, assoc. cancer research scientist, 1967-69, prin. cancer research scientist, 1974-79, dir. computer sci., 1979-83, dir. dept. biomath., 1983-91, dir. mgmt. info. systems, 1988-91; asst. rsch. prof. SUNY, Buffalo, 1966-68, assoc. rsch. prof., 1968-69, rsch. prof., dir. grad. studies in biometry, 1980-91; rsch. prof. Niagara U., 1968-91; cons. in stats. and computing, 1991—; clin. prof. dept. social and preventive medicine SUNY, Buffalo, 1991—; pres. Compustat Assocs., Inc., Buffalo, 1993—; clin. prof. dept. statistics SUNY, Buffalo, 1995—. Cons. Am. Joint Com. on Cancer, 1980-88. Contbr. articles to profl. jours. Mem. Am. Statis. Assn., Soc. for Epidemiol. Rsch., Sigma Xi Office: 342 Dan Troy Dr Buffalo NY 14221-3514

PRIORE, JR. CHARLES FRANK, school librarian; b. Buffalo, July 27, 1953; s. Charles Frank and Faye Marie Priore; m. Harriet Elizabeth Bohnert, Aug. 28, 1982; children: Anna Emily Priore, Caroline Elizabeth Priore. MLS, SUNY-Buffalo, 1976—77. Sci. libr. U. of Calif.-Davis, 1980—84, Carleton Coll., Northfield, Minn., 1984—. Author: (book) Lock Stock and Barrel; contbr. articles to numerous sci. and tech. jours. Republican. Roman Catholic. Avocation: hunting. Office: Carleton Coll 1 North College St Northfield MN 55057 E-mail: cpriore@carleton.edu.

PRIORY, RICHARD BALDWIN, former electric power industry executive; b. Lakehurst, N.J., May 15, 1946; s. Joseph Albert Jr. and Betty (Baldwin) P.; m. Joan Ellen Rourke, May 30, 1968; children: Jennifer Joan, Richard Baldwin Jr. BSCE magna cum laude, W.Va. Inst. Tech., 1969; MS in Engring., Princeton U., 1973; grad. utility exec. program, U. Mich., 1982; grad. advanced mgmt. program, Harvard U., 1991. Registered profl. engr., N.C., S.C. Design engr., project engr. Union Carbide Corp., 1969-72; asst. prof. structural engring. U. N.C., Charlotte, 1973-76; design engr. Duke Power Co., Charlotte, N.C., 1976-78, prin. engr., 1978-81, mgr. project mgmt. divsn., 1981-84, v.p. design engring., 1984-88, sr. v.p. generation and info. svcs., 1988-91, exec. v.p. power generation group, 1991-94, pres., COO, 1994-97; chmn., CEO Duke Energy Corp. (formerly Duke Power Co.), Charlotte, 1997—2003. Bd. dirs. Duke Energy Corp., Dana Corp., EEI, AEIC; mem. Duke Fluor Daniel Mgmt. Com. Bd. visitors U. N.C., Charlotte; past chmn. bd. dirs. Charlotte-Mecklenburg Edn. Found.; pres., bd. trustees Discovery Place, Inc., 1992-93; past mem. Charlotte-Mecklenburg Pub. Broadcasting Found.; vice chmn. campaign drive United Way Ctrl. Carolinas, Inc., 1990; adv. coun. N.C. Alliance for Competitive Technologies. Mem. ASCE, Nat. Acad. Engring, Charlotte Engrs. Club. Avocation: golf.

PRISANT, L(OUIS) MICHAEL, cardiologist; b. Albany, Ga., Dec. 25, 1949; s. Bennie Martin and Mozelle (Cosper) Prisant; m. Rose Corinth Trincher, June 28, 1975; children: Michelle Elizabeth, Louis Michael. BA, Emory U., 1971; MD, Med. Coll. Ga., 1977. Diplomate Am. Bd. Internal Medicine, Am. Bd. Cardiovasc. Diseases, Am. Bd. Clin. Pharmacology, Am. Bd. Forensic Medicine, Nat. Bd. Examiners, Am. Bd. Forensic Examiners, Am. Soc. Hypertension, cert. specialist in hypertension. Intern Med. Coll. Ga., Augusta, 1977-78, resident, 1978-80; chief med. resident, 1979-80; cardiology fellow Med. Coll. Ga., 1980-82, instr., 1982-83, asst. prof. medicine, 1983-89, assoc. prof. medicine, 1989-94, prof., 1994—, dir. cardiology fellowship tng. program, 1996—2001, dir. hypertension and clin. pharmacology, 2001—. Cons. in field; nat. and internat. lectr. in field. Mem. editl. bd. Blood Pressure Monitoring, Jour. Clin. Hypertension, Heart Disease: Jour. Cardiovasc. Medicine, Am. Jour. Therapeutics, Jour. Clin. Pharmacology; contbr. over 162 articles to profl. jours., chapters to books. Grantee, FOE, 1989, Rorer, 1989, Am. Cyanamid, 1988, Sandoz, 1989—93, Merck, 1990—92, Squibb, 1991, Lorex, 1991, NIH, 1991, 1996, 2002, Lederle, 1993, Ciba-Geigy, 1995, Omedha, 1997, Smith-Kline-Beecham, 1997, Apothecon, 1996, Bristol-Meyer-Squibb, 1998, Novartis, 1999, 2002, HDI, 2000, Searle, 2000, Astra-Zeneca, 2002, 2003, Forest Lab., 2001, Sankyo, 2002, Boehringer, 2002, NitroMed, 2003, Pfizer, 2003. Fellow: AMA (Physician's Recognition award 1982—2004), ACP, Am. Heart Assn. (coun. high blood pressure rsch.), Coun. Geriatric Cardiology, Am. Coll. Chest Physicians, Am. Coll. Forensic Examiners, Am. Coll. Cardiology, Am. Coll. Clin. Pharmacology (regent 2002—); mem.: AAUP, Richmond County Med. Soc., Med. Assn. Ga., Ga. Med. Care Found., Assn. for Advancement Med. Instrumentation (co-chmn. sphygmomanometer com.), So. Med. Assn., Am. Soc. Internal Medicine, Am. Soc. Hypertension (CME com. 2000—03, nominating com. 2001—04), Am. Soc. Echocardiography, Am. Fedn. Clin. Rsch., Internat. Soc. on Hypertension in Blacks, Ahlquist Soc. (pres.), Tau Epsilon Phi, Alpha Phi Omega, Phi Delta Epsilon. Jewish. Avocation: Avocation: computers. Office: Med Coll Ga Hypertension & Clin Pharmacology 1120 15th St BI-5084 Augusta GA 30912 Office Phone: 706-721-8474. Business E-Mail: mprisant@mcg.edu.

PRISCHING, MANFRED, sociology educator; b. Bruck Mur, Austria, Dec. 12, 1950; s. Karl and Margareth (Voggenhuber) P.; m. Roswitha Hribernig, Sept. 7, 1978; children: Margareth, Sebastian. JD, U. Graz, Austria, 1974; M Econs., U. Graz, 1977. Univ. asst., then lectr. U. Graz, 1976-87, lectr. dept. sociology, 1988—. Lectr., U. Limburg, Maastricht, The Netherlands, 1987-88; guest prof. Harvard U., 1995-96; sci. dir. Technikum Joanneum, Graz, 1997-2001. Author: Crises. A sociological analysis, 1986, Protest of Unemployed in Economic Crisis, 1988, Sociology Themes, Theories, Perspectives, 3d edit., 1995, Social Partnership, 1996, Pictures of the Welfare State, 1996, The McSociety, 1998; contbr. numerous articles to profl. jours. Mem. Austrian Acad. Scis. Roman Catholic. Home: Carnerigasse 12 A 8010 Graz Austria Office: Dept Sociology U Graz Universitaetsstrabe 15 A 8010 Graz Austria E-mail: manfred.prisching@uni-graz.at.

PRISCO, DOUGLAS LOUIS, physician; b. N.Y.C., Nov. 30, 1945; s. Frank James and Isabel (Gaetano) P.; m. Marianne Paula Mangano, Jan. 8, 1972; children: Jennifer Leigh, Douglas Louis, Dana Lauren, Andrew Michael. AB, Georgetown U., 1967; postgrad., N.Y. U., 1967-68; MD, U. Rome, 1974. Diplomate Am. Bd. Internal Medicine, sub-bd. Pulmonary Diseases. Intern Mt. Sinai Svcs., Elmhurst, NY, 1974-75, resident in medicine, 1975-77, pulmonary medicine fellow, 1977-79; practice medicine specializing in pulmonary medicine New Hyde Park, NY, 1979-81; clin. asst. in medicine Bklyn. Hosp., Bklyn., 1979-81; pulmonary cons. and admitting physician Booth Meml. Hosp. (now N.Y. Hosp. Med. Ctr. of Queens), Pkwy Hosp.; admitting physician L.I. Jewish Hosp., New Hyde Park, Mt. Sinai of Queens, 1999—; chief pulmonary medicine Deepdale Gen. Hosp., 1980-93; clin. asst. Mt. Sinai Sch. Medicine, N.Y.C., 1977-79; physician adviser St. Barnabas Hosp., 1981-82; pres. Met. Pulmonary Assocs., P.C., 1980—, Met. Pulmonary P.C., 1985—; v.p. network devel. Parkway Hosp., 1997. Physician adv. to Queens County Profl. Standards Rev. Orgn., 1979-85; co-chmn. quality assurance com. downstate region Island peer Rev. Orgn., 1990—, vice chmn. pro-tem regional quality assurance com., N.Y., 1993—; chief pulmonary diseases Little Neck Cmty. Hosp. (formerly Deepdale Ge n. Hosp.), 1980-93, pulmonary chief, med. dir., 1993-96; pres. Med. Staff Soc., 1992—, mem. med. bd.; cons. Queens divsn. Island Peer Rev. Orgn., 1985—, Astoria (N.Y.) Med. Group, dir. pulmonary svcs., 1999—; dir. Fresh Meadows Care, 1997. Mem. Rep. Senatorial Inner Cir., 1990. Fellow Am. Coll. Chest Physicians; mem. ACP, Am. Lung Assn. Queens (bd. dirs. 1988—, honoree 1997), Queens County Med. Soc., Port Washington Yacht Club (former chmn. jr. activities 1987-88, fleet surgeon 1991-93, 95-97, bd.d irs. 1995-97), Capitol Hill Club,

Integrated Delivery Systems of N.Y. (vice chmn., chmn. 1995—). Roman Catholic. Address: Ste 201 3003 New Hyde Park Rd New Hyde Park NY 11042-1214 Office Phone: 516-488-2880. Personal E mail: dlpmd@aol.com.

PRISELAC, THOMAS M. health facility executive, educator; BA in Biology, Washington & Jefferson Coll.; MPH Health Svcs. Adminstrn. and Planning, U. Pitts. Asst. adminstr. Cedars-Sinai Med. Ctr., L.A., 1979—81, assoc. adminstr., 1981—82, sr. assoc. adminstr., 1982—83, v.p. adminstrn., 1983—85, sr. v.p. ops., 1985—91, exec. v.p., COO, 1988—94, pres., CEO, 1994—. Adj. prof. UCLA Sch. Pub. Health; tchr., principles of orgn. leadership Master of Pub. Health for Health Professionals; past chmn. Coun. of Teaching Hosp. of Assn. of Am. Med. Coll.; chmn. Calif. Healthcare Assn., Healthcare Assn. of Southern Calif.; bd. dirs. Am. Hosp. Assn., VHA, Inc., Nat. Com. for Quality Healthcare, Calif. Healthcare Found.; lectr. in field. Bd. dirs. Blue Cross Calif. Office: Cedars Sinai Med Ctr 8700 Beverly Blvd Rm 2628 Los Angeles CA 90048 Address: UCLA Sch Pub Health Dept Health Services Box 951772 Los Angeles CA 90095-1772 Office Phone: 310-423-5711, 310-206-3435. Office Fax: 310 423-0120, 310-206-4722. Business E-Mail: tmp@cshs.org.*

PRISSEL, BARBARA ANN, paralegal, law educator; b. Plum City, Wis., July 7, 1946; d. John Henry and Mary Ann Louise (Dankers) Seipel; m. Stephen Joseph Prissel, Dec. 16, 1967; children: Angela, Benjamin. Grad. with honors, Mpls. Bus. Coll., 1966; student, Moraine Park Tech. Coll., Wis., 1983—. Cert. interactive TV, adult edn. instr. Legal sec. Mott, Grose, Von Holtum & Hefferan, Mpls., 1966-67, Whelan, Morey & Morey Attys. at Law, Durand, Wis., 1967-70, Murry Law Office, River Falls, Wis., 1968-70, Potter, Wefel & Nettesheim, Wisconsin Rapids, Wis., 1970-71; sec. to adminstr. Moraine Park Tech. Coll., Fond du Lac, Wis., 1971-72; paralegal Kilgore Law Office, Ripon, Wis., 1985—2004, Grant Law Office, Waupun, Wis., 2004—. Chmn. legal adv. com. Moraine Park Tech. Coll., Fond du Lac, 1996-98, mem. adminstrv. assts. adv. com., 1984-86, mem. legal adv. commn. 1984—. Contbr. poems to newspapers. Ch. rep. Ch. Women United, Ripon, 1984-87; pianist Christian Women's Orgn., Ripon, 1985-95; pianist, organist Our Lady of Lake Ch., Green Lake, Wis., 1987—. Mem.: NAFE, Legal Profls. Assn. (East Ctrl. Wis. pres. 1994—95, sec. 1995—96, chmn. Day-In-Ct. 1999, NALS Fedn. liaison 2000—02, sec. 2001—02, v.p. 2003—, state legal edn. task force 2003—, chmn. ednl. liaison com., Legal award of Excellence 1995—96), Wis. Assn. Legal Secs. (state legal ednl. liaison com. 1997—, state legal edn. task force 2003—), Nat. Assn. Legal Secs. Roman Catholic. Avocations: teaching and playing piano, creative writing, cooking, swimming, exercising. Home: 129 Wolverton Ave Ripon WI 54971-1144

PRITCHARD, CLAUDIUS HORNBY, JR., retired university president; b. Charleston, W.Va., June 28, 1927; s. Claudius Hornby and Katherine (Ellison) P.; m. Marjorie Walker Pullen, Aug. 9, 1952; children: Virginia Aiken, Katherine Winston, Olivia Reynolds, Claudius V. BA, Hampden-Sydney Coll., 1950; MA, Longwood U., 1965; PhD, Fla. State U., 1971. Comml. loan teller Am. Nat. Bank and Trust Co., Danville, Va., 1950-53; asst. cashier Planters Bank & Trust Co., Farmville, Va., 1953-55; asst. to pres. Hampden-Sydney (Va.) Coll., 1955-57, bus. mgr. and treas., 1957-67, v.p. devel., 1967-71; sr. budget analyst-edn. State of Fla., Tallahassee, 1971-72; pres. Sullins Coll., Bristol, Va., 1972-76; v.p. adminstrn. Maryville U., St. Louis, 1976-77, pres., 1977-92, pres. emeritus, 1992—. Adv. dir. Commerce Bank of St. Louis, 1982—92. Author: Col. D. Wyatt Aiken (1828-1887) South Carolina's Militant Agrarian, 1970; contbr. articles to profl. jours. Mem. bd. visitors Charleston So. U., 1993—; chmn. Summerville Comml. Design Rev. Bd., 1999—; bd. dirs. West St. Louis County YMCA, Chesterfield, Mo., 1985—92. With USNR, 1945—46. Fla. State U. fellow, 1969-70, Arthur Vining Davis fellow Am. Council on Edn., 1974. Mem. AAUP, SCV, Am. Assn. Higher Edn., So. Hist. Assn., S.C. Hist. Soc., Mo. Colls. Fund (bd. dirs., chmn. 1987-88), Mil. Order of the Stars and Bars, Ind. Colls. and Univs. Mo., Chesterfield C. of C. (pres. 1987, Chesterfield Citizen of Yr. award 1986), Rotary. Republican. Presbyterian.

PRITCHARD, DALTON HAROLD, retired electronics research engineer; b. Crystal Springs, Miss., Sept. 1, 1921; s. Cecil Harold and Marvie Prudence (Lofton) P.; m. Caroline Ann Hnatuk, Apr. 27, 1947; 1 child, Mary Ann Pritchard Poole. BSE.E., Miss. State U., 1943; postgrad., Harvard, MIT Radar Sch., 1943-44. Mem. tech. staff RCA Labs., Riverhead, N.Y., 1946-50, mem. tech. staff Princeton, N.J., 1950-75, fellow tech. staff, 1975-87. Session chmn., mem. program com. Internat. Conf. on Consumer Electronics, Chgo., 1980-85 Contbr. articles to profl. jours.; patentee in field. Mem. N.J. Gov.'s Sci. Adv. Council, Princeton, 1981-85. Served to capt. U.S. Army Signal Corps Decorated Bronze Star; recipient Eduard Rhein prize Edward Rhein Found., Berlin, Fed. Republic of Germany, 1980; Disting. Engring. fellow Miss. State U., 1991. Fellow IEEE (Vladimir Zworykin award 1977, David Sarnoff award 1981), Soc. Info. Display, Nat. Assn. Engrs., Nat. Acad. Engring., Sigma Xi, Tau Beta Pi, Kappa Mu Epsilon Republican. Baptist. Avocations: amateur radio, tennis. Home: 3 Bent Tree Ln Hilton Head Island SC 29926-1906

PRITCHARD, DAVID EDWARD, physics educator; b. N.Y.C., Oct. 15, 1941; m. Andrea Hasler; children: Orion, Alexander. BS, Calif. Inst. Tech., 1962; PhD, Harvard U., 1968. Postdoctoral fellow MIT, Cambridge, Mass., 1968, instr., 1968-70, asst. prof., 1970-75, assoc. prof., 1975-80, prof., 1980—, Cecil and Ida Chair, 2001—. Vis. scientist Stanford Rsch. Inst., 1975; vis. prof. U. Pais Sud Orsay, 1983; disting. visitor Joint Inst. for Lab., Astrophysics, 1989, 98, mem. subpanel, 1990—94, chmn., 1994; co-chair First Quantum Electronic and Laser Sci. Conf., 1989; chair Internat. Conf. on Atomic Physics, 2002; Selby Travelling lectr. of Australia, 04. Div. assoc. editor Phys. Rev. Letters, 1983-88; contbr. articles to profl. jours. Polaroid fellow Harvard U., 1962-63, NSF predoctoral fellow, 1963-68. Fellow: AAAS, Optical Soc. Am. (bd. dirs. 1998—2001, Max Born award 2004), Am. Acad. Arts and Scis., Am. Phys. Soc. (disting. traveling lectr. laser sci. topical group 1992—94, rep. steering com. laser sci. topical group, rep. joint coun. on quantum electronics, Broida prize 1991, Centennial spkr. 1999, Schawlow prize 2003); mem.: NAS, Effective Educational Tech., Inc. (co-founder), Tiverton Yacht Club (R.I.). Avocations: sailing, carpentry. Home: 88 Washington Ave Cambridge MA 02140-2708 Office: MIT Rm 26-241 Dept Physics Cambridge MA 02139 Office Phone: 617-253-6812. Business E-Mail: dpritch@mit.edu.

PRITCHARD, HUW OWEN, chemist, educator; b. Bangor, Wales, July 23, 1928; s. Owen and Lilian Venetia P.; m. Margaret Ramsden, Nov. 3, 1956; children— Karen, David. B.Sc., U. Manchester, 1948, M.Sc., 1949, PhD, 1951, D.Sc., 1964. Asst. lectr. chemistry Manchester (Eng.) U., 1951-54, lectr., 1954-65; prof. chemistry York U., Ont., Can., 1965-97, prof. emeritus, 1997—. Contbr. articles to profl. jours. Fellow Royal Soc. Can. Office: Chemistry Dept York Univ Toronto ON Canada M3J 1P3 E-mail: huw@yorku.ca.

PRITCHARD, KATHLEEN JO, not-for-profit association administrator; b. Milw., Feb. 6, 1951; d. Owen J. and Madelon (Coogan) P.; m. William A. Durkin Jr., Oct. 22, 1982; children: Elizabeth Durkin, Christine Durkin, W. Ryan Durkin. BA in Anthropology, U. Wis., Oshkosh, 1973; MA in Pub. Adminstrn., U. Wis., 1980; PhD in Polit. Sci., U. Wis., Milw., 1986. Rsch. analyst Wis. Coun. on Criminal Justice, Madison, 1974-77; planning analyst Wis. Dept. Health and Social Svcs., Madison, 1977-80; assoc. lectr. U. Wis., Milw., 1980-89; vis. asst. prof. Marquette U., Milw., 1986, 90-91; policy cons. dept. adminstrn. City of Milw., 1992; Outcomes Project dir. United Way of Greater Milw., 1992-96, dir. impact and evaluation, 1997—; chmn. United Way of Am. Forum on Outcomes II, 1997. Faculty advisor Model OAS, UN advisor, Milw., 1986-91; campus rep. spkr. Wis. Inst. for Study of War, Peace and Global Cooperation, Milw., 1989-90; mem. United Way Am. Task Force on Impact, 1995—; instr. Nat. Acad. Volunteerism, 1996. Contbr. articles to profl. jours., chpts. to books Dir. cmty impact United Way of Greater Milw., 1998; trustee Pub. Policy Forum, 2000—, NonProfit Mgmt. Fund, 2000—03, NonProfit Mgmt. Edn. Ctr., 2000—03; pres. Whitefish Bay Village, 2002—; dir. cmty. impact, product devel. United Way Am.; mem. exec. coun. Met. Milw. Sewerage Dist.; mem. Lakefront Devel. Com., 2004—; mem. exec. steering com. Partnership for Healthy Milw., 2001—; bd. dirs. Counseling Ctr. of Greater Milw., 2004—. Recipient Alice Paul Dissertation award Women's Caucus for Polit. Sci., 1984; Grad. Sch. fellow U. Wis., Milw., 1983, fellow Kenyon Coll. Summer Inst., 1983. Mem. Phi Kappa Phi (chpt. officer 1989). Personal E-mail: pritchardkj@aol.com.

PRITCHARD, LLEWELYN G. lawyer; b. NYC, Aug. 13, 1937; s. Llewelyn and Anne Mary (Streib) P.; m. Joan Ashby, June 20, 1959; children: David Ashby, Jennifer Pritchard Vick, Andrew Harrison, William Llewellyn. AB with honors, Drew U., 1958; LLB, Duke U., 1961. Ptnr. Helsell & Fetterman, Seattle. Trustee, corp. counsel Allied Arts Found.; pres. Allied Arts Seattle, 1974-76; trustee Meth. Ednl. Found., 1970-85, pres., 1991-92; life trustee PONCHO Patrons of Pacific N.W. Civil, Cultural and Charitable Orgns., pres., 1972-73; bd. dirs. Planned Parenthood of Seattle/King County, 1972-78; trustee Seattle Symphony Orch., 1979-83, chmn. bd., 1980-82, hon. trustee; trustee U. Puget Sound., 1972-99, mem. exec. com., chmn. bd. visitors to Law Sch., 1984-88; trustee, exec. com. Mus. of Glass, 2000—; chancellor Pacific N.W. Ann. conf. United Meth. Ch., 1969—. Fellow Am. Bar Found. (life, state chmn. 1988-98); mem. ABA (bd. govs. 1986-89, chmn. program com. 1988-89, exec. com. 1988-89, Ho. of Dels. 1979—, nat. dir. young lawyers divsn. 1971, chmn. sect. of individual rights and responsibilities 1975-76, exec. coun. family law sect. 2002—, chair standing com. on legal aid and indigent defendants 1973-75, chair legal needs study 1995-98, chair adv. com. to pro bono immigration project 1991-2001, dir. Ctr. for Human Rights 2001—), Wash. State Bar Assn. (bd. govs. King County 1972-75), King County Bar Assn. (chair young lawyers sect. 1970). Avocations: reading, art collector. Home: 5229 140th Ave NE Bellevue WA 98005-1024 Office: Helsell & Fetterman 1001 Fourth Ave Ste 4200 Seattle WA 98154 Office Phone: 206-292-1144.

PRITCHARD, SARAH MARGARET, library director; b. Boston, Feb. 8, 1955; d. Wilbur Louis and Kathleen Hunton (Moss) P.; m. Timothy John Brennan, Aug. 20, 1977 (div. 1993). BA, U. Md., 1975; MA in French, U. Wis., 1976, MLS, 1977. Intern Libr. Congress, Washington, 1977-78, reference specialist in women's studies, 1978-88, head microform reading rm., 1988-90; sr. program officer Assn. Rsch. Librs., Washington, 1990-91, assoc. exec. dir., 1991-92; acad. libr. mgmt. intern Coun on Libr. Resources Princeton U., N.J., 1988-89; dir. librs. Smith Coll., Northampton, Mass., 1992-99; univ. libr. U. Calif., Santa Barbara, 1999—. Ednl. advisor Women's Rsch. and Edn. Inst., Washington, 1987-92; bd. dirs. Western Mass. Regional Libr. Sys., 1997-98; bd. dirs. U. Calif. So. Regional Libr. Facility, 1999—, Gold Coast Libr. Network, Libr. of Calif., 2003—. Editor: The Women's Annual, 1984; compiler ARL Stats., 1990-92; contbr. articles to profl. jours.; mem. editl. bd. Jour. Acad. Librarianship, 1993-99, Portal: Librs. and the Acad., 2000—; contbg. editor Libr. Issues, 1994-99. Trustee Leroy C. Merritt Humanitarian Fund, 1991-94. Named Wis. Alumni Rsch. Found. fellow, 1975-77, Outstanding Alumna U. Wis. Sch. of Libr. and Info. Studies, 1997. Mem. ALA (chair machine assisted reference sect. 1986-87, chair women's studies sect. 1989-90, coun. 1990-98, 2000—, chair stds. com. 1998-2002, chair ethics com. 2002—, Equality award 1997), Nat. Women's Studies Assn., Cosmos Club. Democrat. Office: U Calif Davidson Libr Santa Barbara CA 93106

PRITCHARD, WILLIAM ROY, former university system administrator; b. Portage, Wis., Nov. 15, 1924; s. William Roy and Lillian Edith (Roberts) P.; m. Deanna Elaine Pritchard; children: Rosan June, William Roy, Caryl Jean, Alyn Evan, Cynthia Bedeau. Student, U. Wis., 1942-43; DVM, Kans. State U., 1946; PhD, U. Minn., 1953; JD, Ind. U., 1957; DSc (hon.), Kans. State U., 1970, Tufts U., 1988, Purdue U., 1977, U. Guelph, 1998. Asst. prof. U. Wis., 1946-49; assoc. prof. U. Minn., 1949-53; prof. Purdue U., 1953-57; prof., head vet. sci. U. Fla., 1957-61; assoc. dir. Vet. Med. Rsch. Inst., Ia. State U., 1961-62; prof. U. Calif., Davis, 1962—, dean Sch. Vet Medicine, 1962-82; assoc. dir. Agrl. Expt. Sta., 1962-72; coord. internat. agrl. programs U. Calif. system, 1977-81. Vis. fellow Woodrow Wilson Sch. Pub and Internat. Affairs, Princeton, 1968-69; John Thomson lectr. U. Queensland, 1966; co-dir. nat. veterinary edn. program Duke U., 1987-92; spl. research hemmorrhagic diseases animals. Cons. Dept. Agr., Def. Dept., USPHS, VA, Calif. Dept. Health, FDA, 1962-97; bd. cons. agr. Rockefeller Found., 1962-66; nat. med. cons. surgeon gen. USAF, 1962-64; mem. FAO/WHO Expert Panel Vet. Edn., President's Sci. Advisory Com. Panel World Food Supply, 1966-67, President's Sci. Adv. Com. Panel Biology and Med. Sci., 1969-70, Joint Rsch. Com. Bd. Internat. Food and Agr. AID, 1977-81. With U.S. Army, 1942-44. Recipient Gov. Fla. award, 1961, Disting. Svc. award Kans. State U., 1963, Outstanding Achievement award U. Minn., 1976, Disting. Pub. Svc. award U. Calif., Davis, 1991, Gold Headed Cane award Am. Soc. Vet. Epidemiology, 1992. Mem. AAAS, APHA, Am. Vet. Med. Assn. (Internat. Vet. Congress award 1988), Nat. Acad. of Practice in Vet. Medicine (elected 1986), Am. Soc. Vet. Epidemiologists, Conf. of Pub. Health Vets. (hon. life), U.S. Animal Health Assn., Nat. Assn. State Univs. and Land-Grant Colls. (internat. affairs com. 1965-70), Order of Coif, Sigma Xi, Phi Zeta, Gamma Alpha. Home: 2409 Madrid Ct Davis CA 95616-0141

PRITCHARD, WILLIAM WINTHER, lawyer, drilling company executive; b. Bartlesville, Okla, Mar. 20, 1951; s. James Edward and Agnes Kathryn (Winther) Pritchard; m. Susan Jane Parsons, Aug. 12, 1972; children: Jane, Kathryn, Robert. BA(hon.), U. Kans., 1973; JD, U. Tulsa, 1976. Bar: Okla. 1976. With Parker Drilling Co., Tulsa, 1976, v.p. gen. counsel, 1984. Mem.: Okla. Bar Assn., ABA, So. Hills Country Club. Republican. Presbyterian. Office: Parker Drilling Co 1401 Enclave Pkwy Houston TX 77077-2052

PRITCHETT, GIL, III, actor; b. Waco, Aug. 30, 1959; s. Gilbert Pritchett Jr. and Juanita Alexander; m. Rizel Osara Fajardo (div.); 1 child (dec.). AA in Theatre and Comm., Lon Morris Coll., 1979; AA in Theatre, Inner City Cultural Ctr., 1991. Tchr. Dallas Black Dance Theatre, 1984—86, William Grant Still Arts Ctr., L.A., 1981—82, 1988—89, HArlem Children's Zone, 2002—03. Actor: (Broadway plays) Play On, Jelly's Last Jam; singer: (plays) Summer Parade, Fiesta Tropical; actor: (plays) Peter Pan, People's Choice, Dreamgirls; singer: (plays) Eubie; actor: (plays) Ain't Misbehavin; singer: (plays) The All Night Strutt; actor: (plays) The People Could Fly and Still Do, Red Noses, De Obeah Mon, A Christmas Carol, The Tempest, Finian's Rainbow, (numerous commls.). Mem.: AFL-CIO, AFILA, AEA. Home: 302 W 139th St #3F New York NY 10030 Office Phone: 212-765-9564.

PRITCHETT, SAMUEL TRAVIS, finance and insurance educator, researcher, consultant; b. Emporia, Va., Dec. 18, 1938; s. Harvey Eugene and Mary (Brown) P.; m. Bertha Yates, Feb. 20, 1960; children: John Travis, Meri Katherine. BSBA, Va. Poly. Inst. and State U., 1960, MSBA, 1967; DBA, Ind. U., 1969. CLU, ChFC, CPCU. Claim rep. Equitable Life Assurance Soc., Richmond, Va., 1960-64, asst. div. claim mgr., 1964-65; asst. prof. bus. adminstrn. U. Richmond, 1969-70; asst. prof. ins. Va. Commonwealth U., Richmond, 1970-72, assoc. prof. ins., 1972-73; assoc. prof. fin. and ins. U. S.C., Columbia, 1973-76, prof. fin. and ins., 1976-99, J.H. Fellers prof., 1981-83, W.F. Hipp prof. ins., 1983-2000, program dir., chair banking, fin., ins. and real estate, 1977-83, 99-00, acad. dir. MBA program, 1993-95, disting. prof. finance and ins., 1999-2000, disting. prof. emeritus, 2000—. Vis. prof. ins. Ind. U., Bloomington, 1995-96; chmn. Risk Theory Soc., Columbus, Ohio, 1987-88; acad. dir. internat. exec. devel. program Bamerindus Seguros, Curtiba, Brazil, 1995. Author: Risk Management and Insurance, 7th edit., 1996, Stock Life Insurance Company Profitability, 1986, Individual Annuities as a Source of Retirement Income, 2d edit., 1982, An Economic Analysis of Workers' Compensation in South Carolina, 1994; assoc. editor Jour. Risk and Ins., 1982-86, editor, 1987-91; assoc. editor Fin. Svcs. Rev., 1989-95, 97-99; asst. editor Jour. Am. Soc. CLU and ChFC, 1993-98; mem. acad. rev. bd. Jour. Fin. Planning, 1990-91; mem. editl. bd. Jour. Bus. Rsch., 1976-83, Am. Jour. Small Bus., 1975-79; contbr. articles to profl. jours. Active S.C. Joint Ins. Study Com., 1981-86, 89-95. Mem. Am. Risk and Ins. Assn. (pres. 1980-81), Acad. Fin. Svcs. (pres. 1987-88), So. Risk and Ins. Assn. (pres. 1977-78), Fin. Mgmt. Assn., Profl. Ins. Agts. Found. (named Ins. Educator of Yr. 1989), Beta Gamma Sigma (pres. chpt. 1980-81), Gamma Iota Sigma (nat. trustee 1976-92). Home: 709 Marlin Ln Charleston SC 29412-5039 Office: U SC Moore Sch Bus Columbia SC 29208-0001 *Apply to others religious values such as honesty, humility, respect, and service. Cultivate a strong work ethic and select admirable mentors.*

PRITCHETT, THOMAS RONALD, retired metal and chemical company executive; b. Colorado City, Tex., Sept. 2, 1925; s. John Thomas and Meddie Omeira (Terry) P.; m. Mary Margaret Hallenbeck, Dec. 23, 1948; children: Rhonda Jean, Thomas Rand, Rebecca Ann. BS in Chemistry and ChemE., U. Tex., 1948, MS, 1949, PhD, 1951. Registered profl. engr. Calif. Rsch. chemist Def. Rsch. Lab., Austin, Tex., 1948-51, Monsanto Chem. Co., Dayton, Ohio, 1951-52; sect. head, rsch. investigator, asst. dir., tech. mgr. Kaiser Aluminum & Chem. Corp., Pleasanton, Calif., 1952-68, v.p., dir. rsch., 1968-89; metall. and corrosion cons. Alamo, Tex., 1989—. Contbr. articles to profl. jours. Mem. adv. bd. Sch. Engring. U. Calif.-Berkeley. Served with U.S. Army, 1944-46. Fellow Am. Soc. Metals; mem. AIME, Aluminum Assn. (chmn. tech. com. and acad. com.), Nat. Assn. Corrosion Engrs., Am. Chem. Soc., Electrochem. Soc., Materials Properties Council (bd. dirs.), Sigma Xi, Phi Lambda Upsilon. Home and Office: 325 Diana Dr ACC 403 Alamo TX 78516 Office Phone: 956-787-0919.

PRITSKER, IGOR, mathematics professor; PhD, Univ. South Fla., 1995. Assoc. prof. Okla. State U., Stillwater, 1999—. Office: Okla State U Math Sci 401 Stillwater OK 74078

PRITT, FRANK W. computer company executive; Founder, chmn., CEO Attachmate Corp., Bellevue, Wash., 1982—. Address: PO Box 90026 Bellevue WA 98009-9026

PRITTS, ELIZABETH ANNA, medical educator; b. Vallejo, Calif., Apr. 23, 1963; m. David Leon Olive, Sept. 26, 1999; children: Zachary Olive, Mathew Olive, Alexander Olive. BA, U. Calif., Berkeley, 1989; MD, Thomas Jefferson U., 1994. Diplomate Am. Bd. Ob-Gyn. Resident Yale U., New Haven, 1994—98; fellow U. Calif., San Francisco, 2000—02; asst. prof. U. Wis., Madison, 2002—. Co-founder Am. Women's Med. Assn., Phila., 1992; pres. Choice Physicians, Phila., 1993. Contbr. articles to profl. jours., chapters to books. Recipient First prize, World Congress Endometriosis, 2002; Internat. scholar, NIH, 1999. Fellow. ACOG; mem.: Am. Soc. Reproductive Medicine (presenter 2002), Am. Assn. Gynelogic Laparoscopy. Avocations: yoga, ballet, travel.

PRITZKER, NICHOLAS J. diversified services corporation executive; Formerly exec. v.p. devel. Hyatt Corp., Chgo.; pres. Hyatt Devel. Corp., Chgo. Office: Hyatt Devel Corp 200 W Madison St Chicago IL 60606-3414

PRITZKER, PENNY, investor; b. Chgo., May 2, 1959; d. Donald N. and Sue Ann (Sandel) P.; m. Bryan Traubert, Sept. 10, 1988; children: Donald Pritzker Traubert, Rose Pritzker Traubert. B in Econs., Harvard U., 1981; JD, MBA, Stanford U., 1985. Bar: Ill. 1985. Mgr. Hyatt Devel. Corp., Chgo., 1985-87; pres. Classic Residence by Hyatt, Chgo., 1987—; ptnr. Pritzker & Pritzker, Chgo., 1987—; pres. Pritzker Realty Group (formerly Penguin Group, L.P.), Chgo., 1990—. Chmn. exec. com. Encore Sr. Living, Portland, Oreg.; corp. adv. bd. mem. Mayor Daley's Exec. Fellows Program, Chgo.; mem. Mayor Daley's fin. com.; bd. dirs. William Wrigley, Jr. Co., Chgo., Coast-to-Coast Fin. Corp., N.Y.C., Nat. Investment Conf., Washington. Chmn. Mus. Contemporary Art, Chgo.; adv. bd. dirs. Chgo. Cares; mem. dean's coun. Harvard U.; mem. Women's Issues Network, Chgo., 1991—, The Chgo. Network, 1992—, Internat. Women's Forum, Chgo., Coun. Fgn. Rels., N.Y. Recipient Brick & Mortar award Chgo. Equity Fund, 1991, Disting. Svc. award REIA Kellogg, 1995. Mem. Nat. Assn. Sr. Living Industry Execs. (bd. dirs. 1989-91), Urban Land Inst., Young Pres.'s Orgn. Office: Classic Residence by Hyatt 200 W Madison St Ste 3700 Chicago IL 60606-3414

PRITZKER, THOMAS JAY, hotel business executive; b. Chgo., June 6, 1950; s. Jay Arthur and Marian (Friend) P.; m. Margot Lyn Barrow-Sicree, Sept. 4, 1977; children— Jason, Benjamin, David. BA, Claremont Men's Coll., 1971; MBA, U. Chgo., 1976, JD, 1976. Assoc. Katten, Muchin, Zavis, Pearl and Galler, Chgo., 1976-77; exec. v.p. Hyatt Corp., Chgo., 1977-80, pres., 1980—2002, chmn., CEO, 1999—; chmn. Hyatt Internat. Corp., Hyatt Hotels Corp., 1980—2002; ptnr. Pritzker & Pritzker, Chgo., 1980—. Chmn. bd. dirs. The Pritzker Orgn., 1998—; bd. dirs. Royal Caribbean Cruises Ltd. Trustee Art Inst. Chgo. 1988—, U. Chgo. Mem. ABA, Ill. Bar Assn., Chgo. Bar Assn., Standard Club, Lake Shore Country Club. Office: Hyatt Corp 200 W Madison St38th Flr Chicago IL 60606 Office Phone: 312-750-8101.

PRIVES, CAROL, biologist, educator; Prof. biology Columbia U., N.Y.C., NY, chmn. Dept. Biol. Scis. Mem. sci. adv. bd. NIH Virology Study Section; mem. Damon Runyon Fellowship Com.; mem. sci. adv. bd. N.J. Cancer Commn., Howard Hughes Med. Inst. Mem. editl. bd.: Cell, Genes & Devel., Jour. Biology, Chemistry and Cancer Rsch.; editor: Jour. Virology, 1991—99. Fellow: Am. Acad. Arts and Scis. Office: Dept Biological Scis Columbia Univ 816 Fairchild Center MC422 1212 Amsterdam Ave New York NY 10027

PRIVETT, STEPHEN A. academic administrator; b. San Francisco, Calif. BA in Philosophy and Classics, Gonzaga U., 1966; MDiv, U. Calif., Berkeley, 1972; postgrad., U. Calif., Santa Barbara, 1973—74; MA in Catechetics/Religious Edn., Cath. U. Am., 1982, PhD in Catechetics, 1985. Entered Soc. of Jesus, 1960. Instr. Latin, western civilization and religion Jesuit H.S., Sacramento, 1966—69; dir. Project 50 Santa Clara (Calif.) U., 1970—71; asst. dir. novices Coll. Queen of Peace, Santa Barbara, 1972—73; instr. modern European history, Latin and English Bellarmine Coll. Preparatory, San Jose, Calif., 1974—80, prin., 1975—80; asst. prof. religious studies dept. Santa Clara U., 1985—90, assoc. prof. religious studies dept., 1990—2000, co-dir. The Eastside Project, 1985—91, dir. Voice of the Voiceless: Inst. on Human Rights and Social Justice, 1989—91, v.p. acad. affairs, 1991—97, provost, v.p. acad. affairs, 1997—2000; pres. U. San Francisco, 2000—. Mem. U.S. Cath. Conf. on Certification and Accreditation, 1990—99; mem. Strategic Planning Commn. Calif. Province of the Soc. of Jesus, 1996—2002; mem. Nat. Seminar on Jesuit Higher Edn. U. Scranton, 1999—. Contbr. articles to profl. jours.; author: The U.S. Catholic Church and Its Hispanic Members: The Pastoral Vision of Robert E. Lucey, 1988. Vol. pastoral worker Jesuit Refugee Svc., El Salvador, 1988; bd. dirs. Jesuit Vol. Corps S.W., 1987—95, chair, 1988—91; bd. dirs. Christians for Peace in El Salvador, 1997—2000, Fromm Inst. for Lifelong Learning, U. San Francisco, 2000—; trustee Brophy Coll. Preparatory, Phoenix, 1996—, Seattle U., 2000—, U. Iberoamericana, Mexico City, 2001—; hon. mem. San Francisco Host Com., 2000—. Mem.: Assn. Grad. Programs in Ministry, Assn. Profs. and Rschrs. in Religious Edn. (mem. Cath. Assembly), Religious Edn. Assn., Assn. Cath. Colls. and Univs. (bd. dirs. 2002—), Assn. Jesuit Colls. and Univs. (bd. dirs. 2000—), Commonwealth Club Calif. (bd. govs.). Office: Univ San Francisco Office of the Pres 2130 Fulton St San Francisco CA 94117*

PRIVITERA, JOSEPH F. retired foreign service officer, writer-researcher; b. N.Y.C., Feb. 22, 1914; s. Luigi and Grazia (Paparcuri) Privitera; m. Bettina La Marca, June 30, 1935; children: Joseph Henry, Stephen Louis. BS with honors, NYU, 1935, PhD, 1938; cert. phonetics course, U. Paris, 1936; cert., U. Mex., Mexico City, 1939. Instr. French, NYU, N.Y.C., 1938; asst. prof. Romance langs. St. Louis U., 1939-45; dir. Bi-Nat. Cultural Ctr., U.S. Dept. State, Sao Paulo, Brazil, 1945-47; fgn. svc. officer Am. Consulate Gen., Sao Paulo, 1947-50, Am. Embassy, Quito, Ecuador, 1950-52; dir. Italian broadcasts Voice of Am., U.S. Dept. State, N.Y.C., 1955-76; ret., 1976. Author: Charles Chevillet de Chmpmeslé, 1942-1701, 1938, The Latin American Front, 1945, Portrait of America, 1947, Perfil Cultural de America, 1951; author: (with wife) Language as Historical Determinant-The Normans in Sicily, 1060-1200, 1995; author: Luigi Pirandello, His Plays in Sicilian, 1998, Beginner's Sicilian, 1998; author: (in Italian and English) A Treasury of Italian Cuisine, 1998; author: Faustus in Love, and Other Poems in English and Other Tongues, 1998, Italy, An Illustrated History, 2000, Beginner's Italian, 2000, Sicily, An Illustrated History, 2001; editor (translator): Reference Grammar of Medieval Italian with a Dual Language Edition of the Thirty-One Poems of Dante's Vita Nova, 2001; author: If I Were Minister of Education and Other Poems, Mellen, 2001; author: (with Bettina Privitera) The Mystery of the Sanfratellan Dialect, the Sicilians Legos, 2001; author: Sicilian Dictionary and

Phrase Book Hippocrene, 2003, Hippocreue, 2003. Mem.: Diplomats and Consular Officers Ret. Avocations: salon photographer, amateur flutist. Home and Office: 19 Constitution Way Apt 111 Litchfield CT 06759-3426

PRIVMAN, VLADIMIR, physics educator; b. Lvov, Ukraine, Jan. 2, 1955; arrived in Israel, 1971; came to U.S., 1982; s. Lipa and Bronislava Privman; m. Marina Privman, May 22, 1980; children: Lior, Michael, Eve. BSc in Physics summa cum laude, Technion, Haifa, Israel, 1975, MSc in Physics, 1979, DSc in Physics, 1982. Rothschild fellow, rsch. assoc. Cornell U., Ithaca, N.Y., 1982-84; Bantrell rsch. fellow in physics Calif. Inst. Tech., Pasadena, 1984-85; prof. physics Clarkson U., Potsdam, N.Y., 1985—. Royal Soc. Guest Rsch. fellow U. Oxford, 1991-92. Co-author: (with N.M. Svrakic) Directed Models of Polymers, Interfaces and Clusters: Scaling and Finite-Size Properties, 1989; co-author, editor: Finite Size Scaling and Numerical Simulation of Statistical Systems, 1990, Nonequilibrium Statistical Mechanics in One Dimension, 1997. With Israel Def. Forces, 1975-78. Recipient Young investigator award, Petroleum Rsch. Fund, 1986; grantee NSF, Petroleum Rsch. Fund, SRC, USAF, U.S. Army Rsch. Mem. Am. Phys. Soc., Am. Chem. Soc. Jewish. Office: Clarkson U Dept Physics Potsdam NY 13699-5720 Office Phone: 315-268-3891. E-mail: privman@clarkson.edu.

PRIVO, ALEXANDER, finance educator, department chairman; m. Elena Privo. BS, Touro Coll., N.Y.C., 1982; M Profl. Studies, New Sch. for Social Rsch., N.Y.C., 1985; MS in Edn., CUNY, 1988; PhD in Adminstrn. and Mgmt., Walden U., 1991. Cert. govt. fin. mgr.; cert. secondary tchr. math., ESL, social studies, bus., acctg., Russian, N.y. Dir. acctg. and fin. reporting Assoc. Retail Stores Inc., N.Y.C., 1982-85; tchr. acctg. N.Y.C. Bd. Edn., 1985—; prof., dept. bus. and econs. Touro Coll., 1987—; dean CUNY, 1987-90; chmn. dept. bus. econs. Touro Coll., 1991—. Coord. mentoring program CUNY and N.Y.C. Bd. edn., 1985-92; cons. and prof. Russian (former Soviet Union); exec. training program MBA Baruch Coll., CUNY, 1990—; coord. cooperative edn. program NYC BD. Edn./CUNY, 1992—. Curriculum devel. grantee. Mem. ASCD, Am. Acctg. Assn., Assn. Govt. Accts., Nat. Bus. Edn. Assn., Internat. Bus. Edn. Assn., Met. Bus. Edn. Assn., N.Y. Educators (doctorate), Am. Mgmt. Assn., Kappa Delta Pi. Home: 43-33 46th St Apt F15 Sunnyside NY 11104-2036

PRIZIO, BETTY J. volunteer, retired property manager; b. LA, Jan. 23, 1928; d. Harry W. and Irene L. (Connell) Campbell; divorced; children: David P., John W., Robert H., James R. AA in Social Sci., L.A. City Coll., 1949. Owner, mgr. indsl. bldgs. and condominiums, mktg. exec., Tustin, Calif., 1976—; ret. Co-chair silent auction Am. Lung Assn., Santa Ana, 1997-2001, co-chair Big Breath Easy charity event; bd. dirs. Founders Chpt. Aux., Providence Speech and Hearing Ctr., 1986-88, aux. pres., 1986-89; vol. Western Med. Ctr. Aux., 1985-89, chmn. gift shop com., 1987-88, 2d v.p., 1992, aux. pres., 1999, jr. vol. adv., bd. dirs. fundraising group, scholarship com., Focus on Women com. 1990—, buyer for gift shop, 1998—, 4th v.p. gift shop, 1993, pres., 1999-2001; adv. coun. Chapman U., Orange, Calif., 1986-87; bd. dirs. Pres. Assocs., 1985-86, Chapman Music Assocs., 1986—, Santa Ana YWCA, 1976-77; adv. coun. Orange County chpt. Freedoms Found. at Valley Forge, 1985—; active United Meth. Ch., Olive Crest Treatment Ctr.; pres. Western Medicine Ctr. Disciplinary, 1999. Named Vol. of Yr., Gift Shop, 1999, Vol. of Nov., hosp. staff and physicians, 2003. Mem.: Tustin Hist. Soc. (bd. dirs. 1988—90), Western Med. Ctr. Aux. (life; pres. 1999, 2000, 2001, Col. of Yr. 1999). Republican. Avocations: gardening, arts and crafts, travel, photography. Home: 2522 N Tustin Ave Unit D Santa Ana CA 92705

PRIZZI, JACK ANTHONY, investment banking executive; b. Rochester, N.Y., July 5, 1935; s. Samuel Anthony and Mary Ann (Emanuele) P.; m. Geraldine A. Bias, Feb. 16, 1957 (div. 1971); children: Lynne Marie, Michael Vincent, Karen Annette; m. Serafina M. Iacono, Sept. 30, 1995. BS in Chemistry, Va. Mil. Inst., 1956; MS in Phys. Chemistry, U. Va., 1961, MBA, 1963. Chem. engr. E.I. duPont DeNemours & Co., Inc., Niagara Falls, N.Y., 1956-57; engr. Project Mercury, NASA, 1959; mgr. planning and devel. PPG Industries, Pitts., 1963-68; gen. mgr. Process Components Inc., Norfolk, Va., 1968-70; ptrn. Alan Patricof Assocs., N.Y.C., 1970-74, Beacon Ptnrs., N.Y.C., 1974-76, 77-79, Stuart Bros., N.Y.C., 1976-77; v.p. Walter E. Heller & Co.; exec. v.p. Heller Capital Svcs. Inc., N.Y.C., 1979-84; sr. v.p. DnC Am. Banking Corp., N.Y.C., 1984-86; mng. dir. DnC Capital Corp., 1986-89; pres., CEO Jack A. Prizzi & Co., 1989-98. Founder, mng. prin. CoE Assocs., L.L.C., N.Y.C., 1998—; spl. ltd. ptnr. Harvest Ptnrs., 1993-97; instr. advanced grades N.Y. Power Squadron; bd. dirs. Meridian Resource Corp., 1993-2004. Vol. Urban Cons. Group. Capt. U.S. Army, 1958-59. Grantee Office Naval Rsch., 1960, Calif. Rsch. Corp., 1960-61. Mem. Assn. for Corp. Growth, Natl. Assn. of Corp. Dir., Am. Chem. Soc., Raven Soc., N.Y. Athletic Club. Office: CoE Assocs LLC 156 W 56th St Ste 1401 New York NY 10019-3800 Office Phone: 212-265-7474 209. E-mail: info@coeassociatesllc.com.

PRO, PHILIP MARTIN, judge; b. Richmond, Calif., Dec. 12, 1946; s. Leo Martin and Mildred Louise (Beck) P.; m. Dori Sue Hallas, Nov. 13, 1982; 1 child, Brenda Kay. BA, San Francisco State U., 1968; JD, Golden Gate U., 1972. Bar: Calif. 1972, Nev. 1973, U.S. Ct. Appeals (9th cir.) 1973, U.S. Dist. Ct. Nev. 1973, U.S. Supreme Ct. 1976. Pub. defender, Las Vegas, 1973-75; asst. U.S. atty. Dist. Nev., Las Vegas, 1975-78; dep. atty. gen. State of Nev., Carson City, 1979-80; U.S. magistrate U.S. Dist. Ct. Nev., Las Vegas, 1980-87, U.S. dist. judge, 1987—2002, chief U.S. dist. judge, 2002—. Instr. Atty. Gen.'s Advocacy Inst., Nat. Inst. Trial Advocacy, 1992; chmn. com. adminstrn. of magistrate judge system Jud. Conf. U.S., 1993—. Bd. dirs. NCCJ, Las Vegas, 1982—, mem. program com. and issues in justice com. Mem. ABA, Fed. Judges Assn. (bd. dirs. 1992—, v.p. 1997-2001), Nev. State Bar Assn., Calif. State Bar Assn., Nev. Judges Assn. (instr.), Assn. Trial Lawyers Am., Nev. Am. Inn Ct. (pres. 1989-91), Ninth Cir. Jury (instructions com.), Nat. Conf. U.S. Magistrates (sec.). Republican. Office: US Dist Ct 7015 Fed Bldg 300 Las Vegas Blvd S Ste 4650 Las Vegas NV 89101-5883 Office Phone: 702-464-5510. Business E-Mail: Philip_Pro@nvd.uscourts.gov.

PROBASCO, CALVIN HENRY CHARLES, clergyman, college administrator; b. Petaluma, Calif., Apr. 5, 1926; s. Calvin Warren and Ruth Charlene (Winans) P.; m. Nixie June Farnsworth, Feb. 14, 1947; children— Calvin, Carol, David, Ruth BA cum laude, Biola Bible Coll., La Mirada, Calif., 1953; D.D. (hon.), Talbot Theol. Sem., La Mirada, 1983. Ordained to ministry, 1950. Pastor Sharon Baptist Ch., El Monte, Calif., 1951-58, Carmichael Bible Ch., Calif., 1958-97, pastor emeritus, 1997—; pres. Sacramento Bible Inst., Carmichael, Calif., 1968—86. Mem. Ind. Fundamental Chs. Am. (rec. sec. 1978-81, pres. 1981-84, 1st v.p. 1987-88), Delta Epsilon Chi. Republican.

PROBERT, COLIN, advertising executive; Ptnr., pres. Goodby, Silverstein & Ptnrs., San Francisco. Office: Goodby Silverstein & Ptnrs 720 California St San Francisco CA 94108-2404

PROBERT, EDWARD WHITFORD, foundation executive, volunteer; b. Orange, NJ, May 27, 1936; s. George Ernest and Ethel Loring (Whitford) P.; m. Ann Schuyler Linen, July 2, 1960; children: Edward Whitford Jr., Leslie P. Sirbaugh, David Linen. BA, Yale U., 1958; LLB, U. Va., 1961. With Morgan Guaranty Trust Co. of N.Y., N.Y.C., 1961-88, v.p., 1970-88; from v.p. to pres. Fannie E. Rippel Found., Basking Ridge, NJ, 1988—95, CEO, pres., 1996—, chmn., 2004. Sec. Intersearch Inst., Inc., Annandale, N.J., 1989-93; bd. assocs. Whitehead Inst. for Biomed. Rsch., Cambridge, Mass., 1996—. Co-chmn. capital campaign Jersey Battered Women's Svc., Morris Plains, N.J., 1996-99, bd. dirs., 2002—; chmn. capital campaign St. Peter's Episcopal Ch., Morristown, 2001-2003. Mem. Royal Dornoch Golf Club, Mountain Lake Club, Morristown Club and Morristown Field Club, Somerset Hills C.C. (bd. govs., golf chmn. 1981-90). Republican. Episcopalian. Avocations: golf, swimming, scuba diving, reading, singing. Home: 14 Miller Rd New Vernon NJ 07976 Office: Fannie E Rippel Found 180 Mount Airy Rd Ste 200 Basking Ridge NJ 07920-2021

PROBST, JOHN ELWIN, chaplain, minister; b. Klamath Falls, Oreg., Apr. 3, 1940; s. John Albert and Jocelyn Marlia (Tunnell) P.; m. Patty P. Maness, Jan. 13, 1975; children: Marla, Joni, Jessica. BTh, Internat. Bible Sem., Orlando, Fla. Ordained to ministry So. Bapt. Conv., 1969. Pastor 1st Bapt. Ch., Dorris, Calif., 1968-72; evangelist, Tex., 1972-74; youth pastor Salem Bapt. Ch., Rocky, Okla., 1975; pastor Retrop Bapt. Ch., Carter, Okla., 1975-79; supply pastor 1st Bapt. Ch., Hobart, Okla., 1975-79; interim pastor Mountain Heights So. Bapt. Ch., Leadville, Colo., 1979; missionary-evangelist, interim pastor Skyway Bapt. Ch., Glendale, Ariz., 1979-82; pastor 1st So. Bapt. Ch., Monrovia, Calif., 1982-85; chaplain Media Focus, Duarte, Calif., 1982—; interim pastor United Comty. Ch., Glendale, Calif., 1988-90; owner Probst & Assocs., 1991—. Revival leader; former mem. evangelism and search com. Estrella Assn., Ariz.; former br. mgr. Sherwin Williams Co.; writer, casting dir., producer Seven Star Prodn.; assoc. producer, writer, casting dir. Castel Prodns.; writer Esses Films; researcher, writer, asst. producer Nunn Prodns.; filming in Thialand Castel Prodns., 1987, telemarketer White Horse Prodns; pres. L.A. So. Bapt. Pastors Conf., 1983; ch. planter Philippine Crusade, 1983, 85; numerous others. With USAF, 1959-64. Mem. So. Calif. Motion Picture Coun. (life, Golden Halo awards 1985). Office: PO Box 618 Duarte CA 91009-0618 E-mail: mfocus@hotmail.com. *If I am able through sensitivity in prayer and loving devotion, to stay each day in the center of God's Will for my life-then I will accomplish exactly and only what He plans for me to do.*

PROBST, LAWRENCE F., III, computer company executive; BS, U. Del., 1972. Dist. sales mgr. Johnson & Johnson, 1972-80; nat. accounts mgr. The Clorox Co., 1980-82, Mediagenic (formerly Activision Inc.), 1982-84; v.p. sales Electronic Arts, 1984—86, sr. v.p., distbn., 1987—91, pres., 1991—94, dir., 1991—, chmn., CEO, 1994—. Office: Electronic Arts 209 Redwood Shores Pkwy Redwood City CA 94065*

PROBSTEIN, JON MICHAEL, lawyer; b. N.Y.C., June 24, 1953; s. Albert and Lila (Levin) P. BA in Psychology, Syracuse U., 1973; JD, St. John's U., 1976. Bar: N.Y. 1977, U.S. Dist. Ct. (so. dist. and ea. dists.) N.Y. 1982, U.S. Ct. Appeals (2d cir.) 1983. Assoc. Marchi, Jaffe, Cohen, Crystal & Mintz, N.Y.C., 1977-78, Berman & Zivyak, N.Y.C., 1979-80, Graubard, Moskovitz McGoldrick Dannett & Horowitz, N.Y.C., 1981-82; ptnr. Probstein & Napolitano, N.Y.C., 1982-88, Probstein & Weiner, 1988—; instr. legal rsch. and writing Benjamin Cardozo Sch. Law Yeshiva U., N.Y.C., 1976-77. Playwright Radio Roast, 1987; music mgr. That's Mgmt., N.Y.C., 1987—; producer, dir. actor Avner Prodns., N.Y.C., 1985—; editor St. John's Law Rev. Mem. ABA, Assn. Trial Lawyers Am., Assn. of Bar of City of N.Y., N.Y. State Bar Assn. Address: Ste 1100 488 Madison Ave New York NY 10022

PROBSTEIN, RONALD FILMORE, mechanical engineering educator; b. NYC, Mar. 11, 1928; s. Sidney and Sally (Rosenstein) P.; m. Irene Weindling, July 30, 1950; 1 child, Sidney. BME, NYU, 1948; MSE, Princeton (NJ) U., 1950, AM, 1951, PhD, 1952; ScD (hon.), Brown U., 1997. Rsch. asst. physics NYU, 1946-48, instr. engring. mechanics, 1947-48; rsch. asst. dept. aero. engring. Princeton U., 1948-52, rsch. assoc., 1952-53, asst. prof., 1953-54; asst. prof. divs. engring., applied math. Brown U., 1954-55, assoc. prof., 1955-59, prof., 1959-62; prof. mech. engring. MIT, Cambridge, 1962—89, Ford prof. engring., 1989-96, prof. mech. engring., 1996—2001, Ford prof. engring. emeritus, 1997—; Disting. prof. engring. U. Utah, 1973; sr. ptnr. Water Purification Assoc., Cambridge, 1974-82; chmn. bd. Water Gen. Corp., Cambridge, 1982-83; sr. corp. tech. advisor Foster-Miller, Inc., 1983-91. Commr. commn. on engring. and tech. systems NRC, 1980-83, mem. space studies bd., 2004—; sci. advisor to bd. Corrpro Cos., 1993-2001. Author: Hypersonic Flow Theory, 1959, Hypersonic Flow, Inviscid Flows, 1966, Water in Synthetic Fuel Production, 1978, Synthetic Fuels, 1982, Physicochemical Hydrodynamics, 1989, 2d edit., 1994; editor: Introduction to Hypersonic Flow, 1961, Physics of Shock Waves, 1966, Jour. PhysicoChem. Hydrodynamics, 1987-89; contbr. articles to profl. jours.; patentee in field. Guggenheim fellow, 1960-61; R.F. Probstein Lecture Series in Engring. Sci., MIT, established 1999. Fellow Am. Acad. Arts and Sci. (councilor 1975-79), Am. Phys. Soc., ASME (Freeman award 1971), AIAA, AAAS; mem. NAS, NAE, Internat. Acad. Astronautics, AIChE. Home: 5 Seaver St Brookline MA 02445-5714 Office: 77 Massachusetts Ave Cambridge MA 02139-4301 Office Phone: 617-253-2240. Business E-Mail: rfprobst@mit.edu.

PROBUS, MICHAEL MAURICE, JR., lawyer; b. Louisville, Jan. 26, 1963; s. Michael Maurice and Jerilyn Ann (Burks) P.; m. Luz Marie Probus, May 22, 1985; children: Michael Julian, Lauren Michael. BA, U. Dallas, 1985; JD, U. Tex., 1988. Bar: Tex. 1988, U.S. Dist. Ct. (we. dist.) Tex. 1990, U.S. Ct. Appeals (5th cir.) 1993. Jud. law clk. to chief judge U.S. Dist. Ct. Tex., Houston, 1988-90; assoc. Law Offices of Michael A. Wash, Austin, Tex., 1990-97; pvt. practice, Austin, 1997—. Pro bono atty. Vol. Legal Svcs., Austin, 1994—. Mem.: Travis County Bar Assn. Democrat. Roman Catholic. Office: Law Office M Probus 111 Congress Ave Ste 2230 Austin TX 78701 Office Phone: 512-480-9504. E-mail: mprobusjr@msn.com.

PROCHASKA, BOBBY J. apparel executive; Pres. Santa Rosa Resources, Inc.; gen. mgr., sr. v.p. Gerber Childrenswear, Inc., Greenville, S.C., 2000, pres., COO, 2000—. Office: Gerber Childrenswear Inc 7005 Pelham Rd Ste D Greenville SC 29615

PROCHASKA, FRANK JOSEPH, educator; b. Sterling Twp., Mich., Apr. 20, 1939; s. Joseph Frank and Francis Katarina (Machacek) P.; m. Elfi Elisabeth Wortmann, Mar. 9, 1964; children: Gabriele, Stefanie. B.F.A., U. Notre Dame, 1961; postgrad. U. Colo.-Colorado Springs, 1973-78; M.A., Goddard Coll., 1980; Ph.D., Columbia Pacific U., 1982. Indsl. engr. Hq. Norad/Adcom, Colorado Springs, 1974-76, chief mgmt. engr., 1976-79; cons. Pro Systems, Internat., Colorado Springs, 1980—; instr./prof. U. Colo., Colorado Springs, 1983-90; dept. chmn. indsl. mgmt. Colo. Tech. U., Colorado Springs, 1982—, chair of mgmt. emeritus, 1997—; sr. Fulbright Scholar Am. Univ. in Bulgaria and Tech. Univ. in Sofia, 1998-2000; cons. in field. Contbr. articles to profl. jours. Served to capt. USAF, 1962-73. Recipient Pres. Cost Reduction award, Creative Edn. Found. Address: 7648 Thunderbird Ln Colorado Springs CO 80919-2618

PROCHASKA, JAMES O. psychologist, educator; PhD. Dir. cancer prevention rsch. consortium U. R.I., Kingston, prof. clin. and health psychology; chmn. Pro-Change Behavior Sys. Mem. adv. bd. Addiction Letter, 1995—; cons. in field. Author: Changing for Good, 1995, The Transtheoretical Approach: Crossing Traditional Boundaries of Therapy, 1998, Systems of Psychotherapy: A Transtheoretical Analysis, 2002; contbr. articles to profl. jours. Named hon. chair medicine, U. Birmingham, Eng.; named one of Top Five Most Cited Authors in Psychology, Am. Psychology Soc.; recipient medal of honor, Am. Cancer Soc., 2003, Innovators Combating Substance Abuse award, Robert Wood Johnson Found., 2002. Office: Cancer Prevention Rsch Consortium Univ RI 2 Chafee Rd Kingston RI 02881

PROCHNOW, DOUGLAS LEE, lawyer; b. Omaha, Jan. 9, 1952; s. Albert Delmer and Betty Jean (Wood) P. BA with high distinction, U. Nebr., 1974; JD, Northwestern U., 1977. Bar: Ill. 1977, U.S. Dist. Ct. (no. dist.) Ill. 1977, U.S. Ct. Appeals (7th cir.) 1989, U.S. Supreme Ct. 2000. Assoc. Wildman, Harrold, Allen & Dixon, Chgo., 1977-84, ptnr., 1985—. Spl. asst. corp. counsel City of Chgo., 1986—87. Pres. Chgo. chpt. Prevent Child Abuse Am. Mem. ABA, ATLA (assoc.), Ill. Bar Assn., Chgo. Bar Assn., Soc. Trial Lawyers, Def. Rsch. Inst., Am. Health Lawyers Assn., Phi Beta Kappa, Phi Eta Sigma. Home: 1230 N State Pky Apt 6D Chicago IL 60610-2261 Office: Wildman Harrold Allen & Dixon 225 W Wacker Dr Ste 2700 Chicago IL 60606-1224 Office Phone: 312-201-2526. E-mail: prochnow@wildmanharrold.com.

PROCHNOW, HERBERT VICTOR, JR., retired lawyer; b. Evanston, Ill., May 26, 1931; s. Herbert V. and Laura (Stinson) P.; m. Lucia Boyden, Aug. 6, 1966; children: Thomas Herbert, Laura. AB, Harvard U., 1953, JD, 1956; A.M., U. Chgo., 1958. Bar: Ill. 1957, U.S. Dist. Ct. (no. dist.) Ill. 1961. With 1st Nat. Bank Chgo., 1958-91, atty., 1961-70, sr. atty., 1971-73, counsel, 1973-91, adminstrv. asst. to chmn. bd., 1978-81; pvt. practice, 1991—; ret., 2003. Author: (with Herbert V. Prochnow) A Treasury of Humorous Quotations, 1969, The Changing World of Banking, 1974, The Public Speaker's Treasure Chest, 1986, The Toastmaster's Treasure Chest, 1988; also articles in legal publs. Mem.: Am. Soc. Internat. Law, Chgo. Bar Assn. (chmn. com. internat. law 1970—71), Ill. Bar Assn., ABA, Chgo. Club, Lawyers Club (Chgo.), Harvard Club (N.Y.C.), Univ. Club (Chgo.), Econ. Club, Onwentsia, Phi Beta Kappa. Home: 949 Woodbine Pl Lake Forest IL 60045-2275 Office: 155 N Michigan Ave Chicago IL 60601-7511 Office Phone: 312-616-8110.

PROCHNOW, JAMES R. lawyer; b. Hutchinson, Minn., Sept. 22, 1943; BA, Hamline U., 1965; JD, William Mitchell Law Sch., 1969. Bar: Minn. 1969, U.S. Supreme Ct. 1973, Colo. 1975. Staff civil divsn. Dept. Justice, Washington, 1973-74; legal counsel to Pres. The White House, Washington, 1974; ptnr. Baker & Hostetler, Denver, 1974—94, Patton Boggs, Denver, 1994—2003, Greenberg Traurig LLP, Denver, 2003—. Mem.: Direct Selling Assn., Am. Herbal Products Assn., Colo. Bar Assn., Denver Bar Assn. Office: Greenberg Traurig LLP 1200 17th St Ste 2400 Denver CO 80202

PROCKOP, DARWIN JOHNSON, biochemist, physician; b. Palmerton, Pa., Aug. 31, 1929; s. John and Sophie (Gurski) Prockop; m. Elinor Sacks, Apr. 15, 1961; children: Susan Elizabeth, David John. AB, Haverford Coll., 1951; MA, Oxford U., 1953; MD, U. Pa., 1956; PhD, George Washington U., 1962; DSc (hon.) (hon.), U. Oulu, Finland, 1983, U. So. Fla., 1993. Investigator NIH, 1957—61; assoc., asst. prof., asso. prof., prof. medicine and biochemistry U. Pa., Phila., 1961—72; prof., chmn. dept. biochemistry U. Medicine and Dentistry of N.J. (Rutgers Med. Sch.), Piscataway, NJ, 1972—86; prof., chmn. dept. biochemistry and molecular biology Jefferson Med. Coll., Phila., 1986—96, dir. Jefferson Inst. Molecular Medicine, 1986—96; prof., dir. Ctr. for Gene Therapy, MCP/Hahnemann Med. Coll., Phila., 1996—2000; prof., dir. Ctr. Gene Therapy Tulane U. Med. Ctr., New Orleans, 2000—. Contbr. Served with USPHS, 1958—61. Named hon. companion, U. Manchester, 1999; recipient Disting. Alumnus award, George Washington U., 1991, U. Pa., 1994, Hopkins Meml. medal , Brit. Biochem. Soc, 1998; fellow Fulbright Found., 1951—53; grantee, NIH, 1961—. Mem.: NAS, Am. Assn. Physicians, Am. Soc. Clin. Investigation, Am. Soc. Biol. Chemists, Acad. Finland, Inst. Medicine, Alpha Omega Alpha, Phi Beta Kappa. Achievements include research in on collagen and gene therapy. Home: 291 Locust St Philadelphia PA 19106-3913 Office: Ctr Gene Therapy Tulane U Med Ctr 1430 Tulane Ave New Orleans LA 70112-2699 E-mail: dprocko@tulane.edu.

PROCOPID, FRANK A. manufacturing executive; Sr. v.p., pres. comm. bus. Mohawk Industries, Inc., Calhoun, Ga. Office: Mohawk Industries Inc 160 S Industrial Blvd Calhoun GA 30701-3030

PROCTOR, BARBARA GARDNER, advertising agency executive, writer; b. Ashville, NC; d. William and Bernice (Baxter) Gardner; m. Carl L. Proctor, July 20, 1961 (div. Nov. 1963); 1 son, Morgan Eugene. BA, Talladega Coll., Ala., 1954. Music critic, contbg. editor Down Beat Mag., Chgo., 1958—; internat. dir. Vee Jay Records, Chgo., 1961-64; copy supr. Post-Keyes-Gardner Advt., Inc., Chgo., 1965-68, Gene Taylor Assos., Chgo., 1968-69, North Advt. Agt., Chgo., 1969-70; contbr. to gen. periodicals, 1952—; founder Proctor & Gardner Advt. (divsn. Proctor Comm. Network), Chgo., 1970—, pres., CEO. Pres., CEO Proctor Comm. Network, Chgo.; Mem. Chgo. Urban League, Chgo. Econ. Devel. Corp.; cons. pub. rels. and promotion, record industry; bd. dir. Window to the World Comm., Inc.; bd. trustee 98.7WFMT, WTTW11. Author: (TV documentary) Blues for a Gardenia, 1963. Bd. dirs. People United to Save Humanity, Better Bus. Bur., Window to the World Comm., Inc., Ill. Bell Telephone Co., Northwestern Hosp., Mid-City Nat. Bank, Coun. Chgo. Better Bus. Bur., Louisville Courier-Jour., United Way, Econ. Club; Mem. NARAS, USIA, Chgo. Media Women, Women's Advt. Club, NY Art Dirs. Club, Woman's Day Club, Cosmopolitan C. of C. (dir.); bd. trustee 98.7WFMT, WTTW11; co-chair, State Ill. Gannon-Proctor Commn.; governing coun. mem. Ill. State Bar Assn. Inst. for Pub. Affairs. Recipient Armstrong Creative Writing award, 1954; awards Chgo. Fedn. Advt., Frederick Douglas Humanitarian award, 1975, Headliner award, Assn. for Women in Comm., 1978; named Chgo. Advt. Woman of Yr., 1974; named to Smithsonian Instn. "Black Women Achievements Against the Odds" Hall of Fame and the series' poster-calendar traveling exhbn. Mem. Female Execs. Assn., Internat. Platform Assn., Smithsonian Instn. Assn.*

PROCTOR, CONRAD ARNOLD, physician; b. Ann Arbor, Mich., July 14, 1934; s. Bruce and Luena Marie (Crawford) P.; m. Phyllis Darlene Anderson, June 23, 1956; children: Sharon Heimbach Pins, Barbara Jan Brown, David Conrad, Todd Bruce. MD, U. Mich., 1959, MS, 1964. Cert. Am. Bd. Otolaryngology. Intern St. Joseph Mercy Hosp., Ann Arbor, 1959-60; jr. clin. instr. Univ. Hosp., Ann Arbor, 1961-63, sr. clin. instr., 1963-65; chief dept. otolaryngology Munson Army Hosp., Ft. Leavenworth, Kans., 1965-67; mem. attending staff William Beaumont Hosp., Royal Oak, Mich., 1967—. Instr. Am. Acad. Otolaryngology, Washington, 1968-82, guest examiner, Chgo., 1978-79. Author: Current Therapy in Otolaryngology, 1984-85; (booklet) Dietary Treatment of Meniere's Syndrome, 1983, Hyperinsulinemia and Tinnitus, 1988; (manual) Hereditary Sensorineural Hearing Loss, 1978, Etiology, Treatment of Fluid Retention in Meniere's Syndrome, 1992; (med. jour.) Abnormal Insulin Levels and Vertigo, 1981. Dir. Christian edn. Bloomfield Hills (Mich.) Bapt. Ch., 1969-72, fin. chmn., 1975-78, Sunday sch. tchr., 1967—. Served to capt. U.S. Army, 1965-67. Recipient 1st pl. award for med. rsch. Students Am. Med. Assn., 1959, Merit award Am. Acad. Otolaryngology, 1978; holder 6 world records Internat. Game Fish Assn., 4 world records Nat. Fresh Water Fishing Hall Fame. Mem. AMA, Mich. State Med. Assn., Oakland County Med. Assn., Am. Bd. Otolaryngology, ACS, Triological Soc., Otosclerosis Study Group, Internat. Game Fish Assn. (Nat. Fresh Water Fishing Hall of Fame), Am. Legion, U.S. Tennis Assn., U.S. Golf Assn., Panangling Ltd. (Jonesboro, Maine), Victors and Presidents Club (Ann Arbor), Audubon Soc., Phi Eta Sigma, Phi Kappa Phi, Phi Beta Kappa. Republican. Avocations: baseball, football, tennis, arctic exploration, fishing. Home: 3543 Riverside Dr Auburn Hills MI 48326-4309 Office: 3535 W 13 Mile Rd Royal Oak MI 48073-6710

PROCTOR, DICK, member of parliament; Grad. in Journalism, Carleton U. With newspaper, Toronto, Canada, Edmonton, Canada, CBC-TV; mem. 37th parliament House of Commons, Ottawa, Canada. Chair New Dem. Party caucus House of Commons, critic for agr. and agri-food. New Dem. Party. Office: House of Commons Rm 315 East Block Ottawa ON K1A 0A6 Canada also: 11 Hochelaga St W Moose Jaw SK S6H 2E9 Canada

PROCTOR, GEORGANNE C. company executive; b. 1957; m. Robert Proctor. BS in Bus. Mgmt., U. S.D.; MBA in Fin., Calif. State U., Hayward. From fin. analyst Bechtel Financing Svcs. (now part of Bechtel Enterprises), 1982-89; mgr. Bechtel Info. Tech. Group., 1989-91, mgr. project cost controls for Disney MGM Studio project, 1991; dir. fin. and acctg. Internat. Home Video divsn. Disney Co., 1991-93; dir. fin. Walt Disney Imagineering, 1993-94; CFO Bechtel Enterprises, 1994-97; sr. v.p., CFO Bechtel Group, Inc., San Francisco, 1997—2002, senior v.p., 1997—. Amb. Calif. State. U., Hayward. Office: Bechtel Group Inc PO Box 193965 San Francisco CA 94119-3965

PROCTOR, JESSE HARRIS, JR., political science educator; b. Durham, N.C., Sept. 3, 1924; s. Jesse Harris and Rosa Belle (Rogers) P.; m. Ella Jane Callahan, Mar. 27, 1948; children: Edward Sidney, Thomas Christopher, Kenneth Stuart. AB, Duke U., 1948; MA, Fletcher Sch. Law and Diplomacy, 1949; PhD, Harvard U., 1955. Instr., asst. prof. polit. sci. MIT, 1949-56; asst. prof., assoc. prof. polit. sci. Am. U. in Cairo, 1956-58, vis. prof., 1991-92; asst. prof., then assoc. prof. and prof. polit. sci. Duke U., 1958-70; Charles A. Dana prof. polit. sci. Davidson (N.C.) Coll., 1970-91, prof. emeritus, 1991—, chmn. dept. polit. sci., 1972-89. Vis. assoc. prof. polit. sci. U. Coll., Nairobi, Kenya, 1964-65; vis. prof. polit. sci., U Dar es Salaam, Tanzania, 1969-70; Fulbright lectr. St. Stephen's Coll., Delhi U., India, 1982-83 Editor: Islam and International Relations, 1965; contbg. author: Federalism in the Commonwealth, 1963, The Aftermath of Sovereignty, 1973, Prospects for Constitu-

tional Democracy, 1976; Contbr. articles to profl. jours. Served with USAAF, 1943-46. Mem. Phi Beta Kappa, Pi Sigma Alpha, Omicron Delta Kappa. Home: 53 Wagon Trail Black Mountain NC 28711

PROCTOR, KENNETH DONALD, lawyer; b. Balt., Apr. 28, 1944; s. Kenneth Chauncey and Sarah Elizabeth (Kent) P.; m. Judith Danner Harris, Aug. 2, 1969; children: Kenneth Scott, Kent Harris, Janet Cameron BS, Lehigh U., 1966; JD, U. Md., 1969. Bar: Md. 1969, U.S. Dist. Ct. Md. 1970, U.S. Supreme Ct. 1974, U.S. Ct. Appeals (4th cir.) 1980. Law clk. to judge Md. Ct. Appeals, 1969-70; assoc. Miles & Stockbridge, Balt., 1970-73, 74-76, ptnr., 1976-81, Towson, Md., 1981-96; asst. atty. gen. State of Md., Balt., 1973-74. Trustee Gilman Sch., Balt., 1982-85. Mem. ABA, Md. Bar Assn., Baltimore County Bar Assn. Democrat. Episcopalian. Office: Proctor & McKee PA 102 W Pennsylvania Ave Ste 505 Towson MD 21204-4542 E-mail: kdproctor@proctorlaw.com.

PROCTOR, RICHARD J. geologist, consultant; b. L.A., Aug. 2, 1931; s. George Arthur and Margaret Y. (Goodman) P.; m. Ella McLaren, Feb. 12, 1955; children: Mitchell, Jill, Randall. BA, Calif. State U., L.A., 1954; MA, UCLA, 1958. Engring. geologist, Calif.; cert. profl. geologist Am. Inst. Profl. Geologists. Chief geologist Met. Water Dist., L.A., 1958-80; pres., cons. geologist Richard J. Proctor, Inc., Arcadia, Calif., 1980-95. Vis. assoc. prof. Calif. Inst. Tech., Pasadena, 1975-78. Co-author: Citizens Guide to Geologic Hazards, 1993; editor: Professional Practice Guidelines, 1985, Engineering Geology Practice in Southern California, 1992, Pres., dir. Arcadia Hist. Soc., 1993-96. Fellow Geol. Soc. Am. (Burwell Meml. award 1972); mem. Assn. Engring. Geologists (pres. 1979), Am. Inst. Profl. Geologists (pres. 1989, Van Couvering Meml. award 1990, hon. mem. 1992, Parker Meml. medal 2003), Am. Geol. Inst. (sec.-treas. 1979-83), Conf. Calif. Hist. Socs. (pres. 2004—).

PROCTOR, RICHARD JEROME, JR., business educator, accountant, expert witness; b. NYC, Oct. 6, 1941; s. Richard Jerome and Edith (Decker) P.; m. Elfriede N. Neundorfer, Aug. 19, 1967; children: Courtney, John, David. BS, Columbia U., 1963, MBA, 1970. CPA, N.Y., Conn.; cert. valuation analyst, cert. govt. fin. mgr.; cert. forensic acct. Am. Bd. Forensic Acctg. Sr. acct. Arthur Andersen, N.Y.C., 1970-72; dir. acctg. N.Y. Stock Exchange, N.Y.C., 1972-75; chief fin. officer Executrans, Greenwich, Conn., 1975-77; dir. planning Irvin Industries, Stamford, Conn., 1977-79; asst. prof. acctg. and taxation U. Hartford (Conn.), 1979-82; prof. and dept. chairperson Ancell Sch. Bus. Western Conn. State U., Danbury, 1983—. Pvt. practice, 1979—; cons., expert witness in field. Author (textbook): Proli Footwear-A Team Based Audit Simulation, 2002. Mem. AICPA, Conn. Soc. CPAs (Disting. Authors award 1983, 92), Nat. Assn. Cert. Valuation Analysts, Inst. Bus. Appraisers, Am. Acctg. Assn., Inst. Mgmt. Accts., Am. Bd. Forensic Acctg. (diplomate). Home: 31 Cooper Hill Rd Ridgefield CT 06877-5903 Office: Western Conn State U 181 White St Danbury CT 06810-6826 Office Phone: 203-438-7742.

PROCTOR, RICHARD MACFARLANE, art educator, artist, writer, gallery owner; b. Detroit, Feb. 27, 1936; s. Edgar Elmer and Kathryn Isabella (Macfarlane) P. Student, Henry Ford Community Coll., 1954-55; BS in Art Edn., Mich. State U., 1959, MA in Painting, 1962. Teaching credential K-12. Art tchr. Dearborn (Mich.) Pub. Schs., 1959-60; teaching asst. Mich. State U., East Lansing, 1960-61, acting instr., 1961-62; instr. U. Wash., Seattle, 1962-64, asst. prof., 1964-69, assoc. prof., 1970-92, assoc. prof. emeritus, 1992—. Co-owner, gallery dir., design cons. Childers/Proctor Gallery, Langley, Wash., 1983-99. Author: Principles of Pattern for Craftsmen and Designers, 1969; (with others) Surface Design for Fabric, 1984 (Merit prize for tech. writing 1986), Principles of Pattern Design, 1990. Exhibited in group shows at Mus. of Contemporary Crafts, N.Y.C., Seattle Art Mus., Detroit Art Inst., Henry Art Mus., Kresge Art Ctr., East Lansing, Kerns Gallery, Eugene, Oreg., Contemporary Crafts Gallery, Portland, Seattle U., Northwest Craft Ctr. and Gallery, Wichita (Kansas) Art Assn., Kittredge Gallery, Tacoma, Cornell U., Ithaca, N.Y., Alberta Coll. of Art, Cranbrook Acad. of Art, Wash. State Capitol Mus., Yaw Gallery, Birmingham, Mich., Greenville County Art Mus., S.C., Cerulean Blue Gallery, Seattle, Cheney Cowles Meml. Mus., Spokane, Bellevue Art Mus., Richard White Gallery, Seattle, Childers/Proctor Gallery, Smithsonian Instn. (travelling exhibition); represented in collections Seattle/Tacoma Internat. Airport, Unigard Ins. Group Hdqrs., Rainier Bank, Seattle, Peoples Bank, Bellevue, Safeco Ins. Hdqrs., Seattle Waterfront Banners, 1979. Bd. dirs., founding mem. Island Arts Council, Langley, 1979—, Whidbey AIDS Support Fund; chmn. Design Review Bd. City of Langley, 1985-91; mem. Island County AIDS Task Force, 1992-99; vol. docent Palm Springs Desert Mus., Palm Springs, Calif., 2001—. Mem. AAUP, N.W. Designer Craftsmen (pres. 1968-70), Surface Design Assn. (N.W. reg. rep. 1984-87), N.W. Orchid Soc. (v.p. 1987-88, pres. 1989-91), Useless Bay Golf and Country Club (Langley). Democrat. Episcopalian. Avocations: cactus grower, swimmer, diarist. Home: 455 E Avenida Hokona Palm Springs CA 92264-8437 Office: U Wash Sch of Art Dm 10 Seattle WA 98195-0001

PROCTOR, RICHARD OWEN, historian, public health administrator, army officer; b. Austin, Tex., Nov. 18, 1935; s. William Owen and Arlene Gertrude (Holdeman) P.; m. Martha June Whitlock, Nov. 19, 1955; children: Tanya Marie, Sheilia Renee, Michael Lee, Terry Glen, Richard Lowell, Roger Owen. BA, Oklahoma City U., 1957; MS, MD, Baylor U. Coll. Medicine, Houston, 1964; MPH and TM, Tulane U., 1970; diploma, U.S. Army War Coll., 1983; MS in History, Tex. A&M U., Commerce, 2001. Diplomate Am. Bd. Pediatrics, Am. Bd. Preventive Medicine. Commd. capt. U.S. Army, 1964, advanced through grades to brig. gen.; instr. Imperial Ethiopian Coll. A&M Arts, Alemaya, 1957-59; dep. comdr. U.S. Army Hosp., Kagnew Station, Ethiopia, 1967-69, U.S. Army Med. Lab., Ft. Sam Houston, Tex., 1973-75; instr. U.S. Army Acad. Health Scis., Ft. Sam Houston, 1975-77; surgeon U.S. Army VII Corps, Moeringen, Fed. Republic Germany, 1978-81; prof., chmn., comdt. of students Uniformed Svcs. U. of Health Scis., Bethesda, Md., 1981-82; comdr. Raymond Bliss Army Community Hosp., Ft. Huachuca, Ariz., 1983-85; surgeon U.S. Army Tng. and Doctrine Command, Ft. Monroe, Va., 1985-88; comdg. gen. William Beaumont Army Med. Ctr., El Paso, Tex., 1988-91; dir. pub. health Region 6 Tex. Dept. Health, Houston, 1991-96; co-owner, rancher Whispering Oaks, Tex., 1985—. Cons. WHO/PAHO, Bolivia, 1971; lectr. on anthropology and history; past adj. or clin. faculty positions Baylor U., Tulane U., U. Tex., Tex. A&M U.; archaeol. steward Tex. Hist. Commn., Archaeol. Conservancy. Author: (with others) Principles of Pediatrics: Healthcare of the Young, 1978, Current Pediatrics Diagnosis and Treatment, 1978, 80, Primary Pediatric Care, 1987, 3d edit., 1997, Comprehensive Adolescent Health Care, 1992; author multiple articles on viremia with Sabin polio vaccines. Asst. scout master Boy Scouts Am., Bowie, Md., 1971-73; scout committeeman Boy Scouts Am., Moeringen, 1978-81. Decorated D.S.M., Legion of Merit (twice); recipient scholarship Broadhurst Found., Tulsa, 1953-57; rsch. fellow NIH, 1960-61; Tropical Medicine fellow La. State U., 1970. Fellow Am. Acad. Preventive Medicine, Am. Acad. Pediatrics; mem. Nat. Eagle Scout Assn., Tex. State Hist. Soc., Tex. Archaeol. Soc., Okla. Hist. Soc., Okla. Anthrop. Soc., Ark. Archaeol. Soc., Tex. Map Soc. Methodist. Avocations: conservation, living history. Home: RR 4 Box 1193 Paris TX 75462-9708

PROCTOR, SAMUEL, history educator; b. Jacksonville, Fla., Mar. 29, 1919; s. Jack and Celia (Schneider) P.; m. Bessie Rubin, Sept. 8, 1948; children: Mark Julian, Alan Lowell. BA, U. Fla., 1941, MA, 1942, PhD, 1958. Mem. faculty U. Fla., Gainesville, 1946—, prof. history and social scis., 1963-74, disting. service prof. history, 1974—, Julien C. Yonge prof. Fla. history, 1976—, univ. historian, 1953—, dir. Samuel Proctor Oral History Program, 1968—. Curator History Fla. State Mus.; dir. Doris Duke Southeastern Indian Oral History Program, Ctr. for Study of Fla. History and Humanities. Author: Napoleon Bonaparte Broward, Florida's Fighting Democrat, 1950, Florida Commemorates the Civil War Centennial, 1962, Florida One Hundred Years Ago, 1966, Florida History Preservation Planning, 1971, Gator History: History of the University of Florida, 1986, The University of Florida, 1990, N.B. Broward, 1993; editor, author introduction: Dickison and His Men: Reminiscences of the War in Florida, 1962; series editor: Bicentennial Floridiana Facsimile Series; editor: Eighteenth Century Florida and Its Borderlands, 1975, Eighteenth Century Florida and the Caribbean, 1976, Eighteenth Century Florida, Life on the Frontier, 1976, Eighteenth Century Florida and the Revolutionary South, 1977, Eighteenth Century Florida and the Impact of The American Revolution, 1978, Tacachale, Essays on the Indians of Florida and Southeastern Georgia during the Historic Period, Jews of the South; assoc. editor: Fla. Hist. Quar., 1962-64, editor, 1963-93; contbr. articles to profl. jours. Served with U.S. Army, 1943-46. Mem. Fla. Blue Key, Phi Beta Kappa, Tau Epsilon Phi, Pi Kappa Phi, Phi Alpha Theta. Democrat. Jewish. Home: 2235 NW 9th Pl Gainesville FL 32605-5201

PROCTOR, WILLIAM GILBERT, JR., writer, editor; b. Atlanta, Oct. 11, 1941; s. William Gilbert and Maud (Moore) P.; A.B. magna cum laude in History, Harvard U., 1963, J.D., 1966; m. Priscilla Adrian Moore, June 17, 1967. Admitted to Tex. bar, 1966; reporter NY Daily News, 1969-73; editor-in-chief Ch. Bus. Report, NYC, 1976-82; pres. Inkslingers, Inc.; free-lance writer, NYC and Fla., 1973-; writer, lectr.-in-residence Teen Writers Workshop, Vero Beach, Fla., 2000-; works include Survival on the Campus, 1972, Help Wanted: Faith Required, 1974, The Commune Kidnapping, 1975, Women in the Pulpit, 1976, PDA-Personal Death Awareness, 1976, On the Trail of God, 1977, The Born-Again Christian Catalog, 1979, Return of the Star of Bethlehem, 1980, Too Mean to Die, 1982, The Preconception Gender Diet, 1982, Adventures in Immortality, 1982, How to Go From Rags to Riches in Real Estate, 1982, The Templeton Touch, 1983, The Ethical Executive, 1984, Beyond the Relaxation Response, 1984, Forecast 2000, 1984, Beyond Reason, 1984, The Great American Success Story, 1985, Tough Marriage, 1986, The G-Index Diet, 1993, The Terrible Speller, 1993, Work a 4-Hour Day, 1994, Patient Power, 1996, The Resurrection Report, 1998, The Last Star, 2000, The Gospel According to the New York Times, 2000, Moongate, 2002, The Breakout Principle, 2003; writer, collaborator, Kenneth H. Cooper's Controlling Cholesterol, 1989, Charles Schwab's How to Be Your Own Stockbroker, 1991, Art Linkletter's Yes You Can!, 1982, Warren Avis's Take a Chance to Be First, 1987; Served with USMC, 1966-69. Mem. Authors Guild, Tex. Bar, NYC Bar Assn. Address: PO Box 643511 Vero Beach FL 32964

PROCTOR, WILLIAM LEE, college chancellor; b. Atlanta, Jan. 27, 1933; s. Samuel Cook and Rose Elizabeth (Nottingham) P.; m. Pamela Evans Duke; children: Samuel Matthews (dec.), Priscilla Nottingham. BS, Fla. State U., 1956, MS, 1964, PhD, 1968; DHL (hon.), Nova Southeastern U., 2003; LLD (hon.), Flagler Coll., 2004. Tchr. Seminole County Pub. Schs., Longwood, Fla., 1956-57, 58-62, Orange County Fla. Pub. Schs., Orlando, 1957-58; athletic coach Fla. State U., Tallahassee, 1962-65, asst. dean men, 1965-67, grad. fellow, 1967-68; supt. of schs. Rock Hill (S.C.) Sch. Dist. #3, 1968-69; dean of men U. Ctrl. Fla., Orlando, 1969-71; pres. Flagler Coll., St. Augustine, Fla., 1971-2001, chancellor, 2001—. Cons. on higher edn. policy Heritage Found., Washington, 1983—, Fla. Bd. Edn., 2001-03, State Bd. Edn., 2003—; mem. Commn. on Colls., So. Assn. Colls. and Schs., 1995-2000; dir. Tchr. Edn. Accreditation Coun. Vice-chmn. Fla. Edn. Stds. Commn., 1995-2001; bd. dirs. Penney Retirement Cmty., chmn., 1991—; bd. dirs. Vicar's Landing Retirement Cmty., chmn., 1992-95, bd., 1990-96; trustee, chmn. Fla. Sch. for Deaf and Blind, St. Augustine, 1984-2001; mem. adv. coun. Salvation Army, St. Johns County; mem. devel. coun. First Coast Work Force, 1998-2001; mem. Bus./Higher Edn. Partnership, 2000-01; chmn. Cmtys. in Schs., St. Johns County, Fla., 2002—. Recipient Disting. Educator award Fla. State U. Coll. Edn., 1989, Phil Carrol award Soc. for Advancement Mgmt., 1990, Disting. Svc. award Fla. Sch. for Deaf and Blind, 1990, Patrick Henry Medallion patriotic achievement Mil. Order of World Wars, 1991, Stetson S Club Achievement award, 1993, Order of the South So. Acad. Letters, Arts, and Scis., Excellence in Mgmt. award Soc. for Advancement of Mgmt., 2000, Lifetime Edn. Achievement award, 2001, Disting. Svc. award Fla. Assn. Colls. and Univs., 2002, Sec. Jim Horne's Life Edn. Leadership award; named to Fla. State U. Athletic Hall of Fame, 1988, Order of La Florida, 2001. Mem. Am. Assn. Pres. of Ind. Colls., State Hist. Assn., Ind. Colls. and Univs. of Fla. (legis. chmn. 1974-77, vice chmn. 1976-77, chmn. 1978-79, Liberty Bell award 2003), Rotary (pres. 1978-79, bd. govs. dist. 697 1988-89). Republican. Presbyterian. Avocations: history, jogging, Karate. Office: Flagler Coll Office of the Chancellor PO Box 1027 Saint Augustine FL 32085-1027 Office Phone: 904-819-6210. E-mail: proctorw@flagler.edu.

PRODAN, CALIN IOAN, physician; b. Cluj-Napoca, Cluj, Romania, Jan. 9, 1970; s. Gheorghe and Terezia Prodan; m. Angelia C. Kirkpatrick, June 27, 2000. MD, Iuliu Hatieganu U. of Medicine and Pharmacy, Cluj-Napoca, Romania, 1995. Diplomate Am. Bd. of Psychiatry and Neurology, 2002. Resident neurology U. of Medicine and Pharmacy Iuliu Hatieganu, Cluj-Napoca, Romania, 1995—97; intern dept. internal medicine U. Okla. Health Scis. Ctr., Oklahoma City, 1997—98, resident, dept. neurology, 1998—2001, fellow clin. neurophysiology, dept. neurology, 2001—02; asst. prof. Dept Neurology Okla. U. Med. Ctr., Oklahoma City, 2002—. Staff physician, neurology svc. VA Med. Ctr., Okla. City, 2002—; staff physician Presbyn. Hosp., OU Med. Ctr., Okla. City, 2002—; cons. physician Children's Hosp., OU Med. Ctr., Okla. City, 2002—. Author: (med. articles, pub. papers) Jour. of Child Neurology, Neuropsychiatry, Neuropsychology and Behavioral Neurology, Neurology. Mem.: Am. Assn. of Electrodiagnostic Medicine, Am. Acad. of Neurology. Office: OU Med Ctr Dept of Neurology 711 SL Young Blvd PPOB Ste 215 Oklahoma City OK 73104

PRODI, ROMANO, economist, educator, researcher, former prime minister of Italy, international commission executive; b. Scandiano, Reggio Emilia, Italy, Aug. 9, 1939; s. Mario and Erica Prodi; m. Flavia Franzoni; children: Giorgio, Antonio. JD in econs. and commerce, Cath. U. Milan, Italy, 1961; postgrad., London Sch. Econs. Asst. prof. U. Bologna, dept. polit. sci., 1963—66, assoc. prof., 1966—71, prof. econs. and indusl. policy, 1971—99; industry min. Govt. of Italy, 1978—79; founder Nomisma, 1981, chair, scientific com., 1981—95; chmn. Inst. Indusl. Reconstrn. (IRI), Italy, 1982—89, 1993—94; founder Ulivo centre-left coalition, Italy, 1995—98; prime min. Govt. of Italy, Rome, 1996—98; pres. European Commn., 1999—. Vis. prof. Harvard U., 1974, Stanford Rsch. Inst.; chmn. Società Editrice Il Mulino, Bologna, Italy, 1974—78. Author of numerous profl. jours. and pubs. Recipient Schumpeter prize, Schumpeter Soc., Vienna, 1999, of 18 honorary degrees; Hon. Fellow, London Sch. of Econs. and Polit. Scis., 1989. Mem.: Real Academia de Ciencias Morales y Politicas (hon.). Office: European Commn 200 rue Loi/Wetstraat 200 B-1049 Brussels Belgium*

PROEBSTING, EDWARD LOUIS, JR., retired research horticulturist; b. Woodland, Calif., Mar. 2, 1926; s. Edward Louis and Dorothy (Critzer) P.; m. Patricia Jean Connolly, June 28, 1947; children: William Martin, Patricia Louise, Thomas Alan (dec.). BS, U. Calif., Davis, 1948; PhD, Mich. State U., 1951. Asst. horticulturist Wash. State U., Prosser, 1951-57, assoc. horticulturist, 1957-63, horticulturist, 1963-93, supt. Irrigated Agrl. Rsch. and Ext. Ctr., 1990-93; ret., 1993. Vis. prof. Cornell U., Ithaca, N.Y., 1966; vis. scientist Hokkaido U., Sapporo, Japan, 1978, Victoria Dept. Agr., Tatura, Australia, 1986—. Contbr. numerous articles to profl. jours. Scoutmaster Boy Scouts Am., Prosser, 1963-76, dist. chmn., 1976-78. Served to lt. USNR, 1943-46, 52-54. Recipient Silver Beaver award Boy Scouts Am.; fellow Japan Soc. Promotion Sci., Sapporo, 1978, Res. Bank. Australia, 1986. Fellow AAAS, Am. Soc. Hort. Sci. (pres. 1983-84, sci. editor jour. 1993-98). Methodist. Avocations: backpacking, native plants. Home: 1929 Miller Ave Prosser WA 99350-1532

PROEFROCK, CARL KENNETH, academic medical administrator; b. Curtis, Ill., Mar. 30, 1928; s. Carl Robert and Anna Lorraine (Hagel) Proefrock; m. Margaret Muntz (dec. Apr. 1984); 4 children; m. Janelle Dillon, Sept. 8, 1988 (dec. Sept. 2001). BA, Carthage Coll., Kenosha, Wis., 1949; MDiv, Chgo. Luth. Theol. Sem., 1953. Pastor Evang. Luth. Ch. Am., 1953—66; sr. com. orgn. specialist N.Y.C. Housing and Devel. Adminstrn., 1966-68; exec. dir. Model Cities Program, Manchester, NH, 1968-70, Health Assn. Rochester and Monroe (N.Y.), 1970-73, Mahoning Shenango Area Health Edn. Network, Youngstown, Ohio, 1973-78; spl. asst. to dean Northeastern Ohio Univs. Coll. Medicine, Rootstown, 1978-79; v.p. Med. Coll. Ohio, Toledo, 1979-88, sr. v.p. govtl. affairs, 1988-93; pres. KPA Assocs., Inc., 1993—. V.p. Found. for Applied Rsch., Washington, 1976; chmn. adv. bd. Ohio AHEC, Columbus, 1976; program adminstr. Ohio Statewide Area Health Edn. Ctr., Toledo, 1988-93. Chmn. Toledo Area Coun. Tech., 1986; spl. asst. to clergy All Saints Parish, Pawleys Island, S.C., 1998-2000. Mem. Nat. Area Health Edn. Ctrs. Assn. (bd. dirs. 1988-95), Nat. Assn. Univ. Rsch. Adminstrs., Soc. Rsch. Adminstrs., Internat. Assn. Univ. Rsch. Parks, Soc. Univ. Patent Adminstrs., Nat. Assn. Health Manpower Edn. Systems, Northeastern Ohio Med. Educators Assn. (bd. dirs.), Rotary. Episcopalian. Home: 46 Pawleys Pl Dr Pawleys Island SC 29585-7254 Office: KPA Assocs PO Box 194 Pawleys Island SC 29585-0194 E-mail: kenkpa@sccoast.net.

PROEHL, GERALD T. pharmaceutical executive; Grad., SUNY; MA in Exercise Physiology, Wake Forest U.; MBA, Rockhurst Coll., Kansas City, Mo. From product mgr. to v.p. Hoechst Marion Roussel, Inc.; v.p. mktg. and bus. devel. Santarus, Inc., San Diego, 1999—2000, pres., COO, 2000—02, CEO, 2002—. Office: Santarus Inc 10590 W Ocean Air Dr San Diego CA 92130

PROFETA, SALVATORE, JR., chemist; b. Phila., May 1, 1951; m. Catherine Mary Cherry, Sept. 20, 1980; children: Luisa, Theresa. BA, Temple U., 1973; PhD, U. Ga., 1978. Fellow chemistry dept. Fla. State U., Tallahassee, 1979-80; fellow pharm. chemistry dept. U. Calif., San Francisco, 1980-81, teaching fellow, 1981-82; instr. chemistry dept. La. State U., Baton Rouge, 1982-84; sr. scientist Allergan Pharms., Inc., Irvine, Calif., 1984-87; project mgr. computational chemistry Glaxo Rsch. Inst., Research Triangle Park, N.C., 1987-90, head chemistry systems, 1990-93; dir. N.C. Supercomputing Ctr. Rsch. Inst. at MCNC, Research Triangle Park, N.C., 1993-95; prin. computational chemist Monsanto, St. Louis, 1996-2000; dir. computational chemistry and structural biology Millennium Pharm., Cambridge, Mass., 2000—02; assoc. prof. Dept. Pharm. Chemistry U. S.C., Columbia, SC, 2003—. Cons. CADD-CAMM Smith, Kline & French, Phila., 1980-82, Squibb Rsch. Inst., Princeton, N.J., 1982-84; allocation com. N.C. Supercomputing Ctr., 1989-94. Mem. editl. bd. Jour. Molecular Graphics, 1989-2000; contbg. editor Chem. Design Automation News, 1991-2000; contbr. articles to Jour. Am. Chem. Soc. NSF fellow, 1976-78; Petroleum Rsch. Found. grantee, 1984-88. Fellow N.Y. Acad. Scis.; mem. Am. Chem. Soc. Achievements include patents in anticancer drug design; co-author MM1, MM2, MM3 and AMBER molecular mechanical force fields. Office: Basic Pharm Scis COP CLS 514 Univ South Carolina Columbia SC 29208 Office Phone: 803-576-5684. E-mail: sprofetajr@cop.sc.edu.

PROFFIT, WILLIAM ROBERT, orthodontics educator; b. Harnett County, N.C., Apr. 19, 1936; s. Glenn Theodore and Edna Marie (Queener) P.; m. Sara Thomas, Sept. 20, 1953; children: Lola Ann, Edward Thomas, Glenn Theodore. BS, U. N.C., 1956, DDS, 1959; student, Campbell Coll., Buies Creek, N.C., 1952-53; PhD, Med. Coll. Va., 1962; MS, U. Wash., 1963; FDS, Royal Coll. Surgeons, 1990. Am. Bd. Orthodontics. Investigator Nat. Inst. Dental Research, Bethesda, Md., 1963-65; asst. prof. orthodontics U. Ky., Lexington, 1965-68, assoc. prof., 1968-71; prof. U.Ky., Lexington, 1971-73; prof. orthodontics U. Fla., Gainesville, 1973-75; prof., chmn. dept. orthodontics U. N.C., Chapel Hill, 1975—, Kenan prof., 1992. Cons. NIH, Bethesda, 1974, 76— Author: Contemporary Orthodontics, 1986, 3d edit., 2000; co-author: Surgical Correction of Dentofacial Deformity, 1980, Surgical-Orthodontic Treatment, 1990, Contemporary Treatment of Dentofacial Deformity, 2003; contbr. articles to sci. jours. Served to lt. comdr. USPHS, 1963-65. Fulbright research scholar U. Adelaide, Australia, 1972 Mem. ADA, Am. Assn. Orthodontists (coun. on rsch. 1970-76), Internat. Assn. Dental Rsch., Phi Beta Kappa. Democrat. Presbyterian. Home: 620 Rock Creek Rd Chapel Hill NC 27514-6716 Office: U NC Sch Dentistry Dept Orthodontics Chapel Hill NC 27599-7450 E-mail: william_proffit@dentistry.unc.edu.

PROFFITT, DENNIS LEWIS, finance educator; b. St. Louis, Apr. 2, 1949; s. Waldo E. and Madalyn J. (Lewis) P.; m. Judy Carol Laws, Sept. 5, 1970; children: David Gregory, Karen Michelle. BS, Ctrl. Mo. State U., 1971; MBA, Bradley U., 1974; PhD, St. Louis U., 1984. Dir. bus. affairs Mo. Bapt. Coll., St. Louis, 1976-82; asst. prof. Utah State U., Logan, 1982-87; prof. Grand Canyon U., Phoenix, 1987—. Vis. lectr. Russian People's U., Moscow, 1994, Staffordshire U., Stoke-on-Trent, Eng., 1997. Author: Investments, 1991; editor: Financial Management in Transitional Economies, 1993; contbr. 11 articles to profl. jours. Mem. Am. Fin. Assn., Fin. Mgmt. Assn., Christian Bus. Faculty Assn. (dir. 1997-2000, chair 1999-2000), editor newsletter). Avocations: reading, bicycling. Office: Grand Canyon U 3300 W Camelback Rd Phoenix AZ 85017-1097

PROFFITT, JOHN RICHARD, business executive, educator; b. Grand Junction, Colo., Sept. 12, 1930; s. Hillus D. and Joy Elaine (Lindsay) P.; m. Claire Boyer Miller, May 8, 1965 (div. 1992); children: Cameron Lindsay, William Boyer. BA in Edn., U. Ky., 1953, MA in Polit. Sci., 1961; postgrad., U. Mich., 1959-65. Asst. dean of men, instr. polit. sci. dept. U. Ky., Lexington, 1957-59; teaching fellow U. Mich., Ann Arbor, 1961-63, 63-65; asst. dir. Nat. Commn. on Accrediting, Washington, 1966-68; dir. accreditation and eligibility staff U.S. Dept. HEW, Washington, 1968-75; dir. divsn. eligibility and agy. evaluation U.S. Dept. Edn., Washington, 1975-80, dir. divsn. instnl. and state incentive programs, 1980-82; pres. The Clairion Corp., Bethesda, Md., 1982-84, Nat. Asbestos Removal, Inc., Beltsville, Md., 1985-90, Commonwealth Environ. Svcs., Inc., Alexandria, Va., 1987-91, also chmn. bd. dirs.; chmn. Internat. Environ. Engrs., Inc., Alexandria, Va., 1991-92; pres. Canterbury Internat., Vienna, Va., 1992-95; cons., 1995-99; v.p. E-Pass Techs., Inc., McLean, Va., 1999—. Cons. Conn. State Commn. Higher Edn., Hartford, 1967, Am. Coun. Edn., Washington, 1970; cons. U.S. Dept. Hew, 1967, 68; mem. study steering com. Am. Vocat. Assn., Washington, 1968; exec. sec. Nat. Adv. Com. on Accreditation and Instnl. Eligibility, Washington, 1968-80; mem. gen. com. Nat. Study Sch. evaluation, Alexandria, 1970-78; mem. task force Edn. Commn. of the States, Denver, 1972; subcom. chmn. Fed. Interagy. Com. on Edn., Washington, 1974-76; lectr., presenter profl. confs.; chmn. Commn. Accrediting. Co-author: Accreditation and Certification in Relation to Allied Health Manpower, 1971; contbg. author: Health Manpower: Adapting in the Seventies, 1971, Accreditation in Teacher Education, 1975, Transferring Experiential Credit, 1979; contbr. articles to profl. and govtl. agy. publs., 1968-79. Bd. dirs. and chmn. accrediting commn. Nat. Accreditation Coun. for Agys. Serving the Blind, N.Y.C., 1983-89, v.p. and bd. dirs., 1985-89; pres., chmn. bd. dirs. Found. for Advancement of Quality Svcs. for the Blind, Alexandria, 1988. 1st lt. USAF, 1953-55, Japan and Korea. Higher edn. fellow Univ. Mich., 1959. Mem. Optimist Club (Lexington, Ky.), Club Internat. (Chgo.), Island Club (Hobe Sound, Fla.), Thoroughbred Club Am. (Lexington), Tower Club (Vienna, Va.), Sigma Nu, Omicron Delta Kappa. Democrat. Episcopalian. Avocations: conservation, animal welfare, travel, antiques, art. Home: 515 Beall Ave Rockville MD 20850-2106 E-mail: John.Proffitt@e-pass.com.

PROFFITT, WALDO, JR., newspaper editor; b. Plainview, Tex., Oct. 8, 1924; s. Waldo and Susan Ann (Smith) P.; m. Marjorie Baltzegar, Sept. 14, 1946 (div. 1963); children: Ann Herbert, Deborah, Geoffrey Harrison, Laurence Scott; m. Anne Collier Greene, Feb. 6, 1966; 1 child, Robert Waldo. BA cum laude, Harvard U., 1948. Reporter Bangor (Maine) Commercial, 1948-50; assoc. dir. Harvard News Office, Cambridge, Mass., 1952-54; city editor Charlotte (N.C.) News, 1954-58; mng. editor Journal, Lorain, Ohio, 1958-61; editorial dir. Sarasota (Fla.) Herald-Tribune, 1961-84; editor, 1984-98; columnist Sarasota-Herald Tribune, 1998—. Lt. U.S. Army, 1943-46, ETO, lt. USAF, 1950-52. Mem. Am. Soc. Newspaper Editors, Fla. Soc. Newspaper Editors (pres. 1978). Democrat. Unitarian Universalist. Home: 1581 Hillview Dr Sarasota FL 34239-2047 Office: Sarasota Herald-Tribune PO Box 1719 Sarasota FL 34230-1719

PROFUSEK, ROBERT ALAN, lawyer; b. Cleve., Jan. 14, 1950; s. George John and Geraldine (Hobl) P.; m. Linda Gail Schmidt, May 7, 1972; children: Robert Charles, Kathryn Anne. BA, Cornell U., 1972; JD, NYU, 1975. Bar: Ohio 1975, Tex. 1981, NY 1994. Assoc. Jones Day, Cleve., 1975-81, Dallas, 1981-82, ptnr., 1982—, NY, 1993. bd. dir., CTS Corporcitum and Valero, LP; Contbr. articles to profl. jour. Mem. ABA, NY Bar Assn., Assn. Bar City of NY, Tex. Bar Assn., Greenwich Country Club. Republican. Episcopalian. Home: 541 North St Greenwich CT 06830-3424 Office: Jones Day 222 E 41st St 15th Fl New York NY 10017

PROKASY, WILLIAM FREDERICK, academic administrator; b. Cleve., Nov. 27, 1930; s. William Frederick and Margaret Lovinia (Chapman) P.; m. Pamela Pearson; children: Kathi Lynn, Cheryl Anne; stepchildrenm: Lisa Wier Cauthen, Kevin Wier. BA, Baldwin-Wallace Coll., 1952; MA, Kent State U., 1954; PhD, U. Wis., 1957. Grad. asst. Kent State U., 1953-54; W.A.R.F. fellow U. Wis., 1954-55, teaching asst., 1955-57; asst. prof., then asso. prof. Pa. State U., 1957-66; prof. psychology, chmn. dept. U. Utah, 1966-69, Disting. rsch. prof., 1971-72, dean social and behavioral sci., 1968-70; dean U. Utah (Coll. Social and Behavioral Sci.), 1970-79; acting dean U. Utah (Grad. Sch. Social Work), 1979-80; prof. psychology dean Coll. Liberal Arts and Scis., U. Ill., Champaign-Urbana, 1980-88; prof., v.p. for acad. affairs U. Ga., 1988-98. Cons. in field. Editor: Classical Conditioning, 1965, (with A.H. Black) Classical Conditioning II, 1971, (with D. Raskin) Electrodermal Responding in Psychological Research, 1973, Psychophysiology, 1974-77; editor (with I. Gormezano and R. Thompson) Classical Conditioning III, 1986; assoc. editor Learning and Motivation, 1969-76; cons. editor Jour. Exptl. Psychology, 1968-80. Trustee Utah Planned Parenthood Assn., 1977—80; Utah bd. dirs. ACLU, 1978—80; v.p., bd. dirs. Champaign-Urbana Symphony, 1986—88; mem. bd. advisors Ga. Mus. of Art, 1989—, U. Ga. Performing Arts Ctr., 1998—2003; mem. bd. visitors U. Ga. Librs., 1998—; pres. Friends Ga. Mus. Art, 2002—03; mem. Athens-Clarke County Libr. Bd., 1999—, pres., 2003—; treas. Athens Opera Co., 2001—; pres. Friends of Dance, 2003—; v.p. Athena Clarke County Libr. Endowment Bd., 2003—, mem. Classic Ctr. Endowment Bd., 2003—; mem. Classic Ctr. Cultural Found., 2003—; Del. Utah Dem. Conv., 1968—70, 1972—74; bd. dirs. Friends Ga. Mus. Art, 2004—, Athens Regional Libr., 2002—. Recipient Alumni Merit award Baldwin Wallace Coll., 1992, Disting. Alumni award Piedmont Coll., 1998, U. Ga. Alumni award of excellence, 1998; NSF sr. postdoctoral fellow, 1963-64. Fellow AAAS, Am. Psychol. Assn. (chmn. bd. sci. affairs 1977-78, coun. of reps. 1980-86, bd. dirs. 1983-86, bd. ednl. affairs 1993-96); mem. Fedn. Behavioral, Psychol. and Cognitive Scis. (v.p. 1984-85, pres. 1985-87), coun. of Sci. Soc. Pres.'s (exec. bd. 1987-91, chmn. 1990), Psychonomic Soc., Coun. Rsch. Librs. (bd. dirs. 1990-96), NASULGC (exec. com. coun. on acad. affairs 1995-96), Am. Assn. Higher Edn., Soc. Psychophysiol. Rsch. (bd. dirs. 1978-84, pres. 1982-83), Utah Psychol. Assn. (exec. bd. 1968-70, pres. 1971-72), Assn. Advancement Psychology (bd. dirs. 1982-83), Sigma Xi (pres. U. Utah chpt. 1972-73), Phi Kappa Phi. Personal E-mail: wfp@charter.net.

PROKOPIS, EMMANUEL CHARLES, computer company executive; b. Peabody, Mass., July 5, 1942; s. Charles Emmanuel and Stevia (Kassotis) P.; m. Mary Catherine Dudeck, Dec. 6, 1969; children: Peter Matthew, Christina Prokopis Leonard. BBA, U. Mass., 1966. Mgr., pricing, budgeting, acctg. The Mitre Corp., Mass., Va., 1969-74; mgr. contracts liaison Pratt & Whitney Aircraft, Conn., Fla., 1974-78; mgr. fin. planning, corp. office United Techs. Corp., Hartford, Conn., 1978-81, contr. magnet wire and insulation div. Fort Wayne, Ind., 1981-83, v.p. fin., chief fin. officer The Mostek Corp. (subs.) Carrollton, Tex., 1983-85; sr. v.p. fin. and ops., chief fin. officer The Lotus Devel. Corp., Cambridge, Mass., 1985-87, fin. mgr. mfg. and engring., 1987-91; v.p. budgeting Digital Equipment Corp., 1991-92; exec. v.p. MAST Industries, 1992, Ziff Comm., 1992-93; v.p. corp. contr. Digital Equipment Corp., 1994-96; COO, CFO, treas. IONA Technologies, Cambridge, 1996-97, COO, 1997-99. 1st lt. U.S. Army, 1966-69, Vietnam. Decorated Bronze Star. Greek Orthodox.

PROKOPY, JENNIFER GROVER, writer, consultant; d. Robert Lawrence and Eileen Poole Grover; m. Steven C. Prokopy, Aug. 10, 2002. BS in Journalism, Northwestern U., Evanston, IL, 1991—95. Assoc. editor Primedia Bus. Pub., Chicago, Ill., 1995—97; editl. and prodn. assoc. Anixter Ctr., Chicago, Ill., 1997—99; media rels. mgr. Portland Cement Assn., Skokie, Ill., 1999—2002; prin. Orange Grove Media, Chicago, Ill., 2002—. Recipient Hon. Mention Gold Cir. awards, Media Rels. Campaign, Am. Soc. of Assn. Executives, 2001, Hon. Mention Gold Cir. Awards, Spl. Event Promotion, 2001. Mem.: Pub. Rels. Soc. Am., Constrn. Writers Assn. (v.p. 2004—05), Nat. Assn. Real Estate Editors (second v.p. 2000—02). Office: Orange Grove Media PMB628 3712 N Broadway Ave Chicago IL 60613

PROMISEL, NATHAN E. materials scientist, metallurgical engineer; b. Malden, Mass., June 20, 1908; s. Solomon and Lyna (Samwick) P.; m. Evelyn Sarah Davidoff, May 17, 1931; children: David Mark, Larry Jay. BS, M.I.T., 1929, MS, 1930; postgrad., Yale U., 1932-33; D.Engring. (hon.), Mich. Tech. U., 1978. Asst. dir. lab. Internat. Silver Co. Meriden, Conn., 1930-40; chief materials scientist and engr. Navy Dept., Washington, 1940-66; exec. dir. nat. materials adv. bd. Nat. Acad. Scis., Washington, 1966-74; cons. on materials and policy, internationally, Washington, 1974—. Mem., chmn. NATO Aerospace Panel, 1959-71; U.S. rep. (materials) OECD, 1967-70; U.S. chmn. U.S./USSR Sci. Exch. Program (materials), 1973-77); hon. guest USSR Acad. Scis.; permanent hon. pres. Internat. Conf. Materials Behavior; mem. Nat. Materials Adv. Bd.; adv. com. Oak Ridge Nat. Lab., Lehigh U., U. Pa., U.S. Navy Dept. Labs., U.S. Congress Office Tech. Assessment. Contbr. 65 articles to profl. publs.; contbr., editor: Advances in Materials Research, 1963, Science and Technology of Refractory Metals, 1964, Science, Technology and Application of Titanium, 1970; other books. Named Nat. Capitol Engr. of Yr. Coun. Engring. and Archtl. Socs., 1974; recipient Outstanding Accomplishment awards Navy Dept., 1955-64, Nat. Materials Advancement award, Fedn. Materials Socs., 1994; annual hon. lectr. Electrochem. Soc., 1970. Fellow AIME (hon. mem., ann. disting. lectr. Metall. Soc. 1984), Soc. Advanced Materials and Process Engring. (named one of 12 material scientists who contributed most to aerospace in 20th century 2003), Am. Soc. Materials Internat. (pres. 1972, hon. mem., Carnegie lectr. 1967, ann. hon. lectr. 1984), Brit. Inst. Materials; mem. NAE, ASTM (hon., ann. disting. lectr. 1964), Fedn. Materials Soc. (pres. 1972-73, 1st Decennial award 1982), Soc. Automotive Engrs. (chmn. aerospace materials divsn. 1959-74), Alpha Sigma Mu (hon.). Inventor in electroplating, 1930-40; metall. devels., 1941-66. Home and Office: Hyatt Classic Residence 8100 Connecticut Ave Apt 1406 Chevy Chase MD 20815-2820 *Ten key words and phrases for a professional career: identified goals, long range vision, can-do attitude, integrity, objectivity, understanding and tolerance, faith and trust, professionalism, dedication and perseverance, sense of humor.*

PROMISLO, DANIEL, lawyer; b. Bryn Mawr, Pa., Nov. 15, 1932; s. Charles and Pearl (Backman) P.; m. Estelle Carasso, June 10, 1961; children: Mark, Jacqueline, Steven. BSBA, Drexel U., 1955; JD magna cum laude, U. Pa., 1966. Bar: Pa. 1966. Pres., owner Hist. Souvenir Co., Phila., 1957—; assoc. Wolf, Block, Schorr & Solis-Cohen, Phila., 1966-70, ptnr., 1977-94, exec. com., 1987-89; founder, pres. dir. Inst. for Paralegal Tng., Phila., 1970-75, cons., 1975-77; mng. dir. Wolf, Block, Schorr & Solis-Cohen, Phila., 1997-2001, of counsel, 1994—; pres., owner Hist. Documents Co., 1992—. Editor: Corporate Law, 1970, Real Estate Law, 1971, Estates and Trusts, 1971, Civil Litigation, 1972, Employee Benefit Plans, 1973, Criminal Law, 1974; contbr. articles to profl. jours. Bd. dirs. Phila. Drama Guild, 1977-95, chmn., 1982-86; bd. dirs. Phila. Israel Econ. Devel. Program, 1983-88, Inst. for Arts in Edn., 1990-93, WHYY, Inc., 1994-2003, vice-chmn., 1995-96, chmn., 1996-97; bd. dirs. U.S. Physicians, Inc., 1995-98; trustee Resource Asset Investment Trust (now RAIT Investment Trust), 1997—; bd. advisors Drexel U. Coll. Arts and Scis., 2001-. Mem. Order of Coif, Drexel U. 100, Blue Key, Phi Kappa Phi. Democrat. Jewish. Avocations: movies, basketball, tennis, golf. Office: Wolf Block Schorr & Solis-Cohen 1650 Arch St Fl 22 Philadelphia PA 19103-2097 E-mail: dpromislo@comcast.net.

PRONOVOST, PETER J. anesthesiology educator, health facility administrator; b. Waterbury, Conn., Feb. 22, 1965; s. Henry and Ann Pronovost; m. Marlene Rosemary Miller, Oct. 5, 1996; children: Ethan, Emma. BS, Fairfield U., 1987; MD, Johns Hopkins U., 1991, PhD, 1999. Lic. Md., diplomate Am. Bd. Anesthesiology, Md., cert. spl. cert. competency in critical care medicine Md. Intern John Hopkins Hosp., Balt., 1991—92; resident Johns Hopkins U., Balt., 1992—95, fellow, 1994—96, instr., 1997—98, core faculty program for med. tech. and practice assessment, 1998—, asst. prof., 1998—2001; faculty Inst. for Healthcare Improvement, Boston, 2001—; med. dir. Ctr. for Innovations and Quality Care, Balt., 2001—02; assoc. prof. Johns Hopkins U., Balt., 2001—. Co-chair patient safety com. Johns Hopkins Hosp., Balt., 2001—, dir. performance improvement, 1998—, dir. inpatient care, 1997—; chair adv. panel for ICU core measures Joint Commn. on Accreditation of Healthcare Organizations, Oakbrook Terrace, Ill., 2002—; med. advisor The Leapfrog Group, Washington, 2000—; cons. Vol. Hosps. of Am., Irving, Tex., 2000—; adv. bd. mem. grad. tng. program in clin. investigation Johns Hopkins Bloomberg Sch. of Pub. Health, Balt., 1999—; bd. mem. instl. rev. bd. Johns Hopkins U., Sch. of Medicine, Balt., 1999—2002; chair strategic planning com. Soc. of Critical Care Medicine, Chgo., 2002—; presenter Internat. AIDS Conf.; med. advisor purchasing std. for leapfrog group ICU Physician Staffing Std. Contbr. articles pub. to over 100 profl. jours. Recipient Rsch. scholarship in Preventive Cardiology, 1987, MAP-Reader's Digest Internat. fellowship for work in Nigeria, 1991, Ctr. for AIDA Rsch. (CFAR) scholarship, 1991; grantee Impact of Critical Pathways on Reportable Adverse Events and Liability Claims Experience, MCIC Vt., Inc., 1999—2000, Reducing the rate of failed extubation in the ICU, 1998-1999, Assn. between surg. critical pathways and complications and liability claims experience, MCIC, 1998-1999, Intensive Care Unit Safety Reporting Sys., Evaluating the Impact of the Leapfrog Group's Std. for ICU Physician Staffing. Mem.: Soc. of Critical Care Medicine Patient Safety Found. (founding mem., bd. of trustees), Soc. of Critical Care Medicine (chmn. 2002—02, Presdl. citation 2002, Rsch. award 2001), Assn. for Health Svcs. Rsch. (assoc.), Anesthesia Rsch. Soc. (assoc.), Am. Soc. of Critical Care Anesthesiologist (assoc.), Am. Soc. of Anesthesiologists (assoc.), AMA (assoc.), Delta Omega, Alpha Epsilon Delta, Alpha Sigma Nu. Democrat. Achievements include research in Leapfrog Group adopted Health Care Purchasing Standard based on my research; Reducing Catheter Related Blood Stream Infection in the ICU. Office: Johns Hopkins U Meyer 295 600 N Wolfe St Baltimore MD 21287-7294 E-mail: ppronovo@jhmi.edu.

PRONZINI, BILL JOHN (WILLIAM PRONZINI), writer; b. Petaluma, Calif., Apr. 13, 1943; s. Joseph and Helene (Guder) P.; m. Marcia Muller. Coll. student, 2 years. Author: 65 novels (including under pseudonyms), 4 books of non-fiction, 19 collections of short stories, 1971—; first novel, The Stalker, 1971; editor 80 anthologies; contbr. numerous short stories to publs. Recipient 6 scroll awards Mystery Writers Am., Life Achievement award Pvt. Eye Writers Am., 1987. Office: PO Box 2536 Petaluma CA 94953-2536 E-mail: pronhack@sbcglobal.net.

PROPER, MARY, advertising executive; Controller Suissa Miller Advt., L.A. Office: 8687 Melrose Ave Los Angeles CA 90069-5701

PROPER, MICHAEL CHARLES, cardiologist, educator; b. N.Y.C., N.Y., Mar. 26, 1943; s. Morton and Miriam (Gitelson) P.; m. Hope Ann Ratzan, Dec. 20, 1964; children: David Matthew, Diana Ellen. BS magna cum laude, CUNY, 1963; MD, NYU, 1967. Diplomate Am. Bd. Internal Medicine, Am. Bd. Cardiovasc. Diseases. Intern Bellevue Hosp., N.Y.C., 1967-68, resident, 1968-69, Jackson Meml. Hosp., Miami, Fla., 1969-70; fellow in cardiology Mt. Sinai Hosp., Miami Beach, Fla., 1970-71, Yale-New Haven Hosp., 1973-74; cardiologist Cooper Hosp. Univ. Med. Ctr., Camden, N.J., 1975-94; clin. asst. prof. medicine Robert Wood Johnson Med. Sch., Piscataway, N.J., 1980-90, clin. assoc. prof. medicine, 1990-94. Hosp. affiliations include Our Lady of Lourdes Hosp., Camden, 1978—, West Jersey Hosp. Sys., Marlton, Voorhees, Camden, Berlin, 1975—, assoc. chief divsn. cardiology, 1994-96, chief divsn. cardiology Marlton divsn., 1985-95, exec. com. Marlton divsn., 1986-8, 1992-94; Underwood Meml. Hosp., Woodbury, N.J., 1995—; clin. as st. prof. medicine Jefferson Med. Coll., Phila., 1984-90; trustee Cooper Hosp., Camden, 1981-90; mem. various other hosp. svc. coms.; lectr. in field. Contbr. articles to profl. jours. Advisor Heart Day, Greenbriar Restaurant, Cherry Hill, N.J., 1990. Maj. USAF, 1971-73. Jonas Salk scholar CUNY. Fellow Am. Coll. Chest Physicians, Am. Coll. Cardiology; mem. AMA, ACP, Am. Heart Assn., Camden County Heart Assn., Med. Soc. N.J., Camden County Med. Soc., Phila. Coll. Physicians, Alpha Omega Alpha Honor Soc. Avocations: biking, gardening, cooking, sports. Office: Assoc Cardiovasc Cons 63 Kresson Rd Ste 101 Cherry Hill NJ 08034 Office Phone: 856-428-4100. E-mail: mcprop@comcast.net.

PROPP, STEVEN H. benefits compensation analyst; b. Berkeley, Calif., Oct. 2, 1955; s. Harry and Dorothy S. Propp. BA, Calif. State U., Sacramento, 1978. Analyst Pub. Employees' Retirement Sys., Sacramento, 1979—. Author: Work, Death and Taxes, 2000, Tattered Pilgrims, 2001, Inquiries: Philosophical, 2002, Beyond Heaven and Earth, 2003, Utopia On the 6th Floor: Work, Death and Taxes Part 2, 2004. Avocations: music, reading. Personal E-mail: Stevenhpropp@hotmail.com.

PROPST, CATHERINE LAMB, biotechnology company executive; b. Charlotte, N.C., Mar. 10, 1946; d. James Pinckney and Eliza Mayo (Mills) P. BA magna cum laude, Vanderbilt U., 1967; M of Philosophy, Yale U., 1970, PhD, 1973. Head microbiology div. GTE Labs., Waltham, Mass., 1974-77; various mgmt. positions Abbott Labs., North Chicago, Ill., 1977-80; v.p. rsch. and devel. Ayerst (Wyeth) Labs., Plainview, NY, 1980-83; v.p. rsch. and devel. worldwide Flow Gen. Inc., McLean, Va., 1983-85; pres., CEO Affiliated Sci. Inc., Ingleside, Ill., 1985-97; pres., chmn., CEO Tex. Biotech. Found., Hempstead, Tex., 1997—. Vis. prof. genetics U. Ill., Chgo., 1989—90; founder, exec. dir. Ctr. for Biotech., Northwestern U., 1990—95; pres. Ill. Biotech. Ctr., 1995—97; bd. dirs. several cos.; bd. dirs., mem. sci. adv. bd. Keystone Symposia on Molecular and Cellular Biology, 1997—2002. Author and editor: Computer-Aided Drug Design, 1989, Nucleic Acid Targeted Drug Design, 1992; contbr. articles to profl. jours. Named to Outstanding Working Women in the U.S., 1982; recipient many sci. and bus. awards. Fellow Soc. Indsl. Microbiology (bd. dirs. 1990-93), Nat. Coun. Biotech Ctrs. (bd. dirs. 1995-97); mem. AAAS, Nat. Wildlife Fedn., Consortium for Plant Biotech. Rsch. (bd. dirs. 1994-99), Phi Beta Kappa, Sigma Xi. Episcopalian. Avocations: horseback riding, skiing, raising Black Angus and Black Brangus cattle. Office: Texas Biotech Found PO Box 17 Hempstead TX 77445-0017 Fax: 979-826-9710.

PROPST, M. TERESA CARSON, historian; b. Balt., Jan. 7, 1976; d. John Ryan and Maria Patricia (Romagnoli) Carson; m. Anthony Michael Propst, Nov. 10, 2001. BA, Towson U., 1999. Patient svcs. rep. Advanced Radiology, Towson, 1999—. Adult youth ministry vol. St. William of York Cath. Ch., Balt., 2000—. Mem.: Order of Omega, Golden Key Nat. Honor Soc., Alpha Phi Omega, Alpha Xi Delta (chpt. life advisor Towson U. 2003—), Democrat. Roman Catholic. Avocations: hiking, travel, camping, entertaining. Home: 6243 Pimlico Rd Baltimore MD 21209 Office: Advanced Radiology 124 Sister Pierre Dr Towson MD 21204

PROPST, MICHAEL TRUMAN, pathologist; b. Lebanon, Oreg., July 3, 1940; s. Lynn Edward and Vera Ruth (Forbes) P.; m. Susan Jean Joesting, Dec. 26, 1974; children: Christopher M., Andrew J., Matthew A., Michael Jonathan, Edwin Cam. BS, Oreg. State U., 1962; MD, U. Oreg., 1966. Diplomate Am. Bd. Pathology. Pathologist Humana Hosp., Anchorage, 1974—84; med. examiner State of Alaska, Anchorage, 1975—94; med. dir. Physicians Med. Lab., Anchorage, 1984—94; chief med. examiner State of Alaska, Anchorage, 1994—2001; cons. forensic pathology, 2001—. Served to maj. USAF, 1971-74. Fellow Coll. Am. Pathologists, Am. Soc. Clin. Pathologists, Am. Acad. Forensic Scientists, Royal Soc. Medicine (Gr. Britain),; mem. Nat. Assn. Med. Examiners. Lutheran. Office Phone: 541-469-2317.

PROSKY, ROBERT JOSEPH, actor; b. Phila., Dec. 13, 1930; s. Joseph and Helen (Kuhn) Porzuczek; m. Ida Mae Hove, June 4, 1960, children: Stefan, John, Andrew Student, Temple U., Am. Theatre. Appeared at Arena Stage, Washington, 23 years including roles in Death of a Salesman, Twelfth Night, Enemy of the People, Galileo; appeared on Broadway in Moonchildren, View from the Bridge, Glengarry Glen Ross (Tony award nominee 1985), A Walk in the Woods, 1988 (Tony award nominee 1988, Best Actor award Outer Critics Circle, toured USSR and Lithuania 1989), Camping with Henry and Tom, 1997, The Golem, 2002; films include Thief, 1981, Lords of Discipline, 1983, Christine, 1983, The Natural, 1984, Broadcast News, 1987, Outrageous Fortune, 1987, Things Change, 1988, Gremlins II, 1988, Something About Love, 1990, Green Card, 1990, Life in the Food Chain, 1990, Far and Away, 1992, Hoffa, 1992, Life on the High Wire, 1992, Rudy, 1992, Last Action Hero, 1993, Mrs. Doubtfire, 1993, Miracle on 34th Street, 1994, Scarlet Letter, 1995, Dead Man Walking, 1995, The Chamber, 1996, Mad City, 1997, Dudley-Do-Right, 1998, Swing Vote, 1999, Detox, 1999; TV appearances include role of Sgt. Jablonski in Hill Street Blues, The Murder of Mary Phagan, 1988, Home Fires Burning, 1988, From the Dead of Night, 1989, Heist, 1989, Dangerous Pursuit, 1990, Johnny Ryan, 1990, The Love She Sought, 1990, Double Edge, 1992, Teamster Boss: The Jackie Presser Story, 1992; role of Pat in Veronica's Closet, Danny, 2001, D-Tox, 2002, NBC 75th Anniversary Special, 2002; narrator Lifestories; mem. first Am. co. to tour Soviet Union, 1972., former mem. Arena Stage Repertory Company. Joseph Jefferson award nominee, 1985; recipient Drama Desk award, 1985, Helen Hayes award, 1995, Am. Express Tribute to an Am. Actor, 1998.

PROSNICK, KEVIN PAUL, psychologist, researcher; b. New Brighton, Pa., Jan. 29, 1961; s. Paul A. and M. Joanne Prosnick; m. Amy D. Frankel, June 8, 1996. BA, Youngstown (Ohio) State U., 1983, MS in Edn., 1985; PhD, Kent State U., 1996. Lic. psychologist Ohio, 1997, profl. clin. counselor Ohio, 1997, cert. in neurofeedback Calif., 2001. Counselor Kevin Coleman Ctr., Kent, Ohio, 1986—92; instr. Kent (Ohio) State U., 1992—96; pvt. practice psychologist Akron, Ohio, 1997—. Lectr. John Carroll U., Cleve., 1994—97; rsch. cons. U. Akron, 2002—. Author: (psychol. test) Gestalt Inventory of Resistance Loadings, 1997, Transpersonality, 1999; contbr. articles to profl. jours. Named One of Five Outstanding Young Citizens in Ohio, Jaycees, 1979. Avocations: drums, swimming, reading, travel. Home and Office: 977 Hampton Ridge Dr Akron OH 44313

PROSNITZ, LEONARD R. radiologist; b. Apr. 9, 1936; BA, Amherst Coll., 1957; MD, SUNY, N.Y.C., 1961. Prof. Yale U., New Haven, 1969-83, Duke U., N.C., 1983—, chmn. radiol. oncology dept., 1983—96, 2003—. Contbr. articles to profl. jours. Office: Duke U Med Ctr Radiation Oncology Dept PO Box 3085 Durham NC 27710-0001 E-mail: prosnitz@radonc.duke.edu.

PROSPER, PIERRE-RICHARD, federal agency administrator; b. Denver, 1963; BA, Boston Coll.; JD, Pepperdine U. Bar: Calif. Dep. dst. atty. L.A. County, 1989—94; asst. U.S. atty. State of Calif., ctrl. dist., 1994—96; war crimes prosecutor U.N. Internat. Criminal Tribunal for Rwanda, 1996—98; spl. asst. to asst. atty. gen. for criminal divsn. State Dept.; spl. counsel, policy adviser Office of War Crimes, 1999—2001; amb. at large for war crimes issues U.S. Dept. of State, Washington, 2001—. Recipient Alumni award of Excellence, Boston Coll., 1999, Dist. Alumnus award, Pepperdine U. Sch. Law Alumni, 2000; fellow Wasserstein fellow, Harvard U., 2000—01. Office: US Dept of State Ambassador at large for War Crimes Issue 2201 C St NW Washington DC 20520-7512

PROSPERI, DAVID PHILIP, public relations executive; b. Chgo., June 20, 1953; BSBA, U. Ill., 1975; MBA in Internat. Bus., George Washington U., 1983. Moving cons. Fed. Safety Moving & Storage, Elmhurst, Ill., 1975-79; press aide 1980 Reagan for Pres. campaign, Los Angeles, 1979-80, Reagan-Bush Campaign, Alexandria, Va., 1980-81; asst. press sec. to the Pres. White House, Washington, 1981-82; mgr. govt. affairs The Superior Oil Co., Washington, 1982-84; press. sec. U.S. Dept. Energy, Washington, 1985; asst. to sec. dir. pub. affairs U.S. Dept. Interior, Washington, 1985-88; asst. sec. transp. U.S. Dept. Transp., Washington, 1989-90; sr. v.p., asst. to pres. and CEO, Chgo. Bd. Trade, 1990-95, sr. v.p., 1995—2004, sr. v.p., asst. to pres., CEO, 1996—2003; dir. pub. rels. Chgo. Merc. Exch., Inc., 2004—. Bd. dirs. Corp. Pub. Broadcasting, 1992—93. Republican. Roman Catholic. Avocations: basketball, tennis, spending time with family. E-mail: dprosper@cmc.com.

PROSPERI, LOUIS ANTHONY, lawyer; b. Altoona, Pa., Jan. 12, 1954; s. Louis Alfred and Ann Francis (DiDimenico) P.; m. Susan Lynn Irwin, Sept. 14, 1985. BS in Bus. Adminstrn. summa cum laude, Georgetown U., 1975; JD cum laude, Harvard U., 1978. Bar: Pa. 1978, U.S. Dist. Ct. (we. dist.) Pa. 1978, U.S. Ct. Appeals (Fed. cir.) 1985, U.S. Ct. Fed. Claims, 1985, U.S. Tax Ct. 1979. From assoc. to ptnr. Reed, Smith, Shaw & McClay, Pitts., 1978-94; pvt. practice Law Office Louis A. Prosperi, Pitts., 1994—. Mem. Allegheny County Bar Assn., Pitts. Tax Club. Clubs: Longue Vue (Verona, Pa.). Republican. Roman Catholic. Avocations: golf, tennis, paddle tennis, cross country skiing. Home: 3036 Grassmere Ave Pittsburgh PA 15216-1862 Office: Law Office of Louis A Prosperi Grant Bldg 310 Grant St Ste 3601 Pittsburgh PA 15219-2305 E-mail: laprosperi@acba.org.

PROSSER, DAVID THOMAS, JR., state supreme court justice, former state legislator; b. Chgo., Dec. 24, 1942; s. David Thomas, Sr. and Elizabeth Averell (Patterson) Prosser. BA, DePauw U., 1965; JD, U. Wis., 1968. Bar: Wis. 1968. Lectr. Ind. U., Indpls., 1968-69; advisor U.S. Dept. Justice, Washington, 1969-72; adminstrv. asst. to U.S. Rep. Harold V. Froehlich, Washington, 1973-74; pvt. practice Washington, 1975, Appleton, Wis., 1976; dist. atty. Outagamie County, Appleton, 1977-78; state rep. State of Wis., Madison, 1979-96; commr. Tax Appeals Commn., 1997-98; justice Supreme Ct. Wis., 1998—, Jud. Coun., 2002—. Commr. Nat. Conf. Commrs. Uniform State Laws, 1982—96; mem. Wis. Sesquicentennial Commn., Madison, 1993—99; minority leader Wis. Assembly, 1989—94, spkr., 1995—96. Mem.: Outagamie Bar Assn., Milw. Bar Assn., Dane Bar Assn., Wis. Bar Assn. Presbyterian. Avocation: art collector of American prints. Office: Supreme Ct Wis PO Box 1688 Madison WI 53701-1688 Office Phone: 608-266-1882.

PROSSER, FRANKLIN PIERCE, computer scientist; b. Atlanta, July 4, 1935; s. Edward Theron and Eunice (McDaniel) P.; m. Brenda Mary Lau, June 16, 1960; children: Edward, Andrea. BS, Ga. Inst. Tech., 1956, MS, 1958; PhD, Pa. State U., 1961. Prof. computer sci. Ind. U., Bloomington, 1969-99; asso. dir. Wrubel Computing Center, 1969-81, chmn. dept. computer sci., 1971-77, 87-93, spl. asst. for acad. computing, 1979-81; v.p. Logic Design, Inc., 1982-92. Cons. Lockheed Theoretical Physics Lab., Palo Alto, Calif., 1967 Home: 1200 S Longwood Dr Bloomington IN 47401-6072 Office: Ind U Dept Computer Sci Bloomington IN 47405

PROSSER, GEORGE T. utilities executive; m. Nancy Prosser; children: John, Tom. BS in Acctg., U. Tenn., 1971. Various positions including counterterrorism planning FBI; investigative dept. mgr. Office of Insp. Gen. TVA, Knoxville, asst. insp. gen. for investigations, insp. gen., 1994—. Investigator U.S. Ho. of Reps., FBI, Washington. Mem. Laurel Ch. of Christ. With U.S. Army, Vietnam. Decorated Purple Heart, Bronze Star; recipient Paul R. Roucher Pub. Svc. award, 1991. Office: TVA Office of Insp Gen 400 W Summit Hill Dr Knoxville TN 37902-1419 Fax: 908-771-8618.

PROSSER, JOHN MARTIN, architect, educator, urban design consultant; b. Wichita, Kans., Dec. 28, 1932; s. Francis Ware and Harriet Corinne (Osborne) P.; m. Judith Adams, Aug. 28, 1954 (dec. 1982); children: Thomas, Anne, Edward; m. Karen Ann Cleary, Dec. 30, 1983; 1 child, Jennifer. BArch, U. Kans., 1955; MArch, Carnegie Mellon U., 1961. Registered architect, Kans., Colo. Architect Robinson and Hissem, Wichita, 1954-56, Guirey, Srnka, and Arnold, Phoenix, 1961-62, James Sudler Assocs., Denver, 1962-68; ptnr., architect Nuzum, Prosser and Vetter, Boulder, 1969-73; from asst. prof. to prof. U. Colo., Boulder and Denver, 1968—, acting dean, 1980-84, dean, 1984, dir. environ. design Boulder, 1969-72, dir. urban design, 1972-85. Cons. John M. Prosser Assocs., Boulder and Denver, 1974—; vis. prof. urban design Oxford Brooks, Eng., 1979; vis. critic Carnegie Mellon U., U. N.Mex., Colo. Coll.; pres. Denver chpt. AIA, 1983; prin. investigator Fitsimmons-U. Colo. Health Scis. City Rsch. Study, 1997-99; vis. urban design scholar Nat. Univ. Ireland, 2003. Author, narrator: (PBS TV documentary) Cities Are For Kids, Too, 1984; prin. works include (with others) hist. redesign Mus. Western Art, Denver (design honor 1984), Villa Italia, Lakewood, Colo., Denver, Auraria Higher Edn. Ctr., Pueblo C.C. campus plan and new acad. facilities, comprehensive campus plan Denver U., Ft. Lewis Coll., Westminster Golf Course Cmty., Denver Botanic Gardens 20-Yr. Concept Plan, Colo. Coll. Historic Preservation Plan, Buffalo Hills Ranch Golf Course Cmty., Fountain Valley Sch., Urban Design and Campus Planning, Ctrl. Colo. Springs Strategic Urban Design and Planning, 2001—02, Interquest Corp. Park Urban Plan, 1999-2001. Bd. dirs. Denver Parks and Recreation Bd., 1987-93, 96-2003; chmn. design rev. bd. univs. Colo., Boulder, Denver, Aurora, and Colorado Springs,

1981—; archtl. control com. Denver Tech. Ctr., 1984—, Meridian Internat. Bus. Ctr., 1984—, DTC West, 1991—, Denver Internat. Bus. Ctr., 1993—, Nat. Renewable Energy Lab., 1995—; planning cons. Denver Internat. Airport Environs., 1984—; Nucleus co-founder U. Colo. Real Estate Ctr., 1989-2000; sr. advisor, dir. campus planning, Endur Enterprise Computing Campuses, 2002-03. Capt. USAF, 1956—59. Co-recipient 2d pl. award Am. Soc. Interior Designers, 1984, Honor award Colo. Soc. Architects, 1984. Mem. Urban Land Inst. (panel adv. svcs. 1990, 2001-04), Denver Country Club (bd. dirs. 1984-88, pres. 1986-87), Beta Theta Pi. Democrat. Avocation: arlberg ski. Home: 390 Emerson St Denver CO 80218 Office: 1512 Larimer St Denver CO 80202-1610 Office Phone: 303-892-9013. Personal E-mail: jmpros@aol.com.

PROSSER, MICHAEL JOSEPH, college librarian; b. Syracuse, N.Y., May 9, 1948; s. Palmer Adelbert and Viola Mary (Clairmont) P. AA, Riverside (Calif.) City Coll., 1971; BA in History, Calif. State Coll., San Bernardino, 1977; MSLS, U. So. Calif., L.A., 1981. Cert. cmty. coll. instr., librarian, Calif. Libr. clk. Riverside C.C., 1968-81, learning resources asst., 1981—. Author: California and the Pacific Plate: A Bibliography, 1979. Tutor, Queen of Angels Ch., Riverside, 1985—, facilitator/patrons, 1985—; photographer. With U.S. Army, 1969-71. Mem. ASCD, Internat. Soc. Poets, Calif. Libr. Assn. Democrat. Roman Catholic. Home: 6800 Palos Dr Riverside CA 92503-1330 Office: Riverside Cmty Coll 4800 Magnolia Ave Riverside CA 92506-1242

PROSSER, ROBERT ARTHUR, retired research scientist; b. N.Y.C., Mar. 16, 1925; s. Joseph Watrous and Edna Prosser; m. Laila Vittands, Feb. 1958; children: Louise, Thomas, Joseph. BS, Haverford Coll., 1949; PhD, U. Pa., 1960. Rsch. scientist U.S. Army Natick (Mass.) Soldier Ctr., 1962—2001. Contbr. articles to sci. jours., including Textile Rsch. Jour., Analytical Chemistry, Exptl. Mechanics, Jour. Applied Polymer Sci., Jour. Macromolecular Sci., Jour. Applied Physics. Served with inf. U.S. Army, World War II, ETO. Decorated Combat Infantryman's Badge, Purple Heart. Lutheran. Achievements include patents in field. Avocation: gardening. Home: 93 Beatrice Ln Holliston MA 01746

PROSSER, WESLEY LEWIS, advertising and public relations executive; b. Dodge City, Kans., Oct. 28, 1938; s. Wesley Lewis and Sarah Arvilla (Ellis) P.; m. Doris Jean Russell, Apr. 29, 1972 (dec. Nov. 1986). BA, Okla. State U., 1959. Advt. coordinator Aero-Commander, Inc., Oklahoma City, 1962-65; copy coordinator Farmland Industries, Inc., Kansas City, Mo., 1965-72; copy supr. Fletcher/Mayo/Assocs. Inc., St. Joseph, Mo., 1972-74; advt. and pub. relations dir. Agchem Abbott Labs., North Chicago, Ill., 1974-76; account exec. Rumrill & Hoyt, Inc., Rochester, N.Y., 1976-77; account rep. Vangard Communications Inc., St. Louis, 1977-78; v.p., client group supr. Bozell & Jacobs, Inc., Chgo., 1978-84; account supr. McKinney/Mid America, Chgo., 1984-85; mgr. advt. and pub. rels. Inter Innovation LeFebure Inc., Cedar Rapids, Iowa, 1986-89; mgr. bus. devel. Fanning Advt. Agy. Inc., Davenport, Iowa, 1989-91; dir. mktg. comm. Farm Bus. Software Sys., Inc., Aledo, Ill., 1991—. Presenter in field. Prodr. interactive promotional presentation on computer diskette; contbr. articles to profl. jours. Vol. Jackson County Rep. Party, Kansas City, Mo., 1969, Salvation Army, Dodge City, Kans., 1997-2000. 1st lt. USAF, 1959-61. Recipient 1st Place award Nat. Premium Execs., 1969, Objectives and Results award Am. Bus. Press, 1980-81, 83, others. Mem. Nat. Agrimarketers Assn. (1st Place Best in Advt. award 1974), Bus. and Profl. Advertisers Assn., Assn. Agrl. Computing Cos., Sports Car Club Am. Methodist. Avocations: aviation, summer water sports, creative writing. Home: 725 Alpine Dr Sherrard IL 61281-9339 Office: FBS Systems Inc 1855 55th Ave Aledo IL 61231-8610 Office Phone: 309-582-5628. E-mail: wes@fbssystems.com.

PROST, SHARON, federal judge; b. Newburyport, Mass., May 24, 1951; m. Kenneth F. Greene, June 24, 1984; 1 child, Matthew Prost-Greene. BS, Cornell U., 1973; MBA, George Washington U., 1975, LLM in Taxation, 1984; JD, Am. U., 1979. Bar: D.C. Labor rels. specialist Office of Personnel Mgmt., 1973-76; with Gen. Acctg. Office, 1976-79; trial atty. Fed. Labor Rels. Authority, 1980-83; atty. chief counsel's office Dept. of Treasury, 1983-84; assoc. solicitor Nat. Labor Rels. Bd., 1984-89; chief minority labor counsel Senate Com. on Labor and Human Resources, 1989-93; minority chief counsel Senate Com. on the Judiciary, 1993—2001; judge U.S. Court of Appeal, Federal Cir., 2001—. Office: US Court Appeals Fed Cir 717 Madison Pl NW Washington DC 20439

PROTAS, ELIZABETH J. physical therapist, academic administrator; m. Eugene D. Protas, Mar. 6, 1950; 1 child, Mark Jason. PhD, SUNY, Buffalo, 1974—80. Cert. phys. therapist Tex., 1980. Assoc. dean, sch. phys. therapy Tex. Woman's U., Houston, 1980—2002; chair, dept. phys. therapy U. Tex. Med. Br., Galveston, 2002—. Bd. trustees Am. Coll. Sports Medicine, Indpls., 2002—04. Recipient Joseph Valley Gerontologica Profl. of Yr. award, U. Tex. Health Sci. Ctr., 2000; fellow Founding Fellow, Am. Assn. Cardiovasc. and Pulmonary Rehab.; grantee Support Rsch. and Tng. Grad. Students, Dept. of Veterans. Mem.: Am. Phys. Therapy Assn. Achievements include research in Rehabilitation outcomes for persons with chronic disabilities. Office: U Tex Med Branch 301 U Blvd Galveston TX 77555-1144

PROTHRO, EDWIN TERRY, psychologist educator; b. Robeline, La., Dec. 11, 1919; Edwin Thomas and Frances Lillian (Terry) P.; m. Dorothy Kenworthy, Apr. 26, 1943 (div. 1967); children: Martha Carol Wells, Edwin Terry Jr.; m. Najla Salman, July 31, 1968; 1 child, Gwendolyn. PhD, La. State U., 1942. Asst. prof. psychology La. State U., Baton Rouge, 1946-49; assoc. prof. psychology U. Tenn., Knoxville, 1949-51; prof. psychology Am. U. Beirut, Lebanon, 1951-85; prof. emeritus, 1994—; fellow Ctr. for Middle East Studies Harvard U., Cambridge, Mass., 1960; dean, provost Am. U. Beirut, Lebanon, 1965-73; dep. dir. Edn. Abroad Program U. Calif., Sant Barbara, 1975-77; v.p. Hariri Found., Washington, 1986-97. Cons. Middle East Office Ford Found., Beirut, 1973-75; mem. bd. trustee Am. Community Sch., Beirut, 1970-73; mem. edit. bd. Jour. Social Psychology, 1955-70. Co-author: Psychology: A Biosocial Study of Behavior, 1950, 72; Changing Family Patterns in the Arab East, 1974; contbr. articles to profl. jours. Lt. USNR, 1943-46, WWII. Recipient Order of the Cedars Rep. Lebanon, 1969; Nat. Inst. Mental Health grantee, 1966-70, fellow 1963, 64. Mem. Am. Psychology Soc., La. Psychology Assn. (pres. 1949), Sigma Xi (pres. Beirut chpt. 1955). E-mail: prothro@erols.com.

PROTHRO, JERRY ROBERT, lawyer; b. Midland, Tex., Dec. 22, 1946; s. Jack William Prothro and Nita Marie (Stovall) Milligan; m. Leslie Joan Lepar, Aug. 15, 1970 (div. 1994); children: Laura Kay, Evan Jackson. BA, Southwestern U., 1969; JD, U. Tex. Sch. Law, 1972. Lawyer, capt. U.S. Army, JAGC, 1972-76; ptnr. Turpin, Smith & Dyer, Midland, 1975-85, Boyd, Sanders, Wade, Cropper & Prothro, Midland, 1985-91; pvt. practice Dallas and Midland, Tex., 1991—. Mem. admissions com. M/O div. U.S. Dist. Ct. for Western Dist. Tex., 1987—; speaker in field. Treas., v.p. Southwestern U. Alumni Bd., Georgetown, Tex., 1980-90, pres.-elect, 1991, pres., 1992-94; trustee, Southwestern U., 1992-94; adminstrv. bd. First United Meth. Ch., Midland, 1989-96; vice chmn. Permian Basin AIDS Coalition Bd., 1994; active Midland County Hist. Commn., 1980-85. Named Univ. scholar Southwestern U., 1969; recipient Disting. Svc. medal U.S. Army, 1974. Mem. Midland County Young Lawyers (pres. 1979-80), Midland County Bar Assn., 5th Cir. Bar Assn., Pi Kappa Alpha Social Frat., Blue Key Leadership Frat., Pi Gamma Mu Social Sci. Frat. Methodist. Avocations: antique collecting, camping, men's movement activity. Home: Ste 211 4021 Cole Ave Dallas TX 75204 Office: 3626 N Hall Ste 820 Dallas TX 75219 E-mail: prothro@swbell.net.

PROTHROW-STITH, DEBORAH, academic administrator, public health educator; MD, Harvard U., 1979. Resident Boston City Hosp.; state commr. health Pub. Health Commonwealth Mass., 1987; assoc. dean govt. and faculty devel. Sch. Pub. Health Harvard U., Boston, prof. pub. health practice. Author: Peace by Piece: A Guide for Preventing Community Violence, 1995. Mem. Nat. Commn. Crime Control and Prevention, 1995. Recipient Sec. Health and Human Svc. award, 1989, World Health Day award, 1993. Office: Harvard Sch Pub Health Dept Health Policy & Mgmt 718 E Huntington Ave Boston MA 02115 Business E-Mail: dp-s@hsph.harvard.edu.

PROTIGAL, STANLEY NATHAN, lawyer; b. Wilmington, Del., June 3, 1950; s. Bernard Protigal. BS in Aircraft Maintenance Engring., Northrop U., 1973; JD, Vt. Law Sch., 1978. Bar: U.S. Patent Office 1977, D.C. 1978. Assoc. Sixbey F. & L., Arlington, Va., 1978-79, atty., 1979-82; patent atty. Allied-Signal Bendix Aerospace, Teterboro, N.J., 1982-88; patent counsel Micron Tech., Inc., Boise, Idaho, 1988-94; pvt. practice, Boise, Idaho, 1994-96, Seattle, 1996-98; assoc. Sabath and Truong, San Jose, Calif., 1998—. Mem. IEEE, Mensa. Avocations: pvt. pilot, bicycling, skiing.

PROTOPOPESCU, VLADIMIR ALEXANDRU, research scientist, educator; b. Bucharest, Romania, June 28, 1944; arrived in U.S., 1982; s. Radu and Sylvienne Protopopescu; m. Anca Maria Lazarescu, Aug. 6, 1974 (div. Sept. 1980); 1 child, Alexandru. BS, U. Bucharest, 1968; PhD, Inst. Atomic Physics, 1976. Rschr. and sr. rschr. Inst. Atomic Physics, Bucharest, Romania, 1968—80; rschr. Chalmers Inst. Tech., Göteborg, Sweden, 1981, Yale U., New Haven, 1982—83, Boston U., 1984; rschr., sr. rschr., disting. rschr. Oak Ridge Nat. Lab., 1985—. Adj. prof. U. Tenn., Knoxville, 1988—. Co-author: Boundary Value Problems in Abstract Kinetic Theory, 1987, translator several books. Recipient Prize 'Dragomir Hurmuzescu for physics, Romanian Acad., 1978, R&D 100 award, R&D Mag., Chgo., 1998. Achievements include patents for #5,479,513, Dec. 1995, #6,484,132, Nov. 2002. Avocations: music, reading, gardening. Home: 8613 Wimbledon Dr Knoxville TN 37923 Office: Oak Ridge Nat Lab Oak Ridge TN 37831-6016

PROTSCH, ELIOT G. utilities executive, corporate financial executive; BBA in Econs. and Fin., U. S.D., Vermillion, 1975, MBA, 1976. Cert. Fin. Analyst 1981. With Mut. of Omaha Ins. Co., 1976—78; asst. treas. treasury dept. Wis. Power & Light Co. (now Alliant Energy Corp.), Madison, Wis., 1978—85, dist. mgr. Dane County, 1985—89, v.p. and gen. mgr. energy svc., 1989—92, v.p. customer sales and svc., 1992—93, sr. v.p., 1993—98; exec. v.p. energy delivery Interstate Power & Light (now Alliant Energy Corp.), Cedar Rapids, Iowa, 1998—2003, pres., 1998—; sr. exec. v.p. and CFO Alliant Energy Corp., Madison, Wis., 2004—. Bd. dir. Nuclear Mgmt. Co, Am. Family Ins., chair audit com., 2000—; bd. dir. Capstone MicroTurbine Corp., Alliant Energy Found. Mem. Iowa Bus. Coun., 2000—, chair, 2004—; bd. dir. Mercy Med. Ctr., Cedar Rapids, 1997—, Cedar Rapids C. of C., 2002—; bd. dirs. Iowa Natural Heritage Found., Des Moines, 2000—. Office: Alliant Energy Corp 4902 N Biltmore Ln Madison WI 53718

PROUD, ROBERT DONALD (ROBERT PAYTON), broadcast executive; b. Cleve., Nov. 1, 1949; s. Lloyd Donald and Eleanore Matilda (Cihon) Proud; m. K. Diane Siler, Feb. 17, 1979; 1 child, James S. Owen. Grad., Cleve. Inst. Broadcasting, 1969; student, U. N.Mex., 1982, Instituto Bilingue Cultural, 1989-90. Program dir. Sta. WGCL-FM, Cleve., 1972-74; ops. mgr. Sta. WRBR-FM, South Bend, Ind., 1974-75, Sta. XEROK, Juarez, Mexico, 1975-77; program dir. Sta. WZZP-FM, Cleve., 1977-78; gen. mgr. Sta. KELP, El Paso, Tex., 1978-82; sales mgr. Sta. KAMZ-FM, El Paso, 1982-86; gen. mgr. Stas. KAMA/KAMZ-FM, El Paso, 1982-86; dir. nat. sales Thrash Broadcasting, El Paso, Lubbock, Tex., 1987-88; gen. mgr. Sta. KVIV, El Paso, 1987-89; v.p., gen. mgr. Sta. KEZB, El Paso, Tex., 1989-91; gen. mgr. Sta. KFRR, Denver, 1991-92; gen. sta. mgr. Sta. KQQK, Houston, 1992-95; v.p., gen. mgr. Entravision Comm., Dallas, 1995—2003; v.p. sales OM Media Networks, Sacramento, 2003—. Bd. dirs., chmn. comm. Am. Heart Assn. Mem.: Denver Area Radio Broadcasters, Tex. Assn. Broadcasters, El Paso Assn. Radio Stas. (pres. 1981). Office: 3100 Fite Cir Ste 101 Sacramento CA 95827

PROUGH, RUSSELL ALLEN, biochemistry educator, academic administrator; b. Twin Falls, Idaho, Nov. 5, 1943; s. Elza Leroy and Beulah Elsie (Huddleston) P.; M. Betty Marie Ehlers, Dec. 26, 1965; children: Jennifer Sally, Kimberly Marie. BS in Chemistry, Coll. of Idaho, 1965; PhD in Biochemistry and Biophysics, Oreg. State U., 1969. Postdoctoral fellow VA Hosp., Kansas City, Mo., 1969-72; instr. biochemistry U. Tex. Southwestern Med. Sch., Dallas, 1972-73, asst. prof. biochemistry, 1973-77, assoc. prof. biochemistry, 1977-82, prof. biochemistry, 1982-86, U. Louisville Sch. Med., 1986—, chmn. dept., 1986—99, vice dean rsch., assoc. v.p. rsch., 1998—2003. Mem. NIH Toxicology Study Sect., 1984-88, State of Nebr. Smoking Disease and Cancer Rsch. Program, 1984-91, Nat. Insts. Environ. Health Scis. rsch. com., 1999--. Assoc. editor Drug Metabolism and Disposition, 1994—, Drug Metabolism Rev., 2002--. Recipient Rsch. Career Devel. award USPHS. Mem. Am. Soc. Biochemistry and Molecular Biology, Am. Assn. Cancer Rsch., Am. Soc. Pharmacology and Exptl. Therapeutics, Internat. Soc. for Study of Xenobiotics, Sigma Xi. Lutheran. Office: U Louisville Dept Biochemistry and Molecular Biology Louisville KY 40292-0001 Office Phone: 502-852-7249. E-mail: russ.prough@louisville.edu.

PROULX, (EDNA) ANNIE, writer; b. Norwich, Conn., Aug. 22, 1935; d. George Napolean and Lois Nellie (Gill) Proulx; m. James Hamilton Lang, June 22, 1969 (div. 1990); children: Sylvia Marion Bullock Clarkson, Jonathan Edward Lang, Gillis Crowell Lang, Morgan Hamilton Lang. BA cum laude, U. Vt., 1969; MA, Sir George Williams U., Montreal, Can., 1973; DHL (hon.), U. Maine, 1994; LLD, Concordia U., Montreal, 2002; DLitt (hon.), U. Toronto, 2000. Author: Heart Songs and Other Stories, 1988, Postcards, 1991 (PEN/Faulkner award 1993), The Shipping News, 1993 (Chgo. Tribune Heartland award 1993, Irish Times Internat. Fiction award 1993, Nat. Book award for fiction 1994, Pulitzer Prize for fiction 1994), Accordion Crimes, 1996 (Dos Passos prize for lit. 1996), Brokeback Mountain, 1998 (Nat. Mag. award 1998), Brokeback Mountain, 1998, Close Range: Wyoming Stories, 1999, That Old Ace in the Hole, 2002; contbr. more than 50 articles to mags. and jours.; editor: Best American Short Stories of 1997. Recipient Dos Passos prize for Lit., Longwood Coll., 1997, Ambassador Book award English Speaking Union, 2000, Best Fiction 1999 Book award The New Yorker, 2000, Willa award, 2000, Evil Companions Lit. award, 2001; Kress fellow Harvard U., 1974, fellow Vt. Coun. Arts, 1989, NEA, 1991, Guggenheim Found., 1992; rsch. grantee Inter-U. Ctr., 1975; resident Ucross Found., 1990, 92. Mem. PEN Am. Ctr., Phi Beta Kappa, Phi Alpha Theta. Avocations: canoeing, reading, fishing. Office: c/o Simon & Schuster 1230 Ave of Americas New York NY 10020

PROUST, JOYCELYN ANN, retired librarian; d. Merry Aylor and Alice Wilhelmina (Morgan); m. George Edward Proust (dec.); children: Gabrielle Cynara, Bertrand Gerard. BA, U. Denver, 1950, MA, 1955; cert., U. Paris Sorbonne, 1953. Lifetime French tchg. credential Calif. C.C., lifetime libr. credential C.C. Libr. Colo. Sch. Mines, Golden, 1955—62; prof. libr. sci. Long Beach (Calif.) City Coll., 1962—92, prof. emerita, 1992—. Chair Calif. C.C. Libr. Cooperative, 1968—75; exec. dir., pres. Libr./Learning Resources Assn., Calif., 1985—86. Bd. mem. Long Beach Mozart Festival, 1975—95, chair; active 1976 Bicentennial Com., L.A., 1976. Mem.: Alpha Gamma Delta, Phi Sigma Iota, Alpha Lambda Delta. Unitarian. Home: 5249 Village Rd Long Beach CA 90808

PROUT, CARL WESLEY, retired history educator; b. Bakersfield, Calif., Apr. 19, 1941; s. George Hecla and Ruth (King) P. BA, U. Calif., Santa Barbara, 1964, MA, 1965; postgrad., U. Tenn., Knoxville, 1968-71, Am. U., Cairo, 1974, U. So. Calif., 1981, Ain Shams U., Cairo, 1981. Instr. history Santa Barbara Coll., 1965-66, U. Tenn., Knoxville, 1968-71; instr. Orange Coast Coll., Costa Mesa, 1966-68, asst. prof., 1971-73, assoc. prof., 1973-75, prof., 1975-2001, prof. emeritus, 2001—; retired, 2001. Adj. prof. U. at Sea, 1996—; treas. Willmore Corp., 1980-81, sec., 1984-85, v.p., 1985-86, pres., chmn., 1988-89, also bd. dirs.; group facilitator Coastview Meml. Hosp., Long Beach, 1986-89. Research and publs. in field. Pres., chmn. bd. Alamitos Heights Improvement Assn., 1979-80, bd. dirs., 1980-82; mem. Joint Coun., East Long Beach, 1979-80, Local Coastal Planning Adv. Com., 1979-80; preservation bd. Palm Springs Hist. Site, 1994-2002; founding pres. Palm Springs Hist. Site Preservation Found., 1997-2002; bd. govs. Desert Samaritans for the Elderly, 2003—; v.p. Writers Guild, Palm Springs, 1996-98. Recipient Salgo Outstanding Tchr. award, 1974-76. Mem.: Palm Springs Hist. Soc., Palm Desert Hist. Soc. *Personal philosophy: Honesty, Openmindedness, Willingness = How to succeed in life!.*

PROUT, CURTIS, internist, educator; b. Swampscott, Mass., Oct. 13, 1915; s. Henry Byrd and Eloise (Willett) P.; m. Daphne Brooks, June 27, 1939 (div. 1985); children: Diana P. Cherot, Daphne P. Cook, Rosamond P. Warren, Phyllis P. Brosius; m. Diane Neal Emmons, Dec. 7, 1985. AB, Harvard U., 1937, MD, 1941. Diplomate Am. Bd. Internal Medicine. Intern Peter Bent Brigham Hosp., Boston, 1942; resident in internal medicine Johns Hopkins Hosp., Balt., 1943; research fellow Mass. Gen. Hosp., Boston, 1943-45; practice medicine specializing in internal medicine, 1945—; asst. dir. Univ. Health Services Harvard U., Cambridge, Mass., 1961-72; dir. prison health project Office of Econ. Opportunity, 1972-74; asst. dean Harvard Med. Sch., Boston, 1980-94, asst. clin. prof. medicine, 1975-82. Trustee Humane Soc. Mass., Boston, 1975-00; bd. dirs. Nat. Commn. on Correctional Health Care, 1980-98, chmn., 1990; dir., treas. The Med. Found., Boston, 1980-98. Chmn. Bd. Health, Dover, Mass., 1960-75. Fellow ACP, Mass. Med. Soc.; mem. AMA, Am. Clin. and Climatol. Assn., Tavern Club of Boston (pres. 1980-82). Avocations: sailing, writing. Home: 115 School St Manchester MA 01944-1232 Office: 319 Longwood Ave Boston MA 02115-5728

PROUT, ROBERT STEPHEN, higher education consultant, law enforcement consultant; b. June 24, 1944; Degree in law, LaSalle Ext. U., Chgo., 1967; BA, Muskingum Coll., 1969; MEd, Ohio U., 1970; PhD, Ohio State U., 1972. State trooper Ohio Hwy. Patrol, Akron, Ohio, 1965-68; coord. Zane State Coll., Zanesville, Ohio, 1969—72; dept. chair criminal justice St. Cloud (Minn.) State U., 1972—96, 2002—, dir. grad. program criminal justice, 1988—. Adj. faculty St. John's U., Coll. St. Thomas, U. Louisville; chmn. Govs. Com. on Crime Prevention-Region D, Minn., 1976-77. Author: Meeting Ohio's Law Enforcement Needs, 1973; contbr. articles to profl. jours. Recipient Tchr. of Yr. award, 1988. Office: St Cloud State U 241 Stewart Hall Saint Cloud MN 56301 Office Phone: 320-308-5541. Business E-Mail: prout@stcloudstate.edu.

PROUT, WILLIAM C. telecommunications industry executive; B in Math., Kent State U.; MBA, Ashland Coll. With ITT North, United Tel. Co., Ohio, 1980; sr. v.p. network local telecomm. divsn. Sprint Corp., Overland Park, Kans., 1995—98, sr. v.p. broadband local networks local telecomm. divsn., 1998—2000, sr. v.p. customer svc. ops., local telecomm. divsn., 2000—. Office: Sprint Corp 6200 Sprint Pkwy Overland Park KS 66251

PROUTY, CHARLES S. federal agency administrator; b. Jersey City; BS, U.S. Naval Acad., 1967; MA in Econs., George Mason U., 1982, JD, 1991. Bar: Va. Joined as spl. agt. FBI, 1973, supr. hostage rescue team, 1986—87, supr. violent crimes and major offenders sect. criminal investigative divsn., 1987—89, unit chief spl. ops. and rsch. unit tng. divsn. FBI Acad. Quantico, Va., 1989—92, inspector's aide inspection divsn., 1992—93, spl. asst. to the dep. asst. dir. tng. divsn., 1993—94, asst. spl. agt. in charge, 1994—97, sect. chief bur. applicant recruit and selection sect. Washington, 1997—98, spl. agt. in charge Little Rock divsn., 1998—2000, spl. agt. in charge Boston divsn., 2000—02, exec. asst. dir. law enforcement svcs. divsn. Washington, 2002—. With USN, 1967—73, ret. capt. USNR. Office: FBI J Edgar Hoover Bldg 935 Pennsylvania Ave NW Washington DC 20535

PROVENCHER-KAMBOUR, FRANCES, business development advisor; b. Exeter, N.H., Apr. 22, 1947; d. Roger Arthur and Josette Marguerite (Camus) Provencher; m. Benjamin C. Ryder, Apr. 12, 1969 (div. Mar. 1979); 1 child, Tiffany Nicholas; m. Edward S. Kambour, Dec. 27, 1988. BA, U. N.H., 1969; exec. MBA (partial), U. N.C., 1990-91. Clk. typist, editl. asst. U.S. Embassy, Moscow, 1964-65; asst. editor Durham (N.H.) Advertiser, 1965-69; assoc. editor Kaman Aerospace Corp., Bloomfield, Conn., 1970-71; publs. editor The Hartford Ins. Group, Conn., 1974-76; pub. rels. cons. Fran Ryder Assocs., Farmington, Conn., 1976-78; pub. rels. account exec. Shailer Davidoff Rogers, Inc., Fairfield, Conn., 1978-80; sr. account exec. Creamer Dickson Basford, Inc., Hartford, Conn., 1980-83; account group mgr., account exec. Spiro & Assocs., Phila., 1983-84, v.p., assoc. pub. rels. dir., 1984-85; sr. v.p. pub. rels. LSGE Advt. Inc., Avon, Conn., 1985-87; v.p. corp. comm. Wondriska Assocs., Farmington, 1987-88; pres. The Kambour Co., Raleigh, N.C., 1988-92, dir. pub. rels. & mktg. Westmoreland, NH, 1994—2003, The PBM Co., Research Triangle Park, N.C., 1993-94; cons. MEI Search Consultancy, LLC, an MRI affiliate, Keene, NH, 2001—03; bus. devel. advisor Peace Corps, Cameroon, Equatorial Africa, 2003—. Translator: The Cogito in Edmund Husserl's Phenomenology, 1969. Founder The Art Guild, 1975; bd. dirs. Parent's Assn., Hartford Sch. Ballet, 1982-83, U. Conn. Found., 1986-99, dir. emeritas, 1999—, Cheshire Med. Ctr./Dartmouth-Hitchcock Clinic Cmty. Adv. Coun., 1997-2001, trustee, 1999—; incorporator, 1995-97; incorporator Monadnock Cmty. Found., 2000--, Monodnock Family Svcs., 1996--. Recipient Gold Quill awards Internat. Assn. Bus. Communicators, 1974, Nat. Safety Coun. award, 1985, Paul Harris Fellow award, Rotary Internat., 1997. Mem. Pub. Rels. Soc. Am. (accredited, bd. dirs. 1980-88, 90-2001, assembly del. 1987-88, spl. commendation 1985, mem. Counselors Acad. 1982-92, 94-99, Yankee chpt. pres. 1998-99, nat. presdl. citation for leadership 1993), Elm City Rotary Club (bd. dirs. 1995-2000). Republican. Congregationalist. Office: Corps de la Paix BP 215 Yaoundé Cameroon E-mail: fpkambour@hotmail.com.

PROVENCIO, ROBERTO ENRIQUE, music educator, music minister; b. El Paso, Tex., July 14, 1957; s. Jesus Roberto and Velia Rivero Provencio; m. Linda Kay Johnson, Aug. 18, 1984; children: Robert Phillip, Charles Raymond, Elizabeth Anne, Victoria Lynn. MusB, U. Ariz., 1980; MusM, Tex. State U., 1986; D Musical Arts, U. Colo., 1993. Prof. music Calif. State U., Bakersfield, 1988—; min. music First Presbyn. Ch., Bakersfield, 1995—. Pvt. practice cons., Bakersfield, 1980—. Mem. editl. bd. The Choral Jour.; translator: History of the Choral Movement of Venezuela; author: Releasing the Artist Within: Mnemonics for Achieving Artistic Choral Performance. Mem. Adult Rehab. Ctr. Salvation Army, Bakersfield, 1999; bd. dirs. The Beethoven Festival, Bakersfield, 1992—95. Named Outstanding Hispanic Alumnus, Tex. State U., 1994, Outstanding Music Educator, Calif. Music Educators Assn., 1994, Outstanding Prof., 2001;, Calif. State U. fellow, 1988—92, Choral Rsch. fellow, U. of Colo., Boulder, 1986—88. Mem.: Nat. Assn. Ch. Musicians (bd. govs. 1998—, chair publs. com. jour.), Internat. Fedn. Choral Music, Am. Choral Directors Assn. (life; chair multicultural perspectives western divsn. 1992—96, mem. editl. bd. 1995—), Rotary (dir., scholarship chair 1994, Bakersfield East), Pi Kappa Lambda (life). Conservative. Avocations: motorcycle touring, fly fishing, tennis, photography, tobacciana. Home: 101 Camino del Oeste Bakersfield CA 93309 Office: Calif State U 9001 Stockdale Hwy Bakersfield CA 93311 Office Phone: 661-664-3073.

PROVENSEN, ALICE ROSE TWITCHELL, artist, author; b. Chgo., d. Jay Horace and Kathryn (Zelanis) Twitchell; m. Martin Provensen, Apr. 17, 1944; 1 child, Karen Anna. Student, Art Inst. of Chgo., 1930-31, U. Calif., L.A., 1939, Art Student League, N.Y., 1940-41; D.H.L. (hon.), Marist Coll., 1986. With Walter Lanz Studios, Los Angeles, 1942-43; OSS, 1944-45. Author, illustrator Karen's Opposites, 1963, Karen's Curiosity, 1963, What is a Color?, 1967, author, illustrator (with Martin Provensen) Who's in the Egg?, 1970, author, illustrator The Provensen Book of Fairy Tales, 1971, Play on Words, 1972, My Little Hen, 1973, Roses are Red, 1973, Our Animal Friends, 1974, The Year at Maple Hill Farm, 1978, A Horse and a Hound, A Goat and a Gander, 1979, The Owl and Three Pussycats, 1981, Town and Country, 1984, Shaker Lane, 1987, The Buck Stops Here, 1990, Punch in New York, 1991 (Best Books N.Y. Times, 1991), My Fellow Americans, 1995, Count on Me, 1998 (Book of Yr. Parenting Mag., 1998), The Master Swordsman, 2001, The Magic Doorway, 2001, A Day in the Life of Murphy, 2003 (named One of the Three Best Childrens Books, 2003), illustrator (with Martin Provensen) Mother Goose Book, 1976, illustrator Old Mother Hubbard, 1977, A Peaceable Kingdom, 1978, The Golden Serpent, 1980, A Visit to William Blake's Inn, 1981 (Caldecott honor book, 1981), Birds, Beasts and the Third Thing, 1982, The Glorious Flight, 1984 (Caldecott medal, 1984), The Voyage of Ludgate Hill, 1987, also textbooks; exhibitions include with Martin Provensen Balt. Mus., 1954, exhibitions include Am. Inst. Graphic Arts, N.Y., 1959, Botolph

Group, Boston, 1964, one-woman shows include Henry Feiwel Gallery, N.Y.C., 1991, Children's Mus., Washington, 1991, Moscarelle Mus. Art, Williamsburg, Va., 1991; books represented Fifty Book of Yr. selections Am. Inst. Graphic Arts, 1947, 1948, 1952 (The Charge of the Light Brigade named Best Illustrated Children's Book of Yr. N.Y. Times, 1964, co-recipient medal Soc. Illustrators, 1960). Named to Soc. Illustrators Hall of Fame, 2000.

PROVENZANO, DOMINIC, information specialist; b. N.Y.C., Jan. 25, 1951; s. Nicholas Patrick and Evelyn Provenzano; children: Saverio, Carmela, James. BA, Hobart Coll., Geneva, N.Y., 1972; MS in Fgn. Svc., Georgetown U., 1976; MS, L.I. U., 1978; MA, NYU, 1987. CFP; cert. security analyst. Rschr. The White House, Washington, 1981-82, Time, Inc., N.Y.C., 1982-87; asst. prof. Suffolk C.C., Selden, NY, 1987-91; rsch. specialist Wasserstein Perella & Co., N.Y.C., 1991-93, mgr. info. svcs., 1994-96; rsch. assoc. Russell Reynolds, N.Y.C., 1996-97; dir. rsch. D.S. Wolf Assocs. Inc., N.Y.C., 1997-98; fin. advisor Prudential Securities, Melville, NY, 1998—2003, UBS Paine Webber, Melville, NY, 2003—. Contbr. articles to profl. jours. Named to Outstanding Young Men of Am., 1982. Mem. Head of the Bay Club, Beta Phi Mu., Pi Gamma Mu. Roman Catholic. Office: UBS Paine Webber Melville NY 11747

PROVINE, JOHN CALHOUN, retired lawyer; b. Asheville, N.C., May 15, 1938; s. Robert Calhoun and Harriet Josephine (Thoms) P.; m. Martha Ann Monson, Aug. 26, 1966 (div. Jan. 1975); m. Nancy Frances Lunsford, Apr. 17, 1976 (div. Mar. 1996); children: Robert, Frances, Harriet. AB, Harvard U., 1960; JD, U. Mich., 1966; MBA, NYU, 1972, LLM in Taxation, 1975. Bar: N.Y., Tenn., U.S. Dist. Ct. (so. and ea. dists.) N.Y., U.S. Ct. Appeals (2nd and 6th cirs.), U.S. Dist. Ct. (mid. dist.) Tenn., U.S. Supreme Ct. From assoc. to ptnr. White & Case, N.Y.C., 1966—74, ptnr., 1974—82, 1992—94, Jakarta and Ankara, 1982—91; counsel Dearborn & Ewing, Nashville, 1981—82; ret., 1994. Lt. USN, 1960-63. Mem. ABA, N.Y. Bar Assn., Tenn. Bar Assn., Assn. of Bar of City of N.Y. Avocations: bluegrass music, rural activities. Home and Office: 6630 Manley Ln Brentwood TN 37027-3401 E-mail: jprovine@compuserve.com.

PROVINE, LORRAINE, retired mathematics educator; b. Altus, Okla., Oct. 6, 1944; d. Claud Edward and Emmie Lorraine (Gasper) Allmon; m. Joe A. Provine, Aug. 14, 1966; children: Sharon Kay, John David. BS, U. Okla., 1966; MS, Okla. State U., 1988. Tchr. math. U.S. Grant High Sch., Oklahoma City Schs., 1966-69; tchr. East Jr. High Sch., Ponca City (Okla.) Schs., 1969-70; tchr. Ponca City High Sch., 1978-79, 81-96; lectr. dept. math. Okla. State U., Stillwater, 1996-99. Mem.: NEA, Ponca City Assn. Classroom Tchrs. (treas. 1983—86, 1991—96), Assn. Women in Math, Okla. Coun. Tchrs. Math, Okla. Edn. Assn., Sch. Sci. and Math Assn., Nat. Coun. Tchrs. Math, Math Assn. Am., Internat. Soc. Tech. in Edn., Coun. for Exceptional Children, Okla. Hist. . (life), Okla. State U. Alumni Assn. (life), U. Okla. Alumni Assn. (life), Okla. Assn. Mothers Club (life; state bd. dirs. 1977—87, pres. 1984—85), Delta Kappa Gamma (Delta chpt. treas. 1996—98, Gamma state essay com. 1999—2003, Eta chpt. treas. 2000—04, Gamma state comm. com. 2003—, Eta chpt. pres. 2004—). Republican. Baptist. Avocations: reading, knitting, sewing, genealogy. Home: 1019 Greenway Cir Norman OK 73072-6125 E-mail: lorraineprovine@cox.net.

PROVORNY, FREDERICK ALAN, lawyer, educator; b. Bklyn., Sept. 7, 1946; s. Daniel and Anna (Wurm) P.; m. Nancy Ileene Wilkins, Nov. 21, 1971; children: Michelle C., Cheryl A., Lisa T., Robert D. BS summa cum laude, NYU, 1966; JD magna cum laude, Columbia U., 1969. Bar: N.Y. 1970, U.S. Supreme Ct. 1973, D.C. 1975, Mo. 1977, Md. 1987, Calif. 1989; CPA, Md., Mo. Law clk. to Judge Harold R. Medina U.S. Ct. Appeals (2d cir.), N.Y.C., 1969-70; asst. prof. law Syracuse (N.Y.) U., 1970-72; assoc. Debevoise, Plimpton, Lyons & Gates, N.Y.C., 1972-75, Cole & Groner P.C., Washington, 1975-76; with Monsanto Co., St. Louis, 1976-86, asst. co. counsel, 1978-86; pvt. practice Washington, 1986-89; ptnr. Provorny & Jacoby, Washington, 1989-91; counsel Shaw, Pittman, Potts & Trowbridge, Washington, 1991-93; ptnr. Tydings & Rosenberg, Balt., 1993-94; pvt. practice Balt., 1994—98; Harold R. Tyler prof. of law and tech., dir. Sci. and Tech. Law Ctr., Albany (N.Y.) Law Sch., 1998—2004; pres. Empire State Venture Group, Inc., 2001—03. Lect. Bklyn Law Sch., 1973-74; adj. prof. U. Balt. Sch. of Law, 1996-98, Rensselaer Poly Inst., 2004; pres. Sci. and Tech. Assocs., Inc., 1986-91. Contbr. articles to profl. jours. Trustee Christian Woman's Benevolent Assn. Youth Home, 1979-83, Jewish Family Svcs. of N.E. N.Y., 1999—. Mem. ABA, Am. Law Inst., Am. Arbitration Assn. (panel comml. abitrators), Am. Intellectual Property Lawyers Assn., Licensing Execs. Soc. (U.S., Can.), Assn. Univ. Tech. Mgrs., Philo-Mt. Sinai Lodge 968, Masons, Beta Gamma Sigma. Jewish. Home: 11803 Kemp Mill Rd Silver Spring MD 20902-1511 Office: 3rd Fl 126 State St Albany NY 12207 Office Phone: 518-514-2420. E-mail: frederickprovorny@yahoo.com.

PROVOST, CHERYL LOUISE WINTERS, account executive; b. Niagara Falls, N.Y., Apr. 25, 1947; d. William Joseph and Virginia Louise (Greene) W.; children: Christopher Chase, Matthew Chase, Richard Chase. AAS, Adirondack Community Coll., 1975; BS, Charter Oak State Coll., 1999. RN. RN critical care St. Clare's Hosp., Schenectady, N.Y., 1975-79; RN ICU Glens Falls (N.Y.) Hosp., 1979-80; sales and svc. rep. Clin. Data, Inc., Brookline, Mass., 1980-82; dir. regional devel. Med-Care Convalescent Supply Co., Inc., Rhinebeck, N.Y., 1982-85; sales mgr. ea. ops. Vortec Health Care, Cin., 1985-86; diagnostic sales rep., tng. assoc. MallincKrodt, Inc., St. Louis, 1986-94; cardiology sales specialist and tng. assoc. Mallinkrod Med., Inc., 1988-94, regional account mgr. New Eng., 1994-96, northeast regional bus. mgr., 1996-98, northeast ultrasound market devel. mgr., 1998-99, sales tng. mgr., 1999—. Mem. Nat. Assn. Female Execs., Am. Heart Assn. Republican. Presbyterian. Avocations: cross-country and alpine skiing, golf, cooking, sailing, hiking. Home: 7 Horicon Ave Glens Falls NY 12801-2616 Office: Mallinckrodt Inc 675 Mcdonnell Blvd Saint Louis MO 63134-2001

PROVOST, RUTH W. state legislator; Student, U. Mass. Mem. 2d Dist. Mass. Ho. of Reps., Boston, 1997—, mem. election laws com., mem. energy com. Mem. Sandwich Dem. Town Com., Mass. PTA, Citizens for Pub. Schs., Cape and Isla nds Dem. Coun., Plymouth County Dem. League. Mem. Mass. Assn. Schs. Coms. Office: Mass State Legis Rm 26 State House Boston MA 02133

PROVOST, THOMAS TAYLOR, dermatology educator, researcher; b. Pitts., Mar. 21, 1938; s. Charles Thomas and Marcelle K. (Taylor) P.; m. Carol Sara Christie, July 2, 1960; children: Charles T., Christie Lynn, Thomas Wright. AB, U. Pitts., 1958, MD, 1962. Intern Mary Hitchcock Meml. Hosp., Hanover, N.H., 1962-63; resident in dermatology Dartmouth Med. Ctr., Hanover, N.H., 1966-67, U. Oreg. Med. Ctr., Portland, 1967-68; fellow in immunology SUNY, Buffalo, 1969-72, asst. prof. dermatology, 1972-75, assoc. prof., 1975-78, Johns Hopkins U. Med. Sch., Balt., 1978-82, prof. dermatology, 1982—, chmn. dept. dermatology, 1997—. Lt. commdr. USPHS, 1962-64. Mem. Soc. Investigative Dermatology, Soc. Clin. Investigation. Avocation: boating. Home: PO Box 230 Milton DE 19968-0230

PROVUS, BARBARA LEE, executive search consultant; b. Washington, Nov. 20, 1949; d. Severn and Birdell (Eck) P.; m. Frederick W. Wackerle, Mar. 29, 1985. Student, NYU, 1969-70; BA in Sociology, Russell Sage Coll., 1971; MS in Indsl. Rels., Loyola U., Chgo., 1978; postgrad., Smith Coll., 1971. Sec. Booz, Allen & Hamilton, Chgo., 1973-74, mgr. tng., 1974-77, dir. rsch., 1977-79, cons. search, 1979-80; mgr. mgmt. devel. Federated Dept. Stores, Cin., 1980-82; v.p. Lamalie Assocs., Chgo., 1982-86; prin., founder Sweeney, Shepherd, Bueschel, Provus, Harbert & Mummert, Inc., Chgo., 1986-91; founder Shepherd Bueschel & Provus Inc., Chgo., 1992—. Bd. dirs. Anti-Cruelty Soc., Chgo., 1990—, pres., 1996-97; trustee Sage Colls., Troy, N.Y., 1999-2000. Mem. Assn. Exec. Search Cons. (dir. 1989-92), The Chgo. Network (bd. dirs. 1993—, chair 2002-03), Econ. Club Chgo. Avocations: collecting rubber bands, modern art, baseball. Home: 3750 N Lake Shore Dr Chicago IL 60613-4238 Office: Shepherd Bueschel & Provus Inc 401 N Michigan Ave Ste 3020 Chicago IL 60611-4257 Office Phone: 312-832-3020.

PROWN, JULES DAVID, art historian educator; b. Freehold, N.J., Mar. 14, 1930; s. Max and Matilda (Cassileth) P.; m. Shirley Ann Martin, June 23, 1956; children: Elizabeth Anderson, David Martin, Jonathan, Peter Cassileth, Sarah Peiter. AB, Lafayette Coll., 1951, DFA (hon.), 1979; AM, U. Del., 1956, Harvard U., 1953, PhD, 1961. Dir. Hist. Soc. Old Newbury, Newburyport, Mass., 1957-58, Old Gaol Mus., York, Maine, 1958-59; asst. to dir. Harvard U., Fogg Art Mus., Cambridge, Mass., 1959-61; instr. to Paul Mellon prof. history of art Yale U., New Haven, 1961-99, Paul Mellon prof. emeritus history of art, 1999—; curator Am. art Yale U. Art Gallery, New Haven, 1963-68; vis. lectr. Smith Coll., Northampton, Mass., 1966-67; dir. Yale Ctr. for Brit. Art, New Haven, 1968-76, sr. rsch. fellow, 1999—; assoc. dir. Nat. Humanities Inst., New Haven, 1977. Trustee Whitney Mus., N.Y.C., 1975-94; mem. editorial adv. bd. Am. Art-Smithsonian, Washington, 1986-2001, On Common Ground, 1993—; mem. vis. com. Harvard U. Art Museums, 1993-98. Author: John Singleton Copley, 2 Vols., 1966, American Painting from Its Beginnings to the Armory Show, 1969, The Architecture of the Yale Center for British Art, 1977; Art as Evidence: Writings on Art and Material Culture, 2002, (catalogue) American Art from Alumni Collections, 1968; editor (with Kenneth Haltman) American Artifacts: Essays in Material Culture, 2000. Recipient George Washington Kidd award Lafayette Coll., 1986, recipient Iris Found. award for outstanding contbns. to the decorative arts, 2001, Lawrence A. Fleischman award for scholarly excellence in the field of Am. Art History, 2001. Fellow The Athenaeum of Phila. (hon.); mem. Am. Antiquarian Soc., Coll. Art Assn. (Disting. Tchg. of Art History award 1996), Am. Studies Assn., Conn. Acad. Arts & Scis., Walpole Soc., Royal Soc. Arts. Office: Yale Ctr for Brit Art PO Box 208280 New Haven CT 06520-8280 Business E-Mail: jules.prown@yale.edu.

PROZES, ANDREW, publishing executive; b. Jan. 21, 1946; BA in Math, U. Waterloo, Ont., Can.; MBA, York U., Toronto. Former group pres. Southam Inc., Don Mills, Ont., Can.; exec. v.p., COO Westlaw, The West Group (subs. Thomson Corp.), Eagan, Minn., 1997-99; CEO global legal pub. & info. divsn. Reed Elsevier, N.Y.C., 2000—. Mem. bd. dirs. Reed Elsevier Group plc and Reed Elsevier PLC, 2000—. Office: Reed Elsevier 125 Park Ave 23rd fl New York NY 10017

PRPICH, MICHAEL FRANK, food company manager; b. Harbor City, Calif., Sept. 20, 1971; s. Nicholas Frank Prpich and Donna Jean O'Donnell; m. Christina Reneé Prpich, Dec. 18, 1993 (div. Oct. 1997); m. Loretta Faye Prpich, Nov. 28, 1998; children: Eric Glenn Barr, Morgan Destin Barr, Bethany Anna Faye. BS in Math., Ark. Tech. U., 1997. Dock worker Tyson Valley Distbn. Ctr., Russellville, Ark., 1990, checker, 1990-91, inventory control, 1991, 92, forklift operator, 1991-92, 92-95, lead, 1995-97; plant supr. Tyson Dardanelle, Ark., 1997-98, process improvement mgr., 1998—. Republican. Avocations: computers, racquetball, spending time with family. Home: 413 Valley Ave Berryville AR 72616-3021 E-mail: prpichm@tyson.com.

PRUCHA, FRANCIS PAUL, historian, priest; b. River Falls, Wis., Jan. 4, 1921; s. Edward Joseph Prucha and Katharine Schladweiler. BS, State Tchrs. Coll., River Falls, Wis., 1941; MA, U. Minn., 1947; PhD, Harvard U., 1950; STL, St. Louis U., 1959; DHL (hon.), LeMoyne Coll., Syracuse, N.Y., 1974, Creighton U., Omaha, 1978; LLD (hon.), Merrimack Coll., North Andover, Mass., 1985; LittD (hon.), Marquette U., Milw., 1988; DHL (hon.), Loyola U., Chgo., 1992, Holy Cross Coll., Worcester, Mass., 1992. Entered Soc. of Jesus, 1950, ordained priest Roman Cath. Ch., 1957. Tchr. history Amery H.S., Wis., 1941—42; instr. to prof. Marquette U., Milw., 1960—92, prof. history emeritus, 1992—. Vis. prof. history Harvard U., Cambridge, Mass., 1971, U. Okla., Norman, 1974; Gasson prof. Boston Coll., Chestnut Hill, Mass., 1983—85; Bullitt vis. prof. U. Wash., Seattle, 1988. Author: (book) Broadax and Bayonet, 1953, American Indian Policy in the Formative Years, 1962, Guide to the Military Posts of the U.S., 1964, Sword of the Republic, 1969, Indian Peace Medals in American History, 1971, American Indian Policy in Crisis, 1976, The Churches and the Indian Schools, 1979, Indian Policy in the United States, 1981, The Great Father, 2 vols., 1984, Indians in American Society, 1985, Handbook for Research in American History, 1987, 1994, Atlas of American Indian Affairs, 1990, American Indian Treaties, 1994; editor: Army Life on the Western Frontier, 1958, The Dawes Act and the Allotment of Indian Lands, 1973, Americanizing the American Indians, 1973, Documents of United States Indian Policy, 1975, 2000, Cherokee Removal, 1981; contbr. numerous articles to profl. jours., chapters to books. Bd. trustees St. Louis U., 1974—78, Loyola U., Chgo., 1983—88. 1st lt. Air Corps U.S. Army, 1942—46. Fellow Sr. Rsch. fellow, NEH, 1970, 1981; Guggenheim Found. fellow, 1967. Mem.: Orgn. Am. Historians (exec. bd. 1980—83), Western History Assn. (pres. 1983), Am. Hist. Assn. Roman Catholic. Home: Marquette Univ Jesuit Residence 1404 W Wisconsin Ave Milwaukee WI 53233

PRUCHA, JOHN JAMES, geologist, educator; b. River Falls, Wis., Sept. 22, 1924; s. Edward Joseph and Katharine (Schladweiler) P.; m. Mary Elizabeth Helfrich, June 12, 1948; children: David, Stephen, Katharine, Carol, Mark, Barbara, Margaret, Christopher, Anne, Andrew. Student, Wis. State U., River Falls, 1941—43; PhB, U. Wis., 1945, PhM, 1946; MA, Princeton U., 1948, PhD, 1950. Asst. prof. geology Rutgers U., 1948-51; sr. geologist NY State Geol. Survey, 1951-56; rsch. geologist Shell Devel. Co., 1956-63; prof. geology Syracuse (NY) U., 1963-90, prof. emeritus, 1990—, chmn. dept., 1963-70, 88-89, dean Coll. Arts and Scis., 1970-72, vice chancellor acad. affairs, 1972-85; pres. Syracuse U. Press, 1973-85, bd. dirs., 1985-90. Author: Basement Tectonics of Rocky Mountains, 1965, Structural Behavior of Salt, 1967, Stratigraphy and Structure of Southeastern New York, 1959, Fracture Patterns, 1979, Zones of Structural Weakness, 1992, (with Norman A. Foss) Kinnickinnic Years, 1993. Trustee Le Moyne Coll., 1971-78; bd. dirs. Cultural Resources Coun., Syracuse, 1974—, pres., 1978-80; bd. dirs. Everson Mus. Art, Syracuse, 1977-83, v.p., 1980-81; mem. regents vis. com. NY State Mus., 1993-96. Recipient John Mason Clarke medal NY State Geol. Survey, 1990. Fellow AAAS, Geol. Soc. Am.; mem. Am. Assn. Petroleum Geologists, Am. Geophys. Union, NY State Coun. Profl. Geologists. Home: 112 Ardsley Dr Syracuse NY 13214-2110 Office: Syracuse Univ 204 Heroy Geology Lab Syracuse NY 13244-0001 Office Phone: 315-446-0329.

PRUDEN, ANN LORETTE, chemical engineer, researcher, management consultant; b. Norfolk, Va., Sept. 3, 1948; d. James Otis and Elora Maie Pruden; m. Alan Todd Royer, Aug. 13, 1983; children: James Sebastian Royer, Annabelle Grace Royer. BS in Chemistry, Maryville (Tenn.) Coll., 1970; MA in Chem. Engring., Princeton (N.J.) U., 1978; PhD, 1981. Rsch. and develop. chemist and chem. engr. Mobil Corp., Princeton, 1970—92; supr. Mobil Chem. Co., Edison, N.J., 1992-97, lab. mgr., 1997-2000, tech. mgmt. team, 1997-2000; prin. Inventive Strategies, 2000—. Mem. Quality Director's Network, Indsl. Rsch. Inst., Washington, 1992-98. Contbg. author: Photocatalytic Purification and Treatment of Water and Air, 1993; contbr. articles to profl. jours. Fellow Mobil R&D Corp., Princeton, N.J., 1976-79. Mem.: Inst. Mgmt. Cons., Am. Chem. Soc., AIChE. Achievements include research in heterogeneous catalysis, organizational effectiveness, platform speaking. Office Phone: 908-359-4787. Business E-Mail: pruden@inv-strat.com.

PRUDEN, JAMES NORFLEET, III, lawyer; b. Edenton, N.C., Sept. 1, 1948; s. James Norfleet Jr. and Helen (Goodwin) P.; m. Cynthia Haines Gridley, Aug. 7, 1971; children: Matthew Gridley, Haines Goodwin. AB, U. N.C., 1970; JD, U. Va., 1973. Assoc. Kennedy Covington Lobdell & Hickman, Charlotte, N.C., 1973-78, ptnr., 1979—. Author manuscripts for continuing legal edn. programs, 1979—. Mem. county selection com. John Motley Morehead Found., Chapel Hill, N.C., 1990-92, chmn. 1993-95; vestryman Christ Episcopal Ch., 1990-92, 2000-02, sr. warden, 2002. Recipient John Motley Morehead award, 1966-70. Mem. ABA, N.C. Bar Assn. (chmn. bus. law sect. 1991-92, pres. 2002-03). Democrat. Home: 1139 Queens Rd Charlotte NC 28207-1849 Office: Kennedy Covington Hearst Tower 214 N Tryon St 47th Fl Charlotte NC 28202

PRUD'HOMME, ALBERT FREDRIC, securities company executive, financial planner; b. New Rochelle, NY, Dec. 19, 1952; s. Albert O. and Rita R. (Moshier) P.; m. LuAnn Winfield, June 29, 1985 (div.); children: Cherilyn, Alicia. BA, Mercer U., 1975. Chartered underwriter, 1999. Sales rep. Met. Life Ins. Co., N.Y.C., 1975-82; sales agt. Ohio Nat. Life, Cin., 1977-92; pres. Scepter Securities Inc., Charlotte, N.C., 1982-91; with Wall St. Capital, The Advisors Group, and Acacia Fin. Group, Charlotte, 1991-98; mktg. mgr. Ballantyne Planning Group, MetLife, 1998—2004, Round hill Securities, 2004—. Bd. dirs. Lyons Fin. Group Advisors, Inc. Pres. Belmont Abbey Coll. Athletic Found., 1985-87; bd. dirs. Charlotte Youth for Christ. With U.S. Army, 1972-74. Recipient Estate Planning award Winthrop Coll., 1981. Mem. Fin. Planning Assn. (cert. 1985), Nat. Assn. Ins. & Fin. Advisors, Charlotte Soc. Inst. CFPs (pres. 1994-95). Democrat. Presbyterian. Home: 2114 Bon Villa Way Fort Mill SC 29708-8502 E-mail: aprudhomme@metlife.com.

PRUDHOMME, JAMES LARRY, financial consultant, writer; s. Linda Diane Manning and James Larry Prudhomme. Student in Fin. Mgmt., Northwestern State, Natchitoches, L., 1995—97. Fin. dir. Group One, Dallas, 1998—2002, Preston Dodge, Dallas, 2002—. Mem. Jaycees, Natchitoches, La., 1992—97; organizer Ducks Unltd., Natchitoches, La., 1979—96. Mem.: Toys For Tots (assoc.). Republican. Roman Catholic. Avocations: golf, working out, basketball, football, hunting/fishing.

PRUDHOMME, PAUL, chef, restaurant owner; Owner, chef K-Paul's Louisiana Kitchen, New Orleans, 1979—. Creator Chef Paul Prudhomme's Magic Seasoning Blends. Author: (cookbooks) Fork in the Road, Fiery Foods, Kitchen Expedition, Louisiana Kitchen; co-prodr.: Vol. Meals on Wheels, Easter Seals, March of Dimes, Big Brothers/Big Sisters, Chef and the Child. Named Culinarian of Yr., Culinary Diplomat, Am. Culinary Fedn., 1994; recipient Restaurateur of Yr., La. State Restaurant Assn., 1983. Office: K-Paul's Louisiana Kitchen 416 Chartres New Orleans LA 70130

PRUEHER, JOSEPH W. retired military officer, former ambassador; b. Nashville, Nov. 25, 1942; Grad., U.S. Naval Acad., Annapolis, Md., 1964. Commd. ensign USN, advanced through grades to adm.; commdr. in chief U.S. Pacific Command, Camp H.M. Smith, Hawaii, 1996-99; amb. to People's Republic of China Dept. of State, Beijing, 1999—2001; cons. prof. Stanford-Harvard Preventive Def. Project, 2001—. Bd. dirs. Merrill Lynch & Co.; bd. mem. N.Y. Life Ins. Co., Emerson Electric Co., Fluor Corp.; mem. bd. govs. The Nature Conservancy. Home: Apt 30 148 142nd St New York NY 10030-3504*

PRUESSNER, DAVID MORGAN, lawyer; b. Corpus Christi, Tex., May 13, 1955; s. Harold Trebus and Alma (Morgan) P.; m. Becky McKinney, May 21, 1977; children: Jennifer, Daniel, Heather. BA cum laude, Baylor U., 1977, JD cum laude, 1980. Bar: Tex. 1980, U.S. Dist. Ct. (no. dist.) Tex. 1980, U.S. Ct. Appeals (5th cir.) 1986, U.S. Supreme Ct. 1989. Atty. Coke & Coke, Dallas, 1980-83, Shank, Irwin & Conant, Dallas, 1983-90, Pettit & Martin, Dallas, 1990-92, Fletcher & Springer, Dallas, 1992-99; pvt. practice Law Office of David Pruessner, Dallas, 1999—. Instr. legal assts. program So. Meth. U., Dallas, 1989-91. Mem. editl. bd. Baylor Law Rev., 1980. Avocations: world religions, history, chess. Office: Law Offices of David M Pruessner Ste 600 10100 N Central Expy Dallas TX 75231-4156 Office Phone: 214-696-0600. E-mail: david@prulaw.com.

PRUETT, JOYCE H. writer; d. Albert Hernandez and Viola Ellen Hood; m. Leland Harold Pruett, Aug. 24, 1953 (dec. 1978); children: Susan Ann, John Harold, Robert Raymond, Albert Vincent. BA, U. Tex., Arlington, 1969, MA, 1972. Cert. real estate broker U. Fla., 1973, property mgmt. Nat. Assn. Property Mgrs., 1974. Dir. Columbia Coll., Fort Leonardwood, Mo., 1979—82; bus. cons. Pruett Enterprises, East Greenbush, NY, 1983—91, bus. advisor, 2003—; employment specialist Hudson Valley CC, Troy, NY, 1991—99; self-employment coord. Found. for Mental Hygiene, Albany, NY, 2001—03. Bd. dirs. officer Pub. Access Television, Troy, NY; com. mem. Hudson Valley CC AdHoc, Troy, NY; mem. Chancellor's Award Com., Troy, NY, 1996—99. Author: Surprise, 2004. Subcom. chair Job Svc. & Employer's Com., Troy, NY, 1996; bd. dirs. officer N.Y. State Legis. Forum, Albany, 1999—2001, Pub. Access Television, North Greenbush, NY, 1999—2000; aurthor's forum Public Access TV Schenectas, 2003—04. Grantee, Ronald McDonald House, 2000. Home: 18 PInewood Ave East Greenbush NY 12061 Office: Pruett Enterprises 18 Pinewood Ave East Greenbush NY 12061

PRUETZ, ADRIAN MARY, lawyer; b. Nov. 13, 1948; Student, U. Wis., 1966—69; BA, Loyola U., Chgo., 1972, postgrad., 1972—73; JD magna cum laude, Marquette U., 1982. Bar: Wis. 1982, Calif. 1985. With Quinn Emanuel et al, L.A.; assoc. Whyte and Hirschboeck, SC, 1982—84, Morrison and Foerster, 1984—88, ptnr., 1988—94, Quinn Emanuel, 1994—. Spkr., lectr. Price Waterhouse Intellectual Property Forum, Licensing Execs. Soc., Am. Soc. Indsl. Security. Named one of Most Influential Trial Lawyers in Calif., L.A. Daily Jour., 2002—04, State's Top 25 Copyright, Trademark and Patent Legal Minds, head STRONG, 2003, Calif.'s Most Successful Lawyers, Calif. Law Bus. Mem.: ABA (past chair com. U.S. lit. affecting internat. patent problems, past chair com. impact 1991 amendments), Women Lawyer's Assn. L.A., Los Angeles County Bar, State Bar Calif., Fed. Bar Assn. (spkr., lectr.). Office: 865 S Figueroa St 10th Fl Los Angeles CA 90017 Office Phone: 213-443-3134. E-mail: adriapruetz@quinnemanuel.com.

PRUIS, JOHN J. business executive; b. Borculo, Mich., Dec. 13, 1923; s. Ties J. and Trientje (Koop) P.; m. Angeline Rosemary Zull, Sept. 14, 1944; children: David Lofton, Daniel J., Dirk Thomas. BS, Western Mich. U., 1947; MA, Northwestern U., 1949, PhD, 1951; Litt.D. (hon.), Yeungnam U., Taegu, Korea, Ind. State U.; LL.D. (hon.), Ball State U., U. So. Ind.; DHL (hon.), Keuka Coll. Tchr. pub. schs., Mich., 1942-43; supervising tchr. Campus Sch., Western Mich. U., 1947-48; instr. speech U. No Ia., 1951-52; from asst. prof. to assoc. prof. speech So. Ill. U., 1952-55; mem. faculty Western Mich. U., 1955-68, sec. bd. trustees, 1964-68, v.p. adminstrn., 1966-68; pres. Ball State U., 1968-78; v.p. corp. rels. Ball Corp., 1978-88. Cons., examiner North Central Assn., 1959-78; also bd. dirs. N. Central Assn. V.p. Country dr. chmn. Kalamazoo Cmty. Chest, 1964; bd. dirs. Kalamazoo chpt. Am. Cancer Soc., 1963-68, Del. County United Way, Muncie Symphony Assn., Ball Meml. Hosp., Big Bros./Big Sisters, Ind. Legal Found.; trustee U. So. Ind., 1985-90; exec. v.p. George and Frances Ball Found. With USNR, 1943-46; capt. Res., ret. Mem. Am. Assn. Higher Edn., Speech Communication Assn., Muncie C. of C., Blue Key, Rotary, Phi Delta Kappa, Omicron Delta Kappa, Beta Gamma Sigma Presbyterian. E-mail: jjpruis@iquest.net.

PRUITT, ALICE FAY, mathematician, engineer; b. Montgomery, Ala., Dec. 17, 1943; d. Virgil Edwin and Ocie Victoria (Mobley) Maye; m. Mickey Don Pruitt, Nov. 5, 1967; children: Derrell Gene, Christine Marie. BS in Math., U. Ala., Huntsville, 1977; postgrad., Calif. State U., Northridge, 1978—79. Instr. math. Antelope Valley Coll., Quartz Hill, Calif., 1977—78; space shuttle engr. Rockwell Internat., Palmdale, Calif., 1979—81; programmer, analyst sci. support svcs. Combat Devel. and Experimentation Ctr., Ft. Hunter-Liggett, Calif., 1982—85; sr. engring. specialist Loral Vought Sys. Corp., Dallas, 1985—92; dir. concepts and analysis, advanced sys. engring. Nichols Rsch. Corp., Huntsville, Ala., 1992-99; sr. prin. engr. Computer Sci. Corp., Huntsville, 1999—. Mem. DeSoto (Tex.) Coun. Cultural Arts, 1987-89. Mem. AAUW (sch. bd. rep. 1982, legal advocacy fund chairperson 1989-91), Toastmasters, Phi Kappa Phi. Republican. Methodist. Avocations: dance, gourmet cooking. Office: PO Box 400002 4090 S Memorial Pky Ste A Huntsville AL 35815-1502 Personal E-mail: afpruitt@comcast.net. Business E-Mail: apruitt@csc.com.

PRUITT, ANNE LORING, academic administrator, education educator; b. Bainbridge, Ga., Sept. 19, 1929; d. Loring Alphonzo and Anne Lee (Ward) Smith; m. Harold G. Logan; 1 child, Leslie; stepchildren: Dianne, Pamela, Sharon, Ralph Pruitt, Jr., Harold, Minda, Andrew Logan. BS, Howard U., Washington, 1949; MA, Columbia U., N.Y.C., 1950, EdD, 1964; HumD hon., Ctrl. State U., Wilberforce, Ohio, 1982. Counsel for women Howard U., 1950-52; tchr., dir. guidance Hutto H.S., Bainbridge, 1952-55; dean students Albany State Coll., Ga., 1955-59, Fisk U., Nashville, 1959-61; prof. edn. Case Western Res. U., Cleve., 1963-79; prof. ednl. policy and leadership Ohio State U., Columbus, 1979-95, prof. emeritus, 1995—; assoc. dean Ohio State U. Grad. Sch., Columbus, 1979-84; assoc. provost Ohio State U., Columbus, 1984-86, dir. Ctr. for Tchg. Excellence, 1986-94; dean in residence Coun.

Grad. Schs., Washington, 1994-96, scholar in residence, 1996—2002. Cons. So. Regional Edn. Bd., Atlanta, 1967-78, So. Edn. Found., Atlanta, 1978-87; co-dir. Preparing Future Faculty program, 1994-2002. Author: New Students and Coordinated Counseling, 1973, Black Employees in Traditionally White Institutions in the Adams States 1975-77, 1981, In Pursuit of Equality in Higher Education, 1987; co-author: (with Paul Isaac) Student Services for the Changing Graduate Student Population, 1995, (with Jerry Gaff and Richard Weibl) Building the Faculty We Need: Colleges and Universities Working Together, 2000, (with Jerry Gaff and Joyce Jentoft) Preparing Future Faculty in the Sciences and Mathematics, 2002, (with Jerry Gaff, Leslie Sims and Daniel Denecke) Preparing Future Faculty in the Humanities and Social Sciences: A Guide for Change, 2003. Trustee Urban League, Cleve., 1965-71, Ctrl. State U., 1973-82, Case Western Res. U., 1987-02, Columbus Area Leadership Program, 1988-91; bd. dirs. ARC, Cleve., 1978-79, Am. West Airlines Found., 1992-95; mem. adv. com. USCG Acad., New London, Conn., 1980-83; Ohio State U. rep. to AAUW, 1989-94; univ. co-chairperson United Way, 1990-91; trustee Marburn Acad., 1991-95; mem. Columbus 1992 Edn. Com., 1988-92; mem. edn. subcom. Columbus Found., 1991-94; mem. exec. com. Renaissance League, 1992-94; mem. vis. panel on rsch., Edn1. Testing Svc., 1996-02; mem. Commn. on Future Clemson U., 1997-98; bd. dirs. Black Women's Agenda, Inc., 1997-, pres. 1998-2002; deacon Peoples Congregational United Ch. of Christ, 1998—; mem. B.E.S.T. Expert Panel, 2002-04; evaluation external expert NSF Grad. Tchg. Fellows in K-12 Edn. Program, 2002-04. Recipient Outstanding Alumnus award Howard U. Alumni Assn., 1975; Am. Coun. on Edn. fellow, 1977; named one of Am.'s Top 100 Black Bus. and Profl. Women Dollars & Sense Mag., 1986; recipient Disting. Affirmative Action award Ohio State U., 1988; named Sr. Scholar Am. Coll. Pers. Assn., 1989, Woman of Achievement award YMCA, 1993, Godmother of Minority Grad. Edn., Black Issues in Higher Edn., 1995. Mem. NSF (mem. com. on equal opportunities in sci. and engring. 1989-95), Am. Coll. Pers. Assn. (pres. 1976-77), Coun. Grad. Schs. in U.S. (chairperson com. on minority grad. edn. 1980-84), Am. Ednl. Rsch. Assn., Ohio Assn. Counselor Edn. (pres. 1966-67), Links Inc., Cosmos Club, Alpha Kappa Alpha.

PRUITT, BASIL ARTHUR, JR., surgeon, retired military officer; b. Nyack, N.Y., Aug. 21, 1930; s. Basil Arthur and Myrtle Flo (Knowles) P.; m. Mary Sessions Gibson, Sept. 4, 1954; children: Scott Knowles, Laura Sessions, Jeffrey Hamilton. AB, Harvard U., 1952, postgrad., 1952—53; MD, Tufts U., 1957. Intern Boston City Hosp., 1957-58, resident in surgery, 1958-59, 61-62; commd. capt., M.C. U.S. Army, 1959, advanced through grades to col., 1972; resident Brooke Gen. Hosp., Ft. Sam Houston, Tex., 1962-64; chief clin. divsn. Inst. Surg. Rsch., Ft. Sam Houston, 1965-67; chief profl. svcs. 12th Evacuation Hosp., Vietnam, 1967-68; comdr., dir. U.S. Army Inst. Surg. Rsch., Brooke Army Med. Ctr., Ft. Sam Houston, 1968-95, ret., 1995; clin. prof. gen. surgery U. Tex. Health Sci. Ctr., San Antonio, 1975—; prof. surgery Uniformed Svcs. U. of the Health Scis., Bethesda, Md., 1978—. Mem. surgery, anaesthesiology and trauma study sect. NIH, 1978-82; mem. Shriners Burns Adv. Bd., 1985-92, Shriners Med. Adv. Bd., 1992-95, Shriners Rsch. Adv. Bd., 1996—, mem. Shriners Clin. Outcomes Studies Adv. Bd., 1999—; merit rev. bd. for surgery VA, 1990-93. Author med. books; contbr. chpts. to textbooks, articles to profl. jours.; mem. editl. bd. Jour. Trauma, 1975-94, editor, 1995—; mem. edit. bd.: Archives Surgery, 1981-93, Consultations in Surgery, Correspondence Society of Surgeons, Collected Letters, 1978-2000, Circulatory Shock, 1985-93, Jour. Burn Care and Rehab., 1984-87, Jour. Investigative Surgery, 1987-97, Shock, 1993—, Current Opinion in Surg. Infections, 1993-2001, Sepsis, 1996-2002, Injury, 1998-2003, Turkish Jour. Trauma, 2002—, English edit. Chinese Jour. Traumatology, 1998—. Decorated Bronze Star, Legion of Merit, Disting. Svc. medal; recipient ISS/SIC Danis prize, 1995, G. Whitaker Internat. Burns prize, 2000. Fellow: ACS (pre and postoperative care com. 1969—79, vice chmn. 1973—75, gov. 1973—79, com. on trauma 1974—84, internat. rels. com. 1983—93, chmn. 1987—89), Am. Coll. Critical Care Medicine (disting. investigator award 2000); mem.: Western Trauma Assn., Eastern Assn. Surgery Trauma, N.Am. Burn Soc. (pres. 1993—94), Shock Soc. (clin. counselor 1995—98, chmn. 2005 program com.), Internat. Surg. Group, Surg. Infection Soc. (recorder 1980—84, pres. 1985—86), Assn. Acad. Surgery, Internat. Soc. Surgery, Surg. Biol. Club III, Am. Assn. Surgery Trauma (recorder 1976—80, pres. 1982—83), Halsted Soc. (pres. 1985—86), So. Surg. Assn., Western Surg. Assn. (dist. rep. 1984—88, pres. 1993—94), Tex. Surg. Assn., Am. Surg. Assn. (2d v.p. 1980—81, pres. 1999—2000, medallion 1998), Soc. Univ. Surgeons, Am. Trauma Soc. (pres. Tex. divsn. 1974—75, dir. 1974—, sec. 1986—88, v.p. 1988—90, pres.-elect 1990—92, pres. 1992—94), Am. Bd. Surgery (sr.; diplomate, bd. dirs. 1982—88), Smoke Burn and Fire Assn. (adv. coun.), Internat. Soc. Burn Injuries (nat. rep. 1974—82, co-chmn. disaster planning com. 1982—86, pres.-elect 1990—94, pres. 1994—98), Am. Burn Assn. (pres. 1975—76), Mediterranean Club Burns and Fire Disasters (regional rep. Ams.), Surgeons' Travel Club (pres. 2002—03). Home: 402 Tidecrest Dr San Antonio TX 78239-2517 Office: U Tex Health Sci Ctr Dept Surgery 7703 Floyd Curl Dr San Antonio TX 78229-3900 also: Editl Office Jour Trauma 7330 San Pedro Ste 654 San Antonio TX 78216-6236 Office Phone: 210-342-7903. Business E-Mail: pruitt@uthscsa.edu.

PRUITT, DEAN GARNER, psychologist, educator; b. Phila., Dec. 26, 1930; s. Dudley McConnell and Grace (Garner) P.; m. Frances Juliard, Dec. 27, 1959; children: Andre Juliard, Paul Dudley, Charles Alexandre. AB, Oberlin Coll., 1952; MS, Yale U., 1954, PhD, 1957. Postdoctoral fellow U. Mich., 1957-59; rsch. assoc. Northwestern U., 1959-61; asst. prof., then assoc. prof. U. Del., 1961-66; assoc. prof. to prof. SUNY, Buffalo, 1966—96, SUNY Disting. prof., 1996—2001, SUNY Disting. prof. emeritus, 2001—, dir. grad. program in social psychology, 1969—73, 1976—77, 1985—88, 1998—2001; vis. scholar George Mason U., 2001—. Author: Negotiation Behavior, 1981, (with J. Z. Rubin and S.H. Kim) Social Conflict, 1986, 94, 2003, (with P.J. Carnevale) Negotiation in Social Conflict, 1993; editor; (with R.C. Snyder) Theory and Research on the Causes of War, 1969, (with K. Kressel) Mediation Research, 1989. Grantee Office Naval Rsch., 1965, NIMH, 1969, NSF, 1969, 74, 76, 80, 83, 86, 88, 93, Guggenheim Found., 1978-79. Fellow APA, Am. Psychol. Soc., Soc. for Psychol. Study Social Issues; mem. Internat. Assn. for Conflict Mgmt. (pres. 1990-92, Lifetime Achievement award 1997), Internat. Soc. Polit. Psychology (v.p. 1984-85, Harold D. Lasswell award 1992), Phi Beta Kappa, Sigma Xi. Home: 9006 Friars Rd Bethesda MD 20817-3320 Office: George Mason U Inst Conflict Analysis and Resolution Fairfax VA 22030-4444 E-mail: dean@pruittfamily.com.

PRUITT, GEORGE ALBERT, college president; b. Canton, Miss., July 9, 1946; s. Joseph Henry and Lillie Irene (Carmichael) P.; m. Pamela Young; 1 child, Shayla Nicole. BS, Ill. State U., 1968, MS, 1970, DHL (hon.), 1994; PhD, Union Grad. Sch., Cin., 1974; D Pub. Svc. (hon.), MA (hon.), Bridgewater State Coll., 1990; LLD (hon.), Ill. State U., 1994; DHL (hon.), SUNY Empire State Coll., 1996. Asst. to v.p. for acad. affairs Ill. State U., Normal, 1968-70, dir. high potential students program, 1968-70; dean students Towson State U., 1970-72; v.p., exec. asst. to pres., assoc. prof. urban affairs Morgan State U., 1972-75; v.p., prof. Tenn. State U., 1975-81; exec. v.p. Council for Advancement Experiential Learning, Columbia, Md., 1981-82; pres. Thomas A. Edison State Coll., Trenton, 1982—. Commn. on ednl. credit and credentials, labor/higher edn. coun. Am. Coun. on Edn.; advisor group XII, Nat. Fellowship program W.K. Kellogg Found., 1990-94, advisor group XV, 1995-99; bd. dirs. SEEDCO; nat. adv. com. on instnl. quality and integrity U.S. Dept. Edn., 1994—; bd. dirs. Sun Nat. Bank, Vineland, N.J. Past chair Mercer County Chamber of Commerce; chair Union Inst., Cin., 1989—; bd. trustees Rider U., Lawrenceville, NJ; bd. dirs. N.J. Assn. Colls. and Univs. Recipient Resolution of Commendation Bd., Trustees Morgan State U., 1975, Outstanding Svc. to Edn. award Tenn. State U., 1981, Gubernatorial citation Gov. of Tenn., 1981, Good Guy award George Washington coun. Boy Scouts Am., 1991, Humanitarian award NCCJ, 1992, Educator of Yr. award Black N.J. Mag., 1993, Disting. Alumni award Ill. State U., 1996; apptd. hon. mem. Gen. Assembly Tenn., 1981, hon. mem. U.S. Congress from 5th Tenn. dist., 1981; named ofcr. of the Most Effective Coll. Pres. in U.S., Exxon Edn. Found. Study, 1986; named to Coll. of Edn. Hall of Fame, Ill. State U., 1995; named Mercer Co. N.J. Citizen of Yr., Mercer Co. C. of C., 1997. Mem. Coun. for Advancement Exptl. Learning, Am. Assn. State Colls.and Univs., Coun. for Advancement and Support of Edn., Am. Coun. Edn., Mid. States Assn. Colls. and Schs. (accreditation evaluator commn. on higher edn.), Mercer County C. of C. (chmn.). Office: Thomas Edison Coll 101 W State St Trenton NJ 08608-1101

PRUITT, STEPHEN WALLACE, finance educator; b. Indpls., Feb. 3, 1957; s. Harry Wallace and Dorothy (Thorp) P.; m. Mary Melinda Settle, Dec. 19, 1981; children: Rebecca Elizabeth, Victoria Barrick. BS in Mgmt., Purdue U., 1979; MBA in Fin., Ohio State U., 1980; PhD in Fin., Fla. State U., 1987. Internat. cash mgr. Marathon Oil Co., Findlay, Ohio, 1980-81; fin. analyst Nat. Svc. Industries, Crawfordsville, Ind., 1981-83; asst. prof. fin. U. Miss., Oxford, 1986-88, Ind. U., Bloomington, 1988-93; assoc. prof. fin. U. Memphis, 1993-96, prof. fin., 1996-2000; Arvin Gottlieb/Mo. chair in bus. econs. and fin. U. Mo., Kansas City, 2000—03, Arvin Gottlieb/Mo. chair in bus. econs. and fin., chair dept. fin., info. mgmt. and strategy, 2003—. Cons. in field. Contbr. articles to profl. jours. Bd. dirs. Art Mus. U. Memphis, 1995-2000; founder, pres. Memphis Print Club, 1995-2000. Mem. So. Fin. Assn., Fin. Mgmt. Assn. Republican. Baptist. Avocation: collecting art and antiques. Office: U Mo Henry W Bloch Sch Bus & Pub 5100 Rockhill Rd Kansas City MO 64110-2481 Home: 5316 W 140th St Overland Park KS 66224 Office Phone: 816-235-2334.

PRUKESATONKUL, KAMOL, music educator; b. Bangkok, Feb. 14, 1951; s. Richard and Chee Shim Yip. BA, Bangkok Coll., 1974. Piano tchr., L.A., 1977—. Mem.: Music Tchr. Assn. Calif., Music Tchr. Nat. Assn. Avocations: reading, swimming, golf, hiking, travel. Home and Office: 825 Hampton ST Glendora CA 91740

PRUNES, FERNANDO, plastic surgeon, educator; b. Chihuahua, Mex. m. Linda R. Underwood; children: Alexander, Ariadne, Anthony. MD, U. Chihuahua, Mex., 1968. Surg. intern Booth Meml. Med. Ctr., Flushing, N.Y., 1971-72; resident in gen. surgery Tucson Hosps. Med. Edn. Program, 1972-76; resident in plastic surgery Mayo Grad. Sch. Medicine, 1979-81; chief divsn. plastic surgery Kern Med. Ctr., Bakersfield, Calif., 1983—. Asst. clin. prof. surgery U. Calif., San Diego, 1983-98. Mem. Am. Soc. Plastic Surgeons, Mayo Alumni Assn. Avocations: golf, computers. Office: Kern Med Ctr 1830 Flower St Bakersfield CA 93305-4186

PRUSINER, STANLEY BEN, neurology and biochemistry educator, researcher; b. Des Moines, May 28, 1942; s. Lawrence Albert and Miriam (Spigel) Prusiner; children: Helen Chloe, Leah Anne. AB cum laude, U. Pa., 1964, MD, 1968, DS (hon.), 1998; PhD (hon.), Hebrew U., Jerusalem, 1995, René Descartes U., Paris, 1996; DS (hon.), Dartmouth Coll., 1999; DS (hon.), U. Liege, 2000; MD (hon.), U. Bologna, Italy, 2000; DSc (hon.), Pa. State U., 2001. Diplomate Am. Bd. Neurology. Intern in medicine U. Calif., San Francisco, 1968—69, resident in neurology, 1972—74, asst. prof. neurology, 1974—80, assoc. prof., 1980—84, prof., 1984—, prof. biochemistry, 1988—, acad. senate faculty rsch. lectr., 1989—90, prof. virology Berkeley, 1984—, dir. Inst. for Neurodegenerative Diseases, 1999—; founder, chmn. bd. dirs. InPro Biotech. Inc., South San Francisco, Calif., 2001—. Mem. neurology rev. com. Nat. Inst. for Neurodegenerative Diseases, NIH, Bethesda, Md., 1982—86, Bethesda, 1990—92; mem. Coun. Nat. Inst. Aging, NIH, Bethesda, Md., 2001—; mem. sci. adv. bd. French Found., L.A., 1985—, chmn. sci. adv. bd., 1996—; mem. sci. rev. com. Alzheimer's Disease Diagnostic Ctr. & Rsch Grant Program, State of Calif., 1985—89; chmn. sci. adv. bd. Am. Health Assistance Found., Rockville, Md., 1986—2000, hon. mem. bd. dirs., 2001—; mem. spongiform encephalopathy adv. com. FDA, 1997—2001; mem. adv. bd.Family Survival Project for Adults with Chronic Brain Disorders, San Francisco, 1982—90; mem. adv. bd. San Francisco chpt. Alzheimer's Disease and Related Disorders Found., 1985—91; mem. bd. dirs. Fromm Inst. for Lifelong Learning, San Francisco, 2002—; cons. Inst. of Medicine Com. on Advancing Prion Sci., Washington, 2002—03; mem. bd. govs. Found. for Biomed. Rsch., Washington, 2002—; bd. dirs. Internat. Longevity Ctr., N.Y.C., 2003—. Editor: The Enzymes of Glutamine Metabolism, 1973, Slow Transmissible Diseases of the Nervous System, 2 vols., 1979, Prions--Novel Infectious Pathogens Causing Scrapie and CJD, 1987, Prion Diseases of Humans and Animals, 1992, Molecular and Genetic Basis of Neurologic Disease, 3d edit., 2003, Prions Prions Prions, 1996, Prion Biology and Diseases, 2d edit., 2004; contbr. more than 300 articles to profl. jours. Trustee U. Pa., 2000—, Congregation Sherith Israel, San Francisco, 1999—2002. Lt. comdr. USPHS, 1969—72. Recipient Leadership and Excellence for Alzheimer's Disease award, NIH, 1990—97, Potamkin prize for Alzheimer's Disease Rsch., 1991, Med. Rsch. award, Met. Life Found., 1992, Christopher Columbus Discovery award, NIH and Med. Soc. Genoa, Italy, 1992, Charles A. Dana award, 1992, Dickson prize, U. Pitts., 1992, Max Planck Rsch. award, Alexander von Humboldt Found. and Max Planck Soc., 1992, Gairdner Found. Internat. award, 1993, Disting. Achievement in Neurosci. Rsch. award, Bristol-Myers Squibb, 1994, Albert Lasker award for Basic Med. Rsch., 1994, Caledonian Rsch. Found. prize, Royal Soc. Edinburgh, 1995, Paul Ehrlich and Ludwig Darmstaedter award, Germany, 1995, Paul Hoch award, Am. Psychopathol. Assn., 1995, Wolf prize in medicine, 1996, ICN Virology prize, 1996, Victor and Clara Soriano award, World Fedn. Neurology, 1996, Pasarow Found. prize, 1996, Charles Leopole Mayer prize, French Acad. Scis., 1996, Keio Internat. prize, 1996, Baxter award, Am. Assn. Med. Colls., 1996, Louisa Gross Horwitz prize, Columbia U., 1997, Nobel Prize for Medicine, 1997, K.J. Zulch prize, Gertrude Reemtsma Found., 1997, Benjamin Franklin medal, Franklin Inst., 1998, Jubilee medal, Swedish Med. Soc., 1998, Prize Lecture medal, U. Coll. London, 1999, Sir Hans Krebs medal, Fedn. European Biochem. Socs., 1999, Ellen Browning Scripps medal, 2000, Disting. Alumni award, Coll. Arts and Scis., U. of Pa., 2003, Disting. Med. Grad. award, U. Pa. Sch. Medicine, 1991; fellow Alfred P. Sloan Rsch. fellow, U. Calif., 1976—78; grantee Med. Investigator grantee, Howard Hughes Med. Inst., 1976—81, grantee for excellence in neurosci., Senator Jacob Javits Ctr., NIH, 1985—90. Fellow: AAAS, Royal Coll. Physicians, Am. Acad. Arts & Scis., Am. Soc. Microbiology; mem.: NAS (Inst. Medicine, Richard Lounsbery award for extraordinary achievements in biology and medicine 1993), World Jewish Acad. Scis., Serbian Acad. Scis., Polish Acad. Medicine (Golden Medal Medicus Magnus 2003), Protein Soc. (Amgen award 1997), Royal Soc. London, Am. Philos. Soc., Am. Soc. Molecular Biol. Biochemistry, Am. Soc. Cellular Biology, Am. Soc. Cell Biology, Genetics Soc. Am., Am. Soc. Human Genetics, Soc. Neurosci., Am. Chem. Soc., Am. Soc. Biochemistry and Molecular Biology, Am. Soc. Clin. Investigation, Am. Neurol. Assn., Am. Soc. Virology, Am. Soc. Neurochemistry, Am. Soc. Neurochemistry, Am. Assn. Physicians, Am. Acad. Neurology (George Cotzias award for outstanding rsch. 1987, Presdl. award 1993, Disting. Achievement award 1998), Bohemian Club, Concordia Argonaut Club (bd. dirs. 1997—).

PRUSOFF, WILLIAM HERMAN, biochemical pharmacologist, educator; b. N.Y.C., June 25, 1920; s. Samuel and Mary (Metrick) P.; m. Brigitte Auerbach, June 19, 1948 (dec. Apr. 1991); children— Alvin Saul, Laura Ann. BA, U. Miami, Fla., 1941; MA, Columbia U., 1947, PhD, 1949. Research assoc., instr. pharmacology Western Res. U., 1949-53; mem. faculty Yale Med. Sch., 1953—, prof. pharmacology, 1966-90, prof. emeritus. sr. rsch. scientist, 1990—, acting chmn. dept., 1968. Cons. in field, 1965— Mem. Am. Assn. Cancer Rsch., Am. Chem. Soc., Am. Soc. Biol. Chemists, Am. Soc. Pharmacology and Exptl. Therapeutics, Soc. Chinese Bioscientists in Am., Sigma Xi, Internat. Soc. for Antiviral Rsch. Achievements include rsch. in virology, photochemistry, mechanism drug action, synthesis potential drugs; synthesized Idoxuridine; developed (in collaboration with D.T.S. Lin) Stavudine for therapy of AIDS. Home: De Forest Dr Branford CT 06405 Office: Yale U Sch Medicine New Haven CT 06510 Office Phone: 203-785-4378. E-mail: William.Prusoff@yale.edu.

PRUSSIN, JEFFREY A. management consultant; b. Bklyn., Aug. 11, 1943; s. Samuel and Shirley (Solomon) P.; m. Judith H. May; children: Aaron Justin, Leya Monique. AB, UCLA, 1965; MA, Johns Hopkins U., 1967. Dir. edn. and tng. Group Health Assn. Am., Washington, 1971-72; mgr. prog. devel. Health System div. Westinghouse, Columbia, Md., 1972-73; prin. Health Care Orgn., Delivery & Fin. System, Kensington, Md., 1973-80; exec. asst. for policy Bur. Health Facilities, HHS, Washington, 1980-81; exec. v.p. Comprehensive Am. Care, Miami, Fla., 1981-84; sr. v.p. Internat. Med. Ctrs., Miami, 1984-86; pres. Health Sys. Devel. Corp., South Miami, Fla., 1986-99, J&JP Funding Corp., Jacksonville, Fla., 1999—. Cons. in field; lectr. in field; adj. prof. U. Miami, Fla., 1982-99; vis. asst. prof. Oreg. State U., Eugene, 1970; adj. asst. prof. Linfield Coll., Oreg., 1969-70, Portland State U., 1969-70. Contbr. numerous articles to profl. jours., author: Health Maintenance Organization Legislation in 1973-74, 1974, Employee Health Benefits: HMOs and Mandatory Dual Choide, 1976, Results of a State-of-the-Art Review of Health Assurance for the Elderly, 1979, (with Judith M. Prussin), Health Services and the Elderly: A Comprehensive, Annotated Bibliography, 1982, (with Jack C. Wood), Topics in Health Care Financing: Private Third Party Reimbursement, 1975. Mem. Fla. Assn. Health, Maint. Orgns. (pres. 1985-86), Group Health Assn. Am. Office: J & JP Funding Corp PO Box 600580 Jacksonville FL 32260-0580 E-mail: japrussin@aol.com.

PRUSSING, LAUREL LUNT, public interest lobbyist, economist, auditor; b. N.Y.C., Feb. 21, 1941; d. Richard Valentine and Maria (Rinaldi) Lunt; m. John Edward Prussing, May 29, 1965; children: Heidi Elizabeth, Erica Stephanie, Victoria Nicole Johanna. AB, Wellesley Coll., 1962; MA, Boston U., 1964; postgrad., U. Calif., San Diego, 1968-69, U. Ill., 1970-76. Economist Arthur D. Little, Cambridge, Mass., 1963-67, U. Ill., Urbana, 1971 72; mem. county bd. Champaign County, Urbana, 1972-76, county auditor, 1976-92; legis. dir. ERA Ill., 2002—03; founder ERA Yes!, 2003. Mem. local audit adv. bd. Office Ill. Compt., Chgo., 1984-92. Contbr. to Illinois Local Government: A Handbook, 1990. Founding mem. Citizens Forum on Gambling and Campaign Fin. Reform, 1999; downstate program dir. Citizen Action/Ill., 1999; lobbyist AAUW, Ill., Inc., 2001, 2004; mem. Champaign-Urbana Mass Transit Dist. Bd., 2004—; state rep. 103d dist. Ill. Gen. Assembly, 1993—95; Dem. nominee Ill. 15th dist. U.S. Congress, 1996—98. Named Best Freshman Legislator Ind. Voters Ill., 1994; recipient Friend of Agriculture award Ill. Farm Bur., 1994; named to Legis. Honor Roll Ill. Environ. Coun., 1994. Mem. AAUW, NAACP, LWV, Govt. Fin. Officers Assn., U.S. and Can. (com. on acctg., auditing and fin. reporting 1980-88, Fin. Reporting award 1981-91, Disting. Budget award 1986), Nat. Assn. Local Govt. Auditors (charter), Ill. Assn. County Auditors (pres. 1984-85). Democrat. Home: 2106 Grange Dr Urbana IL 61801-6609 Office Phone: 217-328-2071.

PRUTER, KARL HUGO, bishop; b. Poughkeepsie, N.Y., July 3, 1920; s. William Karl and Katherine (Rehling) P.; m. Nancy Lee Taylor, 1943; children: Hugo Jr., Robert, Karl, Stephen, Maurice, Katherine, Nancy Tenney. BA, Northeastern U., 1943; M.Div., Lutheran Theol. Sem., Phila., 1945; MA in Edn., Roosevelt U., 1963; MA in History, Boston U., 1968. Guest lectr. Landerziehungsheim, Stein, Germany, 1964—65; ordained priest Christ Catholic Ch., 1965; pastor Ch. of the Transfiguration, Boston, 1965—70; bishop Christ Cath. Ch., 1967—. Author: The Theology of Congregationalism, 1953, The Teachings of the Great Mystics, 1969, A History of the Old Catholic Church, 1973, The People of God, 1975, The Jewish Christians in the United States, 1985 Mem. Christ Catholic Ch. Address: Cathedral of Prince of Peace Highlandville MO 65669

PRUTER, MARGARET FRANSON, editor; b. Oak Park, Ill., Jan. 16; d. Frederick G. and Margaret K. (Svoboda) Franson; m. Robert D. Pruter, July 22, 1972; 1 child, Robin. AB, Dominican U., 1961; MA, Northwestern U., 1965. Asst. editor Am. People's Ency., Chgo., 1961-62; rsch. assoc. AMA, Chgo., 1962-63; asst. editor New Standard Ency., Chgo., 1964-66, assoc. editor, 1966-75, sr. editor, 1975-96; editl. dir. Elmhurst (Ill.) Editl. Svcs., 1996—; editor McDougal Littell, Evanston, Ill., 1997—. Exec. dir. Militaria Archives, Elmhurst, Ill., 1972—. Co-author: DuPage Roots, 1985 (Ill. State Hist. Publ. award 1986). Mem. Elmhurst Hist. Commn., 1981—, v.p., 1995—2000, pres., 2000—01; mem. Friends of Elmhurst Pub. Libr., Elmhurst Art Mus. Found.; exec. bd. North Ctrl. Coll. Parents Assn., 1995—98; bd. dirs. DuPage County Hist. Soc., Wheaton, Ill., 1982—, DuPage County Sesquicentennial Com., 1988—89. Mem.: AAUW (bd. dirs. Elmhurst br. 1995—99), Nat. Conf. for the Social Studies, Nature Conservancy, Arch. Conservancy, Am. Studies Assn., Nat. Women's History Mus., Nat. Trust Historic Preservation, Orgn. Am. Historians, Nat. Parks and Conservation Assn., Ill. Hist. Soc., Elmhurst Hist. Soc., Chgo. Women in Pub., Sisters in Crime, Byrd's Nest Chapel Questers (pres. 1992—94, 2003—), Chgo. Hist. Soc., Chgo. Architecture Found., World Wildlife Fed., Sierra Club. Office: Elmhurst Editorial Svcs PO Box 768 Elmhurst IL 60126-0768

PRUTER, ROBERT DOUGLAS, librarian; b. Phila., July 1, 1944; s. Hugo Rehling and Nancy Lee (Taylor) P.; m. Margaret Franson; 1 child, Robin Franson. BA, Roosevelt U., 1967, MA, 1976; MLS, Dominican U., 2000. Asst. editor New Std. Ency., Chgo., 1969-74, assoc. editor, 1974-79, sr. editor, 1979-96; sr. rsch. assoc. Planning Comms., 1996-97; asst. editor Charles D. Spencer & Assocs., Chgo., 1997-98, assoc. editor, 1999-2001; govt. documents lib. Lewis U., Romeoville, Ill., 2001—. Author: Chicago Soul, 1991, Doowop: The Chicago Scene, 1996; editor: Blackwell Guide to Soul Recordings, 1993; adv. editor Popular Music and Society, 1995—; rhythm and blues editor Goldmine Mag., 1984—. Mem. adv. com. Chgo. Blues Festival, 1992—. Served U.S. Army, 1967-69, Vietnam. Mem.: NARAS, Soc. Midland Authors, Chgo. Hist. Soc., Ill. Hist. Soc., N.Am. Soc. for Sport History. Democrat. Avocations: collecting records, sports history rsch. Office Phone: 815-836-5664.

PRUZAN, IRENE, arts administrator, music educator, flutist, marketing and public relations specialist; b. Watertown, N.Y., Jan. 3, 1949; d. John Edward and Esther (Coahn) P.; m. Charles G. Ullery, Jan. 30, 1972 (div. 1978); m. Charles Robert Freeman, May 20, 1988. Student, U. Ariz., 1966-68; MusB, U. So. Calif., 1971; postgrad., San Francisco State U., 1972-74, U. Minn., 1976-80. Tchr. flute, coach chamber music MacPhail Ctr. for Arts, U. Minn., Mpls., 1976-85, coordinator instrumental music, 1978-81, program dir. instrumental music, 1982-85, div. head of programs, 1985-86; regional dir. Music On The Move, Inc., Valley Cottage, NY, 1986-87; pres. Music On the Move Minn., Inc., St. Paul, 1987—2002, cons., 2002—. Founding mem. Crocus Hill Trio, 1976—; pub. rels. cons. Sch. of Music, U. Minn., 1991; faculty Nat. Music Camp, Interlochen, Mich., 1983, 84; cons. edn. and festival Ordway Music Theatre, St. Paul, 1985-87; mgr. Sartory String Quartet, Mpls., 1986-93; developer numerous master classes. Writer teaching materials for flute. Bd. directors Twin Cities Friends of Chamber Music, 1982—89; mem. Ariz. Chamber Orch., Tucson, 1967, San Gabriel (Calif.) Symphony, 1968—71; extra player St. Paul Chamber Orch., 1977—91; organizer German jazz residency USIA, Minn. and Wis., 1986; edn. com. Orlando Philharm., 2001—; cons., program dir. Young Audiences Minn., Mpls., 1986—88. Mem.: Orlando Musicians Union, Twin Cities Musicians Union, Nat. Flute Assn. (dir. mktg. 1987—90, dir. pub. rels. 2004—). Avocation: tennis.

PRUZANSKY, JOSHUA MURDOCK, lawyer; b. NYC, Mar. 16, 1940; s. Louis and Rose (Murdock) P.; m. Susan R. Bernstein, Aug. 31, 1980; 1 child, Dina Gabrielle. BA, Columbia Coll., 1960, JD, 1965. Bar: N.Y., 1965, U.S. Dist. Ct. (ea. and so. dists.) N.Y., 1968, U.S. Supreme Ct., 1980. Ptnr. Scheinberg, DePetris & Pruzansky, Riverhead, NY, 1965-85, Greshin, Ziegler & Pruzansky, Smithtown, NY, 1985-2000, Pruzansky & Besunder, LLP, Islandia, NY, 2001—. NY State Bar Assoc., pres., ho. dels. 1982-, exec. com. 1992-99, spl com. women and law 1986-91, task force on small firms 1991-1992, spl. com. on MDP 1999-2000, chair spl. com., fiduciary appts., 2003—, trusts and estates sect., gen. practice, elder law sects.), 1997-98; mem. exec. coun. NY State Conf. Bar Leaders, 1984—, chmn., 1988-89; mem. grievance com. Appellate Divsn. 10th Judicial Dist., 1992-96; mem. adv. bd. Ticor Title Guarantee Co., 1992-2001; mem. LI adv. bd. HSBC Bank, 1995—; dir. NY State Com. for Modern Ct., 1998—; mem. adv. task force NY Dept. State Corps., 1998—. Mem. bd. visitors Columbia Law Sch., 1998-2004; chair bd. visitors Touro Law Sch., 1998—; dir., sec. L.I. Mus., 1998-2004. Fellow ABA Found., NY State Bar Found. (bd. dir. 1994-2003); mem. ABA (ho. of dels. 1997-2003, probate and real property sect., standing com. on solo and small firm practitioners 1998-2000, NY state del. Caucus of State Bar Assns.), Suffolk County Bar Assn. (bd. dir. 1979-89, pres. 1985-86), NY County Lawyers Assn., Nassau County Bar Assn. Office: Pruzansky & Besunder LLP One Suffolk Sq Ste 315 Islandia NY 11749 E-mail: pruzansk@villagenet.com.

PRYCE, DEBORAH D. congresswoman; b. Warren, Ohio, July 29, 1951; BA cum laude, Ohio State U., 1973; JD with honors, Capital U., 1976. Bar: Ohio 1976. Former asst. city prosecutor, asst. city atty., first asst. city prosecutor, Columbus, Ohio; former judge Franklin County Mcpl. Ct., Columbus; mem. U.S. Congress from 15th Ohio dist., Washington, 1993—, mem. rules com., chair subcom. on legis. budget process, mem. select com. on homeland security, chair Ho. Rep. Conf., 2003—. Republican. Presbyterian. Avocation: skiing. Office: US Ho Reps 221 Cannon Ho Office Bldg Washington DC 20515-0001

PRYCE, JONATHAN, actor; b. North Wales, June 1, 1947; Appearences include (stage) Liverpool Everyman, 1972, Nottingham Playhouse, Comedians, 1977 (Tony award, Theatre World award), 1980, Hamlet (Olivier award), 1986, Macbeth, The Caretaker, 1981, Accidental Death of an Anarchist, 1984, The Seagull, 1986, Uncle Vanya, 1989, Miss Saigon, 1991 (Tony award, Olivier award), Oliver, 1995, My Fair Lady, 2001-02, A Reckoning, 2003, The Goat or Who Is Sylvia, 2004; (films) Voyage of the Damned, 1976, Breaking Glass, 1980, Loophole, 1981, Praying Mantis, 1982, The Plowman's Lunch, 1983, Something Wicked This Way Comes, 1983, Brazil, 1985, The Doctor and the Devils, 1985, Haunted Honeymoon, 1986, Jumpin Jack Flash, 1986, Hotel London, 1987, Man On Fire, 1987, The Adventures of Baron Munchausen, 1988, Consuming Passions, 1988, The Rachel Papers, 1989, Glengarry Glen Ross, 1992, The Age of Innocence, 1993, Shopping, 1994, A Business Affair, 1994, Carrington, 1996 (Best Actor award Cannes Film Festival 1995), Evita, 1996, Tomorrow Never Dies, 1997, Regeneration, 1997, Ronin, 1998, Stigmata, 1999, Very Annie Mary, 2001, Unconditional Love, 2001, Bride of the Wind, 2002, The Affair of the Necklace, 2002, What a Girl Wants, 2003, Pirates of the Caribbean, 2003, De Lovely, 2004, The Brothers Grimm, 2004; (TV movie) Barbarians at the Gate, HBO, 1993 (Emmy nomination, Supporting Actor - Miniseries or Special, 1993), David, 1997, Confessions of an Ugly Stepsister, 2002. Recipient BAFTA Cymru spl. award, 2002. Address: Julian Belfrage Assocs 46 Albermarle St London WIX 4pp England also: UTA 9560 Wilshire Blvd Beverly Hills CA 90212

PRYOR, DAVID BRAM, health science association administrator; b. Charleston, SC, Oct. 18, 1951; s. Sydney and Grace Prystowsky; m. Christin Marie Kennedy; children: Rebecca Whitaker, Rachel Celia, Grace Eileen. Attended, U. Mich., Ann Arbor, 1969—72; MD, U. Mich. Med. Sch., 1972—76. Cert. Am. Bd. Internal Medicine, 1979, bd. cert. cardiovascular diseases 1983, lic. Pa., 1976, NC, 1979, Mass., 1994, Minn., 1996. Intern in medicine Pa. Hosp., Phila., 1976—77, resident in medicine, 1977—79; fellow in cardiology Duke U. Med. Ctr., Durham, NC, 1979—81, asst. prof. medicine, 1983—89, assoc. prof. medicine, 1989—94; sr. staff mem. cardiovascular divsn. Duke U., Durham, NC, 1981—94, dir. section clinical epidemiology and biostatistics, 1984—89, dir. clinical program devel., 1993—94; pres. New England Med. Ctr. Hosp., Boston, 1994—95; prof. medicine Tufts U. Sch. Medicine, 1994—97; sr. v.p./chief info. officer Allina Health Sys., Mpls., 1995—2001; sr. v.p. clinical excellence Ascension Health, St. Louis, 2001—. Program com. and biometry track chair 11th Symposium on Computer Applications in Med. Care, 1987; bd. dir. Clinical Rsch. Internat., Inc., 1989—90, PatientKeeper (Virtmed) Inc., 2001—; chmn. task force reducing med. uncertainty Joint Commn. Accreditation Healthcare Orgn., 1989—91, adv. coun. performance measurement, 1995—, chmn. adv. coun. performance measurement, 1998—2003, mem. performance measurement coord. com., 1998—2000; chmn. epidemiology and prevention track Am. Coll. Cardiology Sci. Session Com., 1991—92, chmn. health svc. delivery track, 1991—92; mem. exec. com. and steering com. Health Care Financing Adminstrn., Coop. Cardiovascular Project, 1992—94; chmn. ops. com. Acad. Med. Ctr. Consortium, 1992—94; mem. sci. session program com. Am. Heart Assn., 1994—96; chmn. bd. dir. Strategicare, Inc., 1996—99; bd. gov. Bioengineering Inst., U. Minn., Mpls., 1996—2002; mem. 2000 Spring Congress Sci. Program com. Am. Med. Informatics Assn. (AMIA), 1999—2000; mem. IT expert adv. panel Nat. Quality Forum (NQF) Nat. Forum for Health Care Quality Measurement and Reporting, 2001—02; mem. adv. bd. Ctr. Info. Tech. Leadership (CITL), 2001—; cons. prof. Cardiovascular Inst., Favaloro Found., Buenos Aires, 1994—97; cons. assoc. prof. medicine Duke U. Med. Ctr., 1994—; adj. prof. epidemiology U. Minn. Sch. Pub. Health, Mpls., 1996—2002; pres. New England Med. Ctr., Boston, 1994—95; adj. prof. St. Louis U. Sch. Pub. Health; numerous positions with Allina Health Sys., Mpls., 1995—2001; reviewer numerous jour. and rsch. grants; presenter in field; mem. numerous nat. and internat. com.; cons. in field. Contbr. articles to jour., chapters to books. Named Laureate, Computerworld Smithsonian award, Allina Health Sys., 1999; named one of 100 Most Powerful People in Healthcare, Modern Healthcare, 2002; recipient Innovations in IT awards, 2nd place, HIMMS and Deloitte and Touche (Allina Health Sys.), 1998, Tng. for Future, 3rd place, Allina Health Sys., 1998, Quest for Best award, 2000, Silver award, 2001; fellow, Am. Coll. Med. Informatics, 1986, Am. Soc. Clinical Investigation, 1992. Fellow: Am. Coll. Med. Informatics, Am. Coll. Physicians, Am. Coll. Cardiology; mem.: Am. Med. Informatics Assn., Am. Heart Assn. (fellow coun. on clinical cardiology), Am. Soc. Clinical Investigation, Am. Fedn. Clinical Rsch. Office: Ascension Health 4600 Edmundson Rd Saint Louis MO 63134 Office Phone: 314-733-8192. Office Fax: 314-733-8011. Business E-Mail: dpryor@ascensionhealth.org.

PRYOR, DAVID HAMPTON, former senator; b. Camden, Ark., Aug. 29, 1934; s. Edgar and Susan (Newton) P.; m. Barbara Lunsford, Nov. 27, 1957; children— David, Mark, Scott. BA in Polit. Sci, U. Ark., 1957, LL.B., 1961. Bar: Ark. 1964. Lawyer, Camden; mem. firm Pryor and Barnes; founder, pub. Ouachita Citizen newspaper, Camden, 1957-60; mem. Ark. Ho. of Reps., 1961-65, 89th-92d Congresses from 4th Ark. dist.; gov. of Ark., 1974-79; senator from Ark., 1979-96. Ranking min. mem. Select Com. On Aging, Nutrition and Forestry Subcom. on Prodn. and Price Competitiveness, Fin. Subcom. on Long Term Growth, Debt. and Deficit Reduction; mem. Govt. Affairs, Sen. Dem. Conf. Com., Sen. Dem. Steering and Coord. Com., Dem. Senatorial Campign Com. Bd. trustees William Jefferson Clinton Presdl. Libr. Found. Fellow Inst. Politics Sch. Govt. Harvard U., 1999. Office: 2701 Kavanaugh Blvd Ste 300 Little Rock AR 72205-3800

PRYOR, ERIC JON, minister, writer; b. Suffern, N.Y., July 16, 1959; s. Peter Anthony Pryor and Joanne Carol Roefs, Nancy Long (Stepmother) and Walter Little Brown(Stepfather); m. Renee Borg, July 16, 1998; children: Christopher Borg, Sarah Borg. MFA, N.Y. Ctr. Media Arts, 1986; DDiv (hon.), Earth Star Temple, 1987. Ordained to ministry Jubilee Christian Ctr., 1995. Founder, min. Nefom Temple, Woodstock, NY, 1980—2004, New Earth Temple, San Francisco, 1987—90; founder, CEO Christian Gladiators Ministry, Sparks, Nev., 1991—2004, Peculiar Nation Prodns., Sparks, 1997—. Media cons. Jubilee Christian Ctr., San Jose, Calif., 1990—2004. Author: Book of Pagan Rituals, Crash and Burn, What is a Witch Really, My Testemony From My Own Mouth; The Ruelle Tarot; prodr.: (video) Satan Unvieled, Law Enforcement Guide to Satanic Cults, From Pagan to Pentecost; contbr. video. Spokesperson Pagan Religious Cmty., San Francisco, 1987—90. Conservative. Achievements include first to develope the worlds largest networking temples for the practicing Pagan community, and Occultist. Avocations: fishing, drag racing, horseback riding, scuba diving, skydiving. Home: 3230 Wedekind Road #116 Sparks NV 89431 Office Phone: 408-262-0900. E-mail: ohwiseone1@yahoo.com.

PRYOR, FREDERIC L. economist, educator; b. Apr. 23, 1933; s. Millard H. and Mary S. Pryor; m. Zora Prochazka, Mar. 26, 1964; 1 child, Daniel. BA, Oberlin (Ohio) Coll., 1955; PhD, Yale U., 1962. Prof. econs. Swarthmore (Pa.) Coll., 1967—2002, sr. rsch. scholar, 2003—. Rsch. dir. Pa. Tax Commn., 1979-81. Author: The Political Economy of Poverty, Equity and Growth: Malawi and Madagascar, 1990, The Red and the Green: The Rise and Fall of Collective Agriculture, 1992, Economic Evolution and Structure, 1995, The Future of U.S. Capitalism, 2002; co-author: Who's Not Working and Why, 1999. Trustee Tougoloo Coll., 1981—. Office: Swarthmore College Ave Swarthmore PA 19081-1390 E-mail: fpryor1@swarthmore.edu.

PRYOR, HAROLD S. retired college president; b. Overton County, Tenn., Oct. 3, 1920; s. Hubert S. and Ethel (Stockton) P.; m. LaRue Vaughn, June 26, 1946. BS, Austin Peay State U., 1946; MA, George Peabody Coll., 1947; Ed.D., U. Tenn., 1951. Instr. George Peabody Coll., Vanderbilt U., 1946-47, E. Tenn. State U., 1947-49, U. Tenn., Knoxville, 1949-51; head dept. edn. Austin Peay State U., 1952, dir. tchr. edn., 1954-68; pres. Columbia (Tenn.) State Community Coll., 1968-84, now pres. emeritus, 1984—. Dir. First Farmers and Merchants Nat. Bank, Columbia, 1970—, First Farmers and Mchts. Corp., 1982—; Columbia State Found., 1971—. Contbr. articles to profl. jours. With U.S. Army, 1943-46. Grantee Dept. Labor; Grantee HEW. Mem. NEA, Tenn. Coll. Assn. (past pres.), Tenn. Edn. Assn., Am. Assn. Higher Edn., Comparative Edn. Soc., Graymere Country Club, Kiwanis, Kappa Delta Pi, Phi Delta Kappa. Democrat. Presbyterian.

PRYOR, HUBERT, editor, writer; b. Buenos Aires, Mar. 18, 1916; (parents Am. citizens); s. John W. and Hilda A. (Cowes) P.; m. Ellen M. Ach, 1940 (div. 1959); children: Alan, Gerald, David. Grad., St. George's Coll., Argentina, 1932; student, U. London, Eng., 1934-36. Corr. in S.Am. for United Press, 1937-39; pub. relations rep. Pan Am. Airways in Buenos Aires, 1939-40; reporter N.Y. Herald Tribune, 1940-41; writer, dir. short-wave newsroom CBS, 1941-46; asst. mng. editor Knickerbocker Weekly, 1946-47; sr. editor Look mag., 1947-62; creative supr. Wilson, Haight & Welch, 1962-63; editor Science Digest, 1963-67; mng. editor Med. World News, 1967; editor NRTA Jour. Modern Maturity, 1967-82; editl. dir. Dynamic Years, 1977-82; publs. coord. Modern Maturity, Dynamic Years, 1982-84; editl. cons., writer, 1985—. Author: Soul Talk, 1995, Eleanor of Palm Beach, 2002. Lt. USNR, 1943-46. Mem. Am. Soc. Mag. Editors, Author's Guild, Overseas Press Club. Home: 3560 S Ocean Blvd Palm Beach FL 33480-5772

PRYOR, JERRY DENNIS, corporate professional; b. Cin., Apr. 11, 1952; s. Cicero and Pauline (Estill) P. BA in History, Lincoln U., 1978. Collector, mgmt. trainee Gem Savs. & Loan, Dayton, Ohio, 1978-81; loan mgr. Maj. Fed. Savs. & Loan, Cin., 1981; acct. receivable mgr. Sonitrol of Cin., 1983-84; sr. adjuster Cen. Trust Bank, Cin., 1984-86; collector Robert Half/ Accountemps, Cin., 1986-97; founder Cin. Empowerment Corp., 1998—. Owner J.D. Pryor & Assocs., 1981—. Treas. Avondale Cmty. Coun.; mentor Taft H.S. and Bloom Middle Sch.; bd. dirs. Avondale Redevel. Corp.; vice chmn. cmty. devel. adv. bd. City of Cin., chmn. housing com.; bd. dirs. Nasus Inc. Honoree Am. Chem. Soc., 1969. Mem. Am. Inst. Banking, MBA Execs. Inc., Real Estate Investor Assn., Am. Inst. Constructors Inc., Civitan Club, Dayton Lodge. Democrat. Baptist. Avocations: softball, basketball, reading, chess. Home: 3455 Knott St Cincinnati OH 45229-2930 Office: Robert Half/Accountemps 201 E 5th St Cincinnati OH 45202-4117 E-mail: jdpryor@one.net., jpryor@stpubs.com.

PRYOR, MARK LUNSFORD, senator; b. Fayetteville, Ark. m. Jill Pryor; children: Adams, Porter. BA in History, U. Ark., 1985, JD, 1988. Pvt. practice Wright, Lindsey & Jennings, Little Rock, 1988—97; mem. Ark. Ho. of Reps., 1990—98, chmn. Freshman Caucus, mem. judiciary com., com. on aging and legis. affairs; atty. gen. State of Ark., 1999—2002; U.S. senator from Ark., 2003—. Democrat. Office: US Senate 217 Russell Senate Office Building Washington DC 20510

PRYOR, RICHARD, actor, writer; b. Peoria, Ill., Dec. 1, 1940; s. Leroy and Gertrude (Thomas) Pryor; m. Jennifer Lee, June 8, 2001; children: Elizabeth Ann, Richard, Rain, Stephen, Gelsey, Franklin. Grad. high sch. Appeared on: Ed Sullivan, Merv Griffin and Johnny Carson television shows in 1960s; appeared in motion pictures The Busy Body, 1967, The Green Berets, 1968, Wild In The Streets, 1968, The Phynx, 1970, Dynamite Chicken, 1970, Lady Sings the Blues, 1972, Hit, 1973, Wattstax, 1973, The Mack, 1973, Some Call It Loving, 1973, Uptown Saturday Night, 1974, Adios Amigos, 1976, The Bingo Long Travelling All-Stars and Motor Kings, 1976, Car Wash, 1976, Silver Streak, 1976, Greased Lightning, 1977, Which Way is Up?, 1977, Blue Collar, 1978, California Suite, 1978, The Wiz, 1978, Richard Pryor Live in Concert, 1979, The Muppet Movie, 1979, Wholly Moses, 1980, In God We Trust, 1980, Stir Crazy, 1980, Bustin' Loose, 1981, Some Kind of Hero, 1982, The Toy, 1982, Superman III, 1983, Richard Pryor Here and Now, 1983, Brewster's Millions, 1985, Critical Condition, 1987, Moving, 1988, See No Evil, Hear No Evil, 1989, Harlem Nights, 1989, Another You, 1991, Lost Highway, 1996, Mad Dog Time, 1996; writer, producer, dir. Jo Jo Dancer Your Life Is Calling, 1986; writer scripts for Flip Wilson; co-writer TV spls. for Lily Tomlin, 1973 (Emmy award); movie script Blazing Saddles, 1973 (Am. Writers Guild award, Am. Acad. Humor award), Lily, 1974 (Am. Acad. Humor award); recorded That Nigger's Crazy, 1974 (Grammy award, certified Gold and Platinum album), Bicentennial Nigger, 1976 (Grammy award); star Richard Pryor Show, NBC-TV, 1977; owner Richard Pryor Enterprises, Inc., Los Angeles, 1975—. Served with U.S. Army, 1958-60. Recipient Grammy award, "...and It's Deep Too!", 2002. Mem. Nat. Acad. Rec. Arts and Scis., Writers Guild Am. Office: Indigo Prodns care Jennifer Lee 4900 Valjean Ave Encino CA 91436-1336

PRYOR, RICHARD WALTER, telecommunications executive, retired air force officer; b. Poplar Bluff, Mo., Nov. 6, 1932; s. Walter V. and Mary (Clifford) P.; m. Barbara LeCompte, Feb. 19, 1955; children: Richard, Susan Davis, Robert, William. B in Gen. Studies, U. Nebr., Omaha, 1972; MA, Webster Coll., St. Louis, 1975. Commd. 2d lt. USAF, 1953, advanced through grades to maj. gen., 1982, ret., 1982; instr. U.S. Air Force Acad.; DVMT engr. space and missile systems USAF, chief of staff Comm. Svcs.; dir. worldwide def. comm. sys. Def. Comm. Agy., 1980-81; pres. ITT World Comm., N.Y.C., 1982-84, ITT Indsl. Transmission Co., N.Y.C.; sr. v.p. engrng. ops. ITT Comm. Svcs. GP; pres., gen. mgr. ITT Christian Rovsing-Copenhagen DK, 1984-86; chmn. Christian-Rovsing Inc., Tulsa; exec. v.p. Electronic Data Sys. (EDS) Comm. Corp., Dallas, 1986-89; pres., COO IMM Corp.-Interdigital AMEX, Phila., 1989-92; chmn., CEO. officer Ultranav Corp, Dallas, 1992—; chmn. Prism Video, Dallas, 1994—; pres. Trans-Tech Holdings Corp., Dallas, 1996—; pres., CEO Unison Corp., Dallas, 1998—, Video Net, Addison, Tex.; chmn., CEO Mega Link Tech., L.A., 2003—, MIUSA, L.A., 2003—. Dir. RPost, L.A., 2000—. Contbr. articles to tech. publs. Assoc. dir. Boy Soucts Am., N.Y.C., 1983. Recipient Cert. of Appreciation Okla. Mental Health Assn., 1979, Kansas City Lions Club, 1974. Mem. Armed Forces Communications and Electronics Assn. (pres. N.Y.C. 1983, nat. dir.), Air Force Assn., Oklahoma City Soc. Profl. Engrs., Canoe Brook Country Club, Army-Navy Club, Phi Alpha Theta. Republican. Roman Catholic. Home: 7802 Mason Dells Dr Dallas TX 75230-2418 Office: Video Net Ste 705 16475 Dallas Pkwy Addison TX 75001 also: 3333 Wilshire Blvd Los Angeles CA 90010

PRYOR, TOMMI THORNBURY, marketing professional; b. Pikeville, Ky., Oct. 21, 1950; d. Joe Warren and Francisanna (Huffman) T. BS in Speech and Journalism, U. Wis., 1972; MA in Comms. Studies, U. Mo, Kansas City, 1980. Registered lobbyist Calif., 2001. Various mktg. positions to CEO Infobahn Industries, Inc., Orange County, Calif., 1995—97; CEO TLC Comms., Ltd., Orange County, Calif., 1998—2002. Dir. Family Entertainment Am., Inc., Laguna Beach, Calif., 1988—90. Author, editor: A Complete How-To Guide for Planning and Implementing a Sucessful Direct Mail Program for Student Recruitment, 1981, A Complete Training Program for Recruiting Students by Telephone, 1981. Cons. Reagan-Bush campaign, Washington, 1984; bd. dirs. Inst. for Christian Statesmanship, Washington, 1985—. Named an Outstanding Young Career Woman of Ea. Kans., Kansas City Bus. and Profl. Women's Clubs, 1976; named to Order of Ky. Cols., Gov. of Ky., 1997. Mem. Direct Mktg. Assn. Washington, Women in Leadership, League Rep. Women, Renaissance Women. Evangelical Christian. Club: Capitol Hill. Avocation: writing, gourmet cooking, travel, antiquing.

PRYOR, WILLIAM DANIEL LEE, humanities educator; b. Lakeland, Fla., Oct. 29, 1926; s. Dahl and Lottie Mae (Merchant) P. AB, Fla. So. Coll., 1949; MA, Fla. State U., 1950, PhD, 1959; postgrad., U. N.C., Chapel Hill, 1952—53; pvt. art study with Florence Wilde; pvt. voice study with Colin O'More, Anna Kaskas; pvt. piano study with Waldemar Hille and audited piano master classes of Ernst von Dohnányi. Asst. prof. English, dir. drama Bridgewater (Va.) Coll., 1950-52; grad. tchg. fellow humanities Fla. State U., Tallahassee, 1953-55, 57-58; instr. English U. Houston, University Park, Houston, 1955-59, asst. prof. University Park, 1959-62, assoc. prof., 1962-71, prof., 1971-97, prof. emeritus, 1997. Vis. instr. English, Fla. So. Coll., Lakeland, MacDill Army Air Base, Tampa, Fla., summer 1951, Tex. So. U., 1961-63; vis. instr. humanities, govt. U. Tex. Dental Br., Houston, 1962-63; lectr. The Women's Inst., Houston, 1967-72; lectr. humanities series Jewish Cmty. Ctr., Houston, 1972-73; originator, moderator TV and radio program The Arts in Houston Stas. KUHT-TV and KUHF-FM, 1956-57, 58-63. Contbg. author: National Poetry Anthology, 1952, Panorama das Literaturas das Americas, vol. 2, 1958-60; assoc. editor Forum, 1967, editor, 1967-82; contbr. articles to profl. jours.; dir. Murder in the Cathedral (T.S. Elliot), U. Houston, 1965; performed in opera as Sir Edgar in Der Junge Lord (Henze), Houston Grand Opera Assn., 1967; played the title role in Aella (Chatterton), Am. premiere, U. Houston, 1970. Bd. dirs., founding mem. Contemporary Music Soc., Houston, 1958-63, Houston Shakespeare Soc., 1964-67; bd. dirs., founding mem., program annotator Houston Chamber Orch. Soc., 1964-76; narrator Houston Symphony Orch., Houston Summer Symphony Orch., Houston Chamber Orch., U. Houston Symphony Orch., St. Stephen's Music Festival Symphony Orch., New Harmony, Ind.; narrator world premier of the Bells (Jerry McCathern), 1969, U. Houston Symphony Orch., 1969, Am. premier Symphony No. Seven, Antartica (Vaughn-Williams), Houston Symphony Orch., 1967, L'Histoire du Soldat (Stravinski), U. Houston Symphony Orch., 1957, Am. premier Babar the Elephant (Poulenc-Francais), Houston Chamber Orch., 1967, Le Roi David (Honegger), 1979, Voice of God in opera Noye's Fludde (Britten), St. Stephen's Music Festival, 1981; bd. dirs., program annotator Music Guild, Houston, 1960-67, v.p., 1963-67, adv. bd., 1967-70; mem.-at-large, bd. dirs. Houston Grand Opera Guild, 1966-67; repertory com. Houston Grand Opera Assn., 1967-70; bd. dirs. Houston Grand Opera, 1970-75, adv. bd. 1978-79; cultural adv. com. Jewish Cmty. Ctr., 1960-66; bd. dirs. Houston Friends Pub. Libr., 1962-67, 73-75, 1st v.p., 1963-67; adv. mem. cultural affairs com. Houston C. of C., 1972-75; adv. bd. dirs. The Wilhelm Schole, 1980-98, Buffalo Bayou Support Com., 1985-87, bd. dirs. Moores Sch. Music Soc., 1998—, trustee, 2002-04, advisory bd. dirs., 2004—; bd. dirs. U. Houston Retiree Assn., 1999-2001, v.p., 2000-2001; founding bd. dirs. Internat. Dohnányi Rsch. Ctr., Inc., 2002-. Recipient Master Tchg. award Coll. Humanities and Fine Arts U., Houston, 1980, Favorite Prof. award Bapt. Student Union, U. Houston, 1991. Mem. MLA, AAUP, Coll. English Assn., L'Alliance Francaise, English-Speaking Union, Alumni Assn. Fla. So. Coll., Fla. State U., South Ctrl. MLA, Conf. Editors Learned Jours., Coll. Conf. Tchrs. English, Nat. Coun. Tchrs. English, Am. Studies Assn., Shepard Soc. Rice U., Nature Conservancy, Nat. Trust for Hist. Preservation, Inst. Internat. Edn., Century Club, Fla. So. Coll., President's Club, James D. Westcott Legacy Soc., Fla. State U., Phi Beta (patron), Phi Mu Alpha Sinfonia, Alpha Psi Omega, Pi Kappa Alpha, Sigma Tau Delta (Outstanding Prof. English U. Houston chpt. 1990), 1927 Soc. U. Houston, Houston Philos. Soc., Tau Kappa Alpha, Phi Kappa Phi, Caledonian Club (London). Episcopalian. Avocations: tennis, racquetball, swimming, travel. Home: 2625 Arbuckle St Houston TX 77005-3929 Office: U Houston Dept English U Park 3801 Cullen Blvd Houston TX 77004-2602 *My commitment is to the humanities. I believe that the most important thing that a teacher can do is to help a student to stand on his/her own intellectual hind legs; to help him/her to learn how to aquire facts; to help him/her to learn how to organize and utilize these facts in intelligent, responsible ways.*

PRYOR, WILLIAM HOLCOMBE, JR., federal judge, former state attorney general; b. Mobile, Ala., Apr. 26, 1962; s. William Holcombe Sr. and Laura Louise (Bowles) Pryor; m. Kristan Camille Wilson, Aug. 15, 1987; children: Caroline Elizabeth, Victoria Camille. BA in Legal Studies with honors, U. of La. (now N.E. La. U.), Monroe, 1984; JD with honors, Tulane U., 1987. Law clk. U.S. Ct. Appeals (5th cir.), Judge John Minor Wisdom, New Orleans, 1987—88; assoc. Cabaniss, Johnston, Gardner, Dumas & O'Neil, Birmingham, Ala., 1988—91, Walston, Stabler, Wells, Anderson & Bains, Birmingham, 1991—95; dep. atty. gen. State of Ala., Montgomery, 1995—97, atty. gen., 1997—2004; judge U.S. Ct. Appeals (11th cir.), 2004—. Adj. prof. Samford U. Cumberland Sch. Law, Birmingham, 1989—94. Bd. student editors: Tulane Law Rev., 1985—86, editor-in-chief:, 1986—87, bd. adv. editors:, 1995—. La. nat. com. Young Rep. Nat. Fedn., 1984—86; mem. Ala. Rep. Exec. Com., 1994—95. Mem.: Amer. Law Inst., Washington Legal Found., Federalist Soc. (assoc.), Order of Coif, Omicron Delta Kappa, Phi Kappa Phi. Republican. Roman Catholic. Office: Elbert B Tuttle US Ct Appeals Bldg 56 Forsyth St NW Atlanta GA 30303*

PRYSBY, CHARLES LEE, political science educator; b. Olympia, Wash., May 11, 1945; s. Charles C. and Rose G. Prysby; m. Anita D. Ebert, June 17, 1967; children: Nicole D., Michelle D. BS in Polit. Sci., Ill. Inst. Tech., 1966; PhD in Polit. Sci., Mich. State U., 1973. NDEA fellow Mich. State U., East Lansing, 1966-69, instr., 1969-71, U. N.C., Greensboro, 1971-73, asst. prof., 1973-78, assoc. prof., 1978-92, prof., 1992—, dept. head, 1993—2002. N.C. state mgr. News Election Service, N.Y.C., 1980-92; N.C. state mgr. Voter News Svc., 1996. Co-author: Voting Behavior: 1972 Election, 1975, Voting Behavior: 1976 Election, 1978, Political Choices, 1980, Voting Behavior: 1980 Election, 1981, Voting Behavior: 1984 Election, 1985, Voting Behavior: 1988 Election, 1989, Political Behavior and the Local Context, 1991, Voting Behavior: 1992 Election, 1993, Voting in Presidential Elections 1972-92, 1995, Voting Behavior: 1996 Election, 1997, Voting Behavior: 2000 Election, 2002, Southern Political Party Activists: Patterns of Conflict and Change, 1991-2001, 2004; contbr. articles to profl. jours. and edited vols. NEH summer seminar fellow, 1978, 83. Mem. N.C. Polit. Sci. Assn. (past-pres. 1984-85), Am. Soc. Pub. Adminstrn. (coun. mem. Piedmont Triad chpt. 1984-85), Am. Polit. Sci. Assn., Southern Polit. Sci. Assn., Midwest Polit. Sci. Assn. Home: 1910 Milan Rd Greensboro NC 27410-2948 Office: Univ NC at Greensboro Dept Polit Sci Greensboro NC 27402-6170 E-mail: prysby@uncg.edu.

PRZEMIENIECKI, JANUSZ STANISLAW, engineering executive, former government senior executive and college dean; b. Lipno, Poland, Jan. 30, 1927; came to U.S., 1961, naturalized, 1967; s. Leon and Maria (Sarnacka) P.; m. Stefania (Fiona) Rudnicka, July 17, 1954; children: Anita, Christopher. BS, U. London, 1949, PhD, 1958; diploma in Aeros., Imperial Coll. Sci. and Tech., 1953; DSc in Engring., U. London, 1988; hon. doctorate Honoris Causa, Warsaw U. Tech., 1999. Registered profl. engr., Ohio. Head structural R & D sect. Bristol Aircraft Ltd., Eng., 1954-61; from assoc. prof. to prof. mechanics Sch. Engring., Air Force Inst. Tech., Wright-Patterson AFB, Ohio, 1961-66, from asst. dean, assoc. dean rsch. to dean, 1966-89, sr. dean, 1970-95; pres. Astra Technologies, Inc., Fla., 1996—. Cons. in field. Author: Theory of Matrix Structural Analysis, 1968, Mathematical Methods in Defense Analyses, 3d edit., 2000, Defense Analyses Software, 1991; assoc. editor: Jour. Aircraft, 1970-71; editl. bd.: Internat. Jour. Numerical Methods in Engring., 1969-75; editor: Mechanics of Structural Systems (textbook series) 1973-89; editor: Critical Technologies for Nat. Defense, 1991, Acquisition of Defense Systems, 1993; contbr. articles to profl. jours. Chmn. bd. trustees The Air Force Inst. Tech. Found., Ohio, 1987-88, trustee, 1993-95; trustee Engring. and Sci. Found. of Dayton, 1984-95. Decorated Polish Underground Army Cross, Warsaw Uprising Cross, Armed Forces medal; recipient USAF superior performance award, 1965, exceptional civilian svc. decoration, 1978, Presdl. rank of Meritorious Exec., 1981, Disting. Exec., 1982, Outstanding Engr. award Dayton Engring. and Sci. Found., 1986, Outstanding Civilian Svc. medal, 1995, Comdrs. Cross of the Polonia Restituta Order by Pres. of Poland, 1995, Disting. Svc. award, Am. Inst. of Polish Culture, 1997. Fellow Royal Aeros. Soc. (Usborne Meml. prize 1959), AIAA (editor-in-chief ednl. series 1981—, Pendray medal 1992), City and Guilds of London Inst.; mem. Am. Soc. Engring. Edn., Ohio Acad. Sci., Polish Inst. Arts and Scis., Tau Beta Pi. Home: 510 Pennyroyal Pl Venice FL 34293-7233

PRZYBYLSKI, SANDRA MARIE, speech pathologist; b. Berwyn, Ill. d. Raymond and Julie Marie (Vocelka) Hammers; m. James Przybylski; children: Eric, Sara. BS, U. Iowa, 1968; MA, U. Ill., 1971. Cert. clin. speech pathologist; speech/lang., educable mentally retarded education, learning disabilites and elem. tchr., life, Mo. Speech, lang. pathologist LaPlata (Mo.) Sch. Dist., 1974-87, Maysville (Mo.) Sch. Dist., 1990-92, Bucklin (Mo.) Sch. Dist., 1992—. Named to Disting. Svc. Registry-Speech and Hearing, 1990. Mem. Am. Speech, Lang., Hearing Assn., Autism Soc. Am., Mo. State Tchrs. Assn., Mo. Speech, Lang. and Hearing Assn. E-mail: sprzy02@yahoo.com., sprzybylski@bucklin.k12.mo.us.

PSALTIS, HELEN, medical and surgical nurse; b. Rockford, Ill., Nov. 27, 1931; d. Harry and Martha (Triantafelakis) P. Diploma, St. Margaret Hosp., Hammond, Ind., 1953; BSN, DePaul U., 1961; MS in Health Edn., Purdue U., 1971; MSN, Purdue U., Calumet, Ind., 1988. RN, Ind., cert. sch. nurse, Ind. Staff nurse U. Ill. Hosp., Chgo., 1959—61, U. Chgo. Hosp., Billings, Ill., 1962; sch. nurse Pub. Sch. City of East Chicago, Ind.; asst. supr., staff nurse, instr. St. Catherine Hosp., East Chicago, Ind., 1962—63; instr., head nurse, staff nurse St Margaret Hosp., Hammond, 1953—58, 1989—, 1963; staff nurse U. Ill. Rsch. Hosp./Chgo. Hosp., 1959—61; asst. supr., staff nurse, inst. St. Catherine Hosp., East Chicago, 1981—91. Mem. ANA, AACCN, Soc. of Critical Care Nursing, Nat. League for Nursing, Sigma Theta Tau. Home: 4303 Ivy St East Chicago IN 46312-3026

PSIHARIS, NICHOLAS See HARRICE, CY

PSILLOS, SUSAN ROSE, artist, educator; b. Bethpage, N.Y., Feb. 15, 1960; d. Reginald and Gloria Barbara Psillos; 1 child, Jennifer Rose. Student, Alfred U., 1978-80; Tchg. Degree in Art, L.I. U., Southampton, 1996. Substitute tchr. art Shoreham-Wading River Sch. Dist., Shoreham, N.Y., 1992—; tchr. arts and crafts Round-out Shoreham-Wading River Sch., Shoreham, 1995-96; tchr. art Bellport (N.Y.) H.S., 1997-98; art tchr. Raynor Country Day Sch., Speonk, N.Y., 1998—, Plainview-Old Bethpage Sch. Dist., 1999—. Guest spkr. in field. Exhibited sculptures at Smithtown (N.Y.) Mus., 1995, 96-97, Bellemeade Gallery, 1997, Knickerbocker Gallery, N.Y.C., 1997, Studio 88, Hampton Bays, N.Y., 1999, Hampton Bays Pub. Libr.; exhibited paintings at Ambiente Gallery, 1991-92, Smithtown Twsp. Art Mus., 1995, 96, Doweling Coll., 1997. Advisor Partnership for Survival, Smithtown, 1991—; bd. dirs., pub. rels. person Sexual Abuse Survivors, Smithtown,1991—. Recipient Art Judge's award Parrish Art Mus., 1976, Outstanding award Sch. Visual Arts, 1976, Profl. Recognition Day award, 1996, Child Abuse & Neglect Family Violence Vol. award Town of Brookhaven. Mem. NOW, N.Y. Art Tchrs. Assn., Artist Support Group. Avocations: cooking, gardening, fine arts, painting, sculpture.

PSOMIADES, HARRY JOHN, political science educator; b. Boston, Sept. 8, 1928; s. John and Koula (Yalmanides) P.; m. Dorothy Smith, Aug. 18, 1962 (dec. Aug. 27, 1984); children— Kathy Alexis, Christine Anne. BA, Boston U., 1953; M.Internat. Affairs, Columbia U., 1955; cert., Middle East Inst., 1956, PhD (Ford Found. fellow), 1962; Litt.D. (hon.), Holy Cross/Hellenic Coll., 1985. Lectr. govt. Columbia U., 1959-65, asst. dean Grad. Sch. Internat. Affairs, 1959-65, dir. Carnegie Endowment Fellowships in Diplomacy, 1959-71; assoc. prof. polit. sci. Queens Coll., City U. N.Y., 1965-69, prof., 1970—2003, chmn. dept. polit. sci., 1967-71, dep. exec. officer Ph.D. program in polit. sci., 1975-76, program dir. seminar on the modern Greek state, 1976—2004; dir. Ctr. Byzantine and Modern Greek Studies, 1976—2004. Cons. faculty U.S. Army Command and Gen. Staff Coll., 1968-86; U.S. Dept. State Fgn. Service Inst., 1968-71; mem. screening com. Fgn. Area Fellowships Program for Asia and Middle East Joint Com., Social Sci. Research Council and Am. Council Learned Socs., 1967-69 Author: Greece and Turkey: Mutual Economic Interests, 1964, (with Thomas Spelios) A Pictorial History of the Greeks, 1967, The Eastern Question: The Last Phase, 1968, 2d edition, 2000, Greek edit., 2004, (with T.A. Couloumbis) Foreign Interference in Greek Polics: An Historical Perspective, 1976, (with A. Scourby) The Greek American Community in Transition, 1982, (with R.S. Orfanos) Education and Greek Americans: Proccess and Prospects, 1987, (with S. Thomadakes) Greece, The New Europe and the Changing International Order, 1993, (with Van Coufoudakis) Greece and the New Balkans: Challenges and Opportunities, 1999, (with Sam Tsemberis) Greek American Famiilies: Traditions and Transformations, 1999; editor: Jour. Modern Hellenism, 1984—; contbr. articles to profl. jours. Served with U.S. Army, 1946-50; to col. AUS, 1950-83. Hon. fellow Soc. Macedonian Studies, Thessaloniki, Greece, 1970—; named Comdr. Order of Honor The Republic of Greece, 1996. Fellow Middle East Studies Assn. N.Am.; mem. Am. Polit. Sci. Assn., Middle East Inst., Modern Greek Studies Assn. (mem. exec. com. 1972-76), Phi Beta Kappa. Greek Orthodox. Home: 440 Riverside Dr New York NY 10027-6828

PSUTY, NORBERT PHILLIP, marine sciences educator; b. Hamtramck, Mich., June 13, 1937; s. Phillip and Jessie (Proszykowski) P.; m. Sylvia Helen Zurinsky, June 13, 1959; children: Eric Anthony, Scott Patrick, Ross Phillip. BS, Wayne State U., 1959; MS, Miami U., Oxford, Ohio, 1960; PhD, La. State U., 1966. Rsch. assoc. Coastal Studies Inst., La. State U., Baton Rouge, 1962-64; instr. dept. geography and dept. geology U. Miami, Coral Gables, Fla., 1964-65; asst. prof. geography U. Wis., Madison, 1965-69; assoc. prof. geography and geol. scis. Rutgers U., New Brunswick, N.J., 1969-73, prof., 1973—2002, chmn. dept. marine and coastal scis., 1991-99, prof. marine and coastal scis., geog., geol. scis., 1989—2002, dir. Marine Scis. Ctr., 1972-76, dir. Ctr. for Coastal and Environ. Studies, 1976-90; assoc. dir. Inst. Marine and Coastal Scis., New Brunswick, 1990—2002; prof. emeritus Rutgers U., 2002—; dir. Sandy Hook Coop. Programs, 2002—. Mem. sci. com. Thalassas, Vigo, Spain, 1985—. Co-author: Living with the New Jersey Shore, 1986, Coastal Dunes, 1990, Coastal Hazard Management, 2002, Coastal Dune Ecology, 2004; mem. editl. bd. Coastal Mgmt., 1981—, Jour. Coastal Rsch., 1987—, Jour. of Coastal Conservation, 1996—; contbr. numerous articles to scholarly jours., chapters to books, monographs. Mem. Water Policy Bd., East Brunswick, NJ, 1981—83, N.J. Shoreline Adv. Bd., Trenton, 1984—86; chmn. N.J. Gov.'s Sea Level Rise Com., Trenton, 1987—90; mem. N.J. State Beach Erosion Commn., 1994—99; referee U.S.A. Volleyball. Recipient Disting. Pub. Svc. award Pres. of Rutgers U. 1988; numerous grants including NSF, Nat. Park Svc., EPA, Office Naval Rsch., Nat. Sea Grant Program, NOAA, 1961—. Mem.: AAAS, N.J. Acad. Sci. (pres. 1982), Internat. Geog. Union (editor newsletter 1984—96, vice chair commn. on coastal environment 1988—92, chmn. commn. on coastal systems 1992—96, editor newsletter 2002—), Coastal Soc. (pres. 1980—82), Assn. Am. Geographers (Honors award 1993), Profl. Assn. Volleyball Ofcls. (chair N.J. bd. 2000—). Avocations: gardening, reading. Office: Rutgers U Inst Marine & Coastal Scis 74 Magruder Rd Highlands NJ 07732 E-mail: psuty@imcs.rutgers.edu.

PTAK, FRANK STANLEY, manufacturing executive; b. Chgo., Apr. 23, 1943; s. Frank J. and Stella R. (Los) P.; m. Karen M. Novoselsky, May 2, 1971; children: Jeffrey B., Jacquelyn F., Russell E. BSc, De Paul U., 1965. CPA, Ill. Sr. auditor Arthur Young & Co., Chgo., 1965-69; sr. rsch. cons. Kemper Fin. Svcs., Chgo., 1969-71; asst. sec., mgr. acquisitions Sara Lee Corp., Chgo., 1971-73, asst. treas., 1973-74, asst. to chmn., 1974, v.p. planning, 1974-75; bus. devel. mgr. ITW Conex, Des Plaines, Ill., 1975-77; mktg. mgr. ITW Shakeproof, Elgin, Ill., 1977-78, group pres., 1977-78, ITW Metal Components Cos., Glenview, Ill., 1978-91; exec. v.p. Global Automotive Components ITW Corp., Glenview, 1991-95, vice-chmn., 1996—. Bd. dirs. Snap-On Inc., The Marmon Group, Gen. Growth Properties, Inc.; adv. coun. DePaul U. Coll. Commerce, Chgo., 1998. Patentee in field. Mem. AICPA, Assn. Corp. Growth, ITW Patent Soc. Jewish. Home: 849 Edgewood Ct Highland Park IL 60035-3714 Office: Illinois Tool Works 3600 W Lake Ave Glenview IL 60025-5811 Business E-Mail: fptak@itw.com.

PTAK, JOHN, talent agent; b. San Diego, Sept. 23, 1942; s. John and Doris Elizabeth P.; m. Margaret Elizabeth Black, May 21, 1981; 1 child, Hillary Elizabeth. BA, UCLA, 1967. Theatre mgr., booker Walter Reade Orgn., Beverly Hills, Calif., 1967-69; adminstrv. exec. Am. Film Inst., Beverly Hills, 1968-70; talent agent Internat. Famous Agy. (now ICM), L.A., 1971-75, William Morris Agy., Beverly Hills, 1976-91, Creative Artists Agy., Beverly Hills, 1991—. Co-chmn. Am. Film Inst. Ctr. for Film & Video Preservation, L.A., 1991—; mem. Nat. Film Preservation Bd., Washington, 1992—. Bd. dirs. Motion Pictures and T.V. Fund Found., 1996—, Nat. Film Preservation Found., 1997—. Avocations: tennis, travel. Office: Creative Artists Agy 9830 Wilshire Blvd Beverly Hills CA 90212-1825

PTASHNE, MARK STEVEN, biochemistry educator; b. Chgo., June 5, 1940; s. Fred and Mildred P. BA, Reed Coll., 1961; PhD, Harvard U., 1968. Lectr. biochemistry Harvard U., Cambridge, Mass., 1968-71, prof., 1971—, chmn. dept. biochemistry and molecular biology, 1980-83, Herchel Smith prof. of molecular biology, 1993-97; Ludwig prof. molecular biology Sloan Kettering Cancer Rsch. Ctr., N.Y.C., 1997—. Feodor Lynen lectr. U. Miami, Fla., 1988. Author: A Genetic Switch, 1986; contbr. numerous articles to sci. jours. Recipient Eli Lilly award, 1975, prix. Charles-Leopold Mayer Acad. des Scis., Inst. de France, 1977, Louisa Gross Horwitz prize Bd. Trustees Columbia U., 1985, Gairdner Found. Internat. award, 1985, Albert Lasker award for Basic Med. Rsch., Lasker Found., 1997; co-recipient Ledle award Harvard U., 1986, GM Sloan prize, 1990. Fellow N.Y. Acad. Sci., Am. Acad. Sci.; mem. NAS, Fedn. Am. Scis. (bd. sponsors 1981). Avocations: opera, classical music. Office: Sloan Kettering Cancer Rsch Ctr 1275 York Ave # New York NY 10021-6094*

PTASYNSKI, HARRY, geologist, oil industry executive; b. Milw., May 26, 1926; s. Stanley S. and Frances V. (Stawicki) Ptasynski; m. Nola G. Whitestine, Sept. 15, 1951; children: Rosa F., Lisa Joy. BS, Stanford U., 1950. Cert. profl. geologist, petroleum geologist. Dist. geologist Pure Oil Co., Amarillo, Tex., 1951-55, Casper, Wyo., 1955-58; ind. geologist, oil prodr. Casper, 1958—. With USN, 1943—46, PTO. Mem.: Soc. Petroleum Engrs., Rocky Mountain Oil and Gas Assn. (bd. dirs., mem. exec. com. 1980—96), Ind. Petroleum Assn. Mountain States (v.p., bd. dirs. 1976—80), Ind. Petroleum Assn. Am. (v.p., bd. dirs. 1976—85), Am. Inst. Profl. Geologists, Am. Assn. Petroleum Geologists. Republican. Episcopalian. Avocations: tennis, trout and salmon fishing, western history, golf. Home: 1515 Brookview Dr Casper WY 82604-4895 Office: 123 W 1st St Ste 560 Casper WY 82601-2483 E-mail: hptasyn@trib.com.

PU, CALTON, computer scientist; BS in Physics, U. Sao Paulo, Brazil, 1978, BS in Computer Sci., 1979; MS, U. Wash., 1983, PhD, 1986. From asst. to assoc. prof. dept. computer sci. Columbia U., 1986-92; assoc. prof. dept. computer sci. and engring. Oreg. Grad. Inst. Sci. and Tech., Portland, 1993-96, prof. dept. computer sci. and engring., 1996-99; prof., John P. Imlay Jr. chair in software Ga. Inst. Tech., Atlanta, 1999—. Vis. rsch. scientist IBM T.J. Watson Rsch. Ctr., summer 1990-91; co-gen. chair Internat. Conf. on Data Engring., 1997, co-PC chair, 1999; vice-chair Heterogeneous Sys. Interoperability, 1995, program com. 1993-95; program. com. Internat. Conf. on Partial Evaluation and Program Manipulation, 1997, Internat. Conf. on Distributed Computing Sys., 1989, 91, 93, 97; co-chair program com. Am. and Pacific Rim Internat. Symposium on Reliable Distributed Sys., 1995, 2003; presenter in field. Mem. editl. bd. Internat. Jour. Digital Libr., 1995—, Jour. Brazilian Computer Soc.; patentee apparatus and method for certifying the delivery of information. Grantee NSF, 1991—, DARPA, 1994—. Mem. ACM; sr. mem. IEEE; fellow AAAS. Office: Ga Inst Tech Coll of Computing 801 Atlantic Dr Atlanta GA 30332-0280 Office Phone: 404-385-1106. Business E-Mail: calton.pu@cc.gatech.edu.

PUANGSUVAN, SOMPORN, surgeon, consultant; b. Rajburi, Thailand, 1941; came to U.S., 1967; s. Boon and Sanguan P.; m. Chintana Chanvitayapongs, Mar. 18, 1978; children: Nick, Neesann. MD, Chiengmai (Thailand) Hosp. U., 1966. Diplomate Am. Bd. Surgery. Intern St. Clares Hosp., N.Y.C., 1967-68; resident Aultman Hosp., Canton, Ohio, 1968-69, Tuskegee (Ala.) VA Hosp., 1969-73; pvt. practice, Caruthersville, Mo., 1979—. Attending physician Pemiscot County Meml. Hosp., Hayti, Mo., chief surgery 1994, surg. cons. 1979—. Fellow ACS. Office: Doctors Clinic PO Box 201 Caruthersville MO 63830-0201

PUCCIATTI, SANDRA MILSTEIN, opera company director; b. Phila., June 14, 1952; d. Harvey Jack Milstein and Beverly Goldberg; m. Joseph Robert Pucciatti, Oct. 2, 1977; 1 child, Rachel Shabana. MusB summa cum laude, Temple U., 1974; MA, Coll. N.J., 1980. Co-founder, adminstr. The Boheme Club, Inc., Trenton, N.J., 1981-89; co-founder, music dir. Boheme Opera Co. N.J., Trenton, 1989-95, mng. dir., 1995—. Piano and ensemble coach N.J. Gov.'s Sch. of Arts, Ewing, N.J., summers 1993-2000; program coord. Inside Opera program Boheme Opera N.J., Mercer County, 1999—. Co-dir. Congregation Beth Chaim Choir, Princeton Junction, N.J., 1980—. Mem. Opera Am., N.J. Art Pride, Trenton Torch Club. Avocations: chamber music, gardening, lecturing about opera medium. Home: 108 Fetter Ave Trenton NJ 08610-3510 Office: Boheme Opera NJ 1 Municipal Dr Hamilton NJ 08619-3809 E-mail: jrspuce@aol.com.

PUCCIO, THOMAS P. lawyer; b. N.Y.C., 1944; BA, Fordham U., 1966, JD, 1969. Bar: N.Y. 1969, U.S. Ct. Appeals (2d cir.) 1970, D.C. 1982, U.S. Supreme Ct. 1982, U.S. Ct. Appeals (4th and 9th cirs.) 1993. Lawyer Office U.S. Atty. Ea. Dist. N.Y., 1969—76, chief criminal divsn., 1973—75; exec. asst. U.S. atty., 1975—76; chief U.S. Dept. Justice Strike Force, 1976—82; pvt. practice N.Y.C., 1982—. Mem.: Assn. Bar City N.Y., D.C. Bar, Fed. Bar Coun. Office: Ste 301 230 Park Ave New York NY 10169

PUCEL, ROBERT ALBIN, electronics research engineer; b. Ely, Minn., Dec. 27, 1926; s. Joseph and Theresa (Francel) P.; m. Catherine Ann Silva, June 30, 1952; children: Robert W., James J., Valerie A., Marc R., David J. BS, MS, MIT, 1951, DSc, 1955. With rsch. div. Research div. Raytheon Co., Lexington, Mass., 1955-93, staff mem. microwave tube group, 1951-55, solid state physics group, 1955-65, project mgr. microwave semicondr. group, 1965-70, cons. to microwave semicondr. group, 1970-74, cons. scientist semicondr. group, 1974-93; pres. RCP Cons., Jewett City, Conn., 1994—. Lectr. on monolithic microwave integrated circuits Editor: Monolithic Microwave Integrated Circuits, 1985; contbg. author: Advances in Electronics and Electron Physics, vol. 38, 1975, Gallium Arsenide Technology, 1985. Served with USNR, 1945-46. Recipient Excellence in Technology award Raytheon, 1988. Fellow IEEE (life; Third Millenium medal); mem. Microwave Theory and Techniques Soc. (editl. rev. bd., nat. lectr. 1980-81, Microwave prize 1976), Nat. Acad. Engring. (Microwave Career award 1994), Electron Devices Soc. Inventor low-distortion FET; co-inventor Spacistor, Overlay FET. Home and Office: RCP Cons 45 Vandy Dr Jewett City CT 06351 E-mail: bobpucel@yahoo.com.

PUCHALSKI, CHRISTINA M. physician, medical educator; d. Anthony R. and Krystyna J. Puchalski. BS, UCLA, 1976, MA, 1977; MD, George Washington U., 1994. Rsch. chemist NIH, Bethesda, Md., 1977—84, adj. scientist, 1984—90; intern in internal medicine George Wash. U. Med. Ctr., 1994—95, resident in internal medicine/primary care, 1997—98, fellowship in primary care, 1997—98; dir. edn. NIHR (Nat. Inst. Healthcare Rsch.), Bethesda, Md., 1997—2001; dir., founder George Washington Inst. for Spirituality and Health, 2001—. Asst. prof. medicine George Washington U. Sch. Medicine, Washington, 1998—2003, assoc. prof. medicine, 2003—. V.p. bd. dirs. Virginia Square Condo, Arlington, Va., 1999—2002, pres. bd. dirs., 2002—. Recipient Humanitarian in Medicine award, Pfizer-AAMC, 1999, John Templeton award, John Templeton Found., 2001—, Humanitarian award, N.J. Healthcare Found., 2002; grantee, NIH, 2002. Fellow: ACP. Roman Catholic. Avocations: piano, hiking. Office: George Washington Univ 2150 Pennsylvania Ave NW Washington DC 20037

PUCIE, CHARLES R., JR., public affairs executive; b. Asheville, N.C., Oct. 8, 1943; BSFS in Internat. Affairs, Georgetown U., 1965. Fin. analyst Chase Manhattan Bank, 1969-70; account exec. Doremus, 1970-73, v.p., 1973-80, sr. v.p., regional mgr., 1980-85; sr. v.p., group dir., internat. counseling Hill and Knowlton, 1986-90, exec. v.p., 1991; founder, CEO Capitoline Internat. Group, Washington, 1991-98; chmn., CEO C.I.H. Ltd., 1992-98; CEO Capitoline/MS&L, G.P., 1994-98; v.p. pub. affairs supreme coun. KC, Washington, 1998-2001; sr. counselor Fleishman-Hillard, Washington, 2001—. Capt., aviator U.S. Army, 1966-69, Vietnam. Office: Fleishman Hillard 1615 L St NW Ste 1000 Washington DC 20036-5610

PUCK, JENNIFER M. physician, scientist; b. Denver, Aug. 9, 1949; m. Robert L. Nussbaum. BA, Harvard U., 1971, MD, 1975; MA, U. Pa., 1991. Diplomate Am. Bd. Pediatrics. Assoc. prof. U. Pa. Med. Sch., Phila., 1991-93; chief immunologic genetics Nat. Human Genome Rsch. Inst./NIH, Bethesda, Md., 1993—; asst. prof. pediatrics U. Pa. Med. Sch., Phila., 1984-91. Fellow Am. Acad. Pediatrics. Office: Nat Human Genome Rsch Inst/NIH Bldg 49 Rm 49 Convent Dr Msc 4442 Bethesda MD 20892-0001

PUCK, THEODORE THOMAS, geneticist, biophysicist, educator; b. Chgo., Sept. 24, 1916; s. Joseph and Bessie (Shapiro) Puckowitz; m. Mary Hill, Apr. 17, 1946; children: Stirling, Jennifer, Laurel. BS, U. Chgo., 1937, PhD, 1940. Mem. commn. airborne infections Office Surgeon Gen., Army Epidemiol. Bd., 1944-46; asst. prof. depts. medicine and biochemistry U. Chgo., 1945-47; sr. fellow Am. Cancer Soc., Calif. Inst. Tech., Pasadena, 1947-48; prof. biophysics U. Colo. Med. Sch., 1948—, chmn. dept., 1948-67, disting. prof. dept. medicine, 1986—; founder, dir. Eleanor Roosevelt Inst. Cancer Research, 1962-95; Disting. rsch. prof. Am. Cancer Soc., 1966—; prof. Denver U., 2003—. Nat. lectr. Sigma Xi, 1975-76 Author: The Mammalian Cell as a Microorganism: Genetic and Biochemical Studies in Vitro, 1972. Mem. Commn. on Physicians for the Future. Recipient Albert Lasker award, 1958, Borden award med. rsch., 1959, Louisa Gross Horwitz prize, 1973, Gordon Wilson medal Am. Clin. and Climatol. Assn., 1977, award Environ. Mutagen Soc., 1981, E.B. Wilson medal Am. Soc. Cell Biology, 1984, Bonfils-Stanton award in sci., 1984, U. Colo. Disting. Prof. award, 1987, Henry M. Porter medal, 1992; named to The Colo. 100, Historic Denver, 1992; Heritage Found. scholar, 1983; Phi Beta Kappa scholar, 1985; Fogarty Internat. scholar NIH, 1997. Fellow Am. Acad. Arts and Scis.; mem. Am. Soc. Human Genetics, Am. Chem. Soc., Soc. Exptl. Biology and Medicine, AAAS (Phi Beta Kappa award and lectr. 1983), Am. Assn. Immunologists, Radiation Research Soc., Biophys. Soc., Genetics Soc. Am., Nat. Acad. Sci., Tissue Culture Assn. (Hon. award 1987), Paideia Group, Santa Fe Inst. Sci. Bd., Inst. Medicine, Phi Beta Kappa, Sigma Xi. Achievements include pioneering contributions to establishment of somatic cell approaches to mammalian cell genetics, to the identification and classification of the human chromosomes; measurement of mutation in mammalian cells; demonstration of the camp-induced reverse transformation reaction and the genome exposure defect in cancer; development of quantitative approaches to mammalian cell radiobiology; development of cancer prevention approaches. Office: Eleanor Roosevelt Inst Cancer Rsch 1899 Gaylord St Denver CO 80206-1210 Office Phone: 303-336-5600. Business E-Mail: tpuck@du.edu. *Our age is threatened by distorted emphasis on power, material wealth, and competitiveness, and by an explosive increase in population which exceeds our traditional regulative capacities. But it also holds promise for new and profound understanding of ourselves - of our basic human biological intellectual and emotional needs. There is room for hope.*

PUCK, WOLFGANG, executive chef; b. St. Veit, Austria, July 8, 1949; married; two children. Chef, part owner Ma Maison, L.A., 1973; exec. chef, ptnr. Spago's, 1982, Chinois on Main, Santa Monica, 1983, Postrio, San Francisco, 1989, Granita, Malibu, Calif., 1991. Fund raising Meals on Wheels, A. Cancer Soc. L.A. Author: Modern French Cooking for the American Kitchen, 1982, The Wolfgang Puck Cookbook: Recipes from Spago and Chinois, 1986, Adventures in the Kitchen with Wolfgang Puck, 1991; producer (instructional cooking video) Spago Cooking with Wolfgang Puck. Office: Eolfgang Puck Cafe 8000 W Sunset Blvd Los Angeles CA 90046-2439

PUCKETT, ALLEN EMERSON, aeronautical engineer; b. Springfield, Ohio, July 25, 1919; s. Roswell C. and Catherine C. (Morrill) Puckett; m. Betty J. Howlett; children: Allen W., Nancy L., Susan E.; m. Marilyn I. McFarland; children: Margaret A., James R. BS, Harvard U., 1939, MS, 1941; PhD, Calif. Inst. Tech., 1949. Lectr. aeronautics, chief wind tunnel sect. Jet Propulsion Lab., Calif. Inst. Tech., 1945—49; with Hughes Aircraft Co., Culver City, Calif., 1949—, exec. v.p., 1965—77, pres., 1977—78, chmn. bd., chief exec. officer, 1978—87, chmn. emeritus, 1987—. Tech. cons. U.S. Army Ordnance, Aberdeen Proving Ground, Md., 1945—60; mem. sci. adv. com. Ballistic Rsch. Labs., 1958—65; bd. dirs. Gen. Dynamics, Fluor, Logicon Investment Co. of Am., Am. Mut. Fund, Lone Star Industries; mem. steering group OASD adv. panel on aeros.; cons. Pres.'s Sci. Adv. Com.; chmn. rsch. adv. com. control, guidance and navigation NASA, 1959—64; vice-chmn. Def. Sci. Bd., 1962—66; mem. Army Sci. Adv. Panel, 1965—69, NASA tech. and rsch. adv. com., 1968—72, space program adv. coun., 1974—78; Wilbur and Orville Meml. lectr. Royal Aero. Soc., 1981. Author (with Hans W. Liepmann): Introduction to Aerodynamics of a Compressible Fluid, 1947; editor (with Simon Ramo): Guided Missile Engineering, 1959; contbr. tech. papers on high-speed aerodynamics. Trustee U. So. Calif. Fellow: AIAA (pres. 1972); mem.: AAAS, NAE, NAS, Aerospace Industries Assn. (chmn. 1979), L.A. World Affairs Coun. (pres.), Phi Beta Kappa, Sigma Xi. Office: Hughes Electronic Co c/o PR Dept PO Box 956 El Segundo CA 90245-0956*

PUCKETT, ALLEN WEARE, health care information systems executive; b. Pasadena, Calif., Mar. 17, 1942; s. Allen Emerson Puckett and Betty Jane (Howlett) Ward; m. Joan Adrienne Roth, Apr. 10, 1965 (div. 1980); children: Glenn A., Tod A.; m. Laura Treadgold, July 10, 1992. BS, U. Calif., Berkeley, 1963; JD, Harvard U., 1966. Bar: Calif. 1966. Prin. McKinsey & Co., San Francisco, 1966-78; pres. Atman Corp., San Francisco, 1979-83; v.p. VWR Sci., San Francisco, 1980-83, Univar Corp., Seattle, 1984-85; sr. v.p. fin. VWR Corp., Seattle, 1986-90, Momentum Distbn. Inc., Seattle, 1990; v.p. cen. ops. Eldec Corp., Lynnwood, 1990-92; exec. v.p. Phycom Corp., 1993-2000, HealthGnostics, Inc., 2000—01; prin. Gordian Solutions LLC, 2001—. Bd. dirs. Washington Dental Svcs. Recipient Nathan Burkan prize ASCAP, 1966. Mem.: Wash. Athletic Club. Avocations: skiing, scuba diving, music. Home: 1624 38th Ave E Seattle WA 98112-3134

PUCKETT, CHARLES LINWOOD, plastic surgeon, educator; b. Burlington, N.C., Oct. 19, 1940; s. Harry W. and Lula C. Puckett; m. Florence Elizabeth Loy, June 18, 1961 (div. 1976); children: Loy C., Lisa A., Leslie A.; m. Patricia Louise Wells, June 17, 1984 (div. 1994); 1 child, Harry James; m. Teresa G. Teel, Nov. 24, 1995. Student, Elon Coll., 1959—62; MD, Wake Forest Coll., 1966. Diplomate in plastic surgery and surgery of the hand Am. Bd. Plastic Surgery, Am. Bd. Surgery. Intern Duke U., Durham, NC, 1966—67, jr. asst. resident gen. and thoracic surgery, 1967—68, sr. asst. resident gen. surgery, 1968—70, chief resident, instr. surgery, 1970—71, fellow gen. and thoracic surgery, 1971—72, asst. resident plastic surgery, 1973—75, instr., chief resident plastic surgery, 1975—76; fellow hand surgery U. Louisville Hosps., 1974; assoc. prof. plastic surgery U. Mo. Health Scis. Ctr., 1976—80, prof. plastic surgery, 1980—, vice chmn. dept. surgery, 1986—. Instr. surgery Duke Hosp., 1970—72, assoc. surgery, 1972—73. Contbr. articles to profl. jours. Maj. U.S. Army, 1971—76. Fellow: ACS (gov. 1991—97, Mo. chpt.); mem.: AMA, So. Med. Assn., Plastic Surgery Rsch. Coun., Plastic Surgery Ednl. Found., Lipolysis Soc. N.Am. Inc., Internat. Microsurgical Soc., Assn. Acad. Chmn. Plastic Surgery (bd. dirs. 1985—87, pres.-elect 1986—87, pres. 1987—88), Am. Trauma Soc., Am. Soc. Plastic Surgeons, Inc. (bd. dirs. member-at-large 1985—88, asst. sec. 1988—89, trustee 1989—92, 2003—, chmn. bd. trustees 1991—92, parliamentarian 1992—93, historian 1994—95, sec. 1995—97, v.p. 1997—98, pres.-elect 1998—99, pres. 1999—2000, Spl. Hon. Citation 2002), Am. Soc. Surgery of the Hand, Am. Soc. for Aesthetic Plastic Surgery, Inc. (bd. dirs. 1989—2000, traveling prof. 2002), Am. Cleft Palate Assn., Am. Bd. Plastic Surgery (dir. 1988—94, chmn. 1993—94), Am. Assn. Plastic Surgeons (trustee 1995—98), Am. Assn. Hand Surgery (bd. dirs. 1982—84, 1990, 1991, v.p. 1986—87, pres.-elect 1987—88, pres. 1988—89, parliamentarian 1992), Alpha Omega Alpha, Sigma Xi. Republican. Avocation: cattle and horse farming. Office: Univ Mo Divsn Plastic Surgery One Hospital Dr Columbia MO 65212

PUCKETT, ELIZABETH ANN, law librarian, law educator; b. Evansville, Ind., Nov. 10, 1943; d. Buell Charles and Lula Ruth (Gray) P.; m. Joel E. Hendricks, June 1, 1964 (div. June 1973); 1 child, Andrew Charles; m. Thomas A. Wilson, July 19, 1985. BS in Edn., Eastern Ill. U., 1964; JD, MS in L.S., U. Ill., 1977. Bar: Kans. 1978, Ill. 1979. Acquisitions/reader services librarian U. Kans. Law Library, Lawrence, 1978-79; asst. reader services librarian So. Ill. U. Law Library, Carbondale, 1979-81, reader services librarian, 1981-83; assoc. dir. Northwestern U. Law Library, Chgo., 1983-86, co-acting dir., 1986-87; dir./assoc. prof. South Tex. Coll. Law Library, Houston, 1987-89; dir./prof. South Tex. Coll. Law Libr., Houston, 1990-94, U. Ga. Law Libr., Athens, 1994—. Co-author: Evaluation of System-Provided Library Services to State Correctional Centers in Illinois, 1983; co-editor Uniform Commercial

Code: Confidential Drafts, 1993. Mem. ABA, Am. Assn. Law Librs. (mem. exec. bd. 1993-96). Avocations: reading, antiques. Office: U Georgia Law Libr Athens GA 30602-6018 Office Phone: 706-542-5078. E-mail: apuckett@uga.edu.

PUCKETT, JIM H. school system administrator; b. Charlotte, N.C., Apr. 28, 1957; s. James D. and James A. Puckett; m. Jo Ellen Inman-Pucket. BBA, U. N.C., 1980. Bd. mem. Charlotte Mecklenburg Bd. Edn., NC, 1997—2000, Lake Norman Charter Sch., Huntersville, 2001—04, Mecklenburg County Bd. Commr., 2000—06. Reg. mgr. Electric Painters, Inc. Office Phone: 704-363-1379.

PUCKETT, LAUREN JOY, music educator; b. Cleve., May 29, 1958; d. Joseph Adolph Hlavacek and Joan Florence Baker; m. Mark Alan Puckett, July 12, 1994; 1 child, Halle Baker stepchildren: Hannah Michelle, Melanie Ruth. MusB in Piano Performance, Eastman Sch. Music, 1980; MusM in Piano Performance, Cleve. State U., 1982. Piano tchr. Cleve. Music Sch. Settlement, 1980—90; pianist Top of the Town Restaurant, Cleve., 1990—94; adj. instr. Hardin-Simmons U., Abilene, Tex., 1996—98, instr., 1998—2003, asst. prof., 2003—. Lectr. music Cuyahoga C.C., Cleve., 1987—90; judge various contests and festivals, Tex., 1995—; pvt. piano tchr., Abilene, 1995—; with Puckett & Puckett Duo Piano Team, Abilene, 1995—; pvt. accompanist, collaborator; pianist Abilene Philharm. Orch., 1995—, Abilene Chamber Players, 1995—. Co-prodr.: (CD recording) Mark Puckett, 2000. Bd. dirs. Young Audiences, 2003—. Recipient Nathan Fryer award, Cleve. Music Sch. Settlement, 1974—76. Mem.: Music Tchrs. Nat. Assn. (cert. tchr. 1990, sec. 1978—80), Abilene Music Tchrs. Assn. (coll. liason 1998—2000), Mu Phi Epsilon, Pi Kappa Lambda (pres. 1986—88). Avocations: travel, art, swimming. Home: 2201 Shoreline Dr Abilene TX 79602 Office: Hardin-Simmons Univ Performance Studies Dept 22 Hickory St Abilene TX 79698-0001 Office Phone: 325-670-1427. E-mail: lpuckett@hsutx.edu.

PUCKETT, MARY ALICE, primary school educator, consultant; d. Bernard Louis and Alida Josepha Stork; m. Gary Michael Puckett, Dec. 27, 1981; 1 child, Sean. BS in Edn., North Tex. State U., 1976; MA in Edn., Tex. Wesleyan U., 1989. Cert. tchr. Tex. State Bd. Edn. 1st grade tchr.-Hill Arlington (Tex.) Ind. Sch. Dist., 1977—2000, 1st grade tchr.-Amos, 2000—01, 1st grade tchr.-Goodman, 2001—03, 1st grade tchr.-Pope, 2003—. Author: (video) It Takes Two Mainstreaming, 1989 (Ptnrs. in Mainstreaming award, 1990), (booklet) The Happy Teacher Campaign, 2000. Vol. Riding Unlimited, Keller, Tex., 1991; ednl. cons. Met. Adventist Cmty. Svc., Grand Prairie, Tex., 2000. Mem.: Courage to Teach, Alpha Delta Kappa. Avocations: reading tutor, travel, writing, attending retreats. Home: 1901 Montana Trail Grand Prairie TX 75052

PUCKETT, PHILLIP P. state legislator, insurance agency executive; b. Russell County, Va., Aug. 10, 1947; BS, U. Tenn.; MA, Va. Poly. Inst. and State U. Pres. Lebanon Ins. Agy.; mem. Va. Senate, Richmond, 1999—. Mem. agr., conservation and natural resources com., commerce and labor com., transp. com. Democrat. Office: Va Senate Gen Assembly Bldg 910 Capitol St Rm 318 Richmond VA 23219-3400 also: PO Box 924 Tazewell VA 24651-0924

PUCKETT, RICHARD EDWARD, artist, consultant, former recreation executivve, former hotel executive; b. Klamath Falls, Oreg., Sept. 9, 1932; s. Vernon Elijah P., Leona Belle (Clevenger) P.; m. Velma Faye Hamrick, Apr. 14, 1957 (dec. 1985); children: Katherine Michelle Briggs, Deborah Alison Bolinger, Susan Lin Rowland, Gregory Richard. Student, So. Oreg. Coll. Edn., 1951—56, Lake Forest Coll., 1957—58, Hartnell Jr. Coll., 1960—70; BA, U. San Francisco, 1978. Acting arts and crafts dir., Ft. Leonard Wood, Mo., 1956-57; arts and crafts dir., asst. spl. svcs. officer, mus. dir. Ft. Sheridan, Ill., 1957-59; arts and crafts dir. Ft. Irwin, Calif., 1959-60, Ft. Ord, Calif., 1960-86; dir. arts and crafts br. Art Gallery, Arts and Crafts Ctr. Materials Sales Store, 1960; opening dir. Presidio Monterey Army Mus., 1968; dir. Model Army Arts and Crafts Program. One-man shows include Seaside City Hall, 1967—86, 2002, Ft. Ord Arts and Crafts Ctr. Gallery, 1967, 1973, 1979, 1981, 1984, 1986, Presidio of Monterey Art Gallery, Del Messa Gallery, Carmel, Calif., 1998, So. Oreg. Art Gallery, Medford, 2000, Country Rose Gallery, Hollister, Calif., 2001—03, Walter Avery Gallery Seaside City Hall, 2002, Sasoontsi Gallery, Salinas, Calif., 2004, also pvt. collections, designed and opened first Ft. Sheridan Army Mus., Presidio of Monterey Mus., exhibited in group shows at Salinas Valley Art Gallery, Glass on Holiday, Gatlinburg, Tenn., 1981—82, Internat. Congress on Arts and Comm., 1997, Del Messa Gallery, 2001—04. Recipient 1st pl. Dept. Army and U.S. Army Forces Command awards for programming and publicity, 1979-81, 83-85 (exhibited in Smithsonian), 1st and 3d pl. sculpture awards Monterey County Fair Fine Arts Exhibit, 1979, Comdrs. medal civilian svcs., 1986, Golden Acad. award, Internat. Man of Yr. award, 1991-92, others. Mem.: Ft. Ord Alumni Assn., Salinas Valley Art Assn. (pres. 2000—), Monterey Peninsula Art Mus. Assn. Home: 210 San Miguel Ave Salinas CA 93901-3021

PUCKETT, ROBERT MARION, clergyman; b. June 17, 1926; BA, Mercer U., 1954; BD, Colgate Rochester Div. Sch., 1957; postgrad., U. Chgo., 1957-58; D Ministry, Princeton Theol. Sem., 1980. Ordained minister Am. Bapt. Ch., 1944, Internat. Coun. of Cmty. Chs., 1944. Min. small rural chs., Ga., Tenn., 1947-54; Immanuel Congl. Ch., Ontario, N.Y., 1954-57; 1st Bapt. Ch., East Aurora, N.Y., 1964-67; Norris (Tenn.) Religious Fellowship, cmty. ch., 1967-94; assoc. min. South Ch.-Cmty. Bapt., Mt. Prospect, Ill., 1957-59, Scarsdale (N.Y.) Cmty. Bapt. Ch., 1959-64; min. visitation Tellico Village Cmty. Ch., Loudon, Tenn., 1994—. Pres. Internat. Coun. Cmty. Chs., 1987-89; mem. Morehouse Coll. Preachers, Morehouse Coll., 1988. Editor Pastor's Jour., 1984-94, Inclusive Pulpit, 1996—. Faculty fellow Colgate Rochester Divinity Sch., 1957-58, Melvin Jones fellow Internat. Lions Club, 1994. Home and Office: 177 Chahyga Way Loudon TN 37774-2801 E-mail: tvpuckett@aol.com.

PUCKETT, RUBY PARKER, nutritionist, hospital food service administrator, consultant, author; b. Dora, Ala., Nov. 26, 1932; d. John Franklin Parker and Ethel V. (Short) Tuggle; m. Larry Willard Puckett, July 2, 1955; children: Laurel Lynn Puckett Brown, Hollie Kristina Puckett Walker. BS in Food and Nutrition, Auburn (Ala.) U., 1954; postgrad. in vocat. edn., U. Fla., 1970, 80; MA in Health Sci. Edn., Cen. Mich. U., 1976. Registered dietitian, foodservice adminstr. Dietetic intern Henry Ford Hosp., Detroit, 1955; staff dietitian VA Hosp., Houston, 1955-56; dietitian Matty Hersee Hosp., Meridian, Miss., 1957-58; asst. dir. U. Miss. Med. Ctr., Jackson, 1960-61; dir. dietetics Ft. Sanders Presbyn. Hosp., Knoxville, Tenn., 1961-63, Waterman Meml. Hosp., Eustis, Fla., 1963-68; dir. food and nutrition U. Fla. Shands Hosp., Gainesville, 1968-95; pres. Square One Cons. Service, Gainesville, 1979-85; pres., owner Food Svc. Mgmt. Cons., 1995—. Adv. com. on jr. coll. dietetic programs Fla. Dept. Edn., 1967-69; nominating com. Southeastern Hosp. Conf. for Dietitians, 1969, sec., 1974-75; pres. Field Agy. Nutrition, 1970; instr. U. Fla., 1972-73, 82-85, clin. and cmty. coordinated undergrad. dietetic program adv. bd., 1974-89; instr. Santa Fe Jr. Coll., Gainesville, 1977-81; adv. com. Marquis Libr. Soc., Inc., 1974; health project rev. com. North Ctrl. Fla. Planning Coun., 1974-76; named to White House Conf. on Food and Nutrition, 1976, Senate Select Com. on Food and Nutrition, 1976; com. on animal products NRC Adv. Bd. on Mil. Pers. Supplies, 1978-81; site evaluator dietetic programs in colls and univs., 1998—; mem. Commn. on Accrediation Dietetic Edn., 1999—, program reviewer for dietary mgr. tng., 2003—; adv. bd. various corps.; reviewer abstracts, articles Jour. Am. Dietetic Assn.; apptd. faculty Dept. Family Youth and Cmty. Svcs. Internat. Food Svc. Adminstrs.; spkr. in field. Author: Food Service in Health Care Facilities, 1988, 3d edit., 2004, Basic Nutrition and Diet Modification Shands Hospital, 1992, revised edit., 2002, Managing Foodservice Operations, 1992, HACCP The Future Challenge, 4th edit., Nutrition Diet Modification Meal Patterns, 4th edit., Disaster and Emergency Preparedness for Food Service Operations, 2003, Dietary Managers Course by Correspondence, 9 edits., Nutrition for the Elderly, Safety, Sanitation and Security for Food Services Operation, Topics in Practice: Productivity Measures for Food Service Operations, 2004, Food Service Manual for Health Care Organizations, 2004; mem. editl. adv. com.: Stokes Report, 1980—84, editl. advisor: Food Management, 1986—, Topics in Clinical Nutrition, 1988—, Aspen's Focus, 1984—91, Aspen's Hosp. Nutrition and Foodservice Forms; contbr. articles to profl. jours.; developer nutrition and older adult distance edn.course. Bd. dirs. Campus USA Credit Union, 1978—, v.p., 1980—81, pres.-elect, 1981—82, chmn. bd., 1982—83, 1998; chmn. Shands Hosp. chpt. United Way, 1978, mem. budget and allocations com., 1983—, mem. speakers bur., 1985—86; mem. adv. bd. Harvest Gainesville, 1991—93, Children's Miracle Telethon, 1992—95; adv. bd. Sta. WRUF Pub. Radio, 1988; profl. adv. bd. Shands Home Care; vol. Mothers Supporting Daus. with Breast Cancer, 2000—; bd. dirs. Fla. 4-H Found., 2000—04; mem. Sexual Phys. Abuse Bd.; courtesy faculty appt. Divsn Youth, Family and Ext.; election clk., inspector/dep. Alachua County (Fla.) Elections, 2000—; bd. dirs. North Fla. Regional Vocat. Sch. Named Alumni of Yr., Auburn U. Sch. Home Econs., 1985, Disting. Ind. Study Course award, 1986, 1990, Disting. Woman, Alachua County, Fla., 1992; named to Woodlawn H.S. Hall of Fame, 1982, Fla. Women's Hall of Fame, 1986; recipient Community Leader award, Sta. WRUF-FM, 1972, Ivy award, Restauranteurs of Distinction, 1980, Disting. Pace Setter award, Roundtable for Women in Foodservice, 1984, Award of Distinction, Sch. Human Svc., Auburn U., 1991. Mem.: IFAS (mem. family youth and cmty. svc. sect.), FCSI (mem. task force needs assessment 2003), Fla. Coun. on Aging (sec. nutrition sect. 1974—76, adv. bd. 1974—76, chmn. 1974—76), Nat. U. Continuing Edn. Assn. (disting. ind. study course 1986, 1998), Nutrition Edn. Soc. (liaison with industry com. 1974, legis. com. 1974, charter), Dietary Mgr. Assn. Found. (steering com.), Am. Soc. Hosp. Food Service Adminstrs. (edn. com. 1968—71, nomination com. 1978, chmn. publ. com. 1981—82, chmn. legis. com. 1984, bd. dirs., task force HACCP cert.), Gainesville Dietetic Assn. (v.p. 1969, pres. 1970, 1976), Fla. Dietetic Assn. (sec. 1968—70, pres. 1973—74, chmn. by-laws com. 1985, del. 1985—87, numerous other offices), Am. Dietetic Assn. (pres. practice group 41 1982—84, area III coord. 1985—88, 1989—, chair practice group mgmt. in food and nutrition svc. 2001, numerous other offices, Excellence in Mgmt. Practice award 1994, medal 1996, Medallion for Profl. Cmty. and Career Achievement, Marjorie Hulsizer Copher award 2003), Internat. Gold and Silver Plate Soc. (sec. bd. trustees 1983—85), Ivy Soc., Altrusa, Pi Lambda Beta, Kappa Sigma Phi. Democrat. Mem. Lds Ch. Avocations: whitewater rafting, hiking, gardening. Office: 5200 NW 43d St Ste 102-302 Gainesville FL 32606 Office Phone: 352-371-6160. Personal E-mail: puckerp@juno.com.

PUCKETT, SUSAN, newspaper editor; Exec. food editor features desk Atlanta Jour. and Constn., 1990-97, food editor, 1997—. Office: Atlanta Jour and Constn 72 Marietta St NW Atlanta GA 30303-2804

PUCKO, DIANE BOWLES, public relations executive; b. Wyndotte, Mich., Aug. 15, 1940; d. Mervin Arthur and Bernice Letitia (Shelly) Bowles; m. Raymond J. Pucko, May 22, 1965; children: Todd Anthony, Gregory Bowles. BA in Sociology, Bucknell U., Lewisburg, Pa., 1962. Accredited in pub. rels. Asst. to pub. rels. dir. Edward C. Michener Assocs., Inc., Harrisburg, Pa., 1962-65; advt./pub. rels. coord. Superior Switchboard & Devices, Canton, Ohio, 1965-66; editorial dir. women's svc. Hutchins Advt. Co., Inc., Rochester, N.Y., 1966-71; pres. Editorial Communications, Rochester and Elyria, Ohio, 1971-77; mgr. advt. and sales promotion Tappan Air Conditioning, Elyria, 1977-80; mgr. pub. affairs Kaiser Permanente Med. Care Program, Cleve., 1980-85; corp. dir. pub. affairs Keystone Health Plans, Inc., Camp Hill, Pa., 1985-86; v.p., dir. client planning Young-Liggett-Stashower, Cleve., 1986; v.p., dir. pub. rels. Marcus Pub. Rels., Cleve., 1987-91; sr. v.p. Proconsul, Cleve., 1991-95, also bd. dirs.; sr. ptnr. pub. rels. Poppe Tyson, Cleve., 1995-96; managing dir. Bozell Pub. Rels., Cleve., 1996-97; sr. counsel Pub. Rels. Ptnrs., Inc., Cleve., 1997—2002. Mgr., role model Women in Mgmt. Field Placement program, Cleve. State U., 1983-92; pub. rels. adv. bd. profl. adviser, Pub. Rels. Student Soc. Am., Kent State U., 1988—. Bd. trustees, mem. exec. com., chmn. pub. rels. adv. com. Ronald MacDonald House of Cleve., 1993—2000; bd. dirs., chmn. pub. rels. com. Assn. Retarded Citizens, Cleve., 1987-91; mem. pub. rels.-mktg. com. Beech Brook, 1996—2000; mem. journalism comm. adv. bd. Elon Coll., 1998—2001. Recipient Woman Profl. Excellence award YMCA, 1984, MacEachern award Acad. Hosp. Pub. Rels., 1985, Bell Ringer award Cmty. Rels. Report, 1985, Bronze Quill Excellence award Internat. Assn. Bus. Communicators, 1992, 93, Cleve. Comms. award Women in Comms. Internat., 1993, 95, Tower award Bus./Profl. Advt. Assn., 1993, 95, Creativity in Pub. Rels. award, 1994, Silver Screen award U.S. Internat. Film & Video Festival, 1995, Silver Quill Excellence award Internat. Assn. Bus. Communicators, 1995, 2001, Internat. Assn. Bus. Communicators. Fellow Pub. Rels. Soc. Am. (bd. dirs. 1983-85, 86-94, officer 1991-95, mem. counselors acad. 1986—, Silver Anvil award 1985, Mktg./Consumer Rels. award East Ctrl. dist. 1992, 95, Lighthouse award 1995); mem. Press Club Cleve. (bd. dirs. 1989-96, v.p. 1990-96), Cleve. Advt. Club, Women's City Club Cleve., Nat. Agri-Mktg. Assn. (Nat. Merit award 2000). Republican. Methodist. Avocation: soccer. Home: 656 University Ave Elyria OH 44035-7278 Office: 6100 Rockside Woods Blvd Cleveland OH 44131-2366

PUDWILL GORIE, DOMINIC L. astronaut; b. Lake Charles, La., May 2, 1957; m. Wendy Lu Williams; children: Kimberly, Andrew. BS in Ocean Engring., U.S. Naval Acad., 1979; MS in Aviation Systems, U. Tenn., 1990. Commd. ensign USN, 1981, advanced through grades to capt.; pilot Attack Squadron 46, USS America, 1981—83, Strike Fighter Squadron 132, USS Coral Sea, 1983—86; test pilot Naval Air Test Ctr., 1988—90; with Strike Fighter Squadron 87, USS Roosevelt, 1990—92; with U.S. Pace Command, Colorado Springs, 1992—94; astronaut NASA, Houston, 1994—, with Astronaut Office, spacecraft communicator Mission Control. Decorated DFC with Combat ″V″, 2 Air medals, 2 Space Flight medals, 2 Navy Commendation medals with Combat ″V″, Navy Achievement medal; named Strike Fighter Wing Atlantic Pilot of Yr. Achievements include logged over 5,200 flight hours in over 30 different aircraft; over 600 carrier landings; logged over 32 days in space; pilot STS-91 (1998), STS-99 (2000); crew comdr. STS-108 (2001). Avocations: skiing, bicycling, fishing, golf. Office: Astronaut Office/CB NASA Johnson Space Ctr Houston TX 77058

PUENTE, ANTONIO E. psychologist, educator, scientist; b. Habana, Cuba, Feb. 14, 1956; s. Antonio A. and Sylvia (Llanso) P.; m. Linda Newman, June 11, 1977; children: Kirsta, Antonio, Lucas. AA, Fla. Jr. Coll., Jacksonville, 1971; BA, U. Fla., 1973; PhD, U. Ga., 1978. Diplomate Am. Bd. Profl. Neuropsychology. Asst. prof. neuroanatomy St. George's U. Sch. Medicine, Grenada, W.I., 1978-79; clin. psychologist N.E. Fla. State Hosp., Macclenny, Fla., 1979-81; clin. neuropsychologist Wilmington, NC, 1982—; prof. psychology U. N.C., Wilmington, 1981—. Author: Neuropsychological Assessment of the Spanish Speaker, Handbook of Neuropsychological Assessment, others; editor: Neuropsychology Review. Mem. AMA (current procedural terminology panel 1994—, Ctr. Medicare and Medicade Svcs. medicare coverage adv. com. 1999—), APA (coun. of reps. 1994-2000, pres. divsn. neuropsychology 2002, Karl Heiser award 1995), Nat. Acad. Neuropsychology (pres. 1991, disting. svc. award 2000), N.C. Psychol. Assn. (pres. 1990), N.C. Psychol. Found. (founding pres. 1991). Republican. Roman Catholic. Avocations: surfing, tennis. Home: 1916 Lunar Ln Wilmington NC 28405-4211 Office: U NC Wilmington Dept Psychology Wilmington NC 28403 Office Phone: 910-962-3812. E-mail: puente@uncw.edu.

PUENTE, JOSE GARZA, safety engineer; b. Cuero, Tex., Mar. 19, 1949; s. Roque Leos and Juanita Vela (Garza) P.; m. Francisca Rodriguez Estrada, Sept. 7, 1969; 1 child, Anthony Burk. BA, West Tex. A&M U., 1972; postgrad., U. Ariz., 1980; grad., U.S. Army Transp. Courses, 1972, 78, Command and Gen. Staff Coll., 1992, grad., 1999. Cert. U.S. Coun. Accreditation in Occupl. Hearing, Audiometric Technicians of Am. Indsl. Hygiene Assn.; cert. pub. mgr., Ariz. Asst. gen. mgr. Am. Transit Corp., Tucson, 1972-75; pub. transp. supt. City of Tucson, 1975-77, asst. safety coord., 1977-81; safety coord. City of Mesa, Ariz., 1981-88; corp. safety dir. Am. Fence Corp., Phoenix, 1988-89; safety adminstr. Ariz.-ADOT, Phoenix, 1989-98; safety mgr. ADP Marshall, Raleigh, N.C., 1998, ADP Marshall Lucent Tech., Norcross, Ga., 1998-99; tech. cons. Bell South projects Liberty Mut., Norcross, 1999—. Owner La Paz Gospel Supplies & Gift shop, Tucson, 1979-80. Mem. Tucson Child Care Assn., 1973-74; mem. citizen task force Sunnyside Sch. Bd., 1977; mem. minority selection for Hispanic seatbelt program vendor Gov.'s Office of Hwy. Safety, 1989—; mem. Mayor's Task Force on Seatbelt Awareness, City of Mesa, 1988-89. Lt. Col. USAR, 1971-99. Recipient Excellence award Ariz. Safety Assn., 1984; fellow Advanced Mgmt. Seminar Urban Mass Transp. Adminstrn., Northeastern U., 1976-77. Mem. Am. Soc. Safety Engrs. (pres. Ariz. chpt. 1990-91, Safety Profl. of Yr. 1984), Inc. Mex.-Am. Govtl. Employees (charter), Ariz. Safety Engrs., Ariz. Mcpl. Safety Assn. (Profl. of Yr. 1986), Nat. Coun. of La Raza), Internat. Order DeMolay (charter), Toastmasters. Republican. Baptist. Office: 1750 Beaver Ruin Rd Ste 500 Norcross GA 30093-2805 Home and Office: PO Box 1114 Trussville AL 35173-6100 Fax: 770-831-6504. E-mail: jose.puente@libertymutual.com.

PUERNER, JOHN P. newspaper publishing executive; b. Aruba, Dutch West Indies, Jan. 13, 1952; BA, MBA, U. of Colo. From fin. analyst to v.p. Chgo. (Ill.) Tribune, 1979—89, v.p., dir. mktg. and devel., 1989—93; pres., pub. The Orlando (Fla.) Sentinel, 1993—2000; pres., pub., CEO LA Times, 2000—. Bd. dir. LA (Calif.) Bus. Advisors, YMCA, LA, Town Hall, LA, LA (Calif.) World Affairs Coun., Calif. Sci. Ctr. Found., LA (Calif.) Ednl. Partnership; adv. coun. Leeds Sch. Bus. U. Colo. Bd. dir. United Way, LA, LA (Calif.) County Mus. Art, Pasadena (Calif.) Art Ctr. Coll. Design, Internat. Women's Media Found. Office: Los Angeles Times The Times Mirror Co Times Mirror Sq Los Angeles CA 90053-0001*

PUESCHEL, SIEGFRIED M. pediatrician, educator; b. Waldenburg, Germany, July 28, 1931; came to U.S., 1961; naturalized, 1971; widowed. Student, Braunschweig Coll., Germany, 1953-55, Leibniz Coll., Tubingen, Germany, 1955-56, U. Tubingen, Germany, 1955-57, Free U., Berlin, 1957-58, U. Freiburg, Germany, 1958; MD summa cum laude, Med. Acad., Dusseldorf, Germany, 1960; MPH, Harvard U., 1967; PhD, U. R.I., 1985; JD, So. New Eng. Sch. Law, 1996. Diplomate Am. Bd. Pediatrics, Am. Bd. Med. Genetics. Intern Mercer Hosp., Trenton, N.J., 1961-62; jr. resident in pediatrics Children's Hosp., Honolulu, 1962-63; asst. resident in pediatrics Children's Hosp. Med. Ctr., Boston, 1963-64, asst. in mental retardation, 1967-68, assoc. in mental retardation, 1968-75, dir. Down Syndrome Program, 1970-75, dir. PKU Clinic, 1972-75; sr. resident in pediatrics Montreal Children's Hosp., 1964-65, fellow in biochemical genetics/metabolism, 1965-66; assoc. physician R.I. Hosp., Providence, 1975-79, dir. child devel. ctr., 1975-94, dir. PKU and Amino Acid Program, 1975—, dir. Down Syndrome Program, 1978—, physician, 1979—. Instr. pediatrics Harvard U., Cambridge, Mass., 1968-74, asst. prof. in pediatrics, 1974-75, lectr. in pediatrics, 1975—; asst. prof. in pediatrics Brown U., Providence, 1975-77, assoc. prof. in pediatrics, 1977-85, prof. in pediatrics, 1985—; consulting pediatrician Waltham (Mass.) Hosp., 1968-75; cons. in genetics Lying in Hosp., Boston, 1969-75, Women and Infants Hosp., Providence, 1975—; cons. Devel. Evaluation Clinic Children's Hosp. Med. Ctr., Boston, 1975—; mem. prevention of mental retardation com. Internat. League of Socs. for Persons with Mental Handicaps; mem. rsch., prevention and program svc. com. Assn. for Retarded Citizens U.S.; mem. nat. conf. on rsch. perspectives in down syndrome Nat. Inst. Child Health and Rehab. Svcs.; mem. state-of-the-art conf. on down syndrome Office Spl. Edn. and Rehab. Svcs. U.S. Dept. Edn.; mem. nat. adv. child health and human devel. coun. NIH, Washington; mem. sub-com. on tng., edn. and quality assurance-tech. assistance Devel. Disabilities Coun., R.I.; mem. med. adv. com. Spl. Olympics. Author chpts. to books; mem. editl. bd. Down Syndrome Papers and Abstracts for Profls., Exceptional Parents, Down's Syndrome: Rsch. and Practice; reviewer numerous jours.; contbr. articles to profl. jours. Grantee Mass. Dept. Health, 1968, Vigneron Meml. Fund, 1984-85, Charlotte Taylor Fund, 1985-86, Dept. Health and Human Svcs., 1982-86, March of Dimes Nat. Found., 1987-89, Sigma-Tau Pharm., Inc., 1990-93; recipient Recongnition award March of Dimes, 1976, Recognition award Blackstone Valley chpt. R.I. Assn. for Retarded Citizens, 1979, Fogarty Founders award, 1988, Edn. award Muscular Dystrophy Assn., 1985, 86, Muscular Dystrophy Tchg. award, 1988, Recognition award Devel. Ctr. for Handicapped Personsn-Utah State U., 1986, Down Syndrome Assn. of Greater Cin. award, 1986, Colegion John Langdown Down award Mexico City, 1987, Disting. Rsch. award Assn. for Retarded Citizens of U.S., 1990, Conn. Down Syndrome Assn. award, 1991, Sindrome de Down award Asociación Down de Monterrey (Mexico), 1994. Fellow Am. Acad. Pediatrics, Am. Coll. Med. Genetics (founder); mem. AAAS, Am. Assn. Mental Retardation (Profl. Contbn. award 1991), Am. Acad. Cerebral Palsy and Devel. Medicine, Am. Pediatric Soc., Am. Soc. Human Genetics, Nat. Down Syndrome Congress (past pres., Recognition for Disting. Svc. award 1980, Mid-Hudson Valley award 1983, Achievement in Rsch. award 1988, Outstanding Physician award 1991), N.Y. Acad. Sci., R.I. Med. Soc., New Eng. Regional Genetics Group, Soc. Inherited Metabolic Disorders, Down Syndrome Soc. R.I. (award 1985), Assn. for Children with Down Syndrome (bd. dirs.). Office: RI Hosp Child Devel Ctr 593 Eddy St Providence RI 02903-4923

PUETZ, PAMELA ANN, human resources executive; b. Lawrence, Mass., Aug. 17, 1949; d. Gregory and Eleanor Christine Bedrosian; m. Tracy Barnum Braun, Jan. 26, 1974 (div. 1985); 1 child, Susannah; m. Dan Lee Puetz, May 31, 1986. AS, Fisher Jr. Coll., Boston, 1969; BS in Mgmt. with high distinction, Babson Coll., Wellesley, Mass., 1973. Br. mgr. First Security Bank of Utah, N.A., Salt Lake City, 1974-76; bus. mgr. U.S. Ski Team, Inc., Park City, Utah, 1976-77; banking specialist Tracy Collins Bank, Salt Lake City, 1980-83; instr. Fitness Inst., LDS Hosp., Salt Lake City, 1983-85; owner/operator Grapevine Svcs., Redondo Beach, Calif., 1987-88; human resources adminstr. PacifiCare Health Systems, Inc., Cypress, Calif., 1988-89, human resources analyst, 1989-91, human resources project mgr., 1991-93, human resources mgr., 1993—94; sr. mgr. human resources systems Mattel, Inc., El Segundo, Calif., 1994-95; sr. cons., HRIS mgr. PacifiCare Health Systems, Inc., Cypress, Calif., 1995-96, dir. Employee Svc. Ctr., 1996—. Mem., bd. dir. Human Options, 2004—. Mem. Internat. Human Resources Info. Mgmt. Assn., Soc. for Human Resources Mgmt., World At Work. Avocations: scuba, skiing.

PUFFER, RICHARD JUDSON, retired college chancellor; b. Chgo., Aug. 20, 1931; s. Noble Judson and Lillian Katherine (Olson) P.; m. Alison Foster Cope, June 28, 1952; children— Lynn, Mark, Andrew. Ph.B., Ill. Wesleyan U., 1953; MS in Edn, Ill. State U., 1962; PhD (Roy Clark Meml. scholar), Northwestern U., 1967. Asst. plant supt. J.A. Olson Co., Winona, Miss., 1957-59; tchr. Leroy Community Unit Dist. (Ill.), 1959-60; tchr., prin. Community Unit, Dist. 7, Lexington, Ill., 1960-62; asst. county supt. schs. Cook County, Ill., 1962-65; dean arts and scis. Kirkwood Community Coll., Cedar Rapids, Iowa, 1967-69; v.p. Black Hawk Coll., Moline, Ill., 1969-77, pres., 1977-82, chancellor, 1982-87; pres. The Ark Computer Ctr., 1989-92. Dir. W. Ctrl. Ill. Ednl. TV Corp., Springfield, Ill., 1977-87; cons. examiner North Central Assn., 1978-87. Editor: Cook County Ednl. Digest, 1962-65. Bd. dirs. Cedar Rapids Symphony, 1967-69, United Way of Rock Island and Scott Counties, Ill., 1978-80, Unitarian Universalist Dist. of Mich., 1995-98; bd. dirs., sec. West Shore Unitarian Universalist Congregation, 1996-99; sec., treas. Ill. Ednl. Retirement Cts., 1987-91; vice-chmn. Illini Hosp. Bd., 1988-93, chmn., 1993-95; bd. dirs. Illowa coun. Boy Scouts Am., 1979-83, v.p., 1981-83. With USNR, 1953-57. Mem. Rotary (pres. 1975-76, East Moline, Ill.), Green Medallion, Blue Key, Phi Delta Kappa, Pi Gamma Mu. Home and Office: 6191 Grace Ave Ludington MI 49431-8629

PUGH, ANNE D. state legislator; b. Rye, N.Y., May 21, 1952; BS, Union Coll., 1974; MSW, Washington U., St. Louis, 1975; CAS, U. Vt., 1990; student, Case Western Res. U. Planning commr. City of South Burlington (Vt.), 1986-92; justice of peace, mem. South Burlington Bd. Civil Authority, 1988—; mem. Vt. Ho. of Reps., 1993—; social worker, educator, cons. City of South Burlington. Mem. gov.'s commn. on women Vt. Ho. of Reps.; chmn. South Burlington Dem. Com.; bd. dirs. Vt. Women's Health Ctr. Trustee Ctr. Human Svc.; chmn. South Burlington Dem. Com. Mem. NASW (past pres.), Nat. Assn. Family Based Svc. (bd. dirs.). Address: 67 Bayberry Ln South Burlington VT 05403

PUGH, ARTHUR JAMES (JAY PUGH), retired department store executive, consultant; b. Glen Morrison, W.Va., Sept. 24, 1937; s. Arthur James and Mary Pugh; m. Sharon Hubacher, Sept. 26, 1961; children: James Gregory, Mary Elizabeth. BSBA, W.Va. U., 1959; Master of Retailing, U. Pitts., 1960. Mgmt.

trainee, buyer Woodward & Lothrop, Washington, 1960-71, v.p., 1971-77, sr. v.p., 1977-80, exec. v.p., 1980-87, Coun. of Better Bus. Bur., Arlington, Va., 1987-90, bd. dir.; cons., bd. dir. Fairfax, Va., 1990—. Trustee, chmn. audit com. Calvert Mut. Funds, Washington, 1983—; bd. dirs. Acacia Capital Corp., Washington; bd. dirs., exec. com. compensation com., chmn. investment com. Acacia Fed. Savs. Bank, Falls Church, Va. Chmn. bd. dirs. Better Bus. Bur. Met. Washington, 1987. Mem. Rotary Found. of Washington (pres. 1990-91), Nat. Retail Mchts. Assn. (bd. dirs. 1986), W.Va. U. Alumni Assn. (bd. dirs. 1993-98), Fairfax Country Club (bd. dirs. 1990-92), Rotary Club of Washington (Rotarian of Yr. 1982, pres. 1984). Republican. Presbyterian. Avocations: tennis, running, skiing. Home and Office: 4823 Prestwick Dr Fairfax VA 22030-4533 E-mail: jaypugh@prodigy.net.

PUGH, DOROTHY GUNTHER, artistic director; b. Memphis, May 8, 1951; Grad. magna cum laude, Vanderbilt U., 1973; studied with Raymond Clay, studied with Donna Carver, studied with David Howard; student, Royal Acad. Dancing, London. Founder, artistic dir. Ballet Memphis, 1985—. Named one of city's influential citizens, Memphis Mag.; recipient Woman of Achievement award for Initiative, 1987, Gordon Holl Artistic Adminstr. of Yr. award, State of Tenn., 1999. Office: Ballet Memphis PO Box 3675 Cordova TN 38088-3675*

PUGH, EMERSON WILLIAM, electrical engineer; b. Pasadena, Calif., May 1, 1929; s. Emerson Martindale and Ruth Hazel (Edgin) P.; m. Elizabeth Burnam Russell; children: William Russell, Sarah Elizabeth, David Emerson. BS in Physics, Carnegie Mellon U., 1951, PhD in Physics, 1956. Asst. prof. physics Carnegie Mellon U., Pitts., 1956-57; with IBM, 1957-93, rsch. staff mem. rsch. div., Poughkeepsie, N.Y., 1957-61, engring. mgr. components div., 1962-65, group dir. data processing group, Harrison, N.Y., 1965-66, dir. tech. planning rsch. div., Yorktown Heights, N.Y., 1966-68, asst. to v.p. IBM Corp., Armonk, N.Y., 1968-71, rsch. mgr. rsch. div., Yorktown Heights, 1971-85, mgr. tech. history, 1985-93. Vis. scientist IBM Lab., Zurich, Switzerland, 1961-62; mem. United Engring. Trustees Bd., N.Y.C., 1986-92; mem. Engring. Soc. Libr. Bd., N.Y.C., 1986-89; trustee Chalres Babbage Found., 1990—, Samuel Morse Hist. Site, 1998-99. Author: Principles of Electricity and Magnetism, 1960, Memories That Shaped an Industry, 1984, IBM's Early Computers, 1986, IBM's 360 and Early 370 Systems, 1991, Building IBM, 1995; also articles; 10 patents. Fellow IEEE (v.p. 1986-87, pres. 1989, chmn. friends com. Ctr. for History Elec. Engring. 1991-94, chmn. history com. 1995-98, dir. found. 1996—, pres. found. 2000—), AAAS, Am. Phys. Soc. Home: 3 Rock St Cold Spring NY 10516 2911

PUGH, GEORGE WILLARD, law educator; b. Napoleonville, La., Aug. 17, 1925; s. William Whitmell and Evelyn (Foley) P.; m. Jean Earle Hemphill, Sept. 6, 1952; children: William Whitmell III, George Willard Jr., David Nicholls, James Hemphill. BA, La. State U., 1947, JD, 1950; J.S.D., Yale U., 1952; Dr. h.c., U. Aix-Marseille III, France, 1984. Bar: La. 1950. Instr. La. State U. Law Sch., 1950, mem. faculty, 1952-94, prof. law, 1959-94, Julius B. Nachman prof. law, 1984-94; prof. law emeritus, 1994—. Faculty U. Thessaloniki Greece 1974, Aix-en-Provence, France, 1985, 91; faculty U. San Diego, Paris, 1977; rsch. cons. La. State Law Inst., 1953-54; 1st jud. adminstr. Jud. Coun. Supreme Ct. La., 1954-56; vis. prof. U. Tex., 1961; vis. Doherty prof. law U. Va., 1966-67; faculty orientation program in Am. law Assn. Am. Law Schs., 1968, law teaching clinic, 1969; vis. prof. U. Aix-Marseille III, France, 1983, 1987, U. Catholique de Louvain, Belgium, 1987; cons. La. State U.S. Vietnam Legal Adminstrn. Project, 1969; coord., reporter Code of Evidence for La., 1981-95. Author: Louisiana Evidence Law, 1974, supplement, 1978; co-author: Cases and Materials on the Adminstration of Criminal Justice, 2d edit., 1969, Handbook on Louisiana Evidence Law, 1989, 17th edit., 2004. Bd. dirs. Legal Aid Soc. Baton Rouge, 1965-89, chmn., 1963-64; adv. bd. St. Alban's Episcopal Student Ctr., La. State U., 1965-68, 70-72. Served with AUS, World War II. Named George W. and Jean H. Pugh Inst. for Justice in his honor, La. State U. Law Ctr., 1997; fellow, Comparative Study Adminstrn. Justice, 1962—65. Mem. Am., La., Baton Rouge bar assns., Order of Coif, Omicron Delta Kappa, Lambda Chi Alpha. Democrat. Episcopalian. Home: 167 Sunset Blvd Baton Rouge LA 70808-5073

PUGH, JENNIFER SERAFIN, lobbyist; b. Allentown, Pa., Dec. 28, 1978; d. Earl Paul and Elaine Helen Pugh. Student, Susquehanna U., 1996—99. Intern Am. Enterprise Inst., Washington, 1999; rsch. asst. Pub. Opinion Strategies, Alexandria, Va., 2000; staff asst. Senator Rick Santorum, Washington, 2000—01; govt. rels. coord. NSPE, Alexandria, Va., 2001—02; coord. fed. govt. rels. HDR, Alexandria, 2002—. Member-at-large, pub. chair Alexandria (Va.) Beautification Commn., 2002—; sec. Alexandria (Va.) Young Reps., 2003. Mem.: Am. League Lobbyists, Alexandria (Va.) Young Reps. (sec. 2003—04), Capitol Hill Club, Zeta Tau Alpha (v.p. membership 2001—03, pres. alumnae 2003—04). Republican. Roman Catholic. Office: Hdr 1101 King Street Suite 400 Alexandria VA 22314 Business E-Mail: jpugh@hdrinc.com.

PUGH, JESSIE TRUMAN, minister; b. Noble, La., Oct. 28, 1923; s. Jessie Trulonzer and Lucy (Sanderson) P.; m. Bessie Byrl Halbrooks, Aug. 10, 1944; children: James Terry, Datha Jo, Nathanael Brent. BTh, Tex. Bible Coll., 1971; DD, Berean Christian Coll., 1973; D Christian Lit., Christian Life Coll., 1985. Ordained to ministry United Pentecostal Ch. Internat. Youth sec. Tex. Dist., 1940, pres. youth camps, 1954; instr. Tex. Bible Coll., Houston, 1962-67; pastor various chs., 1944-67; gen. dir. home missions U.S. and Can., 1967-74; pastor 1st Pentecostal Ch., Odessa, Tex., 1974—; pres. Christian Life Coll., Stockton, Calif., 1980-82; dist. supt. Texaco dist. United Pentecostal Ch., 1983—91, mem. gen. bd., 1985—. Speaker camp meetings and convs.; host lectr. Pastor's Round Table, 1997—; overseas lectr. Contbr. articles to profl. jours.; hosy Pastor's Round Table, 1997—. Home: 1500 Tanglewood Ln Odessa TX 79761-1824 *I am increasingly impressed that the real issues of life are moral. All racial and physical maladies have roots in neglected moral and spiritual principles. Thus to uphold and propagate such is to have lived well.*

PUGH, JOHN ROBERT, chancellor, former state health administrator; b. New Orleans, Dec. 20, 1945; s. Edward Nicholls and Yvonne Marie (Duplantier) P.; m. Margaret Louise McMullen, Aug. 26, 1975; children— Margaret Elizabeth, John Robert. BA in Philosophy, Baylor U., 1967; M. in Social Work, U. Tex.-Austin, 1970. Program dir. McLaughlin Youth Ctr., Anchorage, Alaska, 1973-78; dep. dir. Alaska Div. Social Services, Juneau, 1978-80; dir. Alaska Family and Youth Services, Juneau, 1980-83; dep. commr. Alaska Dept. Health and Social Services, Juneau, 1983, commr., 1983-86; dean, Sch. of Education Univ. Alaska Southeast, Juneau, 1986-95, chancellor, 1995—. Cons., lectr. in field Mem., Blue Ribbon Commn. for Revision of Children's Code, 1975-77; supt. Sunday Sch., No. Light United Ch., Juneau, 1979—; mem. Gov.'s Council for Handicapped and Gifted, 1980-84; mem. precinct com. Greater Juneau Democratic Com., 1983—; bd. dirs. Alaska State Fin. Corp., 1985—; coach Juneau Little League, 1984— . Served to capt. USAF, 1969-73 Mem. Nat. Assn. Social Workers (pres. 1975-76), Am. Pub. Welfare Assn., Am. Correctional Assn., Alaska Pub. Employees Assn. (pres. 1977-79), Acad. Cert. Social Workers (cert.) Methodist. Avocations: fishing; outdoor sports. Office: U Alaska Southeast 11120 Glacier Hwy Juneau AK 99801

PUGH, RANDALL SCOTT, lawyer; b. Jamestown, N.Y., Mar. 31, 1950; s. H. Theodore and Jeanne M. (Crossley) P.; m. Christie S., Sept. 3, 1978; 1 child, Theodore Clifford. BA, Hobart Coll., 1972; JD, U. Richmond, 1976. Bar: Va. 1976, U.S. Dist. Ct. Va. 1982, U.S. Bankruptcy Ct. 1982. Law clk. to justice Supreme Ct., Richmond, Va., 1976-77; asst. county atty. Prince William County, Manassas, Va., 1977; assoc., ptnr. Whitticar, Sokol, Ledbetter & Haley, Fredericksburg, Va., 1978-87; prin. R. Scott Pugh, Fredericksburg, 1987—. Pres. Lawyer Assistance and Support Svc., Fredericksburg, 1987—; dep. county atty. Spotsylvania County, Va., 1988-90; instr. criminal law Rappahannock Criminal Justice Acad., 1978-90. Editor: Cir. Writer, 1991—98. Bd. dirs. Rappahannock Boy Scouts Am., Fredericksburg, 1982-86, Big Bros. & Sisters, 1978-81; chmn. Spotsylvania County Dem. Com., 1987-91; mem., chair Spotsylvania County Sch. Bd., 1993-96; mem. Spotsylvania County Bd. of Zoning Appeals, 1997—, chair; TV host and panelist Rappahannock Rev., 1997—2002. Mem. ABA, Va. Trial Lawyers Assn., Fredericksburg Area Bar Assn. (pres.), Fredericksburg C. of C. (legal counsel), Fredericksburg Area Jaycees (bd. dirs. 1978-82), Hobart Coll. Alumni, U. Richmond Alumni Assn. Democrat. Methodist. Avocation: computers. Office: PO Box 999 9108 Courthouse Rd Spotsylvania VA 22553-1902 Office Phone: 540-582-5438.

PUGH, RICHARD CRAWFORD, lawyer, educator; b. Phila., Apr. 28, 1929; s. William and Myrtle P.; m. Nanette Bannen, Feb. 27, 1954; children: Richard Crawford, Andrew Lembert, Catherine Elizabeth. AB summa cum laude, Dartmouth Coll., 1951; BA in Jurisprudence, Oxford (Eng.) U., 1953; LLB, Columbia U., 1958. Bar: N.Y. 1958. Assoc. firm Cleary, Gottlieb, Steen & Hamilton, N.Y.C., 1958—61, ptnr., 1969—89; disting. prof. law U. San Diego, 1989—, univ. prof., 1998—99. Mem. faculty Law Sch. Columbia U., 1961-89, prof., 1964-69, adj. prof., 1969-89; lectr. Columbia-Amsterdam-Leyden (Netherlands) summer program Am. law, 1963, 79; dep. asst. atty. gen. tax div. U.S. Dept. Justice, 1966-68; Cons. fiscal and fin. br. UN Secretariat, 1962, 64. Editor: Columbia Law Rev., 1957—58; co-editor (with W. Friedmann): Legal Aspects of Foreign Investment, 1959; co-author (with others): International Law, 2001, Taxation of International Transactions, 2001; co-editor: Taxation of Business Enterprises, 2002, International Income Taxation: Code and Regulations, 2004. Served with USNR, 1954-56. Rhodes scholar, 1951-53. Mem. ABA, Am. Law Inst., Am. Coll. Tax Counsel, Am. Soc. Internat. Law, Internat. Fiscal Assn. (pres. U.S. br. 1978-79). Home: 7335 Encelia Dr La Jolla CA 92037-5729 Office: U San Diego Sch Law Alcala Park San Diego CA 92110-2429 E-mail: rpugh@sandiego.edu.

PUGH, RODERICK WELLINGTON, retired psychologist; b. Richmond, Ky., June 1, 1919; s. George Wilmer and Lena Bernetta (White) P.; m. Harriet Elizabeth Rogers, Aug. 29, 1953 (div. 1955). BA, Fisk U., 1940; MA, Ohio State U., 1941; PhD, U. Chgo., 1949. Diplomate Am. Bd. Profl. Psychology. Instr. Albany (Ga.) State Coll., 1941-43; psychology trainee VA, Chgo., 1947-49; lectr. Roosevelt U., Chgo., 1951-54; staff clin. psychologist VA Hosp., Hines, Ill., 1950-54, asst. chief psychologist for psychotherapy, 1954-58, chief clin. psychology sect., 1958-60, supervising psychologist, coord. psychol. internship tng., 1960-66; pvt. practice clin. psychology Chgo., 1958—99; assoc. prof. psychology Loyola U., Chgo., 1966-73, prof., 1973-88, emeritus prof. psychology, 1989—. Cons. St. Mary of the Lake Sem., Niles, Ill., 1965-66, Ill. Div. Vocational Rehab., 1965-82, Center for Inner City Studies, Northeastern State U., Chgo., 1966-67, VA Psychology Tng. Program, 1966—, Am. Psychol. Assn. and Nat. Inst. Mental Health Vis. Psychologists Program, 1966-89; juvenile problems research rev. com. NIMH, 1970-74; cons. Center for Minority Group Mental Health Programs, 1975-77, cons. psychology edn. br., 1978-82; lectr. U. Ibadan, Nigeria, 1978; Mem. profl. adv. com. Div. Mental Health, City of Chgo., 1979-82; mem. adv. com. U.S. Army Command and Gen. Staff Coll., 1981-83 Author: Psychology and the Black Experience, 1972; Contbr.: chpt. in Black Psychology, 1972; Cons. editor: Contemporary Psychology, 1975-79; contbr. articles to profl. jours. Sec. bd. trustees Fisk U., 1968-78. Served to 2d lt. AUS, 1943-46, ETO. Vis. scholar Fisk U., 1966, vis. prof. in psychology, 1994. Fellow Am. Psychol. Soc., Am. Psychol. Assn. (nat. adv. panel to Civilian Health and Med. Program of Uniformed Services 1980-83, joint coun. on profl. edn. in psychology 1988-90); mem. Midwestern Psychol. Assn., Ill. Psychol. Assn. (chmn. legis. com. 1961, council mem. 1960-62, Disting. Psychologist award 1988, Outstanding Contbn. to Profession of Psychology award 2001), Soc. for Psychol. Study Social Issues, Assn. Behavior Analysis, AAUP, Sigma Xi, Alpha Phi Alpha, Psi Chi. Home: Unit 25C 5201 S Cornell Ave Chicago IL 60615-4207 Office: Loyola U 6525 N Sheridan Rd Chicago IL 60626-5344 Business E-Mail: 72752.47@compuserve.com.

PUGH, THOMAS WILFRED, lawyer; b. St. Paul, Minn., Aug. 3, 1949; s. Thomas Leslie and Joann Marie (Tauer) P.; m. Susan Elizabeth Beattie, Sept. 12, 1971; children: Aimee Elizabeth, Douglas Thomas. AB cum laude, Dartmouth Coll., 1971; JD cum laude, U. Minn., 1976. Assoc. Thuet & Lynch, South St. Paul, 1976-79; ptnr. Thuet, Lynch & Pugh, South St. Paul, 1980-85; atty., pres. Thuet, Pugh, Rogosheske & Atkins, Ltd., South St. Paul, 1986—; mem. Minn. Ho. of Reps., St. Paul, 1989—, Dem. leader, 1999—2002. Mem. Supreme Ct. Task Force Conciliation Ct., St. Paul, 1992, Dakota County Tech. Coll. Adv. Bd., 1991-96. Bd. dirs. Wakota Arena, South St. Paul, 1984-87; pres. Luther Meml. Ch., South St. Paul, 1983-84. Daniel Webster scholar Dartmouth Coll., 1970, Rufus Choate scholar, 1971. Mem. Minn. State Bar Assn., 1st Dist. Bar Assn., Ducks Unltd., Pheasants Forever, South St. Paul C. of C. (local issues chair 1982, Dedicated Svc. award 1983), South St. Paul Jaycees (pres. 1978-79, Key award 1979), Lions. Lutheran. Avocations: tennis, golf, hunting, fishing, reading. Office: Thuet Pugh & Rogosheske 222 Grand Ave South Saint Paul MN 55075-2237

PUGH, WILLIAM WHITMELL HILL, III, lawyer; b. Baton Rouge, La., June 25, 1954; s. George Willard and Jean (Hemphill) P.; m. Beth Smith, Mar. 12, 1983; children: Brendan Kelly, Bryan Clayton, Katharine Elaine. BA, U. Va., 1976; JD, La. State U., 1979. Bar: La. 1979, U.S. Supreme Ct. 1986, U.S. Ct. Appeals (5th and 11th cirs.) 1983. Law clk. to presiding justice U.S. Ct. Appeals (5th cir.), New Orleans, 1979-80. Editor-in-chief La. Law Rev., 1978-79. Mem. Maritime Law Assn., La. Assn. Def. Counsel, La. State Bar Assn., Coun. of La. State Law Inst. (young lawyers rep. 1988-91, mem. 1992—). Office: Liskow & Lewis One Shell Sq 50th Fl New Orleans LA 70139-5001 Office Phone: 504-556-4149. E-mail: wwpugh@liskow.com.

PUGLIESE, KAREN OLSEN, freelance public relations counsel; b. S.I., N.Y., Aug. 20, 1963; d. Harold Birger and Janet Mildred (Cronk) Olsen; m. John Michael Pugliese Jr., Oct. 21, 1989; children: Emily Olsen, John Michael Pugliese III. BA in Polit. Sci., Union Coll., 1985. Asst. editor Food Mgmt. mag., N.Y.C., 1985-86; account exec. Edelman Pub. Rels., N.Y.C., 1986-87; account exec., sr. v.p., group dir. Creamer Dickson Basford, N.Y.C., 1987-96; freelance pub. rels. counsel, Redding, Conn., 1996—. Recipient Gold Quill, Internat. Assn. Bus. Communicators, 1991, award Internat. Pub. Rels. Soc., 1993, Creativity in Pub. Rels., Inside PR, 1993. Republican. Avocations: tennis, reading, walking.

PUGLIESE, MARIA ALESSANDRA, psychiatrist; b. Phila., Sept. 16, 1948; d. Peter Francis and Ida Agnes (Rosa) Pugliese; m. J. Paul Hieble, Sept. 14, 1985. BS, Chestnut Hill Coll., 1970; MD, U. Pa., 1974. Diplomate Am. Bd. Psychiatry and Neurology; with added qualifications in addiction psychiatry. Intern in pediatrics Children's Hosp. of Phila., 1974-75; resident in psychiatry Inst. Pa. Hosp., Phila., 1975-78, attending psychiatrist, 1978-97, Malvern (Pa.) Inst., 1982—, Pa. Hosp., 1997—. Office: 111 N 49th St Philadelphia PA 19139-2718 E-mail: mariadoc2@cs.com.

PUGSLEY, FRANK BURRUSS, lawyer; b. Kansas City, Mo., Apr. 3, 1920; s. Charles Silvey and Emma (Burruss) P.; m. Aline East, May 7, 1943; children— John, Susan Pugsley Patterson, Nancy Pugsley Young BS in Mech. Engring, U. Tex., Austin, 1942; JD, DePaul U., Chgo., 1950. Bar: Ill. 1950, Tex. 1953, U.S. Supreme Ct. 1960. Engr. Gen. Electric Co., Schenectady, 1946-50, patent atty., 1950-52; assoc. Baker & Botts, Houston, 1952-60, ptnr., 1960-84, sr. ptnr., 1974-84. Lectr. Southwestern Legal Found., Practising Law Inst., Bur. Nat. Affairs Conf. Contbr. articles to legal jours. Trustee West Univ. Methodist Ch., Houston, 1959-65; bd. dirs. St. Stephens Episcopal Day Sch., 1960-62; adminstrv. bd. St. Luke's United Meth. Ch., 1981-83. Served to lt. USNR, 1942-46. Fellow Tex. Bar Found.; mem. ABA (chmn. intellectual property law sec. 1980-81), Am. Intellectual Property Law Assn. (pres. 1966-67), Tex. Bar Assn. (chmn. intellectual property law sect. 1960-61), Houston Bar Assn., Petroleum Club, Frisch Auf! Valley Country Club, Friars. Home: 3602 Nottingham St Houston TX 77005-2221

PUGSLEY, ROBERT ADRIAN, law educator; b. Mineola, NY, Dec. 27, 1946; s. Irvin Harold and Mary Catherine P. BA, SUNY-Stony Brook, 1968; JD, NYU, 1975, LLM in Criminal Justice, 1977. Instr. sociology New Sch. Social Rsch., N.Y.C., 1969-71; coord. Peace Edn. programs The Christophers, N.Y.C., 1971-78; assoc. prof. law Southwestern U., L.A., 1978-81, prof., 1981—, Paul E. Treusch prof. law, 2000-01. Adj. asst. prof. criminology and criminal justice Southampton Coll.-Long Island U., 1975-76; acting dep. dir. Criminal Law Edn. and Rsch. Ctr., NYU, 1983-86; bd. advisors Ctr. Legal Edn. CCNY-CUNY, 1978, Sta. KPFK-FM, 1985-86; founder, coord. The Wednesday Evening Soc., L.A., 1979-86; vis. prof. Jacob D. Fuchsberg Law Ctr. Touro Coll., L.I., N.Y., summers, 1988, 89; lectr. in criminal law and procedure Legal Edn. Conf. Ctr., L.A., 1982-96; prof., dir. Comparative Criminal Law and Procedure Program U. B.C., Vancouver, summers, 1994, 98-2003; chair pub. interest law com. Southwestern U., 1990-2001; lectr. legal profl. responsibility West Bar Rev. Faculty, Calif., 1996-98; legal analyst/commentator for print and electronic media, 1992—. Creative advisor (syndicated TV program) Christopher Closeup, 1975-83; host (cable TV) Earth Alert, 1983-87; prodr., moderator (TV program) Inside L.A., Sta. KPFK-FM, 1979-86, Open Jour. program, Sta. KPFK-FM, 1991-94; contbr. articles to profl. jours. Founding mem. Southwestern U. Pub. Interest Law com., 1992—; mem. L.A. County Bar Assn. Adv. Com. on Alcohol & Drug Abuse, 1991-95, co-chair, 1993-95; mem. exec. com. non-govtl. orgns. UN Office Pub. Info., 1977; mem. issues task force L.A. Conservancy, 1980-81, seminar for law tchrs. NEH UCLA, 1979; co-convenor So. Calif. Coalition Against Death Penalty, 1981-83, convener, 1983-84; mem. death penalty com. Lawyer's Support Group, Amnesty Internat., U.S.A.; founding mem. Ch.-State Coun., L.A., 1984-88; bd. dirs. Equal Rights Sentencing Found., 1983-85, Earth Alert, Inc., 1984-87; mem. adv. bd. First Amendment Info. Resources Ctr., Grad. Sch. Libr. and Info. Scis., UCLA, 1990—; mem. coun. Friends UCLA Libr., 1993—, pres., 1996-2002; mem. adv. bd. Project Prevention, 1998-. Robert Marshall fellow Criminal Law Edn. and Rsch. Ctr., NYU Sch. Law, 1976-78. Mem. ABA (sect. criminal justice 1978-, Ctr. Profl. Responsibility 1995-), Am. Legal Studies Assn., Am. Soc. Polit. and Legal Philosophy, Assn. Am. Law Schs., Inst. Soc. Ethics and Life Scis., Soc. Am. Law Tchrs., Internat. Platform Assn., Internat. Soc. Reform of Criminal Law, The Scribes. Democrat. Roman Catholic. Office: Southwestern U Sch Law 675 S Westmoreland Ave Los Angeles CA 90005-3905 Office Phone: 213-738-6757. Business E-Mail: rpugsley@swlaw.edu.

PUHEKKER, KRISTIN ROSE, music educator; b. Carmel, N.Y., Aug. 14, 1976; d. Joseph and Eileen Puhekker. BS in Music Edn., The Coll. St. Rose, 1998, MS in Music Edn., 1999. Cert. in piano pedagogy The Coll. St. Rose, 1998. H.s. choral dir. Tuxedo Union Free Sch. Dist., NY, 1999—2000; mid. sch. choral dir. Irvington Union Free Sch. Dist., 2000—01; dir. mid. sch. piano program Bedford Ctrl. Sch. Dist., 2001—02; elem. gen. music tchr., choral dir. Port Chester Pub. Schools, 2002—. Music tchr. Putnam Arts Coun., Mahopac, NY, 1999—. Avocations: piano, reading, exercise.

PUIA, GEORGE M. writer, educator; b. Grosse Pointe, Mich., Dec. 19, 1951; s. Grace Puia; m. Lynn M. Puia; children: Michael A., Natalie E. PhD, U. Kans., Lawrence, 1988—93. Asst. prof., dir. small bus. inst. U. Tampa, Fla., 1992—96; assoc. prof. Ind. State U., Terre Haute, 1996—2000; DOW Chem. Co. centennial chair in global bus. Saginaw Valley State U., University Ctr., Mich., 2000—. Author: (textbook) International Business: An applied approach; editor: Case Rsch. Jour., 1996—98; contbr. articles to profl. jours. Chair Saginaw Vision 2020, Mich., 2002—03. Recipient Oustanding Rsch. Award, McGraw-Hill Irwin and S.W. Acad. Internat. Bus., 2001; grantee Bus. Internationalization Grant, U.S. Dept. Edn., 2003—04. Mem.: Acad. Mgmt. (conf. track chair), Acad. Internat. Bus. (assoc.; track chair, reviewer), Beta Gamma Sigma (assoc.). Achievements include development of a mid-range theory to explain the effects of national cultural differences on cross-border acquisitions; a prototype for an environmentally sustainable business along the Saginaw Bay Watershed utilizing waste heat from industrial production. Avocations: reading, travel. Office: Saginaw Valley State Univ 7400 Bay Rd University Center MI 48710

PUICAN, MICHAEL, small business owner, poet; b. Waynesboro, Pa., Oct. 2, 1951; s. Michael and Dolores Estelle Puican; m. Mary Kathleen Hawley, Sept. 10, 1957; children: Susann Elisabeth, Nadia Hawley Miecznikowski. BS in Communication Studies, Northwestern U., Evanston, Ill., 1979. V.p. mktg. Alberto Culver Co., Melrose Park, Ill., 1990—2002, Hedstrom Corp., Arlington Heights, Ill., 2002—03; CEO, owner JossClaude Products, Chgo., 2003—. Author: 30 Seconds, Tia Chucha Press, 2004. Home: 1016 Hull Ter Evanston IL 60202 Office: JossClaude Products 216 S Jefferson Ste 001 Chicago IL 60661 Office Phone: 312-441-0391. Personal E-mail: mpuican@ameritech.net.

PUJOL, ERNESTO, artist; b. Havana, Cuba, 1957; BA in Visual Arts magna cum laude, U. Puerto Rico, 1979; postgrad., Pratt Inst., 1987, Hunter Coll. Artist The Marketplace Program, Bronx Mus. Arts, NY, 1991. One-man shows include Taller D'Jevarez, San Juan, 1984, Cavin-Morris, N.Y.C., 1993, INTAR, 1994, Galeria Ramis Barquet, Monterrey, Mex., 1995, Casa de las Americas, Havana, 1995, Frederic Snitzer Gallery, Miami, Fla., 1995, Iturralde Gallery, L.A., 1996, exhibited in group shows at Galeria Interamericana, P.R., 1984, Nat. Arts Club, N.Y.C., 1990, Hudson Guild Gallery, 1991, Cavin Morris Gallery, 1992, The Space, Boston, 1992, Paine Weber Gallery, N.Y., 1992, Reed Coll. Art Gallery, Portland, Oreg., 1994, Seton Hill Coll., Pa., 1995, Iturralde Gallery, L.A., 1995, Spectrum Gallery, Rochester, N.Y., 1996, PS 122, N.Y.C., 1996, numerous others, Represented in permanent collections Casa de las Americas, Havana, El Museo del Barrio, N.Y., Assn. Artistas Plasticas de Cuba, Havana, Mus. Art, Ft. Lauderdale, Fla., Cintas Found. Fellows Collection, Art Mus., Fla., Internat. U. Miami, Bronx Coun. Arts, Longwood, N.Y. Recipient Breakthrough award for creativity, Acad. Ednl. Devel., Washington, 1990, Cert. of Appreciation, Dept. Cultural Affairs, L.A., 1995; fellow Cintas Found. fellow, Arts Internat., Inst. Internat. Edn., 1991, Visual Arts fellow, Pollock-Krasner Found., 1993, Regional fellow in painting, Mid-Atlantic Arts Found./Nat. Endowment Arts, 1994; scholar Studio scholar, Bronx Coun. Arts, 1991. Office: Galeria Ramis Barquet 41 E 57th St New York NY 10022-1908

PUJOLS, ALBERT, professional baseball player; b. Santo Domingo, Dominican Republic, Jan. 16, 1980; Profl. baseball player St. Louis Cardinals, 2001—. Named Nat. League Rookie of the Yr., 2001; named to Nat. League All-Star Team, 2001, 2003, 2004. Achievements include won the National League in batting title (.359 average) 2003; led the National League in runs (137), 2003; fourth player in MLB history to start career with 4 straight 100 RBI season's, 2004. Office: Busch Stadium 250 Stadium Plaza Saint Louis MO 63102*

PUKEL, CLIFFORD STUART, physician; b. Bronx, N.Y., Nov. 15, 1955; s. Bayas William and Pearl (Buchholtz) P.; m. Victoria Perry; children: Zachariah, Jacob. BA in Biology, Queens Coll. CUNY, 1979; MD, U. Miami, 1991. Rsch. technician Sloan-Kettering Inst. for Cancer Rsch., N.Y.C., 1980-83, rsch. asst., 1983-85; rsch. assoc. dept. medicine U. Miami, Fla., 1985-87; resident dept. internal medicine U. W.Va., Charleston, 1991-94; fellow hematology, oncology, instr. medicine Dartmouth-Hitchcock Med. Ctr., Lebanon, N.H., 1994-97; pvt. practice Wichita, 1998—2000, Eau Claire, Wis., 2000—02, Vince Lombardi Cancer Clinic, Green Bay, Wis., 2002—, Aurora Bay Care Med. Ctr., Green Bay, 2002—; asst. prof. clin. medicine U. Kans. Sch. Medicine, Wichita, 1998-99, U. Wis. Sch. Medicine, Madison, 2000—. Vis. scientist Escola Paulista de Medicina, Sao Paulo, Brazil, 1984. Contbr. articles to profl. jours. Free Sons of Israel scholar, 1974, N.Y. State Regents scholar, 1974, U. Miami Med. Sch. scholar, 1990. Jewish. Achievements include patent for Method for Detecting the Presence of GD3 Ganglioside; notable findings on role of gangliosides in human cancer, on role of cytokines in diabetes mellitus. Office: Vince Lombardi Cancer Clinic Green Bay WI 54308 Office Phone: 920-288-4180.

PULANCO, TONYA BETH, special education educator; b. Portland, Oreg., Apr. 17, 1933; d. Anthony Lorenzo and Adelfa Elizabeth (Dewey) P. BA, San Jose State U., 1955; MA, Columbia U., 1966. Occupl. therapist Langley Porter Hosp., San Francisco, 1958-60; writer ednl. sub-contracts Columbia U., N.Y.C., 1961-64; from tchr. to dir. edn. Gateway Sch. N.Y., N.Y.C., 1965—. Mem. Assn. for Children with Learning Disabilities, Am. Occupl. Therapy Assn., Japanese Am. Citizens League. Avocations: tap dancing, walkathons, silversmithing, jazz, opera. Office: Gateway Sch NY 236 2d Ave New York NY 10003

PULEC, JACK LEE, otolaryngologist; b. Crete, Nebr., July 12, 1932; s. Anton and Antonette (Divoky) Pulec; m. Marlene Berniece Aron, Nov. 10, 1951; 1 child, Marilyn Louise. BA, U. Nebr., 1955, MD, 1957; MS, U. Minn., 1962. Diplomate Am. Bd. Otolaryngolgy. Intern Bishop Clarkson Meml. Hosp., Omaha, Nebr., 1957-58; resident in ob-gyn. U. Nebr., Omaha, 1958-59; resident in otolaryngology Mayo Found., 1959-62; fellow in neurol-otology L.A. Found. Otolarynology, 1963-64; otologist Hosp. Good Samaritan, L.A.; otolaryngologist St. Vincent's Hosp., L.A., Children's Hosp., L.A., Cedars-Sinai Hosp., L.A., Hollywood Presbyn.-Queen of Angels, L.A., L.A. County Gen. Hosp.; clin. prof. otolaryngology Loma Linda Med. Ctr., U. So. Calif. Cons. Mayo Clinic, Rochester, 1963-69; ptnr. Otologic Med. Group, L.A., 1969-76; pres. Pulec Ear Clinic, L.A., 1976—. Editor: Meniere's Disease, 1968; editor-in-chief Ear, Nose and Throat Jour., 1992—. Fellow Am. Acad. of Otolaryngic Allery, Am. Acad. of Otolaryngology-Head and Neck Surgery (Practitioner Excellence award 1998), Am. Coll. Surgeons, Am. Laryngological, Rhinological and Otological Soc., Am. Neurotology Soc., Am. Otological Soc., Royal Soc. of Medicine, L.A. County Med. Assn. (pres. Met. dist. 1990-91, councilor 1993—), Banany Soc. (Sweden), Calif. Med. Assn. (del. 1988—), AMA, Neurotological and Equilibriometric Soc. (Germany), Otosclerosis Study Club (pres.-elect 1996-97, pres. 1997-98). Office: 1245 Wilshire Blvd Ste 503 Los Angeles CA 90017-4805

PULEO, FRANK CHARLES, lawyer; b. Montclair, N.J., Nov. 25, 1945; s. Frank and Kathren (Despenzerie) P.; m. Alice Kathren Leek, June 1, 1968; children— Frank C., Richard James. B.S.E., Princeton U., 1967; J.D., N.Y.U., 1970. Bar: N.Y., 1971. Ptnr., Milbank, Tweed, Hadley & McCloy, N.Y.C., 1970— . Mem. ABA (mem. com. on fed. regulation securities), N.Y. State Bar Assn. Office: Milbank Tweed Hadley & McCloy 1 Chase Manhattan Plz Fl 49 New York NY 10005-1413

PULGRAM, ERNST, linguist, philologist, Romance and classical linguistics educator, writer; b. Vienna, Sept. 18, 1915; came to U.S. 1939, naturalized 1943; s. Sigmund and Gisela (Bauer) P.; m. Frances McSparran, Nov. 29, 1985. Dr. Phil. in Romance and Classical Philology, U. Vienna, 1947, Dr. phil. honoris causa, 1990; PhD in Comparative Linguistics, Harvard U., 1946. Asst. prof. Union Coll., Schenectady, N.Y., 1946; asst. prof. U. Mich., Ann Arbor, 1948-51, assoc. prof., 1951-56, prof., 1956—, H. Keniston disting. prof. romance and classical linguistics, 1979-86, prof. emeritus, 1986—. Vis. prof. U. Florence, Italy, 1956-57, U. Cologne, Germany, 1970, U. Heidelberg, Germany, 1972, U. Regensburg, Germany, 1975, U. Vienna, 1977, Internat. Christian U., Tokyo, 1982, U. Innsbruck, Austria, 1983. U. Munich, Germany, 1987; lectr. numerous univs., internat. linguistic congresses; cons. Sch. Langs. and Linguistics, Georgetown U., Washington Author: Theory of Names, 1951, The Tongues of Italy, 1958, Introduction to Spectrography of Speech, 1959, Syllable, Word, Nexus, Cursus, 1970, Latin-Romance Phonology, Prosodics and Metrics, 1975, Italic, Latin, Italian: 600 B.C.-A.D. 1250, 1978, Practicing Linguist, Essays 1950-1985 (2 vols.), 1986; editor: Studies Presented to Joshua Whatmough, 1957, Romanitas: Studies in Romance Linguistics, 1984; contbr. autobiographical sketch in First Person Singular III, 1998; contbr. articles to profl. jours.; author revs.; mem. editorial bd. Current Issues in Linguistic Theory (Amsterdam), Mich. Germanic Studies, Jour. Linguistics and Philology, Mediterranean Language Rev. Served to pvt. inf. U.S. Army, 1942-44; PTO Fellow Am. Council of Learned Socs., 1951-52, 59-60, Guggenheim Found., 1954-55, 62-63; recipient Henry Russell award U. Mich., 1951, Festschrift, Amsterdam, 1980 Mem. Linguistic Soc. Am. (exec. com., com. on appointment of hon. mems., program com.), Internat. Linguistic Assn., Internat. Phonetics Assn., Linguistic Assn. Can. and the U.S. (founding mem., pres. 1978-79) Avocations: collecting drawings and watercolors; hiking; swimming. Home: 1050 Wall St Ann Arbor MI 48105-1974 E-mail: mcsparra@umich.edu.

PULGRAM, WILLIAM LEOPOLD, architect, space designer; b. Vienna, Jan. 1, 1921; came to U.S., 1940; s. Sigmund and Gisela (Bauer) P.; married, Jan. 12, 1952; children: Deirdre, Laurence, Anthony, Christopher. BS, Ga. Inst. Tech., 1949, BArch, 1950; postgrad., Ecole des Beaux Arts, Fontainebleau, France, 1951. Archtl. designer various firms, Atlanta, 1951-58; assoc., chief interior design FABR&P, Atlanta, 1958-63; exec. v.p., gen. mgr. Associated Space Design Inc., Atlanta, 1963-70, pres., CEO, 1971-85, chmn., CEO, 1985-86, chmn. emeritus, 1986-88; arch., cons. Atlanta, 1988—. Cons. UN, 1986; com. mem. NAS, 1980-84; lectr. at colls., univs., U.S. and abroad. Author: Designing the Automated Office, 1984, Japanese transl., 1985; contbr. articles to jours. in field. Mem., lectr. High Mus. Art, Atlanta, 1970—. With U.S. Army, 1943-46. Named to Hall of Fame Interior Design mag., 1986. Fellow AIA (chmn. interiors 1978-84, archtl. res. coun. AIA Found. 1983-85); mem. Archs., Designers and Planners for Social Responsibility (nat. bd. dirs. 1989-93), Am. Soc. Interior Designers, Atlanta C. of C., Atlanta City Club, Lake Lanier Sailing Club. Mem. Unitarian Universalist Ch. Home and Office: W L Pulgram FAIA Cons 4317 E Conway Dr NW Atlanta GA 30327-3528 Office Phone: 404-255-8514. E-mail: pulgramga@mindspring.com.

PULIAFITO, CARMEN ANTHONY, ophthalmologist, healthcare executive; b. Buffalo, Jan. 5, 1951; s. Dominic F. and Marie A. (Nigro) P.; m. Janet H. Pine, May 19, 1979 AB cum laude, Harvard Coll., 1973, MD magna cum laude, 1978; MBA, U. Pa., 1997. Diplomate Am. Bd. Ophthalmology. Intern Faulkner Hosp., Tufts U. Sch. Medicine, 1978-79; resident Mass. Eye and Ear Infirmary, Boston, 1979-82, retina fellow, 1982-83; instr. Harvard Med. Sch., Boston, 1983-85, asst. prof., 1985-89, assoc. prof., 1989-91, dir. divsn. continuing edn. dept. ophthalmology, 1989-91; dir. Bascon Palmer Eye Inst., Miami, 2001—. Vis. scientist MIT Regional Laser Ctr., Cambridge, 1982—, asst. prof. health scis. and tech. program, 1987-89, assoc. prof., 1989-91; mem. staff Mass. Eye and Ear Infirmary, Boston, 1983; dir. Morse Laser Ctr., Mass. Eye and Ear Infirmary, 1986-91, dir. New Eng. Eye Ctr., 1991-2001; prof., chmn. dept. ophthalmology Tufts U. Sch. Medicine, 1991-2001, prof. ophthalmology and health mgmt., 1997-2001; adj. prof. biomed. engring. Tufts U., 1991—; chmn. med. bd. New Eng. Med. Ctr. Hosps., 1994-95, ophthalmologist in chief, 1991-2001; assoc. examiner Am. Bd. Ophthalmology, 1990—; sr. v.p. for network devel. Lifespan, 1997-2001; prof., chmn. dept. ophthalmology U. Miami Sch. Medicine, 2001—; med. dir. Anne Bates Leach Eye Hosp., 2001—. Author: (with D. Albert) Foundations of Ophthalmic Pathology, 1979, (with R. Steinert) Principles and Practice of Ophthalmic YAG Laser Surgery, 1984, Lasers in Surgery and Medicine: Principles and Practice, 1996, (with M.R. Hee, J.S. Schuman and J.G. Fujimoto) Optical Coherence Tomography of Ocular Diseases, 1996, (with E. Reichel) Atlas of Indocyanine Green Angiography, 1996; editor-in-chief Lasers in Surgery and Medicine, 1987-95, Ophthalmic Surgery and Lasers, 1995—; contbr. about 120 articles to profl. jours. Pres. Am. Soc. for Laser Medicine and Surgery, 1994-95; v.p. Mass. Soc. Eye Physicians and Surgeons, 1994-96; assoc. examiner Am. Bd. Ophthalmology, 1990—; retina trustee Assn. Rsch. in Vision and Ophthalmology, 1995-99, pres., 2000-01. Recipient Richard and Hinda Rosenthal award in visual scis., 1994, Man of Vision award Boston Aid to the Blind, 1993, Leon Goldman award Biomed. Optics Soc., 1993, I Migliori award Pirandello Lyceum of Mass., 1994. Fellow Am. Acad. Ophthalmology, Am. Soc. for Laser Medicine and Surgery (pres. 1994-95); mem. Assn. Rsch. in Vision and Ophthalmology (pres.-elect 1998-99, pres. 1999-2000, immediate past pres. 2000-2001), Mass. Soc. Eye Physicians and Surgeons (v.p. 1994-96). Roman Catholic. Home: 9321 SW 63rd Ct Miami FL 33156-1814 Office: Bascom Palmer Eye Inst 900 NW 17th St Miami FL 33136 Office Phone: 305-326-6303. E-mail: cpuliafito@miami.edu.*

PULIDO, JOSE S. physician; b. Apr. 29, 1956; BA with hons., U. Chgo., 1976, MS, 1977; MD, Tulane U., New Orleans, 1981; MBA, U. Iowa, 1993. Diplomate Am. Bd. Ophthalmology. Intern Tulane Affil. Hosps.-Charity Hosp., New Orleans, 1981-82; resident in ophthalmology U. Ill., Chgo., 1982-85, chief resident in ophthalmology, 1985-86; fellow vitreoretinal surgery Bascome Palmer Eye Inst./U. Miami Sch. Medicine, 1986-87, fellow retina rsch., 1987; fellow ocular oncology Wills Eye Hosp./Thomas Jefferson U. Sch. Medicine, Phila., 1998; head and prof. dept. ophthalmology and visual scis. U. Ill., Chgo., 1996—. Instr. organic chemistry U. Chgo., 1976-77; asst. prof. ophthalmology Coll. of Medicine, U. Iowa, Iowa City, 1987-92, assoc. prof., 1992-97, prof. 1997-98, others. Reviewer numerous jours., including: Archives of Ophthalmology, 1985—, Ophthalmology, 1987—, Am. Jour. of Ophthalmology, 1992—, others; abstract editor: Diabetes 2000 Newsletter, 1992—, Ophthalmology World News, 1994-96, others; editor: Evidence-Based Eye Care, 1998—; contbr. articles to profl. jours. Mem. Am. Diabetes Assn. (del.), Am. Acad. Ophthalmology, Pan-Am. Acad. Ophthalmology, Retina Soc., Vitreous Soc., Fluorescein Reading and Macular Evaluation, Assn. for Rsch. in Vision and Ophthalmology, Am. Coll. Surgeons, Schepens Internat. Soc., Am. Ophthal. Soc., Macula Soc. Office: U Ill Chgo Eye Ctr 1855 W Taylor St Chicago IL 60612-7242

PULIDO, MARK A. pharmaceutical and cosmetics company executive; b. 1952; McKesson Drug Co., 1975-88; exec. v.p. FoxMeyer Drug Co., 1988-89; chmn., pres., CEO, Red Line Healthcare Corp., 1989-96; pres., CEO, Sandoz Pharmaceuticals Corp., 1994-95; pres., chmn., CEO, dir. McKesson Corp., 1996-99; chmn., CEO, pres. BenefitPoint, San Francisco, 2000—. Office: BenefitPoint 801 Montgomery St San Francisco CA 94133-5164

PULIDO, MIGUEL ANGEL, mayor; b. Mexico City, Mex., 1956; m. Laura Pulido; children: Miguel Robert, David, Isabel. BSME, Calif. State U., Fullerton. Dir. computer program McCaughey & Smith Energy Assocs., v.p.; mem. Santa Ana (Calif.) City Coun., 1986—; mayor City of Santa Ana, 1994—. Mem. Santa Ana Redevel. Agy.; bd. dirs. Orange County Transp. Authority, mem. 1st dist. Bd. dirs. Calif. Workforce Investment, Bowers Mus., Discovery Sci. Ctr. Orange County, Pacific Symphony Orch., UCI Found., Fed. Inter-Govtl. Policy Adv. Com. Trade. Avocations: chess, backgammon, tennis, music, guitar. Office: Office Mayor & City Coun 20 Civic Ctr Plaza PO Box 1988 Santa Ana CA 92702-1988 E-mail: mpulido@ci.santa-ana.ca.us.

PULITZER, LILLY (LILLIAN MCKIM ROUSSEAU), apparel designer, writer; b. Nov. 1931; m. Peter Pulitzer, 1952 (div. 1969); 3 children; m. Enrique Rousseau (dec. 1993). Owner Fla. juice stand; dress designer, 1960—84, 1993—. Co-author (with Jay Mulvaney): Essentially Lilly: A Guide to Colorful Entertaining, 2004.

PULITO, FRANCIS N. artist; b. Kensington, Conn., Jan. 12, 1920; s. Daniel I. and Victoria (Zappone) P.; m. Jean L. Lawrence, Nov. 3, 1945 (dec. 1989); children: Randy, Craig, Roger, Derek, Betsy. Grad. high sch., Berlin, Conn. Exhbns. of landscapes and seascapes U.S. and internat., especially along Eastern Seaboard and with galleries in Washington and the Northeast. Charter mem. Cmty. Art League Kensington, 1955—. With U.S. Army, 1942-45, ETO. Decorated Bronze Star, Silver Star. Mem. Lions (Berlin). Democrat. Avocations: outdoors, fishing, hiking, athletics. Home: 737 Lower Ln Berlin CT 06037

PULITZER, ROSLYN KITTY, social worker, psychotherapist; b. Bronx, N.Y., Apr. 25, 1930; d. George and Laura Eleanor (Holtz) P. BS in Human Devel. and Life Cycle, SUNY, N.Y.C., 1983; MSW, Fordham U., 1987; postgrad., Masterson Inst., N.Y.C., 1991. cert. in psychoanalytic psychotherapy of the personality disorders, Masterson Inst., N.Y.C.; lic. clin. social worker, N.Y. Clinic dir. Resources Counseling and Psychotherapy Ctr., N.Y.C., 1985-89; social worker, clin. supr. methadone maintenance treatment program Beth Israel Med. Ctr., N.Y.C., 1989-97; psychotherapist pvt. practice, 1989—. Cons. therapist, clin. supr. Identity House, N.Y.C., 1980-97, exec. dir., 1985, clin. dir., 1993-94. Mem. regional adv. coun. N.Y. State Div. Human Rights, N.Y.C., 1975-76; mem. Community Bd. 6, N.Y.C., 1978-81; founder, legis. chmn. N.Y. State Women's Polit. Caucus, 1978-80. Mem. NASW, Acad. Cert. Social Workers, Soc. Masterson Inst., N.Y. Milton Erickson Soc. for Psychotherapy and Hypnosis (cert.). Avocations: photography, snorkeling. Home: 2742 La Silla Dorada Santa Fe NM 87505-6703 Office Phone: 505-473-9694. Fax: 505-438-2884. E-mail: images-rkp@comcast.net.

PULLEN, PENNY LYNNE, non-profit organization administrator, former state legislator; b. Buffalo, N.Y., Mar. 2, 1947; d. John William and Alice Nettie (McConkey) P. BA in Speech, U. Ill., 1969. Tv technician Office Instnl. Resources, U. Ill., 1966-68; cmty. newspaper reporter Des Plaines (Ill.) Pub. Co., 1967-72; legis. asst. to Ill. legislators, 1968-77; mem. Ill. Ho. of Reps., 1977-93, chmn. ho. exec. com., 1981-82, minority whip, 1983-87, asst. minority leader, 1987-93; pres., founder Life Advocacy Resource Project, Arlington Heights, Ill., 1992—. Exec. dir. Ill. Family Inst., 1993-94; dir. Legal Svcs. Corp., 1989-93; mem. Pres.'s Commn. on AIDS Epidemic, 1987-88; mem. Ill. Goodwill Del. to Republic of China, 1987. Summit conf. observer as mem. adhoc Women for SDI, Geneva, 1985; mem. Nat. Coun. Ednl. Rsch., 1983—88; dir. Eagle Forum of Ill., 1999—2003, pres., 2003—; del. Rep. Nat. Conv., 1984; mem. Rep. Nat. Com., 1984—88; del. Atlantic Alliance Young Polit. Leaders, Brussels, 1977; pres. Maine Twp. Rep. Women's Club, 1997—99, Rep. Women of Park Ridge, 2001—03. Recipient George Washington Honor medal Freedoms Found., 1978, Dwight Eisenhower Freedom medal Chgo. Captive Nations Com., 1977, Outstanding Legislator awards Ill. Press Assn., Ill. Podiatry Soc., Ill. Coroners Assn., Ill. County Clks. Assn., Ill. Hosp. Assn., Ill. Health Care Assn.; named Ill. Young Republican, 1968, Outstanding Young Person, Park Ridge Jaycees, 1981, One of 10 Outstanding Young Persons, Ill. Jaycees, 1981. Mem. DAR, Am. Legis. Exch. Coun. (dir. 1977-91, exec. com. 1978-83, 2d vice chmn. 1980-83), Com. on the Status of Women (sec. 1997—).

PULLER, LINDA TODD, state legislator; b. Cedar Rapids, Iowa, Jan. 19, 1945; d. Robert Grant and Margaret Jean (Threlkeld) Todd; m. Lewis Burwell Puller, Apr. 26, 1968; children: Lewis B. III, Margaret Todd. BA in Art History, Mary Washington Coll., 1967. With campaign Moore for Chmn., Fairfax, Va., 1987; adminstrv. aide Chair Bd. Suprs., Fairfax, 1988; polit. cons. Wilder for Gov., 1989; mem. Va. Senate, 1992—. Democrat. Episcopalian. Office: VA Senate State Capitol Richmond VA 23219

PULLIAM, FRANCINE SARNO, real estate broker, real estate developer; b. San Francisco, Sept. 14, 1937; d. Ralph C. Stevens and Frances I. (Wilson) Sarno; m. John Donald Pulliam, Aug. 14, 1957 (div. Mar. 1965); 1 child, Wendy; m. Terry Kent Graves, Dec. 14, 1974. Student, U. Ariz., 1955-56, U. Nev., Las Vegas, 1957. Airline stewardess Bonanza Airlines, Las Vegas, 1957; real estate agt. The Pulliam Co., Las Vegas, 1958-68, Levy Realty, Las Vegas, 1976-76; real estate broker, owner Prestige Properties, Las Vegas, 1976—. Importer, exporter Exports Internat., Las Vegas, 1984—; bd. dirs. Citicorp Bank of Nev.; mem. adv. bd. to Amb. to Bahamas Chic Hect.; property mgr. Prestigo Properties, 1992—. Bd. dirs. Las Vegas Bd. Realtors, Fedn. Internat. Realtors, Nat. Kidney Found., Assistance League, Cancer Soc., Easter Seals, Econ. Rsch. Bd., Children's Discovery Mus., New Horizons Ctr. for Children with Learning Disabilities, Girl Scouts, Home of the Good Shepard, St. Jude's Ranch for Homeless Children; pres., bd. dirs. Better Bus. Bur.; chmn. Las Vegas Taxi Cab Authority; pres. Citizens for Pvt. Enterprises. Mem. Las Vegas C. of C. (bd. dirs., developer). Republican. Roman Catholic. Office: 2340 Paseo Del Prado Ste D202 Las Vegas NV 89102-4341 Office Phone: 702-382-0700.

PULLIAM, LARRY G. food products executive; b. Grapevine, Tex. m. Cynthia Pulliam; 2 children. With a regional food svc. co., Ft. Worth, 1974—87, Sysco Corp., L.A., 1987—91, v.p. ops., 1991—95, exec. v.p., CEO Balt., 1995—97, v.p., cheif info. officer Houston, 1997—2000, pres., CEO, 2000—02, sr. v.p. mdse. svcs., 2002—. Mem. dirs. coun. Sysco Corp.; bd. dirs. Capital Bank. Bd. dirs. End Hunger Network. Office: Sysco Corp 1390 Enclave Pky Houston TX 77077-2099

PULLIAM, WALTER TILLMAN, newspaper publisher; b. Knoxville, Nov. 5, 1913; s. James Richardson and Jennie Blanche (Badgett) P.; m. Julia Hill Brownlow, Apr. 18, 1970; 1 child, Mary L. Doffermyre. BA, U. Tenn., 1936. Copy editor Knoxville Jour., 1936; reporter Knoxville News-Sentinel, 1936-42, polit. writer, 1946; nat. affairs reporter, asst. city editor Washington Post, 1947-49; editor, pub. Harriman Record, Tenn., also pres.; gen. mgr. Record Printing Co., Inc., 1949-77; pres. La Follette Press, Inc., 1968—. Pub. La Follette Press, Tenn., Jellico Advance-Sentinel, Tenn., Town Crier, Lake City, Tenn. Author: Harriman: The Town that Temperance Built, 1977; contbr. articles to profl. jours. Chmn. Indsl. Devel. Commn. Harriman; mem. Harriman Pub. libr. Bd.; vice chmn. Tenn. Hist. Commn., 1981—; founder, chmn. tenn. Newspaper Hall Fame, 1965—; v.p. Knoxville Opera Co.; pres. Tenn. Newspaper Found., 1980-84, Monteagle Assembly (Tenn.), 1979-83; trustee James White Fort. With Mediterranean edit. Stars and Stripes, U.S. Army, 1942-46. Mem. Tenn. Press Assn. (past pres.), East Tenn. Hist. Soc. (pres.), Tenn. Hist. Soc. (v.p.), Soc. Profl. Journalists, Nat Press Club (Washington), Cherokee Country, LeConte (Knoxville), Rotary (past dist. gov.). Presbyterian. Home: 1400 Kenesaw Ave Knoxville TN 37919-7773

PULLIAM, YVONNE ANTOINETTE, gifted education educator; b. Chgo. d. Virgil D. Sr. and Velma (Hunter) P. BA in Edn., Lane Coll., 1966; MA in Ednl. Adminstrn. and Supervision, Roosevelt U., 1988. Cert. intermediate tchr. Tchr. Howalton Day Sch., Chgo., 1968-69; actress N.Y.C., 1970-75; tchr. gifted Chgo. Bd. Edn., 1975-78, 81—; tutor Broadway play Raisin, N.Y.C., 1977-78, Annie, N.Y.C., 1980-82. Coordinator Adopt-a-Sch. program, Chgo., 1984-85; tchr. rep. PTA O'Keefe Sch., Chgo., 1984-85. Cartoonist 1st Nat. Bank Chgo. newsletter 1969; stand-in for Diana Ross In Mahogany, 1976; appeared on All My Children, The Hosp. and indsl. films and voiceovers; assoc. dir.: (TV comedy) From Chicago. Recipient cert. of merit Glamour mag., 1965, award for innovative teaching Bus.Week, 1990; named featured designer V2 Fashions, Chgo., 1967, Essence mag., 1971. Mem. AFTRA, Chgo. Tchrs. Union, Am. Film. Inst., Phi Delta Kappa. Democrat.

PULLIN, TANYA, state representative; b. South Shore, Ky, Sept. 15, 1957; d. Norman Keith and Mildred Pauline (Williams) P. JD, Univ. of Ky., 1986; MA, Duke Univ., 1985; BS, Univ. of Ky., 1980. Bar: Ky., 1986, U.S. Ct. Appeals Fed. Cir. 1987. State Rep. House of Rep., Dist. 98, Ky., 2000—; employed Baker & McKenzie, Hong Kong, China, 1995—97, Deacons, Hong Kong, China, 1990—95, Morgan & Finnegan, 1986—90. Bd. dirs., State YMCA of Ky., Frankfort, 1987—. Mem. N.Y. Soc. of Ky. Women (treas. 1988—), Kentuckians of N.Y. (dinner chmn. 1989—), Rainbow Girls (majority member). Democrat. Christian. Office: Capitol Capitol Annex Rm 432C Frankfort KY 40601 also: Dist Rural Rt 1 PO Box 486 South Shore KY 41175

PULLING, THOMAS LEFFINGWELL, investment advisor; b. N.Y.C., May 1, 1939; s. T.J. Edward and Lucy (Leffingwell) P.; m. Lisa Canby, Sept. 14, 1962 (div. 1968); children: Elizabeth, Edward L.; m. Sheila Sonne, Mar. 12, 1970 (div. 1980);children: Victoria, Diana, Christopher; m. Eileen Kingsbury-Smith, Dec. 21, 1989. BA cum laude, Princeton U., 1961. Asst. treas. J.P. Morgan & Co. Inc., N.Y.C., 1962-68; v.p. N.Y. Securities Co., N.Y.C., 1968-71, L.M. Rosenthal & Co., N.Y.C., 1971-76; mng. dir. Citigroup Asset Mgmt., N.Y.C., 1976—. Bd. dirs. Henry Luce Found., 1988—, Woodlawn Cemetery, 1980—; trustee Long Island U., 1995—. With USMC, 1962-67. Mem.: Coun. on Fgn. Rels., Pilgrims of U.S. (N.Y.C.), The Bohemian Club (San Francisco), The Brook Club (N.Y.C.), Univ. Club (N.Y.C.), La Gorce Country Club (Miami), Surf Club (Miami, Fla.), Piping Rock Club (Locust Valley, NY). Republican. Episcopalian.

PULLMAN, ALAN, architect; b. N.Y. BArch, Syracuse U. Registered arch., Calif. Design dir. MCG Arch., Beverly Hills, Calif.; joined Perkowitz & Ruth, Long Beach, Calif., 1999, design dir. Studio One Eleven, 1999—, assoc., 2000—. Advisor Long Beach Village Arts Dist.; bd. mem. Lonb Beach Conservation Corp. Mem.: AIA, Smart Growth Network, Calif. Redevelopment Assn., Nat. Main St. Ctr., Urban Land Inst. Office: Studio One Eleven @ Perkowitz & Ruth 18th Fl 111 W Ocean Blvd Long Beach CA 90802

PULLMAN, BILL, actor; b. Hornell, N.Y., Dec. 17, 1953; m. Tamara Pullman, children: Maesa, Jack, Louis. BFA, SUNY, Oneonta; MFA, U. Mass., Amherst. Theatre instr. Mont. State U., Bozeman. Actor: (theatre) The Rover, 1981, Ah, Wilderness!, 1983, The Old Flag, 1983, Dramathon '84, 1984, Curse of the Starving Class, 1985, All My Sons, 1986, Barabbas, 1986, Nanawatai, 1986, Demon Wine, 1988, Control Freaks, 1993, (films) Ruthless People, 1986, Spaceballs, 1987, The Serpent and the Rainbow, 1988, Rocket Gibraltar, 1988, The Accidental Tourist, 1989, Cold Feet, 1989, Brain Dead, 1989, Sibling Rivalry, 1990, Going Under, 1991, Bright Angel, 1991, Newsies, 1992, A League of Their Own, 1992, Singles, 1992, Sommersby, 1993, Sleepless in Seattle, 1993, Malice, 1993, Mr. Jones, 1993, The Favor, 1994, Wyatt Earp, 1994, While You Were Sleeping, 1995, Casper, 1995, Mr. Wrong, 1996, Independence Day, 1996, Lost Highway, 1997, The End of Violence, 1997, The Thin Red Line, 1998, Brokedown Palace, 1998, Zero Effect, 1998, A Man is Mostly Water, 1999, History Is Made at Night, 1999, The Guilt, 1999, Brokedown Palace, 1999, Lake Placid, 1999, (voice) Coming to Light: Edward S. Curtis and the North American Indians, 2000, (voice) Titan A.E., 2000, Numbers, 2000, Ignition, 2001, Igby Goes Down, 2002, 29 Palms, 2002, Rick, 2003; (TV movies) Home Fires Burning, 1989, Crazy in Love, 1992, The Last Seduction, 1994, Mistrial, 1996, Merry Christmas George Bailey, 1997, The Virginian, 2000; (TV) Opening the Tombs of the Golden Mummies: Live, 2000; (TV series) Revelations, 2004. Office: UTA care JJ Harris 9560 Wilshire Blvd Ste 500 Beverly Hills CA 90212-2427 also: Big Town Prodns Ste 80 6201 Sunset Blvd Los Angeles CA 90028-8704*

PULLMAN, MAYNARD EDWARD, biochemist; b. Chgo., Oct. 26, 1927; s. Harry and Gertrude (Atlas) P.; m. E. Phyllis Light, Sept. 12, 1948; children: H. Cydney, B. Valerie, Jacky Leigh. BS, U. Ill., 1948, MS, 1950; PhD (NIH fellow), Johns Hopkins U., 1953. Fellow in pediatrics Johns Hopkins Hosp., 1953-54; asst. Pub. Health Rsch. Inst., City N.Y., 1954-56, assoc., 1956-61, assoc. mem., 1961-65, mem., 1965-89, chief, 1973-87, assoc. dir., 1983-89; sr. rsch. scientist Coll. Physicians and Surgeons Columbia U., 1989-92, cons., 1997—. Vis. prof. biochemistry U. São Paulo (Brazil) Sch. Medicine, 1963-64; research assoc. prof. biochemistry Sch. Medicine NYU, 1966-76, research prof., 1976-90; biochemistry study section mem. NIH, 1969-73. Editorial bd.: Jour. Biol. Chemistry, 1967-71, 78-80. NIH grantee, 1956-85; Shubert Found. grantee, 1972-74. Fellow N.Y. Acad. Scis.; mem. AAAS, Am. Soc. Biol. Chemistry and Molecular Biology, Brit. Biochem. Soc., Am. Chem. Soc. Home and Office: 338 Archer St Freeport NY 11520-4233 E-mail: mep2658@aol.com.

PULLMAN, PHILIP NICHOLAS, author; b. Norwich, Norfolk, Eng., Oct. 19, 1946; s. Alfred Outram and Audrey Evelyn (Merrifield) P.; m. Judith Speller, Aug. 15, 1970; children: James, Thomas. BA, Oxford U., 1968. Tchr. Oxfordshire Edn. Authority, Oxford, Eng., 1972-88; lectr. Westminster Coll., Oxford, 1988-96. Author: The Ruby in the Smoke, 1987 (Best Book award Internat. Reading Assn., 1988), Shadow in the North, 1988, The Tiger in the Well, 1991, Spring-Heeled Jack, 1991, The Broken Bridge, 1992, The White Mercedes, 1993, The Golden Compass (Guardian Children's Fiction award, 1996, Carnegie medal, 1996), The Subtle Knife, 1997, Clockwork or All Wound Up, 1998, I Was a Rat!, 1999, The Amber Spyglass, 2000 (Whitbread Book of Yr.). Avocations: music, drawing.

PULOS, VIRGINIA KATE, communications consultant; b. Dayton, Ohio, Oct. 12, 1947; d. James C. and Mary M. Pulos; m. Georgios S. Georgiou; 1 child, Kate Elizabeth Chiemingo. BFA in Music summa cum laude, U. Cin., 1970. Singer, actor Broadway, Off Broadway, Stock, Film, Regional Theatre, more, 1970-89; founder, pres. Ginny Pulos Comms., Inc., 1989—. Speech, media and tng. cons.; asst. prof comm. NYU Sch. Continuing and Prolf. Studies; speaker confs. in field. Actress: Portrait of Jenny (Eugene O'Neil award, Richard Rodgers award), regular appearances on TV shows: All My Children, As the World Turns, The Doctors, 1982-88; numerous major opera and musical theatre roles, including: (Broadway) A Little Night Music, (Regional) My Fair Lady, others, 1970—; numerous radio and TV commls., 1970-80; guest soloist: Bklyn. Kingsboro Symphony in the Parks, 1984, 85, others. Program chair The Matrix Awards, 1993, 95, 96, others. Named Corbett Found. Internat. Opera fellow, Hamburg, Germany, 1969, N.Y.C., 1970-77. Mem. Screen Actors Guild, Actors Equity Assn., Am. Fedn. TV and Radio Actors, Pub. Rels. Soc. Am., N.Y. Women in Comm. (bd. dirs., 1992-99). Office: Ginny Pulos Comms Inc 4th Fl 1120 Ave of the Americas New York NY 10036-6700 Office Phone: 212-626-6597. Business E-Mail: info@ginnypulos.com.

PULTE, WILLIAM J. construction executive; Chmn. Pulte Homes Corp., 1950—. Office: Pulte Homes Corp 33 Bloomfield Hills Pkwy Bloomfield Hills MI 48304-2946

PULZ, GARY EDWARD, psychologist; b. Lakewood, N.J., Apr. 6, 1951; s. Edward Walter and Helen P.; m. Joanne Miriam Laukshtein, June 24, 1972; children: Kristian, Rein, Karalina, Daggi. BA, Mt. St. Mary's Coll., Emmitsburg, md., 1973; MA in Psychology, Jersey City State Coll., 1978, profl. diploma in Sch. Psychology, 1980. Nat. cert. sch. psychologist, N.J.; lic. profl. counselor, N.J. Probation officer Ocean County Probation Dept., Toms River, N.J., 1974-78; clin. psychologist Ocean County Mental Health Clinic, Toms River, 1978-80; sch. psychologist Howell (N.J.) Twp. Schs., 1980-87; owner, operator Uncle Wills Pancake House, Beach Haven, N.J., 1974-95, Amber Apts. and Morningstar Band B, Beach Haven, 1995—; pvt. practice lic. profl. counselor N.J., 1999—. Sch. psychologist Stafford Twp. Schs., Manahawkin, N.J., 1987—. Contbr. articles to profl. jours. Organizer/mem. juv. conf. Ocean County Juv. Cts., Toms River, 1987—; mem. eucharistic minister com. St. Francis Ch., Beach Haven, N.J., 1995—; coach of softball and basketball Medford Youth Assn., N.J., 1995-97, LBI Youth Assn., Long Beach Island, N.J., 1990-95. Mem. Nat. Assn. Sch. Psychologists, N.J. Assn. Sch. Psychologists, N.Am. Master Psychologists, N.J. Assn. Mental Illness, N.J. Assn. Master Psychologists (pres. 1994—), Beach Haven Bus. Assn. (pres. 1990-95), N.J. Edn. Assn., Internat. Sch. Psychologists Assn., Mon/Ocean Sch. Psychologists Assn. (v.p. 1983-87). Republican. Roman Catholic. Avocations: Aikido, skiing, boating, travel, historical home renovations. Home: 125 Engleside Ave Beach Haven NJ 08008-1762 also: 24 Glen Lake Dr Medford NJ 08055-3104 Office: Stafford Twp Schs 1000 Mckinley Ave Manahawkin NJ 08050-2807 Fax: 609-978-5739. E-mail: garypulz@aol.com.

PUMARIEGA, JOANNE BUTTACAVOLI, mathematics educator; b. Coral Gables, Fla., May 27, 1952; d. Ciro Charles and Rosaria Frances (Calabrese) Buttacavoli; m. Andres Julio Pumariega, Dec. 26, 1975; children: Christina Marie, Nicole Marie. BA in Math. and Edn. magna cum laude, U. Miami, 1973, MA in Math., 1974; postgrad., U. Houston, 1991-92. Cert. secondary math. tchr., Tex., Fla., Tenn., N.C. Grad. tchg. asst. U. Miami, Coral Gables, 1973-74; substitute tchr. Dade County Pub. Schs., Miami, 1975; math. instr. Miami Dade C.C., 1975-76; math. and G.E.D. instr. Durham (N.C.) Tech. Inst., 1976-77; math. instr. Durham H.S., 1977-78, Durham Acad., 1978-80, Univ. Sch. of Nashville, 1980-83; pvt. practice math. instr. Houston, 1984-86; tutor Clear Lake Tutoring Svc., Houston, 1987-90; pvt. practice S.A.T. lang. instr. League City, Tex., 1990-92; pvt practice math. and S.A.T. instr. Johnson City, Tenn., 1996—; lang. instr. Nelson Elem. Sch., Columbia, 1993-96. Instr. fgn. langs. and math. Lonnie B. Nelson Elem. Sch., Columbia, S.C.; adj. faculty math. East Tenn. State U., 1999—. Author (with F. Rodriguez and A. Pumariega): HIV/AIDS in Children and Adolescents, 1999; co-author (with A. Pumariega): Risk Factors of Mental Illness and Addiction Amongst Hispanic Immigrant Youth, 2002; contbr. articles to profl. jours. Chair bd. edn. St. Mary Parish, League City, 1988-90, lector, 1992, v.p. coun. Cath. Women, Johnson City, 1997-99; C.C.E. tchr. St. John Neumann Cath. Ch., Columbia, S.C. & Johnson City, Tenn., 1993-95, lector, 1992-96; lector St. Mary's Ch., Johnson City, 1996—; treas. St. Thomas More Women's Club, Houston, 1985-86; v.p., then pres. housestaff med. wives Duke U., Durham, N.C., 1978-80; mem. Wash./Unicoi/Johnson County Med. Alliance, 1999-2002, 2003-04, chair pub. rels. com., 1999-2002, asst. treas., 2002-03, membership chmn., 2003-04, co-chmn. caring com., 2004—. Recipient Above and Beyond award, East Tenn. State U., 2002. Mem. Newcomers of Greater Columbia (chmn. pub. rels. chpt. 1993,95), Newcomers of Greater Colo. (com. chair coord. 1994-95), Welcome Neighbors of Bay Area (v.p., program chmn. 1991-92), Tex. Med. Aux., Bay Area Med. Wives, East Tenn. State U. Women's Club (v.p. 1997-98, pres. 1998-99, parliamentarian 1999-2000), U. S.C. Faculty Women's Club (v.p. 1993-94, pres. 1994-95, parliamentarian, advisor 1995-96), Phi Kappa Phi, Kappa Delta Pi, Delta Kappa Gamma (corr. sec. Gamma chpt. 2004-), Alpha Lamba Delta (Woman of Yr. 1972). Roman Catholic. Avocations: reading, public speaking, travel. Home: 2 Roundtree Court Johnson City TN 37604-1492 Office: East Tenn State U Dept Math PO Box 70663 Johnson City TN 37614-1701 Office Phone: 423-439-4349. Personal E-mail: pumarieg@aol.com.

PUMP, BERNARD JOHN, finance company executive, consultant; b. Schenectady, N.Y., Feb. 23, 1960; s. Robert Franz and Mary Eileen (Dalton) P.; m. Karen Yi-Shui Kao, May 13, 1989; children: Rachel Elise, Ryan Bernard, Megan Eileen. BS in Econ. cum laude, U. Pa., 1984; MA in Econ., U. Chgo., 1994, MBA, 1995. CPA, Mass. Acct. Coopers & Lybrand, N.Y.C., 1984-87; mgr. fin. analysis Am. Express TRS, N.Y.C., 1987-89; economist Lexecon, Inc., Chgo., 1991-96; ptnr. Deloitte & Touche LLP, Chgo., 1996—. Fl. broker, trader evening session Chgo. Bd. Trade, 1995-97. Co-author: Proving Antitrust Damages, 1996. Mem. Inst. Mgmt. Accts. (cert.), Union League Club. Republican. Roman Catholic. Avocations: restoring antique watches and fountain pens, golf. Home: 1830 W Eddy St Chicago IL 60657 Office: Deloitte & Touche LLP 180 N Stetson Ave Fl 19 Chicago IL 60601-6779 E-mail: bpump@deloitte.com.

PUN, SUZIE, biomedical engineer, educator; d. Fu-Shang and Naomi Mei-Li Hwang; m. Winston Pun, Oct. 6, 2001. BS, Stanford U., Palo Alto, Calif., 1996; MS, Calif. Inst. Tech., Pasadena, 1998, PhD, 2000. Asst. prof. U. Wash., Seattle, 2002—; sr. scientist Insert Therapeutics, Pasadena, Calif., 2000—02. None. Named one of World's 100 Top Young Innovators, MIT Tech. Rev., 2001; fellow, Whitaker Found., 1996. Mem.: Am. Soc. of Gene Therapy, Am. Soc. of Chem. Engring., Tau Beta Pi, Phi Beta Kappa. Achievements include patents for linear cyclodextrin polymers; patents pending for supramolecular complex formation; nanoparticle modification by inclusion complex formation; research in gene delivery.

PUNDMANN, ED JOHN, JR., automotive company executive; b. St. Charles, Mo., Feb. 24, 1939; s. Ed J. Sr. and Ruth O. (Brehme) P.; m. Dolores Anne Lienau, June 15, 1963 (dec.); children: Mary Ann, Steven A., Susan K. BA, Westminster Coll., 1961. Jr. accountant Peat, Marwick & Mitchell, St. Louis, 1961-62; salesman Pundmann Ford, St. Charles, 1962-82, gen. mgr., 1982-92, pres., 1992—. Bd. dirs., chmn. First State Bank; mem. St. Charles City Tax Incremental Financing Commn., 1990-99; mem. Ford Motor Dispute Settlement Bd., 1993-94, St. Charles County Work Force Devel. Bd., 2002—, Ford Motor Co. Nat. Dealer Coun., 2001-2003. Treas. St. Charles City Charter Commn., 1981; mem. St. Charles City Park Bd., 1981-82; chmn. St. Charles City Econ. Devel. Commn.; mem. St. Charles City Park Found. Bd., 1985—, also past pres.; St. Louis Regional Commerce and Growth Assn.; adv. bd. St. Charles County; mem. Handicapped Facilities Bd. St. Charles County, 1986-94, also past pres.; active St. Charles County Road Bd., 1996—; past pres. St. John United Ch. of Christ; bd. dirs. Emmaus Homes, 1981-91, Parkside Meadows Retirement Facility, 1982-2001; chmn. St. Charles City Charter Rev. Commn., 1991; bd. dirs. St. Charles Jaycee Village Retirement Home, 1980-90, Boone Ctr. Workshop, 1982-92, Parkside Found., 2001-, St. Charles City Schs. Found, 1995—, St. Charles Crime Stoppers, 1999—; dist. chmn. Boy Scouts Am., 1979-82. Recipient Gov. of Mo. award, 1989, Mo. Time Quality Dealer award, 1995, United Ch. of Christ award, 1993, Jefferson award TV Sta. KSDK, St. Louis, 1996, Profl. Excellence Achievement award St. Charles C.C., 2002. Mem. Mo. Auto Dealers Assn. (bd. dirs. 1983—, treas. 1997-98, 2d v.p. 1998-99, 1st v.p. 1999-2000, pres. 2000-2001), Greater St. Louis Ford Dealers Assn. (past pres.), St. Charles C. of C. (past bd. dirs., pres., Citizen of Yr. award 1986, Small Bus. Person of Yr. 2002), Rotary (past pres.). Lodges: Rotary. Home: 3304 Lennox Dr Saint Charles MO 63301-0632 Office: Pundmann Ford 2727 W Clay St Saint Charles MO 63301-2566 E-mail: edp@pundmannford.com.

PUNDT, RICHARD ARTHUR, lawyer; b. Apr. 18, 1944; s. Arthur Herman and Johanna Celeste (Pasterik) Pundt; m. Joyce Kay Schoenfelder, Dec. 1, 1968; children: Vincent Arthur, Jennifer Johanna, Heather Ann. BA, State U. Iowa, 1966; JD, Drake U., 1969. Temporary claims dep. Iowa Employment Security Commn., 1968—69; admitted to Iowa bar, 1969; staff atty. Polk County Legal Aid Office Econ. Opportunity, 1969; spl. agt. FBI, 1969—71; prin. Richard A. Pundt. Law Office; pres. and CEO enlighten techs., Inc. (IP video network); pres. Lawchek Ltd. Dir. Cedar Rapids Profl. Football Corp., 1972—73, pres., 1972—73. Exec. dir. Iowans for Rockefeller, 1968, Polk County Republican Com., 1968—69; mem. Linn County Rep. Ctrl. Com., 1972—78; chmn. Linn County Rep. party, 1977—78; asst. prosecuting atty. Linn County, 1972—76. Mem.: Linn County Bar Assn., Iowa Bar Assn., Am. Iowa Bar Assn., Metro Athletic Assn. (dir. 1976—), Sertoma. Roman Catholic. Home: 3851 Hickory Ridge Ln SE Cedar Rapids IA 52403-3765 Office: 330 1st St SE Cedar Rapids IA 52401-1702 Office Phone: 319-363-8800.

PUNNOOSE, ALEX, physics educator; b. Marika, Kerala, India, May 21, 1968; arrived in U.S., 1999; s. Punnoose Chacko and Mary Punnoose; m. Tina Kurian, Apr. 21, 1996; children: Catherine Alex, Paul Alex. BS, Mahatma Gandhi U., India, 1988; MS, Aligarh Muslim U., India, 1990, MPhil, 1992, D in Physics, 1994. Lectr. in physics Mahatma Gandhi U., Kottayam, 1994—97; postdoctoral rsch. assoc. W.Va. U., Morgantown, 1999—2002; asst. prof. of physics Boise State U., 2002—. Mem. of sci. com. and rev. bd. Internat. Cmty. for Composites Engring., New Orleans, 2002—; mem. awards and honors com. Boise State U., 2002—; presenter in field. Contbr. articles to profl. jours. Prayer leader St. Marks Cath. Ch., Boise, 2002—03. Mem.: Asia-Pacific Electron Paramagnetic Resonance Soc. (founding mem.), Am. Phys. Soc., Internat. Electron Spin Resonance Soc. Achievements include discovery of ferromagnetism at room temperature in semiconducting Co doped Titanium Oxide; development of noval procedure to employ electron magnetic resonance to measure magnetic hysteresis of exchange coupled magnetic nanostructures employed in spintronic devices; research in catalysts, magnetic nanostructures, semiconductors, nanoparticles, and magnetic materials; new mechanism based on Four Spin Cyclic Exchange for high temperature superconductors. Office: Boise State U 1910 University Dr Boise ID 83725 E-mail: apunnoos@boisestate.edu.

PUNSHON, TRACY, research scientist; b. Coatbridge, Lanarkshire, Scotland, Mar. 21, 1970; d. Mary Winifred Leech and Harry Punshon; life ptnr. Brian Jackson. BSc, Liverpool John Moores U., England, 1992; PhD, Liverpool John Moores U., 1996. Post-doctoral assoc. Savannah River Ecology Lab., Aiken, SC, 1998—2000; rsch. assoc. Rutgers U. c/o Savannah River Ecology Lab., Aiken, SC, 2000—. Exptl. officer Liverpool John Moores U., Liverpool, England, 1996—98. Contbr. articles various profl. jours., chapters to books various profl. text. Grantee various amounts, Savannah River Site Environ. Restoration Divsn., 2000—03, River Site Environ. Restoration Divsn., 2000—03. Mem.: Soil Sci. Soc. of Am. Labor. Achievements include discovery of metal uptake in trees. Avocations: running, painting, diarist. Office: Savannah River Ecology Lab Drawer E Aiken SC 29802

PUNT, LEONARD CORNELIS, educational services company executive; b. Bongondza, Zaire, Nov. 16, 1940; arrived in US, 1954, naturalized, 1960; s. Harry Marius and Clara VandeGevel Punt; m. Sarah Elizabeth Walton, Dec. 18, 1966; children: John, Amy, Brian. BA, Wheaton (Ill.) Coll., 1964; MEd, Loyola U., Chgo., 1981. Owner, dir. The Reading Tree Inc., Downers Grove, Ill., 1976—; v.p. Am. Bus. Comm., Downers Grove, 1978—. Author: Dyslexia: Definition and Solutions, 2003. Mem.: Naperville C. of C. Office: Reading Tree Inc 5117 Main St Ste D Downers Grove IL 60515-4654 E-mail: Readtrec2@msn.com.

PUNUKOLLU, GOPI KRISHNA, cardiologist; m. Hima B Parupalli, Feb. 4, 1995; children: Maitreya, Sneha. M.B.B.S, Siddhartha Med. Coll., Vijayawada AP India, 1996. Diplomate Am. Bd. of Internal Medicine, 2003. Ho. officer North Western Regional Health Authority, Port Of Spain, Trinidad and Tobago, 1996—2000; sr. resident L.I. Coll. Hosp., Bklyn., 2000—03, staff cardiologist, 2003—. Contbr. articles to profl. jours. Fellow: Am. Coll. of Cardiology (assoc.). A Connecticut Party. Achievements include research in in pulmonary embolism. Office Phone: 718-780-1809.

PUNZO, FRED, science educator; s. Linda D'Agostino and Anthony Punzo. BA, St. Francis Coll., Bklyn, NY, 1964—68; PhD, Iowa State U., Ames, 1972—75. Asst. prof. biology Blackburn Coll., Carlinville, Ill., 1975—81; prof. biology U. Tampa, Fla. Author: (book) Biology of Camel-Spiders, Desert Arthropods. Active mem. Amnesty Internat., NY, NY, 1995—2004, ACLU, Miami, Fla., 1993—2004; active mem., census taker Audubon Soc., Orlando, Fla., 1991—2004; active mem. Entomol. Soc. Am., Leland, Md., 1975—2004. Mem.: Soc. Study Amphibians and Reptiles, Am. Arachnological Soc., Animal Behaviour Soc. (assoc.), Internat. Behavioral Neuroscience Soc. (assoc.), Am. Soc. Mammalogists (life). Avocations: travel, reading, hiking, music.

PUORRO, GERARD E. pharmaceutical executive; Pres. Candela Corp., Wayland, Mass. Office: Candela Corp 530 Boston Post Rd Wayland MA 01778-1833

PUOTINEN, ARTHUR EDWIN, college president, clergyman; b. Crystal Falls, Mich., Sept. 7, 1941; s. Kaleva Weikko and Ines Pauline (Maki) P.; m. Judith Cathleen Kapoun, Aug. 8, 1964; children: Anne, Marjetta, Sara. AA, Suomi Coll., 1961; BA, Augustana Coll., Rock Island, Ill., 1963; MDiv, Luth. Sch. Theology, Chgo., 1967; MA, U. Chgo., 1969, PhD, 1973; MBA, Wake Forest U., 1984. Pastor Trinity Luth. Ch., Chgo., 1968-70; asst. prof. religion Cen. Mich. U., Mt. Pleasant, 1971-74; dean faculty Suomi Coll., Hancock, Mich., 1974-78; v.p. acad. affairs Lenoir-Rhyne Coll., Hickory, N.C., 1978-83; assoc. dean acad. affairs Roanoke Coll., Salem, Va., 1983-84; exec. dir. Luth. Ednl. Conf. of N.Am., Washington, 1984-88; pres. Grand View Coll., Des Moines, 1988-96; v.p., provost Finlandia U., Hancock, Mich., 1996—. Pastor ELCA No. Great Lakes Synod, Evang.-Luth. Ch. Am. Author: Finnish Radicals..., 1979; contbr. articles to books and jours. Grantee NEH, U.S. Dept. Edn. Democrat. Avocations: jogging, reading, travel. Office: Suomi Coll 600 Quincy St Hancock MI 49930-1806 Home: 246 E Genesee Street Iron River MI 49935 E-mail: puotinin@mail.portup.com., apuotinen@accisd.k12.mi.us.

PUPELLO, DENNIS FRANK, cardiac surgeon, educator; b. Tampa, Fla., May 31, 1939; s. Frank and Grace Ann (Torres) P.; m. Lisa Valerie Arcuri, Feb. 23, 1991; children: Ariel, Alana, Alexa, Angela, Dennis, Frank, Bradford, Derek. BS in Biology, U. Tampa, 1961, postgrad., 1962, DSc, 1988; MD, U. Fla., 1967. Diplomate Am. Bd. Surgery. Intern Stanford U. Hosp., Palo Alto, Calif., 1967-68, resident in cardiovasc. surgery, 1968-72; dir. cardiac surgery Tampa (Fla.) Gen. Hosp., 1972-82; chief dept. cardiac surgery St. Joseph's Hosp., Tampa, 1985—; chief cardiac surgery Blake Meml. Hosp., Brandenton, Fla., 1988-99, Wuesthoff Hosp., Rockledge, Fla., 1991-2001. Clin. asst. prof. sugery Univ. S. Fla., 1974- ; mem. courtesy staff Tampa Gen. Hosp., 1982—, Meml. Hosp. Tampa, 1982—, Univ. Cmty. Hosp., Tampa, 1982—; mem. cons. staff MacDill AFB Regional Hosp., Tampa, 1982—, Women's Hosp. Tampa, 1982—; mem. courtesy staff Town and Country Hosp., 1991—; dir. cardiac surgery program St. Joseph's Hosp., Tampa, 1983—. Author: (chpt.) Valvular Heart Disease, 1995; contbr. articles to profl. jours. Capt. USAR. Fellow Am. Coll. Cardiology, Am. Coll. Chest Physicians; mem. AMA, Internat. Assn. Biol. Implants, Fla. Med. Assn., Fla. Heart Assn. (mem. rsch. com. 1973, mem. com. CPR 1974), Fla. Soc. Thoracic and Cardiovasc. Surgeons (sec., treas. 1984, pres. 1986-87, chmn. membership com. 1991), Hillsborough County Med. Assn., Hillsborough County Heart Assn. (bd. dirs. 1973, chmn. profl. edn. com. 1977), Manatee County Med. Assn., Alpha Omega Alpha. Avocations: scuba diving, pianist, boating. Office: Cardiac Surgical Assocs 3003 W ML King Blvd Tampa FL 33607-9213

PURCELL, ANN RUSHING, state legislator, office manager; b. Reidsville, Ga., May 12, 1945; d. William Robert and Katie (Dasher) Rushing; m. Dent Wiley Purcell, May 26, 1966; children: Edwin Wiley, Mieke Ann, Mikki Marie. BS in Edn., Ga. So. Coll., 1966; hon. degree, Ga. Future Farmers Am., 1999. Cert. secondary tchr. Tchr. math. Evans (Ga.) High Sch., 1966 68; tchr. math., earth and sci. Beaumont Jr. High Sch., Lexington, Ky., 1969-70; substitute tchr. Tallahassee, Fla., 1970's; agt. Noblin Realty, Tallahassee, 1970's; office mgr. Radiation Therapy Assocs., PC, Savannah, Ga., 1979—; state legislator Ho. of Reps. Ga. Gen. Assembly, Atlanta, 1991—. Author: Purcells of South Georgia and Other Related Families, 1976. Bd. dirs. Med. Assn. Ga. Polit. Action Com., Atlanta, 1988-89, Girl Scout Coun. Savannah, 1991-93, Ga. So. U. Found., 1992—. Armstrong Atlantic U. Found., 2004—; mem. adv. com. Effingham County Extension Svc., 1992—; Effingham County fin. chmn State YMCA, 1991—, vice chmn. steering com., 1999, bd. dirs., 1999; mem. adv. com. Treutlin Home, 1999-; bd. adv. Claxton Youth Detention Ctr.; bd. dirs. Effingham YMCA, 1999—. Hon. comdr. 165th Ga. Air Guard Airlift, 2000—; hon. mem. Civil Air Patrol, 2001—, Ga. State Patrol, 2001. Decorated WA-PO-HE award Ga. Nat. Air Guard, Minuteman award; named Georgia's Legislator of Yr., Ga. Sch. Counselors Assn., 1996, Ga. Legislator of Yr., Coastal Conservation Assn. Ga., 1998; named to Hon. Ga. State Patrol, 2001; recipient Friend of Medicine award, Med. Assn. Ga., 1991, 1993, 1994, 1996, Guardian of Small Bus. award, Nat. Fedn. Ind. Bus., 1992, 1994, 1996, Commendation cert., Ga. Emergency Mgmt. Agy., 1995, Vol. of Yr. award, Effingham 4-H, 1998, Nat. Am. hon. degree, Future Farmers Am., 1999, Friend of State 4-H award, 1999, svc. award, Effingham Recreation Dept., 2000, cmty. svc. award, Guyton Masonic Lodge, 2000, Hon. Family Consumer Cmty. Leaders of Ga. award, 2001, Ga. Pub. Health award, 2003, Ga. Vet. award, Med. Assn. Ga., 2003, Effingham Jr. Adv. Family Connection award, 2003, 2004, Environ. Leadership award, Ga. Conservation Voters, 2003, 2004, Pub. Rels. award, Ga. Ext. Assn. of Family and Consumer Scis., 2003, Leadership award, Ga. Water Coalition, 2003, 2004, Charles Dick award, U.S. Nat. Guard, 2003, Air Nat. Guardsmen award, Savannah Assn. Flying, 2003. Mem. Aux. to the Med. Assn. Ga. (pres. 1985), Aux. to the Ga. Med. Soc. (pres. 1981-82), Ga. Salzburger Soc., Effingham County Pub. Ofcls. Assn., Rotary Internat. (Paul Harris fellow 2003), Ga. Peace Officers Assn. (hon.), Rincon Noon Lions Club, Exch. Club. Republican. Methodist. Avocations: painting, genealogy, fishing. Home: 410 Willowpeg Way Rincon GA 31326-9137 Office: LOB 508 Atlanta GA 30334-1600

PURCELL, BILL, mayor; b. Phila., Oct. 25, 1953; s. William Paxson Jr. and Mary (Hamilton) P.; m. Deborah Lee Miller, Aug. 9, 1986; 1 child, Jesse Miller. AB, Hamilton Coll., 1976; JD, Vanderbilt U., 1979. Bar: Tenn. 1979, U.S. Ct. Appeals (6th cir.) 1985, U.S. Supreme Ct. 1986. Staff atty. West Tenn. Legal Svcs., Jackson, Tenn., 1979-81; asst. pub. defender Met. Pub. Defender, Nashville, Tenn., 1981-84, sr. asst. pub. defender, 1984-85; assoc. Lionel R. Barrett, P.C., Nashville, 1985-86; ptnr. Farmer, Berry & Purcell, Nashville, 1986-90; mem. Tenn. Ho. of Reps., Nashville, 1986-96, also majority leader, 1990-96; dir. child and family policy ctr. Vanderbilt Inst. for Pub. Policy Studies, Vanderbilt U., Nashville, 1996-99; mayor Met. Govt. of Nashville and Davidson county, 1999—. Hmn. select com. on children and youth Tenn. Gen. Assembly, 1989—96; exec. dir. Vanderbilt Legal Aid Soc., 1978—79; chmn. NCSL Assembly of State Issues, 1995; chmn. policy makers' program adv. bd. Danforth Found., 1993—2002; mem. adv. bd. U.S. Conf. of Mayors, 2001—02, trustee, 2002—, chmn. task force on hunger and homelessness, 2001—. Chmn. coun. on youth, edn. and families Nat. League of Cities, 2003—04; exec. com. 6th Dist. Dems., Nashville, 1986—88; mem. Tenn. State Gen. Assembly, Nashville, 1986—96, majority leader, 1990—96; chmn. human svcs. com. Nat. Conf. State Legislatures, Washington, 1993; mem. exec. com. Dem. Nat. Com., 1994—97; chmn. Dem. Legislative Campaign Com., 1994—96. Toll fellow Coun. State Govts., 1988; named Legislator of Yr. Dist. Attys.' Gen. Conf. 1989, Tenn. Conservation League, 1991; recipient Distinguished Alumnus award, Vanderbilt Law School, 2004. Mem. ABA, Tenn. Bar Assn., Nashville Bar Assn. Methodist. Office Phone: 615-862-6000. Office Fax: 615-862-6040.

PURCELL, BRADFORD MOORE, publishing company executive; b. Garden City, N.Y., Oct. 1, 1929; s. William Lawrence and Margaret (Moore) P.; m. Louise Rauth, July 10, 1954; children: Margaret, Philip, Mark, Louisa, Christopher. BA, Williams Coll., 1951; MBA, Columbia U., 1957. Sr. v.p. devel. McGraw Hill, Inc., 1976-79, sr. v.p., 1979-81; group v.p. tng. systems, 1981-83, sr. v.p. mktg., 1983-85; pres. W.H. Smith Pubs Inc., N.Y.C., 1985-91; v.p. admin. and fin. Rsch. Books Inc., 1992. Served to 1st lt. USAF, 1951-53. Home: 106 Tantumorantum Rd Lyme CT 06371-3137 Office: Rsch Books Inc 38 Academy St # 1507 Madison CT 06443-2600 E-mail: brad@researchbooks.com.

PURCELL, DALE, college president, consultant; b. Baxley, Ga., Oct. 20, 1919; s. John Groce and Agnes (Moody) P.; m. Edna Jean Rowell, Aug. 2, 1944; children: David Scott, Steven Dale, Pamela Jean; m. Mary Louise Gerlinger, Aug. 26, 1962; adopted children: Amelia Allerton, Jon Allerton. BA, U. Redlands, 1948, MA, 1949; postgrad., Northwestern U., 1951-52; LL.D., Lindenwood Colls., 1974. Topographer U.S. E.D., 1939; U.S. counterintelligence agt., 1940-42; assoc. prof. Ottawa U., 1953-54, asst. to pres., 1954-58; gen. sec. Earlham Coll., 1958-61; dir. devel. U. So. Fla., 1961-63; exec. dir. Cancer Research Center, Columbia, Mo., 1963-65; pres. Westminster Coll., Fulton, Mo., 1973-76, Dale Purcell Assocs., 1972-92; a founding dir. Am. Sports Medicine Inst., Birmingham, Ala., 1987-92. Rep. cons. clients Hughston Sports Medicine Found., Columbus, Ga., Berry Coll., Mt. Berry, Ga., Hope Coll., Holland, Mich., William Woods Coll., Fulton, Mo., Eureka (Ill.) Coll., Cranbrook Insts., Bloomfield Hills, Mich., Penrose Hosp., Colorado Springs, Colo., Northwestern Coll., Orange City, Iowa, Centro Medico Docente, Caracas, Venezuela, Wayland Acad., Beaver Dam, Wis., Cen. Coll., Pella, Iowa, U. of Stirling, Scotland, U. Ottawa, Ont., Can., Washington & Lee U., Lexington, Va., Taylor U., Upland, Ind., Menninger Found., Topeka, Kans., Ill. Wesleyan U., Bloomington, Cox Med. Systems, Springfield, Mo., Nat. Council Family Rels. Mpls., Stephens Coll., Columbia, Mo., Hist. Savannah Found., Ga. Bd. visitors Berry Coll. Capt. USMCR, 1942-46, 52-53. Recipient Disting. Achievement award Berry Coll., 1974, medal Pres. of China, 1945, medal Pres. of Korea, 1953. Mem. Pi Kappa Delta (Alpha chpt.). Presbyterian (elder 1964—). Clubs: St. Louis (Clayton), Univ. (St. Louis and N.Y.C.), Litchfield County Ct. Home: Woodlands 120 Belden St Falls Village CT 06031-1124 Office Phone: 860-824-1236. E-mail: mlgp@sbcglobal.net.

PURCELL, FENTON PETER, engineering consultant; b. Paterson, N.J., Nov. 23, 1942; s. Lee Thomas and Dorothy P.; BCE, Rensselaer Poly. Inst., 1965; m. Susan Duggan, Feb. 20, 1971; children: Aimee and Suzie (twins), Jacqueline. Engr., Lee T. Purcell Assocs., cons. engrs., Paterson, 1965-66, partner, 1969—; v.p. Fenton Corp., Paterson, 1970—; partner L.T.P.A. Partnership, Paterson, 1981—. Cons. World Bank, 1997—, Asian Devel. Bank, 1997—; bd. dirs. Ramapo Valley chpt. ARC, 1978—, 1st v.p., 1980. Served to capt. Med. Svc. Corps, U.S. Army, 1966-69. Decorated Army Commendation medal; registered profl. engr., N.J., N.Y. State, Pa., Mass.; lic. profl. planner, N.J.; diplomate Am. Acad. Environ. Engrs., Nat. Acad. Forensic Engrs. Mem. Am. Water Works Assn., Water Pollution Control Fedn., N.J. Cons. Engrs. Coun., Am. Cons. Engrs. Coun., Rensselaer Soc. Engrs., N.J. Water Pollution Control Assn., Nat. Soc. Profl. Engrs., N.J. Soc. Profl. Engrs. Home: 4 Highview Ter Saddle River NJ 07458-2130 Office: Lee T Purcell Assocs Fairfield NJ 07004 Office Phone: 973-227-7200.

PURCELL, GEORGE RICHARD, artist, postal employee; b. Clayton, N.Y., May 4, 1921; s. George Thomas and Katherine Eileen (Eagan) P.; m. Mary Sutter, Apr. 3, 1961. BS, Niagara U., 1947; postgrad., Syracuse U., 1952-53, 55-56. With Eagan Real Estate, Syracuse, 1948-49; claims interviewer N.Y. State Divsn. Unemployment Ins., 1949-50, 52; with U.S. Postal Svc., Syracuse, 1957—, cert. classifier of mails, 1975-77, with registry dept., 1977—. Tutor in philosophy, 1971—; mem. world peace and diplomacy forum Internat. Biog. Ctr., Cambridge, Eng., mem. rsch. coun. Exhibited in Ctrl. N.Y. Art Open, 1981, Drake Gallery, Fayetteville, N.Y., 1982, Assoc. Artists Gallery, Syracuse, 1983, 91, Fayetteville Art Festival, 1984, Recreation Generation Art Exhibit, 1982—, DeWitt (N.Y.) Libr., 1986-94, N.Y. State Fair, 1990, Art Telauc WCNY-TV, Syracuse, 1990-01, Cazenovia Coll. Art Auction, 1994, N.Y. State Fair Fine Art Exhibit, 1999. Founder, pres. Syracuse chpt. Cath. Med. Mission Bd., 1973-76, rep., 1976—; del. Presdl. Trust, 1992; active Cath. Near-East Welfare Assn., Book Mission Program, New Mems. Art Show Manlius Libr., 1991, Rep. Nat. Com., Heritage Found., Washington; dep. dir. gen. Internat. Biog. Assn., Cambridge, Eng. Served with U.S. Army, 1943-46. Decorated Legion de l'Aigle der Mer, Order of Holy Cross of Jerusalem, knight Order of Holy Grail, knight Lofsensischen Ursinius Orden, baron Royal Order of Bohemian Crown; N.Y. State War Svc. scholar, 1955; named to Hall of Fame, Am. Biog. Inst., Raleigh, N.C. Fellow Australian Inst. Coordinated Rsch. (life); mem. Am. Biog Inst. (life assoc., rsch. bd. advisors nat. divsn., apptd. dep. dir.), Internat. Soc. Neplatonic Studies, World Jewish

Congress, Soc. Ancient Greek Philosophy, Inst. des Hautes Etudes, Alliance Universelle pour la Pax (hon. prof.), Osterrichische Albert Sweitzer Gesselshaft, Acad. Maison des Internationale Intellectuels. Roman Catholic.

PURCELL, HENRY, III, real estate developer; b. Watertown, N.Y., Dec. 21, 1929; s. John Cecil and Elizabeth (Hathway) P.; m. L. Betty Collier; children: Robert William, Emmy Purcell Reynolds, Jenny Purcell Hawley. BS in Mil. Engring., U.S. Mil. Acad., 1953; MBA in Econs. and Fin., U. Utah, 1975; postgrad., Princeton, 1960-61; PhD in Bus., Kennedy Western U., 2001. Cert. Middle East specialist, Turkish linguist. Commd. 1st lt. U.S. Army, Augsburg, Republic of Germany, 1953, advanced through grades to lt. col., 1967, commdr. Co. K. 1st regiment, 5th infantry div., 1955-56, chief translation, U.S. Mil. Mission to Turkey Ankara, Turkey, 1957-59, batallion commdr., tng. div. Ft. Ord, Calif., 1965, sr. regimental adv. 7th ARVN regiment, 5th ARVN div., 1966, adv. G3 plans, III Corps ARVN, 1966-67, with Middle East Plans div., U.S. Strike Commd., 1968-70, asst. chief staff, G5 101st Airborne/Ambl div. I Corps, South Vietnam, 1970, with G3Plans, Iv Corps ARVN, 1970, sr. regimental adv. 32d regiment, 1971, with war plans div., deputy chief of staff, ops., The Pentagon, 1971, Middle East Specialist U.S. Readiness command, 1972-74, retired, 1974; Middle East specialist U.S. Attache's Office, Ankara, Istanbul, 1961-63; with Spacos, G3 Plans and nuclear weapons employment div. NATO, Izmir, Turkey, 1963-65; pres. Henry Purcell, Inc., Tampa, 1976—, Warn-a-Prowler Inc., Tampa, 1994—. Personal interpreter/Turkish translator for Lyndon B. Johnson. Author: Valuation of Publicly Traded Companies: Indicating Investment Targets, 2001. Pres. Nat. Sojourners, Tampa, 1969, 70, 72, Wilson Jr. High Sch. PTA, Tampa, 1977; commdr. Heroes of '76, Tampa, Fla., 1969, 70. Decorated DFC, Bronze Star for Valor with two oak leaf clusters, Cross of Gallantry, Gold Star, Silver Star (Vietnam), 10 Air medals, Army Commendation medal for valor with one oak leaf cluster with "V" device. Mem. Unified Constrn. Trades Bd., Nat. Assn. Realtors, Fla. West Coast Roofing Assn., Nat. Builders Assn., Greater Tampa C. of C. (com. of 100 1980—). Office: 825 W Platt St Tampa FL 33606-2251 E-mail: purcellh@aol.com.

PURCELL, JAMES JOSEPH, publishing executive, public relations executive; b. Newark, Mar. 9, 1966; s. James Joseph and Ruth Madeline Purcell; m. Andrea Krasno, May 7, 2000. Diploma/MDS award, US Army Infantry Sch., Ft. Benning, Ga., 1983, U.S. Army Intelligenc Sch., Ft. Huacheca, Ariz., 1985; Airborne Wings, US Army Airborne Sch., Ft. Benning, 1986; AS, Brookdale C.C., Lincrof, N.J., 1987. Mortarman U.S. Army Reserve, Red Bank, NJ, 1983—85; intelligence analyst U.S. Army, Ft. Bragg, NC, 1985—89; tng. officer active reserve NJ Nat. Guard, Freehold, 1989—90; infantryman US Army, Ft. Campbell, Ky., 1990—91; maintenance svc. asst. mgr. JV Basics, Howell, NJ, 1991—93; reporter Tritown News, Jackson, NJ, 1993—94, Wall (NJ) Herald, 1994—96; editor Ocean County Rev., Lavallette, NJ, 1996—98; reporter Greater Media Newspaper, E. Brunswick, NJ, 1998; publisher The Courier, Middletown, NJ, 1998—. Organizer The Ricky Ashmore Fund, Middletown, NJ, 2000—02; vol. pub. rels. agt. NAACP, Long Branch, NJ, 2002—; organizer Middletown Police Widows Support Group, 2003—; active mem. Rep. Party Union Beach, NJ, 2001—. Sgt. U.S. Army, 1985—89. Recipient Cert. Appreciation, US Coast Guard, 2001, Comty. Svc. award, NAACP, Long Branch, N.J., 2003, Cert. Recognition, U.S. Congress/ Rep. F. Pallone, 2003. Mem.: 82d Airborne Divsn. Assn., Elks Lodge, Red Bank, NJ. Republican. Baptist. Avocations: colllecting vintage baseball memorabilia, tai chi. Home: 536 Sydney Ave Keyport NJ 07735 Office: The Courier 320 Kings Hwy E Middletown NJ 07748 E-mail: jim18an@att.net.

PURCELL, JAMES MICHAEL, science educator; b. Phila., Pa., Feb. 23, 1937; s. George Vincent Purcell and Mary Margaret Whalen; m. Sheila Marianne Riley, Nov. 18, 1961; children: James Michael Purcell II, Sean Philip, Liam Thomas More. BS in chemistry, Villanova U., 1959, MS in biochemistry, 1961; grad. edn., Drexel U., 1970. Rsch. chemist U.S. Dep. Agrl., Agrl. Res. Svc., Ea. Regional Res. Ctr., Phila., 1961—91; adj. instr. Phila. Coll. of Textiles & Sci., Phila., 1991—92; chmn., allied health, sci., & math. divsn. Manor Coll., Jenkintown, Pa., 1992—98, sr. assoc. prof., 1998—; corp. sec. The CECON Group, Inc., Wilmington, Del., 1992—97; adj. instr., biochemistry Thomas Jefferson U., Coll. of Health Professions, Phila., 1998—. Mem , adv. bd. Analytical Letters Marcel Dekker Pub., N.Y.C., 1981—; chmn., Del. Valley chpt. Soc. for Applied Spectroscopy, Wilmington, Del., 1983—84; treas. Fedn. of Analytical Chemistry and Spectroscopy Soc., Phila., 1985—88, Rotary Club of Chestnut Hill, Phila., 1998—, treas.; dir., 2000—02. Grant facilitator, tutor Providence Ctr., Phila., 1998—2004. Mem.: NSTA, NY Acad. of Scis., Soc. of Coll. Sci. Tchrs. Avocations: birding, reading mystery novels, acting, theater. Office: Manor Coll 700 Fox Chase Rd Jenkintown PA 19046 Office Phone: 215-885-2360. Office Fax: 215-576-6564. Business E-Mail: jpurcell@manor.edu.

PURCELL, JAMES NELSON, JR., international organization administrator; b. Nashville, July 16, 1938; s. James Nelson and Mary Helen P.; m. Walda Jean Primm, July 16, 1961; children: Deirdre Ann, Carole Elizabeth. BA in Polit. Sci., Furman U., 1961; M.P.A. (Maxwell Grad. Sch. fellow), Syracuse U., 1962. Mgmt. intern U.S. AEC, N.Y.C., Washington, Oak Ridge, 1962, budget analyst Oak Ridge, Washington, 1962-66; mgmt. analyst AID, State Dept., Washington, 1966-68; budget preparation specialist Office Mgmt. and Budget/Exec. Office of the Pres., 1968-69, dept. chief budget preparation, 1969-72, sr. budget examiner Internat. Ednl. Exch. program, 1972-74, chief Justice-Treasury br., 1974-76; chief resources programming and mgmt. div. Bur. Ednl. and Cultural Affairs, Dept. State, Washington, 1976-77; exec. dir. Bur. Adminstrn., Dept. State, Washington, 1978-79; dep. asst. sec. Bur. Refugee Programs, Dept. State, Washington, 1979-82, dir., 1982-87; dir. gen. Internat. Orgn. for Migration, Geneva, 1988-98; internat. cons., 1998—. Bd. dirs. Coun. for Cmty. of Democracies; sr. adv. Inst. for Study of Internat. Migration, Georgetown U. Mem. Am. Soc. Pub. Adminstrn. Home: 5113 W Running Brook Rd Columbia MD 21044 Office Phone: 443-745-2380. Personal E-mail: jpurcellatcol@comcast.net.

PURCELL, JOHN F. lawyer; b. Bellingham, Wash., Apr. 25, 1954; AB with honors, Stanford U., 1976; JD, Lewis and Clark Coll., 1980. Bar: Oreg. 1980. Ptnr. Miller Nash LLP, Portland, 1987—. Mem. Oreg. State Bar. Office: Miller Nash LLP 111 SW 5th Ave Ste 3500 Portland OR 97204-3638

PURCELL, KAREN ANNE, veterinarian; b. Troy, NY, Apr. 18, 1965; d. Joseph Kenneth and Mary Grace Purcell; m. Denis George Parslow, Jan. 17, 1964. BS in biology, Pace U., 1987; Doctorate in vet. medicine, Coll. of Vet. Medicine at Cornell, 1992. Assoc. vet. Wholepet Health Ctr., Everett, Mass., 1999—2003; relief vet. Karen Purcell DVM, Londonderry, NH, 2003—; assoc. vet. Abbott Valley Vet. Ctr., Cumberland, RI, 1999, Abbott Animal Hosp., Worchester, Mass., 1997—99, Uxbridge Animal Hosp., Uxbridge, Mass., 1994—97. Lectr. Becker Coll., Leominster, Mass., Am. Humane Assn., Atlanta, 2000, Tuft's Animal Expo., Boston, 2001, Am. Ferret Assn., Boston, 2002. Author: (textbook) Essentials of Ferrets: A Guide for Practitioners; contbr. articles various profl. jours.; med. reveiwer Ferrets for Dummies. Pres., vet. adv. Mass. Ferret Friends, Mass., 1995—2000. Master: Am. Vet. Med. Assn.; mem.: Lesbian and Gay Vet. Med. Assn., Assoc. of Exotic Mammal Veterinarians, Mass. Vet. Med. Assn. (member-education com. 2002—04), Alpha Psi (rush co-chair 1990—91). Avocations: reading, belly dance, science fiction conventions. Personal E-mail: drkaren@ilk.org.

PURCELL, KAREN BARLAR, physician, nutritionist, vocalist, writer; b. Miami, Fla., Dec. 31, 1947; d. Raymond and Elita (Kitzmiller) Barlar; m. John A. Purcell, June 11, 1977 (div. Dec. 1986); 1 child, Carl; m. Roy Gene Autry, Dec. 31, 1987 (dec. Mar. 2003). MusB, U. Cin., 1969; MusM, New England Conservatory Music, Boston, 1971; post grad tng., Bastyr U., Seattle, WA, 1997-98; D in Naturopathy, Natural Health Acad. Healing Arts, Tenafly, NJ, 1992. Diplomate Am. Bd. Naturopathic Physicians, 1997, cert. master herbalist, Dallas; ordained to mininstry Progressive Universal Life Ch., 1998. Assoc. prof. U. Miami, 1974-77, Dade County Jr. Coll., Miami, 1974-77; pvt. practice, N.Y.C., 1990—. Assoc. prof. NYU, 1988-92, Strasberg Theater Inst., N.Y.C., 1988-92, UN Internat. Sch., N.Y.C., 1992-96; star mgr. Nature's Sunshine Products; profl. spkr. in field, 1990—. Author: Simplified Nutritional Handbook, 1996, How to Survive a Nuclear Disaster, 2002; opera singer, 1970—. Founder WINS Found. for Moderate to Severe Brain Disorders, 1999—. Mem. Am. Naturopathic Med. Assn., Internat. and Am. Assn. Clin. Nutritionists, Internat. and Am. Assn. Counselors and Therapists, Nat. Spkrs. Assn. Avocations: botany, cooking, travel. Office: 666 West End Ave Ste 15S New York NY 10025-7357 Office Phone: 212-580-3051. E-mail: kbpurcell@aol.com.

PURCELL, LEE, actress, film producer; b. N.C., June 15, 1957; divorced; 1 child, Dylan D. Purcell. Studies with Margot Lister, London; studies with Milton Katselas, Jeff Corey, U.S. Pres., owner Silver Strand Entertainment, L.A., 1995—. Appeared in (films) Adam at 6 A.M., 1970, The Toy Factory, 1971, Dirty Little Billy, 1972, Kid Blue, 1973, Mr. Majestyk, 1974, Almost Summer, Big Wednesday, 1978, Stir Crazy, 1980, Valley Girl, Eddie Macon's Run, 1983, Laura's Dream, 1986, Airplane II, 1989, Trackers, 1990, Money & Murder, 1993, The Joke, 1994, Malaika, 1997, Dizzyland, 1998, The Unknown, 2003, (TV) Hijack, 1973, Stranger in Our House, 1978, Howard, The Amazing Mr. Hughes, 1979, Kenny Rogers as the Gambler, 1980, Killing At Hell's Gate, 1981, My Wicked Wicked Ways: The Legend of Errol Flynn, 1986, Betrayed by Innocence, 1989, Long Road Home (Emmy nominee Lead Actress-Special), 1991, To Heal a Nation, 1992, Dazzle, 1994, Secret Sins of the Father (Emmy nominee Supporting Actress-Special), 1994, Due South (recurring role), 1995-96, Promised Land, 1999, (stage) One Flew Over the Cuckoo's Nest, Richard III, A Streetcar Named Desire, The Taming of the Shrew, A Midsummer's Night Dream. Recipient Bronze Star Halo Career Achievement award So. Calif. Motion Picture Council, 1985, Golden Star Halo award, 1986, Silver Medal award N.Y. Film and TV Festival, 1987. Mem. Actors' Equity Assn., Screen Actors Guild, AFTRA, Acad. Motion Picture Arts and Scis., Acad. TV Arts And Scis. Avocations: writing, collecting antiques and art. Office: PO Box 12581 La Crescenta CA 91224-5581

PURCELL, MARY HAMILTON, speech educator; b. Ft. Worth; d. Josseph Hants and Letha (Gibson) Hamilton; m. William Paxson Purcell, Jr., Dec. 28, 1950; children: William Paxson III, David Hamilton. BA, Mary Hardin-Baylor Coll., 1947, HHD (hon.), 1986; MA, La. State U., 1948; HHD (hon.), U. New Eng., 2000. Instr. dept speech and dramatic arts Temple U., Phila., 1948-53, 60-61; part-time instr. speech Cushing Jr. Coll., Bryn Mawr, Pa., 1966-78. Pres. Pa. Program for Women and Girl Offend, 1968—73, Nether Providence Parent Tchr. Orgn., 1975—76; treas. Virginia Gildersleeve Internat. Fund U. Women, 1975—81, bd. dirs., 1987—93; mem. U.S. del. UN Commn. on Status of Women, 1996; co-chmn. NGO Com. for UNICEF, 1994—2000, mem. global forum, 2001—; mem. Wallingford-Swarthmore Dist. Sch. Bd., 1977—83; bd. dirs. Ministers and Missionaries Fund Am. Bapt. Conv., 1985—94, pres., 1995—2003, Internat. Devel. Conf., 1986—; bd. dirs. Nat. Peace Inst. Found., 1983—86; Big Bros./Big Sisters of Am., 1985—90; bd. dirs. Citizens Crime Commn. of Phila., 1976—, Pa. Women's Campaign Fund, 1985—88, 1993—. Named Outstanding Alumna, Mary Hardin-Baylor Coll., 1972, Disting. Dau. Pa., 1982, v.p., 1994—95, pres., 1995—97, Woman of Yr., DECO Women's Conf., 1998; recipient Eleanor Schnurr award, UNA/USA, 2000. Mem. AAUW (Pa. state pres. 1968-70, v.p. mid. Atlantic region, 1973-77, program v.p. 1979-81, pres. 1981-85, rep. to UN 1985-89), Internat. Fedn. Univ. Women (1st v.p. 1986-89, pres. 1989-92, rep. to UN 1992—; pres. UN Dept. Pub. Info. Non Govt. Orgn. ann. conf. 1993), Speech Assn. Am. (Zeta Phi Eta award for excellence in comm. 1983), Pi Kappa Delta, Pi Gamma Mu, Delta Sigma Rho, Alpha Psi Omega, Alpha Chi. Democrat. Baptist. Home: 9 Oak Knoll Dr Wallingford PA 19086-6315 E-mail: mjd1926@aol.com.

PURCELL, MARY LOUISE GERLINGER, retired adult education educator; b. Thief River Falls, Minn., July 17, 1923; d. Charles and Lajla (Dale) Gerlinger; m. Walter A. Kuyawski, June 9, 1950 (dec. July 1954); children: Amelia Allerton, John Allerton; m. Dale Purcell, Aug. 26, 1962. Student, Yankton Coll., 1941-45, Yale Div. Sch., 1949-50, NYU, 1949; MA, Columbia U., 1959, EdD, 1963. Teenage program dir. YWCA, New Haven, 1945-52; dir. program in family rels. Earlham Coll., Richmond, Ind., 1959-62, asst. prof. sociology and psychology, 1959-62, conf. coord. undergrad. edn. for women, 1962; chmn. divsn. home and cmty. Stephens Coll., Columbia, Mo., 1962-73, chmn. family and cmty. studies, 1962-78; dir. continuing edn. women Learning Unltd., 1974-78; prof. Auburn (Ala.) U., 1978-88, head dept. family and child devel., 1978-84, chmn. search com. for v.p. acad. affairs, 1984, spl. asst. to v.p. acad. affairs, 1985-86, prof. emerita, 1988—. Developer course, cons. Contemporary Am. Woman, 1962; vis. prof. Ind. U. Summer Sch., 1970; cons. student pers. svcs. Trenton (N.J.) State Coll., 1958—59, 1961. Contbr. articles to coll. bulls., jours. V.p. Falls Villate-Canaan Hist. Soc., 1998 -2001, pres., 2002—. Recipient Alumni Achievement award, Yankton Coll., 1975; Alumni fellow, Tchrs. Coll. Columbia U., 1959. Mem.: AAUW, Nat. Coun. Family Rels., Groves Conf. Family (nat. program chmn. 1977, dir., chmn.-elect affiliated couns. 1981—82, chmn. 1982—84, chmn. film awards com., chmn. spl. emphases sect., bd. dirs.), Am. Home Econs. Assn. (bd. dirs. 1967—69, chair 1st subject matter unit 1969, family rels. and child devel. sect. 1986—89), Falls Village Can. Hist. Soc. (v.p. 1998—2001, pres. 2002—), Litchfield County Univ. Club (mem. scholarship com. 2001—, bd. dirs. 2001—), Housatonic Camera Club (co-pres. 1996—2000), Delta Kappa Gamma. Congregationalist. Home: 120 Belden St Falls Village CT 06031-1124 E-mail: mlgp@sbcglobal.net.

PURCELL, PATRICK JOSEPH, newspaper publisher; b. N.Y.C., Nov. 9, 1947; s. Patrick Joseph and Sarah (Muller) P.; m. Maureen T. Shuart, Aug. 8, 1970; children: Kathleen, Erin, Patrick, Kerry. BBA, St. John's U., 1969; MBA, Hofstra U., 1977. Various supr. positions N.Y. Daily News, N.Y.C., 1969-80; assoc. pub. Village Voice, N.Y.C., 1980-82; v.p. advt. N.Y. Post, N.Y.C., 1982-83; v.p. sales and mktg. Skyband Inc., N.Y.C., 1983; pres., pub. Boston Herald, 1984—, owner, 1994—; pub. The N.Y. Post, 1986-88; exec. v.p. News Am./Newspapers, 1986-90, pres., 1990-93, CEO, 1993-94; East Coast pres. Am. Ireland Fund, 1996—. Bd. dirs. Bay Bank, MetroWest Sub. Regional Bd., The Genesis Fund. Bd. dirs. NCCJ, Boston, 1984-86, Boy Scouts Am., Boston, 1984-85, Cath. Charitable Bur., Boston, 1984-86, John F. Kennedy Found.; mem. Greater Boston Assn. Retarded Citizens, 1984-86; chmn. Boston Against Drugs, 1988—; mem. White House Conf. for a Drug Free Am., 1987. Mem. Boston Better Bus. Bur., Am. Newspaper Pub. Assn., New Eng. Newspaper Assn., Boston C. of C. (bd. dirs. 1984-86), Downtown Crossing Assn. (bd. dirs.) Clubs: Publicity, Ad (Boston). Roman Catholic. Avocations: jogging; skiing. Office: Boston Herald PO Box 2096 Boston MA 02106-2096

PURCELL, PHILIP JAMES, financial services company executive; b. Salt Lake City, Sept. 5, 1943; m. Anne Marie Mc Namara, Apr. 2, 1964. BBA, U. Notre Dame, 1964; M.Sc. in Econs., London Sch. Econs. and Polit. Sci., U. London, 1966; MBA, U. Chgo., 1967. Mng. dir., cons. McKinsey & Co., Inc., Chgo., 1967-78; v.p. planning and adminstrn. Sears, Roebuck and Co., Chgo., 1978-82; from pres., CEO, to chmn., CEO Dean Witter Discover & Co., N.Y.C., 1982-97; chmn., CEO Morgan Stanley (name changed from Morgan Stanley, Dean Witter & Co. 2002), N.Y.C., 1997—. Dir. N.Y. Stock Exch., 1991-96; mem. coun. U. Chgo. Grad. Sch. Bus. Trustee U. Notre Dame. With USNR. Mem. Econ. Club Chgo., Chgo. Club, Links. Roman Catholic. Office: Morgan Stanley 1585 Broadway Ste 39th New York NY 10036-8200*

PURCELL, ROBERT HARRY, virologist, researcher; b. Keokuk, Iowa, Dec. 19, 1935; s. Edward Harold and Elsie Thelma (Melzl) P.; children: David Edward, John Leslie. BA in Chemistry, Okla. State U., 1957; MS Biochemistry, Baylor U., 1960; MD, Duke U., 1962. Intern in pediatrics Duke U. Hosp., Durham, N.C., 1962-63; officer USPHS, 1963; with Epidemic Intelligence Svc., Communicable Disease Ctr. Atlanta; assigned to vaccine br. Nat. Inst. Allergy and Infectious Diseases, Bethesda, Md., 1963-65; sr. surgeon Lab. Infectious Diseases, NIH, Bethesda, Md., 1965-69, med. officer, 1969-72, med. dir., 1972-74, head hepatitis viruses sect., 1974-2001, co-chief, 2001—. Organizer, invited participant, speaker numerous nat. and internat. symposia, confs., workshops, meetings; temporary advisor WHO, 1967—; expert cons. in hepatitis U.S.—China, U.S.—Taiwan, U.S.—Japan, U.S.—Russia, U.S.—India, U.S.—Pakistan Bilateral Sci. Agreements; lectr. various virology classes. Reviewer numerous sci. jours.; contbr. 600 articles to profl. jours., chpts. to books; 20 patents in field. Recipient Superior Svc. award USPHS, 1972, Meritorious Svc. medal USPHS, 1974, Gorgas medal, 1977, Disting. Svc. medal USPHS, 1978, Disting. Alumni award Duke U. Sch. Medicine, 1978, Eppinger prize 5th Internat. FALK Symposium on Virus and Liver, Switzerland, 1979, Medal of City of Turin, Italy, 1983, Gold medal Can. Liver Found., 1984, King Faisal Internat. prize for Medicine, 1998, Rsch. Sci. award Hepatitis Found. Internats., 1999; named to Alumni Hall of Fame East Okla. State Coll., 1996. Fellow AAAS, Washington Acad. Scis., Am. Acad. Microbiology, Molecular Medicine Soc.; mem. Am. Epidemiology Soc., Am. Soc. Microbiology, Am. Soc. Virology, Soc. Epidemiol. Rsch., Infectious Diseases Soc. Am. (Squibb award 1980), N.Y. Acad. Scis., Am. Soc. Clin. Investigation, Assn. Am. Physicians, Am. Coll. Epidemiology, Am. Assn. Study of Liver Diseases (Disting. Achievement award 2000), Internat. Assn. Study and Prevention Virus Associated Cancers, Internat. Assn. Biol. Standardization, Internat. Assn. Study Liver, Soc. Exptl. Biology and Medicine (Disting. Scientist award 1986), Nat. Acad. Scis. (Washington chpt.). Office: NIH Lab Infectious Diseases 50 S Dr MSC 8009 Rm 6523 Bethesda MD 20892-8009 Office Phone: 301-496-5090. Business E-Mail: rpurcell@niaid.nih.gov.

PURCELL, STUART MCLEOD, III, financial planner; b. Santa Monica, Calif., Feb. 16, 1944; s. Stuart McLeod Jr. and Carol (Howe) P. AA, Santa Monica City Coll., 1964; BS, Calif. State U., Northridge, 1967; grad., CPA Advanced Personal Fin. Planning Curriculum, San Francisco, 1985. CPA, Calif.; CFP. Sr. acct. Pannell Kerr Forster, San Francisco, 1970-73; fin. cons. Purcell Fin. Services, San Francisco, 1973-74, San Rafael, Calif., 1980-81; controller Decimus Corp., San Francisco, 1974-76, Grubb & Ellis Co., Oakland, Calif., 1976-78, Marwais Steel Co., Richmond, Calif., 1979-80; owner, fin. counselor Purcell Wealth Mgmt., San Rafael, 1981—. Exec. dir. www.norforprofits.com, 2000—; guest lectr. Golden Gate U., San Francisco, 1985—; leader ednl. workshops, Larkspur, Calif., 1984; speaker Commonwealth Club Calif., 1989, 91. Contbr. articles to newspapers and profl. jours. Treas. Salvation Army, San Rafael-San Anselmo-Fairfax, Calif., 1987—; chmn. fin. planners div. United Way Marin County, Calif., 1984; mem. fundraising com. Marin County March of Dimes, 1987—, Marin County Arthritis Found., 1988—; mem. Marin Estate Planning Council. Served to lt. (j.g.) USNR, 1968-76. Named Eagle Scout, 1959, Best Fin. Advisor Marin County Independent-Jour. newspaper, 1987, Top Producer Unimarc, 1986; recipient Outstanding Achievement award United Way, 1984; named to The Registry of Fin. Planning Practitioners, 1987. Mem. AICPA, Calif. Soc. CPAs, Nat. Speakers Assn., Internat. Assn. for Fin. Planners (exec. dir. North Bay chpt., San Francisco 1984), Internat. Soc. Pre-Retired Planners, Soc. CPA-Fin. Planners (dist. membership chmn. San Francisco 1986), Registry Fin. Planning Practitioners, Sigma Alpha Epsilon. Presbyterian. Avocations: travel, auto racing, skiing, gardening. Home: 45 Vineyard Dr San Rafael CA 94901-1228 Office: Purcell Wealth Mgmt 45 Vineyard Dr San Rafael CA 94901-1228 E-mail: topbuspro@comcast.net.

PURCHASE-OWENS, FRANCENA, human resources specialist, educator; b. Milw., Nov. 14, 1960; d. Johnny and Arlene (Roberts) Purchase. Cert., Mich. Profl. Sch. Modeling, 1980; AA cum laude, Milw. Stratton Coll., 1982; BS in Applied Liberal Studies, Western Mich. U., 1997, M in Ednl. Leadership, cum laude, 2004. Investment mgmt. sec. M&I Bank, Milw., 1984-85; cons. United Devel. Corp., Milw., 1986-88; paraprofessional Grand Rapids (Mich.) Pub. Schs., 1990-92; temp. helper Dayton Hudson Fortune 500, Grand Rapids, Mich., 1990; customer svc. rep. Kent County Conv. and Visitors Bur., Grand Rapids, 1995; mktg. rschr. Wirthlin Worldwide, Grand Rapids, 1996-98; pres. Creative Works, Grand Rapids, 1988—, Francena Purchase Internat. Honor Soc., Kentwood, Mich., 1999—, Francena Purchase Internat. Applied Studies, Grand Rapids, 1999—, Purchase Bus. Inst., Kentwood, 1999—, Francena Purchase Internat. Applied Profl. Studies Soc., Grand Rapids, Mich., 2000—; prof. U. Wis. (Big 10 U. Sys.); adminstrv. asst. to Elizabeth Kubler-Ross Ga. State U., 1980. Sec. Mich. Nat. Bank, Grand Rapids, 1980-81, Internat. Mktg. dept. Am. Seating, Grand Rapids, 1980-81, Volt Tech. Svcs. engring. firm, Milw., 1980, sec. to various tep. cos. and positions; asst. exec. sec. Manpower Internat. Inc., Milw., 1982-84; cons. NASW; rschr., sec. United Devel. Corp.; human resource asst., computer programmer, sec. Patricia Stevens Coll., Milw., 1985-86; clerk-typist med. recors Spectrum Health (formerly Blodgett Meml. Med. Ctr.), Grand Rapids, 1979, telemarketer Weathermaster Indsutries, Inc., Milw., 1980; computer programming cons. Nat. Assn. Social Workers, Milw., 1980; office asst. to various cos. Access, Milw., 1980; asst.to pres. Alissia Cosmetics, Miss Black Pageant, 1980; legal sec. to attorney David Clowers, Milw., 1980, student asst. Ga. State U. Gerontology dept., Atlanta, 1980; student asst. Maln office, attendance office Ottawa Hills H.S., Grand Rapids, 1976-77, Fed. Govt. contract divsn., Grand Rapids, 19777-78; cashier Helen Smith's Market, Milw., 1972-73; clerk draft typist Ind. Libr. Life Ins. Co. claims dept., Grand Rapids, 1978-79; grad. asst. candidate Dale Carnegie course in Human Rels and Pub. Speaking; grad. student adv. bd. Western Mich. U., Kalamazoo, 2000; mem. Nat. Honor Soc. Iroquois Mid. Sch., 1974-75, Grand Rapids, Ottawa Hills H.S., 1976-79. Co-editor: Smoke Signal, 1975. Vol. United Way, Grand Rapids, 1990, TV (GVSU-TV) fundraiser Grand Valley State U.; reading condr. S.E. Neighborhood Assn., Grand Rapids, 1990; mem. literacy coun. Kent County Literacy Coun., Grand Rapids, 1991—, task force Dwelling Pl., Grand Rapids, 1999, First Call Help United Way, Grand Rapids, 1992; model Miss J. Fashion bd. Jacobson's Dept. store, East Grand Rapids Mich., 1979; finalist Miss Black Wis. pageant, Milw., 1981; bd. dirs. Program and Quality Com., Pers. Com., Fin. Com., Consumer Adv. bd., Touchstone innovaré mental health, Grand Rapids, 2000—, Kent County Cmty. Mental Health, 1999—; mem. Task Force Herkimer Apartment Projects, Weston Apartments Dwelling place of Grand Rapids, 1999; reading program asst. S.E. End Neigborhood Assn., Grand Rapids, 1993; rehab. asst. Kent Comty. Hosp. Complex, Grand Rapids, 1991; intake asst. Baxter Comty. Ctr., Grand Rapids, 1989; tutor Kent County Literacy Coun., Grand Rapids, 1988; facilitator trainer Employers Coalition for Healing Racism, Grand Rapids, 1997, Citizens Cirs. Resource Ctr., Grand Rapids, 1998, Ptnrs. in Pub. Edn., Grand Rapids, 1999, United Way Champions Diversity, Grand Rapids, 1999; project help tutor Iroquois Mid. Sch., Grand Rapids, 1975; student tutor Washington Elem., Kalamazoo, 1974; student rep. Bus. Office Edn. Club, 1978-79 (2nd place Extemporaneous Verbal Coms. 1978, 1st place second divsn. 1979, other leadership awards 1978-79); fundraiser Spl. Olympics Office Edn. Assn. Ottawa Hills H.S., 1978. Recipient shorthand awards taking dictation of 140 words per minute Milw. Stratton Coll., 1981-82, Century award typing 100 words per minute Milw. Stratton Coll., 1982, Machine Transcription award secretarial skills contest seventh place Milw. Area Tech. Coll., 1981, shorthand award Ottawa Hills H.S., 1979; Phillip Morris scholar Alverno Coll., 1981; Nontraditional Student grantee Western Mich. U., 1994, 2000, Thurgood Marshall Profl. Tuition grantee; Thurgood Marshall Assistanship scholar Western Mich. U.1989, 1998; 1st place speaker, 3rd place typist and secretarial job application Office Edn. Assn. Extemporaneous Speaking; 6th place with Letter of Recognition from Senator Berger of Wis. Milw. Area Tech. Coll., 1981; Internat. finalist theatre arts, Milw., 1986; noted as jr. achievement Ottawa Hills H.S., 1978, other different honors, awards, recognitions, accomplishments, etc. Mem. ASCD, ASTD, Am. Mgmt., Am. Cancer Soc., Program Soc. Human Resource Mgmt. (Superior Merit award), Internat. Econ. Assn., Phi Beta Lambda (sec. 1982), Mich. Jaycee, U.S. C of C., Jr. Chamber Internat., Jaycess Networking and Leads, Alzheimers Assn., Am. Cancer Soc. Program, Profl. Bus. Leaders (sec.-elect), Profl. Secs. Internat., Office Edn. Assn., Grand Rapids Econ. Club, Phi Beta Lambda, others. Avocations: modern dancing, reading, tennis. Address: PO Box 7421 Grand Rapids MI 49510

PURCIFULL, DAN ELWOOD, plant virologist, educator; b. Woodland, Calif., July 1, 1935; s. Ernest Lee and Virginia (Margaroli) P.; m. Marcia Ann Weatherby, Sept. 7, 1966; children: Scott, Douglas. BS, U. Calif., Davis, 1957, MS, 1959, PhD, 1964. Asst. prof. plant pathology U. Fla., Gainesville, 1964-69, assoc. prof., 1969-75, prof., 1975-99, prof. emeritus, 2000—. Plant virus subcom. Internat. Com. for Taxonomy of Viruses, 1973-75, mem. potyvirus study group, 1987-93; mem. plant virology adv. com. Am. Type Culture Collection, 1993-99; mem. Internat. Legume Virus Working Group, 1999. Assoc. editor Phytopathology, 1971-73, Plant Disease, 1987-89; contbr. articles to profl. jours. Mem. Morningside Nature Center Commn., City of Gainesville, 1978-81, treas., 1981. With U.S. Army, 1957. Fellow AAAS, Am.

Phytopathol Soc. (Lee Hutchins award 1981, Ruth Allen award 1992); mem. Fla. State Hort. Soc., N.Y. Acad. Sci., Am. Soc. Virology, Phytopathol. Soc. Japan, Brazilian Phytopathol. Soc., U.S. Golf Assn., Nat. Wildlife Fedn., The Nature Conservancy, Nat. Geographic Soc., Smithsonian Instn. (assoc.), Sigma Xi, Gamma Sigma Delta. Home: 3106 NW 1st Ave Gainesville FL 32607-2504 E-mail: depurc@aol.com.

PURCIFULL, ROBERT OTIS, insurance company executive; b. Grinnell, Iowa, July 1, 1932; s. Chauncey O. and Mildred E. (Clendenen) P.; m. Mary G. White, Sept. 12, 1953; children: Jane, Robert Otis, Patricia, Elizabeth. BA, Grinnell Coll., 1954. C.L.U. With Occidental Life Ins. Co., Calif., 1960-78, 1st. v.p. charge agys., 1968-71, exec. v.p. sales, 1971-76; pres., chief exec. officer Transmerica Ins. Mgmt., Inc., Los Angeles, 1972-78, Countrywide Life Ins. Co., Los Angeles, 1973-76, dir., 1973-78; chmn. bd., pres. Plaza Ins. Sales Inc., San Francisco; pres., chief exec. officer Occidental Life of Can., 1977-78; pres., chief operating officer, dir. Penn Mut. Life Ins. Co., Phila., 1979-80. Sr. v.p. life divsn. Am. Gen. Corp., 1981-82; pres. Lincoln Am. Life Ins. Co., Am. Gen. Life Ins. Co. Del., Am. Gen. Life Ins. Co. Tex., Am. Amicable Life Ins. Co., Pioneer Am., 1982-84; vice chmn. Pioneer Security Life Ins. Co., 1982-84; pres., CEO Gulf Life Ins. Co., Interstate Fire Co., Jacksonville, Fla., 1984-88, also dir.; pres. Am. Gen. Group Ins. Co. Fla., 1986-89; vice chmn. Gulf Life Ins. Co., 1988-91; chmn., CEO ROP & Assocs. Past pres. Vols. of Am., LA; trustee Life Underwriters Tng. Coun., Washington, 1975—78; campaign chmn. Jacksonville United Way, 1988, 1989, chmn., 1989—90; pres. Jacksonville U. Coun., 1992, 1993, Jacksonville Symphony Orch., 1993—94; chmn. bus. adv. coun. U. North Fla.; councilman City of Upper Arlington, Ohio, 1962—66; chmn. Conservative Order for Good Govt., San Diego County, Calif., 2001. Mem. Life Ins. Mktg. and Rsch. Assn. (bd. dirs. 1982-85). Home: 12285 Fairway Pointe Row San Diego CA 92128-3230 E-mail: Purcifull@aol.com.

PURDES, ALICE MARIE, retired adult education educator; b. St. Louis, Jan. 8, 1931; d. Joseph Louis and Angeline Cecilia (Mozier) P. AA, Belleville Area Coll., 1951; BS, Ill. State U., Normal, 1953, MS, 1954; cert., Sorbonne U., Paris, 1964; PhD, Fla. State U., Tallahassee, 1976. Cert. in music edn., elem. edn., secondary edn., adult edn. Tchg. and grad. asst. Ill. State U., 1953-54; music supr. Princeton (Ill.) Pub. Schs., 1954-55; music dir. Venice (Ill.) Pub. Schs., 1955-72, secondary vocal music dir., 1955-72; coord. literacy program Venice-Lincoln Tech. Ctr., 1983-86, chmn. lang. arts dept., 1983-96; ret., 1996. Tchr. in space candidate, 1985. Mem. St. Louis chpt. World Affairs Coun., UN Assn., Nat. Mus. of Women in the Arts, Humane Soc. of Am.; charter mem. St. Louis Sci. Ctr., Harry S. Truman Inst.; contbr. Old Six Mile Mus., 1981, Midland Repertory Players, Alton, Ill., 1991; chair Cystic Fibrosis Spring Bike-A-Thon, Madison, Ill., 1981, Granite City, Ill., 1985. Named to Ill. Sr. Hall of Fame, 2001, Gov's Sr. Hall of Fame, 2001; recipient Gold medal, Nat. Senior Olympics, 1989, Gold medal, more than 400 others, Sr. World Games, 1992, Generations of Success Alumni award, Belleville Area Coll., 1998, several scholarships. Mem.: AAUW, Am. Fedn. Tchrs. (pres. 1957—58), Ill. Adult and Continuing Educators Assn., Am. Choral Dirs. Assn., Ill. Music Educators Assn. (Svc. award 2002), Music Educators Nat. Conf., Ill. State U. Alumni Assn., Slavic and East European Friends (life), Fla. State Alumni Assn., Lovejoy Libr. Friends, Nat. Space Soc., Western Cath. Union, Croation Fraternal Union, St. Louis Numis. Assn., Friends St. Louis Art Mus., Archaeol. Inst. Am., Travelers Abroad (pres. 1966—68, 1989—), Madison Rotary Club (internat. amb., Humanitarian award 1975). Roman Catholic. Avocations: bowling, travel. Home: PO Box 274 Madison IL 62060-0274 Office Phone: 618-830-1640.

PURDOM, PAUL WALTON, JR., computer scientist; b. Atlanta, Apr. 5, 1940; s. Paul Walton and Bettie (Miller) P.; m. Donna Armstrong; children: Barbara, Linda, Paul BS, Calif. Inst. Tech., 1961, MS, 1962, PhD, 1966. Asst. prof. computer sci. U. Wis.-Madison, 1965-70, asst. prof., 1970-71; mem. tech. staff Bell Telephone Labs., Naperville, Ill., 1970-71; assoc. prof., chmn. computer sci. dept. Ind. U., Bloomington, 1977-82, prof. computer sci., 1982—. Grant researcher FAW, Ulm, Germany. Author: (with Cynthia Brown) The Analysis of Algorithms; assoc. editor: Computer Surveys; contbr. articles to profl. jours. NSF grantee, 1979, 81, 83, 92, 94. Mem. AAAS, Soc. for Indsl. and Applied Math., Assn. Computing Machinery, Sigma Xi. Democrat. Methodist. Home: 2212 S Belhaven Ct Bloomington IN 47401-6803 Office: Ind U Dept Computer Science 215 Lindley Hall Bloomington IN 47405-4101 Business E-Mail: pwp@cs.indiana.edu.

PURDOM, THOMAS JAMES, lawyer; b. Seymour, Tex., Apr. 7, 1937; s. Thomas Exer and Juanita Florida (Kuykendall) P.; m. Betty Marie Shoemaker, May 31, 1969; 1 son, James Robert. Student, U. Syracuse, 1956—57, U. Md., 1958—59; BA, Tex. Tech. Coll., 1962; JD, Georgetown U., 1966. Bar: Tex. 1966, U.S. Supreme Ct. 1978, U.S. Ct. Appeals (5th cir.) 1983. Ptnr. Griffith & Purdom, Lubbock, Tex., 1966-67; asst. dist. atty. 72d Jud. Dist., Lubbock, 1967-68; county atty. Lubbock County, Tex., 1968-72; pres. Purdom & Atchley, Lubbock, 1972—. Mem. com. for Vol. 5 pattern jury charges, 1988-97. Author: West's Texas Forms Vols. 16, 17, 18, 1984-96, Family Law, Texas Practice and Procedure, 1981. Served with USAF, 1956-60. Recipient Sam Emison award Tex. Acad. Family Law Specialists, 2000. Fellow Tex. Bar Found.; mem ABA, Lubbock County Bar Assn. (bd. dirs. 1970, Disting. Sr. Lawyer award 2000), State Bar Assn. Tex. (sec. family law sect. 1974-75, chmn. family law sect. 1975-76, mem. examining commn. for family law specialization), Am. Acad. Matrimonial Lawyers (cert. family law, Tex. bd. legal specialization), Delta Theta Phi. Democrat. Baptist. Home: 3619 55th St Lubbock TX 79413-4713 Office: Purdom & Atchley 3619 55th St Lubbock TX 79413-5713 E-mail: purdom6@aol.com.

PURDUM, DENNIS R. financial company executive; Chm. regional mgr., ptnr., Ernst & Young LLP, N.Y.C. Office: Ernst & Young LLP 787 7th Ave Fl 14 New York NY 10019-6085

PURDY, ALAN HARRIS, biomedical engineer; b. Mt. Clemens, Mich., Dec. 13, 1923; s. Harry Martin and Elinor (Harris) P.; m. Anna Elizabeth Sohn, Aug. 16, 1968 (dec.); children: Catherine, Charles, Susan, Harry; m. Margaret Josephine Kelley, Mar. 5, 1997. BSME, U. Miami, 1954; MS in Physiology, UCLA, 1967; PhD in Engring., U. Mo., 1970. Cert. clin. engr., Washington. Project engr. in acoustics Arvin Industries, Columbus, Ind., 1954-56, AC Spark Plug Co., Flint, Mich., 1956-60; asst. prof. engring. Calif. Poly. U., Pomona, 1960-62; assoc. dir. biomed. engring. U. Mo., Columbia, 1967-71; dep. assoc. dir., assoc. dir. Nat. Inst. for Occupational Safety and Health, Rockville, Md., 1971-81, scientist, biomed. engr. Cin., 1983-86; asst. dir. Fla. Inst. Oceanography, St. Petersburg, 1981-83; pres. Alpha Beta R & D Corp., San Marcos, Calif., 1986—. Cons. Smithy Muffler Corp., L.A., 1961-62, Statham Instruments, L.A., 1966; cons. faculty, Tex. Tech. U., Lubbock, 1972-73; lectr. U. Cin., 1980. Patentee in diving, acoustical and occupational safety fields. Pilot CG Aux., 1989-98. With USAF, 1942-43. Nat. Heart Inst. spl. fellow, 1963-67; Fulbright scholar, Yugoslavia, 1984. Mem. Acoustical Soc. Am., Biomed. Engring. Soc., Am. Inst. Physics, Exptl. Aircraft Assn., Aircraft Owners and Pilots Assn., DAV. Democrat. Home and Office: 941 Cycad Dr San Marcos CA 92078-5013 E-mail: ahpurdy@nethere.com.

PURDY, DAVID LAWRENCE, medical products executive; b. N.Y.C., Sept. 18, 1928; s. Earl and Mabel (Roberts) Purdy; m. Margaret Helen Rye, July 7, 1951; children: Susan Lee, John F.(dec.), Ross David(dec.), Thomas Griffith. BME, Cornell U., 1951; degree in advanced & creative engring., GE, 1955, degree in profl. bus. mgmt., 1956. Devel. engr. GE, Valley Forge, Pa., 1953-64; mgr. energy conversion divsn. Nuc. Materials and Equipment Corp. (acquired by ARCO), Apollo, Pa., 1964-69, Atlantic Richfield Corp., Apollo, 1969-72; founder, pres., chmn. Biocontrol Tech., Inc., Indiana, Pa., 1972—2000; chmn., treas. Diasense, Inc., Indiana, 1989—2000; pres., founder Purdy Tech., Inc., Marion Center, Pa., 2000—. Contbr. articles to profl. jours. 1st lt. USAF, 1961—63. Fellow: ASME (life); mem.: AAAS. Achievements include 32 patents in field; patents for generator of electrical energy by radioisoptope thermoelectric conversion; radioisotope powered cardiac pacemaker; radioisotope powered artificial heart; thermoelectric apparatus for high thermoelectric efficiency by cascading materials; method of metals joining and articles produced by such method - brazing copper to tungsten; thermelectric apparatus for high thermoelectric efficiency by cascading materials; generator of electrical energy by radioisotope thermoelectric conversion; rate responsive pacemaker; artificial pancreas; noninvasive glucose sensor; multi-leaflet heart valve. Office: Purdy Tech Inc 1482 Ambrose Rd Marion Center PA 15759

PURDY, JAMES, writer; b. 1923; Ed., Spain. Editor, other positions, Cuba, Mexico. Author: Don't Call Me by My Right Name, 1956; 63, Dream Palace, 1956, 180, Color of Darkness, 1957, Malcolm, 1959, 1980, paperback, 1987, The Nephew, 1960,, 1980, paperback, 1987, (play) Children is All, 1962, Cabot Wright Begins, 1964, Eustace Chisholm and The Works, 1967, An Oyster is A Wealthy Beast, 1967, Mr. Evening, 1968, Jeremy's Version, 1970, On the Rebound, 1970, (poems) The Running Sun, 1971, Collected Poems, 1990, (novel) I am Elijah Thrush, 1971; Sunshine is an Only Child, 1973, Sleepers in Moon Crowned Valleys, The House of the Solitary Maggot, 1974, Island Avenue, 1997, (play) Foment, 1997, (selected stories) Color of Darkness, Children is All, The Candles of Your Eyes, 1991, (fairy tale) Kitty Blue, 1993 (Eng. edit. The Netherlands); (novel) In a Shallow Grave, 1976; (plays and stories) A Day After the Fair, 1977; (recordings) Eventide, 63; Dream Palace, 1968, 1980; (novels) Narrow Rooms, 1978, Gertrude of Stony Island Avenue, 1998, Foment, 1997; (poetry) I Will Arrest the Bird that has No Light, 1978, Lessons and Complaints, 1978; Sleep Tight, 1978, Proud Flesh, 4 short plays, 1980; (novel) Mourners Below, 1981, The Berry-Picker, 1981, Scrap of Paper, 1981, Dawn, 1985, The Brooklyn Branding Parlors, 1986; (novel) On Glory's Course, 1983, (poems) Don't Let the Snow Fall, 1985, Are You in the Winter Tree?, 1987, (novel) In the Hollow of His Hand, 1986, (collected stories) The Candles of your Eyes, 1987, Garments the Living Wear, 1989, (fiction) Reaching Rose, 1994, (play) Ruthanna Elder, 1989, Moe's Villa & Other Stories, 2000, A Room All to Itself, 2002, Moe's Villa and Other Stories, 2002; subject of book: James Purdy (Stephen D. Adams), 1976, Collected Poems, 1990, (plays) In The Night of Time and Four Other Plays, 1992, A Day After the Fair, 1993, (novel) Out With The Stars, 1992, In the Night of Time and Four Other Plays, 1992, (plays) Foment, 1994, Brice, 1994, Where Quentin Goes, 1994, Gertrude of Stony Island Avenue, 1998 (novel), (play) Foment, 1998; intro. to Weymouth Sands (by John Cowper POWYS); contbr. article to Life Mag., 1965. Recipient Morton Dauwen Zabel Fiction award Am. Acad. Arts and Letters, 1993, Oscar Williams and Gene Durwood award for poetry and art, 1995; subject of The Not-Right House, Essays on the Books of James Purdy (Bettina Schwarzschild), 1969-70. Address: 236 Henry St Brooklyn NY 11201-4280

PURDY, JAMES AARON, medical physics educator; b. Tyler, Tex., July 16, 1941; s. Walter Bethel and Florence (Hardy) P.; m. Marilyn Janette Coers, Jan. 29, 1965; children: Katherine, Laura. BS, Lamar U., 1967; MA, U. Tex., 1968, PhD, 1971. Asst. rsch. scientist U. Tex., Austin, 1969-71; rsch. asst. M.D. Anderson Hosp. and Tumor Inst., Houston, 1968-69, fellow in med. physics, 1972-73; from instr. physics to prof. Sch. of Medicine, Washington U., St. Louis, 1973—83, prof., 1983—2004, chief physics sect., 1976—2004, assoc. dir. Radiation Oncology Ctr., 1987—2004; prof. U. Calif., Davis, Calif., 2004—, vice chmn. Dept. Radiol. Oncology, 2004—. Mem. NIH Radiaton Study sect. Divsn. Rsch. Grantes, 1991-95; Landauer lectr., Oakland, Calif., 1991. Editor: Three Dimensional Treatment Planning, 1991, Advances in Radiation Oncology, 1992, 3D Radiation Treatment Planning and Conformal Therapy, 1995, A Practical Guide to 3D Planning and Conformal Radiation Therapy, 1999, 3-D Conformal and Intensity Modulated Radiation Therapy: Physics and Clinical Applications, 2001; sr. physics editor: Internat. Jour. Radiation Oncology, Biology, and Physics, 1996—. With USMC, 1961-64. Fellow Am. Assn. Physicists in Medicine (pres. 1985, William D. Coolidge award 1997), Am. Coll. Radiology (ACR Gold Medal 2002), Am. Coll. Med. Physics (chmn. bd. chancellors 1990, Marvin M.D. Williams award 1996); mem. Am. Inst. Physics, Am. Bd. Med. Physics (vice chmn. 1988-92), Am. Bd. Radiology, Am. Soc. Therapeutic Radiology and Oncology (ASTRO Gold medal 2000). Methodist. Avocation: travel. Home: 918 Eucalyptus St Davis CA 95616 Office: Univ Calif Davis Rad Oncology 4501 X Street 6126 Sacramento CA 95817 Office Phone: 916-734-3932. Business E-Mail: james.purdy@ucmdc.ucdavidis.edu.

PURDY, KEVIN MOORE, estate planner; b. Escondido, Calif., Jan. 26, 1952; s. Kenneth C. and Helen M. (Moore) P.; m. Janice M. Cook, May 12, 1982. BA in Philosophy, Psychology, U. Redlands, 1974. Pres. Timeline Pub., San Diego, Calif., 1980-90; estate planner Sagemark Cons., San Diego, Calif., 1990—. Pub. spkr.; digital artist. Author: A Brief History of the Earth and Mankind, 1986, A Brief History of Mankind, 1987. Avocations: photography, music, travel, investment analysis. Office: Sagemark Cons 4275 Executive Sq Ste 400 La Jolla CA 92037-9197 E-mail: kpurdy@home.com.

PURDY, LESLIE, community college president; b. Downey, Calif., Aug. 18, 1943; d. Hubert C. and Janice M. (Harker) Noble; m. Ralph Purdy, Aug. 23, 1969; children: Christopher Hugh, George Colin. BA cum laude, Occidental Coll., L.A., 1965; MAT, Oberlin (Ohio) Coll., 1966; EdD, UCLA, 1973. Tchr. Parma (Ohio) Sr. H.S., 1966; ombudsman/instr. social sci. Raymond Coll., U. of Pacific, Stockton, Calif., 1967-69; coord. spl. svcs. ERIC Clearinghouse for C.C.'s, L.A., 1970-74; sr. instrnl. designer Coastline C.C., Fountain Valley, Calif., 1974-84, adminstrv. dean, 1984-94, pres., 1994—. Bd. dirs. Intelecom, Pasadena, Calif.; bd. dirs., pres. Instrnl. Telecom. Coun., Washington, 1987-94; adv. bd. PBS "Going the Distance" program, Washington, 1993-96; cons. Commn. on Innovation, Calif. Colls. Chancellor's Office, 1993-94. Editor: Reaching New Students Through New Technologies, 1983; instrnl. designer Psychology: The Study of Human Behavior, 1989 (Emmy 1990); exec. prodr. (telecourses): Universe: The Infinite Frontier, 1994 (Emmy 1994), Time to Grow, 1992 (Emmy 1992); contbr. articles to profl. jours. Mem. Orange County Forum, 1994—, Ctr. for Studies of Media and Values, L.A., 1990-95, Bread for the World, Washington, 1980—; bd. mem. West County Family YMCA, 1993-2000; bd. mem. Garden Grove Renaissance Found., 1998—; bd. mem. Orange County Nat. Conf. of Cmty. and Justice, 1997—, Orange County Workforce Investment Bd., 2000—; mem. adv. bd. Calif. C.C. Satellite Network, 2001-02. Recipient Emmy awards Am. Acad. TV Arts and Scis., 1987, 90, 92,. 95, Western Region award Instrn. Telecom. Coun., 1995; named one of Women of Distinction City of Garden Grove, 2001. Mem. Assn. of Calif. C.C. Adminstrs., Assn. Ednl. Comms. and Tech., Am. Assn. of Women in C.C.'s, UCLA Alumni Assn. (Doctoral Award in Edn. 1973). Presbyterian. Avocations: backpacking, gardening, conservation, choral singing. Office: Coastline Cmty Coll Office of Pres 11460 Warner Ave Fountain Valley CA 92708 E-mail: lpurdy@cccd.edu.

PURDY, WILLIAM RICHARD, lawyer; b. Statesville, N.C., May 3, 1946; s. Frank Kerr and Catherine Ritchie Purdy; m. Susan Clark Smith, Aug. 18, 1968; children: Kathryn Blythe Purdy Barton, Susanna Grey. BA, U. N.C., 1972, JD, 1975. Assoc. Smith, Currie & Hancock, Atlanta, 1975—77; v.p. Southeastern Svcs., Inc., Jackson, Miss., 1977—80; founding ptnr., prin. Ott & Purdy, P.A., Jackson, Miss., 1980—2003; founding ptnr., mem. Purdy & Germany, PLLC, Jackson, 2003—. Gen. counsel Miss. Rd. Bldrs. Assn., Jackson, 1993—, Assoc. Gen. Contrs. of Miss., Jackson, 1995—, Miss. Asphalt Pavers Assn., Jackson, 1998—; lectr. in field. Author (editor): Contractor's Desk Book on Mississippi Construction Law, 1996. 1st lt. USMC, 1968—72. Decorated Bronze Star; named Master of the Bench, Charles Clark Inn, Am. Inns of Ct., 1994—; recipient Commendation for Disting. Prof. Achievement, Joint Resolution of Miss. Senate and Ho. of Reps., 2000. Fellow: Miss. Bar Found., Internat. Soc. Barristers, Am. Coll. Constrn. Lawyers; mem.: ABA (mem. pub. contract law sect., state chair 1980—83, mem. forum com. on constrn. law 1980—). Avocations: jogging, rock and roll, golf sports. Office: Purdy & Germany PLLC PO Drawer 1079 Jackson MS 39215-1079 Office Phone: 601-969-4140.

PURE, PAMELA, information technology executive; Various mgmt., product devel. and mktg. positions Shared Med. Sys. (now divsn. Siemens); COO Channel Health Subs. IDX Sys.; group pres. product devel. and support McKesson Corp., San Francisco, 2001—02, COO, McKesson Info. Solutions, 2002—. Office: 1 Post St San Francisco CA 94104

PURI, ISHWAR KANWAR, engineering educator, researcher; b. New Delhi, Feb. 25, 1959; arrived in U.S., 1982; s. Krishan K. and Sushilla Puri; m. Beth R. Levinson, July 15, 1989; children: Shivesh, Sunil Krishan. BSME, U. Delhi, 1982; MS in Engring. Sci., U. Calif., San Diego, 1984, PhD in Engring. Sci., 1987. Postdoctoral rsch. engr. U. Calif., San Diego, 1987-89, asst. rsch. engr., 1989-90; vis. asst. prof. U. Ill., Chgo., 1990-91, from asst. prof. to assoc. prof., 1991-94, prof., 1999—2004, dir. grad. studies, 1994—97, 1999—2000, dir. student transatlantic exch. program, 2000—04, assoc. dean rsch. and grad. studies, 2000-01, exec. assoc. dean engring., 2001—04, dir. Ctr. Internat. Edn. and Rsch., 2001—04; prof., head dept. engring. sci. and mechanics Va. Tech., Blacksburg, 2004—. Disting. guest Inst. Energy Tech. Swiss Fed. Inst. Tech., Zurich, 1998, Zurich, 99. Editor: Environmental Implications of Combustion Processes, 1993, Advanced Thermodynamics Engineering, 2001; contbr. articles to profl. jours. Fellow, Stanford U. Ctr. Turbulence Rsch., 1992; Rsch. grantee, NSF, NASA, U.S. Dept. Edn., Gas Rsch. Inst., EPA, DOE. Fellow: AIAA (mem. terrestrial energy sources com. 1999—2002), AAAS (Environ. fellow 1993), ASME, Combustion Inst.

PURI, MADAN LAL, mathematics professor; b. Sialkot, Feb. 20, 1929; came to U.S., 1957, naturalized, 1973; s. Ganesh Das and S. W. P.; m. Uma Kapur, Aug. 24, 1962; 3 children. BA, Punjab U., India, 1948, MA, 1950, D.Sc., 1975; PhD, U. Calif. at Berkeley, 1962. Head dept. math. D.A.V. Coll., Punjab U., 1955-57; instr. U. Colo., 1957-58; tchg. asst., rsch. asst., jr. rsch. statistician U. Calif. at Berkeley, 1958-62; asst. prof., assoc. prof. math. Courant Inst., NYU, 1962-68; vis. assoc. prof. U. N.C., summers 1966-67; prof. math. Ind. U., Bloomington, 1968—, Coll. Arts and Scis. Disting. Rsch. scholar, 2004—. Guest prof. U. Gottingen, West Germany, 1972, Alexander von Humboldt guest prof., 1974-75; guest prof. U. Dortmund, West Germany, 1972, Technische Hochschule Aachen, West Germany, 1973, U. Goteborg, Chalmers U. Tech., both Sweden, 1974; vis. prof. U. Auckland, N.Z., 1977, U. Calif., Irvine, 1978, U. Wash., Seattle, 1978-79, U. Bern (Switzerland), 1982, Va. Poly. Inst., 1988; disting. visitor London Sch. Econs. and Polit. Sci., 1991; vis. prof. U. Göttingen, Germany, 1991, June-July 1992; rsch. fellow Katholieke U., Nijmegen, The Netherlands, 1992; vis. prof. U. Des Scis. et Tech. de Lille, France, 1994, U. Basel, Switzerland, 1995—, U. New South Wales, Australia, 1996; vis. univ. fellow Australian Nat. U., Canberra, Australia, 1999; guest prof. U. Konstanz, Germany, 2000, U. Gottingen, 2001. Co-author: Non Parametric Methods in Multivariate Analysis, 1971, Non Parametric Methods in General Linear Models, 1985. Editor Stochastic Process and Related Topics, 1975, Statistical Inference and Related Topics, 1975, Non Parametric Techniques in Statistical Inference, 1970; co-editor: Nonparametric Statistical Inference, Vols. I and II, 1982, New Perspectives in Theoretical and Applied Statistics, 1987, Mathematical Statistics and Probability Theory, Vol. A, 1987, Statistical Sciences and Data Analysis, 1993, Recent Advances in Statistics and Probability, 1994, Asymptotics in Statistics and Probability, 2000, Probability, Statistics and their Applications, 2003. Recipient Sr. U.S. Scientist award, Humboldt Preis, 1974-75, 83, Rsch. award Humboldt Found., U. Göttingen, 2001. Fellow Royal Statis. Soc., Inst. Math. Statistics, Am. Statis. Assn.; mem. Math. Assn. Am., Internat. Statis. Inst., Bernoulli Soc. Math. Stats. and Probability. Office: Ind U Dept Math Rawles Hall Bloomington IN 47405

PURI, PRATAP, educator, researcher; b. Lahore, Punjab, India, Mar. 15, 1938; came to U.S., 1968; s. Kidar Nath and Shakuntala Devi (Trehan) P.; children: Amrita, Salil. BA with honors, Punjab U., 1957; MA in Math., Delhi (India) U., 1959; M.Tech., Indian Inst. Tech., Kharagpur, 1960, PhD, 1965. Assoc. lectr. Indian Inst. Tech. Bombay, Maharashtra, India, 1962-63, lectr., 1963-68; asst. prof. dept. math. U. New Orleans, 1968-71, assoc. prof., 1971-76, prof., 1976—2004, rsch. prof., 2004—. Co-author (book): Partial Differential Equations with Mathematica, 1997, Computational Methods for Linear Integral Equations, 2002, Partial Differential Equations and Boundary Value Problems with Mathematica, 2d edit., 2003; contbr. articles to profl. jours. Indian Inst. Tech. scholar, 1959-60; C.S.I.R. rsch. fellow, 1960-61, Polish Acad. Scis. postdoctoral fellow, 1966. Mem. Am. Acad. Mechs., Soc. Indsl. and Applied Maths., Calcutta Math. Soc. (life). Avocation: bridge. Office: U New Orleans Dept Math 2000 Lakeshore Dr New Orleans LA 70148-3520 Office Phone: 504-280-7376.

PURI, RAJENDRA KUMAR, business and tax specialist, consultant; b. Hoshiarpur, Punjab, India, Dec. 22, 1932; came to the U.S., 1965, naturalized, 1969; s. Harbans Lal and Satya Vati (Jerath) P.; children: Neena, Veena, Ram. BS, Agra U., 1952; diploma in Russian lang. and lit., U. Dehli, 1958; BA, U. Wash., 1968, MBA, 1969; MS in Taxation, Golden Gate U., 1982. Customs officer Govt. of India, New Delhi, 1955-60; asst. treas. Merc. Bank Ltd., New Delhi, 1960-65; mem. staff Peat, Marwick, Mitchell & Co., CPAs, Seattle, 1969-70; state examiner State of Wash., Seattle, 1970-72, asst. supervising state examiner, 1972-74, supervising state examiner, 1974-77; sr. internal auditor Lockheed Corp., Sunnyvale, Calif., 1977-79; sci. programming analyst Lockheed Missile and Space Co., Sunnyvale, 1979-80, data processing specialist, 1980-84, sci. programming specialist, 1984-88; chief acct. Tex. Dept. Health, Austin, 1989-90; dir. internal audit, internal auditor Tex. Workers' Compensation Commn., Austin, 1990-95; bus. and tax cons., 1996—2003. Del. Wash. State Rep. Conv., 1976, Snohomish County Rep. Conv., 1976; Rep. nominee for state auditor, Wash., 1976; spl. advisor U.S. Congl. Adv. Bd., 1982-83. Mem. AICPA. Home: 2608 Hunlac Cove Round Rock TX 78681-7107 E-mail: rkpi_2000@yahoo.com.

PURIS, MARTIN FORD, media executive; b. Chgo., Feb. 22, 1939; s. Martin and Virginia Lee (Farmer) Puris; m. Mary M. Herrmann; children: Kimberly Mayo, Jason Patterson, Mary Elizabeth. Student, DePauw U., 1961. With Campbell-Ewald Co., Detroit, 1962—64, Young & Rubicam, Inc., N.Y.C., 1964-66; v.p. Carl Ally, Inc., N.Y.C., 1966-74; pres., CEO Ammirati & Puris, Inc., N.Y.C., 1974-94; chmn., CEO, chief creative officer Ammirati, Puris, Lintas, N.Y.C., 1995—99; chmn., CEO NTM (Not Traditional Media), N.Y.C. Media advisor Pres. George Bush; dir. IPG Group, 1995—99; vice chmn. Sheltering Arms; mng. dir. New Things Investment Group; treasurer Hampton Classic. Author: Comeback: How Seven Straight-Shooting CEO's Turned Around Troubled Companies, 1999. Recipient awards Art Dir. Club, Copy Club, N.Y.C., Cannes Film Festival. Mem.: Devon Yacht Club, Union Club, Am. Yacht Club, Nantucket Yacht Club, N.Y. Yacht Club. Republican. Roman Catholic. Avocations: sailing, tennis, show jumping, hunting.

PURJES, DAN, investment company executive; Chmn. of bd., pres. Josephthal Holdings Inc., N.Y.C., until 2000; chmn., CEO Josephthal Group, Inc., N.Y.C. Office: Josephthal Group Inc Fl 24 200 Park Ave Fl 25 New York NY 10166-2599

PURKAYASTHA, DAS D. biostatistician; s. D. Lal and Nandita Purkayastha. M, PhD, U. Buffalo, 1982—87; MS, Guwahati U., India, 1973—76; BS in physics, math., stats., with honors, GC Coll., Guwahati U., 1970—73; Pre U. Sci., GC Coll., India, 1969—70. Computer Programming IASRI, New Delhi, 1978, Statistical Analysis Systems (SAS) SAS Inst., USA, 1999; Clinical Trial Statistician Course Pharm. Edn. Rsch. Inst., 1998, Clinical Trial Project Management George Wash. U., 2000, Clinical/Drug Development Training Novartis, USA, 1999, FDA Drug Regulatory Requirements Novartis, USA, 1998; Faculty Development Program U. of Buffalo, NY, 1986, Regulatory Studies Mich. State U., East Lansing, MI, 1990. Sr. rsch. fellow IASRI, Indian Statis. Rsch. Inst., New Delhi, 1977—81; tchg./rsch. asst. U. Buffalo, 1982—86, vis. lectr., 1987—88; scientist grade Argonne (Ill.) Nat. Lab., U. Chgo., 1988—89; econometrician/statistician Pub. Svc. Commn., Washington D.C., DC, 1989—94; adj. faculty George Wash. U., Washington DC, 1994; dir., biostatistical applications Cardiology Rsch. Ctr., Washington D.C., DC, 1995—97; sr. biostatstician Novartis Pharmaceuticals, East Hanover, NJ, 1997—99, prin. biostatistician, 1999—2001, assoc. dir., biostatistics, 2001—. Contbr. scientific papers, articles to profl. jours. Cmty. svc., charity, children welfare, edn. Recipient Above and Beyond awards, Novartis, 1997—2003, Social and Cultural Club, Drama and Debating Societies, Art and Theatre, 1960—82, Indian Rsch. Svc. Exam., Indian Agr. Scientist Recruitment Bd. (ISRB), 1980, Indian Stats. Svc. Exam., Union Pub. Svc. Commn., IAS Exam. Excellence Award, Recognition on FDA submission and approval of Pediatric Drug Exclusivity, Clin. Devel. Med. Affair, Novartis, 2003; State Merit

Academic Grant, Guwahati U., 1973—76, Nat. Merit Scholarship, Bd. of Secondary Edn., 1969—73, Sr. Rsch. fellowship, Indian Coun. of Rsch., 1977. Mem.: AAAS, Am. Statis. Assn. Avocations: writing, swimming, yoga. Office: Novartis One Health Plaza East Hanover NJ 07936

PURKERSON, MABEL LOUISE, physician, physiologist, educator; b. Goldville, S.C., Apr. 3, 1931; d. James Clifton and Louise (Smith) P. AB, Erskine Coll., 1951; MD, U. S.C., Charleston, 1956. Diplomate Am. Bd. Pediat. Instr. pediat. Washington U. Sch. Medicine, St. Louis, 1961-67, instr. medicine, 1966-67, asst. prof. pediat., 1967-98, asst. prof. medicine, 1967-76, assoc. prof. medicine, 1976-89, prof., 1989-98, prof. emerita, 1998—, assoc. dean curriculum, 1976-94, assoc. dean acad. projects, 1994-98. Cons. in field. Editl. bd. Am. Jour. Kidney Diseases, 1981-87; contbr. articles to profl. jours. Mem. bd. counselors Erskine Coll., 1971-87; trustee St. Louis Symphony Orch., Erskine Coll., 2000—. USPHS spl. fellow, 1971-72. Mem. Am. Heart Assn. Coun. on the Kidney (exec. com. 1973-81), Am. Physiol. Soc., Am. Soc. Nephrology, Internat. Soc. Nephrology, Ctrl. Soc. Clin. Rsch., Am. Soc. Renal Biochemistry and Metabolism, Am. Osler Soc., Explorer's Club, Sigma Xi (chpt. sec. 1974-76). Home: 20 Haven View Dr Saint Louis MO 63141-7902 Office: Bernard Becker Med Libr Renal Div Dept PO Box 8132 Saint Louis MO 63110-1093 Office Phone: 314-362-4234. E-mail: purkerm@msnotes.wustl.edu.

PURKEY, THOMAS EUGENE, social worker; b. Dallas, Jan. 14, 1969; s. Walter Ross and Elizabeth (Kenner) Purkey. BA, Austin Coll., 1991; MA in Soc. Svcs. Adminstrn., U. Chgo., 1993. Campus mgr. Comtys. in Schs., Dallas, Inc., 1993-96, sr. program coord., 1996-97, network adminstr., 1996-97, United Way of Met. Dallas, 1997—. Recipient Arrow of Light, Boy Scouts of Am., Dallas, 1979, Eagle Scout, 1982. Mem. Nat. Assn. Social Workers, Nat. Eagle Scout Assn. Democrat. Methodist. Avocations: flying, boating, stamp collecting/philately, computers. Home: 7210 Clemson Dr Dallas TX 75214-1719 Office: United Way of Met Dallas 901 Ross Ave Dallas TX 75202-1998

PURL, O. THOMAS, retired electronics company executive; b. East St. Louis, Ill., June 5, 1924; s. Ruthford Keith and Muriel Agnes (Thompson) P.; m. Martha Elaine Smalley, Feb. 21, 1948; children— Thomas Keith, Jeanne Marie Purl Elder. BS, U. Ill., 1948, BS, 1951, MS, 1952, PhD, 1955. Head high-power traveling wave tube sect., mem. tech. staff Hughes Research Lab., Culver City, Calif., 1955-58; sect. head, dept. mgr., group v.p., v.p. shareholder relations and planning coordination Watkins-Johnson Co., Palo Alto, Calif., 1958-86. Contbr. articles to profl. jours.; patentee in field. Chmn. career guidance com. Santa Clara Valley Joint Engring. Council, 1971-73; bd. dirs. Jr. Achievement of Santa Clara County, 1975-79. Served to 1st lt. USAAF, 1943-46. Fellow IEEE (chmn. Santa Clara Valley subsect. 1972); mem. Sigma Xi, Eta Kappa Nu, Phi Kappa Phi, Sigma Tau. Clubs: Commonwealth of Calif. Home: 466 La Mesa Dr Portola Valley CA 94028

PURNELL, CHARLES GILES, lawyer; b. Aug. 16, 1921; s. Charles Stewart and Ginevra (Locke) P.; m. Jane Carter; children: Mimi, Sarah Elizabeth, Charles H., John W. Student, Rice Inst., 1938-39; BA, U. Tex., 1941; student, Harvard Bus. Sch., 1942; LLB, Yale U., 1947. Bar: Tex. 1948. Ptnr. Locke, Purnell, Boren, Laney & Neely, Dallas, 1947-89, Locke, Purnell, Rain & Harrell, Dallas, 1989-90, of counsel, 1990-99, Locke, Liddell & Sapp, Dallas, 1999—. Exec. asst. to Gov. of Tex., Austin, 1973-75. Bd. dirs. Trinity River Authority of Tex., 1975-81; vice chmn. Tex. Energy Adv. Council, 1974. Served to lt. U.S. Navy, 1942-45; PTO. Mem. ABA, Tex. Bar Assn., Tex. Bar Found, Yale Club, Dallas Country Club, Dallas Petroleum Club, La Jolla (Calif.) Beach and Tennis Club. Episcopalian. Home: 1 Saint Laurent Pl Dallas TX 75225-8128 Office: Locke Lidell & Sapp 2200 Ross Ave Ste 2200 Dallas TX 75201-6776

PURNELL, JOHN H. beverage company executive; b. 1941; married. BSChemE, John Hopkins U., 1963; MBA, U. Pa., 1965. V.p. Anheuser-Busch, Inc., St. Louis, 1965-79; with Anheuser-Busch Cos., Inc., St. Louis, 1979—, sr. v.p., 1987-91; chmn., chief exec. officer Anheuser-Busch Internat., Inc., St. Louis, 1991—. Office: Anheuser-Busch Cos Inc 1 Busch Pl Saint Louis MO 63118-1852

PURNELL, MAURICE EUGENE, JR., lawyer; b. Dallas, Feb. 17, 1940; s. Maurice Eugene Sr. and Marjorie (Maillot) P.; m. Diane Blake, Aug. 19, 1966; children: Maurice Eugene III, Blake Maillot. BA, Washington and Lee U., 1961; MBA, U. Pa., 1963; LLB, So. Meth. U., 1966. Bar: Tex. 1966. Ptnr. Locke, Purnell, Boren, Laney & Neely, Dallas, 1966-87; shareholder Locke Purnell Rain Harrell PC, Dallas, 1987-99; ptnr. Locke Liddell & Sapp LLP, Dallas, 1999—2002, of counsel, 2002—. Bd. dirs. Leggett & Platt, Inc. Bd. dirs. Dallas Summer Musicals. Mem. ABA, Tex. Bar Assn., Tex. Bar Found., Dallas Bar Assn. Am. Judicature Soc., Dallas C. of C. Brook Hollow Golf Club. Home: 4409 S Versailles Ave Dallas TX 75205-3044 Office: Locke Liddell & Sapp LLP 2200 Ross Ave Ste 2200 Dallas TX 75201-6776

PURNELL, OLIVER JAMES, III, judge; b. Richmond, Va., Jan. 18, 1949; s. Oliver James Jr. and Margaret Helen (Hodges) P.; m. Cheryl Naomi Williams, June 30, 1973; children: Oliver James IV, Amy Susan. AA, U. Hartford, 1969; AB, Middlebury Coll., 1972; MSLS, Case Western Res. U., 1976; JD, Western New England Sch. Law, 1982. Bar: Conn. 1982, U.S. Dist. Ct. Conn. 1982. Dir., pharmacy libr. U. Conn. Sch. Pharmacy, Storrs, Conn., 1977-81; assoc. Lavitt, Hutchinson & Kaplan, Vernon, Conn., 1981-84, DuBeau & Ryan, Vernon, Conn., 1984-87, Howard, Kohn Sprague & Fitzgerald, Hartford, Conn., 1987-89; pvt. practice Vernon, 1989-92; reference libr. U. Conn. Sch. Law, Hartford, 1992-98; regional info. mgr. Lexis-Nexis, Vernon, 1998—99; judge Ellington Dist. Probate Ct., Vernon, 1999. Adj. prof. U. Hartford. Contbr. articles to profl. jours. Scoutmaster Boy Scouts Am., Rockville, Conn., 1990—; trustee Rockville (Conn.) Pub. Libr.; corporator Ea. Conn. Health Network; mem. U. Hartford Alumni Coun. Mem. Am. Assn. Law Libraries, So. New England Law Libr. Assn. (pres. 1998-99), Conn. Bar Assn. (coun. of bar pres. 1995-96), Tolland County Bar Assn. (pres. 1995-96), Nat. Coll. Probate Judges (chrm. Conn. probate tech. com., Masonic Lodge, A.F. & A.M. (master Fayette Lodge 1970). Avocations: skiing, camping, hiking, church organist. Office: 6 Forestview Dr Vernon Rockville CT 06066-4807 Mailing: PO Box 891 Vernon Rockville CT 06066-0891 E-mail: jpurnell3@att.net.

PURPURA, DOMINICK P. dean, neuroscientist; b. N.Y.C., Apr. 2, 1927; m. Florence Williams, 1948; children: Craig, Kent, Keith, Allyson. AB, Columbia U., 1949; MD, Harvard U., 1953. Intern Presbyn Hosp., N.Y.C., 1953-54; asst. resident in neurology Neurol. Inst., N.Y.C., 1954-55; prof., chmn. dept. anatomy Albert Einstein Coll. Medicine, Yeshiva U., N.Y.C., 1967-74, sci. dir. Kennedy Ctr., 1969-72, dir. Kennedy Ctr., 1972-82, prof., chmn. dept. neurosci., 1974-82, dean, 1984—, Stanford (Calif.) U., 1982-84. Editor-in-chief Brain Rsch. Revs., 1975—2000, Developmental Brain Rsch., 1981—2000, Molecular Brain Rsch., 1985—2000, Cognitive Brain Rsch., 1991—2000, Brain Rsch., 1975—2000, mem. editl. bd., 1965—2000. Served with USAAF, 1945-47. Fellow N.Y. Acad. Scis.; mem. NAS, Inst. Medicine of NAS, Am. Acad. Neurology, Am. Assn. Anatomists, Am. Assn. Neurol. Surgeons, Am. Epilepsy Soc., Am. Physiol. Soc., Assn. Rsch. in Nervous and Mental Disease, Soc. Neurosci., Sigma Xi. Office: Yeshiva U Albert Einstein Coll Medicine 1300 Morris Park Ave Bronx NY 10461-1926

PURSCELL, KEITH WILLIAM, minister; b. Coucil Bluffs, Iowa, Feb. 12, 1931; s. Benjamin William and Marie Esther (Lowe) Purscell; m. Mary Louise Elliott, May 16, 1952 (dec. Jan. 22, 1993); children: Kenneth, Sally, David, Glenda; m. Helen Margaret Duncan, June 17, 1994. Student, Johnson Bible Coll., Knoxville, Tenn., 1949—51; BA, Nebr. Christian Coll., Norfolk, 1953; postgrad. studies, Lincoln Christian Coll. Sem., Ill., 1953—54; MDiv., Phillips Grad. Sem., Enid, Okla., 1970. Ordained Clergy The Christian Ch., 1951. Pastor First Christian Ch., Spencer, Iowa, 1970—79, Broadway Christian Ch., Wichita, Kans., 1979—82, 1st Christian Ch., Independence, Kans., 1982—86, La Junta, Colo., 1986—90, Mankato, Minn., 1990—96; interim pastor Congregational Ch., Webster City, Iowa, 1998—99, St. Lukes, Fairbault, Minn., 1999—2000; retired. Chmn. com. on scholarships for ministry Disciples of Christ, Kans., 1979—86; chmn. com. on ministry Disciples of Christ Colo., and Wyoming, 1989—90; organising pres., v.p. Living at Home Block Nurse Program Disciples of Christ, Mankato, Minn., 1991—. Co-author: (devotional prayer) Secret Place, 1982; contbr. articles to Christian mags., 1955—95. Named Disting. alumus, Phillips U. Alumni, 2001. Disciples Of Christ. Achievements include Helped create senior center and county transportation for Clay County, Iowa, 1976-79; designed regional policy on sexual abuse by clergy or staff for Christian Church in the Central Rockies Region. Avocation: photography. Home and Office: PO Box 3639 Mankato MN 56002

PURSE, CHARLES ROE, real estate investment banker; b. Redhill, Surrey, Eng., May 19, 1960; arrived in U.S., 1960; s. James Nathanial II and Rolande Marie-Louise (Redon) Purse; m. Carole Lynn Sadler, July 5, 1986; children: Hayley Elizabeth, Cameron James, Andrew Lang. BA, Dartmouth Coll., 1982; MBA, Northwestern U., 1985. Account officer No. Trust Bank, Chgo., 1982-85; asst. v.p. Citicorp Real Estate, Inc., Chgo., 1985-88; v.p. Citibank, Ltd., Sydney, Australia, 1988-91, Citibank Realty Investment Advisors, N.Y.C., 1991-94; sr. v.p. Yarmouth Group, N.Y.C., 1994-96; mng. dir. DRA Advisors, Inc., N.Y.C., 1996-2000; dir. real estate pvt. fund group Credit Suisse First Boston, NYC, 2000—. Active alumni bd. We. Res. Acad., Hudson, Ohio, 2002. Mem.: Pension Real Estate Assn., Bald Peak Colony Club, Belle Haven Club, Hillsboro Club (Hillsboro Beach, Fla.), Cromer Golf Club (Sydney), Country Club (Cleve.). Republican. Avocations: golf, photography, skiing, tennis. Office: Credit Suisse First Boston 13th Fl Eleven Madison Ave New York NY 10010 Business E-Mail: charles.r.purse@csfb.com.

PURSER, DONALD JOSEPH, lawyer; b. Chgo., Apr. 21, 1954; s. Donald Cornelius and Mary Alice (Fashingbauer) P.; m. Ludmila Purser. BS, U. Utah, 1975; MS, Reid Coll., 1976; JD, George Mason U., 1980; postdoctoral, Georgetown U., 1981. Bar: Va. 1980, U.S. Tax Ct. 1980, U.S. Ct. Appeals (4th and 10th cirs.) 1980, Utah 1981, U.S. Supreme Ct, 1987; Nat. Bd. Trial Advocacy. Spl. agt. U.S. Dept. of State, Washington, 1976-80; law clk. to judge U.S. Dist. Ct., Alexandria, Va., 1980-81; assoc. Richards, Brandt, Miller & Nelson, Salt Lake City, 1981-83; sole practice Salt Lake City, 1983-85; ptnr. Fowler & Purser, Salt Lake City, 1985-87, Purser & Edwards LLC, Salt Lake City, 1987—; owner Advent Wealth Strategies Group LLC. Judge pro tem Salt Lake County Cir. Ct., 1981-85; adj. faculty U. Phoenix, Salt Lake City, 1984—; advance staff office of v.p. of U.S., Washington, 1986; bd. dirs. Ameralex Risk Retention Group Chgo., Am. Western Life Ins. Co., Tarzana, Calif.; chmn. Rep. Congl. Dist. Utah. Active fin. com. Snelgrove for Congress campaign, 1988. Maj. JAGC, USAR. Mem. ABA (litigation sect., torts and ins. practice sect.), Am. Bd. Trial Advocates, Am. Inn of Ct. II (barrister), Phi Delta Theta, Delta Theta Pi. Clubs: Blue Goose (Salt Lake City), Utah Elephant. Lodges: K.C. Republican. Roman Catholic. Avocations: skiing, stock market, reading, Aikido. Home: 2595 E 3300 S Salt Lake City UT 84109-2727 E-mail: purserlaw@aol.com.

PURSLEY, CAROL ROBERTS, admissions director; b. Montgomery, Ala., Dec. 11, 1965; d. Robert Edwin and Phyllis (Roberts) P. BA, Hartwick Coll., 1988; MEd, Boston U., 1995. Mktg. asst. Christie's, N.Y.C., 1990-95; mktg. assoc. United Distillers, Stamford, Conn., 1995-97; coord. spl. svcs., counselor St. Luke's Sch., New Canaan, Conn., 1997-99, dir. admissions, 1999—. Mem. ASCD, ACA. Roman Catholic. Avocations: running/racing, hiking, travel, mountain biking, baking. Home: 23 Carlton St Greenwich CT 06830-4615 E-mail: carolpursley@msn.com.

PURSLEY, JULIE, newscaster; married. BA in Telecommunications, Ind. U., 1991. Reporter Sta. WBKO-TV, Bowling Green, Ky.; with Sta. WHAS-TV, Louisville; anchor Sta. WRTV-TV, Indpls., 2001—. Office: WRTV TV 1330 N Meridian St Indianapolis IN 46202*

PURSLEY, MICHAEL BADER, electrical engineering educator, communications systems research and consulting; b. Winchester, Ind., Aug. 10, 1945; s. Bader E. and Evelyn L. (Bennett) P.; m. Lou Ann Hinchman, July 6, 1968; 1 child, Jessica Ann. BS, Purdue U., 1967, MS, 1968; PhD, U. So. Calif., 1974. Mem. tech. staff Hughes Aircraft Co., Los Angeles, 1967; engr. Northrop Co., Hawthorne, Calif., 1968; staff engr. Hughes Aircraft Co., Los Angeles, 1968-74; acting asst. prof. UCLA, 1974; asst. prof., then assoc. prof. elec. engring. U. Ill., Urbana, 1974-80, prof., 1980-93; Holcombe prof. elec. and computer engring. Clemson (S.C.) U., 1992—; assoc. Ctr. Advanced Study, 1980-81; vis. prof. UCLA, 1985; cons. U.S. Army, Huntsville, Ala., 1977, Ft. Monmouth, N.J., 1983-86, 91, ITT, Ft. Wayne, Ind., 1979—; pres. SIGCOM, Inc., 1986-90; prin. scientist Techno-Scis. Inc., 1990-96. Introduction to Digital Communications, 2004; author: Random Processes in Linear Systems, 2002, Introduction to Digital Communications, 2005; contbr. chapters to books. Recipient Fred W. Ellersick award Comms. Soc., 1996, Tech. Achievement award Mil. Comm. Conf., 1999, Edwin Howard Armstrong Achievement award, 2002. Fellow IEEE (pres. info. theory group 1983, Centennial medal 1984, Millennium medal 2000); mem. Inst. Math. Stats. Office: Clemson U 303 Fluor Daniel Bldg Dept ECE Clemson SC 29634

PURTELL, LAWRENCE ROBERT, lawyer; b. Quincy, Mass., May 2, 1947; s. Lawrence Joseph and Louise Maria (Loria) P.; m. Cheryl Lynn Tymon, Aug. 3, 1968; children: Lisa Ann, Susan Elizabeth. AB, Villanova U., 1969; JD, Columbia U., 1972. Bar: N.Y. 1973, N.J. 1978, Conn. 1988. Assoc. White & Case, N.Y.C., 1972-73; judge advocate USMC, Washington, 1973-76; assoc. White & Case, N.Y.C., 1977-79; corp. counsel Great Atlantic & Pacific Tea Co., Montvale, N.J., 1979-81; asst. gen. counsel United Techs. Corp., Hartford, Conn., 1981-84, assoc. gen. counsel, 1984-92, sec., gen. counsel, 1989-92; v.p., gen. counsel and sec. Carrier Corp., 1992-93; sr. v.p., gen. counsel and corp. sec. Mc Dermott Internat., New Orleans, La., 1993-96; sr. v.p., gen. counsel Koch Industries, Wichita, Kans., 1996-97; exec. v.p., gen. counsel Alcoa, Pitts., 1997—. Capt. USMC, 1973-76. Roman Catholic. Avocation: running. Home: 637 Shoreline Dr Naples FL 34119 Office: Alcoa 390 Park Ave New York NY 10022

PURTLE, JOHN INGRAM, lawyer, former state supreme court justice; b. Enola, Ark., Sept. 7, 1923; s. John Wesley and Edna Gertrude (Ingram) P.; m. Marian Ruth White, Dec. 31, 1951 (dec. 1995); children: Jeffrey, Lisa K.; m. Phyllis Kelly Purtle. Student, U. Ctrl. Ark., 1946—47; LLB, U. Ark., 1950. Bar: Ark. 1950, U.S. Dist. Ct. (ea. dist.) Ark. 1950. Pvt. practice, Conway, Ark., 1950-53, Little Rock, 1953—78, 1990—; mem. Ark. State Legislature, 1951-52, 69-70; assoc. justice Ark. Supreme Ct., 1979-90. Tchr., deacon Baptist Ch. Served with U.S. Army, 1940-45. Mem. ABA, Ark. Bar Assn., Am. Judicature Soc., Ark. Jud. Coun. Democrat.

PURVES, DALE, neurobiology research educator; b. Mar. 11, 1938; BA summa cum laude, Yale U., 1960; MD, Harvard U., 1964. Prof. physiology Med. Sch. Washington U., St. Louis, 1979-85, prof. neurobiology Med. Sch., 1985-90, co-dir. Javits Ctr. Med. Sch., 1985-90; G.B. Geller prof., chair neurobiology Duke U. Med. Ctr., Durham, 1990—. Author: Principles of Neural Development, 1985, Body and Brain, 1988, Neural Activity and the Growth of the Brain, 1994, Neuroscience, 1997, 2d edit., 2000, Why We See What We Do! The Wholly Empirical Empirical Basis of Vision, 2002. Mem. Nat. Acad. Sics., Inst. Med., Am. Acad. Arts and Scis. Office: Duke U Med Ctr 101 Bryan Rsch Bldg Research Dr Durham NC 27710

PURVES, DENNIS PATRICK, librarian; b. Elizabeth, N.J., Dec. 25, 1970; s. Dennis Patrick and Mary T. Purves. BA, Seton Hall U., 1993; MLS, Rutgers U., 1994. Libr. page Linden (N.J.) Pub. Libr., 1987—95, libr., 1996—; libr. Alexander Libr. Rutgers U., New Brunswick, NJ, 1995; freelance subject cataloger Bowker-Reed Reference, New Providence, NJ, 1996—97. Mem.: ALA, N.J. Libr. Assn. Democrat. Roman Catholic. Home: 38 E Elm Street Apt 3A Linden NJ 07036 Office: Linden Pub Libr 31 E Henry St Linden NJ 07036 Office Phone: 908-298-3830. E-mail: dpurves@lindenpl.org.

PURVIS, GEORGE FRANK, JR., life insurance company executive; b. Rayville, La., Nov. 22, 1914; s. George Frank and Ann Mamie (Womble) P.; m. Virginia Winston Wendt, May 16, 1942; children: Virginia Reese (Mrs. William H. Freshwater), Winston Wendt, George Frank III. AA, Kemper Mil. Sch., 1932; LLB, La. State U., 1935; DHL (hon.), LLD (hon.), U. Southwestern La., 1997; DHL (hon.), U. S.W. La., 1997. Bar: La. 1935. Sole practice, Rayville, 1935-37; atty. Office Sec. State State of La., Baton Rouge, 1937-41, also dep. ins. commr., 1945-49; atty. La. Ins. Dept., also spl. asst. to atty. gen., 1937-41; with Pan-Am. Life Ins. Co., New Orleans, 1949—, exec. v.p., 1962-64, pres., chief exec. officer, 1964—, chmn. bd., 1969—, also bd. dirs. Pres., bd. dirs. Compania de Seguros Panamericana, S.Am.; pres. Pan-Am. de Colombia Compania de Seguros de Vida, S.A.; chmn., bd. govs. Internat. Ins. Seminars, Inc., 1984—; mem. Industry Sector Adv. Com. for Trade Policy Matters, 1986; lectr. ins. law Tulane U., New Orleans, 1949-56; bd. dirs. 1st Nat. Bank Commerce in New ORleans, Republic Airlines, Inc., 1st Commerce Corp., So. Airlines-Republic Airlines, Pan Am de Mex. Cos. de Seguros Sobre la Vida, S.A., 1964-88; dir. Northwest Airlines, 1986-87. Compiler, author: Louisiana Insurance Code, 1948; contbr. articles to profl. jours. Chmn. big donors com. New Orleans Christmas Seal Campaign, 1961, gen. campaign chmn., 1962, chmn. profl. group VIII, 1963; vice chmn. New Orleans United Fund campaign, 1965, gen. chmn., 1967; pres. Tb Assn. Greater New Orleans, 1967, La. State U. Found., 1967, YMCA, New Orleans, 1968—, Internat. House, 1977, Met. Area Com., 1979; geog. chmn. U.S. Savs. Bond Campaign, Greater New Orleans, 1971; mem. Bd. City Park Commrs., 1965-79, mem. bd. commrs. Port of New Orleans, 1979—, pres. bd. commrs., 1982; chmn. S.S. Huebner Found. Ins. Edn., 1977—, Bus. Task Force on Edn., Inc., 1980—; mem. adv. bd. Bapt. Hosp., 1985—, Salvation Army, 1986—; bd. dirs. Family Svc. Soc. New Orleans, Council for a Better La., New Orleans Philharm. Symphony Soc., Summer Pop Concerts, Bur. Govt. Rsch. New Orleans; mem. Govs. Cost Control Commn., 1981-89; trustee Greater New Orleans Found., 1987—, chmn. bd. trustees La. Ind. Coll. Fund Inc., 1987-88, mem. 1987—. Served with USNR, 1941-45. Decorated Order of Vasco Nunez de Balboa (Panama); named Alumnus of Yr., La. State U., 1975, role model Young Leadership Coun., 1993; recipient award Inst. for Human Understanding, 1975, Weiss Meml. award, 1976, Vol. Activist award, 1978, award of excellence Greater New Orleans Fedn. Chs., 1983, Disting. Svc. award Navy League, 1983, Humanitarian award Nat. Jewish Hosp./Nat. Asthma Ctr., 1984, internat. ins. award Internat. Ins. Adv. Coun., 1986, 1st ann. award for outstanding efforts in promoting trade with L.Am., Rotary Club, 1987, Hall of Fame award La. State U., 1987, Man of Yr. award Fedn. Ins. and Corp. Counsel, 1988, Integritas Vitae award Loyola U. of South, 1991, Bus. Hall of Fame award Jr. Achievement, 1993, cert. of appreciation La. Air N.G., 1995, Paul M. Hebert Law Ctr.'s Disting. Alumnus of 1998, La. State U., Exec. of Yr. award Bus. Assn. Latin Am. Studies, 1999, East Jefferson Gen. Hosp. Aux. Great Gentleman's award, 2000, Cert. of Life Membership award Salvation Army Bd., 2000; selected role model Young Bus. Leadership Coun., 1993; honored as a founding mem. in Soc. of St. Ignatius, Loyola U., 1996. Mem.: ABA, Internat. Trade Adminstrn. (industry sector and functional adv. coms. for trade policy matters), New Orleans Assn. Life Underwriters (award for Loyal and Unselfish Svc. to the Ins. Industry 1987), La. Assn. Legal Res. Life Ins. Cos. (pres. 1963—68), Ins. Econs. Soc. Am. (chmn. 1980—81), Health Ins. Assn. Am. (dir., chmn. 1970), Am. Life Conv. (past chmn. legal sect., exec. com., v.p. La., chmn. 1972), Assn. Life Ins. Counsel, Am. Judicature Soc., La. Law Inst., La. Bar Assn., C. of C. Greater New Orleans Area (dir., pres. 1970), Delta Kappa Epsilon (Disting. Alumnus award Zeta Zeta chpt. 2001), Omicron Delta Kappa, Phi Delta Phi. Episcopalian. Home: 5501 Dayna Ct New Orleans LA 70124-1042

PURVIS, HOYT HUGHES, political scientist, academic administrator, educator; b. Jonesboro, Ark., Nov. 7, 1939; s. Hoyt Somervell and Jane (Hughes) P.; m. Marion M. Purvis; children: Pamela R., Camille C. BJ, U. Tex., 1961, MJ, 1963; postgrad., U. Nancy, France, 1962-63, Vanderbilt U., Nashville, 1963-64. Researcher/writer So. Edn. Reporting Svc., Nashville, 1963-64; reporter Houston Chronicle, 1964-65; press sec., spl. asst. Sen. J.W. Fulbright, Washington, 1967-74; dir. pubs. and lectr. LBJ Sch. Pub. Affairs, U. Tex., Austin, 1974-76; fgn./def. advisor and dep. staff dir. Sen. Majority Leader and Sen. Dem. Policy Com., Washington, 1977-80; sr. rsch. fellow LBJ Sch. Pub. Affairs, U. Tex., 1980-82; dir. and prof. Fulbright Inst. Internat. Rels., U. Ark., Fayetteville, 1982—2000; dir. Internat. Rels., prof. journalism and polit. sci. U. Ark., Fayetteville, 2000—. Author: Interdependence, 1992, Media, Politics and Government, 2001; co-author: Legistling Foreign Policy, 1984, Seoul & Washington, 1993; editor: The Presidency and the Press, 1976, The Press: Free and Responsible?, 1982, Media Issues and Trends, 1998; co-editor: Old Myths and New Realities in U.S.-Soviet Relations, 1990; columnist N.W. Ark. Times, 2000—. Mem. adv. coun. Sci. Info. Liaison Office, Ark. Gen. Assembly, Little Rock, 1984-96; chmn. Fayetteville City. Cable Bd., 1991-93; apptd. J. Wm. Fulbright Fgn. Scholarship Bd., 1994-2003, vice chair, 1995, chmn., 1996—99. Rotary fellow, 1962-63, others; recipient Fulbright Coll. Master Tchr. award, Disting. Faculty Achievement award U. Ark. Alumni Assn. Mem. Internat. Studies Assn. (regional v.p. 1984-86), Am. Polit. Sci. Assn., Assn. for Edn. in Journalism and Mass Communication, Phi Beta Delta (named Nat. Outstanding Faculty award 2000), Delta Phi Alpha. Methodist. Home: PO Box 1872 Fayetteville AR 72702-1872 Office: University of Ark 116 Kimpel Hall Fayetteville AR 72701

PURVIS, JEFF, race car driver; Race car driver Joe Gibbs, Richard Childress Racing, Welcome, NC. Named Champion, World Series of Dirt, 1984, NDRA, 1984—85. Office: c/o Richard CHildress Racing 236 Industrial Dr Welcome NC 27374

PURVIS, RONALD SCOTT, financial counselor, real estate professional; b. Cleve., Apr. 17, 1928; s. Samuel Martin Jr. and Dorothea (Scott) P.; m. Lynne Willis, Dec. 20, 1963; children: Ward S., Blair P. Snyder, Heather Leigh Ann. BS, U.S. Naval Acad., 1953; B Individualized Study, George Mason U., 1984. CLU, Chartered Fin. Cons. Enlisted USN, 1946, advanced through grades to lt. comdr., 1966, hon. discharged, 1972; served in destroyer with task force 77 Korea, 1953; flight instr., 1955-56; vx-6 squadron pilot, parachutist in-charge U.S. Naval Support Force Team, Antarctica, 1956-58; to McMurdo and South Pole, 1957-58; in charge of all-weather fighter detachment, 1958-59; with Office of the CNO (Op-007) Navy Dept., 1960-63; aide to pres. Kennedy, 1961-63; in charge of ordnance Handling, Flight Deck of aircraft carrier in the Mediterranean, 1963-64; in charge of Pub. Affairs NAS, Jacksonville, Fla., 1965-67; in charge of 5 Def. Dept. Combat MoPic Teams, U.S. Mil. Assistance Command Vietnam, 1968-69; dir. internal rels. CNO (Op-007), 1969-72; gen. agt. Can. Life Assurance, Washington, 1972-88; pres. RSVP Realty, Annandale, Va., 1985-2000, Purvis Corp., Falls Church, Va., 1986—2003. Del. Rep. Convs., Va., 1975—. Purvis Peak, Antarctic mountain, named in his honor. Mem. D.C. Soc., SAR (asst. registrar 1982-84, chaplain 1989-91, treas. 1991-92, state sec. 1992-94, sr. v.p. 1994-95, state pres. 1995-96, alt. nat. soc. trustee 1996-97, nat. soc. trustee 1997-98, registrar 1998-2000, mgmt. bd. 2000—), Assn. Naval Aviation, Masons, Shriners. Avocations: skiing, flying, scuba diving, golf, dance. Home: 27310 Baylys Neck Rd Accomac VA 23301 Office: 3415 Lakeside View Dr Falls Church VA 22041-2454 Office Phone: 703-820-3832. E-mail: purvispeak@juno.com.

PURYEAR, ALVIN NELSON, management educator; b. Fayetteville, N.C., Apr. 6, 1937; s. Byron Nelson and Gladys (Bizzell) P.; m. Catherine Paulette Wiggins, Aug. 30, 1962; children: Pamela, Susan, Karen. BA, Yale U., 1960; MBA, Columbia U., 1962, PhD, 1966. Employee relations adviser Mobil Oil Corp., N.Y.C., 1965-66, fin. analyst, 1966-67; specialist computational systems Allied Chem. Corp., 1967-68; asso. prof. Grad. Sch. Bus. Adminstrn. Rutgers U., Newark, 1968-69; asso. prof. mgmt. Bernard M. Baruch Coll., N.Y.C., 1970-72, prof. mgmt., 1972—, Lawrence N. Field prof. entrepreneurship, 1999—, chmn. dept., 1978-79, dean coll., 1972-75, dir. Baruch/Cornell Indsl. and Labor Relations program, 1977-81; v.p. for orgn. and mgmt. Ford Found., 1980-82; 1st dep. comptroller City of N.Y., 1983-85. Chmn. bd. Broadcast Capital Fund Inc., 1993-95; bd. dirs. Green Point Fin. Corp., Bank of Tokyo-Mitsubishi Trust, Am. Capital Strategies Ltd.; dir. Greenpoint Savs. Bank, 1992—. Co-author: Black Enterprise, Inc, 1973; also articles. Trustee Barber-Scotia Coll., 1977-82, Loyola coll., Balt., 1976-82, Riverdale Country Sch., Bronx, 1980-92, chmn. bd., 1987-89, Grad. Sch. Polit. Mgmt., 1987-95,

Pitts. Theol. Sem., 1989-92, 96-2000, Yale U., New Haven, 1994-96, Cmty. Svc. Soc. of N.Y., 1997—, Union Theol. Sem. & Presbyn. Sch. Christian Edn., 2001—; bd. dirs. Program Agy. United Presbyn. Ch., 1976-88, pres. 1983-86, Presbyn. Ch. U.S.A., 1987-97, chmn. 1991-93; active Presbyn. Investment and Loan Corp., 1996—, Yale Alumni Fund, 1977-82. John Hay Whitney fellow, 1960-61; Samuel Bronfman fellow, 1960-62 Mem. Acad. Mgmt., Assn. Yale Alumni (vice chmn. 1984-86, chmn. 1986-88), Am. Mgmt. Assn., Smithsonian Nat. Bd., Interracial. Coun. Bus. Opportunity (bd. dirs.). Presbyn. (elder).

PURYEAR, JAMES BURTON, college administrator; b. Jackson, Miss., Sept. 2, 1938; s. Harry Henton and Doris (Smith) P.; m. Joan Copeland, June 13, 1965; children: John James, Jeffrey Burton, Joel Harry. BS, Miss. State U., 1960, MEd, 1961; PhD, Fla. State U., 1969. Lic. profl. counselor, Ga. Assoc. dir. YMCA Miss. State U., Starkville, 1962-64; dir. YMCA, Starkville, Miss., 1964-65; dir. fin. aid Fla. State U., Tallahassee, 1967-69; asst. dir. student affairs Med. Coll. of Ga., Augusta, 1969-70, dir. student affairs, 1970-86, v.p. student affairs, 1986-2000, v.p. emeritus, student affairs, 2000—. Mem. adv. bd. Ga. Fed. Bank, Augusta, 1978-85; deacon, 1971-, chmn. bd. First Bapt. Ch., Augusta, 1978-80; pres. Learning Disabilities Assn., Augusta, 1987, PTA, 1994, Band Assn.,1996; bd. dirs. Augusta Tng. Shop for Handicapped, 1994-98; mem. exec. bd., v.p. Boy Scouts Am., 1996-02. Yearbook Dedication MCG Student Yearbook, 1975; scholar Med. Coll. Ga., 1988; recipient Svc. to Mankind award Sertoma, 1988. Mem. Nat. Assn. Student Pers. (S.E. regional bd. 1985), Am. Coll. Pers. Assn., So. Assn. Coll. Student Affairs, Rotary (pres. 1978, dist. lt. gov. 1997-99, dist. gov. 2001-02, Paul Harris fellow 1985, Will Watt fellow). Baptist. Avocations: golf, photography, scouting.

PURYEAR, JOAN COPELAND, academic administrator; b. Columbus, Miss., May 10, 1944; d. John Thomas and Mamie (Cunningham) Copeland.; m. James Burton Puryear, June 13, 1965; children: John James, Jeffrey Burton, Joel Harry. BA summa cum laude, Miss. State U., Starkville, 1965; MA, Fla. State U., 1969; EdD, U. Ga., 1987. Instr. English, Fla. State U., Tallahassee, 1965-69, Augusta (Ga.) State U., 1987-88; head English dept. Augusta Tech. Coll., 1989-93, chairperson gen. edn. and devel. studies, 1993-96, mem. dean's coun., mgmt. team, 1994—, gen. edn. and devel. studies, 1997—, dean allied health scis., 1997—2004. Chmn. State Exec. Bd. English, Ga., 1990-92, East Ctrl. Consortium English, Ga., 1990-92; facilitator Total Quality Mgmt. Tech. Tng.; mem. exec. steering com. Continous Improvement Coun., 1996-02; mem. and co-chmn. Continuous Improvement Coun., 1996-97. Mem. Cmtys. in Schs., 1996 –; trustee Augusta Tech. Inst. Found. Bd., 1996—; mem. founding bd. Junior Achievement, 2001-02; co-pres. Davidson Fine Arts Sch. PTA, 1995, co-pres. bd. assn., 1996; pres. Med. Coll. Spouse's Club, Augusta, 1972; dir. Women's Mission Orgn., First Bapt. Ch., Augusta, 1982, dir. youth Sunday Sch., 1992-98, chmn. 175th Anniversary, 1992, deacon, 1996—, vice moderator, 1998-99, mem. ministerial adv. com., 1992-2001, chair, 2003, vice chmn. scholarship and edn. com., 2002, chmn. nominating com., 2004; mem. found. bd. Walton Rehab. Ctr. Mem.: Rotary (chmn. dist. membership 2003—), Augusta South Rotary Club (pres. 2002—03), Phi Theta Kappa (advisor 1992—, Horizon regional award for outstanding advisor 1997). Baptist. Avocations: flower arranging, home decorating, reading, travel. Office: Augusta Tech Coll 3200 Augusta Tech Dr Augusta GA 30906-3375

PURYEAR, MARTIN, artist, educator; b. Washington, May 23, 1941; s. Reginald Thomas and Martina Alice (Morse) P. BA, Cath. U., 1963; postgrad., Swedish Royal Acad., Stockholm, 1966-68; M.F.A., Yale U., 1971, Doctorate (hon.), 1994. Mem. Peace Corps, Sierra Leone, 1964—66; asst. prof. Fisk U., Nashville, 1971-73, U. Md., College Park, 1974-77; assoc. prof. art U. Ill., Chgo., 1978-86, prof., 1986-88; staff Calder Atelier, Saché, France, 1992—93; resident Am. Acad., Rome, 1997; represented by Donald Young Gallery, Chgo. Exhibited in group shows at Whitney Biennial Exhbn., 1979, 81, 89, Whitney Mus. Am. Art, N.Y., Guggenheim Mus., N.Y.C., 1978, 85, 87, Mus. Modern Art, N.Y.C., 1984, St. Louis Art Mus., 1988, Donald Young Gallery, Chgo., 2002, 03, McKee Gallery, N.Y.C., 2002, Irish Mus. Modern Art, Dublin, 2004, others; one-man shows include Corcoran Gallery Art, 1977, Joslyn Art Mus., 1980, Univ. Art Mus., 1985, Bklyn. Mus., 1988; commd. sculptures include Bodard Art, Nathan Manila Sculpture Pk., Govs. State U., University Park, Ill., Chevy Chase Garden Pla., Md.; traveling retrospective Art Inst. Chgo., Hirshorn Museum, Washington, D.C., Museum of Contemporary Art, Los Angeles, 1991-92; Documenta IX, Kassel, Germany, 1992. Recipient Purchase prize Balt. Mus. Art, 1962, award Francis J. Greenburger Found., 1988, Best Artist prize Sao Paulo Bienal, 1989, Creative Arts award for sculpture Brandeis U., 1989, medal for sculpture Skowhegan Sch. Painting & Sculpture, 1990, award Coll. Art Assn.; Louis Comfort Tiffany Found. grantee, 1981; Guggenheim fellow, 1982 Mem.: Am. Acad. and Inst. Arts and Letters. Office: Nancy Drysdale Gallery 700 New Hampshire Ave NW # 917 Washington DC 20037-2406*

PUSATERI, LAWRENCE XAVIER, lawyer; b. Oak Park, Ill., May 25, 1931; s. Lawrence E. and Josephine (Romano) P.; m. Eve M. Graf, July 9, 1956; children: Joanne J. Katsis, Lawrence F., Paul L., Mary Ann, Eva M. Campbell. JD summa cum laude, DePaul U., 1953. Bar: Ill. 1953. Asst. state's atty. Cook County, 1957-59; ptnr. Newton, Wilhelm, Pusateri & Naborowski, Chgo., 1959-77; justice Ill. Appellate Ct., Chgo., 1977-78; ptnr. Peterson, Ross, Schloerb & Seidel, Chgo., 1978-95; of counsel Peterson & Ross, Chgo., 1996—2000. Pres. Conf. Consumer Fin. Law, 1984-92, chmn. gov. com., 1993-99; mem. Ill. Supreme Ct. Com. on Pattern Jury Instrns., 1981-96; mem. adv. bd. Ctr. for Analysis of Alt. and Dispute Resolution, 1999—; mem. U.S. Senate Jud. Nominations Commn. State Ill., 1993, 95; exec. dir. State of Ill. Jud. Inquiry Bd., 1995-96; panel chmn. Cook County mandatory arbitration, 1990—, judicate Am. Arbitration; mem. Merit Selection Panel for U.S. Magistrate; lectr. law DePaul U., Chgo., 1962, Columbia U., N.Y.C., 1965, Marquette U., Milw., 1962-82, Northwestern U. Law Sch., Def. Counsel Inst., 1969-70; apptd. by U.S. Senator Paul Simon to Merit Screening Com. Fed. Judges, U.S. Atty. and U.S. Marshal, 1993, others; mem. task force indigent appellate def. Cook County Jud. Adv. Coun., 1992-95; mem. Ill. Gen. Assembly, 1964-68. Contbr. articles to profl. jours. Chmn. Ill. Crime Investigating Commn., 1967-68, chmn. Ill. Parole and Pardon Bd., 1969-70; bd. dirs. Ill. Law Enforcement Commn., 1970-72; chmn. Com. on Correctional Facilities and Svcs.; exec. v.p. and gen. counsel Ill. Fin. Svcs. Assn., 1980-95; chmn. law forum Am. Fin. Svcs. Assn., 1975-76; mem. spl. commn. on adminstrn. of justice in Cook County, Ill. (Greylord Com.) 1984-90, bd. dirs. Chgo. Crime Commn., 1986-91, Cath. Lawyers Guild; mem. Ill. Supreme Ct. Spl. Commn. on the Adminstrn. of Justice, Ill. Supreme Ct. Appointment, 1991; adv. bd. mem. Ctr. for Analysis of Alternative Dispute Resolution Systems, 1998-; past pres. Justinian Soc. Lawyers. Served to capt. JAGC, AUS, 1955-58. Named One of Ten Outstanding Young Men in Chgo., Chgo. Jr. Assn. Commerce and Industry, 1960, 65; recipient Outstanding Legislator award Ill. Gen. Assembly, 1966; named Prin. for a Day Big Shoulders Fund. Fellow Am. Coun. Fin. Svcs. Attys.; mem. ABA (com. consumer fin. svcs. 1975-99, ho. dels. 1981-90, jud. adminstrn. divsn. 1980-95, mem. exec. com. lawyer's conf. 1994-95, mem. bench and bar rels. com. 1994-96, mem. adv. com. to Ill. State Del., Jud. Adminstrn. Divsn. in Recognition of Leadership in Improvement of Adminstrn. of Justice award 1993, 50 Yr. award 2003), Ill. State Bar Assn. (pres. 1975-76, com. on fed. jud. and related appointments, mem. adv. com., state del., 1994-99, bd. dirs., co-chmn. joint com. jud. compensation 2002—, Abraham Lincoln Legal Writing award 1959, Sr. Counsellor award 2003), Chgo. Bar Assn. (bd. mgrs. 1965-66), Fred B. Snite Found. (sec., counsel 1976-90), Gertrude and Walter Swanson Found. (sole trustee 1995—), Mid-Am. Club Chgo. Republican. Roman Catholic.

PUSCHAVER, ERNEST L. finance company executive; BS, Case Inst. Tech., 1969; MBA, Harvard U., 1972. CPA. Dir. fin., chief acctg. officer FleetBoston Fin. Corp., 2000—. Mem.: Am. Inst. CPAs. Office: FleetBoston Fin Corp 100 Federal St Boston MA 02110

PUSCHEL, PHILIP P. textiles executive; m. Roberta J. Green. AB, Hamilton Coll., 1960; MBA, Stanford U., 1962. V.p. F Schumacher & Co., N.Y.C., 1971, pres., CEO, 1981, chmn. bd., 1981—, CEO officer, 1989—99. With USN, 1962-65. Office: F Schumacher & Co 79 Madison Ave Fl 15 New York NY 10016-7802

PUSCHETT, JULES B. medical educator, nephrologist, researcher; b. Hazelton, Pa., Mar. 13, 1934; m. Diane Puschett; children: Mitchell, Lynne. BA magna cum laude, Lehigh U., 1955; MD, U. Pa., 1959. Intern Jackson Meml. Hosp., Miami, 1959-60; resident, fellow endrocrinology and metabolism Univ. Hosp., Balt., 1963-66; postdoctoral fellow in medicine NIH Inst. Arthritis and Metabolic Disease, Bethesda, Md., 1966-68; fellow, renal-electrolyte sect. U. Pa. Sch. Medicine, Phila., 1966-68; rsch. assoc. VA Hosp., Phila., 1968-70, staff to chief renal-electrolyte sect. dept. medicine, 1968-73, clin. investigator, 1970-73; head renal-electrolyte divsn. Allegheny Gen. Hosp., Pitts., 1973-78; dir. renal-electrolyte divsn. fellowship tng. program U. Pitts. Sch. Medicine, 1976-78; chief renal-electrolyte divsn. dept. medicine U. Ark. for Med. Scis., Little Rock, 1979-80, U. Pitts. Sch. Medicine, 1980-90; interim chief sect. nephrology dept. medicine Tulane U. Sch. Medicine, New Orleans, 1990-92, prof. chmn. dept. medicine, 1990—, asst. dean network affairs, 1996—, Harry B. Greenberg, MD chair in internal medicine, 1999—. Instr. medicine U. Pa. Sch. Medicine 1967-79, assoc. in medicine 1969-70, asst. prof. medicine 1970-73; clin. assoc. prof. medicine U. Pitts. Med. Sch. 1973-78; prof. medicine U. Ark. Med. Scis. 1979-80; prof. medicine U. Pitts. Sch. Medicine 1980-90; adj. prof. dept. pharmacology Tulane U. Sch. Medicine, New Orleans, 2002—. Editor: The Diuretic Manual, 1984, Diuretics: chemistry, Pharmacology and Clinical Applications, 1984, Disorders of Fluid and Electrolyte Balance: diagnosis and Management, 1985, Diuretics II: Chemistry, Pharmacology and Clinical Applications, 1986, Diuretics III, 1989, Diuretics IV, 1993; contbr. over 170 articles to profl. jours.; spkr. and presenter in field; editl. bd. Am. Jour. Med. Scis., Am. Jour. Nephrology (sect. editor Physiology for the Nephrologist), Cardiovasc. Risk Factors, Internat. Jour. Artificial Organs, Southern Med. Jour. Chmn. 1st Ann. Kidney Ball, Nat. Kidney Found. of Western Pa., 1988, chmn. 2d Ann. Kidney Ball, 1989. With USN 1960-63. Recipient Gloria P. Walsh award for Tchg. Excellence, Graduating Class/Tulane U. Sch. Medicine, 1998; named Outstanding Tchr. Yr., Owl Club, Tulane U., 1991, 94; Coxe Meml. scholar Lehigh U., 1951. Fellow ACP; mem. AMA, AAAS, Am. Fedn. Clin. Rsch., Am. Soc. Artificial Internal Organs, Am. Soc. Nephrology (chmn. audit com. 1992), Nat. Kidney Found. (pub. policy com. 1989, vol. svc. award 1990), Internat. Soc. Nephrology, Am. Heart Assn. Coun. on the Kidney in Cardiovasc. Disease (chmn. subcom. on scientific confs. 1991-92, exec. com. 1991-95, long-range planning com. 1992-94, vice chair 1998-2000, chair-elect 1999-2000, chair 2000—), Am. Heart Assn. Coun. for High Blood Pressure Rsch., Am. Physiol. Soc., Fedn. Am. Socs. for Exptll. Biology, Am. Geriat. Soc., Ctrl. Soc. for Clin. Rsch., Soc. for Exptl. Biology and Medicine, Am. Soc. Clin. Pharmacology and Therapeutics, Am. Coll. Clin. Pharmacology, Endocrine Soc., Am. Soc. Renal Biochemistry and Metabolism, Am. Soc. Hypertension (Outstanding Tchr. Yr. 1986), Internat. Soc. Nutrition and Metabolism in Renal Disease, Am. Soc. Bone and Mineral Rsch., European Dialysis and Transplant Assn., Nat. Kidney Found. of Western Pa. (med. adv. com. 1981, chmn. 1981-83, Gift of Life award 1991), Nat. Kidney Found. of La. (mem.-at-large, trustee 1991), So. Med. Assn., So. Soc. Clin. Investigation (councilor 1992-94, sec.-treas. 1994-99, pres.-elect 1998-99, pres. 1999-2000), La. State Med. Soc., Orleans Parish Med. Soc. (membership com. 1993, long-range planning com. 1993), La. Soc. Internal Medicine, S.E. Clin. Club, Midwestern Salt and Water Club, Phi Beta Kappa, Alpha Epsilon Delta, Alpha Omega Alpha. Office: Tulane Univ Sch Medicine Dept Medicine SL 12 1430 Tulane Ave New Orleans LA 70112-2699 E-mail: jpusche@tulane.edu.

PUSEY, WILLIAM ANDERSON, lawyer; b. Richmond, Va., Mar. 17, 1936; s. Paul H. and Vernelle (Barnes) P.; m. Patricia Powell, Sept. 3, 1960; children: Patricia Brent, William A. Jr., Margaret Glen. AB, Princeton U., 1958; JD, U. Va., 1962. Bar: Va. 1964. Assoc. McCutchen, Brown, et al, San Francisco, 1962-63; dep. dist. atty. Alameda County, Oakland, Calif., 1963-64; assoc., ptnr., sr. counsel Hunton & Williams, Washington, Fairfax and Richmond, Va., 1964—. Trustee Ea. Mineral Law Found., Morgantown, W.Va., 1985—, pres., 1987-88. Chmn. bd. dirs. Presbyn. Sch. Christian Edn., Richmond, 1984-85. Mem. Am. Hort. Soc. (bd. dirs. and sec. 1995-2002, gen. counsel 2002—), Order of Coif, Phi Beta Kappa, Omicron Delta Kappa. Home: 3910 N Glebe Rd Arlington VA 22207-4340 Office: Hunton & Williams 1900 K St NW Washington DC 20006-1110

PUSHINSKY, JON, lawyer; b. N.Y.C., May 30, 1954; s. Paul and Harriet (Rosenberg) P.; m. M. Jean Clickner, July 31, 1982; children: Matthew Clickner-Pushinsky, Jeremy Clickner-Pushinsky. BA, MA, U. Pa., 1976; JD, U. Pitts., 1979. Bar: Pa. 1979, U.S. Dist. Ct. (we. dist.) Pa. 1979, U.S. Ct. Appeals (3rd cir.) 1980, U.S. Supreme Ct. 1988. Staff counsel W.Va. Legal Svcs. Plan, Wheeling, 1979—80; pvt. practice Pitts., 1980—. Dem. candidate Superior Ct. Pa., 1993, 95; solicitor Cmty. Human Svcs. Corp., Pitts., 1992—; consulting lawyer ARC-Allegheny, Pitts., 1981—. Recipient Civil Libertarian award ACLU of Pa., 1994, Cmty. Citation of Merit Allegheny County Mental Health/Mental Retardation Bd., 1992, Cert. Appreciation Pitts. Commn. on Human Rels., 1992. Mem. Pa. Trial Lawyers Assn., Allegheny County Bar Assn. (appellate practice com., civil rights com.), Acad. Trial Lawyers Allegheny County. Democrat. Avocations: reading, hiking, movies. Office: 429 4th Ave Pittsburgh PA 15219-1500

PUSHKAREV, BORIS S. research foundation director, writer; b. Prague, Czechoslovakia, Oct. 22, 1929; arrived in U.S., 1949, naturalized, 1954; s. Sergei G. and Julie T. (Popov) P.; m. Iraida Vandellos Legky, Oct. 20, 1973. BArch, Yale U., 1954, M.C.P., 1957. Instr. city planning Yale U., New Haven, 1957-61; chief planner Regional Plan Assn., N.Y.C., 1961-69, v.p. rsch., 1969-89, sr. v.p., 1989-90; adj. assoc. prof. NYU, 1969-79; chmn. Russian Rsch. Found. Study of Alternatives to Soviet Policy, 1981—. Bd. dirs. Russian Solidarists; lectr. New Humanitarian U., Moscow, 1993—2002. Author: (with Christopher Tunnard) Man-Made America, 1963; (with Jeffrey Zupan) Urban Space for Pedestrians, 1975, Public Transportation and Land Use Policy, 1977, Urban Rail in America, 1982, Russia and the Experience of the West, 1995; editl. bd. POSSEV; chmn. POSSEV Publ. Assn., Moscow, 1999--; contbr. articles to profl. jours. Recipient Nat. Book award (with C. Tunnard), 1964. Mem. Am. Assn. for Advancement of Slavic Studies. Russian Orthodox. Home: 770 Anderson Ave Apt 20F Cliffside Park NJ 07010-2172 E-mail: posevru@online.ru.

PUSHKARSKY, LOUIS PAUL, retired mathematics educator; b. Slovak Town, Ark., Aug. 17, 1922; s. Erasmm and Yadwiga (Petroczynski) P.; m. Clarice W. Pollard, Jan. 19, 1963; children: Larry, David. BS in Math. and sci., U. Ctrl. Ark., 1951; MA in Math., U. Ark., 1953. Head math. and sci. Bradford (Ark.) Schs., 1952-55; prof. math. North Ctrl. Mo. Coll., Trenton, 1955-89, head math. and sci., 1955-89, prof. emeritus, 1989—. Mem. Trenton City Coun., 1985-91. Sgt. USAAF, 1943-45. Mem. VFW (bd. dirs. Mo. dept. 1976-77, asst. insp. gen. 1980-81. mat. adc 1978, 98, chaplain ritual team 1995—, dist. adj. 1974—), DAV (comdr. 1999-2000), Elks (exalted ruler 1975), Alpha Chi. Avocations: observing nature, collecting music, gardening. Home: 169 E 7th St Trenton MO 64683

PUSKAR, MILAN, pharmaceuticals executive; b. 1935; Grad., Youngstown State U., 1961. V.p. Mylan Pharm. Inc., 1961-72; divsn. v.p. ICN Pharms., Inc., 1972-75; pres., CEO, chmn. Mylan Lab. Inc., 1976-2000, chmn., CEO, 2000—. Vice chmn. bd. dirs. Mylan Lab. Inc., 1980-93, chmn. bd., CEO, 1993—. Office: STE 400 1500 Corporate DR Canonsburg PA 15317-8580

PUSTEJOVSKY, SUSAN F. mathematics educator; b. St. Paul, Minn., Jan. 27, 1951; d. John Orville and Florence Grabowski Sandberg; m. John S. Pustejovsky, Sept. 4, 1976; children: James Eric, Robert John. BA in math. and German, Marquette U., 1973, MA in German lang. and lit., 1976, MS in math., 1987, PhD in math., 1999. Asst. prof. Alverno Coll., Milw., 1991—2002, assoc. prof., 2002—. Mem.: Wis. Math. Coun., Nat. Coun. Tchrs. of Math., Math. Assn. of Am. Home: 5110 N Hollywood Ave Whitefish Bay WI 53217 E-mail: susan.pustejovsky@alverno.edu.

PUSTILNIK, DAVID DANIEL, lawyer; b. N.Y.C., Mar. 10, 1931; s. Philip and Belle (Gerberholtz) P.; m. Helen Jean Todd, Aug. 15, 1959; children: Palma Elyse, Leslie Royce, Bradley Todd. BS, NYU, 1952, JD, 1958, LLM, 1959; postgrad., Air War Coll., 1976. Bar: N.Y. 1959, U.S. Supreme Ct. 1962, Conn. 1964. Legis. tax atty. legis. and regulations div. Office Chief Counsel, IRS, Washington, 1959-63; atty. Travelers Ins. Co., Hartford, Conn., 1963-68, assoc. counsel, 1968-73, counsel, 1973-75, assoc. gen. counsel, 1975-87, dep. gen. counsel, 1987-93. Mem. adv. coun. Hartford Inst. on Ins. Taxation, 1978-93, vice chmn., 1991-92, chmn., 1992-93. Grad. editor NYU Tax Law Rev., 1958-59. Trustee Hartford Coll. for Women, 1985-91; life sponsor Am. Tax Policy Inst.; dir. Congregation Beth Yam, 1996-99. Served to col. USAFR. Kenneson fellow NYU, 1958-59. Fellow Am. Coll. Tax Counsel; mem. ABA (chmn. ins. cos. com. 1976-78), Am. Coun. Life Ins. (chmn. co. tax com. 1982-84), Am. Ins. Assn. (chmn. tax com. 1979-81), Assn. Life Ins. Counsel (chmn. tax sect. 1991-93), Twentieth Century Club, Sea Pines Country Club (co-chair social com. 1997-99).

PUTCHAKAYALA, HARI BABU, engineering company executive; b. Maddirala, India, July 15, 1949; came to the U.S., 1978; s. Seshadri Chowdary and Sambrajyam (Penubothu) P.; m. Vijay Lakshmi, Aug. 9, 1976; children: Sashi Manohar, Gopi Krishna. BS in Chem. Engring., REC, Warangal, India, 1971; MS, BITS, Pilani, India, 1974; PhD, IIT, New Delhi, 1978. Registerd profl. engr., Mich., Md., Calif., Pa., Mo. Trainee Fertilizer Corp., Bombay, 1971; environ. engr. Madison Madison Internat., Detroit, 1978-81, project coord., 1981-84, project mgr., 1984-89, v.p., 1990—2002, total quality officer, 1995—2002, also bd. dirs. Bd. dirs. Spack Inc., Bloomfield Hills, Mich. Contbr. articles to Canadian Jour. Chem. Engring. Rsch. fellow Univ. Grants Commn., 1974-78; recipient Cert. Boiler Efficiency Inst., 1981, U. Wis., 1986, 1992, Mich. State U., 1989, Ctr. for Hazardous Materials Rsch., 1990. Mem. AICE, NSPE, Am. Soc. for Quality Control, Am. Cons. Engrs. Coun., Project Mgmt. Inst. Achievements include development of design modification for incineration plants, O&M manuals for numerous water and wastewater facilities; design of wastewater treatment systems; research into energy and value engineering studies; capital improvement programs for public schools. Home: 654 Fox River Dr Bloomfield Hills MI 48304-1012

PUTH, JOHN WELLS, consulting company executive; b. Orange, N.J., Mar. 14, 1929; s. Leonard G. and Elizabeth R. (Wells) P.; m. Betsey Leeds Tait, Mar.1, 1952; children: David Wells, Jonathan Craig, Alison Leeds. BS cum laude, Lehigh U., 1952. Dir. mktg. Purolator Products, Rahway, N.J., 1955-61; pres., chief exec. officer Bridgeport (Conn.) Hardware Mfg. Co. subs. Purolator, 1962-65; group v.p. H.K. Porter Co., Pitts., 1965-72; pres., CEO Disston Inc., Pitts., 1972-75, Vapor Corp., Niles, Ill., 1975-83; chmn., pres., CEO Clevite Industries Inc., Glenview, Ill., 1983-89; pres. JW Puth Assocs., Skokie, Ill., 1989—; gen. ptnr. BUCF III and BUCF IV venture capital funds, Chgo. Bd. dirs. L.B. Foster, Pitts., A.M. Castle & Co., Franklin Park, Ill., V.J. Growers Inc., Apopka, Fla., George W. Schmidt Inc., Niles, Ill., Adams St. Ptnrs. LLC, Chgo., Guy & O'Neil, Fredonia, Wis.; advisor GTCR Funds, Golfserve Inc., Chgo. Chmn. bd. trustees Hadley Sch. for Blind, Winnetka, Ill., 1982-84; former trustee Lehigh U., Kenilworth Union Ch.; bd. dirs. Iaccoca Inst. With U.S. Army, 1946-47, PTO. Mem. Chgo. Club, Econ. Club, Comml. Club, Indian Hill Country Club, Old Elm Club, Loblolly Pines Club. Republican. Presbyterian. Home: 180 De Windt Rd Winnetka IL 60093-3744

PUTHENPURAKAL, JOSEPH MATHEW, information technology executive; b. Changanacherry, India, Feb. 12, 1949; came to U.S., 1978; s. Mathew Joseph and Teresa Mathew P.; m. Mary Jose Shirly, Aug. 21, 1977; children: Mathew Joseph, Thomas Joseph, Sherin Jose. BS, Kerala U., India, 1976; MS, Kerala U., 1978; AA, Dupage Coll., Glen Ellyn, Ill., 1982; BA, North Cen. Coll., Naperville, Ill., 1984; MBA, Thornewood U., Amsterdam, Netherlands, 1998, PhD, 2001. Software engr. AT&T Tech., Lisle, Ill., 1983-84; mem. tech. staff AT&T Bell Labs., Naperville, Ill., 1984-87; info. systems cons. Indecon, Inc., Chicago, 1987-89; pres. Chicagoland Star Telephone Co., 1988, Global Resources Co., Chgo., 1988—; mgr. Jewel Info. Systems Group, Melrose Park, Ill., 1989—91; pres. Optimum Techs. Inc., Lisle, Ill., 1992—. Trustee Rep. Presdl. Task Force, Washington, 1986. Mem. Data Processing Mgmt. Assn., Am. Entrepreneurs Assn., Internat. Traders. Avocations: reading, travel, swimming. Home: 1230 Golfview Dr Woodridge IL 60517 Office: Optimum Techs Inc 1230 Golfview Dr Woodridge IL 60517

PUTKA, ANDREW CHARLES, lawyer; b. Cleve., Nov. 14, 1926; s. Andrew George and Lillian M. (Koryta) P. Student, John Carroll U., 1944, U.S. Naval Acad., 1945-46; AB, Adelbert Coll., Western Res. U., 1949, JD, 1952. Bar: Ohio 1952. Practice law, Cleve.; instr. govt. Notre Dame Coll.; v.p. Koryta Bros. Coal Co., Cleve., 1952-56; supt. divsn. bldg. and loan assns. Ohio Dept. Commerce, 1959-63; pres., chmn. bd., CEO Am. Nat. Bank, Parma, Ohio, 1963-69; dir. fin. City of Cleve., 1971-74; dir. port control, 1974-78; dir. Cleve. Hopkins Internat. Airport, 1974-78. Mem. Ohio Ho. of Reps., 1953-56, Ohio Senate, 1957-58; dep. auditor, acting sec. Cuyahoga County Bd. Revision, 1970-71; mem. exec. com. Cuyahoga County Democratic Com., 1973-81, Assn. Ind. Colls. and Univs. Ohio, 1983-89; bd. govs. Sch. Law, Western Res. U., 1953-56; mem. exec. com. World Service Student Fund, 1950-52; U.S. rep. Internat. Pax Romana Congress, Amsterdam, 1950, Toronto, 1952; mem. lay advisory bd. Notre Dame Coll., 1968-90, trustee, 1990-93, hon. trustee, 1993—; mem. adv. bd. St. Andrew's Abbey, 1976-88; trustee Case-Western Res. U., Newman Found. No. Ohio, 1980-93, hon. trustee, 1993—; 1st v.p. First Cath. Slovak Union of U.S., 1977-80; pres. USO Council of Cuyahoga County, 1980-83. Voted an outstanding legislator Ohio Press Corrs., 1953; named to All-Star Legislative team Ohio Newspaper Corrs., 1955; named one of Fabulous Clevelanders Cleve. Plain Dealer, John Henry Newman honor Soc. Mem. Cuyahoga County, Cleve. Bar Assn., Nat. Assn. State Savs. and Loan Suprs. (past. nat. pres.), U.S. Savs. and Loan League (mem. legis com, 1960-63), Am. Legion, Ohio Mcpl. League (bd. trustees 1973), Parma C. of C. (bd. dirs., treas. 1965-67), Newman Fedn. (past nat. pres.), NCCJ, Catholic Lawyers Guild (treas.), Am. Ohio Bankers Assn., Am. Inst. Banking, Adelbert Alumni Assn. (exec. com.), Cathedral Latin Alumni Assn. (trustee 1952—), Internat. Order of Alhambra (internat. parliamentarian 1971—, past grand comdr., supreme advocate 1973), Amvets, KC, Pi Kappa Alpha, Delta Theta Phi (past. pres. Cleve. alumni senate, master inspector 1975). Office: 28 Pond Dr Cleveland OH 44116-1062 Office Phone: 440-331-5532.

PUTMAN, DALE CORNELIUS, management consultant, lawyer; b. Ponca, Nebr., Apr. 29, 1927; s. Merle H. and Catherine V. (Sheahan) P.; m. Alice Anselmi, Sept. 8, 1951; children: Mark, Lee, Neil, Bruce, Kirk, Nancy, Wendy. BS, U. Nebr., 1949, LL.D., 1951. Bar: Nebr. 1951, Iowa 1951, Mo. 1977. Mgr. Interstate Assn. Credit Mgmt., Sioux City, Iowa, 1951-52; sec., legal counsel Metz Baking Co., Sioux City, 1953-66, v.p., 1966-69, exec. v.p., 1969-72, pres., 1972-76; chief operating officer Interstate Brands Corp., Kansas City, Mo., 1976-77, pres., dir., 1977-80, pres., chief exec. officer, 1980-84; chmn., chief exec. officer, pres., dir. Interstate Bakeries (formerly DPF, Inc.), 1980-84; pvt. practice mgmt. cons., 1984—. Served with U.S. Army, 1945-46. Knight, Order of the Holy Sepulchre of Jerusalem, knight Order of Malta. Mem. KC (4th degree), Serra Internat. Republican. Roman Catholic. Home: 8405 Reinhardt Ln Shawnee Mission KS 66206-1316 E-mail: putman9752@aol.com.

PUTNAM, ADAM HUGHES, congressman, farmer, rancher; b. Bartow, Fla., July 31, 1974; s. William Dudley and Sara Elizabeth (Hughes) P; m. Melissa Putnam; children: Abbie Anna, Elizabeth Langford, Emma Katherine. BS in Food and Resource Econs., U. Fla., 1995. Co-owner Dudley Putnam, Inc., Bartow, Fla., 1988—; mem. Fla. Ho. of Reps., Tallahassee, 1996—2000, Congress from Fla. 12th dist., Washington, 2001—, mem. agrl. com., 1999—2000; chmn. subcom. on tech., info. policy, intergovtl. rels. and census. V.p. Fla. 4-H Found., 1997—. Mem. Fla. Cattlemen's Assn., Fla. Farm Bur., Bartow Kiwanis Club. Republican. Episcopalian. Avocations: hunting, fishing, reading. Office: US Ho of Reps 506 Cannon HOB Washington DC 20515-0912

PUTNAM, ALLAN RAY, association executive; b. July 16, 1920; s. Carl Eugene and Alice (Atwood) P.; m. Marion S. Witmer, Aug. 8, 1942 (dec. Mar. 1993); children: Judith H., Robert W., Victoria, Christian; m. Ann K. Mossman, Sept. 10, 1994. BS in Econs., U. Pa., 1942. Mem. exec. staff Am. Electroplaters Soc., 1946-49; asst. exec. sec., pub. mag. Tool Engr. Am. Soc. Tool and Mfg. Engrs., 1949-59; mng. dir. ASM Internat., Materials Park, Ohio, 1959-84, sr. mng. dir., 1983-85; sec.-gen. World Materials Congress, 1986—.

Prees. Nat. Assn. Exhibit Mgrs., 1955, Coun. Engring. and Sci. Soc. Execs., 1958; mgr. Am. Soc. Metals Found. Edn. and Rsch., 1963-85. Bd. govs., treas. Cape Cod Conservatory Music and Arts; bd. govs., pres. Cape Cod Symphony Orch. Served to capt. USAAF, 1942-46. Mem. ASTM, AAAS, NSTA (life), Am. Soc. Assn. Execs. (past dir.), Cleve. Conv. and Visitors Bur. (past dir.), Pres.'s Assn., Am. Mgmt. Assn., Metal Properties Coun. (past dir.), Franklin Inst., Internat. Iron and Steel Inst., Am. Iron and Steel Inst., S.E. Asia Iron and Steel Inst., Metals Soc. (London, hon.), Am. Assn. Cost Engrs., Associacao Brasileira de Metals, Italian Soc. Metallurgy, Chinese Soc. Metals, German Soc. Metals, Australasian Inst. Metals, Am. Nuclear Soc., Soc. Automotive Engrs., Soc. Mfg. Engrs., Cyrogenic Soc., Soc. for Advancement Materials and Process Engring., Am. Soc. Engring. Edn., Iron and Steel Inst. Japan (hon.), Metall. Soc., Greater Cleve. Growth Assn., Buckeye Trail Assn., Country Club (Pepper Pike, Ohio), Apalachian Mountain Club, Horseshoe Trail Club, Univ. Club (Washington), Orleans Yacht Club (bd. dirs.), Rotary (sec.). Home: 17 Pride's Path PO Box 2772 Orleans MA 02653-6772 E-mail: arputnam@capecod.net.

PUTNAM, FRANK WILLIAM, biochemistry and immunology educator; b. New Britain, Conn., Aug. 3, 1917; s. Frank and Henrietta (Holzmann) P.; m. Dorothy Alice Linder, Nov. 18, 1942; children— Frank William, Beverly Susan. BA, Wesleyan U., Middletown, Conn., 1939, MA, 1940; PhD, U. Minn., 1942; MA (hon.), Cambridge (Eng.) U., 1973. Instr., research asso. Duke U. Med. Sch., 1942-46; biochemist CWS, Camp Detrick, Md., 1946; asst. prof. U. Chgo., then assoc. prof. biochemistry, 1947-55; Lasdon research fellow Cambridge U., 1952-53; prof. biochemistry, head dept. U. Fla., 1955-65; prof. biology, dir. div. biol. scis. Ind. U., Bloomington, 1965-69, prof. molecular biology and zoology, 1972-74, disting. prof. molecular biology and biochemistry, 1974-88, prof. emeritus, 1989—. Bd. visitors Duke U. Med. Ctr., 1970-75; chmn. com. nomenclature of human immunoglobulins Internat. Union Immunol. Socs., 1971-76; chmn. basic sci. rev. bd. VA, 1972-76; chmn. cancer cause and prevention adv. com. Nat. Cancer Inst., 1974-75; sci. adv. com. Papanicolaou Cancer Research Inst., 1976-82; rsch. rev. com. ARC, 1973-77; sci. com. Brussels Colloquium on Protides of Biol. Fluids, 1970-90; chmn. virus cancer program adv. com. Nat. Cancer Inst., 1975-77; sr. med. adv. group VA, 1976-80; coun. divsn. biol. scis. and Pritzker Med. Sch., U. Chgo., 1977-87; chmn. Assembly Life Scis. Nat. Acad. Scis., 1977-81; mem. U.S. Nat. Com. Biochemistry, 1973-79; pres. sci. adv. com. G.E.R.M.I., Lyon, France, 1981-87. Co-author, editor: The Plasma Proteins, vol. 1, Isolation, Characterization and Function, 1960, vol. 2, Biosynthesis, Metabolism, Alterations in Disease, 1960, The Plasma Proteins, 2d edit., Structure, Function, and Genetic Control, Vol. 1, 1975. Vol. 2, 1975, Vol. 3, 1977, Vol. 4, 1984, Vol. 5, 1987; mem. editorial bd. Archives of Biochemistry and Biophysics, 1954-59, Science, 1968-82, Immunochemistry, 1972-75, Biomed. News, 1969-73, Fedn. Proc, 1958-63; Author numerous research papers. Trustee Argonne Univs. Assn., 1981-82; bd. govs. U. Chgo. Argonne Nat. Lab., 1983-89, chmn. Sci. and tech. com., 1983-87; bd. dirs. Radiation Rsch. Found., 1981-87. Markle scholar med. scis., 1950-56; Guggenheim fellow, 1970; fellow Churchill Coll., Cambridge U., 1973—; recipient Distinguished award teaching and research Wesleyan U., 1964, Distinguished Service award in medicine U. Chgo., 1968; Outstanding Achievement award U. Minn., 1974 Fellow AAAS, N.Y. Acad. Scis.; mem. Nat. Acad. Scis., Am. Acad. Arts and Scis. (Midwest council 1975-84), Pan-Am. Assn. Biomed. Scis. (sec.-gen. 1975-78), Japan Electrophoresis Soc. (hon.), Am. Inst. Biol. Scis. (life), Am. Soc. Biol. Chemists (sec. 1958-63), Soc. Exptl. Biology and Medicine, Am. Assn. Immunologists, Am. Chem. Soc. (chmn. div. biol. chemistry 1966-67), Soc. Peruana de Patologia (hon.), Fedn. Socs. Exptl. Biology (chmn. secs. com. 1958-63), Protein Soc., Internat. Soc. Thrombosis Haemostasis, Phi Beta Kappa, Sigma Xi, Phi Lambda Upsilon, Delta Sigma Rho. Clubs: Cosmos. Address: 11130 Springfield Pike Apt B423 Cincinnati OH 45246-4193

PUTNAM, FRANK WILLIAM, JR., medical researcher; b. Mpls., Feb. 6, 1947; s. Frank William and Dorothy Alice (Linder) P.; m. Karen Elizabeth Thompson, May 30, 1987. BA, Wesleyan U., 1969; MA, Ind. U., 1974; MD, Ind. U., Indpls., 1975. Intern Ind. U. Med. Sch., Indpls., 1975-76; resident in psychiatry Yale U. Med. Sch., New Haven, 1976-79; clin. assoc. NIMH, Bethesda, Md., 1979-82, sr. staff fellow, 1982-86, chief dissociative disorders unit, 1986—; resident in child and adolescent psychiatry Childrens Hosp. Nat. Med. Ctr., Washington, 1986-89; dir. Mayerson Ctr. for Safe and Healthy Children, Cin. Vis. clin. prof. Rush Med. Sch., Chgo., 1985—; cons. City Lights, Washington, 1986—; prof. pediats. and psychiatry Cin. Childrens Hosp.; sci. dir. Every Child Succeeds. Author: The Diagnosis and Treatment of Multiple Personality Disorder, 1986; contbr. articles to profl. jours. Vol. Mobile Med., Kensington, Md., 1982—. Mem. Internat. Soc. for Study of Multiple Personality and Dissociation (founding mem., Morton Prince award 1985), AAAS, Am. Acad. Child and Adolescent Psychiatry, Am. Psychiat. Assn., N.Y. Acad. Sci. Clubs: Cedar Brook (Kensington). Avocation: making guitars and violins. Office: Mayerson Ctr for Safe and Healthy Children ML 3008 Childrens Hosp 3333 Burnet Ave Cincinnati OH 45229-3039 Office Phone: 513-636-7001.

PUTNAM, FREDERICK WARREN, JR., bishop; b. Red Wing, Minn., June 17, 1917; s. Frederick W. and Margaret (Bunting) P.; m. Helen Kathryn Prouse, Sept. 24, 1942; children: James Douglas, John Frederick, Andrew Warren. BA, U. Minn., 1939; M.Div., Seabury-Western Theol. Sem., 1942, D.D., 1963; postgrad., State U. Iowa, 1946-47, Mpls. Coll. of Art & Design, 1984-97. Ordained to ministry Episcopal Ch. as deacon, priest, 1942. Pastor in, Windom and Worthington, Minn., 1942-43, Iowa City, 1943-47, Evanston, Ill., 1947-59, Wichita, Kans., 1960-63; Episc. chaplain State U. Iowa, 1943-47; suffragan bishop Episcopal Diocese, Okla., 1963-79; bishop Episcopal Ch. in, Navajoland, 1979-83; asst. bishop Diocese of N.C., 1983, Diocese of Minn., 1983-89, 96-99; acting rector St. George's Episcopal, Pearl Harbor, Hawaii, 1984-85, 96, St. Clement's, Honolulu, 1986, St. John's, Kula, Maui, Hawaii, 1988, 98, St. Elizabeth's, Honolulu, 1990; interim rector St. Stephen's Episcopal Ch., Edina, Minn., 1991-92, Trinity Episcopal Ch., Pocatello, Idaho, 1994; vis. bishop Diocese of N.J., 1995. Bd. dirs. Kiyosoto Ednl. Experiment Program, 1954-91, Mobile Outreach Ministry, 1998—, v.p., 1989-91; cons. Oklahoma City Community Relation Commn., 1966-70; Pres. Okla. Conf. Religion and Race, 1963-67; v.p. Greater Oklahoma City Council Chs., 1966-67; nat. chaplain Brotherhood of St. Andrew, 1967-79, mem. brotherhood legion, 1972—; priest assoc. Order Holy Cross, 1942—; exec. com. Conf. Diocesan Execs., 1969-76, pres., 1972-74; mem. Okla. Commn. United Ministries in Higher Edn., 1970-79, pres., 1973-75; mem. nat. com. on Indian work Episc. Ch., 1977-80; chaplain Okla. Assn. Alcoholism and Alcohol Abuse, 1974-78; hon. life mem. Oklahoma City and County Criminal Justice Council, 1978—; Bechtel lectr. U. Denver, 1966. Editor: (pub.) Sharers Mag., 1957-63; contbr. articles to profl. pubs. Founder, pres. Oklahoma City Met. Alliance for Safer City, 1971-78; Trustee Seabury-Western Theol. Sem., 1959-65, Episcopal Theol. Sem. Southwest, 1966-69, St. Simeon's Episcopal Home, 1963-79, St. Crispins Episcopal Conf. Ctr., 1963-79, Casady Sch., 1963-79, Holland Hall Sch., 1963-79, Episcopal Soc. Cultural and Racial Unity, 1967-70; trustee Neighborhood Services Orgn., treas., 1969; founder, 1st pres. Friends of Wichita Pub. Libr., 1962; bd. dirs. Minn. Photographic Exbn.; chmn. Mpls.-St. Paul Internat. Photog. Exhbn., 1987, 89; State Bd. Minn. Common Cause, 1989—, state chmn., 1993-95—; bd. dirs. Minn. Com. for Pub. Edn. Recipient Disting. Service award Evanston Jr. C. of C., 1952; Merit award Photog. Soc. Am. Fellow Coll. Preachers; mem. ACLU, Assoc. Parishes (pres. 1960-64), Mpls. Soc. Fine Arts (mem. photo coun.), Photog. Soc. Am., Am. Com. for KEEP (v.p. 1961-70, 90), Walker Art Ctr., Sierra Club, Met. Sr. Fedn., Audubon Club, Am. Assn. Ret. Persons, Minn. Hort. Soc., Hist. Soc. Episcopal Ch., Archaeol. Conservancy, Ancient Bibl. Manuscripts Ctr., Claremont, Calif., World Future Soc., Photographic Soc. Am. (assoc. 1989—, mem. v.p., 1995-97—), Twin Cities Assn. Camera Clubs (v.p. 1987), U. Minn. Alumni Assn., Minn. Hist. Soc., St. Paul Camera Club, Crosstown Camera Club, N.Am. Rights Fund., People for the Am. Way, Episcopal Peace Fellowship, Amnesty Internat., Greenpeace, Liturgical Conf., Living Ch. Found., Worldwatch Inst., Clan Douglas Soc., Northwest Racquet and Swim Club, Explorers Club, Phi Kappa Psi. Clubs: Normandale Tennis and Swim. Episcopalian. Home: 5229 Meadow Rdg Edina MN 55439-1412

PUTNAM, GEORGE W., JR., retired army officer; b. Ft. Fairfield, Maine, May 5, 1920; s. George W. and Rae B. (Merrithew) P.; m. Elaine Anderson (dec. 1973); m. Claudine Mahin (div. 1995); m. Helen Guerin, 1995; children: James M., J. Glenn; stepchildren: Philip Mahin, Leslie Mahin. Enlisted man U.S. Army, 1941-42, commd. 2d lt., 1942, advanced through grades to maj. gen., 1970; comdg. gen. 1st Aviation Brigade, Vietnam, 1970, 1st Cav, Divsn., Vietnam, 1970-71; dir. Mil. Personnel Mgmt., Hdqrs. Dept. Army, Washington, 1971-75; comdg. gen. U.S. Army So. European Task Force, Vicenza, Italy, 1975-77, U.S. Army Phys. Disability Agy., Washington, 1977-81; ret. U.S. Army, 1981. Dir. Army Coun. Rev. Bds., 1977-81; pres. Nat. Capital Retiree Coun., 1982-85. Internat. judge 5th and 6th World Helicopter Championships, 1986, 89, 94, chief judge 7th World Championship, 1992; U.S. mem. Internat. Helicopter com. Fedn. Aeronautique Internationale, 1988-91, 93-95; bd. dirs. Army Aviation Mus. Found., 1987—, pres., 1993-96; chmn. bd. trustees Army Aviation Hall of Fame, 1996-2001. Recipient Elder Statesman of Aviation award, 1998; inducted Army Aviation Hall of Fame, 1980. Mem. Nat. Aero. Assn. (sr. v.p. 1991-98, Fedn. Aero. Internat. (v.p. 1995-98), Army Aviation Assn. Am. (sr. v.p., pres. 1983-87, pres. scholarship found. 1991-93), Helicopter Club Am. (pres. 1988-90). Home: 4106 N Richmond St Arlington VA 22207-4816

PUTNAM, J. STEPHEN, financial executive; 3 children. BA, Bowdoin Coll., 1965. Exec. v.p. Raymond James Fin., Inc.; treas. Meerschaert Mut. Fund; bd. dirs. F.L. Putnam Securities. Former chmn. bd. St. Joseph's Coll., North Windham, Maine; former chmn. Scholarship Am.; former pres. Palm Harbor (Fla.) Cmty. Svc. Agy.; former chmn. Boston Stock Exch., Nat. Assn. Securities Dealers, Inc. Decorated Bronze Star, Army Commendation medal. Office: Raymond James Fin Inc 880 Carillon Pkwy Saint Petersburg FL 33716-1100 Office Phone: 727-567-2195. E-mail: Steve.Putnam@RaymondJames.com.

PUTNAM, MARLENE EVANS, artist; b. Hartford, Conn., Nov. 2, 1941; d. Charles Evans and Adrienne Edmay Levasseur; m. Harold Barnes Putnam, Jr., Mar. 9, 1980. Student, U. Hartford, 1960-63, Mus. of Fine Arts, Boston, 1971-77. Profl. artist Rockport (Mass.) Art Assn., 1986—, North Shore Art Assn., Gloucester, Mass., 1980—, Internat. Soc. of Marine Painters, Bradenton, Fla., 1983—, Art of the Sea, Rockland, Maine, 1995—, Tequesta (Fla.) Galleries, 1986—; fellow Am. Artist Profl. League, N.Y.C., 1996—. One-woman shows include Elliott Mus., 1993, Vero Beach Mus. Art, 1992, Art of the Sea, S. Thomaston, Maine, 1995; permanant collections at Harvard Law Sch., Dartmouth Coll., Nat. Wildlife Refuge, Cape Canaveral, Fla., Fla. Supreme Ct., Elliott Mus., Stuart, Fla., Vero Beach Mus. Art. Recipient over 50 awards in Fla. and Mass. Fellow Am. Artist Profl. League; mem. Rotary. Democrat. Avocations: learning and playing the viola, reading, computers, gardening, hiking.

PUTNAM, MICHAEL COURTNEY JENKINS, classics educator; b. Springfield, Mass., Sept. 20, 1933; s. Roger Lowell and Caroline (Jenkins) P. AB, Harvard U., 1954, AM, 1956, PhD, 1959; LLD (hon.), Lawrence U., 1985. Instr. classics Smith Coll., Northampton, Mass., 1959-60; faculty classics Brown U., Providence, 1960—, prof., 1967—, chmn., 2000-2001, prof. comparative lit., 1980—, MacMillan prof. of classics, 1985—; acting dir. Ctr. for Hellenic Studies, Harvard U., 1961-62, sr. fellow, 1971-86; Townsend prof. classics Cornell U., 1985; Mellon prof.-in-charge Am. Acad. in Rome, 1989-91; Martin classical lectr. Oberlin Coll., 2004. Scholar in residence Am. Acad. in Rome, 1969-70, classical jury, 1982-83, trustee, 1991—; assoc. univ. seminar on classical civilization Columbia U., N.Y.C., 1972—; mem. cath. Commn. on Intellectual and Cultural Affairs, 1969—; adv. coun. dept. classics Princeton U., 1981-87, chmn., 1983-87; cons. Am. Coun. Learned Socs., 1987-89; mem. Inst. for Advanced Study, 1987-88; vis. scholar Phi Beta Kappa, 1994-95; councillor Assn. of Lit. Scholars and Critics, 1996-99. Author: The Poetry of the Aeneid, 1965, Virgil's Pastoral Art, 1970, Tibullus: A Commentary, 1973, Virgil's Poem of the Earth, 1979, Essays on Latin Lyric, Elegy and Epic, 1982, Artifices of Eternity: Horace's Fourth Book of Odes, 1986, Virgil's Aeneid: Interpretation and Influence, 1995, Virgil's Epic Designs, 1998, Horace's Carmen Saeculare, 2000, Maffeo Vegio: Short Epics, 2004; contbr. articles to profl. jours. Trustee Lowell Obs., Flagstaff, Ariz., 1967-87, bd. advisors, 1987—; trustee Bay Chamber Concerts, Camden, Maine, 1972-88, incorporator, 1988-94; mem bd. cons. Portsmouth Abbey Sch., 1985-89; hon. sec. Keats-Shelley Meml. Assn., Rome, 1989-91. Rome Prize fellow Am. Acad. in Rome, 1963-64; Guggenheim Meml. fellow, 1966-67; sr. fellow NEH, 1973-74, cons. 1974-78, 87-90; Am. Council Learned Soc. fellow, 1983-84. Fellow Am. Acad. Arts and Sci. 1996—; mem. Am. Philol. Assn. (bd. dir. 1972-75, mem. com. on award of merit 1975-78, chmn. 1977-78, 1st v.p. 1981, pres. 1982, del. Am. Coun. Learned Soc. 1984-87, Charles J. Goodwin award of merit 1971, fin. trustee 1997-2004), mem. Am. Philosophical Soc., 1998—; Archaeol. Inst. Am., Classical Assn. New Eng., Medieval Acad. Am., Vergilian Soc. Am. (trustee 1969-73, v.p. 1974-76), Accademia Nazionale Virgiliana, Art Club. Office: Brown U Dept Classics Providence RI 02912-1856 E-mail: michael_putnam@brown.edu.

PUTNAM, PAUL ADIN, retired government agency official; b. Springfield, Vt., July 12, 1930; s. Horace Adin and Beatrice Nellie (Baldwin) P.; m. Elsie Mae (Ramseyer) June 12, 1956; children: Pamela Ann, Penelope Jayne, Adin Tyler II, Paula Anna. BS, U. Vt., 1952; MS, Wash. State U., 1954; PhD, Cornell U., 1957. Research animal scientist Agrl. Research Service, USDA, Beltsville, Md., 1957-66, investigation leader beef cattle nutrition, 1966-68, chief beef cattle research br., 1968-72; asst. dir. Beltsville Agrl. Research Ctr., 1972-80, dir., 1980-84; dir. cen. plains area Ames, Iowa, 1984-87; assoc. dir. mid. south area Stoneville, Miss., 1987-88; dir. mid south area, 1988-94; selectman Town of Springfield, Vt., 1996—2002. Contbr. articles to profl. jours. Recipient Kidder medal U. Vt.; Outstanding Performance awards USDA, also cert. merit; Danforth fellow; Borden fellow; Purina Research fellow. Fellow AAAS (rep. sect. O), Am. Soc. Animal Sci. (pres., North Atlantic sect., chmn. various coms., N.E. sect. Disting. Service award); mem. Am. Dairy Sci. Assn., Orgn. Profl. Employees USDA (pres. Beltsville chpt.), Council for Agrl. Sci. and Tech. Home: 36 Putnam Rd Springfield VT 05156-9115 E-mail: pputnam8@vermontel.net.

PUTNAM, RICHARD, dentist, educator; b. Lima, Peru, June 10, 1968; arrived in U.S., 1994; s. Jorge A. and Rosa V. Putnam; m. Cheryl Ordway Putnam, Aug. 21, 1997; children: Carina, Nathaniel. DDS, Cayetano Heredia U., Lima, Peru, 1991; cert., U. Conn., Farmington, 1997; DMD, Boston U., 2000. Dentist Ramon Castillo, MS, DDS, Lima, Peru, 1992—94, Hugo Mantino, DDS; resident U. Conn., Farmington, Conn., 1994—97; intern Robert Lindberg, DMD, Waltham, Mass., 1999—2000; dentist Robert B. Stocks, Vernon, Conn., 2000—02; dentist, faculty U. Conn., 2002—. Dir. dentist site Manchester Cmty. Dental Svcs., Conn., 2003—. Recipient Implant award, Boston U., 2000. Mem.: Conn. State Dental Assn., Acad. of Gen. Dentistry, Am. Dental Assn. Home: 28 Box Mt Dr Vernon Rockville CT 06066 E-mail: rputnam100@hotmail.com.

PUTNAM, ROBERT ERVIN, chemist, consultant; b. Northampton, Mass., Oct. 18, 1927; s. Ervin Earl and Mary Gertrude (Connelly) P.; m. Caroline Wright, Aug. 23, 1952; children: David Earl, Mary Caroline, Robert Edward, Andrew Wright. BS in Chemistry, U. Mass., 1950; PhD in Organic Chemistry, U. Ill., 1953. Rsch. chemist E.I. du Pont de Nemours, Wilmington, Del., 1953-59, rsch. supr., 1959-65, sr. rsch. supr., 1965-67, Parkersburg, W.Va., 1967-78, rsch. lab. supt., 1978-82, rsch. mgr., 1982-85; adj. faculty Washington State C.C., Marietta, Ohio, 1985-95; pvt. practice Marietta, 1985-95. Alumni adv. coun. dept. chemistry U. Mass., Amherst, 1975-78; instr. chemistry Marietta Coll., 1982-89, adv. coun., 1989-95, dir. Inst. for Learning in Retirement, 1995-98. Editor Bull. Am. Friends of Puttenham, 1984—; contbr. 20 articles to profl. jours. With USNR, 1945-46. NSF fellow, U. Ill., 1952-53. Fellow AAAS; mem. Am. Chem. Soc. (chmn. Ohio Valley sect. 1976-78), Rsch. Soc. Am., Valley Renaissance Consort, Mid-Ohio Valley Aviation Assn., Sigma Xi, Gamma Alpha, Phi Lambda Upsilon. Democrat. Mem. Unitarian Ch. Achievements include patents on fluorine containing polymers and monomers, ion exchange resins; research on industrial processes for nylon, polyacetals, acrylics, rubber toughened plastics, fluorinated plastics. Address: 100 Alden Ave Marietta OH 45750-1138 Office Phone: 740-373-4510. E-mail: putnamr@charter.net.

PUTNAM, RUTH ANNA, philosopher, educator; b. Berlin, Sept. 20, 1927; d. Martin and Marie (Kohn) Hall; m. Hilary W. Putnam, Aug. 11, 1962; children: Samuel, Joshua, Maxima. BS in Chemistry, UCLA, 1954, PhD in Philosophy, 1962. Instr. philosophy UCLA, 1957-59; acting asst. prof. U. Oreg., 1959-62; from lectr. to prof. philosophy Wellesley (Mass.) Coll., 1963-98, chmn. dept., 1979-82, 91-93; ret., 1998. Dir. summer seminar NEH, 1986, 89; mem. extramural grad. fellowships Wellesley Coll., faculty benefits com., com. budget, academic review bd., taskforce on affirmative action, bd. of admissions; presenter in field. Editor: Cambridge Companion to William James, 1997; contbr. chpts. to books, articles to profl. jours., and encys. Mem. Am. Philos. Assn. (program com. ea. divsn. 1977). Jewish. Office: Wellesley Coll 106 Central St Wellesley MA 02481-8268 E-mail: rputnam@wellesley.edu.

PUTNAM, WILLIAM LOWELL, science association administrator; b. Springfield, Mass., Oct. 25, 1924; s. Roger Lowell and Caroline Piatt (Jenkins) P.; m. Joan Fitzgerald, Sept. 29, 1951 (dec. April 1993); children: Katherine Elizabeth Putnam Delaney, W. Lowell, Erica A. Broman; m. Katherine E. Flynn, Sept. 18, 1999. Grad., Harvard Coll., 1945. With Springfield C. of C., 1950-52; founder, chmn. Springfield TV Corp., 1952-84; with Carroll Travel Bur., 1984-98. Vice chmn. Assn. Maximum Svc. Telecasters, 1975-84; sec.-treas. NBC Affiliates, 1980-83. Sole trustee Lowell Obs., Flagstaff, Ariz.; chmn. Springfield Park Commn., 1991-95. 1st lt. U.S. Army, 1943-45. Decorated Silver Star, Bronze Star, Purple Heart. Mem. Assn. Canadian Mountain Guides (hon.), Alpine Club Can. (hon.), Appalachian Mountain Club (hon.), Am. Alpine Club (pres. 1974-76, treas. 1977-91, hon.), Internat. Union Alpine Clubs (hon., Am. del., v.p. 2002). Avocation: alpinism. Home and Office: Lowell Obs Flagstaff AZ 86001 E-mail: putnam@lowell.edu.

PUTNEY, LACEY EDWARD, state legislator; b. Big Island, Va., June 27, 1928; m. Elizabeth Harlow; children: Susan Powers, L. Edward Jr. BA, Washington & Lee U. Mem. Va. State Legis., 1962—, spkr. ho., 2000—02, co-chair privileges & elections com., mem. appropriations com., mem. agrl. com., mem. rules com. Independent. Baptist. Office: Gen Assembly Bldg PO Box 406 Richmond VA 23218-0406

PUTNEY, MARK WILLIAM, lawyer, utilities executive; b. Marshalltown, Iowa, Jan. 25, 1929; s. Lawrence Charles and Geneva (Eldridge) P.; m. Ray Ann Bartnek, May 25, 1962 (dec. Feb. 2000); children: Andi Bartnek, William Bradford, Blake Reinhart; m. Linda Phelps, July 21, 2003. BA, U. Iowa, 1951, JD, 1957. Bar: Iowa 1957, U.S. Supreme Ct. 1960. Ptnr. Bradshaw, Fowler, Proctor & Fairgrave, Des Moines, 1961-72, of counsel, 1992-94; chmn., CEO. Bradford & Blake Ltd., Dakota Dunes, S.D., 1992—; pres., chmn., chief exec. officer Iowa Resources, Inc., 1984-90; chmn., chief exec. officer Iowa Power & Light Co., 1984-90, Iowa Gas Co., 1984-85, Midwest Resources Inc., 1990-92. Civilian aide to Sec. Army for Iowa, 1975-77; bd. dirs. Greater Des Moines YMCA, 1976-86, Boys' Home Iowa, 1982-86, Hoover Presdl. Libr. Assn., 1983—, U. Iowa Found., 1984—, Edison Electric Inst., 1986-89, Greater Des Moines Com., 1984—, pres. 1988; bd. dirs. Assoc. Edison Illuminating Cos., 1988-93, pres., 1991-92; chmn. Iowa Com. Employer Support of Guard and Res., 1979-86; bd. dirs. Des Moines Devel. Corp., 1984-92, chmn., 1989-90. With USAF, 1951-53. Recipient Disting. Alumnus award U. Iowa, 1995. Mem. Iowa Utility Assn. (chmn. 1989, dir.), Des Moines Club (pres. 1977), Desert Forest Golf Club (Carefree, Ariz.), Masons, Shriners, Delta Chi, Phi Delta Phi. Republican. Episcopalian. Home: PO Box 1126 Carefree AZ 85377 Personal E-mail: markwputney@aol.com.

PUTNEY, MARY LYNN, bank administrator, educator; b. N.Y.C., Feb. 26, 1948; d. Joseph John Berry and Evelyn Marie (Geoghegan) Schneir; m. Paul Michael McCaffery, May 18, 1968 (div. June 1976); children: Melissa Berry McCaffery, Paul David McCaffery; m. Frederick Bates Putney, May 30, 1992. MBA in Fin., Columbia U., 1982. Various positions Citibank, N.Y.C., 1974-85, v.p. fgn. exch., 1985-88, v.p. leveraged capital, 1988-92, mng. dir. pvt. banking, 1992-95, mng. dir. global equity, 1995—; adj. prof. Columbia Bus. Sch., N.Y.C., 1986—. Dir. Sinter Metal Corp., Cleve.; mem. adv. bd. AIG Millenium Fund, Russia, CVC/Opportunity Ptnrs., Brazil. Contbr. articles to profl. jours. Dir. Project Renewal, N.Y.C., 1995—, Mary Knoll Sch. Theology, Ossining, N.Y., 1994-95. Mem. Emily's List, Women's Campaign Fund, Sleepy Hollow Country Club, Sea Pines Country Club, Beta Gamma Sigma. Avocations: golf, bridge. Office: Citibank NA 153 E 53rd St New York NY 10022-4611

PUTTER, IRVING, French language educator; b. N.Y.C., Dec. 3, 1917; s. Joseph and Anna (Schrank) P.; children— Paul Stephen, Candace Anne Putter. BA, CCNY, 1938; MA, State U. Iowa, 1941; PhD, Yale U., 1949. Mem. faculty U. Calif.-Berkeley, 1947-88; prof. French U. Calif. at Berkeley, 1961-88, chmn. dept., 1968-71, humanities research fellow, 1971-72, 78-79, 84-85. Author: Leconte de Lisle and His Contemporaries, 1951, The Pessimism of Leconte de Lisle: Sources and Evolution, 1954, The Pessimism of Leconte de Lisle: The Work and The Time, 1961, La Dernière Illusion de Leconte de Lisle: Lettres Inédites a Emilie Leforestier, 1968; also numerous articles.; editor, translator: Chateaubriand: Atala, René, 1952. Guggenheim fellow, 1955-56; Fulbright fellow, 1955-56 Home: 115 Saint James Dr Piedmont CA 94611-3603

PUTTERMAN, FLORENCE GRACE, artist, printmaker; b. N.Y.C., Apr. 14, 1927; d. Nathan and Jean (Feldman) Hirsch; m. Saul Putterman, Dec. 19, 1947. BS, NYU, 1947; MFA, Pa. State U., 1973. Founder, pres. Arts Unlimited, Selinsgrove, Pa., 1969—; curator Milton Shoe Collection, 1970—; artist in residence Title III Program Cultural Enrichment in Schs. Program, 1969-70; instr. Lycoming Coll., Williamsport, Pa., 1972-74, Susquehanna U., Selinsgrove, PA, 1984—. One-woman shows include Everson Mus., Syracuse, N.Y., 1976, Hagerstown, Md., 1978, Stuhr Mus., Grand Island, N.B., 1979, Muhlenburg Ctr. for the Arts, Pa., 1985, Harmon Gallery, Fla., 1985, The State Mus. of Pa., 1985-86, Segal Gallery, N.Y., 1986, Canton Inst. Fine Arts, Ohio, 1986, Fla. Biennial Polk Mus., Lakeland, Fla., 1987, 89, Artists Choose Artists, Tampa Mus., 1987, Auburn Works on Paper, 1987, Ala., Ruth Volid Gallery, Chgo., 1989, Polk Mus. Art, Lakeland, Fla., 1989, Lowe Gallery, Atlanta, 1990, Mickelson Gallery, Washington, 1990, Palmer Mus., Pa. State U., 1990, Payne Gallery, Moravian Coll., 1991, Everhart Mus., Scranton, Pa., 1991, Lowe Gallery, L.A., 1992, Center Gallery, Bucknell U., Pa., 1993, Lore Degenstein Gallery, Susquehanna U., Selinsgrove, Pa., 1993, Lowe Gallery, Atlanta, 1993, Down Roll Gallery, Sarasota, Fla., Gallery 10, Washington, Donn Roll Contemporary, Sarasota, Fla., 1996, Grand Central Gallery, Tampa Fla., 1997, Walter Wickiser Gallery, N.Y., Hodges-Taylor Gallery, Charlotte N.C., Ziegenfuss Gallery, Sarasota, Burroughs-Chapin Mus., Myrtle Bend, S.C., Lighthouse Gallery, Tequesta, Fla., 1998, Galerie Lumiere, Savannah, Ga., 1999, Walter Wickiser Gallery, N.Y., 1999, Ellen Noel Art Mus., Odessa, Tex., 1999, Spartansburg County Mus. Art, Spartansburg, S.C., 2000, Saginaw (Mich.) Art Mus., 2000, Art Mus., No. Mich. U., Marquette, Lancaster Mus. Art, 2001, Albany (Ga.) Art Mus., 2002, Walter Wickiser Gallery, N.Y.C., 2003, Mira Mar Gallery, Sarasota, Fla., 2003, Waterworks Visual Art Ctr., Salisbury, N.C., 2003, Robeson Gallery, Pa. State U., 2003; 10-yr. retrospective Susquehanna U., 2003, Baisden Gallery, Tampa, Fla., 2004, Pfenninger Gallery, Lancaster, Pa., 2004, Walter Wickisen Gallery, N.Y., N.Y., 2004; exhibited in numerous group shows including: Libr. Congress, Smithsonian Traveling Exhbn., Sarasota (Fla.) Biennial Ringling Mus., 2000, Tampa Mus. Art, 2001, Springfield (Mo.) Art Mus., 2002, Chattahoochee Valley Art Mus., 2002, Butler Inst. Am. Art, 2002, Appalachian Corridors, Charleston, W.Va., 2003, La. State U., Baton Rouge, 2004others. Recipient award Silvermine Guild Conn. Appalachian Corridors, Arena, 1976, Gold medal of honor Audubon Artists ann. competition, Whitehead award Boston Printmakers, 1985, Shellenberg award Artists Equity, 1985, award N.C. Print & Drawing, 1985, award Chautauqua Nat., 1985, Johnson & Johnson award 3rd Ann. Nat. Printmaking Coun. of N.J., 1985, Purchase award N.J. State Mus., 1987, Disting. Alumni award Pa. State U. Sch. Arts & Architecture, 1988, Ethel

Klassen Meml. award Fla. Artists Group, 1992, Earl Horter award Phila. Watercolor Club, 1992, award of excellence, 1995, Stella Drabkin Meml. award Colorprint Soc., Award for Excellence Phila. Watercolor Club, 1996, Elizabeth Morse Meml. award Fla. Artists Group, 1996, Daniel Serra Y Navas Meml. award Audubon Artists, N.Y., 1996, Purchase award drawing annual Del Mar (Tex.) Coll., 1997, Purchase award Stockton (Calif.) Arts Commn., 1998, LaGrange Nat. Biennial, 2002; Va. Ctr. for the Creative Arts fellow, 1983-84; Nat. Endowment Arts grantee. Mem. Soc. Am. Graphic Artists (v.p., Daniel Serra Badine award 2004), Nat. Assn. of Women Artists (Nat. Medal of Honor, Elizabeth Blake award). Personal E-mail: Flo2@gte.net. *I examine the world through painting. I consider the act of art a spiritual experience. My work is informed by nature and visually recalled and then made permanent on paper or canvas. Maintaining a feeling of being in harmony with the world allows for periods of quiet meditation and creativity.*

PUTTLITZ, DONALD HERBERT, medical microbiologist; b. Kingston, NY, Apr. 21, 1938; s. Adalbert Siegfried and Elizabeth Ann (Barthel) P.; m. Barbara Ann Dingman, July 19, 1969; children: Michelle, Brian, Laura. BS with distinction, SUNY, New Paltz, 1959; MS, SUNY, Albany, 1961; PhD, Cornell U., 1965. Diplomate Am. Bd. Med. Microbiology. Assoc. microbiologist Beth Israel Med. Ctr., N.Y.C., 1967-85; supr. microbiology Jamaica (N.Y.) Hosp., 1985-92; instr. physician asst. program Touro Coll., N.Y.C., 1986-88; supr. microbiology Sound Shore Med. Ctr. of Westchester, New Rochelle, N.Y., 1993-97. Mem. faculty Mt. Sinai Coll. Medicine, 1972-85. Mem. N.Y.C. Bd. Edn., 1997—. Predoctoral traineeship fellow NIH, 1964-65, postdoctoral traineeship fellow USPHS, 1965-67. Mem. Am. Soc. Microbiology, N.Y.C. Soc. Microbiology. Roman Catholic. Home: 116 Horace Harding Blvd Great Neck NY 11020-1107

PUTZEL, CONSTANCE KELLNER, lawyer; b. Balt., Sept. 5, 1922; d. William Stummer and Corinne (Strauss) Kellner; m. William L. Putzel, Aug. 28, 1945; 1 son, Arthur William. AB, Goucher Coll., 1942; LLB, U. Md., 1945, JD, 1969. Bar: Md. 1945. Social worker Balt. Dept. Pub. Welfare, 1945-46; atty. New Amsterdam Casualty Co., Balt., 1947; staff atty. Legal Aid Bur., Balt., 1947-49; mem. Putzel & Putzel, P.A., Balt., 1950-89; pvt. practice Balt., 1989—; instr. U. Balt. Sch. Law, 1975-77, Goucher Coll., 1976-77. Chair character com. Ct. Appeals for 3d Cir., 1976-97. Author: A Practice Guide to Divorce, 1999, Representing the Older Client in Divorce, 1992. Commr. Md. Com. on Status of Women, 1972-76, Com. to Implement ERA, 1973-76; Pres. U. Md. Law Alumni Assn., 1978; bd. dirs. Legal Aid Bur., 1951-52, 71-73. Fellow Am. Acad. Matrimonial Lawyers (chair elder issues com. 1996); mem. ABA (co-chair elder issues com., mem. coun. sr. lawyers divsn. 1996-2000, editl. bd. 1996-99), Md. Bar Assn. (bd. govs. 1972-73, chmn. family law sect. 1978-79, chair sr. lawyers divsn. 2001-03). Home: 7121 Park Heights Ave Unit 401 Baltimore MD 21215-1610 Office: 401 Washington Ave Ste 803 Towson MD 21204 Office Phone: 410-494-7044. Business E-Mail: lawtowson@aol.com.

PUTZEL, MICHAEL, journalist, editor; b. Washington, Sept. 16, 1942; s. Max and Nell (Converse) P.; m. Ann Blackman, Feb. 23, 1974; children: Leila Elizabeth, Christof Blackman. BA, UNC in Polit. Sci., 1967. Reporter Charleston (W.Va.) Gazette, 1963-66; newsman AP, Raleigh, N.C., 1967-68, N.Y.C., 1968-69, war corr., 1969-72, reporter, 1972-79; asst. metro editor Washington Post, Washington, 1979; White House corr. AP, Washington, 1979-84, chief White House corr., 1984-87, chief of bur. Moscow, 1987—90, diplomatic corr. Washington, 1990-91; Washington bureau chief Boston Globe, 1991-92, White House corr., 1993-94; columnist "Plugged In", 1994-95; founder, CEO Trysail, Inc., Washington, 1996—; founder, pres. Milestones Inc., Washington, 1999—2000; v.p. Continental Computer Corp., Washington, 2000—03; book editor Washington, 2003—. Lectr. Georgetown U., Washington, 1999—. With USAR, 1964-65. Recipient AP Mgn. Editors citation, 1975, 81, Merriman Smith Meml. award White House Corr. Assn., 1986. Home: 4938 Quebec St NW Washington DC 20016-3231 Office Phone: 202-362-3133. E-mail: mputzel@trysail.com.

PUYAU, FRANCIS ALBERT, retired physician, radiology educator; b. New Orleans, Dec. 1, 1928; s. Frank Albert and Rose Sue (Jones) P.; m. Geraldine Sally diBenedetto, June 6, 1951; children: Michael, Stephen, Jeanne Marie, Julie, Melissa. BS, Notre Dame U., 1948; MD, La. State U., 1952. Diplomate Am. Bd. Pediat., Am. Bd. Pediat. Cardiology, Am. Bd. Radiology. Intern Charity Hosp., New Orleans, 1952-53, resident in pediat., 1955-57; from instr. pediat. to prof. radiology and pediat. La. State U. Sch. Medicine, New Orleans, 1957-74, acting head dept. radiology, 1971-72, head dept., 1972-74; asst. prof. pediat. Vanderbilt U., 1961-68; fellow dept. diagnostic radiology Charity Hosp., New Orleans, 1968-70; prof. radiology and pediat. Tulane U. Sch. Medicine, New Orleans, 1974-97, prof. medicine, 1974-95, acting chmn. dept. pediat., 1976-78; cons. St. Tammany Hosps., Covington, La., 1968-81; dir. cardiac catherization lab. dept. cardiology Charity Hosp., New Orleans, 1970-85; staff radiologist Our Lady of the Lake Regional Med. Ctr., Baton Rouge, 1986-93. Mem. staff Hotel Dieu, New Orleans, 1973-80; head x-ray dept. Children's Hosp. of New Orleans, 1976-82. Contbr. articles to profl. jours. With USPHS, 1953-55. Fellow Am. Coll. Cardiology, Am. Coll. Radiology; mem. East Baton Rouge Med. Soc., So. Soc. Pediatric Research, Am. Coll. Radiology, La. Radiology Soc., New Orleans Radiology Soc. (pres. 1985), New Orleans Pediatric Soc., Soc. Chmn. Acad. Radiology Depts., Radiol. Soc. N.Am., Am. Roentgen Ray Soc., Assn. Univ. Radiologists, Southern Yacht Club (New Orleans), Alpha Omega Alpha. Roman Catholic. Home: 458 Shady Lake Pkwy Baton Rouge LA 70810-4322

PUZDER, ANDREW F. restaurant executive, lawyer; b. Cleve., July 11, 1950; s. Andrew F. and Winifried M. Puzder; m. Deanna L. Descher, Sept. 26, 1987. BA, Cleve. State U., 1975; JD, Washington U., 1978. Gen. counsel, exec. v.p. Fidelity Nat. Fin., Inc., 1978-96, CKE Restaurants, Inc., 1997-99; CEO, pres. Hardee's Food Systems, Inc., 1997—2000, CKE Restaurants, Inc., Anaheim, Calif., 2000—. Editor Washington U. Law Quarterly, 1977-78. Author of law upheld by U.S. Supreme Ct. in Webster v. Reproductive Health Svcs., 1989; founding dir. Common Ground Network for Life and Choice, 1993. Mem. State Bar Nev., The Mo. Bar, State Bar Calif., Phi Alpha Theta. Address: CKE Restaurants 3916 State St, Ste 300 Santa Barbara CA 93105*

PUZZO, JOSEPH ANTHONY, JR., elementary school educator; b. Red Bank, N.J., May 7, 1959; s. Joseph Anthony Puzzo, Sr. and Rita Ann (Scala) Puzzo. BA, Rutgers U., 1981; MA, Nova Southeastern U., 2003. Lic. English tchr. N.J. Fitness instr. Matawan (N.J.) Athletic Club, 1989—90; fitness instr., personal trainer The Racquetplace, Matawan, 1990—95, Powerhouse Gym, 1995—96; full-time substitute tchr. Middletown Twp. (N.J.) Schs., 1996—99; full-time educator Thorne Middle Sch., Port Monmouth, 1999—. Ednl. advisor Jr. Nat. Young Leaders Conf., Washington, 2003—. Author: (monthly fitness column) Shape Up, 1990—92. Mem.: Middletown Twp. Ednl. Assn., N.J. Ednl. Assn., Nat. Coun. Tchrs. English. Roman Catholic. Avocations: writing, films, music, sports.

PYATT, EVERETT ARNO, government official; b. Kansas City, Mo., July 22, 1939; s. Arno Doyne and Myrl Elizabeth (Osborn) P.; m. Susan Evelyn Kristal, Sept. 28, 1968; children: Jennifer, Laura, Jeffrey. B.E., BS, Yale U., 1962; MBA, U. Pa., 1977. Staff engr. office dir. def. research and devel. Office Sec. Def., Dept. Def., Washington, 1962-72; dir. acquisition planning Office Asst. Sec. Def. for Program Analysis and Evaluation, 1972-75; dir. logistics resources Office Asst. Sec. Def. for Installations and Logistics, 1975-77; prin. dep. asst. sec. for logistics Dept. Navy, Washington, 1977-79, prin. dep. asst. sec. for shipbldg. and logistics, 1981-84, asst. sec. for shipbldg. and logistics, 1984-89; exec. advisor Coopers & Lybrand, 1989—; pres. EV Ventures; dep. chief fin. officer Dept. Energy, 1979-81; dir. Dept. Energy (Office of Alcohol Fuels), 1980. Recipient Disting. Civilian Svc. medal USN, 1980-81, 87, Superior Civilian Svc. medal, 1981, Outstanding Svc. medal Dept. Energy, 1981, Pres.'s award of meritorious excellence, 1983, Disting. Civilian Pub. Svc. award Dept. Def., 1989; Office of Sec. Def. fellow, 1975-77. Mem.: IEEE, Yale Club. Home: 4560 25th Rd N Arlington VA 22207-4147 Office: Coopers & Lybrand 12902 Federal Systems Park Dr Fairfax VA 22033-4421 Office Phone: 703-841-8318. Personal E-mail: epyatt1@comcast.net.

PYATT, KEDAR DAVIS, JR., research and development company executive; b. Wadesboro, N.C., May 20, 1933, s. Kedar D. and Frances (Hales) P.; m. Mary Mackenzie, June 2, 1956; children: Geoffrey, Kira, David, Rebecca. BS in Physics, Duke U., 1955; PhD in Physics, Yale U., 1960. With Gen. Atomic, San Diego, 1959-67; sr. v.p. Fed. sys. divsn. Maxwell Techs., San Diego, 1967—, sr. v.p. just Sys. Divsn. Recipient Exceptional Pub. Svc. medal Dept. Def., 1985, Lifetime Achievement medal DSWA, 1997. Office: Maxwell Tech Sys Divsn 9210 Sky Park Ct San Diego CA 92123-4302 E-mail: bud@maxwell.com.

PYE, GORDON BRUCE, economist; b. Oak Park, Ill., Oct. 30, 1933; s. Harold Charles and Florence Martha P. BS in Chem. Engring, M.I.T., 1955, PhD in Econs, 1963. Asst. prof. bus. adminstrn. U. Calif., Berkeley, 1963-66, assoc. prof., 1966-69, prof., 1969-72; econ. cons. Standard Oil Co. Calif. (name changed to Chevron Texaco Corp.), San Francisco, 1972-74; v.p., sr. economist Irving Trust Co., N.Y.C., 1974-78, sr. v.p., mgr. econ. research and planning div., 1978-89; prin. Gordon B. Pye Assocs., N.Y.C., 1990—. Assoc. editor: Fin. Analysts Jour, 1972-89. Mem. Forecasters Club N.Y. (pres. 1980-81). Home: 230 E 50th St New York NY 10022-7702 E-mail: GBPye@aol.com.

PYE, LENWOOD DAVID, materials science educator, researcher, consultant; b. Little Falls, N.Y., May 16, 1937; s. Lenwood George and Elizabeth Marie Pye; m. Constance Lee Lanphere, Sept. 6, 1958; children: DeAnn, Lorie, Lisa, Brien. BS, Alfred U., 1959, PhD, 1968. Rsch. engr. PPG Industries, Pitts., 1959-60; rsch. scientist Bausch & Lomb, Rochester, N.Y., 1960-61, 62-64; prof. glass sci. N.Y. State Coll. Ceramics Alfred U., 1968—2003, dir. Inst. Glass Sci. and Engring., 1984-96, dir. Industry-Univ. Ctr. Glass Rsch., 1986-96, dean N.Y. State Coll. Ceramics, 1996—2003, dean and prof. emeritus, 2003—. Pres. Internat. Commn. on Glass, 1997-2000. 1st lt. U.S. Army, 1960-62. Recipient Dominick Labino lectr. award 1995, Phoenix award as Glassman of Yr., 1996, award for excellence in tchg. Am. Soc. Engring. Edn., 1980, Presdl. Order of Merit, Alfred U., 2002, Chancellors award for scholarship and creativity SUNY, 2002. Fellow Am. Ceramics Soc. (trustee 1992-95), U.K. Soc. Glass Tech. (hon.); mem. Acad. Ceramics, German Soc. Glass Tech. (hon.). Office: NY State Coll Ceramics Alfred Univ 2 Pine St Alfred NY 14802-1214 E-mail: pye@alfred.edu.

PYERITZ, REED EDWIN, medical geneticist, educator, research director; b. Pitts., Nov. 2, 1947; s. Paul L. and Ida Mae (Meier) P.; m. Jane Ellen Tumpson, May 28, 1972; 2 children. SB in Chemistry, U. Del., 1968; AM, Harvard U., 1971, PhD in Biochemistry, 1972, MD, 1975. Diplomate Am. Bd. Internal Medicine, Am. Bd. Genetics. Intern Peter Bent Brigham Hosp., Boston, 1975-76; resident Peter Bent Bingham Hosp., Boston, 1976-77, Johns Hopkins Hosp., Balt., 1977-78; from instr. to prof. medicine and pediatrics Sch. Medicine, John Hopkins Hosp., Balt., 1977-93, chair dept. human genetics, 1994-00, prof. human genetics, medicine and pediatrics, 1994-01, MCP Hahnemann Sch. Medicine, 1993-00; prof. medicine and genetics U. Pa. Sch. Medicine, Phila., 2001—, chief divsn. med. genetics, 2001—. Dir. Inst. Genetics, Allegheny U. Health Sci., 1993-99; dir. Ctr. for Med. Genetics, Allegheny Gen. Hosp., 1995-2000; chief physician Md. Athletic Commn., Balt., 1978-93; med. adv. bd. Nat. Marfan Found., N.Y.C., 1982—, chmn. 1982-93, clin. care adv. bd., Nat. Neurofibromatosis Found., 1985—; med. adviser Alliance of Genetic Support Groups, 1994-2001; mem. rsch. adv. bd. Nat. Orgn. Rare Disorders, 1989-2000; mem. rsch. adv. com. Am. Heart Assn., 1996-98; mem. genetic adv. bd. Nat. Cancer Inst., 1996-99; mem. med. adv. bd. Can. Marfan Assn., 1999-, chmn., 2003-; mem. sci. adv. bd. Hereditary Hemorrhagic Telangiectasia Found., 2003—, chair med. adv. bd., Canadian Marfan Assn., 2003-. Co-editor Principles and Practice of Medical Genetics, 1992-; mem. editl. bd. New Eng. Jour. Medicine, 1993-96, JAMA, 1997-2001, Circulation, 2004—; contbr. over 300 articles to profl. publs. NIH grantee. Fellow: ACP, Am. Coll. Med. Genetics (dir. 1992—94, pres.-elect 1995—96, pres. 1997—98, past pres. 1999—2000); mem.: AAAS, AMA, Am. Med. Accred. Program (spl. adv. com. 1998—2000), Assn. Profs. Human Med. Genetics (pres. elect 1998—99, pres. 2000—02), Assn. Am. Physicians, Am. Soc. Clin. Investigation, Am. Fedn. Med. Rsch., Physician Consortium for Performance Improvement, Am. Heart Assn., Am. Soc. Human Genetics (chmn. program com. 1994—95). Office: Divsn Med Genetics Maloney 538 U Pa Sch Medicine 3400 Spruce St Philadelphia PA 19104-4283 Office Phone: 215-662-4740. Business E-Mail: reed.pyeritz@uphs.upenn.edu.

PYFER, JOHN FREDERICK, JR., lawyer; b. Lancaster, Pa., July 25, 1946; s. John Frederick and Myrtle Ann (Greiner) P.; m. Carol Trice, Nov. 25, 1970; children: John Frederick III, Carol Lee. Grad. cum laude, Peddie Sch., 1965; BA in Polit. Sci. and Econs., Haverford Coll., 1969; JD, Vanderbilt U., 1972. Bar: Pa. 1972, U.S. Dist. Ct. (ea. dist.) Pa. 1973, U.S. Tax Ct. 1975, U.S. Supreme Ct. 1975, U.S. Dist. Ct. (mid. dist.) Pa. 1984, U.S. Ct. Appeals (3d cir.) 1986. Law clk. to presiding justice Ct. Common Pleas, Lancaster, Pa., 1972-74; assoc. Xakellis, Perezous & Mongiovi, Lancaster, 1972-76; founding ptnr. Allison & Pyfer, Lancaster, 1976-85; pres. Pyfer & Assocs., Lancaster, 1986-88, Pyfer & Reese, Lancaster, 1988—. Prof. para-legal tng. Pa. State Ext. Svc., 1989-93; fed. ct. mediator, 1992-2001. Contbr. articles to law revs., law treatises. Pres. Lancaster-Lebanon Coun., Boy Scouts Am., 1989—93, coun. commr., 1987—89, mem. nat. com., 1996—, exec. bd. N.E. region, 1998—, area pres., 2000—03, v.p., 2004—; bd. dirs. World of Scouting Mus.; achieved Eagle Scout, 1962; named Disting. Eagle Scout, 2001; elder, pres. United Ch. of Christ, 1989, 1995, 2004. Named Pa. Super Lawyer, 2004; recipient Silver Beaver and Silver Antelope, Baden Powel fellow, Boy Scouts Am., Internat. Scouter's award, 2003. Fellow Am. Bd. Criminal Lawyers, Lancaster Heritage Ctr. (vice-chair 2003—); mem. ABA (First prize Howard C. Schwab Nat. Essay Contest in Writing 1972), SAR, Am. Arbitration Assn., Lancaster Bar Assn., Inns Ct. (founder, pres. W. Hensel Brown 1993-94), Christian Lawyers Soc., Train Collector Assn. (divsn. pres. 1984), Am. Orchid Soc. (affiliate pres. 1998), Lions Club (pres. 1980-82, 2000-01) (Willow Street, Pa.), Masons (Lancaster). Republican. Home: 1100 Little Brook Rd Lancaster PA 17603-6116 Office: Pyfer & Reese 128 N Lime St Lancaster PA 17602-2951 Office Phone: 717-299-7342. Business E-Mail: law@pyferreese.com. E-mail: jfpyfer@comcast.net.

PYKE, RONALD, mathematics professor; b. Hamilton, Ont., Can., Nov. 24, 1931; s. Harold and Grace Carter (Digby) P.; m. Gladys Mary Davey, Dec. 19, 1953; children: Darlene, Brian, Ronald, Gordon. BA (hon.), McMaster U., 1953; MS, U. Wash., 1955, PhD, 1956. Asst. prof. Stanford U., Calif., 1956-58; asst. prof. Columbia U., N.Y.C., 1958-60; prof. math. U. Wash., Seattle, 1960-98, prof. emeritus, 1998—. Vis. prof. U. Cambridge, Eng., 1964-65, Imperial Coll., London, 1970-71, Colo. State U., Ft. Collins, 1979, Technion, Israel, 1988, 90, 92; pres. Inst. Math. Stats., 1986-87; mem. bd. math. scis. NRC/NAS, 1984-88, chmn. com. applications and theoretical stats., 1985-88. Editor Ann. Prob., 1972-75; contbr. articles to profl. jours. NSF grantee, 1961-91. Fellow Internat. Statis. Inst. (v.p. 1989-91), Am. Statis. Assn., Inst. Math. Stats. (pres. 1986-87); mem. Bernoulli Soc., Statis. Soc. of Can. Office: U Washington PO Box 354350 Seattle WA 98195-4350

PYKE, THOMAS NICHOLAS, JR., government science and engineering administrator; b. Washington, July 16, 1942; s. Thomas Nicholas and Pauline Marie (Pingitore) P.; m. Carol June Renville, June 22, 1968 (dec. Oct. 2002); children— Christopher Renville, Alexander Nicholas. BS, Carnegie Inst. Tech., 1964; MS in Engring., U. Pa., 1965. Electronic engr. Nat. Bur. Standards, Gaithersburg, Md., 1964-69, chief computer networking sect., 1969-75, chief computer systems engring. div., 1975-79, dir. ctr. for computer systems engring., 1979-81, dir. ctr. programming sci. and tech., 1981-86; asst. adminstr. for satellite and info. services NOAA, Washington, 1986-92, dir. high performance computing and com., 1992-00, dir. The Globe Program, 1994—2002, chief info. officer, dir. high performance computing and comm., 2000—01; chief info. officer U.S. Dept. Commerce, 2001—. Organizer profl. computer confs., 1970-86; mem. Presdl. Adv. Com. on Networking Structure and Function, 1980, Interagy. com. on Info. Resources Mgmt., 1983-84, bd. dirs., 1984-87, vice chmn. 1986-87 (Exec. Excellence award 1991), chmn. Interagy. Working Group on Data Mgmt. for Global Change, 1987-93; speaker in field. Editorial bd. Computer Networks Jour., 1976-86; contbr. articles to profl. jours. Mem. Task Force on Computers in Schs., Arlington, 1982—85; co-pres. Jamestown Elem. Sch. PTA, Arlington, 1984—85; bd. dirs. Glebe Commons Assn., Arlington, Va., 1976—79, v.p., 1977—79. Recipient silver medal Dept. Commerce, 1973, gold medal, 1995; award for exemplary achievement in pub. adminstrn. William A. Jump Found., 1975, 76, Presdl. Rank award of Meritorious Exec., 1988, 99; Westinghouse scholar Carnegie Inst. Tech., 1960-64; Ford Found. fellow U. Pa., 1964-66. Fellow Washington Acad. Scis. (Engring. Sci. award 1974); mem. IEEE (sr. mem.), Computer Soc. of IEEE (bd. govs. 1971-73, 75-77, vice chmn. tech. com. on personal computing 1982-86, chmn. 1986-87), AAAS, Assn. Computing Machinery, Sigma Xi, Eta Kappa Nu, Omicron Delta Kappa, Pi Kappa Alpha (chpt. v.p. 1963-64) Episcopalian. Office: 14th St and Constitution Ave NW Rm 5029 Washington DC 20230 E-mail: tpyke@doc.gov.

PYLE, BENJAMIN MALREY, investor; b. Apple Springs, Tex., Sept. 27, 1927; s. Uria Malrey Pyle, Nora Etta Burran; m. Mary Ellen Hartmann, Jan. 31, 1932; children: Malrey Nathan, Dwight Dana. BBA in Banking/Fin., U. Houston, 1960; postgrad., So. Meth. U., 1965—66; non-traditional degree, Beverly Hills U., 1985; MS in Econs., U. So. Calif.; MA, Liberty U., Lynchburg, Va., 1993. Banking exec., dir. Comml. Banking, Houston and Baytown, Tex., 1960—83; adminstrv. exec. Hill & Hill Transp., Houston, 1983—85; farm credit examiner Farm Credit Adminstrn., McLean, Va., 1986—87, asst. receiver Sugarland, Tex., 1988—91; entrepreneur/investor Baytown, Tex., 1994—. Bus. cons. Pyle Bros., Baytown, Tex., 1992—; adv. bd. So. Partisan Mag., Columbia, SC, 1995—96. Contbr. articles to profl. jours. Polit. activist, precinct chmn. Rep. Party, Trinity County, Tex., 1998—; exec. bd. Episcop. Dioces. of Tex., Camp Allen, 1997—98; pres., bd. dirs. Civil War Round Table, Lufkin, Tex., 1999—; bd. regents Liberty U., 1994; mem. Trinity County Hist. Commn., 1991—; with U.S. Maritime Svc., 1944—46. With U.S. Merchant Marines, 1944—46, with USMC, 1946—57. Recipient Outstanding Leadership award, Mt. Zion Cemetery Assn. Mem.: SPJST (pres. 1977—94), Coll. of Bus. Adminstrn. Alumni U. Houston (charter). Republican. Episcopalian. Avocations: farming, ranching, hunting, lecturing. Mailing: 13529 FM 357 Groveton TX 75845-3203

PYLE, DAVE, newspaper editor; Bur. chief AP, Mpls., 1980—. Office: 511 11th Ave S Ste 404 Minneapolis MN 55415-1568

PYLE, GERALD FREDRIC, medical geographer, educator; b. Akron, Ohio, Dec. 22, 1937; s. Russell Roy and Ruth (Martin) P.; m. Carole Wood, Aug. 29, 1959; children: Eric, Frances. BA, Kent State U., 1963; MA, U. Chgo., 1968, PhD, 1970. Cartographer Rand McNally, Chgo., 1962-64; rsch. geographer Ency. Brit., Chgo., 1964-65; cartographer U. Chgo., 1965-70; from asst. prof. to prof. U. Akron, 1970-80; prof. geography and earth sci. U. N.C., Charlotte, 1980-98, prof. health promotion, 1995—2002, prof. health behavior and adminstrn., 2002—. Vis. fellow Macquarie U., Sydney, Australia, 1988; rsch. dir. Ctr. for Urban Studies, Akron, Ohio, 1973—80; tech. dir. Akron Area Census File, 1974—80; vis. scholar U. SC, 1977; interim dir. health adminstrn. program U. NC, Charlotte, 2001—02. Author: Heart Disease, Cancer and Stroke in Chicago, 1971, Spatial Dynamics of Crime, 1974, Applied Medical Geography, 1979, Diffusion of Influenza: Patterns and Paradigms, 1986, (with Shannon and Bashshur) The Geography of AIDS, 1990, (with shannon) Medical Atlas of the Twentieth Century, 1993; sr. editor Med. Geography, Social Sci. and Medicine, 1977-84; book rev. editor Social Sci. and Medicine, 1990—. Recipient Scholars medal First Citizens Bank, 1992; grantee Ill. Regional Med., 1969, Law Enforcement Adminstrn. Agy., 1972, 74, NSF, 1979, 82, Nat. Geog. Soc., 1988, NRC, 1995, Smart Start 1999-2001. Fellow Ohio Acad. Sci.; mem. APHA, Am. Coll. Epidemiology, Assn. Am. Geographers (Rsch. Honors S.E. divsn. 1994), Phi Kappa Phi. Democrat. Anglican. Achievements include research in spatial diffusion of infectious diseases and the location of health care delivery facilities. Home: 9801 Belt Rd Midland NC 28107-9057 Office: U NC Coll Health and Human Svcs 9201 University City Blvd Charlotte NC 28223-0002 Office Phone: 704-687-4262. E-mail: gfpyle@uncc.edu.

PYLE, HOWARD, lawyer, consultant; b. Richmond, Va., Feb. 1, 1940; s. Wilfrid and Anne Woolston (Roller) P.; m. Victoria M. Sheffield; children: Elizabeth Roller Ross, Howard. AB, Princeton U., 1962; JD, U. Va., 1967. Bar: Va. 1967, D.C. 1969. Career trainee CIA, Washington, 1967-69; adminstrv. asst. to Congressman Odin Langen, U.S. Ho. of Reps., Washington, 1969-70, to Congressman Hastings Keith, 1971; asst. to sec. Dept. Interior, Washington, 1971-73; Washington rep. Std. Oil Co. Ind., 1973-77; mgr. fed. pub. affairs R.J. Reynolds Industries, Inc., Winston-Salem, N.C., 1977-80; dir. fed. rels. Houston Industries, Washington, 1980-99; pres. HPYLE Cons., Alexandria, Va., 1999—. Bd. govs., pres. Episcopal Sr. Ministries, 1986-96; bd. dirs., pres. Friendship Terrace, 1986-96; chair D.C. area ann. giving Princeton U. Capt. USNR, 1962-89, ret. Mem.: SAR, NRA, Va. Bar, DC Bar, Res. Officers Assn., Naval Res. Assn., Princeton Club of Washington (mem. coun. 1998—, chmn. comms. com., chair DC ann. giving), Va. Country Club, Delta Theta Phi. Republican. Episcopalian. Home: 125 N Lee St Alexandria VA 22314-3260 also: PO Box 19645 Alexandria VA 22320-0645 Office: HPYLE Cons PO Box 19645 Alexandria VA 22320-0645 E-mail: hpyle@alumniprinceton.edu.

PYLE, JEAN L. economist, consultant, educator; BA, Bucknell U., 1966; MA, U. Mich., 1967; PhD, U. Mass., 1985. Asst. prof. econ. Smith Coll., Northampton, Mass., 1986—87, U. Mass., Lowell, 1987—91, assoc. prof. and prof. econ., 1991—97, prof. dept. regional econ. and social devel., 1997—2002, prof. emerita, 2002—, sr. assoc. Ctr. for Women and Work, 2002—. Author: The State and Women in the Economy: Lessons From Sex Discrimination in the Republic of Ireland, 1990; editor: Globalization, Universities, and Issues of Sustainable Human Development, 2002, Approaches to Sustainable Development: The Public University in the Regional Economy, 2001; mem. editl. bd.: Globalizations; contbr. chapters to books, articles to profl. jours. Fellow, U. Mich., 1966—67, U. Mass., Amherst, 1980—81, 1981—82; grantee, U. Mass., Lowell, 1987—2002. Mem.: Soc. for Internat. Devel., Assn. for Women in Devel., ASA Sect. on Sex & Gender, Am. Sociol. Assn., Com. on the Status of Women in the Economics Profession, Am. Econ. Assn., Internat. Assn. for Feminist Economics, Phi Beta Kappa. Office: Dept Reg Econ & Social Dev Univ Mass 61 Wilder Lowell MA 01854 Office Phone: 978-934-2792. E-mail: jean_pyle@uml.edu.

PYLE, KENNETH BIRGER, historian, educator; b. Bellefonte, Pa., Apr. 20, 1936; s. Hugh Gillespie and Beatrice Ingeborg (Petterson) P.; m. Anne Hamilton Henszey, Dec. 22, 1960; children: William Henszey, Anne Hamilton. AB magna cum laude, Harvard U., 1958; PhD, Johns Hopkins U., 1965. Asst. prof. U. Wash., 1965-69, assoc. prof., 1969-75, prof. history and Asian studies, 1975—, dir. Henry M. Jackson Sch. Internat. Studies, 1978-88; pres. Nat. Bur. Asian Rsch., 1988—; vice chmn. Japan-U.S. Friendship Commn., 1989-92, chmn., 1992-95. Co-chmn. Joint Com. on U.S.-Japan Cultural and Ednl. Coop., 1992-95; vis. lectr. history Stanford U., 1964-65; vis. assoc. prof. history Yale U., 1969-70, Edwin O. Reischauer Meml. Lectr., 1997; Mansfield Freeman lectr. Wesleyan U., 2002. Author: The New Generation in Meiji, Japan, 1969, The Making of Modern Japan, 1978, rev. edit., 1996; editor: The Trade Crisis: How Will Japan Respond?, 1987, The Japanese Question: Power and Purpose in a New Era, 1992, rev. edit., 1996, From APEC to Xanadu, 1997; founding editor Jour. Japanese Studies, 1974-86, chmn. editl. bd., 1987-89, assoc. editor, 1989—. Bd. dirs. Maure and Mike Mansfield Found., 1979-88; bd. govs. Henry M. Jackson Found., 1983—; adv. bd. Japan Found., 1989-99, Japan-Am. Student Conf., 1991—. Recipient Japanese Imperial award 3d Class, Order of Rising Sun, 1999, The Henry M. Jackson award for disting. pub. svc., 2000; Ford Found. fellow, 1961-64; Fulbright-Hays fellow, 1970-71; Social Sci. Research Council-Am. Council Learned Socs. fellow, 1970-73, 77, 83-84 Mem. Assn. Asian Studies, Am. Hist. Assn., Coun. Fgn. Rels. Presbyterian. Home: 8416 Midland Rd Medina WA 98039-5336 Office: Henry M Jackson Sch Internat Studies U Wash Seattle WA 98195-0001

PYLE, KURT H. lawyer; b. Oakland, Calif., Mar. 11, 1941; s. Thomas H. and Jean W. P.; m. Beth R., Apr. 30, 1977; children: Christopher, Brendan, Hilary. BS, U. Calif., Berkeley, 1962; JD, Hastings Coll. Law, 1965. Bar: Calif. 1966, U.S. Dist. Ct. (ctrl. dist.) Calif. 1966, D.C. 1972, U.S. Ct. Appeals (9th cir.) 1978, U.S. Dist. Ct. (no. and so. dists.) Calif. 1982, U.S. Dist. Ct. (ea. dist.)

Calif. 1983, U.S. Claims Ct. 1984, U.S. Tax Ct. 1984. Capt., judge advocate USAF, Wright-Patterson AFB, Ohio, 1962-65; from atty. to mng. ptnr. Schramm & Raddue, Santa Barbara, Calif., 1965-96; ptnr. Reicker, Pfau Pyle McRoy & Herman LLP, Santa Barbara, 1996—. Bd. dirs. Santa Barbara Counseling Ctr., 1996-2000. Mem. ATLA, Santa Barbara County Bar Assn., Assn. Bus. Trial Lawyers, Consumers Attys. Calif., Santa Barbara Inn of Ct. Home: 520 Grove Ln Santa Barbara CA 93105-2428 Office: Reicker Pfau Pyle McRoy & Herman LLP PO Box 1470 Santa Barbara CA 93102-1470 Office Phone: 805-966-2440. Business E-Mail: kpyle@rppmh.com.

PYLE, R. MICHAEL, wholesale distribution executive, educator; b. Indpls., Oct. 2, 1948; s. Merrill Ernest Pyle Jr. and Virginia Ann (Mitchell) Gilson; m. Margaret Ann Johnson, Aug. 11, 1973; 1 child, Ian Scot. BA in English, Ind. U., 1976. V.p. Nat. Wine & Spirits Corp., Indpls., 1976—. Lectr. on wine, Ind., 1976—. T.V. host (series): Wine, What Pleasure, 1980-82; assoc. prodr. (4-part documentary): The Wines of California, 1981. Mem. Wine Educators Am. Avocation: book and film collecting. Home and Office: 6816 Sargent Rd Indianapolis IN 46256-2167

PYLE, ROBERT MILNER, JR., financial consultant; b. Orange, N.J., Oct. 24, 1938; s. Robert M. and Dorothy (Collings) Pyle; m. C. Page Neville, May 31, 1969; children: Cynthia Neville, Laura Collings. BA, Williams Coll., 1960; JD, U. Va., 1963. Bar: N.Y. 1964. Assoc. Mudge Rose Guthrie & Alexander, N.Y.C., 1963—68; with Studebaker-Worthington, Inc., N.Y.C., 1968—77, sec., 1972—76, assoc. gen. counsel, 1974—77; with Singer Co., N.Y.C., 1977—79; corp. counsel, asst. to sec. Am. Soc. Corp. Secs., N.Y.C., 1977—78; sr. corp. counsel, asst to sec. Am. Express Co., N.Y.C., 1979; v.p., counsel Am. Soc. Corp. Secs., Inc., N.Y.C., 1979—89, v.p., sec., counsel, 1989—91; v.p., sr. asst. sec. Am. Express Co., N.Y.C., 1991—96, cons., 1997—. Career counseling rep. Williams Coll., 1977—. Trustee Pingry Sch., Martinsville, NJ, 1972—74, Arts Coun. Suburban Essex Inc., 1979—84, chmn. bd., 1981—84; trustee Suburban Cmty. Music Ctr., 1985—87; mem. Millburn-Short Hills Rep. Mcpl. Com. Essex County, 1998—2003; bd. govs. Colonial Dances, Ltd., N.Y.C., 1970—74; bd. dirs. Millburn-Short Hills Hist. Soc., 1985—90, v.p., 1985—87. Mem.: ABA, Assn. Bar City N.Y., Am. Soc. Corp. Secs. (hon.), Pilgrims U.S., Pingry Sch. Alumni Assn. (bd. dirs. 1966—78, pres. 1972—74, cert. of merit 1968), Hillsboro Club (Fla.), Short Hills Club, Bay Head Yacht Club (N.J.), No. N.J. Squash Racquets Assn. (sec., trustee), Met. Squash Racquets Assn. (past treas.), Racquet and Tennis Club, Pi Delta Epsilon, Delta Theta Phi, Sigma Phi. Episcopalian. E-mail: rmpylejr@aol.com.

PYLE, ROBERT NOBLE, government relations executive; b. Wilmington, Del., Oct. 23, 1926; s. Joseph Lybr and LaVerne Ruth (Noble) P.; m. Claire Thoron; children: Robert Noble Jr., Mark C., Nicholas A., Louis P. Crosier, Sarah P. Moore. BA, Dickinson Coll., 1948; postgrad., Wharton Sch., U. Pa., 1949, U. Minn. Pres. Robert N. Pyle, Inc., Wilmington, 1949-52; adminstrv. asst. to U.S. Congress, Washington, 1952-63; chmn., bus. and polit. cons. and lobbyist Robert N. Pyle & Assocs., Washington, 1970—; cons. Ind. Bakers Assn., 1981—, chmn. Sec./treas. Bulgarian Am. Bus. Ctr. Contbr. numerous articles to profl. jours.; reporter covering Nurnburg Trials, Paris Peace Conf. for, Stars & Stripes, Europe, 1946. Part-time field man Rep. Nat. Congl. Com., 1959-74. With U.S. Army, 1945-46, ETO. Mem. City Tavern Club, La Quinta Resort and Club, Kenwood Golf and Country Club, Lincoln Club. Presbyterian. Home: 50060 Camino Privado La Quinta CA 92253 Office: 1223 Potomac St NW Washington DC 20007-3212

PYLE, ROLANDA, social worker; b. N.Y.C., June 3, 1955; d. Clarence Leroy and Elnora E. (Harris) P. BA, CCNY, 1977; MA, L.I. U., 1984. Notary pub. N.Y., 1994. Sr. counselor Ctrl. Bklyn. Coord. Coun., 1982-85; project coord. Project Teen Aid, Bklyn., 1985; program dir. Family Dynamics, Bklyn., 1985-89; cmty. coord. N.Y.C. Dept. Health, 1989-91; supr. Child Devel., Bklyn., 1992; program dir. Miracle Makers, Inc., Bklyn., 1992-95; dir. Grandparent Resource Ctr., N.Y.C. Dept. Aging, 1995—. Mem. adv. bd. Family Cons. Svcs., Bklyn., 1996-97; mem. Child Welfare Task Force, Bklyn., 1992-95, Interagy. Coun. Aging, Bklyn., 1993-95, Sr. Citizen Task Force, Bklyn., 1992-95. Author (short story) African Voices, 1996; author of poems. Mem. N.Y. Com. Kinship Family Care, co-chair, 1996-97; mem. N.Y. Kin Care Task Force, Coalition 100 Black women, 1995-97. Fellow Brookdale Ctr. Aging; mem Avocations: travel, reading, writing, art exhibits, music. Home: 1304 Dean St Brooklyn NY 11216-3401 Office: NYC Dept Aging Grandparent Resource Ctr 2 Lafayette St Fl 15 New York NY 10007-1307

PYLE, THOMAS ALTON, instructional television and motion picture executive; b. Phoenix, Sept. 8, 1933; s. Thomas Virgil and Evelyn B. (Redden) P.; m. Victoria K. Bileck, Apr. 21, 1957 (dec.); children: Pamela V., Brett T.; m. Marilyn Ann Miller, May 12, 2001. BA, Ariz. State U., 1956. Freelance unit mgr., casting dir., pay master motion picture industry MGM, Universal, 20th Century Fox, Paramount and others, L.A. and N.Y.C., 1956—60; v.p. sales Depicto Films Corp., NYC, 1960—65; prodr. John Sutherland Prodn., LA, 1965—67; v.p. mktg. Audio Prodn. Ednl. Svc., NYC, 1967—71; exec. v.p. mktg. Data Plex Systems, NYC, 1971—74; divsn. pres., exec. prodr. Sterling Inst. Video Prodns., Washington, D.C., 1974—80; founder and pres. Applied Video Concepts, Inc., Washington, 1980—83; pres./ CEO Nat. Sci. Ctr. Found., Burke, Va., Augusta, Ga., 1983—85, tng. and edn. cons. to industry, govt. and military Washington, 1985—87; exec. dir., CEO Network for Instrnl. TV, Inc., Reston, Va. and Phoenix, 1987—. Built 88 new TV channels for K-12 sch. in 13 states and DC, 1997 started 1st highspeed wireless delivery of Internet to urban pub. sch., 1998 launched TeachersFirst-.com an advertising supported free Internet svc. to K-12 teachers; launched TeachersAndFamilies.com, 2002 for parents, teachers, and pre-school children; founder, pres. New Century Comm., an ITFS/EBS leasing adv. svcs., 2004—; bd. dir. Natl. ITFS Assn., So. Fla. Instrnl. TV, Inc., Del. Valley Ednl. Telecomm. Network, Inc., Instrnl. Opportunities, Inc., St. Louis, Mo., Cons. Wireless Cable Industry. Writer, dir., producer over 200 motion pictures, commd. for film on Pres. John F. Kennedy, 1962; prodr.: (films, on) Pres. Lyndon B. Johnson, 1964; singer: over 1500 performances on Broadway, stock, concerts, opera, radio and TV, appearing with Leonard Berstein, Fred Warring, Robert Shaw, Ralph Hunter, under mgmt. to Red and Enda Skelton, 1951—55, Nat. Artisits Corp., 1955—60. V.p. Dexter Park Assn., Spring Valley, NY, 1968-74, Solaridge Cluster Assn., Reston, Va., 1990-99. Recipient 27 awards from nat. and internat. film and video festivals, 2 Commendation awards White House, 1970, 2 Acad. award nominations. Mem. AAAS, Internat. Platform Assn., NY Acad. of Sci. Republican. Achievements include acknowledged authority on increasing productivity through edn., tng. and info. relay, expert on their effects in critical areas of tech., sci. comm. and defense. Avocation: photography. Office: New Century Communications 34111 N 7th St Phoenix AZ 85085 Office Phone: 623-434-3500.

PYLES, RODNEY ALLEN, archivist, county official; b. Morgantown, W.Va., June 21, 1945; s. Melford John and Luci L. (Scarcella) P.; m. Carol Louise Wrobleski, May 20, 1972; 1 child, Janessa Louise. BA, MA (Benedum scholar 1966-67, grad. research asst. 1967-68, grad. teaching fellow 1968-69), W.Va. U., 1967, 69. Instr. polit. sci. Alderson-Broaddus Coll., Philippi, W.Va., 1969-71; asst. curator W.Va. U. Library, 1971-77; dir. archives and history div. W.Va. Dept. Culture and History, 1977-85; dep. chief Assessor's Office Monongalia County, 1985-88; assessor Monongalia County, 1989—. Mng. editor: W.Va. History quar, 1977-85 Mem. Morgantown (W.Va.) Dem. exec. com., 1966-69, Monongalia County (W.Va.) Dem. exec. com., 1972-74; mem. Morgantown Libr. Bd., 1988-91; pres. Morgantown Hist. Landmarks Commn., 1986—; bd. dirs., trustee W.Va. Pub. Theatre, 1999—, treas., 2003—. Mem. Soc. Am. Archivists, Mid-Atlantic Regional Archives Conf., W.Va. Hist. Soc. (exec. sec. 1977-90), W.Va. Libr. Assn., Am. Assn. State and Local History (state awards chmn. 1980-85, state membership com. 1981-87), Monongalia Hist. Soc. (pres. 1986-88, bd. dirs. 1988—), W.Va. Polit. Sci. Assn. (treas. [illegible]), W.Va. Assessors' Assn. (pres. 1992-93), KC (pres. bowling league [illegible] deg., faithful capt. 1996—, chancellor 1998-2000, dep. Grand Knight [illegible], Grand Knight, 2002-), Sons of Italy (treas. 1995—). Roman Catholic. Home: 536 Harvard Ave Morgantown WV 26505-2157 Office: County Court House Rm 215 Morgantown WV 26505 Office Phone: 304-291-7222. E-mail: rapone@sbccom.com., rpyles@assessor.org.

PYLES, SELMA BROADWAY, music educator; b. Columbus, Ohio, June 7, 1955; d. Norman James and Ruth (Demarest) Broadway; m. Michael Lee Pyles, Aug. 4, 1990. MusB Edn., Ohio State U., 1977. Cert. tchr. Ohio Dept. Edn., 1977. Mid. sch. orch. tchr. South-We. City Sch. Dist., Grove City, Ohio, 1977—88; asst. h.s. orch. tchr. Hilliard City Sch. Dist., Ohio, 1988—2001, mid. sch. orch. tchr., 1988—2001, elem. orch. tchr., 2001—. Orch. condr. Columbus Symphony Cadet Youth Orch., Ohio, 1989—90; orch. tchr. Ohio String Tchrs. Assn. Mid. Sch. Orch. Summer Camp, Columbus, 1988—97. Contbr. book. Choir dir. Westgate Friends Ch., Columbus, 1980—95, Youth Musicale, Canton, Ohio, 1980—82, Sounds of Celebration, Elyria, Ohio, 1984—86; orch. dir. N.W. Bible Ch., Hilliard, Ohio, 1998—2004, interim choir dir., 2002—04. Recipient Pub. Sch. Orch. Tchr. of Yr., Ohio Orch. and String Tchrs. Assn., 2003. Mem.: NEA (assoc.), Am. String Tchr. Assn. (assoc.), Ohio Orch. and String Tchrs. Assn. (assoc. Pub. Sch. Orch. Tchr. of the Yr. 2003), Ohio Edn. Assn. (assoc.). Achievements include Middle School Large Group Contests Superior Ratings 1989-2001. Avocations: church music, bible study, violin. Home: 4266 Ongaro Dr Columbus OH 43204 Office: Hilliard City Sch Dist 4681 Leap Road Hilliard OH 43026 Office Phone: 614-334-1600. Personal E-mail: mspyles@columbus.rr.com. E-mail: selma_pyles@fclass.hilliard.k12.oh.us.

PYLIPOW, STANLEY ROSS, retired manufacturing company executive; b. Coudersport, Pa., Apr. 4, 1936; s. Stanley Edward and Helen L. (Haskins) P.; m. Phyllis Beverly Moore, Dec. 1, 1956; children— David, James, Vicky, Kenneth, Sandra BBA in Acctg. cum laude, St. Bonaventure U., 1957. Various fin. positions Chicopee Mfg., New Brunswick, N.J., 1957-65; various positions to v.p., gen. mgr. Domestic Coatings div. Mobil Chem. Co., N.Y.C., 1965-73; asst. corp. controller Monsanto Co., St. Louis, 1974-76; controller, dir. planning Monsanto Comml. Products, St. Louis, 1976-79; sr. v.p., bd. dirs., chief fin. officer Fisher Controls Internat., Inc., St. Louis, 1979-92; ret., 1992; bd. dirs. RBA Group. Treas. Ulster Project, St. Louis, 1998—2002. Treas., City of Town and Country, Mo., 1980-84; bd. dirs. Ecumenical Housing Prodn. Corp., St. Louis, 1980-90; mem. Acctg. Edn. Change Commn., 1992-96. Served to 1st lt., U.S. Army, 1958. Named Exec. of Yr., Profl. Secs. Internat., 1982 Mem. Inst. Mgmt. Accts. (pres. 1990-91, chmn. 1991-92), Fin. Execs. Inst., Bellerive Country Club, Silverthorn Country Club. Republican. Avocations: golf, exercise, spectator sports. Home: 5085 Golf Club Ln Brooksville FL 34609 also: 14006 Baywood Villages Dr Chesterfield MO 63017-3420 Office Phone: 352-796-6903. Personal E-mail: stanpylipow@aol.com.

PYM, BRUCE MICHAEL, lawyer; b. Alameda, Calif., Sept. 29, 1942; s. Leonard A. and Willamay (Strandberg) P. B.B.A., U. Wash., 1964, J.D., 1967. Bar: Wash. 1967, U.S. Dist. Ct. (we. dist.) Wash. 1968, U.S. Ct. Appeals (9th cir.) 1968, U.S. Tax Ct. 1969, U.S. Supreme Ct. 1971. Law clk. Wash. State Supreme Ct., Olympia, 1967-68; assoc. Graham & Dunn, Seattle, 1968-73, shareholder, 1973-92; ptnr. Heller, Ehrman, White & McAuliffe, Seattle, 1992—; mng. ptnr. Northwest Offices, 1994-99. Bd. dirs. United Way of King County, 1986-92, chmn., 1990. Mem. ABA, Wash. State Bar Assn., King County Bar Assn. (pres. 1984-85). Office: Heller Ehrman White & McAuliffe 701 5th Ave Ste 6100 Seattle WA 98104-7098 E-mail: bpym@hewm.com.*

PYNE, JOSEPH H. marine transportation executive; b. 1947; BA, U. N.C. With Northrop Svcs., Inc., Kirby Inland Marine, 1978-84, exec. v.p., 1984, pres., 1984-99; dir. Kirby Corp., Houston, 1988—, pres., CEO, 1995—. With USN. Office: Kirby Corp 55 Waugh Dr #1000 Houston TX 77007

PYOTT, DAVID EDMUND IAN, pharmaceutical executive; b. London, Eng., Oct. 13, 1953; married; 4 children. MA, U. Edinburgh, 1975; diploma in German and European Law, U. Amsterdam, 1976; MBA, London Bus. Sch., 1980. Numerous positions Sandoz Nutrition, Barcelona, 1980-90, gen. mgr., 1990-92; pres., CEO Sandoz Nutrition Corp., Mpls., 1992-95; head divsn. nutrition Sandoz Internat. AG, 1995—97; mem., exec. com. Novartis AG (merger Sandoz and Ciba), 1995—97; pres., CEO Allergan, Inc., Irvine, Calif., 1998—, chmn., 2001—. Bd. dirs. PhRMA, Avery Dennison Corp., Edwards Lifescis. Corp., Advanced Med. Optics, Inc.; chmn. Calif. Healthcare Inst.; mem. bd. dirs. U. Calif. (Irvine) Grad. Sch. Mgmt.; mem.LA Bus. Advisors; vice chair Chief Exec. Roundtable for UCI Bd. dirs. Internat. Coun. of Ophthalmology Found., Eyecare Am.; pres. Pan-Am. Ophthalmological Found. Mem. Pharm. Rsch. and Mfrs. Am. (bd. dirs., Allergan rep.), Pan Am. Assn. Ophthalmology (bd. dirs.), L.A. Bus. Advisors. Achievements include transforming Botox, an obsure treatment for rare muscular diseases, into a cultural and medical phenomenon. Office: Allergan Inc 2525 Dupont Dr Irvine CA 92612-1531 Address: Allergan Inc PO Box 19534 Irvine CA 92623

PYSHER, ALAN GUY, nurse anesthetist; b. East Stroudsburg, Pa., Sept. 10, 1946; s. Kermit Joseph and Fern Elizabeth (Blake) P.; m. Branda Ann Petraitis, June 3, 1973 (div. 1984); 1 child, Lynn Claire. AAS, Northampton C.C., 1973; BA, Stephens Coll., 1984; MEd, U. So. Miss., 1988. RN; cert. registered nurse anesthetist. Nurse anesthetist Tinker AFB Hosp., Oklahoma City, 1981-84; chief nurse anesthetist Lajes Field Hosp., Azores, Portugal, 1984-85; asst. chief nurse anesthetist Kessler Med. Ctr., Biloxi, Miss., 1985-88; chief nurse anesthetist Cannon AFB Hosp., Clovis, N.M., 1988-91, Wilford Hall Med. Ctr., San Antonio, 1991-95; program dir. David Grant Med. Ctr., Fairfield, Calif., 1995-98; anesthesia element chief Wright-Patterson AFB, Dayton, Ohio, 1998-2000; comdr. surg. ops. squadron, dir. nurse anesthesia edn. Wilford Hall Med. Ctr., Lackland AFB, San Antonio, 2000—02; comdr. edn. and tng. squadron Wilford Hall Med Ctr., Lackland AFB, San Antonio, 2002—. Assoc. clin. prof. Uniformed Svcs. U. Health Scis., Bethesda, Md., 1998—2001. Col. USAF, 1973—. Mem. ANA, Am. Assn. Nurse Anesthetists, Assn. Mil. Surgeons U.S., Aerospace Med. Assn., Air War Coll. Alumni Assn., VFW, Purple Heart Assn. Republican. Lutheran. Avocations: golf, martial arts. Home: 8910 Shady Hls San Antonio TX 78254-5525 Office: 59th Med Wing Lackland AFB San Antonio TX 78233 Office Phone: 210-292-5574. E-mail: pyshera@aol.com.

PYSHER, ZANE KERMIT, counselor; b. Pen Argyl, Pa., Mar. 19, 1943; s. Kermit Joseph and Fern Elizabeth Pysher; m. Marcia Ann Cook, July 9, 1966; children: Erica Ann, Zane-Alan. BA, Albright Coll., 1965; MA, Kean Coll., 1970. Cert. tchr. English, History, N.J., Pa., Mass.; cert. student personnel guidance svcs. N.J., Pa. Tchr. English, reading, libr. sci. Warren Hills Sch., Washington, NJ, 1965—69; counselor, dir. guidance Roxbury Twp. Schs., Succasunna, N.J., 1969—. Sec., pres. bd. edn. com. Good Shepherd Nursery Sch., Easton, Pa., 1996-98 Author: Book of Genealogy, 1997. Mem. ch. coun. Good Shepherd Luth. Ch., Easton, 1992—94, mem. ministry com., 2000—03. Recipient Morris County Tchr. Recognition award Morris County Assn. Sch. Administrators, 1999. Mem.: NEA, Roxbury Edn. Assn. (sch. bldg. rep. 1972—75, mem. scholarship com. 1978—2003, sch. test coord. 1987—2003), Morris County Guidance Assn., NJ Edn. Assn. Democrat. Lutheran. Avocations: photography, golf, bowling, sports cards collecting, coin collecting/numismatics. Home: 2311 Ben Jon Rd Easton PA 18040

PYTELL, ROBERT HENRY, retired lawyer, former judge; b. Detroit, Sept. 27, 1926; s. Henry Carl and Helen (Zielinski) P.; m. Laurie Mazur, June 2, 1956; children: Mary Beth, Mark Henry, Robert Michael. JD, U. Detroit, 1951. Bar: Mich. 1952. Of counsel Pytell & Varchetti, P.C., Detroit, 1952-2001; asst. U.S. atty. Ea. Dist. Mich., 1962-65; judge Mcpl. Ct., Grosse Pointe Farms, Mich., 1967-85. With USNR, 1945-46. Mem. Am. Coll. Trust and Estate Coun., State Bar Mich. (mem. probate coun. probate sect. 1998-2000), Crescent Sail Yacht Club (Grosse Pointe), Delta Theta Phi. Roman Catholic. Office: 18580 Mack Grosse Pointe MI 48236 Office Phone: 313-268-7939.

PYTKA, STEPHEN MILTON, office equipment executive; b. Ludlow, Mass., Apr. 29, 1947; s. Milton Ignatius and Jean Marie (Kmiecik) P.; m. Linda Rachel Madsen, May 25, 1969; children: Jonathan Stephen, Justin Stephen, Brendan Stephen. BSEE, Worcester Poly. Inst., 1968; MBA, Dartmouth Coll., 1977. Design engr. AT&T, Whippany, N.J., 1968-69, Kwajalein, Marshall Islands, 1970-71, Greensboro, N.C., 1969-70, Langdon, N.D., 1971-73; sys. engr. GE, Pittsfield, Mass., 1973-75; planning mgr. Xerox Corp., Rochester, N.Y., 1977-81; mktg. mgr. Wang Labs., Inc., 1982-83; exec. v.p. Cap. Internat., Marshfield, Mass., 1983—. Co-founder P&R Microtech, 1982-83; exec. v.p. BIS Cap Internat., 1983-89; pres., chief ops. officer BISCOM, Inc., 1990-96; v.p. The Onstott Group, 1997-98; chmn., CEO Streamware, Inc., 1998-2000; pres., CEO eChinaLink, 2000-01, Talksender, Inc., 2000-01, Hellotech, 2001-02;, Gazelle Systems, Inc., 2002-03; mem. exec. bd. WPI Venture Forum; trustee MV YMCA; mem. adv. bd. Mt. Vernon Strategies, Touch Applications; panelist MIT Enterprise Forum; trustee Andover YMCA; mng. dir. Consilium Ptnrs., 2004—; spkr. in field. Mem. Am. Mgmt. Assn., Soc. Photog. Scientists and Engrs., Andover Country Club. Republican. Roman Catholic. Home: 9 Langley Ln Andover MA 01810-4259 Office: Consilium Ptnrs 399 Boylston St Boston MA 02116

PYTLINSKI, JERZY TEODOR, physicist, educator, research administrator; b. Warsaw, Apr. 1, 1938; s. Stanislaw and Natalia (Matuszewska) P.; m. Bonnie Laurie Bennett, Dec. 30, 1969; 1 child, Christine Barbara. MS, Tech. U. Warsaw, 1962; PhD in Plasma Physics with distinction, U. Paris, 1967. Program mgr., acting div. head N.Mex. State U., Las Cruces, 1977-80; sr. scientist, div. head U. P.R., Mayaguez, 1981-83, program dir., sr. scientist San Juan, 1983-86, sr. scientist, founding dir. Univ.-Industry Rsch. Ctr. Tampa, Fla., 1986-89; pres. Univ.-Industry Rsch. Ctr., Tampa, Fla., 1989—, prof., 1989—. Mem. adv. bd. on solar energy UNESCO, 1979-85; referee Am. Jour. Physics, 1980—, Solar Energy Jour., 1983-87, 38th Internat. Sci. and Engring. Fair, 1987; mem. U.S. tech. adv. group of ISO TC-180, 1981—. Mem. editl. bd. Internat. Jour. Energy, Environ. Econs., 1990—; co-editor Procs. Internat. Conf. Energy for Ams., 1987; contbr. over 80 articles to profl. jours. and procs. Grantee state and fed. agys., various edn. and rsch.founds.; Postdoctoral fellow U. Liverpool, England, 1968-69; recipient commendation State of Kans., 1977. Mem. Am. Phys. Soc., Nat. Coun. Univ. Rsch. Adminstrs., Soc. Rsch. Adminstrs., Internat. Solar Energy Soc., Internat. Energy Soc. (sci. coun. 1985—), Sigma Phi Sigma. Republican. Roman Catholic. Avocations: reading, tennis, travel. Achievements include research in plasma physics and alternative energy sources; managment and administration.

PYTTE, AGNAR, physicist, retired academic administrator; b. Kongsberg, Norway, Dec. 23, 1932; arrived in U.S., 1949, naturalized, 1965; s. Ole and Edith (Christiansen) Pytte; m. Anah Currie Loeb, June 18, 1955; children: Anders H., Anthony M., Alyson C. AB, Princeton U., 1953; AM, Harvard U., 1954, PhD, 1958. Faculty Dartmouth Coll., 1958—87, prof. physics, 1967—87, chmn. dept. physics and astronomy, 1971—75, assoc. dean faculty, 1975—78, dean grad. studies, 1975—78, provost, 1982—87; pres. Case Western Res. U., Cleve., 1987—99; adj. prof. physics Dartmouth Coll., 1999—. Rschr. in plasma physics; mem. Project Matterhorn Princeton U., 1959—60, 1978—79, U. Brussels, 1966—67. Bd. dirs. Accreditation Coun. for Grad. Med. Edn., 2000—04, Environ. Careers Orgn., 2003—, Sherman Fairchild Found., Inc., 1987—. Mem.: Am. Phys. Soc., Sigma Xi, Phi Beta Kappa. E-mail: agnar.x.pytte@dartmouth.edu.

QAZI, MUJTABA A. ophthalmologist; b. Karachi, Pakistan, Jan. 5, 1971; arrived in US, 1975; s. Asghar H. and Rehana Qazi; m. Erum Qazi, Aug. 3, 1995; children: Amaan, Rida, Ameen. BA, NYU, 1993, MD, 1997. Diplomate Am. Bd. Ophthaalmology. Intern St. Vincent's Hosp., N.Y.C., 1997—98; resident dept. ophthalmology Boston U. Med. Ctr., 1998—2001; chief resident dept. ophthalmology Boston VA Med. Ctr., 2000; fellow in corneal, anterior segment and refractive surgery Pepose Vision Inst., Chesterfield, Mo., 2001—02. Dir. clin. studies Pepose Vision Inst.; clin. instr. Washington U. Sch. Medicine, St. Louis. Author: Principles of Managing Ophthalmic Injury, 2000, Scleral Expansion Band Segments for the Treatment of Presbyopia, 2002; reviewer Am. Jour. Ophthalmology, Jour. of Refractive Surgery; co-editor refractive surgery sect.: Current Opinions in Ophthalmology. Bd. mem. Midwest Cornea Rsch. Found. Finalist Leadership scholarship, Nat. Assn. Asian Am. Profls., 1989; NYU Coll. Arts & Scis. Pres. scholar, 1989—93, Empire State Acad. scholar, 1989—93. Mem.: Internat. Soc. Refractive Surgeons, Am. Soc. Cataract & Refractive Surgery, Am. Acad. Ophthalmology. Home: 294 Hickory Hedge Dr Manchester MO 63021 Office: Pepose Vision Inst PC 16216 Baxter Rd Ste 205 Chesterfield MO 63017 Office Phone: 636-728-0111. E-mail: mqazi@peposevision.com.

QI, JIANWEI, mechanical engineer, researcher; b. Wuxi, Jianhsu, China, Mar. 11, 1967; s. Guoqin Qi and Yaqin Huang; m. Xinwei Dong; children: Yun, Yuan. BS, Nanjing (China) U. Aeronautics and Astronautics, 1989; M.E., Zhejiang U., Hangzhou, China, 1991; PhD, Tsinghua U., Beijing, China, 1996. Rsch. asst. Inst. Fluid Engring., Zhejiang U., Hangzhou, China, 1989—91; rsch. and tchng. asst. Tsinghua U., Beijing, 1992—94, lectr., 1995—96; engr. China Packaging Corp., Beijing, 1996—97; rschr. Nat. Inst. Advanced Indsl. Sci. and Tech., Tsukuba, Japan, 1998—2000; postdoctoral rschr. The Johns Hopkins U., Balt., 2000; rsch. scientist, lab mgr. U. Md., College Park, 2000—. Sci. and tech. cons. Author: The First Prize in Sci. and Tech. Progress by State Edn. Commn. China, 1996; contbr. articles to profl. jours. (The Excellent Engring Prize by Tsinghua U., 1996). Mem.: IMAPS, AAAS, ASME, Japan Sci. and Tech. Corp. Achievements include contributions to developing Advanced Thermal Technology for electronics, energy, advanced materials process and green environmental systems. Office: U Md 2181 Martin Hall College Park MD 20742

QI, XIUJUAN, mathematician, educator; d. Guangxun Qi and Fuyun Hou; m. Xiaofeng Hu, Aug. 8, 1997; 1 child, Harry Hu. MS in Probability and Stats., S.E. U., Nanjing, China, 1997; MS in Applied Math., U. Del., Newark, 2002. Rsch. asst. S.E. U., Nanjing, China, 1994—97; asst. prof. Shanghai Inst. of Elec. Power, China, 1997—99; tchg. asst. U. Del., Newark, 2000—02.

QI, ZHIGANG, materials scientist, chemist; s. Pengling Qi and Fengzhi Jing. BSc in Chemistry, U. Sci. and Tech., Beijing, 1985; PhD, McGill U., 1996. Post-doctoral fellow Meml. U. of Newfoundland, St. John's, Canada, 1996—97; sr. staff scientist H Power Corp., Belleville, NJ, 1997—2003; fellow Plug Power Inc., Latham, NY, 2003—. Contbr. over 50 articles to profl. jours. Mem.: The Electrochem. Soc. Achievements include first to ground breaking research in PEM fuel cells and conductive polymers; patents for. Home: 12 Calif Ave Apt A208 Albany NY 12205 Office Phone: 518-782-7700 1229. Business E-Mail: zhigang_qi@plugpower.com.

QIAN, CHUANXI, mathematics professor; s. Xueshu Qian and Kouzhen Yuan; m. Jiajie Ma; 1 child, Shannon Shuang. PhD, U. of RI, 1993. Vis. asst. prof. math. Miss. State Univ., 1994—95, asst. prof. math., 1995—98, assoc. prof. math., 1998—2003, prof. math., 2003. Author: (over 60 rsch. papers pub.) Math. Rsch. Jours. Mem.: Am. Math. Soc. Office: Dept of Math and Stats Missi State Univ Mississippi State MS 39762 Address: 107 Claudia Dr. Starkville MS 39759

QIANG, XIAO, advocate; BS, U. Sci. and Tech. China; student, U. Notre Dame, 1986—89. Human rights worker Ind. Fedn. Chinese Students and Scholars, Washington; exec. dir. Human Rights in China, N.Y.C. Spkr. Chinese human rights UN Commn. on Human Rights, 1993—; lectr. in field in various countries. Office: Human Rights in China 350 Fifth Ave Ste 3309 New York NY 10118

QIAO, GUILIN, pharmacologist, medical researcher; s. Ronghua (Liu) and Shuanbao Qiao; m. Hongfei Li, Aug. 15, 1987; children: Peter L, Eric L. DVM, Hebei Agrl. U., Baoding, China, 1978—82; MS, NE Agrl. U. Harbin, China, 1982—85; PhD, So. China Agrl. U, Canton, China, 1986—89. Postdoctral fellow/sr. rsch. assoc. NC State U., Raleigh, NC, 1990—95; assoc. prof. NE Agrl. U, Harbin, China, 1991—94; asst. prof. NC State U, Raleigh, NC, 1995—98; team leader Nat. Inst. for Occupl. Safety and Health (NIOSH), Morgantown, W.Va., 1998—2001, Ctr. for Disease Control and Prevention, Morgantown, W.Va., 1998—2001; assoc. prof. W.Va. U., Morgantown, W.Va., 1999—; pharmacologist FDA, Rockvile, Md., 2001—. Expert panel mem. AIBS, Dulles, Va., 2000—02. Chair Chess Club, Chinese Am. Friendship Assn. (CAFA), Raleigh, NC, 1996—98. Recipient Outstanding DVM Student Awards, Hebei Agrl. U., 1979—81, Third Prize for Excellent Sci. Papers, Heilongjiang Sci. & Tech. Com., 1987, Excellent Academic Achievements Awards, Guangdong Grad. Edn. Assn. and Guangdong Student Union, 1987,

Second Prize for Sci. & Technol. Achievements, Heilongjiang Sci. & Tech. Com., 1990, Heilongjiang Edn. Commn., 1996, Outstanding Performance and Lasting Contbn. Achievement Award, NIOSH/CDC, 2000, Team Excellence Award, US-FDA, 2001; grantee PI with $500K equ., Nat. Natural Sci. Found.-China, 1990, COI with $1.2 Million, Fed. gov agencies and industries, 1994—2000, PI with $456K, US-Environ. Protection Agy., 1995, PI with $402K, Centers for Disease Control and Prevention (CDC), 1997, PI with $3.3 million, Nat. Occupl. Rsch. Agenda (NORA), 2000. Master: Dermal Toxicology Splty. Sect., Soc. of Toxicology (SOT) (membership com. chair 2000—02), Am. Chinese Toxicol. Soc. (v.p. 2003—05); mem.: Am. Assn. of Pharm. Scientists, Soc. for Risk Analysis (corr.), Am. Acad. of Vet. Pharm. and Therapeutics (corr.), Assn. of Govt. Toxicologists (corr.), Soc. of Toxicology (corr.), Internat. Soc. of Exposure Analysis (corr.), NIOSH/CDC (animal care and use com. (acuc) 1999—2001), Dermal Toxicology Splty. Sect., Soc. of Toxicology (SOT) (organizing com. 1999—2000). Achievements include research in Theoretical Estimation of in vivo skin metabolism of drugs; development of Dermatopharmacokinetic modeling of chem. penetration; research in Linked pharmacokinetic-pharmacodynamic modeling.

QIU, LARRY DONGXIAO, economics professor; b. Luchun, Guangxi, China, Oct. 6, 1961; s. Peilung Qiu and Meijian Chen; m. Denise Jinglian Qiu, Jan. 9, 1987; children: Alice W., Jennifer Z. BS, Zhongshan U., Guangzhou, China, 1983; MA, U. B.C., Vancouver, Can., 1989, PhD, 1993. Asst. prof. Hong Kong U. Sci. and Tech., 1993-2001, assoc. prof., 2001—. Cons. Hong Kong Govt., 1996 98, Asian Devel. Bank, Manila, 1997-98. Contbr. articles to profl. jours. Mem. Am. Econ. Assn., Royal Econ. Soc., Econometric Soc., European Econ. Assn., Internat. Econs. and Fin. Soc. Avocations: tennis, soccer, music. Office: Dept Econs Hong Kong U Sci & Tech Kowloon Hong Kong Office Fax: (852) 2358 4971.

QIU, LI-HUI, music educator, actress; b. Shanghai; arrived in U.S., 1997; d. Jian-Fei Qiu and Ping-Hua Wan; m. Liang Yun, Jan. 1, 1962; children: Gang, Xiao. BA, Shanghai Music U., China, 1962. Nat. 2nd class actress Shanghai Orch., China, 1962—97; vocal actress Shanghai Ballet Troupe, China, 1975—76; tchr. music Edison (NJ) Chinese Sch., 1998—2001, Everbright Chinese Sch., Edison, NJ, 2001—; pvt. instr. vocal, keyboard and piano, 1990. Benefit performances NJ Chinese Festival, 1999, Montvale High Sch., 1998, Woodbridge (NJ) Housing Auth., 2001—03; adv. The Cultural Festival on Mother's Day, NYC, 1998. Mem.: Shanghai Keyboard Assn., Nat. Musician Soc. of China (Shanghai chapt.), Music Tchrs. Nat. Assn. Home and Studio: Apt 4J 55 Brook St Woodbridge NJ 07095 E-mail: yunliang01@netzero.net.

QIU, PEIHUA, statistician, educator, statistician, researcher; b. Shanghai, Oct. 17, 1965; arrived in U.S., 1991; s. Hongde Ren, Qibao Li; m. Yan Zhang, May 7, 1977; 1 child, Andrew Qiu. BS in Math., Fudan U., China, 1986; PhD, U. Wis., 1996. Asst. prof. Fudan U., Shanghai, 1989—91; sr. rsch. consulting statistician Ohio State U., Columbus, 1996—98; asst. prof. U. Minn., Mpls., 1998—2002, assoc. prof., 2002—. Contbr. chapters to books, articles to profl. jours. Recipient best paper winner of the 5th ISI competition for young statistician, Internat. Statis. Inst., 1991. Mem.: Bernoulli Soc., Inst. Math. Stats., Am. Statis. Assn. Home: 6768 Carlisle Curve Shakopee MN 55379

QU, GANG, education educator, researcher; s. Quanlong Qu and Xiaoya Wang; m. Zhe Jin, 1994; 1 child, Anthony Zhirui. BS(hon.), U. Sci. and Tech. China, Hefei, Anhui, 1992, MS, 1994; MA, U. Okla., 1996; MS (hon.), UCLA, 1998, PhD, 2000. Prof. U. Md., College Park, 2000—. Vis. rschr. Semiconductor Co. of Toshiba Corp., Kawasaki, Japan, 1999; dir. embedded sys. rsch. lab. U. Md., College Park, 2000—; reviewer in field. Author: Intellectual Property Protection inVLSI Designs: Theory and Practice, 2003, (chapter) Energy Efficient Design for Secure Sensor Networks in Handbook of Sensor Networks, 2004; contbr. articles to profl. jours. N/a. Recipient Dimitris N. Chorafas Found. award, 1999; grantee, NSF, 2003; Minta Martin Rsch. Fund grant, Glenn L. Martin Inst. Tech., U. Md., 2001, Scholarships, Assn. for Computing Machinery, IEEE, 1999, NCR fellowship, Nat. Cash Register Co., 1999. Mem.: IEEE, Virtual Socket Interface Alliance, Assn. for Computing Machinery (assoc.). Achievements include first to intellectual property protections in VLSI design; research in low power computer and embedded systems design, wireless ad-hoc sensor networks. Office: Univ Md Dept of ECE 1417 A V Williams Bldg College Park MD 20742 Office Phone: 301-405-6703. Business E-Mail: gangqu@glue.umd.edu.

QUAAL, WARD LOUIS, broadcast executive; b. Ishpeming, Mich., Apr. 7, 1919; s. Sigfred Emil and Alma Charlotte (Larson) Q.; m. Dorothy J. Graham, Mar. 9, 1944; children: Graham Ward, Jennifer Anne. AB, U. Mich., 1941; LL.D. (hon.), Mundelein Coll., 1962, No. Mich. U., 1967; D.Pub. Service, Elmhurst Coll., 1967; D.H.L. (hon.), Lincoln Coll., 1968, DePaul U., 1974. Announcer-writer Sta. WBEO (now sta. WDMJ), Marquette, Mich., 1936-37; announcer, writer, producer Sta. WJR, Detroit, 1937-41; spl. events announcer-producer WGN, Chgo., 1941-42, asst. to gen. mgr., 1945-49; exec. dir. Clear Channel Broadcasting Service, Washington, 1949-52, pres., chief exec. officer, 1964-74; v.p., asst. gen. mgr. Crosley Broadcasting Corp., Cin., 1952-56; v.p., gen. mgr., mem. bd. WGN Inc., Chgo., 1956; exec. v.p., then pres. WGN Continental Broadcasting Co. (now Tribune Broadcasting Co.), 1960-75; pres. Ward L. Quaal Co., 1975—; dir. Tribune Co., 1961-75; dir., mem. exec. com. U.S. Satellite Broadcasting Co., 1982-2000. Bd. dirs. Christine Valmy Inc.; chmn. exec. com., dir. WLW Radio Inc., Cin., 1975-81; co-founder, dir. Universal Resources Inc., 1961-86; mem. FCC Adv. Com. on Advanced TV Sys., 1988-96. Author: (with others) Broadcast Management, 1968, rev. edit., 1979, new edit. 1997; co-prodr. (Broadway play) Teddy and Alice, 1988. Mem., Hoover Commn. Exec. Br. Task Force, 1949-59; mem. U.S.-Japan Cultural Exchange Commn., 1960-70; mem. Pres.'s Council Phys. Fitness and Sports, 1983-93; bd. dirs. Farm Found., 1963-73; bd. trustees Hollywood (Calif.) Mus., 1964-78, MacCormac Jr. Coll., Chgo., 1974-80; chmn. exec. com. Council for TV Devel., 1969-72; mem. bus. adv. coun. Chgo. Urban League, 1964-74; bd. dirs. Broadcasters Found., Internat. Radio and TV Found., Sears Roebuck Found., 1970-73; trustee Mundelein Coll., 1962-72, Hillsdale Coll., 1966-72. Served as lt. USNR, 1942-45. Named Radio Man of Yr., Am. Coll. Radio, Arts, Crafts & Scis., 1961, Laureate in Order of Lincoln, Lincoln Acad. Ill., 1965, Communicator of Yr., Jewish United Fund, 1969, Advt. Club Man of Yr., 1973; named one of Top 100 Mems., Delta Tau Delta, 1999, 1st 100 5th Estaters, Broadcasting 20th Century, 1999, First 50 Giants of Broadcasting, Libr. Am. Broadcasting, 2003; named to Delta Tau Delta Disting. Svc. Chpt., 1970, Broadcasting Mag. Hall of Fame, 1991, Mgmt. Hall of Fame, NATAS/TV Bur. Advt., 2003; recipient Disting. Bd. Gov.'s award, NATAS, 1966, 1987, Inaugural Inductee Mgmt. Hall of Fame, 2003, Freedoms Found. award, Valley Forge, 1966, 1968, 1970, Disting. Alumnus award, U. Mich., 1967, Loyola U. Key, 1970, Advt. Man of Yr. Gold medallion, Chgo. Advt. Club, 1968, Disting. Svc. award, Nat. Assn. Broadcasters, 1973, Ill. Broadcaster of Yr. award, 1973, Press Vet. of Yr. award, 1973, Comm. award of distinction, Brandeis U., 1973, Founder & Leadership award, Broadcast Pioneers Libr., 1991, 1st recipient Sterling medal, Barren Found., 1985, Lifetime Achievement award in broadcasting, Ill. Broadcasters Assn., 1989, Lifetime Achievement award, WGN TV, 1998, 1st person named to Better Bus. Bur. Hall of Fame, Coun. on Better Bus. Burs., Inc., 1975. Mem. NATAS (bd. govs. 1966-76, Silver Circle award 1993), Nat. Press Found. (bd. dirs. 1991-99), Nat. Assn. Broadcasters (bd. dirs. 1952-56), Fed. Comm. Bar Assn., Broadcast Music Inc. (bd. dirs. 1953-70), Assn. Maximum Svc. Telecasters Inc. (bd. dirs. 1952-72), Broadcast Pioneers (pres., bd. dirs. 1962-73), Broadcast Pioneers Libr. (pres. 1981-84), Broadcast Pioneers Ednl. Fund Inc., Broadcasters Found. (chmn. bd. 1996-99). Office: Ward L Quaal Co One Northfield Plaza Ste 300 Northfield IL 60093

QUACKENBUSH, JUSTIN LOWE, federal judge; b. Spokane, Wash., Oct. 3, 1929; s. Carl Clifford and Marian Huldah (Lowe) Q.; m. Marie McAtee; children: Karl Justin, Kathleen Marie, Robert Craig. Student, U. Ill., 1947-49; BA, U. Idaho, 1951; LLB, Gonzaga U., Spokane, 1957. Bar: Wash. 1957. Dep. pros. atty., Spokane County, 1957-59; ptnr. Quackenbush, Dean, Bailey & Henderson, Spokane, 1959-80; dist. judge U.S. Dist. Ct. (ea. dist.) Wash., Spokane, 1980—, now sr. judge. Part-time instr. Gonzaga U. Law Sch., 1960-67 Chmn. Spokane County Planning Commn., 1969-73. Served with USN, 1951-54. Mem. Wash. Bar Assn., Spokane County Bar Assn. (trustee 1976-78), Internat. Footprint Assn. (nat. pres. 1967), Shriners. Episcopalian. Office: US Dist Ct PO Box 1432 Spokane WA 99210-1432

QUACKENBUSH, MARGERY CLOUSER, psychoanalyst, administrator; b. Reading, Pa., Apr. 30, 1938; d. Carl Brumbach and Katherine Elvina (Althouse) Clouser; m. Robert Mead Quackenbush, July 3, 1971; 1 child, Piet Robert. BA, Pratt Inst., 1960; MA, Calif. Grad. Inst., 1982; PhD in Psychoanalysis, Internat. U. Grad. Studies, N.Y.C., 2001. Cert. in psychoanalysis Ctr. for Modern Psychoanalytic Studies, 1992. Instr. Pratt Inst., Bklyn., 1978-79, Fashion Inst. of Tech., N.Y.C., 1980-81; counselor Wiltwyck, Bronx Ctr., 1981-82; exec. dir. Nat. Assn. for Advancement of Psychoanalysis, N.Y.C., 1982—; pvt. practice in psychoanalysis N.Y.C., 1980—. Mem. Lenox Hill Dem. Club, N.Y.C., 1993-95; spkr. various cmty. groups, 1991—. Recipient Maison Blanche award, 1959, Miriam Berkman Spotnitz award, 1992, Am. Bd. Accreditation Profl. Svc. award, 2000-04. Mem. Nat. Assn. for Advancement of Psychoanalysis, Nat. Soc. DAR, Alumni Assn. of the Ctr. for Modern Psych. Studies (sec. 1992-94, Alumni Assn. program dir., v.p. 1995-98). Democrat. Avocations: reading, writing, golf, horseback riding. Home: 460 E 79th St Apt 14E New York NY 10021-1447 Office: Nat Assn Advancement Psychoanalysis 80 8th Ave # 1501 New York NY 10011-5126 Personal E-mail: naap72@aol.com.

QUACKENBUSH, ROBERT MEAD, artist, author, psychoanalyst; b. Hollywood, Calif., July 23, 1929; s. Roy Maynard and Virginia (Arbogast) Q.; m. Margery Clouser, July 3, 1971; 1 child: Piet Robert. B of Profl. Arts, Art Ctr. Coll. of Design, Pasadena, Calif., 1956; grad., Ctr. Modern Psychoanalytic Studies, N.Y.C., 1991; MSW, Fordham U., 1994; PhD, Internat. U. Grad. Studies, 1999. Art dir. Scandinavian Airlines Sys., N.Y.C. and Stockholm, 1956-61; pvt. practice N.Y.C., 1961—; psychoanalyst/psychtherapist New Hope Guild Ctrs. for Emotionally Disturbed Children, Bklyn., 1994-2000. Educator Robert Quackenbush Studios, N.Y.C.; lectr. U.S., Europe, Middle East and South Am.; TV performer Ednl. TV; mem. faculty N.J. Ctr. for Modern Psychoanalysis. Author/artist: more than 180 books for young readers including; author: (novels) Robert Quackenbush's Treasury of Humor, 1990, Benjamin Franklin and His Friends, 1991, Evil Under the Sea, 1992, James Madison & Dolly Madison and Their Times, 1993, Arthur Ashe and His Match with History, 1994, Clara Barton and Her Victory Over Fear, 1995, Batbaby, 1997, (under pen name Richard Gobbletree) Treasure Hunt, 1997, Two Miss Mallard Mysteries: Surfboard to Peril and Stage Door to Terror, 1998, Daughter of Liberty, 1999, Flamenco to Mischief: A Miss Mallard Mystery, 2000, Miss Mallard's Case Book, 2000, Batbaby Finds a Home, 2001, Mishap in Kaiserslautern: A Miss Mallard Mystery, 2001; prodr.: (TV series for children's worldwide programming) Dear Mr. Quackenbush and The Great American Storybook, 1988, The Miss Mallard Mysteries, 1999; Represented in permanent collections Whitney Mus., The Smithsonian Inst., numerous pvt. collections. With U.S. Army 1951-53. Recipient 2 Citations for outstanding Troop Info. & Edn. instrn. from commdg. gen. 31st Inf. Divsn. 1953, 4 time winner Am. Flag Inst. award for outstanding contbn. to field of children's lit., 1976, 77, 81, 99, Edgar Allen Poe Spl. award, 1982, Gradiva award, 1998, Gold medal for disting. achievement by a mem. in art and lit. Holland Soc., 2000. Mem. Mystery Writers of Am., Authors' Guild, Authors' League of Am., Holland Soc. of N.Y., Nat. Assn. for Advancement of Psychoanalysis (trustee, v.p. pub. info., founder and chair Gradiva awards), Soc. Modern Psychoanalysts. Avocations: travel, antique restoration. Home: 460 E 79th St Apt 14E New York NY 10021-1447 Office: Robert Quackenbush Studios 223 E 78th St New York NY 10021-1222 Office Phone: 212-744-3822. Personal E-mail: rqstudios@aol.com. *Humor became a key to survival in my family when I was growing up during the depression and World War II. Thus humor became the keynote of all the books I write and illustrate - I want young readers to know that as long as we keep our sense of humor, our spirits cannot be crushed. In my analytic practice I encourage children to verbalize their conflicts through art and writing projects.*

QUACKENBUSH, ROGER E. retired secondary school educator; b. Cooperstown, N.Y., Jan. 22, 1940; s. Eugene W. and Marion I. (Clark) Q.; m. Cathy E. Quackenbush, Mar. 31, 1973; children: Michele, Stacey, Thomas. BS, SUNY, Albany, 1961, MS, 1966; PhD, Columbia Pacific U., San Rafael, Calif., 1984; postgrad., numerous univs. Cert. permanent biology and gen. sci. tchr., N.Y. Tchr. gen. sci. and math Troy (N.Y.) Pub. Sch. System, 1961-64; tchr. earth sci. and biology Schuylerville (N.Y.) Cen. H.S., 1964-66; tchr. biology Bethlehem Cen. H.S., Delmar, N.Y., 1966-95; cons. advanced placement biology Niskayuna (N.Y.) H.S., 1995-96; instr. anatomy and physiology lab. Russell Sage Coll., Troy, N.Y., 1996-97. Mentor student tchrs., 1968-90; instr. Tchr. Expectation Student Achievement program, 1985-91; lectr. on marine mammals SUNY, Albany, 1986; instr. DNA Sci. and Tech. for h.s. students SUNY, Albany, 1996; lectr. on whales; workshop leader on use microcomputers in classroom; former mem. Mid States Commn. on Evaluation Local H.S.'s; past mem. adv. bd. Upstate N.Y. Jr. Sci. and Humanities Symposium; test writer Regents biology exams. N.Y. State Dept. Edn.; presenter/cons. N.Y. State Edn. Dept. alt. assessment writer's workshop, 1994; leader, naturalist for whale watch trips and Kenya safaris; presenter for DNA-molecular biology lab. techniques; presenter on use of Tex. Instruments calculator and the Calculator Based Lab. sys. in the sci. classroom; mem Select Seminar on Evaluating Tchrs., 1985; mem. Wells Conf. Regents Biology Syllabus Revision, 1991; faculty cons. AP Biology reading Coll. Bd. Advanced Placement Program, 1997-98; cons. DNA molecular biology technology Greater Capital Region Tchr. Ctr., 1988-2001; instnl. animal care and use com. N.Y. State Health Dept., 1999-2001 Author: Once Upon a Yesterday, 2000, Adrift Upon the Air, 2001, Sketches of the Mind, 2002; editor/writer of alternative assessments for N.Y. State Edn. Dept., 1993-94; contbr. articles to profl. jours.; author: Swahili Phrasebook, 1993. Hon. admisssions liaison officer USAF Acad., 1988. Recipient Eagle award Boy Scouts Am., 1956, Excellence in Tchg. award, 1989, letter of commendation U. Chgo., 1978, MIT, 1985, U.S. Army, 1989, Tufts U., 1990, 94, 97, Tchr. of Yr. award Tufts U., 1985, Golub Tchr.-Scholar award SUNY, 1991, 96; Chpt. II grantee N.Y. State Dept. Edn., 1987, NSF grantee, 1965, 67, 68, 72, 87, 90, Future Directions, 1990, Greenwall Found., 1993, hon. mention Tandy Tech. Scholar award, 1994, Tandy Tech. Scholar prize for excellence in sci. tchg., 1995, Outstanding Tchr. award U. Chgo., 1995; named Hon. Grad. Marshal, 1991, 94, hon. N.Y. State Biology Mentor, 1995. Mem. NEA, Nat. Assn. Biology Tchrs., BALSA, Soc. Marine Mammalogy, Am. Cetacean Soc., Cetacean Soc. Internat., Sci. Tchrs. Assn. N.Y. State (past sect. dir., past state bd. dirs.), NEA of N.Y., Phi Delta Kappa. Home: 25 Robinhood Rd Albany NY 12203-5133 E-mail: rquacken@nycap.rr.com.

QUADAY-GRAY, AILENE DIANN, retired speech pathology/audiology services professional; b. Blue Earth, Minn., Aug. 26, 1937; d. Carl Frederick Quaday and Arlene Alice Bunting; m. Maurice Clayton Maine, Aug. 18, 1956 (div. May 1975); children: Keith Mauricé, Kevin Richard; m. Francis Moulton Gray Jr., May 7, 1989 (dec. Dec. 1994). BA, St. Cloud (Minn.) State U., 1971; postgrad., San Diego State U., 1979-81, various colls., 1971-85, West Hills and Fresno Pacific, 1987-94. Lic. speech pathologist, Calif.; cert. presch. tchr., Calif. Speech pathologist Comprehensive Health Ctrs., Inc., San Diego, 1981-82; speech pathologist pilot project Kings Rehab. Ctr., Inc., Hanford, Calif., 1983 summer; tchr., dir. First Luth Ch. Presch., Hanford, 1983-85; speech specialist Fresno (Calif.) County Office of Edn., 1985-87, Kings County Office of Edn., Hanford, 1987-91, Reef-Sunset Unified Sch. Dist., Avenal, Kettleman City, Calif., 1991-94, Kingsburg (Calif.) Joint Union Charter Elem. Schs., 1994-2001; part-time presch. speech therapist Sanger (Calif.) Unified Sch. Dist., 2001—02. Cons. Headstart: Tech. Assistance Mgmt., 1971-72; part-time speech therapist Selma (Calif.) Unified Sch. Dist., 2001-04. Vice chmn. bd. edn. St. James Luth., San Diego, 1979-80; del. Consortium on County Health Needs, Wright County, Minn., 1972-75; advisor Wright County Minn. Commrs. on Handicapped, 1973-75; vol. children's waiting rm. Navy Hosp., Bremerton, Wash., 1976-77. Mem. Calif. Speech, Lang. and Hearing Assn. Democrat. Methodist. Avocations: playing flute, teaching language, reading, poetry. Home: 2132 14th Ave Kingsburg CA 93631-1731

QUADE, MARSHALL ROSS, transportation planner; b. Milw. s. Richard William and Shirley Ann Quade. BA in Polit. Sci., U. Wis., Milw., 1989, M of Urban Planning, 1992; mgmt. cert., Marquette U., 1997. Grad. rsch. asst. dept. urban planning U. Wis., Milw., 1990-91, grad. rsch. asst. Urban Rsch. Ctr., 1991-92; econ. devel./land use planner City of Brookfield, Waukesha, Wis., 1991-94; sr. transp. planner, analyst Wis. Dept. Transp., Waukesha, 1994-2000; dist. planning supr. Madison, 2000—. Adj. asst. prof. U. Wis., Milw., 2004—. Planning, allocations, and monitoring vol. United Way Greater Milw., 1994-96; Future Cities Competition vol. Nat. Engrs. Week, Milw., 1994. Recipient Wis. Downtown Action Coun. Student Project award, 1992, Site Sponsor award Goodwill Industries of S.E. Wis. and Greater Chgo., 1999. Mem. Am. Inst. Cert. Planners, Am. Planning Assn., Inst. Transp. Engrs. (affiliate dir. Wis. sect.), Assn. Commuter Transp.

QUADE, VICKI, editor, writer, playwright, producer; b. Chgo., Aug. 15, 1953; d. Victor and Virginia (Uryasz) Q.; m. Charles J. White III, Feb. 15, 1986 (div. Aug. 1996); children: Michael, David, Catherine. BS in Journalism, No. Ill. U., 1974. Staff reporter news divsn. The News-Tribune, LaSalle, Ill., 1975-77; staff writer news divsn. The News-Sun, Waukegan, Ill., 1977-81; staff writer ABA Jour., Chgo., 1981-85; mng. editor ABA Press, Chgo., 1985-90, editor, 1990-2000, sr. editor, 1994-2000. Author: (poetry) Rain and Other Poems, 1976, Laughing Eyes, 1979, Two Under the Covers, 1981, (biography) I Remember Bob Collins, 2000; playwright Late Nite Catechism, 1993, Room for Advancement, 1994, Mr. Nanny, 1997, (musical) Lost in Wonderland, 1998, (musical) Here Come the Famous Brothers, 2001; prodr. Late Nite Catechism, Mr. Nanny, Here Come the Famous Brothers, Christopher Carter Messes With Your Mind, Forever Plaid, Cast on a Hot Tin Roof, Verbatim Verboten; contbr. to numerous anthologies and publs.; contbd. to: 20th Century Chicago: 100 Years 100 Voices (contbd. the year 1953), owner/operator Crossroads Theater, Naperville, Ill. Recipient numerous awards from Soc. Nat. Assn. Publs., AP, UPI. Mem. Am. Soc. Bus. Press Editors (award); Chgo. Newspaper Guild (award), Am. Soc. Assn. Execs. (Gold Circle award 1989, 90). Avocations: travel, photography.

QUADRACCI, THOMAS A. printing company executive; Co-founder, bd. mem. Quad Graphics, Milw., 2002—, pres., CEO, 2002—. Office: Quad Graphics 555 S 108th St Milwaukee WI 53214

QUADRI, FAZLE RAB, lawyer, government official; b. Dacca, Pakistan, Aug. 5, 1948; came to U.S., 1967; s. Gholam Moula and Jehan (Ara) Q.; children: Ryan F., Tania M. AA, Western Wyo. Coll., 1969; BA, Calif. State U., 1972; JD, Western State U., 1978; postgrad. cert. in criminal advocacy, U. Calif., San Francisco, 1988. Bar: Calif. 1981; cert. program of learning for lawyers, Harvard Law Sch., 2002, 03, 04. Sr. adminstrv. analyst San Bernardino County, Calif., 1978-82, acting legis. adv., 1982, sr. legis. analyst, 1982-90, county legis. analyst, 1990-93, acting pub. defender, 1984; dist. counsel Mojave Desert Air Quality Mgmt. Dist., Victorville, Calif., 1993—; dist. cousnel Antelope Valley Air Pollution Control Dist., 1997—. Local gov. rep. State Hazardous Waste Mgmt. Council, Sacramento, Calif., 1982-84; chmn.'s rep. County Projects Selection Coms., San Bernardino, 1983-91; county rep. South Coast Air Quality Mgmt. Dist., El Monte, Calif., 1983-87. Advisor Mcpl. Adv. Couns., San Bernardino, 1984-87; mem. Law Libr. Bd. Trustees, 1984-85, 93-95. Mem. ABA, Calif. Bar Assn. (mem. exec. com. pub. law section 2000—, chair 2003-04.), Calif. State U. Alumni Assn. (bd. dirs. 1985-86); Masons, Shriners. Republican. Islamic. Avocations: personal computers, reading, music, Karate, water sports. Home: 535 E Mariposa Dr Redlands CA 92373-7351 Office: Mojave Desert AQMD 14306 Park Ave Victorville CA 92392-2310 Office Phone: 760-245-1661. E-mail: quadri@mdaqmd.ca.gov.

QUADROS, PAUL D. health products executive; BA in Fin., Calif. State U., Fullerton; MBA, UCLA. Securities analyst, instnl. portfolio mgr.; asst. treas.The Times Mirror Co.; sr. v.p. Pub. Storage, Inc., 1981—84; exec. v.p. Amreal Securities Corp., 1984—85; officer Tech. Funding, 1985—86, gen. ptnr., 1986—95, dir. rsch. and dir. equity investments, chmn. med. investment com., 1990—94; chmn. bd., CFO and sec. GenStar Therapeutics Corp., San Diego, 1995—97, pres., CEO, 1997—98, chmn. bd., CFO, 1998—. Office: Genstar Therapeutics 6555 Nancy Ridge Dr Ste 200 San Diego CA 92121-3221

QUAGLIA, JORDANO, language educator, writer; s. Jordano Quaglia and Quaglia Zefina; m. Marisa Queiroz de Vilhena; children: Flávia Vilhena, Lívia Vilhena, Gabriel Macarini. B in History, Universidade de Campinas, Brazil, 1988; MA in Latin Am. and Caribbean studies, SUNY, 1990, ArtsD in latin am. studies, 2003. Physical Educator Universidade de Campinas, Brazil, 1992. Instr. Portuguese SUNY, Albany, 1995—97; sr. lectr. Portuguese Yale U., New Haven, 1997—. Author (theatrical dir.): Drama of a Librarian Without Material (Best play, Campinas, 1982). Social awareness Universidade de Campinas, Brazil, 1985—88. Fellow Lindsay Fellowship, YCIAS - African Studies - Yale U., 2002; grantee Malcon Batchelor Fund, Spanish and Portuguese Dept., Yale U., 1998—2002, Latin Am. and Iberian Studies Title VI, YCIAS - LAIS - Yale U., 1999—2003, Travel Grant, Ctr. for Lang. Studies - Yale U., 2000—01, IIG - Instl. Grant, 1999, Hewllet Packard Family Title VI Grant, Yale U., 2000, CLEAR - Lansing WI - Travel Grant, Title VI - Edn. dept., 2000, Travel Grant, Consortium for Lang. and Tchg. - Ivy League, 2001—02. Citizens. Roman Catholic. Office: Yale U - Spanish and Portuguese Dept 82-90 Wall St New Haven CT 06520 Personal E-mail: jordano.quaglia@yale.edu.

QUAID, DENNIS, actor; b. Houston, Apr. 9, 1954; s. William Rudy and Juanita B.; m. P.J. Soles, 1978 (div. 1983); m. Meg Ryan, 1991 (div. 2000); 1 child, Jack Henry; m. Kimberly Buffington, July 4, 2004. Student, U. Houston, 1972-75. Actor(films) Crazy Mama, 1975, I Never Promised You A Rosegarden, 1977, Sept. 30, 1955, 1977, Our Winning Season, 1978, The Seniors, 1978, Breaking Away, 1979, G.O.R.P., 1980, The Long Riders, 1980, Caveman, 1981, All Night Long, 1981, The Night the Lights Went Out in Georgia, 1981, Tough Enough, 1983, Jaws 3-D, 1983, The Right Stuff, 1983, Dreamscape, 1984, Enemy Mine, 1985, Innerspace, 1987, The Big Easy, 1987, Suspect, 1987, D.O.A., 1988, Everybody's All-American, 1988, Great Balls of Fire, 1989, Postcards from the Edge, 1990, Come See the Paradise, 1990, Undercover Blues, 1993, Wilder Napalm, 1993, Flesh and Bone, 1993, Wyatt Earp, 1994, Something to Talk About, 1995, Dragonheart, 1996, Criminal Element, 1997, Going West, 1997, Gang Related, 1997, Savior, 1997, Switchback, 1997, The Parent Trap, 1998, On Any Given Sunday, 1999, Frequency, 2000, Traffic, 2000, The Rookie, 2002, Far From Heaven, 2002, Cold Creek Manor, 2003, The Alamo, 2004, The Day After Tomorrow, 2004; (theatre) The Last of the Knucklemen, 1983, True West, 1984; (TV movies) Are You In the House Alone?, 1978, Amateur Night at the Dixie Bar and Grill, 1979, Bill, 1981, Johnny Belinda, 1982, Bill: On His Own, 1983, Everything That Rises (also dir, prod.), 1998, Dinner with Friends, 2001; (TV appearances) Baretta, 1977. Office: 9034 Sunset Blvd # 200 Los Angeles CA 90069 *An artist must take chances in performing his craft. If he is to succeed he must be willing to fall flat on his face.**

QUAID, RANDY, actor; b. Houston, Oct. 1, 1950; s. William R. and Juanita B. Quaid; m. Ella Marie Jolly, May 11, 1980 (div.); 1 child. Student, Houston Baptist Coll., 1969-70, U. Houston, 1970-71. Film appearances include Targets, 1968, The Last Picture Show, 1971, What's Up Doc, 1972, Lolly Madonna XXX, 1972, The Last Detail, 1973 (Acad. award, Golden Globe nominations for best supporting actor), Paper Moon, 1973, Apprenticeship of Duddy Kravitz, 1974, Breakout, 1974, Missouri Breaks, 1975, Bound for Glory, 1976, The Choirboys, 1977, Three Warriors, 1978, Midnight Express, 1979, Foxes, 1980, Long Riders, 1980, Heart Beeps, 1981, National Lampoon's Vacation, 1983, The Wild Life, 1984, The Slugger's Wife, 1985, Fool for Love, 1986, The Wraith, 1986, Caddyshack II, 1988, Moving, 1988, Parents, 1989, Out Cold, 1989, Blood Hounds of Broadway, 1989, National Lampoon's Christmas Vacation, 1989, Quick Change, 1990, Martians Go Home, 1990, Days of Thunder, 1990, Quick Change, 1990, Texasville, 1990, Freaked, 1993, The Paper, 1994, Bye Bye, Love, 1995, Woman Undone, 1995, Legends of the North, 1995, Last Dance, 1996, Kingpin, 1996, Independence Day, 1996, Vegas Vacation, 1997, P.U.N.K.S., 1998, Bug Buster, 1998, Hard

Rain, 1998, The Debtors, 1999, The Adventures of Rocky & Bullwinkle, 2000, Home on the Range (voice), 2004; appeared in TV films Getting Away From It All, 1972, The Great Niagara, 1974, The Last Ride of the Dalton Gang, 1979, To Race the Wind, 1980, Guayana Tragedy: The Story of Jim Jones, 1980, Of Mice and Men, 1981, Inside the Third Reich, 1982, Cowboy, 1983, A Street Car Named Desire, 1984, LBJ: The Early Years, 1986, Dead Solid Perfect, 1988, Evil in Clear River, 1988, Murder in the Heartland, 1993, Frankenstein, 1993, Next Door, 1994, Ruby Ridge: An American Tragedy, 1996, Moonshine Highway, 1996, Roommates, 1994, Ed McBain's 87th Precinct: Lightning, 1995, Streets of Laredo, 1995, Gun, 1997, Purgatory West of the Pecos, 1998, Msil to the Chief, 1999, TV series Saturday Night Live, 1985-87, Davis Rules, 1991-92, The Magical Legend of the Leprechauns, 1999; off-Broadway play True West, 1983 Mem. Acad. Motion Picture Arts and Scis.

QUAIL, PETER HUGH, biologist, educator; b. Australia, Feb. 4, 1944; BSc, U. Sydney, 1964, PhD, 1968. Rsch. assoc. Mich. State U./AEC Plant Rsch. Lab., East Lansing, 1968—71, U. Freiburg, Biologisches Inst., Germany, 1971—73; rsch. fellow, group leader photobiology lab. Australian Nat. U., Sch. Biol. Scis., Canberra, Australia, 1973—77; sr. fellow dept. biology Stanford (Calif.) U., Carnegie Instn., 1977—79; assoc. prof. botany U. Wis., Madison, 1979—84, prof. botany and genetics, 1984—87; rsch. dir., prof. molecular plant biology U. Calif.-Berkeley, Plant Gene Expression Ctr., 1987—89, rsch. dir., prof. dept. plant biology, 1989—. Cons. Resources Devel. Found., 1988, Rockefeller Found. Internat. Rice Rsch. Program, 1988—89; vis. scientist plant genetics Weizmann Inst. Sci., Rehovot, Israel, 1977; mem. NSF Oversight Panel, 1982; mem. rev. com. dept. energy U. Ga., Complex Carbohydrate Ctr., 1986; mem. NSF Grant Rev. Panel, 1988; mem. biochem. genetics program NSF, 1993; ad hoc mem. Biochem. Genetics/Mechanisms of Gene Expression Program, NSF Panel, 1996—2000; mem. sci. adv. com. Rockefeller Found. Biotech., Breeding and Seed Sys. for African Crops Program, 2001—. Reviewer: Dept. Energy, Plant Molecular Biology, Genes and Devel., others, mem. editl. bd.: Planta, 1980—87, Plant Physiology, 1980—87, Plant Molecular Biology, 1980—87. Recipient Commonwealth scholarship, 1961—64, Sibella MacArthur Onslow Meml. prize, 1964, Commonwealth Rsch. studentship, 1965—68, Fulbright-Hays travel grantee, 1968, Alexander von Humboldt stipend, 1971—73, Romnes Faculty fellow, U. Wis., 1984, Am. Soc. Photobiologists Rsch. award, 1988, award for disting. contbns. to photochemistry/photobiology, LI-COR Inc., 1995, Anton Lang Meml. award, Australian Soc. Plant Physiologists, 2000. Mem.: Internat. Soc. Plant Molecular Biology (bd. dirs. 1992—96), Am. Soc. Plant Physiologists (chmn. phytochrome session 1977). Office: Plant Gene Expression Ctr 800 Buchanan St Berkeley CA 94710

QUAINTANCE, ALICE LYNN, elementary school media specialist; b. Morristown, Tenn., July 20, 1958; d. Celton D. and Mary Lou (Scott) VanCleave; m. David Scott Quaintance, Aug. 2, 1980; children: Jennifer Lee, Allison Marie. BS, East Tenn. State U., 1980. Media specialist Surgoinsville (Tenn.) Elem. Sch., 1980-82, Clearwood Jr. H.S., Slidell, La., 1982-83, 84-86, tchr., 1983-84; media specialist Rose Park Mid. Sch., Nashville, 1987-88, Hermitage (Tenn.) Elem. Sch., 1988—; owner Just Acquaintances. Publicity chairperson Donelson/Hermitage (Tenn.) Neighborhood Assn., 1995-97; parent rep. Nashville Ballet Friends, 1997-99. Recipient Dalcon Arts in Schs. award Nashville Inst. for the Arts, 1992, Merit award Gov. Tenn., 1993, Acts of Excellence award Mayor of Nashville, 1994, Golden Apple award Metro Nashville Pub. Schs., 1996, Vol. of Yr. award Nashville Ballet, 1998, Svc. Above Self Tchr. award Rotary Club, 2003. Mem. NEA, Tenn. Edn. Assn., Met. Nashville Edn. Assn. United Methodist. Avocation: the arts. Home: 3826 Pacifica Dr Hermitage TN 37076-1926 Office Phone: 615-885-8838. Business E-Mail: alice.quaintance@mnps.org.

QUAINTON, ANTHONY CECIL EDEN, diplomat; b. Seattle, Apr. 4, 1934; s. Cecil Eden and Marjorie Josephine (Oates) Q.; m. Susan Long, Aug. 7, 1958; children: Katherine, Eden, Elizabeth. BA, Princeton U., 1955; BLitt, Oxford (Eng.) U., 1958. Rsch. fellow St. Antony's Coll., Oxford, 1958-59; with Fgn. Svc., State Dept., 1959-97; vice consul Sydney, Australia, 1960-62; Urdu lang. trainee, 1962-63; 2d sec., econ. officer Am. embassy, Karachi, Pakistan, 1963-64, Rawalpindi, Pakistan, 1964-66, 2d sec., polit. officer New Delhi, 1966-69; sr. polit. officer for India Dept. State, Washington, 1969-72; 1st sec. Am. embassy, Paris, 1972-73, counselor, dep. chief mission Kathmandu, Nepal, 1973-76; amb. to Ctrl. African Empire, Bangui, 1976-78, Managua, Nicaragua, 1982—84, 1984—87; dir. Office for Combating Terrorism, Dept. State, Washington, 1978-81; dep. insp. gen. Dept. State, 1987-89; amb. Lima, Peru, 1989-92; asst. sec. of state for diplomatic security Dept. State, Washington, 1992-95, dir. gen. fgn. svc., 1995-97. Exec. dir. Una Chapman Cox Found., 1998—99; vis. lectr. Princeton U., 1998—99; pres., CEO Nat. Policy Assn., 1999—2003; diplomat in residence Am. U., 2003—; cons. internat. policy com. U.S. Conf. Cath. Bishops; hon. fellow Washington Coll.; bd. dirs. Washington Theol. Consortium; program dir. Am. Acad. Diplomacy, 2004—. Treas. Washington Lions Found.; v.p. Lions Cmty. Outreach Found., Pub. Diplomacy Found. English Speaking Union fellow, 1951-52; Marshall scholar, 1955-58; recipient Rivkin award, 1972, Herter award, 1984, Disting. Honor award Dept. State, 1997. Fellow Fgn. Policy Assn.; mem. Am. Acad. Diplomacy (program dir. 2004—), Coun. on Fgn. Rels., Am. Fgn. Svc. Assn., Washington Inst. Fgn. Affairs, Lions Internat., Met. Club, Phi Beta Kappa. Home: 3424 Porter St NW Washington DC 20016-3126 E-mail: aquainton@aol.com.

QUALE, JOHN CARTER, lawyer; b. Boston, Aug. 16, 1946; s. Andrew C. and Luella (Meland) Q.; m. Diane Zipursky, Jan. 19, 1992; children: Virginia Ann, Jane Harris, John Andrew; stepchildren: Rachel Goldman, Alisa Goldman. AB cum laude, Harvard U., 1968, JD cum laude, 1971. Bar: Mass. 1971, D.C. 1972. Assoc. Kirkland & Ellis, Washington, 1971-78, ptnr., 1978-83, Wiley, Rein & Fielding, Washington, 1983-96, Skadden, Arps, Slate, Meagher & Flom L.L.P., Washington, 1996—. Spkr. mass media trade groups. Contbr. articles to profl. jours. Trustee Fed. Comm. Bar Assn. Found., 1992-93. Mem. ABA, Fed. Comm. Bar Assn. (treas. 1982-83, 98-99, mem. exec. com. 1993-98), Barristers, Met. Club. Office: Skadden Arps Slate Meagher & Flom LLP 1440 New York Ave NW Ste 600 Washington DC 20005-6000 E-mail: jquale@skadden.com.

QUALLEY, CHARLES ALBERT, art educator; b. Creston, Iowa, Mar. 19, 1930; s. Albert Olaf and Cleora (Dietrick) Q.; m. Betty Jean Griffith, Nov. 26, 1954; children: Janet Lynn, John Stuart. BFA, Drake U., 1952; MA, U. Iowa, 1956, MFA, 1958; EdD, Ill. State U., 1967. Art tchr. Des Moines Pub. Schs., 1952, 1954—55; critic art tchr. U. Iowa, 1955-57; prof. fine arts U. Colo., Boulder, 1958-90, prof. emeritus, 1990—, chmn. dept. fine arts, 1968-71, assoc. chmn., 1981-82. Vis. prof. Inst. for Shipboard Edn., semester at sea, 1979, Ill. State U., 1985. Author: Safety in the Art Room, 1986; contbg. editor Sch. Arts, 1978-85, mem. editl. adv. bd., 1985-87; author column Safetypoint, 1981-85. Served with AUS, 1952-54, Korea. Fellow Nat. Art Edn. Assn. (v.p. 1980-82, pres. 1987-89, dir. conv. svcs. 1990-99, Art Educator of Yr. 1993); mem. Nat. Art Edn. Found. (trustee 1987—, chair bd. trustees 1996-2004), Colo. Art Edn. Assn. (editor 1965-67, 75, pres. 1976- 78), Delta Phi Delta, Omicron Delta Kappa, Pi Kappa Delta. Home: 9025 Natalie Ave NE Albuquerque NM 87111-3131

QUALLS, CHARLES WAYNE, JR., research pathologist; b. Oklahoma City, Feb. 8, 1949; s. Charles Wayne and Mary Opal (Howard) Q.; m. Cheryl Lynn Lightfoot, Aug. 9, 1969; children: Kerry Lynn, Julie Elizabeth. BS, Okla. State U., 1971, DVM, 1973; PhD, U. Calif., Davis, 1980. Diplomate Am. Coll. Vet. Pathologists. Postdoctoral fellow U. Calif., Davis, 1973-77; asst. prof. La. State U., Baton Rouge, 1977-82; assoc. prof. Okla. State U., Stillwater, 1982-87, prof. vet. pathology, 1988-99, acting head dept. vet. pathology, 1991-92, coord. grad. instrn. Coll. Vet. Medicine, 1996-99, adj. prof. vet. pathology, 1999—; sr. prin. pathologist GlaxoSmithKline, Research Triangle Park, N.C., 1999—; dir. molecular pathology and electron microscopy Glaxo Wellcome Inc., Research Triangle Park, N.C., 1999-2001; project dir., pathologist GlaxoSmithKline, Research Triangle Park, NC, 2001—03, dir. molecular and ultrastructural pathology, 2003—. Mem. editl. bd. Jour. Toxicology and Environ. Health, Vet. Pathology, Bull. Environ. Toxicology; contbr. articles to profl. jours., chpts. to books. Grantee Dept. of Def., U.S. Army Rsch. and Engring. Program, EPA, others. Mem AVMA (student sponsor 1983-90), Soc. Toxicologic Pathologists, Soc. Toxicology, Phi Kappa Phi, Phi Zeta. Home: 4722 NC 57 Hurdle Mills NC 27541-9305 Office: GlaxoSmithKline Safety Assessment 5 Moore Dr Rm 9 3013 Research Triangle Park NC 27709 Office Phone: 919-483-6024. Business E-Mail: charles.w.qualls@gsk.com.

QUALLS, RANDALL WADE, music educator; b. Pendleton, Oreg., Nov. 9, 1962; s. Donald Ben and Janet Irene Qualls; m. Suzanne Mecham, July 31, 1985; children: Nicole, Rochelle Offret, Danielle, Madison. BS, Weber State U., 1985. Cert. Music Edn. 7-12 Composite Utah, 1985. Chair performing arts, dir. instrumental music Fremont H.S., Plain City, Utah, 1999—, Box Elder H.S., Brigham City, Utah, 1987—99; dir. instrumental music Carbon H.S., Price, Utah, 1985—87. Coord. Utah all state band Utah Music Educators Assn., Salt Lake City, 1988—94, Utah state band com. mem., 1988—94; curriculum devel. com. mem. Box Elder H.S., Brigham City, 1995—97, academic excellence com. mem., 1994—97; tchr. retention com. mem. Weber Sch. Dist., Ogden, 2001—; chmn.steering com. Ogden City Concert Band, Ogden, 1991—95. Dir.: (guest conductor, ogden honor band); author: Surviving the Trimester System in a Music Program, musician (teacher) music teacher. Mem.: Music Educators Nat. Conf.

QUALLS, ROBERT L. manufacturing executive, banker, former state official, educator; b. Burnsville, Miss., Nov. 6, 1933; s. Wes E. and Letha (Parker) Q.; m. Carolyn Morgan, Feb. 10, 1979 (dec. July 1996); 1 child, Stephanie Elizabeth; m. Nancy Martin, Sept. 11, 1999. BS, Miss. State U., 1954, MS, 1958; PhD, La. State U., 1962; LLD, Whitworth Coll., 1974; DBA (hon.), U. of the Ozarks, 1984. Prof., chmn. div. econs. and bus. Belhaven Coll., Jackson, Miss., 1962-66, asst. to pres., 1965-66; asst. prof. finance Miss. State U., State College, 1967-69, adj. prof., 1969-73; sr. v.p., chmn. venture com. Bancorp South, Tupelo, Miss., 1969-73; v.p. Wesleyan Coll., Macon, Ga., 1974; pres. U. of the Ozarks, Clarksville, Ark., 1974-79; mem. cabinet Bill Clinton Gov. of Ark., 1979-80; exec. v.p. Bank of America, Little Rock, 1980-85, chmn., CEO, dir. Harrison, Ark., 1985-86; pres., dir. First Bank Fin. Services, Inc., 1980-85, Advt. Assocs., Inc., 1980-85; pres., chief oper. officer Baldor Electric Co., Ft. Smith, Ark., 1986-91, CEO, 1992-97, vice chmn., 1998—2000, dir., mem. exec. com., 1987—, presiding non-mgmt. dir., 2004—. Mktg. cons. Ill. Central Industries, Chgo., 1964; mem. faculty, thesis examiner Stonier Grad. Sch. Banking, Rutgers U., 1973-86; mem. faculty Miss. Sch. Banking, U. Miss., 1973-78; course coordinator Sch. Banking of the South, La. State U., 1978-88, Banking Sch., Duke U., 1977; lectr. Southwestern Sch. Banking, So. Meth. U., 1983; adj. prof. bus. adminstrn. U. Central Ark., 1985-86; bd. dirs., mem. audit com., Bank of Ozarks, presiding ind. dir., 2003—. Author: Entrepreneurial Wit and Wisdom, 1986; co-author: Strategic Planning for Colleges and Universities: A Systems Approach to Planning and Resource Allocation, 1979; mem. editorial adv. bd.: Bank Mktg. Mag., 1984-86. Chmn. cmty. svc. and continuing edn. com. Tupelo Cmty. Devel. Found., 1972-73; mem. Miss. 4-H adv. coun., 1969; active Boys Scouts Am.; mem. Lee County Dem. Exec. Com., 1973-74; trustee Walton Family Found., 1975-79, Oklahoma City U., 1990-95; trustee, mem. exec. com. U. Ozarks, 1982-88, chmn. bd., 2000-03; mem. Pres.'s Roundtable U. Ctrl. Ark., 1982-87; mem. exec. com. Coll. Bus. Adv. Bd., U. Ark., Little Rock, 1980-85; bd. dirs. U. Ark. Med. Sch. Found., 1991-97, Ark. Inst., 1991-94; chmn. bd. Petit Jean Youth Found., 2001-03; mem. Clarksville Light and Water Commn., 2000-01; elder Clarksville Presbyn. Ch., 1997-2000; bd. dirs. Vera Lloyd Presbyn. Home and Family Svcs. Lt. AUS, 1954-56. Found. for Econ. Edn. fellow, 1964; Ford Found. faculty research fellow Vanderbilt U., 1963-64; recipient Pillar of Progress award Johnson County, 1977 Mem. Am. Bankers Assn. (mktg. planning and rsch. com. 1972-73), Ark. Coun. Ind. Colls. and Univs. (chmn. 1978-79), Johnson County C. of C. (pres. 1977), Fort Smith C. of C. (dir. 1995-98), Blue Key, Omicron Delta Kappa, Delta Sigma Pi, Sigma Phi Epsilon (citation 1977), Beta Gamma Sigma, Masons (32 deg.), Clarksville Rotary (pres. 1979). Presbyterian. E-mail: nancy_qualls@msn.com.

QUALLS, ROXANNE, mayor; D (hon.), Cin. State Tech. and C.C., 1996. Former exec. dir. Women Helping Women; former dir. No. Ky. Rape Crisis Ctr.; former dir. Cin. office Ohio Citizen Action; councilwoman City of Cin., 1991-93, mayor, 1993-98, founder youth summer jobs program Artworks, Cin. Homeownership Partnership. Former chairperson Cin. City Council's Intergovtl. Affairs and Environment Com.; former vice chairperson Community Devel., Housing and Zoning Com.; mem. Gov.'s Commn. on Storage and Use of Toxic and Hazardous Materials, Solid Waste Adv. Com. of State of Ohio, Gov.'s Waste Minimization Task Force; former chair bd. commrs. Cin. Met. Housing Authority; bd. dirs. Shuttlesworth Housing Found. Hon. chair Friends of Women's Studies; mem. Jr. League Adv. Coun.; bd. dirs. Nat. Underground Railroad Freedom Ctr., Ctr. Voting and Democracy; past bd. didrs. No. Ky. Cath. Commn. Soc. Jusitice. Recipient Woman of Distinction award Girl Scouts U.S., 1992, Woman of Distinction award Soroptomists, 1993, Outstanding Achievement award Cin. Woman's Polit. Caucus, 1993, Women of Achievement award YWCA, 1994, Outstanding Svc. award Ohio Pub. Employees Lawyers Assn., 1996, Pub. Offcl. of Yr. award State of Cinn., 1996, Nat. Assn. Soc. Workers, 1996, Nat. Homebuilders Assn., 1997. Mem. Nat. Assn. Regional Couns. (former pres., 1st v.p., 2d v.p.), Ohio Ky. Ind. Regional Coun. Govts. (1st v.p., 2d v.p.). Office: 93 Perry St #3 Brookline MA 02446-6935 Fax: 513-352-5201.

QUALLS, STEVEN DANIEL, lawyer; b. Detroit, May 24, 1967; s. Hugh Pharris Qualls and Lenora Ann Allen; m. Elizabeth Lynn Crosier, June 21, 1990; children: Joshua Michael, Emily Elizabeth. BS, Tenn. Tech. U., 1992; JD, Nashville Sch. Law, 1996. Law clk. Cameron & Chaffin, Cookeville, Tenn., 1992-96, atty., 1996-98; atty., sr. ptnr. Qualls & Fry PLLC, Cookeville, 1998—. Mem. adv. bd. First Am. Nat. Bank, Cookeville, 1996-98; cons. Jackson Bank and Trust, Cookeville, 1996-98. Bd. dirs. Montessori Childrens Sch., Cookeville, 1993-98, Cancer Care Fund, Inc., 1999-2000, Putnam County Clean Commn., 2000-2001; treas. State Senate Charlotte Burks, Cookeville, 1998; active Dem. Party Putnam County, Cookeville, 1998; mem. Leadership Putnam Class of 2000; vice mayor Cookeville, 2002-. Mem. Noon Day Lions Clu b(v.p. 1996-98). Avocations: racquetball, tennis, golf. Home: 410 Concord Dr Cookeville TN 38501-3069 Office: Qualls Fry & Dunaway PLLC 16 S Washington Ave Cookeville TN 38501-3980 E-mail: squalls@citlink.net.

QUALSET, CALVIN O. plant genetics and agronomy educator; b. Newman Grove, Nebr., Apr. 24, 1937; s. Herman Qualset and Adeline (Hanson) Vakoc; m. Kathleen Boehler; children: Douglas, Cheryl, Gary. BS, U. Nebr., 1958; MS, U. Calif., Davis, 1960, PhD, 1964. Asst. prof. U. Tenn., Knoxville, 1964-67; from asst. prof. to assoc. prof. U. Calif., Davis, 1967, prof., 1973-94, prof. emeritus, 1994—, chmn. dept. agronomy and range sci., 1975-81, 91-94, assoc. dean Coll. Agrl. and Environ. Sci., 1981-86, dir. Genetic Resources Conservation Program, Davis, 1985—2002. Sci. liaison officer U.S. Agy. Internat. Devel., Washington, 1985-93, rsch. adv. com., 1989-92; nat. plant genetic resources bd. USDA, Washington, 1982-88; bd. trustees Am. Type Culture Collection, 1993-99, Internat. Rice Rsch. Inst., 1999-2004, Agronomic Sci. Found., 1999-. Contbr. over 300 articles to profl. jours. and tech. publs. Bd. dirs. Auksuciai Found., 1999—; contbr. to wheat improvement in Mex. citation, 1988. Fulbright fellow, Australia, 1976, Yugoslavia, 1984; recipient Pub. Plant Breeding award U.S. Coun. Comml. Plant Breeders, 1996, Charles Black award Coun. Agrl. Sci. and Tech., 2002, William L. Brown award Mo. Bot. Garden, 2002, Master Alumni award U. Nebr., 1997, Citation for contbns. to agriculture in Lithuania, 2004, Citation for Excellence, U. Calif., Calif. Aggie Alumni Assn., 2003. Fellow AAAS (chmn. agr. sect. 1992), Am. Soc. Agronomy (pres. 1994, agronomy honoree Calif. sect. 2001), Crop Sci. Soc. Am. (pres. 1989, editor-in-chief 1980-84); mem. Soc. Conservation Biology, Soc. Econ. Botany, Genetic Soc. Am., Internat. Union Biol. Scis. (mem. U.S. nat. com. 2000—), Am. Genetic Assn., U. Nebr. Alumni Assn. Achievements include development of more than 15 cultivars of wheat, oat, triticale. Office: U Calif Genetic Res Conserv Prog One Shields Ave Davis CA 95616

QUAM, DORI, music educator, paralegal; b. Estherville, Iowa; BME, S.D. State U., Brookings, 1985; Cert., Minn. Paralegal Inst., Minnetonka, Minn., 1995. Cert.: Nat. Assn. Legal Assts. (legal asst.) 1997. Tchr. Titonka Consol. Schs., Titonka, Iowa, 1985—89, Mallard Cmty. Sch., Mallard, Iowa, 1990—95; paralegal Davenport, Evans, Hurwitz & Smith, L.L.P., Sioux Falls, SD, 1995—; flute instr. S.D. State U., Brookings, SD, 2000—. Mem.: S.D. Paralegal Assn., Nat. Flute Assn., Upper Midwest Flute Assn. Avocations: hiking, reading, music, games, travel. Office Phone: 605-336-2880.

QUAM, LOIS, healthcare company executive; MA in Philosophy, Politics, Econs., U. Oxford, 1985. Dir. rsch. and eval. United HealthCare, 1989-93, v.p. public sector svcs., 1993; sr. advisor White House Task Force Nat. Health Care Reform, 1993-96; CEO AARP/United divsn. United HealthCare, 1996-98; CEO Ovations (formerly Retiree and Sr. Svcs. Co. United HealthCare), Minnetonka, MN, 1998—. Office: Ovations United Health Group 500 Opus Ctr 9900 Bren Rd E Minnetonka MN 55343-9664

QUAN, DENISE ALANE, music educator; b. L.A., Mar. 10, 1959; d. Olin Quan and Lois Wong Patterson. AA, L.A. City Coll., 1991; BA, BMus, U. So. Calif., 1994, MMus, 2001. Cert. tchr., Calif. Piano dept. chair Sat. Conservatory Music, L.A., 1992—; asst. lectr. U. So. Calif., L.A., 1994-96; music dept. chair, orch. and band dir. Virgil Mid. Sch., L.A., 1996—; instr. music dept. L.A. City Coll., 2001—02. Adv. bd. L.A. City Coll. Music Dept., 1998—. Bd. dirs. Sat. Conservatory Music, 2001—. Mem. L.A. City Coll. Alumni Assn., Phi Beta Kappa, Pi Kappa Lambda, Phi Kappa Phi. Avocations: reading, crossword puzzles, gardening, history, baking. Office: Virgil Mid Sch 152 N Vermont Ave Los Angeles CA 90004

QUANDT, JOSEPH EDWARD, lawyer, educator; b. Port Huron, Mich., May 21, 1963; s. Herbert Raymond and Mary Katherine (West) Q.; m. Christine Ann Reilly, Aug. 21, 1993. BA, Oakland U., 1990; JD, Thomas M. Cooley Law Sch., Lansing, Mich., 1993. Bar: Mich. 1994, U.S. Dist. Ct. (ea. and we. dists.) Mich. 1994. Exec. dir. Lord & Taylor, Sterling Heights, Mich., 1985-90; compliance and enforcement specialist Mich. Dept. Environ. Quality, Lansing, 1990-93, adv. bd., 1997—; assoc. Stowe, Draling & Boyd, Traverse City, Mich., 1993-94, Smith & Johnson, Traverse City, 1994-98; ptnr. Menmuir, Zimmerman, Kuhn, Taylor and Quandt, Traverse City, 1998—. Lectr., commentator Inst. CLE, Ann Arbor, Mich., 1994—; adj. prof. Thomas M. Cooley Law Sch., 1997—; co-chair environ. law sect., mem. Environ. Law Coun. State Bar Mich. Contbr. articles to profl. jours. Bd. dirs. Involved Citizens Enterprises, Traverse City, 1995—. Mem. Nat. Honor Soc. for Polit. Scientists, Ancient Order Hibernians, Pi Sigma Alpha. Republican. Roman Catholic. Avocations: ice hockey, golf, fly fishing. Office: Zimmerman Kuhn Darling Boyd Taylor and Quandt PLC 412 S Union St Traverse City MI 49684-2404 Office Phone: 231-947-7900. E-mail: jequandt@zimmerman-kahn.com.

QUANE, JAMES, human services administrator; b. Limerick, Ireland, July 1, 1960; arrived in US, 1983; s. James and Angela Quane. BS, U. Coll. Galway, Ireland, 1980; MA, U. Akron, 1987, PhD, 1992. Civil servant Bd. of Edn., Nigeria, 1980—83; grants admin. Cuyahoga County Comm. Mental Health Bd., Cleve., 1990—93; assoc. dir. Ctr. for Study of Urban Inequality, U. Chgo., Chgo., 1993—96, Joblessness & Urban Pverty Rsch. Program, Harvard U., 1996—; sr. rsch. assoc. Kennedy Sch. of Govt., Harvard U., Cambridge, Mass., 2003—. Contbr. articles various profl. jours. Mem.: Am. Sociological Assn. Avocations: travel, golf. Home: 121 Prospect Ave Quincy MA 02170 Office: Harvard U Jobless Urban Poverty Rsch 79 JFK St Cambridge MA 02138 Office Phone: 617-490-5621.

QUANN, MEGAN, Olympic athlete; b. Tacoma, Wash., Jan. 15, 1984; Recipient Gold medal 100-meter breaststroke, 4 x 100-meter medley (team) Sydney Olympics, 2000, Silver medal 100-meter breaststroke Pan Pacific Championships, 1999; set Am. record for 100-meter breaststroke U.S. Open Swimming Championships, San Antonio, 1999; winner 100-meter breaststroke title U.S. Spring Nats., 1998, 99, 1st pl. 100m breast stroke, Nat. Championships, 2003. Office: USA Swimming 1 Olympic Plz Colorado Springs CO 80909-5746

QUANT, HAROLD EDWARD, retired financial services company executive, rancher; b. Aug. 21, 1948; s. Harold Atwell and Dorothy Ann Quant; m. Michelle Bumpers, June 27, 1982; children: Andrew, Angela, Emily. BSBA, San Jose State U., 1976. Account exec. Dun & Bradstreet, San Jose, Calif., 1970-81; pres. Telecredit Collection Svcs., Inc., L.A., 1981-85; v.p. FCA, Arlington, Tex., 1986-90; pres., CEO Creditwatch, Inc., Arlington, 1990-2000, chmn. bd. dirs.; ret., 2000. Sgt. USMC, 1965—70, Vietnam. Mem.: City Club. Republican. Mem. United Ch. Of God. Avocation: horses.

QUARFORTH, JAMES S. communications executive; b. Annandale, Va. BS Fin., U. Richmond, 1976; MBA, James Madison U., 1982. CEO NTELOS, Inc., Waynesboro, Va., 1999—, also bd. dirs. Office: 401 Spring Ln Ste 300 PO Box 1990 Waynesboro VA 22980

QUARLES, BETH, civil rights administrator; Commr. Civil Rights Commn., Indpls. With presdl. task force, Mits task force, Muncie task force ADA; with Pecso CEO Learning Ctr.; active in youth leadership, employment opportunities and law enforcement ADA; hearing impaired cons.; condr. sign lang. classes. Bd. dirs. Open Door Comty., Muncie (Ind.) Pub. Libr., United Way, County Commty. Partnership on Disability, Muncie Civic Theater; vol. interpreter for deaf; mentor numerous minority bus. Recipient Frieda Dawkins award, Presdl. Points of Light award, also state, nat., and internat. awards for theatrical prodns. Office: Civil Rights Commn 100 N Senate Ave Rm W103 Indianapolis IN 46204-2273

QUARLES, CARROLL ADAIR, JR., physicist, researcher; b. Abilene, Tex., Nov. 24, 1938; s. Carroll Adair and Marguerite Marie (Vollmers) Q.; m. Sonja Gale Bandy, May 14, 1971; children: Jennifer Anne, John Patrick. BA, Tex. Christian U., 1960; PhD, Princeton U., 1964. Rsch. physicist Brookhaven Nat. Lab., Upton, N.Y., 1964-67; mem. faculty Tex. Christian U., Ft.Worth, 1967—, assoc. prof. physics Ft. Worth, 1970-76, prof. Ft.Worth, 1976—, W.A. Moncrief Jr. prof. physics, 1986—, chmn. dept. physics, 1978-84, 96-99, assoc. dean Coll. Arts and Scis. Ft.Worth, 1974-78. Contbr. articles to profl. jours. Mem. AAAS, Am. Phys. Soc. (sec.-treas. Tex. sect. 1993-99, chair Tex. sect. 2003, mem. exec. com. Forum on Physics and Soc., 1999-2002), Am. Assn. Physics Tchrs. (pres. Tex. sect. 1984), Sigma Xi, Phi Beta Kappa (pres. Delta of Tex. chpt. 1982-84). Roman Catholic. Office: Tex Christian U Dept Physics Fort Worth TX 76129-0001 Business E-Mail: c.quarles@tcu.edu.

QUARLES, JAMES LINWOOD, III, lawyer; b. Huntington, W.Va., Oct. 12, 1946; s. James Linwood Jr. and Beatrice (Hardwick) Q.; m. Sharon Taft, Dec. 20, 1969; children: Jessica, Matthew. BS cum laude, Denison U., 1968; JD cum laude, Harvard U., 1972. Bar: Mass. 1974, U.S. Dist. Ct. Mass. 1975, U.S. Ct. Appeals (D.C. cir.) 1975, U.S. Ct. Appeals (6th cir.) 1979, U.S. Supreme Ct. 1980, D.C. 1981, U.S. Ct. Appeals (2d cir.) 1981, U.S. Ct. Appeals (1st and 4th cirs.) 1983, Md. 1985, Va. 2000. Law clk. to presiding justice U.S. Dist. Ct. Md., Balt., 1972-73; with Watergate Spl. Pros. Force, Washington, 1973-75; from assoc. to sr. ptnr. Wilmer Cutler Pickering Hale and Dorr, Boston and Washington, 1975—. Mem. Am. Law Inst. Democrat. Office: Wilmer Cutler Pickering Hale & Dorr Ste 1000 1455 Pennsylvania Ave NW Washington DC 20004-1085 Office Phone: 202-942-8404. E-mail: james.quarles@wilmerhale.com.

QUARLES, ORAGE, III, publishing executive; m. Terry Linda Quarles; 2 children. From apprentice compositor to advt. dir. San Bernardino County (Calif.) Sun, dir. advt., 1984—87; asst. to regional pres. Gannett western region, 1987; pres., pub. Ft. Collins Coloradoan, Stockton (Calif.) Record, 1990—93; pres., pub., dir. Carolina ops. The Herald, Rock Hill, SC, 1993—96; pub. The Modesto (Calif.) Bee, 1996—2000; pres., pub. The News and Observer Pub. Co., Raleigh, NC, 2000—. Bd. dirs. AP; mem. gen. mgmt. adv. bd. Am. Press Inst.; former chmn. Newspaper Assn. of America, Vienna. Bd. trustees Wake County Triangle United Way, Wake Edn. Partnership, Peace Coll., Raleigh; bd. dirs. Carolina Ballet, United Arts Coun., N.C. Mus. of Art Found., Downtown Raleigh Alliance. Mem.: Nat. Assn. Minority Media Execs. Office: News & Observer 215 S McDowell St Raleigh NC 27705

QUARLES, RANDAL KEITH, lawyer, federal official; b. San Francisco, Sept. 5, 1957; s. Ralph Ray and Beverly Kay (Hulse) Q.; m. C. Hope Eccles, Sept. 13, 1997; children: Randal, Spencer. AB, Columbia U., 1981; JD, Yale U., 1984. Assoc. Davis Polk & Wardwell, N.Y.C., 1984-91, ptnr., 1993—2001; spl. asst. to sec. Dept. of Treasury, Washington, 1991-92, deputy asst. sec., fin. insts. policy, 1992-93; dep. undersec. internat. affairs Dept . of Treasury, 2002—. U.S. exec. dir. IMF, 2001—02, European Bank Reconstrn. and Devel., 2002; mem. bd. dirs. Overseas Pvt. Investment Corp., 2004—. Mem. fin. adv. com. Dole Presdl. Campaign, Washington, 1996. Mem. Yale Club, Salt Lake Country Club. Mem. Lds Ch. Avocations: aviation, skiing. Office: Dept Treasury Asst Sec Internat Affairs 1500 Pennsylvania Ave NW Washington DC 20220 Home: 4515 Dexter St NW Washington DC 20007 E-mail: randal.quarles@do.treas.gov.

QUARTERMAN, CYNTHIA LOUISE, lawyer; b. Savannah, Ga., Apr. 6, 1961; d. Rudolph V. and Bernice Q.; m. Pantelis Michalopoulos, Nov. 2, 1993. BS, Northwestern U., 1983; JD, Columbia U., 1987. Atty. Benson & McKay, Kansas City, 1987-88, Steptoe & Johnson, Washington, 1988—93; dep. dir. Minerals Mgmt. Svc., Dept. Interior, Washington, 1993-95, dir., 1995-99; ptnr. Steptoe & Johnson, Washington, 1999—. Mem. adv. bd. Inst. for Energy Law, co-chair ann. inst. Mem. ABA (vice chair sect. on environment, energy, resources, oil and natural gas exploration and prodn. com. 2002—03), Energy Bar Assn. (chair environment and pub. lands com. 2002—03), Women's Coun. Energy and Environment. Home: 1337 21st St NW Washington DC 20036-1503 E-mail: cquarter@steptoe.com.

QUAST, PEARL ELIZABETH KOLB, retired elementary school educator; b. Omro, Wis., Nov. 21, 1934; d. Frank Kolb and Lavon Opal Buchanan; m. Arthur Roman Quast; children: Arthur R. Jr., Robert F., John M. BS in Edn., Edgewood Coll., Madison, Wisconsin, 1956; MA in Edn., Cardinal Stritch Coll., Milw., 1971. Cert. tchr. unlimited 0743, K-3 Wis., remedial reading 42 and 27 (K-12), reading specialist 42 and 27 (K-12). Tchr. grade 2 Deerfield (Ill.) Pub. Schs., 1956—58; tchr. grade 3 Whitefish Bay (Wis.) Pub. Schs., 1958—60; tchr. reading Milw. Pub. Schs., 1969—75; reading specialist Germantown (Wis.) Pub. Schs., 1975—91. Seminar presenter Reading Assn., Milw., 1982—86; vol. coord. The Cath. Ctr., Sun City West, 1998—99; coord. lectors Our Lady of Lourdes Ch., Sun City West, 1996—2003, lector, cantor, choir mem., Sun City West and Phoenix, 1995—2003. Bd. trustees Found. for Sr. Living, Phoenix, 1998—2001; group leader founding com. Cath. Ctr. for Srs.' Needs, Sun City and Sun City West, 1995—2001; coord. lectors Our Lady of Lourdes Ch., 1996—2003, mem.; del. Phoenix Diocesan Synod, 2002—03; Bd. trustees Symphony of the West Valley, Sun City West, 1996—2002. Mem.: AAUW (v.p. membership 1994—96), West Valley Art Mus. (sec. Woman's League 1994—96), Cath. Ctr. (founding officer, v.p. adv. com. 1996—2000, Cert. Appreciation), Found. for Sr. Living, Weavers West Handweaving Guild, Our Lady of Lourdes Church. Roman Catholic. Avocations: handweaving, travel, singing, reading, cultural arts.

QUATE, CALVIN FORREST, engineering educator; b. Baker, Nev., Dec. 7, 1923; s. Graham Shepard and Margie (Lake) Quate; m. Dorothy Marshall, June 28, 1945 (div. 1985); children: Robin, Claudia, Holly, Rhodalee; m. Arnice Streit, Jan. 1987. BS in Elec. Engring, U. Utah, 1944; PhD, Stanford U., 1950. Mem. tech. staff Bell Telephone Labs., Murray Hill, N.J., 1949-58; dir. research Sandia Corp., Albuquerque, 1959-60, v.p. research, 1960-61; prof. dept. applied physics and elec. engring. Stanford (Calif.) U., 1961-95, chmn. applied physics, 1969-72, 78-81, Leland T. Edwards prof. engring., 1986—, assoc. dean Sch. Humanities and Scis., 1972-74, 82-83, rsch. prof. dept. elec. engring., 1995—. Sr. rsch. fellow Xerox Rsch. Ctr., Palo Alto, Calif., 1984—94. Served as lt. (j.g.) USNR, 1944—46. Recipient Rank prize for Opto-electronics, 1982, Pres.'s Nat. medal of Sci., 1992. Fellow: Acoustical Soc., Am. Acad. Arts and Scis., IEEE; mem.: Royal Soc., Royal Microscop. Soc., Am. Phys. Soc., NAS, NAE, Tau Beta Pi, Sigma Xi. Office: Stanford U E L Ginzton Lab Palo Alto CA 94305-4085

QUATRANO, ANNE, chef, restaurant owner; Grad., Calif. Culinary Acad., San Francisco. Chef, co-owner Bacchanalia, Atlanta, Floataway Cafe, Atlanta, Star Provisions, Atlanta; chef Grolier Club, NY, Bimini Twist, La Petit Ferme. Elected mem. James Beard Found. Office: 1198 Howell Mill Rd Atlanta GA 30301

QUATTRONE-CARROLL, DIANE ROSE, clinical social worker; b. N.Y.C., July 18, 1949; d. Mario Anthony and Filomena (Serpico) Quattrone; m. Rene Eugene Carroll Jr., June 7, 1980; children: Jenna Cristine, Jonathan Rene. BA cum laude, Bklyn. Coll., 1971; MSW, Rutgers U., 1974. Lic. marriage and family counselor, lic. clin. social worker, N.J.; bd. cert. diplomate in clin. social work. Clin. social worker, field instr. Essex County Guidance Ctr., East Orange, N.J., 1974-82; exec. dir. Psychotherapy Info. and Referral Svc., Madison, N.J., 1982-87; pvt. practice Sparta, N.J., 1982—. Nat. Assn. Social Workers. Avocation: travel.

QUAY, THOMAS EMERY, lawyer; b. Cleve., Apr. 3, 1934; s. Harold Emery and Esther Ann (Thomas) Q.; divorced; children: Martha Wyndham, Glynis Cobb, Eliza Emery; m. Winnifred B. Cutler, May 13, 1989. AB in Humanities magna cum laude (Univ. scholar), Princeton U., 1956; LLB (Univ. scholar), U. Pa., 1963. Bar: Pa. 1964. Assoc. Pepper, Hamilton & Scheetz, Phila., 1963-65; with William H. Rorer, Inc., Ft. Washington, Pa., 1965—, sec., counsel, 1974-79, v.p., gen. counsel, sec., 1979-88; v.p. legal planning and adminstrn. Rorer Group, 1988-90; counsel Reed Smith Shaw and McClay, Phila., 1991-93; v.p., gen. counsel Athena Inst., Chester Springs, Pa., 1993—. Bd. dirs. Main Line YMCA, Ardmore, Pa., 1971-73, chmn. bd., 1972-73; editor 10th Reunion Book Princeton Class of 1956, 1966, 25th Reunion Book, 1981—, class sec., 1966-71, class v.p., 1971-81, pres., 1981-86. Lt. (j.g.) USNR, 1957-60. Recipient Commendation award, Main Line YMCA, 1984. Mem. ABA, Pa. Bar Assn., Phila. Bar Assn., Pharm. Mfrs. Assn. (chmn. law sect. 1983), Pa. Biotech. Assn. (chmn. legis. com., mem. exec. com. 1991-93), Phila. Drug Exch. (chmn. legis. com. 1975-78), Cannon Club of Princeton U., Sharswood Law Club of U. Pa., Princeton Club of Phila. Democrat. Presbyterian.

QUAYLE, DAN (JAMES DANFORTH QUAYLE), former vice president United States, entrepreneur; b. Indpls., Feb. 4, 1947; s. James C. and Corinne (Pulliam) Q.; m. Marilyn Tucker, Nov. 18, 1972; children: Tucker Danforth, Benjamin Eugene, Mary Corinne. BS in Polit. Sci., DePauw U., Greencastle, Ind., 1969; JD, Ind. U., 1974. Bar: Ind. 1974. Ct. reporter, pressman Huntington (Ind.) Herald-Press, 1965-69, assoc. pub., gen. mgr., 1974-76; with consumer protection divn. Office Atty. Gen., State of Ind., 1970-71; adminstrv. asst. to gov. State of Ind., 1971-73; dir. Ind. Inheritance Tax Div., 1973-74; tchr. bus. law Huntington Coll., 1975; mem. 95th-96th Congresses from 4th Dist. Ind., Washington; U.S. Senator from Ind. U.S. Senate, Washington, 1981-89; v.p. served under Pres. George Bush U.S., Washington, 1989-93; founder BTC, 1994; pres. Quayle & Assoc. Internat. advisor to investment bankers, Cerberus Capital Management; author, speaker, corp. bds.; disting. vis. prof. Am. Grad. Sch. Internat. Mgmt., 1997-99. Author: Standing Firm, 1994, The American Family, 1996, Worth Fighting For, 1999. Chmn. Campaign Am., 1995-99. With Ind. Army N.G., 1970-76. Mem. Huntington Bar Assn., Hoosier State Press Assn., Huntington C. of C. Clubs: Rotary. Republican. Office: Quayle and Associates 7001 N Scottsdale Rd Ste 2010 Scottsdale AZ 85253-3644*

QUAYLE, JACKIE M. artist; b. San Antonio, Feb. 9, 1956; d. John W. and Helen H. Quayle. BA in Piano, U. Ala., 1979, postgrad., 1979—80. Pianist various univs. and chs., 1972—; mgr. Sambos Restaurant, Texas City, 1981. Tchr. music pvt. practice, Tex., Ala. Author (illustrator): Alphabet Zoo, 2000, composer to original poetry songs. Served USMC. Mem.: Phi Beta Kappa. Avocation: crafts.

QUAYLE, MARILYN TUCKER, wife of former vice president of United States, lawyer; b. 1949; d. Warren and Mary Alice Tucker; m. J. Danforth Quayle, Nov. 18, 1972; children: Tucker, Benjamin, Corinne. BA in Polit. Sci., Purdue U., 1971; JD, Ind. U., 1974. Pvt. practice atty., Huntington, Ind., 1974—77; ptnr. Krieg, DeVault, Alexander & Capehart, Indpls., 1993—2001; pres. BTC Inc., Phoenix, 2001—. Author (with Nancy T. Northcott): Embrace the Serpent, 1992; author: The Campaign, 1996. Office: Quayle and Associates Ste 2010 7001 N Scottsdale Rd Scottsdale AZ 85253-3644

QUAZZO, STEPHEN R. investment company executive; Bachelors Degree, MBA, Harvard U. Lic. real estate broker Ill. V.p. real estate dept. Goldman, Sachs & Co. Midwest; pres. Equity Instnl. Investors, Inc., 1991—96; co-founder, CEO Transwestern Investment Co. LLC, Chgo., 1996—. Bd. dirs. Transwestern Comml. Svcs. LLC, Starwood Hotels and Resorts. Trustee The Latin Sch. Chgo.; Chgo. adv. bd. mem. City Year. Mem.: Urban Land Inst. (trustee, chair indsl. and office park devel. coun.). Office: Transwestern Investment Co LLC Ste 800 150 N Wacker Dr Chicago IL 60606*

QUDDUS, MOHAMMED TANVIR, electrical engineer, researcher; b. Comilla, Bangladesh, July 1, 1966;, U.S., 1995; s. Mohammed Abdul Quddus and Khodeja Begum; m. Farhana Hussain. BS, Bangladesh U. Engring. and Tech., Dhaka, 1991, MS, 1993; PhD, Ariz. State U., 1999. Lectr. Bangladesh U. Engring. and Tech., Dhaka, Bangladesh, 1991—93, asst. prof., 1993—95; sr. staff engr. ON Semiconductor, Phoenix, 2000—. Contbr. articles to profl. jours. Pres. Bangladesh Student Assn., Ariz. State U., Tempe, Ariz., 1998—99. Recipient Pres. award, Govt. Bangladesh, 1984; scholar, Ariz. State U., 1997—98, 1999—2000. Mem.: IEEE, Am. Chem. Soc., Phi Kappa Phi. Achievements include patents in field. Office: ON Semiconductor 5005 E Mcdowell Rd Phoenix AZ 85008 Home: 474 W Seagull Dr Chandler AZ 85248-2799 Personal E-mail: tanvir@fastq.com. Business E Mail: tanvir.quddus@onsemi.com.

QUEALLY, PAUL B. venture capitalist; b. Glen Cove, N.Y., Mar. 30, 1964; s. Francis Xavier and Claire (Doyule) Q.; m. Anne-Marie Flinn, Apr. 3, 1990; 1 child, P. Brian. BA, U. Richmond, 1986; MBA, Columbia U., 1990. Analyst Donaldson, Lufkin & Jenrette, N.Y.C., 1986—88, assoc., 1988—90, v.p., 1991—96; gen. ptnr. Welsh, Carson, Anderson & Stowe, N.Y.C., 1996—. Bd. dirs. E & B Marine, Inc., Edison, N.J., Champion Healthcare, Inc., Houston, Alphagraphics, Inc., Tucson, Cardiovascular Ventures, Inc., Stuart, Fla., United Signal Ptnrs., AmComp, Inc., AmeriSafe, Inc., Concentra Managed Care, Inc., Lab One, Inc., MedCath Corp., SHPS, Inc., AmeriPath, Inc., acting chmn., 2004— Mem. Phi Beta Kappa, Omicron Delta Epsilon. Republican. Roman Catholic. Avocations: golf, reading, antique shopping. Office: Welsh Carson Anderson 320 Park Ave Bsmt New York NY 10022*

QUEBE, JERRY LEE, retired architect; b. Indpls., Nov. 7, 1942; s. Charlie Christopher and Katheryn Rosella (Hankins) Q.; m. Mary Lee Darby (div.); children: Chad, Tara; m. Julie Ann Gordon (div.); 1 child, Dana Ann; m. Lisbeth Jane Gray, Mar. 16, 1986. BArch, Iowa State U., 1965. Registered arch., Wis. Mem. staff Hansen Lind Meyer, Iowa City, 1965-70, assoc., 1970-74, prin., 1975-77, prin., v.p. Chgo., 1977-86; exec. v.p. VVKR, Inc., Alexandria, Va., 1986-93; prin., sr. v.p. Perkins & Will, Chgo., 1994-96, also bd. dirs.; sr. v.p. RTKL Assocs. Inc., Chgo., 1996—2002, ret., 2002. Chmn. Cedar Rapids/Iowa City Architects Council, 1974. Author: Drafting Practices Manual, 1978; contbr. articles to profl. jours. Pres. bd. dirs. Mental Health Assn. of Greater Chgo., 1990-95. Fellow AIA, Am. Coll. Healthcare Archs-.(founder); mem. Forum for Health Care Planning (bd. dirs. 1992-99). Avocations: photography, woodworking, gardening. Home: 43495 Trout Creek Road Soldiers Grove WI 54655-7090 E-mail: jlquebe@mwt.net.

QUEEN, ARTHUR JEROME, glass company executive; b. Washington, Apr. 17, 1942; s. Stanley Leo and Marion Sara (Johnson) Q.; m. Mabel Luckett, Dec. 26, 1960 (div. Feb. 1980); children: Tyrone, Sherriane, Belinda, Monica, Jerome; m. Sandra Bernadine Cartwright; children: Robbie, Kelsi. Student, Prince George Community Coll., Largo, Md., 1960-61, Del. State Tchrs. Coll., 1961-62. Asst. mgr. Superior Millwork, Hyattsville, Md., 1963-69; gen. mgr. Gen. Glass Corp., Washington, 1969-85; pres. Ebony Glass and Mirror Co., Norcross, Ga., 1985—. Pres. Decatur (Ga.) United Meth. Men, 1987—, flat schools United Meth. Ch., 1987.; active Atlanta Regional Minority Purchasing Council. Mem. Nat. Glass Assn., Associated Builders and Contractors, Gwinett (Ga.) C. of C., Better Bus. Bur., Nat. Assn. Minority Contractors. Avocations: bowling, basketball.

QUEEN, DOROTHY, distribution company executive; b. Carlsbad, N.Mex., Jan. 23, 1946; m. Bill Queen (dec.); 1 child. BS in Biology, N.Mex. State U.; med. tech., Tex. Tech. Co-founder Queen Oil & Gas Co., Inc., Carlsbad, 1972—, pres. Vol. 4H, Future Farmers of Am. Avocations: being outdoors, skiing, nature, raising horses, bird watcher. Office: Queen Oil & Gas 3202 S Canal St Carlsbad NM 88220 Fax: 505-887-6485.

QUEEN, EVELYN E. CRAWFORD, retired judge; b. Albany, N.Y., Apr. 6, 1945; d. Iris (Jackson) Crawford; m. Charles A. Queen, Mar. 6, 1971; children: Angelia, George. BS, Howard U., 1968, JD, 1975. Bar: N.Y. 1976, D.C. 1977, U.S. Ct. Appeals (D.C. cir.) 1977, U.S. Dist. Ct. (D.C. dist.) 1978, U.S. Supreme Ct. 1980. Park ranger Nat. Park Svc., Washington, 1968-69; pers. specialist NIH, Bethesda, Md., 1969-75; staff atty. Met. Life Ins. Co., N.Y.C., 1975-76; atty. advisor Maritime Adminstrn.-U.S., Washington, 1976-78; asst. U.S. atty.-D.C. Justice Dept., Washington, 1978-81; hearing commr. D.C. Superior Ct., Washington, 1981-86, judge, 1986—2001, ret., 2001. Adj. law prof. Howard U., 1988, Dave Clarke Sch. Law, U. D.C., 1993, 94. Contbr. chpt. to book. Recipient spl. achievement awards HEW, 1975, Trefoil award Hudson Valley Coun. Girl Scouts U.S.A., 1988, Spl. Achievement award Dept. Justice, 1981, Sigma Delta Tau Jud. Svc. award, 2001. Mem. Nat. Bar Assn., Washington Bar Assn. Office: DC Superior Ct 500 Indiana Ave NW Washington DC 20001-2191

QUEEN, JAMES E. automotive executive; b. Zanesville, Ohio, Feb. 4, 1949; B in Aero. and Aerospace Engring., U.S. Naval Acad., 1971. Mgr. customer satisfaction and engring. Buick, 1985—86; sr. staff engr. Buick Car Group Powertrain Divsn., Detroit, 1986—88; asst. chief engr. GM, 1988—91, Bucik-Oldsmobile-Cadillac Lansing Automotive Divsn., 1991—95; engring. dir. N. Am. GM Tech. Ctr., Warren, Mich., 1995—97; group dir. engring. GM Small Car Group, 1997—99; v.p./group dir. engring. GM N. Am., 1999—2001; v.p. GM. N. Am. Engring., 2001—. Served USMC, 1971—77. Office: GM Corp Box 300 300 Renaissance Ctr Detroit MI 48265-3000

QUEEN, JOYCE ELLEN, elementary school educator; b. Cleve., Mar. 17, 1945; d. Wilbur Raynor and Mae (Reid) Closterhouse; m. Robert Graham Queen, Mar. 17, 1973. BA in Biology, Macalester Coll., 1966; MS in Conservation and Natural Resource Mgmt., U. Mich., 1968. Cert. tchr. biol. and earth scis., Ohio. Exhibitor, docent, coord. Grand Rapids (Mich.) Pub. Mus., 1967-68; tchr., naturalist Rose Tree-Media (Pa.) Outdoor Edn., 1967, Willoughby-Eastlake (Ohio) Schs., 1969-70, Independence (Ohio) Schs., 1970-78; sci. tchr. grades 1-7, coord. sci. field trip Hathaway Brown Sch., Cleve., 1970—, primary sci. educator, 1970—, primary sci. dept. chair, 1998—2002, prime sci. dept. head, 2003. Designer Courtland Woods nature trail, 1986, designer sci. greenhouse, 1990-92; designer sci. classroom Van Dyke Architects/Hathaway Brown Sch., 1990-92; designer, coord. Dampeer Primary sci. courtyard, 1993, Oliva Herb Garden, 1998, Colini Landscape Design/Hathaway Brown Sch., Shaker Hts., Ohio; mem. ednl. adv. com. William G. Mather Vessel Mus., Cleve., 1992, Holden Arboretum, Kirtland, Ohio, 1992-97; workshop leader Lake Erie Islands Hist. Mus., South Bass Island, Ohio, 1992, H.B. Winter Sci. Symposium Workshop, 1994—, Sagamore Adirondacks Great Camps Wksh, 2003; presenter Nat. Assn. Ind. Schs., Columbus, Ohio, 1993; workshop leader for schs. on garden design, sci. labs., and sci. discovery programs; youth divsn. judge Cleve. Botanic Garden Show, 1999, 2000, 2002, NOAA (with Betsy Youngman and Art Traverse) Live From Antarctica, 2003. Contbr. articles to profl. jours. Design cons. Cleve. Bot. Garden and Floral Scape, 1998; active Belize (Ctrl. Am.) Tchrs. Workshop, 1994; Sagamore Adirondack Great Camps Workshop, 2003. Catalyst grantee Hathaway Brown Sch. Gt. Lks. Curriculum, 1991; recipient Environ. Edn. award Ohio Alliance for Environment, 1986, Presdl. Excellence in Elem. Sci. Tchg. award NSF, 1992, Sheldon Exemplary Equipment and Facilities award, 1992; Great Lakes Lighthouse Keepers Assn. scholar; Marine Ecology scholar Marine Resources, Inc., 1989; Internat. Space Sta. Conf. scholar, 2000; Maine Salt Marsh Ecology Curriculum scholar, 2001; Calif. Coastal Wetlands and Desert Study scholar, 2002. Mem. NSTA (recipient Exemplary Environ. and Facilities award with Sheldon Mfg. Co. 1992), Cleve. Regional Coun. Sci. Tchrs., Cleve. Coun. Ind. Schs., Cleve. Natural Hist. Mus., Cleve. Zool. Park, Ind. Sch. Assn. Ctrl. Sts., Internat. Pen Pal Exchange Progam. Presbyterian. Avocations: orchardist, naturalist, horticulturist. Office: Hathaway Brown Sch 19600 N Park Blvd Cleveland OH 44122-1899 E-mail: jqueen@hb.edu.

QUEEN LATIFAH, (DANA OWENS), recording artist, actress; b. N.J, Mar. 18, 1970; d. Lance and Rita O. Student, Borough of Manhattan C.C. CEO Flavor Unit Entertainment. TV appearances include: Living Single, Fresh Prince of Bel Air, In Living Color, Ellen, Hangin' with Mr. Cooper, Mad TV, The Arsenio Hall Show, Mama Flora's Family, 1998, The Queen Latifah Show, 1999-2001, Spin City, 2001, (miniseries) Living with the Dead, 2002; film appearances include: House Party 2, 1991, Jungle Fever, 1991, Juice, 1992, Who's the Man, 1993, My Life, 1993, Set It Off, 1996, Hoodlum, 1997, The Wizard of Oz, 1998, Living Out Loud, 1998, Sphere, 1998, The Bone Collector, 1999, (voice) Bringing Out the Dead, 1999, The Country Bears, 2002, Brown Sugar, 2002, (voice) Pinocchio, 2002, Chicago, 2002 (Acad. award best sup. actress nom., 2003), Bringing Down the House, 2003, Scary Movie 3, Barbershop 2: Back in Business, 2004; albums include All Hail the Queen, 1990, The Nature of Sista, 1991, X-tra Naked, 1992, Black Reign, 1994, Order In The Court, 1998, She's a Queen: A Collection of Hits, 2002. Named Best New Artist, New Music Seminar, 1990, Best Female Rapper, Rolling Stone Readers' Poll, 1990; recipient Grammy award nomination, 1990, Soul Train Music award, 1995, Sammy Davis Jr. award, 1995, Entertainer of Yr. award, 1995, Grammy award for best rap solo performance, 1995. Office: Flavor Unit Entertainment 155 Morgan St Jersey City NJ 07302-2932

QUEHL, GARY HOWARD, consultant; b. Green Bay, Wis., Mar. 25, 1938; s. Howard and Virginia Babcock (Dunning) Q.; children: Scott Boyer, Catherine Mary. BA, Carroll Coll., 1960; MS, Ind. U., 1962, EdD, 1965; LHD, Buena Vista Coll., 1977, Davis and Elkins Coll., 1979; EdD (hon.), Columbia (SC) Coll., 1987. Asst. dean students Wis. State U., 1962; asst. dean coll. Wittenberg U., 1965-67; v.p., dean coll. Lindenwood Colls., St. Charles, Mo., 1967-70; exec. dir. Coll. Ctr. of the Finger Lakes, Corning, NY, 1970-74; pres. Coun. of Ind. Colls., Washington, 1974-86, Coun. for Advancement and Support of Edn., Washington, 1986-90, Quehl Assocs., 1990—. Cons. in field, 1990—. Editor, author books in field. Mem. secretariat Nat. Ctr. for Higher Edn.; bd. dirs. St. Norbert Coll., Carroll Coll., Muskingum Coll., Elmira Coll., Nat. Assn. Ind. Colls. and Univs., ind. sector, Cornell Coll. Mem. Am. Coun. Edn., Am. Conf. Acad. Deans, Nat. Panel for Women in Higher Edn., North Ctrl. Assn. Acad. Deans (past pres.) Mem. United Ch. Christ. E-mail: quehl@queasso.com.

QUELER, EVE, conductor; b. N.Y.C. Student, Mannes Coll. Music, CCNY. Music staff N.Y.C. Opera, 1958-70; assoc. condr. Ft. Wayne (Ind.) Philharm., 1970-71; founder, music dir. Opera Orch., N.Y., 1968; condr. Lake George Opera Festival, Glen Falls, N.Y., 1971-72, Oberlin (Ohio) Music Festival, 1972, Romantic Festival, Indpls., 1972, Mostly Mozart Festival, Lincoln Center, 1972, New Philharmonia, London, 1974, Teatro Liceu, Barcelona, 1974, 77, San Antonio Symphony, 1975; guest condr. Paris Radio Orch., 1972, P.R. Symphony Orch., 1975, 77, Mich. Chamber Orch., 1975, Phila. Orch., 1976, Montreal Symphony, 1977, Cleve. Orch., 1977 (Recipient Martha Baird Rockefeller Fund for Music award 1968, named Musician of Month Mus. Am. Mag. 1972), N.Y.C. Opera, 1978, Opera Las Palmas, 1978, Opera de Nice, 1979, Nat. Theatre of Prague, 1980, Opera Caracas, Venezuela, 1981, San Diego Opera, 1984, Australian Opera, Sydney, 1985, Kirov Opera, St. Petersburg, Russia, 1993, Hamburg Opera, Germany, 1994, Pretoria, South Africa, 1995, Hamilton, Ont., 1995, Hawaii Philharmonic, 1997, Hong Kong Sinfonietta, 1998, Hong Kong Philharmonic, 1999, Orch. dello Stato de Mexico, 1999-2002, Macau Festival, 2000, Festival Euro Mediteranneo, Italy, 2002; Opei Bonn, 1994-96; recording CBS Masterworks, 1974, 76, Hungaroton Records, 1982-85. Decorated Chevalier de l'ordre des Arts et des Lettres; named Woman in Music, N.Y.C., 2002; recipient Butterfly award, Licia Albanese-Puccini Foundation, 1995. Office: Opera Orch 239 W 72nd St Ste 2R New York NY 10023-2734*

QUELLA, JAMES ANDREW, merchant banker; b. Chgo., Feb. 3, 1950; s. Andrew Sylvester and Mary (Failla) Q.; children: Lindsay V., James S. BA, U. Wis., 1975; MBA, U. Chgo., 1981. Sales dir. Textron, Inc., Dallas, 1975-79; v.p. Strategic Planning Assocs., Washington, 1981-90; vice chmn. Mercer Mgmt. Consulting, N.Y.C., 1990-2000; bd. dirs. Mercer Mgmt. Cons., N.Y.C., 1996-2000; mng. dir./sr. op. ptnr. DLJ Mcht. Banking Ptnrs./CSFB Pvt. Equity, N.Y.C., 2000—04, Blackstone Group, 2004—. Bd. dirs. Columbia House Corp. Co-author: Profit Patterns, 1999; contbr. articles to profl. jours. Vol./contbr. Hale House, N.Y.C., 1996—. Avocations: golf, skiing, biking, art collection, basketball. Home: 22 W 66th St Apt 12 New York NY 10023-6202 Office: Blackstone Group 345 Park Ave New York NY 10145 Office Phone: 212-538-5019. E-mail: Quella@blackstone.com.

QUELLO, JAMES HENRY, government official; b. Laurium, Mich., Apr. 21, 1914; s. Bartholomew and Mary Katherine (Cochis) Q.; m. Mary Elizabeth Butler, Sept. 14, 1937 (dec. 1999); children: James Michael, Richard Butler. BA, Mich. State U., 1935, D of Humanities (hon.), 1977; D of Pub. Svc. (hon.), No. Mich. U., 1975. V.p., sta. mgr. Goodwill Stas., Inc., Detroit, 1947-72; v.p. Capital Cities Comm. Corp., 1968; commr. FCC, Washington, 1974—98. Comm. cons., Detroit, 1972-74; commr. Detroit Housing and Urban Renewal Commn., 1951-72 Contbr. articles to mags., newspapers. Bd. dirs. Greater Detroit Hosp. Assn.; trustee Mich. Vet. Trust Fund; mem. Gov.'s Spl. Commn. on Urban Problems, Mich., Gov.'s Spl. Study Com. on Legis. Compensation, Mayor's Com. on Human Relations; bd. dirs. Am. Negro Emancipation Centennial; mem. exec. bd. Boy Scouts Am.; TV-radio chmn. United Found. Lt. col. AUS, 1940-45. Decorated Bronze Star with oak leaf cluster, Croix de Guerre (France); recipient Internat. Pres.'s award Nat. Assn. TV Program Execs., 1985, Silver Satellite award Am. Women in Radio and TV, 1988, 93, Sol Taishoff award Washington Area Broadcasters Assn., 1989, 93, Pub. Svc. award Fed. Comm. Bar Assn., 1993, Disting. Svc. award Media Inst., 1993, Golden Eagle Amb. award Pa. Assn. Broadcasters, 1993, Disting. Alumni award Mich. State U., Club Dir. award Detroit Adcraft Club, 1993, L.I. Coalition for Fair Broadcasting award, 1993, Nat. Disting. Svc. award Nat. Assn. Pub. TV, 1993, Obie award Ohio Ednl. TV Stas., 1993, Gold Eagle Leadership award Wireless Cable Assn. Internat., 1993, Pres. award Alaska Broadcasting Assn., 1994, Chmn. award Nat. Religious Broadcasters, 1994, Ga. Broadcasters award Broadcasters of Am., 1994, 1st Amendment award Radio & TV News Dirs. Found., 1994. Mem. Nat. Assn. Broadcaster (gov. liaison com. 1964-72, Keystone award 1990, Disting. Svc. award 1994, Honor award for protecting the technical integrity of radio and TV 1994, Broadcasting Cable Hall of Fame, 1995, Nat. Radio Hall of Fame 1996), Mich. Assn. Broadcasters (pres. 1958, legis. chmn. 1959-72, dir., Outstanding Mich. Citizen 1989, Pioneer award 1994, Ellis Island honor award 1997), Greater Detroit Bd. Commerce, Sigma Alpha Epsilon. Clubs: Adcraft (Detroit); Detroit Athletic, Army and Navy Country; Nat. Press (Washington). Office: FCC Wiley Rein and Fielding 1776 K St NW Washington DC 20006-2304 Office Phone: 202-719-7052. Personal E-mail: j.Quello@wrf.com.

QUENCER, ROBERT MOORE, neuroradiologist, researcher; b. Jersey City, Nov. 14, 1937; s. Arthur Bauer and Isabell (Moore) Q.; m. Christine F. Thomas, Sept. 16, 1972; children: Kevin, Keith. BS, Cornell U., 1959, MS, 1963; MD, SUNY, Syracuse, 1967. Diplomate Am. Bd. Radiology, Nat. Bd. Med. Examiners; cert. of added qualifications in neuroradiology. Intern Jackson Meml. Hosp., Miami, Fla., 1967-68; resident in radiology Columbia U., NYC, 1968-71, fellow in neuroradiology, 1971-72; asst. prof. Downstate Med. Ctr., Bklyn., 1972-76; assoc. prof. U. Miami, 1976-79, prof., 1979 92, chmn., prof., 1992—, chief sect. neuroradiology, 1976-86, dir. divsn. magnetic resonance imaging, 1986-92, Robert Shapiro MD prof. radiology. Vis. prof. U. Tenn. Coll. Medicine, Memphis, 1982, Downstate Med. Ctr. Coll. Medicine, Bklyn., 1992, U. Vt. Coll. Medicine, Burlington, 1983, NY Med. Coll., Valhalla, 1984, U. Va. Sch. Medicine, Charlottesville, 1984, U. Ky. Sch.

Medicine, Lexington, 1985, Yale U. Sch. Medicine, New Haven, 1986, 2000, Columbia U. Sch. Medicine, NYC, 1986, The Mayo Clinic & Found., Rochester, Minn., 1987, Med. Coll. Va., Richmond, 1988, U. Pa. Sch. Medicine, Phila., 1988, Harvard U. Sch. Medicine/Mass. Gen. Hosp., Boston, 1989, U. Conn., Farmington, 1990, Kumamoto, Japan, 1993, U. Man., Can., 1992, Mich. State U., 1996, Mt. Sinai Med. Ctr., 1997, Cornell U. Sch. Medicine, 1998, U. Minn., 2001, U. Ky., 2002; UTMB Galveston, 2003; Dartmouth Hitchcock Med. Sch., 2003; Duke Univ. Sch. of Med., 2003; guest lectr. Asian Oceanic Soc. Neuroradiology, 2001, Internat. Med. Soc. Paraplegic, Lucerne, Switzerland, 2001; Phaler lectr. Phila. Roentgen Soc., 1995; dir. programs in dept. radiology U. Miami Sch. Medicine, 1984, 86, Med. Coll. Wis., 1990, 92, Kauai, Hawaii, 1991, Whistler, B.C., 1990; guest lectr. at ASEAN Congress of Radiology, Malaysia, 1992, Royal Australia Radiology Soc., Brisbane, 1993, Brazilian Congress Neurology, 1996, NY Roentgen Soc., 1997, Somerset MR course, Torquay, UK, 1998, Republic of China, 1999, Yale U., 2000, U. Minn., 2001, U. Tex., 2003, Duke U., 2003; adv. cons. NIH, 1987, 90; sci. merit reviewer V.A., 1987; presenter, lectr. in field. Author: Neurosonography, 1988; dep. editor Am. Jour. Neuroradiology, 1984-96, editor-in-chief, 1998—; assoc. editor for neuroimaging Yearbook of Neurology and Neurosurgery, 1991—; manuscript reviewer Am. Jour. Neuroradiology, 1984—, Paraplegia, 1989—, Radiographics, 1991—, Pediatrics, 1993—, Radiology, 1994—; mem. editl. bd. Jour. Clin. Neuro-Ophthalmology, 1980-90; contbr. articles to profl. jours. Pres. Am. Soc. Neuroadiology, 1994-95; prin. investigator NIH Grant on imaging/pathology of spinal cord injury; chmn. Commn. Neuroradiological Socs. World Fedn. Neuroradiology Soc., 2003-, Neuroradiology Sci. Program Com. Radiological Soc. North Am., Scientific RSNA Program, dir. for neuroradiology, 2004-; Lt. (j.g.) USN, 1959-61. Fellow Am. Coll. Radiology, Am. Soc. Neuroradiology (pres. 1994-95, program com. 1985-89, 92, editl. com. 1984—, publs. com. 1984—); mem. AMA, Radiol. Soc. N.Am. (program subcom. on neuroradiology 1990-94), Southeastern Neuroradiol. Soc. (founder, pres. 1980-81, examiner for bd. certification in radiology and neuroradiology), Fla. Radiol. Soc. (magnetic resonance com. 1991-92), Alpha Omega Alpha. Avocations: golf, travel. Office: U Miami 1150 NW 14th St Miami FL 33136-2137 E-mail: rquencer@med.miami.edu.

QUENEAU, PAUL ETIENNE, metallurgical engineer, educator; b. Phila., Mar. 20, 1911; s. Augustin L. and Jean (Blaisdell) Q.; m. Joan Osgood Hodges, May 20, 1939; children: Paul Blaisdell, Josephine Downs (Mrs. George Stanley Patrick). BA, Columbia U., 1931, BSc, 1932, M of Engring., 1933; postgrad., Cambridge (Eng.) U., 1934; DSc, Delft (Netherlands) U. Tech., 1971. With INCO, 1934-69; rsch. supt. Internat. Nickel Co., 1940-41, 46-48, v.p., 1958-69, chief tech. officer, tech. asst. to pres., 1960-66, asst. to chmn., 1967-69; vis. scientist Delft U. Tech., 1970-71; prof. engring. Dartmouth Coll., 1971-87, prof. emeritus, 1987—, Paul and Joan Queneal prof. in environ. design. Cons. engr., 1972—; vis. prof. U. Minn., 1974-75, U. Utah, 1987-91; geographer Perry River Arctic Expdn., 1949; chmn. arctic rsch. adv. com. USN, 1957; gov. Arctic Inst. N.Am., 1957-62; mem. engring. coun. Columbia U., 1965-70; mem. vis. com. MIT, Cambridge, 1967-70; mem. extractive metallurgy and mineral processing panels NAS; pres. Q-S Oxygen Processes Inc., 1974-79, also bd. dirs. Author: (with Hanson) Geography, Birds and Mammals of the Perry River Region, 1956; Cobalt and the Nickeliferous Limonites, 1971; editor: Extractive Metallurgy of Copper, Nickel and Cobalt, 1961; (with Anderson) Pyrometallurgical Processes in Nonferrous Metallurgy, 1965; The Winning of Nickel, 1967; contbr. articles to profl. jours.; patentee 500 internat. patents, 36 U.S. patents including processes and apparatus employed in the pyrometallurgy, hydrometallurgy and vapometallurgy of nickel, copper, cobalt, lead, zinc, iron and steel, extractive metallurgy oxygen tech. including INCO oxygen flash smelting, oxygen top-blown rotary converter, lateritic ore matte smelting, nickel high pressure carbonyl and iron ore recovery processes; co-inventor Lurgi QSL direct lead-making, QSOP direct coppermaking and nickelmaking reactors, Lurgi direct steelmaking reactors, and Dravo oxygen sprinkle smelting copper furnaces. Bd. dirs. Engring. Found., 1966-76, chmn. bd. dirs., 1973-75. With U.S. Army, 1942-45, ETO; col. C.E., USA ret.1971. Decorated Bronze Star, ETO Medal with 5 Battlestars, Army Commendation Medal USAR, 1937-42; Evans Fellow Cambridge U., 1933-34; recipient Egleston Medal Columbia U., 1965, Fletcher Award Dartmouth Coll., 1991, McGraw-Hill Chem. Engring. Award for Personal Achievement in Chem. Engring., 1996. Fellow Metall. Soc. of AIME (dir. 1964, 68-71, pres. 1969, Extractive Metallurgy Lecture award 1977, Paul E. Queneau TMS Internat. Symposium on Extractive Metallurgy of Copper, Nickel and Cobalt 1993); mem. AIME (Douglas Gold medal 1968, v.p. 1970, dir. 1968-71, Henry Krumb lectr. 1984, keynote lectr. ann. meeting 1990, award for personal achievement in chem. engring.), NAE, NSPE, Can. Inst. Mining and Metallurgy, Inst. Mining and Metallurgy U.K. (overseas mem. council 1970-80, Gold medal 1980), Sigma Xi, Tau Beta Pi. Achievements include 36 U.S. patents and 500 foreign patents. Office: Dartmouth Coll Thayer Sch Engring Hanover NH 03755

QUENNELL, NICHOLAS, landscape architect, educator; b. London, Sept. 30, 1935; s. Cecil William and Beatrice Irene Quennell; m. Grace Tankersley, Apr. 30, 1983. AA, Archtl. Assn., London, 1957; MLA, Harvard U., 1969. Registered architect, N.Y., Pa., N.J., Conn., U.K.; registered landscape architect, N.Y., N.J., Conn., Mass., N.C. Architect London County Coun., 1959-61, Jose Luis Sert, Cambridge, Mass., 1961-62, Lawrence Halprin & Assocs., San Francisco, 1962-65, Vollmer Assocs., N.Y.C., 1965-68; prin. Nicholas Quennell Assocs., N.Y.C., 1968-79, Quennell Rothschild Assocs., N.Y.C., 1979-97, Quennell, Rothschild & Ptnrs., N.Y.C., 1998—. V.p. The Mcpl. Art Soc. (dir. 1978-85), N.Y.C., 1985-92, dir. The Archtl. League, N.Y.C., 1984-89. Bd. dirs. Nat. Assn. for Olmsted Pks., Washington, 1988-90, chmn., 1990-93; mem. Art Commn. of City of N.Y., 1992-97, pres., 1993-97. Fellow Am. Soc. of Landscape Architects; mem. Century Assn. Office: Quennell Rothschild & Ptnrs 118 W 22nd St New York NY 10011-2416 E-mail: quennell@qrpartners.com.

QUENNEVILLE, JOEL, professional hockey coach; b. Windsor, Ont., Can., Sept. 15, 1958; m. Elizabeth Quenneville; children: Dylan, Lily, Anna. Hockey player, player coach St. John's Maple Leafs, 79-92; head coach Springfield Indians, Am. Hockey League, 1993-94; asst. coach Colorado Avalanche, 1995-96; head coach St. Louis Blues, 1997—2004, Colorado Avalanche, 2004—. Named Most Valuable Defensemen, 1985, 86, Coach of Yr., NHL, 1999-2000. Office: c/o Colorado Avalanche Pepsi Center 1000 Chopper Circle Denver CO 80204*

QUENNEVILLE, KATHLEEN, lawyer; b. Mt. Clemens, Mich., July 31, 1953; d. Marcel J. and Patricia (Armstrong) Q. BA, Mich. State U., 1975; JD, Golden Gate U., 1979. Bar: Calif. 1980. Atty. Wells Fargo Bank, San Francisco, 1980-81; staff counsel Calif. State Banking Dept., San Francisco, 1981-83; assoc. Manatt, Phelps, Rothenburg & Tunney, Los Angeles, 1983-84; v.p., assoc. gen. counsel Bank of Calif., San Francisco, 1984-96; sr. v.p., gen. counsel The Mechanics Bank, Richmond, Calif., 1996—. Asst treas. AIDS Legal Referral Panel of the San Francisco Bay Area, 1986-92. Mem. Calif. State Bar Assn. (bus. law sect. corp. law depts. com. 1988-90), Calif. Bankers Assn. (chair regulatory compliance com. 1994-96, legal affairs com. 1996—). Office: The Mechanics Bank 3170 Hilltop Mall Rd Richmond CA 94806-5231

QUENON, ROBERT HAGERTY, retired mining consultant and holding company executive; b. Clarksburg, W.Va., Aug. 2, 1928; s. Ernest Leonard and Josephine (Hagerty) Q.; m. Jean Bowling, Aug. 8, 1953; children: Evan, Ann, Richard. BS in Mining Engring., W.Va. U., 1951; LL.B., George Washington U., 1964; PhD (hon.), U. Mo., 1979, Blackburn Coll., 1983, W.Va. U., 1988. Mine supt. Consol. Coal Co., Fairmont, W.Va., 1956-61; mgr. deep mines Pittston Co., Dante, Va., 1964-66; gen. mgr. Riverton Coal Co., Crown Hill, W.Va., 1966-67; mgr. ops. coal and shale oil dept. Exxon Co., Houston, 1967; pres. Monterey Coal Co., Houston, 1969-76; sr. v.p. Carter Oil Co., Houston, 1976-77; exec. v.p. Peabody Coal Co., St. Louis, 1977-78, pres., chief exec. officer, 1978-83, Peabody Holding Co., Inc., St. Louis, 1983-90, chmn., 1990-91. Bd. dirs. Newmont Mining Co., Denver, Ameren Corp., St. Louis, Laclede Steel Co., St. Louis, Miss. Lime Co., Alton, Ill.; bd. dirs., chmn. Fed. Res. Bank St. Louis, 1993-95, dep. chmn., 1990-92; mem. coal industry adv. bd. Internat. Energy Agy., 1980-97, bd. chmn., 1984-90; chmn. Bituminous Coal Operator's Assn., 1980-83, 89-91. Trustee Blackburn Coll., Carlinville, Ill., 1975-83, St. Louis U., 1981-91; pres. St. Louis Art Mus., 1985-88. Served with AUS, 1946-47. Recipient Eavenson award Soc. Mining, Metallurgy, and Exploration, 1994, Erskine Ramsay award Am. Inst. Mining, Metallurg. and Petroleum Engrs., 1985. Mem. Am. Mining Congress (vice-chmn. 1980-91), Nat. Coal Assn. (chmn. bd. 1978-80), U.S. C. of C. (dir. 1982-88). Office: PO Box 11328 Saint Louis MO 63105-0128

QUENTEL, ALBERT DREW, lawyer; b. Miami, Fla., Nov. 27, 1934; s. Charles Edward Jr. and Alberta Amelia (Drew) Q.; m. Paula Staelin Hagar, Feb. 9, 1957 (dec. Mar. 1998); children: Albert D. Jr., Stephen C., Marshall Lee, Paul G., Peter E., Michael J. BA, U. Fla., 1956, JD with honors, 1959. Bar: Fla. 1959. Assoc. Mershon, Sawyer, Johnston, Dunwody & Cole, Miami, 1959-64, ptnr., 1965-71; prin., shareholder Greenberg Traurig P.A., Miami, 1971—. Editor-in-chief U. Fla. Law Rev., 1959; contbg. author: Florida Real Property Practice, 1965, Real Estate Partnerships Selected Problems and Solutions, 1991, Commercial Real Estate Finance, 1993. Mem. Gov.'s Growth Mgmt. Adv. Com., Tallahassee, 1985-87; bd. dirs. Nat. Parkinson Found., Miami, 1980-98, v.p., 1985-97. Mem. NRA (life 1989—), Am. Coll. Real Estate Lawyers, Fla. Bar Assn. (chmn. pub. rels. com. 1970-72, chmn. editorial com. jour. 1972-73), Lions (pres. Key Biscayne, Fla. club 1973), Miami Club (pres. 1991-92), Bath Club, Blue Key, Beta Theta Pi (pres. local chpt. 1954-55), Phi Eta Sigma, Phi Kappa Phi. Republican. Congregationalist. Avocations: reading, shooting, photography. Home: 825 Algeria Ave Miami FL 33134-2401 Office: Greenberg Traurig 1221 Brickell Ave Miami FL 33131-3224 E-mail: QuentelA@gtlaw.com.

QURESHI, MOHAMMED YOUNUS, psychology educator, consultant; b. Haripur Hazara, Pakistan, Dec. 12, 1929; came to U.S., 1953; s. Mohammed Noor and Meryam Khatoon Q.; m. Nora Jane Knapp, May 27, 1958 (div. Nov. 1979); children: Ahmed, Amna, Shukria, Shawn; m. Farzana Kaukab, May 17, 1980; children: Ajmel, Sabeeha, Azem. PhD, U. Ill., 1958. Lic. psychologist, Wis.; diplomate Am. Bd. Psychol. Spltys. Asst. prof. psychology U. Minn., Duluth, 1960-62, U. N.D., Grand Forks, 1962-64; assoc. prof. psychology Marquette U., Milw., 1964-70, prof., 1970—2003, prof. emeritus psychology, 2003—, chmn. dept. psychology, 1971-77. Cons. psychologist. Author: Statistics and Behavior: An Introduction, 1980, 2d edit., 1991; contbr. articles to sci. and profl. jours. Pres. 81st St. Sch. PTA, 1968-70; merit badge counselor Milw. County coun. Boy Scouts Am., 1973-88; pres. Islamic Assn. Greater Milw., 1978-83. Grantee NIH, 1962-69; Office of Edn., 1970-71, TOPS Club, 1969-76. Mem. Am. Psychol. Assn., Psychometric Soc., Sigma Xi. Home: 15660 Monet Ct Brookfield WI 53005-5125 Office: Marquette U Schroeder Health Complex PO Box 1881 Milwaukee WI 53201-1881 Office Phone: 414-288-7468.

QUERIN, JEFFREY DAVID, theater educator; b. Youngstown, Ohio, Apr. 20, 1973; s. David Jon and Susan Jane Querin. BS in Drama, Evangel U., Springfield, Mo., 1996; BBA in Mktg., Evangel U., 1996; MA, NYU, N.Y.C., 2004. Actor-tchr. Gt. Lakes Theater Festival, Cleve., 1996—97; pub. rels. and performance A.D. Players, Houston, 1997—98; artistic dir. 34west Theater Co., Boardman, Ohio, 2000—. Actor-tchr. Stages Repertory Theatre, Houston, 2003—03. Actor: (performance) Much Ado About Nothing, Folktale Journeys at the Provencetown Playhouse, The Glass Menagerie, Everyman; dir.: The Little Prince. Missions bd. Old North Ch., Canfield, Ohio, 2002—03. Scholar various sch. and deptl. scholarships, Evangel U., 1991—96, Deptl. scholar, NYU, 2003—04. Mem.: Drama League. Home: 7950 Market St #12 Boardman OH 44512 Personal E-mail: jeffquerin@hotmail.com.

QUESENBERRY, KENNETH HAYS, agronomy educator; b. Springfield, Tenn., Feb. 28, 1947; s. James William and Cora Geneva (Moore) Quesenberry; m. Joyce Ann Kaze; children: James Kenneth, Kendra Joyce. BS, Western Ky. U., 1969; PhD, U. Ky., 1975. D.F. Jones predoctoral fellow U. Ky., Lexington, 1972—75; asst. prof. U. Fla., Gainesville, 1975—80, assoc. prof. agronomy, 1980—86, prof. agronomy, 1986—. Contbr. articles to profl. jours. Served with U.S. Army, 1969—71, Vietnam. Fellow: Crop Sci. Soc. Am. (chair divsn. C-8 1993—94), Am. Soc. Agronomy. Achievements include research in germplasm enhancement of forages with release of four cultivars of tropical grasses and three clovers and genetic transformation of clovers; specialist Trifolium species germplasm. Avocations: sports, antique furniture refinishing. Office: U Fla PO Box 110500 Gainesville FL 32611-0500 Office Phone: 351-392-1811 ext. 213. E-mail: clover@ifas.ufl.edu.

QUESINBERRY, BONITA MAE, counselor, writer, editor; d. Perry Bennett Quesinberry and Esta Mae Lamb; children: Contrina Monique Williamson-(dec.), Angelique Desiree Williamson(dec.), Esta Maria Willliamson, James Lee Williamson. Student, U. Tex., 1965, N.E. Tarrant County C.C., Ft. Worth, 1979—82; BA, Real Estate Career Coll., Dallas, 1985. Registered counselor Wash. Exec sec. to pres. Grapevine (Tex.) Nat. Bank, 1977—79; jr. loan officer Meadowbrook Nat. Bank, Ft Worth, 1979—82; legal sec. Earl King, Atty. at Law, Ft Worth, 1982—83; paralegal Edward Sartain, Atty. at Law, Ft Worth, 1983—84; tchr. Real Estate Career Coll., Dallas, 1984—86; fin. officer, adminstrv. mgr. King County Water Dist. No. 19, Vashon Island, Wash., 1987—97; assoc. editor Waltsan Pub., Ft Worth, 2002—. Author: Shades of The Rainbow, 2003; featured author Buzzle eZine. Counselor, author Unicorn Haven, 1997—. Recipient Editor's Choice award, Iliad Press, 1990. Master: Truth Seekers and Spkrs. (life; prin. spkr. 2002); mem.: Authors' Den. Avocations: helping others, reading, crocheting, gardening, interior decorating. Office: Unicorn Haven 60 NE River Rd Tahuya WA 98588-9769 Office Phone: 360-275-5962. E-mail: unicornhaven@earthlink.net.

QUESNEL, GREGORY L. transportation company executive; b. Woodburn, Oreg., May 24, 1948; BA in Finance, U. Oregon; MA in Bus. Adminstrn., U. Portland; grad. Exec. Program in Bus. Adminstrn., Columbia U. Dir. fin. acctg. Consolidated Freightways, Portland, 1975-78, dir. mgmt. and cost acctg., 1978-86; fin. officer CF MotorFreight, Consolidated Freightways, Portland, 1986-89; v.p. acctg. Emery Worldwide, Consolidated Freightways, Scranton, Pa., 1989-91; exec. v.p., CFO CNF Transp. Inc., Palo Alto, Calif., 1991-97, pres., CEO, 1997—. Mem.: Chief Fin. Execs. (conf. bds. coun., conf. bds. coun. of fin. execs.), Fin. Exec. Inst. E-mail: colvert.nancy@cnf.com.

QUEST, DONALD O. neurological surgeon; b. St. Louis, Nov. 20, 1939; s. Oliver Harry and Elaine Elsie (Henderson) Q.; m. Ilona Maris, July 20, 1969; children: Wendy Elaine, Amy Ilona, Susan Elissa. BS, U. Ill., 1961; MD, Columbia U., 1970. Diplomate Am. Bd. Neurol. Surgery. Intern Mass. Gen. Hosp., Boston, 1970-71, resident, 1971-72, Neurol. Inst. N.Y., N.Y.C., 1972-76; attending neurosurgeon Downstate Med. Coll., Bklyn., 1976-78, Columbia U., N.Y.C., 1978—; chair. Am. Bd. Neurological Surgery, Houston. Past pres. Congress Neurosurgery, 1986-87; sec. Am. Bd. Neurosurgery, 1996—. Pres. Bd. Edn., N.J., 1980-86. Lt. USN, 1961-66. Mem. Neurol. Soc. Am., Am. Acad. Neurol. Surgery, Am. Assn. Neurol. Surgery, Congress Neurol. Surgeons, Soc. Neurol. Surgeons. Avocations: literature, music. Office: Neurol Inst NY 710 W 168th St New York NY 10032-2603

QUEST, KRISTINA KAY, art educator, small business owner; b. Fort Atkinson, Wis., Sept. 22, 1952; d. Duane and Kiwa (Kikuchi) Tessman; m. Michael Charles Quest, July 28, 1973; children: Jennifer, Eric, Sarah. BS in Art Edn., U. Wis., 1992; student, U. Wis., Whitewater, 2002—. Lic. tchr., Wis. Substitute tchr., various cities, 1993-97, 99—; summer sch. tchr. Ft. Atkinson Sch. Dist., 1993-97; art tchr. 7th and 8th grade St. Peter's Luth. Sch., Helenville, Wis., 1997; tchr., kindergarten day care tchr. 1st Class Presch., before/after sch. day care at Prospect Elem., Lake Mills, Wis., 1997—99; owner The Oriental Quest, Oshkosh, Wis., 2000—01, Back Acres Mobile Home Park, Oshkosh, Wis., 2000—; art tchr. Wis. Career Acad., Milwaukee, 2002—03; substitute tchr. Lake Mills (Wis.) Sch. Dist., 2003—04; sch. yr. vol. counselor Christian Alpha Life Resource Ctr., 2003—04. Past mem. Jefferson Arts Coun., bd. dirs., 1976-90; workshop fine arts fair judge Lakeside Luth. H.S., Lake Mills, Wis., 1991-92; art fair judge for Fort Fest, Fort Atkinson, Crafters, 1993; owner mobile home park, substitute tchr. Johnson Creek (Wis.) Sch. Dist., Wis. Career Acad., Milw., 2002-03, 6-10th grade art tchr. Author/illustrator: (book) Tiannamen Square, China's Dark Hours, 1987 (Juried Art Show 1993). Participant art donator AIDS Wellness Auction, The Globe, Oshkosh, 1999. Recipient art award Wis. Regional Arts Program/Waukesha Creative Arts League, Madison, 1993. Mem. Wis. Art Edn. Assn., Nat. Art Edn. Assn., Women in the Arts Nat. Mus., Japanese Am. Pub. Mus., U. of Wis.-Whitewater Alumni Assn., Student Tchr.'s Assn. Lutheran. Avocations: watercolor, sculpting, painting, Japanese sumi brush-stroke painting, block printing. Office: 105 Aztalan St Johnson Creek WI 53038-9666 Office Phone: 920-699-8533. Business E-Mail: mkquest@tds.net.

QUESTER, GEORGE HERMAN, political science educator; b. Bklyn., July 14, 1936; s. Jacob George and Elizabeth (Mattern) Q.; m. Aline Marie Olson, June 20, 1964; children: Theodore, Amanda. AB, Columbia U., 1958; MA, Harvard U., 1964, PhD, 1965. Instr., then asst. prof. govt. Harvard U., 1965-70; assoc. prof. govt. Cornell U., 1970-73, prof., 1973-82; prof. polit. sci. U. Md., College Park, 1982—. Vis. prof. U.S. Naval Acad., Annapolis, Md., 1991-93. Author: Deterrence Before Hiroshima, 1966, Nuclear Diplomacy, 1970, The Politics of Nuclear Proliferation, 1973, The Continuing Problem of International Relations, 1974, Offense and Defense in the International System, 1977, American Foreign Policy: The Lost Consensus, 1982, The Future of Nuclear Deterrence, 1986, The International Politics of Television, 1990, Nuclear Monopoly, 2000, Before And After The Cold War, 2002. Served with USAF, 1958-61. Fellow Center Advanced Study Behavioral Scis., 1974-75 Mem. Council Fgn. Relations, Inst. Strategic Studies, Am. Polit. Sci. Assn. Home: 5124 37th St N Arlington VA 22207-1862 Office: Univ Md 3140 Tydings College Park MD 20742-0001 Business E-Mail: gqueste@gvpt.umd.edu.

QUESTROM, ALLEN I. retail executive; b. Newton, Mass., Apr. 13, 1941; s. Irving Allen and Natalie (Chadbourne) Questrom; m. Kelli Questrom. BS, Boston U., 1964. From exec. trainee to div. mdse. mgr. Abraham & Straus, Bklyn., 1965-73; v.p., gen. mdse. mgr. home store Bullock's, L.A., 1973-74, sr. v.p., gen. mdse. mgr. all stores, 1974-77; exec. v.p. Bullock's div. Federated Dept. Stores, L.A., 1977-78, pres. Rich's div. Atlanta, 1978-80, chmn. bd., chief exec. officer, 1980-84, chmn. bd., chief exec. officer Bullock's/Bullocks Wilshire div., 1984-88, corp. exec. v.p. Cin., 1987-88, vice-chmn., 1988; also chmn., CEO Allied Stores Corp., Cin., 1990-97; pres., CEO Neiman Marcus Group Inc., Dallas, 1988-90; chmn., CEO Federated Dept. Stores Inc., Cin., 1990-97; chmn., pres., CEO Barneys New York, 1999—2000; chmn., CEO J.C. Penney Co., Inc., Plano, Tex., 2000—. Prin. AEA Investors Inc.; ptnr. Mellon Ventures. Avocations: skiing; golf; travel. Office: JC Penney Corp Inc 6501 Legacy Dr Plano TX 75024-3698*

QUETGLAS, MOLL JUAN, plastic and maxillofacial surgeon; b. Cuidadela, Menorca, Spain, Feb. 11, 1922; s. Honesto Quetglas Montserrat and Catalina Moll Coll; m. Conception Marimon Alvarez; children: Juan, Alfonso, Carlos. Degree, U. Barcelona, Spain, 1945; MD, U. Madrid, 1970. Diplomate Bd. Plastic Surgery, Bd. Maxillofacial Surgery and Plastic and Reconstructive Surgery, Bd. Gen. Surgery and Traumatology. Gen. practice medicine, Mahon, Spain, 1945-52; resident in gen. surgery Madrid, 1953-55; head surg. svc. Mil. Hosp., Larache, Morocco, 1955-59, Tenerife, Canary Island, 1960-61, Social Security, Madrid, 1962-84; head plastic surgery svc. Ctrl. Mils. Hosp., Madrid, 1962-87; prof. U. Madrid, 1978-87. Dir. hosps. Social Security, 1968-71; mem. exec. com. I.S.A.P.S., 1975-76; prof. anatomy Med. Sch., Salamanca (Spain) U., 1972; asst. plastic surgery svc. Walter Reed Hosp., Washington, 1969. Author: Brief Handbook of Plastic and Aesthetic Surgery of the Face, 1971, Plastic Surgery: Three Steps in its Evolution, 1999; co-author: Treatise of Medical Rehabilitation, 1967, 2d edit., 1970, Iberoamerican Text of Plastic Surgery, 1986, 2d edit., 1994, Art of Aesthetic Plastic Surgery, 1989, Uloracion de las Secuelas Traumaticas en el Aparato Locomotor, 1995, Rehabilitacion Media-Editorial Masson, 1996; dir., founder Spanish Jour. Plastic Surgery, 1968-76; hon. dir. Jour. Plastic Jour., 1983; editor: Facial Traumatology, 1983; dir. Jour. Ibero-L.Am. Jour. Plastic Surgery, 1975-2000; contbr. over 100 articles to med. jours.; co-translator (book) Aesthetic Rhinoplasty (written by Dr. Aiach). Col. M.C., Spanish Army, 1987. Recipient Ex-Combatiente, Donador de Sangre, Cruz de San Hermenegildo, Placa de San Hermenegildo, Cruz del Merito Militar, Spanish Army Min., medal Complutense U. Madrid; named Illustrious Citizen City Coun. Ciudadela, 2002. Mem. Internat. Confedn. Plastic Surgery, Spanish Soc. Plastic Surgery (mem. exec. com. 1969-71, pres. 1972-74), Plastic Surgery Soc. Ecuador (hon.), Plastic Surgery Soc. Argentina (hon.), Plastic Surgery Soc. Chile (hon.), Spanish Soc. Traumatology, Assn. Mil. Plastic Surgeons, Assn. Mil. Surgeons, Acad. Surgery Madrid, N.Y. Acad. Scis., Helenic Soc. Plastic Reconstructive Surgery, Revista Palstic Surgery Am. Ibero-Latinamerican (hon. dir.), Spanish Plastic Surgery Soc. (hon.). appointed Ciudadelono Illustrious by Coun. (ciudodela). E-mail: cirplast@teleline.es., jquet@grupobbva.net.

QUEVEDO, HECTOR ADOLF, operations research specialist, environmental scientist; b. Juarez, Mexico, June 25, 1940; arrived in U.S.A., 1973. s. Robert and Margaret (Urias) Quevedo Endlich; m. Gloria (Guijarro), June 2, 1971; children: Gloria, Hector. BA, U. Tex., El Paso, 1966; MS in Environ. Sci., U. Okla., 1972, PhD in Environ. Sci., 1977. Part time instr. math. U. Tex., El Paso, 1977—80; environ. engr. El Paso Natural Gas Co., El Paso, 1978—79; systems analyst U.S. Army, White Sands Missile Range, N.Mex., 1980—84, Ft. Bliss, Tex., 1985—98; ret., 1998. Instr. environ. engring. and stats., rschr. Univ. Autonoma de Juarez, Juarez, Mexico, 1998. Author: Una Nueva Filosofía Médica Racionalist, 1998. Democrat. Avocations: classical music, reading, outdoor recreation, writing. Home: 11148 Voyager Cove St El Paso TX 79936-3007 Office Phone: 915-594-0896. Personal E-mail: hqnatura@aol.com.

QUIAMBAO, DALISAY LELAY, dietician, consultant, surveyor; b. Catanduanes, The Philippines, July 10, 1945; came to U.S., 1970; d. Patricio and Concepcion (Aldave) Lelay; m. Enrique Quiambao, Dec. 10, 1967 (div. Aug. 1989); children: Larry, Edwin, Cheryl. BS in Nutrition, Philippine Women's U., Manila, 1966; postgrad., U. N.C., Greensboro, 1976-78. Cafeteria mgr. Durham County Schs., Durham, N.C., 1973-78; dietetic technician Murdoch Ctr., Butner, N.C., 1978-80, clin. dietitian, 1980-84, adminstrv. dietitian, 1984-86; dir. food svc. N.C. Spl. Care Ctr., Wilson, 1986-88; dietitian cons. Granville (N.C.) Med. Ctr., 1985-86; dietitian cons. div. facility svcs. N.C. Dept. Human Resources, Raleigh, 1988—. Foodsvc. cons. Classic Food Svcs., Durham, 1989-90; dietary cons. Coordinating Coun. for Sr. Citizens, Durham, 1990-91; dietitian cons. Meals on Wheels, Interim Health Care Corp.; instr. Durham Tech. Community Coll., 1990. Recipient cert. for pub. mgr. program N.C. Office State Pers., 1987, svc. award N.C. Dept. Human Resources, 1988. Mem. Am. Dietetic Assn. (registered), N.C. Dietetic Assn., Am. Heart Assn., Philippine Am. Assn. N.C. Roman Catholic. Avocations: reading, baking, arts and crafts, developing recipes, volunteering. Home: 503 Windcrest Rd Durham NC 27713-6224 Office: NC Dept Human Resources Div Facility Svcs 701 Barbour Dr Raleigh NC 27603-2008

QUIAT, GERALD M. lawyer; b. Denver, Jan. 9, 1924; s. Ira L. and Esther (Greenblatt) Q.; m. Roberta M. Nicholson, Sept. 26, 1962; children: James M., Audrey R., Melinda A., Daniel P., Ilana L., Leonard E. AA, U. Calif., Berkeley, 1942; AB, LLB, U. Denver, 1948, changed to JD, 1970. Bar: Colo. 1948, Fed. Ct. 1948, U.S. Dist. Ct. Colo. 1948, U.S. Ct. Appeals (10th cir.) 1948, U.S. Surpeme Ct. 1970. Dep. dist. atty. City and Co. of Denver, Colo., 1949-52; partner firm Quiat, Seeman & Quiat, Denver, 1952-67, Quiat & Quiat (later changed to Quiat, Bucholtz & Bull, P.C.), 1968; pres. Quiat, Bucholtz & Bull & Laff, P.C. (and predecessors), Denver, 1968-85; pvt. practice Denver, 1985—. Bd. dirs., past chmn. audit com. Guaranty Bank & Trust Co., Denver. Past trustee Holding Co.; pres., chmn. bd. dirs. Rose Med. Ctr., Denver, 1976—79; mem. Colo. Civil Rights Com., 1963—71, chmn., 1966—67, 1969—70, hearing officer, 1963—71; bd. dirs. AMC Cancer Rsch. Ctr., Denver, 1971—, chmn. bd., 1991—93, sec. treas., 2000—; chmn. bd. Am. Med. Ctr., 1993—95; mem. nat. civil rights com. Anti-Defamation League, hon. mem. nat. exec. com., hon. nat. commr.; chmn. Mountain State region, 1980—82; mem. exec. com., bd. mem. Mountain States region Anti-Defamation League. With inf. U.S. Army, 1942—45. Decorated Combat Infantry Badge, Bronze Star. Mem. ABA, Colo. Bar Assn., Colo. Trial Lawyers Assn. (pres. 1970-71), Am. Legion (comdr. Leyden-Chiles-

Wickersham post 1 1955-56, past judge adv. Colo. dept.). Home: 5361 Nassau Cir E Englewood CO 80110-5100 Office: Penthouse Suite 1720 S Bellaire St Denver CO 80222-4304 E-mail: gqph@aol.com.

QUICK, ALBERT THOMAS, lawyer, educator; b. Battle Creek, Mich., June 28, 1939; s. Robert and Vera Quick; m. Brenda Jones; children: Lori, Traci, Becki, Breton, Regan, Leigh. BA, U. Ariz., 1962; MA, Cen. Mich. U., 1964; JD, Wayne State U., 1967; LLM, Tulane U., 1974. Bar: Mich. 1968. Asst. prosecutor Calhoun County, Marshall, Mich., 1968-69; assoc. Hatch & Hatch, Marshall, 1969-70; asst. prof. U. Maine, Augusta, 1970-73; prof. law U. Louisville, 1974-87, spl. asst. to univ. provost, 1983-87; dean, prof. law Ohio No. U., Ada, 1987-95; prof. law, dean U. Toledo, 1995-99, dean and prof. emeritus, 1999—; of counsel Smith Haughey Rice & Roegge, Traverse City, Mich., 2002—. Vis. prof. Mich. State U. Law Sch., 2000, Barry U. Law Sch., 2004. Co-author: Update Federal Rules of Criminal Procedure; contbr. articles to profl. jours. Trustee Traverse Dist. Libr.; sec. bd. Human Rights Commn., co-chair; bd. visitors Wayne State U., 2003—; Mich. Bar standing com. Justice Initiatives, 2003—. Recipient Medallion of Justice Nat. Bar Assn., 1995. Mem. ABA, ACLU, Mich. State Bar Assn., Willis Soc., Ohio State Bar Assn., Phi Kappa Phi, Coif. Episcopalian. Avocations: golf, art, reading. Office: 202 E State St Traverse City MI 49685-0848 Office Phone: 231-929-4878. E-mail: atquick@charter.net.

QUICK, DANNY RICHARD, computer systems engineer; b. Millen, Ga., Aug. 7, 1948; s. John Francis and Olene (Crane) Q.; m. Donna Kay Nobles, Oct. 13, 1973; children: Dexter Brian, Debby Kim. Cert. data processing, Strayer Coll., Arlington, Va., 1989. Enlisted USAF, 1967, advanced through grades to sr. master sgt., 1984; chief Message Processing Br. Orgn. Joints Chiefs of Staff, Pentagon, Washington, 1984-88, ret., 1988; systems analyst Potomac Systems Engring., Annandale, Va., 1988-89; sr. systems cons. Wang Labs., Inc., Bethesda, Md., 1989-93; prin. systems engr. Computer Scis. Corp., Falls Church, Va., 1993—2002; computer specialist Dept. of State, Washington, 2002—. Mem. methods & procedures panel U.S. Mil. Comm.-Electronics Bd., Washington, 1984-88, mem. call signs panel, 1984-88. Recipient Def. Meritorious Svc. medal Sec. Def., Washington, 1987, Meritorious Svc. medal Sec. Air Force, Washington, 1980; named one of 50 Outstanding Airmen of Yr., Airforce Mil. Pers. Ctr., Randolph AFB, Tex., 1983-84. Mem. Am. Legion (exec. com. 1984-86, editor Post-O-Gram, 1983-84). Republican. Methodist. Achievements include the merge of the principal officers e-mail system and the foreign affairs information systems networks; led the Dept. of State test and deploy team in testing and deploying a Lotus Notes locally developed database program, which is installed on a Microsoft Windows NT/2000 LAN, for distributing inbound and transmitting outbound diplomatic telegrams, throughout the Department of State and at American embassies and consulates worldwide. Home: 4 Caledon Ct Stafford VA 22556-1608 Office: Dept of State IRM/OPS/MSO/MSP/TD 7374 Boston Blvd Springfield VA 22153-2804

QUICK, EDWARD RAYMOND, museum director, educator, curator; b. L.A., Mar. 22, 1943; s. Donald Russell Quick and Gertrude Ruth (Albin) Thornbrough; m. Ruth Ann Lessig; children: Jeannette Lee, Russell Raymond. BA, U. Calif., Santa Barbara, 1970, MA, 1977. Adminstr. supr. Civil Service, Santa Ana, Calif., 1971-75; sr. computer operator Santa Barbara Rsch. Ctr., 1975-77; asst. collections curator Santa Barbara Mus. Art, 1977-78; collections mgr. Montgomery (Ala.) Mus. Fine Arts, 1978-80; asst. dir. Joslyn Art Mus., Omaha, 1980-85; dir. Sheldon Swope Art Mus., Terre Haute, Ind., 1985-95, Berman Mus., Anniston, Ala., 1995-97; mus. curator National Archives, Washington, 1998-2000, William Clinton Presdl. Libr. and Mus., 2000—04; staff curator mus. mgmt. Nat. Archives Office Presdl. Librs., Washington, 2004—. Adv. Ind. Arts Commn., Indpls., 1986-91; mem. Arts in Pub. Places Commn., Terre Haute, Ind., 1986-93; pres. Friends Vigo County Pub. Libr., 1988-95, treas., 1990-93. Author: Code of Practice for Couriering Museum Objects, 1985, Gilbert Brown Wilson and Herman Melville's "Moby Dick", 1993, The American West in the Berman Collections, 1997, Cattle Drive, 1997; co-author: Registrars in Record, 1987; contbg. author: Dante Marioni: Blown Glass, 2000. Bd. dirs. Vol. Action Ctr., Terre Haute, 1987-90, Terre Haute Cmty. Relief Effort for Environ. and Civic Spirit, 1989. With USAF, 1961-65, Air N.G., 1979-96. Mem. Am. Assn. Mus. (adv. 1994—, mgmt. and long-range planning com. 1994—), Assn. Ind. Mus., Am. Assn. State and Local History, Internat. Coun. Mus., Rotary Internat., Kiwanis Internat., Alpha Gamma Sigma. Avocation: museum administrative research. Office: Nat Archives Presdl Librs 8601 Adelphi Rd Rm 1320 College Park MD 20740-6001 Office Phone: 301-837-0611.

QUICK, JOAN B. state legislator; b. Rochester, N.Y., Mar. 21, 1946; m. Terry Quick; children: Christopher, Scott, Erin, Brooke, Tom, Tim, Elizabeth. Student, Ashland Coll. Mem. dist. 94 R.I. Ho. of Reps., 1990—, dep. minority leader, 1997—; mem. spl. legis. com.; mem. rules com. and joint com. on accounts and claims; health care adminstr. Mem. Am. Legis. Exchange Coun., Rep. State Ctrl. Com., Nat. Fedn. Rep. Women, R.I. Fedn. Rep. Women. Home: 16 Mullin Hill Rd # G Little Compton RI 02837-1957 Mailing: RI Ho of Reps PO Box 433 Adamsville RI 02801-0433

QUICK, PETER, former brokerage firm executive; married. BS in Engring., U. Va.; postgrad., Stanford U. With U.S. Clearing Corp., 1983-94, pres., 1990-94, Quick & Reilly Group, Inc., 1994-96, Quick & Reilly, Inc., NYC, 1996—2000; pres., dir., firm com. Am. Stock Exch., NYC, 2000—, also bd. govs. Bd. dirs. Securities Industry Automation Corp., Reckson Associates Realty Corp. Bd. dirs. St. Francis Hospital, Good Shepherd Hospice; trustee Securities Industry Inst., Wharton Sch. U. Penn.; mem. nat. selection com. Jefferson scholar program U. Va.; trustee Museum of Am. Financial History. Recipient Ellis Island Medal of Honor award, 2001. Office: The American Stock Exch 86 Trinity Pl New York NY 10006*

QUICK, THOMAS CLARKSON, brokerage house executive; b. Westbury, N.Y., Feb. 26, 1955; s. Leslie Charles and Regina (Clarkson) Q. BS in Bus., Fairfield U., 1977. Br. mgr. Quick & Reilly Inc., Palm Beach, Fla., 1977-81; dir. The Quick & Reilly Group, N.Y.C., 1981-85; v.p. Quick & Reilly Inc., Palm Beach, 1981-86, pres., dir. N.Y.C., 1985-96, also bd. dirs.; pres., COO Quick & Reilly/Fleet Securities, Inc., 1996-98; also bd. dirs.; pres., COO Quick & Reilly Group Inc., 1998-2001. Trustee Security Industry Found. for Econ. Edn., Securities Industry Inst.; bd. dirs. Senesco Techs., corcoran.com., MindArrow Systems.com. Treas. Nat. Corp. Theater Fund, Alcoholism Coun. of N.Y.C; trustee U.S. Com.; bd. trustees Fairfield U.; mem. investment adv. bd. and endowment com. St. Jude Children's Rsch. Hosp., Memphis, 1986—; chmn. com. Wall Street Friends of St. Jude Children's Rsch. Hosp., 1979—, mem. endowment com.; bd. dirs. Best Buddies, Am. Ireland Fund. Mem. The Investment Assn. N.Y., N.Y. Stock Exch., Securities and Industry Assn. (econ. edn. com.), Am. Assn. of Sovereign Mil., Order of Malta, Young Pres.'s Orgn., Univ. Club, Friendly Sons of St. Patrick, Apawamis Country Club (Rye, N.Y.), The Beach Club (Palm Beach, Fla.), Chgo. Athletic Club., New York Yacht Club, Lotus Club, Lost Tree Club. Home: 291 El Vedado Way Palm Beach FL 33480 Office: Quick & Reilly Inc Fleet Securities 26 Broadway Fl 14 New York NY 10004-1801 E-mail: tquick@quick-reilly.com.

QUICK, WALTER CURTIS, music company executive; b. Bklyn., Jan. 10, 1962; s. Clarence and Della (Holder) Q.; 1 child, Sapphire Asia. BS, Fisk U., 1986. Gen. mgr. restaurant, Bklyn., 1982-84; resident dir. Upward Bound U. Pitts., Pitts., 1985-86; pres. Quick Del Music Co., N.Y.C.; C.D.P. Southland Corp., Falls Church, Va., 1987; mgr. Marriott Corp., Alexandria, Va., 1988; marshall, coach football and track Falls Church High Sch., 1989-90; security specialist Downtown EMT dba Live, N.Y.C., 1997—; security specialist internal security Azure, Inc. Cons. security Downtown Enterprises, N.Y.C. Author: poems. Mem. Easter Seals, N.Y., Wilson Cancer Assocs., N.Y., Covenant House, N.Y. Links scholar. Mem. ACLU, Am. Assn. Retired Persons, Am. Fedn. T.V. and Audio Artists, Nat. Park Trust, Nat. Cancer Coalition, Screen Actors Guild, Smithsonian Instn. Office: Quick-Del Music 595A Decatur St Brooklyn NY 11233-2005

QUICKE, JOHN J. aerospace company executive; Grad., U. Mo., 1972. With Arthur Andersen & Co., 1972-77; dir. corp. treas. Wetterau Inc., 1977-79; dir. taxes Chromalloy Am. Corp. (now part of Sequa Capital Corp.), St. Louis, 1979-82, v.p., contr., 1983; v.p. fin. projects Sequa Capital Corp., N.Y.C., 1987-91, pres., COO, 1991—. Office: Sequa Corp 200 Park Ave Fl 44 New York NY 10166

QUICKEL, KENNETH ELWOOD, JR., physician, medical center executive; b. Harrisburg, Pa., Aug. 20, 1939; s. Kenneth E. and Carolyn (Chick) Q.; m. Mary Wickersham Jennings, July 1, 1961; children: Robert Reid, Mary Elizabeth, David Blake. BA, Dartmouth Coll., 1961, B in Med. Sci., 1962; MD, Johns Hopkins U., 1964. Med. resident Johns Hopkins Hosp., Balt., 1964-66; endocrine fellow Duke U., Durham, N.C., 1966-67, 69-71; staff endocrinologist Geisinger Med. Ctr., Danville, Pa., 1971-84, pres., 1982-84; asst. dean Milton S. Hershey Med. Ctr., Hershey, Pa., 1973-77; pres. Geisinger Med. Mgmt. Corp., Danville, 1978-82, NPW Med. Ctr., Wilkes Barre, Pa., 1979-82; exec. v.p. Geisinger Found., Danville, 1981-84; pres. Ramsey Clinic, St. Paul, 1984-87, Joslin Diabetes Ctr., Boston, 1987-99. Bd. dirs. Controlled Risk Ins. Co., Barbados, 1987—. Contbr. articles to sci. jours. Trustee Deaconess Hosp., Boston, 1987—. Surgeon USPHS, 1967-69. Fellow ACP, Am. Coll. Physician Execs. (disting.); mem. Am. Diabetes Assn., Endocrine Soc., Harvard Club. Republican. Home: 435 Elliott Rd Centerville MA 02632-3666 Office: Joslin Diabetes Ctr 1 Joslin Pl Boston MA 02215-5306

QUIE, PAUL GERHARDT, pediatrician, educator; b. Dennison, Minn., Feb. 3, 1925; s. Albert Knute and Nettie Marie (Jacobson) Quie; m. Elizabeth Holmes, Aug. 10, 1951; children: Katie, Bill, Paul, David. BA, St. Olaf Coll., 1949; MD, Yale U., 1953; PhD (hon.), U. Lund, 1993. Diplomate Am. Bd. Pediat., Nat. Bd. Med. Examiners (mem.). Intern Hennepin County Hosp., 1953—54; pediatric resident U. Minn. Hosps., 1957—59; mem. faculty U. Minn. Med. Sch., 1959—, prof. pediatrics, 1968—99, prof. microbiology, 1974—99, assoc. dean of students, 1992—, Am. Legion meml. heart research prof., 1974—91, Regents prof., 1991; Regent's prof. emeritus, 1999—; interim dir. Ctr. for Biomed. Ethics U. Minn. Med. Sch., 1985—86; attending physician Hennepin County Hosp., 1959—91. Cons. U. Minn. Nursery Sch., 1959—91; chief of staff U. Minn. Hosp., 1979—84; vis. physician Radcliffe Infirmary, Oxford, England, 1971—72; mem. Adv. Allergy and Infectious Disease Coun., 1976—80; mem. pediat. com. NRC, 1978; mem. bd. sci. counselors Gamble Inst., 1985—90; vis. prof. U. Bergen, 1991; hon. prof. U. Hong Kong Med. Sch., 1995; vis. prof. pediat. Chubu Hosp., Nagasaki, Japan, 1996; co-dir. internat. med. edn. and rsch. program U. Minn. Med. Sch., 1998—. Editl. bd. Pediat., 1970—76, Rev. Infectious Diseases, 1989—92. Pres. Fairview Found., 1998—99; bd. dirs. Ctr. for Victims of Torture. Med. officer USNR, 1954—57. Recipient E. Mead-Johnson award, Am. Acad. Pediat., 1971, Shotwell award, Hennipen Med. Soc., 2001; fellow Guggenheim, 1971—72, Alexander von Humboldt, 1986; scholar John and Mary R. Markle, 1960—65. Mem.: Eliz Glaser Pediat. AIDS Found., Minn. Acad. Medicine (pres. 1993—94), Assn. Am. Physicians, Am. Acad. Pediat., Minn. Acad. Pediat., Am. Soc. Clin. Investigation, Am. Pediatric Soc. (coun. 1976—83, pres. 1987—88), Soc. Pediatric Rsch., Infectious Diseases Soc. Am. (coun. 1977—82, pres. 1985, Bristol award 1994), Am. Soc. Microbiology, Am. Fedn. Clin. Rsch., Minn. Med. Found. (pres. 1986—88), N.W. Pediat. Soc., Inst. Medicine of NAS. Achievements include research in function of human leukocytes and international medical education and research. Home: 2154 Commonwealth Ave Saint Paul MN 55108-1717 Office: PO Box 293 Minneapolis MN 55440-0293 Business E-Mail: quiex001@umn.edu.

QUIGG, CATHERINE THIEL, writer; b. Evanston, Ill., May 24, 1930; d. Ernest and Dorothy Frances Thiel; m. Paul Stewart Quigg, Nov. 26, 1966; children: Paula, Jeanne, Mary. BS in Journalism, Northwestern U., 1952. Advt. copywriter Sears Roebuck & Co., Chgo., 1953—55, Ruthrauff & Ryan, Inc., Chgo., 1955—57, Foote, Cone & Belding, Inc., Chgo., 1963—66; pub. rels. dir. Inst. Internat. Edn., Chgo., 1958—60; acct. exec. Daniel J. Edelman & Assocs., Chgo., 1961—63. Expert witness on nuc. waste legis. U.S. Congress, 1977, 79. Contbr. articles to profl. jours., books, mags. Rsch. dir. Pollution and Environ. Problems, Inc., Palatine, Ill., 1972—84; founding mem., pres. Ill. Safe Energy Alliance, Chgo., 1973—83; organizer solar energy forum Harper Coll., Ill., 1975; proposer, drafter Ill. Nuc. Power Evaluation Act, 1978; bd. dirs. Fox Valley Mental Health Assn., Elgin, Ill., 1976—78. Mem.: Nat. Resources Def. Coun., Barrington Writers Workshop, Sierra Club. Avocations: music, reading, writing poetry and short stories. Home: 838 Harriet Ln Barrington IL 60010

QUIGLEY, HERBERT JOSEPH, JR., pathologist, educator; b. Phila., Mar. 6, 1937; s. Herbert Joseph and Mary Kathleen (Carney) G.; m. Jacqueline Jean Stocksdale, Nov. 28, 1965 (div. 1974); 1 child, Amelia Anne. BS in Chemistry, Franklin and Marshall Coll., 1958; MD, U. Pa., 1962. Diplomate Am. Bd. Pathology. Intern Presbyterian Hosp., NYC, 1962—66, resident, 1962—66; chief pathology Monroe County Hosp., Key West, Fla., 1966-68; from asst. prof. to assoc. prof. pathology Creighton U., Omaha, 1968-72, prof., 1972—2003, prof. emeritus, 2003; chief pathology svc. VA Med. Cr., Omaha, 1968-88. Bd. dirs. Triton-Chito Inc., Omaha. Contbr. articles to profl. jours.; patentee in field. Bd. dirs., former pres., chmn. Nebr. Assn. Earth Sci. Clubs, Omaha, 1972—. Lt. comdr. USNR, 1966-68. Recipient career devel. award NIH, 1962-66, Borden prize for med. rsch. Borden Co., Inc., 1962; fellow NIH, Nat. Cancer Inst., 1958-62. Fellow Coll. Am. Pathologists, Am. Soc. Clin. Pathologists, Am. Inst. Chemists; mem. Nebr. Assn. Pathologists, N.Y. Acad. Scis. Republican. Roman Catholic. Avocations: paleontology, geology. Home: 9511 Mockingbird Dr Omaha NE 68127-2423 Office: VA Med Ctr 4101 Woolworth Ave Omaha NE 68105-1850

QUIGLEY, JAMES H. finance company executive; b. Utah, 1953; Grad., Utah State U. With Deloitte & Touche USA LLP, 1974—99, nat. dir. mfg., asst. to chmn., sec. to bd. dirs., chief staff to office of chmn., vice chmn., regional mng. ptnr. NY office, 1999—2003, chmn. ptnr. compensation and benefits com. and mergers and acquisitions com., CEO, 2003—. Bd. trustees NYC2012 Com., Lincoln Ctr. Consolidated Corp. Fund; nat. adv. coun. Marriott Sch. Mgmt. Brigham Young U.; bd. mem. Bus. Coun. NY State, Profl. Housing Resources, Southwestern Area Commerce and Industry Assn., Conn., Jr. Achievement, NYC; treas. nat. coun. Better Bus. Bureau, Washington. Mem. task force on role and mission United Way of Tri-State; bd. trustees Cent. Park Conservancy. Mem.: Union League Club, Econ. Club NY. Office: Deloitte & Touche USA LLP 1633 Broadway New York NY 10019-6754 Office Phone: 212-489-1600. Office Fax: 212-489-1687.

QUIGLEY, JAMES R. investment company executive; BS in internat. econ., Elliott Sch. Internat. Affairs, George Wash. U. With Merrill Lynch & Co., 1983—, head global debt markets issuer client group, sr. v.p., head client strategy, 2001—02, vice chmn., exec. client coverage group, 2002—, pres. Merrill Lynch Internat., 2002—. Office: Merrill Lynch 4 World Fin Ctr New York NY 10080

QUIGLEY, JEROME HAROLD, management consultant; b. Green Bay, Wis., Apr. 19, 1925; s. Harold D. and Mabel (Hansen) Q.; m. Lorraine A. Rocheleau, May 3, 1947; children: Kathy, Ross, Michael, Daniel, Mary Beth, Andrew, Maureen. BS, St. Norbert Coll., 1951. Pers. adminstr. Gen. Motors Corp., 1959-64; dir. indsl. rels. Raytheon Co., Santa Barbara, Calif., 1964-67; dir. pers. U. Calif., Santa Barbara, 1967-72; corp. dir. indsl. rels. Gen. Rsch. Corp., 1972-73; dir. indsl. rels. ISS Sperry Univac, 1973-75; corp. dir. indsl. rels. Four-Phase Systems, Inc., Cupertino, Calif., 1975; sr. v.p. human resources UNC, Annapolis, Md., 1975-86; pres. Profl. Guidance Assocs., Inc., 1986—. Aviator with USN, 1943-47. Mem. Am. Electronics Assn., Assn. Former Intelligence Officers, Scottsdale Civilian Police Acad., Assn. Naval Aviation, Tailhook Assn., Ariz. County Attys. and Sheriffs Assn., Ret. Officers Assn., AVCAD/NAVCAD Assn., Navy Aviation Mus. Found., Navy League, The Mist Spa and Tennis Club, Am. Legion, VFW. Republican. Roman Catholic. Office: Profl Guidance Assocs Inc 7789 E Joshua Tree Ln Scottsdale AZ 85250-7962 Office Phone: 480-483-0540.

QUIGLEY, JOHN BERNARD, law educator; b. St. Louis, Oct. 1, 1940; s. John Bernard and Ruth Rosina (Schieber) Q. BA, Harvard U., 1962, MA, LLB, 1966. Bar: Ohio 1973, Mass. 1967, U.S. Dist. Ct. (so. dist.) Ohio 1976, U.S. Ct. Appeals (6th cir.) 1986, U.S. Supreme Ct. 1989. Research assoc. Harvard U. Law Sch., Cambridge, Mass., 1967-69; prof. law Ohio State U., Columbus, 1969—. Author: Basic Laws on the Structure of the Soviet State, 1969, The Soviet Foreign Trade Monopoly, 1974, Palestine and Israel: A Challenge to Justice, 1990, The Ruses for War: American Interventionism since World War II, 1992, Flight into the Maelstrom: Soviet Immigration to Israel and Middle East Peace, 1997, Genocide in Cambodia, 2000. Mem. Nat. Lawyers Guild (v.p. 1977-79), Am. Soc. Internat. Law, AAUP. Avocations: tennis, speed skating, violin. Office: Ohio State U Coll of Law Coll of Law 55 W 12th Ave Columbus OH 43210-1338

QUIGLEY, JOHN MICHAEL, economist, educator; b. N.Y.C., Feb. 12, 1942; BS with distinction, U.S. Air Force Acad., 1964; MSc with honors, U. Stockholm, Sweden, 1965; AM, Harvard U., 1971, PhD, 1972. Commd. 2d lt. USAF, 1964, advanced through grades to capt., 1968; asst. prof. econs. Yale U., 1972-74, assoc. prof., 1974-81; prof. pub. policy U. Calif., Berkeley, 1979—, prof. econs., 1981—, Chancellor's prof., 1997—, I. Donald Terner disting. prof., 1999—, chmn. dept. econs., 1992-95, vis. prof. econs. and stats. U. Gothenberg, 1978. Cons. numerous govt. agys. and pvt. firms; econometrician Hdqrs. U.S. Air Force, Pentagon, 1965-68; research assoc. Nat. Bur. Econ. Research, N.Y.C., 1968-78; mem. com. on nat. urban policy NAS, 1985-93. Author, editor, contbr. articles to profl. jours.; editor in chief Reg. Sci. and Urban Econs., 1987-2003; mem. editl. bd. many sci. and scholarly jours. Fulbright scholar, 1964-65; fellow NSF, 1968-69, Woodrow Wilson, 1968-71, Harvard IBM, 1969-71, NDEA, 1969 71, Thord-Gray Am. Scandinavian Found. 1971-72, Social Sci. Research Council, 1971-72. Mem. Am. Econ. Assn., Econometric Soc., Regional Sci. Assn. (bd. dirs. 1986), Nat. Tax Assn., Assn. for Pub. Policy and Mgmt. (bd. dirs. 1986-89, v.p. 1987-89), Am. Real Estate and Urban Econs. Assn. (bd. dirs. 1987-2001, pres. 1995-97). Home: 875 Hilldale Ave Berkeley CA 94708-1319 Office: U Calif 2607 Hearst Ave Berkeley CA 94720-7305 E-mail: quigley@econ.berkeley.edu.

QUIGLEY, LEONARD VINCENT, lawyer; b. Kansas City, Mo., June 21, 1933; s. Joseph Vincent and Rosemary (Cannon) Q.; m. Lynn Mathis Pfohl, May 23, 1964; children: Leonard Matthew, Cannon Louise, Daniel Pfohl, Megan Mathis. AB, Coll. Holy Cross, 1953; LL.B. magna cum laude, Harvard U., 1959; LL.M. in Internat. Law, NYU, 1962. Bar: N.Y. 1960. Assoc. Cravath, Swaine & Moore, N.Y.C., 1959-67; ptnr. Paul, Weiss, Rifkind, Wharton & Garrison, N.Y.C., 1968—; gen. counsel Archaeol. Inst. Am., Boston. Served to lt. USN, 1953-56. Mem. ABA, Can. Bar Assn., N.Y. State Bar, Coun. Fgn. Rels., Assn. Bar City N.Y., Harvard Club (N.Y.C.), West Side Tennis Club (Forest Hills, N.Y.). Office Phone: 212-373-3320. Business E-Mail: lquigley@paulweiss.com.

QUIGLEY, MARTIN SCHOFIELD, writer, educator; b. Chgo., Nov. 24, 1917; s. Martin Joseph and Gertrude Margaret (Schofield) Q.; m. Katherine J. Dunphy, July 2, 1946; children: Martin, Elin, William, Kevin, Karen, Patricia, John, Mary Katherine, Peter. AB magna cum laude, Georgetown U., 1939; MA, Columbia U., 1973, EdD, 1975. Reporter Motion Picture Herald, N.Y.C. and Hollywood, Calif., 1939-41; with overseas br. OWI, 1942; secret war work U.S. Govt., 1943-45; various editl. and mgmt. posts Quigley Pub. Co., Inc., N.Y.C., 1946—2001, pres., 1964-2001, chmn., 2001—; staff, dept. higher and adult edn. Tchrs. Coll., 1974-75; prof. higher edn. grad. courses Baruch Coll. CUNY, 1977-89; prof. higher edn. grad. courses Tchrs. Coll. Columbia U., 1979-80, 90; prof. higher edn. grad. courses Seton Hall U., 1981-82. Pres. QWS, Inc., 1975-80; ednl. cons.; cons. supt. schs. N.Y. Archdiocese, 1962-70 Author: Great Gaels, 1944, 2d edit. 1997, Roman Notes, 1946, Magic Shadows--the story of the origin of motion pictures, 1948, Government Relations of Five Universities in Washington, D.C., 1975, Peace Without Hiroshima-Secret Action at the Vatican in Spring of 1945, 1991, First Century of Film, 1995, A U.S. Spy in Ireland, 1999, Community College Movement in Perspective, 2003; co-author: Catholic Action in Practice, 1962, Films in America, 1969; editor: New Screen Techniques, 1953. Pres. N.Y. Christian Family Movement, 1960-62, mem. nat. exec. com., 1960-65; founder, chmn. N.Y. Ind. Schs. Opportunity Project, 1965-77; pres. Found. Internat. Coop., 1960-65; bd. dirs. Will Rogers Inst., Motion Picture Pioneers; treas. Religious Edn. Assn. U.S. and Can., 1975-81, chmn., 1981-84; trustee Village of Larchmont, N.Y., 1977-79, mayor, 1980-84; mem. Laymen's Nat. Bible Assn., 1981—; trustee Am. Bible Soc., 1984—; bd. dirs. William J. Donovan Meml. Found., 1994-2001. Mem.: Larchmont Yacht. Roman Catholic. Home: 8 Pheasant Run Larchmont NY 10538-3423

QUIGLEY, PHILIP J. retired telecommunications industry executive; b. 1943; With Advanced Mobile Phone Svc. Inc., 1982-84, v.p., gen. mgr., Pacific region; with Pac Tel Mobile Access, 1984-86, pres., chief exec. officer; with Pac Tel Personal Communications, 1986-87, pres., chief exec. officer; exec. v.p., chief oper. officer Pac Tel Corp., 1987; ret. chmn., pres., chief exec. officer Pacific Telesis Group, San Francisco, 1997—; pres. Pacific Bell, 1987-94; bd. dirs. SRI Internat., Menlo Park, Calif., 1998—. Address: 2241 Forest View Ave Hillsborough CA 94010-6166

QUIGLEY, STEPHEN HOWARD, executive editor; b. Boston, May 29, 1951; s. John Joseph Sr. and Anne Margaret (O'Brien) Quigley; m. Suzanne Elizabeth Daley, July 21, 1980; children: Benjamin Parker, Theodore Hunter, Margaret Hunter. BA in French and Internat. Rels., Dartmouth Coll., 1973. Sales rep. Addison-Wesley Pub. Co., Inc., Reading, Mass., 1973—75, math. editor, 1975—81, regional sales mgr., 1981—85; sr. math. editor Scott, Foresman and Co., Chgo., 1985—88, PWS-KENT Pub. Co., Boston, 1988—95; exec. editor math. and stats. sci., tech. and med. pub. divsn. John Wiley and Sons, Inc., Marblehead, Mass., 1995—. Mem. Independence Day Celebration Commn., 1987—88; mem. Eveleth Sch. liaison Sch. PTA, Marblehead, Mass., 1989—90, vice chair sch. com., 1991—92, chair sch. comm., 1992—93; water safety chmn., bd. dirs. Greater Lynn chpt. ARC, 1978—81; leader Boy Scouts Am., Explorers Group, Marblehead, 1976—79; swim ofcl. Ill. High Sch. Ofcls. Assn., 1984—88; lector Star of Sea Ch., Marblehead, 1988—; dir. Goldthwait Reservation, Marblehead; vol. Marblehead Little Theatre, 2001—. Recipient Club of Yr. award, Darmouth Coll., 1988, Disting. Book award, Assn. Am. Publ., 1999, 2001, 2003. Mem.: ASCD, Nat. Coun. Tchrs. Math., Nat. Fedn. Interscholastic Ofcls. Assn., Am. Math. Assn. Two-Yr. Colls., Am. Statis. Assn., Math. Assn. Am., Am. Math. Soc., Friends of the Performing Arts, North Shore Friends in Pub. (founding group), Glenview C. of C. (mem. accreditation team 1988), Chgo. Dartmouth Club (pres. 1988—89), North Shore (Mass.) Dartmouth Club, Corinthian Yacht Club (rec. chair, operating com. 1997—2000), Rotary (bd. dirs. Boston 1990—95, Svc. award 1988). Republican. Roman Catholic. Avocations: swimming, sailing, tennis, singing, computing. Home: 10 Leicester Rd Marblehead MA 01945-1817 Office: Wiley Pub 2 Hooper St Marblehead MA 01945-3431 Office Phone: 781-631-0062. Business E-Mail: squigley@wiley.com.

QUIGLEY, THOMAS, research scientist; B in Watershed and Range Sci., M in Watershed and Range Sci., Utah State U.; D in Range Sci., Colo. State U.; postgrad. in meteorology, U. Utah. Asst. dir. for rsch. Rocky Mountain Rsch. Sta., Ft. Collins, Colo. and Ogden, Utah, 2001—02; dir. Pacific N.W. Rsch. Sta., Portland, Oreg., 2003—. With USAF. Office: Pacific NW Rsch Sta PO Box 3890 333 SW 1st Ave Portland OR 97208-3890

QUIGNEY, THERESA ANN, special education educator; b. East Cleveland, Ohio, June 19, 1952; d. James and Lenora Mary (McDonald) Q.; m. Joseph Carl Lang, July 23, 1983. BA, Notre Dame Coll., 1974; MEd, Cleve. State U., 1980; PhD, Kent State U., 1992. Cert. tchr. handicapped K-12; cert. ednl. adminstrv. specialist edn. of exceptional pupils; cert. ednl. supr.; cert. elem. prin.; cert. h.s. prin. cert. tchr. French K-12, Ohio. Spl. edn. tchr. Newbury (Ohio) Local Schs., 1974—80; county supr., specific learning disabilities and behavior handicaps Geauga County Bd. Edn., Chardon, Ohio, 1980—86, 1987—88; asst. prof. spl. edn. West Chester (Pa.) U., 1992—93; asst. prof. edn. Heidelberg Coll., Tiffin, Ohio, 1993—94; assoc. prof. spl. edn. Cleve. State U., 1994—, coord. spl. edn. program Coll. Edn., 2000—02. Ednl. rschr.;

presenter in field. Contbr. articles to profl. jours. Vol. cons. Tchrs. for Action Rsch. South Euclid/Lyndhurst (Ohio) Sch. Dist., 1996—; past participant issues task force Ohio Coun. for Exceptional Children; presenter, participant Oxford Round Table, Oxford U., England; past bd. mem. Camp Sue Osborne, Lake County, Ohio; mem. steering com. State Improvement Grant (Edn.), 2000—02. Grantee Ohio State Supt.'s Task Force on Spl. Edn., 1997, Cleve. State U. Coll. Edn., 1997, Am. Sch. Counselor's Assn.; recipient achievement recognition Assn. for Children and Adults with Learning Disabilities, Ohio, 1980. Mem. CEC, ASCD, Am. Ednl. Rsch. Assn., Learning Disabilities Assn., Mid-We. Ednl. Rsch. Assn., Coun. for Learning Disabilities, Kappa Delta Pi, Phi Delta Kappa, Pi Lambda Theta (vol. cons. Gamma Epsilon chpt. 1996—). Avocations: travel, writing, reading, sketching. Office: Cleveland State Univ Euclid Ave at E 24th St Cleveland OH 44115 Business E-Mail: t.quigney@csuohio.edu.

QUILALA, JOANNA CANEDA, physician assistant, researcher; d. Jimmy Ortanez and Filipina Caneda Quilala. BA in Chemistry, Calif. State U., Fullerton, 1994—2000; MS in Physician Asst. Studies, Western U. of Health Scis., Pomona, Calif., 2000—02. Field rschr., phlebotomist RAND, Santa Monica, Calif., 1998—2003; quality mgmt. coord. Beverly Hosp., Montebello, 2004—. Physician asst. helper U. So. Calif./L.A. County Med. Ctr., 1997—2000. Allied Health Careers Scholarship, Kaiser Permanente, 2000—01. Mem.: Calif. Acad. Physician Assts. (assoc.), Western U. Alumni Assn. (life). Roman Catholic. Avocations: travel, dance, singing. Personal E-mail: qtkeylala@aol.com.

QUILLEN, CECIL DYER, JR., lawyer, consultant; b. Kingsport, Tenn., Jan. 21, 1937; s. Cecil D. and Mary Louise (Carter) Q.; m. Vicey Ann Childress, Apr. 1, 1961; children: Cecil D. III, Ann C. BS, Va. Poly. Inst., 1958; LLB, U. Va., 1962. Bar: Va. 1962, N.Y. 1963, Tenn. 1974. Atty. patent dept. Eastman Kodak Co., Rochester, NY, 1962—65; atty. patent sect. Tenn. Eastman Co. (divsn. Eastman Kodak), Kingsport, 1965—69, mgr. patent sect., 1969—72, mgr. licensing, 1972—74, sec. and asst. chief counsel, 1974—76, v.p., chief counsel, 1983—85; dir. patent litigation Eastman Kodak, 1976—82, dir. antitrust litigation, 1978—82, v.p., assoc. gen. counsel, 1986, sr. v.p., gen. counsel, dir., 1986—92; sr. advisor Putnam, Hayes, Bartlett and PHB Hagler Bailly, Washington, 1992—2000, Cornerstone Rsch., Washington, 2000—. Mem. ABA, Va. State Bar, Am. Intellectual Property Law Assn., Va. Poly. Inst. Com. of 100, Assn. Gen. Counsel, Phi Kappa Phi, Omicron Delta Kappa, Tau Beta Pi, Phi Lambda Upsilon. Personal E-mail: cecilquillen@prodigy.net. Business E-Mail: cquillen@cornerstone.com.

QUILLEN, CECIL DYER, III, lawyer; b. Rochester, N.Y., Aug. 15, 1963; s. Cecil Dyer, Jr. and Vicey Ann (Childress) Q.; m. Mary Stuart Humes, Oct. 20, 1990; children: Caroline, James C.D., George. AB magna cum laude, Harvard U., 1985; JD, U. Va., 1988. Bar: N.Y. 1989, D.C. 1991, U.S. Ct. Appeals (4th cir.) 1989. Law clk., Sr. Cir. Judge U.S. Ct. Appeals (4th cir.), Richmond, Va., 1988—89; assoc. Sullivan & Cromwell, N.Y.C., 1989-95, Linklaters, N.Y.C., 1995-96, ptnr., 1996—, ptnr. London office, 2000—. Spkr. various profl. confs. Notes editor Va. Law Rev., 1987-88. Mem. ABA, N.Y. State Bar Assn., Assn. Bar City of N.Y., Raven Soc., Order of Coif, Phi Beta Kappa. Office: Linklaters One Silk St London EC2Y 8HQ England

QUILLEN, WILLIAM TATEM, retired judge, lawyer, educator; b. Camden, NJ, Jan. 15, 1935; s. Robert James and Gladys Collings (Tatem) Quillen; m. Marcia Everhart Stirling, June 27, 1959; children: Carol Everhart, Tracey Tatem. BA, Williams Coll., 1956; LLB, Harvard U., 1959; LLM, U. Va., 1982; LLD (hon.), Widener U. Sch. Law, 2002. Bar: Del. 1959. Assoc. Richards, Layton & Finger, Wilmington, Del., 1963—64; adminstrv. asst. to Gov. of Del., 1965; assoc. judge Superior Ct. of Del., 1966—73; chancellor State of Del., 1973—76; sr. v.p. Wilmington Trust Co., 1976—78; justice Supreme Ct. of Del., 1978—83; ptnr. Potter Anderson & Corroon, Wilmington, 1983—86; gen. counsel, v.p. Howard Hughes Med. Inst., 1986—91; sec. of state State of Del., Dover, 1993—94; assoc. judge Superior Ct. Del., Wilmington, 1994—2000; of counsel Drinker Biddle & Reath, Wilmington, 2003—. Mem. adj. faculty Widener U. Sch. Law, Wilmington, 1976—83, 1985—86, 1995—2000, 2002—, disting. vis. prof. law, 1992—94, 2001—02. Trustee Widener U., 1979—91; Dem. candidate for gov. Del., 1984. With JAGC USAF, 1959—62. Mem.: ABA, Del. State Bar Assn., Wilmington Club, Phi Beta Kappa. Democrat. Presbyterian. Office Phone: 302-467-4219.

QUILLIAN, WARREN WILSON, II, pediatrician, educator; b. Miami, Fla., Jan. 21, 1936; s. Warren Wilson and Rosabel (Brown) Q.; m. Sallie Ruth Creel, July 26, 1958; children: Rutledge, Ruth, Warren C., Frances. MD, Emory U., 1961. Diplomate Am. Bd. Pediat. (examiner 1966—, bd. dirs. 1974-80, 1992-98, treas. 1978, v.p. 1979, pres. 1980). Intern in pediat. Vandertilt U., Nashville, 1961-62; resident Children's Hosp. Med. Ctr., Harvard U., Boston, 1962-63; chief resident Grady Meml. Hosp., Emory U., Atlanta, 1963-64; pvt. practice Coral Gables, Fla., 1966. Instr., asst. clin. prof., assoc. clin. prof., now clin. prof. pediat. U. Miami Med. Sch., 1966—; active staff, bd. dirs. Miami Children's Hosp.; active staff Jackson Meml. Hosp.; past chief pediat. Doctors' Hosp.; mem. courtesy staff Mercy Hosp., Bapt. Hosp., South Miami Hosp.; chmn. health adv. com. Dade County Schs.; bd. dirs., v.p. Am. Bd. Pediat. Found., 1991-98; mem. adv. bd. McGlannon Sch.; cons. Fla. Divsn. Med. Svcs.; bd. dirs. Bank Coral Gables. Contbr. articles to med. jours. Hon. bd. dirs. Soc. for Abused Children of Children's Home Soc., Miami, 1980-84; mem. Coral Gables Code Enforcement Bd., 1986-88; team-sch. physician Coral Gables Sr. H.G., 1980-88; bd. dirs. Dade County March of Dimes, Miami, 1968-72; bd. advisors Dade County Assn. Retarded Children, 1968-76; trustee Emory U., 1991-97; mem. coun. ministries, youth coord., mem. fin. com., Sunday Sch. tchr. United Meth. Ch. Coral Gables, 1966—; chair parish rels. com.; mem. bd. advisors The Growing Place; mem. Citizens Bd. U. Miami, 1997—; v.p. bd. Good Hope Equestrian Tng. Ctr. for Retarded, 1999—. Capt. M.C., U.S. Army, 1964-66. Recipient citation of merit Emory U., 1980, alumni commendation Miami Children's Hosp., 1983, Tchg. award U. Miami Sch. Medicine, 1995, 2002, Winston Churchhill medal, 1999; named to CGHS Athletic Hall of Fame, 1996, Wisdom Hall of Fame, 1998. Fellow Am. Acad. Pediat.; mem. AMA, Fla. Med. Assn. (sch. health com.), Fla. Pediat. Soc. (past chmn. sch. health com.), So. Med. Assn., Dade County Med. Assn. (sch. health com., continuing edn. com.), Empirical Soc. (past pres.), Soc. for Pediat. Rsch., So. Perinatal Soc., Greater Miami Pediat. Soc. (past pres., chmn. legis. and sch. health com., Hall of Fame), Miami Med. Forum (past pres., Haverfield Cup 1985, Mansfield Trophy 1983, 88, 98), Sr. Soc. Emory U., Biscayne Bay Yacht Club (commodore, bd. govs.), DVS Sr. Honor Soc., Alpha Omega Alpha, Omicron Delta Kappa, Alpha Epsilon Upsilon, Phi Delta Theta. Democrat. Avocations: fishing, golf, boating. Office: 305 Granello Ave Coral Gables FL 33146-1806

QUILLIAN, WILLIAM FLETCHER, JR., retired banker, former college president; b. Nashville, Apr. 13, 1913; s. William Fletcher and Nonie (Acree) Q.; m. Margaret Hannah Weigle, June 15, 1940; children— William Fletcher III, Anne Acree, Katherine, Robert. AB, Emory U., 1935, Litt.D. (hon.), 1959; B.D., Yale, 1938, PhD, 1943; postgrad., U. Edinburgh, 1938-39, U. Basel, 1939; Day fellow from, Yale, 1938-39; Rosenwald fellow, 1940-41; LL.D., Ohio Wesleyan U., 1952, Hampden-Sydney Coll., 1978, Randolph-Macon Coll., 1967; D.H.L., Randolph-Macon Woman's Coll., 1978. Ordained to ministry Meth. Ch., 1942. Student asst. Stamford (Conn.) Presbyn Ch., 1936-38; del. Gen. Com. of World Student Christian Fedn., Bievres, France, 1938; discussion leader World Conf. Christian Youth, Amsterdam, Holland, 1939; pastor Clarendon (Vt.) Community Ch., summer 1940; asst. prof. philosophy Gettysburg Coll., 1941-43, prof., 1943-45; prof. philosophy Ohio Wesleyan U., 1945-52; pres. Randolph Macon Woman's Coll., 1952-78, pres. emeritus, 1978—; sr. v.p. Central Fidelity Bank, 1978-88; exec. dir. Greater Lynchburg (Va.) Community Trust, 1988-97; v.p., bd. dirs. Pride of Virginia Meats, Inc. Tchr. Garrett Biblical Inst., summer 1951. Author: The Moral Theory of Evolutionary Naturalism, 1945, Evolution and Moral Theory in America, Evolutionary Thought in America, 1950; Contbr. articles to philos. and religious jours. Pres. bd. dirs. United Way Cen. Va., campaign chmn., 1987; bd. dirs. Alpha Tau Omega Found., Lynchburg Gen. Hosp.; hon. life trustee Va. Found. Ind. Colls., pres., 1958-61. Mem. Assn. Va. Colls. (past pres.), So. U. Conf. (pres. 1967-68), So. Assn. Colls. for Women (pres. 1956), Nat. Assn. United Methodist Colls. and Univs. (pres. 1973), Am. Philos. Assn., Soc. for Values in Higher Edn. (mem. central com. 1945-48, chmn. 1947-48), Nat. Assn. Bibl. Instrs., AAUP, Greater Lynchburg C. of C. (dir. pres. 1979-80), Phi Beta Kappa, Omicron Delta Kappa, Alpha Tau Omega (dir. found.) Home: 501 Ves Rd Lynchburg VA 24503-2503

QUILLIGAN, EDWARD JAMES, obstetrician, gynecologist, educator; b. Cleve., June 18, 1925; s. James Joseph and Maude Elvira (Ryan) Q.; m. Betty Jane Cleaton, Dec. 14, 1946; children: Bruce, Jay, Carol, Christopher, Linda, Ted. BA, MD, Ohio State U., 1951; MA (hon.), Yale, 1967. Intern Ohio State U. Hosp., 1951-52, resident, 1952-54, Western Res. U. Hosps., 1954-56; asst. prof. obstetrics and gynecology Western Res. U., 1957-63, prof., 1963-65; prof. obstetrics and gynecology UCLA, 1965-66; prof., chmn. dept. Ob-Gyn Yale U., 1966-69, U. So. Calif., 1969-78, asso. v.p. med. affairs, 1978-79; prof. Ob-Gyn. U. Calif., Irvine, 1980-83, vice chancellor health affairs, dean Sch. Medicine, 1987-89; prof., chmn. ob.-gyn. dept. U. Wis., 1983-85; prof., chmn. Ob-Gyn Davis Med. Ctr. U. Calif., Sacramento, 1985-87, vice chancellor Health Scis., dean Coll. Med. Irvine, 1987-89, prof. ob-gyn, 1987-94, prof. emeritus ob-gyn., 1994; exec. dir. med. edn. Long Beach (Calif.) Meml. Health Svcs., 1995—. Contbr. articles to med. jours.; co-editor-in-chief: Am. Jour. Obstetrics and Gynecology. Served to 2d lt. AUS, 1944—46. Recipient Centennial award Ohio State U., 1970 Mem. Soc. Gynecologic Investigation, Am. Gynecol. Soc., Am. Coll. Obstetrics and Gynecology, Sigma Xi. Home: 24 Urey Ct Irvine CA 92612-4077 E-mail: equilligan@cox.net.

QUIMBY, FRED WILLIAM, pathology educator, veterinarian; b. Providence, Sept. 19, 1945; s. Edward Harold and Isabel (Barber) Q.; m. Cynthia Claire Connelly, Aug. 21, 1965; children: Kelly Ann, Cynthia Jane. VMD, U. Pa., 1970, PhD, 1974. Diplomate Am. Coll. Lab. Animal Medicine. Hematology fellow New Eng. Med. Ctr., Boston, 1974-75, instr. pathology, 1975-76, asst. prof., 1976-79; assoc. prof. pathology Cornell Med. Coll., N.Y.C., 1979-92, prof. pathology, 1993-2000. Dir. lab. animal medicine Tufts-New Eng. Med. Ctr., Boston, 1975—79; dir. Ctr. Rsch. Animal Resources Cornell U., Ithaca, 1979—2001; assoc. v.p., sr. dir. Lab. Animal Rsch. Ctr. Rockefeller U., 2001—. Editor Animal Welfare, 1992, Lab. Animal Sci., 1992-93, consulting editor, 1993-95; editor: Clinical Chemistry of Laboratory Animals, 2d edit., 1999, Laboratory Animal Medicine, 2d edit., 2002; guest editor Applied Animal Behavior Sci., 1997; chmn. editl. bd. ILAr News, 1988-91; contbr. over 120 sci. papers and abstracts. Recipient Focused Giving award, Johnson and Johnson, 1987—90; Greenfield Trust scholar, 1966—70, N.H. Rural Rehab. Corp. scholar, 1966—70, U. Pa. scholar, 1969—70. Mem. Am. Vet. Med. Assn. (Charles River prize 1995), Am. Assn. Lab. Animal Sci. (pres. N.E. br. 1978-79, B. Trum award 1979), Am. Soc. Lab. Animal Practitioners (Rsch. award 2004), World Vet. Assn. (sec. exec. com. animal welfare 1990-96). Episcopalian. Home: Apt 24P 504 E 63d St New York NY 10021-7919 Office Phone: 212-327-8535. Business E-Mail: quimby@rockefeller.edu.

QUIMBY, JEFFREY YORKE, small business owner; b. Long Beach, Calif., Sept. 22, 1963; s. Terry Yorke Quimby and Mary Jane Rider. Entrepreneur Slangtalkonline.com, Hollywood, Calif., 2000—; bus. cons.' La La Land Devel. LLC, 2000—. Avocation: surfing.

QUIN, JOSEPH MARVIN, chemicals executive; b. Vicksburg, Miss., Aug. 18, 1947; m. Terry Gage, June 12, 1973; children: William C., Elizabeth G. BA in Finance, U. Miss., 1969; MBA, U. Va., 1972. Fin. analyst Ashland Chem. Co., Dublin, Ohio, 1972—74, mgr. project analysis, 1974—79, mgr. planning & analysis & dir. planning and devel., 1979—81, adminstrv. v.p., 1981-83; treas. Ashland Inc., 1983-87, adminstrv. v.p. fin., treas., 1987-92, sr. v.p., CFO, 1992—. Bd. mem. Marathon Ashland Petroleum, Kentucky Electric Steel; trustee Cin. Symphony Orch. Episcopalian. Office: Ashland Inc PO Box 391 Covington KY 41015-0391

QUIN, LOUIS DUBOSE, chemist, educator; b. Charleston, S.C., Mar. 5, 1928; s. Louis DuBose and Olga vonOven (Jatho) Q.; children: Gordon, Howard, Carol. BS, The Citadel, 1947; MA, U. N.C., 1949, PhD, 1952. Research chemist Am. Cyanamid Co., Stamford, Conn., 1949-50; research project leader FMC Corp., South Charleston, W.Va., 1952-54, 56; mem. faculty dept. chemistry Duke U., Durham, N.C., 1956-86, prof., 1967-81, James B. Duke prof. chemistry, 1981-86, chmn. dept., 1970-76; prof. chemistry U. Mass., Amherst, 1986-96, prof. emeritus, 1996—, head dept., 1986-94; adj. prof., disting. vis. prof. chemistry U. N.C., Wilmington, 1996—. Mem. Durham Human Relations Commn., 1978-81 Author: Heterocyclic Chemistry of Phosphorus, 1981, (with J.G. Verkade) Phosphorus-31 NMR Spectroscopy in Stereochemical Analysis, 1987, Phosphorus-31 NMR Spectral Properties in Compound Characterization and Structural Analysis, 1994, A Guide to Organophosphorus Chemistry, 2000. Served to 1st lt. U.S. Army, 1954-56. Fellow AAAS; mem. Am. Chem. Soc. Office: 124 White Oak Bluffs Stella NC 28582

QUINA, MARION ALBERT, JR., lawyer; b. Mobile, Ala., Apr. 18, 1949; s. Marion Albert Sr. and Tallulah (Dunlap) Q.; children: Marion Albert III, Elliott Richardson; m. Jamie Mayhall Curtis, May 2, 1998. BS, U. Ala., 1971; JD, Samford U., 1974. Bar: Ala. 1974, U.S. Dist. Ct. (so. dist.) Ala. 1975, U.S. Ct. Appeals (5th cir.) 1977, U.S. Ct. Appeals (11th cir.) 1981. Assoc. Lyons, Pipes & Cook, Mobile, 1974-77, ptnr., 1978-87; shareholder Lyons, Pipes & Cook, P.C., Mobile, 1988—. Past mem., bd. dirs. Mobile Touchdown Club, Presch. for the Sensory Impaired; mem. United Way, 1989—; chmn. adv. bd. Cumberland Sch. of Law, Birmingham; sec., treas., vice chmn., chmn. Southeastern Admiralty Law Inst., Athens, Ga., 1996-99. 1st lt. U.S. Army. Mem. ABA, Ala. Bar Assn., Mobile Bar Assn. (past chmn. admiralty and maritime law com.), Maritime Law Assn. U.S. (assoc.), Ala. Wildlife Fedn. (past dir.), Mobile Area C. of C. (past vice chmn., gen. counsel), Kiwanis (past dir.), Mobile County Wildlife Assn., Mobile Propeller Club, Mobile Area C. of C. Diplomat Club, among others. Avocations: hunting, fishing. Office: Lyons Pipes & Cook PC 2 N Royal St Mobile AL 36602-3896

QUINBY, HAROLD EUGENE, retired councilman; b. St. Louis, July 19, 1929; s. Porter Harris Quinby and Ruth Elaine Dodendorf; m. Eunice Jean Davis, Mar. 18, 1950; children: Hal Eugene, Constance Louise. Grad. h.s., Seattle, 1947. Cert. leadership tng. Neighborhood commr. Boy Scouts Am., Seattle, 1953-55; lt. vol. fire dept. King County Fire Dist. 11, Seattle, 1962-71; city councilman City of Mukilteo, Wash., 1994—2001; ret., 2001. Adv. bd. Paine Field Cmty. Coun., Mukilteo, 1996-99, Snohomish County Mental Health, Everett, Wash., 1991-99, adv. bd. chmn. 1991-99; sign/advertise chair Save Our Cmty., Mukilteo, 1992-99; city councilman Mukilteo City, 1994-2001. Sgt. USMC, 1947—52, Korea. Democrat. Episcopalian. Avocations: model railroader, model airplanes, motor cycle tourer, antique cars.

QUINBY, WILLIAM ALBERT, lawyer, arbitrator, mediator; b. Oakland, Calif., May 28, 1941; s. George W. and Marge (Diaz) Q.; m. Marion Bach, Nov. 27, 1964; 1 child, Michelle Kathleen. BA, Harvard U., 1963; JD, U. Calif., San Francisco, 1967. Bar: Calif. 1967. V.p., dir., shareholder Crosby, Heafey, Roach & May, Oakland, 1967-96; mediator, arbitrator Am. Arbitration Assn. and AAA Ctr. for Mediation, San Francisco, 1996—. Bd. dirs. Haws Drinking Faucet Co., Berkeley, Calif.; mem. faculty Hastings Coll. Advocacy, San Francisco, 1980, instr. Boalt Hall Sch. Law, 1997; co-moderator Counsel Connect's Calif. ADR Discussion Group; lectr. currents devels. in banking arbitration and mediation; mem. fellowship rev. com. HEW; mem. panel disting. neutrals Ctr. for Pub. Resources, Inc.; mem. mediation panel Nat. Assn. Securities Dealers; trustee Nat. Pre-Suit Mediation Program; adj. prof. Hastings Coll. of the Law, U. Calif., 1998, 99. Author: Six Reasons--Besides Time and Money--to Mediate Rather Than Litigate, Why Health Care Parties Should Mediate Rather Than Litigate, Starting an ADR Practice Group in a Law Firm, Mediation Process Can Amicably Solve Business Disputes and Not a Gold Rush (But Silver, Maybe), ADR Practice in a Large Law Firm Produces No Overnight Bonanzas, Making The Most of Mediation (Effective Mediation Advocacy). Bd. dirs. Big Bros. East Bay, Oakland, 1983-87, Easter Seals Soc. East Bay, 1973; past bd. dirs. Oakland East Bay Symphony, Oakland Pub. Libr. Found.; chmn. bd. dirs. Bay Area Tumor Inst. Scholar Harvard U., 1962-63. Fellow Coll. Comml. Arbitrators; mem. ABA (sect. on dispute resolution, chair programs, mediation coms.), Calif. Bar Assn., Alameda County Bar Assn., San Francisco Bar Assn., Contra Costa County Bar Assn., Calif. Bus. Trial Lawyers Assn., Am. Arbitration Assn. (large, complex case panel, comml. mediation and arbitration panels), Oakland C. of C. (past bd. dirs., exec. com.), Alameda County Barristers Club (bd. dirs., pres. 1972), Harvard Club, San Francisco Calimari Club. Republican. Avocations: running, skiing, tennis, travel, gardening. Office: Wulff Quinby & Sochynsky Dispute Resolution 1901 Harrison St Ste 1420 Oakland CA 94612-3582 Office Phone: 510-663-5220. E-mail: wquinby@aol.com.

QUINCE, PEGGY A. state supreme court justice; b. Norfolk, Va., Jan. 3, 1948; m. Fred L. Buckine; children: Peggy LaVerne, Laura LaVerne. BS in Zoology, Howard U., 1970; JD, Cath. U. of Am., 1975; LLD (hon.), Stetson U., 1999, St. Thomas U., 2004. Hearing officer Rental Accomodations Office, Washington; pvt. practice Norfolk, 1977-78, Bradenton, Fla., 1978-80; asst. atty. gen. criminal divsn. Atty. Gen.'s Office, 1980; apptd. 2d Dist. Ct. of Appeals, 1994-98; state supreme ct. justice Fla. Supreme Ct., 1998—. Lectr. in field. Former asst. Sunday sch. tchr., former mem. #3 usher bd. New Hope Missionary Bapt. Ch.; active Jack and Jill of Am., Inc., Urban League, NAACP, Tampa Orgn. for Black Affairs. Recipient award Cath.'s Neighborhood Legal Svcs. Clinic. Mem. Nat. Bar Assn., Fla. Bar, Va. State Bar, George Edgecomb Bar Assn., Fla. Assn. Women Lawyers, Tallahassee Women Lawyers, Alpha Kappa Alpha. Office: 500 S Duval St Tallahassee FL 32399-6556 Office Phone: 850-922-5624. E-mail: supremecourt@flcourts.org.

QUINDLEN, ANNA, journalist; b. Phila., July 8, 1953; d. Robert V. and Prudence Quindlen; m. Gerald Krovatin; children: Quin, Christopher, Maria. BA, Barnard Coll., 1974. Reporter New York Post, N.Y.C., 1974-77; gen. assignment, city hall reporter New York Times, N.Y.C., 1977-81, columnist About New York, 1981-83, dep. met. editor, 1983-85, columnist Life in the 30's syndicated, 1986-89, columnist Public and Private, 1990-94. Author: Living Out Loud, 1988, Object Lessons, 1991, The Tree That Came to Stay, 1992, Thinking Out Loud, 1993, One True Thing, 1994, Happily Ever After, 1997, Black and Blue: A Novel, 1998, A Short Guide to a Happy Life, 2000, Blessings, 2002, Loud and Clear, 2004. Recipient Mike Berger award for Disting. Reporting, 1983, Pulitzer Prize for commentary, 1992; named Woman of Yr., Glamour mag., 1991. Office: c/o ICM 40 W 57th St New York NY 10019-4001

QUINLAN, EILEEN, nun, literature educator; b. Cleve., Ohio, July 7, 1951; d. Thomas P. Quinlan and Ethel M. Murphy. BA, Notre Dame Coll., Cleve., 1974; MA, Bowling Green State U., 1986; PhD, Loyola U., Chgo., 1999. Prof. English Notre Dame Coll., Cleve., 1999—. Mem.: Coll. English Assn. Ohio (bd. dirs. 2001), Midwest MLA, MLA. Roman Catholic. Office: Notre Dame Coll 4545 College Rd Cleveland OH 44121 E-mail: equinlan@ndc.edu.

QUINLAN, GUY CHRISTIAN, lawyer; b. Cambridge, Mass., Oct. 28, 1939; s. Guy Thomas and Yvonne (Carver) Q.; m. Mary-Ella Holst, Apr. 18, 1987. AB, Harvard Coll., 1960; JD, Harvard U., 1963. Bar: N.Y. 1964, U.S. Dist. Ct. (so. and ea. dists.) N.Y. 1965, U.S. Ct. Appeals (2d cir.) 1967, U.S. Supreme Ct. 1969, U.S. Ct. Appeals (8th cir.) 1973, (10th cir.) 1977, (4th cir.) 1993, (11th cir.) 1995, U.S. Tax Ct. 1977. Assoc. Clifford Chance, N.Y.C., 1963-70, ptnr., 1970—90, of counsel, 1991—. Past pres. Unitarian Universalist Svc. Com., Yorkville Common Pantry; Unitarian Universalist Dist. of Met. N.Y.; mem. adv. council on ministerial studies Harvard U. Div. Sch.; chair nuclear disarmament task force All Souls Unitarian Ch. Mem.: Lawyers Com. on Nuclear Policy, Amnesty Internat. Legal Network, N.Y. State Bar Assn., ABA, Arm Control Assn., Harvard Club. Democrat. Office: Clifford Chance US LLP 31 W 52d St New York NY 10019-6131 Office Phone: 212-878-8219.

QUINLAN, J(OSEPH) MICHAEL, lawyer; b. Rockville Centre, N.Y., Nov. 2, 1941; s. Joseph Charles Quinlan and Harriet Veronica (Gorman) Greene; m. Agnes Mary Quinlan, May 5, 1973; children: Kara Ann, Kristen Quinlan Calder. BS in Social Sci., Fairfield U., 1963; JD, Fordham U., 1966; LLM, George Washington U., 1970. Bar: N.Y. 1966, D.C. 1967, Va. 1993, U.S. Ct. Mil. Appeals 1967, U.S. Supreme Ct. 1970. Exec. asst. to warden U.S. Penitentiary, Leavenworth, Kans., 1973-74; of counsel N.E. region U.S. Bur. Prisons, Phila., 1974-75, exec. asst. to dir. Washington, 1975-78; supt. Fed. Prison Camp, Eglin AFB, Fla., 1978-80; warden Fed. Correctional Inst., Otisville, N.Y., 1980-85; from dep. asst. dir. to dir. U.S. Bur. Prisons, Washington, 1985-92; dir. strategic planning Corrections Corp. Am., 1993-97; dir., bd. dirs. U.K. Detention Svcs., London, 1993-97; vice-chmn., bd. trustees Prison Realty Trust, 1997-99. 1st vice-chmn. bd. dirs. Horton Meml. Hosp., Middletown, N.Y., 1982-85; CEO Prison Realty Trust, 1997-99; pres. Corrections Corp of Am., 1999-2000, exec. v.p., COO, 2000-02, sr. v.p., 2002—. Bd. advisors BI Inc., 2001—. Lt. col. USAFR, 1966-93. Recipient SES Presdl. Disting. Rank award, 1988, SES Presdl. Meritorious Rank award, 1991, Exceptional Leadership award U.S. Atty. Gen., 1991, Nat. Pub. Svc. award Nat. Acad. Pub. Adminstrn./Am. Soc. Pub. Adminstrn., 1992, John Marshall award Dept. Justice, 1993. Fellow Nat. Acad. Pub. Adminstrn.; mem. ABA (corrections and sentencing com. 1985—), Am. Correctional Assn. (mem. prison industries com., E.R. Cass award 2003), Nat. Com. Comm. Corrections, N.Y. Bar Assn., D.C. Bar Assn., Va. Bar Assn. Roman Catholic. Avocations: reading, family activities. Home: 1462 Evans Farm Dr Mc Lean VA 22101-5652

QUINLAN, KATHLEEN, actress; b. Pasadena, Calif., Nov. 19, 1954; Actress: (theatre) Taken in Marriage, 1979 (Theatre World award 1979), Accent on Youth, 1983, Les Liaisons Dangereuses, 1988, (feature films) One is a Lonely Number, 1972, American Graffiti, 1973, Lifeguard, 1976, Airport '77, 1977, I Never Promised You a Rose Garden, 1977, The Promise, 1979, The Runner Stumbles, 1979, Sunday Lovers, 1981, Hanky Panky, 1982, Independence Day, 1982, Twilight Zone: The Movie, 1983, The Last Winter, 1983, Warning Sign, 1985, Wild Thing, 1987, Sunset, 1988, Clara's Heart, 1988, The Doors, 1991, Trial by Jury, 1994, Apollo 13, 1995 (Acad. award nominee for best actress 1996), Zeus and Roxanne, 1997, Event Horizon, 1997, Lawn Dogs, 1997, A Civil Action, 1998, My Giant, 1998; (TV movies) Can Ellen Be Saved?, 1974, Lucas Tanner, 1974, Where Have All the People Gone?, 1974, The Missing Are Deadly, 1975, The Turning Point of Jim Malloy, 1975, The Abduction of Saint Anne, 1975, Little Ladies of the Night, 1977, She's in the Army Now, 1981, When She Says No, 1984, Blackout, 1985, Children of the Night, 1985, Dreams Lost, Dreams Found, 1987, Trapped, 1989, The Operation, 1990, Strays, 1991, An American Story, 1992, Stolen Babies, 1993, Last Light, 1993, Perfect Alibi, 1994, Breakdown, 1996, In the Lake of the Woods, 1996, The Doris Duke Story, 1998. Mem. Actors' Equity Assn., Screen Actors Guild.

QUINLAN, MARK, credit agency executive; BA in Bus. Adminstrn, MBA, U. Rochester. V.p. First Fidelity Bancorp; sr. v.p. Star Bancorp; v.p. info. and human svcs. Union Ctrl. Ins. and Investments; sr. v.p., chief info. officer Charter One Fin. Inc., 2003—. Office: Charter One Fin Inc 1215 Superior Ave Cleveland OH 44114

QUINLAN, MARY LOU, advertising executive; BA, St. Joseph's U., 1975; MBA, Fordham U., 1982; doctorate (hon.), Alvernia Coll., 1996. Dir. comm. St. Joseph's U., 1975-78; dir. advtg. Avon Products, 1978-89; sr. v.p. Ally & Gargan, 1989-91; exec. v.p., mng. ptnr. DDB Needham N.Y., 1991-94; pres N.W. Ayer & Ptnrs., N.Y.C., 1994-99, CEO, 1995—99; vice chairperson The MacManus Group, N.Y.C., 1999; founder, CEO Just Ask a Woman, N.Y.C., 1999—. Bd. dirs. 1800flowers.com, 2002—; lectr. St. John's U., 2004—. Author: Just Ask a Woman: Cracking the Code of What Woman Want and How They Buy, 2003. Bd. dirs. St. Joseph's U., Phila. Named Advt. Woman of Yr., Advt. Women of N.Y., 1995. Mem.: N.Y. Women in Comm. (Matrix Award for Advt. 1997). Office: Just Ask a Woman 670 Broadway Ste 301 New York NY 10012

QUINLAN, MICHAEL ROBERT, fast food franchise company executive; b. Chgo., Dec. 9, 1944; s. Robert Joseph and Kathryn (Koerner) Q.; m. Marilyn DeLashmutt, Apr. 23, 1966; children: Kevin, Michael. BS, Loyola U.,

Chgo., 1967, MBA, 1970. With McDonald's Corp., Oak Brook, Ill., 1966—, v.p., 1974-76, sr. v.p., 1976-78, exec. v.p., 1978-79, chief ops. officer, 1979-80, pres. McDonald's U.S.A., 1980-82, pres., 1982-89, COO, 1982-87, CEO, 1987-97, chmn., 1989-97, also bd. dirs., 1992—. Mem.: Butterfield Country, Oakbrook Handball-Racquetball. Republican. Roman Catholic. Office: McDonald's Corp McDonalds Plaza Oak Brook IL 60523-2275

QUINN, AIDAN, actor; b. Chgo., Mar. 8, 1959; m. Elizabeth Bracco; children: Ava, Mia. Actor: (films) Reckless, 1984, Desperately Seeking Susan, 1985, The Mission, 1986, Stakeout, 1987, Crusoe, 1989, The Handmaid's Tale, 1990, The Lemon Sisters, 1990, Avalon, 1990, At Play in the Fields of the Lord, 1991, The Playboys, 1992, Benny & Joon, 1993, Blink, 1994, Legends of the Fall, 1994, Mary Shelley's Frankenstein, 1994, Out of Ireland (voice), 1994, The Stars Fell on Henrietta, 1994, Haunted, 1994, Michael Collins, 1996, Looking for Richard, 1996, Commandments, 1996, Lumière et compagnie, 1995, The Assignment, 1997, Wings Against the Wind, 1998, Practical Magic, 1998, Blue Vision, 1998, The Impostors, 1998, 50 Violins, 1999, In Dreams, 1999, The Messiah XXI, 2000, Stolen Summer, 2002, Evelyn, 2002, Song for a Raggy Boy, 2003, Proud, 2003, Bobby Jones, Stroke of Genius, 2004, Cavedweller, 2004, Shadow of Fear, 2004; (plays) The Man in 605, Fool for Love, 1983, Hamlet, 1984, A Lie of the Mind, 1985, A Streetcar Named Desire, 1988 (Theatre World award 1988), Scheherazade, The Irish Hebrew Lesson, (TV) An Early Frost, 1985 (Emmy award nominee 1985), Perfect Witness, 1989, Lies of the Twins, 1991, A Private Matter, 1992, Two of Us, 2000, See You in My Dreams, 2000, The Prince and the Pauper, 2000, Benedict Arnold: A Question of Honor, 2003, Plainsong, 2004; actor, prodr.: This Is My Father, 1998. Address: William Morris Agy 151 S El Camino Dr Beverly Hills CA 90212 also: David Seltzer Industry Entertainment 3rd Fl 955 S Carrilo Dr Los Angeles CA 90048*

QUINN, ALICE FREEMAN, literature educator; BA, Manhattanville Coll., 1970; graduate student in English Lit., NYU, 1971. Editor Alfred A. Knopf Pub. Firm, 1976—87; fiction editor The New Yorker, 1987—2001, poetry editor, 1987—. Adj. prof. poetry Columbia U., 1994—; lectr. in field. Contbr. articles to Artforum, The New Yorker, The Forward, and Poetry Ireland. Jury mem. Kingsley & Tate Tufts Poetry Awards, 1994—. Mem.: Poetry Soc. Am. (exec. dir. 2001—) Home: 720 Greenwich St #9F New York NY 10014

QUINN, AMELIA TURNER, writer; b. Crawfordsville, Ark., Apr. 21, 1948; d. George (dec.) and Erma Lee Turner; children: Donald Levelle, Monique Dunell Dominiguez, David Lewis Jr. V.p. Quinn's Exterminating Co., Inc., Lynwood, Calif., 1978—2001. Author: (copyrighted brochures) Volume No. 1 - (various titles). Avocations: benevolent works, travel, reading. Home: 304 N Montgomery St Apt #2 Memphis TN 38104 Office: Mt Truth Christian Fellowship PO Box 40143 Memphis TN 38174-0143

QUINN, ANDREW PETER, JR., lawyer, insurance executive retired; b. Providence, Oct. 22, 1923; s. Andrew Peter and Margaret (Canning) Q.; m. Sara G. Bullard, May 30, 1952 (dec. Feb. 2004); 1 child, Emily H. AB, Brown U., 1945; LLB, Yale U., 1950. Bar: R.I. 1949, Mass. 1960, U.S. Tax Ct. 1960, U.S. Supreme Ct. 1986. Pvt. practice, Providence, 1950-59; ptnr. Letts & Quinn, 1950-59; with Mass. Mut. Life Ins. Co., Springfield, 1959—88, exec. v.p., gen. counsel, 1971-88; of counsel Day, Berry & Howard, Hartford, Conn. and Boston, 1988-99; retired, 1999. Pres., trustee MML Series Investment Fund, 1971-88; bd. dirs. Sargasso Mut. Ins. Co., Ltd., 1986-95, pres., 1986-89, chmn. bd. dirs., 1989-93. Trustee, MacDuffie Sch., 1974-87, chmn. bd., 1978-85; trustee Baystate Med., Springfield, 1977-80. Lt. (j.g.) USNR, 1944-46. Mem. ABA (co-chmn. nat. conf. lawyers and life ins. cos. 1973), Assn. Life Ins. Counsel (pres. 1983-84, Anderson Disting. Svc. award 1998), Am. Coun. Life Ins. (chmn. legal sect. 1971), Life Ins. Assn. Mass. (chmn. exec. com. 1975-77), Brown U. Alumni Assn. (bd. dirs. 1969-72), N.Y. Yacht Club, Longmeadow Country Club, Dunes Club, Hillsboro Club, Colony Club (Springfield, Mass.), Conn. Valley Brown U. (past pres.). Home: 306 Ellington Rd Longmeadow MA 01106-1559

QUINN, ART JAY, veterinarian, retired educator; b. Bennington, Kans., Aug. 2, 1936; s. Arthur Jess and Edith Mae (Reigle) Q. BS, Kans. State U., 1959, DVM, 1961. Diplomate Am. Coll. Vet. Ophthalmologists. Pvt. practice, Albuquerque, 1961-75; field rep. Am. Animal Hosp. Assn., Denver, 1968-69; prof. Coll. Vet. Medicine, Okla. State U., Stillwater, 1975-95, prof. emeritus, 1995—. Contbr. articles to profl. jours. Capt. U.S. Army, 1962-64. Recipient Small Animal Proficiency award, Kans. Vet. Med. Assn., 1961, Upjohn award, 1961, Western Region Practitioner award, AAHA, 1993, Meritorious Svc. award, Western Vet. Conf., 2002; grantee, Sarkey Found. grantee, 1981. Mem.: AVMA, Am. Coll. Vet. Ophthalmologists, Am. Animal Hosp. Assn. Democrat. Home: 210 Cedar Ln Diamond Head Sand Springs OK 74063-5309

QUINN, CHARLES NICHOLAS, journalist; b. Utica, N.Y., July 28, 1930; s. Charles Dunaway and Elsa (Zarth) Q.; children— Diana David, Ben, Jane. BA, Cornell U., 1951; MS, Columbia U. Sch. Journalism, 1954. Reporter Providence Jour., 1954-56, N.Y. Herald Tribune, 1956-62; corr. NBC News, N.Y.C., 1962-66, Washington, 1966-71, Rome, 1971-74; mng. editor, chief corr. NBC Radio News, Washington, 1978-80; corr. Ind. Network News, Washington, 1980-81; electronic media rep. Am. Petroleum Inst., Washington, 1981-91. Reported on hunger in U.S. on: Huntley-Brinkley Report, (co-recipient Emmy 1969). Served with arty. U.S. Army, 1951-53. Mem. Nat. Press Club (bd. govs. 1990-91).

QUINN, CHRISTOPHER CARDINAL, neurobiologist, educator; b. Texarkana, Tex., Jan. 7, 1974; s. John Cardinal and Vivian Ann Quinn; m. Maria Lourdes Chen, May 23, 1999. BA, Rutgers U., 1996; PhD, Yale U., 2001. Ruth Kirschtein fellowship dept. pathology Robert Wood Johnson Med. Sch. Contbr. articles to profl. jours. Recipient Ruth L. Kirschstein Nat. Rsch. Svc. award, NIH, 2003—; fellow, U. Medicine and Dentistry of N.J. Found., 2001, Am. Soc. Pharmacology and Exptl. Therapeutics, 1994; grantee, Sigma Xi, 1994, 1995. Mem.: Soc. Neurosci. Democrat. Roman Catholic. Achievements include discovery of TUC-4b protein and description of its role in neurite growth; role of MIG-10 in signaling downstream of axon guidance cues. Office: Robert Wood Johnson Med Sch Dept Pathology 675 Hoes Ln Piscataway NJ 08854 E-mail: quinncc@umdnj.edu.

QUINN, DAVID W. building company executive; b. 1942; BA, Midwestern U. Ptnr. Arthur Andersen, Dallas, 1967-84; COO Alpert Cos., 1984-87; exec. v.p. Centex Corp., Dallas, 1987-96, vice chmn., 1996—, also bd. dirs. Office: Centex Corp 2728 N Harwood St Ste 200 Dallas TX 75201-1591

QUINN, E. MOORE, linguistic anthropology educator; d. John Douglas Quinn and Lorraine O'Sullivan Gaston. BE, Fitchburg State Coll., 1969; MA in Celtic Langs. and Lit., Harvard U., 1988; MA in Anthropology, Brandeis U., 1994, PhD in Anthropology, 1999. Lectr. English, folklore, history U. Mass., Lowell, 1990; adj. prof. sociology Becker Coll., Worcester, Mass., 1996; adj. prof. anthropology, lang. Bradford Coll., Mass., 1999; adj. prof. anthropology and women's studies MIT, 1999—2001; asst. prof. linguistic anthropology, folklore, reading and rsch. Coll. of Charleston, SC, 2001—. Dir. rsch. Cultural Survival, Cambridge, 1999—2000. Author numerous conf. papers and invited lectrs., (jour. articles) Jour. of the Soc. of Anthropology of Europe, 2001, articles and reviews in several jours. and mags. Recipient Sachar Dissertation award, 1993, Solidarity award, Irish Ctr. for Migration Studies, 1999; Nat. Furniture Fund fellowship, 1997, Brandeis U. Fellowships, 1990—98. Avocation: performance of Irish, Celtic Traditional and contemporary music. Office: Coll Charleston 66 George St Charleston SC 29401 E-mail: quinne@cofc.edu.

QUINN, EUGENE FREDERICK, foreign service officer, clergyman; b. Oil City, Pa., Sept. 16, 1935; s. Frederick Anthony and Wilma (Scott) Q.; m. Charlotte Alison Smith, Aug. 25, 1965 (div. June 2000); children: Christopher Edward Vermilye, Alison Moore; m. Carolyn Tanner Irish, June 14, 2001. AB, Allegheny Coll., 1957; MA in African studies, UCLA, 1966, MA in History, 1969, PhD in History, 1970; diploma in theol. studies, Va. Theol. Sem., 1974. Ordained to ministry Episcopal Ch., 1975. Info. officer Am. Embassy, Rabat, Morocco, 1958-59, cultural affairs officer Port-au-Prince, Haiti, 1959-61; country pub. affairs officer Ouagadougou, Upper Volta, 1961-63; field rep. Joint U.S. Affairs Office, Saigon, Vietnam, 1964-66; country pub. affairs officer Am. embassy, Yaounde, Cameroun, 1966-68, counselor embassy for press and cultural affairs Prague, Czechoslovakia, 1975-78, apptd. career mem. Sr. Fgn. Service with class of counselor, 1981, minister-counselor, 1986; dir. fgn. service personnel Voice of Am., Washington, 1981-83; dep. asst. sec. pub. affairs Dept. Transp., 1983-85; dir. Office Pub. Affairs Voice of Am., 1985-86; internat. coord. for Bicentennial U.S. Constn., dir.'s office U.S. Info. Agy., 1986-91; cons. internat. affairs, 1992—. Dir. rule of law programs, conf. on security and cooperation in Europe, Office of Dem. Instns. and Human Rights, Warsaw, 1993-95. Author: Federalist Papers' Reader, 1992, To Heal the Earth, 1994, Democracy at Dawn, Notes From Poland and Points East, 1998, Human Rights and You, 1998, French Overseas Empire, 2000, To Be A Pilgrim, The Anglican Ethos in History, 2001, African Saints, Martyrs and Holy People, 2002, Courthouse at Indian Creek, 2002; co-author: Pride, Faith and Fear: Islam in Africa, 2003; editor: Diplomacy for the Seventies, 1969; mem. editl. bd. Fgn. Svc. Jour., 1972-75, Dept. State Open Forum Jour., 1982-83; contbr. articles to profl. jours., chpts. to books. Trustee N.J. Ednl. Consortium, 1970-72; coord. USIA Yorktown Bicentennial Activities, 1981; assisting clergyman St. Columba Ch., Washington, 1973-75, 78-81, Nat. Cathedral, Washington, 1981-82, 95-2001, Grace Ch., Silver Spring, Md., 1981-82, Epiphany Ch., Washington, 1983, 86-92; chaplain Anglo-Am. Diplomatic Cmty., Prague, 1975-78, Warsaw, 1993-95; vicar St. James Ch., Bowie, Md., 1983-84; rector Christ Ch., Accokeek, Md., 1985, St. John's Ch., Pomonkey, Md.; assisting clergyman All Saints Ch., Chevy Chase, Md., 1981-82, 86 90; interim pastor Ch. of Holy Communion, Washington, 1992 93, St. Andrews Leonardtown, Md., 1998-99; chair environ. com. Episcopal Diocese of Washington Peace Comm., 1991-92; mem. Environ. Stewardship Team, Episcopal Ch., 1992-95. Recipient Meritorious Honor award USIA, 1964, 66, 85; Merit medal Republic of Vietnam, 1965, medal of honor, 1966 Mem. Cosmos Club (Washington). Clubs: Cosmos (Washington). Home and Office: 48W 300 S # 2601 N Salt Lake City UT 84101

QUINN, FRANCIS A. bishop; b. L.A., Sept. 11, 1921; Ed., St. Joseph's Coll., Mountain View, Calif., St. Patrick's Sem., Menlo Park, Calif., Cath. U., Washington, U. Calif., Berkeley. Ordained priest Roman Cath. Ch., 1946, ordained titular bishop of Numana and aux. bishop of San Francisco Roman Cath. Ch., 1978. Bishop Diocese of Sacramento, 1979—94, bishop emeritus, 1994—. Roman Catholic. Office: 2110 Broadway Sacramento CA 95818-2518

QUINN, FRANCIS F. lawyer; b. Phila., Jan. 22, 1946; AB, St. Joseph's U., 1967; JD, U. Pa., 1971. Bar: Pa. 1972, N.J. 1993, N.Y. 1995, U.S. Supreme Ct. 1985. Law clk. to Hon. Daniel H. Huyett III U.S. Dist. Ct. (ea. dist.) Pa., 1971-73; ptnr. Lavin, Coleman, O'Neill, Ricci, Finarelli & Gray, Phila., 1973—. Mem. Phila. Bar Assn., Def. Rsch. and Trial Lawyers Assn., N.Y. Assn. Def. Counsel, Bar Assn. City of N.Y., N.Y. State Bar Assn. Office: Lavin Coleman Finarelli & Gray 767 3rd Ave Fl 7 New York NY 10017-2023

QUINN, FRANCIS XAVIER, arbitrator, mediator, author, lecturer; b. Dunmore, Pa., June 9, 1932; s. Frank T. and Alice B. (Maher) Q.; m. Marlene Stoker Quinn; children: Kimberly, Catherine, Cameron, Lindsay, Megan, Savannah, Jackson Blair. BA, Fordham U., 1956, MA, 1958; STB, Woodstock Coll., 1964; MS in Indsl. Rels., Loyola U., Chgo., 1966; PhD in Indsl. Rels., Calif. Western U., 1966. Assoc. dir. Inst. Indsl. Rels. St. Joseph's Coll., Phila., 1966-68; Manpower fellow Temple U., Phila., 1969-74, asst. to dean Sch. Bus. Adminstrn., 1972-78. Arbitrator Fed. Mediation and Conciliation Svc., Nat. Mediation Bd., Am. Arbitration Assn., Nat. Assn. Railroad Referees, Dem. Nat. Steering Com.;; apptd. to Rail Emergency Bd., 1975, to Fgn. Service Grievance Bd., 1976, 78, 80. Author: The Ethical Aftermath of Automation, 1963, Ethics and Advertising, 1965, Population Ethics, 1968, The Evolving Role of Women in the World of Work, 1969, Developing Community Responsibility, 1970; editor: The Ethical Aftermath Series; contbr. articles to profl. jours. Chmn. Hall of Fame com. Internat. Police Assn., 1990-92, Tulsa City-County Mayor's Task Force to Combat Homelessness, 1991-92; mem. exec. bd. Tulsa Met. Ministries, 1990-92, Labor-Religion Coun. Okla., 1990-98; pastoral coun. Holy Family Roman Cath. Ch., 2000-03, formation adv. bd., 2002-04. Named Tchr. of Yr. Freedom Found., 1959; recipient Human Rels. award City of Phila.; inducted into Hall of Fame, Internat. Police Assn., 2000. Mem. Nat. Acad. Arbitrators (v.p. 1999-2001), Indsl. Rels. Rsch. Assn., Assn. for Social Econs., Soc. for Dispute Resolution, Am. Arbitration Assn. (arbitrator), Nat. Assn. Railroad Refs. (pres. 2000-04, arbitrator), Internat. Soc. Labor Law and Social Security. Democrat. Home: 4213 Blackhaw Ave Fort Worth TX 76109-1618 E-mail: FXQ@prodigy.com.

QUINN, JACK, congressman, English language educator, coach; b. South Buffalo, N.Y., 1951; s. Jack Sr. and Norma Ide Q.; m. Mary Beth McAndrews, 1974; children: Jack III, Kara. BA, Siena Coll.; MA in Edn., SUNY, Buffalo. English language tchr. Orchard Park (N.Y.) Schs.; town councilman Town of Hamburg, N.Y., also town supv.; mem. U.S. Congress from 30th N.Y. Dist., 1993—2002, U.S. Congress from 27th N.Y. Dist., 2003—; mem. transp. and infrastructure com., chmn. subcom. on railroads, mem. vet. affairs com. Recipient Humanitarian award Erie County for the Disabled, Pub. Svc. award Niagara Frontier Parks and Recreation Soc., Disting. Grad. award Nat. Cath. Elem. Schs. Assn., Bronze Good Citizen medal SAR, New Horizons award Drug Edn. of Internat. Assn. of Lions Club, Red, White and Blue award Am. Legion of N.Y., Honor medal Hilbert Coll., Fin. Reporting award Govt. Fin. Officer's Assn., Disting. Career Svc. award Siena Coll., 1995. Mem. Hamburg C. of C., Greater Buffalo C. of C., Buffalo KC, Hamburg Kiwanis Club. Republican. Roman Catholic. Office: US Ho Reps 2448 Rayburn Ho Office Bldg Washington DC 20515

QUINN, JAMES E. retail products executive; m. Diane Quinn; 2 children. BA in comm., Hofstra U.; MBA in fin. mgmt., Lubin Sch. Bus., Pace U. V.p. corp. sales Tiffany & Co., 1986—90, sr. v.p. corp. divsn., 1990—92, exec. v.p., 1992—98, dir., 1995—, vice chmn., 1998—2003, pres., 2003—. Mem. bd. dirs. BNY Hamilton Funds, Inc., Mutual Am. Capital Mgmt.; chmn. Smurfit Sch. Bus., U. Coll. Dublin, 2003. Mem. adv. com. Bus. Coun. United Nations; N. Am. adv. bd. U. Coll. Dublin; bd. dirs. Fifth Ave. Bus. Improvement Dist.; trustee Mus. City NY, Montclair Art Mus. Office: Tiffany & Co 727 5th Ave New York NY 10022

QUINN, JAMES W. lawyer; b. Bronxville, N.Y., Oct. 1, 1945; s. James Joseph Quinn and Marie Joan (Blossy) Tisi; m. Kathleen Manning, Kellianne, Christopher, Tierney, Kerrin. AB cum laude, U. Notre Dame, 1967; JD, Fordham U., 1971. Bar: N.Y. 1972, U.S. Dist. Ct. (so. and ea. dists.) N.Y. 1973, U.S. Ct. Appeals (2nd cir.) 1976, U.S. Supreme Ct. 1984, U.S. Ct. Appeals (3rd, 7th and 9th cirs.) 1985, U.S. Ct. Appeals (8th cir.) 1991. Assoc. Weil, Gotshal & Manges, N.Y.C., 1971-77, 78-79, ptnr., 1979—, Fleisher & Quinn, N.Y.C., 1977-78. Adj. assoc. prof. law Fordham U., N.Y.C., 1985-87. Co-author: Corporate Counsellors Deskbook, Litigating Complex Careers; editor: Fordham U. Law Rev., 1969—71; contbr. articles to profl. jours. Fellow Internat. Acad. Trial Lawyers, Am. Coll. Trial Lawyers; mem. ABA (litigation sect., co-chmn. subcom. alternate means of dispute resolution of com. corp. counsel, program chmn. trial practice com., sports and entertainment forum), Assn. of Bar of City of N.Y. (com. of state jurisdiction, com. on entertainment sports, com. on anti-trust regulation, chmn. sports law com.). Home: 1 Maple Way Armonk NY 10504-2602

QUINN, JANE BRYANT, journalist, writer; b. Niagara Falls, NY, Feb. 5, 1939; d. Frank Leonard and Ada (Laurie) Bryant; m. David Conrad Quinn, June 10, 1967; children: Matthew Alexander, Justin Bryant. BA magna cum laude, Middlebury Coll., 1960. Assoc. editor Insiders Newsletter, NYC, 1962-65, co-editor, 1966-67; sr. editor Cowles Book Co., NYC, 1968; editor-in-chief Bus. Week Letter, NYC, 1969-73, gen. mgr., 1973-74; syndicated fin. columnist Wash. Post Writers Group, 1974—2001; contbr. fin. column to Women's Day mag., 1974-95, Good Housekeeping, 1995—; contbr. NBC News and Info. Service, 1976-77; bus. corr. WCBS-TV, NYC, 1979, CBS-TV News, 1980-87, ABC-TV Home Show, 1991-93; contbg. editor Newsweek mag., 1978. Host PBS personal fin. series Take Charge!, 1988; dir. bd. dirs. Bloomberg LP. Author: Everyone's Money Book, 1979, 2d edit., 1980, Making the Most of Your Money, 1991, 2d edit., 1997, A Hole in the Market, 1994; co-developer, contbr. (software program) Quicken Financial Planner, 1995. Dean's coun. Harvard Sch. Pub. Health; mem. bd. advisors Jerome Levy Econs. Inst. Bard Coll. Named one of 25 Most Influential Women in US, World Almanac; recipient Emmy award for outstanding coverage fin. on TV, Gerald Loeb award for lifetime achievement and disting. bus. and fin. journalism, John Hancock award for excellence in bus. and fin. journalism, Janus award for excellence in TV and bus. reporting, Journalism award for excellence in personal fin. reporting, ICI-Am. U., three-time winner Nat. Press Club award for consumer journalism, two-time winner Nat. Headliner award, honored for outstanding consumer media svc., Consumer Fedn. Am. Mem. Phi Beta Kappa. Office: Newsweek Inc 251 W 57th St New York NY 10019-1802*

QUINN, JARUS WILLIAM, physicist, former association executive; b. West Grove, Pa., Aug. 25, 1930; s. William G. and Ellen C. (DuRoss) Q.; m. Margaret M. McNerney, June 27, 1953; children: J. Kevin, Megan, Jennifer, Colin, Kristin. BS, St. Joseph's Coll., 1952; postgrad., Johns Hopkins U., 1952-55; PhD, Cath. U. Am., 1964. Rsch. assoc. physics Johns Hopkins U., 1954-55; staff scientist Rsch. Inst. Advanced Study, 1956-57; rsch. assoc. physics Cath. U. Am., 1958-60, instr., 1961-64, asst. prof., 1965-69; exec. dir. Optical Soc. Am., Washington, 1969-93; governing bd. Am. Inst. Physics, 1973-94; pres. Stellar Focus, Sunnyvale, Calif., 1994-95. Bd. govs. Am. Assn. Engring. Socs., 1990-93. Fellow Optical Soc. Am. (Distinguished Service Award, 1993), mem. Am. Phys. Soc., Am. Soc. Assn. Execs., Coun. Engring. and Sci. Soc. Execs. Home: 15 Forsythia Ct Durham NC 27705 E-mail: optics2010@yahoo.com.

QUINN, JOHN ALBERT, chemical engineering educator; b. Springfield, Ill., Sept. 3, 1932; s. Edward Joseph and Marie (Von De Bur) Q.; m. Frances Wilkie Daly, June 22, 1957; children: Sarah D., Rebecca V., John E. BSChemE, U. Ill., 1954; PhDChemE, Princeton U., 1959. Mem. faculty chem. engring. U. Ill., Urbana, 1958-70; prof. U. Pa., Phila., 1971—, Robert D. Bent prof., 1978—, chmn. dept. chem. engring., 1980-85. Vis. prof. Imperial Coll. U. London, 1965-66; vis. scientist MIT, 1980; vis. prof. U. Rome/La Sapienza, 1992; mem. sci. adv. bds. Sepracor, Inc., Marlborough, Mass., 1984—, Whitaker Found., Mechanicsburg, Pa., 1987—; Mason lectr. Stanford U., 1981; Katz lectr. U. Mich., 1985; Reilly lectr. U. Notre Dame, 1987; Michael's lectr. MIT, 2001. Contbr. articles to profl. publs.; editl. advisor Jour. Membrane Sci., 1975—, Indsl. and Chem. Engring. Rsch., 1987-88, Revs. in Chem. Engring., 1980—; pioneer rschr. on mass transfer and interfacial phenomena. Sr. postdoctoral fellow NSF, 1965-66; Sherman Fairchild scholar Calif. Inst. Tech., 1985. Fellow AAAS, Am. Inst. Med. and Biol. Engring.; mem. NAE, AIChE (Allan P. Colburn award 1966, Alpha Chi Sigma award 1978), Am. Acad. Arts and Scis., Am. Chem. Soc., Internat. Soc. Oxygen Transport to Tissue, Sigma X, Phi Lambda Upsilon, Tau Beta Pi. Home: 275 E Wynnewood Rd Merion Station PA 19066-1627 Office: Univ Pa Towne Bldg 220 S 33rd St Philadelphia PA 19104-6393 Office Phone: 215-898-8503.

QUINN, JOHN COLLINS, publishing executive, newspaper editor; b. Providence, Oct. 24, 1925; s. John A. and Kathryn H. (Collins) Q.; m. Lois R. Richardson, June 20, 1953; children: John Collins, Lo-anne, Richard B., Christopher A. AB, Providence Coll., 1945; MS, Columbia U. Sch. Journalism, 1946. Successively copy boy, reporter, asst. city editor, Washington corr., asst. mng. editor, day mng. editor Providence Jour.-Bull., 1943-66; with Gannett Co. Inc., Rochester, N.Y., 1966-90; exec. editor Rochester Democrat & Chronicle, Times-Union, 1966-71; gen. mgr. Gannett News Service, 1967-80, pres., 1980-88, v.p. parent co., 1971-75, sr. v.p. news and info., 1975-80, sr. v.p., chief news exec. parent co., editor USA TODAY, 1983-89; exec. v.p. Gannett Co., Arlington, Va., 1983-90; trustee Gannett Found., Arlington, 1988-91; dep. chmn. Freedom Forum, Arlington, 1991-97, trustee, 1991—. Named to R.I. Hall of Fame, 1975, Editor of Yr. Nat. Press Found., 1986; recipient William Allen White citation, 1987, Women in Communications Headliner award, 1986; Paul Miller/Okla. State U. medallion, 1988. Mem. AP Mng. Editors (past dir., nat. pres. 1973-74), Am. Soc. Newspaper Editors (dir., chmn. editorial bd., chmn. conv. program, nat. pres. 1982-83) Roman Catholic. Home: 365 S Atlantic Ave Cocoa Beach FL 32931-2719 Office: Freedom Forum 1101 Wilson Blvd Ste 2300 Arlington VA 22209-2265 Office Phone: 703-528-0800.

QUINN, JOHN MICHAEL, physicist, geophysicist; b. Denver, May 8, 1946; s. Leonard Simon and Winifred Ruth (Doolan) Q.; m. Pamela Dagmar Shield, May 28, 1983. BS in Physics, U. Va., 1968; MS in Physics, U. Colo., 1982. Physicist U.S. Naval Rsch. Lab., Washington, 1967—73; prin. engr. Singer Simulation Products, Silver Spring, Md., 1973—74; rsch. physicist U.S. Naval Rsch. Lab, Washington, 1979—80; geophysicist U.S. Naval Oceanog. Office, Stennis Space Ctr., Miss., 1974—79, 1982—85, geophysicist, mathematician, 1985—95; rsch. geophysicist U.S. Geol. Survey, Denver, 1995—2002; ret., 2002. Cons. Earth Climate Rsch. Inst., 2002—; investigator Polar Orbiting Geomagnetic Survey Experiment, 1990-94; prin. investigator Def. Meteorol. Satellite Program Polar Orbiting Geomagnetic Survey Ext., 1991-2002; chmn. com. on earth and planetary geomagnetic survey satellites Internat. Assn. Geomagnetism and Aeronomy, 1991-99, mem. internat. geomagnetic ref. field com., 1989-2002; U.S. del. UN Internat. Stds. Orgn., 2000-2002; project coord. USN Project MAGNET; vis. scientist Nat. Oceanic and Atmospheric Adminstrn., 2003-. Author: Epoch World Geomagnetic Model, 1985, 90, 95, 2000. With U.S. Army, 1968—71. Mem. Am. Geophys. Union, Am. Math. Soc., European Geophys. Soc., Math. Assn. Am. Achievements include devel. of official Dept. of Def. world magnetic models which are used by military and civilian agencies for navigational purposes and basic rsch. of earth's magnetic field, specialized remote geomagnetic sensing/modeling techniques to detect, in the lithosphere, magnetization due to meteorite impact shocks and hotspot basalt flows; engaged in geodynamo research, yielding high-resolution fluid-flow models at the core-mantle-boundary. Home: 2732 S Braun Way Lakewood CO 80228-4954 Personal E-mail: p-j_quinn@comcast.net.

QUINN, MARK T. medical educator; b. San Jose, Calif., June 11, 1958; BA in Biology and Chemistry, Point Loma Coll., 1982; PhD in Physiology and Pharmacology, U. Calif., San Diego, 1987. Postdoctoral rsch. assoc. Rsch. Inst. Scripps Clinic, La Jolla, Calif., 1988-89; sr. rsch. assoc. Mont. State U., Bozeman, 1989-90, asst., assoc. rsch. prof., 1991-95, asst. prof., 1995—, assoc. prof., 1998. Contbr. articles to profl. jours. Recipient Investigator award Arthritis Found., 1991, Health FIRST award NIH, 1992—, Charles and Nora Wiley Meritorious Rsch. award, 1993; grantee Am. Cancer Soc., 1989, Am. Lung Assn., 1991-93, Arthritis Found., 1994—, USDA, 1995—; U. Calif. Regents fellow, 1981, Point Loma Coll. Rsch. Assocs. fellow, 1981, San Diego & Grad. Opportunity Rsch. fellow, 1986-87, Arthritis Found. Postdoctoral fellow, 1989-91. Mem. Am. Soc. Cell Biology, Am. Heart Assn. (coun. basic rsch., Established Investigator award 1996—), Soc. Leukocyte Biology. Office: Mont State U Dept Vet Molecular Biology Bozeman MT 59717-0001

QUINN, MAUREEN E. ambassador; b. Spring Lake, N.J. Vice consul, gen. svcs. officer U.S. Consulate Gen., Karachi, Pakistan, 1982—84; econ. officer, comml. attaché Am. Embassy Conakry, Guinea, 1984—86; with Western Hemisphere's Bur. Regional Econ. Affairs, 1986—88, Econ. Bur. Office Internat. Devel. Fin., 1988—90; Pearson fellow U.S. Ho. Reps., Washington, 1990—91; econ. counselor Am. Embassy Dept. of State, Panama, 1991—94, exec. asst., spl. asst. to undersec. for econ., bus. and agrl. affairs, 1994—97, dep. exec. sec., 1997—98, dep. chief of mission Am. Embassy, 1998—2001, U.S. amb. to Qatar, 2001—. Office: DOS Amb 6130 Doha Pl Washington DC 20521

QUINN, MICHAEL DESMOND, diversified financial services executive; b. Balt., Sept. 4, 1936; s. Michael Joseph and Gladys (Baldwin) Quinn; m. Mary Annette McHenry, Apr. 11, 1961; children: Caitlin A., Maureen K., Patricia B., Marianne P. BA, U. Md., 1970. With Weaver Bros., Inc. of Md., Balt., 1960—; investment v.p., corp. dir. interim loan dept. Weaver Bros., Balt., 1978—86; chmn. of bd. Wye Mortgage Co.,L.P., 1977—, Christiana Capital Group, Inc.; chmn., CEO Alliance Recovery Group, Balt., 1990—, Estate Trust Co., Inc., Balt. Mem. faculty evening coll. Johns. Hopkins U., Balt., 1967—, Essex

Cmty. Coll., Balt., 1967—. Mem. Gov.'s task force Md. Housing Ins. Fund; mem. Md. Health Claims Arbitration Panel; bd. visitors U. Md.; dist. adv. coun. U.S. Small Bus.Asminstrn. With USN, 1956—58. Mem.: Soc. Cert. Sr. Advisors, N. Am. Soc. Corp. Planning, Md.Bankers Assn., Home Builders Assn., Real Estate Bd. Greater Balt. (bd. dirs.), Md. Mortgage Bankers Assn. (pres. bd. govs.), Balt. County C. of C. (bd. dirs.), Balt. Jr. Assn. Commerce (Richard Troja Merit award. 1967, Outstanding Young Man of Balt. 1969), Ancent Order Hibernians, Greater Balt. Com., Balt. Econ. Soc. Home: 8207 Robin Hood Ct Baltimore MD 21204-1900 Office: 7400 York Rd Ste 300 Baltimore MD 21204-7502 Office Phone: 800-456-5100. Personal E-mail: eti7400@aol.com. Business E-Mail: mdquinn@estatetrustinc.com.

QUINN, NIGEL WILLIAM TREVELYAN, scientist, engineer; b. Belfast, Northern Ireland, Dec. 28, 1955; arrived in U.S., 1978; s. Stanley Quinn and Elaine Elizabeth Hayes. BSc with honors, Cranfield U., 1977; MS, Iowa State U., 1981; PhD, Cornell U., 1987. Registered profl. engr., Calif. GE fellow Cornell U., 1984—86, sr. rsch. assoc., 1987—90; lead groundwater modeler San Joaquin Valley Drainage Program, 1987—90; geol. scientist, group leader Hydro Ecol. Engring. Advanced Decision Support Berkeley (Calif.) Nat. Lab., 1990—; rsch. engr. U. Calif., Berkeley, 1999—2002. Convener Calif. Water and Environ. Modeling Forum, Sacramento, 2002—; bd. dirs. Internat. Symposium on Environ. Software Sys., Germany; adj. prof. Calif. Water Inst. Contbr. chapters to books, articles to profl. jours. Dir. UN Assn., Ames, 1978—81. Recipient Hunting Challenge Cup, Cranfield U., 1977. Mem.: ASCE, Water Environment Fedn., Am. Water Resources Assn., Am. Geophysical Union, Berkeley Yacht Club, Yolo Polo Club. Unitarian. Avocations: sailing, travel, polo. Home: 1123 Lochbrae Rd Sacramento CA 95815 Office: Berkeley Nat Lab 70A-3317H 1 Cyclotron Rd Berkeley CA 95815 Business E-Mail: nwquinn@lbl.gov.

QUINN, PAT (JOHN BRIAN PATRICK QUINN), professional sports team manager; b. Hamilton, Ont., Can., Jan. 29, 1943; s. John Ernest and Jean (Ireland) Q.; m. Sandra Georgia Baker, May 1, 1963; children: Valerie, Kathleen. BA in Econs., York U., 1972; JD, Del. Law Sch., 1987. Player Toronto Maple Leafs, Ont., 1968-70, Vancouver Canucks, B.C., Can., 1970-72, Atlanta Flames, 1972-77; coach Phila. Flyers, 1977-82, L.A. Kings, 1984-86; head coach Team Canada, 1986; pres., gen. mgr. Vancouver Canucks, 1987-97, head coach, 1990-97, Toronto Maple Leafs, 1997—. Player rep. NHL, Atlanta, 1973-77, bd. govs., 1987-, head coach, Team Can., Salt Lake City Olympic Games, 2002, World Cup of Hockey, 2004 Named Def. Man of Yr., Vancouver Canucks, 1971, Coach of Yr. NHL, 1979-80, Coach of Yr., Sporting News, 1980, 92, Coach of the Yr. Hockey News, 1980, 92, Coach of the Yr. Acad. Awards of Sports, named to the Longest Unbeaten Record in Profl. Sports of 35 Games, 1979-80; recipient Jake Milford award, 1994, Jack Diamond award, 1994. Roman Catholic. Avocations: sports, reading. Office: Toronto Maple Leafs 60 Carlton St Toronto ON Canada M5B 1L1

QUINN, PAT MALOY, engineering company executive; b. Clay Ctr., Kans., May 28, 1932; s. Lawrence Maloy and Lois Shouse (Benjimen) Q.; m. Virginia Lois White, June 1, 1957; children: Michael Maloy, Jennifer Quinn Williams, Patrick Maloy, Amy Anne. BA in Literature, Kans. State U., 1954, BS in Civil Engring., 1960. Licensed engr., Kans., D.C., Va., N.Y., N.J., Pa., N.C., S.C., N.H., Ohio, Ill., Ind., Ky., W.Va. Civil engr. Schuab-Eaton, Manhattan, Kans., 1957-66, Louis Berger Internat., East Orange, N.J., 1966—, v.p., 1976-84, chief structural engr., 1966-68, chief engr., 1968-72, project mgr., 1973, 1974, v.p., 1974-76, group v.p., ptnr., 1984—. 1st lt. U.S. Army, 1954-57, Germany. Mem. ASCE, ASME, NSPE. Office: Louis Berger Internat 1819 H St NE Ste 900 Washington DC 20002-4017

QUINN, PATRICIA K. literary agent; b. Chico, Calif. d. Donald Joseph and Kathleen (Alexander) Q. BA, Bennington Coll., 1971; MFA in Drama, Yale U., 1976. Prodr., devel. exec. various Off-Broadway and regional theatres, 1976-84; devel. cons. Sundance Film Inst., Utah, 1983—85; theatrical agt. I.C.M., LA, 1985-90; v.p. comedy devel. Warner Bros. TV, Burbank, Calif., 1990-92; lit. and packaging agt. Met. Talent Agy., LA, 1995—2000. Instr. UCLA Ext., 1995—; spkr., lectr. Nat. Assn. of TV Programming Execs., Fla. Bar, NATAS, Media Xchange (Internat.); mem. TV com. Brit. Acad. Film and TV Arts, 2002-; prof. reps. peer group com. NATAS, 2002-04. Founding mem. N.Y. Theatre Workshop, N.Y.C., 1980—86. Mem.: Women in Film (v.p. bd. dirs. 1995—2001). Office: Innovative Artists 1505 10th St Santa Monica CA 90401 E-mail: p_quinn@sbcglobal.net.

QUINN, PATRICK, lieutenant governor; b. Sept. 22, 1948; BS, Georgetown U.; JD Northwestern U. Sch. of Law. Commr. Cook County Bd. of Tax Appeal, 1982; treas. State of Ill., 1990—94, lt. gov., 2003—. Chmn. Ill. River Coordinating Counc., Ill. Rural Affairs Counc., Ill. Rural Bond Bank. Office: James R Thompson Ctr 100 W Randolph 15-200 Chicago IL 60601 also: State Capitol 214 State House Springfield IL 62706

QUINN, PATRICK, tranportation executive; BA, U. Nebr., 1968, JD, 1971. From assoc. to ptnr. Nelson & Harding, Lincoln, Nebr., 1971-77; gen. counsel S.W. Motor Freight, Chattanooga, 1977-85; pres., co-chmn. U.S Xpress Enterprises, Inc., Chattanooga, Tenn., 1985—. Office: US Xpress Enterprises Inc 4080 Jenkins Rd Chattanooga TN 37421-1174

QUINN, PHILIP LAWRENCE, philosophy educator; b. Long Branch, N.J., June 22, 1940; s. Joseph Lawrence and Gertrude (Brown) Q. AB, Georgetown U., 1962; MS, U. Del., 1967; MA, U. Pitts., 1968, PhD, 1970; MA (hon.), Brown U., 1972. Asst. prof. philosophy Brown U., Providence, R.I., 1969-72, assoc. prof. philosophy, 1972-78, prof. philosophy, 1978-85, William Herbert Perry Faunce prof. philosophy, 1982-85; John A. O'Brien prof. philosophy U. Notre Dame, South Bend, Ind., 1985—. Author: Divine Command and Moral Requirements, 1978; editor Faith and Philosophy, 1990-95; co-editor: A Companion to Philosophy of Religion, 1997, The Philosophical Challenge of Religious Diversity, 1999; contbr. articles to profl. jours. Fulbright fellow, 1962-63; Danforth fellow, 1967-69. Mem. AAAS, Am Philos. Assn. (sec., treas. ea. divsn. 1982-85, chmn. career opportunities com. 1985-90, exec. com. ctrl. divsn. 1987-90, v.p. ctrl. divsn. 1993-94, pres. 1994-95, chair ctrl. divsn. nominating com. 1995-96, acting chair Nat. Bd. of Officers 1995-96, chair 1996-99), Philosophy of Sci. Assn. (nominating com. 1984-86), Am. Acad. Arts and Scis., Soc. Christian Philosophers (exec. com. 1981-84), Am. Acad. Religion (steering com. philosophy of religion sect. 1999—). Roman Catholic. Avocations: reading, swimming, film, theater. Home: 1645 W Turtle Creek Dr South Bend IN 46637-5660 Office: Univ Notre Dame Dept Philosophy Notre Dame IN 46556 Office Phone: 574-631-7372.

QUINN, R. JOSEPH, district judge; m. Carole Quinn. BA, St. John's U.; JD, Hamline U. Minn. State rep., 1983-90; formerly judge Minn. Supreme Ct., 1991-99; now. judge Dist. Ct., 1999; chief judge 10th judicial dist., Minn. Office: Anoka County Court 325 E Main St Anoka MN 55303-2483

QUINN, TOM, communications executive; b. L.A., Mar. 14, 1944; s. Joseph Martin and Grace (Cooper) Quinn; children: Douglas, Lori, Shelby. BS, Northwestern U., 1965. Reporter, newswriter ABC Radio, Chgo. and L.A., 1965; reporter, prodr. Sta. KXTV, Sacramento, 1966; day editor City News Svc., L.A., 1966-68, chmn., 1980-85; pres. Americom Broadcasting, Inc., L.A., 1985—. Pres. Radio News West, L.A., 1968—70, Reno Radio Reps., 1998—, KFSO Radio, Fresno, 1995—98; dir. Southland News, L.A. Mem. governing bd. Tahoe Regional Planning Agy., 2002—; campaign mgr. Jerry Brown for Sec. State, L.A., 1970; dep. sec. state Calif. Sacramento, 1971—74; campaign mgr. Brown for Gov., L.A., 1974; sec. Calif. Dept. Environ. Affairs, Sacramento, 1975—79; chmn. Calif. Air Resources Bd., Sacramento, 1975—79, Tom Bradley Mayoral Campaign, 1985. Recipient Headliner of Yr. award Greater L.A. Press Club, 1978, Environ. Protection award Calif. Trial Lawyers Assn., 1979. Democrat. Office: 11400 W Olympic Blvd STE 150 Los Angeles CA 90064-1541

QUINN, WILLIAM FRANCIS, lawyer, director; b. Rochester, N.Y., July 13, 1919; s. Charles Alvin and Elizabeth (Dorrity) Q.; m. Nancy Ellen Witbeck, July 11, 1942; children: William Francis, Stephen Desford, Timothy Charles, Christopher Thomas, Ann Cecily, Mary Kaiulani, Gregory Anthony. BS summa cum laude, St. Louis U., 1940; LLB cum laude, Harvard U., 1947. Bar: Hawaii 1948. Ptnr. Robertson, Castle & Anthony, Honolulu, 1947-57; gov. Ter. of Hawaii, Honolulu, 1957-59, State of Hawaii, Honolulu, 1959-62; ptnr. Quinn & Moore, Honolulu, 1962-64; exec. v.p. Dole Co., Honolulu, 1964-65, pres., 1965-72; ptnr. Jenks, Kidwell, Goodsill & Anderson, Honolulu, 1972-73, Goodsill Anderson & Quinn, 1973-82, Goodsill Anderson Quinn & Stifel, 1982-91; ret., 1991. Mem. sr. adv. bd. 9th Cir. Jud. Coun. Served with USN, 1942-45. Decorated knight of Holy Sepulchre Order. Mem. Pacific Club (Honolulu). Republican. Roman Catholic. Home: 4340 Pahoa Ave Apt 13C Honolulu HI 96816-5023

QUINN, WILLIAM FRANCIS, investment company executive, accountant; b. N.Y.C., Jan. 16, 1948; s. Francis Joseph and Kathleen Elizabeth (McHugh) Q.; m. Doreen Jean Vaccarello, June 7, 1970; children: Billy, Bridget, Kristie, Brian. BS in Acctg., Fordham U., 1969. CPA, N.Y. Auditor Arthur Young & Co., N.Y.C., 1969-74; dir. acctg. Sky Chefs, N.Y.C., 1974-77, v.p. controller, 1977-79; asst. treas. cash mgmt. Am. Airlines, Dallas, Ft. Worth, 1979-81, asst. treas. funds mgmt., 1981-86; pres. AMR Investment Services, Dallas, Ft. Worth, 1986—. Com. in investment employee assets Fin. Exec. Inst., Washington, 1986—; chmn. Am. Airlines Federal Credit Union, Dallas, Ft. Worth, 1979—; founder Dallas-Ft. Worth Pension Group, 1983—; spkr. in field; bd. dirs. Crescent Real Estate Equities, Inc. Bd. dirs. United Way Tarrant County, 1988—; advisor ARCO pension fund. Mem. Am. Inst. CPA's, N.Y. Soc. CPA's. Republican. Roman Catholic. Avocations: reading, tennis, skiing, travel. Office: AMR Investment Services Inc PO Box 619003 Dallas TX 75261-9003 also: AMR Investment 4333 Amon Carter Blvd Fort Worth TX 76155

QUINN, YVONNE SUSAN, lawyer; b. Spring Valley, Ill., May 13, 1951; d. Robert Leslie and Shirley Eilene (Morse) Quinn. BA, U. Ill., 1973; JD, U. Mich., 1976, MA in Econs., 1977. Bar: N.Y. 1978, U.S. Dist. Ct. (ea. and so. dists.) N.Y. 1978, U.S. Ct. Appeals (3d, 5th, 9th, 10th and D.C. cirs.) 1982, U.S. Ct. Appeals (2d cir.) 1992, U.S. Ct. Appeals (4th cir.) 1994, U.S. Supreme Ct. 1982. Assoc. Cravath, Swaine & Moore, N.Y.C., 1977-80, Sullivan & Cromwell, N.Y.C., 1980-84, ptnr., 1984—. Mem. ABA, Assn. of Bar of City of N.Y., India House Club. Office: Sullivan & Cromwell 125 Broad St New York NY 10004-2489 Office Phone: 212-558-3736. Business E-Mail: quinny@sullcrom.com.

QUINNAN, GERALD VINCENT, JR., medical educator; b. Boston, Sept. 7, 1947; s. Gerald Vincent and Mary (Lally) Q.; children: Kevin, Kylie, Kathleen, John, Gerald; m. Leigh A. Sawyer. AB in Chemistry, Coll. Holy Cross, 1969; MD cum laude, St. Louis U., 1973. Diplomate Am. Bd. Internal Medicine. Intern, resident, fellow Boston U. Med. Ctr., 1973-77; med. officer Bur. Biologics, USPHS, Bethesda, Md., 1977; advanced through grades to asst. surgeon gen. USPHS, 1992; dir. herpes virus br., dep. dir. div. virology Bur. Biologics, Bethesda, 1980-81; dir. div. virology Ctr. for Drugs and Biologics, Bethesda, 1981-88; dep. dir. Ctr. Biologics Evaluation and Rsch., Bethesda, 1988-93, acting dir., 1990-92; prof. Uniformed Svcs. U. Health Scis., Bethesda, 1993—, chair preventive medicine, 2002—. Contbr. chpts. to books, numerous articles to profl. jours.; editl. bd./reviewer several jours. Fellow Infectious Diseases Soc. Am.; mem. AAAS, Am. Soc. for Microbiology, Am. Soc. for Clin. Investigation, Sigma Xi, Alpha Omega Alpha. Roman Catholic. Office: Uniformed Svcs U Hlth Scis Dept Preventive Medicine & Biometrics 4301 Jones Bridge Rd Bethesda MD 20814-4712 Office Phone: 301-295-3173. Business E-Mail: gquinnan@usuhs.mil.

QUINONES, JOSE RAMON, JR., obstetrician-gynecologist, educator; b. N.Y.C., 1940; MD, U. P.R., 1963. Diplomate Am. Bd. Ob-Gyn. Intern USAF Hosp., Washington, 1963-64; resident in ob-gyn. Kings County-SUNY Downstate Med. Ctr., Bklyn., 1967-71; staff N.Y. Meth. Hosp. Bklyn., 1971—, Brookdale Hosp., Bklyn., 1985—2001. Clin. assoc. prof. SUNY Downstate. Fellow ACOG, ACS; mem. AMA. Office: Ste 103 6410 Veterans Ave Brooklyn NY 11234

QUIÑONES KEBER, ELOISE, art historian, educator; b. LA; d. Rudy Jr. and Margaret Q. BA, Immaculate Heart Coll., 1966; MA, UCLA, 1967, Columbia U., 1979, PhD, 1984. Lectr. Columbia U., N.Y.C., 1984-86; prof. art history Baruch Coll., The Grad. Ctr., CUNY, 1986—. Author: Codex Telleriano Remensis: Ritual, Divination, and History in a Pictorial Aztec Manuscript, 1995 (Getty Grant Program Publ. Subvention award, 1992); co-author: Art of Aztec Mexico: Treasures of Tenochtitlan, 1983; editor: Chipping Away on Earth: Studies in Prehispanic and Colonial Mexico in Honor of Arthur J.O. Anderson and Charles E. Dibble, 1995, In Chalchihuitl in Quetzalli: Mesoamerican Studies in Honor of Doris Heyden, 2000, Representing Aztec Ritual: Performance, Text, and Image in the Work of Sahagún, 2002; co-editor: The Work of Bernardino de Sahagun: Pioneer Ethnographer of 16th-Century Aztec Mexico, 1988, Mixteca-Puebla: Discoveries and Research in Mesoamerican Archaeology and Art, 1994; contbr. articles to profl. jours. Mellon postdoctoral fellow Columbia U., 1984-86, fellow Ford Found./NRC, 1986-87, Am. Coun. of Learned Socs. fellow, 1987-88, 93-94, grantee, 1985, 95, NEH fellow, 1993-94, grantee, 1986, 91; grantee Am. Philos. Soc., 1986; fellow Guggenheim Found., 1998; recipient Ralph Waldo Emerson award Phi Beta Kappa Soc., 1996. Mem. Coll. Art Assn., Assn. Latin Am. Art, Am. Soc. for Ethnohistory. Office: CUNY Grad Ctr Art History Program 365 Fifth Ave New York NY 10016 also: CUNY Grad Ctr and CUNY Baruch Coll Dept Fine and Performing Arts 1 Bernard Baruch Way New York NY 10010-1703 E-mail: Eloise_Quinones-Keber@baruch.cuny.edu., equinones@mindspring.com., EQuinones-Keber@gc.cuny.com.

QUINSON, BRUNO ANDRE, publishing executive; b. Norwich, Conn., Jan. 1, 1938; s. Louis Jean and Suzanne Marie (Richard) Q.; m. Mary Ann Goodman, May 3, 1980; children by previous marriage: Timothy Bruno, Marc Albert (dec.), Christopher Louis; stepchildren: J. Geoffrey Taylor, Luke J. Taylor (dec.), Adam J. Taylor, Joshua P. Taylor. BA, Williams Coll., 1958; postgrad., NYU, 1960-61. Product mgr. Simon & Schuster, N.Y.C., 1960-65; pub., gen. mgr. Golden Press (div. Western Pub. Co., Inc.), 1965-70; pres. Larousse & Co., Inc., N.Y.C., 1970-82, also bd. dirs.; pres. trade and reference div. Macmillan Pub. Co., N.Y.C., 1982-88; pres., chief exec. officer Henry Holt & Co. Inc., N.Y.C., 1988-96. Bd. dirs. Millbrook Press, 1999-2004, The Frost Place, Music & More, Fitzhenry & Whiteside, 1997-2003, Nat. Book Found., chmn., 1993-96; treas. Columbia Univ. Press, 1994-2003, vice chmn., 1997-2003; mem. exec. bd. Macmillan Ltd., 1995-96. Bd. dirs. Rye (N.Y.) Art Ctr., treas., 1973-74; bd. dirs. Northside Ctr. for Child Devel., 1981-89, chmn., 1987-89, mem. adv. bd., 1990—; bd. dirs. 1115 Fifth Ave. Corp., 1983-94, 96-2004, pres., 1998-2003; bd. dirs. Mus. of the City of N.Y., 1999—, Lycee Francais de New York, 1994-96, Vol. Cons. Group, 1997, Each Child a Reader Found., 1996; founding mem. Barrington Stage Co.; founding mem., bd. dirs. Interlaken Sch. Art, 1998-2001; mem. nat. adv. bd. Eudora Welty Found., 2002—; trustee, Leopold Schepp Found., 2001—; bd. dirs., Manhattan Theater Club, 1991-1997, emeritus 1997—; bd. trustees, PEN Am. Ctr., 2003—. Decorated chevalier Des Arts et Lettres (France). Mem. Am. Assn. Pubs. (bd. dirs. 1991-95), Pubs.' Lunch Club (pres. 1990-93), Century Assn., Norfolk Country Club, The River Club. Office: 2 E 93rd St New York NY 10128-0610

QUINT, ARNOLD HARRIS, lawyer; b. Boston, Jan. 3, 1942; s. Milton and Esther (Kirshen) Q.; m. Susan Arenson, July 23, 1967; children: Edward, Michael. AB, Haverford (Pa.) Coll., 1963; LLB, Yale U., 1966. Bar: D.C. 1967. Supervisory atty. Power Commn., Washington, 1967-70; assoc. Hunton & Williams, Washington, 1970-74, ptnr., 1974—. Mem. ABA, Energy Bar Assn. (com. chmn. 1979-83, bd. dirs. 1989-92). Office: Hunton & Williams 1900 K St NW Washington DC 20006-1110 Office Phone: 202-955-1542. E-mail: aquint@hunton.com.

QUINT, DOUGLAS JOSEPH, neuroradiology educator; b. NYC, Apr. 25, 1956; s. George and Barbara (Gilder) Q.; m. Leslie Eisenbud, May 23, 1982; children: Mark Harry, Jason Meyer. BA, Wesleyan U., Middletown, Conn., 1978; MD, Cornell U., 1982. Diplomate Nat. Bd. Med. Examiners, Am. Bd. Radiology. Med. intern U. Mich. Hosps., Ann Arbor, 1982-83, resident in radiology, 1983-86; fellow in neuroradiology, mem. assoc. staff Henry Ford Hosp., Detroit, 1986-88; prof. neuroradiology and MRI U. Mich. Med. Sch., Ann Arbor, 1988—. Contbr. articles to med. jours. Mem. Am. Soc. Neuroradiology (sr.), Radiol. Soc. N.Am., Am. Roentgen Ray Soc., Am. Coll. Radiology, AMA. Avocations: softball, tennis, model trains, photography, baseball. Office: U Mich Hosp Radiology Dept 1500 E Medical Ctr Dr Ann Arbor MI 48109-0030 Office Phone: 734-936-4460.

QUINT, IRA, retail executive; b. N.Y.C., May 29, 1930; s. Theodore Isaac and Rebecca (Ginandes) Q.; m. Carol Ann Goldsmith (div. Feb. 1984); children: Susan Amy, Stephanie Ann. BS, NYU, 1951; MBA, Harvard U., 1954. Group nat. mdse. mgr. Sears Roebuck & Co., Chgo., 1954-78; pres. Colonial Corp. Am., N.Y.C., 1978-79; pres., CEO Venture Stores, St. Louis, 1979-81; exec. v.p. Montgomery Ward, Chgo., 1981-85; pres. Lane Bryant Stores, N.Y.C., 1985-90; pres., chief exec. officer Conston Corp., Phila., 1990-92; pres. Quint Consultancy, N.Y.C., 1992—; dir. Maggie Moos Internat., 2001—. Mem.: Harvard (N.Y.C.). Home and Office: 130 E 67th St New York NY 10021-6136

QUINTANILLA, ANTONIO PAULET, retired physician, educator; b. Feb. 8, 1927; came to U.S., 1963, naturalized, 1974; s. Leandro Marino and Edel Paulet Quintanilla; m. Mary Parker Rodriguez, May 2, 1958; children: Antonio Paulet, Angela, Francis, Cecilia, John. PhD, San Marcos U., 1948, MD, 1957. Assoc. prof. physiology U. Arequipa, Peru, 1960-63; assoc. in physiology Cornell U., N.Y., 1963-64; prof. physiology U. Arequipa, 1964-68; assoc. prof. medicine Northwestern U., 1969-80, prof., 1980-2000; ret., 2000. Chief renal sect. VA Lakeside Hosp., 1976-90; cons. nephrologist Northwestern Meml. Hosp., Evanston Hosp., 1990-98, sr. attending emeritus; lectr. nat. Ctr. Advanced Med. Edn., Chgo.; mem. adv. bd. Am. Fedn. Clin. Rsch. Contbr. articles on renal disease to med. jours.; author books in English and Spanish, poetry, short stories. Fellow ACP; mem. Ctrl. Soc. Clin. Rsch., Internat. Soc. Nephrology, Am. Soc. Nephrology, Am. Physiol. Soc. Home: 650 S River Rd Unit 411 Des Plaines IL 60016-8428 E-mail: a.p.quintanilla@worldnet.att.net.

QUINTANILLA-VILLANUEVA, ROSALINDA, economist; b. Monterrey, Mex., Feb. 22, 1959; came to U.S., 1978; d. Ernesto Quintanilla and Marina Villanueva. BA in Econs. with high honors, Inst. Tech. Monterrey, 1976; MA in Econs., U. Wis., Milw., 1979; PhD in Econs., U. Minn., 1988. Rsch. assoc. Econometric Unit Inst. Tech. Monterrey, 1976; cons. Grupo Indsl. ALFA, Monterrey, 1977; assoc. prof. econs. U. Autonoma Metropolitana, Mexico City, 1977-78; economist, working with countries in L.Am., Asia, Ea. Europe World Bank, Washington, 1991—. Nat. Coun. Sci. and Technology fellow, 1978-82. Avocations: painting, Mexican history, world history. Office: World Bank 1818 H St NW Washington DC 20433-0001

QUINTANS, ALFREDO SISON, JR., thoracic and cardiovascular surgeon; b. Dagupan City, Philippines, Dec. 25, 1937; s. Alfredo L. Quintans, Sr. and Sotera S. Sison; m. Estrellita Tan Quintans: children: Armel, Alfredo III, Arlene Quintans Carr. MD, U. Santo Tomas, Manilla, Philippines, 1961. Diplomate Am. Bd. Gen. Surgery, Am. Bd. Thoracic Surgery; lic. surgeon, N.C., N.Y. Rotating intern St. Luke's Hosp., Newburgh, N.Y., 1963-64, surg. resident, 1964-66, chief surg. resident, 1966-67, 68-69, emergency room physician, 1969-70, attending thoracic and cardiovascular surgeon, 1972—; chief surg. resident Youngstown (Ohio) Hosp. Assocs., 1967-68; resident in thoracic and cardiovascular surgery VA Hosp./Duke U. Hosp., Oteen and Durham, N.C., 1970-72; pvt. practice thoracic and cardiovascular surgeon New Windsor, N.Y., 1972—; attending thoracic and cardiovascular surgeon Cornwall (N.Y.) Hosp., 1972—. Cons. VA. Hosp., Castle Point, N.Y. Fellow ACS, Am. Coll. Chest Physicians; mem. Am. Thoracic Soc. (N.Y. Trudeau Soc. chpt.), Soc. Thoracic Surgeons, N.Y. State Med. Soc., Med. Soc. County Orange, Mid-Hudson Surg. Soc., Inc. Home: 3212 Nys Route 9W New Windsor NY 12553-6756

QUINTERO, RONALD GARY, management consultant; b. Detroit, Jan. 5, 1954; s. John Urdiales and Jean Lorraine (Morton) Q.; m. Barbara Kay McDaniel, June 15, 1985; children: Jean Marie, Alexandra Lisa. AB, Lafayette Coll., 1975; MS, NYU, 1976, APC, 1978. CPA, CFA, CFP, cert. mgmt. acct., cert. fraud examiner, cert. insolvency, cert. turnaround profl.; accreditation in bus. valuation. Sr. mgr. Peat, Marwick, Mitchell & Co., N.Y.C., 1975-85; workout cons. Zolfo, Cooper & Co., N.Y.C., 1985-87; assoc. Bear, Stearns & Co., Inc., N.Y.C., 1987-88; prin. R. G. Quintero & Co., N.Y.C., 1988—. Mng. dir. Chartered Capital Advisers, Inc., N.Y.C., 1988—; adj. prof. New Sch. for Social Rsch., N.Y.C., 1983-85; internat. lectr.; adj. prof. N.Y. Inst. Fin., N.Y.C., 1988—; instr. Ctr. for Profl. Edn., Berwyn, Pa., 1991—; leading provider CFA Sems. Author: (book and cassette) Mergers and Acquisitions, 1990, CFA Review Notes, 2001; contbg. author several books; contbr. articles to profl. jours.; creator: Quintero Index of Bankrupt Stocks. Mem. AICPAs, Am. Bankruptcy Inst., N.Y. Soc. CPAs (chmn. com. 1990-91, Max Block Disting. Article award 1990, Outstanding Discussion Leader 1991), Turnaround Mgmt. Assn. (bd. dirs., exec. com.). Avocations: squash, softball, running, computers, reading. Office: R G Quintero & Co 145 4th Ave New York NY 10003-4906 E-mail: q@rgquintero.com.

QUINTIERE, GARY GANDOLFO, lawyer; b. Passaic, N.J., Nov. 26, 1944; s. Benjamin and Sadie (Riotto) Q.; m. Judy Rosenthal, Aug. 16, 1966; children: Karen, Geoffrey. AB in Govt., Lafayette Coll., 1966; JD, George Washington U., 1969. Bar: Va. 1969, D.C. 1970. Law clk. to Judge Philip Nichols, Jr. U.S. Ct. Appeals (Fed. cir.), Washington, 1969-70; from assoc. to ptnr. Miller & Chevalier, Washington, 1970-85; ptnr. Morgan, Lewis & Bockius, Washington, 1985—. Mem. ABA, D.C. Bar Assn., Va. Bar Assn., Am. Coll. Employee Benefits Counsel. Avocations: tennis, skiing, golf. Home: 14 Mercy Ct Potomac MD 20854-4540 Office: Morgan Lewis & Bockius 1111 Pennsylvania Ave NW Washington DC 20004

QUINT SEHAT, ARLENE, art history educator, curator, museum administrator; b. Chgo., Sept. 4, 1944; d. Milton and Ruth Quint; m. Kourosh Sehat, July 11, 1938. BA in Art History, U. Calif., 1966, MA in Art History, 1969, PhD in Art History, 1974. Asst. prof. Calif. State U., L.A., 1969-76, assoc. prof., 1976-79; fine arts mgmt. specialist, curator of collections U.S. gen. svcs. adminstrn. Washington, 1980-88; assoc. prof. Coll. Notre Dame, Balt., 1988-90; vis. assoc. prof Lincoln U., Pa., 1993-95; lectr. in art history Morgan State U., Balt., 1994—. Vis. assoc. prof. HUC Skirball Mus., L.A., 1975-77; cataloger, rschr. NYU, N.Y.C., 1969; rschr. Los Angeles County Mus. Art, 1964-66; chancellor's tchr. fellow U. Calif., 1966-67; adj. prof. Towson U., Balt. Contbr. articles to profl. jours. R & D grantee Coll. Notre Dame, Balt. Mem. Am. Assn. Museums, Internat. Coun. Museums (mem. documentation working group, internat. coord. conservation documentation), Coll. Art Assn., Arts Club Washington (chmn. edn. and scholarship com., admissions and membership com.).

QUINTYN, CONRAD BEZEKIAH, anthropologist, educator; s. Walter Hezekiah and Joycelyn Orlena Quintyn. BA in Anthropology, Baylor U., 1991; MA in Anthropology, U. Mich., 1993, PhD in Anthropology, 1999. Asst. prof. Washtenaw C.C., Ann Arbor, Mich., 2000—00, Iowa State U., Ames, 2000—01; rsch. scientist U. Mich., Ann Arbor, 2002—. Forensic anthropologist U.S. Army Ctrl. ID Lab, Honolulu, 2001—02; asst. prof. SUNY, Oswego, 2003. Author: The Father of Man: Meeting the True Adam, 2003; editor: Gardens of Youth, 2003, Theatree of the Mind, 2003. With USN, 1983—87. Decorated Good Conduct ribbon, Sea Svc. ribbon, Fleet Marine Force ribbon; fellow Rackham Merit fellow, U. Mich., 1992—97; grantee, 1996, Rackham Dissertation grantee, 1999, Irene Sala Levi Care Archaeological Found., 1997. Mem.: Am. Mus. Natural History (assoc.), Nat. Geog. Soc. (assoc.), Am. Assn. Phys. Anthropologists (assoc.), Am. Anthrop. Assn. (assoc.), VFW (assoc.). Achievements include Recovery and identification of the remains of a U.S. pilot shot down in Rabaul Is, New Guinea in 1942, during WWII. Recovery

and identification of the remains of a U.S. pilot missing in Laos,1971. Office: U Mich Dept Anthropology Ann Arbor MI 48109 Home: 329 Maple St Apt 8 Oswego NY 13126-3416 E-mail: darnoc@umich.edu., CBQuintyn@hotmail.com.

QUIRK, ALFRED P, JR., corporate financial executive; BA in econ., Holy Cross, 1980; MBA, Cornell U., 1984. Investment analyst, bond investment dept. Aetna Inc., 1984—, sr. investment officer, 1988, asst. v.p., corp. fin., 1991, v.p., 1996, v.p., fin., treas., 1999—. Office: Aetna Inc 151 Farmington Ave Hartford CT 06156

QUIRK, FRANK JOSEPH, management consulting company executive; b. NYC, Feb. 27, 1941; s. Frank J. and Madeline B. Quirk; m. Betty Josephine Mauldin, Jan. 7, 1967; children: Laura Josephine, Katherine Elizabeth. BA, Cornell U., 1962, MBA, 1964. Assoc. Booz, Allen & Hamilton, Inc., Chgo. and Washington, 1967-72; exec. v.p. Macro Internat., Inc., Calverton, Md., 1972-79, pres., CEO, 1980-98, chmn., CEO, 1998—; exec. v.p. Opinion Rsch. Corp., Princeton, NJ, 1999—2003, pres., 2003—. Bd. dirs. Profl. Svcs. Coun., Opinion Rsch. Corp., Smithsonian Instn. Librs. Served to capt. U.S. Army, 1964-66. Capt. U.S. Army, 1964—66. Mem. Belle Haven Country Club. Home: 2110 Foresthill Rd Alexandria VA 22307-1128 Office: Macro Internat Inc 11785 Beltsville Dr Beltsville MD 20705-3121 Office Phone: 301-572-0200.

QUIRK, I-FAN, filmmaker; m. Justine Litchman, Aug. 18, 2002. BA with honors, Princeton U., 1991; MFA, N.Y. U., 1996. Dir. Being Claudine Prodn., N.Y.C., 1998—; COO A Dozen Eggs Films, N.Y.C., 2003—. Dir.: (film) Being Claudine (First prize Best Dir., R.I. Film Festival, 2001, Grand prize Telluride Indiefest), Desire (Commendation Two Stars, Can. Internat. Film Festival, 1996), (play) Friendship, (film) Spinnin' Daze, The Hustle. Recipient Post-Prodn. award, Warner Bros., 1999; John B. Lynch scholar, Princeton U., 1987—91. Personal E-mail: ifanquirk@hotmail.com.

QUIRK, JOHN JAMES, investment company executive; b. N.Y.C., July 10, 1943; s. Francis J. and Madeline A. (Meizinger) Q.; m. Kathryn Anne O'Brien, Mar. 21, 1963; children: John James, Ashlin Carter, Merritt Andrew. BA, Georgetown U., 1965; MBA, U. Va., 1967. Asst. treas., mgr. corp. fin. dept. W.R. Grace & Co., N.Y.C., 1967-74; asst. v.p., asst. treas. City Investing Co., N.Y.C., 1974-77, v.p., treas., 1978-81, sr. v.p., treas., 1982-85; chmn. bd. Quirk Carson Peppet Inc., 1985-98; prin. Churchill Capital, Inc., 1999—2001; mng. dir. Morgan, Joseph & Co. Inc., 2001—. Bd. dirs. Environ. Opportunities Fund., Ltd., City Investing Co. Liquidating Trust. Mem.: Racquet and Tennis; Wee Burn (Conn.). Home: 445 Hollow Tree Ridge Rd Darien CT 06820-3030 Office: 600 5th Ave Fl 19 New York NY 10020-2302 E-mail: jquirk@morganjoseph.com.

QUIRK, KATHLEEN L. mining executive; BS in Acctg., La. State U. With Mobil Oil Corp., Dallas; from mem. staff to treas. Freeport-McMoRan Copper & Gold Inc., New Orleans, 1989—2000, treas., 2000—, sr. v.p., 2003—, CFO, 2003—. Office: Freeport McMoRan Copper & Gold Inc 1615 PoydrasSt New Orleans LA 70112*

QUIRK, PETER RICHARD, engineering company executive; b. New Orleans, Dec. 28, 1936; s. Andrew John and Elise (Richard) Q.; m. Marilyn Ann Montalban, Aug. 16, 1958; children: Karen, Cheryl, Brian, Kathleen, Aimee, Elizabeth. BS, La. State U., 1959. Registered profl. engr., La. Sr. staff engr. Continental Oil Co., Ponca City, Okla., 1959-64; pres. Walk, Haydel & Assocs. Inc., New Orleans, 1964—, now pres. and CEO, v.p. bus. devel. Mem. Bur. Govtl. Rsch., Natural Gas Assn. of New Orleans, 1991—. Active World Trade Ctr., 1972—; bd. dirs. Closer Walk Ministries, 1984—, Covenant Ho. New Orleans, 1989—, Met. Area Com., 1989—, La. State U. Found., 1989—, Phi Kappa Theta Nat. Found., 1990—, Cath. Found., 1993—, Xavier U., 1995—; chair bd. dirs. United Way of Greater New Orleans, 1996, chmn. gen. campaign, 1991, co-chair Day of Caring, 1995; bd. dirs. U. New Orleans Higher Edn. Coun., 1992—; mem. adv. bd. U. New Orleans Ctr. for Energy Resources Mgmt., 1992—; chair exec. com. Archbishop's Cmty. Appeal, 1993—, Daughters of Charity Health Svc., 1996—; chair Cystic Fibrosis Found. Ann. Walk, 1993; steering com. LaVitae Found., 1998—; mem. Ursuline Acad. Capital Campaign Adv. Bd. 1998—, Ursuline Acad. Recipient A.E. Wilder Jr. award Cons. Engr. Coun. L.A., 1989, Vol. Activist award, 1993, Man of Achievement award Phi Kappa Theta Nat. Found., 1991, Order St. Louis award. Mem. Instrument Soc. Am., NSPE, Constrn. Mgmt. Assn. Am. (bd. dirs. 1987-90), La. Engring. Soc. (A.M. Lockett medal 1999), Am. Cons. Engrs. Council (trustee polit. action com. 1984-90, fellow 1988, Cmty. Svc. award 1996), Cons. Engrs. Council La. (pres. 1982-83), New Orleans and River Region C. of C., La. Chem. Industry Alliance, Greater New Orleans Bus. Roundtable, Paper Industry Mgmt. Assn., Phi Kappa Theta. Clubs: Serra (New Orleans pres. 1986, 94-95), Engineers (New Orleans pres. 1984-85). Republican. Roman Catholic. Home: 1201 Beverly Gardens Dr Metairie LA 70002-1903 Office: Walk Haydel & Assocs Inc 600 Carondelet St New Orleans LA 70130-3511

QUIRK, RAYMOND R, investment company executive; married; 3 children. Former cty. mgr., regional mgr., divsn. one mgr., COO Fidelity, 1985, now pres., 2003—. Mem. bd. dirs. Fidelity Nat. Title, Alamo Title, Chgo. Title, Home Warranty subsidiaries of Fidelity Nat. Fin. Avocation: golf.

QUIRK, RONALD JOSEPH, language educator; s. Maurice Joseph and Minnie Quirk; m. Virginia Traverso, Sept. 2, 1967; children: Teresa, Maria, Andrew, Thomas. BA, Trinity Coll., Hartford, Conn., 1964; MA, Brown U., Providence, R.I., 1966, PhD, 1971. Instr. R.I. Coll., Providence, 1968; asst. prof. Trinity Coll., Hartford, Conn., 1971—74; prof. Quinnipiac U., Hamden, Conn., 1974—, dept. chmn., 1984—93, assoc. provost, 1993—97. Author: (books) Basic Spanish for Legal Personnel, 1979, Serafín Estébanez Calderón, 1992, Literature as Introspection: Spain Confronts Trafalgar, 1998. Mem. Bristol Bd. Edn., Conn., 1978—83. Woodrow Wilson Hon. Fellow, 1964. Mem.: Phi Beta Kappa. Roman Catholic. Office: Quinnipiac Univ 275 Mt Carmel Ave Hamden CT 06518 Business E-Mail: ronald.quirk@quinnipiac.edu.

QUIRKE, LILLIAN MARY, retired art educator; b. West Haven, Conn., Oct. 1, 1928; d. Mortimer Francis and Ellen Louise (Bird) Q. BS, BA, So. Conn. U., 1950; MA, Long Beach State U., 1953, EdD, Columbia U., 1963. Cert. elem. and art tchr., Conn., Calif. Tchr. Long Beach (Calif.) Pub. Schs., 1950-54; jr. high art tchr. Army Dependents Sch., Frankfurt, Germany, 1954-55; art tchr. Navy Dependents Sch., Naples, Italy, 1955-56; art instr. So. Conn. U., New Haven, 1956-64, Foothill C.C., Los Altos, Calif., 1964-67; from art instr. to prof. DeAnza C.C., Cupertino, Calif., 1967-88; adj. prof. Queens (N.Y.) Coll., 1990-91. Author: The Rug Book, 1979; contbr. articles to profl. jours.; mem. editl. bd. Art Edn. mag., 1985-87. Active Dem. and Rep. Ctrl. Coms., San Jose, Calif., 1968-71; mem. arts rev. com. Cupertino Pub. Libr., 1977-81. Title IV grantee, 1967, grantee State of Calif., 1968, NDEA grantee U.S. Office Edn., 1966. Mem. Nat. Art Edn. Assn. (life, sec. Pacific chpt. 1954—, founder higher edn. sect. 1973), Calif. Art Edn. Assn. (rsch. chair 1969-72), Artists and Tech. (bd. dirs. 1984-88), Fla. Shore and Beach Preservation Assn. (founding bd. dirs. St. Johns First Coast chpt. 1996, sec.-treas. 1996-97, sec. 1996-98). Avocations: quilting, boating, cooking, computer graphics. Home: 5916 Rio Royalle Rd Saint Augustine FL 32080-7304 E-mail: liljim@aug.com.

QUIRMBACH, HERMAN CHARLES, economics professor; b. St. Paul, Minn., Oct. 6, 1950; s. William Herman and Elizabeth Lou (Ziegler) Q. AB in Govt. cum laude, Harvard U., 1972; AM in Econs., Princeton U., 1980, PhD in Econs., 1983. Assoc. economist, cons. Rand Corp., Santa Monica, Calif., 1981—; assoc. prof. econs. Iowa State U., Ames, 1990—. Vis. asst. prof. econs. U. Wis., Madison, 1983—84; mem. numerous coms. Iowa State Senate. Contbr. articles to profl. jours. Treas. Story County Dem. Party, Ames, 1992-94; councilman 4th ward Ames City Coun., 1995-2003; pres. Iowa Civil Liberties Union, 2001-02, bd. dirs., 1996—2002; bd. dirs. Ames Mcpl. Utility Retirement Sys., 1996-2003, Ames Convention and Visitors Bur., 1997-99; Ames mayor pro tem, 2002; mem. Student Aid Commn., Iowa Coll., 2003—; mem. Iowa Property Tax Implementation Com., 2003—; mem. Iowa Senate Dist. 23, 2003—. Recipient Don Biggs award for polit. leadership, 1998-99. Mem. AAUP, ACLU, Ames League of Women Voters, Am. Econ. Assn., Econometric Soc., Ames C. of C., Appalachian Mountain Club, White Mountain Four Thousand Footer Club, Ames Kiwanis Club, Ames Patriotic Coun. Office: Iowa State Univ Econs Dept Heady Hall Ames IA 50011

QUIROGA, ALICIA ESPINOSA, physiatrist; b. Manila; d. Eugenio Rillo and Felisa Padiernos (Espinosa) Q. BS, U. Philippines, 1969, MD, 1973. Rotating intern Philippine Gen. Hosp., Manila, 1973-74, resident dept. pediatrics, 1975-77; resident dept. phys. medicine and rehab. U. Md., Balt., 1977-80; fellow in pediatrics & rehab. Children's Hosp. Nat. Med. Ctr., Washington, 1980-81; fellow George Washington U. Hosp., Washington, 1980-81; attending physiatrist, asst. prof. U. Md. Sch. Medicine, Balt., 1981-86; attending physiatrist Sinai Hosp. of Balt., 1986-87; chief rehab. medicine svc. VA Med. Ctr., Augusta, Ga., 1987—. Fellow Am. Acad. Phys. Medicine and Rehab.; mem. Assn. Acad. Physiatrists. also: Macon Rehab Ctr 3330 Northside Dr Macon GA 31210-2559 Office: Apt 1041 9860 62nd Ter N Saint Petersburg FL 33708-3534 Home: 11899 Marla Ln Seminole FL 33772-2219

QUISENBERRY, NANCY LOU, university administrator, educator; b. Washington, Ind., Jan. 29, 1938; d. Joseph Franklin and Maud Helen (Fitch) Forbes; m. James D. Quisenberry, Feb. 6, 1960; 1 child, James Paul. BS in Home Econs., Ind. State Tchrs. Coll., 1960, MS in Home Econs., 1962; EdD, Ind. U., 1971. Cert. tchr. Ind. Home economics tchr. Honey Creek High Sch., Terre Haute, Ind., 1961-62; third grade tchr. Indpls. Pub. Sch., 1962-64; sustitute tchr. Dep. of Def., Baumholder, Fed. Republic Germany, 1964-65; first grade tchr. Wayne Twp. Schs., Indpls., 1966-67; assoc. faculty lang. arts Ind. U.-Purdue U., Indpls., spring 1970; prof. curriculum and instruction So. Ill. U., Carbondale, 1971—98, assoc. dean Coll. of Edn., 1976-96, interim dean, 1996-98; exec. dir. Orpheum Children's Sci. Mus., Champaign, Ill., 2004—. Cons. U. N.C., Durham, 1977, Ministry Edn., Bangkok, 1980, Bangkok, 84, DePaul U., 1990, Ill. State U., 2002, U. Miss., 2001, Loyola U., 2002, Gov.'s State U., 2002; dir. tech. and tng. assistance grant Head Start-OCD, Carbondale, 1972—74, Cameroon project USAID, Carbondale, 1984—86; mem. Ill. State Tchr. Cert. Bd., 1981—84, 1984—87. Co-author: Early Childhood Education Programs: Developmental Objectives and Their Use, 1975, Play as Development, 1978, Educators Healing Racism, 1999, Racism in the Classroom: Case Studies, 2002. Bd. dirs. Jackson County YMCA, 1988; chair candidacy com. Ctrl. So. Ill. Synod Evang. Luth. Ch. Am., Springfield, 1987—90, sec. multisynodical com. Chgo., 1987—90, synod coun., 1992—95; pres. Epiphany Luth. Ch. Coun., Carbondale, 1984—85, 1989—92, 1994—96. Recipient Dare To Be Great award, Ill. Women Adminstrs. and So. Ill. Region, 1989, Woman of Distinction award, So. Ill. U., 1992; grantee, Bur. Educationally Handicapped, 1979—82, 1990—95. Mem.: World Orgn. for Pre-sch. Edn. (U.S. nat. com., treas. 1997—99, chmn. strategic planning commn. 1999—2002, webmaster 2000—), Assn. Tchr. Educators (chair com. racism from a healing perspective 1995—98), Ill. Assn. Colls. for Tchr. Edn. (pres. 1984—86), Am. Assn. Colls. for Tchr. Edn. (bd. dirs. 1986—88, chair adv. coun. state reps. 1987—88, bd. dirs. 1991—94), Nat. Coun. for Accreditation Tchr. Edn. (bd. examiners 1987—98, new profl. tchr. project elem. edn. stds. drafting com. 1996—98, transition team elem. stds. 1998—2000, chair Rubics devel. com. 2001, exec. bd. 2002—, chair Coun. Profl. Preparation of Educators 2003—), Assn. Childhood Edn. Internat. (chair tchr. edn. com. 1989—93, folio rev. coord. elem. edn. 1989—2001, sec.-treas. 1996—, pres.-elect 1998—2000, pres. 2001—03, folio rev. coord. elem. edn. 2004—, past pres. 2003—04), Internat. Coun. on Edn. for Tchg. (N.Am. v.p. 1992—94, pres.-elect 1997—2000, pres. 2000—02, bd. dirs.). Avocations: gardening, flute, sewing, walking, organ. Home: 1713 E Mumford Dr Urbana IL 61802-8605 Office: So Ill U Coll Edn Carbondale IL 62901-4624 E-mail: nancyq@siu.edu.

QUIST, CAROL BENNION, editor; d. Feramorz Horne Bennion and Flora Melissa Stewart; m. William Woodbury Quist, June 24, 1959; children: William, Douglas, Jerald, Ronald, Kenneth. AB, Stanford U., Calif., 1958; MA, U. Utah, Salt Lake City, 1990. Freelance editor Editorial Svcs. Inc., Salt Lake City, 1980—; instr. Salt Lake CC, Salt Lake City, 1990—2000; assoc. editor Sunstone Edn. Found., Salt Lake City, 1993—. Author essays. Recipient Prix de Paris, Vogue Mag., 1958, First Pl. lightverse, Utah Arts Coun., 1987. Mem.: Utah State Poetry Soc., League Utah Writers, Golden Key Honor Soc. Avocations: travel, gardening, theater. Office: Sunstone Edn Found Inc 343 N Third W Salt Lake City UT 84103

QUIST, GORDON JAY, federal judge; b. Grand Rapids, Mich., Nov. 12, 1937; s. George J. and Ida F. (Hoekstra) Q.; m. Jane Capito, Mar. 10, 1962; children: Scot D., George J., Susan E., Martha J., Peter K. BA, Mich. State U., 1959; JD with honors, George Washington U., 1962. Bar: D.C. 1962, Ill. 1964, U.S. Dist. Ct. (no. dist.) Ill. 1964, U.S. Supreme Ct. 1965, Mich. 1967, U.S. Dist. Ct. (we. dist.) Mich. 1967, U.S. Ct. Appeals (6th cir.) 1967. Assoc. Hollabaugh & Jacobs, Washington, 1962-64, Sonnenschein, Levinson, Carlin, Nath & Rosenthal, Chgo., 1964-66, Miller, Johnson, Snell & Cummiskey, Grand Rapids, 1967-72, ptnr., 1972-92, mng. ptnr., 1986-92; judge U.S. Dist. Ct. (we. dist.) Mich., Grand Rapids, 1992—. Mem. Code of Conduct com. U.S. Cts., 2000—. Bd. dirs. Wedgewood Acres-Ch. Youth Home, 1968-74, Mary Free Bed Hosp., 1979-88, Christian Ref. Publs., 1968-78, 82-88, Opera Grand Rapids, 1986-92, Mary Free Bed Brace Shop, 1988-92, Better Bus. Bur., 1972-80, Calvin Theol. Sem., 1992-93; bd. dirs. Indian Trails Camp, 1970-78, 82-88, pres., 1978, 88. Recipient Disting. Alumnus award George Washington U. Law Sch. 1998 Mem. Am. Indicature Soc., Mich. State Bar Found., Univ. Club Grand Rapids, Order of Coif, Am. Inns Ct. Avocations: reading, travel. Office: 482 Ford Fed Courthouse 110 Michigan St NW Grand Rapids MI 49503-2313 E-mail: Gordon_J_Quist@miwd.uscourts.gov.

QUITTNER, JOSH, editor-in-chief; m. Michelle Slatalla; 3 children. Grad., Grinnell Coll., Columbia U. With Bergen Record, NJ, Albuquerque Jour., Newsday; joined TIME, 1995, mng. editor time.com, mng. editor ON Mag., tech. editor; editor in chief Bus. 2.0, N.Y.C., 2002—. Co-author (with M. Slatalla): Flame Wars: A Cyberthriller, 1995, Masters of Deception: The Gang That Ruled Cyberspace, 1997, Speeding the Net: The Inside Story of Netscape and How It Challenged Microsoft, 1998. Office: Business 2-0 1271 Ave America New York NY 10020

QUIVERS, ERIC STANLEY, physician; b. Winston-Salem, N.C., Oct. 27, 1955; s. William Wyatt and Evelyn Cecelia (Seace) Q.; m. Mara Carlos, Feb. 15, 1987; children: Micah Stanley, Lucas Sorrell. BS, Morehouse Coll., 1979; MD, Howard U., 1983. Cert. pediats., pediat. cardiology. Intern and resident in pediats. Howard U. Hosp., 1983-86, Dist. Columbia Gen. Hosp., 1983-86; staff pediatrician Park W. Med. Ctr., Balt., 1986-88; fellow in pediat. cardiology Mayo Clin., 1988-91; mem. cardiology faculty Children's Nat., Washington, 1991—. Dir. preventive cardiology, Children's Nat., Washington, dir. exercize lab., 1991—, transplant cardiologist, 1997—; adv. bd. Take AIM Prodns. Healthcare Forum Cardiology fellow, 1999. Mem. Am. Coll. Cardiology, Internat. Heart and Lung Transplantation Soc. Assn. of Black Cardiologist, Mid Atlantic Am. Coll. Sports Medicine. Office: Childrens Med Ctr Dept Pediat Cardiology 111 Michigan Ave NW Dept Pediat Washington DC 20010-2916

QUIVERS, ROBIN, radio personality; b. 1953; d. Charles and Louise Quivers. Student, U. Md., 1974. Morning anchor W100, Carlisle, Pa., 1980; joined WWDC, Wash., DC, 1981; radio personality WNBC, N.Y.C., 1982—85, WXRK-FM, N.Y.C., 1985—. Co-author: Quivers: A Life, 1995; actor: (TV films) Deadly Web, 1996; (films) Private Parts, 1997; guest appearance: (TV series) The Fresh Prince of Bel-Air; The Larry Sanders Show. With USAF. Address: WXRK-RADIO 40 W 57th St Fl 14 New York NY 10019-4001

QUON, MALCOLM YEE, defence systems company executive; b. Greenwood, Miss., Sept. 3, 1960; s. Joe Wing and Sandra Quon; m. Melanie Chow; children: Mallery, Joseph. BBA in Computer Info. Systems, Delta State U., 1983. Exec. v.p. Vision Systems Internat. LLC, San Jose, Calif., 1999—. Capt. U.S. Army, 1983-88. Office: Vision Systems Internat LLC 2711 Orchard Pkwy San Jose CA 95134 E-mail: Malquon@cs.com.

QUON, MICHAEL JAMES, medical researcher, internist; b. Oakland, Calif, Apr. 26, 1960; s. Jimmie Earl and Helen (Tang) Quon; m. Huison Kim, June 22, 1985; children: Hana, James. BS in Biomed. Engring., Northwestern U., 1982, PhD in Biomed. Engring., 1987, MD, 1988. Diplomate Nat. Bd. Med. Examiners, Am. Bd. Internal Medicine. Resident in internal medicine U. Chgo., 1988—90; fellow in endocrinology NIH, Bethesda, Md., 1990—93, sr. clin. investigator, 1993—95, sr. investigator Nat. Heart, Lung and Blood Inst., 1995—2002, chief diabetes unit NCCAM, 2002—. Contbr. articles to profl. jours. Capt. USPHS, 1990—. Mem.: ACP, Juvenile Diabetes Found. Internat., Coun. for High Blood Pressure, Am. Heart Assn., Am. Diabetes Assn. (Rsch. award grant 1994—). Avocations: piano, violin. Office: NIH NCCAM Bldg 10 rm 6C 205 Bethesda MD 20892-0001

QURAISHI, MOHAMMED SAYEED, retired health scientist, administrator; b. Jodhpur, India, June 23, 1924; arrived in US, 1946, naturalized, 1973; s. Mohammed Latif and Akhtar Jahan Q.; m. Akhtar Imtiaz, Nov. 12, 1953; children: Rana, Naveed, Sabah. B.Sc., St. John's Coll., 1942; M.Sc., Aligarh Muslim U., 1944; PhD, U. Mass., 1948. Sr. mem. UN, WHO Team to Bangladesh, 1949-51; entomologist Malaria Inst. Pakistan, 1951-55; sr. rsch. officer Pakistan Council Sci. and Indsl. Rsch., 1955-60; sr. sci. officer Pakistan AEC, 1960-64; assoc. prof. entomology U. Man., 1964-66, N.D. State U., Fargo, 1966-70, prof., 1970-74; chief scientist biology N.Y. State Sci. Svc., Albany, 1974-75; entomologist, toxicologist, chief pest control and consultation sect. NIH, Bethesda, Md., 1976-84; health scientist adminstr., exec. sec. microbiology and infectious disease rsch. com. Nat. Inst. Allergy and Infectious Diseases, Bethesda, Md., 1984-88, sci. rev. adminstr. spl. revs., 1988-96, sci. rev. adminstr. AIDS clin. epidemiol. rsch. rev. br., 1996-2000; ret., 2000; sr. scientist Inst. Nuclear Sci., CENTO, Tehran, Iran, 1960-64; program mgr. interdepartmental contract Project THEMIS, Dept. Def., 1968-74. Cons. breast cancer rsch. program UIS Dept. Def., 2001; vis. scientist Harvard Sch. Pub. Health, 1995. Author: Biochemical Insect Control: Its Impact on Economy, Environment and Natural Selection, 1977; mem. editorial bd. Jour. Environ. Toxicology and Chemistry, 1981-84; author numerous sci. papers. Chmn. NIH Asian-Am. Cultural Assn., 1980—81; mem. Montgomery County Bd. Social Svcs., 2002. Recipient Sustained High Quality Performance award, 1980, Merit Pay Performance awards, 1984, 86, 87, Recognition and Appreciation of Spl. Achievement award NIH, 1988, Spl. Recognition award for Svcs. to NIH, Asian Am. Cultural Com., 1989, Appreciation in Recognition of Outstanding Support for Combined Fed. Campaign, 1991. Mem. Am. Chem. Soc., Soc. Environ. Toxicology and Chemistry (mem. publs. com. in charge spl. publs. 1982-84), Sigma Xi, Phi Kappa Phi. Home: 19813 Cochrane Way Gaithersburg MD 20879-1637 E-mail: sayeedquraishi@aol.com.

QURAISHI, NISAR ALI, internist; b. May 15, 1946; s. Jehan Dad and Sahib Jan (Qurashi) Q.; m. Shahida Parveen, June 25, 1970;children: Abid, Zahid. MB BS, Dacca Med. Coll., Pakistan, 1969. Diplomate Am. Bd. Internal Medicine. House surgeon Dacca Med. Coll., 1969, sr. house physician, 1969-70; intern, resident Beekman Downtown Hosp., N.Y.C., 1970-74; pvt. practice N.Y.C., 1974—. Attending physician NYU Downtown Hosp., N.Y.C., 1974—; physician in charge exercise EKG, Mobil Oil Corp., N.Y.C., 1977-86; clin. asst. prof. medicine N.Y. Med. Coll., 1996—; attending physician St. Vincent's Hosp. and Med. Ctr. of N.Y., 1996—. Fellow Am. Coll. Physicians, Am. Soc. Internal Medicine; mem. AMA, N.Y. State Med. Soc., N.Y. County Med. Soc. Office: 303 Greenwich St New York NY 10013-3801 also: 1 Chopin Ct Jersey City NJ 07302-3240

QUREISHI, A. SALAM, computer software and services company executive; b. Aligarh, India, July 1, 1936; s. M.A. Jabbar and Saira (Sattar) Q.; m. Naheed Fatima; children: Lubna, Leila. BS in Physics and Math., Aligarh U., India, 1954; MS in Stats., Patna U., India, 1957. Mgr. applications IBM Corp., Palo Alto, Calif., 1961-67; founder, pres., chmn. bd. Optimum Sys., Inc., Palo Alto, Calif., 1967-71; CEO Sysorex Internat., Inc., Mountain View, Calif., 1972—. Republican. Office: Sysorex Internat Inc 335 E Middlefield Rd Mountain View CA 94043-4028 Home: 925 Mountain Home Rd Woodside CA 94062-2519

QUTUB, EILEEN, state legislator, real estate appraiser; b. York, Nebr., Mar. 2, 1948; m. Abe Qutub. BS in Mgmt. Human Resources, George Fox Coll. Mem. Oreg. Legislature, Salem, 1996—, mem. jud. com., mem. pub. affairs ocm., dep. co-chair ways and means com., mem. subcom. on transp. and econ. devel. com., asst. majority leader. Precinct Com., alt. del. Oreg. Rep. Orgn.; facilitator engring. dept.-real estate divsn. City of Charlotte, N.C. Republican. Home: 11135 Sw Patridge Loop Beaverton OR 97007 Office: S 210 State Capitol Salem OR 97310 E-mail: qutub.sen@state.or.us.

QUTUB, MUSA YACUB, hydrogeologist, educator, consultant; b. Jerusalem, June 2, 1940; came to U.S., 1960; s. Yacub and Sarah Qutub; married; children: Hanhia, Jennan, Sarmad, Muntaser, Aya, Saif, Tasneem. BA in Geology, Simpson Coll., Indianola, Iowa, 1964; MS in Hydrogeology, Colo. State U., 1966; Ph.D in Water Resources, Iowa State U. Sci. and Tech., 1969. Instr. earth sci. Iowa State U., Ames, 1966-69; from asst. prof. to prof. Northeastern Ill., Chgo., 1969-80, prof. geography and environ. studies, 1980—. Cons. hydrogeology, Des Plaines, Ill., 1970—; sr. adviser Saudi Arabian Ministry Planning, Riyadh, 1977-78; leader U.S. environ. sci. del. to People's Republic of China, 1984; pres., founder Islamic Info. Ctr. Am. Author: Secondary Environmental Science Methods, 1973; contbr. numerous articles to profl. jours.; editor Environ. Resource, Directory Environ. Educators and Cons. World. NSF grantee, 1970-71, 71-72, 72-73, 75, 76, Hew grantee, 1974, grantee Ill. Dept. Edn., 1970. Mem. AAAS, NSF (cons.), Am. Waterworks Assn., Am. Men and Women Sci., Nat. Assn. Geology Tchrs. (pres. central sect. 1974), Environ. Sci. Inst. (edn. com.), Internat. Assn. Advancement of Earth and Environ Sci. (pres. 1975—, founder), Ill. Earth Sci. Edn. (pres. 1971-73, founder), Phi Delta Kappa. Moslem. Avocations: tennis, track, cross country, soccer.

QUTUBUDDIN, SYED ABU SHAMS, chemical engineer, educator; b. Dhaka, Bangladesh, Nov. 23, 1952; arrived in U.S., 1976; s. Syed A N M and Gulshan Sakina Nasiruddin; m. Rukiye Benek. BSc, Bangladesh U. of Engring. and Tech., Dhaka; MS, SUNY, Buffalo, 1978; PhD, Carnegie Mellon U., 1982. Lectr. chem. engring. Bangladesh U. Engring. and Tech., Dhaka, 1975—76; prof. chem. engring. Case Western Res. U., Cleve., 1982—. Sr. cons. Saudi Basic Industries Corp., Riyadh, 1990—91; program dir. NSF, Arlington, Va., 1994—96. Contbr. more than 50 articles to profl. jours. Pres. Sakina Enterprise, Cleve., 1987—90. Recipient Presdl. Young Investigator award, NSF, 1986, Young Faculty award, Amoco Found., 1986, LaMer award, Am. Chem. Soc., 1985. Mem.: AIChE. Achievements include patents for polymer composites from microemulsions. Home: 16610 Fernway Shaker Heights OH 44120 Office: Case Western Res U 10900 Euclid Ave Cleveland OH 44106 Office Phone: 216-368-2764. E-mail: sxq@cwru.edu.

RAAB, HARRY FREDERICK, JR., retired physicist; b. Johnstown, Pa., May 9, 1926; s. Harry Frederick and Marjorie Eleanor (Stiff) R.; m. Phebe Ann Duerr, June 16, 1951; children: Constance Diane, Harry Frederick, Cynthia Ann Raab Morgenthaler. Student, Navy Electronics Tech. Sch., 1944-45; SB and SM E.E., MIT, 1951; postgrad., Oak Ridge Sch. Reactor Tech., 1954-55. Reactor control engr. Bettis Atomic Power Lab Westinghouse Electric Corp., West Mifflin, Pa., 1951-54, mgr. surface ship physics, 1956—62, mgr. light water breeder reactor physics, 1962-72; chief physicist Navy Nuc. Propulson Directorate, Washington, 1972-95, ret., 1995. Patentee light water breeder reactor. Active Laymen's Missionary League, Episc. Diocese of Pitts., 1957-72; lay eucharistic min., lay intercessor and lector Episc. Ch. of Good Shepherd, Burke, Va., 1972-, Sunday sch. tchr., 1957-72, dir. liturgy, 1987-97, stewardship chmn., 1979-82, 84, 92-93, chmn. presch. bd., 1994-97, healing

ministry, 1989—, sr. warden, 1983, 85, 97, Stephen Ministry leader, 1998—; mem. stewardship com. Diocese of Va., 1983—, chmn. stewardship, 1995-2002; chaplain for mentally retarded No. Va. Tng. Ctr., 1983—; bd. dirs. Phoenix Cmty. Svcs., 1995-99; lay pediat. chaplain Fairfax Hosp., 1995—. With USNR, 1944-46, PTO. Fellow Am. Nuc. Soc.; mem. Internat. Platform Assn., Masons, Sigma Xi, Tau Beta Pi, Eta Kappa Nu. Republican. Home: 8202 Ector Ct Annandale VA 22003-1342 E-mail: hraabjr@aol.com. *Always treat others with respect. Strive for excellence. Always act with honesty and integrity. Remember Henry Ford's observation: "If you say that you can, or if you say you cannot, you are right".*

RAAB, IRA JERRY, lawyer, judge; b. N.Y.C., June 20, 1935; s. Benjamin and Fannie (Kirschner) R.; m. Regina Schneider, June 4, 1957 (div. 1978); children: Michael, Shelley; m. Katie Rachel McKeever, June 30, 1979 (div. 1991); children: Julie, Jennifer, Joseph; m. Gloria Silverman, Nov. 7, 1996; children: Jill, Todd, John. BBA, CCNY, 1955; JD, Bklyn. Law Sch., 1957; MPA, NYU, 1959, postgrad.; MS in Pub. Adminstrn., L.I. U., 1961; MBA, Adelphi U., 1990. Bar: N.Y. 1958, U.S. Dist. Ct. (so. and ea. dists.) N.Y. 1960, U.S. Supreme Ct. 1967, U.S. Tax Ct. 1976, U.S. Ct. Appeals (2d cir.) 1977. Pvt. practice, Woodmere, NY, 1958-96, 2003—; agt. Westchester County Soc. Prevention of Cruelty to Children, White Plains, 1958; counsel Dept. Correction City of N.Y., 1959, trial commr. Dept. Correction, 1976, asst. corp. counsel Tort divsn. N.Y.C. Law Dept., 1963-70; staff counsel SBA, N.Y.C., 1961-63; counsel Investigation Com. on Willowbrook State Sch., Boro Hall, S.I., N.Y., 1970; gen. counsel Richmond County Soc. Prevention of Cruelty to Children, Boro Hall, 1970-81; pro bono counsel N.Y.C. Patrolmen's Benevolent Assn., 1974-81; rep. to UN Internat. Criminal Ct., 1977-78; arbitrator Small Claims Ct. Day Cts., N.Y.C., 1970-96; arbitrator L.I. Better Bus. Bur., 1976-93, Nassau County Dist. Ct., 1978-93, arbitrator Small Claims Ct., 1978-96; spl. master N.Y. County Supreme Ct., 1977-96; judge N.Y.C. Parking Violations Bur., 1991-93; arbitrator, 2003—; hearing ofcl. Nassau County Supreme Ct., 1982—96, 2003—. Small claims arbitrator N.Y.C. Civil Ct., 1970-96; arbitrator U.S. Dist. Ct. (ea. dist.) N.Y., 1986-96, 2003—; lectr. cmty. and ednl. orgns.; instr. paralegal course Lawrence Sch. Dist., N.Y., 1982-84; law prof. Briarcliff Coll., Bethpage, N.Y., 1997. Chmn. Businessmen's Luncheon Club, Wall St. Synagogue, 1968-79; exec. sec. Cmty. Mediation Ctr., Suffolk County, 1978-80, exec. v.p., 1980-81; vice chmn. Woodmere Inc., Com., 1980-81; mem. adv. bd. Nassau Expressway Com., 1979-80; bd. dirs. Woodmere Mchts. Assn., 1979-80, v.p., 1979-83, chmn., 1984-93; sec. Congregation Aish Kodesh, Woodmere, 1992-2002; candidate for dist. ct. judge Nassau County, 1987, 88, 89, 91, 93, 94, 96; candidate for supreme ct. justice Nassau and Suffolk Counties, 1995, 98; elected judge Nassau County Dist. Ct., 1997-99; candidate for county ct., Nassau County, 1997; elected presiding judge dist. ct., 1999-2000; elected justice Nassau County Supreme Ct., 2000-03. Recipient Consumer Protection award FTC, 1974, 76, 79, Recognition award Pres. Ronald Reagan, 1986, Man of Yr. award L.I. Coun. of Chambers, 1987, N.Y. State Ct. Reporters Assn., 1999. Mem. ABA (chmn. cts. and comty. com. 1988-93, exec. com. jud. adminstrn. divsn. lawyers conf. 1989-95), Am. Judges Assn. (rep. to UN 2000—, bd. govs. 1973-78, 82-88, 89-96, 97-2003, nat. treas. 1978-82, chmn. civil ct. ops. com. 1975-76, chmn. editl. film com. 1974-77, editl. bd. Ct. Rev. mag. 1975-79, 82-86, chmn. spkrs. bur. com. 1976-77, chmn. legis. com. 1983-95, chmn. resolutions com. 1995-98, 2000-2002, chmn. jud. concerns com. 1997-99, historian 1988—, William H. Burnett award 1983), Am. Judges Found. (pres. 1977-79, chmn. bd. trustees 1979-83, treas. 1974-75, 76-77, trustee 1983-97, 2000—), Assn. Arbitrators of Civil Ct. City of N.Y. (past pres.), N.Y. State Bar Assn. (sec. dist., city, town and village cts. com.), Nassau County Bar Assn. (criminal cts. com., matrimonial and family ct. com., ct. com., ethics com., Supreme Ct. com.), Profl. Group Legal Svc. Assn. (past pres.), Internat. Assn. Jewish Lawyers and Jurists (com. to draft Internat. Bill of Rights to Privacy 1982, coun. 1981-95, bd. govs. 1984-95), adv. bd. comty. dispute ctr. 1979-81), K.P. (past chancellor comdr.). Democrat. Home and Office: 375 Westwood Rd Woodmere NY 11598-1624 Address: 9452 Lantern Bay Cir West Palm Beach FL 33411 Personal E-mail: irajraab@yahoo.com.

RAAB, JENNIFER J. city commissioner; AB with distinction, Cornell U., 1977; MPA, Princeton U., 1979; JD cum laude, Harvard U., 1985. Spl. projects mgr. S. Bronx Devel. Org., 1979-81; dir. pub. affairs Planning commn. City of N.Y., 1981-82, chmn. Landmarks Preservation commn., 1994—2001; litigation assoc. Cravath, Swaine & Moore, N.Y.C., 1985-90; campaign dir. Rose State Senate Campaign, 1988; issues dir. Giuliani Mayorial Campaign, 1989; litigation assoc. Paul, Weiss, Rifkind, Wharton & Garrison, N.Y.C., 1990-94; pres. Hunter Coll., 2001—. Bd. dirs. Argus Cmty., Inc., Bronx, N.Y., 1987-94, City Vol. Corps, 1994; active Manhattan Cmty. Bd. 5, 1990-94; pres. E. 154-155th St. Housing Corp., Bronx, 1992-94; vol. arbitrator Small Claims divsn. Bronx Civil Ct., 1993-94; mem. citizen's adv. coun., Mid-Town Cmty. Ct., 1994. Mem. Phi Beta Kappa. Office: Hunter College Room E1700 695 Park Ave New York NY 10021

RAAB, SHELDON, lawyer; b. Bklyn., Nov. 30, 1937; s. Morris and Eva (Shereshevsky) Raab; m. Judith Deutsch, Dec. 15, 1963; children: Michael Kenneth, Elisabeth Louise, Andrew John. AB, Columbia U., 1958; LLB cum laude, Harvard U., 1961. Bar: N.Y. 1961, U.S. Ct. Appeals (2d cir.) 1963, U.S. Dist. Ct. (so. and ea. dists.) 1967. Dep. asst. atty. gen. State of N.Y., 1961—63, asst. atty. gen., 1963—64; assoc. Frank, Harris, Shriver & Jacobson (and predecessor firm), N.Y.C., 1964—69, ptnr., 1970—81, inc. ptnr., 1981—93, of counsel, 1993—. Mem. exec. com. lawyers' divsn. United Jewish Appeal, 1982—93. Mem.: ABA, Assn. of Bar of City of N.Y. (adminstrv. law com. 1968—71, spl. com. electric power and environment 1971—73, chmn. energy com. 1974—79, fed. cts. com. 1981—84, state superior cts. juris. com. 1985—88), N.Y. State Bar Assn. (trial lawyers sect. 1968—), Am. Law Inst. Democrat. Office: Fried Frank Harris Shriver & Jacobson LLP 1 New York Plz New York NY 10004-1980 Office Phone: 212-859-8090. Business E-Mail: raabsh@ffhsj.com.

RAABE, GERHARD KARL, epidemiologist; b. Flushing, N.Y., Feb. 24, 1948; s. Oscar Albert and Eugenie (Loehr) R.; m. Barbara Irene Douglas, Nov. 27, 1969; children: Andrew John, Emily Jean. BA in Biology, Hofstra U., 1969; MS in Computer Sci., Pratt Inst., 1971; DrPH, Columbia U., 1987. Sr. rsch. scientist N.Y. State Dept. Mental Hygiene, N.Y.C., 1970-77; med. systems analyst Mobil Oil Corp., N.Y.C., 1977-79, indsl. med. advisor, 1979-81, mgr. epidemiology and med. info. svcs., 1982-89, dir. epidemiology and med. info. svcs. Princeton, N.J., 1990-97; dir. med. info. and health risk assessment Global Med. Svcs., Mobil Bus. Resources Corp., 1997-99; pres., prin. scientist occupl. and environ. health Health Risk Scis., Inc., New Hope, Pa., 1999—. Cons. spl. studies Cornell U. Med. Ctr., N.Y.C., 1973-77; cons. N.Y.C. Health Systems Agy., 1976; chmn. occupational health com. Fla. Phosphate Coun., Lakeland, 1979-85; reviewer profl. jours.; expert panelist WHO, IARC, U.S. EPA. Contbr. articles to profl. jours., chpts. to books. Fellow Am. Coll. Epidemiology (mem. policy com.); mem. AAAS, Soc. for Epidemiologic Rsch., Internat. Soc. for Environ. Epidemiology, Am. Statis. Assn., Am. Petroleum Inst. (chmn. epidemiology 1985-88, chmn. health and product stewardship 1996-2000), N.Y. Acad. Scis., Soc. for Risk Analysis, Indsl. Epidemiology Forum (chmn. 1991), Internat. Commn. on Occupl. Health. Republican. Lutheran. Avocations: science fiction, tennis. Home: 2215 Aquetong Rd New Hope PA 18938-1149 Office: Health Risk Scis Inc PO Box 189 New Hope PA 18938-0189 Office Phone: 215-862-5718. E-mail: gkraabe@cs.com.

RAABE, WILLIAM ALAN, tax writer, business educator; b. Milw., Dec. 14, 1953; s. William Arthur and Shirley R.; m. Nancy Elizabeth Miller, Mar. 1989; children: Margaret Elisabeth, Martin William. BS, Carroll Coll., 1975; MAS, U. Ill., 1976, PhD, 1979. Wis. Disting. prof. U. Wis., Milw., 1979-96; tax edn. cons. Price Waterhouse Coopers, N.Y.C., 1985—; prof., dir. acctg. programs Samford U., Birmingham, Ala., 1997-2001; founding dean Sch. Mgmt., disting. prof. Capital U., Columbus, Ohio, 2001—02; mem. tax faculty Fisher Coll. Bus. Ohio State U., Columbus, 2002—. Vis. assoc. prof. Ariz. State U., Tempe, 1985; vis. faculty Ernst & Young, N.Y.C., 1990—, Deloitte & Touche, N.Y.C., 1998—, Calif. CPA Found., 1986, AICPA, 1984-94, Wis. Bar Assn., 1992, Capital U. Law Sch., 2002—; developer Estate Tax Planner, McGraw Hill Software, N.Y.C., 1980-88; expert witness, 1985—; cons. corp. income tax State Ala., 1997-01, State of Wis., 1995, 99; dir. Fisher/Ohio State U. Tax Clinic, 2003—. Author West's Federal Taxation, 1985—, West's Federal Tax Research, 1986—, Income Shifting After Tax Reform, 1987, Multistate Corporate Tax Guide, 1985-96, California Income Taxation, 1999—; contbr. articles to profl. jours. Bd. dirs., pres. Luth. High Sch. Assn. Milw., 1991-96, Bethesda Luth. Home, Watertown, Wis., 1989-91, Luth. Counseling and Family Svcs., 1982-88, Concord Chamber Orch., Milw., 1983-88; mem. Econ. Devel. Com., Wauwatosa, Wis., 1986-89; faculty athletic rep. to NCAA from U. Wis. Milw., 1990-96; mem. Milw. Symphony Chorus, Master Singers of Milw., Samford Master Singers, Samford Die Kantorei; vice chair faculty senate Samford U., 2000-01. Fellow Am. Acctg. Assn., Nat. Ctr. for Tax Edn. and Rsch., Wis. Inst. CPAs (Educator of Yr. 1987), Ala. Acctg. Educators Assn. (pres. 1999-2000). Office: Fisher Coll bus 2100 Neil Ave Columbus OH 43210-1144 Office Phone: 614-292-4023. Business E-Mail: raabe.12@osu.edu.

RAACK, RICHARD CHARLES, retired education educator, writer, researcher; b. L.A., July 10, 1928; s. Charles Frank and Virgina Josephine Raack; m. Marilyn Frances Loeffler (div.); 1 child, Elizabeth Hope. BA, U.C.L.A., L.A., 1950, MA, 1953; PhD, Harvard, Cambridge, Mass., 1957. Instr. R. I. Sch. of Design, Providence, 1956—57, Mass. Inst. of Tech., Cambridge, Mass., 1957—59; asst. prof. Long Beach State Coll., Long Beach, Calif., 1961—65; prof. Cal State Univ., Hayward, Calif., 1961—85. Editor: (films) Good Bye Billy; prodr.: (films) Good Bye Billy; editor: (films) America Goes to War 1917-1918; prodr.: (films) America Goes to War 1917-1918; editor: (films) The Frozen War; prodr.: (films) The Frozen War; editor: (films) America and The Russian Civil War 1918-1920; prodr.: (films) America and The Russian Civil War 1918-1920; editor: (films) Will Rogers Storm of Fire; prodr.: (films) Will Rogers Storm of Fire; author: The Fall of Stein, 1965, Stalin's Drive to the West, 1995. Staff sgt. USAF, 1951—52. Office: Calif State Univ History Dept Hayward CA 94542

RAAD, VIRGINIA, pianist, lecturer; b. Salem, W.Va., Aug. 13, 1925; d. Joseph M. and Martha (Joseph) R. BA in Art History, Wellesley Coll., 1947; spl. student, New Eng. Conservatory Music, 1947-48; diplôme, Ecole Normale de Musique, Paris, 1950; Doctorate with honors (French Govt. grantee 1950-52, 54-55), U. Paris, 1955; student, Alfred Cortot, Jeanne Blancard, Berthe Bert, Jacques Chailley. Artist in residence Salem (W.Va.) Coll., 1957-70; ind. concert pianist, 1960—; musician in residenceat cmty. colls. N.C. Arts Coun., 1971—. Adjudicator Nat. Guild Piano Tchrs., Nat. Fedn. Music Clubs; panelist, grant reviewer NEH, 1978-84, 92—; mem. com. Nat. Endowment Arts, 1978; Am. rep. Debussy Centennial Colloque, Paris, 1962. Perfomances, concerts, lectrs. master classes at West Ga. Coll., Carrollton, La Grange (Ga.) Coll., Columbus (Ga.) Coll., Young Harris (Ga.) Coll., U. Fla., Gainesville, Norton Gallery, Palm Beach, Fla., Alliance Française de Rollins Coll., Winter Park, Fla., Dixon Gallery and Gardens, Memphis, St. Jude Children's Rsch. Hosp., Memphis, Cleveland (Tenn.) State C.C., Sampson Tech. Inst., Clinton, N.C., Wayne C.C., Goldsboro, N.C., Brevard (N.C.) Coll., Ctrl. (S.C.) Wesleyan Coll., Ky. Wesleyan Coll., Owensboro, Berea (Ky.), Coll., Alice Lloyd Coll., Pippa Passes, Ky., Coll. of William and Mary, Williamsburg, Va., Eastern Mennonite Coll., Harrisonburg, Va., The Phillips Gallery, Washington, Trinity Coll., Washington, Manhattanville Coll., Purchase, N.Y., Elmira (N.Y.) Coll., Fordham U., N.Y.C., The Piano Tchrs. Congress of N.Y., Middlebury (Vt.) Coll., St. Anselm's Coll., Manchester, N.H., Mount St. Mary's Coll., Hooksett, N.H., Wellesley (Mass.) Coll., Curry Coll., Milton, Mass., So. Conn. State U., New Haven, Slippery Rock (Pa.) U., Seton Hill Coll., Greensboro, Pa., Alliance Française de Pitts. and U. Pitts., Channel 13 WQED (PBS) Pitts., Lincoln U., Oxford, Pa., The Grier Sch., Tyrone, Pa., Mount de Chantal Acad., Wheeling W.Va., Wheeling Jesuit U., among other colls. and univs.; contbg. author: Debussy et l'Evolution de la Musique au XX Siècle, 1965; author: The Piano Sonority of Claude Debussy, 1994; recording artist: EDUCO, 1995—; contbr. articles to profl. jours. Active Amnesty Internat. Urgent Action Network; alumna regional rep. Wellesley Coll.; mem bd. visitors New Eng. Conservatory of Music, 2004—. Named Outstanding W.Va. Woman Educator Delta Kappa Gamma, 1965; presented biography to Schlesinger Library on History of Women in Am. Radcliffe Coll., 1967; grantee Govt. France, Am. Coun. Learned Socs. Mem. Soc. Française de Musicologie, Am. Musicol. Soc. (regional officer 1960-65), Am. Coll. Musicians, Internat. Musicol. Soc., Music Tchrs. Nat. Assn. (adjudicator, musicology program chair 1983-87), W.Va. Music Tchrs. Assn., Coll. Music Soc., Audubon Activist, Alpha Delta Kappa (hon.). Republican. Roman Catholic. Avocations: hiking, gardening, birding. Address: 60 Terrace Ave Salem WV 26426-1116 Office Phone: 304-782-2274. E-mail: virginiaraad@aol.com.

RAAF, JOHN HART, surgeon, health facility administrator, educator; b. Portland, Oreg., Aug. 10, 1941; s. John E. and Lorene (Rardin) R.; m. Heather Neilson, June 15, 1965; children— Jennifer, John, Sabrina AB magna cum laude, Harvard U., 1963, MD cum laude, 1970; D.Phil., Oxford U., 1966. Diplomate Am. Bd. Surgery. Intern Mass. Gen. Hosp., Boston, 1970-71, resident in surgery, 1971-73, 75-77; research fellow Sloan-Kettering Inst., N.Y.C., 1973-75; fellow in immunology Meml. Hosp., N.Y.C., 1973-74; faculty assoc. in surgery M.D. Anderson Hosp. and Tumor Inst., Houston, 1977-78, asst. prof. surgery, 1978-79, Cornell U. Med. Coll., N.Y.C., 1979-81; assoc. prof. surgery Meml. Sloan-Kettering Cancer Ctr., N.Y.C., 1981-85; dir. Cleve. Clinic Cancer Ctr., 1985-90; chmn. dept. surgery Meridia Huron Hosp., Cleve., 1991-94; chief surg. svc. VA Med. Ctr. Cleve., 1994-2001; prof. surgery Case Western Res. U., 1994—, vice chmn. dept. surgery, 1994-2001. Mem. selection coms. for Rhodes scholarships, Vt., 1969-71, New Eng., 1969-71, La., 1977, Tex., 1978, Ohio, 1989-94; mem. soft tissue sarcoma discussion group Nat. Cancer Inst., 1980; mem. clin. trials com. Nat. Cancer Inst., NIH, 1984-88 Co-author Meml. Sloan-Kettering Cancer Ctr. publs., 1980; also numerous articles, chpts., abstracts, letters, short papers, movies, med. photographs; editor: Diagnosis and Treatment of Soft Tissue Sarcomas, 1993; editor-in-chief Primary Care and Cancer, 1981-92; mem. editorial bd. Meml. Sloan-Kettering Cancer Ctr. Clin. Bull., 1979-82; assoc. editor Oncology mag., 1987-92; mem. editorial com. Cleve Clinic Jour. Medicine, 1987-90. Rhodes scholar Oxford U., Eng., 1963; nat. scholar Harvard U. Med. Sch., 1966-70; Am. Cancer Soc. postdoctoral scholar Harvard U. Med. Sch., 1969-70; ACS scholar Mass. Gen. Hosp., Boston, 1975-77; Am. Cancer Soc. jr. faculty clin. fellow, 1980-83. Fellow ACS; mem. Am. Assn. Cancer Research, Am. Assn. Endocrine Surgeons, Am. Soc. Clin. Oncology, Assn. Acad. Surgery, Assn. Am. Rhodes Scholars, Cen. Surg. Assn., Cleve. Surg. Soc., Soc. Surg. Oncology (publs. com. 1981-84, working group on edn. 1982, membership com. 2000), Meml. Hosp. Alumni Soc. (chmn. program com. 1982), Cleve. Skating Club, Charaka Club (N.Y.C.). Home: 12501 Fairhill Rd Cleveland OH 44120-1017

RAAFLAUB, KURT ARNOLD, classics educator; b. Buea, Cameroon, Feb. 15, 1941; s. Fritz and Heidi (Ninck) R.; m. Deborah Dickmann Boedeker, July 14, 1978. MA, U. Basel, Switzerland, 1967, PhD, 1970. Asst. prof. ancient history Free U. Berlin, 1972-78, Brown U., Providence, 1978-80, assoc. prof. classics and history, 1980-83, prof., 1983—, John Rowe Workman Disting. prof. classics and humanistic tradition, 1989-92, David Herlihy Univ. prof., 2001—, chmn. dept. classics, 1984-89; co-dir. Ctr. for Hellenic Studies, Washington, 1992-2000, chmn. program in ancient studies, 2000—. Author: Dignitatis Contentio, 1974, Die Entdeckung der Freiheit, 1985, The Discovery of Freedom in Ancient Greece, 2004; co-author: Studien zum Attischen Seebund, 1984, Aspects of Athenian Democracy, 1990, Ancient History: Recent Work and New Directions, 1997; editor or co-editor: Social Struggles in Archaic Rome, 1986, Between Republic and Empire: Interpretations of Augustus and His Principate, 1990, Athens and Rome, Florence and Venice: City-States in Classical Antiquity and Medieval Italy, 1991, Anfänge politischen Denkens in der Antike: Die nahöstlichen Kulturen und die Griechen, 1993, Studies in the Ancient Greek Polis, 1995, More Studies in the Ancient Greek Polis, 1996, Democracy 2500: Questions and Challenges, 1998, Democracy, Empire and the Arts in Fifth-Century Athens, 1998, War and Society in the Ancient and Medieval Worlds, 1999; contbr. articles to profl. jours. Mem. Historisches Kolleg Munich, 1989-90. Am. Coun. Learned Socs. fellow, 1983-84, Ctr. for Hellenic Studies fellow, 1976-77, NEH fellow, 1989; faculty fellow U. New England, Armidale, Australia, 1996. Mem. Philol. Assn., Assn. Ancient Historians, Am. Inst. Archaeology, German Archaeol. Inst. (corr.). Avocation: music. Home: 495 Lloyd Ave Providence RI 02906-4547 Office: Brown U Dept Classics Providence RI 02912-1856 E-mail: kurt_raaflaub@brown.edu.

RA'ANAN, URI (HEINZ FELIX FRISCHWASSER), international politics educator; b. June 10, 1926; m. Estelle Khan, 1949; children: Gavriel, Michael. BA, MA, MLitt, Oxford U. Polit. journalist, 1950-57; positions in internat. diplomacy, 1958-64; sr. fellow Rsch. Inst. on Communist Afairs, Columbia U., N.Y.C., 1964-66, lectr. in govt., 1965-66; assoc. Ctr. for Internat. Studies MIT, Boston, 1966-76, vis. prof. polit. sci., 1966-68; prof. internat. politics, dir. Internat. Security Studies Fletcher Sch. Law and Diplomacy, Tufts U., Boston, 1967-87; univ. prof. Boston U., 1988—, dir. Inst. for Study of Conflict, Ideology and Policy, 1988—. Assoc. Davis Ctr. for Russian Studies, Harvard U.; cons. Nat. Inst. Justice and Temple U. Rsch. Program on Organized Crime, 1981-83, Battelle Columbus Labs./U.S. Army Ballistic Missile Def. Program, 1976-77, U.S. Senate Subcom. on Nat. Security, 1972; mem. Ronald Reagan's Fgn. Affairs and Def. Adv. Team, 1980. Author, editor 24 books; mem. adv. bd. Polit. Warfare; contbr. chpts. to numerous books, articles to profl. jours.; numerous appearances on TV and radio. Mem. Am. Assn. Advancement of Slavic Studies, Internat. Inst. of Strategic Studies Office: Inst for Study of Conflict Ideology and Policy 141 Bay State Rd Boston MA 02215-1708 Office Phone: 617-353-5815. E-mail: raanan@bu.edu.

RAAS, DANIEL ALAN, lawyer; b. Portland, Oreg., July 6, 1947; s. Alan Charles and Mitzi (Cooper) R.; m. Deborah Ann Becker, Aug. 5, 1973; children: Amanda Beth, Adam Louis. BA, Reed Coll., 1969; JD, NYU, 1972. Bar: Wash. 1973, Calif. 1973, U.S. Dist. Ct. (we. dist.) Wash. 1973, U.S. Ct. Appeals (9th cir.) 1975, U.S. Supreme Ct. 1977, U.S. Tax Ct. 1983, U.S. Ct. Claims 1984. Atty. Seattle Legal Svcs, VISTA, 1972-73; reservation atty. Quinault Indian Nation, Taholah, Wash., 1973-76, Lummi Indian Nation, Bellingham, Wash., 1976-97, spl. counsel, 1997—; mem. Raas, Johnsen & Stuen, P.S., Bellingham, 1982—; judge Tulalip Indian Tribe Ct. Appeals, 2004—. Cons. Falmouth Inst., Fairfax, Va., 1992-2000, Nat. Am. Ind. Ct. Judges Assn., McLean, Va., 1976-80. Rules chmn. Whatcom County Dem. Conv., Bellingham, 1988, 92, 94, 96, 2004; bd. dirs. Congregation Beth Israel, Bellingham, 1985-2000, pres., 1990-92; adv. com. legal asst. program Bellingham Vocat. Tech. Inst., 1985-91; trustee Whatcom County Law Libr., 1978-2002; pres. Vol. Lawyer Program, 1990-93, bd. dirs., 1988-94; pres. Cliffside Cmty. Assn., 1978-80, bd. dirs., 1977-89; bd. dirs. Friends Maritime Heritage Ctr., 1983-86, Samish Camp Fire Coun., 1988-94, pres. 1991-94, v.p., 1989-91, regional v.p. Union Am. Hebrew Congregations, 1986-93, nat. trustee, 1995—, exec. com., 1995-99, sec. Pacific N.W. region, 1993-95, pres., 1995-99. John Ben Snow scholar, NYU, 1969-70, Root-Tilden scholar, NYU, 1970-72. Mem. Wash. State Bar Assn. (trustee Ind. law sect. 1989-95, Pro Bono award 1991), Whatcom County Bar Assn. (v.p. 1981, pres. 1982, Pro Bono award 1991), Grays Harbor Bar Assn. (v.p. 1976). Home: 1929 Lake Crest Dr Bellingham WA 98229-4510 Office: Raas Johnsen & Stuen PS 1503 E St Bellingham WA 98225-3007 Office Phone: 360-647-0234.

RABADEAU, MARY FRANCES, protective services official; b. Elizabeth, N.J., July 13, 1948; d. Russell John and Frances (Hanley) R. Student, Union Coll., 1967-69; MEd, Kean Coll., 1976. Officer City of Elizabeth Police Dept., N.J., 1978-82, detective, 1982-83, sgt., 1983-87, lt., 1987-91, capt., 1991-92, dir., 1993-95, dep. chief, 1994; chief N.J. Transit Police Dept., Maplewood, 1995—. Instr. Union County Police Acad. Trustee Blessed Sacrament Ch., Elizabeth, N.J., 1989-99; bd. acad. advisors N.J. state police grad. studies program Seton Hall U.; bd. trustees Benedictine Acad., Elizabeth, N.J. Named one of Outstanding Young Women in Am., 1983, Woman Leader N.J. Assn. Women Bus. Owners, 1997; recipient John H. Stamler Police Acad. Svc. award, 1992, Cert. of Recognition award YWCA, 1992, Disting. Grad. award Nat. Cath. Ednl. Assn., 1995; honoree Union County Commn. on the Status of Women, 1993, Hispanic Law Enforcement Assn. of Union County, 1995, Women Helping Women Recognition award Soroptimist Internat. Ams., 2001. Mem. NAACP, Internat. Assn. Chiefs of Police, N.J. State Chiefs of Police, Essex County Chiefs Assn., N.E. Assn. Women Police (cert., Merit award), Elizabeth Police Patrolman's Benevolent Assn., Elizabeth Police Superior Officers Assn. (treas. 1983-91, v.p. 1991), Am. Soc. Law Enforcement Trainers, Emerald Soc., Union County Urban League, Italian Law Enforcement Officers Assn., Fellas Inc. (hon.), Union County Men's Svc. Orgn., Nat. Assn. of Women Law Enforcement Execs. Democrat. Roman Catholic. Office: NJ Transit Police Dept 180 Boyden Ave Maplewood NJ 07040-2494 Home: 184 Riveredge Dr Chatham NJ 07928-3112

RABASSA, CLEMENTINE CHRISTOS, humanities educator, translator; b. N.Y.C., July 31, 1932; d. Sotter and Mary (Legatos) Christos; m. Gregory Rabassa; 1 child, Clara C. BA cum laude, Hunter Coll., 1953, MA, 1958; PhD with distinction, Columbia U., 1971. Preceptor, instr. Spanish Columbia U., N.Y.C., 1963-66, instr. Spanish, 1964-66; from asst. prof. to assoc. prof. humanities Medgar Evers Coll., CUNY, 1973-79, prof. humanities, 1979-90, prof. humanities emerita, 1990—, coord. fgn. langs., 1976-79. Author: Demetrio Aguilera - Malta and Social Justice, 1980, En Torno a Aguilera - Malta, 1981, Summer II, a novella, 1999, (poetry) Pollock's Polka, 2004; co-editor Studies in Afro-Hispanic Lit., 1977-79; translator: Canticle for a Memory (Francisco Arriví), 1993, Emotions (Julio Ortega), 1999. Fellow Fulbright-Hays, 1963, NEH, 1971-72, Rockefeller Found., 1979-80, Gulbenkian Found., 1989; named to Hunter Coll. Hall of Fame, 1982. Mem. MLA, Am. Lit. Translators Assn., Alliance Française, PEN Am. Ctr., Phi Beta Kappa, Sigma Delta Pi. Democrat. Greek Orthodox. Avocations: music, painting, writing. Home and Office: 140 E 72d St Apt 10B New York NY 10021-4243 Office Phone: 212-439-6636.

RABASSA, GREGORY, Romance languages educator, translator, poet; b. Yonkers, NY, Mar. 9, 1922; m. Clementine Christos, 1966; children: Kate, Clara. AB, Dartmouth Coll., 1945, LittD. hon., 1982; MA, Columbia U., 1947, PhD in Portuguese, 1954. Instr. Spanish Columbia U., 1947-52, assoc., 1952-58, asst. prof., 1958-63, assoc. prof. Spanish and Portuguese, 1963-68; prof. Romance langs. Queens Coll., CUNY Grad. Sch., Flushing, N.Y., 1968-86, Disting. prof., 1986—. Assoc. editor Odyssey Rev., 1961-64 Contbr. articles to profl. jours.; author If This Be Treason: Translation and Its Dyscontents, 2004. Staff sgt. OSS, 1942-45. Decorated Croce al Merito di Guerra Italy, Order of San Carlos Colombia; recipient Nat. Book award for transl., 1967, transl. prize, PEN Am. Ctr., 1977, Gode award, Am. Transl. Assn., 1980, PEN transl. medal, 1982, Arts award, N.Y. Gov., 1985, transl. prize, Wheatland Found., 1988, lit. award, Am. Acad. and Inst. Arts and Letters, 1989, presdl. medal, Dartmouth Coll., 1991, Ivan Sandrof award, The Nat. Book Critics Cir., 1993, Lit. Lion award, N.Y. Pub. Libr., 1993, Mellon Humanities award, Loyola U., Chgo., 1995, Gabriela Mistral prize, Chile, 1996, Gregory Kolovakos award, PEN, 2001, John Steinbeck Writers award, Southampton Coll., 2002; fellow Fulbright-Hays fellow, 1965—66, NEH fellow, 1979—80, Guggenheim fellow, 1988—89. Mem. Renaissance Soc. Am., MLA, Am. Assn. Tchrs. Spanish and Portuguese, Latin Am. Studies Assn., Am. Lit. Translators Assn., Hispanic Soc. Am., Century Assoc., PEN Club, Phi Beta Kappa. Office: Dept Hispanic Langs & Lits CUNY Queens Coll Flushing NY 11367 Office Phone: 212-439-6636.

RABAUT, THOMAS W. defense industry executive; b. Detroit, 1948; BS, U.S. Mil. Acad., 1970; MBA, Harvard U., 1977. Trainee mfg. dept. dr. divsn., various mfg./mgmt. positions FMC, 1977-81, planning mgr. fluid control divsn., 1982, mfg. mgr., ops. mgr. fluid control divsn., mgr. steel products divsn., 1986-88, dir. ops. ground sys. divsn., 1989; gen. mgr. def. sys. group FMC Corp., 1993, v.p., 1994—; pres., CEO United Defense Industries, Inc., Arlington, Va., 1994—. With U.S. Army, 1970-75. Mem. Am. Def. Preparedness Assn., Assn. of U.S. Army, Navy League, Surface Navy Assn. Office: United Defense Industries Inc 1525 Wilson Blvd Arlington VA 22209

RABB, BRUCE, lawyer; b. Cambridge, Mass., Oct. 4, 1941; s. Maxwell M. and Ruth (Criedenberg) R.; m. Harriet Rachel Schaffer, Jan. 4, 1970; children: Alexander Charles, Katherine Anne. AB, Harvard U., 1962; Cert. d'Etudes Politiques, Institut d'Etudes Politiques, Paris, 1963; LLB, Columbia U., 1966. Bar: N.Y. 1966. Law clk. to judge U.S. Ct. Appeals (5th cir.), 1966-67; assoc.

Stroock & Stroock & Lavan, N.Y.C., 1967-68, 71-75, ptnr., 1976-91, Kramer Levin Naftalis & Frankel LLP, N.Y.C., 1991—2003, counsel, 2003—. Staff asst. to Pres. U.S., 1969-70; vice-chmn. Lawyers Com. Human Rights, 1977-95, nat. coun., 1996—; supr. bd. dirs. Agora-Gazeta, sp.zo.o., 1993-98, Agora-Druk, sp.zo.o., 1995-98; pub. mem. Adminstrv. Conf. U.S., 1982-86, 89-92, spl. counsel, 1986-88. Sec. Lehrman Inst., 1978-88; bd. dirs. Citizens Union of N.Y., 1981-87, 88-94, 95-2001, 02—, treas., 2002—; bd. dirs. Am. Friends of Alliance Israelite Universelle, 1987-2001, Welfare Law Ctr., 1997—, Sabre Found., 2003—, Nat. Com. on Am. Fgn. Policy, 2004—; bd. dirs. Human Rights Watch, 1987-2003, emeritus, 2003—; mem. Human Rights Watch/Ams., 1982—, Human Rights Watch/Helsinki, 1985-97, Fund for Free Expression, 1987-97, Human Rights Watch/Middle East and No. Africa, 1989—, vice chmn., 1990—; mem. internat. adv. com. Internat. Parliamentary Group for Human Rights in the Soviet Union, 1984-88, Prin. of the Coun. for Excellence in Govt., 1990—; mem. adv. coun. Doctors of the World USA, 1996—,; mem. adv. coun. FilmAid Internat., 2000-03, dir., sec., 2003—. Mem. ABA (adv. panel Internat. Human Rights Trial Observer project), Am. Law Inst., Assn. of Bar of City of N.Y. (fed. legis., internat. law chair 1992-95, internat. human rights, civil rights, legal edn. and admission to bar, internat. trade coms., coun. fgn. affairs), Coun. Fgn. Rels., Harvard Club N.Y.C., Met. Club of Washington. Office: Kramer Levin et al 919 3rd Ave New York NY 10022-3852 E-mail: brabb@kramerlevin.com.

RABB, GAEL CAUTION, mental health consultant; b. Nüernberg, Germany, Oct. 24, 1953; U.S. mil. dependent, came to U.S., 1965; d. Gustave Hamilton Jr. and Anne Grace (Richardson) Caution; m. Larry Lebby, Oct. 2, 1970 (div.); children: Lanir, Amanda; m. Moses Rabb Jr., Oct. 16, 1995; children: Mary Anne Grace. BA in Psychology, U. S.C., 1975, PhD in Clin. Psychology, 1984. Lic. ind. social worker. Fellow White House, Washington, 1980-81; dir. psychology Morris Village Alcohol and Drug Tx Ctr., Columbia, S.C., 1985; dir. health and human svcs. Office of the Gov., S.C., 1986; pres. Cautions Consults, Columbia, 1988—. Home and Office: 2324 Washington St Columbia SC 29204-1862

RABB, GEORGE BERNARD, zoologist, conservationist; b. Charleston, S.C., Jan. 2, 1930; s. Joseph and Teresa C. (Redmond) R.; m. Mary Sughrue, June 10, 1953. BS, Coll. Charleston, 1951, LHD (hon.), 1995; MA, U. Mich., 1952, PhD, 1957. Teaching fellow zoology U. Mich., 1954-56; curator, coord. rsch. Chgo. Zool. Park, Brookfield., Ill., 1956-64, assoc. dir. rsch. and edn., 1964-75, dep. dir., 1969-75, dir., 1976—2003, dir. emeritus, 2003—. Rsch. assoc. Field Mus., 1965—; lectr. dept. biology U. Chgo., 1965-89; mem. Com. on Evolutionary Biology, 1969—; pres. Chgo. Zool. Soc., 1976-2003, pres. emeritus, 2004—; mem. steering com. Species Survival Commn., Internat. Union Conservation of Nature/World Conservation Union, 1983—, vice-chmn. for N.Am., 1986-88, dep. chmn., 1987-89, chmn., 1989-96, vice-chmn. comms., 1997—; chmn. policy adv. group Internat. Species Info. System, 1974-89, chmn. bd., 1989-92; pres. bd. dirs. Chgo. Wilderness Mag., 1999—; v.p. Fauna and Flora Internat., 1998—; chmn. bd. Ill. State Mus., 1999—. Bd. dirs. Defenders of Wildlife, 2002—. Fellow AAAS; mem. Am. Soc. Ichthyologists and Herpetologists (pres. 1978), Herpetologists League, Soc. Systematic Zoology, Soc. Mammalogists, Soc. Study Evolution, Ecol. Soc. Am., Soc. Conservation Biology (council mem. 1986), Soc. for Integrative and Comparative Zoology, Soc. Study Animal Behavior, Am. Assn. Museums, Am. Soc. Naturalists, Am. Assn. Zool. Parks and Aquariums (dir. 1979-80), World Assn. Zoos and Aquariums, World Conservation Union (hon. mem.), Chgo. Coun. Fgn. Rels. (Chgo. com.), Sigma Xi. Office: 9236 Broadway Brookfield IL 60513

RABB, HARRIET SCHAFFER, academic administrator, educator, lawyer, government official; b. Houston, Sept. 12, 1941; d. Samuel S. and Helen G. Schaffer; m. Bruce Rabb, Jan. 4, 1970; children: Alexander, Katherine. BA in Govt., Barnard Coll., 1963; JD, Columbia U., 1966. Bar: N.Y. 1966, U.S. Supreme Ct. 1969, D.C. 1970. Instr. seminar on constl. litig. Rutgers Law Sch., 1966-67; staff atty. Ctr. for Constl. Rights, 1966-69; spl. counsel to commr. consumer affairs N.Y.C. Dept. Consumer Affairs, 1969-70; sr. staff atty. Stern Cmty. Law Firm, Washington, 1970-71; asst. dean urban affairs Law Sch., Columbia U., N.Y.C., 1971-84, prof. law, dir. clin. edn., 1984-99, George M. Jaffen prof. law and social responsibility, 1991-99, vice dean, 1992-93; gen. counsel Dept. Health and Human Svcs., Washington, 1993—2001; v.p., gen. counsel Rockefeller U., 2001—. Mem. faculty employment and tng. policy Harvard Summer Inst., Cambridge, Mass., 1975-79. Author: (with Agid, Cooper and Rubin) Fair Employment Litigation Manual, 1975, (with Cooper and Rubin) Fair Employment Litigation, 1975. Bd. dirs. Ford Found., 1977-89, N.Y. Civil Liberties Union, 1972-83, Lawyers Com. for Civil Rights Under Law, 1978-86, Legal Def. Fund NAACP, 1978-93, Mex. Am. Legal Def. and Edn. Fund, 1986-90, Legal Aid Soc., 1990-93, The Hastings Ctr., 2004-; mem. exec. com. Human Rights Watch, 1991-93; trustee Trinity Episcopal Sch. Corp., 1991-93; mem. external adv. bd. Columbia U. Ctr. for Bioethics, 2002-. Office: Rockefeller U 1230 York Ave New York NY 10021 Office Phone: 212-327-8070. Business E-Mail: hrabb@rockefeller.edu.

RABB, THEODORE K. historian, educator; b. Teplice-Sanov, Czechoslovakia, Mar. 5, 1937; came to U.S., 1956, naturalized, 1978; s. Oskar Kwasnik and Rose (Oliner) Rabinowicz; m. Tamar Miriam Janowsky, June 7, 1959; children: Susannah Rabb Bailin, Jonathan Richard, Jeremy David. BA, Queen's Coll. Oxford U., Eng., 1958; MA, Queen's Coll. Oxford U., 1962, Princeton U., 1960, PhD, 1961. Instr. Stanford U., 1961-62; instr. Northwestern U., 1962-63; asst. prof. Harvard U., 1963-67; mem. faculty Princeton U., 1967—, prof. history, 1976—. Vis. assoc. prof. Johns Hopkins U., 1969, SUNY-Binghamton, 1973-74; visitor Inst. Advanced Studies, Princeton, 1973, 82; mem. nat. bd. cons. NEH, Nat. Coun. History Edn. (chair); N.J. Com. for Humanities (chair); chief historian Renaissance Television Series; bd. dirs. Humanities West, Save Venice, Inc.; juror Rome Prize; cons. in field. Author: The Thirty Years War, 2d edit, 1972, Enterprise and Empire, 1967, The Struggle for Stability in Early Modern Europe, 1975, The Origins of Modern Nations, 1981, Renaissance Lives: Portraits of an Age, 1993, rev. edit., 2000, Origins of the Modern West, 1993, Jacobean Gentleman, 1998; co-author: The Western Experience, 8th edit., 2003, Peoples and Nations, 1982; editor: Jour. Interdisciplinary History, 1970—; co-editor: Action and Conviction in Early Modern Europe, 1969, The Family in History, 1973, Marriage and Fertility, 1981, Industrialization and Urbanization, 1981, Climate and History, 1981, The New History, 1982, Hunger and History, 1985, Population and Economy, 1986, Art and History, 1988, La Fame nella storia, 1991, Origin and Prevention of Major Wars, 1988, The Making and Unmaking of Democracy, 2003. Bd. govs. Hebrew U. Fellow and/or grantee Folger Shakespeare Library, Am. Philos. Soc., Social Sci. Research Council, Am. Council Learned Socs., Guggenheim Found., NEH. Mem. Am. Hist. Assn. (chmn. com. quantitative rsch. history, chmn. nominating com.), Social Sci. History Assn. (exec. com., treas.), Am. Assn. Advancement Humanities (dir., sec.-treas.), Nat. Coun. History Stds., C.C. Humanities Assn. (steering com.), Royal Hist. Soc., Internat. Commn. History Parliamentary and Rep. Instns., Renaissance Soc. Am., Hakluyt Soc., Nat. Coun. History Edn. (chair), Historians Early Modern Europe, Conf. Brit. Studies. Office: Princeton University History Dept Princeton NJ 08544-1017

RABBANI, FARHANG, urologic oncologist; b. Tehran, Iran, Dec. 30, 1967; s. Mehdi and Parirokh Rabbani; m. Taghreed Almahmeed, Aug. 24, 1999. BSc in Math. with honors, U. B.C., Vancouver, Can., 1987, MD, 1991. Diplomate Am. Bd. Urology . Rotating intern St. Joseph's Hosp., London, Ont., Can., 1991-92; urology resident U. B.C., 1992-96; urol. oncology fellow Meml. Sloan-Kettering Cancer Ctr., NYC, 1996-99, clin. asst. attending dept. urology, 1999—2002; asst. prof. dept. urology Cornell U., 2003—; asst. attending Meml. Sloan-Kettering Cancer Ctr., NYC, 2003—. Grants reviewer Med. Rsch. Coun., London, 1997-99. Cons. editor Prostate Cancer and Prostatic Diseases; contbr. articles to profl. jours., chpts. to books. Recipient Gov.-Gen. of Can. Gold medal, 1987. Fellow Royal Coll. Physicians and Surgeons Can.; mem. Am. Assn. Cancer Rsch., Am. Urol. Assn. (scholarship award western sect. 1995), Am. Soc. Clin. Oncology. Avocations: skiing, skating, programming. Office: Meml Sloan-Kettering Cancer Ctr Dept Urology 1275 York Ave New York NY 10021-6094 Office Phone: 646-422-4385.

RABBAT, GUY, electronics company executive, inventor; b. Cairo, Jan. 30, 1943; came to U.S., 1972; s. Victor and Alice R.; m. Elfriede Freitag, Aug. 3, 1968; children: Ralph, Shirley; m. Nadia Kobinger, Feb. 8, 1992; children: Richard, Jacques, Laurent. Baccalaureate, France; BS, Queens U., Eng., 1967, MS, 1969, PhD in Elec. Engring. with honors, 1971. Design supr. Siemens AG, Germany, 1964-68; asst. lectr. Queens U., Eng., 1968-72; dir. ops. IBM, 1972-84; v.p. Austin ops., CAE system div. Tektronix, 1984-86; head elec. engring. GM Corp., Mich., 1986-87; pres., chief exec. officer Modular Computer Systems, Inc. (MODCOMP), Ft. Lauderdale, Fla., 1987-92; mng. dir., exec. bd. dirs. Rank Xerox, Ltd., Welwyn Garden City, Herts, England, 1992-96; corp. v.p. Gen. Elec. Co., Milw., 1996-98; chief tech. officer, chief info. officer Gen. Elec. Med. Sys., Milw., 1996-98; sr. v.p. Solectron Corp., 1998—2003; chmn., gen. ptnr. Corcica Tech. Ventures, 2001—; pres., CEO HTC Corp., 2002—. Chmn. Internat. IEEE Conf. on Cirs. and Computers, 1980, Internat. IEEE Conf. on Computer Design, 1983; bd. dirs. indsl. affiliates Mich. State U., 1986-88; pres. Am. Automation Assn., 1984-86; chmn., founder High Tech. Consortium Yr. 2000 and Beyond, 1998-2000. Author: Hardware and Software Concepts in VLSI, 1983, Advanced Semiconductor Technology and Computer Systems, 1988; contbr. numerous scis. tech. papers; patentee in field. Fellow: Royal Engring. Coun. (London), IEEE (Eng. chpt., editor-in-chief, chmn. editl. bd. Circuits and Devices Mag. 1984—86, invention and outstanding contbn. awards). Avocations: history, archeology, poetry, jogging. Office: Solectron Corp 847 Gibraltar Dr Bldg 5 Milpitas CA 95035-6332 Home: 110 W 5th Ave San Mateo CA 94402 Office Phone: 408-218-4393. Business E-Mail: guy.rabbat@htc-corp.com.

RABBITT, DANIEL THOMAS, JR., lawyer; b. St. Louis, Sept. 19, 1940; s. Daniel Thomas and Charlotte Ann (Carpenter) R.; m. Susan Lee Scherger, July 26, 1969. BA in Commerce, St. Louis U., 1962, JD cum laude, 1964. Bar: Mo. 1964, U.S. Supreme Ct. 1970. Assoc. Moser, Marsalek, Carpenter, Cleary, Jaeckel, Keaney & Brown and predecessor, St. Louis, 1964-68; ptnr. Moser, Marsalek, Carpenter, Cleary, Jaeckel, Keaney & Brown, St. Louis, 1969-81, Brown, James & Rabbitt, P.C., St. Louis, 1981-91, Rabbitt, Pitzer & Snodgrass, P.C., St. Louis, 1991—. Recipient Lon Hocker Meml. Trial Atty. award Mo. Bar Found., 1975. Fellow: Am. Coll. Trial Lawyers; mem.: ABA (chmn. young lawyers sect. 1973—74), Mem. prod. Liability Adv. Coun., Bar Assn. Met. St. Louis, Internat. Assn. Def. Counsel (product liability com.), Mo. Bar Assn., Mo. Athletic Club (gov. 1978—81, v.p. 1980—81). Office: 100 S 4th St Ste 400 Saint Louis MO 63102 E-mail: rabbitt@rabbitt.law.com.

RABBITT, LINDA, construction executive; BA, U. Mich., Ann Arbor; MA, George Wash. U. With KPMG (formerly Peat Marwick), 1981—85, dir. mktg., 1982—85; co-founder, co-owner, exec. v.p. Hart Construction Co., Inc.; founder, pres. Rand Contruction, 1989—. Dir. Watson Wyatt & Co., 2002—. Bd. trustees George Wash. U., Federal City Coun. Named Person of Vision, Arlington C. of C., 1995, Bus. Woman Yr., United Cerebral Palsy, 1996, Wash. Woman of Genius, Trinity Coll., 2002, Washingtonian Yr., Washingtonian mag., 2004; named one of 100 Most Powerful Women, 2001; recipient Working Woman 500, 2001. Mem.: Wash. Bd. Trade (past chair), Comml. Real Estate Women (past pres., Annual Achievement award 2003). Office: Rand Construction Corp 2100 Wash Blvd Ste 175 Arlington VA 22204 Office Phone: 703-553-5511. Office Fax: 703-486-3092.

RABE, DAVID WILLIAM, playwright; b. Dubuque, Iowa, Mar. 10, 1940; s. William and Ruth (McCormick) Rabe; m. Elizabeth Pan, 1969 (div.); 1 child; m. Jill Claybrugh, Mar. 1979. BA in English, Loras Coll., 1962; MA, Villanova U., 1968. Feature writer Register, New Haven, 1969-70; asst. prof. Villanova U., 1970-72. Author: (plays) The Basic Training of Pavlo Hummel, 1971 (Obie award disting. playwriting, 1971, Drama Desk award, 1971, Drama Guild award, 1971), Sticks and Bones, 1971 (Elizabeth Hull-Kate Warriner award Dramatists Guild, 1971, Variety Poll award, 1971, Outer Critics' Circle award, 1972, Tony award best play, 1972, N.Y. Drama Critics' Circle citation, 1972), The Orphan, 1973, In the Boom Boom Room, Burning, 1974, Streamers, 1976 (N.Y. Drama Critics' Circle award best Am. play, 1976), Goose and Tomtom, 1976, Hurlyburly, 1985, Those the River Keeps, 1990, Crossing Guard, 1994, A Question of Mercy, 1997, (screenplays) I'm Dancing as Fast as I Can, 1982, Streamers, 1983, Casualties of War, 1989, State of Grace, 1990, The Firm, 1993, (novels) Recital of the Dog, 1992, The Crossing Guard, 1999, (films) Hurlyburly, 1998, In the Boom Boom Room, 1999. With U.S. Army, 1965—67. Recipient AP award, 1970, Am. Acad. Arts and Letters award, 1974, Nat. Inst. and Am. Acad. award, 1976; grantee Rockefeller Found., 1969; Guggenheim fellow, 1976. Address: care United Talent Agy 9560 Wilshire Blvd Fl 5 Beverly Hills CA 90212-2401

RABECS, ROBERT NICHOLAS, lawyer; b. Scranton, Pa., Mar. 19, 1964; s. Nicholas and Anne Marie (Stull) R.; m. Kimberly Ann Rabecs. BA summa cum laude, U. Scranton, 1986; JD cum laude, Georgetown U., 1990. Bar: Pa. 1990, D.C. 1992. Assoc. Reed Smith Shaw & McClay, Washington, 1990-94, Hogan & Hartson, Washington, 1994—. Adj. prof. law George Washington U. Law Sch., Washington, 2002—. Columnist Managed Healthcare News, Belle Meade, N.J., 1994-98. Fulbright scholar, 1986-87; NEH undergrad. fellow, 1985. Mem. ABA, Am. Health Lawyers Assn., Pa. Bar Assn. (health law com.), D.C. Bar Assn. (health law sect.), Alpha Sigma Nu. Roman Catholic. Home: 6809 Rannoch Rd Bethesda MD 20817- Office: Hogan & Hartson 555 13th St NW Washington DC 20004-1161 Office Phone: 202-637-5842. E-mail: rnrabecs@hhlaw.com.

RABENBERG, JOHN, farmer, political organization worker; Chmn. Mont. Rep Party, Helena, Mont., 2003—. Chmn. Mont. Essential Air Svc. Task Force. Mailing: Montana Republican Party Chmn 921 Euclid Ave Helena MT 59601*

RABENSTEIN, DALLAS LEROY, chemistry professor; b. Portland, Oreg., June 13, 1942; 8. Melvin Leroy and Rose Marie (Nelson) R.; m. Gloria Carolyn Duncan, Aug. 30, 1964; children: Mark, Lisa. BS, U. Wash., 1964; PhD, U. Wis., 1968. Lectr. U. Wis., Madison, 1967-68; research chemist Chevron Research Co., Richmond, Calif., 1968-69; from asst. prof. to prof. chemistry U. Alta., Edmonton, Can., 1969-85; prof. U. Calif., Riverside, 1985-97, chmn. dept. chemistry, 1989—92, 1998—2000, 2002—03, dean Coll. Natural and Agrl. Scis., 1993-94, disting. prof. chemistry, 1997—; dean grad. div., 2003—. Vis. prof. U. Oxford, 1976-77, U. Western Ont., 1982; McElvain lectr. U. Wis., 1981; Dow lectr. U. B.C., 1988; Eli Lilly lectr., Ind. U., 1993; faculty rsch. lectr. U. Calif., Riverside, 2000; cons. in field. Contbr. articles to profl. jours. NIH and NSF grantee. Fellow AAAS, Chem. Inst. Can. (Fisher Sci. Lecture award 1984); mem. Am. Chem. Soc., Internat. Soc. Magnetic Resource. Avocations: reading, gardening, music. Home: 5162 Palisade Cir Riverside CA 92506-1521 Office: U Calif Dept Chemistry Riverside CA 92521-0001 Office Phone: 951-827-4302. E-mail: dallas.rabenstein@ucr.edu.

RABIDEAU, MARGARET CATHERINE, retired media center director; b. Chgo., Nov. 24, 1930; d. Nicholas and Mary Agnes (Burke) Oberle; m. Gerald Thomas Rabideau, Nov. 27, 1954; children: Mary, Margaret, Michelle, Gregory, Marsha, Grant. BA cum laude, U. Toledo, 1952, MA in Ednl. Media Tech., 1978. Cert. tchr. K-12 media tech., supr. ednl. media, tchr. English and journalism, specialist in edn. Asst. dir. pub. rels. U. Toledo, 1952-55; publicity writer United Way, Toledo, 1974-75; tchr. Toledo Pub. Schs., 1975-80, libr., media specialist, 1980-90; dir. media svcs. Sylvania (Ohio) Schs., 1990—2002, ret., 2002. Task force to evaluate coll. programs Ohio Dept. Edn., 1987; on-site evaluation team, Hiram Coll., Ohio, 1991; north ctrl. evaluation team Northwestern Ohio, 1985—. Citizen task force Toledo/Lucas County Libr., Ohio, 1991, mem. friends of the libr., 1990—; task force Sta. WGTE-TV PBS Sta., Toledo, 1993; mem. tech. com. strategic plan Sylvania Schs., 1997; instr. U. Toledo, 1990— Recipient Disting. Educator for Art Edn. award N.W. Ohio Art Edn. Assn., 1997; nmamed Educator of Yr., Sylvania Schs., 2001. Mem. ALA, U. Toledo Alumni Assn., Ohio Ednl. Libr. Media Assn. (N.W. dir. 1993—, vocat. dir. 1985-89, Libr. Media Specialist of Yr. 1993, disting. educator art edn. 1999), Am. Ednl. Comm. and Tech., Ednl. Leadership Assn. (bd. dirs.), Maumee Valley Computer Assn. (task force), Phi Delta Kappa (Outstanding Newsletter Nat. award 1990, pres. Toledo chpt., svc. key award, 1998). Avocations: running, travel, cross stitching. Home: 1038 Olson St Toledo OH 43612-2828

RABIDEAU, MARILYN ANN, elementary school educator; b. Green Bay, Wis., Sept. 23, 1939; d. Henry John and Irma Tornow Fink; m. Kenneth Francis Rabideau, June 9, 1962; children: Neil Kenneth Rabideau, Laurie Ann Rabideau Kleisinger. BS in Edn., U. Wis., 1961; MEd, Nat. Louis U., 1996. Life license elem. sch. tchr. grades 1-8 Wis. Dept. Pub. Instrn. Elem. educator Janesville (Wis.) Pub. Schs., 1961-2001, retired, 2001. Pres. Rock County (Wis.) Ext. Homemakers, 1968-70; pres., coun. mem. Faith Luth. Ch., Janesville, 1983-88; officer, bd. dirs. Faith Lutheran Endowment Found., 1996-2002. Recipient Cert. of Excellence, Wis. Ctr. for Academically Talented Youth, Inc., Madison, 1995. Mem. Phi Beta Kappa, Delta Kappa Gamma (chpt. pres. 1998-2000, 02). Avocations: writing, music, drawing, sports, handicrafts.

RABIDEAU, PETER WAYNE, university administrator, chemistry educator; b. Johnstown, Pa., Mar. 4, 1940; s. Peter Nelson and Monica (Smalley) R.; m. Therese Charlene Newquist, Sept. 1, 1962 (div.); children: Steven, Michael, Christine, Susan; m. Jennifer Lee Mooney, Nov. 15, 1986; children: Mark, Leah. BS, Loyola U., Chgo., 1964; MS, Case Inst. Tech., Cleve., 1967; PhD, Case Western Res. U., Cleve., 1968. Postdoctoral asst. U. Chgo., 1968-69, instr., 1969-70; asst. prof. Ind. U.-Purdue U., Indpls., 1970-73, assoc. prof., 1973-76, prof., 1976-90, chmn. dept. chemistry, 1985-90; dean Coll. Basic Scis. La. State U., Baton Rouge, 1990-99; dean Coll. Liberal Arts and Scis. Iowa State U., Ames, 1999—2003; provost, v.p. acad. affairs Miss. State U., 2003—. Program officer NSF, 1988-89. Contbr. numerous articles to profl. jours. Recipient rsch. award Purdue Sch. Sci. at Indpls., 1982, Outstanding Alumnus award chemistry dept. Case Western U., 2001. Fellow AAAS; mem. Am. Chem. Soc. (chmn. Ind. sect. 1974, councilor 1981-90). Home: 105 Derbyshire Rd Starkville MS 39759 Office: Miss State U PO Box BQ Mississippi State MS 39762 E-mail: prabideau@provost.msstate.edu.

RABIL, ALBERT, JR., humanities educator; b. Rocky Mount, N.C., May 8, 1934; s. Albert and Sophie Mae (Safy) R.; m. Janet Spain, Aug. 29, 1956; children: Albert III, J. Alison. BA, Duke U., 1957; MDiv, Union Theol. Sem., 1960; PhD, Columbia U., 1964. Instr. religion Trinity Coll., Hartford, Conn., 1964-65, asst. prof., 1965-68; asst. prof. hist. theology Chgo. Theol. Sem., 1969-71; assoc. prof. SUNY-Old Westbury, 1971-74, prof., 1974-77, disting. tchg. prof. humanities, 1977-98, emeritus prof., 1998. Program dir. NEH Summer Inst., 1992, 94, 95, 96, 98, 2000, 01, 03, 04, 05. Author: Merleau-Ponty, 1967 (Ansley award 1964), Erasmus and the New Testament, 1972, Laura Cereta, 1981, (with others) Her Immaculate Hand, 1983, Erasmus' Paraphrases of Romans and Galatians, 1983, Erasmus' Annotations on Romans, 1994; editor: Renaissance Humanism (3 vols.), 1988; editor, translator: Knowledge, Goodness, and Power, 1991, Henricus Cornelius Agrippa Declamation on the Nobility and Preeminence of the Female Sex, 1996; co-editor Renaissance Quarterly, 1992-97; series co-editor The Other Voice in Early Modern Europe, 1993—; mem. editl. bd. Soundings: An Interdisciplinary Jour., 1992-94. Travelling fellow Union Theol. Sem., 1960, Soc. for Values in Higher Edn., 1961; grantee Fulbright Found., 1961, NEH, 1974, 81, 94, 2002, 03, 04. Mem. Erasmus Rotterdam Soc. (mem. editl. bd. 1980—), Soc. for Values in Higher Edn. (bd. dirs. 1981-90), Renaissance Soc. Am. (bd. dirs. 1991-97). Democrat. Home and Office: 2305 Honeysuckle Rd Chapel Hill NC 27514-1716 Personal E-mail: arabil@nc.rr.com.

RABIL, MITCHELL JOSEPH, lawyer; b. Smithfield, NC, Sept. 19, 1931; s. Albert G. and Eva (Nassif) R.; m. Antoinette M. Olivry, Nov. 25, 1956 (div. Oct. 1986); children: Elizabeth, Nathalie, Marcus, Gregory; m. Dolores E. Bleam, Jan. 21, 1989; children: Susan Starr Vermes, Scott Starr. BS, Wake Forest Coll., 1953; LLB, Georgetown U., 1961. Bar: N.C. 1961, N.J. 1967, D.C. 1980, Pa. 1981, U.S. Tax Ct. 1962, U.S. Supreme Ct. 1979; CPA, N.J., N.C. Supervisory acct. GAO, Washington, 1956-60; fin. analyst, staff acct. SEC, Washington, 1960-62; tax atty. Office of Chief Counsel, IRS, Phila. and N.Y.C., 1962-66; assoc. Archer, Greiner, Hunter & Read, Camden, N.J., 1966-71; ptnr. Myers, Matteo, Rabil, Norcross & Landgraf, Cherry Hill, N.J., 1971-89, Montgomery, McCracken, Walker and Rhoads, Cherry Hill, 1989-95; sole stockholder, pres. Mitchell J. Rabil & Assocs., P.A., Cherry Hill, 1995-2000; mem. Rabil & Harris LLC, Cherry Hill, 1998-2000, Rabil & Ropka, LLC, Cherry Hill, 2000—02, Rabil, Ropka, Kingett & Hatzell LLC, Cherry Hill, 2002—. Mcpl. chmn. Riverton (N.J.) Rep. Com., 1976-83; chmn. area 2 Burlington County Rep. Com., 1976-82; bd. dirs. West Jersey Chamber Music Soc., 1990-91, Zurbrugg Meml. Hosp., 1991-93; active NJ New Capital Sources Bd., 1996-2000. With AUS, 1953-55. Mem. AICPA, N.J. Bar Assn., NJ Soc. CPAs, Am. Assoc. Atty. CPAs (bd. dirs., past pres.) Cherry Hill C. of C. (bd. dirs. 1990-94), World Affairs Council Phila., Union League (Phila.), Riverton Country Club, Rotary (pres. Cherry Hill chpt. 1980-81, past dir.). Roman Catholic. Home: 107 Wayside Ct Delran NJ 08075-2000 Office: Ste B Bldg 2 1010 Kings Hwy S Cherry Hill NJ 08034-2524

RABIN, ALAN A. economics professor; b. N.Y.C., June 16, 1947; s. Sidney and Claire Rabin. BA, Hamilton Coll., 1969; PhD, U. Va., 1977. NSF trainee U. Va., 1970—71, 1971—72; intern Coun. Econ. Advisors, 1971; instr. Calif. State U., Northridge, 1973-74, Georgetown U., Washington, 1975; asst. prof. econs. U. Tenn., Chattanooga, 1977-81, assoc. prof., 1981-86, prof., 1986—. Author: (book) Monetary Theory; contbr. articles to profl. jours. NDEA fellow, 1969-70; U. Tenn.-Chatanooga faculty rsch. grantee, 1982. Mem. Am. Econs. Assn., So. Econs. Assn., Atlantic Econs. Soc., We. Econs. Assn., U. Tenn. Chattanooga Coun. Scholars, Omicron Delta Epsilon. Avocations: sports, stamp collecting/philately, theater. Home: 1175 Pineville Rd Apt 161 Chattanooga TN 37405-2653 Office: U Tenn-Chattanooga Dept Economics Chattanooga TN 37403 E-mail: alan-rabin@utc.edu.

RABIN, DAVID NEAL, radiologist; b. Chgo., Jan. 16, 1956; s. Harold and Nancy Rabin; m. Debbie Lynn Rabin, Apr. 16, 1989; 1 child, Perry. BS in Biology, Loyola U. Chgo., 1978; MD, U. Ill., Chgo., 1982. Lic. physician, Ill. Intern Ill. Masonic, Chgo., 1982-83; resident Rush Presbyn. St. Lukes, Chgo., 1983-87; abdominal imaging fellow Mallinckrodt Inst. of Radiology, Washington U., St. Louis, 1987-88; radiologist Rush Presbyn. St. Luke's Med. Ctr., Chgo., 1988-89; asst. prof. radiology Rush Med. Coll., Chgo., 1988-89; radiologist Highland Park (Ill.) Hosp., 1988-2000; asst. prof. radiology Northwestern U. Med. Sch., Chgo., 1992—; vice chair Evanston Northwestern Healthcare Radiology, 2000—. Mem. cardiac computed tomography med. adv. bd. GE, 1999—; lectr. U. Chgo., 1996—. Contbr. articles to profl. jours.; editor Annals of Improbable Research, 1995—. Mem. profl. edn. com. Am. Cancer Soc., Lake County, Ill., 1993-98; vol. faculty Coll. Lake County, 1990-2000. Mem. Am. Coll. Radiology (com. on edn. for ultrasound 1995-2001, ultrasound accreditation program reviewer 1995—, commn. on stds. and accreditation com. on small and/or rural practices 1998-2000), Radiol. Soc. N.Am. (com. on comm. chair 1997-99), Highland Park Ind. Practice Assn. (bd. dirs. 1994-2000), Evanston Ind. Practice Assn. (compensation com. 2000-02). Avocations: amateur radio, fishing, woodwork, photography, astronomy. Office: Evanston Northwestern Healthcare 718 Glenview Ave Highland Park IL 60035

RABIN, GILBERT, judge, lawyer; b. Tarrytown, NY, June 10, 1923; s. Charles and Jeanette (Kalman) R.; m. Zita Segall, June 18, 1950; children: Jill, Corey, Marni. LLB, N.Y. U., 1948, LLM, 1950; LLD (hon.), Mercy Coll., 1981. Bar: N.Y. 1948. Assoc. Raphael & Conlon, N.Y.C., 1948-50; sr. ptnr. Rabin & Green, N.Y.C., 1950-73; sole practice Yonkers, N.Y., 1974-82; judge, chief judge City of Ct. Yonkers, 1982-94; jud. hearing officer N.Y. Supreme Ct., 9th Jud. Dist., 1994—. Supr. jury selection Supreme Ct., Westchester County, NY; lectr. N.Y. State Jud. Sems.; legis. advisor Mem. N.Y. State Assembly, Yonkers, 1966—70; justice City of Yonkers, 1970—82. Co-founder Children's Hearing Edn. and Rsch., 1979—. Recipient numerous awards Israel Bonds, Big Bros., others. Mem. N.Y. State Bar Assn., West County Bar Assn., Yonkers Lawyers Assn., N.Y. State City Ct. Judges Assn., N.Y. State Magistrates Assn. Jewish. Office Phone: 914-995-4097.

RABIN, HERBERT, physicist, university official; b. Milw., Nov. 14, 1928; 2 children. BS, U. Wis., 1950; MS, U. Ill., 1951; PhD in Physics, U. Md., 1959. Physicist elec. divsn. U.S. Naval Rsch. Lab., 1952-54, physicist solid state physics divsn., 1954-62, head radiation effects sect. optical materials br., 1962-67, head quantum optics sect., applied optics br., 1967-68, head quantum optics br., 1968-71, assoc. dir. rsch. for space sci. and tech., 1971-77, assoc. dir. rsch. for space and comm. sci. and tech., 1977-79; dep. asst. sec. for rsch., applied and space tech. Office of Navy Secretariat, Washington, 1979-83; dir. engring. rsch. ctr., prof. elec. engring., assoc. dean Coll. Engring., U. Md., College Park, 1983—, interim dean coll. engring., 1999-2000. Dir. GRC Internat., 1988—98, Washington Aluminum Co., 1992—95, Yurie Sys. Inc., 1995—98, VT Linx Multimedia Sys., Inc., 2000—02; vis. scientist Technisch Hochschule, Stuttgart, Germany, 1960—61; mem. staff physics dept. George Washington U., 1955—73; cons. Sch. Engring. Sao Carlos U., Sao Paulo, Brazil, 1964, Sao Paulo, 70; trustee Nat. Technol. U., 1984—2000, life trustee, 2000—03; vis. fellow SEEDA, England, 2003. Contbr. articles to tech. jours. Recipient Meritorious Civilian Svc. award, USN, 1969, Disting. Civilian Svc. award, 1976, 1993, Dept. Def., 1979, Cert. of Commendation, NASA, 1986, Centennial medal, U. Md. Coll. Engring., 1994. Fellow: AIAA, AAAS, Optical Soc. Am., Am. Phys. Soc.; mem.: IEEE (sr.), Brazilian Acad. Scis. (corr.). Achievements include patents in field. Home: 7109 Radnor Rd Bethesda MD 20817-6332 Office: U Md Engring Rsch Ctr College Park MD 20742-0001

RABIN, JOSEPH HARRY, marketing research company executive; b. Chgo., Dec. 12, 1927; s. Morris and Libby (Broder) Rabinovitz; m. Barbara E. Leader, Oct. 31, 1954; children: Marc Jay, Michelle Ann, Deborah Susan. BSc, Roosevelt U., 1950; MBA, DePaul U., 1951. Account exec. Gould, Gleiss & Benn, 1951-56; asst. dir. mktg. rsch. Paper Mate Co., Chgo., 1956-63; pres. Rabin Rsch. Co., Chgo., 1963—. Pres. Mather H.S. Coun., 1972-74; mem. adv. coun. U. Toledo, 1976-77, Kellstadt Ctr. DePaul U., 1986-93; mem. adv. com. Bur. of the Census, 1978-83; bd. dirs. Market Rsch. Inst., 1973-75, Ner Tamid Synagogue, 1976—, Jewish Vocat. Svc., 1977-80. With AUS, 1946-47. Mem. Am. Mktg. Assn. (pres. Chgo. chpt. 1961-62, nat. dir. 1973-75, nat. v.p. mktg. rsch. 1978-79, nat. pres. 1981-82), Assn. Consumer Rsch., Am. Statis. Assn. (pres. Chgo. chpt. 1962-63), Am. Assn. Pub. Opinion Rsch. Home: 7061 N Kedzie Ave Chicago IL 60645-2846 Office: Rabin Rsch Co 150 E Huron St Chicago IL 60611-2999 Office Phone: 312-482-8500. Business E-Mail: jrabin@rabin-research.com.

RABINER, LAWRENCE RICHARD, electrical engineer, educator; b. Bklyn., Sept. 28, 1943; s. Nathan Marcus and Gloria Hannah (Bodinger) R.; m. Suzanne Login, June 23, 1968; children: Sheri Lynn, Wendi Beth, Joni Elizabeth BS, MS, MIT, 1964, PhD, 1967. Mem. tech. staff AT&T Bell Labs., Murray Hill, N.J., 1967-70, supr. human machine voice communications group, 1971-85, head speech rsch. dept., 1985-90, dir. info. principles rsch. lab., 1990-95, v.p. user experience rsch. divsn., 1995-96; v.p. Speech and Image Processing Svcs., 1995-98, rsch. v.p., 1998—2002; prof. Rutgers U., 2002—, U. Calif., Santa Barbara, 2003—. Author: Theory and Application of Digital Signal Processing, 1975, Digital Speech Processing, 1979, Multirate Digital Signal Processing, 1983, Fundamentals of Speech Recognition, 1993. Bd. dirs. Summit Jewish Community Ctr., N.J., 1985-90. Fellow NAE, NAS, IEEE (pres. ASSP Soc. 1974-75, Piori award 1980), Soc. award 1980, Centennial award 1984, Kilby medal 1999, Millenium award 2000), Acoustical Soc. Am. (Biennial award 1974, v.p. 1994-95). Republican. Jewish. Avocations: stamp collecting/philately, bridge, racquetball. Home: 58 Sherbrook Dr Berkeley Heights NJ 07922-2346 E-mail: lrr01@comcast.net., lrr01@yahoo.com., lrr@caip.rutgers.edu., rabiner@ece.ucsb.edu.

RABINOVICH, ELIEZER M. retired ceramics engineer; b. Moscow, Apr. 4, 1937; s. Meyer L. and Brokha (Medalié) Rabinovich; m. Gesya Asinovsky, Apr. 25, 1967; children: Asya R. Takken, Irena Rosenblum. Engr. in Ceramic Tech. (equiv. MSc.), Moscow Mendeleev Inst. of Chem. Tech., 1959, Candidate of Tech. Sciences (PhD equivalent), 1964. Sci. Rsch. Inst. of Glass for Electronics, Moscow, 1959—74, group leader, 1969—73; sr. rsch. fellow Israel Ceramic and Silicate Inst., Haifa, Israel, 1974—80; leading investigator Bell Labs. of Lucent Technologies, Murray Hill, NJ, 1981—2001. Adj. prof. of ceramic sci. Technion - Israel Inst. of Tech., Haifa, 1975—80; vis. prof. U. of Paris-Sud, Orsay, France, 1989, U. of Saarland, Saarbrucken, Germany, 2001—02; program chmn. Glass and Optical Materials Divsn. of the Am. Ceramic Soc., 1999—2001; mem. of editl. bd. Jour. of Sol-Gel Sci. and Tech., 1995—2000. Contbr. articles over 91 to profl. jours. Fellow: Am. Ceramic Soc. (mem. of various committees, program chmn. 2001). Jewish. Achievements include patents for 15 in area of technical glass (1966-2000). Home: 52 Evergreen Dr Berkeley Heights NJ 07922 Personal E-mail: emrabin@comcast.net.

RABINOVICH, SERGIO, physician, educator; b. Lima, Peru, Apr. 8, 1928; m. Nelly; children— Gina, Sergio, Norca, Egla. MD, San Fernando Med. Sch., U. San Marcos, Lima, Peru, 1953. Intern San Fernando Med. Sch., U. San Marcos, Lima, 1947-54; resident in medicine Grasslands Hosp., Valhalla, N.Y., 1954-57, Henry Ford Hosp., Detroit; prof., head dept. internal medicine U. Arequipa Med. Sch., 1960-61; asst. prof. dept. internal medicine U. Iowa, Iowa City, 1963-65, asst. prof., 1965-69; attending physician and cons. VA Hosp., Iowa City, 1965-73; assoc. prof. U. Iowa, 1969-73; prof., chief dept. medicine div. infectious disease So. Ill. U. Sch. Medicine, Springfield, 1973-96, prof., chmn. dept. medicine, 1974-88, pres. Faculty Coun., 1992-93, prof. emeritus, 1996. Author: (with I.M. Smith, S.T. Donta) Antibiotics and Infection, 1974. Fellow ACP, Infectious Disease Soc. Am.; mem. AMA, Am. Soc. Microbiology, N.Y. Acad. Sci., Am. Fedn. Clin. Research, AAAS, Am. Thoracic Soc., Ill. Thoracic Soc. (pres. 1978-79), Central Soc. Clin. Research, Sigma Xi. Office: So Ill U Sch Medicine 800 N Rutledge St Springfield IL 62794-9636 Office Phone: 217-545-0181. Personal E-mail: sergiorabinovich@aol.com.

RABINOVITCH, BENTON SEYMOUR, chemist, educator emeritus; b. Montreal, Que., Can., Feb. 19, 1919; came to U.S., 1946; s. Samuel and Rachel (Schachter) R.; m. Marilyn Werby, Sept. 18, 1949; children: Peter Samuel, Ruth Anne, Judith Nancy, Frank Benjamin; m. Flora Reitman, 1980. BSc, McGill U., 1939, PhD, 1942; DSc (hon.), Technion Inst., Haifa, 1991. Postdoctoral fellow Harvard, 1946-48; mem. faculty U. Wash., Seattle, 1948—, prof. chemistry, 1957—, prof. chemistry emeritus, 1985—. Cons. and/or mem. sci. adv. panels, cons. NSF, Nat. Acad. Scis.-NRC; adv. com. phys. chemistry Nat. Bur. Standards. Author Antique Silver Servers, 1991, Contemporary Silver, 2000; co-author: Physical Chemistry, 1964; former editor: Ann. Rev. Phys. Chemistry; mem. editorial bd.: Internat. Jour. Chem. Kinetics, Rev. of Chem. Intermediates, Jour. Phys. Chemistry, J. Am. Chem. Soc. (assoc. editor). Served to capt. Canadian Army, 1942-46, ETO. Nat. Research Council Can. fellow, 1940-42; Royal Soc. Can. Research fellow, 1946-47; Milton Research fellow Harvard, 1948; Guggenheim fellow, 1961; vis. fellow Trinity Coll., Oxford, 1971; recipient Sigma Xi award for original research, Debye award in phys. chemistry, 1984, Polanyi medal Royal Soc. Chemistry; named hon. liveryman Worshipful Co. of Goldsmiths, London, 2000. Fellow Am. Phys. Soc., Am. Acad. Arts and Scis., Royal Soc. London; mem. Am. Chem. Soc. (past chmn. Puget Sound sect., past chmn. phys. chemistry div., editor jour.), Faraday Soc. Achievements include rsch. in Unimolecular gas phase reaction and history and design of silver implements. Home: 12530 42nd Ave NE Seattle WA 98125-4621 Office: Univ Washington Chemistry Box 351700 Seattle WA 98195 Fax: 206-685-8665. Office Phone: 206-543-1636.

RABINOVITCH, NATHAN, pediatrician, educator; b. Montreal, Can., Jan. 15, 1963; MD, McGill U., 1989. Intern Albert Einstein Coll. Medicine, Bronx, NY, 1989—90, resident pediat., 1990—92; fellow allergy and immunology Nat. Jewish Ctr. Immunology and Respiratory Diseases, 1994; asst. prof. pediat. U. Colo. Health Scis. Ctr., Denver, 1996—. Clin. instr. Montefiore Med. Ctr.-Albert Einstein Coll. Medicine, 1993—94; faculty physician, pediat. asthma/allergy specialist Nat. Jewish Med. Ctr. Recipient Future Leaders Devel. award, Am. Acad. Allergy, Asthma and Immunology, 2001. Office: Univ Colo Health Sci Ctr Dept Pediat 1400 Jackson St Denver CO 80206

RABINOVITZ, JASON, film and television consultant; b. Boston, Aug. 17, 1921; s. Morris J. and Martha (Leavitt) R.; m. Frieda Pearlson, July 18, 1948; children: Abby, Judith, Daniel, Jonathan. BA magna cum laude, Harvard U., 1943, MBA with distinction, 1948. With Chase Nat. Bank, N.Y.C., 1948-49; asst. to sec.-treas. United Paramount Theatres, Inc., N.Y.C., 1949-53; dir. Microwave Assocs., Burlington, Mass., 1952-54; asst. controller ABC, N.Y.C., 1953-56; adminstrv. v.p. ABC-TV Network, N.Y.C., 1956-57; with Metro-Goldwyn-Mayer, Inc., N.Y.C., 1957-69, treas., CFO, 1963, financial v.p., 1967-69; dir., exec. v.p., gen. mgr. Ency. Brit. Ednl. Corp., Chgo., 1971-73; sr. v.p., gen. mgr. Am. Film Theatre, N.Y.C., 1974-75; v.p., asst. to pres. Metro-Goldwyn-Mayer, Inc., Culver City, Calif., 1976-79, v.p. fin., 1979-83; sr. v.p. fin. and corp. adminstrn. MGM/UA Entertainment Co., 1983-84; cons. motion picture and TV, 1984—. Dir. Pacific Rim Entertainment, 1993-95. Dir. Am. Jewish Hist. Soc., 1994—96. Capt. U.S. Army, 1942—46. Decorated Bronze Star. Mem. Phi Beta Kappa, Phi Eta Sigma. Home: 1675 Stone Canyon Rd Los Angeles CA 90077-1912 E-mail: frjarab@earthlink.net.

RABINOVITZ, JOEL, lawyer, educator; b. 1939; AB, Cornell U., 1960; LLB, Harvard U., 1963. Bar: N.Y. 1963, Calif. 1981. Asst. prof. U. Fla., Gainesville, Fla., 1966—68; vis. assoc. prof. UCLA, 1968—69, acting prof., 1969—72, prof., 1972—79; vis. prof. NYU, 1976; dep. Internat. Tax Counsel, Dept. Treasury, 1980—81; ptnr. with Irell & Manella LLP, L.A., 1981—. Office: Irell & Manella LLP 1800 Avenue Of The Stars Los Angeles CA 90067-4212

RABINOVITZ, NILI, language educator, consultant; b. Jerusalem, Feb. 20, 1937; d. Haim Eliyahu and Ziporah Goldvasser; m. Ernest Rabinovitz, June 11, 1965 (dec. Apr. 1975); children: Tal, Sherone, Lisa. Tchg. cert., Levinsky Coll., Tel-Aviv, 1955; Diploma in French, Alliance Francaise, Paris, 1964; BA in Music Edn., Tel-Aviv U., 1979; MA in Music Therapy, Haharimam U., Phila., 1982. Lang. and music tchr. Dimona Elem. & Mid. Schs., Tel-Aviv, 1957—73; Hebrew tchr. Consulate Sch., Paris, 1962—64, Adults Ulpam, Jerusalem, 1964—66; programs writer Israeli Radio, Jerusalem, 1964—66; cons. Gratz Coll., Melrose Park, Pa., 1983—90, dir., Hebrew program, 1990—2003. Office: Gratz Coll 7605 Old York Rd Melrose Park PA 19027

RABINOWITSH, STEVE, urban planner educator, city council member; b. L.A., Jan. 17, 1949; s. Jack and Xenia Rabinowtsh; m. Lynnie Shaub Herr, Apr. 19, 1980; children: Ni cholas, Jackson. BA in Polit. Sci., U. Colo., 1970, MA in Polit. Sci., 1973, M in Urban Planning, 1975. City planner City of Longmont, Colo., 1975-76; planning cons. Brisco, Maphis, Murray & Lamont, Boulder, 1976-78; regional planner Denver Regional Coun. of Govts., 1978-82; planning cons., 1983-85; instr. Santa Rosa (Calif.) Jr. Coll., 1986—. City coun. mem. City of Santa Rosa, 1998—; mem., chmn. Sonoma County Open Space Dist., 1990-98; exec. bd. Assn. of Bay Area Govts., Oakland, Calif., 1999—; mem. Santa Rosa Creek Com., 1990-99, chmn., 1997-99. Recipient Conservation Partnership award U.S. Nat. Park Svc., 1996, Merit award City of Santa Rosa, 1992, 99. Avocations: photography, travel, french, aerobics. Home: 1275 4th St PMB 178 Santa Rosa CA 95404-4041 Office: City of Santa Rosa PO Box 1678 Santa Rosa CA 95402-1678

RABINOWITZ, DOROTHY, television critic; b. N.Y.C. BA, Queens Coll., N.Y.C.; postgrad., NYU, Pratt Inst. Freelance writer, syndicated columnist, commentator Sta. WWOR-TV News, N.Y.C.; editl. page writer and television critic Wall St. Jour., mem. editl. bd. Author: Home Life, 1970, New Lives, 1976, No Crueler Tyrannies: Accusation, False Witness, and Other Terrors of Our Times, 2003; columnist Dorothy Rabinowitz's Media Log. Recipient Pulitzer prize for Disting. Commentary, 2001. Office: Wall St Jour 1155 Ave of the Americas 5th fl New York NY 10036

RABINOWITZ, HOWARD K. physician, educator; b. Pitts., Sept. 25, 1946; s. Mac and Anne (Morgan) R.; m. Carol A. Gelles, Feb. 4, 1968; children: Elyse, Daniel J. Student, Rutgers Coll., 1964-67; MD, U. Pitts., 1971. Diplomate Am. Bd. Family Practice, Am. Bd. Pediatrics. From instr. to assoc. prof. Dept. Family Medicine Jefferson Med. Coll., Phila., 1976-90, vice chmn., 1990-95; prof., 1990—. Bd. dirs. Am. Bd. Family Practice, Lexington, Ky., pres., 1992-93. Contbr. articles to profl. jours. With USPHS, 1972-74. RWJ Health Policy fellow, 1993-94. Fellow Phila. Coll. Physicians; mem. AMA, Soc. Tchrs. Family Medicine, Am. Acad. Family Physicians. Office: Jefferson Medical College Dept Family Medicine 1015 Walnut St Ste 401 Philadelphia PA 19107-5005

RABINOWITZ, JACK GRANT, radiologist, educator; b. Monticello, N.Y., July 9, 1927; s. Abraham and Bessie (Sussman) R.; m. Rica Gedalia Arnon, Oct. 19, 1972; children— Antoine, Anne, Pierre, Yaron, Tal. BA, UCLA, 1949; MD, U. Berne, Switzerland, 1955. Diplomate: Am. Bd. Radiology. Intern Kings County Hosp., Bklyn., 1955-56, resident, 1956-59; instr. radiology Downstate Med. Center, Bklyn., 1960-61, asst. prof. radiology, 1967-70, prof. radiology, 1970-73; asst. radiologist Mt. Sinai Sch. Medicine, N.Y.C., 1962-65, asst. prof. radiology, 1965-66, asso. prof. radiology, 1966-67, prof., chmn. dept. radiology, 1978-95, prof., 1995—. Asso. attending radiologist Mt. Sinai Hosp., N.Y.C., 1965-67, dir. radiology, 1978—; radiologist-in-chief Bklyn.-Cumberland Med. Center, Bklyn., 1967-70; dir. diagnostic radiology Kings County Hosp. Center, Bklyn., 1970-73; prof., chmn. dept. diagnostic radiology U. Tenn., Memphis, 1973-78; cons. in radiology VA Hosp., Bronx, N.Y. Author: Pediatric Radiology, 1978, Radiology for the Primary and Emergency Care of Physicians, 1981. Fellow Am. Coll. Radiology; mem. Radiol. Soc. N. Am., Am. Roentgen Ray Soc., Assn. Univ. Radiologists, AMA, Soc. Chmn. Acad. Radiology Depts., Tenn. Radiol. Soc., Tenn. Med. Soc., Memphis and Shelby County Med. Soc., Memphis Roentgen Soc. Office: Mt Sinai Hosp 1 Gustave L Levy Pl New York NY 10029-6500 Office Phone: 212-241-7427. Business E-Mail: jack-rabinowitz@msnyu.health.org.

RABINOWITZ, PETER J. literature educator, music critic; BA, MA, PhD, U. Chgo. Prof. comparative lit. Hamilton Coll., Clinton, NY, 1974—. Author: (book) Before Reading; co-author (with Michael Smith): Authorizing Readers; co-editor (with James Phelan): Understanding Narrative, (book series) Theory and Interpretation of Narrative Series; contbr. editor (magazine) Fanfare. Office: Hamilton Coll 198 College Hill Rd Clinton NY 13323

RABINOWITZ, SAMUEL NATHAN, lawyer; b. Hazleton, Pa., Sept. 16, 1932; s. Morris M. and Bodia (Janowitz) R.; m. Barbara Cohen, Mar. 27, 1955; children— Fredric E., Mark I., Joshua A. BA, Pa. State U., 1955; JD, Temple U., 1959. Bar: D.C. 1959, Pa. 1960. Agt. IRS, Phila., 1956—60; sole practice Phila., 1960—61; ptnr. Blank Rome, LLP, Phila., 1961—. Mem. trust com. Continental Bank, Phila., 1983-91; faculty Temple U. Sch. Law Contbr. articles to profl. jours. Active Phila. Friends Boys Town Jerusalem; bd. dirs. Jerusalem Soc. Boys Town, Phila., Friends of Ben Gurion U. the Negev, Jewish Nat. Fund Coun., Phila., Fellow Am. Coll. Trust and Estate Counsel; mem. ABA, Pa. Bar Assn., Phila. Bar Assn. (chmn. probate and trust sect. 1985-86), Green Valley Country Club, Elkview Country Club, Delaire Country Club (Delray Beach, Fla.), Golden Slipper, Maccabi/USA Sports for Israel (exec. com., counsel). Home: 4454 White Cedar Ln Delray Beach FL 33445 Office: Blank Rome LLP One Logan Sq 8th Fl Philadelphia PA 19103-6998

RABINOWITZ, WILBUR MELVIN, manufacturing executive, consultant; b. Bklyn., Feb. 18, 1918; s. Harry A. and Caroline (Simmons) R.; m. Audrey H. Perlmutter, Apr. 30, 1944; 1 child, Michael B. PhB, Dickinson Coll., 1940; JD, Harvard U., 1943. Gen. mgr. J. Rabinowitz & Sons, Inc., Bklyn., 1945-67, pres., 1967-81, pres. emeritus cons., 1981-95. Pres. Met. Glass & Plastic Containers, 1967-81; trustee Mendeleyev U., Moscow, 1991—. Author: Almost Everywhere. Pres. Rabinowitz Found., N.Y.C., 1967—; trustee Dickinson Coll., Carlisle, Pa., 1975—. With AUS, 1943-45, ETO. Mem. Nat. Assn. Container Distbrs. (past pres.), U.S. Power Squadrons (past comdr.), Explorers Club. Home: 425 E 58 St No 40A New York NY 10022-8332

RABIU, BADRU I.O. federal official; b. Lagos, Nigeria, Aug. 18, 1935; came to U.S., 1972; divorced; six children. Polit., labor specialist Am. Embassy, Lagos, 1951-72; dir. Liberty Immigration and Citizenship Svc., N.Y.C., 1984—. Adminstrv. asst. Arlington (Va.) County, 1981-83; labor writer U.S. Dept. Labor, Washington, 1979-80. Contbr. articles to profl. jours. Mem. Rep. Nat. Com. (life), Rep. Senatorial Inner Circle, Nigeria Muslim Orgn., UN Assn. of U.S. Moslem. Home: 2840 Ocean Pkwy Apt 9E Brooklyn NY 11235-7956 Office: 72 Maiden Ln Ste 312 New York NY 10038

RABKIN, MITCHELL THORNTON, physician, educator, hospital administrator; b. Boston, Nov. 27, 1930; s. Morris Aaron and Esther (Quint) Rabkin; m. Adrienne M. Najarian, June 24, 1956; children: Julia Margaret, David Gregory. AB magna cum laude, Harvard U., 1951, MD cum laude, 1955; DSc (hon.), Brandeis U., 1983; DPharm (hon.), Mass. Coll. Pharmacy, 1983; DSc (hon.), Curry Coll., 1989; DSc (hon.), Northeastern U., 1994; DHumLet (hon.), Salem (Mass.) State Coll., 1995. Intern Mass. Gen. Hosp., Boston, 1955—56, resident in internal medicine, 1956—57, 1959—60, chief resident, 1962, mem. staff, 1963—72, bd. consultation, 1972—80, hon. physician, 1981—; clin. fellow NIH, Bethesda, Md., 1957—59; gen. dir. Beth Israel Hosp., Boston, 1966—80, pres., 1980—96; CEO CareGroup, Boston, 1996—98; now disting. inst. scholar Carl J. Shapiro Inst. for Edn. and Rsch. Harvard Med. Sch. and Beth Israel Deaconess Med. Ctr., Boston, 1996—; principal Washington Advisory Group, 1999—. Asst. prof. medicine Harvard U., 1969—70, assoc. prof., 1971—83, prof., 1983—, pres. med. alumni coun., 2002—03; v.p. NYU Sch. Medicine Found. Bd. With USPHS, 1957—59. Fellow: AAAS, ACP, Am. Acad. Arts and Scis.; mem.: Inst. Medicine of NAS, Conf. Boston Tchg. Hosps. (past chmn.), Assn. Am. Med. Colls. (chmn. 1996—97), Soc. Med. Adminstrs., Mass. Med. Soc., Century Assn. (N.Y.C.), Tavern Club Boston, Harvard Club of Boston. Jewish. Office: Beth Israel Deaconess Med Ctr/Harvard U Shapiro Inst Edn and Rsch 330 Brookline Ave Boston MA 02215-5400 Office Phone: 617-667-9400. Business E-Mail: mrabkin@bidmc.harvard.edu.

RABKIN, PEGGY ANN, retired lawyer; b. Buffalo, Apr. 13, 1945; d. Anthony J. and Margaret G. (Catuzzi) Marano; m. Samuel S. Rabkin, June 29, 1969. BA, SUNY, Buffalo, 1967, MEd, 1970, MA, 1972, JD, PhD, 1975. Tchr. Buffalo Pub. Schs., 1967-69; grad. teaching asst. SUNY, Buffalo, 1969-72; case analyst U.S. Equal Employment Opportunity Com., 1974; dir. affirmative action U. Louisville, 1975-78, adj. prof. of law, 1976-77; atty. office for civil rights HEW, N.Y.C., 1978; sr. atty. for labor and employment Am. Home Products Corp., N.Y.C., 1978-86, sr. atty., 1986—. Author: Fathers to Daughters, 1980; editor: Buffalo Law Rev., 1974-75; contbr. articles to profl. jours. Commr. Louisville & Jefferson Co. Human Relations Com., Louisville, 1977-78. Recipient Christopher Baldy fellow, SUNY at Buffalo Law Sch., 1974-75, Regents Coll. Scholarship N.Y. State Bd. of Regents, 1963-67. Mem. ABA, Assn. of Bar of City of N.Y., Am. Corp. Counsel Assn., Soc. of Human Resources Mgmt., U.S. C. of C. (labor com. 1991—). Avocations: skiing, reading, cooking, and nutrition.

RABO, JULE ANTHONY, chemical researcher, consultant; b. Budapest, Hungary; came to U.S., 1957; m. Sheelagh Ennis; children: Benedict, Sebastian. BSChemE, Poly. U., Budapest, 1946, DSc in Chemistry, 1949, D honoris causa, 1986, U. Veszprem, Hungary, 2002. From asst. prof. to assoc. prof. Poly. U., Budapest, 1946—54; assoc. dir. Hydrocarbon Rsch. Inst., Budapest, 1951—56; rsch. assoc. Union Carbide Corp., Buffalo, 1957-60, rsch. mgr. Tarrytown, N.Y., 1960-72, corp. fellow, 1969-82, sr. corp. rsch. fellow, 1982—, UOP, Tarrytown, 1988—. Cons. in chemsitry and catalysis, Armonk, N.Y.; former mem. adv. bd. Ctr. for Advanced Materials, Lawrence-Berkeley Lab.; mem. adv. bd. dept. chemistry Lehigh U. Author: Zeolite Chemisty and Catalysts; former mem. editorial bd. Jour. Catalysis, Applied Catalysis; contbr. articles to profl. jours.; patentee in field. Recipient Kossuth award Govt. of Hungary, 1953, Excellence in Catalysis award N.Y. Catalysis Soc., 1982, Humboldt award, Fed. Republic of Germany, 1990. Mem. Am. Chem. Soc. (E.V. Murphree award 1988), Am. Catalysis Soc. (Eugene J. Houdry award 1989), Hungarian Acad. Sci. (Varga medal 1991), Am. Inst. Chemists (Chem. Pioneer award 1993).

RABOLD, BARBARA ANN, artist, writer, illustrator, systems analyst; b. Germantown, Ohio, Apr. 15, 1939; d. George Crone and Gertrude Faye (Marshall) Carr; divorced; children: Matthew Theodore, Teresa Marie. Student, Sinclair C.C., Dayton, Ohio, 1990-92. Former saleswoman House of Stuart Cosmetics, McNess Home Products, Sarah Coventry Jewelry, Amway Products. Choir dir. for 14 yrs.; distbr. nutraceuticals Mannatech, 1998; tchr. art W. Carrollton City Recreation. Exhibited in group shows at Miamisburg (Ohio) Art Gallery, 1970-87, Salem and Dayton Malls, Dayton, 1975-78, Beachmont Mall, Cin., 1975-78, Indpls. Mall, 1975-78. Vol. tutor West Carrollton Sch. Sys., 1970-78, Miami Valley Literacy Coun., Dayton, 1988-2000; pub. spkr.; discussion moderator Parents Without Ptnrs., Dayton, 1980-82, 89-90; asst. group leader Alzheimer Assn., Dayton, 1990; pastoral svc. vol. local hosp. Recipient 600 vol. hours. svc. award Miami Valley Literacy Coun., 1991, more than 600 svc. hours Southview Hosp. Avocations: swimming, reading, gourmet cooking, dance, boating. Home and Office: 102 1/2 Home Ave West Carrollton OH 45449-1206

RABON, WILLIAM JAMES, JR., architect; b. Marion, SC, Mar. 7, 1931; s. Williams James and Beatrice (Baker) R.; m. Martha Ann Hibbitts, Mar. 7, 1987. BS in Arch., Clemson Coll., 1951; BArch, N.C. State Coll., 1955; MArch, MIT, 1956; postgrad., Inst. Urbanistico, Rome, 1957-58. Registered architect, Calif., N.C., Ohio, Pa., Ga. Designer archtl. firms, N.Y.C. & Birmingham, Mich., 1958-61; designer, assoc. John Carl Warnecke & Assocs., San Francisco, 1961-63, 64-66, Keyes, Lethbridge & Condon, Washington, 1966-68; prin. archtl. ptnr. A.M. Kinney Assocs. & William J. Rabon, Cin., 1968-85; v.p., dir. archtl. design A.M. Kinney, Inc., Cin., 1977-85; v.p., dir. programming svcs. Design Art Corp., 1977-85; sr. architect John Portman & Assocs., Atlanta, 1985-88; dir. archtl. design Robert & Co., Atlanta, 1988-89; design prin. Carlson Assocs., Atlanta, 1990-93; prin., dir. rsch. & med. facilities programming & design Rosser Internat., 1993-97, William J. Rabon, Arch., 1995—. Lectr. U. Calif., Berkeley, 1963-65; asst. prof. archtl. design Cath. U. Am., 1967-68; planning cons. Nat. Bur. Stds. Lab., China, 1982. Prin. works include Kaiser Tech. Ctr., Pleasanton, Calif., 1970 (Rsch. Devel. Lab. of Yr. award), Clement Nat. Bank, Milford, Ohio, 1971, Pavilion Bldg. Children's Hosp. Med. Ctr., Cin., 1973 (Cin. AIA design award), EG&G, Hydrospace, Inc., Rockville, Md., 1970 (Potomac Valley AIA design award), Mead Johnson Pk., Evansville, Inc., 1973 (Rsch. Devel. lab. of Yr. merit award), Hamilton County Vocat. Sch., Cin., 1972, Hdqrs. Lab. EPA, 1975, Arapahoe Chem. Co. Rsch. Ctr., Boulder, Colo., 1976 (Rsch. Devel. lab. of Yr. award, 1976, Concrete Reinforced Steel Inst. Nat. Design award, Regional AIA design award), Corp. Hdqrs. Ohio River Co., Cin., 1977, Children's Hosp. Therapy Ctr., 1981 (Cin. ALA design award, 1978, award of merit Am. Wood Coun., 1981), Va. Hosp. addition (Cin. ASHRAE Design award, 1980), NALCO Chem. Co. Rsch. Ctr., Naperville, Ill., 1980 (Ohio and Cin. AIA design awards, 1980, 1981), NALCO Chem. Co. Hdqs., 1987, Proctor and Gamble-Winton Hill Tunnel, Cin., 1978 (Ohio AIA design award), Toyota Regional Ctr., Blue Ash, Ohio (Ohio AIA and Ohio Masonry Coun. combined design award, 1981), U. Cin. Med. Ctr. Lab., Cin., 1981, Children's Hosp. Ambulatory Svc. Ctr., 1984, East and West fleethdqrs. and Data Ctr. Librs. of Royal Saudi Arabian Navy, 1985, corp. hdqrs. The Drackett Co., Cin., 1983, corp. hdqrs. Brown & Williamson, Louisville, 1984, Children's Hosp. Med. Ctr. Ambulatory Svcs. Ctr., Cin., 1984, Olin Corp. Rsch. Ctr., Cheshire, Conn., 1985, Inst. Paper Sci. & Tech., Atlanta, 1989, Citicorp. Data Ctr., Napa, Calif., 1992, Sci. Complex, Athens, Ga., 1996, Biocontainment Rsch. Ctr., 1998. 1st lt., co. comdr., Battalion S-2 and Platoon leader AUS, 1951—53, Korean War. Company awarded Presdl. Unit Citation; recipient Silver Star, Bronze Star for Valor, Bronze Star for Meritorious Svc., Purple Heart with bronze cluster; MIT Grad. scholar, 1956; Fulbright scholar, Italy, 1957-58. Mem. AIA, Nat. Coun. Archtl. Registration Bds.

RABOSKY, JOSEPH GEORGE, engineering consulting company executive; b. Sewickley, Pa., May 20, 1944; s. Mary Helen (Mayer) Rabosky; m. Suzanne Lazzelle, Aug. 23, 1969. BS, Pa. State U., 1966; MS in Engring., W.Va. U., 1969; MSCE, U. Pitts., 1973, PhD, 1984. Registered profl. engr., Pa., W.Va., Ohio. Project engr. Chester Engrs., Coraopolis, Pa., 1969-70, mgr., 1989-92; project mgr. Calgon Corp., Pitts., 1970-73, sect. leader, 1979-85, mktg. mgr., 1985-86; sr. environ. specialist Mobay Chem. Corp., Pitts.,

1975-79; project engr. Morris Knowles, Inc., Pitts., 1973-74; project mgr. Penn Environ. Cons., 1974-75; engring. mgr. Baker/TSA, Inc., Pitts., 1986-89; pres. AquaTerra, Inc., Moon Twp., Pa., 1992-95, Rabosky & Assocs., Moon Twp., Pa., 1995—. Adj. prof. U. Pitts., 1985-88, Pa. State U.-Beaver, McKeesport and New Kensington campuses, 1985—, Youngstown State U., 2003-. Mem. Am. Acad. Environ. Engrs. (diplomate, cert. water supply wastewater engr.), Western Pa. Water Pollution Control Assn. (officer 1984-94, pres. 1992-93), Internat. Water Conf. (mem. exec. bd. 1989-94, gen. chmn. 1992-93), Pa. Water Environ. Assn. (pres. 1996-97). Home: 104 Wynview Dr Moon Township PA 15108-1033 Personal E-mail: joeralco@aol.com.

RABOW, MICHAEL WARREN, physician, educator; b. June 30, 1965; BA, Harvard U., 1987; MD, U. Calif., San Francisco, 1993. Diplomate Am. Bd. Internal Medicine. Resident in primary care U. Calif., San Francisco, 1993-96, fellow in gen. medicine, 1996-97, asst. prof. medicine, 1997—. Author: (with others) Current Medical Diagnosis and Treatment, 1998; contbr. articles to profl. jours. Office: U Calif San Francisco 1701 Divisadero St Ste 500 San Francisco CA 94115-3011

RABSON, ALAN SAUL, federal agency administrator, physician, educator; b. N.Y.C., July 1, 1926; s. Abraham and Florence (Shulman) Rabson; m. Ruth L. Kirschstein, June 11, 1950; 1 child, Arnold. BA, U. Rochester, 1948; MD, SUNY, Bklyn., 1950. Intern Mass. Meml. Hosp., Boston, 1951—52; resident in pathology NYU Hosp., 1952—54, USPHS Hosp., New Orleans, 1954—55; pathologist Nat. Cancer Inst., Bethesda, Md., 1955—; prof. pathology Georgetown U. Med. Sch., 1974—, Uniformed Services U. Health Scis., 1978—, George Washington U., 1978—; dep. dir. Nat. Cancer Inst., Bethesda, 1995—, acting dir., 2001—02. Contbr. articles to med. jours. Mem.: Am. Assn. Pathologists, Alpha Omega Alpha, Sigma Xi, Phi Beta Kappa. Address: NIH-Nat Cancer Inst 9000 Rockville Pike Bldg 31 Bethesda MD 20892-0001

RABSTEJNEK, GEORGE JOHN, photomics executive; b. Queens, N.Y., June 14, 1932; s. George John and Rose Anna (Krasa) R.; m. Patsy Kidd, July 17, 1964; 1 child, Marley Ann. B in Indsl. Engring., Ga. Inst. Tech., 1954; postgrad., U. Conn. Sch. Law, 1960, NYU Sch. Bus., 1965-69; advanced mgmt. program, Harvard U., 1975. Dir. material mgmt. svcs. divsn. Harbridge House, Inc., Boston, 1965-69, v.p., group head, 1969-75, exec. v.p., 1975-76, pres., 1976-83, CEO, 1983-92, chmn., 1983-93, ret., 1993. Chmn. bd. dirs. R.P.W., Inc., Bluelight, Inc.; chmn. B.O.D. Ctr. for Tech. Commercialization, 2002; founder, mem. exec. com. Keck Neural Prothesis Rsch. Ctr. Contbr. articles to profl. jours. Vice chmn. World Affairs Coun. Boston, 1988, pres., 1984-87; trustee Internat. Coord. Coun., Boston, 1984-2003; trustee, chmn. of bd. dirs. Mass. Eye and Ear Infirmary, Boston, 1984—, vice chmn. bd. dirs.; mem. Draper Labs. Corp., 1994, chmn. bd. dirs., 2002; mem. adv. bd. Town of Cohasset, Mass., 1975; chmn. nat. adv. bd. Ga. Inst. Tech., 1991-92; mem. exec. adv. bd. Ivan Allen Coll.; mem. bd. visitors Northeastern U.; chmn. bd. dirs. Ctr. for Tech. Commercialization. Comdr. USNR, 1954-75, ret. Recipient Disting. Alumni award Sch. Indsl. and Sys. Engring., Ga. Inst. Tech., named to Acad. Disting. Engring. Alumni. Mem. Am. Inst. Indsl. Engrs., Nat. Security Indsl. Assn. (v.p. 1987—), Nat. Def. Transp. Assn. (Def. Transp. award 1980), Assn. Naval Aviators, Navy League, Reynolds Soc. (chmn.), Nat. Security Industry Assn. (trustee 1990-93), Harvard Club, Algonquin Club (Boston), Cohasset Golf Club (Mass.), Cohasset Yacht Club, Cohasset Tennis and Squash Club, Mill Reef Club, Antigua, B.W.I., Comml. Club, F St. Club (Washington), Phi Kappa Sigma. Republican. Unitarian Universalist. Home: 181 Border St Cohasset MA 02025-2043 Personal E-mail: gjrab@attbi.com.

RABUN, JOHN BREWTON, JR., criminal justice agency administrator; b. Augusta, Ga., Aug. 16, 1946; s. John Brewton and Alsie Imor (Bateman) R.; m. Anna Betsy Park, Dec. 27, 1967; children: Kerry Kristin, John Candler. BA, Mercer U., 1967; postgrad., So. Bapt. Theol. Sem., 1967—70; MSW, U. Louisville, 1971. Cert. social worker, Ky., DC. Exec. dir. Ky. Civil Liberties Union, Louisville, 1971—72; dir. Cmty. Residential Treatment Svcs., Louisville, 1973—78; program mgr. Field Svcs., Louisville, 1978—80, Exploited and Missing Child Unit, Louisville, 1980—84; v.p., COO Nat. Ctr. for Missing and Exploited Children, Washington, 1984—. Mem. Alderman's Task Force on Social Svcs., Louisville, 1982, Mayor's City Youth Commn., Louisville, 1983-84; trainer and/or cons. to numerous agys. in U.S., U.K., Can., Mex., Belgium, Germany, Austria, Netherlands. Contbr. articles to criminal justice and healthcare publs. and books. Recipient Key to City of Louisville, 1983, Disting. Alumnus award U. Louisville, 1985, 2003, Russell L. Colling Lit. award Internat. Assn. for Healthcare Security and Safety, 1991; named hon. chief of police City of Louisville, 1982; Alumni fellow U. Louisville, 1999. Mem. ACLU, NASW, Nat. Sheriff's Assn., Nat. Coun. Juvenile and Family Ct. Judges, Internat. Juvenile Officers Assn., Acad. Cert. Social Workers, Internat. Assn. Healthcare Safety and Security, Am. Soc. Indsl. Security, Internat. Assn. Chiefs of Police. Baptist (deacon). Avocations: photography, hunting, fishing, internet. Home: 13519 Oak Ivy Ln Fairfax VA 22033-1230 Office: Nat Ctr for Missing and Exploited Children 699 Prince St Alexandria VA 22314-3117 Office Phone: 703-837-6216.

RABUZZI, DANIEL D. medical administrator; b. Pitts., June 19, 1935; s. Daniel Ralph and Victoria (Bruni) R.; m. Kathryn Allen, June 11, 1958; children: Daniel, Matthew, Douglas. AB, Harvard Coll., 1957; MD, U. Pa., 1961. Diplomate Am. Bd. Otolaryngology. Instr. otolaryngology U. Md., Balt., 1967-68; asst. prof. SUNY, Syracuse, 1968-71, assoc. prof., 1971-77, prof., 1977-81, clin. prof. otolaryngology, 1984-97, emeritus prof., 1997—; prof., chmn. N.Y. Med. Coll. and N.Y. Eye & Ear Infirmary, N.Y.C., 1981-84. Pres. St. Joseph's Hops. Med. Staff, Syracuse, 1990-92; med. dir. Harrison Surgery Ctr., 1996—. Contbr. 55 articles to profl. jours., chpts. to books. Capt. U.S. Army, 1966-68. Fellow ACS; mem. Am. Soc. Head and Neck Surgery, Am. Acad. Otoloaryngology, Am. Cancer Soc. (pres. County unit 1978-80), Onondaga County Med. Soc. (pres. 1987 88). Avocations: roman archeology, european travel, golf, historical readings. Office: Harrison Outpatient Surgery Ctr 550 Harrison St Ste 230 Syracuse NY 13202-3064 Office Phone: 315-472-4424. Personal E-mail: buzdoc@earthlink.net.

RABY, JOHN CORNELIUS, secondary school educator; b. N.Y.C., May 18, 1944; s. John Cornelius and Adele Lambrose Raby; m. Betty Louise Hays, July 31, 1971; 1 child, John Hays. BA in History, Stanford U, 1966; MA in History, Columbia U Tchr. Coll., 1968. Cert. teach social studies N.Y., N.J., Calif. History tchr. Mountain HS, West Orange, NJ, 1968—71; faculty mem. The. Gov. Sch. of N.J. for Pub. Issues, West Long Branch, 1983—88, 1990, 1992—93, 1995; history tchr. James Caldwell HS, West Caldwell, NJ, 1973—89, The Pingry Sch., Martinsville, NJ, 1989—. Cross-country coach The Pingry Sch., Martinsville, NJ, 1993—. Mem. Dem. Com., Warren, NJ, 1995—, treas., 2002—. Recipient U.S. Presdl. Tchr. award, NEA, 1986, Nat. Tchr. award Finalist, The Disney Corp., 1994; grantee Fellow, Soc. For Values In Higher Edn., 1994—. Mem.: Organization of Am. Historians, Soc. For Values In Higher Edn. (Nat. Bd. Mem. 2003), Am. Historical Assoc. (assoc.). Democrat. Avocations: running, travel, gardening, reading. Office: The Pingry School Box 366 Martinsville Rd Martinsville NJ 08836

RABY, KENNETH ALAN, lawyer, retired army officer; b. Dec. 29, 1935; s. Carl George and Helen Josette (Milne) R.; m. Shirley Rae Nelson, June 2, 1957; children: Randolph Carlton, Shelly Ann. BA, U. S.D., 1957, JD, 1960; grad. with honors, Command and Gen. Staff Coll., 1975, U.S. Army War Coll., 1981. Bar: S.D. 1960, Ga. 1988, Supreme Ct. Ga., Supreme Ct. S.D., Ga. Ct. Appeals, U.S. Supreme Ct. Commd. 2d lt. U.S. Army, 1957, advanced through grades to col. JAGC, 1979, ret., 1987; dep. staff judge adv. Am. Divsn., Chu Lai, Vietnam, 1968-69; chief legal team U.S. Army Inf. Sch., Ft. Benning, Ga., 1969-71; team chief, acting divsn. chief adminstrv. law divsn. Office JAG, Dept. Army, 1971-74; staff judge adv. Hdqs. 24th Inf. Divsn., Ft. Stewart, Ga., 1974-79; staff judge adv. U.S. Army Armor Ctr., Ft. Knox, Ky., 1979; chief criminal law divsn. Office of JAG, Washington, 1981-84; sr. judge Army Ct. Mil. Rev., Falls Church, Va., 1984-87; staff atty. Ga. Ct. Appeals, 1987—; chief mil. def. counsel U.S. vs. Calley (My Lai Massacre) U.S. Army, 1969—71. Former chmn., mem. Joint Service Com. on Mil. Justice, 1981-84; mem. Mil. Justice Act of 1983 Adv. Commn., 1984-87; army liaison to criminal law sect. ABA, 1981-84. Eagle Scout Boy Scouts Am., 1952—53. Decorated Legion of Merit, Bronze Star with oak leaf cluster, Meritorious Svc. medal with 2 oak leaf clusters, Joint Svc. Commendation medal, Air medal, Army Commendation medal with oak leaf cluster, Army Achievement medal. Mem.: FBA (chmn. law enforcement liaison com. 1986—87), Ga. Bar Assn., Assn. U.S. Army, Masons (32d degree, KCCH), Order Ea. Star (grand chpt. Ga. 1999—2000, gen. grand chpt. parliamentarian 2003—, worthy grand patron), Arture Reghine Lodge (Italy) (hon.), Royal Order Scotland (hon.), Theta Xi, Delta Theta Phi. Home: 575 Spender Trace Atlanta GA 30350-5017 Office: Staff Atty Ga Ct Appeals Jud Bldg Rm 336 Capitol Sq Atlanta GA 30334-9003 Office Phone: 404-657-4048. E-mail: alan.raby@juno.com.

RABY, WILLIAM LOUIS, writer, consultant; b. Chgo., July 16, 1927; s. Gustave E. and Helen (Burgess) R.; m. Norma Claire Schreiner, Sept. 8, 1956; children: Burgess, Marianne, Marlene. BSBA, Northwestern U., 1949; MBA, U. Ariz., 1961, PhD, 1971. Ptnr. VAR CPA Firms, 1950-76, Touche Ross & Co., N.Y.C., 1977-87. Pres. Ariz. State Bd. Accountancy, 1993-94; mem. Ariz. State Bd. Tax Appeals, 1994—, chmn., 1997-99, 2003—; prof. acctg. emeritus Ariz. State U.; columnist Tax Notes mag., Arlington, Va., 1990—; cons. on video and audio tax edn. tapes Bisk Pub. Co., 1992—. Author: The Income Tax and Business Decisions, 1964, Building and Maintaining a Successful Tax Practice, 1964, The Reluctant Taxpayer, 1970, Tax Practice Management, 1974, Introduction to Federal Taxation, annually, 1980-91, Tax Practice Management: Client Servicing, 1986; editor: Raby Report on Tax Practice, 1986-96, PPC Guide To Successful Tax Practice, 1991; mem. editorial adv. bd. Practical Tax Strategies; contbr. articles to profl. jours. Mem. AICPA (chmn. fed. tax divsn. 1980-83, v.p. 1983-84, coun. 1983-90), Tax Ct. Bar. Presbyterian (elder, United Presbyn. Ch. chmn. adv. coun. on ch. and soc. 1979-81). Office: PO Box 26846 Tempe AZ 85285-6846 Office Phone: 480-967-1501. E-mail: wlraby@cs.com.

RACCAH, DOMINIQUE MARCELLE, publisher; b. Paris, Aug. 24, 1956; arrived in U.S., 1964; d. Paul Mordechai and Colette Bracha (Madar) R.; m. Raymond W. Bennett, Aug. 20, 1980; children: Marie, Lyron, Doran. BA, U. Ill., Chgo., 1978; MS, U. Ill., Champaign-Urbana, 1981. Rsch. analyst Leo Burnett Advt., Chgo., 1980-81, rsch. supr., 1981-84, assoc. rsch. dir., 1984-87; pres., pub., owner Sourcebooks, Inc., Naperville, Ill., 1987—; co-CEO Login Pubs. Consortium, Chgo., 1990-99. Author Financial Sourcebooks' Sources, 1987. Recipient Blue Chip Enterprise award, 2000, Ernst & Young Entrepreneur of Yr. Ill. and N.W. Ind., 2000; named to Inc. 500 list; inducted into Univ. Ill. Entrepreneurship Hall of Fame, 2001. Mem. Pubs. Mktg. Assn., Am. Booksellers Assn., Am. Assn. Pubs. Avocations: photography, writing, history. Home: 26 N Webster St Naperville IL 60540-4527 Office: Sourcebooks Inc 1935 Brookdale Rd # 139 Naperville IL 60563-9245 E-mail: dominique@sourcebooks.com.

RACE, GEORGE JUSTICE, pathology educator; b. Everman, Tex., Mar. 2, 1926; s. Claude Ernest and Lila Eunice (Bunch) R.; m. Annette Isabelle Rinker, Dec. 21, 1946; children: George William Daryl, Jonathan Clark, Mark Christopher, Jennifer Anne (dec.), Elizabeth Margaret Rinker. MD, U. Tex., Southwestern Med. Sch., 1947; MS in Pub. Health, U. N.C., 1953; PhD in Ultrastructural Anatomy and Microbiology, Baylor U., 1969. Intern Duke Hosp., 1947-48, asst. resident pathology, 1951-53; intern Boston City Hosp., 1948-49; asst. pathologist Peter Bent Brigham Hosp., Boston, 1953-54; pathologist St. Anthony's Hosp., St. Petersburg, Fla., 1954-55; staff pathologist Children's Med. Center, Dallas, 1955-59; dir. labs. Baylor U. Med. Center, Dallas, 1959-86, chief dept. pathology, 1959-86, vice chmn. exec. com. med. bd., 1970-72; cons. pathologist VA Hosp., Dallas, 1955-71; adj. prof. anthropology and biology So. Meth. U., Dallas, 1969; instr. pathology Duke, 1951-53, Harvard Med. Sch., 1953-54; asst. prof. pathology U. Tex. Southwestern Med. Sch., 1955-58, clin. assoc. prof., 1958-64, clin. prof., 1964-72, prof., 1973-94, prof. emeritus, 1994—, dir. Cancer Center, 1973-76, assoc. dean for continuing edn., 1973-94, emeritus assoc. dean, 1994—. Pathologist-in-chief Baylor U. Med. Ctr., 1959-86, prof. biomed. studies Baylor Grad. sch., 1989-94; chmn. Baylor Rsch. Found., 1986-89; prof. microbiology Baylor Coll. Dentistry, 1962-68, prof. pathology, 1964-68, prof., chmn. dept. pathology 1969-73, dean A. Webb Roberts Continuing Edn., 1973-94; spl. advisor on human and animal diseases to gov. State of Tex., 1979-83. Editor: Laboratory Medicine (4 vols.), 1973, 10th edit., 1983; Contbr. articles to profl. jours., chpts. to textbooks. Pres., Tex. div. Am. Cancer Soc., 1970; chmn. Gov.'s Task Force on Higher Edn., 1981. Served with AUS, 1944-46; flight surgeon USAF, 1948-51, Korea. Decorated Air medal. Fellow AAAS, Coll. Am. Pathologists, Am. Soc. Clin. Pathologists; mem. AMA (chmn. multiple discipline research forum 1969), Am. Assn. Pathologists, Internat. Acad. Pathology, Am. Assn. Med. Colls., Explorers Club (dir., v.p. 1993-2000), Sigma Xi, Alpha Omega Alpha. Home: 3429 Beverly Dr Dallas TX 75205-2928 Fax: 214-526-8607. E-mail: georgejrace@yahoo.com.

RACETTE, NANCY KELLY, development company executive, consultant; b. Albany, N.Y., Aug. 4, 1960; d. Barbara Maaloe Kelly-Yeardon and David Peter Kelly; m. John Michael Racette, June 27, 1987; children: Kelly Ann, Casey John. BS, Boston U., 1982. Cert. Fund Raising Exec. Assn. of Fundraising Profls., 1996, JFK Sch. of Govt., Harvard U., 2000. Dir. devel. and mktg. Hudson Valley Girl Scout Coun., Albany, NY, 1990—94; dir. devel. and comm. ARC of Northeastern N.Y., Albany, 1994—96; sr. dir. devel. Am. Nat. Red Cross, Washington, 1996—2001; exec. vice pres., prin. Devel. Resources, Inc., Arlington, Va., 2001—. Directorship AFP Found. for Philanthropy, Alexandria, Va., 1997—. Mem.: AFP/DC (assoc.; edn. chair 2003—). Avocations: swimming, tennis, travel. Home: 3337 Holloman Rd Falls Church VA 22042 Office: Devel Resources Inc 1601 N Kent St Arlington VA 22209 Personal E-mail: racette@dri.cc.

RACHANOW, GERALD MARVIN, lawyer, pharmacist; b. Balt., Aug. 7, 1942; s. Louis and Lillyan (Binstock) R.; m. Sally Davis, July 26, 1964; children: Mindy, Shelly, Gary. BS in Pharmacy, U. Md., 1965; JD, U. Balt., 1972. Bar: Md. 1973, U.S. Dist. Ct. Md. 1977, U.S. Supreme Ct. 1977. Consumer safety officer FDA, Rockville, Md., 1973-96, dep. dir. divsn. OTC drug evaluation, 1978-96, regulatory counsel divsn. OTC drug products, 1996—; ptnr. Rachanow & Wolfson, Owings Mills, Eldersburg, Md., 1975—. Contbr. fed. drug law exam. Nat. Assn. Bds. Pharmacy, 1985. Contbr. articles to profl. jours. Fellow Am. Soc. Pharmacy Law; mem. ABA, Soc. FDA Pharmacists, Heuisler Honor Soc. Avocations: chess, stamp and coin collecting, sports. Home: 6700 Sweet Clover Ct Eldersburg MD 21784-6385 Office: US FDA 5600 Fishers Ln Rockville MD 20857-0001 Office Phone: 301-827-2307. Business E-Mail: geraldrachanow@fda.hhs.gov.

RACHELEFSKY, GARY STUART, medical educator; b. N.Y.C., 1942; BS, Columbia Coll., 1963. Intern Bellevue Hosp. Ctr., N.Y.C., 1967-68; resident in pediatrics Johns Hopkins Hosp., 1968-70, Ctr. Disease Control, 1970-72; fellow UCLA Med. Ctr., 1972-74; clin. prof., assoc. dir. A/I Tng. Program UCLA. Fellow Am. Acad. Allergy, Asthma and Immunology (bd. dirs., past pres.). Office: 11620 Wilshire Blvd Ste 200 Los Angeles CA 90025-1767 Personal E-mail: rachruss@ix.netcom.com. Business E-Mail: gr@allergymedicalclinic.com.

RACHIE, CYRUS, retired lawyer; b. Willmar, Minn., Sept. 5, 1908; s. Elias and Amanda (Lien) R.; m. Helen Evelyn Duncanson, Nov. 25, 1936; children: John Burton Rachie, Janice Carolyn MacKinnon, Elisabeth Dorthea Becker. Student, U. Minn., 1927-28; JD, George Washington U., 1932, William Mitchell Coll. Law, 1934. Bar: Minn. 1934, U.S. Supreme Ct. Atty. Minn. Hwy. Dept., 1934-43; spl. asst. atty. gen. Minn., 1946-50; counsel Luth. Brotherhood (fraternal life ins. co.), 1950-61; pvt. practice law Mpls., 1961-62; v.p., counsel Gamble-Skogmo, Inc., Mpls., 1962-64; v.p., gen. counsel Aid Assn. Lutherans, Appleton, Wis., 1964-70, sr. v.p., gen. counsel, 1970-73; with Rachie & Rachie, 1973-83; pvt. practice Minn., 1983—2001; part-time spl. master Minn. 4th Jud. Dist., 1977; ret., 2001. One of eleven com. mems. planning 1957 Luth. World Fedn. in Mpls. Councillor Nat. Luth. Coun., 1959-66, sec., 1962-64, mem. exec. com., 1965-66; United Luth. Ch. in Am. del. to 4th Assembly Luth. World Fedn., Helsinki, 1963; past pres. Luth. Welfare Soc. Minn.; past chmn. Mpls. Mayor's Coun. on Human Rels.; chmn. finance United Fund drive, 1967-68; past mem. bd. dirs. Mpls. YMCA; trustee emeritus William Mitchell Coll. Law Augsburg Coll. With USNR, 1943-46. Recipient Disting. Alumnus award William Mitchell Coll. Law, 1987. Mem. ABA, Minn. Bar Assn., Am. Legion, Minn. Fraternal Congress (past pres.), Rotary. Lutheran. Home: PO Box 157 Forest Lake MN 55025-0157 *I always try to keep in mind that the Christian Cross consists of both vertical and horizontal lines. The vertical is the longest line and represents a direct line from all of us on the bottom to God on the top and we must commune with Him. The horizontal represents an encompassing line that takes in all of mankind. If my life activities do not include the implementation of both lines of the cross, I will not have a balanced and Christian life.*

RACHKO, MAURICE, cardiologist; arrived in U.S., 1990; s. Hanna and Saydi Rachko; m. Dima Yeshou, Aug. 17, 2001; 1 child, Grace. MD, Aleppo U. Dir. coronary care unit The Bklyn. Hosp. Ctr., 2000—, Beth Israel Med. Ctr., N.Y.C., 2004—; cardiology attending Heart Inst. Heart Inst. Continuum Health Ptnr., 2004—. Asst. prof. clin. medicine Weil Med. Coll. Cornell U., N.Y.C., 2001. Contbr. articles to profl. jours. Recipient Resident Rsch. award, SUNY HSC, 1998. Fellow: ACP, Am. Coll. Cardiology; mem.: Am. Heart Assn. Avocations: basketball, movies. Office: The Brooklyn Hosp Ctr 121 DeKalb Ave Brooklyn NY 11201 Office Phone: 212-844-1835.

RACHLIN, ALAN SANDERS, lawyer; b. N.Y.C., Mar. 14, 1942; s. Irving Louis and Blanche (Klein) R.; m. Gail S. Kaufman, June 11, 1972 (dec. Apr. 1987); m. Charlotte D. Moslander, Aug. 15, 1992. BA, CCNY, 1965; MPA, CUNY, 1971; JD, N.Y. Law Sch., 1975. Bar: N.Y. 1976, U.S. Dist. Ct. (so. and ea. dists.) 1976, U.S. Supreme Ct. 1983. Atty. N.Y. State Dept. Ins., N.Y.C., 1976-79, sr. atty., 1979-81, assoc. atty., 1981-87, supervising atty., 1987-96, prin. atty., 1996—. With U.S. Army, 1966-67. Mem. ABA, Assn. Bar City N.Y., N.Y. State Bar Assn., N.Y. County Lawyers Assn., Med. Jurisprudence, Democrat. Jewish. Avocations: science fiction, mysteries. Office: NY State Ins Dept 25 Beaver St New York NY 10004-2310 E-mail: arachlin@ins.state.ny.us.

RACHLIN, HARVEY BRANT, writer; b. Phila., June 23, 1951; s. Philip and Mazie (Drucker) R.; m. Marla Sivak Goldwert, June 28, 1987; 1 child, Glenn. BA in Biology, Hofstra U., Hempstead, N.Y., 1973. With music pub. cos., 1973—; owner Western Hemisphere Music Co., Ellipsis Music Mgmt. Co., Manhasset Hills, NY, 1975—, pres., 1982-92, mem. faculty Five Towns Coll., Seaford, NY, 1978 84, Manhattanville Coll., Purchase, NY, 1995—. Author: The Songwriter's Handbook, 1977 (N.Y. Pub. Libr. Book for Teen Age 1979-82); The Encyclopedia of the Music Business, 1981 (Outstanding Music Reference Source ALA 1981, ASCAP-Deems Taylor award 1982, Writer's Digest Book Club Spl. Selection, included in Selected Bibliography for Musicians Libr. of Congress); Love Grams, 1983; The Money Encyclopedia, 1984 (Outstanding Fin. Reference Book, Libr. Jour., 1984, Ency. Britannica Home Libr. selection); The Kennedys: A Chronological History 1823--, 1986; The Songwriter's and Musician's Guide to Making Great Demos, 1988 (N.Y. Pub. Libr. Book for Teen Age 1989); The Making of a Cop, 1991 (N.Y. Pub. Libr. Book for Teen Age, 1992), The Songwriter's Workshop, 1991, The TV and Movie Business: An Encyclopedia of Careers, Technologies, and Practices, 1991 (Fireside Theatre Book Club main selection), The Making of a Detective, 1995 (featured on Good Morning America), Lucy's Bones, Sacred Stones, and Einstein's Brain, 1996 (History Book Club selection, named one of best books in print The Reader's Catalog); co-writer, cons. adapted as three-part TV mini-series History's Lost and Found (now daily series on The History Channel, CineGold Eagle award 2000), Jumbo's Hide, Elvis's Ride, and the Tooth of Buddha, 2000 (Book-of-the-Month Club's Quality Paperback Book Club selection); free-lance music journalist; contbr. Songwriter Mag., 1978—, Law and Order Mag., 1992—, Songwriter's Market, 1979, 80, 87, 92; guest on The Joe Franklin Show, 1977, 81, The Dinah Shore Show, 1978, Nine Broadcast Plaza, 1991, The Sally Jessy Raphael Show, 1993, The Late Late Show with Tom Snyder, 1996; compositions performed L.I. Mandolin and Guitar Orch., 1988. Recipient Outstanding Reference Book of Yr. award, ALA, 1981, award, Libr. Jour., 1984, profiled in, N.Y. Times, 1982, 1996, Pro-Music, 1982, Valley Stream Herald, 1995, 1996, 1998, Writer's Market, 1994, Newsday, 1996, 1999, Sarasota Herald-Tribune, 1996, Coral Springs Forum, 1997, Boston Herald, 1997, L.I. Lifestyles, 2000, City Line News, 2001. Mem.: Am. Soc. Journalists and Authors. Home: 878 Warner Rd Valley Stream NY 11580-1526 Office Phone: 516-568-1795.

RACHLIN, LAUREN DAVID, lawyer; b. Buffalo, Feb. 6, 1929; s. Harry A. and Thelma (Goldberg) R.; m. Jean K. Rachlin, June 27, 1954; children: Laura Gail, Ellen Joan, James N. BS, U. Buffalo, 1948; JD, Harvard U., 1951. Bar: NY 1952, U.S. Dist. Ct. (no. and we. dists.) NY 1952, U.S. Tax Ct. 1952, U.S. Supreme Ct. 1958, U.S. Ct. Appeals (2d cir.) 1967, U.S. Ct. Internat. Trade 1978. Ptnr. Rachlin & Rachlin, Buffalo, 1952—81; sr. ptnr. Kavinoky & Cook, Buffalo, 1981—2003; ptnr. Hodgson Russ, LLP, Buffalo and Toronto, 2003—. U.S. appointee to Bi-nat. Dispute Settlement Panel created under U.S.-Can. Free Trade Agreement, 1989-93; U.S. appointee N.Am. Free Trade Agreement Bi-Nat. Dispute Settlement Panel, 1994-96, 2004-; arbitrator Internat. C. of C., Am. Arbitration Assn.; founder and dir. Can./U.S. Border Alliance regionalizing the bi-national trade corridor linking Toronto, Hamilton, Buffalo, Syracuse and Rochester, 1996—; founder, past pres., dir. World Trade Ctr.-Buffalo Niagara, 1986—; lectr. in field. U.S. del. to UN Human Rights Commn., 1970; cons. to temporary commn. NY State Constl. Conv.; mem. Erie County Charter Rev. Commn.; mem.-at-large U.S. Nat. Commn. for UNESCO, 1972-76, chmn. human rights task force; mem. industry functional adv. com. Customs for Trade Policy Matters of U.S. Dept. Commerce, Office U.S. Trade Rep., 1987—. Mem. ABA (fgn. investment in U.S. real estate com., internat. bus. law com., subcom. on trade import), NY State Bar Assn. (founding chmn. internat. sect. 1987-89, chmn. internat. divsn. 1989-94, chair legal edn. and admission to bar com. 1999-2002), World Arbitration Inst. (adv. bd., bd. dirs.), Am. Assn. Exporters & Importers (trade policy com.), Interpacific Bar Assn., Interam. Bar Assn., Customs and Internat. Trade Bar Assn., Erie County Bar Assn, Industry Trade Adv. Commn. on Customs and Trade Facilitation, US Dept. Commerce. Office: Hodgson Russ LLP Ste 2000 1 M & T Plz Buffalo NY 14203-2391 Address: Ste 2309 150 King St W Toronto ON M5H 1J9 Canada Office Phone: 716-856-4000.

RACHLIN, WILLIAM SELIG, retired surgeon; b. Hartford, Conn., May 13, 1929; s. Irving I. and Rose (Saxe) R.; m. Joy B. Loitman; children: Faye, Margo. AB, Princeton U., 1948; MD, Harvard Med. Sch., 1952. Diplomate Am. Bd. Surgery. Intern in surgery Beth Israel Hosp., Boston, 1952-53, asst. resident in surgery, 1953-54, 58-59, chief resident in surgery, 1959-60; pvt. practice surgery, Brookline, Mass., 1960—99. Capt. USAF, 1954 56. Fellow ACS, Am. Coll. Gastroenterology; mem. Mass. Med. Soc. (trustee 1980—), Norfolk Dist. Med. Soc. (pres. 1977-79). Democrat. Jewish.

RACHLIS, ARNOLD ISRAEL, rabbi, religion educator; b. Phila., Apr. 25, 1949; s. Burech and Pauline (Glanzberg) R.; children: Adam, Michael. BA, U. Pa., 1970; MA, Temple U., 1972; ordination, Reconstructionist Rabbinical Coll, 1975; DD, Reconstructionist Rabbinical Coll., 2000; BA (hon.), Ctrl. High Sch., Phila., 1966. Ordained rabbi, 1975. Asst. dir. Hillel Found., Temple U., Phila., 1972-74; lectr. Temple U., 1974-76; mem. faculty Spertus Coll., Chgo., 1976-85; rabbi Jewish Reconstructionist Cong., Evanston, Ill., 1976-91, Univ. Synagogue, Irvine, Calif., 1991—. Host Of Cabbages and Kings Program ABC-TV, Chgo., 1982-91; sr. fgn. affairs advisor Dept. State, Washington, 1985-86; vice-chmn. Mazon, A Jewish Response to Hunger, 1996-98 and 2003-; internat. bd. dir. New Israel Fund; bd. dir. US Interreligious Com. for Peace in the Mid. East, U. Ill. Fund for Gerontology Rsch.; mem. adv. bd. China Judaic Studies Assn., Nanjing U., People's Republic of China, Am. for Peace Now. Contbr. articles to profl. jours.; regular columnist Chgo. Jewish Sentinel; columnist Phila. Jewish Exponent, 1974-76; cons. for Judaica sect. Compton's Ency. Recipient Leadership Citation Jewish Reconstructionist Found., 1980; White House fellow, 1985-86, Leadership Greater Chgo. fellow, 1988-89; subject of award winning documentary film, The Legacy. Mem. Reconstructionist Rabbinical Assn. (pres. 1977-79), Chgo. Bd. Rabbis (pres. 1990-91), Chgo. Action for Soviet Jewry (adv. coun.), Chevra. Avocations: theater, writing, hiking, foreign travel. Home: 4876 Paseo De Vega Irvine CA 92612-3323 Office: University Synagogue 4915 Alton Pkwy Irvine CA 92604-8606 Office Phone: 949-553-3535. E-mail: rabbi@universitysynagogue.org.

RACHOFSKY, DAVID J. lawyer; b. Oceanside, N.Y., Nov. 17, 1936; s. Lester M. and Marjorie A.; m. Faith Allen; children: Robert, Patricia, Edward. BSEE, MIT, 1958; JD, Temple U., 1968. Bar: Pa., U.S. Dist. Ct. (ea. dist.) Pa., U.S. Tax. Ct., U.S. Ct. Fed. Claims, Pa. Supreme Ct. 1968. Ptnr. Dechert LLP, Phila., 1968—. Lectr. law Temple U. Law Sch., 1976-95. Contbr. articles to profl. jours. With USAF, 1969-72. Mem. ABA, Phila. Bar Assn., Internat. Fiscal Assn. (chmn. mid-Atlantic region 1985-87, mem. coun. 1986—, mem. exec. com. 1992—, v.p., sec. 1992-96, exec. v.p. 1996-98, pres. 1998-2000). Office: Dechert LLP 4000 Bell Atlantic Tower 1717 Arch St Lbby 3 Philadelphia PA 19103 2713

RACHOW, LOUIS A(UGUST), librarian; b. Shickley, Nebr., Jan. 21, 1927; s. John Louis and Mable (Dondlinger) R. BS, York Coll., 1948; MS in L.S., Columbia U., 1959. Librarian York Coll., Nebr., 1949-54; instr. library asst. Queens Coll., N.Y.C., 1956-57; serials acquisition asst. Columbia U. Law Library, N.Y.C., 1957-58; asst. librarian Univ. Club, N.Y.C., 1958-62; librarian Hampden-Booth Theatre Library at the Players, N.Y.C., 1962-86, curator, 1986-88; library dir. Internat. Theatre Inst. U.S., N.Y.C., 1989—2002. Cons. theatre sect. U. Calif., San Diego, new campuses program, 1964, Music Ctr. Operating Archives, Los Angeles, 1985; mem. library adv. bd. Eugene O'Neill Meml. Theatre Center, 1966— Editor, compiler: Guide to Performing Arts, 1968; assoc. editor Am. Notes and Queries, 1971-74, asst. editor, 1967-71; mem. editorial adv. bd. Nat. Dir. for Performing Arts and Civic Ctrs.; editor Performing Arts series Gale Info. Guide, 1976-83, Theatre and Performing Arts Collections, 1981; contbr. articles and revs. to profl. jours. Mem. adv. bd. Am. Theatre Co., OKC Theatre Prodns. Served with AUS, 1954-56 Mem. Theatre Libr. Assn. (rec. sec. 1966-67, pres. 1967-72, 81-83, v.p. 1976-80, editor Broadside 1973-81), ALA, Spl. Librs. Assn. (sec.-treas. mus. group N.Y.C. chpt. 1964-66), N.Y. Libr. Club (pres. 1979-80), Am. Theatre Assn., New Drama Forum Assn. (pres. 1983-86), Am. Soc. Theatre Rsch., N.Y. Tech. Svcs. Librs., Archons of Colophon (convener 1982-83), Episcopal Actors Guild Am. (bd. dirs. 1976-2002, v.p. 2002—), Drama Desk, Broadway Theatre Inst. Outer Critics Circle (treas. 1998—), Players Club, The Lambs Club. Home: 528 W 114th St New York NY 10025-7841

RACHOW, SHARON DIANNE, realtor; b. St. Joseph, Mo., Apr. 12, 1939; d. Norman DeLos Zancker and Sylvia Lavina (Hawkins) Trouel; m. Thomas Eugene Rachow, Oct. 22, 1968; children: Todd A., Tiffany K. Student, So. Ill. U., 1969-72. Cert. Quality Svc. 2003. Sec. Westab, Inc. (now Mead), St. Joseph, 1957-60, Seitz Packing Co. (now Sara Lee), St. Joseph, 1960-66; exec. asst. to v.p., gen. mgr. Kansas City (Mo.) Chiefs, 1972; co-owner, mgr. Pool 'N Patio Plus, St. Joseph, 1973-84; realtor Coldwell Banker Gen. Realtors, St. Joseph, 1984-93, RE/MAX, 1993—. Trustee Nat. Multiple Sclerosis Soc., Mid Am. chpt., Midland M.S. Express Br., 1993-98. Mem.: Real Estate Buyer's Agt. Coun. (accredited buyers rep. 1996—), St. Joseph Regional Bd. Realtors (cert. residential specialist 1987, Multi-List com. 1993—2002, dir. 1994, forms com. 1994—2002, Top Residential Sales award 1986—, Top 10), Multi Million Dollar Club (life quality svc. cert. 2003). Republican. Lutheran. Home: 4211 Country Ln Saint Joseph MO 64506-2454 Office: RE/MAX of St Joseph Inc 1119 N Woodbine Rd Saint Joseph MO 64506-2434 Office Phone: 816-262-0022. Business E-Mail: sharonr@stjoelive.com.

RACICOT, MARC F. lawyer, former governor; b. Thompson Falls, Mont., July 24, 1948; s. William E. and Patricia E. (Bentley) Racicot; m. Theresa J. Barber, July 25, 1970; children: Ann, Timothy, Mary Catherine, Theresa, Joseph. BA, Carroll Coll., Helena, Mont., 1970; JD, U. Mont., 1973; postgrad., U. Va., 1973, Cornell U., 1977. Bar: Mont. 1973. Dep. county atty. Missoula (Mont.) County, 1976—77; bur. chief County Prosecutor Svcs. Bur., Helena, Mont., 1977—89; asst. atty. gen. State of Mont., Helena, 1977—89, spl. prosecutor for the Atty. Gen.'s Office, atty. gen., 1989—93, gov., 1993—2001; ptnr. Bracewell & Patterson LLP, Washington, 2001—; chmn. Repub. Nat. Com., Washington, 2002—03, Bush-Cheney Re-election campaign, 2003—. Founder Missoula Drug Treatment Program, 1977; active United Way, Helena; bd. visitors U. Mont. Sch. Law. Capt. U.S. Army, 1973—76. Named to Basketball Hall of Fame, Carroll Coll., 1982. Mem.: Mont. Bar Assn. Republican. Roman Catholic. Office: Bracewell & Patterson LLP 2000 K St NW Ste 500 Washington DC 20006-1872 Home: 901 15th St S Apt 201 Arlington VA 22202-5031

RACINA, THOM (THOMAS FRANK RAUCINA), television writer, editor; b. Kenosha, Wis., June 4, 1946; s. Frank G. and Esther May (Benko) Raucina. B.F.A., Goodman Sch. Drama, Art Inst. Chgo., 1970, M.F.A. in Theatre Arts and Directing with honors, 1971. TV writer Hanna-Barbera Co., Hollywood, Calif., 1973-74, MTM Enterprises, Inc., Hollywood, 1974-76; head writer General Hospital ABC-TV, Hollywood, 1981-84; head writer Days of Our Lives NBC-TV, 1984-86, head writer Another World, 1986-88, co-head writer Generations daytime series, 1988-91, head writer syndicated Dangerous Women night-time TV series, 1991-92; assoc. head writer daytime TV series Santa Barbara, 1992-93. Author: Lifeguard, 1976, The Great Los Angeles Blizzard, 1977, Quincy, M.E., 2 vols., 1977, Kodak in San Francisco, 1977, F.M., 1978, Sweet Revenge, 1978, The Gannon Girls, 1979, Nine to Five, 1980, Tomcat, 1981, Secret Sex: Male Erotic Fantasies (as Tom Anicar), 1976, Magda (as Lisa Wells), 1981, Snow Angel, 1995, Hidden Agenda, 1997, Secret Weekend, 1999, The Madman's Diary, 2000, Never Forget, 2002, Deadly Games, 2003; ghost writer: non-fiction The Happy Hustler (Grant Tracy Saxon), 1976, Marilyn Chambers: My Story (Marilyn Chambers), 1976, Xaviera Meets Marilyn (Xaviera Hollander and Marilyn Chambers), 1977; musical plays A Midsummer Night's Dream, music and lyrics, 1968, Allison Wonderland, music and lyrics, 1970, The Marvelous Misadventure of Sherlock Holmes, book, music and lyrics, 1971; TV scripts Sleeping Over segment of Family, ABC, 1978, Russian Pianist segment, ABC, 1979, 1 Child of the Owl, NBC After-Sch. Spl., 1979; contbr. articles to Playboy, Cosmopolitan, Penhouse, Oui, Los Angeles, Gentleman's Quar., Westways; West Coast editor: Grosset & Dunlap, Inc., N.Y.C., 1978—; lead writer for TV: Family Passions, 1993-94, Life's A Bitch!, 1994, Friends & Lovers, 1994; theatre dir., pianist, organist, composer. Recipient Emmy award nomination 1982, 83, 84, 85, 87; U.S. Nat. Student Assn. grantee, 1965 Mem. Authors Guild Am., Writers Guild Am. West. Democrat. Roman Catholic. Home: 2851 Calle Loreto Palm Springs CA 92264-6702 E-mail: racina@aol.com. *Nearly losing my life to the disease pancreatitis at sixteen years of age certainly opened my eyes to how precious the future was— I had a second chance, and I knew I'd been given talent for a reason: to use. I've since lived wanting to do it all, know it all, feel and experience all that life has to offer. I've no desire to write literature, but rather to entertain, and everything I write has that motivation as a core. If my storytelling ability moves just one person to laughter— or tears— I've accomplished all I set out to do.*

RACINE, DOUGLAS A, former lieutenant governor; b. Burlington, Vt., Oct. 7, 1952; m. Roberta A. Harold. AB, Princeton U., 1974. U.S. senator from Vt., 1983-92; v.p. Racine's Jeep, Eagle, Isuzu, Inc.; lt. gov. State of Vt., Montpelier, 1997—2003. Democrat. Office: Office of the Lt Gov State House Montpelier VT 05633-0001

RACITI, CHERIE, artist; b. Chgo., June 17, 1942; d. Russell J. and Jacque (Crimmins) R. Student, Memphis Coll. Art, 1963-65; BA in Art, San Francisco State U., 1968; M.F.A., Mills Coll., 1979. Assoc. prof. art San Francisco State U., 1984-89, prof., 1989—. Lectr. Calif. State U., Hayward, 1974, San Francisco Art Inst., 1978; mem. artist com. San Francisco Art Inst., 1974-85, sec., 1980-81. One woman shows include U. Calif., Berkeley, 1972, Nicholas Wilder Gallery, L.A., 1975, San Francisco Art Inst., 1977, Marianne Deson Gallery, Chgo., 1980, Site 375, San Francisco, 1989, Reese Bullen Gallery, Humboldt State U., Arcata, Calif., 1990, Mills Coll. Art Mus., Oakland, Calif., 1998; group shows include Whitney Mus. Art, 1975, San Francisco Sci. Fiction, The Clocktower, N.Y.C., Otis-Parsons Gallery, Los Angeles, 1984-85, San Francisco Art Inst., 1985, Artists Space, N.Y.C., 1988, Angles Gallery, Santa Monica, 1987, Terrain Gallery, San Francisco, 1992, Ctr. for the Arts, San Francisco, 1993, Santa Monica Coll., 1998, 25/25 25th Anniversary Exhbn., So. Exposure Gallery, San Francisco, 1999, Santa Cruz Mus., 2003, Thacher Gallery U. San Francisco, 2004. Bd. dirs. New Langton Arts, 1988-92. Eureka fellow Fleishhacker Found., San Francisco; recipient Adaline Kent award San Francisco Art Inst., 1976, Djerassi resident, 1994, Tyrone Guthrie Ctr. resident, Ireland, 1995, Millay Colony for Arts resident 1999, Juror's award Art Coun. Inc. San Francisco. Office: San Francisco State U Art Dept 1600 Holloway Ave San Francisco CA 94132-1722 E-mail: craciti@sfsu.edu.

RACKOW, ERIC C. health facility administrator; Graduate, Franklin and Marshall Coll.; MD, SUNY, Downstate Med. Ctr., Brooklyn, 1971. Bd. cert. internal medicine, cardiovasc. diseases, critical care medicine, internal medicine, 1975, cardiology, 1977, critical care, 1987. Residency Kings County Hosp. Ctr., 1970—72, chief residency, 1972—73, clin. fellow, 1973—75; dir. clin. trials NYU Hosp. Ctr.; prof. heath care mgmt. NYU Med. Ctr., Sch. Medicine; sr. v.p. & chief med. officer NYU Hosp. Ctr., 2000—04, pres., 2004—. Adj. prof. medicine NY Med. Coll.; chmn. emeritus St. Vincent's Hosp. & Med. Ctr. of NY, Dept. Medicine; hon. role, Physician-in-Chief Inst. Critical Care Medicine; past pres. Soc. Critical Care Medicine; past chair Am. Bd. Internal Medicine, Critical Care Medicine Subspecialty Bd. Contbr. numerous articles and abstracts in critical care medicine to profl. jours. Office: NYU Hosps Ctr Sch Med HCC15 550 First Ave New York NY 10016

RACKOW, JULIAN PAUL, lawyer; b. Phila., Dec. 16, 1941; s. Lawrence Lionel and Blanche (Wachman) R.; m. Paulette Schorr, June 23, 1963; children: Jeffrey A., Andrea B. AB, Cornell U., 1963; JD, Harvard U., 1966. Bar: Pa. 1966, U.S. Dist. Ct. (ea. dist.) Pa. 1966. Assoc. atty. Goodis, Greenfield, Narin & Mann, Phila., 1966-69; ptnr., co-chmn. dept. real estate Blank, Rome LLP, Phila., 1970—. Mem. exec. com., bd. dirs. Ctrl. Phila. Devel. Corp., 1990—, pres. 1996-2000, chmn., 2000—; bd. dirs. Ave of the Arts, Inc., 2000—, Parkway Coun. Found., 2004—. Mem. Phila. Bar Assn., Harvard Law Sch. Assn. Phila, Am. Coll. Real Estate Lawyers, Ave. of the Arts, Inc. Avocations: tennis, travel, piano. Office: Blank Rome LLP One Logan Sq Philadelphia PA 19103-6998 Office Phone: 215-569-5671. E-mail: rackow@blankrome.com.

RACTLIFFE, ROBERT EDWARD GEORGE, management executive; b. Hertfordshire, Eng., July 25, 1943; came to U.S., 1965; s. Augustus David John and Veronica Phyllis (Jones) R.; m. Nancy Jane Brumbaugh, June 29, 1968; children: Richard Alban, Tiffany Elizabeth, Courtney Veronica. BS with honors, U. London, 1965; MSEE, U. Pitts., 1969, MBA with honors, 1972; PMD, Harvard U., 1975. Engr. Westinghouse Electric Corp., Pitts., 1965-69, sales mgr. LRA Div., 1969-73, mfg. engr. mgr. LRA Div., 1974-76, dept. mgr. Hydrogenerator Dept., 1976-78, mgr. product mktg. Steam Turbine Generator Div. Phila., 1979-81, mgr. strategic planning Power Generation Bus. Unit, 1981-84, gen. mgr. Power Generation Comml. Div. Orlando, Fla., 1984-86; pres., North Am. Ops. United Tech. Carrier Corp., Syracuse, N.Y., 1986-88; pres., chief exec. officer NORDYNE Inc., St. Louis, 1989—. Patentee in field; contbr. articles to profl. jours. Mem. AAIM (bd. dirs.), Gas Appliance Mfrs. Assn. (co. rep.), Manufactured Housing Inst. (co. rep.), Air Conditioning and Refrigeration Inst. (bd. dirs., v.p. exec. com., com. chmn., co. rep.). Republican. Episcopalian. Avocations: golf, tennis, skiing. Office: NORDYNE Inc PO Box 8809 O Fallon MO 63366-8809

RADA, RUTH BYERS, college dean, author; b. Los Angeles, Oct. 3, 1923; d. George and Gerda Marie (Lihm) Byers; children: Kaaren Ruth, Georgene Melanie. AB, U. So. Calif., 1944, MA, 1945; EdD, Nova U., 1976. Asst. dean instrn. and evening East L.A. Coll., 1964-69, dean instrn., 1969-70; dean student personnel L.A. Harbor Coll., 1970-73, East L.A. Coll., 1973-77, L.A. Mission Coll., 1977-83; prof. biol. sci. East L.A. C.C., 1945-69, ret., 1983. Author: Water Biology, 1950, (with others) Human Body in Health and Disease, 1969, Structure and Function of Human Body, 1970, Laboratory Manual for Introductory Microbiology, 1963. Mem. Calif. Cmty. and Jr. Coll. Assn. (area pres. 1973-74), Calif. Woman Adminstrs. Assn., Los Angeles Coll. Adminstrs. Assn. (sec. 1973-74), Phi Beta Kappa, Phi Kappa Phi, Pi Lambda Theta, Phi Sigma. Republican. Mem. Ch. of Religious Sci.

RADACOVSKÝ, MARIO, dancer; b. Slovaquie; Student, Conservatory of Dance, Bratislava. Soloist Slovak Nat. Theater Ballet, Bratislava, 1988; prin. dancer Slovak Nat. Theater, 1989—91; soloist Czech Nat. Theater, Brno, 1991—92; dancer Nederlands Dans Theater II, 1992, Nederlands Dans Theater I, 1994; prin. dancer Les Grands Ballets Canadiens de Montréal, 1999—. Participant Moscow Internat. Ballet Competition, 1988; guest dancer Nat. Theatre Prague, 1997; participant Internat. Ballet Competition, Osaka, Japan, 1991, The 10 Dancers Ensemble, Austria, 1994. Dancer (ballets) Giselle, Slovak Nat. Theater, Swan Lake, Sleeping Beauty, Giselle, Les Grands Ballets Canadiens de Montréal, The Nutcracker, Approximate Sonata, Without Words, Jardí Tancat, Perpetuum, Concerto Barocco, The Queen of Spades. Recipient 1st prize, Czechoslovakian Ballet Competition, 1990. Office: Les Grands Ballets Canadiens de Montreal 4816 rue Rivard Montreal QC Canada H2J 2N6

RADANOVICH, GEORGE P. congressman; b. Mariposa, Calif., June 20, 1955; s. Joan and George F.; m. Ethie Weaver; 1 child, George King. BS in Agr. Bus. Mgmt., Calif. State Polytechnic U., 1978. Pres. Radanovich Winery, Mariposa, Calif., 1982—; chair County Planning Comm., 1986-87, county supr., 1988-92; mem. U.S. Congress from Calif. 19th dist., Washington, 1995—; mem. energy and com. com., resources com., chmn. natural parks subcom. Mem. Calif. Agrl. Leadership Program Class XXI, Rotary (Paul Harris Fellowship). Republican. Roman Catholic. Office: US Ho Reps 438 Cannon HOB Washington DC 20515

RADCLIFFE, DANIEL, actor; b. London, July 23, 1989; Actor: (films) Tailor of Panama, 2001, Harry Potter and the Sorcerer's Stone, 2001, Harry Potter and the Chamber of Secret's, 2002, Harry Potter and the Prisoner of Azkaban, 2004; appearances (TV) The Today Show, 2001, The Oprah Winfrey Show, 2001, Late Night with Conan O'Brien, 2004, (TV special) David Copperfield, 1999. Office: c/o ICM 4-6 Soho Sq London W1D 3PZ England*

RADCLIFFE, GEORGE GROVE, retired life insurance company executive; b. Balt., Nov. 12, 1924; s. George G. and Elsie (Winter) R.; m. Bettie Howell, Feb. 10, 1951 (div.); 1 child, Cynthia; m. Kathleen Moore Smith, 1991. BA, Johns Hopkins U., 1947; grad. Advanced Mgmt. Program, Harvard U. Grad. Sch. Bus. Adminstrn., 1962. With Balt. Life Ins. Co., 1947-89, v.p. treas., 1963-69, exec. v.p., 1969-72, pres., 1972-89, chief exec. officer, 1974-89, chmn. bd., 1980-89, pres., 1981-86, ret., chmn. bd. dirs. emeritus, 1989. Chmn. bd. trustees Johns Hopkins U., 1984-90, trustee, 1975-93, trustee emeritus, 1993—. Mem. Tred Avon Yacht Club, Talbot Country Club, Delta Upsilon. Methodist. Home and Office: PO Box 409 Oxford MD 21654-0409

RADCLIFFE, GLENA ELOISE, lyricist, poet, composer; b. Washington, June 7, 1941; d. Harold Glenn and Dorothy Dean (McGinnis) Snyder; m. Russell Traverse Radcliffe, Sept. 19, 1963; children: Melanie Christine McCabe, Lori Victoria Meyers. Grad. HS, Bradenton, Fla. Pvt. practice, Colo., 1980—87. Author: (albums) Come'n on Down the Line, 1983. Bd. dirs. North Fork coun. The Arts and Humanities, Read, Colo., 1981—83; bd. dirs. Thunder Mountain Theatre, Paonia, Colo., 1981—83. Democrat. Avocations: piano, guitar, writing poetry and music, birdwatching, ATV riding. Home: 1215 Coronado Rd Corrales NM 87048-3108 Mailing: PO Box 3108 Corrales NM 87048

RADCLIFFE, REDONIA (DONNIE RADCLIFFE), journalist, writer; m. Robert C. Radcliffe; 1 child, M. Donnel Nunes. BA, San Jose (Calif.) State U., 1951. Reporter, women's editor, county editor The Salinas Californian, 1951-59; free-lance writer Europe, 1959—66; reporter Washington Star, 1967-72; White Ho. reporter, columnist Washington Post, 1972-95. Author: Simply Barbara Bush: A Portrait of America's Candid First Lady, 1989, Hillary Rodham Clinton: A First Lady for Our Time, 1993, reissued as Hillary Rodham Clinton: The Evolution of a First Lady, 1999; contbr.: The Fall of a President, 1974, Guide to Washington, 1989. Trustee Calvert County (Md.) Libr.; bd. dirs. Nat. 1st Ladies' Libr. E-mail: redrad@erols.com.

RADDING, ANDREW, lawyer; b. N.Y.C., Nov. 30, 1944; m. Bonnie A. Levinson, Oct. 7, 1972; children: Judith Lynne, Joshua David. BBA, CCNY-Baruch Sch., 1965; JD, Boston U., 1968. Bar: N.Y. 1968, Md. 1977, D.C. 1977, U.S. Supreme Ct. Grad. fellow Northwestern U. Sch. Law, 1968-69; asst. counsel U.S. Ho. of Reps. Select Com. on Crime, 1969-72; asst. U.S. atty. for Dist. Md., 1972-77; ptnr. Francomano, Radding & Mannes, Balt., 1977-80, Burke, Gerber, Wilen, Francomano & Radding, Balt., 1980-85, Blades & Rosenfeld P.A., Balt., 1985-97, Adelberg, Rudow, Dorf and Hendler LLC, Balt., 1997—. Mem. adj. faculty clin. practice skills, criminal law, fed. criminal practice U. Balt. Sch. Law, 1980—; mem. trial experience com. U.S. Dist. ct., 1986-88; apptd. by gov. State Adminstrv. Bd. of Election Laws, 1995-96; instr. professionalism course Md. State Bar Assn., 1999—. Bd. dirs. Copper Hill Condominium, 1979-82, pres., 1981-82; vice chair Lawyers for Erlich for Gov. Com., 2002; mem. subcom. Md. Republican Conv., 1981; sen. C.M. Mathias Jud. Selection com., 1986; chmn. U.S. Dist. Ct. Bicentennial Program, 1989-90; mem. Mayor's Domestic Violence Coord. com., 2001—. Mem.: ABA, Nat. Arbitration Forum (arbitrator), U.S. Arbitration and Mediation (inquiry panel and peer rev. panel atty. grievance com. 1991—), Md. Inst. Continuing Profl. Edn. for Lawyers (bd. govs. 1987—92), U.S. Atty. Alumni Assn. Md. (pres. 1978—), Fed. Bar Assn. (Balt. chpt. pres. 1986—87), Balt. City Bar Assn. (jud. selection com. 1990—92, 1994—, chmn. 1996—97, exec. coun. 1998—99, co-chmn. membership com. 1999—2000, exec. coun. 2000—, chmn. fee arbitration com. 2001—02, co-chmn. 2004—), Md. Bar Assn. (CLE com. 2002—, program com. 2003—). Jewish. Office: Adelberg Rudow et al LLC 2 Hopkins Plz Baltimore MD 21201-2930 Office Phone: 410-539-5195. E-mail: aradding@adelbergrudow.com.

RADEBOLDT-DALY, KAREN ELAINE, medical nurse; b. Bklyn., Mar. 3, 1944; d. Harry Phillip and Lillian Florence (Renton) McAnaney; m. Richard William Radeboldt, Aug. 19, 1968 (dec. Aug. 1985); children: Karyn, Kellianne, Kimberly, Kristi-Jo, Richard; m. William J. Daly, Sr., Jan. 22, 1995. Lic. practical nurse, Wyckoff Heights Sch. Nursing, Bklyn., 1968; RN, Orange County C.C., Middletown, N.Y., 1990. LPN, N.Y., RN, N.Y.; cert. med.-surg. nurse, N.Y. Nurses aide, lic. practical nurse Wyckoff Heights Hosp., Bklyn., 1967-90; staff nurse, med.-surg. nurse Westchester Med. Ctr., Valhalla, N.Y., 1990-96, staff nurse, trauma unit, 1996-98, staff nurse, critical care-trauma ICU, 1998—. Mem. Am. Jour. Nursing. Adventist. Avocations: reading, sewing, bowling, walking, motorcycle riding. Home: 101 Daly Rd Middletown NY 10940-7356

RADEL, EVA, pediatrician, hematologist; b. Vienna, Apr. 10, 1934; came to U.S., 1939; d. Ernest O. and Marian (Feiks) Grossman; m. Stanley Robert Radel, May 31, 1954; children: Carol, Laura. AB, N.Y. U., 1954, MD, 1958. Pediatric intern, resident Bronx Mcpl. Hosp. Ctr., 1958-61; pediatric hematology rsch. fellow Albert Einstein Coll. Medicine, Bronx, 1961-63; pediatrician, head pediatric hematology Morrisania city Hosp., Bronx, 1963-76; assoc. dir. pediatrics North Cen. Bronx Hosp., 1978-82; attending physician pediatric hemetology out patients Montefiore Med. Ctr., Bronx, 1965-79, svc. head pediatric hematology-oncology, 1979—; head pediatric hematology North Cen. Bronx Hosp., 1976-97. Responsible investigator Children's Cancer Study Group, 1980-2001; dir. pediatric hematology-oncology Albert Einstein Coll. Medicine, Bronx, 1980-2000; prin. investigator Children's Oncology Group, 2001—. Fellow Am. Acad Pediatrics; mem. Am. Soc. Hematology, Am. Soc. Pediatric Hematology-Oncology, Soc. for the Study of Blood. Office: Childrens Hosp at Montefiore Sect Pediat Hematology-Oncology 3415 Bainbridge Ave Bronx NY 10467-2401 Office Phone: 718-741-2342. Business E-Mail: eradel@montefiore.org.

RADEMAKER, STEPHEN GEOFFREY, federal agency administrator, lawyer; b. Balt., July 18, 1959; s. Thomas Joseph and Ruth Virginia (Wentz) R.; m. Danielle Pletka; children: Andrew, Olivia, Sophia, Nicola. BA with highest distinction, U. Va., 1981, JD, 1984, MA in Fgn. Affairs, 1985. Bar: Va. 1984, D.C. 1985. Assoc. Covington & Burling, Washington, 1984-86; law clk. to Hon. James L. Buckley U.S. Ct. Appeals (D.C. cir.), Washington, 1986; counsel to vice chmn. U.S. Internat. Trade Commn., Washington, 1986-87; spl. asst. to asst. sec. for Inter-Am. affairs Dept. State, Washington, 1987-89; assoc. counsel to Pres. of U.S. and dep. legal advisor to NSC, Washington, 1989-92; gen. counsel Peace Corps, Washington, 1992-93; Rep. chief counsel Com. Fgn. Affairs U.S. Ho. of Reps., Washington, 1993-95, chief counsel Com. Internat. Rels., 1995—2001, dep. staff dir., chief counsel Com. Internat. Rels., 2001—02, chief counsel Select Com. on Homeland Security, 2002; asst. sec. for arms control Dept. of State, Washington, 2002—. Mem. UN Sec. Gen.'s Adv. Bd. on Disarmament Matters, 2003—. Recipient Raven award U. Va., 1984; S. Philip Heiner scholar U. Va., 1983. Mem. Va. Bar Assn., D.C. Bar Assn., Phi Beta Kappa, Omicron Delta Kappa. Republican. Lutheran. Avocations: skiing, bicycling, scuba diving. Office: US Dept State 2201 C St NW Washington DC

RADER, DAVID, insurance company executive; BA, Ohio State U., 1968. Pres., CEO, dir. First Profls. Ins. Co., Jacksonville, Fla., 1999—. Office: FPIC Ins Group Inc Ste 800 1000 Riverside Ave Jacksonville FL 32204

RADER, DOTSON CARLYLE, author, journalist; b. Minn., July 25, 1941; s. Paul Carlyle and Lois (Schacht) R. Student, Columbia, 1962-68. Editor Defiance: A Radical Rev. (Warner Communications, Inc.), 1969-71; contbg. editor Evergreen Rev., 1969-73, Esquire, N.Y.C., 1973-77, N.Y. mag., 1977-80; cons. Nat. Com. for Lit. Arts at Lincoln Center, N.Y.C., 1980—. Mem. sponsoring bd. New Politics, 1972—; host Free Time Show, WNET-TV, N.Y.C., 1972-73 Author: I Ain't Marchin' Anymore!, 1969, Government Inspected Meat and Other Fun Summer Things, 1971, Blood Dues, 1973, Tennessee: Cry of the Heart; An Intimate Memoir of Tennessee Williams, 1985; screenplay The Bronze Lily, 1974, The Dream's on Me: A Love Story, 1976, Miracle, 1978; novel Beau Monde, 1981; play (with Mike Miller) Shattered Glass, 1990; contbg. editor Parade Mag., 1984— Mem. Student Peace Union, 1961-63, Students for a Democratic Soc., 1964-69, War Resisters League, 1970—; pres. Humanitas, Columbia, 1963-67; vice chmn. Peoples Coalition for Peace and Justice, 1972. Named hon. ambassador State of W. Va., 1982; recipient award for nat. journalism Odyssey Inst., 1982, Spl. Olympics award for nat. journalism Joseph P. Kennedy Found., 1985 Mem. PEN, Overseas Press Club, The Dramatists Guild.

RADER, I. ANDREW, foundation administrator; Chmn. Allen-Bradley Co., Milw.; chmn. bd. dirs. Lynde & Harry Bradley Found., Milw., 1985—. Office: Lynde & Harry Bradley Found Found 1241 N Franklin Pl Milwaukee WI 53202-2901

RADER, LOUIS T. corporation executive, educator; b. Frank, Can., Aug. 24, 1911; came to U.S., 1934, naturalized, 1940; s. Italo and Louise (Bonamico) R.; m. Constance Wayland, Sept. 10, 1938; children— Louis Albert, John Newton. BS, U. B.C., 1933; PhD in Elec. Engring, Calif. Inst. Tech., 1938. Engr. Gen. Electric Co., 1937-45; prof., head dept. elec. engring. Ill. Inst. Tech., 1945-47; with Gen. Electric Co., 1947-59, gen. mgr. splty. control div., 1951-59; v.p., dir. ITT, N.Y.C., 1959-61; group v.p. U.S. Commercial, 1961—; pres. Univac div. Sperry Rand Corp., N.Y.C., 1962-64; v.p., gen. mgr. Indsl. Process Control div. Gen. Electric Co., N.Y.C., 1964-69; prof. elec. engring. U. Va., 1969-82, prof. emeritus, 1982—, prof., Grad. Sch. Bus., 1969-82. Vis. com. div. engring. and applied sci. Calif. Inst. Tech., 1968-75 Recipient Alumni distinguished service award Calif. Inst. Tech., 1966; Va. Engring. Found. award, 1982. Fellow IEEE; mem. Am. Soc. Engring. Edn., Nat. Acad. Engring., Sigma Xi, Tau Beta Pi, Beta Gamma Sigma, Eta Kappa Nu, Omicron Delta Kappa. Office: U Va Prof Emeritus Darden Grad Sch Bus PO Box 6550 Charlottesville VA 22906-6550 Home: 1009 Arapaho Path Schenectady NY 12302-3301

RADER, NANCY LOUISE DE VILLIERS, psychology educator, consultant; b. Danbury, Conn., May 21, 1948; d. Martin Anthony and Elsie Concetta (Lauricella) R.; m. David Strutt de Villiers, Sept. 6, 1975; 1 child, Alyssa Jane. AB magna cum laude, Smith Coll., 1970; PhD, Cornell U., 1976. Asst. prof. psychology UCLA, 1974-82, dir. Infant and Child Lab., 1979-82, scholar Found. for Child Devel., 1982-83, postdoctoral fellow, rsch. psychologist

Neuropsychiat. Inst., 1983-84; vis. scholar Cornell U., Ithaca, N.Y., 1979, rsch. assoc., 1984-85; asst. prof. Ithaca Coll., 1985-90, assoc. prof., 1990—2004, prof., 2004—, chair psychology dept., 2000—03. Contbr. articles to profl. jours., chpts. to books. Bd. dirs. Coddington Community Ctr., Ithaca, 1991-94, Family and Children Svcs., 1999-2002. Fellow NDEA, 1968, 71-74, Ford Found., 1970-74; grantee NIMH, 1982, NSF, 2001—. Mem. APA, Am. Psychol. Soc., Soc. for Rsch. in Child Devel., Internat. Soc. for Study Behavioral Devel., Internat. Soc. for Ecol. Psychology, Ea. Psychol. Assn., Sigma Xi (pres. Ithaca Coll. chpt. 1988-89), Phi Kappa Phi. Avocations: gardening, mystery. Home: 201 Eastman Hill Rd Willseyville NY 13864-1229 Office: Ithaca Coll Psychology Dept Ithaca NY 14850 Office Phone: 607-274-3510.

RADER, PATRICK NEIL, accountant; b. Oak Ridge, Tenn., May 16, 1952; s. Daniel Hurley Jr. and Mary Lou (Arms) R.; m. Deborah Lynn Bryant, Dec. 20, 1975 (div. May 1978); 1 child, Andrew Neil; m. Caroline Elizabeth Snow, Dec. 30, 1983; children: Laura Ashley, Mary Beth, Patrick Samuel. BSBA with high honors, U. Tenn., 1974, MBA, 1986. CPA, Tenn.; CFP; chartered mutual fund counselor; chartered retirement planning counselor; accredited asset mgmt. specialist. Fin. officer Union Carbide Corp., Oak Ridge, 1975-79, fin. mgr., 1979-84; capital acctg. mgr. Martin Marietta Corp., Oak Ridge, 1984-86, materials mgr., 1986-90, bus. mgr., 1990-94, sr. bus. analyst, 1995-97; bus. mgr. Lockheed Martin Energy Rsch. Corp., 1998—. Tech. advisor software devel. Co-author: (user's manual) Subcontract Guidelines, 1986. Mem. AICPA, Fin. Planning Assn. Baptist. Avocations: boating, reading.

RADER, PAUL ALEXANDER, minister, religious organization administrator; b. N.Y.C., Mar. 4, 1934; s. Lyell M. and Gladys Mina (Damon) R.; m. Kay Fuller, May 29, 1956; children: Edith Jeanne, James Paul, Jennifer Kay. BA, Asbury Coll., Wilmore, Ky., 1956; BD, Asbury Theol. Sem., 1959; LLD (hon.), Asbury Coll., Wilmore, Ky., 1984; ThM, So. Bapt. Theol. Sem., Louisville, 1961; D Missiology, Fuller Theol. Sem., 1973; DD (hon.), Asbury Theol. Sem., 1995. Ordained to ministry Salvation Army, 1961. Tng. prin. The Salvation Army, Seoul, 1973-74, edn. sec., 1974-77, chief sec., 1979-83, tng. prin. Suffern, N.Y., 1983-86, divisional comdr. for Ea. Pa. and Del. Phila., 1986-88, chief sec. ea. ter. N.Y.C., 1988, territorial comdr. U.S.A. western ter. Rancho Palos Verdes, Calif., 1989-94, gen., 1994-99; pres. Asbury Coll. 2000—. Adj. prof. Seoul Theol. Sem., 1980-82; trustee Asian Ctr. for Theol. Studies and Mission, 1980-83, Asbury Coll., 1988—; pres. The Salvation Army Calif. Corp., Rancho Palos Verdes, 1989-94. Recipient Alumnus A award Asbury Coll., 1982, Disting. Alumni award Asbury Theol. Sem., 1989; Paul Harris fellow Rotary Internat., 1989. Mem. Am. Soc. Missiology, Internat. Assn. Mission Studies. Address: Asbury Coll 1 Macklem Dr Wilmore KY 40390-1198

RADER, RALPH TERRANCE, lawyer; b. Clarksburg, W.Va., Dec. 5, 1947; s. Ralph Coolidge and Jeanne (Cover) R.; m. Rebecca Jo Vorderman, Mar. 22, 1969; children: Melissa Michelle, Allison Suzanne. BSME, Va. Poly. Inst., 1970; JD, Am. U., 1974. Bar: Va. 1975, U.S. Ct. Customs and Patent Appeals, 1977, U.S. Dist. Ct. (ea. dist.) Mich. 1978, Mich. 1979, U.S. Ct. Appeals (6th cir.) 1979, U.S. Dist. Ct. (we. dist.) Mich. 1981, U.S. Ct. Appeals (fed. cir.) 1983. Supervisory patent examiner U.S. Patent Office, Washington, 1970-77; patent atty., ptnr. Cullen, Sloman, Cantor, Grauer, Scott & Rutherford, Detroit, 1977-88; ptnr. Dykema, Gossett, Detroit, 1989-96; founder, ptnr. Rader, Fishman & Grauer, Bloomfield Hills, Mich., 1996—. Contbr. articles to profl. jours. Mem. adminstrv. bd. 1st United Meth. Ch., Birmingham, Mich., 1980—. With U.S. Army, 1970-76. Mem. ABA, Am. Patent Law Assn., Mich. Patent Law Assn., Mich. Bar (governing coun. patent, trademark and copyright law sect. 1981-84), Engring. Soc. Detroit, Masons, Tau Beta Pi, Pi Tau Sigma, Phi Kappa Phi. Methodist. Home: 4713 Riverchase Dr Troy MI 48098-4186 Office: Rader Fishman & Grauer 39533 Woodward Ave Ste 140 Bloomfield Hills MI 48304-5098 Office Phone: 248-594-0620. Business E-Mail: rtr@raderfishman.com.

RADER, RANDALL RAY, federal judge; b. Hastings, Nebr., Apr. 21, 1949; BA magna cum laude, BYU, 1974; JD with honors, George Washington U., 1978. Bar: D.C., U.S. Ct. Appeals (fed. cir.) 1990, U.S. Claims Ct., U.S. Supreme Ct. Legis. asst. to Congresswoman Virginia Smith U.S. Ho. of Reps., 1975—78; mem. staff Ways and Means Com. U.S. Ho. Reps., 1978—81; chief counsel subcom. on Constn. U.S. Senate Judiciary Com., 1981—86, chief counsel, staff dir. subcom. on patents, copyrights and trademarks, 1987—88; counsel to Senator Orrin Hatch, 1981—88; judge U.S. Ct. Claims, Washington, 1988—90, U.S. Ct. Appeals (fed. cir.), Washington, 1990—. Lectr. patent law U. Va. Sch. Law, 1993—99; lectr. trial advocacy, lectr. George Washington U. Nat. Law Ctr., Washington, 1993—97; lectr. comparative patent law Georgetown U. Law Ctr., Washington, 1998—99. Co-author: Patent Law, 1997; co-editor: Criminal Justice Reform, 1983; contbr. articles to profl. jours. Mem.: FBA. Office: US Ct Appeals Fed Cir 717 Madison Pl NW Ste 913 Washington DC 20439-0002

RADER, STEVEN PALMER, lawyer; b. Charlotte, N.C., Dec. 30, 1952; s. Alvin Marion Jr. and Shirley Ninabelle (Palmer) Rader; m. Victoria Rolinsky, 2001; 1 child, Tudor R. AB, Duke U., 1975; postgrad., Stetson U., 1975-76; JD, Wake Forest U., 1978. Bar: N.C. 1978, U.S. Dist. Ct. (ea. dist.) N.C. 1979. Assoc. Wilkinson and Vosburgh, Washington, N.C., 1978-81; pvt. practice Washington, 1981-88; spl. asst. to sec. N.C. Dept. Human Resources, Raleigh, 1988-89, asst. dir. office legal affairs, 1989-91, gen. counsel, 1991-93; ptnr. Wilkinson & Rader, P.A., Washington, 1993—. Commr. Nat. Conf. Commrs. on Uniform State Laws, 1985-93; gen. counsel N.C. Rep. Party, 1992-97; commr. N.C. Rules Rev. Commn., 1997-99. Mem., sec. City of Washington Human Rels. Coun., 1981-83, chmn. Beaufort County Rep. party, Washington, 1983-87, 1st Congl. Dist. Rep. party, N.C., 1985-92; v.p. East Main St. Area Neighborhood Assn., 1983-85, 1st v.p., Ocean Villas Homeowners Assn., 1999-2003, pres. 2003—; del. Rep. Nat. Conv., 1984, 88, 92; Presdl. elector from N.C., U.S. Electoral Coll., 2000. Mem. N.C. State Bar, 2d Jud. Dist. Bar, Beaufort County Hist. Soc. (v.p. 1981-85, pres. 1985-86). Lutheran. Avocations: boating, classic automobiles, travel. Home: PO Box 1901 Washington NC 27889-1901 Office: Wilkinson & Rader PA PO Box 732 Washington NC 27889-0732 Office Phone: 252-946-7167.

RADFORD, R. S. lawyer, law educator; b. Independence, Kans., July 30, 1945; s. Lloyd Raymond and Arlene (Bacon) R.; m. Sharon L. Browne, Nov. 24, 1992; children: Jessica Siegel, Jacob Siegel. BS in Bus. Adminstrn., Rockhurst Coll., 1974; MA in Econs., U. So. Calif., 1976; JD, 1988. Bar: Calif. 1988, Supreme Ct. 1992. Prin. atty. Pacific Legal Found., Sacramento, Calif., 1988—; dir. progrm for jud. awareness, 1999—. Adj. prof. law U. Pacific McGeorge Sch. Law, Sacramento, 2001—. Contbr. numerous articles to profl. jours. Named Laywer of Yr. Calif. Lawyer, 1997 Office: Pacific Legal Found 10360 Old Placerville Rd Sacramento CA 95827 Fax: (916) 362-2932. E-mail: radford@cal.com., rsr@pacificlegal.org.

RADICE, ANNE-IMELDA, museum director; b. Buffalo, Feb. 29, 1948; d. Lawrence and Anne (Marino) R. AB, Wheaton Coll., 1969; MA, Villa SchiFanoia, Florence, Italy, 1971; PhD, U. N.C., 1976; MBA, Am. U., 1984. Asst. curator Nat. Gallery of Art, Washington, 1972-76; archtl. historian U.S. Capitol, Washington, 1976-80, curator Office of Architect, 1980-85; dir. Nat. Mus. Women in the Arts, 1985-89; chief div. of creative arts USIA, 1989-91; sr. dep. chmn. Nat. Endowment for Arts, Washington, 1991-92; acting chmn., 1992-93; exec. v.p. Gray & Co. II, Miami, Fla., 1993; prodr. World Affairs TV Prodn., 1994; assoc. producer Think Tank, 1994; chief spl. projects, confidential adviser Courtney Sale Ross, 1994-96; v.p., COO ICL Internat., 1996—; exec. dir. Friends of Dresden, 1998—2001; exec. dir. appeal Consci. Found., 2001—03; chief staff U.S. Dept. Edn., 2003—. Cons. in pub. rels. and TV, 1994—. Contbr. articles to profl. jours.

RADICE, FRANK J. communications executive; b. Washington, Dec. 13, 1949; m. Vida S. Radice, July 4, 1995. Student, U. Md., 1968-72. Film editor WRC/NBC-TV, Washington, 1971-72, ABC News, Washington, 1972, assignment editor, 1976, assoc. prodr. Good Morning Am., 1978, ops. prodr. World News Tonight, 1979-80; prodr. Nightline N.Y.C., 1980-83; program prodr. The Last Word ABC News, N.Y.C., 1983; field dir. Entertainment Tonight Paramount Motion Pictures, N.Y.C., 1984; prodr., developer Live At 5:00 WRC/NBC-TV, Washington, 1985; exec. prodr. Entertainment News, Cable News Network, N.Y.C., 1987-89; InterActive sr. producer/product devel., producer advt. and promotion ABC News, N.Y.C., 1989-91; advt. mgr. WCBS-TV, N.Y.C., 1991; v.p. advt. and promotion NBC Entertainment, N.Y.C., 1996; sr. v.p. The NBC Agy., 2000—. Exec. prodr. NBC on Ted, 2004—; pres. V&R Co., 1999; exec. prodr. NBC Inflight on United Airlines, 1984—. Prodr. A Line in the Sand, War of Peace, War in the Gulf; writer, prodr., 1992; co-exec. prodr. (CD): The Best of The Today Show Summer Concerts, Vols. 1 and 2, 2000. Recipient award Coll. Emergency Physicians, 1983, Emmy award NATAS, 1984, 1990, 7 NY Festival awards, 2000-03; Alfred I Dupont grantee Columbia U., NYC, 1984, 91, Mobius award, 1998, Cine Golden Eagle award 2002-03; Brand Builder award, B & C, 2003; named to Promax Hall of Fame, 2004. Mem. Broadcast Music Inc. (writer affiliate), AFTRA, Nat. Assn. Broadcast Employees and Technicians, Internat. Alliance Theatrical and Stage Employees, Writers Guild Am., Dirs. Guild Am., Congressional Country Club, Friars (N.Y.C.). Democrat. Roman Catholic. Office: NBC Ste 1891E 30 Rockefeller Plz New York NY 10112-0002 Office Phone: 212-664-4444. Business E-Mail: frank.radice@nbcuni.com.

RADICE, MARK A. musicologist; b. Passaic, N.J., July 17, 1951; s. Arturo Radice and Claire Harriet Beaven; m. Jean Clay Radice, Sept. 15, 1973; children: Caroline Emily, Elisa Louise, Nicholas Arthur, Peter Andrew. MusB, Boston U., 1973; MusM, U. Cin., 1977; PhD, U. Rochester, 1984. Lectr. San Francisco State U., 1979—87; prof. music history Ithaca Coll., NY, 1987—, curator Karel Husa Archive, 2000—. Organist, music dir. Grace Episcopal Ch., Cortland, NY, 1990—. Author: Opera in Context, 1998, Writing about Music, 1999, Karel Husa: A Composer's Life, 2002, Concert Music of the 20th Century, 2003; composer: (organ solo) Plainchant Christmas Melodies, Kum ba ya, Toccata, Evocation and Fandango. Mem.: Coll. Music Soc., Am. Musicological Soc. Democrat. Episcopalian. Avocation: bodybuilder. Office: Itaca Coll Sch Music 953 Danby Rd Ithaca NY 14850

RADIGAN, FRANK XAVIER, pharmaceutical company executive; b. Paterson, N.J., Apr. 13, 1933; s. John Joseph and Susan Clair (Brett) R.; m. Julia Lou Smith, Aug. 27, 1960 (div. Nov. 1988); children: Francis Gregory, Patricia Louise, Brett Frasier; m. Carol E. Berkley, June 26, 1992; children: Dana, Traci. AB in Sociology, Seton Hall U., 1955; MBA Mktg., U. Hartford, 1968. Asst. mgr. Beneficial Fin. Co., Newark, 1955-57; hosp. rep. Becton-Dickinson Co., Rutherford, N.J., 1957-58; dist. mgr. Merck Human Health Divsn., West Point, Pa., 1958-98, ret., 1998. Horse breeder, 1976—86. Active Greater Balt. SCORE; mem. Passaic County Dem. Com., 1955—56; chmn. St. John the Baptist Social Justice, New Freedom, Pa., 1981—85. Capt. USAR. Mem.: Md. Mental Health Assn. (legis. com. 1969—73), Balt. Pharm. Assn. (hon. pres. 1989), W.Va. Pharm. Soc., Md. Pharmacists Assn. (past chmn. indsl. rels. com., hon. pres. 1999—2000), Am. Mktg. Assn., Am. Pharm. Assn., Hopewell Fish and Game Assn., Bon Air Country Club, Lions (pres. Glen Rock 1975—76, 1986—88), Elks. Roman Catholic. Home: 2440 Bradenbaugh Rd White Hall MD 21161-9661 Personal E-mail: fxr333@msn.com.

RADIN, ALEX, former association executive, consultant; b. Chattanooga, June 14, 1921; s. Joseph and Mollie (Pernat) R.; m. Sara Leah Gordon, Sept. 6, 1943 (dec. Nov. 20, 1964); children— Jay Jacob, William Gordon m. Carol Nita Schuman, Sept. 21, 1979 BA, U. Chattanooga, 1947. Reporter Chattanooga Times, Chattanooga, 1938-42; adminstrv. asst. Office of Price Adminstrn., Washington, 1942-43; adminstrv. analyst Dept. of State, Washington, 1945-48; asst. to gen. mgr. Am. Pub. Power Assn., Washington, 1948-51, exec. dir., 1951-86; pres. Radin & Assocs. Inc., 1986—. Cons. U.S. Senate Com. on Interior and Insular Affairs, Washington, 1959; mem. exec. com. Am. Nuclear Energy Coun., Washington, 1973-88; v.p. Consumer Fedn. Am., Washington, 1978-86; mem. So. States Energy Bd.'s Adv. Com. on TVA, 1986-87; chmn. Monitored Retrievable Storage Rev. Commn., 1988-89; rep., sec. U.S. Dept. Energy, Independent Mgmt. and Fin. Rev. of Yucca Mt. (Nev.) Project, 1994-95; mem. adv. bd. Ford Found. Energy Policy Project, 1973-74; bd. dirs. Consumer Energy Coun. Am., 1999—. Columnist, Pub. Power Mag.; contbr. articles to newspapers and mags.; author Public Power, Private Life, 2003. Mem. adv. bd. Dance Theatre of Harlem, N.Y.C., 1985—. Recipient Leland Olds award Western States Water and Power Consumers Conf., 1970, Philip Hart Disting. Consumer Svc. award Consumer Fedn. Am., 1985, Alex Radin Disting. Svc. award Am. Pub. Power Assn., 1986, named Disting. Alumnus of 2001 U. Tenn. Chattanooga, 2001, Lifetime Achievement award Energy Daily, 2003. Mem. Alpha Soc. Clubs: Nat. Press. Democrat. Jewish. Avocations: photography; music; art; hiking. Home: 2510 Virginia Ave NW Apt 610N Washington DC 20037-1904 Office: Radin & Assocs Inc Ste 609 2510 Virginia Ave NW Washington DC 20037-1904 Office Phone: 202-338-0607.

RADIN, BERYL AVIS, public administration and policy educator; b. Aberdeen, S.D., Nov. 15, 1936; d. Norman and Sophie (Edelman) R. BA, Antioch Coll., 1958; MA, U. Minn., 1963; PhD, U. Calif., Berkeley, 1973. Asst. prof. LBJ Sch. of Pub. affairs U. Tex., Austin, 1973—77; prof. pub. adminstrn. Washington Pub. Affairs Ctr., U. So. Calif., 1978—94, dir., 1982—85; prof. pub. adminstrn. and policy SUNY, Albany, 1994—2001; prof. govt. and pub. adminstrn. Univ. Balt., 2002—. Vis. prof. Fudan U., Shanghai, China, 1985; vis. fellow pub. policy program The Australian Nat. U., Canberra, 1985, 86, 88, 93; vis. prof. Grad. Sch. Pub. Policy, U. Calif., Berkeley, 1987; Fulbright lectr. to India, Indian Inst. Pub. Adminstrn., New Delhi, 1990; speaker, conf. presenter in field; cons. to numerous govt. agys. and govts.; cons. Office Asst. Sec. for Mgmt. and Budget, HHS. Author: Implementation, Change and The Federal Bureaucracy: School Desegretation Policy in HEW (1964-68), 1977, Linkages Between Civil Rights Enforcement and Operating Programs, 1980, Evaluation of the Planning Requirements Reform Demonstration Project, 1981; co-author: New Governance For Rural America: Creating Intergovernmental Partnerships, 1996, The Politics of Federal Reorganization: Creating the U.S. Department of Education, 1988, Serving Children and Families Effectively: How the Past Can Help Chart the Future, 1991, Beyond Machiavelli: Policy Analysis Comes of Age, 2000, The Accountable Juggler, 2002; mng. editor Jour. Pub. Adminstrn. Rsch. and Theory; contbr. chpts. to books and articles to jours. Asst. info. officer U.S. Commn. on Civil Right, 1963-65; policy analyst SSI Study Group, Social Security Adminstrn., 1975; sr. policy analyst Office of Asst. Sec. for Planning and Evaluation, 1977-78, Pres.'s Reorgn. Project, OMB, 1978; asst. edn. dir. Phila. Joint Bd., Amalgamated Clothing Workers of Am., 1960-62; cons. Nat. Urban League, Ford Found., The Urban Inst., Nat. Urban Coalition, Civil Rights Dept., Survey of Race Rels. in Britain; bd. dirs. Human Svcs. Rsch. Inst. Fellow Nat. Assn. Schs. Pub. Affairs and Adminstrn. (mem. stds. com., 1982-85), Nat. Acad. Pub. Adminstrn.; mem. ASPA (program com. 1993, bd. dirs. Nat. Capital Area chpt. 1983-85, Donald Stone award), Assn. Pub. Policy Analysis and Mgmt. (program com. 1991, vice chair program com. 1992, pres. 1995-97), Am. Polit. Sci. Assn. (chair pub. adminstrn. program com. 1992, chair Gaus lecture com. 1994), Pub. Mgmt. Rsch. Assn. (bd. dirs.), Ctr. for Women Policy Studies. Office: U Balt Sch Pub Affairs 1304 St Paul St Baltimore MD 21202

RADIN, SAM, lawyer, estate planner; b. N.Y.C., Aug. 1, 1951; s. Clarence and Marjorie (Rembar) R.; m. Pamela Anderson, Sept. 13, 1981; children: Clarence Anderson, Elizabeth Rebecca. BA, Columbia U., 1973; JD, Boston U., 1976. Bar: N.J. 1976, U.S. Dist. Ct. N.J. 1976, N.Y. 1978, U.S. Dist. Ct. (so. dist.) N.Y. 1978, U.S. Ct. Appeals (D.C. cir.) 1978, U.S. Supreme Ct. 1980. Assoc. Burns, Van Kirk, N.Y.C., 1976-79, Lovejoy Wasson successor to Burns, Van Kirk, N.Y.C., 1979-80; pvt. practice, N.Y.C., 1980-84; v.p., gen. counsel Nat. Madison Group, Inc., N.Y.C., 1984-99, pres., 1999—. Contbg. author: Executive Compensation Answer Book, 1998; contbg. author, editor: Estate and Retirement Planning Answer Book, 1999; also articles. Bd. dirs. Student Athletes Inc., N.Y.C., 1992-98, Westchester Conservatory Music, White Plains, N.Y., 1995-97; trustee Payomet Performing Arts Charitable Trust, 1999—, Nat. Lighthouse Ctr. and Mus., 2000—, pres., 2001—. Recipient Nathan Burkan Meml. prize ASCAP, 1975. Mem. ABA (subcom. on life ins. tax sect. 1996—), N.Y. State Bar Assn., Assn. Bar City N.Y., Assn. Advanced Life Underwriting, Comm. on Estate Taxation. Avocations: salt water fly fishing, collecting books, skiing, running. Home: 71 Greenacres Ave Scarsdale NY 10583-1442 Office: Nat Madison Group Inc 261 Madison Ave New York NY 10016-2401 E-mail: sradin@nationalmadison.com.

RADIN, STEVEN S. lawyer; b. Newark; s. Morris and Sara Radin; m. Karen Burman; children: Jonathan, Elizabeth Radin. AB, Seton Hall U., 1957; LLB, JD, Columbia Law Sch., 1960. Bar: NJ 1961, NY 1980, Colo. 1987. Atty. Sills Cummis Gross & Epstein, Newark, 1971—. 2d lt. U.S. Army. Office: Sills Cummis Gross & Epstein One Riverfront Plaza Newark NJ 07102

RADINSKY, TROY D. assistant principal; s. Alice E. Radinsky; m. Lori M. Schulz, May 22, 2004. BS in Edn., Ashland (Ohio) U., 1990; MS, U. Akron, Ohio, 2001. Cert. edn. (adminstrn., tchg.) Ohio, Pa. Baseball coach Ashland U., 1988—91; tchr., varsity head coach Vila Angela-St. Joseph H.S., Cleve., 1998—2001; asst. prin., athletic dir. Pymatuning Valley H.S., Andover, Ohio, 2001—02; asst. prin. Edison H.S., Richmond, Ohio, 2002—. Sports information assistant Penguin Football Magazine (Vip Sandlini scholar for athletic/acad. achievemnet, 1985). Mem. Ashland U. Alumni Bd., 2003—. Mem.: Ohio HS Baseball Coaches Assn., Ohio Inschoolastic Amateur Athletic Assn., Ohio Assn. Secondary Sch. Adminstrs., Polish Nat. Alliance (life), Am. Legion (life). Avocations: travel, movies, outdoor activities, sports. Office: Edison HS 9890 SR 152 Box 308 Richmond OH 43944 Personal E-mail: radt@stratos.net.

RADKE, JAN RODGER, pulmonologist, physician executive; b. Detroit, Nov. 16, 1942; s. Edward V. and Dorothy M. Radke; m. Judith Hogan, June 20, 1987; children: Jennifer, John, Collin, Cameron. BS, Mich. State U., 1965; MD, U. Wis., 1969. Diplomate Am. Bd. Internal Medicine, Am. Bd. Pulmonary Disease. Intern Henry Food Hosp., 1969-70, resident internal medicine, 1970-71, resident, 1974-75, chief med. resident internal medicine, 1975-76, fellow pulmonary/critical care, 1977-78; v.p. satellite program Henry Ford Health Systems, Detroit, 1989; assoc. v.p. ambulatory program, assoc. prof. medicine Loyola U. Med. Ctr., Maywood, Ill., 1990-93, v.p. health care svcs., 1993-96; pres., CEO Univ. Care Plus, 1996-99; exec. dir. med. svcs. R & D plan and ambulatory care U. Tex. Med. Sch. and Hermann Hosp., Houston, 1996—, assoc. dean clin. affairs, 1997—, assoc. prof. medicine, 1996—; chief med. officer U. Calif., San Diego, 1999—. Lt. comdr. USNR, 1971-73. Fellow ACP, Am. Coll. Chest Physicians; mem. Am. Coll. Physician Execs. Avocation: birding. Office: USCD Healthcare 402 Dickinson St San Diego CA 92103-6902

RADKOSKI, DONALD J. food products company executive; V.p., dir. fin., asst. tres. Bob Evans Farms, Columbus, Ohio, 1980-88, CFO, group v.p. fin., treas., 1988—. Office: Bob Evans Farms Inc 3776 S High St Columbus OH 43207-0863

RADLAUER, STEVE, freelance writer, journalist, producer; b. NYC, Nov. 2, 1948; s. Marvin and Gladys (Steltzer) R.; m. Kerry K. Willis, June 7, 1985; 1 child, Kate. Student, Union Coll., Schenectady, NY; BS, U. State of NY. Dir. A-Space, Toronto, Canada, 1971-73; co-owner The Ritz Cafe, Toronto, Canada, 1973-77; program dir. Dry Salvages Film Group, NYC, 1978-85. Co-author: The Hist. Shops and Restaurants of NY, 2002; editor-in-chief (online news comedy site) Today's Other News on American Online, 1996; co-author: Dan Quayle: Airhead Apparent, 1992, Special Moments, 1984; freelance writer articles for various pubs. incl. N.Y. Mag., Spy, Esquire, N.Y. Times, L.A. Times. Mem. Authors Guild. E-mail: steve@radz.org.

RADLO, EDWARD JOHN, lawyer, mathematician; b. Pawtucket, R.I., Mar. 7, 1946; s. Edward Zygmund and Sue Mary (Borek) Radlo; m. Patricia Jackson, Feb. 22, 1989; children: Heather Sue, Graeme Michael, Connor Andrew. BS, MIT, 1967; JD, Harvard U., 1972. Bar: Calif. 1972, U.S. Dist. Ct. (no. dist.) Calif. 1972, R.I. 1973, U.S. Patent Office 1973, Can. Patent Office 1974. Staff. dir. Atty. Gen.'s Adv. Commn. on Juvenile Code Revision, Boston, 1970—72; law clk. R.I. Supreme Ct., 1972—73; patent atty. Honeywell Info. Systems, Waltham, Mass., 1973—74, Varian Assoc., Palo Alto, Calif., 1974—78, Ford Aerospace Corp., 1978—83, patent counsel, 1983—90; ptnr. Fenwick & West LLP, Mountain View, Calif., 1991—2004, Sonnenschein Nath & Rosenthal LLP, San Francisco, 2004—. Lectr. U. Calif., San Jose State U., U. Santa Clara, 1975—78. Organizer So. Peninsula Emergency Comm. Sys., 1970; mem. Los Altos Hills (Calif.) Emergency Comm. Com, Lawyers' Alliance for Nuclear Arms Control, 1982—83, Environ. Def. Fund, 1979; bd. dir. Tomahawks Lacrosse Club, Menlo Park, Calif.; bd. dirs. No. Calif. Jr. Lacrosse Assn., Corte Modera, Calif. Lt. USPHS, 1967—69. Mem.: ABA, Calif. Bar (intellectual property sect.), Silicon Valley Intellectual Property Law Assn., Assn. Radio Amateurs of So. New England Inc. (sec. 1962—63), No. Calif. Contest Club (pres. 1984—85), Sigma Xi. Home: 28040 Elena Rd Los Altos Hills CA 94022-2454 Office: Sonnenschein Nath & Rosenthal LLP 685 Market St San Francisco CA 94105 Personal E-mail: EddRad@aol.com.

RADLOFF, ROBERT ALBERT, real estate company executive; b. Chgo., Mar. 30, 1947; s. Henry O. and Virginia G. (Grothus) R.; m. Ann Macy Beha, June 21, 1975; children: Macy, Allison. BS in Fin., Boston U., 1969. V.p. Kuras & Co., Inc., Boston, 1971-76; sr. v.p. Boston Co. Real Estate Counsel, Inc., 1976-81, pres., 1981-89, chmn., 1989-91; real estate investments counselor Boston, 1991—. Bd. dirs. Mass. Cultural Coun., 1992, Friends of Vieilles Maison Francais, 1992, The Augustus Saint-Gaudens Meml.; trustee Isabella Stewart Gardner Mus., 1995; chmn., bd. overseers WGBH Ednl. Found. Mem. Am. Soc. Real Estate Counselors (cert.), Somerset Club. Avocations: art, tennis, travel. Office: 33 Kingston St Boston MA 02111-2208

RADMER, MICHAEL JOHN, lawyer, educator; b. Wisconsin Rapids, Wis., Apr. 28, 1945; s. Donald Richard and Thelma Loretta (Donahue) R.; children from previous marriage: Christina Nicole, Ryan Michael; m. Laurie J. Anshus, Dec. 22, 1983; 1 child, Michael John BS, Northwestern U., 1967; JD, Harvard U., 1970. Bar: Minn. 1970. Assoc. Dorsey & Whitney, Mpls., 1970-75, ptnr., 1976—. Lectr. law Hamline U. Law Sch., St. Paul, 1981-84; gen. counsel, rep., sec./asst. sec. 136 federally registered investment cos., Mpls. and St. Paul, 1977—. Contbr. articles to legal jours. Active legal work Hennepin County Legal Advice Clinic, Mpls., 1971—. Mem. ABA, Minn. Bar Assn., Hennepin County Bar Assn., Mpls. Athletic Club. Home: 4329 E Lake Harriet Pky Minneapolis MN 55409-1725 Office: Dorsey & Whitney 50 South 6th St Ste 1500 Minneapolis MN 55402 Office Phone: 612-340-2724. E-mail: radmer.michael@dorsey.com. *A key to a successful and happy life is achieving a balance. Intellectual, academic and vocational goals are important, but their pursuit should be balanced with ample time spent with family and friends, travel and enjoying reading, music, art and sports. Don't be afraid to try something new; realize that education should be a lifelong pursuit. Much frustration can be avoided by realizing that life is full of trade-offs. You can't experience the joy of raising children and have the complete freedom of the child-free. Finally, while you should strive for perfection, be content with less. We are only human, and live in an imperfect, yet wonderful, world.*

RADNER, ROY, economist, educator, researcher; b. Chgo., June 29, 1927; s. Samuel and Ella (Kulansky) R.; m. Virginia L. Honoski, July 26, 1949 (dec. Apr. 1976); children: Hilary A., Erica H. (dec.), Amy E., Ephraim L.; m. Charlotte Virginia Kuh, Jan. 22, 1978. PhB with honors, U. Chgo, 1945, BS in Math., 1950, MS in Math., 1951, PhD in Math. Stats., 1956. Rsch. asst. Cowles Commn. for Rsch. in Econs. U. Chgo., 1951, rsch. assoc., 1951-54, asst. prof., 1954-55; mem. Cowles Found. for Rsch. in Econs. Yale U., New Haven, 1955-57, asst. prof. econs., 1955-57; assoc. prof. econs. and stats. U. Calif., Berkeley, 1957-61, prof. econs. and stats., 1961-79, chmn. dept. econs., 1966-69; Taussig prof. econs. Harvard U., Cambridge, Mass., 1977-78, vis. prof. Kennedy Sch. Govt., 1978-79; mem. tech. staff AT&T Bell Labs, Murray Hill, N.J., 1979-84, disting. mem. tech. staff, 1985-95; rsch. prof. econs. NYU, N.Y.C., 1983-95, prof. econs. and info. sys., 1995-96, L.N. Stern Sch. prof. bus., 1996—. Mem. com. on fundamental rsch. relevant to edn. NRC-NAS, 1976-77, mem. commn. on human resources, 1976-79; mem. assembly of behavioral and social scis. NRC, 1979-82, mem. com. on risk and decision making, 1980-81, mem. working group on basic rsch. in behavioral and social scis., 1985-86, mem. com. on info. tech. workforce, 1999-2000, mem. com. on

geophys. and environ. data, 2001—; mem. panel on contingent valuation methology NOAA, U.S. Dept. Commerce, 1992-93; mem. steering com. Enjeux et Procedures de Decentralization Commisariat du Plan, Paris, 1992-95; mem. Com. on Prevention of Nuclear War; mem. com. on Info. Tech. workforce NRC; also various other profl. coms., bds., panels. Author: (books, monographs) Notes on Theory of Econ. Planning, 1963; co-author (with D. Jorgensen and J.J. McCall): Optimal Replacement Policy, 1967; co-author: (with J. Marshack) Econ. Theory of Teams, 1972; co-author: (with L.S. Miller) Demand and Supply in U.S. Higher Edn., 1975; co-author: (with C.V.Kuh) Mathematicians in Academia, 1980, author also articles on econ. theory, orgn. theory, econs. of edn., co-editor Decision and Orgn., Edn. as an Industry, Info., Incentives and Econ. Mechanisms, Perspectives and Deterrence, Bargaining with Incomplete Info.; assoc. editor: Jour. Econ. Theory, assoc. editor: Info. Sys. Frontier, assoc. editor: Games and Econ. Behavior. 2d lt. U.S. Army, 1945-48, PTO. William Cook scholar U. Chgo., 1944-45; fellow Ctr. Advanced Study in Behavioral Scis., Stanford, Calif., 1955-56, Guggenheim Found. fellow, 1961-62, 65-66, overseas fellow Churchill Coll., Cambridge U., Eng., 1969-70, 89. Fellow AAAS (disting. fellow), Econometric Soc. (v.p. 1970-72, pres. 1972-73), Am. Acad. Arts and Scis., Am. Econ. Assn. (disting. fellow); mem. NAS (chair econ. sect. 1994-97), Inst. Math. Stats. Avocations: music, hiking, cross country skiing. Home: 3203 Davenport St NW Washington DC 20008-2211 Office: Stern Sch Business NYU KMC 8-87 44 W 4th St New York NY 10012-1126 E-mail: rradner@stern.nyu.edu.

RADNER, SIDNEY HOLLIS, retired rug company executive; b. Holyoke, Mass., Dec. 8, 1919; s. William I. Radner; m. Helen Jane Cohen, Dec. 12, 1946; children: William Marc, Richard Scott. Student, Yale U., 1941. Ret. pres. Am. Rug Co., Holyoke. Lectr., cons., investigator on crooked gambling U.S. Armed Forces, Govt. of Can., state and mcpl. police squads; dir. Houdini Magical Hall of Fame, Niagara Falls, Ont., Canada; dir., organizer Ann. Ofcl. Houdini Seance. Author: Radner on Poker, Radner on Dice, Radner on Roulette and Casino Games, How to Detect Card Sharks; contbr. articles to profl. jours.; appeared in (TV series) Turn of a Card, 1953, Tonight Show, 1956, BBC Omnibus: Houdini, 1971, CNN, 1993—94, Today Show, Merv Griffin Show, CNBC, PBS, CBC, In Search Of..., Can. Discovery on magic, 1998, History Channel on Houdini, 2000, Ripley's Believe It or Not, History Channel, 2000, (TV series) Today Show, 2004, BBC History of Magic, 2004, cons. (TV films) Houdini, 1998, cons., participant (TV Spl.) A&E Houdini, 1996, appeared in (TV spl.) E Network Houdini documentary, 1998, cons., participant (TV films) Discovery Channel documentary, 1997. Past pres. Holyoke C. of C.; co-founder Volleyball Hall of Fame; past bd. dirs. Greater Springfield (Mass.) Better Bus. Bur.; hon. curator, dir. Houdini Hist. Ctr., Appleton, Wis. With criminal investigation divsn. U.S. Army, 1942—46. Named to Volleyball Hall of Fame, 1999. Mem.: Acad. Magical Arts, Nat. Assn. Bunco Investigators, Magicians Guild (charter), Magic Cir. London (mem. Inner Magic Cir.), Internat. Brotherhood Magicians, Soc. Am. Magicians (mem. occult investigation com.), Profls. Against Confidence Crime, China-Burma-India Vets. Assn. (life), Magic Collector's Assn. (charter, Honor award 1992), Houdini Club Wis. (hon.), Shriners, Masons, Rotary, Soc. Osaris (hon.). Jewish. Home: 1050 Northampton St Holyoke MA 01040-1321 also: 3200 S Ocean Blvd 203C Palm Beach FL 33480 Office: 1594 Dwight St Holyoke MA 01040-2356 E-mail: HollisRendar@aol.com.

RADNOR, ALAN T. lawyer; b. Cleve., Mar. 10, 1946; s. Robert Clark and Rose (Chester) R.; m. Carol Sue Hirsch, June 22, 1969; children: Melanie, Joshua, Joanna. BA, Kenyon Coll., 1967; MS in Anatomy, Ohio State U., 1969, JD, 1972. Bar: Ohio 1972. Ptnr. Vorys, Sater, Seymour & Pease, Columbus, Ohio, 1972—. Adj. prof. law Ohio State U., Columbus, 1979-99. Author: Cross-Examining Doctors: A Practical Guide, 1999; contbr. articles to profl. jours. Bd. dirs., trustee Congregation Tifereth Israel, Columbus, 1975—, pres., 1985-87; trustee Columbus Mus. Art, 1995-98; pres. The Thurber House., 2004. Named Boss or Yr., Columbus Assn. Legal Secs., 1983. Fellow Am. Coll. Trial Lawyers; mem. ABA, Ohio State Bar Assn., Columbus Bar Assn., Def. Rsch. Inst., Internat. Assn. Def. Counsel. Avocations: reading, sculpture. Home: 400 S Columbia Ave Columbus OH 43209-1629 Office: Vorys Sater Seymour & Pease 52 E Gay St PO Box 1008 Columbus OH 43216-1008

RADO, PETER THOMAS, lawyer; b. Berlin, Nov. 12, 1928; came to U.S., 1931; naturalized, 1937; s. Sandor and Emmy (Chrisler) R.; m. Jacqueline Danenberg, Sept. 11, 1977. AB, HArvard U., 1949, LLB, 1952, LLM, 1953. Bar: N.Y. 1952. Assoc. Ide, Haigney & Rado, N.Y.C., 1956-61, ptnr., 1961—. With U.S. Army, 1953-55. Mem. ABA, N.Y. State Bar Assn., Assn. of Bar of City of N.Y., Internat. Bar Assn., Harvard Club (N.Y.C.). Home: 176 E 71st St New York NY 10021-5159 Office: Ide Haigney & Rado 176 E 71st St New York NY 10021-5159 E-mail: radopandj@aol.com.

RADOCK, MICHAEL, foundation executive; b. Belle Vernon, Pa, July 17, 1917; s. Nicholas M. and Pauline (Radich) R.; m. Helen Adelaide Hower, Sept. 2, 1944; children: Robert Hower, William Michael. AB magna cum laude, Westminster Coll., New Wilmington, Pa., 1942, LittD (hon.), 1965; MS in Journalism, Northwestern U., 1946; postgrad., Case Western Res. U., 1950-52. Reporter Fayette City Jour., Pa., 1937-39; corr. for Pa. newspapers, 1937-39; reporter, sports editor Charleroi Daily Mail, Pa., 1942; dir. news bur., asst. prof. journalism Westminster Coll., 1942-45; dir. pub. rels., prof. journalism Kent State U., Ohio, 1945-53; with corp. pub. relations Ford Motor Co., Dearborn, Mich., 1953-61; established Inst. for Pub. Rels. Kent State U., Ohio, 1947; v.p. univ. relations, prof. journalism U. Mich., Ann Arbor, Mich., 1961-81; sr. v.p. devel. and univ. relations, prof. journalism U. So. Calif., Los Angeles, Calif., 1981-82; v.p. resource devel. Aspen Inst. Humanistic Studies, NYC, 1982-83; advisor to pres. C.S. Mott Found., Flint, Mich., 1983-90, cons., 1990—. Mem. faculty Harvard U. Inst. in Ednl. Mgmt., 1972, 73, Williamsburg Devel. Inst., 1979-81; vis. prof. journalism U. Wyo., Laramie, 1952, U. Kent, Canterbury, Eng., 1989; trustee Westminster Coll., 1972-82; mem. adv. bd. Pub. Rels. News; cons. NSF, 1972-73; mem. adv. bd. Chronicle of Non-Profit Enterprise, 1990—. Contbr. Handbook of Institutional Advancement, 1977, (books) Lesly's Public Relations Handbook, 1978, Public Relations Career Directory, 1987, 88, 89, 93, 95, Lesly's Handbook of Public Relations and Communications, 1990. Mem. Fulbright Bd. Fgn. Scholarships, Washington, 1972-74; mem. exec. bd. U. Mich., 1979-81, mem. bd. in control of intracollegiate athletics, 1961-81; trustee Glacier Hills Retirement Ctr., Ann Arbor, 1988-93, Ann Arbor Area Cmty. Found., 1989-92, Mich. Hist. Ctr. Found., 1990—; chmn. White House Sci. and Tech. Adv. Com. on Black Colls., Washington, 1986-88. Recipient Disting. Service award Kent State U., 1965, Frank Ashmore award for disting. service to edn. Am. Coll. Pub. Relations Assn., 1968-69; Disting. Service award for leadership in institutional advancement for minority colls. and univs., 1980. Fellow Pub. Rels. Soc. Am. (accredited); mem. Inst. for Pub. Rels. Rsch. and Edn. (bd. trustees 1980-84), Soc. of Profl. Journalists, Nat. Soc. Fund Raising Execs., Higher Edn. Roundtable. Republican. Presbyterian. Home: 1200 Earhart Rd Ann Arbor MI 48105-2768

RADOFF, LEONARD IRVING, librarian, consultant; b. Houston, Jan. 9, 1927; s. Morris Aaron and Jenny (Goldberg) R.; m. Lisel Ruth Ephraim, July 25, 1953; 1 child, Lesley Radoff Rappaport BA, Rice U., Houston, 1949; M.L.S., U. Tex., Austin, 1965. Cert. secondary sch. tchr., Tex. Tchr. math Aldine Ind. Sch. Dist., Houston, 1959-61, sch. librarian, 1961-63; head pub. services Abilene Pub. Library, Tex., 1964-65; library dir. Pasadena Pub. Library, Tex., 1966-70; chief br. services Houston Pub. Library, 1971-92, ret., 1992; library bldg. cons. Houston, 1975—. Treas. Literacy Vol. Am., Houston, 1984-85; mem. Northside Interests, Houston, 1982-85. Served with USN, 1945-46 Hoenthal scholar, 1948 Mem. Tex. Library Assn., ALA, Freedom to Read Found., Houston Great Books Council (leader trainer 1953-59, pres. 1967-69) Avocations: tutoring; listening to music; stamp collecting. Home: 4013 Gano St Houston TX 77009-4119

RADOMSKI, MAREK WITOLD, science educator; b. Bochnia, Poland, Aug. 9, 1954; s. Alfons Radomski and Barbara Radomska; m. Anna Socha, Nov. 7, 1975; children: Aleksandra Radomska, Barbara Radomska. MD, Jagiellonian U., Krakow, Poland, 1972—78. Asst. prof. Jagiellonian U., Cracow, Poland, 1978—88; assoc. prof. Polish Acad. of Sciences Med. Rsch. Ctr., Warsaw, 1988—91; scientist Wellcome Rsch. Lab., Beckenham, 1989—94; prof. U. of Alta., Edmonton, Canada, 1994—2002; prof. and dir. U. of Tex., Houston, 2002—. Recipient Alta. Heritage Found. for Med. Rsch. Scholar, Alta. Heritage Found. for Med. Rsch., 1994—2000, Scientist, Can. Institutes of Health Rsch., 2000—, Altapharm Award in Pharmacology, The Pharmacological Soc. of Can., 2001, State Professorship, Pres. of Polish Republic, 2002. Office: Univ of Tex 6770 Bertner Ave Houston TX 77030 Personal E-mail: mradomsk@yahoo.com. Business E-Mail: marek.radomski@uth.tmc.edu.

RADON, JENIK RICHARD, lawyer; b. Berlin, Jan. 14, 1946; arrived in U.S., 1951, naturalized, 1956; s. Louis and Irmgard (Hinz) R.; m. Heidi B. Duerbeck, June 10, 1971 (dec. Sept. 1999); 1 child, Kaara H.D. BA, Columbia Coll., 1967; MCP, U. Calif., Berkeley, 1971; JD, Stanford U., 1971. Bar: Calif. 1972, NY 1975, U.S. Ct. Appeals (2d cir.) 1975, U.S. Dist. Ct. (so. dist.) NY 1975. Atty. Radon & Ishizumi, NYC, 1981—; counsel Walter, Conston, Alexander & Green, NYC, 1991—2000, ptnr., 2000. Lectr. Polish Acad. Scis., 1980, Tokyo Arbitration Assn., 1983, Japan External Trade Orgn., 1983, 86, Japan Mgmt. Assn., 1983, 90, Japan Inst. Internat. Bus. Law, 1983-84, Va. Ctr. World Trade, 1985, UN Indsl. Devel. Orgn., Warsaw, 1987, Wichita World Trade Coun., 1987, Inst. Nat. Economy of Poland, 1987, Hungarian Econ. Roundtable, 1987, Tallinn, 1988, USSR Com. on Sci. and Tech., 1988, USSR Fgn. Trade Ministry, 1988, Tallinn Tech. Inst., 1988, Tartu State U., 1988, U. Ottawa, 1988-89, Palm Beach World Trade Coun., 1988, Fla. Atlantic U., 1988, Bus. Assn. Latin Am. Studies, 1989—, Assn. France-Poland, 1989, Russian and East European Studies Inst. Stanford U., 1989, Ukrainian Profl. Assn. NY and NJ, 1989, Columbia U. Harriman Inst., 1989, Inst. East-West Security Studies, 1989, Friedrich-Schiller U. Jena, East Germany, 1990, East European Inst. Free U. Berlin, numerous others; bd. dirs. Gland Pharma Ltd., India, 1996—, HTM Sport, Estonia, 1993-2004; pub. Baltic Rev., 1993-2004, City Paper (Baltic), 1993—; mem. exec. com. Vetter Pharma, Germany; adj. mem. faculty, lectr. Stanford Sch. of Law, 2000-02, Stanford Bus. Sch., 2000-01, Columbia Sch. Internat. Pub. Affairs, 2002-, Indira Gandhi Inst. for Devel. Rsch., Bombay, 2004-. Editor-in-chief Stanford Jour. Internat. Studies, 1970-71; contbr. The Internat. Acquisitions Handbook, 1987, Negotiating and Financing Joint Ventures Abroad, 1989, How to Form and Manage Successful Strategic Alliances, 1990, Risks Mgmt. in Internat. Bus. 1991, Comrade Goes Pvt., 1992, Investing in Reform, 1991, Fordham Internat. Law Jour., 1996, various jours. in U.S., Germany, Can. Active Am. Coun. on Germany, NYC, 1978—; vice-chmn. U.S.-Polish Econ. Coun., 1989-93; mem. exec. com. Afghanistan Relief Com., NYC, 1980-95; bd. dirs. Columbia Coll. Alumni Assn., 1988-92, nat. coun., 1996-98, Freedom Medicine, 1987-94, chmn., 1989-94; trustee Direct Relief Internat., Santa Barbara, Calif., 1987-89; founder and dir. Eesti and Eurasian Fellowship of Columbia U., 1990—; profl. advisor Harriman Inst., 1993—; advisor Estonian Ministry Economy, Reform and Justice, 1991-95; advisor to Parliament Republic of Georgia, 1996-98, to Pres. of Georgia, 1999-2003; advisor Min. of Fin. of Georgia, 1998-2000, Georgian Internat. Oil Corp., 1998—; chmn. Estonian-Am. C. of C., 1990-93, Deutsche Stiftung fuer internationale rechtliche Zusammenarbeit, Estonia Commn., Beirat, 1992-94, Ctr. for Global Change and Governance at Rutgers U., 2004-. Recipient Order of Honor award Republic of Georgia, 2000. Mem. ABA, Asia-Pacific Lawyers Assn., German-Am. Law Assn. Roman Catholic. Office: Radon & Ishizumi 269 W 71st St New York NY 10023-3701

RADUNZ, PAUL A. transportation executive; BA, St. Olaf Coll. Sr. v.p., chief info. officer GE Card Svcs., GE Capital Fleet Svcs.; v.p., chief info. officer CH Robinson, Eden Prairie, Minn., 2001—. Office: CH Robinson 8100 Mitchell Rd Eden Prairie MN 55344-2248

RADWAY, ROBERT J. lawyer, consultant, law educator; b. Lansing, Mich., June 8, 1940; s. David and Sophie C. (Zidell) Radway; m. Barbara L. Bernstein, June 18, 1967 (div. June 1975); children: Rachel, Theodore. BBA, U. Mich., 1961, MBA, 1962; postgrad., Hague Acad. Internat. Law, The Netherlands, 1966; JD, U. Calif., Hastings, 1969. Bar: Mass. 1970, U.S. Dist. Ct. Mass. 1970, U.S. Ct. Appeals (1st cir.) 1970, Ohio 1973, N.Y. 1978. Various mgmt. positions Gen. Dynamics Corp. and IBM Corp., San Diego, 1962-65, GTE Corp., Calif., 1967-69, internat. contract adminstr., 1969-70; atty. New Eng. Tel., Boston, 1970-72; counsel-internat. Arthur G. McKee & Co., Cleve., 1972-76; counsel and dir. tech. programs Coun. of Americas, N.Y.C., 1976-78; pvt. practice N.Y.C., 1978-82; ptnr. Radway & Dalto, N.Y.C., 1983-85, Radway & Assocs., N.Y.C., 1986-92; pres. Vector Internat., N.Y.C., 1993—. Cons. UN Centre Transnational Corps., UN Indsl. Devel. Orgn., UN Devel. Programme, Ctr. Latin Am., U. Wis., Milw.; adj. prof. NYU, 1983—85, Pace U., Fordham U., 1995—2000; vis. adj. prof., lectr. Europe and Asia, 1988—93; lectr. in field; bd. dirs. WORLDGTL, inc. Co-editor: Reference Manual on Doing Business in Latin America, 1979; mem. editl. bd. Multinational Corporation Law, Vol I - Mexico and Central America, 1981; contbr. articles to profl. jours. Pres. Tenants Assn., 1984—85. Mem.: ABA (sects. internat. and bus./corp. law), Licensing Execs. Soc., Greater Cleve. Internat. Lawyers Group (founder, pres. 1973—76), Dickinson Soc. Internat. Law (founder, pres. 1966—67), Am. Fgn. Law Assn. (bd. dirs. 1985—96), Assn. Bar City of N.Y., Inter-Am. Bar Assn. (coun. 1983—2003, chmn. organizing host com. 1988, mem. exec. com. 1995—2000), Princeton Club N.Y., Hastings Coll. Law Alumni Club N.Y. and New Eng. (founder, bd. dirs. 1979—), U. Mich. Alumni Club N.Y. (bd. dirs. 1977—2000, pres. 1988, dir., chmn. Scholarship Fund, Inc. 1995—). Republican. Jewish. Avocations: sailing, tennis, golf, bicycling. Home and Office: 250 E 73rd St New York NY 10021-4307 E-mail: rjrvector@verizon.net.

RADWIN, JEROME, public health service officer; BA in Polit. Sci., Idaho State U., 1965. Fundraiser March of Dimes Birth Defects Found., NY, 1967, dir., gen. solicitation, dir., devel. Chgo., 1971—74, exec. dir., 1974, exec. dir., nat. field svcs. dir., 1974—78, exec. dir., nat. field svcs. dir., asst. v.p., chpt. programs for nat. office, 1978, dir., chpt., v.p., corp. comms. and v.p., planning and mktg., 1984—88; founder J. Radwin Cons. Svc., 1989—; exec. dir. Nat. Victim Ctr., 1990—93; v.p., opers. Am. Found. for AIDS Rsch., N.Y.C., 1993, sr. v.p., 1993—95, sr. v.p., COO, 1995—97, exec. v.p., CEO, 1997—2000, CEO, 2000—. Office: Am Found for AIDS Rsch 120 Wall St 13th fl New York NY 10005-3902 E-mail: jerry.radwin@amfar.org.

RADYCKI, DIANE JOSEPHINE, art historian; b. Chgo., Dec. 4, 1946; d. Casimir Constantine and Sophie Jeanette Radycki; m. Sidney Tillim, June 27, 1998. BA, U. Ill., 1969; MA, Hunter Coll., 1976; PhD, Harvard U., 1993. Intern Busch-Reisinger Mus., Cambridge, 1984-85; guest-curator Fogg Mus., Cambridge, 1983, 87, 88; tchg. fellow Harvard U., Cambridge, Mass., 1987; instr. U. Houston, 1992-93, asst. prof., 1993-96, Moravian Coll., 1998—; dir. Payne Gallery, Moravian Coll., Bethlehem, Pa., 1999—. Editor, translator: Letters and Journals of Paula Modersohn-Becker, 1980; contbr. hist. articles to jours. in field. Agnes Mongan fellow, 1982-84, Fulbright fellow, 1989-91, AAUW fellow, 1991. Office: Moravian Coll Art Dept Bethlehem PA 18018

RADZIK, ALBIN F. military analyst, consultant; b. Berwyn, Ill., Oct. 21, 1947; s. Albin F. and Evelyn Clara Radzik; children: Melanie Rose, Amy Marie. BS, Northwestern U.; MBA, Georgetown U., 1994; HHD (hon.), Kalinin U., St. Petersburg, 1995. Analyst U.S. Govt., Washington, 1976—, mil. cons., 1978—2001. Author: (poetry) Love and Distance, 1967 (Hole Creative Writing award, 1967). Open space com. City of Redlands, Calif., 1985—86. Served to capt. U.S. Army, 1966—82. Decorated Bronze Star, Purple Heart, DSC, Army Commendation medal, Air medal, Combat Inf. badge; recipient Cold War Recognition cert., U.S. Sec. Def., 2003. Mem.: Royal Order of the Purple Heart. Office Phone: 909-478-0659. Personal E-mail: aradzik@netzero.net.

RADZINOWICZ, MARY ANN, language educator; b. Champaign, Ill., Apr. 18, 1925; d. Arthur Seymour and Ann (Stacy) Nevins; m. Leon Radzinowicz, June 16, 1958 (div. 1978); children: Ann Stacy Radzinowicz Prior, William Francis Henry. BA, Radcliffe Coll., 1945; MA, Columbia U., 1947, PhD, 1953; MA (hon.), U. Cambridge, Eng., 1960. Prof. Vassar Coll., Poughkeepsie, N.Y., 1947-50, 52-59, Girton Coll., Cambridge, Eng., 1960-80, U. Cambridge, 1973-80, Cornell U., Ithaca, N.Y., 1980-90, Jacob Gould Schurman prof. English emeritus, 1990—. Mem. adv. bd. 2d, 3d, 4th Internat. Milton Symposia, 1985—. Author: Toward Samson Agonistes, 1978 (Hanford prize 1979), Milton's Epics and Psalms, 1989, Milton and the Tragic Women of Genesis, 1995 (Hanford prize); editor American Colonial Prose, 1984, Paradise Lost, Book VIII, 1974; mem. editorial bd. Milton Quarterly, 1981—, Christianity and Literature, 1989—. Mem. MLA, Renaissance Soc. Am., Milton Soc. Am. (honored scholar 1987), John Donne Soc. Home: Ballyconry House Ballyvaughan County Clare Ireland Office: Cornell U Dept English Lit Ithaca NY 14850 E-mail: manr@eir.com.

RAE, BARBARA JOYCE, former employee placement company executive; b. Prince George, B.C., Can., May 17, 1930; d. Alfred and Lottie Kathleen (Davis) Holmwood; m. George Suart, Feb. 14, 1984; children: James, Glenn, John. MBA, Simon Fraser U., Burnaby, B.C., 1975, LLD (hon.), 1998. CEO Dekora Staging Inc.; chmn., CEO Adia Can., Ltd., Vancouver, B.C., 1953-95; also bd. dirs. Bd. dirs. emeritus Can. Imperial Bank Commerce, Grosvenor Internat. Ltd., Noranda, Inc., Telus, Xerox Can.; dir. VLINX.Com., Can. Inst. Adv. Rsch., 1995-2001, KTCS Pub. Broadcasting; bd. govs. Multiple Sclerosis Soc., 1995—; mem. Fed. Task Force on Future of Can. Fin. Svcs. Sector, 1997-98; past chmn. B.C. Women's Hosp. Found., 1994-97. Chancellor Simon Fraser U., 1987—93; mem. Jud. Appts. .Com., 1988—90; commr. Triennial Commn. Judges Salaries and Benefits; mem. Premier's Econ. Adv. Coun., 1987—91, Prime Minister's Com. on Sci. and Tech., 1989—94; gen. chmn. United Way Lower Mainland, 1987; chair Salvation Army Red Shield Vancouver Campaign, 1986; bd. dirs. Vancouver Bd. Trade, 1972—76; dir. Royal B.C. Mus.; patron Can. Coun. Christians and Jews; mem. adv. bd. Salvation Army, 1985—. Decorated Order of Can., Order of B.C.; recipient Outstanding Alumnae award Simon Fraser U., 1985, Disting. Alumni Svc. award, 1995, Bus. Women of Yr. award Vancouver YWCA, 1986, West Vancouver Achievers award, 1987, B.C. Entrepreneur of Yr. award, 1987, Nat. Vol. award, 1990, Can. Woman Entrepreneur B.C. award, 1992, Queen's Jubilee medal, 2003, Clan Leader award Simon Fraser U., 2004. Home: 2206 Folkestone Way #3 West Vancouver BC Canada V7S 2X7 E-mail: brae@sfu.ca.

RAE, DOUGLAS WHITING, management educator; b. Indpls., May 2, 1939; s. William Douglas and Katherine (Whiting) R.; m. Ellen Shuman, July 24, 1993; children: Hugh, Katie, Kimberly. BA, Ind. U., 1962; MS, U. Wis., 1964, PhD, 1967; MA (hon.), Yale U., 1974. Instr. U. Vt., Burlington, 1964-65; asst. prof. Syracuse U., N.Y., 1966-67; asst. prof. polit. sci. Yale U., New Haven, 1967-74, prof., 1974—, chmn. dept., 1985-89; Richard Ely prof. of pub. mgmt. Yale Sch. of Mgmt., New Haven, 1989-94; chief adminstrv. officer City of New Haven, 1990—91. Cons. Parliament of Spain, Madrid, 1979-81. Author: Political Consequences of Electroral Laws, 1967, Analysis of Political Cleavages, 1971, Equalities, 1981, City: Urbanism and Its End, 2003. Pres. New Haven Youth Soccer, 1981-84; chmn. Spl. Commn. on Poverty, New Haven, 1983; mem. Youth Planning Coun., 1983-86; bd. mem. Inner City Scholarship Fund, 1983-85; trustee Hamden Hall Sch., 1984-89; bd. dirs. Project More, 1985-2003, New Haven Scholarship Fund, 1987—, New Haven Law Club, 2003—; commr. Pub. Housing Authority New Haven, 1986-89; bd. chair Leeway, Ind. AIDS Care Facility, 1993—; pres. Tweed-New Haven Airport, 1992—. Recipient Hurfurth Prize U. Wis., 1968; Guggenheim Found. fellow, 1969-70; Netherlands Inst. Advanced Study fellow Wasenaar, 1975; Am. Acad. Arts and Sci. fellow Boston, 1983; recipient George Hallett prize Am. Polit. Sci. Assn. Mem. U.S. Soccer Fedn., U.S. Tennis Assn. Democrat. Home: 71 Livingston St New Haven CT 06511-2409

RAE, MATTHEW SANDERSON, JR., lawyer; b. Pitts., Sept. 12, 1922; s. Matthew Sanderson and Olive (Waite) R.; m. Janet Hettman, May 2, 1953; children: Mary-Anna, Margaret Rae Mallory, Janet S. Rae Dupree. AB, Duke, 1946, LLB, 1947; postgrad., Stanford U., 1951. Bar: Md. 1948, Calif. 1951. Asst. to dean Duke Sch. Law, Durham, N.C., 1947-48; assoc. Karl F. Steinmann, Balt., 1948-49, Guthrie, Darling & Shattuck, L.A., 1953-54; nat. field rep. Phi Alpha Delta Law Frat., L.A., 1949-51; research atty. Calif. Supreme Ct., San Francisco, 1951-52; ptnr. Darling, Hall & Rae (and predecessor firms), L.A., 1955—. Mem. Calif. Commn. Uniform State Laws, 1985—, chmn., 1993-94; chmn. drafting com. for revision Uniform Prin. and Income Act of Nat. Conf., 1991-97, Probate and Mental Health Task Force, Jud. Coun. Calif., 1996-2000. Vice pres. L.A. County Rep. Assembly, 1959-64; mem. L.A. County Rep. Ctrl. Com., 1960-64, 77-90, 2000—, exec. com., 1977-90; vice chmn. 17th Congl. Dist., 1960-62, 28th Congl. Dist., 1962-64; chmn. 46th Assy. Dist., 1962-64, 27th Senatorial Dist., 1977-85, 29th Senatorial Dist., 1985-90, sec. 53d Assembly Dist., 2000-; mem. Calif. Rep. State Ctrl. Com., 1966—, exec. com., 1966-67; pres. Calif. Rep. League, 1966-67; trustee Rep. Assocs., 1979-94, pres., 1983-85, chmn. bd. dirs., 1985-87. 2d lt. USAAF, WWII. Fellow Am. Coll. Trust and Estate Counsel; academician Internat. Acad. Estate and Trust Law (exec. coun. 1974-78); mem. ABA, L.A. County Bar Assn. (chmn. probate and trust law com. 1964-66, chmn. legis. com. 1980-86, chmn. program com. 1981-82, chmn. membership retention com. 1982-83, trustee 1983-85, dir. Bar Found., 1987-93, Arthur K. Marshall award probate and trust law sect. 1984, Shattuck-Price Meml. award 1990), South Bay Bar Assn., State Bar of Calif. (chmn. state bar jour. com. 1970-71, probate com. 1974-75; exec. com. estate planning trust and probate law sect. 1977-83, chmn. legis. com. 1977-89; co-chmn. 1991-92; probate law cons. group Calif. Bd. Legal Specialization 1977-88; chmn. conf. dels. resolutions com. 1987, exec. com. conf. dels. 1987-90), Lawyers Club L.A. (bd. govs. 1981-87, 1st v.p. 1982-83), Am. Legion (comdr. Allied post 1969-70), Legion Lex (bd. dirs. 1964-99, pres. 1969-71), Air Force Assn., Aircraft Owners and Pilots Assn., Town Hall (gov. 1970-78, pres. 1975), World Affairs Coun., Internat. Platform Assn., Breakfast Club (law, pres. 1989-90), Commonwealth Club, Chancery Club (pres. 1996-97), Rotary, Phi Beta Kappa (councilor Alpha Assn. 1983—, pres. 1996), Omicron Delta Kappa, Phi Alpha Delta (supreme justice 1972-74, elected to Disting. Svc. chpt. 1978), Sigma Nu. Presbyterian. Home: 600 John St Manhattan Beach CA 90266-5837 Office: Darling Hall & Rae LLP 520 S Grand Ave Fl 7 Los Angeles CA 90071-2645

RAEBER, JOHN ARTHUR, architect, construction consultant; b. St. Louis, Nov. 24, 1947; s. Arthur William and Marie (Laux) R. AA, Jefferson Coll., 1968; AB, Washington U., 1970, MArch, 1973. Registered architect, Calif., Mo.; cert. constrn. specifier; cert. Nat. Coun. Arch. Specification writer Hellmuth, Obata & Kassabaum, St. Louis, 1973-78, constrn. administr., 1978-79; mgr. of specifications Gensler & Assocs., San Francisco, 1979-82; ind. constrn. specifier San Francisco, 1982—. Adj. prof. architecture Calif. Coll. Arts and Crafts, San Francisco, 1986—; access code advisor Constrn. Industry & Owners, 1982—; spkr., instr. seminars orgns., univs., 1982—; mem. Calif. State Bldg. Standards Commn. Accessibility Adv. Panel, Sacramento, 1981, Calif. Subcom. Rights of Disabled Adv. Panel, Sacramento, 1993; cons. Nat. Inst. Bldg. Scis., 1996—. Author: CAL/ABL: Interpretative Manual to California's Access Barriers Laws, 1982; co-author: (with Peter S. Hopf) Access for the Handicapped, 1984; columnist Constrn. Specifier Mag., 1988-95. Vol. Calif. Office Emergency Svcs. Safety Assessment, Sacramento, 1991—. Fellow AIA (San Francisco chpt. codes com., Calif. coun. codes and standards com., nat. masterspec rev. com. 1982-84, nat. codes com. corr.), Contrns. Specifications Inst. (cert., columnist newsletter San Francisco chpt. 1984-95, Ben John Small award for Outstanding Stature as practicing specifications writer 1994, pres. St. Louis chpt. 1978-79, pres. San Francisco chpt. 1993-94, tech. com., edn. com., publs. com., Specifications Proficiency award San Francisco chpt. 1989, Tech. Commendation award 1987); mem. Specifications Cons. in Ind. Practice (nat. pres. 1990-92, nat. sec./treas. 1988-90), Internat. Conf. Bldg. Officials, Phi Theta Kappa. Avocations: history, anthropology, sci. fiction. Home and Office: 3962 26th St San Francisco CA 94131-2002

RAEBURN, ANDREW HARVEY, performing arts association executive, record producer; b. London, July 22, 1933; arrived in U.S., 1964, Can., 1993; s. Walter Augustus Leopold and Dora Adelaide Harvey (Williams) R. BA in History, King's Coll., Cambridge U., Eng., 1958, MA, 1962; diploma (hon.) in music performance, Mt. Royal Coll., Calgary, Can., 1998. Mus. dir. Argo Record Co., London, 1959-64; asst. to music dir., program editor Boston Symphony Orch., 1964-73; dir. artists and repertory New World Records,

N.Y.C., 1975-79; artistic adminstr. Detroit Symphony Orch., 1979-82; exec. dir. Van Cliburn Found. Inc., Ft. Worth, 1982-85; performing arts cons., 1985-93; exec. v.p. The Peter Pan Children's Fund, 1990-91; exec. dir. Esther Honens Internat. Piano Competition Found., 1993-95, pres., 1995-99, vice chmn., artistic dir., 1999-2001, pres., artistic dir., 2001—. Cons. music; radio and TV commentator; mem. faculty Boston U., 1966-67; condr. New World String Orch., 1978; v.p. World Fedn. Internat. Music Competitions, 2003-. Author record liner notes, Argo, RCA, Time-Life records, 1960-79, program notes, Boston Symphony Orch., 1968-73. Served with Royal Arty. Brit. Army, 1952-55; founding dean Prague Mozart Acad. 1992-93. Home: 702 235 Fifteenth Ave SW Calgary AB Canada T2R OP6 Office: 610 8th Ave SW Ste 600 Calgary AB Canada T2P 1G5 E-mail: raeburn@honens.com., araeburn@telus.net.

RAEBURN, JOHN HAY, English language educator; b. Indpls., July 18, 1941; s. Gordon Maurice and Katherine (Calwell) R.; m. Gillian Kimble, Aug. 18, 1963 (div. July 1979); children— Daniel Kennedy, Nicholas Kimble; m. Kathleen Kamerick, July 5, 1986. AB with honors, Ind. U., 1963; A.M., U. Pa., 1964, PhD, 1969. Asst. prof. U. Mich., Ann Arbor, 1967-74; vis. lectr. U. Iowa, Iowa City, 1974-75, assoc. prof., 1976-83, prof. English, 1983—; chmn. Am. Studies dept., 1983-85, 94-2000; chmn. English dept. U. Iowa, Iowa City, 1985-91; assoc. prof. U. Louisville, 1975-76. Author: Fame Became of Him: Hemingway as Public Writer, 1984; editor: (with others) Frank Capra: The Man and His Films, 1975 Mem. Am. Studies Assn., Orgn. Am. Historians. Democrat. Home: 321 Hutchinson Ave Iowa City IA 52246-2407 Office: U Iowa Dept Am Studies Dept English 701 Jefferson Building Iowa City IA 52242-1418 Office Phone: 319-335-0320. E-mail: john-raeburn@iowa.edu.

RAEDER, MYRNA SHARON, lawyer, educator; b. N.Y.C., Feb. 4, 1947; d. Samuel and Estelle (Auslander) R.; m. Terry Oliver Kelly, July 13, 1975; children: Thomas Oliver, Michael Lawrence. BA, Hunter Coll., 1968; JD, NYU, 1971; LLM, Georgetown U., 1975. Bar: N.Y. 1972, D.C. 1972, Calif. 1972. Spl. asst. U.S. atty. U.S. Atty's Office, Washington, 1972-73; asst. prof. U. San Fransisco Sch. Law, 1973-75; assoc. O'Melveny & Myers, L.A., 1975-79; assoc. prof. Southwestern U. Sch. Law., L.A., 1979-82, prof., 1983—, Irwin R. Buchalter prof. law, 1990, Paul E. Treusch prof. law, 2002; mem. faculty Nat. Judicial Coll., 1993—. Prettyman fellow Georgetown Law Ctr., Washington, 1971-73. Author: Federal Pretrial Practice, 3d edit., 2000; co-author: Evidence, State and Federal Rules in a Nutshell, 4th edit., 2003, Evidence, Cases, Materials and Problems, 2d edit., 1998. Recipient Ernestine Stahlhut award, Women Lawyers L.A., 2003. Fellow Am. Bar Found.; mem. ABA (trial evidence com. litigation sect. 1980—, criminal justice sect. 1994-97, vice-chair planning 1997-98, chair elect 1997-98, chair 1998-99, mem. mag. bd., 2000—, adv. to nat. conf. commrs. uniform state laws drafting com. uniform rules of evidence 1996-1999, Commn. Women in the Profession, Margaret Brent Women Lawyers of Achievement award 2002), Am. Law Inst., Assn. Am. Law Schs. (chair women in legal edn. sect. 1982, com. on sects. 1984-87, chair elect evidence sect. 1996, chair 1997), Nat. Assn. Women Lawyers (bd. dirs. 1991-98, pres.-elect 1993, pres. 1994-96), Women Lawyers Assn. L.A. (bd. dirs., coord. mothers support group 1987-96), Order of Coif, Phi Beta Kappa. Office: Southwestern U Sch Law 675 S Westmoreland Ave Los Angeles CA 90005-3905 Business E-Mail: mraeder@swlaw.edu.

RAEDER, WILLIAM MUNRO, publishing executive; b. Boston, Dec. 3, 1935; BA, Boston U., 1960, MA, 1964. Agent Nat. Life Ins. Co. Vt., 1965-69; exec. dir. Fund Urban Negro Devel., Boston, 1969-71; pres., mgr. Aquarius Theatre, Boston, 1971-72; bus. cons. Boston, 1972-75; pres. Nat. Braille Press, Boston, 1975—. Office: Nat Braille Press 88 Saint Stephen St Boston MA 02115-4302

RAEL, HENRY SYLVESTER, SR., retired health administrator, financial and management consultant; b. Pueblo, Colo., Oct. 2, 1928; s. Daniel and Grace (Abeyta) R.; m. Helen Warner Loring Brace, June 30, 1956 (dec. Aug. 1980); children: Henry Sylvester Jr., Loring Victoria, Thomas Warner Bush. AB, U. So. Colo., 1955; BA in Bus. Adminstrn., U. Denver, 1957, MBA, 1958. Sr. boys counselor Denver Juvenile Hall, 1955-58; adminstrv. asst. to pres. Stanley Aviation Corp., Denver, 1958-61; Titan III budget and fin. control supr. Martin Marietta Corp., Denver, 1961-65; mgmt. adv. services officer U. Colo. Med. Center, Denver, 1965-72; v.p. fin., treas. Loretto Heights Coll., Denver, 1972-73; dir. fin. and adminstrn. Colo. Found. for Med. Care, 1973-86. Instr. fin. mgmt., mem. fin. com. Assn. Profl. Standards Rev. orgn., 1980-85; speaker systems devel., design assns., univs., 1967-71. Mem. budget lay adv. com. Park Hill Elem. Sch., Denver, 1967-68, chmn., 1968-69; vol. worker Boy and Girl Scouts, 1967-73; bd. dirs. Community Arts Symphony, 1981-83, 85-87; controller St. John's Episcopal Cathedral, 1982-83; charter mem. Pueblo (Colo.) Coll. Young Democrats, 1954-55; block worker Republican Party, Denver, 1965-68, precinct committeeman, 1978-84; trustee Van Nattan Scholarship Fund, 1974-96; bd. dirs. Vis. Nurse Assn., 1977-84, treas., 1982-84. Served with USAF, 1947-53, res., 1954-61. Recipient Disting. Service award Denver Astron. Soc., 1968, Citation Chamberlin Obs., 1985; Stanley Aviation masters scholar, 1957; Ballard scholar, 1956. Mem.: Nat. Astronomers Assn. (exec. bd. 1965—97), Am. Assn. Founds. for Med. Care (fin. com. 1981—82), Denver Astron. Soc. (pres. 1965—66, bd. dirs. 1982—94), Colo. Pub. Employees Retirement Assn. (bd. dirs. 1993), Budget Execs. Inst. (sec. 1963—64, v.p. chpt. 1964—65), Hosp. Systems Mgmt. Soc., Assn. Systems. Mgmt. (pres. 1971—72), Whispering Pines of Denver Homeowners Assn. (pres. bd. dirs. 1998, dir.-at-large 2001), Brandy Chase Homeowners Assn. (bd. dirs. 1997), Delta Psi Omega, Epsilon Xi. Home: 7755 E Quincy Ave Apt 57 Denver CO 80237-2312

RAESSLER, KENNETH RAY, music educator; b. Highspire, Pa., Aug. 17, 1932; s. Rufus Ray and Grace Mary; m. Joyce Elaine Bond, Aug. 20, 1960; children: Laurie Elaine Raessler Denison, Todd Ray. BS, West Chester U., West Chester, PA, 1954; MM, Temple U., Philadelphia, PA, 1959; PhD, Mich. State U., East Lansing, MI, 1967. Music dir. Belvidere Sch. Dist., Belvidere, NJ, 1954—57; choral music dir. East Stoudsburg (Pa.) Area HS, 1957—61, Hatboro-Horsham H.S., Hatboro, Pa., 1962—63; assoc. prof. music Gettysburg Coll., Gettysburg, Pa., 1963—73; dir. music edn. Williamsport Area Sch. Dist., Williamsport, Pa., 1973—89; dir. sch. music Tex. Christian U., Fort Worth, Tex., 1989—2001, prof. music, 1989—2001. Cons. Wenger Corp., Owatonnia, Minn., 1991, Korg Corp., Los Angeles, Calif., 1991, Yamaha Corp., Grand Rapids, Mich., 1986—96. Author: (book) Aspiring to Excel; contbr. articles to profl. jours. Pres. Willismsport Rotary Club, Williamsport, Pa., 1985. Recipient Cmty. Svc. award, Williamsport Rotary Club, 1989, Disting. Alumni award, West Chester U./ West Chester, Pa., 2003. Mem.: Tex. Assn. of Music Schs. (pres.), Tex. Christian U. Faculty Senate (sec. 1996—98), Van Cliburn Found. (exec. bd. 1989—2002), Phi Mu Alpha Sinfonia (bd. trustees 1998—, v.p. 2000—04). Democrat. Christian. Avocations: golf, swimming. Home: 4900 Westridge Villa #14 Fort Worth TX 76116 E-mail: k.raessler@tcu.edu.

RAETZ, CHRISTIAN R. H. biochemistry educator; b. Berlin, Nov. 17, 1946; BS in Chemistry, Yale U., 1967; MD, Harvard U., 1973, PhD. House officer Peter Bent Brigham Hosp., Boston, 1973-74; research assoc. Nat. Inst. Gen. Med. Scis., USPHS, Bethesda, Md., 1974-76; asst. prof. biochemistry U. Wis.-Madison, 1976-79, assoc. prof., 1979-82, prof., dir. Ctr. for Membrane Biosynthesis Research, 1982—87; exec. dir biochemistry Merck Rsch. Lab., Rahway, NJ, 1987—91, v.p. basic rsch., biochemistry and mircobiology, 1992—93; prof. chmn. of biochemistry Duke Univ. Med. Ctr., Durham, NC, 1993—. Mem. biochemistry study sect. NIH Contbr. numerous articles to profl. jours. Mem. editorial bd. Jour. Biol. Chemistry Recipient James Tolbert Shipley Research prize Harvard U. Med. Sch., 1973, Harry and Evelyn Steenbock Career Advancement award, 1976, Research Career Devel. award NIH, 1978-83, Dreyfus Tchr.-Scholar award, 1979; H. I. Romnes Faculty fellow U. Wis., 1984; NIH grantee Mem. Am. Soc. Biol. Chemists, Japanese Soc. Promotion Sci., Phi Beta Kappa, Alpha Omega Alpha Office: Duke U Dept Biochemistry 225 Nanaline H Duke PO Box 3711 DUMC Durham NC 27710-0001 Home: 7411 Bill Poole Rd Rougemont NC 27572

RAEUCHLE, JOHN STEVEN, application developer; b. Washington, Sept. 21, 1955; s. Richard Frank and Ruth Darlene (Fulton) R. BS, Tex. Christian U., 1978. Programmer Tex. Christian U., Ft. Worth, 1976-78, Warrex Computer Sys., Ft. Worth, 1978-79; sys. programmer Tandy Data Processing, Ft. Worth, 1979 84; sr. programmer, analyst Commodity News Svcs., Leawood, Kans., 1984-86, Logica Data Archs., St. Louis, 1986-89; computer analyst Credit Sys., Inc., St. Louis, 1989-95; sr. software engr. Master Card Internat., St. Louis, 1995—. Mem. St. Louis Ambassadors, 1989—98; active Boy Scouts Am., 1964—95. Recipient awrd of merit Boy Scouts Am., Commrs. Key, 1982. Mem. St. Louis Jaycees Found. (treas. 1990-94, 2001—, sec. 1994-96, 99-2001, pres. 1996-99), U.S. Jr. C. of C. Senate Found., Mo. Jr. C. of C. Internat. Senate (treas. 1997-98, v.p. 1998-99, pres. 1999-2000, chmn. bd. 2000-01, comm. dir. 2004—), Mo. Jaycees (state officer 1989-94), Kansas City Jaycees (bd. dirs. 1985-87), Kansas City Jaycees Found., St. Louis Jr. C. of C. (pres. 1988-89). Democrat. Methodist. Avocations: camping, bowling, hiking. Home: 52 Country Creek Dr Saint Peters MO 63376-3041 Office: Master Card Internat 2200 Master Card Blvd O Fallon MO 63366 Office Phone: 636-722-2342.

RAFAJKO, ROBERT RICHARD, medical research company executive; b. Chgo., Sept. 3, 1931; s. Edward Michael and Mildred Eleanor (Simo) R.; m. Mary Ann Filipi, June 24, 1954 (div. 1979); children: Rorie Rae, Ronald Raymond, Robin Rene, Rod Richard, Rebecca Rae.; m. Anne Thorne Sloan, Jan. 26, 1982; 1 son, Andrew Sloan. BA, Coe Coll., 1953; MS, U. Iowa, 1958, PhD, 1960. Rsch. assoc. Merck Sharp and Dohme, West Point, Pa., 1960-61; rsch. scientist Microbiol. Assos., Bethesda, Md., 1961-66; v.p., gen. mgr. Med. Rsch. Cons., Rockville, Md., 1966-69; v.p. R & D, N.Am. Biols., Rockville, 1969-74; pres. Biofluids, Inc., Rockville, 1974-99, Bonheur Inc., Keswick, Va., 1999—. Pres. Tysan Serum, Inc., Rockville, 1974-2000, Kytaron Inc, Rockville, 1987-99; breeder thoroughbred horses, 1980—. Contbr. 23 articles to profl. jours. Chmn. PVAAU Swimming Program, Washington, Md. and Va., 1973-76; bd. dirs. Montgomery County Swim League, Montgomery County, Md., 1968-76. Served with USAF, 1954-55. Mem. AAAS, N.Y. Acad. Scis., Am. Soc. Microbiology, Tissue Culture Assn., Am. Horse Council, Horsemans Benevolent and Protective Assn. Republican. Presbyterian. Avocations: scuba diving, photography, collecting stamps, travel. Home and Office: 1349 Queenscroft Keswick VA 22947-2731 E-mail: bonheur421@aol.com.

RAFAL, KEITH W.L. physician; b. N.Y.C., June 15, 1955; s. Stanley and Joyce Rafal; m. Teriann S. Rafal, Dec. 27, 1981; children: Lauren E., Allison L. BA in Psychology, SUNY, Albany, 1977; MD, Howard U., 1982. Diplomate Am. Bd. Phys. Medicine and Rehab. Intern Faulkner Hosp., Boston, 1982-83; resident in phys. medicine and rehab. Boston U. Med. Ctr., 1983-85; fellow in geriatric medicine Brown U./Roger Williams Gen. Hosp., Providence, 1986-87; med. dir. Cushing Hosp., Framingham, Mass., 1987-89; chief physiatrist, dir. geriats. Fairlawn Rehab. Hosp., Worcester, Mass., 1989-93; chief physiatrist, med. dir. Wellmark Health Care, Wellesley, Mass., 1993-95; assoc. med. dir. New Eng. Rehab. at Home, Woburn, Mass., 1995-97; med. dir. rehab. Greenery Rehab. Ctr., Boston, 1995—; co-owner, co-founder Alternative Care & Healing Ctr., Franklin, Mass., 1996—; med. dir. fibromyalgia program Rehab. Hosp. R.I., North Smithfield, 1999—. Med. dir. Rehab. Hosp. R.I.; mem. clin. faculty, asst. prof. U. Mass. Med. Sch., Worcester, 1987—93; mem. clin. faculty, instr. Tufts Med. Sch., Boston, 1994—, Harvard U., 1997—98, Brown U., 2003—; pres., founder Healing Choices, P.C., 2001—. Fellow: Am. Acad. Pain Mgmt.; mem.: Am. Acad. Phys. and Med. Rehab., Nat. Ctr. Homeopathy. Avocations: playing the cello, nature walks, spending time with family. Office: Alternative Care and Healing Ctr 326 Union St Ste 2 Franklin MA 02038-2438

RAFALOFF, GARY B. financial company executive; b. Bklyn., Apr. 25, 1952; s. Ralph and Sara R.; m. Roberta Dianne Rafaloff, Aug. 4, 1974; children: Lauren, David, Chelsea. BS in Psychology, SUNY, Cortland, 1974; MS in Orgnl. Psychology, Stevens Inst. Tech., 1979. Sr. ptnr. Person.Paradigms, Inc., 1978-83; assoc. prof. Stevens Inst. Tech., Hoboken, N.J., 1979-83; pres. Rafaloff Assocs., N.Y.C., 1983-86; br. mgr. Advest Inc., N.Y.C., 1986-93; sr. v.p. Shearson Lehman, N.Y.C., 1993-94, Smith Barney Inc., N.Y.C., 1994-96; pres. RGR Fin. Corp., N.Y.C., 1996—. Founder, dir. GoCollect.com Corp., N.Y.C., 1999—. Avocations: various sports, collecting, coaching children's sports. Office: RGR Fin Corp 575 Lexington Ave Fl 7 New York NY 10022-6102

RAFEEDIE, EDWARD, senior federal judge; b. Orange, N.J., Jan. 6, 1929; s. Fred and Nabeeha (Hishmeh) R.; m. Ruth Alice Horton, Oct. 8, 1961; children: Fredrick Alexander, Jennifer Ann. BS in Law, U. So. Calif., 1957, JD, 1959; LLD (hon.), Pepperdine U., 1978. Bar: Calif. 1960. Pvt. practice, Santa Monica, Calif., 1960-69; mcpl. ct. judge Santa Monica Jud. Dist., 1969-71; judge Superior Ct. State of Calif., L.A., 1971-82; dist. judge U.S. Dist. Court (cen. dist.) Calif., L.A., 1982-96, sr. judge, 1996—. With U.S. Army, 1950-52, Korea. Office: US Dist Ct 312 N Spring St Ste 244P Los Angeles CA 90012-4704

RAFELSON, MAX EMANUEL, JR., biochemist, medical school administrator; b. Detroit, June 17, 1921; s. Max Emanuel and Lillian (Kay) R.; m. Trudy Diane Hellem, Mar. 31, 1973; children— Mark Thomas, Anne Elizabeth. BS, U. Mich., 1943; PhD, U. So. Cal., 1951. Postdoctoral rsch. fellow U. Stockholm, Sweden, 1951-52; asst. prof. biol. chemistry U. Ill. Coll. Medicine, Chgo., 1953-55, assoc. prof., 1955-60, prof., 1961-70; assoc. dean biol. and behavioral scis. Rush Med. Coll., Rush-Presbyn.-St. Luke's Med. Center, 1970-71, v.p. info. scis., 1971-77, v.p., 1972—; prof. biochemistry Rush Med. Coll., 1972-90, prof. and chmn. emeritus, 1990—. John W. and Helen H. Watzek meml. chmn. biochemistry Presbyn.-St. Lukes Hosp., Chgo., 1961-70; vis. prof. U. Paris, France, 1960, 77-78, U. Ulm, Fed. Republic Germany, 1986; assoc. mem. commn. influenza Dept. Def., 1961—. Author: Basic Biochemistry, 1965, 68, 71, 80, Concise Biochemistry, 1996; contbr. articles on biochemistry, blood platelets, viruses, protein structure, endothelial cells and metabolism to profl. publs. Served with USNR, 1943-46. Mem. Am. Soc. Biol. Chemists, Biochem. Soc. (London), Am. Chem. Soc., AAAS, Nat. Acad. Clin. Biochemistry, Société de Chemie Biologique, Sigma Xi. Home: 9015 Stoneland Dr San Antonio TX 78230-4576

RAFF, DANIEL MARTIN GORODETSKY, economist, economic and business historian, educator; b. Washington, Sept. 23, 1951; s. Morton Spencer and Miriam Susan (Gore) R.; m. Susan Claire Adelman, May 18, 1986; 1 child, Anna Amelia Gorodetsky. BA, New Coll., Sarasota, Fla., 1973; MPA, Princeton U., 1976; BPhil, Oxford U., 1978; PhD, MIT, 1987. Vis. lectr. econs. Brasenose Coll., Oxford, 1982; lectr. econs. Magdalen Coll., Oxford, 1983-85; rsch. assoc. Harvard U. Grad. Sch. Bus. Adminstrn., Cambridge, Mass., 1986-87, asst. prof. bus. adminstrn., 1987-93; assoc. prof. mgmt. The Wharton Sch., U. Pa., Phila., 1993—. Vis. assoc. prof. bus. adminstrn. Columbia U., N.Y.C., 1992-94, lectr. in law, 1994; faculty rsch. fellow Nat. Bur. Econ. Rsch., Cambridge, 1988—. Contbr. articles to profl. jours., chpts. to books. Mem.: Bus. History Conf., Econ. History Assn., Am. Econ. Assn., Cliometric Soc., Am. Hist. Soc. Office: U Pa Wharton Sch Dept Mgmt Philadelphia PA 19104-6370

RAFF, MARTIN JAY, internist, infectious diseases educator, lawyer; b. Bklyn., Mar. 20, 1937; s. Henry B. and Anne (Regunberg) R.; m. Marjorie A. Rosen (div. 1975); m. Patricia Jean Donnelly; children: Eric Howard, Lori Ellen, Stacy Alison, Jason Hart, Evan Jerome, Joshua Michael. BA, Brandeis U., 1958; MS, U. Vt., 1960; MD with honors, PhD, Med. Br. U. Tex., Galveston, 1965; JD, U. Louisville, 1988. Bar: Ky. 1988; lic. in medicine Tex., N.Y., Pa., Ky., Ind. Intern N.Y. Hosp.-Cornell U. Med. Ctr., N.Y.C., 1965-66, asst. physician, fellow in infectious diseases, 1966-67; asst. physician in medicine N.Y. Hosp., CUMC, Meml. Hosp. Cancer Allied Diseases, N.Y.C., 1969-71; chief sect. infectious diseases, from asst. to assoc. to prof. medicine U. Louisville, 1971—, dir., coordinator clin. diagnosis, 1971-76, assoc. dept. microbiology, 1971-76, mem. grad. faculty, 1974, from asst. to assoc. prof. microbiology, 1977—2002, assoc. chmn. dept. medicine (clin. service), 1979-80; dir. med. teaching program, staff physician, cons. Jewish Hosp., Louisville, 1983-87; clin. chief med. service, staff physician, cons. U. Louisville and Humana Hosp. U., Louisville, 1987—. Physician N.Y. State Narcotics Addiction Control Commn., 1969-71; staff physician Louisville Gen. Hosp., 1971-79, Louisville Meml. Hosp., 1975—; staff physician, cons. VA Med. Ctr., Louisville, 1971—; cons. Bapt. Hosp. Highlands, Humana Hosp. Surburban, Norton-Kosair-Children's Hosp., Sts. Mary and Elizabeth Hosp., St. Anthony Hosp., Clark County (Ind.) Meml. Hosp., Meml. Hosp. Floyd County (Ind.), 1972—, Merrell-Nat. Labs., 1973-81, Bapt. Hosp. East, Inst. Phys. Medicine Rehab. 1975—, Humana Hosp. Audubon, 1979—; chief clin. internal medicine U. Louisville Health Scis. Ctr. Author: infectious diseases sects. in various med. examination rev. books; contrb.various articles to profl. jours., 1968—. Advisor-cons. PRO-POWER, 1987-; mem. Met. Opera Guild, 1978-, City-County Bd. Health com. Swine Flu, 1976-77; sponsor Louisville Orch., 1977-; patron Louisville Ballet, 1979-, Ky. Opera Assn.; mem. Pres.'s Coun., 1982-; physician cons. Actor's Theatre Louisville, 1977-, Louisville Ballet, 1977-. Served with U.S. Army Med. Corps, 1967-69. NIH fellow, 1966-67. Fellow Am. Coll. Physicians, Infectious Diseases Soc. Am., Am. Coll. Chest Physicians, Am. Coll. Legal Medicine, Am. Soc. Legal Medcine, Am. Bd. Internal Medicine; mem. Internat. Soc. Chemotherapy, Internat. Soc. Aquatic Medicine, Inter-Am. Soc. Chemotherapy Inc., AAAS, AAUP, Nat. Found. Infectious Diseases, Ky. Bar.Assn., Ky. Med. Assn., Louisville Bar Assn., Jefferson County Med. Soc., Assn. Trial Lawyers Am. Avocations: japanese antiques, stamp collecting/philately, coin collecting/numismatics, opera, scuba diving. Home: 517 Ridgewood Rd Louisville KY 40207-1324 Office: U Louisville Sch Med Louisville KY 40292-0001 also: Univ Physicians Group 530 S Jackson St Louisville KY 40202 Personal E-mail: oisshasan@aol.com.

RAFFA, JEAN BENEDICT, author, educator; b. Lansing, Mich., Apr. 23, 1943; d. Ernest Raymond and Verna Lois (Borst) Benedict; m. Frederick Anthony Raffa, June 15, 1964; children: Juliette Louise, Matthew Benedict. BS, Fla. State U., 1964, MS, 1968; EdD, U. Fla., 1982. Tchr. Leon County Sch. Sys., Tallahassee, Fla., 1964-69; coord. children's programming WFTV, Orlando, Fla., 1978-80; cons. edn. Tchr. Edn. Ctr. U. Ctrl. Fla., Orlando, 1980-89; writer Orlando, Fla., 1989—; instr. Disney Inst., Orlando, Fla., 1996. Adj. instr. U. Cen. Fla., 1977-85; vis. asst. prof. Stetson U., DeLand, Fla., 1988-89; cons. Lang. Arts Curriculum Com. Orange County Sch. Sys., 1983; inst. The Jung Center, Winter Park, FL, 1997—. Author: Introduction to Television Litcracy, 1989, The Bridge to Wholeness: A Feminine Alternative to the Hero Myth, 1992, Dream Theatres of the Soul: Empowering the Feminine Through Jungian Dreamwork, 1994; contbr. articles to profl. jours., articles and meditations to religious jours. Mistress of ceremonies Young Authors' Conf., Orange and Volusia County Sch. Sys., 1984-85; cons. Young Authors' Conf. Orange and Seminole County Sch. Sys., 1985-89; judge Volusia County Pub. Schs. Poetry Contest, 1983, 84, Seminole County Pub. Schs. Lit. Mag., 1985-89; pres. Maitland (Fla.) Jr. H.S. PTA, 1986-87; pres., bd. dirs. Canterbury Retreat and Conf. Ctr. Episcopal Diocese Ctrl. Fla., 1988-90; chair edn. commn. Episcopal Ch. of the Good Shepherd, 1986-89; sr. warden Vestry of Episcopal Ch. of the Good Shepherd, 1988. Mem. Kappa Delta Pi, Phi Delta Kappa. Democrat. Avocations: antiques, horseback riding, travel, reading. Office: 17 S Osceola Ave Ste 200 Orlando FL 32801-2828 Office Phone: 407 648 5141.

RAFFAY, STEPHEN JOSEPH, manufacturing executive, director; b. McAdoo, Pa., Oct. 25, 1927; s. Stephen John and Stephanie (Severa) R.; m. Audree Eugenia Kuehne, Sept. 12, 1953; children: Andrea, Stephen, Leslie. BA, Columbia, 1950, MS, 1951. C.P.A., N.Y. Sr. accountant Arthur Andersen & Co., N.Y.C., 1951-56; asst. controller Emhart Corp., Farmington, Conn., 1956-61, asst. treas., 1961-63, treas., 1963-67, v.p. internat., 1967-72, v.p., group pres., 1972-79, exec. v.p., 1979-84, vice chmn., chief adminstrv. officer, 1984-87, dir., 1980-87; sr. v.p. Dexter Corp., Windsor Locks, Conn., 1987-90. Bd. dirs. United Plumbing Tech., Inc., Trust Co. Conn., Rossi Enterprises, Inc., EDAC Techs. Inc. Bd. dirs. Hartford Symphony Soc. With AUS, 1946-47. Mem. AICPA, Conn. Soc. CPAs. Home: 93 Westmont St West Hartford CT 06117-2929

RAFFEL, BURTON NATHAN, retired educator, poet, writer, translator; b. N.Y.C., 1928; married, six children. BA cum laude, Bklyn. Coll., 1948; MA, Ohio State U., 1949; JD, Yale U., 1958. Lawyer Milbank, Tweed, Hadley & McCloy, N.Y.C., 1958-60; editor Foundation News, 1960-63; instr. English SUNY, Stony Brook, 1964-65, asst. prof. of English, 1965-66, assoc. prof. English Buffalo, 1966-68; prof. English and Classics U. Tex., Austin, 1969-71; sr. tutor, dean Ont. Coll. Art, Toronto, Can., 1971-72; prof. English U. Denver, 1975-87; dir. Adirondack Mountain Found., 1987-89; Disting. prof. arts and humanitites, prof. English U. La., Lafayette, 1989—2003; assoc. prof. English U. Haifa, 1968—69. Lectr. English dept. Bklyn. Coll., 1950-51; instr. Ford Found. English Lang. Tchr. Tng. program in Indonesia, resident in Makassar, 1953-55; vis. prof. Humanities York U., Toronto, 1972-75, vis. prof. English Emory U., 1974; sr. editor, cons. McDonnell Douglas Computer-Based Systems Tng. Group, Denver, 1985-87; lectr. in law U. Denver, 1986-87. Author: The Development of Modern Indonesian Poetry, 1967, Mia Poems, 1968, The Forked Tongue: A Study of the Translation Process, 1971, Why Re-Create?, 1973, Four Humours, 1979, (film) The Legend of Alfred Packer, 1979, Robert Lowell, 1981, T.S. Eliot, 1982, Changing the Angle of the Sun-Dial, 1984, Grice, 1985, Evenly Distributed Rubble, 1985, Ezra Pound: The Prime Minister of Poetry, 1985, The Art of Translating Poetry, 1988, American Victorians: Exploration in Emotional History, 1984, Possum and Ole Ez in the Public Eye, 1985, After Such Ignorance, 1986, Man as a Social Animal, 1986, Artists All, 1986, Politicians, Poets, and Con Men, 1986, Founder's Fury, 1988, The Art of Translating Poetry, 1988, Founder's Fortune, 1989, From Stress to Stress: An Autobiography of English Prosody, 1992, The Art of Translating Prose, 1994, The Annotated Milton, 1999, Beethoven in Denver and Other Poems, 1999, The Annotated Hamlet, 2003, The Annotated Romeo and Juliet, 2004, numerous translations; mem. editl. bd. Oral Tradition, 1983—, Literature East and West, 1967-70; adv. editor The Lit. Rev., 1987-2003; reviewer/writer Asian Wall St. Jour., 1978-85; contbr. numerous articles to profl. publs. Mem. Bar of the State of N.Y., The Nat. Faculty. Home: 203 S Mannering Ave Lafayette LA 70508-4829 E-mail: bnraffel@cox-internet.com.

RAFFEL, JEFFREY ALLEN, urban affairs educator; b. Bklyn., June 19, 1945; s. George A. and Renee (Lane) R.; m. Joanne Ruth Traum, Aug. 27, 1966; children: Allison, Lori, Kenneth. AB, U. Rochester, 1966; PhD, MIT, 1972. Asst. prof. U. Del., Newark, Del., 1971—76, assoc. prof., 1976—82, dir. M Pub. Adminstrn. program, 1980—86, prof., 1982—, acting assoc. dean Coll. Urban Affairs and Pub. Policy, 1989, chair pub. mgmt. faculty, 1994—97, 1994—, dir. sch. urban affairs and pub. policy, 1997—, Charles P. Messick prof. pub. adminstrn., 2002—. Pub. svc. fellow, spl. asst. to gov. for intergovtl. rels. State of Del., 1979-80; chair urban ednl. policy group Nat. Assn. State Univs. and Land Grant Colls., 1987-93; mem. state supt.'s adv. com. on tchr. recruitment, Del., 1988-91. Author: Politics of School Desegregation, 1980, Historical Dictionary of School Segregation and Desegregation, 1998; co-author: Systematic Analysis of University Libraries, 1969, Selling Cities: Attracting Homebuyers Through Schools and Housing Programs, 1995; mem. editl. bd. Pub. Productivity Rev., N.Y.C., 1984—; contbr. articles to urban affairs publs. Treas. Nottingham Swim Club, Inc., Newark, 1985-88; co-chair Gov.'s Task Force on Enhancing Ednl. Dollar, 1986-87; chair long-range planning com. and membership com. Delmarva coun. Boy Scouts Am., 1988-89; mem. Gov.'s Sch. Reform Partnership, Del, 1990—. Recipient cert. of recognition, NCCJ Greater Wilmington, 1980, Cmty. Builder award, NCCJ, 2002, numerous profl. and civic awards. Mem. ACLU (Del. chpt. sec. 1992—), Del. Assn. Pub. Adminstrn. (pres. 1981-82), Am. Soc. Pub. Adminstrn., Am. Edn. Rsch. Assn. Avocations: golf, reading. Home: 4 High Pond Dr Newark DE 19711-2597 Office: U Del Sch Urban Affairs Pub Policy Newark DE 19716

RAFFEL, LEROY B. real estate development company executive; b. Zanesville, Ohio, Mar. 13, 1927; s. Jacob E. and Anne M. (Oliker) R.; m. Shirley Balbot, Sept. 11, 1949; children: Kenneth, Janet, James, Nancy. BS, U. Pa., 1949. Pres. Raffel Bros., Inc., Youngstown, Ohio, 1949-78, York Mahoning Co., Youngstown, 1950-64, Arby's, Inc., Youngstown, 1964-70, chmn. bd., 1971-79; pres. Brom Equity Devel., Inc., Miami, Fla., 1979—. Served with

USNR, 1945-46. Home: 2141 NE 190th Ter North Miami Beach FL 33179-4352 Office: Brom Equity Devel Inc Ste 207 1380 NE Miami Gardens Dr Miami FL 33179-4709 Office Phone: 305-949-6445.

RAFFELSON, MICHAEL, financial executive; s. Leo and Fay Rebecca Raffelson; m. Eileen Judith, Mar. 23, 1975; 1 dau., Elyse Lauren. BBA, CCNY, 1967; MBA, CUNY, 1969. Acct. Am. Metal Climax Inc., N.Y.C., 1967-69; fin. analyst Anaconda Co., N.Y.C., 1971-74; sr. fin. analyst corp. staff Internat. Paper Co., N.Y.C., 1975-76, bus. analyst white papers group, 1976-79, applications coord. paper and packaging mgmt. sys., 1979-81, mgr. mgmt. svcs. info. sys., 1981-85; mgr. ops. analysis and control info. svcs. The First Boston Corp., N.Y.C., 1986-87, mgr. telecom. analysis and control, 1987-88, asst. v.p., 1988; v.p. Chase Manhattan Bank, N.Y.C., 1988-2000, J.P. Morgan Chase and Co., N.Y.C., 2001—. Instr. fin. mgmt. edn. program Internat. Paper, 1977. Served with AUS, 1969-71. Mem. Phi Epsilon Pi (pres. chpt. 1966). Office: JP Morgan Chase and Co 575 Washington Blvd Jersey City NJ 10041

RAFFERTY, JAMES GERARD, lawyer; b. Boston, July 9, 1951; s. James John and Helen Christine (Kennedy) R.; m. Rhonda Beth Friedman, May 17, 1981; children: Jessica Faith, Evan Louis Quinn. BA, Brown U., 1974; MA, Princeton U., 1980; JD, Georgetown U., 1984. Bar: Md. 1985, D.C. 1985, U.S. Tax Ct. 1988, U.S. Ct. Appeals (4th cir.) 1989, U.S. Ct. Appeals (3d cir.) 1992. Assoc. Piper & Marbury, Washington, 1984-91, Pepper, Hamilton & Scheetz, Washington, 1991-92; founding ptnr. Harkins Cunningham, Washington, 1992—. Contbr. articles to legal jours. Brown U. Club of Boston scholar, 1969-70. Mem. ABA (chmn. com. on affiliated and related corps. tax sect. 1994-95). Roman Catholic. Avocation: golf. Office: Harkins Cunningham 801 Pennsylvania Ave NW Ste 600 Washington DC 20004-2664 E-mail: jrafferty@harkinscunningham.com.

RAFFIN, THOMAS A. physician; b. San Francisco, Jan. 25, 1947; s. Bennett L. and Carolyn M. Raffin; m. Michele Raffin, June 19, 1987; children: Elizabeth S., Ross Daniel, Jason Bennett, Nicholas Ethan. AB in Biol. Sci., Stanford Med. Sch., 1968, MD, 1973. Diplomate Am. Bd. Pulmonary Medicine, Am. Bd. Internal Medicine (also in Critical Care Medicine). Intern Peter Bent Brigham Hosp., 1973-75; fellow in respiratory medicine sch. medicine Stanford U., Stanford, Calif., 1975-78, med. fiberoptic bronchoscopy service dir. med. ctr., 1978—, acting asst. prof. sch. medicine, 1978-80, assoc. dir. med. ctr. intensive care units, med. dir. dept. respiratory therapy hosp., 1978—, assoc. prof. medicine sch. medicine, 1986-95, acting chief div. respiratory medicine, 1988—2004, chief divsn. pulmonary and critical care, 1990—2004, prof. medicine sch. of medicine, 1995—, Colleen and Robert Haas emeritus prof. medicine/biomed. ethics, 1999—; dir. emeritus Stanford U. Ctr. for Biomed. Ethics, 1989—; co-founder Rigel Pharms., Inc. Gen. ptnr. Telegraph Hill Ptnrs., 2002; bd. dirs. Apollo Biotechnology, New Link Genetics. Author: Intensive Care: Facing the Critical Choices, 1988; contbr. articles to profl. jours. V.p. lung cancer com., No. Calif. Oncology Group, 1983-85; com. mem. NIH Workshop, 1984. Recipient Henry J. Kaiser Found. award, 1981, 84, 88, 97, Arthur L. Bloomfield award, 1981. Fellow ACP (rep. coun. subsplty. socs. 1986), Am. Coll. Chest Physicians (program com. mem. 1985-86); mem. AAAS, Am. Fedn. for Clin. Rsch., Am. Thoracic Soc., Santa Clara County Lung Assn. and Med. Soc., Calif. Med. Assn. (chmn. sect. chest diseases 1984-85), Soc. for Critical Care Medicine, Calif. Thoracic Soc. Jewish. Avocations: painting, gardening. Home: 13468 Three Forks Ln Los Altos CA 94022-2432 Office: Stanford U Med Ctr Dept Medicine Div Pul & Crit Care Med # H3151 Stanford CA 94305 Office Phone: 415-765-6980.

RAFIQ, AZHAR, medical educator, researcher; b. Bonn, Germany, Apr. 9, 1956; arrived in U.S., 1967; s. Rafiq Khan and Muqaddas Begum; m. Ghazala Hashmi, June 16, 1990; children: Yasmin, Noor. BSc in Biology, City Coll. of N.Y., N.Y.C., 1977; MA in Neurobiology, Hunter Coll. of N.Y., N.Y.C., 1983; MD, St. George's U., Grenada, 1990; Exec. MBA, Va. Commonwealth U., Richmond, 2003. Rsch. asst., dept. microbiology and immunology Morehouse Coll. Medicine, Atlanta, 1990—91; rsch. asst. Va. Commonwealth U., Richmond, 1991—2001, asst. prof., dept. surgery, 2001—, chief scientific officer NASA Rsch. Partnership Ctr., 2003—. Contbr. chapters to books, articles to profl. jours. Fellow, NIH, 1991—94, 1994—2001; grantee, NASA, 2002—. Mem.: AAAS, Va. Acad. Sci., Am. Telemedicine Assn. Avocations: gardening, bicycling.

RAFI RASHID, MUJAHIDE ABDULLAH See TANKERSLEY, MICHAEL

RAFTER, TRACY, publishing executive; m. Michael Rafter; 1 child, Haley. With advt. sales mgr., Idaho; gen. mgr.; pub.; group pub. Taunton Daily Gazette and The Herald News, Fall River, Mass.; co-owner Valley Times, Milton-Freewater, Oreg., 1999—2002; sr. v.p. advt. and mktg. L.A. Newspaper Group, 2001—04; pub., CEO L.A. Daily News, 2004—. Office: LA Daily News 21221 Oxnard St POBox 4200 Woodland Hills CA 91365

RAFTNER, THOMAS, airport terminal executive; Dir. Atlantic City Internat. Airport, 1992—. Office: Atlantic City Internat Airport c/o South Jersey Transp Authority Civil Terminal Ste 106 Egg Harbor Township NJ 08234

RAFUSE, ETHAN SEPP, historian, educator; b. Washington, Sept. 13, 1968; s. Robert W. Rafuse, Jr. and Diane Nester Rafuse; m. Rachel Lee Rafuse, May 22, 1998; 1 child, Corinne Lee. BA in History, George Mason U., Fairfax, Va., 1991; MA in History, George Mason U., 1993; PhD in History and Polit. Sci., U. of Missouri-Kansas City, 1999. History and polit. sci. instr. Johnson County C.C., Overland Park, Kans., 1996—2001; lectr. U. of Mo.-Kansas City, 1997—2001; pk. ranger Manassas Nat. Battlefield Pk., Manassas, Va., 1998; asst. prof. of history U.S. Mil. Acad., West Point, NY, 2001—03; assoc. prof. of mil. history U.S. Army Command and Gen. Staff Coll., Ft. Leavenworth, Kans., 2004—; pk. ranger Harry S Truman Nat. Hist. Site, Independence, Mo., 1999—2001. Fellow West Point Summer Seminar on Mil. History, West Point, NY, 1999. Author: A Single Grand Victory: The First Campaign and Battle of Manassas; contbr.; author: Fitz John Porter, the Second Manassas Campaign, and the Problem of Command and Control in the 19th Century, George Gordon Meade and the War in the East; co-contributor Oxford Companion to United States Military History, The Civil War Battlefield Guide, co-editor The Ongoing Civil War: New Versions of Old Stories; contbr., articles to profl. jours. Mem.: Gen. Meade Soc. of Pa., Hist. Soc. of Pa., Va. Hist. Soc., Soc. of Civil War Historians, Soc. for Mil. History. Office: Cgsc/Csi Atzl-Swi 1 Reynolds Ave Fort Leavenworth KS 66027-1352

RAGALEVSKY, STANLEY VICTOR, lawyer; b. Everett, Mass., Aug. 31, 1948; s. Stanley G. Ragalevsky. AB, Boston Coll., 1970; JD, Harvard U., 1973. Bar: Mass. 1973, U.S. Dist. Ct. Mass. 1974, U.S. Ct. Appeals (1st cir.) 1979, U.S. Supreme Ct. 1981. Assoc. firm Warner & Stackpole, Boston, 1973-80, ptnr., 1981-99, Kirkpatrick & Lockhart, LLP, Boston, 1999—. Author: Asset Protection Strategies, 2002, Massachusetts Bank Lending Powers Handbook, 1999; contbr. articles to profl. jours. Home: 15 Fuller Farms Rd Topsfield MA 01983-1300 Office: Kirkpatrick & Lockhart LLP 75 State St Ste 6 Boston MA 02109-1807 Office Phone: 617-261-3100.

RAGAN, AMANDA, state senator; b. Sept. 1954; m. James Ragan; children: Edith, Charles. Mem. Iowa State Senate, DesMoines, 2002—, asst. minority leader, ranking mem. human resources com., mem. agr. com., mem. econ. growth com., mem. rules and adminstrn. com., mem. state govt. com. Diplomat Mason City C. of C.; active Mason City Sesquicentennial Com.; mem. Birth Defects Adv. Bd., HAWK-I Bd.; bd. dirs. Buena Vista U. Alumni Assn.; active North Iowa Girl Scout Coun.; exec. dir. Meals on Wheels, Mason City, Cmty. Kitchen North Iowa, Inc., Mason City; active Iowa Dem. Party State Ctrl. Com.; bd. dirs. Kinney Pioneer Mus. Named Diplomat of Yr., Mason City C. of C., 1998, 2001. Mem.: Mason City Sunrise Rotary (bd. dirs.). Office: State Capitol Bldg East 12th and Grand Des Moines IA 50319 Home: 20 Granite Ct Mason City IA 50401

RAGAN, CHARLES OLIVER, JR., lawyer; b. Knoxville, Tenn., Dec. 23, 1935; s. Charles Oliver and Jeanette (Butler) R.; m. Pauline Iona Kimsey, Apr. 19, 1958. BSBA, U. Tenn., 1958, JD, 1963. Bar: Tenn. 1964, U.S. Dist. Ct. (ea. dist.) Tenn. 1965; cert. consumer bankruptcy specialist. Staff atty. State of Tenn., Chattanooga, 1964-69; atty. Bean & Phillips, Chattanooga, 1969-73; sr. ptnr. Ragan & Schulman, Chattanooga, 1973-75, Ragan & Littleton, Chattanooga, 1975-80, Ragan & Wulforst, Chattanooga, 1980-84; pvt. practice Chattanooga, 1984—. Tenn. commnr. Nat. Conf. Commrs. on Uniform State Laws, 1976-80. Campaign treas. for Dem. candidates. Democrat. Methodist. Home: 185 Woodcliff Cir Signal Mountain TN 37377-3142 Office: PO Box 487 Signal Mountain TN 37377-0487

RAGAN, CHARLES RANSOM, lawyer; b. N.Y.C., Aug. 13, 1947; s. Charles Alexander Jr. and Josephine Forbes (Parker) R.; m. Barbara Thiel McMahon, Aug. 30, 1969; children: Alexandra Watson, Madeline McCue. AB, Princeton U., 1969; JD, Fordham U., 1974. Bar: N.Y. 1975, U.S. Ct. Appeals (3d cir.) 1975, Calif. 1976, U.S. Ct. Appeals (9th cir.) 1976, U.S. Dist. Ct. (no. dist.) Calif. 1976, U.S. Supreme Ct. 1981, U.S. Dist. Ct. (so. dist.) N.Y. 1982, U.S. Ct. Appeals (2d cir.) 1984. Law clk. to Hon. R.J. Aldisert U.S. Ct. Appeals (3rd cir.), 1974-76; assoc. Pillsbury, Madison & Sutro, San Francisco, 1976-81, ptnr., 1982-97, Palo Alto, 1997-2000, Pillsbury Winthrop, Palo Alto, San Francisco, 2001—. Mem. exec. com. 9th Cir. Judicial Conf., 1987-91. Avocations: biking, swimming, spectator sports. Office: Pillsbury Winthrop LLP 50 Fremont St San Francisco CA 94105

RAGAN, MARILYN KAY, performing arts educator, costume designer; b. Bartlesville, Okla., July 21, 1961; d. Virginia A. and Robert M. Johnson. Assoc. in Gen. Edn., Rose State Coll., Midwest City, Okla., 1988; BA in Speech/Theatre, Northeastern State U., Tahlequah, Okla., 1991; MFA Drama, U.Okla., Norman, 1998. Pub. affairs asst. USAFR, Okla. City, 1983—85; asst. libr. Cherokee Nation, Tsa-La-Gi Libr., Tahlequah, Okla., 1991—92; costume designer, stage mgr. Okla. Childrens Theatre, Oklahoma City, 1993—95; grad. tchg. asst., costume shop Universtiy of Okla., Norman, Okla., 1994—98; adminstrv. asst. Okla. State Dept. of Edn., Oklahoma City, 2000—02; asst. prof. of theatre Cameron U., Lawton, Okla., 2002—. Resident costume designer Cameron U., Lawton, Okla., 2002—; stage mgr. Okla. Summer Arts Inst., Lone Wolf, Quartz Mountain Resort, Okla., 2003; sch. of drama rep. U. of Okla. Student Senate, Norman, 1996—97; sec. Okla. State Dept. of Edn., Oklahoma City, 2001—02; bd. mem. Blue Moon Productions, Lawton, Okla., 2003—04; costume, make-up and props supr. Okla. Film Inst., 2004. Actor: (live theatre) Talk Radio, As Bees in Honey Drown, (film) Sirens Call Della; author: (short stories) Educated by a Caterpillar, 1988, (poetry, three album collection) The Sound of Poetry, (poetry) The Silence Within, (poetry, the poetry guild) Echoes of the Heart, Voices in the Heart, (poetry) My Unicorn Buddy and The Unicorn, 1987, The Colors of My Dream, 1988, The Meaning of Christmas, 2002, A Butterflies Dream, 2003, My Lovely Mountain Fairy, 2004, Once In a Misty Dream, 2004. Prudential youth leadership trainer Points of Light, Okla. State Dept. of Edn., Oklahoma City, 2001—03; senate mem., okla. collegiate legislators Rose State Coll., Midwest City, Okla., 1986—88; costume cons. Blue Moon Productions, Lawton, Okla., 2003—04. Airman 1st class USAFR, 1983—89, Tinker Air Force Base, 507th Tactical Fighter Group. Recipient Best Actress in a Supporting Role, Tahlequah Cmty. Theatre, Okla., 1990, Best Actress in a Cameo Role, 1991, Best Actress in a Leading Role, Tahlequah Cmty. Theatre, 1991, Award of Excellence for Costume Design & Make-up, Am. Coll. Theatre Festival Region IV, Rsch award for Seminole Light Horsemand and Clothing Worn in Indian Territory 1830 to Statehood, Cameron U.; fellow Am. Indian Grad. Fellowship, Am. Indian Grad. Assn., 1994-95; scholar Delware Tribal Scholarship Award, Del. Tribe of NW Okla., 1995-1996, Jr. Coll. Achievement Scholar, Northeastern State U., Okla., 1988-1990, Ray Heiniky Meml. Scholarship Award, 1989-1990, Mary Clarke Miley Scholarship Award, U. of Okla., 1997-1998. Mem.: Okla. Speech Theatre Commn. Assn., Southwest Theatre Assn., Costume Soc. Am., Davinci Inst. (assoc.), SW Theatre Assn. (assoc.), Alpha Psi Omega, Phi Theta Kappa. Baptist. Achievements include development of Paper Mask Construction. Avocations: painting, sewing, hiking, flute, pool. Office: Cameron Univ 2800 West Gore Blvd Lawton OK 73505 Office Phone: 580-581-2815. Personal E-mail: redstargazermkr@aol.com. E-mail: marilynr@cameron.edu.

RAGAN, ROBERT ALLISON, private investment executive, financial consultant; b. Gastonia, N.C., Aug. 21, 1938; s. Caldwell and Jocelyn (Sikes) R. BS in Bus. Adminstrn., U. N.C., 1961; postgrad., Stonier Grad. Sch. of Banking Rutgers U., 1968. V.p. N.C. Nat. Bank (now Bank of Am.), Charlotte, 1961-81; pres., treas. R.A. Ragan & Co., Inc., Charlotte, 1981—. Dir. Carolina Mills, Inc., Maiden, N.C., 1977—. Author, pub.: The Ragans of Gastonia (1790-1995), 1995, The Textile Heritage of Gaston County, N.C. (1848-2000), 2000. Founder, pres. bd. govs. The Gaston Soc. of Mecklenburg County, Charlotte, NC, 1999—; trustee, bd. visitors Darlington Sch., Rome, Ga., 1981—; mem. bd. visitors Daniel Stowe Bot. Gardens, Belmont, NC, 2001—; pres. bd. trustees Gaston County Mus. Art and History, Dallas, NC, 1978—81, 1997—99. Mem. Charlotte City Club, DeBordieu Colony Country Club (Georgetown, S.C.), Linville (N.C.) Ridge Country Club. Republican. Presbyn. Avocations: preservation and recording of local and North Carolina history, especially industrial history, travel. Home: 227 Fenton Pl Charlotte NC 28207-1913 Office: R A Ragan & Co PO Drawer 6158 Charlotte NC 28207-0001 also: 407 DeBordieu Blvd Georgetown SC 29440

RAGANS, ROSALIND DOROTHY, textbook author, retired art educator; b. Bklyn., Feb. 28, 1933; d. Sidney Guy Gordon and Beatrice (Zuckerman) Safier; m. John Franklin Ragans, July 31, 1965; 1 child, John Lee. BFA, CUNY-Hunter Coll., 1955; MEd, Ga. So. Coll., 1967; EdD, U. Ga., 1971. Cert. tchr. art, Ga. Tchr. art Union City (N.J.) Bd. Edn., 1956-62; tchr. 1st grade Chatham Bd. Edn., Savannah, Ga., 1962-64; instr. art Ga. So. U., Statesboro, 1964-69, asst. prof., 1969-76, assoc. prof., 1976-89, prof. emeritus, 1989—. Keynote speaker art edn. confs., Ind., 1987, 88, Ark., Wis., 1989, Md., 1990, others; presenter GA Art Edn. Conf., 1998, 2000, NAEA, 1999. Author: (textbooks) ArtTalk, 1988, 2d edit., 1994, 3d edit., 1999, Introducing Art, 1997, Exploring Art, 1990, 2d edit., 1997, Understanding Art, 1990, 2d edit., 1997, (sr. author) Art Connections K-5, 1997, 2d edit., 2000. Mem. Nat. Assn. Educators (life), Ga. Assn. Educators (life), Nat. Art Edn. Assn. (Southeastern Art Educator of Yr. 1991, Nat. Art Educator of Yr. 1992), Ga. Art Edn. Assn. (Ga. Art Educator of Yr. 1990), Pilot Club Internat. (Ga. dist., Ga. Profl. Handicapped Woman of Yr. 1988). Jewish. Avocation: painting.

RAGATZ, THOMAS GEORGE, lawyer; b. Madison, Wis., Feb. 18, 1934; s. Wilmer Leroy and Rosanna (Kindschi) Ragatz; m. Karen Christensen, Dec. 19, 1965; children: Thomas Rolf, William Leslie, Erik Douglas. BBA, U. Wis., 1957, LLB, 1961. CPA Wis.; bar: Wis. 1961, U.S. Dist. Ct. (ea. and we. dists.) Wis. 1961, U.S. Tax Ct. 1963, U.S. Ct. Appeals (7th cir.) 1965, U.S. Supreme Ct. 1968. Staff acct. Peat, Marwick, Mitchell & Co., Mpls., 1958; instr. Sch. Bus., U. Wis., Madison, 1958-60; formerly lectr. in acctg. and law Law Sch. U. Wis.; law clk. Wis. Supreme Ct., 1961-62; assoc. Boardman Suhr Curry & Field, Madison, 1962-64, ptnr., 1965-78, Foley & Lardner, Madison, 1978—, mng. ptnr., 1984-93, chmn. budget com., 1994-99. Dir. Sub-Zero Freezer Co., Inc., Mortenson, Matzell & Meldrem, Inc., Norman Bassett Found., Wis. Sports Found., United Way Found.; pres. Courtier Found.; dir., pres. Wis. Sports Devel. Corp.; lectr. seminars on tax subjects. Author: The Ragatz History, 1989; contbr. articles to profl. jours. Formerly dir. United Way, Meth. Hosp. Found; mem. U. Wis. Found.; chmn. site selection com. U. Wis. Hosp. Com.; past pres. 1st Congl. Ch. Found.; bd. dirs. Found. for Madison Pub. Schs.; pres. Bus. and Edn. Partnership, 1983—89, bd. dirs.; past pres. First Congl. Ch. Found.; chmn. site selection com. U. Wis. Hosp.; bd. regents U. Wis., panel provision of legal svcs.; bd. dirs. Met. YMCA, Madison, 1983—90, YMCA Found., Norman Bassett Found., Courtier Found.; pres. Bus. & Edn. Partnership, 1983—89. Fellow: Am. Bar Found.; mem.: ABA, Dane County Bar Assn. (pres. 1978—79, chmn. jud. qualification com., sec.), Wis. Inst. CPA, State Bar Wis. (sec. 1969—70, bd. govs. 1971—75, chmn. fin. com. 1975—80, chmn. tax sect., chmn. spl. com. on econs., chmn. svcs. for lawyers com.), Wis. Bar Found., Seventh Cir. Bar Assn., Am. Judicature Soc., Order of Constantine, Bascom Hill Soc., Order of Coif, Madison Club (pres. 1980—81), Madison Club House Corp. (pres. 1999—, bd. dirs.), Sigma Chi, Beta Gamma Sigma. Republican. Home: 3334 Lake Mendota Dr Madison WI 53705-1469 Office: Foley & Lardner PO Box 1497 Madison WI 53701-1497 also: Foley & Lardner 1st Wisconsin Ctr 777 E Wisconsin Ave Ste 3800 Milwaukee WI 53202-5302

RAGAVAN, ANPALAKI JEYABALASINKHAM, software developer, researcher; arrived in U.S., 1992; d. George Nagularajah and Thangaranee Veluppillai Jeyabalasingham; m. Ragavan Vinasithamby, July 1, 1993. BS(hon.), U. Sri Lanka, 1985, MPhil (hon.), 1989; MS (hon.), U. Nev., 1996, MS in Environ. Engring., student, U. Nev., 2003—. Cert. BASIC computer programmer, geographic info. sys., Visual Basic programmer, GIS and web design, well drilling with LS 100. Asst. prof. U. Sri Lanka, Kilinochchi, 1989—92; rsch. asst. Ind. State U., Tere Haute, 1992—93; software developer Bur. Labor Stats., Washington, 1996—99; rsch. asst. U. of Nev., Reno, 1999—. Grad. fellow U. Nev., Reno, 1993—96; presenter in field. Contbr. articles to profl. jours. (Excellence in Abstract Submission award Am. Jour. Pub. Health, 2001); author: (book) Introductory Statistics, Lab-Guide - SAS, 1st edition., 1993, (Nev. health divsn. quar. report) Impact Of Discharge Planning On Adherence to Treatment for Inmates with HIV/AIDS in Nevada, 2001, Surveillance Update: Discharge Planning For Inmates with HIV/AIDS in Nevada, 2002. Recipient Excellence in Abstract Submission, APHA, HIV/AIDS Sect., 2001, Cert. Of Appreciation, Nev. State Mental Health and Devel. Services, 2000, Overseas Devel. Adminstrn. scholarship, Govt. Of UK, 1986—89; grantee, State of Nev., 2002; scholar, Asian Inst. Of Tech. in Thailand, 1991, Ind. State U., 1992—93, U. of Nev., Reno, 1993—, Soroptimist Internat. of Reno, Sierra Nev. Region, 2000. Mem.: Am. Statis. Assn., Geol. Soc. Am., Alumni Assn. U. Nev. Mem. Lds Ch. Avocations: dance, music, guitar, swimming, sports. Office: U Nev Dept Internal Med Reno NV 89512 Home: 3950 Clear Acre LN #276 Reno NV 89512-1202 Personal E-mail: ragavan@unr.edu. Business E-Mail: ragavan@unr.edu.

RAGGI, REENA, circuit judge; b. Jersey City, May 11, 1951; BA, Wellesley Coll., 1973; JD, Harvard U., 1976. Bar: N.Y. 1977, U.S. Dist. Ct. (ea. dist.) N.Y. 1987, U.S. Ct. Appeals (2d cir.) 2002. U.S. atty. Dept. Justice, Bklyn., 1986; ptnr. Windels, Marx, Davies & Ives, N.Y.C., 1987; judge U.S. Dist. Ct. (Ea. dist.) N.Y., 2002, U.S. Ct. Appeals (2nd Cir.), N.Y.C., 2002—. Office: US Courthouse 225 Cadman Plz E Brooklyn NY 11201

RAGGIO, LOUISE BALLERSTEDT, lawyer; b. Austin, Tex., June 15, 1919; d. Louis F. and Hilma (Lindgren) Ballerstedt; m. Grier H. Raggio, Apr. 19, 1941; children: Grier, Thomas, Kenneth. BA, U. Tex., 1939; student, Am. U. Washington, 1939-40; JD, So. Methodist U., 1952. Bar: Tex. 1952, U.S. Dist. Ct. (no. dist.) Tex. 1958. Intern Nat. Inst. Pub. Affairs, Washington, 1939-40; asst. dist. atty. Dallas County, Tex., 1954-56; shareholder Raggio and Raggio, 1956—. Sec. Gov.'s Commn. on Status of Women, 1970-71; trustee Tex. Bar Found., 1982-86, chmn., 1984-85, chmn. fellows, 1993—, Dallas Women's Found., 1993—, Nat. Conf. Bar Founds., 1986-92. Recipient Zonta award, Bus. and Profl. Women's Club award, So. Meth. U. Alumni award, Woman of Yr. award Tex. Fedn. Bus. and Profl. Women's Clubs, 1985, award Internat. Women's Forum, 1990, Disting. Law Alumni award So. Meth. U., 1992, Disting. Trial Lawyer award, 1993, Outstanding Trial Lawyer award Dallas Bar Assn., 1993, Pacemaker award Nat. Bus. Women Owners Assn., 1994, Thomas Jefferson award ACLU, 1994, Courage award Women Journalists North Tex., 1995, Tex. Lawyer award 1999, Entrepreneur award Fortune Sm. Bus. Mag., 2000, Gillian award 2000, Professionalism award Dallas (Tex.) Bar, 2003; named to Tex. Women's Hall of Fame, 1985; named one of Heroes of Sm. Bus., Fortune Sm. Bus. Mag., 2000. Fellow Am. Bar Found.; mem. ABA (chmn. family sect. 1975-76, Best Woman Lawyer award 1995, Lifetime Achievement award 2002), LWV (pres. Austin 1945-46), State Bar Tex. (chmn. family law sect. 1965-67, dir. 1979-82, citation for law reform 1967, Pres.'s award 1987, Sarah T. Hughes award 1993, named one of 100 Tex. Lawyers of Century, 1999, 50 Yr. Lawyer award 2003), Dallas Bar Found. (pres. fellow com. 1991), Am. Acad. Matrimonial Lawyers (gov. 1973-81, trustee found. 1992—), Bus. and Profl. Women's Club (pres. Town North 1958-59), Phi Beta Kappa (pres. Dallas chpt. 1970-71, 90-92). Unitarian Universalist. Home: 3561 Colgate Ave Dallas TX 75225-5010 Office: Raggio and Raggio 3316 Oak Grove Ave Ste 100 Dallas TX 75204-2338 Office Phone: 214-880-7500. E-mail: louise@raggiolaw.com. *All things are possible in our expanding universe if we can tune in to the infinite power available to all of us. Our ancestors concentrated on the problems— let us be a part of the solutions so desperately needed in our complex and troubled world.*

RAGGIO, WILLIAM JOHN, state legislator; b. Reno, Oct. 30, 1926; s. William John and Clara M. (Cardelli) R.; m. Dorothy Brigman, August 15, 1948 (dec. Apr. 1998); children: Leslie Ann, Tracy Lynn, Mark William. Student, La. Poly. Inst., 1944-45, U. Okla., 1945-46; BA, U. Nev., 1948; JD, U. Calif. at Hastings, 1951. Bar: Nev. 1951, U.S. Supreme Ct. 1959. Atty., Reno and Las Vegas; asst. dist. atty. Washoe County, Nev., 1952-58; dist. atty., 1958-71; ptnr. firm Wiener, Goldwater, Galatz & Raggio, Ltd., 1971-72, Raggio, Walker & Wooster, Reno and Las Vegas, 1974-78, Raggio, Wooster & Lindell, 1978-92; sr. ptnr. Vargas & Bartlett, 1992-98; then Jones-Vargas (formerly Vargas & Bartlett), 1998—; mem. Nev. Senate, Washoe Dist. 3, Carson City, 1973—. Mem. Nev. Senate, 1973—, minority floor leader, 1977-81, 82-87, 91, majority flr. leader, 1987—; mem. legis. commn., vice chmn. criminal law and adminstrn. council State Govts., 1972-75; v.p., dir. Archon Corp. Mem. Nev. Am. Revolutionary Bicentennial Commn., 1975-81; mem. Republican State Cen. Com.; past nat. chmn., current dir. Am. Legislative Exchange Council, dir. Sierra Health Svcs.; republican candidate for U.S. Senate, 1970. Served with USNR, 1944-46; to 2d lt. USMCR, 1946-47. Named Young Man of Yr., Reno-Sparks Jr. C. of C., 1959, Alumnus of Yr. U. Nev. Reno, 2000, Civic Leader of Yr Greater Reno C. of C., Disting. Eagle Scout, 1989; named to Jr. Achievement of Nev. Hall of Fame, 1999, Reg. Trans. Commn. Hall of Fame; recipient Disting. Nevadan award, 1968, Fellows award The Salvation Army, Torch of Liberty award The Anti-Defamation League, SIR award Assoc. Gen. Contractors, 1995, Outstanding Svc. award Airport Authority of Washor County, Pres.'s medal UNLV, 2000. Fellow Am. Bd. Criminal Lawyers; mem. ABA (state chmn. jr. bar conf. 1957-60, ho. dels.) Am. Judicature Soc., Am. Coll. Trail Lawyers, Am. Bd. Trial Advocates, Am. Inns of Ct., Navy League, Air Force Assn., Nat. (nat. pres. 1967-68; named Outstanding Prosecutor 1965), Nev. State (sec. 1959, pres. 1960-63) Dist. Attys. Assn., NCJ (Brotherhood award 1965), Nev. Peace Officers Assn., Internat. Assn. Chiefs Police, Am. Leg. Exch. Coun. (nat. chmn. 1991-92), Coll. of Edn. U. Nev. (life), Am. Legion, Elks, Lion Club, Prospectors Club, Alpha Tau Omega, Phi Alpha Delta. Republican. Roman Catholic. Home: PO Box 281 Reno NV 89504-0281

RAGHAVAN, ASURI, business executive; BSEE, U. Madras; MS in Computer Sci., Temple U. Sr. v.p., pres. equipment divsn. Kulicke & Soffa, until 1998; pres., CEO Gasonics, San Jose, Calif., 1998—. Office: Gasonics Intl 2730 Junction Ave San Jose CA 95134-1909

RAGHAVAN, DEREK, oncologist, medical researcher and educator; b., Aug. 11, 1949; came to U.S., 1991; m. Patricia Harrison; 2 children. MB, BS with honors, Sydney U., 1974; PhD, London U., 1984. Cert. Royal Australian Coll. Physicians, Fgn. Lic. Exam Coun., Ednl. Coun. Fgn. Med. Grads., Gen. Med. Coun. (U.K.), NSW Med. Bd. (Australia). Resident, registrar Royal Prince Alfred Hosp., Sydney, 1974-77; lectr., sr. registrar Royal Marsden Hosp., London, 1978-80; rsch. fellow Ludwig Inst. Cancer Rsch., London, 1978-80; med. rsch. specialist U. Minn., Mpls., 1980-81; sr. specialist med. oncology Royal Prince Alfred Hosp., Sydney, 1981-91; prof., chief solid tumor oncology and investigational therapeutics Roswell Park Cancer Inst. and SUNY, Buffalo, 1991-97; prof. medicine and urology U. So. Calif., L.A., 1997—2003, chief divsn. med. oncology, 1997—2003, assoc. dir. Norris Cancer Ctr., 1997—2004; prof., dir. Cleve. Clinic Taussig Cancer Ctr., 2004—. Pres. med. staff Roswell Park Cancer Inst., Buffalo, 1995—96; chair VA Merit Rev. Bd. in Oncology, 1996—97; mem. oncology drug adv. com. FDA, 1996—2000; chair cancer clin. investigations review com. Nat. Cancer Inst., 1996—97, mem. cancer ctrs. support rev. com., 2000—; prof. medicine SUNY, Buffalo, 1991—97, prof. urology, 1996—97; assoc. dir. U. So. Calif.-Norris Cancer Ctr. U. So. Calif., 1997—2003; mem. VA Merit Rev. Bd. for Prostate Cancer, 1998, NIH Support Cancer Ctr. Rev. Com., 2000—04;

mem. scientific adv. bd. Southwest Oncology Group, 1998—, bd. govs., 1998—, vice chair genitournaiy com., 1998; vice chair genitouring cancer com. Radiation Therapy Oncology Group, 1995—97; mem. sci. adv. com. European Orgn. for Rsch. and Treatment of Cancer, 2000—, mem. external sci. audit com., 2001—; mem. external adv bd. Comprehensive Cancer Ctr. U. Ala., Birmingham, 2002—; mem. external adv. bd. Ohio State U. James Comprehensive Cancer Ctr., 2002—; mem. clin. trials and awards adv. com. Cancer Rsch. UK, 2002—; mem. clin. trials and awards com. Cancer Rsch. U.K., 2002—. Editor: The Management of Bladder Cancer, 1988, Textbook of Uncommon Cancer, 1988, 2d edit. 1999, Principles and Practice of Genitourinary Oncology, 1997, ACS Atlas of Clinical Oncology-Germ Cell Tumors, 2002; assoc. editor Urologic Oncology, 1995—, Clin. Cancer Rsch., 1996—; mem. editl. bd. Jour. Clin. Oncology, 1990-94, European Jour. Cancer, The Prostate, The Breast, Prostate Cancer, Advances in Oncology, Abstracts in Hematology and Oncology, 1998-2000; mem. editl. bd. Oncology; bd. cons. Jour. Urology, 1996—; contbr. numerous articles to profl. jours. Rsch. grantee Nat. Health and Med. Rsch. Coun., Australia, 1983-90; traveling fellow NSW Cancer Coun., Sydney, 1978; named Hospice Physician of Yr., Hospice of Buffalo, 1994. Fellow: ACP (MKSAP XI com. 1997—98, sci. program com. 2000), Royal Australian Coll. Physicians (chair specialist adv. com. in med. oncology 1988—90); mem.: Sydney U. Med. Soc. (pres. 1974), Med. Oncology Group Australia (chmn. 1988—90), Soc. Urologic Oncology, Am. Assn. Cancer Rsch., Am. Soc. Clin. Oncology (liaison Am. joint com. on cancer 1995—2000, AJCC liaison 1995—2000, chair cancer comms. com. 1998—2000, 1998—2000, program com. 1999—2000, mem. pub. issues com. 2000—02, assoc. editor People Living With Cncer Website). Avocations: tennis, squash. Office: Cleve Clinic Taussig Cancer Ctr Euclid Ave Cleveland OH 44195

RAGHAVAN, HARSHA, investment company executive; b. Madras, India, Oct. 10, 1971; s. Ramabadran and Kamala Raghavan; m. Sulakshana Srinivasan, Apr. 7, 1975. MBA, Stanford U., 2004; degree in computer sci., U. Calif., Berkeley, 1994. Sr. assoc. JP Morgan Ptnrs., Bombay, 1996—99; pres., CEO Stario, Inc., Santa Clara, Calif., 1999—. May Ree Clark fellow, Stanford U., 2002—04. Office: Stario Inc 3350 Scott Blvd Santa Clara CA 95054

RAGINSKY, NINA, artist; b. Montreal, Apr. 14, 1941; d. Bernard Boris and Helen Theresa R.; 1 child, Sofya Katrina. BA, Rutgers U., 1962; studied painting with, Roy Lichtenstein; studied sculpture with, George Segal; studied Art History with Allan Kaprow, Rutgers U. Freelance photographer Nat. Film Bd., Ottawa, Ont., Can., 1963-81; instr. metaphysics Emily Car Coll. Art, Vancouver, B.C., Can., 1973-81; painter Salt Spring Island, B.C., 1989—. Sr. artist, jury Can. Coun.; selected Can. rep. in Sweden for Sweden Now Mag., 1979; tchr., lectr. in field, 1973—. One woman shows include Vancouver Art Gallery, Victoria Art Gallery, Edmonton Art Gallery, Art Gallery Ont., San Francisco Mus. Art, Acadia U., Nancy Hoffman Gallery, N.Y.C., Meml. U. Newfoundland Art Gallery; exhibited in group shows at Rutgers U., 1962, Montreal Mus. Fine Arts, 1963, Nat. Film Bd., Ottawa, 1964, 65, 67, 70, 71, 76, 77, Internat. Salon Photography, Bordeaux, France, 1968, Nat. Gallery Ottawa, 1968, Eastman House, Rochester, N.Y., 1969, Vancouver Art Gallery, 1973, 80, Mural for Conf. Ctr. Ottawa, 1973, Field Mus., Chgo., 1976, Edmonton Art Gallery, 1978, 79, Walter Philips Gallery, 1979, Glenbow Mus. Gallery, 1979, Harbour Front Community Gallery, 1980, Hamilton Art Gallery, 1980, Musée Maisil de St. Lambert, 1981, Mendel Art Gallery, 1981, Dunlop Art Gallery, Regina, Can., 1981, Vancouver Art Gallery, 2001; represented in permanent collections Nat. Film Bd. Stills divsn., Ottawa, Ont., Banff (Alta.) Sch. Fine Arts, Nat Gallery Ottawa, Can., George Eastman House, Rochester, NY, Wadsworth Atheneum, Conn., Edmonton Art Gallery, U. Victoria, B.C., various pvt. collections. Bd. dirs. Island Watch, Salt Spring Island, B.C., 1993; founder, coord. Salt Spring Island Ecosys. Stewardship Project, 1993; founder, coord. Salt Spring Island Waterbird Watch Collective, 1994—. Decorated officer Order of Can., 1984; recipient Kees Vermeer award for edn. and conservation Simon Fraser U., 1997. Mem.: Royal Can. Acad. Arts. Avocations: gardening, birding, subject of numerous publs. Home and Office: 272 Beddis Rd Salt Spring Island BC Canada V8K 2J1 Office Phone: 250-537-4515.

RAGLAND, BOB, artist, educator; b. Cleve., Dec. 11, 1938; s. Carey and Violet (English) R. Cert. Completion, Rocky Mount Sch. Art, Denver, 1968. Instr. painting and drawing Denver Pub. Libr., 1969-71, Eastside Action Ctr., Denver, 1969-71; artist-in-residence Model Cities Cultural Arts Ctr. Workshop, 1971-73; artist/tchr. KRMA-TV. Lectr. in field; vis. artist Denver Pub. Sch. for the Arts, 1993-96, Urban Peak Homeless Ctr., Denver, 1996; founding faculty mem. Auraria campus C.C. Denver, 1970-72; lectr. Afro-Am. art of the 60's and 70's; visual arts coord. City Spirit Project, Denver, 1978; instr. Gove Cmty. Sch., 1979-95, Met. State Coll., Denver, Arapahoe C.C., Littleton, Colo.; artist-in-residence Fred N. Thomas Career Edn. Ctr., Denver Pub. Schs., 1997—, Denver Athletic Club, summer 2000; vis. artist Summer Scholars Program, Denver, 1998; founder Non-Starving Artist's Project, Denver, 1996, City Pk. Art Festival, Denver, 2003, Summer Scholars, 2002, Art Students League, 2003; art career coach 1980—; advisor Foothills Art Ctr., 1998; art career coach, 1980—. Exhibited in 16th Ann. Drawing Exhbn., Dallas Mus. Fine Art Traveling Exhbn., 1967, Tubman Gallery, Boston, 1981; one man shows at Cleve. State U., 1968, Denver Nat. Bank, 1980-81, Century Bank Cherry Creek, Denver, 1980-81; works in permanet collections at Denver Pub. Libr., Karamu House, Cleve., Irving St. Ctr. Cultural Arts Program, Denver; group exhbns. include Colo. History Mus., 1993, 94, 95, Savageau Art Gallery, 1995-96, Met. State Coll. Visual Arts Ctr., 1993, The Triumph of the Human Spirit Foothills Art Ctr., Golden, Colo., 1997, 1st Plymouth Congl. Ch., 2000; author: The Artists Survival Handbook or What to do till You're Rich and Famous, 1980; pub.: Colo. Gallery Guide, 1978—; contbr. Black Umbrella/Black Artists Denver. Chmn. Arts and Humanities Com., 1968-69. Inducted in Colo. 100, Denver Post, Colo. Hist. Soc., 1993; recipient Excellence in Arts award Denver Black Arts Festival, 1993, Recognition award KCNC-TV and Denver Ctr. Performing Arts, 1986. Mem. Colo. Black Umbrella. Home: 1723 E 25th Ave Denver CO 80205-5505

RAGLAND, JACK WHITNEY, artist; b El Monte, Calif., Feb. 25, 1938; s. Jack Rider and Dorsey (Whitney) R.; m. Marilee J. Weaver, July 31, 1969; children— Roxanne, Natasha. BA, Ariz. State U., 1960, MA, 1964; postgrad., UCLA, 1961-64. Grad. asst. tchr. Ariz. State U., 1960-61; grad. teaching asst. UCLA, 1961-64; head art dept. Simpson Coll., Indianola, Iowa, 1964-76. Demonstrator Nat. Art Materials Trade Assn., Denver, 1993, Pasadena Conv. Ctr., 1994 One-man shows include Kleine Gallery, Vienna, Austria, Simpson Coll., Internat. Art Svc., Pan Paciific Hotel, San Diego, Lakes Art Center, Okaboji, Iowa, Hilltop Ctr., Fallbrook, 1996-98, Desert Art Source Gallery, 1999-2002; exhibited in group shows, Lyn Kottler Gallery, N.Y.C., Phoenix Art Mus., Tucson Festival Art, Talisman Gallery, Bartlesville, Okla., Exhibiting Artists Fedn., Poultney, Vt., Des Moines Art Center, Joslyn Mus. Art, Omaha, Lagerquist Gallery, Atlanta, Desert Art Source Gallery, Palm Desert, Calif., Desert Pleine Air Show, La Quinta, Calif., San Diego, NAMTA Art Show, San Francisco, 1995, Christian Art Show Jubilee 2000, 04, Fall Brook, Calif., Pleine Air San Diego/Calif. Art Club, La Quinta Festival, 2000, Eagle Gallery, La Jolla, Galerie Internat., Solana Beach, Calif., Encouragment Gallery, Fallbrook, Calif., Show Case Houses, Pasadena, Rancho Santa Fe, Calif., 1995, 96, Palm Springs Paradise, 2000, San Diego, 97, 98, 99; represented in permanent collections, Albertina Museum, Vienna, Kunstmus., Basel, Switzerland, Bibliothèque National, Paris, Los Angeles County Mus., Simpson Coll., Phoenix Art Mus., Ariz. State collection, Graphische Bundes Versuchsanstalt, Vienna, Austria, also pvt. collections, works include stained glass windows, Meth. Ch., Perry, Iowa.; works reproduced Applause mag, 1971, New Woman mag, 1974, Artists of Cen. and No. Calif., Vol. II, San Diego Better Homes and Gardens Lifestyles mag., 1995, San Diego Decorating mag., 1995, 98, Pasadena Showcase House Design Mag., 1995, San Diego Decor and Style, 1996, 97, 98, Sci. of Mind Mag., 1997, Desert Art Scene Mag., 1999-2003; poster artist Vintage Car Show, Fallbrook, 2003. Recipient grand purchase prize Ariz. Ann. Art Show, 1961, 1st prize in prints Iowa State Fair, 1974, 1st prize So. Calif. Expn., Del Mar, 1984, 1st prize Fall Brook Art Assn., 2000, Best of Show, 2003, others; featured in Am. Artist mag. Oct. 1993. Mem. Calif. Art Club. Home: 5555 8th St Fallbrook CA 92028-9619 Office Phone: 760-728-9503. E-mail: jwragland@aol.com. *To capture the spiritual essence of a subject through form and color is the goal of my art.*

RAGLAND, KATHRYN MARIE, dancer, educator; b. Lakewood, Ohio, Nov. 22, 1948; d. Earl Albert and Alice Maxine (Outzs) R.; m. Donald Glen Rubright, Sept. 1, 1973 (div. 1977); m. Jack Victor Rutberg, Mar. 9, 1980 (div. 1988); 1 child, Jessica Erin; m. Johnny Anthony Vergona, Oct. 9, 1988; 1 child, David Sean; stepchildren: Danielle Evelyn Vergona, Jonathan Chaunch Vergona. AA, L.A. Valley Coll., 1971; BFA cum laude, U. Utah, 1973, MFA in Dance, 1975; MA in Marriage, Family and Child Counseling/Clin. Child Devel., Pacific Oaks Coll., 1993; postgrad., Fielding Inst., 2001—. Lic. marriage and family therapist. With Momentum Dance Co., LA, 1975-77; dance spl. pub. sch. LA, 1975-76; instr. Scripps Coll., Claremont, Calif., 1976-77; dir. dance Cypress Coll., Calif., 1978-85, instr. dance, 1978—85, 1986—2002; owner, operator Gymboree, 1985-88. Mem. adj. faculty Antioch U., 1998—; faculty facilitator MA-CEL program Fielding Grad. Inst.; dance instr. Hollywood (Calif.) Little Red Sch. House, 1985-89, sch. coun., 1997—, asst. head of sch., 2000-02, Hollywood Schoolhouse prin., 2002-04; inclusion specialist Milatro Charter Sch., 2004—; spl. products coord. Learning Ctr., 2004—; dance instr. McGroarty Arts Ctr., 1992-97, bd. dirs., 1991-92, 97-2002; mem. arts assistance team L.A. Supt. Schs.; curriculum coun. LA HS Performing Arts, adv. bd., 1986-88, Dance Resource Ctr., 1991-92; intern Julie Ann Singer Ctr. Therapeutic Sch., 1991-92; coord. infant devel. program Santa Clara Valley Child and Family Devel. Ctr., 1992-93; therapist Julia Ann Singer Ctr. Family Stress Program, 1994-95, Verdugo Mental Health Ctr., 1994—; crisis counselor Verdugo Disaster Recovery Program, 1994-95; trainer Project COPE, 1995-96; co-dir. Verdugo Creative Arts Group, 1995-2002; program coord. Atwater Park Ctr., 1996-97; coach LA Odyssey of the Mind, 1998—, LA regional dir., 2002, bd. dirs., 2002--; bd. dirs. L.A. Basin, 2002—. Author/choreographer Kitty Kats, 1986; choreography work includes Man of La Mancha, 1976-80, Pippin, 1981, Fiddler on the Roof, 1981, Music Man, 1983, Spanish Suite, 1983, A Funny Thing Happened on the Way to the Forum, 1984, Skaters Edge, 1984, Cartoon, 1984, Urban Primitive, 1985, Cabaret, 1985, Healings, 1987, Cloud Reveries, 1988, Guys and Dolls, 1988, The Lottery, 1988, Cabaret, 1989, Atmos, 1990, Damn Yankees, 1990, Conflict of Interest, 1990; author, dir., choreographer We Saved the Day, 1987, The Visit, 1988, Where the Wild Things Are, 1991, Evening's After Image, 1992, Hair, 1992, South Pacific, 1993, Hello Dolly, 1993, In Search of Quieter Times and Places, 1993, Fiddler on the Roof, 1994, Pajama Game, 1994, Nine, 1994, Testosteroni Baloney, 1994, Guys and Dolls, 1995, Into the Woods, 1995, Alice in Wonderland, 1996, Pirates of Penzance, 1997, Rags, 1997; dir. Courage of the Heart, 1998; dir./choreographer Bye Bye Birdie, 1998; choreographer Mikado, 1998, Sweeney Todd, 1999, Funny Thing Happened on the Way to the Forum, 1999, Jesus Christ Superstar, 1999, Oklahoma, 2000, Rocky Horror Show, 2000, Man of La Mancha, 2001, Joseph and the Amazing Technicolor Dreamcoat, 2001, Cabaret, 2002. Mem. So. Calif. steering com. Legis. Action Coalition Arts Edn.; den leader Cub Scouts, 1996-2000. Mem. AAHPERD, ASCD, AARP, Dance Resource Ctr., Calif. Dance Educators Assn. (v.p. 1980-82, legis. rep. 1982-86), Calif. Music Educators (legis. com. 1982-86), L.A. Area Dance Alliance, Faculty Assn. C.C., Calif. Assn. Health, Phys. Edn., Recreation and Dance, Calif. Assn. Marriage and Family Therapists, So. Calif. Assn. Edn. Young Children (bd. dirs. South Bay chpt.), Calif. Confedn. Arts, Calif. Learning Disabilities Assn., Calif. Elem. Edn. Assn., Josephson Inst. Ethics (mem. shared leadership coun. Millikin Middle Sch. 1994-96, mem. learn coun. Apperson Sch. 1994-95), Assn. Ednl. Therapists, Learning Disabilities Assn. L.A., Calif. Elem. Edn. Assn., Assn. Supervision Curriculum Devel. Democrat.

RAGLAND, ROBERT ALLEN, lawyer; b. Bartlesville, Okla., Apr. 18, 1954; s. Thomas Martin and Joan Ethel (Murphy) R. BA, U. Md., 1976; JD, George Mason Sch. of Law, 1980. Dir. regulatory reform and govt. org. Nat. Assn. Mfrs., Washington, 1979-82, asst. v.p. taxation, 1983-86; mgr. congl. rels. The Clorox Co., Oakland, Calif., 1982-83; dir. tax rsch. U.S. C. of C., Washington, 1988-93; v.p., officer Wachovia Bank, 1995—2004; v.p. SunTrust Bank, Orlando, Fla., 2004—. Chief tax counsel, mng. dir. Nat. Chamber Found., Washington, 1989-93. Author: Transportation Reform, 1980, Employee Stock Ownership Plans, 1989, Taxation of Foreign Source Income, Distributional Impact of Excise Taxes, 1990; editor Taxation of Intercorporate Profits, 1990, Jour. Regulation and Social Costs, 1992-93, Jour. Regulation, 1992-93. Active Boy Scouts Am., Washington, 1967—, bd. dirs. nat. capital area coun.; dep. dir. duPont for Pres., 1987-88; v.p. Nat. Chamber Found. U.S. C. of C., 1989-93, dir., Liz Lerman Dance Exchange, 1993-2001, dir. Our House, Inc., 1988-2000. Republican. Roman Catholic. Home: The Waverly 803 322 E Central Blvd Orlando FL 32801

RAGLAND, SAMUEL CONNELLY, industrial engineer, management consultant; b. Nashville, July 12, 1946; s. Julian Potter and Stella (Thompson) R.; m. Marilyn Margaret Oppelt, July 15, 1967 (dec.); children: Sherry Anne, David Michael. BSBA, Ariz. State U., 1974; MBA, U. Phoenix, 1991. Indsl. engr. 1st Interstate Bank, Phoenix, 1966-76, Beckman Instruments, Scottsdale, Ariz., 1976-78; mgmt. analyst Ariz. Legis. Budget Com., Phoenix, 1978; indls. engr. mgmt. sys. ITT Courier Terminal Sys., Tempe, Ariz., 1978-81; project control adminstr. Gen. Host Corp., Phoenix, 1981; sr. cons. Arthur Young & Co., Phoenix, 1981-82; ops. analyst City of Phoenix, 1982-84; project leader Garrett Engine divsn. Allied-Signal Corp. (formerly Garrett Turbine Engine Co.), Phoenix, 1984-92; cons., program mgr. TRW, Mesa, Ariz., 1992-93; prin., owner Ragland Assocs., Scottsdale, 1994—; owner Granite Investments, Inc., 2001—. Exec. mgmt. cons. Gov.'s Office Excellence in Govt., State of Ariz., 1995-96, mgr. quality assurance Coxreels, Inc., 1996-97; ind. engring. cons. Boeing Co., 1997-2001; indsl. engr. strategic planning Aviation Mgmt. Sys., 2000-01; owner, Granite Investments, Inc., Bennett Auto. LLC, 2003—; prin. LST Group LLC, 2003—. Contbr. articles to profl. jours. Mem. Inst. Indls. Engrs. (sr. mem. ctrl. Ariz. chpt., dir. cmty. rels. 1983-85, dir. chpt. devel. 1985-86, v.p. 1986-87, pres. 1987-88, 99-2000, nat. chpt. devel. com. 1988-91), Assn. Sys. Mgmt. (divsn. dir. 1989-92, pres. 1992-93), Phoenix Philatelic Assn. Home: 12614 N Cave Creek Rd Ste 106 Phoenix AZ 85022-5860

RAGLAND, THOMAS EUGENE, osteopath, protective services official; b. Dunlap, Kans., Sept. 22, 1936; s. Sylvester Ellis and Edna Mae (Cooper) R.; m. Barbara Jean Royal, Aug. 5, 1961 (dec. June 1977); children: Sheri Elizabeth, Thomas Eugene II, Diedra Elise; m. Tawina Denise Barganier, May 30, 1992. BS, McPherson (Kans.) Coll., 1959; DO, Coll. Osteo. Medicine Surgery, Kansas City, Mo., 1973; doctoral student, Ashland (Ohio) Theol. Sem., 1993—. Cert. med. technologist, Am. Soc. Clin. Pathology, St. Mercy Sch. Med. Tech., Hutchinson, Kans., 1960. Med. intern Youngstown (Ohio) Cafaro Hosp., 1973-74; founder, pres. The Cmty. Health Ctr., Youngstown, 1974—; med. resident Youngstown Hosp. Assn., 1976-77; med. dir. Trumbull Correctional Instn., Warren, Ohio, 1991-93, Belmont Correctional Instn., St. Clairsville, Ohio, 1995—. Assoc. med. cons. So. Ohio Correction Facility, Lucasville, 1993-95; health dir. City of Youngstown, 1975-76; spl. med. task force East Ohio Regional Hosp., Martins Ferry; night clinic Hough Norwood Health Ctr., Cleve. Author: The Faces of Fear, 1989, At the Window of Death, 1996, The Exoffended Home, 1996, (documentary) Seven-Seven-Seven: Personal Autobiography of a Prison Physician, 1996; lectr., spkr., host radio talk show (WGFT) A Unique Ministry, Youngstown. Mem.: AMA, State Med. Bd. of Ohio, Nat. Osteo. Med. Assn., Am. Osteo. Med. Assn., Am. Assn. Christian Counselors. Mem. Holiness Church of God in Christ. Avocations: basketball, track, tennis, fishing. Address: A Unique Ministry PO Box 6218 Youngstown OH 44501-6218 Office: Community Health Ctr 3025 Market St Youngstown OH 44507-1636

RAGLAND, WILLIAM C. accountant; s. Rev. Samuel Emerson and Lillian Harlow Ragland; m. Maria Norma Castro, June 12, 1964 (dec. Mar. 1997); children: Marie Werbel, Michele Dilworth; m. Catherine Graeber Crowe, Jan. 2, 2000. BS, U. Ky., Lexington, 1948—52; MS, U. Mich., Ann Arbor, 1956. CPA Ky., 1958. Staff acct. Lybrand, Ross Bros. & Montgomery, Louisville, 1952—54; agt. IRS, Louisville, 1954—60; with Office Internat. Ops. IRS, 1960—70; tech. advisor Office of Chief Counsel, Washington, 1970—84; auditor Fairfax County, Va., 1988—95. Lt. col. USAR, 1946—78. Mem.: United Methodist Men, Rotary, Beta Alpha Psi. Methodist.

RAGNO, NANCY NICKELL, educational writer; b. Phila., Sept. 2, 1938; d. Paul Eugene and Sara Jane (Mensch) Nickell; m. Joseph Diego Ragno, Aug. 25, 1961; 1 child, Michelle Angela. BA, Lebanon Valley Coll., 1960; MA, NYU, 1968. Cert. tchr., N.J. Tchr. N.J. pub. schs., 1961-68; project editor Prentice-Hall, Inc., Englewood Cliffs, N.J., 1968-70, Harcourt Brace Jovanovich, N.Y.C, 1970-72; sr. editor Silver Burdett Co., Morristown, N.J., 1972-76; editor, writer Houghton Mifflin Co., Boston, 1976-77; sr. editor J.B. Lippincott Co., Phila., 1977-79; sr. author Silver Burdett Ginn, Morristown, 1984—. Author: (textbook series) Silver Burdett English, 1984, World of Language, 1992, (sound filmstrip) The City and the Modern Writer, 1970, Buying on the Installment Plan, 1974. Bassoonist Harrisburg (Pa.) Symphony Orch., 1959, Plainfield (N.J.) Symphony Orch., 1976, Somerset (N.J.) County Orch., 1989, Princeton (N.J.) Community Orch., 1992. Mem. ASCD, Nat. Coun. Tchrs. English, Internat. Reading Assn., Am. Soc. Journalists and Authors, Textbook Authors Assn., Authors Guild, U.S. Power Squadron. Democrat. Mem. Ch. of Christ. Avocations: music, writing, boating. Home: 38 Tortoise Ln Tequesta FL 33469-1552

RAGO, ANN D'AMICO, academic administrator, public relations executive; b. Pitts., Aug. 24, 1957; d. Jack and Florence D'Amico; m. John Rago; children: Annie J., Emily I., John Henry. BA, Duquesne U., Pitts., 1979, MA, 1987. From comm. assoc. to dir. pub. rels. Duquesne U., 1979—89, coord. univ. rels., 1989—93, adj. prof. comm., 1990—2000, exec. dir. pub. affairs, 1993—2002; v.p. instnl. rels. Carlow Coll., Pitts., 2002—. Editor University Record, 1989 (silver medal). Bd. dirs. Support, Pitts., 1989-91; sch. dir. Carylnton Sch. Bd., Pitts., 1989-93, pres. sch. bd., 1990. Recipient Gold award for publs./external prospectus 9th Ann. Admissions Advt. Awards, 1994, Gold award for Total Pub. Rels. Campaign, 10th Ann. Admissions Advt. Awards, 1995, Gold award for Total Pub. Rels. Campaign, 11th Ann. Admissions Awards, 1996, 1st Place award in Category 35, Internal Pub. Rels. Campaign, Pitts. chpt. Women in Comm., Inc., 1996, Bronze Cert. for logo and letterhead for Duquesne U.'s Capital Campaign and cert. merit for Duquesne U.'s internal publ. 14th Ann. Admissions Advt. Awards, 1998, Clarion award Assn. for Women in Communications, 2003. Mem. Pub. Rels. Soc. Am. (1st place award 1993), Internat. Assn. Bus. Communicators (award of excellence 1991, award of honor 1993, award of merit 1994), Am. Mgmt. Assn., Assn. for Women in Comm. (Clarion award 2003), Press Club Western Pa., Sigma Delta Chi. Office: Carlow Coll Institutional Relations 3333 Fifth Ave Pittsburgh PA 15213 Office Phone: 412-578-2090. Personal E-mail: adr824@aol.com. Business E-Mail: arago@carlow.edu.

RAGON, ROBERT RONALD, clergyman; b. Flintstone, Ga., Sept. 10, 1939; s. Robert Emmett and Frances Cora (Stoner) R.; m. Judith Ann Ward, Apr. 27, 1962; children: Ronald Russell, Regina Renee. BS, U. Chattanooga, 1962; BDiv, MDiv, Columbia Theol. Sem., Decatur, Ga., 1967. Ordained to ministry Presbyn. Ch., 1967. Pastor Trion (Ga.) Presbyn. Ch., 1967-72; dir., pastor Chattooga County Presbyn. Ministries, Trion, 1971-72; pastor Brainerd Presbyn. Ch., Chattanooga, 1972—. Moderator Knoxville Presbytery, 1979-80; founder An Order of Slaves of Christ, Chattanooga, 1970; stated clk. Presbytery of S.E., 1990-93, moderator, 1995-96. Author: Covenant Agreement: O.S.C., 1970, The Journey, 1990. Trustee King Coll., Bristol, Tenn., 1983-86. Mem. Masons (Ga. chaplain 1980), KT (sec. 1991), Shriners, Kiwanis (bd. dirs. Chattanooga 1986-90). Republican. Presbyterian. Avocation: investments. Home: 4229 Happy Valley Rd Flintstone GA 30725-2222 Office: Brainerd Presbyterian Church 1624 Jenkins Rd Chattanooga TN 37421-3249 Office Phone: 423-899-2424. E-mail: rjragon@earthlink.net.

RAGONE, DAVID VINCENT, former university president; b. N.Y.C., May 16, 1930; s. Armando Frederick and Mary (Napier) R.; m. Katherine H. Spaulding, Dec. 18, 1954; children: Christine M., Peter V. BS, MIT, 1951, MS, 1952, DSc, 1953. Asst. prof. chem. and metall. engring. U. Mich., Ann Arbor, 1953-57, assoc. prof., 1957-61, prof., 1961-62; asst. dir. John J. Hopkins Lab. for Pure and Applied Sci., also chmn. metallurgy dept. Gen. Atomic divsn. Gen. Dynamics, La Jolla, 1962-67; Alcoa prof. metallurgy Carnegie-Mellon U., Pitts., 1967-69, assoc. dean Sch. Urban and Pub. Affairs, 1969-70; dean Thayer Sch. Engring. Dartmouth Coll., 1970-72; dean Coll. Engring. U. Mich., 1972-80; pres. Case Western Res. U., Cleve., 1980-87; vis. prof., dept. materials sci. and engring. MIT, Cambridge, 1987-88, sr. lectr. dept. materials sci. and engring., 1988-98; gen. ptnr. Ampersand Ventures, 1988-92, ptnr., 1992—. Mem. Nat. Sci. Bd., 1978-84; mem. tech adv. bd. U.S. Dept. Commerce, 1967-75; chmn. adv. com. advanced auto power systems Coun. on Environ. Quality, 1971-75; trustee Henry Luce Found. Named Outstanding Young Engr., Engring. Soc. Detroit, 1957. Mem. Univ. Club (N.Y.C.), Longwood Cricket Club (Boston), Sigma Xi, Tau Beta Pi. Office: Ampersand Ventures 55 William St Wellesley MA 02481-4003 Business E-Mail: ragone@mit.edu.

RAGSDALE, ANN F. state representative; b. Wilkes-Barre, Pa., June 4, 1936; married; children: JoAnn, Fran, Bridget. Attended, Front Range C.C. State rep. dist. 35 Colo. Ho. of Reps., Denver, mem. local govt. and transp. and energy coms. Chmn., 2 terms Adams County (Colo.) Dem. Party; mem. Jud. Dist. 17 Victims Compensation Bd.; adv. bd. Adams County Libr. Mem.: Women in Govt., Downtown Dem. Forum, Ad-Dems Club, Dem Fems. Democrat. Roman Catholic. Avocations: sewing, crafts, cross country skiing, reading, furniture refinishing. Office: State Capitol # 357 200 E Colfax Ave Denver CO 80203

RAGSDALE, GEORGE ROBINSON, lawyer; b. Raleigh, N.C., Mar. 26, 1936; s. George Young and Susan (Jolly) R.; m. Adora Prevost, Oct. 20, 1962; children: John Robinson, George Young II, Adora P. AB, U. N.C., 1958, LLB, 1961. Asst. to chief counsel U.S. Senate Subcom. on Constnl. Rights, Washington, 1961—62; law ptnr. Bailey & Ragsdale, Raleigh, NC, 1962—65; legal counsel to Dan K. Moore, Gov. of N.C., Raleigh, 1965—68; judge Superior Ct. of N.C., Raleigh, 1968—70; ptnr. Moore, Ragsdale, Liggett, Ray & Foley, Raleigh, 1970—86, LeBoeuf, Lamb, Greene & MacRae, N.Y.C. and Raleigh, 1987—93, Ragsdale, Liggett & Foley, Raleigh, 1994—. Lectr. N.C. Assn. Def. Counsel. Trustee U. N.C., Chapel Hill, 1979-87, vice-chmn. bd. trustees, 1983-84, chmn., 1984-85; trustee U. N.C. Endowment, 1980—, chmn., 1984-85; bd. dirs. U. N.C. Instnl. Devel. Found., Inc., 1985—, U. N.C.-Chapel Hill Found.; bd. visitors U. N.C., The Ednl. Found., Inc. Mem. ABA, N.C. Bar Assn., Wake County Bar Assn., Assn. Bar of City of N.Y., Def. Rsch. Inst., Raleigh C. of C., Kiwanis, Sphinx Club of Raleigh, Terpsichorean Club, Raleigh Execs. Club, Carolina Country Club, Biltman Forest Country Club. Episcopalian. Office: Ragsdale Liggett 2840 Plaza Pl PO Box 31507 Raleigh NC 27612

RAGSDALE, RICHARD ELLIOT, healthcare management executive; b. St. Louis, Dec. 20, 1943; s. Billie Oscar and Isabelle (Roques) R.; m. Anne Elizabeth Ward, Aug. 20, 1968; children: Richard, Kevin, Bethany. BBA, Ohio U., 1965; M in Internat. Commerce, Thunderbird Grad. Sch. Internat. Mgmt., 1968. Asst. treas. Chase Manhattan Bank, N.Y.C., 1968-73; v.p., treas. Hosp. Affiliates Internat., Nashville, 1973-80; v.p., treas., chief fin. officer INA Health Care Group, Dallas, 1980-81; sr. v.p., chief fin. officer, dir. Republic Health Corp., Dallas, 1981-83, sr. exec. v.p., dir., 1983-85; chmn. Cmty. Health Systems Inc., Brentwood, Tenn., 1985-96, co-chmn., 1996-98; chmn. Great No. Health Mgmt., Ltd., London, 1986-89. Dir. HealthMont, Inc., 2000-03, chmn., 2002-03; dir. Vanderbilt U. Tech. Co., 2001-2003. Coach Spring Valley Athletic Assn., Dallas, 1985; trustee Watkins Inst., 1988-94; trustee Benton Hall Sch., 1988—, chair, 1991-2002; trustee Maryville Coll., 1990—, chair, 1992—; chmn. Hosp. Authority of Metro Govt. Bd. Trustees, Nashville, 1999—; dir. Nashville Zoo, 2000—. Recipient Thunderbird Disting Alumni award Entrepreneurship, 1990, Jonas Meyer Disting. Alumni award, 1993, Maryville Coll. medallion, 1999. Mem. Fedn. Am. Hosps. (legis. commn. 1984-95) Republican. Avocations: scuba diving, drag racing.

RAGSTER, LAVERNE E. academic administrator; b. St. Thomas, Virgin Islands; BS in Biology and Chemistry, U. Miami, 1973; MS in Biology, San Diego State U., 1975; PhD in Biology, U. Calif., San Diego, 1980. Pres. U. Virgin Islands, St. Thomas, asst. prof. then prof., 1980—90, chair divsn. sci. math., sr. v.p., provost. Trustee U. Virgin Islands, St. Thomas, acting v.p. rsch. land grant affairs, v.p. rsch. pub. svc.; sub-sec. gen. Assn. Caribbean Univs. Rsch. Insts.; coord. Consortium Caribbean Univs. Natural Resource Mgmt. Contbr. articles to profl. jours. Mem.: Caribbean Coun. Sci. Tech. (rep. U.S. Virgin Islands), Nature Conservancy (bd. dirs.), Island Resources Found. (bd. dirs.), Caribbean Conservation Assn. (past v.p.), Caribbean Natural Resources Inst. (bd. dirs., past chair bd. dirs.), Caribbean Studies Assn. (past pres.). Office: Office of Pres U Virgin Islands 2 Hohn Brewers Bay St Thomas VI 00802-9990

RAGUSA, ELYSIA, real estate company executive; V.p. Lincoln Property Co.; pres. S.W. corp. svcs. The Staubach Co., Addison, Tex., pres., COO. Grad. Leadership Dallas; assoc. mem. Dallas Citizens Coun.; bd. dirs. Dallas County C.C. Found., Vis. Nurse Assn.; bd. mem. United Way Met. Dallas, former chmn. ctrl. budget com., former mem. exec. com. Mem.: Internat. Women's Forum, Dallas Breakfast Group. Office: The Staubach Co Ste 400 15601 Dallas Pkwy Addison TX 75001*

RAGUSA, OLGA MARIA, retired Italian language educator; b. Catania, Italy, Feb. 11, 1922; came to U.S., 1932; d. Andrea and Anna (von Weiskopf) R. BA summa cum laude, Hunter Coll., 1943; MA, Columbia U., 1947, PhD, 1954. Instr. French and German Rutgers U., Newark, 1946-47; instr. Italian Vassar Coll., Poughkeepsie, N.Y., 1949-52; asst. prof. Columbia U., N.Y.C., 1955-61, assoc. prof., 1961-65, prof., 1965-79, Da Ponte prof. Italian, 1979—2002, chmn. dept., 1973-92; ret., 2002. Co-owner, editor S.F. Vanni (book dealers), 1974—; mem. exec. coun. MLA, 1972-75; mem. selection com. Am. Coun. Learned Socs., 1976-80; mem. area adv. com. for Western Europe, Coun. Internat. Exchange Scholars, 1983-86. Author: Mallarmé in Italy: Literary Influence and Critical Response, 1957, Verga's Milanese Tales, 1964, Narrative and Drama: Essays in Modern Italian Literature from Verga to Pasolini, 1976, Pirandello: An Approach to His Theatre, 1980; editor: Romance Section: Italian, Columbia Dictionary of Modern European Literature, 1980; editor Italica jour., 1968-84; mem. editorial bd. European Womens Writers Series, U. Nebr. Press, 1984—; contbr. numerous articles, revs. to Am. and European publs. Recipient Disting. Svc. award Am. Assn. Tchrs. of Italian, 1990; Fulbright fellow U. Milan, Italy, 1958-59, Am. Coun. Learned Socs. fellow, 1971-72; decorated knight Order of Merit (Italy), 1982 Mem. Phi Beta Kappa. Roman Catholic. Home: 30 W 12th St New York NY 10011-8635

RAHALL, NICK JOE, II, (NICK RAHALL), congressman; b. Beckley, W.Va., May 20, 1949; s. N. Joe and Alice Rahall; children: Rebecca Ashley, Nick Joe III, Suzanne Nicole. BA, Duke U., 1971. Staff asst. U.S. Senator Robert C. Byrd, 1971-74; sales rep. Sta. WWNR, Beckley, 1974; pres. Mountaineer Travel Co., Beckley, 1975-77, W.Va. Broadcasting, 1980—; mem. U.S. Congress from 3rd W.Va. dist., Washington, 1977—. Mem. transp. and infrastructure com.ranking, mem. resources com.; bd. dirs. Rahall Comm. Corp.; served on U.S. Constn. Bicentennial Commn. of MO. Del. Dem. Nat. Conv., 1972, 74, 78, 80, 84, 88, 92, 96; W.Va. chmn. March of Dimes, 1979; mem. profl. adv. bd. Alsac-St. Jude Children's Rsch. Hosp. Named Young Man of Year, Beckley Jaycees, 1972; Outstanding Young Man in W.Va., W.Va. Jaycees, 1977; recipient Achievement award Logan Cripple Children Soc., 1978; Citizenship award K.C., 1978, Disting. Svc. award Am. Fedn. Govt. Employees W.Va., 1984, Young Dem. of Yr. Dem. Nat. Conv., 1980, Outfitter of Yr. Profl. Outfitters, 1987, Seneca award Sierra Club 1988, River Conservation award Am. River 1988; named Coal Man of Yr. Coal Industry News, 1979, W.Va. Son of Yr., W.Va. Soc. of Washington, 1996. Mem. NAACP, NRA, Elks, Moose, Masons (33d degree) Shriners.Nat. Santa Fe Trail Ambassador, 2001. Democrat. Presbyterian. Office: US Ho of Reps 2307 Rayburn Ho Office Bldg Washington DC 20515-4803 E-mail: nrahall@mail.house.gov.

RAHARINAIVO, ANDRÉ LÉON, research executive, educator; b. Tananarive, Madagascar, Sept. 1, 1940; arrived in France, 1954; s. Ignace Léon and Marthe (Rasoazanamalala) R.; m. Christiane Martine Laurent, May 7, 1966 (div. June 1994); 1 child, Jacques Yves. Engr. mining and metallurgy, Ecole des Mines, Nancy, France, 1964; degree superior scientific studies, U. Nancy, France, 1964; PhD, U. Compiegne, France, 1982. Cert. engr. Head sect. Lab. Ctrl. Ponts et Chaussées, Paris, 1971-80, dep. head dept., 1980-83, sec. sci. coun., 1983-91, rsch. mgr., 1991—. Prof. U. Paris-Sud, Orsay, France, 1981; lectr. Ecole Nat. Ponts et Chaussées, Paris, 1977. Author: Fracture Mechanics and Mechanisms, 1990; patentee in field. Capt. Equipment, 1967-69, France. Mem. Ctr. Français Anticorrosion, Nat. Assn. Corrosion Engrs. Avocation: singing gospel music. Home: 378 rue de Vaugirard F-75015 Paris France E-mail: andraha@aol.com.

RAHE, MARIBETH SEMBACH, bank executive; b. Evanston, Ill., Oct. 3, 1948; d. Daniel F. and Boysie (Beebe) Sembach; m. Martin E. Rahe, May 31, 1975. BA, Bowling Green State U., 1970; postgrad., Ohio State U., 1970-72; MBA, Am. Grad. Sch. Internat. Mgmt., 1974. Internat. banking officer Harris Bank, Chgo., 1974-77, asst. v.p. London, 1977-80; v.p. Morgan Guaranty Trust Co., London, 1980-83, N.Y.C., 1983-84; sr. rep. Sparebanken Oslo Akershus, N.Y.C., 1984-85; v.p. Morgan Guaranty Trust Co., N.Y.C., 1985-87, J.P. Morgan Investment Mgmt., N.Y.C., 1987-88; sr. v.p. Harris Bank, Chgo., 1988-91, dept. exec., 1991-94, sr. exec. v.p., 1994-95, vice chmn. bd., 1995-97; vice chmn. U.S. Trust Co. N.Y., 1997—2001, pres., 2001—02. Bd. dirs. Trustmark Ins. Co., U.S. Trust Co., N.Y. Bd. dirs. Rush Presbyn. Hosp., N.Y. Landmark Conservancy, Nat. Trust, Thunderbird Am. Grad. Sch. Internat. Mgmt.; com. 200 Found. Bd.; chair devel. com. Rush Presbyn. Hosp.; mem. Fin. Svcs. Roundtable, The Chgo. Network, Women's Forum, Inc. Recipient Outstanding Alumni award, Am. Grad. Sch., 1991. Mem.: Chgo. Women's Network, Econ. Club N.Y., Econ. Club Chgo., Am. Bankers Assn., Chgo. Club. Republican. Lutheran. Home: 269 Vine Ave Lake Forest IL 60045-1934

RAHE, RICHARD HENRY, psychiatrist, educator; b. Seattle, May 28, 1936; s. Henry Joseph and Delora Lee (Laube) R.; m. Laurie Ann Davies, Nov. 24, 1960 (div. Dec. 1990); children: Richard Bradley, Annika Lee; m. Sohyon Mir Rahe, Aug. 24, 2003. Student, Princeton U., 1954-57; MD, U. Wash., 1961. Diplomate Am. Bd. Psychiatry and Neurology. Chief resident in psychiatry U. Wash. Sch. Medicine, Seattle, 1965; rsch. psychiatrist USN, San Diego, 1965-75; commdg. officer Naval Health Rsch. Ctr., San Diego, 1976-80; exec. officer Long Beach Naval Hosp., Calif., 1980-82; commdg. officer Guam Naval Hosp., Agana, 1982-84; prof. psychiatry Uniformed Svc. U. of the Health Sci., Bethesda, Md., 1984-86, U. Nev. Sch. Medicine, Reno, 1986—2003. Dir. Mil. Stress Studies Ctr., Bethesda, 1984-86, Nev. Stress Ctr. Vets. Affairs Med. Ctr., Reno, 1986-2003, psychiatrist, Vets. Affairs Puget Sound Health Care Sys., Am. Lake Divsn., Tacoma, Wash. Contbr. numerous articles to sci. jour., chpts. to books; photographic prints and video. Dir. Nev. Mental Health Inst., Sparks, 1991-94. Capt. USN, 1965-86. Recipient Legion of Merit, 1986, Dept. of State award for treatment of Am. hostages held in Iran, 1981. Fellow Am. Psychiat. Assn.; mem. Am. Psychosomatic Soc. (past pres.), World Psychiat. Assn. (past. pres. mil. sect.). Avocations: hiking, skiing, swimming. Office: Veterans Affairs Puget Sound Health Care Sys Am Lake Divsn Tacoma WA 98493 Home: 8301 SW Lafayette Way Wilsonville OR 97070-9433

RAHHAL, DONALD K. obstetrician, gynecologist; b. Clinton, Oklahoma, 1942; MD, U. Okla., 1971. Diplomate Am. Bd. Ob., Gyn. (bd. dir. 1992-2000). Resident Ind. U. Hosp., Indpls., 1971-74; ob-gyn Mercy Health Ctr., Okla. City, 1981—, chief of staff, 2003; ob-gyn Deaconess Hosp., Okla. City, 1981—; clin. prof. U. Okla. Coll. Medicine, Okla. City, 1981—. Mem. ACOG, AMA. Office: 4140 W Memorial Rd Ste 500 Oklahoma City OK 73120-8376

RAHIM, M. AFZALUR, management educator, editor; b. Bangladesh; s. Khalilur and Nazman Nessa (Khatun) R.; m. Masuda Rahim, Mar. 25, 1966; 1 child, Sayeed M. B Commerce with honors, Dhaka (Bangladesh) U., 1960, M Commerce, 1961; MBA, Miami U., Oxford, Ohio, 1968; PhD, U. Pitts., 1976. Assoc. prof. mgmt. Dhaka U., 1970-72, Youngstown (Ohio) State U., 1976-83; prof. mgmt. Western Ky. U., Bowling Green, 1983—; pres. Ctr. for Advanced Studies in Mgmt., Bowling Green, 1988—. Author: Managing Organizational Conflict, 1986, 3d edit., 2001, Current Topics in Management, vol. 1, 1996, vol. 2, 1997, vol. 3, 1998, vol. 4, 1999, vol. 5, 2000, vol. 6, 2001, vol. 7, 2002, vol. 8, 2003; founding editor Internat. Jour. Conflict Mgmt., 1988—, Internat. Jour. Orgn. Analysis, 1990—. Fulbright scholar, 1966-68. Avocations: chess, stamps, soccer. Office: Ctr for Advanced Studies in Mgmt 1574 Mallory Ct Bowling Green KY 42103-1300 E-mail: mgt2000@aol.com.

RAHL, LESLIE, risk advisor, entrepreneur; b. N.Y.C., May 16, 1950; d. Myron and Esther (Botwin) Horwitz; m. Jeffrey Mark Lynn, Dec. 20, 1969 (div. 1981); m. J. Andrew Rahl Jr., Apr. 30, 1989; 1 child, Kevin; stepchildren: Kaitlin, Stephen. SB, MIT, 1971, MBA, 1972. V.p. swaps and derivatives Citibank, N.Y.C., 1972-91; pres. Leslie Rahl Assocs., N.Y.C., 1991-94; founder, pres. Capital Market Risk Advisors, N.Y.C., 1994—. Presenter in field. Contbr. articles to profl. jours. Recipient On the Rise award Fortune; One of Top 50 Women in Fin. Euromoney, 1997. Mem. Internat. Assn. Fin. Engrs. (bd. dirs. 1993—), Madison Beach Club. Avocation: wine tasting. Office: Capital Market Risk Advisors 565 5th Ave New York NY 10017-2413

RAHM, DAVID ALAN, lawyer; b. Passaic, N.J., Apr. 18, 1941; s. Hans Emil and Alicia Katherine (Onuf) R.; m. Susan Eileen Berkman, Nov. 23, 1972; children: Katherine Berkman, William David. AB, Princeton U., 1962; JD, Yale U., 1965. Bar: N.Y. 1966, D.C. 1986. Assoc. Paul, Weiss, Rifkind & Wharton, N.Y.C., 1965-66, 1968-69; asst. counsel N.Y. State Urban Devel. Corp., N.Y.C., 1969-72, assoc. counsel, 1972-75; counsel real estate div. Internat. Paper Co., N.Y.C., 1975-80; ptnr. Stroock & Stroock & Lavan, N.Y.C., 1980-83, sr. ptnr., 1984—2001. Mem. legis. com. Real Estate Bd. N.Y., 1988—92; lectr. Old Dominion Coll., Norfold, Va., 1967—68, NYU, 1986—; mem. editl. bd. Comml. Leasing Law and Strategy, 1988—95; mem. N.Y.C. bd. advisors Commonwealth Land Title Ins. Co., 1996—2000. Contbr. articles. Fund raiser corp. com. N.Y. Philharm., N.Y.C., 1980-84; trustee Manhattan Sch. Music, 1989—, treas., 1991-94, chmn., 1994—; bd. dir. New Dramatists, Inc., 2001-, exec. com., 2001—; v.p., 2002—. Mem. ABA (comml. leasing com. 1987-88, 94-2000, pub./pvt. devel. com. 1989-2000, real property sect.), Assn. of Bar of City of N.Y. (housing and urban devel. com. 1977-80, 81-84, real property com. 1989-92), Princeton Club. Democrat. Presbyterian. Avocations: music, reading, travel, exercise. Office: Stroock Stroock & Lavan 180 Maiden Ln Fl 17 New York NY 10038-4937 E-mail: drahm@stroock.com.

RAHM, SUSAN BERKMAN, lawyer; b. Pitts., June 25, 1943; d. Allen Hugh and Selma (Wiener) Berkman; m. David Alan Rahm, Nov. 23, 1972; children: Katherine, William. BA with honors, Wellesley Coll., 1965; postgrad., Harvard U., 1966-68; JD, NYU, 1973. Bar: N.Y. 1974, D.C. 1988. Assoc. Marshall, Bratter, Greene, Allison & Tucker, N.Y.C., 1973-81, ptnr., 1981-82, Kaye Scholer, LLP, N.Y.C., 1982—, ptnr, chair real estate dept., 1993-98; chair internat. practice group Kaye Scholer, LLP, N.Y.C., 1999—. N.Y. adv. bd., Chgo. Title Ins. Co., 1995. Editor: New York Real Property Service, 1987. Bd. dirs. Girls Inc., 1989-93; mem. aux. bd. Mt. Sinai Hosp., N.Y.C., 1976-78. Recipient cert. of outstanding svc. D.C. Redevel. Land Agy., 1969, She Knows Where She's Going award Girls' Clubs of Am., 1987, Woman of Yr. award CREW.NY, 1999. Mem. ABA, Assn. Bar City N.Y., N.Y. Bar Assn. (real property law com., co-chmn. real-estate devel. . 1987-91), Am. Coll. Real Estate Lawyers, WX formerly known as Comml. Real Estate Women N.Y. (bd. dirs. 1988-94, v.p. 1988-91, pres. 1991-93), Assn. Fgn. Investors in Real Estate, Assn. Real Estate Women (Outstanding Achievement award 2003). Office: Kaye Scholer LLP 425 Park Ave New York NY 10022-3506

RAHMAN, MEZBAHUR, statistics educator; b. Sirajganj, Rajshahi Division, Bangladesh, Jan. 1, 1961; s. Sanwar Hossain Sarkar and Mohila Khatun Khan; m. Tania Rahman, Aug. 4, 1986; 1 child, Sudha. BSc, U. Dhaka, Bangladesh, 1979—84; MSc, U. Dhaka, 1984—86; MS, Mich. State U., East Lansing, 1987—89; PhD, U. Calif., Riverside, 1990—95. Tabulator Nat. Inst. Local Govt., Dhaka, Bangladesh, 1986—86; tabulation officer Rsch. Svcs. Ltd., Dhaka, Bangladesh, 1987—87; tchg. asst. Old Dominion U., Norfolk, Va., 1989—90, U. Calif., Riverside, 1990—95, vis. prof. Davis, 1996; multi-year lectr. Calif. State U., Monterey Bay, 1996—99; asst. prof. Minn. State U., Mankato, 1999—2003, assoc. prof., 2003—; part-time instr. Calif. State U., San Bernardino. Contbr. articles. Mem.: Am. Math. Assn., Am. Statis. Assn., Bangladesh Statis. Assn. (life). Islam. Achievements include research in testimation in regression parameter estimation; quantiles for Shapiro-Francia W' Statistic using exclusive Monte Carlo simulation; moments for order statistics in scale and shift parameter exponential distribution; data-based selection of the smoothing parameter in kernel density estimation using exact and approximate MISE; estimation of parameters of the exponential power family of distributions; semi-parametric estimation of a probability density; estimating the Box-Cox Transformation via Shapiro-Wilk W Statistic. Avocations: travel, bicycling, racquetball. Home: 10 Westminster Rd Mankato MN 56001 Office: Minn State U Wh273 Mankato MN 56001 Office Phone: 507-389-6790. Business E-Mail: mezbahur.rahman@mnsu.edu.

RAHMAN, MOHAMMED SIDDIQUR, environmental engineer, researcher; b. Bogra, Bangladesh, Mar. 22, 1948; came to U.S., 1980; s. Azizar and Samina (Khatun) R.; m. Shahanara Zaman, Aug. 14, 1974; children Sabrina Rahman, Sajedur Amin Rahman. BS, Bangladesh Agrl. U., Mymensingh, 1970; MS, U. of New Castle Upon Tyne, Eng., 1979; PhD, Rutgers U., 1984. Lectr. Bangladesh Agrl. U., Mymensingh, 1972, asst. prof., 1974; rsch. asst. Rutgers U., New Brunswick, N.J., 1980; environ. engr. N.J. Dept. Environ. Protection, Trenton, 1986, rsch. scientist, 1987—. Author, editor: Elevated Radon Area Evaluation Program, 1990. Convener Fedn. Bangladeshi Assns. in N.Am., N.J., 1994; pres. Bangladesh Soc. of N.J., 1992-94. Talent scheme scholar Bangladesh govt., 1964, commonwealth scholar, Eng., 1977. Mem. Conf. Radiation Control Program Dirs. (assoc.), Bangladesh Engring. Inst. Home: 145 Franklin Corner Rd Lawrenceville NJ 08648-2501 Office: Dept of Environ Protection CN415 Trenton NJ 08625

RAHMAN, MUHAMMAD ABDUR, mechanical engineer; b. Sylhet, Assam, India, Mar. 1, 1930; came to U.S., 1950; s. Haji Sajjad Ali Khan and Momtaj Khanom. BSME, U. Toledo, 1953, MSME, 1968; PhD in Engring., Calif. Coast U., 1985. Registered profl. engr., Calif. Mech. design engr. various cons. firms, L.A., 1955-61; aerospace engr. Douglas Aircraft Co., Santa Monica, Calif., 1962-63, N.Am. Aviation, Inc., L.A., 1963-64, NASA Manned Spacecraft Ctr. Gemini & Apollo Program Office, Houston, 1964-70; safety engr. U.S. Dept. Labor, OSHA, Washington, 1975-86; invention researcher Arlington, Va., 1987—. Contbr. articles to profl. jours. Mem. N.Y. Acad. Scis. Democrat. Moslem. Achievements include patent for solar energy collector, supersonic MHD generator system; copyrights for hypothesis on unified field theory and creation of the universe, on the gravitoenergy in the creation of cosmic matters in the space, on the mechanism of superconductivity, a note of caution for superconductivity in reference to permeability and permitivity, concentration on suggesting methods to build superconductors and biomedical engineering instrumentation for cancer in particular, others. Home and Office: 1805 Crystal Dr Apt 1013 Arlington VA 22202-4407

RAHMAN, RAFIQ UR, oncologist, educator; b. Mirali, Pakistan, Mar. 3, 1957; came to U.S., 1985; s. Rakhman and Bibi (Sana) Gul; m. Shamim Ara Bangash; children: Maryam, Hassan, Haider. BS, MB, U. Peshawar, Pakistan, 1980. Bd. cert. internal medicine, med. oncology, hematology; lic. physician Pa., Ala., Ky. House officer in internal medicine Khyber Tchg. Hosp.-U. Peshawar, 1980-81, house officer in gen. surgery, 1981, jr. registrar med. ICU, 1983-84; jr. registrar internal medicine Khyber Tchg. Hosp., 1981-82; sr. registrar internal medicine Khyber Tchg. Hosp.-Lady Reading Hosp. & Postgrad. Inst., Peshawar, 1984-85; Audrey Meyer Mars fellow in med. oncology Roswell Park Cancer Inst., Buffalo, 1985-86; resident in internal medicine SUNY-Buffalo Gen. Hosp.-Erie County Med. Ctr.-VA Med. Ctr., 1986-88; chief resident in internal medicine SUNY-Buffalo-Erie County Med. Ctr., 1988; fellow in hematology and med. oncology SUNY-Buffalo-Roswell Park Cancer Inst., 1989-90; hematologist, med. oncologist Daniel Boone Clinic and Harlan A.R.H., 1991-92; clin. asst. prof. medicine U. Ky., 1991—; attending physician, hematology, med. oncologist Hardin Meml. Hosp., Elizabethtown, Ky., 1993—, chief medicine, 1996, pres.-elect med. staff, 2001—02, pres. med. staff, 2002—03. Tchr. med. students Med. Sch., SUNY; participant CALGB protocol studies Roswell Park Cancer Inst., investigator. Editor English sect. Cenna mag.; contbr. articles to profl. jours. Founder Cmty. Uplift Program, Pakistan; founding dir. Pakistan Human Devel. Fund, Pakistan Am. Liason Ctr., Washington. Mem.: Assn. Pakistan Physicians Ky. and Ind. (pres. 2002—03), Ky. Med. Assn. Avocations: travel, aeromodeling, swimming, studying political science and history. Home: 400 Briarwood Cir Elizabethtown KY 42701 6915 Office: 1107 Woodland Dr Ste 105 Elizabethtown KY 42701-2789 Office Phone: 270-769-6665. E-mail: rahmanrafiq@hotmail.com.

RAHMAN, SHAMIM A. engineering executive; b. Jamshedpur, India, Apr. 22, 1963; arrived in U.S., 1979; s. Habib Ur Rahman and Anis Fatema Ansari; m. Shaheen Janjua Rahman; children: Amnah, Zara. BS, Tex. A&M U., 1984; MS, Calif. Tech., 1985; PhD, Pa. State, 1997. Staff engr. Aerospace Corp., El Segundo, Calif., 1985—92; project engr. TRW Inc., Redondo Beach, Calif., 1997—98; mgr. engring. divsn. NASA, Stennis Space Ctr., Bay St. Louis, Miss., 1998—, chief engring. divsn. propulsion test, 2001—02, chief engr. propulsion test, 2003—. Mem. NASA Engring. Mgmt. Bd., 2000—. Mem.: AIAA (sr.). Democrat. Muslim. Avocations: skiing, tennis. Office: NASA Stennis Space Ctr Bay Saint Louis MS 39529-0001

RAHMAN, YUEH-ERH, biologist; b. Kwangtung, China, June 10, 1928; came to U.S., 1960; d. Khon and Kwei-Phan (Chan) Li; m. Aneesur Rahman, Nov. 3, 1956; 1 dau., Aneesa. BS, U. Paris, 1950; MD magna cum laude, U. Louvain, Belgium, 1956. Clin. and postdoctoral research fellow Louvain U., 1956-60; mem. staff Argonne (Ill.) Nat. Lab., 1960-72, biologist, 1972-81, sr. biologist, 1981-85; prof. pharmaceutics Coll. Pharmacy, U. Minn., Mpls., 1985—, dir. grad. studies, pharmaceutics, 1989-92, head dept. pharmaceutics, 1991-96, 97-98. Vis. scientist State U. Utrecht, Netherlands, 1968-69; adj. prof. No. Ill. U., DeKalb, 1971-85; cons. NIH.; Mem. com. of rev. group, div. research grants NIH, 1979-83 Author; patentee in field. Recipient IR-100 award, 1976; grantee Nat. Cancer Inst., Nat. Inst. Arthritis, Metabolic and Digestive Diseases. Fellow Am. Assn. Pharm. Scientists; mem. AAAS, Am. Soc. Cell Biology, N.Y. Acad. Scis., Radiation Rsch. Soc., Assn. for Women in Sci. (1st pres. Chgo. area chpt. 1978-79). Unitarian Universalist. Home: 939 Coast Blvd Unit 6G La Jolla CA 92037-4115 Office: Coll Pharmacy U Minn Minneapolis MN 55455

RAHMANI, REZA MOSSAVER, writer, retired Iranian Air Force officer, banker, tour operator; b. Tehran, Iran, Jan. 17, 1912; came to U.S., 1963; s. Aliasghar M. and Khadijeh M. R.; m. Behjatmolook Lazgui, 1939 (div. 1947); children: Farhad, Sohrab; m. Poorandokht Amir Fazli, 1949; children: Ali M., Jasmin M. Rahmani Dugan. BS, Mil. Cadet Acad., Tehran, 1934; MS, Air Obs. Acad., Tehran, 1935, Higher Acad. Air Navigation, Cazaux, France, 1949; PhD equivalent, Staff and War Coll., Tehran, 1942; LLB, U. Tehran, 1945; MBA, Columbia U., N.Y.C., 1967. Commd. officer Iranian Air Force, 1948, advanced through grades to col., 1949; tchr., operator 1st Wing Iranian Air Force, Tehran, 1942-45; prof. Mil. Cadet Acad., 1945-46, Staff and War Coll., Tehran, Iran, 1946-48; reorganizer ednl. sys. Iranian Air Force, 1948-52; ret., 1952; air, mil. and naval attache Iranian Embassy, Baghdad, Iraq, 1952-54; mgr. Bank Saderat, Ekbatan, Iran, 1954-55, head internat. dept. Tehran, 1955-60, gen. mgr. Hamburg, Germany, 1961-63, Paris, 1962-63, London, 1962-63; founder head Persepolis Travel, Ltd., N.Y.C., 1967-91; ret., 1991. Ofcl.guest ednl. orgns., U.S., Gt. Britain, France, also aircraft factories in all three countries. Author: The Old Soldier, Vol. 1, 1985, Vol. 2, 1992, Vol. 3, 1993. Active Freedom Party, 1952. Decorated Sci. medal 3, Sci. medal 2 (Iran). Mem. Columbia U. Alumni Assn., Rancho Bernardo Swim and Tennis Club. Democrat. Home: 17199 Prado Pl San Diego CA 92128-2163

RAHN, ALVIN ALBERT, former banker; b. St. Paul, Apr. 8, 1925; s. Albert and Manda (Lau) R.; m. Helen Lyngen, June 10, 1950; children: Jennifer, Karen, Paul. BBA, U. Minn., 1949; postgrad., Stonier Sch. Banking, 1968. C.P.A., Minn. With income tax div. Minn. Dept. Taxation, 1949-61, asst. dir., 1957-61; with 1st Bank System Inc., Mpls., 1961-85, treas., 1969-85, chief fin. officer, 1973-74, sr. v.p., 1974-85; ret. Served with USNR, 1943-46. Mem. Am. Inst. C.P.A.s, Minn. Soc. C.P.A.s, Fin. Execs. Inst. Home: 5601 Dewey Hill Rd Minneapolis MN 55439-1919

RAHNER, JEAN A. performing company executive, educator; b. Schenectady, N.Y., Sept. 28, 1940; d. James A. Pelicone and Margaret Visco; m. Thomas P. Rahner, July 7, 1959; children: Laura A., Philip P. BA, Flagler Coll., St. Augustine, Fla., 1977. Instr. Flagler Coll., St. Augustine, 1986—96; artistic dir. and prodr. Limelight Theatre, Inc., 1992—; interviewer, Kaleidoscope WFCF-FM, 1992—. Mem. St. Augustine Art Assn., St. Augustine Hist. Soc. Mem.: Am. Bus. Women's Assn. Avocations: photography, video. Office: Limelight Theatre Inc 11 Old Mission Rd Saint Augustine FL 32084

RAHR, STEWART, health medical products executive; b. Feb. 19, 1948; BA, N.Y. Univ., 1968. Pres. Kinray, 1978—, CEO, 1984—. Office: Kinray Inc 152-35 10th Ave Whitestone NY 11357-1233

RAI, MAQBOOL AHMAD, civil engineer, consultant; b. Shorkot, Pakistan, Apr. 15, 1937; s. M. Bahadur and Bakht Bhari R.; m. Samra Rubina Rani, Feb. 2, 1966; 4 children. BS, MIE, MAWWA, MASCE. Asst. engr. Karachi Devel. Authority, 1963-68; dist. engr. Dist. Coun., Gujrat, Sargodha, 1968-69, Mianwali, Campbellpur, 1971-72; asst. mcpl. engr. Mcpl. Corp., Lahore, 1972-74, mcpl. engr. Gujranwala, Multan, Lahore, 1975-78; deputy dir. Lahore Devel. Auth.; mcpl. engr. Mcpl. Corp., Lahore, 1978-82; project engr. Hamad M. Al-Qahtany Est., Saudi Arabia, 1982-84; officer on spl. duty Punjab Local Govt. Bd.; mcpl. engr., chief engr. Mcpl. Corp., Lahore, 1984, mcpl. engr. Sialkot, Sheikhupura, 1984-87, Met. Corp., Lahore, 1987-91, superintending engr., 1991-93; chief engr. Mcpl. Corp., Rawalpindi, 1993-94, Faisalabad, 1994-95; additional dir. gen. inspections local govt. dept. Govt. of Punjab, 1995; chief engr. Met. Corp., Lahore, 1995-97. Recipient prizes in English and Perusian, German first class first with distinction, U. Karachi, Higher Level Appreciations and awards for meritorsious svcs. in Engring. Realsm. Home: 232 Pak Block Allama Iqbal Town Lahore Pakistan

RAI, RAJAT, health facility administrator; BSME, Regional Engring. Coll.; MBA in Fin., Wayne State U. From mem. staff to pres. Option Care, Inc., Buffalo Grove, Ill., 1992—2000, pres., 2000—, CEO, 2001—, bd. dirs. Office: Option Care Inc 485 Half Day Rd Ste 300 Buffalo Grove IL 60089*

RAIBLEY, PARVIN RUDOLPH, dentist; b. Boonville, Ind., Nov. 19, 1926; s. Otto Sr. and Hallie Marie (Hedges) R.; m. Mary Helen Holder, Aug. 31, 1946; children: Bruce D., Brian L., Brent A. Student, Purdue U., 1945, U. Evansville, 1946—50; BS in Dentistry, Ind. U., 1951, DDS, 1954. Practice gen. dentistry, Evansville, Ind., 1954—; pres. Parvin Raibley Profl. Dental Corp. Bd. dirs. Health Resources Inc., Evansville, 1986-94; dir. Health Resources, Inc. of Ky., 1988-94; dir. Ill. Dental Plans, 1993-94. Counselor Boy Scouts Am. With U.S. Army, 1944-45. Named Dentist of Yr. Ind. Acad. Gen. Dentistry, 1992. Fellow Acad. Gen. Dentistry, Am. Soc. Dentistry Children, Internat. Coll. Dentists; mem. ADA, First Dist. Dental Soc., Ind. Dental Assn., Am. Acad. Pediatric Dentistry, Ind. Acad. Gen. Dentistry, S.W. Ind. Oral Health Found. (disbursement com.), Masons. Republican. Methodist. Avocations: farming, forestry, fishing, poetry, gardening. Home: 7100 Olive St Evansville IN 47715-3625 Office: 207 S Green River Rd Evansville IN 47715-7334 Business E-Mail: praibley@aol.com.

RAICHLE, MARCUS EDWARD, radiology, neurology educator; b. Hoquiam, Wash., Mar. 15, 1937; m. Mary Elizabeth Rupert, 1964; children: Marcus Edward, Timothy Stephen, Sarah Elizabeth, Katherine Ann. BS, U. Wash., 1960, MD, 1964. Diplomate Am. Bd. Psychiatry and Neurology. Intern Balt. City Hosps., 1964—65, resident, 1965—66; asst. neurologist N.Y. Hosp. Cornell Med. Ctr., N.Y.C., 1966—68, neurologist, chief resident, 1968—69; clin. instr. dept. medicine divsn. neurosci. U. Tex. Med. Sch., San Antonio,

1969—70; rsch. instr. Washington U. Sch. Med., St. Louis, 1971—72, from asst. prof. neurology to assoc. prof. neurology, 1972—78, from asst. prof. radiology (radiation scis.) to assoc. prof. radiology Edward Mallinckrodt Inst. Radiology, 1972—79, from asst. prof. to assoc. prof. biomedical engring., 1974-79, prof. neurology, 1978—, prof. radiology Edward Mallinckrodt Inst. Radiology, 1979—, prof. biomedical engring., 1979—. Instr. dept. neurology Cornell U. Med. Coll., N.Y.C., 1968—69; asst. neurologist Barnes Hosp., St. Louis, 1971—75, assoc. neurologist, 1975—78, neurologist, 1978—; cons. neurologist St. Louis Children's Hosp., 1975—; neurologist Jewish Hosp., St. Louis, 1984—, St. Louis Regional Hosp., St. Louis, 1984—; mem. neurology study sect. A NIH, 1975—79; mem. com. cerebrovascular diseases Nat. Inst. Neurol. Diseases and Stroke, long range planning effort, 1978, basic sci. task force, 78; mem ad hoc adv. panel Nat. Inst. Neurol. Diseases and Stroke, 1983, chmn. PET grants spl. rev. com., 83, chmn. brain imaging ctrs. spl. rev. com., 85; mem. adv. bd. McDonnell-Pew Program cognitive neuroscience, 1989; other coms. Mem. editl. bd.: Stroke, 1982, Neurology, 1976—82, Annals of Neurology, 1979—86, Brain, 1985—90, Journal Cerebral Blood Flow and Metabolism, 1983—86, dep. chief editor:, 1981—83, mem. editl. bd.: Human Neurobiology, 1985—87, Brain Rsch., 1985—90, Synapse, 1987—90, Jour. Neurosci., 1989—95, Jour. Cognitive Neurosci., 1989—, Cerebral Cortex, 1990—, Jour. Nuclear Medicine, 1990—96. Maj. USAF, 1969—71. Recipient umerous awards, lectrs., fellows including Charles A. Dana award for pioneering achievements in health and edn., Dana Found., 1996. Mem.: NAS, Inst. Medicine of NAS.

RAIKES, CHARLES FITZGERALD, retired lawyer; b. Mpls., Oct. 6, 1930; s. Arthur FitzGerald and Margaret (Hawthorne) R.; m. Antonia Raikes, Dec. 20, 1969; children: Jennifer Catherine, Victoria Samantha. BA, Washington U., 1952; MA, Harvard U., 1955, LL.B., 1958. Bar: N.Y. State 1959. Assoc. White & Case, N.Y.C., 1958-69; assoc. gen. counsel Dun & Bradstreet, Inc., N.Y.C., 1969-72, v.p., gen. counsel, 1972-73, The Dun & Bradstreet Corp., N.Y.C., 1973-76, sr. v.p., gen. counsel, 1976-94, of counsel, 1994-95; ret., 1995. Cons. Bd. Govs. Fed. Reserve System, 1958-95. Served with U.S. Army, 1952-54. Woodrow Wilson fellow, 1952 Mem. Assn. Bar City of N.Y., Harvard Club, Phi Beta Kappa. Home: 26 Crooked Trl Norwalk CT 06853-1106

RAIKES, JEFF, information technology executive; B of Engring. and Econ. Systems, Stanford U. Software devel. mgr. Apple Computer Inc.; product mgr. Microsoft, Redmond, Wash., 1981, v.p. Worldwide Sales and Support Group, group v.p. Productivity and Bus. Svcs. Ptnr. Seattle Mariners Baseball Club, 1992—; bd. dirs. XO Comm. Inc.; mem. Sr. Leadership Team, Bus. Leadership Team, Microsoft. Mem. U. Nebr. Found.; trustee Wash. State U. Found.; leader Online Wash. State U. Initiative. Office: Microsoft One Microsoft Way Redmond WA 98052-6399

RAIKHEL, NATASHA V. plant cell biology educator; b. Jan. 11, 1947; MS, Leningrad State U., 1970; PhD, Inst. Cytology, Acad. Scis., Leningrad, 1975. Rschr. Acad. Scis., Inst. Cytology, Leningrad, 1970—75, asst. rsch. scientist lab. cytology of unicellular organisma, 1975—78; postdoctoral assoc. dept. botany U. Ga., Athens, 1979—84, asst. rsch. scientist dept. botany, 1984—86; from asst. prof. to assoc. prof. to prof. Mich. State U., MSU-DOE Plant Rsch. Lab. and Dept. Botany, East Lansing, 1986—94, univ. disting. prof., 1997—2000; Ernst and Helen Leibacher chair prof. plant molecular, cell biology and genetics dept. botany and plant scis. U. Calif., Riverside, Calif., 2001—, dir. Ctr. for Plant Cell Biology dept. botany and plant scis., 2001—, Disting. prof. plant cell biology dept. botany and plant scis., 2001. Sabbatical leave U. Melbourne, Australia, 1996, Nagoya (Japan) U., 1996; mem. adv. panel on Alzheimer's DiseaseUSDA, 92; mem. adv. panel NSF, 1994—97; co-organizer NATO-ASI Course, Maratea, Italy, 1997, 22d Symposium in Plant Biology, 2003. Mem. editl. bd.: Plant Physiology, 1988—92, Jour. Cell Biology, 1995—2000, editor-in-chief: Plant Physiology, 1997—, mem. editl. bd.: Current Opinion in Plant Cell Biology, 1998—. Recipient Guggenheim fellowship, 1996, Fellowship for Rsch. in Japan, 1996. Mem.: Internat. Soc. for Plant Molecular Biology (bd. dirs. 2001), Am. Soc. for Plant Physiologists (mem. publ. com. 1992—93, mem. exec. com. 1996—99), Am. Soc. for Cell Biology (program com. mem. 1998—2000). Office: U Calif Riverside Dept Botany and Plant Scis 2109 Batchelor Hall Riverside CA 92521-

RAIL, KATHY LYNN PARISH, accountant; b. Chewelah, Wash., May 21, 1951; d. John Edward and Margaret Irene (Seefeldt) Rail. BBA, Gonzaga U., 1984. CPA, Wash. Legal sec. Redbook Pub. Co., N.Y.C., 1974-75, Howard Michaelson, Esquire, Spokane, Wash., 1975-76; sec. Burns Internat. Security Svcs., Spokane, 1977-79; sec. to contr. Gonzaga U., Spokane, 1979-81, acctg. asst., 1981-82; staff acct. Martin, Holland & Petersen, CPA's, Yakima, Wash., 1984-87; acct., supr. Strader Hallet & Co., P.S., Bellevue, Wash., 1988-91; acct. Miller & Co., P.S., Woodinville, Wash., 1991-93; pres. Parish Rail, CPA, P.S., Redmond, Wash., 1993—. Treas. White Pass Ski Patrol, Nat. Ski Patrol Systems, Wash., 1987-90; editor, chmn. audit com. Mt. Spokane Ski Patrol, 1983-84. Mem. AICPA, Am. Soc. Women Accts. (charter, editor 1987), Wash. Soc. CPA (sec. Sammamish Valley chpt. 1990-92, pres. 1992-93, 93-94), Washington Soc. of Cert. Pub. Accts. (chair adv. coun. 1995-96, tax com., govt. affairs com., dir. 1996-98), Bus. and Profl. Women of Woodinville (treas. 1994-95), Carnation C. of C. Lutheran. Avocations: skiing, piano, golf.

RAILA, FRANK ARTHUR, radiologist; b. Chgo., July 26, 1925; BS, Loyola U., Maywood, Ill., 1950, MD, 1957; MS, U. Ill., Chgo., 1953. Diplomate Am. Bd. Radiology, subspecialty neuroradiology. Intern Resurrection Hosp., Chgo., 1957-58; resident in radiology VA Hosp., Long Beach, Calif., 1963-66; prof. radiology U. Miss. Med. Ctr., Jackson. Mem. staff U. Miss. Med, Ctr., Jackson; alsp pvt. practice managed care/HMO. Co-author: (CD-ROM) Diagnostic Radiology, 1996; contbr. Youmans Neurological Surgery, 4th edit. Mem. St. Mark's Meth. Ch., Brandon, Miss. Lt. col. U.S. Army Res. Med. Corps., ret. Fellow Am. Coll. Radiology; mem. Am. Univ. Radiologists, New Zealand Med. Assn., Radiol. Soc. N.Am., So. Med. Assn., Am. Inst. of Ultrasound in Medicine, Soc. of Nuclear Medicine, Am. Ex-Prisoners of War, Am. Legion, Veterans of the Battle of the Bulge, Southeastern Neuroradiol. Soc., Am. Soc. Head and Neck Radiology, Am. Soc. Neuroradiology, Am. Soc. Pediat. Neuroradiology, Am. Soc. Spine Radiology, N.Am. Spine Soc. Office: Univ Radiologists Assocs U Miss Med Ctr Dept Rad 2500 N State St Jackson MS 39216-4500 E-mail: frankaraila@aol.com.

RAILSBACK, SHERRIE LEE, educator, adoption search and reunion consultant; b. Phila., Mar. 12, 1942; children: Ricky, Cindy. BBA, U. Ky., 1981. Sales mgr. Marjo Cosmetics, Ft. Wayne, Ind.; asst. dir. patient fin. svcs. Riverside Meth. Hosp., Columbus, Ohio; cons. Railsback and Assocs., Long Beach, Calif.; adoption search/reunion cons., educator Searchers Connection, L.A. Mem.: ASTD, NAFE, Book Publicists So. Calif., Nat. Spkrs. Assn. Office Phone: 310-967-1337.

RAILTON, PETER ALBERT, philosophy educator; b. Elgin, Ill., May 23, 1950; s. Arthur Roy and Marjorie Elizabeth Marks Railton; m. Rebecca Jarvis Scott, Apr. 21, 1978; children: John Scott-Railton, Thomas Scott-Railton. AB magna cum laude, Harvard U., 1971; PhD, Princeton U., 1980. From asst. prof. philosophy to assoc. prof. U. Mich., Ann Arbor, 1979—90, prof. philosophy, 1990—, Nelson prof., 1999—2001, Perrin Collegiate prof., 2001—, dept. chair, 2002—. Vis. prof. U. Calif., Berkeley, 1984-85, Princeton (N.J.) U., 1990; mem. Coun. for Philos. Studies, N.Y.C., 1992-94; rsch. assoc. Ecole Poly., Paris, 1995—. Co-editor, author: Moral Discourse and Practice, 1997; author: Facts, Values and Norms, 2003; mem. editl. bd.: Ethics, Utilitas; contbr. articles to profl. jours. Am. Coun. Learned Socs. fellow, 1988-89, 2000, NEH fellow, 1999, Guggenheim fellow, 2001-2002. Mem. Am. Philos. Assn. (various coms. 1978—), Am. Soc. for Polit. and Legal Philosophy, Philosophy of Scis. Assn. (com. mem. 1978—), Am. Acad. Arts and Sci. Office: U Mich Dept Philosophy 2215 Angell Hall Ann Arbor MI 48109 Office Phone: 734-764-6285.

RAILTON, WILLIAM SCOTT, federal agency administrator; b. Newark, July 30, 1935; s. William Scott and Carolyn Elizabeth (Guiberson) R.; m. Karen Elizabeth Walsh, Mar. 31, 1979; 1 son, William August; children by previous marriage: William Scott, Anne Greenwood. BSEE, U. Wash., 1962; JD with honors, George Washington U., 1965. Bar: D.C. 1966, Md. 1966, Va. 1993, U.S. Patent Office 1966. Assoc., then ptnr. Kemon, Palmer & Estabrook, Washington, 1966-70; sr. trial atty. Dept. Labor, Washington, 1970-71, asst. counsel for trial litigation, 1971-72, chief counsel U.S. Occupational Safety and Health Rev. Commn., Washington, 1972-77, acting gen. counsel, 1975-77; ptnr. Reed Smith LLP, Pitts., 1977—2002, ret., 2002; appointed commr., chmn. U.S. Occupl. Safety and Health Rev. Commn., 2002—. Lectr. George Washington U. Law Sch., 1977-79, seminar chmn. Occupational Safety and Health Act, Govt. Inst., 1979-96; lectr. Practicing Law Inst., 1976-79. Author: (legal handbooks) The Examination System and the Backlog, 1965, The OSHA General Duty Clause, 1977, The OSHA Health Standards, 1977; OSHA Compliance Handbook, 1992; contbg. author: Occupational Safety and Health Law, 1988, 93. Regional chmn. Montgomery County (Md.) Republican party, 1968-70; pres. Montgomery Sq. Citizens Assn., 1970-71; bd. dirs., pres. Foxvale Farms Homeowners Assn., 1979-82; pres. Orchards on the Potomac Homeowners Assn., 1990-92; dir. Great Falls Hist. Soc., 1991-94; scoutmaster Troop 55 Boy Scouts Am., 1993-98. With USMC, 1953-58. Recipient Meritorious Achievement medal Dept. Labor, 1972, Outstanding Service award OSHA Rev. Commn., 1977, elected fell. Coll. Labor and Employment Lawyers, 1998. Fellow Coll. Labor and Employment Lawyers; mem. ABA (mgmt. co-chmn. occupational safety and health law com. 1995-98), Md. Bar Assn., Va. Bar Assn., Bar Assn. D.C. (vice chmn. young lawyers sect. 1971), Order of Coif, Sigma Phi Epsilon, Phi Delta Phi. Home: 10102 Walker Lake Dr Great Falls VA 22066-3502 Office: US Occupational Safety and Health Rev Commn 1120 20th Street NW Washington DC 20036 *Lawsuits are won by pre-trial preparation. A litigator should be candid with his clients and honest in his dealings with associates, opponents and the courts; an attorney should also volunteer his service to the community of which he is a part.*

RAIMI, BURTON LOUIS, lawyer; b. Detroit, May 5, 1938; s. Irving and Rae (Abel) R.; m. Judith Morse, Mar. 31, 1963 (div. Mar. 1985); children: Diane L., and Matthew D. BA, Brandeis U., 1960; JD with honors, U. Mich., 1963; LLM, George Washington U., 1964. Bar: Mich. 1963, DC 1964, Fla. 1991, U.S. Ct. Appeals (4th, 7th, 8th, 9th, 10th, 11th and DC cirs.), U.S. Supreme Ct., U.S. Ct. of Fed. Claims. Atty. appelate ct. sect. NLRB, Washington, 1964-69; assoc. Morgan, Lewis & Bockius, Washington, 1969-71; dep. gen. counsel FDIC, Washington, 1971-78; ptnr. Rosenman and Colin, Washington, 1978-86, Dechert Price & Rhoads, Washington, 1986-93; shareholder McCaffrey & Raimi, P.A., Naples and Sarasota, Fla., 1994—2002, Law Offices of Burton L. Raimi PA, Sarasota, Fla., 2003—. Speaker various insts. Mem. ABA (past chmn. bank receiverships subcom. of banking com.), D.C. Bar Assn. (past chmn. banking law com., com. on interest on lawyers trust accounts), Fla. Bar (bus. law com.). Avocations: travel, golf, fishing. Home: 4452 Staghorn Ln Sarasota FL 34238-5626 Office: 1800 2nd St Ste 753 Sarasota FL 34236-5900 Office Phone: 941-957-0733. Office Fax: 941-957-0449. Business E-Mail: burt@moneylaw.com.

RAIMI, RALPH ALEXIS, mathematics professor; b. Detroit, July 25, 1924; s. Jacob and Sylvia (Krusner) R.; m. Sonya Lenore Drews, June 29, 1947, children: Jessica, Diana. BS in Physics, U. Mich., 1947, MS in Math, 1948, PhD, 1954. Faculty U. Rochester, 1952—, prof. math., 1966—95, chmn. dept. sociology, 1983—86, assoc. dean for grad. studies Coll. Arts and Sci., 1967—75, prof. emeritus math., 1995—. Cons. in Math. Edn. State of Calif. Bd. Edn. and private ednl. founds. Author: Vested Interests, 1982, The Philomathic Debating Club, 1991; contbr. articles to mags., jours., newspapers. Served to 1st lt. USAAF, 1943-46. Fulbright Grad. fellow Paris, 1949-50; Lloyd postdoctoral fellow U. Mich., 1955-56; NSF grantee; Office of Naval Rsch. grantee. Mem.: Nat. Assn. Scholars, Am. Math. Soc., Math. Assn. Am., Philomathic Debating Club, Am. Wine Soc. Home: 46 Glen Ellyn Way Rochester NY 14618-1502 *In my childhood I was told to be like everyone else, and not to take on airs. My relatives and teachers doubtless had a democratic virtue in mind, but their egalitarianism slowed my ambition. Books came from the library and not from the likes of me, I thought, and wealth was theft from the poor. Now I know better, but it is mostly too late.*

RAIMI, SAMUEL M. film director; b. Royal Oak, Mich., Oct. 23, 1959; s. Leonard Ronald and Celia Barbara (Abrams) R. Student in humanities study, Mich. State U., East Lansing, 1977-79. V.p. Renaissance Pictures, Ferndale, Mich., 1979—. Writer, dir. (films) Evil Dead, 1981, Crimewave, 1985 (Best Dir. award 1986), Evil Dead II, 1986, Darkman, 1990, Army of Darkness: Evil Dead 3, 1993; co-writer: (screenplay) The Hudsucker Proxy, 1994; prodr. Hard Target, 1993, Timecop, 1994; dir. (film) The Quick and the Dead, 1995, A Simple Plan, 1998, For Love of the Game, 1999, The Gift, 2000, Spider-Man, 2002, Spider-Man 2, 2004; appeared in films Spies Like Us, 1985, Thou Shall Not Kill...Except, 1987, Maniac Cop, 1988, Miller's Crossing, 1990, Innocent Blood, 1992, Intruder, 1994, Terminal Force, 1995; appeared on TV Journey to the Center of the Earth, 1993, Body Bags, 1993, The Stand, 1994; prodr., writer Mantis, 1993; exec. prodr. syndicated TV series The Legendary Journeys of Hercules, 1994-97, Xena: Warrior Princess, 1995-97, American Gothic, 1995-96, Spy Game, 1997, Young Hercules, 1998, Jack of All Trades, 2000, Cleopatra 2025, 2000-2001. Recipient Best Horror Film, Knokke'heist Film Festival Belgium, 1982, Best Horror Film and Best Spl. Effects, Sitges Film Festival, Spain, 1982, 1st Prize of the Critics, 1st Prize of the Pub., Paris Festival Sci. Fiction, Fantasy and Horror, 1983, Best Horror Film of Yr., Fangoria Mag., 1983. Mem. Mich. State U. Soc. for Creative Film Making (founder, pres. 1978, 79), Calif. Rare Fruit Growers. Office: ICM 8942 Wilshire Blvd Beverly Hills CA 90211-1934

RAIMONDI, RUGGERO, opera singer; b. Bologna, Italy, Oct. 3, 1941; m. Isabel Maier, 1987. Studies with, Teresa Pediconi, Armando Piervenanzi. Debut in La Boheme, Spoleto, Italy, 1964; singer in major houses, Europe and US; Met. debut in Ernani, NYC, 1970; favorite roles include Don Giovanni, Philip II, Boris and Don Quichotte; recorded Verdi Requiem, Vespri Siciliani, La Boheme, Aida, Attila, Don Carlos, Macbeth, Simon Boccanegra, Don Giovanni, Boris Godunov, Tosca, Turandot, Barbiere di Siviglia, Mosè, Nozze di Figaro, Italiana in Algieri, Cenerentola, Il Viaggio a Reims, and others; appeared in films Don Giovanni (Joseph Losey), 1979, Six Characters in Search of a Singer (Maurice Bejart), 1983, Carmen (Francesco Rosi), 1986, Tosca (B. Jaquot), 2001, others; opera prodn. since, 1986—. Decorated Comdr. Arts et Lettres, Officier de la Légion d'Honneur (France), chevalier Ordre de Malte, Grand Ufficiale della Repubblica Italiana, comdr. Mérite Culturel (Monaco), others; named Citizen of Honor, City of Athens, Greece. Office: 140 bis rue Lecourbe F-75015 Paris France

RAINAL, ATTILIO JOSEPH, retired electronics engineer, researcher; b. Marion Heights, Pa., Feb. 14, 1930; m. Violet Dorothy Robel, June 29, 1957; children: Valery, Eric. BS in Engring. Sci., Pa. State U., 1956; MSEE, Drexel U., 1959; D of Elec. Engring., Johns Hopkins U., 1963. Engr. Applied Physics Lab. Johns Hopkins U., Silver Spring, Md., 1955; engr. Martin Co., Balt., 1956-59; mem. rsch. staff Carlyle Barton Lab. Johns Hopkins U., Balt., 1959-64; mem. tech. staff R & D AT&T Bell Labs., Whippany and Murray Hill, N.J., 1964-83, mem. disting. tech. staff R & D, 1983—2003, ret., 2003. Contbr. more than 40 articles to jours. including Rev. of Sci. Instruments, Electronics, Bell Systems Tech. Jour., Bell Labs. Tech. Jour. With USAF, 1948-52. Mem. IEEE (life), Info. Theory, Component, Hybrids and Mfg. Tech. Achievements include research on noise theory, signal detection and estimation, radiometry, radar, FM, first passage times of random processes, crosstalk, voltage breakdown, current carrying capacity of printed wires, performance limits of electrical interconnections; 12 patents, including balanced interconnections, and laser intensity modulation. Home: 28 Woodruff Rd Morristown NJ 07960-4620

RAINALDI, LIDIO G. state senator; Magistrate; Dem. senator dist. 4 N.Mex. State Senate. Mem. judiciary com. N.Mex. State Senate, vice chair Indian and cultural affairs. Home: 1101 Martinelli Gallup NM 87301 Office: NMex State Senate State Capitol Mail Rm Dept Santa Fe NM 87503 E-mail: senate@state.nm.us.

RAINBOLT, H. E. bank executive; b. 1929; BBA in econ. and fin., U. Okla.; grad., Sch. of Banking, U. of Wis.-Madison. With Fed. Nat. Bank & Trust, Shawnee, Okla., 1950-89, chmn. bd. dirs., 1967-89; chmn. BancFirst, Oklahoma City, 1989—. Bd. dirs. Trencor Inc., Oklahoma City, Sentinel Petroleum Co. Inc., Oklahoma City. Office: BancFirst 101 N Broadway Ave Ste 200 Oklahoma City OK 73102-8403

RAINE, MELINDA L. library manager; b. Boston, Feb. 4, 1951; d. James Agee and Marjorie Elizabeth (Gilstrap) Raine; m. Stephen Richard Brogden, Jan. 1, 1983; 1 child, Nathan Raine Brogden. BA, U. Iowa, 1973, MA, 1974. Info. specialist Pub. Libr. Des Moines, 1974-82, libr. mgr., 1982-90; task force coord. Visio 2020 Project, Conejo Future Found., Thousand Oaks, Calif., 1991-92; mgr. engring. libr. Metters Industries, Camarillo, Calif., 1992-94; govt. publs. libr. Pepperdine U., Malibu, Calif., 1994-98, coord. info. resources, 1998—. Author: Options for Our Endangered Environment, 1992, Water: Liquid Gold, 1992, The Housing Crisis, 1992, Solid Ideas for Solid Waste, 1992; co-author (with Elizabeth parang and Trisha Stevenson): Redesigning Freshman Seminar Library Instruction Based on Information Comepetencies in Research Strategies, 2001. Mem. ALA, AAUW (pub. policy chair 1993-96, v.p. programming 1992-93), Calif. Libr. Assn., Calif. Acad. and Rsch. Librs. Office: Pepperdine U 24255 Pacific Coast Hwy Malibu CA 90263-4786

RAINER, REX KELLY, civil engineer, educator; b. Montgomery, Ala., July 17, 1924; s. Kelly Kenyon and Pearl (Jones) R.; m. Betty Ann Page, Aug. 28, 1945; children: Rex Kelly, John Kenyon. BS, Auburn (Ala.) U., 1944, MS, 1946; PhD, Okla. State U., 1967. Asst. engr. L. & N. R.R. Co., Cin., 1944-45; design engr. Polglaze & Basenberg, Birmingham, Ala., 1945-51; pres., chmn. Rainer Co., Inc., Orlando, Fla., 1951-62; prof. civil engring. Auburn U., 1962-67, head civil engring. dept., 1967; exec. v.p., 1980; hwy. dir. State of Ala., 1979-80, fin. dir., 1981-82; spl. asst. to gov. of Ala., 1981-82; dir. Office for Advancement Devel. Industry U. Ala., Birmingham, 1982-86; pres., cons. engr. Rex K. Rainer, Inc., 1982-98, ret., 1998. Cons. to ins. cos., constrn. engring. firms; mem. Ala. Bd. Registration Profl. Engrs. and Land Surveyors, 1977-89. Contbr. articles to profl. jours. Mem. Municipal Planning Bd., 1963-65, Indsl. Park Devel. Bd., 1969-71, So. Regional Edn. Bd., 1982-86. Served with AUS, 1943. Fellow ASCE (sec., treas. 1970, pres. Ala. chpt. 1976-77, chmn. Constrn. Rsch. Coun., chmn. hwy. div. publs. com.; Civil Govt. award 1981); mem. Assn. Gen. Contractors Am. (bd. dirs. 1955), Am. Soc. for Engring. Edn. (chmn. constrn. engring. com.), Am. Pub. Works Assn., Phi Kappa Phi, Tau Beta Pi, Chi Epsilon.

RAINER, WILLIAM GERALD, cardiac surgeon; b. Gordo, Ala., Nov. 13, 1927; s. Jamie Flournoy and Lula (Davis) R.; m. Lois Sayre, Oct. 7, 1950; children: Vickie, Bill, Julia, Leslie. Student, Emory U., Atlanta, Ga., 1943-44, U. Ala., 1944-45; MD, U. Tenn., Memphis, 1948; MS in Surgery, U. Colo., Denver, 1958. Diplomate Am. Bd. Surgery, Am. Bd. Thoracic Surgery. Intern Wesley Hosp., Chgo., 1949; gen. practice medicine Blue Island, Ill., 1950-52; resident Denver VA Hosp., 1954-59; practice medicine specializing in cardiac surgery Denver, 1960—. Bd. dirs. St. Joseph Hosp. Found., Denver; dinsting. clin. prof. surgery U. Colo. Health Sci. Ctr. Contbr. articles to profl. jours. Active Colo. Symphony Assn.; dir. emeritus St. Joseph Hosp. Found. Bd. Lt. U.S. Army, 1952-54. Decorated Bronze Star; recipient Disting. Alumnus award U. Tenn. Health Sci. Ctr., 1992, Florence Sabin award U. Colo. Health Sci. Ctr., 1998, Disting. Svc. award U. Colo., 2004. Mem. Soc. Thoracic Surgeons (sec. 1980-85, pres. 1989, historian 1996—, Disting. Svc. award 1998), Colo. Med. Soc. (pres. 1984-85), Denver Med. Soc. (pres. 1984), Denver Clin. & Pathology Soc. (pres. 1997), Am. Coll. Chest Physicians (pres. 1984), Am. Bd. Thoracic Surgeons (bd. dirs. 1982-88), Am. Surg. Assn., Am. Assn. Thoracic Surgery, Societé Internationale de Chirugie, Cactus Club. Avocations: photography, travel. Office: 2005 Franklin St Ste 380 Denver CO 80205-5411 Office Phone: 303-839-5662. E-mail: wrainer@qwest.net.

RAINES, FRANKLIN DELANO, finance company executive; b. Seattle, Jan. 14, 1949; s. Delno Thomas and Ida Mae Raines; m. Wendy Farrow. BA magna cum laude, Harvard U., 1971, JD cum laude, 1976; postgrad., Oxford U., 1971-73. Assoc. dir. Seattle Model Cities Program, 1972-73; assoc. Preston, Thorgrimson, Ellis, Holman & Fletcher, Seattle, 1976-77; asst. dir. White House Domestic Policy Staff, Washington, 1977-78; assoc. dir. U.S. Office of Mgmt. and Budget, Washington, 1978-79; v.p. Lazard, Freres & Co., N.Y.C., 1979-82, sr. v.p., 1983-84, ptnr., 1985—91; vice-chmn. Fannie Mae, Washington, 1991-96; dir. U.S. Office Mgmt. and Budget, 1996-98; chmn., CEO designate Fannie Mae, Washington, 1998, chmn., CEO, 1999—. Bd. dirs. Pepsico, Pfizer, Inc., Fannie Mae. Former pres. bd. overseers Harvard U.; chmn. Fannie Mae Found.; co-chmn. Bus. Roundtable; Nat. Urban League; Enterprise Found.; Black Student Fund. Rhodes scholar, 1971. Mem. AAAS, Coun. Fgn. Rels., Nat. Acad. Social Ins., Washington State Bar Assn., D.C. Bar Assn., Bus. Coun. Avocations: running, golf.

RAINES, JEFF, biomedical scientist, medical research director; b. NYC, Sept. 5, 1943; s. Otis J. and Mildred C. (Wetzler) Raines; children: Gretchen Christena, Victoria Jean. BSME, Clemson U., 1965; MME, U. Fla., 1967; PhD in Biomed. Engring., MIT, 1972. Mem. staff MIT, Cambridge, 1968—70; biophysicist dept. surgery Mass. Gen. Hosp., Boston, 1972—77, dir. Vascular Lab., 1972—77; instr. surgery Harvard Med. Sch., Boston, 1973—77; preceptor Harvard/MIT Sch. Health Scis., 1976—77; rsch. dir., dir. Vascular Lab. Miami (Fla.) Heart Inst., Miami Beach, 1977—88; adj. prof. bioengring. U. Miami, Coral Gables, 1977—; prof. surgery U. Miami (Fla.) Sch. Medicine, 1977—. Prin. investigator series NIH programs and pharm. firms, 1977—; Harvard Travelling fellow lectr. in Europe, 1975. Contbr. numerous articles on biomechanics, cardiovasc. diagnosis, dynamics and instrumentation to sci. jours. Recipient Apollo Achievement award, NASA, 1969; fellow, NIH, 1972. Fellow: Am. Assn. Physicists in Medicine, Am. Coll. Radiology, Am. Coll. Cardiology; mem.: ASME, AAAS, Cardiovasc. Sys. Dynamics Soc. (founding mem., editor 1976—, pres. 1980—82), Internat. Cardiovasc. Soc., Instrument Soc. Am., Biomed. Engring. Soc., New Eng. Cardiovasc. Soc., Am. Heart Assn., MIT Club, Harvard Club, Coral Gables Club, Kiwanis, Sigma Xi, Tau Beta Pi. Republican. Presbyterian. Achievements include patents for medical devices; development of mathematical models of arterial hemodynamics and clinical use of autotransfusion. Home: 6820 Granada Blvd Coral Gables FL 33146-3824 Office: Univ Miami Dept Surgery R-310 1611 NW 12th Ave Miami FL 33136-1005 Office Phone: 305-585-5371. Business E-Mail: jraines@med.miami.edu.

RAINES, JIM NEAL, lawyer; b. Memphis, Sept. 11, 1943; s. J.E. and Amelia C. Raines; m. Julia Walters, Sept. 1, 1979; 1 dau., Lee Pierceson. BBA, Memphis State U., 1965, JD, 1968. Bar: Tenn. 1968, U.S. Dist. Ct. (we. dist.) Tenn. 1968, U.S. Ct. Appeals (6th cir.) 1970, U.S. Ct. Appeals (5th cir.) 1975, U.S. Supreme Ct. 1974. Trial atty. antitrust divsn. U.S. Dept. Justice, Washington, 1968-70; asst. U.S. atty. We. Dist. Tenn., Memphis, 1970-74; ptnr. Burch, Porter & Johnson, Memphis, 1975-76, Glankler, Brown, Gilliland, Chase, Robinson, Raines, Memphis, 1976—2001; v.p., sec., gen. counsel Thomas & Betts Corp., Memphis, 2001—. Served with USMC, 1960-64. Mem. ABA, Memphis Bar Assn., Shelby County Bar Assn., Univ. Club. Office: Thomas & Betts Corp 8155 T&B Blvd Memphis TN 38125 Business E-Mail: jim_raines@tnb.com.

RAINES, KAREN CORNELL, secondary school educator; b. Columbus, Ohio, Dec. 12, 1956; d. Stanley Buel and Ruth Ellen Cornell; m. Roger Dale Raines, July 5, 1980; children: Mary Katherine, Sandra Beth. MusB, W.Va. U., 1979, MMus, 1983; tchg. cert., William Carey Coll., Gulfport, Miss., 1996. Cert. tchr., Miss. Choral dir. Grace Luth. Ch., Long Beach, Miss., 1992-94, Christ United Meth. Ch., Long Beach, 1994-98; tchr. music Waveland (Miss.) Elem. Sch., 1996-98, North Bay Elem. Sch., Bay St. Louis, Miss., 1996-99; tchr. choral music Robert Smalls Mid. Sch., Beaufort, S.C., 1999—. Mem. dist. curriculum com. Bay/Waveland Schs., Bay St. Louis, 1997-99. Mem. choirs performing at Carnegie Hall, N.Y.C., 1997, internat. choral competition, Verona, Italy, 1999. Mem. Music Educators' Nat. Conf. Democrat. Methodist. Avocations: reading, community choral groups. Home: 109 Lakewood Dr Guyton GA 31312-6562 Office: Robert Smalls Mid Sch 43 W K Alston Dr Beaufort SC 29906-9432

RAINES, LOUIS EDWARD, school administrator; b. Balt., Nov. 24, 1965; s. Clarence William Raines and Nona Ann Raines-Dotson; m. Carmen Benninga, Dec. 29, 1989. BME, Kans. State U., 1994, M of Ednl. Adminstrn., 1996. Cert. instr. grade K-12, Kans.; cert. bldg. level adminstr., Kans. Prin. arranger, composer Frontier, Manhattan, Kans., 1984-89; freelance composer, arranger Manhattan, 1989-94; dir. choral activities Concordia (Kans.) H.S., 1994-98, assoc. prin., 1998-2000, prin., 2000—02, Fort Morgan (Co.) H.S., 2002—. State resource specialist Kans. North Cen. Accreditation, Wichita; vis. team chair N. Ctrl. Accreditation, Wichita; mem. legis. liaison com. United Sch. Adminstrs. Kans., 1998-2002. Composer: (songs) Country Christmas, 1987; arranger: (mus. medley) Nursery Rhyme Parade, 1992; studio arranger: (sound recs.) Won't Let Love Hurt Me Again, Bed of Roses, Second Wind, Something to Remember You By, 1988; performer with Kans. State Opera Theatre; edn. and polit. editor Open Directory Project. Sec./treas., Cloud County Dem. Party, Concordia, Kans., 2000-2002; ordained elder, deacon Presbyn. Ch., Louisville, Ky., 1993—; mem. Kans. State Choir, Manhattan, 1986-88, 92-94. Mem. Nat. Assn. Secondary Sch. Prins., United Sch. Adminstrs. of Kans., Kans. Assn. Secondary Sch. Adminstrs., Kans. Music Educators Assn. (choral chairperson no. cen. dist. 1995-97), Golden Key Nat. Honor Soc., Phi Kappa Phi. Democrat. Presbyterian. Avocations: public speaking, coin collecting/numismatics, writing and arranging music, fishing. Home: 801 Ute Fort Morgan CO 80701 E-mail: eraines@morgan.k12.co.us.

RAINES, SHIRLEY CAROL, academic administrator; b. Jackson, Tenn., Apr. 15, 1945; m. Robert J. Canady; 1 stepchild, Brian Scott Smith. BS, U. Tenn., Martin; MS, EdD, U. Tenn., Knoxville; grad. mgmt. program, Harvard Grad. Sch. of Edn. Dept. head Northeastern State U, 1983—87; assoc. prof. edn. George Mason U., Fairfax, Va., 1987—92; prof. and chmn. dept. of childhood/ lang. arts/ reading U. South Fla., 1992—95; prof. U. Ky. Coll. of Edn., 1995—2001, vice chancellor academic svcs. and dean of coll., 1998—2001; pres. U. Memphis, 2001—. Author books; contbr. articles to profl. jours. Recipient Dist. Svc. to Edn., Phi Delta Kappa, Dist. Paper awards, Ednl. Rsch. Assn. Office: U Memphis 341 Adminstrn Bldg Memphis TN 38152

RAINES, TIM D. real estate corporation executive; b. Everett, Wash., May 8, 1950; s. Richard Thomas and Arvilla Mae (Chick) R.; m. Virginia N. McLaurin, July 21, 1977. BA, U. Ala., Tuscaloosa, 1968-72; MA, U. Ala., Birmingham, 1977; postgrad., U. Calif., Berkeley, 1976-77. Cmty. planner HUD, Birmingham, 1972-77, dir., program planning and eval. Atlanta, 1977-83, dir. regional housing ops. div., 1983-87; exec. v.p., COO Sanbury Corp., Atlanta, 1987-92; prin. Profit, Inc., 1992—. Pres. Stonington Homeowners Assn., Atlanta, 1980-83; patron Atlanta Ballet, 1978—; sponsor Pub. TV (WPBA), Atlanta, 1980—; mem. adv. bd. Salvation Army, 1997—; mem. Ga. Affordable Housing Coalition, 1993—. Recipient Cert. of Recognition William A. Jump Found., 1978. Mem. Am. Soc. Pub. Adminstrs., Am. Mgmt. Assn., Atlanta Zool. Soc. Avocations: travel, gardening, harmonica, juggling, custom cars. Home: 8315 Ison Rd Atlanta GA 30350-3129

RAINESS, ALAN EDWARD, psychiatrist, neurologist, educator; b. NYC, Sept. 24, 1935; s. George W. and Ida Rainess; m. Alice Maree Haber, June 5, 1968; children: Alice Jeanne Rainess Jordan, James Alan (dec.). AB, Columbia Coll., 1957; MD, U. Paris, 1965. Diplomate Am. Bd. Psychiatry and Neurology. Intern Meadowbrook Hosp., East Meadow, L.I., 1965-66; resident in psychiatry NY VA Hosp., NYC, 1966-67; teaching fellow in psychiatry Harvard Med. Sch., Boston, 1967; chief resident in psychiatry Boston City Hosp., 1967; psychiatrist U.S. Army Hosp., Heidelberg, Germany, 1968—70; resident in psychiatry Walter Reed Med. Ctr., Washington, 1970-72; clin. dir. Noyes Divsn. St. Elizabeths Hosp., Washington, 1973-76; asst. chief psychiatry Andrews AFB Hosp., Camp Springs, Md., 1976-80, chief neurology, 1989-91; resident in neurology Wilford Hall USAF Med. Ctr., San Antonio, 1980-83; chief medicine and neuropsychiatry Air Univ. Hosp., Maxwell AFB, Ala., 1983-89, chief neurology, 1991-94; psychiatrist Manhattan Psychiat. Ctr., NYC, 1994—97, 1999—2002, clin. dir., 1997-99; psychiatrist Prison Health Svcs., Riker's Island, NYC, 2002—. Asst. clin. prof. psychiatry Georgetown U. Med. Sch., Washington, 1974-79, NYU Sch. Medicine, 1997-2002; assoc. prof. neurology and asst. prof. psychiatry Uniformed Svcs. U. Health Scis., Bethesda, Md., 1989-94. Maj. U.S. Army, 1968-73, col. USAF, 1976-94, ret. Fellow: Am. Psychiat. Assn. (life); mem.: AMA, NYU-Bellevue Psychiat. Soc., Harvard Club of NYC. Home: 345 E 93d St Apt 22H New York NY 10128-5522 Office: OBCC Riker's Island New York NY E-mail: alan.rainess@verizon.net.

RAINEY, CLAUDE GLADWIN, retired health care executive; b. Enloe, Tex., Apr. 21, 1923; s. Claude C. and Pauline (Whitlock) R.; m. Peggy Ballard, July 27, 1947; children— Kathy Suzanne, David Claude, Mark Jeffery, Joel Allen, Peggy Jan, Susan Elise Student pub. health and adminstrv. medicine, Columbia U., 1961-62. Med. adminstrv., officer dept. medicine and surgery VA, Temple, Tex., 1946-51, med. adminstrv. officer dept. medicine and surgery Muskogee, Okla., 1951-56; med. adminstr. Fite Clinic, Lakeland Med. Ctr., Muskogee, Okla., 1956-59; hosp. adminstr. M.-K.-T. R.R. Employees Hosp. Assn., Denison, Tex., 1959-62, also sec., treas. trustee; hosp. adminstr., cons. Denison Hosp. Authority, Meml. Hosp., 1962-66; adminstr. Seton Hosp., Austin, Tex., 1966-74; exec. v.p. Fort Worth Osteo. Hosp., 1974-83; pres. Health Care of Tex., Inc., Fort Worth, 1983-88, ret. Pres. North Grayson County chpt. Am. Cancer Soc., 1960-66, bd. dirs., Tex., 1961—. Served with USNR, 1942-46. Fellow Am. Coll. Hosp. Adminstrs., Am. Coll. Osteo. Hosp. Adminstrs. (award of merit 1984); mem. Am. Hosp. Assn., Tex. Hosp. Assn., Am. Osteo. Hosp. Assn. (Disting. Svc. award 1985) Home: 915 N Fielder Rd #2206 Arlington TX 76012-3147

RAINEY, GORDON FRYER, JR., lawyer; b. Oklahoma City, Apr. 26, 1940; s. Gordon F. and Esther (Bliss) R.; m. Selina Norman, Aug. 3, 1968; children: Kate, Melissa, Gordon III. BA in English, U. Va., 1962, LLB, 1967. Bar: Okla. 1967, Va. 1968. Assoc. Rainey, Flynn, Wallace, Ross & Cooper, Oklahoma City, 1967-68, Hunton & Williams, Richmond, Va., 1968-75, ptnr., 1975—. Chmn. exec. com. Hunton & Williams; rector U. Va.; bd. dirs. Bon Secours Richmond Health Sys., Inc., SunTrust MidAtlantic, Colonial Williamsburg Co.; bd. visitors, rector U. Va. Past pres. U. Va. Alumni Assn.; trustee Colonial Williamsburg Found., Va. Found. Ind. Colls.; mem. Gov.'s Blue Ribbon Commn. on Higher Edn.; campaign chmn. United Way of Greater Richmond, 1982, trustee, 1981-84; bd. dirs., past pres. Sheltering Arms Hosp., 1984; trustee Sheltering Arms Found.; chmn. Gov.'s Econ. Devel. Adv. Coun. Dist. 12; mem. Gov.'s Adv. Com. for Va. Strategy on Econ. Devel.; mem. Bd. Housing and Cmty. Devel.; past mem. bd. govs. St. Catherine's Sch.; past chmn. bd. dirs. Leadership Met. Richmond.; past pres., bd. dirs. Met. Bus. Found. 1st lt. U.S. Army, 1962-64, Korea. Recipient Disting. Grad. award Casady Sch., Comm. and Leadership award toastmasters Internat., 1983. Mem. ABA (sect. on bus. law, banking law com., mem. com. on devel. in investment svcs.), Richmond Metro C. of C. (bd. dirs., past chmn.), Commonwealth Club, Country Club of Va., The Brook (N.Y.C.), Forum Club (Richmond). Republican. Episcopalian. Office: Hunton & Williams Riverfront Plz East Tower PO Box 1535 Richmond VA 23218-1535 Office Phone: 804-788-8275. Business E-Mail: grainey@hunton.com.

RAINEY, JEAN OSGOOD, public relations executive; b. Lansing, Mich., Apr. 5, 1925; d. Earle Victor and Blanche Mae (Eberly) Osgood; m. John Larimer Rainey, Nov. 29, 1957 (dec. Oct. 1991); children: Cynthia, John Larimer, Ruth. Grad., Lansing Bus. U., 1942. Pub. rels. dir. Nat. Assn. Food Chains, Washington, 1954-59; v.p. pub. rels. Manchester Orgns., Washington, 1959-61; ptnr. Rainey, McEnroe & Manning, Washington, 1962-73; v.p. Manning, Selvage & Lee, Washington, 1973-79, pres. Washington divsn., 1979-84; owner Jean Rainey Assocs., Washington, 1984-86, sr. v.p. Daniel J. Edelman Inc., 1987-96; owner Jean Rainey Assocs., Washington, 1996—. Chmn. bd. Windward Mortgage, 1997—2001. Author: How to Shop for Food, 1972. Pres. Hyde Home and Sch. Assn., Washington, 1969-71; co-chmn. Nat. Adv. Com. for Reelection of the Pres., 1972; chmn. bd. trustees St. John's Presch., 1996-99, vice chair, 2003-04; pres. Sherwood Forest Endowment Fund, 1995-97; adminstr. A Few Good Women-Advancing the Cause of Women in Govt., 1969-74, 97-; bd. dirs. Westchester Corp., 2001-04. Mem. Internat. Women's Forum, Pub. Rels. Soc. Am. (accredited, Hall of Fame 1999), Am. Women in Radio and TV (pres. Washington chpt. 1962-63, mem. nat. bd. 1963-65), Am. News Women's Club (pres. 1973-75), City Tavern Club. Republican. Episcopalian. Home: 4000 Cathedral Ave NW Apt 250B Washington DC 20016-5279 Office: PO Box 251 Main Lobby W 4000 Cathedral Ave NW Washington DC 20016-5249 E-mail: jorainey@aol.com.

RAINEY, JOHN DAVID, federal judge; b. Freeport, Tex., Feb. 10, 1945; s. Frank Anson and Jewel Lorene (Hortman) R.; m. Judy Davis, Aug. 17, 1968; children, John David Jr., Jacob Matthew, Craig Thomas. BBA, So. Meth. U., 1967, JD, 1972. Bar: Tex. 1972, U.S. Dist. Ct. (no. dist.) Tex. 1974, U.S. Tax Ct. 1974, U.S. Ct. Appeals (5th cir.) 1981, U.S. Supreme Ct. 1981, U.S. Dist. Ct. (so. dist.) Tex. 1986. Assoc. Taylor, Mizell, Price, Corrigan & Smith, Dallas, 1973-79; ptnr. Gilbert, Gilbert & Rainey, Angleton, Tex., 1979-82, Rainey & LeBoeuf, Angleton, 1982-86; judge 149th Dist. Ct., Brazoria County, Tex., 1987-90, U.S. Dist. Ct. (so. dist.) Tex., 1990—. Bd. dirs. Angleton Bank of Commerce. Mem. City of Angleton Planning and Zoning Commn., 1981-84; mem. Angleton Charter Rev. Commn., 1984, chmn. 1982. Served with U.S. Army, 1969-70. Mem. State Bar Tex., Brazoria County Bar Assn. (pres. 1983-84). Lodges: Lions (pres. Angleton 1986-87). Methodist. Avocations: hunting, fishing, woodworking. Office: US Dist Ct 312 S Main St Rm 406 Victoria TX 77901

RAINEY, KENNETH TYLER, English language educator; b. Memphis, Feb. 27, 1936; s. Andrew Laughlin Jr. and Gracie Ruth (Mullins) R.; m. Elaine Fitts, Jan. 1, 1960; children: Kenneth Tyler Jr., Timothy Andrew, Kevin Laughlin. BA, Miss. Coll., Clinton, 1958; AM, U. Mich., 1959; ThD, New Orleans Bapt. Sem., 1966; PhD, Ohio State U., 1976. Asst. prof. Eng. Miss. Coll., Clinton, 1965-70, Ohio State U., Lima, 1977-83, U. Memphis, 1983-89; prof., chair humanities and tech. comm. So. Poly. State U., Marietta, Ga., 1989—, disting. prof. tchg. and learning, 1997—98. Presenter, cons. in field; vis. prof. Magdeburg, Germany, 1997, 99, Koethen, Germany, 2001-04; proprietor Atlanta ProCom. Woodrow Wilson fellow, 1958-59; Nat. Endowment Humanities grant, 1981-82; Deutsche Akademisches Austansdienst fellow, 1999. Fellow IEEE Profl. Communication Soc., Soc. Tech. Comm. (Jay Gould award for excellence in tchg. tech. comm. 1999, Disting. Chpt. Svc. award 1999, Excellence in Internat. Tech. Pubs. award 1992, 2001), Nat. Coun. Tchrs. English (conf. coll. composition and comm.), Assn. Tchrs. Tech. Writing. Baptist. Avocations: gourmet cooking, traveling in Europe. Home: 1194 Robert Ln Marietta GA 30062-4929 Office: So Poly State U 1100 S Marietta Pkwy SE Marietta GA 30060-2896 Business E-Mail: krainey@spsu.edu.

RAINEY, MATT, photographer; m. Bernadette Rainey; children: Conner, Brenna. Grad., Mason Gross Sch. of the Arts, Rutgers Univ. Photographer Star Ledger, Newark, 1995—, staff photographer, 2000. Photographer in an assign. on locations Is., Mex. The Star Ledger, Newark. Photographer: series to chronicle the Seton Hall Univ. fire. After the Fire, 2000. Recipient Press Photographer of the Yr., New Jersey, 1998, runner-up for the Press Photographer of the Yr. Office: Newark Star Ledger 1 Star Ledger Plz Newark NJ 07102

RAINEY, SUSAN J. school system administrator; m. Jack Rainey; 1 child, Jordan. BA, MA, U. Redlands; PhD, U. So. Calif. Tchr. Moore Jr. H.S., Redlands Unified Sch. Dist.; tchr. Palo Alto, Calif., Yucaipa H.S., 1972—76, dir. activities, 1976—78; asst. prin. Monrovia H.S.; h.s. prin. Brea, Calif.; asst. supt. for adminstrv. svcs. Helmet Unified Sch. Dist., asst. supt. for personnel svcs., assoc. supt.; supt. Charter Oak Unified Sch. Dist., Covina, Calif., 1991—98; sutp. Riverside Unified Sch. Dist., 1998—. Office: Riverside Unified Sch Dist 3380 14th St Riverside CA 92501

RAINEY, WILLIAM E., II, medical educator; BS in Biology, U. North Tex., 1980, MS in Biology, 1981; PhD in Cell Biology, U. Tex., Dallas, 1985. Assoc. prof. ob-gyn. U. Tex. Southwestern Med. Ctr., 1988—. Vis. scientist Flinders Med. Ctr., Adelaide, Australia, 1995. Grantee NIH, Am. Heart Assn.; Given Inst. Pathobiology fellow, 1984, Noble Found. fellow, 1984-85, Fogarty Internat. fellow, 1987-88. Mem. Fedn. Am. Socs. for Exptl. Biology, Endocrine Soc., Soc. Gynecol. Investigation. Office: 5323 Harry Hines Blvd Dallas TX 75390-7208

RAINEY, WILLIAM JOEL, lawyer; b. Flint, Mich., Oct. 11, 1946; s. Ralph Jefferson and Elsie Matilda (Erickson) R.; m. Cynthia Hetsko, June 15, 1968; children: Joel Michael, Allison Elizabeth. AB, Harvard U., 1968; JD, U. Mich., 1971. Bar: N.Y. 1973, Wash. 1977, Ariz. 1987, Mass. 1992, U.S. Dist. Ct. (so. and ea. dists.) N.Y. 1973, U.S. Ct. Appeals (2nd cir.) N.Y. 1973, U.S. Dist. Ct. (we. dist.) Wash. 1977, U.S. Supreme Ct. 1976, U.S. Ct. Appeals (9th cir.) Wash. 1978, U.S. Dist. Ct. Ariz. 1987, U.S. Dist. Ct. Mass. 1992. Assoc. atty. Curtis, Mallet-Prevost, Colt & Mosle, N.Y.C., 1971-76; atty., asst. corp. sec. Weyerhaeuser Co., Tacoma, 1976-85; v.p., corp. sec., gen. counsel Southwest Forest Industries Inc., Phoenix, 1985-87; sr. v.p., corp. sec., gen. counsel Valley Nat. Corp. and Valley Nat. Bank, Phoenix, 1987-91; v.p., gen. counsel Cabot Corp., Boston, 1991-93; exec. v.p., gen. counsel, corp. sec. Fourth Fin. Corp., Wichita, Kans., 1994-96; sr. v.p., gen. counsel, corp. sec. Payless ShoeSource, Inc., Topeka, 1996—2003, Longs Drug Stores Corp., Walnut Creek, Calif., 2003—. Editor U. Mich. Jour. Law Reform, 1970-71. Bd. dirs. Big Bros./Big Sisters, 1994-96. Maj. USAR, 1970-91. Mem. ABA (chmn. task force 1984-91, com. of corp. gen. counsel, exec. com. 2002-), Wash. State Bar Assn., State Bar of Ariz., Assn. Bank Holding Cos. (steering com. 1989-91, chmn. lawyers com. 1990-91), Am. Corp. Counsel Assn., Harvard Club of Phoenix (bd. dirs. 1989-91). Avocations: backpacking, running, fishing, bicycling. Home: 1208 Bridlewood Ct Clayton CA 94517 Office: Longs Drug Stores Corp 141 N Civic Dr Walnut Creek CA 94596 Office Phone: 925-210-6720. Business E-Mail: brainey@longs.com.

RAINIER, ROBERT PAUL, publisher, consultant; b. Adrian, Mich., Oct. 19, 1940; s. Paul Leslie and Mildred Sofia (Magdefrau) R.; m. Dorothy Krauss, May 28, 1966; children: Michele Carole, Kenneth Charles. BA, Northwestern U., 1962, MA, 1964. From mem. staff to editor-in-chief McGraw Hill Book Co., N.Y.C., 1964—74, editor-in-chief humanities, 1974—79; edit. exec. CBS Coll. Pub., N.Y.C., 1979—86, v.p., editor in chief, 1984-86; dir. publs. AICPA, N.Y.C., 1986-97, dir. prof. devel., 1997-99, sr. cons. strategic devel., 1999—2003; pres. Rainier Assocs., 2003—. Vestryman St. Johns Episcopal Ch., Larchmont, N.Y., 1987-90, fundraiser, 1988-89. Staff sgt. N.Y. N.G., 1964-70. Mem. The Dessoff Choirs (pres. 2000—), Soc. Nat. Assn. Publs. (pres. 1992-93). Democrat. Episcopalian. Avocations: music, sports. Home: 21 Summit Ave Larchmont NY 10538-2913 Office Phone: 914-643-0994.

RAINIS, EUGENE CHARLES, bank executive; b. N.Y.C., Sept. 24, 1940; s. Charles William and Louise Theresa (Nold) Rainis; m. Jane Margaret Micucci, Nov. 28, 1964; children: Ellen, David, Mark. BS, Fordham U., 1962; MBA, U. Pa., 1964. Security analyst trainee Merrill, Lynch Pierce Fenner & Smith, N.Y.C., 1963-65; ptnr. Brown Bros. Harriman & Co., N.Y.C., 1965—. Bd. dirs. Bio-Brite, Inc. Chmn. Xavier H.S., N.Y.C.; trustee Robert Brunner Found., Gregorian U. Found., St. Vincents Cath. Med. Ctrs., Cristo Rey H.S. Mem.: Inst. Chartered Fin. Analysts, Knights of Malta, Down Town Assn. (N.Y.C.), Harbour Ridge Golf Club (Palm City, Fla.). Republican. Roman Catholic. Avocation: fishing, golf. Office: Brown Bros Harriman & Co 140 Broadway New York NY 10005

RAINONE, MICHAEL CARMINE, lawyer; b. Phila., Mar. 4, 1918; m. Ledena Tonioni, Apr. 10, 1944; children: Sebastian, Francine. LLB, U. Pa., 1941. Bar: Pa. 1944, U.S. Dist. Ct. Pa. 1944, U.S. Supreme Ct. 1956. Apptd. arbitrator U.S. Dist. Ct. (ea. dist.) Pa., 2003—. Del. 3d cir. Jud. Conf., 1984—85; apptd. fed. arbitrator U.S. Dist. Ct. (ea. dist.) Pa., 2003; mem. Fed. Cts. Com., 2004. Past pres. Nationalities Svc. Ctr., hon. bd. dirs.; commr. Fellowship Commn., 1973—82; internat. pres. Orphans of Italy, Inc., 1975—83; bd. dirs., mem. govt. rels. com. Mental Health Assn. Southeastern Pa., 1979—91; pres. Columbus Civic Assn. Pa., Inc., 1984—91; regional v.p. Nat. Italian-Am. Found.; pres. Seaview Harbor Civic Assn., 1990—95, pres. emeritus, 1996—; apptd. judge Final Law Sch. Trial Advocacy Program N.E., 1996—; counsel, v.p. Piccola Opera Com., Phila., 1997—; task force chmn. Mazzei Nat. Constn. Ctr., 2001; bd. dirs. C.C., Phila., 1970—85; chmn. lawyers' biog. com. Hist. Soc., U.S. Dist. Ct.; trustee Balch Inst. Ethnic Studies, 1989—92; pres. Grad. Club, bd. dirs., 2000. Recipient Man of the Yr. award, Columbus Civic Assn., 1969, Disting. Svc. award, Nationalities Svc. Ctr., 1975, Legion of Honor, Chapel of Four Chaplains, 1979, Bronze Medallion award, 1982, commendation, Pa. Senate, 1982, Appreciation award, Villanova Law Sch., 1993, Achievement award, Syracuse U., 1994, Hon. Lifetime award, KC, 1997, Resolution of Praise, Pres. City Coun. Phila., 1999, Svc. to Legal Profession and Cmty. award, City Coun. of Phila., 2003. Mem.: ATLA (supr. judge law sch. trial advocacy competition 2000, Phila. chpt. emeritus chmn. Justice Michael A. Musmanno award 2000, Supervising Judge Advocacy award Phila. region 2000), ABA (chmn. U.S. Supreme Ct. admissions com. 2001), Am. Arbitration Assn. (arbitrator 1950—), Nat. Itlaian-Am. Bar Assn. (bd. govs. 1986—2003, historian 1987—90, pres. 1991—93, bd. chmn. 1993—95, chmn. Supreme Ct. admissions com. 2000), Phila. Trial Lawyers Assn. (pres. 1982—83, Disting. Svc. award 2000), Lawyers Club Phila. (pres. 1982—84, chmn. nominating com. 2000—, chmn. Centennial Celebration 2001, Achievement and Svc. award 2003), Phila. Bar Assn. (bd. dirs. 1980—83, asst. sec. 1983, 1984, chmn. emeritus Beccaria award 1993—), Pa. Trial Lawyers Assn. (bd. govs. 1982—84), Pa. Bar Assn., Justinian Soc. (bd. govs. 1980—83, sr. lawyer award 2000), Internat. Acad. Law and Sci., N.Y. Trial Lawyers Assn. (assoc.), Sons of Italy (Man of the Yr. award 1995). Home: 2401 Pennsylvania Ave Philadelphia PA 19130-3010 Office: 1601 Market St 16th Fl Philadelphia PA 19103 Office Phone: 215-557-7066. E-mail: mcrainone@cs.com.

RAINS, BAXTER SMITH, sculptor, consultant; b. Atlanta, July 2, 1938; s. Baxter, Jr. and Elinor (Nelson) Rains; m. Barbara Osmundsen, Sept. 20, 1986; children: Anne Douglass, David Sinclair, Elinor Houston, Holly Christine Delaney. Studied, Ga. Inst. Tech., Atlanta, 1964—65, Atlanta Coll. Art, 1966—68; B of Visual Arts, Ga. State U., Atlanta, 1968; MFA, U. Guanajuato, San Miguel de Allende, Mex., 1975. Tchr. The Westminster Schs., Atlanta, 1969—71; instr. Atlanta Coll. Art, 1969—71, U. Guanajuato, San Miguel de Allende, Mexico, 1972—75, Brevard Art Ctr. and Mus., Melbourne, Fla., 1992; prof. Ctr. for the Arts, Vero Beach, Fla., 2000—02; adj. prof. Indian River CC, Fort Pierce, Fla., 2000—. Dir., evening sch. Atlanta Coll. Art, 1970; founder, exec. dir. Sculptural Arts Mus., Atlanta, 1980—82; cons. U.S. Pres.'s Coun. on Handicapped, 1981—82, Brevard Cultural Alliance, Viera, Fla., 2003, Brevard Mus. Art and Sci., Melbourne, Fla., 2003—04; bd. dirs. Arts Festival of Atlanta, 1982—85; artist-in-charge Hope Dragon Found., Merritt Island, Fla., 1996. One-man shows include Ga. State U., Atlanta, 1967, 1968, The Westminster Schs., 1969, 1971, Galeria Roma, San Miguel de Allende, Mex., 1973, 1974, Pine Valley Ranch, Pine, Colo., 1977, El Rancho, Colo., 1977, Gallery Danielli, Toronto, 1979, Washington World Galleries, 1979, Southside Studio Sculpture Show, Richmond, Va., 1990, 1991, Fifth Ave. Art Gallery, Melbourne, Fla., 1992, Brevard Mus. Art & Sci., 2003, Indian River Sculpture Gallery, Vero Beach, Fla., 2004, exhibitions include High Mus. Art, Atlanta, 1969, Mint Mus. Art, Charlotte, N.C., 1970, Galeria Del Conde, San Miguel de Allende, Mex., 1972, 1973, Fiesta de Santa Fe, 1977, Mus. of Touch, Atlanta, 1980, Christian-Brydon Gallery, Richmond, Va., 1989—91, Brigantine Gallery, Cocoa Beach, Fla., 1993, Raleigh Gallery, Design Ctr. of Ams., Dania, Fla., 1992—95, Gaier Contemp. Gallery, Orlando, Fla., 1994—96, Raleigh Gallery, Boca Raton, Fla., 1995—97, Vero Beach Mus. Art, Fla., 2000—03, Represented in permanent collections Brevard Mus. Art & Sci., Melbourne, Fla., Radford U. Sculpture Garden, Va., The Westminster Schs., Atlanta, Piedmont Hosp., Ga. State U. Mus., The Trane Corp., Our Lady of Perpetual Help Hosp., Bklyn., City of Atlanta, Office of the Mayor, First Presbyn. Ch., Atlanta, commissioned, Child Care Assn. of Brevard, Cocoa, Fla., 2004. Mem. Internat. Sculpture Ctr., Washington, 1988—94; bd. govs. Vector Arts Endowment, Indian Harbour Beach, Fla., 1997—. Avocations: archery, gardening. Home: 135B Tomahawk Dr Indian Harbor Beach FL 32937 Office: Osmundsen-Rains Studios 135B Tomahawk Dr Indian Harbor Beach FL 32937

RAINS, JOANNE WARNER, nursing educator; b. Sioux Falls, S.D., June 27, 1950; d. Arnold D. and Arlene M. (Lawrence) W.; m. Daniel P. Rains, Dec. 13, 1975; children: David Warner, Isaac Daniel. BA, Augustana Coll., 1972; MA, U. Iowa, 1976; D of Nursing Sci., Ind. U., 1990. Vis. nurse Delaware County Vis. Nurse Assn., Muncie, Ind., 1976-77; cons. Ind. State Bd. Health, Indpls., 1977-78; instr. Briar Cliff Coll., Sioux Falls, 1981-82; adj. faculty Okla. Bapt. U., Shawnee, 1985; assoc. prof. Ind. U., Indpls., 1990—. Mem. exec. com. Friends Com. on Nat. Legis., Washington, 1992—; fellow Primary Health Care Policy, Washington, 1996; bd. trustees Earlham Coll. Campaign mgr. Doug Kinser for State Rep. Ind. House Dist. 54, 1988-94; exec. com., mem. New Castle (Ind.) Healthy City Com., 1989-99; chair residential drive Am. Cancer Soc., New Castle, 1989. Mem. ANA, Assn. Cmty. Health Nurse Educators (bd. dirs.), Ind. Polit. Sci. Assn. (v.p. 1993-94,. pres. 1994-95), Mem. Soc. Of Friends. Office: Ind U 2325 Chester Blvd Richmond IN 47374-1220 Home: Apt 420 430 Indiana Ave Indianapolis IN 46202-3243

RAINS, M. NEAL, lawyer; b. Burlington, Iowa, July 26, 1943; s. Merritt and Lucille (Lepper) R.; children: Robert Baldwin, Kathleen Kellogg. BA in Polit. Sci. with honors, U. Iowa, 1965; JD, Northwestern U., 1968. Bar: Ohio 1968. Assoc. Arter & Hadden, Cleve., 1968-76, ptnr., 1976—2001, mem. exec. com., 1981-90, mem. mgmt. com., 1987-90, mng. ptnr., 1990-92; ptnr. Frantz Ward LLP, Cleve., 2001—. Lectr. on profl. topics, including alternative dispute resolution, distbn. law, litigation practice and procedure, and antitrust. Contbr. articles to profl. jours. Former trustee Legal Aid Soc. Cleve., Citizens League Greater Cleve., Cleve. Art Assn. With U.S. Army, 1968-70 Fellow: Am. Bar Found.; mem.: ABA, William K. Thomas Am. Inn Ct. (pres. 1999—2000), Cleve. Bar Found. (trustee 1999—), Bar Assn. Greater Cleve. (chmn. young lawyers sect. 1975—76, chmn. CLE com.), Ohio Bar Assn., Rowfant Club, Cleve. Skating Club, Union Club, City Club, Print Club (trustee 2001—), Phi Delta Phi, Omicron Delta Kappa, Phi Beta Kappa. Home: 18400 Shelburne Rd Shaker Heights OH 44118 Office: Frantz Ward LLP 55 Public Sq Cleveland OH 44113 Office Phone: 216-515-1660. Business E-Mail: nrains@frantzward.com.

RAINS, MARY JO, banker; b. Konawa, Oklahoma, Oct. 27, 1935; d. Albert Wood and Mary Leona (Winfield) Starns; m. Billy Z. Rains, June 17, 1956; one child, Nicky Z. Student, Okla. Sch. Banking, 1969, Seminole Jr. Coll., 1970—72, East Ctrl. State U., 1978—79; diploma, Am. Inst. Banking, 1981—83; student, Okla. State U., 1987, Adult Vocat. Tech. Ctr., Pontotoc County, 1987. With acctg. divsn. Universal C.I.T., Okla. City, 1953—56; cashier Okla. State Bank (now Bancfirst), Konawa, 1957—89, sr. v.p., 1989—95; sr. v.p., br. mgr. Okla. State Bank, Konawa, 1995—2002; bd. sec. Seminole County Election Bd., Okla., 2003—. Sec. First Bapt. Ch., Konawa, Okla. 1969-79, budgeting com., 1982-92, chmn. fin. com., 1994—, lectureship adminstr.; fin. bd. Kennedy Libr., 1997—; bd. dir. Sacred Heart Mission Hist. Soc., Ctrl. Okla. Family Med. Ctr., 2003—, fin. com., 2004. Mem. Okla. Bankers Assn. (dir. women's divsn. 1974-76), Konawa C. of C., Am. Legion, Wewoka C. of C. Home: RR 2 Box 28 Konawa OK 74849-9704 Office: Courthouse Ste 101 Wewoka OK 74884 Office Phone: 405-257-2786.

RAINS, SCOTT WYATT, editor, musician; b. Lawton, Okla., Mar. 13, 1971; s. Ora Russell and Sandra Jean (Elliott) Rains; m. Misty René Marshall, Sept. 26, 1992; 1 child, Chloe Brie. Studied, Okla. State U., Stillwater, 1989—90, U. Ctrl. Okla., Edmond, 1994—96. Print pressman Edmond Evening Sun, Okla., 1994—98; editor, publisher The Cyril News, Okla., 1998—. Pres. Cyril Rotary Club, Okla., 2001. Mem.: Okla. Press Assn. Democrat. Avocations: writing, music, art. Office: The Cyril News PO Box 10 120 Main St Cyril OK 73029 Office Phone: 580-464-2410.

RAINWATER, FREDDIE BARRETT, volunteer worker; b. Pensacola, Fla., Aug. 25, 1947; d. Bernard Sr. and Blanche L. Barrett; m. Crawford Rainwater, Jan. 24, 1970. BS, U. Tex., 1970, postgrad.; MS, U. S.C., 1972. Founder Favor House Spouse Abuse Shelter, Pensacola, Fla., 1979-85; co-organizer Manna Food Bank, Pensacola, 1981—; co-founder Friendship Scholarships, Gulf Breeze, Fla., 1989—. Mem. reorganizing bd. Wildlife Sanctuary N.W. Fla., Pensacola; pres. Panhandle Tiger Bay Club, Pensacola, 1999-2000; chmn.

Escambia and Santa Rosa Counties George Bush for Pres. Campaign, Pensacola, 1979-80; reorganizer Santa Rosa County Rep. Party, Milton, Fla., 1979-80; chmn. Santa Rose County Party Reorgn., Milton, Fla. Recipient Svc. to Mankind award Liberty Sertoma Club, Pensacola, 1986, Liberty Bell award Escambia-Santa Rosa Counties Bar Assn., 1991, Cmty. Leader of Yr. award Pensacola C. of C., 1992, Woman of Yr. award Pensacola YWCA, 1987, Multi County Shelter for Abused Women dedicated to Freddie Rainwater, 1986. Home: 616 Baycliff Rd Gulf Breeze FL 32561

RAINWATER, GARY L. corporate financial executive; BSEE, U. Mo., Columbia; M of Systems Mgmt., U. So. Calif. Engr. electric transmission and distbn. Union Electric Co. (now Ameren Corp.), v.p. corp. planning, 1993—97; pres., CEO Ameren CIPS, 1997, exec. v.p.; pres., CEO Ameren CILCO, Ameren CIPS, Ameren Corp., St. Louis. Mem. dean's adv. coun. U. Mo. Sch. Engring.; mem. adv. coun. engring. mgmt. and engring. tech. Washington U.; bd. dirs. AmerenUE, Ameren CILCO, Ameren CIPS and other Ameren subs., Mo. Hist. Soc., St. Louis USO, Ill. Energy Assn., Urban League Met. St. Louis, US Bank. Recipient Mo. Honor award for disting. svc. in engring., U. Mo.-Columbia Coll. Engring., 2000. Mem.: Engrs.' Club (Knight of St. Patrick 2000). Office: Ameren 1901 Chouteau Saint Louis MO 63166-6149

RAINWATER, JOAN LUCILLE MORSE, investment company executive; b. Chattanooga, Mar. 5, 1943; d. Robert Ora and Alma Lucille (Miller) M.; m. Percy Raymond Rainwater (div. 1987); children: Karen Sue, Steven Jay, Robin Rae, Linda Sue. Student, John Robert Powan Sch. Design, 1977-78, Corcoran Sch. Art, 1985-86, Nova U., 1980, 85, 87. Co-owner Rainwater Concrete, Lorton, Va., 1962-87, Undertaking Gallery, Occoquan, 1977-80; cons. in art edn. Occoquan Elem. Sch., Woodbridge, Va., 1969-73; owner Riverside Gallery, Occoquan, 1980-84, Joamen Investments, Occoquan, 1985—. Author: (poems) At Waters Edge, 1995. Founding mem. Hist. Occoquan, 1970, Women's Mus., Washington; pres., v.p. Woodbridge Art Guild, 1980-82. Recipient numerous awards for paintings, various juried shows Washington area, 1977-87. Mem. Unity Ch. Avocations: hiking, reading, esoteric studies. Home: 1600 Russell Rd Alexandria VA 22301-1926

RAINWATER, R. STEVEN, systems engineer; b. Tyler, Tex., Dec. 13, 1962; s. Clois Miles and Nancy Jane Rainwater; m. Susan C. Chance, May 11, 1991. AA, Northlake Coll., Irving, Tex., 1981-83; student, U. Tex., 1983-88. Programmer Profl. Info. Libr., Dallas, Tex., 1984-89; systems engr. Kimball Computer Video Tech., Irving, Tex., 1989-91; pres. Network Cybernetics Corp., Irving, 1992—. Cons. Chaparal Steel Inc., Midlothian, Tex., 1988-89; sys. operator The Interocitor BBS, Irving, 1990—. Author computer software. Mem. Soc. Motion Picture and TV Engrs. Avocation: artificial intelligence rsch. Home: 2821 Vassar Dr Irving TX 75062-4575 Office: Network Cybernetics Corp 5353 Alpha Rd Ste 205 Dallas TX 75240-7346

RAINWATER, RICHARD, financial consultant, investor; b. Ft. Worth; BA in Math., U. Tex., 1966; MBA in Fin. and Mktg., Stanford U., 1968. With Goldman, Sachs & Co., N.Y.C., Dallas; chief fin. arch. Bass Orgn., Ft. Worth, 1970-86; ind. investor Ft. Worth, 1986-94; founder, chmn. bd. Crescent Real Estate Equities, Inc., Ft. Worth, 1994—; chief investor Mesa Inc., 1994—. Spkr. Harvard Bus. Sch., Stanford U., U. Tex. Bus. Sch. Appeared on cover of Bus. Week mag., Oct. 1986; recipient Man of Yr. award, 1989, Kupfer Disting. Exec. award Tex. A&M U., 1991, Golden Plate award Am. Acad. Achievement, 1992. Office: Crescent Machinery Company 1120 Blue Mound Road Fort Worth TX 76131

RAINWATER, TONYA B. judge; b. Granite City, Ill., Apr. 13, 1956; d. Markus Vernell and Shirley (Pohl) Baccus; m. Giles Dean Rainwater, Oct. 29, 1983; children: Sabrina B., Kali B., Blake B. BS, Fla. State U., 1976; JD, U. Fla., 1978; MBA, Fla. Inst. Tech., 1988. Bar: Fla. 1979. Asst. state atty. Office State Atty., Titusville, Fla., 1979-80; prin. Tonya L. Baccus, P.A., Indian Harbour Beach, Fla., 1981-86; county ct. judge Brevard County, Melbourne, Fla., 1987-91; cir. ct. judge 18th Jud. Cir., Melbourne, 1991—. Adj. prof. Fla. Inst. Tech., Melbourne, 1985-86. Mem. WestShore Jr./Sr. H.S. Improvement Coun., Melbourne, 1999—. Mem.: Civilian-Mil. Coun. Office: 2825 Judge Fran Jamieson Way Viera FL 32940-8006

RAIRDIN, CRAIG ALLEN, software company executive, software developer; b. Cedar Rapids, Iowa, Oct. 23, 1959; s. Ernie W. and Sherryl E. (Asklund) R.; m. Johnna L. Miller, Jan. 9, 1982. BS in Computer Sci. with distinction, U. Iowa, 1981. Software engr. Rockwell Internat., Cedar Rapids, 1982-88; divsn. dir. Parsons Tech., Cedar Rapids, 1988-90, v.p., 1990-98; ind. software developer, 1999—; pres. Laridian, Cedar Rapids, 1999—. Cons. Creative Computer Systems, Cedar Rapids, 1987-90. Author: (software) Juliet, 1987, QuickVerse, 1988, Bible Illustrator, 1990, Standard Template for Electronic Publishing (STEP), 1995, PalmBible, 1998, PocketBible, 2000. Chmn. Area Liaison Com., Campus Bible Fellowship, Iowa City, 1983-90; precinct chmn. Linn. County Rep. Party, Cedar Rapids, 1986-90; founder Bible Software Industry Standards Group, 1995; vol. pilot Angel Flight Ctrl., 2001—. Republican. Christian. Avocations: church, amateur radio, flying.

RAISBECK, DAVID W. food products executive; BS in Indsl. Adminstrn., Iowa State U., 1971; MBA, U. So. Calif., 1991. Joined Cargill, Mpls., 1971, exec. v.p., 1995, vice chmn., 1999—; also bd. dirs. Mem. Chgo. Merc. Exch., Mpls. Grain Exch.; bd. dirs. Cardinal Health, Eastman Chem.; chmn. bd. dirs. Horizon Milling. Gov. Iowa State U. Found.; mem. Order of the Knoll; mem. dean's adv. coun. Iowa State U., Sch. Bus.; bd. dirs. Greater Mpls. YMCA. Recipient Citation of Achievement award, Iowa State U. Coll. Bus., 1998. Office: Cargill PO Box 9300 Minneapolis MN 55440 also: Cargill Inc 15615 McGinty Rd West Wayzata MN 55391

RAISBECK, GORDON, systems engineer, consultant; b. N.Y.C., May 4, 1925; s. Milton Joseph and Marcelle (Ellinger) R.; m. Barbara Wiener, Dec. 22, 1948; children: Michael Norbert, Lucy Margaret, Alison Jane, Timothy Gordon, James Gregory. Rhodes scholar, Oxford (Eng.) U., 1947-48; BA, Stanford U., 1944; PhD, MIT, 1949. Registered profl. engr., Mass., Maine. Instr. M.I.T., Cambridge, 1948-49; mem. tech. staff Bell Telephone Labs., Inc., Murray Hill, N.J., 1949-61; dir. transmission line research Bell Telephone Labs., Inc. (now Lucent), 1954-61; mem. profl. staff research and devel. Advanced Research Projects Agy., Washington, 1959-60; mem. profl. staff Arthur D. Little, Inc., Cambridge, 1961-86, dir. systems engring., 1966-70, dir. phys. systems research, 1970-75, v.p. systems engring., 1973-86, part-time 1982-86; cons. mgmt. of technol. innovation, 1982-94. Instr. Drew U., Stanford U., MIT. Contbr. articles to profl. jours.; author: Information Theory: An Introduction for Engineers and Scientists, 1964; patentee in field (22). Served to lt. (j.g.) USNR, 1944-46, ATO, PTO. Rhodes scholar, 1947 Fellow IEEE, Acoustical Soc. Am.; mem. Oceanic Engring. Soc. IEEE (sec. 1988-92), Engring. Mgmt. Soc. IEEE, N.Y. Acad. Scis., New Coll. Soc., Oxford Soc., Assn. Am. Rhodes Scholars, Amateur Chamber Music Players, Chamber Music Am., Sigma Xi. Democrat. Episcopalian. Home and Office: 4 Drake Ln Scarborough ME 04074-7414 also: Blanche Rd RR #1 Barrington Cape Negro NS Canada B0W 1E0 E-mail: raisbeck7@netscape.net.

RAISBECK, JAMES DAVID, engineering company executive; b. Milw., Sept. 29, 1936; m. Sherry Raisbeck; 1 child, Jennifer Lee; stepchildren: Eric Valpey, Laura Valpey. BS in Aerodynamics, Purdue U., 1961. Rsch. aerodynamist Boeing Comml. Airplane Co., Seattle, 1961-66; new airplane and rsch. outplant mgr. Boeing Airplane Co., Wright-Patterson AFB, Ohio, 1966-68; program mgr. comml. STOL airplane programs Boeing Co., 1968-69; pres., CEO Robertson Aircraft Corp., Seattle, 1969-73; v.p. tech. Am. Jet Industries, Van Nuys, Calif., 1973-74; CEO Raisbeck Group, San Antonio and Seattle, 1974-80, Raisbeck Engring., Inc., Seattle, 1980—, Raisbeck Comml. Air Grp., Inc., Seattle, 1996—. Recipient Outstanding Engr. award Purdue U., 1999; named Disting. Engring. Alumnus 1979, Purdue U. Fellow AIAA (assoc.); mem. Soc. Automotive Engrs., NBAA, Purdue U. Alumni Assn., Tau Beta Pi, Phi Eta Sigma, Sigma Gamma Tau. Achievements include numerous patents in aircraft design. Office: Raisbeck Engring Inc 4411 S Ryan Way Seattle WA 98178-2021 Fax: 206-722-1892.

RAISCH, KEVIN PAUL, research scientist, educator; b. Cedar Rapids, Iowa, Nov. 26, 1957; s. William Raymond and Shirley Ellen Raisch; m. Saeng I. Sengchanthong, Nov. 27, 1993; children: Robin Shao-he, Tamarine Jie. BS, Iowa State U., Ames, 1976—81, MS, 1983—86; PhD, Colo. State U., Fort Collins, 1986—89. Postdoctoral fellow Mayo Clinic and Mayo Found., Rochester, Minn., 1989—92, rsch. assoc., 1992—93; rsch. scientist Med. Coll. Wis., Milw., 1993—98; instr. U. Ala., Birmingham, 1998—2000, asst. prof., 2000—. Mem.: Radiation Rsch. Soc., N.Y. Acad. Scis., Am. Soc. Biochemistry and Molecular Biology, Am. Soc. for Microbiology, Am. Soc. for Gene Therapy, AAAS, Am. Assn. for Virology, Am. Assn. for Cancer Rsch. Achievements include patents for a Human anti-epidermal growth factor receptor single-chain antibodies. Office: Univ Ala 1824 6th Ave S WTI-674 Birmingham AL 35294 Office Phone: 205-934-7077. E-mail: raisch@uab.edu.

RAISH, CAROL BROOKS, anthropologist, archaeologist; b. Tulsa, Okla., Oct. 20, 1946; d. Horace Brooks and Julia Ann (Duff) Gotcher; m. Gordon Kent Raish, Jan. 17, 1970 (div. May 1978); 1 child, Susan Brooks Raish Sehlmeyer. BA in Spanish and Secondary Edn., Washburn U., 1968; MA in Anthropology, U. Nebr., 1979; PhD of Anthropology, U. N.Mex., 1988. Archeologist Midwest Archeol. Ctr. U.S. Nat. Park Svc., Lincoln, Nebr., 1978—79; archeologist Cibola Nat. Forest U.S. Forest Svc., Albuquerque, 1982—86; archeologist, editor Midwest Archeol. Ctr. U.S. Nat. Park Svc., Lincoln, 1988—89; anthropologist, archeologist Heritage Resource Staff Jemez Ranger Dist. Santa Fe Nat. Forest U.S. Forest Svc., Jemez Springs, N.Mex., 1989—95, anthropologist, rsch. social scientist Rocky Mountain Rsch. Sta. Albuquerque, 1995—. Author: Domestic Animals and Stability in Pre-State Farming Societies, 1992; co-editor, Livestock Management in the American Southwest, 2000; contbr. articles to profl. jours. Asst. troop leader Girl Scouts Am., Albuquerque, 1982—87. Mem.: N.Mex. Archeol. Coun. (sec. 1990—91), Soc. Am. Archaeology, Soc. Human Ecology. Democrat. Avocations: hiking, needlecrafts. Home: 10504 Monte Rosso Pl NW Albuquerque NM 87114 Office: Rocky Mountain Rsch Sta USDA Forest Svc 333 Broadway SE Ste 115 Albuquerque NM 87102-3497

RAISH, DAVID LANGDON, lawyer; b. Cleve., Mar. 12, 1947; s. John E. Raish and Roslyn V. (Skeels) Pettibone; m. Roslyn Anne Dinnick, Sept. 12, 1969; children: David Jr., Anne, Julia. BA, Yale U., 1969; JD, Harvard U., 1973. Bar: Mass. 1975, D.C. 1981. Law clk. to hon. James R. Browning U.S. Ct. Appeals-9th Cir., San Francisco, 1973-74; assoc. Ropes & Gray, Boston, 1974-82, ptnr., 1982—. Mem. ABA Tax sect. 1991—, mem. Employee Benefits Com., 1993—, mem. coun., 1999-2004, vice chair, 2002-04. Author: Cafeteria Plans, 2000, Cash or Deferred Arrangements, 1997, Compensation and Benefits for Key Employees of Tax-Exempt Organizations, 1995; bd. advisors Jour. Taxation of Employee Benefits, 1990-2000. Tenor Tanglewood Festival Chorus. Office: Ropes & Gray One International Pl Boston MA 02110 Business E-Mail: draish@ropesgray.com.

RAISH, STEPHEN E, retail executive; m. Jane Raish; children: John, Sarah. BA in physics, Carleton Coll., 1972. Various store positions J.C. Penney Corp., 1972—91, mgr. store systems and inventory, 1991, dir. geog. markets, 1993, dir. stores coord., 1996, divisional v.p., home and leisure divsn., 1997—; pres., home and leisure divsn., 1998—; pres., ACT divsn. J.C. Penney Corp., 1999—, exec. v.p., CIO, 2001—. Office: JC Penney Corp Inc 6501 Legacy Dr Plano TX 75024-3698

RAISIAN, JOHN, academic administrator, economist; b. Conneaut, Ohio, July 30, 1949; s. Ernest James and Ruby Lee (Owens) Raisian; m. Joyce Ann Klak, Aug. 17, 1984; children: Alison Kathleen, Sarah Elizabeth. BA, Ohio U., 1971; PhD, UCLA, 1978; LLD (hon.), Albertson Coll. Idaho, 1995. Rsch. assoc. Human Resources Rsch. Ctr., U. So. Calif., L.A., 1972—73; cons. Rand Corp., Santa Monica, Calif., 1974—75; vis. asst. prof. econs. U. Wash., Seattle, 1975—76; asst. prof. econs. U. Houston, 1976—80; sr. economist Office Rsch. and Evaluation, U.S. Bur. Labor Stats., Washington, 1980—81; spl. asst. for econ. policy Office Asst. Sc. for Policy, U.S. Dept. Labor, Washington, 1981—83, dir. rsch. and tech. support, 1981—84; pres. Unicon Rsch. Corp., L.A., 1984-86; sr. fellow Hoover Instn., Stanford, Calif., 1986—, assoc. dir., dep. dir., 1986—90, dir., 1990—. Advisor Nat. Coun. on Handicapped, Washington, 1985—86, Nat. Commn. on Employment Policy, Washington, 1987—88; chmn. minimum wage bd. Calif. Indsl. Welfare Commn., 1987; mem. nat. adv. com. Student Fin. Assistance, Washington, 1987—89; corp. mem. Blue Shield Calif., 1994—96; bd. dirs. Sentinel Groups Fund, Inc., 1997—; mem. Pacific Coun. Internat. Policy; nat. adv. bd. City Innovation. Editor (editl. bd.): (jour.) Jour. Labor Rsch., 1983—; contbr. articles to profl. jours. Exec. dir. Presdl. Task Force on Food Assistance, Washington, 1983—84. Recipient Best Publ. of Yr. award, Econ. Inquiry, Western Econ. Assn., 1979, Disting. Tchg. award, U. Houston Coll. Social Scis., 1980, Disting. Svc. award, U.S. Dept. Labor, 1983; fellow predoctoral fellow, Rand Corp., 1976. Mem.: Nat. Assn. Scholars, Coun. on Fgn. Rels., Mont Pelerin Soc., World Affairs Coun., Commonwealth Club of Calif., We. Econs. Assn., Am. Econs. Assn., Phi Beta Kappa. Republican. Avocation: wine collecting, sports enthusiast. Office: Hoover Instn Stanford Univ Museum Way & Lomita Stanford CA 94305

RAISIG, PAUL JONES, JR., lawyer; b. Jamestown, N.Y., June 21, 1932; s. Paul Jones and Marian Elizabeth (Christian) R.; m. Carolyn Virginia Sides, June 12, 1955; children: Dawn Virginia, Paul Christian, Anne Sibley. B.G.E., U. Nebr., 1961; MBA, U. Ala., 1965; JD, Campbell U., 1989. Bar: N.C., 1989, D.C. 1991, U.S. Supreme Ct. 1992. Commd. 2d lt. U.S. Army, 1953, advanced through grades to col., 1973, ret., 1977 served in Vietnam, 1963, bn. comdr., Vietnam, 1968; dep. dir. U.S. Army Reorganization, 1973; v.p. Armed Forces Relief and Benefit Assn., Washington, 1977-79; sr. cons. Dept. Def., Washington, 1979-80; exec. dir. Am. Fedn. Info. Processing Socs., Arlington, Va., 1980-84; v.p., dir. Designs, Ltd., Alexandria, Va., 1985-86; ptnr. Barrington, Herndon & Raisig, P.A., Fayetteville, N.C., 1989-92. Adj. prof. bus. law and bus. mgmt. Campbell U., 1992-2004; cons. in field; mediator for Superior Ct. and arbitrator for Dist. Ct. Decorated Legion of Merit (3), Bronze Star medal (2), Air medal (5), Purple Heart (2), Meritorious Service medal, Army Commendation medal with V Device (3), Combat INf. badge. Mem. U.S. Council for World Communications, Beta Gamma Sigma. Home and Office: Buffalo Lake 325 Mallard Rd Sanford NC 27332-1142 E-mail: pjr4u2@aol.com. *As we go about climbing the mountains in our lives, we must always remember to take the high road - for that is the only way to truly reach the top.*

RAISLER, KENNETH MARK, lawyer; b. New Rochelle, N.Y., May 15, 1951; s. Herbert A. and Norma (Glaubach) R.; m. Sara Ann Kelsey, June 11, 1978; children: Alison Elisabeth, Katharine Kelsey, David Mark. BSBA, Yale Coll., 1973; JD, NYU, 1976. Bar: N.Y. 1977, D.C. 1977, U.S. Dist. Ct. (so. dist.) N.Y. 1977, U.S. Dist. Ct. D.C. 1977, U.S. Ct. Appeals (2d cir.) 1977, U.S. Ct. Appeals (D.C. cir.) 1977, U.S. Ct. Appeals (7th cir.) 1982, U.S. Ct. Appeals (10th cir.) 1983, U.S. Supreme Ct. 1985. Law clk. U.S. Dist. Ct. (so. dist.) N.Y., N.Y.C., 1976-77; asst. U.S. atty., Washington, 1977-82; dep. gen. counsel Commodity Futures Trading Commn., Washington, 1982-83, gen. counsel, 1983-87; ptnr. Rogers & Wells, N.Y.C., 1987-92, Sullivan & Cromwell, N.Y.C., 1992—. Mem. Assn. of Bar of City of N.Y. (chair futures regulation com. 1988-91). Office: Sullivan & Cromwell 125 Broad St 33d Fl New York NY 10004-2489 E-mail: raislerk@sullcrom.com.

RAISLER, MARY E. nurse; b. May 13, 1955; BSN, U. South Ala., 1998. RN, Fla. Med. svcs. mgr. Med. Ctr. Health Plan, Pensacola, Fla., 1987-90; quality assurance coord. Blue Cross/Blue Shield Fla., Pensacola, 1990-95; managed care dir. West Fla. Med. Ctr. Clinic, Pensacola, 1995-98; dir. managed care Bapt. Health Care, Inc., Pensacola, 1998—, clin. appeals coord., 2000—02, dir. resource mgmr., 2002—. Vol. Big Bros./Big Sisters of Pensacola, 1996-03. Mem. Nat. Assn. Healthcare Quality, Am. Case Mgmt. Assn., Fla. Assn. Health Care Quality (pres.-elect 1997-98, pres. 1998-99). Office: 1000 W Moreno St Pensacola FL 32501-2316 Office Phone: 850-469-2089.

RAISYS, VIDMANTAS A. toxicology educator, clinical chemist; b. Telsiai, Lithuania, Nov. 3, 1934; came to U.S., 1956; s. Vladas A. and Jadvyga Raisys; m. Maria Nijole Galbuogis, Aug. 4, 1962; children: Victor A., Rasa K. BS, Roosevelt U., 1962; MS, U. Ill., Chgo., 1965; PhD, SUNY, Buffalo, 1969. Diplomate in clin. and toxicological chemistry Am. Bd. Clin. Chemistry. Postdoctoral fellow U. Pa., Phila., 1969—71; prof. toxicology, dir. toxicology U. Wash., Seattle, 1971—, Wash. State toxicologist, 1976—90, head chemistry divsn., 1996—2001, prof. emeritus, 2001—. Contbr. over 100 articles and abstracts to sci. jours. Fellow Nat. Acad. Clin. Biochemistry, Am. Acad. Forensic Scis.; mem. Acad. Clin. Physicians and Scientists, Am. Assn. Clin. Chemistry, Internat. Assn. Therapeutic Drug Monitoring and Clin. Toxicology. Avocations: reading, skiing, classical music, fishing.

RAITT, BONNIE LYNN, blues singer, guitarist; b. Burbank, Calif., Nov. 8, 1949; Student, Radcliffe Coll. Performer: blues clubs, East Coast, concert tours in Britain, 1976, 1977; albums include Bonnie Raitt, 1971, Give It Up, 1972, Takin' My Time, 1973, Streetlights, 1974, Home Plate, 1975, Sweet Forgiveness, 1977, The Glow, 1979, Green Light, 1982, Nine Lives, 1986, Nick of Time, 1989 (Grammys 1990, Rock-Best Vocal Performance, Female, Pop-Best Vocal Performance, Female, Album of Yr., 1990), I'm in the Mood (with John Lee Hooker) (Grammy 1990, Blues-Best Traditional Record, 1990), The Bonnie Raitt Collection, 1990, Luck of the Draw, 1991 (Grammy, Rock-Best Vocal Performance, Female, Grammy for Best Duet with Delbert McClinton, 1992), Longing In Their Hearts, 1994 (Grammy award Best Pop Album, 1994), Road Tested, 1996, Fundamental, I Can't Make You Love Me, 1998, Silver Lining, 2002, songs include Something to Talk About (Grammy, Best Pop Vocal Performance, Female, 1992), Good Man, Good Woman (with Delbert McClinton) (Grammy, Rock-Best Vocal by a Duo or Group, 1992). Founding mem. Musicians United for Safe Energy, Rhythm and Blues Found.*

RAIZEN, SENTA AMON, educational administrator, researcher; b. Vienna, Oct. 28, 1924; came to U.S., 1940; d. John and Helen (Krys) Amon; m. Abraham A. Raizen, Apr. 18, 1948; children: Helen S., Michael B., Daniel J. BS, Guilford Coll., 1944; MA, Bryn Mawr, 1945; Tchr. Cert., U. Va., 1960. Rsch. chemist Sun Oil Co., Norwood, Pa., 1945-48; rsch. asst. NAS, Washington, 1960-62; assoc. program dir. NSF, Washington, 1962-69, spl. asst., 1969-72; sr. researcher The Rand Corp., Washington, 1972-74; assoc. dir. Nat. Inst. Edn., Washington, 1974-78; ind. cons. Washington, 1978-80; study dir. NAS, Washington, 1980-88; dir. Nat. Ctr. for Improving Sci. Edn., Washington, 1988—. Cons. Nat. Ctr. for Edn. Stats., Washington, 1987—, Ednl. Testing Svc., Princeton, N.J., 1988—, Nat. Goals Panel, Washington, 1990-2000, Third Internat. Math. and Sci. Study, Internat. Assn. Evaluation Ednl. Achievement, The Netherlands, 1990—, SRI Internat., 1998—, Orgns. for Econ. Cooperation and Devel., Paris, 1998—. Contbr. articles to profl. jours., encys., books, reports in field. Pres. Cooperative Nursery Sch., Arlington, Va., 1953-57; leader Brownies, Girl Scouts, U.S. and Cub Scouts, Boy Scouts, Am., Arlington, 1958-64. Recipient Disting. Lifetime award WestEd, 2000; grantee NSF, U.S. Dept. Edn., U.S Dept. Energy, pvt. founds., 1988-2000, fellowship for grad. study NSF, 1944-45, Meritorious Svc. award, 1968, The Network Pres.' award, 1991. Fellow AAAS; mem. Am. Chem. Soc., Am. Ednl. Rsch. Assn. Avocations: dance, swimming, reading, knitting, stitchery, grandchildren. Home: 5513 31st St N Arlington VA 22207-1532 Office: Nat Ctr Improving Sci Edn 1726 M St NW Ste 704 Washington DC 20036-4524

RAJA, KRISHNAN SELVA, materials engineer; b. Tiruchirappalli, Tamilnadu, India, July 30, 1965; s. Somasundaram and Meena Krishnan; m. Kalyani Ramanathan, May 11, 1989; children: Santosh Somu, Ramakrishnan. B.E, Coll. of Engring., Guindy, Anna U., Chennai, 1986; M.Tech, Indian Inst.Tech., Madras, Chennai, India, 1988—88, Ph.D, 1993. Rsch. exec. Larsen & Toubro Ltd., Mumbai, India, 1993—97; rsch. assoc. Tohoku U., Sendai, Japan, 1998—2000; rsch. scientist U. of Nev., Reno, 2001—. Mem.: Nat. Assn. Corrosion Engineers (Internat.), Am. Soc. Metals (corr.). Achievements include development of a non-destructive electrochemical evaluation method to detect intergranular susceptibility of Ni-Cr-Mo-W alloy which will be used for construction of nuclear waste containers; research in Charecterized semiconductor properties of passive film of stainless alloys and correlated to SCC susceptibility; Recommended optimal post weld heat treatment cycles for better corrosion properties of PH stainless steels; development of a low cost weld overlay material for flux cored arc weld deposits for better abrasive wear resistant coatings; research in Observed that yield strength of the material does not affect the passive film properties. Dislocation dynamics at metal/oxide interface affects cracking in SCC. Office: Univ Nevada Coll of Engring Reno NV 89557 Office Phone: 775-784-7789. Personal E-mail: rajacorr@yahoo.com. E-mail: ksraja@unr.edu.

RAJA, RAJENDRAN, physicist; b. Guruvayur, Kerala, India, July 14, 1948; arrived in U.S., 1974; s. P.K. Sreeveerarayan and Chandramathi Raja; m. Selitha Barbara Freundorfer, 1976; 1 child, Anjali. BA with honors, Cambridge (Eng.) U., 1970, MA with honors, 1974; PhD, Cambridge (Eng.)U., 1974. Rsch. assoc. Fermilab, Batavia, Ill., 1975—78, assoc. scientist, 1978—83, scientist I, 1983—88, scientist II, 1988—. Monte Carlo convenor DO Expt., 1986—97, top quark physics convenor, 1990—94; head DO Software Support Group, 1986—93, DO Electron ID Group, 1989—94; head, emittance exch./ring coolers group Muon Collider/Neutrino Factory Collaboration, 2001—; spokesman Mipp Expt. Fermilab, Batavia, 2001—; fellow Trinity Coll., Cambridge U., 1973. Contbr. over 300 articles to profl. jours. Pres. Cambridge U. India Soc., 1969—70. Mem.: AAAS, Planetary Soc., Am. Phys. Soc. Achievements include discovery of top quark. Home: 1304 Margate Ct Naperville IL 60540 Office: Fermi Nat Accelerator Lab PO Box 500 Batavia IL 60510 Office Phone: 630-840-4092. Business E-Mail: raja@fnal.gov.

RAJAB, MOHAMMAD HASAN, biostatistician, educator; b. Oct. 8, 1955; married; 2 children. BS in Agrl. Scis., Damascus (Syria) U., 1976; MS in Quantitative Genetics, Tex. A&M U., 1983, MS in Stats., PhD in Quantitative Genetics, Tex. A&M U., 1987, MPH, 2002. Instr. Coll. Agr., Damascus U., 1976-80, asst. prof. quantitative genetics, 1987-90; tchg. asst. dept. stats. Coll. Sci., Tex. A&M U., College Station, 1986-87; vis. asst. prof. Tex. A&M U., College Station, 1990; rsch. sci. dept. stats. Coll. Sci., Tex. A&M U., College Station, 1990-93, asst. prof. dept. psychiatry-behavioral scis. Coll. Medicine, 1993-99, assoc. prof. dept. psychiatry, behavioral scis., 1999—. Vis. asst. prof. Inst. für Tierenranhrung, U. Bonn, Germany, 1990; co-investigator Coordinating Ctr. Partial Hospitalization of High-Risk Suicidal Youth Study, NIH, 1990-94, statistician ctrl. vein occlusion study, 1994-96; epidemiologist biostats. dept. Scott and White Hosp., Temple, Tex., 1993—; dir. effectiveness registry outcome rsch. unit Scott and White Hosp., 1997-2003, dir. biostats., 2003-; presenter in field. Contbr. articles to profl. jours. Acad. scholar USAID, 1980; recipient Govt. award Damascus U., 1976. Mem. Am. Stats. Assn., Soc. Clin. Trials, Sigma Xi. Office: Texas A&M U Health Sci Ctr Biostatistics 2401 S 31st St Temple TX 76508-0001 E-mail: mhrajab@yahoo.com.

RAJASEKAR, ARCOT, computer scientist; s. Kuppuswamy and Sakunthala Arcot; m. Malini Govindaraj Purasawalkam, Aug. 21, 1989; 1 child, Bhairavi. B with honors in engring., Coll. of Engring., U. of Madras, India, 1979; MS, Indian Inst. of Tech., India, 1982; PhD, U. Md., 1984. Post doctoral rsch. assoc. U. Md. Inst. for Advanced Computer Studies, Coll. Pk., Md., 1989—90; asst. prof. U. Ky., Lexington, 1990—96; scientist to principle scientist San Diego Supercomputer Ctr., La Jolla, Calif., 1996—2001, dir., data grid technologies group, 2001—. Vice thrust area liaison Nat. Partnership for Advanced Computational Infrastructure, La Jolla, Calif., 1997—; reviewer NSF, Washington, 2000—02. Author: (research monograph) Foundations of Disjunctive Logic Programming; guest editor Annals of Mathematics and Artificial Intelligence; contbr. articles various profl. jours., chapters to books various profl. text. Various scientific grants, NSF, 1991—2007, Storage Resource Broker Performance Optimization grant, Dept. of Def., 2000-2001, Biomedical Imaging Rsch. Network Coordinating Ctr. grant, NIH, 2001-2004, Portal Web Services: Support of DOE SciDAC Collaborations grant, Dept. of Energy, 2002-2005, Rsch. in String-oriented Databases grant, Dept. of Def., 1996. Mem.: Global Grid Forum. Hindu. Achievements include development

of storage resource broker; patents pending for collection-based persistent digital archive; development of MCAT - a metadata catalog; research in data grid technology; logic programming. Avocations: reading, fish-breeding, web-surfing, camping, hiking. Office: San Diego Supercomputer Ctr UCSD 9500 Gilman Dr La Jolla CA 92014-0505 E-mail: sekar@sdsc.edu.

RAJASEKARAN, KANNIAH, agricultural biotechnologist, researcher; BS in Agr., Tamil Nadu Agrl. U., India, 1973, MS in Agr., 1975; PhD, U. of Sydney, Australia, 1982. Project dir. Phytogen Inc., Pasadena, Calif., 1985—95; rsch. biologist USDA, Agrl. Rsch. Svc., New Orleans, 1996—. Mem.: Am. Chem. Soc., Internat. Assn. for Plant Tissue Culture, Internat. Assn. for Plant Molecular Biology, Am. Soc. of Plant Biologists, Soc. for In Vitro Biology. Achievements include patents for cotton biotechnology; genetic engineering for disease resistance in plants. Office: USDA ARS 1100 Robert E Lee Blvd New Orleans LA 70124 Office Phone: 504-286-4482.

RAJEWSKY, KLAUS, immunologist, educator; b. Frankfurt, Germany, Nov. 12, 1936; arrived in U.S.A., 2001; MD, U. Frankfurt, 1962. Diplomate 62. Postdoctoral fellow Inst. Pasteur, Paris, 1962—63, head immunology unit, 1964—66; sr. fellow Nat. Inst. Med. Rsch., London, 1969; prof. molecular genetics U. Cologne, France, 1970—2001; sr. investigator Ctr. Blood Rsch. Harvard Med. Sch., Boston, 2001—, prof. pathology, 2001—. Program coord. Inst. Genetics, Monterotondo, Italy, 1996; sci. adv. bd. European Molecular Biology Lab., 1977—79, 1995—, Gesellschart fur Naturrorscher und Arzte, 1979—81, Max Planck Inst. Immunobiology, Freiburg, Germany, 1983—87; sci. adv. bd. Immunology Dept. Inst. Pasteur, Paris, 1984; sci. adv. bd. Ctr. Immunologie de Marseille-Luminy, 1985—92; sci. adv. bd. Immunology Dept. Cancer Rsch. Inst., N.Y.C., 1987—; external adv. bd. Centro de Biologica Molecular, Madrid, 1995—96; sci. adv. bd. German Rheumatism Rsch. Ctr., Berlin, 1997—, Umea Ctr. Molecular Medicine, 1999—; fgn. mem. Conseil de la Biologie Ecole Normale Superiere, Paris, 1987—; chmn. symposium com. Internat. Union of Immunological Socs., 1974—77; mem. sci. and tech. adv. com. UNDP/ World Bank/ Who Spl. Programme for Rsch. and Tng. in Tropical Diseases, 1990—94; adv. bd. Robert Koch Ctr. Rsch. in Autoimmune Diseases Weizmann Inst., Rehovot, Israel, 1993—; sci. adv. bd. Ctr. for Molecular Biology U. Heidelberg, Germany, 1994—; internat. adv. bd. Rsch. Inst. Biol. Scis. Sci. U. of Tokyo, 1995—2000. Mem. exec. com.: European Jour. Immunology, 1971—91, mem. editl. bd.: Immunogenetics, 1974—82, Cell Biophysics, 1979—82, Annales d'Immunologie, 1980—88, Hoppe Seyler's Zeitschrift fur Physiologisch Chemie, 1978—86, The EMBO Jour., 1982—86, Jour. Molecular and Cellular Immunology, 1982—90, The Internat. Immunology, 1989—, Proceedings of the Royal Soc. (Series B), 1990—91, Cell, 1992—, The Jour. of Exptl. Medicine, 1992—, Current Opinion in Immunology, 1993—, Immunity, 1994—97, Mouse Knockouts and Mutants, 1996—, Genes and Function, 1996—97; contbg. editor: Molecular Medicine, 1995—. Mem.: Gesellschaft fur Biologische Chemie, Brit. Soc. Immunology, Gesellschaft fur Immunologie. Office: Center for Blood Research 200 Longwood Ave Boston MA 02115

RAJKUMAR, LAKSHMANASWAMY, biologist, researcher; s. Padmanabhan Conjeevaram and Saraswathi Lakshmanaswamy; m. Selvapriya Thangaraj, June 9, 1993; children: Divya, Preetha. MS, U. Madras, 1988, MPhil, 1990, PhD, 1997. Hon. prin. Saraswathi Coll., Madras, India, 1993—97; asst. rsch. endocrinologist U. Calif., Berkeley, 2002—. Contbr. scientific papers. Fellow, U. Calif., Berkeley, 1997—2002. Mem.: AAAS (assoc.), N.Y. Acad. Scis. (assoc.), Am. Assn. Cancer Rsch. (assoc.), Soc. Reproductive Biology and Comaparative Endocrinology (life). Achievements include research in Developed a short-term prevention treatment against breast cancer. Avocations: cricket, tennis, travel. Office: University of California at Berkeley 491 Life Sciences Addition Berkeley CA 94720 Personal E-mail: preetharaj@yahoo.com. E-mail: rajkumar@berkeley.edu.

RAJLICH, VACLAV THOMAS, computer science educator, researcher, consultant; b. Prague, Czech Republic, May 3, 1939; came to U.S., 1980; s. Vaclav and Marie Rajlich; m. Ivana M., Aug. 6, 1968; children: Vasik, Paul, John, Luke. MS, Czech Tech. U., Prague, 1962; PhD, Case Western Res. U., 1971. Rsch. engr. Rsch. Inst. for Math. Machines, Prague, 1963-67, scientist, 1971-75, mgr., 1975-79; vis. assoc. prof. computer sci. Calif. State U., Fullerton, 1980-81; assoc. prof. computer and communication sci. U. Mich., Ann Arbor, 1982-85; prof. Wayne State U., Detroit, 1985—, chair dept. computer sci., 1985-90. Vis. scientist Carnegie-Mellon U., Pitts., 1987, Harvard U., Cambridge, Mass., 1988. Contbr. articles to profl. jours. Recipient Chrysler Challenge Fund, 1988. Mem. Computer Soc. of IEEE, Assn. for Computing Machinery. Roman Catholic. Achievements include development of tools for software maintenance, program comprehension, software design methods, parallel grammars, graph rewriting, abstract state machines. Office: Wayne State U Dept Computer Sci Detroit MI 48202 E-mail: rajlich@cs.wayne.edu.

RAJSKI, PEGGY, film director, film producer; b. Stevens Point, Wis. Attended, U. Wis. Films include: (prodn. mgr.): Lianna, 1982, Almost You, 1984; (prodr., prodn. mgr.) The Brother From Another Planet, 1984, Matewan, 1987, (co-prodr., prodn. mgr.) Eight Men Out, 1988; (co-prodr.) The Grifters, 1990, (prodr.) Little Man Tate, 1991 (also 2nd. unit dir.), Used People, 1992, Home for the Holidays, 1995; (prodr. video) Bruce Springsteen's Glory Days; (dir.) Trevor, 1994 (Acad. award for Best Live Action Short Film).

RAJTAR, STEVEN ALLEN, lawyer; b. Cleve., Aug. 16, 1951; s. Steve and Rose (Golembiewski) R.; m. Gayle Prince, June 15, 1974; children— Jason Paul, Kelly Rose. B.A. in Anthropology, U. Central Fla., Orlando, 1973, B.S. in Math., 1973; J.D., U. Fla., 1976, LL.M., 1977. Bar: Fla. 1976, Tenn. 1977, U.S. Dist. Ct. (no. dist.) Fla. 1977, U.S. Tax Ct. 1977, U.S. Dist. Ct. (ea. dist.) Tenn. 1978, U.S. Dist. Ct. (middle dist.) Fla. 1980. Assoc. Clayton, Duncan, Johnston, Quincey, Ireland & Felder, Gainesville, Fla., 1976-77, Gearhiser & Peters, Chattanooga, 1977-79; assoc. Matthias & Matthias, Orlando, 1979-84, ptnr., 1985-85; sole practice law, 1985—. Contbr. articles to Tenn. Bar Jour. Mem. Fla. Bar, Orange County Bar Assn., U. Central Fla. Alumni Assn. (dir. 1979-82, 83-85). Unitarian. Home: 1614 Bimini Dr Orlando FL 32806-1512 Office: 1063 Maitland Ctr Commons Maitland FL 32751

RAJYAGURU, VRAJLAL LALJIBHAI, anesthesiologist; b. Jam Raval, India, Nov. 24, 1961; arrived in U.S., 1987; s. Laljibhai Kanji and Devkiben L. (Joshi) Rajyaguru; m. Kalpana S. Thanki, Mar. 12, 1986; children: Neal, Parth. MB, BS, M.P. Shah Med. Coll., India, 1986; MD, N.Y. Med. Coll., 1994. Diplomate Am. Bd. Anesthesiology (fellow). Intern in surgery St. Vincent's Hosp., N.Y.C., 1989-90; resident in surgery L.I. Jewish Med. Ctr., New Hyde Pk., NY, 1990-91; resident in anesthesiology and pain mgmt. N.Y. Med. Coll., Valhalla, 1991-94; pvt. practice. Rschr. laser application in vascular surgery, 1989. Co-chmn. physician adv. bd. Nat. Rep. Congl. Com., 2001. Named Fla. Businessman of the Yr., Nat. Rep. Congl. Com., 2001. Fellow: Am. Bd. Disability Analysis, Am. Acad. Pain Mgmt., Am. Bd. Pain Medicine; mem.: AMA, Neuromodulation Soc. (advisor). Address: Advanced Pain Clin PO Box 3129 Kissimmee FL 34742

RAK, LINDA MARIE, elementary education educator, consultant; b. Dunkirk, NY; d. Felix Joseph and Helen (Dudek) Ruzycki; m. Joseph John Rak, Oct. 11, 1969; children: Joel, Seth. BA in Edn., SUNY, Fredonia, 1969, MS in Edn., 1974; postgrad., SUNY, Brockport, 1980-84, SUNY, Buffalo, 1988-90. Cert. reading and spl. edn. tchr., NY. Tchr. 1st grade Webster Central Sch. Dist., NY, 1969-72; tchr. kindergarten and reading Williamson Central Sch. Dist., 1973-76; instr. in GED Orleans County Job Devel. Agy., Albion, 1979-83; adult basic edn. coord. SUNY, Brockport, 1980-85; tchr. remedial reading, lang. arts coord. Kendall Central Sch. Dist., 1985—, spl. edn. tchr., 1988—. In-svc. presenter Kendall Elem. Sch., NY, 1984—2002; workshop presenter Monroe #2 Orleans BOCES, Spenceport, 1988—91, Genesee Wyoming Bd. of Coop. Ednl. Svcs. (BOCES), 1988—91, NY State Whole Lang. Conf., 1993; reading recovery tchr. Kendall Elem. Sch., 1996—2003; adj. prof. dept. edn. and human devel. SUNY, Brockport, 2001—; early intervention tchr., cons. Kendall Elem. Sch., Kendall, 2003—. Nursery sch. treas. AAUW, Orleans and Niagara Counties, NY, 1977-79; tchr. Sunday sch. St. Joseph's Ch., Lyndonville, NY, 1978-95, mem. parish coun., 1996—. Recipient Cert. of Appreciation, Congressman John J. La False, 1985; named Religious Educator of the Yr., Diocese of Buffalo, 1987. Mem. Internat. Reading Assn., Rochester Area Reading Coordinators (pres. 1992-96), Genesee Valley Devel. Learning Group (satellite rep. 1987-88), Lit. Vols. Orleans County (v.p. 1981-84, Outstanding Leadership award 1984), Somerset Hist. Soc., Reading Recovery Coun. Roman Cath. Avocation: home restoration. Home: 64 N Main St # 329 Lyndonville NY 14098-9672 Office: Kendall Cen Sch Dist 1932 Kendall Rd Kendall NY 14476-9775 E-mail: lrak@kendallcsd.org.

RAKAS, JASENKA MILAN, aviation engineer; b. Belgrade, Yugoslavia, 1965; arrived in US, 1992; d. Milan and Bisa Rakas. BS, Belgrade U., 1990; MS, U. Md., 1997, PhD, 2001. Rsch. engr. U. Md., College Park, 1996—97, rsch. asst., 1998—2000, rschr., 2001, U. Calif., Berkeley, 2002—. Prin. investigator CSSI, Inc., Washington, 1994—95; cons. Sohar, Inc., Beverly Hills, Calif., 1998—99, Gellman Rsch. Assocs., Inc., Jenkintown, Pa., 1999—2003, JDA Aviation Tech. Solutions, Washington, 2001; vice-chair airfield and airspace capacity and delay com. Transp. Rsch. Bd. Editor: Airports in the 21st Century, 2001, Airport-Airspace Simulation for Capacity Evaluation, 2001, Airport-Airspace Simulations: A New Outlook, 2002, Airport Modeling and Simulation for Environmental Analysis, 2002; contbr. articles to profl. jours. Harkins Group fellow, U. Md., 2001. Mem.: ASCE, N.Am. Simmod Users Group, Inst. for Ops. Rsch. and the Mgmt. Scis. Office: Univ Calif Berkeley Nat Ctr Excellence for Aviation Ops Rsch Berkeley CA 94720 Business E-Mail: jrakas@ce.berkeley.edu.

RAKEL, ROBERT EDWIN, internist, educator; b. Cin., July 13, 1932; s. Edwin J. and Elsie (Machino) R.; m. Peggy Klare; children: Barbara, Cindy, Linda, David. BS in Zoology, U. Cin., 1954, MD, 1958. Diplomate Am. Bd. Family Practice. Intern St. Mary's Hosp., Cin., 1958-59; resident in internal medicine USPHS Hosp., Seattle, 1959-61; resident in gen. practice Monterey County Hosp., Salinas, Calif., 1961-62; practice medicine Newport Beach, Calif., 1962-69; chmn. family practice program U. Calif., Irvine, 1969-71; prof., head dept. family practice U. Iowa, 1971-85; assoc. dean acad. and clin. affairs, Richard M. Kleberg, Sr. prof., chmn. dept. family medicine Baylor Coll. Medicine, Houston, 1985-97, prof. dept. family and cmty. medicine, 1997—. Dir. family practice residency program Hoag Meml. Hosp., Newport Beach, 1969-71; med. staff Mercy Hosp., Iowa City, 1971-85; chief family practice svc. St. Luke's Episc. Hosp., The Meth. Hosp., Houston, 1985-97; trustee The Hospice of Tex. Med. Ctr., 1986-97, Inst. of Religion Tex. Author: elected References in Family Medicine, 1973; author: (with H.F. Conn & T.W. Johnson) Family Practice, 1973; author: (with H.F. Conn) Textbook of Family Practice, 1978; editor: Textbook of Family Practice, 3d edit., 1984, Textbook of Family Practice, 5th edit., 1995, Textbook of Family Practice, 6th edit., 2002, Principles of Family Medicine, 1977; author forward: Neurology for the Everyday Practice of Medicine, R.G. Feldman, 1984; contbr. Dictionary of Am. Med. Biography Vols. I and II, 1984; editor: Conn's Current Therapy, 1984—, Yearbook of Family Practice, 1977—90, (series) Procedures for Your Practice Patient Care, Vol. 18, Essentials of Family Practice, 1992, 2d edit., 1998, Saunders Manual Med. Practice, 1996; mem. 13 editorial bds. med. jours.; contbr. articles to med. jours., Encyclopedia Britannica, 1995; editor: Saunders Manual Med. Practice, 2d edit., 2000. Served with USPHS, 1959-61. Recipient Mead-Johnson Scholar award in Gen. Practice, 1971. Fellow Am. Acad. Family Physicians (pres. Orange County chpt. Calif. 1969, commn. on edn. 1970-76, Thomas W. Johnson award 1973); mem. AMA (sect. on med. schs. 1985-97, gov. coun. of sect. 1986-88), Tex. Med. Assn., Am. Bd. Family Practice (bd. dirs. 1973-79, v.p. 1977-79, chmn. exam. com. 1974-79, recert. com. 1973-79, others), Am. Bd. Med. Spltys. (com. splty. evaluation 1978-81), Nat. Bd. Med. Examiners (bd. dirs. 1975-79), Soc. Tchrs. Family Medicine (dir. 1971-79, sec. 1971-73), Coun. Acad. Socs., Assn. Am. Med. Colls., History of Medicine Soc. (founder, chmn. U. Iowa 1978-85, founder, chmn. Baylor Coll. Medicine 1986—), Am. Osler Soc. (bd. dirs. 1989-96, pres. 1994). Home: 2420 Underwood St Houston TX 77030-3506 Office: Baylor Coll Medicine 1 Baylor Plz Houston TX 77030-3411 E-mail: rrakel@bcm.tmc.edu.

RAKER, IRMA, judge; b. Bklyn. m. Samuel K. Raker. BA, Syracuse U., 1959; cert. of attendance (hon.), Hague (The Netherlands) Acad. Internat. Law, 1959; JD, Am. U., 1972. Bar: Md. 1973, D.C. 1974, U.S. Dist. Ct. Md. 1977, U.S. Ct. Appeals (4th cir.) 1977. Asst. state's atty. State's Atty.'s Office of Montgomery County, Md., 1973-79; ptnr. Sachs, Greenebaum & Tayler, Washington, 1979-80; judge Dist. Ct. Md., Rockville, 1980-82, Cir. Ct. for Montgomery County, Md., 1982-94, Ct. of Appeals of Md., 1994—. Adj. prof. Washington Coll. Law, Am. U., 1980—; mem. faculty Md. Jud. Inst., Nat. Criminal Def. Inst., 1980, 81, 82; instr. litigation program Georgetown Law Ctr.-Nat. Inst. Trial Advocacy; mem. legis. com. Md. Jud. Conf., mem. exec. com., 1985-89, mem. commn. to study bail bond and surety industry in Md.; mem. spl. com. to revise article 27 on crimes and punishment State of Md., 1991—; mem. inquiry com. atty. Grievance Commn. Md., 1978-81; chairperson jud. compensation com. Md. Jud. Conf., 1997—. Past editor Am. U. Law Rev. Treas., v.p. West Bradley Citizens Assn., 1964-68; mem. adv. com. to county exec. on child abuse Montgomery County, 1976-77, mem. adv. com. to county exec. on battered spouses, 1977-78, mem. adv. com. on environ. protection, 1980; mem. citizens adv. bd. Montgomery County Crisis Ctr., 1980. Recipient Robert C. Heeney award Md. State Bar Assn., 1993, Dorothy Beatty Meml. award Women's Law Ctr., 1994, Rita Davidson award Women's Bar Md., 1995, Margaret Brent Trailblazers award ABA Commn. on Women in the Profession/Women's Bar Assn. Md., 1995, Elizabeth Dole Woman of Achievement award ARC, 1998, Leadership in Law award The Daily Record, 2001, Nat. Assn. Social Workers' Pub. Citizen of Yr. award, 2001, others; named of Md.'s Top 100 Women Warfield's Bus. Record, 1997, 99, 2001. Fellow Md. Bar Found.; mem. ABA (chair criminal justice stds. com. 1995-96, mem. coun. criminal law sect. 1997—, del. nat. conf. state trial judges, active various coms.), Md. State Bar Assn. (chair coun. criminal law and practice sect., mem. bd. govs. 1981, 82, 85, 86, 90, mem. coun. litigation sect., active coms., chair com. to draft pattern jury instrns. in civil and criminal cases 1980—), Nat. Assn. Women Judges, Internat. Acad. Trial Judges, Am. Law Inst., Montgomery County Bar Assn. (chair criminal law sect. 1978-79, mem. exec. com. 1979-80, active other coms., Outstanding Jurist award 2000), Montgomery County Bar Leaders, Women's Bar Assn. Md., Women's Bar Assn. D.C., Hadassah Women's Orgn. (life), Pioneer Women Na'amat (Celebration of Women award 1985), Pi Sigma Alpha. Office: Ct of Appeals of Md 50 Maryland Ave Rockville MD 20850-2320

RAKIC, PASKO, neuroscientist, educator; b. Ruma, Yugoslavia, May 15, 1933; came to U.S., 1969; m. Patricia Goldman, 1969. MD, U. Belgrade, 1959, PhD in Devel. Biology and Genetics, 1969. With inst. path. physiology Med. Sch. U. Belgrade, 1959-61, resident in neurosurgery, 1961-62; NIH research fellow neuropathology Harvard Med. Sch., Boston, 1962-66; asst. prof. Inst. Biol. Rsch., Belgrade, 1967-68; from asst. prof. to assoc. prof. neuropathology and neuroscience Harvard Med. Sch., 1969-77; prof. neurosci. Yale Med. Sch., New Haven, 1977-78, Dorys McConnell Duberg prof. neurosci., 1978—, also chmn. neurobiology dept. Author of 300 sci. papers and gen. books on brain orgn. and devel. Mem.: AAAS, NAS, Inst. Med., Am. Phys. Soc. (Lashley award 1986, Fyssen Internat. Sci. prize 1992, Gerard prize, Pasarw award, Henry Gray award), Soc. Neurosci. (pres. 1996). Office: Yale U Sch Medicine Sect Neurobiology 333 Cedar St New Haven CT 06510-3289

RAKITA, LOUIS, cardiologist, educator; b. Montreal, Que., Can., July 2, 1922; came to U.S., 1951, naturalized, 1962; s. S. and Rose (Weinman) R.; m. G. Blanche Michlin, Dec. 4, 1945; 1 son, Robert M. BA, Sir George Williams Coll., Montreal, 1942; MD, C.M., McGill U., 1949. Diplomate: Am. Bd. Internal Medicine. Intern Montreal Gen. Hosp., 1949-50; resident in medicine Jewish Gen. Hosp., Montreal, 1950-51; fellow in medicine Alton Ochsner Med. Found., New Orleans, 1951-52; chief resident in medicine Cleve. City Hosp., 1952-53, Am. Heart Assn. fellow, 1954-55, Inst. for Med. Research, Cedars of Lebanon Hosp., Los Angeles, 1953-54; practice medicine specializing in internal medicine and cardiology Cleve., 1954—; instr. medicine Western Res. U., Cleve., 1954-55, sr. instr., 1955-57, asst. prof., 1957-61, asso. prof., 1961-71; asst. vis. physician Cleve. City Hosp., 1954-57, vis. physician, 1957—; advanced fellow Cleve. Met. Gen. Hosp., 1959-61, dir. cardiology, 1966-87, immediate past dir., div. cardiology, 1987—; asso. div. of research in med. edn. Case Western Res. U., Cleve., 1969-75, prof. medicine, 1971-93, prof. emeritus medicine, 1993. Chmn. Phase IIA Cardiovascular com. Case Western Res. U., 1965-70, Faculty Senate Subcom. for Devel. and Evaluation of Ednl. Methods, 1969, chmn. Univ. Com. on Ednl. Planning, 1971-73, Faculty Coun. Sch. Medicine, 1979-80, Faculty Coun. Steering Com. Sch. Medicine, 1979-80, mem. bd. trustees Com. on Univ. Plans, 1971-73, Faculty Senate, Exec. Coun.; cons. in cardiology Luth. Med. Ctr., Cleve., 1970—, Crile VA Hosp., Cleve., 1969—; vis. cardiologist Sunny Acres Hosp., Cleve., 1973—; cardiologist rep. of del. to USSR, 1973. Author: (with M. Broder) Cardiac Arrhythmias, 1970, (with M. Kaplan) Immunological Diseases, 1972; Contbr. (with M. Kaplan) articles on cardiovascular diseases to profl. publs. Served with RCAF, 1942-45. Recipient Research Career Devel. award USPHS, 1962-69, Saltzman award Mt. Sinai Med. Health Found., 1997. Fellow ACP (Laureate award Ohio chpt. 1992), Am. Coll. Cardiology, Royal Coll. Physicians and Surgeons Can. (cert.), Am. Heart Assn. (mem. exec. com. N.E. Ohio chpt. 1972—, trustee 1969—, pres. N.E. Ohio chpt. 1972-74, coun. on clin. cardiology 1972—, chmn. various coms., v.p. North Ctrl. Region 1985-86, bd. dirs. 1985-86, hon. life trustee Northeast Ohio affiliate, vice chmn. task force on product licensing feasibility 1987—, Award of Merit 1987, Gold Heart award 1989); mem. AAUP, Am. Fedn. Clin. Rsch., Ctrl. Soc. Clin. Rsch., Soc. Exptl. Biology and Medicine, Cleve. Med. Libr. Assn. (trustee 1972—), Nat. Bd. Med. Examiners, The Press of Case Western Res. U. (adv. com. 1970), Nat. Heart and Lung Inst., Nat. Insts. Health (left ventricular assist device clin. trial program divsn. extramural affairs, data rev. bd. 1981—, adv. com. med. devices applications program 1971-75), Sigma Xi. Home: 24151 S Woodland Rd Cleveland OH 44122-3315 Office: 2500 Metrohealth Dr Cleveland OH 44109-1900 E-mail: lrakita@earthlink.net.

RAKO, SUSAN, psychiatrist, author; b. Springfield, Mass., Sept. 4, 1939; d. Robert and Ann (Melnikoff) Mandell; 1 child, Jennifer Sarah. Student, Wellesley Coll., 1957-60; BS, U. Cin., 1961; MS in Film, Boston U., 1988; MD, Albert Einstein Coll. Medicine, 1966. Med. rsch. asst. neuroendocrinology Worcester Found. Exptl. Biology, Shrewsbury, Mass., 1959; med. rsch. asst. May Inst., Cin., 1961-62; intern in medicine, surgery Mt. Auburn Hosp., Cambridge, Mass., 1966-67; resident in adult psychiatry Mass. Mental Health Ctr., Boston, 1967-69; tchg. fellow in psychiatry Harvard Med. Sch., Boston, 1967-69, clin. fellow in psychiatry, 1969-70; pvt. practice Newton, Mass., 1970—; clin. instr. psychiatry Harvard Med. Sch., Boston, 1970-75; resident in child and adult psychiatry Beth Israel Hosp., Boston, 1969-70; psychiatrist Mass. Mental Health Ctr., Boston, 1970-77, Newton-Wellesley Hosp., 1982. Cons. Cutler Counseling Ctr., Norwood, Mass., 1983, VA Hosp., San Juan, PR, 1990—94; pres. Women's Health on Alert, Inc., 2003—; spkr. in field. Author: No More Periods? The Risks of Menstrual Suppression, 2003; The Hormone of Desire: The Truth About Testosterone, Sexuality, and Menopause, 1996, 2d edit., 1999, No More Periods? The Risks of Menstrual Suppression, 2003; co-editor: Semrad: The Heart of a Therapist, 1980, (paperback) 2004; film maker Susan and Jenni, 1987. E-mail: susanrako@aol.com.

RAKOFF, JED SAUL, federal judge, author; b. Phila., Aug. 1, 1943; s. Abraham Edward and Doris Tobiah (Michell) R.; m. Ann Rosenberg, Aug. 4, 1974; children: Jena Lynn, Elana Beth, Keira Jan. BA, Swarthmore Coll., 1964, LLD (hon.), 2003; MPhil, Balliol Coll., Oxford U., Eng., 1966; JD, Harvard U., 1969. Bar: N.Y. 1971, D.C. 1983, U.S. Supreme Ct. 1986. Law clk. U.S. Ct. Appeals (3rd cir.), Phila., 1969-70; assoc. Debevoise, Plimpton, Lyons & Gates, N.Y.C., 1970-73; asst. U.S. atty. So. Dist. N.Y., N.Y.C., 1973-80, chief bus. and securities fraud prosecutions U.S. Atty.'s Office, 1978-80; ptnr. Mudge Rose Guthrie Alexander & Ferdon, N.Y.C., 1980-90, Fried Frank Harris Shriver & Jacobson, N.Y.C., 1990-96; judge U.S. Dist. Ct. (so. dist.) N.Y., 1996—. Lectr. in law Columbia Law Sch., 1988-; mem. bd. mgrs. Swarthmore Coll., 2003-. Author: (with S. Arkin et al) Business Crime, 6 vols., 1982, Criminal Defense Techniques, 6 vols., 1982, (with H. Goldstein) RICO: Civil and Criminal Law and Strategy, 1989, (with L. Blumkin and R. Sauber) Corporate Sentencing Guidelines,: Compliance and Mitigation, 1993; editor-in-chief Bus. Crimes Bull., 1994-95; columnist N.Y. Law Jour., 1985-95; contbr. numerous articles to law revs. Mem. exec. bd. N.Y. chpt. Am. Jewish Com., 1971-95. Fellow Am. Coll. Trial Lawyers (chmn. N.Y. State 1993-94), Am. Bd. Criminal Lawyers; mem. ABA, N.Y. State Bar Assn., Assn. of Bar of City of N.Y. (chmn. criminal law com. 1986-89), Fed. Bar Coun., N.Y. Coun. Def. Lawyers (dir. 1990-94). Democrat. Jewish. Office: US Courthouse 500 Pearl St Rm 1340 New York NY 10007-1316 Office Phone: 212-805-0401. Business E-Mail: Jed_S_Rakoff@nysd.uscourts.gov.

RAKOLTA, JOHN, JR., construction executive; b. Detroit, May 26, 1947; BSCE, Marquette U. Design engr. Bendix Machine Tool; mem. sr. staff aerospace sector engring. Allied Signal; chmn., CEO Walbridge Aldinger Co., Detroit. Mem. NAACP, Automotive Industry Action Group (bd. dirs.), Detroit Urban League, Engring. Soc. Detroit. Office: Walbridge Aldinger 613 Abbott St Ste 300 Detroit MI 48226-2521

RAKOV, BARBARA STREEM, marketing executive; b. Bklyn., Jan. 4, 1946; d. Harold B. and Claire (Colbert) Streem; m. Harris J. Rakov, Nov. 20, 1970 (div. Mar. 1972). BS, Boston U., 1967; postgrad. NYU, 1972-74. Market rsch. analyst, product mgr., mktg. mgr. J.B. Williams, N.Y.C., 1967-77; mktg. dir. Del Labs., Farmingdale, N.Y., 1977-78; product mgr., sr. product mgr., asst. to office of pres., dir. mktg. and sales Benelux countries, v.p. group mktg., dir., dir. new products, v.p. bus. devel. Joseph E. Seagram & Sons, 1978-90; pres. BSR Assocs., N.Y.C., 1990-92; v.p. mktg. Del Labs., 1992-94; v.p. mktg. Tsumura Internat., Secaucus, N.J., 1994-96; v.p. mktg. Franco Mfg. Co., Inc., Metuchen, N.J., 1996—. Mem. L'Ordre des Coteaux de Champagne, Les Gastronomes de la Mer, Am. Mgmt. Assn. Avocations: tennis, skiing, squash, reading, water skiing. Home: 415 E 52d St New York NY 10022-6424 Office: Franco Mfg Co Inc 555 Prospect St Metuchen NJ 08840-2271

RAKOVE, JACK NORMAN, history professor; b. Chgo., June 4, 1947; s. Milton Leon and Shirley (Bloom) R.; m. Helen Scharf, June 22, 1969; children: Robert, Daniel. AB, Haverford Coll., 1968; PhD, Harvard U., 1975. Asst. prof. history Colgate U., Hamilton, N.Y., 1975-80; from asst. to assoc. prof. history Stanford (Calif.) U., 1980-90, prof., 1990—, Coe prof. history and Am. studies, 1996—, prof. polit. sci., 1999—. Author: Beginnings of National Politics, 1979, James Madison and The Creation of the American Republic, 1990, Original Meanings, 1996 (Pulitzer prize for History, 1997), Declaring Rights, 1997; editor: Interpreting the Consitution, 1990, James Madison Writings, 1999, The Unfinished Election of 2000, 2001, The Federalist, 2003. Commr. Calif. Bicentennial Commn., 1986-87. With USAR, 1968-74. NEH fellow, 1985-86, Stanford Humanities Ctr. fellow, 1988-89, 2000-01. Mem. Am. Hist. Assn., Orgn. Am. Historians, Soc. Am. Historians, Am. Polit. Sci. Assn., Am. Acad. Arts & Scis., Am. Antiquarian Soc., Soc. History of Early Am. Rep (pres. 2002). E-mail: rakove@stanford.edu.

RAKOWER, JOEL A. business appraiser, litigation consultant; b. 1958; BA in Acctg., U. South Fla., 1980. CPA, N.Y., Fla. Ptnr. Goodman, Rakower & Agiato, Commack, N.Y., 1989-93; pres. Fin. Appraisal Svcs. Ltd., Commack, 1993—. Testified as expert witness numerous times in N.Y. and Conn.; lectr., seminar presenter to profl. and ednl. orgns. Author: Enhanced Earning Capacity: Understanding the Computations, 1993, Quantifying Celebrity Status, 1995, Reality, What a Concept, 2001; contbr. articles to profl. jours. Mem. Nat. Assn. Cert. Fraud Examiners (cert.), Fla. Inst. CPAs, Am. Soc. Appraisers, Inst. Bus. Appraisers, N.Y. State Soc. CPAs, Nat. Assn. Forensic Economists. Office: Fin Appraisal Svcs Ltd 366 Veterans Memorial Hwy Commack NY 11725-4387 Office Phone: 631-543-1333.

RAKSIN, ALEX, reporter; b. Nov. 9, 1960; m. Victoria Hendrick; children: Tobias, Leonid. BA in Journalism, U. So. Calif., 1984. Columnist LA Times, 1985—93, dep. book editor, 1993—96, editl. writer, 1996—. Freelance writer, 1984—93; instr. UCLA Ext., 1986—89; dir. Lit. awards PEN USA West, 1998—2000. Recipient Outstanding Media award for Editl. Writing, Nat. Alliance for Mentally Ill, 2001, Nat. Headliner award for Editl. Writing, Calif. Alliance for Mentally Ill, 2001, 1999, Aaron Price Child Health and Welfare

Scholarship and Journalism award, 1999, Sigma Delta Chi award for editl. writing, 2002, Pulitzer prize for editl. writing, 2002. Mem.: Nat. Conf. Editl. Writers, Nat. Com. Concerned Journalists, Nat. Book Critics Cir. Office: LA Times 202 W 1st St Los Angeles CA 90012

RALEIGH, CECIL BARING, geophysicist; b. Little Rock, Aug. 11, 1934; s. Cecil Baring and Lucile Nell (Stewart) R.; m. Diane Lauster, July 17, 1982; children: Alison, Marianne, Lawrence, David. BA, Pomona (Calif.) Coll., 1956; MA, Claremont (Calif.) Grad. Sch., 1958; PhD, UCLA, 1963. Fellow Research Sch. Phys. Sci., Australian Nat. U., Canberra, 1963-66; geophysicist U.S. Geol. Survey, Menlo Park, Calif., 1966-80, program mgr. for earthquake prediction research program, 1980-81; dir. Lamont-Doherty Geol. Obs. and prof. geol. scis. Columbia U., Palisades, N.Y., 1981-89; dean Sch. Ocean and Earth Sci. and Tech. U. Hawaii, Honolulu, 1989—2003. CEO Ctr. for a Sustainable Future, Inc., 1996—; mem. Gov.'s Task Force on Sci. Tech., 1996-98; mem. NAS/NRC Ocean Studies Bd.; chmn. NAS/NRC Yucca Mountain Panel, High Tech. Devel. Corp.; bd. dirs. JOI, Inc. Author papers control earthquakes, rheology of the mantle, mechanics of faulting, crystal plasticity. Trustee Bishop Mus., 1997—2003. Recipient Interdisciplinary award U.S. Nat. Com. Rock Mechanics, 1969, 74; Meritorious Service award Dept. Interior, 1974; Barrows Dist. Alumnus award Pomona Coll. Fellow Am. Geophys. Union, Geol. Soc. Am. Democrat. Inventor formation fracturing method. Office: U Hawaii Sch Ocean Earth Sci & Tech Honolulu HI 96822

RALES, MITCHELL P. automotive parts company executive; b. 1956; married Pres. Danaher Corp., Washington, 1984—, also bd. dirs., ptnr. Equity Group Holdings, Washington, 1979 ; chmn. exec. com. Danaher Corp., Washington. Office: Danaher Corp 1250 24th St NW Washington DC 20037-1124

RALES, STEVEN M. automotive parts company executive; b. Pitts., Mar. 31, 1951; married BA, DePauw U., 1973; JD, America U., 1978. Ptnr. Equity Group Holdings, Washington, 1979—; chmn. bd., chief exec. officer Danaher Corp., Washington, 1984—, now chmn. bd. Office: Danaher Corp 2099 Pennsylvania Ave NW Washington DC 20006-6800

RALEY, BENNETT W. federal agency administrator; BS in Agrl. Bus., Colo. State U., 1979, JD, 1983. From assoc. to ptnr. Davis, Graham & Stubbs, Denver; shareholder Trout & Raley, P.C., 1983—90; gen. counsel No. Colo. Water Conservancy Dist.; spl. asst. atty. gen. N.Mex. Office of the State Engr. and Interstate Stream Commn.; asst. sec. water and scis. U.S. Dept. Interior, Washington, 2001—. Staff counsel U.S. Senator Hank Brown; chief counsel U.S. Senate Judiciary Subcom. on the Constn., Federalism and Property Rights; co-chair Fed. Water Rights Task Force. Office: US Dept Interior Water and Sci 1849 C St NW Washington DC 20240

RALEY, JOHN W., JR., lawyer; b. May 23, 1932; s. John Wesley and Helen Thames; children: John Wesley III, Robert Thames. AB, Okla. Baptist U., 1954; JD, U. Okla., 1959. Bar: Okla. 1959, U.S. Supreme Ct. 1973, U.S. Ct. Appeals (10th cir.), 1962, U.S. Dist. (we. dist.) 1961, U.S. Dist. Ct. (no. dist.) Okla. 1988, U.S. Dist. Ct. (ea. dist.) Okla. 1989. Asst. U.S. atty. We. Dist. Okla. U.S. Dept. Justice, 1961-69; ptnr. Northcutt, Raley, Clark and Gardner, Ponca City, Okla., 1969-90; U.S. atty. Ea. Dist. Okla. U.S. Dept. Justice, 1990-97; of counsel Northcutt, Clark, Gardner & Hron, Ponca City, 1997—; mcpl. ct. judge Ponca City, 2001—. Mayor of Ponca City, Okla., 1980-83; mem. Okla. Ethics Commn., 2003—. Capt. USNR, 1950-84, ret. Recipient George Washington Honor medal Freedoms Found. at Valley Forge, 1971, Spl. Initiative award U.S. Dept. Justice, 1994, Outstanding Alumni Achievement award Okla. Bapt. U., 1981, Outstanding Citizen award Ponca City, 1984. Fellow Am. Coll. Trial Lawyers; mem. ABA, Am. Bd. Trial Advs., Okla. Bar Assn. (mem. bd. govs., 1989-90), Kay County Bar Assn. (pres. 1980), Am. Legion, Mason, Reserve Officers Assn., Naval Reserve Assn., VFW. Republican. Southern Baptist. Office: 400 E Central Ave Ste 401 Ponca City OK 74601-5428 Address: PO Box 1412 Ponca City OK 74602-1412

RALEY, JOHN WESLEY, III, lawyer; b. Oklahoma City, Oct. 19, 1959; s. John Wesley Raley Jr. and Mary Lane Mallett; m. Kelly Elaine Williams, Sept. 22, 1984; children: Katherine Elise, William Thomas, James Wesley. BA summa cum laude, U. Okla., 1981, JD, 1984; LLM, U. Aberdeen, Scotland, 1988. Bar: Tex. 1985, U.S. Dist. Ct. (so. dist.) Tex. 1985, U.S. Ct. Appeals (5th cir.) 1985; bd. cert. personal injury trial law Tex. Bd. Legal Specialization. With Fulbright & Jaworski, LLP, Houston, 1985-96, ptnr., 1996-2000; shareholder, mng. ptnr. Cooper & Scully, P.C., Houston, 2001—. Lectr. civil litigation U. Houston CLE, 1995—; bd. dirs. Houston Pub. TV, on-air spokesman, 1996—. Vol. Habitat for Humanity, Houston, 1998. Fellow Tex. Bar Found. (life); mem. ABA, State Bar Tex., Houston Bar Assn. (interdisciplinary ednl. alliance, spkrs. bur.), U. Okla. Varsity O Club, Phi Beta Kappa. Avocations: basketball, golf, tennis, local amateur drama performances. Home: 5 Falling Leaf Ln Houston TX 77024-4513 Office: 2700 Chase Tower 600 Travis St Houston TX 77002-3009

RALL, JOSEPH EDWARD, physician; b. Naperville, Ill., Feb. 3, 1920; s. Edward Everett and Nell (Platt) R.; m. Caroline Domm, Sept. 28, 1944 (dec. Apr. 1976); children: Priscilla, Edward Christian. BA, North Central Coll., 1940, D.Sc. (hon.), 1966; MS, Northwestern U., 1944, MD, 1945; PhD, U. Minn., 1952; Dr. honoris causa, Faculty of Medicine, Free U. Brussels, Belgium, 1975; MD (hon.), U. Naples, 1985. Assoc. mem. Sloan Kettering Inst., N.Y.C., 1950-55; chief clin. endocrinology br. Nat. Inst. Arthritis, Metabolism and Digestive Diseases, NIH, 1955-62; dir. intramural research Nat. Inst. Arthritis, Diabetes, Digestive and Kidney Diseases, 1962-83; dep. dir. intramural research NIH, 1983-91; sr. investigator Nat. Inst. Diabetes and Digestive and Kidney Diseases, NIH, 1991; scientist emeritus NIH, 1995. Mem. NRC, 1960-65 Author numerous articles, chpts. in books on thyroid gland nuc. hormone receptors, and radiation. Chmn. Coun. of Scientists for Internat. Human Frontier Sci. Program, 1989-93. Served to capt. M.C. AUS, 1946-48. Recipient Van Meter prize Am. Goiter Assn., 1950, Fleming award, 1959, Outstanding Achievement award Mayo Clinic and U. Minn., 1964; Disting. Service award Am. Thyroid Assn., 1967; Disting. Service award HEW, 1968, Disting. Exec. rank, sr. exec. service, 1980, R.H. Williams Disting. Leadership award in endocrinology, 1983, Disting. Achievement award N.Y. Hosp., Cornell Med. Ctr., 1987; named Outstanding Alumnus N. Central Coll., 1966 Mem. NAS, AAAS, Am. Acad. Arts and Scis., Am. Soc. Clin. Investigation, Am. Phys. Soc., Endocrine Soc., Assn. Am. Physicians, Societe de Biologie (France), Royal Acad. Medicine (Brussels). Home: 3947 Baltimore St Kensington MD 20895-3913 Office: NIH Bldg 10 Rm 7C432 Bethesda MD 20892 Office Phone: 301-401-2486. Business E-Mail: joseph_rall@nih.gov.

RALLI, CONSTANTINE PANDIA, lawyer; b. Bronxville, N.Y., Apr. 6, 1948; s. Pandia C. and Mary (Motter) R.; m. Alison Rhoads, Aug. 11, 1973; children: Pandia C., Christopher A. BA, Middlebury Coll., 1970; JD, Fordham U., 1973; LLM in Taxation, NYU, 1986. Bar: N.Y. 1974, U.S. Ct. Appeals (2nd cir.) 1974, U.S. Dist. Ct. (so. and ea. dists.) N.Y. 1975, U.S. Tax Ct. 1977, Fla. 1985, Conn. 1985, U.S. Dist. Ct. Conn. 1987. Assoc. Davis Polk & Wardwell, N.Y.C., 1973-81; ptnr. Hall, McNicol, Hamilton & Clark, N.Y.C., 1981-88, LeBoeuf, Lamb, Greene & MacRae, N.Y.C., 1988—. Sec., bd. dirs. Fairfield-Maxwell Ltd., Campo Tankers SA, N.Y.C., 1987-95. Bd. dirs. Samaritan Counseling Ctr., Rye, N.Y., 1987-90, Rye Free Reading Room, 1990-93, Rye Presbyn. Ch., 1986-89. Mem. Union Club, Am. Yacht Club, Ekwanok Country Club (Manchester, Vt.). Republican. Presbyterian. Home: 11 Rockridge Rd Rye NY 10580-4130 Office: LeBoeuf Lamb Greene & MacRae 125 W 55th St New York NY 10019-5369 also: 411 Pequot Ave Southport CT 06490-1386

RALLO, JAMES GILBERT, management company executive; b. Balt., Mar. 1, 1942; s. James Vincent and Thelma Mary (Hannahs) R.; m. Frances Elaine Petro, June 13, 1965; children: James Michael, Robert Francis. BS, U. Md., 1965; postgrad., George Washington U., 1967—. Mktg. trainee Chessie Sys., Balt., 1965—66; market analyst Bendix Corp., Balt., 1966—68, contract adminstr. N.Y.C., 1968—70; account exec. Peterson, Howell & Heather, Inc. (name changed to PHH Arval) PHH Vehicle Mgmt. Svcs., Hunt Valley, Md., 1970—75; regional mgr. Peterson, Howell & Heather, Inc., Hunt Valley, 1975—80, v.p. sales, 1980—83, v.p. sales and client rels., 1983—87, sr. v.p. sales and client rels., 1987—91, sr. v.p. client and industry rels., 1991—94, v.p. industry rels., 1994—2003, v.p. strategic partnership, 2003—. Bd. dirs., mem. fin. com. Towson YMCA, Md., 1981-93, mem. fundraising com., mem. budget com.; coach Cockeysville-Springlake Recreation Coun., 1973-82; advisor Jr. Achievement, 1975-76; fund solicitor United Way, 1983-84; v.p. NAFA Found., 1995—. Mem.: Am. Automotive Leasing Assn., Automotive Fleet and Leasing Assn. (dir. lessors 1993—95, conf. com. 1993—2001, v.p. 1999—2000, exec. v.p. 2000—01, pres. 2001—02, bd. dirs., ednl. com.), Nat. Assn. Fleet Adminstrs. (affiliate chmn. intercounty chpt. 1978—80, nat. affiliate com. 1990—2000, editl. com. 1992—96, bd. govs. 1993—, chmn. affiliates com. 1995—97, co-chair edn. com. 1999—2001, affiliate trustee 2000—03, mem. conf./program com. 1993—98, Hon. award for disting. svc. 1997), Optimists Club (v.p. Springdale-Cockeysville 1982—84, chmn. fundraising com.). Avocations: skiing, coaching youth sports, antique/classic cars, reading, golf. Office: PHH Arval 940 Ridgebrook Rd Sparks MD 21152 Office Phone: 410-771-2371. Business E-Mail: jim.rallo@phh.com.

RALPH, DAVID CLINTON, communications educator; b. Muskogee, Okla., Jan. 12, 1922; s. Earl Clinton and Rea Jane (Potter) R.; m. Kathryn Juanita Wicklund, Nov. 29, 1947; children: David Randall, Steven Wicklund. AA, Muskogee Jr. Coll., 1941; BS in Theatre, Northwestern U., 1947, MA in Theatre, 1948, PhD in Speech, 1953. Lectr. Ind. U., Hammond, 1947-48; instr. speech U. Mo., Columbia, 1948 53; tchr. debate forensics summer program for high sch. students Northwestern U., Evanston, Ill., 1949-51; asst. prof. speech Mich. State U., East Lansing, 1953-57, assoc. prof., 1957-64, prof. speech and theatre, 1964-68, prof. communication, 1968-94, prof. emeritus, 1994—, dir. comm. undergrad. program, 1968-88. Cons. in field. Co-author: Group Discussion, 1954, 2d edit., 1956, Principles of Speaking, 1962, 3d edit., 1975; contbr. articles to profl. jours., chpts. to books. Coach Jr. League Boys' Baseball, Lansing, Mich., 1958-74; mem. civilian aux. to Lansing Fire Dept., 1987—. Lt. USNR, 1942-46, PTO, ETO. Named Hon. State Farmer, Future Farmers Am., 1965; recipient Community Svc. award Mich. State U. Sr. Class Coun., 1979, Outstanding Faculty award, 1987, 91; Teaching Excellence award State of Mich., 1990. Mem. AAUP, Nat. Communication Assn., Cen. States Communication Assn., Golden Key (hon., faculty advisor), Omicron Delta Kappa. Democrat. Methodist. Avocation: model trains and fire engines. Office: Mich State U Dept Communication East Lansing MI 48824

RALSTON, ANTHONY, computer scientist, mathematician, educator; b. N.Y.C., Dec. 24, 1930; s. Alfred Joseph and Ruth (Bien) R.; m. Jayne Madeleine Reenthal, Feb. 14, 1958; children: Jonathan, Geoffrey, Steven, Elizabeth. BS, MIT, 1952, PhD, 1956. Mem. tech. staff Bell Tel. Labs., 1956-59; lectr. U. Leeds, 1959-60; mgr. tech. computing Am. Cyanamid Co., 1960-61; assoc. prof. math. Stevens Inst. Tech., 1961-64, prof., 1964-65; dir. computer svcs. SUNY, Buffalo, 1965-70, prof., 1965-95, chmn. dept. computer sci., 1967-80, prof. emeritus, 1995—. Bd. examiners Grad. Record Exam in Computer Sci., 1976-82; mem. computer sci. and tech. bd. NRC, 1976-79, math. sci. edn. bd., 1985-89; acad. visitor Imperial Coll., London, 1995-2003. Author: A First Course in Numerical Analysis, 1965, 2d edit., 1978, Introduction to Programming and Computer Science, 1971, Discrete Algorithmic Mathematics, 1991, 3d edit., 2004, Algorithms, 1997; editor: Ency. of Computer Science, 1976, 2d edit., 1982, 3d edit., 1992, 4th edit., 2000, concise edit., 2004, ABACUS, 1983-88; co-editor: Mathematical Methods for Digital Computers, Vol. 1, 1960, Vol. 2, 1967, Vol. 3, 1977, The Influence of Computers and Informatics in Mathematics and Its Teaching, 1993. 2d lt. U.S. Army, 1957. Fellow AAAS, Royal Soc. of Arts, Assn. Computing Machinery (pres. 1972-74, mem. coun. 1968-76, Disting. Svc. award 1982); mem. Math. Assn. Am. (bd. govs. 1984-87), Am. Fedn. Info. Processing Soc. (pres. 1975-76), Com. Concerned Scientists (bd. dirs.). Home: Flat 4 58 Prince Consort Rd London SW7 2BA England Office Phone: 44-20-75892195. E-mail: ar9@doc.ic.ac.uk.

RALSTON, BARBARA JO, bank executive; b. Youngstown, Ohio, Apr. 11, 1940; d. Fred Kenneth and Juanita Ruth (Welch) Roof; m. Donald Gene Ralston, Jan. 9, 1960; children: Mark David, Lori Sue. Cert., Pacific Coast Banking Sch. U. Wash., Seattle, 1981; AA in fin., Maricopa County CC. Sec. Bank of Scottsdale, Ariz., 1962-66; adminstrv. asst. Talley Industries, Mesa, Ariz., 1966-73; asst. mgr. Continental Bank, Phoenix, 1973-77; exec. v.p. Continental Bank Service Corp., Phoenix, 1977-85, pres., dir., 1985—86; chmn., pres. to sr. v.p. electronic and convenience banking to exec. v.p. personal banking group Chase Bank of Ariz., exec. v.p., COO; exec. v.p., mgr. northeast Ariz. retail area First Interstate Bank, 1994—95, Phoenix area pres., 1995—96; sr. v.p., mgr. in-store banking Wells Fargo Bank, Ariz., 1996—97; founder, pres., CEO Camelback Cmty. Bank, Phoenix, 1998—. Pres. Ariz. Bus. Leadership. Bd. dirs. Valley Big Bros.-Big Sisters, Phoenix, 1986; mem. Ariz. Acad., Phoenix, 1984; treas. Phoenix Together Town Hall, 1986; chair Am. West Airlines Edn. Found.; immediate past chair, Fresh State Women's Found.; past chair Ariz. Town Hall; past internat. pres. Financial Women Internat. Recipient You Too Can Make A Difference award Valley Christian Ctrs., Phoenix, 1985. Mem. Nat. Assn. Bank Women (state pres. 1981-82), Am. Inst. Banking (state edn. chmn. Ariz. chpt. 1984), Tumbleweed (pres. 1983); Am. Bankers Assn. (state membership chair for Ariz., chair ABA Edn. Found, 2003-), Ariz Bankers Assn. (bd. dirs., 2001-03, pres., 2001-02. Lodges: Soroptimists (pres. 1982, Women Helping Women award 1984). Republican. Methodist. Avocations: reading, travel, sewing. Office: Camelback Cmty Bank 2777 E Camelback Rd Ste 100 Phoenix AZ 85016

RALSTON, J. FRED, JR., internist; b. Fayetteville, Tenn., Apr. 25, 1954; s. Joseph Frederick Ralston and Clara Robertson Ralston-Wolfhard; m. Farris Lynch, Feb. 17, 1990; children: James David, Willis Farris. BA in Polit. Sci., Yale U., New Haven, Conn., 1976; MD, U. Tenn., Memphis, 1980. Diplomate Am. Bd. Internal Medicine. Resident in internal medicine Bapt. Meml. Hosp., Memphis, 1980—83; pvt. practice Fayetteville, Tenn., 1983—; dir. CCU Lincoln Med. Ctr., Fayetteville, 1984—. Active Lincoln County unit Am. Cancer Soc., Fayetteville, 1984-97, bd. dirs., pres., 1988-89; deacon, elder First Presbyn. Ch., Fayetteville, 1988-99; trustee Lincoln Regional Hosp., Fayetteville, 1989-2001. Fellow ACP (publ. com. 2001-03, vice-chmn. 2002-03, parliamentarian select 2002-03, parliamentarian 2003—, vice-chmn. health pub. policy com. 2003-04, chmn.-elect bd. govs., vice-chmn. fin., exec. com. bd. regents 2004—,); mem. AMA (Tenn. del., chair young physicians sect. 1991-92), Tenn. Med. Assn. (rural caucus 1984—, chair 1991-92, 97-98, del. 1985—, comm. com. 1988-99, co-chair 1992-95, chair 1995-99, judicial coun. 1988-92, chair 1990-92, legis. com. 1992—, bd. trustees 1998-2001, chmn. bd. trustees 2000-01, chair Tenn. care reform task force). Home: 51 Timberlake Dr Fayetteville TN 37334 Office: Fayetteville Med Assocs PC 207 S Elk Ave Fayetteville TN 37334 Office Fax: (931) 438-0069. E-mail: ralston@fayelectric.com.

RALSTON, JOANNE SMOOT, public relations executive; b. Phoenix, May 13, 1939; d. A. Glen and Virginia (Lee) Smoot; m. W. Hamilton Weigelt, Aug. 15, 1991 (dec.). BA in Journalism, Ariz. State U., 1960. Reporter The Ariz. Rep., Phoenix, 1960-62; co-owner, pub. rels. dir. The Patton Agy., Phoenix, 1962-71; founder, pres., owner Joanne Ralston & Assocs., Inc., Phoenix, 1971-87, 92—. Pres. Nelson Ralston Robb Comm., Phoenix, 1987—91, Joanne Ralston & Assocs., Inc., Scottsdale, 1991—, Kapaau, Hawaii, 2000—. Contbr. articles to profl. jours. Bd. dirs. Ariz. Parklands Found., 1984-86, Gov.'s Coun. on Health, Phys. Fitness and Sports, 1984-86; mem. task force Water and Natural Resources Coun., Phoenix, 1984-86; mem. Hawaii Gov.'s Adv. Bd., 2003—, others. Recipient Lulu awards (36) L.A. Advt. Women, 1964—, Gold Quill (2) Internat. Assn. Bus. Communicators, Excellence awards Fin. World mag., 1982-93, others; named to Walter Cronkite Sch. Journalism Hall of Fame, Coll. Pub. Programs Ariz. State U., 1987; named one of 25 Most Influential Arizonians, Phoenix Mag., 1991. Mem. Pub. Rels. Soc. Am. (counselor sect.), Internat. Assn. Bus. Communicators, Phoenix Press Club (pres. bd.), Investor Rels. Inst., Phoenix Met. C. of C. (bd. dirs. 1977-84, 85-91), Rotary Internat. Republican. Avocations: horses, dog training. Address: PO Box 808 Kapaau HI 96755-0808 Office Phone: 808-889-6433.

RALSTON, JOSEPH W. career officer; b. Hopkinsville, Ky., Nov. 4, 1943; m. Diane Dougherty; children: Christopher, Paige, David, Sarah. Grad., Miami (Ohio) U., 1965; M in Pers. Mgmt., Ctrl. Mich. U.; student, Army Command and Gen. Staff Coll., Nat. War Coll. at Fort McNair, Harvard U. Commd. 2d lt. res. officer tng. corps. program USAF, 1965, advanced through grades to gen., 1995; comdr. in chief U.S., European Command, NATO Supreme Allied Force. Achievements include operational command at squadron, wing, numbered air force and major command, as well as a variety of influential staff and management positions including two terms as vice chairman of the Joint Chiefs of Staff. Office: Supreme Allied Comdr Europe CMR Box 7100 APO AE 09705

RAM, CHITTA VENKATA, physician; b. Machilipatnam, India, Oct. 24, 1948; s. Chitta M. Row and Chitta (Cheruvu) Sarojini; m. Ashalata Ram, Feb. 17, 1979; children: Gita, Radha. B.Sci, Marathwada U., Aurangabad, India, 1966; MD, Osmania U., Hyderabad, India, 1972. Diplomate Am. Bd. Internal Medicine. Resident in internal medicine Brown U., R.I. Hosp., Providence, 1974-76; fellow in hypertension Hosp. U. Pa., Phila., 1976-77; faculty assoc. U. Tex. Southwestern Med. Ctr., Dallas, 1977-78, asst. prof., 1978-83, assoc. prof., 1983-89, prof. internal medicine, 1989—. Dir. Tex. Blood Pressure Inst., Dallas; dir. rsch. and edn. Dallas Nephrology Assocs.; dir. hypertension clinic Parkland Meml. Hosp., Dallas, hypertension unit St. Paul Med. Ctr., Dallas, dir. continuing med. edn. dept., 1996-98, chmn. instnl. rev. com., 1996-98, pres. med. staff, 1997-98; dir. Tex. Blood Pressure Inst., Dallas. Contbr. numerous articles to profl. jours. and chpts. to textbooks; editl. cons., reviewer numerous nat. and internat. jours. and pubs. Pres. Tex. IndoAm. Physician Soc., Dallas, 1988; trustee Dallas/Ft. Worth Hindu Temple Soc., Dallas, 1988. Named Outstanding Tchr. St. Paul Med. Ctr., 1982; recipient Mother of India award, 1992. Master ACP; fellow Am. Coll. Cardiology, Am. Coll. Chest Physicians (regent), Am. Coll. Clin. Pharmacology; mem. Am. Assn. Physicians from India (pres.-elect 1994-95, pres. 1995-96), Tex. Indo-Am. Physicians Soc.

RAMACHANDRAN, VENKATANARAYANA DEEKSHIT, electrical engineering educator; b. Mysore, India, May 3, 1934; s. K.C. Venkatanarayana Deekshit and Subbamma Deekshit R.; m. Kamala Visweswaraiya, June 12, 1960; 1 child, Ravi P. BS, U. Mysore, 1953; B in Engring., Indian Inst. Sci., Bangalore, 1956, M in Electronics, 1958, PhD, 1965. Registered profl. engr. Sr. research asst. Indian Inst. Sci., 1958-59, lectr., 1959-66; asst. prof. N.S. Tech. Coll., Halifax, Can., 1966-69; prof. elec. engring. Concordia U. (formerly Sir George Williams Univ.), Halifax, Can., 1971—; acting chmn. dept. elec. and computer engring. Montreal, various times; grad. program dir. dept., 1969-84. Adj. prof. U. Windsor, Ont., Can., 1983—, Ecole Tech. Superieure U. Quebec, Montreal, 1989—; mem. program com. Internat. Symposium on Operator Theory of Networks and Systems, 1975; vice chmn. Internat. Symposium on Circuits and Systems IEEE, Montreal, 1984, mem. tech. program com., 1987; internat. coordinator Internat. Conf. on Computers, Systems and Signal Processing, Indian Inst. Sci., 1984. Author papers in profl. jours., over 125 papers presented to confs., others. Named to Order of Engrs. of Que.; recipient Merit award Concordia Council on Student Life, 1981-82, Outstanding Contbn. award Engring. and Computer Sci. Assn., Concordia U., 1996. Fellow Inst. Electronics and Telecomms. India (edit. bd. jour. 1986), Inst. Engrs. India, Inst. Elec. Engrs. Eng., Engring. Inst. Can. (sec. Montreal chpt. 1979-80, centennial bd. 1983-84), IEEE (Outstanding Engring. Educator award IEEE Can. 2003); mem. Circuits and Systems chpt. IEEE (chmn. Montreal sect. 1978-84), Can. Soc. Elec. Engrs. (editor jour. 1983-85, editor bull. 1981-83), Am. Soc. Engring. Edn. (chmn. awards com. St. Lawrence chpt. 1987-88, Western Elec. Fund award 1983, Myril B. Reed Best Rsch. Paper award 1984, Outstanding Svc. 1993) Office: Concordia U Faculty of Engring 1455 de Maisonneuve Blvd W Montreal QC Canada H3G 1M8 Office Phone: 514-848-2424 3078. E-mail: kamala@ece.concordia.ca.

RAMADAN, NABIH M. pharmaceutical company official, educator; b. Beirut, Feb. 3, 1960; came to U.S., 1985; s. Manih Fawzi Ramadan and Nadia Shaar; m. Cynthia Ann Ramadan, Mar. 26, 1988. BS in Biology and Chemistry, Am. U. of Beirut, Lebanon, 1980, MD, 1985. Resident in neurology U. Cin., Ohio, 1985-88; fellow in cerebrovascular disease Henry Ford Hosp., Detroit, 1988-90, dir. Ambulatory Headache Clinic, 1990-96, dir. Cerebrovascular Diseases Lab., 1990-96; dir. Cin. Headache Ctr., 1996-99; assoc. prof. neurology U. Cin., 1996-99; med. dir. Eli Lilly & Co., Indpls., 1999, rsch. advisor, 1999—. Adj. prof. neurology Ind. U. Med. Ctr., Indpls. Office: Eli Lilly & Co Lilly Corp Ctr Indianapolis IN 46285-0001

RAMAGE, MARTIS DONALD, JR., banker; b. Tupelo, Miss., Oct. 6, 1957; s. Martis Donald and Helen Frances (Estes) R. AA, Itawamba Jr. Coll., Fulton, Miss., 1978; BBA in Banking and Fin., U. Miss., 1980; grad., Mid South Sch. of Banking, 1989. Mgmt. trainee Peoples Bank & Trust Co., Tupelo, 1981-82, asst. cashier, 1983-89, asst. v.p., 1989-90, v.p., 1990-93, 1st v.p., 1993-2000, sr. v.p., 2000—02, divsn. v.p., 2002—. Sec. Peoples Holding Co., 1993-96, v.p., 1996—. Author: Our Ramage Family, 1986, Mississippi Society SAR 1909-1993, Tupelo, Mississippi, Tornado 1936, 1997; co-editor: The Peoples Bank & Trust Co-In Partnership with the Community, 1989; editor N.E. Miss. Hist. Geneal. Soc. Quar. Treas. United Way of Greater Lee County, Tupelo, 1991-2000, sec., 1991-2001, Leadership Lee; pres. Friends of Lee County Libr., 1995-97; bd. dirs. Brice's Battlefield Commn., Inc., 1995—, Tupelo Cmty. Concert, 1998—, Regional Rehab. Ctr., 2003-; trustee Miss. Dept. Archives and History, 1996—, Lee/Itawamba County Libr., 1998—; chmn. Christmas Festival Com., Tupelo, 1990-91; mem. Miss. rev. bd. Nat. Register Hist. Places, 1999-2002. Mem. SAR (trustee 1992-94, pres. Miss. 1991-92, Silver Good Citizenship medal 1990, sr. v.p. 1994—), SCV, Mil. Order of Stars and Bars, Am. Inst. Banking (pres. Tupelo chpt. 1986-87), Ole Miss. Alumni Assn. (bd. dirs. 1991-94), Bank Adm. Inst. (v.p. North Miss. chpt. 1990-94, pres. 1994-95), Tupelo Artist Guild (bd. dirs. 1993-98, sec. 1996-98), Miss. Hist. Soc. (bd. dirs. 1995-97), Itawamba Jr. Coll. Alumni Assn. (pres. 1982-83), Itawamba C.C. Alumni Assn. (bd. 2002—), Regional Rehab. Ctr. (bd. dirs. 2003—), Civitan Club, Masons. Home: 4218 Ridgemont Dr Belden MS 38826-9785 Office: Peoples Bank & Trust Co 209 Troy St Tupelo MS 38804-4827 Office Phone: 662-680-1306. Personal E-mail: martyr@tsixroads.com. Business E-Mail: martyr@thepeopleplace.com.

RAMAKRISHNAN, VENKATASWAMY, civil engineer, educator; b. Coimbatore, India, Feb. 27, 1929; came to U.S., 1969, naturalized, 1981; s. Venkataswamy and Kondammal (Krishnaswamy) R.; m. Vijayalakshmi Unnava, Nov. 7, 1962; children: Aravind, Anand. B.Engring., U. Madras, 1952, D.S.S., 1953; D.I.C. in Hydropower and Concrete Tech, Imperial Coll., London, 1957; PhD, Univ. Coll., U. London, 1960. From lectr. to prof. civil engring., head dept. P.S.G. Coll. Tech., U. Madras, 1952-69; vis. prof. S.D. Sch. Mines and Tech., Rapid City, 1969-70, prof. civil engring., 1970—, dir. concrete tech. research, 1970-71, head grad. div. structural mechanic and concrete tech., 1971—, program coordinator materials engring. and sci. Ph.D. program, 1985-86, disting. prof., 1996—. Emeritus mem. TRB. Author: Ultimate Strength Design for Structural Concrete, 1969; also over 200 articles. Recipient Outstanding Prof. award S.D. Sch. Mines and Tech., 1980, 1st Rsch. award, 1994; Colombo Plan fellow, 1955-60. Mem. Internat. Assn. Bridge and Structural Engring., ASCE (vice chmn. constrn. div. publs. com. 1974), Am. Concrete Inst. (chmn. subcom. gen. considerations for founds., chmn. com. 214 on evaluation of strength test results, sec.-treas. Dakota chpt. 1974-79, v.p. 1980, pres. 1981, Robert Philio Rsch. Excellence award), Instn. Hwy. Engrs., Transp. Rsch. Bd. (chmn. com. on admixtures and curing, chmn. com. on mech. properties concrete), Am. Soc. Engring. Edn., NSPE, Internat. Coun. Gap-Graded Concrete Rsch. and Application, Sigma Xi. Address: 5260 Autumn Place Rapid City SD 57702 Office Phone: 605-394-2403. Business E-Mail: vramakri@silver.sdsmt.edu. E-mail: vramakrishnan@rushmore.com. *To me, success is a coin with hard work on one side and perseverance with devotion on the other. No matter what—head or tails—the message is the same: keep on working. Goals in my life were pursuit of truth and beauty. The structures I have created, and my writings based on research have given me greater satisfaction than any wealth, position, or power.*

RAMALEY, JUDITH AITKEN, former university president, endocrinologist; b. Vincennes, Ind., Jan. 11, 1941; d. Robert Henry and Mary Krebs (McCullough) Aitken; m. Robert Folk Ramaley, Mar. 1966 (div. 1976); children: Alan Aitken, Andrew Folk. BA, Swarthmore Coll., 1963; PhD, UCLA, 1966; postgrad., Ind. U., 1967-69. Rsch. assoc., lectr. Ind. U., Bloomington, 1967-68, asst. prof. dept. anatomy and physiology, 1969-72; asst. prof. dept. physiology and biophysics U. Nebr. Med. Ctr., Omaha, 1972-74, assoc. prof., 1974-78, prof., 1978-82, assoc. dean for rsch. and devel., 1979-81; asst. v.p. for acad. affairs U. Nebr., Lincoln, 1980-82; prof. biol. scis. SUNY, Albany, N.Y., 1982-87, v.p. for acad. affairs, 1982-85, acting pres., 1984, exec. v.p. for acad. affairs, 1985-87; exec. vice chancellor U. Kans., Lawrence, 1987-90; pres. Portland (Oreg.) State U., 1990-97, U. Vt., Burlington, 1997—2001; asst. dir. edn. and human resources NSF, 2001—. Mem. endocrinology study sect. NIH, 1981-84; cons.-evaluator North Cen. Accreditation, 1978-82, 89-90; regulatory panel NSF, 1979-82, bioadv. com., 1994-98; mem. Ill. Commn. Scholars, 1980-90; Vt. tech. coun. Gov.'s Bus. Adv. Coun., Vt. Bus. Roundtable, Com. on Econ. Devel., 1997-2001; presdl. prof. biomed. scis. U. Maine, Orono, 2001—; subcom. on coll. drinking Nat. Inst. Alcohol Abuse & Alcoholism, 1998-01. Co-author: Progesterone Function: Molecular and Biochemical Aspects, 1972; Essentials of Histology, 8th edit., 1979; editor: Covert Discrimination, Women in the Sciences, 1978; contbr. articles to profl. jours. Bd. dirs. Family Svc. of Omaha, 1979-82, Albany Symphony Orch., 1984-87, mem. exec. com., 1986-87, 2d v.p., exec. com., 1986-87, Capital Repertory Co., 1986-89, Assn. Portland Progress, 1990-97, City Club of Portland, 1991-92, Metro Family Svcs., 1993-97, Campbell Inst. for Children, Portland Met. Sports Authority, 1994; vice-chair Ore. Campus Compact, exec. com. 1996-97, nat. adv. coun. Sch.-Work Opportunities, 1996—; bd. dirs. NCAA Pres. Commn., 1991, chair divsn. II subcom., 1994, joint policy bd., 1994; chmn. bd. dirs. Albany Water Fin. Authority, 1987; exec. com. United Way Douglas County, 1989-90; adv. bd. Emily Taylor Women's Resource Ctr., U. Kans., 1988-90; mem. Portland Opera Bd., 1991-92, Portland Leaders Roundtable, 1991-97; bd. devel. com. United Way of Columbia-Willamette, 1991-95; active Ore. Women's Forum, 1991-97, Portland Met. Sports Authority, Greater Burlington Industry Corp., 1998—; progress bd. Portland-Multnomah County, 1993-97; trustee Wilmington Coll. Ohio, 1998—. NSF grantee, 1969-83; fellow Margaret Chase Smith Ctr. for Pub. Policy. Fellow AAAS; mem. Nat. Assn. State Univs. and Land Grant Colls. (exec. com., mem. senate 1986-88, vice-chair commn. urban agenda 1992-94, chair 1995-97), Am. Assn. for Higher Edn. (bd. dirs. 2003—), Assn. Am. Colls. and Univs. (bd. dirs. 1995-98, chair nat. panel on greater expectations 2000-02), ACE (commn. on govt. rels. 1996-2000), Kellogg Commn. on Future of State and Land-Grant Univs., Assn. Governing Bds. Coll. & U. (pres.'s coun. 1998-2000), Endocrine Soc. (chmn. edn. com. 1980-85), Soc. Study Reprodn. (treas. 1983-85), Soc. for Neurosci., Am. Physiol. Soc., Am. Assn. Schs. and Colls., Am. Coun. on Edn. (chmn. commn. on women in higher edn. 1987-88, commn. on govt. rels., bd. dirs. 1999-2001), Assn. Portland Progress (bd. dirs.), Portland C. of C. (bd. dirs. 1995), Western Assn. of Schs. and Colls. (commr. 1994-97). Office: Edn and Human Resources Directorate Nat Sci Found 4201 Wilson Blvd Arlington VA 22230

RAMANI, RAJA VENKAT, mining engineering educator; b. Madras, India, Aug. 4, 1938; came to U.S., 1966; s. Natesa and Meenakshi (Srinivasan) Rajaraman; m. Geetha V. Chalam, July 9, 1972; children: Deepak, Gautam. BSc with honors, Indian Sch. Mines, Dhanbad, Bihar, 1962, DSc (hon.), 1997; MS, Pa. State U., 1968, PhD, 1970. Registered profl. engr., Pa., 1971; lic. first class mine mgr., 1965. Mining engr., mgr. Andrew Yule & Co., Asansol, West Bengal, India, 1962-66; grad. asst. Pa. State U., University Park, 1966-70, asst. prof., 1970-74, assoc. prof., 1974-78, prof. mining engring., 1978—, chmn. mineral engring. mgmt. sect., 1974—, head dept. mineral engring., 1987-98, George and Anne Deike chair in mining engring., 1997—. Chmn. com. post-disaster survival/rescue NAS, Washington, 1979-81; mem. health rsch. panel NAS Com. on the Rsch. Programs of the U.S. Bur. of Mines, 1994; mem. NAS Com. on Techs. for the Mineral Industries, 2000-01; mem. NAS Com. on Coal Waste Impoundments, 2001-02; chmn. Gov.'s Commn. on Mine Voids and Mine Safety, Pa., 2002; cons. UN, UN Devel. Program, Dept. Econ. and Social Devel., N.Y.C., 1983-97, World Bank, 1998-99, Nat. Safety Coun., 2003-; cons., expert panels U.S. Dept. Labor, 1979, 92, 96, HHS, 1977, 92, U.S. Dept. State, 1986, 87, U.S. Dept. Interior, 1995, Dept. Environ. Resources, Commonwealth of Pa., 1990, 92; co-dir. Generic Mineral Tech. Ctr. on Respirable Dust, U.S. Bur. Mines, 1983—, Nat. Mines/Land Reclamation Ctr., 1988—, Std. Oil Ctr. of Excellence on Longwall Tech., 1983-89; presenter in field. Sect. editor, author: Computer Methods for the Eighties, 1979, SME Mining Engineering Handbook, 1992; editor State-of-the-Art in Longwall-Shortwall Mining, 1981, Longwall Thick Seam Mining, 1988, Computers in Mineral Industry, 1994, Internat. Mine Ventilation Congress, 1997. Recipient Disting. Alumni award Indian Sch. Mines, Dhanbad, 1978, Ednl. Excellence award Pitts. Coal Mining Inst., 1986, Environ. Conservation award AIME, N.Y.C., 1990, Howard N. Eavenson award SME/AIME, N.Y.C., 1991, Robert Stefanko Best Paper award, 1993, Coal Divsn. Disting. Svc. award, 1993, Howard L. Hartman award, 1997, Percy H. Nicholls award AIME/ASME Joint Soc., 1994, Mineral Industry Edn. award Am. Inst. Mining Engrs., 1999, The Thornton medal Instn. Mining and Metallurgy, 2000; Fulbright scholar to Soviet Union Coun. Internat. Exch. of Scholars, Washington, 1989-90; Henry Krumb lectr. AIME, 1994. Mem. Internat. Coun. for Application of Computers in the Mineral Industry (chmn. 1984-87, Disting. Achievement award 1989), Soc. Mining, Metall. and Exploration (Disting. Mem. 1989, pres. 1995), Mine Ventillation Soc. South Africa, Inst. for Ops. Rsch. and Mgmt. Scis. Achievements include research in health, safety, environmental and productivity aspects in underground and surface mining engineering. Home: 285 Oakley Dr State College PA 16803-1349 Office: Dept Mineral Engring Pa State U University Park PA 16802 Office Phone: 814-863-1617. Business E-Mail: RVR@PSU.edu.

RAMANUJA, TERALANDUR KRISHNASWAMY, retired structural engineer; b. Mysore, India, June 23, 1941; came to U.S., 1967, naturalized, 1979; s. Teralandur R. and Padmammal Krishnaswamy; m. Jayalakshmi Ramanuja, Jan. 18, 1971; children: Srinivasan, Rekha. BSCE, U. Mysore, 1962; MS in Structural Engring., U. Notre Dame, 1969. Registered profl. engr., Ill., Mich., Ind., N.Y. Sub-divisional officer Mil. Engring. Svcs., Bangalore, India, 1962-67; structural engr. Clyde E. Williams and Assocs., South Bend, Ind., 1969-73; head structural engring. dept. Ayres, Lewis, Norris & May, Cons. Engrs., Ann Arbor, Mich., 1973-76; sr. project mgr. Johnson & Anderson Cons. Engrs., Pontiac, Mich., 1976-78; supr. Bechtel Power Corp., Ann Arbor, 1978-85; supr. Shoreham Nuclear Power Sta. Lilco, N.Y.C., 1985-89; engring. supr. Clinton (Ill.) Power Sta. Ill. Power Co., 1989—2000; ret. Fellow ASCE; mem. Am. Concrete Inst.; mem. Chi Epsilon. Achievements include structural and foundation design of facilities for fossil and nuclear power plants, water/waste treatment plants, petrochemical plants, pulp and paper mills and for heavy equipment/machinery for these plants; seismic and dynamic analysis of structures, systems and components in nuclear power plants. Home: 307 Birchwood Crossing Ln Maryland Heights MO 63043

RAMAPRASAD, KACKADASAM RAGHAVACHAR, physical chemist; b. Dec. 8, 1938; came to U.S., 1965, permanent resident, 1971; s. Kackadasam Raghavachar and Saroja (Narasimhachar) R.; m. Rukmani Raghavachari, July 14, 1968; children: Saroja, Venkat. BS in Chemistry (hon.), U. Mysore, Bangalore, 1958; MS in Phys. Chemistry, NYU, 1971; PhD, 1972. Trainee Bhabha Atomic Rsch. Ctr. Tng. Sch., Bombay, India, 1958-59; rsch. asst., jr. sci. officer chemistry divsn., 1959-65; teaching fellow N.Y.C., 1965-71; duPont teaching asst., 1967-68; maitre-asst. dept. de chimie physique U. Geneva, 1972-73; chemist Ecole Poly-Technique Federale de lausanne, Switzerland, 1974; rsch. assoc. dept. chemistry Princeton (N.J.) U., 1974-77; rsch. assoc., mem. profl. rsch. staff dept. chem. engring., 1977-79; sr. scientist Chronar Corp., Princeton, 1979-89, Electron Transfer Techs., Inc., Princeton, 1990-93; staff scientist TRI-Princeton, 1993-96, sr. scientist, 1996-2001, sr. scientist, group leader, 2001—. Contbr. articles to profl. pubs. Recipient Founder's Day award N.Y.U., 1972. Mem. Am. Chem. Soc., Sigma Xi. Office: TRI/Princeton PO Box 625 Princeton NJ 08542-0625

RAMAT, CHARLES S. apparel executive; Chmn. bd., pres., CEO, asst. sec. Aris Industries Inc., N.Y.C. Office: 1411 Broadway New York NY 10018*

RAMBERG, PATRICIA LYNN, college president; b. Melrose Park, Ill., June 15, 1951; d. Roy Andrew and Elsie Elaine (Lossau) Fricke; children: Richard Lynn II, Caitlyn Elizabeth. BS in Bus. Adminstrn. magna cum laude, Elmhurst Coll., 1976; MA in Edn., U. St. Thomas, 1989. Assoc. dir. ops. Bank Mktg. Assn., Chgo., 1972-75; exec. dir. Soc. Tchrs. Family Medicine, Kansas City, Mo., 1975-78, Minn. Assn. Children with Learning Disabilities, St. Paul, 1979-80; sr. instrnl. designer Applied Learning Systems, Mpls., 1989-90; dir. Upper Midwest Conservation Assn., Mpls., 1990-92; account exec. Dean Witter Reynolds, Inc., Bloomington, Minn., 1992-94; investment specialist FBS Investment Svcs., Inc., Mpls., 1994; v.p., dir. profl. devel. US Bank, Mpls., 1994-98; pres., CEO Alfred Adler Grad. Sch., Hopkins, Minn., 1998—. Adj. faculty U. St. Thomas, St. Paul, 1990. Lutheran. Avocations: photography, horses. Office: Alfred Adler Grad Sch 1001 Highway 7 Hopkins MN 55305-4723 Home: 230 Chicago Ave N Wayzata MN 55391-1125

RAMBERG, WALTER DODD, architect; b. Charlotte, N.C., Feb. 17, 1932; s. Walter Gustav Charles and Julia Elisabeth (Lineberger) R.; m. Lucinda Jenifer Ballard, Nov. 25, 1961 (dec. 1989); children: Lucinda E.G., Jenny S.F., Julia E.L.; m. Seska Peck Dunne, Sept. 14, 1996. BA, Yale U., 1953, M.Arch., 1956. Fulbright fellow Kyoto (Japan) U., 1956-58; apprentice architect Paul Rudolph, New Haven, 1958-61; project designer Meyer & Ayers, Balt., 1961-63; partner Howe & Ramberg, Washington, 1963-65; prin. Walter Dodd Ramberg (Architect), Washington, 1965—. Prof. architecture Cath. U. Am., 1977—; mem. design adv. panel Balt. Dept. Housing and Community, 1973—; mem. bd. architecture rev. Baltimore County, 1986-89. Designer: N.W. Balt. High Sch, 1963 (P.A. Excellence in Design award); architect: Bridge for Washington Cathedral, 1965 (Excellence in Design award Washington Bd. Trade, AIA), Kidder Guest House, 1965 (1st Honor award Balt. AIA), Azrael House, 1969 (Honor award Balt. AIA), Cutts House, 1973 (Honor award Balt. AIA), Woody House, 1975 (Merit award Balt. AIA), Lineberger Meml. Library, 1976 (Merit award Nat. AIA, ALA); contbr. articles to profl. publs. Served to lt. USCGR, 1958-59. Mem. AIA (corp.), AAUP, Soc. Archtl. Historians. Clubs: Met. (Washington). Episcopalian. Home: 1651 Belfast Rd Sparks MD 21152-9788 Office: 1830 T St NW Washington DC 20009-7138

RAMBO, JAMES EDMONDSON, lawyer, corporate executive; b. Dayton, Ohio, July 26, 1923; s. Thomas Buchanan and Anna (Dopf) R.; m. Sylvia Yvonne Lower, Nov. 2, 1957; children— Eric S., Todd C., Bradley C. A.B., Ohio U., 1947; LL.B., U. Cin., 1949. Bar: Ohio 1949, U.S. Dist. Ct. (so. dist.) Ohio 1950, U.S. Ct. Appeals (6th cir.) 1954. Assoc. Coolidge, Becker, Wall & Wood, Dayton, 1949-54; asst. U.S. atty. So. Dist. Ohio, Dayton, 1954-57; asst. gen. counsel NCR Corp., Dayton, 1957-65, v.p., sec. and gen. counsel, 1965—, dir., 1971— . Trustee Dayton Art Inst., 1970-73; bd. visitors U. Dayton Coll. Law, 1977-81; trustee Good Samaritan Hosp., Dayton, 1977— . Served with 1st lt. C.E., U.S. Army, 1943-46. Mem. Dayton Bar Assn., Ohio State Bar Assn., ABA, Assn. Gen. Counsel. Republican. Clubs: Dayton Country; N.Y. Athletic (N.Y.C.). Office: NCR Corp 1700 Patterson Blvd Dayton OH 45479-0001

RAMBO, SYLVIA H. federal judge; b. Royersford, Pa., Apr. 17, 1936; d. Granville A. and Hilda E. (Leonhardt) R.; m. George F. Douglas, Jr., Aug. 1, 1970. BA, Dickinson Coll., 1958; JD, Dickinson Sch Law, 1962; LLD (hon.), Wilson Coll., 1980, Dickinson Sch. Law, 1993, Dickinson Coll., 1994, Shippensburg U., 1996, Widener U., 1999. Bar: Pa. 1962. Atty. trust dept. Bank of Del., Wilmington, 1962-63; pvt. practice Carlisle, 1963-76; from public defender to chief public defender Cumberland County, Pa., 1974-76; judge Ct. Common Pleas, Cumberland County, 1976-78, U.S. Dist. Ct. (mid. dist.) Pa., Harrisburg, 1979—, chief judge, 1992-99; federal judge U.S. Dist. Ct., Harrisburg, 2000—. Asst. prof., adj. prof. Dickinson Sch. Law, 1974—76; former mem. Jud. Conf. Com. on Adminstrn. of Magistrate Judges Sys., 1996—2002; mem. Pa. Bar Assn. Task Force on Legal Svcs. to the Needy, 2000—03. Bd. govs. Dickinson Sch. Law., Pa. State U., 2000—. Mem. Phi Alpha Delta. Democrat. Presbyterian. Office: US Dist Ct Federal Bldg PO Box 868 Harrisburg PA 17108-0868 Office Phone: 717-221-3960.

RAMER, BRUCE M. lawyer; b. Teaneck, N.J., Aug. 2, 1933; s. Sidney and Anne S. (Strassman) R.; children: Gregg B., Marc K., Neal I. BA, Princeton U., 1955; LLB, Harvard U., 1958. Bar: Calif. 1963, N.J. 1958. Assoc., Morrison, Lloyd & Griggs, Hackensack, N.J., 1959-60; ptnr. Gang, Tyre, Ramer & Brown, Inc., L.A., 1963—. Exec. dir. Entertainment Law Inst., Law Ctr. of U. So. Calif.; bd. of councilors Law Ctr. U. So. Calif.; chmn., nat. bd. govs. Am. Jewish Com., 1995-98, nat. v.p., 1982-88, pres., 1998—, L.A. chpt., 1980-83, chair Western region, 1984-86, comty. svc. award, 1987, nat. pres., 1998—, adv. bd. Skirball Inst. on Am. Values, 1998—; chmn. Asia Pacific Rim Inst., 1989-98; trustee Loyola Marymount U., L.A. Children's Mus., 1986-89; vice chair United Way, 1991-93, corp. bd. dirs., 1981-93, chair coun. pres. 1989-90, mem. cmty. issues coun., 1989-90, chair discretionary fund distbn. com., 1987-89; bd. dirs., chair Geffen Playhouse, 1995-98, founding chair, 1998—; bd. dirs. L.A. Urban League, 1987-93, 96—, Jewish Fedn. Coun. of Greater L.A. (mem. Cmty. Rels. com., bd. dirs., exec. com.), Jewish TV Network, Sta. KCET-TV; mem., bd. dirs. Rebuild L.A., 1992-96; mem. bd. govs. Calif. Cmty. Found., 1988-98; recipient Ann. Brotherhood award NCCJs, 1990; mem. Fellows of Am. Bar Found.; mem. econ. strategy panel State Calif., 1997—; bd. dirs. Shoah Visual History Found., Righteous Persons Found., L.A. 2012 Bid Com. for the So. Calif. Olympic Games; bd. dirs. Jewish Fedn. Coun. Greater L.A., mem. exec. com., cmty. rels. com. Pvt. U.S. Army, 1958-59, 2d lt., 1961-62. Mem. ABA (mem. spl. com. jud. ind.), L.A. County Bar Assn., Calif. Bar Assn., Beverly Hills Bar Assn. (Exec. Dirs. award 1988, Entertainment Lawyer of Yr. award 1996), L.A. Copyright Soc. (pres. 1974-75), Calif. Copyright Conf. (pres. 1973-74), Princeton Club (pres. 1975-78). Office: Gang Tyre Ramer & Brown Inc 132 S Rodeo Dr Beverly Hills CA 90212-2415

RAMER, HAL REED, academic administrator; b. Kenton, Tenn., June 8, 1923; s. Claude Orion and Dixie Clayton (Carroll) R. BS, George Peabody Coll., 1947; MSW, U. Tenn., 1952; PhD, Ohio State U., 1963. Asst. dean men Ohio State U., Columbus, 1953-58, dir. internat. house, 1958-60, staff asst. to pres., 1960-62; asst. commr. State Dept. Edn., Nashville, 1963-70; founding pres. Vol. State C.C., Gallatin, Tenn., 1970—2003, pres. emeritus, 2003—. Bd. dirs. Sumner Regional Health Sys., Inc. Com. mem. March of Dimes, Gallatin; Mem. adv. bd. First Union Bank Mid. Tenn., First Union Bank Mid. Tenn., Hendersonville; trustee Nashville United Way, 1970, Hiwassee Coll., 2001; bd. advisors Aquinas Coll., Nashville, 1967—; former chmn. Tenn. Fulbright-Hays Sch. Commn.; YMCA. With U.S. Army Air Corps, 1943—45. Recipient Distinctive Svc. award Devel. Coun. Peabody Coll., Nashville, 1960s, Disting. Svc. award Tenn. Dept. Edn., 1970, Outstanding Leader award Vanderbilt U. chpt. Phi Delta Kappa, 1987, Gov.'s Svc. award State of Tenn., 1993, Sertoma Club Svc. to Mankind award, 1995-96, Disting. Alumnus award Peabody Coll., 1996, Disting. Svc. award Tenn. Bd. Regents, 1997, Svc. award Am. Assn. Cmty. Col., 1999, Otis Floyd Jr. award for excellence Tenn. Coll. Pub. Rels. Assn., 1999, Lifetime Achievement award Peabody Coll. of Vanderbilt U., 2003; named Rotarian of the Yr., 1979; Paul Harris fellow Rotary Internat., 1981. Mem. Am. Legion, Coun. Pres. C.Cs. (chmn. state Tenn. 1988-89), Tenn. Coll. Assn. (pres. 1985-86), Nat. Alumni Assn. Peabody Coll. (pres. 1970-71, trustee), Tenn. Acad. Sci., Tenn. and Sumner County Hist. Socs. (bd. dirs.), English Speaking Union Internat. (Nashville chpt.), So. Assn. Colls. and Schs., Univ. Club Nashville, Gallatin and Hendersonville C. of C., St. Thomas Aquinas Soc., Torch Club, Alpha Tau Omega, Kappa Phi Kappa, Alpha Phi Omega, Phi Delta Kappa. Methodist. Avocations: antiques, antique cars, photography. Home: 120 Abbottsford Nashville TN 37215-2440

RAMER, JAMES LEROY, civil engineer; b. Marshalltown, Iowa, Dec. 7, 1935; s. LeRoy Frederick and Irene (Wengert) Ramer; m. Jacqueline L. Orr, Dec. 15, 1957; children: Sarah T., Robert H., Eric A., Susan L. Student, U. Iowa, 1953-57; MCE, Washington U., St. Louis, 1976, MA in Polit. Sci., 1978; postgrad., U. Mo., 1984—. Registered profl. engr., land surveyor. Civil and constrn. engr. U.S. Army C.E., Tulsa, 1960-63; civil and relocations engr. U.S. State Dept., Del Rio, Tex., 1964; project engr. H.B. Zachary Co., San Antonio, 1965-66; civil and constrn. engr. U.S. Army C.E., St. Louis, 1967-76, tech. advisor for planning and nat. hydropower coord., 1976-78; project mgr. for EPA constrn. grants Milw., 1978-80; chief arch. and engring. HUD, Indpls., 1980-81; civil design and pavements engr. Whiteman AFB, Mo., 1982-86; project mgr. maintenance, 1993—; soil and pavements engr. Hdqrs. Mil. Airlift Command, Scott AFB, Ill., 1986-88. Project mgr. AF-1 maintenance hangar; cattle and grain farmer, 1982—; pvt. practice civil-mech. engr., constrn. mgmt., estimating, cost analysis, cash flow, project scheduling, expert witness, profl. land surveying, Fortuna, Mo., 1988—2001; chief constrn. inspector divsn. design and constrn. State of Mo., 1992—93; project engr. Mil. Housing, 2001—; adj. faculty civil engring. Washington U., 1968—78, U. Wis., Milw., 1978—80, Ga. Mil. Coll., Whiteman AFB, Longview Coll., Kansas City; adj. rsch. engr. U. Mo., Columbia, 1985—86; project engr., quality control officer Korte Constrn. Co. Author (tech. writing operation and maintenance manuals,); fin. reports and environ. control plans, designs & builds tech. and indsl. models. Mem.: AAUP, NSPE, ASCE, Soc. Am. Mil. Engrs., Optimists Internat. Lutheran. Achievements include patents for in diverse art, 9 copyrights; development of solar waterstill, deep shaft hydropower concept. Home: 11147 Angel Rd Fortuna MO 65034-2167 Office Phone: 660-337-6335.

RAMER, LAWRENCE JEROME, corporation executive; b. Bayonne, N.J., July 29, 1928; s. Sidney and Anne (Strassman) R.; m. Ina Lee Brown, June 30, 1957; children: Stephanie Beryl, Susan Meredith, Douglas Strassman. BA in Econs, Lafayette Coll., 1950; MBA, Harvard U., 1957; LLD (hon.), Lafayette Coll., 1992. Sales rep., then v.p. United Sheet Metal Co., Bayonne, 1953-55; with Am. Cement Corp., 1957-64; v.p. mktg. div. Riverside Cement Co., 1960-62, v.p. mktg. parent co., 1962-64; vice chmn. bd., chief exec. officer Clavier Corp., N.Y.C., 1965-66; exec. v.p., vice chmn. bd. Pacific Western Industries, Los Angeles, 1966-70; pres., chief exec. officer Nat. Portland Cement Co. Fla., 1975-89; chmn. bd. Sutro Partners, Inc., Los Angeles, 1977-89, Somerset Mgmt. Group, 1975-92, Luminall Paints Inc., Los Angeles, 1972-95; chmn. bd., CEO Bruning Paint Co., Balt., 1979—2000; chmn. bd., chief exec. officer Pacific Coast Cement Co., Los Angeles, 1979-90; pres., CEO Ramer Equities, Inc., 1990—2000, chmn., 2000—; chmn. bd. Scott Paint Co., Sarasota, Fla., 2000—. Chmn. Lee and Lawrence J. Ramer Family Found., 1986—; bd. dirs. Orbis Internat., N.Y.C., The Music Ctr., L.A., Canyon Ranch, Tucson, Music Ctr. Found., L.A.; bd. dirs. Ctr. Theatre Group-Mark Taper Ahmanson Theatres, L.A., pres. and chmn., 1987-97. Chmn. bd. trustees Lafayette Coll., Easton, Pa., 1992—2001, chmn., 1976—2001, bd. trustees; trustee, chmn. bd. trustees Calif. Inst. Arts, Valencia, Calif.; nat. bd. govs. Am. Jewish Com., NY, assoc. treas., trustee; trustee Facing History and Ourselves; bd. dirs. United Friends of Children, L.A. (Calif.) World Affairs Coun.; bd. govs. Hebrew Union Coll.; bd. dir. Pacific Coun. Internat. Policy, 2004. Office: Ramer Equities Inc 10900 Wilshire Blvd Ste 550 Los Angeles CA 90024-6501 Office Phone: 310-209-0442. Personal E-mail: lj.ramer@verizon.net.

RAMEY, CRAIG T. psychology educator; BA in Psychology, W.Va. U., 1965, MA in Psychology, 1967, PhD in Devel. Psychology, 1969; postdoctoral in Devel. Psychology, U. Calif., Berkeley, 1969. Asst. prof. psychology Wayne State U., 1969-71; assoc. prof., dept psychology U. N.C., Chapel Hill, 1971-78; sr. investigator, dir. infant rsch. Frank Porter Graham Child Devel. Ctr., U. N.C., Chapel Hill, 1971-74, dir. rsch., 1975-89, assoc. dir., 1978-89; prof. psychology U. N.C., Chapel Hill, 1979-90, prof. pediatrics, Sch. Medicine, 1984-90; dir. Civitan Internat. Rsch. Ctr., U. Ala., Birmingham, 1990—, Sparks Ctr. for Devel. and Learning Disorders, U. Ala., Birmingham, 1990—; prof. depts. sociology, psychology, pediatrics, maternal and child health and neurobiology U. Ala., Birmingham, 1990—. Contbr. to profl. jours. including Journal of the American Medical Association, American Journal of Public Health, Am. Psychologist, Educational Psychology. Office: U Ala Birmingham 1719 6th Ave S Ste 137 Birmingham AL 35294-0001

RAMEY, DENNY L. bar association executive director; b. Portsmouth, Ohio, Feb. 22, 1947; s. Howard Leroy and Norma Wylodine (Richards) R.; m. Jeannine Gayle Dunmyer, Sept. 24, 1971 (div. Nov. 1991); children: Elizabeth Michelle, Brian Michael. BBA, Ohio U., 1970; MBA, Capital U., 1976. Cert. assn. exec. Adminstrv. mgr. Transit Warehouse div. Elston Richards Storage Co., Columbus, Ohio, 1970-73; mgr. continuing profl. edn. Ohio Soc. CPA's, Columbus, 1973-79; exec. dir. Engrs. Found. of Ohio, Columbus, 1979-80; asst. exec. Ohio State Bar Assn., Columbus, 1980-86, exec. dir., sec., treas., 1986—. Treas., exec. com., bd. dirs. Ohio Bar Liability Ins. Co., Columbus, 1986—; treas. Ohio State Bar Found., 1986—; treas. Ohio Legal Ctr. Ins., Columbus, 1988-91; sec. Ohio Printing Co., Ltd., 1991; v.p. Osbanet, Inc., 1993—; chmn. Lawriter LLC, 2000—; bd. dirs. OSBA.com, LLC. Mem.: Ohio Soc. Assn. Execs., Am. Soc. Assn. Execs., Nat. Assn. Bar Execs., Brookside Golf & Country Club, Scioto Country Club. Methodist. Avocations: tennis, golf, sports, music, wine appreciation. Office: Ohio State Bar Assn 1700 Lake Shore Dr PO Box 16562 Columbus OH 43216-6562 E-mail: dramey@ohiobar.org.

RAMEY, SAMUEL EDWARD, bass soloist; b. Colby, Kans., Mar. 28, 1942; s. Robert Guy and Grace Irene (Mallory) R.; m. Carrie Tanate, Jan. 10, 1970. Student, Kans. State U., 1960-62; B.Mus., Wichita State U., 1968. Debut in Carmen, N.Y.C. Opera, 1973, leading bass, 1973—, European debut, Glyndebourne Festival, 1976, debut, Hamburg Staatsoper, 1978, Paris Opera, 1979, Houston Grand Opera, 1975, San Francisco Opera, 1978, Chgo. Lyric Opera, 1979, Festival International Aix-en-Provence, 1979, 80, Teatro della Scala, 1981, Vienna Staatsoper, 1981, in Rinaldo, Met. Opera, 1984; recording artist opera and oratorio, Philips, Angel, RCA, Deutsche Grammophone, London, CBS Records. Named Kansan of the Year Native Sons and Daughters of Kansas, 1994. Office: Columbia Artists Mgmt Inc Arbib Div 165 W 57th St New York NY 10019-2201

RAMI, JANET SIMMONS, university dean, nursing educator; b. Washington, La. BSN, Dillard U., 1970; MS in Cross-Cultural Nursing, U. So. Miss., 1979; PhD in Edn. Rsch. Methodology, La. State U., 1992. Dir. nursing staff edn. Earl K. Long Hosp., Baton Rouge, 1977-83; coord. nurse staff edn. State La., Office of Hosps., Baton Rouge, 1983-84; asst. prof. So. U. and Agrl. and Med. Coll., Baton Rouge, 1984-85, acting dean, asst. prof., 1985-86, dean, assoc. prof., 1986—. Contbr. articles to profl. jours. Coun. mem. (hon.) city of Baton Rouge, 1984; rep. (hon.) to State of La., 1984. Mem. ANA, Baton Rouge Dist. Nurses Assn., Coun. Acad. Nurse Educators, La. State Nurses Assn., Nat. League for Nursing, Sigma Theta Tau, Alpha Kappa Alpha, Lambda Phi Alpha. Office: S U Sch Nursing Office Dean PO Box 11794 Baton Rouge LA 70813-1794

RAMI, PEMON, theatrical company executive, theater producer; m. Masequa Myers. Co-founder Lamont Zeno Theatre and Cultural Arts Program, Chgo., 1973; appeared in, provided casting svcs. for 14 feature films and TV movies including Mahogany, 1973, The Spook Who Sat By the Door, 1973; co-prodr., co-dir., co-host series of radio dramas A Taste of Culture, WBMX Radio, Chgo., 1980; gen. mgr. Maria Gibbs' Crossroads Nat. Edn. and Arts Ctr. of L.A., 1990; mgr. med. media and conf. svcs. dept. Cedars-Sinai Med. Ctr., L.A., 1992—2001. Cons. Govt. Trinidad and Tobago. Dir.: (romantic comedy) Miss Dessa (Best Dir. award Beverly Hills/Hollywood NAACP Theatre); prodr.: (video) Take a Close Look; dir.: (TV talk shows for series) Getting It Right; prodr., dir., creative cons., costume designer: (video) It's OK to Say No Way; Follow Your Dream; cons., prodr., dir., co-writer (touring prodn. and video) Give Life a Chance; multimedia conf. facility, Emergency Dept. and Transfusion Ctr., Cedars-Sinai Med. Ctr. Named one of Top 100 Prodrs. in Nation, AV Video Multimedia Prodr. mag.; recipient award, Joseph Jefferson Com. Chgo., Chgo. Black Theatre Alliance, Ariz. Commn. on Arts, Ariz. Health Edn. Media Makers award, award, Am. Advt. Fedn., Internat. TV Assn., Nat. Assn. Audio Visual Communicators, Key to City of Detroit. Office: Masequa Myers & Assocs 6100 So Dorchester 1 W Chicago IL 60637

RAMIL, MARIO R. retired state supreme court justice; b. Quezon City, The Philippines, June 21, 1946; came to U.S., 1956; s. Quintin A. and Fausta M. (Reyes) R.; m. Judy E. Wong, Nov. 6, 1971; children: Jonathan, Bradley. BA in Polit. Sci., Calif. State U., Hayward, 1972; JD, U. Calif., San Francisco, 1975. Bar: Calif. 1976, Hawaii 1976, U.S. Dist. Ct. Hawaii, U.S. Dist. Ct. (no. dist.) Calif., U.S. Ct. Appeals (9th cir.). Law clk. San Francisco Neighborhood

Legal Aid Found., 1973-75; legal counsel Sandigan-Newcomers Svcs., Inc., San Francisco, 1975-76; dep. atty. gen. Dept. Labor and Indsl. Rels., 1976-79; dep. atty. gen. cen. adminstrn. U. Hawaii, 1979-80; staff atty. house majority atty.'s office Hawaii Ho. of Reps., 1980; pvt. practice, 1980-82; dep. atty. gen. adminstrv. div. State of Hawaii, 1982-84, ins. commr., 1984-86; dir. Hawaii State Dept. Labor and Indsl. Rels., Honolulu, 1986-91; of counsel Lyons, Brandt, Cook and Hiramatsu, 1991-93; assoc. justice Hawaii Supreme Ct., Honolulu, 1993—2003. Bd. dirs. Hawaii Youth-At-Risk, 1989; co-chair state conv. Dem. Party State of Hawaii, 1984; mem. Adv. Coun. on Housing and Constrn., State of Hawaii, 1981; pres., bd. dirs. Hawaii Non-Profit Housing Corp.; exec. sec., chmn. adminstrv. budget com. Oahu Filipino Community Coun.; bd. dirs, legal advisor Oahu Filipino Jaycees, 1978-81.

RAMIREZ, ARCHIMEDES, neurosurgeon, educator; b. Binakayan, The Philippines, Nov. 26, 1938; came to U.S., 1947; s. Francisco Mendoza and Mercedes (Parales) R.; m. Carol Domush, Mar. 19, 1944. BS in Chemistry, Va. Mil. Inst., 1961; MD, U. Va., 1966. Diplomate Am. Bd. Neurol. Surgery. Intern Saginaw (Mich.) Gen. Hosp., 1967; resident in gen. surgery Saginaw Coop. Hosps., Inc., 1971-72; resident in neurosurgery Walter Reed Army Med. Ctr., Washington, 1972-76; commd. 2d lt. U.S. Army, 1961, advanced through grades to col., 1984, gen. med. officer, 1968-69, 1969-70; chief neurol. surgery Letterman Army Med. Ctr., San Francisco, 1976-79; chief neurosurgery svc. Marin Gen. Hosp., Greensbrae, Calif., 1981—; neurosurgeon "Desert Storm", Letterman Army Med. Ctr., San Francisco, 1990—91; ret. U.S. Army M.C., 1991. Cons. Letterman Army Med. Ctr., 1979-92; mem. admission com. U. Calif.-San Francisco Med. Sch., 1978-79; mem. clin. faculty dept. neurosurgery U. Calif. San Francisco Med. Ctr., 1978—; cons. neurosurgeon Kaiser Hosp. Terra Linda, San Rafael, Calif., 2000—. Mem. AMA, Am. Assn. Neurol. Surgeons, Congress Neurol. Surgeons, Pan Pacific Neurosurgery Congress (adv. coun. 1986—), Calif. Assn. Neurol. Surgeons, San Francisco Neurol. Soc., Calif. Med. Assn., Marin Med. Soc. Avocation: golf. Office: Archimedes ramirez Md #A 1125 Sir Frances Drake Blvd Kentfield CA 94904-1418 E-mail: abackdoc@mail.MSN.com.

RAMIREZ, ARNULFO GONZALEZ, language educator, linguist; b. Tex. BA, Tex. A&M, 1965, MA, 1968; PhD, Stanford U., 1974. Fulbright prof. U.Thessaloniki, Salonika, Greece, 1968—69; asst. prof. UCLA, 1975—76, Stanford U., Palo Alto, Calif., 1976—79; assoc. prof. SUNY, Albany, NY, 1980—85, prof., 1985—89, La. State U., Baton Rouge, 1989—, dir. linguistics, 2002—. Adv. bd. Nat. Ctr. Lang. and Culture, U. Calif., Santa Cruz, 1990—95. Author: (book) Bilingualism Through Schooling, 1985, Spanish in the USA, 1992, Contexts for Second Language Acquistion, 1995. Named to Knight Order of Queen Isabel, Spanish Govt., 1992. Office: La State Univ Baton Rouge LA 70803

RAMIREZ, ARTHUR P. physicist; BS in physics, Yale U., 1978, PhD in physics, 1984. Post doctoral mem. of tech. staff AT&T Bell Lab., 1984—86; mem. of tech. staff Bell Labs., 1986—99, disting. mem. of tech. staff, 1999—2000; leader, condensed matter and thermal physics group Los Alamos Nat. Lab., 2001—. Mem. reverse site rev. panel Materials Rsch. Sci. and Engring. Ctrs., 2000; mem. adv. com. Conf. on Strongly Correlated Electrons 2001, 2000; mem. proposal adv. com. Nat. High Magnetic Field Lab., 1999—; mem. rev. panel Inst. for Atomic and Molecular Physics; mem. site rev. panel U. of Wis., Materials Rsch. Science and Engring. Ctr., 1999; mem. adv. com. Highly Frustrated Magnetism 2000 Conf., 1999; mem. preproposal panel Materials Rsch. Sci. and Engring. Ctrs., 1999; sci. grant com. for minorities Bell Labs., 1997—; mem. Bell Labs High Sch. Sci. grant program, 1997—2000; co-chair Colossal Magnetoresistance APS Focused Session, 1998; mem. GMAG nominating com., 2001; co-organizer Physics of Frustration from Proteins to Pyrochlores workshop, 2002. Fellow: Am. Physical Soc. Achievements include research in experimental condensed matter physics. Office: Condensed Matter and Thermal Physics Group Los Alamos Nat Lab MS K764 Los Alamos NM 87545

RAMIREZ, CARLOS MOISES, former mayor; b. El Paso, Tex., May 1, 1951; m. Maria Eugenia Kenna. Disting. grad., U.S. Army Field Artillery Sch., 1973; BS in Civil Engring., U. Tex., 1977, MS in Civil Engring., 1986. Registered profl. engr. Tex. Field artillery surveyor U.S. Army, U.S., Europe, 1972-75; plant design engr. Texaco USA, Port Arthur, Tex., 1977-79; export purchasing agt. Exxon Co., USA, Houston, 1979-82; project engr. Ariz. nuclear power project, spl. projects engr., fuels engr., environ. engr. El Paso (Tex.) Electric Co., 1982-88; asst. v.p. Indsl. Devel. Corp., El Paso, 1989-91; interim exec. dir. Greater El Paso Civic, Convention and Tourism Dept., 1991-92; exec. asst. to mayor City of El Paso, 1991-92; prin. Kistenmacher Engring. Co., Inc., 1993-95; v.p. Neologic Internat., Inc., 1995-96; pres. Univer Industries, 1996-97; mayor City of El Paso, 1997—2001. Chmn. met. social planning com. City of El Paso, 1988, mem. airport archtl. rev. com., 1989, chmn. border rels. commn., 1996-97. Prodr., creater TV program Enfoque Hispano. Co-founder Career Awareness Exploring Program, El Paso, 1990; candidate for mayor City of El Paso, 1992-93, 95; El Paso rep. Nat. Com. Employer Support of the Guard and Reserve, U.S. Dept. Def., 1993—; founding mem. World Trade Ctr. El Paso/Juarez. Mem. ASCE (pres. El Paso chpt. 1987), Tau Beta Pi, Chi Epsilon.

RAMIREZ, EDWARD ANTHONY, information technology manager; b. Sterling, Ill., Apr. 26, 1964; s. Louis John and Mariam Dean Ramirez; m. Cheri Ann Butler, Sept. 16, 1995; children: Paige, Bryce. AAS in elec. engring. tech., Hamilton Coll., Davenport, Iowa, 1989; BS in computer and info. sci., U. Phoenix, 1999; MS in project mgmt., George Washington U., 2000. Engring. mgr. / sr. program mgr. Intel Corp., Chandler, Ariz., 1999—; engr. and sr. project mgr. Motorola Inc., Schaumburg, Ill., 1989—99. Staff sgt. USAF, 1983—87. Recipient Disting. Grad., Profl. Mil. Edn. Sch., 1986, Honor Grad., USAF Tech. Schools, 1983, Commander's Top Six, SJAFB, 1985. Mem.: PMI. Home Fax: 480-917-3976. E-mail: tony_ramirez@cox.net.

RAMIREZ, JANICE L. assistant school superintendent; b. Dodge City, Kans., July 16, 1947; d. Chris William and Lois (Moore) Langvardt; 1 child, Jessica. BS, Emporia State U., 1969, MA, 1970; PhD, Kans. State U., 1982. Div. prin. Highland Park High Sch./Topeka (Kans.) pub. schs.; prin. Topeka pub. schs., Mesa (Ariz.) pub. schs., asst. supt. Mem. mid. level task force Ariz. Dept. Edn. Contbr. articles to profl. jours. Bd. dirs. Maricopa County Sports Commn.; chair merit sys. bd. City of Mesa. Recipient Kamelot award; named one of Top 100 Bus. Women in Ariz., Today's Ariz. Woman Success Mag., 1996—. Mem. Am. Assn. Sch. Pers. Adminstrs., Ariz. Sch. Pers. Adminstrs. Assn., Nat. Assn. Ednl. Negotiators, Ariz. Sch. Adminstrs. Assn., Phi Delta Kappa. Office: 63 E Main St # 101 Mesa AZ 85201-7204 Office Phone: 480-472-0412.

RAMIREZ, MANUEL ARISTIDES (MANNY RAMIREZ), professional baseball player; b. Santo Domingo, Dominican Republic, May 30, 1972; Grad. high sch., N.Y.C. Outfielder Cleve. Indians, 1993—2000, Boston Red Sox, 2001—. Named to The Sporting News Am. League Silver Slugger team, 1995, Am. League All-star team, 1995, 1998—2004; recipient Players Choice award for Am. League Outstanding Player, 1999, Am. League Batting Title, 2002. Achievements include leading the Am. League in RBI's, 1999. Office: Boston Red Sox Fenway Park 4 Yawkey Way Boston MA 02215

RAMIREZ, MARIO EFRAIN, physician; b. Roma, Tex., Apr. 3, 1926; s. Efren M. and Carmen (Hinojosa) R.; m. Sarah B. Aycock, Nov. 25, 1949; children: Mario, Patricia Ann, Norman Michael, Jaime Eduardo, Roberto Luis. Student, U. Tex., 1942-45; MD, U. Tenn., 1948. Diplomate Am. Bd. Family Physicians. Intern Shreveport (La.) Charity Hosp., 1949, resident; practice medicine specializing in family practice; pvt. family practice Roma, 1950-75, Rio Grande City, Tex., 1975-93; owner, adminstr. Ramirez Meml. Hosp., Roma, 1958-75. Assoc. med. dir. South Tex. Blue Cross Blue Shield Tex., McAllen, 1993-95. County judge Starr County, Rio Grande City, 1969-78; chmn. South Tex. Devel. Coun., 1975-76, Tri-County Cmty. Action Coun., 1971-78; mem. coordinated bd. Tex. Colls. and Univs., 1979-85; mem. devel. bd. U. Tex., 1986—; presdl. appointee bd. regents Uniformed Svcs. U. Tex. Health Scis., 1985-92; mem. bd. regents U. Tex. Sys., 1989-95, vice chmn. bd., 1991-92. Recipient Spl. citation Surgeon Gen., 1967, Disting. Alumnus award U. Tex., 1975, 78, Achievement award Lab World, 1978, Presdl. citation U. Tex., 1979, Outstanding Alumnus award U. Tenn., 1991, Mirabeau B. Lamar medal Assn. Tex. Colls. and Univs., 1997; named Family Dr. of Yr., Good Housekeeping mag. and Am. Acad. Family Physicians, 1978, Border Texan of the Yr., 1995; honoree Founder's Day for contbns. to higher edn. U. Tex. Pan Am., 1989. Fellow Am. Acad. Family Physicians; mem. AMA (vice chmn. com. health care of poor 1971-75, Benjamin Rush Bicentennial award 1976, Council of Med. Services 1985-94), Tex. Med. Assn. (chmn. com. health care of poor 1971, Disting. Service award 1972, pres. 1979-80), Tex. Acad. Family Physicians (v.p. 1973, pres. 1975, Distinguished Service award 1967, Outstanding Leadership award 1975-76, v.p. Valley chpt. 1960-61, pres. 1961-62), Hidalgo-Starr Counties Med. Soc. (pres. 1964) Clubs: Lions, K.C, Rotary, Alhambra. Address: 212 W Pine Ridge Ln Mcallen TX 78503-3129 E-mail: mramirezmd@aol.com.

RAMIREZ, MARTIN RUBEN, architect, engineer, educator, cognitive scientist, consultant; b. San Luis Potosi, Mex., Aug. 17, 1962; s. Victorio Niño and Concepcion (Zuñiga) R.; m. Maureen Therese McDermott, July 27, 1991. BS, Northwestern U., 1984, MS, 1986, PhD, 1991. Asst. to v.p. engring. Perkins & Will, Chgo., 1980-84; cons. engr. Alfred Benesch & Co., Chgo., 1985-86, Teng & Assocs., Chgo.; prof. engring. Johns Hopkins U., Balt., 1990-94; pres. I.D.E.A.S., Chgo., 1994—99; pres., chief product officer 5Ps, Chgo., 1999; chief info. officer Metric Interface Sarbanes-Oxley Compliance, 2002—. Cons. Wiss-Jenney Elstner, Northbrook, Ill., 1985—86, Mitsubishi Heavy Industries, Hunt Valley, Md.; cons. to forune 500 corps., govts., dists. and instns.; founder, dir. program on engring. Johns Hopkins U., Balt., 1993. Reviewer for several jours.; editor Needs Database. Recipient Fazlur Khan Meml. prize, 1986, Young Investigator award NSF, 1993; Lilly fellow, 1992; NSF grad. fellow, 1985. Mem.: ASME, ASCD, ASCE (assoc.), Am. Acad. Mechanics, IEEE Computer Soc., U.S. Assn. for Computational Mechanics, Am. Soc. Engring. Edn. (chair Frontiers in Edn. Conf. 1993), Am. Edn. Rsch. Assn., Tau Beta Pi. Achievements include major innovations e-business usability, business strategy, learning, integration; orbitz.com, Sprint PCS vision designer. Avocations: bicycling, cars, travel, music. Office Phone: 312-446-9487. E-mail: martin@metricinterface.com., martin@5Ps.biz.

RAMIREZ, MARY CATHERINE, retired secondary school educator; b. McLeansboro, Ill., Feb. 16, 1921; d. George Washington and Mary Margaret (Lane) Tousley; m. John Ramirez, Oct. 30, 1948 (dec. 1975). BS, Ctrl. U., Edmond, Okla., 1942; MA, U. Okla., 1945. Tchr. Bradley (Okla.) High Sch., 1942-43, McLeansboro (Ill.) High Sch., 1943-46, No. Okla. Jr. Coll., Tonkawa, Okla., 1946-47, Draughon Bus. Coll., Springfield, Mo., 1947-48, VA Hosp., Springfield, Mo., 1948-52, Madison, Wis., 1952-63, Madison pub. sch., 1963-85. Mem. AAUW (publicity chmn. Madison br. 1954-60)., NEA, Madison Civics Club. Avocations: travel, photography, coin and stamp collecting, needlecrafts. Home: 971 Wellington Ct Nekoosa WI 54457-9040

RAMIREZ, RALPH HENRY, nurse, corporate executive; b. Oakland, Calif., Sept. 25, 1949; s. Hector Ramirez and Genevieve (Figueroa) Ingraham. BS in Nursing, San Jose State U., 1974; M in Health Svcs. Adminstrn., St. Joseph's Coll., 1995. RN; cert. critical care nurse. DON nursing Chgo. Ctr. Hosp., 1980-84; adminstr. Med. Profls. Supplemental Staffing, Chgo., 1984-85; pres. Progressive Svcs., Chgo., 1985-92; v.p. Seville Internat. Tours, Inc., 1990—; pres. Progressive Health Svcs. Ctrs., Inc., 1992-94, Merchants Nat. Fin. and Mgmt., Houston, 1994-95; ops. mgr. Ravenswood Home Care, Chgo., 1995-98; adminstr. United Home Health Svcs., Homewood, Ill., 1998—2003; br. mgr. Patient Care, Inc., Chgo., 2003—. Contbr. articles to profl. jours. Sponsor nursing symposium, Chgo., 1991—; bd. dirs. AIDS Found. of Chgo., 1991—, chmn. Gala com., 1993, 94, Chase House, Chgo., 1998—; co-chair Bonaventure House Benefit, 1993. Mem. Am. Biog. Inst. (Disting. Leadership award for Outstanding Svc. to Nursing Profession, Golden Acad. award), Chgo. Nurses Assn., Ill. Nurses Assn., Sigma Theta Tau. Democrat. Episcopalian. Avocations: swimming, weightlifting. Home: 5218 N Kenmore Ave Apt 1N Chicago IL 60640-2400 Office: United Home Health Care 1806 Gottschalk Homewood IL 60430 E-mail: rhr950@rcn.net.

RAMIREZ, TINA, artistic director; b. Caracas, Venezuela; d. Gloria Maria Cestero and Jose Ramirez Gaonita. Studied dance with Lola Bravo, Alexandra Danilova, Anna Sokolow. Toured with Federico Rey Dance Co.; founder, artistic dir. Ballet Hispanico, N.Y.C., 1970—. Panelist NEA N.Y. Sate Coun. on Arts; mem. advisory panel N.Y.C. Dept. Cultural Affairs; bd. dirs Dance Theater Workshop. Appearances (Broadway plays) Kismet, Lute Song, (TV series) Man of La Mancha. Recipient Arts and Culture Honor award, Mayor of N.Y.C., 1983, Ethnic New Yorker award, N.Y.C., 1986, Gov.'s Arts award, N.Y. State Gov. Mario Cuomo, 1987, honoree Nat. Puerto Rican Forum, Hispanic Inst. for Performing Arts. Office: Ballet Hispanico 167 W 89th St New York NY 10024-1901

RAMIREZ, W. FRED, chemical engineering educator; b. New Orleans, Feb. 19, 1941; s. Walter Frederick and Elza Welch Ramirez; m. Marion Kneipp; children: Jennifer Louise, Karen Elizabeth, Ellen Christine. BS, Tulane U., 1962, MS, 1964, PhD, 1965. Asst. prof. dept. chem. engring. U. Colo., Boulder, 1965-70, assoc. prof., 1970-75, prof., 1975—, chmn. dept. chem. engring., 1971-79, 89-92, 1997-98, 2002—03. Vis. scientist Institut Francaise du Petrole, Rueil-Malmaison, France, 1976-77; vis. prof. dept. chem. engring., MIT, Cambridge, Mass., 1985-86, depts. engring. and chem. engring. Cambridge (Eng.) U., 1992-93, dept. chem. engring. U. Newcastle, Australia, 2001-02; cons. Marathon Oil Co., Littleton, Colo., 1968-72, Dowell divsn. Dow Chem., Tulsa, 1980-85, Adolph Coors Co., Golden, Colo., 1988-89, others. Author: Process Simulation, Applications of Optimal Control Theory to Enhanced Oil Recovery, 1987, Comp. Methods for Process Simulation, 1989, 2d edit., 1997. Process Control and Identification, 1994; contbr. articles to profl. jours. Singer several local choral groups, Boulder, 1980—. Faculty fellow U. Colo., 1985, 92, 2001, Exch. fellow Acad. Sci., USSR, 1987, rsch. fellow Fulbright Found., France, 1976. Fellow AIChE; mem. Am. Soc. Engring. Educators. Avocations: jogging, travel. Office: U Colo Dept Chem Engring Boulder CO 80309-0424

RAMIREZ-BETANCES, BEATRIZ EUGENIA, student activist; b. Madrid, Jan. 20, 1972; d. Wallace Ramírez-Acarón and Beatriz Zahyde Betances-Fradera; m. Manuel Elías Cardoza-Soriano, Feb. 17, 2000; 1 child, Laura Ester Cardoza-Ramírez. BA, U. P.R., 1994—94; MA, postgrad., U. Mich., 2002—. Grad. student instr. Residential Coll., U. Mich., Ann Arbor, Mich., 2000—02; tchg. fellow Ctr. Rsch. on Learning and Tchg. U. Mich, 2003, grad. tchg. cons., 2004—. V.p. Puerto Rican Lit. Students Assn., Rio Piedras, PR, 1996—97; conf. co-chair, comparative lit. intra faculty-student forum 2002 U. of Mich., 2001—02, conf. chair for the 13th ann. grad. and profl. nat. student of color of rackham conf., 2002—, grad. student rep. program in comparative lit., 2002—. Dir.: (play) Historias para ser contadas. Residential Coll., U. of Mich.; actor: (performances) Calibanismo. Taller de Imágenes en Puerto Rico, Oiste el chiste del dominicano. Taller de Imágenes en Puerto Rico, Trilogía/Suicide note from a cockroach in a low income housing project. Taller de Imágenes en Puerto Rico; asst. editor Ediciones Huracán. Rep. univ. child care oversight com. Rackham Student Govt., U. Mich.; union rep. com. on student-parent's issues, steward, contract enforcer in the grievance com. Grad. Employee Orgn., U. Mich., 1999—2003. Mem.: AAUW, Asociación Puertorriqueña de Estudiantes de Literatura (v.p. 1996—97), Student of Color of Rackham Assn. (conf. chair 2001—02), Latin Am. Studies Assn., Am. Comparative Lit. Assn., MLA, ACLU. Home: 2418 Arrowwood Trail Ann Arbor MI 48105 Office: University of Michigan 2015 Tisch Hall Ann Arbor MI 48109-1003 Office Phone: 734-763-2351. Business E-Mail: beatrize@umich.edu.

RAMIREZ-MIRELES, FERNANDO, electrical engineer; s. Fernando Ramirez Matuk and Maria Elia Mireles Tabares; m. Gina Miroslava Guerrero Barja; children: Tania Fernanda Ramirez Guerrero, Thalia Miroslava Ramirez Guerrero. BSc in Electronics Comm., Met. Autonomous U., Mexico City; MScEE, Ctr. for Rsch. and Advanced Studies of Nat. Politechnic Inst., Mexico City; PhDEE, U. So. Calif. Intern Mex. Tel. Co., Mexico City, 1987—88; rschr. Ctr. for Rsch. and Advanced Studies Nat. Politechnic Inst., Mexico City, 1988—92; rsch. asst. U. So. Calif., L.A., 1996—98; summer intern Torrey Sci. Corp., San Diego, 1997; mem. tech. staff Glenayre/Wireless Access, Santa Clara, Calif., 1998—99; comm. sys. engr. Aware, Inc., Lafayette, Calif., 1999—2001; sr. comm. sys. engr. Ikanos Comms., Fremont, Calif., 2001—. Cons. Nat. Bank Mex., Mexico City, 1991; invited spkr. at tech. confs. Referee: profl. jours.; contbr. articles to profl. jours. and confs. Named Candidate to Nat. Rschr., Nat. Sys. Rschrs., Mex., 1993—94; named one of Best Students of Mex., Best Students of Mex. Orgn., 1989; recipient Fulbright Scholarship, Fulbright-Garcia Robles Commn., 1992—97, Universitarian Merit medal, Met. Autonomous Univ., Mex., 1987, Honorific Mention, IV Ericsson's Nat. Prize of Sci. and Tech., Mex., 1990. Mem.: IEEE (sr.), Soc. Hispanic Profl. Engrs., Tau Beta Pi. Achievements include patents in field of DSL communications. Avocation: travel. Office: Ikanos Comms 47709 Fremont Blvd Fremont CA 94538 Home: 6604 SE 38th Ave Portland OR 97202-7707 Personal E-mail: fernandomireles@yahoo.com. Business E-Mail: ramirezm@ieee.org.

RAMIREZ-RIVERA, JOSE, physician; b. Mayaguez, P.R., June 26, 1929; s. Jesus Ramirez and Nieves Rivera; m. Leila Suner, May 14, 1971; children: Federico, Steven, Sally, Juliette, Natasha, Leila. BA, Johns Hopkins U., 1949; MD, Yale U., 1953. Diplomate Am Bd Internal Med. Intern U. Md. Hosp., 1953-54; resident in medicine Univ. Hosp., Balt., 1954-55, fellow in hematology, 1958-59, resident, 1959; staff physician VA Hosp., Balt., 1960-67, assoc. chief of staff, 1962-68; asst. in medicine Johns Hopkins U., 1960-67, instr. in medicine, 1967-68; asst. prof. medicine U. Md., 1961-68; assoc. prof. Duke U., Durham, N.C., 1968-70; dir. med. edn. and clin. investigation Western Region P.R., 1970-80; chief medicine Mayaguez (P.R.) Med. Ctr., 1971-82. Prof med Univ PR, San Juan, 1974—, dir univ med servs Med Sci Campus, 1982—86; prof med Univ Cent del Caribe, 1998—; dir Rincon Rural Health Project, 1975—82; assoc chief staff educ VA Med Ctr, San Juan, 1990—92; dir clin investigation La Concepcion Hosp, San German, 1996—. Contbr. articles to med jours. Bd dirs Soc Educ Suroeste. With USPHS, 1955—57. Decorated comendador Imperial Orden Hispanica de Carlos V. Fellow: ACP (pres. PR chpt. 1986—88), Coll. Chest Physicians, Royal Soc. Med (London); mem.: Imperial Orden Hispanica de Carlos V, Puerto Rican Fedn Bioethics (bd. dirs. 1999—2002, pres. 2002—), Soc. Autores Puertorriguenos, PR Lung Assn. (bd. dirs. 1975—80), Casa Espanã (bd. dirs. 1998—), Alliance Francaise PR (v.p. 1995—96, pres. 1996—2000), PEN Club. Roman Catholic. Office Phone: 787-793-6576. Personal E-mail: ramirj@hotmail.com.

RAMJI, AL-NOOR, telecommunications industry executive; BSc in electronics, U. of London. Cert. chartered fin. analyst. Head of treasur ops. Credit Suisse First Boston, 1984—90; mng. dir., COO Swiss Bank Corp., 1990—96; global chief info. officer Dresdner Kleinwort Wasserstein, 1996—2000; exec. v.p., chief info. officer Qwest Commn. Internat., Inc., 2001—. Office: Quest Communications International Inc 1801 California St Denver CO 80202

RAMKRISHNA, DORAISWAMI, chemical engineering educator, researcher; b. Trichur, Kerala, India, Oct. 29, 1938; came to U.S., 1974; s. M.R. and Ponnu (Raman) Doraiswami; married, 1966; children: Sriram, Arvind. B in Chem. Engring., Bombay U., 1960; PhD in Chem. Engring., U. Minn., 1965, DSc (hon.), 2004. From asst. to assoc. prof. chem. engring. Indian Inst. Tech., Kanpur, 1967-75, prof., 1975-76; prof. chem. engring. Purdue U., West Lafayette, Ind., 1976—, Harry Creighton Peffer disting. prof., 1994—. Vis. assoc. prof. U. Wis., Madison, 1974-75; vis. prof. U. Minn., Mpls., 1975-76, George T. Piercy disting. vis. prof., 1988; Kane vis. prof. dept. chem. tech. Bombay U., 1983; Melchor vis. prof. U. Notre Dame, Ind., 1994. Author: (with Neal R. Amundson) Linear Operator Methods in Chemical Engineering, 1985, Population Balances, 2000; contbr. over 175 papers to profl. jours. Named Disting. Engring. alumnus Bombay U., 1994. Fellow Am. Inst. Med. and Biol. Engring.; mem. AIChE (Alpha Chi Sigma award 1987, RH Wilhelm award in Chem. Reaction Engring., 1998, Thomas Baron award, 2004), Am. Chem. Soc. (Sr. Humboldt award 2001). Hindu. Achievements include application of operator theory, population balances and stochastic methods to numerous chemical engineering problems. Home: 3517 Woodwind Pl West Lafayette IN 47906-8861 Office: Purdue U Sch Chem Engring Northwestern Ave Purdue University IN 47907 Office Phone: 765-494-4066. Business E-Mail: ramkrish@ecn.purdue.edu.

RAMM, DOUGLAS ROBERT, psychologist; b. New Haven, Dec. 11, 1949; s. Robert Frederick and Gladys (Torgrimson) R.; m. Barbara Stephens, Aug. 10, 1974; children: Jennifer, Jessica. BA, Ithaca Coll., 1972; MA, Duquesne U., 1974, PhD, 1979. Diplomate Am. Bd. Profl. Psychology; bd. cert. clin. psychologist Am. Bd. Profl. Psychology. Staff psychologist Westmoreland Hosp., Greensburg, Pa., 1976-79, chief clin. psychologist, dir. child & adolescent psychiat., 1979-82; pvt. practice Greensburg, Pa., 1980—. Pres. Ethics, Inc., Ctr. for Sci. Study of Values and Morality, 1995-98; cons. U. Pitts., Pa. Bur. Vocat. Rehab., Westmoreland County Ct. of Common Pleas; past pres. Mental Health Assn. Westmoreland County. Author: Clinically Formulated Principles of Morality, 1996, The Formula for Happiness, 2004. Mem. APA, ASCD, Am. Philos. Assn., Pa. Psychol. Assn., Acad. Clin. Psychology, Soc. Personality Assessment, Nat. Acad. Neuropsychologists, Nat. Register Health Svc. Providers in Psychology, Am. Coll. Forensic Examiners (diplomate), Soc. Bus. Ethics, Rotary Club. Methodist. Office: 225 Humphrey Rd Greensburg PA 15601-4571 Office Phone: 724-832-9096. Personal E-mail: plato1211@aol.com.

RAMM, LOUISE, administrator; b. Manchester, N.H., June 22, 1945; BS, Marquette U., 1967; MS, U. Va., 1971, PhD, 1974, postgrad., 1974-77. Rsch. tech. Adenovirus Lab., Rockville, Md., 1967-68; rsch. asst. Marine Biol. Lan., Woods Hole, Mass., 1974-76; rsch. scientist microbiology dept. Johns Hopkins U. Sch. Medicine, Balt., 1977-82, rsch. assoc. faculty, subdept. immunology, 1982-87; rsch. assoc. faculty dept. pathology U. Md. Sch. Medicine, Balt., 1987; health scientist adminstr. Nat. Ctr. Rsch. Resources, Bethesda, MD, 1987-94, dep. dir., 1994—. Contbr. articles to profl. jours. Office: Nat Ctr Rsch Resources Msc 2128 Bldg 3b11 Bethesda MD 20892-0001 also: Nat Ctr Rsch Resources 6705 Rockledge Dr Rm 5158 Bethesda MD 20892-0001

RAMMING, MICHAEL ALEXANDER, retired school system administrator; b. St. Louis, Feb. 4, 1940; s. William Alexander and Emily Louise (Reingruber) Ramming; m. Susan Ray Oliver, July 9, 1962; children: Michael Murray, Todd Alexander. BS, Centenary Coll., 1963; MA, Washington U., St. Louis, 1968. Cert. adminstr. secondary schs. Mo. Tchr., coach Ladue Sch. Dist., St. Louis, 1963-88, adminstr., 1988—2002; ret., 2002. Adj. prof. Lindenwood U., 2002—; cons. Ladue Sch. Dist., St. Louis, 2002—. Vol. Sr. Olympics, St. Louis, 1992, 1993. Mem.: Mo. Interscholastic Athletic Adminstrs. Assn. (25 Yr. Svc. award), Nat. Interscholastic Athletic Adminstrs., Mo. Assn. Secondary Sch. Prins., Nat. Assn. Secondary Sch. Prins. Avocations: tennis, walking, travel. Home: 18128 Dawns Trail Wildwood MO 63005 Office: Ladue Horton Watkins High Sch 1201 S Warson Rd Saint Louis MO 63124-1266 *As I look back I feel that participation in sports as a player, coach, and fan provided me with a wealth of leadership, community building, daring, sharing, and the ability to accept success and failure.*

RAMO, ROBERTA COOPER, lawyer; b. Denver, Aug. 8, 1942; d. David D. and Martha L. (Rosenblum) Cooper; m. Barry W. Ramo, June 17, 1964. BA magna cum laude, U. Colo., 1964; JD, U. Chgo., 1967; LLD (hon.), U. Mo., 1995, U. Denver, 1995; LHD (hon.), U. Colo., 1995; JD (hon.), Golden Gate U., 1996; LLD (hon.), U. S.C., 2001. Bar: N.Mex. 1967, Tex. 1971. With NC. Fund, Durham, 1967-68; nat. tchg. fellow Shaw U., Raleigh, N.C., 1968-70; mem. Sawtelle, Goode, Davidson & Troilo, San Antonio, 1970-72, Rodey, Dickason, Sloan, Akin & Robb, Albuquerque, 1972-74; sole practice law Albuquerque, 1974-77; dir., shareholder Poole, Kelly & Ramo, Albuquerque, 1977-93; shareholder Modrall, Sperling, Roehl, Harris & Sisk, Albuquerque, 1993—. Lectr. in field., bd. dirs. Merrill Lynch Asset Mgmt., Ednl. Credit Mgmt. Corp. Co-author: New Mexico Estate Administration System, 1980; editor: How to Create a System for the Law Office, 1975; contbg. editor: Tex. Probate Sys., 1974; contbr. articles to profl. jours., chpts. to books. Mem. steering com. World Conf. Domestic Violence, 1996—99; mem. Am. Law Inst. Coun., 1997—, exec. com., 2000—; mem. Martindale-Hubbell Legal

Adv. Bd., 1996—2000; bd. dirs., past pres. N.Mex. Symphony Orch., 1977—86; bd. dirs. Albuquerque Cmty. Found., N.Mex. First, 1987—90, Santa Fe Opera, Santa Fe, 2001—; bd. regents U. N.Mex., 1989—94, pres., 1991—93; founding bd. mem. Think N.Mex., 1998—; mem. Civitas Initiative, 1997—; chmn. bd. Cooper's Inc., 1999—. Recipient Disting. Pub. Svc. award Gov. of N.Mex., 1993. Fellow: Am. Bar Found.; mem.: ABA (pres. 1995, bd. govs. 1994—97, chmn. London 2000 com., Asia Law Initiatives Coun. 1999—, others), Am. Arbitration Assn. (bd. dirs. 1997—, bd. trustees Global Ctr. Dispute Resolution Rsch. 1999—), Law Inst. Coun., Am. Judicature Soc. (bd. dirs. 1988—91), Am. Bar Retirement Assn. (bd. dirs. 1990—94), N.Mex. Bar Assn. (Outstanding Contbn. award 1981, 1984), Albuquerque Bar Assn. (bd. dirs., pres. 1980—81), Greater Albuquerque C. of C. (bd. dirs., exec. com. 1987—91). Address: Modrall Sperling Roehl Harris & Sisk PO Box 2168 Albuquerque NM 87103-2168

RAMO, SIMON, retired engineering executive; b. Salt Lake City, May 7, 1913; s. Benjamin and Clara ((Trestman)) Ramo; m. Virgina Smith, July 25, 1937; children: James Brian, Alan Martin. BS, U. Utah, 1933, DSc (hon.), 1961; PhD, Calif. Inst. Tech., 1936; DEng (hon.), Case Western Res. U., 1960, U. Mich., 1966, Poly. Inst. N.Y., 1971; DSc (hon), Union Coll., 1963, Worcester Polytechnic Inst., 1968, U. Akron, 1969, Cleve. State U., 1976; LLD (hon.), Carnegie-Mellon U., 1970, U. So. Calif., 1972, Gonzaga U., 1983, Occidental Coll., 1984, Claremont U., 1985. With Gen. Electric Co., 1936—46; v.p. ops. Hughes Aircraft Co., 1946—53; with Ramo-Woolridge Corp., 1953—58; dir. U.S. Intercontinental Ballistic Missile Program, 1954—58, TRW Inc., 1954—85, exec. v.p., 1958—61, vice chmn. bd., 1961—78, chmn. exec. com., 1969—78, cons., 1978—; pres. The Bunker-Ramo Corp., 1964—66; chmn. bd. TRW-Fujitsu Co., 1980—83. Bd. dirs. Arco Power Techs.; vis. prof. mgmt. sci. Calif. Inst. Tech., 1978—; Regents lectr. UCLA, 1981—82, U. Calif. at Santa Cruz, 1978—79; chmn. Ctr. for Study Am. Experience, U. So. Calif., 1978—80; Faculty fellow John F. Kennedy Sch. Govt., Harvard U., 1980—84; mem. White House Energy Rsch. and Devel. Adv. Coun., 1973—75; chmn. Pres.'s Com. on Sci. and Tech., 1976—77; bd. advisors for sci. and tech. Repu. of China, 1981—84; chmn. bd. Aetna, Jacobs & Ramo Venture Capital, 1987—90, Allenwood Ventures, Inc., 1987—; advisor Axiom Venture Ptnrs., 1997—. Author: (novels) The Business of Science, 1988, other sci., engring. and mgmt. books. Life trustee Calif. Inst. Tech., Nat. Symphony Orch. Assn., 1973—83; trustee emeritus Calif. State U.; bd. govs., pres. Performing Arts Coun. Mus. Ctr. LA, 1976—77; co-chair bd. overseers Keck Sch. Medicine, U. So. Calif., 1999—; bd. dirs. W. M. Keck Found., 1983—, LA World Affairs Coun., 1973—85, Mus. Ctr. Found., LA, LA Philharm. Assn., 1981—84. Named to Bus. Hall of Fame, 1984; recipient IAS, 1956, award, Am. Inst. Elec. Engrs., 1959, Am. Iron and Steel Inst., 1968, Disting. Svc. medal, Armed Forces Comm. and Electronics Assn., 1970, medal of achievement, WEMA, 1970, awards, U. So. Calif., 1971, 1979, Kayan medal, Columbia U., 1972, award, Am. Cons. Engrs. Coun., 1974, medal, Franklin Inst., 1978, Aesculapian award, UCLA, 1984, Durand medal, AAIA, 1984, John Fritz medal, 1986, henry Townley Heald award, Ill. Inst. Tech., 1988, Nat. Engring. award, Am. Assn. Engring. Socs., 1988, Franklin-Jefferson medal, 1988, Howard Hughes meml. award, 1989, Air Force Space and Missile Pioneers award, 1989, Pioneer award, Internat. Coun. on Sys. Engring., 1997, Disting. pub. Svc. medal, NASA, 1999, Lifetime Achievement trophy, Smithsonian Inst., 1999, John F. Kennedy Astronautics award, Am. Astronautical Soc., 2000, John R. Alison award for indsl. leadership, Air Force Assn., 2000, Presdl. Medallion, U. So. Calif., 2002, Founders award, USC Thornton Sch. of Music, 2003, Medal of Achievement, AEA, 1970. Fellow: Am. Acad. Polit. Sci., Am. Acad. Arts and Scis., IEEE (Electronic Achievement award 1953, Golden Omega award 1975, Founders medal 1980, Centennial medal 1984); mem.: Nat. Acad. Engring. (founder, coun. mem. Bueche award), Internat. Acad. Astronautics, Pacific Coun. Internat. Policy, Coun. Fgn. Rels., Inst. advancement Engring., Am. Philos. Soc., Am. Phys. Soc., N.Y. Acad. Scis., Theta Tau (Hall of Fame laureate), Eta Kappa Nu (eminent mem. award 1966). Office: 9200 W Sunset Blvd Ste 801 Los Angeles CA 90069-3603

RAMO, VIRGINIA M. SMITH, civic worker; b. Yonkers, N.Y. d. Abraham Harold and Freda (Kasnetz) Smith; m. Simon Ramo; children: James Brian, Alan Martin. BS in Edn., U. So. Calif., DHL (hon.), 1978. Nat. co-chmn., ann. giving U. So. Calif., 1968-70, vice chmn., trustee, 1971—, co-chmn. bd. councilors Sch. Performing Arts, 1975-76, co-chmn. bd. councillors Schs. Med. and Engring. Vice-chmn. bd. overseers Hebrew Union Coll., 1972-75; bd. dirs. The Muses of Calif. Mus. Sci. and Industry, UCLA Affiliates, Estelle Doheny Eye Found., U. So. Calif. Sch. Medicine; mem. adv. coun. L.A. County Heart Assn., chmn. com. to endow Chair in cardiology at U. So. Calif.; vice chmn., bd. dirs. Friends of Libr. U. So. Calif.; bd. dirs., nat. pres. Achievement Rewards for Coll. Scientists Found., 1975-77; bd. dirs. Les Dames L.A., Cmty. TV So. Calif.; bd. dirs., v.p. Founders L.A. Music Ctr.; v.p. L.A. Music Ctr. Opera Assn.; v.p. corp. bd. United Way; v.p. Blue Ribbon-400 Performing Arts Coun.; chmn. com. to endow chair in gerontology U. So. Calif.; vice chmn. campaign Doheny Eye Inst., 1986; co-chair, bd. overseers Keck Sch. Medicine U. So. Calif., 1999—. Recipient Svc. award Friends of Librs., 1974, Nat. Cmty. Svc. award Alpha Epsilon Phi, 1975, Disting. Svc. award Am. Heart Assn., 1978, Svc. award U. So. Calif., Spl. award U. So. Calif. Music Alumni Assn., 1979, Life Achievement award Mannequins of L.A. Assistance League, 1979, Woman of Yr. award Pan Hellenic Assn., 1981, Disting. Svc. award U. So. Calif. Sch. Medicine, 1981, U. So. Calif. Town and Gown Recognition award, 1986, Asa V. Call Achievement award U. So. Calif., 1986, Phi Kappa Phi scholarship award U. So. Calif., 1986, Vision award Luminaires of Doheny Eye Inst., 1994, Presdl. medallion U. So. Calif., 2002, USC Thornton Sch. of Music Founder's award, 2003. Mem. UCLA Med. Aux., U. So. Calif. Pres.'s Cir., Commerce Assocs. U. So. Calif., Cedars of Lebanon Hosp. Women's Guild (dir. 1967-68), Blue Key, Skull and Dagger.

RAMON, EMILIO, language educator; s. Emilio Ramon and Gemma Garcia; MA(hon.), U. Aberdeen, 1992; BA, U. Alicante, 1993; MA, U. Houston, 1999; postgrad., U. Tex., 1999—2004. Asst. instr. U. Houston, 1997—99, U. Tex., Austin, 1999—. English tchr. Colegio Inmaculada Jesuitas, Alicante, 1993—97, Studio 3. Sch. of English, Alicante, 1993—94; rsch. asst. Arte Publico Press, Houston, 1996; adminstrv. asst. Inst. Valencia de la Vivenda, Alicante, 1996—97; chair com. for pub. procs. of the coloquium, dept. Spanish and Portuguese U. Tex., Austin, 2002, Austin, 03; presenter in field. Contbr. articles to profl. jours. Erasmus scholar, European Coun. of Edn., 1991—92. Mem.: MLA. Office: Dept Spanish and Portuguese U Tex at Austin 1 University Austin TX 78712 E-mail: unioneuropeasp@hotmail.com.

RAMONI, MARCO F. computer scientist; b. Milan, Apr. 13, 1963; arrived in U.S., 2000; s. Giulio Ramoni and Mariarosa Bassi. PhD, Poly. Milan, 1993. Rsch. assoc. Children's Hosp. Boston, 2000—; asst. prof. Harvard Med. Sch., Boston, 2000—; assoc. dir. of bioinformatics Harvard-Ptnrs. Ctr. for Genetics and Genomics. Pres. Bayesware LLC, Boston, 2000—. Recipient Philips award for Young Investigators, Philips Corp. 1983, biomed. and bioengring. grant, NSF, 2002—05; fellow, Helvetic Confedn., 1989. Mem.: Assn. for Computer Machinery (Knowledge Discovery Cup 1999), Am. Med. Informatics Assn., Am. Assn. for Artificial Intelligence. Achievements include research in Artificial Intelligence and Bioinformatics. Office: Harvard Med Sch 71 Ave Louis Pasteur #255 Boston MA 02115

RAMOS, ALBERT A. electrical engineer; b. L.A., Feb. 28, 1927; s. Jesus D. and Carmen F. (Fontes) R.; B.S. in Elec. Engring., U. So. Calif., 1950, M.S. in Systems Mgmt., 1972; Ph.D., U.S. Internat. U., 1975; m. Joan C. Pailing, Sept. 23, 1950; children— Albert A., Richard R., James J., Katherine. With guided missile test group Hughes Aircraft Co., 1950-60; with TRW DSG, 1960-91, sr. staff engr. Norton AFB, San Bernardino, Calif., 1969-91, ret., 1991. Served with USNR, 1945-46. Registered profl. engr., Calif. Mem. IEEE, NSPE, Air Force Assn., Mexican-Am. Engring. Soc., Mexican-Am. Profl. Mgmt. Assn. (mem. administering commn. dept. community svcs.), Sigma Phi Delta, Eta Kappa Nu, Tau Beta Pi. Home: 8937 Napoli Dr Las Vegas NV 89117-1182

RAMOS, ALICE M, education educator; b. NYC, June 18, 1948; d. Alejo Ramos and Dominga Mendez de Ramos. BA in French and Spanish, Marymount Manhattan Coll., 1970; MA in French lang. and lit., NYU, 1971, PhD in French Lit., 1979; PhD in Philosophy, U. Navarra, 1985. Spanish instr. Marymount Manhattan Coll., NYC, 1971—72; tchg. asst. in French NYU, 1972—74; instr./asst. prof. in French Coll. of Mt. St. Vincent, Riverdale, NY, 1975—80; lectr. in French U. Navarra, Pamplona, Spain, 1980—85, lectr. in philosophy, 1985—86; asst. prof. philosophy St. John's U., Jamaica, NY, 1987—93, assoc. prof. philosophy, 1993—2002, prof. philosophy, 2002—. Bd. dirs. Murray Hill Inst., 2000—. Author: (book) Signum: De la Semiotica Universal a la Metafísca del Signo, 1987; editor: Beauty, Art and the Polis, 2000; co-editor: Faith, Scholarship and Culture in the 21st Century, 2002; contbr. articles to profl. jours. Roman Cath. Avocations: art, music. Office: St John's U Dept Philosophy 8000 Utopia Pkwy Jamaica NY 11439

RAMOS, FLAVIA SALES, education educator, consultant; b. Recife, Pernambuco, Brazil, May 20, 1960; d. Feliciano Sales Ramos and Maria de Fatima Volpini; m. Hedi Mattoussi, June 28, 1996; 1 child, Yasmine Vivian Mattoussi. BA in Art Edn., Universidade Fed. do Rio de Janeiro, Brazil, 1982; MEd in Internat. Edn., U. of Mass., 1989, EdD in Internat. Edn., 1999. Cert. Family and School Bilingual Mediator Ctr. for Human Devel. Springfield, Mass., 1989. Rsch. asst. U. of Mass., Amherst, 1986—96; asst. prof. and dir. of the internat. tng. and edn. program Am. U., Washington, 2002—; vis. asst. prof. of internat. edn. George Wash. U., Washington, 2000—02. Dir. of internat. tng. programs Inst. for Tng. and Devel., Amherst, Mass., 1990—96; rsch. cons. Johns Hopkins U./ USAID, Mogadishu, Somalia; adj. prof. program in intercultural mgmt. Sch. Internat. Tng., Brattleboro, Vt., 1990; outreach network devel. cons. Ptnr. for a Healthier Cmty., Inc, Springfield, Mass., 1996—97; rsch. & edn. cons. Mass. Ctr. for Sudden Infant Death Syndrome, Boston, 1997—; adj. faculty internat. studies U. Conn., Storrs, 2002; ednl. cons. Us Dept. Of Labor, Washington, 2002. Author (illustrator): (children's books) E O Vento Contou Series, (health info. booklets) Read This if You Want to Feel Good and Look Good About Your Baby, Read this if you want your baby to grow happy, safe, and healthy., When a Baby Dies.; contbr. articles to profl. jour. Mem.: Comparative and Internat. Edn. Soc., The Assn. for Women's Rights in Devel., Nat. Assn. of Multicultural Edn. (NAME). Baha'I. Achievements include development of The FotoDialogo Method. Avocation: travel. Office: American University 4400 Massachusetts Ave NW Washington DC 20016 Office Phone: 202-885-3723. Business E-Mail: framos@american.edu.

RAMOS, JOHN C., JR., protective services official, educator; s. John C. and Helen Barbara Ramos; m. Kathryn Elizabeth Fisher, July 16, 1967; children: John C. III, Joeseph Michael, Amanda Ann. Grad. high sch., Munster, IN. Indiana Law Enforcement Academy Basic Course: Ind. Law Enforcement Tng. Bd. 1990, Basic SWAT Team Tactics: Muncie Police Dept. 1996, Sub-machinegun Instructor: Singleton Internat. 1997, Advanced Handgun, Shotgun, Machinegun and High Risk Entry: Singleton Internat. 1999, Diversionary Devices & Less Lethal Munitions: Tng. Resource Group, Inc. 1999, High Risk Entry: HSS Internat. 2001, GSG-9 Tactics: HSS Internat. 2001, Basic SWAT Tactics & Operation: Lake County Sheriffs Police 2001, SWAT Training: US Dept. of Justice Fed. Bur. of Investication 2002, Managing Civil Actions in Threat Incidents Command Course: US Dept. of Homeland Security 2003, Instructor Development: Ind. Law Enforcement Tng. Bd. 1995, Police Rifle & Carbine: NW Ind. Law Enforcement Acad. 2002, Firearms Instructor: Ind. Law Enforcement Tng. Bd. 1996, Firearms Training Systems: NW Ind. Law Enforcement Tng. Bd. 1994, Hostage Negotiator Seminar: NW Ind. Law Enforcement Tng. Bd. 1993, Police Officer Survival Tactics: NW Traffic Inst. 1989, Street Survival: Calibre Press 1989; Haz-Mat Operations East Chgo. Fire Dept., 2003, ASP Tactical Baton Instructor Armament Systems and Procedures, Inc., 1992, Sexual Assault Awareness FBI, 1989. Profl. motorcross National #127, 1981—83; part time police office Cedar Lake Police Dept., Ind., 1987—89; police officer East Chicago Police Dept., 1989—. Dept. instr. East Chicago Police Dept., 1995—. Author: The Book of Room Domination and Assault Techniques, The Book of Cop Rules and Patrol Tactics. Recipient 2nd Pl. Expert Duty Class, State FOP Elkhart, 1989, 5th Pl. B Class, Ind. Law Enforcement Acad. League, 1990, Mr. VCO, East Chgo. Police Dept., 1990, 1st Pl. Sharpshooter Team, Ill. Police Combat Assn., 1990, 2nd Pl. Marksman, Ill. Police Combat League, 1990, Outstanding Performance, Lake County Task Force Against Drunk Driving, 1991, Outstanding Dedication and Svc., Am. Legion Post 369. Mem.: Nat. Tactical Officers Assn. Conservative. Penticostal. Avocations: bicycling, shooting, gaming. Office: East Chgo Police Dept 2301 E Columbus Dr East Chicago IN 46312 Office Phone: 219-680-7122. Personal E-mail: reeper351@prodigy.net.

RAMOS, JOSE A. engineering educator; b. San Juan, P.R., Apr. 29, 1957; s. Luis R. and Lydia Ramos. BSCE, U.P.R., Mayaguez, 1978; MSCE, Ga. Inst. Tech., 1979, PhD, 1985. Registered profl. engr., P.R. Rsch. engr. United Techs. Optical Systems, West Palm Beach, Fla., 1986—90; postdoctoral fellow Katholieke U. Leuven, Belgium, 1990—93; cons. Sci. Studies Co., Palm Beach Gardens, Fla., 1993—95; assoc. prof. elec. engring. Ind. U./Purdue U., Indpls., 1995—2000, 2002—; assoc. prof. U. Miami, Coral Gables, Fla., 2000—02. Vis. summer rsch. scholar U. Montpellier II, France, 1998—2000. Contbr. articles to profl. jours. Ford Found. fellow, 1983—85. Mem.: IEEE (assoc.; faculty advisor 1997—2003), Soc. Indsl. and Applied Math. (assoc.). Office: Ind U Purdue U 723 W Michigan St SL 164 - E Indianapolis IN 46202 Office Phone: 317-274-0044. Business E-Mail: jaramos@iupui.edu.

RAMOS, LEONNA ANNE (LEONNA ABRAHAM-BRANDAO), writer; b. Barnstable, Mass., Jan. 20, 1947; d. Arthur Brandao and Lillian Jeanne Abraham; 1 child, John Anthony. Student, Fisher Jr. Coll., 1970, Cape Cod C.C., 1982—84, U. Mass., 1984—88. With C.C. Hosp., Hyannis, Mass., 1961—64, King's Dept. Store, Hyannis, 1967—68, A& P Grocery Store, Osterville, Mass., 1968—78; sr. social worker Dept. Social Svcs., Cape Islands, 1980—94; missionary New Vision Organ Ghana, 1995—96; med. provider numerouse home health care agys., Cape Code, 1996—2002; writer, 2002—. Founder New Vision Orgn., Ghana, West Africa, 1995—, Mashpee, Mass., 1996—; coord. svcs. to prisoners through numerous ministries, 2002—04. Author: Prison Poetry with Untold Stories, 2003, World of Healing and Hope, 2003, Touching Lives, 2003, Inspired By the Holy Spirit, 2003, No Redemption, No Existence, 2003, How can I Make It Through, 2003, No Voice, No Hope, 2003, Knock and The Doors Shall Open, 2003, The Lord Forgave You, 2003, Never Judge A Book By Its Cover, 2003. Democrat. Avocations: Bible, writing.

RAMOS, PETER, religious studies educator, minister; b. New York, NY, Jan. 7, 1958; s. Pedro Ramos and Edith Silva; m. Maria Teresa Jimenez, July 26, 2003; m. Ivette Roman, June 28, 1979 (div.); children: Priscilla, Peter Jr., Pearl. Cert., Blanton-Peale Inst. of Religion, 1994—95; PhD, New Covenant U., 2001—03. Lic. Marriage Therapist Am. Assn. of Christian Counselors / Va., 2003. Pres. The Christian U., Paterson, NJ, 2003—; prof. Farleigh Dickinson Univ., Teaneck, NJ, 2003. Exec. dir. Inst. for Latino Studies, Paterson, NJ, 2001—; founder and dir. Youth Impact Ministries, 1987—95; prodr., host Radio Program, U.S. (East Coast), Carribean, Ctrl. and South Am., 1991—95. Author: (book) Matrimonio, Divorcio y Recasamiento: Que Dice la Biblia?, (manual) El Cuidado Pastoral en el Area del Matrimonio. Min. Paterson Christian Ctr., Paterson, NJ, 2003—04. Mem.: Am. Assn. of Christian Therapists (licentiate), Am. Assn. of Christian Counselors (licentiate). Christian. Office: The Christian University 553 Main Street - Suite 1 Paterson NJ 07011 Personal E-mail: drpeterramos@aol.com.

RAMOS, RAUL, surgeon; b. Sabinas, Coahulla, Mex., Oct. 30, 1942; s. Raul and Carmen (Lopez) R.; m. Hilda Muzquiz de Ramos, Mar. 1, 1992; children by previous marriage: Raul, Maria, Ana, Veronica. MD, U. Nuevo Leon, Mex., 1966. Diplomate Am. Bd. Surgery, Am. Bd. Colon and Rectal Surgery. Intern Bapt. Meml. Hosp., San Antonio, 1966-67, mem. active staff, chmn. dept. surgery, 1983-84, 89-90; clin. asst. prof. surgery U. Tex. Health Sci. Ctr., San Antonio, 1973-78, head divns. proctology, 1973—, clin. assoc. prof. surgery, 1978-89, dir. residency program colon and rectal surgery, 1979-82, clin. prof. surgery, 1989—. Mem. active staff Santa Rosa Med. Ctr., S.W. Tex. Meth. Hosp., Audie Murphy Meml. VA Hosp., San Antonio Humana Hosp., St. Luth's Luth. Hosp., Bexar County Hosp. Dist.; vis. prof. U. Nuevo Leon, Monterrey, Mex., 1976, 80, Assemblea Nacional de Cirjuanos, Mexico City, 1976, Mil. Med. Sch., Mexico City, 1980, 81, Socieda Mex. Cirjanos Puebla, 1990, Loyola Univ., 1992, U. Guanajuato, mex., 1992, Institutos Technologico Estudios Superiores en Monterrey, 1993; examiner Am. Bd. Surgery, 1990; presenter numerous seminars. Mem. AMA, ACS, Am. Soc. Colon and Rectal Surgeons (mem. coun. 1981-82), Tex. Med. Assn., Tex. Soc. Colon and Rectal Surgeons (pres. 1977, 78), Tex. Soc. Colo-Rectal Surgeons (sec. 1977)Associacion de Cirujanos de Noreste A.C., Sociedad Colombiana de Gastroenterologia, Sociedad Colombiana de Cirujanos de Colon y Recto, Sociedad Chilena de Cirugia, Sociedad Chilena de Proctologia, Sociedad mexicana de Cirjuanos de Colon y Recto, Collegium Internatcionale Chirurgia Digestivae, Internat. Soc. Univ. Colon and Rectal Surgeons, So. Med. Assn. (v.p. sect. colo-rectal surgery 1979, chmn. 1980, sec. 1981, 82, 83), Priestly Surg. Soc., Bexar County Med. Soc. (bd. dirs. 1990-92, chmn. exhibits com.), Gen. Surg. Soc. San Antonio (v.p. 1979, pres. 1980), Sociedad Medica Hispano-Americano de Tejas (sec. 1979, pres. 1986), San Antonio Surg. Soc. (pres. 1986-87), Aust Soc., Mayo Alumni. Avocations: tennis, golf, reading. Office: Colon and Rectal Assocs San Antonio 7950 Floyd Curl Dr Ste 101 San Antonio TX 78229-3916

RAMOS, ROSE MARY, elementary school educator; b. San Antonio, Aug. 8, 1942; d. Henry Barbosa and Bertha Alice (Cuellar) Gonzalez; m. Jesus Ramos Jr., Sept. 11, 1965; children: Rebecca Anne, Veronica Anne. BS in Elem. Edn., Our Lady of Lake U., San Antonio, 1965; MA in Edn., U. Houston, 1992. Cert. elem. educator, kindergarten, reading specialist, bilingual and ESL. Tchr. San Antonio (Tex.) Ind. Sch. Dist., 1965-89, Ft. Bend County Ind. Sch. Dist., 1989-2001, 2002—. Acad. adv. com. Ft. Bend I.S.D., 1996; sales cons. Mary Kay. Mem. Fort Bend Women's Tex. Dem. Party; charter mem., v.p. U.S. Congressman Henry B. Gonzalez Found. Mem. San Antonio Conservation Soc. Democrat. Roman Catholic. Avocations: reading, life sciences, writing. Home: 3614 Belle Grove Ln Sugar Land TX 77479-2257 E-mail: rmramos@houston.rr.com.

RAMOS-MOLL, ERVIN, career officer, federal agency administrator; b. Utuado, P.R., Apr. 4, 1947; s. Carlos Ramos and Balbina Moll; m. Ruth E. Ruiz-Aceuedo, June 6, 1972; children: Ervin, Jr., Carlos S., Mary M. BBA in Econs., InterAm. U., 1969, MBA in Mktg. Mgmt., 1974, MEd in Guidance, Counselling, 1976. Commd. 1st lt. U.S. Army, 1975, col., 1968—; mil. personnel supr. ROTC, RUM, Mayaguez, P.R., 1972-75; revenue officer IRS, Mayaguez, 1975-80, group mgr., 1980-86, Hato Rey, P.R., 1986-91, chief field br. Ft. Lauderdale, Fla., 1991-95, Miami, Fla., 1995-99, chief special procedures br. Ft. Lauderdale, Fla., 1999—, SBSE terr. mgr. Miami, Fla. Dep. chief staff logistics 65 ARCOM, Ft. Buchanan, P.R., 1995-97; commdr. 265th USARF Sch. Brigade, Caquas, P.R., 1997-99, asst. chief of staff 143rd TRANSCOM, Orlando, Fla. Recipient Bronze Star, 1970. Avocations: stamp collecting/philately, computers, electronics, science fiction. Office: IRS 51 SW 1st Ave Miami FL 33130 E-mail: ermoll@bellsouth.net, ervin.ramos@ml.irs.gov.

RAMPE, KEVIN M. real estate developer; m. Christine Rampe. BA cum laude, Union Coll.; JD magna cum laude, Albany U.; grad. in Sr. Exec. Program, Harvard U. Litig. assoc. Shearman & Stearling, 1992—96; first asst. counsel Gov. Pataki's Office, 1996—99; from dep. supt. and gen. counsel to first dep. supt. Ins. Dept. N.Y. State Ins. Dept., N.Y., 1999—2004, first dep. supt. Ins. Dept., 2004—. Office: Lower Manhattan Development Corp One Liberty Plaza 20th Fl New York NY 10006*

RAMPERSAD, PEGGY A. SNELLINGS, sociologist, consultant; b. Fredericksburg, Va., Jan. 12, 1933; d. George Daniel and Virginia Riley (Bowler) Snellings; m. Oliver Ronald Rampersad, Mar. 19, 1955; 1 child, Gita. BA, Mary Washington Coll., Fredericksburg, 1953; student, Sch. Art Inst. Chgo., 1953—55; MA, U. Chgo., 1965, PhD, 1978. Grad. admissions counselor U. Chgo., 1954-57, adviser to fgn. students, 1958, dir. admissions Grad. Sch. Bus., 1959-63, rsch. project specialist, 1970-78, pers. mgr., 1979-80, mgr. organizational devel., 1980-82, adminstr. dept. econs., 1983-95; cons. PSR Consulting, Chgo., 1995—. Cons. North Ctrl. Assn. Colls. and Secondary Schs., Chgo., 1964—70, Orchestral Assn. Chgo. Symphony Orch., 1982, Chgo. Ctr. Decision Rsch., 1982, Harvard U., 1993—97. Exhibitions include Va. Mus. Fine Arts, Art Inst. Chgo., others; editor: North Ctrl. Assn. Quar., 1972; contbr. articles to profl. jours. Grad. fellow, U. Chgo., 1963—67. Mem.: AAUW, Am. Acad. Polit. and Social Sci., Am. Econ. Assn., Art Inst. Chgo. (assoc.), Pi Lambda Theta (past pres.). Episcopalian. Avocations: painting and drawing, opera, reading, walking. Home and Office: 28 Seneca Ter Fredericksburg VA 22401-1115

RAMPHELE, MAMPHELA A. medical educator; MD, U. Natal, 1972; PhD in Social Anthropology, U. Cape Town; B in Adminstrn., U. South Africa; diploma in tropical health and hygiene and pub. health, U. Witwatersrand. Sr. rsch. officer U. Cape Town, South Africa, 1986—91, dep. vice chancellor, 1991—95, vice chancellor, 1996—2000; mng. dir. human devel. World Bank, Washington, 2000—. Immediate past chmn. bd. trustees Ind. Devel. Trust; adv. bd. World Bank Econ. Devel. Inst. Author: Across Boundaries; contbr. articles to profl. jours. Student activist Black Consciousness Movement. Recipient of numerous nat. and internat. awards including 17 hon. doctorates, awards for svc. to cmty. Mem.: Inst. of Medicine of NAS. Office: The World Bank 1818 H St NW Washington DC 20433

RAMPINO, MICHAEL ROBERT, earth and environmental science educator; b. N.Y.C., Feb. 8, 1948; s. Michael A. and Annette (Cohen) R. BA, Hunter Coll., 1968; PhD, Columbia U., 1978. Rsch. assoc. Goddard Inst. NASA, N.Y.C., 1978-85; asst. prof. NYU, 1985-91, assoc. prof. dept. biology, earth and environ. sci. program, 1991—. Rsch. cons. NASA Goddard Inst. for Space Studies, N.Y.C., 1985—; cons. Discovery Channel, 1995—, Readers Digest, 1985—, Planetary Soc., 1996—, BBC, 1996—, York Films, Eng., 1997, PBS, 1993, ON Comm. TV, 1997—, Psudo NET-TV, 1999—, Pioneer Prodns., 2004; vis. prof. NYU, Florence, Italy, 1999, 2001, 2003, Yamaguchi U., Japan, 2000, U. Vienna, 2002, U. Urbino, Italy, 2003. Author: Evolution of the Universe, 2004; editor: Climate: History, Periodicity and Predictability, 1987, Debates About the Earth, 1996; co-editor: Encyclopedia of Earth Sciences, 1998—; editor-in-chief: Earth Science Encyclopedia Online; mem. editl. bd. Jour. Coastal Rsch., Jour. Earth Sys. Sci. Edn.; contbr. articles to profl. jours. Mem. Internat. Assn. Volcanology, Nat. Assn. Geosci. Tchrs., Am. Geophys. Union, Geol. Soc. Am., Meteoritical Soc., Internat. Soc. Study Origins of Life, N.Y. Acad. Scis. (chair geol. scis. sect. 1990-91), Sigma Xi. Achievements include developer of galactic theory of periodic comet impacts and mass extinctions; research in planetary sci., impact centers, geologic boundaries, climate change and volcanic eruptions. Home: 110 Bleecker St Apt 26F New York NY 10012-2107 Office: Earth and Environ Sci Program NYU 100 Washington Sq E New York NY 10003-6688 Office Phone: 212-998-3743. E-mail: mrr1@nyu.edu.

RAMSAUR, ALLAN FIELDS, lawyer, lobbyist; b. Rocky Mount, NC, Dec. 30, 1951; s. Carl Hamilton and Celestine (Fields) R.; m. Jimmie Lynn Brewer, Sept. 2, 1972; children: Katherine Celeste, Benjamin Allan. BA in Polit. Sci., Lambuth U., 1974; JD, U. Tenn., 1977. Bar: Tenn. 1977. Staff atty. Tenn. Dept. Mental Health, Nashville, 1977-80; dir. Tenn. Assn. Legal Services, Nashville, 1980-86; campaign dir. Steve Cobb, Nashville, 1986; exec. dir. Nashville Bar Assn., 1986-98, Tenn. Bar Assn., 1999—. Pres. Woodland-in-Waverly Neighborhood Assn., Nashville, 1985; bd. dirs. SAGA, Nashville, 1984-86, Bethlehem Center, Nashville, 1990-96 (sec. 1992, v.p. 1994-95). Recipient Leadership Nashville award, 1988. Mem. ABA (liaison to standing com. on legal aid and indigent defendants 1984-86, spl. com. on prepaid legal svcs. 1988-89, standing com. on lawyer referral and info. svc. 1990-92), Nat. Assn. Bar Execs. (chair edn. com.), Tenn. Bar Assn. (pres. young lawyers divsn. 1985-86), Nat. Legal Aid and Defender Assn. (chmn. legis com. 1984-86), Tenn. Soc. Assn. Execs. (pres. 2000). Democrat. Methodist. Home: 1417 Beddington Park Nashville TN 37215-5815 Office Phone: 615-383-7421. Business E-Mail: aramsaur@tnbar.org.

RAMSAY, DAVID LESLIE, physician, dermatologist, medical educator; b. Rochester, N.Y., Apr. 25, 1943; s. Joseph Walter and Jean (Eastwood) R. AB in English with honors, Ind. U., 1965, MD, 1969; MEd, U. Ill., 1973. Diplomate Am. Bd. Dermatology. Assoc. faculty mem. Ind. U., Indpls., 1965-69; intern in medicine George Washington U. Med. Ctr., 1969-70; resident in dermatology NYU Med. Ctr., 1970-73; dir. dermatology residency tng. Nat. Naval Med. Ctr., Bethesda, Md., 1973-75; asst. prof. medicine Georgetown U., Washington, 1974-75; asst. prof. dermatology NYU, 1974-78, assoc. prof. dermatology, 1978-95, prof. dermatology, 1995—2003, clin. prof. dermatology, 2003—, senator, 1986-94, pres. faculty coun., 1988-90, dir. ednl. affairs dermatology, 1975—, dir. cutaneous lymphoma sect., 1975—. Author: Simulations in Dermatology, 1974; contbg. author: Adolescent Dermatology, Basic Mechanisms of Physiologic and Aberrant Lymphoproliferation in the Skin, Hematology and Oncology Clinics in North America; sr. editor: Jour. of Drugs in Dermatology, 2003-; contbr. more than 25 articles to profl. jours. Pres., bd. dirs. One Fifth Ave. Apt. Corp., N.Y.C., 1978-80; trustee Bklyn. Acad. Music, 1989—. Lt. comdr. USN, 1973-75. NIH fellow U. Ill., 1972-73. Fellow ACP, Internat. Soc. Cutaneous Lymphomas, Am. Acad. Dermatology; mem. Am. Dermatologic Assn. Roman Catholic. Avocations: collecting visual art, swimming, reading. Home: One Fifth Ave New York NY 10003 Office: NYU Med Ctr 530 5th Ave New York NY 10036-5101

RAMSAY, DONALD ALLAN, physical chemist; b. London, July 11, 1922; s. Norman and Thirza Elizabeth (Beckley) Ramsay; m. Nancy Brayshaw, June 8, 1946 (dec. July 25, 1998); children: Shirley Margaret, Wendy Kathleen, Catharine Jean, Linda Mary; m. Marjorie Craven Findlay, Apr. 13, 2000. BA, Cambridge (Eng.) U., 1943, MA, PhD, Cambridge (Eng.) U., 1947, ScD, 1976; D honoris causa, U. Reims, France, 1969; Filosofie hedersdoktor, U. Stockholm, Sweden, 1982. With divsn. chemistry Nat. Rsch. Coun. Can., Ottawa, 1947-49, with divsn. physics, 1949-75; with Herzberg Inst. Astrophysics, 1975-87, sr. research officer, 1961-68, prin. research officer, 1968-87, guest worker, 1987—2001, Steacie Inst. Molecular Scis., rschr. emeritus, 2002—. Vis. prof. U. Minn., 1964, U. Orsay, 1966, U. Stockholm, 1967, 71, 74, U. Calif., Irvine, 1970, U. Sao Paulo, 1972, 78, U. Bologna (Italy), 1973, U. We. Australia, 1976, Australian Nat. U., 1976, East China Normal U., Shanghai, 1987, Tex. Christian U., 1988, U. Wuppertal, Germany, 1988, U. Canterbury, Christchurch, New Zealand, 1991, 96, U. Ulm, Germany, 1992, Germany, 96, Germany, 97. Editor: (with J. Hinze) Selected Works of Robert S. Mulliken, 1975; contbr. numerous articles on molecular spectra and molecular structure to profl. jours. Recipient commemorative medal for 125th anniversary Confederation Can., 1992, Alexander von Humboldt Rsch. award, 1993-95; decorated Queen Elizabeth Silver Jubilee medal. Fellow: Chem. Inst. Can. (Chem. Inst. Can. medal 1992), Am. Phys. Soc., Royal Soc. London, Royal Soc. Can. (life; treas. 1976—79, 1988—91, Centennial medal 1982); mem.: Order of Can. Mem. United Ch. of Canada (organist 1954-97). Club: Leander (Henley-on-Thames, Eng.). Home: 400 Laurier Ave E Apt 11 Ottawa ON Canada K1N 8Y2 Office: Nat Rsch Coun 100 Sussex Dr Ottawa ON Canada K1A 0R6 E-mail: donald.ramsay@nrc.ca.

RAMSAY, GUSTAVUS REMAK, actor; b. Balt., Feb. 2, 1937; s. John Breckinridge and Caroline V. (Remak) R. BA, Princeton U., 1958. Appeared in plays Hang Down Your Head and Die, 1964, Half A Sixpence, 1965, Lovely Ladies, Kind Gentlemen, Sheep on the Runway, 1970, On the Town, 1971, The Real Inspector Hound, After Magritte, 1972, Jumpers, 1974, Private Lives, 1975, Landscape of the Body, Dirty Linen, 1977, The Rear Column, 1978, All's Well That Ends Well, 1978, Every Good Boy Deserves Favor, 1980, Save Grand Central, 1980, The Winslow Boy, 1980-81, The Dining Room, 1982, as St. John Quartermaine in Quartermaine's Terms, 1983— (Obie award), Woman in Mind, 1988, The Devil's Disciple, 1988, Love Letters, 1989, Prin, 1990, Nick & Nora, 1991, St. Joan, 1993, The Moliere Comedies, 1995, The Heiress, 1995, Misalliance, 1997, Thief River, 2001; appeared in movies The Tiger Makes Out, The Stepford Wives, The Great Gatsby, The Front, Class, Simon, The House on Carroll Street, Mr. and Mrs. Bridge, Shadows and Fog, King of the Hill, Addicted to Love, Fever, 1998; TV movies The Dining Room, Heartbreak House, Kennedy, Liberty, Concealed Enemies, Dream House, Mellon, Lincoln and Seward, Dead Ahead: The Exxon Valdez Disaster, Truman. With U.S. Army, 1959-62. Democrat. Presbyterian. Home: 115 Central Park W New York NY 10023-4153

RAMSAY, KARIN KINSEY, publisher, educator; b. Brownwood, Tex., Aug. 10, 1930; d. Kirby Luther and Ina Rebecca (Wood) Kinsey; m. Jack Cummins Ramsay Jr., Aug. 31, 1951; children: Annetta Jean, Robin Andrew. BA, Trinity U., 1951. Cert. assoc. ch. edn., 1980. Youth coord. Covenant Presbyn. Ch., Carrollton, Tex., 1961-76; dir. ch. edn. Northminster Presbyn. Ch., Dallas, 1976-80, Univ. Presbyn. Ch., Chapel Hill, N.C., 1987-90, Oak Grove Presbyn. Ch., Bloomington, Minn., 1990-93; coord. ecum. ministry Flood Relief for Iowa, Des Moines, 1993; program coord. 1st Presbyn. Ch., Green Bay, Wis., 1994-95; owner, sole proprietor Hist. Resources Press, Corinth and Denton, Tex., 1994—. Dir. Godspell tour Covenant Presbyn. Ch., 1972-75; mem. Presbytery Candidates Com., Dallas, 1977-82, Presbytery Exams. Com. Dallas, 1979-81; clk. coun. New Hope Presbytery, Rocky Mount, N.C., 1989-90; creator, dir. Thee Holy Fools mime/musical group and This Is Me retreats. Author: Ramsay's Resources, 1983—; pub., editor: Patton's Ill-Fated Raid, 2002, Angel Kisses, 2004, My Beating Heart, 2004; contbr. articles to jours. in field. Design cons. Brookhaven Hosp. Chapel, Dallas, 1977-78; elder Presbyn. Ch. U.S.A., 1982—; coord. Lifeline Emergency Response, Dallas, 1982-84. Mem. Internat. Platform Assn., Small Publisher's Assn. of N. Am.,Pub. Marketing Assoc., Writer's League of Tex. Office Phone: 940-321-1066. *Yesterday taught me the lessons which made today possible. Today is the challenging link between yesterday and tomorrow. Tomorrow is an opportunity built on the foundation of today. Today is special.*

RAMSAY, LINDA, architect; Grad., Clemson U., Ga. Inst. Tech. Prin. Ramsay Sherrill Arch., Savannah, Ga., 1985—. Chair Hist. Dist. Bd. Rev., Savannah, Ga. Fellow: AIA (pres.). Office: Ramsay Sherrill Arch 221 E York St Savannah GA 31401

RAMSAY, MICHAEL, information technology executive; BSEE, U. Edinburgh, Scotland. Sr. v.p. silicon Desktop Group Silicon Graphics, Inc., 1996—97; pres. TiVo Inc., Alviso, Calif., 1997—, CEO, 1997—, chmn. bd., 1997—. Bd. dir. Netflix. Office: TiVo Inc 2160 Gold St Alviso CA 95002-2160

RAMSAY, MICHAEL ANTHONY, anesthesiologist; b. Dublin, Feb. 5, 1945; came to U.S., 1976; MD, U. London, 1968. Diplomate Am. Bd. Anesthesiology. Intern London Hosp., 1968-69, resident in anesthesiology, 1969-70, 71-72, Northampton Gen. Hosp., 1970-71; fellow in pediat. anesthesiology Hosp. for Sick Children, London, 1972-74; cons. anesthesiologist London Hosp., 1974-76; attending staff Baylor U. Med. Ctr., Dallas, 1976-88, chief anesthesiology, 1988—2004; clin. prof. U. Tex. S.W. Med. Sch., 1989—2004; pres. Baylor Rsch. Inst., 2000—04. Mem.: AMA, Inst. Anethesia Rsch. Soc., Am. Soc. of Transplanation, Liver Transplant Soc., Am. Soc. of Anesthesia Inst., Dallas County Medical Soc., Dallas County Anesthesiology Soc. Home: 7135 Elmridge Dr Dallas TX 75240 Office: Baylor Univ Med Ctr 2nd Flr Roberts Hosp 3500 Gaston Ave Dallas TX 75246

RAMSAY, WILLIAM CHARLES, writer, composer; b. N.Y.C., Nov. 6, 1930; s. Claude Barnett and Myrtle Marie (Scott) Ramsay; m. Jane Coutant Evans, July 7, 1997; children from previous marriage: Alice, John, Carol Ramsay Scott, David. BA in English Lit., U. Colo., 1952; MA in Physics, UCLA, 1957, PhD in Physics, 1962. NFS postdoctoral fellow U. Calif., San Diego, 1962-64, asst. prof. Santa Barbara, 1964-67; tech. mgr. Sys. Assocs., Inc., Long Beach, Calif., 1967-72; sr. environ. economist U.S. AEC, Bethesda, Md., 1972-75; tech. adviser U.S. Nuc. Regulatory Agy., Washington, 1975-76; sr. fellow Resources for the Future, Washington, 1976-83, Ctr. Strategic and Internat. Studies, Washington, 1983-85; sr. staff officer NAS, Washington, 1985-86; freelance writer, editor, publ. Washington, Santa Barbara, 1986—. Cons. Vols. Tech. Assistance, Arlington, Va., 1987—90, Arlington, 1998—. Internat. Resources Group, Washington, 1991. Author: (book) Unpaid Costs of Electrical Energy, 1979, Bioenergy and Economic Development, 1985, (plays) Agamemnon, 2000; co-author: (book) Managing the Environment, 1972, Energy in America's Future, 1979; composer: Glory Road, 2003, The Hawk, Genesis, Spring Dawn. Bd. dirs. Santa Barbara Symphony. Buenos Aires Conv. fellow, 1952, NSF fellow, 1962, NATO scholar, 1960, 1962. Mem.: Internat. Assn. Energy Economists, Am. Astron. Soc., Am. Phys. Soc. Avocation: piano. Home and Office: 115 Summit Ln Santa Barbara CA 93108-2323

RAMSBY, MARK DELIVAN, lighting designer and consultant; b. Portland, Oreg., Nov. 20, 1947; s. Marshall Delivan and Verna Pansy (Culver) R.; married; children: Aaron Delivan, Venessa Mercedes. Student, Portland (Oreg.) State U., 1966-67. With C.E.D., Portland, 1970-75; minority ptnr. The Light Source, Portland, 1975-78, pres., 1978-87; prin. Illume Lighting Design, Portland, 1987-90; ptnr. Ramsby, Dupuy & Seats, Inc., Portland, 1990-91; dir. lighting design PAE Cons. Engrs., Inc., Portland, 1991—. Pvt. practice cons. Portland, 1979—. Recipient Top 100 Outstanding Achievement award Metalux Lighting, 1981-85, 100% award, 1985, Edwin F. Guth award of merit, 1990, 95, 96, 99, 2001, Edison award of excellence, 1990, Edwin F. Guth award of excellence, 1993, 94, Paul Waterbury award of Merit, 1995. Mem. Illuminating Engring. Soc. Am. (sec.-treas. Oreg. sect. 1978-79, Oreg. sect. pres. 2002—, Oreg. Section and Regional and Internat. awards 1989, 90, 93, 94, Lighting Design awards), Internat. Assn. Lighting Designers. Lutheran. Avocations: lighting design, historical restoration, flyfishing, downhill skiing. Office: PAE Cons Engrs 808 SW 3d Ave Ste 300 Portland OR 97204-2426

RAMSDELL, BRUCE D. music educator; b. Winona, Minn., 1956; s. H. James and Claran Ramsdell; m. Carol J. Ramsdell. BA, Winona State U., 1974—77; MA, U. of Iowa, 1982. Cert. tchr. Minn. State Bd. Edn. Music tchr. Crestwood Jr. H.S., Cresco, 1977—80; choir dir. Crestwood Sr. H.S., 1980—83, Hempstead Sr. H.S., Dubuque, 1983—86, Winona Sr. H.S., 1986—. Dir. Pavan, Winchester, Va., 1986—97, spkr. Edn. Minn., St. Paul, 2000—; tchr. edn. partnership Winona State U., 2001—. Bd. mem. Winona Symphony Assn., 1987—96, Winona Cmty. Theater, 1988—2000. Recipient Tchr. of Yr, Winona Edn. Assn., 1999 and 1992, Minn. Tchr.-Honor Roll, Edn. Minn., 1999, Minn. Tchr. of Excellence, 1999. Mem.: Music Edn. Nat. Conf., Am. Chora Directors Assn., NEA. Avocations: genealogy, travel. Office: Winona Senior School 901 Gilmore Ave Winona MN 55987

RAMSDEN, WILLA OLDHAM, retired organization executive, columnist, historian, consultant; b. San Diego, Nov. 27, 1911; d. William Henry Stillwell and Martha Ellen Estell; m. Clifton John Oldham (dec. Feb. 1984); m. Percy Herbert Ramsden (dec. Oct. 1993). Field dir. Girl Scout Coun., San Diego, 1934—39, asst. exec., 1945—49, exec. dir. Fresno, Calif., 1939—41, San Jose, Calif., 1942—44, Riverside, Calif., 1949—56; ret., 1956; self-employed feature writer, columnist, 1957—59; feature writer, columnist Boulder City, Nev., 1960—69, Carson City, Nev., 1970—; staff substitute City of Carson City, 1974—92, cons. pers., adminstrn., orgn., 1974—. Spkr. various civic and svc. clubs, schs., Nev., 1960—2001, Hannah Clapp Lecture Series, Carson City, 1999—2000; mem. panel Landmark Soc. series, Carson City, 2001; pres. Region XII Girl Scout Profls.; nat. bd. dirs. Girl Scout Profls. Contbr. over 500 articles to profl. jours., mags. and newspapers; weekly columnist: Mayor of Boulder City, Nev., 1963—64; author: Carson-Tahoe Hospital: The Story of a Caring Community, 1987, Carson City - Nevada's Capital City, 1991; Represented in permanent collections Getchell Libr. U. Nev. Active Nev. State Mus., Carson City, 1972—; organizer Appaloosa Club Clark County, Las Vegas, 1960; docent Nev. State Mus., Carson City, 1972—75; mem. bicentennial commn. Carson City Centennial, 1974—78; mem. organizing com. Friends in Svc. Helping, Carson City, 1977; chmn. All Carson City Ch. Women Leadership Conf., 1978, Western Nev. Sr. Conf., Carson City, 1985; promotion staff for bd. suprs. Marriage Bur., 1991; mem. planning com. Nev. Women's Project, 1997—98; sustaining mem. Rep. Nat. Com., Washington, 1970—2002; mem. Rep. Presdl. Task Force; mem. election bd. Riverside, 1956—59, Carson City, 1971—72; chmn. election bd., 1973—81; dep. election bd., 1982—92; active local Rep. campaigns; bd. deacons 1st Presbyn. Ch., Carson City, 1978—80, chair, 1979—80, 1986—88, organizer sr. Serving Others Loving Others program, deacon, 1978, founder sr. assistance program, 1982, chair social action com., 1982. Nominee Nev. Woman of Yr., 1970; named Hon. Life mem., Nat. Presbyn. Ch. USA, 1976; recipient Thanks badge, Nat. Bd. Girl Scouts U.S., 1957, cert. of appreciation, Nat. Appaloosa Horse Club, 1960, commendation cert., Carson City Centennial/U.S. Bicentennial Commn., City of Carson City, 1979, Ad hoc Recreational Vehicle Com, City of Carson City, 1987. Mem.: Rep. Presdl. Task Force, Heritage Found. Presbyterian. Avocations: gourmet food study, classical music, travel, reading, computer contacts.

RAMSER, WANDA TENE, library and information scientist, educator; b. Atlanta, June 4, 1951; d. Galen Eugene Ramser and Christine Elizabeth Owen; children: Catherine Nicole Hannabach, David Richmond Hannabach. BA in History with honors, U. Calif., Santa Barbara, 1973; MLIS with honors, UCLA, 1976, MA in Latin Am. Studies, 1977. With UCLA Latin Am. Ctr., 1973—78; literacy coord. County of Los Angeles Libr., 1978—83; assoc. faculty South Orange County C.C. Dist., Mission Viejo, Calif., 1986; libr. youth svcs. County Orange, Calif., 1986—87; libr. City of San Diego Libr., 1993—2001, City of Oceanside, Calif., 2001—. Pres. San Diego chpt. Svcs. to Latinos/REFORMA; bd. dirs. UCLA Club San Diego, Palomar Coll. Libr. Tech. Bd. Active Chicano Fedn. San Diego County, 1993—, Chicano Pk./Barrio Sta. San Diego, 1993—; mem. spkr.'s bur. City of Hope Nat. Cancer Ctr., 2000—. Mem.: AAUW, ALA, Calif. Libr. Assn., City San Diego Latino Employees Assn. (bd. dirs.). Address: PO Box 1484 Beverly Hills CA 90213-1484

RAMSEUR, T. MICHAEL, social worker; b. Princeton, N.J., Aug. 18, 1947; s. Thomas Michael and Suzanne T. Ramseur; life ptnr. Annette D. N/A; 1 child, Georgia Anne Bennett-Ramseur. Degree, Trinity Coll., Hartford, Conn., 1970; MSW, Simmons Sch. of Social Work, Boston, 1991. LCSW Mass., 1993. Dir. of social svcs. Baldpate Hosp., Georgetown, Mass., 1999—. Illustration in The New Yorker, Picture for Strange Love, flash films, Vortex and The Ghost of the Witch Judge; author: The Eye of Danvers, 2004, (CD) The Haunted Palace, 2004. Mem.: NASW (assoc.). Home: 11 Riverside Dr Newbury MA 01951 Office: Baldpate Hospital 83 Baldpate Road Georgetown MA 01833 Office Phone: 978-352-2131. Office Fax: 978-352-6755. Personal E-mail: mramseur@yahoo.com.

RAMSEY, CATHERINE LOUISE, secondary school educator, horse trainer; b. Rahway, NJ, July 14, 1945; d. Hugo George and Ida Marie Bischoff; 1 child, Edward H. Schremp. BA, Douglass Coll., New Brunswick, NJ, 1963—67; MA, Tenn. Tech. U., Cookeville, 1983. Cert. TW Career Ladder II. Tchr. Crossroads Sch., South Brunswick, NJ, 1967—77, Payson Mid. Sch., Ariz., 1978, Jackson County HS, Gainesboro, Tenn., 1978—2004. Adj. Tenn. Tech. U., Cookeville, 1987—91, Vol. State Cmty. Coll., Livingston, Tenn., 1992—2004. Mem.: NEA, Tenn. Edn. Assn. Avocations: horse training, trail riding. Home: 2330 Hilham Highway 85 Livingston TN 38570 Office: Jackson County High School 190 Blue Devil Lane Gainesboro TN 38562 Office Phone: 931-268-2334.

RAMSEY, CHARLES EUGENE, sociologist, educator; b. Paragon, Ind., Apr. 24, 1923; s. Sarcefield Dodson and Stella (Goss) R.; m. Alberta Mae Jordan, July 19, 1943; children— James D., Charles W., Jane E., Suzanne. BS, Ind. State Tchrs. Coll., 1947; MS, U. Wis., 1950, PhD, 1952. Faculty U. Wis., 1951-52, U. Minn., 1952-54, Cornell U., 1954-62, Colo. State U., 1962-65; prof. sociology U. Minn., Mpls., 1965-77; chmn. dept. sociology U. Tex., Arlington, 1977-83. Vis. prof. Inter-Am. Instn. Agrl. Sci., Costa Rica, 1961, Exptl. Sta., U. P.R., 1961-62; research cons. to various univs., agys. Author: (with Lowry Nelson and Cooley Verner) Community Structure and Change, 1960, (with David Gottlieb) The American Adolescent, 1965, Understanding the Deprived Child, S.R.A, 1967, Problems of Youth, 1967, (with D.J. McCarty) The School Managers: Power and Conflict in American Public Education, 1971, (with William A. Stacey) Social Statistics, 1992; also articles. Achievements include developing and testing theory of variations in community power structure, types of sch. bds., and roles of sch. supt., developed method of comparative measurement of level of living for different countries. Home: 1102 De Pauw Dr Arlington TX 76012-5339 Office: U Tex Dept Sociology Arlington TX 76004

RAMSEY, CHARLES H. police chief; B in Criminal Justice, M in Criminal Justice, Lewis U.; grad., FBI Nat. Acad., Nat. Exec. Inst. Cadet Chgo. Police Dept., 1968, police officer, 1971, promoted through the to commdr. of patrol, detectives and narcotics units, dept. supt. bur. staff svcs., 1994; chief police Met. Police Dept., Washington, 1998—. Spkr. in field; adj. faculty mem. Northwestern U. Traffic Inst. Sch. Police and Command, Lewis U. Recipient Gary P. Hayes award, Police Exec. Rsch. Forum, 1994, Robert Lamb Humanitarian award, Nat. Orgn. Black Law Enforcement Exec., 2001, Civil Rights award, Internat. Assn. Chiefs of Police, 2001. Office: Govt of DC John A Wilson Bldg 1350 Pennsylvania Ave NW Washington DC 20004

RAMSEY, DAVID SELMER, retired health facility administrator; b. Mpls., Feb. 19, 1931; s. Selmer A. and Esther D. (Dahl) R.; m. Betty Seiler, May 15, 1953; children— Scott, Stewart, Thomas BS, U. Mich., 1953, MS in Microbiology, 1954, M.H.A., 1962. Research asst. Detroit Inst. Cancer Research, 1954-60; asst. adminstr. Harper Hosp., Detroit, 1962-68, assoc. adminstr., 1968-72; exec. v.p. Iowa Meth. Med. Ctr., Des Moines, 1972-83, pres., 1983-93, Iowa Health Sys., 1993-95, Fine Wood Designs, 1996—. Avocations: golf, tennis, photography. Home: 25213 N Quail Haven Dr Rio Verde AZ 85263-7108

RAMSEY, FORREST GLADSTONE, JR., retired engineering company executive; b. Wichita, Kans., Oct. 25, 1930; s. Forrest Gladstone and Anastasia Ruth (Linot) R.; m. Gwendolyn Moreton, June 22, 1953 (div. Jan. 1982); children: Deborah Jenkins, Rebecca Johnson, Susan Klopp, Diane Hayes, Forrest G. III, Mark, Kenneth; m. Carmen Bergen, Apr. 30, 1988. BS in Engring., U.S. Naval Acad., 1952, postgrad., Wichita State U., 1957-58, U. Colo., 1958-64. Commd. ensign USN, 1952, res., 1957; planner, engr. Boeing Corp., Wichita, Kans., 1957-58; engr., logistician Martin-Marietta, Denver, 1959-65; div. dir. Computer Scis., Washington, 1965-73; program dir. Systems Cons., Washington, 1973-76; CEO Am. Sys. Corp., Washington, 1976-92, chmn., bd. dirs., 1992-97; ret., 1997. Mem. Profl. Svcs. Coun. (vice chmn. 1990), Naval Submarine League (bd. dirs. 1982-90). Roman Catholic. Home: 1700 Stony Brook Rd Bedford VA 24523 E-mail: forrest.ramsey@1952.usna.com.

RAMSEY, FRANK ALLEN, veterinarian, retired army officer; b. Rocksprings, Tex., May 1, 1929; s. Reynolds Allen and June (Burdette) R.; m. Lucette C. Reboul, Jan. 1958; children: Randal R., Ramsay A.; m. 2d, Mary Lou Cain, June 1991. D.V.M., Tex. A & M U., 1954; grad., U.S. Army Command and Gen. Staff Coll., 1965, U.S. Army War Coll., 1972. Commd. 1st. lt. U.S. Army Vet. Corps, 1955, advanced through grades to brig. gen., 1980; chief vet. service Ft. Leonard Wood, Mo., 1958-61; acad. vet. U.S. Mil. Acad., West Point, N.Y., 1962-64; vet. staff officer U.S. Army Combat Devel. Command Med. Service, Ft. Sam Houston, Tex., 1965-67; asst. chief profl. programming and planning br. Office Surgeon Gen., Washington, 1967-68, chief profl. programming and planning br., 1968-71, chief food inspection policy office, 1972-73, sr. vet. staff officer, 1973-77; asst. chief of staff Vet. Service, 7th Med. Command, Army Europe and 7th Army, Heidelberg, W. Ger., 1977-80; asst. for vet. services to surgeon gen. and chief U.S. Army Vet. Corps, Hdqrs. Dept. Army, Washington, 1980-85; ret., 1985. Decorated Army Commendation medal, Legion of Merit with oak leaf cluster, D.S.M. Mem. AVMA, Assn. Fed. Veterinarians, Assn. Mil. Surgeons U.S., Assn. Equine Practitioners, Am. Assn. Food Hygiene Veterinarians, Conf. Pub. Health Veterinarians, Tex. Vet. Med. Assn. Lodges: Masons (32 degree). Presbyterian. Home: 8 El Norte Cir Uvalde TX 78801-4021

RAMSEY, INEZ LINN, librarian, educator; b. Martins Ferry, Ohio, Mar. 25, 1938; d. George and Leona (Smith) Linn; m. Jackson Eugene Ramsey, Apr. 22, 1961; children: John Earl, James Leonard. BA in History, SUNY, Buffalo, 1971, MLS, 1972; EdD in Audiovisual Edn., U. Va., 1980. Libr. Iroquois Ctrl. H.S., Elma, N.Y., 1971-73, Lucy Simms Elem. Sch., Harrisonburg, Va., 1973-75; instr. James Madison U., Harrisonburg, 1975-80, asst. prof., 1980-85, assoc. prof., 1985-91, prof., 1991-98; ret., 1998. Mem. Va. State Library Bd., Richmond, 1975-80; cons. in field. Author: (with Jackson E. Ramsey) Budgeting Basics, Library Planning and Budgeti;g; contbr. to Ency., articles to profl. jours.; project developer Internet Sch. Libr. Media Ctr.; project dir. Oral (tape) History Black Community in Harrisonburg, 1977-78; storyteller, puppeteer. Recipient Pierian Press's Libr. Hi Tech (periodical) award, 1998; rsch. grantee James Madison U., Harrisonburg, 1981, Commonwealth Ctr. State Va., 1989. Mem. ALA, Am. Assn. Sch. Librs., Assn. Edn. Comm. Tech. (exec. bd. DSMS 1989-98, DSMT Meritorious Svc. award 1998), Va. Ednl. Media Assn. (sec. 1981-83, citation 1983, pres. 1985-86, Educator of Yr. award 1984-85, Meritorious Svc. award 1987-88), Phi Beta Kappa (pres. Shenandoah chpt. 1980-81), Beta Phi Mu, Phi Delta Kappa. Home: 3215 S Torrey Pines Dr Las Vegas NV 89146-6529

RAMSEY, IRA CLAYTON, retired pipeline company executive; b. Quitman, Ga., May 13, 1931; s. James Redding and Ruth Frances (Treadaway) R.; m. Marianne Vinzant, Dec. 23, 1962; children: Clayton Hamilton, Robin Leigh. BBA, U. Ga., Atlanta, 1954; LLB, Atlanta Law Sch., 1950; postgrad., U. Tex., 1968, U. Pitts., 1973. With Plantation Pipe Line Co., Atlanta, 1948-96, asst. sec., 1967-70, treas., contr., 1970-90, v.p. fin., 1990-96. Life trustee Ga. Found. for Ind. Colls.; chmn. bd. trustees KingsBridge Retirement Ctr., Inc. Baptist. Home: 780 Wesley Oak Rd NW Atlanta GA 30328-4738

RAMSEY, JANET LOUISE, public health service officer; d. Frank Leslie Huston and Eunice Fern Huston(Maiden: Rife); m. Bill Gene Ramsey, Aug. 1, 1958; children: Anthony Lee, Gary Dean. Adminstrv. asst. Clark County Health Dept, Kahoka, Mo., 1968—2001, adminstr., 2001—. Singer (songwriter) country songs. Co-founder, charter mem. County Assn. Recreation, Kahoka, 1990—2002; leader Boy Scouts Am., 1989; active PTO; Sunday sch. tchr., Bible sch music dir., choir. Mem.: Tuesday Club (assoc.; sec. 2003—04). Avocations: poetry, travel.

RAMSEY, JAROLD WILLIAM, English language educator, author; b. Bend, Oreg., Sept. 1, 1937; s. Augustus S. and Wilma E. (Mendenhall) R.; m. Dorothy Ann Quinn, Aug. 16, 1959; children: Kate, Sophia, John. BA with honors, U. Oreg., 1959; Ph. D., U. Wash., 1966. Acting instr. U. Wash., Seattle, 1963-65; asst. prof. English U. Rochester, (N.Y.), 1965-70, assoc. prof., 1970-81, prof., 1981-97; prof. emeritus, 1997—; dir. undergrad. rsch. U. Rochester, (N.Y.), 1990-96. Vis. prof. English U. Victoria, B.C., Can., 1974, 75-76; dir. NEH summer seminars on Indian lit., 1985, 88. Author: The Space Between Us, 1970, Love in an Earthquake, 1973 (Lillian Fairchild award 1973), Dermographia, 1982, Reading the Fire, 1983, rev. edit., 1999, Hand-shadows, 1989, (play) Coyote Goes Upriver, premier 1985, (cantata) (with Samuel Adler) The Lodge of Shadows, premiere 1988; editor: Coyote Was Going There, 1977, Nehalem Tillamook Tales, 1990, The Stories We Tell: Oregon Folk Literature (with Suzi Jones), 1994, New Era: Reflections on the Human and Natural History of Central Oregon, 2003. Recipient Don Walker award Western Am. Lit., 1979, Borestone Mount Found. Best Poems award, 1972, 75, 76; Helen Bullis prize, 1984, Poetry prize Quar. Rev., 1989; Alumni Achievement award U. Oreg. Alumni Assn, 1990; Nat. Endowment Arts writing grantee, 1974, 76; Ingram Merrill Found. writing grantee, 1976 Mem. MLA (chair com. on lits. and langs. of Am. 1991-92), Assn. Study Am. Indian Lit. (pres. 1981), Am. Folklore Soc., Phi Beta Kappa Democrat. Home: 5884 NW Highway 26 Madras OR 97741-9543 E-mail: jwr1937@madras.net.

RAMSEY, JOANNE MARIE, financial services representative; d. Erwin P. and Erna M. (Green) Forrest; 1 child, Cheryl. BS, Monmouth Coll., 1967; MS, Stevens Inst. Tech., 1971. Mem. tech. staff Bell Telephone Labs., Holmdel, N.J., 1967-71; programmer analyst Cooper Electric Supply Co., Middletown, N.J., 1971-73; sr. programmer Insco Systems Corp., Neptune, N.J., 1973-78; sr. programmer analyst Internat. Flavors and Fragrances, Hazlet, N.J., 1978-79; mgr. Bristol-Myers Squibb Co., Plainsboro, NJ, 1980—2002, Primerica Fin. Svcs., NJ, 2002—, sr. fin. svcs. rep., 2002—. Mem. NAFE, AAUW, Am. Prodn. and Inventory Control Soc., N.J. Assn. Women Bus. Owners. E-mail: jmramsey4@comcast.net.

RAMSEY, JOHN ARTHUR, lawyer; b. Apr. 1, 1942; s. Wilbert Lewis and Lillian (Anderson) R.; m. Nikki Ann Ramsey, Feb. 9, 1943; children: John William, Bret Anderson, Heather Nicole. AB, San Diego State U., 1965; JD, Calif. Western Sch. Law, 1969. Bar: Colo. 1969, Tex. 1978. Assoc. Henry, Cockrell, Quinn & Creighton, 1969-72; atty. Texaco Inc., 1972-80; asst. to pres. Texaco U.S.A., 1980-81, asst. to divsn. v.p., 1981-82, divsn. atty. Denver, 1982-88; ptnr. Holland & Hart, 1989—. Editor-in-chief: Calif. Western Law Rev., 1969. Bd. dirs. Selective Svc., Englewood, Colo., 1972-76; chmn. coun. Bethany Luth. Ch., Englewood, 1976; mem. exec. bd. Denver Area coun. Boy Scouts Am., 1999—. Mem. ABA (vice-chmn. oil, natural gas exploration and prodn. com. sect. natural resource law 1983-88, chmn. 1989, coun. sect. natural resources, energy and environ. law 1990-93). Republican. Office: Holland & Hart 8390 E Crescent Pkwy Ste 400 Greenwood Village CO 80111-2822

RAMSEY, LLOYD BRINKLEY, retired savings and loan executive, retired army officer; b. Somerset, Ky., May 29, 1918; s. William Harold and Mary Ella (Barnett) R.; m. Glenda Burton, Feb. 22, 1941 (dec. Oct. 20, 2000); children: Lloyd Ann (Mrs. Kyle D. Wallace), Larry Burton, Judi Ramsey (Mrs. David E. Derr). AB, U. Ky., 1940; postgrad., Yale U., 1946, Command and Gen. Staff Coll., Ft. Leavenworth, Kans., 1949-50, U.S. Army War Coll., Carlisle Barracks, Pa., 1953-54, Harvard, 1961. Adc. HRLG Alexander, 1943; Commd. 2d lt. U.S. Army, 1940, advanced through grades to maj. gen., 1968; bn. comdr. 7th Inf., 3d Inf. Div., 1944-45; instr. Inf. Sch., Ft. Benning, Ga., 1946-49; assigned Office G-2 Dept. Army Gen. Staff, 1950-53; sec. joint staff UN Far East Command, 1954-57; comdg. officer 1st Inf. Brigade, Ft. Benning, Ga., 1957-58; adv. Korean Army War Coll., 1959-60; with Office Chief Legis. Liaison, Dept. Army Gen. Staff, 1960-63, Office Asst. Chief Staff Force Devel., 1963-64; dep. comdr. Ft. Leonard Wood, Mo., 1964—65; dep. chief information, 1966-67; chief of staff Third Army, Ft. McPherson, Ga., 1967-68; div. comdr. Americal 23d Div., Vietnam, 1969-70; provost marshall gen. Army, Washington, 1970-74, ret., 1974; chmn. bd. McLean Savs. & Loan Assn., Va., 1974-88. Decorated D.S.M. with oak leaf cluster, Silver Star medal with two oak leaf clusters, Legion of Merit with oak leaf cluster, D.F.C., Bronze Star medal with V and three oak leaf clusters, Air medal with 16 oak leaf clusters, Purple Heart with four oak leaf clusters, Combat Inf. badge; mem. Order Brit. Empire; Croix de Guerre France; Vietnamese Nat. Order; Vietnamese Armed Forces Honor medal; Vietnamese Gallantry Cross with palm. Mem. Sigma Chi, Omicron Delta Kappa. Baptist. Home: 3624 Bowling Dr Salem VA 24153-8806 *Accept a man for what he is, not for what you want him to be.*

RAMSEY, LYNN ALLISON, trade association, public relations professional; b. Phila., July 31, 1944; d. Charles Edward and Edna Berry (Whetstone) R. Student, Inst. European Studies, Vienna, Austria, 1964-65; BA, Boston U., 1967. Copy editor Am. Heritage Pub. Co., N.Y.C., 1969-71; prodr., writer Rick Carrier Film Prodns., N.Y.C., 1971-72; mng. editor New Ingenue mag., N.Y.C., 1973-75; freelance writer N.Y.C., 1975-80; mgr. pub. rels. Cunningham and Walsh (acquired by Ayer Pub. Rels. 1987), N.Y.C., 1981—; v.p., mgr. Ayer Pub. Rels., N.Y.C., 1988-95; pres., CEO Jewelry Info. Ctr., N.Y.C., 1995—. Author: Gigolos; The World's Best-Kept Men, 1978; photographer: FLY: The Complete Book of Sky Sailing, 1974; contbr. articles to profl. jours. Mem. Fgn. Policy Assn. 1982-87; mem. Chelsea Cmty. Ch. Bd., 1996—, chair, 1999—; sec. U.S.A. Bald Eagle Command, 1975—. Mem. Pub. Rels. Soc. Am. (accredited, bd. dirs. N.Y. chpt. 1993-95), Fashion Group Internat., Women's Jewelry Assn. (bd. dirs. 1993—, treas. 2000—, Award for Excellence 1993), Soc. Jewelry Historians. Avocations: cross country skiing, travel, cooking, reading.

RAMSEY, MARGIE, librarian; b. Bay City, Tex., Aug. 29, 1921; d. Cyrus Otis Lansford and Myra Lenore Ferrell; m. Joe Bryan Ramsey, July 29, 1945; children: Ronald Lansford, Kevin Bryan. BA in Libr. Sci., Tex. State U., 1942. Cert. tchr., Tex. Libr. Talco (Tex.) Ind. Sch. Dist., 1942-44; sec. Consolidated Aircraft, San Diego, summer 1943; bookkeeper Lockheed Aircraft, Dallas, 1944; libr. Dallas Pub. Libr., 1944-45; sec. Steck Co., Austin, Tex., 1946-48; libr. U. Tex., Austin, 1948-51. Author, poet:. Vol. libr. Hyde Park United Meth., Austin, 1963-2002, Leander (Tex.) Ind. Sch. Dist., 1982-92; mem. The Internat. Libr. of Poetry. Named Outstanding Vol., Nat. Assn. Ptnrs. in Edn., Kraft-Disney, 1989. Fellow AAUW. Democrat. Avocations: teaching, camping, computers, reading, collecting rare books. Home: 1105 Church St Georgetown TX 78626 E-mail: mramsey@verizon.net.

RAMSEY, NATALIE D. lawyer; b. Greeneville, Tenn., Dec. 6, 1959; d. William Trent and Nancy Elizabeth (Maupin) R. BS, U. Del., 1981; JD, Villanova U., 1984. Bar: Pa. 1984, U.S. Dist. Ct. (ea. dist.) Pa. 1985, U.S. Ct. Appeals (3rd cir. and 11th cirs.) 1989. Assoc. atty. Frederick L. Reigle, Esq. and Assocs., Reading, Pa., 1984-85, Montgomery, McCracken, Walker & Rhoads, LLP, Phila., 1985-93; ptnr. Montgomery, McCracken, Walker & Rhoads, Phila., 1993—, chair bankruptcy and reorgn. group, 1997—. Vice chair Ea. Dist. of Pa. Bankruptcy Conf., 2000—; dir. Consumer Bankruptcy Advocacy Project. Contbr. articles to profl. jours. Bd. pres. Habitat for Humanity, 1997-2002. Mem. Comml. Law League, Turnaround Mgmt. Assn. Presbyterian. Avocations: travel, reading. Office: Montgomery McCracken Walker & Rhoads LLP 123 S Broad St Ste 2538 Philadelphia PA 19109-1099 Office Phone: 215-772-1500. E-mail: nramsey@mmwr.com.

RAMSEY, NORMAN F. physicist, researcher; b. Washington, Aug. 27, 1915; s. Norman F. and Minna (Bauer) Ramsey; m. Elinor Jameson, June 3, 1940 (dec. Dec. 1983); children: Margaret, Patricia, Janet, Winifred; m. Ellie Welch, May 11, 1985. AB, Columbia U., 1935; BA, Cambridge (Eng.) U., 1937, MA, 1941, DSc, 1954; PhD, Columbia U., 1940; MA (hon.), Harvard U., 1947; DSc (hon.), Case Western Res. U., 1968, Middlebury Coll., 1969, Oxford (Eng.) U., 1973, DCL (hon.), 1990; DSc (hon.), Rockefeller U., 1986, U. Chgo., 1989, U. Sussex, 1990, U. Houston, 1991, Carleton Coll., 1991, Lake Forest Coll., 1992, U. Mich., 1993, Phila. Coll. Pharmacy & Sci., 1995, Colby Coll., 1998. Kellett fellow Columbia U., 1935—37, Tyndall fellow, 1938—39; Carnegie fellow Carnegie Inst. Washington, 1939—40; assoc. U. Ill., 1940—42; asst. prof. Columbia U., 1942—46; assoc. MIT Radiation Lab., 1940—43; cons. Nat. Def. Research Com., 1940—45; expert cons. sec. of war, 1942—45; group leader, asso. div. head Los Alamos Lab., 1943—45; assoc. prof. Columbia U., 1945—47; head physics dept. Brookhaven Nat. Lab. of AEC, 1946—47; assoc. prof. physics Harvard U., 1947—50, prof. physics, 1950—66, Higgins prof. physics, 1966—86, Higgins prof. emeritus, 1986—. Sr. fellow Harvard Soc. Fellows, 1970—; Eastman prof. Oxford U., 1973—74; Luce prof. cosmology Mt. Holyoke Coll., 1982—83; prof. U. Va., 1983—84; dir. Harvard Nuc. Lab., 1948—50, 1952—53, Varlan Assocs., 1963—66; mem. Air Forces Sci. Adv. Com., 1947—54; sci. advisor NATO, 1958—59; mem. Dept. Def. Panel Atomic Energy; exec. com. Cambridge Electron Accelerator; gen. adv. com. AEC. Author: Nuclear Moments and Statistics, 1953, Nuclear Two Body Problems, 1953, Molecular Beams, 1956, 1985, Quick Calculus, 1965, Spectroscopy with Coherent Radiation, 1998; contbr. articles Phys. Rev., other sci. jours. on nuclear physics, molecular beam experiments, radar, nuclear magnetic moments, radiofrequency spectroscopy, masers, nucleon scattering. Trustee Assoc. Univs., Inc., Brookhaven Nat. Lab., Carnegie Endowment Internat. Peace, 1962—85, Rockefeller U., 1977—90; pres. Univs. Rsch. Assocs., Inc., 1966—72, 1973—81, pres. emeritus, 1981—. Recipient Presdl. Order of Merit for radar devel. work, 1947, award, E.O. Lawrence and AEC, 1960, Columbia award for excellence in sci., 1980, medal of honor, IEEE, 1983, Rabi prize, 1985, Monte Ferst award, 1985, Compton medal, 1985, Rumford premium, 1985, Oersted medal, 1988, Nat. medal of Sci., 1988, Nobel prize for Physics, 1989, Pupin medal, Columbia Engring. Sch. Alumni Assn., 1992, Sci. for Peace prize, 1992, Einstein medal, 1993, Vannevar Bush award, 1995; fellow Guggenheim, Oxford U., 1954—55. Fellow: Am. Phys. Soc. (coun. 1956—60, pres. 1978—79, Davisson-Germer prize 1974), Am. Acad. Sci.; mem.: AAAS (chmn. physics sect. 1977), NAS, Am. Inst. Physics (chmn. bd. govs. 1980—87), Am. Philos. Assn., French Acad. Sci., Sigma Xi, Phi Beta Kappa (senator 1979—88, v.p. 1982—85). Home: 24 Monmouth Ct Brookline MA 02446-5634 Office: Harvard U Lyman Physics Lab Cambridge MA 02138

RAMSEY, PAUL GLENN, dean, internist; b. Pitts., 1949; MD, Harvard U., 1975. Diplomate Am. Bd. Internal Medicine. Intern Cambridge Hosp., 1975-76; resident in medicine Mass. Gen. Hosp., Boston, 1976-78, U. Wash., Seattle, 1980-81, fellow infectious diseases, 1978-80, prof., 1991—, chmn. dept. medicine, 1992-97; physician-in-chief U. Wash. Med. Ctr., 1992-97; v.p. for med. affairs, dean Sch. Medicine U. Wash., Seattle, 1997—. Mem.: Inst. Medicine, AAAS, Assn. Am. Physicians, Am. Fedn. Clin. Rsch., ACP. Office: U Wash Sch Medicine PO Box 356350 Seattle WA 98195-6350

RAMSEY, ROBERT LESLIE, oncologist; b. Vienna, Va., June 15, 1946; MD, U. Chgo., 1972. Diplomate Am. Bd. Internal Medicine. Intern UCLA Med. Ctr., 1972-73, resident in Medicine, 1973-75, fellow in Hematology-Oncology, 1975-77; asst. dep. for health policy, asst. sec. of the Army The Pentagon, Washington. Office: The Pentagon Washington DC 20905

RAMSEY, RONALD L. state legislator, realtor; b. Johnson City, Tenn., Nov. 20, 1955; married; three children. BS in Indsl. Tech., East Tenn. State U., 1978. Real estate broker/auctioneer; mem. Tenn. Ho. of Reps. 98th-99th Gen. Assemblies, Tenn. Senate 100th Gen. Assembly, Senate asst. rep. floor leader, mem. govt. ops. com., mem. select com. on children and youth; chmn. environment, conservation and tourism com. Tenn. Senate 100th Gen. Assembly & 101th Gen. Assembly. Mem. Elizabeth Chapel United Meth. Ch.; mem. adv. bd. Farm Credit Assn. Mem. Bristol Tenn.-Va. Assn. Realtors (past pres.), Blountville Ruritan, Blountville Bus. Assn. (past pres.). Republican. Address: 1626 Highway 37 Blountville TN 37617-4701 Office: 306 War Memorial Bldg Nashville TN 37243-0202 E-mail: sen.ron.ramsey@legislature.state.tn.us.

RAMSEY, S. ROBERT, education educator; b. Memphis, Tenn., July 27, 1941; s. Samuel Robert and Ida Shelton (Taylor) R.; m. Younghi Kim, Dec. 24, 1969; children: James William, Julia Kim. PhD, Yale U., 1969—75. Asst. prof. Columbia U., 1975—84; assoc. prof., prof. U. of Md., 1984—, prof. and chair, dept. of Asian and East European Languages and Cultures, 1996—. Vis. lectr. in Chinese U. Pa., 1983-84; guest lectr. linguistics USIS, Korea, 1973-74; mem. adv. bd. Nat. Fgn. Lang. Ctr., Washington, 1990, 92—; presenter papers in field, 1974—; lectr. in field, 1979—; cons. N.J. Dept. Higher Edn., 1978; scholar in residence Ind. U., 1982; mem. panel NSF, 1989, U.S. Dept. Agriculture, 1988, U. Pitts., 1991, others; organizer, chair seminars; participant, speaker confs., symposia; course evaluator; expert witness U.S. Dist. Ct., Md., 1992. Author: Accent and Morphology in Korean Dialects, 1978, The Languages of China, 1989, Chugoku no shogengo, 1990, (with Iksop Lee) The Korean Language, 2000; contbr. chpts. to books, numerous articles to profl. jours. With U.S. Army, 1966-68. Recipient Outstanding Achievement award Am. Cong. Surveying and Mapping, 1985; Fulbright-Hays fellow Seoul U., 1972-74, Kyoto U., 1978-79; Social Sci. Rsch. Coun. grantee, 1976, 79, Nat. Mus. Ethnography Travel grantee, 1987, Travel and Rsch. grantee Korea Rsch. Found., 1993, Rsch. grantee Seoul Nat. U., 1993. Mem. Linguistic Soc. Am., Assn. Asian Studies, Assn. Tchrs. Japanese (exec. com. 1983-85, 92-94), Internat. Cir. Korean Linguistics (pres. 1992-95), Am. Assn. Tchrs. Korean (sec. 1994—), Tau Beta Pi. Home: 6909 Dartmouth Ave College Park MD 20740 Office: U of Md Asian/East European 2106G Jimenez Hall College Park MD 20742 Office Phone: 301-405-4256. E-mail: ramsey@umd.edu.

RAMSEY, SALLY ANN SEITZ, retired state official; b. Columbus, Ohio, Feb. 15, 1931; d. Albert Blazier and Mildred (Dodson) Seitz; m. Edward Lewis Ramsey, Apr. 11, 1953 (div. 1962); children: Edward Lewis, Sylvia Ann Mitchell. BA, Ohio State U., 1952, MA, 1955, postgrad., 1963-66; postgrad. St. Mary Coll.-Xavier, Kans., 1962. Rsch. engr., then sr. rsch. engr. N.Am. Aviation, Inc., Columbus, Ohio, and Downey, Calif., 1962-67; legis. intern State of Ohio, 1964-65; rsch. and info. officer Ohio Dept. Urban Affairs, Columbus, 1967-68; adminstrv. specialist Ohio Dept. Devel., Columbus, 1968; assoc. planner, then sr. planner Div. State Planning, Fla. Dept. Adminstrn., Tallahassee, 1968-76; econ. analysis supr., then econ. analyst Fla. Dept. Commerce, 1976-93; ret., 1993; congl. campaign cons., 1966. U.S. Econ. Devel. Adminstrn. fellow, 1978-79. Mem. ASPA, DAR, Fla. Econs. Club, Kappa Kappa Gamma, Pi Sigma Alpha. Episcopalian. Home: 2963 Golden Eagle Dr E Tallahassee FL 32312-4056

RAMSEY-GOLDMAN, ROSALIND, physician; b. N.Y.C., Mar. 22, 1954; d. Abraham L. and Miriam (Colen) Goldman; m. Glenn Ramsey, June 29,1 975; children: Ethan Ramsey, Caitlin Ramsey. BA, Case Western Res. U., 1975, MD, 1978; MPH, U. Pitts., 1988, DPH, 1992. Med. resident U. Rochester (N.Y.), 1978-81; chief resident Rochester Gen. Hosp., 1981-82; staff physician Univ. Health Svc., Rochester, 1982-83; rheumatology fellow U. Pitts., 1983-86, instr. medicine, 1986-87, asst. prof., 1987-91, co-dir. Lupus Treatment and Diagnostic Ctr., 1987-91; asst. prof. medicine Northwestern U., Chgo., 1991-96, assoc. prof. medicine, 1996—2001, prof. medicine, 2001—. Dir. Chgo. Lupus Registry, Northwestern U., Chgo., 1991—, chairperson Systemic Lupus Internat. Collaborating Clinics Group, 2003—. Contbr. rsch. articles to profl. jours. Recipient Finkelstein award Hershey (Pa.) Med. Ctr., 1986. Fellow ACP, Am. Coll. Rheumatology; mem. Soc. for Epidemiologic Rsch., Ctrl. Soc. Clin. Rsch. Office: Northwestern U Feinberg Sch Medicine McGaw Pavilion 240 E Huron Ste 2300 Chicago IL 60611 Office Phone: 312-503-8003. Business E-Mail: rgramsey@northwestern.edu.

RAMSIER, PAUL, composer, psychotherapist; b. Louisville, Sept. 23, 1927; s. Paul and Lucie (Herrmann) R. PhD., N.Y.U., 1972; MSW, SUNY, Stony Brook, 1976. Composer, N.Y.C., 1950—; psychotherapist in pvt. practice, 1977—. Adj. prof. music N.Y.U., 1970—. Composer numerous musical compositions including Divertimento Concertante on a Theme of Couperin, 1965, Road to Hamelin, 1978, Eusebius Revisited, 1980, Silent Movie, 1985, Zoo of Dreams, 2002, Stargazer, 1995, Homage to Rafael, 1995, Pavane, 1998, Lullaby, 1999, Three Lyric Pieces, 2000, Walrus Bird, 2002, Cheetah Departs, 2002, Sahara Rainforest, 2003, Swallowtail Bridge, 2004; pub. Boosey and Hawkes, G. Schirmer. Huntington Hartford fellow, 1960, MacDowell fellow, 1963, Yaddo fellow, 1970; NEA grantee, 1975; recipient Disting. Alumnus award U. Louisville, 1983, Composer award Internat. Soc. Bassists, 1995. Mem. ASCAP. Home and Office: 2323 Goldenrod St Sarasota FL 34239-5334

RAMSTAD, JAMES, congressman, lawyer; b. Jamestown, N.D., May 6, 1946; s. Marvin Joseph and Della Mae (Fode) R. BA, U. Minn., 1968; JD with honors, George Washington U., 1973. Bar: N.D. 1973, D.C. 1973, U.S. Supreme Ct. 1976, Minn., 1979. Adminstrv. asst. to L.L. Duxbury, Minn. Ho. Reps., 1969; spl. asst. to Congressman Tom Kleppe, 1970; pvt. practice law, Jamestown, 1973, Washington, 1974-1978, Mpls., 1978-90; mem. Minn. Senate, 1981-91, asst. minority leader, 1983-87; mem. U.S. Ho. of Reps.from 3rd Minn. dist., 1991-; adj. prof. Am. U., Washington, 1975-78. Bd. dirs. Children's Heart Fund, Lake Country Food Bank. Served as 1st lt. U.S. Army Res., 1968-74. Mem. Minn. Bar Assn., D.C. Bar Assn., N.D. Bar Assn., Hennepin County Bar Assn., U. Minn. Alumni Assn. (nat. dir.), Am. Legion, Wayzata C. of C., TwinWest C. of C., Com. Ways & Means, U. Minn. Alumni Club (past pres. Washington), Lions, Phi Beta Kappa, Phi Delta Theta. Republican. Office: 103 Cannon Ho Office Bldg Washington DC 20515-0001

RAMUNNO, THOMAS PAUL, management consultant; b. Chgo., Sept. 13, 1952; s. Anthony Michael and Dorothy (Buriak) R.; m. Deborah G. Pauline Benton, Jan. 31, 1976 (div. 1991); 1 child, Michael Thomas. BBA, U. Ga., 1974, MBA, 1978. Treas. Concept Inc., Atlanta, 1974-77; product mgr. Johnson-Johnson, Inc., Atlanta, 1978-80; dir. Rollins Inc., Atlanta, 1979-80; cons. Chase Econometrics, Atlanta, 1980-83; v.p. comml. svcs., dir. corp. product mgmt./mktg. Union Trust Co. Md., 1983-84; prin., exec. v.p. Mktg. Scis. Group, Inc., Hunt Valley, Md., 1984-85; v.p., dir. Citicorp, Chgo., 1985-86; sr. mgr. fin. instns. consulting group Deloitte & Touche, Chgo., 1987-90; dir. cons. svcs. FSA, Inc., 1990-92; CEO Adv. Scis. Group, 1991-98; pres. IASG, 1990-98; ptnr. Info. Scis., Inc., 1996-98; v.p., practice leader Metagroup Cons., 1998-2000; ptnr. KPMG Cons., 2000—01; mng. ptnr. Scient, Inc., 2001—02; CEO, mng. ptnr. EVP/Chicago, 2001—; mng. ptnr. St. Charles Group, 2002—03, Enterprise Performance Solutions, 2002—, Fox Glen Performance Techs., 2002—. Home: 675 N Hidden Prairie Ct Palatine IL 60067

RAMUS, JOSEPH S. marine biologist; b. Grosse Pointe Farms, Mich., May 7, 1940; married; three children. BA, U. Calif., Berkeley, 1963, PhD in Botany, 1968. From asst. prof. to assoc. prof. biology Yale U., New Haven, 1968-78; from assoc. prof. to prof., asst. dir. marine lab. Duke U., Beaufort, NC, 1978-90, dir. marine lab., 1990-99, prof. marine lab., biological oceanography, coastal system sci. and policy divsn., 1999—. Mem. AAUP, Am. Soc. Limnology & Oceanology, Phycol. Soc. Am., Am. Geophys. Union. Office: Duke U Marine Lab Marine Lab BRL 220 135 Duke Marine Lab Rd Beaufort NC 28516 also: Duke U Marine Lab Piver's Island Beaufort NC 28516

RAN, SHULAMIT, composer; b. Tel Aviv, Oct. 21, 1949;, U.S. m. Abraham Lotan, 1986. Studied composition with, Paul Ben-Haim, Norman Dello, Joio, Ralph Shapey; student, Mannes Coll. Music, N.Y.C., 1963—67. With dept. music U. Chgo., 1973—, William H. Colvin prof. music; composer-in-residence Chgo. Symphony Orch., 1990—97, Lyric Opera of Chgo., 1994—97. Compositions include 10 Children's Scenes, 1967, Structures, 1968, 7 Japanese Love Poems, 1968, Hatzvi Israel Eulogy, 1969, O the Chimneys, 1969, Concert Piece for piano and orch., 1970, 3 Fantasy Pieces for Cello and Piano, 1972, Ensembles for 17, 1975, Double Vision, 1976, Hyperbolae for Piano, 1976, For an Actor: Monologue for Clarinet, 1978, Apprehensions, 1979, Private Game, 1979, Fantasy-Variations for Cello, 1980, A Prayer, 1982, Verticals for piano, 1982, String Quartet No. 1, 1984, (for woodwind quintet) Concerto da Camera I, 1985, Amichai Songs, 1985, Concerto for Orchestra, 1986, (for clarinet, string quartet and piano) Concerto da Camera II, 1987, East Wind, 1987, String Quartet No. 2, 1988—89, Symphony, 1989—90, Mirage, 1990, Inscriptions for solo violin, 1991, Chicago Skyline for brass and percussion, 1991, Legends for orch., 1992—93, Invocation, 1994, Yearning for violin and string orch., 1995, (opera) Between Two Worlds (The Dybbuk), 1995—97, Soliloquy, 1997, Vessels of Courage and Hope for orch., 1998, (flute concerto) Voices, 2000, Three Scenes for solo clarinet, 2000, Supplications for chorus and orch., 2002, Violin Concerto, 2003, commd. pieces include for Am. Composers Orch., Phila. Orch., Chgo. Symphony, Balt. Symphony, Chamber Soc. of Lincoln Ctr., Mendelssohn String quartet, Da Capo Chamber Players, Sta. WFMT, Lyric Opera Chgo., composer and soloist for 1st performances Capariccio, 1963, Symphonic Poem, 1967, Concert Piece, 1971. Named Guggenheim fellow, 1977, 1990; recipient Acad. Inst. Arts and Letters award, 1989, Pulitzer prize for music, 1991, Friedheim award for orchestral music, Kennedy Ctr., 1992. Office: U Chgo Dept Music 1010 E 59th St Chicago IL 60637-1512

RANALD, MARGARET LOFTUS, English literature educator, author; b. Auckland, N.Z., Sept. 5, 1927; came to U.S., 1952; d. Leonard R. and Geraldine (McGrath) Loftus; m. Ralph Arthur Ranald, Feb. 26, 1955; 1 child, Caroline Margaret. AB, U. N.Z., Wellington, 1949, MA honors, 1951; MA, UCLA, 1954, PhD, 1958. Jr. asst. Dept. Prime Min. Govt. N.Z., Wellington, 1944-52; asst. to sec. Princeton (N.J.) U., 1956-57; from instr. to asst. prof. Temple U., Phila., 1957-61; from asst. prof. to prof. CUNY, N.Y.C., 1961—. Assoc. bibliographer MLA, N.Y.C., 1958—; mem. assoc. faculty, mem. adv. com. Columbia U., N.Y.C., 1976—; vis. prof. UCLA, 1970-85, 98, tchg. asst., 1953-55. Author: The Eugene O'Neill Companion, 1984, Shakespeare and his Social Context, 1987, John Webster, 1989; assoc. editor (book series): International Bibliography of Theatre, 1985—. Fulbright fellow, 1952-54; sr. fellow Folger Shakespeare Libr., 1970-72. Mem. MLA, Am. Soc. Theatre Rsch. (exec. sec., v.p. 1976-83), Eugene O'Neill Soc. (coun., pres. 1996-2000), Shakespeare Soc. Am. (former rsch. asst.), Princeton Club N.Y. Avocations: music, drama, theatrical history, travel. Office: CUNY Dept of Eng 65-30 Kissena Blvd Flushing NY 11367

RANALD, RALPH ARTHUR, former government official, educator; b. N.Y.C., Nov. 25, 1930; s. Josef A. and Pearl R.; m. Margaret Florence Loftus, Feb. 26, 1955; 1 dau., Caroline. AB, UCLA, 1952, MA, 1954; AM, Princeton U., 1958; postgrad. (Carnegie fellow) Law Sch., Harvard U., 1961-62, 76-77, 99-2000; grad., Exec. Program Nat. and Internat. Security, 1978; PhD, Princeton U., 1962; JD, Fordham U., 1997. Bar: N.Y. Teaching asst. UCLA, 1952-54; univ. fellow, rsch. asst. Princeton (N.J.) U., 1956-59; asst. prof. Fordham U. Grad. Sch., N.Y.C., 1959-65; asst. dean acad. affairs, prof. Coll. Arts and Scis. NYU, N.Y.C., 1965-69; prof. CUNY, 1969—; spl. policy asst. HEW, Washington, 1968-69, Office of Mgmt. and Budget, 1976-77; sr. cons. U.S. Dept. Def., 1969-70, 77-78; mem. staffs Dept. Def. and Army Gen. Staff U.S. Govt. Long Com., 1989, U.S. Dept. Def., 1995-96. Vis. prof. and cons. univs. including U. So. Calif., summers 1968-74, Calif. State U., UCLA, summers 1985, 98; vis. scholar Harvard Law Sch., 1999—2003. Author: Management Development in Government, 1979, George Orwell, 1965; contbr. reports, articles to publs. in law, govt. and edn. Treas. N.Y. State Com. for Pub. Higher Edn., 1975-78, mem. com., 1970—. 1st lt. U.S. Army, 1953-56, to col., 1977-78, res., 1978—. Recipient U.S. Legion of Merit, 1983; sr. fellow Am. Soc. Pub. Adminstrn. (selection com. for fellows, 1970-74); mem. Res. Officers Assn. U.S. (life), Harvard U. Law Sch. Assn., Assn. of Princeton U. Grad. Alumni, U.S. Army War Coll. Alumni Assn., John F. Kennedy Sch. of Govt. Alumni Assn., Princeton Club of N.Y., Army and Navy Club, Phi Beta Kappa. Home and Office: 239 Central Park W New York NY 10024-6038

RANCE, QUENTIN E. interior designer; b. St. Albans, Eng., Mar. 22, 1935; came to U.S., 1981. s. Herbert Leonard and Irene Ann (Haynes) R.; m. India Adams, May 17, 1974. Grad., Eastbourne (Eng.) Sch. Art, 1960. Soft furnishings buyer Dickeson & French Ltd., Eastbourne, 1960-61, outside sales mgr., 1961-62; design dir. Laszlo Hoenig, Ltd., London, 1962-73; mng. dir. Quentin Rance Interiors Ltd., London, 1973-81; pres. Quentin Rance Enterprises, Inc., Encino, Calif., 1981—. Works featured in Designers West, 1983, Design House Rev., 1983, Profiles mag., 1987, Nat. Assn. Mirror Mfrs. Jour., 1988, Designer Specifier, 1990. Mem. Founders for Diabetic Research/City of Hope. Served with RAF, 1953-55. Recipient Hon. Mention award Nat. Assn. Mirror Mfrs., 1987, 1st Pl. Nat. Pub. Svc. award, Designer Specifier, 1990. Fellow Chartered Soc. Designers (Eng.); mem. Am. Soc. Interior Designers (profl., chpt. bd. dirs. 1983-87, 89-91, chmn. Avanti 1983-85, admissions chmn. 1985—, Presdl. citations 1984, 87, 91, 95, 97), Knights of Vine. Avocations: bicycling, antiques, fine wines, stamp collecting/philately, theater. Home and Office: 18005 Rancho St Encino CA 91316-4214 Office Phone: 818-705-8111. Personal E-mail: qer@earthlink.net. *Personal philosophy: Good design is always there to be seen, there to be appreciated, and there for expanding one's own boundaries of creativity.*

RANCK, EDNA RUNNELS, academic administrator, researcher; b. Waterville, Maine, Aug. 24, 1935; d. Everett Elias and Edna May (King) Runnels; m. James Gilmour Ranck, June 30, 1971 (dec. May 1979); children: Matthew, Christopher, Joshua Duggan; m. Martin Fleischer, Apr. 19, 1982; stepchildren: Christina, Laura Ranck. BA cum laude, Fla. State U., Tallahassee, 1957; MDiv magna cum laude, Drew U. Theol. Sch., Madison, NJ, 1971, MEd in Edn. Adminstrn., 1978; EdD in Curriculum and Tchg., Columbia U., NYC, 1986. Dir. Collinsville Child Care Ctr., Morristown, NJ, 1971-78; exec. dir. Children's Svcs. Morris County, Morristown, 1980-84; co-mgr. NJ Child Care Clearinghouse, Trenton; coord. NJ Child Care Adv. Coun., Trenton, 1987-92; dir. NJ Office Child Care Devel., Trenton, 1992; child care coord. NJ Dept. Human Svcs., Trenton, 1992-98, Nat. Assn. Child Care Resource & Referral Agys., Washington, 1998—2002, Westover Consultants, Inc., Silver Spring, Md., 2002—. Adj. faculty Kean U. NJ, Union, 1983; dir. Sprout House Presch., Chatham, NJ, 1984-87; mem. Morris County Human Svcs. Adv. Coun., Morristown, NJ, 1986-87, spkr. in field. Author: Dodge Foundation Project, 1984, Young Children, 1987, Our History, Our Vision: A History of the National Association of Child Care Rsource and Referral Agencies, 1997, monthly Policy Perspectives column, 2000-02; contbr. chapters to books, articles to profl. jours. Exec. bd. Drew U. Alumni Assn. Theol. Sch., 1986-92; active Drew U. Alumni Study Commn., 1993, Non-Govt. Orgn. rep. to UN Internat. Fedn. Educative Cmtys., 1992-99; moderator history/archives panel Nat. Assn. for Edn. of Young Children, 1999-2001. Recipient Volpe Commitment in Child Care award, NJ Child Care Assn., 1991, Essex C.C. Early Childhood award, 1997, Aletha Wright award for Excellence in Early Edn., 1998. Mem. Internat. Assn. Presch. Edn. N.Am. (bd. dirs.), Child Care Action Campaign Panel, Acad. Child and Youth Care Workers, Nat. Assn. of Regulatory Adminstrn. (bd. dirs. 2000—), World Orgn. Presch. Edn. (bd. dirs.

2000—), Tchrs. Coll. Columbia U. Washington Alumni Assn. (co-chmn.), Phi Beta Kappa, Pi Sigma Alpha, Sigma Delta Pi. Republican. United Methodist. Avocations: writing, travel, clothing design, art collecting, benefit walks. Home: 4447 MacArthur Blvd NW Washington DC 20007-2564 E-mail: edna.ranck@verizon.net.

RANCOURT, JOHN HERBERT, retired pharmaceutical company executive, marine engineer; b. Troy, N.Y., Aug. 10, 1946; s. Charles Dennis and Helen Mary (Keadin) R.; divorced; children: Karen Mary, John Herbert, Alison Jane, Elizabeth Anne, Maureen Ellen. BS in Mgmt., Rensselaer Poly. Inst., 1968, MS in Mgmt., 1972, MBA, 1981. CPA, Ill.; cert. mgmt. acct. From asst. to dir. rsch. Rensselaer Poly. Inst., 1968-69; mgmt. trainee, buyer/purchasing agt., contr. rsch. divsn. Huyck Corp., Rensselaer, N.Y., 1969-74, corp. internat. project mgr. Wake Forest, N.C., 1974-76, adminstrv. svc. mgr. Formex divsn., 1976-77; sr. fin. analyst Abbott Labs., North Chicago, Ill., 1977-79, sect. mgr. sales acctg., 1979-80, mgr. fin. analysis, materials mgmt. divsn., 1980-82, mgr. fin. planning and analysis, pharm. products divsn., 1982-84, contr. TAP Pharms. subs., 1984-97; mng. prin. The Rancourt Group Internat., Libertyville, Ill., 1997—; dir. adminstrn. and fin. Jered Industries, Chelsea, Mass., 1999-2000, dir. adminstrn. and fin. marine svcs. divsn. Vancleave, Mass., 2000; prin. John H. Rancourt & Assocs. - CPA and Cons., 2001—. Fin. cons. to entrepreneurs and Fortune 500 cos.; instr. acctg. Coll. of Lake County, Grayslake, Ill., part-time, 1981-85. Indian Guide/Princess Tribal leader YMCA, 1980-90; solicitor United Way, 1981, 83, 85, 87, 88-89, 90-91, mem. allocation panel, 1990-92. Mem. Nat. Assn. Accts., Am. Inst. CPAs, Ill. CPA Soc., Wis. Inst. CPAs, Fin. Execs. Inst., Liberty Road and Track Club. Roman Catholic. Home: 220 Wildflower Ln La Grange IL 60525 Office Phone: 708-214-4692. E-mail: john@johnhrancourt.com.

RAND, A. BARRY, financial services executive; m. Donna (Rand); children: Christopher and Allison. BA, Am. Univ.; MBA, M in Mgmt. sci., Stanford U.; various degrees (hon.). Exec. v.p. worldwide ops. Xerox Corp., until 1999; chmn. bd. dirs., CEO, Avis Group Holdings, Inc., Garden City, NY, 1999—2001; chmn., CEO Equitant Corp., 2003—. Bd. dirs. AT&T Wireless, Abbott Laboratories, Agilent Technologies, Equitant Corp., Aspect Communications Corp. Bd. dir. Urban Family Inst.; Garth Fagan Dance Theater; bd. trustees Howard U., mem. adv. coun. Stanford U. Grad. Sch. Bus. Recipient Image Award NAACP, 1993; inducted into Nat. Sales Hall of Fame, 1993; Stanford Sloan fellow, Stanford U. Office: Equitant Corp Stamford Ctr Six Landmark Sq, 4th Fl Stamford CT 06901-2792*

RAND, ANTHONY EDEN, lawyer; b. Garner, N.C., Sept. 1, 1939; s. Walter and Geneva R., Jr.; m. Karen Skarda; children: Ripley E., Craven M. AB, U. N.C., 1961, LLB, 1964; LLD (hon.), Fayetteville State U., 2000. Ptnr. Mitchiner, Andrews, Rand, Raleigh, N.C., 1965-68, Rose, Thorp, Rand & Ray, Fayetteville, N.C., 1968-81, Rose, Rand, Winfrey & Gregory, Fayetteville, 1982-89, Rand, Finch & Gregory, Fayetteville, 1989-93; mem. from 12th dist. N.C. Senate, Fayetteville, 1982—88, mem. from 24th dist., 1995—2002, mem. from 19th dist., 2003—, chmn. rules and operations, 1995—, majority leader, 1987—88, 2001—; mem. Senate 12th Dist., 1982—88; ptnr. Rand and Gregory, Fayetteville, 1993—. Sec., legal counsel, cons. Lithotripters, Inc.1989-96; cons., Prime Med. Svcs., 1996-2000, Sonorex, Inc., 2001—. Mem. N.C. State Dem. Exec. Com., 1975-77; chmn. exec. com. Cumberland County Dem. party (N.C.), 1977-81; bd. visitors U. N.C.-Chapel Hill, Meth. Coll.; bd. dirs., founding mem. Pub. Sch. Forum; bd. dirs. Fayetteville Area Sentencing, 1985; mem. adv. bd. Mus. Cape Fear, 1989-95; mem. nat. adv. panel Child Care Action Com., 1989—; pres. Med-Tech Investments, 1989-97. Named Legis. of Yr., ARC of N.C., 2003, N.C. Nurses' Assn., 2003, Autism Soc., 2004; recipient Legis. Leadership award, N.C. Coun. Cmty. Progress, 2000, Fayetteville C. of C., 2000, Hon. Trustee award, Fayetteville Tech. C.C., 2003, Disting. Svc. award, N.C. State, 2002, Chancellor's medallion, Fayetteville State U., 2001, N.C. Gun Violence Prevention Citizen of Yr. award, 2003. Mem. ABA, ATLA (state commiteeman 1968-72), N.C. Bar Assn., Alpha Tau Omega, Delta Theta Phi. Episcopalian. Office: 2014 Litho Pl Fayetteville NC 28304 Office Phone: 910-733-9892. E-mail: Tonyr@ncleg.net.

RAND, CALVIN GORDON, arts and education consultant; b. Buffalo, May 15, 1929; s. George Franklin and Isabel (Williams) R.; m. Patricia Clemens Andrew, Aug. 18, 1951; children: Robin, Melissa, Jennifer, Lucinda, Elizabeth BA, Princeton U., 1951; MA, Columbia U., 1954; LHD (hon.), York U., Can., 1984. Head history dept. Riverdale Sch., N.Y.C., 1955-60; lectr. philosophy SUNY-Buffalo, 1961-68, acting dir. cultural affairs, 1968-71; founder, pres. The Niagara Inst., Niagara-on-the-Lake, Can., 1971-79; pres. Am. Acad. in Rome, N.Y.C., 1980-84; ind. producer, theatre and film cons., N.Y.C., 1985-90. Founding chmn., dir. Shaw Festival Theatre, Niagara-on-the-Lake, 1964-78,. bd. govs., 1979—; trustee Playwrights Horizons Theatre, N.Y.C., 1982-92; bd. dirs. Arts in Edn. Inst.; mem. N.Y. State Coun. on Arts, 1978-82, Arts Coun. Western N.Y., 1987-93; chmn. World Ency. Contemporary Theater; chmn. arts coun. SUNY, Buffalo, 1987-94, adj. prof. theater, 1988—. Contbr. articles to profl. jours. Bd. dirs. Burchfield-Penney Art Ctr., Buffalo, 1991—, vice-chair, 1999—; bd. dirs. Irish Classical Theater, 1993—, pres., 1998-2004; trustee Albright-Knox Gallery, Buffalo, 1976-80, 84-88, 90-94. Recipient spl. citation Ont. Arts Coun., 1976, Fellowship Fund award Niagara Inst., 1980, Centennial Arts award Nichols Sch., 1992, Red Jacket award, Erie County Hist. Soc., 2000; named Man of Yr., Coun. World Affairs, 1976, Buffalo Courier Express, 1976, Arts Patron of Yr., Western N.Y. Arts Coun. and C. of C., 1989; Disting Non-Alumni, SUNY, Buffalo, Man of Yr., 1997, YMCA of Western NY, 1999; Vanier Coll. fellow York U. Mem. Princeton Club, Saturn Club.

RAND, DEBORAH, lawyer; b. Wasington, Sept. 16, 1944; d. Harry I. and Anna T. Rand. BA, Carleton Coll., 1964; MAT, Harvard U., 1966; JD, Rutgers U., 1974. Bar: N.Y. 1975, U.S. Ct. Appeals (2d cir.) 1975, U.S. Dist. Ct. (so. dist.) N.Y. 1977, U.S. Dist. Ct. (ea. dist.) N.Y. 1995. Tchr. social studies N.Y. h.s., 1966-71; staff atty. EEOC, Washington, 1974-76; sr. atty. MFY Legal Svcs., N.Y.C., 1976-81; project dir. West Side Single Rm. Occupancy Law Project, N.Y.C., 1981-85; staff Rutgers Urban Legal Clinic, 1985-86; coord. cmty. housing project Bklyn. Legal Svcs., 1986-87; dep. chief Office of Corp. Counsel, N.Y.C., 1987—2002, sr. coun., 2003—. Office: Office Corp Counsel NYC Law Dept 100 Church St New York NY 10007-2601

RAND, DUNCAN DAWSON, retired librarian; b. Biggar, Sask., Can., Oct. 28, 1940; s. Dawson Ellis and Elizabeth Edna (Gabie) R.; m. Nancy Jean Daugherty, Sept. 7, 1963; children: Jacqueline Nancy, Duncan Dawson, Thomas Nelson, John David, Jennifer Nancy. BA, U. Sask., 1963; B.L.S., McGill U., 1964. Young adult librarian Regina Pub. Library, Sask., 1964-65; coordinator library services Regina Separate Sch. Bd., 1965-68; asst. chief librarian Regina Pub. Library, 1968-71; dep. dir. London Pub. Library and Art Mus., 1971-73, acting dir., 1973-74; chief librarian Lethbridge Pub. Library, Alta., 1974-2000, ret., 2001. Dir. So. Alta. Art Gallery, Alberta Libr., 1996—. Editor: Sask. Geneal. Soc. Bull, 1968-71. Vice pres. Alta. council Boy Scouts. Mem. Libr. Assn. Alta (dir., pres. 1986-87), Can. Libr. Assn. (dir.), Can. Assn. Pub. Librs. (chair 1976-77), Sask. Geneal. Soc. (pres.), Assn. Profl. Librs. of Lethbridge (chmn. 1982-84), So. Alta. Regional Info. Network (chmn. 1996-2000), Samaritans (pres. 1998-2001), Allied Arts Coun. (bd. dirs. 1993-98), Southern Alberta Regional Info. Network (chmn.), Rotary, Ipalosh (archivist, sec. 1980-94). Office: 810 5th Ave S Lethbridge AB Canada T1J 4C4

RAND, HARRY ISRAEL, lawyer; b. NYC, July 27, 1912; s. Samuel and Rose (Hirth) R.; m. Anna Tulman, Oct. 22, 1938; children: Steven, Deborah, Naomi. BS, CCNY, 1932; JD, NYU, 1936. Bar: NY 1936, US Supreme Ct. 1943, DC 1947, US Dist. Cts. (so. and ea. dists.) NY 1959, 60, US Ct. Appeals (2d cir.) 1966. Atty. US Pub. Works Adminstrn., 1938-39, US Dept. Interior, 1939-43, US Dept. Justice, 1943-48; pvt. practice Washington, 1948-58; mem. Weisman, Celler, Allan, Spett & Sheinberg, NYC, 1959-67, Botein, Hays & Sklar, NYC, 1967-89; counsel Herrick, Feinstein, NYC, 1990—. Mem. Assn. Bar City NY, Am. Law Inst. Home: 66 Hillandale Rd Westport CT 06880-5319 also: 320 W 86th St New York NY 10024-3139 Office: Herrick Feinstein LLP Two Park Ave New York NY 10016 Office Phone: 212-592-1420. Business E-Mail: hrand@herrick.com

RAND, HARRY ZVI, art historian, poet; b. N.Y.C., Jan. 10, 1947; m. Jennifer Rand; 1 child, Leah Zoë. BA, CCNY, 1969; AM, Harvard U., 1971, PhD, 1974. Contbg. editor Arts mag., N.Y.C., 1975-91, 1975—; assoc. curator Nat. Mus. Am. Art, Washington, 1977-79, curator, 1979-93, chmn. dept., 1978-84, sr. curator, 1993-97; sr. curator cultural history Nat. Mus. Am. Hist., Smithsonian Inst., Washington, 1997—. Mem. adv. bd. Awards in Visual Arts, Winston-Salem, N.C., 1982-92, Austrian Internat. Art Inst., 1989—; arts advisor Virlane Found., New Orleans, 1980—; cons. NAS, 1983, Cosanti Found., 1989—, Exodus Found., 1992—, World Econ. Forum, 1992-94, World Bank, 1994-96. Co-author: The Genius of American Painting, 1973, Still Working, 1993, Vincent Pepi, 1995; author: Seymour Lipton, 1979, Arshile Gorky, 1981, 91, Recent Trends in Collecting, 1982, The Beginning of Things, 1983, Martha Jackson Meml. Collection, 1985, Der Maler Hundertwasser, 1986, 2001, Manet's Contemplation at the Gare Saint-Lazare, 1987, paperback edit. 1991, Paul Manship, 1989, Julian Stanczak, 1990, Hundertwasser, 1991, 92, Jochen Seidel, 1992, Color, 1993, The Clouds, 1996; hon. editor Leonardo mag., 1983—; patentee in field. N.Y. State Regents scholar, 1965-68; travelling fellow Harvard U., 1973, Andrew W. Mellon Found. fellow, 1976-77; Rockefeller Found. devel. grantee, 1982-83, Rsch. Opportunities grantee Smithsonian Instn., 1985, 86, 87, 88, 89, 90, 91, 92, 94, 95, Spl. Scholarly Studies grantee, 1987-95, Ednl. Outreach grantee, 1995; Getty Found. Curatorial fellow, 2003. Fellow Explorers Club; mem. World Art Coun. (steering com. Geneva 1992-96), World Soc. to Stop Trade Stolen Art (bd. dirs. 1994—99). Home: 5511 Greystone St Chevy Chase MD 20815-5556 Office: Nat Mus Am History Washington DC 20560-0616

RAND, JOELLA MAE, retired nursing educator, counselor; b. Akron, Ohio, July 9, 1932; d. Harry S. and Elizabeth May (Miller) Halberg; m. Martin Rand (dec.); children: Craig, Debbi Stark. BSN, U. Akron, 1961, MEd in Guidance, 1968; PhD in Higher Edn. Adminstrn., Syracuse U., 1981. Staff nurse Akron Gen. Hosp., 1953-54; staff-head nurse-instr. Summit County Receiving, Cuyahoga Falls, Ohio, 1954-56; head nurse psychiat. unit Akron Gen. Hosp., 1956-57; instr. psychiatric nursing Summit County Receiving, Cuyahoga Falls, 1957-61; head nurse, in-service instr. Willard (N.Y.) State Hosp., 1961-62; asst. prof. Alfred (N.Y.) U., 1962-76, assoc. prof., assoc. dean, 1976-78, acting dean, 1978-79, dean, 1979-90, dean coll. profl. studies, 1990-91, prof. counseling, 1991-2000; ret., 2000. Cons. N.Y. State Regents Program for Non-Collegiate Sponsored Instrn., 1984; cons. collegiate programs N.Y. State Dept. Edn., 1985, Elmira Coll., 1991, U. Rochester, 1992-93; accreditation visitor Nat. League for Nursing, 1984-92; ednl. cons. Willard Psychiat. Hosp., 1992-93; mem. profl. practice exam. subcom. Regents Coll., 1990-95. Vol. Williard Drug Treatment Ctr., 1997—, bd. dirs., Romulus Zoning Bd., 2002—; vol. Red Cross, 2003—, co-capt. disaster team, 2004—; bd. dirs. Five Point Correctional Facility, Willard Drug Treatment Ctr. Recipient Tchg. Excellence award Alfred U., 1977, Mary E. Gladwin Outstanding Alumni award Akron U. Coll. Nursing, 1983, Alfred Alumni Friends award, 1989, Grand Marshall commencement Alfred U., 1993, Vol. of Yr. award Willard Drug Treatment Ctr., 1999. Mem.: ACA (NAR rep. 2000—04, co-capt. disaster team Red Cross-Finger Lakes chpt. 2003—, pres.-elect, NYCA 2004), Genesee Valley Edn. Com. (chair 1984—86), Western N.Y. League Nursing (bd. dirs. 1991—93), Genesee Regional Consortium (v.p.), N.Y. State Coun. of Deans (treas. 1984—88), N.Y. State Counseling Assn. (v.p.-elect profl. svcs. 1995—96, v.p. profl. svcs. 1996—98, v.p.-elect profl. svcs. 1998—99, v.p. profl. svcs. 1999—2000), Sigma Theta Tau (treas. Alfred chpt. 1984—85). Avocations: boating, fishing, public speaking in areas of family and child abuse. E-mail: drand@rochester.rr.com.

RAND, LAWRENCE ANTHONY, investor, financial relations executive; b. Bklyn., Nov. 19, 1942; s. Gerald M. and Elaine Shirley Rand; m. Madelon L., July 4, 1942; children: Allan, Joshua, Emily. AB with honors, Brown U., 1964; MA, NYU, 1965, PhD, 1998. Lectr. NYU, 1967, CUNY, 1968; analyst CIA, Langley, Va., 1967-68; account supr. Ruder & Finn Inc., N.Y.C., 1968-71; co-founder, sr. v.p. Kekst & Co., N.Y.C., 1971—, also bd. dirs. Chmn., bd. dirs. ALS Assn., L.A., 1987-92. Bd. dirs. N.Y. United Hosp., Port Chester; chmn. ethics com. Village Rye Brook, NY, 1993—2000, village trustee, 2000—02, mayor, 2004—; bd. dirs. U.S. Tennis Assn. Tennis and Edn. Found. Mem. Brown U. Club, Bailiwick Club (Greenwich, Conn.). Office: Kekst & Co 437 Madison Ave 19th Fl New York NY 10022-7195 Office Phone: 212-521-4800. E-mail: lar@kekst.com.

RAND, LEON, academic administrator; b. Boston, Oct. 8, 1930; s. Max B. and Ricka (Muscanto) Rakisky; m. Marian L. Newton, Aug. 29, 1959; children: Debra Ruth, Paul Martin, Marta Leah. BS, Northeastern U., 1953; MA, U. Tex., 1956, PhD, 1958. Postdoctoral fellow Purdue U., 1958-59; asst. prof. to prof. U. Detroit, 1959-68; prof., chmn. dept. chemistry Youngstown (Ohio) State U., 1968-74, dean grad. studies and research, 1974-81, acting acad. v.p., 1980; vice chancellor acad. affairs U. N.C., Pembroke, 1981—85; chancellor Ind. U.-S.E., New Albany, 1986-96; chancellor emeritus Ind. U., 1996—, prof. emeritus, 1999—; spl. asst. to chancellor IUPUI, 1996-98. Bd. dirs. Floyd Meml. Hosp., New Albany, 1987—90, Jewish Hosp., Louisville, 1991—96. Bd. dirs., mem. exec. com. Louisville (Ind.) area chpt. ARC; docent Indpls. Mus. Art, 1998—. Mem.: Metroversity (bd. dirs.), Am. Inst. Chemists, Am. Chem. Soc., Sigma Xi, Phi Kappa Phi. Home: 1785 Arrowwood Dr Carmel IN 46033-9019 E-mail: LRand7658@sbcglobal.net.

RAND, PETER, writer, editor, educator; b. San Francisco, Feb. 23, 1942; s. Christopher T.E. Rand and Margaret Aldrich Demott; m. Bliss I. Rand, Dec. 19, 1976; 1 child, James. Student, U. Calif., Berkeley; MA, Johns Hopkins U., 1975. Adv. fiction editor Antaeus, NYC, 1970-73; editor Washington Monthly, 1974-75; instr. Columbia U., NYC, 1976-91; preceptor Harvard U., Cambridge, Mass., 1997-98, Boston U., 1999—. Freelance editor, Belmont, Mass., 1994—. Author: Firestorm, 1969, The Time of the Emergency, 1977, The Private Rich, 1984, Gold from Heaven, 1988, China Hands, 1995; editor: Deng Xiaoping, Chronicle of an Empire (by Ruan Ming), 1994, Scarlet Memorial, Tales of Cannibalism in Modern China (by Zheng Yi), 1996, Tiananmen Follies (by Dai Qing), 2003. Trustee Belmont Citizens Forum, 1999—2002. Grantee Creative Artists Performing Svc., NYC, 1977. Mem. PEN, J.K. Fairbank Ctr. for East Asian Rsch. (affiliate), Tavern Club. Avocation: tennis. Home: 35 Falmouth St Belmont MA 02478

RAND, PETER ANDERS, architect; b. Hibbing, Minn., Jan. 8, 1944; s. Sidney Anders and Dorothy Alice (Holm) R.; m. Nancy Ann Straus, Oct. 21, 1967; children: Amy, Dorothy. BA, St. Olaf Coll., 1966; cert., Oslo Internat. Summer Sch., Norway, 1964, U. Minn. Sch. Architecture, 1969-72. Registered architect, Minn. Designer, architect, dir. pub. rels. Setter, Leach & Lindstrom, Inc., Mpls., 1972-78; dir. bus. devel, head Eden Prairie (Minn.) office Archtl. Design Group, Inc., 1979-80; dir. mktg. and publs. Minn. Soc. AIA, 1981-82, exec. dir., 1982-85, exec. v.p., CEO, 1986-98, v.p., 1999—. Pub. Architecture Minn. mag.; bd. dirs. MSAADA Architects & Engrs.; cons., archtl. designer. Bd. dirs. Project for Pride in Living, 1979-88, chmn., 1980-86; trustee Bethlehem Luth. Ch., 1980-86, chmn. bd. trustees, 1985, chmn. com. on worship, 1993-96, mem. ch. coun., 1993-96; mem. Minn. Ch. Ctr. Commn., 1981-89, chmn., 1985-88; sec. Coun. Archtl. Component Execs. of AIA, 1987, 92, pres., 1997-98; bd. dirs. Minn. Coun. Chs., 1985-89, sec., 1989; bd. dirs. Mpls. Coun. Chs., 1985-88; bd. dirs. Arts Midwest, 1987-96, treas., 1989, v.p., 1990-91, chmn., 1992-93; bd. dirs. Nordic Ctr., Preservation Alliance Minn., 1995—. Served with U.S. Army, 1966-69. Fellow AIA (jour. honor awrd 1981, Nat. Svc. award 1993); mem. Minn. Soc. AIA, Nat. Trust Hist. Preservation, Torske Klubben. Home: 1728 Humboldt Ave S Minneapolis MN 55403-2809

RAND, ROBERT STEPHEN, electrical engineer, physicist, statistician; b. Worcester, Mass., Nov. 10, 1953; s. Raymond Stephen and Dorothy May Rand; m. Maria Elisa Rand; 1 child, Christine Allie. PhD in Engring. Physics, U. Va., Charlottesville, 2001. Scientist U.S. Army ERDC, Alexandria, Va., 1977—. Mem.: SPIE, IEEE-Geosci. and Remote Sensing Soc., Sigma Xi. Business E-Mail: robert.s.rand@erdc.usace.army.mil.

RAND, ROBERT WHEELER, neurosurgeon, educator; b. L.A., Jan. 28, 1923; s. Carl W. and Catherine (Humphrey) R.; m. Helen L. Pierce, Dec. 17, 1949; children: Carl W., Richard P. Student, Harvard U., 1940-42, UCLA, 1942-44; MD, U. So. Calif., 1947; MS, U. Mich., 1951, PhD in Anatomy, 1952; JD, U. West L.A., 1974. Intern, resident in neurosurgery U. Mich., Ann Arbor, 1947-52; from instr. to prof. neurol. surgery UCLA, 1953-89; assoc. med. dir. John Wayne Cancer Inst., Santa Monica, Calif., 1989—. Expert witness malpractice cases Superior Ct. Author: Spinal Cord Tumors in Childhood, 1960, Microneurosurgery, 3d edit., 1985; contbr. articles to profl. jours.; inventor neuropledgets, thermomagnetic surgery coil system, microballoon for aneurysm occlusion, Malcolm-Rand graphite cranial frame, cobalt scalpel. Lt. comdr. USNR, 1943-46, 54-56. Recipient Profl. award UCLA, 1973. Fellow ACS; mem. AMA, Calif. Med. Assn., L.A. County Med. Assn., Am. Surg. Assn., Internat. Coll. Surgeons, Am. Assn. Neurol. Surgeons, Assn. Neurol. Surgeons, Soc. Neurol. Surgeons, Western Neurosurg. Soc., L.A. Country Club. Office: John Wayne Cancer Inst St John's Hosp 2200 Santa Monica Blvd Santa Monica CA 90404-2302

RAND, WILLIAM, lawyer, former state justice; b. N.Y.C., Oct. 11, 1926; s. William and Barbara (Burr) R.; married; children: Alicia, Carley Coudert, William Coudert, Paula Burr. AB, Harvard U., 1948; LLB, Columbia U., 1951. Bar: N.Y. 1951, U.S. Dist. Ct. N.Y. 1951, U.S. Supreme Ct., 1958, U.S. Ct. Appeals (2d cir.) 1961, U.S. Ct. Appeals (4th cir.) 1985, U.S. Ct. Appeals (3rd cir.) 2004. Asst. dist. atty. New York County, 1954-59; asst. counsel to gov. of State of N.Y., 1959-60; assoc. Coudert Bros., N.Y.C., 1961-62, ptnr., 1963-98; justice N.Y. State Supreme Ct., 1962. Justice Village of Cove Neck, Oyster Bay, N.Y., 1974-98. Mem. exec. com. New York County Reps., 1968-72. Served with USN, 1944-46, PTO. Mem.: Racquet and Tennis Club (N.Y.C.), Piping Rock Club (Locust Valley, N.Y.). Home: 73 Cove Neck Rd Oyster Bay NY 11771-1821 Office: Coudert Bros Fl 43 1114 Avenue of the Americas New York NY 10036-7710 E-mail: randw@coudert.com.

RAND, WILLIAM MEDDEN, biostatistics educator; b. Seneca Falls, N.Y., June 26, 1938; s. Austin Loomer and Rheua Vaughn (Medden) R.; m. Patricia Ann Gooding, Oct. 7, 1967; 1 child, Toby Stewart. BA, Ind. U., 1959; MA, Brandeis U., 1961; PhD, UCLA, 1969. Rsch. engr. Jet Propulsion Lab., Pasadena, Calif., 1962-65; rsch. assoc. U. So. Calif., L.A., 1965-67; asst. prof. MIT, Cambridge, 1969-74, assoc. prof., 1974-76, lectr., 1976-88; prof. biostats. Tufts U. Sch. Medicine, Boston, 1988—, dir. biometry div., 1988—; prof. veterinary medicine Tufts U., Boston, 1995—, prof. gen. dentistry, 1998—. Rsch. coord. world hunger program UN U., Tokyo, 1979-82 Editor: Protein-Energy Requirement Studies in Developing Countries, 1984, Food Composition Data, 1987. Mem. Am. Statis. Assn., Biometric Soc., Am. Inst. Nutrition, Am. Soc. for Clin. Nutrition. Office: Tufts U Sch Medicine 136 Harrison Ave Boston MA 02111-1800 Business E-Mail: william.rand@tufts.edu.

RANDA, JAMES PAUL, physicist, electrical engineer; b. Chgo., Jan. 26, 1947; s. John Joseph and Catherine Anne (Baier) R.; m. Susan Bulmann, June 12, 1980; 1 child, David. BS, Ill. Benedictine Coll., 1969; MS, U. Ill., 1970, PhD, 1974. Vis. asst. prof. Tex. A&M U., College Station, 1974-75; postdoctoral fellow U. Manchester, Eng., 1975-78; asst. prof. U. Colo., Boulder, 1978-83; physicist, sr. project leader Nat. Inst. of Stds. and Tech., Boulder, 1983—. Lectr. physics dept. U. Colo., Boulder, 1985-89; lectr., cons. Productivity and Stds. Bd., Singapore, 2000; U.S. rep. to working group on radiofrequency quantities Internat. Com. of Weights and Measures, Sevres, France, 1999—, chmn., 2002—. Editor: Quantum Flavordynamics, Quantum Chromodynamics, and Unified Field Theories, 1980; contbr. articles to profl. jours. Recipient Bronze medal, U.S. Dept. Commerce, 1992, 1999, award for best paper, IEEE Transactions on Electromagnetic Compatibility, 1992. Mem. IEEE, MTT Soc., EMC Soc. (tech. com., chair 1990-94), Am. Phys. Soc., Automated RF Techniques Group, Geoscience and Remote Sensing Soc. of IEEE. Avocations: reading, hiking, gardening, writing. Office: NIST 818-01 325 Broadway Boulder CO 80305-3328 Business E-Mail: randa@boulder.nist.gov.

RANDALL, ARTHUR RAYMOND, building contractor; b. Hamden, Conn., May 14, 1927; Cert. consultant, Consultants Inst., Columbus, Ohio, 1986. Pres., owner Sherman Constrn. Co, Orange, Conn., 1949—; ptnr. Shoreline Shelving Co., Orange, 1985—. Cons., pres. N.E. Bldg. Cons., Orange, 1978—; environ. insp., mem. Environ. Assessment Assn. Mem. Am. Cons. League, Am. Soc. Home Insps. Office: Sherman Constrn Co 61 Hampton Close Orange CT 06477-1934

RANDALL, CHANDLER CORYDON, church rector; b. Ann Arbor, Mich., Jan. 22, 1935; s. Frederick Stewart and Madeline Leta (Snow) R.; m. Marian Archias Montgomery, July 2, 1960; children: Sarah Archais, Elizabeth Leggett, Rebekah Stewart. AB in History, U. Mich., 1957; S.T.B. in Theology, Berkeley Divinity at Yale U., 1960; PhD in Hebraic Studies, Hebrew Union Coll., 1969; D.D. (honoris causa), Berkeley Divinity at Yale U., 1985. Rector St. Paul's Episcopal Ch., Richmond, Ind., 1967-71; rector Trinity Episcopal Ch., Ft. Wayne, Ind., 1971-88, St. Peter's Episcopal Ch., Del Mar, Calif., 1988-00. Bd. dirs. Living Ch. Found., Milw.; bibl. theologian Episcopal Ch. Stewardship, N.Y.C., 1985; alumni coun. Berkeley Divinity at Yale, New Haven, Conn., 1981-87; bishop's cabinet Diocese of No. Ind., South Bend, 1983-87. Author: Satire in the Bible, 1969, An Approach to Biblical Satire, 1990; contbr. articles to profl. jours. Founder Canterbury Sch., Ft. Wayne, 1977; commr. Ind. Jud. Qualifications Commn., Indpls., 1981-87; pres. Ft. Wayne Plan Commn., 1977; bd. dirs. Ft. Wayne Park Found., 1983-88; platform com. Ind. Republican Party, Indpls., 1974. Recipient Disting. Svc. medal U. Mich., 1981, Scheuer scholar Hebrew Union Coll., 1963-66, Liberty Bell award Ft. Wayne Bar Assn., 1988; named Sagamore of the Wabash, Gov. Ind., 1987. Mem. Am. Schs. Oriental Research, Yale U. Alumni Club (pres. 1982-88), Quest Club (pres.), Rotary Club, Chi Psi (nat. chaplain 1982). Republican. Episcopalian. Avocations: college recruiting, genealogy. Office: St Peters Episcopal Church PO Box 336 Del Mar CA 92014-0336

RANDALL, CLAIRE, church executive; b. Dallas, Oct. 15, 1919; d. Arthur Godfrey and Annie Laura (Fulton) R. AA, Schreiner Coll., 1948; BA, Scarritt Coll., 1950; DD (hon.), Berkeley Sem., Yale U., 1974; LHD (hon.), Austin Coll., 1982; LLD (hon.), Notre Dame U., 1984. Assoc. missionary edn. Bd. World Missions Presbyn. Ch., U.S., Nashville, 1949-57, dir. art Gen. Coun. Atlanta, 1957-61; dir. Christian World Mission, program dir., assoc. dir. Ch. Women United, N.Y.C., 1962-73; gen. sec. Nat. Coun. Ch. of Christ in U.S.A., N.Y.C., 1974-84, ret., 1985; nat. pres. Ch. Women United, N.Y.C., 1988-92. Mem. Nat. Commn. on Internat. Women's Yr., 1975-77, Martin Luther King Jr. Fed. Holiday Commn., 1985. Recipient Woman of Yr. in Religion award Heritage Soc., 1977; Empire State Woman of Yr. in Religion award State of N.Y., 1984; medal Order of St. Vladimir, Russian Orthodox Ch., 1984. Democrat. Episcopalian. Avocations: golf, swimming, painting, reading, music. Home: 9965 W Royal Oak Rd # 1214 Sun City AZ 85351-6116

RANDALL, CLIFFORD WENDELL, civil engineer, educator; b. Somerset, Ky., May 1, 1936; s. William Lesbert and Geneva (James) R.; m. Phyllis Amis, Aug. 15, 1959; children: Andrew Amis, William Otis. BSCE, U. Ky., 1959, MS in Sanitary Engring., 1963; PhD in Environ. Health Engring., U. Tex., 1966. Asst. prof. civil engring. U. Tex., Arlington, 1965-68; mem. faculty Va. Poly. Inst. and State U., 1968—2001, prof. civil engring., 1972-81, Charles Lunsford prof., 1981—2001; vis. prof. U. Cape Town, South Africa, 1983; chmn. environ. engring. and scis. program Va. Poly. Inst. and State U., 1979-97, Charles Lunsford prof. emeritus, 2001—. Lectr. Shanghai Archtl. and Mcpl. Engring. Inst., Wuhan Tech. U., 1987; dir. Occoquan Watershed Monitoring Program, 1971-2001; mem. Occoquan watershed monitoring subcom. Va. State Water Control Bd., 1971—, chair, 1971-85, 2001—, vice chair, 1986-2001; mem. U.S. nat. com. Internat. Water Quality, 1976-88, chair 1986-88, mem. 1992 IAWQ Biennial Conf. Com., chair conf. arrangements, Washington; tng. grant cons. EPA, 1970-71; cons. to industry, 1969—; WHO cons. to Nat. Environ. Engring. Rsch. Inst. India, 1983-84; Va. gov. appointee sci. and tech. adv. com. Chesapeake Bay Program; mem. sci. and tech. adv. com. Chesapeake Bay Program, 1984—, chmn. 1993-97; mem. nitrogen tech. adv. com. N.Y.C. Dept. Environ. Protection, 1994—; mem. blue ribbon panel

wastewater treatment City of Atlanta, 1997-2001. Author tech. papers in field; co-author: Biological Process Design for Wastewater Treatment, 1980, Stormwater Management in Urbanizing Areas, 1983, Design and Retrofit of Wastewater Treatment Plants for Biological Nutrient Removal, 1992. Troop com. chmn. local Boy Scouts Am., 1978-82, chmn. dist. Camporee com., 1977; camp pres. Gideons Internat., 1976-78, 80, 95-97, state cabinet mem., 1985-88; vice moderator Highlands Bapt. Assn., 1980-81, moderator, 1982-83; mem. bd. deacons Blacksburg Bapt. Ch., 1971-74, 79-82, chmn., 1974. Lt. U.S. Coast and Godetic Survey, 1959-62. Ford Found. fellow, 1964-65; recipient citation Engring. News-Record, 1988, Disting. Svc. award U.S. nat. com. Internat. Assn. Water Quality, 1989, Salute to Excellence Gov. of Md., 1994, Alumni Pub. Svc. award Va. Tech., 1996, Mathias medal for sci. excellence Chesapeake Rsch. Consortium and the Sea Grant Offices of Md. and Va., 1996, Dean's award Excellence Pub. Svc., Va. Tech. Engring., 1997; named Conservationist of Yr. Chesapeake Bay Found., 1986; AEC trainee U. Tex., 1963-65. Mem. ASCE (chmn. water resources mgmt. com. 1977, environ. engring. rsch. coun. 1989-90, svc. award 1978, 80, meritorious tech. paper award 1969), Am. Water Works Assn. (cert. recognition for acad. excellence 1980, 89), Water Environ. Fedn. (bd. dirs. 1981-84, Morgan cert. of merit for full scale rsch. 1982, Bedell award 1983, svc. award 1984, Gordon M. Fair medal for excellence in engring. edn. 1998), Internat. Water Assn. (governing bd. 1986-88, USA rep. on sci. and tech. com. 1994-98, mem. nutrient removal specialist group mgmt. com. 1990—, chmn. 1994-98), Va. Water Environment Assn. (v.p. 1974-75, pres. 1975-76), Assn. Environ. Engring. Profs. (sec.-treas. 1979-80, bd. dirs. 1978-80, 93-97, v.p. 1994-95, pres. 1995-96, past pres. 1996-97). Home: 1302 Crestview Dr Blacksburg VA 24060-5609 Office: Va Poly Inst & State U Dept Civil Engring 330 Norris Hall Blacksburg VA 24061

RANDALL, CRAIG, financial and business management consultant, accountant, computer specialist; b. Santa Monica, Calif., Oct. 29, 1957; s. Les Shepard and Marian Hand; m. Jeanne Runsvold, July 14, 1984. Student, Pierce Coll., 1975-76, Calif. State U.-Northridge, 1977-79. Asst. controller Becker CPA Rev., Encino, Calif., 1979-81; sr. staff acct. Kress and Goldstein, CPAs, Sherman Oaks, Calif., 1981-84; pres., chief exec. officer Bus. Computers Network, Inc., Woodland Hills, 1984—, Randall Accountancy Corp., Woodland Hills, 1984—. Office: Randall Accountancy A Profl Corp 21031 Ventura Blvd Ste 1101 Woodland Hills CA 91364-2254

RANDALL, DAVID JOHN, physiologist, zoologist, educator; b. London, Sept. 15, 1938; BSc, U. Southampton, 1960, PhD, 1963, FRSC, 1981. From asst. to assoc. prof. U. B.C., 1963-73, prof. zoology, 1973—, assoc. dean grad. studies, 1990-96, 2000; head biology and chemistry City U. Hong Kong, 2000—; univ. grants coun. mem. Hong Kong Govt. Spl. Adminstrv. Region, 2000—03. Vis. lectr. Bristol U., 1968-69; vis. sci. Marine Labs U. Tex., 1970, Zool. Sta., Naples, Italy, 1973; NATO vis. sci. Acadia U., 1975, Marine Lab U. Tex., 1977; chief sci. Alpha Helix Amazon Expedition, 1976; mem. adv. bd. J. Comp Physiology, 1977-92, J. Exp. Biol., 1981-84; chmn. animal biol. comt. Nat. Res. Coun., Can., 1974; vis. prof. U. Nairobi, 1988, George Washington U., 1988-89, City U. Hong Kong, 1997; concurrent prof. Nanjing U., China, 1993—; external examiner U. Singapore, 1990-91, 2000-02; mem. UGC, Hong Kong, 2001-03. Assoc. editor: Marine Behavior Physiology. Recipient Award of Excellence Am. Fisheries Soc., 1994. Fellow Royal Soc. Can.; mem. Can. Soc. Zoologists (Fry medal 1993), Soc. Exp. Biologists. Office: City U Hong Kong Biol Chem Tat Chee Ave Kowloon Hong Kong Fax: 2788 7406. Business E-Mail: bhrand@cityu.edu.hk.

RANDALL, FRANCIS BALLARD, historian, educator, writer; b. N.Y.C., Dec. 17, 1931; s. John Herman, Jr. and Mercedes (Moritz) R.; m. Laura Regina Rosenbaum, June 11, 1957; children: David R., Ariane R. BA, Amherst Coll., 1952; MA, Columbia, 1954, PhD, 1960. Instr. history Amherst Coll., 1956-59; from instr. to asst. prof. history Columbia, 1959-61, vis. prof., 1967-68; humanities faculty Sarah Lawrence Coll., Bronxville, NY, 1961—2002, chmn., 1985—89, 1998—2001, trustee, 1971-76. Author: (with others) Essays in Russian and Soviet History, 1963, Stalin's Russia, an Historical Reconsideration, 1965, N.G. Chernyshevskii, 1967, Vissarion Belinskii, 1987, History Papers: A Teaching Life, 2000. Freedom rider civil disobedience to racism, 1961, war draft resistance arrests, 1967, 70. Fulbright fellow for study in India, 1965, Wye fellow, 1986. Mem.: AAUP (chpt. chmn. 1966—69), Am. Assn. for Advancement Slavic Studies, Am. Hist. Assn., Sigma Xi, Phi Beta Kappa. Home: 425 Riverside Dr Apt 10I New York NY 10025-7730

RANDALL, HERBERT EUGENE, photographer, consultant; b. Riverhead, N.Y., Dec. 16, 1936; s. Herbert Eugene Randall and Jane Margaret Paul; m. Rosalind Norma Singho, May 1, 1965; 1 child, Dana Singho. AS, N.Y.C. C.C., 1957. Photographic cons. South Bronx (N.Y.) Youth Village, 1968—70; coord. photography multi-media project N.Y.C. Bd. Edn., N.Y., 1974—81; workshop presenter in field; lectr. U. Ala., 2001, State U. NY, Old Westbury, 2001, U. So. Miss., 2002, Jackson State U., 2004, Miami U., 2004. Co-author: Faces of Freedom Summer, 2001; photographer: People Mag., 1999, The N.Y. Times, 2001, The Parrish Art Mus., Mus. Modern Art, Met. Mus. Art, U. So. Miss., George Eastman House, exhibitions San Francisco (Calif.) Mus. Modern Art, Internat. Ctr. Photography, Bklyn. (N.Y.) Mus., Art Inst. Pitts., The Corcoran Gallery Art, The High Mus. Art, The Studio Mus. Fellow Whitney fellowship, John Hay Whitney Found., 1964—65; grantee, Creative Artists Pub. Svc. Program, 1971—72. Avocations: reading, movies, hiking, sports.

RANDALL, KAREN, film company executive; BA cum laude, Vassar Coll., 1973; JD, UCLA, 1976. Ptnr. Wyman Bautzer Kuchel & Silbert, 1976; mng. ptnr. Katten Muchin & Zavi, LA; sr. v.p., gen. counsel Universal Studios, 1996—2000; exec. v.p., gen. counsel Vivendi Universal Entertainment, Universal City, Calif., 2000—. Bd. mem. United Internat. Pictures, Hollywood Sign Trust, Hollywood Canteen Found. Named to, YWCA Acad. Women Achievers, The Am. Lawyer's 1995 edit. of "Forty-Five Under 45"; recipient Women of Distinction award, Hollywood C. of C., Pursuit of Justice award, Calif. Women's Law Ctr., Corp. Leadership award, Big Sisters L.A. Mem.: Motion Picture Assn. Am. (Universal's liaison, bd. dirs., mem. spl. policy group), Am. Corp. Counsel Assn. (nat. bd. dirs.). Office: Vivendi Universal Entertainment 100 Universal City Plaza Universal City CA 91608-1002

RANDALL, KARL W. aviation executive, lawyer; b. Mount Pleasant, Mich., Feb. 12, 1951; s. Herbert J. and Wilma E. (Worstell) R.; m. Natalie Kilmer Randall, Dec. 17, 1971; children: Adam B., Kara J. AA, Mich. Christian Coll., Rochester, 1971; BA, Oakland U., Rochester, 1977; JD, Wayne State U. Law Sch., Detroit, 1981. Bar: Mich., 1981, U.S. Dist. Ct., 1981, U.S. Ct. Appeals, 1983; cert. airport mgr., Mich., 1993. Quality contr. Staley SNO BOL Corp., Pontiac, Mich., 1971-72; engring. tech. Oakland Co. Drain Comm., Pontiac, 1972-83; sr. asst. corp. counsel Oakland County Corp. Counsel, Pontiac, 1983-93; mgr. aviation Oakland County Internat. Airport, Waterford, Mich., 1993—. Dir. Integrity Jour., Mt. Pleasant, 1980-98, Oakland County Coord. Child Care Coun., Waterford, 1992-97. Author, editor: (religious jour.) Integrity, 1982, 94-95. Mem. Rep. Com. Oakland County, 1988—, Exec. Club Oakland County, 1993—. Mem. Mich. Assn. Airport Execs. (exec.). Republican. Mem. Ch. of Christ. Avocations: physical fitness, motorcycling, jogging, golf, piano. Office: Oakland County Internat Airport 6500 Highland Rd Waterford MI 48327-1607 E-mail: randallk@co.oakland.mi.us.

RANDALL, KAY TEMPLE, accountant, retired real estate agent; b. Chattanooga, Sept. 23, 1952; d. James H. Temple and Hortense N. (Dailey) Goodner; m. Gary F. Goodner, Feb. 9, 1968 (div. July 1972); 1 child, Jeffrey F. Goodner; m. Rodney B. Randall, Oct. 3, 1987. Student, Chattanooga State Coll., 1970-77, 82-83, Am. Inst. Banking, 1977-79. Lic. real estate agt., Tenn., ret.; notary public, Tenn. Ins. rep. Colonial Life Accident and Health, Columbia, S.C., 1980-82; real estate appraiser, agt. Chattanooga, 1983-88; acct. Mr. Transmission of Chattanooga, Inc., 1987—; real estate agt. Chattanooga, 1988—99. Adminstrv. asst. to legal profession, Chattanooga, 1972-75. Adv. bd. United Meth. Ch., Chattanooga, 1979-82, tchr., 1979-83; fellow cen. br. YMCA, Chattanooga, 1977-97. Fellow Walden's Club. Republican. Episcopalian. Avocation: collecting art. Home: 1858 Rivergate Ter Soddy Daisy TN 37379-5947 Office: Mr Transmission of Chattanooga Inc PO Box 1395 Soddy Daisy TN 37384-1395 E-mail: rodkayj@aol.com.

RANDALL, KENNETH C. dean, law educator; JD, Hofstra U., 1981; Master's, Yale U., 1982, Columbia U., 1985, Doctorate, 1988. Practice law Simpson Thacher & Bartlett, N.Y.C., 1982-84; with faculty U. Ala. Sch. Law, Tuscaloosa, 1985—, vice dean, 1989-93, dean, 1993—. Author book on international law; contbr. articles to law jours. and revs. W. Bayard Cutting Jr. fellow of internat. law Columbia U. Sch. Law, 1984-85. Office: U Ala Law Sch PO Box 870382 Tuscaloosa AL 35487-0001

RANDALL, LILIAN MARIA CHARLOTTE, museum curator; b. Berlin, Feb. 1, 1931; came to U.S., 1938; d. Frederick Henry and Elizabeth Agnes (Ziegler) Cramer; m. Richard Harding Randall, Apr. 11, 1953; children: Christopher, Julia, Katharine. BA cum laude, Mount Holyoke Coll., 1950; MA, Radcliffe Coll., 1951, PhD, 1955; LHD (hon.), Towson State U., 1993; D of Arts (hon.), Mt. Holyoke Coll., 1998. Asst. dir. Md. State Arts Coun., 1972-73; curator manuscripts and rare books Walters Art Gallery, Balt., 1974-85, rsch. curator manuscripts, 1985-95; rsch. cons., 1995-97. Vis. lectr. dept. art history Johns Hopkins U., 1964-68; hon. vis. lectr. U. Mich., Ann Arbor; lectr. in field; bd. dirs. Digital Scriptorium: Electronic Access to Medieval Manuscripts; advisor Union Manuscript Computer Catalogue, 1996—. Author: Images in the Margins of Gothic Manuscripts, 1966; co-editor: Gatherings in Honor of Dorothy Miner, 1974, The Diary of George A. Lucas: An American Art Agent in Paris, 1909-1957, 1979, Illuminated Manuscripts: Masterpieces in Miniature, 1984, Medieval and Renaissance Manuscripts in the Walters Art Gallery, Vol. I, France, 875-1420, 1989, Vol. II, France, 1420-1540, 1992, Vol. III, Belgium, 1250-1530, 1997; contbr. articles to profl. jours. Mem. Williston Libr. com., 1988-89; reviewer, panelist NEH, 1980—; mem. vis. com. Art of Europe dept. Mus. Fine Arts, Boston, 2002—. Grantee AAUW, 1953-54, ACLS, 1960, 65, Bunting Inst., 1961-63, Ford Found., 1967-69, Am. Philos. Soc., 1971, NEA, 1975, Samuel H. Kress Found., 1979, 81-84, NEH, 1977-84, 89-95; grantee publ. subsidy Md. State Arts Coun., 1972, Mcpl. Art Soc. Balt., 1972, Andrew W. Mellon Found., 1988, Getty Grant program, 1990-92, NEA Mus. program, 1992-93; recipient Festschrift, Walters Art Gallery, ed. Elizabeth Burin, 1996, Sesquicentennial award Mount Holyoke Coll., 1987. Fellow Medieval Acad. Am. (libr. preservation com., various coms. 1985-87, 90-93); mem. Internat. Ctr. Medieval Art (bd. dirs. 1978-82, 96-99), Coll. Art Assn. (Arthur Kingsley Porter prize 1957), Balt. Bibliophiles (bd. dirs. 1966-80, pres. 1980-83), Pyramid Atlantic (bd. dirs. 1985-88), Mus. Fine Arts Boston (vis. com. Art of Europe dept. 2002—), Grolier Club, Phi Beta Kappa. Home: 370 Adams St Milton MA 02186-4233

RANDALL, LINDA LEA, biochemist, educator; b. Montclair, N.J., Aug. 7, 1946; d. Lowell Neal and Helen (Watts) R.; m. Gerald Lee Hazelbauer, Aug. 29, 1970. BS, Colo. State U., 1968; PhD, U. Wis., 1971. Postdoctoral fellow Inst. Pasteur, Paris, 1971—73; asst. prof. Uppsala (Sweden) U., 1975—81; assoc. prof. Wash. State U., Pullman, 1981—83, prof. biochemistry, 1983—2000; Wurdock prof. biochemistry U. Mo., Columbia, 2000—. Guest scientist Wallenberg Lab., Uppsala U., 1973-75; study section NIH, 1984-88. Mem. edtl. bd. Jour. of Bacteriology, 1982-96; co-editor: Virus Receptors Part I, 1980; contbr. articles to profl. jours. Recipient Eli Lilly Award in Microbiology and Immunology, Am. Soc. Microbiology, Am. Assn. Immunologists, Am. Soc. Exptl. Pathology, 1984, Faculty Excellence Award in Rsch., Washington State U., 1988, Disting. Faculty Address, 1990, Parke-Davis award, 1995. Fellow AAAS, Am. Acad. Microbiology; mem. NAS, Am. Microbiol. Soc., Am. Soc. Biol. Chemists, Protein Soc. Avocation: dance. Office: Univ Mo Dept Biochemistry 117 Schweitzer Hall Columbia MO 65211 Office Phone: 573-884-4160.

RANDALL, LYNN ELLEN, librarian; b. Chgo., Oct. 10, 1951; d. Ward W. and Hazel A. (Nettles) R. BA, King's Coll., 1970; MA, Seton Hall U., 1973; MLS, Rutgers U., 1978. Libr. asst. Newark Coll. Engring, Newark, 1970-75; libr. dir. N.E. Bible Coll., Essex Fells, N.J., 1975-81; reference libr. Seton Hall U., South Orange, N.J., 1983-85; dir. libr. svc. Berkeley Coll., NJ, 1985-89; with Caldwell Coll., NJ, 1989—, exec. dir. libr. svcs. Reference libr., instr. Morris (N.J.) County Coll., 1981-83; panelist/facilitator Middle States Self-Study Inst., 1996, 97, Evaluator, Middle States, 1994-. Mem. N.J. Libr. Assn. (pres. 1996-97), Am. Libr. Assn. Office: Jennings Libr Caldwell Coll 9 Ryerson Ave Caldwell NJ 07006-6109 Office Phone: 973-618-3314. Business E-Mail: lrandall@caldwell.edu.

RANDALL, MALCOM, health care administrator; b. East St. Louis, Ill., Aug. 9, 1916; s. John Leeper and Merle Dorothy Randall; m. Christine Sheppard, Nov. 10, 1972 AB, McKendree Coll., 1939; M.H.A., St. Louis U., 1955; D of Pub. Svc. with honors, U. Fla., 1996. Chief br. office VA, St. Louis, 1946-49, asst. area dir. area office, 1949-53; spl. asst. to dir. VA Hosp., St. Louis, 1953-56, hosp. adminstr. Spokane, Wash., 1956-57, Chgo., 1957-58, Indpls., 1958-60, Wood, Wis., 1960-64, hosp. dir. Miles City, Mont., 1964-66; med. ctr. dir. and med. dist. dir. VA, Gainesville, Fla., 1966—, regional rep., 1991—; prof. health and hosp. adminstrn. U. Fla., Gainesville, 1966—. Pres. N. Cen. Fla. Health Planning Council; mem. Fla. State Health Planning Council; chmn. Gov.'s Commn. on Alzheimer's Disease; mem. Alachua County Emergency Med. Svcs. Coun.; bd. dirs. emeritus 1st Union Nat. Bank Fla., Regional Med. Programs; mem. editorial bd. Jour. Am. Coll. Health Care Execs.; cons. on health care Univ. Clin. Ctr., Ljubljana, Slovenia, 1982—, Ministry of Health, Hungary and Med. U. Debrecen, 1989—. Contbr. numerous articles to profl. jours. Bd. dirs. Civitan Regional Blood Ctr., Gainesville, 1970. Served to capt. USN, 1942-46 Recipient Presdl. Rank award Pres. U.S., 1983, Meritorious Svc. award U. Fla., 1984, Exceptional Svc. award, 1985, Exec. Performance award, 1986, all VA; named Citizen of Yr., Gainesville, 1977. Fellow Am. Coll. Health Care Execs. (council regents, VA liaison); mem. Inst. Medicine, Nat. Acad. Sci., Assn. Am. Med. Colls. (bd. dirs., council tchg. hosps.), Am. Health Planning Assn. (bd. dirs.), Am. Hosp. Assn. (governing council mem. et and fed. hosp. sect.). Clubs: Heritage. Lodges: Rotary. Home: 1617 NW 19th Cir Gainesville FL 32605-4092 Office: VA Med Ctr Archer Rd Gainesville FL 32608 E-mail: mran268075@aol.com. *A core set of values should be the base for all of your activities, both professional and personal.*

RANDALL, MARILYN MAE, writer; d. Dice A. and Margaret L. Hartman; m. Charles D. Randall, Aug. 24, 1991; children: Philip E. Marechal, Cheryl L. Pittman. BA magna cum laude, Trinity Coll., Washington, 1988. Vis. author/lectr. various elem. and mid. schs., Tenn., 2002—; participant Clemson (SC) U. First Ann. Summer Booksigning, 2002, Ea. Tenn. State U. Celebration of Books and Authors, Johnson City, 2002; featured lectr./workshop presenter Christian Writers' Conf., Memphis, 2002, Ea. Tenn. State U. Celebration Books and Authors, 2004; featured local author Fall for the Book George Mason U., 2004; workshop presenter U. Tenn., 2004. Author: (children's books) Southern Christmas, 2001, Wishes for Christmas, 2002, Wellington's Windows, 2003, The Three Wives of Hero the Second, 2004, A Marine Salute (endorsed by USMC and Young Marine Orgn.); editor: The Forty Days of Lent. Pres. Good Samaritan chpt. Daus. of the King, Knoxville, 1998—2004. Mem.: Alpha Sigma Lambda, Phi Beta Kappa. Episcopalian. Avocations: composing, poetry. Home: 1550 Scenic View Dr Loudon TN 37774

RANDALL, MARLENE DIETRICH, councilwoman, retired school system administrator; b. Norfolk, Va., Oct. 18, 1934; d. James E. West and Gladys Daniels (West) Pretlow; m. Vernon Lee Randall, Aug. 26, 1958; children: Ricardo C., Veronica Randall Williams, Michelle Randall Bryant. BS, Va. State U., Petersburg, 1954; MA, Columbia U., N.Y.C., 1968; postgrad., U. Va., 1980, Nova U., Washington, D.C., 1986. Elem. sch. tchr. Portsmouth Pub. Schs., Va., 1955—66, reading specialist, 1966—71, asst. prin., 1971—74, prin., 1976—89, adminstrv. asst. to supt., 1989—93. Bd. dirs. Portsmouth C. of C., Va.; bd. dirs., Tidewater chpt. Am. Red Cross, Norfolk, Va.; bd. dirs. Effingham St. YMCA, Portsmouth, Va. Empowerment coord. Norfolk/Portsmouth Empowerment Ctr., 2000—; sec. NAACP, Tidewater Cluster, 2000—; bd. dirs. Girl Scouts Coun. of Colonial Coast; councilwoman Portsmouth City Coun., Va., 2002—. Baptist. Office: City Council PO Box 820 Portsmouth VA 23705-0820 Home: 206 Wynn St Portsmouth VA 23701 Office Phone: 757-393-8639. Fax: 757-465-3804.

RANDALL, NEIL WARREN, gastroenterologist; b. White Plains, N.Y., Mar. 24, 1957; s. Leroy Bruce and Libby Cynthia (Brandt) R.; m. Linda Ilene Zell, Oct. 31, 1992. BA, U. Va., 1978; MD, U. Md., 1983. Diplomate Am. Bd. Internal Medicine with subspecialty in gastroenterology, geriat. Resident in internal medicine Ochsner Clinic, New Orleans, 1983-86; fellow in gastroenterology Tufts U., Boston, 1986-88; staff gastroenterologist Cleve. Clinic Fla., Fort Lauderdale, 1988-92, Geisinger Clinic, Danville, Pa., 1992-97, Pa. State Geisinger Health Sys., Danville, 1997-98; med. dir. gastrointestinal endoscopy Geisinger Health Sys., 1999-2000; gastroenterologist Gastroenterology Group of Naples, 2001—. Fellow ACP, Am. Coll. Gastroenterology; mem. Am. Soc for Gastroent. Endoscopy. Avocations: theater, travel, wine. Office: Gasterenterology Group Naples 1064 Goodlette-Frank Rd Naples FL 34102-5449 Office Phone: 239-649-1186.

RANDALL, PETER, plastic surgeon; b. Phila., Mar. 29, 1923; s. Alexander and Edith Tilghman (Kneedler) R.; m. Rose Gordon Johnson, May 1, 1948; children: Deborah K., Peter G., Julia B., Susanna T. BA, Princeton U., 1944; MD, Johns Hopkins U., 1946; MS (hon.), U. Pa., 1969. Diplomate Am. Bd. Plastic Surgery. Intern Union Meml. Hosp., Balt., 1946-47; asst. resident in surgery Hosp. of U. of Pa., Phila., 1949-50; fellow in plastic surgery Barnes Hosp.-St. Louis Childrens Hosp., 1950-52, resident in plastic surgery, 1952-53; asst. instr. plastic surgery Washington U., St. Louis, 1950-53; from asst. prof. to assoc. prof. plastic surgery U. Pa. Hosp., Phila., 1953-69, prof. plastic surgery, 1969-92; emeritus prof. plastic surgery, 1992—; chief div. plastic surgery sch. medicine U. Pa., Phila., 1979-87. Sr. surgeon Children's Hosp. Phila., 1965—. Contbr. articles to profl. jours. Pres. Plastic Surgery Edn. Found., 1972-73. Lt. (j.g.) USNR, 1947-49. Fellow: ACS (bd. govs., chmn. 1982—84, 1st v.p. 1985—86), Am. Assn. Plastic Surgeons (hon. Clinician of Yr. award 1987, disting. fellow 1994); mem.: AMA, Am. Cleft Palate Assn. (pres. 1965—66, Honors award 1986), Plastic Surgery Rsch. Coun. (founder, chmn. 1964—65), Phila. Acad. Surgery, Phila. County Med. Soc., Northea. Soc. Plastic Surgery (founder), Am. Surg. Assn., Coll. Physicians of Phila., Am. Soc. Plastic Surgeons (pres. 1978—79, Spl. Achievement award 1987), Am. Bd. Plastic Surgery (vice-chmn. 1976—77), Am. Cleft Palate Ednl. Found. (founder, pres. 1972—73), Robert H. Ivy Soc. (founder, pres. 1966—67), Halsted Soc., others, Sigma Xi. Office: U Pa Hosp 3400 Spruce St Philadelphia PA 19104-4206

RANDALL, PRISCILLA RICHMOND, retired travel company executive; b. Arlington, Mass., Mar. 19, 1926; d. Harold Bours and Florence (Hoefler) Richmond; m. Raymond Victor Randall, Mar. 2, 1946; children: Raymond Richmond, Priscilla Randall Middleton, Susan Randall Geery. Student, Wellesley Coll., 1943-44; Assoc., Garland Coll., 1946; student, Winona State U., 1977-81. Pub. relations dir. Rochester Meth. Hosp., Rochester, Minn., 1960-69; dir. pub relations Sheraton Rochester, 1969-71; pres. Med. Charters, Rochester, 1970-75, Ideas Unltd., Rochester, 1969-77; chief exec. officer Randall Travel, Rochester, 1977-89; pres. Randall Travel Delray, Delray Beach, Fla., 1989—2002; ret., 2002. Pres. Bar Harbour Apts. Inc., Delray Beach, 1989, sec., bd. dirs., 2002; social com. chmn., 1999—, sec., 1993-99. Editor, Inside Story, 1960-69, Rochester Meth. Hosp. News, 1960-69; producer Priscilla's World, 1972-75. Pres. Rochester Meth. Hosp. Aux., 1957-59, Downtown Bus. Assn., Rochester, 1985; treas. Class of 1947 Wellesley (Mass.) Coll., 1997-2002. Recipient Woman of Achievement Bus. YWCA, Rochester, 1983, Golden Door Knob, Bus. and Prfl. Women, Rochester, 1979. Mem. Inst. Cert. Travel Agts. (life), Assn. Retail Travel Agts. (life, nat. bd. 1988-90, sec. to bd. 1988-90, sec.-treas. Arlington, Va. nat. bd. 1990), Am. Soc. Travel Agts., Pacific Area Travel Agts., Minn. Exec. Women in Travel, Cruise Line Internat. Assn. (master cruise counselor), Little Club (sec. 2002, v.p. 2003- Gulfstream, Fla.) (sec. women's golf com. 1993-99, sec. bd. govs. 2002, treas. 2002), Hibiscus Garden Club (Delray Beach, Fla.) (pres., corr. sec.), Travelors Century Club (bd. govs.), Circumnavigator Club, Little Club (v.p. 2003—). Avocation: travel writing. Home: 86 Macfarlane Dr Apt 2C Delray Beach FL 33483-6901

RANDALL, RICHARD RAINIER, geographer; b. Toledo, July 21, 1925; s. Robert Henry and Maree (Gard) R.; m. Patricia Lee Spencer, June 9, 1962; children: Allison Maree, Susan Rebecca, Richard Rainier Jr. BA, George Washington U., 1949, MA, 1950; PhD, Clark U., 1955; postgrad., Graz U., Austria. Geog. analyst CIA, Washington, 1955-61; Washington rep. Rand McNally & Co., Washington, 1961-72; owner Randall Assocs., Washington, 1972-73; exec. sec. U.S. Bd. Geog. Names, Washington, 1973-93; geographer Def. Mapping Agy., Washington, 1973-93; ret., 1993; cons. on geog. names, 1993—. Convenor UN Working Group on Undersea and Maritime Feature Names, 1975-84; mem., prin. U.S. tech. advisor U.S. and U.K. Conf. on Geog. Names, 1976, 79, 81, 84, 86, 88, 92; dep. head U.S. del. UN Conf. on Geog. Names, 1977, head, 1982, 87, 92; 1st v.p. of 6th UN Conf. 92; prin. U.S. expert UN Group Experts on Geog. Names, 1975, 77, 79, 82, 84, 86, 87, 89, 92; pres. com. on geog. terminology Pan Am. Inst. Geography and History, 1973-77, pres. working group on geog. names and gazetters, 1981-94. Author: Place Names: How they Define the World—And More, 2001; contbr. articles to profl. jours.; inventor flexible fishhook V.p. North Cleveland Park Citizens Assn., Washington, 1968. With U.S. Army, 1943-46, ETO. Fulbright scholar, NRC, Austria, 1953-54; decorated ETO ribbon with 4 battle stars, Bronze Star, Combat Infantryman's badge, others. Mem. Am. Congress on Surveying and Mapping (dir. cartography divsn. 1973-75, dir. press rels. 1961-72, program dir. cartography divsn. ann. meeting 1967), Am. Geog. Soc., Assn. Am. Geographers (chmn. Mid-Atlantic divsn. 1978, dir. press rels. ann. conf. 1968), Am. Names Soc., Am. Austrian Soc. (v.p. 1955-57), Explorers Club, Cosmos Club. Republican.

RANDALL, ROBERT L(EE), ecological economist; b. Aberdeen, SD, Dec. 28, 1936; s. Harry Eugene and Juanita Alice (Barstow) R. MS in Phys. Chemistry, U. Chgo., 1960, MBA, 1963. Market devel. chemist E.I. du Pont de Nemours & Co., Inc., Wilmington, Del., 1963-65; chem. economist Battelle Meml. Inst., Columbus, Ohio, 1965-68; mgr. market and econ. rsch. Kennecott Copper Corp., N.Y.C., 1968-74, economist, 1974-79, dir. new bus. venture devel., 1979-81; pres., mng. dir. R.L. Randall Assocs., Inc., 1981—; economist U.S. Internat. Trade Commn., Washington, 1983—. Founder, pres., exec. dir. RainForest ReGeneration Inst., 1986—, ind. internat. press corr., 1997—, indsl. panel policy rev. of effect of regulation on innovation and U.S.-internat. competition U.S. Dept. Commerce, 1980-81; participant preparatory com. UN Conf. on Environ. and Devel., Rio de Janeiro, 1991; del. observer internat. negotiating com. UN Framework Conv. on Climate Change, 1991—. Contbg. author: Computer Methods for the 80's; sect. lead author, editor: World Energy Assessment, 2000; pub. reviewer intergovtl. panel on climate change Third Assessment Report; addresser 4th Internat. Greenhouse Gas Tech. conf., Interlaken, Switzerland, 1998; contbr. articles to profl. jours. Mem. Gay Activists Alliance, N.Y.C., 1971-75, chmn. state and fed. legislation com., 1975. Mem. AAAS (organizer ann. meeting Tropical Forest Regeneration Symposium), AIME (econ. coun., mineral econ. subsect.), Internat. Soc. Ecol. Health, Internat. Soc. Ecol. Economists, Am. Econ. Assn., Am. Statis. Assn., Am. Chem. Soc., Soc. Mining Engrs., Chemists Club of N.Y.C., Metall. Soc., N.Y. Acad. Scis., Nat. Econs. Club Washington (sec., reporter), Assn. Environ. and Resource Economists, Marine Biol. Assn. (Plymouth, Eng.), Wanderbirds Hiking Club (hike leader, treas.), Capital Hiking Club (hike leader, Washington). Home: 1727 Massachusetts Ave NW Washington DC 20036-2153 Office: US Internat Trade Com 500 E St NW Washington DC 20436-0003 E-mail: randall@usitc.gov. *Like thousands of organizations around the world, The RainForest ReGeneration Institute is trying to find a practical and effective way forward, through United Nations-sponsored treaty negotiations, appropriate national actions, and imaginative project work, on the ground, in local communities. Tropical rainforests must have recognizable community value if they are to be viable. Global value is not enough for the conservation of the tropical rainforests. Ultimate wisdom does not reside in any individual or organization. All must work together through every available forum and mechanism, and to create new modalities where those presently in existence are inadequate or ineffective.*

RANDALL, ROGER DAVID, publishing executive; b. St. Charles, Minn., Dec. 24, 1953; s. Curtis Clark and Virginia Mae (Tollefson) Randall; m. Mary Barnard, Aug. 25, 1979; children: Sara Louise, Clark Robinson. BA, Morn-

ingside Coll., 1976. Advt. dir. Nutra-Flo Chem. Co., Kay Dee Feed Co., Sioux City, Iowa, 1976-78; agrl. account svc. Lewis & Gilman, Phila., 1978-80, Creswell, Munsell, Fultz & Zirbel, Cedar Rapids, Iowa, 1980-81, Richardson, Myers & Donofrio, Inc., Balt., 1981-84; mktg. mgr. Farm Jour., Inc., Phila., 1984-85, v.p., 1986-89, v.p., pub., 1989-95, pres., 1995-99, CEO, 1999-2000, also bd. dirs.; pres., CEO AgWeb.com, 1999-2001; exec. v.p. Miller Meester, Inc., 2001—03. Mem. bus. adv. com. Nat. Assn. Conser. Dist. Bd. dirs. Planned Parenthood Sioux City, 1977-78, Iowa Planned Parenthood Fedn., 1978, Sioux City Pub. Mus., 1977-78; trustee Old 1st Reformed Ch., 1994-95. Recipient Disting. Alumni award, Morningside Coll., 1997. Mem. Nat. Agri-Mktg. Assn. (pres. Chesapeake chpt. 1984, nat. awards agri. excellence 1988, exec. com. 1990-92, sec.-treas. 1992-93), Queen Village Neighbors Assn. (dir., treas. 1987-90, pres. 1994-95), Preservation Alliance of Minn. (dir., vice chair, commn. com. co-chair) Mem. United Ch. Of Christ. Home: 4270 Norwood Ln N Minneapolis MN 55442

RANDALL, WILLIAM SEYMOUR, leasing company executive; b. Champaign, Ill., July 5, 1933; s. Glenn S. and Audrey H. (Honnold) R.; m. Sharon Larsen; children: Steve, Cathy, Mike, Jennifer. BS, Ind. State U., 1959. Controller Amana Refrigeration Co., Iowa, 1966-70; div. controller Trane Co., Clarksville, Tenn., 1970-74, corporate controller La Crosse, Wis., 1974-79; v.p., chief fin. officer Sta-Rite Industries, Milw., 1979-82; pres., owner Profl. Staff Resources, Inc., Milw., 1982—. Served with AUS, 1953-55. Mem. Financial Execs. Inst. Lodges: Rotary. Home: 13365 Tulane St Brookfield WI 53005-7141 Office: 14430 W Bluemound Rd Ste 103 Milwaukee WI 53226 Office Phone: 414-778-5100. E-mail: wmrandall@msn.com.

RANDALL JOUBERT, LORRIE BOULLION, science educator; d. Thomas Loris and Nancy Ann Fontenot Boullion; m. Lonnie G. Randall, Jr, June 21, 1986 (div. Oct. 24, 1994); m. Bryan K. Joubert, Mar. 26, 2004; children: Tyler Cole, Jacob Hunter. BS, La. State U., 1989; MS, U. La., Lafayette, 1995. Tchr. Breaux Bridge (La.) H.S., 1996—98; from instr. to asst prof. La. State U., Eunice, 1998—. Com. mem., advisor La. State U., 1998—; conf. presenter. Mem.: Am. Math. Assn., La.-Miss. Math. Assn. Two-Yr. Colls. (sec. 2002—03). Avocations: reading, children's sports, travel. Office: La State U P O Box 1129 Eunice LA 70535

RANDAZZO, GARY WAYNE, newspaper executive; b. Georgetown, Tex., Sept. 23, 1947; s. Frank Birchmans and Edna Earle (Forbis) R.; m. Joyce Sue McNorton, Oct. 7, 1966; children: Gary Wayne Jr., Vanessa Rene, Michael Jason, Daniel Paul. BBA, U. Tex., 1974; MBA, Tex. A&I U., Corpus Christi, 1976. Instr. Del Mar Coll., Corpus Christi, 1974-76; bus. mgr. Corpus Christi Caller-Times, 1976-81; pres., pub. Huntsville (Tex.) Item, 1981-83; pres. Am. Property Data, Houston, 1984-87; gen. mgr. Health Care News, Houston, 1987-89; sr. v.p. sales and mktg. Houston Chronicle, Houston, 1989—2002; exec. v.p., gen. mgr. San Francisco Chronicle, 2002—. Chmn., bd. dirs. Leadership Houston; bd. dirs. Downtown Houston Assn., treas.; bd. dirs. Better Bus. Bur.; chmn. Big Bros./Big Sisters; mem. adv. coun. San Francisco Unified Sch. Dist. Mem. Kiwanis (bd. dirs.). Home: 72 Novara Ct Danville CA 94526 Office: San Francisco Chronicle 901 Mission San Francisco CA 94103 Office Phone: 415-777-8124. Business E-Mail: grandazzo@sfchronicle.com.

RANDEL, DON MICHAEL, academic administrator, musicologist; m. Carol Randel; children: Amy Elizabeth Keating, Julia, Emily Catherine Pershing, Sally Randel Eggert. AB magna cum laude, Princeton U., 1962, MFA, 1964, PhD, 1967. With dept. music, dept. chair, vice provost Cornell U., 1968, assoc. dean Coll. Arts and Scis., dean Coll. Arts and Scis., 1991—95, provost, Given Found. prof. musicology, 1995—2000; pres. U. Chgo., 2000—. Editor: New Harvard Dictionary of Music, 1986, Harvard Biographical Dictionary of Music, 1996, Harvard Concise Dictionary of Music and Musicians, 1999, The Harvard Dictionary of Music, 2003. Recipient Fulbright award; Hon. Woodrow Wilson fellow, Danforth Grad. fellow. Fellow: Am. Acad. Arts and Scis.; mem.: Am. Philos. Soc. Office: U Chgo Adminstrn 502 5801 S Ellis Ave Chicago IL 60637-5418

RANDELL, CORTES W. news service executive; b. Wash., D.C., 1935; m. Joan. V. (Wirz) 1968; children: Cortes John, Christina Alexis. BSME, U. Va., 1959; student, Darden Sch., U. Va., 1962. Engr. Gen. Electric, N.Y., 1959-61, Internat. Telephone & Telegraph, Chgo., 1962-64; pres. Nat. Student Mktg., N.Y., 1964-71; cons. and trustee Wash. Trust, 1972-84; pres. Federal News Svc., Wash., D.C., 1984—. Author: Taking the Stand, Testimony of Oliver North, 1987, The National Press Club's Best Contemporary Speakers, 1995. Mem. Nat. Press Club, Yale Club. Avocations: offshore performance boating, ballooning, advising startup companies. Office: 9017 Swift Creek Rd Fairfax Station VA 22039-2815 E-mail: cort.randell@verizon.net.

RANDELS, DAVID GEORGE, retired secondary school educator; b. Bryan, Ohio, Feb. 6, 1943; s. George D. and Doris L. Randels; 1 child, Kellie R. BS in Edn., Bowling Green State U., 1965, MusM, 1971. Instr., counselor Culver (Ind.) Mil. Acad., 1962-67; instr. music Port Clinton (Ohio) City Schs., 1965—2004; ret., 2004. Tchr., drummer various jazz bands, 1960—; drummer Jamie Wight New Orleans Joymakers, 1980—. Musician (drummer): (albums) 6 recordings. Named Outstanding Bandsman, Bowling Green State U., 1965; recipient John Phillips Sousa Band award, Bryan HS, 1961, Dist. Svc. award, Ottawa County, Ohio, 2004, Mayor's Svc. award, Port Clinton, Ohio, 2004. Mem.: Music Educators Nat. Conf., Port Clinton Fedn. Tchrs. (Lifetime Achievement award 1984), U.S. Capital Hist. Soc., Nat. Sch. Orch. Assn. (Disting. Svc. award 1994), Port Clinton Model R.R. Club (pres. 1965), Elks, Phi Kappa Psi, Phi Delta Kappa, Kappa Kappa Psi. Democrat. Avocations: model railroading, music, antique cars, camping, fishing. Home: PO Box 182 Port Clinton OH 43452-1901 Office: 8060 W Mud Creek Rd Oak Harbor OH 43449-9642 Office Phone: 419-898-2442. Personal E-mail: drandels@hotmail.com. Business E-Mail: davidranels@cnos.net.

RANDHAWA, BIKKAR SINGH, psychologist, educator; b. Jullundur, India, June 14, 1933; came to Can., 1961, naturalized, 1966; s. Pritam S. and Sawaran K. (Basakhi) R.; m. Leona Emily Bujnowski, Oct. 8, 1966; children: Jason, Lisa. BA in Math., Panjab (India) U., 1954, BT in Edn., 1955, MA in History, 1959; BEd, U. Alta., Can., 1963; MEd in Measurement and Evaluation, U. Toronto, 1967, PhD, 1969. Tchr. secondary sch. math., Panjab, 1955-61; asst. headmaster, then headmaster, 1955-61; tchr. h.s. math. and sci. Beaver County, Riley, Canada, 1961—64, Camrose County, 1964—65, Beaver County (Alta.) Pub. Schs., 1965-67; tutor in math. for social sci. Ont. Inst. Studies in Edn., Toronto, 1968-69; mem. faculty U. Sask., Saskatoon, Canada, 1969—76, 1977—, prof. ednl. psychology, 1977-2000, prof. emeritus, 2000—, asst. dean rsch. and field svcs., 1982-87. Prof., coord. Visual Scholars' Program, U. Iowa, 1976-77; adj. prof. edu. psychology, U. Alta., 2002-; cons. in field. Contbr. articles to profl. jours. Treas. St. Albert Crime Stoppers, 2002—. Fellow APA, Am. Psychol. Soc. (charter), Can. Psychol. Assn.; mem. Can. Ednl. Rsch. Assn. (pres. 1997-99), Can. Soc. Study Edn., St. Albert Rotary Club (treas. 2003-), Phi Delta Kappa (pres. Saskatoon chpt. 1971, 85). Home: 14 Harwood Dr Saint Albert AB Canada T8N 5V5 E-mail: randy.randhawa@shaw.ca.

RANDI, JAMES (RANDALL JAMES HAMILTON ZWINGE), magician, writer, educator; b. Toronto, Aug. 7, 1928; naturalized U.S. citizen, 1987; s. George Randall and Marie Alice (Paradis) Zwinge. Student, Oakwood Collegiate Inst., Toronto, 1940-45; LittD (hon.), U. Indpls., 1995. Internationally known conjuror, lectr., author, investigator. Regent's lectr. UCLA, 1984; skeptical lectr. on paranormal subjects. Author: The Magic of Uri Geller, 1975 (with Bert Sugar) Houdini, His Life and Art, 1978, Flim-Flam, 1982, Test Your ESP Potential, 1983, The Faith Healers, 1987, The Magic World of the Amazing Randi, 1989, The Mask of Nostradamus, 1990, James Randi: Psychic Investigator, 1991, Conjuring, 1992, An Encyclopedia of Claims, Frauds, and Hoaxes of the Occult and Supernatural, 1995 (English, Chinese, French, Italian, Japanese, Korean, Norwegian, Punjabi, Polish and Spanish edits.); host TV spls. Recipient Blackstone award Internat. Platform Assn., 1983, 87, Forum award Am. Phys. Soc., 1988, Nat. Consumer Svc. award Nat. Coun. Against Health Fraud, 1988, Gold medal U. Ghent, Belgium, 1989, Humanist Disting. Svc. award Am. Humanist Assn., 1990, medal with golden wreath Hungarian Soc. for Dissemination of Scientific Knowledge, 1992; MacArthur Found. fellow, 1986, Spl. fellow Acad. Magical Arts and Scis., 1987; inducted into Soc. Am. Magicians Hall of Fame, 1988. Founding fellow Com. for Scientific Investigation of Claims of the Paranormal (exec. bd. dirs. 1973-91). Achievements include performing at White House, 1974. Home: 12000 NW 8th St Fort Lauderdale FL 33325-1406 Office: James Randi Ednl Found 201 SE 12th St Fort Lauderdale FL 33316-1815 Office Phone: 954-467-1112. Personal E-mail: randi@randi.org. *We are well into the third millennium with quack medicine, "Creation Science," and other pseudo-scientific matters heedlessly and increasingly embraced by the public, and major TV programs feature performers who claim to "speak to the dead." These con artists, feeding on the grief and vulnerability of their victims, are ignored, even tolerated, by our state and federal agencies.. Medieval notions and an anti-science movement threaten our very survival. We must reach out to our youth and develop in them a respect and understanding for real science. Acceptance of "politically correct" attitudes as standards, and of unquestioning belief in obviously crackpot theories, have brought us to a crisis in education. We need to adopt higher standards for our young people in respect to critical thinking, and encourage them to question the claims of the quacks and scam artists. The one-million dollar prize offered by my Foundation for proof of any paranormal power is still unclaimed. Why?.*

RANDINELLI, TRACEY ANNE, magazine editor; b. Morristown, N.J., Apr. 6, 1963; d. Andrew R. and Patricia Ann (Brenner) R. BA in Comm., U. Del., 1985. Copywriter Macy's N.J., Newark, 1985-86; editl. asst. Globe Comms. Corp., N.Y.C., 1986-87; from asst. editor to assoc. editor Scholastic Math and DynaMath Mags. Scholastic, Inc., N.Y.C., 1987-89, editor Scholastic Math Mag., 1989-93; mng. editor Zig Zag Mag. Games Pub. Group, N.Y.C., 1995; sr. editor Contact Kids Mag./ Sesame Workshop, N.Y.C., 1996-2001; freelance writer, 2001—02; sr. editor Pearson Learning Group, 2002—. Mem. Soc. Children's Book Writers, Ednl. Press Assn. Am. (Disting. Achievement award feature articles divsn. 1991, 95, coverdesign 1996, how-to feature divsn. 1998, 99). E-mail: pen4kidz@aol.com.

RANDISI, ELAINE MARIE, accountant, educator, writer; b. Racine, Wis., Dec. 19, 1926; d. John Dewey and Alveta Irene (Raffety) Fehd; m. John Paul Randisi, Oct. 12, 1946 (div. July 1972); children: Jeanine Randisi Manson, Martha Randisi Chaney (dec.), Joseph, Paula, Catherine Randisi Carvalho, George, Anthony (dec.); m. John R. Woodfin, June 18, 1994. AA, Pasadena Jr. Coll., 1946; BS cum laude (Giannini scholar), Golden Gate U., 1978. With Raymond Kaiser Engrs., Inc., Oakland, Calif., 1969-75, 77-86, corp. acct., 1978-79, sr. corp. acct., 1979-82, sr. payroll acct., 1983-86; accts. payable coord. Crosby, Heasfey, Roach & May, Oakland, Calif., 1989—96; acctg. mgr. Lilli Ann Corp., San Francisco, 1986-89; accounts payable coord. Crosby, Heafy, Roach & May, Oakland, 2003—. Initiated Minority Vendor Purchasing Program for Kaiser Engrs., Inc., 1975-76; corp. buyer Kaiser Industries Corp., Oakland, 1975-77; lectr. on astrology Theosophical Soc., San Francisco, 1979-99; mem. faculty Am. Fedn. Astrologers Internat. Conv., Chgo., 1982, 84. Mem. Speakers Bur., Calif. Assn. for Neurologically Handicapped Children, 1964-70, v.p., 1969; bd. dirs. Ravenwood Homeowners Assn., 1979-82, v.p., 1979-80, sec., 1980-81, mem. organizing com. Minority Bus. Fair, San Francisco, 1976; pres., bd. dirs. Lakewood Condominium Assn., 1984-87; mem. trustee Ch. of Religious Sci., 1992-95; treas. First Ch. Religious Sci., 1994-98, lic. practitioner, pres., 1990-91, sec., 1989-90. Mem. Am. Fedn. Astrologers, Calif. Scholarship Fedn. (life), Alpha Gamma Sigma (life). Home: 742 Wesley Way Apt 1C Oakland CA 94610-2339

RANDLE, BERNADETTE, musician, composer, graphics designer; b. St. Louis, Jan. 8, 1947; d. William George Randle and Louise Robinmae Randle-Ware. BA summa cum laude, Concordia U. Wis., 1993; MA, Lindenwood U., 1994. Dir. employment programs YMCA of Greater St. Louis, 1980—83; freelance studio musician Platinum Chess Record, Englewood, NJ, 1983—86; office clk. Def. Contract Audit Agy. & HUD, St. Louis, 1986—87; mktg. specialist Tailored Software Corp., Maryland Heights, Mo., 1987—89; graphic illustrator The Bionetics Corp., St. Louis, 1989—97; concept developer/tech. writer Bus. Blueprints, St. Louis, 1997—2000; composer, arranger ReMembered/The Gozz Ensemble; creative dir. Prosit Media Group; min. music Third United Presbyn. Ch., St. Louis. Mktg. cons. The Enterprise Found., St. Louis, 2002—03. Author: (short story) Chicken Soup for the Surviving Soul; pianist, arranger, composer numerous recs., 1974—. Vol. counselor CanSurmount, St. Louis, 1991—96; vol. visitor Am. Heartland Hospice, St. Louis, 1994. Grantee, Mo. Arts Coun., 1991. Mem.: Broadcast Music Inc., Mensa, Sigma Phi Omega. Avocations: reading religious histories, surfing the web, collecting baseball caps and kaleidoscopes. Office: Prosit Media Group 11621 Olive Street Rd Creve Coeur MO 63141 Personal E-mail: bernadettrandle@sbcglobal.net.

RANDLE, JOHN, professional football player; b. Hearne, Tex., Jan. 12, 1967; Student, Trinity Valley C.C., Tex., Tex. A&I U. Defensive tackle Minn. Vikings, 1990—2000, Seattle Seahawks, 2001. Selected to Pro Bowl, 1993, 94; named to The Sporting News NFL All-Pro Team, 1994. Achievements tied AFC record for most sacks, 1994. Office: Seattle Seahawks 11220 NE 53rd St Kirkland WA 98033-3825 Office Phone: 1-888-NFL-HAWK.

RANDLETT, MARY WILLIS, photographer; b. Seattle, May 5, 1924; d. Cecil Durand and Elizabeth (Bayley) Willis; m. Herbert B. Randlett, Oct. 19, 1950 (div.); children: Robert, Mary Ann, Peter, Susan. BA, Whitman Coll., Walla Walla, Wash., 1947. Freelance photographer, 1949—. One-woman shows include Seattle Sci. Ctr., 1971, Western Wash. State U., 1971, Seattle Art Mus., 1971, Art Gallery Greater Victoria, 1972, Alaska State Mus., 1972, State Capitol Mus., 1983, Whatcom Mus. History and Art, Bellingham, Wash., 1986, Janet Huston Gallery, LaConner, Wash., 1990, Gov.'s Gallery, Office of Gov., Olympia, Wash., 1991, Stonington Gallery, Seattle, 1992, Valley Mus. Art, LaConner, 1992, Grad. Sch. Design Dept. Landscape Arch. Harvard U., Cambridge, Mass., 1996, Mus. N.W. Art, LaConner, 1998, others, exhibited in group shows at Am. Soc. Mag. Photographers, 1970, Whatcom Mus., Bellingham, Henry Gallery, Seattle, 1971, 1974, Royal Photg. Soc., 1979, Heard Mus., Phoenix, 1979, State Capital Mus., Olympia, Wash., 1983, 1984, 1988, 1989, 1993, Santa Fe Ctr. for Photography, 1987, Tacoma Art Mus., 1989, Helen Day Art Ctr., Stowe, Vt., 1989, Valley Mus. N.W. Art, LaConner, 1991, 1994, 1996—98, Allen Libr. U. Wash., Seattle, 1991, Wing Luke Asian Mus., 1991, Cheney Cowles Mus., Spokane, 1991, 1998, Security Pacific Gallery, Seattle, 1992, Benham Gallery, 1993, Stonington Gallery, 1993, 1998, Rainier Club, Seattle, 1994, Port Angeles (Wash.) Fine Arts Ctr., 1994, Mus. History and Industry, Seattle, 1994, Whatcom Mus., Bellingham, 1994, Pacific N.W. Annual Bellevue Art Mus., Wash., 1995, Skagit Valley Hist. Mus., LaConner, 1995, Seattle Art Mus., 1996—98, Kirkland (Wash.) Arts Ctr., 1997, Bainbridge Arts and Crafts, Bainbridge Island, Wash., 1997, Lucia Douglas Gallery, Bellingham, 1997, Anchorage Mus. History & Art, 1997, Burke Mus. Natural History and Culture, Seattle, 1998, Henderson House, Turnwater, Wash., 1998, Whatcom Arco Exhibit Gallery, Bellingham, 1998, Sea First Gallery, Seattle, 1998, 1999, Citizens Cultural Ctr., Fujinomita, Japan, 1999, Mus. Am. Indian, N.Y.C., 1999, Cheney Cowels Mus., Spokane, 1999, J. Paul Horiuchi Seattle Asian Art Mus., 2000, Mus. NW Art, 2000, Seattle Art Mus., 2002, Whitney Mus. Am. Art, N.Y.C., 2002, High Mus., Atlanta, 2002, and numerous others, Represented in permanent collections Met. Mus., Nat. Collection of Fine Arts, Nat. Portrait Gallery, Washington State Libr., Manuscript divsn. U. Wash., Pacific Northwest Bell, Seattle, Swedish Med. Ctr., Whatcom Mus., Bellingham, Henry Gallery, Seattle, Wash. State Capitol Mus., Olympia, Phillips Collection, Wash.; works appeared in books The Master and His Fish (Roderick Haig-Brown), 1982, Theodore Roethke: The Journey to I and Otherwide (Neal Bowers), 1982, Mountain in the Clouds (Bruce Brown), 1982, Masonry in Architecture (Louis Redstone), 1982, Writings and Reflections from the World of Roderick Haig-Brown, 1982, Pike Place Market (Alice Shorett and Murray Morgan), 1982, The Dancing Blanket, (Cheryl Samuel), 1982, Collected Poems of Theodore Roethke, 1982, Spires of Form (Victor Scheffer), 1983, Assault on Mount Helicon (Mary Barnard), 1983, New as a Wave (Eve Triem), 1983, Sketchbook: A Memoir of the '30's and the Northwest School (William Cumming), 1983, Good Intentions (Jane Adams), 1985, Blackbirds of the Americas (Gordon Orians and Tony Angell), 1985, Historic Preservation in Seattle (Larry Kreisman), 1985, Down Town Seattle Walking Tours (Mary Randlett and Carol Tobin), 1986, Seattle, the Seattle Book, 1986, When Orchids Were Flowers (Kate Knap Johnson), 1986, Jacob Lawrence, American Painter, (Ellen Wheat), 1986, Manic Power: Robert Lowell and His Circle (Jeffrey Meyers), 1987, The Isamu Noguchi Garden Museum (Isamu Noguchi), 1987, Washington's Audacious State Capitol an its Builders (Norman Johnston), 1988, The Bloedel Reserve: Gardens in the Forest (Lawrence Kreisman), 1988, Washingtonians: A Biographical Portrait of the State on the Occasion of its Centennial, 1988, Directory of Literary Biography: Canadian Writers 1920-59, 2d series, 1989, Crafts of America, 1989, The Lone Tree Tragedy (Bruce Brown), 1989, Northwest Coast Handbook of North American Indians, 1990, Dancing on the Rim of the World, 1990, Openings, Original Essays by Contemporary Soviet and American Writers (eds. Robert Atwan, Valeri Vinokurov), 1990, George Tsutakawa (Martha Kingsbury), 1990, Contemporary American Poetry (ed. Al Polin Jr.), 1991, Natural History of Puget Sound Country (Arthur Kruckberg), 1991, Bones (Joyce Thompson), 1991, Cebu (Peter Basho), 1991, Catalogue of Historic Preservation Publications, 1992, Art in Seattle's Public Places (James Rupp), 1992, The Olympic Rainforest (Ruth Kirk with Jerry Franklin), 1992, Steelhead Fly Fishing (Trey Combs), 1992, Illustrated Guidelines for Rehabilitation Historic Buildings, 1993, A History of African American Artists (Bearden and Henderson), 1994, Childrens Literature Review Vol. 1, 1994, Invisible Gardens: The Search for Modernism the American Landscape (Walker and Simo), 1994, Seeing Seattle (Roger Sale), 1994, Reaching Home (Jay and Matson), 1994, Redesigning the American Lawn: A Search for Environmental Harmony (Gordone Geballe, Diana Balmari and F. Herbert Bormann), 1995, Reaching Home: Pacific Salmon, Pacific People (Foyes, Jay and Matson), 1995, Carl F. Gould: A Life in Architecture and the Arts (T. William Booth and William H. Wuksib), 1995, Destination Zero (Sam Hamill), 1996, Market Sketchbook, 25th Anniversary Edition, 1996, Spririts of the Ordinary, 1997, Instrument of Change: Jim Schoppert 1947-1992, 1997, Looking for Edulabee Dix (Joann Ridley), 1997, Jack Lenor Larsen: A Memoir, 1998, Museo Nacional Centro de Arte Reina (Mark Tobey), 1998, Fountains Splash, and Spectacle: Water and Design from the Renaissance to Present (ed. Marilyn Symmes), 1998, Ghost Dancing (Anna Linzer), 1998, The Flower in the Skull (Kathleen Alcala), 1998, This Great Unknowing: Last Poems (Denise Levertov), 1999, Building Washington (Paul Dorpat, Genevier McCoy), 1999, The Wright Collection, Seattle Art Museum, 1999, Made to Last: Historic Preservation in Seattle and King County (Larry Kreisman), 1999, Isamu Noguchi: A Study of Space (Ana Maria Torres), 2000, The Tiger Iris (Joan Swift), 2000, The Eighth Lively Art (Wesley Wehr), 2000, All Powers Necessary and Convenient (Mark F. Jenkins), 2000, Ice Breakers: Alaska's Most Innovative Artists (Julie Decker), 2000, Over the Line: The Life and Art of Jacob Lawrence (Peter Nesbett and Michelle Dubois), 2000, Iridescent Light: The Emergence of Northwest Art (Delores Tarzan Ament), 2001, Messages from Frank's Landing, 2000, Leo Kenney: A Retrospective, 2000, Building for Learning: Seattle Public Schools History 1860-2000, 2001, Geology and Plant Life, 2001, and numerous others; works also appeared in newspapers and mags., one-woman shows include Iridescent Light: The Emergence of Northwest Art, Mary Randlett Portraits in the Arts Cmty., Wright Exhbn. Space, Seattle, 2002—03, book, Maritime Seattle, 2002, Picture Bainbridge Island: A Pictorial History, Distant Corner, 2003, Child of the Oemulgee. Recipient Wash. State Gov.'s award for spl. commendation for contbns. in field of photography, 1983, Individual Artist award, King County Arts Commn., 1989, Lifetime Achievement award, Artist Trust, 2001, Matrix Table, Seattle Women of Achievement, 1999, Nancy Blankenship Pryor award, 2001, Alumnus of Merit award, Whitman Coll, 2003; grantee, Nat. Endowment for Arts, 1976, Allied Arts Found., 2000. Mem. AIA (hon.), Am. Soc. Mag. Photographers. Home: PO Box 11238 Olympia WA 98508-1238 Office Phone: 360-352-1716.

RANDMAN, BARRY I. real estate developer; b. Cin., Apr. 1, 1958; s. David I. and Marilyn June (Garfinkel) F. BBA in Fin., U. Denver, 1980. With acctg. dept. Rookwood Pottery & Celestial Restaurants, Cin., 1976-80; asst. to pres., head mktg. and real estate branching Great Am. Banks Inc., Miami, 1980-83; pres. Tower Mgmt. Inc., Cin., 1983-85, bd. dirs.; pres. Ohio Jet Svcs. Inc., Cin., 1983-85; v.p. Home State Fin. Svcs. Inc., Cin., 1984-85; pres. East Hill Devel. Corp., Cin., 1985—, B.I.R. Properties Inc., Cin., 1985—. Pres. Golden Devel. Corp., 1988-91, SRB Food Corp., 1988-92, Scarborough Devel. Corp., 1989, Redmont Devel Corp., 1990—, Eastridge, Inc., 1993-99, 613 Roce LLC, Hale Justis, LLC, 1999—. Mem. Jewish Welfare Fund, Cin., 1980. Avocations: skiing, tennis, gardening. Home: 9 Hill and Holow Ln Cincinnati OH 45208-3357 Office: 2321 Kemper Ln Cincinnati OH 45206-2610

RANDOLPH, A(RTHUR) RAYMOND, federal judge; b. Riverside, N.J., Nov. 1, 1943; m. Eileen J. O'Connor, May 18, 1984; children: John Trevor, Cynthia Lee. BS, Drexel U., 1966; JD summa cum laude, U. Pa., 1969. Bar: Calif. 1970, D.C. 1973, U.S. Supreme Ct. 1973. Law clk. to Hon. Henry J. Friendly U.S. Ct. Appeals (2d cir.), N.Y.C., 1969—70; asst. to solicitor gen. U.S. Dept. Justice, Washington, 1970—73, dep. solicitor gen., 1975—77; ptnr. Sharp, Randolph & Green, Washington, 1977—83, Randolph & Truitt, Washington, 1983—87, Pepper, Hamilton & Scheetz, Washington, 1987—90; judge U.S. Ct. Appeals (D.C. cir.), Washington, 1990—. Spl. asst. atty. gen. State of Mont., 1983—90, State of N.Mex., 1985—90, State of Utah, 1986—90; adv. panel Fed. Cts. Study Com., 1989—90; spl. counsel Com. on Stds. Ofcl. Conduct, U.S. Ho. of Reps., 1979—80; adj. prof. Georgetown U. Law Ctr., 1974—78; exec. sec. Atty. Gen.'s Com. on Reform of Fed. Jud. Sys., 1975—77; com. on fed. rules evidence U.S. Justice Dept., 1972; chmn. Com. on Govtl. Structures, McLean, Va., 1973—74; adj. prof. law sch. George Mason U., 1992, disting. prof., 1998—; com. codes conduct Jud. Conf. U.S., 1992—95, chmn., 1995—98. Recipient Spl. Achievement award, U.S. Dept. Justice, 1971. Mem.: D.C. Bar Assn., Calif. Bar Assn., Am. Law Inst., Order of Coif. Office: US Court of Appeals 333 Constitution Ave NW Washington DC 20001-2866

RANDOLPH, CARL LOWELL, chemical company executive; b. Pasadena, Calif., May 30, 1922; s. Carl L. and Lulu (McBride) R.; m. Jane Taber, June 25, 1943; children: Margaret, Stephen. BA, Whittier Coll., 1943; MS, U. So. Calif., 1947, PhD, 1949; LLD, Whittier Coll., 1982; D in Pub. Svc. (hon.), U. Alaska, 1983. Prin. chemist Aerojet-Gen. Corp., 1949-57; v.p. U.S. Borax Rsch. Corp., Anaheim, Calif., 1957-63; asst. to pres. U.S. Borax & Chem. Corp., L.A., 1963-66, v.p., 1966-68, exec. v.p., 1968-69, pres., 1969-86, vice chmn., 1983-87. Trustee, chmn. bd. Whittier Coll., emeritus, 1969—; bd. dirs., chmn. Ind. Colls. So. Calif., 1982—. Lt. (j.g.) USNR, 1944-46. Mem. Phi Beta Kappa, Sigma Xi. Home: 3836 Bay Ln Anacortes WA 98221-8413

RANDOLPH, CHRISTINE ERIS, elementary school educator, consultant; b. San Diego, Dec. 7, 1970; d. Joseph Paul and Alice Contogenis; m. Paul William Randolph, Sept. 14, 1996; children: Alicia, Alec. BA in Psychology, San Diego State U., 1997, MA in Ednl. Leadership, 2004. Tchr. Cajon Valley Sch. Dist., El Cajon, Calif., 1997—2001, San Ysidro Sch. Dist., San Diego, 2001—. Ednl. cons. for tchrs. of English learners Writing for Excellence, San Diego, 2001—; spkr. in field. Author: Writing for Excellence-An Essay Writing Guide, 2002. Mem.: Greater San Diego Reading Assn. (award for excellence in tchg. of lang. arts 2003).

RANDOLPH, DAVID, conductor; b. NYC, Dec. 21, 1914; s. Morris and Elsie (Goodman) R.; m. Mildred Greenberg, July 18, 1948. BS, CCNY, 1936; MA, Tchrs. Coll., Columbia U., 1942. Music specialist OWI, N.Y.C., 1943-47. Adj. prof. music NYU, 1948-85, Mostly Mozart course, 1976-85; lectr. Town Hall, N.Y.C., 1955-60, Columbia U., 1957, Cosmopolitan Club, N.Y.C., 1962-63; pre-concert lectr. N.Y. Philharm., Avery Fisher Hall, 1964-86,Cleve. Orch., 1981, Vienna Symphony Orch., 1988; tchr. conducting Dalcroze Sch., 1948-49; music commentator Little Orch. Soc. Concerts and Broadcasts, 1950-62, Met. Opera Intermission Broadcasts, 1951, 52; intermission commentator Lewisohn Stadium Concert Broadcasts, 1952-58; vis. prof. music SUNY, New Paltz, 1970-72, Fordham U., 1972-73; lectr. New Sch. for Social Rsch., 1973-90, IBM, N.Y.C., 1978-86, Beethoven Soc., 1977, 83; prof. music Montclair State Coll., Upper Montclair, N.J., 1973-87; guest condr. Rockland County (N.Y.) Ann. Choral Festival, 1972, 73; adviser film Music to Live By, mem. N.J. Arts Coun., 1967-70; mem. music comm. Gov. N.J.'s Commn. to

Study Arts, 1965; honored guest Handel Festival, Halle, Germany, 1991. Condr. Randolph Singers, 1944-62 (appeared on NBC Today, and Tonight Shows), concerts Town Hall, NYC, Carnegie Recital Hall, recs. for Columbia, Vanguard, Westminster, Monteverdi's Lagrime d'amante, Satie's Mass for the Poor, Concert Hall Soc., CRI, Esoteric Records, United Choral Soc., LI, NY, 1961-86, NJ Ballet Orch., 1977, 83, Masterwork Chamber Orch., 1982-83, Philharmonia Orch. in Brahms' Requiem, London, 1988, Barge Concert, NYC, 1987, 89; guest condr., Conn. Symphony Orch., 1961; condr. concert tour Spain with Am. choruses and Radio TV Orch. of Moscow, 1992; music annotator, CBS, NYC, 1947-48; choral seminar leader Mohonk Mountain House, 1986-95; music dir., condr. Masterwork Chorus and Orch., 1955-93, St. Cecilia Chorus and Orch., NYC, 1965—; performances at Carnegie Hall, Avery Fisher Hall, Lincoln Ctr., Kennedy Ctr. including Brahms' Requiem, Schicksalslied, Nänie, Gesang der Parzen, Mozart's Requiem, C Minor Mass, Vesperae de Confessore, Beethoven's Missa Solemnis, Symphony No. 9, Mass in C Major, Choral Fantasy, Bach's Mass in B Minor, St. John Passion, St. Matthew Passion, Christmas Oratorio, Magnificat, Haydn's St. Cecilia Mass, Theresienmesse, Paukenmesse, Lord Nelson Mass, Heiligmesse, Schöpfungsmesse, Michael Haydn's Requiem, Bruckner's Mass in E Minor, Requiem, Vaughan Williams' A Sea Symphony, Dona Nobis Pacem, Mass in G Minor, Hodie, Verdi's Requiem, Four Sacred Pieces, Honegger's King David, Elgar's The Music Makers, Corigliano's Fern Hill, Salieri's Mass in D, Purcell's The Fairy Queen, Mendelssohn's Elijah, Die erste Walpurgisnacht, Lobgesang, Lauda Sion, Poulenc's Gloria, Rutter's Gloria, Dvorak's Requiem, Te Deum, Kodaly's Te Deum, Berlioz' Requiem, Messe solennelle, Cherubini's Requiem, Schubert's Masses 5 and 6, Stabat Mater, Vivaldi's Gloria, Dixit Dominus, Zelenka's Missa Dei Patris, Gounod's St. Cecilia Mass, Handel's Solomon, Israel in Egypt, Judas Maccabaeus, Dixit Dominus and 171 complete performances of Handel's Messiah, Orff's Carmina Burana, Saint-Saëns' Requiem, Puccini's Messa di Gloria, Zimmermann's Psalmkonzert, Finzi's For St. Cecilia, In Terra Pax, Rachmaninoff's The Bells, others; broadcaster: David Randolph Concerts, WNYC and radio stas. of Nat. Assn. Ednl. Broadcasters, 1946-79, Young Audience telecasts, CBS-TV, 1958-59, series of candid rehearsals of Bach's Mass in B minor, PBS, 1967; host: weekly broadcasts Lincoln Ctr. Spotlight, Sta. WQXR, NYC, 1966-67; regular guest critic First Hearing program Sta. WQXR, NYC, and 68 other stas., 1986-95; author: This Is Music, 1964, 98, numerous album jacket notes; A New Music Made with a Machine, Horizon Magazine, 1959; editor: David Randolph Choral Series; writer, narrator: Instruments of the Orchestra, 1958, compact disc 1995, Stereo Review's Guide to Understanding Music, 1973; music critic, High Fidelity Mag., 1952-57; composer: A Song for Humanity, 1968, Andante for Strings, 1937, Edward, 1937; contbg. author: NY Times Guide to Listening Pleasure, 1968; analyzed Mendelssohn's Symphony No. 3 on records for Book of Month Club. Recipient 1st award for edn. by radio Ohio State Inst., 1948, 50, 51, Sylvania TV award, 1959, Disting. Alumni award Columbia U., 1982, cert. of appreciation Mayor of City of N.Y. at Carnegie Hall, 1991, Townsend Harris medal CCNY, 1996, Lifetime Achievement award Carnegie Hall, MidAmerica Prodns., 2000; St. Cecilia Chorus endowed David Randolph Disting. Artist-in-Residence Program at New Sch. in N.Y., 1996. Home: 420 E 86th St Apt 4-c New York NY 10028-6456 Office Phone: 212-744-1444.

RANDOLPH, DONALD PHILLIP, nurse anesthetist; b. Cedar Rapids, Iowa, Jan. 24, 1957; s. Eugene George Randolph and Shirley Jean Mathieson. B, Mt. Marty Coll., 1981; PhD in Religion, U. Calif., 2002. Cert. nurse anesthetist, Am. Assn. Nurse Anesthetists, 1981. Staff nurse anesthetist Tucson Anesthesia, 1981—89, Mayo Clinic, Scottsdale, 1989—94; nurse anesthetist pvt. practice, 1995—. Coord. and polit. action coord. A.B.A.T.E., Mesa, Ariz., 2000—02. Mem.: League Am. Bicyclists (effective cycling instr. 1986—), Sportbike Riders Assn., Motorcycle Riders Found., Am. Brotherhood Aimed Toward Edn. (life), Am. Motorcyclist Assn. (life; field rep. 2001—03), Modified Motorcycle Assn. (life), Harley Owner's Group (life). Independent-Republican. Christian. Avocations: motorcycle rights, bicycle education. Personal E-mail: dprcrna@sprintmail.com.

RANDOLPH, JACKSON HAROLD, utility company executive; b. Cin., Nov. 17, 1930; s. Dward Bradley and Cora Belle (Puckett) R.; m. Angelina Losito, June 20, 1958; children: Terri, Patti, Todd, Craig. BBA, U. Cin., 1958, MBA, 1968. C.P.A., Ohio. Acct. Arthur Andersen & Co., Cin., 1958-59; with Cin. Gas & Electric Co., 1959—, v.p. fin. and corp. affairs, 1981-85, exec. v.p., 1985-86, chmn., pres., CEO, from 1986, now chmn., also dir.; chmn. CINergy Corp., 1994—, now chmn.; former pres., now chmn. Union Light Heat and Power Co., Covington, Ky. Bd. dirs. Cen. Trust Bank, N.A., Cin. Fin. Corp., PNC Corp.; CEO CINergy Corp., 1994-95, chmn., 1995—. V.p., bd. dirs. Gen. Protestant Orphan Home, Cin., 1981-86; treas., bd. dirs. Cin. chpt. ARC, 1975—; mem. adv. com. Catherine Booth Home, 1980—, Dan Beard council Boy Scouts Am., 1985. Served with USN, 1951-55. Mem. Cin. Country Club, Queen City Club, Met. Club, Bankers Club, Delta Sigma Pi, Phi Eta Sigma, Beta Gamma Sigma. Home: 414 Bishopsbridge Dr Cincinnati OH 45255-3900 Office: CINergy Corp 139 E 4th St Cincinnati OH 45202-4003 also: Union Light Heat & Power Co 107 Brent Spence Sq Covington KY 41011-1433*

RANDOLPH, JENNINGS, JR., (JAY RANDOLPH), sportscaster; b. Cumberland, Md., Sept. 19, 1934; s. Jennings and Mary Katherine (Babb) R.; m. Sue Henderson, May 28, 1966; children: Jennings, Brian Robert, Rebecca Sue. BA, Salem (W.Va.) Coll., 1963. Sports and promotion dir. Sta. WHAR, Clarksburg, W.Va., 1958-61; sportscaster Sta. KLIF, Dallas, 1963-66; Sta. KMOX, St. Louis, 1966-68; with Sta. KSDK-TV, St. Louis, 1968—, sports dir., 1968-88, spl. sports corr., 1988—, also on nationally televised broadcasts for various sports events including Sr. PGA tour; TV announcer Fla. Marlins Baseball Club, Ft. Lauderdale, 1993—2002. Interviewer analyst Champions Tour on Golf Channel and CNBC; broadcaster coll. basketball ESPN regional TV; TV announcer St. Louis Cardinals, 1970-87, Cin. Reds., 1988; mem. NBC's broadcast staff for 1988 Olympics, Seoul, Korea and 1992 Summer Games, Barcelona, Spain; host nationally syndicated The Golf Show. Trustee Salem Coll., 1976-89. With U.S. Army, 1954-56. Inducted into Boys and Girls Clubs of Am. Hall of Fame, 1990 Mem. Nat. Assn. Sportscasters, Delta Tau Delta. Achievements include being an amateur golf champion. Home: 12021 Charter Oakpky Saint Louis MO 63146

RANDOLPH, JESSE See CASTILE, RAND

RANDOLPH, JUDSON GRAVES, pediatric surgeon; b. Macon, Ga., July 19, 1927; s. Milton Fitz and Abigail Theresa (Graves) R.; m. Susan Comfort Adams, June 14, 1952; children: Somers, Garrett, Judson, Adam, Comfort. BA, Vanderbilt U., 1950, MD, 1953. Intern in surgery U. Rochester, N.Y., 1953-54; asst. resident in pathology Vanderbilt U., 1954-55; asst. resident, then sr. resident in surgery Mass. Gen. Hosp., Boston, 1956-58; asst. resident in surgery Children's Hosp., Boston, 1955-56, sr. resident, then chief resident, 1958-61, asst. surgeon, 1961-63; teaching fellow to instr. surgery Med. Sch. Harvard U., 1960-63; jr. assoc. in surgery Peter Bent Brigham Hosp., Boston, 1961-63; surgeon-in-chief Children's Hosp., Washington, 1964-91; mem. faculty Med. Sch. George Washington U., 1964-91, prof. surgery and child health, 1968-91; prof. surgery Meharry Med. Coll., 1992-96. Cons. Nat. Naval Med. Ctr., NIH, Walter Reed Army Med. Ctr.; trustee Vanderbilt U., 1980—. Editor: Pediatric Surgery, 3d edit., 2 vols., 1979, 4th edit., 2 vols., 1985, The Injured Child, 1980; mem. editl. bd. Surgery, 1978-92; contbr. numerous articles to med. jours. With USNR, 1945-46, PTO. Mem. ACS (gov. 1969-75), AMA, Am. Acad. Pediats. (chmn. exec. com. surg. sect. 1974-75), Am. Assn. Thoracic Surgery, Am. Pediat. Surg. Assn. (gov. 1980—, pres. 1984), Washington Acad. Surgery (pres. 1989), Soc. U. Surgeons, Am. Surg. Assn., So. Surg. Assn., Am. Bd. Surgery (bd. dirs. 1973-79, diplomate), Alpha Omega Alpha (faculty), Cosmos Club (Washington), Belle Meade Club. Methodist. Office Phone: 615-383-3757. Personal E-mail: jrpedsurg@aol.com.

RANDOLPH, KENNETH E. retired lawyer; Sr. v.p., gen. counsel Dynegy Inc. (formerly NGC Corp.), Houston, 1987—2003.

RANDOLPH, KEVIN HOWARD, marketing executive; b. Seattle, July 6, 1949; s. Howard Amos and Betty Elaine (Leahy) R.; children: Heather, Lyndsay. BA, Wash. State U., 1972. Mgr. Computers for Mktg., L.A., 1972-74; data processing mgr. Parker Rsch., Pasadena, Calif., 1974-77; prin. Randolph & Assocs., L.A., 1977-79; v.p. Bank Am. Corp., San Francisco, 1979-87, Interactive Network, Mountain View, Calif., 1987-91; sr. v.p. ICTV, Santa Clara, Calif., 1991-93; pres. Randolphs.Com., Ephrata, Wash., 1993—; v.p. U.S. West Mrg., Inc., Benicia, Calif., 1993-94; exec. v.p., COO Interactive Video Enterprises, Inc., San Ramon, 1994-95; founder, pres., CEO Asia Online, Ltd., Hong Kong, 1999-2000. Cons. Randolph Home Ctr., Ephrata, Wash., 1972—. Home: 309 3rd Ave SE Ephrata WA 98823 Office Phone: 415-999-6804. E-mail: kevin@randolphs.com.

RANDOLPH, LEONARD MCELROY, JR., career officer; b. Washington, Sept. 22, 1943; s. Leonard McElRoy and Jessie Marshall (Stockton) R.; m. Linda Fleming Raney, Aug. 1, 1987; children: Nathaniel Randolph, Brion Randolph, Holly Tocknell, Chad Muterspaw, Judd Muterspaw. BS in Biology, Marietta (Ohio) Coll., 1965; MS in Microbiology, Howard U., Washington, 1967; MD, Meharry Med. Coll., Nashville, 1972; DHL (hon.), Meharry Med. Coll., 2001. Diplomate Am. Bd. Surgery, Am. Bd. Med. Mgmt., Am. Coll. Physician Execs.; cert. physician exec. Grad. tchg. asst. Howard U., Washington, 1966-67; rsch. microbiologist Georgetown U., Washington, 1966-67; chemistry tchr. Ballou H.S., Washington, 1967-68; Commd. 2d lt. USAF, 1972, advanced through grades to maj. gen., 1998, intern, 1972-73, resident, 1973-77, gen. surgeon Bergstrom AFB, Tex., 1977-78, chief gen. surgery, 1978-80, chief surg. svcs., 1980-83, attending surgeon Wright-Patterson AFB, Ohio, 1983-84, dir. med. edn., 1984-85, chief med. officer Minot AFB, N.D., 1985-86, hosp. cmdr. George AFB, Calif., 1988-90, dep. command surgeon HQ Tactical Air Command Langley AFB, Va., 1990-91, forward command surgeon Desert Storm Riyahd, Saudi Arabia, 1990-91, med. ctr. comdr. Travis AFB, Calif., 1994-97; asst. prof. surgery Wright State U. Sch. Medicine, Dayton, Ohio, 1983-88; command surgeon U.S. Ctrl. Command, MacDill AFB, Fla., 1991-94, U.S. Transp. Command and Air Mobility Command, Scott AFB, Ill., 1997-99. Lead agt. DOD Health Svc. Region 10, 1994-97; spec. asst. to USAF Surg. Gen., 1999, dep. surgeon gen., 1999-2001; dep. exec. dir. Tricare Mgmt. Activity, Office of Under Sec. Def., Washington, 2001-03; assoc. prof. surgery U. Calif. Davis Sch. Medicine, 1995-97; assoc. prof. mil. medicine and emergency medicine Uniformed Svcs. U. of Health Scis., 1995—; acting dep. asst. sec. def. Health Plan Adminstrn., TRICARE Mgmt. Activity, 2003—, COO, 2003—. Contbr. articles to profl. jours. Bd. trustees Marietta Coll., 2001—. Decorated Def. Superior Svc. medal for Operation Restore Hope, Legion of Merit Operation Desert Storm, Disting. Svc. medal USAF; selected for Boys State (Georgetown U.); recipient Excellence award Fed. Healthcare Execs., 1997, Disting. Alumni of Yr. award Nat. Assn. for Equal Opportunity in Higher Edn., 1999, Disting. Alumnus award Marietta Coll. Alumni Assn., 2000, Exceptional Svc. award Uniformed Svcs. U. of the Health Scis., 2003; named to Hall of Excellence, Ohio Found. Ind. Colls., 2003. Fellow ACS (bd. govs. 1996—2002), Am. Coll. Physician Execs. (disting. pres. 2000-2001), Am. Acad. Med. Adminstrs. (hon.); mem. Soc. Air Force Clin. Surgeons (bd. govs. 1996-2002), Soc. Med. Adminstrs., Soc. Med. Cons to Armed Forces, Assn. Mil. Surgeons of the U.S., Air Force Assn. (life), Christian Med. Assn., Aerospace Med. Assn., Alpha Omega Alpha, Beta Kappa Chi, Beta Beta Beta. Avocations: reading, lecturing, sports, writing. Office: Tricare Mgmt Activity Skyline 5 Ste 810 5111 Leesburg Pike Falls Church VA 22041-3206 Fax: 703-681-3665. E-mail: caprand@aol.com., randy.randolph@tma.osd.mil.

RANDOLPH, ROBERT DEWITT, lawyer; b. Sligo, Pa., Mar. 6, 1929; s. DeWitt Lyman and Hazel Irene (McCall) R.; m. Betty Ann McElhattan, May 8, 1953 (dec. Aug. 1979); children: Douglas, Andrew; m. Susan Denise Hopkins, Oct. 15, 1988 BA, Westminster Coll., 1951; LLB, Harvard U., 1957. Bar: Ohio 1958, Pa. 1960, U.S. Supreme Ct. 1981. Assoc. Buckingham, Doolittle & Burroughs, Akron, Ohio, 1957-59, Rose, Houston, Cooper & Schmidt, Pitts., 1959-60, 61-65; fgn. svc. officer U.S. Dept. State, Washintgon, 1960-61; ptnr. Houston, Cooper, Spear & German, Pitts., 1965-70, Randolph & O'Connor, Pitts., 1970-74, Buchanan Ingersoll P.C., Pitts., 1974-93. Pres. Assn. Retarded Citizens Allegheny, Pitts., 1990-92; mem. Allegheny County Mental Health/Mental Retardation Bd., 2002—. With U.S. Army, 1951-54. U.S. Army, 1951—54. Mem. St. Clair Country Club. Democrat. Presbyterian. Avocations: golf, skiing. Home: 750 Washington Rd Pittsburgh PA 15228-2051

RANDOLPH, ROBERT MORRISON, literature educator; b. Paterson, N.J., Nov. 29, 1944; s. John Lillard Randolph; m. Barbara Ann Burr (div.); children: Anna, Brittany; m. Amy Theresa Stoeltje, June 20, 1994; 1 child, Pilar 1 stepchild, Elijah. BA, Wilmington (Ohio) Coll., 1966; MA, So. Ill. U., 1968, PhD, 1976; MA, Louisville Presbyn. Theol. Sem., 1986. Instr. So. Ill. U., Carbondale, 1966—76; from lectr. to prof. Tex. State U., San Marcos, 1986—. Author: R. Cory in Winter, 1997 (Saddle Mountain Poetry prize, 1997); contbr. to lit. jours.; co-editor: The Lit. Rev. Fulbright scholar, Finland, 1990, Greece, 1994. Democrat. Presbyterian. Avocations: Ju Jitsu, Aikido. Office: English Dept Tex State U San Marcos TX 78666

RANDOLPH, SOMERS, sculptor; b. Boston, May 25, 1956; s. Judson Graves and Susan Comfort (Adams) R.; m. Hillary Allen Fitzpatrick, Oct. 8, 2000; 1 child, Comfort Avery. BA, Princeton U., 1979. Mem. adv. bd. Nashville African Am. Art Assn., 1994—; pres. bd. dirs. Visual Arts Assn. Nashville, 1995-96. Creator sculptures in stone for more than 25 yrs. Mem. Leadership Nashville, 1996—. Recipient Gov.'s award for Cmty. Svc., State of Calif., 1990. Mem. Nat. Sculpture Assn. Home: 1889 Conejo Dr Santa Fe NM 87505 Studio: 1889 Conejo Dr Santa Fe NM 87505-6114

RANDOLPH, STEVEN, financial advisor; b. Nebr., Oct. 14, 1946; m. Sherri Hamrick, 1980 (div. 1989); children: David, John, Michelle; m. Kathleen Riley, 1991. BS, U. Nebr., 1971. Registered rep. Nat. Assn. Securities Dealers, SEC; lic. in variable annuities, ins. and disabilities. Rep. Real Estate Consulting Svcs., Inc., Newport Beach, Calif., 1971-86; fin. advisor Agy. Fin. Svcs., Newport Beach, Calif., 1986—. With USMC, 1964-68, Vietnam. Mem. Nat. Assn. Securities Dealers, Nat. Assn. Life Underwriters (Nat. Sales Achievement award, Nat. Quality award), Million Dollar Round Table Club, Pres.'s Club (awards). Avocations: cooking, travel, watersports, sports cars. Home and Office: PO Box 9612 Newport Beach CA 92658-9612

RANDS, ROBERT LAWRENCE, archaeologist; b. Washington, May 13, 1922; s. John and Una Alice (Clingan) R.; m. Barbara Rathbone Cornett, Aug. 1948 (div. 1977); 1 child, Gordon Phillips; m. Elizabeth Lowry Vaughan, May 26, 1977 (dec. Oct. 18, 1990). BA in Anthropology, U. N.Mex., 1949; MA in Anthropology, U. Calif., L.A., 1949; PhD in Anthropology, Columbia U., 1952. Asst. prof. to prof. U. Miss., University, 1952-63; prof., asst. dir. rsch. lab. anthropology U. N.C., Chapel Hill, 1963-66; prof., curator Mesoamerican archaeology So. Ill. U., Carbondale, 1966-91; rsch. prof. So. Ill. U., Ctr. Archeol. Investigations, Carbondale, 1993—2002; adj. prof. So. Ill. U., Ctr. Archeol. Investigations, Carbondale, 2002—. Rsch. assoc. Univ. Mus., U. Pa., Phila., 1960-82; vis. scholar Dumbarton Oaks, Washington, 1975; rsch. collaborator Smithsonian Instn. Ctr. Materials Rsch. & Edn., Washington, 1987-93, 95-2000, Brookhaven Nat. Lab. Dept. of Chemistry, Upton, 1974-77, 80-83; ceramicist Proyecto de las Cruces Palenque Pre-Columbian Art Rsch. Inst., San Francisco, 1997-98. Co-editor: Man Across The Sea, 1971; co-author: Maya Sculpture, 1972. Fellow John Simon Guggenheim Found., 1956; grantee Inst. Andean Rsch., 1951, 59, Am. Philos. Soc., 1959, NSF, 1963, 67, 70, 75, Found. Advancement Mesoamerican Studies, 1998. Mem.: Am. Anthrop. Assn., Soc. Am. Archaeology (Excellence in Ceramic Studies award 1998), Sigma Xi. Achievements include research in ceramic technology as a means of investigating trade and interaction in ancient Maya society; major archaeological expeditions Chiapas and Tabasco, Mexico. Home: 27898 Old Village Rd Mechanicsville MD 20659-4286

RANDT, CLARK THORP, JR., ambassador, lawyer; b. Cleve., Nov. 24, 1945; s. Clark Thorp and Mary-Louise (Mitchell) R.; m. Sarah Talcott, Nov. 3, 1979; children: Clark Thorp III, Paull Mitchell, Clare Talcott. BA, Yale U., 1968; JD, U. Mich., 1975; People's Republic China law diploma, U. East Asia, 1988. Bar; N.Y. 1976. Assoc. Milbank, Tweed, Hadley & McCloy, N.Y.C., Hong Kong and Tokyo, 1975-82; 1st sec., comml. attache Am. Embassy, Beijing, 1982-84; ptnr. Heller, Ehrman, White & McAuliffe, San Francisco and Hong Kong, 1985-87; former resident ptnr. Gibson, Dunn and Crutcher, Hong Kong; US amb. to China US Dept. State, 2001—. Cons. People's Republic China Ministry Fgn. Econ. Rels. and Trade joint legal seminars U.S. Dept. Commerce, 1983-85; legal advisor Nat. Coun. U.S.-China Trade, 1974. Contbr. articles to profl. jours. and books. Mem. nat. steering com. George Bush for Pres., 1988; vice chmn. Reps. Abroad Com., Hong Kong, 1988—. With USAF, 1968-72. Recipient Disting. Svc. medal U.S. Dept. Commerce, 1984. Mem. ABA, Am. Soc. Internat. Law, Am. C. of C. in Hong Kong (v.p., gov.), Yale Club, Univ. Club, Am. Club in Hong Kong, Ladies Recreation Club. Office: 7300 Beijing Pl Washington DC 20521-7300 also: US Embassy 3 Xiu Shui Bei Jie Beijing 100600 China

RANEY, MIRIAM DAY, actress; b. Florence, SC, Sept. 30, 1922; d. Lewie Griffith and Iola Lewis (Edwards) Day; m. Robert William Raney, Mar. 31, 1946 (div. Sept. 1976); children: Robert William Jr., Miriam, Kevin Paige, Megan. *Great-great-great grandfather, William Lewis of Horry County, South Carolina, ran supplies in his sloops, the Rattlesnake, the Scorpion and the Centipede, to Colonel, later Brigadier General, Francis Marion, during the Revolutionary War. Great-great-great grandfather, Richard Edwards, formerly of Virginia, was with General Washington at Valley Forge during the Revolutionary War. He received a head wound and had gold trepanned into his skull. From then on, he was known as "Gold Dick" Edwards. After mustering out, he settled in the South Carolina Low Country. Grandsons of both fought for the Confederacy in the Civil War.* BSM in Voice, Music Edn., U. N.C., Greensboro, 1939-43; student, Julliard Sch. Music, 1942-43; BA in Music History and Lit., U. Ark., Little Rock, 1978-81; cert., Adam Roarke Film Actors Lab., Irving, Tex., 1989. Singing chorus N.Y.C. Ctr. Opera Co., 1943-44; understudy, singing chorus Oklahoma, Theater Guild, N.Y.C., 1944-45; ingenue lead Connecticut Yankee, Geosan Subway Cir., N.Y.C., 1945; understudy, singing chorus Up In Central Park, Michael Todd, N.Y.C., 1945-46. Beauty cons. Mary Kay Cosmetics, Inc., Dallas, 1993-98. Author: slide sound synchronized show Ark. Women in Music, 1982; composer, lyricist: The Bend and the Willow, 1982, Ballad of Petit Jean, 1983; stage appearances include Hedda Gabler (Reponde de Capite repertory), 1990, Time of Your Life (Cmty. Theatre of Little Rock), 1991, Our Town, 1991, Evening with Women II (Regional Theatre of Ctrl. Ark.), 1991; appeared in TV program Unsolved Mysteries, 1988; film Killing Time with Aunt Olene, 1988; also commercials tng. films, 1987-99; print model, Little Rock, Memphis, Ft. Worth, 1988-98. Named Illustrious Alumna, U. NC, 1945; recipient Thanks Badge, Girl Scouts USA, Oachita Coun., Little Rock, 1965. Mem. AAUW (Little Rock br. legis. com. 1973-79, program com. 1973-79, cultural interest rep. 1975-77, 96-98, state rep. for cultural interests 1976-78), Mus. Coterie, Cen. Ark. Guild of Organists (pres. student chpt. 1977-80). Democrat. Avocations: walking, birding, gardening, reading, movies. Home: 25 Valley Forge Dr Little Rock AR 72212-2613 Office Phone: 501-225-3460. E-mail: mimraney@comcast.net.

RANGEL, CHARLES BERNARD, congressman; b. Harlem, N.Y., June 11, 1930; s. Ralph and Blanche (Wharton) R.; m. Alma Carter, July 26, 1964; children: Steven, Alicia. BS, NYU, 1957; JD, St. John's U. Sch. Law, 1960; LLD (hon.), Wagner Coll., 1982, Atlanta U., 1983, St. John's U., Mt. Sinai Sch. Medicine, NYU, Howard U., 1988, Hofstra U., 1989. Bar: N.Y. 1960. Asst. U.S. atty., So. Dist. N.Y., 1961-62; mem. N.Y. State Assembly, 1966-70, U.S. Congress from 15th N.Y. dist., Washington, 1971—. Ranking mem. ways and means com., subcom. on trade; mem. joint com. on taxation.; dep. Dem. whip Served with AUS, 1948-52, Korea. Decorated Bronze Star, Purple Heart (U.S.); Korean presdl. citations. Democrat. Home: 40 W 135th St New York NY 10037-2504 Office: US Ho of Reps 2354 Rayburn Ho Office Bldg Washington DC 20515-0001

RANICK, MARVIN, retail sales executive; b. 1940; With Deb Shops, Inc., 1961—, v.p. ops., gen. mdse. mgr., pres., CEO, bd. dirs., 1979—. Office: DEB Shops Inc 9401 Blue Grass Rd Philadelphia PA 19114

RANIS, GUSTAV, economist, educator; b. Darmstadt, Germany, Oct. 24, 1929; s. Max and Bettina (Goldschmidt) R.; m. Ray Lee Finkelstein, June 15, 1958; children: Michael Bruce, Alan Jonathan, Bettina Suzanne. BA summa cum laude, Brandeis U., 1952, hon. degree, 1982; MA, Yale U., 1953, PhD, 1956. Asst. adminstr. program and policy AID/Dept. of State, 1965-67; dir. Econ. Growth Ctr. Yale U., New Haven, 1967-75, prof. econs., 1964—, Frank Altschul prof. internat. econs., 1981—; dir. Yale Ctr. Internat. and Area Studies, 1996—2004. Ford Found. vis. prof. U. De Los Andes, Bogota, Colombia, 1976-77; Ford Found. vis. prof. Colegio de Mex., 1971-72; fellow Inst. for Advanced Study, Berlin, 1993-94; cons. World Bank, AID, Ford Found., ILO, FAO, Inter-Am. Devel. Bank. Author: (with John Fei) Development of the Labor Surplus Economy: Theory and Policy, 1964,; (with Fei and Shirley Kuo) Growth with Equity: The Taiwan Case, 1979; (with Keijiro Otsuka and Gary Saxonhouse) Comparative Technology Choice in Development, 1988; (with F. Stewart and E. Angeles-Reyes) Linkages in Developing Economies: A Philippine Study, 1990; (with S.A. Mahmood) Political Economy of Development Policy Change, 1992; (with John C. H. Fei) Growth and Development from an Evolutionary Perspective, 1997; editor: Taiwan: From Developing to Mature Economy, 1992, En Route to Modern Economic Growth: Latin America in the 1990s, 1994, Japan and the U.S. in the Developing World, 1997,; co-editor: The State of Development Economics, 1988, Science and Technology: Lessons for Development Policy, 1990; mem. editl. bd. Jour. of Internat. Devel., 1995—, Oxford Devel. Studies, 1996—. Trustee Brandeis U., 1967-93, chmn. acad. affairs com., 1986-93. Social Sci. Rsch. Coun. fellow, Japan, 1955-56, Carnegie scholar, 2004-. Mem. Am. Econ. Assn., Coun. Fgn. Rels., Overseas Develop. Coun. (mem. adv. com.). Home: 7 Mulberry Rd Woodbridge CT 06525-1716 Office: Econ Growth Ctr Yale 27 Hillhouse Ave New Haven CT 06520 Office Phone: 203-432-3609. Business E-Mail: gustav.ranis@yale.edu.

RANK, EVERETT GEORGE, government official; b. Fresno, Calif., Dec. 1, 1921; s. Everett George and Evelyn Lydia (Dawson) R.; m. Evelyn Ingeborg Karschen, Apr. 30, 1948; children— Patricia, Judy, Ginny Student pub. sch., Clovis, Calif. Farmer, Fresno, 1946-81; chmn. Fresno County Agrl. Stblzn. and Conservation Service, 1959-69, Calif. Agrl. Stblzn. and Conservation Service, Berkeley, 1969-73; western regional dir. Agrl. Stblzn. and Conservation Service, Dept. Agr., Washington, 1974-76, adminstr., 1981-86. Pres. Clovis Unified Sch. Bd., 1959-72; bd. govs. U. Calif.-Fresno, 1977-81. Served with USN, 1941-45, PTO Mem. Masons (32 degreer), Shriners. Republican. Baptist. Avocation: golf. Home: 11868 Old Friant Rd Fresno CA 93720-9701

RANK, LARRY GENE, retired bank executive; b. Auburn, Ind., July 14, 1935; s. Lloyd R. Rank and Elizabeth M. (Williamson) Jackson; m. Bette Whitehurst, May 2, 1959; children: Kevin, Karen Grad., Am. Inst. Banking, 1962, U. Balt., 1969, Grad. Sch. Banking, Brown U., 1975, Nat. Council Savs. Instns., 1985. Exec. v.p. Provident Bank Md., Balt., 1982-85, pres., COO, 1985-90, dir., 1984-90; mng. dir. Jannotta, Bray & Assocs. Inc., Balt., 1991-92; exec. dir. Big Bros. and Big Sisters Ctrl. Md. Inc., 1993-96. Assoc. cons. Drake, Beam, Morin, 1997-98. Bd. dirs. ARC, Ctrl. Md. chpt., 1984-98, chmn. bd., 1990-92, bd. dirs. Ctrl. Ariz. chpt., 1998—, nat. com. on nominations; bd. dirs. United Way of Ctrl. Md., Balt., 1990-92; chair Gov.'s Vol. Awards Selection com., 1989; chmn. Am. Heart Assn.-Heart Ball, 1989-98, bd. dirs. Am. Heart Assn.; chmn. bd. Neighborhood Housing Svcs.; bd. dirs. Goodwill Industries, 1989-98; vol. Valley Big Bros./Big Sisters, Phoenix; bd. dirs. N.W. Hosp. Ctr., 1985-98, chair sys. bd., 1997-98; bd. dirs. Big Bros./Big Sisters Ctrl. Md. Mem.: Wildcat Club Villanova U., Foothills Golf Club (Phoenix), Deacon Club Wake Forest. Lutheran. Avocations: golf, sports, books, travel. Fax: (480) 753-9437. E-mail: rank37@msn.com.

RANKAITIS, SUSAN, artist; b. Cambridge, Mass., Sept. 10, 1949; d. Alfred Edward and Isabel (Shimkus) Rankaitis; m. Robbert Flick, June 5, 1976. BFA in Painting, U. Ill., 1971; MFA in Visual Arts, U. So. Calif., 1977. Rsch. asst., art dir. Plato Lab., U. Ill., Urbana, 1971-75; art instr. Orange Coast Coll., Costa Mesa, Calif., 1977-83; chair dept. art Chapman Coll., Orange, Calif., 1983-90; Fletcher Jones chair art Scripps Coll., Claremont, Calif., 1990—. Represented by Robert Mann Gallery, NYC; overview panelist visual arts Nat. Endowment for Arts, 1983, 84; selector Bingham Ednl. Trust, 1997-2002; scholar-in-

residence Borchard Found., Missillac, France, 2004. One-woman shows include Los Angeles County Mus. Art, 1983, Internat. Mus. Photography, George Eastman House, 1983, Gallery Min. Tokyo, 1988, Ruth Bloom Gallery, Santa Monica, 1989, 90, 92, Schneider Mus., Portland, Ore., 1990; Ctr. for Creative Photography, 1991, Robert Mann Gallery, NYC, 1994, 97, Mus. Contemporary Photography, Chgo., 1994, Mus. of Photographic Arts, 2000; represented in permanent collections MOCA, LA, U. N.Mex. Art, Ctr. for Creative Photography, Mus. Contemporary Photography, Chgo., Santa Barbara Mus. Art, Los Angeles County Mus. Art, Mpls. Inst. Arts, St. Louis Art Mus., San Francisco Mus. Modern Art, Art Inst. Chgo., Mus. Modern Art, Lodz, Poland, Princeton U. Art Mus., Stanford U. Art Mus., Contemporary Art Mus., Honolulu, Mus. Contemporary Photography, Art Inst. Chgo., St. Louis Art Mus., others. Active art auction Venice Family Clinic, 1980—. Recipient Graves award in Humanities, 1985; fellow NEA, 1980, 88, US, France, 1989, Agnes Bourne fellow Djerassi Found., 1989, Award in the Visual Arts, Flintridge Found., 2004; Durfee Chinese/Am. grantee, 2000-2001, Cultural Affairs grantee City L.A., 2001; Borchand Found. scholar-in-residence, France, 2004. Mem. Coll. Art Assn., Los Angeles County Mus. Art, Santa Monica Mus. Art. Home: 3117 N Lansbury Ave Claremont CA 91711-4146 Office Phone: 909-607-4439., 213-683-9679. Business E-Mail: srankait@scrippscollege.edu.

RANKIN, ALEX C. management executive; B in Commerce, BA in Psychology, MBA. With Agra Industries, Ltd., 1976-94; pres., CEO Nex-Cycle, Inc., Irving, Tex., 1994—. Office: Nexcycle Inc 1672 Railroad St Corona CA 92880-2502 E-mail: arankin@nexcycle.com.

RANKIN, ALFRED MARSHALL, JR., manufacturing executive; b. Cleve., Oct. 8, 1941; s. Alfred Marshall and Clara Louise (Taplin) R.; m. Victoire Conley Griffin, June 3, 1967; children: Helen P., Clara T. BA in Econs. magna cum laude, Yale U., 1963, JD, 1966. Mgmt. cons. McKinsey & Co., Inc., Cleve., 1970-73; with Eaton Corp., Cleve., 1974-81, pres. materials handling group, 1981-83, pres. indsl. group, 1984-86, exec. v.p., 1986, vice chmn., chief oper. officer, 1986-89; pres., COO NACCO Industries, Inc., Cleve., 1989-91, pres., CEO, 1991-94, also bd. dirs., chmn., pres., CEO, 1994—; bd. dirs. The Goodrich Corp., Vanguard Group. Former pres., trustee Hathaway Brown Sch.; trustee Univ. Hosps. Cleve., Mus. Arts Assn., Univ. Circle, Inc., Cleve. Mus. Art, John Huntington Art Trust, Cleve. Tomorrow; past chairperson The Cleve. Found. Mem. Ohio Bar Assn. Clubs: Chagrin Valley Hunt, Union, Tavern, Pepper Pike, Kirtland Country (Cleve.); Rolling Rock (Ligonier, Pa.); Met. (Washington). Republican. Office: NACCO Industries Inc 5875 Landerbrook Dr Ste 300 Mayfield Heights OH 44124

RANKIN, CLYDE EVAN, III, lawyer; b. Phila., July 3, 1950; s. Clyde Evan, Jr. and Mary E. (Peluso) R.; m. Camille Cozzone, Aug. 24, 1997; A.B., Princeton U., 1972; J.D., Columbia U., 1975; postgrad. Hague Acad. Internat. Law, 1975. Bar: N.Y., N.J., D.C., U.S. Supreme Ct. Law clk. to judge U.S. Dist. Ct. So. Dist. N.Y., 1975-77; assoc. Debevoise, Plimpton, Lyons & Gates, N.Y.C., 1977-79; assoc. Coudert Bros., N.Y.C., 1979-83, ptnr., 1984—. Trustee The Rensselaerville (N.Y.) Inst., 1989—, Coun. on Fgn. Rels., 1996—. Stone scholar, 1974. Mem. ABA, Assn. of Bar of City of N.Y., N.Y. State Bar Assn., D.C. Bar Assn., N.J. Bar Assn. Roman Catholic. Club: Amateur Comedy (N.Y.C.). Contbr. article to legal jour. E-mail: rankinc@coudert.com. Office: Coudert Bros 1114 Ave of Americas New York NY 10036-7703 Office Phone: 212-626-4740.

RANKIN, JACQUELINE ANNETTE, communications expert, educator; b. Omaha, Nebr., May 19, 1925; d. Arthur C. and Virdie (Gillispie) R. BA, Calif. State U., L.A., 1964, MA, 1966; MS in Mgmt., Calif. State U., Fullerton, 1977; EdD, U. LaVerne, Calif., 1981. Tchr. Rowland H.S., La Habra, Calif., 1964-66, Lowell H.S., La Habra, Calif., 1966-69, Pomona (Calif.) H.S., 1969-75; program asst. Pomona Adult Sch., 1975-82; dir. Child Abuse Prevention Program, 1985-86; exec. dir. child abuse prevention Calif. Dept. Pub. Svc., 1985-87; instr. Ind. U., Purdue U., 1993; assoc. prof. speech Ball State U., Muncie, Ind., 1993-94; instr. No. Va. U., 1994—, trainer Loudoun campus, 1996. Faculty evening divsn. Mt. San Antonio C.C., 1966-72; asst. prof. speech Ball State U., Muncie, Ind., 1993; instr. No. Va. U., Alexandria, Annandale, Manassas, Woodbridge, 1995—; assoc. faculty dept. comm. and theatre, Ind. U., Purdue U., Indpls., 1993; trainer internat. convs., sales groups, staffs of hosps., others; spkr., writer, trainer, lectr., cons. in field. Columnist: Jackie's World, Topics Newspapers; author: Body Language: First Impressions, Body Language in Negotiations and Sales, Body Language in Love and Romance, Body Language of the Abused Child, 1999, Using body Language That Kids Trust, Ten Tips for Evaluating Body Language of the Abused Child; contbr. articles to Child Law Practice, ABA and other profl. jours. Mem. Fairfax County Dem. Com.; mem. adv. coun., mem. nat. capital chpt. bd. dirs. ARC. Mem. Internat. Platform Assn., Pi Lambda Theta, Phi Delta Kappa. Home and Office: 7006 Elkton Dr Springfield VA 22152-3330 Office Phone: 703-866-0084. E-mail: jackie.rankin@cox.net.

RANKIN, JAMES, financial services company executive; b. Morris Plains, N.J., Jan. 25, 1957; s. Bernard James and Carol Joyce (Cooper) R.; m. Rebecca R. Samuel, May 11, 1989. BS, U. Calif., Davis, 1980; postgrad., U. Calif., Berkeley, 1981-83; MBA, Harvard U., 1986. Asst. v.p. Wells Fargo Bank, San Francisco, 1979-88; v.p. T. Rowe Price, L.A., 1988-93; v.p., chmn. oper. com. Founders Asset Mgmt., Denver, 1993-98; v.p. customer support FOLIOfn Investments, LLC, Vienna, Va., 1999-2000; sr. mng. dir. product mgmt. EquiServe, Jersey City, N.J., 2000—. Mem. Harvard Bus. Sch. Club of So. Calif. Avocations: skiing, bicycling, travel. Office: EquiServe 150 Royal St Canton MA 02021 Home: 120 Sidney Bay Dr Newport Coast CA 92657-2112 E-mail: rankinjp@yahoo.com.

RANKIN, JAMES WINTON, lawyer; b. Norfolk, Va., Sept. 9, 1943; s. Winton Blair and Edith (Griffin) R.; m. Donna Lee Carpenter, June 25, 1966 (dec.); children— Thomas James, William Joseph, Elizabeth Jeanne; m. JoAnne Katherine Murray, Feb. 11, 1978. AB magna cum laude, Oberlin Coll., 1965; JD cum laude, U. Chgo., 1968. Bar: Ill. 1968, U.S. Dist. Ct. (no. dist.) Ill. 1969, U.S. Ct. Appeals (7th cir.) 1971, U.S. Ct. Appeals (5th cir.) 1979, U.S. Supreme Ct. 1975, Calif. 1986. Law clk. U.S. Dist. Ct. (no. dist.) Ill., 1968-69; assoc. Kirkland & Ellis, Chgo., 1969-73, ptnr., 1973—. Mem. ABA, Order of Coif, Mid-Am. Club, Univ. Club, Mich. Shores Club, Kenilworth Club, Ephriam Yacht Club. Presbyterian. Home: 633 Kenilworth Ave Kenilworth IL 60043-1070 Office: Kirkland & Ellis 200 E Randolph St Fl 54 Chicago IL 60601-6636

RANKIN, JOHN KARL, retired minister, retired theology studies educator; b. Texhoma, Okla., Apr. 14, 1921; s. James Hubert Rankin and Alice Fletcher Boston-Rankin-Gens; m. Elizabeth Ryan Rankin, Mar. 3, 1927; children: Philip Henry, John Mark. BA, Univ. Okla., Norman, 1949; ThM, Perkins Sch. of Theology, So. Meth. univ., Dallas, Tex., 1954. Cert. Profl. Chaplains Assn., 1964, supr. Assoc. Clin. Pastoral Edn., 1963. Pastor Tex. Conf. Dist. Missions, Tex., 1950—59; chaplain student supr. Okla. State Hosp., Norman, 1960—67, dir. clin. pastoral edn., 1967—72, Chgo. State Hosp., Alexian Bros. Med. Ct., Elk Grove Village, Ill., 1972—84; ret. United Meth Ch., Chgo., 1984. Tech. sgt. USMC, 1942—45. Recipient Disting. Svc. award, Assn. for Clin. Pastoral Edn., 1986. Mem.: Blue Bonnet Masonic Lodge 1219 (chaplain). Independent. Methodist. Avocations: photography, gardening. Home: 1214 Sutton Dr San Antonio TX 78228-4013

RANKIN, RACHEL ANN, retired media specialist; b. High Point, N.C., Mar. 8, 1937; d. Benjamin Carl and Anne Jane Mixson; m. Thomas M. Rankin, July 30, 1961; 1 child, Rachel Roxanne Lineberry. AA, Mars Hill Coll., 1957; BA, Wake Forest U., 1959; MLS, U. S.C., 1977. Caseworker Rockingham County Welfare, Reidsville, N.C., 1959-61, Berlin Am. Sch., 1967-69, Albemarle County Schs., Charlottesville, Va., 1970-72, Lexington County Schs., Ballentine, S.C., 1973-76; tchg. asst., student tchr. supr. Sch. Edn. U. S.C., Columbia, 1976-77; sch. media specialist Montgomery County Schs., Rockville, Md., 1977-99; ret., 1999. Mentor for new librs./media specialists Montgomery Pub. Schs., 2001—03. V.p. Berlin Am. PTA, 1967—68; del. European Conf. PTAs, Garmisch, Germany, 1968; mem. planning com. N.C. Cherry Blossom Ball, Washington, 1983; co-coord. support group Am. Cancer Soc., 1988—89; People to People del. to China, 1998; bd. dirs. Fourth Presbn. Sch., Potomac, 2001—03. Named Most Outstanding Tchr., Jackson Burley Sch., Charlottesville, 1972; recipient ofcl. citation Ho. of Dels., Md. Gen. Assembly, 1983, 96. Mem. NEA (life), Soc. Sch. Librs. Internat. (del. 1983), Am. Assn. Sch. Librarians (del. Montgomery County 1982, 90, 92, 97), Am. Cancer Soc. (dist. chair crusades 1988-90), Md. Ednl. Media Orgn., Montgomery County Ednl. Media Specialists Assn. (treas. 1981-82, v.p. 1982-83, pres. 1983-84), Montgomery County Edn. Assn., N.C. State Soc. of Washington (bd. govs. 1984-86), Delta Kappa Gamma (sec. Sigma chpt. 1988-91, v.p. 1996-98, pres. 1998-2000). Democrat. Presbyterian. Home: 15219 Red Clover Dr Rockville MD 20853-1645

RANKIN, ROBERT ARTHUR, journalist; b. Richmond, Va., May 31, 1949; s. Arthur Norton and Martha Louise (Rountree) Rankin; m. Janis Johnson, May 11, 1979 (div. May 2001); 1 child, Benjamin John. BA in Polit. Sci., Randolph Macon Coll., 1971; MA in Govt., U. Va., 1974; Walter Bagehot fellowship, Columbia U., 1978-79. Reporter Richmond News Leader, Va., 1972-75; reporter Congl. Quar., Washington, 1975-78; editorial writer Miami Herald, Fla., 1980-85, Phila. Inquirer, 1985-87; nat. corr. Washington bur. Knight Ridder Newspapers, 1987-99, govt. and politics editor, 2000—01. V.p. Civic Assn. Hollin Hills, Alexandria, Va., 1991—92. Co-recipient Pulitzer prize for editl. writing, 1983; recipient Olive Br. award, NYU Ctr. War, Peace and News Media, 1990, 1st prize, Va. Press Assn., 1974, Best Editl. award, Phila. chpt. Sigma Delta Chi, 1987. Mem.: Nat. Press Club, White House Corr. Assn. (bd. govs. 1996—98). Office: Knight Ridder Newspapers 700 12th St NW Ste 1000 Washington DC 20005-3994 Business E-Mail: rrankin@krwashington.com.

RANKIN, SCOTT ANTHONY, food scientist, researcher; b. Fullerton, California, June 2, 1965; s. Vance George and Ina Rankin; m. Teresa Hendrickson, Dec. 19, 1988; children: Adriana Renee, Madeline Paige, Harrison Scott, Dylan Scott. BS, Brigham Young U., Provo, UT., 1988—90, MS, 1990—91; PhD, Oreg. State U., Corvallis, 1991—95. Asst. prof. U. of Md., Coll. Pk., Md., 1996—2001, U. of Wis., Madison, 2001—. Mem. Stake High Coun., LDS Ch., Madison, Wis., 2003—. Recipient rsch. grant, USDA, 2003-2005. Mem.: Am. Dairy Sci. Assn. (program chair 2003—), Inst. of Food Technologists (divsn. chair 2003—), Am. Chem. Soc. Office: Univ Wis Madison 1605 Linden Dr Madison WI 53706 Office Fax: 608-262-6872. Business E-Mail: sarankin@wisc.edu.

RANKIN, WILLIAM PARKMAN, communications educator, academic administrator; b. Boston, Feb. 6, 1917; s. George William and Bertha W. (Clowe) Rankin; m. Ruth E. Gerard, Sept. 12, 1942; children: Douglas W., Joan W. BS, Syracuse U., 1941; MBA, NYU, 1949, PhD, 1979. Sales exec. Redbook mag., N.Y.C., 1945-49, This Week mag., N.Y.C., 1949-55, adminstrv. exec., 1955-60, v.p., 1957-60, v.p., dir. advt. sales, sales devel. dir., 1960-63, exec. v.p., 1963-69; gen. exec. newspaper divsn. Time Inc., N.Y.C., 1969-70; gen. mgr. feature svc. Newsweek Inc., N.Y.C., 1970-74, fin. and ins. advt. mgr., 1974-81; prof., asst. to dir. Walter Cronkite Sch. Journalism & Telecom., Ariz. State U., Tempe, 1981-98, prof. emeritus, 1998—, also bd. dirs. Lectr. Syracuse U., NYU, N.Y.C., Berkeley Sch. Author: Selling Retail Advertising, 1944, The Technique of Selling Magazine Advertising, 1949, Business Management of Consumer Magazines, 1980, 2d edit., 1984, The Practice of Newspaper Management, 1986. Mem.: Dutch Treat Club (N.Y.C.). Home: 2625 E Southern Ave C-18 Tempe AZ 85282-7615 Office: Ariz State U Walter Cronkite Sch Journalism and Mass Communication Tempe AZ 85287-1305 Office Phone: 480-831-3316.

RANKINE, V.V. sculptor, painter; b. Boston, July 27, 1920; d. Auguste and Hetty (Hemenway) Richard; m. John Magruder, 1945 (div. 1950); 1 child, John Magruder; m. Paul Scott Rankine, 1952 (div. 1969); 1 child, David Scott; m. Rufus King, Nov. 23, 1973. Student, Amedee Ozenfant Sch., N.Y.C., 1940-41, Black Mt. Coll., 1942-43. Dir. dept. art Madeira Sch., Greenway, Va., 1967-70; artist-in-residence Inst. Man and Sci., Rensselaer, N.Y., summer 1968; instr. humanities art Hunter Coll. H.S., N.Y.C., 1970-71; instr. painting and drawing U. Md., College Park, 1979-81. One-woman shows include Fraser's Stable Gallery, Washington, 1978, Corcoran Gallery Art, Washington, 1978, No. Va. C.C., 1978, Women Artists Ea. L.I., East Hampton, N.Y., 1979; group exhbns. include Corcoran Gallery Art, Washington, 1954, 55, 58, 67, Betty Parsons Gallery, N.Y.C., 1966-81, Mus. Modern Art, N.Y.C., 1966, 30th Corcoran Biennial, Washington, 1967-68, Four Americans, Axiom Gallery, London, 1968, Painting and Sculpture Today, Indpls., 1965; work rep. in Nat. Mus. Am. Art, Washington, Corocoran Gallery Art, Washington, Oklahoma City Mus., Indpls. Mus. Art, Woodward Found., Washington, Guild Hall Mus., East Hampton, N.Y. Recipient Painting prize Corcoran Gallery, 1955, Maurice Tuchman Juror award Corcoran Gallery Art, 1978. Home: 5 Centre St Dover MA 02030-2203

RANN, ROBERT KENNEDY, humanities educator; b. Detroit, Mich., Oct. 2, 1953; s. Robert Earle and Mary Ann Rann; m. Satoko Yamakawa; children: Jennifer Nishio, Evan Kentaro. PhD, U. Mich., 1987. Assoc. prof. humanities Madonna U., Livonia, Mich., 1987—. Editor: Japanese Studies Across the Curriculum, 1992. Recipient Fulbright-Hays Doctoral Dissertation award, 1984, Japan Found. Doctoral Dissertation fellowship, 1984, Nat. Endowment for Humanities Dist. Tchg., 2003—05. Mem.: Assn. for Asian Studies.

RANNEY, AUSTIN (JOSEPH RANNEY), political science educator; b. Cortland, N.Y., Sept. 23, 1920; s. Frank Addison and Florence Edith (Ranney) R.; m. Elizabeth Mackay (div. Oct. 1975); m. Nancy Boland; children: Joseph, Douglas, Gordon, David. BS, Northwestern U., 1941, LLD (hon.), 1995; MA, U. Oreg., 1943; PhD, Yale U., 1948, DSS (hon.), 1985; LLD (hon.), SUNY, 1986, Northwestern U., 1995. Statistician Douglas Aircraft Corp., Chgo., 1942-44; instr. Yale U., New Haven, 1945-47; from instr. to prof. U. Ill., Urbana, 1947-63; prof. U. Wis., Madison, 1963-76; resident scholar Am. Enterprise Inst., Washington, 1976-86; prof. U. Calif., Berkeley, 1986-91, prof. emeritus, 1991—, chmn. dept. polit. sci., 1987-90. Author: The Doctrine of Responsible Party Government, 1954, Governing, 1958, Curing the Mischiefs of Faction, 1975, Channels of Power, 1983. Mem. Presdl.-Congl. Commn. on Polit. Activity Govtl. Employees, Washington, 1967-68, Dem. Nat. Com. Commn. on Party Structure, Washington, 1969-72, Commn. on Presdl. Debates, Washington, 1980-88; chmn. Gov.'s Commn. on Registration and Voting Participation, Madison, Wis., 1964, social sci. rsch. coun. Com. on Govtl. Processes, 1964-71, coun. on social scis. policy Yale U., 1983-88. Recipient Wilbur Lucius Cross medal Yale U. Grad. Sch., 1977; sr. rsch. fellow NSF, 1970, John Simon Guggenheim fellow, 1974, fellow Ctr. for Advanced Study in Behavioral Scis., 1974. Fellow Brit. Acad. (corr.); mem. Am. Polit. Sci. Assn. (pres. 1975-76), Am. Acad. Arts and Scis. (v.p. 1981-84). Home: 990 Regal Rd Berkeley CA 94708-1430 Office: Univ Calif Dept Polit Sci Berkeley CA 94720-0001 E-mail: austin@ranneyberkeley.com.

RANNEY, CARLETON DAVID, retired plant pathology researcher, administrator; b. Jackson, Minn., Jan. 23, 1928; s. Carleton Oran and Ada Elizabeth (Harriman) R.; m. Mary Kathryn Ransleben, July 16, 1949; children: David Clayton, Mary Elizabeth. AA, Chaffey Jr. Coll., Ontario, Calif., 1952; BS, Tex. A&M U., 1954, MS, 1955, PhD, 1959. Plant pathologist Crops Rsch. Divsn. Agrl. Rsch. Svc. USDA, College Station, Tex., 1955-58, Stoneville, Miss., 1958-70, investigations leader Beltsville, Md., 1970-72; area dir. Ala. No. Miss. area Agrl. Rsch. Svc. USDA, Starkville, Miss., 1973-78, area dir. Delta States area Stoneville, Miss., 1978-84, area dir. Mid-South area, 1984-87; asst. dir. Miss. Agrl. and Forestry Exptl. Stas., Stoneville, 1987-94, head Delta br. sta., 1987-94, emeritus plant pathologist, 1994—. Adj. prof. agronomy Miss. State U., 1970-94; sr. exec. svc. USDA, Stoneville, 1984-87; adv. bd. Belt Wide Meetings Nat. Cotton Coun., Memphis, 1987-96. Contbr. articles to profl. jours. Sect. advisor SE2 Order of Arrow, Eagle Scout, Boy Scouts Am., Miss. and West Tenn., 1973-83; pres. Delta Area coun. Boy Scouts Am., Clarksdale, Miss., 1990-91; v.p. Leland Habitat for Humanity, 1995-2000, bd. dirs. 2000—. Served with USAAC, 1946-49. Recipient Silver Beaver Boy Scouts Am., 1981, Disting. Svc. Order of Arrow Boy Scouts Am., 1983, Superior Svc. award USDA, 1981, Cert. of Merit USDA, 1983. Mem. Agron. Soc. Am., Nat. Cotton Disease Coun. (sec. 1959-60, chmn. 1961-62), Lions (pres. Leland club 1995-96), Sigma Xi, Alpha Zeta, Phi Kappa Phi. Methodist. Achievements include development of fungicide control seedling diseases; definition of relationship of microclimate to boll rot of cotton; development of non-mercurial seed treatments. Office: Delta Rsch & Ext Ctr PO Box 226 Stoneville MS 38776-0226 E-mail: cdmkranney@tecinfo.net.

RANNEY, DANIEL ANTHONY, minister, language educator; b. Rutland, Vt., July 28, 1956; s. Philip Clayton and Jeanette Gabriele Ranney. BA, Bob Jones U., Greenville, SC, 1989; MDiv, Mid Am. Bapt. Theological Sem., Schenectady, NY, 1996. Cardiac monitor tech. Greenville Meml. Hosp., 1986—92, Ellis Hosp., Schenectady, 1992—95; deskman/Bible instr. City Mission of Schenectady, 1995—98; pastor Mont Pleasant Bapt. Ch., Schenectady, 1995, Tupper Lake Bapt. Ch., NY, 2001—02; French tchr. Fair Haven Grade Sch., Vt., 2002; adminstr. Truthville (NY) Christian Acad., 2004—. Pastoral instr. Internat. Ch. Planters, Tumbling Shoals, Ark., 2002; del. Billy Graham Evang. Assn., Amsterdam 2000, Netherlands. Author: (book) Perfect War, 2002; lyricist: songs Perfect War Won, 2004; author: (poem) Perfect War, 2004. Sgt. E5 U.S. Army, 1980—84, US, Germany. Avocations: running, classical music, Mediterranean cuisine. Home: 235 County Rte 12 Granville NY 12854 Office Phone: 518-642-4662. Personal E-mail: John330_2000@yahoo.com.

RANNEY, HELEN MARGARET, retired internist, hematologist, educator; b. Summer Hill, NY, Apr. 12, 1920; d. Arthur C. and Alesia (Toolan) Ranney. AB, Barnard Coll., 1941; MD, Columbia U., 1947; ScD, U. S.C., 1979, SUNY, Buffalo, 1996. Diplomate Am. Bd. Internal Medicine. Intern Presbyn. Hosp., N.Y.C., 1947—48, resident, 1948—50, asst. physician, 1954—60; practice medicine specializing in internal medicine, hematology N.Y.C., 1954—70; instr. Coll. Phys. and Surg. Columbia, N.Y.C., 1954—60; from assoc. prof. to prof. medicine Albert Einstein Coll. Medicine, N.Y.C., 1960—70; prof. medicine SUNY, Buffalo, 1970—73, U. Calif., San Diego, 1973—90, chmn. dept. medicine, 1973—86, Disting. physician vet. adminstr., 1986—91; cons. Alliance Pharm. Corp., San Diego, 1991—2004; ret., 2004. Master: ACP; fellow: AAAS; mem.: NAS, Am. Acad. Arts and Scis., Am. Assn. Physicians, Harvey Soc., Am. Soc. Hematology, Am. Soc. for Clin. Investigation, Inst. Medicine, Alpha Omega Alpha, Sigma Xi, Phi Beta Kappa.

RANNEY, RICHARD RAYMOND, periodontist educator, researcher, dean; b. Atlanta, July 11, 1939; s. Russell Ballou and Maureen Joan (Bannon) R.; m. Beverly Anne Toton, June 10, 1961 (div.); children: Christine Marie, Kathleen Anne; m. Patricia Marie DeNoto, Feb. 25, 1969; children: Maureen Frances, Russell Christopher. DDS, U. Iowa, 1963; MS, U. Rochester, 1969; D (hon.), U. Buenos Aires, 1995. Asst. prof. periodontology U. Oreg., 1969-72; assoc. prof. periodontics Va. Commonwealth U., Richmond, 1972-78, prof., 1978-86, dir. grad. periodontics, 1972-76, chmn. dept. periodontics, 1974-77, asst. dean rsch. and grad. affairs, 1977-84, asst. dean rsch., 1984-86; dir. Clin. Rsch. Ctr. Periodontal Diseases, Richmond, 1978-86; prof. Sch. Dentistry U. Ala., Birmingham, 1986-91, dean, 1986-89; prof. U. Md., Balt., 1991—2004, dean, 1991—2002; Sr. Policy Fellow Am. Dental Edn. Assn., 2003—04. Contbr. chpts. to books, articles to profl. jours. With USPHS, 1963-66. Nat. Inst. Dental Rsch. grantee, 1970-86. Fellow: AAAS, Am. Coll. Dentists, Internat. Coll. Dentists; mem.: ADA, Am. Dental Edn. Assn. (sr. policy fellow 2003—04), Am. Assn. Dental Rsch. (pres. 1990—91), Internat. Assn. Dental Rsch. (pres. 1995—96, basic rsch. periodontology award 1985), Am. Acad. Periodontology, Omicron Kappa Upsilon, Sigma Xi. Office: U Md 666 W Baltimore St Baltimore MD 21201-1510 Business E-Mail: rranney@dental.umaryland.edu.

RANNEY, SANDRA KAY, artist, fine arts and humanities educator; b. Tucson, June 17, 1948; d. Gail Hamilton and Beverly Jean (Crawford) Cowell. BA in Social Scis., Nyack Coll., 1972; M in Humanities, U. Richmond, 1985; PhD of Comparative Arts, Ohio U., 1995. Tchg. assoc., lectr. Ohio U., Athens, 1985—90; prof. Pittsburg State U., Kans., 1990—96, Ind. Wesleyan U., 1999—. Exec. dir. Kokomo (Ind.) Art Assn., 1999. Scholar U. Richmond, 1984-85, Ohio U., 1987; doctoral fellow Ohio U., 1985-89; grantee Pittsburg State U., 1994, NEH, 1982. Mem. Assn. for Integrated Studies, Coll. Art Assn. Avocations: art, music, drama. Home: 503 Rainbow Cir Kokomo IN 46902 E-mail: drsranney@mymailstation.com.

RANNEY-MARINELLI, ALESIA, lawyer; b. Ithaca, N.Y., 1952; BA, Mich. State U., 1973; JD cum laude, Harvard U., 1977. Bar: Del. 1977, N.Y. 1986. Ptnr. Skadden Arps Slate Flom & Meagher, N.Y.C. Office: Skadden Arps Slate Meagher & Flom 4 Times Sq Fl 24 New York NY 10036-6595

RANNIGER, LESLIE JEAN, lawyer; b. Dallas, Mar. 5, 1957; BA, U. Colo., Boulder, 1979; MBA, U. Denver, 1982, JD, 1985. Bar: Colo. 1985, U.S. Dist. Ct. Colo., 1985. Atty. Cosgiff Dunn & Abplanalp, Vail, Colo., 1985—87, Frascona & Joiner, Boulder, 1987—89; in-house counsel Ameralq Inc., Boulder, 1989—90; pvt. practice Boulder, 1990—. V.p., bd. dirs. Boulder County YWCA, 1985-87; dir. Cherryvale Fire Protection Dist., 1982-83. Office: PO Box 15 Boulder CO 80306-0015

RANSEL, DAVID LORIMER, history professor; b. Gary, Ind., Feb. 20, 1939; s. Joseph A. and Patricia (Lorimer) R.; m. Therese Holma; children: Shairstin, Annaliisa. BA, Coe Coll., 1961; MA, Northwestern U., 1962; PhD, Yale U., 1969. Instr. Tollare Folkhogskola, Boo, Sweden, 1959-60; asst. instr. Yale U., New Haven, 1966-67; instr. U. Ill., Urbana, 1967-69, asst. prof., 1969-73, assoc. prof., 1973-81, prof., 1981-85, Ind. U., Bloomington, 1985—, Robert F. Byrnes prof. history, 2001—, dir. Russian and East European Inst., 1995—. Author: The Politics of Catherinian Russia, 1975, Mothers of Misery, 1988, Village Mothers: Three Generations of Change in Russia and Tataria, 2000; editor: The Family in Imperial Russia, 1978, Imperial Russia: New Histories for the Empire, 1998; editor/translator: Village Life in Late Tsarist Russia, 1993; editor Slavic Rev., Urbana, 1980-85, Am. Hist. Rev., Bloomington, 1985-95; bd. editors The History of the Family: An International Quarterly, Historisk Tidskrift, Forum for Anthropology and Culture, Kritika: Explorations in Russian and Eurasian History. Guggenheim fellow, 1989-90, Wilson fellow, 1989-90, NEH fellow, 1998-99; Fulbright-Hays grantee, 1979, 90, Irex grantee, 1990, 93. Mem. Am. Hist. Assn. (mem. gov. coun. 1985-95, mem. fin. com. 1989-95), Am. Assn. for Advancement of Slavic Studies (bd. dirs. 1979-85, mem. fin. com. 1980-85, chmn. com. on status of women 1991-93, v.p., pres.-elect 2003, pres. 2004—), Irex (program com. 1995-99). Avocations: classical guitar, sailing, running. Office: Ind Univ Russian/East European Inst 565 Ballantine Hall Bloomington IN 47401-5017 Office Phone: 812-855-7309. Business E-Mail: ransel@indiana.edu.

RANSOHOFF, RICHARD MILTON, neurologist, researcher; b. Cin., Aug. 18, 1946; s. Jerry Nathan and Sue (Westheimer) R.; m. Margaret Seidler, Mar. 26, 1988; children: Amy Julia, Lena Jane. BA, Bard Coll., 1968; MD, Case Western Reserve U., 1978. Diplomate Am. Bd. Psychiatry and Neurology, Am. Bd. Internal Medicine. Resident in internal medicine Mt. Sinai Hosp., Cleve., 1978-81; resident in neurology The Cleve. Clinic Found., 1981-83, chief resident in neurology, 1983-84, mem. assoc. staff in neurology, 1984-93, mem. asst. staff in molecular biology Rsch. Inst., 1989-94, mem. staff neurology dept., 1993—, mem. staff in molecular biology Lerner Rsch. Inst., 1994—97, mem. staff in neuroscis. Lerner Rsch. Inst., 1994—; prof. dept. med. virology, immunology and molecular genetics Ohio State U. Health Sci. Ctr., Cleve. Clinic Found., 1997—2001; postdoctoral fellow in molecular biology Case Western Reserve U., Cleve., 1984-89. Mem. neurology C study sect., Washington, 1995—98; cons. Rsch. Ctr. for AIDS Dementia, Johns Hopkins U., 1998—2002; mem. clin. adv. bd. LeukoSite, Inc., Cambridge, Mass., 1998—2000; project dir. Nat. Inst. Neurol. Diseases and Stroke, Washington, 1999—; mem. sci. adv. bd. ChemoCentryx, Santa Clara, Calif., 2001—; cons. Ctr. Neurobiology & Neurodegeneration U. Nebr. Med. Ctr. Co-author: Transcriptional Regulation in the Interferon System, 1997; co-editor: Cytokines in the CNS, 1996; editor: Chemokines in the CNS, 2002; sect. editor: Jour. Immunology, 2002—, editl. bd.: Jour. of Neuroimmunology, 1998—, Ency. Neurol. Scis., 2003, mem. editl. adv. bd.: Trends in Immunology; contbr. more than 160 articles to profl. jours. Chair profl. adv. com. Nat. Multiple Sclerosis Soc., N.E. Ohio, 1985-95, trustee, 1985-97, mem. med. adv. bd. Nat.

Multiple Sclerosis Soc., N.Y.C. 1996—, mem. peer rev. com. B, 2003—; mem. corp. Hathaway Brown Sch., Shaker Heights, Ohio; ad hoc reviewer Charles Dana Fund, N.Y.C., Wellcome Trust, U.K. Grantee NIH, Washington, 1988—, Harry Weaver Neurosci. scholar Nat. Multiple Sclerosis Soc., N.Y.C., 1987-92; recipient Physicians Rsch. Tng. award Am. Cancer Soc., N.Y.C., 1984-86, Clin. Investigator Devel. award Nat. Inst. Neurol. and Communicative Diseases and Stroke, Washington, 1988-93, John and Samuel Bard award for Sci. and Medicine, 2002. Mem.: Am. Assn. Immunologists, Am. Assn. Neurology, Am. Neurol. Assn. (mem. sci. program com. 1996—98). Office: Lerner Rsch Inst NC-30 Cleve Clinic Found 9500 Euclid Ave Cleveland OH 44195-0001 E-mail: ransohr@ccf.org.

RANSOM, BRYAN KENNETH, music educator; b. Columbus, Ohio, Mar. 8, 1967; s. Robert Leigh and Sylvia Sue Ransom; m. Christina Jalene Snodgrass, June 25, 1994; 1 child, Alysa Noelle. BA in music, San Diego State U., 1987—92. Tchg. State of Calif., 1992. Dir. of athletic bands San Diego State U., 1992—. Entertainment coord. San Diego Chargers, 1994—. Recipient Directors award, San Diego State U. Bands, 1992. Mem.: So. Calif. Sch. Band and Orch. Assn. (assoc.). Office: San Diego State U 5500 Campanile Dr San Diego CA 92182-7902 Personal E-mail: bransom@mail.sdsu.edu.

RANSOM, EVELYN NAILL, language educator, linguist; b. Memphis, Apr. 20, 1938; d. Charles Rhea and Evelyn (Goodlander) Naill Ransom; m. Gunter Heinz Hiller, June 7, 1960 (div. Mar. 1964). AA, Mt. Vernon Jr. Coll., 1958; BA, Newcomb Coll., 1960; MA, N.Mex. Highlands U., 1965; PhD, U. Ill., 1974. Cert. secondary tchr., N.Mex. Instr. Berlitz Sch. Langs., New Orleans, 1961; tchr. MillerWall Elem. Sch., Harvey, L.A., 1961-62; teaching asst. N.Mex. Highlands U., Las Vegas, 1963-64; instr. U. Wyo., Laramie, 1965-66; teaching asst. U. Ill., Urbana, 1966-70; prof. English lang. Ea. Ill. U., Charleston, 1970-93; vis. prof. in linguistics No. Ariz. U., Flagstaff, 1990-91, adj. faculty, 1993-94, Ariz. State U., Tempe, 1995-98; retired. Referee Pretext: Jour. of Lang. and Lit., Ill., 1981, S.W. Jour. Linguistics, 1999; co-chair roundtable Internat. Congress of Linguistics, 1987; linguistics del. People to People, Moscow, St. Petersburg, Prague, 1993, China, 1998; dissertation reader SUNY, Buffalo, 1982; vis. scholar UCLA, 1977; conductor workshop LSA summer inst. Author: Complementation: Its Meanings and Forms, 1986; contbr. articles to profl. publs. Organizer Prairie Women's Cir., Champaign, 1981-83. Nat. Def. Fgn. Lang. fellow, 1969; grantee Ea. Ill. U., 1982, 87, 88, NSF, 1988. Mem. Linguistic Soc. Am., Linguistic Assn. S.W. (jour. referee 1999). Avocations: computer applications for the humanities, chess, motorhoming. Home: 201 E Southern Ave # 135 Apache Junction AZ 85219-3740

RANSOM, GAYLORD RICK, structural engineer; b. Redwood City, Calif., Feb. 3, 1953; . Gaylord Pat and Yola Grace (Old) R.; m. Linette Diane Pauls, June 25, 1984 (d ec. Sept., 1992); children: Anna, Brent, Sarah, Kimberly, Amy, Rebecca; m. Karla Jean Lauck, Feb. 7, 1993. BS in Civil Engring., Calif. State U., Fresno, 1977. Civil engr. intern III City of Fresno, Calif., 1973-75, engr. aide II, 1975-76, civil engineer I, 1976-78, structural engr. III, 1978-80, chief structural engr., 1980-83, dep. city engr., 1982-83, asst. dep. dir. inspections, 1980-83; prin. Ransom, Boone & Assocs., Fresno, 1976-83; assoc. William Brooks Assocs., Fresno, 1983-95; pres. Brooks, Ransom & Assocs., Fresno, 1995—. Chmn. CSUF Engring. adv. com., Fresno, 1995—. Mem. Structural Engrs. of Calif. (bd. dirs.), Calif. Soc. Profl. Engrs. (pres. 1981-82), Nat. Soc. Profl. Engrs., Internat. Conf. of Bldg. Officials. Republican. Baptist. Avocations: firearms, hunting, fishing, 4-wheel drive. Office: # 100 7415 N Palm Ave Fresno CA 93711-5730

RANSOM, MICHAEL T. counselor; b. Fullerton, Calif., Apr. 15, 1975; s. Gary D. and Carol S. Ransom; m. Angela D. Ransom, Jan. 18, 2002. BS magna cum laude, Westminster Coll., 1998—2003. Cert. nurse asst. LDS Hosp., Salt Lake City, 1997—2002; undergraduate tchg. asst. Westminster Coll., Salt Lake City, 1999—2000; grad. rsch. assisstant U. of ND, Dept. of Counseling, Grand Forks, ND, 2002—; psychiat. technician McKay-Dee Hosp. Ctr., Ogden, Utah, 2002. Mem.: Clin. Neuropsychology, Divsn. 40 of APA, Student Mem., APA Student Affiliate, APA of Grad. Students (APAGS), Psi Chi - The Nat. Honor Soc. in Psychology (vice-president 2001—02), Beta Beta Beta - The Nat. Honor Soc. in Biology. Office: University of North Dakota Dept of Counseling PO Box 8255 c/o Michael Ransom Grand Forks ND 58202

RANSOM, TASHA ELANA, news production assistant; b. Evanston, Ill., Aug. 24, 1973; d. Vincent Allen and Mary Geraldine Ransom. BS, Drake U., Des Moines, 1995; postgrad., Valparaiso U., Ind., 1996—97; MA, Columbia Coll., Chgo., 2002. Law clk. Vickie Pasley & Assocs., Chgo., 1992, 1994; product mgr. Zachs Investment & Rsch., Chgo., 1996; law clk. Hoeppner Wagner & Evans, Valparaiso, Ind., 1997—98; intern Lawyers for the Creative Arts, Chgo., 1999—2000; asst. Linda S. Mensch P.C., Chgo., 1999—2001; intern, prodn. cmty. affairs Fox News Chgo., 2000—01, asst. to news dir., 2001—. Recipient Alumni of the Yr., Outstanding Contbn. in the African Am. Cmty., Youth Action Ministry, 2003; Chuck Suber scholarship, Columbia Coll., 2001—02. Mem.: Nat. Assn. Black Journalists, Phi Alpha Delta, Delta Sigma Pi.

RANSOME, ERNEST LESLIE, III, retail company executive; b. Riverton, N.J. s. Percy A. and Clarice (Frishmuth) R.; m. Nancy Ellis Clark, Aug. 16, 1947 (div. Jan. 1984); children: Leslie Ransome Hudson, Elizabeth Ransome, Jane Ransome Bromley; m. Myradean Alcott, Feb. 12, 1984. AB in Econs., Princeton U., 1947; LLD, U. St. Andrews, Scotland, 2001. Ins. exec. Johnson & Higgins, Phila., 1947-48; asst. to dean Princeton (N.J.) U., 1948-50; asst. treas. Giles & Ransome, Bensalem, Pa., 1950-55, v.p. adminstrn., 1955-69, exec. v.p., 1969-82, vice chmn., 1982-88, chmn. bd., 1988—; v.p. Ransome Airlines, Bensalem, Pa., 1966-86. With Mannington Mills, Salem, N.J., chmn., 1991-92. Mem. Zoning Bd. Borough of Riverton, N.J., 1965-69; bd. trustees Riverton Library, 1959-79; campaign chmn. Zurbrugg Hosp., Riverside, N.J., 1971. 2d lt. USMC, 1944-46. Mem. Pine Valley Golf Club (pres. 1977-88, chmn. 1988-2001), Royal and Ancient Golf Club (St. Andrews, Scotland). Republican. Episcopalian. Avocation: golf.

RANTA, RICHARD ROBERT, university dean; b. Virginia, Minn., Nov. 18, 1943; s. V. Robert and Bernice (Smith) R.; 1 child, Erick H.; m. Carol Crown. AS, Hibbing (Minn.) Community Coll., 1963; BS, U. Minn., 1965; MA, Cornell U., 1967; PhD, U. Iowa, 1974. Floor dir. Sta. KDAL-TV, Duluth, Minn., 1964-65; asst. prof. U. Va., Charlottesville, 1969-72, U. Memphis, 1972-75, assoc. prof., 1975-91, prof., 1991—, interim dean Univ. Coll., 1975, asst. v.p. academic affairs, 1976-78, dean Coll. Comm. and Fine Arts, 1977—; gen. mgr. High Water Records, Memphis, 1980—. Bd. dirs. Concerts Internat., Memphis, pres., 1988-90; TV cons., free-lance producer, 1973—; mem. Rec. Hall of Fame selection panel Nat. Rec. Acad., L.A., 1986-2000. Assoc. prodr.: (TV program) Nat. Arthritis Telethon, 1985-90; Rec. Acad. graphics and prodn. coord. Grammy Awards TV program, 1983—; author articles in Communication Adminstrn. Bull., 1977—, editl. bd., 1991—, exec. com., 1996-2000. Chmn., v.p. Tenn. Humanities Coun., Nashville, 1980-82; v.p. Memphis Devel. Found., 1983-86; bd. dirs. Leadership Memphis, 1987-90, 94-97, chmn. mktg. com., 1987-90, chmn. selection com., 1994-95; bd. dirs. Life Blood, Memphis, 1984-92; treas. Memphis-Shelby County Film and TV Commn., 1986-98, chair, 1999-2002, bd. dirs., 2002-; mem. Tenn. Film, Entertainment and Music Commn., Nashville, 1987-97, chmn., 1993-95; chmn. bd. dirs. Crime Stoppers Memphis Assn., 1993-95; chmn. Memphis Arts Festival, 1992-94;bd. dirs. Tenn. Arts Commn., 2000--. Recipient Edn. Operational Models grant Ednl. Testing Svc., 1975, Communication Lab. grant HEW, 1976, Disting. Alumnus award Minn. Cmty. Coll. System, 1984, Alumni Cmty. Svc. award Leadership Memphis, 1997. Mem. NARAS (v.p. 1986-88, 92-93, chmn. edn. com. 1983—, trustee 1982-86, 88-92, 93-97, pres. Memphis chpt. 1984-86, bd. govs. 1978-98), So. States Comm. Assn. (pres. 1987-88, fin. bd. 1985-87, 93-95, exec. dir. 1995—), Tenn. Speech Comm. Assn. (pres. 1986-87, editor Communicator 1993—), Nat. Comm. Assn. (vice chmn., then chmn. exptl. learning com. 1979-83, mem. fin. and adminstrn. coms. 1989-93, chmn. fin. com. 1991-93), So. Arts Fedn. (bd. dirs. 1994-2000), Internat. Coun. Fine Arts Deans (parliamentarian 1996-2000), Tenn. Arts and Scis. Deans Assn. (chair 1997-98), Advt. Fedn. (bd. dirs.), Delta Sailing Assn. Club (sec. 1984-2000), Rotary (pres.-elect Memphis). Avocations: sailing, tennis, photography. Office: U Memphis Coll Communication & Fine Ar Memphis TN 38152-0001 E-mail: rranta@memphis.edu.

RANTS, CAROLYN JEAN, college official; b. Hastings, Nebr., Oct. 3, 1936; d. John Leon and Christine (Helzer) Halloran; m. Marvin L. Rants, June 1, 1957 (div. July 1984); children: Christopher Charles, Douglas John. Student, Hastings Coll., 1954—56; BS, U. Omaha, 1960; EdM, U. Nebr., 1968; EdD, U. S.D., 1982. Elem. sch. tchr. Ogallala (Nebr.) Cmty. Sch., 1956-58, Omaha Pub. Schs., 1958-60, Hastings Pub. Schs., 1960-64, Grosse Pointe (Mich.) Cmty. Schs., 1964-67; asst. prof., instr. Morningside Coll., Sioux City, Iowa, 1974-82, dean for student devel., 1982-84, v.p. for student affairs, 1984-94, interim v.p. for acad. affairs, 1992-94, v.p. enrollment and student svcs., 1994-96, v.p. adminstrn., 1996-99; exec. dir. enrollment svcs. Western Iowa Tech C.C., 1999—, dean of students, 2000—. Mem. new agy. com., chmn. fund distbn. and resource deployment com. United Way, Sioux City, 1987-94, co-chair, United Way Day of Caring, 1996; mem. Iowa Civil Rights Commn., 1989-97; bd. dirs. Leadership Sioux City, 1988-93, pres., 1992-93; bd. dirs. Siouxland Y, Sioux City, 1985-90, pres., 1988; bd. dirs. Girls, Inc., 1995-2000, Red Cross, 2002—; bd. dirs. New Perspectives, Inc., 1996-2000, pres. 1999, 2000; mem. Vision 2020 Cmty. Planning Task Force, 1990-92; pres. bd. dirs. Siouxland Youth Chorus, 2001—; bd. dirs. Sioux City Symphony, 2001—; treas. Trees of Siouxland Youth Chorus, 2002—. Mem. Iowa Women in Ednl. Leadership (pres. Sioux City chpt. 1986), Nat. Assn. Student Pers. Adminstrs.(region IV-E adv. bd.), Nat. Assn. for Women Deans, Adminstrs. and Counselors, Iowa Student Pers. Adminstr. (chmn. profl. devel. Iowa chpt. 1988-89, pres. 1991-92, Disting. Svc. award 1992), AAUW (corp. rep., coll./univ. rep. 1994-96), P.E.O. (pres. Sioux City chpt., Tri-State Women's Bus. Conf. (treas., planning com. Sioux City chpt. 1987-89), Quota Club (com. chmn. Sioux City 1987-89, v.p. 1992-94, pres. 1994-95, Siouxland Woman of Yr. award 1988), Sertoma (officer, bd. govs., regional dir.), Omicron Delta Kappa (faculty dir. province X 1996-99), Delta Kappa Gamma (state 1st v.p. 1993-95, state pres. 1995-97, internat. com. 1998-2000, 2002-04, N.W. regional dir. 2004—), Phi Delta Kappa (pres. 1988-89, Excellence in Leadership award 1998, Spl. Commendation Bessie Gabbard award 2001). Republican. Methodist. Avocations: handbells, cross-stitching. Home: 2904 S Cedar St # 4 Sioux City IA 51106-4246 Office: Western Iowa Tech Comm Coll PO Box 5199 4647 Stone Ave Sioux City IA 51102-5199 E-mail: rantsc@witcc.com.

RANTS, CHRISTOPHER C. state representative; b. Grosse Point, Mich., Sept. 16, 1967; m. Trudy Rants; 2 children. BA, Morningside Coll., 1989. Coord. Metz Baking Co., 1990—98; cons. Susan Pierce & Assocs., 1998—; mem. Iowa Ho. Reps., Des Moines, 1993—, mem. adminstrn. and rules com., asst. majority leader, 1997—98, majority leader, 1999—, spkr. pro tempore, 1999, spkr., 2003—. Active United Way Loaned Exec. Program, Grace United Meth. Ch. Mem.: Nat. Fedn. Ind. Bus. (Iowa affiliate), Omicron Delta Kappa. Republican. Methodist. Office: State Capitol East 12th and Grade Des Moines IA 50319 also: 2740 S Glass St Sioux City IA 51106

RANU, HARCHARAN SINGH, biomedical scientist, administrator, orthopaedic biomechanics educator; b. Lyallpur, India; came to U.S., 1976; s. Jodh Singh and Harnam Kaur R. BSc, Leicester Poly., Eng., 1963; MSc, U. Surrey, Guilford, Eng., 1967, Cambridge (Eng.) U., 1972; PhD, Middlesex Hosp. Med. Sch. and Poly. of Cen. London, 1975; diploma, MIT, 1984. Chartered engr., Eng. Med. scientist Nat. Inst. Med. Rsch. of the Med. Rsch. Coun., London, 1967-70; rsch. fellow Middlesex Hosp. Med. Sch. and Poly. of Cen. London, 1971-76; rsch. scientist Plastics Rsch. Assn. of Great Britain, Shawbury, Eng., 1977; asst. prof. Wayne State U., Detroit, 1977-81; prof. biomed. engring./orthopaedic biomechanics biomaterials La. Tech. U., Ruston, 1982—; prof., chmn. dept. biomechanics N.Y. Coll. Osteo. Medicine, Old Westbury, 1989-93; prof., asst. to pres. and dir. doctoral program Life Coll., Marietta, Ga., 1993—; dir. tng. Rehab. Rsch. and Devel. Ctr., 1983-85; mem. La. Tech. U. Libr. Com., 1983-85; chmn. design competition Assn. Biomed. Engrs.; mem. steering com. So. Biomed. Engring. Confs., 1983—; chmn. tech. in health care conf. U. Cambridge, 1985; chmn. Internat. Symposium on Bioengring., Calcutta, India, 1985; dir. orthopaedic biomechanics rsch. labs., staff Nassau County Med. Ctr., Long Island, 1989—; prof., asst. to pres., dir. doctoral program Life Coll., Marietta, Ga., 1993—. Mem. biomed. engring. faculty com. La. Tech. U., faculty com., rsch. awards com., grad. studies com., grad. faculty, acad. bd. dirs; vis. scientist Dryburn Hosp., Durham, Eng., 1985-87, cons., 1988—; vis. prof. U. Istanbul, 1982, Lab. de Recherch Orthopediques, Paris, 1985—, Kings Coll. Med. Sch. U. London, 1989—, Indian Inst. Tech., New Delhi, Postgrad Inst. Med. Edn. and Rsch., Chandigarh, India, 1989—, Inst. Biol. Physics USSR Acad. Sci., Moscow, 1990, Polytech. Ctrl. London, 1991—; adj. prof. Coll. Physicians and Surgeons Columbia U., N.Y.C., 1988—, Inst. Biol. Physics USSR Acad. Sci., Moscow, 1990, N.Y. Coll. Podiatric Medicine, 1991—, CUNY, 1992—; cons. Lincoln Gen. Hosp., Ruston, La., 1982-85, La. State U. Med. Ctr., Shreveport, 1982—, St. Luke's and Roosevelt Hosp. Ctr., N.Y., 1988—, Foot Clinics N.Y., 1991—, Vets. Affairs Med. Ctr., N.Y., 1992—, various biomed. rsch. & legal corps., U.S., U.K.; mem. media resource svc. Inst. Pub. Info., N.Y., 1989—; med. scientist, cons. NATO, 1982—; presenter, lectr., dir. organizer numerous sci. orgns. and nat. & internat. confs.; external examiner for doctoral candidates All India Inst. Med. Scis., New Delhi, Indian Inst. of Tech., New Delhi, Banaras Hindu U., Varanasi, India, 1994—; vis. prof. U. Buenos Aires, Pontific Cath. U. Chile, Fed. U. Rio de Janeiro, numerous others. Author: Rheological Behavior of Articular Cartiliage Under Tensile Loads, 1967, Effects of Ionizing Radiation on the Mechanical Properties of Skin, 1975, Effects of Fractionated Doses of X-irradiation on the Mechanical Properties of Skin--A Long Term Study, 1980, Effects of Ionizing Radiation on the Structure & Physical Properties of the Skin, 1983, 3-D Model of Vertebra for Spinal Surgery, 1985, Application of Carbon Fibers in Orthopaedic Surgery, 1985, Relation Between Metal Corrision & Electrical Polarization, 1989, The Distribution of Stresses in the Human Lumbar Spine, 1989, Medical Devices & Orthopaedic Implants in the United States, 1989, Spinal Surgery by Modeling, 1989, Multipoint Determination of Pressure-Volume Curves in Human Intervertebral Discs, 1993, Evaluation of Volume-Pressure Relationship in Lumbar Discs Using Model and Experimental Studies, 1994, A Mechanism of Laser Nuclectomy, 1994, Microminiaturization in Laser Surgery in Vivo Intradiscal Pressure Measurements in Lumbar Intervertebral Discs, 1994, An Experimental and Mathematical Simulation of Fracture of Human Bone Due to Jumping, 1994; editor The Lower Extremity, 1993—; guest editor IEEE Engring. in Medicine & Biology, 1991; mem. editl. bd. Med. Instrumentation, 1988—, Jour. Biomed. Instrumentation & Tech., 1988—, Jour. Med. Engring. & Tech., 1989—, Jour. Med. Design & Material, 1990—, Jour. Long-Term Effects Med. Implants, 1991—, Biomed. Sci. & Tech., 1991—; reviewer Jour. Biomechanics, 1981—, Clin. Biomechanics, 1984—, Jour. Biomed. Engring., 1981, Phys. Therapy, 1990—, IEEE Biomed. Transactions, 1991—, Jour. Engring. in Medicine, 1989—; contbr. articles to profl. jours. Faculty advisor India Students Assn. Wayne State U., 1980. Recipient Edwin Tate award U. Surrey, 1968, Third Internat. Olympic Com. World Congress On Sprots Scis. award, Atlanta, 1995; numerous rsch. grants. Fellow ASME (bioengring. com. 1990—, award L.I. chpt. 1991), Biol. Engring. Soc. (London) (President's prize 1984), Instn. Mech. Engrs. (chmn. revv. bd. for corp. memberships, James Clayton awards 1974-76); mem. AAAS, Am. Coll. Sports Medicine, Am. Soc. Biomechanics (edn. com. 1990—), Orthopaedic Rsch. Soc., Biomed. Engring. Soc., India Assn., India Assn. North La., Inst. Physics and Engring. in Medicine, Chartered Scientist, The Sci. Coun., England. Sikh. Achievements include research in microfracture simulation of human vertebrae under compressive loading, laserectomy of the human nucleus pulposus and its effect on the intradiscal pressure, pressure-volume relation in human intervertebral discs, in vitro and in vivo intradiscal pressure measurements before and after laserectomy of the human nucleus pulposus, gait analysis of a diabetic foot, bioengineering in the millennium, bioengineering-building the future of biology and medicine, bioengineering the cutting edge of biology and medicine in the millennium, in vivo micro-fracture simulation in Indian Olympic field hockey players, relief from low-back pain in sports by infusion of saline into the human nucleus pulposus and establishing the pressure-volume relationship, clinical applications of bioinstrumentation for better health, fifth IOC World Congress on sports sciences, micro-fracture simulation in tennis players, human gait analysis normal and pathological, simulation of micro-fracture injury in female gymnasts-an in vivo study, pattern recognition in human gait, identification of ethnicity from human gait; micro-fracture injury simulation in pole-vaulting and female gymnasts; 3-D simulation of drop in intradiscal pressure in spinal discs due to laserectomy; Ranu's principle and laserectomy to relieve low back pain; Rranu's cumulative gait effect phenomenon. Micro-Fracture injury simulation in skiers. Office: Life Coll Sch Grad Studies Marietta GA 30060 Personal E-mail: drhsranu@yahoo.com.

RANUM, JANE BARNHARDT, state senator, lawyer; b. Charlotte, N.C., Aug. 21, 1947; d. John Robert and Gladys Rose (Swift) B.; m. James Harry Ranum, Mar. 29, 1972; 1 child, Elizabeth McBride. BS, East Carolina U., 1969; JD, Hamline U., 1979. Bar: Minn. 1979, U.S. Dist. Ct. Minn. 1979. Tchr. elem. sch. Durham County, Durham, N.C., 1960-70; tchr. Dept. Def., Baumholder, Germany, 1970-72, Dist. 196, Rosemount, Minn., 1972-76; law cclk. Hennepin County Dist. Ct., Mpls., 1982; asst. county atty. Hennepin County, Mpls., 1982—; mem. Minn. Senate, St. Paul, 1991—. Chmn. legislature commn. on children, youth and their families, 1993—, mem. rep. chem. abuse and prevention resource coun., 1993. Mem. exec. com., lobbying coord. Dem. Farmer Labor Feminist Caucus, St. Paul, 1980-84; bd. dirs. Project 13 for Reproductive Rights, Mpls., 1981-82; state del. Minn. Dem. Farmer Labor Party Conv., 1982, 84, precinct del., 1974—. Named Feminist of Yr., Minn. NOW, 1994, Legislator of Yr., Minn. Assn. for Retarded Citizens, 1994. Mem. Minn. Bar Assn., Minn. Women Lawyers, Minn. Family Support and Recovery Coun., Hennepin County Bar assn. Democrat. Home: 5045 Aldrich Ave S Minneapolis MN 55419-1207 Office: Minn Senate State Capitol Saint Paul MN 55155-0001

RAO, DABEERU C. epidemiologist, educator; b. Apr. 6, 1946; came to U.S., 1972; s. Ramarao Patnaik and Venkataratnam (Raghupatruni) R.; m. Sarada Patnaik, 1974; children: Ravi, Lakshmi. BS in Stats., Indian Statis. Inst., Calcutta, 1967, MS, 1968, PhD, 1971. Rsch. fellow U. Sheffield, Eng., 1971-72; asst. prof., geneticist U. Hawaii, Honolulu, 1972-78, assoc. prof., geneticist, 1978-80; assoc. prof., dir. divsn. biostats. Washington U. Med. Sch., St. Louis, 1980-82, prof. depts. biostats., psychiatry and genetics, 1982—. Adj. prof. math., 1982—, dir. div. biostats., 1980—. Author: A Source Book for Linkage in Man, 1979, Methods in Genetic Epidemiology, 1983, Genetic Epidemiology of Coronary Heart Disease, 1984; editor-in-chief Genetic Epidemiology jour., 1984-91; contbr. articles to profl. jours. Grantee NIH, 1978—. Mem. Am. Statis. Assn., Am. Soc. Human Genetics, Internat. Genetic Epidemiology Soc. (pres. 1996), Behavior Genetics Assn., Soc. Epidemiol. Rsch., Biomed. soc. Office: Washington U Sch Medicine Divsn Biostats Box 8067 660 S Euclid Ave Saint Louis MO 63110-1010 E-mail: rao@wubios.wustl.edu.

RAO, JAGANMOHAN BOPPANA LAKSHIMI, electrical engineer; b. Raghavapuram, India, Aug. 6, 1936; came to U.S. 1961; s. Satyanarayana and Subbarao (Challagulla) Boppana; m. Krishna K. Koganty, May 18, 1960; children: Ravi, Madhu, Sushma. MSEE, U. Wash., 1963, PhD in Elec. Engring., 1966. Asst. rsch. engr. Radiation Lab., U. Mich., Ann Arbor, 1966-68; staff engr. Northrop Corp., McLean, Va., 1968-70; asst. prof. Savannah (Ga.) State Coll., 1970-71; rsch. assoc. NASA Goddard Space Flight Ctr., Greenbelt, Md., 1971-73; electronics engr. Naval Rsch. Lab., Washington, 1974—. Contbr. articles to profl. jours. Pres. Greater Washington Telugu Cultural Soc., 1977-78. Recipient Spl. Achievement award IEEE/Antennas and Propagation Soc., 1969, pub. award, Naval Rsch. Lab., 1998. Fellow IEEE (chpt. chmn. 1986-87), Sigma Xi. Achievements include patents on bicollimated dual reflector antenna and on voltage controlled ferroelectric lens phased array. Home: 9004 Acredale Ct College Park MD 20740-4001 E-mail: rao@radar.nrl.navy.mil.

RAO, JIAN YU, physician, cancer biologist, educator; b. Xingguo, Jiangxi, China, Feb. 16, 1964; s. Youfar Rao and Yuanqiao Ding; m. Pingping Shuang Gu, Jan. 20, 1987; children: Andrew William, Elizabeth Ann. MD, Shanghai Med. U., 1984. Diplomate Am. Bd. Pathology. Rsch. investigator Cancer Inst. Chinese Acad. Med. Scis., Beijing, 1984-87; asst. rsch. prof. U. Okla. Health Scis. Ctr., 1993-94; intern, resident, cytopathology fellow UCLA Med. Ctr., 1994-98, asst. rschr., 1995-99, asst. prof., 1999—2003, assoc. prof., 2003—. Co-author: Molecular Epidemiology, 1993, Moleculary Pathology of Early Cancer, 1999; contbr. articles to profl. jours. Recipient Young Investigator award Internat. Soc. Analytic Cytology, 1992, Richard F. Dwyer and Elaine W. Dwyer award Jonsson Comprehensive Cancer Ctr., 1995; Provost's Rsch. fellow U. Okla. Health Scis. Ctr., 1987; Rsch. grantee Nat. Cancer Inst. NIH, 1993. Mem. AMA, Internat. Soc. Preventive Oncology, Am. Soc. Clin. Pathologists, Sigma Xi. Achievements include patent for Cell Analysis Method Using Quantitative Fluorescence Image Analysis. Office: UCLA 10833 Le Conte Ave Los Angeles CA 90095-3075 Fax: 310-206-5178.

RAO, K.V.R. MOHAN See KOTTAMASU, MOHAN

RAO, NANNAPANENI NARAYANA, electrical engineer; b. Kakumanu, Andhra Pradesh, India; m. Sarojini Jonnalagadda, June 10, 1955; children: Vanaja, Durgaprasad, Hariprasad. BSc in Physics, U. Madras, India, 1952; DMIT in Electronics, Madras Inst. Tech., 1955; MSEE, U. Wash., 1960, PhD in Elec. Engring, 1965. Acting instr. elec. engring. U. Wash., 1960-64, acting asst. prof., 1964-65; asst. prof. elec. engring. U. Ill., Urbana, 1965-69, asso. prof., 1969-75, prof., 1975—, Edward C. Jordan prof., 2003—, assoc. head elec. and computer engring., 1987—. Cons. Fakultas Teknik, Univ. Indonesia, Jakarta, 1985-86, 87. Author: Basic Electromagnetics with Applications, 1972, Elements of Engineering Electromagnetics, 6th edit., 2004; contbr. numerous articles to profl. jours. Recipient Engring. award Telugu Assn. N.Am., 1983, Excellence in Edn. award, 1999, Fakultas Teknik award Universitas Indonesia, 1986. Fellow IEEE (Undergrad. Teaching award 1994); mem. Am. Soc. Engring. Edn. (AT&T Found. award for excellence in instrn. engring. students 1991), Internat. Union Radio Sci. (U.S. Commn. G). Achievements include contributions to engineering education in the United States and abroad. Home: 2509 S Lynn St Urbana IL 61801-6841 Office: U Ill Dept Elec & Computer Engring 1406 W Green St Urbana IL 61801-2918 E-mail: rao@ece.uiuc.edu.

RAO, P. SYAMASUNDAR, pediatric cardiologist; b. Ullibhadra, India, Sept. 21, 1941; came to U.S., 1966; s. P.V.B. Krishna Rao and P. Savithramma; m. P. Hymavathi, Mar. 27, 1966; children: Vijay K. Patnana, Madhavi Patnana, Radkhika N. Patnana. Intermediate degree in Arts and Scis., Andhra U., Visakhapatnam, India, 1958; MBBS, Andhra Med. Coll., Visakhapatnam, 1964, diploma in child health, 1966. Diplomate Am. Bd. Pediats, Am. Bd. Pediat. Cardiology. Asst. prof. Med. Coll. Ga., Augusta, 1972-75, assoc. prof., 1975-79, prof. pediats., 1979-82, assoc. dir. pediat. cardiology, 1976-82; cons. pediat. cardiologist King Faisal Specialist Hosp., Riyadh, Saudi Arabia, 1982-87, chmn. pediats., 1986-87; prof., head pediat. cardiology U. Wis. Med. Sch., Madison, 1987-94; prof., dir. pediat. cardiology St. Louis U. Sch. Medicine, 1994-98, prof. pediats., 1998—2002; prof., dir. pediat. cardiology U. Tex.-Houston Med. Sch., Houston, 2002—. Author: Tricuspid Atresia, 1982, 1992, Transcatheter Therapy in Pediatric Cardiology, 1993, Catheter-Based Devices, 2003; contbr. 40 chpts. to books, over 300 articles to profl. jours. Recipient award for outstanding contbn. to pediat. cardiology Telugu Assn. N.Am., John Lind's Lectr. award Swedish Pediat. Assn.,1992, Meritorious Svc. award Wis.-Nicaragua Ptnr., 1993, Outstanding Scientist award Am. Assn. Cardiologists of Indian Origin, 1996. Fellow Am. Coll. Cardiology (councillor Mo. chpt. 1997), Am. Acad. Pediats., Soc. Cardiac Antiography (mem. pediat. cardiology com. 1996); mem. Am. Pediat. Soc., Soc. Pediat. Rsch., Am. Heart Assn. Avocations: tennis, movies. Office: UT Houston Medical School 6431 Fannin MSB 3130 Houston TX 77030 E-mail: p.syamasundar.rao@uth.tmc.edu.

RAO, POSINASETTI NAGESWARA, manufacturing engineering educator; b. Palakol, Andhra, India, June 15, 1947; s. Kondaiah and Suramma P.; m. Venkata Rama Lakshmi, Aug. 18, 1976; children: Prasant, Praveen. BSc, The Narsapur (India) Coll., 1967; B of Engring., Govt. Engring. Coll., Anantapur, India, 1970; M of Engring., Birla Inst. Tech. & Sci., Pilani, India, 1973; PhD, Indian Inst. Tech., New Delhi, 1981. Asst. lectr. Birla Inst. Tech. & Sci., Pilani,

India, 1973-75; lectr. Indian Inst. Tech., New Delhi, 1975-81, asst. prof., 1981-90, prof., 1990-97; vis. faculty MARA U. Tech., Shah Alam, Malaysia, 1997—2001; assoc. prof. U. No. Iowa, Cedar Falls, Iowa, 2001—. Dir. Rasmi Diecastings Ltd., Hyderabad, India, 1988—; vis. faculty Asian Inst. Tech., Bangkok, Thailand, 1993. Author: Numerical Control and Computer Aided Manufacturing, 1985, Manufacturing Technology Foundry, Forming & Welding, 1987, Computer Aided Manufacturing, 1993, AutoCAD 14 for Engineering Drawing Made Easy, 1999, Manufacturing Technology Metal Cutting and Machine Tools, 2000, CAD/CAM Principles and Application, 2002; editor: Emerging Trends in Manufacturing, 1986; contbr. numerous articles to profl. jours. Mem.: ASME, Nat. Assoc. of Indsl. Tech., Am. Soc. Engring. Edn., Soc. Mfg. Engr., Indian Soc. Mech. Engrs. Home: 319 E St Cedar Falls IA 50613 Office: U No Iowa Dept Indsl Tech Cedar Falls IA 50614-0178 Office Phone: 319-273-6429. Personal E-mail: pnageswara@hotmail.com. Business E-Mail: rao@uni.edu.

RAO, POTARAZU KRISHNA, environmental consultant; b. Andhra Pradesh, India, Mar. 26, 1930; s. Satyanarayana and Annapooma (Mullapudi) Rao; m. Rukmani Krutivinti, Aug. 5, 1954; children: Ramanarayan, Sreedhar. BS, Andhra U., 1950, MS, 1952, Fla. State U., 1957; PhD, NYU, 1968. Meteorologist Can. Meteorol. Svc., Montreal, Can., 1960-61; rsch. phys. scientist Nat. Oceanic and Atmospheric Adminstrn./Nat. Environ. Satellite Data and Info. Svc., Washington, 1961-74, chief atmospheric energetics br., acting dir., 1976-80, chief satellite applications lab., 1980-86, dir. office of rsch. and applications, 1986-96; chief scientist for satellite and info. svcs. Nat. Oceanic and Atmospheric Adminstrn., Washington, 1996—2002; program dir., weather modification NSF, Washington, 1971 72; advisor on satellite programs World Meteorological Orgn., Geneva, 1974-76; cons. TRW, ITT. Bd. dirs. Climate and Global Change Program Nat. Oceanic and Atmospheric Adminstrn., Washington; mem. adv. bd. Coop. Inst. for Rsch. in Atmospheres, Ft. Collins, 1986—. Editor: Weather Satellites, 1990; contbr. articles to profl. jours. Founder, trustee Sri Siva Vishnu Temple, Lanham, Md. Fellow: N.Y. Acad. Scis., Royal Meteorol. Soc. U.K., Am. Meteorol. Soc. Hindu. Avocations: tennis, photography. Home: 15824 Buena Vista Dr Rockville MD 20855-2658

RAO, PRASAD, electronics executive; Pres., CEO, Cybertech Sys., Inc., Oak Brook, Ill. Office: Cybertech Systems Inc 1250 E Diehl Rd Ste 403 Naperville IL 60563-9389

RAO, PRASADA, engineering educator; arrived in U.S., 1997; s. Seshaghiri Rao. PhD, Indian Inst. of Tech., Mumbai, 1997. Rsch. assoc. Duke U., Durham, NC, 2000—02; asst. prof. Calif. State U., Fullerton, 2002—. Rsch. assoc. U. of Ky., Lexington, 1997—2000. Contbr. articles to profl. jours. Grantee, Office of Naval Rsch., 2001—04, NAVO PET and Logicon, 2001, Miss. State U., 2001—02. Achievements include development of Parallel version of TABS-MDS model; Parallel version of RMA-2 model; research in Water security modeling. Office: Calif State U Civil and Environ Engring Fullerton CA 92831 E-mail: prasad@duke.edu.

RAO, RAMA KRISHNA R. pharmaceutical company executive; b. Tanuku, Andhra Province, India, Nov. 20, 1955; came to U.S., 1998; s. R.R. and Satyavani R. (Gudipati) R.; m. Kavitha Advikolanu, May 19, 1996. B in Tech., Indian Inst. Tech., Delhi, 1977; postgrad. diploma in mgmt., Indian Inst. Mgmt., Calcutta, 1981; MBA, INSEAD, Fontainebleau, France, 1989. Asst. mgr. Metal Box India, Calcutta, 1977-84; exec. asst. to gen. mgr. Bank of Bahrain & Kuwait, Bahrain, 1985-88; fin. assoc. Eli Lilly, Geneva, credit and customer svc. mgr., 1993-94, fin. mgr. Africa, 1994-95; mgr. (global treasury) Gems Eli Lilly, Brussels, 1995-97; fin. advisor corp. fin. and investment banking Lilly Corp. Ctr., Indpls., 1998-99; CFO, fin. mgr. PC/NS Lilly USA, Indpls., 1999—2001; fin. dir. intercontinental region Novartis Oncology Bus. Unit, East Hanover, NJ, 2001—04; CFO, v.p. fin. Novartis Can., Dorval, Canada, 2004—. Alumni mem. panel for INSEAD interviews, Belgium, U.S., 1995-99. Contbr. journalist Students' Newsletter, IIT, Delhi, co-editor Students' Newsletter, I.I.M., Calcutta, INSEAD, Fontainebleu, France. Vol. Samaritans/Befrienders, Bahrain, 1987, 88; donor of blood Red Cross/Crescent, India, Belgium, U.S., Bahrain, 1974-97. Recipient First prize Nat. Young Mgrs. Competition, All India Mgmt. Assn., 1983. Mem. AMA, Assn. Investment Mgmt. and Rsch., Inst. Mgmt. Accts. Hindu. Avocations: travel, military history, foreign policy. E-mail: rama.rao@pharma.novartis.com.

RAO, SETHURAMIAH LAKSHMINARAYANA, demographer, United Nations official; b. Mysore, Karnataka, India, Apr. 28, 1942; came to U.S., 1967; s. Ramakrishniah Sethuramiah and Bhageerathi; m. Sudha Bagur Viswanath, Aug. 1, 1971; children: Rekha, Kumar. MSc, U. Mysore, 1963; MPH, U. N.C., 1968; cert., U. Mich., 1969; PhD, U. Pa., 1971. Cert. Demographic Tng. and Rsch. Ctr., Bombay. Asst. prof. Brown U., Providence, 1971-73; UN adviser Govt. of Sri Lanka, Colombo, 1974-77; chief population and devel. UN Population Fund, N.Y.C., 1978-82, chief policy br., 1982-90, country dir. Addis Ababa, Ethiopia, 1991-92, dep. dir. info. & extern rels. N.Y.C., 1992-95, dir. tech. and evaluation divsn., 1995-97, dir. divsn. adminstrn. fin. and mgmt., 1998-2000, dir. strategic planning & coord. divsn., 2001—. Sec. UN Population Fund segment of UN Devel. Program/UN Population Fund exec. bd.; leader UN tech. missions to several countries. Author: Socio-Religious Factors in Fertility, 1973; co-author: Population Problems of Sri Lanka, 1977, Population Program Experience, 1991; contbr. articles to profl. jours. V.p. Mysore Self Reliance Assn., Mangalore, 1963-65, Indo-Am. Forum for Polit. Edn., N.Y., 1989-90; founder, pres. New Eng. Kannada Koota, Providence, 1972-73. Recipient several acad. honors and gold medals, U. Pa., 1971, U. Mysore, 1961, 63. Mem. Delta Omega, Internat. Union for the Scientific Study of Population. Avocations: travel, debate, bridge playing. Home: 143 Nelson Rd Scarsdale NY 10583-5811 Office: UN Population Fund 220 E 42nd St New York NY 10017-5806 E-mail: rao2108@aol.com.

RAO, VIJAYENDRA, economist; s. Surendra L. and Vasanthi Rao; m. Sita Reddy. PhD, U. Pa., 1990. Asst. prof. Williams Coll., Williamstown, Mass., 1994—98; lead economist The World Bank, Washington, 1999—. Editor (bds.): Culture and Public Action; assoc. editor: Economic Development and Cultural Change: Journal of Development Studies; contbr. articles to profl. jours. Recipient Aguiar award for Best Undergraduate, St. Xavier's Coll., Mumbai, 1984; Hewlett fellow, U. Chgo., 1990—92, Mellon fellow, U. Mich., 1992—94, Brown U., 1998. Mem.: Am. Econ. Assn. Achievements include research in Methods to Mix Anthropological and Economic Techniques to Study problems of Poverty and Deprivation in Developing Countries; Studies on the economics and sociology of dowries in India; Studies on festivals and social status in India; Econs. of prostitution; Rsch. on domestic violence in India. Office: The World Bank 1818 H St NW Washington DC 20433

RAOOF, AMEED MOHAMMED SAEED, anatomist; b. Baghdad, Iraq, Aug. 20, 1952; s. Mohammed Saeed and Selima Shaker (Mahmood) R.; m. Samar Ghanim Ismail, Apr. 10, 1978; children: Saja, Duna, Khalid, Sarah. Diploma med. edn., U. Dundee, 1991, PhD in Anatomy, 1984; MSc in Anatomy, U. Baghdad, 1980, MB ChB, 1977. Lectr. Coll. of Medicine, Baghdad, 1978-80; tutor U. Dundee, 1983-84; asst. prof. Coll. of Medicine, Abha, Saudi Arabia, 1985-95, assoc. prof., 1996-98; lectr. U. Mich. Sch. Medicine, Ann Arbor, 1998—. Head med. edn. Office Coll. Medicine, Abha, 1988-92; mem. coll. rsch. com., 1994—, mem. acad. com., 1986—, head computer ctr., 1990—. Contbr. articles profl. jours. Jour. Histochemistry and Cytochemistry, profl. jours. Med. Edn., profl. jours. Jour. Helminthology, profl. jours. Parasitology Rsch., profl. jours. Internat. Jour. Plastination. Recipient Cert. of Recognition, Deanship of Admission, 1990, 1991, 1992, 1993, Elizabeth Crosby award, 2001, U. Mich. award for humanism in med. edn., 2001. Mem.: Assn. Am. Med. Colls., Internat. Soc. Plastination, Am. Assn. Clin. Anatomy, Am. Assn. Anatomy, Internat. Assn. Med. Sci. Educators, Assn. Med. Edn. Europe, Internat. Brain Rsch. Orgn., Royal Microscopical Soc., Assn. for Study of Med. Edn., AAAS. Achievements include description for the first time the complete histochemical profile of the Ochocerca fasciata worm; description of human fetal spinal cord length changes using room-temperature plastination technique; distribution of acetylcholinesterase enzyme in the camel's brain, histology and ultrastructure of the camel's lacrimal gland; choice factor for med. students' admission to U. Mich. Med. Sch., intro. of integrated clin. tchg. to anatomy. Address: 3808 Med Sci II Ann Arbor MI 48109-0608

RAPAPORT, SAMUEL I. educator, physician; b. Los Angeles, Nov. 19, 1921; s. Hyman and Bertha (Krupnick) R.; m. Joyce Mildred Cooperman, Oct. 3, 1951; children: Susan Rapaport Braunwald, Sally Rapaport Hartinian, Mark Hyman, Bruce Allen. Student, UCLA; MD, U. So. Calif., 1945. Diplomate: Am. Bd. Internal Medicine (mem. bd. 1973-80, bd. govs. 1976-80, sec.-treas., chmn. hematology subcom. 1978-80). Intern Los Angeles County Hosp., 1945; resident medicine VA Hosp., Long Beach, Calif., 1948-50, chief hematology sect., 1950-57; asso. prof. medicine U. Calif. at Los Angeles Med. Center, 1957-58; mem. faculty U. So. Calif. Sch. Medicine, 1958-74, head hematology div. dept. medicine, 1958-74, prof. medicine, 1964-74; head hematology div. Los Angeles County-U. So. Calif. Med. Center, 1958-74; chief med. service San Diego VA Hosp., 1974-78; prof. medicine U. Calif., San Diego, 1974-96; prof. emeritus, 1996—; vice chmn. dept. medicine U. Calif., 1974-78, co-head hematology-oncology div., 1978-87, prof. pathology, 1980-93; dir. Hematology Lab., U. Calif.-San Diego Med. Ctr., 1980-87. Cons. hematology tng. grants study sect. Nat. Inst. Arthritis and Metabolic Diseases, 1968-71; mem. med. adv. coun. Nat. Hemophilia Found., 1970, 77—; chmn. adv. com., div. blood diseases and resources Nat. Heart, Lung and Blood Inst., 1980-82, mem. adv. coun., 1989-93; mem. hematology study sect. NIH, 1984-88, chmn. study sect., 1977-88. Author: Introduction to Hematology, 1971, 2d edit., 1987; also papers in field. Chmn. coun. on thrombosis Am. Heart Assn., 1995-97. Served with USAAF, 1946-48. Spl. fellow Nat. Heart Inst., U. Oslo, 1964-65; Fulbright research scholar U. Oslo, 1953-54; fellow Sackler Inst. for Advanced Study, Tel Aviv U., 1983; recipient Disting. Sci. Achievement award Coun. on Arteriosclerosis, Thrombosis, and Vascular Biology Am. Heart Assn., 2001. Master ACP (John Phillips Meml. award for outstanding work on clin. medicine 1996); mem. Assn. Am. Physicians, Am. Soc. Hematology (pres. 1977), Western Soc. Clin. Rsch. (pres. 1966), Am. Fedn. Clin. Rsch. (chmn. Western sect. 1960), Am. Soc. Clin. Investigation, Western Assn. Physicians (pres. 1973) Home: 7887 Lookout Dr La Jolla CA 92037-3951

RAPER, CHARLES ALBERT, retired management consultant; b. Charleston, W.Va., Aug. 18, 1926; s. Kenneth B. and Louise (Williams) R.; m. Margaret Ann Weers, Dec. 26, 1947; children: Kathleen, Josephine, Charles. Student, Okla. State U., 1945; BS, U. Ill., 1949. Sales mgr. Meyer Furnace Co., Peoria, Ill., 1949-54; v.p. mktg. Master Consol., Inc., Dayton, Ohio, 1954-61; mgmt. cons. McKinsey & Co., Inc., Chgo., 1961-67; v.p. mktg. Gen. Portland Inc., Dallas, 1967-69, pres., also dir., 1969-75; v.p., gen. mgr. Scholl Inc., Chgo., 1975-81; pres. Oxford Group of Sara Lee, 1981-84; mgmt. cons. McKinsey & Co., 1984—. Vice-chmn. devel. bd. U. Tex., Dallas; exec. bd. Circle 10 coun. Boy Scouts Am.; Svc. Corp. of Ret. Execs. counselor. With USN, 1944-46. Mem. Dallas C. of C. (chmn. bd. dirs. 1974—), Sales Execs. Club, Cherokee Country Club, Chattooga Club, Atlanta Mallet Club (pres.), Phi Gamma Delta. Methodist. Home: 301 Townsend Pl NW Atlanta GA 30327-3035

RAPER, KELLIE CURRY, education educator, researcher; BSA Economics, Okla. State U., Stillwater, Okla.; MSA Economics, Okla. State Univ., Stillwater, Okla.; DAgr Economics, Tex. A&M U., Coll. Stat., Tex., 1996. Asst. prof. U. Mass., Amherst, Mass., 1995—98, Mich. State U., East Lansing, Mich., 1998—. Editl. bd. Agrl. and Resource Economics Rev., 1997—; sec. USDA Regional Rsch. Project NE-165, 1996—2003; editl. rev. bd. Jour. of Food Distbn. Rsch., 2001—. Author: (dissertation) Empirical Measurement of Market Power (Hon. Mention Am. Agrl. Economics Assn., 1997); contbr. articles pub. to profl. jour. Grantee Rsch. Grant, Livestock Mktg. Info. Ctr., 2003, USDA, 2003, 1996. Mem.: Food Distbn. Rsch. Soc. (v.p. for membership 2002—), Am. Assn. of Agrl. Economics. Office: Mich State Univ 211 C Agrl Hall East Lansing MI 48824-1039

RAPER, MARK IRVIN, public relations executive; b. Greensboro, N.C., Aug. 26, 1954; s. James Crawford and Jean Elizabeth (Willick) R.; m. Martha Jefferson Taylor, Sept. 17, 1977; children: Carter Jefferson, Martha Stuart, Lucy Colston. Student, U. Richmond, 1972-75; pharmacy cert., Baylor U., 1976; BS in Mass Communications, postgrad., Va. Commonwealth U., 1981. Cert. pharmacy specialist. Dir., pub. relations Stuart Circle Hosp., Richmond, Va., 1980-81, Leigh Meml. Hosp.- Alliance, Norfolk, Va., 1981-82; dir. mktg. Alliance Health Services Corp., Norfolk, 1982-84; mgr. advt., pub. relations Figgie Internat. Holding Co., Richmond, 1984-86; dir. pub. rels. Ford & Westbrook Agy., Richmond and Atlanta, 1986-88; pres. Earle Palmer Brown Pub. Rels., Richmond, 1988-94, mng. ptnr., 1994—. Asst. editor Va. Family Physician (quarterly), Richmond, 1981; coordinator communications In-Vitro program Norfolk Gen. Hosp., 1982. Creator Legends Festival Program, 1987. Rep. Va. 1st Amendment Congress, 1981; dir. Children's Miracle Network, ctrl. Va., 1987; bd. dirs. Richmond Forum, 1987, Carpenter Ctr. for Performing Arts, Richmond, 1988. Recipient Top Student Scholarship Richmond Pub. Relations Assn., 1980, Gold Quill award Internat. Assn. Bus. Communicators, 1983; named one of Best in East Am. Soc. Hosp. Pub. Relations, 1983, Outstanding Young Men in Am., 1987. Mem. Pub. Rels. Soc. Am. (cert. of achievement 1983), L. Ginter Recreation Assn. Richmond (treas. 1987-90), Phi Kappa Phi, Kappa Tau Alpha. Avocations: tennis, golf, basketball, travel, music. Home: 3740 Titan Dr Richmond VA 23225-1247

RAPER, WILLIAM BURKETTE, retired college president; b. nr. Wilson, N.C., Sept. 10, 1927; s. William Cecil and Beulah Maybelle (Davis) R.; m. Rose Mallard, Aug. 19, 1951; children: Olivia, Kristie, Burkette, Elizabeth, Stephen (dec.), Laura. AB, Duke U., 1947, MDiv, 1951; MS (Kellogg fellow), Fla. State U., 1962; LLD, Atlantic Christian Coll. (now Barton Coll.), 1960. Ordained to ministry Free Will Baptist Ch., 1946; pastor Hull Rd. Free Will Bapt. Ch., Snow Hill, N.C., 1951-55; pres. Mt. Olive (N.C.) Coll., 1954-95, ret. pres. emeritus, 1995. Dir. Wachovia Bank and Trust Co., 1979-97; promotional dir. Free Will Bapt. State Conv. N.C., 1953-54; pres. council Ch.-Related Colls. N.C., 1966-67; mem. N.C. Edn. Assistance Authority, 1972-76; sec. Ind. Coll. Fund of N.C., 1976-78; Mem. N.C. Gov.'s Com. on Hwy. Traffic Safety, 1968; regional coordinator U.S. Office Edn. Program with Developing Instns., 1968-70; dir. Edn. Professions Devel. Act Grant for Strengthening Devel. in Pvt. Two-Year Colls., 1970-72; trustee N.C. Coll. Found., 1977-94; adv. com. Ind. Coll. Presidents, U. N.C. Recipient Disting. Service award Mt. Olive Jr. C. of C., 1961; named N.C. Young Man of Year, 1961 Mem. Am. Assn. Community and Jr. Colls. (commn. on legislation 1963-66, cons. 1968-71, chmn. commn. on student personnel 1970-71), N.C. Assn. Ind. Colls. and Univs. (exec. com. 1967-70, 76-77, 83-85), N.C. Assn. Colls. and Univs. (pres. 1969-70), Masons. Democrat. Office: Mt Olive Coll Office of Pres Emeritus Mount Olive NC 28365 E-mail: wraper@moc.edu.

RAPER, WILLIAM CRANFORD, lawyer; b. Asheville, N.C., Aug. 17, 1946; s. James Sidney and Kathryn (Cranford) R.; m. Patricia Dotson, Sept. 28, 1974; children: Kimber-leigh, Heather, James. AB, U. N.C., 1968; JD, Vanderbilt U., 1972. Bar: N.C. 1972, U.S. Ct. Appeals (4th cir.) 1972, U.S. Supreme Ct. 1977, U.S. Ct. Appeals (fed. cir.) 1985. Law clk. to Senator Sam Ervin Jr., Washington, 1970; law clk. to presiding justice U.S. Ct. Appeals (4th cir.), Richmond, Va., 1972-73; ptnr. Womble, Carlyle, Sandridge & Rice, Winston-Salem, N.C., 1974—. Fellow Am. College Trial Lawyers; mem. ABA, N.C. Bar Assn., N.C. Assn. of Def. Attys. (charter). Office: Womble Carlyle Sandridge & Rice One Wachovia Ctr 301 S Coll St Ste 3300 Charlotte NC 28202-6025 E-mail: braper@wcsr.com.

RAPHAEL, ALBERT ASH, JR., retired lawyer; b. N.Y.C., June 4, 1925; s. Albert Ash and Clare (Schindler) R.; m. Dorothy Buck, Oct. 7, 1960; 1 child, Bruce William. AB, Yale U., 1947; LL.D., Harvard U., 1950. Bar: N.Y. 1950, Vt. 1972. Mem. firm Gallert, Hilborn & Raphael, N.Y.C., 1950-60, Alter, Lefevre, Raphael, Lowry, and Gould, N.Y.C., 1960-78; pvt.practice Waitsfield, Vt., 1972—86; pvt. practice, 1995—2002; ptnr. Raphael and Ware, Waitsfield, 1986-95; ret. Waitsfield, 2002. Dir. various real estate cos. Mem. bd. zoning appeals, Waitsfield, 1974-83, selectman, 1976-82, chmn. bd. selectmen, 1981-82 Mem. Waitsfield Planning Commn., 1996-2003. Served with F.A., AUS, 1943-46. Mem. Vt. Bar Assn., Assn. of Bar of City of N.Y. Home: PO Box 113 Warren VT 05674-0113 Personal E-mail: aar@madriver.com.

RAPHAEL, COLEMAN, business consultant; b. N.Y.C., Sept. 16, 1925; s. Morris and Adella (Leav) R.; m. Sylvia Moskowitz, Feb. 28, 1948; children—Hollis, Gordon. B.Civil Engring., CCNY, 1945; M.C.E., Poly. Inst. Bklyn., 1951, PhD in Applied Mechanics, 1965. Structural research engr., test research engr. Republic Aviation Corp., 1945-47; instr. mech. engring. Pratt Inst., Bklyn., 1947-51; from sr. research engr. to mgr. space systems div. Republic Aviation Corp., 1951-65; gen. mgr. space and electronics systems div., then v.p. Fairchild Hiller Corp., Germantown, Md., 1965-70; with Atlantic Rsch. Corp., Alexandria, Va., 1970-86, chmn. bd., 1980-86, SJI Industries, 1968-70; dean bus. sch. George Mason U., Fairfax, Va., 1986-91; ret., 1991; bd. mem., prin. owner Applied Bus. Systems, Bethesda, Md., 1990-98; dir. GEICO, Envipco. Bd. dirs. ENVIPCO (chmn. 1995), Fairfax, Va.; founder, chmn. Night Owl Security, Landover, Md., Geico, Chevy Chase, Md., 1981-92; mem. engring. adv. com. Montgomery Coll., Md., 1968-69, George Washington U., 1977-82; mem. Gov. Va. Task Force Nuclear Power Plants, 1969; chmn. energy com. Gov. Md. Sci. Adv. Coun., 1974-76; bd. visitors U. Pitts., 1980-82. Author textbook, papers, reports in field. Chmn. U.S. Bond drive, Alexandria, 1975-76; chmn. adv. com. Montgomery County Bldg. Codes, 1976-77. Recipient Citizenship award Montgomery County Press Assn., 1967, Disting. Service award Montgomery County C. of C., 1969, Disting. Citizenship award State of Md., 1970, Washington Bus. Hall of Fame, 1998. Mem. AIAA (chmn. mgmt. com. 1976), Aircraft Industries Assn., Nat. Space Club, disting Alumus, Poly. Inst. of Bklyn., 1982. Home: 508 Hermleigh Rd Silver Spring MD 20902-1608 E-mail: colesyl@att.net.

RAPHAEL, LOUISE ARAKELIAN, mathematician, educator; b. N.Y.C., Oct. 24, 1937; d. Aristakes and Antionette (Sudbeaz) Arakelian; m. Robert Barnett Raphael, June 12, 1966 (div. 1985); children: Therese Denise, Marc Philippe. BS in Math., St. John's U., 1959; MS in Math., Cath. U., Washington, 1962; PhD in Math, Cath. U., 1967. Asst. prof. math. Howard U., Washington, 1966-70, vis. prof., 1981-82, assoc. prof., 1982-86, prof., 1986—; assoc. prof. Clark Coll., Atlanta, 1971-79, prof., 1979-82. Vis. assoc. prof. MIT, Cambridge, 1977-78, vis. prof., 1989-90; vis. mem. Courant Inst. Math. Scis., NYU, 1996-97; vis. scholar Cornell U., 2004. Contbr. over 40 rsch. articles to profl. jours. Program dir. NSF, Washington, 1986-88; acting adminstrv. officer Conf. Bd. Math. Scis., 1985-86. Grantee NSF, 1975-76, 79-81, 89-91, Army Rsch. Office, 1981-89, Air Force Sci. Rsch., 1981-82, 91-95, Nat. Security Agy., 1994-96. Mem.: Soc. Indsl. and Applied Math., Math. Assn. Am. (1st v.p. 1996—98, chmn. minorities in math. task force 1988), Am. Math. Soc. (coun. 2001—04, com. mem.), Sigma Xi. Democrat. Roman Catholic. Office: Howard U Dept Math Washington DC 20059-0001

RAPHAEL, SALLY JESSY, talk-show host; b. Easton, Pa., Feb. 25, 1942; children: Allison (dec.), Andrea; m. Karl Soderlund; 2 step-daughters, 1 adopted son, also foster children. BFA, Columbia U. Anchored radio program Jr. High Sch. News Sta. WFAS-AM, White Plains, N.Y., 1955; host of cooking program WAPA-TV, San Juan, P.R., 1965-67; radio and television broadcaster Miami and Ft. Lauderdale, Fla., 1969-74; host Sta. WMCA-Radio, N.Y.C., 1976-81; talk show host NBC Talk-net, N.Y.C., 1982-88, ABC Talkradio, N.Y.C., 1988-91; syndicated TV talk-show host N.Y.C., 1983—. Part-time owner of a perfume factory, 1964-68; owner of an art gallery, 1964-69; owner, The Wine Press, N.Y.C., 1979-83; ind. producer TV films, 1991 Author: (with M.J. Boyer) Finding Love, 1984, (with Pam Proctor) Sally: Unconventional Success, 1980; film appearances include: She-Devil, 1989, Resident Alien, 1990, The Addams Family, 1991, The Associate, 1996, Meet Wally Sparks, 1996, (TV movie) No One Would Tell, 1996; TV appearances include: Murphy Brown, Dave's World, The Nanny, The Tonight Show, Nightline, Diagnosis Murder, Conspiracy of Silence, Touched By An Angel, Sabrina the Teenage Witch, John LaRoquette Show; co-exec. producer (mini-series) The 3rd Twin, 1997 (film cameo) Double Whammy, 2000. Recipient Bronze medal, Internat. Film & Television Festival of NY, 1985; Emmy award as outstanding talk-show host, daytime, 1988, Emmy award for outstanding talk show, 1989. Office: USA Studios The Sally Show Fl OF2 15 Penn Plz New York NY 10001-2010

RAPHAELSON, ARNOLD HERBERT, economist educator; b. Worcester, Mass., Oct. 13, 1929; s. Louis and Celia (Ostroff) Raphaelson; m. Ruth Camaan, July 4, 1951; children: Marc, Jonathan, Joshua. BA in English, Brown U., 1950; MS in Journalism, Columbia U., 1951; MA in Econs., Clark U., 1956, PhD, 1960. City staff reporter Worcester Telegram, 1953—55; lectr. part-time Clark U., 1957—58; asst. prof. econs. U. Maine, 1958—60, assoc. prof., 1960—66; assoc. prof. econs. Temple U., Phila., 1966—70, prof., 1970—. Counsel Subcom. on Intergovtl. Rels. U.S. Senate, 1964—65; cons. to govt. agys., 1964—. Contbr. articles on health econs. to profl. jours. Mem. Upper Dublin Ednl. Adv. Com., Upper Dublin, Pa., 1972—78. With U.S. Army, 1951—53. Mem.: Health Econs. Rsch. Orgn., Am. Econ. Assn. Jewish. Office Phone: 215-283-1463.

RAPHAELSON, JOEL, retired advertising agency executive; b. N.Y.C., Sept. 27, 1928; s. Samson and Dorothy (Wegman) R.; m. Mary Kathryn Hartigan, Aug. 20, 1960; children: Matthew, Katherine, Paul. BA, Harvard U., 1949. Copywriter Macy's, N.Y.C., 1950-51, BBDO, N.Y.C., 1953-58; with Ogilvy & Mather, Inc., N.Y.C., 1958-94, sr. v.p., dir., 1966-75, mem. exec. com., 1970-75; creative cons. Ogilvy & Mather, Inc., Europe, 1975-76; exec. creative dir. Ogilvy & Mather, Inc., Chgo., 1976—82; sr. v.p. internat. creative svcs. Ogilvy & Mather Worldwide, 1982-92, spl. assignments as editor, writer, speechwriter, cons., 1993-94, ret., 1995. Lectr. Am. Assn. Advt. Agys., other bus. orgns., writers groups, schs. Author: (with Kenneth Roman) How To Write Better, 1978, Writing That Works, 1981, rev. expanded edit., 1992, 00; editor: The Unpublished David Ogilvy, 1986, Viewpoint (co. jour.), 1983-94; contbr. Harvard Bus. Rev., other bus. publs. Cons. Lyric Opera Chgo., Exec. Svc. Corps, Chgo. With U.S. Army Signal Corps, 1951-53. Home: 20 E Cedar St Apt 8A Chicago IL 60611-5115 Personal E-mail: joelr28@aol.com.

RAPHEL, ROBIN, ambassador; b. Vancouver, Wash., Sept. 16, 1947; 2 children. BA, U. Wash.; Diploma in Hist. Studies, Cambridge U., Eng.; MA, U. Md. Lectr. history Damavand Coll., Tehran, Iran, 1970-72; analyst CIA, 1974-75, USAID, Islamabad, Pakistan, 1975-78; with office investment affairs bur. econs. Dept. of State, 1978-80, staff asst. to asst. sec. Near East and South Asian affairs, 1980-81, econ. officer Israel desk, 1981-82, spl. asst. to under sec. polit. affairs, 1982-84; 1st sec. polit. affairs London, 1984-88; polit. counselor Pretoria, South Africa, 1988-91, New Delhi, 1991-93; asst. sec. South Asian affairs Dept. of State, Washington, 1993-97; U.S. amb. to Tunisia Tunis, 1997-2000; sr. v.p. Nat. Def. U., 2000—. Mem. Am. Econ. Assn., Am. Fgn. Svc. Assn., Phi Beta Kappa. Office: Nat Def U Marshall Hall Fort McNair Washington DC 20319

RAPIER, DAVID, electronics executive; Studied, Brigham Young U. Gen. mgr., regional dir., area dir. Avnet, Inc., 1976—90, cons., AvnetDirect, Avnet Computer Mktg. Group, 1996—99, v.p., opers., Avnet Applied Computing, 1999—2001, sr. v.p., chief of staff, Avnet Applied Computing, 2001—02, sr. v.p., Strategic Planning, Avnet Applied Computing, 2002, v.p., 2002—, sr. v.p., bus. opers., Global Info. Solutions, 2003—. Office: Avnet Inc 2211 S 47th St Phoenix AZ 85034

RAPIN, ISABELLE, physician; b. Lausanne, Switzerland, Dec. 4, 1927; d. Rene and Mary Coe (Reeves) R.; m. Harold Oaklander, Apr. 5, 1959; children: Anne Louise, Christine, Stephen, Peter. Physician's Diploma, Faculte de Medicine, U. Lausanne, 1952, Doctorate in Medicine, 1955. Diplomate Am. Bd. Psychiatry and Neurology. Intern in pediatrics N.Y. U. Bellevue Med. Center, 1953-54; resident in neurology Neurol. Inst. of N.Y., Columbia-Presbyn. Med. Center, 1954-57, fellow in child neurology, 1957-58; mem. faculty Albert Einstein Coll. Medicine, Bronx, N.Y., 1958—, prof. neurology and pediatrics, 1972—; attending neurologist and child neurologist Einstein Affiliated Hosps., Bronx. Mem. Nat. Adv. Neurol. and Communicative Disorders and Stroke Coun., NIH, 1984-88. Contbr. chpts. to books, articles to

med. jours. Recipient award Conf. Ednl. Adminstrs. Serving the Deaf, 1988. Fellow: Am. Acad. Neurology (exec. bd. 1995—99); mem.: AAAS, Assn. for Rsch. in Nervous and Mental Diseases (v.p. 1986), Internat. Neuropsychology Soc., Child Neurology Soc. (Hower award 1987), Am. Neurol. Assn. (v.p. 1982—83), Internat. Child Neurology Assn. (sec.-gen. 1979—82, v.p. 1982—86, Frank R. Ford lectr. 1990). Office: Albert Einstein Coll Medicine 1410 Pelham Pky S Bronx NY 10461-1101 Business E-Mail: rapin@aecom.yu.edu.

RAPINI, RONALD PETER, dermatology educator; b. Akron, Ohio, Feb. 15, 1954; s. Vincent Thomas and Joann Irene (Tufexis) R.; m. Mary Jo Beigel, June 16, 1979; children: Brianna Marie, Sarina Elizabeth. BS in Biology, U. Akron, 1975; MD, Ohio State U., 1978. Diplomate Am. Bd. Dermatology (bd. dirs. 1996-2004, pres. 2004), Am. Bd. Dermatopathology. Assoc. prof. U. Tex. Med. Sch., Houston, 1983-93; prof. and chair dermatology dept. Tex. Tech. U., Lubbock, 1994—2002; prof., chair dept. dermatology U. Tex. Med. Sch., Houston, 2002—. Author (with K.G. Gross and H.K. Steinman): Mohs Surgery, 1000; author: (with J. Bolognia and J. Jorizzo) Dermatology, 2003. Fellow Am. Acad. Dermatology, Am. Soc. Dermatol. Surgery (bd. dirs. 1995-98), Soc. Investigative Dermatology; mem. AMA, Am. Soc. Dermatopathology (pres. 1998-99), Am. Soc. Mohs Surgery (pres. 2003), Internat. Soc. Dermatopathology. Avocations: tennis, entomology, piano, running, bicycling. Office: U TEx Med Sch 6431 Fannin St Houston TX 77030-0001 E-mail: ronrapini@aol.com.

RAPKE, JACK, agent; Co-head of motion picture divsn., then co-chmn. Creative Artists Agy., Beverly Hills, Calif.; prodr. Image Movers, Universal City, Calif. Office: Image Movers 100 Universal City Plz Bldg 484 Universal City CA 91608-1002

RAPOPORT, ANATOL, peace studies educator, mathematical biologist; b. Lozovaya, Russia, May 22, 1911; emigrated to U.S., 1922, naturalized, 1928; s. Boris and Adel (Rapoport) R.; m. Gwen Goodrich, Jan. 29, 1949; children: Anya, Alexander, Charles Anthony. PhD, U. Chgo., 1941; DHL, U. Western Mich., 1971; LLD, U. Toronto, 1986; DS, Royal Mil. Coll. Can., 1995; Ehrendoktor, U. Bern, Switzerland, 1995. Faculty dept. math. Ill. Inst. Tech., 1946-47; com. math. biology U. Chgo., 1947-54; fellow Ctr. Advanced Study Behavioral Scis., Stanford, 1954-55; asso. prof. Mental Health Research Inst., prof. math. biology U. Mich., 1955-70; prof. psychology and math. U. Toronto, 1970-80; dir. Inst. for Advanced Studies, Vienna, 1980-83; prof. peace studies U. Toronto, 1984—. Author: Science and the Goals of Man, 1950, Operational Philosophy, 1953, Fights, Games, and Debates, 1960, Strategy and Conscience, 1964, Prisoner's Dilemma, 1965, Two-Person Game Theory, 1966, N Person Game Theory, 1970, The Big Two, 1971, Conflict in Man Made Environment, 1974, Semantics, 1975, The 2 x 2 Game, 1976, Mathematische Methoden in den Sozialwissenschaften, 1980, Mathematical Models in the Social and Behavioral Sciences, 1983, General System Theory, 1986, The Origins of Violence, 1989, Decision Theory and Decision Behavior, 1989, Canada and the World, 1992, Peace: An Idea Whose Time Has Come, 1992, Gewissheiten and Zweifel, 1994, Uverennost' i Somnenia, 1999, Certainties and Doubts, 2000, Skating on Thin Ice, 2002; editor: General Systems, 1956—77. Served to capt. USAAF, 1942-46. Fellow Am. Acad. Arts and Scis.; mem. Am. Math. Soc., Internat. Soc. Gen. Semantics (pres. 1953-55), Canadian Peace Research and Edn. Assn. (pres. 1972-75), Soc. for Gen. Systems Research (pres. 1965-66), Sci. for Peace (pres. 1984-86) Home: 38 Wychwood Park Toronto ON Canada M6G 2V5

RAPOPORT, BERNARD, life insurance company executive; b. San Antonio, July 17, 1917; s. David and Riva (Feldman) Rapoport; m. Audre Jean Newman, Feb. 15, 1942; 1 child, Ronald B. BA, U. Tex.-Austin, 1939. Chmn. bd., CEO Am. Income Life Ins. Co., Waco, Tex., 1951-99, cons., 1999—, founder and chmn. emeritus, 2002—; pres., chmn. bd., 2000-01. Chmn bd regents Univ Tex, 1991; apptd by pres adv comt for trade policy and negotiations, 1994—. Mem Nat Coun Crime and Delinquency, San Francisco, 1979—, Union Am Hebrew Congreagations, 1981—, Nat Hispanic Ctr Advanced Studies and Policy Analysis, Oakland, Calif., 1981—, Jerusalem Found, New York, NY, 1979—, Hebrew Union Col, Cincinnati, Ohio, 1980—; assoc mem Univ Cancer Found, Houston, 1976—, Jt Ctr Polit and Econ Studies, 1987—; chmn Negro Col Fund, Waco, 1979—80, United Way Waco, 1982—83; trustee Paul Quinn Col, Waco, 1963—90, Boy's Club Waco, 1982—; chmn bd regents Univ Tex, 1993—97; bd dirs Library of Congress Trust Fund, Washington, 1998—; bd. dirs. LBJ Found. Recipient Horatio Alger Award, 1999. Fellow: City of Jerusalem. Democrat. Jewish. Avocations: tennis, politics, reading. Home: 2332 Wendy Ln Waco TX 76710-2011 Office: PO Box 21900 Waco TX 76702-1900 E-mail: brapoport@ailife.com.

RAPOPORT, BERNARD ROBERT, lawyer; b. N.Y.C., Jan. 18, 1919; s. Max and Rose (Gerard) R.; m. Robyrta Wechter, May 31, 1959; 1 son: Michael. AB, Cornell U., 1939, JD, 1941. Bar: N.Y. 1941, Fed. Ct. (so. dist.) 1946. Assoc. firm Proskauer, Rose, Goetz, Mendelsohn, N.Y.C., 1941-50; gen. counsel M. Lowenstein Corp., N.Y.C., 1950-86, bd. dirs., 1961-86, treas., 1975-86, sec., 1970-86; dir., treas., sec. Leon Lowenstein Found. Served to capt. Signal Corps, U.S. Army, 1942-45. Mem. ABA, Assn. of Bar of City of N.Y. Address: 910 5th Ave New York NY 10021-4155

RAPOPORT, DAVID E. lawyer; b. Chgo., May 27, 1956; s. Morris H. and Ruth (Teckteil) R.; m. Andrea Gail Albun; children: Alyson Faith, Steven Andrew. BS in Fin., No. Ill. U., 1978; JD with high honors, Ill. Inst. Tech., 1981; cert. trial work, Lawyers Postgrad. Inst., Chgo., 1984; cert. civil trial specialist, Nat. Bd. Trial Adv., 1991. Bar: Ill. 1981, Wis. 1995, U.S. Dist. Ct. (no. dist.) Ill. 1981, U.S. Dist. Ct. (trial bar) Ill. 1993, U.S. Dist. Ct. (so. and ctrl. dists.) Ill., U.S. Ct. Appeals (7th cir.) 1981, U.S. Ct. Appeals (4th cir.) 1996. Assoc. Katz, Friedman, Schur & Eagle, Chgo., 1981-90, of counsel, 1990—; ptnr. Baizer & Rapoport, Chgo., of counsel Highland Park, Ill., 1990-95; founder, pres. Rapoport Law Offices, P.C. (formerly Rapoport & Kupets P.C.), 1995—. Instr. legal writing Ill. Inst. Tech.-Kent Coll. Law, Chgo., 1981, guest lectr., 1985-92; instr. Ill. Inst. CLE, 1995—; arbitrator Million Dollar Advs. Forum, 1995—; state coord. Nat. Bd. Trial ADvocacy; lead trial counsel, mem. plaintiff's steering com. In Air Disaster at Charlotte Douglas Airport, 1994; mem. lead counsel com. In Air Disaster at Morrisville, N.C., 1994; lead trial counsel, In The Air Disaster at Sioux Gateway Airport, 1989. Fellow Roscoe Pound Found.; mem. ABA, ATLA (sustaining mem.), Ill. Bar Assn., Ill. Trial Lawyers Assn., Chgo. Bar Assn., Ill. Inst. for CLE, Trial Lawyers for Pub. Justice, Trial Lawyers for Pub. Justice, Trial Lawyers for Civil Justice, Lake County Bar Assn. Office: Rapoport Law Offices PC 20 N Clark St Ste 3500 Chicago IL 60602-2801

RAPOPORT, JUDITH, psychiatrist; b. N.Y.C., July 12, 1933; d. Louis and Minna (Enteen) Livant; m. Stanley Rapoport, June 25, 1961; children: Stuart, Erik. BA, Swarthmore Coll., 1955; MD, Harvard U., 1959. Lic. psychiatrist. Cons., child psychiatrist NIMH/St. Elizabeth's Hosp., Washington, 1969—72; clin. asst. prof. Georgetown U. Med. Sch., Washington, 1972—82, clin. assoc. prof., 1982—85, clin. prof. psychiat., 1985—; med. officer biol. psychiatry br. NIMH, Bethesda, Md., 1979—82, chief, child psychiatry lab. of clin. scis., 1982—84, chief, child psychiatry div. intramural rsch. programs, 1984—; prof. psychiatry George Washington U. Sch. Med., Washington, 1979—; prof. pediat. Georgetown U., Washington, 1985—. Cons. in field. Author: (non-fiction) The Boy Who Couldn't Stop Washing, 1989 (best seller literary guild selection, 1989), Childhood Obsessive Compulsive Disorder, 1989. Fellow: Am. Acad. Arts & Sci., Am. Acad. Child Psychiatry, Am. Psychiat. Assn.; mem.: Inst. Medicine, D.C. Psychiat. Assn. Home: 3010 44th Pl NW Washington DC 20016-3557 Office: NIMH Rm 3N202 10 Center Dr Bldg 10 Bethesda MD 20892-0001 E-mail: rapoport@helix.nih.gov.

RAPOPORT, MILES S. former state offical; m. Sandra Luciano; children: Jeff, Ross. BA in Polit. sci., N.Y. U., 1971. Exec. dir. Conn. Citizen Action Group, 1979-84; mem. Conn. Ho. of Reps., asst. majority leader, 1987-92, house chmn. govt. adminstrn. and elections com., mem. fin., revenue and bonding com.; sec. of state State of Conn., 1994-98; exec. dir. Democracy Works, Hartford, Conn., 1999—2001. Office: President Demos 5th Fl 220 Fifth Ave New York NY 10001

RAPOPORT, NANCY B. dean, law educator; b. Bryan, Tex., June 29, 1960; m. Jeffrey D. Van Niel, Oct. 13, 1996. BA in legal studies, honors psychology summa cum laude, Rice U., 1982; JD, Stanford Law Sch., 1985. Bar: Calif. 1987, U.S. Dist. Cts. (no., ea., ctrl., and so. dists.) Calif. 1987, U.S. Ct. Appeals (9th cir.) 1987, Ohio 1993, Nebr. 1999, U.S. Dist. Ct. (no. dist.) Tex. Jud. clerk Hon. Joseph T. Sneed, United States Ct. Appeals for Ninth Cir., San Francisco, 1985—86; assoc. bus.dept. of bankruptcy and workouts group Morrison & Foerster, San Francisco, 1986—91; asst. prof. Ohio State U. Coll. Law, Columbus, Ohio, 1991—95, tenured assoc. prof., 1995—98, assoc. dean student affairs, 1996—98, prof., 1998; dean, prof. law U. Nebr. Coll. Law, Lincoln, 1998—2000, U. Houston Law Ctr., 2000—. Invited spkr., panelist, and presenter in field. Co-editor (with Bala G. Dharan): Enron: Corporate Fiascos adn Their Implications, 2004. Bd. trustees Law Sch. Admissions Coun., 2001—04; bd. dirs. Friends of Girl Scouting Adv. Bd., 2001—, Pro Bono Rsch. Group, 2000—, St. Elizabeth Found., 1999—2000, ADL Southwest Regional Bd., 2001—, Houston Area Women's Ctr. Named Legal Pioneer for Women in Law (first woman to serve as dean of Nebr. Law Sch.), Nebr. State Bar Assn., 2000, Outstanding Prof. of Yr., Ohio State U. Coll. Law., 1997; named to Louis Nemzer meml. lectr., 1998; fellow 1998 Fellowship, Am. Bankruptcy Law Jour. Fellow: Am. Bar Found.; mem.: ABA (task force on law student debt 2001—03), Assn. Am. Law Sch.'s Prof. Develop. Com., Ohio State Bar Assn. (legal edn. com. 1997—98), Am. Bankruptcy Inst. (law sch. com. 1994—), Bar Assn. San Francisco, Nebr. Continuing Legal Edn. (long-range planning com. 1998—2000), Nat. Assn. Coll. and U. Attys., Nebr. State Bar Assn. (bankruptcy sect. 1998—2000, exec.com., bankruptcy sect. 1999—2000, access to profession com. 1999—2001), Houston Bar Found. (selection com. Best Article award 2000—), Houston Bar Assn., Am. Law Inst. Avocations: tae kwon do, ballroom dancing, Latin dancing, black and white photography, music. Office: U Houston Law Ctr 100 Law Ctr Houston TX 77204-6060 Office Phone: 713-743-2100. Business E-Mail: nrapoport@uh.edu.

RAPOPORT, ROBERT MORTON, medical educator; b. Oakland, Calif., Nov. 20, 1952; married; 2 children. BA in Biological Scis., U. Calif., Santa Barbara, 1974; PhD in Pharmacology, U. Calif., L.A., 1980; postdoc. studies in Pharmacology, U. Va., 1980-81, Stanford U., 1981-83. Rsch. pharmacologist VA Med. Ctr., Palo Alto, Calif., 1983-84, Cin., 1984—. Asst. prof. dept. pharmacology and cell biophysics U. Cin., 1984-91, assoc. prof., 1991—; asst. dir. med. pharmacology, 1994; spkr. in field. Reviewer manuscripts. various jours., grants various assns.; contbr. over 100 articles to profl. publs. Grantee U. Calif., 1977, VA, 1983-86, 85-86, 87-90, NIH, 1985-87, 88-93, Am. Heart Assn. S.W. Ohio, 1985-86, 86-87, 88-89, 89-91, 91-92, U. Cin., 1985-86, Am. Heart Assn., 1987-90, 1995—, Veterans Affairs, 1994-95, 95—, Univ. Rsch. Coun., 1994-95, Parke-Davis, 1994, 95; recipient Rsch. Career Devel. award, 1986-91. Office: Dept Pharmacology Univ Cincinnati 231 Bethesda Ave Cincinnati OH 45267-0001

RAPOPORT, RONALD JON, journalist; b. Detroit, Aug. 14, 1940; s. Daniel B. and Shirley G.; m. Joan Zucker, Sept. 2, 1968; children— Rebecca, Julie. BA, Stanford U., 1962; MS, Columbia U., 1963. Reporter Mpls. Star, 1963-65; asso. editor Sport mag., 1965-66; sports reporter AP, N.Y.C., San Francisco, 1966-70, Los Angeles Times, 1970-77; sports columnist Chgo. Sun-Times, 1977-88, Los Angeles Daily News, 1988-95; sports commentator Weekend Edit. Nat. Pub. Radio, 1986—; dep. sports editor Chgo. Sun-Times, 1996-98, sports columnist, 1998—. Author: (with Chip Oliver) High for the Game, 1971, (with Stan Love) Love in the NBA, 1975, (with Jim McGregor) Called for Travelling, 1979; editor: A Kind of Grace: A Treasury of Sportswriting by Women, 1994, (with Betty Garrett) Betty Garrett and Other Songs, 1998, See How She Runs: Marion Jones and the Making of a Champion, 2000. Served with U.S. Army Res., 1963.

RAPP, GEORGE ROBERT (RIP RAPP), geology and archeology educator; b. Toledo, Sept. 19, 1930; s. George Robert and Gladys Mae (Warner) R.; m. Jeannette Messner, June 15, 1956; children: Kathryn, Karen. BA, U. Minn., 1952; PhD, Pa. State U., 1960. Asst. then assoc. prof. S.D. Sch. Mines, Rapid City, 1957-65; assoc. prof. U. Minn., Mpls., 1965-75, prof. geology and archeology Duluth, 1975-95, dean Coll. Letters and Sci., 1975-84, dean Coll. Sci. and Engring., 1984-89, dir. Archeometry Lab., 1975—; Regents' prof. geoarchaeology, 1995—. Prof. Ctr. for Ancient Studies, U. Minn., Mpls., 1970-93, prof. interdisciplinary archaeol. studies, 1993—; cons. USIA, Westinghouse Corp., Exxon Corp., Ford Found. Author, editor: Excavations at Nichoria, 1978, Troy: Archeological Geology, 1982, Archeological Geology, 1985, Excavations at Tel Michal, 1989, Encyclopedia of Minerals, 1989, Phytolith Systematics, 1992, Geoarchaeology, 1998, Artifact Copper Sources, 2000, Archaeomineralogy, 2002; mem. editl. bd. Jour. Field Archeology, 1976-85, Jour. Archeol. Sci., 1977-79, Geoarcheology Jour., 1984-92, Am. Jour. Archeology, 1985-92. NSF postdoctoral fellow, 1963-64, Fulbright-Hayes sr. rsch. fellow, 1972-73. Fellow AAAS (chmn. sect. E, 1987-88, nat. coun. 1992-95), Geol. Soc. Am. (Archeol. Geology award 1983), Mineral. Soc. Am.; mem. Nat. Assn. Geology Tchrs. (pres. 1986-89), Soc. for Archeol. Sci. (pres. 1983-84), Assn. Field Archeology (pres. 1979-81), Archaeol. Inst. Am. (Pomerance medal 1988), Sigma Xi (bd. dirs. 1990-98). Avocations: classical music, exercise, nutrition. Office: U Minn-Duluth Dept Geol Scis Duluth MN 55812

RAPP, GERALD DUANE, lawyer, manufacturing executive; b. Berwyn, Nebr., July 19, 1933; s. Kenneth P. and Mildred (Price) R.; children: Gerald Duane Jr., Gregory T., Amy Frances Wanzek. BS, U. Mo., 1955; JD, U. Mich., 1958. Bar: Ohio bar 1959. Practice in, Dayton, 1960—; ptnr. Smith & Schnacke, 1963-70; asst. gen. counsel Mead Corp., Dayton, 1970, v.p. human resources and legal affairs, 1973, v.p., corp. sec., 1975, v.p., gen. counsel, corp. sec., 1976, v.p., gen. counsel, 1979, sr. v.p., gen. counsel, 1981-91, counsel to bd. dirs., 1991-92; of counsel Bieser, Greer & Landis, 1992—. Pres. R-J Holding Co., Weber Canyon Ranch, Inc. Sr. editor U. Mich. Law Rev., 1957-58. Past chmn. Oakwood Youth Commn.; past v.p., bd. dirs. Big Bros. Greater Dayton; mem. pres.'s visitors com. U. Mich. Law Sch.; past trustee Urbana Coll.; past pres., trustee Ohio Ctr. Leadership Studies, Robert K. Greenleaf Ctr., Indpls.; past pres. bd. trustees Dayton and Montgomery County Pub. Libr.; past. mem. bd. visitors Law Schs. of Dayton. 1st lt. U.S. Army, 1958-60. Mem. ABA, Ohio Bar Assn., Dayton Bar Assn., Moraine Country Club, Dayton Racquet Club, Dayton Lawyers Club, Met. Club Washington, Phi Kappa Psi, Phi Delta Phi, Beta Gamma Sigma. Presbyterian. Office: 108 Green St Dayton OH 45402-2835

RAPP, LARRY P. financial advisor; b. Ravenna, Ohio, Feb. 20, 1948; s. George P. and Marie A. (Kormos) R.; m. Francine M. Koneval. BS, U. Dayton (Ohio), 1970. CPA. Sr. mgr. Price Waterhouse, Cleve. and N.Y., 1970-83; v.p. fin. Rotek Inc., Cleve., 1983-84; contr. Omnicare Inc., Cin., 1984-87; v.p. fin., chief fin. officer Animed Inc., Roslyn, N.Y., 1987-89; CFO Hawk Group/Weinberg Capital Corp., Cleve., 1989-93; pres. Sanctuary Fin. Group, Akron, 1993-96; CFO LCA-Vision Inc., Cin., 1996-2000; exec. v.p., CFO SLT-Japan Co., Ltd., Tokyo, 2000—; CEO, CFO IHD, Inc., Cin., 2000—. Assoc. editor Ohio CPA Jour., 1987-88, manuscript rev. com., 1995—; mem. nat. com. Career Svcs., FEI. Mem. Am. Inst. CPAs, Ohio Soc. CPAs, Fin Execs. Inst. Home and Office: Sanctuary Fin Group 3596 Sanctuary Dr Akron OH 44333-1748 E-mail: netfao@yahoo.com.

RAPP, LYNN BLAIR, obstetrician-gynecologist, educator; b. N.Y.C., Mar. 25, 1950; MD, U. Padova, Italy, 1983. Diplomate Am. Bd. Ob-Gyn. Resident ob-gyn. S.I. (N.Y.) U. Hosp., 1984-88, attending ob-gyn., 1988—. Attending St. Vincent's Med. Ctr., Richmond, 1992—; attending ob-gyn. Victory Meml. Hosp., Bklyn.; clin. instr. ob-gyn. SUNY Health Sci. Ctr., Bklyn. Fellow ACOG, ACS, Bklyn. Gynecol. Soc.; mem. AMA, Med. Soc. State N.Y., Acad. Medicine Richmond. Office Phone: 718-351-6265.

RAPP, MELANIE L. state legislator, primary school educator; b. Lake Worth, Fla., Sept. 5, 1964; BA in Internat. Culture and Commerce, Christopher Newport U., 1990. Substitute tchr.; state del. dist. 96 Va. House Dels., 2001. Elected mem. York County Bd. Suprs., 2000; mem. Watermen's Mus., Concerned Women for Am.; ea. vice-chmn. Rep. Party Va. Mem.: York Ruritan, York Rep. Women's Club, Va. Soc. Human Life. Republican. Baptist. Office: Gen Assembly Bldg Rm 520 PO Box 406 Richmond VA 23218 Address: Dist Office PO Box 1529 Yorktown VA 23692 E-mail: Del_Rapp@house.state.va.us.

RAPP, RICHARD TILDEN, economist, consultant; b. Miami, Fla., Nov. 30, 1944; s. Melville Benjamin and Rachel (Marx) R.; m. Wilma J. Levin, Aug. 20, 1967; children: Ethan, Sandra. BA cum laude, Bklyn. Coll., 1965; MA, U. Pa., 1966, PhD, 1970. Asst. prof. SUNY, Stony Brook, 1970-75, assoc. prof. econ. history, 1976-77; pres., chief exec. officer Nat. Econ. Rsch. Assocs., Inc., White Plains, NY, 1977—. Cons. on internat. trade and competition econs. Author: Industry and Economic Decline in Seventeenth-Century Venice, 1976, Trade Warfare and the New Protectionism, 1986; co-author: European Economic History, 1975. Nat. adv. bd. Santa Fe Opera, 1989—. Kent fellow Danforth found., 1968-70; Fulbright fellow, 1968-69. Mem. Am. Econ. Assn., Inst. for Advanced Study. Home: 52 Whippoorwill Lake Rd Chappaqua NY 10514-2314 Office: Nat Econ Rsch Assocs Inc 50 Main St White Plains NY 10606-1901

RAPP, ROBERT ANTHONY, metallurgical engineering educator, consultant; b. Lafayette, Ind., Feb. 21, 1934; s. Frank J. and Goldie M. (Royer) R.; m. Heidi B. Sartorius, June 3, 1960; children: Kathleen Rapp Raynaud, Thomas, Stephen, Stephanie Rapp Surface. BSMetE, Purdue U., 1956; MSMetE, Carnegie Inst. Tech., 1959, PhDMetE, 1960; D (hon.), Inst. Polytech., Toulouse, France, 1995. Asst. prof. metall. engring. Ohio State U., Columbus, 1963-66, assoc. prof., 1966-69, prof., 1969—, M.G. Fontana prof., 1988-95, Univ. prof., 1989-95, disting. univ. prof. emeritus, 1995—. Vis. prof. Ecole Nat. Superior d'Electrochimie, Grenoble, France, 1972-73, U. Paris-Sud, Orsay, 1985-86, Ecole Nat. Superior de Chimie, Toulouse, France, 1985-86, U. New South Wales, Australia, 1987; Acta/Scripta Metallurgica lectr., 1991; rsch. metallurgist WPAFB, Ohio, 1960-63. Editor: Techniques of Metals Research, vol. IV, 1982, High Temperature Corrosion, 1984; translator Metallic Corrosion (Kaesche), 1986; bd. rev. jour. Oxid. Metals; contbr. numerous articles to profl. jours. Decorated chevalier des Palmes Academiques; recipient Disting. Engring. Alumnus award Purdue U., 1988, B.F. Goodrich Collegiate Inventor's award, 1991, 92, Ulrick Evans award Brit. Inst. Corrosion, 1992; Guggenheim fellow, 1972; Fulbright scholar Max Planck Inst. Phys. Chemistry, 1959-60, Linford award for Disting. Tchg.,The Electrochem. Soc., 1998. Fellow: Nat. Assn. Corrosion Engrs. (W.R. Whitney award 1986), Electrochem. Soc. (HTM Divsn. Outstanding Achievement award 1992, Linford Tchr. award 1998), Mining Metals and Materials Soc. (R.F. Mehl medal 2000, Educator award 2003), Am. Soc. Metals Internat. (B. Stoughton award 1968, Howe gold medal 1974, Gold medal 2000); mem.: Nat. Acad. Engring., French Soc. Metals and Materials (hon.). Lutheran. Home: 1379 Southport Dr Columbus OH 43235-7649 E-mail: rapp.r@att.worldnet.net., rapp.4@osu.edu.

RAPP, ROBERT NEIL, lawyer; b. Erie, Pa., Sept. 10, 1947; m. Sally K. Meder; 1 child: Jeffrey David. BA, Case Western Res. U., 1969, JD, 1972; MBA, Cleve. State U., 1989. Bar: Ohio 1972, U.S. dist. Ct. (no. dist.) Ohio 1973, U.S. Ct. Appeals (6th crct.) 1981, U.S. Supreme Ct. 1980. Assoc. Metzenbaum, Gaines & Stern, Co., L.P.A., Cleve., 1972-75; ptnr. Calfee, Halter & Griswold, Cleve., 1975—. Adj. prof. law Case Western Res. U., 1975—78, 1994—98, Cleve. Marshall Coll. Law, Cleve. State U., 1976—82; practitioner-in-residence Cornell U. Law Sch., 1993; mem. legal adv. bd. Nat. Assn. Securities Dealers, 1992—96; mem. market ops. rev. com. Nasdaq Stock Market, 1996—; arbitrator, practitioner mediator Nat. Futures Assn. Author: Blue Sky Regulation, 2d edit., 2003; contbr. numerous articles to law jours. Mem. ABA (sect. bus. law: mem. com. fed. regulation of securities, subcom. broker-dealer regulation, sect. litigation: mem. com. securities litigation), Am. Arbitration Assn. (securities arbitrator, mem. comml. adv. coun. Cleve. region), Ohio State Bar Assn. (elected mem. coun. dels. 1976-82, corp. law com. 1980—), Cleve. Bar Assn. (chmn. young lawyers sect. 1976-77), assoc. mem. cert. grievance com., sect. securities law: exec. coun. 1980-85, chmn. govt. liaison com. 1980-81). Office: Calfee Halter & Griswold LLP 1400 McDonald Investment Ct Cleveland OH 44114-2688

RAPP, STEPHEN JOHN, international prosecutor; b. Waterloo, Iowa, Jan. 26, 1949; s. Spurgeon John and Beverly (Leckington) R.; m. Donna J.E. Maier, 1981; children: Alexander, Stephanie. AB cum laude, Harvard U., 1971; JD with honors, Drake U., 1973. Bar: Iowa 1974, U.S. Dist. Ct. (no. and so. dists.) Iowa 1978, U.S. Ct. Appeals (8th cir.) 1979, U.S. Supreme Ct. 1979. Rsch. asst. Office of U.S. Senator Birch Bayh, Ind., 1970; community program asst. HUD, Chgo., 1971; mem. Iowa Ho. Reps., 1972-74, 79-83, Coun. to Majority Caucus, Iowa Ho. Reps., 1975; staff dir., counsel subcom. on juvenile delinquency U.S. Senate, Washington, 1977-78; ptnr. Rapp & Gilliam, Waterloo, 1979-83; pvt. practice Waterloo, 1983-93; U.S. atty. U.S. Dist. Ct. (no. dist.) Iowa, 1993—2001; sr. prosecuting atty. United Nations Internat. Crime Tribunal for Rwanda, 2001—. Del., mem. com. Dem. Nat. Conv., 1976, 80, 84, 88, 92; mem. Dem. Nat. Adv. Com. on Econ., 1982-84, chmn. Black Hawk Dem. Com., 1986-91; mem. Iowa Dem. Com., 1990-93, chair 2d C.D. Dem. Com., 1991-93. Mem. ABA, Iowa Bar Assn., Order of Coif. Methodist. Home: 219 Highland Blvd Waterloo IA 50703-4229 Office: K-708 UN-ICTR PO Box 6016 Arusha Tanzania E-mail: rapp@un.org.

RAPPAPORT, ALAN FRED, clinical psychologist; b. NYC, Nov. 20, 1946; s. Sol and Edith (Drutman) R.; m. Liza E. Peguero, Dec. 27, 1981. BA, Seton Hall U., 1968; MA, U. Conn., 1969; PhD, Pa. State U., 1971. Cert. clin. psychologist, marital therapist, N.J.; cert. in treatment of alcohol and other psychoactive substance abuse disorders. Assoc. prof. Montclair (NJ) State Coll., 1971-73; psychotherapist NYC, 1973-78; clin. dir. Cmty. Mental Health Assocs., Parsippany, NJ, 1978—. Cons. psychologist Stress Release Ltd., NYC, 1972-75; adj. prof. Montclair State Coll., 1978-79. Author: (with others) Marriage and Family Therapy, 1974, Couples in Conflict, 1974, Treating Relationships, 1976. Program dir. Holistic Health Inst. NJ, 1983-85. Fellow: Am. Coll. Psychology; mem.: APA, NJ Psychol. Assn. Office: Cmty Mental Health Assoc 3599 Route 46 Parsippany NJ 07054-1015 Office Phone: 973-263-8070. E-mail: DrRapp@att.net.

RAPPAPORT, ANNA M. actuary; b. New Orleans, Sept. 15, 1940; d. Ludwig Guckenheimer, Gertrude Guckenheimer; m. Peter Plumley; 1 child, Jennifer Rappaport Royce. MBA, U. Chgo., 1985. Actuarial analyst NY Life, NYC, 1958—62; sr. v.p. Standard Security Life, NYC, 1962—73; v.p. Equitable Life Assurance Soc. of the US, NYC, 1976; prin. Mercer Human Resource Cons., Chgo., 1976—. Pres. Soc. Actuaries, Schaumburg, Ill., 1997—98; bd. dirs. Nat. Acad. Social Ins., Washington; mem. Social Security Adv. Bd. Tech. Panel, 2003. Bd. adv. Pension Rsch. Coun.; active Chgo. Network, 1994; bd. dirs. Wiser Bd., Profit Sharing Coun. Am., Metro Chgo. Info. Ctr., 1997—, Actuarial Found., Schaumburg, Ill., 2000—. Avocation: Watercolor painting; snorkeling, bridge. Office: Mercer Human Resource Cons 10 South Wacker Drive Chicago IL 60606-7485 Office Phone: 312 902-7518. Office Fax: 312 902-7626. Business E-Mail: anna.rappaport@mercer.com.

RAPPAPORT, GARY BURTON, defense equipment executive; b. Mpls., Apr. 27, 1937; s. Max and Beatrice (Berkinsky) R.; m. Susan Heller, Nov. 26, 1961; children: Debra Lynn, Melissa Ellen. BS, U. Pa., 1959. Asst. to pres. Napco Industries, Inc., Hopkins, Minn., 1959-61, v.p., 1961-65, exec. v.p., 1964-65, pres., 1965-74, CEO, 1974-84, Venturian Corp., Hopkins, 1984—, also chmn. bd. dirs. Dir. La Maur, Inc., Mpls., 1980-87. Chmn. bd. govs. Mt. Sinai Hosp., Mpls., 1979-81. Served with Air N.G., 1960-64. Jewish. Office: Venturian Corp 11111 Excelsior Blvd Hopkins MN 55343-3434

RAPPAPORT, JAMES WYANT, lawyer, real estate developer; b. Boston, May 9, 1956; s. Jerome Lyle and Nancy (Vahey) R.; m. Cecelia Catherine Ewald; children: James, Jessica, Joshua. BS in Econs., Wharton, U. Pa., 1977; JD, Boston U., 1980. Assoc. Law Offices of Alan Jacobs, Boston, 1980-81; atty. Rappaport and Rakov, Boston, 1981-93; ptnr. Rappaport, Aserkoff & Rappaport, Boston, 1994-2000, New Boston Fund Inc, 2000—. Gen. ptnr. Charles River Park, Boston, 1982-2001; prin. New Boston Funds, 1992—; pres. Charles River Properties, Ltd., 1986-93, Charles River Hawaii Devel. Corp., 1987-90; chmn. Park Transit Displays, 1992-2000, Silent Sys., Inc., 1994-98; dir. Jillians Holding Co., 1998—. Class chmn. Roxbury Latin Sch., 1978-95; vice chmn. Rep. 3d ward, Boston, 1978-83, chmn., 1988-89; mem. Young Eagle sect. Rep. Nat. Com., Boston, 1985-88, Rep. state fin. com., Boston, 1985—, Concord (Mass.) Rep. Town Com., 1985-87, 1989—; bd. dirs. Mass. Taxpayers Com., Needham, Mass., 1984-91, chmn., 1988-91; gen. ptnr. Charles River Hawaii L.P., Kauai, 1986-89; Rep. candidate U.S. Senate, 1990; chmn. Mass. Rep. Party, 1992-97; mem. Rep. Nat. Com., 1992-97; bd. dirs. Jewish Vocat. Svcs., Jewish Community Rels. Coun., Dana Farber Cancer Inst., 1998—, Children's Hosp., 2000—; mem. fin. com. Rep. Nat. Com., 1992-2000. Mem. ABA, Mass. Bar Assn., Vt. Bar Assn., Boston Bar Assn., Greater Boston Real Estate Bd., King David Soc. (chmn. 1999—). Jewish. Avocations: hiking, golf. E-mail: jwrappinc@aol.com.

RAPPAPORT, JONATHAN C. composer, educator, conductor; s. Benjamin and Aletha D. Rappaport; m. Rana Gladstone, Nov. 8, 1946; children: Netta B., Maya J. BMusEd, U. Denver, 1969; Diploma, Kodaly Musical Tng. Inst., Wellesley, Mass., 1975; Kodály Cert., Franz Liszt Acad. of Music, Budapest, Hungary, 1975; MMus, New Eng. Conservatory, Boston, 1983; PhD studies, U. Mass., Amherst, 2000—04. Music tchr. Haldane Ctrl. Sch., Cold Spring, NY, 1969—73, Millbury Pub. Schools, Millbury, Mass., 1976—81; academic coord. Kodaly Ctr. of Am., Newton, Mass., 1982—85; music dir. Broadmoor Chamber Singers, Natick, Mass., 1983—98; music tchr. Worcester (Mass.) Pub. Schs., 1985—94, performing arts liaison, 1994—; co-dir. Kodaly Music Inst. @ New Eng. Conservatory, Boston, 1998—; head of sch. Conservatory Lab Charter Sch., Brighton, Mass., 2004—. Composer: (18 choral compositions) Mother Goose Hushabye, Hanukah Candles Burning Bright, and 16 others; author: (music pedagogical books) New Pathways to Art Music Listening; The Kodály Weave, Vol. I and II; contbr. Mass. Arts Curriculum Framework, articles to music edn. publs. Pres. Beth Tikvah Synagogue, Westborough, Mass., 1997—2000. Recipient Horace Mann Tchr. Award, Mass. Dept. of Edn., 1988, Moss Hart Award, New Eng. Theatre Conf., 2000; grantee Mini Grant, Worcester Alliance for Edn., 1987, 1992. Mem.: Orgn. Am. Kodaly Educators (exec. sec.), Mass. Alliance Arts Edn. (chmn. 1997—98, Irene Buck Svc. to Arts Edn. award 2004), Boston Area Kodaly Educators Assn. (pres.), Mass Music Educators Assn. (K-9 rep. 1999—2003, Lowell Mason award 2004). Avocations: genealogy, antiques. Home: 7 Brady Rd Westborough MA 01581

RAPPAPORT, LAWRENCE, plant physiology and horticulture educator; b. N.Y.C., May 28, 1928; s. Aaron and Elsie R.; m. Norma, Nov. 21, 1953; children: Meryl, Debra Kramer, Craig. BS in Horticulture, U. Idaho, 1950; MS in Horticulture, Mich. State Coll., 1951; PhD in Horticulture, Mich. State U., 1956. Lectr. U. Calif., Davis, 1956-67, jr. olericulturist, dept. vegetable crops, 1956-58, asst. olericulturist, 1958-63, assoc. olericulturist, 1963-67, prof., 1968—, prof. emeritus, 1991—, dir. plant growth lab., 1975-78, chairperson dept. vegetable crops, 1978-84. Vis. scientist Calif. Inst. Tech., 1958; co-dir. Horticulture Subproject, Calif./Egypt project, 1978-82. Contbr. articles to profl. jours. 1st pres. Davis Human Rels. Coun., 1964-66; v.p. Jewish Fedn. Sacramento, 1969; pres. Jewish Fellowship, Davis, 1985-89; founder, 1st dir. Hillel Counselership at Davis, 1965-76. Decorated Bronze star; Guggenheim Found. fellow, 1963, Fulbright fellow, 1964, USPHS Spl. fellow, 1970, Am. Soc. Horticulture Sci. fellow, 1987, Sir Frederick McMaster fellow, 1991. Achievements include discovery of evidence for gibberellin-binding protein in plants; evidence for the signal hypothesis operating in plants, positive evidence for phytochrome-mediated gibberellin metabolism and stem growth; isolation of somaclonal variants of celery bearing stable resistance to Fusarium oxysporum f. sp. apii. Home: 637 Elmwood Dr Davis CA 95616-3514 Office: U Calif Dept Vegetable Crops Asmundson Hall Rm 237 One Shields Ave Davis CA 95616 Business E-Mail: rappaport@vegmail.ucdavis.edu.

RAPPAPORT, LINDA ELLEN, lawyer; b. Freeport, N.Y., Jan. 12, 1952; d. William Jay and Marcia Ann (Wiland) Rappaport; m. Leonard Chazen, June 1, 1980; 1 child, Matthew Ross Chazen. BA, Wesleyan U., Middletown, Conn., 1974; JD, NYU, 1977. Bar: N.Y. 1977. Law clk. Chief Judge James S. Holden U.S. Dist. Ct. Vt., Rutland, 1978; assoc. Shearman & Sterling, N.Y.C., 1979-85, ptnr., 1986—, elected mem. policy com., 1995—. Bd. dirs. N.Y. Women's Found., N.Y.C., 1995—2001, AIESEC Internat., N.Y.C., 1994—2000; bd. govs. Mannes Coll. Music, 2004—. Fellow: Am. Coll. Employee Benefits Coun.; mem.: Bar Assn. City of N.Y. (employee benefits com. 1986—, employment law com. 1986—). Office: Shearman & Sterling 599 Lexington Ave Fl 13 New York NY 10022-6069 E-mail: lrappaport@shearman.com.

RAPPAPORT, MARGARET M.W.E. psychologist, physician, writer, pilot, consultant; b. Nov. 16, 1947; d. Leo J. and Marie L. (Rischle) Williams; m. Herbert Rappaport (div.); children: Amanda, Alexander. BA, U. Buffalo; MA, SUNY; PhD, MD, U. Colo. Zone Perfect cert. instr. Prof., rschr. U. Dar es Salaam, Tanzania; with Rappaport Assocs., Phila., 1974-94; exec. dir. Inst. for Parent/Child Svcs., Phila., 1978-94; pres., CEO, Diabetes Edn. Ctr. of Cape Cod, Inc. Mem. adj. faculty Temple U., Phila., 1974-94; aviation safety counselor FAA; aviation cons.; chair devel. com. Vis. Nurse Assn. Cape Cod; trustee Cape Cod Healthcare Found.; nat./internat. spkr. Pres. Reach New Heights, Inc.; founder Fit to Fly. Mem. adv. coun. VNA Am. Mem. AAUP, Nat. Profl. Spkrs. Assn., Cosmopolitan Club, Orleans Yacht Club. Home: PO Box 1845 Orleans MA 02653-1845 Office Phone: 508-255-9570. Personal E-mail: rappaportmm@prodigy.net.

RAPPAPORT, MARTIN PAUL, internist, nephrologist, educator; b. Bronx, N.Y., Apr. 25, 1935; s. Joseph and Anne (Kramer) R.; m. Bethany Ann Mitchell; children: Karen, Steven; stepchildren: Aaron Cole, Kevin Cole. BS, Tulane U., 1957, MD, 1960. Diplomate Am. Bd. Internal Medicine, Nat. Bd. Med. Examiners. Intern Charity Hosp. of La., New Orleans, 1960-61, resident in internal medicine, 1961-64; pvt. practice internal medicine and nephrology, Seabrook, Tex., 1968-72, Webster, Tex., 1972-98; internist Univ. Med. Group, Houston, 1998; mem. courtesy staff Mainland Ctr. Hosp. (formerly Galveston County Meml. Hosp.), Texas City, 1968-96, Bapt. Meml. System, 1969-72, 88-98; mem. staff Clear Lake Regional Med. Ctr., 1972-98; cons. staff St. Mary's Hosp., 1973-79; cons. nephrology St. John's Hosp., Nassau Bay, Tex.; fellow in nephrology Northwestern U. Med. Sch., Chgo., 1967—68; clin. asst. prof. in medicine and nephrology U. Tex., Galveston, 1969—; part-time physician dept. family medicine outpatient clinics U. Tex. Med. Br., Galveston, 2000; locum tenens, 2000—. Lectr. emergency med. technician cours e, 1974-76; adviser on respiratory therapy program Alvin (Tex.) Jr. Coll., 1976-82; cons. nephrology USPHS, 1979-80. Served to capt. M.C. U.S. Army, 1961-67. Fellow ACP, Am. Coll. Chest Physicians; mem. Internat., Am. Socs. Nephrology, So. Med. Assn., Tex. Med. Assn., Tex. Soc. Internal Medicine (bd. govs. 1994-96), Am. Soc. Artificial Internal Organs, Tex. Acad. Internal Medicine, Harris County Med. Soc., Am. Geriatrics Soc., Bay Area Heart Assn. (bd. govs. 1969-75), Clear Lake C. of C., Rotary, Phi Delta Epsilon, Alpha Epsilon Pi, Tulane Alumni Assn. Home: 15913 Malibu W Willis TX 77318-6784

RAPPAPORT, MICHAEL PAUL, columnist; b. San Diego, Dec. 11, 1949; s. Norman Lewis and Yvonne Naomi Rappaport; m. Leslie Ann Rappaport, Apr. 19, 1975 (div. May 1982); m. Nicole Jacqueline Rappaport, Nov. 2, 1992; children: Pauline Nicole Borderies, Virgile Georges Borderies. AS, No. Va. C.C., Annandale, 1976; BS, George Mason U., 1981. Asst. sports editor Alexandria (Va.) Gazette, 1979-81, Gastonia (N.C.) Gazette, 1982-83; sportswriter Anderson (S.C.) Ind. Mail, 1983-84, St. Louis Globe Dem., 1984-86; sports editor, columnist Greeley (Colo.) Tribune, 1986-88; sportswriter, columnist Reno Gazette Jour., 1988-90; sportswriter Inland Valley Daily Bull., Ontario, Calif., 1990-96, metro columnist, 1996—. Co-author: (e-book) The Woman in the Box, 2000; creator website mikerappaport.com, 2000. Recipient Sweepstakes Writing award Soc. Profl. Journalists Inland Calif. Chpt., 1997, Writing award for best local column, 2001-; named Sportswriter of Yr., South Atlantic League, 1982, 83. Mem. Nat. Soc. Newspaper Columnists, Nat. Press Club, Greater L.A. Press Club, Sigma Phi Epsilon (life, chpt. pres. 1981). Roman Catholic. Avocations: reading, golf, films, rotisserie baseball. Home: 1234 Fernside Dr La Canada Flintridge CA 91011 Office: 2041 E 4th St Ontario CA 91764-2605 E-mail: m_rappaport@msn.com.

RAPPAPORT, STUART RAMON, lawyer; b. Detroit, Apr. 13, 1935; s. Reuben and Zella (Golechen) R.; m. Anne M. Plotnick; children: Douglas, Erica Rappaport Witt. BA in History, U. Mich., 1956; JD, Harvard U., 1959. Bar: Calif. 1962. Trial lawyer, chief trials, bur. chief, chief. asst. pub. defender L.A. County Pub. Defender's Office, L.A., 1962-87; pub. defender Santa Clara County, San Jose, Calif., 1987-95; pvt. practice, 1995—. Mem. standing adv. com. on criminal law Jud. Coun. Calif., San Francisco, 1993—; mem. discipline evaluation com. State Bar of Calif. Contbr. articles to profl. jours. Recipient Lifetime Achievement award Calif. Attys. for Criminal Justice. Mem. Calif. Pub. Defenders Asn. (pres. 1982-83, Lifetime Achievement award), L.A. County Pub. Defenders Assn. (pres.). Democrat. Jewish. Address: 1415 Arch St Berkeley CA 94708 E-mail: sturap@mcn.org.

RAPPAPORT, SUSAN ELIZABETH, English language educator; b. Wakeenie, Kans., Feb. 15, 1953; d. Fred and Susan Louise (Gwin) Thornburg; m. Ronald Irvin Rappaport, Feb. 16, 1977; children: Erick, Scott. BA, U. Okla., 1975. Cert. English tchr. Tchr. English Washington (Okla.) H.S., 1975-77, Highland East Mid. Sch., Moore, Okla., 1978-83, June Shelton Sch. and Evaluation Ctr., Dallas, 1984-89; content mastery aide Coppell (Tex.) Mid. Sch., 1991-92; tchr. English Lakeview Mid. Sch., The Colony, Tex., 1992-95; tchr. English and reading Arbor Creek, Carrollton, Tex., 1995—. Multicultural activities coord. Lakeview Mid. Sch., The Colony, 1994-95; mentor tchr. Arbor Creek Mid. Sch., Carrollton, 1995—, bldg. leadership team, 1995—, sponsor Nat. Jr. Honor Soc., 1996-98. Active Project Graduation, Coppell (Tex.) H.S., 1998, Culture Dept., Soka Gakkai Internat., Dallas, 1998. Grantee Lewisville Ind. Sch. Sys., 1997. Mem. ASCD, Internat. Reading Assn., Nat. Coun. Tchrs. English, Nat. Mid. Sch. Assn. Avocations: reading, gardening.

RAPSON, RICHARD L. history professor, b. N.Y.C., Mar. 8, 1937; s. Louis and Grace Lillian (Levenkind) R.; m. Susan Burns, Feb. 22, 1975 (div. June 1981); m. Elaine Catherine Hatfield, June 15, 1982; 1 child, Kim Elizabeth. BA, Amherst Coll., 1958; PhD, Columbia U., 1966. Asst. prof. Amherst (Mass.) Coll., 1960-61, Stanford (Calif.) U., 1961-65, U. Calif., Santa Barbara, 1965-66; from assoc. prof. to prof. history U. Hawaii, Honolulu, 1966—, founder, dir. New Coll., 1968-73. Bd. dirs. Semester at Sea, U. Pitts.; psychotherapist, Honolulu, 1982—. Author: Individualism and Conformity in the American Character, 1967, Britons View America, 1971, The Cult of Youth, 1972, Major Interpretations of the American Past, 1978, Denials of Doubt, 1980, Cultural Pluralism in Hawaii, 1981, American Yearnings, 1989, Amazed By Life: Confessions of a Non-Religious Believer, 2003; co-author: (with Elaine Hatfield) Love, Sex and Intimacy: Their Psychology, Biology and History, 1993, Emotional Contagion, 1994, Love and Sex: Cross-Cultural Perspectives, 1995, Rosie, 2000, Recovered Memories, 2003, Darwin's Law, 2003; mem. editl. bd. Univ. Press Am., 1981—. Woodrow Wilson fellow Wilson Found., Princeton, 1960; Edward Perkins scholar, Columbia U., 1961; Danforth tchr. Danforth Found., St. Louis, 1965; recipient E. Harris Harbison for Gifted Tchg. award Danforth Found., 1973, Outstanding Tchr. award Stanford U. 25th Reunion Class, 1992. Mem. Am. Hist. Assn., Orgn. Am. Hist., Nat. Womens Hist. Project, Phi Beta Kappa, Outrigger Canoe Club, Honolulu Club. Avocations: squash, travel, classical music. Office: U Hawaii Dept History 2530 Dole St Honolulu HI 96822-2303 Office Phone: 808-956-6801.

RAQUET, MAUREEN GRAHAM, protective services official, educator; b. Seaford, Del., Jan. 28, 1955; d. Robert James and Helen Mary Graham; m. William Jameson Raquet; 1 child, Patrick. BA in Psychology, Lafayette Coll., 1976; MS in Juvenile Justice Adminstrn. and Criminal Justice, Shippensburg U., 1989. Cert. police officer Pa. Police officer Lower Merion Twp. Police Dept., Ardmore, Pa., 1978—80; foster care cons. The Impact Project, Allentown, Pa., 1993—94; juvenile probation officer Montgomery County Juvenile Probation Dept., Norristown, Pa., 1980—92; secure detention coord. Montgomery County Youth Ctr., Norristown, 1992—2000, exec. dir., 2000. Adj. prof. criminal justice West Chester (Pa.) U., 1994—, Montgomery County C.C., Blue Bell, Pa., 1997; mem. adv. bd. Foster Grandparent Program, Norristown, 1998—; bd. dirs. Plays For Living, Norristown, 1995—2000. Recipient Outstanding Scholarship in Juvenile Justice, Pa. Juvenile Ct. Judges' Commn., Ctr. Juvenile Justice Tng. and Rsch., 1989; scholar, Charles A. Dana Found., Lafayette Coll., 1973—76. Mem.: Pa. Assn. Probation, Parole and Corrections, Nat. Coun. Juvenile and Family Ct. Judges, Am. Corrections Assn., Nat. Juvenile Detention Assn., Montgomery County Juvenile Adv. Assn. (v.p. 1991—92), Juvenile Detention Ctrs. Assn. Pa. (mental health adv. bd. 1999—, bd. dirs. tng. commn. 2001—), Alpha Phi Sigma. Office: Montgomery County Youth Ctr 540 Port Indian Rd Norristown PA 19403

RARDON, LARRY L. lawyer; b. Arcadia, Fla., Oct. 4, 1946; s. Wayne V. and Nellie Rardon; m. Hilda M. Rardon, Dec. 12, 1986; children: Shawn, Adria. BA, U. South Fla., 1968; JD, Stetson U., 1971. Bar: Fla. 1971. Specializist in trial work Rardon, Rodriguez & Assocs. PA, Tampa, Fla. Office: 3918 N Highland Ave Tampa FL 33603

RARICK, PHILIP JOSEPH, judge; b. Collinsville, Ill., Nov. 10, 1940; s. Philip J. and Mary (Buckman) R.; m. Janet N. Arnovitz, Feb. 1, 1963; 1 child, Philip J. IV. BA, So. Ill. U., 1962; JD, St. Louis U., 1966. Bar: Ill. 1966, U.S. Dist. Ct. Ill. 1966. Twp. atty. Collinsville & Jarvis, Collinsville, Ill., 1966-75; asst. state's atty. Madison County, Edwardsville, Ill., 1966-75; city atty. City of Collinsville, 1967-75; cir. judge Third Jud. Cir., Edwardsville, 1975-88; presiding judge Criminal Div. in Madison County, Ill., 1982—85; chief cir. judge Third Jud. Cir., Edwardsville, 1985-87; mem. exec. com. Ill. Jud. Conf., Springfield, 1985—; presiding judge Criminal Div. in Madison County, Ill., 1987—88; elected judge Appellate Ct., Fifth Dist., Ill., 1988; mem., chmn. complex litigation com. Ill. Jud. Conf., Springfield, 1988—96; judge indsl. commn. divsn. Ill. Appellate Ct., 1988—; served Industrial Comm. Div. of the Appellate Ct., 1992; mem. Ill. Cts. Commn. State of Ill., Springfield, 1992—99; mem. Courts Comm., Ill., 1992—99; elected judge, retained Appellate Ct., Fifth Dist., Ill., 1998; alt. mem. Courts Comm., Ill., 1999—; mem., chmn. complex litig. com. Springfield, Ill., 1999—2001. Chmn. (manual) Illinois Manual for Complex Litigation. Mem. Ill. State Bar Assn., Ill. Judges Assn. (dir. 1977—), Madison County Bar Assn., Tri-City Bar Assn. Office: Supreme Ct Bldg Springfield IL 62701 also: State of Ill Bldg 160 N LaSalle St Chicago IL 60601

RARIDON, RICHARD JAY, computer specialist; b. Newton, Iowa, Oct. 25, 1931; s. Jack Allison and Letha Helen (Woods) R.; m. Mona Marie Herndon, May 28, 1956; children— Susan Gayle, Ann Chaney. BA, Grinnell Coll., 1953; MA, Vanderbilt U., 1955, PhD, 1959. Assoc. prof. phys. sci. Memphis State U., 1958-62; rsch. scientist Oak Ridge Nat. Lab., 1962-92; cons. ORNL, 1992—. Environ. specialist Coop. Sci. Edn. Center, Oak Ridge, 1971-72 Contbr. articles to profl. jours. Radiol. Physics fellow AEC, 1953-55 Fellow AAAS, Tenn. Acad. Sci. (pres. 1971); mem. Assn. Acads. Sci. (sec.-treas. 1972-76, pres. 1977), Sigma Xi. Home: 111 Columbia Dr Oak Ridge TN 37830-7720 Office: Oak Ridge Nat Lab Oak Ridge TN 37831 Personal E-mail: raridon@hotmail.com.

RASCH, ELLEN MYRBERG, cell biology educator; b. Chicago Heights, Ill., Jan. 31, 1927; d. Arthur August and Helen Catherine (Stelle) Myrberg; m. Robert W. E. Rasch, June 17, 1950; 1 son, Martin Karl. PhB with honors, U. Chgo., 1945, BS in Biol. Sci., 1947, MS in Botany, 1948, PhD, 1950. Asst. histologist Am. Meat Inst. Found., Chgo., 1950-51; USPHS postdoctoral fellow U. Chgo., 1951-53, rsch. assoc. dept. zoology, 1954-59; rsch. assoc. Marquette U., Milw., 1962-65, assoc. prof. biology, 1965-68, prof. biology, 1968-75, Wehr disting. prof. biophysics, 1975-78; rsch. prof. biophysics East Tenn. State U., James H. Quillen Coll. Medicine, Johnson City, 1978-94, interim chmn. dept. cellular biophysics, 1986-94, prof. anatomy and cell biology, 1994—. Mem. Wis. Bd. Basic Sci. Examiners, 1971-75, sec. bd., 1973-75. Contbr. articles to various publs. Recipient Rsch. Career Devel. award, 1967-72, Tchg. Excellence and Disting. award Marquette U., 1975, Kreeger-Wolf vis. disting. prof. in biol. sci. Northwestern U., 1979. Mem. Royal Microscopic Soc., Am. Soc. Cell Biology, The Histochem. Soc. (Outstanding Svc. award), Phi Beta Kappa, Sigma Xi. Home: 1504 Chickees St Johnson City TN 37604-7103 Office: East Tenn State Univ Dept Anatomy & Cell Biology PO Box 70582 Johnson City TN 37614-0582 Office Phone: 423-439-2015.

RASCH, KAREN, film editor; b. St. Clair Shores, Mich., Sept. 25, 1946; d. John Peter Jr. and Louise Mabel Rasch. BA in Theater Arts, UCLA, 1968. Freelance prodn. coord., L.A., 1968—73; script supr. IATSE Local # 871, L.A., 1973—78; sound editor, film editor, asst. IATSE Local # 700, L.A., 1978—, bd. dirs., 1991—2004. Mem.: IATSE, Women in Film, Acad. TV Arts and Scis. (Emmy award 1983). Avocations: sailing, skiing, horseback riding, bicycling, skating. Home: 5516 Wiseburn Ave Hawthorne CA 90250 E-mail: raschacts@yahoo.com.

RASCH, STEPHEN CHRISTOPHER, lawyer; b. Cambridge, Mass., Jan. 20, 1962; s. Philip John and Lynne (Whiteman) R.; m. Ellen Rasch; children: Lauren Byrne, Hilary Daniel, Stephen Charles. BA, U. Notre Dame, 1983; JD, U. Tex., 1986. Bar: Tex. 1986, U.S. Dist. Ct. (no., so., west & ea. dists.) Tex., U.S. Ct. Appeals (5th cir.). Law clk. Hon. Joseph T. Sneed U.S. Ct. Appeals (9th cir.), San Francisco, 1986-87; assoc. Thompson & Knight, Dallas, 1987-92, ptnr., 1993—. Mem. Tex. Bar Assn., Dallas Bar Assn., Order of Coif, Phi Beta Kappa. Republican. Roman Catholic. Office: Thompson & Knight 1700 Pacific Ave Ste 3300 Dallas TX 75201-4693 Office Phone: 214-969-1700. E-mail: raschs@tklaw.com.

RASCHE, ROBERT HAROLD, banker, retired economics educator; b. New Haven, June 29, 1941; s. Harold A. and Elsa (Bloomquist) R.; m. Dorothy Anita Bensen, Dec. 28, 1963; children: Jeanette Dorothy, Karl Robert. BA, Yale U., 1963; A.M., U. Mich., 1965, PhD, 1966. Asst. prof. U. Pa., Phila., 1966-72; assoc. prof. econs. Mich. State U., East Lansing, 1972-75, prof., 1975-98, prof. emeritus, 1999—; sr. v.p., dir. rsch. St. Louis Fed. Res. Bank, 1999—. Vis. scholar St. Louis Fed. Res., 1971-72, 76-77, 94-98, San Francisco Fed. Rsch. Bank, 1985, Bank of Japan, Tokyo, 1990; disting. vis. prof. econs. Ariz. State U., Tempe, 1986; rsch. assoc. Nat. Bur. Econ. Rsch., Cambridge, Mass., 1982-91; mem. Mich. Gov. Coun. Econ. Advisers, 1992-96; mem. Shadow Open Market Com., 1973-98. Mem. Am. Econs. Assn. Lutheran. Home: 14531 Radcliffeborough Ct Chesterfield MO 63017-5626 Office: Fed Res Bank St Louis Rsch Divsn PO Box 442 Saint Louis MO 63166-0442 Business E-Mail: rasche@msu.edu.

RASCON, ALFRED, federal agency administrator; B Mgmt. and Liberal Studies. Commd. 2d lt. U.S. Army, ret.; with immingration and naturalization svc. Dept. Justice, with drug enforcement adminstrn., with internat. criminal police orgn.; dir. Selective Svc. System, Arlington, Va., 2001—. Decorated medal of Honor. Office: Selective Svc System 1515 Wilson Blvd Arlington VA 22209-2425

RASCON, ARMANDO, artist; b. Calexico, Calif., Dec. 9, 1956; s. Reynaldo and Maria (Herrera) R. BFA Coll. Creative Studies, U. Calif., Santa Barbara, 1979. Owner Terrain Gallery, San Francisco, 1988—. Guest faculty dept. art U. Calif., Davis, 1988, Calif. Coll. Arts and Crafts, Oakland, 1991, dept. art practice U. Calif., Berkeley, 1995; juror, panelist Artist Trust Fellowship Grants, Visual Arts, Seattle, 1994; lectr. N.Y. Mus. Modern Art, 1995; panelist LEF Found. Orgn. Grants, Cambridge, Mass., 1996, Nev. State Coun. on the Arts Grants, Carson City, 1996, 97; v.p. San Francisco Art Commn., 1996-97; presenter various lectrs., panels, workshops, confs. One-man shows include Randolph Street Gallery, Chgo., 1991, INTAR, N.Y., 1994, San Diego Mus. Contemporary Art, 1997, Blue Star Art Space, San Antonio, 1998, Newark Mus., 2002, Galeria de la Raza, San Francisco, 2003. Bd. dirs. New Langton Arts, San Francisco, 1988-92; vice-chair Art Commn. City of San Francisco, 1997. Recipient Hazel S. Lagerson scholarship U. Calif., Santa Barbara, 1975, fellowship grant in painting Nat. Endowment for Arts, Washington, 1987, Adaline Kent award San Francisco Art Inst., 1994, Goldie award in visual art San Francisco Bay Guardian, 1994; U.S. Mexico Fund for Culture grantee, 1999; Calif. Arts Coun. Artist fellow, 1999. Home and Office: 165 Jessie St Fl 3 San Francisco CA 94105-4010

RASEY, PATRICIA A. writer; b. Napoleon, Ohio, July 3, 1963; d. Bernard E. and Arlene (Wellman) Miller; m. Mark L. Rasey, Nov. 25, 1983; children: Nicholas T., Tory C. Grad HS, Napoleon. Author: (novels) Kiss of Deceit, 2000, Facade, 2000 (Rio, 2001), Eyes of Betrayal, 2003. Personal E-mail: parasey@earthlink.net.

RASH, MARTIN S. health facility administrator; Various adminstrv. and fin. pos. various cmty. hosps.; exec. v.p., COO Cmty. Health Systems, Inc.; co-founder Province Healthcare, Brentwood, Tenn., 1996—, chmn., 1997—. Bd. dirs. Nashville Health Care Coun.; chmn., bd. dirs. Fedn. Am. Hosps. Office: Province Health Care 100 Westwood Pl Ste 400 Brentwood TN 37027

RASH, WAYNE, JR., journalist; b. Erie, Pa., Mar. 2, 1948; s. Wayne and Elizabeth Rash; m. Carolyn Louise Hall, Nov. 25, 1972; children: Julia Leigh, Wayne III, Brittany Lynne. BA, Lynchburg (Va.) Coll., 1980. Dep. commr. revenue City of Lynchburg, 1976-80; prin. Am. Mgmt. Systems, Inc., Arlington, Va., 1984-92; pres. Wayne Rash & Assocs., 1990—; columnist InternetWeek, 1992—2002, mng. editor tech., 1998-2000, editor/events, 2000-01, sr. contbg. editor, 2001—02; contbg. editor CNet/ZDNet, 2001—02, SD Times, 2001—02; sr. analyst Infoworld, 2002—. Mem. review bd. Infoworld, 1990-94, contbg. editor, 2002. Author: The Novell Connection, 1989, The Executive Guide to Local Area Networks, 1989, WordPerfect Office 3.0: The Basics, 1991, Politics on the Nets, 1997; columnist Byte Mag., 1988-92, cons. editor, 1992-95; columnist The Star Ledger, Newark, 1996-98, OS/2 Mag., 1994-96, Windows NT Mag., 1995-96; cons. editor Byteweek, 1988-92, Computer Digest, 1986-91; editor Byte Information Exchange, 1984-2001, The Washington Post Computer Showcase, 1992-93; contbr. The Washington Post, 1994—; editor Tech Report/The Washington Post, 1996-97; sr. tech. editor, columnist InternetWeek, 1996-98; contbg. editor Plane and Pilot, 1995—, CNet.ZDNet, 2001-02, SD Times, 2001-02. Pres. Kings Park West Civic Assn., Fairfax, Va., 1986-88; active Citizens Adv. Coun. on Nat. Space Policy, Studio City, Calif., 1986—; dir. tech. policy Commonwealth Policy Inst. Network. Lt. USN, 1980-84. Mem. Nat. Press Club, Lions (program chmn. Brookville-Timberlake chpt., Lynchburg 1976-80), Aircraft Owners and Pilots Assn., Am. Flying Club, Exptl. Aircraft Assn., Am. Radio Relay League, Va. Amateur Radio Emergency Svc. Episcopalian. Avocations: amateur radio, scuba diving, writing, foreign travel, flying. E-mail: wayne@rash.org.

RASHAD, PHYLICIA, actress, singer, dancer; b. Houston; m. Ahmad Rashad; children: William Bowles, Condola Phylea. Grad. magna cum laude, Howard U., N.Y. Mem. Negro Ensemble Co., founder Phylicia Rashad and Co., 1990. Actor: (plays) The Cherry Orchard, 1973, Zora, 1981, A Raisin in the Sun, 1984, (Off-Broadway) The Duplex, 1972, Zooman and the Sign, 1980—81, Weep Not for Me, 1981, In an Upstate Motel, 1981, Puppetplay, 1983, Sons and Fathers of Sons, 1983; (Broadway plays) Ain't Supposed to Die a Natural Death, 1971, The Wiz, 1975, Dreamgirls, 1981, Into the Woods, 1988, Jelly's Last Jam, 1992—93, A Raisin in the Sun, 2004 (Tony award best actress in a play, 2004, Drama Desk award best actress in a play, 2004); (films) The Broad Coalition, 1972, The Wiz, 1978, Once Upon a Time When We Were Colored, 1995, Free of Eden, 1999, Loving Jezebel, 1999, The Visit, 2000; (TV films) We're Fighting Back, 1981, Uncle Tom's Cabin, 1987 (Cable ACE award nom. best sup. actress, 1987), False Witness, 1989, Polly, 1989, Polly: Comin Home, 1990, Jailbirds, 1991, Hallelujah, 1993, David's Mother, 1994, The Possession of Michael D., 1995, The Babysitters Seduction, 1996, Free of

Eden, 1999, The Old Settler, 2001, Murder, She Wrote: The Last Free Man, 2001; (TV series) One Life to Live, 1983—84, The Cosby Show, 1984—92 (NAACP Image award best actress, 1987, Emmy award nom. best actress, 1985, 1986), Santa Barbara, 1985, Cosby, 1996—2000, (voice) Little Bill, 1999—; (TV guest appearances) The Love Boat, 1985, A Different World, 1988—90, Blossom, 1991, Touched by an Angel, 1994, 2002, The Cosby Mysteries, 1994, In the House, 1995, Bull, 2001. Office: Care Jim Cota Artisits Agency 10000 Santa Monica Blvd Los Angeles CA 90067-7007

RASHID, ISMAIL O. D. historian, educator; s. Osman Dowdu Rashid and Houratu Iyatunde Martin; m. Anifatu Ayodele Gibrill, Dec. 3, 1994; 1 child, Nafisa Iyatunde. BA with honors, U. of Ghana, Accra, 1988; MA, Wilfrid Laurier U., Waterloo, Ont., Can., 1992; PhD, McGIll U., Montreal, 1998. Lectr. McGill U., Montreal, Canada, 1993—98; asst. prof. Vassar Coll., Poughkeepsie, NY, 1998—. Editor: (book) West Africa's Security Challenges: Building Peace in a Troubled Region. Mem.: Can. Assn. for African Studies, African Studies Assn., Am. Hist. Assn. Office: Vassar College 124 Raymond Ave Poughkeepsie NY 12604 E-mail: israshid@vassar.edu.

RASHID, KAMAL A. university administrator, research educator; b. Sulaimania, Kurdistan, Iraq, Sept. 11, 1944; came to U.S., 1972; s. Ahmad Rashid and Habiba M. Muhiedin; m. Afifa B. Sabir, May 23, 1970; children: Niaz K., Neian K., Suzanne K. BS, U. Baghdad, Iraq, 1965; MS, Pa. State U., 1974, PhD, 1978. Lab. instr. U. Baghdad, Iraq, 1966-72; mem. faculty U. Basrah, Iraq, 1978-80, U. Sulaimania, Iraq, 1980-83; sr. rsch. assoc., vis. prof. Pa. State U., University Park, 1983-86, rsch. assoc. prof. dept. biochemistry and molecular biology, 1992-2000; assoc. dir., prof. biotechnology ctr. Utah State U., Logan, 2000—. Dir. Biotech. Tng. Program program Pa. State U., 1989-2000, dir. summer symposium molecular biology, 1991-92; v.p. Cogenic Inc., State College, Pa., 1989-90; cons., spkr. biotech. tng. program developer. Contbr. articles to profl. jours. Iraqi Ministry Higher Edn. scholar. Mem. AAAS, Soc. for Indsl. Microbiology, Am. Soc. Microbiology, Am. Chem. Soc., Environ. Mutagen Soc., Rotary. Avocations: travel, swimming, reading. Home: 2835 N 2050 E Logan UT 84341-8327

RASHID, MUSHFIQUR M, statistician; s. Abul Abdur and Abeda Rashid; m. Nazrin Joarder, Sept. 3, 1981; children: Naim U., Shafique A., Alma A., Raheem A. BA with honors, Rajshahi U., Bangladesh, 1976; MSc in math., Carleton U., Can., 1984; PhD, Ohio State U., 1988. Lectr., asst. prof. Rajshahi U., Bangladesh, 1977—81; asst. prof. SUNY, Albany, NY, 1988—92, Worcester Poly. Inst., Mass., 1992—96; math. statistician Divsn. of Biometrcs II/CDER/FDA, Rockville, Md., 1996—. Reviewer NIH, Bethesda, Md., NSF, Arlington, Va., 1988—; referee Jour. of the Am. Statis. Assn., Alexandria, Va., 1988—. Author: (encyclopedia article) Encyclopedia of Biopharmaceutical Statistics (Recognized as an Internat. Expert, 2000). Pres. Bangladesh Students' Assn., Ohio State U., Columbus, 1986—87. Recipient Excellent Reviewer award, Divsn. of Biostatistics/CDER/FDA, 2000; Merit scholarship, Bangladesh Govt., 1970-1976. Mem.: Am. Statis. Assn., Phi Kappa Phi. Achievements include research in small area estimation; non-inferiority trials; robust analysis of cross-over designs; repeated measures designs; mixed models. Avocations: gardening, travel, swimming. Office: Divsn Biometrics II/CDER/FDA HFD-715 5600 Fishers Ln Rockville MD 20857 Office Phone: 301-827-3121.

RASHID, RICHARD F. information technology executive; Degree with hon., Stanford U., 1974; MSc in Computer Sci., U. Rochester, 1977, PhD in Computer Sci., 1980. Prof. computer sci. Carnegie Mellon U., Pitts., 1979—91; from mem. staff to v.p. rsch. Microsoft, Redmond, Wash., 1991—94, v.p. rsch., 1994—. Office: One Microsoft Way Redmond WA 98052-6399

RASHKIN, MITCHELL CARL, internist, pulmonary medicine specialist; b. N.Y.C., June 1, 1951; m. Karen B. Ohlbaum, Aug. 8, 1982. BS in Computer Sci., U. Mich., 1973, MD, 1977. Diplomate Am. Bd. Internal Medicine, subspecialty Pulmonary Disease, Nat. Bd. Med. Examiners; cert. in critical care medicine Am. Bd. Internal Medicine; instr. Advanced Cardiac Life Support. Intern U. Cin. Med. Ctr., 1977-78, resident, 1978-80, fellowship in pulmonary medicine, 1980-82, dir. med. intensive care unit, 1982—, program dir. critical care medicine, 1989-95, co-dir. pulmonary care unit, 1990-93, dir. respiratory therapy, 1993—, dir med. stepdown unit, 1993—, asst. prof. medicine, 1982-89, assoc. prof. medicine, 1989—. Asst. prof. clin. emergency medicine U. Cin. Hosps., 1988-90, assoc. prof. 1990—; fellowship dir. Pulmonary/Critical Care U. Cin. Med. Ctr., 1995—; mem. numerous hosp. coms. Fellow ACP, Am. Coll. Chest Physicians; mem. Am. Thoracic Soc., Ohio Thoracic Soc. Office: U Cin Med Ctr PO Box 670564 231 Bethesda Ave Rm 6004 Cincinnati OH 45229-2827 E-mail: mitchell.rashkin@uc.edu.

RASHKIND, ALAN BRODY, lawyer; b. NYC, June 6, 1947; s. Julian and Eleanor (Brody) R.; m. Suzette DeBell, July 9, 1972; children: Graham Brody, Douglas Cormack. BA, Randolph-Macon Coll., 1969; JD, U. Va., 1972. Bar: Va. 1972, U.S. Dist. Ct. (ea. dist.) Va. 1972, U.S. Ct. Appeals (4th cir.) 1980, U.S. Supreme Ct. 1992. Assoc. Furniss, Davis and Sachs, Norfolk, Va., 1972-75; ptnr., shareholder Furniss, Davis Rashkind and Saunders P.C. and predecessors, Norfolk, 1976—. Mem. faculty Va. State Bar Law Sch., 2000—, State Bar Professionalism Course, 1996-99; adj. prof. law William and Mary Law Sch., 2003—. Co-author: Virginia Insurance Case Finder, 1st edit., 1994, 2d edit., 2002; contbr. articles to profl. jours. Trustee Randolph-Macon Coll., Ashland, Va., 1991-2003, vice-chair, 2000-03, pres. Soc. of Alumni, 1987-89; trustee, mem. exec. com. Chesapeake Bay Acad., Virginia Beach, Va., 1989—, vice chmn., 1996-2002, chmn., 2002—. Fellow Va. Law Found., Am. Coll. Trial Lawyers; mem. ABA, Va. State Bar Assn., Va. Bar Assn., Fed. Bar Assn., Norfolk-Portsmouth Bar Assn., Virginia Beach Bar Assn., Va. Assn. Def. Attys., Def. Rsch. Inst., Fedn. Def. and Corp. Counsel, Boyd-Graves Conf., (chmn. 1995-97), I'Anson-Hoffman Inn of Court (master of the bench 1987-94). Office: Furniss Davis et al 6160 Kempsville Cir Norfolk VA 23502-3933 Office Phone: 757-461-7100.

RASI, HUMBERTO MARIO, editor, lecturer; b. Buenos Aires, Mar. 23, 1935; came to U.S., 1962, naturalized, 1968; s. Mario and Gertrudis Frida (Heyde) R.; m. Julia Cuchma, Feb. 28, 1957; children: Leroy Mario, Sylvia Beatrice. BA, Instituto Superior del Profesorado, Buenos Aires, 1960; MA, San Jose State U., 1966; PhD, Stanford U., 1971; D honoris causa, U. Peruana Union, Peru, 1999, U. Adventista del Plata, Argentina, 2001, U. Montemorelos, Mex., 2003. Ordained to ministry Seventh-day Adventist Ch., 1980. Mem. faculty Instituto Florida, Buenos Aires, 1957-61; asst. editor Pacific Press Publ. Assn., Mountain View, Calif., 1962-66; asst. prof., assoc. prof. modern langs. Andrews U., 1969-76, prof., dean Sch. Grad. Studies, 1976-78; chief editor internat. publs. Pacific Press Publ. Assn., 1978-83, v.p. editorial devel., 1984-86; assoc. world dir. edn. Gen. Conf. Seventh-day Adventists, Silver Spring, Md., 1987-90, world dir. edn., 1990—2002; ret., 2002. Exec. dir. Inst. for Christian Teaching, 1987—. Author: The Life of Jesus, 3 vols., 1984—85; contbg. editor: Handbook of L.Am. Studies, Libr. of Congress, 1972—82; editor: Comentario Biblico Adventista, 7 vols., 1978—90; co-editor: Meeting the Secular Mind, 1985; founder, editor-in-chief: Coll. and Univ. Dialogue, 1989—, compiler: Christ in the Classroom, 31 vols., 1991—; contbr. articles on modern Hispanic lit., cultural issues, and religious trends. NEH postdoctoral fellow Johns Hopkins U., 1975-76. E-mail: 102555.2215@compuserve.com.

RASIC, JANKO, architect; b. Zagreb, Croatia, Nov. 2, 1938; came to U.S., 1951; m. Carol Van Brunt, May 30, 1968; children: Timothy, Carolyn. BA, Princeton U., 1959, MFA in Arch., 1961. Registered architect, N.Y., N.J. Architect archeol. excavations NYU, 1961-64; archtl. designer Harrison & Abramovitz, N.Y.C., 1964-67; prin. architect Janko Rasic Assocs., N.Y.C., 1969—. Cons. Met. Coun. Housing, N.Y.C., 1968-75, UN Orgn. for Overseas Office Facilities, 2000—. Prin. works include renovation of Henri Bendel bldg., N.Y.C., Coca-Cola bldg., Maxim's Restaurant, Pierre Cardin Gallery and the design of numerous facilities for over forty internat. and domestic banking instns. Mem. mayor's panel architects, N.Y.C., 1968-72; assoc. Real Estate Bd. N.Y., 1978—; mem. N.Y.C. Com. on Water Conservation, 1989—. Recipient design award Hackley Sch., Builders Assn. Westchester, 1970, Nat. Design award Monsanto Corp., 1993; Guggenheim fellow, 1964-65. Mem. AIA (chmn. ednl. facilities com., 1973-74), Adminstrv. Mgmt. Soc. (bd. dirs. 1982-83), Park Assn. N.Y. (design com. 1970), Quogue Assn. (bd. dirs. 1984-86, pres.), Group for South Fork (L.I., N.Y) (bd. dirs. 1986—).

RASIN, RUDOLPH STEPHEN, corporate financial executive; b. Newark, July 5, 1930; m. Joy Kennedy Peterkin, Apr. 11, 1959; children: Rudolph Stephen, James Stenning, Jennifer Shaw Denniston. BA, Rutgers Coll., 1953; postgrad., Columbia U., 1958-59. Mgr. Miles Labs., Inc., 1959-61; devel. mgr. Gen. Foods Corp., White Plains, N.Y., 1961-62; asst. to pres., chmn. Morton Internat. Inc., Chgo., 1962-72; pres. Rasin Corp., Chgo., 1971—, Alliance Brands, LLC. Bd. dirs. Facets Media. Bd. dirs. Geneva Lakes Conservancy, Gatherings Waters Land Trust, Poetry Found. With USAF, 1954—56. Mem. Hinsdale Golf Club, Mid Am. Club (Chgo.), Lake Geneva Country Club, Williams Coll. Club (N.Y.C.), Casino Club (Chgo.), Chgo. Club. Mem. United Ch. of Christ. Home: 64 Snake Rd Lake Geneva WI 53147 Office: Alliance Brands LLC 21 S Clark St Chicago IL 60603

RASKA, KAREL, internist, cardiologist; b. Praha, Czechoslovakia, Feb. 7, 1963; MD, Harvard U., 1989. Diplomate Am. Bd. Internal Medicine, Am. Bd. Cardiology. Intern Mass. Gen. Hosp., Boston, 1989-90, resident in internal medicine, 1990-92; fellow in cardiology Johns Hopkins Hosp., Balt., 1992-95; pvt. practice Morristown, N.J. Mem. ACP, Am. Coll. Cardiology. Office: Morristown Cardiol Assocs 182 South St Morristown NJ 07960-5350

RASKA, KAREL FRANTISEK JULIAN, JR., pathologist, virologist, educator; b. Prague, Czech Republic, May 26, 1939; arrived in U.S., 1965; s. Karel Raska and Helena (Heller) Raskova; m. Jana Dostalova, Feb. 18, 1960; children: Karel III, Francis. MD, Charles U., Prague, 1962; PhD in Biochemistry, Czechoslovak Acad. Scis., Prague, 1965. Diplomate Am. Bd. Pathology (anatomic and clin., immunopathology). Fellow Yale U. Sch. Medicine, New Haven, 1965—66; assoc. Waksman Inst. Microbiology, New Brunswick, NJ, 1966—67; scientist Czech Acad. Sci., Prague, 1967—68; prof. microbiology and pathology Rutgers Med. Sch., Piscataway, NJ, 1968—82; profl. pathology, lab. medicine, microbiology U. Medicine and Dentistry-Robert Wood Johnson Med. Sch., New Brunswick, 1982—; prof., chmn. dept. lab medicine and pathology U. Medicine and Dentistry NJ Med. Sch., Newark, 1989—92; chmn. dept. lab medicine and pathology St. Peter's U. Hosp., New Brunswick, 1992—. Bd. dirs. U. Diagnostic Labs., Piscataway, 1984—96; cons. Newark Beth Israel Med. Ctr., Newark, 1991—2001, E. Orange (NJ) VA Med. Ctr., 1991—; vis. prof. Charles U. Med. Sch., Prague, 1993—94. Contbr. articles to profl. jours., chapters to books. Trustee NJ Organ Sharing Network, Springfield, 1991—2000. Lt. Czechoslovak Air Force, 1962—63. Grantee, NIH, 1975—93, Damon Rynyon-Walter Winchell Cancer Rsch. Fund, 1975, NJ Commn. Cancer Rsch., 1985—86, 1994—95. Mem.: Learned Soc. of the Czech. Republic, Am. Soc. Cell Biologists, Am. Soc. Virology, NJ Soc. Pathology, Assn. Univ. Pathologists, Internat. Acad. Pathology, Am. Assn. Cancer Rsch., Am. Soc. Clin. Immunology, Am. Assn. Immunology, Am. Soc. Investigative Pathology. Avocations: skiing, boating. Office: St Peters Univ Hosp Dept Lab Medicine & Pathology 254 Easton Ave New Brunswick NJ 08901

RASKIN, FRED CHARLES, transportation and utility holding company executive; b. N.Y.C., Sept. 11, 1948; s. Harry and Isabel (Wexler) R.; m. Lorraine Mary Sabourin, Apr. 25, 1974; children: Elizabeth Harris, Alexander Eastwood. BS, Syracuse U., 1970; JD, NYU, 1973. Bar: R.I. 1973, Mass. 1974; CPA, Ohio. Assoc. counsel Fleet Nat. Bank, Providence, 1973-75, Bank of Boston, 1975-78; asst. gen. counsel Eastern Enterprises, Boston, 1978-79, treas., 1979-81, v.p., treas., 1981-84; sr. v.p. fin. Eastern Assoc. Coal Co., Pitts., 1984-87; exec. v.p. Midland Enterprises, Inc., Cin., 1987-90, pres., 1991-98; pres., COO Eastern Enterprises, Weston, Mass., 1998-2000; CEO Woods Hole, Martha's Vineyard and Nantucket Steamship Authority, 2002—. Instr. Boston U., 2001—. Mem. Boston Heart Found., Greater Boston Diabetes Soc. Office: PO Box 284 Railroad Ave Woods Hole MA 02543 Personal E-mail: derfniksar@aol.com.

RASKIN, ILYA, biology professor; b. Moscow, Jan. 16, 1956; Student, Med. Sch. #23, 1973—76; BS, Brandeis U., 1980; PhD, Mich. State U., 1984. Assoc. plant physiologist Shell Agrl. Chem. Co., Modesto, Calif., 1984—86; rsch. biologist agrl. products dept. DuPont Co., Wilmington, Del., 1986—88, prin. investigator cen. R&D dept., 1988—89; assoc. prof. Rutgers U., Ctr. for Agrl. Molecular Biology, New Brunswick, NJ, 1989—94, orif, 1994—2000, prof., 2000—. Lectr. and presenter in field; founder, dir. Phytotech Inc., Monmouth Junction, NJ, 1993—98; founder, chmn., chief scientist Phytomedics Inc., Daton, NJ, 1996—. Ad hoc reviewer: manuscripts for sci. jours. and grants. Named Century Innovator in Botany, Outlook 2000 Issue of U.S. News and World Report, 2000; recipient World Tech. award for biotech., 1999. Mem.: Am. Soc. Plant Physiologists (Charles A. Shull award 1993), Internat. Plant Growth Regulator Soc., Internat. Soc. for Plant Molecular Biology. Office: Rutgers the State U of NJ Cook Coll Biotech Ctr 59 Dudley Rd New Brunswick NJ 08901-8520

RASKIN, JOSHUA R. financial analyst, researcher; b. N.Y.C., June 12, 1973; s. William and Ruth Raskin; m. Melissa Anne Raskin, Nov. 16, 2002. BS in Acctg., Lehigh U., 1995. Auditor Price Waterhouse, N.Y.C., 1995—98; rsch. analyst Morgan Stanley Dean Witter, 1998—99, Lehman Bros., 1999—. Office: Lehman Bros 745 7th Ave New York NY 10019 E-mail: krasjin@lehman.com.

RASKIN, KEITH B. surgeon; Assoc. chief hand surgery NYU Med. Ctr./Hosp. for Joint Diseases, N.Y.C., 1997—. Office: Drs Raskin and Rettig Hand Surgery PC 317 East 34th St New York NY 10016

RASKIN, MICHAEL A. retail company executive; b. N.J., Feb. 26, 1925; s. Harry and Elizabeth Rose (Furstenberg) R.; m. Mary Bonetta Whalen, June 12, 1948; children: Robin Raskin Crowell, Hillary Raskin Maass, Mary Allison Sullivan. AB, Pa. State Coll., 1947; MBA, Columbia U., 1948. With Abraham & Straus, 1949-65; successively mdse. v.p., dir. stores, sr. v.p. Abercrombie & Fitch, N.Y.C., 1966-68; exec. v.p. Dayton's div. Dayton Hudson Corp.; pres. Jos. Magnin Co., San Francisco, 1978—. Chmn., CEO, bd. dirs. Imnar Corp., San Francisco, Info. Please; chmn. exec. com. Acajoe Internat.; bd. dirs. Fortune Almac, Canterbury Cuisine, Cultural Devel. Assocs., HELP Inc., Express Yourself Through Art, Inc., Munsingwear, Inc., B&B Acceptance Corp. Bd. dirs. Amyotrophic Lateral Sclerosis Assn.

RASKIN, MICHAEL NEIL, psychologist, writer; b. Jersey City, Sept. 16, 1945; s. Max and Ruth Shapiro Raskin. BA, Fairleigh Dickinson U., 1968, MA, 1969; PhD, U.S. Internat. U., 1975. Lic. psychologist Maine. Staff psychologist Greystone Park (N.J.) Psychiat. Hosp., 1972—73; dir. psychol. svcs. Tri-County Mental Health Ctr., Lewiston, Maine, 1976—2000; pvt. practice Lisbon Falls, Maine, 2000—. Instr. psychology Fairleigh Dickinson U., Teaneck, NJ, 1969—95, Union Coll., Elizabeth and Cranford, NJ, 1969—95, County Coll. Morris, Dover, NJ, 1969—95, U. Maine, Topsham, Lewiston and Arburn, Maine, 1969—95; pres. Etc-Mfg. Inc, Lisbon Falls, Maine. Author: (textbook) Islands of Certainty in an Ocean of Fear, 2002. Mem.: Maine Soc. Forensic Psychologists, Maine Psychol. Assn. (treas. 1995—). Avocations: writing, needlecrafts, poetry. Home: 752 Newell Brook Rd Durham ME 04222 Office: Michael N Raskin PhD PA 16 Main St Lisbon Falls ME 04252

RASKIN, NEIL HUGH, neurology educator; b. N.Y.C., Jan. 16, 1935; s. Sidney and Bette Raskin; children: Keith, Alexis. AB, Dartmouth U., 1956; MD, Harvard U., 1959. Diplomate Am. Bd. Psychiatry and Neurology. Intern in medicine Bellevue Hosp./Columbia Med. Divsn., N.Y.C., 1959-61; asst. resident, resident, chief resident Neurol. Inst. N.Y., N.Y.C., 1961-64, rsch. fellow in metabolic brain disease, 1964-65; rsch. assoc. NIH, 1966-68; asst. in neurology Coll. Physicians and Surgeons, Columbia U., N.Y.C., 1963-65; chief neurology U.S. Naval Hosp., Phila., 1965-66; sr. surgeon USPHS, Bethesda, Md., 1966-68; asst. prof. neurology U. Calif., San Francisco, 1968-73, assoc. prof. neurology, 1973-79, prof. neurology, 1979—. Attending neurologist Moffitt, San Francisco Gen., Ft. Milley VA Hosps., San Francisco, 1968—; dir. outpatient svcs. Moffitt Hosps., San Francisco, 1977-87; vice chmn. dept. neurology U. Calif., San Francisco, 1977—; vis. prof. U. Mich., U. Oreg., 1991, Cornell U., Harvard U., U. Chgo., Northwestern U., UCLA, 1992, Case Western Res. U., Montreal Neurol. Inst., U. Man., U. B.C., U. N.Mex., Hahnemann U., 1993, St. Louis U., U. Colo., 1994, Dartmouth Med. Sch., U. Pitts., Ind. U., 1996, U. Ark., U. Utah, 1997; invited lectr., Pan-Am. Neurol. Congress, 1975, Headache, Florence, Italy, 1980, World Fedn. Neurology, Kyoto, Japan, 1981, Internat. Symposium on Migraine, London, 1982, Internat. Headache Congress, Munich, 1983, Brazilian Neurol. Congress, Sao Paolo, 1988, Leeds Castle Workshop on Migraine, 1985, World Fedn. Neurology, Buenos Aires, 1997, among others. Author: Headache, 1988, (with O. Appenzeller) Headache: Major Problems in Internal Medicine, 1980; mem. editl. bd. Archives Neurology, 1969—, Neurology, 1969—, New Eng. Jour. Medicine, 1969—, Archives Internal Medicine, 1969—, Rsch. and Clin. Studies in Headache, 1976-81, Comprehensive Therapy, 1976-93, Headache, 1980—, The Medicine Group, 1986—, Cephalalgia, 1986—; contbr. articles to profl. jours. Fellow Am. Acad. Neurology; mem. AAAS, Am. Soc. for Neurochemistry, Am. Neurol. Assn., San Francisco Neurol. Soc., Assn. for Rsch. in Nervous and Mental Diseases, Internat. Assn. for the Study of Pain (panel on headache 1981—), Rsch. Group on Migraine and Headache of the World Fedn. Neurology, Am. Assn. for the Study of Headache (pres. 1994-96, bd. dirs. 1985—), Internat. Headache Soc., Stroke Coun., Am. Heart Assn., Phi Beta Kappa. Office: U Calif San Francisco 505 Parnassus Ave San Francisco CA 94143-0001

RASKIND, LEO JOSEPH, law educator; b. Newark, Nov. 2, 1919; s. Isaac and Fannie (Michelson) R.; m. Mollie Gordon, June 14, 1948; children—Carol Inge, John Richard. AB, UCLA, 1942; MA, U. Wash., 1949; PhD (Fulbright fellow), London Sch. Econs., 1952; LL.B., Yale, 1955. Faculty Stanford Law Sch., 1955-56; lectr., research asso. Yale Law Sch., 1956-58; faculty Vanderbilt Law Sch., 1958-64, Ohio State U. Coll. of Law, 1964-70, U. Minn., 1970-90. Vis. tchr. NYU, 1964, 83, U. Tex., 1964, U. Utah, 1967, So. Meth. U., 1973, U. N.C., 1978, Lyon III, 1984, Kiel U., 1988; vis. prof. Bklyn. Law Sch., 1991—2004, Coll. Law, U. Tenn., Knoxville, 1994, Law Sch., U. Calif., Davis, 1995, U. Minn., 1998. Co-author: Casebook Corporate Taxation, 1978, Casebook Antitrust Law, 2001; mem. adv. bd. BNA jour. Served to capt. AUS, 1942-46. Mem. Am. Law Inst. Office: Bklyn Law Sch 250 Joralemon St Brooklyn NY 11201-3700 Office Phone: 718-780-7911.

RASKY, HARRY, producer, director, writer; b. Toronto, Ont., Can., May 9, 1928; emigrated to U.S., 1955; s. Louis Leib and Pearl (Krazner) R.; m. Ruth Arlene Werkhoven, Mar. 21, 1965; children: Holly Laura, Adam Louis. BA, U. Toronto, 1949, LLD, 1984. Reporter No. Daily News, Kirkland Lake, Ont., 1949; news editor-producer Sta. CHUM, Toronto, 1950, Sta. CKEY, 1951-52; co-founder new documentary dept. CBC, 1952-55; assoc. editor Saturday Night Mag., 1955; producer-dir-writer Columbia Broadcasting Corp., 1955-60, NBC-TV, N.Y.C., 1960-61, ABC-TV, N.Y.C., 1963-69, CBC-TV, Toronto, 1971-78; pres. Harry Rasky Prodns., N.Y.C. and Toronto, 1971—, Maragall Prodns., Toronto, 1978—. Guest lectr. film and TV at various univs., colls.; lectr. U. Toronto, York U. Creator (films) Raskymentary (Emmy 1978, 86, San Francisco Film Festival 1978, Grand prize N.Y. TV-Film Festival 1978, Jerusalem medal 1975), Travels Through Life with Leacock, 1976, The Peking Man Mystery, 1978, Arthur Miller on Home Ground, 1979, (TV films) Hall of Kings (Emmy, 1965), producer, dir., writer (films) Next Year in Jerusalem, 1973, The Wit and World of G. Bernard Shaw, 1974, Tennessee Williams South, 1975, Homage to Chagall-The Colours of Love, 1977 (200 internat. prizes including Oscar nomination Emmy, 1986), Stratasphere, The Mystery of Henry Moore, Karsh: The Searching Eye, (plays) Tiger Tale, 1978, The War Against the Indians, 1992 (Humanities prize, Great Plains Film Festival, Lincoln, Nebr., Golden Hugo award Chgo. Film Festival), Prophecy, 1994 (Golden Angel, honored by Smithsonian, Jerusalem Found.), William Hutt: A Fortunate Man, 1997, Christopher Plummer: King of Players, 1988; author: (memoirs) Nobody Swings on Sunday-The Many Lives of Harry Rasky, 1980, Tennessee Williams a Portrait in Laughter and Lamentation, 1986, Karsh: The Searching Eye, 1986, To Mend the World, 1987, Stratas: An affectionate tribute, 1988, Book 2001: The Song of Leonard Cohen, The Great Teacher, 1989, Robertson-Davies-The Magic Season, 1989; (19 hour retrospective of films including documentaries) Rasky's Gallery: Poets, Painters, Singers and Saints, CBC, 1988, The War Against the Indians, 1993 (12 Internat. awards, adopted Huron Nation title Keeper of the Flame, The Three Harrys, 1999). Mem. YMCA; mem. adv. coun. Univ. Coll./U. Toronto. Decorated Order of Can.; recipient honors City of Venice, Italy, 1970, Golden Eagle, Grand prize N.Y. Intenat. TV and Film Festival of N.Y., 1977, Cert. of Merit, Acad. Motion Picture Arts and Scis., 1984, Red Ribbon, Am. Assn. Film and Video, N.Y.C., 1988, Blue Ribbon, Am. Film Festival, Emmy award, 1990, Moscow award for cultural contbn. to 20th Century USSR, 1991, Retrospective of Films, 1990, Golden Hugo award Chgo. Film Festival, 1993; named Best Non-Fiction Dir., Dirs. Guild Am., N.Y.C. and L.A., 1988, hon. Mayor N.Y.C., 1977, City of Toronto, 1979; Harry Rasky Day named in his honor, City of Toronto, 1988; Moscow Film Festival honoree, 1991; adopted by Huron Indians, named Keeper of the Spirit, adopted by Ojibway Tribe, named Mountain Eagle; presented to Her Royal Majesty Queen Elizabeth, 2002. Mem. Writers Guild Am. (best non-fiction dir. 1986), Dirs. Guild Am., Writers Union Can., Am., Acad. TV Arts and Scis., Assn. Can. TV and Radio Artists, Producers Assn. Can., Acad. Motion Picture Arts and Scis., Overseas Press Club, Acad. of Can. TV and Film Can. (lifetime achievement award 1992), PEN (Toronto), Nat. Arts Club. Jewish. Avocations: swimming, lecturing. Home: 15 Gregory Ave Toronto ON Canada M4W 2X7 Office: care CBC Box 500 Terminal A Toronto ON Canada M5W 1E6 *I have tried to find the positive forces in life and out of them create works of art of a lasting nature with the idea of improving the lives of others. This, plus the adventure of passing on the tradition of my father and his, is my life.*

RASLEAR, THOMAS GREGORY, psychologist; b. N.Y.C., Nov. 25, 1947; s. John W. and Catherine (Turchin) R.; m. Lois T. Keck, Aug. 7, 1971. BS, CCNY, 1969; PhD, Brown U., 1974. Asst. prof. Wilkes Coll., Wilkes-Barre, Pa., 1975-79; rsch. psychologist Walter Reed Amy Inst. Rsch., Washington, 1979-89, sr. rsch. psychologist, 1989-93; engring. psychologist Fed. R.R. Adminstrn., Washington, 1993—. Lectr., presenter in field. Bd. editors Jour. of the Exptl. Analysis of Behaviour, 1989-92; author numerous publs. in field including Proceedings of the XXIV Internat. Congress of Psychology, Vol. 6: Learning; co-author: Understanding Economic Behavior, Animal Learning and Behaviour, 16, Physiology and Behavior, 43, others; contbr. articles to profl. jours.; guest reviewer Jour. of Exptl. Psychology: Animal Behavior Processes, Animal Learning and Behavior, Jour. of Comparative Psychology. Maj. U.S. Army, 1979-89. Rsch. fellow USPHS, 1970-72, N.Y. State Regents fellow, 1969-70. Mem. IEEE, Am. Psychol. Soc. (charter), Am. Psychol. Assn., Acoustical Soc. Am., Ea. Psychol. Assn., AAAS, Sigma Xi, Phi Beta Kappa. Achievements include development and validation of procedures for measuring subjective magnitudes in non-verbal subjects, including non-human animals; testing for toxic effects of drugs and electromagnetic radiation in non-humans; management of research program on human factors and safety in railroad operations; represents the Federal Railroad Adminstration as a human factors expert on the North American Rail Alertness Partnership, the Railroad Safety Advisory Committee (Locomotive Cab Working Conditions Group), The Department of Transportation Human Factors Coordinating Committee, and the Transportation Research Board Human Factors Workshop Planning Committee. Home: 1408 Woodman Ave Silver Spring MD 20902-3905 Office: Fed RR Adminstrn Office of Rsch and Devel RDV-32 400 7th St SW Washington DC 20590-0001

RASMUS, JOHN CHARLES, trade association executive, lawyer; b. Rochester, N.Y., Dec. 27, 1941; s. Harold Charles and Myrtle Leota (Dybevik) R.; m. Elaine Green Reeves, Mar. 19, 1982; children: Kristin, Stuart, Karin. AB, Cornell U., 1963; JD, U. Va., 1966. Bar: Va. 1970, U.S. Supreme Ct. 1974. Spl. agt. Def. Dept., Washington, 1966-70; v.p., adminstrv. officer, legis. rsch. counsel U.S. League Savs. Instns., Washington, 1970-83; asst. to exec. v.p. Nat. Assn. Fed. Credit Unions, 1983-84; sr. fed. adminstrv. counsel, mgr. regulatory & trust affairs Am. Bankers Assn., 1985—. Bd. trustees The

Appraisal Found. Mem. ABA, FBA (disting. svc. award 1980, 82, past chmn. long range planning com., past chmn. coun. fin. instns. and economy), Univ. Club, Exchequer Club, Masons. Home: 303 Kentucky Ave Alexandria VA 22305-1739 Office: Am Bankers Assn 1120 Connecticut Ave NW Washington DC 20036 Business E-Mail: jrasmus@aba.com.

RASMUSON, BRENT J. photographer, graphic artist, lithographer; b. Logan, Utah, Nov. 28, 1950; s. Eleroy West and Fae (Jacobsen) R.; m. Tess Bullen, Sept. 30, 1981 (div. Jan. 2003); children: John, Mark, Lisa. Grad. auto repair and painting sch., Utah State U. Pre-press supr., ptnr. Herald Printing Co., Logan, 1969—80; profl. drummer, 1971-75; owner, builder auto racing engines Valley Automotive Specialties, 1971-76; exec. sec. Herald Printing Co., 1980—89; owner Brent Rasmuson Photography, Logan, 1986—, Temple Picture Classics, Logan, 1996—. Author photo prints of LDS temples: Logan, 1987, 95, 98, 2000, Manti, 1989, 2000, Jordan River, 1989, 96, 98, 2000, Provo, 1990, 2001, Mesa, Ariz., 1990, 96, Boise, Idaho, 1990, 96, 2000, Salt Lake Temple, 1990, 96, 2001, Idaho Falls, 1991, 94, 2000, St. George, 1991, 93, 2000, Portland, Oreg., 1991, 96, 97, 2000, LA, 1991, 96, 97, 2000, Las Vegas, Nev., 1991, Seattle, 1992, Oakland, Calif., 1993, 94, Ogden, 1992, 2001, Bountiful, 2002, Mt. Timpanogos, 2002; author photo print: Statue of Angel Moroni, 1994; author photos used to make neckties and watch dials of LDS temples: Salt Lake, Manti, Logan, LA, Oakland, Seattle, Las Vegas, Mesa, Portland, St. George, Jordan River, scenic tie Mammoth Hot Springs in Yellowstone Park, 1995; landscape scenic photographs featured in Best of Photography Ann., 1987-89, also in calendars and book covers; author photo print of Harris Rsch., Inc. Internat. Hdqrs. (recipient 1st prize nat. archtl. photo competition); designer several bus. logos. Mem.: Internat. Freelance Photographers Orgn., Assoc. Photographers Internat. Platform Assn., Nat. Air and Space Soc., Nat. Trust Hist. Preservation. Republican. Mem. Lds Ch. Avocations: automobiles, travel, reading, coin collecting/numismatics, stamp collecting/philately. Home and Office: 66 W 100 N Logan UT 84321-4506 Office Phone: 435-755-0668.

RASMUSON, EDWARD BERNARD, banker; b. Aug. 27, 1940; s. Elmer Edwin and Lile Vivian Rasmuson; m. Cathryn Elaine Robertson, Sept. 11, 1969; children: Natasha Ann, Laura Lile, David Edward. BA, Harvard U., 1962. Mgmt. trainee Brown Brothers Harriman, 1963, Chem. NY, 1964; asst. cashier Nat. Bank Alaska, Anchorage, 1964—66, asst. v.p., 1966—68, v.p., 1968—73, pres., 1973—85, chmn. bd. dirs., 1986—2001; chmn. adv. bd. Wells Fargo Bank, Anchorage, 2001—02. Bd. regents U. Alaska, 1975—89; mem. Rasmuson Found., 1973—; past trustee Sheldon Jackson Coll.; past pres. Anchorage United Way; Hon. Consul of Sweden State of Alaska. Mem.: World Bus. Coun., Young Pres.'s Orgn., Harvard Club (N.Y.C.), Rainier Club, Seattle Yacht Club, Wash. Athletic Club, Metropolitan Club, Pioneers Club Am., Explorers Club, Elks, Rotary. Office: Wells Fargo Bank Alaska PO Box 196127 Anchorage AK 99519

RASMUSSEN, CAREN NANCY, hospital executive; b. Ft. Riley, Kans., July 7, 1950; d. Stanley Junior and Katherina Wilhelmina R. AAS, Grand Rapids Jr. Coll., 1970; BS, U. Md., 1977; MS, Johns Hopkins U., 1997. Cert. profl. contracts mgr. Contract specialist Kadena Air Base, Okinawa, 1979-81; med. sec. Walter Reed Army Med. Ctr., Washington, 1970-72, sec. procurement, 1972-76, contract specialist, 1976-79, 81-84, procurement analyst, 1984—, sr. contracting specialist, 1988—2001, Nat. Cancer Inst., 2001—. Fellow NAFE; mem. Nat. Contract Mgmt. Assn. Democrat. Avocations: photography, stamp collecting/philately, gardening, travel. Home: 18632 Clovercrest Cir Olney MD 20832-3057 Office: Nat Cancer Inst Rsch Contracts br Rockville MD 20852

RASMUSSEN, EARL R, lumber company and home improvement retail executive; CFO Menard Inc, Eau Claire, Wis. Office: Menard Inc 4777 Menard Dr Eau Claire WI 54703-9625

RASMUSSEN, HARRY PAUL, horticulture and landscape educator; b. Tremonton, Utah, July 18, 1939; s. Peter Y. and Lorna (Nielsen) R.; m. Mary Jane Dalley, Sept. 4, 1959; children: Randy Paul, Lorianne, Trent Dalley, Rachelle. AS, Coll. of So. Utah, 1959; BS, Utah State U., 1961; MS, Mich. State U., 1962, PhD, 1965. Rsch. scientist Conn. Agr. Expt. Sta., New Haven, 1965-66; rschr., instr. Mich. State U., East Lansing, 1966-81; chmn. dept. horticulture and landscape architecture Wash. State U., Pullman, 1981-88; dir. Utah Agrl. Expt. Sta. Utah State U., 1988—. Assoc. v.p. Utah State U., Logan, 1992-99, 2002—. Contbr. articles to profl. jours., chpts. to books. Mem. bd. control YMCA, Lansing, Mich., 1976; mem. coun. Boy Scouts Am., Lansing, 1980; stake pres. Ch. of Jesus Christ of Latter Day Saints, Lansing, 1973-81. NDEA fellow, 1961-65. Fellow Am. Soc. Horticulture Sci.; mem. AAAS, Scanning Electron Microscopy (chmn. plant sect. 1976-83, chmn. exptl. sta. com. on orgn. and policy 1996-97). Home: 1949 N 950 E Logan UT 84341-1813 Office: Utah State U 225 Agr Sci Bldg Logan UT 84322-0001

RASMUSSEN, HOWARD, retired medical educator; b. Harrisburg, Pa., Mar. 1, 1925; s. Frederick and Faith (Elliott) R.; m. Jane Claire Spence, June 10, 1950; children: Gail, Paul, Jane, Craig. AB in Chemistry and Physics, Gettysburg Coll., 1948; MD, Harvard U., 1952; PhD in Biochemistry and Physiology, Rockefeller U., 1959; DSc, Gettysburg Coll., 1964. Asst. prof. physiology Rockefeller U., N.Y.C., 1959-61; assoc. prof. biochemistry U. Wis., Madison, 1961-64; prof. sch. medicine U. Pa., Phila., 1964-75, Benjamin Rush prof. biochemistry, 1964-75, prof. biochemistry and biophysics, 1964-76, chmn. dept. biochemistry, 1964-70, prof. pediatrics, 1975-76; Guggenheim fellow Cambridge U., 1971-72; prof. medicine and cell biology sch. medicine Yale U., New Haven, 1976-93; prof. medicine, surgery, cell biology, anatomy Med. Coll. Ga., Augusta, 1993-2000, Dir. SCOT Urolithiasis Ctr., Sch. Medicine, Yale U., 1977-82, chief divsn. endocrinology, 1980-86, dir. med. scientist tng. program, 1983-91; dir. Inst. for Molecular Medicine and Genetics, Med. Coll. Ga., 1993-98; Wellcome vis. prof. U. Va., Richmond, 1988; Klenk lectr. U. Koln, West Germany, 1989; Lily lectr. XI Internat. Conf. Calcium Regulation, Florence, Italy, 1992. Author: Calcium and cAMP as Synarchic Messengers, 1981, The Physiological and Cellular Basis of Metabolic Bone Disease, 1984. Bd. trustees Gettysburg Coll., 1985-93. Staff sgt. U.S. Army, 1942-44. Recipient Cotlove award Acad. Clin. Lab. Physicians and Scientists, 1993, Andre Lichtwitz prize, 1971. Fellow AAAS. Avocations: opera, hiking.

RASMUSSEN, JOHN OSCAR, nuclear research scientist; b. St. Petersburg, Fla., Aug. 8, 1926; s. John Oscar and Hazel (Ormsby) R.; m. Louise Brooks, Aug. 27, 1950; children— Nancy, Jane, David, Stephen. BS, Calif. Inst. Tech., 1948; PhD, U. Calif. at Berkeley, 1952; MA (hon.), Yale U., 1969. Mem. faculty dept. chemistry U. Calif., Berkeley, 1952-68, 73-91, prof. chemistry, 1971-91, ret., 1991, mem. research staff, 1952-68; sr. rsch. assoc. Lawrence Berkeley Nat. Lab., 1972—. Prof. chemistry Yale U. 1969-73; asso. dir. Yale Heavy Ion Accelerator Lab., 1970-73; vis. research prof. Nobel Inst. Physics, Stockholm, 1953; vis. prof. Inst. Nuclear Sci. U. Tokyo, 1974, Fudan U., Shanghai, 1979, hon. prof., 1984. Contbr. articles to profl. jours. Served with USN, 1944-46. Recipient E.O. Lawrence Meml. award AEC, 1967; NSF sr. postdoctoral fellow Niels Bohr Inst., Copenhagen, 1961-62, NORDITA fellow, 1979, Guggenheim Meml. fellow, 1973, Alexander von Humboldt sr. rsch. fellow Tech. U. Munich, 1991. Fellow Am. Phys. Soc., AAAS; mem. Am. Chem. Soc. (Nuclear Applications in Chemistry award 1976), Fedn. Am. Scientists (chmn. 1969). Office: Lawrence Berkeley Nat Lab MS 70 319 Berkeley CA 94720-0001

RASMUSSEN, MARILYN, state legislator; b. Seattle; m. Don Rasmussen; 7 children. Livestock and timber farmer; mem. Wash. Senate, Dist. 2, Olympia, 1992—; chair agr. and rural econ. devel. com. Wash. Senate, mem. commerce, trade, housing and fin. instns. com.; mem. edn. com. Wash. Legislature, Olympia, mem. ways and means capital subcom., mem. vets. and mil. affairs com., mem. Agy. Coun. on Coord. Transp., mem. Nat. Conf. State Legislatures. Mem. Eatonville Sch. Bd., 1980-87; bd. dirs. Marymount Assn. for Sr. Housing, Nisqually River Interpretive Ctr. Found.; mem. Rocky Mountain Elk Found.; mem. adv. com. Women of Vision; mem. Gov.'s Prayer Breakfast Com.; mem. adv. com. Harborview Vis.; past bd. dirs. Good Samaritan Mental Health Bd.; eucharistic min. Our Lady of Good Counsel. Mem. Wash. State Dairy Fedn., Kiwanis (Spanaway-Parkland), Am. Agri-Women, Wash. Women for the Survival Agr., Wash. Cattlemen's Assn., Wash. Cattlewomen's Assn., South Pierce County C. of C., Vladivostok Sister City Assn., Am. Tree Farm Sys., Tacoma Sportsmen's Club, Delta Kappa Gamma. Democrat. Office: 409 Legislative Bldg Olympia WA 98504-0001

RASMUSSEN, MARK WILLIAM, restaurant owner and chef; b. Wausau, Wis., Dec. 29, 1954; s. William David and Victoria Ann Rasmussen; m. Elizabeth Basatemor, Sept. 7, 1996; 1 child, Erik Ates; m. Nancy Marie Brossa, Oct. 1976 (div. May 1979); children: Maegan Marie, Temperance Kim. AS, Cleve. Inst. Tech., 1991. Chef Kona Surf Hotel, Kailua, Hawaii, 1974—76, Rosalies Italian Restaurant, Hot Springs, Ariz., 1977—79; property mgr. Monarch Realty, Eatontown, NJ, 1979—93; chef, owner Veggie Works Inc., Belmar, NJ, 1994—. Author: Veggie Works Vegan Cookbook, 2001. Avocations: guitar, golf, writing. Home: 114 Riveredge Rd Tinton Falls NJ 07724-2737 Office: Veggie Works Inc 817 Belmar Plaza Belmar NJ 07724 Office Phone: 732-280-1141. E-mail: mwrasmussen@hotmail.com.

RASMUSSEN, NICHOLAS ROBERTS, insurance company executive; b. Medford, Oreg., Aug. 20, 1946; s. George Paul and Mary Lee (Roberts) R.; m. Gail Iown Cunningham, Mar. 28, 1970 (div. Jan. 1988); 1 child, Nicole Roberts; m. Julia Spencer Tucker, May 7, 1988. BS, Stanford U., 1968, MBA, 1974. C.P.A., Tex. Investment analyst Am. Gen. Capital Mgmt. Inc., Houston, 1974-75; asst. dir. planning Am. Gen. Corp., Houston, 1975-76, asst. to pres., 1976-78, 2d v.p., asst. treas., 1978-80, v.p., asst. treas., 1980-81, v.p., treas., 1981-83, sr. v.p., treas., 1983-85, exec. v.p. investments, 1986-88, vice chmn fin. policy, 1988—, CFO, 1999—. Dir. Brookstone Co., 1987—. Dir., treas. San Jacinto Girl Scouts U.S.A., 1976—, bd. dirs., 1981—, mem. audit com., 1981—, investment com., 1981—. Served with USN, 1969-72. Fellow Life Mgmt. Inst.; mem. Am. Inst. C.P.A.s, Tex. Soc. C.P.A.s, Stanford Bus. Sch. Alumni Assn. (bd. dirs. 1983—) Home: 5139 Institute Ln Houston TX 77005 Office: Am Gen Corp 2929 Allen Pkwy Houston TX 77019-7100

RASMUSSEN, RICHARD ROBERT, lawyer; b. Chgo., July 5, 1946; s. Robert Kersten Rasmussen and Marisa Bruna Batistoni; children: Kathryn, William. BS, U. Oreg., 1970, JD, 1973. Bar: Oreg. 1973. Atty. U.S. Bancorp, Portland, Oreg., 1973-83, 95-00, v.p. law divsn., 1983-87, mgr. law divsn., 1983-95, sr. v.p., 1987-95, mgr. corp. sec. divsn., 1990—95; exec. v.p., gen. counsel, sec. West Coast Bancorp, Lake Oswego, Oreg., 2000—. Mem. editl. bd. Oreg. Bus. Law Digest, 1979-81, Oreg. Debtor/Creditor newsletter, 1980-84; contbr. articles to profl. jours. Chmn. mgmt. com. YMCA of Columbia-Willamette, Portland, 1978-79; bd. dirs. Camp Fire, 1988-89, v.p., 1990-91; bd. dirs. Portland Repertory Theatre, 1994-96. Mem.: ABA, Am. Bankers Assn. (bank counsel com. 1996—99), Multnomah County Bar Assn., Oreg. State Bar Assn. (chmn. corp. counsel com. 1979—81, debtor/creditor sect. 1982—83, sec. com. on sects. 1982—83, award of merit, debtor/creditor sect. 2003), Beta Gamma Sigma. Avocations: mountain climbing, white-water rafting, tennis, basketball. Office: West Coast Bancorp 5335 Meadows Rd Ste 201 Lake Oswego OR 97035

RASMUSSEN, ROBERT CARL, lawyer; b. Oelwein, Iowa, Aug. 22, 1949; s. Leo Lyle and Gloria Servoin (Ballinger) R.; m. Marlene Francis Schneider, June 30, 1990. BSBA, The Am. U., 1971; JD, U. Iowa, 1974. Bar: Iowa 1974, Fla. 1975. Dir. edn. mktg. svcs. div. Nat. Student Mktg. Corp., Washington, 1968-70; dir. youth activity div. and spl. projects Distributive Edn. Clubs of Am., Falls Church, Va., 1970-72; assoc. Holland & Knight, Tampa, Fla., 1974-78, ptnr., 1979-83; founding ptnr. Glenn, Rasmussen, Fogarty & Hooker, P.A., Tampa, 1983—. Ex-officio mem. Pres.'s Task Force on Edn. and Tng. for Minority Bus. Enterprises, Washington, 1971-72. Chmn. Leadership Tampa Alumni, 1992; founding chmn. Tampa Heights Neighborhood Revitalization Alliance, 1991-93; mem. Regional Telephone Svc. Steering Com., Tampa, 1991. Recipient Golden Eagle award Am. Acad. of Achievement, 1968. Mem. Fla. Bar, Iowa Bar Assn., Hillsborough County Bar Assn., Greater Tampa C. of C., Tampa Club, Harbour Island Athletic Club,Palma Ceia Golf and Country Club. Republican. Methodist. Office: Glenn Rasmussen Fogarty & Hooker PA 100 S Ashley Dr Ste 1300 Tampa FL 33602-5309

RASMUSSEN, ROBERT DEE, retired real estate appraiser; b. Lincoln, Kans., Dec. 24, 1936; s. Sam and Kristena (Andersen) R.; m. Beverly Bert Rowden, Mar. 22, 1959; children: Robert Denis, Kay Lynn. B Gen. Edn., U. Nebr., 1965; MA, Ariz. State U., 1970. Cert. gen. real estate appraiser, Fla. Commd. USAF, 1957, advanced through grades to col., 1978, fighter pilot various locations, 1956-75, comdr. 59th Tactical Fighter Squadron, 1975-77, chief Europe/Nato Plans Washington, 1978-80, vice-comdr. 474th Tactical Fighter Wing Nellis AFB, Nev., 1980-81; chief of plans U.S. European Command Joint Chiefs of Staff, Stuttgart, Germany, 1981-84; dir. joint matters Hdqrs. Tactical Air Command USAF, Langley AFB, Va., 1984-86, ret., 1986; appraiser, cons. Appraisal House Inc., Ft. Walton Beach, Fla., 1987-94; gen. appraiser Niceville, Fla., 1994-2000; ret., 2000. Dir. U.S. Power Squadrons, Ft. Walton Beach, 1988-90. Decorated Defense Superior Svc. Medal, Legion of Merit, D.F.C. Mem. Ret. Officers Assn., Am. Assn. Ind. Investors, Porsche Club Am. (v.p. Germany region 1983-84, pres. North Fla. region 1989, 97, dir. 1988-94), Mid-Bay Rotary Club (charter, dir. 1995-96). Avocations: boating, fishing, sports cars. Home: 2421 Duncan Dr Niceville FL 32578-2915

RASMUSSEN, STEPHEN S. diversified financial services company executive; BS in Bus. Adminstrn., U. Iowa. Underwriting & mktg. Allied, 1974—82, regional v.p., pacific coast regional office, 1982—86, v.p., underwriting, 1986—98, exec. v.p., product mgmt., 1998—2001; pres., COO CalFarm Ins., 2001—03; pres., COO, property casualty ins. opers. Nationwide, Allied and Farmland, 2003—. Trustee Grand View Coll.; 2002 Walk corp. chair, ctrl. Iowa chpt. Juvenile Diabetes Rsch. Found. Office: Nationwide One Nationwide Pl Columbus OH 43215-2220

RASMUSSEN, THOMAS VAL, JR., lawyer, small business owner; b. Salt Lake City, Aug. 11, 1954; s. Thomas Val and Georgia (Smedley) R.; m. Donita Gubler, Aug. 15, 1978; children: James, Katherine, Kristin. BA magna cum laude, U. Utah, 1978, JD, 1981. Bar: Utah 1981, U.S. Dist. Ct. Utah 1981, U.S. Supreme Ct. 1985, U.S. Ct. Appeals (10th cir.) 1999. Atty. Salt Lake Legal Defender Assn., Salt Lake City, 1981-83, Utah Power and Light Co., Salt Lake City, 1983-89; of counsel Hatch, Morton & Skeen, Salt Lake City, 1989-90; ptnr. Morton, Skeen & Rasmussen, Salt Lake City, 1991-94, Skeen & Rasmussen, Salt Lake City, 1994-97; pvt. practice, Salt Lake City, 1997—. Co-owner, developer Handi Self-Storage, Kaysville, Utah, 1984-93; instr. bus. law Brigham Young U., Salt Lake City, 1988-90. Adminstrv. editor Jour. Contemporary Law, 1980-81, Jour. Energy Law and Policy, 1980-81. Missionary Ch. of Jesus Christ of Latter-Day Sts., Brazil, 1973-75. Mem. Utah, Salt Lake County Bar Assn., Intermountain Miniature Horse Club (pres. 1989, 2d v.p. 1990), Phi Eta Sigma, Phi Kappa Phi, Beta Gamma Sigma. Avocations: tennis, scuba diving, showing horses, travel, collecting art. Home: 3094 Whitewater Dr Salt Lake City UT 84121-1561 Office: 4659 Highland Dr Salt Lake City UT 84117-5137 Office Phone: 801-484-3000.

RASMUSSON, THOMAS ELMO, lawyer; b. Lansing, Mich., Dec. 5, 1941; s. William and Mary Jane Rasmusson; m. Alice Wolo, Oct. 1, 1989; children: David, Jane. BA, Mich. State U., 1963; JD, U. Mich., 1966; MA, Fletcher Sch., 1988. Bar: Mich. 1967, U.S. Ct. Appeals (6th cir.) 1982, U.S. Supreme Ct. 1982. Law clk. to presiding justice Mich. Supreme Ct., Lansing, 1966-68; asst. prosecutor Ingham Prosecutor's Office, Lansing, 1968-72, criminal divsn. chief, 1972-75; spl. prosecutor Ingham County, Lansing, 1975-76; pvt. practice Lansing, 1975—. Trustee Lansing Cmty. Coll., 1998-; Fulbright prof. U.S. Info. Svc., Washington, 1986-88; cons. U.S. AID, Monrovia, Liberia, 1989-90; contractor U.S. Dept. of State, Monrovia, 1987-90; adj. prof. Cooley Law Sch., Lansing, 1991-97; rsch. assoc. program on negotiation Harvard U., Cambridge, 1987-88; mem. Ct. Rule Com., Lansing, 1979-81; dir. Capital Area Sch. Employees Credit Union, 1996-, Educated Solutions, LLC, 2000-. Editor: Jurisprudence and System Science, 1986, Interactive Systems, 1988, (series) Liberian Law Reports, 1988-90; contbr. articles to profl. jours. Chair fin. Ingham Rep. Party, Lansing, 1994-98, mem. exec. com., 1994—; mem. 8th Congl. Com., Lansing, 1997—; trustee Lansing C.C., 1998—; dir. Case Credit Union, Lansing, 1996; dir. MyWebConnect ISP, Lansing, 1998—. Recipient Outstanding Svc. award U.S. Edn. Found., 1987; grantee U.S. Edn. Found., 1987. Mem. AAAS, State Bar Mich. Republican. Methodist. Avocations: physics, history of science. Office: Rasmusson and Assoc 2201 E Grand River Lansing MI 48912 Home: 1713 Willow Creek Dr Lansing MI 48917-7815

RASOR, DINA LYNN, investigator, journalist; b. Downey, Calif., Mar. 21, 1956; d. Ned Shaurer and Genevieve Mercia (Eads) R.; m. Thomas Taylor Lawson, Oct. 4, 1980. BA in Polit. Sci., U. Calif., Berkeley, 1978. Editorial asst. ABC News, Washington, 1978-79; researcher Pres.'s Commn. on Coal, Washington, 1979; legis. asst. Nat. Taxpayers Union, Washington, 1979-81; founder, dir. Project on Mil. Procurement, Washington, 1981-89; investigative reporter Lawson-Rasor Assocs., El Cerrito, Calif., 1990-92; pres., CEO, investigator Bauman & Rasor Group, El Cerrito, Calif., 1993—. Author: The Pentagon Underground, 1985; editor: More Bucks, Less Bang, 1983; contbr. articles to profl. jours. Recipient Sigma Delta Chi Outstanding Leadership award Soc. Profl. Journalists, 1986; named to register Esquire Mag., 1986, Nat. Jour., 1986. Mem. United Ch. Christ.

RASPBERRY, BRENDA, pre-school educator; d. Brenda Raspberry. Student, Ind. U.; diploma in early childhood edn. and sign lang., Monterey (Calif.) Pennisula Coll., 1988; diploma in elem. behavior mgmt., Chapman Coll., Calif., 1980; diploma in child devel. and edn., Cabrillo Coll., Calif., 1997; diploma in computer bus. and data entry, Regional Occupl. Program, Calif., 1999, diploma in early childhood edn. and devel., Hartnell Coll., 2000. Cert. parent educator. Interpreter for deaf Monterey County Interpreting Svcs., Salinas, Calif., 1996—; interpreter Fin. Adminstrv. Secretarial and Transl. Svc., Salinas, Calif., 1998; assistance to adminstrs., sec. Montery County Broadcasting, Inc., Salinas, Calif., 1998—99. Actor: (plays) Yesterday and Today. Pub. rels. Mayor Richard G. Hatcher, Gary, Ind., 1974; spl. adv. Monterey County. Avocations: writing, painting.

RASSBACH, HERBERT DAVID, marketing executive; b. Glen Ridge, N.J., Mar. 23, 1944; s. Merrill Augustus and Ruth Bruce (Sims) Rassbach. BS, Del. State Coll., 1971; MBA, Drexel U., 1979. Prodn. planning mgr. Standard Brands Chem. Industries, Edison, N.J., 1971-74; order fulfillment mgr. P Q Corp., Valley Forge, Pa., 1974-77, mkt. devel. project mgr., 1977-82; market mgr. Willson Safety Products, Reading, Pa., 1983-85; pres. HDR Group, mktg. and mgmt. cons., Wayne, Pa., 1986—. Guest speaker Wharton Sch. U. Pa., 1988, Temple U., Phila., 1989, Wharton Club, 1995. Media comms. bd. Upper Merion Twp., 1989, vice-chmn., 1990, 1992—, chmn., 1991, committeeman, 1977. Mem. Drexel U. Alumni Assn. (v.p. Montgomery County chpt. 1988-91), Alpha Kappa Mu, Delta Mu Delta. Avocations: golf, tennis, running, travel, american history. Home: 635 Mallard Rd Wayne PA 19087-2346 Office: HDR Group PO Box 2164 Southeastern PA 19399-2164 E-mail: hdrassbach@hdrgroup.com.

RASSIDAKIS, GEORGE Z. pathologist, researcher; b. Athens, Greece, Jan. 12, 1968; s. Zacharias M Rassidakis and Ioanna A Vardava. MD, PhD, U. of Patras Med. Sch., Greece, 1991. Pathologist Greek Min. of Health, Greece, 1997. Resident in pathology U. of Athens, Athens, Greece, 1992—96; clin. fellow in cytopathology Sotiria Gen. and Chest Dis. Hosp., Athens, Greece, 1996—97; attending pathologist 401 Army Hosp., Athens, Greece, 1998—99; rschr. in hematopathology MD Anderson Cancer Ctr., Houston, 2000—. Rsch. fellow Karolinska Hosp., Stockholm, 1998—98. Author: scientific articles (medical journals) Mechanisms of Lymphomagenesis and Prognostic Implications. Scholar ICRETT fellowship, UICC, 1997, Alexander S. Onassis Found. Scholarship, Alexander S. Onassis Found., 2000—02. Mem.: Am. Soc. of Hematology, US and Can. Acad. of Pathology, Am. Assn. for Cancer Rsch. (assoc.). Achievements include research in Lymphoma Biology And Prognosis. Office: MD Anderson Cancer Ctr 1515 Holcombe Blvd Houston TX 77030 E-mail: gzrassidakis@mail.mdanderson.org.

RASSIN, DAVID KEITH, nutrition educator, researcher; b. Liverpool, Eng., Dec. 1, 1942; came to U.S., 1974; s. Meyer and Ella Rosetta (House) R.; m. Mildred Glennda McConnell, Feb. 5, 1965; children: Meya Glynne, Keith David, Heather Kareen. AB, Columbia U., 1965; PhD, CUNY, 1974. Rsch. scientist IV Inst. Basic Rsch. in Mental Retardation, Staten Island, N.Y., 1977-79, rsch. scientist V, 1979-80; with U. Tex. Med. Br., Galveston, 1980—, dir. devel. nutrition and metabolism, 1980—, prof. perinatal pediatrics, 1985—, dir. office faculty devel. and comm., 1991—, asst. dean office continuing edn., 1999—. Editor: Basic and Clinical Aspects of Nutrition and Brain Development, 1987, Neural Control of Reproductive Function, 1988; mem. editl. bd. Jour. Neurosci. Rsch., Internat. Jour. Devel. Neurosci. Mem. Soc. Pediatric Rsch., Am. Inst. Nutrition, Am. Soc. for Neurochemistry, Soc. for Neurosci., Am. Soc. Pharmacology and Exptl. Therapeutics, Internat. Soc. for Devel. Neurosci., Am. Soc. for Clin. Nutrition. Avocation: tennis. Home: 2801 Beluche Dr Galveston TX 77551-1509 Office: U Tex Med Br Dept Pediatrics Rte 44 Br Galveston TX 77555-0001 Office Phone: 409-772-1139. Business E-Mail: drassin@utmb.edu.

RASSMAN, JOEL H. real estate company executive, accountant; b. N.Y.C., May 16, 1945; BBA, CUNY, 1967. CPA, N.Y. Ptnr. Ernst & Young (formerly Kenneth Leventhal & Co.), N.Y.C., 1967-84; exec. v.p., CFO, bd. dirs. Toll Bros., Inc., Huntingdon Valley, Pa., 1984—. Mem. AICPA, N.Y. State Soc. CPA's.

RASSMAN, WILLIAM R. plastic surgeon; BS in Biology, L.I. U., 1962; MD, Med. Coll. Va., 1966. Diplomate Am. Bd. Surgery, lic. Calif., Fla., N.Y., Hawaii, Va., Pa., Ill., Nev., Ga., N.C., Wash., Colo., Md., N.J. Intern U. Minn., 1966—67; fellow in cardiovascular surgery Cornell Med. Ctr., 1968—69, resident in orthop. surgery, 1967—69; resident in gen. vascular surgery Dartmouth Med. Ctr., 1971—73; founder, mng. ptnr. N.E. Kingdom Surg. Assocs., 1973—79; staff surgeon, bus. advisor Hilo Med. Group, 1979—83; pres. Bosley Med. Group, 1988—90; CEO IntelliMED Corp., 1984—; pres., founder RW2 Med. Group, 2001—; founder, pres. Maven Technologies, 2001—, New Hair Inst. Med. Group, L.A., 1991—. Cons. IBM, Hosp. Corp. Am., Control Data Corp., E.I. DuPont; lectr. in field. Achievements include patents for hair transplant harvesting device and method for its use; development of and design of heart valves, intra-aortic balloon pump and balloon technology, safety chamber for intra-aortic balloon; and design pulsatile assistance device; design of sophisticated commercial point of transaction clinical information systems for surgery; software scheduling system with application in real time. Office: 9911 W Pico Blvd Ste 301 Los Angeles CA 90035*

RASTEGAR-DJAVAHERY, NADER E. private equities investor; b. Tehran, Iran, May 12, 1953; came to U.S., 1982; s. Morteza and Rabe'eh (Baghai-Kermani) R.; m. Soheila Gharai, Apr. 1979; children: Roya Z., Scheherazade B., Maryam A. BSc, U. Wis., 1976; MBA, Iran Ctr. Mgmt. Studies, 1979. Pres. Shahgard Indsl. Co., Tehran, 1977, Renafa, Inc., Atlanta, 1984—. Contbr. articles to various publs. Active various profl., historical, philatelical and environ. socs. and groups. Lt. Iranian Armed Forces, 1977-78. Avocations: historical research, social welfare, environmental issues, philatelics.

RASTETTER, WILIAM H. biotechnology company executive; BS in Chemistry, MIT; MA, PhD in Chemistry, Harvard U. Faculty MIT, Cambridge, Mass., 1975—82; scientist/rschr. biocatalysis and chem. scis. groups Genentech, 1982—84, dir. corp. ventures, 1984—86; CEO IDEC Pharms. Corp., San Diego, 1986—, pres., 1986—2002, CFO, 1988—93, dir., 1986—, chmn. bd. dirs., 1996—. Dir. Argonaut Technologies, Inc., Illumina, Inc. Office: IDEC Pharmaceuticals Corp 3030 Callan Rd San Diego CA 92121

RASTOGI, ANIL KUMAR, medical device manufacturer, executive; b. India, July 13, 1942; came to U.S., 1969, naturalized, 1978; s. R.S. and K.V. Rastogi; m. Anjali Capur, Mar. 18, 1970; children: Priya, Sonya. BS with honors, Lucknow U., 1963, MS, 1964; PhD in Polymer Sci., McGill U., 1969. From staff to dir. corp. diversification portfolio Owens-Corning Tech. Ctr.,

Granville, Ohio, 1969—87; v.p. Mead Imaging, Miamisburg, Ohio, 1987-89; pres. Mead Cycolor Divsn., Dayton, Ohio, 1989-92; v.p., gen. mgr.infusion systems div. Pharmacia Deltec, Inc., St. Paul, 1992-93, exec. v.p., 1993-94; COO SIMS Deltec, Inc., St. Paul, 1994-95; pres., COO Sabratek Corp., Niles, Ill., 1995—98; pres., CEO NOMOS Corp., Sewickley, Pa., 1998—2002; v.p. entrepreneurship and tech. commercialization Drexel U., Phila., 2002—. Mem. adv. bd. Central Ohio Tech. Coll.; lectr., cons. in field. Author of 15 bus. and tech. publs.; patentee in field. Bd. dirs. Licking County Family Services Assn.; bd. dirs. Tech. Alliance of Central Ohio; v.p. local United Way; bd. dirs. and treas. Columbus Bus. Tech. Ctr.; mem. Overview Adv. Com. Strategic Hwy. Research Program. Fellow NRC Can., 1966-69 Mem. AAAS, Am. Mgmt. Assn., Am. Chem. Soc., Soc. Plastics Engrs., Comml. Devel. Assn., Med. Alley (bd. dirs.), Health Ind. Mfrs. Assn., Nat. Infusion Therapy Alliance (bd. dirs.), Toastmasters (past pres.), Rotary, Sigma Xi. Office: Drexel U 3141 Chestnut St Philadelphia PA 19104-2875 Home: 3131 Walnut St Apt 550 Philadelphia PA 19104-3421 Office Phone: 215-895-0303. Business E-Mail: arastogi@drexel.edu.

RASULO, JAMES A. parks director; Grad. in Econs., Columbia U., 1978; MA in Econs., U. Chgo., 1982, MBA, 1984. Exch. rate/interest rate forecaster Chase Manhattan Bank; mgr. corp. planning Marriott Corp.; from dir. to sr. v.p. corp. strategic planning Walt Disney Co., Lake Buena Vista, Fla., 1986—93, sr. v.p. corp. alliances, 1993—95; exec. v.p. Euro Disney S.C.A., Paris, 1998—2000, also pres., COO, 1999—2000, chmn., CEO, 2000—02; pres. Walt Disney Pks. and Resorts, Walt Disney Co., Lake Buena Vista, Fla., 2002—. Mem.: Am. C. of C. (France), Columbia U. Club France. Office: Walt Disney Co 1375 N Buena Vista Dr Lake Buena Vista FL 32830-8402

RAS-WORK, ANDENET T. software company executive; b. Addis Ababa, Ethiopia, May 28, 1963; s. Terrefe Ras-Work and Berhane Asfaw; m. Eleni Zaude Gabre-Hadhin, Sept. 17, 1993; children: Zega, Yared. Internat. baccalaureate, Internat. Sch. Geneva, Switzerland, 1981; BSEE, UCLA, 1985; MBA, INSEAD, Fontainebleau, France, 1989. Engr., project mgr. Ascom, Bern, Switzerland, 1986-89; European program mgr. Hewlett Packard, Geneva, 1990-95, E-commerce group mgr. Santa Clara, Calif., 1995-2000; pres., CEO Semantix Corp., Herndon, Va., 2000—. Founde,r pres., African Enterprise Group, Geneva, 1992-95. Inventor, innovator, patentee Writing Utensils, 1998. Coun. mem., Leadership Mountain View, Calif., 1997-99. Recipient cert. Congl. Recognition, 1997. Mem. Scharnhorst Racing Club (exec. 1989—). Home: 3842 Macomb St NW Washington DC 20016 Office: Semantix Inc Ste 150 13530 Dulles Technology Dr Herndon VA 20171 Fax: (703) 793-1937; (202) 244-5941. E-mail: araswork@yahoo.com.

RATCHESON, ROBERT ALLAN, neurological surgeon; b. Chgo., Aug. 24, 1940; s. Maurice and Kate (Davidow) Ratcheson; m. Peggy Steiner, June 20, 1964; children: Alexey, Rachael Weissman, Abigail. Student, Miami U., 1961; BS, Northwestern U., 1962, MD, 1965. Diplomate Am. Bd. Neurol. Surgery. Asst. prof. Washington Sch. of Medicine, St. Louis, 1973-77, assoc. prof., 1977-81; Harvey Huntington Brown, Jr. prof., dir. divsn. neurol. surgery Univ. Hosps. of Cleve., 1981-91, Harvey Huntington Brown prof., chmn. dept. neurol. surgery, 1991—. Editl. bd. Jour. of Neurosurgery, 1992—, chmn. 2000-01; contbr. articles to profl. jours. With USPHS, 1967-69. Mem. Am. Assn. Neurol. Surgeons (pres.-elect 2003—, bd. dirs. 1997—, sec. 1997-2003, William P Van Wagenen fellow 1972-73), Soc. Neurol. Surgeons (treas. 1996-2001, pres. 2001-2002), Neurol. Soc. Am. (pres. 2000-2003), Congress Neurol. Surgeons (pres. 1985-86), Assn. Neurol. Surgeons (pres. 2004-2005). Avocation: fly fishing. Office: Univs Hosps of Cleve 11100 Euclid Ave Cleveland OH 44106-1736 E-mail: rar@case.edu.

RATCLIFF, CARTER GOODRICH, writer, art critic, poet; b. Seattle, Aug. 20, 1941; s. Francis Kenneth and Marian Elizabeth (Carter) R.; m. Phyllis Derfner, Jan. 28, 1976. BA, U. Chgo., 1963. Dir. poetry workshop St. Mark's Poetry Project, N.Y.C., 1969-70; editorial assoc. Artnews, N.Y.C., 1969-72; advisory editor Art Internat., Lugano, Switzerland, 1970-75; instr. modern and contemporary art and art theory The Sch. of Visual Arts, N.Y.C., 1972-83; instr. modern and contemporary art Phila. Coll. of Art, 1973; instr. art history NYU Sch. of Continuing Edn., 1973-75; contbg. editor Saturday Review, N.Y.C., 1980-82, Art in America, N.Y.C., 1976—; mem. editorial adv. com. Sculpture, Washington, 1992—. Vis. prof. post-war Am. art SUNY, Purchase, 1983-84, Pratt Inst., Bkyn., 1984-85, Hunter Coll., CUNY, 1985-89, 95-99, 2002; lectr. in field. Author: (books, poetry), Fever Coast, 1973, Give Me Tomorrow, 1983; (books) John Singer Sargent, 1982, Andy Warhol, 1983, Robert Longo, 1985, Komar and Melamid, 1989, Gilbert and George: The Singing Sculpture, 1993, The Fate of a Gesture: Jackson Pollock and Post War American Art, 1996, paperback edit., 1998, Out of the Box: The Reinvention of Art, 1965-1975, 2001; (essays) Joseph Cornell, 1980, Willem de Kooning: The North Atlantic Light, 1983, Roy Lichtenstein, 1989, Barnett Newman, 1991, Gilbert & George, 1993, Ellsworth Kelly, 1996, Francis Bacon, 1998, William Blake, 2001; contbg. editor Art in America, 1976—, Art on Paper, 2001—, Sculpture Mag., 2001—; mem. editl. bd. Sculpture Mag., 1992—; contbr. over 500 articles on art to mags. and catalogs. Recipient of the Frank Jewett Mather award for art criticism Coll. Art Assn., 1987; Poets Found. grantee, 1969, NEA Arts Critics grantee, 1972, 76; Guggenheim fellow, 1976. E-mail: ratcliff1@earthlink.net.

RATCLIFF, DONALD EARL, minister, educator; s. Clarence Earl and Lois Anna R.; m. Brenda Sue Campbell. BA, Spring Arbor Coll., 1973; MA, Mich. State U., 1975; EdS, U. Ga., 1986, PhD, 1995. Ordained to ministry Christian Nation Ch., 1978. Asst. prof. Circleville Bible Coll., 1975—78; tchr., adminstr., dean of men Christian Union Bible Sch., Roseau, Dominica, W.I., 1978-79; dir. Christian edn. Vinton Bapt. Ch., Ohio, 1981-82; interim pastor Mt. Pleasant Bapt. Ch., Toccoa, Ga., 1983-84; assoc. prof. Toccoa Falls (Ga.) Coll., 1982—2001, Biola U., La Mirada, Calif., 2001—04; prof. Vanguard U., Costa Mesa, Calif., 2004—. Spkr. in field. Author: Using Psychology in the Church, 1984, Handbook of Preschool Religious Education, 1988, Handbook of Youth Ministry, 1991, Introduction to Psychology and Counseling, 1991, Handbook of Children's Religious Education, 1992, The Complete Guide to Religious Education Volunteers, 1993, Bruised and Broken, 1992, Child-Rearing and Personality Development, 1993, Handbook of Family Religious Education, 1995, Raising Your Child From Birth to Age Twelve, 1999, Children's Spirituality, 2004, Children's Spirituality, 2004; contbr. articles to profl. jours. Mem. Nat. Assn. Profs. Christian Edn., Christian Assn. Psychol. Studies. Office: Vanguard Univ Dept Psychology 55 Fair Dr Costa Mesa CA 92626 Office Phone: 714-556-3610 306. *Children are perhaps the most undervalued treasure of the church. They are the key to both short-term and long-term growth of the church; they are the church of the future.*

RATCLIFF, JAMES LEWIS, consultant; b. Indpls., Mar. 3, 1946; s. Perry Albert and Viola Ruth (Hall) R.; m. Carol Rocklin Kay, Dec. 24, 1984 (dec.); m. Barbara Marie Montgomery, Aug. 31, 1995. Student, Raymond Coll.; B of History, Polit. Sci., Utah State U., 1968; MA in History, Wash. State U., 1972, PhD, 1976. Prof., sr. scientist Ctr. for the Study of Higher Edn. Pa. State U., University Pk., 1989-2000, dir. Ctr. for the Study of Higher Edn., 1990-97; prof., leader higher edn. sect. Iowa State U., Ames; assoc. prof. Fla. Atlantic U., Boca Raton; asst. prof. Wash. State U., Pullman; prof., sr. scientist Pa. State U., State College; chmn. bd., CEO Rowpar Pharms., Inc., Scottsdale, Ariz., 2000—. Author: Assessment and Curriculum Reform, 1992, Community Colleges, 1994, Realizing the Potential of Postsecondary Education, 1995, (with J. Gaff) A Handbook of Undergraduate Curriculum, 1996. U.S. Dept. Edn. grantee. Mem. AAAS, Am. Assn. Community Jr. Colls., Assn. Study Higher Edn. (bd. dirs.), Coun. Universities Colls. (past pres., bd. dirs.), European Assn. for Inst. Rsch.,Consortium Higher Edn. Rschs., Phi Delta Kappa, Phi Kappa Phi, Phi Alpha Theta. E-mail: jlr7@compuserve.com.

RATCLIFFE, DAVID M. utilities executive; b. Tifton, Ga. B in Biology, Valdosta State U., 1970; JD, Woodrow Wilson Coll. Law, 1975. Bar: Ga. Biologist Ga. Power, 1971; v.p. fuel svcs. So. Co. Svcs., 1986, exec. v.p., 1989—91, pres., CEO Miss. Power, 1991—95, sr. v.p. external affairs, 1995—98, exec. v.p., treas., CFO Ga. Power, 1998—99, CEO Ga. Power, 1999, chmn., pres, CEO, 2004—. Bd. dirs. Edison Electric Inst., CSX Transp., Ga. Rsch. Alliance, Ctrl. Atlanta Progress, Ga. Partnership for Excellence in Edn., chair, 2001—04; bd. dirs. Fed. Res. Bank Atlanta, chair, 2004. Trustee Woodruff Arts Ctr.; mem. adv. bd. Salvation Army. Mem.: Metro Atlanta C. of C. (chair econ. devel.), Ga. Bar Assn. Office: Southern Co 270 Peachtree St NW Atlanta GA 30303*

RATH, ALAN T. sculptor; b. Cin., Nov. 25, 1959; s. George and Carolyn R. BSEE, MIT, 1982. One-man exhbns. include San Jose (Calif.) Art Mus., 1990, Dorothy Goldeen Gallery, Santa Monica, Calif., 1990, 92, Walker Art Ctr., Mpls., 1991, Mus. Contemporary Art, Chgo., 1991, Carl Solway Gallery, Cin., 1991, Inst. Contemporary Mus., Honolulu, 1992, Ctr. Fine Art, Miami, Fla., 1992, Galerie Hans Mayer, Dusseldorf, Germany, 1992, Hiroshima (Japan) City Mus. Contemporary Art, 1994, Worcester (Mass.) Art Mus., 1994, John Weber Gallery, N.Y.C., 1994, Haines Gallery, San Francisco, 1995, 96, 98, Contemporary Art Mus., Houston, 1995, Aspen Art Mus., Colo., 1996, Dorfman Projects, N.Y.C., 1998, Yerba Buena Ctr. for the Arts, San Francisco, 1998, Site Santa Fe (N.Mex.), 1998, Mus. of Art, Austin, Tex., 1999, Scottsdale Mus. of Contemporary Art, 1999; group exhbns. include Visiona, Zurich, 1989, Ars Electronica, Linz, Austria, 1989, L.A. Contemporary Exhbns., 1989, Mus. Folkwang, Essen, Germany, 1989, Cite des Arts et des Nouvelles Technologies, Montreal, 1990, Stadtmuseum Siegburg, Siegburg, Germany, 1990, San Francisco Mus. Modern Art, 1990, 95, 98, Denver ArtMus., 1991, Whitney Am. Art, N.Y.C., 1991, Alvar Alto Mus., Jyvaskyla, Finland, 1992, Internat. Ctr. Photography, N.Y.C., 1992, Padigilione d'Arte Contemporanea, Ferrara, Italy, 1992, John Weber Gallery, N.Y.C., 1993, Spiral Art Ctr., Tokyo, 1994, Aldrich Mus. of Contemporary Art, Ridgefield, Conn., 1995, Otso Gallery, Espo Finland, 1996, LaLonja, Palma de Malloren, Spain, 1996, Kunsthalle, Vienna, 1998, L.A. Mus. Contemporary Art, 1999, Taipei ICA, Taiwan, 2001, Bienal de Valencia, Spain, 2001. Grantee NEA, 1988; Guggenheim fellow, 1994. Office: IKON 830 E 15th St Oakland CA 94606-3631

RATH, HOWARD GRANT, JR., lawyer; b. L.A., Sept. 2, 1931; s. Howard Grant and Helen (Cowell) R.; m. Peyton McComb, Sept. 13, 1958 (dec. Apr. 1984); children: Parthenia Peyton, Francis Cowell; m. Dorothy Moser, Aug. 29, 1986. BS, U. Calif., 1953; JD, U. So. Calif., 1958. Bar: Calif. 1959, U.S. Dist. Ct. (cen. dist.) Calif., 1959, U.S. Ct. Claims 1974, U.S. Tax Ct. 1960. Assoc. O'Melveny & Myers, L.A., 1959-66; tax counsel, dir. tax adminstrn., asst. treas. Northrop Corp. L.A., 1966-74; sr. tax ptnr. Macdonald, Halsted & Laybourne, L.A., 1974-86, Hill & Weiss, L.A., 1986-90; ptnr. Lewis Brisbois Bisgaard & Smith, L.A., 1990—; dir. Rath Packing Co., Waterloo, Iowa, 1966-81. 1st lt. U.S. Army, 1953-55. Mem. State Bar Calif., L.A. County Bar Assn., L.A. Yacht Club, The Athenaeum, Order of Coif, Phi Beta Kappa. Republican. Episcopalian. Office: Lewis Brisbois Bisgaard & Smith 221 N Figueroa St Ste 1200 Los Angeles CA 90012-2646 E-mail: rath@lbbslaw.com.

RATH, MARY LOU, state legislator; b. Buffalo, June 17; d. George Lewis and Margaret M. Whetzle; m. Edward A. Rath, Jan. 10, 1959; children: Allison, Melinda, Edward A., III. BS, Buffalo State U., 1956; Ins. Broker's lic., U. Buffalo, 1965. Home service rep. Nat. Feul Gas, Buffalo, 1958-61; communications affiliate Cummunications Affiliates of N.Y.C., 1961-67; legislator Erie County, N.Y., 1978-93; senator N.Y. State Senate, Albany, 1993—. Mem. N.Y. State Senate, chmn. Senate Local Govt. com., 1982, Buffalo Better Bus. Bur., 1983—, Adminstrv. Regulations Rev. Commn., mem. Alcohol & Drug Abuse, Children & Families, Civil Svc. & Pensions, Edn., Higher Edn. & Taxation, Investigations & Govt. Ops. Coms., various other legis. coms. 1979—. Vice pres. Research and Planning Council, Buffalo and Erie County, 1973-74; pres. Jr. League, 1973-74, mem. admissions com., 1974-78; chmn. Theodore Roosevelt Inaugural Site Restoration com., 1974-78; vol. WBEN "Call for Action", 1974-78; moderator candidates night Coalition for Better Edn., community adv. council SUNY-Buffalo, 1974—, arts adviser, 1981—; mem. Regan Dinner com., 1975; appointed Republican com. woman 8th Dist., Town of Amherst, N.Y., 1979—; trustee Buffalo Sem., 1975-79; bd. dirs. United Way of Buffalo and Erie County, 1977-78; pres. Landmark Soc. of Niagara Frontier, 1977-78; trustee, mem. vestry Calvary Episcopal Ch., Williamsville, N.Y., 1975-78; founding mem. Amherst "Lunch and Issues" program, 1980; bd. dirs. Daemen Coll. Assocs., 1980-81, Buffalo Better Bus. Bur., 1981—, Buffalo Soc. Natural Scis., 1984—; mem. commn. adv. com. State U. of N.Y. at Buffalo, 1985. Recipient Disting. Community Service award Crisis Services, 1984; named Pub. SServant of Yr., Erie County Fedn. Sportsmen's Clubs, 1981, Outstanding Women in Western N.Y., SUNY, 1984; Participant Am. Gas Assn. Lab. Tour, Cleve., 1982 (one of 8 persons invited-nationwide). Mem. Buffalo Philharm. Orchestra Soc., Buffalo Zool. Soc., Erie County Hist. Soc., Landmark Soc. Niagara Frontier, Williamsville Hist. Soc., Amherst C. of C., Buffalo C. of C., Alpha Hon. Soc. Office: 5500 Main St Ste 260 Williamsville NY 14221-6737

RATH, MAURICE MONROE, retired physician; b. Newark, Oct. 2, 1914; s. Sigmund and Lena (Marenus) R.; m. Lydia Harke, Nov. 17, 1940; 1 child, Roger. AB, Ind. U., 1936, MD, 1943; MS, NYU, 1941; PhD, U. Md., Balt., 1942. Diplomate Am. Bd. Family Practice. Pvt. practice, Short Hills, N.J., 1946-63; with FDA, Washington, 1963-65; med. dir. Carter-Wallace Pharm. Co., Cranbury, N.J., 1965-70; dir. restoration ctr. VA Hosp., East Orange, N.J., 1970-73; med. staff physician VA Hosps., Tampa, St. Petersburg, Fla., 1973-80. Assoc. prof. clin. pharmacology Med. Coll. u. N.J., Newark, 1970-75; assoc. prof. medicine U. South Fla. Med. Sch., Tampa, 1973-80; rschr. in field. With USPHS, 1943-46. Fellow Am. Coll. Cardiology, Am. Coll. Therapeutics and Clin. Pharmacology, Stroke Coun., Am. Heart Assn., Phi Beta Kappa, Alpha Omega Alpha. Home: 641 Via Milano Circle Apopka FL 32712

RATH, RICHARD CULLEN, history professor; BA, Millersville U., 1991; PhD, Brandeis U., 2001. Vis. lectr. Oberlin Coll., Oberlin, Ohio, 1998—99, Hamilton Coll., Clinton, NY, 1999—2000; vis. asst. prof. NYU, 2001; asst. prof. U. Hawaii at Manoa, Honolulu, 2002—. Recipient Clio award history, Millersville U., 1990, Richard Keller award Am. history, 1991, Richard L. Morton award, William and Mary Quar., 1993, Webb-Smith award, U. Tex., 1997, Louis Pelzer award, Orgn. Am. Historians, 1997; Kate B. and Hall J. Peterson fellow, Am. Antiquarian Soc., 1998, Crown fellow, Brandeis U., 1991-1996, Rsch. fellow, Smithsonian Instn., 1997, Assoc. fellow, John Carter Brown Libr., 1997, Gest fellow, Quaker Collection at Haverford Coll., 1998, Mellon fellow, Va. Hist. Soc., 1998, fellow, Inst. Advanced Study Religion at Yale U., 2003. Mem.: Omohundro Inst. Early Am. History and Culture, Orgn. Am. Historians, Am. Hist. Assn. Office: Dept History U HI at Manoa Sakamaki Hall 2530 Dole St Honolulu HI 96822 Office Phone: 808-956-7139. Office Fax: 808-956-9600.

RATH, THOMAS DAVID, lawyer, former state attorney general; b. East Orange, N.J., June 1, 1945; s. Harvey and Helen R.; m. Christine Casey, Dec. 18, 1971; children— Erin, Timothy. AB, Dartmouth Coll., 1967; JD, Georgetown U., 1971. Bar: N.J. 1971, N.H. 1972, U.S. Supreme Ct. 1978. Law clk. Judge Clarkson Fisher, U.S. Dist. Ct. N.J., 1971-72; atty. criminal div. Office of Atty. Gen., State of N.H., 1972-73, asst. atty. gen., 1973-76, dep. atty. gen., 1976-78, atty. gen., 1978-80; ptnr. Orr & Reno, P.A., Concord, N.H., 1980-87, Rath & Young, P.A., Concord, 1987-91; founding ptnr. Rath, Young, Pignatelli & Oyer, P.A., Concord, 1991—. Polit. analyst WHDH-TV, Boston, WGBH Pub. TV, Boston, WENH, N.H. Pub. TV, WBUR-Boston Radio; chief strategist Alexander for Pres.; vice chmn. of bd. Primary Bank, 1995-97; pres. Play Ball, N.H., 1994—; commentator, polit. analyst WMUR-TV and Yankee Network; bd. dirs. Assoc. Grocers New England, Chubb Am. Fund. Host State of the State, Yankee Cable Network; co-host Close-Up, WMUR-TV. Chmn. campaign Warren B. Rudman for U.S. Senate, 1980, 86; bd. overseers Aquinas House, Dartmouth Coll., com. on trustees Rockefeller Ctr. Bd. Visitors; bd. oversers Dartmouth Med. Sch.; nat. dir. Baker Exploratory Com., 1986-87; sec. bd. trustees Concord Hosp.; treas. N.H. Rep. party, 1981-93; trustee DWC, 1981-87, chmn., 1982-86; mem. Baker Exploratory Com., 1986-87; trustee Concord Hosp., 1980-86; sr. nat. cons. Dole for Pres.; del. Rep. Nat. Conv., 1984, 88, 92, rules com., 1988, 92, N.H. committeeman, 1996—; Rep. nat. committeeman State of N.H., 1996; bd. dirs. New Eng. Coun., 1997. Mem. Nat. Assn. Attys. Gen. (vice-chmn. Eastern region, vice chmn. standing com. on energy), N.H. Bar Assn. (Spl. Pres. award 1992). Clubs: Dartmouth Coll. (v.p. Merrimack County). Roman Catholic. Office: Rath Young and Pignatelli One Capital Plaza PO Box 1500 Concord NH 03302-1500 E-mail: tdr@rathlaw.com.

RATHEMACHER, ANDRÉE JESSICA, librarian; b. Long Branch, N.J., Aug. 12, 1970; d. Richard Andrew and Shirley Fittro Rathemacher; m. Debashish Mukhopadhyay, Jan. 18, 2004. AB, Brown U., 1992; MLS, U. R.I., 1995, MBA, 2000. Libr. reference, bibliographer, bus. U. R.I. Libr., Kingston, 1995—2003, serials libr., bibliographer, bus., 2003—. Mem. bd. trustees South Kingstown Pub. Libr., RI, 2003—; webmaster R.I. Libr. Assn., Warwick, 1997—2003. Author: Teaching Information Literacy: 35 Practical, Standards-based Exercises for College Students. Recipient Outstanding Paper Excellence award, Reference Services Rev., MCB U. Press, 2000. Mem.: ALA, Assn. Coll. and Rsch. Librs. (chair bus. librs. interest group 1998—2002), Beta Phi Mu, Beta Gamma Sigma. Home: 22 East Park Lane Kingston RI 02881-1799 Office: University Library 15 Lippitt Road Kingston RI 02881-2011 Office Phone: 401-874-5096. E-mail: andree@uri.edu.

RATHER, DAN, broadcast journalist; b. Wharton, Tex., Oct. 31, 1931; m. Jean Goebel; children: Dawn Robin, Dan M. BA in Journalism, Sam Houston State Tchrs. Coll., Huntsville, Tex., 1953; student, U. Houston, South Tex. Sch. Law. Instr. journalism Sam Houston State Coll., for 1 year; later worked for U.P.I. and Houston Chronicle; with CBS, 1962—; joined staff of radio Sta. KTRH (CBS affiliate), Houston; staying about 4 years as news writer, reporter, and later, as news dir.; became dir. news and pub. affairs with CBS Houston TV affiliate KHOU-TV, in the late 1950's; became White House corr., 1964; and then transferred to overseas burs., including chief of London bur., 1965-66; then worked in Vietnam; returned to White House position in fall of 1966; appearing nightly on segments of CBS Evening News; became anchorman-corr. for CBS Reports, 1974-75; co-editor 60 Minutes, CBS-TV, 1975-81; anchorman Dan Rather Reporting, CBS Radio Network, 1977—; anchorman, mng. editor CBS Evening News with Dan Rather, 1981—; corr. 60 Minutes II, 1998—. Co-editor show Who's Who, CBS-TV, 1977; anchor 48 Hours, 1986—; anchored numerous CBS News spl. programs. Author: (with Gary Gates) The Palace Guard, 1974, (with Mickey Herskowitz) The Camera Never Blinks, 1977, The Camera Never Blinks Twice: The Further Adventures of a Television Journalist, 1994, The American Dream, 2001, (with Peter Wyden) Memoirs, I Remember, 1991; editor Our Times, 1994. Recipient numerous Emmy awards; honors include dedication of Dan Rather Comm. Bldg., classroom facility Sam Houston State U., Huntsville, Tex. Office: CBS News 524 W 57th St New York NY 10019-2924

RATHER, LUCIA PORCHER JOHNSON, library administrator; b. Durham, N.C., Sept. 12, 1934; d. Cecil Slayton and Lucia Lockwood (Porcher) Johnson; m. John Carson Rather, July 11, 1964; children: Susan Wright, Bruce Carson. Student, Westhampton Coll., 1951-53; AB in History, U. N.C., 1955, MS in Library Sci., 1957; PhD in History, George Washington U., 1994. Cataloger Library of Congress, Washington, 1957-64, bibliographer, 1964-66, systems analyst, 1966-70; group head MARC Devel. Office, 1970-73, asst. chief, 1973-76, acting chief, 1976-77, dir. for cataloging, 1976-91. Chmn. standing com. on cataloguing Internat. Fedn. Library Assns., 1976-81; sec. Working Group on Content Designators, 1972-77; chmn. Working Group on Corp. Headings, 1978-79, Internat. ISBD Rev. Com., 1981-87. Co-author: the MARC II Format, 1968. Recipient Libr. Congress Disting. Svc. award, 1991, Disting. Alumnus award U. N.C. Sch. Libr. and Info. Sci., 1992. Mem. ALA (Margaret Mann award 1985, Melvil Dewey award 1991), Phi Beta Kappa. Democrat. Presbyterian. Home: 438 Heron Point Chestertown MD 21620-1680

RATHJEN, JON LAURENCE, lawyer, arbitrator, mediator; b. Elizabeth, N.J., June 28, 1951; s. Theodore A. Rathjen and Marie Betty Ahrendtsen; 1 child, Daniel Laurence. AB, Brown U., 1973; JD, U. Calif., Berkeley, 1977. Bar: Calif. 1978, U.S. Dist. Ct. (no. dist.) Calif. 1980. Atty. Paul & Baker, Oakland, Calif., 1979-81, Warwick, Gardner & Rathjen, Oakland, 1981-88, Pearce & Rathjen, Walnut Creek, Calif., 1988—. Cons. Bay Area Lawyers for the Arts, San Francisco, 1981-85; bd. dirs. Dancer's Repertory Theater, Oakland, 1978-81. Mem. Contra Costa County Bar Assn. (family law sect., mediation sub-sect.). Office: 1333 N California Blvd Ste 540 Walnut Creek CA 94596-4576

RATHJENS, GEORGE WILLIAM, political scientist, educator; b. Fairbanks, Alaska, June 28, 1925; s. George William and Jennie (Hansen) R.; m. Lucy van Buttingha Wichers, Apr. 5, 1950; children: Jacqueline, Leslie, Peter. BS, Yale U., 1946; PhD, U. Calif., Berkeley, 1951. Instr. chemistry Columbia U., 1950-53; staff weapons systems evaluation group Dept. Def., 1953-58; research fellow Harvard U., 1958-59; staff spl. asst. to Pres. U.S. for sci. and tech., 1959-60; chief scientist Advanced Research Projects Agy., Dept. Def., 1961, dep. dir., 1961-62; dep. asst. dir. U.S. ACDA, 1962-64, spl. asst. to dir., 1964-65; dir. weapons systems evaluation div. Inst. Def. Analyses, 1965-68; prof. dept. polit. sci. MIT, 1968-96, prof. emeritus, 1996—; sec.-gen. Pugwash Confs. on Sci. and World Affairs, 1997—. Fellow Am. Acad. Arts and Scis.; mem. Fedn. Am. Scientists (sponsor), Inst. Strategic Studies. Office: Mass Inst Tech 77 Massachusetts Ave Cambridge MA 02139-4301 also: Pugwash Am Acad Arts/Scis 136 Irving St Cambridge MA 02138-1929 E-mail: pugwash@amacad.org., gwrathje@mit.edu.

RATHKE, DALE LAWRENCE, retired aerospace executive, management consultant; b. Rangely, Colo., Mar. 16, 1950; s. Edmann Jacob and Cornelia Ruth (Ratliff) R. BA, Yale U., 1971; MA, Princeton U., 1974, ABD, 1977. Dir. internal ops. Assn. of Cmty. Orgns. for Reform Now (ACORN), New Orleans, 1977—; CFO Citizens' Cons. Inc., New Orleans, 1979—; fin. dir. ACORN Housing Corp., New Orleans, 1984—, Affiliated Media Found. Movement, 1979—. Sec.-treas. Broad St. Corp., New Orleans, 1986—, Elysian Fields Corp., New Orleans, 1986—, Greenwell Springs Corp., New Orleans, 1989—, ACORN Fund, Inc., New Orleans, 1991—, ACORN Beneficial Assn., Inc., New Orleans, 1991—, Houston Orgn. and Support Ctr., 1992—, St. Louis Orgn. and Support Ctr., 1992—. Pres. Assn. for Rights of Citizens, New Orleans, 1980—, ACORN Cultural Trust, Inc., 1988—; active Overture to Cultural Season, 1987—, treas., 1999—; active New Orleans Mus. Art, 1990—; dirs., assoc. treas. Raintree Svcs., Inc., 1998—, Sante Fe Opera Guild, 1995—, Metrolitan Opera Guild, 1998—. Mem. Yale Club of N.Y.C., Princeton Club of N.Y.C., Metairie County Club. Avocations: 18th century french furniture, english country homes. Office: ACORN 1024 Elysian Fields Ave New Orleans LA 70117-8454

RATHKE, DIETER B. construction company executive; Pres. Philipp Holzmann U.S.A. Ltd., Charlotte, N.C., also bd. dirs. Chmn. bd. Regent Ptnrs., Inc., Atlanta, Matrix, LLP, Atlanta; bd. dirs. Germania Am., Inc., Atlanta. Bd. dirs. various cmty. orgns. Office: Ja Jones Dr Charlotte NC 28287-0001

RATHKE, SHEILA WELLS, strategic and marketing consultant; b. Columbia, S.C., Aug. 9, 1943; d. Walter John and Betty Marie (McLaughlin) Wells; m. David Bray Rathke, Sept. 1966 (dec. 1997); 1 child, Erinn Michele. BA summa cum laude, U. Pitts., 1976, postgrad., 1976-77. Loan coord. Equibank, Pitts., 1961-65; office mgr. U.S. Steel Corp., Pitts., 1966-70; various account and mgmt. positions Burson-Marsteller, Pitts., 1977-87, exec. v.p., gen. mgr., 1987-94, CEO Can. ops. Toronto, Montreal, Ottawa, Vancouver, 1994-95; sr. v.p., dir. corp. devel. Young and Rubicam, Inc., N.Y.C., 1995-99, COO, 1999-2000; asst. provost strategic and program devel. U. Pitts., 2001—. Instr. Slippery Rock Coll., Pitts., 1984-85; adviser Exec. Report Mag., Pitts., 1986-88, A Better Chance, N.Y.C., 1996-2000, N.Y. Philharm., 1997-99. Trustee U. Pitts., 1976-80, mem. alumni bd. dirs., 1990-94; trustee Robert Morris Coll., 1992-95; bd. dirs. Vocat. Rehab. Ctr., 1987-93, Freewheelers, 1989-92, Pitts. Hist. Soc., River City Brass Band, Quantam Theatre, 2003-. Named Disting. Alumnus, U. Pitts., 1992, Legacy Laureate, 2000. Mem. Female Execs. Am., Am. Assn. Advt. Agys. (chair ea. region 1994-95), Pitts. Advt. Club (bd. dirs. 1988-91, pres. 1990), Alpha Sigma Lambda (charter).

Avocations: skiing, reading, gardening, travel, photography. Home: 1819 Sarah St Apt 2 Pittsburgh PA 15203 Office: U Pitts Cathedral of Learning Pittsburgh PA 15260- E-mail: sheilarathke@msn.com.

RATHMAN, WILLIAM ERNEST, retired lawyer, minister; b. Middletown, Ohio, Jan. 10, 1927; s. Ernest Daniel and Marguerite (Sebald) R.; m. Constance Schedler, Nov. 28, 1958; children: Marchie, William E. Jr. Grad., Phillips Exeter Acad., 1944; BA, Kenyon Coll., 1948; postgrad., Harvard U., 1950, Ohio State U. Coll. of Law, 1951, United Theol. Seminary, Dayton, Ohio, 1975. Bar: Ohio 1952; ordained to ministry Episc. Ch., 1975. Pvt. practice law, Middletown, Ohio, 1952-78; sr. ptnr. Rathman, Elliott & Boyd, Middletown, 1979-84, Rathman, Combs, Schaefer, Valen & Kaup, Middletown, 1985-88, Rathman, Combs, Schaefer & Kaup, Middletown, 1989-95, ret., 1995—. Spl. counsel to County of Butler, 1956-64, City of Middletown, 1965-66, Ohio Atty. Gen., 1967-69; acting judge Middletown Mcpl. Ct., 1969-74. Pres. Middletown Community Found., 1972-76, Middletown Chamber Found., 1977-80, Butler County Park Commn., 1986-90; trustee-at-large Ohio Found. of Ind. Colls., Columbus, 1972-90; trustee, mem. exec. com. Middletown United Way, 1963-90; trustee Middleton Req. Hosp. Found., 1986-90; adv. bd. Middletown campus Miami U., 1984-90. With USN, 1944-46, capt. USAF, 1959, comdr. Am. Legion, 1965. Named Exec. Yr., Middletown chpt. Nat. Secs. Assn., 1969; recipient Outstanding Community Svc. award Middletown post Am. Legion, 1975, Outstanding Svc. award Parstoral Counselling Svc., 1983, Vol. of Yr. award Middletown Area United Way, 1986. Fellow Am. Coll. Trust and Estate Counsel; mem. ABA (estate tax com. 1966-69), Ohio Bar Assn. (coun. del. 1980-93), Butler County Bar Assn. (pres. 1980), Middletown Bar Assn. (pres. 1967), Fed. Bar Assn. (pres. Cin. chpt. 1975), Ohio State Bar Found. (trustee 1992-96, Ohio Supreme Ct. bd. commrs. on grievances and discipline 1996-99), Browns Run Country Club, Masons (Jefferson lodge, master 1959-60), Scottish Rite Valley of Cin. (treas. 1986, chmn. bd. 1990, 33d degree mason 1988—). Episcopalian. Home: 501 Thornhill Ln Middletown OH 45042-3750 also: 1924 S Beach Club Hilton Head Island SC 29928-3750 E-mail: crathman@aol.com.

RATHMANN, PEGGY, writer, illustrator; b. St. Paul; BA in Psychology, U. Minn.; student, Am. Acad. Chgo., Atelier Lack, Mpls., Otis Parsons Sch. Design, L.A. Author: Ruby the Copycat (Most Promising New Author Cuffie award Pubs. Weekly 1991), Good Night, Gorilla (ALA Notable Children's Book 1994), Officer Buckle and Gloria (Caldecott medal 1996), Ten Minutes Till Bedtime, 1998 (ALA Notable Children's Book 1998), The Day The Babies Crawled Away, 2003; illustrator: Bootsie Barker Bites, 1992. Office: Penguin Putnam Inc 345 Hudson St Fl 15 New York NY 10014-4502

RATHOD, MULCHAND, mechanical engineering educator; b. Pathri, India, Mar. 3, 1945; came to U.S., 1970, naturalized, 1981; s. Shamjibhai Laljibhai and Ramaben Rathod; m. Damayanti Thakor, Aug. 15, 1970; children: Prerana, Falgun, Sejal. BS in Mech. Engring., Sardar Patel U., India, 1970; MS, Miss. State U., 1972, PhD, 1975. Rsch. grad. asst. Miss. State U., 1970-75; cons. engr. Bowron & Butler, Jackson, Miss., 1975-76; asst. prof. Tuskegee Inst., Ala., 1976-78; assoc. prof., coord. MET program SUNY, Binghamton, 1979-87; dir. engring. tech. divsn. Wayne State U., Detroit, 1987—. Cons. Interpine, Hattiesburg, Miss., 1977-79, Jet Propulsion Lab., 1980-83, IBM Corp., 1982-85; pres. Shiv-Parvati, Inc. 1982—. Contbr. articles to profl. jours.; patentee in field. Den leader Susquahanna coun. Boy Scouts Am., Vestal, N.Y., 1983-84. Recipient award NASA, 1981; grantee SUNY Found., 1984, Dept. Energy, 1978, GM, 1988-92, UAW Chrysler, 1990-91, Hudson-Webber Found., 1991-92, Ford, 1992-93, Kellogg Found., 1993-94, SME Found., 1994, Mich. Dept. Edn., 1994, NSF, 1995-2001. Fellow: ASME (cert. of appreciation 1991—2001, Dedicated Svc. award 1995, Ben C. Sparks medal 1998, cert. of appreciation 1982—89, BMW award 2001); mem.: ASHRAE, Profl. Order Engring. Tech., N.Y. State Engring. Tech. Assn., Am. Soc. Engring. Edn. (reviewer), India Assn. Miss. State U. (pres. 1972—73), Tau Beta Pi, Tau Alpha Phi (founder, faculty advisor 1989—), Pi Tau Sigma. Home: 1042 Woods Ln Grosse Pointe Woods MI 48236-1157 Office: Wayne State U Div Engring Tech Detroit MI 48202

RATHORE, NAEEM GUL, retired United Nations official; b. Lahore, Punjab, Pakistan, Nov. 21, 1931; arrived in country, 1950; s. Jalaluddin and Zohra (Butt) R.; m. Carol Salima, Sept. 19, 1951; 1 child, Amna Elona. BS, Mich. U., 1952; MA in Polit. Sci., Columbia U., 1955, PhD in Internat. Affairs, 1965. Dir. personnel and adminstrn. UNRWA, Beirut, 1975-76; exec. sec. Internat. Civil Svc. Commn. UN, N.Y.C., 1980-81, sec. First Com., 1980-84, asst. dir. Office Under-Sec. Gen./Dept. Polit. Affairs, 1984-87, chief Divsn. of Palestinian Rights, 1987-89; spl. advisor, spkr. Punjab Assembly, Pakistan, 1994-95; coord. Pakistan Expatriates in UN Systems UN, N.Y.C., 1992-93, adviser to the Pakistan amb., and permanent rep. of Pakistan, 1994—95; corporator Emerson Hosp., Concord, Mass., 1996—. Lectr. Pakistan studies Near and Middle East Inst., Columbia U., N.Y., 1954-55; prof., head dept. internat. affairs U. Islamabad, 1974; active numerous UN coms., panels and task forces with Office of Human Resources Mgmt., UN, including chmn. N.Y. Gen. Svc. Classification Appeals and Rev. Com., 1986-92; pres. FICSA, 1971-74; chmn. UN staff com., 1971-74; active External Exam. in Polit. Affairs (France, Japan, others); counselor, Minuteman Regional Program, Serving Health Info. Needs of Elders, Mass. Exec. Office of Elder Affairs, 1996—; mem. adv. bd. Maynard (Mass.) Adult Learning Ctr., 1997-98; discussion leader Concord Current Affairs Group, 1997—; discussant Great Decisions Coun. on Aging Town of Concord, 1997— advisor spl. projects, 1999—; advisor The Pakistani-Am. Congr., 1999—; del. Overseas Pakistani's Conv., Islamabad, Pakistan, 1999, Russian-Am. Seminar, Ufa, Bashkortostan, 1999; prin. advisor Pakistan Millineum, 2000—; mem. Nat. Campaign for Tolerance, 2002—, Carter Ctr., 2003—, Interfaith Alliance, 2003—, Union Concerned Scientists, 2003—; facilitator Internat. Affairs Discussion Group, Lexington, Mass., 2002—, Masta Mason, 2003-. Author: In Defense of the International Civil Service: Statements and Submission, 1974, United Nations Secretariat: Problems and Prospects, 1974, other publs. in field; contbr. articles to profl. jours. Chmn. internat. svc. projects Rotary Club Concord; adv. Carlisle Cmty. Chest, 2001—. Mem. Fedn. of Internat. Civil Svcs. (pres. 1971-74), Rotary Club Concord (chmn. internat. projects com.), Sierra Club, Mass. Human Devel. Fund, Inc. (chmn. 2004—). Moslem. Avocations: reading, writing newspaper columns, horseback riding, scuba diving, swimming. Home: 1305 Elm St Concord MA 01742-2103 Fax: (978) 369-9548. E-mail: nrathore@aol.com.

RATHORE, UMA PANDEY, utilities executive; b. Mar. 5, 1950; d. O Nath and R Devi Pandey; m. Ram N.S. Rathore, Dec. 18, 1978; children: Dinesh, Rana. BS, Kanpur U., 1967, MS, 1969. Adviser Consul Gen. of Iceland to India, 1976-85; v.p. Nevaid Cons., 1974-82; with North Jersey Utilities, Mount Freedom, N.J., 1983—, pres. Sr. ptnr. Translantic Cons.; founder Maxim Imports, 1994—; ind. mgmt. cons.; bd. dirs. Revel Inc., N.Y. Mem. ethics bd. Randolph Twp., N.J., 1986-91, county and state rep. Shongum Sch. PTA, 1989—, mem. multicultural com., 1993-94; membership chmn. LWV, 1979-81, com. person Dem. dist. 3 Randolph Twp., 1992, 94, mem. ethics com., 1994, mem. com., 1995; mem. drug action com. Randolph Twp., 1994, 95, 96—; mem. Dem. task force N.J. Women's Polit. Caucus, 1994; county and state rep. Randolph Intermediate Sch. PTA, 1993-94, bd. edn. rep., 1996—; mem. PTA coun. Randolph Twp. Schs.; legis. chair Morris County Coun. PTA, 1997—, counselor Region I; mem. Morris Mus., Macculloch Hall, Frelinghuysen Arboretum; mem. Ctr. for Study of Presidency, 1997; mem. DBE, 1999. Mem. Internat. Platform Assn., Dau. Brit. Empire, Acad. Polit. Sci., Kiwanis Club Smithsonian, Libr. of Congress, Fgn. Policy Assn., N.Y. Acad. Scis., Nat. Trust Hist. Preservation, Nat. Wildlife Fedn. Democrat. Avocations: reading, jogging, hiking, mountain climbing. Home and Office: 3 Hickory Pl Randolph NJ 07869-4528

RATIIS, BARBARA, political organization worker; b. Maine; BA in Rhetoric with highest honors, Bates Coll., 1996. Various positions in polit. campaigns, Maine; legis. aide, senate caucus dir.; exec. dir., then coordinated campaign dir. Maine Dem. Party, 2000; dep. Sec. of State, Maine; campaign dir. Baldacci for Gov., Michaud for Congress, Dem. State Senate Campaign Com., Dem. State House Campaign Com., Maine AFL-CIO, AFL-CIO, Dem. Nat. Com.; chairwoman Maine Dem. Party, 2002—. Active Valley St. Organic Cmty. Garden, Portland, Maine, Alumni Coun., Bates Coll., Wayside Soup Kitchen, Portland. Office: Maine Dem Party Main Office PO Box 5258 Augusta ME 04332

RATHWELL, PETER JOHN, lawyer; b. Windsor, Ont., Can., Aug. 20, 1943; came to U.S., 1947; s. Harold Wilfred and Jean Isabel (Lucas) R.; m. Ann Wickstrom Williams, Sept. 10, 1977; 1 child, James Michael. BA, U. Ariz., 1965, JD, 1968. Bar: Ariz. 1968. Assoc. Boettcher, Crowder & Schoolitz, Scottsdale, Ariz., 1972-73; ptnr. Snell & Wilmer, Phoenix, 1973—. Seminar lectr. Nat. Bus. Inst., Inc., 1987—90, Ariz. Ann. Bankruptcy Symposium, 1995, 97, Am. Agrl. Lawyers Assn., 1997, 99, Lormans Bus. Seminars, 2000—, Sterling Edn. Sems., 2001—. Mem. exec. com. Jr. Achievement Ariz., Phoenix, 1980-92, 2000—, bd. advisors, 1980—; chmn. scholarship fund St. Mary H.S., 1982-91; mem., chmn. Phoenix Parks Bd., 1982-87; trustee Orme Sch., 1991—, chair devel. com., 1994—; treas., trustee Smith Scholarship Trust U. Ariz. Law Sch., 1985—; bd. advisors ABI S.W. Bankruptcy Conf. 1995—, co-chair, 2003-. Capt. JAGC, USAF, 1969-72. Fellow State Bar Ariz. Found. (founding mem.), Maricopa County Bar Found. (founding mem.); mem. Am. Bankruptcy Inst., Ariz. Bar Assn. (bar counsel 1982-87, 97, chmn. discipline hearing com. 1987-93, mem. bankruptcy sect.), Maricopa County Bar Assn. (seminar lectr. 1987), Comml. Law League Am., Phoenix Zoo Wildest Club in Town (founding mem. 1972). Republican. Avocations: fishing, raising cattle. Home: 4523 E Mountain View Rd Phoenix AZ 85028-5213 Office: Snell & Wilmer 1 Arizona Ctr Phoenix AZ 85004 Office Phone: 602-382-6203.

RATI, ROBERT DEAN, data processing executive; b. Pittsburg, Kans., Jan. 8, 1939; s. Steve Julius Rati and Dorothy Bill (Rodebush) McWilliams; m. Margaret Fort Henry, June 7, 1969; children: Susan Margaret, Robert Henry. BA, U. Kans., 1961; MA, Northeastern U., Boston, 1970; MBA, Columbia U., 1973. Systems engr. IBM Corp., Boston, 1965-72; mgr. mgmt. services Arthur Young and Co., N.Y.C., 1973-75; mgr. client systems Touche Ross and Co., N.Y.C., 1975-76; mgr. systems and programs Walker Mfg. div. Tenneco, Racine, Wis., 1976-78; mgr. data processing Schwitzer div. Household Internat., Indpls., 1979-87; mgr. mgmt. info. systems Nat. Machinery Co., Tiffin, Ohio, 1988-90; pres. Dunhill Profl. Search of Carmel (Ind.), 1990-97; mgr. Muncie MIS Power Transformer div. Asea Brown Boveri, Muncie, Ind., 1991-94; dir. info. svcs. State Lottery Commn. Ind., Indpls., 1995-97; mgmt. cons. Aerotek-Maxim Group, Indpls., 1998-2000; project mgr. corp. info. tech. SBC Comms., Indpls., 2000—. Contbr. articles to fraternal orgs. publs. Mem. Rep. Com., Ramsey, N.J., 1972-74; treas. Rep. Club Ramsey, 1972-75; vice chmn. Swimming Pool Commn., Ramsey, 1972-74; bd. dirs., exec. com. Near Eastside Multi-Svc. Ctr., Indpls., 1984-87; fin. com. Carmel (Ind.) United Meth. Ch., 1984-87, adminstrv. bd., 1987-90. Lt. (j.g.) USN, 1961-64. Recipient Regional Mgrs. award, IBM Corp., 1967. Mem. SAR (pres. 1979), Soc. Ind. Pioneers (pres. 1996-98), Huguenot Soc. Ind. (pres. 1985-89), S.R. in State of Ill. (pres. 1980-82), Ind. Soc. Colonial Wars (gov. 1995-98), Gen. Soc. Sons of the Revolution (chmn. awards com. 1983-91, Gen. Pres. Commendation award 1985, 91), Pi Mu Epsilon. Republican. Avocations: genealogy, home computer. Home: 4919 Regency Pl Carmel IN 46033-5959 Office: SBC Comms 220 N Meridian St Rm 652 Indianapolis IN 46204

RATICA, ERIC DAVID, music educator; b. Painesville, Ohio, Feb. 3, 1978; s. David Andrew and Margaret Jane Ratica; m. Leanne Nicole Burkey, June 23, 2001. BA, Youngstown (Ohio) State U., 2000. Cert. music tchr. Ohio Dept. Edn., 2000. Instr. percussion Crestwood HS, Mantua, Ohio, 1998—2000, Canfield (Ohio) HS, 1999—2000; dir. bands Norwayne HS, Creston, Ohio, 2000—. Cons. percussion Willoughby (Ohio) South HS, 1996—2000. Recipient Billy Mitchell award, Civil Air Patrol, 1993, Eagle Scout, 1995. Mem.: Ohio Music Edn. Assn. Conservative. Russian Orthodox. Avocations: travel, sports, golf. Home: 428 East Paradise St Orrville OH 44667 Office: Norwayne High School 350 South Main Street Creston OH 44217 Office Phone: 330-435-4276. Business E-Mail: nrcn_ratica@tccsa.net.

RATKOWSKI, DONALD J. mechanical engineer, consultant; b. Cleve., July 29, 1938; m. Joyce Ellen Kotlarczyk, July 15, 1961; children: Rhonda, Tamyra, Cheryl, Randall. Student, Ariz. State U.; AAS, Alliance Coll., 1959, DSc (hon.), 1986. Sr. project engr. semiconductor products div. Motorola, 1960-70, 75-77; v.p. engring. Danker & Wohlk, 1970-75; founder, pres. Paragon Optical Inc., 1976-90; exec. v.p. Pilkinton Vision Care, 1987-90, cons., 1990-91; pres. DJR Resources Inc., Paradise Valley, Ariz., 1990—. Mem. adv. bd. Am. Sec. Coun., 1988-89; mem. steering com. Optometry Coll., Marcinkowski Acad. Medicine, Poland, 1989-91; founder Rigid Gas Permeable Lens Inst., 1985; speaker Nat. Contact Lens Examiners, 1984-91. Contbr. articles to profl. jours.; patentee in field. Sustaining mem. Rep. Nat. Com., 1983-90; mem. U.S. Congl. Adv. Bd., 1990. Recipient Alumnus of Yr. award Alliance Coll., 1985. Mem. Opticians Assn. Am. (assoc. mem. adv. coun. 1987-88), Contact Lens Soc. Am. (bd. dirs. 1986-88, founder scholarship program 1988, hon. chmn. steering com. edn. fund 1989-91), Contact Lens Mfrs. Assn. chmn. external communication com. 1981-90, bd. dirs. 1982-84, Trailblazer award 1987, program chmn. 1989-90, Leonardo DaVinci award 1990), Ariz. Soc. Plastic Engrs. bd. dirs. 1976-78, 83, v.p. 1980-81, pres. 1981-82), Sigma Tau Gamma (Outstanding Alumni award 1985). Home and Office: DJR Resources Inc 8105 N 47th St Paradise Valley AZ 85253

RATLIFF, CHARLES EDWARD, JR., economics professor; b. Morven, NC, Oct. 13, 1926; s. Charles Edward and Mary Katherine (Liles) R.; m. Mary Virginia Heilig, Dec. 8, 1945 (dec. Oct. 2000); children: Alice Ann, Katherine Virginia, John Charles. BS, Davidson Coll., 1947; AM, Duke U., 1951, PhD, 1955; postgrad., U. N.C., Harvard, Columbia. Instr. econs. and bus. Davidson Coll., 1947-48, asst. prof., 1948-49; scholar econs. Duke, 1949-51; faculty Davidson (N.C.) Coll., 1951-60, prof., 1960—, chmn. dept. econs., 1966-83, Charles A. Dana prof., 1967-77, William R. Kenan prof., 1977-92, Kenan prof. emeritus, 1992—; prof. econs. Forman Christian Coll., Lahore, Pakistan, 1963-66, 69-70. Summer vis. prof. U. N.C. at Charlotte, 1958, 60, Appalachian State U., 1962, Punjab U., Pakistan, 1963-64, Kinnaird Coll., Pakistan, 1965, Fin. Svcs. Acad., Pakistan, 1966, NDEA Inst. in Asian History, 1968; lectr. U.S. Cultural Affairs Office, East and West Pakistan, 1969-70. Author: Interstate Apportionment of Business Income for State Income Tax Purposes, 1962, A World Development Fund, 1987, Economics at Davidson: A Sesquicentennial History, 1987; co-author textbooks; contbg. author: Dictionary of the Social Sciences, 1964, Distinguished Teachers on Effective Teaching, 1986, Those Who Teach, 1988, Britain-USA: A Survey in Key Words, 1991, Soldiers and Sentinels: Davidson's World War II Veterans Speak, 2003; mem. editl. bd. Growth and Change: A Journal of Urban and Regional Policy, 1993-99; contbr. articles to profl. jours. Active Mayor's Com. on Affordable Housing, Davidson, 1996-97, Mayor's Com. Comty. Rels., Davidson, 1973-80, chmn., 1973-78; mem. Mecklenburg County Housing and Devel. Commn., 1975-81; exec. com. Mecklenburg Dem. Com., 1967-69, precinct com., 1967-69, 72-74, 89-99, issues com., 1979-99, nat. bd. dirs. Rural Advancement Fund Nat. Sharecroppers Fund, Inc., 1978-94, exec. com., 1981-94, treas., 1981-94; mem. Mecklenburg County Cmty. and Rural Devel. Exec. Com., 1981-99; bd. dirs. Bread for the World, Inc., 1983-84, Pines Retirement Comty., 1990-99, Crisis Assistance Ministry, 1992-96, Davidson Coll. Devel. Corp., 1992-95, Our Towns Habitat for Humanity, 1996-98, Davidson Coll. Alumni Assn., 1997-99, Davidson Affordable Housing Coalition, 1997-99; bd. advisors Mecklenburg Ministries, 1992-99, Drs. for Global Health, 1996—; doner rels. vol. Lakeland Habitat for Humanity, 1999—; planning com. Fla. Presbyn. Homes, Inc., 2000—, spiritual life com., 2000—, fine arts com, 2001—; holder various local, global and conf. positions United Meth. Ch. With USN, 1944-46. Rsch. grant Ford Found., 1960-61, Fulbright-Hays grant, 1973; Rsch. fellow Inter-Univ. Com. Econ. Rsch. on South, 1960-61; recipient Thomas Jefferson award Davidson Coll., 1972, Gold medalist Prof. of Yr. award Coun. Advancement and Support of Edn., 1985, Tchg. Excellence and Campus Leadership award Sears Roebuck Found., 1991, Hunter-Hamilton Love of Tchg. award, 1992, Disting. Svc. award Davidson Coll. Alumni, 2002. Mem. AAUP, So. Econ. Assn. (exec. com. 1961-63, v.p. 1975-76, N.C. corr. So. Econ. Jour.), Am. Econ. Assn., So. Fin. Assn. (exec. com. 1966-68), Nat. Tax Assn. (chmn. interstate allocation and apportionment of bus. income com. 1972-74), Assn. Asian Studies, Fulbright Alumni Assn., Old Catawba Soc., Phi Beta Kappa, Omicron Delta Kappa (Teaching award 1991). Methodist. Home: 29 Lake Hunter Dr Lakeland FL 33803-1288 E-mail: ceratliff@msn.com.

RATLIFF, LOUIS JACKSON, JR., mathematics professor; b. Cedar Rapids, Iowa, Sept. 1, 1931; s. Louis Jackson and Ruth Sara (Sidlinger) R.; m. Georgia Lee Smith, May 9, 1996. BA, State U. Iowa, 1953, MA, 1958, PhD, 1961. Lectr. Ind. U., Bloomington, 1961-63, U. Calif., Riverside, 1963-64, asst. prof. math., 1964-67, assoc. prof., 1967-69, prof., 1969—. Author: Chain Conjectures in Ring Theory, 1978; assoc. editor Procs. of AMS, 1987-92, Comm. in Algebra, 1990-95; contbr. articles to profl. jours. 1st lt. USAF, 1953-57. NSF fellow, 1960-62, grantee, 1965-69, 71-88; recipient Disting. Teaching award, U. Calif.-Riverside, 1983. Mem. Am. Math. Soc., Phi Beta Kappa. Democrat. Seventh Day Adventist. Home: 22344 San Joaquin Dr W Sun City CA 92587-7849 Office: U Calif Dept Math Riverside CA 92521-0001 Business E-Mail: ratliff@math.ucr.edu.

RATLIFF, ROBERT J. farm equipment manufacturing executive; With Internat. Harvester Co., Chgo., 26 years; pres. Uniroyal Tire Co., Worldwide, Troy, Mich.; pres. & CEO Deutz-Allis, Duluth, Ga., 1988-90; co-founder AGCO Corp., Duluth, 1990—, CEO, chmn., 1990-99, now exec. chmn. bd. dirs. Office: AGCO Corp 4205 River Green Pkwy Duluth GA 30096-2584

RATLIFF, THOMAS ASBURY, JR., retired engineer; b. Phila., May 5, 1919; s. Thomas Asbury and Edna Dorothy (Overman) R.; m. Lucy Lila Graydon, Aug. 15, 1942; children: Deborah Ratliff Miller, Anne Ratliff Naberhaus. Test technician GE, Cin., 1951; quality engr. Am. Standard Corp., Cin., 1951-54, asst. dir. tech., 1956-58; chief inspector Gruen Watch Co., Cin., 1954-58; cons. Hyde Engring. Co., Cin., 1958-60, Badgett & Smith, Inc., Cin., 1963-67; sales mgr. Lehmann Corp., Cin., 1960-63; purchasing mgr. Access Corp., Cin., 1967-70; pres. Ratliff & Assoc., Inc., Cin., 1970-96; ret. Adj. prof. engring. U. Cin., 1998-2000. Author: Basic Statistics for Lab Workers, 1992, The Laboratory Quality Assurance System, 1993, 3d. edit., 2003. Col. U.S. Army, 1940-72. Fellow Am. Soc. for Quality (various coms.). Republican. Mem. Soc. Of Friends. Avocation: collecting model cannons. Home: 755 Greenville Ave Cincinnati OH 45246-4608

RATLIFF, WILLIAM, former stae senator; lieutenant governor, civil engineer; b. Aug. 16, 1936; BS in Civil engring., U. Tex., 1960. City mgr., Copperas Cove, Tex.; pvt. practice civil engr. Mt. Pleasant, Tex.; mem. Tex. Senate Dist. 1, 1989—2003, chair fin. com., mem. edn. com., mem. adminstrn. com.; mem. internat. rels., trade and tech. com.; lt. gov. of Tex., 2000—; Dist. 1 State Senator, 2003—. Pres. Mt. Pleasant Indsl. Found.; mem. exec. com. N.E. Tex. Econ. Devel. Dist., Inc.; Sunday sch. tchr.; lay reader; chair fin. com.; bd. trustees Tennison Meml. United Meth. Ch.; Sgt. USAR. Recipient Outstanding State Leader Award, 2001 Mem. Am. Consulting Engr. Coun. (past pres.). Republican. Office: PO Box 12068 Austin TX 78711-2068

RATNATHICAM, CHUTTA, transportation executive; b. Colombo, Sri Lanka; married; 3 children. Grad., Royal Coll., Sri Lanka, 1967; MBA, U. Portland, 1973; grad. exec. program in bus. adminstrn., Columbia U. Corp. auditor CNF Transp. Inc., Palo Alto, Calif., 1977-78, various positions, 1978-91, v.p. Emery Subs., 1991-97; sr. v.p., CFO CNF Inc., Palo Alto, Calif., 1997—2000, 2001—; interim CEO Menlo Worldwide Forwarding, 2000—01. Mem. Am. Inst. Cert. Mgmt. Accts., Sri Lanka Inst. Chartered Accts., Fin. Execs. Inst. (San Francisco chpt.). Office: CNF Inc 1717 NW 21st Ave Palo Alto CA 94304-1297*

RATNER, ALBERT B. building products company executive, land developer; b. Cleve., 1927; Grad., Mich. State U., 1951. With Forest City Enterprises, Inc., Cleve., 1964—, sec., 1960-68, exec. v.p., from 1968, now pres., chief exec. officer, dir., also co-chmn brd. Mem. exec. com., dir. Univ. Circle Devel. Corp.; dir. Am. Greetings Corp. Mem. Internat. Council Shopping Ctrs. Office: Forest City Enterprises Inc 1100 Terminal Tower 50 Public Sq # 1170 Cleveland OH 44113-2202

RATNER, BRUCE, professional sports team executive; b. 1945; 2 children. BA cum laude, Harvard U., 1967; JD, Columbia U., 1970. Dir. Model Cities Program, head Consumer Protection Divsn. John Lindsay Adminstrn., NY, 1970—73; tchr. Law Sch. NYU, 1974—78; commr. consumer affairs, 1978—82; pres. Forest City Ratner Cos., N.Y.C., 1982—, CEO, 1982—; owner N.J. Nets, 2004—. Bd. dir. Mus. Jewish Heritage, Met. Mus. Art, NY, Bklyn. (N.Y) Acad. Music, City Pks. Found., Internat. Rescue Com., Bklyn. C. of C., N.Y.C. Partnership. Named The Top N.Y.C. Exec., Crain's N.Y. Bus., 1992; named one of N.Y.'s Most Influential Business Leaders, 2002; recipient N.Y. State Gov.'s Arts award, 1994. Office: 390 Murray Hill Pkwy East Rutherford NJ 07073*

RATNER, BUDDY DENNIS, bioengineer, educator; b. Bklyn., Jan. 19, 1947; s. Philip and Ruth Ratner; m. Cheryl Cromer; 1 child, Daniel Martin. BS in Chemistry, Bklyn. Coll., 1967; PhD in Polymer Chemistry, Polytech. Inst. Bklyn., 1972. From fellow to prof. U. Wash., Seattle, 1972—86, prof., 1986—. Dir. U. Wash. Engineered Biomaterials NSF Engring. Ctr.; founder Asemblon, Inc. Editor: Surface Characterization of Biomaterials, 1989, Plasmas and Polymers, 1994-99, Biomaterials Science: An Introduction to Materials in Medicine, 2d edit., 2004, Characterization of Polymeric Biomaterials, 1997; mem. editl. bds. 9 jours. and book series; editor Jour. Undergrad. Rsch. in Bioengring., 1998—; contbr. over 300 articles to profl. jours. Recipient Faculty Achievement/Outstanding Rsch. award, Burlington Resources Found., 1990, Perkin Elmer Phys. Electronics award for excellence in surface sci. Fellow Internat. Acad. Med. and Biol. Engring., Am. Inst. Med. Biol. Engring. (founder, pres. 2002-03), Am. Vacuum Soc. (Medard Welsh medal 2002); mem. AAAS, AIChE (C.M.A. Stine award 1998), Nat. Acad. Engring., Am. Chem. Soc., Internat. Soc. Contact Lens Rsch., Materials Rsch. Soc., Soc. for Biomaterials (pres. 1991-92, Clemson award 1989, fellow 1994, Founders award 2004), Biomed. Engring. Soc. Achievements include 15 patents in field. Office: U Wash Dept Bioengring PO Box 351720 Seattle WA 98195-1720 Office Phone: 206-685-1005. Business E-Mail: ratner@uweb.engr.washington.edu.

RATNER, CARL JOSEPH, theater director; b. Memphis, Tenn., Sept. 17, 1957; MusB, Oberlin Conservatory of Music, 1980. Intern Juilliard Sch., N.Y.C., 1980-81, N.Y.C. Opera, 1981-82; asst. dir. Lyric Opera Chgo., 1982-84; prodn. asst. San Francisco Opera, 1985-86; asst. dir. Metropolitan Opera, N.Y.C., 1989-90; artistic dir. Chamber Opera Chgo., 1985-93, Chgo. Opera Theater, 1994-99. Home: 421 W Melrose St Apt 22A Chicago IL 60657-3881 Office: Chicago Opera Theater 70 E Lake St Ste 540 Chicago IL 60601-5990

RATNER, DAVID LOUIS, retired law educator; b. London, Sept. 2, 1931; AB magna cum laude, Harvard U., 1952, LLB magna cum laude, 1955. Bar: N.Y. 1955. Assoc. Sullivan & Cromwell, N.Y.C., 1955-64; assoc. prof. Cornell Law Sch., Ithaca, N.Y., 1964-68, prof., 1968-82; prof. law U. San Francisco Law Sch., 1982-99, dean, 1982-89, prof. emeritus, 1999—. Exec. asst. to chmn. SEC, Washington, 1966-68; chief counsel Securities Industry Study, Senate Banking Com., Washington, 1971-73; vis. prof. Stanford (Calif.) U., 1974, Ariz. State U., Tempe, 1974, U. San Francisco, 1980, Georgetown U., Washington, 1989-90, U. Calif., Hastings, San Francisco, 1992, U. Ariz., 2004; mem. Larkspur (Calif.) Planning Commn., 1992-2004. Author: Securities Regulation: Cases and Materials, 6th edit., 2002, Securities Regulation in a Nutshell, 7 edit., 2002, Institutional Investors: Teaching Materials, 1978. Fulbright scholar Monash U., Australia, 1981. Mem. Cosmos Club (Washington), Harvard Club of San Francisco (pres. 1999-2000), Phi Beta Kappa. Home and Office: 84 Polhemus Way Larkspur CA 94939-1928 E-mail: dlratner@aol.com.

RATNER, ELLEN FAITH, radio talk show host, writer; b. Cleve., Aug. 28, 1951; d. Harry Ratner and Anne Spott. BA, Goddard Coll., 1974; EdM, Harvard U., 1978. Coord. women's svcs. Homophile Comty. Health Svc., Boston, 1971-73; co-dir., co-founder Boundaries Therapy Ctr., Acton, Mass.,

1973-86; dir. psychiat. day treatment program South Shore Mental Health Ctr., Quincy, Mass., 1974-81; v.p. rsch., devel. and svc., dir. ARC Rsch. Found. Addiction Recovery Corp., Rockville, Mass., 1986-90; health care cons., dir. Found. for Addiction Rsch., 1990-94; pres. Talk Radio News Svc., White House corr. Good Day USA "The Washington Reality Check", Washington, 1991—; pres. Talk Radio News Svc. White House corr. Good Day USA "Washington Day", 1995; polit. analyst Fox News Channel, 1997—; Washington bur. chief Talkers Mag., 1996—; CEO Coll. Media News Co. Tchr. Curry Coll., Milton, Mass., 1979-80; cons. program devel. Addiction Recovery Corp., 1984-86; developer, planner The Art's in Mileau Treatment of Phychiatric Outpatients, Quincy, 1980, New Eng.'s first conf. on Chem. Dependency and AIDS, 1988. Author: The Other Side of the Family: A Book for Recovery from Abuse, Incest and Neglect, 1990, 101 Ways to Get Your Progressive Issues on Talk Radio, 1997; appeared on nat. TV and radio shows including C-SPAN, The Oprah Winfrey Show, CNN, Nat. Empowerment TV, others; mem. adv. bd. The Counselor Mag., 1987-90. Bd. trustees, mem. exec. com., vis. com. presdl. search com. Goddard Col., Plainfield, Vt. 1977-81; bd. trustees Samaritan Coll., L.A., 1988-90; bd. dirs. Nat. Lesbian and Gay Health Found., Washington, 1985-92, pres., exec. com., program com., program chair; v.p. Harry Ratner Human Svcs. Fund, Cleve., 1991—; mem. adv. bd. Women of Washington, Inc., 1992—; bd. dirs. Theater Chamber Players, Kennedy Ctr., Washington, 1988-91, An Uncommon Legacy Found., N.Y.C., 1993—, The Ctr. for Spiritual Enlightment, Falls Church, Va., 1994—. Recipient Comty. Svc. award Lesbian and Gay Counseling Svc., Boston, 1985, The Addams-Brown award Nat. Lesbian and Gay Health Found., 1993. Mem. Nat. Assn. Radio Talk Show Hosts, Mass. Assn. Day treatment Adminstrs. (chair regulations and standards com. 1979-81), Lily Dale Assembly. Democrat. Jewish. Avocation: writing works on spiritualism. Office: Talk Radio News Svc 2514 Mill Rd NW Washington DC 20007-2950

RATNER, GAYLE, special education educator; b. Bronx, N.Y. BS, SUNY, Plattsburgh, 1991, MS in Edn., 1993. Cert. spl. edn. grades K-12 and elem. edn. grades N-6. Spl. edn. tchr. Chazy (N.Y.) Ctrl. Rural Sch., 1991—. Asst. chief reader N.Y. State Tchr. Cert. Examinations, mem. students with disabilities content adv. com.; instr. N.Y. State United Tchrs. Effective Tchg. Program, 1999—; mem. edn. bias and sensitivity com. for 4th and 8th grade state assessments CTB/McGraw Hill and N.Y. State, 2001—. Mem.: N.Y. State United Tchrs., Chazy Tchrs. Assn. (pres. 1995—), Nat. Bd. for Profl. Tchg. Stds. (bd. mem., spl. edn. and elem. edn. com. 2000—), Phi Delta Kappa. Office: Chazy Ctrl Rural Sch 609 Route 191 Chazy NY 12921

RATNER, GERALD, lawyer; b. Chgo., Dec. 17, 1913; s. Peter I. and Sarah (Soreson) R.; m. Eunice Payton, June 18, 1948. PhB, U. Chgo., 1935, JD cum laude, 1937. Bar: Ill. 1937. Since practiced in, Chgo.; sr. ptnr. Gould & Ratner and predecessor firm, 1949—. Officer Henry Crown & Co., CC Industries, Inc., Material Svc. Corp., Freeman United Coal Mining Co., Mineral and Land Resources Corp.; lectr., writer on real estate law. Capt. U.S. Army, 1942—46. Gerald Ratner Athletics Ctr. named in his honor, U. Chgo. Mem. ABA, Ill. Bar Assn., Chgo. Bar Assn., Order of Coif, Phi Beta Kappa. Home: 180 E Pearson St Apt 6205 Chicago IL 60611-2191 Office: 222 N La Salle St Ste 800 Chicago IL 60601-1086 Office Phone: 312-236-3003.

RATNER, HANK J. broadcast executive; BA, JD with distinction, Emory U. Assoc. Sullivan & Cromwell; asst. gen. counsel Cablevision Sys. Corp., Bethpage, NY, 1987—88; vice chmn. Rainbow Media, Cablevision Sys. Corp. Office: Cablevision Systems Corp 1111 Stewart Ave Bethpage NY 11714-3581

RATNER, LEE, medical educator; Prof. medicine, prof. molecular microbiology Washington U., St. Louis, 1993—, prof. pathology, 1996—. Office: Box 8069 10049 Clin Scis Rsch Bldg Saint Louis MO 63110

RATNER, LORMAN ALFRED, history professor; b. N.Y.C., July 23, 1932; s. Mortimer Ratner and Lillian Becker; m. Nina V. Nutt, June 20, 1953 (dec. Feb. 1989); children: Wendy Ratner MacMullen, Todd, Joseph, Matthew; m. Paula T. Kaufman, Sept. 17, 1989. AB, Harvard Coll., 1954; MA, Cornell U., 1958, PhD, 1961. Asst. prof. Ithaca (N.Y.) Coll., 1959-61; from asst. prof. to assoc. prof. to prof. Lehman Coll., CUNY, Bronx, 1961-70, dept. chair, 1970-72, dean of planning and social scis., 1972-77; vice chancellor U. Wis., Kenosha, 1977-83; chancellor U. Wis. Ctrs., Madison, 1983-86; dean of arts and scis., prof. U. Tenn., Knoxville, 1986-96, prof. history, 1996-99, prof. emeritus, 1999; adj. prof. U. Ill., Urbana-Champaign, 1999—. Author: Powderkeg, 1968, James Kirke Paulding, 1993, Andrew Jackson and His Tenn. Lieutenants, 1997, others. Mem., pres. Bd. of Edn., N.Y., 1971-76. Home: 1609A Lakeside Dr Champaign IL 61821-5557

RATNER, MARCIA, research scientist; b. Hartford, Conn., June 24, 1960; d. William and Gertrude Chorches Ratner. BA in Psychology, Boston U., 1995, PhD, 2004. Project mgr. Boston U., 1998—2004; rsch. assoc. in neurology Boston U. Sch. Medicine, 1998—, instr. toxicology and forensic toxicology, 2000—04, rsch. assoc. pharm., 2004—. CEO, v.p. Chem. Safety Net, Inc., 2002—; counselor Specialized Housing, Brookline, Mass., 1995—. Mem.: N.Y. Acad. Sci., Am. Conf. Govt. Indsl. Hygiene, Soc. Occupl. Environ. Health, Soc. Occupl. Health, Soc. for Neurosci., Mass. Neuropsychol. Soc., Am. Acad. Clin. Toxicology, Internat. Neurotoxicol. Assn., Combined Jewish Philanthropies, Psi Chi, Alpha Phi Omega. Jewish. Avocations: horseback riding, guitar, running, skiing. Office: Boston U Sch Medicine C-329 715 Albany St Boston MA 02118-2526 E-mail: marcia@bu.edu.

RATNER, MARINA, mathematician, educator, researcher; b. Moscow, Oct. 30; MA, PhD, Moscow State U. Asst. High Tech. Engrng. Sch., Moscow, 1969-71; lectr. Hebrew U., Jerusalem, 1971-74, sr. tchr. pre-acad. sch., 1974-75; from acting asst. prof. to assoc. prof. U. Calif., Berkeley, 1975-82, prof., 1982—. Alfred P. Sloan rsch. fellow, 1977-79, Miller rsch. prof., 1985-86, John Simon Guggenheim fellow, 1987-88; recipient John J. Carty medal for the Advancement of Science Nat. Acad. of Sciences, 1994. Mem. NAS (John J. Carty Medal for the Advancement of Science, 1994), AAAS. Office: Univ Calif Berkeley Dept Math 970 Evans Hall Berkeley CA 94720-3841

RATNOFF, OSCAR DAVIS, physician, educator; b. N.Y.C., Aug. 23, 1916; s. Hyman L. and Ethel (Davis) Ratnoff; m. Marian Foreman, Mar. 31, 1945; children: William Davis, Martha. AB, Columbia U., 1936, MD, 1939; LLD (hon.), U. Aberdeen, 1981; ScD (hon.), Case Western Res. U., 1996. Intern Johns Hopkins Hosp., Balt., 1939—40; Austin fellow in physiology Harvard Med. Sch., Boston, 1940—41; asst. resident Montefiore Hosp., N.Y.C., 1942; resident Goldwater Meml. Hosp., N.Y.C., 1942—43; asst. in medicine Columbia Coll. Physicians and Surgeons, N.Y.C., 1942—46; fellow in medicine Johns Hopkins, 1946—48, instr. medicine, 1948—50, instr. bacteriology, 1949—50; asst. prof. medicine Western Res. U., Cleve., 1950—56; assoc. prof. Case Western Res. U., 1956—61, prof., 1961—; asst. physician Univ. Hosp., Cleve., 1952—67, physician, 1967—. Author: Bleeding Syndromes, 1960; mem. editl. bd.: Jour. Lab. Clin. Medicine, 1956—62, assoc. editor:, 1986—91, bd. rev. editors:, 1991—95, editl. adv. bd.:, 1995—; editor: Treatment of Hemorrhagic Disorders, 1968; editor: (with C.D. Forbes) Disorders of Hemostasis, 1984, Disorders of Hemostasis, 3rd edit., 1996; mem. editl. bd.: Circulation, 1961—65, Blood, 1963—69, 1978—81, Am. Jour. Physiology, 1966—72, Jour. Applied Physiology, 1966—72, Jour. Lipid Rsch., 1967—69, Jour. Clin. Investigation, 1969—71, Circulation Rsch., 1970—75, Annals Internal Medicine, 1973—76, Perspectives in Biology and Medicine, 1974—, Thrombosis Rsch., 1981—84, Jour. Urology, 1981—88, Internat. Jour. Hematology, 1991—; contbr. articles to med. jours. Career investigator Am. Heart Assn., 1960—86. Maj. USMC, 1943—46. Named to Heart Hall of Fame, N.E. Ohio Heart Assn., 1989; recipient Henry Moses award, Montefiore Hosp., 1949, Disting. Achievement award, Modern Medicine, 1967, James F. Mitchell award, 1971, Murray Thelin award, Nat. Hemophilia Found., 1971, H.P. Smith award, Am. Soc. Clin. Pathology, 1975, Joseph Mather Smith prize, Columbia Coll. Physicians and Surgeons, 1976, Disting. Achievement in Med. Sci. award, U. Hosps. of Cleve., 1992, Saltzman award, Mt. Sinai Hosp. of Cleve., 1994. Master: ACP (John Phillips award 1974); fellow: AAAS; mem.: AMA, NAS (Kovalenko award 1985), Am. Soc. Biol. Chemists, Am. Physiol. Soc., Internat. Soc. Thrombosis (Grant award 1981, Spl. award 1993), Internat. Soc. Hematology, Am. Soc. Hematology (Dameshek award 1972), Assn. Am. Physicians (Kober lectr. 1985, Kober medal 1988), Ctrl. Soc. Clin. Rsch. (Disting. Svc. award 1992), Am. Soc. Clin. Investigation, Soc. Scholars Johns Hopkins U., Am. Fedn. Clin. Rsch. Home: 1801 Chestnut Hills Dr Cleveland OH 44106-4643 Office: Univ Hosps of Cleve Dept Medicine Cleveland OH 44106

RATOFF, MICHAEL BARTON (NICO RATOFF), writer, poet, publishing executive; b. White Plains, NY, Oct. 12, 1966; s. Steven Bernard and Doris Ratoff; 1 child, Xavier Sabine. Student(hon.), Meeting Sch., NH, 1983—84. Dir. Rebel Butterfly Press, Tucson, 1990—. Author: Caspar And The Sun, 2001, Silver And Shiny, 1997, Silent Noisy Spring, 2001, (poetry) Poems From The Wreckage, 1990, Mad's Black Book, 1992, Life As it's Own Reward, 1991, Insurrection, 1988, (poetry/graphic art public exhibition) Mad Poet Project. Founder, dir. Mad Poet Project; chief creative dir. Fractal Chaos Collective, Tucson, 1990—2003. Mem.: Araki Mujinsai Ryu-iaido (corr.). Avocations: Japanese studies, iado. Home: 3875 N Country Club Rd #220 Tucson AZ 85716 Office: Rebel Butterfly Press 3875 N Country Club Apt 220 Tucson AZ 85716 Personal E-mail: nico@rebelbutterfly.com. E-mail: nico@rebelbutterfly.com.

RATO FIGAREDO, RODRIGO, international official; b. Madrid, Mar. 18, 1949; married; 3 children. MBA, U. Calif., Berkeley; law degree, Madrid Complutense U.; PhD in Economics, Universidad Complutense, 2003. Mem. Nat. Exec. Com. of AP, 1979-86; co-founder Econ. Commn. of AP, 1979; spokesman for the econ., 1984-86; asst. gen. sec. AP, 1983-86; mem. Parliament for Cádiz in the 2d Legislature; v.p. of def. and security commn. NATO, 1987, 88, mem. spl. com. for strategy and control of armaments, 1988; asst. gen. sec. IXth Party Congress; nat. mem. Parliament for Madrid; spokesman for Grupo Parlamentario Popular Parliament in the IVth and Vth Legislatures; mem. Parliament in the VIth Legislatures; vice gen. sec. of Partido Popular XIIth Nat. Congress, 1996—; 2d v.p. of govt. Ministry Econs. and Fin, Madrid, 1996—2000; 2nd v.p. of govt. and min. of the economy, 2000—04; chmn. Internat. Monetary Fund, 2004—. Office: IMF 700 19th St NW Washington DC 20431

RATTAZZI, SERENA, retired art association administrator; b. Taranto, Italy, Aug. 20, 1935; came to U.S., 1969; d. Umberto and Ligetta (Maresca) Bardelli; m. Mario Cristiano Rattazzi, Jan. 15, 1962; 1 child, Claudia. BA, Liceo Umberto I, Naples. Italy, 1953; MSW, U. Naples, 1958; postgrad. in legal problems of mus. adminstrn., Am. Legal Inst., ABA, 1985, 86, 87, 89. Pub. rels., publs. asst. Albright-Knox Art Gallery, Buffalo, 1974-76, coord. pub. rels., 1976-82, asst. dir. for adminstrn., 1982-84, The Bklyn. Mus., 1984-85, vice dir. for adminstrn., 1985-89, assoc. dir., 1989-90; dir. Am. Fedn. Arts, N.Y.C., 1990—2000. Adv. bd. The Pitts. Ctr. for Arts, 1989-92, A.I.R. Gallery, N.Y.C., 1990-93; field reviewer Inst. Mus. Svcs., Washington, 1990; adv. coun. dept. art history and archaeology Columbia Univ., 1992—. Mem. ArtTable Inc. (bd. dirs. 1986-88, pres. 1986-88), Am. Assn. Museums (standing profl. com. on pub. rels. mgmt. 1978-82, bd. 1990-96). Avocation: reading.

RATTI, RICARDO ALLEN, lawyer; b. Humacao, P.R., Sept. 3, 1922; s. Augustus Peter and Gertrude Alice (Allen) R.; m. Ruth Anne Holland, Aug. 15, 1947; children— Carolyn, Christine, Steven, Julia; m. Jean E. Royer, May 26, 1991. B.S. in Marine Engring., USCG Acad., 1944; J.D., George Washington U., 1956. Bar: U.S. Ct. Appeals (D.C. cir.) 1956. Chief counsel U.S. Coast Guard, Washington, 1973-76; dep. asst. chief counsel FAA, Washington, 1976-78; chief counsel subcom. on Mcht. Marine, U.S. Ho. of Reps., Washington, 1978-85. Served to rear adm. USCG, 1972-76. Decorated Legion of Merit; recipient John Ordronaux prize George Washington Law Sch., 1954, John B. Larner medal, 1956. Mem. Fed. Bar Assn., Ret. Officers Assn., Nat. Assn. Uniformed Services (dir. 1981-84). Republican.

RATTI, RONALD ANDREW, economics professor; b. Neath, West Glamorgan, Wales, Oct. 10, 1948; came to U.S., 1970; s. Ronald Rudolph and Janet (Marshall) R. BA, U. Lancaster, 1970; MA, Case Western Res. U., 1972; PhD, So. Meth. U., 1975. Asst. prof. to assoc. prof. U. Mo., Columbia, 1975-85, prof. econs., 1985—, chmn. dept., 1982-89. Vis. scholar Fed. Res. Bank Kansas City, Mo., 1978, Fed. Res. Bank St. Louis., 1984-85; acad. visitor London Sch. Econs., 1985; vis. Fulbright prof. Korea U., Seoul, 1996, Korea Inst. Fin., 1997. Contbr. articles to profl. jours. Office: U Mo Dept Econs 118 Profl Bldg Columbia MO 65211-0001

RATTIE, MARGARET ELIZABETH (BETH RATTIE), elementary school educator; b. Mount Airy, N.C., Feb. 11, 1951; d. Joseph Jackson and Margaret Adelaide (Hill) R.; divorced; 1 child, Heather Elizabeth Cooke. BS, North Tex. State U., 1972; MS, Radford (Va.) U., 1986; Specialist, Appalachian State U., 1983. Cert. tchr., adminstr. Tchr. Patrick County Schs., Stuart, Va., 1972-79; asst. prin. Surry County Schs., Mount Airy, N.C., 1980-84; tchr. Osceola County Schs., Kissimmee, Fla., 1984-88, asst. prin., 1988—99, prin., 1999—2000; dir. alternative programs Osceola County, 2000—. Mem. Found. for Osceola Edn., Kissimmee, 1998—; mem. Arts for Complete Edn., Kissimmee, 1997—; facilitator So. Assn. Colls. and Schs., Atlanta, 1994—. Mem. Nat. Assn. Secondary Sch. Prins., Beta Sigma Phi (pres., treas.), Alpha Delta Kappa (pres. 1994-96), Phi Delta Kappa. Democrat. Baptist. Avocation: bowling. Home: 2733 Scarborough Dr Kissimmee FL 34744-5485

RATTMAN, WILLIAM JOHN, electronics and electro-optic engineer; b. Springfield, Mass., Nov. 16, 1933; s. Frank William and Sylvia Mary (Berry) R.; m. Jayne Winona Crockett, Aug. 19, 1954; children: Joy Diane, Beth Jayne, Amy Cathryn. BSEE, U. Mass, 1955; MSEE, Northeastern U., 1961. Sr. engr. Raytheon Co., Bedford, Mass., 1955-63; prin. engr., 1967-72; engring. specialist Sylvania Applied Rsch. Lab., Waltham, Mass., 1963-67; mgr. R&D Electro Signal Lab., Inc., Rockland, Mass., 1972-86. Cons. electronics, electro-optics to mfg. firms. Patentee optical depth finder, contrast detector, low drive power wideband optical modulator, laser ablative printing system, photoelectric smoke detector, self diagnostic smoke detector. Co-chmn. Town of Needham United Way Campaign, 1973. Mem. Soc. Photo-Optical Instrumentation Egnrs., S. Yarmouth Hist. soc. (pres. 1974-75). Home and Office: 303 Bellingrath Ter Deland FL 32724 Office Phone: 386-736-3232. E-mail: wrattman@cfl.rr.com.

RATTRAY, JAMES BAILEY, lawyer; b. Watertown, N.Y., July 26, 1950; s. Clifford M. and Dora M. (Bailey) R.; m. Paula Cataldi, Nov. 30, 1998. AB cum laude, Syracuse U., 1972; JD, Coll. William and Mary, 1975, MLT, 1982. Bar: Va. 1975, D.C. 1976. Assoc. firm Ernest C. Consolvo, Norfolk, Va., 1975; dep. city atty. City of Hampton, Va., 1976—92; exec. dir. Hampton Redevel. and Housing Authority, 1992—2001; asst. office dir. Ga. Dept. Cmty. Affairs, Atlanta, 2002—03; exec. dir. East Point (Ga.) Housing Authority, 2004—. Instr. St. Leo Coll., Tidewater Center, Langley AFB, Va., 1982-99, Golden Gate U., Resident Ctr., Langley AFB, 1978-82, Hampton U., Va., 1985-90. Contbr. articles to profl. jours. Mem. ABA, D.C. Bar Assn., Va. Bar Assn., Local Govt. Attys. of Va., Nat. Assn. Housing and Redevel. Ofcls., Pub. Housing Authority Dirs. Assn. Episcopalian. Home: 1015 Lake Windward Overlook Alpharetta GA 30005-9010 Office: East Point Housing Authority PO Box 91363 East Point GA 30364 E-mail: jimbrattray@aol.com.

RATZLAFF, RUBEN MENNO, religion educator, minister; b. Burrton, Kans., Jan. 8, 1917; s. Henry and Julia (Foth) R.; m. Frances Irene King, Sept. 7, 1941; children: Keith Lowell, Paul Dennis, Mark Henry, Loren Lee; m. Doris Carr Arneson, Aug. 1, 1992. BA, Johnson Bible Coll., 1940; BD, Butler U., 1955, MA, 1959. Ordained to ministry Chs. of Christ, 1938. Min. Pleasant Hill Christian Ch., Hall, Ind., 1948-50, Christian Ch., Clermont, Ind., 1950-55, Kennard, Ind., 1955-59; prof. San Jose (Calif.) Christian Coll., 1959-98, prof. emeritus, 1998—. Ann. vis. lectr. Springdale Coll., Selly Oak Colls., Birmingham, Eng., 1985-97; vis. lectr. Zimbabwe Christian Coll., Harare, 1995, Philippine Coll. Ministry, Baguio City, 1998. Author: Ezra Nehemiah, 1982; contbr. articles to profl. jours. Recipient Hebrew award Hebrew Synagogue, 1950. Mem. Theta Phi. Home: 5340 Elgin St SE Turner OR 97392-9607 *What amazes me most is that God the Almighty sends His Son to knock at our door, and wait with His hat in His hand while we decide whether to follow Him.*

RATZMAN, ZACHARY M. lawyer, consultant; b. Cin., June 28, 1972; s. Norman A. and Francine N. Ratzman. BA in Polit. Sci. and Sociology summa cum laude, Ohio U., Athens, 1995; at, Ohio State U. Coll. of Law, Columbus, 1995—96; JD magna cum laude, U. Mich. Law Sch., Ann Arbor, 1998. Bar: N.Y. State 1998, U.S. Dist. (so. dist.) N.Y. 2001, U.S. Dist. Ct. (ea. dist.) N.Y. 2001; lic. min. Universal Life Ch., 2003, cert. perform marriages Ohio Sec. of State, 2003. Summer assoc. Crowell & Moring LLP, Washington, 1997; dir. advance Campaign to Elect Lee Fisher Gov. of Ohio, Columbus, 1998—98; law clk. to the hon. Harold Baer, Jr. U.S. Dist. Ct. (so. dist.) N.Y., N.Y.C., 1999—2000; assoc. Patterson Belknap Webb & Tyler LPP, N.Y.C., 2000—02; assoc. white collar criminal def. group Skadden Arps Slate Meagher & Flom LLP, N.Y.C., NY, 2002—03; assoc. Goodkind Labaton Rudoff & Sucharow LLP, N.Y.C., 2004—. Cons., N.Y.C., 2003. Finalist, Harry S. Truman Scholarship Found., 1993; recipient Joel S. Rudy Outstanding Undergrad. Student Leader, Ohio U., 1994, Hardest Working Student Senator, Ohio U. Undergrad. Student Senate, 1994. Mem.: Bar Assn. of City of N.Y., Order of the Coif, Phi Beta Kappa. Jewish. Avocations: international travel, running, domestic politics & policy. Home: #12 172 East 85th St New York NY 10028 Office: Goodkind Labaton Rudoff & Sucharow LLP 100 Park Ave New York NY 10017 Office Phone: 212-907-0881. Home Fax: 212-883-7081; Office Fax: 212-883-7081. Personal E-mail: zratzman@yahoo.com. E-mail: zratzman@glrslaw.com.

RAU, DAVID EDWARD, financial and real estate consultant; b. Lincoln, Nebr., Sept. 27, 1956; s. Leo George and Anne Marie (Pavel) R.; divorced; children: Andrew David, Peter Nicholas, Victoria Anne. BBA, U. Ariz., 1978. CPA, Ariz., N.Mex. Sr. Peat Marwick Main, Albuquerque, 1978-82, supervising sr. Phoenix, 1982-83; asst. treas. Kroy Inc., Scottsdale, Ariz., 1983-85; acct. Zolondek & Blumenthal, Phoenix, 1985; v.p., controller Del Webb Corp., Phoenix, 1985—2002. Bd. dirs. Ariz. Tax Rsch. Assn. Chmn. Phoenix chpt. walk Juvenile Diabetes Found., 1990, pres. 1992, 93, 94; mem. Ariz. Town Hall; advisor Phoenix Sky Harbour Ctr. Tech. Adv. Panel, 1987; treas. Drugs Don's Work in Ariz., 1994—. Mem. Ariz. Soc. CPAs, Albuquerque Jaycees (treas. 1981-82), Nat. Assn. Real Estate Cos. (tax com.), Ariz. C. of C. (bd. dirs.), Beta Alpha Psi. Republican. Roman Catholic. Avocations: skiing, fishing, family. E-mail: drau52611@aol.com.

RAU, LEE ARTHUR, lawyer; b. Mpls., July 22, 1940; s. Arthur W. and Selma A. (Lund) R.; m. Janice R. Childress, June 27, 1964; children: Brendan D., Patrick C., Brian T. BSB, U. Minn., 1962; JD, UCLA, 1965. Bar: Calif. 1966, D.C. 1972, Va. 1986, U.S. Dist. Ct. D.C. 1973, U.S. Dist. Ct. (ea. dist.) Va. 1988, U.S. Ct. Mil. Appeals 1966, U.S. Ct. Appeals (D.C. cir.) 1972, U.S. Ct. Appeals (3d cir.) 1975, U.S. Ct. Appeals (6th cir.) 1980, U.S. Ct. Appeals (4th cir.) 1988, U.S. Supreme Ct. 1971. Trial atty. evaluation sect. antitrust div. U.S. Dept. Justice, Washington, 1965-66, appellate sect., 1970-72; assoc. Reed Smith Shaw & McClay, Washington, 1972-74, ptnr., 1975—2002; commr. Fairfax County Redevel. and Housing Authority, 2002—. Former mem. constl. and adminstrv. law adv. com. Nat. Chamber Litigation Ctr. Inc.; sec., bd. dirs. Old Dominion Land Co., Inc. Contbr. articles to profl. jours. Sec. bd. dris. Reston Found., 1982-93; bd. dirs. Reston Interfaith Inc., 1973-89, pres, 1984-88; bd. dirs. Greater Reston Arts Ctr., 1988-96, pres., 1989-91, sec., 1991-95; mem. Washington Dulles Task Force, 1982-91; mem. exec. com. and ops. com. Fairfax-Falls Ch. United Way, mem. regional coun., 1988-92. Capt. JAGC, U.S. Army, 1966-70. Named Restonian of Yr., 1990; decorated Commendation with oak leaf cluster; recipient Best of Reston award. Mem.: D.C. Bar Assn. (past chmn. energy study group). Democrat. Lutheran. Home: 11654 Mediterranean Ct Reston VA 20190-3401

RAUB, DONALD WILMER, minister, author; b. Quakertown, Pa., Dec. 24, 1931; s. Harvey Wilmer and Estella Martha (Bleam) R.; m. Dolores Jean Kern, Oct. 20, 1951; children: Diane, Donald, Deborah, Devlyn. DRE, Evang. Bible Sem., Lake Worth, Fla., 1987, ThD, 1999. Ordained minister Evang. Ch. Alliance, 1951. Evangelist Evang. Ch. Alliance, Bradley, Ill., 1951-58; pastor Troy (Ohio) Gospel Tabernacle, 1959-60; writer and photographer Quakertown (Pa.) Free Press, 1963-73; pastor East Rockhill Chapel, 1965—; with Merck & Co., West Point, Pa., 1968-94; ret., 1994. Advisor Lebanon (Pa.) Gospel Assn., 1992-94; lectr. in field. Author: I, Being of Sound Mind, 1988, 2d edit., 1989, Unusual Experiences and Special Moments, 1990, The Value of Christian Holiness, 1992; inventor fin. game: Independence, 1976; patentee in field; contbr. articles to profl. jours. Bd. dirs. Transylvania Bible Sch. (now Biblical Life Inst.), Freeport, Pa., 1957—, North Penn Symphony Orch. Soc., Lansdale, Pa., 1980-90; v.p. Transylvania, Inc., 1994-97, chmn. bd. dirs., 1997-2003. Mem. Songwriters of N.Am. (founder). Republican. Avocation: horticulture. Address: PO Box 224 Tylersport PA 18971-0224

RAUBICHECK, CHARLES JOSEPH, lawyer; b. N.Y.C., Oct. 9, 1946; s. Walter Alan and Catherine Gertrude (Fordrung) R.; A.B., Georgetown U., 1968; J.D., Georgetown U., 1971; m. Ann S. Macdonald, Feb. 18, 1978. Admitted to D.C. bar, 1971, N.Y. State bar, 1976; atty. Office Gen. Counsel FDA, Washington, 1971-75; ptnr. Frommer Lawrence & Haug LLP, N.Y.C., 2000—; adj. prof. N.Y.U. Sch. Law, N.Y.C., 1976—; elder Lafayette Ave. Presbyn. Ch., Bklyn., 2000—; trustee Riverside Ch., N.Y.C., 1993-94. Mem. Fed. Cir. Bar Assn., N.Y. Intellectual Property Bar Assn., N.Y. State Bar Assn. (chair food, drug, cosmetic law sect. 1986-88, 98-2000, vice-chair 1996—), Union League Club (N.Y.C.). Office Phone: 212-588-0800.

RAUCH, ARTHUR IRVING, management consultant; b. N.Y.C., Sept. 18, 1933; s. David and Miriam (Frankel) R.; m. Roxane M. Spiller, Aug. 19, 1962 (div. 1977); children: David S., Janine B.; m. Lynn R. Saidenberg, Oct. 11, 1987. BA magna cum laude, Dartmouth Coll., 1954, MS, 1955. Chartered fin. analyst. Security analyst Lionel D. Edie & Co., N.Y.C., 1959-64; group dir. rsch. Eastman Dillon, Union Securities & Co., N.Y.C., 1964-68; v.p., sr. analyst Laird, Inc., N.Y.C., 1968-69, dir. rsch., 1969-71, sr. v.p., 1970-73; ptnr. Oppenheimer & Co., N.Y.C., 1973-77; v.p. corp. devel. Rorer Group, Inc., Ft. Washington, Pa., 1977-84; v.p. corp. fin. Arnhold & S. Bleichroeder, Inc., N.Y.C., 1984-88; cons. corp. devel. ICN Pharms., Inc., N.Y.C., 1988-89. Mem. investment com. Becker Fund, 1969-73. Exec. com. Dartmouth Class of 1954, 1968-79, 94—. Lt. (j.g.) USNR, 1956-59. Rufus Choate scholar Dartmouth Coll., 1951. Mem. N.Y. Soc. Security Analysts, Assn. Corp. Growth, Fin. Analysts Fedn. (corp. fin. com.), Phi Beta Kappa. Home and Office: 115 Central Park W Apt 9D New York NY 10023-4153 Personal E-mail: arauch@spitfire.net.

RAUCH, CHARLES FREDERICK, JR., retired university official and business educator; b. Lancaster, Ohio, Oct. 24, 1925; s. Charles Frederick and Mary Catherine (Getz) R.; m. Diane Matilda Wilcox, Jan. 1, 1951 (div. July 1974); 1 child, Frederick Whitman; m. Esther Eleze Nettles, Apr. 25, 1975. BS, U.S. Naval Acad., 1947; MSME, U.S. Naval Postgrad. Sch., Monterey, Calif., 1957; MBA, Ohio State U., 1980, PhD, 1981. Commd. ensign USN, 1947, advanced through grades to rear adm., 1972; comdg. officer nuclear submarines, New London, Conn., 1962-66; systems analyst, sr. naval advisor, spl. asst. Office Chief Naval Ops., Washington and Saigon, Vietnam, 1967-71, dir. human resource mgmt. programs Washington, 1971-76; ret., 1976; asst. prof. U. Maine, Orono, 1981-84, dir. fin. mgmt., 1984-92, v.p. bus. and fin., 1992-96, part-time faculty, 1999-2000; acting pres. Am. Univ., Bulgaria, 1992. Cons. to dep. asst. sec. def., Washington, 1976; cons. Maine Maritime Acad., Castine, 1982—84; bd. dirs. Audubon Expdn. Inst., treas., 1998—2003; mem. coun. Am. U., Bulgaria, 1997—2000. Contbg. author: Leaders and Managers: International Perspectives on Managerial Behavior and Leaderships, 1984. Bd. dirs. Bangor Symphony Orch., pres., 2001-04. Decorated D.S.M. with gold star. Mem. Maine Audubon Soc., Greater Bangor C. of C. (chmn. com. on univ.-cmty. rels. 1986-89, bd. dirs. 1988-92), Navy League (pres. Penobscot coun. 1998-2000), Bangor Rotary (treas. 1999—), Phi Kappa Phi, Beta Gamma Sigma. Episcopalian. Avocations: wildlife photography, woodcarving. Home: 74 Luckey Landing Rd Glenburn ME 04401 E-mail: CFR@maine.edu.

RAUCH, GEORGE WASHINGTON, lawyer, director; b. Marion, Ind., July 18, 1919; s. George W. and Emma Asenath (Nolen) R.; m. Audrey M. Cranfield, Feb. 28, 1943 (div.); children: George Washington III, Nancy Lynn, Jane Nolen; m. Dorothy D. Farlow, June 26, 1970. BS, Ind. U., 1941; LL.B., U. Va., 1947. Bar: Ind. 1948, Ill. 1957, Mass. and Fla. 1972. Practice law Batton, Harker and Rauch (and predecessor firms), Marion, Ind., 1948-57; v.p., gen. counsel The Greyhound Corp., Chgo., 1957-61; mem. firm Hubachek & Kelly Ltd. and predecessor firms, Chgo., 1961-82; pres. Hubachek & Kelly Ltd., 1972-80; of counsel firm Chapman and Cutler, Chgo., 1982-95; gen. counsel Household Internat., 1967-78, dir., 1967-92, mem. fin. com., 1969-92, exec. com., 1972-92; dir. Edwards Engring. Corp., Constrn. Materials Co., Indsl. Air & Hydraulics Co., 1976-90, Burch Co., 1972-97, pres., 1975-97; dir. 1242 Lake Shore Dr. Corp., 1971-83, pres., 1973-74. Mem. Nat. Conf. Commrs. on Uniform Laws, 1955-57. Served as aviator USNR, 1941-45; lt. comdr. Mem. Raven Soc., Sankaty Head Golf Club (Nantucket, Mass.), Casino Club (Nantucket), Beach Club (Palm Beach, Fla.), Masons, Shriners, Phi Delta Phi, Delta Tau Delta. Home: 455 Australian Ave Palm Beach FL 33480-4532 also: PO Box 149 83 Baxter Rd Siasconset MA 02564

RAUCH, IRMENGARD, linguist, educator; b. Dayton, Ohio, Apr. 17, 1933; d. Konrad and Elsa (Knott) R.; m. Gerald F. Carr, June 12, 1965; children: Christopher, Gregory. Student, Nat. U. Mex., summer 1954; BS with honors, U. Dayton, 1955; MA, Ohio State U., 1957; postgrad. (Fulbright fellow), U. Munich, Fed. Republic Germany, 1957-58; PhD, U. Mich., 1962. Instr., German and linguistics U. Wis., Madison, 1962-63, asst. prof., 1963-66; assoc. prof. German U. Pitts., 1966-68; assoc. prof. German and linguistics U. Ill., Urbana, 1968-72, prof., 1972-79, U. Calif., Berkeley, 1979—. Author: The Old High German Diphthongization: A Description of a Phonemic Change, 1967, The Old Saxon Language: Grammar, Epic Narrative, Linguistic Interference, 1992, Semiotic Insights: The Data Do the Talking, 1998, The Gothic Language: Genetic Provenance and Typology, Readings, 2002; editor (with others): Approaches in Linguistic Methodology, 1967; editor: Spanish edit., 1974, Der Heliand, 1974, Linguistic Method: Essays in Honor of Herbert Penzl, 1979, The Signifying Animal: The Grammar of Language and Experience, 1980, Language Change, 1983, The Semiotic Bridge: Trends from California, 1989, On Germanic Linguistics: Issues and Methods, 1992, Insights in Germanic Linguistics I: Methodology in Transition, 1995, Across the Oceans: Studies from East to West in Honor of Richard K. Seymour, 1995, Insights in Germanic Linguistics II: Classic and Contemporary, 1996, Synthesis in Diversity: Semiotics Around the World, 1997, New Insights in Germanic Linguistics I, 1999, II, 2001, III, 2002; editor of three series: Berkeley Insights in Linguistics and Semiotics, Berkeley Models of Grammars, Studies in Old Germanic Languages and Literatures; founder, co-editor Interdisciplinary Jour. for Germanic Linguistics and Semiotic Analysis; contbr. articles to profl. jours. Named outstanding woman on campus U. Ill. Sta. WILL, 1975; recipient Disting. Alumnus award U. Dayton, 1985; research grantee U. Wis., summer 1966, U. Ill., 1975-79, Eastern Ill. U., 1976, Nat. Endowment Humanities, 1978, U. Calif., Berkeley, 1979—; travel grantee NSF, Linguistics Soc. Am., 1972; Guggenheim fellow, 1982-83; IBM Distributed Acad. Computing Environment, 1986; NEH grantee, 1988; Festschrift: Interdigitations: Essays for Irmengard Rauch, 1999. Mem. Linguistics Soc. Am., MLA, Am. Assn. Tchrs. German (hon.), Society for Germanic Philogy, Philogical Assn. of the West Coast, Phonetics Assn., Semiotic Soc. Am. (pres. 1982-83), Semiotic Circle of Calif. (founder), Internat. Assn. for Semiotic Studies (pres., dir. 5th congress 1994), Alpha Sigma Tau, Delta Phi Alpha. Home: 862 Camden Ct Benicia CA 94510-3633 Office: U Calif Dept German Berkeley CA 94720-0001

RAUCH, JOHN KEISER, JR., architect; b. Phila., Oct. 23, 1930; s. John Keiser and Marjorie (Gretz) R.; m. Carol Pfaff, Mar. 11, 1953 (div. June 1978); children: John David, Charles Daniel, Kathryn Mari, Peter, Carol Anne; m. Carol A. McConochie, Jan. 10, 1981. Student, Wesleyan U., Middletown, Conn., 1948-51; BArch., U. Pa., 1957; grad. cert. program, Pa. Acad. Fine Arts, 2001. Draftsman Cope & Lippincott, Phila., 1957-60; architect Venturi and Short, Phila., 1960-64; partner Venturi and Rauch (Architects and Planners), Phila., 1964-79, Venturi, Rauch and Scott Brown, 1980-82, v.p., mng. prin., 1982-87, mem. cons., mediator, arbitrator, 1988-96; instr. U. Pa. Grad. Sch. Fine Arts, 1969-70, 89. Lectr. dept. architecture Princeton (N.J.) U., 1990-94. Trustee Found. for Architecture, 1977-84, mem. adv. com., 1994-2002; treas. Phila. Rehab., Inc., 1984-94; pres. Reading Terminal Market Pres. Fund, 1988-93, bd. dirs. 1994-2001; bd. dirs. United Cerebral Palsy Assn., 1988-91. Recipient Good Neighbor award Mellon/PSFS Bank, 1992. Fellow AIA (emeritus; Firm award 1983, John Harbeson Disting Svc. Phila. Chpt. award 1992); mem. Pa. Soc. Architects. Democrat. Home: 620 Gate House Ln Philadelphia PA 19118-4303

RAUCH, LAWRENCE LEE, aerospace and electrical engineer, educator; b. L.A., May 1, 1919; s. James Lee and Mabel (Thompson) R.; m. Norma Ruth Cable, Dec. 15, 1961; children: Lauren, Maury Rauch. AB, U. So. Calif., 1941; postgrad., Cornell U., 1941; AM, Princeton U., 1948, PhD, 1949. Instr. math. Princeton U., 1943- 49; faculty U. Mich., 1949—, prof. aerospace engring., 1953-79, emeritus, 1979, chmn. instrumentation engring. program, 1952-63, chmn. computer, info. and control engring. program, 1971-76, asso. chmn. dept. elec. and computer engring., 1972-75; chief technologist telecommunication sci. and engring. div. NASA/Calif. Inst. Tech. Jet Propulsion Lab., 1979-85. Vis. prof. Ecole Nationale Supérieure de L'Aéronautique et de l'Espace, Toulouse, France, 1970, Calif. Inst. Tech., Pasadena, 1977-85, U. Tokyo, 1978; cons. govt. and industry, 1946—; chmn. telemetering working group, panel test range instrumentation Research and Devel. Bd. Dept. Def., 1952-53; mem. exec. com. (Nat. Telemetering Conf.), 1959-64; Western Hemisphere program chmn. (1st Internat. Telemetering Conf.), London, 1963, program chmn., U.S.A., 1967; supr. air blast telemetering, Bikini, 1946; mem. project non-linear differential equations Office Naval Research, 1947-49; mem. research adv. com. on communications, instrumentation and data processing NASA, 1963-68. Author: Radio Telemetry, 1956; also numerous sci. articles and papers on radio telemetry. Recipient award for outstanding contbn. to WWII Army and Navy, 1947, award for outstanding contbn. to telemetering field Nat. Telemetering Conf., 1960; Donald P. Eckman award for disting. achievement in edn. Instrument Soc. Am., 1966; Pioneer award Internat. Telemetering Conf./USA, 1985. Fellow IEEE (spl. award contbns. radio telemetry 1957, adminstrv. com. profl. group space electronics and telemetry 1958-64), AAAS, Explorers Club; mem. Am. Math. Soc., AIAA, U. Mich. Research Club, Phi Beta Kappa, Sigma Xi, Phi Eta Sigma, Phi Kappa Phi. Achievements include patent in field; development of first electronic time-division multiplex radio telemetering system, of pre-detection recording; radio telemetry of first U.S. jet aircraft, of air blast over pressure for Operation Crossroads at Bikini Atoll; analysis of optimum demodulation of frequency-modulated signals. Address: 5231 N Citrus Ave Los Angeles CA 90038-3401 E-mail: lawrence.l.rauch@jpl.nasa.gov.

RAUCH, MICHAEL H. lawyer; BA, Princeton U., 1960; LLM, Harvard U., 1963. Bar: N.Y., U.S. Supreme Ct., U.S. Ct. Appeal (2d, 4th, 5th, 7th, 9th, and 10th cirs.). With Fried Frank Harris Shrivers & Jacobson, N.Y.C., 1968, ptnr., 1972—. Office: 1 New York Plz New York NY 10004

RAUCH, PAUL DAVID, television producer; b. Jersey City, N.J. s. Harry and Ruth (Reyman) R.; children— Stacie Jennifer, Tyler Meade. Classical music corr. Yomiuri Shimbun, 1956-58; corr. Voice of Am., 1958; Supr. prodn. TV programs CBS-TV, 1958-59; supr. prodn. TV programs Procter & Gamble Co., 1960-70; v.p. in charge daytime and east coast primetime programming CBS-TV, 1970-72; exec. producer Another World, others NBC-TV, 1972-82; exec. TV producer Twentieth Century Fox, 1982-83; executive producer One Life To Live ABC-TV, 1983-91; exec. producer Santa Barbara NBC-TV, 1991-93; exec. producer 919 Fifth Ave CBS, 1994-95; producer Lover's Knot (feature film), 1995-96; developer Columbia-Tristar TV, FOX TV, USA cable TV, 1994-96; exec. producer Guiding Light CBS, 1996—. Exec. prodr., Run The Wild Fields (Showtime feature film, Emmy award 2001), 1999. Served with AUS, 1956-58 Recipient Emmy award Nat. Acad. TV Arts and Scis., 1975, 76, Emmy award nomination for Another World, NBC-TV, 1976-77, NBC Bicentennial Special, Rachel Jackson, 1976.

RAUCH, RUDOLPH STEWART, III, periodical editor, arts education executive; b. Bryn Mawr, Pa., July 5, 1943; s. Rudolph Stewart and Frances (Brewster) R.; m. Sheila Prentice, Oct. 31, 1972; children: Edward Prentice, Michael Brewster. BA, Princeton U., 1965. Corr. Time mag., N.Y.C., 1969-70, Bonn, W. Ger., 1970-71, Saigon, Vietnam, 1971-72, Rio De Janeiro, Brazil, 1972-74, Buenos Aires, Argentina, 1974-76, Atlanta, 1976-79, dep. chief of corrs. N.Y.C., 1979-80; asst. to chmn. bd. Time Inc., N.Y.C., 1981-84, internat. dir. mag. devel., 1984-85; exec. editor N.Y. N.J. Conn. Real Estate, 1986-87; mng. editor Constitution, 1989-94; mng. dir. Met. Opera Guild, Inc., N.Y.C., 1994—; pub. Opera News, N.Y.C., 1994—, editor, 1998—. Editor, pub. Opera News, 1998—. Edward R. Murrow Press fellow Council on Fgn. Relations, 1980-81 Mem. Coun. Fgn. Rels. Office: Met Opera Guild 70 Lincoln Center Plz Fl 6 New York NY 10023-6577 E-mail: rrauch@metguild.org.

RAUCHER, HERMAN, novelist, screenwriter; b. Bklyn., Apr. 13, 1928; s. Benjamin Brooks and Sophie (Weinshank) R.; m. Mary Kathryn Martinet, Apr. 20, 1960; children: Jacqueline Leigh, Jennifer Brooke. BS, NYU, 1949. Asst. trade ad mgr. 20th Century Fox Films, N.Y.C. and Los Angeles, 1950-54; copy dir. Walt Disney Studios, N.Y.C., 1954-55; copy supr. Calkins & Holden Advt., N.Y.C., 1955-57; copy dir., v.p., dir. Reach McClinton Advt., N.Y.C., 1957-63; v.p., creative dir. Maxon Advt., N.Y.C., 1963-64; creative supr. Gardner Advt., N.Y.C., 1964-65; v.p. advt., cons. Benton & Bowles Advt., N.Y.C., 1965-67; freelance novelist, screenwriter, 1967—; pres. Bearfilm Prodns., 1971-96. Author: (novels and screenplays) Watermelon Man, 1970, Summer of '42 (nominated Acad. award for best original screenplay 1971, Writers Guild award nomination, Photoplay award), Ode to Billy Joe, 1976, A Glimpse of Tiger, 1972, (novel) Maynard's House, 1979, (screenplays) Sweet November, 1968, The Other Side of Midnight, 1977, Class of 44, 1972, Hieronymus Merkin (Best Original Screenplay award Writers Guild of Great Britain 1969), There Should Have Been Castles, 1978, Ginger, 1995, ARA/Froom, 2001 also various dramas appearing on TV in Alcoa Hour, Studio One, Matinee Theatre, Goodyear Playhouse, (TV mini-series under pseudonym) Master of the Game, 1984, (TV pilot) Remember When, 1974; playwright: Harold, 1962, Two Weeks Somewhere Else, 1967, Red Lights and Dragons, 1996, Kitty Hawk (musical), 2000; contbg. editor: Greenwich Time; contbr. to book revs. to N.Y. Times. Served with U.S. Army, 1950-52. Mem. Writers Guild Am., Authors League Am., Am. Film Inst., Dramatists Guild, Acad. of Motion Picture Arts and Scis. Office Phone: 203-869-3194. E-mail: hraucher@optonline.net.

RAUCINA, THOMAS FRANK See RACINA, THOM

RAUE, JORG EMIL, electrical engineer; b. Stettin, Germany, June 13, 1936; came to U.S., 1952; s. Ludwig and Liselotte (Barth) R.; m. Anke Volkmann, June 29, 1957; children: Monika Kay, Jennifer Faye. BSEE, Milw. Sch. Engring., 1961; MSEE, Marquette U., 1965, PhDEE, 1968. Mem. faculty Milw. Sch. Engring., 1961-68, chmn. dept., 1968-69; research engr. TRW Systems, Redondo Beach, Calif., 1969-76, mgr. dept., 1976-79; sr. research scientist TRW Electronic Systems, Rendondo Beach, Calif., advanced systems mgr., 1980-93; tech. cons. Calif., 1993—; chmn. dept. elec. engring. Calif. Polytech State U., San Luis Opispo, 1979-80. Mem. faculty Marquette U., Milw., 1968-69, Loyola U., Los Angeles, 1970-72, U. So. Calif., Los Angeles, 1983—. Contbr. articles to profl. jours. Served with U.S. Army, 1955-58. Recipient Disting. Tchr. award Milw. Sch. Engring., 1968; named Outstanding Alumnus Milw. Sch. Engring., 1985. Fellow IEEE; mem. Microwave Soc. of IEEE (sec. adminstrn. com. 1985—), Sigma Xi. Avocations: tennis, bicycling, flying, bridge. Home and Office: 28813 Rothrock Dr Palos Verdes Estates CA 90275-3060 E-mail: raue@cox.net.

RAUENHORST, MARK, property manager, real estate company executive; BA, Creighton U.; MBA, U. Notre Dame. With Am. Linen Supply, Graco; joined Opus, 1982—; exec. v.p. Opus U.S.; pres., COO Opus US Corp., 1990—91, Opus Corp., 1991—96, pres., CEO, 1996—. Bd. mem. ConAgra Foods. Mem.: Urban Land Inst., Nat. Assn. Indsl. and Office Properties, Internat. Coun. Shopping Ctrs., Young Pres. Orgn. Office: Opus Property Mgmt Corp 10350 Bren Rd W Minnetonka MN 55343*

RAUGHTER, JOHN B. editor; Contbg. editor The Am. Legion, Indpls. Office: The Am Legion 5561 W 74th St Indianapolis IN 46268-4184

RAUGHTON, JIMMIE LEONARD, education consultant, public administrator, urban planner; b. Knoxville, Tenn., Oct. 9, 1943; s. George L. and Ann (Simotes) R. BA in Urban and Regional Planning, U. No. Colo., 1974, MA, 1976; PhD, U. Colo., 1993. Mgr. Flexitran divsn. Gathers, De Vilbliss Archs. and Planners, 1966-68; asst. dir. planning City of Aurora, Colo., 1968-71; planner City of Lakewood, Colo., 1971-73, City of Boulder, Colo., 1973-74; instr. urban planning C.C. of Denver, 1974-76, divsn. dir. human resources and svcs., 1976-81, divsn. dir. sci. and tech., 1981-85; v.p. State of Colo. C.C., 1985—99; pres. Golden Sq. Consulting Group, Denver, 1999—. Chmn. profl. adv. com. to Colo. Gov.'s Land Use Adviser, 1973; cons. Denver Regional Coun. of Govts. for Model Sign Code, 1973, City of Boulder Transp. Dept., 1975—; coord. devel. Rocky Mountain Energy and Environ. Tech. Ctr., 1980; exec. dir. Edn. Found. Colo., 1989-98; spkr. in field. Mem. exec. bd. Civic Ctr. Assn., Denver, 1973-75; supervisory com. Colo. State Employees Credit Union, 1986—; mem. bd. Support Sys. Consol., 1984, Bridge Industry, 1985, 2003; candidate Denver City Coun., 1975; bd. dirs. Plan Metro Denver, 1975-76, Four Corner Art Collection, 1973—. Recipient Citizen award of honor Assn. Beautiful Colo. Roads, 1972. Mem. ASTD, Am. Inst. Planners (exec. bd. Colo. 1970-75, treas. 1972-73), Am. Soc. Planning Ofcls., Am. Vocat. Assn., Pi Alpha Alpha, Colo. City Mgrs. Assn. Home: 2501 High St Denver CO 80205-5565

RAUH, CARL STEPHEN, lawyer; b. Washington, Dec. 14, 1940; s. Joseph L. and Olie (Westheimer) R. AB, Columbia U., 1962; LL.B., U. Pa., 1965; LL.M., Georgetown U., 1968. Bar: D.C. 1966, U.S. Supreme Ct. 1969. Asst. U.S. atty. for D.C., 1966-69; atty. Dep. Atty Gen.'s Office Dept. Justice, Washington, 1969-71; 1st asst. atty. gen. U.S. V.I., 1971-73; prin. asst. U.S. atty. for D.C., 1974-79; U.S. atty. for D.C., 1979; ptnr. Dunnells, Duvall, Bennett & Porter, Washington, 1980-90, Skadden, Arps, Slate, Meagher & Flom, Washington, 1990—. Mem. D.C. Jud. Nomination Commn., 1985-90. Recipient Dir.'s award Dept. Justice, 1976; Atty. Gen.'s Disting. Service award, 1980 Fellow Am. Coll. Trial Lawyers; mem. ABA, D.C. Bar Assn., Nat. Assn. Former U.S. Attys., Asst. U.S. Attys. Assn. (Harold J. Sullivan award 1980). Office: 1440 New York Ave NW Washington DC 20005-2111

RAUH, JOHN DAVID, manufacturing executive; b. Cin., May 28, 1932; s. Carl J. and Grace (Stix) R.; m. Elizabeth Gibbons, June 19, 1954; children: Carol Miller (dec. 1991), Daniel Gibbons.; m. Mary Stoner, Dec. 23, 1984; children: Brooks Tomb, Howard Tomb. AB, Harvard U., 1954, MBA, 1956. Gen. mgr. Rauh Shirt Co., Cin., 1959-61, Clopay Corp., Cin., 1961-85, pres., 1972-75, chmn., CEO, 1975-85, also chmn. Adj. faculty mktg. Colby-Sawyer Coll., New London, N.H., 1989-92; fellow Kennedy Sch., Harvard, 1989. Pres. Charter Com. Greater Cin., 1969-76; canidate U.S. Senate, N.H., 1990, 92, 96; trustee Franklin Pierce Coll., 1993-2000; chair Childrens Alliance N.H., 1997-2002, treas., 2002—; bd. dirs. Common Cause, 1998-2002; chair Ams. for Campaign Reform, 2003—. 1st lt. Fin. Corps. AUS, 1956-59. Home: 57 Old Bay Rd PO Box 2124 New Castle NH 03854 Office Phone: 603-227-0626. E-mail: jdrauh5@aol.com.

RAUL, ALAN CHARLES, lawyer; b. Bronx, N.Y., Sept. 9, 1954; s. Eugene and Eduarda (Müller-Mañas) R.; m. Mary Tinsley, Jan. 30, 1988; children: Caroline Tinsley, William Eduardo Tinsley, Alexander Tinsley. AB magna cum laude, Harvard U., 1975, MPA, 1977; JD, Yale U., 1980. Bar: N.Y. 1982, D.C. 1982, U.S. Ct. Appeals (D.C. cir.) 1982, U.S. Supreme Ct. 1988. Law clk. to judge U.S. Ct. Appeals (D.C. cir.), Washington, 1980-81; assoc. Debevoise & Plimpton, N.Y.C., 1981-86; White House assoc. counsel Pres. Reagan, Washington, 1986-88; gen. counsel Office Mgmt. and Budget, Washington, 1988-89, USDA, Washington, 1989-93; prin. Beveridge & Diamond P.C., Washington, 1993-97; ptnr. Sidley Austin Brown & Wood LLP, Washington, 1997—. Cons. Reagan-Bush campaign, N.Y.C., 1984; mem. implementation task force Internet Corp. for Assigned Names and Numbers, 2000—. Author: (book) Privacy and the Digital State, 2001. Co-chairperson, co-founder Lawyers Have Heart; chmn. bd. USDA Grad. Sch., 1991-93; bd. dirs. Nation's Capital affiliate Am. Heart Assn., 1993-97, 2003—. Greater Washington region, 2002—; treas., dir. Citizens Assn. Georgetown, 1993-97; mem. Nat. Policy Forum's Environ. Policy Coun.; mem. adv. coun. Atlantic Legal Found., 2001—. Recipient Disting. Achievement award Am. Heart Assn., 1991, Vol. of Yr. award, 1993, Lifetime Achievement award, 1999. Mem. ABA (chmn. com. on nat. security and internat. law 1990-92, coun. sect. internat. law and practice 1992-98, standing com. on election law 1995-99, sect. internat. law and practice govt. affairs officer 1996-98, coun. sect. adminstrv. law and regulatory practice 2004—), Assn. of Bar of City of N.Y. (chmn. subcom. on Cen. Am. issues 1985, mem. com. on inter-Am. affairs 1983), Federalist Soc. (mem. nat. practitioners adv. coun., chair environ. and property rights practice group 1996-99), Coun. on Fgn. Rels. Office: Sidley Austin Brown & Wood LLP 1501 K St NW Washington DC 20005 E-mail: araul@sidley.com.

RAULINAITIS, PRANAS ALGIS, electronics executive, consultant; b. Kaunas, Lithuania, May 13, 1927; came to U.S., 1954, naturalized, 1960; s. Pranas Viktoras and Paulina (Gervaite) R.; m. Angele Staugaityte, Oct. 4, 1952; 1 son, Pranas Darius. With Commonwealth Rys. of Australia, Melbourne, 1949-53; asst. to fin. acct. Kitchen & Sons, Pty. Ltd., Melbourne, 1953-54; v.p. photo divsn. Interphoto Corp., L.A, 1954-71; sr. v.p., sec. Craig Corp., L.A., 1971-87; pres. PAR Enterprises, Burbank, Calif., 1987—; asst. sec. M&F Corp. Enterprises Ltd. Adviser Ministry Fgn. Affairs Republic of Lithuania, 1992; asst. sec. M & F Corp. Enterprises, Ltd., Chgo., 2004 . Former pres. Lithuanian Am. Coun., Inc. of Calif., bd. dirs. Lithuanian-Am. Assns.; founder, former dir., v.p. Baltic Am. Freedom League; former mem. Am. Soc. Internat. Law. Home and Office: PAR Enterprises 1501 W Riverside Dr Burbank CA 91506-3027 E-mail: raulalgis@juno.com.

RAUM, MARY BETH, ballet educator; b. Takoma Park, Md., Oct. 14, 1957; d. Lawrence Arthur and Catherine Tompkins Raum. BS cum laude, U. Md., College Park, 1979; MAS magna cum laude, Johns Hopkins U., Balt., 1979; PhD summa cum laude, U. Wash., Seattle, 1992. Adminstr. Johns Hopkins U./APL, Laurel, Md., 1976—82; adj. faculty/tech. mgmt U. Md. Open Univ., College Park, 1980—84; cons. Lawrence A. Raum & Assocs., Inc., Tacoma, 1982—92; doctoral rsch. assoc. George Wash. U., Washington, 1983; grad. faculty, adj. Chapman U., Bangor, Wash., 1984—; adj. faculty/mgmt. City U., Silverdale, Wash., 1986—88; corps de ballet/instr. Pacific Regional Ballet, Bremerton, Wash., 1996—; doctoral rsch. assoc. U. Wash., Seattle; ballet instr. MK Ballet Studio, Bremerton, Wash. Ballet mistress Pacific Regional Ballet, Bremerton, Wash., 2002—. Classical dance pointe, Raymonda (High Second Pl. Regional Dance Competition, 2002); author: (academic) An Overview of Federal Research Evaluation Activities (NSF Grant George Wash. Univ, 1985); character dance, Untitled (Internat. Dance Competition Sterling Silver Champion, 2001), classical ballet pointe, Raymonda (Dance Magic Regional High Score 2nd Pl., 2002), spanish character dance, Voz de la Referencia (Regional lst Pl. & Championship High Score Adult Trophy, 2002); author: (academic dissertation) The Decision Anatomies of Three Technology Based Public Bodies in the State of Washington; author: (alaska oil spill commission) (policy study) General Study of Key Events Surrounding the Aslaka Oil Spill; author: (basic research) Field Survey of Industrial Company Needs Related to Graduate Academic Programs in Business and Technical Managment (Rsch. Grant, 1990), (government study nas) A New Look at National Policy for Marine Resources and Engineering Development, (encylopedia) Notable Twentieth Century Scientists (contbr. to Gale Rsch. Inc.). Mem.: Phi Kappa Phi. D-Conservative. Methodist. Avocation: free lance writer. Office: Chapman Univ Naval Submarine Base Bangor Silverdale WA 98370 Personal E-mail: maryraumphd@aol.com.

RAUP, DAVID MALCOLM, paleontology educator; b. Boston, Apr. 24, 1933; s. Hugh Miller and Lucy (Gibson) R.; m. Susan Creer Shepard, Aug. 25, 1956; 1 son, Mitchell D.; m. Judith T. Yamamoto, May 30, 1987. BS, U. Chgo., 1953; MA, Harvard U., 1955, PhD, 1957. Instr. Calif. Inst. Tech., 1956-57; mem. faculty Johns Hopkins U., 1957-65, assoc. prof., 1963-65; mem. faculty U. Rochester, 1965-78, prof. geology, 1966-78, chmn. dept. geol. scis., 1968-71, dir. Center for Evolution and Paleobiology, 1977-78; curator geology, chmn. dept. geology Field Mus. Natural History, Chgo., 1978-80, dean of sci., 1980-82; prof. geophys. sci. U. Chgo., 1980-95, chmn. dept., 1982-85, Sewell L. Avery disting. service prof., 1984-95; prof. emeritus, Sewell L. Avery disting. svc. prof. emeritus, 1995—. Geologist U.S. Geol. Survey, part-time, 1959-77; vis. prof. U. Tubingen, Germany, 1965, 72 Author: (with S. Stanley) Principles of Paleontology, 1971, 78, The Nemesis Affair, 1986, 2d edit., 1999, Extinction: Bad Genes of Bad Luck?, 1991; editor: (with B. Kummel) Handbook of Paleontological Techniques, 1965; contbr. articles to profl. jours. Recipient Best Paper award Jour. Paleontology, 1966; Schuchert award Paleontol. Soc., 1973; grantee Calif. Rsch. Corp., 1955-56, Am. Assn. Petroleum Geologists, 1957, Am. Philos. Soc., 1957, NSF, 1960-66, 75-81, Chem. Soc., 1965-71, NASA, 1983-95. Mem. AAAS, Am. Acad. Arts and Scis., Nat. Acad. Sci., Paleontol. Soc. (pres. 1976-77, medal 1997), Am. Soc. Naturalists (v.p. 1983), Am. Philos. Soc. Home: RR 1 Box 168-y Washington Island WI 54246-9753 Personal E-mail: draup@itol.com.

RAUSCH, HOWARD, information service executive; b. N.Y.C., June 29, 1928; s. Sol and Helen (Kartiganer) R.; m. Sidra Levine Cohn, Apr. 22, 1979. AB, Syracuse U., 1950. Reporter Phila. Bull., 1961; copy editor Wall St. Jour., 1961-63, N.Y. Times, 1963-64; editor, fgn. corr. McGraw-Hill, N.Y.C. and Moscow, 1964-68; pres. Advanced Tech. Publs., Inc., Newton, Mass., 1968-80; editor, pub. Laser Focus mag., 1968-80; editor, founder Energy Research, 1975-80; editor Electronic Business, 1980-82; founder, pub. Lightwave Jour., 1983-90; tech. dir. Optical Soc. Am., Washington, 1991-93; pres. Capital Access Info. and Cons. Svcs., Washington, 1993—. Home and Office: 2541 Waterside Dr NW Washington DC 20008-2820 E-mail: hrausch@capaccess.org.

RAUSCHENBERG, BRADFORD LEE, museum researcher; b. Atlanta, Sept. 11, 1940; BS in Archaeology and Biology, Ga. State Coll., 1963; MA in History, Wake Forest U., 1995. Archaeologist Ga. Hist. Commn., 1963-64; site supr., asst. Stanley South, State Archaeologist of N.C., 1964-66; antiquarian, asst. dir. Restoration Old Salem, Inc., Winston-Salem, N.C., 1966-73; asst. to dir. Mus. Early So. Decorative Arts, Winston-Salem, 1973-76, rsch. fellow, 1976-87, dir. rsch., 1987-93, Mus. Early So. Decorative Arts and Old Salem, Inc., Winston-Salem, 1993—, sr. fellow emeritus. Cons., lectr. in field. Author: British Regional Carving (1600-1640), and Furniture (1600-1800), 1984, Wachovia Historical Society: 1895-1995, 1995, Charleston Furniture, 1680-1820, 3 vols., 2003. With USCG, 1964-72. Recipient Halifax Resolves award, 1986; grantee NEH, 1972-81, Kaufman Americana Found., 1981-82. Mem. Am. Ceramic Circle (grantee), Orgn. Am. Historians, No. Ceramic Soc., So. Hist. Assn., Friends of Swiss Ceramic Circle, Regional Furniture Soc., Furniture History Soc., Soc. Hist. Archaeology, Soc. Post-Medieval Archaeology, Soc. Historians Early Am. Republic. Address: 221 Harmon Ct Winston Salem NC 27106-4613 Office: Mus Early So Decorative Arts PO Box 10310 Winston Salem NC 27108-0310

RAUSCHENBERG, ROBERT, artist; b. Port Arthur, Tex., Oct. 22, 1925; m. Sue Weil, 1950 (div. 1952); 1 child, Christopher. Student, U. Tex., Kansas City Art Inst., Academie Julian, Paris, Black Mountain Coll., N.C., Art Students League, N.Y.C.; LHD (hon.), Grinnell Coll., 1967; DFA (hon.), U. So. Fla., 1976. Neuropsychiat. tech. Calif. Naval Hosps. Originator Overseas Culture Interchange traveling exhn., 1985—. One-man shows include Parsons Gallery, N.Y.C., 1951, Stable Gallery, 1953, White Chapel Art Gallery, London, 1964, Galerie Ileana Sonnabend, Paris, 1971, 1972, 1973, Leo Castelli Gallery, N.Y.C., 1972, 1973, Ace Gallery, L.A., 1973, Nat. Collection Fine Arts, Smithsonian Inst., Washington, 1976, Mus. Modern Art, N.Y.C., 1977, Albright Knox Gallery, 1977, Art Inst. Chgo., 1977, San Francisco Mus. Modern Art, 1977, Vancouver Art Gallery, 1978, Staatliche Kunsthalle, Berlin, 1980, Kunstalle, Düsseldorf, 1980, Louisiana Mus., Copenhagen, 1980, Stadelsches Kunstinst., Frankfurt, 1981, Tate Galery, London, 1981, Städtische Galerie im Lembacchaus, Munich, 1981, Phoenix Art Mus., 1982,

G.H. Dalsheimer Gallery, Balt., 1983, Castelli Graphics, 1984, Galerie Bayeler, Basle, 1984, Juan March, Madrid, 1985, L.A. County Mus. Art, 1987, Inst. Contemporary Art, London, 1987, Galerie Alfred Kren, Cologne, 1988—89, Tretyakov Gallery, Moscow, 1989, Nat. Art Gallery, Kuala Lumpur, Malaysia, 1990, Mus. Contemporary Art, L.A., 1995—97, Pace Wilder Stein Gallery, N.Y.C., 1996, L.A., 1996—97, Guggenheim Mus., 1998, others, exhibited in group shows at Sao Paulo Biennial, 1959, Exposition Internat. Surrealisme, Paris, 1959—60, Mus. Modern Art, 1959, Guggenheim Mus., 1961, 1992, Mus. South Tex., Corpus Christi, 1974, N.Y. Collection in Stockholm, 1972, Whitney Mus. Am. Art, N.Y.C., 1972, 1973, Garage Show, Rome, 1973, Automme Festival d'Artes, Paris, 1973, N.Y. Cultural Ctr., 1973, Represented in permanent collections Albright-Knox Art Gallery, Whitney Mus. am. Art, Wadsworth Atheneum, Tate Gallery, Mus. Modern Art, Neue Galerie Aachen, Germany, Hirshhorn Mus., Moderna Museet, Stockholm, others, prin. works include electronic sculpture Soundings, prin. works include painting Tut-Scape; set and costume designer, lighting expert, stage mgr. Merce Cunningham Dance Co., 1964; choreographer dance Pelican, others. Served USNR, WWII. Recipient 1st Prize, Internat. Exhbn. Prints Gallery Modern Art, Ljubljana, Yugoslavia, 1963, Venice Biennale, 1964, Corcoran Biennal Contemporary Am. Painters, 1965, Skowhegan Sch. Painting and Sculpture medal, 1982, Grammy award, 1984. Mem.: NAD (assoc.), Am. Acad. and Inst. Arts and Letters. Gallery: Pace Wildenstein Gallery 32 E 57th St New York NY 10022-2513

RAUSCHENBUSCH, STEPHANIE, artist, educator, poet; b. Washington, July 27, 1942; d. Stephen and Josephine Burns Raushenbush; m. Joseph Marchant Hayman, Dec. 29, 1984; m. Louis R. Rowan, June 20, 1964 (div. June 20, 1979); 1 child, Quentin Rowan. BA magna cum laude, Radcliffe Coll., Cambridge, Mass., 1964; MA summa cum laude, Columbia U., NYC, 1966. Treas. Noho Gallery, NYC, 1999—. One-woman shows include Noho Gallery, NYC, 1983, 1987, 1989, 1991, 1993, 1995, 1997, 1999, 2002, exhibited in group shows at Woodstock (NY) Guild, 1986, Art and the Law traveling exhibit, 1988—1889, Biennale d'Arte Contemporanea, Florence, 2001, in pvt. collections; author: (book of poetry) The Heart's Ice Thaws, 1999; contbr. poetry to lit. jours.; exhibitions include, 1986—90, 2003. Trustee Friends Sem., NYC, 1998—2001. Fellow, Woodrow Wilson Found., 1964—65; grantee Kent fellowship grad. studies, Danforth Found., 1966—70. Mem.: NY Soc. of Women in the Arts, Women's Caucus for Art, Catherine Lorillard Wolfe Art Club. Democrat. Mem. Soc. Of Friends. Avocation: gardening. Home: 46 Sherman St Brooklyn NY 11215

RAUSCHER, JAMES FRANCIS, music educator; b. Menomenie, Wis., Apr. 30, 1957; s. Shirley Mae and Francis James Rauscher; m. Vanessa Ann Bourg, June 22, 1984; children: John Gilbert, Ann Marie. MusB in Edn., U. Wis., Eau Claire, 1979; MusM in Piano Performance and Lit., U. Ill., 1981; Ph.D in Fine Arts, Tex. Tech U., 1991. Prof. piano Amarillo Coll., Tex., 1981—, chmn., dept. music, 1988—; dir. music, organist St. Mary's Cath. Ch., 1988—. Prin. keyboardist Amarillo Symphony Orch., 1981—. Musician solo pianist; chamber musician. Recipient Amarillo Music Tchr. Yr., 1986. Mem.: Tex. Music Educators Assn., Tex. C.C. Tchrs. Assn., Amarillo Music Tchrs. Assn. (pres. 1992—94), Tex. Music Tchrs. Assn., Music Tchrs. Nat. Assn. Roman Catholic. Avocations: reading, travel. Office: Amarillo College PO Box 447 Amarillo TX 79178 E-mail: rauscher-jf@actx.edu.

RAUSEN, AARON REUBEN, pediatric hematologist, oncologist; b. Jersey City, June 30, 1930; s. David and Ruth (Schwartz) R.; m. Emalou Watkins, Apr. 7, 1968; children: David, Susan, Elisabeth. Degree, Dartmouth Coll., 1950; MD, SUNY, Bklyn., 1954. Intern, then resident in pediatrics Bellevue Hosp. Ctr., N.Y.C., 1954-56; chief resident in pediatrics Mt. Sinai Hosp., N.Y.C., 1958-59, asst. assoc. and attending pediatrician, 1961-81; fellow in hematology Children's Hosp. and Harvard Med. Sch., Boston, 1959-61; chief of pediatrics City Hosp. Ctr., Elmhurst, N.Y., 1964-72; dir. pediatrics Beth Israel Med. Ctr., N.Y.C., 1972-81; dir. pediatric oncology NYU Med. Ctr., N.Y.C., 1981-97; prof. pediatrics NYU Sch. Medicine, N.Y.C., 1981—. Prof. pediat. Mt. Sinai Sch. Medicine, N.Y.C., 1971—81, professorial lectr., 1981—; dir. Stephen D. Hassenfeld Children's Ctr. for Cancer and Blood Disorders, N.Y.C., 1990—97, founding dir., 1997—; cons. Lenox Hill Hosp., N.Y.C., 1981—; vis. prof. Dartmouth Med. Sch., Hanover, NH, 1984—86; prin. investigator Children's Oncology Group, 1999—. Contbr. articles to profl. jours. Bd. dirs. N.Y.C. chpt. Am. Cancer Soc., 1984—, Nat. Childhood Cancer Found., 1992—, Children's Oncology Soc. N.Y., 1993—, Ovarian Cancer Rsch. Fund, 1994-99. Capt. Med. Corps, U.S. Army, 1956-58. Fellow Am. Acad. Pediatrics; mem. Am. Pediatric Soc., Am. Soc. Hematology, Am. Soc. Clin. Oncology, Am. Assn. Cancer Rsch., Am. Soc. Pediatric Hematology-Oncology, N.Y. Pediatric Soc. (pres. 1974), Yale Club N.Y.C., Phi Beta Kappa, Alpha Omega Alpha. Office: 317 E 34th St Fl 8 New York NY 10016-4974 Office Phone: 212-263-7144. E-mail: aaron.rausen@med.nyu.edu.

RAUSHER, DAVID BENJAMIN, internist, gastroenterologist; b. Bklyn., Sept. 15, 1952; s. Herbert and Shirley Ruth R.; m. Judy A. Steinlauf, Aug. 8, 1976; children: Scott, Michael, Steven. BA, Hamilton Coll., 1973; MD, SUNY, Bklyn., 1977. Diplomate Am. Bd. Internal Medicine, Am. Bd. Gastroenterology. Resident Emory U. Hosps., Atlanta, 1977-80, fellow in gastroenterology, 1980-82; pres. Atlanta Ctr. for Gastroenterology, Decatur, Ga., 1982—; med. dir. Atlanta Endoscopy Ctr., Decatur, 1994—. Chmn. diagnostic treatment ctr. DeKalb Med. Ctr., Decatur, Ga., 1985—, co-chief gastroenterology, 1995-97, chief sect. gastroenterology, 1998—. Office: Atlanta Ctr Gastro 2665 N Decatur Rd Decatur GA 30033-6125 Office Phone: 404-296-1986.

RAUSSER, GORDON C(LYDE), agricultural and resource economics educator; b. Lodi, Calif., July 21, 1943; s. Elmer A. and Doyve Ester (Meyers) R.; children: Sloan, Stephanie, Paige. BS summa cum laude, Calif. State U., 1965; MS with highest honors, U. Calif., Davis, 1968, PhD with highest honors, 1971. Prof. econs. and agrl. econs. U. Calif., Davis, 1969-74; vis. prof. U. Chgo., 1972-74; prof. econs. and stats. Iowa State U., 1974-75; prof. bus. adminstrn. Harvard U., 1975-78; prof., chmn. dept. agrl. and resource econs. U. Calif., Berkeley, 1979-85, 93-94, Robert Gordon Sproul disting. prof., 1985—, dean nat. resources, 1994-2000; dir. Giannini Found., Berkeley, 1984-86. Vis. prof. Hebrew U. and Ben-Gurion U., Israel, 1978; Ford Found. vis. prof., Argentina, 72; spl. cons. and sr. economist Coun. Econ. Advisors, 1986—87; chief economist AID, 1988—90; advisor econ. rsch. svc. USDA, 1978—80, 1986—88, Agr. Can., 1977—79, Bur. Agrl. Econs., Australia, 1987, U.S. Office Mgmt. and Budget, 1986; mem., chmn. planning com. Sch. Bus. Adminstrn. U. Calif., Berkeley, 1986—87, mem. adv. com. Agrl. Issues Ctr., 1984—85, mem. planning com. Agrl. and Natural Resources Program, 1986, mem. econs. programs evaluation com., 1987—88; mem. Citrus Planning Commn., Brazil, 1984; pres. Inst. for Policy Reform, Washington, 1989—94; prin., founder Law & Econ. Cons. Group, Berkeley, Washington, Chgo., NYC, 1990—2000; sr. cons. Charles River Assocs., 2000—. Author: Macroeconomic Environment for U.S. Agricultural Policy, Alternative Agricultural and Food Policies and the 1985 Farm Bill, The Emergence of Market Economies in Eastern Europe, New Directions in Econometric Modeling and Forecasting, Dynamics of Agricultural Systems: Economic Prediction and Control, Quantitative Methods in Agricultural Economics, GATT Negotiations and the Political Economy of Policy Reform; co-editor: Handbook of Agricultural Economics, Vol. 2A, 2002, Vol. 2B, 2002, Vol. 1A, 2001, Vol. 1B, 2001; editor Decision-Making in Business and Economics, 1977-79, Am. Jour. Agrl. Econs., 1983-86. Mem. western nutrition ctr. coordinating com. USDA, 1980-83; mem. Arab-Am. Coun. for Cultural and Econ. Exch., 1979-81; bd. dirs. Giannini Found. Agrl. Econs., 1979-84, mem. exec. com., 1979-84; mem. planning com. Berkeley Food Coop., 1980-83, planning com. for food policy Resources for the Future, 1984-85; mem. adv. com. Calif. State Dept. Agr., 1982-84; bd. dirs. Am. Agrl. Econs. Awards. Grantee USDA, NSF, World Bank, Chgo. Merc. Exch., U.S. Bur. Mines; Fulbright scholar, Australia, 1987; Sr. fellow Resources for Future, 1984-85. Fellow: AAAS, Am. Agrl. Econs. Assn. (oustanding enduring rsch. contbn. com. 1982—84, outstanding PhD dissertation com. 1974—76, chmn. outstanding article com. 1983—86, rsch. awards of merit 1976, 1978, 1980, 1982, 1986, 1989, 1992, Pub. Enduring quality award 1993, rsch. awards of merit 1993, Disting. Policy Contbn. award 1993, rsch. awards of merit 1994, 2000, 2001), Am. Statis. Assn.; mem.: Western Agrl. Econ. Assn. (Best Pub. Rsch. award 1978, Outstanding Pub. Rsch. award 1994), Ops. Rsch. Soc., Math. Assn. Am., Econometric Soc., Am. Acad. Polit. and Social Sci., Am. Econ. Assn., Commonwealth Club (dir. agr. study group 1983—84), Alpha Zeta, Alpha Gamma Rho. Home: 661 San Luis Rd Berkeley CA 94707-1725 Office: U Calif Berkeley ARE 207 Giannini Hall Berkeley CA 94720-3310 Business E-Mail: rausser@are.berkeley.edu.

RAUTAHARJU, PENTTI MATTI, research scientist, educator; b. Tuusniemi, Finland, Dec. 23, 1932; s. Emil Matti Rautaharju and Ellen Raatikainen; m. Meeri Maria Rautaharju, Aug. 5, 1956 (div. 1977); children: Anu, Tina, Mia; m. Farida Swaliha Razack, Oct. 14, 1982; children: Satu, Sherene, Riza. MD, Helsinki Sch. Medicine, Finland, 1957; PhD, U. Minn., 1962. Prof. dir. Heart Disease Rsch. Ctr., Dalhousie, Halifax, Can., 1963-90, Epicare Ctr., U. Alberta, Can., 1990-94, Winston Salem, N.C., 1994—. Contbr. articles to profl. jours. With Finnish Army, 1954. Fellow RCP, Am. Coll. Cardiologists; mem. Can. Cardiovascular Soc. (Outstanding Scientist 1984), Order of Finland. Avocations: poetry, woodcarving, gardening. Office: Epicare Ctr 2000 West First St Winston Salem NC 27104 Home: 737 Vista Meadows Dr Weston FL 33327-1835 E-mail: frautaha@wfubmc.edu.

RAUWERDINK, WILLIAM JAY, accountant; b. Sheboygan, Wis., Mar. 3, 1950; s. Harvard M. and Dorothy M. (Duenk) R.; m. Ann Catherine Geske, July 14, 1979; 1 child, Margaret Allene. BBA, U. Wis., 1972; MBA, Harvard U., 1974. CPA, N.Y., Mich., Mass. Ptnr. Deloitte & Touche, Detroit, 1978—93; exec. v.p., CFO, treas., sec. The MEDSTAT Group, Inc., Ann Arbor, Mich., 1994—96, Lason, Inc., Troy, Mich., 1996—2000; exec. v.p., CFO, treas. Hotwire.com, San Francisco, 2001; interim pres., CFO, Gyricon, LLC, Ann Arbor, 2002—04. Bd. dirs. Trinity Health Svcs., Novi, Mich. Mem. Wis. Bus. Alumni Assn. (bd. dirs. 1980-89, 92—, pres. 1984-85), Harvard Club (Boston). Mailing: 5382 Pembrooke Crossing West Bloomfield MI 48322

RAUZI, HAROLD RAY, lawyer, respiratory therapist; b. Litchfield, Ill., Oct. 1, 1953; s. Harold Ray and Eileen Ione (Keck) R.; m. Mary Elizabeth Draper, Aug. 8, 1987. AS, Lewis & Clark C.C., Godfrey, Ill., 1973; diploma in Respiratory Therapy, Meml. Med. Ctr., Springfield, Ill., 1974; BA, Ottawa U., 1984; JD cum laude, Case Western Reserve U., 1989. Bar: Ohio 1989, U.S. Dist. Ct. (no. dist.) Ohio 1990, U.S. Ct. Appeals (6th cir.) 1990; Registered Respiratory Therapist, Nat. Bd. for Respiratory Care. Clin. instr., critical care respiratory therapist U. Kans. Med. Ctr., Kansas City, 1974-80; clin. edn. coord. Parkview Meml. Hosp., Ft. Wayne, Ind., 1980-82; sr. respiratory therapist Luth. Hosp., Ft. Wayne, 1982-86; respiratory therapist Mt. Sinai Hosp., Cleve., 1986-88; assoc. Armstrong & Di Santis Law Firm, Cleve., 1990, Buckley King, Cleve., 1990—98, ptnr., 1998—. Mem. editl. bd.: Health Matrix, 1987—89; contbr. articles to profl. jours. Mem.: Coun. Appellate Lawyers, Cleve. Bar Assn., Ohio Bar Assn., Am. Assn. for Respiratory Care, Am. Mensa Ltd. Office: Buckely King LPA 1400 Fifth Third Ctr Cleveland OH 44114 Office Phone: 216-363-1400. Business E-Mail: rauzi@bucklaw.com.

RAVAIOLI, UMBERTO, electrical engineer, educator; b. Forli, Italy, Oct. 8, 1955; arrived in U.S., 1983; s. Ademaro Ravaioli and Saura Bacchini; m. Ann Lucia Chan, Jan. 2, 1987; children: Umberto Jay, Linda Selene. Diploma in Trombone, Conservatory of Ferrara, Italy, 1976; Laurea in Electronics Engring., U. Bologna, Italy, 1980, Laurea in Physics, 1982; PhD in Elec. Engring., Ariz. State U., 1986. Asst. prof. elec. and computer engring. U. Ill., Urbana, 1986—91, assoc. prof. elec. and computer engring., 1991—95, prof. elec. and computer engring., 1995—. Fellow: IEEE, Inst. of Physics. Office: U Ill Urbana-Champaign 405 N Mathews Ave Urbana IL 61801 Office Phone: 217-244-5765. E-mail: ravaioli@uiuc.edu.

RAVDEL, BORIS, electrochemist, researcher; b. St.Petersburg (Leningrad), Russia, Sept. 20, 1952; arrived in US, 1996; s. Adolf and Eugenia Ravdel; m. Elena Varshavskaya, Nov. 5, 1971; children: Anna, Polina. PhD, Inst. Tech., Russia, 1981; MS, St. Petersburg Inst. Tech., 1974. Rschr. Inst. of Tech., St.Petersburg, Russia, 1974—93; asst. prof. Northwestern Poly. Inst., St.Petersburg, 1993—96; vis. rschr. NCSU, Raleigh, NC, 1996—98; rschr. ECO/Tracer Technologies, Somerville, Mass., 1998—2000; rsch. scientist Lithion/Yardney Tech. Products, Pawcatuck, Conn., 2000—. Voting surveyor Dem. Elections, St.Petersburg, Russia, 1990—93. Grantee Ministry for Highest Edn. of Russia fellow, Rsch. found., 1991-1993. Mem.: The Electrochem. Soc. Inc. Achievements include patents pending for thermostable electrolyte for lithium-ion batteries. Office: Lithion/Yardney Tech Product 82 Mechanic St Pawcatuck CT 06379 Home: 95 James Rd Voluntown CT 06384 Office Phone: 860-599-1100 467. Personal E-mail: varrav@myprimus.com. E-mail: bravdel@lithion.com.

RAVECHÉ, HAROLD JOSEPH, university administrator, physical chemist; b. N.Y.C., Mar. 18, 1943; s. Harold Edward Raveche and Helen Patricia (DeVincent) Gravino; m. Elizabeth Marie Scott, Jan. 26, 1974; children— John Vincent, Justin Blaise, Bernice Helen, Elizabeth Ann. BA in Chemistry, Hofstra U., 1963; PhD in Phys. Chemistry, U. Calif.-San Diego, 1968. NRC postdoctoral assoc. Nat. Bur. Standards, Gaithersburg, Md., 1968-70, research chemist, 1970-78, chief thermophysics div., 1978-85; dean Sch. of Sci., prof. chemistry Rensselaer Poly. Inst., Troy, N.Y., 1985-88; pres. Stevens Inst. Tech., Hoboken, N.J., 1988—. Bd. dirs. Nat. West N.J. and Bancorp, Atlantic Energy Inc.; commr. of sci. and tech., N.J. Editor: Perspectives in Statistical Physics, 1980; contbr. articles to profl. jours. Pres. Potomac Highlands Citizens Assn., Md., 1978-80 Recipient Disting. Young Scientist of Yr. award Md. Acad. Scis., 1975, U.S. Sr. Exec. Service award Nat. Bur. Standards, 1983, Equal Employment Opportunity award Nat. Bur. Standards, 1984 Mem. AAAS (commn. on sci. edn. 1972-75), Am. Phys. Soc. (adv. council 1975-78), Soc. for Indsl. and Applied Math. (adv. bd. conf. on large-scale computational problems 1984-88), Am. Chem. Soc., Sigma Xi Roman Catholic. Avocations: hiking, swimming, skiing, music, theater. Office: Stevens Inst Tech Office of Pres Castle Point On Hudson Hoboken NJ 07030*

RAVEN, ABBE, broadcast executive; b. New York, 1953; 1 child. BA in Theater, U. Buffalo, 1974; MA in Cinema and Theater, Hunter Coll. Prodn. mgr., stage mgr. Manhattan Theater Club, Bklyn. Acad. Music, N.Y.C.; mgr. prodn. Hearst/ABC Video Svcs.; dir. prodn. svcs. A&E TV Networks, 1984-88, sr. v.p. prodn., 1988—; sr. v.p. programming and prodn. The History Channel and HTV Prodns., 1995-97; sr. v.p. programming The History Channel, 1997—2000, gen. mgr., exec. v.p., 2000—. Instr. various ednl. instns. Active Competition Com. CableACE Awards, chair 12 Ann. Ceremonies; active coms. focusing on violence in TV. Named to, Hunter Coll. Hall of Fame; recipient U. Buffalo Alumni award, National History Day Org. Corp. Leadership Award, 2000. Mem. NATAS, Women in Cable, Am. Women in Radio and TV, PROMAX, Nat. Acad. Cable Programming. Office: A&E TV Networks The Hearst Corp 235 E 45th St 9th Fl New York NY 10017-3305

RAVEN, BERTRAM H(ERBERT), psychology educator; b. Youngstown, Ohio, Sept. 26, 1926; s. Morris and Lillian R.; m. Celia Cutler, Jan. 21, 1961; children: Michelle G., Jonathan H. BA, Ohio State U., 1948, MA, 1949; PhD, U. Mich., 1953. Rsch. assoc. Rsch. Ctr. for Group Dynamics, Ann Arbor, Mich., 1952-54; lectr. psychology U. Mich., Ann Arbor, 1953-54; vis. prof. U. Nijmegen, U. Utrecht, Netherlands, 1954-55; psychologist RAND Corp., Santa Monica, Calif., 1955-56; prof. UCLA, 1956—, chair dept. psychology, 1983-88. Vis. prof. Hebrew U., Jerusalem, 1962-63, U. Wash., Seattle, U. Hawaii, Honolulu, 1968, London Sch. Econs. and Polit. Sci., 1969-70; external examiner U. of the W.I., Trinidad and Jamaica, 1980—, rsch. assoc. Psychol. Rsch. Ctr., 1993—; participant Internat. Expert Conf. on Health Psychology, Tilburg, Netherlands, 1986; cons., expert witness in field, 1979—. Author: (with others) People in Groups, 1976, Discovering Psychology, 1977, Social Psychology, 1983, Social Psychology: People in Groups (Chinese edit.), 1994; editor: (with others) Contemporary Health Services, 1982, Policy Studies Rev. Ann., 1980; editor: Jour. Social Issues, 1969-74; mem. editl. bd. Jour. of Criminology and Social Psychology, 2001-, Revista de Psicologia de la Salud, 1995-; mem. adv. bd. Jour. Entrepreneurship, 2004-; contbr. articles to profl. jours. Co-dir. Tng. Program in Health Psychology, UCLA, 1979-88; cons. WHO, Manila, 1985-86; cons., expert witness various Calif. cts., 1978—. Guggenheim fellow, Israel, 1962-63; Fulbright scholar Netherlands, 1954-55, Israel, 1962-63, Britain, 1969-70; recipient Citation from L.A. City Coun., 1966, Rsch. on Soc. power by Calif. Sch. of profl. psychology, L.A., 1991; NATO sr. fellow, Italy, 1989. Fellow APA (chair bd. social and ethical responsibility 1978-82, ethics com. 2003—), Am. Psychol. Soc., Soc. for Psychol. Study of Social Issues (pres. 1973-74, coun. 1995-97, Kurt Lewin award 1998), Soc. for Personality and Social Psychology; mem. AAAS, Am. Sociol. Assn., Internat. Assn. Applied Psychology, Soc. Exptl. Social Psychology, Assn. Advancement of Psychology (founding, bd. dirs. 1974-81), Internat. Soc. Polit. Psychology (governing coun. 1996-98), Interam. Psychol. Soc., Am. Psychology-Law Soc., Psychologists for Social Responsibility. Avocations: guitar, travel, international studies. Home: 2212 Camden Ave Los Angeles CA 90064-1906 Office: UCLA Dept Psychology Los Angeles CA 90095-1563 Office Phone: 310-825-2296. Business E-Mail: raven@ucla.edu.

RAVEN, FRANCIS HARVEY, mechanical engineer, educator; b. Erie, Pa., July 29, 1928; s. Frederick James and Eleanor Elizabeth (Sopp) R.; m. Therese Mary Strobel, June 21, 1952; children: Betty, Ann Raven McCarthy, Paul, John, Mary Raven Mansmann, Cathy, Linda. BS in Math., Gannon Univ., 1948; BSME, Pa. State U., 1950, MSME, 1951; PhD, Cornell U., 1958. Design engr. Hamilton Standard div. United Techs., Hartford, Conn., 1951-54; instr. Cornell U., Ithaca, N.Y., 1954-58; asst. prof. mech. engring. U. Notre Dame, 1958-62, assoc. prof., 1962-66, prof., 1966—. Cons. microprocessor and computer control of robots and mech. systems; devel. Vector Loop Method (first analytical method for the design of mechanisms and cam systems.). Author: Automatic Control Engineering, 1961, 5th edit., 1995, Mathematics of Engineering Systems, 1966, Engineering Mechanics, 1973; pub. McGraw-Hill Book Co. Mem. ASME, Am. Soc. for Engring. Edn. (AT&T Teaching award 1968-69), Sigma Xi. Roman Catholic.

RAVEN, HYACINTHE L. publishing executive, editor; b. Garfield Hts., OH, Oct. 27, 1976; d. Gary Lee and Deborah Ann (Fox) Steely. BA Linguistics, Anthropology, Cleveland State Univ., Cleveland, OH, 2001—; Phil. Concentration, Shimer Coll., Waukegan, Ill, 1994—95. Owner/editor Via Dolorosa Press, Cleveland, Ohio, 1994—. Editor: (magazine) Erased, Sigh, Sigh, 1994—. Mem.: Linguistic Soc. of Am. (mem. 2002), Modern Lang. Assoc. (mem. 2002). Independent. Achievements include Founded via Dolorosa Press at age 17, now heading into it's 10th yr. with over 50 books pub. Office: Via Dolorosa Press 701 E Schaaf Rd Cleveland OH 44131-1227

RAVEN, LUISA ANTONIA, nurse, psychotherapist; b. N.Y.C., Sept. 25, 1939; d. Joseph A. and Mary Louise (Swann) R. BSN, St. Louis U., 1976; BA in Edn., Caldwell (N.J.) Coll., 1970; MSN, Columbia U., 1982. RN, N.J. Joined Order Sisters of St. Joseph of Peace, Roman Cath. Ch., 1962. Pvt. practice nurse psychotherapist, Englewood Cliffs, N.J.; instr. nursing Felician Coll., Lodi, N.J.; clin. specialist psychiat. nursing Greystone Park (N.J.) Psychiat. Hosp.; staff nurse med./surg. psychiat. unit St. Mary's Hosp., Passaic, NJ. Adj. faculty Bergen C.C., Paramus, N.J. Mem. N.J. Nurses Assn. (Psychiat. Nurse of Yr. award 1984), Sigma Theta Tau, Alpha Sigma Nu. Home: 5 Oakdale Manor Apt B18 Suffern NY 10901-5700

RAVEN, PETER HAMILTON, botanical garden director, botany educator; b. Shanghai, June 13, 1936; s. Walter Francis and Isabelle Marion (Breen) R.; children— Alice Catherine, Elizabeth Marie, Francis Clark, Kathryn Amelia. AB with highest honors, U. Calif.-Berkeley, 1957; PhD, UCLA, 1960; DSc (hon.), St. Louis U., 1982, Knox Coll., 1983, So. Ill. U., 1983, Miami U., 1986, U. Goteborg, 1987, Rutgers U., 1988, U. Mass., 1988, Leiden U., The Netherlands, 1990; HHD (hon.), Webster U., 1989; D.Sc. (hon.), Universidad Nacional de La Plata, Argentina, 1991, Westminster Coll., 1992, U. Mo., 1992, Washington U., 1993, U. Conn., 1993; DSc (hon.), U. Cordoba, Argentina, 1993. Taxonomist, curator Rancho Santa Ana Botanic Garden, Claremont, Calif., 1961-62; asst. prof., then assoc. prof. biol. scis. Stanford U., Calif., 1962-71; dir. Mo. Bot. Garden, St. Louis, 1971—; adj. prof. biology St. Louis U., 1973—; Engelmann prof. botany Washington U., St. Louis, 1971—; adj. prof. biology U. Mo., St. Louis, 1976—. Sr. rsch. fellow New Zealand Dept. Sci. and Indsl. Rsch., 1969-70; v.p. XIII Internat. Bot. Congress, Sydney, 1981; Home Sec. Nat. Acad. Scis., 1987—; chmn. report rev. com. NRC, 1989—; mem. pres. com. Adv. on Sci. and Tech., 1994—; hon. vice-chair 27th Internat. Geographical Cong., 1992; hon. v.p. XV Internt. Bot. Cong., Tokyo, 1993; mem. Nat. Sci. Bd., 1990-94; mem. jury Internat. St. Francis Prize for Environment, 1990-93; mem. exec. com. Joint Appeal by Religion and Sci. for Environment, 1991—; mem. external adv. bd. Com. on Peabody Mus., Yale U., 1992-94; mem. coun. World Resources Inst., 1992—; mem. adv. com. Africa Ctr. for Resources and Environment, 1992—, Third World Found. N.Am., 1993; mem. adv. com. to biodiversity com. Chinese Acad. Scis., 1993—; mem. Exec. Com. Round Table, St. Louis, 1993—; mem. hon. fgn. adv. bd. Botanical Garden Orgn. Thailand, 1993—. Author: Native Shrubs of Southern California, 1966, (with P.R. Ehrlich, R.W. Holm) Papers on Evolution, 1969, (with H. Curtis) Biology of Plants, 1971, 4th edit., 1986, (with R.F. Evert and S.E. Eichhorn) 5th edit., 1992, (with B. Berlin and D. Breedlove) Principles of Tzeltal Plant Classification, 1974, (with G.B. Johnson) Biology, 1986, 3d edit., 1992, Understanding Biology, 1988, 3d edit., 1995; editor: (with L.E. Gilbert) Coevolution of Animals and Plants, 1981, (with F.J. Radovsky & S.H. Sohmer) Biogeography of the Tropical Pacific, 1984, (with others) Topics in Plant Population Biology, 1979, (with K. Iwatsuki and W.J. Bock) Modern Aspects of Species, 1986; editor-in-chief Brittonia, 1963-66; mme. editorial bd. Flora Neotropica, 1965-84; editor (with D.E. Osterbrock) Origins and Extinctions, 1988, paperback, 1992, (with R.M. Polhill) Advances in Legume Systematics, 1981 (with L. Berg and G.B. Johnson) Environment, 1995; mem. editorial bd. Evolution, 1963-65, 76-79, Memoirs of N.Y. Botanical Garden, 1966-84, N.Am. Flora, 1966-84, Am. Naturalist, 1967-70, Annual Rev. Ecology and Systematics, 1971-75, Flora of Ecuador, 1974—, Evolutionary Theory, 1975—, Adansonia, 1976—, Jour. Biogeography, 1978—, Science, 1979-82, Proceedings of U.S. Nat. Acad. Scis., 1980-87, World Book, Inc., 1982-86, Diversity, 1985-90, Bothalia, 1985—, Serie Botánica of the Anales del Instituto de Biología UNAM, 1989, Ecol. Applications, 1989-92, others; mem. adv. bd. Applied Botany Abstracts, 1981—, Tropical Plant Sci. Research, 1982—, Darwiniana, 1985—; mem. internat. editl. com. Acta Botánica Mexicana, 1987—; mem. internat. editl. adv. bd. Candollea, 1995—; mem. editl. bd. Botanical Bulletin Academia Sinica, 1988—, Botanical Mag., 1988-92, Chinese Jour. of Botany, 1991—, Edinburgh Jour. of Botany, 1994—; co-chmn. editl. com. Flora of China, 1988—; advisor Plants Today, 1988-89; contbr. over 400 articles to profl. jours. Bd. curators U. Mo., 1985-90; commr. Tower Grove Park, St. Louis, 1971—; mem. Arnold Arboretum Vis. Com., 1974-81, chmn. 1976-81; bd. overseers Morris Arboretum, 1977-81; mem. sci. adv. bd. Nat. Tropical Botanical Garden, 1975—; mem. Smithsonian Council, 1985-90; chmn. St. Louis Area Mus. Collaborative, 1985-91, Commn. for Flora Neotropica, 1985—; mem. Commn. on New Century, 1981-84; mem. sci. and engring. panel Com. on Scholarly Communication with People's Republic China, 1981-85; chmn. com. to visit dept. organismic and evolutionary biology Harvard U., 1982-84, mem. 84-85; ednl. adv. bd. John Simon Guggenheim Meml. Found., 1986—; research assoc. botany Bernice P. Bishop Mus., 1985—; hon. trustee Acad. Sci. of St. Louis, 1986—; chmn. Internat. Union for the Conservation of Nature, World Wildlife Fund, 1984-87, hon. chmn. 1987-90; mem. adv. and tech. bd. Fundación de Parques Nacionales and Fundación Neotrópica, Costa Rica, 1988—; mem. Nat. Coun. World Wildlife Fund and Conservation Foun., 1989—, U.S. bd. dirs. 1983-88, bd. dirs. Conservation Found., 1985-88, sci. adv. com. Conservation Internat., 1988—, chmn's. coun., 1989, World Wildlife Fund, 1987-90, Conservation Found., 1989—, Found. Flora Malesianna, 1992—, Sci. Svc., 1993—; hon. scientific adv. com. XVII Pacific Sci. Congress, 1990-91; adv. bd. The Winslow Found., 1993—, The Internat. Sci. Camp The Earth We Share, 1993—; exec. bd. Internat. Sci. Found. for the Former Soviet Union, 1992—; internat. adv. bd. Fifth ICSEB Congress, Hungary, 1994—. Commn. mem. U.S. MAB, 1994-95. Recipient A.P. DeCandolle prize, Geneva, 1970; Disting. Service award Japan Am. Soc. So. Calif., 1977; award of Merit, Bot. Soc. Am., 1977; Achievement medal Garden Club Am., 1978; Willdenow medal Berlin Bot. Garden, 1979; Disting. Service award Am. Inst. Biol. Scis., 1981; Joseph Priestly medal,

Dickinson Coll., 1982; Gold Seal medal Nat. Council of State Garden Clubs, 1982; Internat. Environ. Leadership medal UN Environ. Program, 1982; Spl. citiation Doña Doris Yankelewitz de Monge, 1985, Internat. Prize for Biology, Govt. Japan, 1986, Hutchinson medal Chgo. Hort. Soc., 1986, Archie F. Carr medal, 1987, Global 500 Honor Roll UN Environ. Program, 1987, Am. Fuchsia Soc. Achievement Medal, 1987, George Robert White Medal of Honor Mass. Horticultural Soc., 1987, Robert Allerton Medal Nat. Tropical Bot. Garden, 1988, Nat. Conservation Achievement award Nat. Wildlife Fedn., 1989, Delmer S. Fahrney medal Franklin Inst., Phila., 1989, (with E.O. Wilson) Environ. prize Institut de la Vie (Paris), 1990, Order of Golden Ark (officer), The Netherlands, 1990, award for Support of Sci. Coun. Sci. Soc. Pres., 1990, (with Norman Myers) Volvo Environ. prize, 1992, Pres.'s Conservation Achievement Awd., 1993, Nature Conservancyvement award TNC, 1993, Internat. award Internat. Inst. of St. Louis, 1994, Founder's Coun. Centennial Merit award The Field Mus. of Natural History, 1994, Sword of St. Ignatius Loyola award St. Louis U., 1994, Tyler Environ. Achievement prize, 1994, and numerous other botanical awards and honors; Guggenheim fellow, 1969-70; John D. and Catherine T. MacArthur Found. fellow, 1985-90, NSF postdoctoral fellow, Brit. Mus. London, 1960-61. Fellow Am. Acad. Arts and Scis. (com. on membership 1980-82), Linnean Soc. London (fgn. mem.), Calif. Acad. Scis. (CAS Fellow, Fellows' medal 1988), AAAS, Indian Nat. Sci. Acad., Third World Acad. Scis., World Acad. Art & Sci.; mem. NSF (systematic biology panel 1973-76, chmn. adv. com. for biol. behavioral and social scis. 1984-90), NAS (com. on human rights 1984-87, home sec. 1987—), Royal Danish Acad. Scis. and Letters (fgn. hon.), Royal Swedish Acad. Scis. (fgn.), Royal Soc. New Zealand (hon.), NRC (gov. bd. 1983-86, 87-88, chmn. com. on research priorities in tropical biology 1977-79, assembly life scis. 1979-81, com. on selected research problems in humid tropics 1980-82, commn. internat. relations 1981-82), Calif. Bot. Soc. (v.p. 1968-69), Am. Soc. Plant Taxonomists (pres. 1972), Assn. Systematics Collections (pres. 1980-82, Fed. Council Arts and Humanities, Nat. Geographic Soc. (com. on research and exploration 1982—), Internat. Orgn. Plant Biosystematists (v.p. 1989-92, pres. 92-95), Internat. Assn. for Plant Taxonomy (council 1981—), Orgn. Tropical Studies (treas. 1981-84, v.p. devel. 1984-85, pres. 1985-88, past pres. 1988-90, bd. dirs. 1981-91), Am. Soc. Naturalists (pres. 1983), Miller Inst. Basic Research in Sci. (adv. bd. 1983-89), Am. Inst. Biol. Scis. (pres. 1983-84), Mo. Acad. Scis., Geol. Soc. Am., Bot. Soc. Am. (pres. 1975, chmn. com. on sci. exchange with People's Republic China 1978-84), Assn. Tropical Biology (bd. dirs. 1981-85), Am. Assn. Mus. (exec. com. 1980-83), Assn. Sci. Mus. Dirs., Assn. Pacific Systematists, Sociedad Argentina de Botanica (socio honorario), Fundación Miguel Lillo (hon.), Soc. Systematic Zool., Sociedad Botánica de México (life), Assn. pour l'Etude Taxonomique de la Flore d'Afrique Tropicale, Orgn. for Phyto-Taxonomic Investigation of Mediterranean Area (council 1975-89), All-Union Botanical Soc. USSR (hon. fgn. mem.), Accademia Nazionale delle Scienze detta dei XL (fgn.), Am. Philosophical Soc, Russian Acad. Scis. (fgn. mem.), Nat. Acad. Scis. India (fgn. fellow 1990—), Academia de Ciencias Exactas, Físicas y Naturales, Austrian Acad. Scis., Academia Chilena de Ciencias, Academia Nacional de Ciencias, Academy Scis. Ukraine, Chinese Acad. Scis., Nature Conservancy (Pres. Conservation Achievement Awd., 1993), Phi Beta Kappa, Sigma Xi Office: Mo Bot Garden 4344 Shaw Blvd Saint Louis MO 63110-2226

RAVENAL, EARL CEDRIC, international relations educator, author; b. NYC, Mar. 29, 1931; s. Alan M. and Mildred S. (Sherman) R.; m. Carol Bird Myers, May 26, 1956; children: Cornelia Jane, John Brodhead, Rebecca Eliza. BA, Harvard U., 1952; postgrad., U. Cambridge, Eng., 1952-53; M.M.P. diploma, Harvard Bus. Sch., 1958; MA, Johns Hopkins U., 1971, PhD, 1975. Treas. Elbe File & Binder Co., Inc., Fall River, Mass., 1955-64, pres., 1965-67; dir. Asian div. systems analysis Office Sec. Def., Washington, 1967-69; prof. internat. relations Johns Hopkins U. Sch. Advanced Internat. Studies, Washington, 1973-78, Georgetown U. Sch. Fgn. Service, Washington, 1976—. Bd. advisors Ctr. for Def. Info., Washington, 1971-97, Ctr. for Study Conflict, 1983—; bd. dirs. Critical Rev. Author: (with others) Peace with China?, 1971, (with others) Atlantis Lost, 1976, Never Again, 1979, Toward World Security, 1978, Strategic Disengagement and World Peace, 1979, NATO's Unremarked Demise, 1979, Defining Def., 1984, NATO: The Tides of Discontent, 1985, Large-Scale Foreign Policy Change, 1989, Designing Defense, 1991, Defending America in an Uncontrollable World, 2002; contbg. editor Inquiry Mag., 1976-85, Critical Rev., 1987—; contbr. articles to profl. jours. Advisor Democratic Presdl. Campaign, 1972; advisor Jerry Brown Presdl. Campaign, 1976, Libertarian Presdl. Campaigns, 1980, 84. Served with JAGC U.S. Army, 1953-55. Henry fellow U. Cambridge, 1952-53; mem. faculty Salzburg Seminar in Am. Studies, 1977; fellow Bellagio Ctr. Rockefeller Found., 1975, Woodrow Wilson Internat. Ctr. for Scholars, 1973, Washington Ctr. of Fgn. Policy Research, 1974; sr. fellow Cato Inst., 1985-91, 97—. Mem. Council Fgn. Relations, Am. Polit. Sci. Assn., Internat. Inst. Strategic Studies, Fed. Am. Scientists, Internat. Studies Assn. Clubs: Cosmos (Washington); Fed. City (Washington); Harvard (N.Y.C.); Signet (Cambridge, Mass.); Tred Avon Yacht (Oxford, Md.). Libertarian. Home and Office: 4439 Cathedral Ave NW Washington DC 20016-3562

RAVENEL, SHANNON, book publishing professional; b. Charlotte, NC, Aug. 13, 1938; d. Elias Prioleau and Harriett Shannon (Steedman) R.; m. Dale Purves, May 25, 1968; children: Sara Blake, Harriett. BA, Hollins Coll., 1960. Mktg. asst., sch. dept. Holt, Rinehart & Winston, Inc., NYC, 1960-61; editl. asst. Houghton Mifflin Co., Boston, 1961-64, editor, 1964—70; editl. cons. pvt. practice, St. Louis, 1973-90; sr. editor, co-founder Algonquin Books of Chapel Hill, NC, 1982-91, editl. dir., 1992-2000; dir. Algonquin imprint Shannon Ravenel Books, 2001—. Series editor: Best American Short Stories, 1978-90; editor: Best American Short Stories of the Eighties, 1990, New Stories From the South, 1986—. Recipient Disting. Achievement award Coun. Lit. Mags. & Presses, NYC, 1990. Mem. PEN Am. Ctr. Democrat. Office: Algonquin Books of Chapel Hill PO Box 2225 Chapel Hill NC 27515-2225 E-mail: shannonr@algonquin.com.

RAVENHOLT, REIMERT THOROLF, epidemiologist, researcher; b. Milltown, Wis., Mar. 9, 1925; s. Ansgar Benedikt and Kristine Henriette (Petersen) R.; divorced; children: Janna, Mark, Lisa, Dane; m. Betty Butler Howell, Sept. 26, 1981. BS, U. Minn., 1948, MB, 1951, MD, 1952; MPH, U. Calif., Berkeley, 1956. Bd. cert. preventive medicine. Intern USPHS Hosp., San Francisco, 1951-52; epidemic intelligence service officer USPHS Communicable Disease Ctr., Atlanta, 1952-54; dir. epidemiology and communicable disease div. Seattle-King County Health Dept., 1954-61; epidemiology cons. European area USPHS, Paris, 1961-63; assoc. prof. preventive medicine U. Wash. Med. Sch., Seattle, 1963-66; dir. Office of Population, AID, Washington, 1966-79, World Health Surveys, Ctrs. for Disease Control, 1980-82; asst. dir. epidemiology and research Nat. Inst. Drug Abuse, Rockville, Md., 1982-84; chief epidemiology br. FDA, Rockville, Md., 1984-87; dir. World Health Surveys, Inc., Seattle, 1987-93; pres. Population Health Imperatives, Seattle, 1993—. Author/designer website dealing with epidemiology. Served with USPHS, 1951-54, 61-63. Recipient Disting Honor award AID, 1973, Hugh Moore Meml. award IPPF and Population Crisis Com., 1974. Fellow Am. Coll. Epidemiology, APHA (Carl Schultz award 1978), mem. Am. Coun. on Sci. and Health (bd. dirs.); mem. Cosmos Club (Washington). Independent. Home: 3156 E Laurelhurst Dr NE Seattle WA 98105-5333 E-mail: ravenrt@oz.net.

RAVETCH, IRVING, screenwriter; b. Newark, Nov. 14, 1920; s. I. Shalom and Sylvia (Shapiro) R.; m. Harriet Frank Jr., Nov. 24, 1946. BA, UCLA, 1941. Screenwriter: (films) (with La Cava) Living in a Big Way, 1947, The Outriders, 1950, Vengeance Valley, 1951; (with Harriet Frank, Jr.) The Long, Hot Summer, 1958, The Sound and the Fury, 1959, Home from the Hill, 1959, The Dark at the Top of the Stairs, 1960, House of Cards, 1969, The Cowboys, 1972, Conrack, 1974, The Spikes Gang, 1974, Norma Rae, 1979 (Academy award nomination best adapted screenplay 1979), Murphy's Romance, 1985, Stanley and Iris, 1990; writer, prodr.: (with Frank) Hud, 1963 (Academy award nomination best adapted screenplay 1963, N.Y. Film Critics Circle award best screenplay 1963), Hombre, 1967, The Reivers, 1969; story: (with Frank) Ten Wanted Men, 1955. Recipient N.Y. Film Critics award, 1963, Writers' Guild Am. award, 1988; Oscar nomination for Hud, Acad. Motion Picture Arts and Scis., 1963, Norma Rae, 1979.

RAVID, KATYA, medical educator; m. Shmuel Ravid; children: Yinon Arie, Noga Leah, Jonathan David. BSc, Technion-Israel Inst. Tech., Haifa, Israel, 1979, PhD, 1985. Postdoctoral fellow dept. biochemistry Brandeis Univ., Waltham, Mass., 1986-88; postdoctoral assoc. dept. biology Mass. Inst. Tech., Cambridge, 1988-91; instr. molecular medicine Harvard Medical Sch., Boston, 1992; asst. prof. biochemistry Boston Univ. Sch. Medicine, Boston, 1993-95, assoc. prof. biochemistry rsch. assoc. prof. medicine, 1993—, investigator Whitaker Cardiovascular Inst., 1993—, scientific dir. Core Transgenic facility, 1993—. Peer reviewer Am. Heart Assn. 1995—. Contbr. articles to profl. jours. With Israeli Def. Forces, 1977-79. Recipient numerous rsch. grants. Mem. The Am. Soc. Hematology, Am. Soc. Cell Biology, Am. Soc. Biochemistry and Molecular Biology, Am. Assn. Advancement of Sci. Office: Boston U Sch Medicine Dept Biochemistry 715 Albany St # K724 Boston MA 02118-2526

RAVIN, CARL ERIC, radiologist, educator, department chairman; m. Alison Bingham Ravin; children: David, Adam, Todd. AB, Cornell U., 1964, MD, 1968. Diplomate Am. Bd. Radiology. Instr. diagnostic radiology Yale U. Sch. Medicine, New Haven, 1975, asst. prof. radiology, 1976—78, U. Utah Med. Ctr., Salt Lake City, 1975—76; assoc. prof. radiology Duke U. Med. Ctr., Durham, NC, 1978—82, prof. radiology, 1982—, chmn. dept. radiology, 1985—. Bd. dirs. Duke U. Health Sys. Inc., Durham, NC, Duke U. Affiliated Physicians Inc., Durham, NC, Durham Casualty Co., Durham, NC. Editor: (textbook) Textbook of Diagnostic Imaging, 1988, 1994. With U.S. Coast Guard, 1970—71. Fellow: Am. Coll. Chest Physicians, Am. Coll. Radiology; mem.: AMA, Soc. Chmn. Acad. Radiology Depts., Am. Roentgen Ray Soc., Soc. Thoracic Radiology, Radiol. Soc. N.Am., Fleischner Soc. (pres. 1997—98). Office: Duke Univ Med Ctr Erwin Rd Durham NC 27710

RAVIN, LINDA, actress; b. N.J., Oct. 21, 1956; d. Frank and Sophie Genevieve (Adams) Ravinsky. BA, Jersey City State Coll.; studies with Ann Countryman, Gene Frankel, Phil Black, Bob Audy. Dancer various prodns. including Salute to Armed Forces, Dance Festival in Park; actress numerous plays including West Side Story, 1977, Sugar Babies, 1979-82, When the Kids Are Away, One Flew Over the Cuckoo's Nest, Detective Story, House of Blue Leaves, My Fair Lady, Pippin, (films) Don Juan, 1975, The Cellar, Dino's Case, Four Friends, 1981, (TV shows) Let's Talk to the Stars, Ryan's Hope, Edible Capra Mystery, A Little Sex, 1982, The Hamptons. Mem. Actors' Equity Assn., AFTRA, Screen Actors Guild.

RAVITCH, DIANE SILVERS, historian, educator, author, government official; b. Houston, July 1, 1938; d. Walter Cracker and Ann Celia (Katz) Silvers; m. Richard Ravitch, June 26, 1960 (div. 1986); children: Joseph, Steven (dec.), Michael. BA, Wellesley Coll., 1960; PhD, Columbia U., 1975; LHD (hon.), Williams Coll., 1984, Reed Coll., 1985, Amherst Coll., 1986, SUNY, 1988, Ramapo Coll., 1990, St. Joseph's Coll., N.Y., 1991, Middlebury Coll., 1997, Union Coll., 1998. Adj. asst. prof. Tchrs. Coll., Columbia U., N.Y.C., 1975-78, assoc. prof., 1978-83, adj. prof., 1983-91; asst. sec. office ednl. rsch. and improvement U.S. Dept. Edn., Washington, 1991-93, counselor to the sec. edn., 1991-93. Vis. fellow Brookings Instn., Washington, 1993-94, non-resident sr. fellow, 1994-, editor papers on edn. policy, 1997-, Brown chair in edn. policy, 1997-; rsch. prof. NYU, 1994-; mem. Nat. Assessment Governing Bd., 1997-; mem. com. on edn. policy Nat. Acad. Scis., 2003-. Author: The Great School Wars, 1974, The Revisionists Revised, 1977, The Troubled Crusade, 1983, The Schools We Deserve, 1985, National Standards in American Education, A Citizens Guide, 1995, Left Back, 2000, The Language Police, 2003; author: (with others) Educating an Urban People, 1981; author: The School and the City, 1983, Against Mediocrity, 1984, Challenges to the Humanities, 1985, What Do Our 17 Year Olds Know?, 1987; editor: The American Reader, 1990; co-editor: New Schools for a New Century, 1997, City Schools, 2000, The Democracy Reader, 1992, Making Good Citizens, 2001; editor: Learning from the Past, 1995, Debating the Future of American Education, 1995; co-editor: Kid Stuff, 2003. Chair Ednl. Excellence Network, 1988—91, 1994—96; trustee Nat. Humanities Ctr., 1999—2000, N.Y. Pub. Libr., N.Y.C., 1981—87, hon. life trustee, 1988—; trustee N.Y. Coun. on Humanities, 1996—; mem. Landmarks Preservation Commn., Southold, NY, 2000—02; bd. dirs. Woodrow Wilson Nat. Fellowship Found., 1987—91, Coun. Basic Edn., 1989—91, Thomas B. Fordham Found., 1998—, New Am. Found., 2000—, Albert Shanker Inst., 2002—, Core Knowledge Found., 2003—, Hunt Inst. Ednl. Policy and Leadership, 2002—. Recipient Award for Disting. Svc., N.Y. Acad. Pub. Edn., 1994, Wellesley Coll. Alumnae Achievement award, 1989; Guggenheim fellow, 1977-78; Phi Beta Kappa vis. scholar. Mem. Nat. Acad. Edn., Am. Acad. Arts and Scis., Soc. Am. Historians, N.Y. Hist. Soc. (trustee 1995-98), PEN Internat. Office: NYU 82 Wash Sq E New York NY 10003-6644

RAVITZ, LEONARD J., JR., physician, scientist, consultant; b. Cuyahoga County, Ohio, Apr. 17; s. Leonard Robert and Esther Evelyn (Skerball) R. BS, Case Western Res. U., 1944; MD, Wayne State U., 1946; MS, Yale U., 1950. Diplomate Am. Bd. Psychiatry and Neurology, 1952, Am. Bd. Forensic Examiners, 1996, Am. Coll. Forensic Examiners; bd. cert. forensic examiner. Rsch. asst. EEG to A.J. Derbyshire, PhD Harper Hosp., Detroit, 1943-46; spl. trainee in hypnosis to Milton H. Erickson, MD Wayne County Gen. Hosp., Eloise, Mich., 1945-46, 46-80; rotating intern St. Elizabeth's Hosp., Washington, 1946-47; jr. asst. resident in psychiatry Yale-New Haven Hosp., 1947-48; asst. in psychiatry and mental hygiene Yale Med. Sch., 1947-48, assoc. in psychiatry and mental hygiene, sr. asst. resident, 1948-49, rsch. fellow to Harold S. Burr, PhD, sect. neuro-anatomy, 1949-50, sr. resident in neuropsychiatry Richard S. Lyman svc., 1950-51; instr. Duke U. Med. Sch., Durham, 1950-51; assoc. to R. Burke Suitt, MD, Pvt. Diagnostic Clinic, Duke Hosp., Durham, 1951-53; assoc. Duke U. Med. Sch., 1951-53; vis. asst. prof. neuropsychiatry and asst. to vis. prof. Richard S. Lyman, MD, Meharry Med. Ctr., Nashville, 1953; asst. dir. profl. edn. in charge tng. U. Wyo. Nursing Sch. Affiliates; chief rsch. rehab. bldg. Downey VA Hosp. (now called VA Hosp.), N. Chicago, Ill., 1953-54; assoc. psychiatry Sch. Medicine and Hosp., U. Pa., Phila., 1955-58; electromagnetic field measurement project office dep. asst. sec. def. in charge health & med. E.H. Cushing MD Dept. Def., Pentagon, 1958; dir. tng. and rsch. Ea. State Hosp., Williamsburg, Va., 1958-60; pvt. practice neuropsychiatry specializing in hypnosis Norfolk, Va., 1961-69. Psychiatrist, cons. Divsn. Alcohol Studies and Rehab. Va. Dept. Health (later Va. Dept. Mental Health and Mental Retardation), 1961-81; psychiatrist Greenpoint Clinic, Bklyn., 1983-87, 17th St. Clinic, N.Y.C., 1987-92, Downstate Mental Hygiene Assocs., Bklyn., 1983—; sec.-treas. Euclid-97th St. Clinic, Inc., Cleve., 1957-63, pres., 1963-69; spl. tng. in epistemology and methodologic foundations of sci. knowledge F.S.C. Northrop, PhD, 1973-92; electrodynamic field rschr. with Harold S. Burr, PhD, sect. neuro-anatomy Yale Med. Sch., 1948-73; cons. hypnosis with Milton H. Erickson, MD, 1945-80; clin. asst. prof. psychiatry SUNY Health Sci. Ctr. Med. Sch., 1983—; pvt. cons., Cleve., 1961-69, Upper Montclair, N.J., 1982-90; lectr. sociology Old Dominion U., Norfolk, 1961-62, cons. to Ruth Harrell, 1978-90; spl. med. cons. Frederick Mil. Acad., Portsmouth, Va., 1963-71; cons. Tidewater Epilepsy Found., Chesapeake, Va., 1962-68, USPH Hosp. Alcohol Unit, Norfolk, 1980-81, Nat. Inst. Rehab. Therapy, Butler, N.J., 1982-83; participant 5th Internat. Congress for Hypnosis and Psychosomatic Medicine, Gutenburg U., Mainz, Germany, 1970; organizer symposia on hypnosis in psychiatry and medicine, field theory as an integrator of knowledge, hypnosis in gen. practice, history of certain forensic and psychotherapeutic aspects of the study of man, Eastern State Hosp., Coll. William and Mary, James City County Med. Soc., Va. Soc. Clin. Hypnosis, Williamsburg, Va., 1959-60. Asst. editor Jour. Am. Soc. Psychosomatic Dentistry and Medicine, 1980-83; mem. editorial bd. Internat. Jour. Psychosomatics, 1984—; contbr. sects. to books, articles, book revs., abstracts to profl. publs. Sr. v.p. Willoughby Civic League, 1971-75. ASTP AUS, 1946-48. Lyman Rsch. Fund grantee, 1950-53. Fellow AAAS, Am. Psychiat. Assn. (life), N.Y. Acad. Scis., Am. Soc. Clin. Hypnosis (charter, life, cons. cert. program), Royal Soc. Health (London); mem. Va. Soc. Clin. Hypnosis (founding pres. 1959-60), Norfolk Acad. Medicine, Soc. for Investigation of Recurring Events, Va. Med. Soc., Sigma Xi, Nu Sigma Nu. Achievements include discovery of electromagetic field correlates of hypnosis, emotions, psychiatric/medical disorders, aging, and electrocyclic phenomena in humans which parallel those of other life forms, earth and atmosphere underwriting beginning short- and long-range predictions preceding clinical changes, such seemingly disparate phenomena united under a single regulating principle defined in terms of measurable field intensity and polarity. Office: SUNY Health Sci Ctr Dept Psyc Box 1203 450 Clarkson Ave Brooklyn NY 11203-2056 also: PO Box 9409 Norfolk VA 23505-0409

RAVIV, GABRIEL, medical products executive; BS, Hebrew U., Jerusalem, Israel, 1973; MSEE, PhD in Elec. Engring. and Computer Sci., Northwestern U. From officer to pres., CEO Bio-Logic Sys. Corp., Mundelein, Ill., 1979—81, pres., 1981—99, CEO, 1981—, bd. dir. Adj. prof. Northwestern U. Office: Bio Logic Systems Corp 1 Bio Logic Plaza Mundelein IL 60060*

RAVNIKAR, VERONIKA A. reproductive endocrinologist, educator; b. Bklyn., Jan. 13, 1950; m. Dr. Leonard Sicilian; 3 children. AB in premedicine magna cum laude, Immaculata (Pa.) Coll., 1971; MD, SUNY Upstate, 1975. Diplomate Am. Bd. Ob-gyn. Resident in ob-gyn Prentice Women's Hosp. of Northwestern Med. Ctr., Chgo., 1975-79; fellow in reproductive endocrinology and infertility Brigham and Women's Hosp.-Harvard Med. Sch., Boston, 1979-81, obstetrician-gynecologist, 1981-89; asst. prof. ob-gyn, and reproductive biology Harvard Med. Sch., 1987-92, part-time lectr., 1992—; prof. U. Mass. Med. Ctr., 1992—, obstetrician-gynecologist, 1993—, dir. divsn. reproductive endocrine and infertility and menopause, 1992—. Cons. in field. Mem. editl. bd. Women's Health Digest Med., 1994. Recipient rsch. paper award Dist. VI meeting, Milw., 1979, rsch. paper award Boston Obstetrical Soc., 1981; Bristol Myers grantee, NIH grantee; Grace La Gendre fellow Com. of Nat. Bus. and Profl. Women's Club in N.Y., 1973. Fellow Am. Coll. Obstetricians and Gynecologists; mem. Am. Fertility Soc., Soc. Reproductive Endocrinologists, The Endocrine Soc., Assn. Gynecologic Laparoscopists, Am. Heart Assn., North Am. Menopause Soc. (founding mem.), others. Home: 423 Commonwealth Ave Newton MA 02459-1301 Office: U Mass Med Ctr Ss4-717 55 Lake Ave N Worcester MA 01655-0002

RAWA, MANNEE JEAN, writer; b. Chgo., Sept. 22, 1944; d. Ernest and Melicent Alice Hoover Van Duser; m. Edward Gerald Rawa, Apr. 30, 1966; children: Edward Jason, Julie Meltrese. AA, Stephens Coll., 1964; BS, Fla. State U., 1966; MA, Rollins Coll., 1974; postgrad., Moscow State U., 1992, postgrad., 1997, postgrad., 2004. Instr. So. Coll., Orlando, Fla., 1974—75; archivist Rollins Coll., Winter Park, Fla., 1975—85; test adminstr. U. Ctrl. Fla., Orlando, 1986; tutor Chinese, Russian and Biblical Hebrew, 2000—. Author: A Chinese Japanese Comparative Radical Etymology, 1993, Faraway Places: The Travels and Travails of an Innkeeper's Daughter, 2001, An Etymological Study of Selected Words in the Orthodox New Testament, 2002, Lev: The Detinko Diaries, 2004. Avocations: language research, reading, writing, adventure travel, foreign languages. Home: 141 Spring Ln Winter Park FL 32789

RAWAL, DARSHAN LAL, civil engineer, structural engineer, consultant; b. India, Nov. 12, 1934; arrived in U.S., 1966; s. Saudagar Mal and Kaushalya Devi Rawal; m. Raj Kumari, Dec. 5, 1956; children: Upma, Bela, Neeru. BSCE, M.U. Aligarh, U.P. India, 1957; MSCE, Utah State U., 1967; M in Engring. Adminstrn., Ill. Inst. Technology, Chgo., 1977. Registered profl. engr., Ill., structural engr., Ill. Sr. civil engr. Ill. Dept. of Transp., 1967-73; sr. structural engr. Sargent & Lundy, Chgo., 1974-86, Brown & Root, Lombard, Ill., 1979-81, Stone & Webster Engring. Corp., N.Y.C., 1986—87; sr. engr. Ambitech Engring. Corp., Downers Grove, Ill., 1988—99, John Brown Engrs. & Constructor's, Chgo., 1991—94. Pres. Hindu Soc., Chgo., 1971—72, chmn. bd. trustees Medinah, Ill., 1994—97. Mem.: ASCE (life). Hindu. Achievements include design of drawings related to fossil/nuclear power plants, highways/bridges, petro chemidal, steel industries and automobile dealership buildings. Home: 2078 Audubon Dr Glendale Heights IL 60139-1808

RAWAL, VIRESH, education educator; married. BS in Chemistry, U. of Conn., 1980; PhD in Chemistry, U. of Pa., 1986. Postdoctoral fellow Columbia U., N.Y.C., 1986—88; asst. prof. chemistry Ohio State U., Columbus, 1988—94, assoc. prof. chemistry, 1994—95, U. of Chgo., 1995—98, prof. chemistry, 1999—. Cons. Various Pharm. Cos., 1996—. Mem. editl. bd.: Jour. Organic Chemistry. Recipient DuPont Young Faculty award, DuPont Corp., 1988—89, Faculty award, Am. Cyanamid Corp., 1994, Merck Young Investigator award, Merck & Co., 1995, Pfizer Rsch. award, Pfizer Inc., 1995—98; grantee, Eli Lilly Corp., 1993—95; Douty Found. fellow, U. Pa., 1981, Rohm and Haas Chemistry fellow, 1981—83, Dean's fellow, 1983—85. Fellow: AAAS; mem.: Am. Chem. Soc. (Jr. Faculty award 1990, Arthur C. Cope Scholar award 2003). Achievements include research in Organic synthesis; development of Catalysts for asymmetric synthesis. Office: Dept Chem U of Chgo 5735 South Ellis Ave Chicago IL 60637

RAWDEN, DAVID, financial services company executive; CFO, Peregine, Southfield, Mich., until 1999; prin. Jay Alix & Assocs., Southfield, 1999—. Office: Jay Alix and Associates 2000 Town Ctr Ste 2400 Southfield MI 48075-1250

RAWDING, MICHAEL, information technology executive; BA in Polit. Sci. & German, Middlebury Coll., Vt. With Unisys; from mgr. to corp. v.p. Microsoft, Redmond, Wash., corp. v.p. Asia region. Avocations: tennis, reading, travel, spending time with family. Office: One Microsoft Way Redmond WA 98052-6399

RAWITCH, ALLEN BARRY, medical educator, academic administrator; b. Chgo., Dec. 29, 1940; s. Sam and Jean Rawitch; m. Patricia Nan Rawitch, July 21, 1962; children: Bruce, David. BS in Chemistry, UCLA, 1963, PhD in Biol. Chemistry, 1967. Rsch. fellow U. Ill., Urbana, 1967-69; asst. prof. Kent (Ohio) State U., 1969-73, assoc. prof., 1973-75, U. Kans. Med. Ctr., Kansas City, 1975-80, prof., 1980—, asst. dean student affairs, 1999-2000, vice chancellor acad. affairs, dean grad. studies, 2000—, chmn. biochemistry and molecular biology, 2002—03. Vice chair biochemistry U. Kans. Med. Ctr., 1977-95, chair edn. coun., 1995-99 Editor Med. Biochemistry Question Bank, 1985-94; contbr. articles to profl. jours. Res. police officer capt. Overland Park Police Dept., 1979—. Rsch. grant NIH, 1971-2000, NSF, 1970, Am. Heart Assn., 1998-2002. Mem. Am. Soc. for Biochemistry and Molecular Biology, The Protein Soc., Am. Thyroid Assn., Sigma Xi. Avocations: amateur radio, woodworking, target shooting. Office: Office Acad Affairs U Kans Med Ctr 3901 Rainbow Blvd Kansas City KS 66160-0001

RAWITCH, ROBERT JOE, journalist, educator; b. L.A., Oct. 11, 1945; s. Sam and Jean (Reifman) R.; m. Cynthia Z. Knee, Oct. 27, 1968; children: Dana Leigh, Jeremy Aaron, Joshua Eric. BA in Journalism, Calif. State U., Northridge, 1967; MS in Journalism, Northwestern U., 1968. Reporter L.A. Times, 1968-80, asst. met. editor, 1980-82, editor Valley sect., 1982-83, suburban editor, 1983-89, exec. editor Valley and Ventura County edits., 1989-93; dir. editl. ops. Valley and Ventura County edits., 1993-95; sr. v.p. Winner and Assocs., 1996—. Lectr. Calif. State U., Northridge, 1971-83, 95-96, 2003, 04. Co-author: Adat Ari El, The First Fifty Years, 1988. Chmn. Calif. Freedom of Info. Com., 1978-79; pres. Calif. First Amendment coalition, 1991-93; bd. dirs. Temple Adat Ari El, 1987-92; bd. dirs. Calif. State U. Northridge Found., Univ. Corp. Recipient Greater L.A. Press Club award, 1973, 75, 79, L.A. Jewish Youth of Yr. award United Jewish Fund, 1963, Clarence Darrow Found. award, 1979. Mem. Soc. Profl. Journalists (nat. bd. dirs. 1979-82), Calif. Soc. Newspaper Editors (pres. 1995-96), Medill Alumni Assn. (bd. dirs. 1994-2000), CSUN Journalism Alumni Assn. (bd. dirs. 2002—). Office: Winner & Assocs 16501 Ventura Blvd Encino CA 91436-2007 Office Phone: 818-385-1900. Personal E-mail: bobrawitch@aol.com.

RAWL, ARTHUR JULIAN (LORD OF CURSONS), retail executive, accountant, consultant, author; b. Boston, July 6, 1942; s. Philip and Evelyn (Rosoff) R.; m. Karen Lee Werby, June 4, 1967; 1 child, Kristen Alexandra. BBA, Boston U., 1967, postgrad, 1972-74; DBA, St. George's U., 2000. CPA,

Mass., N.Y., La. Audit mgr. Touche Ross & Co., Boston, 1967-77, N.Y.C., 1977-79, ptnr., 1979, Newark, 1980-88, N.Y.C., 1988-89, Deloite & Touche, N.Y.C., 1989-90; exec. v.p., CFO Hanlin Group, Inc., Linden, NJ, 1990-94, United Auto Group, Inc., NYC, 1994-97; pres., CEO, bd. dirs. Brazil Internat. Motors, Brazil Am. Auto Group, Sao Paolo, 1999—2003; chmn., CEO Auto Alliance, Englewood, NJ, 2003—. Bd. dirs. BiakalInterPlast (USSR), Kuperwood Enterprises, Hanlin Group, Inc., Quipp, Inc.; mem. adj. faculty Boston U., 1971-75. Contbr. articles to profl. journals, mags. and trade publs. Mem. Newton Upper Falls (Mass.) Hist. Commn., 1977; bd. dirs. Sherburne Scholarship Fund Boston U., 1977-80; mem. Englewood (N.J.) Planning Bd., 1981-83; trustee Englewood Bd. Edn., 1983-85, 89-93, pres., 1991-92; trustee, treas. exec. com. Englewood Econ. Devel. Corp., 1986-89; fin. and compensation com. Dwight Englewood Sch., 1985-90; mem. parent devel. com. Mt. Holyoke Coll., 1991-94; treas. Brit. Meml. Garden Trust, 2003. Served to 2d class petty officer USN, 1960-63. Fellow AICPA, Mass. Soc. CPAs, N.Y. Soc. CPAs; mem. VFW, Am. Legion, Navy League U.S., N.J. Hist. Soc. (bd. govs., exec. com., nominating com., treas. 1987-99), St. George's Soc. N.Y. (treas. exec. com. 1998—), H.M. Sovereign Order of St. John, Coll. Arms Found. (v.p. 2001—), The Most Venerable Order of the Hosp. of St. John of Jerusalem, Univ. Club, Essex Club, Sloane Club (London). Home: 1200 W Ave PH-2 Miami Beach FL 33139 E-mail: a.rawl@att.net.

RAWLEY, CHARLES E., III, food service executive; Pres., COO Tricon Global Restaurants Inc., Louisville. Office: Tricon Global Restaurants Inc 1441 Gardiner Ln Louisville KY 40213

RAWLEY, JAMES ALBERT, history professor; b. Terre Haute, Ind., Nov. 9, 1916; s. Frank S. and Annie B. (Vanes) R.; m. Ann F. Keyser, Apr. 7, 1945; children: John Franklin, James Albert. AB, U. Mich., 1938, A.M., 1939; PhD, Columbia U., 1949. Instr., Columbia U., 1946-48; Instr. N.Y. U., 1946-51, Hunter Coll., 1951-53; asso. prof. to prof. Sweet Briar Coll., 1953-64, chmn. history dept., 1953-57, chmn. div. social studies, 1962-64; prof. U. Nebr., 1964-87, prof. emeritus, 1987—, chmn. history dept., 1966-67, 73-82, acting dean univ. libraries, 1984-85, honors MASUA lectr., 1984-85, Carl Happold Disting. prof., 1986-87; resident scholar Rockefeller Study and Conf. Center, Italy, 1977. Vis. prof. U. Hanover, 1990; mem. adv. bd. Salmon P. Chase Papers, Abraham Lincoln Prize. Author: Edwin D. Morgan: Merchant in Politics, 1811-1883, 1955, Turning Points of the Civil War, 1966, Race and Politics, 1969, The Politics of Union, 1974, The Transatlantic Slave Trade, 1981, Secession: The Disruption of the American Republic, 1844-1861, 1989, Abraham Lincoln and a Nation Worth Fighting For, 1996, 2d edit., 2003, London, Metropolis of the Slave Trade, 2003; editor: The American Civil War: An English View, 1964; editor: Lincoln and Civil War Politics, 1969; contbr.: Essays in American Historiography, 1960. Served to 1st lt. AUS, 1942-46. Recipient Outstanding Research and Creativity award U. Nebr., 1983, George Howard-Louise Pound Disting. Career award U. Nebr., 1991; NEH fellow Huntington Library, 1979 Fellow Royal Hist. Soc., Soc. Am. Historians; mem. Am. Hist. Assn., So. Hist. Assn., Nebr. State Hist. Soc. (past pres.), Orgn. Am. Historians, Abraham Lincoln Assn. (bd. dirs.), Civil War Round Table Nebr. (charter pres. 1989-90), Lincoln Country Club, Phi Beta Kappa. Home: 2300 Bretigne Dr Lincoln NE 68512-1910 E-mail: jcanningalunl@as.unl.edu.

RAWLINGS, BOYNTON MOTT, lawyer; b. El Paso, Tex., Dec. 6, 1935; s. Junius Mott and Laura Bassett (Boynton) R.; m. Nancy Mary Peay, Aug. 24, 1962 (div. 1973); children: Laura Bassett, James Mott; m. Judith Reed, Dec. 10, 1977; 1 child, William Reed. AB, Princeton U., 1958; LLB, Stanford U., 1961; diploma, U. Strasbourg, France, 1963. Bar: Calif. 1962, D.C. 1980, Conseil Juridique Paris, 1973, Avocat Paris, 1992. Assoc. Broad, Busterud & Khourie, San Francisco, 1963-65, Homer G. Angelo, Brussels, 1966; assoc., ptnr. S.G. Archibald, Paris, 1967-74; ptnr. Boynton M. Rawlings, Paris, L.A., 1974-84, Kevorkian & Rawlings, Paris, 1984-90, Oppenheimer, Wolff and Donnelly, Paris, 1990-99, Rawlings & Giles LLP., Paris, 2000—. Contbr. articles to profl. jours. Mem. L.A. Bar Assn. (bd. dirs. sect. internat. law 1975-82), French Am. C. of C. L.A. (bd. dirs. 1985—). Republican. Episcopalian. Avocations: music, tennis, skiing, hiking. Office: Rawlings & Giles 53 Ave Montaigne 75008 Paris France also: The Farragut Bldg 500 17th St NW Ste 700 Washington DC 20006-4804 Home: 38 Elliott St Charleston SC 29401-2529

RAWLINGS, GREGORY OWEN, science educator, consultant; b. Roswell, N.Mex., Jan. 29, 1951; s. Vernon Keith and Mildred Mary Rawlings; m. Virginia Lee Murphy, Oct. 25, 1985; 1 child, Stephanie Janiece. BS, U. of Kans., 1973. Cert. edn. Kans. State Dept. of Edn. Intermediate sci. tchr. Unified Sch. Dist. #497, Lawrence, Kans., 1973—78, Unified Sch. Dist. #305, Salina, Kans., 1978—82; asst. mgr., cashier supr. Wal-Mart #558, Salina, 1983—84; account rep. Burroughs Computer Corp., Rochester, NY, 1984—85; tchr. 8th grade earth sci. and algebra Unified Sch. Dist. 469, Lansing, Kans., 1986—. Resource person Harvard-Smithsonian Ctr. for Astrophysics - Project ESTEEM. Mem. Dist. Site Coun., Lansing, 1995—2002, Dist. Steering Com., Lansing, 1986—94; mem. blue ribbon adv. bd. ShareNet Pan Ednl. Inst., Independence, Mo., 1989—93. Mem.: NEA, Kans. Nat. Edn. Assn. (adminstrv. bd. dirs. 2003—04), Nat. Sci. Tchrs. Assn. Home: 210 Jayhawk Ct Lansing KS 66043-1811 Office: USD 469 - Lansing Mid Sch 509 Ida Lansing KS 66043-1522 Personal E-mail: rawlingsg@usd469.net. E-mail: rawlingsg@usd469.net.

RAWLINGS, HUNTER RIPLEY, III, academic administrator, classicist; b. Norfolk, Va., Dec. 14, 1944; married; 4 children. BA, Haverford Coll., 1966; PhD Classics, Princeton U., 1970. Asst. prof. U. Colo., Boulder, 1970—75, assoc. prof., 1975—80, prof. classics, 1980—88, v.p. acad. affairs, rsch., dean System Grad. Sch., 1984—88; pres. U. Iowa, 1988—95; pres., prof. greek classics Cornell U., Ithaca, NY, 1995—2003. Chair Iowa Commn. Fgn. Lang. Studies and Internat. Edn., 1988—91; bd. dirs. Tokpkins County Trust Co.; bd. dirs. Brookhaven Sci. Assocs. Author: The Structure of Thucydides' History, 1981; editor-in-chief: Classical Jour., 1977—83; contbr. articles to profl. jours. Bd. dirs. Norwest Bank Iowa N.A., 1988—95. Fellow, Ctr. Hellenic Studies, 1975—76. Fellow: Am. Acad. Arts and Scis.; mem.: Nat. Fgn. Lang. Ctr. (mem. nat. adv. bd. 1995—), Am. Coun. Edn. (bd. dirs. 1994—97), Assn. Am. Univs. (exec. com. 1990—92). Address: 54 Woodard RD Newfield NY 14867-9267

RAWLINGS, PAUL C. retired government official; b. Cave City, Ark., June 21, 1928; s. Otha A. and Leona (King) R.; m. Catherine Terral, 1951 (div. 1970); children: William A., Rebecca, Neal; m. Erma Martin, June 20, 1971 (div. Jan. 1997). Grad., Little Rock Jr. Coll.; LL.B., Ark. Law Sch., 1950. Bar: Ark. 1950. Practiced in, Little Rock, 1950, 52-73; adminstrv. law judge Office Hearings and Appeals, Social Security Adminstrn., HEW, Hattiesburg, Miss., 1973-92; ret. adminstrv. law judge sr. status, 1992; partner firm Terral, Rawlings, Matthews & Purtle, until 1973. Asst. atty. gen., Ark., 1955-56 Bd. dirs. Ark. Enterprises for Blind, 1964-67. Served with AUS, 1950-52. Mem. Ark. Bar Assn., Law Sci. Acad. Methodist (past chmn. bd. adminstrn., trustee). Club: Lion (past pres.). Home: 100 # 14 Swinging Bridge Dr Heber Springs AR 72543-8717

RAWLINS, CHRISTOPHER JOHN, publishing executive, director; b. Stoke-on-Trent, Staffordshire, Eng., Aug. 20, 1945; s. Jack and Evelyn Daphne (Douglas-Hamilton) R.; m. Mary Joan Goodchild, May 31, 1969; children: Sarah Elizabeth, Jeremy Mark, Penelope Jane. BSc (with honors), London U., 1968. Editorial asst. Soc. of Chem. Industry, London, 1968-71; asst. editor Acad. Press Ltd., London, 1971, IPC Sci. and Tech. Press, Guildford, Eng., 1971-75, mng. editor, 1976-79, pub., 1979-80, pub. dir., 1980-82, Butterworth Scientific Ltd., Guildford, Eng., 1982-86; v.p., pub. dir Butterworth Pubs., Stoneham, Mass., 1987-92; pub. Kluwer Acad. Pub., London, 1992-93; v.p., jours. pub. Appleton & Lange, Norwalk, Conn., 1993-97; pub. specialist Jours. divsn. Nature Pub. Group, N.Y.C., 1997-2000. Independent pub., 2001—. Chmn. North Farnham Liberal Assn., Hale, Eng., 1973-75, 79-81, chmn. bd. of govs. Hale and Folly Hill First Schs., Eng., 1983-85. Mem.: Royal Soc. Chemistry, Inst. of Materials, Minerals and Mining, Pubs. Assn. (vice chmn. serials pubs. exec. 1985—86), Assn. of Am. Pubs. (jour. com. 1987—92, Sci., Tech. and Med. Pubs. Group serials com. 1988—92, jour. com. 1997—, Best New Jour. Sci., Tech., Medicine award 1991, 2002), Internat. Soc. Cancer Gene Therapy (mem. exec. coun. 1999—, v.p. membership affairs 2001—). Anglican. Avocations: sports, gardening, music, current affairs, photography.

RAWLINS, DONALD RAY, lawyer; b. Dyersburg, Tenn., Apr. 28, 1965; s. Dal M. and Rebecca S. Rawlins. BBA, U. Memphis, 1987; JD, Am. U., 1990. Bar: Tenn., 1990. V.p., asst. gen. counsel, asst. sec. AutoZone, Inc., Memphis, 1990—2004; asst. gen. counsel Thomas & Betts Corp., Memphis, 2004—, asst. sec., 2004—, chief compliance officer. Recipient Best Brief award ATLA, 1990. Office: Thomas and Betts Corp 8155 T&B Boulevard Memphis TN 38125

RAWLINS, JOSEPH T. music educator; b. Lakeland, Fla., Nov. 7, 1936; s. Joseph T. and Dora C. Rawlins; m. Elizabeth Johnson, Jan. 27, 1960; children: Michelle Elizabeth Freeman, Melanie Elaine Wiggins. AA, U. Fla., 1957; MusB, La. State U., 1959, MusM, 1961, D in Musical Arts, 1972. Choral dir. Charlotte H.S., Punta Gorda, Fla., 1961—63; choral dir., instr. Millsaps Coll., Jackson, Miss., 1963—65; assoc. prof. music Auburn (Ala.) U., 1965—74; prof. music U. West Fla., Pensacola, 1974—. Nat. voice com. Music Tchrs. Nat. Assn., 1968—70. Contbr. articles to profl. jours.; musician: Pensacola Symphony Orch., Memphis Symphony, Pensacola Oratorio Soc. and Symphony, East Tenn. U. Choral Union and Symphony, U. Fla. Opera, La. State U. Opera Theatre, State Symphony Fla., Columbus (Ga.) Symphony, Jackson (Miss.) Opera Co., Jackson Choral Soc., Miss. Fine Arts Festival, Auburn U. Sympony and Choral Union, Okaloosa-Walton C.C. Symphony and Choral Union, Fla. State Music Tchrs. Conv., Fla. League of the Arts State Convs., Nat. Assn. Tchrs. Singing, Am. Musicol. Soc. Conv., Nat. Opera Assn. Conv., Music Educators Nat. Conf., Music Tchrs. Nat. Assn. Conv. Pvt. U.S. Army, 1961. Rsch. Grant-in-Aid, Auburn U., 1973. Mem.: Fla. League of the Arts (bd. dirs. 1980—82, 1996—2000, v.p. 1998—2002), Pi Kappa Lambda, Phi Kappa Phi, Phi Mu Alpha Sinfonia. Avocations: walking, gardening, listening to talk radio. Home: 8339 Pilgrim Rd Pensacola FL 32514 Office: Univ West Fla Art/Music/Theatre Dept 11000 University Pkwy Pensacola FL 32514-5750

RAWLINS, V. LANE, university president; b. Rigby, Idaho, Nov. 30, 1937; m. Mary Jo Rawlins, three children. BA in Economics, Brigham Young U., 1963; PhD in Economics, U of Calif., Berkeley, 1969. Faculty Wash. State U., Pullman, 1968-86, chair. economics, 1977-82, vice provost, 1982—86; vice chancellor, academic affairs U. of Alabama, 1986-91; pres. Memphis St. U., Memphis, 1991-00, Wash. State U., Pullman, Wa., 2000—. Office: Washington State U Office Pres PO Box 641048 Pullman WA 99164-1048

RAWLINSON, GAYLA, director, consultant; d. Perry Dale and Marie Arrington Rawlinson. B of Social Work, Stephen F. Austin State U., 1984; M in Sociology, Social Rsch., Sam Houston State U., 1994. LCSW Tex., 1985. Dir., on-campus activities cmty. svcs. Lufkin State Sch., Tex., 1985—90; residential social worker Tri-County MHMR, Conroe, 1990—93; flood recovery worker Montgomery County Emergency Assistance, 1994—96; collaborative respite coord. NANNI, Inc., Houston, 1996—96; mgr. funding source U. Houston, 1996—99; dir. resource devel. Harris County Dept. Edn., 1999—. Cons. Gayla Rawlinson Cons., Houston, 1997—2004. Bd. mem. Coalition Homeless, Houston, 2002—04. Recipient Commendation from then Gov. George W. Bush, State of Tex. Office of Gov., 1994—95. Mem.: Assn. Fundraising Profls. (assoc.). Avocations: basket weaving, pets - dog, cats and iguanas, travel. Office: Harris County Department of Education 6300 Irvington Blvd Houston TX 77022-5618

RAWLINSON, HELEN ANN, librarian; b. Columbia, S.C., Mar. 30, 1948; d. Alfred Harris and Mary Taylor (Moon) R. BA, U. S.C., 1970; MLS, Emory U., 1972. Asst. children's librarian Greenville (S.C.) County Library, 1972-74, br. supr., 1974-76, asst. head extension div., 1976-78; children's room librarian Richland County Pub. Library, Columbia, 1978-81, sr. adult services librarian, 1981-82, chief adult services, 1982-85, dep. dir., 1985—. Mem. adv. com. S.C. Pre-White House Conf. on Libr. and Info. Svcs., chmn. program com. Recipient Outstanding S.C. Librarian award by S.C. Library Assn., 1998. Mem. ALA, S.E. Libr. Assn., S.C. Libr. Assn. (2d v.p. 1987-89, editl. com. 1993, chmn. pub. libr. sect. 1995), U. S.C. Thomas Cooper Soc. (bd. dirs., v.p., pres.-elect, pres.). Baptist. Home: 1316 Guignard Ave West Columbia SC 29169-6137 Office: Richland County Pub Libr 1431 Assembly St Columbia SC 29201-3101 Office Phone: 803-799-9084. E-mail: harawlin@richland.lib.sc.us.

RAWLINSON, JOHNNIE BLAKENEY, federal judge; b. Concord, N.C., Dec. 16, 1952; BS in Psychology summa cum laude, NC A&T State U., 1974; JD, U. of Pacific, 1979. Private practice, Las Vegas, 1979—80; staff atty. Nevada Legal Services, 1980; from dep. dist. atty. to asst. dist. atty. Clark County Dist. Atty.'s Office, 1980—98; judge U.S. Dist. Ct. Nev., 1998—2000, U.S. Ct. Appeals (9th cir.), 2000—. Office: 333 Las Vegas Blvd S Rm 7072 Las Vegas NV 89101

RAWLINSON, JOSEPH ELI, foundation executive, lawyer; b. Delta, Utah, May 9, 1915; s. Eli Wilford and Dora Pearl (Day) R.; m. Elaine Millicent Andersen, June 2, 1947; children: James, Jolene, Nancy, Rex, Anina, Cheryl, Mark, Lisa, David. BS, U. Utah, 1936; JD, Loyola U., 1958. Bar: Calif. 1959; CPA, Calif. Agt. IRS, Wichita, Kans., 1938-52; acct. Serene Koster, Barbour, Calif., 1952-62; lawyer in pvt. practice Calif., 1959; pres., CEO Fritz B. Burns Found., Burbank, Calif., 1980—. Recipient Silver medal Am. Inst. Accts., 1942. Office: Fritz B Burns Found 4001 W Alameda Ave Ste 203 Burbank CA 91505-4338 Office Phone: 818-840-8802. E-mail: josepheli@sbcglobal.net.

RAWLS, CHARLES RICHARDSON, lawyer, government official; b. Wilmington, N.C. m. Deanne Elizbeth Maynard. BA in Bus. Mgmt., N.C. State U., 1979; JD, Campbell U., 1982. Bar: N.C. 1982. Counsel to subcom. on forests, family farms, and energy Ho. of Reps., Washington, 1983—85, assoc. gen. counsel com. on agr., 1985—88, legis. dir. Congressman Martin Lancaster, 1988—90, adminstrv. asst., 1991—93; asst. to dep. sec. agr. Richard Rominger USDA, Washington, 1993—98, gen. counsel, 1998—2001; gen. counsel, v.p. for legal, tax, and acctg. Nat. Council of Farmer Cooperatives, 2002—03; gen. counsel FCA, McLean, Va., 2003—. Office: Farm Credit Admin 1501 Farm Credit Dr Mc Lean VA 22102-5090

RAWLS, FRANK MACKLIN, lawyer; b. Suffolk, Va., Aug. 24, 1952; s. John Lewis and Mary Helen (Macklin) R.; m. Sally Hallum Blanchard, June 26, 1976; children: Matthew Christopher, John Stephen, Michael Andrew. BA in History cum laude, Hampden Sydney Coll., 1974; JD, U. Va., 1977. Bar: Va. 1977, U.S. Dist. Ct. (ea. dist.) Va. 1977, U.S. Ct. Appeals (4th cir.) 1977. Assoc. Rawls, Habel & Rawls, Suffolk, 1977-78, ptnr., 1978-91, Ferguson & Rawls, Suffolk, 1991-96, Ferguson, Rawls, MacDonald, Overton & Grissom PC, Suffolk, 1996-98, Ferguson, Rawls, MacDonald & Overton PC, Suffolk, 1999—2002, Ferguson, Rawls & Raines, P.C., 2002—. Sec., Suffolk Title Ltd., 1986-95; bd. dirs Old Dominion Investors Trust, Inc., Secure Title, Inc. Deacon Westminster Reformed Presbyn. Ch., Suffolk, 1979-83, elder, clk. of session, 1984-91, 94-99; chmn. bd. dirs. Suffolk Crime Line, 1982-90, Suffolk Cheer Fund, 1982—, Covenant Christian Schs., Suffolk, 1982-84; bd. dirs. Norfolk Christian Schs., 1990-2004, v.p., 1998-99, pres., 1999-2004; pres. Parent Tchr. Fellowship, 1995-97, vice-chmn. steering com. for capital campaign, 1996-98, v.p., 1997-98; adv. bd. dirs. Salvation Army, Suffolk, 1977-95, chmn., 1989-90; chmn. Suffolk Com. on Affordable Housing, 1989-90; bd. dirs. Suffolk YMCA, 1988-90, Suffolk Youth Athletic Assn., 1999-2000. Mem. ATLA, Suffolk Bar Assn. (past pres.), Va. State Bar, Va. Bar Assn., Christian Legal Soc., Va. Trial Lawyers Assn., Suffolk Bar Assn. E-mail: frawls@frrlaw.com.

RAWN, WILLIAM LEETE, III, architect; b. Berkeley, Calif., Aug. 8, 1943; s. William Leete Jr. and Betsy (Blanckenburg) R. BA, Yale U., 1965; JD, Harvard U., 1969; MArch, MIT, 1979. Bar: D.C., 1969. Assoc. Arent, Fox, Kintner, Plotkin & Kahn, Washington, 1969-71; asst. to pres. U. Mass., Boston, 1971-73, asst. chancellor phys. planning, 1973-75; architect Davis Brody & Assocs., N.Y.C., 1979-83, William Rawn Assocs., Boston, 1983—. Vis. prof. urban design Harvard U. Grad. Sch. Design, 1993, 94. Designer serigraphs, 1971-79; contbr. articles to profl. jours., newspapers. Mem. Boston Civic Design Com., 1990; Inst. Contemporary Art, Boston, 1994. Recipient Urban Design citation Progressive Architecture, U. Va./City of Charlottesville Urban Plan, 1995. Fellow AIA (hon., Nat. AIA Award of Excellence, 1993, AIA Award in Urban Design, 1996-2000, Nat. AIA Honor Award in Arch. 1994, 95, 2000, Louis Sullivan award 1995); mem. Boston Soc. Architects (37 regional and local AIA design awards 1985-96), D.C. Bar Assn., Yale Club of N.Y.C., Harvard Club (Boston). Office: William Rawn Assocs Archs Inc 101 Tremont St Ste 204 Boston MA 02108-5004

RAWNSLEY, HOWARD MELODY, pathologist, educator; b. Long Branch, N.J., Nov. 20, 1925; s. Walter A. and Elizabeth (Melody) R.; m. B. Eileen Fiddes, Sept. 5, 1967; children: Virginia Ingram, Elizabeth Sue. AB, Haverford Coll., 1949; MD, U. Pa., 1952. Diplomate Am. Bd. Pathology (trustee 1988-96). Intern Hosp. U. Pa., 1952-53, resident, 1953-57; practice medicine, specializing in pathology Phila., 1957-75; mem. Wm. Pepper Lab., U. Pa., 1957-75, asst. dir., 1960-68, dir., 1968-75; assoc. dir. Clin. Research Ctr., 1962-67, acting dir., 1969— 70, asst. prof. pathology and medicine, 1960-65, assoc. prof., 1965-69, prof., 1969-75; prof. pathology Dartmouth Hitchcock Med. Ctr., Hanover, N.H., 1975-95, chmn. dept., 1980-87, sr. v.p. med. affairs, 1987-94. Cons. VA Hosp.; mem. exec. com. Am. Bd. Med. Spltys., 1998-2001. Chmn. bd. dirs. New Eng. Blood Svcs. ARC, 1996—2000, 2002—05. With U.S. Army, 1944—46. Woodward fellow in chemistry, 1953-55 Mem. AMA, ARC (biomed. svcs. com. 1990-92), Pathology Soc. Phila. (pres.), Coll. Am. Pathologists (bd. govs. 1985-93), Am. Soc. Clin. Pathologists (Disting. Svc. award 1995). Home: 7 Haskins Rd Hanover NH 03755-2204 E-mail: hrawn@valley.net.

RAWSKI, CONRAD H(ENRY), humanities educator, medievalist; b. Vienna, May 25, 1914; came to U.S., 1939, naturalized, 1944; s. Stanislaus and Johanna (Buberl-Maffei) R.; m. Helen Orr, July 5, 1957; children: Thomas George, Judith Ellen Rawski Kleen. MA, U. Vienna, 1936, PhD, 1937; postgrad., Péter Pázmány Egyetem, Budapest, 1938-39, Harvard U., 1939-40; MS in Libr. Sci., Western Res. U., 1957. Lectr. in music U. Louisville, 1940; from asst. prof. to prof. music Ithaca (N.Y.) Coll., 1940-56; dir. grad. studies, dean Ithaca (N.Y.) Coll. Sch. Music, 1951-56; head fine arts dept. Cleve. Public Library, 1957-62; assoc. prof., prof. library sci., coordinator Ph.D. program in info. sci. M.A. Baxter Sch. Info. and Libr. Sci., Case Western Res. U., Cleve., 1957-80, prof., sr. rsch. scholar, 1980-85, prof. emeritus for life, dean emeritus, 1985. Music columnist Boston Evening Transcript, 1939-40, Ithaca Jour., 1943-50; lectr. in musicology, medieval studies, info. sci. Fellow Fund for the Advancement of Edn., Ford Found., 1952-53, Nat. Endowment for Humanities, 1979 Author: Petrarch: Four Dialogues for Scholars, 1967, Toward a Theory of Librarianship, 1973, Petrarch's Latin Prose Works and the Modern Translator, 1977, Introduction to Research in Information Science, 1982; translator, editor: Petrarch's Remedies for Fortune Fair and Foul, 5 vols., 1991, Petrarch to Boccaccio: The Griseldis Letters, 1994, Francisci Petrarchae lectoris Adminiculum: Late Antique and Medieval Latin Words in the Works of Petrarch, 1998; originator: A Petrarch System, 1994-2002; contbr. articles to profl. jours. and encyclopedias. Mem. Renaissance Soc. Am., Medieval Acad. Am., Soc. for Medieval Latin, ALA (nat. Beta Phi Mu award 1979), Rowfant Club of Cleve. Address: 17877 Lost Trl Chagrin Falls OH 44023-5835 E-mail: hrawski@earthlink.net.

RAWSKI, EVELYN SAKAKIDA, history professor; b. Honolulu, Feb. 2, 1939; d. Evan T. and Teruko (Watase) Sakakida; m. Thomas G. Rawski, Dec. 16, 1967. BA, Cornell U., 1961; MA, Radcliffe Coll., 1962; PhD, Harvard U., 1968. Asst. prof. history U. Pitts., 1967-72, assoc. prof., 1973-79, prof. history, 1980—; univ. prof., 1996—. Author: Agricultural Change and the Peasant Economy of South China, 1972, Education and Popular Literacy in Ch'ing China, 1979, The Last Emperors: A Social History of Qing Imperial Institutions, 1998; co-author: Chinese Society in the Eighteenth Century, 1987, Worshiping the Ancestors: Chinese Commemorative Portraits, 2001; co-editor: Popular Culture in Late Imperial and Modern China, 1985, Death Ritual in Lake Imperial and Modern China, 1988, Harmony and Counterpoint: Chinese Music in Ritual Context, 1996. Grantee Am. Coun. Learned Socs., 1973-74; NEH fellow, 1979-80, Chinese Studies fellow Am. Coun. Learned Socs./Social Sci. Rsch. Coun., 1989, Guggenheim fellow, 1990, Woodrow Wilson Internat. Ctr. fellow 1992-93. Mem. Assn. Asian Studies (China-Inner Asia coun., bd. dirs. 1976-79, v.p. 1994-95, pres. 1995-96). Home: 5317 Westminster Pl Pittsburgh PA 15232-2120 Office: U Pitts Dept History Pittsburgh PA 15260 Business E-Mail: esrx@pitt.edu.

RAWSON, CLAUDE JULIEN, English educator; b. Shanghai, Feb. 8, 1935; came to U.S., 1985; m. Judith Ann Hammond, July 14, 1959; children: Hugh, Tim, Mark, Harriet, Annabel. BA, Oxford (Eng.) U., 1955, MA, BLitt, 1959. English lectr. U. Newcastle, Eng., 1957-65; from lectr. to prof., chmn. dept. U. Warwick, Coventry, Eng., 1965-85, hon. prof., 1986—; George Sherburn prof. English U. Ill., Urbana, 1985-86; George M. Bodman prof. English Yale U., New Haven, Conn., 1986-96, Maynard Mack prof. English, 1996—. Vis. prof. U. Pa., Phila., 1973, U. Calif., Berkeley, 1980; chmn. Yale Boswell Papers, 1990—2001; del. for lang. and lit. Oxford U. Press, NY. Author: Henry Fielding and the Augustan Ideal, 1972, 2d edit., 1991, Gulliver and the Gentle Reader, 1973, 2d edit., 1991, The Charater of Swift's Sahir, 1983, Order from Confusion Sprung, 1985, 2d edit., 1992, (with F.P. Lock) Collected Poems of Thomas Parnell, 1989, Satire and Sentiment 1660-1830, 1994, 2d edit., 2000, (with H. B. Nisbet) Cambridge History of Literary Criticism, vol. 4: The Eighteenth Century, 1997, God, Gulliver, and Genocide, 2001, 2d edit. 2002, Basic Writings of Jonathan Swift, 2002; editor: Modern Lang. Rev. and Yearbook of English Studies, London, 1974-88; gen. editor: Cambridge (Eng.) History of Literary Criticism, 1983—, Unwin Critical Libr., London, 1974—, Blackwell Critical Biographies, 1985—, Cambridge Edition of the Works of Jonathan Swift, 2001—. Recipient Cert. of Merit for Disting. Svc. Conf. of Editors of Learned Jours., 1988; Andrew Mellon fellow Clark and Huntington Libr., 1980, 90, Guggenheim fellow, 1991-92, Sr. Faculty fellow Yale U., 1991-92; NEH grantee, 1991. Fellow Am. Acad. Arts and Scis.; mem. Modern Humanities Rsch. Assn. (life mem., com. mem. 1974-88), Internat. Soc. 18th Century Studies, Am. Soc. for 18th Century Studies, Brit. Soc. for 18th Century Studies (pres. 1973-74), Grolier Club. Office: Yale U Dept English PO Box 208302 New Haven CT 06520-8302

RAWSON, ELEANOR S. publishing company executive; m. Kennett Longley Rawson (dec.); children: Kennett Longley, Linda. V.p., exec. editor David McKay Co.; pres., editor-in-chief Rawson, Wade Publishers, Inc.; v.p. Scribner Book Cos.; pub. Rawson Assocs. (divsn. Macmillan Pub. Co.); v.p., chmn., pub. Rawson Assocs./Scribner/divsn. Simon & Schuster Consumer Grp; teaching staff Columbia U. Lectr. NYU, New Sch., N.Y.; organizer, panelist various writers' confs.; mem. exec. coun., nominating chair Am. Assn. Pubs., 1970-74. Former editorial staff writer Am. mag.; free-lance writer radio and mags., newspaper syndicates; fiction editor Collier's mag., Today's Woman. Trustee, past v.p. Museums at Stony Brook. Mem. Women's Nat. Book Assn., P.E.N., Am. Assn. Museums, Yale Club, Cosmopolitan Club, Old Field Club, Women's Forum, Women In Media, Women in Comms. Office: Rawson Associates 150 E 69th St New York NY 10021-5704

RAWSON, ERIC GORDON, optical engineer; b. Saskatoon, Sask., Can., Mar. 4, 1937; s. Donald Strathern and Hildred Iantha (Patton) R.; m. Zivile Anne Nalivaika, May 5, 1966; children: Carol, Dalia, Cliff. BA, U. Saskatchewan, 1959, MA, 1960; PhD, U. Toronto, Ont., 1966. Mem. tech. staff Bell Telephone Labs., Murray Hill, N.J., 1966-73; mem. rsch. staff Xerox PARC, Palo Alto, Calif., 1973-78, area mgr., 1978-94; prin. Rawson Optics, Inc., Brentwood, Calif., 1994-99, pres., CEO, 1999—. Bd. dirs., sec. Alamed. Corp., Palo Alto, 1991—. Editor: Book of Milestones Fiber Optics Local Area Networks, 1994; contbr. over 65 articles to profl. jours. Fellow Optical Soc. Am. (mem. engring. coun. 1995—, Engring. Excellence award 1990), Soc. Photo-Instrumentation Engrs.; mem. IEEE (sr.). Achievements include over 30 patents for optics and biomedical monitoring. Office: 763 Franklin Dr Brentwood CA 94513-6463 E-mail: ericrawson@rawsonoptics.com.

RAWSON, HARVE E. psychologist, writer; b. Webb CIty, Mo., July 25, 1934; s. Paul Charles and Florence Landon Rawson; m. Joyce Elaine Blossom, June 9, 1961; children: Paul Gerald, Reed Harve. BA, Antioch Coll., 1957; MA, Ohio State U., 1959, PhD, 1961. Rsch. specialist N.Am. Aviation Inc., Columbus, Ohio, 1961—63; prof. psychology Hanover (Ind.) Coll., 1963—94, prof. emeritus, 1994—; dir. children's svcs. Englishton Pk., Lexington, Ind., 1969—93; dean faculty Franklin (Ind.) Coll., 1994—96; vis. prof. psychology Miss. State U., Starkville, 1998. Grant reviewer Coun. Internat. Exch. Scholars, Washington, 2000—04. Author: Webb City, 2000, Around the World in 30 Years, 2001, Purposeful Parenting, 2002, A Delightful Ordeal, 2003; contbr. over 40 articles to profl. jours. Pres. Lide White Boys and Girls Club, Madison, Ind., 1969, 1974, 1978, 1999—2001; v.p. Jefferson County Youth Shelter, Madison, 1992. Recipient Sagamore of the Wabash award, Gov. Ind., 1993; scholar, Fulbright Found., Bahrain, 1988—89, Fulbright Found., 1994. Mem.: Ind. Psychol. Assn. (pres. 1974—76, Cmty. Svc. award 1991, Disting. Acad. Psychologist award 1986—87), Traveler's Century Club. Avocation: travel. Home: 1820 Crozier Ave Madison IN 47250 Office Phone: 812-265-4554.

RAWSON, JIM CHARLES, business executive; b. Houston, Apr. 20, 1947; s. Charles Manly and Georgie (Kearse) R.; m. Linda Eidman, Apr. 12, 1968; children: John Erich, Susan Margaret. BBA, Tex. Christian U., 1969. CPA, Tex. Acctg. clk. Tenneco, Inc., Houston, 1969-71, Projects Am. Corp., Houston, 1971-74, office mgr., 1974-77, v.p., gen. mgr., 1977-82, pres., 1982—. Recipient Gold award, Am. Land Devel. Assn., 1983, Silver award, 1983, Bronze award, 1985. Mem. Am. Inst. CPA's, Tex. Soc. CPA's (Houston chpt.), Sports Car Club of Am. Methodist. Avocations: sports car racing, salt water fishing. Office: Projects Am Corp 6124 Beverlyhill St Houston TX 77057-6610

RAWSON, JOHN ELTON, neonatologist, educator; b. Okolona, Miss., Jan. 31, 1938; s. Elton Phlemuel and Marjorie Morgan Jones Rawson; m. Mary Crouch Rawson, June 23, 1962; children: Katherine Asbury Rawson Kronzer, Edwin Lauderdale. BS in Chemisty, Millsaps Coll., 1960; MD, U. Miss., 1965. Diplomate Am. Bd. Pediat., Am. Bd. Neonatology and Perinatal Medicine; lic. physician, Miss. Clin. assoc. prof. pediat. U. Miss. Sch. Medicine, Jackson, 1972—; attending neonatologist, chief newborn medicine Ctrl. Miss. Med. Ctr., Jackson, 1978—; attending neonatologist Miss. Bapt. Med. Ctr., Jackson, 1982—. Chmn. bd. dirs. Health Choice of Miss., Jackson, 1991-98, Integrity Health Plan, Inc., Jackson, 1995-98, State Watch, Inc., Jackson, 1988-96; chief of staff Meth. Healthcare, Inc., Jackson, 1994-95. Editor: Newborn Ventilation, 1976. State chmn. March of Dimes, Jackson, 1972-82; mem. vestry St. James Episcopal Ch., Jackson, 1975-78; trustee St. Andrew's Day Sch., Madison, Miss., 1978-89, Meth. Lebouner Found., Memphis, 1991-2000. Capt. USAF, 1968-70. Mem. Rotary (Paul Harris fellow 1984). Office: Ctrl Miss Med Ctr 1850 Chadwick Dr Jackson MS 39204 Home: 632 Lake Cavalier Rd Madison MS 39110-7155 Office Phone: 601-376-1700. E-mail: jackrawson@hotmail.com.

RAWSON, RACHEL L. lawyer; BA magna cum laude, Kenyon Coll., 1987; JD, Columbia U., 1990. Bar: N.Y. 1991, Ohio 1995. With Jones Day, Cleve., 1992—, ptnr., 2003—. Mem.: ABA (bus. law sect.), Cleve. Bar Assn. (banking and bus. law sect.). Office: Jones Day North Point 901 Lakeside Ave Cleveland OH 44114-1190

RAWSON, RAYMOND D. dentist, state legislator; b. Sandy, Utah, Nov. 2, 1940; s. James D. and Mable (Beckstead) R.; m. Linda Downey, July 23, 1959; children: Raymond Blaine, Mark Daniel, Pamela Ann, David James, Kristi Lynn, Kenneth Glenn, Richard Allen. BS, U. Nev. at Las Vegas, 1964; DDS, Loma Linda U., 1968; MA, U. Nev., 1978. Diplomate Am. Bd. Forensic Odontology (pres. 1984), Am. Bd. Oral Medicine. Gen. practice dentistry, Las Vegas, 1968—. Instr. dental hygiene, dental dir. Clark County Community Coll., 1977—, dep. coroner, chief dental examiner, 1977—; adj. prof. U. Nev., 1977—, adj. assoc. prof. oral diagnosis and forensic dentistry Northwestern U., Chgo., 1985—. Contbr. articles to profl. jours. Active Boy Scouts Am., 1968—; chmn. youth and family health comm. assembly on fed. issues, Nat. Conf. State Legislators, mem. steering comm. Reforming STates Group, coun. of State Govts.; pres. Red Rock Stake; bishop Ch. Jesus Christ Latter-day Saints, 1978-84; asst. majority leader Nev. State senator. Recipient Cmty. Heroes award Nat. Conf. Christians and Jews, Las Vegas, 1994. Fellowo Am. Acad. Forensic Scis. (pres., chmn.), ADA (editl. rev. bd. jour.), Fedn. Dentaire Internat., Omicron Kappa Upsilon (commr. edn. commn. of the states). Republican. Office: 6375 W Charleston Blvd Las Vegas NV 89146-1139 Address: Nev Senate 401 S Carson St Rm 213A Carson City NV 89701-4747

RAWSON, RICHARD J. corporate lawyer; b. Florham Park, N.J. BS, Notre Dame U.; JD, Rutgers U. Formerly with Sullivan & Cromwell, N.Y.C. and Washington; various positions with Law Divsn. AT&T, 1984—96, sr. v.p., gen. counsel, 1995, Lucent Technologies, Murray Hill, NJ, 1996—. Mem. ABA, Am. Corp. Counsel Assn. Office: Lucent Technologies 600 Mountain Ave New Providence NJ 07974-2008

RAWSON, WILLIAM ROBERT, lawyer, retired manufacturing company executive; b. Montclair, N.J., Mar. 14, 1925; s. William Howard and Maude Elizabeth (Wheeler) R.; m. Elizabeth S. Crandall, Sept. 30, 1949 (dec. Oct. 2001); children— Shirley, Jean, Elizabeth. AB, Brown U., 1947; LL.B., N.Y. U., 1950. Bar: N.J. 1950, Ill. 1974. Practice of law, Bloomfield, N.J., 1950-52; legal asst. Thomas A. Edison Industries, West Orange, N.J., 1952-57; asst. counsel T.A. Edison div. McGraw-Edison Co., Elgin, Ill., 1957-67, v.p. adminstrn., div., 1967-72, asst. gen. counsel, 1972-77, corp. v.p. adminstrn., 1977-80, v.p. law, adminstrn. also corporate sec., 1980-85; corp. counsel L. Kaiser/Estech div. Vigoro Industries, Inc., Savannah, Ga., 1985-89. Dir. Chgo. Econ. Devel. Corp. Chmn. Millburn (N.J.) Planning Bd. and Bd. Adjustment, 1962-70, Millburn Red Cross, 1969-70; mem. twp. coun., dep. mayor Twp. of Millburn, 1970-72; v.p. Elgin (Ill.) United Way, 1978-79; bd. dirs. United Way Suburban Chgo., 1981-85; pres. Regional Adult Literacy Partnership, Savannah, 1990-91; pres., bd. dirs. The Landings Homeowners Assn., 1995-96, pres., 1992-93. Lt. (j.g.) USN, 1943-46. Mem. ABA, Ill. State Bar Assn., Am. Arbitration Assn. (arbitrator constrn. industry panel 1985—), Elgin C. of C. (v.p. 1978-79) Republican. Episcopalian. Home: 4 Sandsfield Way Savannah GA 31411-2511

RAY, ALBERT, family physician, educator; b. N.Y.C., Aug. 8, 1948; s. Herman and Stella (Meritz) R.; m. Cheryl Antecol, Oct. 8, 1977; children: Heather, Erin, Samantha. BA, Bklyn. Coll., 1969; MD, Cath. U. Louvain, Belgium, 1976. Diplomate Am. Bd. Family Practice, Can. Coll. Family Physicians. Intern Meml. U. of Nfld., St. John's, Can., 1976; resident McGill U., Montreal, 1978; family physician SCPMG, San Diego, 1978—. Clin. prof. U. Calif., San Diego, 1978—; mem. cmty. faculty UCLA, USD, U. Calif., Davis, USC; mem. clerkship cmty. adv. bd. U. Calif., San Diego, 1995—; pres. profl. staff Kaiser Found. Hosp.; bd. dirs. So. Calif. Permanente Med Group; asst. chief family medicine Kaiser Permanente, San Diego. Author: Lecons d'Histologie, 1973; contbr. to profl. jours. Program chair adult edn. Congregation Beth Israel, 1995; bd. dirs. Temple Emanuel, San Diego, 1990, Agy. for Jewish Edn.; expert reviewer Med. Bd. Calif., 1995; spl. med. cons. Calif. Dept. of Corps., 1996; hon. chmn. physician's adv. bd. Nat. Rep. Congl. Com. Named Family Physician of Yr., Calif. Acad. Family Physicians, 2002. Fellow: Am. Acad. Family Physicians; mem.: Calif. Acad. Family Physicians, San Diego Acad. Family Physicians, San Diego County Med. Soc. (councilor 2002—03, treas. 2004), Calif. Med. Assn. (ho. of dels.), AMA. Avocations: golf, tennis, travel, antiques, gardening. Office: Kaiser Permanente 4405 Vandever Ave San Diego CA 92120-3315 Office Phone: 619-516-7400.

RAY, AMRIT, pharmaceuticals strategist, company executive; s. N.K. Ray. BS with honors, MD, U. Edinburgh; MBA, Dartmouth Coll. Physician Full Registration Gen. Med. Coun., U.K.; Fellow Chartered Mgmt. Inst., U.K. Bus. strategy cons. McKinsey & Co., Inc., London; cardiology resident physician Edinburgh Royal Infirmary, Edinburgh, England; med. rsch. collaborator Mayo Clinic, Rochester, Minn.; tropical medicine rschr. All-India Inst. Med. Sciences, New Delhi; med. rsch. collaborator Veterans Assn. Med. Ctr., Roanoke, Va.; strategic mgmt. group Pfizer, Inc., New London, Conn., 2002—. Strategy cons. Dartmouth-Hitchcock Med. Ctr., NH, Polaroid Corp., Mass., Pfizer Global Rsch. & Devel., Groton, Conn. Exec. coach to the dir. Garde Theater and Arts Ctr., New London, Conn. Recipient Myre-Sim Award, Royal Coll. Physicians, U.K., 1997, Global Healthcare Practice - Top 5 Bus. Plan, McKinsey & Co., Inc., 1998, Faculty Medicine Rsch. Award, U. Edinburgh; scholar Reuben Cohen Award, Dartmouth Coll., 2000, Med. Rsch. Award, Med. Rsch. Coun. U.K., Breast Cancer Rsch. Scholarship, Zeneca Pharmaceuticals. Mem.: No. New Eng. Soc. Healthcare Risk Mgmt., Internat. Pharm. Fedn., Am. Soc. Pharmacology and Exptl. Therapeutics, Am. Mgmt. Assn., Brit. Med. Assn., Tuck Biotechnology & Healthcare Soc. (pres.).

RAY, ANNETTE D. executive secretary; b. Decatur, Ind., Mar. 24, 1950; d. Gilbert O. and Florence L. Hoffman; m. Richard M. Ray, Nov. 28, 1975 (dec. June 1999); children: Michelle Ann, Ellen Marie, Laura Leigh, David Richard, Ruth Anne. AA, Concordia Jr. Coll., Ann Arbor, Mich., 1970; BS, Concordia Tchrs. Coll., Seward, Nebr., 1972; attended, Ctrl. Fla. C.C., Ocala, 1974. Lic. real estate, Ind.; lic. tchr., Ind., Fla. Elem. tchr. St. John's Luth., Ocala, 1972-74; mgr. apt. complex Victoria Sq. Apts., Ft. Wayne, Ind., 1974-75; substitute tchr. East Allen County Schs., Allen County, Ind., 1976-79, Circut A Luth. Schs., Adams and Allen County, Ind., 1977-81; corp. sec., treas., office mgr. Heritage Wire Die, Monroeville, Ind., 1987—. Co-author, co-editor: 1928-1988 A Rememberance, 1988, Coming to America--32 Families 1597-1997; author, collator Madison Township portion 2005 Allen County History, 1990-2000. Vol. Monroeville C. of C., 1987—, Concerned Area Residents Quality Edn., Allen County, 1990—, Am. Cancer Soc., Allen County, 1991—, chairperson Celebrity Bagger Day, 1995, 96; bd. dirs. Hoagland (Ind.) Hist. Soc., 1983—, sec. 2002; bd. dirs. Hoagland Area Advancement Assn., 1999—, sec. 2003; contbr. 2005 Allen County (Ind.) History. Lutheran. Avocations: remodeling old homes, reading, genealogy, gardening, floral arranging. Home: 16901 Berning Rd Hoagland IN 46745-9753 Office: Heritage Wire Die Inc 19819 Monroeville Rd Monroeville IN 46773-9113 E-mail: heritagewiredie@yahoo.com.

RAY, ARLISS DEAN, retired environmental consultant; b. Hot Springs, Ark., Apr. 3, 1929; s. Clyde E. and Gladys Lorraine (Wofford) R.; m. Ardyth Lee Sharman, Aug. 23, 1952 (dec. Feb. 1992); children: Sandra Lee, Nancy Lynn, Laurie Jean, James Clyde; foster child, Joseph T. Yannetti. BEngring., Yale U., 1951; MS, Oreg. State U., 1957; PhD, U. Calif.-Berkeley, Berkeley, 1962. Asst. prof. environ. engring. Vanderbilt U., 1961-63; assoc. prof., then prof. U. Mo., Columbia, 1963-71; v.p. Woodward-Envicon, also Woodward Clyde Cons., Clifton, N.J., 1972-75; pvt. cons., 1975-77; co-founder, 1978; exec. officer environ. mgmt. and cons. EMANCO Inc., Houston, 1978-94; ret., 1994. Adv. EPA, NSF. Contbr. articles to profl. jours. Lt. (j.g.) USN, 1951—55, Korea. Recipient award merit Mo. Water Pollution Control Assn., 1967. Mem. ASCE, Am. Water Works Assn., Air Pollution Control Assn., Water Pollution Control Fedn., Sigma Xi, Tau Beta Pi, Chi Epsilon, Pi Mu Epsilon. Home: 500 Pakis St Apt 2B Hot Springs National Park AR 71913-6556 E-mail: adrsprings@prodigy.net.

RAY, BILLY JOHN, JR., music educator; b. Puyallup, Wash., Apr. 9, 1964; s. Billy John, Sr. and Leone Dorothy Ray; m. Claudette Ann Laycock, Mar. 31, 1990; children: Jazmyn, Kierstyn. BA in Edn., Ctrl. Wash. U., 1987. Instrumental music tchr. Ellensburg (Wash.) Sch. Dist., 1987—88, Endicott (Wash.) Sch. Dist., 1988—. Mid. sch. football asst. coach Endicott-St. John Mid. Sch., 1993—95, mid. sch. football head coach, 1996—; baseball asst. coach St. John (Wash.)-Endicott HS, 1996—97, softball asst. coach, 1997—2002, mid. sch. asst. coach baseball, 2003—. Mem.: Wash. Interscholastic Activities Assn. (mem. music com. 1997—), Wash. Music Educators Assn. Home: 104 E St Endicott WA 99125 Office: Endicott Sch Dist 308 School Dr Endicott WA 99125 E-mail: bray@endicott.wednet.edu.

RAY, BRADLEY STEPHEN, petroleum geologist; b. Ada, Okla., Feb. 15, 1957; s. Walter Lloyd and Betty Louise (McCurley) R. BS in Geology, Baylor U., 1980; MS in Geology, U. Tex., 1985. Cert. geologist. Asst. geologist Hunt Oil Co., Dallas, 1978, geologist, 1979-81; ind. oil and gas producer Dallas, 1981—. Chmn. adv. bd. Geol. Info. Libr. Dallas, 1988—; bd. dirs. Global Mapping Internat. Trustee Dallas Bapt. U., 1988-94, Criswell Coll., 1990-92; chmn. The Habitats Project, 1993—; mem. Peoples Info. Network. Mem. Am. Assn. Petroleum Geologists, Ind. Petroleum Assn. Am., Soc. Ind. Profl. Earth Scientists, Dallas Geol. Soc., Tex. Ind. Producers and Royalty Owners, Okla. Ind. Petroleum Assn., Geol. Soc. Am., Computer Oriented Geol. Soc., Nat. Stripper Well Assn., Energy Club, Oklahoma City Geol. Soc., Colbert-Tracht Club. Republican. Baptist. Home: 4925 Greenville Ave Ste 1348 Dallas TX 75206-4021 Office: 1348 One Energy Sq Dallas TX 75206

RAY, BRUCE DAVID, lawyer, writer; b. Denver, Dec. 19, 1955; s. John Denver Ray and Jane (Guiney) Mitchell; m. Faith Theofanus, Aug. 20, 1978 (div. 2001); children: Ellena, Constance, Christian, Zoe. BA magna cum laude, U. Colo., 1978; JD, Union U., Albany, N.Y., 1981. Bar: Colo. 1981. Spl. environ. counsel URS-Berger, San Bernardino, Calif., 1982-84; asst. regional counsel EPA, Denver, 1984-90; spl. asst. U.S. atty. U.S. Dept. Justice, Denver, 1987-90; assoc. gen. counsel Johns-Manville Corp., Denver, 1990—. Asst. editor Natural Resources and Environment, 1989—; contbr. articles to legal jours. First v.p. St. Catherine Greek Orthodox Ch. of S.E. Denver, 1994-95. Recipient bronze medal EPA, 1986, 91, gold medal, 1989, Environ. Excellence award, 1987, Best Article award, 1988, Roasch prize Albany Law Sch., 1981. Mem. ABA (sect. on environment, energy and resources law), Colo. Bar Assn. (environ. law coun. 1987—, chmn. 1995-96), Aurora Bar assn., Environ. Law Inst., Air and Waste Mgmt. Assn., Phi Beta Kappa. Avocations: german language and literature, modern greek, writing. Office: Johns-Manville 717 17th St Denver CO 80202-3330 E-mail: rayb@jm.com.

RAY, CARLOS See NORRIS, CHUCK

RAY, CHARLES AARON, foreign service officer; b. Center, Tex., July 5, 1945; m. Myung Wook Soe, Nov. 3, 1973; children: David Edward, Denise Ellen, Gayle Denene, Jason Andre. BSBA, Benedictine Coll., 1972; MS in Sys. Mgmt., U. So. Calif., 1981; MS in Nat. Security Strategy, Nat. War Coll., 1997. Commd. 2d lt. U.S. Army, 1965, advanced through grades to maj., ret., 1982; consular officer U.S. Consulate Gen., Guangzhou, China, 1983-84, chief consular sect. Shenyang, China, 1985-87, chief adminstrv. sect. Chiangmai, Thailand, 1988-91; spl. asst. to dir. Office Def. Trade Controls, Washington, 1991-93; dep. chief of mission Am. Embassy, Freetown, Sierra Leone, 1993-96; detailed to Nat. War Coll., Washington, 1996-97, Nat. Fgn. Affairs Tng. Ctr., Arlington, Va., 1997-98; consul gen. U.S. Consulate Gen., Ho Chi Minh City, Vietnam, 1998-2001; sr. seminar Nat. Fgn. Affairs Tng. Ctr., 2001—02; amb. U.S. Embassy, Phnom Penh, 2002—. Editl. cartoonist Spring Lake News, 1975-79; contbr. articles to Asia Mag., 1974-79; editor mag. Psyop Digest, 1976-78; exec. editor Def. Trade News, 1992-93. Avocations: golf, taekwondo, softball, tennis, painting, poetry. Office: US Embassy Box P Apo AP 96546 Office Phone: (855) 23 218 926. E-mail: rayc@state.gov.

RAY, CHARLES ALBERT, photojournalist; b. Franklin County, Tenn., Feb. 9, 1928; s. Sherman Peaturney and Sona Arlena Ray; m. Betty Heringa, Dec. 10, 1950 (div. June 1965); m. Deborah Freshwater, Apr. 7, 1972 (div. Apr. 1980); m. Theresa Ann Bailey, Dec. 20, 1997; children: David Charles, Thomas Wesley. Student, Grand Rapids (Mich.) Jr. Coll., 1951—53, Bay City (Mich.) Jr. Coll., 1956—61. News cinematographer Sta. WWTV-TV, Cadillac, Mich., 1953—54, Sta. KWWL-TV, Waterloo, Iowa, 1955, Sta. WNEM-TV, Bay City, 1956—61, Sta. WGN-TV, Chgo., 1961—65, NBC News, Chgo., 1965—87; ret., 1987. Author: The Life of a Network Newsreel Cameraman, 2001; exhibitions include Charles Ray Photo Archives, Florida Gulf Coast U., 2002. Named Chgo. Cameraman of Yr., 1963, 1965, 1967; recipient numerous news awards. Mem.: Internat. Cinematographers Guild Local 600, Chgo. Press Photographers Assn., Nat. Press Photographers Assn. (News Film award). Avocations: photography, reading, writing, fishing. Office: PO Box 449 Sanibel FL 33957

RAY, CHARLES DEAN, neurosurgeon, spine surgeon, bioengineer, inventor; b. Americus, Ga., Aug. 1, 1927; s. Oliver Tinsley and Katherine (Broadfield) R.; children: Bruce, Marlene. AB, Emory U., 1950; MS, U. Miami, 1952; MD, Med. Coll. Ga., 1956. Diplomate Am. Bd. Neurol. Surgery, Am. Bd. Spine Surgery. Intern Bapt. Meml. Hosp., Memphis, 1956-57; resident, rsch. assoc. neurosurgery U. Tenn. Hosp., Memphis, 1957-62; fellow, rsch. asst. Mayo Clinic and Found., Rochester, Minn., 1962-64; asst. prof. neurosurgery, lectr. bioengring. Johns Hopkins U. Med. Sch., Balt., 1964-68; chief dept. engring. F. Hoffmann-LaRoche, Basel, Switzerland, 1968-73; clin. assoc. prof. medicine U. Minn., Mpls., 1973; practice medicine specializing in neurosurgery Norfolk, Williamsburg, Va., 1973—. Lectr. U. Basel (Switzerland), 1968—73; dir. emeritus Inst. Low Back and Neck Care; med. dir. The Spine Program Ea. Va. Med. Sch., Norfolk, Va.; pres. Am. Coll. Spine Surgery; mem. staff Sentara Hosps., Norfolk; chmn. bd. pres. Cedar Devel. Corp., Cedar Surg., Inc., 1985—; v.p. med. rsch. Medtronic, Inc., Mpls., 1972—79; bd. dirs. Herman Miller, Inc.; chmn. emeritus, med. dir. Raymedia, Inc., Mpls.; cons. in field; adj. prof. orthopedics Ain Shams U., Cairo, 2002—, U. Colo., Denver, 2002—. Author: Principles of Engineering Applied to Medicine, 1964, Medical Engineering, 1974, Lumbar Spine Surgery, 1988; contbr. over 350 articles to profl. publs. Chmn. com. materials and devices World Fedn. Neurosurg. Socs., 1977—, Cosmos Club, 1976—; vestry St. Martin's Episcopal Ch., Wayzata, Minn., 1976-79. With USN, 1945-49. Named Disting. Alumnus, Med. Coll. Ga., 1999; recipient Gold award for Best Med. Device Design of Yr. R&D 100, 2000. Fellow: ACS, Royal Soc. Health, Am. Coll. Spine Surgery (pres.); mem.: ASTM, AMA (sr.), IEEE (sr.), Internat. Spine Arthroplasty Soc. (pres.), N.Am. Spine Soc. (past pres., chmn., Wiltse award 1999), Internat. Orgn. Standardization, Pan-Am. Med. Assn. (life), Am. Assn. Neurol. Surgeons (sr.), Internat. Soc. Stereotaxic and Functional Neurosurgery, Internat. Fedn. Med. Biol. Engring., West Germany Armed Forces Med. Soc., Congress Neurol. Surgeons, Mpls. Club, Sigma Xi. Achievements include over 50 U.S. patents and over 100 foreign patents. Home: 4320 Via Presada Santa Barbara CA 93110 Office: PO Box 2219 Yorktown VA 23692 Office Phone: 757-988-0600. Personal E-mail: InveRay@aol.com.

RAY, CHARLES KENDALL, retired university dean; b. Boise City, Okla., Mar. 15, 1928; s. Volney Holt and Mamie (Burton) R.; m. Doris Derby, Aug. 26, 1951. BA, U. Colo., 1951; MA, Columbia, 1955, Ed.D., 1959. Teaching prin. Bur. Indian Affairs, Savoonga, Alaska, 1951-54; mem. faculty U. Alaska, 1957-93, prof. edn., 1960-93, dean Sch. Edn., 1961-80, dir. summer sessions, 1980-93. Author: A Program of Education for Alaska Natives, 1959, Alaskan Native Secondary School Dropouts, 1961. Mem. N.E.A., Phi Delta Kappa. Home: 2000 1st Ave Apt 2204 Seattle WA 98121-2171

RAY, CREAD L., JR., retired state supreme court justice; b. Waskom, Tex., Mar. 10, 1931; s. Cread L. and Antonia (Hardesty) R.; m. Janet Watson Keller, Aug. 12, 1977; children: Sue Ann (dec.), Robert E., Glenn L., David B., Marcie Lynn, Anne Marie. BBA, Tex. A&M U., 1952; JD, U. Tex., 1957; L.H.D. (hon.), Wiley Coll., Marshall, Tex., 1980. Bar: Tex. 1957. Practiced in, Marshall, 1957-59; judge Harrison County, 1959-61; justice 6th dist. Ct. Civil Appeals, Texarkana, 1970-80, Supreme Ct. Tex., 1980-90, ret., 1990; prin. C.L Ray, Austin, 1991—. Past pres. Marshall Jaycees, Marshall C. of C.; mem. Tex. Ho. of Reps., 1966-70; active local, regional, nat. Boy Scouts Am.; trustee Wiley Coll. Lt. col. USAF, 1952-54, Korea; ret. Recipient various Boy Scouts awards. Mem. State Bar Tex., N.E. Tex. Bar Assn. (past pres.), Rotary, Tex. Aggies. Democrat. Methodist. Home and Office: 604 Beardsley Ln Austin TX 78746-4929 Office Phone: 512-328-9238. E-mail: judgeclray@aol.com, judgeclray@msn.com.

RAY, DOUGLAS KENT, newspaper executive; Pres., CEO Daily Herald/Sunday Herald, Arlington Heights, Ill., 1970—. Office: Daily Herald/Sunday Herald Paddock Publs PO Box 280 Arlington Heights IL 60006-0280

RAY, ELISE, gymnast; b. Tallahassee, Feb. 6, 1982; d. Bill and Ellen Ray. Mem. U.S. Gymnastics Team, 1996-2001, U.S. Olympic Team, 2000. Recipient 1st team Internat. Team Championships, 1997; 1st pl. uneven bars, John Hancock U.S. Gymnastics Championships, 1998; 1st pl. fixed bars, John Hancock U.S. Gymnastics Championships, 1999; 1st pl. All Around uneven bars, John Hancock U.S. Gymastics Championships, 2000; 1st pl. All Around vault, uneven bars, fixed bars, Aussie Haircare Gymnastics Invitational, 2000; 1st team All-Around Champion, Sr. Pacific Alliance Championship, New Zealand, 2000, All-Around Champion, NCAA Championships, 2001, 1st pl. balance beam, NCAA Championships, 2002. Mem. Hill's Angels Club. Avocations: shopping, arts and crafts, movies, family. Address: Womens Gymnastics 1000 S State St Ann Arbor MI 48109

RAY, EVELYN LUCILLE, arts facilitator, small meetings planner; b. Phila., Oct. 15, 1949; d. William and Erma Lucille (Chadrick) Ray. Sec. City of Phila., 1967, Free Libr. of Phila., 1972-77, Office of City Solicitor, Phila., 1977-81, Water Dept., Phila., 1981-87; program devel. creative cons. Accoutrements for the Arts, Phila., 1989, creative dir., 1993—, meeting planner for small meetings specializing in theme and site selection, 1995—. Comms. support Pa. Acad. of Fine Arts, Phila., 1987-88; creative cons. West Phila. Cultural Alliance, Phila., 1988-89; mem. adv. bd. Internat. Biog. Ctr., Cambridge, Eng., 1995—, Am. Biog. Inst., Raleigh, N.C., 1995—. Republican. Baptist. Avocations: travel, real estate: interior design and preservation, entertaining, classical music. Office: Accoutrements for the Arts 341 N Robinson St Philadelphia PA 19139-1125

RAY, FRANK ALLEN, lawyer; b. Lafayette, Ind., Jan. 30, 1949; s. Dale Allen and Merry Ann (Fleming) R.; m. Carol Ann Olmutz, Oct. 1, 1982; children: Erica Fleming, Robert Allen. BA, Ohio State U., 1970, JD, 1973. Bar: Ohio 1973, U.S. Dist. Ct. (so. dist.) Ohio 1975, U.S. Supreme Ct. 1976, U.S. Tax Ct. 1977, U.S. Ct. Appeals (6th cir.) 1977, U.S. Dist. Ct. (no. dist.) Ohio 1980, U.S. Dist. Ct. (ea. dist.) Mich. 1983, U.S. Ct. Appeals (1st cir.) 1986; cert. civil trial adv. Nat. Bd. Trial Advocacy. Asst. pros. atty. Franklin County, Ohio, 1973-75, chief civil counsel, 1976-78; dir. econ. crime project Nat. Dist. Attys. Assn., Washington, 1975-76; assoc. Brownfield, Kosydar, Bowen, Bally & Sturtz, Columbus, Ohio, 1978, Michael F. Colley Co., L.P.A., Columbus, 1979-83; pres. Frank A. Ray Co., L.P.A., Columbus, 1983-93, 2000—, Ray & Todaro Co., LPA, Columbus, 1993-94, Ray, Todaro & Alton Co., L.P.A., Columbus, 1994-96, Ray, Todaro, Alton & Kirstein Co., L.P.A., Columbus, 1996, Ray, Alton & Kirstein Co., L.P.A., Columbus, 1996—98; sr. ptnr. Ray & Alton, L.L.P., Columbus, 1998—2000; adj. prof. Moritz Coll. of Law, Ohio State U., 2003—. Mem. seminar faculty Nat. Coll. Dist. Attys., Houston, 1975-77; mem. nat. conf. faculty Fed. Jud. Ctr., Washington, 1976-77; bd. editors Man. for Complex Litigation, Fed. Jud. Ctr., 1999—; bd. mem. bar examiners Ohio Supreme Ct., 1992-95, Rules Adv. Com., 1995-99. Editor: Economic Crime Digest, 1975-76; co-author: Personal Injury Litigation Practice in Ohio, 1988, 91. Mem. fin. com. Franklin County Rep. Orgn., Columbus, 1979-84; trustee Ohio State U. Humanities Alumni Soc., 1991-93, Nat. Coun. Ohio State U. Coll. Law Alumni Assn., 1998—; mem. Legal Aid Soc. of Columbus Capital Campaign Fund Cabinet, 1998. Capt. inf. U.S. Army, 1976. Named to Ten Outstanding Young Citizens of Columbus, Columbus Jaycees, 1976; recipient Nat. award of Distinctive Svc., Nat. Dist. Attys. Assn., 1977. Fellow: Ohio Acad. Trial Lawyers (pres. 1989—90, Pres.'s award 1986), Ohio State Bar Found., Roscoe Pound Found., Am. Coll. Trial Lawyers, Internat. Soc. Barristers, Columbus Bar Found. (trustee 2003—); mem.: ATLA (state del. 1990—92), ABA, Franklin County Trial Lawyers Assn. (pres. 1987—88, Pres.'s award 1990), Ohio State Bar Assn. (com. negligence law 1990—97, mem. com. jury instrns. 2002—), Million Dollar Advs. Forum, Columbus Bar Assn. (pres. 2001—02, Profl. award 1987), Am. Bd. Trial Advs. (pres., Ohio Chpt. 2004), Inns. of Ct. (pres. Judge Robert M. Duncan chpt. 1993—94). Presbyterian. Home: 2030 Tremont Rd Columbus OH 43221-4330 Office: 175 S 3rd St Ste 350 Columbus OH 43215-5188 Office Phone: 614-221-7791. E-mail: far@raylaw.com.

RAY, GENE WELLS, industrial executive; b. Murray, Ky., Apr. 23, 1938; s. Terry Lee and Loreen (Lovett) R.; m. Becky Huie, Mar. 5, 1956 (dec. 1976); m. Taffin Ray; children: Don Dickerson, Kathy Pratt, Nancy Solomon. BS in Math., Physics and Chemistry, Murray State U., 1956; MS in Physics, U.

Tenn., 1962, PhD in Theoretical Physics, 1965. With tech. staff Aerospace Corp., San Bernardino, Calif., 1965-68; mgr. strategic div. USAF (OA), Washington, 1968-70; scientist, sr. v.p., systems group mgr. Sci. Applications Inc., La Jolla, Calif., 1970-81, also bd. dirs.; pres., chief exec. officer Titan Systems Inc., San Diego, 1981-85, CEO, 1985—, CEO, pres., chmn.; assoc. prof. Carson Newman Coll., Tenn., 1964-65. Inventor mass flow meter. 1st lt. USAR, 1963-68. Republican. Avocations: tennis, wine collecting. Home: PO Box 2464 Rancho Santa Fe CA 92067-2464 Office: Titan Corp 3033 Science Park Rd San Diego CA 92121-1199

RAY, GILBERT T. lawyer; b. Mansfield, Ohio, Sept. 18, 1944; s. Robert Lee Ray and Renatha (Goldie) Washington; m. Valerie J. Reynolds, June 14, 1969; children: Tanika, Tarlin. BA, Ashland Coll., 1966; MBA, U. Toledo, 1968; JD, Howard U., 1972. Assoc. O'Melveny & Myers, L.A., 1972-79, ptnr., 1980-2000, ret. ptnr., 2000—. Bd. dirs. Sierra Monolithics, Inc., Watson, Wyatt & Co., Advance Auto Parts, Automobile Club of So. Calif., Haynes Found., Anchor Pathway Fund, Seasons Series Fund, SunAmerica Series Trust. Mem. The Calif. Club, L.A. Country Club. Democrat. Office: 400 S Hope St Ste 1900 Los Angeles CA 90071-2899

RAY, H. M. lawyer; b. Rienzi, Miss., Aug. 9, 1924; s. Thomas Henry and Isabelle (Dunlap) R.; m. Merle Burt, Nov. 28, 1953 (dec. Dec. 1993); children: Howard Manfred, Mark Andrew. JD, U. Miss., 1949. Bar: Miss. 1949. U.S. atty. No. Dist. Miss., Oxford, 1961-81; pvt. practice law Corinth, Miss., 1949-61, Jackson, Miss., 1981-85, 90—; asst. atty. gen. State of Miss., Jackson, 1986-90. Mem. Atty. Gen.'s Adv. Com. U.S. Attys., 1973-78, chmn., 1976; vis. lectr. UN, Asia and Far East, UN (Inst. for Prevention Crime and Treatment of Offenders), Tokyo, 1977; pros. atty. Alcorn County, Miss., 1956-57, 58-61; mem. Miss. Ho. of Reps., 1948-51; mem. Miss. Gov.'s Com. to Study Laws Regarding Use of Deadly Force on Fleeing Felons, 1982-83, Miss. Gov.'s Constl. Study Commn., 1985-86. Co-author: Miss. Workmens' Compensation Act, 1948. Chmn. Corinth-Alcorn County Airport Bd., 1959-61; trustee Alcorn County Public Library, 1959-62. Served with USAAC, 1943-45, ETO; with USAF, 1951-53. Recipient Corinth's Young Man of Yr. award, 1958 Presbyterian (elder). Clubs: Kiwanis (lt. gov. 1955-56, dist. chmn. 1956-57, pres. Corinth 1953-54). Home: 12 Windy Ridge Cove Jackson MS 39211-2904

RAY, HUGH MASSEY, JR., lawyer; b. Vicksburg, Miss., Feb. 1, 1943; s. Hugh Massey and Lollie Landon (Powell) R.; m. Carroll Robertson, Sept. 7, 2002; children: Hugh, Hallie. BA, Vanderbilt U., 1965, JD, 1967. Bar: Tex. 1967, U.S. Dist. Ct. (so. dist.) Tex. 1967, U.S. Dist.Ct. (we. dist.) La. 1979, U.S. Dist. Ct. (we. dist.) Tex. 1979, U.S. Dist Ct. (no. dist.) Tex. 1980, U.S. Ct. Appeals 1st, 5th, 9th, 11th cirs.) 1982, U.S. Dist. Ct. (no. dist.) Calif. 1989, N.Y. 1992; cert. Tex. Bd. Legal Specialization. Asst. U.S. atty. So. Dist. Tex., 1967-68; assoc. Andrews & Kurth, Houston, 1968-77, ptnr., 1977—. Lectr. Ctrl. and Ea. European Law Initiative, Vilnius, Lithuania, 1996. Co-author: Bankruptcy Investing, 1992, Creditor's Rights in Texas, vol. 1 & 2, 1998; contbr. articles to profl. jours. Mem.: ABA (chmn. real property practice com. 1975—77, chmn. cont. legal edn. com. young lawyers divsn. 1976—78, vice-chmn. 1979, chmn. oil and gas subcom. bus. bankruptcy com. 1985—89, chmn. executory contracts subcom. 1989—93, chmn. bus. bankruptcy com. 1993—96, chmn. com. on trust indentures and indenture trustees 1995—97, mem. standing com. on jud. selection, tenure and compensation 1996—97, chmn. ad hoc com. on bankruptcy ct. structure 1996—2001, coun. mem. bus. law sect. 1997—2001, chair energy gus. com. 2001—), South Tex. Coll. Law (trustee 2003—), Houston Symphony Orch. (trustee 2004—), Am. Coll. Bankruptcy., Am. Law Inst., Tex. Bar Assn. (chmn. bankruptcy com. 1985—88), Houston Bar Assn., Tex. Club, River Oaks Country Club, Houston Country Club. Episcopalian. Home: 3036 Locke Ln Houston TX 77019-Office: Andrews & Kurth 600 Travis St Ste 4200 Houston TX 77002-2910

RAY, JOHN WALKER, otolaryngologist, educator, broadcast commentator; b. Columbus, Ohio, Jan. 12, 1936; s. Kenneth Clark and Hope (Walker) R.; m. Susanne Gettings, July 15, 1961; children: Nancy Ann, Susan Christy. AB magna cum laude, Marietta Coll., 1956; MD cum laude, Ohio State U., 1960; postgrad., Temple U., 1964, Mt. Sinai Hosp., Columbia U., 1964, 66, Northwestern U., 1967, 71, U. Ill., 1968, U. Ind., 1969, Tulane U., 1969. Diplomate Am. Bd. Otolaryngology. Intern Ohio State U. Hosps., Columbus, 1960-61, clin. rsch. trainee NIH, 1963-65, resident dept. otolaryngology, 1963-65, 66-67, resident dept. surgery, 1965-66, instr. dept. otolaryngology, 1966-67, 70-75, clin. asst. prof., 1975-82, clin. assoc. prof., 1982-92, clin. prof., 1992-2000, clin. prof. emeritus, 2000—; hon. staff, past chief of staff Good Samaritan Hosp., also Bethesda Hosp., Zanesville, Ohio, 1967—. Hon. active staff Meml. Hosp., Marietta, Ohio, 1992—; radio-TV health commentator, 1982—. Contbr. articles to profl. jours.; collaborator with surg. motion picture: Laryngectomy and Neck Dissection, 1964. Past pres. Muskingum chpt. Am. Cancer Soc. Capt. USAF, 1961-63. Recipient Barraquer Meml. award, 1965; named to Order of Ky. Col., 1966, Muskingum County Country Music Hall of Fame. Fellow ACS, Am. Soc. Otolaryn. Allergy, Am. Acad. Otolaryngology-Head and Neck Surgery (past gov.), Am. Acad. Facial Plastic and Reconstructive Surgery; mem. AMA, Nat. Assn. Physician Broadcasters, Muskingum County Acad. Medicine (past pres.), Ohio Med. Assn., Columbus Ophthalmol. and Otolaryn. Soc. (past pres.), Ohio Soc. Otolaryngology (past pres.), Am. Soc. Contemporary Medicine and Surgery, Acad. Radio and TV Health Commentators, Fraternal Order of Police Assocs., Internat. Bluegrass Music Assn., Phi Beta Kappa, Alpha Omega Alpha, Beta Beta Beta, Alpha Tau Omega, Alpha Kappa Kappa. Presbyterian. Home: 1245 East Dr Zanesville OH 43701-1445

RAY, MICHAEL EDWIN, lawyer; b. Charlotte, N.C., Dec. 13, 1949; s. Daniel Shaw Ray and Jane (Horne) Keziah; m. Janet Langston Jones, July 14, 1973; children: John Daniel, Jennifer Marjory. BA, Furman U., 1972; JD, U. S.C., 1978. Bar: N.C. 1978, S.C. 1978, U.S. Dist. Ct. (ea., mid. and we. dists.) N.C. 1978, U.S. Ct. Appeals (4th cir.) 1981, U.S. Ct. Appeals (Fed. cir.) 1989. Legal adminstr. Wyche Burgess Freeman & Parham, Greenville, S.C., 1973-75; assoc. Womble Carlyle Sandridge & Rice, PLLC, Winston-Salem, N.C., 1978-85, mem., 1985—. Editor-in-chief S.C. Law Rev., 1977-78. Bd. dirs. Piedmont Opera Theatre, Inc., 1997-98; S.C. Manpower Planning Coun., Columbia, 1971-72. T.B. Clarkson scholar Furman U., 1971-72. Mem. ABA, Internat. Bar Assn., N.C. Bar Assn., S.C. Bar Assn., Fed. Cir. Bar Assn. (bd. govs. 1994-97), Am. Intellectual Property Law Assn., Forsyth County Bar Assn., Furman U. Alumni Assn. (bd. govs. 1995-2000), Lex Mundi, Ltd. (dir. 1995-99, sec. 1996-97, chair-elect 1997-98, chair 1998-99, chair emeritus 1999-2000). Democrat. Presbyterian. Avocations: sailing, woodworking, music. Home: 4269 Stonehenge Ln Winston Salem NC 27106-3535 Office: Womble Carlyle Sandridge & Rice PLLC One W Fourth St Winston Salem NC 27101 E-mail: mray@wcsr.com.

RAY, PAUL RICHARD, JR., executive recruiter, consultant; b. Columbus, Ga., Nov. 6, 1943; s. Paul Richard and Sarah (Campbell) R.; m. Elizabeth Richards, June 29, 1968; children: Paul Richard III, John Ray, Alice Ray. BSBA, U. Ark., 1966; JD, U. Tex., 1969. Bar: Tex. 1970. Dir. mktg., various mktg. positions tobacco divsn. R.J. Reynolds Tobacco Co., Winston-Salem, N.C., 1969-78; cons. Paul R. Ray & Co., Ft. Worth, 1978, v.p., 1978-79, sr. v.p., 1979-83, exec. v.p., 1983-84, pres., 1984—, COO, 1984-86; CEO Ray & Berndtson, Ft. Worth, 1986-98, chmn. bd., CEO, 1998—. Bd. dirs. Cook-Ft. Worth Children's Med. Ctr., United Way Met. Tarrant County; liberal arts adv. bd. U. Tex.; dean's exec. adv. bd. U. Ark. Recipient Brite Divinity award Tex. Christian U. Mem. ABA, Assn. Exec. Search Cons. (chmn. 1995-98), Tex. Bar Assn., Young Pres.' Orgn., River Crest Country Club, City Club. Office: Ray & Berndtson Inc PO Box 901012 Fort Worth TX 76101

RAY, PAUL S. engineering educator, researcher; b. Bengal, India, Feb. 1, 1933; arrived in U.S., 1974; s. Suresh Chandra and Radha Rani Ray; m. Sudha Karmakar, Apr. 29, 1961; children: Steve S., Sumit S. B of Mech. Engring. with honors, Jadavpur U., Calcutta, India, 1956; M of Mech. Engring., Indian Inst. Tech., Kharagpur, India, 1961; MBA in Mgmt., Golden Gate U., 1978; PhD in Indsl. Engring., U. Okla., 1988. Registered profl. engr., Tex., chartered engr., Engring. Coun., London; cert. safety profl. Bd. Cert. Safety Profls. Sr. indsl. engr. Hindustan Motors Ltd., India, 1960—63; sr. asst. Union Carbide (I) Ltd., India, 1963—72; mgr. mgmt. svcs. Hindustan Copper Ltd., India, 1972—74; project plan-scheduling engr. Bechtel Corp., San Francisco, 1974—87; asst. prof. U. Ala., Tuscaloosa, 1989—95, assoc. prof., 1995—. Presenter in field. Contbr. chapters to books, articles to profl. jours. Gordon fellow, U. Okla., 1985, recipient numerous rsch. grants. Mem.: Campus Safety Assn., Nat. Safety Coun., Sys. Safety Soc. (Educator of the Yr. 2003, 2004), Human Factors and Ergonomics Soc. (newsletter editor indsl. ergonomics tech. group 1990—91), Internat. Soc. Occupl. Ergonomics & Safety (pres. elect 2002—03, pres. 2003—04), Am. Soc. Safety Engrs. (Safety Rsch. award 1999), Internat. Soc. Engring & Safety, Inst. Indsl. Engrs. (sr.; v.p. publ. Okla. chpt. 1988—89, 2d v.p. Birmingham chpt. 1992—93, sec. 1994—95, bd. dirs. 1995—96). Achievements include patents pending for. Avocations: travel, TV, reading. Office: Univ Ala PO Box 870288 Tuscaloosa AL 35487 Business E-Mail: pray@coe.eng.ua.edu.

RAY, RACHAEL, chef; Mgr. fresh foods dept. Macy's Marketplace, NY; store mgr., buyer Agata & Valentina, NY; mgr., pub and rest. Sagamore Resort, Lake George, NY; food buyer Cowan & Lobel, Albany; host 30 Minute Meals, Albany, 30 Minute Meals, Food Network, $40 a Day, Food Network. Author: 30-Minute Meals, 1999, Veggie Meals, 2001, Comfort Foods, 2001, 30-Minute Meals 2, 2003, Get Togethers: Rachael Ray's 30-Minute Meals, 2003. Office: Food Network Studios 604 W 52nd St New York NY 10019

RAY, RAYMOND B. federal judge; b. 1943; BA, U. South Fla., 1965; JD, U. Fla., 1971. Bar: Fla. Asst. U.S. atty. Dept. Justice, So. Dist. Fla., Miami, 1971-74; bankruptcy judge U.S. Bankruptcy Ct. (so. dist.) Fla., Ft. Lauderdale, 1993—. Comdr. USNR, 1961—85, ret. Office: US Courthouse Rm 306 299 E Broward Blvd Fort Lauderdale FL 33301-1944

RAY, ROGER BUCHANAN, retired communications executive, lawyer; b. Tampa, Fla., Aug. 12, 1935; s. Ralph Jackson and Virginia Marie (Stewart) R.; m. Mary Frye Gaillard, Dec. 27, 1957; children: Mary Katherine, Roger Buchanan Jr. BA in Acctg., U. South Fla., 1967; MBA with honors, U. Notre Dame, 1984; JD, Stetson U., 1991. Bar: Fla. 1992. Acct. Gen. Telephone Co. Fla., Tampa, 1959-67; internal audit mgr. GTE Service Co., N.Y.C., 1967-69; budget dir. Gen. Telephone Co. of S.E., Durham, N.C., 1969-74; v.p., controller Gen. Telephone Co. Mich., Muskegon, 1974-78; regional v.p. fin. GTE Service Corp., Westfield, Ind., 1978-82; v.p. fin. Gen. Telephone Co. Wis., 1982-84, Gen. Telephone Co. Ohio, 1982-84, Gen. Telephone Co. Pa., 1982-84, Gen. Telephone Co. Ill., 1982-84; v.p. fin., bd. dirs. Gen. Telephone Co. Mich., 1982-84, Gen. Telephone Co. Ind., 1982-84; v.p. fin., mem. exec. com., bd. dirs. GTE Communications Systems, Phoenix, 1985-87; asst. state's atty. 13th jud. cir. Tampa, Fla. bar, 1992; asst. state atty. 6th Jud. Cir., Pinellas County, Fla., 1992-96; ret., 1996. Lay eucharistic min., former vestry mem., former sr. warden Ch. of Ascension, Clearwater, Fla.; treas., bd. mem. Monaco Travelers. Mem. Fin. Execs. Inst., Notre Dame Alumni Assn., Kappa Alpha. Republican. Episcopalian. Avocations: jogging, motorhome travel, golf, reading, church work. Home: 2337 Kings Point Dr Largo FL 33774-1010

RAY, RONALD DUDLEY, lawyer; b. Hazard, Ky., Oct. 30, 1942; BA in Psychology and English, Centre Coll., 1964; JD magna cum laude, U. Louisville, 1971. Assoc. Greenebaum, Doll & McDonald, 1971-75, ptnr., 1975-84, 85-86, Ray & Morris, Louisville, 1986-89; mng. ptnr. Ronald Ray Attys., Louisville, 1990—; dep. asst. sec. def. Pentagon, Washington, 1984-85. Adj. prof. law U. Louisville Sch. Law, 1972-80; commr. Presdl. Commn. on Assigment of Women in Mil., 1992. Author: Military Necessity & Homosexuality, 1993; sr. legal editor: Personnel Policy Manual, Bank Supervisory Policies, The Bank Employee Handbook, 1985-86; mil. historian. State fin. chmn. Nat. Fin. Com. for George Bush for Pres.; chmn. Vietnam Vets. Leadership Program in Ky., 1982-85, Ky. Vietnam Vets. Meml. Fund, 1985-91; trustee Marine Corps Command and Staff Found., 1985-92; mem. exec. com. State Cen. Com., Ky. Rep. Party, 1986-90; mem. Am. Battle Monuments Commn., 1990-94; chmn. Vets. for Bush in Ky., 2000; mem. Nat. Com. Vets. for Bush, 2000; spokesman Coalition of Am. Vets., 1998—, chmn., 1999—; spl. coun. Naval Aviation Found., 1994—. With USMC, 1964-69; col. USMCR (ret.). Decorated Silver Star medal with gold star, Bronze Star medal, Purple Heart, Vietnamese Cross of Gallantry, Vietnamese Honor Medal; recipient Nat. Eagle award Nat. Guard Assn., 1985. Mem. Naval Inst. (life), Marine Corps Res. Officers' Assn. Home: Halls Hill Farm 3317 Halls Hill Rd Crestwood KY 40014-9523 E-mail: euniceray@aol.com.

RAY, ROSABELL HARRIET See BATTIN, R.

RAY, ROY LEE, state legislator, public finance consultant; b. Akron, Ohio, July 16, 1939; s. Charles Henry Ray and Geneva Lee (Edwards) Kendall; m. Frances Margaret Jordan, Aug. 24, 1968; children: Christopher Lee, Brian Edward. BS, Akron U., 1962. Sales rep. internat. div. Goodyear Tire & Rubber Co., Akron, 1962-68; stockbroker Francis I. DuPont & Co., Akron, 1968-69; rsch. analyst City of Akron, 1969-72, dep. dir. pub. svc., 1972-73, commr. pub. utilities, 1973-74, budget dir., 1974-79, fin. dir., 1977-79, mayor, mgr., safety dir., 1980-83; pres. Albrecht, Inc., Akron, 1983-85; cons. Ohio Co., Akron, 1988—; mem. Ohio Senate from 27th dist., Columbus, 1986—; fin. chmn. Ohio Senate, Columbus, 1996—. State sen. Ohio Senate, 1986—. Pres. Ohio Mcpl. League, 1982-83; chmn. Conf. Ohio Big-City Mayors, 1981-83, N.E. Ohio Four-County Coord. Orgn., 1981-82; bd. trustees local United Way, Akron Gen. Med. Ctr., Am. Cancer Soc. Recipient Alumni Honor award U. Akron, 1987, Freshman of Yr. award Columbus Monthly mag., 1988. Mem. Kiwanis, Phi Kappa Tau (Ray C. Bliss award 1983), Omicron Delta Kappa. Office: 692 Sunnyside Ave Akron OH 44303-1756 also: Ohio Senate 1st Fl Rm 127 Senate Bldg Columbus OH 43215

RAY, RUTH ALICE YANCEY, retired rancher, real estate developer; b. Birmingham, Ala., July 26, 1931; d. John Grayson and Ruth Ethel (Lutman) Yancey; (div. July 1986); children: Virginia Ruth, John Edward, William Arthur. Student, Fla. State U., 1949-50; BS, Appalachian State U., 1954; postgrad., Stetson U., 1966-67, Appalachian State U., 1962-63, Stetson U., 1964-67. Tchr. pub. schs., Nenana, Alaska, 1955-56; tchr. 1st Christian Ch., Clermont, Fla., 1965-67, Lake County Sch. Bd., Clermont, 1969-70; rancher Rays' Ranch, Clermont, 1963-97; pvt. real estate developer Clermont, 1990—; substitute tchr. Buncombe County Asheville City Sch. Sys., 1999—. Chmn. Clermont Planning and Zoning Commn., 1973-81; mem. Heart of Fla. Girl Scout Coun., 1988—, life mem. Ctr. Fla. Girl. Scout Coun.; life mem. Friends of Cooper Mem. Libr., South Lake Art League; assoc. Sisters of St. Mary. Named Conservation Farmer of Yr., State of Fla., 1982. Mem. Lake County Farm Bur. (bd. dirs. 1977-81), Lake County Cattlemen's Assn. (v.p. 1979-81), Lake County Farmer's Home Adminstrn. (bd. dirs. 1984-88, 1990—, chmn. 1985, 88, 90-91), Nat. Cutting Horse Assn. (life), Am. Quarter Horse Assn., Am. Paint Horse Assn., E.S.A. Internat., Daus. of King (pres., sec.), Sigma Kappa. Republican. Episcopalian (sr. warden, eucharistic min.). Avocations: needlepoint, fishing, hiking, reading. Home and Office: 4575 NW Continental Pl Beaverton OR 97006 E-mail: raray415@aol.com.

RAY, SIBA PRASAD, materials scientist, ceramics scientist; b. Dinhata, India, Jan. 4, 1944; came to U.S., 1969; s. Nilmony P. and Bina Pani Ray; m. Liplka Ray, May 28, 1977; children: Sourav, Leena. B of Engring., Calcutta (India) U., 1964; MS, Columbia U., 1970, D of Engring. Sci., 1974. Sci. officer Bhabha Atomic Rsch. Ctr., Bombay, 1964-68; rsch. assoc. Pa. State U., University Park, 1974-76; scientist Alcoa Labs., Alcoa Ctr., Pa., 1977-78, sr. scientist, 1978-82, sci. assoc. Alcoa Center, Pa., 1982-91, sr. sci. assoc., 1991-98; program mgr. materials devel. NGAP, Alcoa, Alcoa Center, 1999—. Cons. Alcoa Separations Tech., Warrendale, Pa., 1991, Electro Metallurgy and Electrochemistry Cons., New Kensington, Pa., 1992. Contbr. articles to Jour. Solid State Chemistry, J. Am. Ceramic Soc., Light Metals, Bull. Am. Ceramic Soc. Pres. Bengali Assn. Pitts., 1988. Mem. The Metall. Soc., Am. Ceramic Soc., Sigma Xi. Achievements include 29 patents in the area of inert elctrodes, ceramic composites and reaction sintering. Home: 6007 Pilgrim Ct Murrysville PA 15668-8533 Office: Alcoa Labs Alcoa Tech Ctr Alcoa Center PA 15069

RAY, STEPHEN M. health services executive; BA, U. Tenn. CPA. With Health Mgmt. Assocs., Inc., Naples, Fla., v.p., contr., treas., 1987—. Office: Health Mgmt Assocs Inc Ste 500 5811 Pelican Bay Blvd Naples FL 34108-2710

RAY, SUSANNE GETTINGS, counselor; b. Marietta, Ohio, July 20, 1937; d. Lewis B. and Reina Ashton Gettings; m. John W. Ray; children: Nancy Ann, Susan Christy. BS in Nursing, Case Western Res. U., 1960; MEd in Cmty. Counseling, Ohio U., 1987. Nat. cert. counselor, registered adv. Nat. Bd. Cert. Counselors. Staff nurse Cleve. Vis. Nurse Assn., 1960-61; sr. nurse Columbus (Ohio) Pub. Health Nursing Svc., 1962-64; founder, mgr. healthcare program Muskingum County (Ohio) Children's Svcs., 1972-76; spl. svcs. coord. Muskingum County Head Start, Zanesville, Ohio, 1979-85; clin. counselor Six County Mental Health Ctr., Zanesville, 1987-94; edn. coord. Safe/Response, Zanesville, 1995-97; counselor Paula Colman & Assocs., 1999—. Stephen min. Ch. Sch. tchr. Ctrl. Presbyn. Ch., elder, 1996-99; founder, coord. SAFE; bd. dirs. Eastside Cmty. Ministry; mem. Grads. and Headstart Health Adv. Bd.; bd. dirs., legis. chair Ohio Coalition of Sexual Assualt; mem. edn. and svc. com. Cmty. Against Rape. Recipient various profl. and cmty. awards. Mem. Am. Counseling Assn., Ohio Counseling Assn., Sigma Theta Tau, Chi Sigma Iota. Office: Paula Colman & Assocs 860 Bethesda Dr Zanesville OH 43701-1800

RAY, TIMOTHY BRITT, social worker, lawyer, administrator; b. New Orleans, June 13, 1939; s. Archibald Cole and Eliza Owen (Britt) R.; m. Constance Helen Abbott, Nov. 27, 1964; children: Michael Gregory Owen, Mary Eliza Rebecca. BA, Davidson Coll., 1961; MA, La. State U., 1963; MSW, W. Va. U., 1968; JD, Santa Clara U., 1976. Bar: Ohio 1981. Chief psychiatric social worker Alameda County, Oakland, Calif., 1974-77; exec. dir. Toledo Legal Aid Soc., 1977-82; counselor youth Fla. Health and Rehabilitative Svcs., Miami, 1983-84; exec. dir. Dist. Ill. Mental Health Bd., Gainesville, Fla., 1984, Older Americans Coun., Gainesville, 1984-90; elderly housing mgr. Gainesville Housing Authority, 1990-92, med. social work supr. Olsten-Kimberly Quality Care, 1993-94; med. social worker Hospice of Marion County, Gainesville, 1994—. Chmn. health care services adv. com. Upjohn Co., Gainesville, 1986. Contbr. articles in profl. jours. Chmn. United Way Exec. Dirs. Coun., Gainesville, 1985; Alachua County rep. Dist. III Alcohol, Drug Abuse and Mental Health Planning Coun.; chmn. Adult and Elderly Svcs. Com., 1987-88; pres. Interagy. Coun., Gainesville, 1986; pres. bd. Bread of Mighty Food Bank, Inc., 1987-90; elder 1st Presbyn. Ch., Gainesville; bd. dirs. Alzheimers Assn., 1989-90, Cmty. with a Heart, Ocala, Fla., 1995—; mem. Gainesville Human Rels. Adv. Bd., 1989-91; mem. Children's Def. Fund; grad. Leadership Gainesville XVII. Bd. govs. fellow, 1967. Mem. ABA, NASW, ACLU, Acad. Cert. Social Workers, Sierra Club, Phi Alpha Delta. Democrat. Presbyterian. Avocations: swimming, tennis. Home: 3321 NW 45th Ave Gainesville FL 32605-1459 E-mail: timandconnieray@sbcglobal.net.

RAY, VIRGINIA H. S. columnist, writer; b. Chgo., Aug. 4, 1931; d. Russell Horton and Cora Virginia Stafford; m. Wilson K. Ray, Nov. 8, 1952 (dec. Oct. 14, 2000); 1 child, Virginia Ray Bouchillon. Writer, reporter South Bend (Ind.) Tribune, 1953—58; freelance writer Lausanne, Switzerland, 1963—68, Tokyo, 1973—79; freelance writer, corr. York County Coast Star, Kennebank, Maine, 1989—2002, Biddeford (Maine) Jour. Tribune, 1990—. Newsletter editor Jr. League Pitts., 1969—70, Tokyo Am. Club, 1974—78; founder libr., Fox Chapel, 1st Internat. Fair, Japan, 1974. Active Pitts. Jr. League, 1958—73; chmn. Three Rivers Art Festival, Pitts., 1962; active Kennebankport Hist. Soc., 1990. Mem.: Portland Jr. League, Brick Store Mus. Republican. Avocations: reading, history, travel, tennis. Home: #15 Pt Arundel PO 1144 Kennebunkport ME 04046-1144 Office Phone: 207-967-4227. Personal E-mail: vsr@gwi.net.

RAY, WAYNE ALLEN, epidemiologist, educator; b. Yakima, Wash., July 2, 1949; s. Allen and Patsy (McKay) R.; m. Janine Elise Thorson, June 11, 1972; children: Lily Amelia, Lea Camille. BS, U. Washington, 1971; MS, Vanderbilt U., 1974, PhD, 1981. Research assoc. Vanderbilt U. Sch. Medicine, Nashville, 1974-75, research instr., 1975-78, research asst. prof., 1979-83, asst. prof., 1984-85, dir. div. pharmacoepidemiology, 1984—, assoc. prof., 1985-90, prof., 1991—. Contbr. articles to profl. jours. Recipient Burroughs Wellcome scholar in Pharmacoepidemiology Am. Coll. Preventive Medicine, 1984. Mem. Am. Statis. Assn., Assn. Computing Machinery, Computer Soc. of IEEE, Soc. Epidemiologic Research, Am. Pub. Health Assn., Phi Beta Kappa. Avocation: gardening. Office: Vanderbilt U A-1124 Medical Ctr N 1211 22d Ave S Nashville TN 37232-2637

RAY, WILLIAM JACKSON, psychologist; b. Birmingham, Ala., Sept. 3, 1945; s. Norman M. and Mary K. Agnew; m. Judith Mebane, Aug. 22, 1987; children from previous marriage: Adam, Lauren. BA, Eckerd Coll., 1967; MA, Vanderbilt U., 1969, PhD, 1971; Fellow in med. psychology, Langley Porter Neuropsychiat. Inst., U. Calif. Med. Center, San Francisco, 1971-72. Prof., dir. clin. psychology tng. program Pa. State U., 1972—, dir. clin. trng., 1991-97. Author: (with R.M. Stern) Biofeedback, 1977, (with others) Evaluation of Clinical Biofeedback, 1979, (with R.M. Stern and C.M. Davis) Psychophysiological Recording, 1980, 2d edit. (with R.M. Stern and K. Quigley), 2000, Methods Toward a Science of Behavior and Experience, 1981, 7th edit., 2003, (with E. Susman & L. Feajous) Emotion, Cognition, Health and Development in Children and Adolescents, 1992, (with L. Michelson) Handbook of Dissociation, 1996 (Cornelia Wilbur award ISSD); series editor: Plenum Series in Behavioral Psychophysiology and Medicine. Recipient Nat. Media award Am. Psychol. Found., 1976, 78, Rsch. award Best Empirical Paper, Soc. Clin. Experimental Hypnosis. Mem. AAAS, APA, APS, Soc. Psychophysiol. Rsch. Office: Dept Psychology Pa State U University Park PA 16802 Office Phone: 814-863-1726. Business E-Mail: wjr@psu.edu.

RAY, WILLIAM MELVIN, newsletter publishing consultant; b. Dutch Mills, Ark., Mar. 13, 1935; s. William Estes and Verda Lou (Robbins) R.; m. Janet Drachman, June 6, 1969; children: Matthew Stephen, Susannah Brett. BA, U. Redlands, 1959. Reporter Sun-Telegram, San Bernardino, Calif., 1959-60; sports editor Times-Delta, Visalia, Calif., 1961-62; reporter Progress-Bull., Pomona, Calif., 1962-63; copy editor, reporter Newsday, Garden City, N.Y., 1963-65; news editor Nat. Petroleum News, McGraw-Hill, N.Y.C., 1966-71; Washington editor/chief editor Energy Newsletters, McGraw-Hill, 1972-80, v.p., gen.mgr., 1980-98, newsletter cons., 1998—. New product champion McGraw-Hill, N.Y.C., 1989-92, chmn. newsletter editl. bd., 1985-88, seminar spkr., 1985—. Author: Newsletter Publishing, 1990, Business Newsletter Promotion, 1991.

RAYBECK, DOUGLAS, anthropologist, educator; b. Jamestown, N.Y., Mar. 8, 1941; s. Joseph Anthony Raybeck and Evelyn (Jackson) Warfield; m. Peggy Ann Root, June, 1964 (div.); m. Karen Lynne Jones, Mar. 11, 1967; 1 child, Alethea Joy. Student, Freiburg U., 1962; BA, Dartmouth Coll., 1964; postgrad., Sch. Oriental African Studies, 1967, London Sch. Econs., 1967; PhD, Cornell U., 1975. Instr. in anthropology Kirkland Coll., Clinton, N.Y., 1970-75, asst. prof., 1975-76, assoc. prof., 1976-78, Hamilton Coll., Clinton, 1978-84, prof., 1984—, Christian A. Johnson Excellence in Tchg. prof., 1993-96. Various adminstrv. positions Hamilton Coll., 1978—; co-dir. Cognitive Assocs., Clinton, 1988-2003; cons. Bur. Labor Statistics, Washington, 1990. Author: Mad Dogs, Englishmen and the Errant Anthropologist, 1996, Looking Down the Road: A Systems Approach to Future Studies, 2000; co-author: Improving Student Memory, 1993, A Clash of Scientific Cultures, 1998, Improving Memory and Study Skills: Theory and Practice, 2002; co-editor: Deviance, 1991; mem. editl. adv. bd. Ethnic Groups, 1988-94, Cross Cultural Rsch., 1995—, Cognitive Technology 1996—; contbr. articles to profl. jours. Active E. Timor Action Network, 1992—. Rsch. grantee NIMH, 1968-70, Fulbright-Hays teaching and rsch. grantee, 1977; recipient Samuel & Helen Lang prize, 2003. Mem. Am. Anthrop. Assn., Soc. for Cross Cultural Rsch. (pres.-elect 2002-03, pres. 2003-04), Soc. for Psychol. Anthropology, Sigma Xi. Democrat. Avocations: biking, science fiction, computers. Office: Hamilton Coll 198 College Hill Rd Clinton NY 13323-1218 E-mail: draybeck@hamilton.edu.

RAYBOURN, ELAINE MARIE, research scientist; BA, Eckerd Coll., 1985; MA, U. Miami, 1993; PhD, U. N.Mex, 1998. Sr. mem. tech. staff Advanced Concepts Group Sandia Nat. Labs., Albuquerque, 1998—; prin. mem. tech. staff computational initiatives divsn. Sandia Nat. Labs., Albuquerque, 2001—. Nat. lab. prof. dept. comms. and journalism U. N.Mex., Albuquerque, 1999—; European Consortium Informatics and Math. postdoctoral rschr. French Nat. Inst. Rsch. in Computer Sci. and Control, Rocquencourt, 2003—, Fraunhofer Gesellschaft Inst. Applied Info. Tech., Sankt Augustin, Germany, 2002—03, guest rschr., 2001—02; rsch. fellow Brit. Telecom. Rsch. and Advanced Communication Tech. Ctr., Martlesham Heath, Ipswich, England, 1999—2002. Mem. editl. bd. Internat. Jour. Interactive Tech. and Smart Edn.; contbr. articles to profl. jours. Scholar, U. of N.Mex, 1995—98. Mem.: Assn. of Computing Machinery (mem. spl interest group on computer supported group work, mem.spl. interest group on human computer interaction). Achievements include contributed to innovations in intercultural communication training by designing computer simulation game for multiple users in which they explore cultural issues i.e. power and identity; research in design of technologies by focusing on intercultural communication and culture in her research and development of training and learning applications. Office: Sandia Nat Labs PO Box 5800 MS 1188 Albuquerque NM 87185 Office Phone: 505-844-7975. E-mail: emraybo@sandia.gov.

RAYBURN, CAROLE ANN (MARY AIDA RAYBURN), psychologist, researcher, writer, consultant; b. Washington, Feb. 14, 1938; d. Carl Frederick and Mary Helen (Milkie) Miller; m. Ronald Allen Rayburn (dec. Apr. 1970). BA in Psychology, Am. U., 1961; MA in Clin. Psychology, George Washington U., 1965; PhD in Ednl. Psychology, Cath. U. Am., 1969; MDiv in Ministry, Andrews U., 1980. Lic. psychologist, Md. Psychometrician Columbian Prep. Sch., Washington, 1963, clin. psychologist Spring Grove State Hosp., Catonsville, Md., 1966-68; pvt. practice, 1969, 71—; staff clin. psychologist Instl. Care Svcs. Div. D.C. Children's Ctr., Laurel, Md., 1970-78; psychologist Md. Dept. Vocat. Rehab., 1973-74; psychometrician Montgomery County Pub. Schs., 1981-85. Lectr. Strayer Coll., Washington, 1969-70; forensic psychology expert witness, 1973—; guest lectr. Andrews U., Berrien Springs, Mich., 1979, Hood Coll, Frederick, Md., 1986-88; instr. Johns Hopkins U., 1986, 88-89; adj. faculty Profl. Sch. Psychology Studies, San Diego, 1987; adj. asst. prof. Loyola Coll., Columbia, Md., 1987; cons. Julia Brown Montessori Schs., 1972, 78, 82—, VA Ctr., 1978, 91-93. Editor: (with M.J. Meadow) A Time to Weep and a Time to Sing, 1985; contbg. author: Montessori: Her Method and the Movement (What You Need to Know), 1973, Drugs, Alcohol and Women: A National Forum Source Book, 1975, The Other Side of the Couch: Faith of the Psychotherapist, 1981, Clinical Handbook of Pastoral Counseling, 1985, An Encyclopedic Dictionary of Pastoral Care and Counseling, 1990, Religion Personality and Mental Health, 1993; co-editor (with Violet Franks) Springer Focus on Women series; author copyrighted inventories Religious Occupational and Stress Questionnaire, 1986, Organizational Relationships Survey, 1987, Attitudes Toward Children Inventory, 1987, State-Trait Morality Inventory, 1987, Body Awareness and Sexual Intimacy Comfort Scale (BASICS), 1993, Inventory in Religiousness, 1996, Inventory on Spirituality, 1997, Sports, Exercise, Leadership and Friendship Questionnaire, 1997, Peacefulness Inventory, Life Choices Inventory, 1998, Inventory on the Supreme and Work, 1999, Children's and Adolescents' Peace Inventory, 2002; cons. editor Profl. Psychology, 1980-83; assoc. editor Jour. Pastoral Counseling, 1985-90, guest editor, 1988; co-proposer (with Lee Richmond) The Theory and Field of Theobiology: interfacing of theology and the sciences, 1998; mem. editl. bd. Internat. Jour. Ethics, 2004—; contbr. numerous articles to profl. jours. Bd. dirs. Psychologists Ethical Treatment of Animals, 1998-2000. Recipient Svc. award Coun. for Advancement Psychol. Professions and Scis., 1975, cert. D.C. Dept. Human Resources, 1975, 76, cert. recognition D.C. Psychol. Assn., 1976, 1985; AAUW rsch. grantee, 1983. Fellow: APA (mem. editl. bd. Jour. Child Clin. Psychology 1978—82, divsn. psychology women chair task force on women and religion 1980—81, chair equal opportunity affirmative action divsn. clin. psychology 1980—82, clin. psychology women's sect. 1984—86, divsn. psychology issues in grad. edn. and clin. tng. 1988—, program chair 1991—94, pres. divsn. psychology of religion 1995—96, fellow, divsn. on internat. psychology, divsn. psychology of religion, psychology of women, clin. psychology, cons. psychology, gen. psychology, psychotherapy, state assn. affairs, divsn. media psychology, divsn. family psychology, Mentoring award divsn. clin. psychology, sect. of clin. psychology of women 1997, divsn. psychology of religion 1997, William C. Bier rsch. award divsn. psychology of religion 2000), Md. Psychol. Assn. (editor newsletter 1975—76, chair ins. com. 1981—83, pres. 1984—85, exec. adv. com. 1985—, chpt. recognition 1978), Am. Assn. Applied & Preventive Psychology (sec. 1992—93, chair fellows com. 1992—93), Am. Orthopsychiat. Assn.; mem.: Balt. Assn. Cons. Psychologists (pres. 1991—92), Assn. Practicing Psychologists Montgomery-Prince George's Counties (pres. 1986—88, editor newsletter 1990—, treas. 1996—98), Internat. Soc. Polit. Psychology, Psi Chi (hon.). Achievements include research on stress in religious professionals, women and stress, women and religion, pastoral counseling, state-trait morality inventory, leadership, mentoring, clergy stress, psychotherapy, children, body image, intimacy, peacefulness, spirituality, life choices, religiousness, work. Address: 1200 Morningside Dr Silver Spring MD 20904-3149

RAYBURN, S. T. lawyer; b. Brookhaven, Miss., Aug. 26, 1947; s. Harry Newton and Margaret Elaine (Zeigler) R.; m. Elizabeth Hooker, June 6, 1970 (div. Nov. 1990); children: Andrew Newton, Thomas McCarver, Shelby Hooker; m. Paige Bruce, Feb. 1, 1992; children: Samuel Taylor, Samath Paige. BA, Miss. State U., 1970; JD cum laude, U. Miss., 1972. Bar: Miss. 1972, U.S. Dist. Ct. (no. dist.) Miss. 1972, U.S. Ct. Appeals (5th cir.) 1973, U.S. Supreme Ct. 1976, U.S. Ct. Appeals (11th cir.) 1981, U.S. Dist. Ct. (so. dist.) Miss. 1984. Assoc. Sumners & Hickman, Oxford, Miss., 1972-75; ptnr. Sumners, Hickman & Rayburn, Oxford, Miss., 1975-89, Hickman, Rayburn & Goza, Oxford, Miss., 1989-92; shareholder Mitchell, McNutt, Threadgill, Smith & Sams, Oxford, Miss., 1992-97; ptnr. Rayburn Law Firm, Oxford, 1997—. Mem. character & fitness com. Miss. State Bd. Bar Examiners, 1990-99. Sec. Lafayette County Dem. Exec. Com., Oxford, 1976-80, chmn., 1980-88; chmn. Miss. Commn. Wildlife Conservation, Jackson, Miss., 1984-89. Mem. Miss. Bar Assn. (commr.), Miss. Def. Lawyers Assn., 3rd Cir. Bar Assn. (pres.), Intern Assn. of Def. Counsel, Def. Rsch. Inst., Oxford-Lafayette County C. of C. (pres.). Presbyterian. Avocations: boating, motorcycles. Home and Office: Rayburn Law Firm PO Box 430 Oxford MS 38655-0430

RAYEVSKY, ROBERT, illustrator; b. Moscow, Nov. 7, 1955; came to U.S., 1979; s. Igor G. and Pauline (Rubin) R.; m. Kimberley Colton, Dec. 29, 1994; children: Miriam, Claire, Rafael. BFA in Graphic Design, Moscow Polygraphic Inst., 1978; BFA in Illustration, Parsons Sch. of Design, N.Y.C., 1982. Lectr. various schs. and univs. Illustrator: Two Fools And A Horse, 2003, Under New York (Linda Oatman High), 2000, Joan of Arc (Margaret Hodges), 1999, Squash It! (adapted by Eric A. Kimmel), 1997, The Sleepy Men (Margaret Wise Brown), 1996, The Talking Tree (hardcover reprint), 1995, Our King Has Horns, 1995, Three Sacks of Truth (adapted by Eric A. Kimmel), 1993, Belling the Cat and Other Aesop's Fables, 1990, The Riddle (Adele Vernon), 1987, others; profl. publs. include Applied Arts, 1997, Step-By-Step Graphics, 1997, N.Y. Art Rev., others; shows include Illustrators Only Awards Show, N.Y.C., 1996, 99, R. Michelson Galleries, Mass., Child-At-Heart Gallery, Mass., Bologna Illustrators Annual, Italy, others; set designer The Strange Games, N.Y.C., Illustration W. Annual Show, 1995, 98-99, Soc. of Illustrators Exhibition's 1992, 94-96, 99, 2001, 2003, Illustrators 38, N.Y.C., 1996, Illustrators 41, N.Y.C., 1999; contbr. commercial illustrations newspapers and magazines, including N.Y. Times, Chgo. Tribune, Working Mother, Individual Investor. Home: 76 Marian St Northampton MA 01060-1119 E-mail: rayevsky@earthlink.net.

RAYLESBERG, ALAN IRA, lawyer; b. N.Y.C., Dec. 6, 1950; s. Daniel David and Sally Doris (Mantell) R.; m. Caren Thea Coven, Nov. 20, 1983; children: Lisa Maris, Jason Todd. BA, NYU, 1972; JD cum laude, Boston U., 1975. Bar: N.Y. 1976, U.S. Dist. Ct. (so. dist.) N.Y. 1976, U.S. Dist. Ct. (ea. dist.) N.Y. 1978, U.S. Tax Ct. 1981, U.S. Ct. Appeals (2d and 5th cirs.) 1982, U.S. Ct. Appeals (1st cir.) 1986, U.S. Ct. Appeals (9th cir.) 1996. Assoc. Orans, Elsen & Polstein, N.Y.C., 1975-77, Guggenheimer & Untermyer, N.Y.C., 1977-83, ptnr., 1983-85, Rosenman & Colin, N.Y.C., 1985—2002, co-chmn. litig. dept., 1998-99, chmn. litig. dept., 1999—2002; ptnr., sect. head litig. group Vinson & Elkins, N.Y.C., 2002—04; ptnr. Chadbourne & Parke, N.Y.C., 2004—. Adj. instr. N.Y. Law Sch., 1980-83; instr. Nat. Inst. of Trial Advocacy; mem. adv. group comml. divsn., mem. mediation panel N.Y. State Supreme Ct.; mem. arbitration panel U.S. Dist. Ct. (ea. dist.) N.Y.; mem. CPR Panel of Disting. Neutrals, N.Y.C.; judge Nat. Moot Ct. Competition, 1980—. Author: Case Evaluation, Commercial Litigation in New York State Courts, 2004. Bd. dirs. Fund for Modern Cts., 1994—. Mem. ABA, Fed. Bar Coun., Assn. Bar City N.Y., N.Y. County Lawyers Assn. (bd. dirs. 1995-98, 99-2002, fed. ct. com. 1988—, appellate ct. com. 1990—, co-chmn. appellate ct. com. 1992-93, chair appellate ct. com. 1993-96), N.Y. County Lawyers Assn. Found. (bd. dirs. 1998—), N.Y. State Bar Assn. (ho. dels. 1996-2000), Securities Industry Assn. (legal and compliance divsn) N.Y. Coun. Def. Lawyers, Town Club of New Castle (mem. exec. com. 1987-91). Democrat. Jewish. Office: Chadbourne & Parke 30 Rockefeller Plz New York NY 10112 Office Phone: 212-408-5198. Personal E-mail: alan.raylesberg@verizon.net. Business E-Mail: araylesberg@chadbourne.com.

RAYMO, MAUREEN ELIZABETH, geologist, researcher; b. L.A., Dec. 27, 1959; d. Chester Theodore and Maureen Dorothy (Sterett) R.; m. Chris James Marone, May 24, 1986; children: Victoria Ray, Daniel Chester. ScB, Brown U., 1982; MA, Columbia U., 1985, MPhil, 1988, PhD, 1989. Rsch. asst. Lamont-Doherty Geol. Obs., Palisades, N.Y., 1982-83, adj. assoc. rsch. scientist, 1989—; assoc. scientist dept. geology U. Melbourne, Australia, 1989-90; asst. prof. dept. geology and geophysics U. Calif., Berkeley, 1991-92; asst. prof. dept. earth, atmospheric and planetary scis. MIT, Cambridge, 1992—. Prin. investigator rsch. grants NSF, 1991—; mem. ocean history panel Joint Oceanographic Instns. for Deep Earth Sampling, 1992—. Co-author (with C. Raymo): Written In Stone, 1989; contbr. articles to profl. jours. Named Nat. Young Investigator, NSF, 1992. Mem. AAAS, Am. Geophys. Union, Sigma Xi. Democrat. Office: MIT Earth Atmospheric & Planetary Scis E34-254 Cambridge MA 02139

RAYMOND, BARBARA, writer, educator; b. Buffalo, July 26, 1947; d. Peter and Eileen Bisantz; m. Robert Raymond, Jan. 16, 1971 (div.); children: Beth, Timothy. BS in English Edn., SUNY, Buffalo, 1969, MS in English Edn., 1974. Tchr. Sweet Home Jr. H.S., Amherst, NY, 1969—71, Maryvale Jr. H.S., Cheektowaga, NY, 1971—77; instr. - mag. writing, writing for publ. and news writing Notre Dame Coll. of Ohio, South Euclid, 1990—93; instr. - pub. speaking John Carroll U., University Heights, Ohio, 2000—02; instr. English The Acad. of Ct. Reporting, Cleve., 1999—2002. Contbr. articles to mags. incl. Good Housekeeping, Redbook, McCall's, Reader's Digest, others. Mktg. chairperson Adoption Network, Cleve., 1996—99. Recipient Ace Award for Excellence in Feature Writing, Women in Comm., Akron Chpt., 1991. Mem.: Adoption Network, Am. Adoption Congress. Avocations: reading, attending concerts. Home: 2508 24th Ave Astoria NY 11102

RAYMOND, BRUCE ALLEN, medical association administrator; b. Aberdeen, S.D., Dec. 8, 1924; s. Samuel A. and Pearl (Blackstone) R.; m. Virginia Stratton, Apr. 2, 1948 (div. 1969); children: Judith Ann, Jaqueline Marie, Bruce Allen Jr., Brian Andrew; m. Jane Molnar, Nov. 15, 1969; children: Douglas A., Andrew D., Colin K. BS, Leland Stanford U., U.S.D., 1945; MD, Washington U., St. Louis, 1949. Diplomate Am. Bd. Surgery, Am. Bd. Thoracic Surgery. Intern U. Ored. Med. Sch. Hosps., Portland, 1949-50; resident in surgery Walter Reed Gen. Hosp., Washington, 1953-57, resident in thoracic surgery, 1957-59, asst. chief thoracic surgery, 1959-60; chief thoracic and cardiovascular surgery Letterman Gen. Hosp., San Francisco, 1960-64, Fitzsimmons Gen. Hosp., Denver, 1967-69, chief dept. surgery, 1969-71; pvt. practice surgery Warwick, R.I., 1975-86; sr. med. dir. Health Care Compare Corp., Downers Grove, Ill., 1986—89, Equicor Corp. Healthcare Mgmt., Pitts., 1989—90; med. dir. The Health Plan of the Upper Ohio Valley, 1996—2003. Asst. clin. prof. U. Colo., 1967-71; assoc. clin. prof. surgery Northwestern U., Chgo., 1973-80; mem. staff Kent County Med. Mem. Hosp., Warwick, 1975-86, Miriam hosp., Providence, 1975-86; cons. in field. Contbr. articles to profl. jours. Elder, Prebyn. Ch.; various offices, bd. dirs. Boy Scouts Am., R.I., Pa., and Ill. Col.M.C. U.S. Army, 1949-72. Decorated Legion of Merit. Fellow ACS, Am. Coll. Cardiology, Am. Coll. Chest Physicians; mem. Soc. Thoracic Surgeons, Pan Pacific Surg. Assn., Am. Heart Assn., AMA, Am. Assn. Med. Instrumentation, Am. Acad. Med. Dirs., Uniformed Svcs. Univ. Surg. Assocs., New Eng. Vascular Soc. Republican. Avocation: downhill skiing. Home: 218 Salem Dr Upper Saint Clair PA 15241-2226 E-mail: braymond66@adelphia.net.

RAYMOND, DAVID WALKER, lawyer; b. Chelsea, Mass., Aug. 23, 1945; s. John Walker and Jane (Beck) R.; m. Sandra Sue Broadwater, Aug. 12, 1967 (div.); m. Margaret Byrd Payne, May 25, 1974; children: Pamela Payne, Russell Wyatt. BA, Gettysburg Coll., 1967; JD, Temple U., 1970. Bar: Pa. 1970, D.C. 1971, Ill. 1975, U.S. Dist. Ct. (no. dist.) Ill. 1981, U.S. Supreme Ct. 1974. Govtl. affairs atty. Sears, Roebuck and Co., Washington, 1970-74, atty. Sears Hdqrs. law dept. Chgo., 1974-80, asst. gen. counsel advt., trademarks and customs, 1981-84, asst. gen. counsel adminstrn., 1984-86, mgr. planning and analysis corp. planning dept., 1986-89, sr. corp. counsel pub. policy corp. law dept., 1989-90; assoc. gen. counsel litigation and adminstrn. law dept. Sears Mdse. Group, 1990-92, dep. gen. counsel, 1992-93, v.p., gen. counsel, 1993-95; v.p. law Sears Roebuck and Co., 1996; of counsel Winston & Strawn, Washington, 1996-2001; v.p., gen. counsel C-NAV Systems, Inc., Gettysburg, Pa., 2001—03. Mem. staff Temple Law Quar., 1968-69, editor 1969-70. Trustee No. Ill. U., 1996—98; bd. vis. Christopher Newport U., 1999—2003; bd. fellows Gettysburg Coll., 1999—2003; bd. dirs. ATO House Corp., 1997—, pres., 2004—. Mem.: ABA, Phi Alpha Delta. Presbyterian.

RAYMOND, DOROTHY SARNOFF, communications consultant, former actress and singer; b. N.Y.C. d. Jacob and Belle (Roossin) S.; m. Milton Harold Raymond, Mar. 15, 1957. BA, Cornell U., 1935. Cons. 5 adminstrns., over 12 years; cons. 5 adminstrns. U.S. Dept. State; founder, chmn. Dorothy Sarnoff Speech Dynamics and Communications Svcs. Inc. subs. Oglivy & Mather, N.Y.C., 1975—2000. Lectr., cons. nat. and internat. orgns., 1975—. Appeared in Broadway plays: Rosalinda, 1942, Magdalena, 1948, The King and I, 1951, My Darling Aida, 1953; debut in opera as Marquerite in Faust, Phila. Opera, 1942; leading roles with N.Y.C., Phila., L.A. and San Francisco Civic Light, New Orleans, St. Louis Mcpl., Salt Lake City operas include La Boheme, Tosca, Tales of Hoffmann, Carmen, Merry Widow, Fleidermaus, Pagliacci, New Moon, Chocolate Soldier, Great Waltz, Vagabond King; soprano soloist with various symphony orchs., soloist and guest on numerous TV programs incl. Ed Sullivan Shows, 1951—; author: Speech Can Change Your Life, 1970, Make the Most of Your Best, 1981, Never Be Nervous Again, 1988, contbr. articles to profl. jours. and mags. Mem. spl. med. adv. bd. N.Y. Cornell Hosp. Recipient Gold Medal of Honor award for disting. svc. to humanity Nat. Inst. Social Scis.; named Woman of Achievement Albert Einstein Med. Coll. Mem. Women's Forum, Women in Communication, Mortar Bd., Tower Club (Cornell U. chpt.), Lotos Club, N.Y. Hosp. Med. Adv. Bd. Home: 150 E 69th St New York NY 10021-5704

RAYMOND, EUGENE THOMAS, technical writer, consultant, retired aircraft engineer; b. Seattle, Apr. 17, 1923; s. Evan James and Katheryn Dorothy (Kranick) R.; m. Bette Mae Bergeson, mar. 1, 1948; children: Joan Raymond Hibbs, Patricia, Robin Raymond Flashman. BSME, U. Wash., 1944, postgrad., 1953-55. Registered profl. engr., Tex. Rsch. engr. The Boeing Co., Seattle, 1946-59, sr. group engr., 1959-63, 66-71, sr. specialist engr., 1971-81, prin. engr. flight control tech., 1982-88; project design engr. Gen. Dynamics, Fort Worth, 1963-66. Author: (book) Aircraft Flight Control Actuation System Design, 1993; aircraft editl. adv. bd. Hydraulics and Pneumatics mag., 1960-70; contbr. over 20 tech. papers and articles to profl. jours. Lt. USNR, 1943-46, 49-52. Recipient prize Hydraulics and Pneumatics mag. 1958. Mem. SAE Internat., Engring. Soc. for Advancing Vehicle Mobility on Land, Sea, Air and Space (cert. of appreciation, chmn. adv. bd. com. A-6 nat. com. for aerospace fluid power, actuation, and control tech. 1983-88, vice-chmn. com. 1986-88, cons.), Fluid Power Soc. (dir. N.W. region 1973-74), Puget Sound Fluid Power Assn., AIAA, Meridian Valley Country Club, Masons, Shriners, Beta Theta Pi. Lutheran. Achievements include 5 patents in Fluid Sealing Arrangements, Quasi-Open-Loop Hydraulic Ram Incremental Actuator with Power Conserving Properties, Rotary Digital Electrohydraulic Actuator, Two-Fluid Nonflammable Hydraulic System and Load-Adaptive Hydraulic Actuator System and Method for Actuating Control Surfaces; designed and developed mechanical systems for the XB-47 and B-52 jet bombers, 707 airliner and many other aircraft, including the X-20 Dyna-Soar manned dynamic soaring hypersonic space plane, the American SST, the rewinged Navy A-6 attack plane the B-2 Stealth Bomber and the Chinese XAC Y-7 commuter. Home: 13816 SE 251st St Kent WA 98042-6629 *Personal philosophy: I have always tried to act correctly, fairly, and truthfully and to set a good example for my children and my peers.*

RAYMOND, GEORGE EDWARD, JR., (CHIP RAYMOND), operations research analyst; b. Monterey, Calif., Dec. 26, 1947; s. George Edward and Madeleine (Gordon) R.; m. Elizabeth B. Dees, Aug. 26, 1968 (div. Dec. 1980); children: Madeleine, Anna Marie, Katie; m. Barbara Ann Sullivan, July 7, 1990. BS, N.C. State U., 1972; MBA, George Mason U./Oxford U., 1995; grad., Naval Postgrad. Sch., 1993. Served to maj. U.S. Army, Ft. Belvoir, Va., 1972-82; sr. cons. KPMG Peat Marwick, Washington, 1982-85; sr. product mgr. Magnavox, Ft. Wayne, Ind., 1985-87; dir. econ. analysis U.S. Army Info. Sys. Software Ctr., Ft. Belvoir, 1987—. Adj. prof. George Mason U., 1997—. Editor: Resource Management for Software Development, 1990. Mem. Army Acquisition Corps. Recipient meritorious svc. award U.S. Army, 1982. Mem. IEEE, Am. Soc. Mil. Comptrollers, Assn. Computing Machinery, Order Ky. Cols. Republican. Roman Catholic. Avocations: skiing, scuba diving, sailing. Home: 11471 Meath Dr Fairfax VA 22030-5449 Office: USAISSC Software Ctr 6000 6th St Fort Belvoir VA 22060-5506

RAYMOND, GEORGE MARC, city planner, educator; b. Odessa, Russia, Jan. 1, 1919; came to U.S., 1937, naturalized, 1942; s. Mark J. and Rachelle (Schneiderman) R.; m. Kathleen E. Waid, Oct. 3, 1942 (div. Mar. 1978); 1 dau., Valerie M.; m. Lois Jean Gainsboro, Mar. 26, 1979. BArch, Columbia, 1946. Planning dir. Harrison, Ballard & Allen, Inc., N.Y.C., 1952-54; founder, pres. Raymond, Parish, Pine & Weiner, Inc., 1954-83; pres. George M. Raymond Assocs., 1983—; prof. planning, chmn. dept. city and regional planning Pratt Inst., Bklyn., 1959-75; founder, dir. Pratt Ctr. for Community Improvement, Bklyn., 1963-70. Lectr. planning Columbia U., 1955-58; lectr. planning and urban renewal New Sch. Social Rsch., 1967-72; pres. Assn. Collegiate Sch. Planning, 1968-69; chmn. Westchester County Housing Implementation Commn., 1992-93. Editor: Pratt Planning Papers, 1963-73, (with Astrid Monson) Pratt Guide to Housing, Planning and Urban Renewal for New Yorkers, 1965. V.p. Citizens Housing and Planning Coun. N.Y.C., 1967-86, N.Y. Assn. Environ. Profls., 1977-79; pres. Westchester Citizens Housing Coun., 1964-66, Met. Com. on Planning, 1950-51; founder, pres. Friends of Music Concerts, 1954-57, Spoken Arts Soc., 1966-67; past 1st v.p. Federated Conservationists Westchester County; past dir. Nat. Housing Conf., Phipps Houses, Wave Hill, Settlement Housing Fund; chmn. Westchester County Housing Opportunity Commn., 1994—; land use adv. com. N.Y. State Legis. Commn. on Rural Resources, 1992-98. Fellow: Am. Inst. Cert. Planners; mem.: Am. Planning Assn. (pres. NY met. chpt. 1983—85), Am. Soc. Cons. Planners (pres. 1968—70). Home: 192 Locust Ln Irvington NY 10533-2315 Office: 101 Executive Blvd Elmsford NY 10523-1316

RAYMOND, JACK, journalist, public relations executive, foundation executive; b. Lodz, Poland, Oct. 6, 1918; s. Harry and Anna (Lange) R.; m. Gertrude Silverman, Oct. 6, 1946; children: David Alan, Judith. Student, CCNY, 1939. Sports writer N.Y. World-Telegram, 1934-38; ct. reporter, city editor, columnist N.Y. Daily North Side News, 1938-40; Corr. N.Y. Times, 1940-66, 1946-47, Frankfurt, 1947-49, Bonn, 1949-52, Balkans, Belgrade, 1952-56, Moscow, 1956, Pentagon corr. Washington, 1956-66; pub. rels. exec., pres. Thomas J. Deegan Co., Washington and N.Y.C., 1966-70; v.p. Bryan Publs., N.Y.C., 1970-74; founding pres. Internat. Inst. for Environ. Devel., 1970—73; pres. Dialog divsn. J. Walter Thompson Co., 1973-75; pres. Jack Raymond & Co., Inc., N.Y.C., 1975-87, chmn., 1987-92; pres. JR Cons. Svc., Inc., 1987-96; acting comm. dir. Commonwealth Fund, 1987. Book reviewer The Villager, N.Y.C., 1970-74; cons. UN Conf. on Human Environment, 1972, Aspen Inst. Humanistic Studies, HABITAT, UN Conf. Human Settlements; adv. com. Ctr. for Environ. Info. UN Assn. U.S., 1975-78; mem. Rumanian-U.S. econ. coun. U.S. C. of C., 1973-75; project dir. 1987 Workshop Internat. Environ. Bur. Internat. C. of C.; cons. INFORM, 1989, Rene Dubos Ctr. for Human Environments, 1989-2000; adv. bd. Volvo Journalists Retreat Duke U., 1992; internat. adv. bd. Ctr. for Social Policy in Mid-East, 1983-91; exec. bd. Ency. of Environment. Author: How to Serve and Get Ahead in the Armed Forces, 1963, reissued as Your Military Obligations and Opportunities, 1964, Power at Pentagon, 1964, Robert O. Anderson: Oil Man/Environmentalist, 1988; co-author: This is Germany, 1950; editor Upton Nooz, 1942-43; combat corr. Stars and Stripes, news editor Naples and Rome edits., mng. editor Marseilles edit.; combat corr., war editor, editor Stars and Stripes mag. Paris edit., combat corr., news editor Frankfurt edit., 1943-45; contbr. articles to profl. jours. Trustee N.Y. Urban League, 1969-72; bd. dirs. Internat. Inst. Environ. Affairs, N.Y.C., 1970-74, pres., 1970-73; bd. dirs. Internat. Inst. Environment and Devel., London, 1974-89, mem. adv. coun., 1978-82, mem. exec. com., 1982-89; bd. dirs. Epoch B. Found., La Jolla, Calif., acting pres., 1977-85; trustee Moroccan-Am. Found., 1982-88; bd. overseers Heller Grad. Sch., Brandeis U., 1981-88; founding assoc. John J. McCloy Internat. Ctr., N.Y.C., 1986, bd. dirs., 1987-99; mem. adv. bd. Ctr. for East-West Dynamics, 1992-95, Volvo JNLSTS Retreat, Williamsburg, Va., 1992; With U.S. Army, 1942-45. Decorated 5 Battle Stars, Bronze Star, Purple Heart. Mem. Coun. on Fgn. Rels. Clubs: Overseas Press Am. (N.Y.C.) (pres. 1972-76), Century Assn. (N.Y.C.), Nat. Press (Washington). Office: 340 E 57th St New York NY 10022

RAYMOND, KAY E. (KAY ENGELMANN RAYMOND), Spanish language educator, consultant; b. Cin., Feb. 1, 1939; d. Gerson Silas and Pauline Coleman (Early) Engelmann; m. Ralph Raymond II, Feb. 1, 1964 (div. Nov. 1977); 1 child, Jennifer Kay Raymond-Judy. AB magna cum laude, Radcliffe Coll., 1961; MA, Brown U., 1964; PhD, Ind. U., 1983. Lectr. Boston U., 1965-68; lectr. Assumption Coll., Worcester, 1965-67; instr. Regis Coll., Weston, 1967-71; assoc. instr. Ind. U., Bloomington, 1972-83; lectr. Emporia (Kans.) State U., 1983-84; asst. prof. U. Ala. at Huntsville, 1984-89, Sam Houston State U., Huntsville, Tex., 1989-94, assoc. prof., 1995—, coord. fgn. langs., 1995-98. Advisor Internat. Hispanic Assn., Sam Houston State U. 1990—. Sigma Delta Pi, 1990—; vol. translator City of Huntsville, 1993-98. Named Top Prof Sam Houston State U. Bapt. Student Ministry, 1996, Outstanding Advisor Internat. Hispanic Assn., 1996-97, Sammy award Sam Houston State U. Student Activities, 2003. Mem.: Tex. Fgn. Lang. Assn., Tex. Assn. Coll. and Univ. Lang. Suprs., Tex. Assn. Coll. Tchrs., Am. Coun. on the Tchg. of Fgn. Langs., Harvard Univ. Club Houston (schs. and scholarship com. 1997—), Sigma Delta Pi, Pi Delta Phi, Phi Sigma Iota. Home: 3644 Youpon Ln Huntsville TX 77340-8920 Office: Sam Houston State U Dept Fgn Langs PO Box 2147 Huntsville TX 77341-2147 Office Phone: 936-294-1444. E-mail: fol_ker@shsu.edu.

RAYMOND, KENNETH NORMAN, chemistry educator, research chemist; b. Astoria, Oreg., Jan. 7, 1942; s. George Norman and Helen May (Dunn) R.; m. Jane Galbraith Shell, June 19, 1965 (div. 1976); children: Mary Katherine, Alan Norman; m. Barbara Gabriele Sternitzke, June 17, 1977; children: Gabriella Petra, Christopher Norman. BA, Reed Coll., 1964; PhD, Northwestern U., 1968. Asst. prof. chemistry U. Calif.-Berkeley, 1967-74, assoc. prof., 1974-78, prof., 1978—; vice chmn. dept. U. Calif. Berkeley, 1982-84, 1999—2000, chmn., 1993-96; faculty sr. scientist Lawrence Berkeley Lab., 1996—; interim dir. Seaborg Ctr., 2002—. Mem. study sect. NIH, 1983; adv. com. NSF, 1985—87; co-chmn. bd. chem. scis. & tech. NRC, 2000—; co-founder Lumiphere, Inc., 2001. Editor: Bioinorganic Chemistry II, 1977; assoc. editor Biology of Metals, 1987-91; editl. bd. Inorganic Chemistry, 1976-86, Accounts Chem. Rsch., 1982-90, Inorganica Chemica Acta f-Block Elements, 1984-90, Jour. Coordination Chemistry, 1981—, Jour. Inorganic and Nuclear Chemistry, 1974-81, Jour. Am. Chem. Soc., 1983-95, Topics in Current Chemistry, 1981-97, Metals in Biology, 1993—, Jour. Supramolecular Chemistry, 1992—, Jour. Biol. Inorganic Chemistry, 1996—, Procs. NAS USA, 2002--; U.S. editl. advisor Springer-Verlag in Chemistry, 1972-91; contbr. articles to profl. jours.; author more than 400 papers, 11 patents in field.

Alfred P. Sloan rsch. fellow, 1971-73; Miller rsch. prof., 1977-78, 96; Guggenheim fellow, 1980-81; recipient E.O. Lawrence award Dept. Energy, 1984, Humboldt Rsch. award for U.S. Scientists, 1992, 2000, Alfred R. Bader award Am. Chem. Soc., 1994, Vollum award Reed Coll., 2002. Mem. NAS, Am. Acad. Arts and Scis., Am. Chem. Soc. (chair divsn. inorganic chemistry 1996), Am. Crystallographic Soc., Sigma Xi. Democrat. Office: U Calif Berkeley Dept Chemistry Berkeley CA 94720-1460 E-mail: raymond@socrates.berkeley.edu.

RAYMOND, LEE R. oil company executive; b. Watertown, S.D., Aug. 13, 1938; m. Charlene Raymond. BSChemE, U. Wis., 1960; PhD ChemE, U. Minn., 1963. Joined Exxon Corp., Tulsa, Okla., 1963; various positions Exxon Co. USA and Creole Petroleum Corp., Houston and Caracas, Venezuela, 1963—72; mgr. planning Exxon Internat. Co., N.Y.C., 1972—75; v.p. Lago Oil, Aruba, 1975—76, pres., dir., 1976—79; pres. Exxon Nuc. Co., Bellevue, Wash., 1979—81; exec. v.p. Exxon Enterprises Inc., N.Y.C., 1981—83; pres., dir. Esso Inter-Am. Inc., Coral Gables, Fla., 1983—84; sr. v.p., dir. Exxon Corp., N.Y.C., 1984—86, pres., dir., 1987—93, chmn., CEO, 1993—99, pres., 1996—99; chmn., CEO Exxon Mobil Corp., Irving, Tex., 1999—. Bd. dirs. J.P. Morgan and Co., Inc., N.Y.C., Morgan Guaranty Trust Co. of N.Y., N.Y.C.; bd. dirs., mem. exec. and policy coms. Am. Petroleum Inst. Dallas Citizens Coun.; bd. dirs. United Negro Coll. Fund, 1991—; mem. adv. bd. Project Shelter Pro-Am; trustee Wis. Alumni Rsch. Found., 1987—; bd. dirs., hon. trustee bus. coun. Internat. Understanding, Inc.; mem. U. Wis. Found.; mem. innovations in medicine leadership coun. Southwestern Med. Ctr.; ptnr. emeritus N.Y.C. Partnership; mem. Am. Coun. on Germany, Dallas Com. Fgn. Rels.; vice chmn., bd. trustees Am. Enterprise Inst., Washington. Mem.: Trilateral Commn., Occupl. Physicians Scholarship Fund (chmn. fundraising campaign 1995), Am. Soc. Engring. Edn. (nat. adv. coun.), Singapore-U.S. Bus. Coun., Coun. Fgn. Rels., Nat. Petroleum Coun. (mem. nom. and natural gas coms.), Bus. Roundtable, Bus. Coun., NAE.*

RAYMOND, LISA, professional tennis player; b. Norristown, Pa., Aug. 10, 1973; d. Ted and Nancy Raymond. Student, U. Fla. Profl. tennis player WTA Tour, 1993—. Mem. U.S. Fed Cup Team, 1997—98, 2000, 2002—03. Recipient 1 Career singles title, 42 Career Doubles Titles, WTA Tour; winner U.S. Open, 1996, 2002, Wimbledon, 1999, Australian Open Grand Slam doubles, 2000, Wimbledon, 2001, U.S. Open Grand Slam doubles, 2001, WTA Doubles Championship, 2001, Mixed Doubles Roland Garros, 2003; named NCAA Singles Champion, 1992, 93. Avocations: shopping, hanging out with friends, watching television, football, volleyball. Office: US Tennis Assn 70 W Red Oak Ln White Plains NY 10604-3602

RAYMOND, PAWLICKI, pharmaceutical executive; Mgr. info. tech. dept. PepsoCo Internat., Citibank, Hewlett Packard; v.p. info. tech. Cytec Industries; v.p. info. tech. & CIO Novartis Pharm. Mem. Novartis Pharm. Corp. Exec. Com. Office: Novartis Pharm One Health Plaza East Hanover NJ 07936-1000

RAYMOND, URAL WAYNE, retired retail executive; b. Missoula, Mont., May 20, 1944; s. Ural Daniel and Fayetta Arilla Raymond. Student, U. N.C., 1969-70, U. Mont., 1962-66, 93-94. Enlisted man U.S. Army, 1966-69, 70-89; advanced through grades to master sgt. U.S. Army, 1985; ret., 1989; advt. mgr. Sears & Roebuck, Missoula, 1993-99; ret., 1999. Chmn. western dist. Am. Legion Baseball, Missoula, 1997—; pres. Friends of the Libr., Missoula, 1997-99. With U.S. Army, 1966-69. Decorated Bronze Star. Mem. Nev. Internat. Lic. Plate Soc. (treas. state br. 1998—). Democrat. Evangelical. Avocations: collecting license plates, collecting flags, baseball, collecting stamps, collecting coins.

RAYMOND, USHER (USHER), vocalist, actor; b. Chattanooga, Tenn., Oct. 14, 1978; s. Jonnetta Patton and Usher Raymond. Singer: (albums) Usher, 1994, My Way, 1997 (Soul Train award Best R&B/Soul Single for "You Make Me Wanna", 1998), Live, 1999, All About U, 2000, 8701, 2001 (Grammy award Best Male R&B Vocal Performance, 2001, 2002, Platinum 7 times), Confessions, 2004 (MTV Video Music award Best Dance Video for song "Yeah!", 2004, MTV Video Music award Best Male Video for the song "Yeah!", 2004); actor: (films) The Faculty, 1998, She's All That, 1999, Light It Up, 1999, Texas Rangers, 2001; (TV films) Gepetto, 2000; (TV series) Moesha, 1997—98, The Bold and the Beautiful, 1998, (TV guest appearances) The Famous Jett Jackson, 2000, Sabrina the Teenage Witch, 2002, The Twilight Zone, 2002, American Dreams, 2002, 7th Heaven, 2002, Soul Food, 2003. Named Artist of the Year, Billboard Music Awards, 1998; recipient Pop Music award, ASCAP, 2003. Achievements include First place on the Star Search TV talent series, 1992. Mailing: c/o JPat Mgmt 3996 Pleasantdale Rd # 104A Atlanta GA 30340*

RAYMOND, WILFRED J. priest, educator; b. Old Town, Maine, Mar. 5, 1944; s. Joseph Raymond and Lydia Belanger. BA in Phil., Stonehill Coll., 1967; MTh, U. Notre Dame, 1971. Ordained priest Roman Cath. Ch., 1971. Tchr. St. Joseph's, South Bend, Ind., 1970-71, Notre-Dame H.S., Bridgeport, Conn., 1972-74; recruiter Congregation of Holy Cross, Bridgeport, Conn., 1974-79; campus minister Stonehill Coll., Easton, Mass., 1979-92, adminstr., 1985-90, asst. dean, 1985-90; asst. provincial Congregation of Holy Cross, Bridgeport, Conn., 1994-98; pastor St. Francis de Sales, Bennington, Vt., 1993-94; provincial supr. Congregation of Holy Cross, Bridgeport, Conn., 1998—; nat. dir. Family Theater Prodns., Hollywood, 2000—. Contbr. articles to profl. jours.; guest spkr. Bd. dirs. King's Coll., Wilkes Barre, Pa., 1998—, Stonehill Coll., Easton, Mass., 1998—; chmn. bd. dirs. Holy Cross Family Ministries. Democrat. Home and Office: 7201 W Sunset Blvd Los Angeles CA 90046-3405 E-mail: wraymond@familytheater.org.

RAYMUND, STEVEN A. computer company executive; b. 1955; BS, U. Oreg., 1978; MA Internat. Polit., Georgetown U. Sch. Fgn. Svc., 1980. With Tech Data Corp., 1981—, COO, 1984—86, CEO, 1986—, Chmn., 1991—. Bd. Dir. Jabil Circuit. Office: Tech Data Corp 5350 Tech Data Dr Clearwater FL 33760-3122*

RAYNAULD, ANDRE, economist, educator; b. Quebec, Que., Can., Oct. 20, 1927; s. Léopold and Blanche (Gauthier) R.; m. Michelle Nolin, Oct. 15, 1951; children: Francoy, Olivier, Dominique, Isabelle. BA cum laude, U. Montreal, 1948, MA in Indsl. Rels. magna cum laude, 1951; D. in Econs., U. Paris, 1954; D. in Econs. (hon.), U. Ottawa, 1976, U. Sherbrooke, 1976. Mem. faculty U. Montreal, 1954-71, founder, dir. Ctr. Econ. Research and Devel., 1970-72; vis. prof. U. Toronto, 1962-63; chmn. Economic Council Can., Ottawa, 1971-76; mem. Que. Nat. Assembly, Montreal, 1976-80; prof. U. Montreal, 1980-93, prof. emeritus, 1993—. Exec. com. Can. Social Sci. Rsch. Coun., 1961-63, 64-65; pres. Inst. Canadien Affaires Publiques, 1961-62; bd. govs. Can. Labour Coll., 1962-66; dir., exec. com. CBC, 1964-67; trustee CBC Pension Fund, 1967-70; pres. Soc. Canadienne de Sci. Economique, 1967-69; mem. Royal Commn. Bilingualism and Biculturalism, 1969-70, Can. Coun. Urban and Regional Rsch., 1971, Quebec Coun. Planning and Devel., 1971; chmn. com. inquiry French-lang. tchr.-tng. Western provinces Dept. Sec. State, 1971; mem. interfutures study group OECD, Paris, 1976-78; mem. bd. Inst. Rsch. Pub. Policy, 1980—; rsch. fellow Devel. Ctr. OECD, Paris, 1986—; invited prof. College de France, Paris, 1987. Author: Economic Growth in Quebec, 1961, The Canadian Economic System, 1967, La propriete des entreprises au Quebec, 1974, Institutions Economiques Canadiennes, 2d edition, 1977, Le financement des exportations, 1979, Government Assistance to Export Financing, 1984, The External Financing of Tunisia's Imports, OECD, 1988, Financing Exports to Developing Countries, OECD, 1992; co-editor: Economic Integration in Europe and North America, 1992, Labour Standards and International Competitiveness, 1998; co-author: L'Etat Providence des Entreprises, 1999; editor Can. Jour. Econs., 1965-70. Recipient ann. award des Diplomes de l'U. de Montreal, 1974; apptd. Officer of Order of Can., 1986; fellow Walter Levy Coun. on Fgn. Rels., Boston, 1977. Fellow Royal Soc. Can.; mem. Can. Econs. Assn. (pres. 1983-84), Am. Econs. Assn., Atlantic Econ. Soc. (disting. assoc.). Liberal. Roman Catholic. Home: 4820 Roslyn St Montreal QC Canada H3W 2L2

RAYNER, ARNO ALFRED, investment company executive, consultant; b. San Francisco, Sept. 23, 1928; BS in Econs., U. Calif., Berkeley, 1949, MBA, 1954. Security analyst Bank of Calif., San Francisco, 1950-54; various positions to sr. v.p. Indsl. Indemnity, San Francisco, 1954-74; v.p. internat. svcs. Bechtel Group, San Francisco, 1975-76; pres. Rayner Assocs., Inc., Mill Valley, Calif., 1977-99, chmn. bd., 1999—. Recipient Investment prof. of the yr., San Francsico Bond Club, 1999, Disting. Citizen of the Yr., Marin Coun. Boy Scouts of Am., 2000. Home: 7 Venado Dr Belvedere Tiburon CA 94920-1625 E-mail: arnorayner@aol.com.

RAYNER, ROBERT MARTIN, financial executive; b. London, Sept. 21, 1946; s. Henry John and Kathleen Mary (Edwards) R.; m. Mindy S. Miller, May 28, 1979. BSc with honors in Eng., Bristol (Eng.) U., 1968; MBA, London Bus. Sch., 1976. Sr. engr. Halcrow and Ptnrs., London, 1968-74; fin. dir. Pepsico Inc., Purchase, N.Y., 1976-88; pres. constrn. materials group, sr. v.p., CFO ESSROC Corp., Nazareth, Pa., 1988-94, pres., COO, 1994—. Bd. dirs. Essroc Cement Corp., Nazareth, San Juan Cement Co., P.R., Ciment Quebec Inc., St. Basile. Mem. Inst. Civil Engrs. Avocations: running, golf, theater, music. Office: Essroc Italcementi Group 3251 Bath Pike Nazareth PA 18064-8999

RAYNER, VICTORIA LEIGH, medical educator, estheticist, consultant; b. Sacramento, Mar. 6, 1954; d. Harold Edward Rayner and Angela Jane Allitore; m. Vallucci, July 20, 1997. Degree in bus. studies, Highline CC, Seattle, 1976; BA, Coll. of Marin, 1974. Lic. post-secondary instr. Calif., 1995, continuing edn. instr. Calif. Bd. of Registered Nursing, 1996. Founder and pres. Bay Area Skin Assn., San Francisco, 1981; founder and dir. Ctr. Appearance and Esteem, 1987; founder Camouflage Therapy Clinic Dermatology Dept. San Francisco Gen. Hosp., 1987, clin. assoc. Camouflage Therapy Clinic, 1986—; clin assoc. Alta Bates, Berkeley; founder Rayner Inst. Career Advancement, Washington. Contbg. mem. and presenter U. Calif. Arts and Lectrs., San Francisco, 1988—; adv. bd. Dermascope, Sunnyvale, Tex., 1990—, Les Nouvelle Esthetique, Coral Gables, Fla., 1990—; adv. com. rsch. divsn. Almay Cosmetics, Oxford, NC, 1992—93; cons. and rep. Nat. Assn. Women in Bus., mem. public rels. com., 1993—95; founder Women's Forum for Discussion Group, San Francisco, 1996; lectr. on medical esthetics; presenter to physicians, hospital and clinics. Author: Clin. Cosmetology; A Med. Approach to Aesthetic Procedures, 1993, A Survival Guide for Today's Career Woman, 1994; contbr. chapters to books. Leader medical esthetics trng. and care Task Force Legis. Reform of Patients' Rights, Sacramento, 1993—95; bd. dir. Alissa Ann Ruch Burn Found., San Francisco, 1991—93. Recipient For Those Who Care Vol. award, KRON-TV, 1989, award of Merit, Commn. on Status of Women of City and County of San Francisco, 1993, Contribn. to Cosmetology, Internat. Congress of Esthetics, 2003. Mem.: NAFE, Nat. Cosmetology Esthetic Assn., Am. Soc. of Plastic Surgery Skin Care Specialists, Dermatology Nursing Assn. Independent. Roman Catholic. Achievements include development of long distance learning programs in esthetic procedures; women over forty, reentry career devel. programs; four outpatient cosmetic rehabilitation clinics for women and children. Avocations: interior design, cooking, reading, painting. Office: Rayner Inst for Career Advancement #300 1201 Penn Ave NW Washington DC 20004 Fax: 202-667-6297. E-mail: victoriarayner@hotmail.com.

RAYNER, WILLIAM ALEXANDER, retired newspaper editor, author; b. Winnipeg, Man., Can., Nov. 7, 1929; s. William and Annie Mitchell (McDonald) R.; divorced; 1 child, Robert William. Student Can. schs. Sports editor Trail Times, B.C., 1954-55; sportswriter Victoria (B.C.) Times, 1955-57, Vancouver (B.C.) Herald, 1957; copy editor, reporter Montreal (Que.) Star, 1957-58; asst. sports editor Vancouver Sun, 1958-62, copy editor, then slotman, 1962-74, news editor, 1974-83, systems mgr., 1983-88, ret., 1988; copy editor Toronto Globe & Mail, 1962. Author: Vancouver Sun Style Guide, 1976, Images of History - Twentieth Century British Columbia Through the Front Pages, 1997, British Columbia's Premiers in Profile-The Good, The Bad and the Transient, 2000, Scandal! 130 Years of Damnable Deeds in Canada's Lotus Land, 2001. Dir. B.C. Newspaper Found. Mem. Writers Union Can. E-mail: v3n4w5@aol.com.

RAYNOLDS, DAVID ROBERT, buffalo breeder, writer; b. N.Y., Feb. 15, 1928; s. Robert Frederick and Marguerite Evelyn (Gerdau) R.; m. May (Kean) Raynolds, May 12, 1951; children: Robert, Linda, Martha, Laura, David A.F. AB, Dartmouth Coll., 1949; MA, Wesleyan U., Middletown, Conn., 1955; predoctoral, Johns Hopkins Sch. Advanced Internat. Studies, Washington, 1956; grad., Nat. War Coll., Washington, 1973. Account exec. R.H. Morris Assoc., Newtown, Conn., 1949-50; fgn. svc. officer Dept. of State, Washington, 1956-76; pres. Ranch Rangers, Inc., Lander, Wyo., 1976—. Pres. Nat. Buffalo Assn., Ft. Pierre, S.D., 1987-88. Author: Rapid Development in Small Economies (Praeger); contbr. articles to profl. jours. Trustee, bd. dirs. Liberty Hall Found.; mem. steering com. Wyo. Bus. Alliance; mem. planning bd. Mus. of the Am. West. With U.S. Army, 1950—53. Recipient Meritorious Svc. Award, Dept. of State, Washington, 1966. Mem. The Explorers Club, Fremont County Farm Bur., Fgn. Svc. Assn., Am. Legion, Rotary, Elks. Republican. Episcopalian. Avocation: travel. Office: Table Mountain Group PO Box 1310 Lander WY 82520-1310

RAYNOLDS, HAROLD, JR., retired state education commissioner; b. Chgo., Feb. 7, 1925; s. Harold and Dorothy (Smith) R.; m. Ann Richards Ellis, June 1950 (div. 1968); children— Christopher, Timothy, Madeline, Dorothy, m. Patricia Adele Miller, Jan. 20, 1973 (dec. 1996). BS, Cornell U., 1948, MA, 1953; postgrad., NYU, 1968-69. Cert. supt. schs., N.Y., Maine, Alaska. Supt. schs. Cape Elizabeth Sch. Dist., Maine, 1969-74; supt. schs. Portland Sch. Dist., Maine, 1974-79; commr. edn. State of Maine, Augusta, 1979-83, State of Alaska, Juneau, 1983-86, Commonwealth of Mass., 1986-91; interim supt. Windsor Ctrl. Supervisory Union Sch. Dist., Woodstock, Vt., 1991-92; supt. Springfield (Vt.) Sch. Dist., 1994-97, Addison Ctrl. Supervisory Union, Middlebury, Vt., 2003—04. Contbr. articles to ednl. jours. Mem. sch. com., Pomfret, Vt., 1993—; mem. Vt. Senate, 1965-66; chmn. Vt. Bd. Edn., Montpelier, 1963-68; trustee U. Maine, Orono, 1979-83; Dem. candidate for U.S. Congress, Vt., 1962. Staff sgt. U.S. Army, 1943-45, ETO. Mem. Am. Assn. Sch. Adminstrs., Chief State Sch. Officers, Hemlock Soc. of Vt. (pres. 2002—), Phi Delta Kappa. Unitarian-Universalist. Avocations: reading; gardening; cross-country skiing; theater; music.

RAYNOLDS, WILLIAM F., II, lawyer; b. San Antonio, Feb. 7, 1948; s. William F. and Doris Raynolds; m. Kathryn Raynolds, July 11, 1987; children: Lisa Chipman, Mike Chipman, Casey Raynolds. BS, U. Tulsa, 1973, JD, 1976. Atty. Hood & Raynolds, Tulsa, 1987—. Adj. prof. legal assistant program U. Tulsa, 1993—, adj. prof. coll. law, 1995—. Editor Okla. Family Law Jour., 1995. Fellow Am. Acad. Matrimonial Lawyers; mem. ABA (family law sect.), Tulsa County Bar Assn. (family law sect., pres. 1993-97), Okla. Bar Assn. (family law sect.). Roman Catholic. Office: Hood & Raynolds 1914 S Boston Ave Tulsa OK 74119-5222 E-mail: hood_raynalds@compuserve.com.

RAYNOR, BRUCE S. labor union administrator; m. Joan Raynor; children: Alvin Carter, Kudjo Sogadzi, Candice, Robin Sydney. Grad., Cornell U., 1972. Edn. dir. edn. dept. Textile Workers Union Am., 1973, edn. dir., 1974; so. regional dir., internat. v.p. Amalgamated Clothing and Textile Workers Union, 1981, exec. v.p., 1993, Union Needletrades, Indusl., and Textile Employees, 1995, sec.-treas., 1998, pres., 2001—. Mem. bd. trustees N.Y. State Statutory Affairs Com. Cornell U., 1989; v.p. AFL-CIO, mem. exec. bd. Mem.: Cornell Sch Indusl. and Labor Rels. (mem adv. com.). Office: 275 7th Ave FL 11 New York NY 10001-6708

RAYNOR, EILEEN MARGOLIES, otolaryngologist, educator; b. N.Y.C., Feb. 11, 1965; d. Allan Fred and Noemi (Schmerz) Margolies; m. Dewey Lee Raynor, Jr., Nov. 9, 1991; children: Stephanie Dianne, Logan Foster. AB in Chemistry, Duke U., 1987; MD, U. N.C., 1993. Cert. Am. Bd. Otolaryngology. Resident otolaryngology Med. Coll. Ga., Augusta, 1993—98; asst. prof. otolaryngology U. Fla., Jacksonville, 1998—. Cons. Medimetrics Corp., Jacksonville, Fla., 1999—; med. dir. Pediat. Hearing Program, Jacksonville, 2000—; mem. Cleft Palate Team Childrens Med. Svcs., Jacksonville, 2000—. Contbr. articles to profl. jours., chapters to books. Recipient Nat. Leadership award, 2003; Deafness Rsch. Found. rsch. grantee, 1991. Fellow: Am. Acad. Otolaryngology (cmty., acad. rels. com. 2002—); mem.: AMA, Assn. for Rsch. in Otolaryngology, Triological Soc. (James Harrell award So. sect. 1997), Am. Acad. Facial Plastic Surgery, Duke Alumni Club (bd. dirs. 2000—). Avocations: cooking, skiing, photography, jewelry design. Home: 1031 River Oaks Rd Jacksonville FL 32207 Office: U Fla Jacksonville 655 W 8th St Jacksonville FL 32209 E-mail: eileen.raynor@jax.ufl.edu.

RAYNOR, RICHARD BENJAMIN, neurosurgeon, educator; b. N.Y.C., Aug. 16, 1928; s. Murray and Mildred (Pitt) R.; m. Barbara Golob; children: Geoffrey, Michele. BSME, U. Mich., 1950; MD, U. Vt., 1955. Diplomate Am. Bd. Neurol. Surgery. Intern Mt. Sinai, N.Y.C., 1955-56; residency Neurol. Inst. Presbyn. Hosp., N.Y.C., 1956-57, Nat. Hosp., London, 1957; residency neurosurgery Neurol. Inst. Presbyn. Hosp., 1958-62; assoc. in neurosurgery Coll. Physicians and Surgeons Columbia U., N.Y.C., 1965-77; clin. assoc. prof. NYU, N.Y.C., 1977-2000, clin. prof., 1984—. Pvt. practice neurosurgery, N.Y.C., 1965—. Cons. editor Spine; contbr. over 50 articles to profl. jours., chpts. to books. Served as capt. U.S. Army, 1962-64. Fellow Am. Coll. Surgeons; mem. Cervical Spine Research Soc. (pres. 1986-87), Am. Assn. Neurol. Surgeons, Congress Neurol. Surgeons. Clubs: University (N.Y.C.). Avocations: skiing, squash. Office: 112 E 74th St New York NY 10021-3535 Office Phone: 212-535-1255.

RAYSON, EDWIN HOPE, lawyer; b. Earlville, Ill., Jan. 13, 1923; s. Edwin H. and Lillian (Astley) R.; m. Evelyn Sherry Kirkland, Oct. 1, 1983; children: Jane Rayson Young, Edwin Hope III, G. Scott. AB, U. Tenn., 1944, LL.B., 1948. Bar: Tenn. 1948. Pvt. practice, Knoxville, 1948—; ptnr. Kramer, Rayson, Leake, Rodgers & Morgan, 1949—. Lectr. labor law U. Tenn. Coll. Law, 1951-71 Served to lt. (j.g.) USNR, 1944-46. Mem. Order of Coif, Sigma Chi, Omicron Delta Kappa. Home: 501 River Rd Loudon TN 37774-5583 Office: 25th Fl 1st Tennesse Plaza Knoxville TN 37901 Office Phone: 865-525-5134.

RAYSON, GLENDON ENNES, internist, preventive medicine specialist, writer; b. Oak Park, Ill., Dec. 2, 1915; s. Ennes Charles and Beatrice Margaret (Rowland) R. AB, U. Rochester, 1939; MD, U. Ill., Chgo., 1948; MPH, Johns Hopkins U., 1965; MA, Northwestern U., 1965. Diplomate Am. Bd. Internal Medicine, Am. Bd. Preventive Medicine, Am. Bd. Forensic Medicine, Am. Bd. Forensic Examiners. Resident in internal medicine Presbyn.-St. Luke's Hosp., Chgo., 1953-56; physician-in-charge Contagious Disease Hosp., Chgo., 1956-58, asst. med. supt., 1958-64; rsch. assoc. Sch. Hygiene and Pub. Health Johns Hopkins U., Balt., 1966-71; internist Johns Hopkins Hosp., 1971-82, Columbia Free State Health Plan, Balt., 1984-91; pvt. practice Balt., 1984—; with Neurodiagnostics Assocs., 1990—2001. Attending internist emergency rm. South Balt. Gen. Hosp., 1982-84; asst. prof. health sci. U. Ill., Chgo., 1958-64; fellow in gastroenterology and endocrinology Presbyn.-St. Luke's Hosp., 1956-58. Contbr. articles to med. jours., chpt. to book. Vol. physician, Vietnam, 1968, 71, 72, 73; mem. Citizens Amb. Program Delegation to Vietnam, 1993. Capt. M.C., USAF, 1951-53. Fellow: Am. Geriatrics Soc., Am. Col. Preventive Medicine; mem.: APHA, ACP-ASIM, AMA. Avocations: poetry, short stories, composing songs. Home: 337 Poplar Point Rd Perryville MD 21903-1803 Office: 218 N Charles St Apt 1407 Baltimore MD 21201-4024

RAYWARD, WARDEN BOYD, librarian, educator; b. Inverell, NSW, Australia, June 24, 1939; s. Warden and Ellie Rayward. BA, U. Sydney, 1960; diploma in libr., U. NSW, 1964; MS in L.S, U. Ill., 1965; PhD, U. Chgo., 1973. Asst. state library, NSW, 1961-64; research librarian planning and devel., 1970; lectr. Sch. Librarianship U. NSW, Sydney, 1971-72, head sch. Info., Libr. and Archive Studies, 1986-92, prof., 1986-00, dean Faculty Profl. Studies, 1993-96, prof. emeritus, 2000—; asst. prof. U. Western Ont., 1973-74, Grad. Library Sch. U. Chgo., 1975-77, assoc. prof., 1978-80, prof., 1980-86; dean U. Chgo. Grad. Library Sch., 1980-86; rsch. prof. U. Ill., Champaign, 2000—. Cons. NEH, 1976-79, U.S. Dept. Edn., 1981; bd. govs. Charles Stuart U., 1994-96; bd. dirs. Internat. House-U. NSW, 1992-97; George A. Miller vis. prof. U. Ill., 1997-98; Leverhulme Trust vis. prof. Leed Met. U., 2002; vis. prof. Leeds Met. U., 2004—. Author: The Universe of Information: The Work of Paul Otlet for Documentation and International Organization, 1975 (also transl. Russian and Spanish), Hasta la documentacion electronica, 2002; editor: The Variety of Librarianship: Essays in Honour of John Wallace Metcalfe, 1976, The Public Library: Circumstances and Prospects, 1978, Library Quar., 1975-79, Library History in Context, 1988, Libraries and Life in a Changing World: the Metcalfe Years 1920-1970, 1993; editor, translator: International Organization and the Dissemination of Knowledge: Selected Papers of Paul Otlet, 1990; editor Confronting the Future, University Libraries in the Next Decade, 1992, Developing a Profession in Librarianship in Australia: Travel Diaries and Other Papers of John Wallace Metcalfe, 1996, Aware and Responsible: Papers of The Nordic-International Colloquium (Scarlid), 2004; mem. editl. bd. World Book of Encyclopedia, 1990-97; contbr. articles to profl. jours. Coun. on Library Resources fellow, 1978, vis. fellow U. Coll. London, 1986, 90, Mortenson fellow U. Ill., 1992-93, Garfield fellow in hist. sci. lit., 2000. Mem.: ALA, Union Interant. Assns., Am. Soc. Info. Sci., Australian Libr. and Info. Assn. (hon.). Office: U Ill Grad Sch Libr and Info Scis 501 E Daniel St Champaign IL 61820-6211 E-mail: wrayward@alexia.lis.uiuc.edu.

RAZ, HILDA, editor-in-chief, educator, English educator; b. Rochester, N.Y., May 4, 1938; d. Franklyn Emmanuel and Dolly (Horwich) R.; m. Frederick M. Link, June 9, 1957 (div. 1969); children: John Franklin Link, Aaron Link; m. Dale Nordyke, Oct. 4, 1980. BA, Boston U., 1960. Asst. dir. Planned Parenthood League of Mass., Boston, 1960-62; edit. asst. Prairie Schooner, Lincoln, Nebr., 1970-74, contbg. editor, 1974-77, assoc. editor, 1977-87, acting editor, 1981-83, 85, poetry editor, 1980-87, editor-in-chief, 1987—; prof. dept English U. Nebr., Lincoln, 1990—, Luschei editor-in-chief. Lectr., reader, panelist in field; participant many workshops, symposia, confs.; panelist creativity arts com. NEA, 2000; judge Kenyon Rev., 1990, Ill. Art Coun./NEA fellowships, 1987; bd. govs. Ctr. for Great Plains Studies, U. Nebr., 1989-95. Author: The Bone Dish, What Is Good, Divine Honors, 1998, Trans, 2001; editor: Best of Prairie Schooner: Fiction and Poetry, 2001, Best of Prairie Schooner: Essays, 2000, Living on the Margins, 1999, other books; editor Nebr. Humanist, 1990. Pres. Assoc. Writing Programs, bd. dirs., 1988-89, ex-officio pres., 1989-90, v.p., 1987-88; bd. dirs. Nebr. Libr. Heritage Assn., 1988-91; mem. Mayor's Blue Ribbon Com. on Arts, 1985-88; bd. dirs. Planned Parenthood League Nebr., 1978-83, sec. bd. dirs., 1979-80, chairperson long-term planning com., 1980-81, 81-82. Recipient Literary Heritage award, Mayor's Art award, Lincoln, 1988, 2002; Bread Loaf scholar editors, 1974, poetry, 1985; Robert Frost fellow, 1988, 89, Mag. Panel fellow, 1993, 94. Avocation: gardening. Home: 960 S Cotner Blvd Lincoln NE 68510-4926 Office: Univ of Nebraska Lincoln Prairie Schooner 201 Andrews Hall Lincoln NE 68588-0334 E-mail: HRaz1@unl.edu.

RAZA, ASIM, psychiatrist; b. Rawalpindi, Pakistan, Apr. 27, 1958; s. Kamal and Sughra Raza. FSc, Sir Syed Sch. and Coll., Rawalpindi, 1975; BSc, B Medicine and Surgery, Rawalpindi Med. Coll., 1983. Diplomate Am. Bd. Psychiatry and Neurology. Intern dept. medicine Rawalpindi Gen. Hosp., 1983; med. officer dept. medicine Cantonment Gen. Hosp., Rawalpindi, 1984—91, med. officer outpatient dept., 1991—92; resident dept. psychiatry U. Mo. Sch. Medicine, Kansas City, 1993—97, chief resident dept. psychiatry, 1996—97; attending psychiatrist North Ark. Human Svcs., Kensett (Ark.) Family Med. Ctr., 1998—; cons. in field. Treas. Residents Assn. Western Mo., Kansas City, 1994—95, v.p., 1995—96, pres., 1996—97. Recipient Psychiatry Resident of Yr. award, Pfizer, 1997; fellow, Eli Lilly, 1994. Mem.: Ark. Psychiat. Soc., Am. Psychiat. Assn. (Wyeth Ayerst Resident Reporter 1996, mem.-in-tng. rep. Western Mo. br. 1996—97).

RAZAVI, HOSSEIN, bank executive; b. Esfahan, Iran, Feb. 12, 1947; arrived in U.S., 1971; s. Mostafa and Sarvvar (Amiri) R.; m. Nahid Najafi; 1 child, Pouneh. BS, MS, Tehran Polytech., Iran, 1970; PhD, U. Md., 1974. Economic Planning Orgn., Tehran, Iran, 1975-78, dir., 1978-81; supr. Ernst & Whiney, Washington, 1981-84; energy economist World Bank, Washington, 1984-93,

chief oil & gas divsn., 1993-97, dir. energy dept., 1997—2001, dir. infrastructure and energy djept., 2001—. Author: Fundamental of Petroleum Trading, 1991, Financing Energy Projects, 1996. Lt. Iran Air Force, 1970-71. Mem. Internat. Assn. Energy Economist (v.p. 1997—), Harvard Bus. Sch. Club. Avocations: tennis, wind-surfing, ballroom dancing, writing. Office: World Bank 1818 H St NW Washington DC 20433-0001 Office Phone: 202-458-5300. E-mail: hrazavi@worldbank.org.

RAZEK, EDWARD G. retail executive; Exec. v.p., creative dir. Shelly Berman Communicators; v.p. mktg. Ltd. Stores, 1983—87, exec. v.p., 1987—92; v.p., dir. mktg. Ltd., Inc., Columbus, Ohio, 1993—97, pres. creative svcs., 1997—. Office: Ltd Brands Three Ltd Pkwy Columbus OH 43230

RAZOUK, RASHAD ELIAS, retired chemistry educator; b. Dumiat, Egypt, Aug. 22, 1911; arrived in U.S., 1968; s. Elias A. and Martha A. (Israfil) R.; m. Emily S. Habib, Aug. 24, 1946 (dec. Dec. 1988); children: Reda R., Rami R.; m. Henrietta Doche, July 8, 1990. BSc with honors, Cairo U., 1933, MSc, 1936, PhD, 1939. Asst. prof. Cairo U., 1939-46, assoc. prof., 1946-50; prof. chemistry, chmn. dept. Ain Shams U., Cairo, 1950-66; prof. Am. U. Cairo, 1966-68, Calif. State U., L.A., 1968-78, emeritus prof., 1978—; vice dean Faculty Sci. Ain Shams U., Cairo, 1954-60. Acting dir. divsn. surface and coll. chem. Nat. Rsch. Ctr., Cairo, 1954-68; vis. rsch. prof. U. So. Calif., 1965; cons. Lockheed Aircraft Co., L.A., 1971-73. Contbr. articles on adsorption, active solids, wetting and wettability, solid reactions, surface tension, and contact angles to profl. jours. Fellow Am. Inst. Chemists (emeritus); mem. Am. Chem. Soc. (emeritus), Royal Soc. Chemistry (life). Democrat. Roman Catholic. Home: 2721 W Willow St #G14 Burbank CA 91505

RAZZANO, FRANK CHARLES, lawyer; b. Bklyn., Feb. 25, 1948; s. Pasquale Anthony and Agnes Mary (Borgia) R.; m. Stephanie Anne Lucas, Jan. 10, 1970; children: Joseph, Francis, Catherine. BA, St. Louis U., 1969; JD, Georgetown U., 1972. Bar: N.Y. 1973, U.S. Dist. Ct. (so. dist.) N.Y. 1973, U.S. Dist. Ct. (es. dist.) N.Y. 1973, N.J. 1976, D.C. 1981, Va. 1984, U.S. Dist. Ct. N.J. 1976, U.S. Dist. Ct. Md. 1977, U.S. Dist. Ct. (no. dist.) Calif. 1981, U.S. Dist. Ct. D.C. 1982, U.S. Dist. Ct. (ea. dist.) Va. 1989, U.S. Dist. Ct. (we. dist.) Va. 1990, U.S. Ct. Appeals (2d cir.) 1973, U.S. Ct. Appeals (3d cir.) 1975, U.S. Ct. Appeals (D.C. and 5th cirs.) 1983, U.S. Ct. Appeals (4th cir.) 1984, U.S. Ct. Appeals (6th cir.) 1990, U.S. Ct. Appeals (8th and 9th cirs.) 2000, U.S. Supreme Ct. 1976. Assoc. Shea & Gould, N.Y.C., 1972-75; asst. U.S. atty. Dist. of N.J., Newark, 1975-78; asst. chief trial atty. SEC, Washington, 1978-82; ptnr. Shea & Gould, Washington, 1982-94, mng. ptnr., 1991-92; ptnr. Camhy Karlinsky Stein Razzano & Rubin, Washington, 1994-96, Dickstein, Shapiro, Morin & Oshinsky, Washington, 1996—. Lectr. in field; adv. bd. Securities Litigation Reform Act Reporter, Securities Regulation Law Jour.; adj. prof. law U. Md. Sch. Law. Civil law editor Rico Law Reporter, mem. adv. bd. Corp. Confidentiality and Disclosure Letter; hon. adv. com. Jour. Internat. Law and Practice, Detroit Coll. Law; contbr. articles to legal jours. Scoutmaster Vienna coun. Boy Scouts Am., 1984. Recipient spl. achievement award Justice Dept., 1977, spl. commendation, 1978, Outstanding Achievement award Detroit Coll. of Law, 1993. Mem. ABA (chmn. criminal law com., sect. bus. law 1996—), Va. Bar, D.C. Bar (chmn. litigation sect. 1987-89, vice-chmn. coun. sects. 1988-89), Assn. Securities & Exch. Commn. Alumni (pres. 1993-95), Phi Beta Kappa, Eta Sigma Phi. Roman Catholic. Home: 1713 Paisley Blue Ct Vienna VA 22182-2326 Office Phone: 202-828-2229. E-mail: razzanof@dsmo.com.

RAZZANO, PASQUALE ANGELO, lawyer; b. Bklyn., Apr. 3, 1943; s. Pasquale Anthony and Agnes Mary (Borgia) R.; m. Maryann Walker, Jan. 29, 1966; children: Elizabeth, Pasquale, Susan, ChristyAnn. BSCE, Poly. Inst. Bklyn., 1964; student law, NYU, 1964-66; JD, Georgetown U., 1969. Bar: Va. 1969, N.Y. 1970, U.S. Ct. Appeals (2d, 3d, 7th, 9th and fed. cirs.), U.S. Supreme Ct., U.S. Dist. Ct. (so., ea. and western dists.) N.Y., U.S. Dist. Ct. (we. dist.) Tex., U.S. Dist. Ct. Hawaii, U.S. Dist. Ct. Conn. Examiner U.S. Patent Office, 1966-69; assoc. Curtis, Morris & Safford, P.C., 1969-71, ptnr., 1971-91, Fitzpatrick, Cella, Harper & Scinto, 1991—. Guest lectr. U.S. Trademark Assn., Am. Intellectual Property Law Assn., Practicing Law Inst., NYU Law Ctr., ABA, N.Y. Intellectual Property Law Assn. Mem. bd. editors Licensing Jour., 1986—; mem. bd. editors Trademark Reporter, 1987—, book rev. editor, 1989-91, pub. articles editor, 1991-94, domestic articles editor, 1992-93, 95, editor-in-chief 1996-98. Rep. committeeman Rockland County. Recipient Robert Ridgeway award, 1964. Mem.: FBA (chmn. patent law com. 1999—2002, bd. govs. 2002—), ABA (guest lectr.), Columban Laws Assn., Bar Assn. City N.Y., Italian Am. Bar Assn., Va. Bar Assn., N.Y. Coun. Bar Leaders (exec. coun. 1993—94), N.Y. Bar Assn., Am. Intellectual Property Law Assn., Internat. Trademark Assn. (bd. dirs. 1996—99), Licensing Exec. Soc. (chmn. N.Y. chpt. 1996—99), N.Y. Intellectual Property Law Assn. (bd. dirs. 1985—93, sec. 1988—91, pres. 1994—95), Shorehaven Golf Club, Minute Man Yacht Club, N.Y. Athletic Club. Republican. Roman Catholic. Address: 21 Covlee Dr Westport CT 06880-6407 also: 14 Deerwood Trl Lake Placid NY 12946-1834 Office Phone: 212-218-2253. E-mail: prazzano@fchs.com.

RE, EDWARD DOMENIC, law educator, retired federal judge; b. Santa Marina, Italy, Oct. 14, 1920; s. Anthony and Marina (Maetta) R.; m. Margaret A. Corcoran, June 3, 1950; children: Mary Ann, Anthony John, Marina, Edward, Victor, Margaret, Matthew, Joseph, Mary Elizabeth, Mary Joan, Mary Ellen, Nancy Madeleine. BS cum laude, St. John's U., 1941, LLB summa cum laude, 1943, LLD (hon.), 1968; JSD, NYU, 1950; DPed (hon.), Aquila, Italy, 1960; LL.D. (hon.), St. Mary's Coll., Notre Dame, Ind., 1968, Maryville Coll., St. Louis, 1969, N.Y. Law Sch., 1976, Bklyn. Coll., CUNY, 1978, Nova U., 1980, Roger Williams Coll., 1982, Dickinson Sch. Law, Carlisle, Pa., 1983, Seton Hall U., 1984, Stetson U., 1990, William Mitchell Coll. Law, 1992, St. Francis Coll., Bklyn., 1993; L.L.D. (hon.), St. Thomas U., Miami, 2003; L.H.D. (hon.), DePaul U., 1980, Coll. S.I., CUNY, 1981, Pace U., 1985, Am. U. of Rome, 1995; D.C.S. (hon.), U. Verona, Italy, 1987; JD (hon.), U. Bologna, Italy, 1988, U. Urbino, 1994. Bar: N.Y. 1943. Appointed faculty St. John's U., N.Y., 1947, prof. law, 1951-69, adj. prof. law, 1969-80, Disting. prof., 1980—2002, ret., 2003; vis. prof. Georgetown U. Sch. Law, 1962-67; adj. prof. law N.Y. Law Sch., 1972-82, Martin disting. vis. prof., 1982-90; spl. hearing officer U.S. Dept. Justice, 1956-61; chmn. Fgn. Claims Settlement Commn. of U.S., 1961-68; asst. sec. ednl. and cultural affairs U.S. Dept. State, 1968-69; judge U.S. Customs Ct. (now U.S. Ct. Internat. Trade), N.Y.C., 1969-91, chief judge, 1977-91, chief judge emeritus, 1991—. Mem. Jud. Conf. U.S., 1986-91, adv. com. on appellate rules, 1976-88, com. on internat. jud. rels., 1994-97; chmn. adv. com. on experimentation in the law Fed. Jud. Ctr., 1978-81; mem. bd. higher edn. City of N.Y., 1958-69, emeritus, 1969—; Jackson lectr. Nat. Coll. State Trial Judges, U. Nev., 1970. Author: Foreign Confiscations in Anglo-American Law, 1951, Selected Essays on Equity, 1955, (chpt., freedom in internat. soc.) Concept of Freedom, 1955, Cases and Materials on Equitable Remedies, 1975, Cases and Materials on Remedies, 1982; co-author (with Joseph R. Re), 2000, Law Students' Manual on Legal Writing and Oral Argument, 1991, Brief Writing and Oral Argument, 1999; co-author: (with Lester D. Orfield) Cases and Materials on International Law, 1965; co-author: (with Zechariah Chafee Jr.) Cases and Materials on Equity, 1967; contbr. articles to legal jours. Served with USAAF, 1943-47; col. JAGD, ret. Decorated Grand Cross Order of Merit Italy; recipient Am. Bill of Rights citation; Morgenstern Found. Interfaith award; USAF commendation medal; Distinguished service award Bklyn. Jr. C. of C., 1956 Mem. ABA (ho. of dels. 1976-78, chmn. sect. internat. and comparative law 1965-67), Am. Fgn. Law Assn. (pres. 1971-73), Am. Law Inst., Fed. Bar Coun. (pres. 1973-74), Am. Soc. Comparative Law (pres. 1969-91), Am. Justinian Soc. Jurists (pres. 1974-76), Internat. Assn. Jurists: Italy-USA (pres. 1991—), Internat. Assn. Judges (prin. rep. to UN 1993-), Scribes Am. Soc. Writers on Legal Subjects (pres. 1978). Home: 305 B 147th St Neponsit NY 11694 Office: 305 B 147th St Neponsit NY 11694

RE, RICHARD NOEL, endocrinologist; b. Palisade, N.J., Sept. 4, 1944; m. Martha Jean Macdonald, 1979; children: Richard Macdonald, Christopher Moran, Gregory Noël. AB summa cum laude, Harvard U., 1965, MD cum laude, 1969. Diplomate Am. Bd. Internal Medicine, Am. Bd. Endocrinology and Metabolism. Med. intern Mass. Gen. Hosp., Boston, 1969-70, med. resident, 1970-71, clin. and rsch. fellow in endocrinology, 1971-74, clin. asst. in medicine, 1974-76, chief Hypertension Clinic, 1975-79, asst. in medicine, 1976-79; rsch. fellow Harvard Med. Sch., Boston, 1971-74, instr. in medicine, 1975-76, asst. prof. medicine, 1977-79; mem. staff Ochsner Med. Instns., New Orleans, 1979—; assoc. clin. prof. medicine Tulane U. Sch. Medicine, New Orleans, 1980—; head sect. on hypertensive diseases Ochsner Clinic, New Orleans, 1981—; v.p., dir. rsch. Alton Ochsner Med. Found., New Orleans, 1985—. Adj. prof. biology U. New Orleans, 1984—; chmn. clin. investigations com. Alton Ochsner Med. Found., 1980-86; mem. sci. rev. panel VA, 1988—; chmn. sci. resources com. Blood Rsch. Ctr., New Orleans, 1989-91, trustee, 1989-91; mem. adv. bd. Internat. Consortium for the Study of Tissue Renin Angiotensin Systems, 1990-92; mem. rsch. com. Am. Heart Assn.-La., Inc., 1990, mem. sci. peer rev. com., 1990-91; mem. rsch. adv. com. Medicare Clinics Pilot Project, 1990-92; bd. dirs. Health Care tech. Leadership Forum, 1999—. Author: Bioburst: The Impact of Modern Biology on the Affairs of Man, 1986; author: (with others) Clinical Pharmacy and Clinical Pharmacology, 1976, Biological Handbook II, 1977, Methods in Immunodiagnosis, 1981, Prostaglandins, Platelets, and Salicylates: Basic and Clinical Aspects, 1982, Systemic Disease in Dental Treatment, 1982, Kidney in Essential Hypertension, 1984, Current Clinical Practice, 1987, Current Advances in ACE Inhibition, 1989, Advances in Vascular Pathology, 1990; contbr. numerous articles to profl. jours. including Am. Jour. Hypertension, New Eng. Jour. Medicine, Jour. Inorganic Biochemistry, Current Opinion in Cardiology, Contemporary Internal Medicine, Lancet, Modern Medicine, Am. Jour. Cardiology. Fellow coun. on high blood pressure rsch. Am. Heart Assn. Quentee Nat. Heart and Lung Inst. NIH, 1981-85, La. Heart Assn., 1981-83, Indsl. Support, 1981-91, Dept. of Energy, 1995—. Fellow Am. Coll. Physicians; mem. AAAS, Am. Fedn. for Clin. Rsch., Assn. Am. Med. Colls. Group on Med. Edn., N.Y. Acad. Scis., Cen. Soc. for Clin. Investigation, So. Soc. for Clin. Investigation (Tinsley Harrison award 1996), So. Med. Assn., Internat. Soc. Hypertension, Endocrine Soc., Soc. for Exptl. Biology and Medicine, Phi Beta Kappa. Achievements include research on growth factors and cardiovascular structure, on angiotensin and regulation of cellular growth, and on hypertension. Office: Alton Ochsner Med Found 1516 Jefferson Hwy New Orleans LA 70121-2429 E-mail: rre@ochsner.org.

REA, ANN W. librarian; b. Jefferson City, Mo., Aug. 3, 1944; d. William H. and Ruby (Fogleman) Webb; m. Glen N. Rea, Sept. 28, 1974; children: Sarah, Rebecca. BA, U. Mo., 1966; MLS, U. So. Calif., 1968. Libr. St. Charles (Mo.) County Libr., 1967-71; libr. adult svcs. Paterson (N.J.) Free Pub. Libr., 1971-74; libr. Beal Coll. Libr., Bangor, Maine, 1983—. Pres. Bairnet. Mem ALA, Maine Libr. Assn.(scholarship and loan com.). Office: Beal Coll Libr 99 Farm Rd Bangor ME 04401 Office Phone: 207-947-4591.

REA, ANNE E. lawyer; b. 1959; AB, Brown U., 1981; JD, U. Chgo., 1984. Bar: Ill. 1984. With Sidley Austin Brown & Wood, Chgo., 1984—, ptnr., 1992—. Selected as one of 15 Rising Stars You Won't Want to Oppose in Ct., Ill. Legal Times. Mem.: ABA, Leadership Greater Chgo., Chgo. Bar Assn., Ill. State Bar Assn. Office: Sidley Austin Brown and Wood Bank One Plz 10 S Dearborn St Chicago IL 60603

READ, JAMES CARROLL, geneticist educator; b. Stephenville, Tex., Aug. 28, 1940; s. Edgar L. and LaRUe (Webber) R.; m. Patricia Ann Higgins, Mar. 24, 1969 (dec.); children: Tambria L., Heather L., Pattillo H., Jeannette L.; m. Bonnie Kay Zimmerman, Nov. 3, 2001. BS in agrl. edn., Tex. A&M Univ., 1966, MS plant breeding, 1969, PhD in genetics, 1971. Rsch. geneticist USDA ARS, Salinas, Calif., 1971-74; asst. prof. Tex. A&M Univ., Dallas, 1974-81, assoc. prof., 1981-99, prof., 1999—. Higher pvt. edn. task force Dallas Ind. Sch. Dist., 1978-81; cons. B. Johnson, Inc.,Dallas, 1987. Contbr. articles to profl. jours. Pres. Plano Lions Club, 1984, election judge Collin County, Plano, 1995; bd. dirs. Tex. Forage & Grassland Coun., 1992-95. Recipient NDEA fellowhip U.S. Gov., 1969. Mem.: Tex. Forage Workers (pres. 1994—95), Am. Forage and Grassland Coun. (merit award 1999, Vice Chancellor award in Excellence, The Agriculture Program of Tex. A&M U. Sys.), Soc. for Range Mgmt., Crop. Sci. Soc. Am., Am. Soc. Agronomy, Gamm Sigma Delta, Phi Kappa Phi, Alpha Zeta. Republican. Baptist. Avocations: golf, hunting. Office: Tex A&M Univ 17360 Coit Rd Dallas TX 75252-6502

READ, JOHN CONYERS, non-profit management; b. N.Y.C., May 21, 1947; s. Edward Cameron Kirk and Louise (Geary) R.; m. Alexandra Gould, Mar. 30, 1968; children: Cameron Kirk, Trevor Conyers, Alexandra. AB, Harvard, 1969, MBA, 1971; LHD (hon.), Centenary Coll., 2004. Ops. rsch. analyst HEW, Washington, 1971-72; exec. asst. to dir. Cost of Living Council, Washington, 1973; chief econ. adviser to Gov. Mass., 1974; exec. asst., counselor to sec. labor Washington, 1975; asst. sec. labor for employment standards, 1976—77; dir. corp. employee rels., pers. Cummins Engine Co., Columbus, Ind., 1977-80, plant mgr., 1980-85; v.p. Midrange Engines, 1986-90; v.p., gen. mgr. engine group Donaldson Co., Inc., Mpls., 1990-92; exec. v.p., 1992-94; ptnr. Hidden Creek Industries, Mpls., 1996—2000; pres., CEO Heavy Duty Holdings, Mpls., 1997-2000; pres. Read Ptnrs. Inc., Mpls., 2001—02, Outward Bound U.S.A., Garrison, NY, 2002—. Cons. nat. productivity and energy policies; chmn. NAM Task Force on Wage and Price Policies, 1978-80; bd. dirs. MAC Equipment Co., Active Leasing Co. Author Ford Found. monograph on occupational disease and workers' compensation; contbr. articles to newspapers and mags. Trustee Nat. Ctr. Occupl. Readjustment, 1984-87; trustee N.C. Outward Bound Sch., dir., 1995—, chmn., 1997-2000; chmn. Charleston Pvt. Industry Coun., 1985; mem. plant closing task force U. S. Dept. Labor, 1986, mfg. task force NRC, 1989, critical industries task force Def. Dept., 1989. Mem. Nat. Assn. Mfrs. (bd. dirs., chair employee rels. com. 1993-95). Home: 111 Marlborough Rd Briarcliff Manor NY 10510

READ, JOHN O. state legislator, pharmacist; b. Bunkie, La., July 8, 1941; m. Pat Yelverton. Student, Miss. Gulf Coast C.C., N.E. La. U. Mem. Miss. Ho. of Reps., 1993—; mem. appropriations, fees and salaries, labor coms.; mem. pub. health, judiciary B coms. Mayor City of Gautier, mem. city coun. Democrat. Baptist. Home: 2307 Highway 90 Gautier MS 39553-5231 Office: State Capitol Bldg PO Box 1018 Jackson MS 39215-1018

READ, MICHAEL OSCAR, editor, consultant; b. Amarillo, Tex., July 11, 1942; s. Harold Eugene and Madeline (Welch) R.; m. Jill Kay Vanderby, July 6, 1963 (div. Apr. 1967); 1 child, Rebecca Anne; m. Fawn Dale Barby, Apr. 10, 1977; 1 child, Nathan Michael. AA in Chemistry, Amarillo Coll., 1962; BA in Journalism, Tex. Tech. U., 1965. News editor Olton (Tex.) Enterprise, 1963-64; reporter, photographer Lubbock (Tex.) Avalanche-Jour., 1964-67, copy editor, 1967-70, city editor, 1970-72; copy editor Houston Post, 1972-74, systems editor, 1974-89, dir. news tech., 1989-95; electronic media content coord. Houston Chronicle, 1995-2000, web ops. and devel. editor, 2000—. Bd. dirs. Shell Employees Fed. Credit Union, Houston, 2001—, vice chmn., 2002—, supervisory com., 1996-2001; tchr. Let's Compute!, Stafford, Tex., 1985—; cons. Newspaper Pub. Sys., Stafford, 1989—; mem. joint Newspaper Assn. Am.-Internat. Press. Telecomm. Coun. Com. Wire Svc. Standards; mem. adv. bd. Found. for Am. Comms. FACSNET; chmn. adv. com. Sch. of Mass. Comm., Tex. Tech U. Author weekly newspaper column, 1977—. Vol. United Way, Houston, 1973—; bd. dirs. Meadows (Tex.) Community Improvement Assn., 1985-95, Meadows Utility Dist., 1988-93, Meadows Econ. Devel. Corp., 1994-99. Named among Outstanding Alumni, Tex. Tech U. Sch. Mass Comms., 2001; Eldon Durrett scholar, 1961-65. Mem. Am. MENSA, Am. Philatelic Soc., Am. 1st Day Cov. Soc. (life), U.S. Chess Fedn. (life), Soc. Profl. Journalists (conv. com. 1989-90), Press Club of Houston. Avocations: stamp collecting/philately, photography, gardening. Office: Houston Chronicle 801 Texas St Houston TX 77002-2996 Home: 215 Lakeside Blvd Sugar Land TX 77478-3957 E-mail: mike.read@chron.com.

READ, PIERS PAUL, author; b. Beaconsfield, Eng., Mar. 7, 1941; s. Herbert Edward and Margaret (Ludwig) R.; m. Emily Albertine Boothby, July 29, 1967; children: Albert Nathaniel, Martha Marianna, William Edward, Beatrice Mary. BA, St. John's Coll., Cambridge U., 1962, MA, 1963. Sub-editor Times Lit. Supplement, 1963-64. Adj. prof. writing Columbia U., 1980; lit. panel mem. Arts Coun. Gt. Britain, 1974-76; gov. Cardinal Manning Boys Sch., 1985; chmn. Cath. Writers Guild, 1993-97. Author: (novels) Game in Heaven with Tussy Marx, 1966, The Junkers, 1968 (Sir Geoffrey Faber Meml. prize, 1969), Monk Dawson, 1970 (Somerset Maugham award, Hawthornden prize, 1970), The Professor's Daughter, 1971, The Upstart, 1973, Polonaise, 1976, A Married Man, 1980, The Villa Golitsyn, 1982, The Free Frenchman, 1986, A Season in the West, 1988 (James Tait Black Meml. prize), On the Third Day, 1990, The Patriot, 1995, Knights of the Cross, 1997, (non-fiction) Alive: The Story of the Andes Survivors, 1974 (Thomas More medal), The Train Robbers, 1978, Ablaze: The Heroes and Victims of Chernobyl, 1993, The Patriot, 1996, (songs) Knights of the Cross, 1997, The Templars, 1999, The Gospel of St. John: The Story of the Son of God, 1999, Alice in Exile, 2001, Alec Guiness: The Authorised Biography, 2003, (TV plays) Coincidence, The Family Firm, The House of Highburgh Hill. Mem. Brit. bd. of Aid to Church in Need, 1988. Ford Found. fellow, 1963-64; Harkness fellow, 1967-68 Fellow Royal Soc. Lit.; mem. Soc. Authors (com. mgmt. 1972-74), Inst. Contemporary Arts (com. mgmt. 1972-74) Roman Catholic. Address: 50 Portland Rd W11 4LG London England E-mail: piersread@dial.pipex.com.

READ, RICHARD EATON, newspaper reporter; b. St. Andrews, Scotland, Sept. 3, 1957; s. Arthur H. and Katharine (Eaton) R.; m. Kim R. Kunkle, July 26, 1986; 1 child, Nehalem Kunkle-Read. BA in English, Amherst Coll., 1980; postgrad., Harvard U., 1996—97; LHD (hon.), Williamette U., 2003. Press sec. Mass. Commn. on State and County Bldgs., 1980; staff writer The Oregonian, 1981-86; fellow The Henry Luce Found./The Nation, Bangkok, 1986-87; freelance writer Tokyo, 1987-89; Asia bur. chief The Oregonian, Tokyo, 1989-94; sec., 1st dir., 1st v.p. Fgn. Corrs. Club of Japan, 1990-93, internat. bus. writer The Oregonian, Portland, 1994-99, sr. writer internat. affairs, 1999—. V.p., bd. dirs. The Internat. Sch., Portland, 2002—. Recipient Pulitzer prize for explanatory reporting, 1999, Overseas Press Club award for bus. reporting from abroad, 1999, Scripps Howard Found. award for bus. reporting, 1999, Blethen award for enterprise reporting Pacific Northwest Newspaper Assn., 1999, 2001, Pacific Northwest Soc. Prof. Journalists first place award for social issues, 2001, bus. 1998, spot news 1997, edn. 1990, Oreg. Gov.'s award for achievement in internat. bus., 2000, Pulitzer prize for pub. svc., 2001, Unity award in media investigative reporting, Lincoln U., 2001, Blethen award, 2001, Bruce Baer award, 2001, Media Leadership award Am. Immigration Lawyers Assn., 2001; named Internat. Citizen of Yr. 1999 World Affairs Coun. Oreg., named Internat. Citizen of Yr. 2002 Oreg. Assn. Consuls Eisenhower Exch. fellow, Peru, 1997; Nieman fellow, 1996-97; U. Md. CASE fellow, 2002.

READ, ROBERT ALLEN, music educator; b. Pottstown, Pa., Dec. 16, 1958; s. Kenneth Edward Read; m. Ruth Ann Radakovic, Nov. 17, 1984; children: Brian William, Stephanie Lynne, Rachel Ann. B of Edn., Ind. U. Pa., 1980; MEd in Music, U. Pa., 1990. Dir. bands Churchill Area H.S., Pitts., 1980—82, Gateway Sr. H.S., Monroeville, 1982—. Marching activities cons. Casavant Cavalcade, Indiana, Pa., 1976—; marching band drill cons., prodn. design pvt. practice, Harrison City. Mem.: Nat. Band Assn., Pa. Music Educators Assn., Music Educators Nat. Conf., Phi Mu Alpha (sec. 1978—79). Achievements include development of Curriculum/National Standards adaptability. Home: 127 Cool Springs Lane Harrison City PA 15636 Office: Gateway Senior High School 3000 Gateway Campus Boulevard Monroeville PA 15146 Office Phone: 412-373-5751. Personal E-mail: read5@comcast.net. E-mail: rread@gator.gasd.k12.pa.us.

READ, SARAH J. lawyer; BA cum laude, Yale U., 1978; JD, U. Wis., 1981; postgrad., Ctr. for Conflict Resolution, Chgo., MIT-Harvard U. Bar: Wis. 1981, Ill. 1981, U.S. Dist. Ct. (we. dist.) Wis. 1981, U.S. Dist. Ct. (no. dist.) Ill. 1981. Ptnr. Sidley & Austin, Chgo., also mem. telecom., energy and petrochems. practice goup, mem. alternative dispute resolution resource group. Mem. Ohio Telecom. Adv. Bd., 1984. Mem. ABA, Wis. Bar Assn., Chgo. Bar Assn., Order of Coif. Office: Sidley & Austin 1 S First National Plz Chicago IL 60603-2000 Fax: 312-853-7036.

READ, SUSAN PHILLIPS, state appeals court judge; b. Gallipolis, Ohio, June 27, 1947; d. Gomer Wesley and Elizabeth Molineaux Phillips; m. Howard John Read. BA summa cum laude, Ohio Wesleyan U., 1969; JD Floyd R. Mechem Prize Scholar, U. Chgo., 1972. Asst. counsel SUNY, 1974—77; in-house counsel GE Co., 1977—88; ptnr. Bond, Schoeneck & King, Albany, NY, 1988—94; dep. counsel to Gov. Pataki, 1995—97; judge Ct. of Claims, 1998—; assoc. judge N.Y. State Ct. Appeals, Schenectady, 2003—. Mem.: Phi Beta Kappa. Office: NY State Ct Appeals 20 Eagle St Albany NY 12207-1095

READ, THOMAS LAWRENCE, music educator, composer; b. Erie, Pa., July 3, 1938; s. Thomas Albert and Virginia Leonore Read; m. Evelyn Doris Rosenbaum, Sept. 1, 1964; children: Thomas F., Rebecca D. Calos, Benjamin R. MusB, Oberlin Conservatory, 1960; MusM, New Eng. Conservatory, 1962; Mus D., Peabody Conservatory, 1971. Violinist Balt. Symphony, 1962—63; adj. faculty Peabody Conservatory, Balt., 1963—64; asst. prof. West Chester (Pa.) State Coll., 1965—67; prof. of music U. Vt., Burlington, 1967—. Condr. Vt. Youth Orch., Burlington, 1973—75; clinician and lectr. New Eng. area. Composer over 100 compositions. Grantee, U. Vt., 1975, 1979, 1984; vis. composing fellow, Johnson Composers Conf., 1975, 1978, MacDowell Colony, 1975, 1978, Ives Ctr. Am. Music, 1982, Composition grantee, Vt. Coun. on Arts, 1981, 1984. Mem.: Am. Composers Alliance (regional chmn.), Vt. Composers Consortium (bd. dirs. 1988—90). Avocations: hiking, running, book collecting. Office: U Vt Dept Music Burlington VT Personal E-mail: tread@uvm.edu.

READ, VIRGINIA HALL, retired biochemistry educator; b. Louisville, Miss., Oct. 15, 1937; d. Angus R. and Hassie (Bowie) Hall; m. Dale Gilbert Read Sr., Mar. 5, 1960; children: Laura Read Sprabery, Dale Gilbert Jr., Eva Read Warden. BS, U. Miss., 1959; MS, U. Miss., Jackson, 1962, PhD, 1964. Instr. biochemistry U. Miss., Jackson, 1965-66, asst. prof. biochemistry, 1966-68, 70-74, assoc. prof. biochemistry, 1974-2000, assoc prof. pathology, 1979-2000; asst. prof. medicine U. Ala., Birmingham, 1968-70. Contbr. articles to Jour. Clin. Investigation, Jour. Clin. Endocrinology and Metabolism, Nature, Biochem. Pharmacology. Grantee U.S. Pub. Health Svc., 1960-62, fellow, 1968-70. Mem. Am. Assn. Clin. Chemistry, Acad. Clin. Biochemistry, Endocrine Soc., Sigma Xi. United Methodist. Personal E-mail: dread@was.net.

READ, WILLIAM B. business educator; b. Springfield, Mass., June 24, 1935; s. William and Elinor Read; m. Jean E. Read, May 17, 1980; 1 child, Thomas W. BA, Am. Internat. Coll., 1961; MA, U. Conn., 1963. Prof. Bus. Law Bay Path Jr. Coll., Longmeadow, Mass., 1963—64, Andover Inst. Bus., Springfield, Mass., 1964—66, Husson Coll., Bangor, Maine, 1966—. Editor in chief Bus. Law Rev., 1968—73, 1981—. Mem.: North Atlantic Regional Bus. Law Assn. Avocation: swimming. Office: Husson Coll Bangor ME 04401

READE, CLAIRE ELIZABETH, lawyer; b. Waltham, Mass., June 2, 1952; d. Kemp Brownell and Suzanne Helen (Dorntge) R.; m. Earl Phillip Steinberg, Nov. 22, 1980; children: Evan Samuel, Emma Miriam. BA, Conn. Wesleyan U., 1973; JD, Harvard U., 1979; MA in Law and Diplomacy, Tufts U., 1979. Bar: Mass. 1980, D.C. 1983. Sheldon fellow Harvard U., Cambridge, Mass. and, Republic of China, 1979-80; assoc. Ropes & Gray, Boston, 1980-82, Arnold & Porter, Washington, 1982-86, ptnr., 1987—. Exec. editor: International Trade Policy: The Lawyer's Perspective, 1985; contbr. articles to profl. jours. Mem. ABA (co-chair internat. trade com.), DC Bar Assn., Coun. on Foreign Rels. Office: Arnold & Porter 555 12th St NW Washington DC 20004-1206 Office Phone: 202-942-5566. E-mail: readecl@aporter.com.

READE, LEWIS POLLOCK, business executive, retired diplomat, engineer; b. N.Y.C., Nov. 1, 1932; s. Herman Ross and Dorothy Stella (Pollock) R.; m. Anne Carol Kulka, July 3, 1953 (div. Feb. 1968); children: Steven Gordon, Nicholas Edward; m. Margaret Ann Kilpatrick, Mar. 30, 1968; 1 child, Jonathan Collins. BS in Mech. Engrin., U. Miami, 1953; postgrad., Hofstra U., 1953-54, U. Balt., 1957-59, U. N.Mex., 1997—. Product engr. Sperry Gyroscope, Lake Success, N.Y., 1953-54; project engr. ARMA, Garden City,

N.Y., 1954-55; field engr. Westinghouse Electric Corp., Balt. & Rome, 1957-66; v.p. Westinghouse Learning Corp., Washington & Pitts., 1966-70; v.p. corp. planning & devel. Tyco Labs., Waltham, Mass., 1970-71; chmn., chief exec. officer, treas. Kellett Corp., Willow Grove, Pa., 1971-72; exec. v.p. Big Bros./Big Sisters of Am., Phila., 1973-80; mission dir. U.S. Agy. Internat. Devel., Kingston, Jamaica, 1982-85; sr. dep. asst. adminstr. Pvt. Enterprise Bur., Washington, 1985-86; mission dir. U.S. Agy. Internat. Devel., Amman, Jordan, 1986-90, Jakarta, Indonesia, 1990-92; dir. gen. U.S.-Asia Environ. Partnership, Washington, 1992-97; ret., 1997; pres., CEO Jordan-U.S. Bus. Partnership, Amman, 1998—2000. Sgt. USAR, 1955—57. Mem. Am. Fgn. Svc. Assn. Home: 92 Vista Montana Loop Placitas NM 87043-9518

READER, GEORGE G. retired internal-public health medicine educator; b. Bklyn., 1919; m. Helen Brown, May 23, 1942; 4 children. BA in Animal Biology, Cornell U., Ithaca, N.Y., 1940; MD, Cornell U., N.Y.C., 1943; ScD (hon.), Drew U., 1988. Intern in medicine N.Y. Hosp., N.Y.C., 1944-45, resident and fellow in medicine, 1946—50, resident in hematology, 1950—51; instr. medicine Cornell U. Med. Ctr., 1951—52, from asst. prof. to prof., 1952—89, emeritus prof. medicine, 1989—, Livingston Farrand prof. pub. health, 1989—. Former advisor Social Security Adminstrn.; former chmn. human ecology study sect. NIH; former chmn. tech. com. on tng. White House Conf. on Aging; former cons. OEO, Office Sec. of HEW, Health Svcs. and Mental Health Adminstrn.; head transition task force health adv. coun. N.Y. State Dept. Health, 1974—84; former chmn. N.Y. State Task Force on Health of Sch. Age Child and Health Manpower; rep. Cornell U. Med. Ctr. in Health Planning for N.Y.C.; mem. master plan com. N.Y.C. Hosp. Coun. Mem. N.Y.C. Mayor's Organized Task Force for Health Planning; mem. local planning bd. representing N.Y. Hosp., Health Sys. Agy., N.Y.C. Scholar Regents scholar, Cornell U., 1940. Mem.: ADA, Inst. of Medicine (sr.), Skulls. Office: Cornell U/Weill Med Coll Dept Pub Health 1300 York Ave # 73 New York NY 10021-4805

READER, JONATHAN WHITTIER, sociology educator, consultant; b. N.Y.C., July 19, 1944; s. George Gordon and Helen (Brown) R. BA in Govt., Cornell U., Ithaca, N.Y., 1966, PhD in Sociology, 1981; MPA, N.Y.U., 1969. Lt. USPHS, Washington, 1968-70; cons. project office Linton, Mields & Costen, Washington, 1969-70; rsch. adminstr. Cornell U., Ithaca, 1972-80; prof. sociology Drew U., Madison, N.J., 1980—. Cons. Trans Century Corp., El Paso, Tex., 1969-70, Conf. Mayors, Washington, 1970, Stockton (N.J.) State U., 1970, Local 32B and J, N.Y.C., 1982-84, 88. Author, co-author some 20 scholarly articles, papers, revs. and rsch. reports on local govt. fiscal policy, corp. mergers, innovations in med. tech., other subjects; appeared in movie Meeting the Beautiful People, 1994. Bd. dirs. N.J. Cheetah, Mendham, 1998—, Conservation Fund. Dissertation fellow U.S. Dept. Housing and Urban Renewal. Mem. Am. Sociology Soc. Democrat. Avocations: tennis, dance, theater, american presidents, birding. Home: 42B Loantaka Way Madison NJ 07940 Office: Drew U 36 Madison Ave Madison NJ 07940 E-mail: JReader@Drew.edu.

READER, JOSEPH, physicist; b. Chgo., Dec. 1, 1934; BS, Purdue U., 1956, MS, 1957; PhD in Physics, U. Calif., 1962. Rsch. assoc. physics Argonne Nat. Lab., 1962-63; staff physicist Nat. Inst. Standards and Tech., Gaithersburg, Md., 1963-99, group leader atomic spectroscopy group, 1999—. Recipient Gold medal Dept. Commerce, 1989. Fellow Am. Phys. Soc., Optical Soc. Am. (William F. Meggers award 1992). Achievements include research in experimental atomic physics, optical spectroscopy, hyperfine structure, electronic structure of highly ionized atoms, wavelength standards, and ionization energies of atoms and ions. Office: Natl Inst Of Stds & Tech Gaithersburg MD 20899-0422

READING, ANTHONY JOHN, accountant; b. London, Aug. 8, 1943; came to U.S., 1993; m. Myra Elizabeth Steer, Aug. 27, 1966; 1 child, Jason. Chartered acct. Mng. dir., dir. mfg., dir. fin. Donaldson Co. Inc., Brussels, 1970-80; group exec. Thomas Tilling Plc, London, 1980-83; divisional group chief exec. BTR Plc, London, 1983-87; group mng. dir. Polly Peck Internat., London, 1987-89, Pepe Group Plc, London, 1989-90; divisional dir. Tomkins Plc, London, 1990-92, also bd. dirs.; chmn., CEO Tomkins Corp., Dayton, Ohio, 1992—. Chmn. Orgn. Internat. Investment, Washington, 2002. Named Mem. of Most Excellent Order of Brit. Empire, Her Majesty Queen Elizabeth II, 1978. Fellow Inst. Chartered Accts. Eng. and Wales; mem. Naval and Mil. Club London. Avocations: music, golf, water sports. Office: Tomkins Corp 4801 Springfield St Dayton OH 45431-1084 E-mail: areading@tomkins-industries.com.

READING, JAMES EDWARD, transportation executive; b. Milw., June 26, 1924; s. James Edwards and Helen Marie (Boehm) R.; m. Ada Irene Kelly, May 24, 1944; children: Wendy Irene, James David, Christopher Kelly, Mary Katherine, Kevin Sinclair. Student, San Diego State U., 1942, Ga. Inst. Tech., 1944. With Union-Tribune Pub. Co., San Diego, 1942-59, dist. mgr., 1953-58, circulation promotion mgr., 1958-59; adminstrv. asst. to v.p. Copley Newspapers, La Jolla, Calif., 1959-60; dir. advt. and pub. rels. San Diego Transit System, 1960-67; dir. mktg. Calif. Motor Express, 1967-68; asst. to exec. v.p. Am. Transit Assn., Washington, 1968; v.p. Nat. City Mgmt. Co.; resident mgr. Regional Transit Service, Rochester, N.Y., 1968-74; asst. gen. mgr. ops. Regional Transit Dist., Denver, 1974-77; gen. mgr. Central Ohio Transit Authority, Columbus, 1977-85; dir. Santa Clara County Transp. Agy., San Jose, Calif., 1985-90; ind. cons. San Diego, 1990—. Lectr. in field. Treas. Contg. Edn. Ctr., Rancho Bernardo. With ETO U.S. Army, 1943—46. Named Public Relations Man of Yr. Public Relations Club, San Diego, 1962; recipient Urban Mass Transp. Adminstrs. award for outstanding pub. service, 1980, 82; charter mem. Herbert Hoover H.S. Achievement Hall of Fame, San Diego, 1998; named to Rancho Bernardo Hall of Fame, 2000. Mem. Am. Pub. Transit Assn. (bd. dirs., past v.p., elected Hall of Fame 1995), Am. Legion, Rotary Club Rancho Bernardo (past pres., treas.), Press Club of Rancho Bernardo (past pres.), Rancho Bernardo Spirit of Fourth (past pres., treas.), Tau Kappa Epsilon. Republican. Roman Catholic. Home: 11728 Caminito Corriente San Diego CA 92128-4548

READING, PHYLLIS ANN, social welfare administrator; b. Seattle, Apr. 21, 1954; ADN, Shoreline C.C., Seattle, 1975; BSN, Seattle U., 1979; M Nursing in Adminstrn., U. Wash., 1988. RN, Wash., Calif. Relief charge nurse CCU Group Health Hosp., Redmond, Wash., 1979-81; relief supr. pheresis unit Puget Sound Blood Ctr., Seattle, 1981-83; coord. critical care Snoqualmie (Wash.) Valley Hosp., 1983-85, asst. adminstr., 1985-89; staff devel. specialist U. Wash. Med. Ctr., Seattle, 1989-93; edn. specialist AACN, Aliso Viejo, Calif., 1993-94, program devel. and meeting svcs. dir., 1994-96, dir. profl. devel., 1996-97, exec. dir., 1997-2000, program dir. Ctr. for Leadership Excellence, 1994-96, exec. prodr. satellite video confs., 1994-96; exec. dir. Nat. Assistance League, L.A., 2000—02; dir., patient and family services ALS Assn., San Francisco, 2002—. Mem. nat. faculty tchg. improvement project sys. Kellogg Found., 1992. Mem. adv. bd. N.W. Emergency Physicians, Seattle, 1985-89; bd. dirs. Am. Cancer Soc., Kirkland, Wash., 1988-89. Mem. AACN, Am. Soc. Assn. Execs., Sigma Theta Tau. Avocation: tennis. Office: 140 Geary St 4th Fl San Francisco CA 94108

READY, CHRISTOPHER JAMES, accountant; b. Somerset, Mass., Aug. 3, 1966; s. Daniel F. and Dorothy T. (McViney) R.; m. Mary E. Durand, May 30, 1992. BS in Acctg. cum laude, U. Mass. Dartmouth, 1992; MBA with honors, Bryant Coll., 1998. Sr. acct. Furon Co., Bristol, RI, 1992-95; cost acct. Uvex Safety, Inc., Smithfield, RI, 1995-99; contr. Invensys Position Sensors, Woonsocket, RI, 1999—2001; fin. mgr. Honeywell Sensing and Control, Pawtucket, RI, 2001—. Mem. Inst. Mgmt. Accts., Beta Gamma Sigma. Avocations: golf, drums, drawing. Home: 92 Log Rd Harrisville RI 02830-1884 Office: Honeywell Seinsing and Control 500 Narragansett Park Dr Pawtucket RI 02861

READY, ELIZABETH M. state legislator; b. Burlington, Vt., Oct. 7, 1953; m. John H. McLain; 3 children. BA, U. Vt. Selectman Town of Lincoln, Vt.; mem. Vt. Senate, Montpelier, 1989—. Regional planning commr.; educator. Home: Box 2018 RR 1 Box 5146 Bristol VT 05443 Office: State House 115 State St Montpelier VT 05633-0001

READY, ROBERT JAMES, financial company executive; b. Bridgeport, Conn., June 26, 1952; s. John Edward and Anne (Salata) R.; m. Margaret S. Neale, Aug. 23, 1975; children: Carolyn, Christopher and Steven (twins). AS, Housatonic Community Coll., 1972, BS, Babson Coll., 1974. CLU; chartered fin. cons.; registered fin. cons.; cert. ins. cons; cert. retirement cons.; cert. retirement adminstr. Agt. John Hancock Mut. Life Ins. Co., Hamden, Conn., 1975-77; broker Beardsley, Brown & Bassett Inc., Bridgeport, Conn., 1977-80; agt. Aetna Life and Casualty Ins. Co., Trumbull, Conn., 1980-83; v.p. Crestview Fin. Services Inc., Westport, Conn., 1983-2000, Crestview Securities Inc., Westport, Conn., 1983-2000, Crestview Investment Advisors Inc., Westport, Conn., 1983-2000; sr. v.p. ins. RDM Ins. Svcs. Inc., Westport, Conn., 2000—. Mem. Nat. Assn. Life Underwriters, Conn. Assn. Life Underwriters, Bridgeport Life Underwriters (bd. dirs. 1977), New Haven County CLU and Chartered Fin. Cons., Soc. of Fin. Svc. Profls. (Fairfield county chpt.). Roman Catholic. Avocations: golf, tennis, softball. Office: RDM Financial Group Inc 1555 Post Rd E Westport CT 06880-5602 Office Phone: 203-255-0222. E-mail: bready@rdmfinancial.com.

REAGAN, GARY DON, state legislator, lawyer; b. Amarillo, Tex., Aug. 23, 1941; s. Hester and Lois Irene (Marcum) R.; m. Nedra Ann Nash, Sept. 12, 1964; children: Marc Kristi, Kari, Brent. BA, Stanford U., 1963, JD, 1965. Bar: N.Mex. 1965, U.S. Dist. Ct. N.Mex. 1965, U.S. Supreme Ct. 1986. Assoc. Smith & Ransom, Albuquerque, 1965-67; ptnr. Smith, Ransom, Deaton & Reagan, Albuquerque, 1967-68, Williams, Johnson, Houston, Reagan & Porter, Hobbs, N.Mex., 1968-77, Williams, Johnson, Reagan, Porter & Love, Hobbs, N.Mex., 1977-82; pvt. practice pvt. practice, Hobbs, N.Mex., 1982—; city atty. City of Hobbs, 1978—80, 1997—2004, City of Eunice, N.Mex., 1980—; mem. N.Mex. State Senate, 1993-96. Instr. N.Mex. Jr. Coll. and Coll. of S.W., Hobbs, 1978-84; N.Mex. commr. Nat. Conf. Commrs. Uniform State Laws, 1993-96; adv. mem. N.Mex. Constl. Revision Commn., 1993-95. Mayor City of Hobbs, 1972-73, 76-77, city commr., 1970-78; pres., dir. Jr. Achievement of Hobbs, 1974-85; pres., trustee Landsun Homes, Inc., Carlsbad, N.Mex., 1972-84; trustee Lydia Patterson Inst., El Paso, Tex., 1972-84, N.Mex. Conf. United Meth. Ch., 1988—, Coll. S.W. Hobbs, 1989-2001; chmn. County Dem. Com., 1983-85. Mem. ABA, State Bar N.Mex. (coms. 1989-96, v.p. 1992-93, pres. 1994-95), Lea County Bar Assn. (pres. 1976-77), Hobbs C. of C. (pres. 1989-90), Rotary (pres. Hobbs 1985-86), Hobbs Tennis Club (pres. 1974-75). Home: 200 E Eagle Dr Hobbs NM 88240-5323 Office: 1819 N Turner Ste G Hobbs NM 88240-3834 Office Phone: 505-397-6551. E-mail: lglregan@nm.net.

REAGAN, HARRY EDWIN, III, lawyer; b. Wichita, Kans., Sept. 9, 1940; s. Harry E. II and Mary Elizabeth (O'Steen) R.; m. Marvene R. Rogers, June 17, 1965; children: Kathleen, Leigh, Mairen. BS, U. Pa., 1962, JD, 1965. Bar: Pa. 1965, U.S. Dist. Ct. (ea. dist.) Pa. 1965, U.S. Ct. Appeals (3d cir.) 1965. From assoc. to ptnr. Morgan, Lewis & Bockius, Phila., 1965-98. Chmn. Northhampton Twp. Planning Commn., Bucks County, Pa., 1974-79; mem. Warwick Twp. Planning Commn., 1980-95, chmn., 1994; supr. Warwick Twp., 1996-98; mem. San Miguel County (Colo.) Open Space Commn., 1998—, chmn., 2001—, San Miguel County Planning Commn.; mem. Town of Telluride Open Space Commn., 1999-2002, San Miguel County Planning Commn., 2002—. Mem. ABA (labor sect.), Pa. Bar Assn. (labor sect.), Phila. Bar Assn. (labor sect.), Indsl. Rels. Assn. (pres. Phila. chpt. 1990-91). Republican. Presbyterian. Avocations: coaching rugby, skiing, raising horses, bicycling. Home and Office: Box 530 12350 McKenzie Springs Rd Placerville CO 81430

REAGAN, JAMES RAYMOND, safety and ergonomics consultant; b. Camden, N.J., Aug. 24, 1926; s. James Raymond and Anne Frances R.; m. Gloria Ann Smith Reagan, Jan. 2, 1950; children: Michael, Stephen, John, James, Elizabeth. BME, U. Del., Newark, 1949. Reg. profl. engr., Del.; cert. profl. ergonomist. Student opr., engr. DuPont, Chattanooga, 1949-53, line supv. Seaford, Del., 1953-56, sr. engr., 1956-58, group supv. of design, 1958-65, area supv., 1965-78, safety, health & environ. supv., 1978-88, ergonomics mgr. Wilmington, Del., 1988-91, sr. cons., 1992—. Pres., prin. cons. Reagan Ergonomics, Jacksonville, Fla., 1991—. Author: Ergonomics Overview, 1998. Pres. Bulldog Boosters, Laurel. Del., 1974, Sussex (Del.) Engring. Soc., 1968. 1st lt. U.S. Army, 1944-47, WWII, 51-52, Korea. Recipient Environ. Respect awards (2) DuPont, Wilmington, 1990. Mem. VFW, KC, Am. Indsl. Hygiene Assn., Nat. Safety Coun., Human Factors and Ergonomics Soc., Am. Legion. Achievements include development of criteria for selecting ergonomist and training DuPont leaders and engineers in ergonomics. Home and Office: 408 Chipley Place W Jacksonville FL 32259-4330 also: DuPont Safety Resources 131 Continental Dr Ste 307 Newark DE 19713-4324

REAGAN, JANET THOMPSON, psychologist, educator; b. Sept. 15, 1945; d. Virgil Joe and Carrie mae (Alexander) Thompson; children: Natalia Alexandria, Robert Barry. BA in Psychology, Berea Coll., 1967; PhD in Psychology, Vanderbilt U., 1972. Mgr. rsch. and eval. Nashville Mental Health Ctr., 1971-72; mgr. eval. Family Health Found., New Orleans, 1973-74; asst. prof. dept. health systems mgmt. Tulane U., New Orleans, 1974-77; dir. eval. Project Heavy West, L.A., 1977-78; asst. prof. health adminstrn. Calif. State U.-Northridge, 1978-83; assoc. prof., dir. health adminstrn., 1983-87; prof., dir. health adminstrn., 1987—. Cons. in field. Contbr. to books, articles to profl. jours., papers to profl. assns.; mem. editl. adv. bd. Jour. Long Term Care Adminstrn., Healthcare Papers. Mem. Am. Pub. Health Assn., Am. Coll. Health Care Adminstrn., Assn. Health Svcs. Rsch., Am. Coll. Health Care Execs. (com. on higher edn. 1987, chmn. 1991), Assn. Univ. Programs in Health Adminstrn. (task force on undergrad. edn. 1985-90, chmn. 1988-90, mem. bd. dirs. 1995, chmn. bd. dirs. 1998-99), Psi Chi, Phi Kappa Phi. Home: 9354 Encino Ave Northridge CA 91325-2414 Office: Calif State U Dept Health Sci Northridge CA 91330-0001 Office Phone: 818-677-2298. Business E-Mail: janet.reagan@csun.edu.

REAGAN, JOSEPH BERNARD, retired aerospace executive, management consultant; b. Somerville, Mass., Nov. 26, 1934; s. Joseph B. and Helen Lowry R.; m. Dorothy Hughes; children: Patrick, Michael, Kevin, Kathleen, Brian, John, Maureen. BS in Physics, Boston Coll., 1956, MS in Physics, 1959; PhD in Space Sci., Stanford U., 1975; postgrad. exec. mgmt., Pa. State U., State College, 1981. Staff scientist, rsch. scientist, sr. scientist, scientist Lockheed Rsch. & Devel. Div., Palo Alto, Calif., 1959-75, mgr., 1975-84, dir., 1984-86, dep. gen. mgr., 1986-88, v.p., asst. gen. mgr., 1988-90; v.p. gen. mgr. Lockheed Missle and Space Co., 1991-96. Bd. dirs. Southwall Techs. Inc., Palo Alto. Contbr. articles to profl. jours. Bd. dirs. Tech. Mus., San Jose. Capt. U.S. Army, 1956-64. Recipient Career Achievement in Sci. award Boston Coll. Alumni Assn., 1993. Fellow AIAA (outstanding engr. San Francisco chpt. 1988); mem. Am. Geophys. Union, Nat. Acad. of Engring., Nat. Rsch. Coun. (mem. naval studies bd.). Republican. Roman Catholic. Avocation: computer and woodworking hobbies. Home and Office: 13554 Mandarin Way Saratoga CA 95070-4847

REAGAN, LAWRENCE PAUL, JR., systems engineer; b. Honolulu, Nov. 5, 1957; s. Lawrence Paul Sr. and Laura Louise (Sears) R.; m. Ann Marie Decker, Apr. 15, 1989; children: Lawrence P. III, Andrew Scott, Kelly Rene, Ryan Joshua. BS in Mech. & Aerospace Engring., Ill. Inst. Tech., 1979; MS in Acquisition & Contract Mgmt., West Coast U., Santa Barbara, Calif., 1986. Product engr. R.G. Ray Corp., Schaumburg, Ill., 1978-80; launch integration mgr. USAF Hqrs. Space Divsn., L.A. AFB, 1980-84; chief Titan program mgmt. USAF Aerospace Test Group, Vandenberg AFB, Calif., 1984-89; chief joint comm. br. USAF Pentagon, Washington, 1989-91; sr. sys. engr. Dynamics Rsch. Corp., Arlington, Va., 1992-96, dir. Md. ops. California, Md., 1996-97; fed. programs mgr. Info. Builders, Inc., Arlington, 1997-98, dir. fed. programs, 1998—2003; v.p. PRICE Systems LLC, Arlington, 2003—. CEO Jacob's Well, Inc., Lexington Park, Md., 1993—. Contbr. papers to profl. publs. Named Outstanding Young Engr., Air Force Assn. Mem. AIAA, Soc. Logistics Engring., Air Force Assn., Armed Forces Comms. Electronics Assn. Home: PO Box 22 Lusby MD 20657-0022 Office: PRICE Systems LLC 1700 N Moore St Ste 1100 Arlington VA 22209 Office Phone: 703-740-0078. Business E-Mail: larry.reagan@pricesystems.com.

REAGAN, NANCY DAVIS (ANNE FRANCIS ROBBINS), former First Lady of the United States, volunteer; b. N.Y.C., July 6, 1921; d. Kenneth and Edith (Luckett) Robbins; step dau. Loyal Davis; m. Ronald Reagan, Mar. 4, 1952 (dec. 2004); children: Patricia Ann, Ronald Prescott; stepchildren: Maureen (dec. 2001), Michael. BA, Smith Coll., 1943; LLD (hon.), Pepperdine U., 1983; LHD (hon.), Georgetown U., 1987. First Lady of the U.S., Washington, 1981—89. Contract actress, MGM, 1949-56; films include Portrait of Jennie, 1948, East Side, West Side, 1949, Doctor and the Girl, 1949, Shadow on the Wall, 1950, The Next Voice You Hear, 1950, Night into Morning, 1951, It's a Big Country, 1951, Shadow in the Sky, 1952, Talk About a Stranger, 1952, Donovan's Brain, 1953, Hellcats of the Navy, 1957, Crash Landing, 1958, You Can't Hurry Love, 1988, Lunar: Silver Star Story, 1992; TV credits include Schlitz Playhouse of Stars, 1951, Climax, 1954, General Electric Theater, 1953, Zane Grey Theater, 1956, The Tall Man, 1960, 87th Precint, 1961, Wagon Train, 1957, Different Strokes, 1978, Dynasty, 1981; Author: Nancy, 1980; formerly author syndicated column on prisoner-of-war and missing-in-action soldiers and their families; author: (with Jane Wilkie) To Love a Child, 1982, (with William Novak) My Turn: The Memoirs of Nancy Reagan, 1989. Civic worker, visited wounded Viet Nam vets., sr. citizens, hosps. and schs. for physically and emotionally handicapped children, active in furthering foster grandparents for handicapped children program; hon. nat. chmn. Aid to Adoption of Spl. Kids, 1977; spl. interest in fighting alcohol and drug abuse among youth: hosted first ladies from around the world for 2d Internat. Drug Conf., 1985; hon. chmn. Just Say No Found., Nat. Fedn. of Parents for Drug-Free Youth, Nat. Child Watch Campaign, President's Com. on the Arts and Humanities, Wolf Trap Found. bd. of trustees, Nat. Trust for Historic Preservation, Cystic Fibrosis Found., Nat. Republican Women's Club; hon. pres. Girl Scouts of Am. Named one of Ten Most Admired Am. Women, Good Housekeeping mag., ranking #1 in poll, 1984, 85, 86; Woman of Yr. Los Angeles Times, 1977; permanent mem. Hall of Fame of Ten Best Dressed Women in U.S.; recipient humanitarian awards from Am. Camping Assn., Nat. Council on Alcoholism, United Cerebral Palsy Assn., Internat. Ctr. for Disabled; Boys Town Father Flanagan award; 1986 Kiwanis World Service medal; Variety Clubs Internat. Lifeline award; numerous awards for her role in fight against drug abuse. Republican. Address: 2121 Avenue Of The Stars Fl 34 Los Angeles CA 90067-5062*

REAGAN, PAUL TERRENCE, retired social worker; b. Potsdam, N.Y., Jan. 23, 1938; s. Leo Mark and Helen Mc Carthy Reagan; 1 child, Siobhan. BA, MA, MSW, SUNY, Albany. Cert. social worker N.Y. Staff social worker Poughkeepsie (N.Y.) Continuing Treatment Ctr., 1989—2002. Pres. Panda pub. access TV sta., Rhinebeck, NY, 1995—2001. Participant 1st Eathiopia program Peace Corps, 1962—64; vol. ARC, Poughkeepsie, 1989—2002; nominee N.Y. State Senate Dutchess and Columbia County Dem. Coms., Poughkeepsie, 2002. Fellow, N.Y. State United Teachers, 1970—73; grantee, N.Y. State Edn. Dept., 1973—74, 1980—81; scholar, Syracuse Teachers Assn., 1957—58. Mem.: Albany Alumni Assn., Dutchess County Coalition for the Homeless. Home: PO Box 211 Staatsburg NY 12580

REAGON, BERNICE JOHNSON, cultural historian, educator, curator, singer, composer; b. Oct. 4, 1942; Student, Albany State Coll., 1959-61; BA in History, Spelman Coll., 1970; PhD, Howard U., 1975. With African Diaspora Program, Festival of Am. Folklife Smithsonian Instn., Washington, 1974-76, dir. Program in Black Am. Culture, Nat. Mus. Am. History, 1976-88, mus. curator, 1988—; disting. prof. history dept. Am. U., Washington, 2000—. Founder, artistic dir. Sweet Honey in the Rock, Washington, 1973—; vocal dir. Black Repertory Theatre, Washington, 1972-77; mem. Freedom Singers, 1962-63; founder, dir. Harambee Singers, Atlanta, 1968-70. Author: Black People and Their Culture: Selected Writings from the African Diaspora, 1976, Compositions One: The Original Compositions of Bernice Johnson Reagon, 1986; author, programmer Voices of Civil Rights Movement, Black American Freedom Songs, 1960-65, three-record album and book Smithsonian Coll. Recs., 1980; recs. include Songs of the South, 1964, Sound of Thunder, 1967, Give Your Hands to Struggle, 1975, River of Life, 1987; (with the Freedom Singers) We Shall Overcome, 1963, (with Sweet Honey in the Rock) B'Lieve I'll Run On, See What the End's Gonna Be, 1978, Good News, 1981, We All...Everyone of Us, 1983, The Other Side, 1985, Feel Something Drawing Me On, 1985, Live at Carnegie Hall, 1988, All for Freedom, 1989, others; mus. cons., composer for films including Eyes on the Prize-I, 1987, We Shall Overcome, 1988, Roots of Resistance, 1990. Program chair Albany (Ga.) Movement, 1961-62; field sec. Student Non-Violent Coord. Com., 1962-64. MacArthur Found. fellow; recipient Charles Frankel prize NEH, 1995. Achievements include pioneering in the development of a focus on African American culture in exhibition and programming at Smithsonian Instn. Office: Smithsonian Instn Nat Mus Am History Div Community Life Washington DC 20560-0001 Address: Am U Dept History 4400 Massachusetts Ave NW Washington DC 20016

REAM, BOB, political organization administrator; Chmn. Mont. Dem. Party, Helena, 1997—. Prof. emeritus Sch. Forestry U. Mont. Office: Mont Dem Party PO Box 802 Helena MT 59624-0802 Fax: 406-442-9534.

REAM, JAMES TERRILL, architect, sculptor; b. Summit, N.J., Sept. 8, 1929; s. Merrill Jay and Catherine Ada (Terrill) R.; m. Joyce Kimball Johnson, June 9, 1953 (div. Dec. 1976); children— Claudia, Sarah, Benjamin, m. Nancy Ann Buford, Jan. 1, 1980; stepchildren— Kathleen, Ann Maguire BArch, Cornell U., 1953; postgrad., Pratt Inst., 1953-54, U. Rome, 1956-57. Registered architect. Assoc. W. C. Muchow Assocs., Denver, 1959-62; prin. Ream, Quinn & Assocs., Denver, 1962-66; v.p. design John Carl Warnecke & Assocs., San Francisco, 1966-69; prin., pres. James Ream & Assocs., Inc., San Francisco, 1969-78, Robbins and Ream Inc., San Francisco, 1978-83; prin. James Ream Architect, San Francisco, 1983—. Prin. archtl. works include Denver Convention Ctr., Currigan Hall, Pasadena Conf. Ctr., Stapleton Plaza Hotel, Vail Transp. Ctr. Bd. dirs. San Francisco Planning and Urban Rsch. Assn., 1977—; chmn. bd. dirs. San Francisco Heritage, 1984-91, pres., 1983-84. Served to 1st lt. USAF, 1954-56. Recipient citation for design in steel Am. Iron and Steel Inst., 1975; Honor award Am. Concrete Inst., 1975; Nat. Design award Prestressed Concrete Inst., 1983; Honor award for design in steel Am. Inst. Steel Constrn., 1970 Fellow AIA (honor award western region 1969, fellowship in design 1979, honor award for design excellence 1983, design cons. San Jose Arena). Democrat. Avocations: opera, theater, hiking, tennis. Office: 3385 Clay St San Francisco CA 94118-2006

REAMAN, GREGORY HAROLD, pediatric hematologist, oncologist; b. Akron, Ohio, Sept. 9, 1947; s. Harold J. and Margaret U. (D'Alfonso) R.; m. Susan J. Pristo, Sept. 7, 1974; children: Emily Margaret, Sarah Elizabeth. BS in Biology, U. Detroit, 1969; MD, Loyola U., Chgo., 1973. Diplomate Nat. Bd. Med. Examiners, Am. Bd. Pediats. with subspecialty in pediat. hematology and oncology. Pediatric intern Loyola U. Med. Ctr., 1973-74; resident in pediatrics Montreal Children's Hosp., McGill U., 1974-76; clin. assoc. pediatric oncology br. Nat. Cancer Inst., NIH, Bethesda, Md., 1976-78, investigator pediatric oncology br., 1978-79; assoc. dept. hematology/oncology, attending physician Children's Nat. Med. Ctr., Washington, 1979—, chmn. dept. hematology/oncology, 1985—2003, dir. med. spl. svcs., 1995—99, exec. dir. Ctr. for Cancer and Blood Disorders, 1999—2002; asst. prof. pediats. Sch. Medicine and Health Scis. George Washington U., 1979—82, assoc. prof. pediats., 1982—87, prof. pediats., 1987—. Assoc. chmn. Children's Cancer Group; chmn. Children's Oncology Group;chmn. bd. dirs. Nat. childhood Cancer Found.; strategic planning com. Children's Oncology Svcs. of Met. Washington; exec. v.p. for sci. and med. affairs Nat. Childhood Cancer Found., 2002—; mem. oncologic drugs adv. com., FDA, 2002—. Mem. editl. bd. Cancer Data Query, Nat. Cancer Inst., Jour. Clin. Oncology, Am. Jour. Pediat. Hematology Oncology, Cancer, The Oncologist; reviewer Blood, Jour. Clin. Oncology; assoc. editor: Cancer, 1990-2000; contbr. articles to profl. publs. Trustee Nat. Childhood Cancer Found., Arcadia,

Calif.; bd. dirs. Am. Cancer Soc., Atlanta; trustee, chmn. patient care and profl. edn. coms. Leukemia Soc. Am. Lt. comdr. USPHS, 1976-79, Res., 1979—. Folger Summer scholar Am. Cancer Soc.; recipient Spl. Fellowship Rsch. award Leukemia Soc. Am., 1980-82; grantee DHHS, Nat. Cancer Inst., 1987—. Mem. Soc. Pediat. Rsch., Am. Soc. Hematology, Am. Pediat. Soc., Am. Fedn. Clin. Rsch., Am. Soc. Clin. Oncology, Am. Assn. Cancer Rsch., Am. Soc. Pediat. Hematology/Oncology, Children's Oncology Group, Washington Blood Club, Alpha Omega Alpha. Democrat. Roman Catholic. Home: 7306 Brennon Ln Chevy Chase MD 20815-4064 Office: Children's Nat Med Ctr 111 Michigan Ave NW Washington DC 20010-2916

REAME, NANCY, nursing educator; BSN, Mich. State U., 1969; MSN, Wayne State U., Detroit, 1974, PhD, 1977. RN. Postdoctoral fellow U. Mich., Ann Arbor, prof. dept. nursing. Mem.: Inst. of Medicine of NAS. Achievements include research in in brain aging and menopause; long-term satisfaction and outcomes after surrogate pregnancy; bioethics of assisted reproduction; gender and health. Office: Univ Mich Sch Nursing 400 N Ingalls Bldg Rm 2238 Ann Arbor MI 48109-0482

REAMER, SHIRLEY JEAN, minister; b. South Bend, Ind., Aug. 15, 1935; d. John Lewis and Vivian Leora (Hammer) Helvey; m. Thomas Charles Reamer, June 22, 1956; children: Thomas Darwin, Trent Alan, Terry Michael, Traci Sue, Tricia Ann. Grad. high sch., South Bend, 1953; ThD, Shalom Bible Coll. and Sem., West Des Moines, Iowa, 1992. Ordained to ministry Full Gospel Fellowship, 1974. Dir. children's ministry Calvary Temple, South Bend, 1972-73; evangelist Full Gospel Fellowship, 1976—; founder, pastor Maranatha Temple, South Bend, 1981-83. Founder, pres. Women's Aglow Fellowship, Michiana, Ind., 1976-79; founder, dir. Prison Ministry-Aglow, Westville, Ind., 1976-77; founder, dir. Soup Kitchen/Care Ctr., Maranatha Temple, 1982—, Supplied Facilities for Ctr. for Homeless, 1984-87, dir. City March, 1989; mem. United Religious Community Task Force, South Bend, 1985. Author: Ministerial Ethics, 1984, Teaching Syllabus, 1985, Recruits for Christ, 1987, Teaching Syllabus, Genesis, The Beginning, 1994. Pres. In His Glorious Image, 1998. Recipient Spirit of Am. Women award J.C. Penneys, South Bend, 1988; named one of 16 Best Pastors, Charisma Mag., 1988. Home: 313 Sherwood Ave South Bend IN 46614-1869 *Life, when valued as our most treasured possession, will be held as sacred and will always be found on a lighted path to direct the way of another.*

REAMS, BERNARD DINSMORE, JR., lawyer, educator; b. Lynchburg, Va., Aug. 17, 1943; s. Bernard Dinsmore and Martha Eloise (Hickman) Reams; m. Rosemarie Bridget Boyle, Oct. 26, 1968 (dec. Oct. 1996); children: Andrew Dennet, Adriane Bevin; m. Lee Anne Oberhofer, Apr. 19, 2003. BA, Lynchburg Coll., 1965; MS, Drexel U., 1966; JD, U. Kans., 1972; PhD, St. Louis U., 1983. Bar: Kans. 1973, Mo. 1986, N.Y. 1996, Tex. 2002. Instr., asst. librarian Rutgers U., 1966-69; asst. prof. law, librarian U. Kans., Lawrence, 1969-74; mem. faculty law sch. Washington U., St. Louis, 1974-95, prof. law, 1976-95, prof. tech. mgmt., 1990-95, librarian, 1974-76, acting dean univ. libraries, 1987-88; prof. law, assoc. dean, dir. Law Libr. St. John's U. Sch. Law, Jamaica, N.Y., 1995-97, assoc. dean acad. affairs, 1997-98; prof., dir. law libr. and info. tech. St. Mary's U., San Antonio, 2000—03, prof. law, 2000. Vis. fellow Max-Planck Inst., Hamburg, 1995, 97-98, 2001; vis. prof. law Seton Hall U., 1998-2000. Author: Law For The Businessman, 1974, Reader in Law Librarianship, 1976, Federal Price and Wage Control Programs 1917-1979: Legis. Histories and Laws, 1980, Education of the Handicapped: Laws, Legislative Histories, and Administrative Documents, 1983, Internal Revenue Acts of the United States: The Revenue Act of 1954 with Legislative Histories and Congressional Documents, 1983, Congress and the Courts: A Legislative History 1978-1984, 1984, University-Industry Research Partnerships: The Major Issues in Research and Development Agreements, 1986, Deficit Control and the Gramm-Rudman-Hollings Act, 1986, The Semiconductor Chip and the Law: A Legislative History of the Semiconductor Chip Protection Act of 1984, 1986, American International Law Cases, 2d series, 1986, Technology Transfer Law: The Export Administration Acts of the U.S., 1987, Insider Trading and the Law: A Legislative History of the Insider Trading Sanctions Act, 1989, Insider Trading and Securities Fraud, 1989, The Health Care Quality Improvement Act of 1989: A Legislative History of P.L. No. 99-660, 1990, The National Organ Transplant Act of 1984: A Legislative History of P.L. No. 98-507, 1990, A Legislative History of Individuals with Disabilities Education Act, 1994, Federal Legislative Histories: An Annotated Bibliography and Index to Officially Published Sources, 1994, Electronic Contracting Law, 1996, Health Care Reform, 1994, The American Experience: Clinton and Congress, 1997, The Omnibus Anti-Crime Act, 1997, The Law of E-SIGN: A Legislative History of the Electronic Signature in Global and National Commerce Act, 2001; co-author: Segregation and the Fourteenth Amendment in the States, 1975, Historic Preservation Law: An Annotated Bibliography, 1976, Congress and the Courts: A Legislative History 1787-1977, 1978, Federal Consumer Protection Laws, Rules and Regulations, 1979, A Guide and Analytical Index to the Internal Revenue Acts of the U.S., 1909-1950, 1979, The Numerical Lists and Schedule of Volumes of the U.S. Congressional Serial Set: 73d Congress through the 96th Congress, 1984, Human Experimentation: Federal Laws, Legislative Histories, Regulations and Related Documents, 1985, American Legal Literature: A Guide to Selected Legal Resources, 1985, U.S.A. Patriot Act: A Legislative History, 2002. Bd. trustees Quincy Found. for Med. Rsch. Charitable Trust, San Francisco. Fellow Am. Bar Foun.; recipient Thornton award for excellence Lynchburg Coll., 1986, Joseph L. Andrews Bibliog. award, 1995; named to Hon. Order Ky. Cols., 1992. Mem. ABA, Am. Law Inst., ALA, Am. Soc. Law and Medicine, Nat. Health Lawyers Assn., Am. Assn. Higher Edn., Spl. Librs. Assn., Internat. Assn. Law Libr. Coll. and Univ. Attys., Order of Coif, Phi Beta Kappa, Sigma Xi, Beta Phi Mu, Phi Delta Epsilon, Kappa Delta Pi, Pi Lambda Theta. Office: St Marys U Sch Law One Camino Santa Maria San Antonio TX 78228 Office Phone: 210-431-5030. E-mail: breams@stmarytx.edu.

REAMY, MICHAELIN, marriage and family therapist, educator, consultant; b. N.Y.C., Feb. 20, 1938; d. Judson Reamy and Eleanor Stevens (McMichael) R.; m. James Donald Cowie, Aug. 29, 1959; children: Jennifer D., James J., David K., Laura S.; m. Richard Ward Stephenson, Aug. 31, 1979. B.S. with Distinction in Human Ecology, Cornell U., 1960; M.S.W., U. Ga., 1979; student of Carolyn Myss and Norm Shealy, cert. program in intuition and energy medicine. Cert. primordial sound meditation instr. with Deepak Chopra, 1996. Tchr. swimming, Conn., E. Africa, Lebanon, 1968-75; social work intern, grad. asst., Atlanta, 1978-79; dir. social services, assoc. dir. and coordinator family therapy adult treatment program Brawner Psychiat. Inst., Atlanta, 1980-82; dir. extramural tng., marriage and family therapist Atlanta Inst. Family Studies, 1982-87; Perspective Ctr. for Psychotherapy, 1988-98; Natural Color & Design, 1988—. Mem. Atlanta Com. Children, 1983-85; instr. Water Safety ARC, 1957—. Recipient DAR Citizen award, 1956; YMCA Service Award, White Plains, N.Y., 1958. Diplomate NASW; mem. Nat. Assn. Social Workers, Am. Assn. Marriage and Family Therapy (com. on supervision), Cornell U. Human Ecology Alumni Assn., Mortar Bd., Omicron Nu, Phi Kappa Phi, Phi Kappa Phi. Contbr. articles to profl. jours. Kappa Phi. Contbr. articles to profl. jours. Office: Natural Color & Design PO Box Q Menlo Park CA 94026-6218 Home: 1115 Santa Cruz Ave Menlo Park CA 94025-5002

REANEY, JAMES CRERAR, dramatist, poet, educator; b. South Easthope, Ont., Can., Sept. 1, 1926; s. James Nesbit and Elizabeth Henrietta (Crerar) R.; m. Colleen Thibaudeau, Dec. 29, 1951; children: James Stewart, Susan Alice. BA, U. Toronto, 1948, MA, 1949, PhD, 1957; DLitt, Carleton U., 1975. Asst. prof. English U. Man., Canada, 1949-60; prof. English U. Western Ont., London, Canada, 1960—. Author: Killdeer, 1960 (Massey award 1960), Poems, 1972, Colours in the Dark, 1969, Masks of Childhood, 1972, Listen to the Wind, 1972, Apple Butter and Other Plays for Children, 1973; plays include The St. Nicholas Hotel, 1975 (Chalmers award for best Can. play 1975), Sticks and Stones: The Donnellys Part I, 1973, The Donnellys Part II, 1974, Handcuffs: The Donnellys Part III, 1977, 14 Barrels from Sea to Sea, 1975, The Dismissal, 1978, Wacousta, 1980, King Whistle, 1982, I the Parade, 1983, The House by the Churchyard, 1985, Alice Through the Looking-Glass, 1994, Serinette (opera libretto), 1986, Crazy to Kill (opera libretto), Performance Poems, 1991; novels for children include: The Boy with an R on his Hand, 1963, Take the Big Picture, 1986, Box Social & Other Stories, 1996, Taptoo (opera libretto) 1999, Zamorna: The Story of Branwell Bronte (play) 1999; editor, pub.: Alphabet, 1960-70; contbr. articles to profl. jours. Decorated Order of Can. Fellow Royal Soc. Can.; mem. Playwrights Union Can., Can. Poetry League. Mem. New Democratic Party. Home: 276 Huron St London ON Canada N6A 2J9 Office: care agt David Johnston 932 Logan Ave Toronto ON Canada M4K 3E4

REAP, SISTER MARY MARGARET, college administrator; b. Carbondale, Pa., Sept. 8, 1941; d. Charles Vincent and Anna Rose (Ahern) R. BA, Marywood Coll., Scranton, Pa., 1965; MA, Assumption Coll., Worcester, Mass., 1972; PhD, Pa. State U., 1979; Doctorate (hon.), U. of Scranton, 1997, Allentown Coll., 1999. Elem. tchr. St. Ephrem's, Bklyn., 1966-67; secondary tchr. South Catholic High, Scranton, Pa., 1967-69, Maria Regina High Sch., Uniondale, N.Y., 1969-72; mem. faculty Marywood U., Scranton, Pa., 1972-86, dean, 1986-88, pres., 1988—. Tchr. Mainland China, Wuhan, 1982, Marygrove Coll., Detroit, 1979; bd. dirs. Moses Taylor Hosp., Scranton Prep. Sch., Mid-Valley Hosp.; mem. Middle States Commn. for Higher Edn., 1998—; bd. dirs. Coun. Ind. Colls., Assn. Ind. Colls. and Univs. of Pa. Contbr. articles to profl. jours. Recipient Local Chpt. Svc. award UN, 1984, Woman of Yr. award Boy Scouts Am., 1993, Humanitarian award Easter Seals, 1998, Country Club Woman of Yr., 1999; named Outstanding Alumna, Pa. State Coll. Edn., 1989. Mem. Am. Assn. Cath. Colls., Phi Delta Kappa (Northeast Woman 1986, 96, Educator of Yr. award 1990). Office: Marywood U Office of the President Scranton PA 18509-1598

REARDEN, CAROLE ANN, clinical pathologist, educator; b. Belleville, Ont., Can., June 11, 1946; d. Joseph Brady and Honora Patricia (O'Halloran) R. BSc, McGill U., 1969, MSc, MDCM, 1971. Diplomate Am. Bd. Pathology, Am. Bd. Immunohematology and Blood Banking, Am. Bd. HIstocompatibility and Immunogenetics. Resident and fellow Children's Meml. Hosp., Chgo., 1971-73; resident in pediatrics U. Calif., San Diego, 1974, resident then fellow, 1975-79, asst. prof. pathology, 1979-86, dir. histocompatability and immunogenetics lab., 1979-94, assoc. prof., 1986-92, prof., 1992—, head divsn. lab. medicine, 1989-94; dir. med. ctr. U. Calif. Thornton Hosp. Clin. Labs., San Diego, 1993—. Prin. investigator devel. monoclonal antibodies to erythroid antigens, recombinant autoantigens; dir. lab. exam. com. Am. Bd. Histocompatibility and Immunogenetics. Contbr. articles to profl. jours.; patentee autoantigen pinch. Mem. Mayor's Task Force on AIDS, San Diego, 1983. Recipient Young Investigator Rsch. award NIH, 1979; grantee U. Calif. Cancer Rsch. Coordinating Com., 1982, NIH, 1983; scholar Nat. Blood Found. Mem. Am. Soc. Investigative Pathology, Am. Soc. Hematology, Am. Assn. Blood Banks (com. organ transplantation and tissue typing 1982-87, tech. com. 13 and 14 edit. tech. manual 1996-2002). Office: U Calif San Diego Dept Pathology 0612 9500 Gilman Dr La Jolla CA 92093-0612 E-mail: arearden@ucsd.edu.

REARDON, FRANK EMOND, lawyer; b. Providence, May 22, 1953; s. J. Clarke and Dorothy (Emond) R.; m. Deborah Walsh, Sept. 30, 1978; children: Kathleen Elizabeth, Brendan Francis, William James, Sean Patrick. BA, Holy Cross Coll., Worcester, Mass., 1975; JD, Suffolk U., 1978; MS, Harvard U., 1981. Bar: Mass. 1978, R.I. 1978, U.S. Dist. Ct. Mass. 1980, U.S. Dist. Ct. R.I. 1980, U.S. Supreme Ct. 1986. Counsel Nat. Assn. Govtl. Employment and Internat. Brotherhood Police Officers, Cranston, R.I., 1978-81; asst. gen. counsel Brigham and Women's Hosp., Boston, 1981-84; litigation counsel Risk Mgmt. Found. Harvard Med. Instns., Cambridge, Mass., 1984-87; ptnr. Hassan and Reardon, Boston, 1987—. Chmn. bd. dirs. St. Monica's Nursing Home, 1984-89, Med. Area Fed. Credit Unon, 1984-89; clk., trustee Deaconess Glover Hosp., Needham, Mass.; ethics com. Boston Children's Hosp., 1993-96. Contbr. articles to profl. jours. Chmn. fin. com. Town of Needham, Mass.; mem. pres.'s council Coll. Holy Cross, 1985—. Beuilacqua scholar, 1978. Mem. ABA, Mass. Bar Assn. (chmn. health law sect. 1987—), Assn. Trial Lawyers Am., Am. Soc. Law and Medicine (cmty. rep. children's hosp. ethics com.). Democrat. Roman Catholic. Avocations: tennis, sailing, golf, writing. Home: 44 Sargent St Needham MA 02492-3434 Office: Hassan & Reardon 535 Boylston St Boston MA 02116-3720

REARDON, JAMES G. lawyer; b. Worcester, Mass., Apr. 24, 1928. A.B., Coll. Holy Cross, 1950; LL.B., George Washington U., 1953. Bar: Mass. 1953, D.C. 1953, U.S. Dist. Ct. Mass. 1953, U.S. Dist. Ct. R.I. 1975, U.S. Ct. Appeals (1st cir.) 1980. Ptnr. Reardon & Reardon, Boston; mem. Joint Com. on Bench and Bar, 1978-79, Gov.'s Task Force on Juvenile Crime, 1980-81; bd. advisors Legis., Jud. and Constl. Officers' Compensation, 1982. Fellow Mass. Bar Found., Inc. (mem. Jud. council 1978—, defenders com., 1978—); mem. Worcester County Bar Assn. (chmn. grievance com. 1969, pres. 1970-71), Mass. Bar Assn., Bar Assn. D.C., Mass. Trial Lawyers Assn. (1st v.p. 1973-74), Mass. Acad. Trial Lawyers (pres. 1974-78). Office: 69 Beacon St Boston MA 02108-3422

REARDON, NANCY ANNE, human resource executive; b. Little Falls, N.Y., Sept. 19, 1952; d. Warren Joseph and Elizabeth Owen (Tiel) Reardon; m. Steven Jonathan Sayer, Aug. 28, 1976; children: Scott Jason, Kathryn Anne. BS in Psychology, Union Coll., Schenectady, N.Y., 1974; MS in Social Psychology, Syracuse U., 1978. With GE Co., N.Y.C., 1979-85, Avon Products Inc., N.Y.C., 1985-89, Am. Express, N.Y.C., 1989-91; sr. v.p. human resources Borden Internat., Inc., Bethel, Conn., 1991-97; sr. v.p. corp. affairs & human resources Borden Inc., Columbus, OH, 1997—. Adv. bd. mem. Catalyst, 1995. Mem. Human Resource Planning Soc. (bd. dirs. 1991-94, treas. 1992-93), N.Y. Human Resource Planners (bd. dirs., pres. 1989-91), Sr. Pers. Execs. Forum, Nat. Fgn. Trade Coun. (bd. dirs. 1995). Office: Borden Inc 180 E Broad St Columbus OH 43215-3799

REARDON, PATRICK THOMAS, reporter; b. Chgo., Nov. 22, 1949; s. David Joseph and Audrey Joanne (Thomas) Reardon; m. Catherine Shiel, Oct. 30, 1982; children: David Joseph Shiel, Sarah Catherine Shiel. BA in English, St. Louis U., 1971. Reporter, photographer Austinite/N.W. Passage, Chgo., 1972-73; reporter, editor City News Bur. Chgo., 1973-76, Suburban Trib, Chgo., 1976-81, Chgo. Tribune, 1981-91, book reviewer, 1985—, columnist, 1990—92, 2001—02, urban affairs writer, 1991-97, feature writer, 1997—. Co-author: Chicago Schools: "Worst in America", 1988, The American Millstone, 1986, Chicago Days, 1997, Christmas Presence, 2002, Hidden Presence, 2003; author: Daily Meditation (with Scripture) for Busy Dads, 1995, Starting Out: Reflections for Young People, 2000. Recipient Lisagor award, Headline Club, Chgo., 1988, 1991, 1992, 2003, Feature Writing award, Minn. Soc. Profl. Journalists, 2000. Roman Catholic. Home: 6220 N Paulina St Chicago IL 60660-1119 Office: Chgo Tribune 435 N Michigan Ave Ste 500 Chicago IL 60611-4066

REARDON, ROBERT IGNATIUS, JR., lawyer; b. N.Y.C., Nov. 28, 1945; s. Robert I. and Mildred (Lomax) R.; m. Lise Hofffman; children: Colleen Brooke, Kelly Elizabeth. BS in Econs., Boston Coll., 1967; JD, Fordham U., 1970. Bar: Conn. 1970, U.S. Dist. Ct. Conn. 1974, U.S. Ct. Mil. Appeals 1971, U.S. Ct. Appeals (2d cir.) 1974, U.S. Supreme Ct. 1974, U.S. Ct. Claims 1986. Ptnr. Shapiro & Reardon, P.C., New London, Conn., 1973-83; pres. Reardon Law Firm P.C., New London, 1983—. State trial referee Conn. Superior Ct., 1985—. Chmn. Bd. Fin. Town of Waterford, Conn., 1974-79; mem. Bd. Edn. Town of East Lyme, Conn., 1981-84; trustee Eugene O'Neill Meml. Theater, Inc., 1978-84; active Conn. Commn. Pub. Trust, 1998-2000. Served as capt. USMC, 1970-73. Mem. ABA (award of achievement young lawyers sect. 1975), ATLA (bd. dirs. 1998—), Conn. Trial Lawyers Assn. (pres. 1997-98), Conn. Bar Assn. (bd. govs. 1979-81, ho. of dels. 1975-79), New London County Bar Assn. (mem. exec. com. 1975-79). Office: 160 Hempstead St New London CT 06320-5638

REARDON, STEPHEN JAMES, JR., retired English speech educator; b. Butte, Mont., Nov. 6, 1929; s. Stephen James and Myrtle Agnes (MacKillican) R. PhB, Carroll Coll., 1952; MA in English, U. Wash., 1963. Tchr. English, speech Butte Jr. H.S., 1957-65; instr. English, speech Mont. State U., Bozeman, 1965-67; upward bound tchr. St. Michael's Coll., Colchester, Vt., summers 1968, 69; tchr. English West Jr. H.S., Butte, spring 1969, Butte H.S., Sch. Dist. No. 1, 1972-92. Speech coach Butte H.S., Sch. Dist. No. 1, 1973-85. Mem. Am. Legion Post No. 1, Butte, 1976—. With U.S. Army, 1955-57. Named Class AA Mont. Speech Coach of Yr., Mont. Forensic Educators Assn., 1978-79, 83-84, named to Hall of Fame, 1997; recipient Gold Star Excellence Tchg award Rivendell Psychiat. Ctr. and Mont. Eagle Comm., 1990-91, Golden Apple Excellence in Edn. award Butte C. of C., 1992; torchbearer in Bozeman for Winter Olympics, 2002. Mem. U.S. Judo Assn. (5th degree black belt 1999), U.S. Judo, Inc. (5th degree black belt 1999), U.S. Tomiki Aikido Black Belt Fedn. (1st degree black belt 1998), Butte Tchrs. Union Local 332, Butte Judo Club (dir. 1972-80, 82—), Butte Karate Club N.W. Tae Kwon Do Assn. (hon. black belt 1989). Democrat. Roman Catholic. Avocations: martial arts, skiing, swimming, writing. Home: 616 W Gold St Butte MT 59701-2363 E-mail: sreardonj@aol.com.

REARDON, TARA G. state legislator; b. Concord, N.H., Jan. 12, 1956; 2 children. AAS, Westbrook Coll., 1976; JD, 1989. Mem. N.H. Ho. of Reps. (dist. 23), Concord, 1996—; pvt. practice Concord. Mem. N.H. Bar Assn., Maine Bar Assn., Concord Area Home Builders. Roman Catholic. Office: NH State Legis State House Concord NH 03301

REARDON, THOMAS R. physician, medical association administrator; m. Elizabeth Reardon. MD, U. Colo., 1959. Intern Balt. City Hosp.; pvt. practice Portland, Oreg. Apptd. Congrl. Physician Payment Rev. Commn., 1986-94; mem. Pres. Commn. on Patient Rights and Quality Care. Chair of judges Portland Rose Festival Parade. With USAF, 1960-63. Mem. AMA (pres., chair bd. trustees 1997, mem. 1990—, exec. com. 1994—, sec. treas. 1994 95, vice chair bd. trustees 1995-97, hosp. med. staff sect. in ho. of dels. 1983-90, steering com.), Am. Rose Soc., Portland Rose Soc. (past pres.), Multnomah County Med. Soc. (pres. 1980-81, Disting. Svc. award 1982), Oreg. Med. Assn. (pres. 1983-84). Avocation: horticulture. Office: AMA 515 N State St Chicago IL 60610-4325

REARDON, WILLIAM J. state representative; b. Kansas City, Kans., June 24, 1941; m. Kathy Reardon. AA, Donnelly Jr. Coll.; BA, Rockhurst Coll.; MA, U. Mo. Tchr.; mem. Kans. Ho. of Reps., 1975—. Mem.: Nat. Assn. H.S. Social Studies Tchr., Quindro Dem. Club. Roman Catholic. Office: 272-W State Capitol 300 SW 10th Ave Topeka KS 66612 Home: 2206 Everett Kansas City KS 66102-2602

REARICK, ANNE, photographer, educator; BA in English with honors, U. Mass., 1982; MFA in Photography with honors, Mass. Coll. Art, 1990. Photographer, instr. photography Cambridge Sch. Weston, 1994—. One-woman shows include Dean's Gallery, MIT, Cambridge, 1997, Salle Buscaillet, Bordeaux, France, 2000, exhibited in group shows at Erector Sq. Gallery, New Haven, 1997, Conant Gallery, Groton, Mass., 1997, 1999, Photographic Resource Ctr., Boston, 1997, Tufts U., Aidekman Arts Ctr., Medford, Mass., 1997, Whistler Mus., Lowell, Mass., 1999, Galerie Vu, Paris, 1999, Boise (Idaho) Art Mus., 1999, S.E. Mus. Photography, Daytona, Fla., 2001, Soc. Contemporary Photography, Kansas City, Mo., 2001, FNAC, Paris, 2002, Photographic Ctr., Skopelos, Greece, 2002, exhibited in group shows, Represented in permanent collections St. Botolph's Club Found. Collection, Boston, S.E. Mus. Photography, Daytona, Rose Art Mus., Brandeis U., Waltham, Mass., Internat. Polaroid Collection, Cambridge, Boise Art Mus., Bibliotheque Nationale, Paris. Recipient Blanche E. Colman award, 1992, Golden Lights award, 1996; fellow, New Eng. Found. for the Arts/Mass. Cultural Coun., 1995, John Simon Guggenheim Meml. Found., 2003; grantee, Polaroid Film, 1990, Somerville Arts Coun., 1990, 1993, 1997, 2003, Janet Wu, 1993, St. Botolph's Club Found., 1995; Fulbright fellow, 1990—91. Office: Cambridge Sch Weston 45 Georgian Rd Weston MA 02493

REASON, J. PAUL, naval officer; b. Washington, Mar. 22, 1941; s. Joseph Henry and Bernice (Chism) R.; m. Dianne Lillian Fowler, June 12, 1965; children: Rebecca, Joseph. BS, U.S. Naval Acad., 1965; MS, USN Postgrad. Sch., 1970. Cert. nuclear propulsion engr. Commd. ens. USN, 1965, advanced through grades to adm., 1996; naval aide to pres. The White Ho., Washington, 1976-79; exec. officer USS Miss., 1979-81; comdg. officer USS Coontz, 1981-83, USS Bainbridge, 1983-86; comdr. Naval Base, Seattle, 1986-88, Cruiser-Destroyer Group 1, 1988-90, Naval Surface Force Atlantic, 1991-94; dep. chief naval ops. plans, policy and ops. Dept. Navy, Washington, 1994-96; comdr.-in-chief U.S. Atlantic Fleet, 1996-99; retired, 1999; v.p. Syntek, Inc., Arlington, Va., 1999-2000; pres. Metro Machine Corp., Norfolk, Va., 2000—. Decorated DSM, Legion of Merit, other mil. awards. Avocations: fishing, tennis. Address: 201 W Tazewell St Apt 319 Norfolk VA 23510-1319

REASONER, HARRY MAX, lawyer; b. San Marcos, Tex., July 15, 1939; s. Harry Edward and Joyce Majorie (Barrett) Reasoner; m. Elizabeth Macey Hodges, Apr. 15, 1963; children: Barrett Hodges, Elizabeth Macey Reasoner Stokes. BA summa cum laude in Philosophy, Rice U., 1960; JD with hons., U. Tex., 1962; postgrad., U. London, 1962—63. Bar: Tex., DC, NY. Law clk. U.S. Ct. Appeals (2d cir.), 1963—64; assoc. Vinson & Elkins, Houston, 1964—69, ptnr., 1970—, mng. ptnr., 1992—2001. Vis. prof. U. Tex. Sch. Law, 1971, Rice U., 1976, U. Houston Sch. Law, 1977; chair adv. group U.S. Dist. Ct. (so. dist.) Tex.; mem. adv. com. Supreme Ct. Tex. Author (with Charles Alan Wright): Procedure: The Handmaid of Justice, 1965. Trustee U. Tex. Law Sch. Found., Ctr. Am. and Internat. Law, Baylor Coll. Medicine; chair Tex. Higher Edn. Coordinating Bd., 1991; chair. Houston A+ Challenge, Houston, 1997—; mem. Supreme Ct. of U.S. Bd. Hist. Soc. 2000—; bd. dirs. Houston Music Hall Found. Bd., 1996—, Tex. So. Univ. Found., 2001—; mem. Tex. Supreme Ct. Hist. Soc. Bd., 1997—. Named Disting. Alumnus, U. Tex., 1997, U. Tex. Sch. Law, 1998, Rice U., 2003; recipient Professionalism award, US Court Appeals, Fifth Circuit, Am. Inns Court Found., 2004; fellow, Rotary Found., 1962—63. Fellow: Tex. Bar Found., ABA Found., Internat. Soc. Barristers, Am. Coll. Trial Lawyers, Internat. Acad. Trial Lawyers; mem.: ABA (chmn. antitrust sect. 1989—90), Am. Bd. Trial Advocates, Philos. Soc. Tex., Houston Philos. Soc., Am. Law Inst., Assn. Bar City of NY, Houston Bar Assn., Century Assn. N.Y.C., Chancellors, Cosmos Club (DC), Phi Delta Phi, Phi Beta Kappa. Office: Vinson & Elkins 2800 First City Tower 1001 Fannin St Houston TX 77002-6760 Office Phone: 713-758-2358.

REASONER, STEPHEN M. federal judge; b. 1944; BA in Econs., U. Ark., 1966, JD, 1969. Mem. firm Barret, Wheatley, Smith & Deacon, Jonesboro, Ark., 1969-88; from judge to chief judge U.S. Dist. Ct. (ea. dist.) Ark., Little Rock, 1991-98, dist. judge. Bd. dirs. U. Ark. Law Rev.; mem. judicial coun. 8th cir., 1990-93. Trustee Craighead-Jonesboro Pub. Libr., 1972—, chmn. 1984-88; bd. dirs. Jonesboro C. of C., 1981-84, Ark. IOLTA, 1987—. Abilities Unltd., 1974-81; mem. St. Marks Episcopal Ch. Vestry, 1976-79, sr. warden, 1979. With USAR, 1969-73. Mem. ABA, Am. Counsel Assn., Am. Judicature Soc., Ark. Bar Assn. (exec. com., ho. of dels. 1984-87), Craighead County Bar Assn. (pres. 1983-84). Avocation: flying. Office: Courthouse 600 W Capitol Ave Ste 560 Little Rock AR 72201-3327

REASONER, WILLIS IRL, III, lawyer; b. Hamilton, Ohio, Dec. 24, 1951; s. W. Irl Jr. and Nancy Jane (Mitchell) R.; m. Lana Jean Mayes, Apr. 19, 1975 (div. Sept. 1985); 1 child, Erick; m. Joan Marie Mogil, Dec. 30, 1985; children: Scott, Sally. BA in History, Ind. U., 1974; JD cum laude, U. S.C., 1978. Bar: Ohio 1978, U.S. Dist. Ct. (so. dist.) Ohio 1978, U.S. Dist. Ct. (no. dist.) Ohio 1979, U.S. Ct. Appeals (6th cir.) 1988, U.S. Ct. Appeals (1st cir.) 1991, U.S. Ct. Appeals (7th cir.) 1999. Assoc. Porter, Wright, Morris & Arthur, Columbus, Ohio, 1978-83; ptnr. Baker & Hostetler, Columbus, 1983-94, Habash, Reasoner & Frazier, 1994—. Mem. ABA, Ohio Bar Assn., Columbus Bar Assn. Home: 4005 Redford Ct New Albany OH 43054-9500 Office: Habash, Reasoner & Frazier 471 E Broad St Ste 800 Columbus OH 43215-3854

REATEGUI, LISA J. lawyer; b. 1966; BA magna cum laude, Princeton U., 1988; MA in Latin Am. Studies, Stanford U., 1990; JD magna cum laude, Northwestern U., 1995. Atty. Sidley Austin Brown & Wood, Chgo.,

1995—2003, ptnr., 2003—. Chmn. major gifts fund raising Princeton U.; mem. women's bd. The Field Mus., mem. young profl.'s bd. Mem.: ABA, Chgo. (Ill.) Bar Assn. Office: Sidley Austin Brown & Wood Bank One Plz 10 South Dearborn St Chicago IL 60603

REATH, GEORGE, JR., lawyer, mediator, arbitrator; b. Phila., Mar. 14, 1939; s. George and Isabel Duer (West) Reath; m. Ann B. Rowland, 1990; children from previous marriage: Eric(dec.), Amanda. BA, Williams Coll., 1961; LLB, Harvard U., 1964. Bar: Pa. 1965, U.S. Dist. Ct. (ea. dist.) Pa. 1966, U.S. Ct. Appeals (3d cir.) 1996. Assoc. Dechert Price & Rhoads, Phila., 1964-70, Brussels, 1971-74; atty. Pennwalt Corp., Phila., 1974-78, mgr. legal dept., asst. sec., 1978-87, sr. v.p. law, sec., 1987-89; sr. v.p., gen. counsel, sec. Elf Atochem N.Am., Inc. (formerly Pennwalt Corp.), Phila., 1990-92; sr. v.p., gen counsel, sec. Legal Triage Svcs., Inc., Phila., 1993-98; sr. v.p., gen. counsel, sec. Triage Mediation Svcs., Inc., Phila., 1999—. Trustee Children's Hosp., Phila., 1974—2003, sec., 1980—81, vice chmn., 1984—97, trustee emeritus, 2003; bd. mgrs. Phila. City Inst. Libr., 1974—, treas., 1981—88, pres., 1989—99; bd. dirs. Phila. Festival Theatre New Plays, 1983—94, Ctrl. Phila. Devel. Corp., 1987—93, Bach Festival Phila., 1990—98, v.p., 1992—93; bd. dirs. Citizens Crim Commn. Delaware Valley, 1st vice chmn., 1992—94, chmn., 1994—96, exec. com., 1996—; bd. trustees Episcopal Cmty. Svcs., 1999—, treas., 2000—. Mem.: ABA, Assn. Conflict Resolution, Am. Corp. Counsel Assn., Phila. Bar Assn., Pa. Bar Assn., Penn Club, Winter Harbor Yacht Club, Penllyn Club, Phi Beta Kappa. Office Phone: 215-235-7711. Personal E-mail: gr@mindspring.com. Business E-Mail: gr@triagemediation.com.

REAUGH, ORLAND H. oil industry executive; b. Hanford, Wash., June 19, 1913; s. Harry Wallace Reaugh and Anna Charlotte Magnuson; m. Ruth Verne Davis, July 8, 1941 (dec. Sept. 1999); children: Dianne Reaugh Bauman, Harry Coleman; m. Mary Ann McMillan, June 17, 2000. BSChemE, Wash. State U., 1933. Reg. profl. engr., Tex. Engr. Gulf Oil Corp., 1933-48; dist. supt. McElroy Ranch Co., Breckenridge, Tex., 1948-51; ptnr. Ibex Co., Breckenridge, 1951-54; v.p. Graridge Corp., Breckenridge, 1954-66; sr. v.p. Petroleum Corp. Tex., Breckenridge, 1966-83, States Inc., Breckenridge, 1983—2003, co-chmn., 1998—2004; sr. v.p. Breck Oper. Corp., 2004—. Mem. sch. bd. Breckenridge Ind. Sch. Dist.; trustee Breckenridge Libr. & Fine Arts Found., 1989—. Capt. USAF, 1942-46. Mem. West Central Tex. Oil and Gas Assn. (dir., v.p.), Breckenridge C. of C. (pres. 1978). Republican. Methodist. Home: 304 N Harding St Breckenridge TX 76424-3219 Office: Breck Operating Corp PO Box 911 Breckenridge TX 76424-0911

REAULO, ARTHUR ROBERT, mental health specialist, advocate; b. Troy, N.Y., May 11, 1952; s. Arthur R. Reaulo and Barbara Joyce Doyle. BA, SUNY, Albany, 1976; postgrad., Ctrl. Tex. U., 1978-80, Boston U., 1998-99. Cert. case mgr. Resident counselor Rehab. Support Svcs., Albany, 1988-91, case coord., 1991-93, sr. resident counselor, 1993-95, residential mgr., 1995-99; case mgr. Homeless and Travelers Aid Soc., Albany, 1999—. Residential mgr., cons. Rehab. Support Svcs., Albany, 1995—. Mem. Albany County Sexual Abuse Task Force, 1997—; advocate to lobby legislators to mental health issues Rehab. Support Svcs., Albany, 1988—. Mem. Internat. Assn. Psychosocial Practitioners. Democrat. Avocations: basketball, historical documentaries, watching classical movies/c-span, attending monlthy county sessions. Home: 19th house Kaine Dr Albany NY 12203-3803

REAVES, BARRY RECO, minister; b. June 25, 1951; s. Millard Ray Reaves and Gertrude E. Burney; m. Darla Gilliam, May 25, 1990 (div. Sept. 1995); children: Derrick Pace, Barry II, Roberto Vito, Renika Darla; m. Glenda Ree Reaves, June 21, 1996. Lic. min. Maranatha House of Prayer, 1999; lic. ins. MBA & TWA Assurance. Pers. specialist U.S. Army, 1971-73; letter carrier U.S. Postal Svc., Richmond and Washington, 1984-98; ins. agt. Mil. Benefit Assn., Clarksville, Tenn., 1989-90; preacher Mem. of the Ministry, 1999—. Cons. Gospel Ministry, Clarksville, 1999-2001. Composer gospel music. Avocations: reading, writing, gospel music, singing. Home: 405 Cunningham Ln Clarksville TN 37042

REAVES, CHARLES DURHAM, investment company executive, lawyer; b. Florence, S.C., June 1, 1935; s. Howard Meacham and Kathleen (Durham) R.; m. Gretchen Wuerdeman, May 4, 1963; 1 son, Mark Charles. BA magna cum laude, Furman U., 1956; LLB, U. Ala., 1961; LLM, Georgetown U., 1966; MBA, Emory U., 1981. Bar: Ala. 1961, Mass. 1967, D.C. 1970. Legal adv. to chmn. FTC, Washington, 1963-67; sec., assoc. counsel Paul Revere Life Ins. Co., Worcester, Mass., 1967-70; v.p., sec., gen. counsel Saunders Leasing System, Inc., Washington, 1970-74, Birmingham, Ala., 1974-80, sr. v.p. fin., sec., 1981-86; pres. Southeastern Asset Mgmt. Funds Trust, Memphis, 1986-93; exec. v.p., gen. counsel, chief compliance officer Longleaf Ptnrs. Funds, 1993—2002; of counsel Armstrong Allen PLLC, 2002—. Bd. dirs. ICI Mut. Ins. Co., Burlington, Vt. Bd. trustees Memphis Opera, 1993—. Capt. USAR, 1961-63. Decorated Army Commendation medal. Mem. ABA, FBA, Mass. Bar Assn., D.C. Bar Assn., Ala. Bar Assn., Tenn. Bar Assn., Ala. Assn. Corp. Counsel (pres. 1981-82), Fin. Execs. Inst. (dir. 1983-84), Rotary, The Club (Birmingham), Westwood Country Club (Vienna, Va.), Econ. Club of Memphis (dir. 1993-96, 2004), Southwind Country Club (Memphis). Office: Brinkley Plaza Ste 700 80 Monroe Ave Memphis TN 38103 E-mail: creaves@armstrongallen.com.

REAVES, KAREN JAMIL, communications educator; b. Portsmouth, Va., May 7, 1966; d. Timothy Lawrence and Berdie Davis Reaves; 1 foster child, George N Boykins. BS in internat. studies, Norfolk State U., 1991; MS in edn., Old Dominion U., 1997, MS in reading, 2003. Reading specialist Va., 2003. Tchr. Faith Acad. Sch., Norfolk, Va., 1993—2000; 4th chairperson/tchr. West Clayton Elem., Clayton County, Ga., 2000—01; dept. chair English/reading Norview Mid. Sch., Norfolk, Va., 2001—03; commn. skills specialist Dreamkeepers Acad. and JJ Roberts, Norfolk, 2003—. Cons. Let Us Present, Ports, Va., 2000—; reading specialist The Reading Pl., Ports, Va., 2003—. Mem.: Norfolk Teachers of English, Norfolk Reading Coun. Home: 806 Bold St Portsmouth VA 23701 Office Phone: 757-628-2555.

REAVES, MELVIN JUNIOR, retired small business owner; b. Benson, N.C., May 4, 1919; s. Edgar Washington and Bess Ann (Rowsey) Reaves; m. Cynthia Thomas, Nov. 18, 1937; children: Sherwood, Sharon, Dennis, Jackie. Owner Reaves Music Co., Odessa, Tex., San Angelo, Tex., House Beautiful, Odessa, Tex., Austin Piano Co., Austin P&O Inc., Seguin (Tex.) Piano Co., Mel Reaves Realty, Austin, Tex. Author: What Color Blue. Mem. C. of C., Odessa, Tex. With USN, WWII. Mem.: DAV, VFW, Am. Legion, Lions Club. Presbyterian. Home: 512 Green Valley Dr Unit A Bastrop TX 78602-6873 E-mail: melreaves@academicplanet.com.

REAVES, MICHAELA CRAWFORD, history educator; d. Alvin Clegg and Mary Henry Crawford; m. James Alan Reaves, May 21, 1988; children: David James, Katherine Rose. BA, Calif. Luth. U., 1979; MA, Calif. State U., Northridge, 1987; PhD, U. Calif., Santa Barbara, 1996. Assoc. prof. Calif. Luth. U., Thousand Oaks, Calif., 1987—. Contbr. chapters to books Wilma Pearl Mankiller; author: (periodical) Cephas Little Bard: Soldier, Pioneer, Doctor. Mem.: Org. of Am. Historians (assoc.), Am. Hist. Assn. (assoc.), Phi Kappa Phi. Roman Catholic. Avocations: reading, gardening, camping. Office: Calif Luth U 60 West Olsen Rd Thousand Oaks CA 91360 Personal E-mail: reaves@clunet.edu. E-mail: reaves@clunet.edu.

REAVES, RAY DONALD, civil engineer; b. Jacksonville, Ala., Aug. 6, 1935; s. William Ozzie and Josephine (Jackson) R.; m. Annette Baird, Dec. 18, 1959; children: Tanya Ann Walker, Ronald Ray. BS in Civil Engring., Auburn (Ala.) U., 1960; MBA, U. Utah, 1976; postgrad., U. Mo., Kansas City. Registered profl. engr., Okla.; diplomate Am. Acad. Environ. Engrs. Commd. 2d lt. USAF, 1961, advanced through grades to col., 1981; comdt. Airlift Ops. Sch., Scott AFB, Ill., 1980-82; dep. base comdr. Little Rock AFB, 1982-83; base comdr. Kunsan Air Base, Korea, 1983-84, Tinker AFB, Oklahoma City, 1984-85; dir. environ. mgr. Oklahoma City Air Logistics Ctr., Tinker AFB, 1985-89; ret. USAF, 1989; mgr. environ. engring. Oklahoma County, Oklahoma City, 1989-95, Okla. county engr., 1995—. Bus. Tech. Delegation Citizen to Citizen ambassador to Russia and Ukraine, 1992. Mem. ASCE, NSPE, Okla. Soc. Profl. Engrs. (citizen ambassador to Russia and Ukraine 1992), Midwest City C. of C., Rotary, Masons, Shriners. Avocations: golf, boating, tinkering.

REAVES, RICHARD BRUCE, music educator; s. Clarence Wyman and Jeanne Marie Reaves; m. Nancy June Johnson, Nov. 26, 1977; children: Jason Kristofor, Jasmine Elizabeth, Jenny Anna. B in Music Edn. (cum laude), Union Coll., Ky., 1977. Cert. EMT; music educator K-12 Va., vol. fire instr. Va. Asst. band dir. Jefferson HS, Shenandoah, W.Va., 1983—89; adj. prof. of brass Shepherd Coll., Shepherdstown, W.Va., 1986—94; asst. band dir. James Wood HS, Winchester, Va., 1989—91, Aylor Mid. Sch., Stephens City, Va., 1991—94; asst. condr. Loudoun Symphonic Winds, Loudoun County, Va., 1989—; band dir. Park View HS, Sterling, Va., 1994—99, Loudoun Valley HS, Purcellville, Va., 1999—. Prin. tubist Milbrook Orch., Shepherdstown, W.Va., 1986—94; condr. bass trombonist Martinsburg Jazz Orch., Martinsburg, W.Va., 1988—2004. Composer: (musical play) Mary and Joseph, 1975, (musical score) Good Woman of Setzuan, 1976, (work for piano) The Child, 1975—2003. Pres. Purcellville (Va.) Vol. Fire Co., 1983—2004. Mem.: Va. Band and Orch. Dirs. Assn. (dist. rep. 2002—04), Va. Music Educators Assn. Avocations: composing and performing music, farming, fire and rescue, coaching youth baseball. Office: Loudoun Valley HS 340 N Maple Ave Purcellville VA 20132 Office Phone: 540-338-6800. Office Fax: 540-338-6815. E-mail: rreaves@loudoun.gov.

REAVIS, HUBERT GRAY, JR., retired metal products executive; b. Winston-Salem, N.C., May 4, 1945; s. Hubert Gray and Marie (Long) R.; m. Brenda Todd, Oct. 19, 1969; children: Anna Caroline, Jennifer Rebecca. BS in Engring., N.C. State U., 1967. Metall. engr. Alumninun Co. Am., Alcoa, Tenn., 1967-73; divisional metall. engr. Aluminum Co. Am., Newburgh, Ind., 1973-79, product metall. engr. Pitts., 1979-86; quality assurance mgr. Aluminun Co. Am., Newburgh, Ind., 1986-88; tech. mgr. Aluminum Co. Am., Newburgh, Ind., 1988-96, mgr. materials devel. group, 1997—2002, sr. mgr. tech., 2002—04, ret., 2004. Patentee in field. Mem. Alumninum Co. Am. Polit. Action, Pitts., 1979-86, Newburgh, 1986—. Recipient (3) Arthur Vining Davis awards. Mem. Am. Soc. for Metals, N.C. State Alumni Loyalty Fund, Phi Kappa Phi, Theta Tau, Alpha Sigma Mu, Tau Beta Pi.

REAVLEY, THOMAS MORROW, federal judge; b. Quitman, Tex., June 21, 1921; s. Thomas Mark and Mattie (Morrow) Reavley; m. Florence Montgomery Wilson, July 24, 1943; children: Thomas Wilson, Marian, Paul Stewart, Margaret. BA, U. Tex., 1942; JD, Harvard U., 1948; LLD, Austin Coll., 1974, Southwestern U., 1977, Tex. Wesleyan, 1982; LLM, U. Va., 1983; LLD, Pepperdine U., 1993. Bar: Tex. 1948. Asst. dist. atty., Dallas, 1948—49; mem. Bell & Reavley, Nacogdoches, Tex., 1949—51; county atty. Nacogdoches, Tex., 1951; with Collins, Garrison, Renfro & Zeleskey, 1951—52; mem. Fisher, Tonahill & Reavley, Jasper, Tex., 1952—55; sec. state Tex., 1955—57; mem. Powell, Rauhut, McGinnis & Reavley, Austin, Tex., 1957—64; dist. judge Austin, Tex., 1964—68; justice Tex. Supreme Ct., Tex., 1968—77; counsel Scott & Douglass, 1977—79; judge U.S. Ct. Appeals (5th cir.), Austin, Tex., 1979—90, sr. judge, 1990—. Lectr. Baylor U. Law Sch., 1976—94; adj. prof. U. Tex. Law Sch., 1958—59, 1978—79, 1988—95; mem. Am. Bar Assn., Am Bar Found., Tex. Bar Assn, Am. Law Inst., Am. Judicature Soc. Chancellor S.W. Tex. conf. United Meth. Ch., 1972—93. Lt. USNR, 1943—45. Mem.: Masons (33 degree). Office: US Ct Appeals Homer Thornberry Judicial Bldg 903 San Jacinto Blvd Ste 434 Austin TX 78701-2450

REBACK, JOYCE ELLEN, lawyer; b. Phila., July 11, 1948; d. William and Sue (Goldstein) R.; m. Itzhak Brook, Aug. 2, 1981; children: Jonathan Zev, Sara Jennie. BA magna cum laude, Brown U., 1970; JD with honors, George Washington U., 1976. Bar: D.C. 1976, U.S. Dist. Ct. D.C. 1976, U.S. Ct. Appeals (D.C. cir.) 1976, U.S. Ct. Appeals (3d cir.) 1983, U.S. Ct. Appeals (Fed. cir.) 1985. Assoc. Fulbright & Jaworski, Washington, 1976—84, ptnr., 1984—87; legal cons. IMF, Washington, 1987—. Contbr. articles to profl. jours. Mem. ABA, D.C. Bar Assn., Phi Beta Kappa. Jewish. Office: Internat Monetary Fund 700 19th St NW Washington DC 20431-0001

REBAR, ALAN H. dean; b. Stillwater, Okla. DVM, Purdue U., 1973, PhD, 1975. Diplomate Am. Coll. Vet. Pathologists. Asst. prof. clin. pathology Purdue U., West Lafayette, Ind., 1976; assoc. dean for rsch. Purdue U. Sch. Vet. Medicine, West Lafayette, Ind., 1989—, head dept. vet. pathology, 1995—, dean, 1996—, prof. vet. clin. pathology. Recipient Award of Merit, Am. Animal Hosp. Assn., Gaines Cycle Fido award. Mem.: Am. Coll. Vet. Pathologists (diplomate). Office: Purdue U Sch Vet Medicine 1240 Lynn Hall Purdue U West Lafayette IN 47907-1240 Office Phone: 765-494-7608. Office Fax: 765-496-1261. Business E-Mail: rebara@vet.purdue.edu.*

REBAY, LUCIANO, Italian literature educator, literary critic; b. Milan, Apr. 23, 1928; came to U.S., 1955; s. Angelo and Pierina (Doniselli) R.; m. Martha Virginia Krauss, Aug. 2, 1952; children: Alexandra, Ilaria. Maturita classica Liceo Manzoni, Milan, 1946; Licence es lettres, U. Aix-en-Provence, France, 1951; PhD, Columbia U., 1960. Instr. Italian Columbia U., N.Y.C., 1957-60, asst. prof., 1960-63, assoc. prof., 1963-65, prof., 1965-73, Giuseppe Ungaretti prof. Italian lit., 1973—, chmn. Italian Dept., 1970-73; dir. Ctr. Italian Studies, 1985-88. Cons. to scholarly jours.; mem. Nat. Bd. Translators, Columbia U. Transl. Ctr. Author: Le origini della poesia di Giuseppe Ungaretti, 1962, Invitation to Italian Poetry, 1969, Alberto Moravia, 1970, Giuseppe Ungaretti, Gli scritti egiziani, 1909-1912, 1980, Montale, Clizia e l'America, 1982, Montale per amico, 1994, Montale: del dire e del non dire, 1998; editor: Giuseppe Ungaretti, Saggi e interventi, 1974, Jean Paulhan-Giuseppe Ungaretti, Correspondance, 1921-68, 1989. Guggenheim fellow, 1966-67; Am. Council Learned Socs. fellow, 1970-71; NEH fellow, 1980-81; Am. Philos. Soc. research grantee, 1970, 75 Mem. MLA, Am. Assn. Tchrs. of Italian, Associazione Internazionale per gli Studi di Lingua e Letteratura Italiana

REBEIZ, CONSTANTIN A. plant biochemist, educator, lab administrator; b. Beirut, July 11, 1936; arrived in U.S., 1969, naturalized, 1975; s. Anis C. and Valentine A. (Choueyri) Rebeiz; m. Conness Carole Louise, Aug. 18, 1962; children: Paul A., Natalie, Mark J. BS, Am. U., Beirut, 1959; MS, U. Calif., Davis, 1960, PhD, 1965. Dir. dept. biol. scis. Agrl. Rsch. Inst., Beirut, 1965-69; rsch. assoc. biology U. Calif., Davis, 1969-71; assoc. prof. biochemical plant physiology U. Ill., Urbana-Champaign, 1972—76, prof., 1976—, dir. Lab. Plant Biochemistry and Photobiology, 1973—. Adj. prof. U. Limerick, Ireland, 2003. Contbr. articles to profl. jours. Named one of 100 Outstanding Innovators, Sci. Digest, 1984—85; recipient Beckman Rsch. award, 1982, 1985, Funk award, 1985, Sr. Rsch. award, U. Ill., 1994, Presdl. Green Chemistry Challenge award, 1999, Outstanding Sci. Achievement award, Faculty of Agrl. and Food Sci., Am. U. Beirut, 2002; grantee John P. Trebellas Rsch. Endowment, 1986, C.A. and C.C. Rebeiz Endowment for basic rsch., 2000. Mem.: AAAS, Lebanese Assn. Advancement Scis. (mem. exec. com. 1967—69), Am. Soc. Photobiology, Am. Soc. for Biochemistry and Molecular Biology, Am. Soc. Plant Physiologists. Achievements include research in pathway of chlorophyll biosynthesis; chloroplast development; bioengineering of photosynthetic reactors; first to biosynthesis of chlorophyll in vitro; duplication of greening process of plants in test tube; development of demonstration of operation of multibranched chlorophyll biosynthetic pathway in nature; formulation of a blue-print chloroplast bioengineering in green plants aimed at improving plant productivity; formulation and design of laser herbicides, insecticides and cancer chemotherapeutic agents. Home: 301 W Pennsylvania Ave Urbana IL 61801-4918 Office: U Ill 240A Pabl Urbana IL 61801 Office Phone: 217-333-1968. Business E-Mail: crebeiz@uiuc.edu. *Meaningful scientific discoveries are those that help humans achieve a better understanding of themselves, of their environment or of the universe at large, as well as those that contribute to the betterment of the human spiritual, psychological and physical condition.*

REBEK, JULIUS, JR., chemistry educator, consultant; b. Beregszasz, Hungary, Apr. 11, 1944; came to U.S., 1949; s. Julius and Eva (Racz) R.; divorced; children: Eva Louise, Anna Elizabeth. BA, U. Kans., 1966; PhD, MIT, 1970. Asst. prof. chemistry UCLA, 1970-76; assoc. prof. U. Pitts., 1976-80, prof., 1980-89, MIT, Cambridge, 1989-96; dir. Skaggs Inst. for Chem. Biol. Scripps Rsch. Inst., 1996—. Cons. Cubist, Inc., Cambridge, Mass., Darwin, Seattle. Contbr. over 150 articles to rsch. publs. NSF fellow 1967-70, A. P. Sloane fellow, 1977, A. V. Humboldt fellow, 1981, Guggenheim fellow, 1986; recipient James Flack Norris award in physical chemistry, 1997. Fellow Am. Acad. Arts and Sci.; mem. Am. Chem. Soc. (A.C. Cope scholar 1991), Nat. Acad. Sci. Achievements include discoveries in reaction mechanisms, molecular recognition and a self-replicating system. Office: Scripps Rsch Inst 10550 N Torrey Pines Rd La Jolla CA 92037-1000

REBELL, ARTHUR L. corporate financial executive; Past prof., mergers & acquisitions Stern Grad. Sch. Bus., NYU; various positions Schroder Wertheim & Co., N.Y.C.; mng. dir. High View Cap. Corp., Strategic Mgmt. Co., LLC, N.Y.C., 1997—98; sr. v.p., chief investment officer Loews Corp., N.Y.C., 1998—. Office: Loews Corp 667 Madison Ave New York NY 10021-8087

REBENACK, JOHN HENRY, retired librarian; b. Wilkinsburg, Pa., Feb. 10, 1918; s. Charles Lewis and Carrie (Fielding) R.; m. Dorothy Merle Treat, Oct. 31, 1942 (dec. Apr. 1971); children: Charles Edwin, Christine (Mrs. Clair N. Hayes III); m. Frances Strabley Krieger, May 6, 1972. AB, U. Pitts., 1942; BS in L.S, Carnegie Library Sch., 1947. Reference asst. Carnegie Library, Pitts., 1947-50; librarian Salem (Ohio) Pub. Library, 1950-53, Elyria (Ohio) Library, 1953-57; asst. librarian Akron (Ohio) Public Library, 1957-65, asso. librarian, 1965-67, librarian-dir., 1967-80. Dir. U.S. Book Exchange, Inc., 1972 Mem. United Community Council, Citizens' Com. Pub. Welfare, 1965-66, chmn. group work and recreation div., 1963-66, v.p., 1967-68, pres. conf. of execs., 1975-76; mem. steering com., planning div. United Way; mem. Akron Mayor's Task Force on Human Relations, 1962; mem. library com. President's Com. on Employment of Handicapped, 1967-80, chmn., 1973-80, mem. sch. library manpower adv. com., 1967-73; mem. coll. adv. com. U. Akron, 1972-85; mem. adv. council on fed. programs State Library of Ohio, 1975-79; Bd. visitors Grad. Sch. Library and Info. Sci., U. Pitts., 1968-74; mem. exec. bd. Gt. Trail council Boy Scouts Am., 1977-80; bd. dirs. Summit County unit Am. Cancer Soc., 1976—, pres., 1979-81; bd. dirs. Ohio div., 1981-91, chmn. pub. info. com., 1989-90, exec. com. 1988-91. With AUS, 1942-45. Recipient Newton D. Baker citation, 1968 Mem. ALA (chmn. personnel adminstrv. sect. 1966-67, chmn. bldgs. and equipment sect. 1971-73, chmn. legislation assembly 1976-77), Ohio Library Assn. (exec. bd. 1957-60, chmn. adult edn. round table 1963, chmn. legis. com. 1965-66, 70-72, 76-80, pres. 1966-67, Librarian of Year 1979, named to Hall of Fame 1989), Ohio Library Found. (privileged mem. 1980, privileged dir. 1988—), Carnegie Library Sch. Assn. (pres. 1961-63), U. Pitts. Grad. Sch. Library and Info. Sci. Alumni Assn. (exec. com. 1978-79, Disting. Alumnus award 1980), Am. Assn. UN (v.p. Akron chpt. 1960), Kiwanis Internat. Found. (Tablet of Honor 1997, George F. Hixson fellow 1998), Beta Phi Mu. Clubs: Torch (pres. 1968-69), Kiwanis (pres. Akron 1978-79). Congregationalist. Home: 2095 Brookshire Rd Akron OH 44313-5323

REBER, CALVIN HENRY, theological studies educator, minister; b. Lebanon, Pa., Apr. 30, 1915; s. Calvin Henry Reber and Stella Elizabeth Mease; m. Audrie Eleanora Fox, June 6, 1939 (dec. Dec. 1987); children: Vera Blinn, James. BA, Lebanon Valley Coll., 1936, DD, 1959; MDiv, United Theol. Sem., Dayton, Ohio, 1939; PhD, Columbia U., 1958. Ordained to ministry Meth. Ch., 1939. Missionary to China, United Brethren Ch., Hong Kong, 1939-41; pastor Evang.-United Brethren Ch., Palmyra, Pa., 1942-46, Missionary to China, Canton, 1946-48; assoc. exec. sec. Kwangtung Synod Ch. of Christ, Canton, 1948-51; mission prof. United Theol. Sem., 1951-83, adj. faculty, 1983-88. Vis. prof. Chung Chi Coll., Chinese U. Hong Kong, 1970-71. Author: Renewal Thru Mission, 1966; editor Telescore Messenger, 1990-94. Fellow Am. Assn. Theol. Schs., 1973. Mem. Assn. Profs. of Missions, Ea. Pa. Conf. of United Meth. Chs. Democrat. Avocations: photography, travel. Home: 248 Village Sq Chambersburg PA 17201-4000

REBER, DAVID JAMES, lawyer; b. Las Vegas, Nev., Mar. 1, 1944; s. James Rice and Helen Ruth (Cusick) R.; m. Jacqueline Yee, Aug. 31, 1968; children: Emily, Brad, Cecily. BA, Occidental Coll., L.A., 1965; JD, Harvard U., 1968. Bar: Calif. 1969, Hawaii 1975, U.S. Dist. Ct. Hawaii, U.S. Ct. Appeals (9th cir.), U.S. Supreme Ct. Asst. prof. law U. Iowa, Iowa City, 1968-70; assoc. Sheppard Mullin Richter & Hampton, L.A., 1970-75, Goodsill Anderson Quinn & Stifel, Honolulu, 1975-76, ptnr., 1976—. Bd. dirs. Enterprise Honolulu; bd. dirs., pres. Legal Aid Soc. Hawaii. Mem. ABA (bus. and pub. utilities sects.), Hawaii Bar Assn. Avocations: golf, tennis, softball, travel. Office: Goodsill Anderson Et Al 1099 Alakea St Ste 1800 Honolulu HI 96813-4511 Office Phone: 808-547-5611. E-mail: dreber@goodsill.com.

REBERT, JEPHREY LEE, transportation planner, musician; b. Carlisle, Pa., June 10, 1959; s. John Alton and Mary Anna (Feeman) R. BS, Pa. State U., 1982. Residential appraiser County of York, Pa., 1984-85; phys. and environ. planner York County Planning Commn., 1985-87, transp. planner, 1987-93, sr. transp. planner, 1993—. Musician, prodr.: audiotape Peace of Mind (Loose Cannons), 1995; musician: (CD) Colonial Pagoda (Namaste), 1997. Alumni mem. Pa. State Blue Band; treas., bd. dirs. Ctr. for Ind. Living Opportunities. Mem.: Inst. Transp. Engrs., Am. Planning Assn., Victory Athletic Assn., Phi Mu Alpha Sinphonia (Alpha Zeta chpt., alumnus). Avocations: anthropology, racquet sports, coin collecting/numismatics. Home: 59 N Lehman St York PA 17403-1116 Office: York County Planning Commn 100 W Market St York PA 17401-1332

REBHUN, JOSEPH, allergist, immunologist, medical educator; b. Przemysl, Poland, Oct. 7, 1921; came to U.S., 1950; s. Baruch and Serel R.; m. Maria Birkenhejm, Aug. 10, 1945; children: Lillian Friedland, Richard B.R., Donald. MD, U. Innsbruck, Austria, 1950; MS in Medicine, Northwestern U., 1954. Diplomate Am. Bd. Allergy and Immunology. Intern Barnert Meml. Hosp., Patterson, N.J.; resident in internal medicine Tompkins County Meml. Hosp. and Cornell U., N.Y., 1951-52; fellow in allergy Northwestern U. Med. Sch./Children's Meml. Hosp., Chgo., 1952-54; fellow instr. Northwestern U. Med. Sch., 1954; asst. clin. prof. medicine Loma Linda U., 1957-93; clin. prof. medicine U. So. Calif., L.A., 1965-91, ret., 1998. Chief allergy Chgo. Eye, Ear, Nose and Throat Hosp., 1953-55; cons. Pacific State Hosp., Spadra Pomona Valley Cmty. Hosp., Pomona Casa Colina Hosp. Author: SOS, 1946, The Cry of Democracy for Help, God and Man in Two Worlds, 1985, The Embers of Michael, 1993, Crisis of Morality and Reaction to the Holocaust, 1998, Leap to Life: Triumph Over Nazi Evil, 2000; contbr. numerous articles to med. jours. Pres. Am. Congress Jews from Poland, 1969-70. Capt., U.S. Mil., San Francisco. Recipient honors City and County of L.A., L.A. Office Dist. Atty., Senate of State of Calif., all 1985. Fellow Am. Acad. Allergy (rsch. coun. 1960-65), Am. Coll. Allergy, Assn. Clin. Allergy and Immunology; mem. West Coast Allergy Soc., Calif. Allergy Assn., L.A. Soc. Allergy, L.A. Med. Assn., Calif. Med. Assn. E-mail: joerebhun@aol.com.

REBOLLO-LOPEZ, FRANCISCO, state supreme court justice; Justice Supreme Ct. of Puerto Rico, San Juan, 1992—. Office: Supreme Court PO Box 2392 San Juan PR 00902-2392

REBSTOCK, THEODORE LYNN, chemist, educator, retired research scientist; b. Elkhart, Ind., June 24, 1925; s. Adolph Rebstock and Redna Dunkelberger; m. Barbara Jean Lee, Nov. 30, 1957; children: David Lynn, Donald Lee. BA, North Crtl. Coll., Naperville, Ill., 1949; MS, Mich. State U., 1951, PhD, 1956. Instr. rsch. Mich. State U., East Lansing, 1951—56, asst. prof. agrl. chemistry, 1956—59, vis. prof., 1965; assoc. prof. chemistry Westmar Coll., Le Mars, Iowa, 1959—66, prof. chemistry, 1966—83, chmn. chemistry dept., 1963—83; mgr. R&D Lab. Harkers, Inc., Le Mars, Iowa, 1984—90; ret., 1990. Dir. divsn. natural scis. Westmar Coll., Le Mars, Iowa, 1970. Contbr. articles to profl. jours. Fellow: AAAS; mem.: Am. Chem. Soc., Kiwanis Club (pres. 1993), Sigma Xi. Methodist. Avocations: golf, bowling, gardening, woodworking. Home: 1026 Sixth Ave SE Le Mars IA 51031

REBUELTA, AVELINO LUIS, public administration educator; b. June 22, 1944; MPA, Am. U., Washington, 1982; M in Ednl. Adminstrn., U. Tex., Edinburg, 1999. Prof. Universidad Nacional Autonoma De Mexico, Mexico

City, 1962—, Instituto Politecnico Nacional, Mexico City, 1962—, Universidad Pedagogica Nacional, Mexico City, 1982—. Home: 701 Hibiscus Ave Apt 5 Mcallen TX 78501-1858 Office Phone: 956-630-6417. E-mail: al.rebuelta@hotmail.com.

RECANATI, DINA, artist; b. Cairo, Jan. 15, 1928; Student with Jose de Creft, Art Students League, N.Y.C., 1959—62. Represented by Julie M. Gallery, Tel Aviv. Exhibitions include Julie M Gallery, Tel Aviv, Israel, 1981—84, Jewish Mus. Sculpture Garden, NY, 1981—84, Am-Israel Cultural Found., 1984, Hebrew Coll., Boston, 1985, Julie M. Basel Art Fair, 1986, Bklyn. Mus., 1988, Mus. Contemporary Art, Ramat Gan, Israel, 1989, Barbican Art Gallery, London, 1990, Berlin Shafir Gallery, NY, 1990, Tel Aviv Mus. Art, 2001; artist (prin. works) Israel Mus. Jerusalem, Tel Aviv Mus., Ben Gurion Airport, Tel Aviv, Tel Aviv U., Israel, Jewish Mus., N.Y., Herzliya Mus., Continental Grain Collection, N.Y., Israel Embassy, Wash.; prin. works include Hudson Valley, N.Y., NYU, Artomi Fields Sculpture Pk., Hudson Valley, N.Y., Represented in permanent collections Gate (bronze), Ministry of Transportation, Israel, Gates (spl. bronze edit.), Am.-Israel Cultural Found., N.Y., Israel Chancellery, Wash., President's Garden Collection, Jerusalem, Beit Ariella Public Library, Tel Aviv, Weizmann Inst. Sci., Rehovot, Israel; (bibliography) Recent Works by Dina Recanati, 2001, Dina Recanati, From the Artists' Notebook, 2001; contbr. pubs. to Artist's Notebook, Gordon Galleries, Israel, 1975, Tel Aviv Mus. Art, 2001. Recipient Knickerbocker award, Nat. Arts Club, 1961, King Solomon award, Am.-Israel Found., 1977, Louise Waterman Wise award, Am. Jewish Congress, 1976. Address: 136 Grand St #6E New York NY 10013-3127

RECCHI, MARK, professional hockey player; b. Kamloops, BC, Can., Feb. 1, 1968; Right wing Pitts. Penguins, 1988—92, Phila. Flyers, 1992—95, Montreal Canadiens, 1995—99, Phila. Flyers, 1999—2004, Pitts. Penguins, 2004—. Named Most Valuable Player, All-Star Game, 1997; named to NHL All-Star Game, 1991, 1993, 1994, 1997—2000. Achievements include mem. of Stanley Cup Championship Teams, 1991, 1992. Office: c/o Pittsburgh Penguins Mellon Arena 1 Chatam Center Pittsburgh PA 15219

RECENDEZ, ELIJIO MARCO, personal care industry executive, small business owner; s. Remijio and Manuella Recendez; life ptnr. Richard J. Lampton B, U. So. Calif., 1983. Lic. cosmetologist Calif. St. stylist Joseph Martin, Beverly Hills, Calif., 1980—; image counsultat Elijio Salon And Spa Inc., Santa Monica, Calif., 1986—. Colorist Matrix Internat., L.A., 1990—; bus. advisor Santa Monica Coll., 1999—2003. Recipient award of excellence, Cosmetology for United Latinos, 1979. Mem.: So. Calif. Cosmetology Assn. (10 Years of Excellence award). Avocations: travel, walking, hiking, jet skiing. Office: Elijio Salon And Spa Inc 1620 26th St Ste 1005 N Santa Monica CA 90404 E-mail: elijiosalon @aol.com.

RECH, LINDSAY FAITH, writer; b. Phila., Pa., Mar. 30, 1978; d. Ivan Blaine and Hillary-Sue Resnick; m. Scott Rech, Oct. 21, 2000. BFA in Theater and English summa cum laude, Rider U., 2000. Writing tutor Rider U., Lawrenceville, NJ, 2000; columnist Pennington (NJ) Post, 2000—01; freelance reporter, theater critic Times Pub. Newspapers, Inc., Yardley, Pa., 2000, asst. editor, 2000—02; author Red Dress Ink, N.Y.C., 2003—. Spkr. Northampton Writers Group, Richboro, Pa., 2003. Columnist: A Different Voice, 2000—01; author: Losing It, 2003, Joyride, 2004. Acad. achievement scholar, presdl. scholar, Rider U., 1996—2000, Clayton Family scholar, 1997—2000. Mem.: Authors Guild, Phi Beta Kappa, Sigma Tau Delta, Alpha Lambda Delta. Jewish. Avocations: 1980s pop culture, vegetarian cooking, travel. E-mail: lindsayfaithrech@yahoo.com.

RECHARD, PAUL ALBERT, retired civil engineering company executive, consultant; b. Laramie, Wyo., June 4, 1927; s. Ottis H. and Mary R. (Bird) R.; m. Mary Lou Roper, June 26, 1949; children: Robert Paul, Karen Ann. BS, U. Wyo., 1948, MS, 1949, CE, 1955. Registered land surveyor, Wyo.; registered profl. engr., Wyo.; cert. profl. hydrologist Am. Inst. Hydrology. Hydraulic engr. U.S. Bur. Reclamation, Cody, Wyo. and Billings, Mont., 1949-54; dir. water resources Natural Resource Bd., Cheyenne, Wyo., 1954-58; prin. hydraulic engr. Upper Colorado River Commn., Salt Lake City, 1958-64; dir. Water Resources Rsch. Inst. U. Wyo., Laramie, 1964-81, mem. faculty dept. civil engring., 1964-82, prof., 1964-82; pres. Western Water Cons., Laramie, 1980-2001, Hydrology Assocs., Laramie, 1978-80; ret. Western Water Consults., Inc., 2001. Owner Paul A. Rechard, P.E., Laramie, 1964-1978, 2001-. Editor: Compacts, Treaties and Court Decrees Affecting Wyoming Water, 1956; contbr. articles to tech. publs. Pres., Thayer Sch. PTA, Laramie, 1965; mem. Laramie City Planning Commn., 1974-80. Served with USNR, 1945-46. Recipient Wyo. Eminent Engr. award Tau Beta Pi, 1993; named Disting. Alumnus U. Wyo., 1998; named Outstanding Engr. Wyo. Engring. Soc., 1999. Fellow ASCE (life mem., pres. Wyo. sect. 1968); mem. NSPE (life), Am. Geophys. Union, Wyo. Engring. Soc. (pres. 1976, hon.), U.S. Com. on Irrigation and Drainage, Lions (pres. Laramie 1968), Masons, Sigma Xi (pres. Wyo. chpt. 1973), Phi Kappa Phi (pres. Wyo. chpt. 1969), Gamma Sigma Delta, Sigma Tau (pres. Wyo. chpt. 1948, selected Wyo. Eminent Engr. 1993). Republican. Presbyterian. Home and Office: 316 Stuart St Laramie WY 82070-4866 Office Phone: 307-745-7477. Personal E-mail: prechard@msn.com. E-mail: prechard@wwcengineering.com.

RECHCIGL, JACK EDWARD, soil and environmental sciences educator; b. Washington, Feb. 27, 1960; s. Miloslav and Eva (Edwards) R.; m. Nancy Ann Palko, Sept. 30, 1983; children: Gregory John, Kevin Thomas, Lindsey Nicole. BS, U. Del., 1982; MS, Va. Poly. Inst. and State U., 1983, PhD, 1986. Asst. prof. soil sci. U. Fla. Agrl. Rsch. and Edn. Ctr., Ona, 1986-91, assoc. prof. soil and environ. scis., 1991-96, prof. soil and environ. scis., 1996—; assoc. dir. Gulf Coast Rsch. and Edn. Ctr., U. Fla., Bradenton, 2000-01, dir., 2001—. Hon. prof. Czech Agrl. U., Prague, 1999. Editor: Soil Amendments and Environmental Quality, 1995, Soil Amendments: Impact on Biotic Systems, 1995, Use of By-Products and Wastes in Agriculture, 1997, Environmentally Safe Approaches to Crop Disease Control, 1997, Biological and Biotechnological Approaches to Insect Pest Management, 1999, Environmentally Safe Approaches to Insect Pest Management, 1999; assoc. editor: Jour. Environ. Quality, 1994-97, Soil and Crop Science Society of Florida, 1999; editor-in-chief: (book series) Agriculture and Environment, 1999—; contbr. chpts. to books, articles to Environ. Quality, Soil Sci., Soil Fertility, Water Quality. Recipient rsch. achievement award U. Fla., 1991, Rsch. Found. Professorship, 1999—, U. Del. Disting. Alumni award, 1999; rsch grantee TVA, 1984-86, Allied Signal, 1987—, So. Fla. Water Mgmt. Dist., 1987-90, 1999—, Fla. Inst. Phosphate Rsch., 1990—, USDA, 1992—. Fellow Am. Soc. Agronomy, Soil Sci. Soc. Am.; mem. Soil Sci. Soc. Am., Sigma Xi, Gamma Beta Phi, Gamma Sigma Delta, Phi Sigma. Achievements include research leading to the reduction of fertilizer recommendations in Florida, thereby helping to improve water quality; utilization of industrial organic and inorganic wastes (ex. phosphogypsum and granular biosolids) as potential fertilizers in agriculture. Home: 13511 4th Plz E Bradenton FL 34212-9682 Office: U Fla Gulf Coast Rsch and Edn Ctr 5007 60th St E Bradenton FL 34203-9511 E-mail: rechcigl@mail.ifas.ufl.edu.

RECHLER, SCOTT, real estate company executive; married; 2 children. Grad., Clark U.; M in Fin., NYU. Joined Reckson Assocs. Realty Corp., Melville, NY, 1989—, pres., CEO, 2003—. Chmn. capital campaign com., bd. dirs. L.I. Children's Mus. Mem.: Nat. Assn. Real Estate Investment Trusts (bd. govs.). Office: Reckson Assocs Realty Corp 225 Broadhollow Rd Melville NY 11747-4833*

RECHT, ARTHUR, former state supreme court justice; b. Feb. 4, 1938; m. Karen Markham, June 10, 1962; children: Jason Markham, Judd Samuel. BA in Polit. Sci., U. Pitts., 1959; JD, W.Va. U., 1962. Ptnr. Schrader, Miller, Stamp & Recht, Wheeling, W.Va., 1962—81; judge 1st Jud. Cir., Hancock, Brooke and Ohio Counties, W.Va., 1981—83; ptnr. Recht & Johnson, Wheeling, 1984—87, Volk, Frankovich, Anetakis, Recht, Robertson & Hellerstedt, Wheeling, 1987—93, Schrader, Recht, Byrd, Companion & Gurley, Wheeling, 1993—95; justice W.Va. Supreme Ct. Appeals, Charleston, 1995—96; judge Ohio County Cir. Ct., Wheeling, 1996—. Asst. solicitor City of Wheeling, 1963—64; chair com. legal ethics West Va. State Bar, 1985—91; mem. Gov.'s Com. Selection of Jud. Candidates for Circuit Ct., 1990—95. Active Wheeling Human Rights Commn., 1974—79; pres. Police Civil Svc. Commn., Wheeling, 1984—91. Named West Virginian of Yr., Sunday Gazette Mail, 1982, Woodland Scholar Inst., 1986; recipient cert. of merit, W.Va. State Bar, 1991. Home: 30 Forest Hills Dr Wheeling WV 26003-6643 Office: Ohio County Courthouse Rm 504 Wheeling WV 26003

RECHTIEN, JAMES JOSEPH, osteopath, educator; b. St. Louis, June 4, 1938; s. Joseph Elmer and Celene Margaret (LeClere) R.; m. Mary Ann Ryan, Nov. 2, 1968; children: Catherine, Matthew, Timothy. BSMetE, Purdue U., 1960; PhD, Northwestern U., Evanston, Ill., 1966; DO, Kirksville Osteopathic Coll., 1976. Diplomate Am. Bd. Osteopathic and Rehab. Medicine. Asst. metallurgist Argonne Nat. Lab., LeMont, Ill., 1966-72; asst. instr. Kirksville (Mo.) Osteopathic Coll., 1972-76; intern Detroit Osteopathic Hosp., 1976-77; pvt. practice Rogers City (Mich.) Med. Group, 1977-80; resident U. Mich., Ann Arbor, 1983-86; assoc. prof. osteopathic medicine Mich. State U., East Lansing, 1980-91, prof. osteopathic medicine, 1991—. Fellow Am. Acad. of Phys. Medicine and Rehab., Am. Osteopathic Coll. of Rehab. Medicine. Avocation: railroad history. Home: 2947 Crestwood Cir East Lansing MI 48823-6500 Office: Mich State U A434 E Free Hall East Lansing MI 48824 E-mail: rechtien@msu.edu.

RECHTIN, EBERHARDT, retired aerospace executive, retired educator; b. East Orange, N.J., Jan. 16, 1926; s. Eberhardt Carl and Ida H. (Pfarrer) R.; m. Dorothy Diane Denebrink, June 10, 1951; children: Andrea C., Nina, Julie Anne, Erica, Mark. BS, Calif. Inst. Tech., 1946, PhD cum laude, 1950. Dir. Deep Space Network, 1958-67; asst. dir. Calif. Inst. Tech. Jet Propulsion Lab., 1960-67; dir. Advanced Rsch. Projects Agy., Dept. Def., 1967-70, prin. dep. dir. def. rsch. and engring., 1970-71, asst. sec. def. for telecom., 1972-73; chief engr. Hewlett-Packard Co., Palo Alto, Calif., 1973-77; pres., CEO Aerospace Corp., El Segundo, Calif., 1977-87, pres.-emeritus, 1988; prof. U. So. Calif., 1988-94, emeritus prof., 1994—. Author: Systems Architecting. Creating & Building Complex Systems, 1991, The Art of Systems Architecture, 1997, Systems Architecting of Organizations, Why Eagles Can't Swim, 2000. Served to lt. USNR, 1943-56. Recipient maj. awards NASA, Dept. Def., USN, Disting. Alumni award Calif. Inst. Tech., 1984. Fellow AAAS, AIAA (Robert H. Goddard Astronautics award 1991), IEEE (Alexander Graham Bell award 1977), Internat. Coun. Sys. Engrs. (Pioneer award 1999); mem. Nat. Acad. Engring. (C&C prize Japan 1992), Tau Beta Pi, Eta Kappa Nu (eminent mem.). Home: 8 Aurora Dr Palos Verdes Peninsula CA 90274-4202 Personal E-mail: ebrechtin@cox.net.

RECHY, JOHN FRANCISCO, writer; b. El Paso, Tex. s. Roberto Sixto and Guadalupe (Flores) R. BA, U. Tex., El Paso; student, New Sch. Social Research. Instr. creative writing UCLA, Occidental Coll., U. So. Calif. Author: City of Night, 1963, Numbers, 1967, this Day's Death, 1969, The Vampires, 1971, The Fourth Angel, 1973, The Sexual Outlaw, 1977, Rushes, 1979, Bodies and Souls, 1983, Marilyn's Daughter, 1988, The Miraculous Day of Amalia Gómez, 1991, Our Lady of Babylon, 1996, The Coming of the Night, 1999, The Life and Adventures of Lyle Clemens, 2003; (plays) Momma As She Became-Not As She Was, 1968, Rushes, 1978, Tigers Wild, 1986; (CD-Rom) Mysteries and Desire: Exploring the Worlds of John Rechy, 2000; contbr.: short stories and articles to Tex. Observer, The Nation, Village Voice, London mag., Saturday Rev., N.Y. Times Book Rev., L.A. Times, San Francisco Chronicle Books, Washington Post Book World, Phila. Inquirer, Contemporary Fiction, Big Table, others; also anthologies Chicano Voices, Black Humor, Urban Reader, Evergreen Rev. Reader, New Am. Story, The Moderns, Rediscoveries, Men on Men, others; trans.: stories and articles for Tex. Quar., Evergreen Rev. Served with AUS. Recipient Lifetime Achievement award PEN-USA-West, 1997, Pub. Triangle's William Whitehead award for lifetime achievement in lit., 1999, Longview Found. award for short story The Fabulous Wedding of Miss Destiny, 1960; Nat. Endowment for Arts grantee, 1976. Mem. Authors Guild, Tex. Inst. Letters, PEN, Nat. Writers Union.

RECK, ANDREW JOSEPH, philosopher, retired educator; b. New Orleans, Oct. 29, 1927; s. Andrew Gervais and Katie (Mangiaracina) R.; m. Elizabeth Lassiter Torre, June 17, 1987. BA, Tulane U., 1947, MA, 1949; postgrad., U. St. Andrews, Scotland, 1952—53; PhD, Yale U., 1954; student, U. Paris, 1962, student, 1964. Instr. English U. Conn., 1949-50; instr. philosophy Yale U., 1951-52, 55-58; faculty Tulane U., 1958—2003, prof. philosophy, 1964—2003, chmn. dept., 1969-89, dir. Master Liberal Arts program, 1984—2003, ret., 2003. Thomasfest lectr. Xavier U., Cin., 1970; Suarez Lectr. Spring Hill Coll., 1971; Niebuhr lectr. Elmhurst (Ill.) Coll., 1976; vis. prof. Fordham U., 1979; vis. scholar Hastings Ctr. (N.Y.), 1981; Woodruff lectr. Emory U., 1982; Fairchild lectr. U. So. Miss., 1982, 87; Matchette Found. lectr. Cath. U. Am., 1991, 95; Sr. Scholar Inst. Humane Studies, Menlo Park, Calif., 1982; vis. scholar Poynter Ctr., Ind. U., Bloomington, 1983; Tulane U. faculty rep. to bd. adminstrs. Tulane Ednl. Fund., 1988-91. Author: Recent American Philosophy, 1964, Introduction to William James, 1967, New American Philosophers, 1968, Speculative Philosophy, 1972; co-author: Die Philosophie des 18. Jahrhunderts 1, 2004; editor: George Herbert Mead Selected Writings, 1964, 2d edit., 1981, Knowledge and Value, 1972, (with T. Horvath, T. Krittek and S. Grean) American Philosophers' Ideas of Ultimate Reality and Meaning, 1993; co-editor Ultimate Reality and Meaning, Interdisciplinary Studies in the Philosophy of Understanding, 1990-; mem. adv. editl. bd. Internat. Jour. World Peace, Trans. Charles Peirce Soc., Santayana edit. So. Jour. Philosophy, Library of Living Philosophers; editor History of Philosophy Quar., 1993-98. Served with AUS, 1953-55. Howard fellow, 1962-63, Liberty Fund grantee, 1982, Newcomb fellow, 1991-93; Fulbright scholar, 1952-53, Am. Coun. Learned Socs. grantee, 1961-62, Am. Philos. Soc. grantee, 1972, Huntington Libr. grantee, 1973, La. Ednl. Quality State Found. grantee, 1994-96, U.S. Info. Agy. grantee, Brazil, 1993. Mem.: La. Endowment for Humanities (bd. dirs. 1990—96), Internat. Soc. for Study of Human Ideas of Ultimate Reality and Meaning (bd. dirs. 1989—, treas. 2001—03, sec./treas. 2003—), Charles S. Peirce Soc. (sec.-treas. 1985—86, v.p. 1986—87, pres. 1987—88), Soc. Advancement Am. Philosophy (exec. com. 1980—82, pres.-elect 1997—98, pres. 1998—2000, exec. com. 2001—03, chair nominating com. 2002—04), Metaphys. Soc. Am. (councillor 1971—75, pres. 1977—78, program com. 1989—90, chair program com. 1995—96), Coun. for Internat. Rsch. Scholars (philosophy screening com. 1974—77), Am. Coun. Learned Socs. (Am. studies adv. com. 1972—76), So. Soc. Philosophy and Psychology (treas. 1968—71, pres. 1976—77), Southwestern Philos. Soc. (exec. com. 1965—69, v.p. 1971—72, pres. 1972—73), Am. Philos. Assn. (program com. ea. divsn. 1969, nominating com. western divsn. 1975—76, 1981—82, adv. com. to program com. ea. divsn. 1994—97, chair ad hoc com. on history 1996—), Tulane U. Emeritus Club (Outstanding Grad. of Class of 1947 award 1997), Omicron Delta Kappa, Alpha Sigma Lambda (hon. Theta chpt. of La.), Phi Beta Kappa (pres. Alpha of La. 1966—67). Home: 6125 Patton St New Orleans LA 70118-5832 E-mail: areck@cox.net.

RECKER, PATRICIA BULLION, secondary school educator; b. San Antonio, Tex., May 29, 1953; d. Richard Wood and Vera Williams Bullion; m. Steven Isadore Recker, Aug. 20, 1983; children: Noah James, Samantha Jo. AS in biology, San Antonio Coll., 1971—73; BS in biology, Southwest Tex. State U., 1973—75; MS in biology, Incarnate Word Coll., 1977—79; PhD, Bowling Green State U., 1980—82. Chemistry/biology tchr. Meml. H.S., San Antonio, 1975—77; instr. zoology Incarnate Word Coll., San Antonio, 1979—80; instr. anatomy Owens Tech. Inst., Toledo, 1983; biology tchr. Upward Bound, San Antonio, 2000—02, John Jay H.S., San Antonio, 1984—. Recipient Subaru Nat. Sci. Tchg. award, 2001. Mem.: Tex. Assn. of Biology Teachers, Nat. Sci. Tchr. Assn., Nat. Assn. Biology Teachers. Avocation: travel. Home: 112 Miller Cove La Vernia TX 78121 Office: John Jay H S 7611 Marbach Rd San Antonio TX 78227 Personal E-mail: jay187@nisd.net.

RECKER, THOMAS EDWARD, fraternal organization executive; b. Livonia, Mich., Feb. 28, 1960; s. Peter Edward and Patricia Ann (Heidenwolf) R. BA in Ednl. Psychology, U. Mich., 1982; MA in Coll. Student Personnel, Bowling Green State U., 1985. Asst. exec. dir. Grand Chpt. of Phi Sigma Kappa, Indpls., 1985-87, exec. dir., 1987-90; exec. v.p. Grand Chpt. of Phi Sigma Kappa and Phi Sigma Kappa Found., Indpls., 1990—. Mem. Am. Soc. Assn. Execs., Assn. Frat. Advisers, Frat. Execs. Assn. Office: Phi Sigma Kappa Frat 2925 E 96th St Indianapolis IN 46240-1368

RECKERS, PHILIP MERLE, accounting and business educator; b. Quincy, Ill., May 1, 1946; s. Merle Joseph and Frances Adelaide (Friye) R.; m. Patricia Anne Polchinski, May 12, 1979; children: Brian, Colleen, Ashley. BS, Quincy Coll., 1968; MBA, Washington U., St. Louis, 1972; PhD, U. Ill., 1978. Asst. prof. U. Md., College Park, 1976-80; assoc. prof. Ariz. State U., Tempe, 1980-83, prof. acctg. and bus., 1983—; dir. Sch. Accountancy, 1993—2002; dir. rsch. Ctr. for Advancing Bus. through Info. Tech., 2002—. Assoc. editor: Advances in Acctg., 1985—93, mem. editl. bd.: Auditing, 1987—2003, Behavioral Rsch. in Acctg., 1992—2002, Intl. Jour. Auditing, 1999—2004; editor: Advanes in Acctg., 1994—; author: Intermediate Accounting, 1994—, 3d edit., 2000, SAP Account Managerial Acctg., 2003; contbr. articles to profl. jours. With U.S. Army, 1970—72, Viet Nam. Recipient Am. Acctg. Assn. Innovations in Acctg. Edn. award, 2003; grantee Peat Marwick Found. auditing rsch. grantee, 1976, 1985, 1989, 1990, 1991, Ernst and Young Found. tax rsch. grantee, 1991, Am. Acctg. Assn. edn. rsch. grantee, 1982. Mem. Am. Acctg. Assn., Fedn. Schs. Accountancy (pres. 2002), Am. Inst. CPAs (mem. pre-cert. edn. exec. com.). Roman Catholic. Home: 7461 S Rita Ln 4-779 Tempe AZ 85283 Office: Ariz State U Coll Bus Sch Accountancy Ba 301D Tempe AZ 85287

RECKTENWALD, FRED WILLIAM, city financial official; b. Fremont, Ohio, Dec. 24, 1946; s. Harold Louis and Geraldine Fern (Worthington) R.; m. Elaine Marie Denman, July 3, 1982. Acct. Henry Packing Co., Perrysburg, Ohio, 1969-70, Edward R. Moyer, CPA, Bellevue, Ohio, 1970-71; ptnr. Singer and Recktenwald Acctg., Fremont, Ohio, 1971-79; compt. Shortway Bus Lines, Inc., Toledo, 1979-80; city auditor City of Fremont, 1980—. Mem. Coastal Resources Adv. Coun., 1992-93. Pres. Sandusky County Improvement Bd., Fremont, 1988-89, sec., 1990-95; chmn. Fremont Revolving Loan Fund Bd., 1989—; adv. bd. Terra Tech. Coll., Fremont, 1985-98, Vanguard Vocat. Sch., Fremont, 1988-93; fin. com. St. Joseph's Parish, Fremont, 1986-88; v.p. Terra C.C. Found. Bd., 1999-2001, pres., 2001; mem. cen. com. Sandusky County Dems., 1996—. Mem. North Ctrl. Ohio Fin. Officers (pres. 1985), Ohio Govt. Fin. Officers Assn., Govt. Fin. Officers Assn. U.S. and Can. (Fin. Reporting Achievement award 1989, 90, 91, 92, 93) Mcpl. Treas. Am., Ctrl. Cath. Boosters (trustee 1977-78, treas. 1997-2001), KC, Elks, Moose, Ft. Clinton Yacht Club, Fremont Country Club. Democrat. Roman Catholic. Avocations: bowling, golf. Office: City of Fremont 323 S Front St Fremont OH 43420-3037 E-mail: fremontauditor@ezworks.net.

RECORD, DONALD D. music educator, literature educator; b. Enid, Okla., Mar. 31, 1952; s. Joe Neil and Lois Elaine Record; m. Anna-Karin Höglund, May 1, 1976 (div. May 1981). BSc in English Edn., Phillips U., 1976; EdM, Northwestern U., 2003. Songwriter Swedish Broadcasting Co., Stockholm, 1976—80; prof. musician Tree Pub. Corp., Nashville, 1979—82, Naked Ear Music, Mendocino, Calif., 1980—90; prof. music Phillips U., Enid, Okla., 1990—99, No. Okla. Coll., Tonkawa, 1999—, prof. English Enid, 1999—. Author: Meet Don Record, 1978; singer: One More Goodbye, One More Hello, 1981; singer, songwriter: Reservation, 1977. V.p. Enid Arts and Humanities Coun., 2001. Mem.: Moose Lodge. Avocations: horseback riding, Bocce, surfing, skiing. Home: Ste 5 1510 E Broadway Enid OK 73701 Office: No Okla Coll 100 S University Ave Enid OK 73701

RECORD, PHILLIP JULIUS, journalist; b. Fort Worth, Jan. 12, 1929; s. Phillip Cross and Frances Virginia (McElwee) R.; m. Patricia Ann Edwards, Sept. 29, 1954; children: Christopher Phillip, Gregory Edwards, Timothy James. BA in Journalism, U. Notre Dame, 1950. Gen. reporter Lubbock Avalanche-Jour., Tex., 1950-54; copy editor, reporter Fort Worth Star-Telegram, 1954-67, asst. city editor, 1967-68, city editor evening edit., 1968-76, mng. editor, 1976-80, assoc. exec. editor, 1980-91, spl. asst. to pub., ombudsman, 1991-97, columnist, 1997—2001. Mem. mass comms. com. Tex. Tech. U., 1971—2000, chmn., 1990—92, bd. dirs., 1992—; journalism profl. in residence Tex. Christian U., 1999—. Mem. Friends of Ft. Worth Pub. Libr.; bd. visitors Tex. Christian U.; conciliation/arbitration bd. Cath. Diocese of Ft. Worth, 1994—, chair, 1996—, publs. adv. com., 1982—; bd. dirs. Tarrant County Mental Health Assn., 1990—95; dir. Freedom Info. Found., Tex., 1987—93; founding mem. Ft. Worth Theatre. With U.S. Army, 1950—52. Recipient Ethics award Tex. Christian U., 1991, others for reporting, photography and headline writing; named to Tex. Tech U. Mass Comms. Hall of Fame. Mem. ABA (nat. commn. on pub. understanding about law 1984-90, commn. on partnership programs 1990-93), Investigative Reporters and Editors Inc., Soc. Profl. Journalists (pres. 1983-84, bd. dirs. Found. 1980-2001, v.p. Found., 1991-94, bd. chair 1994-01, Wells Key 1991), Creative Thinking Assn., Orgn. News Ombudsmen (dir. 1994—, v.p. 1995-96, pres. 1996-97). Avocation: tennis. Home: 6144 Walla Ave Fort Worth TX 76133-3557 Office: 6144 Walla Ave Fort Worth TX 76133 *As a journalist, I strive to be a servant of the truth and a servant of the people. As a follower of Jesus, I try to live my life as he would. But, being human, I fail frequently. But I try and I care. I think that makes me OK in God's eyes.*

RECTOR, JOHN MICHAEL, association executive, lawyer; b. Seattle, Aug. 15, 1943; s. Michael Robert and Bernice Jane (Allison) R.; m. Mary Kaaren Sueta Jolly, Feb. 8, 1977 (div. 1994); m. Carmen De Ortiz, 1994; children: Christian Phillip, Ciera Rose, Zachary Ryan. BA, U. Calif., Berkeley, 1966; JD, U. Calif., Hastings, 1969; PharmD (hon.), Ark. State Bd. Pharmacy, 1991. Bar: Calif. 1970, U.S. Supreme Ct. 1974. Trial atty. civil rights divsn. Dept. Justice, 1969-71; dep. chief counsel judiciary com. U.S. Senate, 1971-73, counsel to Sen. Birch Bayh, 1971-77, chief counsel, staff dir., 1973-77; confirmed by U.S. Senate as assoc. adminstr. to Law Enforcement Assistance Adminstrn. and adminstr. of Office Juvenile Justice Dept. Justice, 1977-79; spl. counsel to U.S. Atty. Gen., 1979-80; dir. govt. affairs Nat. Assn. Retail Druggists, Washington, 1980-85; sr. v.p. govt. affairs, gen. counsel Nat. Cmty. Pharmacists Assn., 1986—. Chmn. adv. bd. Nat. Juvenile Law Ctr., 1973-77; mem. Hew panel Drug Use and Criminal Behavior, 1974-77; mem. cons. panel Nat. Commn. Protection Human Subjects of Biomed. and Behavioral Rsch., 1975-76; mem. bd. Nat. Inst. Corrections, 1977-79; chmn. U.S. Interdepartmental Coun. Juvenile Justice, 1977-79; mem. bd. com. civil rights and liberties Am. Dem. Action, 1976-80, Pres.'s Com. Mental Health-Justice Group, 1978; com. youth citizenship ABA, 1978-84; mem. Pharm. Industry Adv. Com.; exec. dir., treas. polit. action com. Nat. Pharmacists Assn., 1981—; exec. dir. Retail Druggist Legal Legis. Def. Fund, 1985—, founder, chmn. Washington Pharmacy Industry Forum; mem. numerous fed. narcotic and crime panels and coms.; owner Second Genesis, an antique and furniture restoration co. Mem. editl. bd. Managed Care Law; contbr. articles to profl. jours. Exec. com. small bus. and fin. couns. Dem. Nat. Com., 1988-92; dir. Dem. Leadership Coun.'s Network, 1989-92, bd. advisers, 1992-94, Clinton-Gore Washington Bus. adv. com.; bd. dirs. Small Bus. Legis. Coun., 1987—, sec., 1999, treas., 2000, chmn. elect, 2001, chmn., 2002; bd. dirs. Nat. Bus. Coalition for Fair Competition, 1984—. Perry E. Towne scholar, 1966-67; mem. U.S. Atty. Gen.'s Honors Program, 1968-71; recipient Children's Express Juvenile Justice award, 1981, John W. Dargavel medal, 2003, J. Leon Lascoff Meml. award, 2004. Mem. Calif. Bar Assn., Nat. Health Lawyers Assn., Am. Soc. Assn. Execs. (govt. affairs sect.), Washington Coun. Lawyers, Assn. of Former Sr. Senate Aides (exec. com.), Vinifera Wine Growers Assn. Va. (life), Health R Us, Am. League of Lobbyists, Theta Chi. Democrat. Avocations: collecting antique furniture, books and documents. Office: Nat Cmty Pharmacists Assn 205 Daingerfield Rd Alexandria VA 22314-2885

RECTOR, M. EUGENE, community pharmacist; b. Sequin, Tex., Aug. 16, 1950; m. Marcia A. Rector, May 15, 1982. AA, Blinn Coll., 1970; BS in Pharmacy, U. Tex., Austin, 1972; BA in Philosophy, U. Tex., Dallas, 1982; MS in Mgmt. and Adminstrn. Scis., 1985; PharmD, Broadmoore U., Belize City, Belize, 1998. Staff pharmacist Baylor U. Med. Ctr., Dallas, 1973-81, Presbyn. Hosp., Dallas, 1981-86; dir. pharmacy Madison St. Joseph Health Ctr., Madisonville, Tex., 1986—2001; pharmacist Walgreens #4999. Fellow Am. Coll. Apothecaries (assoc.); mem. Am. Soc. Health-Sys. Pharmacists, Tex.

Soc. Health-Sys. Pharmacists, Lions Club of Hilltop Lakes, Masons (Vickery Lodge 1351, Rogers Prairie Lodge 540 past master). Republican. Methodist. Avocations: hunting, ranching. Home: 16584 Fm 3 S Normangee TX 77871-3511 E-mail: gener@txcyber.com.

RECTOR, SUSAN DARNELL, lawyer; b. Wilmington, Del., Feb. 14, 1959; d. W. Thomas and Barbara Joan (Shafer) Darnell; m. Neil Kenyon Rector, Aug. 7, 1982. BA in Economics, Wake Forest U., Winston-Salem, N.C., 1981; JD, U. N.C., Chapel Hill, 1984. Bar: Ohio 1984. Lawyer Ohio Legislative Svc. Commn., Columbus, Ohio, 1984-87; assoc. Schottenstein, Zox & Dunn, Columbus, Ohio, 1987-93, ptnr., 1993—. Bd. trustees Firstlink, Inc., 1990-95, v.p., 1993, pres., 1994; apt. to Ohio Small Bus. and Entrepreneurship Coun., 1991-95; bd. dirs. The Wilds. Contbr. articles to profl. jours. Allocation com. United Way, Columbus, 1990-96, campaign cabinet, 1991, co-chair planning, evaluation and allocation com., 1993-94, bd. trustees, 1996—, chair health vision coun., 1996-99; trustee Columbus Zool. Park Assn., 2001—, v.p., 2002-03; chmn. devel. com., 2001-03, chmn. zoo fund, 2000; bd. dirs., sec., treas. Cmty. Rsch. Ptnrs., 2000-02. Named Harry S. Truman scholar, Truman Scholarship Found., 1979, 1 of 10 Outstanding Young Citizens, Columbus Jaycees, 1993, 1 of 40 under 40, Business (Columbus); grad. Columbus Area Leadership program; Best Lawyers in Am., 2003. Mem. ABA, Ohio Bar Assn., Columbus Bar Assn. (Cmty. Svc. award 1997), Columbus Bar Found. (trustee 1995—, pres. 2003), Women Lawyers of Franklin County, Jr. League of Columbus (bd. trustees, sec. 1989-90, 95-98, pres. 1997-98), Columbus Met. Club, Columbus Women's Network (Cmty. Leader award), Mortar Bd., Phi Beta Kappa, Omicron Delta Kappa. Home: 67 E Deshler Ave Columbus OH 43206-2655 Office: Schottenstein Zox & Dunn 250 West Street Columbus OH 43215 Office Phone: 614-462-2219. E-mail: srector@szd.com.

RECUPERO, PATRICIA RYAN, hospital administrator, psychiatrist, lawyer, health facility executive; m. Joseph Recupero. AB, SUNY, 1969; JD, Boston Coll. Law Sch., 1973; MD, Brown U., 1985. Bar: Mass. 1973, RI 1974, Fed. Bar: Dist. of Mass. 1975, Dist. of RI 1975; lic. Mass., 1989, RI, 1989, cert. Am. Bd. Psychiatry and Neurology, 1990, in Addiction Psychiatry RI, 1993, cert. in Forensic Psychiatry RI, 1994. Assoc. dir. edn./tng. Brown U. Dept. Psychiatry /Human Behavior, Providence, 1989—94; clin. instr. psychiatry Brown U. Dept. of Psychiatry/Human Behavior, 1989—91, clin. asst. prof. psychiatry, 1991—2000; asst. prof. medicine Tufts U., 1995—98; vice chair, dept. psychiatry St. Elizabeth's Med. Ctr., Boston, 1995—97, dir. clin. svcs., 1995—97, dir. residency tng. psychiatry, 1996—97; dir. managed care Butler Hosp., Providence, 1990—95, dir. alcohol/drug inpatient svcs., 1991—94, chief forensic psychiatry, 1994—95, med. dir., med. adminstrn., 1997—98, v.p. systems integration/managed care, assoc. med. dir., med. adminstrn., 1998—98, exec. v.p., 1998—98, pres., CEO, 1999—; exec. v.p. behavioral health Care New Eng., Providence, 1999—; clin. assoc. prof. psychiatry Brown U. Dept. Psychiatry/Human Behavior, 2000—. Mem. resource utilization com. Health Advantage, 1993—95; mem. contract for competency to stand trial evaluation program RI Dept. Mental Health Retardation and Hospitals, 1993—95; mem. utilization mgmt. com. Blue Chip RI, 1995—98; forensic evaluations Dept. Disabled Persons Protection Commn., 1995—; ind. med. evaluations Northwestern Ins. Co., 1995—; spl. master RI Supreme Ct., 1996; gender equity/sexual harrassment officer Brown U. Program in Medicine (Office of Women in Medicine), 1997—98; chairperson Butler Hosp. Profl. Lecture Series; mem., ho. delegates RI Bar Assn., 1976—77, mem., confidential assistance com., 1992—95; chair, bylaws revision com. RI Psychiat. Soc., 1989—90, deputy legis. rep., 1989—94, sec./treas., 1991—95, pres. elect., 1995—97, pres., 1997—99, dep. rep. to apa assembly dist. branches, 1999—2003, assembly rep., 2003—; addiction psychiatry splty. com. Am. Acad. Psychiatry and the Law, 1997—2000, edn. com., 1997—, chair, gender issues com., 1999—, geriatric psychiatry com., 2000—, counselor, 2002—, am. dir. forensic psychiat. fellowships com., 2003—; coun. on psychiatry and law corr. mem. Am. Psychiat. Assn., 1994—2002, mem. com. on quality indicators, 2000—02, chair, workgroup on cyber medicine, 2000—, assembly liaison to coun. psychiatry and law, 2000—02, guttmacher award com. mem., 2003—, task force to rev. guidelines on seclusion/restraint mem., 2003—, coun. on psychiatry and law mem., 2003—; bd. mem. Nat. Assn. Psychiat. Health Systems, 2002—, planning com. mem., 2002—, third v.p., 2003—, membership com., 2003—. Author: (articles) PTSD Substance Abuse Co-morbidity and Treatment Utilization, A Double-blind, Placebo-controlled Pilot Study of Carbamazepine for the Treatment of Alcohol Dependence, Risk Mgmt. and the Dual Diagnosis Patient, Gender and Forensic Psychiatry, The Shipper's Right to Recover Under COGSA for Damage to Containerized Cargo, Student Comment: Tax Preparation Agencies: What is Needed for the Public's Protection, Eating Pathology and Sexual Abuse, Trauma, Dissociation, Impulsivity, and Self-Mutilation Among Substance Abuse Patients, Marital Violence Victimization and Perpertration Among Women Substance Abusers, Neurosychiatry & Clin. Neuroscience, An Act to Assure Fair and Effective Utilization Rev. of Health Care Svc., Depression and Substance Abuse, Diagnosis and Treatment of Alcoholism in Women; editor: (article) Managed Care; author: (binder) Mandatory Outpatient Treatment, a Resource Document of the Am. Psychiat. Assn., (newsletter) e-Health: Enhanced Treatment or Legal Quagmire?, Women in Forensic Psychiatry, (book chpt.) The Psychology of Female Violence: Crimes Against the Body, (abstracts) Carbamazepine for Alcohol Dependence - A Pilot Study, Traumatic Exposure and PTSD Symptomatology Among Substance Abusers, Seduction: Legal and Psychol. Dilemmas, Impact of Treatment for Substance Abuse on Marital Violence, Informed Consent: Patient Perspectives of Info. Required for SSRI's, Therapy On-Line: Opportunities and Risks, Modifying Adminstrv. Procedures to Reduce Suicide Risk in Police Officers, Undue Influence: What's Psych Got To Do With It?, Psychiatry on Trial: Fact and Fantasy in the Courtroom; contbr. numerous presentations in field. Parole bd. mem. Parole Bd. State of RI, RI, 1993—98; bd. mem. RI Coalition Against Domestic Violence, 1994—95, mem., 1993—98; merit selection panel US Dist. Ct., Dist. of RI, 1998; forensic psychiatry com. on re-cert. Am. Bd.Psychiatry/Neurology, 2000—03; governor's coun. on mental health RI State, 1998—2001; corp. mem. Blue Cross/Blue Shield of RI, 1999—2003; bd. mem. Vis. Nurse Assn./Care New Eng., 1999—2003. Recipient Ann. Exemplary Psychiatrist Award, Nat. Alliance for the Mentally Ill, 2000, Teaching Recognition award, Brown U. Sch. Med., 2001; fellow, Am. Psychiatric Assn., 2003. Fellow: Am. Psychiat. Assn.; mem.: Internat. Acad. Law and Mental Health, RI Medial Women's Assn., RI Med. Soc., Assn. of Women Psychiatrists, Mental Health Assn. of RI, Alliance for the Mentally Ill. Office: Butler Hosp 345 Blackstone Blvd Providence RI 02906

RECUPERO-FAIELLA, ANNA ANTONIETTA, poet; b. Boston, Nov. 22, 1966; d. Vittorio and Anna Maria Recupero; m. Mark Stephan James Faiella, May 30, 1998. Cert. early edn., Wheelock Coll. Tchr. N. Bennet St. Sch., Boston, 1981-87; clk. Post Office, Boston, 1988—. Art coord. N. Bennett Sch., Boston, 1985-87; acting extra films and commls. Author: (poems) A View From the Edge, 1992, Dusting Off Dreams, 1994, Echoes From the Silence, 1995, Treasure the Moment, 1996, Whispers, 1996, Sensations, 1997; co-author: (poems) Distinguished Poets of Amercia, 1993, Outstanding Poets of 1994, 1994, Treasured Poems of America, 1995, Treasured Poems of America, 1996, Best Poems of the 90's, 1996, Best Poems of '97, 1997, Ten Years of Excellence, 1998. Co-chair Wall of Tolerance, 2003. Recipient Editors Choice award, Nat. Libr. Poetry, 1993—97, semifinalist Discover G'Vanni's 500th Art Awd., 1992, semifinalist Internat. Soc. Photography award, 2003, semifinalist Shadows of Tomorrow award, Internat. Soc. Photography, 2003, Internat. Writer Yr. award, Internat. Biographical Ctr., 2003, Outstanding Writer award, Internat. Soc. Poetry, 2004; scholar Mass. State Gen. Scholarship, 1985. Mem. Internat. Soc. Poets (disting. mem. adv. com. 1994), Nat. Mus. Women Arts, Point of Pines Assn. Democrat. Roman Catholic. Avocations: painting, writing poems, travel, nascar racing, comedy. Home: 40 Bickford Ave Revere MA 02151-1723

REDA, JAMES FRANCIS, business consultant; b. Bklyn., Aug. 27, 1953; s. Ralph Charles and Evelyn Susan (Buchan) R.; m. Susan Rosemary Hisnay, June 10, 1982 (div. Oct. 1993); 1 child, Jennifer Beryl; m. Deborah Linda Grannis, July 4, 1994; children: Jennifer Rose, James Francis Jr., Linda Victoria. BS in Indsl. Engring., Columbia U., 1981; MS in Mgmt., MIT, 1983. 1st class FCC lic. Indsl. engr. IBM Corp., Bklyn., 1980, East Fishkill, NY, 1981; process engr. Hewlett-Packard Co., Andover, Mass., 1982; bus. mgr. Wang Labs., Inc., Lowell, Mass., 1983-85; sr. product mgr. Honeywell Fed. Systems, Inc., McLean, Va., 1985-87; assoc. cons. Touche Ross & Co., N.Y.C., 1987; v.p., cons. The Bachelder Group, N.Y.C., 1987-96; cons. Buck Cons., N.Y.C., 1996-97, Hewitt Assocs., Atlanta, 1997-99; sr. mgr. Arthur Andersen LLP, Atlanta, 1999-2000; prin., regional practice leader Buck Cons., Inc., Atlanta, 2000—04; mng. dir. James F. Reda & Assocs., LLC, N.Y.C., 2004—. Campaign advisor Friends of Vincent Gentile, Bklyn., 1994. With USN, 1971-77; lt. comdr. USCGR. Mem. Internat. Inst. Indsl. Engrs. (sr. mem., chpt. pres. 1979-81, Walter Rautenstrauch award 1981), Res. Officers Assn. (Top Grad. award 1983), Am. Compensation Assn., N.Y. Soc. Security Analysts (mem. com. corp. governance), Assn. for Investment Mgmt. Rsch., Internat. Assn. Fin. Engring., U.S. Naval Inst., Armed Forces Comms. Assn., Ret. Officers Assn., Nat. Assn. Stock Plan Profls., Nat. Assn. Corp. Dirs. (chmn. Atlanta chpt.), Naval War Coll. Found., Am. Legion, Tau Beta Pi, Alpha Pi Mu. Republican. Methodist. Avocations: spectator sports, exercise, travel, history, current events. Office: 780 3d Ave New York NY 10017 Home: 5 Howard DR Princeton Junction NJ 08550-2150 Office Phone: 212-751-2178. E-mail: jfreda@jfreda.com.

REDD, CHARLES APPLETON, lawyer; b. Quincy, Ill., Aug. 13, 1954; s. Charles Lambert and Julia (Harrell) R.; m. Susan Backer, June 2, 1978; children: Elizabeth Appleton, Christopher O'Leary, Thomas Charles, Daniel Louis. BA, St. Louis U., 1976, JD, 1979. Bar: Wis. 1979, U.S. Dist. Ct. (ea. and we. dists.) Wis. 1979, Mo. 1980, Ill. 1991. Trust adminstr. First Wis. Trust Co., Milw., 1979-80; asst. counsel Centerre Trust Co. of St. Louis (now Bank of Am., N.A.), 1980-83; assoc. Armstrong, Teasdale, Schlafly & Davis, St. Louis, 1983-85; ptnr. Armstrong, Teasdale LLP and predecessor firm, St. Louis, 1986-94; chmn. trust and estates dept., 1993-94. Adj. prof. law in fed. estate tax and estate planning Northwestern U. Mem. Estate Planning Coun. of St. Louis; bd. dirs. Make-A-Wish Found. of Metro. St. Louis; mem. planned giving and endowment coun. Archdiocese of St. Louis. Recipient Pres.'s award, Mo. Bar, 1991. Fellow Am. Coll. of Trust and Estate Counsel (mem. fiduciary litig. commn., estate and gift tax com.); mem. ABA (real property, probate and trust law sect.), Wis. Bar Assn., Mo. Bar Assn. (probate and trust com.), Ill. State Bar Assn., Bar Assn. Met. St. Louis (past chmn. probate and trust sect.). Home: 7245 Maryland Ave University City MO 63130-4419 Office: Sonnenschein Nath & Rosenthal LLP Ste 3000 1 Metropolitan Sq Saint Louis MO 63102-2741 Office Phone: 314-259-5819. E-mail: credd@sonnenschein.com.

REDD, J. DIANE, professional fundraiser and grants management executive; b. Apr. 10, 1945; d. Robert Fountain and Lillian (Fitts) Redd. BS, W.Va. State Coll., 1967. Instr. bus. subjects Paterson (N.J.) Bus. Edn., 1967—89; with U. Medicine and Dentistry, Newark, 1968—69; adminstrv. asst. rsch. and sponsored programs, 1968—73; asst. dir. health edn., 1973—76; sr. devel. officer, 1976—79; asst. dir. devel., 1979—83; chief devel. and alumni affairs, 1983—89; dir. devel. founds., corps. and major gifts Planned Parenthood Fedn. Am., Inc., N.Y.C., 1989—2002; dir. devel. NAACP-LDF, Inc., N.Y.C., 2002—. Mem. priorities com., devel. com. United Way of Essex and West Hudson, Newark, 1983-85; chmn. human resources com. Cmty. Adv. Bd., U. Medicine and Dentistry N.J., Newark, 1978-82; mem. rsch. bd. advisors Am. Biographical Inst., 1992—. Recipient Recognition of Achievement award Young Women of Am., Inc., Montgomery, Ala., 1979, Black Achiever award YMWCA, 1986. Mem. Nat. Soc. Fund Raising Execs., Ind. (cert., trustee, v.p., parliamentarian, sec.), Exec. Women N.J. (trustee, chmn. scholarship com.), Women in Fin. Devel. Democrat. Office: NAACP Legal Def Fund Inc 99 Hudson St Ste 1600 New York NY 10013

REDD, MARIE E. state legislator, criminal justice educator; b. Huntington, W.Va., Aug. 5, 1954; m. William Redd; 2 children. RBA in Criminal Justice, Marshall U., 1989, MS in Criminal Justice, 1995. Various positions IBM, 1973-92; instr. criminal justice Marshall U., Huntington, W.Va., 1996-97, mem. adj. faculty, 1997—; mem. W.Va. Senate, Charleston, 1999—. Mem. edn. com., govt. orgn. com., health and human resources com., interstate cooperation com., judiciary com., transp. com. Mem. W.Va. Women's Commn.; pres. Women's Orgn., 1st Bapt. Ch., Huntington. Mem. Am. Criminal Justice Assn., Links, Lambda Alpha Epsilon, Alpha Kappa Alpha. Democrat. Office: WVa Senate 1900 Kanawha Blvd E Rm 209W Charleston WV 25305-0009

REDDEL, CARL WALTER, educational administrator; b. Gurley, Neb., May 31, 1937; s. Walter Julius and Friedora Regina (Sorge) R.; m. Colette Marie Antoinette Mansuy, Oct. 26, 1963; children: Eric, Damien. BSED, Drake U., 1959; MA in Russian Studies, Syracuse U., 1962; PhD in Russian History, cert. Russian Studies, Ind. U., 1973. Lectr. U. Md., Toul-Rosieres, France, 1963-66; instr. U.S.A.F. Acad., Colorado Springs, Colo., 1967-68, 71-72, from asst. prof. to assoc. prof., 1972—80, prof., head dept. history, 1982—99; prof., head dept. history, fellow U. Edinburgh, 1980—82; pres., CEO, Eisenhower World Affairs Inst., 1999—2000; pub. svc. fellow Gettysburg (Pa.) Coll., 2000-01; cons. coord. Dwight D. Eisenhower Meml. Commn., Washington, 2001—02, exec. dir., 2002—. Nat. coord., regional World History Assn., Phila., 1990-95; bd. editors, mem. Joun. Slavic Mil., London, 1988—; series editor Military Hist. Symposium Series, Colorado Springs, 1993-2001. Editor: Transformation in Russian and Soviet Military History, 1990; contbr. articles to profl. jours. Mem. Rotary Internat., 1994—. Served to brig. gen. U.S. Air Force, 1962-99. Recipient Young Faculty exch. Internat. Rsch. Exchs. Bd., Moscow State U., 1975; Woodrow Wilson fellow, 1959-60, Danforth Found. fellow, 1959-61. Mem.: Ctrl. Slavic Assn., World History Assn., Am. Assn. Advancement of Slavic Studies, Am. Hist. Assn., Phi Alpha Theta. Lutheran. Home: 420 7th St NW Apt 809 Washington DC 20004-2214 Office: 1629 K St NW Ste 801 Washington DC 20006-3837 Office Phone: 202-296-0005. E-mail: creddel@eisenhowermemorial.org.

REDDEN, HARRAL ARTHUR, JR., broker; b. Neptune, N.J., Aug. 14, 1936; s. Harral A. and Evelyn Redden; m. Bernadine Tenreiro, July 30, 1983; children: Stephen D., Scott H. BA, Ursinus Coll., 1958. Owner, mgr. Redden Agy. (merged into Connelly, Campion, Wright, Inc.), Fair Haven, NJ, 1958-97; producing agt. Connelly, Campion, Wright, Inc., Belmar, NJ, 1997—. Instr. Brookdale CC, 1972—80. Pres. Little Silver (N.J.) Cmty. Appeal, 1971—. 1st lt. USAR, 1963—70. Mem.: Ind. Ins. Agts. N.J. (pres. 1982—83), Soc. CPCUs (pres. Ctrl. Jersey chpt. 1968—69), Monmouth County Ind. Ins. Agts. Assn. (pres. 1966—67), Sea Bright Lawn Tennis Club (Rumson, N.J.). Republican. Methodist. Office: 186 Woods End Dr Little Silver NJ 07739 Business E-Mail: hal@halredden.com.

REDDEN, JAMES ANTHONY, federal judge; b. Springfield, Mass., Mar. 13, 1929; s. James A. and Alma (Cheek) R.; m. Joan Ida Johnson, July 13, 1950; children: James A., William F. Student, Boston U., 1951; LL.B., Boston Coll., 1954. Bar: Mass., 1954, Oreg., 1955. Pvt. practice, Mass., 1954-55; title examiner Title & Trust Ins. Co., Oreg., 1955; claims adjuster Allstate Ins. Co., 1956; mem. firm Collins, Redden, Ferris & Velure, Medford, Oreg., 1957-73; treas. State of Oreg., 1973-77; atty. gen., 1977-80; U.S. dist. judge, now sr. judge U.S. Dist. Ct. Oreg., Portland, 1980—. Chmn. Oreg. Pub. Employee Relations Bd.; mem. Oreg. Ho. of Reps., 1963-69, minority leader, 1967-69. With AUS, 1946-48. Mem. ABA, Mass. Bar Assn., Oreg. State Bar. Office: US Dist Ct 1527 US Courthouse 1000 SW 3d Ave Portland OR 97204-2902 Office Phone: 503-326-8370.

REDDEN, LAWRENCE DREW, lawyer; b. Tallassee, Ala., Dec. 16, 1922; s. A. Drew and Berta (Baker) R.; m. Christine U. Cunningham, Dec. 20, 1943. AB, U. Ala., 1943, LL.B., 1949. Bar: Ala. bar 1949. Since practiced in, Birmingham; asst. U.S. atty. No. Dist. Ala., 1949-52; partner firm Rogers, Howard, Redden & Mills, 1952-79, Redden, Mills & Clark, 1979—; Civilian aide for Ala. to sec. army, 1965-69. Mem. Ala. Democratic Exec. Com., 1966-74 Editor-in-chief: Ala. Law Rev, 1948. Trustee Ala. Law Sch. Found.; adv. council Cumberland Law Sch. Served with AUS, 1943-46; maj. gen. ret. Decorated D.S.M.; recipient Outstanding Civilian Service medal Dept. Army, 1970 Fellow Am. Coll. Trial Lawyers, Internat. Soc. Barristers; mem. ABA, Am. Judicature Soc., Ala. Bar Assn. (pres. 1972-73), Birmingham Bar Assn. (past pres.), Ala. Law Inst. (mem. coun.), U. Ala. Law Sch. Alumni Assn. (past pres.), Phi Beta Kappa, Alpha Tau Omega, Omicron Delta Kappa. Baptist. Home: 2513 Beaumont Cir Birmingham AL 35216-1301 Business E-Mail: ldr@rmclaw.com.

REDDEN, TAYLOR TILGHMAN, musician; b. Swarthmore, Pa., Mar. 2, 1946; s. O. Tilghman Redden and Virginia Dare (Martin) Martin-Redden. Artist diploma, Phila. Conservatory of Music, 1965; BA, BFA in Music, Phila. Music Acad., 1967. Artist, tchr. Phila. Settlement Music Schs., 1968—70; prof. piano Bryn Mawr Conservatory of Music, Bryn Mawr, Pa., 1971—. Mem.: Music Tchrs. N. Am. Home: 539 Cornell Ave Swarthmore PA 19081

REDDICK, CATHERINE ANNE (CAT REDDICK), Olympic athlete; b. Richmond, Va., Feb. 10, 1982; Majoring in comm., U. N.C., 2000—. Mem. Under-16 Nat. Team, 1998, Under-18 Nat. Team, 1998—99, capt., 2000; mem. Under-21 Nat. Team, 2003; soccer player, defender U.S. Women's Nat. Team, 2000—; mem. U.S. Olympic Soccer Team, Athens, 2004. Co-recipient U-18 Soccer Gold medal, Pan Am. Games, 1999, Nordic Cup, Denmark, 2000, 2001, 2002, 2003; named Defensive MVP, NCAA Final Four, 2000, Freshman All-Am. Team, NSCAA, 2000, Second Team All-Am., 2001, First Team All-Am., 2002; named to First Team All-ACC, 2002. Achievements include mem. Gold Medal, U.S. Women's Soccer Team, Athens Olympic Games, 2004. Office: US Soccer Fedn 1801 S Prairie Ave Chicago IL 60616

REDDICLIFFE, STEVEN, periodical editor-in-chief; BS in Journalism, Northwestern U. Assoc. editor Self Mag., 1988—89; mng. editor US Mag., 1988; founding sr. editor Entertainment Weekly, 1989—92; editor-in-chief Parenting Mag., 1992—95, TV Guide, N.Y.C., 1995—2002; mag. devel. Reader's Digest, Pleasantville, NY, 2003—. TV critic (newspaper) Dallas Times Herald, The Miami Herald, Balt. News Am. Office: Readers Digest Box 200 Pleasantville NY 10572-0200

REDDIEN, CHARLES HENRY, II, lawyer, diversified financial services company executive, consultant; b. San Diego, Aug. 27, 1944; s. Charles Henry and Betty Jane (McCormick) R.; m. Paula Gayle, June 16, 1974; 1 child, Tyler Charles. BSEE, U. Colo., Boulder, 1966; MSEE, U. So. Calif., 1968; JD, Loyola U., L.A., 1972. Bar: Calif. 1972, Colo. 1981, U.S. Dist. Ct. 1981. Mgr. Hughes Aircraft Co., 1966-81; pvt. practice, 1972—. Pres., broker R&D Realty Ltd., 1978-91; mem. spl. staff, co-dir. tax advantage group OTC Net Inc., 1981-82; pres., chmn. Heritage Group Inc., investment banking holding co., 1982-84, Plans and Assistance Inc., mgmt. cons., 1982-83, Orchard Group Ltd., investment banking holding co., 1982-84, J.W. Gant & Assocs., Inc., investment bankers, 1983-84; mng. ptnr., CEO J.W. Gant & Assocs., Ltd., 1984-85; chmn. bd. Kalamath Group Ltd., 1985-87, Heritage group Ltd. Investment Bankers, 1985-87; dir. Virtusonics Corp., 1985-92; v.p., dir. Heritage Fin. Planners Inc., 1982-83; pres., chmn. PDN Inc., 1987-89; pub., exec. v.p., dir. World News Digest Inc., 1987-90, LeisureNet Entertainment, Inc., 1989-90; chief exec. officer, Somerset Group Ltd., 1988-93, Inland Pacific Corp., 1989-91, World Info. Network, Inc., 1990-92, pres., CEO, chmn., Europa Cruises Corp., 1992-94; CEO, chmn. Casino World Inc., 1993-97, Miss. Gaming Corp., 1993-97; pres., chmn., CEO Chart Group Ltd., 1997—, SkyData Corp., 2000—; pres., Miss. Corrections, L.L.C. 2000—; COO Internat. Asset Group, Ltd., 2004—. Contbr. articles to profl. jours. Pres. Diamondhead Business and Profl. Assn.; commr. Diamondhead Fire Dist.; dir. Internat. Trade Club South Miss. Recipient tchg. internship award, 1964. Mem. AIAA, IEEE (chmn. U. Colo. chpt. 1965), Calif. Bar Assn., Nat. Assn. Securities Dealers, Phi Alpha Delta, Tau Beta Pi, Eta Kappa Nu. Office: PO Box 6133 Diamondhead MS 39525-6002 E-mail: chartgroup@aol.com.

REDDIG, WALTER EDUARD, architect, master cabinet maker; b. Meldorf, Holstein, Fed. Republic Germany, Apr. 3, 1936; came to U.S., 1960; s. Ernst and Frieda (Probst) R.; m. Irma Andresen, May 6, 1961; children: Sara Birgit, Ralph Edward. Student, Trade Sch., Meldorf, 1953-56; cert. design technician, Masters Sch., Flensburg, Fed. Republic Germany, 1959, cert. interior architect, 1960. Registered architect, Mich., Va., Md., Tex., Ill., Pa., N.H., Fla. Interior designer J. Holleman Assocs., Birmingham, Mich., 1963-66; project coordinator Levine-Alpern Assocs., Detroit, 1966-69; design and project dir. F. Stickel Assocs., Troy, Mich., 1969-73; project designer Greimel, Malcomson & James, Detroit, 1973; pvt. practice architecture Farmington Hills, Mich., 1973—. Instr. Lawrence Tech. U. Coll. of Architecture and Design, Southfield, Mich., 1992— Contbr. articles to mags.; artist water colors. Appointed to Ad Hoc Hist. Dist. Com., Farmington Hills, 1979-81; vice chmn. Hist. Dist. Commn., Farmington Hills, 1981-91; artist in residence Farmington Area Arts Commn., 1984. Mem. AIA, Mich. Soc. Architects, Nat. Council Archtl. Registration Bd. (cert.). Clubs: Farmington Artist (pres. 1983-85). Lutheran. Avocations: painting, photography, music. Home and Office: 24003 Inkster Rd Farmington Hills MI 48336-3855

REDDING, BOBBIE NEWMAN, lawyer; b. Guilford County, N.C., Mar. 30, 1935; d. John J. Newman and Flora Pearl (Kirkman) Brower; m. Marshall S. Redding, June 2, 1957 (div. 1982); children: Joan Lucile, Rebecca Marie Redding Greene. Student, U. N.C., Greensboro, 1952-54; BA in Edn., U. N.C., 1956, MSLS, 1957; JD, Campbell U., 1985. Bar: N.C. 1986. Staff atty. Lumbee River Legal Svcs., Fayetteville, N.C., 1986-88, Cumberland County Dept. Social Svcs., Fayetteville, 1988—. Mem. ABA, N.C. Bar Assn., N.C. Assn. Social Svcs. Attys., N.C. State Bar Assn., Cumberland County Bar, Twelth Judicial Bar. Home: Box F 1100 Clarendon St Fayetteville NC 28305-4800 Office: Cumberland County DSS 1225 Ramsey St Fayetteville NC 28302 Office Phone: 910-677-2667. E-mail: lg2@dss.co.cumberland.nc.us.

REDDING, EVELYN A. dean; b. Gulfport, Miss., Mar. 13, 1945; d. Arthur Edward and Rebecca (Morris) R. BSN, U. Ala., 1967; MS, Fla. State U., 1971; EdD, Okla. State U., 1974; cert. PNP, Tex. Women's U., 1974; MSN, Wichita State U., 1980. Psychiat. nurse Camp Ponderosa, Mentone, Ala., 1967; dir. health svcs. Community Action Agy., Head Start, Dadeville, Ala., 1967-68; pediatric nurse All Children's Hosp., St. Petersburg, Fla., 1968-69; instr. A&M U. Sch. Nursing, Tallahassee, 1969-71; coord. mater and child health Western Ky. U., Bowling Green, 1971-72; dir. grad. program U. Tex. Health Sci. Ctr., Houston, 1974-78; prof., assoc. dean Coll. Nursing U. Tulsa, 1978-81; dean, prof. Coll. Nursing U. Southwestern La., Lafayette, 1981-97, prof., 1997—. Presenter in field. Contbr. articles to profl. jours. Policy adv. bd. Northwest Fla. Family Planning Project, 1969-71, Nurses Coalition for Action in Politics; mem. exec. com. Hospice of Acadiana, 1982-85, pres., bd. dirs., 1984; cons. big Bend Comprehensive Svcs. Clinic, Tallahassee, 1970-71; cons. family planning nurse practitioner program Planned Parenthood Ctr., Houston, 1975-78; cons. grad. edn., nurse clinician program Madigan Army Med. Ctr., Washington, 1975; pres. Dirs. Nursing Edn. and Nursing Svc. Acadiana, 1982-83; docent intern Gilcrease Mus.; chair Tulsa Area Dirs. Nursing Svc. and Nursing Edn. Mem. AAUW (cultural affairs and community com.), ANA, Nat. League for Nursing, ANA Coun. Nurse Researchers, Soc. for Rsch. Nursing Edn., La. State Nurses Assn. (program com. dist. IV 1986), Okla. Nurses Assn. (nurse edn. com. dist. 2 1978-79, by-laws com. 1978-80), Tex. Nurses Assn. (chairperson task force for profl. self-determination 1976-78), Coun. Adminstrs. Nursing Edn. La. (presenter 1987-88), Sigma Theta Tau, Omicron Nu. Avocations: bike riding, reading, fishing, yard work. Office: U Southwestern La Coll Nursing PO Box 42490 Lafayette LA 70504-0001 Home: 14336 Dalton Rd Kaplan LA 70548-6729

REDDING, ROBERT ELLSWORTH, lawyer; b. South Bend, Ind., Mar. 23, 1919; s. Harry Ellsworth and Lorraine (Livengood) R.; m. Blanche Breisch, Apr. 14, 1941 (div.); children: Rosemary, Robert Ellsworth, Douglas; m. A. Virginia Boender, July 22, 1972. AB, Ohio State U., 1940; LLB, JD, Georgetown U., 1946. Bar: D.C. 1946, Md. 1949, U.S. Supreme Ct. 1951. Legal asst. to judge U.S. Tax Ct., Wash., 1947—48; legal asst. to mem. CAB, Washington, 1949-51; mem. Bradshaw Shearin Redding & Thomas, Silver Spring, Md., 1951-59; v.p., gen. counsel Transp. Assn. Am., Washington, 1960-69; dir. Office Facilitation Dept. Transp., 1970-76; sole law practice Washington, Md., 1976—. Sec. Cert. Claims Profl. Accreditation Council, Washington, 1981-85; chief judge Appeal Tax Ct., Rockville, Md., 1953-55;

internat. cons., G.E. Co., 1977; cons. Ford Motor Co., 1978-79; dir. fed. affairs Shippers Nat. Freight Claim Council, Washington, 1979-89; cons. UN Devel. Program, N.Y.C., 1980-81, Montgomery County, Md. Office of Inspector Gen., 1997-2004. Author: Community Planning for Air Transportation, 1960; Washington editor Handling and Shipping mag., 1976 81. Pres. Allied Civic Group (50 assns.), Silver Spring, 1956-58; chmn. rsch. com. Md. Rep. Com., 1965-70; chmn. fin. adv. com. to county coun., Rockville, 1965-70; exec. dir. Montgomery County Taxpayers League, 94-97. 2d lt. U.S. Army, 1943-46. Mem. Assn. of Former Intelligence Officers (v.p. corp. devel.), Univ. Club (bd. govs., Washington), 33 Degree Scottish Rite Mason, Phi Beta Kappa, Phi Alpha Delta (supreme justice 1966-68, exec. v.p. Pub. Svc. Ctr. 1984-91), Wash. counsel for Japan Airlines. Achievements include while dir. Office Facilitation Dept. Transp., principal negotiator of bilateral transport agreements with U.S.S.R., Canada and U.K; chairman, U.S. delegation attending 13 U.N. transportation conferences, also U.S. delegate to similar conferences in Chile, Africa, Thailand and World Bank. Home: 9105 Falls Chapel Way Potomac MD 20854-2452 Fax: 301-340-6468.

REDDING, ROGERS WALKER, physics educator, university official; b. Louisville, July 15, 1942; s. George Walker and Carolyn Lorraine (Rogers) R.; m. Jennie Ruth Fincher, Sept. 6, 1966 (div.); children: Jeffrey Walker, Jonathan Hull; m. Shirley Rubrecht, Aug. 24, 1991. BS, Georgia Tech., 1965; PhD, Vanderbilt U., 1969. Rsch. assoc. Nat. Bur. Standards, Washington, 1969-70; from asst. prof. to assoc. prof. North Tex. State U. (name now U. North Tex.), Denton, 1970-78, prof. physics, 1978-94, dept. chmn., 1980-87, dir. Tex. Acad. Math. and Sci., 1987-89, assoc. dean arts and scis., 1990-94; prof. physics, dean Coll. Arts and Scis. No. Ky. U., Highland Heights, 1994—, v.p. acad. affairs, provost. Disting. vis. prof. USAF Acad., 1989-90. Author: Exploring Physics, 1984; contbr. articles to profl. jours. Mem. Am. Phys. Soc., Am. Assn. Physics Tchrs., AAAS, Optical Soc. Am. Lodges: Kiwanis. Democrat. Avocations: handball, jogging, referee college football, little league coach. Home: 1243 Lawn Lake Trl Colorado Springs CO 80921-3673 E-mail: redding@nku.edu.

REDDY, ERAGAM PREMKUMAR, medical educator; b. Madanapalli, India, Jan. 2, 1944; married; 2 children. BS in Chemistry, Botany, Zoology, Osmania U., India, 1962, MS in Chemistry, 1965, PhD in Molecular Biology, 1971. Rsch. scholar Indian Coun. Sci. and Indsl. Rsch., Hyderabad, 1965-72; NIH postdoctoral fellow UCLA, 1972-73; Fogarty Internat. postdoctoral fellow Nat. Cancer Inst., 1974-75; head viral immunology program Microbiol. Assocs., Bethesda, Md., 1975-78; vis. scientist Lab. Cellular and Molecular Biology, Nat. Cancer Inst., 1978-82, chief molecular genetics sect., 1982-84; rsch. leader dept. molecular oncology Hoffman-LaRoche, Inc., Nutley, N.J., 1984-85; full mem. Roche Inst. Molecular Biology, Nutley, 1985-86; prof. The Wistar Inst., Phila., 1986-91; Wister prof. pathology U. Pa., Phila., 1987-91; dep. dir. Wistar Inst., Phila., 1991-92; dir. Fels Inst. for Cancer Rsch. and Molecular Biology, Phila., 1992—. Bd. dirs. Nat. Inst. Environ. Health Scis., NIH, 1990-95, mem. cell biology, physiology study sect.-2, 1984-89; invited participant nat. and internat. sci. meetings, workshops and symposia; Laura H. Carnell prof. medicine Temple U., Phila., 1993—. Editor: Oncogene, 1987—, The Oncogene Handbook, 1988; assoc. editor Jour. Cellular Biochemistry, 1994. Adv. com. State of N.J. Commn. on Cancer Rsch., 1987—; adv. com. on cell and developmental biology Am. Cancer Soc., 1984. Recipient Sci. Achievement award Am. Cancer Soc., 1993. Mem. AAAS, Internat. Assn. for Comparative Rsch. on Leukemia and Related Diseases. Office: Fels Inst Cancer Rsch 3420 N Broad St Philadelphia PA 19140-5104

REDDY, J. N. mechanical engineering educator; b. Warangal, AP, India, Aug. 12, 1945; m. Aruna Reddy; children: Anita, Anil. BE in Mech. Engring., Osmania U., 1968; MS in Mech. Engring, Okla. State U., 1970; PhD in Engring. Mechanics, U. Ala., 1973. Rsch. scientist Lockheed Missiles & Space Co., 1974-75; asst. prof. U. Okla., 1975-78, assoc. prof., 1978-80; prof. mech. engring. Va. Poly. Inst. and State U., Blacksburg, Va., 1980-85, Clifton G. Garvin prof., 1986-92; Oscar S. Wyatt Jr. chair Tex. A&M U., College Station, 1992—, Univ. Disting. prof., 1998—. Author: Energy Principles and Variational Methods in Applied Mechanics, 1984, 2nd edit., 2002, Applied Functional Analysis and Variational Methods in Engineering, 1986, An Introduction to the Finite Element Method, 2d edit., 1993, Mechanics of Laminated Composite Plates and Shells: Theory and Analysis, 2d edit., 2004, Theory and Analysis of Elastic Plates, 1999, (with others) Variational Methods in Theoretical Mechanics, 1976, A Mathematical Theory of Finite Elements, 1976, Advanced Engineering Analysis, 1982, Finite Element Analysis of Composite Laminates, 1992, The Finite Element Method in Heat Transfer and Fluid Dynamics, 1994, 2d edit., 2001, Practical Analysis of Laminated Composite Structures, 1995, Introduction to Nonlinear Finite Element Analysis, 2004; editor-in-chief Mechanics of Materials and Structures, Internat. Jour. Computational Methods Engring. Sci. Mechanics, Internat. Jour. Structural Stability and Dynamics; mem. editl. bd. Jour. Applied Mechanics, Internat. Jour. Numerical Methods in Engring., Internat. Jour. Numerical Methods in Fluids, others; contbr. over 300 papers to profl. jours. Recipient Ralph R. Teetor Edn. award Soc. Automotive Engrs., 1976, Technical Achievement award NAE, 1995, Archie Higdon Disting. Educator award Am. Soc. Engring. Edn., 1997. Fellow ASME (Worcester Reed Warner medal 1992, Charles Russ Richards Meml. award 1995), ASCE (Walter L. Huber Civil Engring Rsch. prize 1983, Nathan M. Newmark medal 1998), AIAA (assoc.), Am. Acad. Mechanics, Aeronautical Soc. India, U.S. Assn. Computational Mechanics (Computational Solid Mechanics award 2003), Internat. Assn. Computational Mechanics, Am. Soc. Composites (Excellence in the Field of Composite award 2000). Office: Texas A&M Univ Dept Mech Engring College Station TX 77843-3123 Fax: 979-862-3989. Business E-Mail: jmreddy@tamu.edu.

REDDY, JANARDAN K. medical educator; b. Moolasaal, India, Oct. 7, 1938; MB, BS, Osmania U., Hyderabad, India, 1961; MD in Pathology, All India Inst. Med. Scis., 1965. Lic. physicain, Mo., Kans., Ill.; diplomate Am. Bd. Pathology. Rotating house officer Osmania Gen. Hosp., 1961-62; instr. pathology Kakatiya Med. Coll., Warangal, India, 1962-63, asst. prof., 1965-66; resident fellow pathology U. Kans. Med. Ctr., 1966-68, rsch. fellow pathology, 1968-70, asst. prof., 1970-73, assoc. prof., 1973-76, prof., 1976; prof. pathology Northwestern U. Med. Sch., Chgo., 1976—, dir. med. scientist tng. program, 1990-93, chmn. pathology, 1993—. Dir. anatomic pathology Northwestern Meml. Hosp., 1978-81, mem. med. staff, 1976—; mem. Northwestern U. Cancer Ctr., 1976—; mem. med. staff VA Lakeside Hosp., 1990—; group leader Chem.Carcinogenesis Rsch. Group, Northwestern U. Cancer Ctr., 1990—, assoc. dir. cancer edn., 1991—; mem. Task Force on an Environ. Sci./Policy Initiative, Northwestern U., 1991—; chmn. NIH clin. scis. study sect., 1990-91; mem. NIH spl. study sect., 1992; mem. com. on comparative toxicity of naturally occurring carcinogens, 1993—; mem. Nat. Toxicology Program Rev. Com., 1992—; mem. monograph com. WHO, Internat. Agy. on Cancer Rsch., Lyon, France, 1994. Mem. editl. bds. Jour. Histochemistry and Cytochemistry, 1973-76, Exptl. Pathology, 1982—, Toxicologic Pathology, 1983—, Internat. Jour. Pancreatology, 1986—, Lab. Investigation, 1988—, Carcinogenesis, 1989—, The Jour. Northwestern U. Cancer Ctr., 1990—, Gene Expression, 1990—, Internat. Jour. Toxicology, Occupational and Environ. Health, 1992—, Life Sci. Advanced, Oncology, 1991—; assoc. editor Jour. Toxicology and Environ. Health, 1984—, Cancer Rsch., 1985-90. Grantee Joseph Mayberry Endowment Fund, Cancer Rsch. Found., 1991-93, NIEHS, 1995—, NIGMS, 1992-2001, NIDDK, 1995—, NIGMS, 1992-97; merit scholar Osmania U., 1954-61, Govt. of Andhra Pradesh merit scholar, 1963-65; WHO Yamagiwa-Yoshida Internat. Cancer fellow in Japan, 1985; recipient NIH merit award, 1987, UN Devel. Programme-Tokten award, 1988, Fletscher scholar award, 1991; named George H. Joost Outstanding Basic Sci. Tchr., 1995, 97. Fellow AAAS, Assn. Scientists of Indian Origin in Am. (pres. 1983-84, sr. scientist award 1991), Soc. Toxicology (v.p. molecular toxicology speciality sect. 1990-91, pres. 1991-92, pres. carcinogenesis specialty sect. 1990-91, Kenneth P. Dubois award 1990), Am. Pancreatic Assn., Am. Assn. Pathologists (mem. program com. 1989-93), Am. Assn. Cancer Rsch. (mem. program com. 1990-91), Internat. Acad. Pathology, Am. Soc. Cell Biology, Histochem. Soc., Soc. Exptl. Biology and Medicine, Biochem. Soc. London, Soc. Toxicology Pathologists, Internat. Assn. Pancreatology, N.Y. Acad. Scis. Home: 1212 Asbury Ave Evanston IL 60202-1102 Office: Northwestern U Med Sch Dept Pathology Ward 6-204 303 E Chicago Ave Chicago IL 60611-3072

REDDY, KAMBHAM RAJA, plant physiology educator; b. Ambuvari Palli, India, July 1, 1953; s. Kambi Kambham and Ammannamma (Reddy) R.; m. Anasuya Reddy, Feb. 9, 1982; 1 son, Sasank. BSc in Biology, S.V. U., Tirupati, India, 1975, MSc in Botany, 1977, PhD in Botany, 1984. Curator in botany S.V. U., 1977-88; prof. plant physiology Miss. State U., 1991—. Vis. scientist Govt. of India, 1988. Editor: Climate Change and Global Crop Productivity, 2000; contbg. author: Climate Change and Agriculture: Analysis of Potential International Impacts, 1995; contbr. articles to profl. jour., chpt. to books. Recipient Rsch. award of merit, 1995. Mem. Agronomy Soc. Am., Crop Sci. Soc. Am., Biol. Sys. Simulation Work Group, Gamma Sigma Delta (Rsch. award of merit 1995). Achievements include development of new theories and concepts in plant growth regulation and incorporated into a cotton simulation model GOSSYM, used by cotton producers, consultants and rschr. across the cotton belt; extensive contributions to the field of climate change, environmental plant physiology, ethnobotany, remote sensing and crop simulation modeling. Home: 505 Banyan Rd Starkville MS 39759-4348 Office: Mississippi State U Box 9555 Mississippi State MS 39762-9555 Office Phone: 662-325-9463.

REDDY, KRISHNA NARAYANA, artist, educator; b. Chittoor, India, July 15, 1925; s. Narayana B. and Laksmamma R.; m. Judith Blum, June 30, 1967; 1 child, Aparna. Diploma in Fine Arts, Internat. U. Santiniketan, India, 1947; cert. in Fine Arts, Slade Sch. Fine Arts, U. London, 1952; student of Zadkine in sculpture, Academie Grande Chaumière, Paris, 1952—55; student of Marino Marini in sculpture, Academia di Belle Arti di Brera, Milan, 1956—57; specialist in Gravure, Internat. Ctr. for Graphics, Atelier 17, Paris, 1953—55; DLitt (hon.), S.V. Univ., India, 1984. Asst. dir. Internat. Ctr. for Graphics, Atelier 17, Paris, 1957—64, prof., co-dir., 1964—76; from prof. art to prof. emeritus NYU, N.Y.C., 1977—2001, prof. emeritus art and art edn., 2001—. Dir. dept. art Coll. Fine Arts, Kalakshetra, Madras, India, 1947—49; lectr. art Arundale Montessori Tchrs. Tng. Ctr., 1948—49; vis. prof. Am. U., 1964; prof. U. Calif., Davis, 1970—71, U. Wis., Madison, 1973; guest prof. Yale U. Summer Sch. Music and Art, 1973; Andrew Mellon vis. prof. Cooper Union Sch. Art and Arch., 1977; vis. prof. Yale U. Summer Sch. Music and Art, 1978, Kala Inst. Graphics, Berkeley, Calif., 1979, U. Calif., Santa Cruz, 1979. Author: Intaglio Simultaneous Color Printmaking: Significance of Materials and Processes, 1989, New Ways of Colour Printmaking, 1997; retrospective exhbns., Bronx Mus. Arts, 1981-82, Indian Council for Cultual Relations, Ministry of Culture and India Nat. Acad. Fine Arts, 1984-85, Museo del Palacio de Bellas Artes, Mexico City, 1988-89. Recipient Gagan-Abani Puraskar Nat. award Viswa-Bharati, 1983, Printmaker Emeritus award So. Graphics Coun. of Am., 2000; named Featured Guest Artist-Printmaker at the Northwest Print Coun. Ann. Meeting, 1985; Title of Padma Shree awarded by Pres. of India, 1972. Home: 80 Wooster St New York NY 10012-4347

REDDY, THIKKAVARAPU RAMACHANDRA, electrical engineer; b. Nellore, India, June 4, 1944; came to the U.S., 1979; s. Thikkavarapu Kota and Saraswathi T. (Sivareddy) R.; m. Padmavathi Reddy Kakuturu Thikkavarapu, Aug. 17, 1973; children: Lavanya T., Samatha T. BSEE, Osmania U., 1968; diploma in computer sci., Coll. Engring., Madras, India, 1978. Cert. profl. engr., chartered engr. Supervising engr. APSE Bd., Hyderabad, India, 1969-79; elec. design engr. Sargent & Lundy, Chgo., 1979-80; engr. Bechtel Corp., San Francisco, 1980-82, supr. Athens, Ala., 1989-92; sr. project engr. EGS, Inc., Huntsville, Ala., 1983-84; sr. start-up engr. Gilbert Commonwealth Co., Reading, Pa., 1984-86; cons. Quantum Resources, Decatur, Ala., 1986-87; prin. engr. Ebasco Svcs. Inc., N.Y.C., 1987-89; pres. LSP Internat. Inc., Huntsville, 1992—, LASA Internat., Huntsville, 1992—; project engr. Sargent & Lundy, Chgo., 1997—. Guest lectr. gen. interest and wide range of engring. issues; pres. Lasa Internat. Inc., Huntsville, 1992—. Author: Qualification of Electrical Distribution Components, 1984, Thermal Aging Techniques of Organic Materials, 1984, and others; contbr. articles to profl. jours.; guest lectr. on wide range of engring. issues. Mem. NSPE (Outstanding Profl. award 1991, Profl. Engr. of Yr. award 1996), IEEE (Meritorious Svc. award 1985), Commonwealth Engrs. Coun., Project Mgmt. Inst., Am. Telugu Assn. (life), Telugu Assn. N.Am. (life), Internat. Platform Assn., C. of C. Avocations: journalism, ping pong/table tennis, anthropology, archaeology, classic and modern art, literature. Home and Office: 100 Jersey Ln Rockville MD 20850-7757 Personal E-mail: trr2020@yahoo.com.

REDDY, VARDHAN JONNALA, surgeon; b. Kollipara, India, Nov. 26, 1960; MBBS, Guntur Med. Coll., Andhra U., 1985. Diplomate Am. Bd. Surgery, Am. Bd. Thoracic Surgery. Internist Robert Packer Hosp., Sayre, Pa., 1990-91; res. L.I. Jewish Med. Ctr., New Hyde Park, N.Y., 1991-95; fellowship Tex. Heart Inst., Houston, 1995-96; staff surgeon Glades Gen. Hosp., Belle Glade, Fla., 1996-98, chief surgery, 1998—99; cardiothoracic surgeon U. Miss., Jackson, Miss., 1999—2001, Shadyside Hosp., Pitts., 2001—. V.p. Med. Staff Assocs. of Glades Inc., 1998, pres., CEO Heartcom Inc., 1999. Mem. AMA, Internat. Coll. Angiology, Royal Coll. Surgeons Edinburgh (diplomate), Am. Coll. Angiology. Home and Office: 504 Greenbrier Ct Steubenville OH 43953-3335 E-mail: vardhanreddy@usa.net.

REDDY, VENKAT NARSIMHA, ophthalmologist, researcher; b. Hyderabad, India, Nov. 4, 1922; came to U.S., 1947; s. Malla and Manik (Devi) R.; m. Alvira M. DeMello, Dec. 10, 1955; children: Vinay Neville, Marlita Alvira. BSc, U. Madras, 1945; MS, PhD, Fordham U., 1952. Rsch. assoc. Coll. of Physicians and Surgeons Columbia U., N.Y.C., 1952-56, Banting and Best Inst., Toronto, Can., 1956; asst. and assoc. prof. ophthalmology Kresge Eye Inst. Wayne State U., Detroit, 1957-68; prof., biomed. scis., asst. dir. Eye Rsch. Inst. Oakland U., Rochester, Mich., 1968-75, prof., dir., 1975-98, Disting. prof. biomed. scis., dir., 1996-98; prof. ophthalmology Kellogg Eye Ctr. U. Mich., Ann Arbor, 1998—. Mem. study sect. NIH, Bethesda, 1966-70, nat. adv. eye coun., 1982-87, mem. bd. sci. counselors Nat. Eye Inst., 1977-81 Mem. editl. bd. Investigative Ophthalmology and Visual Scis., 1969-72, 78-88, Ophthalmic Research, 1978-90, Experimental Eye Research, 1985-2000; contbr. articles to profl. jours. Recipient Friendenwald award Assn. Rsch. in Ophthalmology, 1979, Rsch. award Cataract Rsch. Found., 1987, Merit award Nat. Eye Inst., 1989; named Scientist of Yr. State of Mich., 1991, Disting. Faculty Mem. Mich. Assn. Governing Bds. State Univs., 1994. Mem. AAAS, Internat. Soc. Eye Rsch., The Biochem. Soc., Assn. Rsch. in Vision and Ophthalmology (pres. 1985), Am. Soc. for Biochemistry and Molecular Biology, Soc. Free Radicals, Oxygen Soc. Sigma Xi. Achievements include research on cataract etiology, intraocular fluids dynamics relating to glaucoma, cell biology of lens, ciliary body and retinal pigment epithelium, cell differentiation. Office: U Mich Kellogg Eye Ctr 1000 Wall St Ann Arbor MI 48105-1912 Office Phone: 734-763-7246. Business E-Mail: venreddy@umich.edu.

REDDY, YENAMALA RAMACHANDRA, metal processing executive; b. Polavaram, Andhra, India, Feb. 12, 1939; came to U.S., 1974; s. Y. Venkata and Y. Lakshamamma Reddy; m. Y. Uma Reddy, May 30, 1965; children: Y. Sharath, Y. Jay. BME, S.V. U., Andhra, 1961; M in Tech., IIT, Bombay, 1966, PhD, 1970. Lic. profl. engr., Wis. Asst. prof. IIT, Bombay, 1966-69; research and devel. mgr. Jyoti Pumps, Baroda, 1973-74; chief engr. Patterson Pumps, Toccoa, Ga., 1974-80; pres. R.B. Pump Co., Baxley, 1980—, U.B. Cons., Ga., 1980—. Pres. Falcon Castings, Inc., 1996, Eagle Motors, Inc., 1996. Contbr. articles to tech. jours. Postdoctoral fellow U. of Tech., Loughborough, Eng., 1970-73. Mem. ASME, IEEE, Am. Foundryman's Soc., Nat. Fire Protection Assn. Office: R B Pump Co 1 Dixie Dr # 557 Baxley GA 31513-6947

REDFERN, JOHN D. manufacturing executive; b. 1935; Grad., Queen's U., Kingston, Ont., 1958; DEng. honoris causa (hon.), Carleton U., 1992. With Lafarge Can. Inc. (formerly Can. Cement Lafarge Ltd.), Montreal, 1977—, pres., CEO, 1977—84, chmn., 1985—; chmn. bd. parent co. Lafarge Corp., Reston, Va., 1985—88, vice chmn., 1989—96. Office: Lafarge Can Inc 606 Cathcart Ste 800 Montreal QC Canada H3B 1L7 Office Phone: 514-861-2581.

REDFIELD, CAROL ANN LUCKHARDT, engineering educator; b. Greencastle, Ind., July 19, 1958; d. Robert Buek and Helen (Brown) K.; m. Josiah Beckley Redfield, Mar. 17, 1990. BS in Edn., U. Mich., Ann Arbor, 1980, MS in Math, MS in Computer & Controls, U. Mich., Ann Arbor, 1982, PhD in Computer Sci. & Engring., 1989. Secondary Teaching Cert. Tchg. asst. U. Mich., Ann Arbor, Mich., 1979-87; rsch. engr. Southwest Rsch. Inst., San Antonio, 1987-94; sr. scientist Mei Tech. Corp., San Antonio, 1995-98; asst. prof. St. Mary's U., San Antonio, 1998—2003, assoc. prof., 2003—. Chair Internat. Space Devel. Conf., San Antonio, 1991. Author: AI and Game Playing, 1986; editor, author: Intelligent Tutoring Systems, 1991, 98; editor: 1991 ISDC Proceedings, 1991, AI in Education, 2001. Internet team dir. Landmark Edn.; founder Radiance Acad. West Charter Sch. Mem. AIAA, Nat. Space Soc., San Antonio Space Soc. (pres. 1988—). Mem. Soc. Of Friends. Avocations: science fiction, games. Home: 609 Ridge View Dr San Antonio TX 78253-5348 Office: St Marys U 1 Camino Santa Maria St San Antonio TX 78228-8524 Office Phone: 210-436-3298.

REDFIELD, JEAN M. electric power company executive; With McKinsey & Co., Inc.; mgr. corp. stratety Detroit Edison Co., 1994-97; pres. Detroit Edison Co. Am., 1997—. Office: Detroit Edison Co 2002 2d Ave Detroit MI 48226

REDFIELD, PAMELA A. state legislator; b. Chicago, Ill., Aug. 11, 1948; m. Jerry Redfield; 6 children. BS in Edn., U. Nebr., 1969. Exec. dir. Omaha-Millard Rotary; libr. spcl.; election cons.; banker; mem. Nebr. Legislature from 12th dist., Lincoln, 1998—. Mem. Ralston Bd. Edn. 1992-1998. Coun. State Govt.; Nat. Conf. State Legislatures; Am. Legis. Exch. Conf.; Nat. Coun. Ins. Legislators Office: State Capitol (Dist 12) Rm 1404 PO Box 94604 Lincoln NE 68509-4604

REDFIELD, ROBERT HORACE, mathematician, educator; b. Schenectady, N.Y., Feb. 24, 1945; s. Robert Horace Redfield and Elizabeth (Carlson) Cherrett; m. Rosemary Jeanne Gagne, Dec. 1970 (div. 1979); 1 child, Signe Anne; m. Mary Eleanor Javorski, Aug. 18, 1984; children: Lisbeth Ellen Sarah, Catherine Mairi Sophia. BA, Reed Coll., 1967; MA, U. Oreg., 1969; PhD, Simon Fraser U., Can., 1973. Rsch. fellow Monash U., Clayton, Victoria, Australia, 1974-77, vis. assoc. prof., 1989-90; vis. asst. prof. math. U. Kans., Lawrence, 1977-78; instr. Okanagan Coll., Kelowna, 1978-86; assoc. prof. math. Hamilton Coll., Clinton, N.Y., 1986 93, prof., 1993-96, Samuel F. Pratt prof.math., 1996—. Vis. lectr. McMaster U., Hamilton, Ont., Canada, 1980; vis. assoc. prof Simon Fraser U., Burnaby, B.C., Canada, 1985, Monash U., Victoria, Australia, 1989. Reviewer: for math reviews, published: textbook on abstract algebra; contbr. rsch. papers to math. publs. Organizer, tchr., Kelowna Internat. Dancers, 1981-86, Clinton Internat. Folk Dancers, 1992—. Grantee, Australian Rsch. Grants Com., 1974-77. Mem. Am. Math. Soc., Can. Math. Soc., Can. Soc. History and Philosophy of Math., Math. Assn. Am., Kelowna Scottish Country Dance Group (treas. 1981-86), Sigma Xi. Office: Hamilton Coll Dept Math Clinton NY 13323

REDFIELD, ROBERT R. virologist, medical educator; b. Chgo., 1951; BS, Georgetown U., 1973; MD, Georgetown U. Sch. Med., 1977; degree (hon.), N.Y. Med. Coll. Intern Walter Reed Army Med. Ctr. 1977—78, resident in med., 1978—80, fellow infectious diseases, 1980—82, fellow tropical med., 1982; project dir. HIV immunotherapy Walter Reed Army Inst. Rsch., chief dept. retroviral rsch.; project dir. HIV vaccine devel. for treatment and prevention Military Med. Consortium for Applied Retroviral Rsch., Dept. Def.; co-founder, assoc. dir. Inst. Human Virology U. Md., Baltimore, dir. clin. care & rsch. div. Inst. Human Virology; prof. med., immunology, microbiology, dept. infectious disease U. Md. Sch. Med.; dir. adult HIV program U. Md. Med. Mem. adv. bd. Fogarty Internat. Ctr.; mem. AIDS rsch. adv. coun. NIH. Bd. dirs. The Pendulum Project. Recipient Lifetime Science award, Inst. Advanced Studies in Immunology and Aging, Highest Achievement in Clinical Virology award, Ortho Diagnostic Systems Inc., Physician Recognition award, Surgeon Gen., multiple medals in virology, U.S. Army. Achievements include being the first to demonstrate the heterosexual transmission of the HIV virus; development of the first clinical staging system, now used around the world; originated efforts to examine viral replication and viral load at all of stages of disease. Office: Inst Human Virology 725 W Lombard St Baltimore MD 21201

REDFORD, DONALD BRUCE, historian, archaeologist; b. Toronto, Ont., Can., Sept. 2, 1934; s. Cyril Fitzjames and Kathleen Beryl (Coe) R.; m. Susan Pirritano, Jan. 30, 1982; children: Alexander, Aksel; children by previous marriage: Christopher, Philip. BA, U. Toronto, 1957, MA, 1958; PhD, Brown U., 1965. Lectr. Brown U., 1960-61; lectr. U. Toronto, 1961-64, asst. prof. Egyptian history and language, 1965-67, asso. prof., 1967-69, prof., 1969-98; site supr. Brit. Sch. Archaeol. Excavations, Jerusalem, 1964-67; dir. Soc. Study Egyptian Antiquities Expdn. to, Karnak, Egypt, 1970-72, Akhenaten Temple Project, Luxor, Egypt, 1972—; research assoc. Univ. Museum, U. Pa., Royal Ont. Mus.; prof. classics Pa. State U., 1998—. Vis. prof. Ben Gurion U., Beersheva, Israel, 1986, U. Pa., 1995-96; dir. excavations Mendes and Ted Kedwa, Egypt, 1991—. Author: History and Chronology of the Egyptian 18th Dynasty, 1967, A Study of the Biblical Joseph Story, 1970, Papyrus and Tablet, 1973, The Akhenaten Temple Project, vol. I, 1977, Akhenaten, the Heretic King, 1984; Annals, King-Lists and Daybooks, 1986, The Akhenaten Temple Project, vol. II, 1988, Egypt, Canaan and Israel in Ancient Times, 1992, The Wars in Syria and Palestine of Thutmose III, 2003; From Slave to Pharaoh: The Black Experience of Ancient Egypt, 2003. Killam grantee, 1975-79; Smithsonian Fgn. Currency grantee, 1973-76, 1979, Social Scis. Humanities Research Council Can. grantee, 1980—. Fellow Royal Soc. Can. Achievements include discovering Temple of Akhenaten at Luxor, 1976. Office: CAMS Weaver Bldg State College PA 16803 also: Pa State U Dept Classics & Mediterranean Studies 108 Weaver Bldg University Park PA 16802-5500 E-mail: dbr3@psu.edu.

REDFORD, ROBERT (CHARLES ROBERT REDFORD), actor, director; b. Santa Monica, Calif., Aug. 18, 1937; m. Lola Van Wegenen (div.); children: Shauna, Jamie, Amy. Student, U. Colo., Pratt Inst. Design, Am. Acad. Dramatic Arts; LHD (hon.), U. Colo., 1987; D (hon.), U. Mass., 1990. Owner ski resort Sundance, Provo, Utah. Pres., founder The Sundance Inst., 1981—. Stage appearances include: Tall Story, The Highest Tree, Sunday in New York, Barefoot in the Park; Films include: (actor) War Hunt, 1961, Situation Hopeless But Not Serious, 1965, Inside Daisy Clover, 1965, The Chase, 1966, This Property Is Condemned, 1966, Barefoot in the Park, 1967, Butch Cassidy and the Sundance Kid, 1969, Tell Them Willie Boy is Here, 1969, Little Fauss and Big Halsey, 1970, The Hot Rock, 1972, Jeremiah Johnson, 1972, The Way We Were, 1973, The Sting, 1973 (Academy award nominee), The Great Gatsby, 1974, The Great Waldo Pepper, 1975, Three Days of the Condor, 1975, A Bridge Too Far, 1977, The Electric Horseman, 1979, Brubaker, 1980, The Natural, 1984, Out of Africa, 1985, Legal Eagles, 1986, Havana, 1990, Sneakers, 1992, Indecent Proposal, 1993, Up Close and Personal, 1996, Anthem, 1997, Enredando sombras, 1998, Forever Hollywood, 1999, Spy Game, 2001, The Last Castle, 2001; actor, exec. prodr. Downhill Racer, 1969, The Candidate, 1972, All The President's Men, 1976; exec. prodr. Promised Land, 1988, Some Girls, 1988, She's the One, 1996, The Dark Wind, 1991, Slums of Beverly Hills, 1998, How to Kill Your Neighbor's Dog, 2000; exec. prodr., narrator Yosemite: The Fate of Heaven, 1989, Incident at Oglala, 1992 (TV) Independent's Day, 1998, Visions of Grace: Robert Redford and 'The Horse Whisperer' 1998 (Audience award); dir. Ordinary People, 1980 (Academy and Golden Globe Awards, Best Director), Quiz Show, 1994; dir., prodr. The Milagro Beanfield War, 1988, A River Runs Through It, 1993 (narrator); prodr. A Civil Action, 1998, The Legend of Bagger Vance, 2000. Recipient Audubon medal, 1989, Dartmouth Film Soc. award, 1990; Cecil B. Demille Golden Globe Award for Lifetime Achievement, 1994, Screen Actors Guild Awards for Life Achievement, 1996, Honorary award, Academy Awards, 2002. Office: 1223 Wilshire Blvd # 412 Santa Monica CA 90403-5400 also: Creative Artists Agy c/o David O'Conner 9830 Wilshire Blvd Beverly Hills CA 90212-1804

REDGRAVE, MARTYN ROBERT, hotel, food service executive; BA in Economics, Princeton U.; MBA in Finance, N.Y.U. CPA Minn. Various fin. and gen. mgmt. positions PepsiCo, 1980—90; exec. v.p. fin., CFO Kentucky

Fried Chicken Corp., 1990—94; CFO, exec. v.p Carlson Cos. Inc., Mpls., 1994—. Vol. United Way. Office: Carlson Cos Inc 1405 Xenium Lane N Plymouth MN 55441-8215 Business E-Mail: mredgrave@carlson.com.

REDGRAVE, VANESSA, actress; b. London, Jan. 30, 1937; d. Michael and Rachel (Kempson) Redgrave; m. Tony Richardson, 1962 (div. 1967); children: Joely Kim, Natasha; 1 child, Carlo. Student, Central Sch. Speech and Drama, London, 1955-57. First stage appearances include: Reluctant Debutante, Frincton Summer Theater, 1957, Come On Jeeves, Arts Theater, Cambridge, 1957, A Touch of the Sun, Saville Theater, London, 1958, Major Barbara, Royal Court, 1958, Mother Goose, Leatherhead, 1958; Prin. theatrical roles include Helena in Midsummer Night's Dream, 1959, Stella in Tiger and the Horse, 1960, Katerina in The Taming of the Shrew, 1961, Rosalind in As You Like It, 1962, Imogene in Cymbeline, 1962, Nina in The Seagull, 1969, Miss Brodie in The Prime of Miss Jean Brodie, 1966, Cato Street, 1971, Threepenny Opera, 1972, Twelfth Night, 1972, Antony and Cleopatra, 1973, Design for Living, 1973, Macbeth, 1975, Lady from the Sea, 1976, 78, 79, The Aspern Papers, 1984 (Laurence Olivier award for actress of yr. in a revival, 1985), The Seagull, 1969, 85, Chekhov's Women, 1985, The Taming of the Shrew, Ghosts, 1986, Touch of the Poet, 1988, Orpheus Descending, 1989, A Madhouse in Goa, 1989, Chekov's Women, 1989, Three Sisters, 1990, When She Danced, 1991, Heartbreak House, 1991, Maybe, 1993, Brecht in Hollywood, 1994, Vita and Virginia, 1994, Long Days Journey Into Night, 2003 (Tony award for best actress, 2003); films include Behind The Mask, 1958, A Man For All Seasons, 1966, Morgan: A Suitable Case for Treatment, 1966 (Best Actress award, Cannes Film Festival, 1966), Blow-Up, 1966, Red And Blue, 1967, Camelot, 1967, The Sailor from Gibralter, 1967, Isadora, 1968 (Best Actress award, Cannes Film Festival, 1969), The Charge of the Light Brigade, 1968, The Seagull, 1968, A Quiet Place in the Country, 1969, Oh! What a Lovely War, 1969, Daniel Deronda, 1969, Dropout, 1969, The Trojan Women, 1970, The Devils, 1970, The Holiday, 1971, Mary, Queen of Scots, 1971, Murder on the Orient Express, 1974, Winter Rates, 1974, 7 per cent solution, 1975, Julia, 1977 (Academy award for best supporting actress, 1978, Golden Globe award for best supporting actress, 1978), Agatha, 1978, Yanks, 1978, Bear Island, 1979, Playing for Time, 1980, My Body My Child, 1981, Wagner, 1981, The Bostonians, 1983 (Best Actress Nat. Film Critics, Best Actress New Delhi Internat. Film Festival), Wetherby, 1985, Steaming, 1985, Prick Up Your Ears, 1987, Comrades, 1987, Consuming Passions, 1988, Diceria dell'Untore, 1989, The Ballad of the Sad Café, 1990, Young Catherine, 1990, Howard's End, 1992, Crime and Punishment, 1993, The House of the Spirits, 1994, Mother's Boys, 1994, A Month by the Lake, 1995, Little Odessa, 1995, Mission Impossible, 1996, For The Love Of Tyler, 1996, Smilla's Sense of Snow, 1996, Deep Impact, 1998, Celebrity, 1998, Lulu on the Bridge, 1998, Uninvited, 1999, Toscano, 1999, A Rumor of Angels, 1999, Mirka, 1999, An Interesting State, 1999, If These Walls Could Talk 2, 1999, The Cradle Will Rock, 1999, Girl, Interrupted, 1999, A Rumor of Angels, 2000, Crime and Punishment, 2000, The 3 Kings, 2000, The Pledge, 2001, Crime and Punishment, 2002, Good Boy!, 2003; TV movies and miniseries appearances include Playing for Time, 1980 (Emmy award for outstanding lead actress in a limited series or spl., 1981), Snow White and the Seven Dwarfs, 1985, Three Sovereigns for Sarah, 1985, Peter the Great, 1986, Second Serve, 1986 (Emmy award, Golden Globe award), A Man for All Seasons, 1988, Young Catherine, 1990, Whatever Happened to Baby Jane, 1990, The Three Sisters, 1990, When She Danced, 1991, Playing for Time (Emmy award, TV Times award), The Wall, 1992, Heartbreak House, 1992, Great Moments In Aviation, 1993, Down Came A Blackbird, 1994, The Young Indiana Jones Chronicles, 1992, If These Walls Could Talk 2, 2000 (Emmy award for outstanding supporting actress in a miniseries or movie, 2000, Golden Globe award for best supporting actress in a series, mini-series or motion picture made for TV, 2001, Screen Actors Guild award for best supporting actress in a TV movie or miniseries, 2001) The Gathering Storm, 2002, The Locket, 2002, Byron,2003; Author: Pussies and Tigers, 1964, (autobiography) Vanessa, 1991, Vanessa Redgrave: An Autobiography, 1994. Bd. govs. Central Sch. Speech and Drama, 1963— . Decorated comdr. Order Brit. Empire; recipient 4 times Drama award Evening Standard, 1961-91, Best Actress award, Variety Club, Gt. Brit., 1961, 66, Best Actress award, Brit. Guild TV Producers and Dirs., 1966, Variety Club of Great Britain award, 1992, Laurence Olivier award Actress of the Yr. in a Revival for A Touch of the Poet; fellow Brit. Film Inst., 1988. Office: ICM 8942 Wilshire Blvd Ste 219 Beverly Hills CA 90211*

REDHEAD, PAUL AVELING, physicist; b. Brighton, Eng., May 25, 1924; m. Doris Packman, 1948; children: Janet, Patricia. BA with honors in Physics, Cambridge (Eng.) U., 1944, MA, 1948, PhD, 1969. Sci. officer dept. naval ordnance Brit. Admiralty, 1944-45, svcs. electronics rsch. lab., 1945-47; rsch. officer NRC Can., Ottawa, Ont., 1947-69, dir. planning group, 1970-72, dir.-gen. planning, 1972-73, dir. div. physics, 1973-86, chmn. com. of lab. dirs., 1981-86, sec. sci. and tech. policy com., 1986-89, researcher emeritus, 1989—. Author: Physical Basis of Ultrahigh Vacuum, 1968, 2d edit., 1993; editor: Jour. Vacuum Scis. and Tech., 1969-74; contbr. numerous articles to profl. jours.; patentee in field. Fellow IEEE, Royal Soc. Can., Am. Phys. Soc., Am. Vacuum Soc. (past pres., Medard W. Welch award 1975); mem. Can. Assn. Physicists (medal for achievement in physics 1989). Home: 1958 Norway Crescent Ottawa ON Canada K1H 5N7 Office: Nat Rsch Coun Can Inst Microstructural Scis Ottawa ON Canada K1A OR6

REDINBO, MATTHEW R. science educator, researcher; b. Lafayette, Ind., Oct. 14, 1966; m. Liz Redinbo; 1 child. BS in Biochemistry, Minor in English Literature, U. Calif., Davis, 1990; PhD in Biochemistry, U. Calif., Los Angeles, 1995; postdoctoral fellow, Lab. of Wim G. J. Hol, Biomolecular Structure Ctr., U. Wash., 1995—99. Dir. structural biology, program in molecular biology and biotechnology U. NC, 2002, joint appointed assoc. prof., dept. biochemistry and biophysics, sch. of medicine, 2002—, assoc. prof., dept. of chemistry, 1999—. U. Calif. Lineberger Comprehensive Cancer Ctr. Recipient Career award in Biomedical Sciences, Burroughs Wellcome Fund, 1999—. Office: Dept Chemistry/Dept Biochemistry & Biophysics Univ NC at Chapel Hill C748 Kenan Labs Campus Box #3290 Chapel Hill NC 27599-3290 Office Phone: 919-843-8910. Office Fax: 919-966-3675. Business E-Mail: redinbo@unc.edu.

REDING, JOHN ANTHONY, lawyer; b. Orange, Calif., May 26, 1944; AB, U. Calif., Berkeley, 1966, JD, 1969. Bar: Calif. 1970, U.S. Dist. Ct. (no., ctrl., ea. and so. dists.) Calif., U.S. Claims Ct., U.S. Supreme Ct. Formerly mem. Crosby, Heafey, Roach & May P.C., Oakland, Calif.; now ptnr. Paul, Hastings, Janofsky & Walker, LLP, San Francisco, global chmn. litigation dept. Mem. ABA (sects. on litigation, intellectual property, and natural resources, energy and eviron. law, coms. on bus. torts, internat. law, trial practice and torts and insurance), Am. Intellectual Property Law Assn., State Bar Calif. (sect. on litigation), Bar Assn. San Francisco, Assn. Bus. Trial Lawyers. Office: Paul Hastings Janofsky & Walker LLP 55 2d St 24th Fl San Francisco CA 94105-3441 E-mail: jackreding@paulhastings.com.

REDING, ROBERT W. air transportation executive; m. Sherrill Reding. BS in Aero. Engring. with honors, Calif. State Poly. U.; MBA, So. Ill. U. Various positions Air Fla.; v.p., flight opers. Midways Airlines, Chgo.; pres., CEO Reno Air, Canadian Regional Airlines; COO Am. Eagle Airlines; sr. v.p., tech. opers. Am. Airlines, 2003—. Mem. Pres.'s Coun., Calif. State Poly. U. With USAF, 1972—79. Office: AMR Corp 4333 Amon Carter Blvd Fort Worth TX 76155

REDISH, EDWARD FREDERICK, physicist, researcher; b. N.Y.C., Apr. 1, 1942; s. Jules and Sylvia Redish; m. Janice Copen, June 18, 1967; children: A. David, Deborah. AB, Princeton U., 1963; PhD, MIT, 1968. CTP fellow U. Md., College Park, 1968-70, from asst. prof. to assoc. prof., 1970-79, prof., 1979—, chmn. dept. phys. astronomy, 1982-85. Vis. scholar, U. Calif., Berkeley, 1999-00; vis. prof. Ind. U., Bloomington, 1985-86, U. Washington, Seattle, 1992-93; vis. fgn. collaborator CEN, Saclay, France, 1973-74; co-dir. Md. U. Project in Physics and Ednl. Tech., 1983-93, Comprehensive Unified Physics Learning Environment, 1989-96; mem. Nuclear Sci. Adv. Com., Dept. of Energy/NSF, 1987-90; mem. program adv. com. Ind. U. Cyclotron Facility, 1985-89, chmn., 1986-89; mem. Internat. Commn. on Physics Edn., 1993-2002, sec., 1999-2002. Author: Teaching Physics with the Physics Suite, 2003, (textbook) Understanding Physics, 2003, (software) Orbits, 1989, The M.U.P.P.E.T. Utilities, 1994, The Comprehensive Unified Physics Learning Environment, 1994; editor: (conf. procs.) Computers in Physics Instrn., 1990, Internat. Conf. Undergrad. Physics Edn., 1997, Physics Edn. Rsch. Supplement to Am. Jour. Physics, 1999—2004. Named Sr. Resident Rsch. Assoc., NAS-NRC, 1977-78; recipient Inst. medal Ctrl. Rsch. Inst. for Physics, 1979, Leo Schubert award Wash. Acad. Sci., 1988, Educator award Md. Assn. Higher Edn., 1989, Glover award Dickinson Coll., 1991, Forman award Vanderbilt U., 1996. Fellow AAAS, Am. Phys. Soc. (mem. com. edn. 2004—), Wash. Acad. Sci.; mem. Am. Assn. Physics Tchrs. (Robert A. Millikan medal 1998). Office: U Md Dept Physics College Park MD 20742-4111

REDLICH, NORMAN, lawyer, educator; b. N.Y.C., Nov. 12, 1925; s. Milton and Pauline (Durst) R.; m. Evelyn Jane Grobow, June 3, 1951; children: Margaret Bonny-Claire, Carrie Ann, Edward Grobow. AB, Williams Coll., 1947, LLD (hon.), 1976; LLB, Yale U., 1950; LLM, NYU, 1955; LLD (hon.), John Marshall Law Sch., 1990. Bar: N.Y. 1951. Practiced in, N.Y.C., 1951-59; assoc. prof. law NYU, 1960-62, prof. law, 1962-74, assoc. dean Sch. Law, 1974-75, dean Sch. Law, 1975-88, dean emeritus, 1992—. Judge Edward Weinfeld prof. law, 1982—; counsel Wachtell, Lipton, Rosen & Katz, N.Y.C., 1988—. Editor-in-chief Tax Law Rev., 1960-66; mem. adv. com. Inst. Fed. Taxation, 1963-68; exec. asst. corp. counsel, N.Y.C., 1966-68, 1st asst. corp. counsel, 1970-72, corp. counsel, 1972-74; asst. counsel Pres. Commn. on Assassination Pres. Kennedy, 1963-64; mem. com. on admissions and grievances U.S. 2d Circuit Ct. Appeals, 1978—, chmn., 1978-87. Author: Professional Responsibility: A Problem Approach, 1976, Constitutional Law, Cases and Materials, 1983, rev. edit., 1996, 2001, Understanding Constitutional Law, 1995, rev. edit., 1999; contbr. articles in field. Chmn. commn. on law and social action Am. Jewish Congress, 1978—, chmn. governing coun., 1996; mem. Borough Pres.'s Planning Bd. Number 2, 1959-70, counsel N.Y. Com. to Abolish Capital Punishment, 1958-77; mem. N.Y.C. Bd. Edn., 1969; mem. bd. overseers Jewish Theol. Sem., 1973—; trustee Law Ctr. Found. of NYU, 1975—, Freedom House, 1976-86, Vt. Law Sch., 1977-99, 2003—, Practicing Law Inst., 1980-99; trustee Lawyers Com. for Civil Rights Under Law, 1976—, co-chmn., 1979-81; bd. dirs. Legal Aid Soc., 1983-88, NAACP Legal Def. Fund, 1985—, Greenwich House, 1987—. Decorated Combat Infantryman's Badge. Mem. ABA (coun. legal edn. and admissions to bar 1981—, vice chmn. 1987-88, chmn. 1989-90, equal opportunities in legal profession 1986-92, ho. of dels. 1991—), Assn. of Bar of City of N.Y. (exec. com. 1975-79, professionalism com. 1988-92), com. on capital punishment 1998—). Office: 51 W 52nd St Fl 30 New York NY 10019-6119

REDLIN, BRUCE MICHAEL, financial consultant; b. Milwaukee, June 13, 1952; s. Raymond Elmer and Elizabeth June R.; m. Lynn Marie, Aug. 7, 1976; children: Joseph, David. B in Bus. Adminstrn., U. Wisc., 1974, M in Bus. Adminstrn., 1975. CPA; cert. govt. fin. officer. Acct. Krueger, Feld & Co. CPA, Milwaukee, 1974-78; mgr. Kirchow, Krause & Co. CPA, Milwaukee, 1978-80; ptnr. Hafner, Jurack & Co., Milwaukee, 1980-82, Redlin & Co. CPA, Milwaukee, 1982—; fin. tech. dir. City of Merrill, Wisc., 1996—. Mem. coms., City of Merrill, Wisc., 1996—. Mem. Am. Inst. CPA's, Wisc. Inst. CPA's, Govt. Fin. Officers Assn., Lion's Club, Rotary Club, Kiwanis Club, Optimists Club. Avocation: physical fitness. Home: PO Box 146 Antigo WI 54409-0146 Office: Redlin CPA 2323 S 109th St Milwaukee WI 53227-1909 E-mail: bredlin@dwave.net.

REDMAN, BARBARA KLUG, nursing educator; b. Mitchell, S.D. d. Harlan Lyle and Darlien Grace (Bock) Klug; m. Robert S. Redman, Sept. 14, 1958; 1 child, Melissa Darlien. BS, S.D. State U., 1958; MEd, U. Minn., 1959, PhD, 1964; LHD (hon.), Georgetown U., 1988; DSc (hon.), U. Colo., 1991; MA in Bioethics, MBE, U. Pa., 2004. RN. Asst. prof. U. Wash., Seattle, 1964-69; assoc. dean U. Minn., Mpls., 1969-75; dean Sch. Nursing U. Colo., Denver, 1975-78; VA scholar VA Cen. Office, Washington, 1978-81; postdoctoral fellow Johns Hopkins U., Balt., 1982-83; exec. dir. Am. Assn. Colls. Nursing, Washington, 1983-89, ANA, Washington, 1989-93; prof. nursing Johns Hopkins U., Balt., 1993-95; dean, prof. Sch. Nursing U. Conn., Storrs, 1995-98; dean Coll. Nursing Wayne State U., Detroit. Vis. fellow Kennedy Inst. Ethics, Georgetown U., 1993-94; fellow in med. ethics Harvard Med. Sch., 1994-95. Author: Practice of Patient Education, 1968—; contbr. articles to profl. jours. Bd. dirs. Friends of Nat. Libr. of Medicine, Washington, 1987—. Recipient Disting. Alumnus award S.D. State U., 1975, Outstanding Achievement award U. Minn., 1989. Fellow Am. Acad. Nursing. Home: 12425 Bobbink Ct Potomac MD 20854-3005 Office: Wayne State U 5557 Cass Ave Detroit MI 48202-3615

REDMAN, CLARENCE OWEN, lawyer; b. Joliet, Ill., Nov. 23, 1942; s. Harold F. and Edith L. (Read) R.; m. Barbara Ann Pawlan, Jan. 26, 1964 (div.); children: Scott, Steven; m. 2d, Carla J. Rozycki, Sept. 24, 1983. BS, U. Ill., 1964, JD, 1966, MA, 1967. Bar: Ill. 1966, U.S. Dist. Ct. (ea. dist.) Ill. 1970, U.S. Ct. Appeals (7th cir.) 1973, U.S. Ct. Appeals (4th cir.) 1982, U.S. Supreme Ct. 1975. Assoc. Keck, Mahin & Cate, Chgo., 1969-73, ptnr., corp. ptnr., 1973—, CEO, 1986-97; of counsel Lord, Bissell & Brook, Chgo., 1997—. Spl. asst. atty. gen. Ill., 1975-8; bd. dirs. AMCOL Internat. Corp. Mem. bd. visitors U. Ill. Coll. of Law, 1991-95. Capt. U.S. Army, 1967-69. Decorated Bronze Star. Mem. Ill. State Bar Assn. (chmn. young lawyers sect. 1977-78, del. assembly 1978-81, 84-87), Seventh Cir. Bar Assn. Office: Lord Bissell & Brook 115 S Lasalle St Ste 3200 Chicago IL 60603-3902 Office Phone: 312-443-0528.

REDMAN, ERIC, lawyer; b. Palo Alto, Calif., June 3, 1948; s. M. Chandler and Marjorie Jane (Sachs) R.; children: Ian Michael, Graham James, Jing; m. Heather Bell, 1996. AB, Harvard U., 1970, JD, 1975; BA, Oxford U., 1972, MA, 1980. Bar: Wash. 1975, U.S. Dist. Ct. (we. dist.) Wash. 1975, D.C. 1979, U.S. Ct. Appeals (9th cir.) 1981, U.S. Supreme Ct. 1983. Asst. U.S. senator W.G. Magnuson, Washington and Seattle, 1968-71, 74-75; assoc. Preston, Thorgrimson et al, Seattle, 1975-78, ptnr., 1979-82, Heller, Ehrman, White & McAuliffe, Seattle, 1983—. Author: Dance of Legislation, 1973; also book revs., articles. Office: Heller Ehrman White & McAuliffe 701 5th Ave Ste 6100 Seattle WA 98104-7098

REDMAN, ROBERT SHELTON, pathologist, dentist; b. Fargo, N.D., Aug. 1, 1935; s. Kenneth and Elizabeth Francis (McMillan) R.; m. Barbara Darlien Klug, Sept. 14, 1958; 1 child, Melissa Darlien Redman Johnson. Student, S.D. State U., 1953-55; BS, DDS, U. Minn., 1959, MSD, 1963; PhD, U. Wash., 1969. Cert. Am. Bd. Oral and Maxillofacial Pathology. Clin. asst. prof. sch. dentistry U. Minn., Mpls., 1963-64, assoc. prof., 1969-75; assoc. prof. sch. dentistry U. Colo., Denver, 1975-78; staff dentist, chief oral pathology rsch. lab. Dept. VA Med. Ctr., Denver, 1975-78, Washington, 1978—. Clin. assoc. prof. Balt. Coll. Dental Surgery U. Md., 1989—; cons. Children's Orthop. Hosp., Seattle, 1966-69; program specialist in oral biology Dept. VA, Washington, 1982-86; adj. scientist Nat. Inst. Dental and Craniofacial Rsch., NIH, 1997—. Contbr. 14 chpts. to books, over 95 articles to profl. jours.; mem. editl. bd. Jour. Dental Rsch., 1995-98, Biotech. and Histochemistry, 2000—; bd. reviewers Anatomical Record, 2004—. Mem. Biol. Stain Commn., 1999—. (bd. trustees, 2002-) Capt. U.S. Army, 1959-61. Recipient Carl A. Schlack award Assn. Mil. Surgeons U.S., 1997. Fellow Am. Acad. Oral and Maxillofacial Pathology; mem. ADA, Am. Assn. Anatomists, Internat. Assn. Dental Rsch. (program chmn. salivary rsch. group 1982-86, sec.-treas. 1995-2001, Salivary Rschr. of the Yr., Salivary Rsch. Group 2001), Soc. for In Vitro Biology, Omicron Kappa Upsilon. Presbyterian. Achievements include discovery and naming of an unique minor salivary gland in the rat; documentation of the relationship between weaning and maturation of salivary glands, of mitotic division of well-differentiated salivary gland cells of all types, including acinar, ductal and myoepithelial cells, of constant cell cycle length and very low rate of apoptosis in salivary glands during development and into maturity; determination of mode of inheritance of benign migratory glossitis, co-developer method to maintain salivary gland acinar cells in culture and several cell lines of these cells. Office: Dept VA Med Ctr (151-I) Oral Pathology Rsch Lab 50 Irving St NW Washington DC 20422-0001 Personal E-mail: oralpath@erols.com.

REDMAN, TIMOTHY PAUL, English language educator, author, chess federation administrator; b. Elmhurst, Ill., June 26, 1950; s. William Charles and Eileen Marie (Keenan) R. BA, Loyola U., Chgo., 1973; MA, U. Chgo., 1974, PhD, 1987. Instr. Loyola U., Rome, 1977, Ill. Inst. Tech., Chgo., 1980-84; lectr. English dept. Loyola U., Chgo., 1982-84, DePaul U., 1982—84; lectr. U. Wis., Parkside, 1984-85; instr. Ohio State U., Lima, 1985-87, asst. prof., 1987-89, U. Tex., Dallas, 1989-91, assoc. dean, coll. master, 1991-92, assoc. prof., 1991-98, prof., 1998—. Author: Ezra Pound and Italian Fascism, 1991; editor: Official Rules of Chess, 3d edit., 1987. Whiting fellow, 1981-82, NEH fellow, 1992-93. Mem. MLA, World Chess Fedn. (gen. sec. Chess in Schs. com.), U.S. Chess Fedn. (past pres.), Nat. Coun. Tchrs. English, PEN U.S.A. West. Roman Catholic. Office: U Tex Dallas Sch Arts & Humanities JO31 PO Box 830688 Richardson TX 75083-0688 also: US Chess Fedn 3054 US Rte 9W New Windsor NY 12553-7624 Office Phone: 972-883-2775. E-mail: redman@utdallas.edu.

REDMAN, WALTER DEWEY, musician, educator; b. Ft. Worth, Tex., May 17, 1931; s. George Dewey Redman and Odessa Wilson-Redman McMullan; m. Lidija Pedenska Redman, Oct. 9, 1967; m. Pennie Wyse Redman, Mar. 17, 1969 (div. 1995); children: Tarik, Kenthony Curtis, Joshua Redman Shedroff. BS, No. Tex. State Coll., 1959, Prarie View A & M, 1953. Tchr. Plainview Sch. Dist., Tex., 1956—57, Bastron Sch. Dist., Tex., 1958—60; jazz musician/performer Self-Employed, San Francisco, 1961—67, Ornette Coleman/Keith Jarrett, NYC, 1967—. Musician: 12solo jazz albums and with many others such as Ornette Coleman, Keith Jarrett, Pat Methen. Prostate cancer activist Bklyn. Borough Pres. Men's Health Initiative, 1992—. PFC U.S. Army, 1953—55, Ft. Bliss, Tex. Grant, John Simon Guggenheim Meml. Found., 2002. Mem.: Am. Fedn. Musicians. Meth. Avocations: travel, writing, teaching.

REDMAN, WILLIAM WALTER, JR., realtor; b. Statesville, N.C., Oct. 15, 1933; s. William Walter and Mildred (Huie) R.; m. Elizabeth Ann Wilhelm, Dec. 28, 1956; children: Lisa Dawn, Kathryn Marlene, Adrienne Ann. Student, U. So. Calif., 1966; BS, Embry-Riddle Aeronat. U., 1972; postgrad., Jud. Coll., 1987. Enlisted U.S. Army, 1954, advanced trhough grades to lt. col., 1974, ret., 1974; dir. pub. rels. Northwestern State Bank, Statesville, 1974-76; pres. Redman Realty, Statesville, 1976-92; mem. N.C. Senate from 26th Dist., 1978-87, minority leader, 1986-87; commr. pub. utilities State of N.C., 1987-95; chmn. N.C. Utilities Commn., 1995—2001. Exec. dir. N.C. Telecomm. Industry Assn.; exec. v.p. carolina Vas. Telephone Membership Assn.; mem. exec. com., vice chmn. com. on adminstrn., comm. com. Nat. Assn. Regulatory Utility Commrs.; chmn. bd. dirs. Nat. Regylatory Rsch. Inst., Ohio State U., 1993; mem. exec. com. Southeastern Assn. Regulatory Utilities Commrs.; past trustee Gardner-Webb Coll.; mem. bd. advisors Sch. Bus. Pub. Utility Regulatory Bd., N.Mex. State U.; dir. N.C. Solar Ctr.; past mem. N.C. Energy Policy Coun., N.C. Tax Rev. Bd.; bd. dirs. N.C. Child Advocay Inst., 1997, Assn. Excs. N.C. 1997—. Decorated DFC with oak leaf cluster, Bronze Star medal with two oak leaf clusters, Air medal with sixteen oak leaf clusters, Meritorious Svc. medal; recipient Valand award N.C. Mental Assns.; named to Inf. Officers Sch. Hall of Fame, Ft. Benning Ga., Disting. Mem. Regt., U.S. Transp. Corps, 1990; recipient 2 Long Leaf Pine award, N.C. Mem. VFW (life), Ret. Officers Assn. (life), Nat. Assn. Adminstrv. Law Judges, Am. Legion (life), Raleigh Exec. Club, N.C. State U. Faculty Club, Rotary Club. Republican. Baptist. Address: 1320 Royalty Cir Statesville NC 28625-8230

REDMANN, JOHN WILLIAM, lawyer, consultant; b. New Orleans, Sept. 10, 1963; s. William Vincent and Ana Maria (Macouzet) R. BA in Psychology, BA in French, Loyola U. of the South, 1986, JD, 1989. Bar: La. 1990, U.S. Dist. Ct. (ea. dist.) La. 1990; cert. notary pub., La. Litigation law clk. Orleans Sewerage and Water Bd., New Orleans, 1989—90; law clk. to Hon. Judge Connolly Orleans Civil Dist. Ct., New Orleans, 1990—92; assoc. Exnicios & Nungesser, New Orleans, 1992—94; prin. Law Offices of John W. Redmann, New Orleans, 1994—. V.p., gen counsel Meridian Group, LLC, New Orleans, 1999—, 5 Lights, LLC, 2000—; v.p. L'Ecole Maternelle, 1998, also bd. dirs.; charter mem. alumni com. Loyola Law Sch. Moot Ct., 1991-96, chmn. 1980's decade ann. fund campaign. Chmn. 1995 Loyola Law Ann. Fund Campaign, New Orleans; charter mem./officer Lawyers Against Crime, Inc., New Orleans, 1995—. Mem. ATLA (traumatic brain injury litigation group 1997-2000), Nat. Inst. Trial Advocacy (diplomate), La. Trial Lawyers Assn. (leadership and membership coms. 1994-96, treas. Bench and Bar sect. 2001—), Assn. of New Orleans Trial Lawyers, Supreme Ct. of La. Hist. Soc. (charter), So. Trial Lawyers Assn. (bd. dirs. 1998-2000), La. Hispanic C. of C. (bd. dirs., sec. 1999, gen. counsel 1999—, 1st v.p. 1999—), Young Leadership Counsel, Bards Bohemia (exec. bd. 1998-99, 2001—), Celtic Club of New Orleans (pres. 1997-98). Roman Catholic. Avocations: travel, foreign languages. Home: 1327 Short St New Orleans LA 70118-4043 Office: Law Office John W Redmann PLC 9701 Lake Forest Blvd Ste 103 New Orleans LA 70127-5403 Office Phone: 800-240-1995. E-mail: advice@redmannlaw.com., john@redmannlaw.com.

REDMON, AGILE HUGH, JR., allergist; b. Dec. 17, 1924; s. Agile H. and Natalie Mary (Collins) R.; m. Dora Mary Bastiani, May 18, 1957 (dec. Apr. 1996); children: James Joseph, John Gerard. Student, Tex. A&M U., 1942-43, U. Southwestern La., 1943-44; MD, Baylor U., 1948. Diplomate Am. Bd. Allergy and Immunology. Intern U.S. Naval Hosp., San Diego, 1948-49, resident in allergy, 1955-56; resident in internal medicine Baylor/VA Hosp., Houston, 1950-53; assoc. prof. medicine Baylor U., Houston, 1957—. Sr. ptnr. Allergy Asthma Assocs., Houston, 1970—; exec. dir. S.W. Allergy Forum, 1996—. With M.C., USN, 1943-48, 53-57. Fellow Am. Acad. Allergy, Asthma, and Immunology (chmn. coun. local soc. pres.'s, Outstanding Vol. Faculty award 1998), Am. Coll. Allergy, Asthma, and Immunology; mem. AMA, Houston Acad. Medicine (pres. 1986), Tex. Med. Assn., Harris County Med. Soc. (v.p. 1984), Tex. Allergy Soc. (pres. 1984-88), Tex. Allergy and Immunology Soc. (founder), Houston Allergy Soc. (past pres). Republican. Roman Catholic. Home: 5223 Contour Pl Houston TX 77096-4117 Office: 7505 Fannin St Ste 515 Houston TX 77054-1913

REDMON, ROSE MARIE, secondary school educator; b. Pasadena, Calif., Sept. 24, 1952; d. Earl Eugene and Rose Ellen (Jackson) R.; 1 child, Matthew Eugene. AA, Midway Jr. Coll., 1972; BS, SUNY, Brockport, 1973; MS, Emporia State U., 1981. Cert. secondary edn. tchr., Minn., N.Y. Educator Kansas City (Kans.) Pub. Schs., 1974-81; instr. U. Minn., Morris, 1981-82; educator Spl. Sch. Dist. 1, Folwell Jr., Mpls., 1982-83; educator, mid. sch. coord. Webster Open Sch., Mpls., 1983-2000; mid. sch. coord. Jordan Park Sch. Extended Learning, Mpls., 2000—. Bd. dirs. Grace Meth. Pre-sch., Mpls., 1988-96. Mem. NEA, ASCD, Am. Fedn. Tchrs., Mpls. Fedn. Tchrs., Nat. Coun. Tchrs. Math., Nat. Youth Leadership Coun., Secondary Edn. Task Force Mpls., Minn. Ednl. Effectiveness Project, Mpls. Edn. Assn. Democrat. Home: 2958 Knox Ave N Minneapolis MN 55411-1250 Office: Mpls Pub Schs 807 Broadway St NE Minneapolis MN 55413-2332 E-mail: rredmon@mpls.k12.mn.us.

REDMOND, ARTHUR J, insurance company executive; BBA, MBA, U. Wis. Mng. dir. global consumer insights and market info. Citibank, 1997—99; exec. dir. global consumer insights office Ford Motor Co., 1999—2002; sr. v.p., strategic mktg. Aetna Inc., 2002—. Bd. trustees Mktg. Sci. Inst. Mem.: U.S. Census Adv. Com., Am. Mktg. Assn., European Soc. of Mktg. and Rsch. Office: Aetna Inc 151 Farmington Ave Hartford CT 06156

REDMOND, BILL, former congressman, minister; m. Shirley Raye Robertson; children: Bethany Joy, Jordan Andrew. BA in Ministry and Adminstrn., Lincoln Christian Coll., 1979, MDiv, 1988. Spl. edn. instr., 1980-83; past tchr. and adminstr. handicapped adults; past min. Santa Fe Christian Ch.; mem. Ho. of Reps. from N.Mex. 3d congl. dist., 1997-98, mem. nat. security com., mem. banking and fin svcs. com., mem. vet. affairs com. Past instr. adulty basic edn. U. N.Mex. Active Boy Scouts Am., numerous youth drug prevention programs, Big Brother program; past foster parent. Served USAR. Republican. Office: PO Box 1226 Los Alamos NM 87544-1226 Fax: 202-226-1331.*

REDMOND, DAVID DUDLEY, lawyer; b. Hartford, Conn., May 12, 1944; s. Robert LaVere and Dorothy Iva (Mylchreest) R.; m. Eugenia Blount Scott, Aug. 24, 1968; children: R. Scott, Sarah D. BA, Washington and Lee U., 1966, LLB, 1969. Bar: Va. 1970, U.S. Dist. Ct. (ea. dist.) Va. 1972, U.S. Ct. Appeals (4th cir.) 1972. Ptnr. Christisn & Barton LLP, Richmond, Va., 1972—. Editl. bd. Washington and Lee U. Law Rev., 1968-69. Chmn. bd. trustees St. Joseph's Villa, 2004—. Capt. U.S. Army, 1970—71. Decorated Bronze Star; named to Washington and Lee U. Athletic Hall of Fame. Mem.: Richmond Bar Assn. (exec. com. 1980), Va. Bar Assn., Va. State Bar, Washington and Lee Law Alumni Assn. (bd. dirs. 1993—2002, pres. 1995—96), Washington and Lee U. Alumni Assn. (pres. Richmond chpt. 1980—82, bd. dirs. 1997—99, 2003—), Omicron Delta Kappa. Office: Mutual Bldg Ste 1200 Richmond VA 23219 E-mail: dredmond@cblaw.com.

REDMOND, DONALD EUGENE, JR., neuroscientist, educator; b. San Antonio, June 17, 1939; s. Donald Eugene and Viola (Kellum) R.; m. Patricia Welder (Robinson), Dec. 22, 1972; one child Andy J. BA, So. Meth. U., 1961; MD, Baylor U., 1968; MAH, Yale U., 1987. Diplomate Am. Bd. Psychiatry and Neurology. With Lab. of Clin. Sci., NIMH, Bethesda, Md., 1973-74; asst. prof. psychiatry Yale U., New Haven, 1974-77; assoc. chief clin. neurol. sci. unit Conn. Mental Health Ctr., New Haven, 1974-87; assoc. prof. psychiatry Yale U., New Haven, 1978-87; pres. St. Kitts Bio Med. Rsch. Found., St. Kitts, West Indies, 1983—, Axion Rsch. Found., Hamden, Conn., 1985—; prof. psychiatry, dir. neurol. behavior lab. Yale U., New Haven, 1987—, dir. neurol. transplant program for neurol. diseases, 1987—; prof. neurol. surgery, 1993—; with Yale Univ., New Haven, 1993. Contbr. articles to profl. jour.; patentee in field. With USPHS, 1972-74. Recipient Rsch. Scientist Award NIMH, 1980-2001; Found. Fund Prize, Am. Psychiatric Assoc., 1981; grantee NIMH, 1974-91, Nat. Inst. Neurol. Diseases and Stroke, 1986—; others. Mem.: Internat. Soc. Motor Disturbances, Am. Soc. Neural Transplantation and Repair (coun. mem. 1994—98, pres. 2002), Am. Coll. Neuropsychopharmacology (fellow 2002—03). Office: Neurobehavior Lab PO Box 3333 New Haven CT 06510-0333

REDMOND, KELLY THOMAS, climatologist; b. Wausau, Wis., Jan. 5, 1952; s. Clarence James and Joyce Alice (Sagstetter) R. BS in Physics, MIT, 1974; MS in Meteorology, U. Wis., 1977, PhD in Meteorology, 1982. Asst. state climatologist Oreg. State U., Corvallis, 1982-84, state climatologist, 1984-89; reg. climatologist Western Reg. Climate Ctr., Desert Rsch. Inst., Reno, Nev., 1989—, reg. climatologist, dep. dir., 1992—. Mem. Am. Assn. State Climatologists (pres. 1989-90). Home: 2570 Polk St Reno NV 89503-1328 Office: Western Reg Climate Ctr Desert Rsch Inst 2215 Raggio Pkwy Reno NV 89512-1095 Office Phone: 702-674-7011. Business E-Mail: kelly.redmond@dri.edu.

REDMOND, MARK LEROY, secondary school educator; b. Warren, Ohio, Sept. 1, 1953; s. Eugene Kenneth and Maude Marcelyn Redmond; m. Donna Susan Rosser, May 28, 1974; children: Benjamin Mark, Melody Dianne. BS in Secondary Edn., Tenn. Temple U., 1975. Tchr. Calvary Bapt. Sch., Kingston, Tenn., 1975—76; audio technician Sword of the Lord Pubs., Murfreesboro, Tenn., 1976—77; tchr. Granger (Ind.) Christian Sch., 1978—. Author: Arty Goes West, 1999, Arty and the Hunt for Phantom, 2001, Arty and the Texas Ranger, 2002, Arty's Long Day, 2003. Mem.: Soc. Children's Book Writers and Illustrators, Western Writers Am. Avocations: single-action shooting, reading, collecting Western memorabilia. Home: 52441 Prescott Ave South Bend IN 46637 Office Phone: 574-272-5815. E-mail: sheriffredmond@aol.com.

REDMOND, MICHAEL R. ophthalmologist; b. Sterling, Ill. MD, St. Louis U., 1968. Diplomate Am. Bd. Ophthalmology. Intern St. Louis U. Group Hosps., 1968—69, resident ophthalmology, 1971—74; fellow pediat. ophthalmology U. Iowa Hosps.-Clinics, Iowa City, 1974—75; opthalmologist Ophthalmology Group Practice, Pensacola, Fla., 1975—. Attending physician West Fla. Hosp., Pensacola, Sacred Heart Hosp., Pensacola. Mem.: AMA, Am. Coll. Surgery, Am. Acad. Ophthalmology (bd. trustees 1993—99, pres. 2003—, chmn., vice chmn. coun.). Office: 8333 N Davis Hwy Pensacola FL 32514-6050

REDMOND, PATRICIA ANN, lawyer; b. Phila., Mar. 17, 1950; d. John Charles and Mildred Muriel (Smith) R.; m. Jerry M. Markowitz, Oct. 19, 1985; 1 child, Lisa Dawn. BA, U. Miami (Fla.), 1975, JD, 1979. Bar: Pa. 1979, Fla. 1979, U.S. Dist. Ct. (so. dist.) Fla. 1980, U.S. Ct. Appeals (11th cir.) 1985. Assoc. Britton, Cohen, Kaufman, et al, Miami, 1980-81; pvt. practice law Miami, 1981-92; atty., shareholder Stearns, Weaver Miller et al, 1992—. Lectr., advisor Legal Svcs., Greater Miami, 1985—; ethics panelist Nat. Conf. of Bankruptcy Judges, 1990; adj. prof. St. Thomas U. Sch. Law, U. Miami Sch. Law, 1999—; co-founder So. Dist. Fla. Bankruptcy Assistance Clinic, 2000-01. Recipient Fla. Bar Pres.'s Pro Bono award for the 11th Jud. Cir., 2002, Richard Hausler Gold Apple award, 2003, Milstein Pro Bono award, Dade County Bar, 2004. Mem. ABA (co-chair subcom. on data collection and bankruptcy, bus. law sect., vice chair secured creditors subcom.), Bankruptcy Bar Assn. So. dist. Fla. (pres. 1988-89, chmn. legal edn. com. 1990-91, chair pro bono clin. programs, vice-chair secured creditors subcom.), Norton Inst., Am. Bankruptcy Inst. (bd. dirs. 2003—), Comml. Law League (vice chmn. speaker bur.). Democrat. Avocations: bicycling, running. Fax: 305-789-3395. Office Phone: 305-789-3553. E-mail: predmond@swmwas.com.

REDMONT, BERNARD SIDNEY, dean, communications educator; b. NYC, Nov. 8, 1918; s. Morris Abraham and Bessie (Kamerman) R.; m. Joan Rothenberg, Mar. 12, 1940; children: Dennis Foster, Jane Carol. BA, CCNY, 1938; M.J., Columbia U., 1939; D.H.L., Fla. Internat. U., 1980. Reporter, book reviewer Bklyn. Daily Eagle, 1936-38; free lance corr. Europe, 1939, 1939-40; telegraph editor, editorial writer Herkimer (N.Y.) Evening Telegram, 1941-42; newswriter U.S. Office of Inter-Am. Affairs (Washington shortwave radio newscasts to Latin Am.), 1942-43, dir. News div., 1944-46; staff corr., bur. chief U.S. News & World Report, Buenos Aires and Paris, 1946-51; columnist Continental Daily Mail, Paris, 1951-53; chief corr. English Lang. World News Service Agence France-Presse, Paris, 1953-65; European corr. Paris news bur. chief Westinghouse Broadcasting Co., Paris, 1961-76; corr., bur. chief CBS News, Moscow, 1976-79, corr. Paris, 1979-81; prof. journalism, dir. broadcast journalism program, dean Boston U. Coll. Communication, 1982-86, dean emeritus, prof. journalism, 1986—, mem. adv. bd. Latin Am. journalism program, 1989—. Cons. Exec. Svc. Corps. of New Eng., 1991—, Internat. Exec. Svc. Corps, 1992—. Author: Risks Worth Taking: The Odyssey of a Foreign Correspondent, Univ. Press of Am., 1992, Friendly Moderation, 1997. Served with USMCR, 1943-44. Decorated Purple Heart, chevalier Legion of Honor (France); recipient award for advancement of journalism Columbia U., 1986, Townsend Harris medal for life achievement, 1991, Yankee Quill award for disting. contbns. to betterment of journalism, 1995; Pulitzer travel fellow; named to Commns. Hall of Fame CCNY, 2002 Mem. Overseas Press Club (award best radio reporting from abroad 1968, 73), Soc. Profl. Journalists, Nat. Press Club, Anglo-American Press Assn. of Paris (pres. 1961, treas. 1970-73, sec. 1974-76) Unitarian Universalist. *Life has more meaning when it affirms, with grace, the Yang and the Yin, reconciling opposites--independence, yet cooperative effort and community caring; courage and hard work, yet moderation and generosity; hatred of injustice, yet kindness,fairness and compassion.*

REDO, DAVID LUCIEN, investment company executive; b. Lakewood, Ohio, Sept. 1, 1937; s. Joseph L. and Florence M. (Morse) R.; m. Judy L. Ijams, Aug. 4, 1962; children: Jenny, Mark. BSEE, U. Calif., Berkeley, 1961; MBA, U. Santa Clara, 1967. Registered investment advisor. Asst. engring. mgr. AT&T, N.Y.C., 1968-71; pension fund mgr. Pacific Telephone, San Francisco, 1971-77; mng. dir. Fremont Group (formerly Bechtel Investments Inc.), San Francisco, 1977—2002; chmn., CEO Fremont Investment Advisors, Inc., San Francisco, 1986—2000; mng. dir. FremontInvestment Advisers, San Francisco, 2000—03; chmn. emeritus Fremont Mutual Funds, 2000—03; prin., portfolio mgr. Wetherby Asset Mgmt., San Francisco, 2003—; dir. Cellan Assoc., San Francisco, 2004—. Bd. dirs. Sit/Kim Internat. Investments; chmn., CEO Fremont Mutual Funds, 1998—2000, chmn. emeritus, 2000—03. Chmn. investment com. U. Calif. Found., 1988—2001; mem. bd. advisors Sentinel Pension Inst., 1978—2001; trustee U. Calif., Berkeley, 1988—2001, trustee emeritus, 2001—. Mem.: Internat. Assn. Fin. Planners. Avocations: golf, travel, reading, walking. Office: Wetherby Asset Mgmt 417 Montgomery San Francisco CA 94104 Personal E-mail: davidredo@sbcglobal.net.

REDO, S(AVERIO) FRANK, surgeon; b. Bklyn., Dec. 28, 1920; s. Frank and Maria (Guida) R.; m. Maria Lappano, June 27, 1948; children— Philip, Martha. BS, Queens Coll., 1942; MD, Cornell U., 1950. Diplomate: Am. Bd. Thoracic Surgery, Am. Bd. Surgery (pediatric surgery). Intern in surgery N.Y. Hosp., N.Y.C., 1950-51, asst. resident surgeon, 1951-56, resident surgeon, 1956-57, asst. attending surgeon, 1958-60, assoc. attending surgeon, 1960-66, surgeon in charge pediatric surgery, 1960, attending surgeon, 1966—; practice medicine specializing in surgery; clin. asso. prof. surgery Cornell U. Med. Coll., 1963-72, prof., 1972—. Author: Surgery in the Ambulatory Child, 1961, Principles of Surgery in the First Six Months of Life, 1976, Atlas of Surgery in the First Six Months of Life, 1977; contbr. articles to profl. jours.; patentee in field. Served to capt. USAAF, 1942-46. Fellow A.C.S., Am. Coll. Chest Physicians; mem. Harvey Soc., Pan Am. Med. Assn., Soc. Univ. Surgeons, Am. Acad. Pediatrics, Am. Fedn. for Clin. Research, Internat. Cardiovascular Soc., Am. Surg. Assn., Am. Assn. Thoracic Surgery, Soc. for Surgery Alimentary Tract, Am. Soc. Artificial Internat. Organs, Am. Acad. Pediatrics, Assn. Advancement Med. Instrumentation, Soc. Thoracic Surgeons, Internat. Soc. Surgery, N.Y. Gastroent. Soc., N.Y. Acad. Sci., N.Y. Cardiovascular Soc., N.Y. Acad. Medicine, N.Y. Soc. Thoracic Surgery, N.Y. Pediatric Soc., Med. Soc. County N.Y., Queens Coll. Alumni Assn. (gov. 1962—), Sigma Xi. Home: 435 E 70th St New York NY 10021-5342 Office: 525 E 68th St New York NY 10021-4870 E-mail: sfredo@aol.com. *My life is based on the principles of doing as much for others as possible and doing no harm; to offer advice only when asked; to apply myself unstintingly, but not selfishly, to my work; to learn from my mistakes; to strive for perfection; and to always have a project and a dream.*

REDSHAW, JAMES DOUGLAS, neurologist; b. Montreal, Aug. 5, 1952; s. Robert Leslie Redshaw and Dorothy Ann Levine; m. Evelyn Lee Downs, Dec. 28, 1979; children: Jeffrey Devin, Timothy Douglas. BSc in Biology, Laurentian U., 1975; PhD in Med. Sci., McMaster U., 1980; MD, U. Calgary, 1986. Postdoctoral fellow Alta. Heritage Found. for Med. Rsch., Calgary, 1980-86; med. resident internal medicine U. Calgary Med. Sch., 1986-87; resident in neurology U. Western Ont., London, 1987-89; clin. fellow in neurology U. Alta., Edmonton, 1989-91; neurologist Boise (Idaho) Neurol. Cons., 1991—. Mem. med. staff St. Alphonsus Med. Ctr./St. Lukes Med. Ctr., Boise, 1991—, chmn. dept. neurology/neurosurgery, Boise, 1997-99. Contbr. articles to profl. jours. Mem. profl. adv. bd. Epilepsy Found. Idaho, Boise, 1991—. Mem. Am. Acad. neurology, Idaho Med. Assn., Idaho Neurol. Inst. (bd. dirs. 1994-2000), Nat. Stroke Assn. Avocations: photography, skiing, water-skiing. Home: 4155 W Quail Ridge Dr Boise ID 83703 Office: Boise Neurol Cons 999 N Curtis Rd Ste 506 Boise ID 83706 Office Phone: 208-367-2800.

REDSTONE, SUMNER MURRAY, entertainment company executive, lawyer; b. Boston, May 27, 1923; s. Michael and Belle (Ostrovsky) R.; children: Brent Dale, Shari Ellin. BA, Harvard U., 1944, LLB, 1947; LLD (hon.), Boston U., 1994; LHD (hon.), N.Y. Inst. Tech., 1996. Bar: Mass. 1947, U.S. Ct. Appeals (1st cir.) 1948, U.S. Ct. Appeals (8th cir.) 1950, U.S. Ct. Appeals (9th cir.) 1948, D.C. 1951, U.S. Supreme Ct. 1952. Law sec. U.S. Ct. Appeals for 9th Circuit, San Francisco, 1947-48; instr. law and labor mgmt. U. San Francisco, 1947; spl. asst. to U.S. Atty. Gen., Washington, 1948-51; ptnr. Ford, Bergson, Adams, Borkland & Redstone, Washington, 1951-54; CEO Nat. Amusements Inc., Dedham, Mass., 1967—, pres., 1967—99, chmn. bd., 1986—, Viacom, Inc., N.Y.C., 1987—, CEO, 1996—. Prof. Boston U. Law Sch., 1982, 85-86; bd. dirs. TV Acad. Arts and Scis. Found.; vis. prof. Brandeis U., Waltham, Mass.; lectr. Harvard Law Sch., Cambridge, Mass.; Judge on Kennedy Libr. Found., (sel. comm. John F. Kennedy Profile in Courage award). Chmn. met. divsn. NE Combined Jewish Philanthropies, Boston, 1963; mem. exec. bd. Combined Jewish Philanthropies of Greater Boston; mem. corp. New Eng. Med. Ctr., 1967—, Mass. Gen. Hosp. Corp.; trustee Children's Cancer Rsch. Found.; founding trustee Am. Cancer Soc.; chmn. Am. Cancer Crusade, State of Mass., 1984-86; Art Lending Libr.; sponsor Boston Mus. Sci.; chmn. Jimmy Fund Found., 1960; v.p., mem. exec. com. Will Rogers Meml. Fund; bd. dirs. Boston Arts Festival; bd. overseers Dana Farber Cancer Ctr., Boston Mus. Fine Arts; mem. presdl. adv. com. on arts John F. Kennedy Libr. Found., also judge ann. John F. Kennedy Profile in Courage Award com.; chmn. Corp. Commn. on Edn. Tech., 1996—, presdl. apptd. chmn., 1996. 1st lt. AUS, 1943-45. Decorated Army Commendation medal; named 1 of 10 Outstanding Young Men in New Eng., Boston Jr. C. of C., 1958; recipient William J. German Human Rels. award Am. Jewish Com. Entertainment/Comm. Divsn., 1977, Silver Shingle award Boston U. Law Sch., 1985, Variety New Eng. Humanitarian award, 1989, Golden Plate award Am. Acad. Achievement, 1993, 32d Ann. Salute to Excellence Program, 1993, Bus. Excellence award U. So. Calif. Sch. Bus. Adminstrn., 1994, The Stephen S. Wise award The Am. Jewish Congress, 1994, Man of Yr. award MIPCOM, the Internat. Film and Programme Market for TV, Video, Cable and Satellite, 1994, The Legends in Leadership award Emory U., 1995, Allan K. Jonas Lifetime Achievement award Am. Cancer Soc., 1995, Humanitarian award Variety Club Internat., 1995, Expeditioner's award N.Y.C. Outward Bound Ctr., 1996, Patron Arts award Songwriter's Hall Fame, 1996, Vision 21 award N.Y. Inst. Tech., 1996, Trustees award NATAS, 1997, Ripple of Hope award Robert F. Kennedy Meml., 1998, Humanitarian award Nat. Conf. Christians and Jews, 1998; named Communicator of Yr., B'nai B'rith Comm./Cinema Lodge, 1980, Man of Yr., Entertainment Industries Divsn. of UJA Fedn., 1988, Pioneer of Yr., Motion Picture Pioneers, 1991, Grad. of Yr., Boston Latin Sch., 1989, Honoree 7th ann. fundraiser Montefiore Med. Ctr., 1995, Hall of Fame award Broadcasting and Cable mag., 1995. Mem. ABA, Nat. Assn. Theatre Owners (chmn. bd. dirs. 1965-66, exec. comm. 1995—), Theatre Owners Am. (asst. pres. 1960-63, pres. 1964-65), Motion Picture Pioneers (bd. dirs.), Boston Bar Assn., Mass. Bar Assn., Harvard Law Sch. Assn., Am. Judicature Soc., Masons, Univ. Club, Harvard Club. Home: 200 Elm St Dedham MA 02027-9126 Office: Nat Amusements Inc PO Box 9126 Dedham MA 02027-9126*

REDWINE, ROBERT PAGE, physicist, researcher; b. Raleigh, N.C., Dec. 3, 1947; s. Robert Word and Hazel Virginia (Green) R.; m. Jacqueline Nina Hewitt, Nov. 22, 1986; children: Keith Hewitt, Jonathan Hewitt. AB, Cornell U., 1969; PhD, Northwestern U., 1973. Rsch. assoc. Los Alamos (N.Mex.) Nat. Lab, 1973-77, staff sci., 1977-79; rsch. assoc. U. Berne, Switzerland, 1974-75; asst. prof. physics MIT, Cambridge, Mass., 1979-82, assoc. prof., 1982-89, prof., 1989—, dir. lab. nuclear sci., 1992-2000, dean for undergrad. edn., 2000—. Contbr. articles to profl. jours. Fellow AAAS, Am. Phys. Soc. Office: MIT Undergrad Edn Bldg 4-110 Cambridge MA 02139

REECE, E. ALBERT, dean, obstetrician, gynecologist, perinatologist; b. Spanishtown, Jamaica, Jan. 3, 1950; came to U.S., 1969; s. Wilfred Anderson Reece and Daisy Lucinda (Price) Reece Batten; m. Sharon Andrea Blake, July 28, 1974; children: Kelie, Brynne, Sharon-Andrea II. BS with honors, L.I. U., 1973; MD, NYU, 1978; ob/gyn specialty diploma, Columbia U., 1982; maternal-fetal subspecialty diploma, Yale U., 1984. Diplomate Am. Bd. Ob-Gyn.; bd. cert. maternal-fetal medicine. Intern, resident Columbia U., Presbyn. Med. Ctr., N.Y.C., 1978-82; materal-fetal medicine fellow Yale U. Sch. Medicine, 1982-84, asst. prof. ob-gyn, 1984-87, assoc. prof. ob-gyn, 1987-90; prof., chmn. ob-gyn Temple U. Sch. Medicine, Phila., 1991—2001; dean, v.p. for med. sciences U. of Arkansas for Med. Sciences, Coll. of Med., 2002—. Elected IOM (chair pediatrics, obstetrics & gynecology, 2003-), NAS, 1998. Co-editor Diabetes Mellitus in Pregnancy: Principles and Practice, 1st edit., 1988, 2nd edit., 1995, Medicine of the Fetus and Mother, 1992, 2nd edit., 1999, A Study Guide for Medicine of the Fetus and Mother, 1992, A Handbook of Medicine of the Fetus and Mother, 1995; co-author. Fundamentals in Obstetric and Gynecologic Ultrasonography, 1993; contbr. articles, abstract to profl. jours. in excess of 400. Mem. sci. adv. com. March of Dimes, 1993—; mem. sci. adv. bd. NIH-DC Infant Mortality Initiative, 1993—; mem. adv. com. Nat. Inst. Child Health and Human Diseases, NIH, 1994—; trustee Reading Rehab. Hosp., 1992—; mem. bioeffects com. AIUM, 1992-95. Grantee March of Dimes, 1985-87, Friedman Found., 1990-92, William Penn Found., 1989-93, Am. Diabetes Assn., 1991-93, NIH, 1992—; named one of Top 100 Black Physicians in Am., Black Enterprise Mag., 2001. Fellow Am. Coll. Ob-Gyn., Coll. Physicians Phila.; mem. Am. Diabetes Assn. (coun. on diabetes in pregnancy), Am. Inst. Ultrasound in Medicine, Hellenic Perinatal Soc. Greece (hon.), Nat. Med. Assn. (exec. com. 1987-88, chmn. ob-gyn. sect. 1991-93), Nat. Acad. Scis. (Inst. Medicine), New Haven Obstet. Soc., Soc. for Gynecol. Investigation, Soc. Perinatal Obstetricians (leader diabetes spl. interest 1992-94, bd. mem. 1995—), Phila. Perinatal Soc. (program chair 1993—), Phila. Obstet. Soc. (mem. coun. 1992-94). Seventh-Day Adventist. Office: Univ Ark for Med Sciences 4301 W Markham Slot 550 Little Rock AR 72205*

REECE, MAYNARD FRED, artist, writer; b. Arnolds Park, Iowa, Apr. 26, 1920; s. Waldo H. and Inez V. (Latson) R.; m. June Carman, Apr. 7, 1946; children: Mark A., Brad D. Privately educated. Artist Meredith Pub. Co., Des Moines, 1938-40; artist, asst., mus. dir. Iowa Dept. History and Archives, Des Moines, 1940-50. Artist: Fish and Fishing, 1963, Waterfowl of Iowa, 1943; watercolor Trout, Saturday Evening Post (award of Distinctive Merit 1962); watercolors 73 Fish, Life mag. (cert. of merit 1955); print of Water's Edge Canada Geese for Am. Artist Collection, Am. Artist Mag., 1985; author, artist: The Waterfowl Art of Maynard Reece, 1985, The Upland Bird Art of Maynard Reece, 1997. Chmn. Gov.'s Com. Conservation of Outdoor Resource, 1963-64; trustee Iowa Natural Heritage Found., Des Moines, 1979—; hon. trustee Ducks Unltd., Inc., 1983—; trustee J.N. "Ding" Darling Conservation Found., Inc., Des Moines, 1962—. Served with AUS, 1943-45. Recipient awards for duck stamps and others Dept. Interior, 1948, 51, 59, 69, 71; recipient award Govt. Bermuda, 1963, award Iowa Conservation Commn., 1972, 77, 80, 81, award Fish and Game Commn., Little Rock, 1982, 88, award Tex. Parks and Wild Life Dept., 1983, award Nat. Fish & Wildlife Found., 1988, award Wash. State Dept. Wildlife, 1989, award Idaho Dept. Fish & Game, 1998, 4 awards Ill. Dept. of Natural Resources, 1997-2000; named Artist of Yr. Ducks Unltd. Inc., 1973; chosen Master Artist 1989, Leigh Yawkey Woodson Art Mus., Wausau, Wis., 1989. Mem. Nat. Audubon Soc., Nat. Wildlife Fedn., Izaak Walton League Am. (hon. pres. 1974-75). Home and Office: 5315 Robertson Dr Des Moines IA 50312-2133

REECE, SHEILA MARLENE, health facility administrator, writer; b. Evansville, Ind., Sept. 3, 1965; d. Ralph Samuel and Marie Annette (Seitz) Truelove; m. Larry A. Reece, Sept. 2, 1995 (div. May 13, 2003); children: Brett M. Cargal, Bailey E. Cargal, Kathryn A., Trevor A. AS in Nursing, Vincennes U., Ind., 1986. RN Ind., 1986. Staff nurse Good Samaritan Hosp., Vincennes, Ind., 1986—92, Jasper Meml. Hosp. and Healthcare, Ind., 1992—99; dir., nursing Chandler Healthcare, Ind., 2000—01; med. staff mgr. Beverly Corp., Newburgh, Ind., 2001—04. Author: (children's book) A Pig For Kate. Vol. Dream Ctr., Evansville, Ind., 2003; youth leader United Meth. Ch., Loogootee, Ind., 1993—96. Achievements include invention of Temper Tamer. Personal E-mail: book_baby2002@hotmail.com.

REECE, THOMAS L. manufacturing executive; Pres., CEO, chmn. Dover Corp., N.Y.C. Office: Dover Corp 280 Park Ave New York NY 10017-1216

REECE, WANDA G. space station training engineer, writer; b. Tuscaloosa, Ala., June 21, 1956; d. James Elton and Mattie Lou (Keating) R. BA, U. Ala., Tuscaloosa, 1977; MA, U. Ala., 1981. News corr. Birmingham (Ala.) Post-Herald, The New York Times, N.Y.C.; assoc. editor Kentron Internat., Houston, Pickens County (Ala.) Herald, Sumter County (Ala.) Jour.; Spacelab tng. engr. and tng. adminstr. Teledyne Brown Engring., Huntsville, Ala.; engine ops. engr. Tec-Masters, Inc., Huntsville. Contbr. numerous news and feature articles to profl. jours. Recipient Scripps-Howard Found. award, 1981, 1st place writer's contest Randall House Publs., 1982, Internat. Cultural Diploma of Honor, 1990, Huntsville/Madison County Conv. and Visitors Bur. award, 1995; first recipient of Paul "Bear" Bryant Acad. scholar U. Ala., 1974. Assoc. fellow AIAA (first woman chmn. of Ala./Miss. sect., chmn. AIAA/ASTD tng. and simulation conf., missile and space reunion com., spl. citation award 1990, Martin Schilling award 1990, Engr. of Yr. 1988, Profl. of Yr. 1992, Ala./Miss. sect.); mem. NAFE, Nat. Space Soc., Am. Soc. Tng. and Devel., Soc. Profl. Journalists, Internat. Soc. Logistics, Kappa Tau Alpha, Sigma Delta Chi. Home: 6315D Madison Blvd Huntsville AL 35806

REECE-PORTER, SHARON ANN, international human rights educator; b. Cin., Nov. 28, 1953; d. Edward and Claudia (Ownes) Reece; divorced, 1981; children: Erika Lynn, Melanie Joyce. BS in Textiles and Clothing, Edgecliff Coll., 1975; cert. clerical computer, So. Ohio Coll., 1984; MEd in Gen. Edn., SUNY, Buffalo, 1994; PhD in Internat. Human Rights Devel., Brentwick U., London, 2000; EdD in Global Edn. (hon.), Australian Inst. Coordinated Rsch., Victoria, 1995; postgrad. in photojournalism/profl. photography, NY Inst. Photography, 2002—. Cert. tchr., Ohio. Dept. supr., asst. buyer Mabley & Carew, Cin., 1975—76; claims adjuster Allstate Ins. Co., Cin., 1976—78; sales merchandiser Ekco Houseware, Cin., 1979—80; sales rep. Met. Life Inc., Cin., 1981—83; info. processing specialist GPA/Robert Half/Word Source, Cin., Dallas, 1985—87; tchr. adult edn. Princeton City Schs., Cin., 1984—90; with Rainbow Internat. Non-Profit Adult Ednl. Rsch. Ctr., Honolulu, 1990—98, Norfolk, Va., 1998—; specialist edn. rsch. found. SUNY, Buffalo, 1993. Prof. computer sci. So. Ohio Tech. and Bus. Coll., Cin., 1986-90; computer software tng. cons., 1987-89; part-time tchr. adult GED classes Adult Learning Ctr. Buffalo Bd. Edn., 1994-95; participant Am. Forum for Global Edn., Honolulu; lectr. photography N.Y. Inst. Photography, N.Y.C., N.Y., 2002—. Tutor U.S. divsn. Internat. Laubach Lit., Clermont County, Ohio, 1984; coordinate workshops Dianetics Found., Virginia Beach, Va. Fellow Australian Inst. for Coordinated Rsch. (life); mem. NAFE, ASTD, Internat. DOS Users Group, Am. Ednl. Rsch. Assn., Nat. Assn. Women Bus. Owners, UN Assn., World Assn. Women Entrepreneurs, Assn. Baha'i Studies in Australia, Boston Computer Soc., Cin. Orgn. Data Processing Educators and Trainers, Internat. Platform Assn., Cin. C. of C. (cert. minority supplier devel. coun.), Dianetics Found. (co-coord. workshops). Baha'I. Home: 2941 Chilton Pl Virginia Beach VA 23456 Office: Rainbow Cinema Global Human Rights Inst Apt 172 4221-125 Pleasant Valley Rd Virginia Beach VA 23464 E-mail: Sharaocean@aol.com., SharonAnHumanRts@aol.com.

REED, ALFRED, composer, conductor; b. N.Y.C., Jan. 25, 1921; s. Carl Mark and Elizabeth (Strasser) Friedman; m. Marjorie Beth Deley, June 20, 1941; children: Michael Carlson, Richard Judson. Student, Juilliard Sch. Music, 1946—48; MusB, Baylor U., 1955, MusM, 1956; MusD, Internat. Conservatory of Music, Lima, Peru, 1968. Exec. editor Hansen Publs., N.Y.C., 1955-66; prof. music U. Miami (Fla.) Sch. Music, 1966-93. Composer, arranger, N.Y.C., 1941-60; condr. Tri-State Music Festival, Okla., 1956-57, 60-66, 70, 73, Midwest Nat. Band Clinic, 1960-91, Bemidji (Minn.) Summer Music Camp, 1970-71, 75, Mid-East Instrumental Music Conf., Pitts., 1957-60, Can. Music Educators Assn., Edmonton, Alta., 1975; composer: Russian Christmas Music, 1944, Symphony for Brass and Percussion, 1952, Rhapsody for Viola and Orch, 1956, Choric Song, 1966, Titania's Nocturne, 1967, A Festival Prelude, 1962, Passacaglia, 1968, Music for Hamlet, 1973, Armenian Dances, 1974-75, Punchinello, Overture to a Romantic Comedy, 1974, Testament of an American, 1974, First Suite for Band, 1975, Othello, A Symphonic Portrait in Five Scenes, 1976, Prelude and Capriccio, 1977, Second Symphony, 1978, Siciliana Notturno, 1978, Second Suite for Band, 1978, The Enchanted Island, 1979, The Hounds of Spring, 1980, Third Suite for Band, 1981, Queenston Overture, 1982, Viva Musica!, 1983, A Little Concert Suite, 1983, El Camino Real, 1985, Centennial!, 1985, Three Revelations from the Lotus Sutra, 1985, Golden Jubilee, 1986, A Christmas Celebration, 1986, Praise Jerusalem!, 1987, Third Symphony, 1988, Eventide, 1988, Golden Eagle, 1989, Curtain Up!, 1990, A Springtime Celebration, Hymn Variants, 1991, With Trumpets and Drums, 1991, Concertino for Marimba and Winds, 1991, 4th Symphony, 1992, Fourth Suite for Band, 1993, Evolutions, A Concert Overture, 1993, 5th Symphony, 1994, Fifth Suite for Band, 1995, Two Bagatelles, 1997, Concerto for Trumpet and Winds, 1997, Divertimento for Flute and Winds, 1997, Sixth Suite for Band, 1998, Millenium III, 1999, Sumus Futuro, 1999, Carto e Camdombe, 1999, Jidai (Year of Years!), 1999, Acclamation!, 1999, Children's Suite, 2001, Five Cameos for Saxophone Ouartet, 2002, Joyeux Nöel, 2002, Music in the air, 2002, Seventh suite for Band, 2002, Fanfare and Processional, 2003, Rosalind

in the Forest of Arden, 2003, others. With AUS, 1942-46. Mem. ASCAP, Am. Bandmasters Assn., Am. Fedn. Musicians, Nat. Band Assn., Music Educators Nat. Conv. Home: 1405 Ancona Ave Miami FL 33146-1903 *As a composer, my desire has always been to achieve both a depth and intensity of communication between myself, my music and my audiences that would enable me to express something of value as regards myself and my time that, hopefully, would give rise to a deeply felt response on the part of my fellow human beings. I suppose this is true of the arts in general, and all artists, regardless of their medium of expression, but music, for me at least, has been the supreme expression of all time, for all men.*

REED, ALFRED DOUGLAS, retired academic administrator; b. Bristol, Tenn., July 18, 1928; s. Roy Theodore and Elizabeth Brown (Tuft) R.; m. Emily Joyce Freeman, Mar. 18, 1950; children: Roy Frederick, Robert Douglas, David Clark, Timothy Wayne, Joseph William. AB, Erskine Coll., Due West, S.C., 1949. Reporter Citizen-Times, Asheville, N.C., 1949-51, city editor, 1953-60, mng. editor, 1962-63, assoc. editor, 1963-66, capital corr., 1959-66; asst. editor The Presbyn. Jour., Weaverville, N.C., 1951-52; assoc. editor Shelby (N.C.) Daily Star, 1961-62; dir. pub. info. Western Carolina U., Cullowhee, NC, 1966-96, asst. to the chancellor, 1996—2002. Cons. Devel. Office, East Carolina U., Greenville, 1980; bd. dirs. Wachovia Bank, Sylva, N.C., 1969-2003. Author: Prologue, 1968, Decade of Development, 1984; exec. editor: Western, The Mag. of Western Carolina University, 1991-96. Mem. Asheville City Bd. Edn., 1958-62; vice chmn. bd. dirs. Sta. WCQS FM, Western N.C. Pub. Radio Inc., Asheville, 1978-88; bd. dirs., mem. exec. com. Cherokee Hist. Assn., 1985—, Western N.C. Assn. Cmtys., 1985-2001, Jackson County Fund of N.C. Cmty. Found., 1991-93; mem. Hunter Libr. Adv. Bd., 1991-98, Pack Place Adv. Coun., Asheville, 1991-95. Recipient Paul A. Reid Disting. Svc. award Western Carolina U., 1980, Disting. Svc. award, 1996. Mem. Pub. Rels. Assn. Western N.C. (bd. dirs. 1988-98, treas. 1966-86), Coll. News Assn. Carolinas (bd. dirs. 1968-71, 80-82), Smoky Mountain Host Assn. (bd. dirs., 1st v.p. 1994-96, pres. 1996-98), Great Smoky Mountains Assn. (bd. dirs. 1998-2002). Democrat. Presbyterian. Avocations: travel, stamps, gardening. Home: 931 University Heights Rd Cullowhee NC 28723-6953 Personal E-mail: douglasreed@earthlink.net.

REED, ANGELICA DENISE, sculptor, writer, illustrator; b. Murfreesboro, Tenn., Dec. 16, 1955; d. Keith Kenyon and Lester Faye (Todd) Reed; m. David Earl Myers, Apr. 19, 1975 (dec. Mar. 1978); m. John Gregory Bettis, May 11, 1979. Student, Mid. Tenn. State U., 1973-75, 77-78, UCLA, 1981-82, Venice Sculpture Studio, 1983-85, Brucchion Sch. of Art, Culver City, Calif., 1987-90. Artist-in-residence Reed Studio and Gallery, Venice, Calif., 1990-95, The Jerry Solomon Gallery, L.A., 1997, Belle Art Galleries, Inc. at Bel Age Hotel, West Hollywood, Calif., 2000—. Cons. Sweet Harmony Music, Sunset Beach, Calif., 1978-83, Bettis Paradise Music, Sunset Beach, 1978-85, John Bettis Music, L.A., 1983—, John Bettis Property Mgmt., L.A., 1986—. Sculptures, illustrations, home landscapings and pencil drawings exhibited in Calif., 1985—. Fundraiser Children's Hosp./Santa Monica Bay Aux., 1991, Nat. Acad. Songwriters, 1985, SEA Environ. Assn., Bonaventure Hotel, L.A., 1990, 91; mem. L.A. com. P.E.T.A. People for the Ethical Treatment of Animals, 1992; vol. St. John Hosp., 1998. Avocations: gymnastics, scuba diving, travel, animals, ballet. Home and Office: 1153 E Main St Murfreesboro TN 37130-3950 E-mail: angelicadenise@comcast.net.

REED, ANNE F. THOMSON, government official; BA, Goucher Coll., 1973; MPA, Harvard U., 1981. Devel. rschr. Office of Alumni Devel. Vanderbilt U., Nashville, 1973-74; jr. cmty. planner Nashville City Planning Commn., 1974-76; staff asst. to asst. dean for adminstrn. Kennedy Sch. Harvard U., Cambridge, Mass., 1976-77, registrar, admissions officer John F. Kennedy Sch. Govt., 1977-80; presdl. mgmt. intern Dept. Navy, Washington, 1981-83, budget analyst for Naval Sea Sys. Command, 1983-86, numerous mgmt. positions Office Comptroller, 1986-93; dep. asst. sec. agr. for adminstrn. USDA, Washington, 1993-96, chief info. officer, 1997—. Office: USDA 14th & Independence Ave SW Washington DC 20250-0001

REED, BERENICE ANNE, art historian, artist, government official; b. Memphis; d. Glenn Andrew and Berenice Marie (Kallaher) R. BFA, St. Mary-of-the-Woods Coll., Ind., 1955; MFA in Painting and Art History, Istituto Pio XII, Villa Schifanoia, Florence, Italy, 1964; ind. art history rsch., Ctr. for Advanced Study in the Visual Arts, Nat. Gallery of Art, Washington, 1998—. Cert. art tchr., Tenn. Comml. artist Memphis Pub. Co., 1955-56; arts adminstr., educator pub. and pvt. instns., Washington, Memphis, 1957-70; arts adminstr. Nat. Park Svc., 1970-73; mem. staff U.S. Dept. of Energy, Washington, 1973-81, U.S. Dept. Commerce, Washington, 1983-84, Exec. Office of the Pres., Office of Mgmt. and Budget, Washington, 1985; with fin. mgmt. svc. U.S. Treasury Dept., Washington, 1985—. Ind. art history rschr. Nat. Gallery of Art, Ctr. Advanced Study in Visual Arts, Washington, 1998—; cons. on art and architecture in recreation AIA, 1972-73; artist-in-residence St. Mary-of-the-Woods Coll., Ind., 1965; guest lectr. instr. Nat. Sch. Fine Arts, Tegucigalpa, Honduras, 1968; exec. com. Parks, Arts and Leisure Project, Washington, 1972-73; rschr. art projects, Washington, 1981-83. Developer (video) In Your Interest, 1992; TV interviewer Am. Fin. Skylink satellite programs, 1996-98. Bd. dirs. Am. Irish Bicentennial Com., 1974-76; advisor Royal Oak Found. Recipient various awards for painting; installed as Dama of Merit, Sacred Mil. Constantinian Order of St. George, Naples, 1997, awarded Star, 2001, installed as Dama, Order of St. Maurice and St. Lazarus, 2000; named one of 150 Women Who Made A Difference in 150 years of St. Agnes Acad., 2001. Mem. Soc. Woman Geographers, Nat. Soc. Arts and Letters, Ctr. for Advanced Study in Visual Arts, Art Barn Assn. (bd. dirs. 1973-83), Patrons of the Arts in the Vatican Mus., Irish Georgian Soc. Roman Catholic. Avocations: photography, performing arts. Home: PO Box 34253 Bethesda MD 20827-0253

REED, BEVERLY MARIE, mathematician, educator; b. Cleve., Apr. 1, 1952; d. Edward Francis and Helen Marie Bruss; m. James Robert Reed, July 5, 1975; children: Joseph Nicholas, Jennifer Lynn. BA, John Carroll U., 1975, MA, 1979; postgrad., Kent State U., 1999—. Secondary sch. math. permanent tchg. cert. Ohio. Math. tchr. Villa Angela Acad., Cleve., 1975—86; math. instr. math. dept. Kent (Ohio) State U., 1986—90, course coord., instr. math. dept., 1990—. Textbook reviewer several pub. firms, 1991—2001; MATHCOUNTS coach Holy Family Sch., Stow, Ohio, 1992—97; chair course redesign com. math. dept. Kent State U., 2002; presenter in field. Contbr. articles to profl. jours. Fundraising chair, advancement chair Boy Scouts Am. Troop 177, Stow, 1992—97; activities and civic svc. com. chair Boy Scouts Am. MOE Dist., Akron, Ohio, 1997—99; vol. trailblazer Cuyahoga Valley Nat. Park, 2003—; lector, commentator, children's liturgy tchr. Holy Family Ch., Stow, 2001—. Recipient George Eisenman award for cmty. svc., Boy Scouts Am., 1998. Mem.: Ohio Coun. Tchrs. Math., Math. Assn. Am., Nat. Coun. Tchrs. Math. Roman Catholic. Avocations: swimming, bicycling, hiking. Office: Kent State Univ Dept Math Scis PO Box 5190 Kent OH

REED, CHARLES BASS, chief academic administrator; b. Harrisburg, Pa., Sept. 29, 1941; s. Samuel Ross and Elizabeth (Johnson) R.; m. Catherine A. Sayers, Aug. 22, 1964; children: Charles B. Jr., Susan Allison. BS, George Washington U., 1963, MS, 1964, EdD, 1970; postgrad. Summer Inst. for Chief State Sch. Officers, Harvard U. Grad Sch. Edn., 1977; D of Pub. Svc. (hon.), George Washington U., 1987; LLD (hon.), Stetson U., 1987; LHD (hon.), St. Thomas U., 1988; LittD (hon.), Waynesburg Coll., 1990; d of the U. (hon.), British Open U., 2000. From asst. prof. to assoc. prof. George Washington U., Washington, 1963—70; asst. dir. Nat. Performance-Based Tchr. Edn. Project, Am. Assn. Colls. for Tchr. Edn., Washington, 1970—71; assoc. for planning and coordination Fla. Dept. Edn., Tallahassee, 1971—75, dir. Office Ednl. Planning, Budgeting, and Evaluation, 1975—79; edn. policy coord. Exec. Office of Gov., Tallahassee, 1979—80, dir. legis. affairs, 1980—81, dep. chief of staff, 1981—84, chief of staff, 1984—85; chancellor State Univ. System Fla., Tallahassee, 1985—98, Calif. State U. Sys., Long Beach, 1998—. Mem. Nat. Commn. on H.S. Sr. Yr., Pres. Leadership Group, Higher Edn. Ctr. for Alcohol and Other Drug Prevention, Coll. Edn. Nat. Bd., Policy Bd., EdVoice; mem. Rand Edn. Adv. Bd; bd. dirs. Nat. Ctr. for Ednl. Accountability, Mem. Coun. for Advancement and Support of Edn., Coun. on Fgn. Rels., Bus.-Higher Edn. Forum. Disting. fellow,Fullbright Commn. 50th Anniversary, Peru, 1996. Mem. Am. Assn. State Colls. and Univs., Am. Assn. for Higher Edn., Am. Coun. on Edn., Assn. Governing Bds. of Univs. and Colls., Nat. Assn. State Univs. and Land-Grant Colls., Nat. Assn. Sys. Heads, Internat. Assn. Univ. Presidents, Hispanic Assn. Colls. and Univs. Democrat. Roman Catholic. Office: Calif State U Office Chancellor 401 Golden Shore St Fl 6 Long Beach CA 90802-4210 E-mail: creed@calstate.edu.

REED, CHARLES ELI, retired chemist, chemical engineer; b. Findlay, Ohio, Aug. 11, 1913; BS, Case Inst. Tech., 1934; ScD in Chem. Engring., MIT, 1937. Asst. prof. chem. engring. MIT, Cambridge, Mass., 1937—42; rsch. assoc. rsch. lab. GE, 1942—45, engring. mgr. chem. divsn., 1945—52, gen. mgr. silicone products dept., 1952—59, gen. mgr. metall. products dept., 1959—62, v.p., gen. mgr. chem. and metall. divsn., 1962—68, v.p., group exec. components and materials group, 1968—71, sr. v.p. corp. tech., 1979; ret., 1979. Recipient Nat. Medal of Technology, U.S. Dept. of Commerce Technology Admin., 1991. Fellow: Am. Inst. Chemists, AICE; mem.: NAE, AAAS, Am. Chem. Soc. Achievements include research in in colloid chemistry, high polymers, distillation. Home: 3030 Park Ave Bridgeport CT 06604-1138

REED, CHRISTOPHER ROBERT, civil engineer; b. Charleston, W.Va., Feb. 12, 1948; s. Clarence Milton and Anne (Schaffner) R.; m. Mary Dandridge Kennedy, Mar. 4, 1983. Student, W.Va. Inst. Tech., 1966-70, 76-77, Ga. State U., 1973-74. Designer Sverdrup & Parcel, Charleston, 1970-72; assoc. project engr. Mayes, Sudderth & Etheredge, Atlanta, 1973-76; project mgr. Sverdrup & Parcel, Washington, 1976-79; estimator Deleuw, Cather/Parsons, Washington, 1979-80; project mgr. Parsons Brinckerhoff, McLean, Va., 1980-85; assoc. Lolederman Assocs., Inc., Rockville, Md., 1985-86, Post Buckley Schuh and Jernigan, Inc., Arlington, Va., 1986-89; assoc., dir. mcpl. engring. Lolderman Assocs., Inc., Rockville, 1989-90; mgr. CRS Donohue and Assocs., Inc., Fairfax, Va., 1990-92; asst. dist. location and design engr. VDOT, Fairfax, 1992-95, dist. location and design engr., 1995, Culpeper, Va., 1996-98, program mgr. Alexandria, Va., 1998-2001, urban program mgr. Fairfax, Va., 2003—; v.p. Michael Baker Jr., Inc., Richmond, Va., 2001—03. Bd. dirs. Ashland Bassats. Mem. Inst. Transp. Engrs., Capital Yacht Club (sec. 1988-89, vice commodore 1990, commodre 1991, chair com. 1999-2003), Project Mgmt. Inst., Corinthian Yacht Club (fleet capt. 1992, rear commodore 1993, vice-commodore 1998), Potomac River Yacht Club Assn. (sec. 2000-01, del. 2002-03), Internat. Order Blue Gavel. Home: 320 Culpeper St Warrenton VA 20186-3001 Office: Hillcrest Bldg Ste 101 1801 Bayberry Ct Richmond VA 23226 E-mail: piperreed@starpower.net.

REED, CYNTHIA S. manufacturing executive; b. Springfield, Mass., Oct. 29, 1955; Student, Dartmouth Coll., 1976; BA, Wellesley Coll., 1977; JD, Northeastern U., 1980. Bar: R.I., Mass. Assoc. Edwards & Angell, Providence, 1980-86; sr. atty. Hasbro, Inc., Pawtucket, RI, 1986-88, asst. v.p., sr. atty., 1988-92, v.p., 1992-95, sr. v.p., gen. counsel, 1995—2002; pres., CEO LTR Holdings, Providence. Sec., trustee In-Sight R.I.; trustee New Eng. Legal Found./R.I. Adv. Bd.; mem. Wellesley Bus. Leadership Coun.; past pres. Wessley Club R.I., Ocean State Adoption Resource Exch. Wellesley scholar, 1977. Mem. ABA (bus. law sect.), Am. Corp. Counsel Assn., Mass. Bar Assn., R.I. Bar Assn. Office: LTR Holdings 275 Promenade St Providence RI 02908

REED, D. GARY, lawyer; b. Covington, Ky., June 4, 1949; m. Mary Elizabeth Goetz, May 20, 1972; children: Mark, Stacey. BA, Xavier U., 1971; JD, Catholic U. Am., 1974. Bar: Ohio 1974, Ky. 1975, U.S. Ct. Appeals (6th cir.) 1975, U.S. Dist. Ct. (so. dist.) Ohio 1974, U.S. Dist. Ct. (ea. dist.) Ky. 1977, U.S. Dist. Ct. (we. dist.) Ky. 1980. Law clk. to judge U.S. Dist. Ct. (so. dist.) Ohio, Cin., 1974-75; assoc. Dinsmore & Shohl, Cin., 1976-82, ptnr., 1982-90; dir. legal svcs. Choice Care Health Plans, Inc., Cin., 1991-96; asst. gen. coun., 1996-97; ins. counsel Humana, Inc., Louisville, 1998—. Asst. sec. Choice Care Found., 1996-97. Contbg. author: Woodside, Drug Product Liability, vol. 3, 1987. Asst. sec. The Choice Care Found., 1996-97. Mem. ABA, Ky. Bar Assn., Ohio Bar Assn., Nat. Health Lawyers Assn., No. Ky. C. of C. (Leadership award 1988), Greater Cin. Coun. for Epilepsy (bd. dirs. 1990-97), Leadership No. Ky. Alumni Assn. Office: Humana Inc Insurance Cons-Law Dept 500 W Main St Ste 300 Louisville KY 40202-4268 E-mail: dgaryreed@aol.com., greed@humana.com.

REED, DAVID ANDREW, managed health care company executive; b. Butler, Pa., Feb. 24, 1933; s. Sherman W. and Caroline (Janner) R.; m. Virginia Rogers, Dec. 1, 1956; children: Kristine Lynn, Katherine Louise, Elizabeth Anne, Amy Janner. AB, Allegheny Coll., 1955; MS, U. Pitts., 1961. Adminstrv. resident Titusville (Pa.) Hosp., 1959, Cin. Gen. Hosp., 1960-61; asst. adminstr. Warren (Pa.) Gen. Hosp., 1961-62, Western Pa. Gen. Hosp., Pitts., 1962-63; with Cin. Gen. Hosp., 1963-69, adminstr., 1964-69; asso. prof. hosp. adminstrn. U. Cin. Coll. Medicine, 1966-69; preceptor program med. and hosp. adminstrn. U. Pitts. Grad. Sch. Pub. Health, 1966-69; pres. Lenox Hill Hosp., N.Y.C., 1969-78; v.p., chief exec. officer Good Samaritan Hosp., Phoenix, 1978-82; pres. SamCor/Samaritan Health Service, Phoenix, 1982-89; pres., chief exec. officer The Samaritan Found., Phoenix, 1989, St. Joseph Health System, Orange, Calif., 1990-95; pres. DAR Consulting Group, Dana Point, 1995—; chmn. PacifiCare Health Systems Inc., Santa Ana, Calif., 1999—. Instr.; past pres. Greater Cin. Hosp. Council, Phoenix Regional Hosp. Council; bd. govs. Greater N.Y. Hosp. Assn.; chmn. Am. Hosp. Assn., also trustee; cons. Hosp. Devel. and Research Inst. Contbr. articles to profl. jours. Bd. dirs. Urban League Cin. Served with AUS, 1955-57. Fellow Am. Coll. Hosp. Adminstrs. (life); mem. Catalina Island Yacht Club, Dana West Yacht Club, Marbella Country Club, Ctr. Club, Phi Gamma Delta. Presbyterian. Office: PacifiCare Health Sysytems Inc 3120 Late Ctr Dr Santa Ana CA 92704 E-mail: consultdar@aol.com.

REED, DAVID BENSON, bishop; b. Tulsa, Feb. 16, 1927; s. Paul Spencer and Bonnie Frances (Taylor) R.; m. Susan Henry Riggs, Oct. 30, 1954 (div.); children: Mary, Jennifer, David, Sarah, Catherine; m. Catherine Camp Luckett, Apr. 15, 1984. AB, Harvard U., 1948; M.Div., Va. Theol. Sem., 1951, D.D., 1964, U. of South, 1972, Episc. Theol. Sem., Ky., 1985. Ordained deacon Episcopalian Ch., 1951. Missionary, Panama, 1951—58, 1951—58; with Nat. Ch. Exec. Office, 1958—61; mission priest SD, 1961—63; bishop of, 1964—72, 1964—70; bishop coadjutor Diocese of Ky., Louisville, 1972—74, bishop of Ky., 1974—94; asst. bishop of Conn. Episcopal Diocese of Conn., Hartford, 1994—95; 1st pres. Anglican Council Latin Am., 1969—72; chmn. standing commn. on ecumenical relations Episcopal Ch., 1979—82; pres. Ky. Coun. Chs., 1988—91; exec. dir. Global Episcopal Mission, 1998—99. Mem. governing bd. Nat. Coun. of Chs. of Christ in U.S.A., 1982-91, mem. exec. com., 1985-91, sec., 1988-91; Anglican co-chmn. Anglican Orthodox Theol. Cons., 1984-94. Bd. dirs. Alliant Health Systems (formerly Norton Kosair Children's Hosp.), Louisville, 1979-94; trustee U. of the South, 1972-94, regent, 1979-82; chmn. Louisville United Against Hunger, 1980-84, 86-87; chmn. Presiding Bishop's Com. on Interfaith Rels., 1991-97. Mem. Harvard Club of Western Ky. (pres. 1992-94). Democrat. Episcopalian. Home: 5226 Moccasin Trail Louisville KY 40207-1634

REED, DAVID GEORGE, entrepreneur; b. Alameda, Calif., July 19, 1945; s. David Francis and Anna Amelia Vangeline (Paulson) R.; m. Marianne Louise Watson, Apr. 7, 1971 (div. June 1975); m. Michele Ann Hock, June 28, 1989; 1 child, Casey Christine Michele. AA in Bus. Adminstrn., Diablo Valley Coll., Pleasant Hill, Calif., 1965; BA in Design and Industry, San Francisco State U., 1967, MBA in Mktg., 1969; cert. res. police officer, Los Medanos Coll., Pittsburg, Calif., 1977. Owner Western Furs, Ltd., Walnut Creek, Calif., 1963-72; mgmt. cons. Controlled Interval Scheduling, Rolling Hills Estates, Calif., 1972-73; owner Dave Reed's Texaco, Concord, Calif., 1973-76; mgmt. cons. Mgmt. Scheduling Systems, Houston, 1974-76, Thomas-Ross Assocs., Mercer Island, Wash., 1972-82; plant mgr. Bonner Packing, Morgan Hill, Calif., 1981; mfg. engr. Systron Donner, Concord, 1982-84, Beckman Instruments, San Ramon, Calif., 1984-90; owner Dave Reed & Co. Water Ski Sch., White Water Rafting, Chiloquin, Oreg., 1987—, Dave Reed & Co., design, market, mfg. Contender boats, Chiloquin, Oreg., 1976—. Lectr. wildlife mgmt. Dave Reed & Co., Chiloquin, 1965—, lectr. mgmt. seminars, 1982—; coach Japanese Water Ski Team, Bluff Water Ski Club, Tokyo, 1984; fin. mgr. Japanese investors Dave Reed & Co., Chiloquin, 1986—, design and supply solar electric power sys., 1994—. Res. dep. sheriff Contra Costa County Sheriff's Dept., Martinez, Calif., 1977-80. With U.S. Army, 1969-71, Vietnam. Recipient Gold medal internat. freestyle wrestling Sr. Olympics, Fullerton, Calif., 1983. Mem. Am. Water Ski Assn. (Calif. state water ski champion 1977, 86, western region water ski champion 1977, silver medal nat. water ski championships 1977), Bay Area Tournament Assn. (chmn. 1968—), Diablo Water Ski Club (bd. dirs. 1968—). Republican. Avocations: water-skiing, skiing, surfing, camping, fly fishing. Home: PO Box 336 Chiloquin OR 97624-0336

REED, DAVID PATRICK, infosystems specialist; b. Portsmouth, Va., Jan. 30, 1952; s. Sherman Clark and Bernice Lois (Maul) R.; m. Lynn Susan Schwartz, June 10, 1973 (div. Mar. 1979); 1 child, Colin Alexander; m. Jessica Amy Kenn, Sept. 4, 1983; children: Katherine Anne, Carly Diana. BS, MIT, 1973, SM, 1975, Degree in Elec. Engring., 1976, PhD, 1978. Asst. prof. computer sci. and engring. MIT, Cambridge, 1978-84, lectr., 1984-86; chief scientist Software Arts, Wellesley, Mass., 1983-84, v.p. R&D, 1984-85; v.p. R&D, chief scientist Lotus Devel., Cambridge, 1985-92; sr. scientist Interval Rsch. Corp., 1992-96; pvt. practice, 1996—; mem. adv. bd. Vanguard, 1991—. Fellow Diamond Tech. Ptnrs. Exch. program, 1997—; vis. scientist MIT Media Lab., 2001-02; adj. prof. MIT Media Lab., 2003—. Contbr. articles to profl. jours. Recipient Tchg. award MIT Elec. Engring. Dept., 1975; fellow Hewlett-Packard Labs., 2003-, FCC Tech. Adv. Coun., 2003-. Mem. IEEE, Assn. Computing Machinery, Computer Soc., Sigma Xi. Democrat. Home and Office: 8 Old Greendale Ave Needham MA 02492-4424 E-mail: dpreed@reed.com.

REED, DIANE MARIE, psychologist; b. Joplin, Mo., Jan. 11, 1934; d. William Marion and Olive Francis (Smith) Kinney; m. William J. Shotton; children: Wendy Robison, Douglas Funkhouser. Student, Art Ctr. Col., L.A., 1951-54; BS, U. Oreg., 1976, MS, 1977, PhD, 1981. Lic. psychologist. Illustrator J.L. Hudson Co., Detroit, 1954-56; designer, stylist N.Y.C., 1960-70; designer, owner Decor To You, Inc., Stamford, Conn., 1970-76; founder, exec. dir. Alcohol Counseling and Edn. Svcs., Inc., Eugene, Oreg., 1981-86, clin. supr., 1986, Christian Family Svcs., Eugene, 1986-87; pvt. practice Eugene, 1985-94; co-founder Reed Consulting, Bend, Oreg., 1995—2000; pvt. practice Bend, Oreg., 2000—. Evaluator Vocat. Rehab. Div., Eugene, 1982—; alcohol and drug evaluator and commitment examiner Oreg. Mental Health Div., 1981—86. Named Disting. Alumnus, Ctrl. Oreg. region U. Oreg. Coll. Edn., 2003. Mem.: APA, Sunriver Area C. of C. (bd. dirs. 1997—98), Bend C. of C., Lane County Psychol. Assn. (pres. 1989—90), Oreg. Psychol. Assn., Ctrl. Oreg. Llama Assn. (pres. 1999—2000), Sunriver Women's Club (comm. chair), Toastmasters Internat., Rotary (pres. 1997—98, Rotarian Yr. 1996—97, 1997—98), U. Oreg. Nat. Alumni (bd. dirs., outstanding alumnus for ctrl. Oreg. 2003). Avocations: photography, skiing, running, hiking, backpacking.

REED, DONNA MARIE, editor, newspaper; b. Dayton, Ohio, Mar. 29, 1950; d. Andrew Levi and Golda Mabel (Branham) Tatman; m. Donald Ray Newsome, May 12, 1973 (div. Sept. 1985); 1 child, Amanda Marie; m. James A. Reed, Sept. 26, 1987. BA, Morehead State U., 1973, MA, 1974. From reporter to state editor Tampa (Fla.) Tribune, 1974-90; dir. comm. Hillsborough County Schs., Tampa, 1990-96; dep. mng. editor Tampa Tribune, 1996—. Bd. dirs. Tampa Edn. Channel; com. mem. Hillsborough Edn. Found., Tampa, 1990—. Recipient Sunshine Medallion award Sunshine State Sch. PR Assn., 1991-96, Prin.'s award Armwood H.S., 1994-95. Mem. Fla. Press Assn., Fla. Soc. Newspaper Editors, Hillsborough Assn. Sch. Adminstrs. (Pub. Rels. award 1991, 95), Plant City Little League, Delta Gamma Alumni Assn. Baptist. Avocations: reading, needlecrafts, sports, bike riding. Office: Tampa Tribune 202 S Parker St Tampa FL 33606-2395

REED, DOUGLAS H. editor, publishing executive; b. Chelsea, Vt., Aug. 24, 1939; s. Herbert William and Gladys Eileen Reed; m. Phyllis E. Bacon, May 31, 2001; children: William, Jennifer Fiorentino, Kellie Lentz. Student, Boston U., 1958—59. Reporter, sports editor Daily Messenger, St. Albans, Vt., 1957—58; reporter Attleboro (Mass.) Daily Sun, 1965—68; copy writer Blue Cross-Blue Shield, Concord, NH, 1968—70; mng. editor Sun Chronicle, Attleboro, 1970—83; chief night copy desk Patriot Ledger, Quincy, Mass., 1984—85; exec. editor Evening Times, Pawtucket, RI, 1985—87; pub., editor The Free Press, North Attleborough, Mass., 1987—. Pres. North Attleboro/Plainville C. of C., North Attleborough, 1991; officer Jaycees; mem. various coms. Plymouth Bay Coun., Girl Scouts Am.; mem. exec. com. Annawon Coun., Boy Scouts Am.; mem., dir. North Attleborough/Plainville Rotary Club; co-founder, first pres. Hillside Adult Day Health Care Ctr., Attleboro; incorporator United Way Greater Attleboro/Taunton; mem. 20th Century Celebration Com.; former coach, umpire, pres. Little Attleboro Baseball League; coach Little All-Am. Football League, Attleboro; former N.H. state bd. dirs. Am. Cancer Soc.; bd. dirs. United Way No. Bristol County, Downtown Assocs. North Attleborough. Lt. cpl. USMC, 2001—03. Named to Cmty. Hall of Fame, N.E. Press Assn., Boston, 2000. Democrat. Methodist. Avocations: reading, golf, bowling, hiking. Office: The Free Press 31 N Washington St North Attleboro MA 02760

REED, EDDIE, pharmacologist; b. Hughes, Ark., Dec. 17, 1953; married; 1 child. BS magna cum laude, Philander Smith Coll., Little Rock, 1975; MD, Yale U., 1979. Diplomate Am. Bd. Internal Medicine, Nat. Bd. Med. Examiners. Commd. USPHS, 1978, advanced through grades to capt.; intern in internal medicine Stanford U. Hosp., Palo Alto, Calif., 1979-80, resident, 1980-81; clin. assoc. div. cancer treatment Nat. Cancer Inst., Bethesda, Md., 1981-83, investigator detailed to lab. cellular carcinogenesis, 1983-85, spl. asst. for pre-clin. sci. Office Dir., 1985-87, sr. investigator clin. pharmacology and med. br., 1987—2001, coord. ovarian cancer studies, 1988-91, head med. ovarian cancer sect. clin. oncology program, 1991—2001, chief clin. pharmacology br., 1993—2001, chief peritoneoscopy svc. med. br., 1987—, sr. attending physician clin. pharmacology and medicine brs., 1987—, sr. med. cons. medicine br., 1987—; dir. Mary Babb Randolph Cancer Ctr./W.Va. U., Morgantown, 2001—. Participant numerous seminars in field, 1984-95; chmn. ambulatory care com. NIH Clin. Ctr., 1989-93; mem. protocol com. Gynecologic Oncology Coop. Study Group, 1989-96, mem. tumor biology and applied sci. com., 1990-95; mem. com. on status of minorities in the intramural NIH, 1992-2001; mem. NIH Inter-Inst. Working Group on Breast and Gynecologic Tumors, 1993-2001; mem. sci. adv. bd. Nat. Ctr. for Toxicological Rsch., FDA, Jefferson, Ark., 1988-96; reviewer Jour. Nat. Cancer Inst., Cancer Rsch., Jour. Clin. Oncology, Jour. Clin. Investigation, Jour. Biol. Chemistry, Gynecologic Oncology. Mem. editl. bd. Yale Jour. Biology and Medicine, 1976-79, Oncology Reports, 1993—, Jour. Nat. Med. Assn., 1994—; contbr. numerous articles to med. jours. Recipient commendation medal USPHS, 1993; EEO spl. achievement award NIH, 1993, tech. transfer award, 1995. Mem. AAAS, Am. Fedn. Clin. Rsch., Am. Assn. Cancer Rsch., Nat. Med. Assn. (sci. coun., head basic sci. subsect. 1994—), Assn. for Acad. Minority Physicians, Environ. Mutagen Soc., Internat. Assn. Environ. Mutagen Socs., Ark. Med., Dental and Pharm. Assn., Gynecologic Oncology Group, Soc. Gynecologic Oncology, Alpha Kappa Mu, Beta Kappa Chi. Home: 901 Suncrest Pl Morgantown WV 26505-3310 Office: Mary Babb Randolph Cancer Ctr WVa U 1801 Health Scis S Morgantown WV 26506-9300

REED, EDWARD CORNELIUS, JR., federal judge; b. Mason, Nev., July 8, 1924; s. Edward Cornelius Sr. and Evelyn (Walker) R.; m. Sally Torrance, June 14, 1952; children: Edward T., William W., John A., Mary E. BA, U. Nev., 1949; JD, Harvard U., 1952. Bar: Nev. 1952, U.S. Dist Ct. Nev. 1957, U.S. Supreme Ct. 1974. Atty. Arthur Andersen & Co., 1952-53; spl. dep. atty. gen. State of Nev., 1967-79; judge U.S. Dist. Ct. Nev., Reno, 1979—, chief judge, now sr. judge. Former vol. atty. Girl Scouts Am., Sierra Nevada Council, U. Nev., Nev. Agrl. Found., Nev. State Sch. Adminstrs. Assn., Nev. Congress of Parents and Teachers; mem. Washoe County Sch. Bd., 1956-72, pres. 1959, 63, 69; chmn. Gov.'s Sch. Survey Com., 1958-61; mem. Washoe County Bd. Tax Equalization, 1957-58, Washoe County Annexation Commn., 1968-72, Washoe County Personnel Com., 1973-77, chmn. 1973; mem. citizens adv. com. Washoe County Sch. Bond Issue, 1977-78, Sun Valley, Nev., Swimming Pool Com., 1978, Washoe County Blue Ribbon Task Force

Com. on Growth, Nev. PTA (life); chmn. profl. div. United Way, 1978; bd. dirs. Reno Siver Sox, 1962-65. Served as staff sgt. U.S. Army, 1943-46, ETO, PTO. Mem. ABA (jud. adminstrn. sect.), Nev. State Bar Assn. (adminstrv. com. dist. 5, 1967-79, lien law com. 1965-78, chmn. 1965-72, probate law com. 1963-66, tax law com. 1962-65), Am. Judicature Soc. Democrat. Baptist. Named in his honor Edward C. Reed H.S., Sparks, Nev., 1972. Office: US Dist Ct 400 S Virginia St Ste 606 Reno NV 89501-2182

REED, ELLEN BETH, librarian; b. Albany, Calif., Aug. 1942; d. Howard Ben Reed and Lillian Margaret Vanlandingham; life ptnr. Rita Bea Miller. BS, Moorhead State Coll., Minn., 1960—64; MA in Theatre, U. of Denver, 1979—81, MA in Librarianship and Info. Mgmt., 1984—85. English teacher, drama dir. Pine River (Minn.) HS, 1965—67; with Strawhat Theatre, Moorhead, 1966—66; english-speech instr., dir. of theatre Milbank (SD) HS, 1967—79; artistic & mng. dir. Pied Pipers Theatre, Inc, Milbank, 1968—70; grad. tchg. asst. theatre dept. U. Denver, 1979—81; asst. to the dir. Picketwire Players, Lajunta, Colo., 1979—79; stack maintenance unit dept. head Penrose Libr., U. of Denver, 1981—85; with Las Vegas-Clark County Libr. Dist., 1985—; stage mgr. Actor's Reperatory Theatre, Las Vegas, 1991—91; sr. libr., spl. collections Clark County Libr., Las Vegas, 1996—2003, reference dept. head, 2003—. Exec. sec. Alpha Lambda Epsilon, Moorhead, Minn., 1961—64, Pine River Edn. Assn., Minn., United States, 1965—67; past pres. Las Vegas-Clark County Libr. Dist. Staff Assn., 1981—92; trustee Sumi Laetz Found., Las Vegas, 1995—; conduct workshops statewide on the subject of nonprofit funding Clark County Libr., 1996—2004, compiler of Nev. funding directory, 1996—. Dir.: (stage plays) various productions including The Diary of Anne Frank, The Crucible, Hello Dolly, The Fantastiks, Antigone, and over 50 more, Including Barefoot in the Park, Cinderella, Bye-Bye Birdie, Including Medea, Stephen Vincent Benet's Stories of America, School for Scandal, (stage play) The Lady Patriot: A Story of Abigail Adams (Gov. & Bicentennial Commn. Medal for Outstanding Svc., 1976), (author, producer) (video) A New World Of Books (Cert. of Recognition, Libr. Dist. Bd. of Trustees, 1994); author (compiler): (bibliography) An Annotated Bibliography Of The Nev. Collection At The Clark County Libr. (LVCCLD Bd. of Trustees Incentive Award, 1996). Mem.: Teamsters local #14 LVCCLD (shop steward). Avocations: cross country skiing, horseback riding, swimming, reading, fishing. Office: Clark County Libr 1401 E Flamingo Las Vegas NV 89119

REED, FRANCES BOOGHER, writer, actress; b. Marion, Ky., May 29, 1938; d. Charles Boogher and Evelyn Shelby (Roberts) R.; m. José Joaquín Solís, June 1, 1957 (div. Sept. 1964); children: Julie, Michael Charles; m. Arnold Haslund, Jan. 30, 1965 (div. May 1967); 1 child, Elizabeth Evelyn Marie; 1 adopted child, Leni Ellis. BA in English and Spanish, U. Houston, 1960; MPH, U. P.R., 1970. Tchr. English as 2d lang. Author: A Dream With Storms, 1979, Thoughts, Feelings and Dreams, 1985, Black Mexican Necklace, 1990, TOEIC Test Guide, 1997, Miguel's Aztec Calendar, 1997, (with Koji Shimada) From Chocolate Bars to CEO, A MacArthur's Kid, 2000, (with Francisco Diaz Infante M.) Pockets and Jingles: Something for His Pockets, 2000, Love Blooms in Mazatlan, 2004; actress (television shows) General Hospital, Rescue-911, others, also movies. Mem. Am. Pub. Health Assn., Screen Actors' Guild, Mensa, Phi Kappa Phi. Democrat. Methodist. Avocations: teaching, dance, reading. Home: 239 Beach City Rd Apt 2113 Hilton Head Island SC 29926-4713 also: PO Box 23481 Hilton Head Island SC 29925-3481 Office Phone: 843-684-8277. E-mail: ML888888@aol.com.

REED, FRANK FREMONT, II, retired lawyer; b. Chgo., June 15, 1928; s. Allen Martin and Frances (Faurot) Reed; m. Jaquelin Silverthorne Cox, Apr. 27, 1963; children: Elizabeth Matthiessen Mason, Laurie Matthiessen Stern, Mark Matthiessen, Jeffrey, Nancy, Sarah Reed Farmer. AB, U. Mich., 1952, JD, 1957. Bar: Ill. 1958. Assoc. Byron, Hume, Groen & Clement, Chgo., 1958-61, Marks & Clerk, Chgo., 1961-63; pvt. practice law Chgo., 1963-78; dir. Western Acadia (Western Felt Works), Chgo., 1960-75, chmn. exec. com., 1969-71; ret., 1978. Author: History of the Silverthorn Family, 4 vols., 1982, Allen Family of Allen's Grove, 1983, Goddard and Ware Ancestors, 1987, Faurot Family, 1988; contbr. articles to The Am. Genealogist, 1972-73, 76-77. Rep. precinct capt., 1972-78; candidate for 43d ward alderman, 1975; bd. dirs., sec. Chgo. Found. Theater Arts, 1959-64; vestryman St. Chrysostom's Ch., 1975-79, mem. ushers guild, 1964-79, chmn., 1976-78; bd. dirs. North State, Astor, Lake Shore Dr. Assn., 1975-78, pres., 1977-78; bd. dirs. Cmty. Arts Music Assn. Santa Barbara, 1984-93, treas., 1988-93; bd. dirs. Santa Barbara Arts Coun., 1987-89. Cpl. AUS, 1952-54. Mem. ABA, Ill. Bar Assn., Racquet Club, Wausaukee Club (sec., dir. 1968-71, 92-94) (Chgo.), Birnam Wood Golf Club (Santa Barbara), Phi Alpha Delta. Episcopalian. Home: 1944 E Valley Rd Santa Barbara CA 93108-1428

REED, FRANK METCALF, bank executive, director; b. Seattle, Dec. 22, 1912; s. Frank Ivan and Pauline B. (Hovey) R.; m. Maxine Vivian McGary, June 11, 1937; children: Pauline Reed, Frank Metcalf. Student, U. Alaska, 1931-32; BA, U. Wash., 1937. V.p. Anchorage Light and Power Co., 1937-42; pres. Alaska Electric & Equipment Co., Anchorage, 1946-50; sec., mgr. Turnagain, Inc., Anchorage, 1950-56; mgr. Gen. Credit Corp., Anchorage, 1957; br. mgr. Alaska SBA, Anchorage, 1958-60; sr. v.p. First Interstate Bank of Alaska, Anchorage, 1960-87, also dir., corp. sec. Dir. First Interstate Corp. of Alaska, First Nat. Bank of Fairbanks; pres., dir. Anchorage Broadcasters, Inc.; past pres., chmn. Microfast Software Corp.; dir., treas. RM.R., Inc.; dir. Anchorage Light and Power Co., Turnagain, Inc., Alaska Fish and Farm, Inc., Life Ins. Co. Alaska. Pres., Anchorage Federated Charities, Inc., 1953-54; mem. adv. bd. Salvation Army, 1948-58; mem. Alaska adv. bd. Hugh O'Brian Youth Found., 1987-91; trustee Anchor Age Endowment Fund, 1988-96, chmn., 1991; mem. City of Anchorage Planning Commn., 1956; mem. City of Anchorage Coun., 1956-57; police commr. Territory of Alaska, 1957-58; chmn. City Charter Commn., 1958; mem. exec. com. Greater Anchorage, Inc., 1955-65; mem. Sch. Bd., 1961-64; mem. Gov.'s Investment adv. com., 1997-72; mem. Alaska State Bd. Edn.; mem. citizens adv. com. Alaska Meth. U.; chmn. Anchorage Charter Commn., 1975; chmn. bldg. fund dr. Cmty. YMCA, 1976 dir., 1976-97, hon. dir. 1998—; sec.-treas. Breakthrough, 1976-78; bd. dirs. Alaska Treatment Ctr., 1980-87, pres. 1985-86; trustee Marston Found., Inc., 1978, exec. dir. 1988. Served as lt. USNR, 1942-46. Elected to Hall of Fame, Alaska Press Club, 1969; named Outstanding Alaskan of Yr. Alaska C. of C., 1976, Alaskan of Yr., 1990, Outstanding Vol. in Philanthropy Alaska chpt. Nat. Soc. Fundraising Execs., 1991; laureate Jr. Achievement's Alaska Bus. Hall of Fame, 2000. Mem.: Alaska Bankers Assns. (pres. 1970—71), Nat. Assn. State Bds. Edn. (sec.-treas. 1969—70), Am. Inst. Banking Am. (exec. coun. 1971—72), Navy League (pres. Anchorage coun. 1961—62), Pioneers of Alaska, Anchorage C. of C. (presl 1966—67, dir.), San Francisco Tennis Club, Tower Club (life), Elks (life), Lions (life; sec. Anchorage 1953—54, pres. 1962—63, dir. 1988, treas. 2002—04, Melvin Jones fellow 2000). Home: 1361 W 12th Ave Anchorage AK 99501-4235 Business E-Mail: freed@acsalaska.net.

REED, GEORGE ELLIOTT, surgeon, educator, dean; b. NYC, Aug. 4, 1923; s. Morris and Mary R. Reed; m. Anne Miller Moore, 1995; children from previous marriage: Elizabeth E., George E. Jr. DVM, Cornell U., 1944; MD, NYU, 1951. Diplomate Am. Bd. Surgery, Bd. Thoracic Surgery. Successively intern, resident, chief resident NYU Bellevue Med. Ctr., N.Y.C., 1951-56, Berg fellow in cardiovascular surgery, 1956-59; from asst. prof. to assoc. prof. surgery NYU, N.Y.C., 1959-69, prof., 1969-78; prof. surgery, chief cardiothoracic surgery NY Med. Coll., Valhalla, 1978—2004, vice dean, 1996—2004; pres. med. staff Westchester County Med. Ctr., Valhalla, NY, 1989-93, from acting med. dir. to med. dir., 1992—2004, dir. George E. Reed Heart Ctr., 1994—2002; pres. Med. Faculty Health Alliance, Valhalla, 1994—2004; also bd. dirs. Westchester Health Care Corp., 1998—. Bd. dirs. Mid-Hudson Family Health Inst.; cons. surgery N.Y. State Dept. Health, Albany, 1963—90, VA, N.Y.C., 1969—78, Lenox Hill Hosp., N.Y.C., 1971—91, Kingston (N.Y.) Hosp., 1971—90; pres. Federated Faculty Practice Plan, 1996—99; adv. bd. Asian Cardiovasc. Thoracic Annals; presenter in field; med. adv. bd. Columbia Meml. Hosp., Hudson, NY, 2002—; pres. Eastview Found., 1992—. Sect. editor: Heart Disease, mem. editl. bd.: Heart and Health Reports; contbr. articles to profl. jours., chapters to books. Fellow: ACS, Am. Coll. Cardiology; mem.: Internat. Soc. Artificial Internal Organs, Am. Soc. Artificial Internal Organs, N.Am. Soc. Pacing and Electrophysiology, Internat. Assn. Cardiac Biol. Implants, Am. Trauma Soc., Soc. Thoracic Surgeons, Am. Assn. Thoracic Surgery, Harvey Soc., Am. Trudeau Soc., Alpha Omega Alpha (faculty). Avocations: woodworking, landscape architecture. Office: Westchester Med Ctr Macy 128 Valhalla NY 10595 Office Phone: 914-493-7676. Personal E-mail: georgereed23@hotmail.com. Business E-Mail: reedg@wcmc.com.

REED, GEORGE FORD, JR., investment executive; b. Hollywood, Calif., Dec. 26, 1946; s. George Ford and Mary Anita Reed; B.A. in Econs. with honors, U. So. Calif., 1969, M.A., 1971; m. Kathryn Nixon, 1981. Analyst planning and research Larwin Group, Beverly Hills, Calif., 1971-72; with Automobile Club So. Calif., Los Angeles, 1972-76, supr. mgmt. info., research and devel., 1973-74, mgr. fin. and market analysis, 1975-81, group mgr. fin. analysis and forecasting, 1981-86; pres. Reed Asset Mgmt. Co., Inc., Los Angeles, 1986—; instr. bus. and econs. Los Angeles Community Coll. Mem. population task force Los Angeles C. of C., 1974; mem. Gov. Calif. Statewide Econ. Summit Conf., 1974. Served with U.S. Army, 1969. Mem. Assn. Corp. Real Estate Execs., Fin. Execs. Inst., Nat. Assn. Bus. Economists, Western Regional Sci. Assn., Am. Mgmt. Assn., Am. Fin. Assn., So. Calif. Planners Assn., Rotary Internat., Omicron Delta Epsilon. Home: 1001 S Westgate Ave Los Angeles CA 90049-5905 Office: 10940 Wilshire Blvd Ste 1600 Los Angeles CA 90024-3940

REED, GLEN ALFRED, lawyer; b. Memphis, Sept. 24, 1951; s. Thomas Henry and Evelyn Merle (Roddy) Reed; m. Edith Jean Renick, June 17, 1972; children: Adam Christopher, Alec Benjamin. BA, U. Tenn., 1972; JD, Yale U., 1976. Bar: Ga. 1976. Project dir. Tenn. Rsch. Coordinating Unit, Knoxville, 1972-73; assoc. Alston Miller & Gaines, Atlanta, 1976-77, Bondurant Miller Hishon & Stephenson, Atlanta, 1978-81, ptnr., 1981-85, King & Spalding, Atlanta, 1985—. Author: (book) Practical Hospital Law, 1979. Gen. counsel Assn. Retarded Citizens, Atlanta, 1979—, bd. dirs., 1986—, pres., 1992—96; mem. adv. bd. CARE Atlanta, 1992—, chmn., 1994—99; v.p. Ga. Network People with Devel. Disabilities, 1991—92; legal advisor Ga. Gov.'s Commn. on Healthcare, 1994; bd. dirs. Ga. Partnership for Caring, 1999—2002, Ga. Comm. Support and Solutions, 2000—, Healthcare Ethics Consortium Ga., 2002—, MedShare Internat., vice chmn., 1999—; bd. dirs. Ctrl. Health Ctr., 1989—95, Vis. Nurse Health Sys., 1992—, chmn., 1996—99; mem. dean's coun. Sch. Pub. Health Emory U., Atlanta, 1998—. Mem.: ABA, Ga. Acad. Hosp. Attys. (pres. 1981—82), Am. Health Lawyers Assn. (bd. dirs. 1997—2000, pres. 1998—99), Am. Acad. Hosp. Attys. (bd. dirs. 1991—97, pres.-elect 1997), Ga. Bar Assn., Phi Beta Kappa. Methodist. Office: King & Spalding 191 Peachtree St NE Ste 40 Atlanta GA 30303-1740 Office Phone: 404-572-3393. Business E-Mail: gareed@kslaw.com.

REED, HAROLD WAYNE, university program coordinator; b. Punxsutawney, Pa., Nov. 30, 1942; s. Wayne Allen and Ethel Naomi (Balls) Reed; m. Edna Ruth Coleman; children: Harold Wayne Jr., Mercedes Adrian. BS in Secondary Edn., Clarion (Pa.) State Coll., 1964; MS in Botany, Ohio U., 1973, PhD in Microbiology, 1978. Vis. asst. prof. U. South Fla., Tampa, 1978—79; postdoctoral assoc. Boston Coll., 1979—82; asst. prof. Ind. U., Kokomo, 1982—87; grad. coord. Ga. Coll. and State U., Milledgeville, 1987—. Cons. Englehard, McIntyre, Ga., 1985—2000. Served with USN, 1968—72. Mem.: Am. Soc. Microbiology. Democrat. Avocation: woodworking. Home: 385 Old Monticello Rd NW Milledgeville GA 31061 Office: Ga Coll and State U 231 W Hancock St Milledgeville GA 31061 Office Phone: 478-445-0815.

REED, HELEN SKUGGEDAL, law librarian, musician; b. Halifax, N.S., Can., June 19, 1948; came to U.S., 1971; d. Johan Martin Skuggedal and Anna Gurine (Ringdal) Burns; m. Robert Douglas Reed, Aug. 14, 1971 (div. 1996); 1 child, Eric Douglas Reed. BA with honors, Dalhousie U., Halifax, 1969; MM, U. Mich., 1971. Libr. Hochstein Sch. Music, Rochester, 1972-75; organist Neu Chapel U. Evansville, 1976-83; acting archivist U. So. Ind., Evansville, 1978-80; organist Washington Ave. Presbyn., Evansville, 1984-90; prin. harpsichordist Evansville Philharm., 1984—; law libr. William H. Miller Law Libr., Evansville, 1985—. Archival cons. Evansville Mus. of Arts and Scis., 1984-85; exec. bd. mem. Four Rivers area Libr. Svcs. Authority, Evansville, 1988-91; bd. dirs., mem. adv. coun. Ind. Coop. Libr. Svcs. Authority, 1995-2000. Recitalist Royal Can. Coll. of Organists Conv., 1973; artist-fellow Bach Aria Festival and Inst., 1992. Founding mem. Evansville Chamber Orch., 1981—; organist Eastminster Presbyn. Ch., Evansville, 1991—. Grantee Nova Scotia Talent Trust, 1969-70. Mem. Am. Assn. Law Librs., Am. Guild Organists (Evansville chpt. exec. 1982-91, 94—), Evansville Area Librs. Consortium, Friends of UE Music (sec., treas. 1988-91), Ohio Regional Assn. Law Librs., Midwestern Hist. Keyboard Soc., Evansville Philharmonic Youth Orch. (mem. adv. coun.). Home: 1435 Brookside Dr Evansville IN 47714-2043 Office: William H Miller Law Libr 825 Sycamore St Ste 207 Evansville IN 47708-1849 Office Phone: 812-435-5175. E-mail: hsr@evansville.net.

REED, HOWARD ALEXANDER, historian, educator; b. Izmir, Turkey; s. Cass Arthur and Rosalind Christine (MacLachlan) R.; m. Shafiga Daulet, May 25, 1985; children from previous marriage: Seth Olcott, Heather MacLachlan, Deborah Lamont; stepchildren: Aylin, Sibel. Student, Phillips Acad., Andover, Mass., 1935-37, Wellington Coll., Berkshire, Eng., 1937-38; BA with honors, Yale U., 1942; MA, Princeton U., 1949, PhD, 1951; PhD (hon.), Hacettepe U., 1997. Instr. history Princeton U., 1949-50, Yale U., New Haven, also dir. Internat. Student Ctr., 1950-52; co-founder, asst. dir., prof. Grad. Inst. Islamic Studies, McGill U., 1952-55; dir. Inst. Internat. and Intercultural Studies, U. Conn., 1967-71, prof. history, 1966—89, prof. emeritus, cons., 1989—. Del. UNRRA and World Student Svc., Greece, 1946-47; program specialist internat. tng. and rsch. Ford Found., 1955-57; dir. coll. and youth programs Am. Friends Svc. Com., 1958-60; assoc. dir. Danforth Found., St. Louis, 1960-64; dir. Nat. Survey Non-Western Studies in Liberal Arts Colls. Dept. Edn., Assn. Am. Colls., 1963-64; exec. assoc. Edn. World Affairs, N.Y.C., 1964-67; participant internat. confs.; cons. Dept. State, U.S. A.I.D., World Bank, India, Oman, Turkey, various unvis., lectr. Author: Non-Western Studies in the Liberal Arts College, 1964, Issues and Opportunities in Turkish Education, 1991; contbr. author: Ency. Islam, 2d edit., 1954—, Foreign Affairs Bibliography, 1942-52, 55, Islam and the West, 1957, A Guide to Historical Literature, 1961, Ency. Americana, 1964-, General Education, Current Ideas and Concerns, 1964, The Emergence of the Modern Middle East, 1970, Expanding Dimensions of World Education, 1976, Internat. Ency. Higher Edn., 1977, Social and Economic History of Turkey (1071-1920), 1980, Islam in the Contemporary World, 1981, 2d edit. 1986, Contributions à l'histoire économique et sociale de l'empire ottoman, 1980, 83, The Oxford Encyclopedia of the Modern Islamic World, 1995; adv. editor: Muslim World, 1970-95; bd. adv. editors: The Middle East Jour, 1977-2002, Jour. Am. Studies Turkey, 1995—, Bull. of the Internat. Conf. on Higher Edn., 1997—; contbr. articles to profl. jours. Bd. dirs. Assn. Princeton Grad. Alumni, 1961-63, Lisle Fellowship, 1948-52, 58-60, 65-70, Pendle Hill, Wallingford, Pa., 1958-73, 75-86, Campus Christian Found., 1969-73, Univ. Senate, 1969-72, Am. Research Inst. Turkey, 1969-74, 77-79; co-founder Middle East Studies Assn., 1966, bd. dirs. 1977-80; trustee Friends World Coll., 1976-87; bd. overseers Moses Brown Sch., 1975-77; mem. exec. council Conf. Peace Research in History, 1972-75. Served to lt. (s.g.) USNR, 1942-46. Decorated Legion of Merit; D.S.C. (Gt. Britain); fellow Internat. Scholboy, 1937-38, Mid. East Inst., 1948-49, Rockefeller Found., 1949-50, 52, Ford Found., 1954, Fulbright fellow, 1970, 81, fellow Am. Coun. Learned Socs.-Social Sci. Rsch. Coun., 1977. Fellow Mid. East Studies Assn. (charter), Soc. Values in Higher Edn., Turkish Studies Assn. (co-founder 1970, sec.), Inst. Turkish Studies (hon.), AHEPA (hon.); mem. Am. Hist. Assn., Conf. on Peace Rsch. in History, Mid. East Inst. (Year 2000 award), Internat. Soc. Oriental Rsch., Brit.-Am. Alumni, Turkish Hist. Soc. (hon.), Assn. Turkish Am. Scientists (adv. bd.), Am.-Turkish Friendship Coun. (nat. adv. bd., Chmn.'s award in edn. 1991), Am.-Turkish Coun., Atatürk Soc. Am., Phi Beta Kappa, Phi Kappa Phi. Mem. Soc. Of Friends. Office: U Conn Dept History U-103 241 Glenbrook Rd Unit U-103 Storrs Mansfield CT 06269-2103

REED, ISHMAEL SCOTT (EMMETT COLEMAN), writer; b. Chattanooga, Feb. 22, 1938; s. Bennie Stephen (stepfather) and Thelma (Coleman) R.; m. Priscilla Rose, 1960 (div. 1970); children: Timothy, Brett; m. Carla Blank; 1 child, Tennessee Maria. Co-founder Yardbird Pub. Co. Inc., Berkeley, 1971, editorial dir., 1971-75; editor Yardbird Reader, 1972-76; co-founder Reed, Cannon & Johnson Comm. Co., Berkeley, 1973—, Before Columbus Found., Berkeley, 1976—; editor-in-chief Y'Bird mag., 1978-80; co-founder Ishmael Reed and Al Young's Quilt, Berkeley, 1980—; co-editor Quilt mag., 1981—. Co-founder East Village Other, 1965, Advance, 1965; tchr. St. Mark's in the Bowery prose workshop, 1966; guest lectr. U. Calif., Berkeley, 1968—, U. Wash., 1969-70, SUNY, Buffalo, 1975, 79, Yale U., 1979, Dartmouth Coll., 1980-81, Sitka Cmty. Assn., 1982, U. Ark., Fayetteville, 1982, Columbia U., 1983, Harvard U., 1987; assoc. fellow Calhoun Coll., Yale U., 1982—, Harvard Signet Soc., 1987—; regents lectr. U. Calif., Santa Barbara, 1988; mem. usage panel Am. Heritage Dictionary. Author: (novels) The Free-Lance Pallbearers, 1967, Yellow Back Radio Broke-Down, 1969, Mumbo Jumbo, 1972 (Nat. Book award nomination 1973), The Last Days of Louisiana Red, 1974 (Richard and Hinda Rosenthal Found. award Nat. Inst. Arts and Letters 1975), Flight to Canada, 1976, The Terrible Twos, 1982, Reckless Eyeballing, 1986, Cab Calloway Stands In for The Moon, 1986, The Terrible Threes, 1989, Japanese By Spring, 1993; (poetry) Catechism of d neoamerican hoodoo church, 1970, Conjure: Selected Poems 1963-70, 1972 (Nat. Book award nomination 1973, Pulitzer prize nomination 1973), Chattanooga, 1973, A Secretary to the Spirits, 1978, Ishmael Reed: New and Collected Poems, 1989, Another Day ath the Front: Dispatches from the Race War, 2003; (essays) Shrovetide in Old New Orleans, 1978, God Made Alaska for the Indians, 1981, Airing Dirty Laundry, 1993, Multi-America, 1996; (play) (with Carla Blank and Suzushi Hanayagi) The Lost State of Franklin, 1976; editor: The Rise, Fall, and...? of Adam Clayton Powell, 1967, 19 Necromancers from Now, 1970 (Calif. Assn. Eng. Tchrs. certificate of merit 1972), Yardbird Lives!, 1978, Calafia: The California Poetry, 1979, Writin' Is Fightin': Thirty-seven Years of Boxing on Paper, 1988; exec. prodr.: (TV pilot) Personal Problems. Chmn. Berkeley Arts Commn., 1980, 81; bd. dirs. chmn. Coordinating Council Lit. Mags., 1975-79, adv. bd. chmn., 1977-79. Recipient John Simon Guggenheim Meml. Found. award for fiction, 1974, Lewis Michaux award, 1978, ACLU award, 1978, Pushcart prize, 1979; Wis. Arts Bd. fellow, 1982; Nat. Endowment for Arts writing fellow, 1974; Guggenheim fellow, 1975. Mem. Author's Guild Am., PEN, Celtic Found. Office: Penguin Putnam Inc 375 Hudson St New York NY 10014-3658

REED, JAKE, professional football player; b. Sept. 28, 1967; m. Vinita; 2 children, Jake Rashann, Jarvin O. Degree in Criminal Justice, Grambling State. Wide receiver New Orleans Saints, Metairie, La., 1991—. Named NFC Offensive Player of Month of Sept., 1997. Office: New Orleans Saints 5800 Airline Dr Metairie LA 70003

REED, JAMES C., JR., lawyer; b. 1945; BS, Abilene Christian U., 1967; JD, So. Methodist U., 1970. Asst. gen. counsel Tesoro Petroleum Corp., San Antonio, 1982—90, v.p., asst. gen. counsel, asst. sec., 1990—93, v.p., gen. counsel, sec., 1993—94, sr. v.p., gen. counsel, sec., 1994—95, exec. v.p., gen. counsel, sec., 1995—. Office: Tesoro Petroleum Corp 300 Concord Plaza Dr San Antonio TX 78216-6999*

REED, JAMES DONALD, journalist, writer; b. Jackson, Mich., Oct. 7, 1940; s. Clair and Esther (Bryden) R.; m. Christine Flowers, June 14, 1969; children: Phoebe C., Alicia M., Gabrielle A. Student, Albion Coll., 1958-60; BA, Mich. State U., 1962; postgrad., SUNY-Stony Brook, 1967-69; MFA, U. Mont., 1970. Mem. faculty dept. creative writing U. Mass., 1970-75; dir. M.F.A. program, 1974; staff writer Sports Illustrated, N.Y.C., 1975-80; assoc. editor Time mag., 1980-90; sr. writer People mag., N.Y.C., 1990-91, sr. editor, 1991-93, sr. assoc. editor spl. issues, 1993—2001; contbg. editor Time Digital mag., 1997—; freelance journalist, 2001—. Author: (poetry) Expressways, 1970, Fatback Odes, 1973; (fiction) Free Fall, 1980; (with Christine Reed) Exposure, 1987, contr. articles to NY Times, Smithsonian, Modern Maturity, et. al. Guggenheim fellow, 1971

REED, JAMES ELDIN, consultant, historian; b. Walla Walla, Wash., Mar. 13, 1945; s. Eldin Wallace and Mary Ellen (White) R.; m. Deborah Jane Addis, Apr. 14, 1983. AB, Ripon Coll., 1967; AM, Harvard U., 1968, MTS, 1971, PhD, 1976. Cert. mgmt. cons., 1984-89. Tchg. fellow Harvard U., Cambridge, Mass., 1972-77, dir. summer writing program, 1977-78; founder, pres., chmn. Addis & Reed Cons., Inc., Boston, 1977—; pub. ARC Publs., Boston, 1995—99; Fulbright scholar Acad. Coun. on UN System, 2004—; Fulbright rsch. chair in pub. policy U. Waterloo, 2004—; sr. rsch. fellow Ctr. on Internat. Governance Innovation, 2004—. Vis. scholar Harvard U., 1992-94, 96-98, 99—; rsch. assoc. North Pacific program Fletcher Sch. Law and Diplomacy, Medford, Mass., 1994-96; v.p., pres. Assn. Mgmt. Cons., Boston, 1985-89; founder, bd. dirs. Nat. Coun. Pub. History, Washington, 1980-83; participant internat. confs. in field. Author: The Missionary Mind and American East Asia Policy, 1983; contbg. author: Enhancing Global Governance, 2002; editor: American Canada Watch, 1995—99; contbr. numerous articles, papers, and revs. to profl. publs., Christian Sci. Monitor, Boston Globe and other newspapers. Cons. House Agr. Com. Washington, 1978, House Judiciary Com., 1999-2000, invited witness Senate Judiciary Com., 1990, Ontario Coun. on Grad. Studies, 1999-2000; legis. dir. Asbestos Victims Campaign, Boston, 1987-90. Woodrow Wilson fellow, 1967-68, Harvard Grad. Prize fellow, 1967-68, fellow Newberry Libr., Chgo., 1965, Ctr. for Internat. Affairs, Harvard U., 1993-94, James Luther Adams Soc., Harvard Div. Sch., 2001—. Mem. Am. Hist. Assn., Can. Inst. Internat. Affairs (pres. Boston br. 1998—), Boston Athenaeum, Harvard Club Boston, Phi Beta Kappa. Unitarian Universalist. Achievements include book on traditional Far East policy of U.S., subscription newsletter on Can. and World Affairs, presentations and articles on Am. civilization, 25-year consultancy and creation of several nonprofit organizations. Home: 25 Holly Ln Brookline MA 02467-2156 Office: Addis & Reed Cons PO Box 85 Chestnut Hill MA 02467 E-mail: jimreed@post.harvard.edu.

REED, JAMES WESLEY, social historian, educator; b. New Orleans, Oct. 17, 1944; married. BA, U. New Orleans, 1967; AM, Harvard U., 1968, PhD, 1974. Research fellow in history Schlesinger Library, 1973-75; prof. history Rutgers U., New Brunswick, N.J., 1975—; dean Rutgers Coll., Rutgers U., New Brunswick, 1985-94. Author: From Private Vice to Public Virtue: The Birth Control Movement and American Society Since 1830, 1978. Office: Rutgers U Dept History Van Dycke Hall Rm 118 New Brunswick NJ 08901 E-mail: reed@history.rutgers.edu.

REED, JAMES WHITFIELD, physician, educator; b. Pahokee, Fla., Nov. 1, 1935; s. Thomas Reed and Chineater (Grey) Whitfield; married; children: David M., Robert A., Mary I., Katherine E. BS, W.Va. State Coll., 1954; MD, Howard U., 1963. Diplomate Am. Bd. Internal Medicine, Am. Bd. Endocrinology and Metabolism; cert. specialist Am. Soc. Hypertension. Commd. U.S. Army, 1963; advanced through grades to col., 1981; resident in internal medicine Madigan Army Med. Ctr., Tacoma, 1966-69, chief endocrinology and metabolism, 1971-76, chief dept. clin. rsch., 1976-78; chief dept. medicine Eisenhower Army Med. Ctr., Augusta, Ga., 1978-81; assoc. prof. internal medicine edn. for FP program U. Tex. at Dallas, 1981-84; prof. medicine Morehouse Sch. Medicine, Atlanta, 1985—, chmn. dept., 1985-92, chmn. grad. med. edn., 1992-96, activity chmn., 1986-88, dir. internal medicine residency, 1992-98, dir. Clin. Rsch. Ctr., 1998-2000; postdoctoral fellow in endocrinology and metabolism U. Calif. Med. Ctr., San Francisco, 1969-71; assoc. chair, prof. medicine Morehouse Sch. Medicine, 1992—, chief endocrinology, 1992—. Dir. endocrinology, fellow Madigan Army Med. Ctr., 1976-78; dir., chief medicine internal medicine residency program Eisenhower Army Med. Ctr., 1978-81, chmn. directorate of clin. investigation, 1978-81, dir. endocrinology fellowship program; med. cons. Tuskgee (Ala.) VA Hosp., 1985—; mem. nat. high blood pressure edn. com. NHLBI/NIH, Nat. Diabetes Mellitus Adv. Coun., Nat. Diabetes Adv. Bd., NHLBI working Com. on Hypertension and Diabetes; chmn. Sub Com. Special Population and Situations, chmn. subcom., mem. exec. com. Joint Nat. Commn. for Detection Evaluation and Treatment of High Blood Pressure; mem. diabetes epidemic action coun. Am. Diabetes Assn. Author: Black Man's Guide to Good Health, 1994, rev. edit., 2000, High Blood Pressure: The Black Man and Woman's Guide to Living with Hypertension, 2002; contbr. articles to profl. publs. Med. advisor, chmn. March of Dimes, Pierce County, Tacoma, 1976-78; pres.

Charles Drew Sickle Cell and Health Bd., Tacoma, 1976-78; mem. task force on cardiovascular risk reduction Am. Heart Assn. Decorated Legion of Merit; recipient Disting. Alumni award Nat. Assn. for Equal Opportunity in Higher Edn., 1988, Nat. Alumnus of Yr. award W.Va. State Coll., 1987; inducted into ROTC Hall of Fame, W.Va. State Coll., 1987. Master ACP; fellow Am. Coll. Clin. Endocrinologist; mem. Assn. Profs. Medicine, Endocrine Soc., Internat. Soc. Hypertension in Blacks (v.p. 1986-92, pres. 1992—2001), Assn. of Program Dirs. in Internal Medicine, Am. Heart Assn. Task Force on Cardiovascular Risk, Alpha Phi Alpha. Democrat. Avocations: bowling, skiing. Home: 380 Mcgill Pl NE Atlanta GA 30312-1069 Office: Morehouse Sch Medicine 720 Westview Dr SW Atlanta GA 30310-1458 Office Phone: 404-756-5788. E-mail: reedj@msm.edu. *One cannot control the circumstance of one's birth, but with keen alertness and honest hard work there are no limits to what one can achieve. So hitch your wagon to a star and never lose sight of it.*

REED, JANE GARSON, eldercare/disability consultant; b. Cleve., Jan. 11, 1948; d. Joseph John Guzowski and Irene Sophie (Dominic) Garson; children: Craig Michael, Kevin Matthew. BBA magna cum laude, Baldwin Wallace Coll., 1977; MBA in Mgmt., Case Western Res. U., 1983; postgrad., Cleve. State U., 1991-97. CPA, Ohio. Sr. asst. acct. Deloitte, Haskins & Sells, Cleve., 1977-78; sr. corp. auditor White Motor Corp., Beachwood, Ohio, 1979-81; instr. acctg. Cuyahoga C.C., Parma, Ohio, 1981-82; ind. contractor State of Wash., Olympia, 1982-84; dir. fin. Nonprofit SNF, Cleveland Heights, Ohio, 1985-86; controller Proprietary SNF, Akron, Ohio, 1986-87; lectr. mgmt. acctg. U. Akron, 1987-88; asst. prof. Baldwin-Wallace Coll., Berea, Ohio, 1989-94; pres. Athena Music, Inc., 2002. Lectr. advocacy and health policy change Cleve. State U., 2001—02. Asst. editor Ohio CPA Jour., 1997-99. Chair Trinity (Marymount) H.S. Reunion Com., 1990-91; vice-chair Com. for Advanced Edn. in Brunswick, 1995-96; mem. acctg. curriculum adv. com. Lorain County C.C.; bd. dirs. Greater Cleve. Brain Injury Coalition, 1997-2000; mem. Ohio Brain Injury Assn., 1996—, 2d v.p., 1999-2001. Mem. AICPA, Ohio Soc. CPAs (editl. bd. jour. com. 1992-95, task force on implementing quality edn. 1992-94, assurance svcs. com. 1998-2000, adv. coun. M.A.P. sect. 1999-2000), Inst. Mgmt. Accts. (faculty advisor to Baldwin-Wallace student chpt. 1990-94), Am. Soc. Women Accts. (pres. 1993-94), Medina County Writers Group (treas. 1998-2003), Delta Mu Delta. Methodist. Avocation: woodworking. Home and Office: 1254 Hadcock Rd Brunswick OH 44212-3018 E-mail: reed@brightdsl.net.

REED, JANET, dance educator, choreographer; b. Shelby, Tenn., Feb. 22, 1955; d. Robert and Mary Evelyn Reed; 1 child, Malik Isaiah Griffin. BS in Phys. Edn., SUNY, Brockport, 1977; MA in Theatre and Dance, U. Buffalo, 1997. Artistic dir. Buffalo City Ballet Co., 1988—; asst. prof. dance State U. Coll. at Buffalo, 1993—. Dir. Janet Reed and Dancers, Buffalo, 1998—. Choreographer (contemporary African dance) Standing on Shaky Ground: yet, she dances with abandon against the turbulent sea, dancer, costume designer I-Woman-I, Mask. Fellow, N.Y. Found. for the Arts, 2002; grantee, N.Y. State Coun. on the Arts, 1991, Barbara Demming Meml. Fund for Women, 1993. Republican. Avocations: travel, sewing, costume design, reading. Office: SUNY at Buffalo 1300 Elmwood Ave Buffalo NY 14222-1095 Personal E-mail: janetreeddancer@aol.com. E-mail: reedj5420usa@netscape.net.

REED, JOAN-MARIE, special education educator; b. St. Paul, Sept. 8, 1960; d. William Martin Reed and Diana-Marie (Miller) Reed Moss. BA, U. Minn., 1982, BS, 1983; MEd, Tex. Woman's U., 1986. Cert. tchr., Tex. Tchr. emotionally disturbed Birdville Ind. Sch. Dist., Ft. Worth, 1984-86, Goose Creek Ind. Sch. Dist., Baytown, Tex., 1986-92, ctr. leader, 1992-93, dept. chairperson, 1987-91; tchr. emotionally disturbed Conroe (Tex.) Ind. Sch. Dist., 1993-94, Willis (Tex.) Ind. Sch. Dist., 1994-95, Jefferson County Pub. Schs., 1995—. Co-editor: New Teacher Handbook, 1986-87, Behavior Improvement Program Handbook, 1987-88, New Teacher Mentor, 1997—, Student Teacher Supervisor, 1997, 99-2000. Mem. NEA, Coun. for Exceptional Children. Congregationalist. Avocations: reading, cooking, travel, running. Office: Drake Mid Sch 12550 W 52nd Ave Arvada CO 80002

REED, JOHN ALTON, lawyer; b. Washington, June 29, 1931; s. John Alton and Emma Powers (Ball) R.; m. Louisa Wardman, June 6, 1953; children: Donna, Joanne, Deborah. AB, Duke U., 1954, LLB, 1956. Bar: Fla. 1956. Assoc. Fowler-White, Tampa, Fla., 1956-57; ptnr. Rush, Reed & Marshall, Orlando, Fla., 1957-67; judge Fla. 4th Dist. Ct. Appeal, 1967-73, chief judge, 1971-73; judge U.S. Dist. Ct. for Middle Dist. Fla., Orlando, 1973-84; ptnr., chmn. dept. litigation Lowndes, Drosdick, Doster, Kantor & Reed, Orlando, 1985-99. Com. on standard civil jury instructions Fla. Supreme Ct., 1986-90. Bd. visitors Duke U. Law Sch., 1983—. Mem. ABA, Fla. Bar Assn., Orange County Bar Assn. Republican. Episcopalian. Office: PO Box 2809 215 N Eola Dr Orlando FL 32802 Home: 1600 US Hwy 64 W Sapphire NC 28774-9513 Office Phone: 407-843-4600.

REED, JOHN CASH, music educator, researcher; b. Jacksonville, Oct. 22, 1957; s. William Franklin and Ann Penney Reed; m. Susie Marie Hand Ates, June 12, 1995; 1 stepchild, Justin Wayne Ates. MusB, Fla. State U., 1979; MusM, Troy (Ala.) State U., 1991. Cert. T-5 Ga. State Bd. Edn. Band dir. Irwin County Schs., Oclla, Ga., 1979—81, Toenbs County Schs., Lyons, Ga., 1981—82, Johnson County Schs., Wrightsville, Ga., 1982—84, Wilkinson County Schs., Irwinton, Ga., 1984—93, Jeff Davis County Schs., Hazelhurst, Ga., 1993—. Composer: over 50 works, 1974—2004. Founder,dir. Dublin (Ga.) Cmty. Jazz Band, 1988—92; pres. Friends of Liberty, Hazlehurst, Ga., 2001—02. Mem.: Internat. Trumpet Guild, Music Educators Assn., Music Educators Nat. Conf. Avocations: astronomy, bibliophile. Home: 66 Georgia Cir Hazlehurst GA 31539 E-mail: jcneed57@yahoo.com.

REED, JOHN FRANCIS (JACK REED), senator; b. Providence, Nov. 12, 1949; s. Joseph Anthony and Mary Louise (Monahan) R. BS, U.S. Mil. Acad., 1971; M in Pub. Policy, Harvard U., 1973, JD cum laude, 1982. Bar: D.C. 1982, R.I. 1983. Commd. 2d. lt. U.S. Army, 1971, served with 82d Airborne Div., 1973-77; asst. prof. U.S. Mil. Acad., West Point, N.Y., 1977-79; resigned U.S. Army, 1979; assoc. Sutherland, Asbill & Brennan, Washington, 1982-83, Edwards & Angell, Providence, 1983-89; mem. R.I. Senate, 1984-90, 102nd-104th Congresses from 2d R.I. dist., 1991—97; mem. judiciary com., mem. econ. and ednl. opportunity com., appropriations com., regional whip for New Eng. Dem. del.; U.S. senator from R.I., 1997—. Co-chair N.E.-Midwest Congl. Coalition.; mem. appropriations com. Armed Svcs. Banking, Housing, and Urban Affairs, Health, Edn., Labor and Pensions, vice-chmn. joint econ. com.; mem. Coun. Fgn. Rels. Author: (with others) American National Security, 1981. Recipient Disting. Svc. award AARP, 1989, John Fogarty award, 1990, Disting. Legislator award United Way Southeastern New Eng., 1988. Mem. ABA, R.I. Bar Assn., D.C. Bar Assn., Environ. and Energy Study Inst., Phi Kappa Phi. Democrat. Roman Catholic. Avocations: reading, hiking. Office: US Senate 728 Hart Senate Ofc Bldg Washington DC 20510-0001

REED, JOHN HATHAWAY, former ambassador; b. Fort Fairfield, Maine, Jan. 5, 1921; s. Walter and Eva Ruth (Seeley) R.; m. Cora Mitchell Davison, Mar. 24, 1944; children— Cheryl, Ruth. BS, U. Maine, 1942, LL.D. (hon.), 1960, Ricker Coll.; grad., Harvard Naval Supply Sch., 1944. Officer Reed Farms, Inc., Fort Fairfield, Maine, 1948-98; pres. Aroostook Raceway, Inc., 1958-59; adv. com. Fort Fairfield br. No. Nat. Bank of Presque Isle; mem. Nat. Transp. Safety Bd., Washington, 1967-75, chmn., 1969-75; ambassador to Sri Lanka Colombo, 1975-77; dir. govt. rels. Assoc. Builders & Contractors, Inc., Washington, 1978-81; ambassador to Sri Lanka and Republic of Maldives, 1982-85; cons. Dept. State, 1985-90; pvt. practice cons. Washington, 1990—. Chmn. Nat. Govs. Conf. Rep., 1966; rep. Fort Fairfield to Maine Legislature, 1954-56; mem. Senate, 1957-59, pres., 1959-60; gov. State of Maine, 1960-67. Pres. bd. Community Gen. Hosp., Fort Fairfield, 1952-54, No. Maine Fair, 1953-59; trustee Ricker Coll., 1953-60, Oak Grove Sch., Vassalboro, Maine; bd. advisors Coll. of Democracy, 1986—, chmn., 1991-2000. Served to lt. (j.g.) USNR, 1942-46. Mem. Am. Fgn. Svc. Assn., Coun. Am. Abassadors, Soc. Sr. Aerospace Execs. Inc. (bd. dirs. 1987-99, pres. 1988-91), Nat. Inst. Former Govs. (bd. dirs. 1992—), Am. Legion, VFW, Grange, Maine Assn. Agrl. Fairs (pres. 1956), Mil. Order of Carabao, Capitol Hill Club, Driving Club (Ft. Fairfield) (pres. 1950-53), Aeroclub of Washington, Internat. Aviation Club, Rotary, Masons, KP, Anah Temple Shrine. Republican. Congregationalist. Office: 410 O St SW Washington DC 20024-2239

REED, JOHN SHEDD, former railway executive; b. Chgo., June 9, 1917; s. Kersey Coates and Helen May (Shedd) R.; m. Marjorie Lindsay, May 4, 1946; children: Ginevra, Keith, Helen, Peter, John Shedd Jr. Student, Chgo. Latin Sch., Hotchkiss Sch.; BS in Indsl. Adminstrn., Yale U., 1939; grad., Advanced Mgmt. Program, Harvard U., 1955. With A.T. & S.F. Ry., 1939-83; test dept. asst., successively spl. rep. to gen. supt. transp. Chgo.; transp. insp. Amarillo, Tex.; trainmaster Slaton, Tex., Pueblo, Colo.; supt. Mo. div., Marceline, Mo.; asst. to v.p. Chgo., 1957-59; exec. asst. to pres., 1957-59; v.p. finance, 1959-64; v.p. exec. dept., 1964-67; pres., 1967-78; chief exec. officer, 1968-82; chmn. bd., 1973-83. Pres. Santa Fe Industries, Inc., 1968-78, chmn. bd. dirs., CEO Santa Fe So. Pacific Corp., 1987, chmn., 1987-88. Dir. Nat. Merit Scholarship Corp., 1996, past chmn.; trustee Shedd Aquarium, Chgo., 1996, past pres.; vice chmn., dir. Alliance Francaise de Chicago. With USNR, 1940-45. Mem. Chgo. Club, Old Elm Club, Shoreacres Club, Onwentsia Club (Lake Forest). Home: 301 W Laurel Ave # 112 Lake Forest IL 60045-1180 Office: 224 S Michigan Ave Ste 200 Chicago IL 60604-2591

REED, JOHN SHEPARD, stock exchange executive; b. Chgo., Feb. 7, 1939; divorced; 4 children; m. Cindy McCarthy, 1994. BA and BS, Washington and Jefferson Coll., MIT, 1961; MS, Sloan Sch. MIT, 1965. With Citicorp/Citibank, 1965—2000, chmn., CEO, 1984-98; co-chmn. CitiGroup, Inc., N.Y.C., 1998—2000; interim chmn. N.Y. Stock Exch., 2003—, interim CEO, 2003—04; Robert S. Hatfield Fellow, Econ. Edn. Cornell Univ., Ithaca, 1998; sr. visiting fellow Princeton Univ., Bendheim Ctr. for Finance, 2002. Bd. dirs. Citicorp/Citibank, 1975-2000, Altria (formerly Philip Morris Inc.), Monsanto Co.; mem. Bus. Coun.; mem. policy com., Bus. Roundtable; chmn. Coalition of Svc. Inds.; svcs. policy adv. com. to the U.S. Trade Rep. Mem. bd. MIT, Meml. Sloan-Kettering Cancer Ctr., Rand Corp., Spencer Found., Am. Mus. Nat. History. Served with C.E. U.S. Army, Korea, 1962-64. Office: NY Stock Exch Inc 11 Wall St New York NY 10005

REED, JOHN SQUIRES, II, lawyer; b. Lexington, Ky., Mar. 20, 1949; s. John Squires and Mary Alexander (O'Hara) R.; m. Nancy Claire Battles, Dec. 29, 1973; children: Alexandra Simmons, John Squires III. AB in Polit. Sci., U. Ky., 1971; JD, U. Va., 1974. Bar: Ky. 1974, U.S. Dist. Ct. (we. dist.) Ky. 1975, U.S. Ct. Appeals (6th cir.) 1975, U.S. Dist. Ct. (ea. dist.) Ky. 1979, U.S. Supreme Ct. 1980, U.S. Ct. Appeals (fed. cir.) 1985. Assoc. Greenbaum Doll & McDonald, Louisville, 1974-79, ptnr., 1979-87, Hirn, Doheny, Reed & Harper, Louisville, 1987-96, Reed Weitkamp Schell & Vice PLLC, Louisville, 1996—. Mem. Leadership Louisville, 1982, treas., mem. exec. com. Leadership Louisville Alumni Assn., 1984, pres., 1985; bd. dirs. Econs. Am. in Ky., 1985-2002, Nat. Assn. Cmty. Leadership, 1986-91, treas., 1987-88, v.p., 1988-89, pres., 1989-90, Leadership Louisville Found., Inc., 1986-92, Greater Louisville Econ. Devel. Partnership, 1987-97; chair Leadership USA, Inc., 1997—, Louisville Collegiate Sch., 1996—. 1st lt. U.S. Army, 1974. Mem. ABA (antitrust, intellectual property, litig. sects.), Ky. Bar Assn., Louisville Bar Assn. (bd. dirs. 1985-86, treas. 1988, sec. 1989, v.p. 1990, pres. 1992), Louisville Boat Club, Valhalla Golf Club, Phi Beta Kappa. Democrat. Presbyterian. Office: Reed Weitkamp Schell & Vice PLLC 500 W Jefferson St Ste 2400 Louisville KY 40202 Office Phone: 502-589-1000. E-mail: jreed@rwsvlaw.com.

REED, JOHN THEODORE, writer, publisher; b. Camden, NJ, July 5, 1946; s. Theodore and Marion Theresa (Simonsick) R.; m. Margaret Ogden Tunnell, May 31, 1975; children: Daniel Tunnell, Steven Tunnell, Michael Tunnell. BS, U.S. Mil. Acad., West Point, NY, 1968; MBA, Harvard U., 1977. Salesman Pritchett & Co., Pine Hill and Collingswood, NJ, 1972-74; property mgr. Fox & Lazo Inc., Cherry Hill, NJ, 1974-75; writer Harcourt Brace Jovanovich, Boston, 1976-86; bank exec. Crocker Nat. Bank, San Francisco, 1977-78; writer, pub. Alamo, Calif., 1977—. Author: Apartment Investing Check Lists, 1978, Aggressive Tax Avoidance for Real Estate Investors, 1981, Aggressive Tax Avoidance for Real Estate Investors, 16th edit., 1998, How to Manage Residential Property for Maximum Cash Flow and Resale Value, 1995, How to Manage Residential Property for Maximum Cash Flow and Resale Value, 5th edit., 1998, How to Use Leverage to Maximize Your Real Estate Investment Return, 1984, 1986, How to Increase the Value of Real Estate, 1986, Office Building Acquisition Handbook, 1982, 1985, 1987, Residential Property Acquisition Handbook, 1991, How to Buy Real Estate for at Least 20% Below Market Value, 1993, How to Buy Real Estate for at Least 20% Below Market Value, 2d edit., 1996, Coaching Youth Football Defense, 1994, Coaching Youth Football Defense, 2d edit., 1996, John T. Reed's Real Estate Investor's Monthly Newsletter, 1986—, Coaching Youth Football, 1995—, Coaching Youth Football, 3d edit., 2000—, Football Clock Management, 1997—, Football Clock Management, 2d edit., 2001—, Aggressive Tax Avoidance for Real Estate Investors, 17th edit., 2001—, Youth Baseball Coaching, 2000—, How to Get Started in Real Estate Investment, 2000—, Gap-Air-Mirror Defense for Youth Football, 2000—, How to Buy Real Estate for Little or No Money Down, 2001—, Single-Wing Offense for Youth Football, 2001—, Fixers, 2002, Succeeding, 2003. Coach Youth Flag Football, 1999. 1st lt. U.S. Army, 1968-72, Vietnam. Mem. Nat. Assn. Real Estate Editors, Am. Baseball Coaches Assn., Am. Football Coaches Assn., Nat. Youth Sports Coaches Assn., Nat. Fedn. Interscholastic Coaches Assn., Calif. Coaches Assn., Football Writers Assn., Profl. Football Rschrs. Assn., Nat. Single-Wing Coaches Assn. Avocations: reading, activities with family. Home and Office: 342 Bryan Dr Alamo CA 94507-2858 Office Phone: 925-820-6292. E-mail: johnreed@johntreed.com.

REED, JOHN WESLEY, lawyer, educator; b. Independence, Mo., Dec. 11, 1918; s. Novus H. and Lilian (Houchens) R.; m. Imogene Fay Vonada, Oct. 5, 1946 (div. 1958); m. Dorothy Elaine Floyd, Mar. 5, 1961; children: Alison A., John M. (dec.), Mary V., Randolph F., Suzanne M. AB, William Jewell Coll., 1939, LLD, 1995; LLB, Cornell U., 1942; LLM, Columbia U., 1949, JSD, 1957. Bar: Mo. 1942, Mich. 1953. Assoc. Stinson, Mag, Thomson, McEvers & Fizzell, Kansas City, Mo., 1942-46; assoc. prof. law U. Okla., 1946-49; assoc. prof. U. Mich., 1949-53, prof., 1953-64, 68-85, Thomas M. Cooley prof., 1985-87, Thomas M. Cooley prof. emeritus, 1987—; dean, prof. U. Colo., 1964-68, Wayne State U., Detroit, 1987-92, prof. emeritus, 1992—. Vis. prof. NYU, 1949, U. Chgo., 1960, Yale U., 1963-64, Harvard U., 1982, U. San Diego, 1993; dir. Inst. Continuing Legal Edn., 1968-73; reporter Mich. Rules of Evidence Com., 1975-78, 83-84; mem. faculty Salzburg Sem., 1962, chmn., 1964. Author: (with W.W. Blume) Pleading and Joinder, 1952; (with others) Introduction to Law and Equity, 1953, Advocacy Course Handbook series, 1963-81; editor in chief Cornell Law Quar., 1941-42; contbr. articles to profl. jours. Pres. bd. mgrs. of mins. and missionaries benefit bd. Am. Bapt. Chs. U.S.A., 1967-74, 82-85, 88-94; mem. com. visitors JAG Sch., 1971-76; trustee Kalamazoo Coll., 1954-64, 68-70. Recipient Harrison Tweed award Assn. Continuing Legal Edn. Adminstrs., 1983, Samuel E. Gates award Am. Coll. Trial Lawyers, 1985, Roberts P. Hudson award State Bar Mich., 1989. Fellow Internat. Soc. Barristers (editor jour. 1980—); mem. ABA (mem. coun. litigation sect.), Assn. Am. Law Schs. (mem. exec. com. 1965-67), Am. Acad. Jud. Edn. (v.p. 1978-80), Colo. Bar Assn. (mem. bd. govs. 1964-68), Mich. Supreme Ct. Hist. Soc. (bd. dirs. 1991—), Sci. Club Mich., Order of Coif. Office: U Mich Sch Law Ann Arbor MI 48109-1215 Office Phone: 734-763-0165. E-mail: reedj@umich.edu.

REED, JOSEPH WAYNE, American studies educator, artist; b. St. Petersburg, Fla., May 31, 1932; s. Joseph Wayne and Gertrude (Cain) R.; m. Kit Craig, Dec. 10, 1955; children: Joseph McKean, John Craig, Katherine Hyde Maruyama. BA, Yale U., 1954, MA, 1958, PhD, 1961. Rsch. asst. Yale Libr., 1956-57; instr. English Wesleyan U., Middletown, Conn., 1960-61, assoc. prof., 1967-71, prof., 1971—, chmn. dept., 1971-73, 75-76, 85-86, prof. English and Am. studies, 1987. Vis. lectr. Yale U., New Haven, 1974; lectr. U.S. dept. State and USIS, Can., India, Nepal, 1974; coord. cultural exch., New Delhi, Bombay, 1992; coord. music and writing workshop U. Va., Georgetown U., others. Author: English Biography in the Early Nineteenth Century, 1801-38, 1966, Faulkner's Narrative, 1973, Three American Originals: John Ford, William Faulkner, Charles Ives, 1984, American Scenarios, 1989; editor: Barbara Bodichon's American Diary, 1972, (with W.S. Lewis) Horace Walpole's Family Correspondence, 1975, (with F.A. Pottle) Boswell, Laird of Auchinleck, 1977, 2d edit., 1994; one-man shows include Portal Gallery, London, 1971, USIS Libr., New Delhi, 1974, 92, Addison/Ripley Gallery, Washington, 1987, 92, 95, 98, Sterling Meml. Libr., Yale U., 2004. Chmn. Wesleyan Sesquicentennial, 1982; chmn. bd. trustees Yale Libr. Assocs., 1984-2000, hon. trustee, 2000—. Lt. (j.g.) USNR, 1954-56. Mem. Elizabethan Club, The Johnsonians (chmn. 1988). Democrat. Episcopalian. Home: 45 Lawn Ave Middletown CT 06457-3135 Business E-Mail: jreed@wesleyan.edu.

REED, JOYLYNN HAILEY, communications educator, consultant; b. Austin, Tex., Oct. 5, 1959; d. James Leon and Carol Massey Hailey; m. Richard Reed, Jan. 17, 1986. PhD ednl. psychology, U. of Tex., Austin, TX, 1984—89, M.A. comm. studies, 1981—83, B.S. comm. studies, 1977—81, B.A. English, 1977—80. ACE Group Fitness Instructor Am. Coun. on Exercise/ Calif., 2003. Program coord./asst. prof. St. Edward's U., Austin, Tex., 1991—97; lectr., communication studies U. of Tex., Austin, Tex., 1990—99, faculty devel. specialist, ctr. for tchg. effectiveness, 1997—2000, program coord., grad. studies, 1998—2000; online instrnl. devel. mgr. 3M NSI, Austin, Tex., 2000—01; pres. MacDermott & Reed, Inc., Austin, Tex., 1997—; sr. lectr., grad. studies U. of Tex. at Dallas, Dallas, 2001—. Bd. of directors Alpha Delta Pi Housing Corp., Austin, Tex., 2000—; adv. bd. Acad. of Oriental Medicine, Austin, Tex., 1994—; bd. of trustees sec. Dispute Resolution Ctr., Austin, Tex., 2000—01; bd. of trustees Finding Our Voice, Austin, Tex., 1999—. Author: (jour. article) Jour. of Ednl. Psychology, Ednl. Psychologist. Mem.: Nat. Reading Conf., Nat. Communication Assn., Am. Ednl. Rsch. Assn., Kappa Delta Pi, Alpha Delta Pi (life). Christian. Avocations: exercise, playing classical piano, sewing.

REED, KATHLYN LOUISE, occupational therapist, educator; b. Detroit, June 2, 1940; d. Herbert C. and Jessie R. (Krehbiel) R. BS in Occupl. Therapy, U. Kans., 1964; MA, Western Mich. U., 1966; PhD, U. Wash., 1973; MLIS, U. Okla., 1987. Occupl. therapist in psychiatry Kans. U. Med. Ctr., Kansas City, 1964-65; instr. occupl. therapy U. Wash., Seattle, 1967-70; assoc. prof. dept. occupl. therapy U. Okla. Health Scis. Ctr., Oklahoma City, 1973-77, prof., 1978-85, chmn. dept. occupl. therapy, 1973-85; libr. edn. info. svcs. Houston Acad. Medicine Tex. Med. Ctr. Libr., 1988-97. Cons. to Okla. State Dept. Health, 1976-77, Children's Convalescent Ctr., Oklahoma City, 1977-80, Oklahoma City Pub. Schs., 1980-81; vis. scholars program Tex. Woman's U., 1991-94, adj. prof. Sch. Occupl. Therapy, 1992-97, vis. prof., 1997—; prof. Houston Ctr. Author: (with Sharon Sanderson) Concepts of Occupational Therapy, 1980, 2d edit., 1983, 3rd edit., 1992, 4th edit., 1999, Models of Practice in Occupational Therapy, 1983, Quick Reference to Occupational Therapy, 1991, 2d edit., 2000, (with Julie Pauls) Quick Reference to Physical Therapy, 1996, 2d edit., 2004, (with S. Cunningham) Internet Guide for Rehabilitation Professionals, 1997, (with Sally Pore) Quick Reference to Speech-Language Pathology, 1999. Vol. crisis counselor Open Door Clinic, Seattle, 1968-72; mem. exec. bd. Seattle Mental Health Inst., 1971-72; Mem. Citizen Participation Liaison Coun., Seattle, 1970-72. Recipient Award of Merit, Can. Assn. Occupl. Therapists, 1988. Fellow Am. Occupl. Therapy Assn. (Merit award 1983, Slagle lecture award 1985, Svc. award 1985, 2001); mem. N.Am. Riding for Handicapped Assn., World Fedn. Occupl. Therapists, Coun. Exceptional Children, Okla. Occupl. Therapy Assn. (pres. 1974-76), Tex. Occupl. Therapy Assn. (Roster of Merit award 2002), Med. Libr. Assn. (Rittenhouse award 1987, Acad. Health Info. Professions), Am. Occupl. Therapy Found., Assn. Advancement Rehab. Tech., Neuro-Devel. Treatment Assn., Tex. Occupl. Therapy Found. (pres. 1998—), Pi Theta Epsilan, Sigma Kappa (Colby award 1994). Democrat. Home: 6699 De Moss Dr Houston TX 77074-5003 Personal E-mail: klreed3@juno.com.

REED, KEITH ALLEN, lawyer; b. Anamosa, Iowa, Mar. 5, 1939; s. John Ivan and Florence Lorine (Larson) R.; m. Beth Illana Kesterson, June 22, 1963; children: Melissa Beth, Matthew Keith. BBA, U. Iowa, 1960, JD, 1963. Bar: Ill. 1963, Iowa 1963. Ptnr. Seyfarth Shaw, Chgo., 1963—. Co-author: Labor Arbitration in Healthcare, 1981; co-editor: Chicagoland Employment Law Manual, 1994, Employment and Discrimination, 1996, Federal Employment Law and Regulations, 1989-99, 2001-; co-contbr. articles to Am. Hosp. Assn. publs., 1986-89. Trustee Meth. Hosp. Chgo., 1985—; mem. ad hoc labor adv. com. Am. Hosp. Assn., Chgo., 1980—; bd. dirs. Lyric Opera Chgo. Ctr. for Am. Artists, pres., 1983-86. Mem. ABA (dir. health law forum 1979-82), Chgo. Bar Assn. (chair labor and employment law com. 1996-), Union League Club Chgo. (bd. dirs. 1985-88), Sunset Ridge Country Club (Northfield, Ill.). Republican. Methodist. Avocations: music, community theater, tennis, golf. Office: Seyfarth Shaw 55 E Monroe St Ste 4200 Chicago IL 60603-5863

REED, KENNETH G. petroleum company executive; b. 1917; married. Ed., U. Tex. With Amerada Petroleum Corp., Tulsa, 1948-70, sr. v.p., 1967-70; exec. v.p. internat. operations Amerada Hess Corp., N.Y.C., 1970; pres., chief exec. officer APEXCO, Inc., Tulsa, 1971-77, Natomas Internat. Corp., 1977, also dir.; exec. v.p. energy, dir. Natomas Co., San Francisco, 1977-83, vice chmn., pres., 1983—; pres., dir. Natomas Energy Co., 1979—; chmn., chief exec. officer Overseas Petroleum Ltd., San Francisco, 1984—. Dir. Natomas N.Am. Inc., 1st Nat. Bank & Trust Co., Tulsa, Oneok Inc., Tulsa. Office: Apt 1518 3840 Rimrock RD Billings MT 59102-0107

REED, LELAND, lawyer; b. Hector, Ark., Sept. 17, 1921; s. Albert McCain and Hattie Mae (Hogins) R.; 1 child, Starla Jacobs. BS, U. So. Calif., 1948; JD, Van Norman U., 1969. Bar: Calif. 1976, D.C. 1994, U.S. Ct. Appeals (9th cir.) 1976, U.S. Supreme Ct. 1980. Pub. acct. Haskings Sells-Arthur Young, L.A. and N.Y.C., 1948-55; plant contr. Dunlop Rubber Co., Buffalo, N.Y., 1955-60; acct. cons. Kirk Mayer Engrng. Co., L.A., 1960-62, Daniel, Mann, Johnson, L.A., 1963-65; contract specialist USN, Long Beach, Calif., 1966-73; contracting officer USAF, L.A., 1973-80, Europe and Middle East, 1980-83; pvt. practice L.A. and Washington, 1983—. Mem. State Bar Calif., D.C. Bar Assn., L.A. County Bar Assn. Avocations: fishing, travel. Home and Office: 4223 Verdugo Rd Ste 2 Los Angeles CA 90065

REED, LEON SAMUEL, writer, photographer; b. Warren, Ohio, July 6, 1949; s. Walter Charles and Lois Avalene (Botroff) R.; m. Margaret Smith, Dec. 27, 1975 (div.); m. Lois S. Lembo, Aug. 5, 1997; children: Samuel, Stephen, Catherine. BA in Econs. and Journalism, Antioch Coll., 1971. Project dir. Coun. on Econ. Priorities, N.Y.C. and Washington, 1970-75; sr. mem. profl. staff Joint Com. on Def. Prodn., U.S. Congress, Washington, 1975-77; mem. profl. staff Com. on Banking, Housing and Urban Affairs, U.S. Senate, Washington, 1977-81; analyst TASC, 1981-82, mgr. contingency planning, 1982-85, mgr. instl. resources dept., 1985-91, dir. indsl. and mfg. scis. divsn., 1991-97; rsch. staff Inst. Def. Analyses, 1998—2003; freelance writer, photographer, 2000—. Author: Military Maneuvers, 1975, Resource Management: A Historical Perspective, 1988; co-author: Guide to Corporations, 1973, Report of the National Critical Technologies Panel, 1991; contbr. Strategic Survey, 1981-82, The American Defense Mobilization Infrastructure, 1983; corr. Potomac Almanac; author numerous congressional and exec. br. reports, also mag. and jour. articles. Del. White House Conf. on Youth, 1971; writer, photographer Md. Soccer News, 1996—; pres. Randolph Civic Assn., 1978—80; v.p. North Bethesda Congress of Citizens Assns., 1983—84, pres., 1984—86; v.p. Md. State Youth Soccer Assn., 1998—; bd. dirs. Coun. on Econ. Priorities, 1971—73, Montgomery Soccer, Inc., 1994—, pres., 2001—. Named to Warren HS Alumni Hall of Fame, 1997.

REED, LESTER JAMES, biochemist, educator; b. New Orleans, Jan. 3, 1925; s. John T. and Sophie (Pastor) R.; m. Janet Louise Gruschow, Aug. 7, 1948; children: Pamela, Sharon, Richard, Robert. BS, Tulane U., 1943; D.Sc. (hon.), 1977; PhD, U. Ill., 1946. Rsch. asst. NDRC, Urbana, Ill., 1944-46; rsch. assoc. biochemistry Cornell U. Med. Coll., 1946-48; faculty U. Tex., Austin, 1948—, prof. chemistry, 1958—, Ashbel Smith prof., 1984-99, prof. emeritus, 1999—; rsch. sci. Clayton Found. Biochem. Inst., 1949—. Assoc. dir., Clayton Found. Biochem. Inst., 1962-63, dir., 1963-96. Contbr. articles profl. jours. Mem. NAS, Am. Acad. Arts and Scis., Am. Soc. for Biochemistry and Molecular Biology (Merck award 1994), Am. Chem. Soc. (Eli Lilly & Co.

award in biol. chemistry 1958), Phi Beta Kappa, Sigma Xi. Home: 3502 Balcones Dr Austin TX 78731-5802 Office: Dept Chem and Biochem 1 Univ Station A5300 Austin TX 78712 Business E-Mail: lreed@mail.utexas.edu.

REED, LOU, musician; b. Bklyn., Mar. 2, 1942; s. Sidney Joseph and Toby (Futterman) R. BA, Syracuse U., 1964. Songwriter Pickwick Records, N.Y.C., 1965; rec. artist Verve, MGM, Atlantic, Arista, RCA, Sire Warner Bros., Reprise, Record Cos, N.Y.C., 1965—. Solo albums include Lou Reed, 1972, Transformer, 1972, Berlin, 1973, Rock 'N' Roll Animal, 1974, Sally Can't Dance, 1974, Metal Machine Music, 1975, Lou Reed Live, 1975, Coney Island Baby, 1976, Rock and Roll Heart, 1976, Street Hassle, 1978, Live, Take No Prisoners, 1978, The Bells, 1979, Growing Up in Public, 1980, Blue Mask, 1982, Legendary Hearts, 1983, New Sensations, 1984, Mistrial, 1986, New York, 1989, Songs for Drella, 1990, Magic and Loss, 1992, Between Thought and Expression: The Lou Reed Anthology, 1992, Different Times: Lou Reed In The 70's, 1996, Set The Twilight Reeling, 1996, Perfect Night Live in London, 1998, Ecstasy, 2000; founding mem. (band) The Velvet Underground, 1966-70, touring with Andy Warhol's The Exploding Plastic Inevitable; albums include The Velvet Underground and Nico, 1967, White Light White Heat, 1968, The Velvet Underground, 1969, Loaded, 1970; albums after Velvet Underground include Live at Max's Kansas City, 1972, Velvet Underground Live MCM XCIII, 1993, VU, 1985, Another View, 1986; exhibited series of photographs Photographic Resource Ctr., 1997, Soho Triad Gallery, 1998, Le Printemps de Cahors, France, 1999, Closure, 1998; photos pub. in photographic mag. Blind Spot; author: Between Thought and Expression, 1991, Pass Thru Fire, 2000; actor in some film roles. Decorated chevalier comdr. Arts and Letters (France); recipient Best New Poet award Coun. on Small Lit. Mags., 1977, Heroes award N.Y. chpt. NARAS, 1997, inducted into Rock and Roll Hall of Fame as member of Velvet Underground, 1996; designated Am. Master, PBS Documentary Series, 1998. Mem. Musician's Union Local 802, Screen Actors Guild Jewish. Office: Sister Ray Enterprises 584 Broadway Rm 609 New York NY 10012-3229

REED, LOWELL A., JR., federal judge; b. Westchester, Pa., 1930; s. Lowell A. Sr. and Catherine Elizabeth R.; m. Diane Benson; four children. BBA, U. Wis., 1952; JD, Temple U., 1958. Bar: Pa. 1959, U.S. Dist. Ct. (ea. dist.) Pa. 1961, U.S. Ct. Appeals (3d cir.) 1962, U.S. Supreme Ct. 1970. Corp. trial counsel PMA Group, Phila., 1958-63; assoc. Rawle & Henderson, Phila., 1963-65, gen. ptnr., 1966-88; judge U.S. Dist Ct., Phila., 1988-99; sr. judge U.S. Dist. Ct., Phila., 1999—. Lectr. law Temple U., 1965-81, faculty Acad. Advocacy, 1988—, Pa. Bar Inst., 1972—. Contbr. articles to profl. jours. Elder Abington (Pa.) Presbyn. Ch.; past. mem. Pa. Senate Select Com. Med. Malpractice; past pres., bd. dirs. Rydal Meadowbrook Civic Assn.; bd. dirs. Abington Sch. Bd., 1971, World Affairs Coun. Phila., 1983-88; trustee Abington Health Care Corp., 1983-88, 90-93. Lt. Comdr. USNR, 1952-57. Recipient Alumni Achievement award Temple U. 1988, Cert. of Honor, 2001, A. Sherman Christensen award Am. Inns. of Ct. Found., 2003. Mem. ABA, Phila. Bar Assn. (chmn. medico legal com. 1975, constl. bicentennial com. 1986-87, commn. on jud. selection and retention 1983-87), Temple Am. Inn of Ct. (pres. 1990-93, master of bench 1990—), Am. Judicature Soc., Temple U. Law Alumni Assn. (exec. com. 1987-90, 99—), Hist. Soc. U.S. Supreme Ct., Hist. Soc. U.S. Dist. Ct. Ea. Dist. Pa. Republican. Office: US Dist Ct US Courthouse Independence Mall W Philadelphia PA 19106

REED, M. SCOTT, accounting company executive; CFO Grant Thornton LLP, Chgo., 1997-99, CEO, 1999-2000. Office: Grant Thornton LLP 175 W Jackson Blvd #20 Chicago IL 60604-3033

REED, MARK ARTHUR, educator, researcher; b. Suffern, N.Y., Jan. 4, 1955; s. Arthur Julius and Rita Margaret Reed; m. Elizabeth J. Schaffer; 1 child, Victor. BS in Physics with honors, Syracuse U., 1977, MS in Physics, 1979, PhD in Solid State Physics, 1983; MA (hon.), Yale U., 1990. Mem. tech. staff Ctrl. Rsch. Labs., Tex. Instruments, Dallas, 1983-88, sr. mem. tech. staff, 1988-90; prof. elec. engring. and applied physics Yale U., New Haven, 1990—, chmn. elec. engring. dept., 1995—2001, Harold Hodgkinson prof. engring. and applied sci., 1999—; chief tech. officer, dir. Molecular Electronics Corp., 1999—2001. Chmn., organizer numerous confs.; speaker in field. Author 5 books; contbr. articles 150 pub. to profl. jours., chapters to books. Recipient Kilby Young Innovator award, 1994, Disting. Alumni award Syracuse U., 2000, Fujitsu Internat. Symposium on Compound Semicondrs. Quantum Device award, 2001, Yale Sci. and Engring. Assn. award for advancement of basic and applied sci., 2002; named one of Fortune Mag.'s 12 most promising young Am. Scientists. Fellow: Am. Phys. Soc.; mem.: IEEE (sr.), Sigma Xi. Achievements include pioneered investigation of "Quantum Dots" and Quantum devices; invention of resonant tunneling transistor; 23 patents for novel quantum effect and heterojunction devices; pioneered research on molecular electronic systems. Office: Yale U PO Box 208284 New Haven CT 06520-8284

REED, MARY ANN, writer; d. Lonnie Oliver and Mary Irene Green; m. James H. Reed Sr., Aug. 20, 1960; children: James A. Reed Jr., Brian. Grad., Collinsville (Ill.) H.S. Sec. Collinsville Sch. Dist., 1967—72, H.H. Wright Constrn. Co., Fairmont City, Ill., 1972—77, Child Fab Co., Cahokia, Ill., 1978—80, Monsamo Chem. Co., Savget, Ill., 1981—84, Shelter Ins. Co., Collinsville, 1981—84; writer. Author: Love Child, 2000, Mistaken Identity, Mission Accomplished, 2002, Bitter Sweet Memories, 2003. Democrat. Baptist. Avocations: reading, bowling, writing, walking, fishing. Home: 2914 N 61st St East Saint Louis IL 62201-2501

REED, MICHAEL HAYWOOD, lawyer; b. Phila., Jan. 17, 1949; s. Soloman Taylor and Vivian (Haywood) Reed; m. Yalta Gilmore, Aug. 12, 1978; children: Alexandra Haywood, Michael Haywood Jr. BA in Polit. Sci., Temple U., 1969; JD, Yale U., 1972. Bar: Pa. 1972, U.S. Dist. Ct. (ea. dist.) Pa. 1972, U.S. Dist. Ct. (ea. dist.) Mich. 1982, U.S. Supreme Ct. 1982, U.S. Ct. Appeals (3d cir.) 1985. Assoc. Pepper, Hamilton & Scheetz, Phila., 1972-80, ptnr., 1980—. Co-adj. prof. law Rutgers U., Camden, N.J., 1983, 85; adj. prof. sch. law Temple U., Phila., 1989; mem. Pa. Judicial Inquiry and Rev. Bd., 1990-93; mem. steering com. Ea. Dist. Pa. Bankruptcy Conf., 1992—. Contbr. articles to profl. jours. Advisor Post 913 Law Explorers, Phila., 1974-84; trustee Acad. Natural Scis., Phila., 1988—, Episcopal Hosp., Phila., 1986—; mem. bd. advisors Pub. Interest Law Ctr., Phila., 1992—; mem. exec. bd. Com. of Seventy, Phila., 1985—. Recipient cert. of honor Alumnus of Yr. Coll. of Arts and Scis. Temple U., 1995, Award of Excellence, Thurgood Marshall Scholarship Fund, Inc., 2003. Fellow Am. Coll. Bankruptcy; mem. ABA (chmn. subcom. labor and employment law, bus bankruptcy com. sect. bus. law 1991-97, chmn. subcom. on labor and employment law 1997-2002), Nat. Bar Assn., Pa. Bar Assn. (mem. ho. of dels. 1985—, chmn. minority bar com. 1988-90, mem. bd. govs. 1993-96, co-chairperson 1994, v.p. 2002-03, pres.-elect 2003-, ann. meeting, Spl. Achievement award 1989, Cert. of Honor award 1995), Barristers Assn. Phila. (1st v.p. 1974-76), Alpha Phi Alpha, Yale Club (Phila.). Democrat. Baptist. Avocations: racquetball, film, theater, biking, piano. Home: 225 N 23rd St Philadelphia PA 19103-1005 Office: Pepper Hamilton & Scheetz 3000 Two Logan Sq 18th and Arch Streets Philadelphia PA 19103-2799

REED, MICHAEL JOHN, dentist, dean, oral biology educator; b. Wednesbury, Eng., Dec. 25, 1940; came to U.S., 1967, naturalized, 1972; s. Harry Ernest and Ida Veva (Heywood) R.; m. Pamela Twycross, July 4, 1965 (div. Feb. 1976); children: Justine Marianne, Helena Clare; m. Ingrid Liepins, Sept. 8, 1978; children: Kathryn Anne, Matthew Harrison. BS with honors, U. Durham, Eng., 1963; B in Dental Surgery, U. Newcastle-Upon-Tyne, Eng., 1967; PhD, SUNY, Buffalo, 1971. Lic. dentist U.K., N.Y., Miss. Instr. oral biology SUNY, Buffalo, 1971-72, asst. prof. oral biology, 1972-77, assoc. prof., 1977-79; asst. dean Sch. Dentistry, U. Miss., Jackson, 1980-85, assoc. dean, 1985; dean, prof. oral biology Sch. Dentistry, U. Mo., Kansas City, 1985—. Cons. Nat. Inst. Dental Rsch., Washington, 1975-85. Contbr. numerous articles to profl. jours. Recipient rsch. career devel. award NIH, 1975-80. Fellow Acad. Dentistry Internat., Internat. Coll. Dentists, Am. Coll. Dentists; mem. ADA (cons. 1982—, joint com. on nat. dental exam., 1988-93, chair 1992-93), Am. Assn. Dental Schs. (sect. chair 1985-86. chmn. schs. coun. of deans, 1992-93, pres. 1997-98), Am. Assn. Dental Rsch. (councillor 1974-76), Fedn. Dentaire Internat., Am. Assn. for Microbiology, Mid-Am. Masters Club, Omicron Kappa Upsilon. Episcopalian. Avocations: running, European current affairs. Office: U Mo-Kansas City Sch Dentistry 650 E 25th St Kansas City MO 64108-2716*

REED, MICHAEL ROBERT, agricultural economist; b. Lawrence, Kans., July 11, 1953; s. Robert Stanley and Marian Lucille (Karr) R.; m. Patricia Gail Gurtler, Mar. 16, 1973; children: Laura Gail, Brian Michael. BS, Kans. State U., 1974; MS, Iowa State U., 1976, PhD, 1979. Asst. prof. U. Ky., Lexington, 1978-83, assoc. prof., 1983-89; prof., 1989—; exec. dir. Ctr. for Export Devel., 1988-95; dir. office of internat. affairs U. Ky., Lexington, 1994-98, dir. office of internat. programs for agr., 1998—. Cons. USDA, 1994-97, 2002—, U.S. AID, Washington, 1983-86, 99-2001. Author: (textbook) International Trade in Agricultural Products, 2000; mem. editl. coun. So. Jour. of Agrl. Econs., 1983-86; contbr. articles to profl. jours. Recipient Outstanding Jour. Article award Soc. Farm Mgrs. and Rural Appraisers, 1986, Jour. Agrl. and Applied Econs., 2002; grantee Farmer Coop. Svcs., 1982-84, 87-88, TVA, 1982-85, Fed. Crop Ins. Corp., 1985-87, USDA, 1986—. Mem. Am. Agrl. Econs. Assn., So. Agrl. Econs. Assn., Gamma Sigma Delta. Home: 2216 Bonhaven Rd Lexington KY 40515-1150 Office: U Ky Dept Agrl Econs 308 Barnhart Bldg Lexington KY 40546-0001 Office Phone: 859-257-7259. Business E-Mail: mrreed@uky.edu.

REED, MIRIAM BELL, legislative staff member; b. N.Y.C., May 31, 1930; d. Samuel Dennis and Miriam Wilkes Bell; m. John Grady Reed, May 1, 1954; children: Roberta, Christine, Karen, Laura, Margaret, Abigail, Elisabeth. BA, Mount Holyoke Coll., 1952. Asst. to adminstrv. asst. Rep. Harlan Hagan, Washington, 1953-54; asst. to econ. prof. Littauer Sch. Pub. Adminstrn., Cambridge, Mass., 1954; producer, treas. Video Ed Prodns., Inc., Hyattsville, Md., 1974-90; Singapore testing coord. Malaysian Am. Commn. on Ednl. Exch., Singapore, 1991-92; legis. aide Del. Constance A. Morella, Annapolis, Md., 1978-86; legis. asst. Hon. Constance A. Morella, Washington, 1987-90, 92, 94-97; staff Friends of Connie Morella for Congress, 1999-2000. Cons. Acad. Arrangements Abroad, N.Y.C., 1974-99. Rsch. and writing of ednl. hist. videotapes, 1974-90 (Pratt Libr. award 1986). V.p., pres. bd. LWV, Bronxville, N.Y., 1957-74; mem. Montgomery County Commn. on the Humanities, 1985-88; mem. Montgomery County Com. to Celebrate Md.'s 350th Birthday. Mem. Montgomery County Hist. Soc. (dir. 1998—), C&O Canal Assn. (dir. 2000—). Avocations: swimming, hiking, backpacking. Home: 8221 Burning Tree Rd Bethesda MD 20817-2908 E-mail: mreed8221@aol.com.

REED, PATSY BOSTICK, former academic administrator; b. Holland, Tex., Dec. 1, 1936; d. William T. and Evelyn R. (Smith) Bostick; m. F. DeWitt Reed, Sept. 6, 1958. BS, U. Tex., 1959, MS, 1967, PhD, 1969. Tchr. pub. schs., Austin and Port Arthur, Tex., 1959-65; fellow U. Va., Charlottesville, 1969-70; rsch. chemist U. Heidelberg, W.Ger., 1970-72; assoc. prof. nutrition Idaho State U., Pocatello, 1973-79; prof. nutrition, adminstr. No. Ariz. U., Flagstaff, 1979-94; dean Coll. Design and Tech., 1981-85; asst. v.p. acad. affairs U. N.C., Asheville, 1985-87, v.p. acad. affairs, 1987-93, interim pres., 1994, chancellor, 1994-99; ret., 1999. Author: Nutrition: An Applied Science, 1980. Mem. AAAS, Am. Chem. Soc., Am. Dietetic Assn., Phi Kappa Phi, Sigma Xi. Office: U NC 1 University Hts Asheville NC 28804-3299

REED, PAUL ALLEN, artist; b. Washington, Mar. 28, 1919; s. Charles Miler and Lula Rachael (Annadale) R.; m. Esther Kishter, July 10, 1939; children—Jean Reed Roberts, Thomas, Robert. Student, San Diego State Coll., 1936, Corcoran Sch. Art, 1937. Asst. art dir. USAF mag., N.Y.C., 1942-44; artist B.D. Adams Advt. Agy., Montclair, N.J., 1944-48; asst. art dir. M.F. Dreher Advt. Agy., N.Y.C., 1948-50; free lance graphics designer Washington, 1950-62; graphics dir. U.S. Peace Corps, Washington, 1962-71; asst. prof. Corcoran Sch. Art, Washington, 1971-81. Artist in residence Phoenix Art Mus., 1976; vis. artist Ariz. State U., Tempe, 1980. One-man shows include Corcoran Gallery Art, 1966, Washington U., 1967, Ariz. State U., 1971, Phoenix Art Mus., 1977, Am. U., 1997, Marymount U., 2002, Represented in permanent collections Hirshhorn Mus., Nat. Mus. Am. Art, N.C. Mus. Art, Corcoran Gallery, San Francisco Mus. Art, Detroit Inst. Art, The New American Abstraction from 1950-1970. Home: 3541 N Utah St Arlington VA 22207-4444

REED, RALPH EUGENE, JR., political party official; b. Portsmouth, Va., June 24, 1961; s. Ralph Sr. and Marcy R.; m. Jo Anne Young, 1987; children: Brittany, Ralph III, Christopher, Nicole. BA in History, U. Ga., 1985; D in Am. History, Emory U., 1991. Exec. dir. Christian Coalition, Chesapeake, Va., 1989-97; founder, pres. Century Strategies, Strategies Cons. Co., Duluth, Ga., 1997—; chmn. Ga. Republican Party, 2001—03; southeast regional campaign chmn. George Bush re-election campaign, 2003—. Founder Students for Am., Raleigh, N.C., 1984; lobbyist; spkr. in field. Office: Century Strategies 3235 Satellite Blvd Ste 575 Duluth GA 30096-9017

REED, RAYMOND DERYL, architect; b. Alturas, Calif., Mar. 29, 1930; s. Russell Jacob and Nita Ferne (Wilcox) R.; m. Patricia Reinerth, Apr. 30, 1954; children— Kathryn, Russell, Ann, Andrea. B.Arch., Tulane U., 1953; M.Arch., Harvard U., 1958. Chmn. architecture and interior design dept. U. Southwestern La., 1958-64; head dept. architecture Iowa State U., 1964-70, dir. grad. research in architecture, 1970-73; mem. faculty Tex. A&M U., 1973—, prof. architecture, 1973—96, dean Coll. Architecture and Environ. Design, 1973-80, prof. emeritus, 1996—. Dir. Internat. Ctr. for Cybernetics and Informatics, 1990. Author: Sustainable Architecture, 1988, rev. edit, 1990; contbr. numerous articles on energy conservation and post petroleum architecture to research publs. Served with USNR, 1953-58. Mem. AIA, Nat. Council Archtl. Registration Bds., Am. Collegiate Schs. Architecture, Tex. Soc. Architects, La. Architects Soc. Home: 1601 Wolf Pen Ct College Station TX 77840-3169 Personal E-mail: rayreed@verizon.net.

REED, ROBERT A. performing arts executive; Gen. mgr. Buffalo (N.Y.) Philharmonic; exec. dir. Tulsa Philharmonic Orch., Tulsa, Okla. Office: Tulsa Philharmonic 2901 S Harvard Ave Ste A Tulsa OK 74114-6100

REED, ROBERT DANIEL, publisher; b. Pottsville, Pa., May 24, 1941; s. Robert Daniel R.; children: Robert Duane, Alan Andrija, Tanya. Purchasing mgr. Ogden Tech. Labs., Sunnyvale, Calif., 1962-69; mktg. mgr. Plaza Press, Sunnyvale, 1969-94; pub. R & E Pubs., Saratoga, Calif., 1966-94; founder Bob Reed Studios; ptnr. Reed's Mktg. Svcs.; co-founder Ceasefire USA; founder, pres. Green PR Internat. Mktg. Cons.; pres. Robert D. Reed Pubs. Co-founder Monterey Pacific Pub., 1997. Author: We Care Cookbook, 1974; pub. over 1150 books on human rights, ethnic history edn., criminology, AIDS, Alzheimers disease, teen suicide, also how-to, trade, and humor books; co-author 50 books on poverty, hunger, homelessness, abuse, sexual assault. With U.S. Army, 1959-61. Mem. Ctr. for Dem. Instns., Nat. Fedn. Ind. Bus., Calif. Inventors Coun., Smithsonian Instn., Soc. for Scholarly Pub., World Future Soc. Inventor electro mech.-electronics devices, creative humor products. Home: 750 La Playa St # 647 San Francisco CA 94121-3262 E-mail: 4bobreed@msn.com. *Spend your life doing what you like to do, by putting all your efforts into it. Don't be afraid to take a chance. Remember, if life gets dull-Risk it a bit.*

REED, ROBERT FREDERICK, physician; b. Rochester, Ind., Jan. 4, 1921; s. Robert Rush Reed and Margaret Cecilia Keesey; m. Barbara Maxine Rigby, June 2, 1947; children: Tamara Leigh Asher, Robert Joseph, Michele Raymonde McClead, Tracy Ann Case, John Fredrick. BS, Ind. U., 1949, MD, 1952. Designated aviation med. examiner, cert. flight instr. Intern VA Hosp., Long Beach, Calif., 1952; family physician St. Joe Co., Mishawaka, Ind., 1952—90. Pres. hosp. staff St. Joseph Hosp., Mishawaka; pres. and founder Mishawaka Airport Realty Corp., Mishawaka Pilots Airport, 1957—2003; flight examiner FAA, 1960—2003; flight instr.; conservator family farm. Author: Hit 'Em High Hit 'Em Low, 1998, A Drop in the Bucket, 1999. City com. mem., Mishawaka. Master sgt. USMC, 1942—45, PTO. Mem.: VFW, Exptl. Aircraft Assn., Aircraft Owners and Pilots Assn. Republican. Methodist. Avocations: reading, aviation, military literature, teaching flying. Home: 1312 Honan Dr South Bend IN 46614 Office Phone: 574-299-9559. E-mail: rfreedmd@SBCglobal.net.

REED, SALLY GARDNER, cultural organization administrator; BA in English, Colo. State U., 1979; MLS, No. Ill. U., 1981. Dir. North Hampton (H.H.) Pub. Libr., 1981-85, Ilsley Pub. Libr., Middlebury, Vt., 1985-93, Ames (Iowa) Pub. Libr., 1993-95; dir. librs. Norfolk (Va.) Pub. Libr., 1995—2001; exec. dir. Friends of Librs. USA, Phila., 2001—. Adv. com. product devel. Rsch. Pub., Inc., 1993-94; bd. trustees Bibliographic Ctr. Rsch., Aurora, Colo., 1994-95. Author: Small Libraries: A Handbook for Successful Management, 1991, 2d edit., 2002, Saving Your Library: A Guide to Getting, Using and Keeping the Power You Need, 1992, Library Volunteers: Worth the Effort!, 1994; editor: Creating the Future: Essays on the Future of Librarianship in an Age of Great Change, 1996, Speaking Out: Voices in Celebration of Intellectual Freedom, 1999, Making the Case for Your Library, 2001, 101+ Great Ideas for Libraries and Friends, 2004; contbr. articles to profl. jours. Bd. dirs. Sheldon Art History Mus., Middlebury, 1988-93, United Way Story County, Ames, 1994-95; mem. cabinet United Way Norfolk, 1996-97, chair city campaign, 1997. Recipient Recognition award Tidewater Area Minority Libr. Network, 1997, Am. Libr. Assoc. Herb & Virginia White award for Promoting Librarianship, 2000. Mem. ALA (intellectual freedom roundtable 1991—, chpt. coun. 1989-93, promotion task force 1989-91, planning budget assembly 1991, adv. com. office libr. outreach svcs. 1993-94, nat. libr. week com. 1993-95, presdl. com. pub. awareness 1994-96, councilor at large 1995-99, chair membership com. 1996, resolutions com. 1997, exec. bd. 1997 2001). Office: Friends Libraries USA 1420 Walnut Ste 450 Philadelphia PA 19102 Office Phone: 215-790-1674.

REED, SAM, secretary of state; b. Portland, Oreg. m. Margie Reed, 1963; children: David, Kristen. BA, MA, Wash. State U. Cert. profl. elections officer. Exec. dir. Gov. Evans' Urban Affairs Coun.; Thurston County auditor; asst. sec. of state State of Wash.; dir. State Constl. Reform Commn.; sec. of state State of Wash., 2001—. Bd. mem. Fed. Election Commn. Voting System; internat. election observer, Rwanda, Uganda; mem. Wash. State Archives Adv. Com., Americorps Adv. Coun., Wash. State Election Admin. & Cert. Bd. Recipient Gov.'s Disting. Vol. award, Thurston County Citizen of the Year Disting. Svc. award. Mem.: Mainstream Reps. of Wash., Wash. State Assn. County Auditors, Olympia Kiwanis. Republican. Avocations: running, piano, arts, tennis. Office: 520 Union Ave SE PO Box 40220 Olympia WA 98504 E-mail: sreed@secstate.wa.gov.

REED, SAMUEL LEE, lawyer; b. Selma, Ind., July 29, 1934; s. Merritt C. and Ivy Jane (Williams) R.; m. Joan C. Guinn, Aug. 27, 1955; children: Scott, Craig, Steven, Jennifer. BS in Bus., Ind. U., 1956; JD, 1959. Bar: Ind. 1959, U.S. Dist Ct. (so. dist.) Ind. 1959. Ptnr. DeFur, Voran, Hanley, Radcliff & Reed, Muncie, Ind., 1959-2003, mng. ptnr., 1981-89; dep. pros. atty. Delaware County, Ind., 1961-63; magistrate U.S. Dist. Ct. (so. dist.) Ind., 1978-85; mem. Ind. Gen. Assembly, 1973-77; former chmn. bd. dirs. Westminster Village Muncie, Inc. Mem. Muncie Community Sch. Bd., 1969-73, pres., 1973; pres. Ind. Pub. Broadcasting Soc., 1979-82; bd. dirs. Muncie Children's Mus., 1980-84; elder First United Presbyterian Ch., Muncie; mem. Community Adv. Council Med. Edn., Muncie; chmn. Delaware County Coalition for Legis. Interests, 1984-85; chmn. Delaware County Rep. Fin. Com., 1984-86; mem. nominating com. Ind. Pub. Service Commn., 1984-86. Recipient Big Ten medal Ind. U., 1956, Disting. Service award Muncie Jaycees, 1968. Mem. ABA, Ind. Bar Assn., Muncie Bar Assn. (pres. 1966), Muncie-Delaware C. of C. (vice chmn. bd. dirs. 1986-89), Exch. Club (pres. club 1969). Republican. Office: 201 E Jackson St Suite 400 Muncie IN 47305

REED, SANDY, former magazine editor; m. Bob Ingle. B Journalism, Kans. State U. Reporting and sr. editing positions San Jose (Calif.) Mercury News, Miami (Fla.) Herald, Billings (Mont.) Gazette, Oakland (Calif.) Tribune; exec. editor news ops. InfoWorld, San Francisco, 1984-90, exec. editor Pers. Computing mag., 1985-90, editor-in-chief, 1990-00, exec. editor PC/Computing, 1991-00. Founding editor Macintosh Bus. Rev.; founding editl. dir. New Media Age mag. (now NewMedia mag). Named one of most influential journalists covering computer industry Mktd. Computers mag. Avocations: surfing the web, reading, travel. Office: Infoworld 155 Bovet Rd Ste 800 San Mateo CA 94402-3150

REED, SCOTT C. music educator, writer; b. Chgo., Aug. 28, 1957; s. Vernon C. Reed and Betty M. Ryan. MusB, U. of So. Calif., 1981. Adj. prof. Gov.'s State U., U. Pk., Ill., 1989—95, Prarie State Coll., Chgo. Heights, Ill., 1994—2004. Author: Getting Into Guitar Improvising: A Systematic Approach To Soloing, 2002, Getting Into Guitar Styles, 2004. Fellow, NEA, 1992—93. Office: Prarie State College 202 South Halsted Chicago Heights IL 60411

REED, SHERMAN KENNEDY, chemical consultant; b. Chgo., Apr. 11, 1919; s. Frank Hynes and Helen Louise (Kennedy) R.; m. Octavia Bailey, Oct. 11, 1943; children: Martin Bailey, Holly Anne Johnson, Julie Marie Reed. BS with honors, U. Ill., 1940; PhD, Cornell U., 1949. Asst. instr. chemistry Cornell U., 1940-43; asst. rsch. scientist Manhattan Project, N.Y.C., 1942-46; asst. prof. Bucknell U., Lewisburg, Pa., 1946-50; with FMC Corp., 1950—, mgr., asst. dir. rsch., 1950-60, divisional dir. rsch. and devel., ctrl. rsch. dir., 1960-76, v.p., 1976-82, cons., 1983—; dir. Avicon, Inc., 1970-82; pres., dir. FMC Gold Corp.; mng. dir. COGAS Devel. Co., 1975—; dir. Indsl. Rsch. Inst., N.Y.C., Franklin Inst., Phila., 1976-83; chmn. bd. Franklin Rsch. Ctr., Phila., 1976-83. Fellow Am. Inst. Chemists; mem. AAAS, Am. Chem. Soc., Assn. Rsch. Dirs. (pres. 1973), Vero Beach Country Club, Union League Club (Phila.), Nassau Club (Princeton, N.J.). Republican. Home and Office: 2300 Indian Creek Blvd W #C211 Vero Beach FL 32966-2400 Personal E-mail: shermankreed@aol.com.

REED, STANLEY FOSTER, editor, writer, publisher, lecturer; b. Bogota, N.J., Sept. 28, 1917; s. Morton H. and Beryl (Turner) R.; m. Stella Swingle, Sept. 28, 1940 (div. 1978); children: Nancie, Beryl Ann, Alexandra; m. Shirley Weihman, Sept. 28, 1985 (dec. Feb. 1988); m. Catherine Case Commander, Dec. 16, 1989 (div. 1991). Student, George Washington U., 1939-40, Johns Hopkins, 1940-41; MBA, Loyola U., Md., 1981. Registered profl. engr., D.C. With Bethlehem Steel Corp., Balt., 1940-41; cons. engr., 1942-44; founder, pres. Reed Research, Inc., Washington, 1945-62; pres. Reed Research Inst. Creative Studies, from 1951; founder, chmn. LogEtronics, Inc., 1955; founder, pres., chmn. Tech. Audit Corp., 1962; assoc. Mgmt. Analysis Corp., 1978-81; sr. cons. Hay Assocs., Phila., 1980-83; entrepreneur-in-residence Coll. Charleston, S.C.; prin., owner mergercentral.com. Co-chmn. semi-ann. Merger Week Northwestern U.; lectr. numerous U.S. and fgn. groups and instns. including Union Theol. Sem., U. Pa., Pa. State U., U. Colo., Georgetown U., Rensselaer Poly. Inst., Am. U., Claremont Coll., So. Meth. U., Pace U., Wayne State U., U. Oreg., U. Conn., St. John's U., Pepperdine U., Loyola Coll. of Md., San Francisco State U., U. Pitts., U. R.I., Marquette U., Vanderbilt U., Boston U., U. Cin., Gustavus Adolphus Coll., U. Mo., Mich. State U., Lehigh U., Calif. Inst. Tech., Denver U., George Washington U., Elmhurst Coll.; vis. fellow Wilton Pk. Conf., Eng., 1968 Author: The Art of M&A: A Merger/Aquisition/Buyout Guide, 1989, 3d edit., 1999, The Toxic Executive, 1993, The Art of M&A Deskbook, Dictionary and Casebook, 2000; founder, editor, pub.: Mergers and Acquisitions mag., 1965—, Dirs. and Bds. mag., 1976—; founder, editor, pub.: Campaigns and Elections mag., 1980; founder, pub. Global Bus. mag., 1985; contbr. articles to leading jours., chpts. to books; patentee. Bd. dirs. Nat. Patent Coun., 1970—; founder, chmn. ann Merger Week, Washington, 1973-77, Northwestern U., 1977-87; Entrepreneur-in-Residence, mem. adv. bd. Tate Ctr. Entrepreneurship, Coll. Charleston, S.C. Mem. Soc. Naval Architects and Marine Engrs. (life), Am. Econ. Assn., Dictionary Soc. of N.Am., La Confrerie des Chevaliers du Tastevin (chef de protocol), N.Y. Yacht Club. E-mail: reeds@cofc.edu.

REED, STEVEN I. science association director; BSc, Williams Coll.; PhD, Dartmouth Coll. Co-founder Immunex; CEO Corixa, Seattle, 1994—, dir., 1994—, chmn. bd. dirs., 1999—. Dir. Micrologix Biotech, Genesis R&D

Corp.; mem. sci. adv. bd. Medarex. Office: Corixa Corp 1124 Columbia Street Ste 200 Seattle WA 98104 Mailing: Micrologix Biotech Inc BC Rsch Bldg 3650 Wesbrook Mall Vacouver BC V6S 2l2 Canada

REED, SUELLEN KINDER, school system administrator; BA in History, Polit. Sci. and Secondary Edn., Hanover Coll., 1967; MA in Elem. Edn. and History, Ball State U., 1970, EdD in Adminstrn. and Supervision, LLD (hon.), 1997; EdD (hon.), Vincennes U., 1996; LittD (hon.), U. Indpls., 1997; LHD (hon.), St. Joseph Coll., 1999, Hanover Coll., 2003; postgrad., Fla. Atlantic U., U. Scranton, Purdue U., Earlham Coll., Ind. U., Ind. State U., U. So. Ind., Butler U., U. Alaska, U. Va. at Edinburgh (Scotland) U., Oxford (Eng.) U. Lic. supt., life lic. in elem. edn., U.S. history, world history, govt., adminstrn. and supervision and endorsement in edn. for gifted and talented K-12, Ind.; lic. adminstr., U.S. history, world history, govt., middle sch. lang. arts, social studies, elem. edn., gifted edn., Fla. Tchr. 5th and 6th grades Rushville (Ind.) Consol. Sch. Corp., 1967-70; tchr. Shelbyville (Ind.) High Sch., 1970-71; tchr. 6th, 7th and 8th grade social studies, curriculum Broward County (Fla.) Sch. Corp., 1971-76; tchr. Rushville Jr. High Sch., 1976-77; asst. prin. Rushville Elem. Sch., 1977-79; prin. Frazee Elem. Sch., Connersville, Ind., 1979-87; asst. supt. Rushville Consolidated Schs., 1987-90, supt., 1991-93; supt. pub. instrn., chairperson bd. edn., CEO dept. edn. State of Indiana, Indpls., 1993—. Pres. N. Ctrl. Regional Edn. Lab., Oak Brook, Ill., 1993—97, Oak Brook, 2002; mem. The Ctr. on Congress Outstanding Tchr. Award Selection Com. Contbr. articles to profl. jours. Bd. trustees Hanover Coll., Commn. Drug-Free Ind., Ind. Commn. Cmty. Svc., Ind. Higher Edn. Telecom. Sys., Ctr. Agrl. Sci. Heritage; hon. bd. mem. Rush County Cmty. Found.; alumni bd. Ball State U. Tchrs. Coll., 1999-; bd. dirs. Nat. Children's Film Festival; trustee, mem. New Salem United Meth. Ch.; bd. dirs. Ind. Historic Landmarks Found., Agy. for Instrnl. Tech., Project Lead the Way, Virtual H.S., 2003—; bd. visitors Ind. U.; hon. bd. mem. Indpls. Zool. Soc. Named Outstanding Sch. Edn. Alumnus, Ball State U., 1994, Govt. Leader Yr., Ind. C. of C., 2001; recipient Pres. award, Ind. Assn. Sch. Prins., 1996, Achievement award, Ind. Network Women Adminstrs., 1996, Alumni award, Hanover Coll., 1997, Legis. award, Ind. Assn. for the Edn. Young Children, 1998, Pres. award, Ind. Middle Level Edn. Assn., 2001, Elizabeth Heywood Wyman award for alumnae, Alpha Omicron Pi, 2001, Friend Youth award, Ind. Sch. Counselors, 2001, Hoosier Heritage Civic Leadership award, 2002, Turn Off the Violence award, Ind. Crime Prevention Coalition, 2002, Ind. Sch. Safety Leadership award, 2002, Citizen's award, Ind. Libr. Fedn., Counselor's award, Assn. for Ind. Media Educators. Mem. ASCD (nat. and Ind. chpts.), Internat. Reading Assn., Nat. Coun. for Accreditation Tchr. Edn. (mem. exec. bd.), Nat. Assn. Elem. and Mid. Sch. Prins. (assoc.), Nat. Assn. Gifted Children (nat. adv. bd.), Internat. Tech. Edn. Assn. (mem. adv. com.), Ind. Assn. Pub. Sch. Supts., Ind. Assn. Elem. and Mid. Sch. Prins. (assoc.), Women's Coun. on Literacy for the Ind. Literacy Found., Rose Hulman Inst. Tech., Network Woman Adminstrs., Indpls. Zoo, Indpls. Art Mus., Indpls. Bd. Assocs., Bus. and Profl. Women of Rushville, Connersville Area Reading Coun., Smithsonian, Rushville Rotary Club, Monday Cir., K-12 Compact Learning and Citizenship (chairwoman), Edn. Commn. States (commr., mem. exec. com. 1994-98, 2002—), Council Chief State Sch. Officers (pres.-elect., 2000-01, pres., 2001-02, v.p., 2002-03), Ind. Hist. Soc., Ind. State Mus., Conner Prairie Farm, Order of Ea. Star (Andersonville chpt.), Delta Kappa Gamma (past pres.), Phi Lambda Theta, Phi Delta Kappa (Conner Prairie). Office: Superintendent Edn Dept 229 State House Indianapolis IN 46204-2798

REED, SUSAN D. prosecutor; m. Robert D. Reed; 1 child. B in Econs., U. Tex., JD, 1974. Bar: Tex., U.S. Dist. Ct. (we. dist.) Tex., Fed. Ct., U.S. Supreme Ct., bd. cert. criminal law: Tex. Bd. Legal Specialization. Judge 144th Dist. Ct.; pvt. practice Souls and Reed; chief pros. 144th and 187th Dist. Cts.; adminstrv. judge Dist. Cts. Bexar County, 1996—97; asst. dist. atty. Bexar County, San Antonio, 1974—82, criminal dist. atty., 1998—. Mem. Criminal Justice Policy Coun., Govs. Juvenile Justice Adv. Bd., Bush-Cheney Transition Team for Dept. Justice, Nat. Adv. Coun. on Violence Against Women. Mem. Regional Anti-Terrorism Task Force; co-chair Anti-Crime Commn., 2002. Recipient Judge of Yr. award, Tex. Gang Investigators Assn. Mem.: Nat. Dist. Attys. Assn., Tex. Dist. and County Attys. Assn. Office: Bexar County Criminal Dist Atty 5th Fl 300 Dolorosa San Antonio TX 78205-3630

REED, SUSAN K, editor-in-chief; d. John and Helen Reed. AB, Vassar Coll. Editor Saturday Review, NYC, 1979—82; writer People Mag., NYC, 1982—96; editor Conde Nast Women's Sports, NYC, 1996—2000; literary agent IMG, NYC, 2000—02; editor in chief Golf for Women, NYC, 2002—. Bd. mem. Student Conservation Assn., 1998—; bd. dirs. Union Theological Seminary, NYC, 2003—. Office: Golf for Women 4 Times Square New York NY 10036 Business E-Mail: susan.reed@golfforwomen.com.

REED, THOMAS W. secondary school educator; b. San Jose, Calif., July 25, 1961; s. Marshall Walker and Joy Collette R.; m. Anna, Sept. 1, 1991; 1 child, Adam. BA in Phys. Edn., Calif. State U., 1986, MA in Edn., 1990. Long-term substitute tchr. Stateline (Nev.) Pvt. Sch., 1988; substitute tchr. Clovis (Calif.) Unified Sch. Dist., 1988-89, various sch. dists., Calif., 1989-90; 6th grade tchr. Sylvan Union Sch. Dist., Modesto, Calif., 1990-92; 7th grade tchr. Waterford (Calif.) Sch. Dist., 1992—. Coach football, 1992-99, basketball, 1992—; mentor tchr. 1997, 98; mem. negotiation team Calif. Mid. Sch. Phys. Edn. Workshop, Sacramento, 1996—, mentor leader, 1997, co-dir., 1999, mem. curriculum com., 2000—; instr., coord. Advancement Via Individual Determination. Mem. Cyclists Across U.S.A., 1987; CPR instr. Meml. Hosp., Modesto, 1998—; speech coord., scholarship chair Waterford Lions Club; vol. Habitat for Humanity. Mem. Calif. Assn. Health, Phys. Edn. & Dance (pub. rels. chair), Am. Alliance Health, Phys. Edn. & Dance, Nat. Ski Patrol (first aid instr.). Avocations: reading, skiing, family time. Office: Waterford Unified Sch Dist 12916 Bentley St Waterford CA 95386-9017 Home: 1500 Kingfield Dr Modesto CA 95350-4616

REED, TRAVIS DEAN, public relations executive; b. Trinity, Tex., Sept. 27, 1930; s. Travis and Alma (Rains) R.; m. Caroline M. McDonald, June 15, 1957; children: Anne Reed Adams, Lisa Reed Lettau. Student, Tex. A&M U., 1948-51, U. Houston, 1951-53. Reporter Houston Post, 1951-53; Washington Bur. corr. McGraw-Hill Pub. Co., 1955-61, Boston Herald-Traveler, 1961-62; with Newhouse News Svc., Washington, 1962-79, chief corr., 1964-67, editor, 1967-79; pub. rels. cons. Washington, 1979—. 1st lt. U.S. Army, 1953-55. Mem. Nat. Press Club, Federal City Club, Gridiron Club, Army and Navy Club. Home: 37277 Branchriver Rd Purcellville VA 20132-1922 Office: T Dean Reed Co PO Box 65276 Washington DC 20035

REED, VASTINA KATHRYN (TINA REED), child and adolescent psychotherapist, family development specialist; b. Chgo., Mar. 5, 1960; d. Alvin Hillard and Ruth Gwendolyn (Thomas) R.; 1 child, Alvin J. BA in Human Svcs. magna cum laude, Nat.-Louis U., Chgo., 1988; MA, Ill. Sch. Profl. Psychology, 1991; tng. cert., Appelbaum Inst. Child Devel.; cert. family devel. specialist, U. Iowa, 2002; fashion cons. of Evangelist Audrey Donson, Good Shepherd Grace Min., 2002—. First aid/CPR cert., ARC. Tchr. early childhood edn. Kendall Coll. Lab. Sch., Evanston, Ill., 1983-85, Rogers Park Children's Learning Ctr., Chgo., 1983-85; child life therapist Mt. Sinai Hosp., Chgo., 1988; child psychotherapist Nicholas Barnes Therapeutic Day Sch., Chgo., 1989-90; presch. instr. YMCA, 1999-2000; crisis line counselor Washington Security Corp., 2000—02; family support Maywood (Ill.) Head Start, 2000—03; health care rep. Care Entrée, 2002—. Den leader Boy Scouts Am., Chgo., 1989-92, scoutmaster, 1992-2000, merit badge counselor, 1999—, troop advisor for Order of the Arrow; vision ptnr., co-labourers Christ Ministry; editor, mem. praise and worship team Christ Outreach Deliverance Ctr. Ministry, 2001—. Recipient Cub Scouter award Boy Scouts Am., 1990, Scoutmaster award of merit, 1993, 94, Scouters Vet. award, 1994, Scouters Tng. award, 1995, Scoutmasters Key award, 1996, Okpik Cold Weather Camping cert., 1994-95, Outstanding Women of 20th Century medal, 2000, Boy Scout Woodbadge Tng. award, 2001. Mem. APA, Nat. Orgn. for Human Svc. Edn., Order of the Arrow, Ea. Stars (Hon. Lady status 1999—), Charles F. Menninger Soc. (patron), Phi Theta Kappa, Kappa Delta Pi. Democrat. Roman Catholic. Avocations: camping, cruising, classic movies, performing in ministry's ensemble, gospel music. Home: 1872 S Millard Ave Chicago IL 60623-2542 Office Phone: 773-612-1567.

REED, W. ALLEN, automotive executive; b. Nashville, Tenn., Apr. 4, 1947; B in Engring., Auburn U., 1970; M in Bus. Adminstrn., Ga. State U., 1975. Cert. Chartered Fin. Analyst. Asst. treas. Delta Airlines, 1981—84; staff v.p., pres. investment mgmt. co. Hughes Aircraft Co., Hughes Investment Mgmt. Co., 1984—91; v.p., treas. Hughes Aircraft, 1991, Hughes Electronics, 1992; chmn. HIMCO, 1984—92; v.p. GM, 1994—; pres., CEO GM Asset Mgmt., 1994—. Mem. investment adv. com. N.Y. State Retirement Sys.; mem. editl. bd. Morgan Stanley Capital Internat.; bd. dirs. GMAC, GMAC Ins. Holdings, iShares, Inc., Temple-Inland Inds. Office: GM Asset Mgmt 767 Fifth Ave 15th Fl New York NY 10153

REED, W. FRANKLIN, lawyer; b. Louisville, Dec. 30, 1946; s. William Ferguson and Stella Elizabeth (Richardson) R.; m. Sharon Ann Coss, June 16, 1973; children: Jonathan Franklin, William Brian, Carrie Ann. BA, Williams Coll., 1968; JD, Columbia U., 1971. Bar: N.Y. 1972, U.S. Dist. Ct. (so. dist.) N.Y. 1975, U.S. Ct. Appeals (2d cir.) 1975, Pa. 1982, U.S. Dist. Ct. (we. dist.) 1983. Assoc. Milbank, Tweed, Hadley & McCloy, N.Y.C., 1971-82, Reed Smith Shaw & McClay, Pitts., 1982-83; ptnr. Reed, Smith, Shaw & McClay, Pitts., 1984—. Mem. instnl. devel. com. The Pitts. Cultural Trust; bd. dirs. Steel Industry Heritage Corp. Mem. ABA, Pa. Bar Assn., Allegheny Bar Assn., Carnegie 100, Williams Coll. Alumni Soc. W. Pa. (sec. 1983—), Rivers Club (Pitts.), St. Clair Country Club (Upper St. Clair, Pa.), Duquesne Club (Pitts.), Phi Beta Kappa. Democrat. Presbyterian. Avocations: fishing, golf. Home: 525 Miranda Dr Pittsburgh PA 15241-2039 Office: Reed Smith LLP 435 6th Ave Pittsburgh PA 15219-1886 E-mail: wreed@reedsmith.com.

REED, WALLACE ALLISON, anesthesiologist; b. Covina, Calif., May 19, 1916; s. Wallace Allison and Mary Julia (Birdsall) Reed; m. Maria Eva Wiemers, Jan. 20, 1938; children: Ellen E., Barbara R., Wallace J., Michael E., Kathryn L., Vikki T. AB, UCLA, Los Angeles, 1937; postgrad., U. Cologne, 1937-38; U. Freiburg, Breisgau, 1938-39; MD, U. So. Calif., 1944. Diplomate Am. Bd. Anesthesiology. Intern Santa Fe Coast Lines Hosp., Los Angeles, 1943-44; resident Precept Sanders-Valley Forge Hosp., 1944—46, Los Angeles County Gen. Hosp., 1946-47; asst. to head dept. anesthesiology Precept Dillon-Los Angeles County Gen. Hosp., 1946-47; clin. instr. surgery U. So. Calif. Sch. Medicine, 1946-47; practice medicine, specializing in anesthesiology Phoenix, 1948-89. Hon. staff mem. Good Samaritan Hosp., St. Joseph Hosp., Maricopa County Gen. Hosp.; mem. hon. staff Children's Hosp.; co-founder John L. Ford, M.D., Surgicenter, 1970; vice pres. Maricopa Found. for Med. Care, 1970-74, pres., 1975-76; mem. House Ways and Means Adv. Com.; adv. coun. Nat. Health Inst., 1975-76; mem. accreditation coun. for ambulatory health care Joint Commn. on Accreditation of Hosps., 1975-79; vice-chmn. Accreditation Assn. for Ambulatory Health Care, 1979-81, pres., 1981-83; mem. panel for study Nat. Health Ins., Congl. GAO; chmn. bd. Alterna Care Corp., 1984-87, now chmn. bd. emeritus; mem. adv. bd. Kino Inst., 1994-95. Bd. dirs. South Phoenix Montessori Sch., pres. bd., 1971-75, Alzheimer's Assn., Greater Phoenix chpt. 1998-2000, co-v.p. 2000; bd. dirs. Ctrl. Ariz. Health Sys. Agy., 1975-78; exec. dir. Surgictr. of Phoenix, 1987-97. Capt. M.C., AUS, 1944-46. Recipient Pinal award Ariz. Psychiat. Soc., 1967-68, Gerard B. Lambert Merit award for innovative ideas that improve patient care; John L. Ford M.D., 1972; recipient spirit of philanthropy award Alzheimer's Assn., 1996, Samba Disting. Svc. award, 2000; Disting. Svc. award Ariz. Soc. Anesthesiology, 2003. Fellow: Am. Coll. Anesthesiologists; mem.: AMA, Soc. for Advancement Geriatric Anesthesia (charter mem.), Guedel Assn. (pres. 1972), Am. Assn. Founds. for Med. Care (dir. 1970—74), Central Ariz. Physicians Svc. Assn. (pres. 1982—83), Maricopa County Med. Soc. (pres. 1964, dir., Salsbury medal 1967, 1971, Thomas Dooley medal 1970), Internat. Assn. Amb. Surgery (hon.), Soc. for Ambulatory Anesthesia (bd. dirs. 1985—87), Federated Amb. Surgery Assn. (pres. 1974—75, dir.), Acad. Anesthesiology (dir. 1966—72, pres. 1969), Ariz., Maricopa County Socs. Anesthesiologists, Am. Soc. Anesthesiologists, WarMer Rsch. Found., Seed Money for Growth Found. (pres. 1984—). Methodist. Home: 4716 N Dromedary Rd Phoenix AZ 85018-2939 Office: 1040 E Mcdowell Rd Phoenix AZ 85006-2622 E-mail: somnus4@cox.net.

REED, WALTER GEORGE, JR., osteopathic physician; b. Ardmore, Okla., Sept. 10, 1928; s. Walter George and Lillian Dorene (Gee) Reed; children: Jay Walter, David George, Kimberly Sue. BA, Phillips U., 1955; DO, Kansas City Coll. Osteopathy, 1959. Intern Des Moines Gen. Hosp., 1959—60; pvt. practice Oklahoma City, 1960-63, Atoka, Okla., 1963-80; flight surgeon USAF, Omaha, 1980-84, Lubbock, Tex., 1984-86; chief med. officer Army Health Clinic, McAlester, Okla., 1986-96; ret. USAF, 1996. Mayor City of Atoka, 1970s; v.p. Atoka Bd. Edn., 1970. Lt. col. USAF, 1980—86. Mem.: Assn. Mil. Surgeons U.S., Air Force Assn. (life), Okla. Osteo. Assn. (life; life), Assn. Mil. Osteo. Physicians and Surgeons (life; life), Ret. Officers Assn. (life; life), Masons (32d degree). Avocation: Avocations: flying, hunting, computers, auto mechanics, plate collecting. Home: 9921 N 110th East Ave Owasso OK 74055-4358 Address: PO Box 119 Owasso OK 74055-0119 Office: Slim Care Owasso OK 74055 also: Slim Care Tulsa OK 74135

REED, WILLIAM EDWARD, government official, educator; b. Columbia, La., July 15, 1914; s. William Reed and Virginia (Barnes) R.; m. Mattye Marie Scott, Aug. 27, 1942; children: Edwarda Marie (Mrs. Lucien L. Johnson), Carol Ann, Beverlyn Bernetiae. BS, So. U., 1937; MS, Iowa State U., 1941; PhD, Cornell U., 1946. County agrl. agt. Agr. and Home Econs. Extension Service, La. State U., 1937-41; lectr. soil sci. and chemistry So. U., 1942-47; agrl. research specialist U.S. Econ. Mission to Liberia, 1947-49; dean agr. Agrl. and Tech. Coll. N.C., 1949-61; mem. U.S. del. Russia; rep. ICA in Togo, 1961; asst. dir. AID Mission to Nigeria, 1961-68; mem. U.S. del. to UN Conf. on Application Sci. and Tech., 1963; dep. dir. AID Mission to Ethiopia, 1968-72; fgn. service officer in residence N.C. A. & T. State U., Greensboro, 1972-74, spl. asst. to chancellor for internat. programs, 1974-76, asso. dean research and spl. projects, 1976-78, dir. internat. programs, 1978-84; cons. in field, 1984—. State rep. Sisters Cities Internat. Mem. Nat. Planning Assn., Am. Fgn. Svc. Assn., Sigma Xi, Phi Kappa Phi, Beta Kappa Chi, Sigma Pi Phi, Gamma Sigma Delta, Beta Epsilon (trustee Boulé Found. 1964—). Episcopalian. Home: 2711 Mcconnell Rd Greensboro NC 27401-4534

REEDE, JOAN YVONNE, academic administrator, medical educator, pediatrician; b. Boston, 1953; 1 child, Loretta Jackson. BS, Brown U., 1977; MD, Mt. Sinai Sch. Med., 1980; MPH, Harvard Sch. Pub. Health, 1990, MS in Health Policy and Mgmt, 1992. Intern Johns Hopkins Hosp., Baltimore, 1980—81, pediat. resident, 1981—83; child psychology fellow Children's Hosp., Boston, 1986—88; med. dir. Cmty. Health Ctr., Boston, Commonwealth of Mass. Dept. Youth Services; dean diversity and cmty. partnership Harvard Med. Sch., 2002—, dir. minority faculty devel. program, faculty dir. cmty. outreach programs, assoc. prof. med.; asst. prof. maternal and child health Harvard Sch. Pub. Health; asst. in health policy Mass. Gen. Hosp. Founder Biomedical Sci. Careers Program, 1991; mem. bd. govs. Warren Grant Magnuson Clin. Ctr.; mem. adv. com. on minority health US Dept. Health and Human Services, 2000—, mem. adv. com. on genetics, health and soc., 2002—; bd. dirs. Mass. Tech. Park. Corp. Named a Ctr. for Disease Control and Prevention/U. Calif. Public Health Leadership Inst. Scholor; recipient Boston NAACP Health award, 1986, Community Service award, Epilepsy Assn. Mass., 1993, Exemplary Models Adminstrv. Leadership award, Am. Assn. U. Adminstrs., 1996. Achievements include being included in the Changing the Face of Medicine exhibit honoring women physicians. Office: Harvard Med Sch 25 Shattuck St Rm 152 Boston MA 02115

REEDER, CLINTON BRUCE, economist, public policy consultant, farmer; b. Pendleton, Oreg., Apr. 22, 1939; s. O. Howard and Rachel B. (Porter) R.; n. Karen J. Durham, June 19, 1960; children: Jeffrey T., Lori J., Paul D. BS, Oreg. State U., 1961, MS, 1963; PhD, Purdue U., 1966; postgrad., U. Oreg. Instr. agrl. econs. Purdue U., West Lafayette, 1963-66; contract mgmt. trainer Nat. Food Mfg. Corp., 1972-78; farmer Pendleton, Oreg., 1978—; mgmt. cons., 1968—; mktg. economist, bus. mgmt. specialist Dept. Agrl., Econs. & Extension Svc, Oreg. State U., Corvallis, 1966-78; econ. & pub. policy cons. Clinton B. Reeder & Assocs., 1968—; dir. Northwest Wheat Policy Project, 1992—, WestFork Natural Resources Rsch. Ctr., 1995—. Ombudsman Oreg. Agrl. Water Quality Mgmt. Program, 2000. Recipient Disting. Svc. award Oreg. Wheat Growers League, 1998, County Points of Light award Nat. Assn. Counties, 1992, Voice of Industry award, 1989, OFS Unity award, 1988; inducted into Hall of Fame, Coll. Agr., Oreg. State U., 1998. Republican. Avocations: reading, public service, writing, research. Home and Office: 47647 Reeder Rd Pendleton OR 97801-9226

REEDER, F. ROBERT, lawyer; b. Brigham City, Utah, Jan. 23, 1943; s. Frank O. and Helen H. (Heninger) R.; m. Joannie Anderson, May 4, 1974; children: David, Kristina, Adam. JD, U. Utah, 1967. Bar: Utah 1967, U.S. Ct. Appeals (1oth cir.) 1967, U.S. Ct. Appeals (D.C. and 5th cirs.) 1979, U.S. Ct. Mil. Appeals 1968, U.S. Supreme Ct. 1972. Shareholder Parsons, Behle & Latimer, Salt Lake City, 1968—. Bd. dirs. Holy Cross Found., 1981-90, chmn., 1987-90; bd. dirs. Holy Cross Hosp., 1990-93, treas., 1986-87, vice chmn., 1987-93; bd. dirs. Holy Cross Health Svcs. Utah, 1993-94, treas., 1993-94; bd. dirs. Sale Lake Regional Med. Ctr., 1995—, vice chmn., 1995-2000, chmn., 2000—; trustee Univ. Hosp. Found.; hon. col. Salt Lake City Police, Salt Lake County Sheriff. Served with USAR, 1967-73. Mem. ABA, Utah State Bar, Salt Lake County Bar (ethics adv. com. 1989-94), Cottonwood Country Club (bd. dirs. 1978-82, 83-86, pres. 1981-82), Rotary. Office: Parsons Behle & Latimer PO Box 45898 Salt Lake City UT 84145-0898

REEDER, HUBERT, elementary school educator; b. Plainfield, NJ, Mar. 17, 1948; s. Henry M. Reeder Sr. and Algaelee Reeder. BS, Rutgers U., 1988. Supr. Arthur Young and Co., Newark, 1976—86; accounts payable Coopers Lybrand, Newark, 1986—92; youth team coord. East Orange YMCA, NJ, 1992—94; substitute tchr. Plainfield Bd. of Edn., NJ, 1994—; resident poet Plainfield Pub. Lib., 1997—; fitness specialist Plainfield YMCA, 2001—, recreation specialist, 2001—. Author: (various) works of poetry, 1999—2002. Named Man of Year, African Am. Group, 1989; recipient Golden Poet award, World of Poetry, 1989. Fellow: Internat. Biog. Org., Am. Biog. Inst.; mem.: Acad. of Am. Poets. Avocations: road racing, basketball, bicycling. Home: P O Box 1132 Plainfield NJ 07062

REEDER, JAMES ARTHUR, lawyer; b. Baton Rouge, June 29, 1933; s. James Brown and Grace (Britt) R.; m. Mary Leone Guthrie, Dec. 30, 1958; children: Mary Virginia, James Jr., Elizabeth Colby. BA, Washington and Lee U., Lexington, Va., 1955; LLB, U. Tex., 1960; JD, La. State U., 1961. Ptnr. Booth, Lockard, Jack et al, Shreveport, La., 1961-72; pres. and mgng. ptnr. Shreveport Broadcasting Co., 1972-86; CEO, mng. gen. ptnr. Radio USA Limited, Houston, 1986-89; pres. SW subsidiaries Sun Group, Inc., Houston, 1990-92; atty. Patton & Boggs, LLP, Washington, 1991-94; ptnr. Patton, Boggs LLP, Washington, 1994—. Dir. ABC Radio Sta. Affiliates adv. bd., N.Y.C., 1978-84. Dir. Boys Country, Houston, 1986-90; pres. Holiday in Dixie, Shreveport, 1968; chmn. Ambassadors Club, Shreveport, 1979. 1st Lt. U.S. Army, 1955-57. Named La. Outstanding Young Man, La. Jaycees, 1969. Mem. ABA (bd. dirs. young lawyers sect. 1967-68, Gavel awards com. 1980), La. Bar Assn. (pres. young lawyers sect. 1966, La. Outstanding Young Lawyer award 1968), D.C. Bar Assn., Tex. Bar Assn., Nat. Assn. Broadcasters, Houston Country Club, Allegro Club (Houston). Roman Catholic. Office Phone: 202-457-5616.

REEDER, OLIVER HOWARD, paint products manufacturing executive; b. Balt., Sept. 19, 1916; s. Charles Howard and Nannie Dryden (Kensett) R.; m. Nancy Hardcastle Fisher, Apr. 18, 1942; children: Nancy Fisher, Ellen Dryden. AB, Princeton U., 1939. With Balt. Copper Paint Co., Balt., 1939—, tech. dir., treas., 1939-47, pres., 1947—, chmn., 1959—; v.p. Balt. Copper Paint div. Glidden-Durkee Div. SCM Corp., 1969—; pres. Jotun-Balt. Copper Paint Co., Inc., 1974-76, v.p., 1976-81. Pres. Hosp. for Consumptives of Md., 1968-84, trustee, 1951-95, trustee emeritus, 1995—; trustee Gilman Sch., Balt., 1948-65, Walters Art Gallery, 1978-83, U.S. Frigate Constellation Found., 1976-89; trustee Johns Hopkins Hosp., 1957-87, trustee emeritus, 1987—, vice chmn. bd., 1986-87; trustee Md. Hosp. Laundry, 1970-89, pres., 1975-84. Fellow Am. Inst. Chemists; mem. Am. Chem. Soc., Soc. Naval Architects and Marine Engrs., Phi Beta Kappa, Sigma Xi. Home: 1300 Dulaney Valley Rd Baltimore MD 21286-1308

REEDER, ROBERT HARRY, retired lawyer; b. Topeka, Dec. 3, 1930; s. William Harry and Florence Mae (Cochran) R. AB Washburn U., 1952, JD, 1960. Bar: U.S. Dist. Ct. Kans. 1960, Kans. 1960, U.S. Supreme Ct. 1968. Rsch. asst. Kans. Legis. Council Rsch. Dept., Topeka, 1955-60; asst. counsel Traffic Inst., Northwestern U., Evanston, Ill., 1960-67, gen. counsel, 1967-92; exec. dir. Nat. Com. on Uniform Traffic Laws and Ordinances, Evanston, 1982-90; ret. Co-author: Vehicle Traffic Law, 1974; The Evidence Handbook, 1980. Author: Interpretation of Implied Consent by the Courts, 1972. Served with U.S. Army, 1952-54. Mem. Com. Alcohol and Other Drugs (chmn. 1973-75). Republican. Methodist.

REEDY, DAVID H. music educator, musician; b. Arcadia, Wis., Dec. 28, 1963; s. Howard H. and Barbara J. Reedy. BS in Applied Piano, U. Wis., LaCrosse, 1987. Owner Reed Music Studios, Onalaska, Wis., 1987—. Chmn. Rising Stars concerto competition LaCrosse Symphony Orch., 2000—. Mem.: Music Tchr.'s Nat. Assn. (cert. music tchr.), Wis. Music Tchr.'s Assn. (award of excellence 1991, 1998, 2001, 100 Pont Award 2003). Office: Reed Music Studios 2700 National Dr Ste 104 Onalaska WI 54650

REEDY, EDWARD K. retired academic administrator; Dir. rsch. ops. Ga. Tech. Rsch. Inst., Atlanta, 1993—97, v.p., dir., 1997—2003, ret., 2003.

REEDY, HARRY LEE, financial services executive; b. Lebanon, Pa., Dec. 25, 1945; s. Harry Lee and Charlotte (Weedmark) R.; m. Linda Bartley, Nov. 7, 1970; children: Jennifer Beth, Sara Emily. BS in Indsl Engring., Pa. State U., 1967; MBA, U. Conn., 1977. Mgmt. asst. Bell Telephone Pa., Phila., 1967-70; field engring. rep. Travelers Cos., Hartford, Conn., 1971-72, ops. analyst, 1972-76, supervising ops. analyst, 1976-79, sr. mgmt. cons., 1979-83, adminstr. consumer affairs, 1983-85, asst. dir. consumer affairs, 1985-90; dir. corp. customer svc. John Hancock Fin. Svcs., Boston, 1990-91, dir. Ctr. for Quality, 1991-96; asst. v.p. quality State St. Corp., North Quincy, Mass., 1997-98, v.p., dir. quality, 1998—. Mem. consumer affairs com. Ins. Info. Inst., N.Y.C., 1988-90. Contbr. articles to trade publs. Participant Leadership Greater Hartford, 1985; bd. dirs., treas. Woodland Manor Condominium Assn., Manchester, Conn., 1986-87; bd. mgrs. Auburn Ct. Condominimum Assn., 2001—; bd. examiners Malcolm Baldridge Nat. Quality award, 1995-2000, sr. examiner, 1997-2000, panel of judges, 2002—, chairperson, 2003—; sr. examiner Mass. State Quality award, 1995-99, judge, 1999; judge New Hampshire Quality Award, 2002. With U.S. Army, 1968-70. Fellow Ins. Consumer Affairs Exch. (treas. 1985-87, v.p. 1987-88, pres. 1988-90), Soc. Consumer Affairs Profls. (v.p. New Eng. chpt. 1991-92); mem. Am. Coun. Life Ins. (consumer affairs com. 1987), Am. Soc. Quality Control, Am. productivity & Quality Ctr., Internat. Benchmarking Clearing House, Strategic Planning Inst., Mass. Coun. Quality (bd. dirs. 1998—, treas. exec. com. 1999-2001), Benchmarking Coun., Assn. Quality and Participation, Beta Gamma Sigma. Democrat. Avocations: photography, racquetball, swimming, reading. Home: 3 Auburn Ct # 2 Brookline MA 02446-6302 Office Phone: 617-985-3070. E-mail: hlreedy@statestreet.com.

REEDY-DEWEY, MADELINE ANNE, retired occupational therapist; b. Milw., Jan. 25, 1954; d. Samuel Smith and Louise Rita (Thomas) Reedy; m. Craig D. Dewey, Sept. 28, 1989. BS in Occupl. Therapy, U. Wis., Milw., 1978. Registered occupl. therapist Wis. Dir. occupl. therapy Hillhaven, Shorewood, Wis., 1978-83, Colonial Manor, Glendale, Wis., 1983-85; Saturday/on-call occupl. therapist Northwest Gen. Hosp., Milw., 1981-84; chief occupl. therapist Silver Spring Convalescent Ctr., Glendale, 1985-86; dir. occupl. therapy Colonia Manor, Glendale, 1986-91; rehab. clin. cons. Therapy Mgmt. Inc. Facilities, various locations, 1991-92; cons./instr. in edn. program W.H. Carter, Inc., Milw., 1994-95; instr. med. terminology and anatomy/physiology Concordia U., Mequon, Wis., 1996; ret., 1996. Clin. supr. practicum students occupl. therapy program U. Wis., Milw. Area Tech. Coll., 1978—83; bd. dirs.

Toner Tech Cartridge Svcs., Inc., Panama City, Fla. Vol. Gulf Coast Cmty. Hosp., Panama City, 1985, St. Michael's Hosp., Milw., 1994, St. Francis Children's Ctr., Milw., 1996, Humane Soc. Bay County, Fla., 2000—01, Vocat. Rehab., Panama City, 2001. Mem.: Wis. Occupl. Therapy Assn., Am. Occupl. Therapy Assn. Roman Catholic. Avocations: volunteer work, gardening, cooking, animal husbandry. Home: 314 Massalina Dr Panama City FL 32401 E-mail: cdeweybc@att.net.

REEF, GRACE, government official; b. Portland, Maine; m. Don Green, Nov. 9, 1991; children: Megan, Jamie, Ryan. BA, Colby Coll., 1984. Legis. asst. Sen. George Mitchell U.S. Senate, Washington, 1984-94, legis. asst. Sen. Tom Daschle, 1995-97; dir. intergovt. affairs Children's Def. Fund, Washington, 1997-2001; subcom. staff dir. children and families Office of Senator Chris Dodd, Washington, 2001—. Office: Office of Senator Chris Dodd 448 Russell Bldg Washington DC 20510 E-mail: grace_Reef@labor.senate.gov.

REEFER, RUSSELL CHARLES, music educator; b. Indiana, Pa., Dec. 14, 1956; s. Russell Charles Reefer and Pauline Louise Simonds; m. Cathie Sue Fehlman, May 18, 1979; children: Allison Nicole, Ashley Marie. BS in Music Edn., Clarion U. of Pa., 1978; MA in Music Edn., Indiana U. of Pa., 1988; postgrad., Shenandoah Conservatory of Music, Winchester, VA, 2003—04. Cert. music tchr. K-12 Pa., 1981. Woodwind clinician Clarion U. Summer Band Clinic, Clarion, Pa., 1978—91; adj. saxophone prof. Ind. U. of Pa., Indiana, Pa., 1995—97; band dir. Redbank Valley Sch. Dist., New Bethlehem, Pa., 1978—. Guest condr. Dist. 2 PMEA Jazz Band Festival, Saint Marys, Pa., 2001; pvt. music tchr., New Bethlehem, Pa., 1978—; guest condr. Dayton Fair Band Night, Dayton, Pa., 1986; saxophone, saxophone soloist Keystone Wind Ensemble, Indiana, Pa., 1996—99. Musician: (saxophone soloist) Women Composer's Concert. Saxophone soloist, music arranger Zion Bapt. Ch., Clarion, Pa., 1991—2004, worship leader, 1992—2000. Recipient Superior Rating, Adjudication Festival for Concert Band, PMEA, 1993, 1994, 1996, 1998, 1999, 2001, 2003, Excellent Rating, Adjudication Festival for Concert Band, PMEA, 1995, 1997, 2002. Mem.: Tech. Inst. for Music Educators (assoc.), Music Educator's Nat. Conf. (assoc.), Pa. State Edn. Assn. (assoc.). Avocations: music, computers. Home: 220 Garfield St New Bethlehem PA 16242 Office: Redbank Valley School District 920 Broad St New Bethlehem PA 16242 Office Phone: 814-275-2680. Personal E-mail: rcreefer@usachoice.net.

REEP, EDWARD ARNOLD, artist; b. Bklyn., May 10, 1918; s. Joseph and Elsie (Abramson) R.; m. Karen Patricia Stevens, Dec. 9, 1942; children— Susan Kay, Cristine Elyse, Janine J., Mitchell Jules. Student, Art Center Coll. Design, 1936-41. Instr. painting and drawing Art Center Coll. Design, Los Angeles, 1946-50, Chouinard Art Inst., Los Angeles, 1950-69; prof. painting, chmn. dept., artist in residence E. Carolina U., 1970-85, prof. emeritus, 1985—. Cons. editor Van Nostrand Reinhold Pub. Co.; ofcl. war artist-corr. WWII, Africa and Italy. Author: The Content of Watercolor, 1968, A Combat Artist in World War II, 1987; shows include Whitney Mus. Am. Art Ann., N.Y.C., 1946-48, Los Angeles County Mus. Ann., 1946-60, Corcoran Gallery Art Biennial, Washington, 1949, Nat. Gallery Art, Washington, 1945, They Drew Fire, 2000, Mus. Modern Art, N.Y.C.; represented in permanent collections Los Angeles County Mus., U.S. War Dept., Grunwald Graphic Arts Collection, UCLA, Nat. Mus. Am. Art, Washington, Lytton Collection, Los Angeles, State of Calif. Collection, Sacramento. Guggenheim fellow, 1945-46; Nat. Endowment for Arts grantee, 1975 Mem. AAUP, Nat. Watercolor Soc. (past pres., Lifetime Achievement award 2002), Watercolor USA Honor Soc. (lifetime achievement gold medal 1997). Democrat. Home: 9021 Crowningshield Dr Bakersfield CA 93311-1901 *I once was consumed by the desire to become an artist. I feel no differently today. There is work ahead. If I had set goals for myself I no longer can recall what they may have been; I go along painting as well or as inventively as I can. Never have I sacrificed living life as I feel I must for my art. My work is a reflection of my life— experiences real and imagined.*

REES, CHARLES H. G. retired finance company executive, investor, consultant; b. Trenton, N.J., Mar. 6, 1922; s. Albert H. and Helen (Gallagher) R.; m. Nancy Thomas, Oct. 30, 1954; children: Liberty, Camilla, Nancy, Hilleary. BA, Princeton U., 1948. Salesman John A. Roebling's Sons Co., Trenton, 1948-50; staff officer CIA, Washington, 1951-54; assoc. J.H. Whitney & Co., N.Y.C., 1954-59; gen. ptnr. Whitcom Investment Co., N.Y.C., 1967-85; with Whitney Comm. Corp., N.Y.C., 1960-85, pres., 1982-85; ret., 1985. Trustee Riverside Rsch. Inst., N.Y.C. With U.S. Army, 1942—46, capt. U.S. Army, 1950—51. Decorated Bronze Star. Mem.: Union Club, Wadawanuck Yacht Club, Misquamicut Club, Ivy Club, Brook Club, Pilgrims N.Y.C. Republican. Home: 215 Farmholme Rd Stonington CT 06378-2205

REES, CLIFFORD HARCOURT, JR., (TED REES), retired association executive, retired air force officer; b. Newport News, Va., Dec. 11, 1936; s. Clifford Harcourt Sr. and Mary Evelyn (Brooks) R.; m. Joan Elizabeth Mittong, July 26, 1958; children— Clifford Harcourt III, Steven M., Daniel B., William B. BS in Fgn. Svc., Georgetown U., 1958; MS in Polit. Sci., Auburn U., 1969; grad., Air War Coll., Montgomery, Ala., 1978. Commd. 2d lt. U.S. Air Force, 1958; advanced through grades to lt. gen., 1988; comdr. 421st Tactical Fighter Squadron, Udorn Royal Thai AFB, 1974-75; chief, house liaison office U.S. Ho. Reps., Washington, 1978-80; asst. col. assignments Randolph AFB, 1980-82; vice-comdr. Air Force Manpower and Personnel Ctr., 1982; dep. dir. legis. liaison Office Sec. Air Force, 1982-84, dir. legis. liaison, 1984-86; comdr. USAF Air Defense Weapons Ctr., Tyndall AFB, Fla., 1986-88; vice comdr. in chief USAF in Europe, Ramstein AB, Federal Republic of Germany, 1988-92, ret., 1992; founder, pres. Rees Group Cons.; pres. Air Conditioning and Refrigeration Inst., Arlington, Va., 1992—2002. U.S. rep. to v.p. Internat. Coun. Mil. Sports, Brussels, 1982-94. Decorated D.S.M. with one oak leaf cluster, DFC with one oak leaf cluster, Legion of Merit with one oak leaf cluster, Meritorious Svc. medal with one oak leaf cluster, Air medal with 11 oak leaf clusters USAF, Das Grosse Verdienstkreuz Mit Stern, Pres. Fed. Republic Germany, 1993; named Commander Order of Meritorious Svc. Mil. Sports Coun., 1993. Mem. Delta Phi Epsilon (v.p. membership 1957-58, nat. pres. 1984-86) Methodist. Home: 2487 Oakton Hills Dr Oakton VA 22124-1530 E-mail: ted@thereesgroup.com.

REES, FRANK WILLIAM, JR., architect; b. Rochester, N.Y., June 5, 1943; s. Frank William and Elizabeth R. (Miller) R.; m. Joan Mary Keevers, Apr. 1, 1967; children: Michelle, Christopher. BS in Architecture, U. Okla., 1970; postgrad., Harvard U., Boston, 1979, 90; OPM, Harvard U., 1990; DArch, U. Hawaii, 2001. Registered architect, 39 states & D.C.; cert. Nat. Coun. Archtl. Registration Bds.; registered interior designer. Sales mgr. Sta. KFOM, Oklahoma City, 1967-70; project architect Benham-Blair & Affiliates, Oklahoma City, 1970-75; pres., CEO, founder Rees Assocs., Inc., Oklahoma City, 1975—. Pres., chmn. bd. Weatherscan Radio Network, Oklahoma City, 1973-78; chmn. bd. Weatherscan Internat., Oklahoma City, 1972-78; pres. Frontier Communications, Oklahoma City, 1980-84; chmn. architecture bd. U. Okla., Norman, 1988-91; bd. dirs. Century, Inc., Oklahoma City. Past pres. Lake Hefner Trails, Oklahoma City, Hosp. Hospitality House, Oklahoma City, Oklahoma City Beautiful; mem. Leadership Oklahoma City. Mem. AIA, Am. Assn. Hosp. Architects, Am. Healthcare Assn., Tex. Hosp. Assn., World Pres. Orgn. (chmn. 1997-98), Assisted Living Fedn. of Am., Am. Assn. Homes and Svcs. for the Agig. Home: 1104 Stone Gate Dr Irving TX 75063-4676 Office: Rees Associates Inc 3102 Oak Lawn Ave Ste 200 Dallas TX 75219-4279

REES, JAMES CONWAY, IV, historic site administrator; b. Richmond, Va., May 5, 1952; BA, Coll. William & Mary, 1974; MPA, George Washington U., 1978. Reporter, photographer Newport News Daily-Press, 1974; coord. radio and television programming The Coll. William & Mary, 1974-78; mng. editor The William & Mary Mag., 1978-82; promotions dir. Va. Shakespeare Festival, 1980; dir. annual giving and pub. info. The Coll. William & Mary, 1978-80, dir. annual support and corp. rels., 1980-81, dir. capital support, 1981-82; asst. dir. devel. Nat. Trust Historic Preservation, 1982-83, assoc. dir. devel., 1983; dir. devel. and comms. Historic Mount Vernon, 1983-85, assoc. dir., 1985-94, exec. dir., 1994—. Bd. dirs. Va. Shakespeare Festival, Washington Area chpt. William and Mary Alumni Soc. Mem. Nat. Trust for Historic Preservation, Friends of the Nat. Symphony, WETA Pub. TV; bd. dirs. Va. Shakespeare Festival, Nt. Parks and History Found. Mem. Am. Film Inst., Va. Assn. Mus. (pres. 1991-94), William and Mary Alumni Soc. (bd. dirs. Washington area chpt.). Methodist. Home: 710 A St NE Washington DC 20002-6032 Office: Mount Vernon Ladies Assn Mount Vernon VA 22121

REES, JAY CARLYLE, conductor, composer, music educator; b. Detroit, Apr. 17, 1961; s. Carlyle Williams and Sharon Gates Rees; m. Wendy Sue Garfield, Nov. 14, 1992; children: Evan Carlyle, Sean Dalby. MusB in Music Edn., U. of Miami, Coral Gables, Fla., 1984; MusM in Performance/Conducting, U. of Ariz., Tucson, 1995. Profl. musician, Miami and L.A., 1984—92; musical dir./performer The Lettermen, 1991—92; dir. of music Granada Hills H.S., Calif., 1989—91; assoc. dir. of bands/ prof. of music U. of Ariz., Tucson, 1995—. Dir. Pride of Ariz. Marching and Pep Bands U. of Ariz., Tucson, 1995—. Composer: (musical compositions/arrangements) various works for wind ensembles, jazz bands, and marching bands; prodr.: (compact disc) Legacy Lane (new works for bands), The Pride of Arizona (new works for marching bands). Designer/choreographer Tucson's Human Flag, 2001. Recipient Golden Rule Award/Vol. of the Yr., J.C.Penney Corp., 1999, Tchr. Appreciation award, U. of Ariz. Young Alumni, 2000, Fight Wildcats Fight award, U. of Ariz. Band Alumn i Bd. of Dirs., 1997; grantee multiple grants and commns., various univs. and founds., 1997—. Office: University of Arizona Sch of Music and Dance/Bands Tucson AZ 85721 Office Phone: 520-621-7027. Business E-Mail: jrees@u.arizona.edu.

REES, LANE CHARLES, industrial relations consultant; b. Longview, Tex., June 23, 1951; s. Holly Elias and Charlene Elizabeth (Quin) R.; m. Brenda Faye Anderson, July 1, 1978; children: Brian Andrew, Lauren Catherine. BBA in Mgmt. magna cum laude, Tex. A&M U., 1973, MEd in Ednl. Adminstrn., 1978. Pers. rep. Tex. A&M U., College Station, 1973-77; v.p. Brazos Gen. Svcs., Bryan, Tex., 1977-78; successively pers. office supr., wage and salary adminstr., employee rels. rep., sr. employee rels. rep. ARCO, various cities, Tex., 1979-83, from sr. employee rels. rep. to employee rels. dir. Anchorage and Kuparuk, Alaska, 1983-87, dir. employee rels. Prudhoe Bay, Alaska, 1987-90, dir. human resources dept. engring., 1990-94; sr. human rels. advisor Algeria and engring. exploration Arco Internat. Oil and Gas, Plano, Tex., 1994-99; pres. Human Resources Solutions, Inc., Dallas/Santa Rosa Beach, Tex., 1999—. Ptnr. Rees and Assocs., Anchorage, Tex., Fla., 1978—. Mem. editl. staff Conf. Leadership, 1978. Vice chmn. Rep. Party of Alaska, 1993-94, chair, 1994; vice-chmn. Walton Co. GOP exec. com., 1999—; mem. ctrl. com. State of Alaska, 1990-94; chmn. utility regulatory commn. municipality of Anchorage, 1989-91; mem. com. sec. United Meth. Com. Commn., Nashville, 1988-97; evangelism chmn., mem. adv. coun. St. John United Meth. Ch., Anchorage, 1986-91, chmn. adminstrv. bd., 1991-93; trustee Nat. Found. Evangelism, Lake Junaluska, NC, 1988—, exec. com., 1995—, chmn. 2002—; conf. lay leader Ala. Missionary Conf.-Meth. Ch., 1992-94; chmn. evangelism and mem. adminstrv. bd. 1st United Meth. Ch., Allen, Tex., 1995-97; mem. adminstrv. bd. Suncreek (Tex.) United Meth. Ch., 1997-99, adv. bd. Freeport United Meth. Ch., lay del. to ann. conf., 1995-2001; active Port Washington United Meth. Ch., 2001-, mem. ch. coun. 2003-, del. ann. conf., 2004-; mem. internat. bd. George Bush Ctr., Tex. A&M U., 1996—; bd. dirs. Walton Co. C. of C., 1999—, Fla. Assn. Counties, 2002—, Fla. Assn. Counties Trust, 2001—, vice chair, 2002—; commr. Walton County, 2000—; vice chair Walton Bd. County Commrs., 2000-01, chair, 2001-02; mem. adv. bd. Walton Tourist Devel. Coun., 2001—; mem. adv. coun. U. West Fla. Coll. Bus., 2002-. Recipient Denman award Alaska Missionary Conf. United Meth. Ch., 1989, Legis. citation State of Alaska, 1989. Mem. Acad. Mgmt., Tex. A&M U. Assn. Former Students (nat. councilman 1987-91, bd. dirs. 1996—), Am. Numis. Assn., Alaska Soc. SAR (pres. 1989-90, trustee Nat. Soc. 1991-94, Silver Good Citizenship award 1989), Phi Eta Sigma, Phi Kappa Phi, Sigma Iota Epsilon (pres. 1972-73), Beta Gamma Sigma. Avocations: golf, racquetball, reading, travel, coin collecting/numismatics. Home: 323 Lakeview Dr Santa Rosa Beach FL 32459-6604 Office Phone: 850-231-0735. E-mail: solutionhr@aol.com.

REES, MARTIN JOHN, astronomy educator; b. York, Eng., June 23, 1942; s. Reginald and Joan (Bett) R. MA, PhD, Cambridge (Eng.) U., 1967; DSc (hon.), Sussex (Eng.) U., 1990, Leicester (Eng.) U., 1993, Uppsala (Sweden) U., 1995, Keele (Eng.) U., 1995, Newcastle (Eng.) U., 1995, Copenhagen U., 1995, Toronto (Can.) U., 1997, Durham (Eng.) U., 1999, Oxford (Eng.) U., 2000. Rsch. fellow Calif. Tech. Inst., 1968; vis. rsch. fellow Inst. for Advanced Study, Princeton, NJ, 1969, 82, 96, 97; vis. scientist Harvard U., Cambridge, Mass., 1972, 87-90; Regents fellow Smithsonian Instn., 1984-87; prof. Sussex U., 1972-73; Plumian prof. astronomy Cambridge U., 1973-91; dir. Inst. Astronomy, Cambridge, 1977-91; rsch. prof. Royal Soc. Cambridge U., England, 1992—2003, prof. cosmology and astrophysics, 2002—; master Trinity Coll., Cambridge, 2004—; astronomer royal, 1995—. Fellow King's Coll., Cambridge U., England, 1969—2003; hon. fellow Trinity Coll., 1995—, master, 2004—; hon. fellow Jesus Coll., 1996—, Cardiff U., Wales, 1998; vis. prof. Harvard U., Princeton U., Calif. Tech., Imperial Coll., London, Leicester U., hon. prof., Imperial Coll., London; bd. trustees Brit. Mus., 1996—2002, Nat. Endowment for Sci., Tech. and Arts, 1998—2001, Inst. for Advanced Study, Princeton, 1998—, Kennedy Meml. Trust, England, 1999—, Inst. for Pub. Policy Rsch., 2001—, Nat. Mus. of Sci. and Tech., 2003—. Author: (with M.C. Begelman) Gravity's Fatal Attraction, 1995, Perspectives in Astrophysical Cosmology, 1995, Before the Beginning, 1997, Just Six Numbers, 1999, Our Cosmic Habitat, 2001, Our Final Century?, 2003. Decorated officer Order of Arts and Letters (France); recipient Heinemann prize, Am. Inst. Physics, 1984, Gold medal, Royal Astron. Soc., 1987, Balzan prize, 1989, Robinson prize, 1990, Bruce medal, 1993, Knight Bachelor, 1992, Sci. Writing award, Am. Inst. Physics, 1996, Bower award, Franklin Inst., 1998, Rossi prize, AAS, 2000, Cosmology prize, Gruber Found., 2001, Einstein award, World Sci. Coun., 2003. Fellow AAAS, Royal Soc. London, Royal Netherlands Acad. Arts and Scis., Indian Acad. Scis. (hon.), Russian Acad. Scis. (hon.), Swedish Acad. Scis., Am. Philosophy Soc.; mem. NAS (fgn. assoc.), Pontifical Acad. Scis., Academia Europea, Inst. Physics (Eng.) (Guthrie prize 1990—), Royal Astron. Soc. (pres. 1992-94), Brit. Assn. Advancement Sci. (pres. 1994-95), Norwegian Acad. Sci., Acad. Lincei (Rome), Finnish Acad. Arts and Sci. Anglican. Office: Inst Astronomy Cambridge England CB3 0HA also: Trinity Coll Cambridge CB2 1TQ England

REES, NINA SHOKRAII, federal official, writer; b. Iran; BS in Psychology, Va. Polytech and State U., 1989; MS in Internat. Transactions, George Mason U., 1991. Mem. staff Rep. Porter Gross, Washington, 1990—92; dir. outreach programs Inst. for Justice, Washington, 1992—94; policy analyst Ams. for Tax Reform, Washington, 1994—96; chief edn. analyst The Heritage Found., Washington, 1997—2001; aide to v.p. U.S. Govt., Washington, 2001—02. Contbr. commentaries in newspapers, TV, radio on ednl. issues, 1995. Education adviser to Bush Campaign, Phila., 2000; contbr. to Rep. platform in edn. area Rep. Paty, 2000. Recipient Rita Ricardo Campbell award, Heritage Found., 1999. Office: US Dept Edn 400 Maryland Ave SW Washington DC 20202

REES, NORMA S. academic administrator; b. N.Y.C., Dec. 27, 1929; d. Benjamin and Lottie (Schwartz) D.; m. Raymond R. Rees, Mar. 19, 1960; children— Evan Lloyd, Raymond Arthur BA, Queens Coll., 1952; Ma, Bklyn. Coll., 1954; PhD, NYU, 1959; D of Arts and Letters honoris causa, John F. Kennedy U., 2001. Cert. speech-language pathology, audiology. Prof. communicative disorders Hunter Coll., N.Y.C., 1967-72; exec. officer, speech and hearing scis. grad. sch. CUNY, N.Y.C., 1972-74, assoc. dean for grad. studies, 1974-76, dean grad. studies, 1976-82; vice chancellor for acad. affairs U. Wis., Milw., 1982-85, from 1986, acting chancellor, 1985-86; vice chancellor for acad. policy and planning Mass. Bd. Regents for Higher Edn., Boston, 1987-90; pres. Calif. State U., Hayward, 1990—. Chmn. Commn. Recognition of Postsecondary Accreditation, 1994-96; mem. adv. com. quality and integrity U.S. Dept. Edn., commn. on internat. edn. Coun. on Higher Edn. Accreditation, 2003—. Contbr. articles to profl. jours. Trustee Citizens Govtl. Rsch. Bur., Milw., 1985-87; active Task Force on Wis. World Trade Ctr., 1985-87; bd. dirs. Am. Assn. State Colls. and Univs., 1995-97, Coun. of Postsecondary Accreditation, Washington, 1985-94, Greater Boston YWCA, 1987-90; mem. Calif. Sch. to Career Coun.; bd. dir. Econ. Devel. Alliance for Bus., Alameda County, 1995—; sec. edn. Nat. Adv. Com. Institutional Quality and Integrity, 1998-2002; bd. dirs. Bay Area World Trade Ctr., 2001—, Alameda County Health Care Found., 2002-. Fellow Am. Speech-Lang-Hearing Assn. (honors); mem. Am. Coun. Edn. (com. internat. edn. 1991-93), Am. Assn. Colls. and Univs. (chair task force on quality assessment 1991-92), Nat. Assn. State Univs. and Land Grant Colls. (exec. com. divsn. urban affairs 1985-87, com. accreditation 1987-90), Hayward C. of C. (bd. dirs. 1995-98), Oakland C. of C. (bd. dirs. 1997—). Office: Calif State Univ Hayward 25800 Carlos Bee Blvd Hayward CA 94542-3001 Office Phone: 510-885-3877. E-mail: nrees@csuhayward.edu.

REES, RAYMOND F. military officer; b. Pendleton, Oreg., Sept. 29, 1944; s. Raymond Emmett and Lorna Doone (Gemmell) R.; m. Karen Kristine Young, Nov. 1966 (div. Mar. 1974); children: Raymond Gordon, Christian Frederick; m. Mary Len Middleton, Dec. 30, 1977; 1 child, Carrie Evelyn. BS, U.S. Mil. Acad., 1966; JD, U. Oreg., 1976. Commd. 2d lt. U.S. Army, 1966; platoon leader, troop exec. officer, co. comdr. 2d Armored Cavalry Regiment, Bamberg, Fed. Republic Germany; troop comdr. 2-17 Cavalry 101 Airborn divsn., Camp Eagle, Vietnam, 1969; troop exec. officer 1-17 Cavalry 82 Airborn divsn., Ft. Bragg, N.C., 1972; resigned U.S. Army, 1973; with Oreg. Army Nat. Guard, 1973—, advanced through grades to maj. gen., 1990; asst. ops. officer Infantry Brigade; co. comdr. 2d Battalion, 162d Infantry, Corvallis, Oreg.; with 116th Armored Calvary Regiment, 1976-87; comdr. 116th cavalry regiment, adjutant gen. Oreg. Army Nat. Guard, 1987-91; dir. Army N.G., 1991-92; vice chief N.G. Bur., Washington, 1992-94; adjutant gen. Oreg. N.G., 1994-99; acting chief N.G. Bur., Washington, 1999—2004; chief of staff Hdqrs. NORAD and U.S. No. Command, 2004—. Decorated Bronze Star, Legion of Merit, D.S.M., Def. Disting. Svc. medal. Mem. VFW, Adjutant Gen. Assn. U.S., Nat. Guart Assn. U.S., Assn. of U.S. Army, Oreg. Nat. Guard Assn., U.S. Armor Assn., Oreg. Bar Assn., Am. Legion, Mil. Order World Wars, West Point Soc. Oreg., 101st Airborne Div. Assn., 116th Armored Cavalry Assn., 41st Infantry Div. Assn., Elks. Office: Hdqrs NORAD/USNORTHCOM/CS 250 Vandenberg St Ste B016 Peterson AFB CO 80914-3804

REES, THOMAS DYNEVOR, lawyer; b. S.I., N.Y., Sept. 25, 1949; s. Thomas and Caroline (Bridgman) Rees; m. Josephine Stephanie Madej, Apr. 8, 1978; 1 child, Thomas D. III. AB in Polit. Sci., Stanford U., 1971; JD, U. Pa., 1975. Bar: N.Y. 1976, Pa. 1977, U.S. Supreme Ct. 1982. Assoc. Lovejoy, Wasson, Lundgren & Ashton, N.Y.C., 1975-77, Morgan, Lewis & Bockius, Phila., 1977-81; dep. gen. counsel Office of Gov. of Pa., Harrisburg, 1981-85; counsel High, Swartz, Roberts & Seidel, Norristown, Pa., 1985-86, ptnr., 1987—. CLE course planner, author, faculty mem. Pa. Bar Inst., 1990—; employment panel arbitrator Am. Arbitration Assn., Phila., 1991—. Contbr. Solicitor Upper Merion Twp., King of Prussia, Pa., 1987—88, 1990—95, Abington Twp., Pa., 1986—87; pres. Gladwyne Civic Assn., Pa., 1995—97. Mem.: ABA, Montgomery County Bar Assn. (co-chair employment law com. 1996—2000), Pa. Bar Assn. (chair mcpl. law sect. 1993—95), King of Prussia C. of C. (solicitor 1996—, v.p., gen. counsel 1999—). Republican. Episcopalian. Office: High Swartz Roberts & Seidel LLP 40 E Airy St Norristown PA 19401-4803 Office Phone: 610-275-0700. E-mail: trees@highswartz.com.

REESE, ALFERD GEORGE, retired army civilian logistics specialist; b. Granville, N.D., Apr. 5, 1934; s. Ferdinand Emil and Iola May (Boulds) R.; m. Donna Mae Berger, 1955 (div. 1972); children: Rick, Denise, Roxanna; m. Nelda Cecilia Pena, May 31, 1985; children: Nancy, Joyce, Alfred, Jeffrey, Jessica, James, Alicia. AS, Humphreys Coll., 1963; BS, U. State of N.Y., Albany, 1983; MPA, U. Colo., Colorado Springs, 1985; postgrad., Ga. State U., 1987-88; PhD, Columbia Pacific U., 1994. Inspector, mechanic Sharp Army Depot, Lathrop, Calif., 1958-66; equipment specialist various stations U.S. Army Aviation Systems Command, 1966-84, supervisory equipment specialist, 1984-88, supervisory logistics specialist St. Louis, 1988-93; ret. Civil Svc., 1993. Mem. com. Boy Scouts Am., Fed. Republic Germany, 1979-81. With USAF, 1953-57. Mem. Army Aviation Assn. Assn. (USAEUR Dept. Army Civilian of Yr. 1980, 81), Ctr. for the Study of the Presidency, Acad. Polit. Sci., Am. Soc. for Pub. Adminstrn., Nat. Rifle Assn. Avocations: golf, skiing, photography, painting. Home: 1590 Fairmount Dr Florissant MO 63033-2645

REESE, ANNETTE EVELYN, music educator; b. Waynesville, N.C., Sept. 23, 1958; d. James F. and Shirley Sharpe Robertson; m. Mark A. Reese, Nov. 22, 1980; children: Alana Riggle, Emily Riggle. MusB Edn., Mars Hill Coll., 1980; MEd, Belmont Abbey Coll., 1996. Cert. music educator K12. Elem. music specialist Marlboro County Schs., Bennettsville, SC, 1980—81; choral dir. North Gaston H.S., Dallas, NC, 1981—85; dir. of bands East Gaston High/Stanley Mid. Sch., Mt. Holly/Stanley, NC, 1985—95, Belmont Mid. Sch., Belmont, NC, 1995—98, Olympic High/Kennedy Mid. Sch., Charlotte, NC, 1998—. Pres. NC Bandmasters Assn., Charlotte, NC, 2000—, South Ctrl. Dist. Bandmasters, NCBA, Charlotte, NC, 1996—98; sec. NC Bandmasters Assn., Charlotte, NC, 1998—2000; band sect. chair, exec. bd. mem. NC Music Educators Assn., Raleigh, NC, 2000—. Contbr. articles to profl. jours. Troop leader Pioneer Girl Scout Coun., GSUSA, Gastonia, NC, 1996—2002. Mem.: NEA, N.C. Assn. Educators, Music Educators Nat. Conf., N.C. Bandmasters Assn. (pres. 2000—02, Excellence award 1996), N.C. Music Educators Assn. (band sect. chair 2000—02), Delta Omicron Profl. Music Frat. Mem. Evangelical Lutheran Ch. Of America. Avocations: needlework, music, travel. Office: Olympic High/Kennedy Mid Sch 4301 Sandy Porter Rd Charlotte NC 28273 E-mail: mrmsyuba@aol.com.

REESE, CHARLES WOODROW, JR., lawyer, real estate developer; b. San Antonio, June 21, 1944; s. Charles Woodrow and Mary Ruth (Gott) R.; m. Jill Fritschi, Aug. 10, 1979; children: Clarissa, Alexandra. BA cum laude, Washington and Lee U., 1966; JD, U. Calif., Berkeley, 1969. Bar: Calif. 1970, U.S. Sup. Ct. 1976. Assoc. McCutchen, Doyle, Brown & Enersen, San Francisco, 1969-75; staff atty. Kaiser Industries Corp., Oakland, Calif., 1975-78; asst. gen. csl. Kaiser Cement Corp., Oakland, 1978-86; mng. dir. Reese Interests, Houston, 1978—; mng. trustee Clotilde deMartini Trusts, San Francisco, 1977-; prin Lempres & Wulfsberg PC, Oakland, 1986-98; exec. v.p. Wulfsberg Reese & Sykes PC, 1998-2002; pres., CFO Wulsberg Reese Colvig & Firstman PC, 2002—. Hon. trustee Orinda Found., 1976—; bd. dirs. Planned Parenthood Alameda/San Francisco, 1981-83, Brown and Caldwell, Walnut Creek, 1987-, PLA Holdings, Inc., Port Costa, 1991-2000. Robert E. Lee Rsch. scholar, 1965-66. Mem. State Bar Calif., ABA, Bar Assn. San Francisco, Alameda County Bar Assn. (coms.), Omicron Delta Upsilon, Pacific Union Club (San Francisco), Orinda (Calif.) Country Club. Republican. Episcopalian. Home: 89 La Salle Piedmont CA 94611 Office: 300 Lakeside Dr 24th Fl Oakland CA 94612-3534 E-mail: creese@wulfslaw.com.

REESE, CLAUDIA, artist; b. Des Moines, May 1, 1949; d. William Lewis and Louise (Weeks) R.; 1 child, Taylor. Student, SUNY, Albany, summer 1967, 68, RIT, summer 1969; BA, Conn. Coll., 1971; MFA, Ind. U., 1974. Vis. artist Iowa Wesleyan Coll., Mt. Plesant, 1974-75, U. No. Colo., Greeley, 1976-77, The Sch. of the Art Inst. of Chgo., 1980, Purdue U., West Lafayette, Ind., 1980-81, La. State U., Baton Rouge, 1981, Brookhaven Coll., Dallas, 1990, N.Mex. State U., Las Cruces, 1992; dir., designer Cera-Mix Studio, Austin, Tex., 1982—. Subject of various articles in profl. jours.; one woman shows include Purdue U., West Lafayette, Ind., 1981, Objects Gallery, San Antonio, 1982, Willingheart Gallery, Austin, Tex., 1984, R.S. Levy Gallery, Austin, 1987, S.W. Craft Ctr., San Antonio, 1988, Everson Mus., Syracuse, N.Y., 1988, Tokyo, 1989, 90, 91, Lyons-Matrix Gallery, Austin, 1997; exhibited in group shows Edits Ltd., Indpls., 1981, Berkeley-Lainson Gallery, Denver, 1981, Renwick Gallery, Smithsonian Instn., Washington, 1981, Wichita Art Mus., Kans., 1981, St. Mary's Coll., South Bend, Ind., 1981, Herron Sch. Art, Indpls., 1981, Craftsman's Gallery, Scarsdale, N.Y., 1982, ACVAA Juried Show, Austin, 1982, Elements Gallery, N.Y.C., 1982, Greenwich, Conn., 1983, Mattingly Baker Gallery, Dallas, 1983, Adesso, Chgo., 1983, Coll. Mainland, Tex. City, 1983, S.W. Tex. State U., 1983, New Stone Age Gallery, 1984, Willingheart Gallery, 1984, Maple Hill Gallery, Portland, Maine, 1984, Tex. Christian U., Ft. Worth, 1984, Laguna Gloria Art Mus., Austin, 1985, Carol Hooberman Gallery, Birmingham, Mich., 1985, John Michael Kohler Arts Ctr., Sheboygan, Wis., Elizabeth Fortner Gallery, Santa Barbara, Calif., 1985,

86, Kimbell Art Mus., Ft. Worth, 1986, Contemporary Arts Ctr., New Orleans, 1986, Aeteilers D'Art, Paris, 1986, Mendocino (Calif.) Arts Ctr., 1986, Kimbell Art Mus., Ft. Worth, 1986, N.Mex. State U., Carlsbad, 1987, Aspen (Colo.) Art Mus., 1987, Longview (Tex.) Mus. Invitational, 1988, North Hampton, Mass., 1988, Huntington Gallery at U. Tex., Austin, 1989, S.W. Univ. in Georgetown, 1989, Nat. Mus. Women in the Arts, Washington, 1989, Nat. Mus. Ceramic Art, Balt., 1990, La. State U., Baton Rouge, 1990, Laguna Gloria Art Mus., Austin, 1990, 91, Twist Gallery, Portland, Oreg., 1991, Virginia Breier gallery, San Francisco, 1991, Art Options, Santa Monica, Calif., 1991, Virginia Brier Gallery, San Francisco, 1991, Twist Gallery, Portland, Oreg., 1991, U. Tex., El Paso, 1992, Renwick Gallery, 1992, Mindscape Gallery, Evanston, Ill., 1992, Pittsburg Ctr. for the Arts, 1992, IO Gallery, New Orleans, 1993, Ruskin Place, Seaside, Fla., 1993, Martin Rathburn Gallery, San Antonio, 1995, Farmington Valley Art Ctr., Conn., 1996, Lyons-Matrix Gallery, 1997, Arlington Mus. Art, 1998, Irving Arts Ctr., Tex., 1998, U. Tex. San Antonio, 1999, San Antonio Mus. Art, 2000, Am. Craft Mus., N.Y.C., 2002, Dallas Ctr. Contemporary Arts, 2002, numerous others; represented in permanent collections The Crescent Collection, Dallas, June Mattingly, Dallas, Bill Bostleman, Ft. Worth, Laurence Miller, Austin, Hadley Sleight, Austin, Marilyn Maxwell, Ft. Worth, Archer Huntington Mus. (now Blanton Mus. of Fine Art); commissioned work displayed at Austin Bergstrom Internat. Airport, S.E. Comm. Libr., Westbank Libr., St. Francis Hosp. Children, Los Angeles, Ch. of Conscious Harmony, Austin, Tex., Carver Mus., Austin, Tex., Sean Bldg. (3 lobbies) U. Tex., Austin. Mem. Tex. Fine Arts Assn., Women and Their Work, Austin Visual Artists Assn. Democrat. Avocations: skiing, sailing, windsurfing, gardening. Office: Cera-Mix Studio 709 N Tumbleweed Trl Austin TX 78733-3240 Fax: 512-263-5019. E-mail: ceramix@io.com.

REESE, CYNTHIA DENE, psychologist, educator, quality assurance professional, risk management consultant; b. Milledgeville, Ga., July 19, 1958; d. Robert Weyman, Sr. and Sara Powers (Neal) Reese. BS in Criminal Justice Adminstrn., Ga. Coll. & State U., Milledgeville, 1994; MA in Psychology, Ga. Sch. Profl. Psychologists, Atlanta, 1998; postgrad., N. Ctrl. U., Prescott, Ariz., 2002—. Investigator, social svcs. supr. Dept. of Family and Children Svcs., Ga.; program dir. Ga. Children's Home, Macon, 1998—2001; risk mgmt., quality assurance dir. Nat. Mentor, Inc., Macon, 2001—; adj. prof. Macon State Coll., 2000—. Clin. cons. Ga. Children's Home, Macon, 1998—99; legal child abuse cons. Recipient Excellence award, Houston County Dist. Atty., 1994, Houston County Sheriff's Office, 1994, Houston County Dept. Family and Child Svcs., 1994. Mem.: Nat. Assn. Forensic Counselors, Am. Soc. Trial Cons. Avocations: physical fitness, travel. Home: 1175 Chisholm Trail Macon GA 31220 Office: The Mentor Network 2987 Clairmont Rd Atlanta GA 30329 Office Phone: 478-737-2466. E-mail: samanthatreese@yahoo.com.

REESE, DELLA (DELOREESE PATRICIA EARLY), singer, actress; b. Detroit, July 6, 1931; d. Richard and Nellie Early; m. Vermont Adolphus Bon Taliaferro (div.); m. Leroy Basil Gray (div.); m. Franklin Thomas Lett, Jr. Student, Wayne U. Ordained to ministry Ch. Understanding Principles for Better Living Inc., April, 1987. Choir singer, 1938—, with Mahalia Jackson troupe, 1945-49, Erskine Hawkins, N.Y.C.; solo artist, 1957—; organized gospel group at Wayne U.; appearances include: (radio shows) with Robert Q. Lewis; (TV series) Della, 1969, The Voyage of the Yes, 1972, Twice in a Lifetime, 1974, Cop on the Beat, 1975, Chico and the Man, 1974, 76-78, Nightmare in Badham County, 1976 (Emmy nomination), Roots: The Next Generation, 1979, It Takes Two, 1982, Charlie & Co., 1985, 86, The Kid Who Loved Christmas, 1990, The Royal Family, 1991, You Must Remember This, 1992, Touched By an Angel, 1994-2003, A Match Made in Heaven, 1997, Miracle in the Woods, 1997, Emma's Wish, 1998, The Secret Path, 1999, Having Our Say: The Delany Sisters' First 100 Years, 1999; spl. appearances with Jackie Gleason, Ed Sullivan, McCloud, 1971, Sanford and Son, 1972, Welcome Back, Kotter, 1975, The A-Team, 1983, Night Court, 1984, MacGyver, 1985, Designing Women, 1986, L.A. Law, 1986, Married People, 1990, Dream On, 1990, Picket Fences, 1992, Promised Land, 1996, Anya's Bell, 1999, The Moving of Sophia Myles, 2000; guest host The Tonight Show; actress (films) Let's Rock, 1958, Psychic Killer, 1975, Harlem Nights, 1989, A Thin Line Between Love and Hate, 1996, (plays) Same Time Next Year, Ain't Misbehavin, Blues in the Night, The Last Minstrel Show; recs. for Jubilee, RCA Victor Records, ABC Paramount Records, Jazz Ala Carte, AIR Co. (Grammy nomination 1987); author: Angels Along the Way, 1997, (voice) Dinosaur, 2000. Voted Most Promising Singer of Yr. 1957; recipient Image awards, 1996, 98-2000, Star on Walk of Fame, 1994. Office: William Morris Agy c/o Jeff Kolodny 151 S El Camino Dr Beverly Hills CA 90212-2775

REESE, FRANCIS EDWARD, retired chemical company executive, consultant; b. Monaca, Pa., Nov. 3, 1919; s. Francis Edward and Vivian Iris (Hancuff) R.; m. Katherine Mary McBrien, June 29, 1946; 1 son, Francis Edward III. BS in Chem. Engring, Purdue U., 1941. Registered profl. engr., Pa. With Monsanto Co., St. Louis, 1941, research engr. plastics div., 1941-48, chief devel. engring. plastics div., 1948-53, asst. engr. plastics div., 1953-56, dir. engring. plastics div., 1956-59, asst. gen. mgr. plastics div., 1959-61, asst. gen. mgr. hydrocarbons div., 1961-65, asst. gen. mgr., hydrocarbons and polymers div., 1965-66, gen. mgr. internat. div., 1966-68, corp. v.p., 1968-74, gen. mgr., hydrocarbons and polymers div., 1968-71, gen. mgr. polymers and petrochems. div., 1971-73, gen. mgr. internat. div., 1973-74, dir., 1973-84, group v.p., 1974-79, sr. v.p., 1979-84. Pres. FTR Assocs., Inc.; mem. engring. found. adv. coun. U. Tex. Fellow AAAS, Am. Inst. Chem. Engrs.; mem. Am. Chem. Soc., Nat. Soc. Profl. Engrs., Soc. Chem. Industry, Tau Beta Pi, Phi Lambda Upsilon. Home: Rydal Park 271W 1515 The Fairway Rydal PA 19046-1435 Office: Rydal Park 544H 1515 The Fairway Jenkintown PA 19046 Office Phone: 215-886-9251. E-mail: FTRAssoc@aol.com.

REESE, GEORGE W. federal agency administrator; b. Detroit; married; 2 children. BS, Lincoln U.; JD, George Washington U.; postgrad., U. Pitts. Sr. atty., atty. advisor Office Gen. Counsel NASA, Washington, with Office Gen. Counsel, 1977—, dep. gen. counsel, 1993—97, assoc. adminstr. equal opportunity programs, 1997—. Officer U.S. Army, Vietnam. Office: NASA Hdqrs Mail Code E 300 E St SW Washington DC 20546

REESE, GLENN G. state legislator, food products executive; b. Greenville, S.C., Jan. 6, 1942; s. Wilford William and Geneva Margaret (Lamb) R.; m. Janis D., June 19, 1970; children: Glenn Jr., David, Kathryn, Michael. AA, Mars Hill Coll.; BA, Auburn U.; MA, Converse. Tchr., S.C., 1963-85; food products exec. Krispy Kreme Doughnut Co., Spartenburg, S.C., 1979-92; senator State of S.C., Columbia, 1991—. Internat. official AIA, Colorado Springs, Co., 1977-92. Democrat. Baptist. Avocation: sports officiating. Office: 117 Sun Valley Dr Inman SC 29349-7458 also: State Senate 510 Gressette Bldg Columbia SC 29302

REESE, HARRY EDWIN, JR., electronics executive; b. Balt., Oct. 27, 1928; s. Harry Edwin and Margery Lee (Stroud) R.; m. Elizabeth Syra Pfeiffer, Oct. 15, 1955; children: Clifford Owen, Susan Syra, Peter Eyre. BSEE, Tufts U., 1950; MS in Stats., Villanova U., 1960. Engr. Philco Corp., Phila., 1950-54; project engr. Burroughs Corp., Paoli, Pa., 1956-59, dept. mgr., 1959-65, GE Co., King of Prussia, Pa., 1965-69; group staff mgr. Burroughs Corp., Paoli, Pa., 1969-75, gen. mgr. Plainfield, N.J., 1975-82, corp. staff dir. Detroit, 1982-83; v.p. quality assurance Am. Electronic Labs., Inc., Lansdale, Pa., 1984—90, ret., 1990. Chmn. Charlestown Twp. Planning Commn., Pa., 1973-75. With U.S. Army, 1954-56. Fellow IEEE (life, pres. Reliability Soc. 1969-70, gen. chmn. Rams symposium 1968, chmn. bd. 1969, Centennial medal 1984); mem. Nat. Mgmt. Assn. (life, chmn. formation com. Am. Electronics Labs. chpt. 1985, Leadership award 1973, 86), Lake Hopatcong Yacht Club (commodore 2000-01), Masons, Rotary (Paul Harris fellow, treas.). Republican. Episcopalian. Avocations: carpentry, architecture, boating, antiques, travel. Home: 17 Bass Rock Rd Hopatcong NJ 07843-1901

REESE, HAYNE WARING, psychologist, educator; b. Comanche, Tex., Jan. 14, 1931; s. Tom F. and Marion (Waring) R.; m. Patsy Atwood, Aug. 24, 1957 (div. Apr. 1967); children: Anne, William, Margaret; m. Nancy Mann, Dec. 16, 1967; 1 child, Bradley. Student, So. Meth. U., 1949-50; BA, U. Tex., 1953, MA, 1955; PhD, U. Iowa, 1958. Asst. prof. U. Buffalo, 1958-62; assoc. prof. SUNY-Buffalo, 1962-66, prof., 1966-67, U. Kans., Lawrence, 1967-70; Centennial prof. psychology W.Va. U., Morgantown, 1970-2000, dir. grad. tng. in life-span devel. psychology, 1973-2000, Centennial prof. emeritus, 2000—. Mem. initial rev. groups div. research grants NIH, Washington, 1969-71, 74-78, 79-84; vis. prof. SUNY, Buffalo, 1970, U. Iowa, 1972, U. Hawaii, 1975, S.W. China Normal U., 1997, 2000. Author: Perception of Stimulus Relations, 1968, Basic Learning Processes in Childhood, 1976; co-author: Life-Span Developmental Psychology, 1977, 1988, Child Development, 1979; editor: Advances in Child Development and Behavior, 26 vols., 1969-2001; co-editor: Life-Span Developmental Psychology, 8 vols., 1973-97; assoc. editor: Jour. Exptl. Child Psychology, 1975-83, editor, 1983-97, mem. editl. bd. 1965-74, 98-2000. Served with U.S. Army, 1954. Fellow AAAS, Am. Psychol. Soc.; mem. Soc. for Rsch. in Child Devel., Psychonomic Soc., Assn. for Behavior Analysis, Internat. Soc. for Study Behavioral Devel. Personal E-mail: haynereese@aol.com.

REESE, JERRY WAYNE, music educator, band director; BS in Edn., Ind. State U., Terre Haute, 1970—75, MS in Edn., 1977—78. Band dir. Warrick County Schools/Castle sch. sys., Newburgh, Ind., 1978—. Mem.: Phi Beta Mu (Band Dir. Frat.). Home: 5055 East Timberwood Dr Newburgh IN 47630 Office: Castle Jr High Band Box 677 Newburgh IN 47629 Personal E-mail: jerryreese@aol.com.

REESE, JODY SUNRAY KIERAN, reporter; b. Hampton, N.S., Can., Mar. 29, 1974; d. Raymond Allan Reese and Jennifer Kieran; 1 child, Jake. BA in Polit. Sci., McGill U., 1996. Editor Leslie County Times, Thousand Sticks Times, Hyden, Ky., 1996—97; reporter Citizen Voice and Times, Irvine, Ky., 1997—99, Keene Sentinel, NH, 1999—2000, Union Leader, Manchester, NH, 2000—01, Hippo Press, Manchester, NH, 2001—. Mem.: Soc. Profl. Journalists, Kiwanis. Roman Catholic. Avocation: extreme sports.

REESE, JOHN ROBERT, lawyer; b. Salt Lake City, Nov. 3, 1939; s. Robert McCann and Glade (Stauffer) R.; m. Francesca Marroquin Gardner, Sept. 5, 1964 (div.); children: Jennifer Marie, Justine Francesca; m. Robin Ann Gunsul, June 18, 1988. AB cum laude, Harvard U., 1962; LLB, Stanford U., 1965. Bar: Calif. 1966, U.S. Dist. Ct. (no. dist.) Calif. 1966, U.S. Ct. Appeals (9th cir.) 1966, U.S. Dist. Ct. (ctrl. dist.) Calif. 1974, U.S. Supreme Ct. 1976, U.S. Dist. Ct. (ea. dist.) Calif. 1977, U.S. Ct. Appeals (6th cir.) 1982, U.S. Ct. Appeals (8th cir.) 1985, U.S. Ct. Appeals (10th cir.) 1992, U.S. Ct. Appeals (Fed. cir.) 1994. Assoc. McCutchen, Doyle, Brown & Enersen, San Francisco, 1965—74, ptnr., 1974—2002, Bingham McCutchen, San Francisco, 2002—. Adj. asst. prof. law Hastings Coll. of Law, 1991; lectr. U. Calif., Berkeley, 1987, 92. Mem. editl. and adv. bds.: Antitrust Bull., Jour. Reprints for Antitrust Law and Econs., 1981—99. Bd. dirs. Friends of San Francisco Pub. Libr., 1981-87; bd. vis. Stanford U. Law Sch., 1983-86. Capt. U.S. Army, 1966-68. Decorated Bronze Star. Mem. ABA, Am. Acad. Appellate Lawyers, State Bar Calif., San Francisco Bar Assn., U.S. Supreme Ct. Hist. Soc., Ninth Jud. Cir. Hist. Soc., Calif. Acad. Appellate Lawyers, Order of Coif. Avocation: gardening. Home: 9 Morning Sun Dr Petaluma CA 94952-4780 Office: Bingham McCutchen 3 Embarcadero Ctr San Francisco CA 94111-4003 Office Phone: 415-393-2225.

REESE, KATHERINE ROSE, music educator; b. Mannington, W.Va., July 27, 1937; m. Wallace Reese, July 29, 1955; children: Kyla O'Dell, Ann Landers. BA, W.Va. U., 1986. Cert. profl. music tchr. Artist tchr. of piano Fairmont (W.Va.) State Coll., 1986—. Address: RR 1 Box 122 Mannington WV 26582-9801

REESE, LYMON CLIFTON, civil engineering educator; b. Murfreesboro, Ark., Apr. 27, 1917; s. Samuel Wesley and Nancy Elizabeth (Daniels) R.; m. Eva Lee Jett, May 28, 1948; children: Sally Reese Melant, John, Nancy. BS, U. Tex. at Austin, 1949, MS, 1950; PhD, U. Calif. at Berkeley, 1955; D in Civil Engring. (hon.), Inst. Bucharest, Romania, 1994. Diplomate: Registered profl. engr., Tex. Internat. Boundary Commn., San Benito, Tex., 1939-41; surveyor U.S. Naval Constrn. Bns., U.S., Aleutian Islands, Okinawa, 1942-45; field engr. Assoc. Contractors & Engrs., Houston, 1945; draftsman Phillips Petroleum Co., Austin, 1946-48; research engr. U. Tex., Austin, 1948-50; asst. prof. civil engring. Miss. State Coll., 1950-51, 53-55; asst. prof. U. Tex., Austin, 1955-57, assoc. prof., 1957-64, prof., 1964—, chmn. dept., 1965-72, Taylor prof. engring., 1972-81, assoc. dean engring. for program planning, 1972-79, Nasser I. Al-Rashid Chair, 1981-84; prin. Ensoft, Inc., 1985—, Lymon C. Reese Assocs. Contbr. articles to profl. jours. Recipient Thomas Middlebrooks award ASCE, 1958; Joe J. King Profl. Engring. Achievement award, 1977, Offshore Tech. Conf. Disting. Achievement award for Individuals, 1985, Disting. grad. Coll. of Engring., U. Tex., Austin., 1985. Mem. ASCE (Karl Terzaghi lectr. 1976 Terzaghi award, 1983, Tex. sect. award of Hon. 1985, hon. mem. 1984—), Nat. Acad. Engring. Baptist (deacon). Office: U Tex Dept Civil Engring Austin TX 78712-1104 Home: 11110 Tom Adams Dr Apt F2 Austin TX 78753-3302 E-mail: lymonreese@aol.com.

REESE, MARTHA GRACE, minister, lawyer; b. Newark, Ohio, Feb. 27, 1953; d. John Gilbert and Louella Catherine (Hodges) R.; 1 child, Elizabeth Lang Harman. BA with high distinction, DePauw U., 1975; JD magna cum laude, Ind. U., 1980; MDiv magna cum laude, Christian Theol. Sem., 1989. Bar: Ind. 1980, U.S. Dist. Ct. (so. dist.) Ind. 1980, U.S. Ct. Appeals (7th cir.) 1981; ordained to ministry Christian Ch. (Disciples of Christ), 1989. Law clk. U.S. Dist. Ct. (so. dist.) Ind., 1980-82; assoc. Baker & Daniels, Indpls., 1982-83; ptnr. Wilson, Hutchens & Reese, Greencastle, Ind., 1984-86; interim assoc. regional min. The Christian Ch. in Ind. (Disciples of Christ), 1988-89; sr. min. Carmel (Ind.) Christian Ch. (Disciples of Christ), 1989-96; dir. The Bethany Project of the Christian Chs., 1996—. Cons. Lilly Endowment, Inc., 1989, 90. Steering com. Ind. Leadership Celebration, 1983-98; trustee Christian Theol. Sem., 1995-99. Mem. Phi Beta Kappa, Theta Phi. Home: 867 Tuxedo Blvd Saint Louis MO 63119-2044

REESE, MICHAEL, mathematics professor; b. Salt Lake City, Utah; SM in Elec. Engring. and Computer Sci., SB in Elec. Engring., MIT, 1985; MA in Math., U. of Calif., Santa Barbara, 1994, MA in Spanish, 1996; MA in Secondary Edn., Adams State Coll., Alamosa, Colo., 1999. Single subject profl. clear credential in math. Commn. on Credentialing, Calif. Elec. engring. intern Hewlett-Packard Co., Sunnyvale, Calif., 1982—85, Tex. Instruments, Dallas, 1985—85; elec. engr. Delco Sys. Ops., Goleta, Calif., 1986—88, Digital Sound Corp., Santa Barbara, 1988—90; writing instr. U. of Calif., Santa Barbara, 1990—94, grad. student rschr., 1994—96; tutor counselor Ind. U., Bloomington, 1996—97; vis. prof. Adams State Coll., Alamosa, 1998—99; classroom tchr. Castle Pk. H.S., Chula Vista, Calif., 1999—2000; assoc. prof. San Diego Mesa Coll., 2000—. Contbr. articles and papers to profl. jours. Reserve police officer Santa Barbara Police Dept., 1992—96; posse and rescue unit mem. Alamosa County Sheriff's Dept., 1998—99; team mem. Alamosa Vol. Search and Rescue, 1999; missionary Ch. of Jesus Christ of Latter-day Saints, Concepcion, Chile, 1979—81. Mem.: Math. Assn. of Am. Ch. Of Jesus Christ Of Latter-Day Saints. Office: 7250 Mesa College Dr San Diego CA 92111-4998

REESE, MONTE NELSON, agricultural association executive; b. Mooreland, Okla., Mar. 31, 1947; s. James Nelson and Ruby Edith (Bond) R.; m. Treisa Lou Bartow, May 25, 1968; children: Bartow Allan, Monica Lynnelle. BS in Agrl. Econs., Okla. State U., 1969. Staff asst. Wilson Cert. Foods, Oklahoma City, 1969-71; assoc. farm dir. Sta. WKY Radio and TV, Oklahoma City, 1971-73; radio-TV specialist Tex. A&M U., College Station, 1973; dir. agrl. devel. Oklahoma City C. of C., 1973-76; asst. exec. dir. Am. Morgan Horse Assn., Westmoreland, N.Y., 1976-77; v.p. pub. affairs Farm Credit Banks of Wichita, Kans., 1977-87; exec. dir. Coffey County Econ. Devel., Burlington, Kans., 1987-88; farm dir. Mid-Am. Ag Network, Wichita, 1988-89; CEO Cattlemen's Beef Promotion and Rsch. Bd., Englewood, Colo., 1989-96; exec. dir. Cattlemen's Beef Promotion & Rsch. Bd., Englewood, CO, 1996-98, COO, 1998—. Lt. col. USAR, 1969—. Office: Cattlemens Beef Promotion Rsch Bd 9110 E Nichols Ave 303 Englewood CO 80112

REESE, PATRICIA ANN, retired editor, columnist; b. Superior, Nebr., Mar. 14, 1954; d. Robert John and Billie Jo (Gooch) R. BS in Wildlife Ecology, Communications, Okla. State U., 1976. Proofreader Ada (Okla.) Evening News, 1976-77, reporter, 1977-81, wire editor, 1981-85, city editor, 1985-92, sects. editor, 1992, ret., 1992. Bd. dirs. Ada Arts and Humanities Coun., 1981-85, 92—, historian, 1982-83, sec., 1983-85, 92—, newsletter editor, 1996—, webmaster, 1998—; tech. adv., editor, webmaster Upward Bound Regional Math./Sci. Ctr., Ada, 1996—; webmaster Okla. Horseshoe Pitchers Assn., 1999—; charter mem. Seekers dept. Tanti Study Club, Ada, 1982. Recipient Carl Rogan News Excellence award Associated Press/Okla. News Execs., 1986, 90-92, Best Column award Okla. Natural Gas, 1991, Outstanding Adan in Arts award, 2000. Mem. Am. Mus. Natural History, Archaeology Inst. Am., Okla. Lupus Assn., Ada Cmty. Theatre II, Okla. Press Assn., Internat. Ceramic Inst., Soc. Environ. Journalists, Okla. Horseshoe Pitchers Assn. (webmaster 1999—). Democrat. Avocations: ceramics, painting, gardening, horses, the environment. Home: 17331 County Rd 1580 Ada OK 74820-0419 E-mail: fantasyfactory@compworldnet.com.

REESE, ROBERT M. retired lawyer; AB, Harvard U., 1972; JD, Georgetown U., 1976. Bar: Pa. 1976, D.C. 1977. Asst. counsel, staff asst. Ways & Means Com. U.S. House of Reps., 1975-76; assoc. Reed, Smith Shaw & McClay, 1976-78; counsel Hershey Foods Corp., 1978-79, staff counsel, 1979-82, sr. counsel, 1982-87, v.p., gen. counsel, 1993-98, sr. v.p., gen. counsel, sec., 1999—2004, retired, 2004. Office: Hershey Foods Corp 100 Crystal A Dr Unit 8 Hershey PA 17033-9702

REESE, STUART HARRY, insurance company executive; b. Richmond, Va., May 3, 1955; s. Allison and Virginia (Saul) R.; m. Elizabeth Garr, Aug. 21, 1976; children: Katharine, Elizabeth, Jillian, Thomas. BA, Gettysburg (Pa.) Coll., 1977; MBA, Dartmouth Coll., 1979. Securities analyst investment pvt. placements Aetna Bond, Hartford, Conn., 1979-81, sr. securities analyst dept. fin. guaranty, 1981-82, dir. treas. investment planning, 1982-83; sr. investment officer Aetna Pub. Bond Rsch., Hartford, Conn., 1983-84, asst. v.p., 1984-85; mng. dir. Aetna Pub. Bond Rsch. & Tng., Hartford, 1985-89; v.p., mng. dir. Aetna Pub. Bond, Hartford, 1989-90; v.p. Capital Markets Investment Mgmt., 1991—. Mem. investment com. Vis. Nurses Assn., Simsbury, Conn., 1991—. Mem. Hartford Soc. Fin. Analysts (v.p. bd. 1991—). Office: Aetna Life & Casualty 185 Asylum St Hartford CT 06103-3408

REESE, THOMAS FRANK, lawyer; b. Feb. 21, 1953; s. William David and Elsa Edith (Bluhm) R.; m. Laurie Ann Evans, Jan. 10, 1976. BA, U. Wyo., 1975; JD, 1981. Bar: Colo. 1982, Wyo. 1981, U.S. Dist. Ct. Wyo. 1981, U.S. Dist. Ct. Colo. 1982. Tchr. Natrona County, Casper, Wyo., 1976-78; mem. Sherman & Howard, Denver, 1981-82, Brown & Drew, Casper, Wyo., 1983—. Wyo. editor Law Rev., 1980-81. Chmn. allocations and admissions com. Natrona County United Way, 1986, bd. dirs., 1984-87, chmn. allocations and admissions com., 1986-88, campaign chmn., 1987, v.p., 1988; pres. United Fund of Natrona County Found., 1987. L.W. Maxfield scholar, 1979-80; Bugas Law scholar, 1980. Mem. Wyo. Bar Assn., ABA, Phi Kappa Phi. Presbyterian. Home: 3520 Valley Rd Casper WY 82604-4906 Office: Brown Drew Massey LLP 159 W Wolcott Ste 200 Casper WY 82601-2486 Office Phone: 307-234-1000. E-mail: tfr@browndrew.com.

REESE, WILLIAM ALBERT, III, psychologist, clinical neuropsychologist; b. Tabor, Iowa, Nov. 23, 1932; s. William Albert and Mary-Evelyn Hope (Lundeen) R.; m. Barbara Diane Windermere, Dec. 22, 1954 (dec. Jan. 1995); children: Judy, Diane William IV, Sandra-Siobhan, Debra-Anne, Robert-Gregory, Barbara-Joanne; m. Ruth Alice Moller, Sept 12, 1996. BA, U. Wash. Reed Coll., 1955; MEd, U. Ariz., 1964, PhD, 1981; postgrad., Fielding Inst. Clin. Neuropsychology, 2000. Diplomate Am. Bd. Christian Psychology, Am. Bd. Forensic Psychologists, Am. Coll. Advanced Practice Psychologists, Prescribing Psychologists Register; cert. in clin. neuropsychology. Clin. psychology cons. Nogales Pub. Schs., Nogales-Tucson, Ariz., 1971-79; clin. psychologist Astra-Found., NYC, 1979-86, chief psychology svc., neuropsychiatry, 1980-89; chief psychologist Family Support Ctr. Cmty.-Family Exception Mem. Svcs., Sonoita, Ariz., 1986-89, Psychol. Svc. Ctr., Mount Tabor, Iowa, 1989-95, Calif. Ctr. Health and Wellness, 1995—; clin. psychologist Calif. Dept. Corrections, 1997—. Dir. religious Marriage and Family Life Wilderness Ctr., Berchtesgaden, Germany, 1981-82; exec. sec. Astra Ednl. Found, 1975-79, bd. dirs, 1979—, EEO officer, 1978—. Author: Developing a Scale of Human Values for Adults of Diverse Cultural Backgrounds, 1981, rev. edit., 1988. Served with USAF, 1967-71, Vietnam. Decorated Bronze Star; fellow in cons. psychology and holistic medicine Clin. Svcs. Found., Ariz., 1979—. Fellow Am. Psychol. Soc., Am. Coll. Forensic Examiners, Clin. Neuropsychiatry and Neuropsychology, 1998; mem. APA, ACA, Internat. Neuropsychol. Assn., Calif. Psychol. Assn., Iowa Psychol. Assn., KC, Los Padres Wilderness Ctr., Outdoor Club, Sierra Club, Skyline Estates Golf and Country Club (Tucson). Office: AstraWorldMedicineUSA com 798 Lighthouse Ave Ste 323 Monterey CA 93940-1010 Office Phone: 831-238-3910. Personal E-mail: psylawreese@aol.com.

REESE, WILLIAM LEWIS, philosophy educator; b. Jefferson City, Mo., Feb. 15, 1921; s. William Lewis and Lillian Amelia (Fisher) R.; m. Louise Weeks, June 11, 1945; children: Claudia, Patricia, William Lewis III. AB, Drury Coll., 1942; B.D., U. Chgo., 1945, PhD, 1947; postdoctoral, Yale U., 1955-56. Asst. prof. philosophy Drake U., 1947-49, assoc. prof. philosophy, 1949-57, head dept., 1954-57; asso. prof. philosophy Grinnell Coll., 1957-60; vis. prof. philosophy Iowa State U., 1958; prof. philosophy, chmn. dept. U. Del., Newark, 1960-67, dir. seminar in philosophy of sci., 1960-66, H. Rodney Sharp prof. philosophy, 1965-67; prof. philosophy SUNY-Albany, 1967-99, chmn. dept., 1968-74, 84, prof. philosophy emeritus, rsch. prof. philosophy, 1999—. Tully Cleon Knoles lectr. U. Pacific, 1962; del. U.S. Nat. Commn. for UNESCO, 1963; gen. mem. 4th East-West Philosophers Conf., 1964 Author, contbr.: Studies in C.S. Peirce, 1952, (with Charles Hartshorne) Philosophers Speak of God, 1953, 2d edit., 2000, The Ascent from Below, 1959, 2d edit., 2000, (with Eugene Freeman) Process and Divinity, 1964, Dictionary of Philosophy and Religion: Eastern and Western Thought, 1980, 3d edit., 1999, Freedom, 2000, Values, 2000; gen. editor: Philosophy of Science, The Delaware Seminar, vols. 1, 2, 1963, vol. 3, 1967; editor: Philosophy and World Religions: The Reader's Adviser, vol. 4, 1988, Fundamental Issues in Philosophy Series, 2000-75; editl. bd.: State of N.Y. Press, 1968-78; contbr. articles to profl. jours. Recipient Ford Found. Study award Argentina, 1967; Fulbright lectr. Argentina, summer 1971; Inst. Humanistic Studies fellow, 1977— Mem.: AAUP, Metaphysical Soc. Am. (sec. 1962—65, treas. 1962—65), Am. Philos. Assn. Mem. Christian Ch. (Disciples Of Christ). Home: Font Grove Rd Slingerlands NY 12159 Office: SUNY Dept Philosophy Albany NY 12222-0001 Business E-Mail: wlr@albany.edu. E-mail: reesewl@cs.com. *To have before one always the realistic sense that if one has been successful in one way one has failed in others, and that one's failures surely outnumber one's successes.*

REEVE, CHRISTOPHER, actor; b. NYC, Sept. 25, 1952; s. Franklin D. and Barbara (Johnson) R.; children: Matthew, Alexandra; m. Dana Morosini, 1 son, Will. BA, Cornell U., 1974; student, Juilliard Sch., N.Y.C.; studies with, Austin Pendleton, Sandra Seacat; Ph.D (hon.), Boston U., 1997, Pace U., 1998. Chmn. Christopher Reeve Paralysis Found., 1999—. Founder, pres., The Creative Coalition, 1989-91 Performed in theaters including Boothbay (Maine) Playhouse, The Williamstown (Mass.) Theatre, San Diego Shakespeare Festival, The Loeb Drama Center; appeared on Broadway with Katherine Hepburn, A Matter of Gravity, 1976, Fifth of July, 1980, The Winter's Tale, 1989; films include Gray Lady Down, 1978, Superman, 1978, Somewhere in Time, 1980, Superman II, 1980, Deathtrap, 1982, Monsignor, 1982, Superman III, 1983, The Bostonians, 1984, The Aviator, 1984, Street Smart, 1987, Superman IV, 1987, Switching Channels, 1988, Noises Off, 1992, The Remains of the Day, 1993, Morning Glory, 1993, Speechless, 1994, The Rhinehart Theory, 1994, Village of the Damned, 1995, A Step Toward Tomorrow, 1996; appeared in over 110 plays including My Life, 1977, The Greeks, Williamstown Theatre Festival prodn., 1981, The Aspern Papers, London prodn., 1984, Marriage of Figaro, 1985, Summer and Smoke, Los Angeles prodn., 1988, also The Royal Family, Holiday, Richard Corey, Mesmer, Cherry Orchard; appeared in John Brown's Body (Stephen Vincent

Benet), Williamstown Theatre Festival, 1989; TV appearances include: (series) Love of Life, 1968-76; (TV movies) Anna Karenina, 1985, The Great Escape II: The Untold Story, 1988, The Rose and the Jackal, 1990, Bump in the Night, 1991, Death Dreams, 1991, Mortal Sins, 1992, Nightmare in the Daylight, 1992, The Sea Wolf, 1993, Above Suspicion, 1995, The Black Fox, 1995, Black Fox: Good Men and Bad, Nine (voice), 1996, A Step Toward Tomorrow, 1996, Rear Window (also exec. prodr.), 1998, The Toughest Break: Martin's Story, 1998; (TV appearances):Frasier, 1993, The Practice, 2002, Smallville, 2002, 03; dir. (movies) In the Gloaming, 2000; exec. prodr. Freedom: A History of Us, 2002. author: Still Me, 1998, (Grammy award, 1999), Nothing Is Impossible: Reflections on A New Life, 2002. Co-founder Christopher and Dana Reeves Paralysis Ctr., 2002. Spl. Obie award, 1998, Annual award, Walter Briehl Human Rights Found., 1998, Albert Lasker award for Service in Support of Medical Rsch., Lasker Found, 2003. Mem., bd. dirs., Save the Children, 1976- Amnesty Internat., 1976-, Nat. Resources. Def. Coun., 1976-, Environmental Air Force, 1976-, America's Watch, 1976-, Nat. Org. on Disability, 1997. Office: Christopher Reeve Paralysis Found 500 Morris Ave Springfield NJ 07081 also: William Morris Agy care Scott Henderson 151 S El Camino Dr Beverly Hills CA 90212-2775 Office Phone: 800-225-0292.*

REEVE, FRANKLIN D. writer, literature educator; b. Phila., Sept. 18, 1928; m. Laura C. Stevenson, 1997; children: Christopher, Benjamin, Alison, Brock, Mark, Katharine, Margaret. AB, Princeton U., 1950; PhD, Columbia U., 1958; AM (hon.), Wesleyan, 1964; LittD (hon.), New Eng. Coll., 2004. Instr., asst. prof. Columbia U., N.Y.C., 1952-61; assoc. prof. Wesleyan U., Middletown, Conn., 1962-66, adj. prof., 1967-87, prof., 1988—2002, prof. emeritus, 2002—. Founding editor The Poetry Rev., 1982—84; bd. govs., v.p. Poetry Soc. Am., 1976—84; sec. Poets House, NYC, 1985—99; bd. govs. Transl. Ctr., NYC, 1980—94; vis. prof. Oxford (Eng.) U., 1964, Columbia U., 1988, Marlboro Vt. Coll., 1999; bd. dirs. Marlboro Rev.; vis. scholar, Moscow, 1961; vis. lectr. Yale U., New Haven, 1972—84; assoc. fellow Saybrook Coll., 1972—; program scholar Vt. Coun. on Humanities; faculty MFA program in creative writing New Eng. Coll., 2003—; lectr. poetry Ctr., N.Y.C., 1980—84; lectr. USAID, 1999; cons. in field. Author: Aleksandr Blok: Between Image and Idea, 1962, 2d edit., 1981, Robert Frost in Russia, 1964, 2d edit., 2001, The Russian Novel, 1966, The Red Machines, 1968, In the Silent Stones, 1968, Just Over the Border, 1969, The Brother, 1971, The Blue Cat, 1972, White Colors, 1974, The White Monk, 1989; author: (edited with Jay Meek) After the Storm, 1991; author: Concrete Music, 1992; editor: Winged Sprits, 1995, A Few Rounds of Old Maid and Other Stories, 1995, The Moon and Other Failures, 1999, (poetry) A World You Haven't Seen, 2001, The Urban Stampede and Other Poems, 2002; translator: Five Short Novels by Turgenev, 1961, Anthology of Russian Plays, 2 vols., 1961, 1963, 1975, 1991, Contemporary Russian Drama, 1968, The Garden by Bella Akhmadulina, 1990, The Trouble with Reason by Alexander Griboyekov, 1993, The King and the Fool by Alexander Borschagovsky, 2001; mem. editl. bd. Marlboro Rev. Trustee Pettee Meml. Libr. Recipient Lit. award Am. Acad.-Nat. Inst., 1970, Lifetime Golden Rose award New Eng. Poetry Soc., 1994, Binswanger Excellence in Tchg. award Wesleyan U., 2002, May Sarton award, 1999. Mem.: New Eng. Poetry Club (bd. dirs. 1996—). Home: PO Box 14 Wilmington VT 05363-0014

REEVE, IVAN LEON, physician; b. Sept. 2, 1930; BA, Pacific Union Coll., 1957; MD, Loma Linda U., 1961. Diplomate Am. Bd. Family Physicians, Am. Bd. Managed Care Medicine. Clin. asst. prof. family medicine Coll. Osteopathic Medicine, Pomona, Calif., 1998; mem. faculty Loma Linda (Calif.) U., 1998; physician Loma Linda Family Med. Group, 1999—. Fellow Am. Acad. Family Physicians (charter). Office: Loma Linda Family Med Group 11370 Anderson St Ste 1050 Loma Linda CA 92354-3450

REEVE, JOHN NEWTON, molecular biology and microbiology educator; b. Wakefield, W. Yorkshire, Eng., June 21, 1947; came to U.S., 1979; s. Arthur Newton and Lilian Elsworth (Tallant) R.; m. Patricia Margaret Watson, Sept. 21, 1967; children: Simon Arthur, Daniel John. BS with 1st class honors, U. Birmingham, Eng., 1968; PhD, U. B.C., Vancouver, Can., 1971. Rsch. scientist U. Ariz., Tucson, 1971-73, Nat. Inst. Med. Rsch., Mill Hill, London, 1973-74; rsch. dir. Max-Planck Inst., Berlin, 1974-79; prof. microbiology Ohio State U., Columbus, 1979—, chmn. dept., 1985—, Rod Sharp prof. microbiology, 1999—. Cons. Battelle Rsch. Lab., Columbus, 1982-87, Govt. of Bulgaria, Sofia, 1987, Promega Corp., Madison, Wis., 1990, Procter and Gamble Co., Cin., 1990; mem. sci. adv. bd. BioTrol. Inc., Chaska, Minn., 1986-90; Disting. vis. prof. U. Adelaide, Australia, 1984, U. Wyo., Laramie, 1988, U. Calcutta, India, 1989, Frei U., Berlin, 1991, U. Karachi, Pakistan, 1995, U. Concepcion, Chile, 1995; governing coun. So. Petrochems. Corp., Chennai, India, 1999—; chmn. biosci. coun. Dept. of Energy, 2001—; mng. editor Extremophiles, 2003—. Named Disting. Rsch. Scholar Ohio State U., 1989. Mem. Am. Soc. for Microbiology (lectr. Found. for Microbiology 1987-88, 94-96. chmn. divsn. K, microbial physiol. 1998-99, coun. 2000-2002, US nat. organizing com. for 2005 Internat. Congress of Microbiology Socs., 2002—). Office: Ohio State U Dept of Microbiology 484 W 12th Ave Columbus OH 43210-1214 Office Phone: 614-292-2301. Office Fax: 614-292-8120. Business E-Mail: reeve.2@osu.edu.

REEVE, LEE M. farmer; married; 3 children. BS in Agr. Econs., Kans. State U. Group mgr., owner Reeve Cattle Co., Garden City, Kans. Bd. dirs. Fidelity State Bank, Garden City, Garden City C. of C., Beef Empire Days, Garden City Fed. Land Bank. Mem. Agr. Value Added Processing Leadership Coun.; bd. dirs. Agrl. non-Food Use Task Force; mem. Kans. Coun. Vocat. Edn., Alt. Agr. Rsch. & Commercialization bd. Recipient Innovator of Yr. award State Bd. Agr., Environ. Achievement award Nat. Environ. Awards Coun., Wheeler McMillan award New Uses Coun., Disting. Agrl. Econs. Alumnus Kans. State U. Office: Reeve Cattle Co PO Box 1036 Garden City KS 67846-1036

REEVE, PAMELA, communications executive; MBA with distinction, Harvard Bus. Sch.; BA with honors, U. Ga. Pres., CEO Lightbridge, Burlington, Mass., 1989—. Bd. trustees Mass. Software Coun. Office: Lightbridge Inc 67 S Bedford St Burlington MA 01803-5152 Fax: 781-359-4500.

REEVES, ALAN M. automotive company executive; Pres. Spalding Ford-Lincoln-Mercury, Inc., Griffin, Ga., 1982, Spalding Automotive Group, Griffin, 1982—. Recipient Award Black Enterprise, 1991. Office: Spalding Ford O Box 819 Experiment GA 30212-0819

REEVES, BARBARA ANN, lawyer; b. Buffalo, Mar. 29, 1949; d. Prentice W. and Doris Reeves; m. Richard C. Neal; children: Timothy R. Neal, Stephen S. Neal (dec.), Robert S. Neal, Richard R. Neal. Student, Wellesley Coll., 1967-68; BA (NSF fellow, Lehman fellow), New Coll., Sarasota, Fla., 1970; JD cum laude, Harvard U., 1973. Bar: Calif. 1973, D.C. 1977. Law clk. U.S. Ct. Appeals, 9th Circuit, Portland, Oreg., 1973-74; assoc. firm Munger, Tolles and Rickershauser, L.A., 1977-78; trial atty. spl. trial sect. Dept. Justice (Antitrust div.), 1974-75; spl. asst. to asst. atty. gen. Antitrust div. Dept. Justice, Washington, 1976-77; chief antitrust div. L.A. field office, 1978-81; ptnr. Morrison & Foerster, L.A., 1981-94, Fried, Frank, Harris, Shriver & Jacobson, L.A., 1995-97, Paul, Hastings, Janofsky & Walker, L.A., 1997—. Mem. exec. com. state bar conf. of dels. L.A. Delegation, 1982-91; del. 9th Cir. Jud. Conf., 1984-88; mem. Fed. Ct. Magistrate Selection Com., 1989; bd. dirs. Pub. Counsel, 1988-92, Western Ctr. Law and Poverty, 1992-98; lectr. in field. Editor: Federal Criminal Litigation, 1994; contbg. author: World Antitrust Law, 1995; contbr. articles to profl. jours. Mem. ABA (litigation sect., antitrust sect.), Fed. Bar Assn. (officer 1998—), Assn. Bus. Trial Lawyers (officer 1997—), Am. Arbitration Assn. (arbitrator, mediator, mem. adv. panel large complex case program), L.A. County Bar Assn. (antitrust sect. officer 1980-81, litigation sect. officer 1988-93 trustee 1990-92, chair alternative dispute resolution sec. 1992-95, L.A. County Ct. ADR com.). Home: 1410 Hillcrest Ave Pasadena CA 91106-4503 Office: Paul Hastings Janofsky & Walker 555 S Flower St Fl 23D Los Angeles CA 90071-2300

REEVES, DANIEL EDWARD, former professional football coach; b. Rome, Ga., Jan. 19, 1944; m. Pam Reeves; children: Dana, Laura, Lee. Grad., U. S.C. Running back Dallas Cowboys, NFL, 1965-72, player-coach, 1970-71, asst. coach, 1972, 74-80; head coach Denver Broncos, NFL, 1981-92, also v.p.; head coach N.Y. Giants, 1993-96, Atlanta Falcons, 1997—2003. Recipient NFL Coach of the Year award, 1984, 1989, 1991, 1993, 1998; named to S.C. Hall Fame.*

REEVES, DANIEL MARTIN, computer scientist; s. Laurie Kalkman and Martin Reeves. PhD, U. Mich., 2004. Mem. staff U. Mich., Ann Arbor. Mem.: Am. Assn. Artificial Intelligence. Avocations: skiing, inline skating, hiking, philosophy. Home: 1915 Pointe Ln #301 Ann Arbor MI 48105 Office: U Mich 1101 Beal Ave Ann Arbor MI 48109 Personal E-mail: dreeves@umich.edu. E-mail: dreeves@umich.edu.

REEVES, EDMUND HOFFMAN, III, food products executive; b. Easton, Pa., Sept. 14, 1949; s. Edmund Hoffman Jr. and Constance Irene (Bartholomew) R.; children: Courtney Ann, Edmund Hoffman IV, Brendan Gill. BA in Econs., Lynchburg Coll., 1972; MBA in Food Mktg., St. Joseph's U., Phila., 1979. With Am. Stores, Inc., 1972-81, Shaffer Clarke & Co., Inc., Old Greenwich, Conn., 1982—88, R.W. Frookies, Inc., 1988—90, Yankee Food Distributors, Ayer, Mass., 1990-92; v.p., gen. mgr. Am. Specialty Brands, Fargo, N.D., 1992-96; dir. U.S. sales Billy Bee Honey Products, Ltd., 1997-2000; v.p. sales & mktg. ZBI Foods, Inc., 2001—. Alumni bd. dirs. Lynchburg Coll., 1989—91; asst. cubmaster, com. chmn. Boy Scouts Am., Trumbull, Conn. Mem. Nat. Food Distbr. Assn., Nat. Assn. Splty. Food Trade Republican. Episcopalian. Avocations: pvt. piloting, boating, woodworking, photography, antiques. Home: PO Box 320537 Fairfield CT 06825-0537 E-mail: reeves3@attglobal.net.

REEVES, GENE, judge; b. Meridian, Miss., Feb. 27, 1930; s. Clarence Eugene and May (Philyaw) R.; m. Brenda Wages, Sept. 26, 1980. JD, John Marshall U., 1964; cert. judge spl. ct. jurisdiction; postgrad., U. Nev., 1995. Bar: Ga. 1964, U.S. Ct. Appeals (11th cir.) 1965, U.S. Supreme Ct. 1969. Ptnr. Craig & Reeves, Lawrenceville, Ga., 1964-71; sole practice Lawrenceville, 1971-85; prin. Reeves Law Firm, 1985-94; judge City Ct., Lawrenceville, 1969-70, Magistrate Ct. of Gwinnett County, Ga., 1994—. Sgt. USAF, 1951-54. Mem. ABA, ATLA, GTLA, Am. Jud. Soc., Gwinnett County Bar Assn. (pres. 1970-72), Criminal Def. Lawyers Assn., Atlanta Bar Assn. Baptist. Home: 221 Pineview Dr Lawrenceville GA 30045-6035 Office: 75 Langley Dr Lawrenceville GA 30045-6935 Office Phone: 770-822-8087. E-mail: GREEV@mindspring.com.

REEVES, JOHN DRUMMOND, English language professional, writer; b. Troy, N.Y., Dec. 8, 1914; s. Robert Brockway and Emma Caroline (Mausert) R.; m. Mary Markwick Moore, Sept. 1, 1951. AB, Williams Coll., Williamstown, Mass., 1937; AM, Columbia U., 1941. Instr. in Eng. Irving Sch., Tarrytown, N.Y., 1937-40, Horace Mann Sch., N.Y.C., 1940-41, 46-47; asst. prof. of classics and Eng. Whitman Coll., Walla Walla, Wash., 1956-62; assoc. prof. English Millikin U., Decatur, Ill., 1962-65; lectr. in Eng. Hofstra U., Hempstead, N.Y., 1965-73, ret., 1973. Author: Windows on Melville, 2001; contbr. articles to profl. jours. Lt. USNR, 1941-45, PTO. Mem. AAUP, Coll. Eng. Assn., Am. Coun. Learned Soc. (reg. assoc. 1957-59), Walla Walla Archaeol. Assn. (pres. 1959-62), SR (N.Y. state chpt.), Masons. Home: 20 Devonwood Dr Apt 161 Farmington CT 06032-1422

REEVES, KATHLEEN WALKER, English and French language educator; b. Mt. Pleasant, Mich., Dec. 7, 1950; d. John J. and Gladys M. W.; m. Daniel H. Reeves, Mar. 10, 1972; children: Sheila, Michael. BA, Ctrl. Mich. U., 1973, MA, 1984. Cert. early adolescent English language arts tchr. English and French tchr. Shepherd (Mich.) High Sch., 1973-76, Chippewa Hills High Sch., Remus, Mich., 1978-79, Onekama (Mich.) Pub. Sch., 1983-86; English tchr. Seaholm High Sch., Birmingham, Mich., 1986—. Field test participant Nat. Bd. Profl. Tchg. Stds., Detroit, 1993—; adv. liaison Instrn. and Devel. of Mich. Ednl. Assn., Lansing, 1994—; bd. dirs. Mich. Assn. Tchr. Edn., Lansing, 1996-97. Troop leader Girl Scouts U.S., Dearborn, Mich., 1988-90; asst. gen. Boy Scouts Am., Dearborn, 1990—. Mem. Nat. Coun. Tchrs. of English (pres. 1973), Assn. for Supervision & Curriculum Devel., Mich. Assn. Tchrs. of French, Birmingham Ednl. Assn. (v.p. 1994—, disting. svc. award 1989, 91, 93). Democrat. Roman Catholic. Avocations: gardening, camping, reading, cooking. Home: 1020 N York St Dearborn MI 48128-1754 Office: Seaholm High Sch 2436 W Lincoln St Birmingham MI 48009-1898

REEVES, KEANU, actor; b. Beirut, Sept. 2, 1964; Stage appearances: Wolf Boy (debut), For Adults Only, Romeo and Juliet; films: Flying, 1986, Youngblood, 1986, River's Edge, 1987, Permanent Record, 1988, The Night Before, 1988, The Prince of Pennsylvania, 1988, Dangerous Liaisons, 1988, BIll and Ted's Excellent Adventure, 1989, Parenthood, 1989, I Love You to Death, 1990, Tune in Tomorrow, 1990, Bill and Ted's Bogus Journey, 1991, Point Break, 1991, My Own Private Idaho, 1991, Bram Stoker's Dracula, 1992, Much Ado About Nothing, 1993, Little Buddha, 1994, Even Cowgirls Get the Blues, 1994, Speed, 1994, Johnny Mnemonic, 1995, A Walk in the Clouds, 1995, Feeling Minnesota, 1996, Chain Reaction, 1996, Devil's Advocate, 1997, The Last Time I Committed Suicide, 1997, The Matrix, 1999, The Replacements, 2000, The Watcher, 2000, The Gift, 2000, Hard Ball, 2001, Sweet November, 2001, The Matrix Reloaded, 2003, The Matrix Revolutions, 2003, Something's Gotta Give, 2003; TV films: Letting Go, 1985, Act of Vengeance, 1986, Young Again, 1986, Babes in Toyland, 1986, Under the Influence, 1986, Brotherhood of Justice, 1986, Children Remember the Holocaust, 1995, Me and Will, 1998; TV special: Save the Planet, 1990. Office: Creative Artists Agy care Kevin Houvane 9830 Wilshire Blvd Beverly Hills CA 90212-1825

REEVES, LUCY MARY, retired secondary school educator; b. Pewamo, Mich., July 2, 1932; d. Lavaldin Edgar and Marian S. (Lee) Hull; m. Walter Emery Reeves, Jan. 21, 1922. BS, Western Mich. U., Kalamazoo, 1965; postgrad., Western Mich. U., 1965-75. Tchr. Country Sch. One Room, Matherton, Mich., 1956-57, Ionia, Mich., 1957-58, Belding, Mich., 1958-62, Saranac, Mich., Belding, Mich., 1965, Belding (Mich.) Area Schs., 1965-89; ret., 1989. Vol. Frederick Meijers Garden, Grand Rapids, Point Man Internat. Ministries, Shiloh Cmty. Ch., United Meml. Health Ctr., Shiloh Cmty. Ch.; vol. United Meml. Health Ctr., Greenville. Mem. NEA, Mich. Edn. Assn., Belding Area Edn., Profl. Businesswomen's Assn. Avocations: computers, reading, travel, sewing.

REEVES, PAMELA, lawyer; b. Marion, Va., July 21, 1954; BA, U. Tenn., 9176, JD, 1979. Bar: Tenn. 1979, U.S. Dist. Ct. (ea. and mid. dists.) Tenn. 1979, U.S. Ct. Appeals (6th cir.), U.S. Supreme Ct. Ptnr. Watson Hollow & Reeves, PLC, Knoxville. Lectr. employment related issues, ethics, and professionalism and civil procedure Knoxville Bar Assn., Tenn. Bar Assn., 1991—. Mem. U. Tenn. Law Rev., 1976; contbr. articles to profl. jours. Mem. ABA, Tenn. Bar Found., Tenn. Bar Assn. (pres. 1998, pres. young lawyers cons. 1989-90, ho. dels. 1987-92), Knoxville Bar Assn. (pres. Knoxville barristers 1983, sec. 1994-96), Am. Inns of Ct. (master of the bench, adminstr. 1994), Phi Beta Kappa. Office: Watson Hollow & Reeves PC 1700 First Tennessee Plz PO Box 131 Knoxville TN 37901-0131 E-mail: swaneeves@mindpsring.com.

REEVES, PEGGY, state legislator; b. Macon, Feb. 20, 1941; m. F. Brent Reeves. BS, Dominican Coll., 1963. Neurophysiology rsch. technician, 1963-64; sci. tchr., 1964-65, sales and broker-assoc. Bartran Homes, 1978-80; broker-assoc. Wheeler Realty, 1983—; mem. Colo. Ho. of Reps., Denver, 1982-84, 87-96, Colo. Senate, Dist. 14, Denver, 1996—; mem. appropriations com., mem. legis. audit com.; mem. health, environment, welfare and instns. com.; mem. local govt. com. Mem. Ft. Collins City Coun., 1973-77, 79-82, Ft. Collins Water Bd., 1977-79; mem. Women's Econ. Devel. Coun., 1988X; mem. One West Art Ctr., Ft. Collins Cmty. Found., Alliance for Children with Disabilities; mem. adv. bd. Colo. Mcpl. Bond Supervision, Vet. Medicine. Mem. AAUW, Colo. State U. Women's Assn., Nat. Assn. Realtors, Colo. Assn. Realtors, Ft. Collins Bd. Realtors. Office: State Capitol 200 E Colfax Ave Ste 274 Denver CO 80203-1716

REEVES, RALPH BERNARD, III, publisher, editor; b. Raleigh, N.C., Apr. 2, 1947; s. Ralph Bernard Reeves Jr. and Frances Rhoda (Campbell) M.; m. Caroline Holton Green, Apr. 24, 1971 (div. 1986); children: Ralph B. IV, Daniel MacQuarrie; m. Katherine Drewry Reid, June 20, 1998. AB in History, U. N.C., 1970. Field coord. FMI Mgmt. Group, Raleigh, N.C., 1972-76; gen. mgr., v.p. The Leader Newspaper, Rsch. Triangle Pk., N.C., 1976-78; pres., pub., founder Spectator Pubs. Inc., Raleigh, N.C., 1978-98, Triad Bus., Greensboro, N.C., 1986-88, Triangle Bus., Raleigh, 1985-91, Spectator Pub., N.C. Architect, 1981-84; pres. Reeves Media, 1998—; pub., editor Raleigh Metro Mag., 1999—. Editor: Mr. Spectator, 1978—98; author: (monthly column) My Usual Charming Self in Metro Mag. 1st v.p. Mordecai Square Hist. Soc., Raleigh, NC, 1980—83; pres. Hilltop Home, 1982—84; coun. mem. N.C. Mus. Art; founder Raleigh Internat. Spy Conf.; chmn. Downtown Adv. Com., 1983—85; bus. adv. com. N.C. Sec. of State, Raleigh, 1992—; bd. dirs. N.C. State U. Friends of Libr., Carolina Ballet. Gov.'s. Bus. award in the Arts and Humanities, 1986, Benjamin Fine award, 1991, AABP award Triangle Bus., 1st place award Feature Writing, 1991. Mem. Fifty Group, English Speaking Union (past pres. RTP br. 1988—), Carolina Co. Club, Sphinx Club. Republican. Episcopalian. Avocations: golf, history, travel. Home: 3066 Granville Dr Raleigh NC 27609 E-mail: reevesmedia@msn.com

REEVES, ROSSER SCOTT, III, retired investment company executive; b. N.Y.C., Aug. 20, 1936; s. Rosser and Elizabeth (Street) R.; m. Colin McRae Squibb, Dec. 14, 1963; 1 dau., Elizabeth Robinson. Acad. degree with honors, Westminster Sch., 1954; postgrad., Yale, 1954-55; BS with honors in architecture, U. Va., 1961. Assoc. real estate firm Douglas L. Elliman & Co., N.Y.C., 1961-62; investment banker Lazard Freres & Co., N.Y.C., 1962-67; founder, mng. partner R.S. Reeves & Co., N.Y.C., 1967-68; sr. mng. partner Bacon, Stevenson & Reeves, N.Y.C., 1968-70; chmn. bd. Quantum Corp., N.Y.C., 1970-75; pres. Rosser Reeves Holdings, Ltd., N.Y.C., 1975—; pres., chief exec. officer dir. Rosser Reeves, Inc., N.Y.C., 1976—; pres. Charlie O Co., 1980-82; pres., chief exec. officer Tiderock Corp., Little Rock, Ark., 1990—. Founder, CEO The Recovery Found., 1992—; mem. N.Y. Stock Exch., 1967-69; mng. ptnr. Wall St. Leasing Assn., 1968-70; chmn. bd. Internat. Subsea Devel. Corp., N.Y.C., 1969-75, Mil. Armament Corp., N.Y.C., 1969-75. Trustee Youth Consultation Service, N.Y.C., 1968-72; bd. dirs. Ark. Symphony Orch., 1982-85, St. Charles Cmty. Assn., 1997—; chmn. St. Charles Lighting Improvement Dist., 1998—. Mem. Scarab. Clubs: Union League (N.Y.C.), Racquet and Tennis (N.Y.C.), N.Y. Stock Exchange Lunch (N.Y.C.); Little Rock (Ark.). Home: 14201 Orleans Dr Little Rock AR 72211-5549 E-mail: scottr@spiritus.org.

REEVES, SAMANTHA, professional tennis player; b. Redwood City, Calif., Jan. 17, 1979; d. Jack and Jill. Profl. tennis player, 1995—. Recipient Ranked #1 in U.S. 18-and-under divsn., 1996, WTA Tours Doubles Titles, Quebec City, 2001, 2002, Ranked #76, WTA, Ranked #12 Among U.S. Players, Highest Season Ending Singles Ranking #101, 2002, 2 Women's Circuit Singles Titles, ITF, Rookie of the Yr., 2002, World Team Tennis MVP, 2003. Office: WTA Tour Corporate Headquarters One Progress Plz Ste 1500 Saint Petersburg FL 33701

REEVES, VAN KIRK, lawyer; b. N.Y.C., May 14, 1939; arrived in France, 1967; s. William Harvey and Caroline (Buck) R.; m. Ann Murchison, June 24, 1967; children: Daisy Fiona, Evander James. BA, Harvard U., 1961, JD, 1964. Ptnr. Coudert Frères, Paris, 1973-95, Coudert Bros., N.Y.C., 1973-95, Porter & Reeves, Paris, 1995—. Mem. Ctr. du Droit de l'Art, Geneva, 1998—, Mona Bismark Found. Author: Confessions of an Art Lawyer, 1997, The Structure and Financing of Art Transactions, 1994; co-author: (with Dr. J. Boll) Auction Sales and Conditions, 1991. Bd. mem., v.p. Internat. Coun. Muss. Found., Paris, 1972-95; bd. suprs. Am. Tax Inst., London, 1978; bd. mem. Fabergè Arts Found., Washington, 1992. Mem. Inst. Internat. Bus. Law and Practice (assoc. mem.). Avocations: projects for the preservation of cultural heritage, hiking. Home: 8 Cité Nicolas Poussin 240 Blvd Raspail 75014 Paris France Office: Porter & Reeves 5 Rue Cambon 75001 Paris France

REEVY-MANNING, GRETCHEN MARIA, psychology educator; b. Cortland, N.Y., Oct. 17, 1964; d. William Robert and Carole May Reevy; m. Todd Royal Manning. AB in Psychology, U. N.C., 1986; PhD in Psychology, U. Calif., Berkeley, 1994. Lectr. psychology dept. Dominican Coll., San Rafael, Calif., 1993—98; lectr. U. Calif., Davis, 1994, Profl. Sch. Psychology, San Francisco, 1995; lectr. psychology dept. Calif. State U., Hayward, 1994—. Grantee, Rand Corp., 1993. Mem.: APA, Soc. Psychol. Study of Social Issues, Western Psychol. Assn., Phi Beta Kappa, Psi Chi. Avocations: swimming, reading. Office: Calif State U Psychology Dept Hayward CA 94542 Office Phone: 510-885-3421. Business E-Mail: greevy@csuhayward.edu.

REFAI, SHAHID, history professor; b. Baroda, Gujarat, India, Dec. 17, 1936; s. Zainulabedin Badruddin and Afzal Banu R.; m. Shama Banu Nagamia, May 19, 1963 (div. Mar. 1998); children: Irfan, Saba, Farah, Aslam; m. Sartaj Banu Kazi, Aug. 16, 1998. BA magna cum laude, MS U., Baroda, India, 1959, MA summa cum laude, 1962; PhD, Cambridge U., 1968. Asst. prof. Cen. Wash. U., Ellensburg, 1971-77; assoc. prof. Coll. St. Rose, Albany, NY, 1977-82, 84-88, prof. of history, 1988—. Vis. lectr. UCLA, 1969-70, U. Calif. Berkeley, 1971; adj. assoc. prof. Cen. Wash. U., Ellensburg, 1983-84; pres. N.Y. Conf. on Asian Studies, New Paltz, N.Y., 1999-2001, chmn. 2000. Contbr. essays to profl. publs. Gen. sec. Tri-City India Assn., Albany, 1985-88, bd. dirs., 1988-91; organizer and coord. Sunday Urdu Sch. of Albany, 1990-95; judge Nat. History Day, Inc., Seattle, 1984; panelist Assn. for Asian Studies, U. Mich., Ann Arbor. Recipient Lady Mountbatton award Cambridge, 1967, scholarship Bombay-Cambridge Soc., 1964-66, others. Avocations: rare book collecting, computers, indian music, videography. Office: Coll of St Rose 432 Western Ave Albany NY 12203-1419 E-mail: refais@mail.strose.edu.

REGALA, DEBBIE, state senator; b. Tacoma, Apr. 27, 1945; m. Leo Regala; children: Alisa, Tim, Jonathan. BA in Fgn. Lang., Edn., U. Puget Sound. Dem. rep. dist. 27 Wash. Ho. of Reps., 1994-2000; Dem. senator dist. 27 Wash. State Senate, 2000—. Mem. edn., labor, commerce and fin. instns. and ways and means coms. Wash. State Senate, vice chair environ., energy and water com.; mem. Joint Legis. Audit and Review Com. Mem. bd. dirs. Nature Conservancy, Point Defiance Zool. Soc.; mem. exec. com. Wash. Cmty. Forestry Coun., Puyallup River Watershed Coun.; parent vol. McCarver Elem.; mem. activities coun. Tacoma Art Mus., docent; lector St. Patrick's Cath. Ch., mem. Parish Coun. Marriage Preparation Team; work site supr. 4 environ. restoration projects; commr. Met. Pk. Sits. Tacoma, 1986-92, pres., 1989, 91. Office: PO Box 40427 405 John A Cherberg Bldg Olympia WA 98504-0427 Fax: 360 786-1999. E-mail: regala_de@leg.wa.gov.

REGALADO, RAUL L. airport executive; b. L.A., Jan. 31, 1945; s. Raul and Antonia (Estavillo) R.; m. Helen Sutcliffe; children: Stephanie, Jennifer, Horst. BS, Embry-Riddle Aero. U., 1972. Mgr. airport city of Klamath Falls, Oreg., 1972-74, City of Fresno, Calif., 1974-79, Orange County, Santa Ana, Calif., 1979-80; dir. aviation San Jose (Calif.) Airport, 1980-89; aviation and parking cons. Raul Regalado & Assocs., 1989-2001; dep. dir. aviation Houston Dept. Aviation, 1991-95; market pres. airport properties APCOA, Inc., Vancouver, Wash., 1995-97, market pres. nat. sales Dallas, 1997-98; pres., CEO Nashville Airport Authority, 2001—. Bd. dirs. Nashville Conv. Visitors Bur., 2003—, Nashville chpt. ARC, 2002—, chmn.-elect, 2004. Capt. U.S. Army, 1966-71; col. USAR, 1972-95, ret. Decorated Legion of Merit, Bronze Star, DFC, Air medal with 49 oak leaf clusters, Meritorious Svc. medal, Army Commendation medal with 3 oak leaf clusters. Mem. Am. Assn. Airport Execs., Calif. Assn. Airport Execs. (pres. 1980-81), Airport Operators Coun. Internat. (bd. dirs. 1986-88), Vietnam Helicopter Pilots Assn., Ret. Officers Assn., Aero. Club No. Calif. (bd. dirs. 1982-91, pres. 1987-89), Quiet Birdmen, Nashville C. of C. (bd. govs. 2003-), Soaring Soc. Am. E-mail: raul_regalado@nashintl.com.

REGALMUTO, NANCY MARIE, small business owner, psychic consultant, therapist; b. Bay Shore, N.Y., Aug. 24, 1956; d. Antonio J. Jr. and Agnes C. (Dietz) R. Student, SUNY, Stony Brook. Sales mgr. Fire, Inc., Hempstead, N.Y., 1976-78; sports handicapper Red Hot Sport, J. Dime Sports, Diamond Sports, Hicksville, N.Y., 1978—; small bus. owner, pres. Synergy (vitamin/nutritional product mfr. and distributor), Bellport, N.Y., 1981—. Cons. on medicine, fin., past life, bus. readings, hypnosis, substance abuse, archeology, law enforcement investigations, family, counseling, inter-species comm., animal therapy, psychic surgery, healing, 1989—; lectr. in field, specializing in holistic remedies and therapies, 1989-91. Columnist Daily Racing Form, 1989-91; appeared on numerous TV programs, worldwide radio, mags., newspapers. Lectr., seminar leader, written about in numerous books. Min. Universal Life Ch., 1996, 97, Ch. of Inner Wisdom, 1996, 97. Mem. NAFE, Internat. Platform Assn., Horse Protection Assn., Therapeutic Riding for the Handicapped, World Wildlife Fedn. Office: 18 Woodland Park Rd Bellport NY 11713-2315

REGAN, DAVID, brain researcher; b. Scarborough, Eng., May 5, 1935; arrived in Can., 1976; s. Randolph and Muriel Frances (Varley) R.; m. Marian Pauline Marsh, Aug. 15, 1959; children: Douglas Lawrence, Howard Michael. BSc, London U., 1957, MSc, 1958, PhD, 1964, DSc, 1974. Lectr. physics London U., 1960-65; reader neurosci. Keele U., Eng., 1965-75; prof. psychology Dalhousie U., Can., 1976-80, prof. physiology, 1980-84, assoc. prof. medicine, 1978-84, prof. medicine, 1984-87, prof. ophthalmology, 1980-87, prof. otolaryngology, 1980-84, Killam rsch. prof., 1978-82; prof. engring. Rutgers U., 1985-86; prof. psychology York U., 1987—2003, prof. biology; prof. ophthalmology U. Toronto, Ont., Can., 1987—. Retained inventor Wilkinson-Graviner Group, Eng., 1970-75; cons. Westinghouse, Pitts., 1980-86; co-dir. human performance in space lab. Inst. for Space and Terrestrial Sci., York U., 1989-2002, disting. rsch. prof., 1991-93, emeritus, 1993—; indsl. rsch. chair aviation vision Natural Sci. and Engring. Rsch. Coun. Can./Can. Aviation Electronics, 1993-2003; Spinoza profl. U. Amsterdam, The Netherlands, 1999. Author: Human Evoked Potentials, 1972, Human Brain Electrophysiology, 1989, Human Perception of Objects, 2000; editor: Spatial Vision, 1989, Binocular Vision, 1989, Vision Research, 1992; contbr. over 250 articles to profl. jours.; holder 8 patents. Recipient Forman prize for med. rsch., 1983, Prentice medal, 1990, Sir J.W. Dawson Medal, Royal Soc. Can., 1997, award of excellence Nat. Sci. and Engring. Rsch. Coun. Can., 2000, Proctor medal, 2000, Queen Elizabeth II medal, 2002, Hebb medal, 2003; rsch. grantee NIH, NRC, Air Force Office Sci. Rsch., Nat. Scis. and Engring. Rsch. Coun. Can., Med. Rsch. Coun.; mem. Order of Can., 2001; Killam fellow, 1990. Fellow: Optical Soc. Am., Royal Soc. Can.; mem.: Netherlands Royal Acad. (fgn.), Am. Acad. Optometry, Royal Coll. Sci. (London) (assoc.), Assn. Rsch. in Vision and Ophthalmology, Soc. Clin. Electroretinography, Exptl. Psychology Soc. Avocations: cricket, walking, modern european history. Office: York U Dept Psychology 4700 Keele St North York ON Canada M3J 1P3 E-mail: dregan@yorku.ca.

REGAN, ELIZABETH ANNE, bail bond agent; b. Portland, Oreg. d. David H. and Carmen M. (Nazario) Regan. AA, Clark Coll., Wash. Bail bond agt. Metro Bail Bonds, 1998—2002. Mem.: Profl. Bail Agts. of U.S., Wash. Bail Assn. Home: 612 W Evergreen Blvd Vancouver WA 98660 Office: A-1 Bail Bonds 612 W Evergeeen Blvd Vancouver WA 98660

REGAN, ELLEN FRANCES (MRS. WALSTON SHEPARD BROWN), ophthalmologist, educator; b. Boston, Feb. 1, 1919; d. Edward Francis and Margaret (Moynihan) R.; m. Walston Shepard Brown, Aug. 13, 1955. AB, Wellesley Coll., 1940; MD, Yale U., 1943. Intern Boston City Hosp., 1944; asst. resident, resident Inst. Ophthalmology, Presbyn. Hosp., NYC, 1944-47, asst. ophthalmologist, 1947-56, asst. attending ophthalmologist, 1956-84; instr. ophthalmology Columbia Coll. Physicians and Surgeons, 1947-55, assoc. ophthalmology, 1955-67, asst. clin. prof., 1967-84; ret., 1984. Mem. AMA, Am. Ophthal. Soc., Am. Acad. Ophthalmology, NY Acad. Medicine, NY State Med. Soc., Mass. Med. Soc., River Club, Tuxedo Club. Home: PO Box 632 Tuxedo Park NY 10987-0632

REGAN, FREDERIC DENNIS, cardiologist; b. Newburyport, Mass., Aug. 21, 1921; s. Dennis and Catherine R. (Haley) Regan; m. Margaret Regan; children: Denise, Frederic, Michael. Student, Syracuse U., 1940—42; MD, U. Buffalo, 1945. Diplomate Am. Bd. Internal Medicine. Intern USPHS Hosp., SI, NY, 1945—46, rsch. fellow in cardiology, 1947; chief med. officer Flagship USS Northwind-Naval Nanook Artic Expedition, 1947; resident in medicine, dep. chief medicine, chief cardiac clinic, 1950—52; practice medicine specializing in cardiology and internal medicine; chief of medicine Richmond Meml. Hosp. and Health Ctr. (now S.I. Univ. Hosp.), dir. medicine. Instr. medicine NY Hosp.; organizer Gateway State Bank. Fellow: ACP, NY Cardiology Soc., Am. Coll. Cardiology; mem.: Richmond County Med. Soc. (pres. 1961—62).

REGAN, GEOFF, Canadian government official; b. Windsor, N.S., Can., Nov. 22, 1959; m. Kelly Regan; 3 children. BA, St. Francis Xavier U.; LLB, Dalhousie U. Mem. Can. Parliament, 1993—, parliamentary sec. to the leader of the govt. in the House of Commons, 2001—03; min. fisheries and oceans Govt. Can., Ottawa, Canada, 2003—. Office: House of Commons Ottawa ON Canada K1A 0A6 also: Fisheries and Oceans Centennial Towers Ste 1570 200 Kent St Ottawa ON Canada K1A 0E6 Office Phone: 613-992-3474.

REGAN, HELEN BROOKS, education educator, educational consultant; b. Wilmington, Del., Jan. 13, 1945; d. Richard Ensign and Helen Townsend (Lewis) Brooks; m. Richard James Regan, Nov. 22, 1980; 1 child, Katherine Helen. BA magna cum laude, Randolph-Macon Woman's Coll., 1966; MA in Teaching, Yale U., 1967; PhD, U. Conn., 1981. Cert. chemistry tchr., intermediate supr., supt., Conn. Tchr. chemistry Glastonbury (Conn.) High Sch., 1967-75; asst. prin. Daniel Hand High Sch., Madison, Conn., 1975-78, 81-83, acting prin., 1979-80; prin. Amity Sr. High Sch., Woodbridge, Conn., 1983-85; assoc. prof. Conn. Coll., New London, 1985—. Cons. Conn. Dept. of Edn., Hartford, 1985—. Co-author: The Staff Development Manager, 1991; contbr. articles to profl. jours. Mem. ASCD, AAUP, Am. Ednl. Rsch. Assn., New Eng. Coalition Ednl. Leaders (pres. 1983-85). Avocations: hiking, stitchery, biking.

REGAN, J. THOMAS, architecture educator; BArch, Auburn U., 1964; grad. diploma, Archtl. Assn. Grad. Sch. Arch., London, 1973. Founding dean Sch. Arch. U. Miami, 1984—90; dean Sch. Design N.C. State U., 1990; with dept. arch. Auburn U.; dean, prof. dept. arch. Tex. A&M U., College Station. Mem.: AIA, Assn. Collegiate Schs. Arch. (pres. 1989). Office: A 202 Langford A Dept Arch Tex A&M Univ College Station TX 77843-3137*

REGAN, JAMES P. technology services executive; b. 1940; BSEE, Villanova U.; MSEE, MIT; grad. exec. mgmt. program, Pa. State U. Exec. dir. Arleigh Burke Ship Acquisition Program; dir. ops. AEGIS Program; dir. sys. engring. and prodn. functions at various levels USN; v.p., div. gen. mgr. Advanced Tech., Inc.; sr. v.p. Litton PRC; pres., CEO CVSI, Inc.; chmn., pres., CEO Dynamics Rsch. Corp., 1999—. Office: Dynamics Rsch Corp 60 Frontage Rd Andover MA 01810-5498

REGAN, JUDITH TERRANCE, publishing executive; b. Leominster, Mass., Aug. 17, 1953; d. Leo James and Rita Ann (Imprescia) Regan; children: Patrick, Lara. BA, Vassar Coll., 1975. Reporter Nat. Enquirer; sr. editor, v.p. Simon & Schuster, N.Y.C., 1989—94; pres., pub. Regan Books imprint of HarperCollins, N.Y.C., 1994—. TV prodr. Entertainment Tonight, N.Y.C., Geraldo, N.Y.C.; prodr. 20th Century Fox Films, Fox TV; anchor Full Disclosure, Fox TV; host Judith Regan Tonight, Fox News Channel. Editor, pub. (books) The Way Things Ought to Be (Rush Limbaugh), 1992, Rogue Warrior (Richard Marcinko), 1992, She's Come Undone (Wally Lamb), 1992, Shampoo Planet and Life After God (Douglas Coupland), 1992, Private Parts, Miss America (Howard Stern), 1993, Judge Robert Bork, Slouching Towards Gomorrah, 1993, I Can't Believe I Said That (Kathie Lee Gifford), 1994, Microserfs, 1996, Shabby Chic (Rachel Ashwell), 1996, The Zone (Dr. Barry Sears), 1996, Brain Lock (Dr. Jeffrey Schwartz), 1997, Wicked, 1997, Confessions of an Ugly Stepsister (Gregory Maguire), 1997—2000, Girlfriend in A Coma, 1998, I Know This Much is True, 1998, Marilu Henner's Total health Makeover, 1998, Story (Robert McKee), 1998, Have a Nice Day, Mick Foley (Mankind), 1999, The Rock Says, 2000, and others, —; exec. prodr.: (TV series) Growing Up Gotti, 2004—. Office: Regan Books 10 E 53rd St New York NY 10022-5244

REGAN, MICHAEL PATRICK, lawyer; b. Bklyn., N.Y., Feb. 22, 1941; s. Cornelius Francis and Marguerite (Cann) Regan; m. Susan Ann Light, July 13, 1974; children: Michael Patrick, Brian Christopher, Mark Dennis. BA in English, U. Notre Dame, 1963; LLB, Union U., Albany, 1967, JD, 1968. Bar: N.Y. 1967, Va. 1975. Assoc. Medwin & McMahon, Albany, NY, 1967—69; asst. dist. atty. Albany County, NY, 1969; corp. atty. Mohasco Corp., Amsterdam, NY, 1969—79; asst. gen. consel Dan River, Inc., Danville, Va., 1975, assoc. gen. counsel, 1981—84, acting gen. counsel, asst. sec., 1988, gen. counsel, asst. sec., 1989; assoc. gen. counsel, asst. sec. Dan River Svc. Corp. of Va., Danville, 1984—88; gen. counsel Wunda Weve Carpets, Inc., Greenville, SC, 1990—93; pvt. practice Danville, 1990—. Clarinetist, saxophonist Tightsqueeze Philharm. Band, 1981—; mem. Danville Symphony Orch., 1981—, prin., 1997—; leader The DanceNotes, 1986—; mem. Starmont Swing Band, 1999—; sec. DanPac Polit. Action Com., 1976—89. Mem.: ABA, ATLA, Va. Trial Lawyers Assn., Danville Bar Assn., Va. Bar Assn., N.Y. State Bar Assn. Republican. Roman Catholic. Home: 236 Cambridge Cir Danville VA 24541-5233 Office: 703 Patton St Danville VA 24541-1905

REGAN, PAUL JEROME, JR., manufacturing company executive, consultant; b. Ithaca, N.Y., Mar. 13, 1940; s. Paul Jerome and Mildred (Dempsey) R.; m. Barbara Ann Easton, Feb. 4, 1962 (dec. Nov. 1996); children: Paul J. III, Timothy Andrew, Allison Ann; m. Susan Margaret Mulcair, Sept. 7, 2002. BS, Cornell U., 1962, MBA, 1965. Pers. asst. Corning (N.Y.) Glass Works, 1963, pers. mgr., 1964-68, dept. mgr. mfg. State College, 1968-70, personnel devel. cons. Corning, 1970-72, prodn. supt. Wilmington, N.C., 1972-74, devel. mgr. Corning, 1974-77, corp. dir., 1977-83, v.p. human resources, 1983-86; sr. v.p. Corning Inc., Corning, 1986-93; ret. Mem. adv. bd. Cornell U., Ithaca, N.Y., 1970-82, lectr., 1977—; founding mem. Human Resource Planning Soc., 1974-93; dir. Corning Can. Inc., Toronto, 1983-93. Contbr. articles to books and profl. jours. including Human Resource Planning Soc. jour.; expert comment on exec. compensation and succession including Wall St. Jour., N.Y. Times, Bus. Week, Forbes. Mem. exec. bd. Thousand Islands Assn., Gananoque, Ont., Can., 1988—, pres., 1999—; chmn. Blue Ribbon Fund, Corning Hosp., 1989-93; mem. Rep. Nat. Com., Washington, 1984—; dir. State College C. of C., 1967-73, Half Moon Bay Found., dir. Friends of the 1000 Islands Mus., Inc., 2000—; chair Museums of 1000 Islands, Inc., 2002—; chmn. Historic Thousand Islands Village Found., 1998—. Johnson Soc. fellow Cornell U., 1991; named Ky. Col., State of Ky., 1984, Adm. Thousand Islands Navy, 1999. Mem. Am. Compensation Assn. (regional chair 1978-81), Am. Acad. Polit. and Social Sci., Heron Soc. (life.), Cornell Club, Nat. Mus. Am. Indian (charter, membership com. 1991—), Antique Boat Mus., Canadian Antique Boat Soc. (dir. 2004—), Save the River Com. (adv. 1982—), Menninger Found. (patron), Trust for Historic Preservation, Delta Phi (past pres.). Avocations: antique wooden boats, decoys, photographs, Inuit art, poetry.

REGAN, RICHARD JOSEPH, political science professor, writer; b. Morristown, NJ, Oct. 26, 1930; s. Joseph Michael and May Catherine (Cella R.). A.B., St. Peter's Coll., 1952; PhL, Woodstock Coll., Md., 1957; STL, 1964; PhD in Polit. Sci., U. Chgo., 1967. Assoc. prof. Fordham U., Bronx, 1968—87, prof., 1987—. Author: American Pluralism and The Catholic Conscience, 1963, Conflict and Consensus, 1967, Private Conscience and Public Law, 1972, Moral Dimensions of Politics, 1986, On Laws, Morality and Politics, 1988, God and Creation, 1994, Just War, 1996, A Summary of Philosophy, 2003; translator: The De Malo of Thomas Aquinas, 2001. Roman Catholic. Avocation: running. Home and Office: Spellman Hall Fordham Univ Bronx NY 10458 Office Phone: 718-817-3950.

REGAN, TIMOTHY JAMES, grain company executive; b. Atchison, Kans., July 31, 1956; s. Vincent James and Phyllis (Brull) R.; m. Veronica Sue Kasten, June 25, 1977; children: Katrina Sue, Brian James. BS, Kans. State U., 1978. Corp. acct. Lincoln Grain Co., Atchison, 1978-80; acctg. supr. Pillsbury Co., St. Joseph, Mo., 1980, br. account mgr., 1980-82, Omaha, 1982, internal auditor Mpls., 1983, regional account mgr. Huron, Ohio, 1983-84, Scoular Grain Co., Omaha, 1984-87, controller, 1987-91, v.p., mem. exec. com., 1990-99, CFO, 1991—. Fin. advisor Grace Abbott Sch. PTO, Omaha, 1987, treas., 1990-91. Fin. adviser Grace Abbott Sch. PTO, Omaha, 1987, treas., 1990-91; bd. dirs. Cath. Charities, 1994-2000, treas., 1997-99; coach Little League Baseball and Soccer. Mem. KC, Elks. Republican. Roman Catholic. Avocations: jogging, basketball, coaching little league baseball and soccer. Office: Scoular Co 2027 Dodge St Omaha NE 68102 Home: PO Box 1331 Tulare CA 93275-1331

REGAN, WILLIAM JOSEPH, JR., energy company executive; b. Bronx, N.Y., Mar. 7, 1946; s. William Joseph and Eleanor F. (Malone) R.; m. Mary Lee Wynn; children— Katrina Lee, Thomas Wynn, James William BS, U.S. Air Force Acad., 1967; MBA, U. Wis.-Madison, 1969, PhD, 1972. Asst. prof. Wayne State U., Detroit, 1971-75; with Nat. Bank Detroit, 1975-77; sr. bus. planner Am. Natural Resources Co., Detroit, 1977-78, dir. fin. planning, 1978-82, v.p., treas., 1982-85; v.p. corp. fin. United Svcs. Automobile Assn., San Antonio, 1986-88, sr. v.p., treas., 1988-95; v.p., treas. Entergy Corp., New Orleans, 1995-99; CFO Calif. Ind. Sys. Operator Corp., Folsom, Calif., 1999—. Home: 15181 De La Pena Cir Rancho Murieta CA 95683-9798 Office: 151 Blue Ravine Rd Folsom CA 95630 E-mail: wregan37@earthlink.net.

REGAN GOSSAGE, MURIEL, librarian; b. N.Y.C., July 15, 1930; d. William and Matilda (Riebel) Blome; m. Robert Regan, 1966 (div. 1976); 1 child, Jeanne Booth; m. Wayne Gossage, 2003. BA, Hunter Coll., N.Y.C., 1950; MLS, Columbia U., 1952; MBA, Pace U., N.Y.C., 1982. Post libr. US Army, Okinawa, 1952-53; researcher P.F. Collier, N.Y.C., 1953-57; asst. libr. to libr. Rockefeller Found., N.Y.C., 1957-67; dep. chief libr. Manhattan Community Coll., N.Y.C., 1967-68; libr. Booz Allen & Hamilton, N.Y.C., 1968-69, Rockefeller Found., N.Y.C., 1969-82; prin. Gossage Regan Assocs., Inc., N.Y.C., 1980-95; pub. svcs. libr. Carlsbad (N.Mex.) Pub. Libr., 1995-2000. Dir. N.Y. Met. Reference and Rsch. Libr. Agy., 1988-95, Coun. Nat. Libr. and Info. Assns., 1991-95; cons. Librs. Info. Ctrs., Gossage Sager Assocs., 2001—. Elder First Presbyn. Ch. of Carlsbad, 1997-99, Stephan min., 2000—, deacon, 2002-03. Mem. Spl. Librs. Assn. pres. 1989-90), Archons of Colophon. Avocations: cats, reading, playing piano, travel. Home: 604 N Lake St Carlsbad NM 88220-5014 E-mail: murielregan@hotmail.com.

REGAN-STANTON, CHRISTA MARIA, artist; b. Stuttgart, Germany, Dec. 30, 1930; arrived in U.S., 1952; d. Friedrich Wilhelm and Anna Katharina (Schiller) Hohnhausen; m. James Allen Stanton (dec.); m. James Dale Regan, Apr. 27, 1955 (div. 1983); children: Jessica Ute, Jeffrey William. M Interpretive Dance, Tanzmeister Sch. Vock, Stuttgart, Germany, 1950. Tchr. Christa Studio Dance, Stuttgart, Germany, Athens, Ohio, 1952—54, Miami U., 1955—56; mgr. Treehouse Gallery, Oak Ridge, Tenn., 1983—95; studio potter Oak Ridge, Tenn. Bd. dirs. Upstairs Gallery, Oak Ridge, Tenn.; show dir. Foothills Craft Guild, Oak Ridge, Tenn., 1985. Recipient Honorable Mention award, Oak Ridge Mus. Fine Arts, 1982, First Place award, 1983, Second Place award, 1985. Mem.: Nat Mus. Women in Arts, Southern Highland Crafts Guild, Tenn. Arts and Crafts Assn., Am. Craft Coun., Foothills Craft Guild. Home: 119 Cooper Cir Oak Ridge TN 37830-7156

REGAZZI, JOHN HENRY, retired electronic distributor executive; b. N.Y.C., Jan. 4, 1921; s. Caesar B. and Jennie (Moruzzi) R.; m. Doris Mary Litzau, Feb. 16, 1946; children: Mark, Dale BBA, Pace Coll., 1951. CPA, N.Y. Mgr. Price Waterhouse, N.Y.C., 1946-62; comptroller ABC, N.Y.C., 1962-70; sr. v.p., CFO Avnet, Inc., N.Y.C., 1970-93; retired, 1993. Contbr. articles to profl. jours. Pres. bd. River Dell Regional High Sch., Oradell, N.J., 1962-65; trustee, treas. Oradell Pub. Library, 1970-79; councilman Borough of Oradell, 1979-88. Served as staff sgt. USAF, 1942-45 Mem. AICPA, Fin. Execs. Internat. Republican. Roman Catholic. Home: 8980 King John Ct Las Vegas NV 89149-3221

REGAZZI, JOHN JAMES, III, publishing executive; b. Bklyn., June 8, 1948; s. John James Jr. and Theresa Cecil (Fiore) R.; m. Marie Louise Ford, May 30, 1971; children: John James IV, Thomas Paul, Michael Rees. BS, St. John's U., Queens, N.Y., 1970; MA, U. Iowa, 1972; MS, Columbia U., 1974; PhD, Rutgers U., 1983. Systems mgr. No. Ill. U., De Kalb, Ill., 1974-76; dir. pub. Found. Ctr., N.Y.C., 1976-79; assoc. prof. Rutgers U., New Brunswick, N.J., 1979-81; v.p. The H.W. Wilson Co., N.Y.C., 1981-88; pres., chief exec. officer Engring. Info., Inc., N.Y.C., 1988-99; pres. Elsevier Inc., N.Y.C., 2000—. Chmn. Article Express Internat., 1992-94; bd. dirs. ICSTI, NTLS, NFALS, CAB Internat.; adj. prof. SUNY, Albany, Columbia U., Rutgers U. Author: Guide to Periodicals in Religion, 1974. Mem. AAAS, IEEE, ALA, Am. Assn. Pubs. (bd. dirs. N.Y.C. chpt. 1987-88), Nat. Info. Standards Orgn. (vice chmn. 1989-90), Nat. Fedn. of Abstracting and Info. Svcs. (bd. dirs. 1980-81, 88, 2004), Assn. Computing Machinery, N.Y. Acad. Sci. Avocation: cycling. Office: Elsevier Inc 360 Park Ave S #11 New York NY 10010-1710

REGELBRUGGE, ROGER RAFAEL, steel company executive; b. Eeklo, Belgium, May 22, 1930; arrived in U.S., 1953, naturalized, 1961; s. Victor and Rachel (Roesbeke) Regelbrugge; m. Dorcas Merchant; children: Anita, Marc, Laurie, Jon, Craig, Kurt, Christiane, Lauren, Lauren, Roger Rafael Jr. BSME, State Tech. Coll., Ghent, 1951; BS in Indsl. Engring, Gen. Motors Inst., Flint, Mich., 1955; MSME, Mich. State U., 1964. Supr. product engring. dept. Gen. Motors Corp., Antwerp, 1955—58; chief devel. engr., then gen. mgr. Airmaster div. Hayes Industries Inc., Jackson, Mich., 1958—66; with Koehring Co., 1966—74, group v.p. internat. ops., 1969—74; exec. v.p. Korf Industries, Inc., Charlotte, NC, 1974—77, chmn.; chmn., pres., CEO Georgetown Industries, Inc. (formerly Korf Industries, Inc.), 1977—95; chmn., CEO GS Industries Inc. (formerly Georgetown Industries), 1995—97, chmn., 1997—. Bd. dirs. GS Industries. Mem. adv. coun. Coll. Engring. U. Notre Dame; trustee Belmont (N.C.) Abbey Coll. Mem.: Am. Soc. Automotive Engrs., ASME, Georgetown Club, Carmel Country Club. Roman Catholic.

REGENSTREIF, HERBERT, lawyer; b. N.Y.C., May 13, 1935; s. Max and Jeannette (Hacker) R.; m. Patricia Friedman, Dec. 20, 1967 (div. July 1968); m. Charlotte Lois Levy, Dec. 11, 1980 (div. Sept. 2002); 1 child, Cara Rachael. BA, Hobart Coll., 1957; JD, N.Y. Law Sch., 1960; MS, Pratt Inst., 1985. Bar: N.Y. 1961, Ky. 1985, U.S. Dist. Ct. (ea. and so. dists.) N.Y. 1962, U.S. Dist. Ct. (ea. dist.) Ky. 1998, U.S. Tax Ct. 1967, U.S. Ct. Appeals (2d cir.) 1962, U.S. Supreme Ct. 1967. Ptnr. Fried & Regenstreif, P.C., Mineola, N.Y., 1963—; reservist atty. Fed. Emergency Mgmt. Agy., 1998-99. Cons. in field; arbitrator Dist. Ct., Nassau County, N.Y., 1989—, N.Y.C. Civil Ct., 1984-86; sec.-treas. Sta. WAHY-FM, Inc., 1998-2000. Contbr. articles to profl. jours. County committeeman Dem. Com., Queens County, N.Y., 1978-79. Mem. Bar Assn. Nassau County, Ky. Bar Assn., Phi Delta Phi, Beta Phi Mu, Hobart Club of N.Y. (gov. 1968-69). Office Phone: 516-294-6442.

REGENSTREIF, S(AMUEL) PETER, political scientist, educator; b. Montreal, Que., Can., Sept. 9, 1936; s. Albert Benjamin and Miriam Lillian (Issenman) R.; children: Anne Erica, Mitchell Chester, Jeffrey Gershon, Gail Aviva. BA, McGill U., 1957; PhD, Cornell U., 1963. Mem. faculty U. Rochester, 1961—, prof. polit. sci., 1971—; coordinator Can. studies program, 1967—. Editl. cons. Toronto Star, 1968-82, Chgo. Sun-Times, 1988-89; polit. cons. Bunting Warburg, Toronto, 1973-90, Coopers & Lybrand, Ltd., 1981-89, Loewen, Ondaatje, McCutcheon, 1991-94; prin. Policy Concepts, Inc., Toronto; broadcaster CKO Radio Network, 1983-89; pvt. polit. cons. Author: The Diefenbaker Interlude: Parties and Voting in Canada, 1965; syndicated columnist: Toronto Star, 1963-82; contbr. articles to profl. jours. Served to lt. Canadian Army, 1957. Ford. Found. fellow, 1960; Can. Council fellow, 1960, 65; Canadian Royal Commn. on Bilingualism and Biculturalism grantee, 1964-66; recipient Edward Peck Curtis award U. Rochester, 1979 Mem. AAAS, Am. Polit. Sci. Assn., Can. Polit. Sci. Assn., Assn. Can. Studies in U.S., Phi Beta Kappa. Jewish. Home: 438C Browncroft Blvd Rochester NY 14609 Office: Univ Rochester Dept Polit Sci Rochester NY 14627 Office Phone: 585-275-5466. E-mail: peter.regenstreif@rochester.edu.

REGER, LAWRENCE LEE, trade association administrator; b. Lincoln, Nebr., June 23, 1939; s. Lawrence John and Bertha (Hergenrader) R. Student, U. Nebr., 1961; LL.B., Vanderbilt U., 1964. Bar: Nebr 1964. Asso. firm Crosby, Guenzel & Binning, Lincoln, 1964-70; gen. counsel Nat. Endowment Arts, 1970-72, dir. program devel. and coordination, 1972-78; dir. Am. Assn. Mus., Washington, 1978-86; pres. Heritage Preservation, Washington, 1988—. Mem. visual arts vis. com. U. Del., 1995—; mem. cultural property adv. com. USIA, 1996—2000; mem. bd. trustees St. Petersburg Internat. Preservation Ctr., 1996—; bd. dirs. Peck Stacpoole Found. Chmn. Nat. Humanities Alliance, 1982-86; bd. dirs. Nat. Musical Arts, 1990—. Recipient Forbes medal Am. Inst. Conservation, 2000, Alumni Achievement award Hixon-Leid Coll. Fine and Performing Arts, U. Nebr., 2004. Home: 5010 Garfield St NW Washington DC 20016-3469 Office: Heritage Preservation 1012 14th St NW Ste 1200 Washington DC 20005 Office Phone: 202-233-0800.

REGES, MARIANNA ALICE, marketing executive; b. Budapest, Hungary, Mar. 23, 1947; arrived in U.S., 1956, naturalized, 1963; d. Otto H. and Alice M. Reges; children: Rebecca, Charles III. AAS with honors, Fashion Inst. Tech., N.Y.C., 1967; BBA magna cum laude, Baruch Coll., 1971, MBA in Stats., 1978. Media rsch. analyst Doyle, Dane, Bernbach Advt., N.Y.C., 1967—70; rsch. supr. Sta. WCBS-TV, N.Y.C., 1970—71; rsch. mgr. Woman's Day mag., N.Y.C., 1971—72; asst. media dir. Benton & Bowles Advt., N.Y.C., 1972—75; mgr. rsch. and sales devel. NBC Radio, N.Y.C., 1975—77; sr. rsch. mgr. Ziff-Davis Pub. Co., N.Y.C., 1977—84; media mgr. Bristol-Myers Squibb Co., 1984—2001, Procter & Gamble Co., 2001—. Mem. Spanish Radio Adv. Coun., N.Y.C., 1986—88, Pan-European TV Audience Rsch. Mgmt. Com., 1988—. Mem. advisor Baruch Coll. Advt. Soc., 1975—; active First Presbyn. Ch., N.Y.C. Mem.: Advt. Rsch. Found., Radio and TV Rsch. Coun., Media Rsch. Dirs. Assn., Am. Advt. Fedn., Am. Mktg. Assn., Anthroposophical Soc., Nature Conservancy, Baruch Alumni Assn., Gilda's Club, Beta Gamma Sigma. Home: 626 E 20th St New York NY 10009-1509 E-mail: marianna10009@hotmail.com.

REGGIE, DORIS BOUSTANY, volunteer; b. Lafayette, La., July 18, 1930; d. Frem Frem and Beatrice (Joseph) Boustany; m. Edmund Michael Reggie, June 17, 1951; children: Ed Michael, Victoria, Denis, Gregory, Alicia, Raymond, Reggie. BS with honors, U. Southwestern La., 1950. Vice chairperson La. State Mus., 1984-88, 92-96, La. Endowment for Humanities, 1982-90, La. Gov.'s Mansion Commn.; mem. adv. com. Boustany Chair in Home Econs., U. Southwestern La.; chairperson Cleanest City Contest, Crowley, 1983, 84; chmn. Crowley, la. city lighting contest, 1980; mem. Dem. Nat. Com. La.; exec. com. La. Dem. Ctrl. Com.; mem. Acadia Parish Dem. Exec. com., 1976-92, La. Dem. State Ctrl. Com., 1976-92; mem. resolution com. Dem. Nat. Conv., 1984, mem. final platform com., 1988; mem. Dem. Nat. Fin. Com., 1980, 84, 88, 92; del. Dem. Nat. Conf., 1976, 80, 84, 88, 92, 96, La. Dem. Conv., 1976—; mem. La. Gov.'s Commn. on Children. Inducted in La. Ctr. for Women and Govt.'s Hall of Fame, 1997. Mem. Equestrian Order of Holy Sepulchre, Crowley Garden Club (pres. 1992-94), Crowley Tree Bd.

REGGIO, VITO ANTHONY, management consultant; b. Rochester, N.Y., Dec. 17, 1929; s. Salvatore and Carrie Angela (LoRe) R.; m. Mary Ann Dolores Pippie, Sept. 28, 1957; children: Salvatore, Angela. BS, Purdue U., 1952; postgrad. sch. modern langs., Middlebury Coll., 1948; postgrad. fellowship, U. Ky., U. Tenn. and U. Ala., 1952-53. Jr. engr. Rochester (N.Y.) Gas and Electric Co., 1950; designer/drafter Globe Constrn. Co., Rochester, 1951; rsch. analyst Commonwealth of Ky., Frankfort, 1952; orgn. & methods analyst, then wage adminstrn. specialist USN Dept. Indsl. Rels., Indpls., 1955-56; cons. mgmt. engr. to project mgr. to account exec. Bus. Rsch. Corp., Chgo., 1956-60; sr. cons. econ. feasibilities Ebasco Svcs., Inc., Chgo., 1960-63, dir. pers. mgmt. cons. dept., 1970-77; regional mgr., orgn. and pers.

mgmt. svcs. EBS Mgmt. Cons., Chgo., 1963-65, nat. dir. orgn. and pers. mgmt. svcs., 1965-70; pres., bd. dirs. Reggio and Assocs., Inc., Chgo., 1977—; mng. dir. Pay Data Svc., 1977—. Bd. dirs. Pay Data Svcs., Chgo. Contbr. papers to profl. publs. With U.S. Army, 1953-55. Named Solco Cultural Soc. fellow, Rochester, N.Y., 1948. Mem. Am. Compensation Assn., Am. Mgmt. Assn., Chgo. Compensation Assn., Soc. Human Resources Profls., Soc. Human Resources Mgmt., Human Resources Mgmt. Assn. Chgo., Western Soc. Engrs. Office: Reggio and Assocs Inc 4365 Lawn Ave Western Springs IL 60558-1465

REGIER, DARCY JOHN, professional hockey team coach; b. Swift Current, Sask., Can., Nov. 27, 1956; came to U.S., 1977; s. John Melvin and Helen (Neufeld) R.; m. Katherine Opyr, June 30, 1979; children: Jonathan, Justin. Student, U. Lethbridge (Alta., Can.), 1980-85. Profl. hockey player, 1976-83; head coach Indpls. Checkers, 1984-85; dir. hockey adminstrn. N.Y. Islanders, Uniondale, 1985-89, asst. coach, 1989-91; gen. mgr., v.p. Buffalo Sabres, 1997—. Mem. all-star team Cen. Hockey League, 1983. Mem. Profl. Hockey Players Assn. (chmn. exec. com. 1980-83). Avocations: bicycling, video productions on sports. Office: Buffalo Sabres One Seymour H Knox III Plz Buffalo NY 14203

REGIS, NINA, librarian, educator; b. Corinth, Miss., Oct. 19, 1928; d. W.C. and Mary Isabelle (Rushing) Hanner; m. George Regis, Sept. 5, 1949 (dec. Jan. 6, 1990); 1 child, Simonne Marie. BA, Bridgewater (Mass.) State U., 1971, MEd, 1975; MALS, U. South Fla., 1981. tchr., Fla., Mass. Geneal. libr., asst. rschr. to curator New Bedford (Mass.) Pub. Libr., 1963-71; assoc. libr. New England Hist. Geneal. Soc., Boston, 1972-73; media specialist, libr. Brevard County Schs., Port Malabar Elem. Sch., Palm Bay, Fla., 1978-90; libr., faculty Brevard C.C., Palm Bay, 1990-96, Melbourne, Fla., 1996—. Developer and organizer libraries, 1968, 80, 91—. Mem. ALA, Fla. Assn. C.C.s, Libr. Assn. of Brevard County, Phi Kappa Phi, Beta Phi Mu. Avocations: creative writing, genealogical research. Office: Brevard C C Melbourne Campus Libr 3865 N Wickham Rd Melbourne FL 32935-2310

REGIS, SUSAN, food service executive; b. N.H. Grad., Skidmore Coll. Worked with Lydia Shire Seasons restaurant, 1983; opened Four Seasons Hotel, Beverly Hills, Calif.; exec. chef Biba, Boston, Pignoli, Boston. Named Best Chef in Boston, Improper Bostonian, Am.'s Best Chef N.E., James Beard Found., 1998. Office: Biba 272 Boylston St Boston MA 02116

REGNIER, JAMES, state supreme court justice; b. Aurora, Ill., July 22, 1944; m. Linda Regnier; 3 children. BS, Marquette U., 1966; JD, U. Ill., 1973. Judicial Fellow ACTL, Internat. Soc. Barristers; completed atty. mediator tng., Atty.-Mediator Tng. Inst., Dallas, 1993. Lawyer pvt. practice, Rochelle, Ill., 1973-78; co-founder, ptnr. Regnier, Lewis and Boland, Great Falls, Mont., 1979-91; lawyer pvt. practice, Missoula, Mont., 1991-97; justice Mont. Supreme Ct., Helena, 1997—. Appt. Mont. Supreme Ct. Commn. on Civil Jury Instrn.; appt. lawyer-rep. to 9th Cir. Judicial Confs., 1987, 88, 89, chair Mont. lawyer delegation, 1989; lectr. U. Mont. Sch. Law, numerous continuing legal edn. seminars. Contbr. Mont. Pattern Jury Instrns. for Civil Cases, 1985. Co-founder Mont. chpt. Am. Bd. Trial Advocates, 1989—, pres. Officer USN, Vietnam. Office: Montana Supreme Ct Justice Bldg 215 N Sanders St Helena MT 59601-4522 also: PO Box 203001 Helena MT 59620-3001 Office Phone: 406-444-5494. Business E-Mail: Howard.Kirschenbaum@rochester.edu.

REGO, CESAR, science educator, researcher; b. Porto, Portugal, Apr. 9, 1963; s. Julio and Amelia Rego; 1 child, Bruno. PhD, U. of Versailles, 1996. Assoc. prof. Universidade Portucalense, Porto, Portugal, 1991—99, U. of Miss., Oxford, 1999—; invited prof. Instituto Superior Tecnico (IST-UTL), Lisbon, Portugal, 1996—98; asst. prof. Faculdade de Ciencias (FCUL), Lisbon, Portugal, 1998—99. Recipient IFORS-Lisbon Best Internat. Paper, IFORS/APDIO, Best Master Thesis, Portuguese Ops. Rsch. Soc.; PhD Scholarship, JNICT, Portugal, Rsch. Grant, Office of Naval Rsch. Mem.: INFORMS (assoc.). Home: 405 Whitney Oxford MS 38655 Office: University of Mississippi Oxford MS 38677 E-mail: crego@bus.olemiss.edu.

REGULA, RALPH, congressman, lawyer; b. Beach City, Ohio, Dec. 3, 1924; s. O.F. and Orpha (Walter) R.; m. Mary Rogusky, Aug. 5, 1950; children: Martha, David, Richard. BA, Mt. Union Coll., 1948, LLD, 1981; LLB, William McKinley Sch. Law, 1952; LLD, Malone Coll., 1976. Bar: Ohio 1952. Sch. adminstr. Stark County Bd. Edn., 1948-55; practiced law Navarre, 1952—; mem. Ohio Ho. of Reps., 1965-66, Ohio Senate, 1967-72, U.S. Congress from 16th Ohio dist., 1973—; vice chmn. appropriations com., chmn. subcom. depts. Labor, HHS, Edn.; ptnr. Regula Bros. Mem. Pres.'s Commn. on Fin. Structures and Regulation, 1970-71. Mem. Ohio Bd. Edn., 1960-64; hon. mem. adv. bd. Walsh Coll., Canton, Ohio; Trustee Mt. Union Coll., Alliance, Ohio, Stark County Hist. Soc., Stark County Wilderness Soc. With USNR, 1944-46. Recipient Community Service award Navarre Kiwanis Club, 1963; Meritorious Service in Conservation award Canton Audubon Soc., 1965; Ohio Conservation award Gov. James Rhodes, 1969; named Outstanding Young Man of Yr. Canton Jr. C. of C., 1957, Legis. Conservationist of Yr. Ohio League Sportsmen, 1969 Republican. Episcopalian. Office: US Ho of Reps 2306 Rayburn House Off Bldg Washington DC 20515-3516

REH, SHEILA NATKINS, humanities educator; b. New York, NY, Apr. 7, 1926; d. Benjamin F. Natkins and Bertha North; m. William S. Reh, Nov. 25, 1944 (dec. Dec. 21, 1969); 1 child, Virginia A. BA-English, NYU -Wash. Sq. Coll., New York, NY, 1942—45; MS-education, Wagner Coll., Staten Island, N Y, 1964—65. Tchr. Bd. of Ed., New York, NY, 1964—89. Actor: (acting) Emerson Little Theatre-Staten Island. Bd. of directors, exec. comm. Snug Harbor Cultural Ctr., Staten Island, NY, 1993—96, lead docent-dept. of ed., co-chair b ook fair, 1996—98. Recipient, N ew York State Assembly, 1998, Vol. of the Yr., Snug Harbor Cultural Ctr., 2001, Vol. Of The Week, SI Advance, 2001 (Year of the Volunteer-UN). Avocations: tennis, drama.

REH, THOMAS EDWARD, radiologist, educator; b. St. Louis, Sept. 12, 1943; s. Edward Paul and Ceil Anne (Golden) R.; m. Benedette Texada Gieselman, June 22, 1968; children: Matthew J., Benedette T., Elizabeth W. BA, St. Louis U., 1965, MD, 1969. Diplomate Am. Bd. Radiology, Nat. Bd. Med. Examiners. Intern St. John's Mercy Med. Ctr., St. Louis, 1969-70; resident St. Louis VA Hosp., 1970-73; fellow in vascular radiology Beth Israel Hosp., Boston, 1973-74; radiologist St. Mary's Health Ctr., St. Louis, 1974—, chmn. dept. radiology, 1986—; clin. asst. prof. radiology St. Louis U. Sch. Medicine, 1978-98, clin. prof. radiology, 1998—; clin. assoc. prof. radiology, 1989—. Fellow Am. Coll. Radiology; mem. AMA, Radiol. Soc. N.Am., St. Louis Met. Med. Soc., Alpha Omega Alpha, Alpha Sigma Nu, Delta Sigma Phi. Republican. Roman Catholic. Clubs: St. Louis, Confrerie des Chevaliers du Tastevin. Home: 9850 Waterbury Dr Saint Louis MO 63124-1046 Office: Bellevue Radiology Inc 4 Sunnen Bus Park Saint Louis MO 63143

REHA, ROSE KRIVISKY, retired finance educator; b. N.Y.C., Dec. 17, 1920; d. Boris and Freda (Gerstein) Krivisky; m. Rudolph John Reha, Apr. 11, 1941; children; Irene Gale, Phyllis. BS in Bus. and Music Edn., Ind. State U., 1965; MA in Bus. and Psychology, U. Minn., 1967, PhD in Ednl. Psychology and Counseling, 1971. With U.S. and State Civil Svc., 1941-63; tchr. pub. schs., Minn., 1965-66; teaching assoc., instr. U. Minn., Mpls., 1966-68, 68-85; prof. coll. bus. St. Cloud (Minn.) State U., 1968-85, prof. emeritus, 1985—, chmn. bus. edn. & office adminstrn. dept., 1982-83. Advisor Small Bus. Inst., 1972-85, SBA, 1972-85; ct. advocate for women in distress St. Cloud Women's Shelter, 1986-89; adj. prof. profl. and bus. comm. Fla. Atlantic U., Boca Raton, Fla., 1989-90; substitute tchr. Broward County, 1990—; tutor (reading) Lauderdale, Fla., 1990-92; moderator, counselor Posnack Jewish Cmty. Ctr., Davie, Fla.; lectr. in com. Soref Jewish Cmty. Ctr. Continuing Edn. for sr. groups, Sunrise, Fla., 1994—; cons., lectr. in field; small bus. cons. Small Bus. Inst. Coll. Bus. St. Cloud St. U. Minn. Reviewer of bus. comm. and consumer edn. textbooks. Contbr. articles to profl. jours. Camp dir. Girl Scouts U.S., 1960-62; active various cmty. fund drives; sec., mem. relicensure rev. Com. Minn. Bd. Teaching Continuing Edn., 1984-85. Recipient Achievement award St. Cloud State U., 1985, St. Cloud State U. Rsch. and Faculty Improvement grantee, 1973, 78, 83. Mem. Am. Vocat. Assn. (cert.), Am. Counseling Assn. (cert.), Am. Mental Health Counselors Assn. (cert.), Minn. Econ. Assn., Minn. Women of Higher Edn., NEA, Minn. Edn. Assn. (pres. women's caucus 1981-83, award 1983), St. Cloud U. Faculty Assembly (pres. 1975-76), St. Cloud State U. Grad. Coun. (chmn. 1983-85), Fifty-five-plus Sr. Group (moderator North Broward, Ft. Lauderdale moderation counselor for PWP Chptr., 1994-97), Pi Omega Pi (sponsor St. Cloud State U. chpt. 1982-85), Phi Chi Theta, Delta Pi Epsilon, Delta Kappa Gamma. Jewish. Home: Apt 465 3671 Environ Blvd Fort Lauderdale FL 33319-4221 Office: Coll Bus St Cloud State U Saint Cloud MN 56301

REHAK, JAMES RICHARD, orthodontist; b. Chgo., Jan. 2, 1938; s. James Joseph and Lydia Ann (Thomas) R.; m. Joann Marie Tabbert, Oct. 15, 1969; 1 child, Suzanne Therese. BS, U. Ill., 1960, DDS cum laude, 1962, MS, 1967, cert. in orthodontics, 1965. Pvt. practice dentistry, Chgo., 1962-63; pvt. practice orthodontics Chgo., Arlington Heights, Ill., Cape Coral, Naples, Fla. Asst. prof. U. Ill. Coll. Dentistry, 1966-68. Pres. bd. trustees St. Ann Sch. Foun.; chmn. bd. dirs. St. John Neumann H.S.; organizer, dir. 1st Nat. Bank, Naples; trustee Catholic Cultural Ctr., Washington. Served to capt. U.S. Army Res., 1962-69. Kellogg Found. fellow, 1958. Fellow Royal Soc. Health; mem. ADA, Ill. Dental Assn., Chgo. Dental Soc., Fla. Dental Assn., West Coast Dental Soc., Collier County Dental Assn., Am. Assn. Orthodontists, Am. Assn. Lingual Orthodontists, Fedn. Dentaire Internationale, Psi Omega, Omicron Kappa Upsilon. Office: 5100 Tamiami Trl N Ste 101 Naples FL 34103-2810

REHBEIN, EDWARD ANDREW, minister, geologist, consultant; b. Aug. 13, 1947; s. Edward Louis and Marjorie Ann (Simshaw) R.; m. Phyllis Jean Boyer, June 23, 1973; children: Matthew Louis, Angela Mae. BS in Geology, Calif. Inst. Tech., 1969. Geologist U. S. Forest Svcs., Elkins, W.Va., 1972—74, U.S. Geol. Survey, Billings, Mont., 1974—76; coal geologist W.Va. Geologic Survey, Morgantown, 1977; cons. Morgantown, 1978; geologist Allied Corp., Beckley, W.Va., 1979; sr. exploration geologist Kerr-McGee Corp., Beckley, W.Va., 1980—82, regional mgr. exploration Reno, 1983—85, exploration geologist Oklahoma City, 1985—88; assoc. min. Ch. of Christ, Beckley, 1989—90, min., 1990—; pres. M&R Computer Sales and Svc., Inc., Beckley, 1989—90. Author: Rememberich God's Word, 1991, Overcome by the Cross, 2003; contbr. articles. Mem.: Am. Assn. Petroleum Geologists, Shotokan Karate Am. Office: N Beckley Ch of Christ PO Box 951 Beckley WV 25802-0951 *So God created man in his own image. (Genesis 1:27). Search the Scriptures, find the full meaning of this, and your life will never be the same.*

REHBERG, DENNIS R. congressman; b. Billings, Mont., Oct. 5, 1955; m. Janice; 1 child. Student, Mont. State U., Wash. State U. Rancher and businessman; legis. aide, 1977; fin. dir. Congl. Campaigns, 1980-82; Mont. state rep. Dist. 88, 1985-89; lt. gov. Mont., 1991-96; mem. U.S. Congress from Mont. at large, Washington, 2001—; mem. agr. com., resources com., transp. and infrastructure com. Republican. Office: US Ho Reps 516 Cannon Ho Office Bldg Washington DC 20515

REHBERG, KITTY, state legislator; b. Cedar Rapids, Iowa, Oct. 16, 1938; m. Franklin Rehberg; 3 children. Student, Rowly C.C. Mem. Iowa Senate from 14th dist., Des Moines, 1996—; mem. appropriations com., mem. rules and adminstrn. com.; vice chair edn. com.; mem. natural resources and environment com. Republican. Office: State Capitol 9th And Grand Ave Des Moines IA 50319-0001 E-mail: kitty_rehberg@legis.state.ia.us.

REHG, KENNETH LEE, linguistics educator; b. East St. Louis, Ill., Nov. 21, 1939; s. Theophil Albert and Kathryn Louise (George) R.; m. Kimi Miyagi; 1 child, Laura Le'olani. BA, U. Ill., 1962, MA, So. Ill. U., 1965; PhD, U. Hawaii, 1986. Tng. officer Internat. Ctr. for Lang. Studies, Washington, 1966-67; lang. officer U.S. Peace Corp, Saipan, Micronesia, 1967-70; asst. rschr. social sci. rsch. inst. U. Hawaii, Honolulu, 1974-83, assoc. prof., 1984—. Cons. Micronesian govt., 1973-76, 97, 2000, 2003, 2004, Samoa Dept. Edn., Pago Pago, 1978, U.S. Geol. Survey, Menlo Park, Calif., 1979-81, Japan Nat. Mus. Ethnology, Osaka, 1986; participant Fulbright-Hays Study Group, Ea. Indonesia, 1991. Author: Ponapean Reference Grammar, 1981; co-author: Kitail Lokaiahn Pohnpei, 1969, Ponapean-English Dictionary, 1979; co-editor: Issues in Austronesian Morphology; mng. editor.: jour. Oceanic Linguistics; contbr. papers to profl. publs. Rsch. fellow U. Hawaii, 1981-82; recipient Excellence in Teaching award Hawaii Tchrs. ESL, 1984, Mortar Bd., 1990, Presdl. Citation for meritorious tchg., 1996. Mem. Linguistic Soc. Am., Linguistic Soc. Hawaii. Office: U Hawaii Dept Linguistics Moore Hall 569 1890 E West Rd Honolulu HI 96822-2318 Office Phone: 808-956-3277. E-mail: rehg@hawaii.edu.

REHM, PATRICE KOCH, radiologist, educator; b. DeSoto, Mo., Nov. 23, 1954; d. James Clarence and Eleanor (Koch) R. BA in Chemistry, U. Mo., 1977; MD, Yale U., 1981. Diplomate Am. Bd. Radiology, Am. Bd. Nuclear Medicine. Intern in medicine Waterbury (Conn.) Hosp., 1981-82; resident in radiology Yale New Haven Hosp., 1982-83, 84-85, fellow in neuroradiology, 1985-86, fellow in nuclear medicine, 1986-87; resident in radiology SUNY Upstate Med. Ctr., Syracuse, 1983-84; clin. assoc. Cleve. Clinic, 1987-88, staff physician, 1988-89, Presbyn. Hosp., Charlotte, N.C., 1989-91, Georgetown U. Med. Ctr., Washington, 1992—; now. assoc. prof. radiology U. Va. Health System, Charlottesville, Va. Mem. Am. Coll. Radiology, Radiologic Soc. N.Am., Soc. Nuclear Medicine. Office: U Va Health System PO Box 800170 Charlottesville VA 22908

REHM, SUSAN, physician; b. 1954; BS, U. Nebr., 1975; MD, U. Nebr., Omaha, 1978. Diplomate Am. Bd. Internal Medicine with subspecialty in infectious disease. Resident in internal medicine The Cleve. Clinic Found., 1978—81, fellow in infectious diseases, 1981—83, assoc. chief of staff, 1997—. Clin. asst. prof. Case Western Res. U., Cleve.; clin. assoc. prof. Ohio State U., Columbus. Mem.: AMA, ACP, Am. Coll. Physician Execs., Infectious Diseases Soc. Am., Am. Soc. Microbiology, Nat. Found. for Infectious Diseases (pres.). Office: The Cleveland Clinic 9500 Euclid Ave Cleveland OH 44195

REHM, SUSAN J. social services professional; b. Yorktown, Va., May 17, 1945; d. Gilbert F. and Jeradean Dolly (Field) R. BA, U. Redlands, 1967; MSW, San Diego State U., 1969. Diplomate in clin. social work; lic. social worker, Calif.; cert. tchr., Calif. Dir. clin. social work home health care and child devel. depts. UCLA Med. Ctr.; dir. social work svcs. Mercy Hosp. and Med. Ctr., San Diego, Calif.; lectr. Sch. Social Work San Diego State U.; exec. dir. Family Svc. Agy., Santa Barbara, Calif. Named state scholar, Calif., 1963-67, U.S. Children's Bur. Fellow, 1968-69. Mem. NASW, Family Svc. Am. (exec. coun.), Santa Barbara Sunrise Rotary, Nat. Found. Infectious Diseases (pres.). Office: Family Svc Agy 123 W Gutierrez St Santa Barbara CA 93101-3424

REHMAN, SAIFUR, web site design company executive; b. Lahore, Pakistan, Sept. 9, 1965; s. Mohammad Makhdoom and Naseem Akhtar; m. Sana Rehman. BSBA, Ctrl. Mo. State Univ., 1993; MS in MIS, U. Balt., 1995. Analyst Accenture (formerly Andersen Consulting), Washington, 1996—97; sr. assoc. IBM (formerly PricewaterhouseCoopers), Fairfax, Va., 1997—99; mgr. Midwest Consulting Group, Kansas City, Mo., 1999—2000; dir. KPMG Consulting Inc., Mountain View, Calif., 2000—; chmn., CEO WebBiz Inc., Palo Alto, Calif., 2001—. Mem.: Am. Soc. Quality, Data Processing Mgmt. Assn., Soc. Info. Mgmt., Project Mgmt. Inst., Delta Sigma Pi. Office: WebBiz Inc P O Box 61034 Palo Alto CA 94306 E-mail: info@irisfirm.com.

REHMUS, CHARLES MARTIN, law educator, arbitrator; b. Ann Arbor, Mich., June 27, 1926; s. Paul A. and Amy D. (Martin) R.; m. Carolyn Brown, Dec. 21, 1948 (div. July 1982); children— Paul, James, Jon, David; m. Laura Carlson, Sept. 4, 1982 AB, Kenyon Coll., 1947; MA, Stanford U., 1951, PhD, 1955. Commr. Fed. Mediation and Conciliation Service, San Francisco, 1952-58; staff dir. Presdl. R.R. Commn., Washington, 1959-61; prof. polit. sci. U. Mich., Ann Arbor, 1962-80, dir. Inst. Labor and Indsl. Relations, 1962-76; chmn. Mich. Employment Relations Commn., Detroit, 1976-80; dean N.Y. State Sch. Indsl. and Labor Relations, Cornell U., Ithaca, 1980-86; prof. law U. San Diego, 1988-97. Author: Final-Offer Arbitration, 1975, The Railway Labor Act at Fifty, 1977, Labor and American Politics, 1967, rev. edit., 1978, The National Mediation Board, 1984, Emergency Strikes Revisited, 1990. Chmn. 4 Presdl. emergency bds. at various times. Served to lt. USNR, 1943-45; PTO Mem. Internat. Inst. Labor Studies (bd. govs. 1984-92), Indsl. Rels. Rsch. Assn. (exec. bd. 1984-88), Nat. Acad. Arbitrators (bd. govs. 1979-82, v.p. 1993-95). Home: 18755 W Bernardo Dr Apt 1027 San Diego CA 92127-3011

REHNKE, MARY ANN, academic administrator; b. Faribault, Minn., Jan. 23, 1945; d. Wesley Arthur and Sarah Frances (Smith) Rehnke; m. Charles Orin Willis, Apr. 18, 1924. BA in English, Cornell Coll., 1967; MA in English, U. Chgo., 1968, PhD in Lit., 1974; MS in Ednl Adminstrn., U. Wis., 1975. Head resident Elizabeth Waters Hall, U. Wis., Madison, 1970-73; asst. prof. English No. Ky. U., Highland Heights, 1973-82, acad. adminstr., 1976-77, dir. summer sessions, 1977-80; dir. conf. planning Am. Assn. Higher Edn., Washington, 1980-82; assoc. dean for faculty relations and acad. programs Coll. St. Catherine, St. Paul, 1982-83; assoc. dean of coll. Daemen Coll., Buffalo, N.Y., 1983-85; v.p. ann. programs Council of Ind. Colls., Washington, 1986—. Mem. planning com. nat. identification program Am. Council Edn., Washington, 1978-85; mem. program com. Nat. Conf. Women Student Leaders and Women of Distinction, Washington, 1985-88. Author: Women in Higher Education Administration: A Brief Guide for Conference Planners, 1982, Guide to Spiritual Retreats in the Washington, D.C. Area, 1997; editor: Creating Career Programs in a Liberal Arts Context, 1987; editor newsletter N. Ctl. Regional Women's Studies, 1978-80; columnist Teaching and Learning, The Independent. Vestry mem Ch. of St. Clement, Alexandria, Va., 1982, vice chair search com., 1986-87. Named one of Outstanding Young Women Am., 1976. Mem. Am. Assn. Higher Edn. (coordinator nat. conf. roundtable 1982-86), Nat. Assn. Women Deans, Adminstrs. and Counselors, N.Am. Assn. Summer Sessions (rsch. chair 1979-80), Soc. for Values in Higher Edn., Jane Austen Soc. N.Am., Phi Beta Kappa, Phi Delta Kappa. Democrat. Episcopalian.

REHNQUIST, WILLIAM HUBBS, United States supreme court chief justice; b. Milw., Oct. 1, 1924; s. William Benjamin and Margery (Peck) Rehnquist; m. Natalie Cornell, Aug. 29, 1953; children: James, Janet, Nancy. BA, MA, Stanford U., 1948, LLB, 1952; MA, Harvard U., 1949. Bar: Ariz. Law clk. to former justice Robert H. Jackson, U.S. Supreme Ct., 1952-53; with Evans, Kitchel & Jenckes, Phoenix, 1953-55; mem. Ragan & Rehnquist, Phoenix, 1956-57; ptnr. Cunningham, Carson & Messenger, Phoenix, 1957-60, Powers & Rehnquist, Phoenix, 1960-69; asst. atty.-gen. office of legal counsel Dept. of Justice, Washington, 1969-71; assoc. justice U.S. Supreme Ct., 1971-1986, chief justice, 1986—. Mem. Nat. Conf. Commrs. Uniform State Laws, 1963—69. Author: The Supreme Court: How It Was, How It Is, 1987, Grand Inquests: The Historic Impeachments of Justice Samuel Chase and President Andrew Johnson, 1992, All the Laws But One, 1999, Centennial Crisis, The Disputed Election of 1876, 2003; contbr. articles to profl. jours. With USAF, 1943—46. Mem.: Nat. Conf. Lawyers and Realtors, State Bar Ariz., Am. Maricopa County Bar Assn., Fed. Bar Assn., Order of Coif, Phi Delta Phi, Phi Beta Kappa. Lutheran. Office: Supreme Ct US 1 First St NE Washington DC 20543-0001

REHNS, MARSHA LEE, magazine editor, writer; b. Balt., Dec. 23, 1946; d. Fred and Ruth (Lieber) R.; m. Walter Richard Arnheim, Sept. 5, 1971; children: Ethan, Phillip. BS, U. Pitts., 1967; MPhil, Yale, 1970. Editor Sci. Med. Pub., N.Y.C., 1972-75, Haymarket Pub., London, 1975-76; mng. editor Harcourt Brace Jovanovich, N.Y.C., 1977-79; editor Sta. WGBH-TV, Boston, 1979-80; columnist Weightwatchers Mag., N.Y.C., 1979-81; editor Am. Baby, N.Y.C., 1981—; cons. Cradle Pub., N.Y.C., 1990-94; writer Kids Discover, N.Y.C., 1991—97, Nat. Mus. Natural History, 1994—; editor Educating Our Children, N.Y.C., 1996; writer U.S. Geol. Surv., Reston, 1999, Newark Mus., 1999—2002; instrnl. designer Nat. Mus. Natural History, 2002—03. Co-author: Seeds of Change: Learning from the Garden, 2000, Brain Attack, 2001. Docent Nat. Mus. Natural History, Washington, 1990—. Home: 10712 Barn Wood Ln Potomac MD 20854-1326

REHORN, LOIS M(ARIE) (LOIS MARIE SMITH), nursing administrator; b. Larned, Kans., Apr. 15, 1919; d. Charles and Ethel L. (Canaday) Williamson; m. C. Howard Smith, Feb. 15, 1946 (dec. Aug. 1980); 1 child, Cynthia A. Huddleston; m. Harlan W. Rehorn, Aug. 25, 1981. RN, Bethany Hosp. Sch. Nursing, Kansas City, Kans., 1943; BS, Ft. Hays Kans. State U., Hays, 1968, MS, 1970. RN, N.Mex.; lic. pvt. pilot. Office nurse, surg. asst. Dr. John H. Luke, Kansas City, Kans., 1943-47; supr. nursing unit Larned (Kans.) State Hosp., 1949-68, dir. nursing edn., 1968-71, dir. nursing, 1972-81, ret., 1981. Recipient Order of the Blue Key, 1942-43; named Nurse of Yr. DNA-4, 1986. Mem. Am. Nurses Assn., Kans. Nurses Assn. (dist. treas.), N.Mex. Nurses Assn. (dist. pres. 1982-86, dist. bd. dirs. 1986-88). Avocation: flying (pilot). Home: 1436 Brentwood Dr Clovis NM 88101-4602 *Keep within you a place where dreams may grow. The fountain of understanding is the willingness to listen.*

REHORN, RICK, state representative; b. Denver, Apr. 28, 1961; m. Jane Rehorn; 1 child. BS in History, U. Kans., 1984, PhD, 1987. Atty.; mem. Kans. Ho. of Reps., 1999—. Democrat. Methodist. Office: 278-W State Capitol 300 SW 10th Ave Topeka KS 66612 Home: 4151 Cambridge Kansas City KS 66103

REIBACK, EARL MARTIN, artist; b. Bklyn., May 30, 1948; s. Sidney Marshall and Beatrice (Rubeinstein) R.; m. Elizabeth M. Meneses, Feb. 24, 1993. BA in English, BS in Engring. Physics, Lehigh U., 1963; MS in Nuclear Engring., MIT, 1967. Lectr. in field. One-man shows include Howard Wise Gallery, N.Y.C., 1965, 66, 68-70, Met. Mus. Art, N.Y.C., 1967, Chapman Kelley Gallery, Dallas, 1969, Moos Gallery, Montreal, Can., 1969-70, Waddell Gallery, N.Y.C., 1972-73, Colibri Gallery, San Juan, P.R., 1974, Esther Robles Gallery, L.A., 1975, 82, Elec. Gallery, Toronto, Can., 1971, 76, 84, Whitney Mus. Am. Art, 1994, O.K. Harris Gallery, N.Y.C., 1995, Cite des arts et des nouvelles techs. de Montreal, 1996, Images du Future, Montreal, 1996, San Jose Mus. Art, 1997-98, Long Beach (Calif.) Mus. Art, 1997, Cinema de Baile, Amsterdam, 2003; represented in permanent collections Whitney Mus. Am. Art, Mus. Modern Art, Phila. Mus. Art, Newark Mus., Flint Inst. Art, Balt. Mus. Art, Milw. Art Ctr., Phoenix Art Mus., Krannert Art Mus., New Orleans Mus. Art, Portland Mus. Art, La Jolla Mus., Long Beach Mus. Contemporary Art, Aldrich Mus. Contemporary Art, Worcester Mus., Wichita Art Mus., Mus. Art, Carnegie Inst., Musee de Art Contemporian, Montreal, Art Mus. Windsor, Can., Lannan Found.Mus., Walker Art Ctr., Art Mus. South Tex., Franklin Inst., U.S. Cultural Ctr., Tel Aviv, Taft Mus., Alexandria Jus., Huntsville Mus. Art, Lawton Gallery, Mus. N.C. Home: 20 E 9th St Apt 80 New York NY 10003-5944 Office Phone: 212-477-6030. E-mail: ereiback@nyc.rr.com.

REIBEL, KURT, physicist, researcher; b. Vienna, May 23, 1926; came to U.S., 1938; s. Michael and Regina (Pak) R.; m. Eleanor Elvira Mannino, June 10, 1954; children— Leah, Michael, David BA, Temple U., 1954; MS, U. Pa., 1956, PhD, 1959. Jr. research assoc. in physics Brookhaven Nat. Lab., 1957-59; research assoc. U. Pa., Phila., 1959-61; asst. prof. Ohio State U., Columbus, 1961-64, assoc. prof., 1964-70, prof. physics, 1970-92, prof. emeritus, 1992—. Vis. scientist CERN, Geneva, Switzerland, 1968-69, 75-76 Author research papers on nuclear and elementary particle physics NSF fellow, 1954-56 Mem. Am. Phys. Soc., AAUP, Fedn. Am. Scientists, Union Concerned Scientists, Sigma Xi Jewish. Office: Ohio State U Dept Physics 174 W 18th Ave Columbus OH 43210-1106

REIBLE, DANNY DAVID, environmental chemical engineer, educator; b. Rantoul, Ill., Dec. 21, 1954; s. George Anthony and Mavis Otilla (Prause) R.; m. Susanne Cecilia Schulte, Mar. 17, 1979; children: Kristin Nicole, Monica Lynn. BS, Lamar U., 1977; MS, Calif. Inst. Tech., 1979, PhD, 1982. Registered profl. engr., La. Asst. prof. La. State U., Baton Rouge, 1981-86, assoc. prof., 1986-92, prof. chem. engring., 1992—, Chevron prof. chem. engring., 1998—, dir. Hazardous Substance Rsch. Ctr., 1995—; Shell prof. environ. engring. U. Sydney, Australia, 1993-95. Vis. rschr. U.S. Army Engr.

Waterways Experiment Sta., Vicksburg, Miss., 1990; sr. visitor Cambridge (Eng.) U., 1992; cons. in field. Author: Fundamentals of Environmental Engineering, 1999, Diffusion Models of Environmental Transport, 2000; contbr. articles to profl. publs. Environ. Sci. and Engring. fellow AAAS, 1987. Mem. AIChE (exec. bd. 1990-95, mem. nat. programming com., chair Baton Rouge sect. 2000, L.K. Cecil award 2001), Am. Chem. Soc., Am. Geophys. Union, Am. Soc. Engring. Edn. (New Engring. Educator Excellence award 1985), Coms. Nat. Rsch. Coun., Sigma Xi. Achievements include identification and evaluation of new mechanisms for contaminant release in the environment; further quantitative modeling of fate and transport contaminants in environmental systems. Home: 2112 Oakcliff Dr Baton Rouge LA 70810-1856 Office: La State U HSRC/S&SW 3418 Ceba Baton Rouge LA 70803-0001

REIBMAN, JEANETTE FICHMAN, retired state senator; b. Ft. Wayne, Ind., Aug. 18, 1915; d. Meir and Pearl (Schwartz) Fichman; m. Nathan L. Reibman, June 20, 1943; children: Joseph M. Edward D., James E. AB, Hunter Coll., 1937; LLB, U. Ind., 1940; LLD, Lafayette Coll., 1969; hon. degree, Lehigh U., 1986, Wilson Coll., 1974, Cedar Crest Coll., 1977, Moravian Coll., 1990. Bar: Ind., 1940, U.S. Supreme Ct. 1944. Pvt. practice law, Ft. Wayne, 1940; atty. U.S. War Dept., Washington, 1940-42, U.S. War Prodn. Bd., Washington, 1942-44; mem. Pa. Ho. of Reps., 1956-66, Pa. State Senate, Harrisburg, 1966-94, chmn. com. on edn., 1971-81, minority chmn., 1981-90, majority caucus adminstr., 1992-94. Mem. Edn. Commn. of the States. Trustee emeritus Lafayette Coll.; bd. mem. Pa. Higher Edn. Assistance Agy., Pa. Coun. on Arts, Camphill Schs. Recipient Disting. Dau. of Pa. award and medal Gov. Pa., 1968, citation on naming of Jeanette F. Reibman Adminstrn. Bldg., East Stroudsburg State Coll., 1972, Early Childhood Learning Ctr. Northampton Community Coll., 1992, Pub. Svc. award Pa. Psychol. Assn., 1977, Jerusalem City of Peace award Govt. Israel, 1977; named to Hunter Coll. Alumni Hall of Fame, 1974; U. Ind. Law Alumni fellow, 1993. Mem. Hadassah (Myrtle Wreath award 1976), Sigma Delta Tau, Delta Kappa Gamma, Phi Delta Kappa, Order Ea. Star. Democrat. Jewish. Office: 711 Lehigh St Easton PA 18042-4325 Home: 1332 Kirkland Village Cir Bethlehem PA 18017-4759

REICE, SYLVIE, columnist, editor, author; b. N.Y.C. d. Samuel and Dora (Weinstock) Wolshine; m. Albert Reice, July 15, 1962; children: Milo, Naomi, Seth, Andrew, Richard. BA cum laude, CUNY; postgrad., New Sch. for Social Rsch., N.Y.C. Mng. editor Co-ed mag. Scholastic Publs., N.Y.C., 1955-59; editor-in-chief Ingenue mag. Dell Pub. Co., N.Y.C., 1959-67; columnist The Swinging Set, Pubs. Hall Syndicate, 1965-70; sr. editor McCalls mag., N.Y.C., 1967-71; editor-in-chief Family Health mag., N.Y.C., 1971-74; exec. editor Newspaper books Chgo. Tribune-N.Y. News Syndicate, N.Y.C., 1975-76; sr. editor Grosset & Dunlap Books, N.Y.C., 1976-79; columnist United Features Syndicate, N.Y.C., 1980—2003. Freelance writer, 1946—; adj. prof. mag. journalism SUNY-Stony Brook, 1970. Author: (short story collections) For Girls Only, 1957, Season of Love, 1962; columnist United Feature Syndicate, NYC, 1980-2003, Adventures in Art, Prime Times, 1998—; contbr. articles to various publs., including McCalls, Health, Seventeen, Ladies Home Jour. Guest editor Taproot mag. for elder citizens, L.I., N.Y., 1986-87. Recipient Penney Missouri award for best article of yr., 1970, award for best short story Bur. of Intercultural Edn., 1952. Mem. PEN, Poetry Soc. Am., Newswomens Club N.Y. (v.p. 1984-94, pres. 1983-84), Phi Beta Kappa. Home and Office: 401 E 81st St New York NY 10028-5811 E-mail: sylvierite@aol.com.

REICH, ABRAHAM CHARLES, lawyer; b. Waterbury, Conn., Apr. 17, 1949; s. Samuel and Esther (Gurvitz) Reich; m. Sherri Engelman, Aug. 15, 1971; children: Spencer, Alexander. BA, U. Conn., 1971; JD, Temple U., 1974. Bar: Pa. 1974, U.S. Supreme Ct. 1979. Assoc. Fox Rothschild LLP, Phila., 1974-81, ptnr., 1981—, mng. ptnr., 2001—. Chair lawyers adv. com. U.S. Ct. Appeals (3d cir.), 1998. Fellow: Am. Coll. Trial Lawyers; mem.: ABA (ho. of dels. 1997—2002, 2004—), Phila. Bar Assn. (chair profl. responsibility com. 1983—84, chair bench-bar com. 1985, chair profl. guidance com. 1987—88, bd. govs. 1987—89, chair bd. govs. 1989, chancellor 1995, del. ABA 1996—2000). Home: 2224 Mount Vernon St Philadelphia PA 19130-3115 Office: Fox Rothschild LLP 2000 Market St Ste 10 Philadelphia PA 19103-3231 Office Phone: 215-299-2090. Business E-Mail: areich@foxrothschild.com.

REICH, ALAN ANDERSON, foundation administrator; b. Pearl River, N.Y., Jan. 1, 1930; s. Oswald David and Alma Carolyn (Anderson) R.; m. Gay Ann Forsythe, Dec. 19, 1954; children: James, Jeffrey, Andrew, Elizabeth. BA, Dartmouth Coll., 1952; diploma in Slavic Studies, Oxford U., 1953; MA, Russian Inst., Middlebury Coll., 1953; MBA, Harvard U., 1959; LLD (hon.), Gallaudet Coll., 1981, Dartmouth Coll., 1992. Exec. Polaroid Corp., Cambridge, Mass., 1960-70; dep. asst. sec. ednl. and cultural affairs Dept. State, Washington, 1970-75; spl. asst. to sec. HEW, 1976-77; dep. asst. sec. commerce, dir. Bur. East-West Trade, Dept. Commerce, Washington, 1977-78; pres. U.S. Coun. for Internat. Yr. of Disabled Persons, Washington, 1978-81, Nat. Orgn. Disability, Washington, 1982—, Bimillennium Found., 1982—, Disability 2000 CEO coun., 1991—. Co-editor: Russian Proverbs, 1998. Chmn. Sudbury (Mass.) Community United Fund, 1962, 66; mem. U.S. del. WHO Gen. Assembly, 1970; pres. Nat. Paraplegia Found.; chmn. bd. dirs. Paralysis Cure Research Found., bd. dirs. of the Healing Community, chmn. People-to-people Com. for Handicapped; Impact Found., 1986—; chmn. World Com. on Disability, 1985—. Served to 1st lt. inf. AUS, 1953-57. Named to U.S. Army Inf. OCS Hall of Fame, 1994; recipient Server award for svc. to handicapped, 1994. Mem. Paralyzed Vets. Washington Inst. Fgn. Affairs, Am., Cosmos Club, Achilles Club (London), Beta Theta Pi. Republican. Methodist. Home: 6017 Copely Ln Mc Lean VA 22101-2507 Office: Nat Orgn on Disability 910 16th St NW Ste 600 Washington DC 20006-2916

REICH, ALLAN J. lawyer; b. Chgo., July 9, 1948; s. H. Robert and Sonya (Minsky) R.; m. Lynne Susan Roth, May 23, 1971; children: Allison, Marissa, Scott. BA, Cornell U., 1970; JD cum laude, U. Mich., 1973. Bar: Ill. 1973, U.S. Dist. Ct. (no. dist.) Ill. 1973. Ptnr. McDermott, Will & Emery, Chgo., 1973-93; vice chmn. D'Ancona & Pflaum LLC, Chgo., 1993—2003; ptnr. Seyfarth Shaw LLP, Chgo., 2003—. Trustee Oakmark Family of Mutual Funds, 1994—. V.p., mem. exec. com. Coun. for Jewish Elderly, 1989—97; mem. men's coun. Mus. Contemporary Art, Chgo., 1988—89; mem. Chgo. exec. bd. Am. Jewish Com., 1989—, nat. bd. govs.; mem. met. Chgo. bd. Am. Heart Assn.; bd. dirs. Young Men's Jewish Coun., Chgo., 1974—84, Coun. for Jewish Elderly, 1986—97. Fellow: Am. Bar Found.; mem.: ABA, Chgo. Bar Assn., Econ. Club Chgo., Northmoor Country Club (Highland Park, Ill.), Standard Club (Chgo.). Home: 936 Skokie Ridge Dr Glencoe IL 60022-1434 Office: Seyforth Shaw LLP 55 E Monroe St Ste 4200 Chicago IL 60603-5803 Office Phone: 312-781-8650. E-mail: areich@seyfarth.com.

REICH, BERNARD, retired telecommunications engineer; b. N.Y.C., Jan. 7, 1926; s. Adolph and Rose (Gluck) R.; m. Sylvia Greenberg, June 15, 1947; children: Robin Reich Murphy, Richard. BS in Physics, CCNY, 1948; MSc, Rutgers U., 2002. Electronic engr., supervisory electronic engr. U.S. Army Electronics R & D Command, Ft. Monmouth, N.J., 1948-81; unit mgr. Semcor, Farmingdale, N.J., 1981-88; telecommunications engr. Telos Corp., Shrewsbury, N.J., 1988-99, retired, 1999. Chmn. spl. working group on semicondrs. and microelectronics NATO, Brussels, 1959-80, chmn. group experts on electronic parts, 1972-80; adv. editor Microelectronics and Reliability, 1970—. Contbr. over 100 articles to tech. jours.; patentee in field. Mem. Juvenile Conf. Com., Ocean Twp., N.J., 1964—; pres. Manor at Wayside Condominium Assn., Ocean Twp., 1990-91. Sgt. U.S. Army, 1945-46, ETO. Recipient decoration for meritorious civilian svc. U.S. Army Electronics R & D Command, 1981. Fellow IEEE (chartered,), IEE (Eng.). Avocations: walking, grandparenting. Home: 45 Gimbel Pl Ocean NJ 07712-2565

REICH, CHARLES, manufacturing executive, research scientist; b. Mpls., Aug. 2, 1942; BS in Chemistry, U. Minn.; PhD in Organic Chemistry, U. Wis. Rsch. chemist 3M Co., 1968—73, various tech. mgmt. positions, 1973—82, mng. dir., Switzerland opers., 1982—89, v.p., dental products divsn., 1989—97, v.p., occupl. health and environ. safety divsn., 1997—98, group v.p., chem. markets group, 1998, group v.p., specialty material markets group, 1999, exec. v.p., specialty material markets and corp. svcs., 1999—2001, exec. v.p., elec. and comm. markets, 2001—02, exec. v.p., health care bus., 2002—. Office: 3M Co 3M Ctr Saint Paul MN 55144

REICH, DAVID LEE, library director; b. Orlando, Fla., Nov. 25, 1930; s. P.F. and Opal Katherine (Wood) Reichelderfer; m. Kathleen Johanna Weichel, Aug. 2, 1954 (div. Sept. 1964); 1 son, Robert Weichel. PhB magna cum laude, U. Detroit, 1961; AM in LS, U. Mich., 1963. Tchr. English Jefferson Davis Jr. Sch., San Antonio, 1961-62; dir. engring. library Radiation Inc., Melbourne, Fla., 1963-64; asst. to dir. libraries Miami-Dade Jr. Coll., Miami, Fla., 1964-65; dir. learning resources Monroe County C.C., Monroe, Mich., 1965-68; dep. dir. Dallas Pub. Library, 1968-73; dep. chief librarian Chgo. Pub. Library, 1973-74, commr., 1975-78; dir. Bd. Libr. Commrs., Commonwealth of Mass., Boston, 1978-80; exec. sec. New Eng. Libr. Bd., Augusta, Maine, 1980-82, vice chmn., 1979-80; dir. Lakeland (Fla.) Pub. Libr., 1983-99, ret., 1999; exec. sec. Soc. Fla. Archivists, 1999—2001, ret., 2001. Libr. cons. Macomb County C.C., Warren, Mich., 1967; chmn. adv. com. to libr. tech. asst. program El Centro Coll., Dallas, 1969-71; mem. inter-task working group Goals for Dallas, 1968-70, mem. Dallas Area Libr. planning coun., 1970-73; mem. adv. coun. dept. libr. sci. No. Ill. U., 1975-78; v.p., pres.-elect Tampa Bay Libr. Consortium, 1985-86, pres., 1986-87. Co-author: The Public Library in Non-traditional Education, 1974; editor The Villas II News, 1999—; contbr. articles to library jours. Bd. dirs. The Villas II Homeowners Assn., 1994-96, 98-2001; steering com. Friends of Tampa Bay Libr. Consortium, 2000—. Sgt. U.S. Army, 1952-55. Recipient Disting. Alumnus award U. Mich., 1978; William B. Calkins Found. scholar Orlando, 1963; Carnegie L.S. Endowment scholar, 1963. Mem. ALA (coun.-at-large 1968-72, 75-79), S.E. Libr. Assn., Fla. Libr. Assn. (sec.-treas. coll. and spl. librs. divsn. 1965, steering com. mcpl. librs. caucus 1983-84, chmn. 1984-85, exec. bd. 1984-87), Soc. Fla. Archivists (exec. bd. 1994-96, sec. 1996-97, exec. sec. 1999-2001, treas. 2000-01), Fla. Pub. Libr. Assn. (pres. 1987-88, exec. bd. 1988-89, 94-95, pres. emeritus 1996-98, editor newsletter 1992-93, 96-97, chmn. libr. adminstrn. divsn. 1992, friends and trustees divsn. 1993, 95), Soc. Automotive Historians, Alumni Assn. U. Mich. (pres. Libr. Sch. alumni 1973), Nat. Soc. SAR (2d v.p. 2004-). Home: 4011 Heron Ave Lakeland FL 33813-1123 E-mail: dreich@tampabay.rr.com.

REICH, ELLEN JUDITH, actress, writer; b. Newark, Apr. 30, 1957; d. Mortimer and Lucretia Pzygucki Reich; m. Richard S. Glaser, May 26, 1985; children: Joseph E. Glaser-Reich, Daniel C. Glaser-Reich. AB, Vassar Coll., 1974—78; JD, Nat. Law Ctr., George Wash. U., 1979—82. Attorney: Md. Bar Assn. 1982. Author: (book) Waiting: A Diary Of Loss & Hope In Pregnancy, (poetry & historic archive photographs) Gershwin & Apricot Silk; actor: (commercials) Hurricane Damage, 1996; (plays) Who Will Carry The Word, Laundry & Bourbon. Bd. mem. HADASSAH, Charlotte, NC, 2000—, Mecklenburg Mental Health Assn., Charlotte, NC, 2000—02, Temple Beth El, Charlotte, NC, 2003—, Judea Reform Congregation, Durham, NC, 1989—92. Mem.: Assn. Of Personal Historians, Nat. Assn. Of Poetry Therapy. Independent. Jewish. Avocations: reading, theater, walking, swimming, weightlifting, bicycling.

REICH, HERB, editor; b. N.Y.C. s. Herman S. and Hattie (Davis) R.; m. Gerri Toog, Aug. 7, 1960; children: Amanda Suri, Elizabeth Jo. BA, Bklyn. Coll., 1950; MA, Bklyn. Coll. and Kings County Hosp., 1951; postgrad., Columbia U., 1951-54. Author sketches and lyrics Tamiment Revues (Pa.), 1951; staff writer NBC-TV, N.Y.C. and Los Angeles, 1955-57; research coordinator Inst. for Motivational Research, Croton-on-Hudson, N.Y., 1958-59; research dir. Scientist and Engr. Technol. Inst., N.Y.C., 1960-64; mng. editor SETI Pubs. Inc., N.Y.C., 1961-64; sr. editor Odyssey Press, N.Y.C., 1964-65; editorial dir. Profl. and Tech. Programs Inc., N.Y.C., 1966-72; dir. Behavioral Sci. Book Service, N.Y.C., 1966-72; dir. behavioral scis. program Basic Books Inc., N.Y.C., 1973-79; editor intersci. div. John Wiley & Sons. Inc., N.Y.C., 1979-87, sr. editor profl. and trade divsn., 1987-95; pres. H&G Reich, Cons., Hastings Hdsn., NY, 1980—. Publ., rsch., advt. and polit. cons.; rschr., statistician, rsch. cons. Am. Found. for Blind, Pepsi Cola Co., Nowland and Co., Comms. and Media Rsch. Svcs. Mng. editor: Odyssey Science Library Ency. of Engring., Signs and Symbols, 1965, Dictionary of Physics and Mathematics Abbreviations, Signs and Symbols, 1965, Dictionary of Electronics Abbreviations, Signs and Symbols, 1965, Dictionary of Computers and Control Systems Abbreviations, Signs and Symbols, 1965; contbr. Random House Dictionary of the English Language, 1967, rev. edit., 1987, The Greatest Revue Sketches, 1982, Ency. of Psychology, 2d edit., 1994; TV writer: Broadway Open House, 1951, Olsen and Johnson Show, 1951, Milton Berle Texaco Star Theatre, 1952, All-Star Revue, 1952, Mel Torme Show, 1952, Eddie Cantor Show, 1953, Red Buttons Show, 1954, Summer Colgate Show, 1954, Jerry Lester Show, 1954, Jan Murray Time, 1955, Howdy Doody Show, 1955-56, Tonight Show, 1956, NBC Comedy Hour, 1956, Wayne and Schuster Hour, 1957. Co-founder, vice chmn. Mt. Vernon United for Better Edn., N.Y., 1970-73; mem. Westchester County Democratic Com., 1972-76; exec. com. Mt. Vernon Dem. City Com., 1973-76; mem. supt.'s adv. com. Hastings Schs., Hastings-on-Hudson, N.Y., 1981-82. Recipient Gold award of excellence for radio advt. Advt. Club of Westchester, 1980; recipient Gold and Bronze awards of excellence for radio advt. Advt. Club of Westchester, 1981 Mem. AAAS, APA, Alpha Phi Omega. Office: PO Box 38 Hastings On Hudson NY 10706 Office Phone: 914-478-4042. E-mail: hgreich@aol.com.

REICH, JACK W. health products executive; BA in Biology, Washington and Jefferson Coll.; BS in Pharmacy, Creighton U.; MS in Hosp. Pharmacy Adminstrn., PhD in Pharms.-Internat. Pharm. Adminstrn., Temple U. V.p. regulatory affairs and quality ops. Gensia, Inc. (now Gensia Sicor, Inc.), 1987—94; sr. v.p. Enterprise Ptnrs., Calif., 1994—95; co-founder MyoTech, Inc., 1995—96; pres. Collateral Therapeutics, Inc., San Diego, 1995—99, bd. dirs., CEO, 1995—, chmn. bd. dirs., 1999—; bd. dirs., chmn. CIStem Molecular Corp. Office: Collateral Therapeutics Inc 11622 El Camino Real San Diego CA 92130

REICH, JILL, dean; B.A., Regis College; Ph. D. in Psychology, Dartmouth Coll. Fmr. dept. chair, assoc. dean Grad. school Loyola; fmr. dean of faculty Trinity College; fmr. exec. dir. of education American Psychology Assoc.; prof., dept. of psychology Bates Coll., v.p. of academic affairs, dean of faculty, 2000—. Office: Bates Coll Lane Hall Rm 120A 2 Andrews Rd Lewiston ME 04240

REICH, KENNETH IRVIN, journalist; b. Los Angeles, Mar. 7, 1938; s. Herman and Ruth Alberta (Nussbaum) R.; children: Kathleen, David. BA, Dartmouth Coll., 1960; MA (Woodrow Wilson fellow), U. Calif., Berkeley, 1962. With UPI, Sacramento, 1962-63, Life mag., 1963-65; with Los Angeles Times, 1965—, polit. writer, 1972-77, 1984 Olympics writer, 1977-84, investigative reporter ins. law, ins. politics & fin. sports, 1985-92. Covering earthquakes, volcanoes, and other issues relating to geology, 1980—; columnist of consumer affairs, 1998-2001; lectr. in field. Author: Making it Happen, Peter Ueberroth and the 1984 Olympics, 1985; contbr. articles to mags. Meml. chmn. Dartmouth Class of 1960, 1993-95, class sec. 1995—. Daniel Webster Nat. Honor scholar Dartmouth Coll., 1956-60. Office: LA Times 202 W 1st St Los Angeles CA 90012 Office Phone: 213-237-7060. Business E-Mail: ken.reich@latimes.com.

REICH, LAURENCE, lawyer; b. Jersey City, Jan. 22, 1931; s. Victor and Miriam (Gross) R.; m. Doris Rita Diamond, Oct. 21, 1965 (dec. Apr. 15, 2002). BA, U. Chgo., 1951, JD, 1953. Bar: N.J. 1954, N.Y. 1982, U.S. Dist. Ct. N.J. 1954, U.S. ct. appeals (3rd cir.) 1958, U.S. Supreme ct. 1963, U.S. Tax Ct. 1971, U.S. Dist. Ct. (so. dist.) N.Y. 1982, U.S. Ct. Appeals (2nd cir.) 1987. From mem. firm to sr. ptnr. Carpenter, Bennett & Morrissey, Newark, 1957—2003, sr. counsel, 2004—. Mem. Bur. Nat. Affairs Tax Adv. bd., 1972—; lectr. in field. Author: N.J. Corporation Law and Practice; contbr. articles to profl. jours. With U.S. Army, 1955-57. Fellow Am. Coll. Tax Counsel, Am. Bar Found.; mem. ABA (com. chmn. sect. taxation 1972-74, 85-86, mem. coun. 1991-94), N.J. Bar Assn. (chmn. taxation sect. 1975-76), Assn. Fed. Bar State N.J. (v.p. 1982-94, bd. trustees 1994-99), Essex County Bar Assn. Office: 3 Gateway Ctr Newark NJ 07102-4079 E-mail: lr@carpben.com.

REICH, MERRILL DRURY, intelligence consultant, writer; b. Washington, Aug. 28, 1930; s. Merrill Dale Reich and Evelyn Merle Wright; m. Georgia Ann Ewing, Aug. 28, 1953; 1 child, Alexandra Therese. BA in History, Govt., Rollins Coll., 1954; postgrad., U. Vienna, 1954-55, Naval War Coll., 1973-74; MA in Mgmt., Cen. Mich. U., 1981. Commd. ensign USN, 1956, advanced through grades to capt., ret., 1982; dir. systems mgmt. BDM Corp., Columbia, Md., 1982-92; cons. Crytec, Inc., 1992-95. Fulbright scholar, 1954-55. Mem. SAR, Nat. Trust for Hist. Preservation, U.S. Naval Inst., Naval War Coll. Found., Assn. Former Intelligence Officers, Navy Cryptologic Vets. Assn., Fulbright Assn., New Eng. Hist. Geneal. Soc., Omicron Delta Kappa, Pi Gamma Mu, Phi Kappa Tau. Avocations: genealogy, lapidary, antiques, swimming, sailing. Home: 1605 Stern Ct Annapolis MD 21401 E-mail: mreich@comcast.net.

REICH, MICHAEL, economics professor; b. Poland, Oct. 18, 1945; came to U.S., 1949; s. Melvin and Betty (Mandelbaum) R.; children: Rachel, Gabriel. BA, Swarthmore Coll., 1966; PhD, Harvard U., 1974. Asst. prof. Boston U., 1971-74, U. Calif., Berkeley, 1974-81, acting assoc. prof., 1981-82, assoc. prof., 1982-89, prof., 1989—. Rsch. dir. Nat. Ctr. for the Workplace, 1993-96, Inst. Labor and Employment, 2001—04, Inst. Industrial Relations, 2004-. Author: Segmented Work, Divided Workers, 1982, Racial Inequality, 1981, The Capitalist System, 1986, Social Structures of Accumulation, 1994, Work and Pay in the U.S. and Japan, 1997; editor: Indsl. Rels. Jour., 1986-94; contbr. articles to profl. jours. Mem. Am. Econ. Assn., Indsl. Rels. Rsch. Assn., Phi Beta Kappa, Sigma Xi. Office: Dept of Econs U Calif 611 Evans Hl Berkeley CA 94720-0001

REICH, MICHAEL IRA, obstetrician/gynecologist; b. N.Y.C., Mar. 31, 1951; s. Mark and Esther (Friedman) R.; m. Ann Bennett Terry, Apr. 27, 1991; children: Hannah Gallogley, Thomas Felix BS in Physics, Cooper Union, 1972; MD, Albert Einstein Coll., 1976. Diplomate Am. Bd. Ob-gyn. Intern N.Y. Med. Coll., N.Y.C., 1976-77; resident in ob/gyn. U. Cin., 1978-81; pvt. practice Salem (Mass.) Women's Health Assocs.; staff North Shore Med. Ctr., Salem. Vol. physician to No. Nigeria World Health Mission, Allison Park, Pa., 1996—98, 2000—03. Fellow Am. Coll. Ob-gyn., Am. Soc. Reproductive Medicine. Jewish. Office: 400 Highland Ave Salem MA 01970-7003 E-mail: terreich@massmed.org.

REICH, NATHANIEL EDWIN, internist, educator, poet, artist; b. N.Y.C., May 19, 1907; s. Alexander and Betty (Feigenbaum) R.; m. Joan Finkel, May 22, 1943; children: Andrew, Matthew. BS, NYU, 1927; student, Marquette U. Coll. Medicine, 1927-29; MD, Rush Med. Coll., U. Chgo., 1932. Diplomate Am. Bd. Internal Medicine. Intern, resident pathologist City Hosp., N.Y.C., 1931-33; emeritus attending physician Kingsbrook Jewish Med. Center Hosp.; vis. physician Kings County Hosp., Bklyn.; attending physician State U. Hosp.; faculty SUNY Downstate Med. Center, 1938—, asso. clin. prof. medicine, 1952-74, clin. prof., 1974-77, emeritus prof., 1977—. Vis. prof. San Marcos U. Coll. Medicine, Lima, Peru, 1968, U. Afghanistan, 1970, U. Indonesia, 1972, U. Sri Lanka, 1975; asst. attending physician N.Y. Postgrad. Hosp., Columbia U., 1940; cons. Dept. H and HS; cardiac cons. U.S. R.R. Retirement Bd., 1965—; program cons. Acad. Family Physicians, 1973, N.Y. State Disability Determinations; lectr. univs., Rome, Moscow, Rijeka, Haiti, Jerusalem, Cairo, Athens, Bangkok, Bucharest, Manila, Lisbon, Beijing, Shanghai, Romania, Taiwan, Madras, Dakar, Senegal, Durban, Witwatersrand, Capetown, Natal, Lima, Buenos Aires, Rio de Janeiro, Quito; 1st Am. physician invited to lecture in USSR, 1956; lectr. univs. U. Madras (India), 1969, Spain, 1971, Auckland, N.Z., Sydney, Australia, Senegal, Portugal; lectr. Japan Med. Assn., Philippine Heart Assn., Royal Thai Air Force Med. Svc., China Med. Assn., Shanghai, 1978, Nat. Taiwan U., Taipei, 1978, Beijing Cardiac Inst., 1986; chmn. internat. cardiology sect. Congress Chest Diseases, Cologne, Germany, 1956; impartial specialist U.S. Fed. Employees; cons. N.Y. State Bur. Disability Determinations, N.Y.C., Office Vocat. Rehab., Dept. Health and Human Svcs., 1965—; chief med. examiner SSS, 1942-44 (Presdl. commendation). One-man shows include L.I. U., 1961, NYU Loeb Ctr., 1962, 72, 74, Greer Gallery, 1963, 64, St. Charles, La., 1964, Nyack, N.Y., 1986, Prospect Park Ctrl. Art Show, 1966, Art Inst. Boston, 1970, 76, George Wiener Gallery, 1972; exhibited in group shows at Little Studio, 1952, Mus. Modern Art, Paris, 1970, Bodley Gallery, 1965, 69, Nyack, N.Y., 1987, others; represented in permanent collections at Huntington Hartford collection N.Y. Cultural Ctr., 1969, Washington County Mus. of Fine Arts, Hagerstown, md.; author 3 textbooks on cardiology; author chpts. in 3 encys.; author: A Renaissance Man at Large; author: (collected poems) Reflections, 1993, (essays) The Facts of Life, 1999. Served from 1st lt. to maj. M.C., AUS, 1944-47. Recipient St. Gaudens award, 1923, 1st prize Art Assn. AMA, 1948, 1st prize Art Assn. Literary Soc., 1949, Disting. Achievement award Boys' H.S. Alumni Assn., 1988, Am. Poetry Assn. Hon. mention World of Poetry, 1990; named Best New Poets of 1989, 94, 95; named Internat. Man of Yr. in Medicine, 2000-2001. Fellow ACP, Royal Soc. Medicine (London), Am. Coll. Cardiology, Am. Coll. Angiology (med. honor award 1956, 59), Am. Coll. Legal Medicine (founder), Am. Coll. Chest Physicians (chmn. exhibits com. 1961, cardiovascular rehab. com. 1965, coronary disease com. 1968, pres. N.Y. state chpt. 1970); mem. N.Y. State Med. Soc. (vice chmn. space med. sect. 1967, 75, chmn. chest sect. 1972), Internat. Soc. Internal Medicine, World Med. Assn., Am. Heart Assn. (coun. on thrombosis), N.Y. Heart Assn., N.Y. Cardiol. Soc. (exec. bd., pres.), Explorers Club (5 explorations described in jour. 1966—, Internat. Man of Yr. for Medicine 1999-2000), Temple Club (v.p.), Doctors Club Bklyn. (vice chmn. bd. govs.), Circumnavigators. Home: 1620 Avenue I Brooklyn NY 11230-3050

REICH, OTTO JUAN, political analyst, business consultant; b. Havana, Cuba, Oct. 16, 1945; came to U.S., 1960; s. Walter and Graciela Maria (Fleites) R.; m. Connie Lynn Dillinger, Apr. 19, 1975; children: Adrienne Michelle, Natalie Lauren BA, U. N.C., Chapel Hill, 1966; MA, Georgetown U., 1973; grad., Officers Candidate Sch., U.S. Army, 1967. Civil affairs officer U.S. Army, Panama, 1967-69; staff asst. U.S. Ho. Reps., Washington, 1970-71; v.p. Cormorant Enterprises, Miami, Fla., 1972-73; internat. rep. Fla. Dept. Commerce, Coral Gables, 1973-75; community devel. coordinator City of Miami, Fla., 1975-76; dir. Washington ops. Council of the Americas, 1976-81; asst. adminstr. U.S. AID, Washington, 1981-83; spl. adv. for pub. diplomacy to sec. state with rank of ambassador U.S. Dept. State, Washington, 1983-86, ambassador to Venezuela, Caracas, 1986-89; sr. assoc. Ctr. for Strategic and Internat. Studies, Washington, 1989—2002; asst. sec. for We. Hemisphere Affairs U.S. Dept. State, 2002—03; spl. envoy to Latin Amer., 2003—04. Ptnr. Brock Group, 1990-96; mem. alt. U.S. rep. UN Human Rights Commn., Geneva, 1991-92. Lst lt. U.S. Army, 1966-69. Decorated Order of Liberator grand cordon class (Venezuela); recipient Superior Honor award U.S. State Dept., 1986-89, 91, Exemplary Svc. award U.S. State Dept., 1988. Mem. Coun. Am. Ambs., Nat. Leadership Coun. (vice chmn.), Ctr. for Strategic and Internat. Studies.*

REICH, PETER LESTER, legal educator, legal and historical consultant; b. L.A., Mar. 20, 1955; s. Jack Edward and Lillian (Lerner) R.; m. Alisa Schulweis, Sept. 8, 1985; children: Gabriel, Eli. BA in History, UCLA, 1976, PhD in History, 1991; JD, U. Calif., Berkeley, 1985. Bar: Calif. 1985, U.S. Dist. Ct. (ctrl. dist.) Calif. 1986. Rsch. atty. Calif. Ct. Appeal, Ventura, 1985-86; assoc. Parker, Milliken et al, L.A., 1986-88; asst. prof. law Whittier Law Sch., L.A., 1988-91, assoc. prof. law, 1991-93, prof. law Costa Mesa, Calif., 1993—. Vis. prof. of history U. Calif., Irvine, 1999—2004. Author: Statistical Abstract of the U.S.-Mexico Borderlands, 1984, Mexico's Hidden Revolution, 1995; mem. editl. bd. Western Legal History, 1995—; contbr. articles to profl. jours. Recipient Hubert Herring Meml. award Pacific Coast Coun. on Latin Am. Studies, 1991, Ray A. Billington award Western History Assn., 1995; Fulbright-Hays fellow, 1979-80; Rocky Mountain Mineral Law Found. rsch. grantee, 1993, 95, 99; Huntington Libr. fellow Andrew Mellon Found., 1997. Mem. Am. Soc. for Legal History, Assn. Am. Law Scs. (sec.-treas. immigration sect., treas., chair elect legal history sect.), Calif. Supreme Ct. Hist. Soc. Democrat. Jewish. Avocations: sea kayaking, hiking, ice skating. Office: Whittier Law Sch 3333 Harbor Blvd Costa Mesa CA 92626-1501

REICH, ROBERT BERNARD, former federal official, political economics educator; b. Scranton, Pa., June 24, 1946; s. Edwin Saul and Mildred Dorf (Freshman) R.; m. Clare Dalton, July 7, 1973. BA, Dartmouth Coll., 1968, MA (hon.), 1988; MA, Oxford (Eng.) U., 1970; JD, Yale U., 1973. Asst. solicitor gen. U.S. Dept. Justice, Washington, 1974-76; dir. policy planning FTC, Washington, 1976-81; mem. faculty John F. Kennedy Sch. Govt. Harvard U., Cambridge, Mass., 1981-92; sec. Dept. of Labor, Washington, 1993-97; Maurice B. Hexter prof. econ. and social policy Brandeis U. Heller Grad. Sch., 1997—. Chmn. biotech. sect. U.S. Office Tech. Assessment, Washington, 1990-91. Author: The Next American Frontier, 1983, Tales of a New America, 1987, The Work of Nations, 1991, Locked in the Cabinet, 1997, The Future of Success, 2001, I'll Be Short: Essentials for a Decent Working Society, 2002, Reason, 2004; co-author: The Power of Public Ideas, 1987; contbg. editor The New Republic, Washington, 1982-93; co-founder, nat. editor, chmn. editl. bd. The Am. Prospect, 1990—. Mem. governing bd. Common Cause, Washington, 1981-85; bd. dirs. Bus. Enterprise Trust, Palo Alto, Calif., 1989-93; trustee Dartmouth Coll., Hanover, N.H., 1989-93. Rhodes scholar, 1968; recipient Louis Brownlow award ASPA, 1983.*

REICH, ROBERT SIGMUND, landscape architect; b. N.Y.C., Mar. 22, 1913; s. Ulysses S. and Adele G. R.; m. Helen Elizabeth Adams, May, 1945; children: Barbara, Betsy, Bob, Bill. BS, Cornell U., 1934, PhD, 1941; postgrad., U. So. Calif., 1951. Instr. landscape design Cornell U., 1936-39, 40-41; instr. landscape design U. Conn., 1939-40; Inst. Land Design La. State U., 1941-46, asst. prof. landscape architecture, 1946-49, asso. prof., 1949-60, prof., 1960—, Alumni prof., 1967—, head dept. landscape architecture, 1964-79, dir. Sch. Landscape Architecture, 1979-83; prof. Landscape Architecture, 1992— Instr. Shrivenham (Eng.) Am. U., 1946, Biarritz (France) Am. U., 1947; vis. lectr. Tulane U., 1958-67; judge, instr. Nat. Council Garden Clubs, 1956—; mem. task force on parks, recreation and tourism Goals for La. Program; mem. com. to establish Chicot State Park Arboretum, Ville Plate, La., 1964, mem. steering com., 1964-75; examiner La. Bd. Examination for Landscape Architects, 1957-77 Co-author: Landscape and You, 1953. Mem. com. to establish City/Parish Beautification Commn., 1961-82; mem. area and facilities com. Baton Rouge Recreation and Pk. Commn., 1957-83; bd. dirs. Hubbard Edn. Trust, Weston, Mass., 1967—; adv. com. Friends of Frederick Law Olmsted Papers, 1983-95. With U.S. Army, 1942-45; in charge alter arrangements U. United Meth. Ch., 1945—. Recipient Tchg. award of merit Gamma Sigma Delta, 1963, Baton Rouge Green Individual Honor award, 1996. Fellow Am. Soc. Landscape Architects (trustee 1968-71, 83-86, 3d v.p. 1971-73, Medal 1992); mem. AIA (hon.), S.W. Park and Recreation Tng. Inst. (dir. 1975-77, award of merit 1968), Phi Kappa Phi, Pi Alpha xi, Omicron Delta Kappa, Sigma Lambda Alpha. Home: 333 E Boyd Dr Baton Rouge LA 70808-4507 Office: La State U Sch Landscape Architecture Coll Design Bldg Baton Rouge LA 70803-0001

REICH, STANLEY BENJAMIN, radiologist, medical educator; b. NYC, Feb. 20, 1921; s. Harry Max Reich and Bessie Bangel; m. Adele Axelrod, Dec. 15, 1944; children: Linda, James, Judi. AB, Cornell U., 1941; MD, NYU, 1944. Diplomate Am. Bd. Radiology, Am. Bd. Nuclear Medicine. Intern Bellevue Hosp., N.Y.C., 1944-45, resident in radiology, 1946-49; asst. prof. NYU/Bellevue Hosp., N.Y.C., 1949-50; clin. prof. radiology U. Calif., San Francisco, 1952-72, 77—; prof. radiology U. Colo., Denver, 1972-77, U. Calif. Davis, Sacramento, 1977—; chief radiology No. Calif. VA Clinics, Martinez, 1979-98. Contbr. articles to profl. jours. Pres. Concordia-Argonaut Club, San Francisco, 1963-65; cons. Travis AFB, Fairfield, Calif., 1977—, Exec. Svc. Corps., San Francisco, 1997—. Lt. (sr.) USN, 1944-47, 50-52. Fellow Am. Coll. Radiology; mem. Am. Soc. Thoracic Radiology (sec. 1967), Am. Radium Soc. Avocations: travel, photography. Home: 2 Abbott Way Piedmont CA 94618-2610

REICH, STEVE, composer; b. N.Y.C., Oct. 3, 1936; m. Beryl Korot; children: Ezra, Michael. Studies in percussion with Roland Kohloff, 1950—53; BA in Philosophy with honors, Cornell U., 1957; studies in composition with Hall Overton, 1957—58; studies with Bergsma and Persichetti, Julliard Sch. Music, 1958—61; MA in Music studies with Berio and Milhaud, Mills Coll., 1963; studies in drumming, Inst. for African Studies, U. Ghana, 1970; student, Am. Soc. for Ea. Arts, Seattle and Berkeley, 1973—74, Cantillation of Hebrew Scriptures, N.Y.C. and Jerusalem, 1976—77; D (hon.), Calif. Inst. Arts, 2000. Organized ensemble Steve Reich and Musicians, 1966; performed throughout the world, 1971—; recs. with various cos. including Columbia Records, Deutsche Grammophon, Nonesuch, Disques Shandar, Hungaraton, Angel, ECM, Phillips, Virgin Classics, Argo. Regents lectr. U. Calif., Berkeley, 2000. Composer, performer: (albums) Come Out, 1967, It's Gonna Rain, 1969, Violin Phase, 1969, Four Organs, 1970, Phase Patterns, 1970, Drumming, 1971, Four Organs, 1973, Six Pianos, 1973, Music for Mallet Instruments, Voices, and Organ, 1973, Music for Eighteen Musicians, 1978 (Grammy award 1999), Octet, 1980, Music for a Large Ensemble, 1980,Tehillim, 1982, The Desert Music, 1984, Sextet, 1986, Six Marimbas, 1986, Electric Counterpoint, 1987, Different Trains, 1988 (Grammy award 1989), The Four Sections, 1987, The Cave, 1994, City Life, 1995, Proverb, 1996, Triple Quartet, 1999, Three Tales, 2002, others; recordings include (10 CD boxed set) Steve Reich Works: 1965-1995; composer: Vermont Counterpoint, Variations for Winds, Strings and Keyboards, Eight Lines for Chamber Orchestra, Piano Phase, Clapping Music, Pendulum Music, Music for Pieces of Wood, Nagoya Marimbas, other works performed by major orchs. and ensembles; commd. to compose for Holland Festival, 1978, Radio Frankfurt, 1979, San Francisco Symphony, 1980, Rothko Chapel, 1981, West German Radio, Cologne, 1984, Fromm Music Found., 1985, Richard Stoltzman, 1985, Bklyn. Acad. Music, 1987, Kronos Quartet, 1988, St. Louis Sympnony, 1987, (with Beryl Korot) The Cave video opera commd. by Vienna Festival, Holland Festival, Festival d'Automne à Paris, Theatre de la Monnaie, Brussels, Hebbel Theatre, Berlin, South Bank Centre/Serious Speakout, London and the Brooklyn Acad. Music, Next Wave Festival, 1993; 4-concert retrospective Lincoln Ctr. Festival, N.Y.C., 1999, video opera (with Beryl Korot) Three Tales, commd. by Vienna Festival, Barbican Ctr., London, SPoleto Festival, Bklyn. Acad. Music, Music Strassbourg, Hebbel Theater, Berlin. Recipient Koussevitzky Found. award, 1981, 2002, Schuman prize Columbia U., 2000; named Composer of Yr., Musical Am., 2000; Rockefeller Found. grantee 1975, 78, 81, 90, Nat. Endowment for the Arts grantee, 1974, 76, 91, N.Y. State Coun. on the Arts grantee, 1974; Guggenheim fellow, 1978, Montgomery fellow Dartmouth Coll., 2000; elected to Am. Acad. Arts and Letters, 1994, Bayerische Akademie der Schönen Künst, 1995; named Commr. dans l'Ordre des Arts et des Lettres, 1999. Office: c/o Boosey & Hawkes Inc 35 E 21st St New York NY 10010-6212

REICH, VICTORIA J. consumer products company executive; b. Southborough, Mass., 1958; BS in Applied Math. and Econs., Brown U. With GE Co.; v.p., contr. Brunswick Corp., Lake Forest, Ill., 1996-2000, sr. v.p., CFO, 2000—. Office: Brunswick Corp 1 N Field Ct Lake Forest IL 60045-4811

REICHARD, GARY WARREN, university administrator, history educator; b. Phila., Nov. 23, 1943; s. David Carl and Gabrielle Rosalind (Doane) R.; m. Marcia Ann King, Aug. 7, 1965 (div. 1978); children: Jennifer D., James J. BA, Coll. of Wooster (Ohio), 1965; MA, Vanderbilt U., Nashville, 1966; postgrad., Ohio U., 1966-67; PhD, Cornell U., 1971. Instr. history Coll. of Wooster, 1967-69; asst. prof. to assoc. prof. history, chmn. dept. Ohio State U., Columbus, 1971-82; assoc. prof. history and dir. univ. honors program U. Del., Newark, 1983-85; assoc. vice chancellor for acad. affairs, assoc. prof. hist. U. Md., College Park, 1985-89; prof. history and dean undergrad. studies Fla. Atlantic U., Boca Raton, Fla., 1989-92, chmn. dept. history, 1992-94; assoc. vice pres. acad. affairs Calif. State U., Long Beach, 1994—2002, provost, sr. v.p. acad. affairs, 2002—. Assoc. editor Ency. of Am. Legislative System; reviewer numerous comml. and univ. presses; author: The Reaffirmation of Republicanism, 1975, Politics as Usual, 1988, 2d edit., 2004; co-author: America: Changing Times, 1979, 2d edit., 1982; co-editor: Reshaping America, 1982, American Choices, 1986, American Issues, 1988, 3d edit., 2002; contbr. articles to profl. jours. Moody rsch. grantee Lyndon B. Johnson found., 1977, Harry S. Truman Libr. Inst. rsch. grantee, 1979, Congl. Leadership rsch. grantee, 1981, Carl Albert Congl. rsch. grantee, 1993, Minn. Hist. Soc. grantee, 1993. Mem. AAUP, Am. Assn. Higher Edn., Am. Hist. Assn., So. Hist. Assn., Orgn. Am. Historians, Immigration Hist. Soc., Phi Beta Kappa, Phi Kappa Phi. Office: Calif State U Long Beach Divsn Acad Affairs 1250 N Bellflower Blvd Long Beach CA 90840-0006 Business E-Mail: reichard@csulb.edu.

REICHARD, LARRY A. biologist, educator; s. Fred J. and Joyce L. Reichard. AS, Delta Coll., 1972; BS, Ctrl. Mich. U., 1974; MS, Mich. State U., 1977; D in Higher Edn. Adminstrn., W.Va. U./Mich. U., 1990. Rsch. assoc. Northwestern U. Med. Sch., Chgo., 1977—79, Med. U. S.C., Charleston, 1979—80; prof. Mt. Senario Coll., Ladysmith, Wis., 1980—81; instr. biology and chemistry Consumer Power Co., Midland, Mich., 1981—82; rsch. assoc. St. Louis U. Med. Sch., 1982—83; lectr. biology U. Mich., Flint, 1983—85; prof. biology W.Va. Inst. Tech., Montgomery, 1985—90, Maple Woods C.C., Kansas City, Mo., 1990—. Contbr. articles to profl. jours. Active Northland Symphony, Kansas City, 2001—. Mem.: Midwest Coll. Tchrs. Biology, Human Anatomy and Physiology Soc., Mo. Acad. Scis. Achievements include research in somatomedin's role in diabetes mellitus; epidemial growth factor and hyaline membrane disease in newborns; cytogenics of langerhans cells of the pancreas. Office: Maple Wood Cmty Coll 2601 NE Barry Rd Kansas City MO 64156

REICHARDT, PAUL BERNARD, provost, chemistry educator; b. St. Louis, Aug. 15, 1943; s. Bernard George and Elaine Charlotte (Schmudde) R.; m. Cordelia Morris (Hufnagel), Apr. 27, 1968; children: Laura, Rebecca, Daniel. BS, Davidson Coll., 1965; PhD in Organic chemistry, U. Wis., 1969. Post doctoral rsch. assoc. Yale U., New Haven, 1969-71, instr., 1971; asst. prof. Ohio State U., Columbus, 1971-72; asst. prof. chemistry U. Alaska, Fairbanks, 1972 75, assoc. prof. chemistry, 1975-81, prof. chemistry, 1981—, dean coll. natural sci., 1991-96, dean coll. sci., engring. and math., 1996-98, provost, 1998—. Head dept. chemistry, U. Alaska, Fairbanks, 1978-82, 88-90; interim dean coll. natural sci., 1990-91; interim provost, 1993-94; interim dir. U. Alaska Mus., 1992-93; NASCU commr. on colleges and universities, 2003-; mem. Gov. Sci. and Engring. Adv. Com., 1986-90; Alaska 2000 Sci. Standards Com., 1992-93. Contbg. articles to profl. jour.; chpts. to books and monographs. Named one of Outstanding Young Men of Am., Jaycees, 1980; recipient Inspirational Tchr. Award, U. Alaska, Fairbanks Alumni Assn., 1982. Mem. AAAS; Am. Chem. Soc.; Phi Beta Kappa; Sigma Xi (pres. local chpt. 1994-95); Phi Kappa Phi. Presbyterian. Avocations: fishing, camping, hiking. Office: U Alaska Office Provost Signers Hall Fairbanks AK 99775-7580 E-mail: fnpbr@uaf.edu.

REICHART, STUART RICHARD, lawyer; b. N.Y.C., Nov. 18, 1924; s. Stanley and Rae (Wein) R.; m. Joan Feirtag, Mar. 28, 1981. LLB, Bklyn. Law Sch., 1948; LLM, NYU, 1951. Bar: N.Y. 1949, D.C. 1971, U.S. Supreme Ct. Adminstrv. judge Armed Services Bd. Contract Appeals, Washington, 1966-72; asst. gen. counsel for procurement USAF, Washington, 1972-75, dep. gen. counsel, 1975-78, gen. counsel, 1978-81; of counsel Fried, Frank, Harris, Shriver & Jacobson, Washington, 1982-90; ind. cons., 1991—. Instr. govt. procurement Ohio State U., U. Dayton, U. Md., 1960-70. Contbr. legal articles on govt. procurement to profl. jours. Served with AUS, 1942-45; served to col. USAF, 1951-71. Decorated Legion of Merit, D.F.C., Air medal with silver oak leaf cluster, Purple Heart; recipient Disting. Civilian Service medals Dept. Air Force, 1979, Dept. Def., 1982, Stuart R. Reichart award USAF, 1982. Mem. Masons. Avocations: bridge, tennis, golf. Home and Office: 16873 C Isle of Palms Dr Delray Beach FL 33484-7008

REICHBACH, GUSTIN LEWIS, state supreme court justice; b. Bklyn., Oct. 9, 1946; s. Herman and Lee (Klein) R.; m. Ellen Meyers, Oct. 24, 1984; 1 child, Hope Isadora. BA in Polit. Sci. with high honors(hon.), SUNY, Buffalo, 1967; JD, Columbia U., 1970. Bar: N.Y. 1972, U.S. Dist. Ct. (ea. and so. dists.) N.Y. 1972, Calif. 1975, U.S. Dist. Ct. (ea. and no. dists.) Calif. 1975, U.S. Supreme Ct. 1984. Pvt. practice, NY, 1972-90, 1975-90; judge Civil Ct. City of N.Y., Bklyn., 1991-98; justice Supreme Ct. N.Y., Bklyn., 1998—; internat. judge UN Interim Mission in Kosovo, 2003; permanent internat. judge Supreme Ct. of Kosovo, 2003—04. Counsel to commr. Calif. Agrl. Labor Rels. Bd., Sacramento, 1975-76. Co-author: The Bust Book, 1970, (Grove Press, NY); Litigating Electronic Surveillance Claims in Criminal Cases, 1977. (Lakes Law Books, S.F.) Recipient David Michael award N.Y. State Bar Assn., 1992. Mem. Phi Beta Kappa. Office: Supreme Ct State NY 120 Schermerhorn St Brooklyn NY 11201-5108

REICHBLUM, AUDREY ROSENTHAL, public relations executive, publishing executive; b. Pitts., June 28, 1935; d. Emanuel Nathan and Willa (Handmacher) Rosenthal; m. M. Charles Reichblum, Jan. 25, 1956; children: Robert Nathan, William Mark. Student, Bennington Coll., 1952-53; BS, Carnegie Mellon U., 1956. Founder, creator, chmn. Pitts. Children's Mus., 1970-73; mag. writer Pitts. Mag., 1978; dir. pub. rels. Pitts. Pub. Theater, 1978-79; pres. arPR audrey reichblum PUB. RELS. inc., Pitts., 1980—, arpr, inc., 1996—; pub. "Knowledge in a Nutshell" Series, 1996—99, "The Edible Game A Smart Cookie", 1996—, "Sweet Smarts The Candy With A Brain", 2004. Pub. rels. cons., bd. mem. Pitts. Planned Parenthood, 1980-84, United Jewish Fedn., Bus. and Profl. Women, Pitts., 1980-85, Pitts. City Theater, 1985-94, Pa. Coun. on Aging, 1996—; chmn. Villa de Marillac Nursing, 1999, Vincencian Collaborative Svcs. Bd. Recipient Gold Cindy award Info. Film Producers Am., 1982, award of excellence Internat. Assn. Bus. Communicators, Pitts., 1986, Matrix award for Three Rivers Arts Festival, Lifetime Achievement award NAWBO-YWCA, Y-Tribute to Women in Comms. award, 1998. Mem. Pub. Rels. Soc. Am. (accredited; award of merit 1983, G. Victor Barkman award for excellence 1984, 1st place award Race For The Cure), Women in Comm. (Matrix-sales promotion award 1987), Nat. Assn. Women Bus. Owners (Life Time Achievement award 1995). Office: 1420 Centre Ave Ste 2213 Pittsburgh PA 15219-3536

REICHE, FRANK PERLEY, lawyer, former federal commissioner; b. Hartford, Conn., May 8, 1929; s. Karl Augustus and LaFetra (Perley) R.; m. Janet Taylor, Sept. 26, 1953; children: Cynthia Reiche Schumacker, Dean S. AB, Williams Coll., 1951; LLB, Columbia U., 1959; MA, George Washington U., 1959; LLM in Taxation, NYU, 1966. Bar: N.J. 1960, D.C. 1981. Assoc. Stryker, Tams & Dill, Newark, 1959-61, Smith, Stratton, Wise & Heher, Princeton, NJ, 1962-64, ptnr., 1964-79; commr. Fed. Election Commn., Washington, 1979-85, chmn., 1982; ptnr. Katzenbach, Gildea & Rudner, Lawrenceville, NJ, 1986-93; pvt. practice law Princeton, 1993-97; of counsel Schragger, Lavine & Nagy, West Trenton, NJ, 1997-2000, Archer & Greiner, Princeton, 2001—. Trustee Westminster Choir Coll., Princeton, 1974-86, Ctr. Theol. Inquiry, Princeton, 1991-97, Wells Coll., Aurora, N.Y., 1994-2003; mem. planned giving com. Williams Coll., Williamstown, Mass., 1973-87, nat. chmn. planned giving, 1983-87; dir., Ctr. Responsive Politics, Washington, 2002—. Lt. USN, 1952-56. Mem. ABA, D.C. Bar Assn., N.J. Bar Assn., Am. Coll. Trust and Estate Counsel (N.J. state chair 1995-2000, bd. regents 2001—). Clubs: Washington Golf and Country, Capitol Hill. Republican. Presbyterian.

REICHEK, JESSE, artist; b. Bklyn., Aug. 16, 1916; s. Morris and Celia (Bernstein) R.; m. Laure Guyot, May 16, 1950; children— Jonathan, Joshua. Student, Inst. Design, Chgo., 1941-42; diploma, Academie Julian, Paris, 1951. Instr. dept. architecture U. Mich., Ann Arbor, 1946-47; prof. Inst. Design Ill. Inst. Tech., Chgo., 1951-53; prof. dept. architecture U. Calif., Berkeley, 1953-87, prof. emeritus, 1987—. Cons. Nat. Design Inst. Ford Found. project, Ahmedabad, India, 1963, San Francisco Redevel. Agy. Embarcadero Center, 1966—; lectr. Nat. Inst. Architects, Rome, 1960, U. Florence, 1960, U. Naples, 1960, Israel Inst. Tech., 1960, Greek Architects Soc., Athens, 1960, U. Belgrade, 1960, MIT, 1965, U. N.Mex., 1964, Am. Cultural Center, Paris, 1960, 64, Gujarat Inst. Engrs. and Architects, 1963, U. Colo., 1961, Harvard, 1962, U. Minn., 1962, U. Coll. London, 1967, Inst. Contemporary Arts, London, 1967, Ecole Nationale des Beaux-Ats, 1967, artist in residence Tamarind Lithography Workshop, 1966, Am. Acad. in Rome, 1971-72; research prof. Creative Arts Inst. U. Calif., 1966-67; artist in residence IBM Los Angeles Sci. Center, 1970-71 Exhibited one man shows at, Galerie Cahiers d'Art Paris, 1951, 59, 68, U. Calif. at Berkeley, 1954, Betty Parsons Gallery, N.Y.C., 1958, 59, 63, 65, 67, 69, 70, Molton Gallery, London, 1962, Am. Culture Center, Florence, Italy, 1962, Bennington Coll., 1963, U. N.Mex., 1966, U. So. Calif., 1967, Axiom Gallery, London, 1968, Yoseido Gallery, Tokyo, 1968, Los Angeles County Mus. Art, 1971; exhibited in group shows, Bklyn. Mus., 1959, Mus. Modern Art, N.Y.C., 1962, 65, 69, Knox-Albright Art Gallery, 1962, Art Inst. Chgo., 1963, Cin. Art Mus., 1966, Balt. Art Mus., 1966, Yale Art Gallery, 1967, Grand Palais, Paris, 1970, Nat. Mus. Art, Santiago, Chile, 1970, art and tech. exhibit, Los Angeles County Mus. Art, 1971, Maeght Found., St. Paul de Vence, France, 1971, Mus. Modern Art, Paris, 1971; represented in permanent collections, Mus. Modern Art, Art Inst. Chgo., Bibliotheque Nationale, Paris, Victoria & Albert Mus., London, Los Angeles County Art Mus., Grunwald Graphic Arts Found., U. Calif. at Los Angeles, San Diego Mus. Art, Amon Carter Mus., Fort Worth; Author: Jesse Reichek-Dessins, 1960, La Monte de la Nuit, 1961, Fontis, 1961, Etcetera, 1965, Le Bulletin Des Baux, 1972; e.g., 1976. Served to capt. C.E. AUS, 1942-46. Home: 5925 Red Hill Rd Petaluma CA 94952-9437

REICHEK, MORTON ARTHUR, retired magazine editor, writer; b. N.Y.C., Nov. 2, 1924; s. Meyer and Katherine (Rabinowitz) R.; m. Sybil Green, June 13, 1953; children: Amy, Marjorie (dec.), James. BS, NYU, 1948; postgrad., Am. U., 1948-50. Press officer, editor U.S. Fish & Wildlife Svc., Washington, 1948-49, U.S. Br. Labor Statistics, Washington, 1949-51, U.S. Nat. Prodn. Authority, Washington, 1951-52; Washington corr. McGraw-Hill Publs., 1952-63, Newhouse Newspapers, 1963-65; assoc. editor Forbes, N.Y.C., 1965-66, Bus. Week, N.Y.C., 1966-76, sr. editor, writer, 1978-88; dir. editorial svcs. Gulf & Western. Industries, Inc., N.Y.C., 1976-78. U.S. rep. NATO journalist program U.S. Dept. State, France, 1957; adj. lectr. Columbia U. Graduate Sch. Journalism, N.Y.C., 1981. Contbr. articles to N.Y. Times Mag., New Republic, others. Staff sgt. U.S. Army, 1943-46, China-Burma-India. Journalist fellow Carnegie-Mellon U. Grad. Sch. Indsl. Adminstrn., 1979; grantee NEH, 1980. Avocations: tennis, computers, music. Home: 1 Worchester Dr Concordia Monroe Township NJ 08831-4723 also: The Cascades 6975 Lismore Ave Boynton Beach FL 33437-6441 E-mail: iankev@att.net.

REICHEL, WALTER EMIL, advertising executive; b. Irvington, N.J., Dec. 12, 1935; s. Walter Edwin and Flora Maria (Pfister) R.; m. Priscilla Tedesco, Feb. 1, 1969; 1 son, Bradley Joseph. BA, Columbia U., 1959; MA., NYU, 1971, M Philosophy, 1989, postgrad., 1989—. With Benton & Bowles, N.Y.C., 1959 67, v.p., 1965-67, asso. media dir., 1965-67; with Ted Bates & Co., Inc. N.Y.C., 1967-87; sr. v.p. Ted Bates & Co., Inc., N.Y.C., 1973-82, exec. dir. media and programs, 1974-82, exec. v.p., 1982-87, dir.; cons., 1987-91; mng. ptnr. A.S. Link Inc., N.Y.C., 1991-2000; sr. v.p., dir. client svcs. KSL Media, 2000—01; prof. advt. and comm. Fashion Inst. of Tech., 2002—. Mem. Advt. Rsch. Found. Home and Office: 449 1/2 Henry St Brooklyn NY 11231-3011 E-mail: aslreichel@aol.com.

REICHENSTEIN, MURRAY L. electronics executive; CFO, v.p. Pitney Bowes Inc., Stamford, Conn., 1996—, chief devel. officer. Office: Pitney Bowes Inc One Elmcroft Rd Stamford CT 06926-0700

REICHERT, AVIRAM, concert pianist, educator; b. Tel-Aviv, Oct. 3, 1971; s. Avner Reichert and Sophia Ashkenazy. MA, Rubin Acad., Tel-Aviv, 1995. Assoc. prof. music Grand Valley State U., Allendale, Mich., 2001—. Soloist pianist Jerusalem Broadcast Symphony Orch., Israel Philharm. Orch., Haifa Symphony Orch., Israel Chamber Orch., Israel Sinfonietta, Rishon Lezion Symphony Orch.; pianist Tokyo Symphony Orch., Dessau Symphony Orch.; numerous orch. engagements Spokane and Yakima Orch., Wash.; recitals Herkules-Saal, Munich; numerous orch. engagements Chgo. Sinfonietta, Ft. Worth Symphony Orch., Nat. Symphony of Dominican Republic, Tokyo City Symphony Orch., Tokyo Philharm. Orch., Eugene (Oreg.) Symphony Orch., Traverse Symphony Orch., S.C. Philharmon. Orch., Grand Rapids (Mich.) Symphony Orch.; piano recitals Ruhr and Epinal Music Festivals, Paris, Frankfurt, Cologn, Lisbon, Milan, Rome, Herkules-Saal, Munich, Washington, San Francisco, Austin, Tex., Scottsdale, Ariz., others. CDs, Harmonia Mundi CD, others. Recipient Bronze medal, Van Cliborn Piano Competition, Ft. Worth, Tex., 1997, 1st prize, Dong-Xa Piano Competition, Seoul, Korea, 1996, Epinal Piano Competition, Epinal, France, 1995. Office: Grand Valley State Univ 1 Campus Dr Allendale MI Home: 2118 Lacrosse St SW Wyoming MI 49509-3635

REICHERT, DAVID, lawyer; b. Cin., Nov. 23, 1929; s. Victor E. and Louise F. Reichert; m. Marilyn Frankel, May 31, 1959; children— James G., Steven F., William M. BA, Bowling Green State U., 1951; JD, U. Cin., 1954. Bar: Ohio 1954, U.S. Supreme Ct. 1963. Ptnr. firm Porter, Wright, Morris & Arthur, formerly sr. ptnr. Reichert, Strauss & Reed and predecessors, Cin. Dir. numerous corps. Monthly columnist: Scrap Age mag, 1966-74; bd. editors: U. Cin. Law Rev, 1953-54. Pres. brotherhood Rockdale Temple, Cin., 1960-61, temple treas., 1973-75, v.p., 1975-79, pres., 1979-81; mem. Amberley Village Planning Commn. & Zoning Bd. Appeals, 1972-79, Ohio Solid Waste Adv. Group, 1974; treas. Contemporary Arts Ctr., Cin., 1973-75, pres., 1976-77, trustee, 1982-88; trustee Cin. Art Mus., 1978-93, v.p., 1992-93, chmn. vis. com. for contemporary art, 1990-92; trustee Jewish Publ. Soc., 1980-86, Cin. Sculpture Coun., 1984-87; mem. acquisitions com. Miami U. Art Mus., 1982-85. Mem. Cin. Print and Drawing Cir. (pres. 1974-76), The Literary Club (sec. 1988-91, v.p. 1991-92, pres. 1992-93), Losantiville Country Club (bd. govs. 1985-92, sec. 1986-90, pres. 1990-92), ISRI 20th Century Club (hon. 1998), Omicron Delta Kappa, Sigma Tau Delta, Phi Delta Phi, Zeta Beta Tau. Office: Porter Wright Morris & Arthur 250 E 5th St Ste 2200 Cincinnati OH 45202-5177

REICHERT, LEO EDMUND, JR., biochemist, endocrinologist; b. N.Y.C., Jan. 9, 1932; s. Leo and Anne (Holsten) R.; m. Gerda Sihler, July 20, 1957; children: Leo, Christine, Linda, Andrew. *Wife Gerda Reichert retired after a career with the IRS. Son Leo Eugene, a graduate of Georgetown University (Government) and Emory University (Law) is a partner with the firm Parker, Hudson, Rainer & Dobbs in Atlanta. Son Andrew Peter is a graduate of Manhattan College (Electrical Engineering) and is Operations Manager, Trader Voice Services with AT&T Solutions in NY. Daughter Christine Ann Reichert Jones, a graduate of Emory University (Psychology) is director of Volunteer Services for Children's Health Care of Atlanta. Daughter Linda Marie Reichert Petmecky, a graduate of Emory University (Business), is former Regional Manager for Riviera Finance in Atlanta.* BS, Manhattan Coll., N.Y.C., 1955; PhD, Loyola U., Chgo., 1960. Asst. prof. biochemistry Emory U. Med. Sch., Atlanta, 1960-66, assoc. prof., 1966-72, prof., 1972-79; prof., chmn. dept. biochemistry Albany (N.Y.) Med. Coll., 1979-88, prof. biochemistry and molecular biology, 1988-99; dir. Tucker Endocrine Rsch. Inst., Atlanta, 2000—. Dir. human and animal hormone isolation and distbn. program (NIH), Emory U. Med. Sch., 1960-75; mem. med. adv. bd. Nat. Pituitary Agy., 1971-74; com. on glycoprotein hormones Nat. Hormone and Pituitary Program, 1968-86; mem. reproductive biology study sect. NIH, 1971-75; mem. adv. panel on cellular physiology NSF, 1983-86, divsn. of integrative and neuro biology, 1992; mem. WHO Expert Adv. Panel on Biol. Standardization, 1984—, Nat. Bd. Med. Examiners, Part I, 1989-91. *Dr. Reichert developed methods for purification of a variety of hormones from human pituitary glands. This made possible use of these hormones in treatment of clinical problems related to human growth and fertility. His studies also facilitated development of techniques for quantitative measurement of pituitary hormones in trace amounts in human blood, an analysis basic to diagnosis in most areas of contemporary clinical endocrinology. Related studies with farm animal pituitary glands contributed significantly to improved fertility and growth of such commercially important food species as cow, sheep, and pig. Students and Fellows trained by Dr. Reichert have achieved prominent positions in academics, industry, and clinical teaching and research.* Mem. editl. bd. Endocrinology, 1967-75, Molecular and Cellular Endocrinology, 1977-83, 90-94, Biology of Reproduction, 1968-70, 86-90, Andrology, 1983-86, Molecular Andrology, 1989-99; contbr. more than 275 articles to profl. jours.; patentee in field. Served with USMC, 1950—53. List among 75 endocrinologists, 1000 scientists most cited, 1965-78. Mem.: AAAS, Soc. for Study of Reprodn., Andrology Soc. (coun. 1983—87), Endocrine Soc. (ethics adv. com. 2000—01, Ayerst award 1970), Am. Soc. Biol. Chemists. Home: 1974 Mountain Creek Dr Stone Mountain GA 30087-1018 Personal E-mail: lerjr@aol.com.

REICHGOTT JUNGE, EMBER D. former state senator, lawyer, writer, broadcast analyst, radio personality; b. Detroit, Aug. 22, 1953; d. Norbert Arnold and Diane (Pincich) Reichgott; m. Michael Junge. BA summa cum laude, St. Olaf Coll., Minn., 1974; JD, Duke U., 1977; MBA, U. St. Thomas, 1991. Bar: Minn. 1977, D.C. 1978. Assoc. Larkin, Hoffman, Daly & Lindgren, Bloomington, Minn., 1977-84; counsel Control Data Corp., Bloomington, Minn., 1984-86; ptnr. The Gen. Counsel, Ltd., 1987—; mem. Minn. State Senate, 1983-2000, chmn. legis. com. on econ. status of women, 1984-86, vice chmn. senate edn. com., 1987-88, senate majority whip, 1990-94, chmn. property tax divsn. senate tax com., 1991-92, chmn. senate judiciary com., 1993-94, senate asst. majority leader, 1995-2000, chmn. spl. subcom. on ethical conduct. Dem. endorsed candidate Minn. Atty. Gen., 1998; instr. polit. sci. St. Olaf Coll., Northfield, Minn., 1993; bd. dirs. Citizens Ind. Bank, St. Louis Park, Minn. Host cable TV monthly series Legis. Report, 1985-92. State co-chair Clinton/Gore Presdl. Campaign, Minn. Dem. Farmer-Labor Party, 1992, 1996; del. Nat. Dem. Conv., 1984, 1992, 1996; pres. Minn. Women's Polit. Caucus, 2002—04; trustee, bd. dirs. N.W. YMCA, New Hope, Minn., 1983—88, United Way Mpls., 1989—, Greater Mpls. ARC, 1988—, chair, 2001—03. Recipient Woman of Yr. award North Hennepin Bus. and Profl. Women, 1983, award for contbn. to human svcs. Minn. Social Svcs. Assn., 1983, Clean Air award Minn. Lung Assn., 1988, Disting. Svc. award Mpls. Jaycees, 1984, Minn. Dept. Human Rights award, 1989, Myra Bradwell award Minn. Women Lawyers, 1993, Disting. Alumnae award Lake Conf. Schs., 1993, Disting. Alumnae award St. Olaf Coll., 1998, awards for leadership Am. Lung Assn., 1999, Am. Heart Assn., 1997, Everyday Hero award Up with People, 1995, Unsung Hero award United Way of Mpls., 1999, 1st recipient of award named in her honor for prevention of sexual assault, 2000; charter inductee Robbinsdale H.S. Hall of Fame, 2000; author of Minn. charter sch. law, winner of "2000 Innovations in Am. Govt. award" Harvard U. and Ford Found., others; named One of ten Outstanding Young Minnesotans, Minn. Jaycees, 1984, Policy Adv. of Yr., NAWBO, 1988, Woman of Achievement, Twin West C. of C., 1989, Marvelous Minn. Woman, 1993; youngest woman ever elected to Minn. Senate, 1983. Mem. Minn. Bar Assn. (bd. govs. 1992-96, Pro Bono Publico Atty. award 1990), Hennepin County Bar Assn., Corp. Counsel Assn. (v.p. 1989-96). Home: 7701 48th Ave N Minneapolis MN 55428-4515 Fax: 763-536-1447. E-mail: emberrj@msn.com.

REICHL, RUTH MOLLY, editor; b. N.Y.C., Jan. 16, 1948; d. Ernst and Miriam and (Brudno) R.; m. Douglas Wilder Hollis, Sept. 5, 1970 (div. 1985); m. Michael Singer, 1985; 1 child, Nicholas Singer. BA, U. Mich., 1968, MA in History of Art, 1970. Chef, owner The Swallow Restaurant, Berkeley, Calif., 1973-77; food writer, editor New West mag., San Francisco, 1978-84; editor restaurant column L.A. Times, 1984-93, food editor, 1990-93; restaurant critic N.Y. Times, 1993-99; editor-in-chief Gourmet Mag., 1999—. Author: Mmmm: A Feastiary, 1972, The Contest Book, 1977, Tender at the Bone: Growing Up at the Table, 1998, Comfort Me with Apples: More Adventures at the Table, 2001; editor: Modern Library Food Series, 2000—, Endless Feasts: Sixty Years of Writing from Gourmet, 2002, Remembrance of Things Paris, 2004, The Gourmet Cookbook, 2004. Office: 4 Times Sq New York NY 10036-6518 Business E-Mail: ruth.reichl@gourmet.com.

REICHLEY, A. JAMES, political scientist; b. St. Clair, Pa., Mar. 3, 1929; s. Grant G. and Mary (Thompson) R.; m. Mary Donohue, Apr. 15, 1961; children: Douglas G., Richard J., Susan M. BA, U. Pa., 1950; MA, Harvard U., 1956. Reporter Pottsville (Pa.) Republican, 1957-61; legis. asst. Senator Kenneth Keating, Washington, 1961-62; legis. sec. Gov. William Scranton, Harrisburg, Pa., 1962-67; polit. editor Fortune, N.Y.C., 1967-76; spl. asst. Pres. Gerald Ford, Washington, 1976; sr. fellow Brookings Instn., Washington, 1977-91, Georgetown U., Washington, 1992—2003. Author: Conservatives in an Age of Change, 1981, Religion in American Public Life, 1985 (Benchmark award 1986), The Life of the Parties, 1992, rev. edit., 2000, The Values Connection, 2001, Faith in Politics, 2002; others; editor: Elections American Style, 1987; contbr. articles to profl. jours. Served with U.S. Army, 1951-53. Congl. fellow, 1959. Mem. Am. Polit. Sci. Assn., Cosmos Club. Republican. Presbyterian. Home: 11912 Gregerscroft Rd Potomac MD 20854-2145 E-mail: j.reichley@worldnet.att.net.

REICHLIN, SEYMOUR, physician, educator; b. N.Y.C., May 31, 1924; s. Henry and Celia (Rosen) R.; m. Elinor Thurman Dameshek, June 24, 1951; children: Seth David, Douglas James, Ann Elise. Student, CCNY, 1940-41; AB, Antioch Coll., 1945; MD, Washington U., St. Louis, 1948; PhD, U. London, 1954. Intern N.Y. Hosp., 1948-49; asst. resident Barnes Hosp., St. Louis, 1949-50, N.Y. Hosp., 1950-51; chief resident Barnes Hosp., 1951-52; research fellow physiology dept. Maudsley Hosp., London, Eng., 1952-54; instr. psychiatry Washington U., 1954-55, asst. prof. psychiatry and medicine, 1955-60; asso. prof. medicine U. Rochester, 1960-66, prof., 1966-69; prof., head dept. med. and pediatric spltys. Sch. Medicine U. Conn., 1969-71, prof., head dept. physiology, 1971-72; prof. medicine Tufts U., 1972-97, prof. emeritus, 1997—; rsch. prof. U. Ariz., 1994-2000. Sr. physician New Eng. Med. Ctr., 1972-93, sr. endocrinologist, 1993-96; mem. endocrinology study sect. NIH, 1966-70; mem. adv. panel FDA, 1977-79; mem. coun. Nat. Inst. Kidney, Diabetes, Digestive Diseases, 1987-90. Mem. editl. bd. Endocrinology, 1969-74, New Eng. Jour. Medicine, 1976-79, Jour. Psychoneuroendocrinology, 1979-83, Brain, Behavior and Immunity, 1990—; contbr. articles to profl. jours., also monographs. Bd. dirs. Founds. Fund, New Haven, 1968-70; med. adv. bd. Med. Found., Boston, adv. bd. MacArthur Found., 1988. Served with AUS, 1943-44. Commonwealth Fund fellow, 1952-54, Lowell M. Palmer fellow, 1954-56. Master ACP-Am. Soc. Internal Medicine (award 2002); fellow AAAS, Am. Acad. Arts and Scis.; mem. Ctrl. Soc. Clin. Rsch., Am. Soc. Clin. Investigation, Assn. Am. Physicians, Am. Physiol. Soc., Endocrine Soc. (Eli Lilly award 1972, Disting. Leadership award 1986, pres. 1975-76), Brit. Soc. Endocrinology, Am. Psychosomatic Soc., Am. Thyroid Assn., Internat. Brain Orgn., Assn. for Rsch. in Nervous and Mental Disease (pres. 1976), Pituitary Soc. (pres. 1994-95), Sigma Xi, Alpha Omega Alpha. Home: X-9 Ranch 6480 South Upper Valley Rd Vail AZ 85641 E-mail: reichlin@dakotacom.net.

REICHMAN, JOEL H. retail executive; With The GAP, San Francisco, 1971-76, Slak Shak Inc., Boston, 1971-76, Designs, Inc., 1976—, exec. v.p., 1985-93, dir., 1987, pres., COO, 1993-94; pres., CEO, 1994—. Home: Designs Inc 555 Turnpike St Canton MA 02021-2724

REICHMAN, LEE BRODERSOHN, physician; b. NYC, June 25, 1938; s. Theodore and Elinore (Brodersohn) R.; m. Rose Ehrinpreis, Oct. 9, 1965; children: Daniel Mark, Deborah Gar. AB, Oberlin Coll., 1960; MD, NYU, 1964; MPH, Johns Hopkins U., 1971. Intern Bellevue Hosp., I Med. Divsn., N.Y.C., 1964-65, resident, 1967-68, Harlem Hosp. Ctr., N.Y.C., 1968-69, fellow in pulmonary medicine, 1969-70; dir. Bur. Tb, Bur. Chronic Disease, N.Y.C. Health Dept., 1971-73, asst. commr. health, 1973-74; assoc. prof. medicine U. Medicine and Dentistry N.J. Med. Sch., Newark, 1974-78; prof. medicine N.J. Med. Sch., Newark, 1978—, prof. preventive medicine, cmty. health, 1993—; dir. pulmonary div. U. Medicine and Dentistry N.J.-N.J. Med. Sch. Univ. Hosp., 1974-92; founding exec. dir. N.J. Med. Sch. Nat. Tuberculosis Ctr., 1993—. Cons. CDC, Atlanta, 1970—; prin. investigator pulmonary complications of HIV infection NHLBI, 1987—95; prin. investigator Model Tb Ctr. CDC, 1993—, prin. investigator Nat. Tb Trials Consortium, 1994—99, adv. coun. for elimination of Tb, 2002—. Editor: Tuberculosis-A Comprehensive International Approach, 2d edit., 2000; author: Timebomb-The Global Epidemic of Multi-Drug Resistant Tuberculosis, 2002; contbr. articles to profl. jours. Bd. dirs. Art Ctr. No. N.J., 1979-86; chmn. N.J. Commn. on Smoking of Health, 1986-87; mem. N.J. TB Adv. Coun., 1976—, chmn. 1991—; chair Nat. Coalition for Elimination of Tb, 1992—2004; mem. N.J. Clean Air Coun., 1987. With USPHS, 1965-67. Recipient Nat. Heart Lung and Blood Inst., Pulmonary Acad. career award, 1975-80, Preventive Pulmonary Acad. career award, 1987-92, Tb Acad. career award, 1993—98, 1st prize trade category Am. Med. Writers Assn., 2002, Solomon A. Berson Med. Alumni Achievement award NYU, 2003. Fellow ACP, Am. Coll. Chest Physicians (gov. 1984-90, pres. N.J. chpt. 1982-84, Simon Rodbard Meml. lectr. 2000), Acad. Medicine of N.J.; mem. Am. Thoracic Soc. (hon. life), Internat. Union Against Tb and Lung Disease (exec. com. 1982-92, vice chair exec. com. 1989-91, N.Am. Region Disting. Svc. award 2001), Am. Lung Assn. (hon. life, nat. bd. dirs. 1980-94, pres. elect 1991-92, pres. 1992-93, past pres. 1993-94, Will Ross medalist 1999), N.J. Thoracic Soc. (pres. 1982-84), Am. Lung Assn. N.J. (hon. life), bd. dirs. 1976—86, pres. 1984-86), Global Alliance for Tb Drug Devel. (pres.). Office: PO Box 1709 225 Warren St Newark NJ 07101-1709 Office Phone: 973-972-3270. E-mail: reichmlb@umdnj.edu.

REICHMANIS, ELSA, chemist; b. Melbourne, Victoria, Australia, Dec. 9, 1953; arrived in U.S., 1962; d. Peteris and Nina (Meiers) R.; m. Francis Joseph Purcell, June 2, 1979; children: Patrick William, Elizabeth Anne, Edward Andrew, Thomas Alexander. BS in Chemistry, Syracuse U., 1972, PhD in Chemistry, 1975. Postdoctoral intern Syracuse (N.Y.) U., 1975-76, Chaim Weizmann rsch. fellow, 1976-78; mem. tech. staff AT&T Bell Labs., Murray Hill, N.J., 1978-84, supr. radiation sensitive materials and applications, 1984-94, head organic and polymer materials, 1994-95; head polymer and organic materials Lucent Techs., Bell Labs., New Providence, NJ, 1996—2000, dir. materials rsch., 2001—. Panel on advanced materials. Japanese Tech. Evaluation Prog., NSF, Washington, 1986, com. to survey materials. rsch. opportunities and needs for electronic industry Nat. Rsch. Coun., 1986, Nat. Materials Adv. Bd., 1993-98, U.S. Nat. Com. for Internat. Union for Pure and Applied Chemistry, 1996-2001. Editor: The Effects of Radiation on High Tech Polymers, 1989, Polymers in Microlithography, 1989, Irradiation of Polymer Materials, 1993, Microelectronics Technology: Polymers for Advanced Imaging and Packaging, 1995, Micro and Nano Patterning Polymers, 1998; patentee in field; assoc. editor Chemistry of Materials, 1996—; contbr. numerous articles to profl. jours. Recipient Soc. of Women Engrs. Achievement award, 1993, Engring. Materials award ASM, 1996, Arents Pioneer medal Syracuse U., 2001. Fellow: AAAS; mem.: IEEE, Soc. Women Engrs., Am. Phys. Soc., Soc. for Photo-optical Engrs., Soc. Chem. Industry (Perkin medal 2001), Am. Chem. Soc. (mem.-at-large 1986—90, sec. 1991—92, polymer materials sci. and engring. divsn. 1991—, vice chair 1993, chair-elect 1994, chmn. 1995, pres.-elect 2002, pres. 2003, award in applied polymer sci. 1999), Nat. Acad. Engring. (elected mem.). Avocations: music, reading, needlepoint.

REICHMANN, PÉTER IVAN, mathematics professor; b. Budapest, Hungary, Feb. 10, 1942; came to U.S., 1959; s. Rezsö Rudolf and Margit (Grünberger) R. BSEE, Ill. Inst. Tech., 1967, MS in Math., 1973, PhD in Math., 1986. Elec. engr. Zenith Military and Motorola Comm. and Govt. divsns., various cities, 1967—69; instr. math. and elec. engring. depts. Chgo. Tech. Coll., 1973—74; asst. prof. of math. Cath. U. Am., Washington, 1987—89; ind. distbr. Brain Garden Co., American Fork, Utah, 2001—; instr. math. Star Sch. Technol. U., Laguna, N.Mex., 2004—; chief mathematician Psitronics Group Sys. Internat., 2002—. Grantee NASA, 1982. Achievements include research on the introduction of a novel geometry for individual cell for negative Poisson's ratio foam and computing its volume. Home: 1305 Coloma Way Roseville CA 95661-4604 Office: Star Sch Tech Univ 2901 State Hwy 6 HC 77 Box 42 Laguna NM 87026 E-mail: pireichmann@hotmail.com., pireichmann@msn.com.

REICHWEIN, JEFFREY CHARLES, archaeologist; b. Cleve., June 10, 1950; s. Gordon Charlton and Grace Leonarda (Tesmer) R.; m. Jean Mabel Brainard, Sept. 16, 1985; 1 child, Juliet Jean Brainard-Reichwein; 1 child from previous marriage, Alyssa L. BA, Ohio U., 1972; MA in Anthropology, Miami U., Oxford, Ohio, 1975; PhD in Anthropology, Ohio State U., 1988. Lectr. Cuyahoga C.C., Parma, Ohio, 1975-83, archaeology field/sch. dir., 1976; grad. tchg. assoc. Ohio State U., Columbus, 1981-86; archaeologist State of Ohio, Dept. Natural Resources, Columbus, 1986—. Adminstrv. asst. ACLU, Cleve., 1978-79; tribal archaeologist Colville Confederated Tribes, Nespelem, Wash., 1979-81, consulting archaeologist, 1982—; vis. instr. Kenyon Coll., Gambier, Ohio, 1986. Author: Emergence of Native American Nationalism in the Columbia Plateau, 1990. Mem. coll. scholarship com. Am. Fedn. State, County and Mcpl. Employees, Columbus, 1995—. Instrnl. Improvement grantee Cuyahoga C.C., Cleve., 1976, Phillips Fund grantee Am. Philos. Soc., Phila., 1984. Mem. ACLU, Ohio Archaeol. Coun. (trustee 1997—), Phi Kappa Phi. Avocations: hiking, canoeing, movies, golf. Office: Divsn Mineral Resources Mgmt Ohio Dept Natural Resources Bldg H-3 Fountain Sq Columbus OH 43224

REICIN, ERIC DAVID, lawyer; b. Chgo. s. Ronald Ian and Alyta Reicin; m. Jodi Reicin, 1994. Student, Regent Coll., Eng., 1990; AB in Econs. and Polit. Sci., U. Mich., 1991; JD cum laude, U. Ill., 1994. Bar: Ill. 1994, U.S. Dist. Ct. (no. dist.) Ill. 1994, DC 1995, U.S. Dist. Ct. DC 1995, U.S. Ct. Appeals (DC cir.) 1995, U.S. Ct. Appeals (4th cir.) 1997, U.S. Supreme Ct. 1998, Va. Intern US Senator Robert W. Kasten, Washington, 1989; intern Office of Policy Devel. White House, Washington, 1990; intern U.S. Congressman Carl Pursell, Washington, 1991; law clk. State's Atty.-Champaign County, 1994; assoc. Laner Muchin Dombrow Becker Levin and Tominberg, Chgo., 1994-95, Birch Horton Bittner and Cherot, Washington, 1995-99; asst. gen. counsel Sallie Mae, Inc., Reston, Va., 1999-2000, assoc. gen. counsel, 2001—03, assoc. gen. counsel, officer, 2003—. Chpt. editor: Employment Discrimination Law, 3d edit., 1999, 2000, 4th edit. 2003. Harno scholar, 1993-94, Congrl. scholar, 1986; Pub. Interest Law Found. fellow. Mem. ABA (exec. lt. gov. 1993-94, EEO com. nat. co-chmn. regional liaison program 1997-98, nat. co-chmn. govt. liaison program 1998-2001, nat. co-chmn. ABA/EEOC joint tng. partnership 1997-2001, nat. chmn. EEO com., corp. coun. 2001—), DC Bar Assn. (litig., labor and employment sect.), Met. Washington Employment Lawyers Assn. (sec., bd. dirs. 1997-99), Washington Met. Area Corp. Counsel Assn. (labor and employment com. chair 1999—, bd. mem. 2003-, v.p. 2004-), Mortar Bd., Pi Sigma Alpha, Omicron Delta Epsilon, Sigma Iota Rho, Alpha Epsilon Pi (Arnold B. Hoffman award 1990). Republican. Office: Sallie Mae Inc 12061 Bluemont Way Reston VA 20190 Office Phone: 703-810-3000.

REICIN, RONALD IAN, lawyer; b. Chgo., Dec. 11, 1942; s. Frank Edward and Abranita (Rome) R.; m. Alyta Friedland, May 23, 1965; children: Eric, Kael. BBA, U. Mich., 1964, MBA, JD cum laude, U. Mich., 1967. Bar: Ill. 1967, U.S. Tax Ct. 1967; CPA, Ill. Mem. staff Price Waterhouse & Co., Chgo., 1966; ptnr. Jenner & Block, Chgo., 1967—. Bd. dirs. Nat. Kidney Found., Ill., 1978—, v.p., 1992-95, pres., 1995-98; bd. dirs. Ruth Page Found., 1985—, v.p., 1990—; bd. dirs. Scoliosis Assn. Chgo., 1981-90, Kohl Children's Mus., 1991-95, River North Chgo. Dance Co., 1999—. Mem.: Ill. State Bar Assn., Chgo. Mortgage Attys. Assn., Chgo. Bar Assn., ABA, Lawyers Club (Chgo.), Exec. Club, Beta Alpha Psi, Beta Gamma Sigma, Phi Kappa Phi. Office: Jenner & Block LLP 1 E IBM Plz Fl 38 Chicago IL 60611-3586 Office Phone: 312-923-2687. E-mail: rreicin@jenner.com.

REID, ALLISTON KING, psychology educator, researcher; m. Leonor G. Reid; children: Rebecca, Caroline. BS, Wofford Coll., 1975; PhD, Duke U., 1981. Assoc. prof. psychology Nat. Autonomous U. of Mex., Mexico City, 1981-84; prof. computer sci. Ea. Oreg. U., La Grande, 1985-91, prof. psychology, 1991-96; prof., chmn. dept. psychology Wofford Coll., Spartanburg, S.C., 1996—. Editl. bd. Jour. of the Exptl. Analysis of Behavior, 1995-97, 2000-2003; contbr. articles to profl. jours. Mem. Am. Psychol. Assn., Am. Psychol. Soc., Assn. for Behavior Analysis, Soc. for the Quantitative Analysis of Behavior, Sigm Xi. Office: Wofford Coll Dept Psychology 429 N Church St Spartanburg SC 29303-3612 E-mail: Reidak@wofford.edu.

REID, ANDY, professional football coach; b. Los Angeles, Mar. 19, 1958; m. Tammy Reid; 5 children. Coach BYU, 1982, San Francisco state, 1983—85; head coach Northern Arizona, 1986, Texas-El Paso, 1987—88; asst. coach U. Mo., Columbia, 1989—91, Green Bay Packers, 1992-99; head coach Philadelphia Eagles, 2000—. Named NFL Coach of the Yr., 2002. Achievements include asst. coach Super Bowl XXXI Champion Green Bay Packers, 1997. Office: Philadelphia Eagles Nova Care Complex 1 Nova Care Way Philadelphia PA 19145-5298*

REID, ANTONIO (L.A. REID), music company executive; With musical group The Deele; co-founder La Face Records, 1989; pres., CEO Arista Records, N.Y.C., 2000—04; chmn. Island Def Jam Music Group, 2004—. Songwriter with Kenny Edmonds, also occasionally with Darryl Simmons. Songs include Girlfriend, 1987, Rock Steady, 1987, Two Occasions, 1987, Don't Be Cruel, 1988, Love Saw It, 1988, Lover In Me, 1988, Every Little Step, 1988 (Grammy award nomination for R&B Song of Yr. 1989), Dial My Heart, 1988, Way You Love Me, 1988, Secret Rendezvous, 1988, Superwoman, 1988, Roses Are Red, 1988, Can't Stop, 1989, My Kinda Girl, 1989, It's No Crime, 1989, On Our Own, 1989, Ready or Not, 1989, Tender Lover, 1989, Giving You the Benefit, 1990, I'm Your Baby Tonight, 1990, Shock Dat Monkey, 1992, End of the Road, 1996. Recipient three Grammy awards. Office: Island Def Jam Music Group 825 8th Ave, 28th fl New York NY 10019*

REID, BELMONT MERVYN, brokerage house executive; b. San Jose, Calif., May 17, 1927; s. C. Belmont and Mary Irene (Kilfoyl) R.; m. Evangeline Joan Rogers, June 1, 1952. BS in Engring., San Jose State U., 1950, postgrad. Pres. Lifetime Realty Corp., San Jose, 1969—77, Lifetime Fin. Planning Corp., San Jose, 1967—77; founder, chmn. bd. Belmont Reid & Co., Inc., San Jose, 1960—77; pres. JOBEL Fin. Inc., Carson City, Nev., 1980—; pres., chmn. bd. Data-West Systems, Inc., 1984—85. Chmn. Carson City Debt. Mgmt. Commn., 1986—99; mem. Carson City Charter Rev. Com., 1986—91, chmn., 1988—91; rural county chmn. Nev. Rep. Cen. Com., 1984—88; County chmn. Carson City Rep. Cen. Com., 1982—85, treas., 1979—81; Carson City Coun. No. 347, Navy League of U.S., 1987—. With USN, 1945—46, with USN, 1951—55. Decorated Air medals. Mem.: Carson City C. of C. (pres. 1986—87, bd. dir. 1982—88), Mcpl. Securities Rulemaking Bd., Nat. Assn. Securities Dealers, Rotary (chpt. sec. 1983—84, 1986—87, pres. 1988—89, Paul Harris fellow), Capital Club of Carson City. Home: 610 E Bonanza Dr Carson City NV 89706 Office: 711 E Washington St Carson City NV 89701-4063

REID, CHARLES ADAMS, III, lawyer; b. Plainfield, N.J., Apr. 21, 1947; s. Charles Adams Jr. and Gertrude C. (Egan) R.; m. Teresa Keenan, May 11, 1974. BA, Colgate U., 1969; JD, Columbia U., 1974. Bar: N.Y. 1974, N.J. 1976, U.S. Ct. Appeals (3d cir.) 1983, U.S. Ct. Appeals (fed. cir.) 1989, U.S. Ct. Appeals (2d cir.) 1991, U.S. Ct. Appeals (9th cir.) 2002, Calif. 2002. Law clk. to hon. John R. Bartels U.S. Dist. Ct. (ea. dist.) N.Y., Bklyn., 1974-75; assoc. Coudert Bros., N.Y.C., 1975-77, Shanley & Fisher, Newark, 1977-82, ptnr. Newark and Morristown, N.J., 1983-99, Drinker Biddle & Reath LLP, Florham Park, N.J. and San Francisco, 1999—. Mem. planning bd. Peapack-Gladstone, N.J., 1984-88, chmn., 1987-88; bd. dirs. Morris Ctr. YMCA, Cedar Knolls, N.J., 1986-93. Served with U.S. Army, 1970-72, Vietnam. Mem. ABA (litigation sect.), N.J. Bar Assn., Morris County Bar Assn., Essex County Bar Assn., Calif. State Bar, Park Avenue Club (Florham Park). Home: 1150 Greenwich St Apt 3 San Francisco CA 94107 Office: Drinker Biddle & Reath LLP 500 Campus Dr Florham Park NJ 07932-1047 also: Drinker Biddle & Reath LLP 225 50 Fremont St 20th Fl San Francisco CA 94105-2235 Office Phone: 973-360-1100., 415-591-7500. Business E-Mail: Charles.Reid@dbr.com.

REID, DANIEL JAMES, public relations executive; b. Grand Rapids, Mich., Sept. 7, 1960; s. Robert Alexander and Janette Helen (Hickey) R.; m. Meredith Christine Ryan, Apr. 30, 1994; children: Ryan Paul, Katherine Baxter, Charles William Edward. BA, Mich. State U., 1983. Sr. account exec. Burson-Marsteller, Chgo., 1983-88; group dir. Ogilvy & Mather, Chgo., 1988-90; sr. ptnr. FRB/BSMG Worldwide (subs. True North Comms.), Chgo., 1990-98; sr. nat. mng. ptnr. BSMG Worldwide, Chgo., 1998-2000, pres. fin. svcs., 2000—; exec. v.p. Weber Shandwick Worldwide, Chgo., 2001—. Contbr. articles to profl. publs. and newspapers. Bd. dirs. Prospect Fin., L.A., Opportunity, Inc., Chgo., LEC Ltd. Mem. Pub. Rels. Soc. Am., Union League Club Chgo., Execs.'s Club Chgo. Republican. Roman Catholic. Office: Weber Shandwick 676 St Clair Chicago IL 60611

REID, DAVID G. lawyer; b. N.Y.C., Oct. 28, 1948; s. Donald D. and Charlotte A. (Marois) R. BA, McGill U., Montreal, 1970; JD, Boston U., 1973. Bar: Vt. 1973, U.S. Dist. Ct. Vt. 1973, Mass. 1977, U.S. Supreme Ct. 1978, U.S. Ct. Appeals (2d cir.) 1978, U.S. Dist. Ct. Mass. 1991. Pub. defender Orleans, Caledonia, Essex counties, St. Johnsbury, Vt., 1973-75, Bennington (Vt.) County, 1975-79, Windham County, Brattleboro, Vt., 1979-89; ptnr. Reid & Rodgers, Brattleboro, 1989—. Office: Reid & Rodgers 47 Williston St Brattleboro VT 05301-3202 E-mail: drj@sover.net.

REID, DEMETRA ADAMS, insurance company executive; b. Chattanooga, May 13, 1968; d. Willie George Adams, I and Janice Martha Beard; 1 child, Kala Marie. Assoc. in Pre-Nursing, St. Phillip's Coll., San Antonio, 1993; BSN registered nurse, U. of Tex. Health Sci. Ctr., San Antonio, 1994; MS in Health Adminstrn., Columbia So. U., Orange Beach, Ala., 2001. Cert. case mgr., CCM/TN, 2001. Dir. nursing H&H Home Health, San Antonio, 1996—98; case mgr. NextCare Hosp., San Antonio, 1999—2000, Blue Cross Blue Shield of Tenn., Chattanooga, 2000—01, sr. health underwriter, 2001—02, supr., health underwriting dept., 2002—03. Cons. Guidance Home Health, San Antonio, 1997—98, Bexar Necessities Home Health, San Antonio, 1997—98; dir., case mgmt. S.E. Bapt. Hosp., San Antonio, 2003—. Author: (novels) Circle With Three Sides, (book of poems) No Rhyme or Reason and No Particular Season. Adopt a family outreach programs mem. Happy Home Bapt. Ch., LaFayette, Ga., 2000—02, choreographer youth dance group. With USAF, 1987—91. Grantee WIN Winners In Nursing grantee, U. of Tex. Health Sci. Ctr., 1993; AMA grantee, 1994. Mem.: Case Mgmt. Soc. of Am., Sigma Theta Tau (life). Christian. Avocations: reading, music, writing. Home: 13031 Pk Crossing Apt #4104 San Antonio TX 78217 Personal E-mail: twodeelite@sbcglobal.net.

REID, DONNA JOYCE, small business owner; b. Springfield, Tenn., June 25, 1954; d. Leonard Earl Reid and Joyce (Robertson) Kirby; m. Kenneth Bruce Sadler, June 26, 1976 (div. Apr. 1980); m. John Christopher Moulton, Oct. 18, 1987 (div. Dec. 1992); m. Peter Leatherland, Apr. 3, 1993. Student, Austin Peay State U., Clarksville, Tenn., 1972-75. Show writer, producer WTVF-TV (CBS affiliate), Nashville, 1977-83, promotion producer, 1983-85, on-air promotion mgr., 1985-86; gen. mgr. Steadi-Film Corp., Nashville, 1986-90; co-owner Options Internat., Nashville, 1990—2003, Shanti's, Inc., Hermitage, 2003—. Big sister Buddies of Nashville, 1981-87. Named to Honorable Order of Ky. Cols. John Y. Brown, Gov., 1980; recipient Significant Svc. award ARC, 1982, Clara Barton Communications award, 1983. Mem. NAFE, Nat. Assn. TV Arts and Scis., Nat. Film Inst., Nat. Assn. Broadcasters, Internat. Platform Assn., Am. Soc. Prevention of Cruelty to Animals, Humane Soc. U.S. Methodist. Avocations: reading, outdoor sports, travel. Office: Shantis Inc 4715 Andrew Jackson Pkwy Hermitage TN 37076 Office Phone: 615-391-4144. Personal E-mail: optionspi@aol.com.

REID, EDWARD SNOVER, III, lawyer; b. Detroit, Mar. 24, 1930; s. Edward S. Jr. and Margaret (Overington) Reid; m. Carroll Grylls, Dec. 30, 1953; children: Carroll Reid Highet, Richard Gerveys, Jenny Reid McTigue, Margaret Reid Boyer. BA, Yale U., 1951; LL.B. magna cum laude (Sheldon fellow), Harvard U., 1956. Bar: Mich. 1957, N.Y. 1958, D.C. 1982, Gaikokuho jimu-bengoshi, Tokyo 1991-96. Asso. Davis, Polk & Wardwell, N.Y.C., 1957-64, partner, 1964-95, sr. counsel, 1996—; dir. Gen. Mills, Inc., 1974-89. Mem. N.Y.C. Bd. Higher Edn., 1971—73; trustee Bklyn. Inst. Arts and Scis., 1966—93, chmn., 1974—79; trustee Bklyn. Mus. Art, 1973—93, 1994—; bd. dirs. Bklyn. Bot. Garden Corp., 1977—92, 1996—, Bargemusic Ltd., 1990—93. Active duty USMCR, 1951—53. Mem. ABA, N.Y. State Bar Assn., Assn. of Bar of City of N.Y., Am. Law Inst., Internat. Bar Assn., Heights Casino Club, Rembrandt Club, Century Assn. Club, Yale Club, Quogue Beach Club, Shinnecock Yacht Club, Quogue Field Club. Home: PO Box 39 Quogue NY 11959-0039 Office: Davis Polk & Wardwell 450 Lexington Ave New York NY 10017-3982 E-mail: ereid@dpw.com.

REID, FRANCES EVELYN KROLL, cinematographer, director, film company executive; b. Oakland, Calif., Mar. 25, 1944; d. William Farnham and Marion Storm (Teller) Kroll. BA, U. Oreg., 1966. Tchr. secondary sch., Los Angeles, 1968-69; sound recordist Churchill Films, Los Angeles, 1971; freelance sound recordist Los Angeles, 1972-75; freelance producer, dir., 1975-78; freelance cinematographer Berkeley, Calif., 1978—; pres. Iris Films, Berkeley, 1977—. Vol. Peace Corps, Malawi, Africa, 1969-70. Producer/dir.

Long Night's Journey Into Day, 2000 (Grand Jury award Sundance 2000); dir. (film) In The Best Interests of the Children, 1977 (Blue Ribbon Am. Film Festival 1978), The Changer: A Record of the Times, 1991, Skin Deep, 1995, Talking About Race, 1994, Straight from the Heart, 1994 (Acad. award nominee 1995); cinematographer: (film) The Times of Harvey Milk, 1984 (Oscar 1985), Living with AIDS, 1986 (Student Acad. award 1987), Common Threads: Stories from the Quilt, 1989 (Oscar award 1990), Complaints of a Dutiful Daughter, 1994 (Acad. award nominee 1995). Mem. Film Arts Found., Assn. Ind. Video and Filmmakers, Acad. Motion Picture Arts and Scis. Office: Iris Films 2600 10th St # 413 Berkeley CA 94710-2522

REID, GERALDINE WOLD (GERALDINE REID SKJERVOLD), artist; b. Apr. 11, 1944; d. Alden Elroy and Verna (Kocinski) Wold BA in Fine Art, Calif. State U., Sacramento, 1972, MFA, 1975; postgrad., Ind. U. - Purdue U. Instr. dental aux. edn. U. Minn., 1966-70, anthropol. rsch. asst., 1976-78; mng. editor Nat. Arts Guide, Chgo., 1978-80; freelance artist Chgo., 1981-94; pres. Chgo. Art Emerging Inc., 1983-85; graphic artist Reid Design & Illustration, Chgo., 1981-94; dir. show coordination Circle Fine Art, Chgo., 1981. Instr. comm. art and design Alexandria Tech. Coll., Minn., 1994—; seminar lectr., 1977, 86; lectr., art and math. Dept. Math. U. Ill., 1987-88; guest lectr. women's art history AAUW, Alexandria, 1997. One-woman shows include Artists' Coop. Gallery, Santa Fe, 1976, Artlink, Ft. Wayne, Ind., 1979, 84—, D.E.O. Fine Arts, Inc., Chgo., 1982-83, Union League Gallery, Chgo., 1989, Brodsky Gallery, 1993, Second Floor Gallery, Cen. Square, Glenwood, Minn., 1999, Ann Bickle Heritage House, Glenwood, 2000, Pope County Mus., Glenwood, 2004; group exhbns. include Crocker Art Mus., Sacramento, 1975, Ft. Wayne Mus. Art, 1978, Artists Guild Chgo., 1982, Charles A. Wustum Mus., Racine, Wis., 1983, Limelight, Chgo., 1986, 87, 88, Neville-Sargent Gallery, 1986, 87, Beacon Street Hull House Gallery, 1988, McDonalds Corp., Chgo., 1988, Prairie Ave. Gallery, Chgo., 1990, Peace Mus., Chgo., 1990, Hyde Park Art Ctr., Chgo., 1990, Lettuce Entertain You Enterprises, Inc., 1990, Olive Tree Gallery, Daley Coll., Chgo., 1991, Crown Ctr. Gallery, Loyola U., Chgo., 1992, Agora Syndicate, Inc., 1992, Kieffer-Nolde/TIC, 1992, Flora '92, 1992, Chgo. Bot. Garden, 1992, Open Spectrum, David Adler Cultural Ctr., 1994, August House Studio, Chgo., 1994—, Upper West Gallery, Alexandria Tech. Coll., Minn., 1995, Plains Art Mus., Fargo, N.D., 1997, Regional Art Exhibit, New York Mills, Minn., 1997, Runestone Mus., Alexandria, 1997-98, Art on the Plains, 3d Ann. Regional Exhbn., Plains Art Mus., Fargo, 31st Ann. Fergus Falls Cmty. Coll. Invitational Art Show, Fergus Falls, Minn., 2002, 03, Pope County Artists Exhibit, Lake Region Arts Coun. Gallery, Fergus Falls, Minn., 2002, Prairie Renaissance Cultural Alliance Gallery, Morris, Minn., 2002-03, Celebration of Lake Region Arts Coun., Fergus Falls, 2002-2003, Fergus Falls C.C. Ann. Invitational, 2003, New York Mills (Minn.) Ann. Regional Exhbn., 2003, Minn. State Cmty. & Tech. Coll., Fergus Falls, 2004; contbr. artwork to 2 ann. 1994 calendars. Mem. New York Mills Cultural Ctr., Mpls. Art Inst., Am. Inst. Graphic Arts, Mpls. Inst. Arts, Glacial Ridge Artists. Business E-Mail: gerrir@alx.tec.mn.us.

REID, HARRY, senator; b. Searchlight, Nev., Dec. 2, 1939; s. Harry and Inez Reid; m. Landra Joy Gould; children— Lana, Rory, Leif, Josh, Key AS, Southern Utah State U., 1959; LLD (hon.), U. So. Utah, 1984; BA, Utah State U., 1961; JD, George Washington U., 1964. City atty., Henderson, Nev., 1964—66; mem. NV state assembly, 1969—70; lt. gov. state of NV, 1971—75; chmn. NV gaming commission, 1977—81; U.S. rep. Nev., 1983—87; U.S. senator from Nev. Washington, 1987—; asst. minority leader U.S. Senate, 2003—. Mem. appropriations, ethics/environment & pub. works, Indian affairs coms.; ranking mem. environ. pub. works. Democrat. Office: US Senate 528 Hart Senate Office Bldg Washington DC 20510-0001

REID, HELEN VERONICA, dean; b. Reading, Eng., Sept. 25, 1956; d. Alan A. and Teresa H. (Thatcher) Ware; m. Gary B. Reid, May 29, 1976; children: Robert, Jennifer, Kristen. BA in Biology, U. Tex., 1976; BSN, U. Tex., Arlington, 1978; MSN, Tex. Women's U., 1983; EdD, U. North Tex., 2000. CCRN, 1980; cert. CPR instr. Asst. nurse coord., staff nurse, float pool nurse Parkland Meml. Hosp., Dallas, 1979-83, float pool nurse, 1987-93; instr. Trinity Valley Community Coll., Kaufman, Tex., 1983-86, freshman team leader, 1986-90; dean health occupations Trinity Valley C.C., Kaufman, Tex., 1990—. Mem.: Tex. C.C. Tchrs. Assn., Nat. Orgn. ADN (pub. rels. dir. 1998—2002), Tex. Orgn. for ADN (sec. 1988—92, nominating com. chair 1995—96, pres.-elect 2002—03, pres. 2003—), Tex. Assn. Vocat. Nurse Educators, Phi Kappa Phi, Sigma Theta Tau. Home: 4332 Crestover Dr Mesquite TX 75150-4452 Office Phone: 972-932-4309. Business E-Mail: reid@tvcc.edu.

REID, INEZ SMITH, lawyer, educator; b. New Orleans, Apr. 7, 1937; d. Sidney Randall Dickerson and Beatrice Virginia (Bundy) Smith. BA, Tufts U., 1959; LLB, Yale U., 1962; MA, UCLA, 1963; PhD, Columbia U., 1968. Bar: Calif. 1963, N.Y. 1972, D.C. 1980. Assoc. prof. Barnard Coll. Columbia U., N.Y.C., 1972-76; gen. counsel youth divsn. State of N.Y., 1976-77; dep. gen. counsel HEW, Washington, 1977-79; inspector gen. EPA, Washington, 1979-81; chief legis. and opinions, dep. corp. counsel Office of Corp. Counsel, Washington, 1981-83; corp. counsel D.C., 1983-85; counsel Laxalt, Washington, Perito & Dubuc, Washington, 1986-90, ptnr., 1990-91; counsel Graham & James, 1991-93, Lewis, White & Clay, P.C., 1994-95; assoc. judge D.C. Ct. Appeals, 1995—. William J. Maier, Jr. vis. prof. law W.Va. U. Coll. Law, Morgantown, 1985-86. Contbr. articles to profl. jours. and publs. Trustee emeritus Lancaster Sem., Pa., 2002—; bd. dirs. Homeland Ministries bd. United Ch. of Christ, N.Y.C., 1978—83, vice chmn., 1981—83; chmn. bd. govs. Antioch Law Sch., Washington, 1979—81; chmn. bd. trustees Antioch U., Yellow Springs, Ohio, 1981—82; trustee Tufts U., Medford, Mass., 1988—98, trustee emeritus, 1999—; trustee Lancaster (Pa.) Sem., 1988—2001; bd. govs. D.C. Sch. Law, 1990—96, chmn., 1991—95. Recipient Emily Gregory award Barnard Coll., 1976, Arthur Morgan award Antioch U., 1982, Service award United Ch. of Christ, 1983, Disting. Service (Profl. Life) award Tufts U. Alumni Assn., 1988. Office: DC Ct Appeals 500 Indiana Ave NW Fl 6 Washington DC 20001-2138

REID, IRVIN D. academic official; BS, MS in Exptl. Psychology, Howard U.; MA, PhD, U. Pa. Head dept. mktg. & bus. law U. Tenn., Chattanooga, 1979-83; assoc. prof. mktg. Howard U., Washington, 1978-79; cons. U.S. Consumer Product Safety Commn., 1977-78; sr. staff specialist in mktg. & econ. rsch. NASA, 1976-77, 78-79; asst. prof. mktg. coll. bus. Drexel U., 1970-78; pres. Montclair State Coll., Upper Montclair, N.J., 1989-97, Wayne State U., Detroit, 1997—. Bd. dirs. Detroit 300 Com., 1998—; exec. com. Detroit Med. Ctr., 1997—, Karmanos Cancer Inst., 1997—, New Detroit, 1998—, N.J./Israel Trade Commn., 1994-97, NCAA Pres.'s Commn., 1994-99, Nat. Conf. Christians and Jews, 1992-97, Mich. Econ. Devel. Corp., 1999—, Detroit Urban League, 1999—, Mich. Opera Theater, 1998—; steering com. Mich. Life Sci. Initiative, 2000—. Mem. Econ. Club Detroit, Univ. Cultural Ctr. Assn., Upper Montclair (N.J.) Country Club. Office: Wayne State U Office of the Pres Detroit MI 48201

REID, JACKSON BROCK, psychologist, educator; b. Honea Path, S.C., Sept. 18, 1921; s. Alexander Mack and Ann Orr (Brock) R.; m. Avis Boykin Long, Jan. 12, 1947; step-children: Jules Heywood Long, Barbara Banning Long. BS, The Citadel, 1942; postgrad., Ariz. State Coll., Flagstaff, 1948; PhD, UCLA, 1951, postgrad., summer 1951. Cert., lic. psychologist, Tex. Asst. prof. ednl. psychology U. Tex., Austin, 1951-55, assoc. prof., 1955-59, prof., 1959-93, prof. emeritus, 1993—, assoc. dean for grad. studies in edn., 1965-73; coordinator ESEA programs U.S. Office Edn., 1969—, chmn. dept. ednl. psychology, 1972-84. Cons. in field. Served to capt. U.S. Army, 1942-47. Office Edn. grantee, 1966-73 Fellow Am. Psychol. Assn. (exptl. and ednl. divs.); mem. AAAS, Am. Ednl. Research Assn., Interam. Soc. Psychology, AAUP, Southwestern Psychol. Assn. (sec.-treas. 1965-66, pres. 1967-68), Tex. Psychol. Assn., Ret. Officers Assn., Nat. Psoriasis Found., ACLU, Common Cause, Fund for Peace, Planned Parenthood of Am., Sigma Xi. Clubs: U. Tex. Faculty Center; Lighthouse Resort and Club (Sanibel Island, Fla.). Achievements include research, publs. in learning theory, behavioral effects of radiation and drugs, child and adolescent behavior, programmed instn., computer-assisted instn. Home: 3801 Westlake Dr Austin TX 78746-1617 Office: U Tex Dept Ednl Psychology Austin TX 78712 *The principal goal in my career has been to preserve psychology as an academic discipline devoted to objective inquiry into the etiology of behavior on the basis of logically directed empirical investigation as opposed to rationalistic - mystical - doctrinaire approaches.*

REID, JAMES EDWARD, lawyer; b. Balt., Aug. 8, 1951; s. Edward Kessinger and Jane Kathryn (Fraver) R.; m. Linda Susan Peterson, Sept. 14, 1979; children: Edward Kessinger, Griffin Arthur, Andrew James. BA, Utica Coll. of Syracuse U., 1973, JD, 1976. Bar: N.Y. 1978, U.S. Ct. Mil. Appeals 1979, U.S. Dist. Ct. (no. dist.) N.Y. 1980, U.S. Ct. Appeals (2d cir.) 1979, U.S. Supreme Ct. 1983, U.S. Dist. Ct. (we. dist.) N.Y. 1988. Assoc. firm Davoli & McMahon, Syracuse, N.Y., 1979-82; ptnr. Greene & Reid, LLP, Syracuse, 1982—; instr. civil practice and litigation paralegal program Syracuse U., 1984-87; adj. prof. advanced trial practice Syracuse U., 1987—. Author: Service of Process Desk Reference Manual, 1984, Legal Implications of Fire Apparatus Color Selection-Its Impact on Liability Consideration, 1987, Jury Instructions in the Civil Law Suit, 1987, Handling the Plaintiff's Personal Injury Case, 1989, Uninsured MVAIC and Underinsured Claims and Problems under New York Law: What They Are and How to Avoid Them, 1992, Personal Injury Chapter: General Practice, 1998. Life mem. bd. visitors Syracuse U. Coll. Law. Maj. USMC, 1972-86. Mem. Onondaga County Bar Assn. (chmn. legis. com. 1983—, bd. dirs. 1985-87), N.Y. State Bar Assn. (chmn.-elect gen. practice sect. 1989, ho. of dels. 1990-92), Upstate Trial Lawyers Assn. (pres. 1988-90, 1997—, N.Y. State Trial Lawyers Assn. (bd. dirs. 1987-88, 1997—, asst. dist. atty. Wayne County, N.Y. 1992—), Order of Barristers, Phi Delta Phi. Republican. Roman Catholic. E-mail: jereid@greenereid.com. Home: 123 Grant St Newark NY 14513-1738 also; 330 East Ave Newark NY 14513-1743

REID, JAMES SIMS, JR., former automobile parts manufacturer; b. Cleve., Jan. 15, 1926; s. James Sims and Felice (Crowl) R.; m. Donna Smith, Sept. 2, 1950; children: Sally, Susan, Anne (dec.), Jeanne. AB cum laude, Harvard U., 1948, JD, 1951. Bar: Mich., Ohio 1951. Pvt. practice law, Detroit, 1951-52, Cleve., 1953-56; with Standard Products Co., Cleve., 1956-99, dir., 1959, pres., 1962-89, chmn., chief exec. officer, 1989-99; ret., 1999. Trustee John Carroll U., 1967—, chmn., 1987-91, Musical Arts Assn. of Cleve. Orch., 1973—. Office: Hanna Bldg Ste 545 1422 Euclid Ave Cleveland OH 44115-1901

REID, JENNIFER IRENE MCPHERRAN, religious studies educator; b. Arnprior, Ont., Canada, Mar. 5, 1962; d. William David Cooper Reid and Irene Marie Michaud; m. Mark L. McPherran, Nov. 17, 1999; children: Kate I. M., Margaret I. PhD, U. of Ottawa, Ont., Can., 1994. Asst. prof. of religion U. of Maine Farmington, 1995—2001, assoc. prof. of religion, 2001—. Dir. Yearly UMF Consultation on the Religious Imagination of Matter, Farmington, Maine, 2001—. Author: (scholarly book) Worse Than Beasts: An Anatomy of Melancholy and the Literature of Travel in 17th and 18th Century England; editor: Religion and Global Culture: New Terrain in the Study of Religion and the Work of Charles H. Long; author: Myth, Symbol, and Colonial Encounter: British and Mi'kmaw in Acadia, 1700-1867. Grantee, Maine Humanities Coun. grantee, 2001. Mem.: Can. Soc. of Ch. History, Can. Soc. for the Study of Religion, Am. Acad. of Religion. Office: University of Maine at Farmington 270 Maine St Farmington ME 04938

REID, JOHN MITCHELL (JACK REID), biomedical engineer, researcher, consultant; b. Mpls., June 8, 1926; s. Robert Sherman and Meryl (Mitchell) R.; m. Virginia Montgomery, Dec. 31, 1949 (div.); children: Donald, Kathryn, Richard; m. Shadi Wang, June 30, 1983. BS, U. Minn., 1950, MS, 1957; PhD, U. Pa., 1965. Engring. assoc. U. Minn., Mpls., 1950-54; rsch. engr. St. Barnabas Hosp., Mpls., 1954-57; assoc. U. Pa., Phila., 1957-66; rsch. asst. prof. U. Wash., Seattle, 1966-72; rsch. engr. Providence Hosp., 1972-74; dir. bioengring. Inst. of Applied Physiology & Medicine, 1973-81; Calhoun prof. Drexel U., Phila., 1981-94, prof. emeritus, rsch. prof., 1994—. Adj. prof. radiology Thomas Jefferson Med. Sch., Phila., 1982—; affiliate prof. U. Washington, 1995—; cons. Inst. Applied Physiology and Medicine, Seattle. Contbr. numerous articles to profl. jours.; 5 U.S. patents on devel. of ultrasonic med. imaging. Scoutmaster Boy Scouts Am., Mpls., 1955-57, Phila., 1960-65, cub and scoutmaster, Seattle, 1965-70. With USN, 1944—46. Recipient Pioneer award Soc. Vascular Technologists, 1994; grantee NIH; Professorship in his named established at Drexel U. Sch. Biomed. Engring. and Health Sys., Phila., 2004. Fellow IEEE, Am. Inst. Ultrasound in Medicine (bd. govs., Pioneer award), Acoustical Soc. Am., Engring. in Medicine and Biology Soc. (Lifetime Achievement award 1993), Am. Inst. Med. and Biol. Engrs.; mem. World Fedn. Ultrasound in Medicine and Biology (hon.). Home: 16711 254th Ave SE Issaquah WA 98027-6973 also: Inst Applied Physiology and Medicine 701 16th Ave Seattle WA 98122-4525 Business E-Mail: jmreid@u.washington.edu.

REID, JOHN PHILLIP, law educator; b. Weehawken, N.J., May 17, 1930; s. Thomas Francis and Teresa Elizabeth (Murphy) R. BSS., Georgetown U., 1952; LL.B., Harvard U., 1955; MA, U. N.H., 1957; J.S.D., NYU, 1962. Bar: N.H. 1955. Law clk. U.S. Dist. Ct. N.H., 1956; instr. NYU, N.Y.C., 1960-62, asst. prof. law, 1962-64, assoc. prof., 1964-65, prof. Sch. Law, 1966—. Author: Chief Justice: The Judicial World of Charles Doe, 1967, A Law of Blood: The Primitive Law of the Cherokee Nation, 1970, In a Defiant Stance, 1977, In a Rebellious Spirit, 1979, Law for the Elephant: Property and Social Behavior on the Overland Trail, 1980, In Defiance of the Law, 1981, Constitutional History of the American Revolution: The Authority of Rights, 1986, Constitutional History of the American Revolution: The Authority to Tax, 1987, The Concept of Liberty in the Age of the American Revolution, 1988, The Concept of Representation in the Age of the American Revolution, 1989, Constitutional History of the American Revolution: The Authority to Legislate, 1991, Constitutional History of the American Revolution: The Authority of Law, 1993, Policing the Elephant: Crime, Punishment, and Social Behavior on the Overland Trail, 1997, Patterns of Vengeance: Crosscultural Homicide in the North American Fur Trade, 1999, Contested Empire: Peter Skene Ogden and the Snake River Expeditions, 2002, Controlling the Law: Legal Politics in Early National New Hampshire, 2004. Fellow Guggenheim Found., 1980, Huntington Library-NEH, 1980, 84; hon. fellow Am. Soc. Legal History, 1986. Fellow Am. Acad. Arts and Scis. Republican. Roman Catholic. Office: NYU Law Sch 40 Washington Sq S New York NY 10012-1099 Office Phone: 212-998-6230. E-mail: john.reid@nyu.edu.

REID, JOSEPH BROWNING, retired architect; b. Flint Hill, Va., June 24, 1924; s. Charles Garrison and Grace Pearl (Bradley) R.; m. Maria Aida Amadounian, July 5, 1957; children: Charles, Avedis, Robert. Student, U. Va., 1948; BS in Forestry with highest honors, N.C. State U., 1952; postgrad., Columbia U., 1955; cert. in architecture, Cooper Union, 1960. Registered architect, N.Y., Va., Md., Pa., D.C.; cert. Nat. Coun. Archtl. Registration Bds.; lic. interior designer, D.C. Staff architect Charles Luckman & Assocs., N.Y.C., 1956-63; sr. architect Clive Entwistle & Assocs., N.Y.C., 1963-64; sr. assoc. Perkins & Will, Washington, 1964-74; v.p. John Carl Warnecke FAIA, Washington, 1974-82; founding ptnr. Kemnitzer Reid & Haffler, Washington, 1982-89; prin. Einhorn Yaffee Prescott, Washington, 1989-98; cons. McLean, Va., 1998—. Advis0r interior design program Marymount Coll., 1982-85; profl. coord. off-campus work program for architecture students Va. Poly. Inst., 1975-81; lectr. No. Va. C.C.; a juror for residential awards Washingtonian mag., 1986; advisor, organizer archtl. awards program Washington Mayor's Award Program. With Mcht. Marine, 1942-47. Recipient Disting. Svc. cert. USO, Washington, 1976, Presdl. Design award Nat. Endowment for Arts, 1987, Hist. Preservation Honor award, 1988, Design award Washington Metro chpt. Am. Soc. Interior Designers, 1989, 2 awards GSA, 1992; Hilda Johnson Cox scholar N.C. State U., 1950. Mem. AIA (sr. dir. Washington Met. chpt. 1979-80, treas. 1981-82, sec. 1982-83, v.p. 1983-84, pres. 1984-85, cert. of deep appreciation 1984, cert. of appreciation 1984, Centennial medal Washington chpt. 1998), Constrn. Specifications Inst. (bd. dirs. 1979-81, 91-92, citation for disting. svc. 1982, nat. honor awards 1992), Soc. Archtl. Adminstrs. (co-founder Washington chpt.), Phi Eta Sigma, Alpha Zeta, Xi Sigma Pi, Alpha Sigma Pi. Democrat. Methodist. Avocations: surf fishing, greek history, travel in greece. E-mail: mariareid@mindspring.com.

REID, JOSEPH WILLIAM, consultant; b. Gainesville, Ga., Apr. 23, 1955; s. William Lowell and Barbara Ann (Trowbridge) R.; m. Elizabeth Chara Sudduth, July 12, 1986; children: Patrick Bennett, Alexandra Mackenzie. BBA in Acctg., U. Ga., 1977. CPA, Ga. Staff acct. KPMG, Atlanta, 1977-81, mgr., 1981-83, sr. mgr., 1983-88, ptnr., 1988—. Active Atlanta Alliance on Devel. Disabilities, bd. dirs., former treas., mem. fin. com., 1990—; mem. adv. coun. Salvation Army Adult Rehab. Ctr., 1998—. Mem. Am. Inst. CPAs, Ga. Soc. CPAs. Avocations: tennis, golf, hiking, water sports. Home: 575 Leather Hinge Trl Roswell GA 30075-4184 Office: KPMG LLP 303 Peachtree St NE Ste 2000 Atlanta GA 30308-3261

REID, KAREN DENISE, aerospace transportation executive, writer; b. Memphis, Jan. 17, 1961; d. L.C. and Shirley (Spencer) Reid. BS in Edn., Memphis State U., 1992. Journeyman trainee Memphis Pub. Co., 1977—2000; exec. sec., treas., trustee Raleigh Ch., Memphis, 1985—94; acctg. clk. Nat. Hardwood Lumber Assn., Memphis, 1996—98; customer svc. agt. Pinnacle Airlines divsn. Northwest Airlines, Memphis, 1998—; owner K.K.'s Express Boutique, 1998—. Author: From Mistress to Ministry, 2003, (manual) Strageic Management Survival Kit for Church Leaders, 2004. Bd. dirs., CEO Twin Ministries, 2000—; pres. Twin Ministries Singles Fellowship, 2004. Avocations: travel, bowling, writing. Office: Twin Ministries PO Box 752613 Memphis TN 38175 Fax: 901-542-0144. E-mail: thetwinministries@yahoo.com.

REID, KATHARINE LEE, museum director; d. Sherman E. and Ruth Lee; m. Bryan S. Reid. BA magna cum laude, Vassar Coll.; postgrad., Sorbonne, Paris, 1963, Instiut d'Art et Archaeologie, 1963; MFA, Harvard U., 1966. Mem. curatorial staff Toledo Mus. Art, David and Alfred Smart Mus., U. Chgo., Ackland Art Mus., U. NC, Chapel Hill; asst. dir. Art Inst. Chgo., 1982—86, dep. dir., 1986—91; dir. Va. Mus. Fine Arts., 1991—2000, Cleve. Mus. Art, 2000—. Bd. dirs. Van Gogh Mus., Amsterdam, Netherlands, Nat. Conf. Cmty. and Justice, Am. Fedn. Arts; chmn. vis. com. Frances Lehman Loeb Art Ctr., Vassar Coll., Poughkeepsie, NY. Fulbright scholar, 1963. Mem.: Am. Assn. Mus. (bd. dirs., former mem. accreditation commn.), Am. Assn. Mus. Dirs. (pres. 2000—01, trustee). Office: Cleve Mus Art 11150 East Blvd Cleveland OH 44106*

REID, KATHERINE LOUISE, artist, educator, author; b. Port Arthur, Tex., Mar. 25, 1941; d. Clifton Commodore and Helen Ross (Moore) Reid. BA, Baylor U., 1963; postgrad. in design and illustration, Kans. City Art Inst., 1964; MEd, U. Houston, 1973; cert. supervision, U. Houston-Clear Lake City, 1980; postgrad., San Jacinto Coll., 1982. Litho reprodn. artist Hallmark Cards, Kansas City, Mo., 1963-64; tchr. art high sch. Pasadena (Tex.) Ind. Sch. Dist., 1964-77, supr. art, gifted and talented and photography, 1977-85, supr. art and photography InterAct, 1985-90, instrnl. specialist, 1990-2000, photography and art, 1990-93, instrnl. specialist in art and spl. programs, 1993 96, rsch. planning, data disaggregation, 1996-2000; internet tchr. recruiter, 2001—02; mural artist Old Car Barn, Edna, Tex., 2000—. 4 MAT learning styles trainer DuPont Leadership Devel. Process Trainer, Selective Rsch., Inst., tchr. perceiver specialist, performance quality sys. trainer, coop. learning trainer, outcome based edn. trainer, integrated unit devel. and authentic assessment trainer The Greater Gulf Coast Adminstr. Assessment Project, Assessor, 1990-2000; head crafts, asst. dir., dir. summer, winter discovery program-ski camp Cheley Colo. Camps, Denver, Estes Park, 1967-75; mem. awards com. John Austin Cheley Found., 1990-92; staff artist, media workshop Tex. Edn. Agy., Austin, summer, 1961; art enrichment tchr. Port Arthur Ind. Sch. Dist. (Tex.), summer, 1961; head crafts Camp Waluta, Silsbee, Tex., summer, 1960; mem. Tex. Edn. Agy., Art Leadership Inst., 1989, 90, Tracking Rsch. Com., 1991, Core Strategic Planning Team, 1992-2000, Outcome Based Edn. Dist. Planning Com., 1991-92, Quality Sys. Improvement Team, 1991-92, Outcome Based Edn. Com. Exit Outcomes, 1991; Region IV data disk trainer, 1998-2000, target teach coord., 1993-2000, multiple intelligence trainer, 1997-2000, data disaggregation trainer, 1997-2000, supt.'s rsch. com., 1999. Author: Through Their Eyes, 1989; inventor, patentee Pet Car Seat, U.S.A. and Can. Mem. Friends of Fine Arts-Baylor U., Waco, Tex., 1981—; mem. Scholastic Art awards Regional Bd., Houston, 1978-84, Tex. Edn. Agy.; bd. dirs. Houston Coun. Student Art Awards, Inc., 1984-90. Named Outstanding Secondary Educator of Am., 1975, Tex. Art Educator of Yr., 1985. Mem. ASCD, Tex. ASCD, Tex. Art Edn. Assn. (rep. editor newsletter 1982-85, chmn. supervision divsn. 1982-83, v.p. membership 1978-80, chmn. pub. info. com., regional chmn. youth art month 1980-82; regional chmn. membership com. 1976-78, pres. elect 1986, sec. 1991-93, Disting. Fellows award 2004), Tex. Alliance for Arts Edn. (bd. vice chmn. 1984-86, treas. 1988-90), Nat. Art Edn. Assn. (conv. com. 1977, 85), Tex. Assn. Sch. Adminstrs., Houston Art Edn. Assn. (sec. 1969), Tex. Ret. Tchrs. Assn. (Dist. IV historian 2001-03), Pasadena Area Ret. Sch. Employees (parliamentarian 2002—), Delta Kappa Gamma (2d v.p. 1984-86, pres. 2002-2004, state leadership devel. for chpt. pres. com., 2003-2005, state banner com., 2004, named Tex. Outstanding Vol. 2004). Baptist. Home: 106 Ravenhead Dr Houston TX 77034-1520 Personal E-mail: klreid@mail.esc4.com. Business E-Mail: artist@oldcarbarn.com.

REID, LANGHORNE, III, merchant banker; b. Dallas, Apr. 3, 1950; s. Langhorne Jr. and Mary Anne (Beasley) R.; m. Sally Wolf, Dec. 26, 1972 (div. Aug. 1977); m. Eve Catherine Murphy, Sept. 6, 1986 (div. 1996); 1 child, Claire Hart Reid; m. Vera Anderson Reid, 1999. BA in Psychology, U. Tex., 1972, JD, 1975; MBA, U. Pa., 1977. Bar: Tex. 1975. V.p. Dillon, Read & Co., Inc., N.Y.C., 1977-82; mng. dir. Drexel Burnham Lambert Inc., N.Y.C., 1982-87; co-dir. mergers and acquisitions Paine Webber Group, N.Y.C., 1987-89; ptnr. Gordon Investment Inc., N.Y.C., 1989-93; pres. Beacon Advisors, Inc., Dallas, 1993-99. Bd. dirs. Windmill Holdings; pres. Partnership Svcs., 1992-93; chmn. Cedco Sys., Inc., 1997—, Amtex Holdings, Inc., 1996—, Garland Broadcast Investors, Inc., 1997—, Pogesa SA, 2002-. Trustee, treas. Animal Med. Ctr., N.Y.C., 1981—; trustee St. Mark's Sch. of Tex., 2002-. Mem. Tex. Bar Assn. Home: 4109 Windsor Pkwy Dallas TX 75205-1670 Office: Arcady Capital Inc Ste 330 100 Highland Park Village Dallas TX 75205-2726

REID, LAURETTA GLASPER, retired principal; b. Balt., Sept. 6, 1931; BS, Coppin State Coll., 1953; MA, Columbia U., 1957; postgrad., Peabody Consevatory of Music, 1962; MS, Johns Hopkins U., 1980. Cert. elem. and middle sch. supr., prin., Md. Asst. prin., edn. specialist, master tchr. Balt. City Pub. Schs., prin. Recipient Senator's Cert. of Merit Tenure; Gov's. Citation. Mem. NAFE, ASCD, Nat. Assn. Elem. Sch. Prins., Md. Assn. Elem. Sch. Prins., Assn. of Tchr. Educators, Phi Delta Kappa. Office: 6405 Laurel Dr Baltimore MD 21207-6326

REID, LEONARD N. academic administrator; BS, Va. Commonwealth Univ., 1973; MS, U. Ill., 1975, PhD, 1978. Prof. advertising Univ. Ga., 1997—, assoc. dean rsch. and grad. studies, 1997—. Cons. Henderson Advt., Inc., BBDO/Atlanta, Caterpiller Tractor Co., Standard Telephone Co., Major League Baseball, RJR-McDonald/Can.; faculty positions Univ. Ill., Ariz. State Univ., Mich. State Univ. Co-author: Advertising: Its Role in Modern Marketing; contbr. articles to profl. jours. Recipient Outstanding Contribution to Rsch. in Advt. award Am. Acad. of Advertising. Office: U Ga Coll Journalism & Mass Comm Athens GA 30602-3018

REID, LORENE FRANCES, middle school educator; b. St. Louis, May 28, 1946; d. Frank Bernard and Marcella Marie (Froechtenigt) Niemeyer; m. Patrick Joseph Reid, Aug. 11, 1967; 1 child, Christina Marie. BA in Spanish, Maryville U., 1968; MEd in Secondary Edn., U. Mo., St. Louis, 1990; PhD in Edn., St. Louis U., 1995; MA in English, Southeast Mo. State U., 1996. Cert. Spanish, social studies, ESL tchr., reading specialist K-12, sch. psychologist, Mo.; cert. early adolescence/English lang. arts Nat. Bd. for Profl. Tchg. Stds. Spanish tchr. Rosary H.S., Spanish Lake, Mo., 1968-69, Taylor Sch., Clayton, Mo., 1969-70, Roosevelt H.S., St. Louis, 1988-89, Cleve. Jr. Naval Acad., St. Louis, 1989-90, Thomas Dunn Meml. Adult Edn., St. Louis, 1992-95; social studies tchr. St. Luke's Sch., Richmond Heights, Mo., 1981-88; ESL tchr. Grant Mid. Sch., St. Louis, 1990-92, Fanning Mid. Sch., St. Louis, 1992-98; tchr. leader Mid. Sch. Initiative, 1998-99; Schs. for Thought coord. MEGA Magnet Cluster, St. Louis, 1999-2000; psychol. examiner Student Support Svcs.-Gifted and Talented, St. Louis, 2000—03, sch. psychologist, 2003. Adj.

prof. U. Mo.-St. Louis, 2000—; tutor Sylvan Learning Ctr., Crestwood, Mo., 1990-92; mem. St. Louis Ednl. Leadership Inst., 1994-97. Mem. Cmty. Leadership Program for Tchrs., St. Louis, 1993-94. Recipient Emerson Electric Excellence in Teaching award, 1994; named Tchr. of Yr., St. Louis Pub. Schs., 1994-95; named as one of 60 tchrs. recognized by Disney Channel Salutes the Am. Tchr., 1995-96. Mem. ASCD, Tchrs. English to Spkrs. of Other Langs., Nat. Coun. Tchrs. English, Midam. Tchs. English to Spkrs. of Other Langs., Internat. Reading Assn., Nat. Assn. Sch. Psychologists, Mo. Assn. Sch. Psychologists, Phi Delta Kappa. Home: 15449 Ardmore Creek Dr #8 Chesterfield MO 63017 E-mail: lorenereid@aol.com.

REID, LYNNE MCARTHUR, pathologist; b. Melbourne, Australia, Nov. 12, 1923; d. Robert Muir and Violet Annie (McArthur) R. MD, U. Melbourne, 1946; MA (hon.), Harvard U., 1976. Reader in exptl. pathology London U., 1964-67, prof. exptl. pathology, 1967-76; dean Cardiothoracic Inst., 1973-76; pathologist-in-chief Children's Hosp., Boston, 1976-89, pathologist-in-chief emeritus, 1990—; S. Burt Wolbach Disting. prof. pathology Harvard Med. Sch., Boston, 2001—. Fellow Royal Coll. Physicians (U.K.), Royal Australian Coll. Physicians, Royal Coll. Pathologists, Royal Coll. Radiologists (hon.), Royal Soc. Medicine, Royal Inst. Gt. Britain, Pathol. Soc. Gt. Britain and Ireland, Thoracic Soc., Assn. Clin. Pathologists, Brit. Thoracic Soc., Fleischner Soc., Can. Thoracic Soc., Neonatal Soc., Am. Thoracic Soc., Am. Soc. Pathologists, Fedn. Am. Socs. Exptl. Biology. Office: 300 Longwood Ave Boston MA 02115-5724

REID, MARY WALLACE, retired secondary school educator; b. Charlotte, N.C., Oct. 21, 1922; d. Isaac and Mamie Maude (Torrence) Wallace; m. James Samuel Reid, Feb. 13, 1946; 1 child, Virginia Anne. BA, Johnson C. Smith U., 1945; MEd, Temple U., 1970, Secondary Adminstrn. cert., 1982, EdD, 1983. Cert. English, secondary adminstr., French, reading, lang. arts tchr., Pa. Tchr. English, lang. arts, reading Sch. Dist. Phila.; ret., 1988. Title I reading coord., 1976-82; mem. pupil progress com.; past assn. student gov., mem. PFT Bldg. com. Mem. Internat. Reading Assn., Nat. Coun. Tchrs. of English. Home: 1704 Stenton Ave Philadelphia PA 19141-1433

REID, MONA GAY, education educator; b. Port Townsend, Wash., May 12, 1961; d. Warren and Bobbie Nell Reid. BS in math., Okla. State U., 1983; MSc in math., U. of Ctrl. Okla., 1990. Math tchr. Duncan Pub. Schools, Duncan, Okla., 1983—86, Irving Ind. Sch. Dist., 1986—89, Colo. Springs Pub. Schools, 1987—88, Moore Pub. Schools, Okla., 1988—90; adj. math faculty Pines Peak Cmty. Coll. and U. Colo., 1990—92; prof. of math. Jackson Cmty. Coll., Mich., 1992—. Office: Jackson Cmty Coll 2111 EmmonsRd Jackson MI 49203

REID, ORIEN, former medical association administrator; b. Oct. 1945; BA, Clark Coll., Atlanta. MSW. Anchor WCAU-TV, Phila., 1979—98; chmn., bd. dirs. Alzheimer's Assn.'s Nat. Bd. Dirs., 1999—2002. Former mem. bd. govs. Nat. Acad. Television Arts and Scis.; former pres. Phila. Consumer Coun. Recipient Best Investigative Reporting, Phila. Press Assn., Excellence in Journalism award, Inst. Food Technologists.*

REID, ROB, information technology executive; Grad., Stanford U., Harvard U. With Silicon Graphics, 1994—96; prin. 21st Century Internet Venture Ptnrs., 1997; founder Listen.com, San Francisco, 1999—, CEO, 1999—2001, exec. chmn., 2001—. Author: (book) Architects of the Web, 1996; contbr. articles to profl. jours. Scholar Fulbright scholar. Office: Listen.com 2012 16th St San Francisco CA 94103

REID, ROBERT ALFRED, physician; b. Milan, June 8, 1939; BA in English Lit., U. Colo., 1961, MD, 1965. Intern U. Colo. Med. Ctr., 1965-66, resident, 1968-71; dir. med. affairs Santa Barbara (Calif.) Cottage Hosp., 1992—. Mem. AMA, Am. Coll. Ob-gyn., Calif. Med. Assn. (pres. 1998). Office: Cottage Health Sys PO Box 689 Pueblo at Bath St Santa Barbara CA 93102 Business E-Mail: rreid@sbch.org.

REID, ROBERT CLARK, chemical engineering educator; b. Denver, June 11, 1924; s. Frank B. and Florence (Seerley) R.; m. Anna Marie Murphy, Aug. 26, 1950; children: Donald M., Ann Christine. Student, Colo. Sch. Mines, 1946-48; BS, Purdue U., 1950, MS, 1951; ScD, MIT, 1954. Prof. chem. engring. MIT, Cambridge, from 1954, now prof. emeritus chem. engring.; Olaf A. Hougen prof. chem. engring. U. Wis., 1980-81. Author: (with J.M. Prausnitz and B.E. Poling) Properties of Gases and Liquids, 1966, 4th edit., 1987, (with M. Ohara) Modeling Crystal Growth Rates from Solution, 1973, (with M. Modell) Thermodynamics and Its Applications, 1974, 2d edit., 1983; Contbr. articles to profl. jours. Recipient Warren K. Lewis award, 1976; Chem. Engring. award Am. Soc. Engring. Edn., 1977; research fellow Harvard U., 1963-64 Mem. Am. Inst. Chem. Engrs. (Ann. lectr. 1967, council 1969-71, editor jour. 1970-76, Founders award 1986), Nat. Acad. Engring., Blue Key, Sigma Alpha Epsilon, Tau Beta Pi. Home: 22 Burroughs Rd Lexington MA 02420-1908 Office: MIT 66-409 Cambridge MA 02139

REID, ROBERT LELON, engineering educator, dean; b. Detroit, May 20, 1942; s. Lelon Reid and Verna Beulah (Custer) Menkes; m. Judy Elaine Nestell, July 21, 1962; children: Robert James, Bonnie Kay, Matthew Lelon. ASE, Mott C.C., Flint, Mich., 1961; BChemE, U. Mich., 1963; MME, So. Meth. U., 1966, PhDME, 1969. Registered profl. engr., Tenn., Tex., Wis. Asst. rsch. engr. Atlantic Richfield Co., Dallas, 1964-65; assoc. staff engr. Linde Divsn., Union Carbide Corp., Tonawanda, NY, 1966-68; from asst. to assoc. prof. U. Tenn., Knoxville, 1969-75; assoc. prof. Cleve. State U., 1975-77; from assoc. to full prof. U. Tenn., Knoxville, 1977-82; prof., chmn. U. Tex., El Paso, 1982-87; dean Coll. Engring., Marquette U., Milw., 1987-98, prof. mech. engring., 1998-2001; dean emeritus, 2001. Summer prof. NASA Marshall Space Ctr., Huntsville, Ala., 1970, EXXON Prodn. Rsch., Houston, 1972, 73, NASA Lewis Space Ctr., Cleve., 1986; cons. Oak Ridge Nat. Lab., 1974-75, TVA, 1978, 79, State of Calif., Sacramento, 1985, Tex. Higher Edn. Coordinating Bd., Austin, 1987. Contbr. articles 100 articles on heat transfer and solar energy. Grantee NSF, DOE, TVA, NASA, DOI, 1976-87; named Engr. of Yr. Engring. Socs. El Paso, 1986. Fellow ASME (Centennial medallion 1980, chmn. cryogenics com. 1977-81, chmn. solar energy divsn. 1983-84, chmn. Rio Grande sect. 1985-87, John Yellott award, 1997, Dedicated Svc. award 1998); mem. ASHRAE, Engrs. and Scientists Milw. (bd. dirs. 1988-93, v.p. 1989-90, pres. 1991-92), Wis. Assn. Rsch. Mgmt. (pres. 1996-97). Lutheran. Avocations: travel, classic car restoration.

REID, ROBERT OSBORNE, oceanographer; b. Milford, Conn., Aug. 24, 1921; married, 1947; 6 children. BE, U. So. Calif., 1946; MS, U. Calif., 1948; DSc, Old Dominion U., 1988. Asst. Scripps Inst. U. Calif., 1946-47, oceanographer Scripps Inst., 1948-51; asst. prof. to assoc. prof. oceanography & meteorology Tex. A&M U., College Station, 1951-59, emeritus disting. prof. oceanography, 1987—. Cons. U.S. Army Corps Engrs., 1965-78, Hydraulic Divsn., Waterways Exptl. Sta., Vicksburg, Va., 1975—; mem. ad hoc panel Computing Resources & Facilities Ocean Circulation Modeling, NAS, 1979-80, com. Coastal Flooding, 1980-84, U.S. Nat. Com. Internat. Union Geodynamics & Geophys., 1980-84, Storm Surge Program Rev. Bd., NOAA, 1981-83, subcom. Nat. Marine Bd., NAS, 1986-88, Coastal Engring. Rsch. Bd., U.S. Army Corps Engrs., 1988-92. Assoc. editor Jour. Geophys. Rsch., 1961-73, Jour Marine Rsch., 1961-73, 83-85; contbr. numerous articles to profl. tech. publs. Fellow Am. Meteorol. Soc. (editor-in-chief Jour. Phys. Oceanography 1970-80, Spl. award 1975), Am. Geophys. Union; mem. NAE (elected), Internat. Assn. Hydraulic Rsch., Sigma Xi. Office: Tex A&M U Dept Oceanography College Station TX 77843-3146

REID, ROBERT TILDEN, medical association administrator, internist; b. Dallas, Feb. 20, 1931; s. Robert Tilden and Gldays Tressy (King) R.; divorced; children: Robert Tilden, Richard Thomas, Annette Marie, Randolph Young. BS, So. Meth. U., Dallas, 1957; MD, U. Tex.-Southwestern, Dallas, 1959. Diplomate Am. Bd. Internal Medicine, Am. Bd. Rheumatology, Am. Bd. Allergy and Immunology. Intern Parkland Meml. Hosp., Dallas, 1959-60, resident, 1960-63; with Scripps Clinic and Rsch., La Jollla, Calif., 1963-70; pvt. practice La Jollla, Calif., 1970—; chief staff Scripps Meml. Hosp., La Jollla, Calif., 1976-78; scientific dir. Erik and Ese Banck Clinical Rsch. Ctr., San Diego, 1994—. Mem. San Diego County Med. Soc. (pres. 1991), Calif. Med. Assn. (trustee 1992-95). Office: PO Box 910236 San Diego CA 92191 Office Phone: 858-646-0757. Personal E-mail: banckcrc@pacbell.net.

REID, RORY, former political organization administrator; b. Alexandria, Va., 1963; BA Internat. Rels., Spanish; JD, Brigham Young U. Sr. v.p., gen. counsel Lady Luck Gaming Corp., Nev.; state chmn. Nev. Dem. Party, 1999—; ptnr. Lionel Sawyer & Collins, 2002—. Mem. Dem. Nat. Com. 1999—; nominee Clark County Commr. Address: 1700 Bank Am Plz 300 S Fourth St Las Vegas NV 89101 Office: Nev Dem Party 1785 E Sahara Ave Ste 496 Las Vegas NV 89104-3712 also: 3790 Paradise Rd Ste 130 Las Vegas NV 89109-4648

REID, ROSALIND, magazine editor; b. Iowa City, Nov. 16, 1954; d. Isaac Errett and Eleanor Mary Reid; children: Sarah C. Herndon, Kathryn A. Herndon. AB in Journalism, Polit Sci., Syracuse U., 1975; MA in Pub. Policy Scis., Duke U., 1981. Reporter and columnist Lewiston (Maine) Daily Sun, 1975-77; staff writer The News and Observer, Raleigh, N.C., 1979-80, The Cary (N.C.) News, 1981-84; asst. news dir. N.C. State U., Raleigh, 1984-90; assoc. editor Am. Scientist, Research Triangle Park, N.C., 1990-91, mng. editor, 1991-92, editor, 1992—. Adv. bd. Dragonfly Mag., 1995—2000. Recipient Best Local Column award Maine Press Assn., 1977, HEW Pub. Svc. fellowship, Duke U., 1977-78. Mem. Nat. Assn. Sci. Writers, Phi Beta Kappa. Office: Am Scientist 3106 E NC Hwy 54 Research Triangle Park NC 27709

REID, ROSEMARY ANNE, insurance agent; b. Portland, Maine, June 15, 1951; d. Kenneth Bruce and Mary (Hollywood) R.; m. Ronald E. Walls, May 7, 1977 (div. Mar. 1986); children: Rachel A., Tate A. BS in Edn., U. South Maine, Portland, 1973. V.p. ins. Gruntal and Co., Inc., Portland, 1987-91; pvt. practice Portland, 1973—. Mem. Cape Elizabeth Town Coun., 1990, 95-99; mem. Cape Elizabeth Sch. Bd., 1991-94, fin. chair, 1992-93. Recipient 10 Yrs. Nat. Quality, 10 Yrs. Nat. Sale Achievement award, 1979-89, Nat. Assn. of Life Underwriters, 1974—, Am. Hometown Leadership award WalMart, 1998. Mem. Million Dollar Round Table (life and qualifying mem., Top of Table 1984, 86), South Maine Assn. Life Underwriters (bd. dirs. 1985-91, officer 1987-91, pres. 1989-90, regional v.p., pub. svc. chair, others), Life Underwriter Tng. Coun. (chair 1986-87), Maine Assn. Life Underwriters (bd. dirs. 1988-92, v.p. 1991-92, pres. elect 1992). Roman Catholic. Avocations: skiing, swimming, biking. Office: PO Box 927 Portland ME 04104-0927

REID, RUST ENDICOTT, lawyer; b. NYC, Dec. 31, 1931; Atty. firm Thompson & Knight, Dallas. Trustee Child Care Group, Dallas, 1968-72, 1996-2002, Hockaday Sch., Dallas, 1972-82, chmn., 1976-78; trustee Tex. coun. Girl Scouts U.S.A., l982-83, Vis. Nurse Assn., Dallas, l984-93, chmn., l991-93; trustee Grace Presbyn. Village Fedn., 1996—. Lt. (j.g.) USNR, l954-57. Fellow Am. Coll. Probate Counsel; mem. Tex. Bar Found., Dallas Estate Planning Coun. (pres. l988-89). Office: Thompson & Knight 1700 Pacific 1700 Pacific 3300 Dallas TX 75201 Home: 6715 Golf Dr Dallas TX 75205-1213

REID, SUE TITUS, law educator; b. Bryan, Tex., Nov. 13, 1939; d. Andrew Jackson Jr. and Lorraine (Wylie) Titus. BS with honors, Tex. Woman's U., 1960; MA, U. Mo., 1962, PhD, 1965; JD, U. Iowa, 1972. Bar: Iowa 1972, U.S. Ct. Appeals (D.C. Cir.) 1978, U.S. Supreme Ct. 1978. From instr. to assoc. prof. sociology Cornell Coll., Mt. Vernon, Iowa, 1963-72; assoc. prof., chmn. dept. sociology Coe Coll., Cedar Rapids, Iowa, 1972-74; assoc. prof. law. U. Wash., Seattle, 1974-76; exec. assoc. Am. Sociol. Assn., Washington, 1976-77; prof. law U. Tulsa, 1978-88; dean, prof. Sch. Criminology, Fla. State U., Tallahassee, 1988-90; prof. pub. adminstrn. and policy Fla. State U., 1990—. Acting chmn. dept. sociology Cornell Coll., 1965-66; vis. assoc. prof. sociology U. Nebr., Lincoln, 1970; vis. disting. prof. law and sociology U. Tulsa, 1977-78, assoc. dean 1979-81; vis. prof. law U. San Diego, 1981-82; mem. People-to-People Crime Prevention Del. to People's Republic of China, 1982; George Beto Vis. Disting. Prof. criminal justice Sam Houston U., Huntsville, Tex., 1984-85; lecture/study tour of Criminal Justice systems of 10 European countries, 1985; cons. Evaluation Policy Rsch. Assocs., Inc., Milw., 1976-77, Nat. Inst. Corrections, Idaho Dept. Corrections, 1984, Am. Correctional Inst., Price-Waterhouse. Author (with others): Bibliographies on Role Methodology and Propositions Volume D - Studies in the Role of the Public School Teacher, 1962, The Correctional System: An Introduction, 1981, Crime and Criminology, 10th edit., 2003, Criminal Justice, 6th edit., 2002; author: Criminal Law, 6th edit., 2004; editor (with David Lyon): Population Crisis: An Interdisciplinary Perspective, 1972; contbr. articles to profl. jours. Recipient Disting. Alumni award Tex. Woman's U., 1979; named One of Okla. Young Leaders of 80's Oklahoma Monthly, 1980. Mem. ABA, Am. Soc. Criminology, Acad. Criminal Justice Scis., Soc. Criminal Jus. Assn. Avocations: walking, reading, cooking, skiing. Office: Fla State Univ Dept Pub Adminstrn Tallahassee FL 32306 E-mail: suetreid@adelphia.net.

REID, SUSAN L. conductor; b. Charlottesville, Va., Apr. 4, 1958; d. L. Leon and Jane S. Reid, Roseann B. Reid. BM, Westminster Choir Coll., 1980; MS, Okla. State U., 1987; MMus, U. Surrey, Guildford, Eng., 1990; DMA, Ariz. State U., 1995; Cert., Royal Coll. of Church Music, Croydon, Eng., 1980. Tchg. asst. U. Surrey, Guildford, England, 1989—90, Ariz. State U., Tempe, 1990—94; dir. of music First United Meth. Ch., Edwardsville, Ill., 1980—83, First Christian Ch., Stillwater, Okla., 1983—89; faculty assoc. in music Ariz. State U., Tempe, 1994—95; dir. of choral activities S.D. Sch. of Mines and Tech., Rapid City, SD, 1995—2000, James Madison U., Harrisonburg, Va., 2000—. Prin., owner Integrated Conducting Inc. Bd. dirs., U.S. corr. Internat. Fedn. Choral Music. Office: James Madison U MSC 7301 Harrisonburg VA 22807

REID, S.W. English educator; b. Neptune, N.J., Nov. 24, 1943; s. Sidney Webb and Mary Cook (Bennett) R.; m. Judith Wright, Aug. 22, 1969; 1 child, Laura. BA, Duke U., 1965; MA, U. Va., 1966, PhD, 1972. Grad. tchg. fellow U. Va., Charlottesville, 1968-70; asst. prof. English, Kent (Ohio) State U., 1970-75, assoc. prof., 1975-84, prof., 1984—, dir. Inst. Bibliography and Editing, 1985—. Vis. fellow Clare Hall, Cambridge (Eng.) U., 1992-93, life mem., 1993—. Textual editor Bicentennial Edition of Charles Brockden Brown, 6 vols., 1977-87; editor-in-chief: (Cambridge edits. of Joseph Conrad) The Secret Agent, 1990, Almayer's Folly, 1994, Notes on Life and Letters, 2004. NDEA fellow U. Va., 1965-68; Rsch. grantee NEH, 1977-84. Office: Kent State University Inst Bibliography-Editing 1118 Library Kent OH 44242-0001 Office Phone: 330-672-2092.

REID, TRACY, professional basketball player; b. Nov. 1, 1976; B.Comm., U. N.C., 1998. Forward Charlotte Sting, 1998—. Named Atlantic Coast Conf. Player of the Yr., Player of the Week, 1998; named to 1997 and 1998 Kodak All-Am. First Team, 1998 AP All-Am. First Team; recipient First team All-Am. selection, U.S. Basketball Writers Assn., Women's Nat. Basketball Assn. Rookie of Yr. award, 1998. Office: Charlotte Sting 3308 Oak Lake Blvd Ste B Charlotte NC 28208-7707

REID, VIRGINIA ANNE, school nurse; b. Phila., Sept. 14, 1950; d. James Samuel and Mary Virginia R. BA in History, Beaver Coll., 1973, MA in Edn., 1976; BSN, Thomas Jefferson U., 1986. RN; cert. tchr., Pa. Tchr. Sch. Dist. Phila., 1973-82; nurse VA Med. Ctr., Phila., 1986-87, Einstein Med. Ctr., Phila., 1987-90, Sch. Dist. Phila., 1989—. Active Girl Scouts Am., 1960; Sunday sch. tchr. House of Prayer Episcopal Ch., Phila. 1960. Mem. Nat. Assn. Sch. Nurses, Order Ea. Star, Phi Delta Kappa, Alpha Kappa Alpha. Avocations: travel, cooking, reading, concerts.

REID, WILLIAM JAMES, mining executive; b. Cowdenbeath, Scotland, Jan. 18, 1941; arrived in U.S., 1968; s. William and Sheila (Davidson) Reid; m. Thelma Rear, Sept. 27, 1969; children: Judith, Robert. Nat. cert. Mining Engring, Ashington County Tech. Coll., Northumberland, Eng., 1961. Student apprentice Brit. Coal, England, 1958-63; sales engr. Huwood Ltd., England, 1964-68; mining engr. Huwood-Irwin Co., Irwin, Pa., 1968-71, mgr. mining sales, 1971-74, gen. sales mgr., 1974-77, v.p., 1977-79; internat. sales dir. Huwood Ltd., England, 1979-81; exec. v.p. Am. Longwall Mining Corp., Abingdon, Va., 1981-83, pres., 1983-95, Am. Longwall Face Conveyors Inc., Abingdon, 1993-95, Internat. Longwall Cons., Abingdon, 1996-98, Internat. Entertainment Assocs., 1996-98; v.p. mktg. Long Airdox Co., Blacksburg, Va., 1998-99; pres. Eimco LLC, Bluefield, W.Va., 1999-2001, Internat. Longwall Cons., Bluefield, 2001—. Apptd. to Nat. Coal Coun. by Sec. Energy, 1994—; dir. Ea. Coal Coun., 1994—. Editor (mng.): Coal Leader, 2001—04; editor: (mng., pub.) Coal News, 2004—. Trustee Sullins Acad., Bristol, Va., 1984. Recipient Overseas medal, Brit. Instn. Mining Engrs., 1992. Mem.: AIME (treas. 1978), Nat. Mining Assn. (bd. govs. mfrs. divsn. 1991—96, 1999—2001), N. Eng. Inst. Mining and Mech. Engrs. (assoc.), Greater Irwin Area C. of C. (bd. dirs. 1977). Presbyterian. Avocations: travel, tennis, wine tasting. Home and Office: Internat Longwall Cons 106 Tamarack St Bluefield WV 24701-4573 Office Phone: 304-327-6777.

REID-ANDERSON, JAMES, diagnostic equipment company executive; BS in Commerce with honors, U. Birmingham, Eng. Exec. level positions with Pepsico Inc., Grand Met. PLC, Mobil Oil Corp.; COO, chief adminstrv. officer Wilson Sporting Goods, Chgo., 1994-96; exec. v.p., CFO Dade Behring, Deerfield, Ill., 1996-97, exec. v.p., CFO, chief adminstrv. officer, 1997-99, pres., COO, 1999—. Fellow Chartered Assn. Cert. Accts.

REID-BILLS, MAE, magazine editor, historian; b. Shreveport, La. d. Dayton Taylor and Bessie Oline (Boles) Reid; m. Frederick Gurdon Bills (div.); children: Marjorie Reid, Nancy Hawkins, Frederick Taylor, Virginia Thomas, Elizabeth Sharples. AB, Stanford U., 1942, MA, 1965; PhD, U Denver, 1977. Mng. editor Am. West mag., Tucson, 1979-89, cons. editor, 1989—. Gen. Electric fellow, 1963; William Robertson Coe fellow, 1964. Mem. Orgn. Am. Historians, Am. Hist. Assn., Phi Beta Kappa, Pi Alpha Delta. Home and Office: 10 Town Plz #159 Durango CO 81301-5104

REIDEL, ART, health products executive; BS in Math., MIT. Pres., CEO Sunrise Test Systems, Inc., 1992—94; v.p. bus. devel. Viewlogic Systems, Inc., 1994—95; pvt. investor, cons., 1995—96; dir., pres. Pharsight Corp., Mountain View, Calif., 1995, pres., CEO, 1996—2002, chmn. bd. dirs., 1995—. Dir. Insightful Corp. Office: Pharsight Corp 800 W El Camino Real #200 Mountain View CA 94040

REIDELBACH, LINDA, state representative; b. Cin., Apr. 1, 1949; BS, Miami U. Ohio. Exec. v.p. MJR Enterprises, Inc.; state rep. dist. 21 Ohio Ho. of Reps., Columbus, vice chair, banking pensions and securities com., chair, children's healthcare and family svcs. subcom., mem. edn., health, human svcs. and aging, and juvenile and family law coms., and fed. grant rev. and edn. oversight subcom. Mem. Columbus team Abstinence Educators Network; mem. Franklin County Rep. Ctrl. Com., Ohio; bd. dirs. Destiny Training Camp. Mem.: Worthington Christian Ch., Worthington League for Decency. Office: 77 S High St 12th fl Columbus OH 44321-6111

REIDENBAUGH, LOWELL HENRY, retired sports editor; b. Lititz, Pa., Sept. 7, 1919; s. Harry Martin and Marian Marie (Nies) R.; m. Ruth Elizabeth Cameron, Nov. 23, 1944; children: Karen Lee (Mrs. William Rogers), Kathy Jean (Mrs. William J. Schuchman). AB, Elizabethtown (Pa.) Coll., 1941. Gen. reporter Lancaster (Pa.) Intelligencer Jour., 1941-42; sports writer Phila. Inquirer, 1944-47; mem. staff The Sporting News, St. Louis, 1947-89, mng. editor, 1962-79, sr. editor, 1980-83, corp. editor, 1983-89. Author: National League History, 1976, The Super Bowl Book, 1981, Cooperstown, Where Baseball's Legends Live, 1983, Take Me Out to the Ballpark, 1983, The Sporting News, First 100 Years, 1985, The 50 Greatest Games, 1986, History 33d Va. Infantry Regiment, CSA, 1987, 25 Greatest Pennant Races, 1987, 25 Greatest Teams, 1988, History 27th Va. Infantry Regiment, CSA, 1993, The Battle of Kernstown, 1997. Served with AUS, 1942-43.

REIDENBERG, MARCUS MILTON, physician, educator; b. Phila., Jan. 3, 1934; m. June Wilson, July 14, 1957; children: Bruce, Joel, Julie. Student, Cornell U., 1951-54; MD, Temple U., 1958. Diplomate Am. Bd. Internal Medicine. Intern Community Gen. Hosp., Reading, Pa., 1958-59; resident Temple U. Hosp., Phila., 1962-65; from instr. to assoc. prof. Temple U. Med. Sch., Phila., 1962-75; assoc. prof. Cornell U. Med. Coll., N.Y.C., 1975-76, prof. pharmacology, head div. clin. pharmacology, 1976—, prof. medicine, 1980—, prof. pub. health, 2002—, acting assoc. dean, 1981-82, asst. dean, 1988—; attending physician N.Y. Hosp., 1980—. Vis. physician Rockefeller U. Hosp., N.Y.C., 1980—; mem. project adv. group FDA, Rockville, Md., 1977-82; vice chmn. Joint Commn. on Prescription Drug Use, Washington, 1977-80; mem. study sect. NIH, Bethesda, Md., 1980-86; del. U.S. Pharmacopeal Conv., 1975-80. Author: Renal Function and Drug Action, 1971; editor: various books, Clin. Pharmacology and Therapeutics, 1985—2001; contbr. articles to profl. jours. Served to lt. M.C., USNR, 1960-62. Recipient Research Career Devel. award NIH, 1970, Julius Sturmer award Phila. Coll. Pharmacy and Sci., 1982. Fellow ACP; mem. Am. Soc. Clin. Investigations, Assn. Am. Physicians, Am. Soc. Clin. Pharmacology and Therapeutics (pres. 1984-85, Rawls Palmer award 1981), Am. Soc. Pharmacology and Exptl. Therapeutics (award 1983, Harry Gold award 1999), Internat. Union Pharmacology (vice chmn. sect. clin. pharmacology 1984-87, chmn. 1987-89), World Health Organization Expert Com. on the Selection and Use of Essential Drugs, 1989, 1994, 1993, 1995, 2002, 2003. Office: Cornell U Med Coll Dept Clin Pharmacology 1300 York Ave New York NY 10021-4805

REIDER, RICHARD GARY, geographer, educator; b. Denver, Feb. 7, 1941; s. Alexander and Natalie Alice (Frick) R. BA, Colo. State Coll., 1963, MA, 1965; PhD, U. Nebr., 1971. Instr. geography Indiana U. of Pa., 1965-66, U. Wyo., Laramie, 1969-71, asst. prof. geography, 1971-77, assoc. prof. geography, 1977-83, prof. geography, 1983—2001, prof. emeritus, 2001—. Cons. Smithsonian Inst., Washington, 1975-77, Office Wyo. Archaeologist, Laramie, 1975—, dept. anthropology U. Wyo., Laramie, 1975—, various firms, Wyo., 1977—. Contbg. author: The Agate Basin Site, 1982, The Horner Site, 1987; contbr. articles to profl. jours. NSF grantee, 1975-76, Smithsonian grantee, 1975-77, 79. Mem. Assn. Am. Geographers, Geol. Soc. Am., Am. Quaternary Assn., Plains Anthrop. Soc., Sigma Xi.

REIDHAAR, DONALD LAVERNE, lawyer; b. Grangeville, Idaho, Sept. 22, 1933; s. Jacob Joseph and Lois Bernice (Heimark) R.; m. Dolores Mae Ferchalk, Mar. 18, 1956; 1 dau., Lisa Ann. A.B. cum laude, U. Wash., 1957; LL.B., U. Calif.-Berkeley, 1960. Bar: Calif. 1961, Oreg. 1960, U.S. Supreme Ct. 1968, U.S. Ct. Appeals (9th cir.) 1960, (10th cir.) 1980, U.S. Dist. Ct. (no. dist.) Calif. 1960, (ce. dist.) Calif. 1966. Law clk. Assoc. Justice, Oreg. Supreme Ct., 1960-61; assoc. Pillsbury, Madison & Sutro, San Francisco, 1961-62; asst. counsel The Regents of U. Calif.-Berkeley, 1962-71, assoc. counsel, 1971-73, gen. counsel, 1973— . Bd. visitors Hastings Coll. Law, 1974-75. Served with AUS, 1954-55. Fellow Am. Bar Found.; mem. Am. Bar Assn., Am. Judicature Soc., Nat. Assn. Coll. and Univ. Attys. (mem. exec. bd. 1976—, pres. 1983-84), State Bar Calif., Oreg. State Bar. Democrat. Lutheran. Clubs: Berkeley Faculty, City Commons (dir.) (Berkeley); Commonwealth (San Francisco); Order of Golden Bear. Office: 590 University Hall 2200 University Ave Berkeley CA 94720

REIDHEAD, SARAH JOSEPHINE, writer; d. Albert Perkins and Sarah Jane (Froehlich) Reidhead. Student, Clemson U., SC, 1972—74. Exec. dir., founder Piedmont Advocacy for Space, Seneca, SC, 1983—90; exec. dir., co-founder Women's Space Network, Seneca, 1984—90; owner The Mill Gallery, Seneca, 1989—94. Mem. Nat. Coordinating Com. for Space, Wash., DC, 1983—89; sec. Oconee County Rep. Party, Seneca, SC, 1992—93, chmn., 1993—95; dir. So. Space Conf., Atlanta, 1996—97; bd. advisors Wyatt Earp Birthplace Mus., Monmouth, Ill., 2001—; co-founder Women's Space Network; founder Piedmont Advocacy Space. Author: Dust Devil, 2000, Travesty, 2004, Sunflowers and Thistle, 2004. Bd. dirs. Oconee Sertoma Club, Seneca, 1990—95; pres. Noisy Waters Sertoma Club, Ruidoso, N.Mex., 1999—2000; mem. Lincoln County Rep. Party, Ruidoso, N.Mex., 1998—2003. Mem.: UDC, DAR, Western Outlaw Lawman Assn., Western Writers Am. (assoc.), Daughters of the King, Jr. Daughters of the King (dir. 1999—2003). Republican. Episcopalian. Avocations: politics, art. Personal E-mail: sjreidhead@hotmail.com.

REIDINGER, RUSSELL FREDERICK, JR., fish and wildlife scientist; b. Reading, Pa., June 19, 1945; BS, Albright Coll., 1967; PhD in Zoology, U. Ariz., 1972. Asst. prof. biology Augustana Coll., 1971-74; rsch. physiologist The Philippines, 1974-78; asst. mem., wildlife biologist Monell Chem. Senses Ctr., 1978-86; dir. Denver Wildlife Rsch. Ctr. U.S. Dept. Agr., Denver, 1987-93; dir. Ctr. Excellence Wildlife Mgmt. Lincoln U., Jefferson City, Mo., 1993—. Vis. prof. dept. zoology U. Philippines, 1975-78; cons. Bangladesh Agr. Rsch. Coun., USAID, 1977, Ministry Agrl. Devel. & Agrarian Reform, Nicaragua, 1981, CID, Uganda, 1996. Mem. Am. Soc. Mammalogists, Wildlife Soc., Nat. Animal Damage Control Assn. Office: Lincoln U Dept Ag Nat & Home Econ Jefferson City MO 65102-0029

REIDY, CAROLYN KROLL, publisher; b. Washington, May 2, 1949; d. Henry August and Mildred Josephine (Mencke) Kroll; m. Stephen Kroll Reidy, Dec. 28, 1974. BA, Middlebury Coll., 1971; MA, Ind. U., 1974, PhD, 1982. Various positions to mgr. subs. rights Random House, Inc., N.Y.C., 1975-83, assoc. pub., 1987-88; dir. subs. rights William Morrow & Co., N.Y.C., 1983-85; v.p., assoc. pub. Vintage Books, N.Y.C., 1985-87, pub., 1987-88, Anchor Books, Doubleday & Co., N.Y.C., 1988; pres., pub. Avon Books, N.Y.C., 1988-92; pres., pub. trade divsn. Simon & Schuster, N.Y.C., 1992—2001, pres. adult publ. divsn., 2001—. Bd. dirs. NAMES Project, 1994—98, Literacy Partners, Inc., 2000—, Nat. Book Found., 2001—. Mem.: NY Women in Comm., Pubs. Lunch Club (recipient Matrix award 2003), Women's Media Group. Office: Simon & Schuster 1230 Avenue Of The Americas New York NY 10020-1586 E-mail: carolyn.reidy@simonandschuster.com.

REIDY, MIKE, food products executive; CFO LePrino Foods, Denver. Office: LePrino Foods 1830 W 38th Ave Denver CO 80211-2200

REIDY, THOMAS MICHAEL, financial executive; b. Elmira, N.Y., Dec. 22, 1951; s. Bernard Thomas and Betty Pauline Reidy; m. Rosemarie Stella, June 12, 1982; 1 child, Carla. AS, Corning C.C., 1971; BA, St. John Fisher Coll., 1973. Cert. fin. planner. Exec. br. dir. YMCA, Rochester, N.Y., 1975-84; fin. planner IDS/Am. Express, Rochester, 1984-86; pres., CEO TMR Adv. Group, Rochester, 1986-95; divsn. mgr. Waddall & Reed, Rochester, 1995-98; pres. Morgan & Alexander Ltd., Rochester, 1998—. Pres. CPA/Bus. Forum, Rochester, 1988—90; prin. Sandler Sales Inst., Pittsford, NY, 2002—. Author: (tng. manual) The NOW Client System, 1996, The True Wealth Revolution, 1999, Quality Life Management System, 1999. Recipient Outstanding Young Man Am. Jaycees, 1979, Businessman of Yr. Nat. Rep. Congrl. Com., 2003. Mem. Rotary Club, C. of C. Profl. Sales Soc. (bd. dirs. 1988-89).

REIF, DAVID (FRANK DAVID REIF), artist, educator; b. Cin., Dec. 14, 1941; s. Carl A. and Rachel L. (Clifton) R.; m. Ilona Jekabsons, July 30, 1966; 1 child, Megan Elizabeth. BFA, Art Inst. Chgo., 1968; MFA, Yale U., 1970. Asst. prof. art U. Wyo., Laramie, 1970-74, assoc. prof., 1974-81, U. Mich., Ann Arbor, 1980-81; prof. U. Wyo., Laramie, 1981—2004, acting head dept. art, 1986—87, Disting. prof. emeritus, 2004—. Selection cons. Ucross Found. Residency Program, Wyo., 1983—; exhibit juror Artwest Nat., Jackson, Wyo., 1986; panelist Colo. State U., Ft. Collins, 1981; lectr. U. Mich., 1980; apptd. Wyo. Arts Coun., 1993-96; vis. artist lectr. Colo. State U., 1996; vis. artist Colo. State U., Ft. Collins, 1996; 3-D juror, art exhbn. Colo. State Fair, Pueblo, 2001. One-man shows include U. Wyo. Art Mus., 1993, Dorsky Galleries, NYC, 1980, No. Ariz. U., 1977, 87, U. Mich., 1980-81, One West Ctr. Contemporary Art, Ft. Collins, 1991, West Wyo. C.C., Rock Springs, 1999, Casper Coll. Goldstein Gallery, 2003; exhibited in group shows at First, Second and Third Wyo. Biennial Tour, 1984-88, U.S. Olympics Art Exhbn., LA, 1984, Miss. Mus. Art and NEA Tour, 1981-83, LA Invitational Sculpture Tour Exhbn., 1991-92, Nicolaysen Art Mus., Casper, Wyo., 1994. Apptd. chair Wyo. Arts Coun., 1995-96. With USAR, 1963-69. Recipient F.D. Pardee award Yale U., 1970; Best Sculpture award Joslyn Art Mus. Omaha, 1978; grantee Nat. Endowment Arts, 1978-79, Wyo. Basic Rsch., 1983-84, 86-87; Tchg. Excellence grantee U. Wyo., 1996-97. Mem. Coll. Art Assn., Internat. Sculpture Ctr. Democrat. Home: 3340 Aspen Ln Laramie WY 82070-5702 Office: U Wyo Dept Art PO Box 3138 Laramie WY 82071-3138 Office Phone: 307-745-3110.

REIF, JOHN STEVEN, epidemiologist, veterinarian; b. N.Y.C., Sept. 18, 1940; s. Hans V. and Anne (Marie) R. DVM, Cornell U., 1963; MSc in Epidemiology, U. Pa., 1966. NIH postdoctoral fellow U. Pa., Phila., 1966-68, asst. prof., 1969-73, assoc. prof., 1974-78; prof., chief comparative medicine sect. Inst. Rural Environ. Colo. State U., Ft. Collins, 1979-95, chmn. dept. environ. health, 1995—. Prof. U. Otago Sch. Medicine, Wellington, N.Z., 1987-88. Contbr. numerous articles to profl. jours. Mem., pres. Larimer County Bd. Health, Ft. Collins, 1980-85; mem. Colo. Bd. Health, Denver, 1982-87. Fogarty fellow NIH, 1987-88; recipient Recognition award Tchrs. Preventive Medicine, 1989. Fellow Am. Coll. Epidemiology; mem. Internat. Epidemiology Assn., Internat. Soc. Environ. Epidemiology, Soc. for Epidemiologic Rsch. Office: Colo State U Dept Environ Health Fort Collins CO 80523-0001 E-mail: jreif@cvmbs.colostate.edu.

REIF, LOUIS RAYMOND, lawyer, utilities executive; b. Buffalo, July 4, 1923; s. John Dennis and Sadie (Wilkenson) R.; m. Nancy C. Heuer, Apr. 12, 1958; children: Tracey Lynn, Christopher Louis. Student, Mich. State U., 1941-42, The Citadel, 1943; AB, U. Buffalo, 1948; JD, U. Mich., 1951. Bar: N.Y. 1953. Pvt. practice, Chgo., 1951-52, Buffalo, 1953—; atty. Continental Ill. Nat. Bank, Chgo., 1951-52; from atty. to sr. v.p. Iroquois Gas Corp., Buffalo, 1952-71, pres., 1971—, also bd. dirs.; from v.p. to pres., CEO Nat. Fuel Gas Co., N.Y.C., 1960-87, chmn., CEO, 1988—; asst. to chmn. Del. North Cos., Buffalo, 1988, COO, 1989—, also bd. dirs., 1989. Chmn. Bio-Quest Inc., Houston, 1996; bd. dirs. Goldome Bank; chmn. N.Y. Gas Group, 1973—; chmn. 17th World Gas Conf., Internat. Gas Union, 1986-88. Pres., dir. Buffalo Better Bus. Bur., 1970; trustee SUNY-Buffalo Found. Served with C.E. AUS, 1943-46, ETO. Mem. ABA, N.Y. Bar Assn., Fed. Power Bar Assn., Erie County Bar Assn., Barrister Soc., Am. Gas Assn. (chmn. dir. 1984-85, Disting. Svc. award 1986), Nat. Alliance Businessmen (dir., chmn. 1967-68), Buffalo C. of C. (dir. 1973—), chmn. nat. affairs com. 1969—), Buffalo Club (bd. dirs. 1988, pres. 1991-92), Phi Alpha Delta. Office: Biokeys Pharmaceuticals Inc 9948 Hibert St Ste 100 San Diego CA 92131

REIFF, DANIEL D. art history educator; b. Potsdam, N.Y., Aug. 17, 1941; s. Henry and Ione Drake Reiff; m. Janet Madej Reiff, June 28, 1975; children: Nicholas Andrew, Michael Christopher. BA, Harvard U., 1963, MA, 1964, PhD, 1970. Instr. art history Baylor U., Waco, Tex., 1964-65, 66-67; acting asst. sec. U.S. Commn. Fine Arts, Washington, 1969-70; asst. prof. art history SUNY, Fredonia, 1970-72, assoc. prof. art history, 1972-77, prof. art history, 1977—2003, disting. svc. prof., 2003—04, disting. svc. prof. emeritus, 2004—. Author: Washington Architecture, 1791-1861, 1971, Architecture in Fredonia, 1811-1972, 1972, Small Georgian Houses in England and Virginia, 1986, Architecture in Fredonia, New York, 1811-1997, 1997, Houses from Books...1738-1950, 2000; contbr. articles to profl. jours. Pres. Fredonia Preservation Soc., 1995-98. Recipient Archtl. Heritage award Preservation League of N.Y. State, Albany, 1986, Ruth Emery award Victorian Soc. in Am., Phila., 1999, Hist. Preservation Book prize Ctr. for Hist. Preservation, Mary Washington Coll., 2001; grantee Graham Found. for Advanced Studies in Fine Arts, Chgo., 1991; fellow Rotary Internat., Evanston, Ill., 1965-66, NEH, 1985. Mem.: Fredonia Preservation Soc., Inc. (pres. 1995—98), Preservation League of N.Y. State, Nat. Trust Historic Preservation, Soc. Archtl. Historians, Nature Conservancy. Avocations: photography, canoeing, hiking, camping, travel. Office: Visual Arts Dept SUNY Coll at Fredonia Fredonia NY 14063

REIFF, JAMES STANLEY, osteopathic physician, addictions and psychiatric physician, surgeon; b. Mar. 17, 1935; s. Nathan Edgar and Freda Matilda (Imhoff) R.; m. Sharon Ann Kraybill, June 9, 1956 (div. April 1970), children: Gregory James, James Stanley II, Cynthia Diane, Jeffery Cameron. BA in Chemistry, Goshen Coll., 1957; DO, Chgo. Coll. Osteo Medicine, 1961. Biochemist Miles/Ames Pharm. Co., Elkhart, Ind., 1955-57; pvt. practice Mich. City, Ind., 1962-69; addictions physician Oaklawn Psychiat. Ctr., Elkhart, 1974-84; med. dir. Life Recovery Ctr., Elkhart, 1987-90, Substance Abuse Coun., St. Joe County, Mich., 1990-95, Am. Plasma Mgmt., Inc., various, Mich., Ind, 1991-97; mem. staff Cmty. Mental Health Svcs., St. Joe County, 1993-97. Bd. dirs. Home for Runaway Kids - Victory House, Elkhart, Ind., 1974-76, 12 Step House Meth. Ch.-Halfway House, Elkhart, 1974-77; bd. dirs., treas. Caldwell Home Corp.-Social Rehab. Ctr. for Alcoholism, Elkhart, 1984-87; bd. dirs. Hope House, Jonesville, Mich. Organist First Presbyn. Ch., Sturgis, Mich., 1993-97. Mem. AMA, Am. Osteopathic Assn., Am. Soc. Addiction Medicine (com. on addiction medicine in correctional facilities 1993—), Mich. State Med. Soc., St. Joe County Med. Soc. Avocation: organ and piano playing. Home and Office: 1301 E Congress St Sturgis MI 49091-9181

REIFF, PATRICIA HOFER, space physicist, educator; b. Oklahoma City, Mar. 14, 1950; d. William Henry and Maxine Ruth (Hoffer) R.; m. Thomas Westfall Hill, July 4, 1976; children: Andrea Hofer Hill, Adam Reiff Hill, Amelia Reiff Hill. Student, Wellesley Coll., 1967-68; BS, Okla. State U., 1971; MS, Rice U., 1974, PhD, 1975. Cert. secondary tchr., Okla., Tex. Resident rsch. assoc. Marshall Space Flight Ctr., Huntsville, Ala., 1975-76; rsch. assoc. space physics and astronomy dept. Rice U., Houston, 1975, asst. prof. space physics and astronomy dept., 1978-81, asst. chmn. space physics and astronomy dept., 1979-85, assoc. rsch. sci., 1981-87, sr. rsch. scientist, 1987-90. Adj. asst. prof. Rice U., 1976-78, disting. faculty fellow, 1990-92, prof. 1992—, chmn. dept. space physics and astronomy, 1996-99, dir. Rice Space Inst., 1999—; mem. sci. team Atmosphere Explorer Mission, Dynamics Explorer Mission; co-investigator Global Geospace Sci. Mission, ESA/Cluster Mission, IMAGE Mission; prin. investigator The Public Connection NASA, Mus. Tchg. Planet Earth, cons. Houston Mus. Natural Sci., 1986—; adv. com. on atmospheric scis. NSF, Washington, 1988-92; mem. stategic implementation study panel NASA, Washington, 1989-91; mem. space sci. adv. com. NASA, 1993-98, mem. space sta. utilization subcom., 1995-98; mem. adv. com. Los Alamos Non-Proliferation Divsn., 1998-2001; univ. rep. U. Space Rsch. Assn., Washington, 1993—, chair Coun. of Instns., 2001—; exec. com. George Observatory, Houston, 1989-92, others. Designer Cockrell Sundial/Solar Telescope, 1989; editor EOS (sci. newspaper), 1986-89; contbr. articles to profl. jours. Trustee, Citizens' Environ. Coalition, Houston, 1978-98, pres. 1980-85, adv. com. 1998-2000; mem. air quality com. Houston/Galveston Area Coun., 1980-83, Green Ribbon Com., City of Houston, 1981-83; active coms. Macedonia United Meth. Ch., 1988—. Named rsch. fellow NAS/NRC., 1975, an Outstanding Young Woman Am., 1977, '80, to Houston's Women on the Move, 1990; named Outstanding Aerospace Educator, Women in Aerospace, 1999; NASA grantee 1993, 94, 95, 98, 99; recipient NASA Group Achievement award. Fellow Am. Geophys. Union (fin. com. 1980-82, editor search com. 1992, pub. edn. com.); mem. Cosmos Club, Wellesley Club, Internat. Union of Geodesy and Geophysics (del. 1975, 81, 83, 89, 91, 93, 95, chair working group 2F, 1991-95). Avocations: organic gardening, beef ranching, scouting. Office: Rice U Dept Physics and Astronomy 6100 S Main St Houston TX 77251 E-mail: reiff@rice.edu.

REIFFEL, JAMES, cardiologist, educator; b. N.Y.C., Sept. 20, 1943; s. Martin Lawrence and Roslyn (Siskind) R.; m. Bonnie Geffen, Mar. 18, 1967; children: Gabrielle, Jamie. BA, Duke U., 1965; MD, Columbia U., 1969. Diplomate NASPE, Am. Bd. Internal Medicine, subsplty. bd. Cardiovascular Disease, subsplty. bd. Clin. Cardiovascular Electrophysiology; cert. Nat. Bd. Examiners. Intern Presbyn. Hosp., N.Y.C., 1969-70, resident, 1970-72, asst. physician, 1974-76, asst. attending physician, 1976-80, assoc. attending physician, 1980-88, attending physician, 1988—, assoc. dir. electrophysiology lab., 1979-91; dir. electrophysiology programs Coll. Physicians & Surgeons, Columbia U., N.Y.C., 1991-99, dir. electrocardiography lab., 1999—, assoc. in clin. medicine, 1974-76, asst. prof. clin. medicine, 1976-80, assoc. prof. clin. medicine, 1980-88, prof. clin. medicine, 1988—. Pres. Soc. of Practioners Columbia Prebyn. Med. Ctr., 2003—. Author numerous abstracts, sci. papers; contbr. articles to profl. jours. With USAR, 1970-76. Cardiology fellow Presbyn. Hosp., 1972-74. Fellow ACP, Am. Heart Assn., Coun. Clin. Cardiology, Am. Coll. Cardiology, N.Y. Cardiol. Soc.; mem. N.Y. Heart Assn., Med. Soc. County of N.Y., Med. Soc. State of N.Y., Am. Fedn. Clin. Rsch., Cardiac Electrophysiologic Soc., N.Am. Soc. Pacing & Electrophysiology. Office: 161 Ft Washington Ave New York NY 10032-3713

REIFFEL, LEONARD, physicist, medical physicist, scientific consultant; b. Chgo., Sept. 30, 1927; s. Carl and Sophie (Miller) R.; m. Judith Eve Blumenthal, 1952 (div. 1962); children— Evan Carl, David Lee; m. Nancy L. Jeffers, 1971. B.Sc., Ill. Inst. Tech., 1947, M.Sc., 1948, PhD, 1953. Physicist Perkin-Elmer Corp., Conn., 1948; engring. physicist U. Chgo. Inst. Nuclear Studies, 1948-49; with Ill. Inst. Tech. Research Inst., Chgo., 1949-65, dir. physics research, 1956-63, v.p., 1963-65; cons. to Apollo program NASA Hdqrs., 1965-70; pvt. practice cons., 1970—; tech. dir. manned space flight expts. bd. NASA, 1966-68; chmn. bd. Instructional Dynamics, Inc., 1966-81, Interand Corp., 1969-91, Telestrator Industries, Inc., 1970-73; sci. editor Sta. WBBM-CBS radio, Chgo.; sci. cons./commentator WBBM-TV, 1971-72; host Backyard Safari, 1971-73; sci. feature broadcaster WEEI-CBS radio, Boston, 1965-75; syndicated newspaper columnist World Book Ency. Sci. Service, Inc. (later Universal Sci. News, Inc.), 1966-72, Los Angeles Times Syndicate, 1972-76; sci. cons. CBS Network, 1967-71; chmn., CEO Exelar Corp., Chgo., 1991—; chmn. bd., pres., CEO Ameraine Corp., Chgo., 1992-95; bd. overseers Armour Coll., bd. advisors engring. depts. Ill. Inst. Tech., 1995—; founder, chmn. Luxelar Corp., 2001—; founder Exelar Med. Corp., 2004, chmn., CT0, 2004—. Cons. Korean Govt. on establishment atomic energy rsch. program; mem. adv. com. isotope and radiation devel. AEC; com. rsch. reactors NAS, 1958-64; cons. U.S. Army, 1976—. Author: (book) The Contaminant, 1979; author numerous sci. papers; patentee in field. Bd. dirs. Student Competitions on Relevant Engring. Named Outstanding Young Man of Year Chgo. Jr. C. of C., 1954, 61; recipient Merit award Chgo. Tech. Socs., 1968; Peabody award for radio edn., 1968; IR-100 award for inventing Telestrator CBS Chalkboard, 1970; award for coverage space events Aviation Writers Assn., 1971; IR-100 award for invention underwater diver communications system, 1972, IR-100 award for DISCON video teleconferencing systems, 1985, Third Annual High Tech Entrepreneur award, 1986, IR-100 award for invention Audiografix, 1973; Disting. Alumni Achievement award Ill. Inst. Tech., 1974, named to Hall of Fame IIT, 1984. Fellow Am. Phys. Soc.; mem. AAAS, Chgo. Literary Club, Sigma Xi, Tau Beta Pi, Eta Kappa Nu. Achievements include being responsible for world's 1st indsl. nuclear reactor, 1956. Home: 602 W Deming Pl Chicago IL 60614-2618 Office Phone: 773-871-0171. E-mail: lreiffel@aol.com.

REIFLER, STEWART, lawyer; b. Poughkeepsie, N.Y., May 5, 1954; s. Aaron and Sally Reifler; m. Sheryl Louise Perry, Sept. 19, 1982; 1 child, Jonathan Perry. Student, McGill U., 1972—75; BA, Bard Coll., 1979; JD magna cum laude, NY Law Sch., 1992. Bar: N.Y. 1992, Conn. 1992, U.S. Tax Ct. 1992, U.S. Supreme Ct. 2004. Assoc. Law Offices of Joseph E. Bachelder, N.Y.C., 1992—95, Weil, Gotshal & Manges, 1995—98; dir. Pricewaterhouse-Coopers, 1998—2001; ptnr. Vedder, Price, Kaufman & Kammholz, 2001—. Steering com. mem., exec. compensation AICPA. Co-author: Compensation Committee Handbook, 2d edit., 2004; contbr. articles to profl. jours. Trustee Westport Pub. Libr., Conn. Recipient Outstanding Editl. Contbn., NY Law Sch. Law Rev., 1991, Law Rev., NY Law Sch., Am. Jurisprudence award, 1991. Mem.: ABA, N.Y. State Bar Assn., Conn. State Bar Assn., Assn. of Bar of City of N.Y., WorldatWork, Nat. Assn. Stock Plan Profls., Minuteman Yacht Club, The Sky Club. Home: 8 Brightfield Ln Westport CT 06880 Office: Vedder Price Kaufman & Kammholz 805 Third Ave New York NY 10022 Office Phone: 212-407-7700. E-mail: sreifler@vedderprice.com.

REIFSNIDER, KENNETH LEONARD, metallurgist, educator; b. Balt., Feb. 19, 1940; s. David Leonard and Daisy Pearl (Hess) R.; m. Loretta Lieb, June 15, 1963; children: Eric Scott, Jason Miles. BA, Western Md. Coll., 1963; BS in Engring., Johns Hopkins U., 1963, MS in Engring., 1965, PhD, 1968. Jr. instr. Johns Hopkins U., Balt., 1966-67; asst. prof. Va. Poly Inst. and State U., Blacksburg, 1968-72, assoc. prof., 1972-75, prof., 1975-83, Reynolds Metals prof. engring. sci. and mechanics, 1983-90, Alexander Giacco prof., 1990—, also chmn. materials engring. sci. Ph.D. program, 1974-92; chmn. adminstrn. bd. Ctr. Composite Materials and Structures, 1984, 1994-97. Dir. Va. Inst. for Material Systems, 1988-2001, assoc. provost for interdisciplinary programs, 1996-2001; engr. Lawrence Livermore Nat. Lab., 1981; mem. Nat. M aterials Adv. Bd., 1996—; cons. in materials sci. NATO, 1969, 75. Editor in chief Internat. Jour. of Fatigue; editor, co-editor, author books, book chpts, articles for profl. publs. Mem. troop 44 com. Boy Scouts Am., Blacksburg, Va. Recipient Va. Acad. Sci. J. Shelton Horsley award, 1978, Va. Poly Inst. Alumni award, 1982, Disting. Rsch. award Am. Soc. Composites, 1992. Fellow ASTM (founder Jour. of Composites Tech. and Rsch., vice chmn. standing com. on publs., award of merit 1982); mem. ASME, Coun. on Engring. Home: 13 Quail Run Rd Storrs Mansfield CT 06268-2768

REIG, JUNE WILSON, scriptwriter, television director, television producer; b. Schenectady, N.Y., June 1, 1933; d. Wallace John and Lillian Lucy (Gay) Wilson; m. Robert Maxwell, Nov. 26, 1969. BA summa cum laude, N.Y. State U., 1954; MA in Dramatic Arts, NYU, 1962. Instr. NYU, N.Y.C., 1962—67; prodr., dir. NYU Theater, N.Y.C., 1963—67; dir.-prodr., writer news and pub. affairs NBC TV Network, N.Y.C., 1963—67; dir., writer, prodr. divsn. entertainment NBC-TV Network, N.Y.C., 1967—73; pres. Bunny/Chord Prodns., N.Y.C., 1972—97. Author: (book) Dairy of the Boy King Tut-Ankh-Amen, Charles Scribner's Sons, 1978; writer: (music spl.) The Heart of Christmas, 1965; An Afternoon at Tanglewood (Peabody award); writer, dir. (TV spl.) Stuart Little, 1966 (Peabody award, Prix Jeunesse); writer The Reluctant Dragon, 1968 (Brotherhood award); writer, dir., prodr. Rabbit Hill, 1966 (ALA award); Bill Cosby As I See It, 1970 (Ohio State award); A Day with Bill Cosby, 1971; Jennifer & Me, 1972; prodr., writer Little Women, the ballet, 1976; Tut, the Boy King, 1978 (Peabody award); writer, dir., prodr.: (TV series) Watch Your Child - The Me Too Show, 1973 (Action for Children's TV Achievement award); films in permanent collections Mus. Broadcasting, N.Y.C. Nominee Emmy award, 1966, 1976; recipient Christopher award. Mem.: NATAS, Dirs. Guild Am., Writers Guild Am., Audubon Soc., NYU Alumni Assn., Internat. Soc. Animal Rights, Friends of Animals, Alan Devoe Bird Club (Old Chatham, N.Y.). Avocations: photography, music, animals. Office: care Howard Comart 450 7th Ave Ste 1701 New York NY 10123-1701 *Whether I am working on a teleplay or book, I write about things I believe children are interested in: feelings, aspirations, caring, animals, loving. As I see it, too much of the fare for young people gives them a distorted view of how much violence there is in the world, and I want to counteract that impression. I want to write about things that create a sense of worth, warm security, and an absence of unnecessary anxiety. When I do write about the darker things that happen in life, it is to help the young person understand himself and the world a little better.*

REIGROD, ROBERT HULL, manufacturing executive; b. N.Y.C., Mar. 26, 1941; s. David and Beatrice (Simon) R.; children: Sandra, Donald. BA in Anthropology, Calif. State U., Long Beach, 1973. With Brother Internat. Corp., Irvine, Calif., 1970-77, gen. mgr. west region, 1977-82, v.p., 1982-86, dir., sr. v.p., 1986—; pres. Brother Internat. de Mexico, S.A. de C.V., 1992—, Brother Internat. do Brasil, Sao Paulo, 1999—. Trustee Leukemia Soc. Am., 1982-84; bd. dirs. Irvine Children's Fund, 1988-90. Mem. Japan Soc. South Fla. (dir. 1994—, trustee). Office: Brother Internat Corp Alameda Nothmann 354 01216000 Sao Paulo Brazil

REILEY, MAME CARRIGAN, political consultant; b. Newport News, Va., Dec. 24, 1952; d. Bernard Campbell and Joan (Carrigan) R. BA in Liberal Arts, Sacred Heart Coll., 1974; cert., Cornell U., 1977. Asst. mgr. Watergate Hotel, Washington, 1975-83; real estate agt. Watergate Mgmt., Washington, 1980-84; dir. mktg., producer spl. events Courtesy Assocs., Washington, 1983-90; campaign mgr. Jim Moran for Congress, Alexandria, Va., 1990—; chief of staff Congressman James Moran, 1991—. Guest lectr. Am. U., Washington, 1987; bd. dirs. Rte One Corridor Housing. Mem. fin. com. Dem. Nat. Com., Washington, 1983, Va. State Cen. Com., 1989—; pres. Washington chpt. Internat. Spl. Events Soc. Mem. Washington Performing Arts Soc. (chmn. pub. relations com. 1985-89). Clubs: Nat. Dem. Avocations: swimming, tennis. Office: 501 Slaters Ln Apt 17 Alexandria VA 22314-1114 Home: 7923 Jackson Rd Alexandria VA 22308-1430

REILEY, T. PHILLIP, systems analyst, consultant; b. Ft. Lewis, Wash., May 5, 1950; s. Thomas Phillip and Anne Marie (Russick) R. BSc in Biophysics, Pa. State U., 1973; postgrad. in Bus. Adminstrn., Rutgers U.; MBA, NYU, 1991. Cert. prodn. and inventory mgmt., cert. integrated resource mgmt. Inventory supr. Leland Tube Co., South Plainfield, NJ, 1973-76; prodn. inventory control supr. Bomar Crystal Co., Middlesex, NJ, 1976-79; prodn. control mgr. Codi Semiconductor Inc., Linden, NJ, 1979-81; mfg. systems analyst Western Union Info. Systems, Mahwah, NJ, 1981-85; bus. analyst Nabisco Brands Biscuit Divsn., Parsippany, NJ, 1985-91, sr. systems analyst, 1991-94, tech. advisor, 1994-97; applications cons. SAP Am., Parsippany, 1997—. Mem. Am. Prodn. and Inventory Control Soc. (past chmn. ednl. com. Raritan Valley chpt.), NY Acad. Scis., Coun. Logistics Mgmt., Am. Inst. Mgmt. Accts., Mensa. Republican. Home: 1308 Centennial Ave #111 Piscataway NJ 08854 Office Phone: 610-661-7603. Personal E-mail: phillip.reiley@sap.com. Business E-Mail: preiley@world.std.com.

REILING, HENRY BERNARD, business educator; b. Richmond, Ky., Feb. 5, 1938; s. Henry Bernard and Lucille Frances (Fowler) R.; m. Carol-Lina Maria Schuetz, June 4, 1962; children: Christina Lucille Reiling Breiter, Maria Hays, Carol-Lena Alexis Reiling Lessans. BA, Northwestern U., 1960; MBA, Harvard U., 1962; JD, Columbia U., 1965. Bar: N.Y. 1965. Mem. faculty Columbia U. Bus. Sch., 1965-76, prof., 1974-76; vis. prof. Stanford U. Bus. Sch., 1974-75; vis. asso. prof. Harvard U. Bus. Sch., 1972-73, prof., 1976—, Eli Goldston prof. bus. adminstrn., 1978—. Contbr. articles to profl. jours. Trustee Riverside Ch., NYC, 1976-77; bd. advisors Northwestern U. Coll. Arts and Scis., 1989—, alumni regent, 1997—. Recipient Alumnus Merit award, Northwestern U., 1996, Svc. award, 2002. Mem. ABA, N.Y. Bar Assn., Bar Assn. City N.Y., Am. Fin. Assn., Fin. Mgmt. Assn., Nat. Tax Assn., Tax Inst. Am., Union Club (N.Y.C.), Beta Gamma Sigma (hon.). Home: 28 Meriam St Lexington MA 02420-3618 Office: Harvard U Bus Sch Boston MA 02163

REILLEY, DENNEN, research agency administrator, educator; b. Greenwich, Conn., Mar. 1, 1937; s. Philip Francis and Florence Rita (Junkersfield) R.; m. Margaret Randall, Dougherty, Dec. 26, 1976; children: Philip F., Christopher J., Diane L., Elizabeth S., Katherine M. BSS, Fairfield U., 1959; MEd, U. Hartford, 1965; postgrad., U. Conn., 1965-70, CAGS, 1970. Tchr. New Britain (Conn.) Pub. Schs., 1960-65; tchr., adminstr. West Hartford (Conn.) Pub. Schs., 1965-69, 72-73; mem. faculty Central Conn. State Coll., New Britain, 1969-72; dir. field svcs. Edn. Devel. Ctr., Newton, Mass., 1973-82; sr. assoc., CEO Applied Rsch. Assocs., Sharon, Mass., 1980—. Adj. faculty U. Wyo., U. Minn.; cons. Am. Humane Assn., Edn. Devel. Ctr.; particip. Intl. Wannsee Conf., Berlin, Germany, 2002. Author: Training Program for Animal Care and Control Professionals, Sources: A Resource Guide to Funding Assistance for Parenting Programs, Education for Parenthood Conference Report; the Tri-State Parenting Collaborative, (with Jan Mokros) Summary of Exploring Childhood Evaluation Findings, The Animal Welfare Board of Directors, Total Quality Management: Implications for Animal Care and Control Professionals, Management Perspectives for Animal Care and Control Professionals, Board Perspectives for Nonprofit Organizations, Long Range Planning for Nonprofit Organizations; contbr. articles to profl. jours. Mem. New Britain Rep. town com., 1961-65; conductor mgmt. seminars nationally Not-for-profit orgns., 1982—. Recipient Rosemary Ames award Am. Humane Assn., 1983. Mem. Nat. Coun. Social Studies (conv. spkr. 1963-79, curriculum com. 1974-77, field svcs. bd. 1977-80), Conn. Coun. Social Studies (pres. 1965-66), NEA (life), ASCD, Am. Humane Assn., HSUS (conv. spkr. 1980-94, cons. 1994—). Office: 57 Brook Rd Sharon MA 02067-1415

REILLEY, DENNIS H. chemicals executive; m. Cindy Reilley; children: Jason, Michael. BS in Fin, Okla. State U., 1975. With Conoco, 1974-80, mgr. adminstrn. surface transp., 1980-81; exec. asst. to pres. petroleum ops., 1981-83, gen. mgr. planning and adminstrn. N.Am. mktg., 1983-84; v.p. ops. Kayo Oil Co., Chattanooga, 1984-87; pres., mng. dir. Conoco, 1987-89; dir. ops. white pigment and mineral products divsn. DuPont, 1989-91, v.p., gen. mgr. white pigment and mineral products, 1991-95, v.p., gen. mgr. specialty

chems., 1995-96, v.p., gen. mgr. Lycra/Terathane, 1996-97, sr. v.p., 1997-99, exec. v.p., COO, 1999-2000; pres., CEO Praxair, Danbury, Ct., 2000—. Address: Praxair Inc 39 Old Ridgebury Rd Danbury CT 06810-5103

REILLEY, GAIL GOODWIN, soprano, music educator, musician; d. Luther Reid Goodwin and Kathryn F.U. Adams; m. Robert Joseph Reilley, Sr., Dec. 10, 1960; children: Robert Jr., Steven Wayne. BA, Temple U., 1960, MusM, 1964. Bus. mgr., asst. condr. choral dept. Temple U., Phila., 1961—66, music instr., choral dir. Tyler Art Sch., 1963—70; co-founder, assoc. dir., accompanist, soprano soloist The Mastersingers, Pa., 1967—; pvt. voice tchr. Norristown, Pa., 1969—; voice tchr. Wyomissing Inst. Fine Arts, West Reading, Pa., 1972—77; musical dir. Plymouth-Whitemarsh H.S., Plymouth Meeting, Pa., 1977—93. Soprano soloist St. Stephen's Episcopal Ch., Phila., 1964—75; accompanist, asst. dir. Univ. Glee Club, Gladwyne, Pa., 1977—; choral dir. Main Line Unitarian Ch., Devon, Pa., 1989—96. Author: Mmm...Cooking for Company, 2001. Avocations: photography, cooking, swimming, exercising, reading. Home: 120 Glenn Oak Rd Norristown PA 19403-2927

REILLEY, MARGARET RANDALL, secondary school educator; b. Atlanta, Feb. 7, 1948; d. Guy Randall and Margaret Olivia (Ross) Dougherty; m. Dennen Reilley, Dec. 27, 1975; stepchildren: Philip F., Christopher J., Diane L. Reilley Waitkus, Elizabeth S. Reilley-Matthews, Katherine M. Reilley Lawn. BA in History, Stanford U., 1970; MA in Edn., Tufts U., 1971. Cert. tchr., adminstr., Mass. Tchr. social studies Norwood HS, Mass., 1971—. Founder, chmn. Norwood Law-Related Edn. Adv. Com., 1987-90; vice chmn. law related edn. com. Mass. Bar Assn., Boston, 1989-93; trainer Nat. Inst. for Citizen Edn. in the Law, Washington, 1990—; cons., reviewer Street Law, 4th edit., 1990-91; bd. dirs. Mass. Assn. for Law-Related Edn., 1990-98; mentor for new tchrs., 2000-; particip. Intl. Wannsee Conf., Berlin, Germany, 2002. Contbr. articles to legal jours. Recipient Horace Mann award Norwood Pub. Schs., 1989, Sch.-Cmty. Bar Partnership award ABA, 1990, Law-Related Edn. Tchr. of Yr. award Mass. Assn. for Law-Related Edn., 1990, Excellence in Tchg. award Harriet Goldin Found., 1993, Superior Tchr. of Law-Related Edn. award Norfolk County Bar Assn., 1994, Mass. Team Dist. Team fellow, 1996—, edn./rsch. fellow, JFK Libr. Mem. Nat. Coun. for Social Studies, Mass. Coun. for Social Studies (bd. dirs. 1993-95), South Shore Coun. for Social Studies (pres. 1993-95) Delta Kappa Gamma, Alpha Iota (pres. 1990-92). Avocations: walking, travel, gardening. Office: Norwood Pub Schs Nichols St Norwood MA 02062

REILLY, CHARLES EDMUND, JR., communications company executive; b. Phila., Nov. 4, 1928; s. Charles Edmund Sr. and Kathryn (McHugh) R.; m. Joan Emily Hunter; children by previous marriage: Lynn, Susan, Kathryn, Charles III. BS in Bus., St. Joseph's U., Phila., 1950; postgrad., U. Pa., 1955; MA in Liberal Studies, Villanova U., 2002. Med. rep. Stuart Pharms., Phila., 1954-56; mgr. newsstand promotion TV Guide Mag., Radnor, Pa., 1956—64, rep. ea. coast NYC, 1959—63; asst. to v.p., dir. corp. relations Young & Rubicam Inc., N.Y.C., 1964-66; exec. dir. Nat. Cath. Office for Radio-TV, N.Y.C., 1966-71; exec. v.p. Patrick Carr Assocs., N.Y.C., 1971-72; corp. exec. J. Walter Thompson, N.Y.C., 1972-74; v.p. Ogilvy and Mather, N.Y.C., 1975-76; founder In-Person Communications Inc., N.Y.C., 1976—. Cons. Pontifical Commn. Social Communications, Vatican City, Italy, 1968-71; adj. assoc. prof. St. John's U., N.Y.C., 1971-72; mem. vis. com. Loyola U., New Orleans, 1987—. Author: (book) You Speak..They Listen, 1984, You and A Life of Reilly, 1987, Special Delivery, 1998, Korea 1950-1953--The War That Never Was, 2000, others; newspaper columnist Suburban and Wayne, 1991—93, Main Line Life, 1994—. Lt. col. Valley Forge Mil. Coll., 1995—2003. 1st lt. U.S. Army, 1950—53. Inducted into Hall of Fame, The Inf. Sch., Ft. Benning, Ga., 1996. Mem.: Union League (Phila.) (former mem.), Princeton (NYC) (former mem.), Merion Cricket (Haverford, Pa.), St. Davids Golf Club (Wayne, Pa.). Republican. Office Phone: 610-687-3122. E-mail: crinperson@aol.com.

REILLY, DANIEL PATRICK, retired bishop; b. Providence, May 12, 1928; s. Francis E. and Mary (Burns) R. Student, Our Lady of Providence Sem., 1943—48, Grand Seminaire, St. Brieuc, France, 1948—53, Harvard U., 1954—55, Boston Coll., 1955—56; D (hon.), Providence Coll., St. Michael's Coll., Holy Apostles Coll. and Sem., Salve Regina Coll., Our Lady of Providence Coll., Sacred Heart U., Assumption Coll., 1995, Anna Maria Coll., 1995, Holy Cross Coll., 1996. Ordained priest Roman Cath. Ch., 1953. Asst. pastor Cathedral Saints Peter and Paul, Providence, 1953—54; asst. chancellor Diocese of Providence, 1954—56, sec. to bishop, 1956—64; became monsignor, 1964; chancellor Diocese of Providence, 1964—72, adminstr., 1971—72, vicar gen., 1972—75; consecrated bishop, 1975; bishop, 1975—94; Conn. state chaplain K.C., 1976—94; Episcopal moderator Nat. Cath. Cemetery Corp., 1977—87; bishop of Worcester Mass., 1994—2004. Ad hoc mem. to aid ch. in Ea. Europe, adminstrv. com. mem. NCCB/U.S. Cath. Conf., 1976—86, 1992—; pro-life com. mem. NCCB, 1989—92, chmn. 10th anniversary peace pastoral com., 1992—93, chmn. internat. policy com., 1993; mem. Priestly Life and Ministry Commn., 1991—94; past pres. New Eng. Consultation Ch. Leaders; drafting com. mem. U.S. Cath. Conf. Pastoral Letter on Peace, 1983, mem. com. on coms.; active Holy See Pontifical Coun.-Cor Unum, 1984—89. Trustee Cath. Mut. Relief Soc., Omaha, 1979—, St. John's Sem., Brighton, Mass., 1987—, Am. Coll., Louvain, Belgium, St. Mary's Sem., Balt.; chmn. bd. Cath. Relief Svcs. Cath. Relief Svcs., 1978—86; mem. fin. and budget com. U.S. Cath. Conf. U.S. Cath. Conf., 1985—87; chancellor Holy Apostles Coll. and Sem., Cromwell, Conn., 1982—94; pres. Conn. Interfaith Housing, 1975—94; cons. Pontifical Coun. Justice and Peace, 1995; bd. dirs. United Way Southeastern Conn., 1976—94, Conn. Drug and Adv. Coun., 1978—80. Mem.: KC (R.I. state chaplain 1964—75), Rotary. Roman Catholic. E-mail: breilly@worcesterdiocese.org. *If you would make a true success of your life for time and for eternity, never forget that it will be achieved by your willingness to make countless efforts that will be known only to God.*

REILLY, DAVID HENRY, university dean; b. Paterson, N.J., Nov. 7, 1936; s. David Henry and Ethel Taylor (Alt) R.; m. Jean Lockwood, July 2, 1960; children— David Scott, Chris Robert, Sandra Jean. BA, U. Vt., 1959; Ed.M., Rutgers U., 1962, Ed.D., 1965. Diplomate: Am. Bd. Profl. Psychology. Remedial reading instr. Drake Sch. of N.J. Neuro-Psychiat. Inst., Princeton, 1959-62, jr. fellow psychol. services at inst., summer 1962-63; research asst. N.J. Bur. Research Neurology and Psychiatry; also sch. psychologist Woodbridge (N.J.) sch. system, 1962-63; clin. psychologist, then research asso. N.J. Bur. Research Neurology and Psychiatry, 1963-64, 65; sch. and research psychologist Woodbridge sch. system, 1964-65; post doctoral fellow clin. child psychology Devereux Found., Devon, Pa., 1965-66; mem. faculty U. N.C., Chapel Hill, 1966-74, prof. psychology, 1974—, chmn. dept. sch. psychology program, 1966-74; dean U. N.C. (Sch. Edn.), Greensboro, 1974-86; dean Coll. of Grad. and Profl. Studies The Citadel, Charleston, 1992—. Mem. N.C. Bd. Examiners Practicing Psychologists, 1973—, treas., 1975, chmn., 1976 Contbr. articles to profl. jours. Research grantee NIMH, 1963; Fulbright Vis. scholar Republic of Cyprus, 1986-87, USSR, 1990. Fellow APA; mem. Am. Acad. Sch. Psychology (pres.-elect 1996-97, pres. 1997-98), Southeastern Psychol. Assn., N.C. Psychol. Assn. (pres. 1980-81), N.C. Assn. Coll. Tchr. Edn. (pres. 1981), N.C. Sch. Psychology Assn. (pres. 1976-77), S.C. Grad. Deans Assn. (pres. 1998-99). Home: 8644 Timbermarsh Ln North Charleston SC 29420 Personal E-mail: skipreilly@knology.net.

REILLY, EDWARD ARTHUR, lawyer; b. NYC, Dec. 17, 1943; s. Edward Arthur and Anna Marguerite (Sautter) R.; children: M. Teresa, Edward A. AB, Princeton U., 1965; JD, Duke U., 1968. Bar: NY 1969, NC 1971, Fla. 1979, Conn. 1983. Asst. dean law sch. Duke U., 1970-72; assoc. Shearman & Sterling, NYC, 1972-80, ptnr., 1980-87, Harlow, Reilly, Derr & Stark, Rsch. Triangle Park, NC, 1988-90; counsel Morris & McVeigh, NYC, 1991-93, ptnr., 1993—. Pres. Am. Friends Paris Opera Ballet, Inc.; sec. Camille and Henry Dreyfus Found., Inc.; sec. Owen Cheatham Found. Decorated Knight of Order of Arts and Letters, French Govt.-Ministry of Culture and Comm., 1992. Fellow Am. Coll. Trust & Estate Counsel; mem. NY State Bar Assn., Fla. Bar Assn., Conn. Bar Assn. Episcopalian. Office: Morris & McVeigh 767 3rd Ave New York NY 10017-2023 Home: 5 Old Field Pl Norwalk CT 06853-1116

REILLY, EDWARD FRANCIS, JR., federal agency administrator, former state senator; b. Leavenworth, Kans., Mar. 24, 1937; s. Edward F. and Marian C. (Sullivan) R. BA, U. Kans., 1961. V.P. Reilly & Sons, Inc., Leavenworth, 1967-92; pres. Yllier Lake Estates, Inc., Easton, Kans., 1965-89; mem. Kans. Ho. of Reps., 1963-64, Kans. State Senate, 1964-92, asst. majority leader, 1977-80, vice-chmn. govtl. orgn., chmn. ins. subcom., chmn. fed. and state affairs com.; chmn. U.S. parole comn. U.S. Dept. Justice, Chevy Chase, Md. Chmn. U.S. Parole Commn. Mem. Nat. Commn. on Accreditation of Law Enforcement Agys.; chmn. U.S. Parole Commn. Dept. of Justice, Md., 1992—; commr. ex officio U.S. Sentencing Commn., Washington; del. to Rep. Nat. Conv., Miami Beach, Fla., 1968; chmn. Leavenworth County Radio Free Europe Fund, 1972; bd. dirs. St. John's Hosp., Leavenworth, 1970-79, sec.; bd. dirs. Leavenworth Assn. for Handicapped, 1968-69, ARC, Leavenworth chpt., Kans. Blue Cross/Blue Shield, 1969-72; apptd. by Pres. Reagan Nat. Hwy. Safety Adv. Com.; active Trinity Nat. Leadership Roundtable, Cath. Campaign Am., Kans. Adv. Bd. Juvenile Offenders, Nat. Com. Cmty. Corrections. Recipient Cmty. Leaders of Am., 1971, 85, 86, Hallpac Pub. Svc. award, 1988, Am. Police Hall of Fame award, 1990, Good Samaritan award Order of Michael the Arch Angel Police Legion, 1990, Commendation award mayor and city commn. of Leavenworth, Kans., 1990, Carnegie Hero Fund Commn. award and medallion, 1991, Silver Angel award Kans. Cath. Conf., 1992; named Outstanding Young Men Am., 1965-76. Mem. Nat. Inst. Corrections (adv. bd.), Advisory Bd., Dept. of Philosophy, Catholic Univ. of America, Am. Paroling Authorities Internat., Am. Correctional Assn., Am. Probation and Paroling Assn., Leavenworth C. of C. (hon. dir. 1970-73), No. Assn. Chiefs Police, Assn. U.S. Army (Henry Leavenworth award 1960), Kansas City (Kans.) C. of C., Leavenworth Hist. Soc. (dir. 1968-73), John Carroll Soc., Native Sons of Kansas City, Ancient Order of Hibernians, U.S. Supreme Ct. Hist. Soc., Kiwanis (dir. 1969-70, Connelly award 1991, Legion of Honor award 1996), K.C., Elks, Eagles, Order of Malta, Equestrian Order Holy Sepulchre Jerusalem, Sacred Military Constantinian Order of Saint George. Republican. Roman Catholic.

REILLY, EDWARD T., JR., advertising executive; b. N.Y.C., Oct. 21, 1946; s. Edward Thomas and Dorothy (Comba) R.; m. Susan M. Brooke, June 28, 1969; children: Kristen, Greg. BBA, St. Francis Coll., N.Y.C., 1968. Editor-in-chief Gregg div. McGraw Hill Book Co., N.Y.C., 1974-76; controller CTB, Monterey, Calif., 1976-78; gen. mgr. Instructo, Palli, Pa., 1978-79; group v.p. for Europe, Africa, Mideast McGraw Hill U.K. Ltd., Maidenhead, U.K., 1980-83; exec. v.p. McGraw-Hill Internat. Book Co., N.Y.C., 1983-84; sr. v.p. fin., planning and adminstrn. McGraw-Hill Broadcasting Co., N.Y.C., 1985-86, exec. v.p., chief operating officer, 1986-87, pres., 1987—; CEO Big Flower Holdings, 1997-2000. Mem. corp. adv. council Nat. Council La Raza; mem. local carriage task force Nat. Assn. Broadcasters; mem. adv. com. on local excellence in TV programming Mus. of Broadcasting; bd. dirs. Internat. Radio and TV Found., Nat. Assoc. of Broadcasters, 1990-94, TV Bur. of Advt., 1988-95, chmn. 1990-93, assoc. of Max Svc. TV, 1987—, chmn. 1994—, Gov.- ABC TV network affiliates assoc., chmn. gov. rel., 1993-95. Chmn. Monterey County Overall Econ. Devel. Com., Monterey, Calif., 1977; bd. govs. Carmel Unified Sch. Dist. (Calif.), 1977. Fellow Inst. Dirs. Great Britain Office: Big Flower Holdings Inc 345 Park /ave New York NY 10154-0004

REILLY, FRANK KELLY, business educator; b. Chgo., Dec. 30, 1935; s. Clarence Raymond and Mary Josephine (Ruckrigel) R.; m. Therese Adele Bourke, Aug. 2, 1958; children: Frank Kelly III, Clarence Raymond II, Therese B., Edgar B. BBA, U. Notre Dame, 1957; MBA, Northwestern U., 1961, U. Chgo., 1964, PhD, 1968; LLD (hon.), St. Michael's Coll., 1991. CFA. Trader Goldman Sachs & Co., Chgo., 1958-59; security analyst Tech. Fund, Chgo., 1959-62; asst. prof. U. Kans., Lawrence, 1965-68, assoc. prof., 1968-72; prof. bus., assoc. dir. divsn. bus. and econ. rsch. U. Wyo., Laramie, 1972-75; prof. fin. U. Ill., Champaign-Urbana, 1975-81; Bernard J. Hank prof. U. Notre Dame, Ind., 1981—, dean Coll. Bus. Adminstrn., 1981-87. Bd. dirs., chmn. Brinson Funds, Assn. Investment Mgmt. and Rsch.; past chmn. Inst. Chartered Fin. Analysts; past chmn. bd. dirs. NIBCO Corp.; bd. dirs. Internat. Bd. CFPs, Discover Bank, Ft. Dearborn Income Securities, Battery Park High Yield Fund., Morgan Stanley Trust Fed. Savs. Bank (FSB). Author: Investment Analysis and Portfolio Management, 1979, 7th edit., 2003, Investments, 1982, 6th edit., 2003; co-editor: Ethics and the Investment Industry, 1989; editor: Readings and Issues in Investments, 1975, High Yield Bonds: Analysis and Risk Assessment, 1990; assoc. editor Fin. Mgmt., 1977-82, Quar. Rev. Econs. and Bus, 1979-87, Fin. Rev., 1979-87, 92—, Jour. Fin. Edn., 1981—, Jour. Applied Bus. Rsch., 1986—, Fin. Svcs. Rev., 1989-96, Internat. Rev. Econs. and Fin., 1992—, European Jour. Fin., 1994—. Arthur J. Schmidt Found. fellow, 1962-65; U. Chgo. fellow, 1963-65; recipient faculty award U. Notre Dame, 1999. Fellow Fin. Mgmt. Assn. (pres. 1983-84, chmn. 1985-91, bd. dirs.); mem. Midwest Bus. Adminstrn. Assn. (pres. 1974-75), Am. Fin. Assn., Western Fin. Assn. (exec. com. 1973-75), Ea. Fin. Assn. (exec. com. 1979-84, pres. 1982-83), Midwest Fin. Assn. (pres. 1993-94), Fin. Analysts Fedn., Acad. Fin. Svcs. (pres. 1990-91), Inst. Chartered Fin. Analysts (coun. of examiners, rsch. and edn. com., edn. steering com.), Internat. Assoc. Fin. Planners (edn. resource com., bd. dirs.), Assn. of Investment Mgmt. and Rsch. (C. Stewart Sheppard award 1991, Daniel J. Forrestal III Leadership award for profl. ethics 2001), Investments Analysts Soc. Chgo. (bd. dirs. 1988-89), Beta Gamma Sigma. Roman Catholic. Office: U Notre Dame Mendoza Coll Bus Notre Dame IN 46556-5646 E-mail: reilly.1@nd.edu. *Any success I have enjoyed is due to the talents God has given me and my belief that I have an obligation to maximize the output from those talents by hard work, while never forgetting that my family comes first because they have always provided me with the love and support necessary for success and happiness.*

REILLY, GEORGE, lawyer; b. Waukegan, Ill., Nov. 29, 1934; s. James M. and Hilda Clara (Van Heirseele) R.; m. Dadee Bruce, Dec. 23, 1957; children: Laurene Beth, Theresa Ann. BA, Ill. Coll., 1956; MS, S.D. State U., 1958; JD, U. Minn., 1964. Bar: Minn. 1964, U.S. Dist. Ct. Minn. 1964, U.S. Ct. Appeals (8th cir.) 1965. Assoc. Leonard, Street and Deinard, Mpls., 1964-70, ptnr., 1973-82, mng. ptnr., 1983-91, ptnr., chair of bus. divsn., 1991-96; chief dep. atty. gen. State of Minn., St. Paul, 1971-72. Chief counsel Minn. Housing and Fin. Agy., St. Paul, 1972-80. Campaign chair Spannaus for Atty. Gen. com., 1974, 78, Spannaus for Gov., 1982. Mem. ABA, Minn. State Bar Assn., Citizens League, Variety Childrens Assn. (bd. dirs.). Democrat. Avocations: travel, sports. Office: Leonard Street & Deinard 150 S 5th St Ste 2300 Minneapolis MN 55402-4238

REILLY, JILL MARLENE, school system administrator; b. Chgo., Jan. 27, 1951; d. Jack Louis and Leah M. Cappels; m. Patrick Duane Reilly, May 29, 1971; children: Elizabeth M. Brama, Joseph D., Heather von Mering. BA in English, U. Cin., 1974; MA in Curriculum, U. Minn., 1985; D in Edn. Leadership, U. St. Thomas, St. Paul, 1992. Co-ptnr. Featherstone-Reilly Ednl. Cons., Apple Valley, Minn., 1984-95; mentor program coord. Intermediate Sch. Dist. # 917, Apple Valley, 1985-93; sr. cons. Honeywell, Inc., Mpls., 1993-95; adj. asst. prof. St. Mary's U., Mpls., 1994—; pres. Acad. Holy Angels, Richfield, Minn., 1995—. Author: Mentorship: The Essential Guide for Schools and Business, 1992; co-author: College Comes Sooner Than You Think, 1987. Bd. dirs. guidance div. Nat. Assn. Gifted Children, Mpls., 1988-93; bd. dirs., chair elect Minn. Coun. Gifted and Talented, Mpls., 1991-94. Office: Acad Holy Angels 6600 Nicollet Ave Richfield MN 55423-2498 Office Phone: 612-798-2611. E-mail: jreilly@ahastars.org.

REILLY, JOHN B. lawyer; b. Bangor, Maine, Sept. 12, 1947; s. Louis J. and Evelyn I. (Lindsay) R.; children: Carolyn, Bridget. BA, U. R.I., 1970; JD cum laude, Suffolk U., 1976. Bar: R.I. 1976, Mass. 1985, U.S. Dist. Ct. R.I. 1976, U.S. Dist. Ct. Mass. 1985, U.S. Dist. Ct. Conn. 1995, U.S. Claims Ct. 1980, U.S. Ct. Appeals (1st and 2d cirs.) 1984, U.S. Ct. Appeals (3d cir.) 1985, U.S. Supreme Ct. 1983; cert. fraud examiner. Sole practice, Providence, 1976-81, Warwick, RI, 1981-83; sr. ptnr. John Reilly & Assocs. and predecessor firms, Warwick, RI, 1984—89, 2002—, Reilly & Nikolyszyn, LLP, Warwick, RI, 2000—01. Mem. Gov.'s Automobile Ins. Task Force, 1992-93. Mem. ABA, R.I. Bar Assn., Def. Rsch. Inst., R.I. Assn. Auth Theft and Arson Investigators (sec. 1995-96, pres. 1997—), Trucking Ind. Def. Assn., Pi Sigma Alpha, Phi Kappa Psi. Home: 80 Paterson Ave Warwick RI 02886-9110 Office: John Reilly & Assocs 300 Centerville Rd Warwick RI 02886-0200 E-mail: jreilly@lawyers-nline.us.

REILLY, JOHN C. actor; b. Chgo., Ill., May 24, 1965; m. Alison Dickey. BFA, DePaul U., 1987. Actor: (films) Casualties of War, 1989, We're No Angels, 1989, Days of Thunder, 1990, State of Grace, 1990, Shadows and Fog, 1992, Out on a Limb, 1992, Hoffa, 1992, What's Eating Gilbert Grape, 1993, The River Wild, 1994, Georgia, 1995, Dolores Claiborne, 1995, Sydney, 1996, Boys, 1996, Boogie Nights, 1997, The Thin Red Line, 1998, Never Been Kissed, 1999, For Love of the Game, 1999, Magnolia, 1999 (Nat. Bd. Rev. award for Best Ensemble, 1999), The Settlement, 1999, The Perfect Storm, 2000, The Anniversary Party, 2001, Frank's Book, 2001, The Good Girl, 2002, Gangs of New York, 2002 (Las Vegas Film Critics Award for Best Supporting Actor, 2003), Chicago, 2002 (Golden Globe for Best Supporting Actor, Acad. award nomination for Best Actor, Las Vegas Film Critics Award for Best Supporting Actor, 2003), The Hours, 2002 (Las Vegas Film Critics Award for Best Supporting Actor, 2003), Anger Management, 2003; (plays) True West, 2000 (Spl. Outer Critics Cir. Award, 2000). Roman Catholic.

REILLY, KEVIN C., SR., radiologist; Fellow in neuroradiology U. Pa. Med. Ctr., Phila.; resident in diagnostic radiology Honolulu; with Army Med. Corps, Tripler Army Med. Ctr., Honolulu. Major U.S. Army, Med. Corps. Mem.: AMA (resident trustee, bd. trustees 2003—), Hawaii Med. Assn., Med. Soc. State NY (MSSNY). Office: Tripler Army Med Ctr 1 Jarrett White Rd Honolulu HI 96859-5000 Office Phone: 808-433-6661.

REILLY, KEVIN DENIS, computer scientist, educator; s. Brian Augustine and Dorothy Evelyn Reilly; m. Jo Ann Grace Caniglia, Feb. 4, 1961; children: Martin Louis, Dennis Patrick(dec.), Ann Marie(dec.), Eileen Marie, Shannon Denise Ray. BS summa cum laude, Creighton U., 1959; MS, U. of Nebr., 1962; PhD, U. of Chgo., 1966. Tchr. U.Calif., L.A., 1966—70; sr. lectr. U. of So. Calif., L.A., 1968—70; prof. U. Ala., Birmingham, Ala., 1970—. Spkr. in field; cons. in field. Contbr. over 250 articles to profl. jours. Judge various sci. fairs, Birmingham; participant in ecumenical dialogs Greek Orthodox-Cath. Discussion Group, Birmingham. Fellow, Woodrow Wilson Found., 1959, NIH, 1962—66, Mobusho fellow, Ministry of Internat. Trade and Industry, Japan, 1989; grantee, NSF, 1966—70, U.S. Office of Edn., 1968—70, NIH, 1972—77, 1977—78, US Army, 1987—90, NSF, 1993, NIH, 1998—2000, 2000—. Mem.: IEEE, Soc. for Modeling and Simulation, European Acad. Sci., Assn. for Computing Machinery. Independent. Roman Catholic. Avocations: travel, philosophy, history, poetry. Home: 304 N Burbank Dr Bluff Park AL 35226-1608 Office: U Ala Birmingham University Station Birmingham AL 35294-1170 E-mail: reilly@cis.uab.edu.

REILLY, KEVIN P. academic administrator; BA, U. Notre Dame, 1971; MA, U. Minn., 1974, PhD in English, 1979. Teaching asst. dept. English U. Minn., Mpls., 1974-79, asst. to dir. undergrad. study dept. English, 1976-77; coord. project on ednl. advisement in the work setting N.Y. State Bd. Regents, 1979-80, dir. Teaching and Beyond project, 1983-84, dir. nat. program non-coll. sponsored instrn., 1979-84, dir. div. coll. and univ. evaluation, 1984-92; assoc. provost for acad. programs, sec. of the univ. SUNY Sys., Albany, 1992—96; also sr. fellow in univ./sch. rels. SUNY Systems, Albany, 1992—96; provost, vice-chancellor U. Wis.-ext., 1996—2000, chancellor, 2000—04, U. Wis. System, Madison, 2004—. Mem. vis. del. Am. educators to rev. sch. system in No. Ireland, 1990; lectr. and presenter in field. Editor: (with Carol Wolfe) A Guide to Educational Programs in Noncollegiate Organizations, 1983, (with Sheila Murdick) Teaching and Beyond: Nonacademic Career Programs for Ph.D.'s, 1984; contbr. numerous articles to profl. jours. Tutor, Literacy Vols. of Am., Schenectady, 1988-90. Recipient Mgmt. Performance awards N.Y. State, 1989, 90; recipient fellowships at U. Minn. Mem. MLA, Am. Assn. for Higher Edn., Am. Conf. for Irish Studies, Am. Ednl. Rsch. Assn., Assn. for Continuing Higher Edn., Irish Am. Cultural Inst. Office: U Wis System 1720 Van Hise Hall 1220 Linden Dr Madison WI 53706-1557 E-mail: kreilly@uwsa.edu.*

REILLY, KEVIN PATRICK, psychology educator; b. Boston, July 11, 1969; s. Stephen Thomas and Mary Lou Reilly; m. Dina Lynn Diamondis, Nov. 7, 1998. BS, Bridgewater (Mass.) State Coll., 1987, MA, 1994; PhD, Lehigh U., 2002. Counselor/mgr. Ctr. for Health and Devel., Weymouth, Mass., 1991—97; grad. asst. Lehigh U., Bethlehem, Pa., 1996—2002; asst. prof. psychology Ferrum (Va.) Coll., 2002—. Counselor Lehigh U., 1999—2002; cons. Medfield (Mass.) State Hosp., 1995—97; tchr. edn. faculty advisor Ferrum Coll., 2002—03; vis. lectr. Bridgewater State Coll., 1994—97, Lehigh U., 1997—2002, Lehigh Carbon C.C., Allentown, Pa., 2001—02. Sci. fair judge Intel Corp., Phila., 1999, Lehigh U., 1999—2002; anxiety disorders workshop leader Franklin County Workforce Consortium, Rocky Mount, Va., 2003; 5th grade career day presenter Ferrum Coll., 2003. Grantee, Dattilio Scholarship Fund, 2000. Mem.: APA (corr.), Am. Psychol. Soc. (corr.), Psi Chi. Avocations: jogging, reading, skiing, music. Home: 50 Buckner St Rocky Mount VA 24151 Office: Ferrum Coll 1 Ferrum Mountain Rd Ferrum VA 24151 E-mail: kpreilly@ferrum.edu.

REILLY, MICHAEL ATLEE, financial company executive, venture capital investor; b. Ft. Worth, Dec. 10, 1948; s. Thomas William and Alma Margaret (Cox) R.; m. Beverly Ann Yates, Dec. 27, 1974; children: Atlee Michael, Asher Yates, Anson Marcus, Austin Thomas, Axton Carter. BA, U. Tex., 1971. Ptnr. Michael A. Reilly Co., Dallas, 1971—80; pres., CEO Ryan Cos., Arlington, Tex., 1980—90, Reilly Bros., Arlington, 1990—. Trustee Childrens Trust Fund State of Tex; vice chmn. Troy Aikman Found. Mem.: Urban Land Inst. Office: Reilly Bros Property Co 1017 So F M Rd 5 Aledo TX 76008-5169

REILLY, NANCY (ANNE CAULFIELD REILLY), painter; b. Bryn Mawr, Pa., Mar. 29, 1927; d. Ralph Caulfield and Claire Helena (Roesch) Goodman; m. Donald Elliott Reilly, May 14, 1949; children: Kevin Caulfield, William Stockbridge, Peter Elliott. Studied with Samuel E. Brown, Westport, Conn., 1955-63; studied with Mimi Jennewein, Larchmont, N.Y., 1964-65. Lectr., demonstrator portrait painting Bridgeport (Conn.) Art League, Milford (Conn.) Art League, Pen and Brush Club, New Haven, Conn. Classic Arts Assn., Allied Artists Am., Kent (Conn.) Art Assn., SCAN, Newtown, Conn. Exhibited in group shows at Nat. Acad. Design, N.Y.C., 1964, 1965, 1969, 1970, Stamford (Conn.) Mus., 1965, Wadsworth Antheum, Hartford, Conn., 1966, 1972, Nat. Acad. Arts and Letters, N.Y.C., 1971, Mus. Sci. and Industry, Bridgeport, 1972, Salmagundi Club, N.Y.C., Nat. Arts Club, Butler Inst. Am. Art, Youngstown, Ohio, 2001, New Britain (Conn.) Mus. Am. Art, 2001, exhibitions include invitational travelling exhbn. Allied Artists Am., 2003—; included in slide collection Smithsonian Instn., Washington, U. Conn. Health Ctr., Farmington. Vol. artist rehab. unit Norwalk Hosp., 1984—95. Recipient Gold medal for oil painting, Catherine Lorillard Wolfe Art Club, 1965, Silver medal for oil painting, Nat. Arts Club, 1969, George Height award for portrait, 1969, Blanche Farr award, 1991. Fellow: Am. Artists Profl. League (Claude Parsons Meml. award 2003); mem.: Conn. Pastel Soc. (signature, J.D. Altobello Meml. award, Honors award 2003, 2004), Artists' Fellowship N.Y., Acad. Artists Assn. Springfield, Kent Art Assn. (Best in Show 1991, Gordon C. Aymar award for oil 1993, Mabel Rowe Aiken award for oil 1995, Frances B. Townley award for portrait 1998, 1999), Hudson Valley Art Assn. (Bronze medal for oil painting 1981, Thora M. Jensen award 1989), Pastel Soc. Am., Nat. Arts Club (Silver medal for oil painting 1969, Bruce Stevenson award for portrait 1971, 1988, 1991), Allied Artists Am. (bd. dirs. 1991—99, participant in travelling exhibn. 2003—), New Haven Paint and Clay Club (Merit award 1992, 1997). Home: 9 Marilane Westport CT 06880-1008

REILLY, PAUL C. consulting company executive; V.p. Southeast Capital Corp., 1986; ptnr. Southeast Capital Assocs. Twelve Ltd. Cons., City of St. Petersburg, 1986.

REILLY, PAUL J. finance company executive; b. Jan. 13, 1957; BS, St. John's U., 1979. Audit mgr. KPM & Peat Marwick, New York, 1979-90; v.p. fin. Arrow Electronics, Inc., Melville, N.Y., 1991—. Office: 25 Hub Dr Melville NY 11747-3503

REILLY, PETER JOHN, chemical engineer, educator; b. Newark, Dec. 26, 1938; s. Edward Thomas and Anita (Galdieri) Reilly; m. Rae Georgine Messer, July 3, 1976; children: Diane Joyce, Karen Elizabeth. AB, Princeton U., 1960; PhD, U. Pa., 1964. Rsch. engr. E.I. Dupont & Co., Deepwater, NJ, 1964—68; asst. prof. U. Nebr., Lincoln, 1968—74; assoc. prof. Iowa State U., Ames, 1974—79, prof., 1979—92, disting. prof., 1992—. Invited prof. Ecole Poly. Federale, Lausanne, Switzerland, 1983—84, 1992—93. Contbr. chapters to books, articles to profl. jours. Fellow: AIChE; mem.: AAUP, Am. Chem. Soc., Sigma Xi. Home: 1807 Wilson Ave Ames IA 50010-4957 Office: Iowa State U 2114 Sweeney Hall Dept Chem Engring Ames IA 50011-2230 Office Phone: 515-294-5968. Business E-Mail: reilly@iastate.edu.

REILLY, PHILIP RAYMOND, medical research administrator; b. Albany, N.Y., Oct. 3, 1947; MD, Yale U., New Haven, 1981. Diplomate Am. Bd. Clin. Genetics. Intern Boston City Hosp., 1983-85, resident, 1983-85; staff Mass. Gen. Hosp., Boston; dir. Eunice Kennedy Shriver Ctr. for Mental Retardation, Waltham, Mass. Mem. Am. Assn. for the Advancement of Sci., Am. Soc. of Human Genetics. Office: Eunice Kennedy Shriver Ctn 200 Trapelo Rd Waltham MA 02452-6332

REILLY, ROBERT FREDERICK, valuation consultant; b. N.Y.C., Oct. 3, 1953; s. James J. and Marie (Griebel) Reilly; m. Janet H. Steiner, Apr. 16, 1975; children: Ashley Lauren, Brandon Christopher, Cameron Courtney. BA in Econs., Columbia U., 1975, MBA in Fin., 1976. CPA Ohio, Ill., cert. mgmt. acct.; CFA, cert. real estate appraiser, rev. appraiser, gen. appraiser Ill., Va., Utah, Oreg., N.Y., bus. appraiser, accredited bus. valuator. Sr. cons. Booz, Allen & Hamilton, Cin., 1975-76; dir. corp. planning Huffy Corp., Dayton, Ohio, 1976-81; v.p. Arthur D. Little Valuation, Inc., Chgo., 1981-85; ptnr., nat. dir. valuation svcs. Deloitte & Touche, Chgo., 1985-91; mng. dir. Willamette Mgmt. Assocs., Chgo., 1991—. Adj. prof. acctg. U. Dayton Grad. Sch. Bus., 1977—81; adj. prof. econs. Elmhurst (Ill.) Coll., 1982—87; adj. prof. fin. Ill. Inst. Tech. Grad. Sch. Bus., Chgo., 1985—91; adj. prof. taxation U. Chgo. Grad. Sch. Bus., 1985—87. Co-author: (book) Valuing Small Businesses and Professional Practices, 1993, Business Valuation Video Course, 1993, Valuing a Business, 1995;: 4th edit., 2000, Valuing Accounting Practices, 1997, Valuaing Professional Practices--A Practitioner's Approach, 1997, Valuing Intangible Assets, 1998, Handbook of Advanced Business Valuation, 1999, Handbook of Business Valuation and Intellectual Property Analysis, 2004; editor, columnist: Ohio CPA Jour., 1984—86, 1991—, Small Bus. Taxation, 1989—90, Bus. Valuation Rev., 1989—90, Jour. Real Estate Acctg. and Taxation, 1991—93, Jour. Property Taxation Mgmt., 1993—, Jour. Am. Bankruptcy Inst., 1993—, Valuation Strategies, 2003—; co-editor: (book) Financial Valuation-Valuation of Business and Business Interests, 1997; contbr. articles to profl. jours. Mem.: AICPA (mem. ABV exam. com. 2002—), Appraisal Inst., Nat. Assn. Bus. Economists, Am. Econ. Assn., Am. Bankruptcy Inst., Inst. CFAs, Chgo. Soc. Investment Analysts, Bus. Valuation Assn., Accreditation Coun. Accountancy (accredited fed. income taxation), Ohio Soc. CPAs (chpt. dir. 1978—81), Ill. Soc. CPAs, Inst. Property Taxation, Inst. Cert. Mgmt. Accts. (chpt. dir. 1976—), Nat. Assn. Real Estate Appraisers, Am. Soc. Appraisers (mem. bd. examiners 1985—89), Inst. Bus. Appraisers (life). Home: 310 Algonquin Rd Barrington IL 60010-6109 Office: 8600 W Bryn Mawr Ave Chicago IL 60631-3579

REILLY, ROBERT JOSEPH, counselor; b. Spokane, Wash., Mar. 7, 1936; s. John Francis and Vivian Helen (White) R.; m. Joan Steiner, June 20, 1960; children: Sean Michael, Patrick Joseph, Bridget Colleen. BA in Psychology, Seattle U., 1985; postgrad., Infantry Officer Candidate Sch., Ft. Benning, 1960, EOAC, Ft. Belvoir, 1968, Leadership Inst. Seattle/City U., 1991—92. Ordained Congl. Ch. Practical Theology, 1992. Enlisted U.S. Army, 1953, advanced through grades to maj., 1981, served in, 1961-62, 1966-67, 69-70, ret., 1981; counseling supr. Schick Shadel Hosp., Seattle, 1984-89; dir. Canyon Counseling, Puyallup, Wash., 1987-92, 95—; social worker Wash. State Employee Adv. Svc., Olympia, 1992-99. Exec. v.p. Coll. Therapeutic Hypnosis, Puyallup, 1989-94; mem. adj. faculty Pierce Coll., Tacoma, 1991-92; mem. Wash. State Chem. Dependency Counselor Cert. Bd., sec., 1995-2003. Editor: The Update, 2003—. Pres. Irish Cultural Club, Tacoma, 1983-85, 93-94; sec. Tacoma chpt. Ret. Officers Assn., 1983-87, pres., 1993-96, bd. dirs., 1982-97; bd. dirs. Tacoma Mus. Playhouse Theater Co., 1997-2000, adv. bd., 2000—; adv. bd. Friends of the Ctrl. Highlands, Vietnam, 1999—; mem. vestry St. Luke's Episcopal Ch., Wenatchee, 2003—. Decorated Vietnamese Cross of Gallantry with silver star, Bronze Star with oak leaf cluster, Meritorious Svc. medal, Army Commendation medal with 2 oak leaf clusters; named Profl. of Yr. Chem. Dependency Profls. Wash., 1994. Mem. Nat. Bd. Hypnotherapy and Hypnotic Anesthesiology (v.p. 1991-97, pres. Wash. chpt. 1991-94, Mem. of Yr. 1994), Nat. Guild Hypnotists, Nat. Assn. Alcohol and Drug Abuse Counselors (mem. del. Russia & Czech Republic 1996), Am. Congress Hypnotist Examiners, Nat. Assn. Tobacco Addiction Counselors, Army Engrs. Assn., Nat. 4th Inf. Divsn. Assn. (sec.-treas. N.W. chpt. 1993-2003, chapt. pres., 2002-03, nat. svc. offer, 2004—), Mil. Officers Assn. Am., The Ret. Enlisted Assn. (pres. Wehatchee chpt. 2001-02, chaplain 2002—, editor Appleland 86er), Assn. for Addiction Profls., Wash. West Home Owners Assn. (pres. 2001-02), La Soc. des Quarante Hommes et Huit Chevaux (Aumonier 2001—). Avocations: volksmarching, symphony music, theater. E-mail: joans.bob@verizon.net.

REILLY, THOMAS F. state attorney general; b. Springfield, Mass. m. Ruth Reilly; 3 children. BA, Am. Internat. Coll., 1964; JD, Boston Coll., 1970. Atty. Civil Rights divsn. Atty. Gen.'s Office; dist. atty. Middlesex County Dist. Atty. Office, 1991—99; atty. gen. State of Mass., Springfield, 1999—. Founder The Cmty. Based Justice Program. Democrat. Office: One Ashburton Pl Boston MA 02108-1698 also: 436 Dwight St Springfield MA 01103 also: One Exchange Place Worcester MA 01608

REILLY, WILLIAM FRANCIS, media company executive; b. N.Y.C., June 8, 1938; s. William F. and Genevieve Reilly; m. Ellen Chapman, Nov. 19, 1966; children: Anthony Chapman and Jane Wasey (twins). AB cum laude, U. Notre Dame, 1959; MBA, Harvard U., 1964. Mgr. fin. analysis W.R. Grace & Co., N.Y.C., 1964-67, asst. to pres., 1969-71, CEO Bekaert Textile Divsn., 1971-74; pres., CEO Herman's World of Sporting Goods, Carteret, N.J., 1974-77; v.p., pres. W.R. Grace and Co., 1978; pres., CEO Home Ctr. Div., 1979-80; pres. Macmillan, Inc., N.Y.C., 1980-90; chmn., CEO Primedia Corp., N.Y.C., 1990-2000; founder, chmn., CEO Aurelian Comm., 2000—. Dir. FMC Corp., Chgo., Barnes & Noble.com; trustee U. Notre Dame, South Bend, Ind., WNET, Channel 13, N.Y.C. 1st lt. U.S. Army, 1959-61. Home: 7 Sutton Sq New York NY 10022-2407 Office: Aurelian Comm LLC 375 Park Ave New York NY 10152

REILLY, WILLIAM THOMAS, lawyer; b. Passaic, N.J., Feb. 25, 1949; s. Thomas Edwin and Edna May (Dorritie) R.; m. Sheila Mary Brogan, Aug. 1, 1981; children: Kathleen Anne, Brendan Thomas, Timothy John. BS, Boston Coll., 1971; JD, Harvard U., 1974. Bar: N.J. 1974, U.S. Dist. Ct. N.J. 1974, U.S. Supreme Ct. 1979, U.S. Ct. Appeals (3rd cir.) 1984, U.S. Ct. Claims, 1996, U.S. Ct. Appeals (fed. cir.) 1997. Assoc. McCarter & English LLP, Newark, 1974-81, ptnr., 1982—. Trustee United Hosps. Med. Ctr., Newark, 1983-89, One-to-One/N.J., Inc., 1990-97, chmn., 1993-97. Mem. ABA, N.J. State Bar Assn., Harvard Law Sch. Assn., Eastward Ho Country Club. Avocation: golf. Home: 302 Kensington Dr Ridgewood NJ 07450-1822 Office: McCarter & English LLP Four Gateway Ctr 100 Mulberry St Newark NJ 07102-4004 Office Phone: 973-622-4444. E-mail: wreilly@mccarter.com.

REIMAN, DONALD HENRY, English language educator; b. Erie, Pennsylvania, May 17, 1934; s. Henry Ward and Mildred Abbie (Pearce) R.; m. Mary (Warner), 1958 (div. 1974); one child, Laurel Elizabeth Reiman Henneman; m. Hélène Liberman (Dworzan), Oct. 3, 1975. BA, Coll. of Wooster, 1956; MA, U. Ill., 1957, PhD, 1960; LittD., Coll. of Wooster, 1981. Instr. English, Duke U., Durham, NC, 1960—62, asst. prof., 1962—64; assoc. prof. U. Wis., Milw., 1964—65; adj. assoc. prof. grad. program in English City Univ. of N.Y., 1967—68; adj. prof. Columbia U., N.Y.C., 1969—70, sr. rsch. assoc. in English, 1970—73; vis. prof. St. John's U., Jamaica, NY, 1974—75; editor Shelley and His Cir., Carl H. Pforzheimer Libr., N.Y.C., 1965—86, N.Y. Pub. Libr., 1986—92; with Carl and Lily Pforzheimer Found., 1992—. Vis. lectr. U. Ill., 1963; vis. prof. U. Wash., Seattle, 1981, N.Y. U., 1992; Lyell reader in bibliography Oxford U., 1988-89; adj. prof. English, U. Del., 1992—; cons. Harvard U. Press, Yale U. Press, Princeton U. Press, Johns Hopkins U. Press, Garland Pub., Inc., W.W. Norton, Oxford U. Press, others. Author: Shelley's The Triumph of Life, A Critical Study, 1965, 2d edit., 1979, Percy Bysshe Shelley, 1969, 2d edit., 1990, (with D.D. Fischer) Byron on the Continent, 1974, English Romantic Poetry, 1800-1835, 1979, Romantic Texts and Contexts, 1987, Intervals of Inspiration: The Skeptical Tradition and the Psychology of Romanticism, 1988, The Study of Modern Manuscripts, 1993; editor: Shelley and His Circle, Vols. V-VI, 1973, Vols. VII-VIII, 1986, IX-X, 2002, The Romantics Reviewed: Contemporary Reviews of English Romantic Writers, 9 vols., 1972, (with S.B. Powers) Shelley's Poetry and Prose: A Norton Critical Edit., 1977, (with Neil Fraistat) 2nd rev. edit., 2002, The Romantic Context: Poetry, 128 vols., 1976-79, (with M.C. Jaye and B.T. Bennett) The Evidence of the Imagination, 1978; gen. editor: Manuscripts of the Younger Romantics, 1985-98; I The Esdaile Notebook: A Facsimile, 1985, II The Mask of Anarchy: Facsimiles, 1985, III Hellas, 1985, V The Harvard Shelley Poetic Manuscripts, 1991; (with M. O'Neill) VIII Fair-Copy Manuscripts of Shelley's Poems, 1997; editor-in-chief: The Bodleian Shelley Manuscripts, 1986-99, I Peter Bell The Third and the Triumph of Life, 1986, VII Shelley's Last Notebook and Other MSS, 1990, (with M.J. Neth) XVI The Hellas Notebook, 1994, The Complete Poetry of Percy Bysshe Shelley Vol. I (with N. Fraistat), 2000; mem. editl. com. adv. bd. Keats Shelley Jour., 1968-73, Milton and the Romantics, 1975-80, Studies in Romanticism, 1977—, Romanticism Past and Present, 1980-86, Text, 1981—, Nineteenth Century Literature, 1986—, Nineteenth Century Contexts, 1987-90; co-founder, editor (with others) Romantic Circle,s. Website; contbr. articles to encyclopedias, books, and profl. journals. Active in Common Cause. Am. Coun. Learned Soc. Fellow, 1963-64, Wesleyan Ctr. Advanced Studies Fellow, 1963-64, NEH Fellow, 1978; grantee Am. Coun. Learned Soc., 1961, NEH, 1983—. Mem. AAUP, MLA, Modern Humanities Rsch. Assn., (life), Wordsworth Coleridge Assn. Am. (founder), Byron Soc. (Am. com. 1973—, treas. 1999-2002, pres. 2003-), Keats Shelley Assn. Am. (bd. dir., treas. 1973-91, v.p. 1991—, Disting. Scholar Award 1987), Bibliog. Soc. Am., Soc. Textual Scholarship (exec. com. 1981-93, pres. 2004-), Charles Lamb Soc., Assn. Documentary Editing, N.Am. Soc. Study of Romanticism. Democrat. Presbyterian. Office: NY Pub Libr Fifth Ave at 42nd St Rm 226 New York NY 10018 Business E-Mail: dhreiman@udel.edu.

REIMAN, RICHARD A. historian, educator; b. Cin., Feb. 27, 1956; s. Richard J. and S. Marilyn Reiman; m. Cathie M. Hawthorne, Aug. 1, 1992; 1 child, Gina M. B, Miami U., 1978; M in History, U. Cin., 1980, PhD in History, 1984. Asst. prof. history U. Mo., St. Louis, 1990—91; assoc. prof. history South Ga. Coll., Douglas, 1993—2001, chair divsn. bus. and social scis., 2001—. Author: The New Deal and American Youth: Ideas and Ideals in a Depression Decade (U. Cin. award Best Book by a Former Grad. Student, 1993); contbr. instructional learning objects, articles and revs. to profl. jours. Mem., mem.-at-large Douglas Lions Club, Ga., 1993, star student coord., 1994—. Fellow, U. Sys. Ga., 1997—98; grantee, 1999—2000. Mem.: Orgn. Am. Historians (assoc.). Achievements include design of Designer of instructional technology learning objects.

REIMAN, ROY J. publishing executive; Pub., founder Reiman Publs., Greendale, Wis., 1964—. Office: Reiman Publs 5400 S 60th St Greendale WI 53129-1404

REIMANN, ARLINE LYNN, artist; b. St. Louis, Nov. 25, 1937; d. Albert Robbins and Bess (Kagan) Miller; m. Hans Reimann, Feb. 24, 1957; 1 child, Robert. BA, Rutgers U., 1974; MA, Montclair State U., 1980. Exhibited in group shows at Hunterdon Nat. Print Exhbn., Hunterdon Art Ctr., Clinton, N.J., 1982, Celebration of Women's Week, Galeria San Jeronimo, San Juan, P.R., 1987, Audubon Artists Ann. Exhbn., Nat. Arts Club, N.Y.C., 1988, 90—, Celebration 89, Interch. Ctr., N.Y.C., Nat. Assn. Women Artists Traveling Printmaking Exhbn., Butler Inst. Am. Art, Youngstown, Ohio, 1989, 395 West Broadway Gallery, N.Y.C., 1994, 420 West Broadway Gallery, Soho, N.Y., 1995, Audubon Artists Invitational, Lever House Gallery, N.Y.C., 1995, Selected N.J. Mems. Nat. Assn. Women Artists, Hunterdon Art Ctr., Clinton, N.J., 1996, Art Ctr. Municipality of Athens, Greece, 1996, West Beth Gallery, Montclair in Manhattan, N.Y.C., 1996, ISE Art Found. N.Y.C., 1996, Soc. Am. Graphic Artists, New Rochelle, N.Y., 1997, Gallery Art 54, N.Y.C., 1997, Jane Voorhees Zimmerli Art Mus., New Brunswick, N.J., 1998, 99, Soc. Am. Graphic Artists, N.Y.C., 1999, 2004, Worldwide Feminist Expo, Balt., 2000, Millenium Collection, Nat. Assn. of Women Artists, United Nations, 2002; represented in permanent collections at Jane Voorhees Zimmerli Art Mus., New Brunswick, N.J., Newark Pub. Libr. Fine Print Collection, Newark, Montclair State U., Bailey Matthews Mus., Sanibel, Fla. Recipient Best in Show award Salute to Women in Arts, Lincoln Ctr., 1981, Hon. mention award Nat. Juried Exhbn. Small Works Montclair State U., N.J., 1995. Aida Whedon Meml. award Nat. Assn. Women Artists, 1996. Mem. Nat. Assn. Women Artists (bd. dirs., chair traveling print exhbn. 1984-89, printmaking jury 1987-89, 95-97), Audubon Artists (bd. dirs., rec. sec. 1991-97), Soc. Am. Graphic Artists, Phi Beta Kappa. Home: 546 Hillrise Pl Walnut Creek CA 94598-4064

REIMANN, HELGA LUISE, sociologist; b. Berlin, July 6, 1937; d. Hans and Renata (Von Radinger) Feick; m. Horst Reimann, July 30, 1963 (dec. Oct. 1994). Dipl.rer.pol., U. Heidelberg (Germany), 1962, DrPhil., 1966; DrHabil., U. Augsburg, 1974. Asst. prof. U. Heidelberg, 1962-70; asst. prof., dir. gen. studies U. Augsburg, 1970-74, privatdozent in sociology, 1976-80, prof. sociology, 1980-2000, ret., 2000; interim prof. U. Würzburg (Germany), 1975-76. Guest prof. U. Pitts., 1968, 98, U. Salzburg (Austria), 1998. Author: Globalisierung, 2002; editor: Weltkultur und Weltgesellschaft, 1997; co-author: Sizilien, 1985, Das Alter, 3d edit., 1994; watercolor exhbns. in Germany, Malta, Italy. Mem.: Internat. Sociol. Assn., Free German Soc. for Scis. and Arts (hon.), Rotary, Order of Merit Malta. Achievements include developments in international and transnational communication and globalization. Home: Cuvilliésstr 10 Munich 81679 Germany Fax: 49 (0) 89 99 88 7941. E-mail: Prof.Helga.Reimann@t-online.de.

REIMER, BENNETT, music educator, writer; b. N.Y.C., June 19, 1932; s. George and Sarah (Talkofsky) R.; children: Jan Ellen, Terry. BM, State Tchr.'s Coll. (now SUNY-Fredonia), 1954; MM, U. Ill., 1955, EdD, 1963. Asst. prof. music edn. U. Ill., Urbana, 1960-65; Kulas prof., chmn. dept. music edn. Case Western Res. U., Cleve., 1965-78; John W. Beattie prof. emeritus Northwestern U., Evanston, Ill., 1978-97. Author: A Philosophy of Music Education, 1970, 2d edit., 1989, Developing the Experience of Music, 1985; editor: Toward an Aesthetic Education, 1971, The Arts, Education and Aesthetic Knowing, 1992, On the Nature of Musical Experience, 1992; co-author: The Experience of Music, 1972, Silver Burdett Music Grades 1-8, 1974, 4th edit., 1985; contbr. over 100 articles on music and arts edn. to profl. jours. Mem. Music Educators Nat. Conf., Music Edn. Research Council, Edn. Aesthetic Awareness (bd. dirs.). Office: Northwestern U Sch Music Evanston IL 60208-0001

REIMER, DENNIS J. retired career military officer; b. Medford, Okla., July 12, 1939; m. Mary Jo Powers; 2 children. BS, U.S. Mil. Acad., 1962; MS, Shippensburg State Coll. Gen. U.S. Army, Ft. McPherson, Ga., chief of staff Washington, 1995—99; ret., 1999; dir. Nat. Meml. Inst. for Prevention of Terrorism, Oklahoma City, 2000—. Bd. mem. Plato Learning Inc., Minn. Decorated Def. Disting. Svc. medal, Disting. Svc. medal, two Legions of Merit, Disting. Flying Cross, six Bronze Star medals, Purple Heart, Combat Infantryman badge, Parachutist badge, Aircraft Crewman badge, Ranger Tab; recipient Nat. Vets. award, 1999. Office: Nat Meml Inst for Prevention of Terrorism Chief of Staff PO Box 889 Oklahoma City OK 73101-0889*

REIMER, JUDY MILLS, pastor, religious executive; m. George G. Reimer, 1964; children: Todd, Troy. BA, Emory and Henry Coll., 1962; MDiv, Bethany Theol. Sem., 1994. Ordained into Set Apart Ministry, Ch. of the Brethren, 1994. Vol. Brethren Vol. Svc. NIH, Bethesda, Md., 1962-64, Hessish Lichtenau, Germany, 1964-65; elem. sch. tchr. Pub. and Private Schs., various cities, 1965-76; deacon Ch. of the Brethren, 1966—; mem Virlina Dist. Bd., 1978-90; chair of nurture com. Ch. of the Brethren Virlina Dist., 1979-82, chair of outdoor ministry, 1983-84, conf. speaker, 1992; founding pastor Ch. of the Brethren, Smith Mountain Lake, Va., 1996-98, gen. bd. exec. dir., 1998—; owner, sr. v.p. Harris Office Furniture Co., Roanoke, Va., 1976—. Co-chair and vice-chair of two Virlina Fin. Campaigns, Ch. of the Brethren, 1980s, mem. Gen. Bd., Ch. of Brethren, 1977-90; mem. PTA, United Way Allocation Com., Roanoke Valley Women Owners Assn. (charter mem.); adult advisor Nat. Youth Cabinet. 1991, 92; worship coord. Nat. Youth Conf. 1994 numerous other coms. for Ch. of Brethren; official observer for Nat. Coun. of Chs. at Nicaraguan Election, Feb., 1990; rep. of Ch. of the Brethren, 1989, Atlanta, The Torch of Conscience Campaign to sensitize congregation to the campaign to abolish death penalty; workshop leader across the denomination on leadership devel., pastor/spouse retreats, women's rallies, etc.; ann. conf. moderator elect, 1993-94. Mem. Inst. Indsl. Comml. Chaplains (chmn. bd. dirs. local unit, asst. treas. nat. bd.). Office: Church of the Brethren General Offices 1451 Dundee Ave Elgin IL 60120-1694

REIN, BERT WALTER, lawyer; b. Bklyn., Feb. 7, 1941; s. Moe and Florence (Fishman) Rein; m. Jennifer Christin Bulson, July 11, 1966 (dec. Mar. 1989); children: Joanna, Benjamin, Samantha; m. Barbara Jean Kahn, Oct. 8, 1992. BA, Amherst Coll., 1961; LLB, Harvard U., 1964. Bar: DC 1965, U.S. Dist. Ct. DC 1965, U.S. Ct. Appeals (DC cir.) 1968, U.S. Ct. Appeals (2d cir.) 1973, U.S. Ct. Appeals (8th cir.) 1974, U.S. Ct. Appeals (4th cir.) 1976, U.S. Ct. Appeals (11th cir.) 1982, U.S. Supreme Ct. 1982. Law ck. to Justice John M. Harlan U.S. Supreme Ct., Washington, 1966-67; assoc. Kirkland & Ellis, Washington, 1967-69, ptnr., 1973-83; spl. asst. U.S. Dept. State, Washington, 1969-70, dep. asst. sec., 1970-73; ptnr. Wiley, Rein & Fielding, Washington, 1983—. Bd. dirs., chmn. govt. and regulatory affairs com. U.S. C. of C., 1986—90; bd. dirs. Nat. Chamber Litig. Ctr.; advisor Reagan Dept. Justice Transition, Washington, 1980; mem. adv. com. U.S. Sentencing Comm., 1988—89; edn. gen. counsel Cmty. Learning and Info. Network, 1992—. Contbr. articles to profl. jours. Mem. capitol area adv. bd. Salvation Army. Capt. USAR, 1964—68. Mem.: ABA, Internat. Trade Commn. Trial Lawyers Assn. (pres. 1990—91), Am. Law Inst., Aviation Club. Republican. Jewish. Home: 6423 Shadow Rd Chevy Chase MD 20815-6613 Office: Wiley Rein & Fielding 1776 K St NW Washington DC 20006-2304 Office Phone: 202-719-7080. Business E-Mail: brein@wrf.com.

REIN, CATHERINE AMELIA, insurance company executive, lawyer; b. Lebanon, Pa., Feb. 7, 1943; d. John and Esther (Scott) Shultz. BA summa cum laude, Pa. State U., 1965; JD magna cum laude, NYU, 1968. Bar: N.Y. 1968, U.S. Supreme Ct. 1971. Assoc. Dewey, Ballantine, Bushby, Palmer & Wood, N.Y.C., 1968-74; with Continental Group, Stamford, Conn., 1974-85, sec., sr. atty., 1976-77, v.p., gen. counsel, 1980-85; sec., asst. gen. counsel Continental Diversified Ops., 1978-80; v.p. human resources Met. Life Ins. Co., N.Y.C., 1985-88, sr. v.p. human resources, 1988-89, exec. v.p. corp. and profl. svcs. dept., 1989—98, sr. exec., v.p. bus. svcs. group and corp. svcs., 1998-99; pres, CEO Met. Life Auto and Home, Warwick, RI, 1999—. Bd. dirs. Bank of N.Y., First Energy Corp. Bd. trustees NYU Sch. Law Found. Mem. ABA, Assn. of Bar of City of N.Y. Episcopalian. Avocations: decorating, restoration, cooking. Office: Met Life Ins Co 1 Madison Ave New York NY 10010-3603

REIN, JEFFREY A. retail executive; BA in Acctg., U. Ariz., 1974, MSc in Pharmacy, 1980. From asst. mgr. to pres., COO Walgreen Co., Deerfield, Ill., 1982—2003, pres., 2003—, COO, 2003—. Office: Walgreen Co 200 Wilmot Rd Deerfield IL 60015

REIN, MICHAEL FRANK, physician, medical educator; b. Washington, Jan. 17, 1943; s. Charles Robert and Norma (Spitalny) R.; m. Marjorie Ann Josephson, Feb. 24, 1968; children: Andrew Charles, Allen Jeffrey. BA, Harvard Coll., 1965; MD, Harvard Medical Sch., 1969. Residency in medicine Mt. Sinai Hosp., N.Y.C., 1969-71, Univ. Va. Hosp., Charlottesville, Va., 1971-72, fellow in infectious disease, 1972-73; chief clin. rsch. sect. venereal disease control div. Ctr. for Disease Control, Atlanta, 1973-75; asst. prof. medicine Univ. Va., Charlottesville, 1975-80, assoc. prof. medicine, 1980-89, prof. medicine, 1989—. Chair coun. med. edn. U. Va. Sch. Medicine, 1995-99, assoc. chair undergrad. med. edn. dept. internal medicine, 1997—; chair AIDS therapeutic data safety monitoring bd NIH, 2002—. Editor: Teaching Atlas of Sexually Transmitted Diseases, 1996; contbr. over 32 articles to profl. jours. Fellow: Infectious Disease Soc. Am., Am. Coll. Physicians; mem.: Am. Sexually Transmitted Disease Assn. (pres. 1980—81). Jewish. Avocation: amateur radio. Home: 109 Sturbridge Rd Charlottesville VA 22901-2113 Office: Univ Va Health Scis Ctr PO Box 800592 Charlottesville VA 22908-0592

REIN, STANLEY MICHAEL, lawyer; b. St. Paul, Apr. 15, 1946; s. Clayton George Rein and Rose Gertrude (Mintz) Brown; m. Linda. R. Arnold; children: Gabriel Todd, Leah Suzanne. BA, U. Minn., 1968; JD cum laude, Harvard U., 1973. Bar: Minn. 1973, U.S. Tax Ct. 1973. Assoc. Dorsey & Whitney, LLP, Mpls., 1973-78; ptnr. Dorsey & Whitney LLP, Mpls., 1979—. Mem. planned giving adv. coun. ARC Mpls. chpt., 1986, 88, planned giving adv. com. Minn. Pub. Radio, 1988-89; bd. dirs. South Metro Airport Action Council, Mpls., 1986, 87. With U.S. Army, 1968-70, Vietnam. Named in Best Lawyers in Am. Fellow Am. Coll. of Trust and Estate Counsel; mem. Minn. Bar Assn. (probate and trust law sect.), Hennepin County Bar Assn. (probate and trust law sect.), Phi Beta Kappa. Jewish. Avocations: reading, travel. Office: Dorsey & Whitney LLP 50 S 6th St Ste 1500 Minneapolis MN 55402-1498 E-mail: rein.stan@dorseylaw.com.

REINALDA, DAVID ANTHONY, elementary school educator; b. Lynwood, Calif., May 17, 1966; s. Robert Aarlen and Marie Antoinette (Presicci) R. AA, Riverside (Calif.) City Coll., 1989; BA, Calif. State U., San Bernardino, 1992; cert. elem. tchr., U. Calif., Riverside, 1994. Instrnl. aide Jurupa Unified Sch. Dist., Riverside, 1985, 89-93, substitute tchr., 1993—; day care worker Our Lady of Perpetual Help, 1988-89; substitute tchr. Riverside Unified Sch. Dist., 1996—; adult edn. tchr. Jurupa Unified Sch. Dist., 1999—. Vol. aide Jurupa Unified Sch. Dist., 1989-91; home tutor, 1987-89. Author: ABC, What's at School for Me, 1997; author children's stories Stone Soup, 1981. Little League coach, Riverside, 1980-82, scorekeeper, 1982-84; Sunday sch. tchr., supr. Hope Cmty. Ch., Riverside, 1988-98. Winner 1st pl. Lions Club speech contest, 1984; named Christian Youth of Yr. Kiwanis Club, 1985, Outstanding Young Man Am., 1992, 96. Mem. Phi Lambda Omega. Democrat. Mem. Christian Reformed Ch. Avocations: bowling, dance, writing, acting.

REINBERG, DANNY, biochemist, educator; BA in Biology, Cath. U.; PhD in Biochemistry and Molecular Biology, Albert Einstein Coll. Medicine. Postdoctoral work Rockefeller U.; mem. faculty SUNY, Stony Brook; prof. biochemistry U. Medicine and Dentistry of N.J.-Robert Wood Johnson Med. Sch., 1986—. Contbr. articles to profl. jours. Achievements include research in understanding the mechanisms by which genes are turned on and off. Office: U Medicine and Dentistry NJ Dept Biochemistry 663 Hoes Ln Research Annex Piscataway NJ 08854-5635

REINBOLT, PAUL C. oil industry executive; b. Chapel Hill, NC; B in Acctg., MBA, Miami U., Oxford, Ohio. Sr. fin. analyst Marathon Oil Corp., Pitts., 1984—86, short-term investment mgr. New York, 1986—87, mgr. treasury, 1987—91, dir. corp. fin. analysis Pitts., 1991—94, asst. treas., corp. fin., 1994—98, mgr. fin. and adminstrn. prodn., UK London, 1998—2000; comptr. US Steel, Pitts., 2000—01; v.p. fin. and treas. Marathon Oil Corp., Houston, 2001—. Office: Marathon Oil Corp Corp Headquarters 5555 San Felipe Rd Houston TX 77056-2723

REINDL, JAMES, newspaper editor; Bur. chief AP, Chgo., 2000—. Office: 10 S Wacker Dr Ste 2500 Chicago IL 60606-7491

REINECKE, MANFRED G. chemistry professor; b. Milw., May 19, 1935; s. Fritz Wilhelm and Erna (Rittmeyer) R.; m. Marlene Zwisler, June 15, 1957; children: Kurt, Kryn, Claire. BS in Chemistry, U. Wis., 1956; PhD in Organic Chemistry, U. Calif., 1960. Asst. prof. U. Calif., Riverside, 1959-64, Tex. Christian U., Ft. Worth, 1964-68, assoc. prof., 1968-73; vis. prof. U. Tubingen, Fed. Republic of Germany, 1971-72; prof. Tex. Christian U., Ft. Worth, 1973—; vis. prof. U. British Columbia, Vancouver, Can., 1987. Chmn. health professions adv. com. Tex. Christian U., 1974-91; mem. sci. adv. bd. Univera Pharm., Inc., 1996-2002; cons. in field. Contbr. more than 80 articles on natural product, organic chemistry and chem. edn. to profl. jours. Recipient W.T. Doherty award Ft. Worth, Dallas sect. Am. Chem. Soc., 1984; NSF Tchg.fellow, 1971-72, NAS fellow, 1979, 90. Mem. Am. Chem. Soc. (chmn. Ft. Worth, Dallas sect. 1976), So. Assn. Advisors Health Professions (bd. dirs. 1986-89), Alpha Epsilon Delta (dir. SW region 1985-2002). Office: Tex Christian Univ Dept of Chemistry PO Box 298860 Fort Worth TX 76129-0001 E-mail: m.reinecke@tcu.edu.

REINECKE, WILLIAM T. conductor, educator; b. New Rochelle, N.Y., Oct. 12, 1959; s. Betty Baltz and Ralph James Reinecke. BS, Lebanon Valley Coll., 1980; M in Music Edn., U. S.C., 1986. Profl. edn. cert. Va. Dir. bands Fieldale-Collinsville (Va.) HS, 1980—84, asst. wrestling coach, 1982—84; dir. bands Apopka (Fla.) HS, 1986—. Guest dir. FBA Dist. 19 Honors Jazz Band, 1999, Orange County Pub. Schs. Honor Jazz Band, Orlando, Fla., 2001. Conductor: Boyertown Alumni Marching Unit Spring Concert, 2002—03. Mem.: Fla. Bandmasters Assn. (dist. sec. 2000—01, mem. adjudication com. 2001, guest dir. dist. 19 jazz band 1999, dist. chmn.). Home: 517 Oakcrest St Altamonte Springs FL 32714 Office: Apopka HS 555 W Martin St Apopka FL 32712 E-mail: reinecw@ocps.net.

REINEMUND, STEVEN S. food products executive; b. Queens, N.Y., Apr. 6, 1948; s. Ott and Dora (Kramer) R.; m. Gail Timbers, Dec. 14, 1974; children: Steven S. Jr., Jonathan Craig. BS in Naval Sci., U.S. Naval Acad., 1970; MBA, U. Va., 1978. Commd. 2d lt. USMC, 1970, advanced through grades to capt., 1974, resigned, 1975; mktg. rep. IBM Corp., 1975-76; v.p., gen. mgr. Marriott-Roy Rogers, 1978-84; sr. v.p., field operator Pizza Hut, Inc., Wichita, Kans., 1984-86, exec. v.p., 1986, pres., CEO, 1986—92, Frito-Lay N.Am., 1992—96; chmn., CEO Frito-Lay, 1996—99; pres., COO PepsiCo, 1999—2001, chmn., CEO, 2001—. Bd. dirs. Bank IV, Wichita. Sec., treas. bd. dirs. U. Va., Darden Sch. Alumni Assn. Named one of Outstanding Young Men Am. Mem. Wichita Area C. of C. (bd. dirs.). Republican. Presbyterian. Avocations: tennis, running. Office: PepsiCo 700 Anderson Hill Rd Purchase NY 10577*

REINER, CARL, director, actor, writer; b. Bronx, N.Y., Mar. 20, 1922; s. Irving and Bessie (Mathias) R.; m. Estelle Lebost, Dec. 24, 1943; children: Robert, Sylvia A., Lucas. Student, Sch. Fgn. Service, Georgetown U., 1943. Appeared on Broadway and with road co.: Call Me Mister, 1947-48; on Broadway in:Inside U.S.A, 1948-49, Alive and Kicking, 1950; TV actor, 1950—; appeared: YourShow of Shows, 1950-54, Caesar's Hour, 1954-58 (Emmy award 1956, 57); master ceremonies: Keep Talking, 1958-59; writer-actor: Dinah Shore Show, 1960; producer, writer: The Dick Van Dyke Show (Emmy awards as writer 1962, 63, 64, as producer 1965, 66), The New Dick Van Dyke Show, Enter Laughing, written 1958, directed 1967, The Comics, 1968; dir.: (films) Enter Laughing, The Comic, 1967, The Comic, 1969, Where's Poppa, 1970, Oh, God!, 1977, The One and Only, 1978, The Jerk, 1979, Dead Men Don't Wear Plaid, 1982, The Man With Two Brains, 1983, All of Me, 1984, Summer Rental, 1985, Summer School, 1987, Bert Rigby, You're a Fool, 1989, Sibling Rivalry, 1990, Fatal Instinct, 1993; appeared in: movie Happy Anniversary, 1959, The Gazebo, 1960, Gidget Goes Hawaiian, 1961, It's a Mad, Mad, Mad, Mad World, 1963, The Russians Are Coming, 1966, The End, 1978, Dead Men Don't Wear Plaid, 1982, (TV movie) Danny Kaye: A Legacy of Laughter, 1996, The Right to Remain Silent, 1996, The Slums of Beverly Hills, 1998; writer, dir.: Something Different, 1967; writer: Sid Caesar, Imogene Coca, Carl Reiner, Howard Morris Special (Emmy award, 1967); producer: TV series Good Heavens, 1976 (recipient Emmy award 1957, 58, 62, 63); Author: (novel) All Kinds of Love, 1993, (novel) Continue Laughing, 1995; author: short stories; screenplay The Thrill of It All; (with Mel Brooks) albums The 2000 Year Old Man, The 2001 Year Old Man, The 2013 Year Old Man; exec. producer: film Heaven Help Us, 1976; dir. The Man with Two Brains, 1983. Served with AUS, 1942-46. Recipient Guest Actor in a Comedy Series Emmy award for Mad About You, 1995. Achievements include receiving the greatest number of Emmys (12) for any individual. Office: care George Shapiro Shapiro-West 141 S El Camino Dr Ste 205 Beverly Hills CA 90212-2718

REINER, GARY M. diversified technology and services company executive; BA, Harvard U., 1976, MBA, 1980. Rsch. analyst Boston Consulting Group, 1980—86, ptnr., 1986—91; v.p. corp. bus. devel. GE, Fairfield, Conn., 1991-96, sr. v.p., chief info. officer, 1996—. Office: GE 3135 Easton Tpke Fairfield CT 06431-0002

REINER, MARK ALLEN, surgeon, educator; b. N.Y.C., Jan. 12, 1949; married; two children. BS, NYU, 1969; MD summa cum laude, SUNY-Downstate, 1974. Diplomate Am. Bd. Surgery. Resident gen. and vascular surgery Mt. Sinai Med. Ctr., N.Y.C., 1974-78, chief resident, 1978-79, clin. asst., 1979—. Sect. chief laparascopic surgery Bronx Vets. Hosp.; attending physician Doctors Hosp., 1982; clin. instr. Mt. Sinai Sch. Medicine Dept. Surgery. Recipient Arthur H. Aufses Sr. award, 1979. Mem.: SAGES, ACS, AMA, N.Y. Surg. Soc., N.Y. Laparoscopy Club, N.Y. Met. Breast Group, N.Y. Acad. Scis., N.Y. Soc. Surgeons, N.Y. State Med. Soc., Am. Geriatric Soc. Home: 1010 5th Ave New York NY 10028-0130 Office Phone: 212-879-6677. E-mail: mdreiner@aol.com.

REINER, ROB, director, writer, actor; b. Bronx, Mar. 6, 1947; s. Carl and Estelle (Lebost) R.; m. Penny Marshall, 1971 (div.), m. Michele Singer, May 19, 1989. Student, UCLA. Co-founder Castle Rock Entertainment, Beverly Hills, Calif. Actor: (TV series) All In the Family, 1971-78 (Emmy award 1974, 78), (TV movie) Thursday's Game, 1974 (films) Enter Laughing, 1967, Halls of Anger, 1970, Summertree, 1971, The Jerk, 1979, This is Spinal Tap, 1984, Throw Momma From the Train, 1987, Postcards From the Edge, 1990, The Spirit of '76, 1990, Sleepless in Seattle, 1993, Bullets Over Broadway, 1994, Mixed Nuts, 1994, Bye Bye, Love, 1995, First Wives Club, 1996, Mad Dog Time, 1996, I Am Your Child (TV), 1997, Primary Colors, 1998, EDtv, 1999, The Muse, 1999, The Story of Us, 1999, (theatre) The Roast, 1980; actor, writer: (films) Halls of Anger, 1970, Where's Pappa?, 1970, Summertree, 1971, Fire Sale, 1971; actor, co-writer, prodr. (TV) More Than Friends, 1978, Million Dollar Infield, 1982; actor, co-writer, dir. (film) This Is Spinal Tap, 1984; dir. (films) The Sure Thing, 1985, Stand By Me, 1986; dir. prodr. (films) The Princess Bride, 1987, When Harry Met Sally, 1989, Misery, 1990, A Few Good Men, 1992, North, 1994, The American President, 1995, Ghosts of Mississippi, 1996, The Story of Us, 1999, Alex & Emma, 2003; co-creator (TV series) The Super, 1972; co-creator, actor (TV series) Free Country, 1977-78. Mem. SAG, AFTRA, Dir. Guild Am., Writers Guild Am. Office: Castle Rock Entertainment 335 N Maple Dr Ste 135 Beverly Hills CA 90210-3867

REINER, THOMAS KARL, manufacturing executive; b. Budapest, Hungary, Dec. 29, 1931; came to U.S., 1959; s. Pál and Jozefa (Keller) R.; m. Joyce Reiner (div.); children: Paul A., Reneé K. Hedsand; m. Eleanor Ruth Aldredge (div.). Diploma optics trade sch., Budapest, 1952; MSME, Tech. U., Budapest, 1955; postgrad., London Coll., 1958, U. Pitts., Carnegie Inst. Tech., 1964.; PhD, U. Wethford, 2001. Engr. Cen. Power Generating Sta., Hungary, 1954-56; cons. engr., test engr. Blaw-Knox Co., London, 1956-57; sr. engr. Eubank & Ptnrs., London, 1957-59; rsch. engr. Pitts. Plate Glass Co., 1959-60, product mgr. Copes-Vulcan divsn., 1960-62; chief engr. J.W. Fecker divsn. Am. Optical Co., 1962-66; product mgr. Carco Electronics, Menlo Park, Calif., 1966-68; chief engr. Fairchild Camera Space and Def., El Segundo, Calif., 1968-70; dir. engring. Templeton, Kenly & Co., L.A. and Chgo., 1970-72; gen. mgr. Foremark Corp., Gardena, 1972-74; sys. pres., prin. owner Kinetron, Inc., Long Beach, Calif., 1974-76; pres., prin. owner GRW, Inc., Hawthorne, Calif., 1977-97, Aircargo Sys./Hydraulics. Adj. prof. Tech. U., Budapest, 1951-54. Patentee in post tension device for concrete, spherical air bearing and gimballed slave connector, synchronization of hydraulic jacking sys., bending of automotive side windows; inventor tug/barge latching sys., membrane type loadcell, ultra low profile platform and truckscales. Bd. pres. Peacock Ridge Homeowners Assn., Palos Verdes, Calif. Lt. Hungarian Army, 1951-57. Mem. Internat. Soc. Weighing and Measurements. Home: 14110 Valley Vista Blvd Sherman Oaks CA 91423-4657

REINERT, JAMES A. entomology educator; b. Enid, Okla., Jan. 26, 1944; s. Andrew J. and Emma Reinert; m. Anita Irwin; children: Travis J., Gina N., Mindy K., Melanie B., Gregory W., Teresa J. BS, Okla. State U., 1966; MS, Clemson U., 1968, PhD, 1970. Asst. state entomologist U. Md., College Park, 1970; asst. prof. entomology to prof. entomology Ft. Lauderdale Rsch. and Edn. Ctr., U. Fla., 1970-84; resident dir., prof. entomology Tex. A&M Univ. Sys., Dallas, 1984-94, prof. entomology, 1994—2003, prof. entomology, faculty fellow, 2004—. Contbr. over 400 articles to profl. jours. Recipient Vice Chancellor's award for team rsch., Tex. A&M Univ. Sys., 2004; grantee, NDEA, 1968. Mem. Inter-Turfgrass Soc., Entomol. Soc. Am. (S.W. br. sec./treas. 1998, pres.-elect 1999, pres. 2000, sec. sect. F 2003, vice-chair 2004, award in urban entomology 2002), So. Nurserymen's Assn. (Porter Henegar Meml. award 1982), Fla. Entomol. Soc. (v.p. 1983, pres. 1984, Entomologist of Yr. 1985), Fla. State Hort. Soc. (v.p. 1982), S.C. Entomol. Soc. (J.H. Cochran award 2002, Rsch. Ctr. Adminstrs. Soc. (v.p. 1994, state rep. 1991-92, sec. 1993), Dallas Agr. Club (bd. dirs. 1989, v.p. 1990, pres. 1991). Roman Catholic. Home: 3805 Covinton Ln Plano TX 75023-7731 Office: Tex A&M Univ Rsch and Ext Ctr 17360 Coit Rd Dallas TX 75252-6599 Office Phone: 972-231-5362. Business E-Mail: j-reinert@tamu.edu.

REINERT, NORBERT FREDERICK, patent lawyer, retired chemical company executive; b. Hamilton, Ohio, Apr. 12, 1928; s. Fred F. and Jennie A. R.; m. Ida Elizabeth Barickman, Jan. 26, 1956; children: Matthew W., Paul H. B.Ch.E., Ohio State U., 1951; LL.B., Cleve.-Marshall Law Sch., 1959. Bar: Ohio 1959, D.C. 1961. Patent agt. Standard of Ohio, Cleve., 1957-59, patent lawyer, 1959-60, E.I. duPont de Nemours & Co., Wilmington, Del., 1960-91, dir. investor relations, 1981-84, mng. counsel, 1985-91; v.p., gen. counsel Endo Labs, Inc. subs. DuPont, Garden City, N.Y., 1971-73, exec. v.p., 1973-77, pres., 1977-81; pvt. practice patent law, 1991—2002. Served with Chem. Corps AUS, 1955-56. Mem. Am. Patent Law Assn., Tau Beta Pi. Republican. Roman Catholic. Home: PO Box 311 Mendenhall PA 19357-0311

REINERTSEN, NORMAN, retired aircraft systems company executive; b. Bklyn., Mar. 27, 1934; s. Berthin and Malene Katherine (Dahl) R.; m. Elizabeth T. O'Shea, Aug. 30, 1958; children: Michael, Christopher, Katherine. BEE, CCNY, 1960; postgrad., Harvard U., 1982. Registered profl. engr., Calif. Various positions Grumman Aerospace Corp., 1960-75; gen. mgr. Grumman Aerospace Corp. (Great River ops.), 1975-77; v.p. automotive Grumman Allied Industries, Melville, N.Y., 1977-83, sr. v.p. vehicle div., 1983-94; sr. v.p. Olson Bodies, Inc., 1977-79; exec. v.p. Grumman Flexible, Delaware, Ohio, 1979-82; pres. Grumman Olson, Mellville, 1983-85; sr. v.p. Vehicle div. Grumman Allied, 1985-87; v.p. quality ops. Grumman Aircraft Sys. div. Northrop Grumman, 1987-94; ret., 1994. With U.S. Army, 1955-57. Mem. Air Force Assn., Northport Yacht Club. Home: 7 Oleander Dr Northport NY 11768-3438

REINGANUM, MARC RICHARD, finance educator; b. Chgo., June 17, 1953; s. Carrol Harrison Jr. and Maurine Judith (Scheckman) R.; m. Jennifer Freidel, Aug. 22, 1978 (div. 1987); m. Alison Fox, May 13, 1989; children: Daniel Louis, Michael Issac, Margaret Elizabeth, Claire Alexandra. AB, Oberlin Coll., 1975; MBA, U. Chgo., 1977, PhD, 1979. Asst. prof. U. So. Calif., 1979-82, assoc. prof., 1982-87; vis. assoc. prof. fin. U. Chgo., 1985-86; Phillips prof. fin., dir. fin. markets inst. U. Iowa, Iowa City, 1987-95; Mary Jo Vaughn Raucher chair of investments, dir. Fin. Markets Inst., 1995—2002; chairperson dept. fin. So. Meth. U., 1995-2000; dir. quantitative rsch., portfolio strategist for equities Oppenheimer Funds, N.Y.C., 2002—. Mem. investments com., bd. trustees So. Meth. U. Contbr. articles, revs. to profl. publs.; mem. editorial bd. various jours. in field. Coach soccer YMCA, 1995-99; coach chess club East Dallas Cmty. Sch., Iowa City Montessori Bd., 1992-95, Huer Sch.; mem. fin. com. Tex. Internat. Theatrical Arts Soc., 1998-2003. Bank Am. Rsch. scholar, 1984-87. Mem. Am. Fin. Assn., Western Fin. Assn., United Way Bd., Iowa City Community Sch. Dist. Found., Phi Beta Kappa, Beta Gamma Sigma. Office: Oppenheimer Funds 489 7th Ave 10th Fl New York NY 10018 Home: 287 Edgerstoune Rd Princeton NJ 08540-6717 E-mail: mreinganum@oppenheimerfunds.com.

REINGLASS, MICHELLE ANNETTE, lawyer; b. L.A., Dec. 9, 1954; d. Darwin and Shirley (Steiner) R. Student, U. Calif., Irvine, 1972-75; BSL, Western State U., 1977; JD, Western State U., Coll. Law, 1978. Bar: Calif. 1979, U.S. Dist. Ct. (ctrl. dist.) Calif. 1979, U.S. Ct. Appeals (9th cir.) 1981, U.S. Dist. Ct. (so. dist.) Calif. 1990. Pvt. practice employee litig., Laguna Hills, Calif., 1979—. Instr. Calif. Continuing Edn. of Bar, 1990—, Western State Coll., 1991, Rutter Group, 1994—; chmn. magistrate selection com. U.S. Dist. Ct. (ctrl. dist.) Calif., L.A., 1991, 93, 94, 95, mem. com., 1997; lectr. in field. Contbr. articles to profl. jours. Pres., bd. dirs. Child or Parental Emergency Svcs., Santa Ana, Calif., 1982-92; bd. dirs. Pub. Law Ctr., Santa Ana, Coalition for Justice, Working Wardrobes; mem. exec. com. and cast CHOC Follies. Recipient Jurisprudence award Anti-Defamation League, 1997; named to Hall of Fame, Western State U., 1993; named one of Best Lawyers, Bestlawyers.com, 2001, 02, 03, one of Top 100 Most Influential Lawyers in Calif., L.A. Daily Jour., 2001, one of Top 30 Female Litigators in Calif., L.A. Daily Jour., 2002. Mem. State Bar Calif., Orange County Bar Assn. (del. to state conv. 1980-94, bd. dirs. 1983-94, chmn. bus. litigation sect. 1989, sec. 1990, treas. 1991, pres.-elect 1992, pres. 1993), Orange County Trial Lawyers Assn. (bd. dirs. 1987-89, Bus. Trial Lawyer of Yr. award 1995), Orange County Women Lawyers (Lawyer of Yr. award 1996), Vols. in Parole (chmn. adv. com. 1990-91), Peter Elliot Inns Ct. (master), Am. Bd. of Trial Advocates. Avocations: distance running, skiing. Office: 23161 Mill Creek Dr Ste 170 Laguna Hills CA 92653-1650 E-mail: michelle@reinglasslaw.com.

REINGOLD, ARTHUR LAWRENCE, epidemiologist, educator; b. Chgo., Oct. 31, 1948; married AB, U. Chgo., 1970, MD, 1976. Diplomate Am. Bd. Internal Medicine. Resident in internal medicine Mount Auburn Hosp., Cambridge, Mass., 1976-78; instr. dept. medicine (epidemiology) U. Conn., Hartford, 1979; epidemic intelligence svc. officer Conn. State Dept. Health Svcs., Hartford, 1979-80; epidemic intelligence svc. officer spl. pathogens br., bacterial diseases divsn. Ctr. Disease Control, Atlanta, 1980-81, resident in preventive medicine, 1980-82, asst. chief respiratory & spl. pathogens epidemiology br. Ctr. Infectious Disease, 1981-85, liaison officer, 1985-87; vis. lectr. dept. biomed. and environ. health scis. (epidemiology) U. Calif., Berkeley, 1985-87, prof. epidemiology, 1987—, head epidemiology program, 1990—, prof. dept. epidemiology & biostatistics San Francisco, 1989—, clin. prof. dept. medicine, 1991—; dir. UCB-UCSF Fogarty Internat. AIDS Training Program; co-dir. Calif. Emerging Infections Program. Cons. in field. Contbr. articles to profl. jours. Fellow Am. Coll. Epidemiology, Infectious Disease Soc. Am.; mem. ACP, Am. Epidemiological Soc., Am. Soc. Microbiology, Soc. Epidemiologic Rsch., Sigma Xi, Inst. Medicine, 2004.

REINGOLD, DAVID AMI, sociologist, educator; b. Chgo., Oct. 30, 1968; s. Haim and Badonna Reingold. BA in Sociology and Social Welfare, U. Wis., 1990; MA in Sociology, U. Chgo., 1992, PhD in Sociology, 1996. Asst. prof. Ind. U., Bloomington, 1997—2003, assoc. prof., 2003—; dir. rsch. and policy devel. Corp. for Nat. and Cmty. Svc., Washington, 2002—04. Rsch. assoc. Ctr. for the Study of Urban Inequality, Chgo., 1990—94; program assoc. Govs. Task Force on Human Svcs. Reform, Chgo., 1993; rsch. assoc. Dept. Children and Family Svcs., Chgo., 1996; field assoc. Rockefeller Inst. Govt., Albany, NY, 1996—98. Contbr. articles to profl. jours.; co-editor: Journ. of Policy Analysis and Management, 2004—. Mem. famliy self sufficiency com. Bloomington Housing Authority, 1997—2002, chmn. family self-sufficiency com., 1998—2002; housing commr. Bloomington Housing Authority Bd., 1999—2002, vice chmn., 2000—02; mem. task force for disadvantaged youth White House, 2002—03; mng. editor, co-editor Journ. Policy Analysis and Mgmt., 2004. Fellow fellwship on race, poverty and social policy, NSF/U. Chgo., 1992—96; grantee rsch. grantee, Ind. Family Social Svcs. Adminstrn., The Joyce Found., Ind. Twp. Assn., 1998—2000, The Joyce Found., 2001—02; scholar Century scholar, U. Chgo., 1990—92. Mem.: Assn. for Pub. Policy Analysis and Mgmt. (policy com. 2003—), Urban Affairs Assn., Am. Sociol. Assn. Office: Ind Univ, Sch Pub & Environ Affairs 1315 E 10th St Bloomington IN 47405 Business E-Mail: reingold@indiana.edu.

REINHARD, CHRISTOPHER JOHN, merchant banking, venture capital and biotechnology executive; b. Bridgeport, Conn., Nov. 11, 1953; s. Warren John and Marian Louise (Dutter) R.; m. Maureen Francis, Sept. 24, 1977; 1 child, Griffin John. BS, Babson Coll., 1976, MBA, 1977. Sr. fin. analyst Gen. Motors Corp., Detroit and N.Y.C., 1977-81; asst. sec. Wheelabrator-Frye Inc., N.H., 1981-83; asst. sec., asst. treas. The Signal Cos., Inc., La Jolla, Calif., 1983-86; mng. dir., v.p. The Henley Group, Inc., La Jolla, 1986-90; mng. dir. Fisher Sci. Group, Inc., La Jolla, 1986-90; mng. dir., v.p. Wheelabrator Tech. Inc., Henley Mfg. Corp., 1987-90; founder, pres. Colony Group Inc., Rancho Santa Fe, 1990—, Reinhard Assocs., Rancho Santa Fe, 1990-95; founder, v.p., CFO Advanced Access, Inc., San Diego, 1995-97. Pres. Direct Feedback, Inc., 1990, Dairy Queen Ventures, 1990-94, Winsor Sport Fencing, 1993—; CEO, founder, pres. Collateral Therapeutics Inc., 1995—; gen. ptnr. Cabrillo Ventures, 1995-96; founder, pres. ihumon, 2000—. Mem. Boston Athenaeum, N.Y. Athletic Club, San Diego Polo Club, Rancho Santa Fe Polo Club. Office: Collateral Therapeutics 11622 El Camino Real San Diego CA 92130-2049

REINHARD, DIANE L. university president; B in elem. edn., M in ednl. psychology, U. Wis.; PhD ednl. evaluation, Ohio State U. Faculty mem., assoc. dean, acting dean U. of Oreg.; prof., dept. of ednl. psychology W.Va. U., dean, coll. of human resources and edn., acting pres.; pres. Clarion U., 1990—2003; interim pres. Ind. U. of Pa., 2004—. Office: Clarion U Office of the President Clarion PA 16214

REINHARD, JOAO PEDRO, chemicals company executive; b. Sao Paulo, Brazil, Aug. 4, 1945; BA, MBA, Escola de Administracao de Empresas da Fundacao Vargas, Sao Paulo, Brazil, 1967. Fin. planning supr. Squibb do Brazil, Sao Paulo, 1968; credit mgr. Dow Quimica, Sao Paulo, 1970-72; fin. asst. Dow Latin Am., Miami, Fla., 1973; treas. Latin Am. Dow Lepetit Latin Am., Miami, Fla., 1974-76; corp. fin. planning mgr. The Dow Chem. Co., Midland, Mich., 1976-77; fin. dir. Dow Quimica S.Am., Sao Paulo, Brazil, 1978-80; treas. Dow Chem. Europe, Horgen, Switzerland, 1981-85; mng. dir. Dow Italy, Milan, 1985-87; v.p. Dow Europe, Horgen, Switzerland, 1985-87; treas. The Dow Chem. Co., Midland, Mich., 1988—, exec. v.p., CFO, 1995—. Bd. dirs. Royal Bank of Canada, Dow Corning Corp., Sigma-Aldrich Corp., Coca-Cola Co., Liana Ltd., Midland, Mich., Dorinco Reinsurance Co., Midland, Dow Chem. Internat. BV, Midland, DCOMCO Inc., Midland, Dow Chm. Inter-Am. Ltd., Midland, Dow Chem. Internat. Inc. (Panama), Midland,, Dow Chem. Internat. Ltd., Midland, Midland Pipeline Corp., Dow Chem. Overseas Capital N.V., Midland, Bank Mendes Gans nv, Amsterdam, The Netherlands. Mem. Fin. Execs. Inst., Fin. Mgmt. Assn., Nat. Assn. Corp. Treasurers, Corp. Fin. Inst. Office: The Dow Chemical Co 2030 Dow Ctr Midland MI 48674-0001 E-mail: preinhard@dow.com.*

REINHARD, KEITH LEON, advertising executive; b. Berne, Ind., Jan. 20, 1935; s. Herman L. and Agnes V. R.; m. Rose-Lee Simons, Nov. 7, 1976; children: Rachel, Elizabeth; children by previous marriage: Christopher, Timothy, Matthew, Geoffrey, Jacqueline. Student public schs., Berne. Comml. artist Kling Studios, Chgo., 1954-56; mgr. tech. communications dept. Magnavox Co., Ft. Wayne, Ind., 1957-60; creative/account exec. Biddle Co., Bloomington, Ill., 1961-63; exec. v.p., dir. creative services, pres. Needham, Harper & Steers, Inc., Chgo., from 1964; then chmn., chief exec. officer Needham, Harper & Steers Worldwide, Chgo.; chmn., chief exec. officer DDB Worldwide Inc., N.Y.C., 1986—, chmn., CEO, 1989—. Episcopalian. Office: DDB Worldwide Inc 437 Madison Ave New York NY 10022-7001

REINHARD, PHILIP G. federal judge; b. LaSalle, Ill., Jan. 12, 1941; s. Godfrey and Ruth R.; married Virginia Reinhard; children: Bruce, Brian, David, Philip. BA, U. Ill., Champaign, 1962, JD, 1964. Asst. state atty. Winnebago County, 1964-67; atty. Hyer, Gill & Brown, 1967-68; state atty. Winnebago County, 1968-76; judge 17th Jud. Cir., 1976-80, Appellate Ct., 1980-92, U.S. Dist. Ct. (no. dist.) Ill., 1992—. Mem. Am. Acad. Jud. Edn., Winnebago County Bar Assn. Office: US Courthouse 211 S Court St Rockford IL 61101-1219

REINHARDT, GEORGE ROBERT, lawyer; b. Tifton, Ga., Mar. 1, 1954; BBA magna cum laude, U. Ga., 1975; JD, U. Va., 1978. Bar: Ga. 1979. Atty. Reinhardt, Whitley, Wilmot, Summerlin & Pittman, PC, Tifton, Ga. Mem.: Tifton Bar Assn., State Bar Ga. (program com. 1998—, chair fin. com. 1999—2000, fin. com. 1996—, exec. com. 1998—, bd. govs. 1992—, state disciplinary bd. review panel 1993—98, chmn. 1996—98, treas. 2000—01, pres.-elect 2003—), Sphinx Soc. Office: Reinhardt Whitley Wilmot et al PO Drawer 1287 1001 N Central St Tifton GA 31794

REINHARDT, JOHN EDWARD, former international affairs specialist; b. Glade Spring, Va., Mar. 8, 1920; s. Edward Vinton and Alice (Miller) R.; m. Carolyn Lillian Daves, Sept. 2, 1947; children: Sharman W. Reinhardt Lancefield, Alice N., Carolyn C. Reinhardt Fenstermaker. AB, Knoxville Coll., 1939; MS, U. Wis., 1947, PhD, 1950. Prof. English Va. State Coll., Petersburg, 1950-56; cultural affairs officer USIS, Manila, 1956-58; dir. Am. Cultural Ctr., Kyoto, Japan, 1958-63; cultural attache USIS, Tehran, Iran, 1963-66; dep. asst. dir. Office East Asia and Pacific, USIA, Washington, 1966-68, 70-71, asst. dir. Office for Africa, 1968-70; ambassador to Nigeria, 1971-75; asst. sec. state for pub. affairs, 1975-77; dir. USIA, Washington, 1977-78, U.S. Internat. Communication Agy., Washington, 1978-81; acting dir. Smithsonian Mus. African Art, Washington, 1981-83; asst. sec. for history and art Smithsonian Instn., Washington, 1983-84, dir. directorate internat. activities, 1984-87; prof. polit. sci. U. Vt., Burlington, 1987-90, prof. emeritus, 1990—. Served as officer AUS, 1942-46. Mem. MLA, Am. Fgn. Svc. Assn. (v.p. 1969-71). Clubs: Cosmos. Methodist. E-mail: john.reinhardt3@verizon.net.

REINHARDT, JOHN W. dean, dental educator; b. Nashville, Ill. m. Claudia Reinhardt. B in biology, Ill. Wesleyan U., 1971; DDS, Loyola U., 1975; MS in operative dentistry, U. Iowa, 1979; MPH in health services rsch., Harvard U., 1988. Diplomate Am. Bd. Operative Dentistry . With US Army Dental Corps; asst. prof. U. Iowa Coll. Dentistry, 1980—84, assoc. prof., 1984—90, head dept. operative dentistry, 1988—2000, prof., 1990—2000; dean U. Nebr. Med. Ctr. Coll. Dentistry, 2000—, prof. dept. adult restorative dentistry, 2000—. Rschr. in field; cons. NIH, ADA, US Navy, Am. Dental Edn. Assn., Consortium Operative Dentistry Educators, Internat. Assn. Dental Rsch., others.; chair Children's Amalgam Trial Data and Safety Monitoring Bd. Nat. Inst. Dental and Craniofacial Rsch., 1997—. Contbr. articles to profl. pubs., scientific papers, chapters to books. Fellow: Internat. Coll. Dentists, Am. Coll. Dentists; mem.: ADA, Am. Bd. Operative Dentistry, Acad. Operative Dentistry (pres. 1997, chair. bd. dirs. founder's fund 2000—, Award of Excellence 2002). Office: U Nebr Med Ctr Coll Dentistry 40th and Holdrege Streets Box 830740 Lincoln NE 68583-1301*

REINHARDT, STEPHEN ROY, federal judge; b. NYC, Mar. 27, 1931; s. Gottfried and Silvia (Hanlon) Reinhardt; children: Mark, Justin, Dana. BA cum laude, Pomona Coll., 1951; LLB, Yale, 1954. Bar: Calif. 1958. Law clk. to Hon. Luther W. Youngdahl U.S. Dist. Ct., Washington, 1956—57; atty. O'Melveny & Myers, L.A., 1957—59; ptnr. Fogel Julber Reinhardt Rothschild & Feldman LC, L.A., 1959—80; judge U.S. Ct. Appeals (9th cir.), L.A., 1980—. Adj. prof. Loyola Law Sch., LA, 1988—90. Pres. LA Recreation and Parks Commn., 1974—75; active Coliseum Commn., 1974—75, LA Police Commn., 1974—78, pres., 1978—80; sec., exec. organizing com. LA Olympics, 1980—84; exec. com. Dem. Nat. Com., 1969—72; nat. Dem. committeeman State of Calif., 1976—80; bd. dirs. Amateur Athletic Found. L.A, 1984—92. 1st lt. USAF, 1954—56. Mem.: ABA (labor law coun. 1975—77), Calif. Bar Assn., LA County Bar Assn.

REINHARDT, UWE ERNST, economist, educator; b. Osnabrueck, Germany, Sept. 24, 1937; came to U.S., 1964; s. Wilhelm and Edeltraut (Kehne) R.; m. Tsung-mei Cheng, May 25, 1968; children— Dirk, Kara, Mark B.Comm. in Econs. with honors, U. Sask., Saskatoon, Can., 1964; MA in Econs., Yale U., 1965, M.Ph. in Econs., 1967, PhD, 1970; DSc (hon.), Med. Coll. of Pa., 1987, CUNY, 1994, SUNY, 1998. Asst. prof. econs. and pub. affairs Princeton (N.J.) U., 1968-74, assoc. prof., 1974-79, prof., 1979—, James Madison prof. polit. economy, prof. econs., 1984—. Bd. dirs. McAllister Holdings; trustee Tchrs. Ins. and Annuity Assn., 1978-93, H&Q Health Fund; cons. Urban Inst., Washington, 1971-75, HEW, 1974—, HHS, Math., Inc., Princeton, 1970-80, AT&T, Basking Ridge, N.J., 1976-82, Nat. Westminster Bank USA, N.Y.C., 1979—, mem. Nat. Leadership Commn. Health Care, 1986—; mem. spl. adv. bd. VA, 1981-85; mem. U.S. Physicians' Payment Rev. Commn., U.S. Congress, 1986—; pres. Assn. for Health Svcs. Rsch., 1989-90, Found. Health Svcs. Rsch., 1990-91; mem. bd. advisors Nat. Inst. Healthcare Mgmt., 1993—, Pew Health Professions Commn., 1997—; mem. Coun. Econ. Impact Health Reform, 1994—; mem. external adv. panel health and nutrition World Bank, 1997—; chair coordinating com. Commonwealth Fund Internat. Program Health Policy, 1998—; commr. Kaiser Commn. Medicaid and Uninsured; trustee Duke U. Health Sys., Triad Hosps., Inc., Medcast/WebMD. Author: Physician Productivity and the Demand for Health Manpower, 1975; mem. editorial bd. Health Affairs, 1982—, New Eng. Jour. Medicine, 1989-92, Health Mgmt. Quar., Health Policy and Edn., Milbank Meml. Quar., Jour. AMA, 1991—; assoc. editor Jour. Health Econs., 1980-85, mem. editorial bd., 1981-83; contbr. articles to profl. jours. Bd. dirs. Nat. Acad. Aging, 1993—. Mem. Nat. Inst. Health Care Mgmt., Inst. Medicine Nat. Acad. Scis. (gov. council 1979-82) Office: Princeton U Woodrow Wilson Sch Prof of Economics & Public Affairs 412 Robertson Hl Princeton NJ 08544-0001

REINHARDT, WILLIAM PARKER, chemical physicist, educator; b. San Francisco, May 22, 1942; s. William Oscar and Elizabeth Ellen (Parker) R.; m. Katrina Hawley Currens, Mar. 14, 1979; children: James William, Alexander Hawley. BS in Basic Chemistry, U. Calif., Berkeley, 1964; AM in Chemistry, Harvard U., 1966, PhD in Chem. Physics, 1968; MA (hon.), U. Pa., 1985. Instr. chemistry Harvard U., 1967-69, asst. prof. chemistry, 1969-72, assoc. prof., 1972-74; prof. U. Colo., Boulder, 1974-84, chmn. dept. chemistry, 1977-80; prof. chemistry U. Pa., Phila., 1984-91, chmn. dept., 1985-88, D. Michael Crow prof., 1987-91; prof. chemistry U.Wash., Seattle, 1991—, assoc. chmn. undergrad. program, 1993-96, Adj prof. physics U. Wash., Seattle, 1998—; vis. fellow Joint Inst. for Lab. Astrophysics of Nat. Bur. Stds. and U. Colo., 1972, 74, fellow, 1974-84; dir. Telluride Summer Rsch. Ctr., 1986-89, treas., 1989-93; com. on atomic, molecular and optical scis. NRC, 1988-90; sub com. Internat. Union Pure and Applied Physics, Atomic Molecular Physics, 2002—; vis. scientist Nat. Inst. Stds. and Tech., summers 1993—; vis. prof. chemistry U. Melbourne, Australia, 1997, Harvard U., 1998, Davidson Lectr., U. Kans., 2000; Kohler lectr. U. Calif., Riverside, 2002; R.S. Berry pub. lectr. Telluride, Colo., 2004. Mem. editl. bd. Phys. Rev. A., 1979-81, Chem. Physics, 1985-94, Jour. Chem. Physics, 1987-89, Jour. Physics B (U.K.), 1992—, Internat. Jour. Quantum Chemistry, 1994-2001, Digital Libr. of Math. Functions, 1999—; rschr. theoretical chem. physics, theoretical atomic and molecular physics for numerous publs. Recipient Camille and Henry Dreyfus Tchr. Scholar award, 1972; Alfred P. Sloan fellow, 1972; J.S. Guggenheim Meml. fellow, 1978; Coun. on Rsch. and Creative Work faculty fellow, 1978; Wilsmore fellow U. Melbourne (Australia), 1997; J.W. Fulbright sr. scholar, Australia, 1997. Fellow AAAS, Am. Phys. Soc., Inst. Physics (U.K.), Phi Beta Kappa; mem. Am. Chem. Soc., Sigma Xi (nat. lectr. 1980-82), Phi Lambda Upsilon (Fresenius award 1977), Phi Beta Kappa (vis. scholar 2002-03). Office: U Wash Dept Chemistry Box 351700 Seattle WA 98195-1700 E-mail: rein@chem.washington.edu.

REINHART, ANNE CHRISTINE, special education educator, consultant; b. Detroit, Mar. 9, 1950; m. Charles Reinhart; children: Kim Meredith, Ted Justin. BS, Ea. Mich. U., 1972; MA, U. Detroit, 1977. Cert. spl. edn., Mich. Spl. edn. tchr. for emotionally impaired State of Mich. Hosp., Pontiac, Berkley (Mich.) Sch. Dist, 1976—. Co-chair ASSET (support group for gifted and talented students), Birmingham, Mich., 1996-98; com. mem. Mich. Dept. of Edn., Office of Spl. Edn.; particpant Mich Pilot Study grant Quality Assurance Rev., 2000-03. Grantee, Dept. Spl. Edn., Mich., 2000—03. Mem. Kappa Delta Pi. Avocations: writing, tutoring, visiting other sch. sites in country. Home: 25925 Romany Way Franklin MI 48025-1909

REINHART, CHARLES LAWRENCE, performing company executive; b. Summit, N.J., Dec. 5, 1930; s. Albert and Rose Belle (Goldstein) R.; m. Molly Moore, Jan., 1967 (div. 1974); children: Taylor, Adam; m. Stephanie Reinhart, July, 1987; 1 child, Ariane; m. Patricia Reinhart, 1953 (div. 1962); 1 child, Scott. BA, Rutgers U., 1952; postgrad., U. Copenhagen, 1955-56; DFA (hon.), Duke U., 2003. Pres. Am. Dance Festival, Durham, NC, 1968—, co-dir., 1993—2002; co-artistic dir. for dance Kennedy Ctr., Washington, 1996—2002, artistic dir. for dance, 2002—04. Mem. dance panel Guggenheim Found., 1973-85; producer numerous NYC dance events including City Ctr. Spring Dance Festival, 1969-73, dance seasons at Anta Theater & City Ctr. for Music and Drama, 1968-73, Dance Repertory Season at Billy Rose Theatre, 1969; developer, nat. coord. NEA Dance Touring Program, 1967-78, NEA Artists-in-Schs. program, 1970-81; organizer cultural presentation program U.S. Dept. State, 1966; mem. adv. com. Asia Soc. Performing Arts program, 1970; dir. Jacob's Pillow Dance Festival, 1974; bd. dirs. Theatre Devel. Fund, Anglo-Am. Contemporary Dance Found., Internat. Theatre Inst., Japan Soc. Performing Arts Com.; co-exec. prodr. PBS Series Free to Dance: The African American Presence in Modern Dance, 2001 (Emmy award, 2001). Cpl. U.S. Army, 1952-53, Korea. Decorated officer Order Arts and Letters comdr. Order Arts and Letters (France); recipient Morrison award, 1985, Dance/USA Honors for lifetime achievement in dance, 1994, Capezio Dance award, 1996, Diaghilev award, 1997, Dance Notation Bur. Svc. award, 1999, Dance Mag. award, 2003. Office: Am Dance Festival 1697 Broadway Rm 900 New York NY 10019 Office Phone: 212-586-1925. E-mail: clr@americandancefestival.org.

REINHART, DIETRICH THOMAS, academic administrator, social studies educator; b. Mpls., May 17, 1949; s. Donald Irving and Eleanor Therese (Noonan) R. BA in History, St. John's U., Collegeville, Minn., 1971; AM in History, Brown U., 1976, PhD in History, 1984. Benedictine monk St. John's Abbey, 1971—; prof. history St. John's U., 1981—, dean of the coll., 1988-91, pres., 1991—. Dir. liturgy St. John's Abbey, 1983-88. Bd. dirs. Minn. Pvt. Coll. Coun., 1991—, George A. MacPherson Fund, 1991—, Hill Monastic Manuscript Library, 1991—, Inst. for Ecumenical and Cultural Rsch., 1991—, First Am. Nat. Bank St. Cloud., 1992—; bd. overseers St. John's Prep. Sch., 1990—. Home: St Johns Abbey Collegeville MN 56321 Office: St John's U Office of Pres Collegeville MN 56321

REINHART, JOHN BELVIN, retired child and adolescent psychiatrist, educator; b. Merrill, Wis., Dec. 22, 1917; s. Dabney Belvin and Ann (Toomey) R.; m. Helen Elsen Reinhart, Jan. 3, 1949; children: Peter, Catherine, Ann, John, Frederick, Andrew. BA, Duke U., 1939; MD, Bowman Gray Sch. Medicine, Winston-Salem, N.C., 1943. Diplomate Am. Bd. Pediatrics, Am. Bd. Psychiatry in child and adolescent psychiatry. Instr. pediatrics Bowman Gray Sch. Medicine, Winston-Salem, 1950-52; asst. prof., assoc. prof., prof. pediatrics and psychiatry U. Pitts. Sch. Medicine, 1956-83, emeritus prof. pediatrics, 1983—; clin. prof. psychiatry Bowman Gray Sch. Medicine, Winston-Salem, 1986-99, ret., 1999—. Co-Author: A Baby's First Year, 1956. Capt. M.C. AUS, 1946-48. Roman Catholic. Avocations: reading, golf, tennis, travel. Home: 34 Hunters Ln Hendersonville NC 28791-1665

REINHART, KELLEE CONNELY, journalist; b. Kearney, Nebr., Dec. 15, 1951; d. Vaughn Eugene and Mary Jo (Mullen) Connely; m. Stephen Wayne Reinhart, June 15, 1974; children: Keegan Connely, Channing Mullen. BA, U. Ala., 1972, MS, 1974. Advt. copywriter Stas. WTBC-AM, WUOA-FM, 1970-72; asst. mgr. Ala. Press Assn., 1972-74; asst. to the editor Antique Monthly mag., 1974-75, mng. editor, 1975-77; editorial dir. Antique Monthly and Horizons mags., 1977-89; dir. univ. rels. U. Ala. System, Tuscaloosa, 1989—. Editor: Wild Birds of America: The Art of Basil Ede, 1991, Centennial Memories, Millennial Hopes, 2000, The People's City, 2003. Bd. dirs. Ala. Humanities Found.; bd. dirs. Ala. Writers Forum, pres., 1999—2001. Recipient Druids Arts award, 1995. Mem. Soc. Profl. Journalists, Am. Soc. Mag. Editors, Newcomen Soc. U.S., Art Table, XXI/U. Ala. Women's Hon. Soc. Office: 401 Queen City Ave Tuscaloosa AL 35401 1551 Office Phone: 205-348-5938. Business E-Mail: kreinhar@uasystem.ua.edu.

REINHART, MARY ANN, medical board executive; b. Jackson, Mich., Aug. 14, 1942; d. Herbert Martin and Josephine Marie (Keyes) Conway; m. David Lee Reinhart, Dec. 28, 1963; children: Stephen Paul, Michael David. MA, Mich. State U., 1983, PhD, 1985. Rsch. asst. Mich. State U., East Lansing, 1979-82, 85, teaching asst. dept psychology, 1982-84, asst. prof. Office Med. Edn. R&D, Coll. Human Medicine, 1985-88; assoc. exec. dir. Am. Bd. Emergency Medicine, East Lansing, 1988-95, dep. exec. dir., 1995-2000, exec. dir., 2000—. Cons. Am. Bd. Emergency Medicine, 1985—88; chairperson collegewide evaluation com. Coll. Human Medicine, Mich. State U., East Lansing, 1985—88; adj. asst. prof. Office Med. Edn. R&D, Coll. Human Medicine, 1988—2000. Reviewer Annals of Emergency Medicine, 1987-95, Acad. Emergency Medicine, 1995-99. Bd. dirs. Neahtawanta Rsch. and Edn. Ctr., Traverse City, Mich., 1991—. Mem. APA (divsn. indsl./orgnl. psychology, health psychology), Phi Kappa Phi. Achievements include application of chart stimulated recall method of assessment in a national medical recertification examination; development and implementation of national longitudinal study of emergency medicine residents and emergency physicians. Office: Am Bd Emergency Medicine 3000 Coolidge Rd East Lansing MI 48823-6319

REINHART, PETER SARGENT, corporate executive, lawyer; b. Mineola, N.Y., May 17, 1950; s. Charles Woodham and Martha Way (Sargent) R.; m. Susan Stockwell, Aug. 29, 1970 (div. Jan. 1976); 1 child, Amy Lynn; m. Gale McElroy, Oct. 16, 1976 (div. May 1985); 1 child, James Gharrett; m. Carol O. Gaffney, Jan. 4, 1992 (div. Jan. 2001). BA, Franklin and Marshall Coll., 1971; JD, Rutgers U., 1975. Bar: N.J. 1975. Atty. Pillsbury and Russell, Atlantic Highlands, N.J., 1975-78; corp. counsel K. Hovnanian Enterprises, Inc., Red Bank, N.J., 1978-81, sr. v.p., gen. counsel, 1981—; also bd. dirs. Pres. Inst. Multi-Family Housing, Plainsboro, N.J., 1989-90. Trustee, mem. editorial bd. Housing N.J. mag., 1991—. Trustee Community Assns. Inst., Arlington, Va., pres. N.J. chpt., 1988; trustee Assn. for Children of N.J., Newark, 1988-93, Keep Middlesex Moving, New Brunswick, 1990-93, Bayshore Cmty. Hosp., Holmdel, N.J., 1992-01, v.p., 1995, chmn., 1997, Meridian Hosp. Corp., 2002—; chmn. Jersey Shore Partnership, 2003—; pres. Greater Red Bank Jaycees, 1978-79, Atlantic Highlands Rep. Club, 1978; v.p. Monmouth coun. Boy Scouts Am., Oakhurst, N.J., 1987-94, pres., 1994-95; v.p. Garden State Games, Edison, N.J., 1991-94; mem. Coun. Affordable Housing, Trenton, N.J., 1993—. Named to Community Assns. Inst. Hall of Fame, 1988; named Jaycee of Yr. Greater Red Bank Jaycees, 1977. Mem. N.J. State Bar Assn., N.J. Shore Builders Assn. (pres. 1989-90, Builder of Yr. 1987, Hall of Fame 1991), Nat. Assn. Indsl. and Office Parks (bd. dirs. 1990-92), N.J. Builders Assn. (v.p. 1992-94, pres. 1995-96, Builder of Yr. award 1995, Shore Athletic Club (Oakhurst), Ea. Monmouth C. of C. (trustee 1992-98, Vol. of Yr. 1995). Avocations: road racing, marathon running, golf. Office: Hovnanian Enterprises Inc PO Box 500 10 Hwy 35 Red Bank NJ 07701-5902

REINHART, RICHARD PAUL, lawyer; b. Cleve., Sept. 1, 1954; s. Richard A. and Carole F. (Kaspar) R.; m. Debra Rae Hitchcock, June 20, 1976; children: Geoffrey, Richelle Marie. BA with honors, Rollins Coll., 1976; JD with distinction, Emory U., 1979. Bar: Ga. 1979, Fla. 1980. Ptnr. Morris, Manning & Martin, Atlanta, 1979-89; officer McMillen Reinhart and Voght, P.A., Orlando, Fla., 1989—, also bd. dirs. Mem. ABA, ATLA, Fla. Bar Assn., Ga. Bar Assn., Orange County Bar Assn., Acad. Fla. Trial Lawyers, Order of Coif, Omicron Delta Kappa. Office: McMillen Reinhart and Voght PA PA 111 N Orange Ave Ste 1450 Orlando FL 32801-4641 E-mail: reinhart@floridamalpractice.com.

REINHART, ROBERT ROUNTREE, JR., lawyer; b. Chgo., Oct. 21, 1947; s. Robert Rountree and Ruth (Duncan) R.; m. Elizabeth Aileen Plews, July 26, 1969; children: Andrea Jean, Jessica Elizabeth, Rebecca Jill. BA, Northwestern U., 1968; JD, U. Mich., 1971. Bar: Ill. 1971, Mich. 1972, Minn. 1973, U.S. Supreme Ct. 1976. Law clk. to judge U.S. Dist. Ct. (we. dist.) Mich., Grand Rapids, 1971-73; assoc. Oppenheimer Wolff & Donnelly, Mpls., 1973-77, ptnr., 1978-96, chair labor and employment bus. group, 1985-92; ptnr. Dorsey & Whitney, Mpls., 1996—, chair labor and employment practice group, 2000—. Co-chmn. Upper Midwest Employment Law Inst., Mpls., 1984—; gen. counsel Minn. Empoyment Law Coun., 1990—. Mem. ABA (labor and employment, civil litigation sects.), Minn. Bar Assn. Office: Dorsey & Whitney Ste 1500 50 S 6th St Minneapolis MN 55402-1498 E-mail: reinhart.robert@dorseylaw.com.

REINHART, WALTER JOSEF, finance educator; b. N.Y.C., Oct. 9, 1943; s. Julius J. and Augusta M. R.; children: Aaron, Kyle, Richard, Sadie. A of Engring. with honors, Bridgeport Engring. Inst., 1967; BSAE, BSME, Okla. State U., 1969, MBA, 1971; PhD in Fin., U. N.C., 1977. Mgmt. trainee IBM, Armonk, N.Y., 1964-66; engr. Pitney Bowes, Stanford, Conn., 1967-68; supr. Corning Glass, Muskogee, Okla., 1969-70; cons. Theodore Barry & Assocs., L.A., 1971-72; instr. Duke U., Durham, N.C., 1974-75; asst. prof. Va. Tech., Blacksburg, 1975-78; assoc. prof. Fla. State U., Tallahassee, 1978-84, Loyola Coll., Balt., 1984—, academic dir. Master of Sci. in Fin. prog. Prin. Reinhart & Assocs., Hunt Valley, Md., 1971—; vis. prof. Assumption U., Bangkok, Thailand, 1994, 95; Fulbright scholar U. Passau, Germany, 2003-04. Author: Portfolio Management Theory and Application, 1997; contbr. articles to profl. jours. Organizer Top of Fla., Tallahassee, 1981-84; leader Boy Scouts Am., Balt., 1984-97. English Speaking Union fellow, Oxford, England, 1989; named Vol. of Yr., Tallahassee, 1984. Mem. Am. Fin. Assn., Am. Inst. Decision Scis., Fla. Econs. Club, Fla. Govt. Fin. Officers Assn., So. Fin. Assn. (v.p. 1997-98, 2003—, bd. dirs. 2000-02), Engring. Soc. Balt. (life), Fin. Mgmt. Assn., Ea. Fin. Assn. (v.p. 2001-02), Elks, Tallahassee C. of C., Beta Gamma Sigma. Office: Loyola Coll 2034 Greenspring Dr Timonium MD 21093-4114 E-mail: Reinhart@Loyola.edu.

REINHARZ, JEHUDA, academic administrator, history educator; b. Haifa, Israel, Aug. 1, 1944; came to U.S., 1961; s. Fred and Anita (Weigler) R.; m. Shulamit Rothschild, Nov. 26, 1967; children— Yael, Naomi BS, Columbia U., 1967; BRE, Jewish Theol. Sem., 1967; MA, Harvard U., 1968; PhD, Brandeis U., 1972; LHD (hon.), Hebrew Union Coll., 1995; DHL (hon.), Jewish Theol. Soc. Am., 1996, Fairfield U., 1999. Prof. modern Jewish history U. Mich., Ann Arbor, 1972—82; Richard Koret prof. modern Jewish history Brandeis U., Waltham, Mass., 1982—84, dir. Tauber Inst. Study of European Jewry, 1984—94; provost, sr. v.p. for acad. affairs Brandeis U., Waltham, Mass., 1992—94; pres. Brandeis U., Waltham, Mass., 1994—. Mem. internat. acad. bd. Annenberg Rsch. Inst., 1986-90; bd. dirs. Yad Chaim Weizmann, 1990-2000, Internat. Editl. Bd. Pardès, 1996—; pres. Israel Prize, 1990, Akiba award, Am.-Jewish Com., 1996. Author: Fatherland or Promised Land: The Dilemma of the German Jew 1893-1914, 1975, Chaim Weizmann: The Making of a Zionist Leader, 1985 (Present Tense Literary award 1985, Kenneth B. Smilen Literary award 1985, Nat. Jewish Book award 1986, Shazar prize in history Israel, 1988), (in Hebrew) Hashomer Hazair in Germany, 1931-39, 1989, Chaim Weizmann: The Making of a Statesman, 1993 (Nat. Jewish Book award 1994); also numerous articles in French, German, Hebrew and English; co-author: Zionism and the Creation of a New Society, 1998, 2d edit., 2000, The Era of Political Zionism, 2000; gen. editor: Studies in Jewish History, 1984, European Jewish History, 1985; co-editor: The Jew in the Modern World, 1980, 2d edit. 1995, Mystics, Philosophers and Politicians, 1982, Israel in the Middle East 1948-83, 1984, The Jewish Response to German Culture, 1985, The Jews of Poland Between Two World Wars, 1989, The Impact of Western Nationalisms, 1992, Zionism and Religion, Hebrew edit., 1994, Essential Papers on Zionism, 1996; editor: The Letters and Papers of Chaim Weizmann, 1918-20, 1977, Dokumente zur Geschichte des deutschen Zionismus, 1882-1933, 1981, Living with Antisemitism, 1987. Bd. govs. United Israel Appeal/Jewish Agy., 1994, 2000; bd. dirs., mem. exec. com. Am. Joint Distbn. Com., 1994-2002; mem. acad. com. U.S. Holocaust Mus., 1990-2003, mem. com. on conscience nat. adv. forum, 1996—; mem. Presdl. Adv. Commn. on Holocaust Assets in U.S., 1998-2000; mem. Commn. on Israel-Diaspora Rels., 1996-97; trustee Am. Hebrew Acad., Greensboro, N.C., 2000—. Recipient Akiba award, Am. Jewish Com., 1996. Fellow Leo Baeck Inst., Royal Hist. Soc., Am. Acad. Jewish Rsch., Am. Acad. Arts and Scis.; mem. Yad Vashem Soc. (adv. bd. 1983), Nat. Coun. Shazar Ctr., Assn. for Jewish Studies (sec. 1986-88, treas./sec., 1988-94), Coun. on Fgn. Rels. Home: 66 Beaumont Ave Newton MA 02460-2331 Office: Office Of The Pres Irving Enclave 113 415 South St # Ms100 Waltham MA 02453-9110 E-mail: jreinharz@brandeis.edu.

REINHERZ, HELEN ZARSKY, researcher, social services educator; b. Boston, Aug. 4, 1923; d. Zachary and Anna (Cohen) Zarsky; m. Samuel E. Reinherz, Aug. 29, 1943; 1 son, Ellis. AB magna cum laude, Wheaton Coll., 1944; MS, Simmons Coll., 1946; S.M., Harvard U., 1962, Sc.D., 1965. Social worker Newton Family Service, Mass., 1946-49, Mass. Gen. Hosp., Boston, 1949-51; supr. psychiat. social work State Hosp., Waltham, Mass., 1958-61; faculty mem. Simmons Coll., Boston, 1965—, prof. methods rsch., 1972—, dir. research Sch. Social Work, 1968-93, dir. PhD program, 1993-96. Prin. investigator Identifying Children at Risk, 1976—84, Adaption in Adolescence, 1987—93, Adult Rsch. Project, 1998—2001, Early Adulthood Rsch. Project, 1993—97, Simms Longitudinal Study, 2001—, Study Adolescent Drug Abuse, 1971—73; rsch. cons. Dept. Mental Health, 1970—80; chmn. Gov.'s Adv. Coun. on Mental Health and Retardation, 1972; mem. adv. com. Mental Health Manpower fo Fed. Govt., 1980—82. Author (with H. Wechler, D. Dobbins): Social Work Research in the Human Services, 1976; author: (with M. Heywood, J. Camp) A Community Response to Drug Abuse, 1976; cons., assoc. editor: Jour. Prevention, 1980—91, mem. fed. adv. com.: Rsch. in Prevention Rev., 1984—87, editl. bd., Jour. Early Adolescence, cons. editor. NASW Jour.; contbr. articles to profl. jours. Recipient Maida H. Solomon award Simmons Coll. Alumni, 1961; NIH tng. fellow, 1961-65; Grant Found. grantee, 1963; Med. Found. grantee, 1967-69; NIMH grantee, 1975-84, 87—. Fellow Am. Orthopyschiat. Assn.; mem. Acad. Cert. Social Workers, Am. Pub. Health Assn., Council Social Work Edn., Harvard Sch. Pub. Health Alumni Assn. (sec.-treas. 1965-68), Phi Beta Kappa, Delta Omega. Home: 17 Corey Rd Malden MA 02148-1116 Office: Simmons Sch Social Work 300 The Fenway Boston MA 02115 Office Phone: 617-521-3934. E-mail: helen.reinherz@simmons.edu. *As a teacher and researcher my efforts have been directed towards encouraging students to formulate the right questions about human problems as a first step to understanding and change.*

REINHOLD, RICHARD LAWRENCE, lawyer; b. Buffalo, Feb. 24, 1951; s. Richard J. and Ann J. R.; m. Beth Stacey Grossman, May 11, 1991; children: Elizabeth Jane, Eleanor Terese, Rebecca Hope. AB, Cornell U., 1973; JD, SUNY, Buffalo, 1976. Bar: N.Y. 1977, Fla. 1977. With office of tax legis. counsel U.S. Dept. Treasury, Washington, 1982-84; ptnr., head tax dept. Willkie Farr & Gallagher, N.Y.C., 1985—. Contbr. articles to profl. jours. Bd. dirs. The Adirondack Coun.; mem. dean's adv. coun. sch. of law SUNY, Buffalo. Fellow Am. Coll. of Tax Counsel; mem. N.Y. State Bar Assn. (chair tax sect. 1996-97), Internat. Fiscal Assn., Tax Forum, Tax Club, Am. Alpine Club. Office: Willkie Farr & Gallagher 787 7th Ave New York NY 10019-6099

REINHORN, ANDREI M. civil structural engineering educator, consultant; b. Bucharest, Romania, Oct. 23, 1945; s. Moritz A. and Dina (Rosenfeld) Reinhorn; m. Tova A. Waldman, Oct. 15, 1968; children: Michael, Gad. BSc, Technion - Israel Inst. Tech., Haifa, 1968, DSc, 1978. Registered profl. engr., N.Y., Israel. Structural engr. Milstein & Singer, Cons. Engrs., Tel Aviv, 1972-73, Haifa, 1973-79, Buffalo, 1980-85, Reinhorn Consulting Engrs., 1990—; vis. asst. prof. U. Buffalo, 1979-81, asst. prof., 1981-86, assoc. prof., 1986-90, prof., 1990—2002; chmn. dept. civil engring. SUNY, Buffalo, 1996-99, eminent prof., 2002—. Assoc. editor: Structures Jour., 2000—; Spectra Jour., 2002; author: conf. procs.; contbr. chapters to books. Capt. Israel Def. Force, 1968—72. Grantee rsch., NSF, 1983—84, 1986—95, 1994—. Fellow: ASCE (faculty advisor 1981—83, bd. dirs. 1986—96, pres. Buffalo sect. 1993—94, Outstanding Svc. award 1982, 1983); mem.: G.E. Brown Jr. Network Earthquake Engring. Simulation (bd. dirs. 2003—), N.Y. State Profl. Engring. Assn. (Engring. Educator of Yr. award 1991, Hist. Achievement award 1995, Engr. of Yr. 2002), Nat. Ctr. for Earthquake Engring. Rsch. (Outstanding Achievement award L.A. Tall Bldg. Coun. 1995), Earthquake Engring. Rsch. Inst., Am. Concrete Inst. Achievements include invention of press brake deflection compensation structure, automatic diagnosic sys. for elec. cir. breakers; patents for. Avocations: photography, skiing, bicycling, scuba diving. Home: 12 Troy View Ln Buffalo NY 14221-3522 Office: SUNY Buffalo Civil Struct/Environ Engrg 231 Ketter Hall Buffalo NY 14260-4300 E-mail: reinhorn@buffalo.edu.

REINHOUDT, JOHANNES FEIKE, pharmaceutical industry executive; b. Kamperland, Zeeland, The Netherlands, Nov. 24, 1962; s. Isaak and Atje (Van Netten) R.; m. Jacomina Apolonia Maria Huige, Oct. 28, 1983; 1 child, Jurgen Raymond. Student nursing, Sch. voor Verpleegkundigen, The Netherlands, 1984; Nurse Anesthetist, Acad. Hosp. Leiden, The Netherlands, 1987. RN, RN anesthetist. Nurse trainee Found. Oosterschelde Hosps., Goes, The Netherland, 1980-85; nurse anesthetist trainee Acad. Hosp. Leiden (The Netherlands), 1985-88; rsch. nurse Pharma Bio-Rsch. Internat., Zuidlaren, The Netherlands, 1988; hosp. product specialist Rhône-Poulenc Pharma B.V., Amstelveen, 1988-89; clin. rsch. assoc., clin. rsch. assoc.-mgr. Rhône-Poulenc Rorer B.V., Amstelveen, The Netherlands, 1989-92; area rsch. cons. Medinet, Breda, The Netherlands, 1992-93; mgr. affiliate liaison, coordination Rhône-Poulenc Rorer SA, Antony, France, 1993-96, sr. mgr. world-wide affiliate liaison and coordination, 1996-97, sr. mgr. world-wide clin. devel. ops., 1997—2000; dir. corp. clin. ops. Aventis Behring GmbH, LLC, King of Prussia, Pa., 2001—03; dir. men's and women's health, clin. ops. TAP Pharmaceutical Products, Inc., Lake Forest, Ill. Initiator Good Clin. Practice platform, The Netherlands, 1991-92. Mem. Am. Mgmt. Assn., Am. Soc. Law, Medicine and Ethics, Drug Info. Assn., Assn. Clin. Rsch. Profls., Am. Soc. of Law Medicine and Ethics Avocation: reading. Address: 510 Capital Ln Gurnee IL 60031-4495

REINICHE, DOMINIQUE, food products executive; With Procter & Gamble, Kraft Jacobs Suchard, Coca-Cola Enterprises, 1992—, pres. French divsn., 1998—2003, sr. v.p., pres. European group, 2003—. Office: Coca-Cola Enterprises 2500 Windy Ridge Pkwy Atlanta GA 30339

REINIKE, IRMA, retired writer, artist, poet, lyricist; b. White Harbor, Long Beach, Miss., Oct. 20, 1927; d. Chester Henry and Edna Claire (Latille) R.; children: Harvey Franklin Linn Shows Jr., George David Shows, Thelma Jewell Shows Hoffman. Student, St. Mary's Dominican Coll.; grad., North Light Art Sch., Cin., 1996, 97, 99. Freelance writer, student Famous Writers Sch., Westport, Conn., 1965—69; freelance writer New Orleans, Long Beach, Miss. Author: Mystery, 1940—41, Long Beach Movie Personality, 1949, My Beach, 1990, Thelma, 1991, (poetry) My Lady of Medjugorje, 1987—88, Irma Reinike Poetry-Book 1, 2000—01, I Love My Flag, 2000, numerous poems; columnist Round the Town, Long Beach, Miss., 1963—66, The Illustrated Press, Irma Reinike's Personality Parade, New Orleans, 1952; composer: (songs) See You Tomorrow, 1995—96, Days of Love, 1997, The Blue of Your Eyes, 1997, others, (stage play) Ethel Chichester, Peg O' My Heart, Kaye Hamilton, Stage Door, 1949, Song, Dance Dixieland Minstrel and Variety Artists, 1950—52, Charity Performer, Le Petit Theatre de Vieux Carre' Sunday Salon, 1996, Destruction by Hurricane Camille, Times Picayune, 1970; Introduction Camille Book-Hurricane, 1969, exhibitions include Artworks books, St. Thomas, 1992, Represented in permanent collections St. Thomas Ch. Mem. Nat. Rep. Senatorial Com., 1994-97; mem. Nat. Rep. Congl. Com., 2000; mem. La. Libr. Found., New Orleans Friends of Pub. Libr., 1994-96; charter mem. World War II Monument Meml., Washington. Honored Author, La. Libr. Assn., 1994, 96, La. State Librarian, 1995, Friends Fest New Orleans Pub. Libr., 1994-96, Patron Le Petit Theatre de Vieux Carre, 1996. Mem.: Long Beach Hist. Soc. Republican. Roman Catholic. Avocations: fine arts, songwriting, poetry, lyricist.

REINING, PRISCILLA COPELAND, anthropologist; b. Chgo., Mar. 11, 1923; d. Kenneth Bayard and Mary Elsie (Weser) Copeland; m. Conrad Copeland Reining, June 26, 1944 (dec. Oct. 1984); children: Robert Cushman, Anne Elizabeth, Conrad Copeland Schilling. AB, U. Chgo., 1945, AM, 1949, PhD, 1967. Lectr. U. Minn., Mpls., 1956-60, Howard U., Washington,

1960-65; rsch. assoc. Cath. U. Am., Washington, 1966-68; assoc. Smithsonian Instn., Washington, 1966, 68, 70; cons. The World Bank, 1972, USAID, 1973, AAAS, Washington, 1971-73, project dir., 1974-81, program dir., 1982-90; vis. prof. African Studies U. Fla., Gainesville, 1994—. Mem. bd. on sci. and tech. for internat. devel. NAS, Washington, 1976-80; mem. arid ecosys. interation Internat. Geosphere/Biosphere Program, Boulder, 1989—; mem. adv. bd. Population and Environ., N.Y.C., 1990—; bd. dirs. Renewable Natural Resources Found., Bethesda, Md., 1991—, Pub. Interest mem. Renewable Natural Resources Found. (RNRF) bd., 1999.; mem. U.S. del. UN Conf. on Desertification, Nairobi, Kenya, 1977. Author: Challenging Desertification, 1980; author, editor: Village Women, 1977; editor: Village Viability, 1980, Resource Inventory, 1984. Mem. Peace Commn. Washington Cathedral, 1986-91. Grantee NIMH, 1966, NSF, 1967, Nat. Geographic Soc. Com. for Rsch. and Exploration, 1994 Fellow AAAS (sec. 1978-89), Am. Anthrop. Assn. (task force on AIDS, task force on environ., Disting. Svc. award 1990), African Studies Assn. (bd. dirs. 1978-80); mem. Anthrop. Soc. Washington (pres. 1976-77), Soc. Women Geographers (triennial presenter 1996); chairperson planning com. renewable natural resources found. Congress, 1998. Home: 3601 Rittenhouse St NW Washington DC 20015-2413

REININGHAUS, RUTH, retired artist; b. NYC, Oct. 4, 1922; d. Emil William and Pauline Rosa (Lazarik) R.; m. George H. Morales, Feb. 20, 1944; children: George James, Robert Charles; m. Allan Joseph Smith, May 28, 1960. Student, Hunter Coll., NYU, Nat. Acad. Sch. of Design, 1960-61, Frank Reilly Sch. of Art, 1963, Art Students League, 1964, 68; studied oil painting, with Robert Beverly Hale and Robert Philips, with Morton Roberts and Frank Reilly, Robert Maione, with Rudy Colao. Instr. art Banker's Trust, N.Y.C., 1971-77, 79-99, Kittredge Club for Women, N.Y.C., 1967-77. Exhibited in group shows at Berkshire Art Mus., 1970s, Hammer Galleries, Inc., N.Y.C., 1974, Far Gallery, N.Y.C., 1974, Mufalli Gallery, N.Y. and Fla., 1983-90, Pen and Brush Club, 1985—, Petrucci Gallery, Saugerties, N.Y., 1988-94, Pastel Soc. Am., 1988—, John Lane Gallery, Rhinebeck, N.Y., 1992-97, Regianni Gallery, N.Y.C., 1994, Catherine Lorillard Wolfe Club, Salmagundi Club, Allied Artists Am., Heidi Newhoff Gallery, N.Y.C., Hudson Valley Art Assn., Knickerbocker Artists, N.Y.C., Pen & Brush Club Inc., Pastel Soc. Am., Heritage Mus.; represented in permanent collections at US Navy Art, US Coast Guard Art Program, Hon. Murtogh D. Guinness; contbr. to popular mags. Recipient 3d prize in Oils, Murray Hill Art Show, 1966, 68; Washington Sq. Outdoor Art Exhibit scholar Nat. Acad., 1960, Frank Reilly Sch. Art, 1963, NYU, 1968, Talens award, 1963, Robert Lehman award, 1968, Richtone Artists award, 1968, Baker Brush award, 1969, Salmagund scholar, 1969; subject NBC TV show You Are an Artist, 1950s. Fellow: Hudson Valley Art Assn. (Claude Parson's Meml. award 1970), Am. Artists Profl. League (Claude Parsons Meml. award 1974, 2d prize oils 1992, 3d prize pastel 1993, Pres. award 1994); mem.: Knickerbocker Artists (Flora B. Giffuni PSA Pres.' award 1990), Oil Pastel Assn. (Pen and Brush award 1987, Strathmore award 1989, Pen and Brush award 1990, Salmagundi Club award 1991), Washington Sq. Outdoor Art Assn. (bd. dirs. 1983—90), Allied Artists Am. (assoc.), Nat. Arts Club (Reciprocal) Artists Fellowship, Soc. Illustrators (hon. 1983—87), Pastel Soc. Am. (bd. dirs. 1988—90, J. Giffuni purchase award 1988, Pastel Soc. of West Coast award 1997), Salmagundi Club N.Y (pres. 1983—87, curator 1989—97, Philip Isenberg award 1974, Salmagundi Club prize 1985, Franklin B. Williams Fund prize 1987, Tom Picard award 1987, Mortimer E. Freehof award 1988, John N. Lewis award 1988—89, Philip Isenberg award 1989—90, Medal of Honor 1989, Helen S. Coes award 1990, Flora B. Giffuni Pres. award 1990, Thomas Moran award 1990, Samuel T. Shaw award 1990, Alice B. McReynolds award 1991, Alphaeus Cole Meml. award 1991, Salmagundi award 1991, Alice B. McReynolds Meml. award 1991, Philip Isenberg award 1992, 1995, Harry Ballinger Meml. award 2000—01, Philip Isenberg award 2001, Jane Impastato award 2003), Pen and Brush Club (Helen Slotman award 1986, OPA Internat. award 1987, Gene Alden Walker award 1988, Pen and Brush Solo award 1992, Margaret Sussman award 1996, 1998, Merit award 2000), Catharine Lorillard Wolfe Art Club (bd. dirs. 1987—, Anna Hyatt Huntington award 1978, Coun. Am. Artists award 1985, Pastel award 1992, Still Life award 1993, 1st prize 2001), Alpha Delta Pi. Lutheran. Avocations: travel, technical illustration, oil, pastel and watercolor painting, collecting antique music boxes and watches. Home: 222 E 93rd St Apt 26A New York NY 10128-3758

REINISCH, JUNE MACHOVER, psychologist, educator; b. N.Y.C., Feb. 2, 1943; d. Mann Barnett and Lillian (Machover) R. BS cum laude, NYU, 1966; MA, Columbia U., 1970, PhD with distinction, 1976. Asst. prof. psychology Rutgers U., New Brunswick, N.J., 1975-80, assoc. prof. psychology New Brunswick, N.J., 1980-82, adj. assoc. prof. psychiatry, 1981-82; prof. psychology Ind. U., Bloomington, 1982-93, dir. Kinsey Inst. Rsch. in Sex, Gender, and Reprodn., 1982-93; prof. clin. psychology Sch. Medicine, Indpls., 1983-93; dir. emeritus Kinsey Inst., 1993—. Dir., prin. investigator Prenatal Devel. Projects, Copenhagen, 1976—, sr. rsch. fellow, trustee The Kinsey Inst., 1993—; pres. R2 Sci. Comms., Inc., Ind., N.Y., 1985—; vis. sr. rschr. Inst. of Preventive Medicine, Copenhagen Health Svcs., Kommunehospitalet, Copenhagen, 1994—; cons. SUNY; sr. cons. Mus. of Sex, N.Y.C., 1998, dir. acquisitions and new exhbns., 2003—, v.p. sci. affairs, 2003. Author: The Kinsey Institute New Report on Sex, 1990, 94, pub. 8 fgn. edits.; editor, contbr. books Kinsey Inst. series; syndicated newspaper columnist: The Kinsey Report; contbr. rsch. reports, revs., articles to profl. jours.; appeared on TV shows including PBS, BBC, ABC and NBC sci. spls., Discovery, ABC Science Specials, 20/20, Oprah Winfrey, Geraldo Rivera, Charles Grodin, Montel Williams, Sally Jessy Rafael, Good Morning Am., Today Show, CBS This Morning; guest host TV shows including CNBC Real Personal, TalkLive, also fgn. appearances. Founders day scholar NYU, 1966; NIMH trainee, 1971-74; NIMH grantee, 1978-80, Ford Found. grantee, 1973-75, Nat. Inst. Edn. grantee, 1973-74, Erikson Ednl. Found. grantee, 1973-74, grantee Nat. Inst. Child Health and Human Devel., 1981-88, Nat. Inst. on Drug Abuse, 1989-95; recipient Morton Prince award Am. Psychopath. Assn., 1976, medal for 9th Dr. S.T. Huang-Chan Meml. Lectr. in anatomy Hong Kong U., 1988, Dr. Richard J. Cross award Robert Wood Johnson Med. Sch., 1991, Award First Internat. Conf. on Orgasm, New Delhi, 1991, Disting. Alumnae award Tchrs. Coll. Columbia U., 1992, award for su contbn. Profl. al Conocimiento dela Sexualidad Humana, Assn. Mexicana de Sexologia, Mexico City, 1996; named Regents lectr. UCLA, 1999. Fellow AAAS, APA, Am. Psychol. Soc., Soc. for Sci. Study Sex; mem. Internat. Acad. Sex Rsch. (charter), Internat. Women's Forum, Women's Forum. Inc., Internat. Soc. Psychoneuroendocrinology, Internat. Soc. Rsch. Aggression, Internat. Soc. Devel. Psychobiology, Am. Assn. Sex. Educators, Counselors and Therapists, Sigma Xi. Office: SUNY HSCB PBL Box 120 450 Clarkson Ave Brooklyn NY 11203-2056 also: The Kinsey Inst Prenatal Devel Project Ind U Bloomington IN 47405 E-mail: DrReinisch@aol.com.

REINITZ, NEALE ROBERT, retired literature educator; b. N.Y.C., Sept. 16, 1923; s. Bertram Reinitz and Sonia Bromberg; m. Beverly Gene Landay, June 24, 1948 (dec. Oct. 26, 2000); 1 child, John Bertram. BA, U. of Wis., 1947; MA, Harvard U., 1949; PhD, U. of Calif., 1958. From instr. to prof. of english The Colo. Coll., Colo. Springs, Colo., 1953—66, prof. of english, 1966—91, chmn. Dept. of English, 1971—80, ret., 1991. Editor: The Higher Jazz, 1998, I Thought of Daisy, 2001; contbr. Edmund Wilson: Centential Reflections, 1997, articles to profl. jours. Sgt. Air Forces U.S. Army, 1943—45, Gander, Newfoundland. Fulbright fellow, 1960—61, faculty fellow, Newberry Libr., Chgo., 1971—91. Mem.: MLA (life), Assn. of Lit. Scholars and Critics (assoc.), Colo. Mountain Club (assoc.). Home: 1928 North Nevada Ave Colorado Springs CO 80907-6913 Personal E-mail: nreinitz.hux@worldnet.att.net.

REINIUS, MICHELE REED, executive recruiter; b. San Diego, Jan. 17, 1948; d. Wallace Alvin Reed and Dorothy Louise Austin; m. Robin Patric Reinius, Aug. 4, 1990; 1 child, Joselyn Ann Andrews. Supr. Asosa Personnel, Tucson, 1981-83; recruiter TAD Tech., Tucson, 1983-85; co-cowner Migar Personnel, Tucson, 1985-90; mgr. Temps by Encore, Tucson, 1990-2000; pres. Ariz. Recruiting Source, Tucson, 2000—. Democrat. Jewish. Avocations: reading, swimming. Office: Ariz Recruiting Source 7483 E Broadway Tucson AZ 85710 Office Phone: 520-751-0067.

REINKE, DORIS MARIE, retired elementary school educator; b. Racine, Wis., Jan. 12, 1922; d. Otto William Reinke and Louise Amelia Goehring. BS, U. Wis., Milw., 1943; MS, U. Wis., Whitewater, 1967. Tchr. kindergarten Elkhorn (Wis.) Area Sch. Sys., 1943-69, bldg. prin., 1968-70, summer sch. dir., 1974-75, grade 2 tchr., 1970-84, primary dept. chmn., 1971-84, administr. asst., supervising tchr., 1957-83, student tchr., 1984, ret., 1984; oriented experience tchr. Program Area Sch. Sys., Elkhorn, 1966. Pres. Elkhorn Edn. Assn., 1949-50; rep. dist. State Kindergarten Conf., Oshkosh, Wis., 1966; participant early edn. conf. State Early Edn. Conf., Eagle River, Wis., 1968; tchr. Covenant Harbor Elderhostel, 1997, 98; established Doris M. Reinke Resource Ctr., 2002. Author: Doris' Corner newsletter Walworth County Geneal. Soc., 1992—; author: (with Charlotte and William Gates) Guide to Beckwith's History of Walworth County, 2000; author: Images of America-Elkhorn, 2004; contbr. weekly newspaper column Webster Notes, 1989, monthly column in The Week, 1991. Chmn. Sch. Centennial, Elkhorn, 1987; mem. Elkhorn Hist. Preservation Com., 1991—; chmn. Sesquicentennial com., 1997—; dir. Webster House Mus., 1991—; mem. Walworth County Sesquicentennial Com., 1997—98; mem. sesquicentennial com. Walworth County Fair, 1998—; archivist Sugar Creek Luth. Ch., 1992—, mem. ch. coun., 2003; choir mem. Luth. Ch., 1995—2001; del. dist. constn. conv. Evang. Luth. Ch. Am., Beloit, Wis., 1987; com. mem. Luth. Ch., Elkhorn, 1987; RSVP Vol. Food Pantry, Elkhorn, 1985—2002, bd. dirs., 1985—88, 1995—. Recipient Wis. Edn. Rsch., West Bend, Wis., 1966, Outstanding Elem. Tchrs., Wash., 1973, Wis. Dept. Edn., Madison, 1980, Local History award State Hist. Soc. Wis., 1993, Outstanding Sr. Citizen award Walworth County Fair, 1999, Cmty. Svc. award, Masons, 2000. Mem.: Walworth County Ret. Tchrs. Assn. (v.p. 1988, pres. 1991), Nat. Ret. Tchrs. Assn., Walworth County Geneal. Soc. (bd. dirs. 1991—92), Walworth County Hist. Soc. (treas. 1985—89, v.p. 1990—91, pres. 1991—96, v.p. 1999—2000, pres. 2000—03), Elkhorn Women's Club (sec. 1999—2000, v.p. 2003), Alpha Delta Kappa (state pres. 1968—70, 1976—78, chpt. pres. 2002—03). Avocations: reading, baseball, bird watching, travel. Home: 516 N Wisconsin St Elkhorn WI 53121-1119

REINKE, RALPH LOUIS, retired academic administrator; b. Elmhurst, Ill., June 22, 1927; s. Louis Fred and Malinda Marie (Beckmann) R.; m. Lois Hermine Borneman, Aug. 28, 1948 (dec. Mar. 1984); children: Janice Reinke Eisenloeffell, Stephan, Sharon Reinke Holaway; m. Carole Louise Rediehs, June 14, 1986 Student, U. Ill., 1945—46; BS, Concordia U., River Forest, Ill., 1949; MA, Northwestern U., 1952; postgrad., U. Chgo., 1956—63; LittD, Concordia Sem., 1972. Prin. St. John Elem. Sch., Houston, 1949-56; assoc. prof. psychology and edn. Concordia U., River Forest, Ill., 1956-68, CEO, 2003—04; pres., chief exec. officer Concordia Pub. House, St. Louis, 1968-86; pres. Concordia U., Seward, Nebr., 1986—90; ret., 1990. Author: Christian Spelling Series, 2d edit, 1971. Mem. sch. bd. selecting com., Oak Park, Ill., 1965-67, chmn. lit. commn. Mo. Synod Luth. Ch., 1967-69; bd. dirs. Concordia U., 1992-2004, chair, 1999-2002. With USNR, 1944-46. Mem. Protestant Ch. Owned Pubs. Assn. (dir. 1969-84, pres. 1982-84), St. Louis Printing Assn. (bd. dirs. 1975-77), Am. Assn. Indsl. Mgmt. (bd. dirs. 1981-85), Assn. Ind. Colls. and Univs. of Nebr. (pres. 1988-89), Luth. Edn. Assn. (pres. 1967-69), Rotary, Phi Delta Kappa. Lutheran. E-mail: rlreinke@aol.com. *Life is a most precious and finite gift of God to man. Those who would lead must make a commitment to devote their full energies and intellects to the improvement of the quality of life of their fellowmen. In the highest sense, leadership is the integrity to heed the quiet voice of conscience from within in the quest of that quality.*

REINKE, WILLIAM JOHN, lawyer; b. South Bend, Ind., Aug. 7, 1930; s. William August and Eva Marie (Hein) R.; m. Sue Carol Colvin, 1951 (div. 1988); children: Sally Sue Taelman, William A., Andrew J.; m. Elizabeth Beck Lockwood, 1991. AB cum laude, Wabash Coll., 1952; JD, U. Chgo., 1955. Bar: Ind. 1955. Assoc. Barnes & Thornburg and predecessors, South Bend, Ind., 1957-61, ptnr., 1961—, of counsel, 1996—, former chmn. compensation com. Trustee Stanley Clark Sch., 1969-80, pres., 1977-80; life mem. adv. bd. Salvation Army, 1973—, pres., 1990-92; bd. dirs. NABE Mich. chpt., 1990-94, pres. 1993-94, Isaac Walton League, 1970-81; bd. dirs. United Way, 1979-81; pres. South Bend Round Table, 1963-65; trustee First Meth. Ch., 1976-70; bd. dirs. So. Bend Civic Theatre, 1997-2003. Served with U.S. Army, 1955-57. Recipient Outstanding Local Pres. award Ind. Jaycees, 1960-61, Boss of Yr. award, 1979, South Bend Outstanding Young Man award, 1961. Mem. ABA, Ind. State Bar Assn., St. Joseph County Bar Assn., Ind. Bar Found. (patron fellow), Am. Judicature Soc., Summit Club (founders com.), Rotary (bd. dirs. 1970-73, 94-97). Home: 51795 Waterton Square Cir Granger IN 46530-8317 Office: Barnes & Thornburg 1st Source Bank Ctr 100 N Michigan St Ste 600 South Bend IN 46601-1632

REINKER, MARY STEFANICH, musician, music educator; b. Joliet, Ill., Aug. 12, 1947; d. Anthony Edward and Mary Vidmar Stefanich; m. Myron Edward Reinker, Oct. 20, 1984; children: Meryt Antonia Reinker Dean, Molly Elizabeth. MusB, U. St. Francis, Joliet, IL, 1969; MusM, Roosevelt U., Chicago, Ill., 1971. Teaching Certificate Chgo. Bd. of Edn., 1972. Organist St. John's Ch., Joliet, Ill., 1958—65; tchr. Chgo. Pub. Schools, 1971—84; pianist/organist St. Edward's Ch., Dana Point, Calif., 1989—94, Gloria Dei Ch., Dana Point, Calif., 1985—89, St. Frances Cabrini Ch., Littleton, Colo., 1994—, St. Mary's Ch., Littleton, Colo., 2004—; private piano instr. Laguna Beach & Dana Point, 1984—94; founder/dir. Forte Acad. of Music, Littleton, Colo., 1997—, Centennial, Colo., 2004—. Clinician & pedagogy advisor Colo. State Music Teachers Assn., Colo., 1996—, Forte Acad. of Music, Littleton, Colo., 1997—. *Mary S. Reinker has successfully developed a standardized piano curriculum and a method for teaching an injury-free natural hand/arm technique used by all piano instructors at the Forté Academy. This "Forté Method" includes a structured testing program called "Certificate of Achievement" that rewards successful students for their accomplishments.* Musician: (performance) Requiem by John Rutter; musician: (organist/pianist) St. Peter's Basilica, Rome, Salzburg Music Festival (Medal, 2002), St. Mark's Cathedral, Venice, Notre Dame, Chartres; musician: Cathedrals of Madrid and Barcelona. Vol. St. Frances Cabrini Ch., Littleton, Colo., 1994—2004; vol. for local retirement and nursing homes Littleton, Colo., 1995—2004. Scholar Ill. State Scholarship, State of Ill., 1965. Mem.: Music Teachers Assn. of Calif., Colo. State Music Teachers Assn., Music Teachers Nat. Assn., Delta Mu Theta Music Honor Soc. Avocations: horseback riding, travel, reading. Office: Forte Acad Music 10143 W Chatfield Ave Ste 15 Littleton CO 80127 Office Phone: 303-948-9221 305. Personal E-mail: maryreinker@qwest.net. E-mail: forteacademy@att.net.

REINKING, ANN H. dancer, actress; b. Seattle, Nov. 10, 1949; d. Walter Floyd and Francis Holmes (Harrison) R.; m. Larry Small, 1970; m. Herbert A. Allen; Aug. 25, 1982; (stepchildren): Leslie, Christie, Herbert, Charlie. Student public schs. Guest tchr. NYU, Duke U., Durham, N.C., Rutgers, N.J., Harvard, Cambridge, Mass.; choreographer Pal Joey, Goodman Theater, Chgo., 1988. Broadway appearances include Coco, 1970, Wild and Wonderful, 1972, Pippin, 1973, Over Here, 1974, Goodtime Charlie, 1975, Chicago, 1977, A Chorus Line, 1976, Dancin', 1978, Sweet Charity, 1986-87; TV appearances include Ellery Queen, Doug Henning: Magic on Broadway, 1982, Parade of Stars, 1983, American Treasury, 1985, Salute to Jules Styne, Broadway Salutes Washington, An Introduction to the Dance Gala of the Stars; film appearances include Movie, Movie, 1978, All That Jazz, 1979-80, Annie, 1982, Micki and Maude, 1984; play Ann Reinking ... Music Moves Me, 1984; actor, choreographer Broadway shows: Chicago, 1996 (Tony award 1997), Annie Get Your Gun, 1999 (Tony award 1999), Fosse, 2001; choreographer Broadway shows: Annie Get Your Gun, 1999, Look of Love, 2003 Recipient Clarence Derwent award, 1974, Outer Critics Circle award, 1974, Theatre World award, 1974, Dance Educators Am. award, 1979, Harkness Dance award, 1979, two Tony award nominations, Tony award for Choregraphy, 1997; Ford Found. scholar, 1964-66; Robert Joffery scholar, 1967; Harkness scholar; Nat. Dance Educators award. Mem. Actors Equity, AFTRA, Stage Actors Guild. Avocations: horseback riding, skiing, swimming, hiking. also: Steps Contemporary & Classical Dance 2121 Broadway Fl 3 New York NY 10023-1786

REINL, HARRY CHARLES, economist; b. Muttersdorf, Suden, Germany, Nov. 13, 1932; arrived in U.S., 1946; s. Carl and Angela (Plass) Reinl. BS, Fordham U., 1953; MA, George Washington U., 1968; cert. in career English, USDA, Washington, 1966; HHD, London Inst. Applied Rsch., 1992; PhD, Brownell U., 1993. Head market rsch. Timex Mfg., Waterbury, Conn., 1955-58; jr. observer Sperry-Rand Corp., N.Y.C., 1958-62; labor economist manpower adminstrn. U.S. Dept. Labor, Washington, 1962-68; labor economist Office Pers. Mgmt. U.S. Civil Svc. Commn., Washington, 1968—. Mgr. N.Y. br. Willmark Svc., N.Y.C., 1971; prof. rsch. Haute Ecole Rsch. Alliance Universelle pour la Paix par la Connaissance, Paris, 1992; rsch. bd. advs. Am. Biog. Inst., Raleigh, NC, 1991; mem. adv. coun. Internat. Biog. Ctr., Cambridge, England, 1992. Author (on microfilm): The Story of My Life, 1984. Founding mem. Nat. Campaign Tolerance, Montgomery, Ala., 2004; with Willmental health testing VA Med. Ctr., Washington, 1989—; life mem. Rep. Nat. Com., Washington, 1979—; mem. Rep. Nat. Senatorial Com., Washington, 1990; founding mem. Wold Peace and Diplomacy Forum, Cambridge, 2003; host N.Y.C. com. Rep. Nat. Conv., 2004. Decorated Knight Templar Bur. Internat.; recipient John Edgar Hoover Meml. award, Police Assn., 1983, HIR citation of Leadership, Rep. Nat. Conv., 1996, medal of Freedom, Rep. Nat. Senatorial Inner Cir., 1999; fellow, AA, 1988—. Mem.: London Diplomatic Acad., Academic Coun., N.Y. Acad. Scis., George Mason U. Mercatus Ctr. (contbr.), Collegiate Network, Inc. (hon. sponsor), Family Immigration History Ctr. Ellis Island, Pres.'s Club, Fordham Univ. Club Washington. Mem. Lds Ch. Home: 2425 Mount Vernon Ave Alexandria VA 22301-1347

REINLEITNER, KATHERINE MINDLIN, psychologist, foundation administrator; b. Scarsdale, N.Y., May 10, 1948; m. Theodore B. Day, Aug. 25, 1968 (div. Sept. 1980); children: Eleanor Day, T. Eugene Day, Jennifer Day, David A.; m. Lee A. Reinleitner, Sept. 15, 1990; children: Mark A., Paul H. BA, Barnard Coll., 1967; MA, Columbia U., 1968; PhD, U. Wash., 1974. Diplomate Am. Bd. Psychopharmacology and Forensic Psychology, Am. Bd. Advanced Practice Psychologists. Intern Astor Home for Children, Reinbeck, NY; psychologist Children's Hosp., Seattle, 1974-83; pvt. practice, Mercer Island and Bellevue, 1976-2000; pvt. practice Bainbridge Island, 1983—2000; adminstr. The Mindlin Found., Bellevue, 1994—. Lectr., asst. prof. U. Wash., 1975-83; gov.'s coun. on abuse and neglect State of Wash., Olympia, 1978-80; bd. dirs. Prescribing Psychologists Register, 1996—, curriculum com., 1996—. Author childrens books; author: What To Do After You've Seen the Zoo, 1983. Tng. fellowship IV, VA, 1970-71, 73-74, NIMH, 1969-70. Mem. AAAS, Internat. Coll. of Prescribing Psychologists, Am. Psychol. Assn., Wash. State Psychol. Assn. Office: The Mindlin Found 146 128th Ave NE Bellevue WA 98005 E-mail: drkathyday@aol.com.

REINOEHL, RICHARD LOUIS, artist, scholar, martial artist; b. Omaha, Oct. 11, 1944; s. Louis Lawrence and Frances Margaret (Robinson) R.; 1 child, Joy Margaret Iroff-Reinoehl. BS in Sociology, Portland State U., 1970; MSW, U. Minn., Duluth, 1977; postgrad., Cornell U., 1984-88. Acting dir. Vanguard Group Homes, Virginia, Minn., 1976-77; dir. Minn. Chippewa Tribe Group Home, Duluth, 1978, Human Devel. Consortium, Minn., N.Y., Ohio, 1978—. Faculty Social Work Program U. Wis., Superior, 1981-84; adv. bd. Computers in Social Svcs. Network, 1982-85; mem. Com. on Internat. Social Welfare Edn., 1982-86, Am. Evaluation Assn., 1986-89; affiliate scholar Oberlin Coll., 1991—; artist-in-residence Ohio Arts Coun., 1996-97. Editor: Computer Literacy in Human Services Education, 1990, Computer Literacy in Human Services, 1990, Men of Achievement, 16th edit., 1993; mem. editl. bd. Computers in Human Svcs., 1983-96, 99, Jour. Technology in Human Svcs., 1999—; assoc. editor book rev., 1996-99; contbr. numerous articles to profl. jours. Mem. Legis. Task Force Regional Alcoholism Bd., 1972-73, Assn. Drug Abuse, Prevention and Treatment, 1973-74, Minn. Pub. Health Assn., 1976-78, Minn. Social Svc. Assn., 1976-83, Wis. Coun. Social Work Edn., 1983-84, N.Y. State Coun. Family Rels., 1986-89, Nat. Coun. Family Rels., 1986-89; exec. bd. Duluth Community Action Program, 1982-83; Dem. precinct chair, Portland, Oreg., 1972-74; precinct vice-chair Dem. Farmer-Labor Party, Duluth, 1979-81, chair, 1981-83, 2d vice-chair exec. bd., 1981-83; mem. Zoning Appeals Bd., New Russia Twp., Ohio, 1996—; mem. art edn. com. Fireland Assn. Visual Arts, 1996-99; mem. land use planning com. New Russia Twp., Ohio, 1998—; chair Lorain County Comprehensive Plan Growth Mgmt. Com., 1999—; mem. Smart Devel. Coalition of Lorain County, 1998—, Lorain County Multi-Modal Transp. Planning Steering Com., 2000—, airport subcom., 2000—, roadways sub-com., 2000—, transit subcom., 2000—, info. tech. sub-com., 2000—; field spl. projects field coord., nat. coord. rural issues Kucinich for Pres. campaign, 2003-; chmn. Smart Devel. Coalition Lorain County, 1996-98, Lorain County Growth Mgmt. Com., mem. Environ. Sub.-Com., 1997-98; mem. Lorain County Multi-Modal Transp. Plan Steering Com., sub-coms. transit, roadways, airports, rail, and info. tech., 1999-2001, New Russia Township Zoning Bd. Appeals, 1995-2000, New Russia Township Land Use Planning Com., 1996-98. Mem. NASW (exec. com., chair program com. Arrowhead Region Minn. chpt., 1980-81, co-chair task force on computers in social work, 1981-82), Acad. Cert. Social Workers, Cornell U. Sailing Club (pres. 1990). Avocations: canoeing, antique volkswagens, wilderness hiking. Office: Human Devel Consortium Inc 46180 Butternut Ridge Rd Oberlin OH 44074-9778 Office Phone: 440-315-0121. Business E-Mail: richard.reinoehl@oberlin.edu. *It's noteworthy that the most sought-after items in a society cannot be bought or sold. Included are wisdom, respect, generosity, truthfulness, and the love of family and friends.*

REINOLD, CHRISTY DIANE, school counselor, consultant; b. Neodasha, Kans., July 21, 1942; d. Ernest Sherman and Faye Etta (Herbert) Wild; m. Willaim Owen Reinold, Dec. 20, 1964; children: Elizabeth, Rebecca. BA Edn., MA in Edn. and Psychology, Calif. State U., Fresno, 1964. Cert. counselor, Family Wellness instr.; lic. mental health counselor, Fla. Tchr. Clovis (Calif.) Unified Sch. Dist., 1965-66, Santa Clara (Calif.) Unified Sch. Dist., 1966-67, Inst. Internat. Chateaubriand, Cannes, France, 1968-69; tchr., vice prin. Internat. Sch., Sliema, Malta, 1969-70; elem. sch. counselor Duval City Schs., Jacksonville, Fla., 1977-82, Lodi (Calif.) Unified Sch. Dist., 1982—. Cons. Calif. Dept. Edn.; mem. Calif. Commn. on Tchr. Credentialing, Sacramento, 1986—, mem. adv. panel, 1998—; mem. stds. rev. com. Nat. Bd. Cert. Sch. Counselors, 2002—. Co-author: The Best for Our Kids; Counseling in the 21st Century; contbr. articles. Chmn. bd. dirs. Oak Crest Child Care Ctr., Jacksonville, 1979-81. Named Anne Upton Sch. Counselor of Yr. for Calif., 1995; named to H.B. McDaniel Hall of Fame, Stanford U., 2003; recipient H.B. McDaniel Individual award, 1986, James Saum Legis. award, 1991, Donald Hayes Lifetime Achievement award, 2002. Mem.: AAUW (3rd v.p. 1974, 1st v.p. 1980, by-laws chmn. 1990, chmn. pub. policy 1991—93, pres. 1993), Lodi Pupil Pers. Assn. (pres. 1986—87), Calif. Alliance Pupil Svcs. Orgns. (bd. dirs. 1988—95), Fla. Sch. Counselors Assn., Calif. Assn. Counseling and Devel., Calif. Sch. Counselor Assn. (legis. chmn. 1985—90, pres. 1991), Am. Sch. Counselor Assn. (govt. rels. specialist 1993—94). Republican. Avocations: history, travel, politics. Home: 1180 Northwood Dr Lodi CA 95240-0443

REINSCH, WILLIAM ALAN, association executive, educator; b. Evanston, Ill., Jan. 15, 1946; s. Bert and Kathleen (Penn) R.; m. Susan Polley Reinsch, Jan. 3, 1970; children: Andrew, Christian. BA, Johns Hopkins U., 1968; MA in Internat. Rels., Johns Hopkins U.-Sch. Advanced Internat. Studies, 1969. Legis. asst. Congressman Gilbert Gude, Washington, 1973-76, Congressman Richard Ottinger, Washington, 1976; chief legis. asst. Senator John Heinz, Washington, 1977-91; legis. asst. Senator John D. Rockefeller IV, Washington, 1991-93; cons., under sec. for export adminstrn. Dept. Commerce, Washington, 1994-2001; pres. Nat. Fgn. Trade Coun., Washington, 2001—; mem. U.S.-China Econ. and Security Rev. Commn., 2001—. Tchr. Landon Sch., Bethesda, Md., 1968-73; adj. assoc. prof. U. Md. U. Coll. Grad. Sch. Mgmt. and Tech., College Park, Md., 1990—; acting staff dir. Environmental Study Conf. U.S. Ho. Reps., 1976. Contbr. articles to profl. jours. Pres. St. Mark Elderly Housing Corp., Rockville, Md. Mem. Phi Beta Kappa, Omicron Delta Kappa, Alpha Delta Phi. Democrat. Presbyterian. Office: Nat Fgn Trade Coun 1625 K St NW Ste 200 Washington DC 20006 E-mail: breinsch@nftc.org.

REINSDORF, JERRY MICHAEL, professional sports teams executive, real estate executive, lawyer, accountant; b. Bklyn., Feb. 25, 1936; s. Max and Marion (Smith) Reinsdorf; m. Martyl F. Rifkin, Dec. 29, 1956; children: David Jason, Susan Janeen, Michael Andrew, Jonathan Milton. BA, George Washington U., 1957; JD, Northwestern U., 1960. CPA Ill., registered mortgage underwriter; bar: DC, Ill. 60; cert. specialist real estate securities, rev. appraiser. Atty. staff regional counsel IRS, Chgo., 1960—64; assoc. law firm Chapman & Cutler, 1964—68; ptnr. Altman, Kurlander & Weiss, 1968—74; of counsel firm Katten, Muchin, Gitles, Zavis, Pearl & Galler, 1974—79; gen. ptnr. Carlyle Real Estate Ltd. Partnerships, 1971—72; chmn. bd. Balcor Co., 1973—87; mng. ptnr. TBC Films, 1975—83; chmn. Chgo. White Sox, 1981—, Chgo. Bulls Basketball Team, 1985—; ptnr. Bojer Fin., 1987—. Lectr. John Marshall Law Sch., 1966—68; former bd. dirs. Project Academus of DePaul U., Chgo., Sports Immortals Mus., 1987—89, Com. Commemorate U.S. Constn., 1987; bd. dirs. LaSalle Nat. Bank; bd. overseers Inst. for Civil Justice, 1996—98; lectr. in real estate, sports and taxation. Author (with L. Herbert Schneider): Uses of Life Insurance in Qualified Employee Benefit Plans, 1970. Mem. Chgo. region bd. Anti-Defamation League, 1986—2001; mem., trustee Ill. Inst. Tech., 1991—96; mem. Ill. Commn. on African-Am. Males, 1992—; bd. dirs. Chgo. Youth Success Found, 1992—, Corp. for Supportive Housing, 1995—; nat. trustee Northwestern U., 1993—; bd. govs. Hugh O'Brian Youth Found.; mem. internat. adv. bd. Barrow Neurol. Found., 1996—97; active Chgo. Baseball Cancer Charities, 1994, 1998; bd. trustees Equity Office Properties, 1997—2004. Named to inductee B'nai B'rith Nat. Jewish Am. Sports Hall of Fame, 1994, Chgo. Sports Hall of Fame, 1997; recipient Hallmark award, Chgo. Baseball Cancer Charities, 1986, Corp. Superstar award, Ill. chpt. Cystic Fibrosis Found., 1988, portsman of Yr. award, 1994, Chicagoan of Yr. award, Chgo. Park Dist., 1990, Kellogg Excellence award, 1991, Cmty. Hero award, Interfaith Organizing Project, 1991, Operation Push Bridgebuilder award, 1992, Alumni Merit award, Northwestern U., 1992, Ellis Island Medal of Honor award, Nat. Ethnic Coalition of Orgns., 1993, Lifetime Achievement award, March of Dimes, 1994, Hallmark Hall of Fame Civic award, Ind. Sports Charities, 1994, Am. Spirit award, USAF, 1995, Alpha Epsilon Pi Arthur and Simiteich Outstanding Alumnus award, 1995, Order of Lincoln, 1997, Mayor's medal Hon., 1997, Bklyn. Businessman of Yr., 1997, Guardian of Children award, Jewish Coun. for Youth Svc., 1998. Mem.: FBA, ABA, Nat. Sports Lawyers Assn., Chgo. Bar Assn., Ill. Bar Assn., Northwestern U. Law Sch. Alumni Assn. (bd. dirs.), Order of Coif, Comml. Club Chgo., Omega Tau Rho. Office: Chgo White Sox 333 W 35th St Chicago IL 60616-3651

REINSMA, HAROLD LAWRENCE, design consultant, engineer; b. Slayton, Minn., Sept. 6, 1928; s. Frank and Ida M. (Zabel) R.; m. Julia A. Tusek, Oct. 18, 1958; children: Frank, Michael, Diane. Student, Macalester Coll., 1948-50; BCE, U. Minn., 1953. Registered profl. engr., Ill. Cons. engr. GM Orr Engring. Co., Mpls., 1953-54; rsch. test engr. Caterpillar Tractor Co., Peoria, Ill., 1955-58, rsch. design engr., 1958-71, rsch. project engr., 1971-73, rsch. supervising engr., 1973-76, rsch. staff engr., 1976-91; design cons. Dunlap, Ill., 1991—. Achievements include patents for 44 including 1st viable sealed and lubricated track, fundamental to success of a new generation of large high performance elevated sprocket tractors; described in Caterpillar's 2004 annual report as a high-risk creative technology breakthrough; include sealed maintenance-free linkage and large diameter high speed pressure balanced oil cooled brake wheel seals for mining trucks, all used in abrasive environments. Avocations: skiing, bicycling, hiking, gardening. Home and Office: 13600 Lucerne Dr Dunlap IL 61525-9619

REINSTEIN, KATHI-ANNE, state representative, state legislator; BS, Suffolk Univ.; MA, Emerson Coll. State rep. legis., Mass., 1999—. Com. Revere Dem. City, Ins., Pub. Safety. Mem.: Saugus River Watewrshed Coun., Revere C. of C., WILL/WAND, Santa Fund, Revere 1st, Revere Beach Partnership, Moose. Democrat. Office: State Ho Rm 236 Boston MA 02133

REINTHALER, RICHARD WALTER, lawyer; b. N.Y.C., Feb. 27, 1949; s. Walter F. and Maureen C. (Tully) R.; m. Mary E. Maloney, Aug. 8, 1970; children: Brian, Scott, Amy. BA in Govt. magna cum laude, U. Notre Dame, 1970, JD summa cum laude, 1973. Bar: N.Y. 1974, U.S. Dist. Ct. (so. and ea. dists.) N.Y. 1974, U.S. Ct. Appeals (2d cir.) 1974, U.S. Ct. Appeals (9th cir.) 1976, U.S. Supreme Ct., 1977, U.S. Ct. Appeals (5th cir.) 1978, U.S. Ct. Appeals (11th cir.) 1981, U.S. Ct. Appeals (1st cir.) 2004. Assoc. White & Case, N.Y.C., 1973—81, ptnr., 1981—95, Dewey Ballantine LLP, N.Y.C., 1995—, co-chmn. litigation dept., 2002—03. Mem. adv. group U.S. Dist. Ct. (ea. dist.) N.Y., 1992—, chairperson subgroup on ethics, 1993—. Contbr. articles to profl. jours. Served to 1st lt. U.S. Army, 1974. Fellow Am. Bar Found.; mem. ABA (2d cir. chmn. discovery com. 1982-87, program coord. 1986, ann. meeting litigation sect., vice chmn. com. on fed. procedure 1988-89, co-chmn. com. on profl. responsibility 1989-92, vice chmn. securities litigation com. 1993-94, vice chair Hong Kong meeting 1995, co-chair energy litigation com. 1996-97, co-chair antitrust litigation com. 1997-2000, mem. Ethics 2000 task force 1999-2000), N.Y. State Bar Assn., Assn. of Bar of City of N.Y. (mem. com. to enhance diversity in the profession 1990-95, mem. Orison S. Marden Meml. Lectrs. com. 1994-2000, chair 1997-2000, spl. com. on mergers, acquisitions and corp. control contests 1995-2002), Scarsdale Golf Club (Hartsdale, N.Y., bd. govs. 1994—2003, pres. 2002-2003), Capital Hill Club (Washington). Republican. Roman Catholic. Avocations: golf, tennis. Office: Dewey Ballantine LLP 1301 Avenue Of The Americas New York NY 10019-6022 Office Phone: 212-259-6090.

REINTZEL, WARREN ANDREW, trust company executive; b. Phila., Jan. 4, 1945; s. Warren H. and Lorna (Geibel) R.; m. Susan Rodgers, Dec. 20, 1969; children: Lisa S., Kurt W. BA with high honors, U. Del., 1967; MA in History, Rutgers U., 1968; JD, U. Pa., 1971. Trust adminstrn. trainee First Pa. Bank, Phila., 1971, trust adminstr., 1972-73, trust officer, 1973-79, sr. trust officer, 1979-81; v.p. Provident Nat. Bank, Phila., 1981-86; v.p., head trust adminstrn. dept. Glenmede Trust Co., Phila., 1986—, sr. v.p., 1994—. Trustee Wanamaker Inst., Phila., 1986—, 1st v.p., 1995-2000, pres., 2000-; trustee Meml. Fund, Luth. Ch. of our Saviour, Haddonfield, N.J., 1989-2000, Haddonfield Hist. Soc., 1997—, Haddonfield Cmty. Found., 1998-. Mem. Phila. Bar Assn., Phila. Fin. Assn. (treas. bd. trustees 1987-89), Phila. Estate Planning Coun. (trustee 1991, sec. 1994-95, treas. 1995-96, v.p. 1996-97, pres. 1997-98), Corp. Fiduciaries Assn. Phila. (mem. personal trust com. 1986-89, pres. 1996-98), Phi Beta Kappa. Republican. Office: Glenmede Trust Co 1650 Market St Ste 1200 Philadelphia PA 19103-7391

REIS, DON, publishing executive; b. N.Y.C., Nov. 19, 1927; m. Barbara Weinberg, 1949; children: Robert, Richard. AB, Princeton U., 1947; MA, NYU, 1955. Rsch. editor Bantam Books, 1952-55, edn. editor, 1955-66; editor-in-chief Washington Square Press Divsn. Simon & Schuster, 1966-68; v.p., editorial dir. Ednl. Directions Inc., Westport, Conn., 1968-85; mng. editor Barron's Ednl. Series, 1985-87; gen. and ednl. editor Barron's, 1987-93, sr. cons. editor, 1993-99; editorial dir. Reis Assocs., Forest Hills, N.Y., 1993—. Author (with A. Butman and D. Sohn) Paperback Books in the Schools, 1962; editor The Collected Essays of Aldous Huxley, 1958. Home and Office: 57 Summer St Forest Hills NY 11375-6035 E-mail: reis@att.net., donjreis@yahoo.com.

REIS, HAROLD F. lawyer; b. July 22, 1916; s. Bernard and Rose (Frank) Reis; m. Ruthanne Abram, June 11, 1951; children: Alan B., Kate Reis Grogan, Deborah Reis Kennedy. BS, CCNY, 1937; LLB, Columbia U., 1940. Bar: NY 1941, DC 1953. With U.S. Dept. Justice, Washington, 1942—67; 1st asst. Office of Legal Counsel, 1960—63, exec. asst. to Atty. Gen., 1963—67; pvt. practice Washington, 1967—83; ptnr. Newman Holtzinger, P.C., Washington, 1983—94; sr. advisor Morgan, Lewis & Bockuis, Washington, 1994—96. Recipient Rockefeller Pub. Svc. award in law, legislation and adminstrn., 1964. Mem.: ABA, DC Bar Assn., Cosmos Club (Washington). Personal E-mail: reis8508@aol.com.

REIS, JEAN STEVENSON, administrative secretary; b. Wilburton, Okla., Nov. 30, 1914; d. Robert Emory and Ada (Ross) Stevenson; m. George William Reis, June 24, 1939 (dec. 1980). BA, U. Tex., El Paso, 1934; MA, So. Meth. U., 1935; postgrad., U. Chgo., 1937-38, U. Wash., 1948-49. Tchr. El Paso H.S., 1935-39; safety engr., trainer Safety and Security Divsn., Office of Chief Ordnance, Chgo., 1942-45; tchr. Lovenberg Jr. H.S., Galveston, Tex., 1946; parish sec. Trinity Parish Episcopal Ch., Seattle, 1950-65; adminstrv. sec., asst. Office Resident Bishop, United Meth. Ch., Seattle, 1965-94. Observer Africa U. installation, Mutare, Zimbabwe, 1994; com. on legislation for 1996 gen. conf. Hist. Soc. of United Meth. Ch. Recipient Bishop's award, 1980. Mem. AAUW, Beta Beta Beta. Home: 9310 42nd Ave NE Seattle WA 98115-3814

REISBERG, BARRY, geropsychiatrist, neuropsychopharmacologist; b. Bklyn., Dec. 3, 1947; s. Harry and Claire (Cohen) R.; m. Rosalie DePaola, Feb. 23, 1974 (dec. Oct. 1975); m. Nancy A. Minich, May 7, 1988. BA, CUNY, Bklyn., 1968; MD, N.Y. Med. Coll., 1972. Diplomate Am. Bd. Psychiatry and Neurology, Am. Bd. Geriatric Psychiatry. Intern N.Y. Med. Coll./Met. Hosp., N.Y.C., 1972-75, resident in psychiatry, 1972-75; fellow dept. psychiatry Middlesex Hosp. Med. Sch. U. London, 1975; staff psychiatrist Franklin D. Roosevelt VA Hosp., Montrose, NY, 1975-78; staff psychiatrist Neuropsychopharmacology Rsch. Unit NYU Med. Ctr., N.Y.C., 1978-80, asst. attending psychiatrist, 1978—2001, attending psychiatrist, 2002—, clin. dir. William and Sylvia Silberstein Aging and Dementia Rsch. Ctr., 1978—. Adj. prof. Ctr. for Studies in Aging McGill U., Montreal, Que., 1993—; clin. instr. dept. psychiatry N.Y. Med. Coll., Valhalla, 1975—78; asst. prof. NYU Sch. Medicine, N.Y.C., 1978—84, assoc. prof., 1984—90, prof., 1990—; rsch. collaborator, vis. clinician Brookhaven Nat. Labs., Upton, NY, 1979—90; dir. clin. core NIMH Clin. Rsch. Ctr., 1989—93, Nat. Inst. Aging Alzheimer's Disease Ctr., 1990—; dir. Zachary and Elizabeth M. Fisher Alzheimer's Disease Edn. and Resources Program NYU Sch. Medicine, 1995—; med. and sci. adv. bd. Alzheimer's Assn., Chgo., 1993—97; med. and sci. panel Alzheimer's Disease Internat., 1997—; cons. psychiatrist N.Y. VA Hosp., 1980—89; chmn. work group WHO, Copenhagen, 1984; mem. aging sect. NIH, 1986—90; vis. prof. Palmerston North Postgrad. Med. Soc., New Zealand, 1991; rsch. adv. bd. WHO Project on Alzheimer's Disease, 1995; Bayer vis. prof. St. Louis U. Sch. Medicine, 1999; Barry Reisberg lectr. Hearthstone Alzheimer's Family Found., 2002—. Author: Brain Failure, 1981; editor: Alzheimer's Disease, 1983; editor: (with others) Diagnosis and Treatment of Senile Dementia, 1989; guest editor Drug Devel. Rsch., Internat. Psychogeriat., mem. editl. bd. Jour. Am. Aging Assn., 1985—, Alzheimer's Disease and Associated Disorders, 1985—2004, Jour. Geriat. Psychiatry and Neurology, 1986—, Am. Jour. Alzheimer's Disease, 1986—, Internat. Psychogeriat., 1989—96, Am. Jour. Geriat. Psychiatry, 1992—2001, Rsch. and Practice in Alzheimer's Disease, 1999—; contbr. over 250 articles to med. and sci. jours. and books. Recipient Home Care award Vis. Nurse Svc. of N.Y., 1985, Lifetime Achievement award for rsch. on Alzheimer's Disease and Related Disorders, 9th Internat. Conf. on Alzheimer's Disease and Related Disorders, 2004; fellow NSF, 1963, Coun. on Internat. Ednl. Exch.-Japan Soc., Tokyo, 1968; grantee NIH, 1979-81, 82-85, 87—, 90-95, 92-95, NIMH, 1983-85, Adminstrn. on Aging, 1998—. Mem. Internat. Psychogeriat. Assn. (bd. dirs. 1985-93, treas. 1993-95, pres.-elect 1995-97, pres. 1997-99, Disting. Svc. award 2001), Am. Aging Assn (bd. dirs. 1990-92), Alzheimer's and Related Disorders Soc. India (hon.), Am. Assn. Geriatric Psychiatry (sec. 1991-92, bd. dirs. 1992-96), Am. Coll. Neuropsychopharmacology. Achievements include patents for treatment for memory impairment; method for assessment of dementia; system for diagnosis and staging of dementia; staging of dementia severity by joint function examination; method for diagnosis of incontinence of corticocerebral origin by neurologic examination; method and apparatus employing motor measures for early diagnosis and staging of dementia; worldwide approval of Alzheimer's medications based in part on work and measures in pivotal trials of rivastigmine, memantine and risperidone; mandated usage of work (measures) in U.S.(center for medicare services 1998), parts of Can. (e.g. Nova Scotia 2003—) and Europe (Catalonia, Spain, 1998-). Office: NYU Sch Medicine William and Sylvia Silberstein Aging and Dementia Rsch Ctr 550 1st Ave New York NY 10016-6402 Office Phone: 212-263-8550. Business E-Mail: barry.reisberg@med.nyu.edu. *Our studies have demonstrated that Alzheimer's disease (AD) recapitulates normal human development inversely in terms of cognition, functioning, neurologic reflexes and in other ways. These findings, termed retrogenesis, appear to represent a new mechanism of disease. Retrogenesis implies that a better understanding of AD can improve understanding of normal human development and behavior and vice versa.*

REISCH, MARC, publishing executive; Exec. v.p., CFO World Color Press, Greenwich, Conn., vice chmn., group pres., 1997-99, pres., 1999-2000; pres., CEO Quebecor World, Greenwich, 2000—. Office: Quebecor World 340 Pemberwick Rd Greenwich CT 06831-4240

REISCHAUER, ROBERT D. research organization executive; AB, Harvard U., 1963; MIA, Columbia U., 1966, PhD, 1971. Spl. asst. to dir., dep. dir., asst. dir. human resources and cmty. devel. Congressional Budget Office, 1975-81; sr. v.p. Urban Inst., 1981-86; chmn. bd. trustees MDRC, 1999—2000; dir. Congressional Budget Office, 1989-95; pres. Urban Inst., 2000—; vice chair Medicare, Payment Advisory Commission, 2001. Author: (with Henry J. Aaron) Countdown to Reform: The Great Social Security Debate, 2001 (revised and updated); editor: Setting National Priorities: Budget Choices for the Next Century, 1997; co-editor: Medicare: Preparing for the Challenges of the 21st Century, 1998, Setting National Priorities: The 2000 Election and Beyond, 1999; contbr. articles to profl. jours., chpts. to books. Sr. Fellow econ. studies Brookings Inst., 1970-75, 86-89, 95-2000. Office: Urban Inst 2100 M St NW Washington DC 20037 Office Phone: 202-261-5400.

REISER, BRIAN SYDNEY, economist, statistician; b. Bklyn., Feb. 28, 1937; s. Eugene N. and Ruth (Cohen) R. BA, Syracuse U., 1961; postgrad. Am. U., 1962, U.S. Dept. Agr. Grad. Sch., 1963. Econ. statistician Bur. of Census, Washington, 1962-69, 1979-88; economist, econ. statistician IRS, Washington, 1969-79; econ. cons., 1988—; exec. sec. Soc. Govt. Economists, 1980-81, adv. com., 1982, dir., 1984-85. Vice pres. Springfield Stamp Club, Va., 1982. Mem. Am. Econ. Assn., Am. Topical Assn., Am. Philatelic Soc., Am. Numismatic Assn., Am. Polit. Items Collectors, Masons, Shriners. Home and Office: 7505 Democracy Blvd Apt 439 Bethesda MD 20817-1284

REISERT, CHARLES EDWARD, JR., real estate executive; b. New Albany, Ind., Apr. 5, 1941; s. Charles Edward Sr. and Jane. W. (Willcox) R.; m. Mary Lynn Nunemacher, Nov. 9, 1963; children: Perry G., Heidi L. BS in Edn., Ind. U., 1963, MA, 1968. Tchr. Ind. Pub. Schs., 1963-67; mgr. Ind. Bell Tel. Co., Indpls., 1967-70; trust officer Ind. Nat. Bank, Indpls., 1970-72; ptnr. R.F.R. Prodns. Inc., Zionsville; dir. Wichita (Kans.) Art Assn., 1972-73; Realtor Century 21 Realty Group-Reisert, Jeffersonville, Ind., 1973—. Mem. Ind. Real Estate Commn., 1982—90, pres., 1990; past pres. Clark County Youth Shelter; bd. dirs., past pres. United Way Clark County; bd. dirs. New Hope, Inc., Sagamore of Wabash; mem. Leadership So. Ind., Leadership Louisville, Clark County Redevel. Commn., Jeffersonville Housing Authority; trustee, pres. Jeffersonville Twp. Pub. Libr.; trustee Clark Meml. Hosp. Found. Recipient Pinnacle award, Sales Mgmt. and Mktg. Assn. of Louisville. Mem. So. Ind. Realtors Assn., (past pres., Realtor of Yr., Realtor Hall of Fame 1998) Nat. Assn. Realtors, Ind. Assn. Realtor, Realtors Nat. Mktg. Inst., So. Ind. C. of C. (past bd. dirs., Profl. of Yr. 1990), Rotary (past pres., Paul Harris fellow). Roman Catholic. Home: 14 Abby Chase Jeffersonville IN 47130-9762 Office: Century 21 Reisert & Assocs 1302 E 10th St Jeffersonville IN 47130-4299 Office Phone: 812-285-5000. Personal E-mail: charleyre@aol.com.

REISIN, EFRAIN, nephrologist, researcher, educator; b. Cordoba, Argentina, Feb. 25, 1943; came to U.S., 1979; s. Maximo and Elisa Reisin; m. Ilana Hershkovitz, Sept. 6, 1971; children: Eyal, Thalia Alexis. MD, Nat. U., Cordoba, 1966. Intern internal medicine Nat. U. Cordoba-Clinicas Hosp., 1966; resident Jimenes Diaz Found., Madrid, 1966-68, Chaim Sheba Med. Ctr., Tel Hashomer, Israel, 1968-71, fellow in nephrology, 1971-74, staff physician nephrology, 1974-77; rsch. fellow in hypertension Health Sci. Ctr., Winnipeg, Man., Can., 1977-78; vis. scientist in hypertension Nat. Health Welfare Can., Winnipeg, Man., 1978-79; Ochsner vis. scientist in hypertension Ochsner Found. Hosp., New Orleans, 1979-82; from asst. prof. to assoc. prof. medicine La. State U., New Orleans, 1982-89, prof. medicine, 1985—, chief sect. nephrology, 1999—. Panelist Consensus Conf., NIH, Bethesda, Md., 1991. Author over 100 articles and book chpts. on hypertension and nephrology; conducted 1st research study documenting positive effects of weight reduction in treatment of hypertension, 1978 (citation classic Inst. Sci. Info. 1988). 1st lt. Israel Army, 1971-72. Grantee Nat. Health and Welfare Can., 1978-79, Am. Heart Assn., 1980-81, also several pharm. cos., 1984—. Fellow ACP, Am. Coun. High Blood Pressure Rsch., Am. Heart Fund, Am. Coll. Clin. Pharmacology (counselor south ctrl. regional chpt. 1991-92), Am. Fedn. Clin. Rsch., So. Soc. for Clin. Investigation; mem. Internat. Soc. Nephrology, Internat. Soc. Hypertension, Am. Soc. Nephrology, Am. Soc. Hypertension, Coun. Nephrology, Am. Heart Assn., Inter-Am. Soc. Hypertension, Orleans Parish Med. Soc. Avocations: tennis, reading, movies. Office: La State U Sch Medicine 1542 Tulane Ave New Orleans LA 70112-2825

REISING, JULIET M. information systems executive; m. Lance Reising; children: Nicholas, Michelle. B in Bus. summa cum laude, U. Ga. cert. CPA. Mgmt., CPA Ernst & Young; CFO AvData, Inc, Composit Comms., Inc., InterServ Svcs. Corp.; exec. v.p., CFP MindSpring Enterprises, Inc.; exec. v.p. Cereus Tech. Ptnrs.; exec. v.p., CFP Verso Tech., Inc., 2000—. Office: Verso Technologies Inc 400 Galleria Pkwy Atlanta GA 30339

REISING, RICHARD P. lawyer; BA, Stanford U.; JD, U. Mo. Bar: Ill. 1970. Asst. gen. counsel, sec. Archer-Daniels-Midland Co., Decatur, Ill., v.p., sec., gen. counsel, 1991-97, sr. v.p., 1997—. Office: Archer-Daniels-Midland Co 4666 E Faries Pky Decatur IL 62526-5666

REISING, RONALD, utilities executive; BA in Econs., Lawrence U.; MA in Mgmt., Northwestern U. CPA. Sr. dir. Deloitte & Touche, 1985—88; v.p. North Am. Venture Group Ltd., 1988—91; various sr. mgmt. positions Ameritech, 1991—2000; CFO Focal Comms., 2000—02; v.p. fin. Cinergy Corp., Cin., 2002—. Office: Cinergy Corp 139 E 4th St Cincinnati OH 45202

REISINGER, RONALD BUSCH (BARON OF INNERYNE, BARON OF CULBIN, LAIRD OF ASCOG CASTLE, LAIRD OF EILEAN NA BEITHE, EARL OF CRAWFORD-LINDSAY, LORD AND BARON OF GARLIES, BARON OF CARSTAIRS), bank executive; b. NYC, Jan. 4, 1943; s. Walter Chalmers and Osa-Lisa Bernadotte (Pearson) Reisinger; m. Carolyn Gall, Dec. 17, 1989; children: Christopher, Hope, Abigail, William, Timothy. Pres., CEO The Reisinger Corp. LLC, Grand Haven, Mich., 1990—. Advisor The Kingdom of Biffeche, Biffeche City, 1965—97; v.p. Central Highland Park Assn., Grand Haven, Mich., 1971—. Decorated knight Grand Cross Order of the Great White Leopard The Kingdom of Biffeche, knight Grand Cross Order of the Palm, knight Grand Cross of The Military Order the Sword of St. Michael, knight G.C. of the Most Illustrious Order of the Raven, knight Grand Crescent the Order of the Crescent, knight Grand Cross of the Order of The Elephant, knight of Saint Germain Scotland's House of Stuart, knight Grand Cross and Grand Prior for N.Am. the Order of The Holy Trinity Ukraine, comdr. the Military and Hospitaller Order of St. Lazarus of Jerusalem Duc de Brissac, knight of Moravian Order St. Wrastislav and St. Columba. Mem.: Celtic Soc., Monarchist League, Traveler's Century Club, Circumnavigators Club, Carlouel Yacht Club, Royal Yacht Club of Biffeche, Bayou Club, Atlanta Polo Club, Spring Lake Country Club, St. Louis Country Club, Kyles of Bute Angling Club (hon.), Convention of the Baronage of Scotland (life). Home: 9441 Beachberry Pl Pinellas Park FL 33782 Office: The Barony of Inneryne Ascog Castle Argylle Tighnabruaich PA21 2BY Scotland Personal E-mail: rreisin1@tampabay.rr.com.

REISINGER, SANDRA SUE, columnist; b. Washington Court House, Ohio, Feb. 27, 1946; d. Dale E. and Elinor Jean (McMurry) R. BS, Ohio State U., 1968, MA, 1969; JD, U. Dayton, Ohio, 1980. Bar: Ohio 1980. Tchg. asst. Ohio State U., 1968-69; with Dayton Daily News, 1969-81, asst. mng. editor, 1976-81; mng. editor The Miami (Fla.) News, 1981-89, Broward Miami (Fla.) Herald, 1989-93, mng. editor, asst. mng. editor, 1994-98, viewpoint editor, 1998-99; columnist The Herald, Ft. Lauderdale, 1999—. Adj. prof. Sinclair (Ohio) C.C., 1971-74, U. Dayton, Ohio, 1980-81. Mem. ABA, AP Mng. Editors Assn. (bd. dirs. 1982-87, exec. com. 1987-94, pres. 1992). Office: The Herald 1520 E Sunrise Blvd Fort Lauderdale FL 33304-2327

REISLER, HELEN BARBARA, public relations executive; b. NYC, June 21; d. George and Elizabeth Lois (Schultz) Gottesman; m. Melvin Reisler, June 5, 1955; children: Susan O'Brien, Karen Reisler, Keith James. BS in Edn., NYU, 1954; MS in Edn. and Reading, L.I. U., 1978. Elem. tchr., N.Y.C., 1954-78; instr. grad. sch., adj. lectr. L.I. U., Bklyn., 1978; acct. exec. N.Y. Yellow Pages, Inc., N.Y.C., 1979, personnel mgr., 1979, adminstrv. dir., 1980-83, v.p. personnel, 1983-84, v.p. adminstrn./personnel, 1984-85, also dir.; staff specialist sales and market support Southwestern Bell Publs., 1985-88; N.Y. mgr. pub. rels. and recruitment N.Y. Yellow Pages/Mast Advt. and Publs., Inc. of Southwe. Bell, 1988; cons. human resources devel. and product promotion, 1989—. Recruiter N.E. Region, N.Y. area cmty. rels. rep.; moderator weekly cable TV show New York Business Forum, N.Y.C., 1983-85. Founder Firefighters Vacation com., 2001—02; bd. dirs. Park Slope Geriatric Ctr., 2002—, Heritage Hills Condo. Assn., 2000—. Named Ptnr. in Edn., N.Y.C. Bd. Edn., 1984, Golden Poets Award; Paul Harris award, 2003. Mem. Internat. Assn. Sales Profls. (bd. dirs. 1993, 94), UN Assn., Sales Execs. Club NY (bd. dirs., reception, membership and mem. rels. coms., chmn. youth edn., v.p. 1987-88, chmn. internal com. 1989), Execs. Assn. Greater NY (chmn. com. Sec. Day), Heritage Hills Country Club Westchester (bd. dirs. 2000—), Sales Exec. Club (v.p.), N.Y. Rotary (chmn. environ. com. 1991—, bd. liaison to pub. rels. and membership coms. 1994—, interviewering com.scholarship candidates 1993-2003, mentor Japanese amb. scholars, 1992-93, divsn. chmn. cmty. svcs., chmn. pub. rels. com., bd. liaison, 1996-2001, 03, bd. dirs., co-chmn. advt. com. chmn. pub. rels. 1996-2004, coord. Gift of Life, 2d v.p. bd. dirs. 1998—, 1st v.p., bd. dirs. 1999—, pres. 2001, prodr. cable TV series N.Y. Rotary-A Club That Works, exec. prodr. Gift of Life-A Child's Story, apptd. media liaison to N.Y. 1998—, creator 9/11 disaster fund 2001-02, chmn. 9/11 adv. com., chmn. publicity and pub. rels., dist. leadership com. 2002, 2004, #7230 dist. gov.-elect, 2004, Paul Harris fellow 1992, 2001, 03, Disting. Pres. award 2001-02, Pub. Rels. award, 1905 Silver Nickel award 2003, Global History fellowship, bd. dirs. 2003—, 4x Dist. P.R. award, Svc. Above Self award), Dutch Treat Club, 100 Club. Office: 47 Plaza St W Brooklyn NY 11217-3905 Personal E-mail: helenbreisler@aol.com.

REISMAN, JUDITH ANN GELERNTER, media communications executive, educator; b. Hillside, N.J., Apr. 11, 1935; MA in Speech Comm., Case Western Res. U., 1976, PhD in Speech Comm., 1980. Faculty dept. anthropology and sociology Haifa U., Israel, 1981—83; rsch. prof. sch. edn. Am. U., Washington, 1983—85; founder, pres. Inst. Media Edn., 1985—. Cons., reviewer grant proposals audio-visual drug programs for youth Dept. Edn., 1987; rsch. design cons. Alcohol and Tobacco Media Analysis in Mainstream Mags., Dept. HHS, 1987—90; cons., field reviewer Drug Free Youth Sch. Candidates Dept. Edn., 1988; lectr., adj. prof. George Mason U., Va., 1990; expert witness Pres.'s Commn. on Assignment of Women in Armed Forces, 1992, U.S. Atty. Gen. Commn. on Pornography, 1985—86, U.S. Atty. Gen. Task Force on Domestic Violence, Washington, 1985, Mapplethorpe Trial, Cin., 1990, Australian Parliament, 1992, Ga. State Senate, 1992; nominated to panel on sex harassment in the Air Force U.S. Inspector Gen., 2003; sci. advisor Protective Parents Assn.; subcom. junk sci. Am. Legis. Exchange Coun. Edn. Task Force, 1999—2004. Author: Images of Children, Crime and Violence in Playboy, Penthouse and Hustler, 1989, Kinsey, Sex and Fraud, 1990, Softport Plays Hardball, 1991, Kinsey, Crimes and Consequences, 1998, 2003; contbr. preme Ct. cases to profl. jours. Co-recipient Scholastic Mag. awards, Dukane award, 1982; recipient Gold Camera award, 1982, Silver Screen award, 1982, Filmstrip of Yr. award, 1981—82, Silver Plaque award, 1982, Family Svc. Assn. Am. 1st pl. award local TV series, 1974, Best of 1965 award, 1965, Scientist of Yr. for Children award, 1993. Mem.: AAAS, Women in Neurosci., Nat. Black Child Devel. Inst., Soc. Sci. Study Sex, N.Y. Acad. Scis., Internat. Comm. Assn., Am. Statis. Assn., Am. Assn. Composers, Authors and Pubs., Nat. Assn. Scholars. Office: 4120 Douglas Blvd 508 Granite Bay CA 95746-9562

REISMAN, RICHARD S. publisher; b. Spring Valley, N.Y., Nov. 6, 1953; s. Herbert and Phyllis Sharon (Hendler) R.; children: Marisa, Kimberly. BA, SUNY, Binghamton, 1975; JD, George Washington U., 1978; MBA, UCLA, 1985. Assoc. McCandless & Barrett, Washington, 1978-80, Donahue, Gallagher, Thomas & Woods, Oakland, Calif., 1980-83; mgr. corp. strategy Times Mirror, L.A., 1985-87; dir. mktg. L.A. Times/Orange County Edit., Costa Mesa, Calif., 1987-90; pub. Orange County Bus. Jour., Irvine, Calif., 1990—. Bd. dirs. Employers Group, 1996—; adv. bd. Orange County Com. for the Arts, 1993—; mem.bd. counselors Chapman U., 1998—; bd. dirs. Orange County Bus. Coun., 1995—; bd. dirs., membership chair, Calif. Coast chpt. YPO; chief exec. roundtable U. Calif., Irvine, 1995—. R.C. Baker Found. fellow UCLA Sch. Mgmt., 1984. Mem. Partnership 2010 (bd. dirs. 1992—). Avocations: tennis, reading, pub. affairs. Office: Orange County Bus Jour 2600 Michelson Dr Ste 170 Irvine CA 92612-6595 E-mail: Reisman@ocbj.com.

REISMAN, ROBERT E. physician, educator; b. Buffalo, Nov. 1, 1932; s. Harry S and Jessie (Goldberg) Reisman; m. Rena Estry, Sept. 5, 1954; children: Jeanne, Linda, Nancy, David. MD, SUNY-Buffalo, 1956; Dr.h.c., U. Montpellier (France), 1982. Diplomate (bd dirs 1984-86) Am Bd Internal Med, (bd dirs 1981-86, chmn 1985, mem residency rev comt allergy and immunology 1988-93, chmn 1990-91 Am Bd Allergy and Clin Immunology. Intern Buffalo Gen. Hosp., 1956-57, resident in medicine, 1957-59; practice medicine specializing in allergy and clin. immunology Buffalo, 1961—; clin. prof. pediatrics and medicine SUNY, Buffalo, 1978—. Co-dir Allergy Research Lab Buffalo Gen Hosp, 1970—90; mem panel allergenic extracts Bur Biologists FDA. With U.S. Army, 1968—69. Master: ACP; fellow: Am Acad Allergy (pres 1980—81). Home: 113 Carriage Cir Buffalo NY 14221-2163 Office: 295 Essjay Rd Williamsville NY 14221-8216 also: 85 High St Buffalo NY 14203-1149 Office Phone: 716-630-1130. E-mail: rreisman@buffalomedicalgroup.com.

REISMAN, ROSEMARY MOODY CANFIELD, writer, retired humanities educator; b. Des Moines, Nov. 18, 1927; d. V. Alton and Lois Gloria (Slee) Moody; m. Michael Ellison Canfield, Sept. 6, 1952 (div. May 1961); children: Michael, John Charles, Celia Catherine, Christopher James; m. Maurice Reisman, May 10, 1986 (dec. 1990). BA in English, U. Minn., 1949, MA in English, 1952; PhD in English, La. State U., 1971. Reporter Ames (Iowa) Tribune, summer 1944; writer, actor Sta. WOI Pub. Radio, Ames, 1944-48; dir., writer children's plays Sta. KASI, Ames, 1949; tchg. asst. U. Minn., 1949-52; writer Sta. WOI-TV, Ames, summer 1952; writer, show host Sta. WDGY, Mpls., 1952-54; instr. La. State U., 1961-69, NDEA fellow, 1969-71; asst. prof. English Troy (Ala.) State U., 1971-80, assoc. prof., 1980-90, chairperson dept. English, 1985-90, prof., 1990-94. Mem. honors coun. Troy State U., 1985-94, mem. honors faculty, 1986-94, mem. acad. coun., 1989-92, mem. faculty adv. coun., 1990-92, Rhodes scholar instnl. rep., 1987-91; adj. prof. Charleston So. U., 1996-99, vis. prof., 1999—; coord. sr. honors seminar Coll. of Charleston, 1996-98; writer, cons. Baton Rouge State Times—Morning Adv., 1963-70; prodr., writer Perspectives project films Ala. ETV, 1977-80; chairperson conf. sessions South Ctrl. Soc. for 18th-Century Studies, 1988, Southeastern Am. Soc. for 18th Century Studies, 1991, 93; chairperson workshop Ala. Coun. Tchrs. of English, fall 1987; grant writer, project dir. Ala. Humanities Found., 1980, 89, asst. project dir. summer grad. course, 1990, presenter various instns., 1985-94; grant writer, project dir. Ala. Pub. Libr. Sys., 1977-80; lectr., presenter various pub. librs. for Auburn Ctr. for Arts and Humanities, 1989-97; presenter numerous lectures and lectr. series, various instns., 1970—, resident Richland Co., SC, 2002-. Author: Perspectives: The Alabama Heritage, 1978; co-author: Contemporary Southern Women Fiction Writers, 1994, Southern Men Fiction Writers, 1998; chairperson editl. adv. bd. Ala. Lit. Rev., 1986-94; mem. editl. bd. Biog. Guide to Ala. Lit., 1985—; guest editor spl. issue Ala. English 7, spring 1995; contbr. essays, articles and revs. to lit. pubs. Baldwin County Humanities scholar Ala. Humanities Found., 1983, 84; finalist Ingalls award for Outstanding Tchg., 1991. Mem.: AAUW (past br. pres., mem. steering com.), NEA, Thomas Cooper Soc. (bd. dirs. 2001—), English Spkg. Union (bd. dirs. Charleston 1997—98, pres. 1998—2002, Sourcelist spkr. 1999—2000), Troy State U. Edn. Assn. (pres. 1990—93), Ala. Edn. Assn., Assn. Coll. English Tchrs. Ala., Assn. Depts. English (state pres. 1986—88), South Atlantic MLA, Soc. of Mary, Soc. of Mary, Gamma Beta Phi (nat. pres. 1978—79, cert. of merit 1979), Phi Beta Kappa (del. to nat. triennial coun. 1991, alt. 1994, pres. Low Country Assn. 1996—98, del. 1997, bd. dirs. 1998—2001, alt. del. 2000, bd. dirs. 2003—, past pres. S.E. Ala. assn.), Confrat. of the Blessed Sacrament. Anglican. Home and Office: 121 Innisbrook Bend Summerville SC 29483-5084

REISMAN, WILLIAM M. lawyer, educator; b. 1939; LL.B., Hebrew U., 1963; LL.M., Yale U., 1964, J.S.D., 1965. Bar: Conn. 1964. Assoc. prof. Yale U. Law Sch., New Haven, 1969-72, prof., 1972-82, Hohfeld prof. jurisprudence, 1982-98, McDougal prof. internat. law, 1998—. Mem. Inter-Am. Commn. on Human Rights, 1990—95, chmn., 1994—95; vice-chmn. Policy Scis. Ctr., Inc., 1992—; assoc. Inst. Droit Internat., 1999; pres. Arbitration Tribunal Bank for Internat. Settlements, 2001—; mem. Eritrea-Ethiopia Boundary Commn., 2001—; pres. Anglo-Irish OSPAR Convention Tribunal, 2001—03. Author: Nullity and Revision, 1971, Art of the Possible: Diplomatic Alternatives in Middle East, 1970, Puerto Rico and the International Process, 1974, Folded Lies: Bribery, Crusades and Reforms, 1979, (with Weston) Toward World Order and Human Dignity, 1976, (with McDougal) International Law in Contemporary Perspective, 1981, (with McDougal) International Law Essays, 1981, (with McDougal) Power and Policy in Quest of Law: Essays in Honor of Eugene V. Rostow, 1985, (with Schreiber) Jurisprudence: Understanding and Shaping Law, 1986, (with Willard) International Incidents: The Law that Counts in World Politics, 1988, (with James E. Baker) Regulating Covert Action: Practices, Contexts and Policies of Covert Coercion Abroad in International and American Laqw, 1991, Systems of Control in International Adjudication and Arbitration: Breakdown and Repair, 1992, (with Westerman) Straight Baselines in International Maritime Boundary Delimitation, 1992, (with C. Antoniou) The Laws of War, 1994, The Supervisory Jurisdiction of the International Court of Justice: International Arbitration and International Adjudication, 1997, (with Craig W. Park and J. Paulsson) International Commercial Arbitration: Cases, Materials and Notes on the Resolution of International Business Disputes, 1997, Law in Brief Encounters, 1999, Jurisdiction in International Law, 1999; editor-in-chief Am. Jour. Internat. Law, 1998-2003. Decorated 1st class Order of Bahrain; Fulbright grantee, 1966-67 Mem. Fgn. Policy Assn. (bd. dirs. 1997—), Coun. Fgn. Rels, Am. Soc. of Internat. Law (Manley O. Hudson Medal). Office: Yale U Law Sch PO Box 208215 New Haven CT 06520-8215 Fax: 203-432-7247. E-mail: michael.reisman@yale.edu.

REISMANN, HERBERT, engineer, educator; b. Vienna, Jan. 26, 1926; s. Henrik and Olga (Pokorny) R.; m. Edith Falber, Aug. 14, 1952; children—Sandra Jean, Barbara Anne. BS in Aero. Engring., Ill. Inst. Tech., 1947, MS, 1949; PhD in Engring., U. Colo., 1962. Project engr. Convair, Ft. Worth, 1951-53; prin. structures engr. Republic Aviation Corp., Hicksville, N.Y., 1954-56; chief engr. systems analysis, chief solid mechanics Martin Marietta Corp., 1957-64; prof., dir. aerospace engring. SUNY, Buffalo, 1964—2001, prof. emeritus, 2002—. Cons. NASA, Bell Aero Systems Corp. Co-author: Elastokinetics, 1974, Elasticity, 1980; author: Elastic Plates, 1988; contbr. articles to profl. jours. Assoc. fellow AIAA (award best tech. paper 1962, oustanding aerospace achievement award 1987); mem. ASME, Internat. Assn. Bridge and Structural Engring., AAUP, Sigma Xi, Tau Beta Pi. Home: 71 Chaumont Dr Buffalo NY 14221-3511 Office: SUNY-Buffalo 605 Furnas Hall Buffalo NY 14260-4200 Office Phone: 716-634-5862. E-mail: herreis@msn.com.

REISNER, LORIN L. lawyer; b. Bklyn., Dec. 30, 1961; s. Ira Aaron and Roberta Goldglit. AB in Politics, Brandeis U., 1983; JD, Harvard U., 1986. Bar: N.Y. 1987, U.S. Dist. Ct. (so. dist.) N.Y. 1987, U.S. Ct. Appeals (2d cir.) 1991. Law clk. to judge U.S. Dist. Ct. (so. dist.) N.Y., NYC, 1986-87; assoc. Debevoise & Plimpton, NYC, 1987-90; asst. U.S. atty. for so dist. N.Y. U.S. Atty.'s Office, NYC, 1990—94; ptnr. Debevoise & Plimpton. Author: (with Bruce P. Keller) Tademark Related Causes of Action and Defenses, 1989. Mem. alumni admissions coun. Brandeis U., 1987—. Mem. ABA, Assn. of Bar of City of N.Y. Democrat. Jewish. Office: Debevoise & Plimpton 919 Third Ave New York NY 10022 Office Phone: 212-909-6191. Office Fax: 212-909-6836. Business E-Mail: llreisner@debevoise.com.

REISNER, MILTON, psychiatrist, psychoanalyst; b. N.Y.C., Jan. 30, 1934; s. Maximillian and Dora Reisner; m. Linda Ellis, Mar. 3, 1959 (div. 1975); children: Margaret Ann, Amanda Lee. BA, NYU, 1954; MD, Downstate Med. Ctr., 1958. Diplomate Am. Bd. Forensic Examiners, Nat. Bd. Med. Examiners, Am. Bd. Forensic Medicine, N.Y. State Bd. Psychiat. Examiners. Resident in psychiatry Kings County Hosp., Bklyn., 1959-62; sr. psychiatrist Manhattan VA Hosp., N.Y.C., 1962-66; assoc. dir. psychiatry Westchester Community Mental Health Bd., White Plains, N.Y., 1966-69; dir. psychiatry Westchester Mental Health Bd., White Plains, 1969-74; pvt. practice N.Y.C., 1976—. Cons. Cath. Charities, N.Y.C., 1965-66, H.I.P., N.Y.C., 1973-74, NYU Med. Ctr., 1963-68. Contbr. articles to profl. jours. Lt. j.g. USPHS, 1958-59. Fellow Am. Soc. Psychoanalytic Physicians; mem. Am. Assn. Psychoanalytic Physicians (pres. 1985-86, 87-88, Plaque 1988), Nat. Arts Club, Phi Beta Kappa. Achievements include research in mirroring as a technique for treating delusions. Office: 200 E 84th St New York NY 10028-2906

REISS, DALE ANNE, accounting executive, investment company executive; b. Sept. 3, 1947; d. Max and Nan (Hart) R.; m. Jerome L. King, Mar. 5, 1978; children: Matthew Reiss, Mitchell, Stacey. BS, Ill. Inst. Tech., 1967; MBA, U. Chgo., 1970. CPA, Fla., Ill., Mich., Mo. Cost acct. First Nat. Bank, Chgo., 1967; asst. contr. City Colls. of Chgo., 1967-71; dir. fin. Chgo. Dept. Pub. Works, 1971-73; prin. Arthur Young & Co., Chgo., 1973-80; sr. v.p., contr. Urban Investment & Devel. Co., Chgo., 1980-85; mng. ptnr. Ernst & Young LLP, Chgo., 1985-98, Ernst & Young, N.Y.C., 1998-99; global dir. real estate, hospitality and constrn. Ernst & Young LLP, N.Y.C., 1999—. Bd. dirs. Ill. Inst. Tech., Urban Land Inst.; adv. bd. Kellogg Real Estate, Northwestern U., U. Chgo. Grad. Sch. of Bus. Mem. AICPA, Fin. Execs. Inst., Chgo. Network (bd. dirs.), Econ. of Chgo. Club, Met. Club, Chgo. Yacht Club, N.Y. Athletic Club. Office: Ernst & Young 5 Times Sq 16th Fl New York NY 10036-6530 E-mail: dale.reiss@ey.com.

REISS, GEORGE RUSSELL, JR., physician; b. Phila., Dec. 25, 1928; s. G. Russell Sr. and Mary Ellen (Brogan) R.; m. Rosemarie Theresa Curcillo, Sept. 19, 1959; children: Mary Elizabeth, Stephanie, G. Russell III, Charlene. BA, LaSalle U., 1953; MD, Temple U., 1957. Diplomate Am. Bd. Pediatrics. Intern Misericordia Hosp., Phila., 1957-58; resident pediatrics St. Christopher Hosp. for Children, Phila., 1958-60; pvt. practice Glenside, Pa., 1960—. With USCG, 1946-49. Mem. Montgomery County Med. Soc., Pa. Med. Soc., Am. Acad. Pediatrics, AMA, Am. Assn. Pro-Life Pediatricians. Roman Catholic. Office: 2220 Mount Carmel Ave Glenside PA 19038-4610 Office Phone: 215-884-7861. E-mail: grcreissjr@aol.com.

REISS, HOWARD, chemistry professor; b. N.Y.C., Apr. 5, 1922; s. Isidor and Jean (Goldstein) R.; m. Phyllis Kohn, July 25, 1945; children: Gloria, Steven. AB in Chemistry, NYU, 1943; PhD in Chemistry, Columbia U., 1949. With Manhattan Project, 1944-46; instr., then asst. prof. chemistry Boston U., 1949-51; with Ctrl. Rsch. Lab., Celanese Corp. Am., 1951-52, Edgar C. Bain Lab. Fundamental Rsch., U.S. Steel Corp., 1957, Bell Telephone Labs., 1952-60; asso. dir., then dir. rsch. div. Atomics Internat., div. N.Am. Aviation, Inc., 1960-62; dir. N.Am. Aviation Sci. Ctr., 1962-67, v.p. co., 1963-67; v.p. rsch. aerospace systems group N.Am. Rockwell Corp., 1967-68; vis. lectr. chemistry U. Calif. at Berkeley, summer 1957; vis. prof. chemistry UCLA, 1961, 62, 64, 67, prof., 1968-91, prof. emeritus, 1991—; vis. prof. U. Louis Pasteur, Strasbourg, France, 1986, U. Pa., 1989; vis. fellow Victoria U., Wellington, New Zealand, 1989. Vis. fellow Princeton (N.J.) Materials Inst., 1996; cons. to chem.-physics program USAF Cambridge Rsch. Labs., 1950-52; chmn. editor Procs. Internat. Conf. Nucleation and Interfacial Phenomena, Boston; mem. USAF Office Sci. Rsch. Physics and Chemistry Rsch. Evaluation Groups, 1966—, Oak Ridge Nat. Lab. Reactor Chemistry Adv. Com., 1966-68; adv. com. math. and phys. scis. NSF, 1970-72, ARPA Materials Rsch. Coun., 1968—; chmn. site rev. com. NRC Associateships Program, Naval Rsch. Lab., 1989. Author: Methods of Thermodynamics, 1965; author articles; editor in field.; editor: Progress in Solid State Chemistry, 1962-71, Jour. Statis. Physics, 1968-75, Jour. Colloid Interface Sci; mem. editorial adv. bd. Internat. Jour. Physics and Chemistry of Solids, 1955, Progress in Solid State Chemistry, 1962-73, Jour. Solid State Chemistry, 1969, Jour. Phys. Chemistry, 1970-73, Ency. of Solid State, 1970, Jour. Nonmetals, 1971—, Jour. Colloid and Interface Sci., 1976-79, Langmuir, 1985—. Guggenheim Meml. fellow, 1978; Howard Reiss chair in chemistry and biochemistry established named in his honor, UCLA, 1999. Fellow AAAS, Am. Phys. Soc. (exec. com. div. chem. physics 1966-69); mem. NAS, Am. Chem. Soc. (chmn. phys. chemistry sect. N.J. sect. 1957, Richard C. Tolman medal 1973, Kendall award in colloid and surface chemistry 1980, J.H. Hildebrand award in theoretical and exptl. phys. chemistry of liquids 1991, Van Arkel hon. chair in chemistry U. Leiden, The Netherlands, 1994), Am. Assn. for Aerosol Rsch. (David Sinclair award 1997), Phi Beta Kappa, Sigma Xi, Phi Lambda Upsilon. Office: U Calif Dept Chemistry And Biochemis Los Angeles CA 90095-0001

REISS, IRA LEONARD, retired sociology educator, writer; b. N.Y.C., Dec. 8, 1925; s. Philip and Dorothy (Jacobs) R.; m. Harriet Marilyn Eisman, Sept. 4, 1955; children: David, Pamela, Joel. BS cum laude, Syracuse U., 1949; MA, Pa. State U., 1951, PhD, 1953. Instr. in sociology Bowdoin Coll., Brunswick, Maine, 1953-55; asst. prof. sociology Coll. William and Mary, Williamsburg, Va., 1955-59; asst. prof. Bard Coll., Annandale-0n-Hudson, N.Y., 1959-61; assoc. to full prof. U. Iowa, Iowa City, 1961-69; prof. U. Minn., Mpls., 1969-96, prof. emeritus, 1996—. Rsch. evaluator U.S. Dept. Edn. and Nat. Inst. Child Health and Human Devel., Washington, 1966-78; rsch. dir. Family Study Ctr., U. Minn., 1969-74; ednl. advisor Kimberly-Clark Corp., Neenah, Wis., 1971-75; chair planning com. and bd. dirs. Inst. for Child, Adolescent Sexual Health, 1992-93; lectr. at 200 univs., 150 profl. mtgs., 100 civic groups, 1953-96; vis. prof. Uppsala Univ., Sweden, 1975-76. Author: Premarital Sexual Standards in America, 1960, The Social Context of Premarital Sexual Permissiveness, 1967, Family Systems in America, 1971, 4th edit., 1988, Journey into Sexuality: An Exploratory Voyage, 1986, An End to Shame: Shaping Our Next Sexual Revolution, 1990, Solving America's Sexual Crises, 1997, At the Dawn of the Sexual Revolution: Reflections on a Dialogue, 2002; editor: 3 textbooks; contbr. over 150 papers to jours. and textbooks in field. Mem. ACLU, 1948—, Planned Parenthood, 1960—, Nat. Abortion Rights Action League 1975—, Amnesty Internat., 1984—. With U.S. Army, 1944-46, ETO. Mem. Midwest Sociol. Soc. (pres. 1971-72), Am. Sociol. Assn. (chair family sect. 1975-76), Nat. Coun. on Family Rels. (pres. 1979-80, Reuben Hill award 1980, E.W. Burgess award 1984), Polish Acad. Sexual Sci. (hon., Internat. Sexual Sci. award 1989), Soc. for Sci. Study Sex (pres. 1980-81, Disting. Sci. Achievement award 1982, Alfred Kinsey award 1990), Internat. Acad. Sex Rsch. (pres. 1984-85), Am. Assn. Sex Educators, Counselors and Therapists (leadership award 1993). Democrat. Jewish. Avocation: good conversations with family and friends. Home: 5932 Medicine Lake Rd Minneapolis MN 55422-3328 E-mail: Reiss001@atlas.socsci.umn.edu.

REISS, JEROME, retired lawyer; b. Bklyn., Dec. 7, 1924; s. William and Eva (Marenstein) Reiss; m. Naomi Betty Plutzik, June 15, 1947; children: Robert Scott, Harlan Morgan, Andrea Ellen, Samantha Glynis. BA, Bklyn. Coll., 1948; JD, Harvard U., 1951. Bar: N.Y. 1951, U.S. Dist. Ct. (so. dist.) N.Y. 1954, U.S. Ct. Claims 1960, U.S. Dist. Ct. (ea. dist.) N.Y. 1964, DC 1967, U.S. Dist. Ct. (we. dist.) N.Y. 1979, U.S. Supreme Ct. 1989. Staff atty. civil br. Legal Aid Soc., N.Y.C., 1951—54; asst. corp. counsel City of N.Y., 1954—58; assoc. Max E. Greenberg, 1958-67; sr. ptnr. Max E. Greenberg, Trayman, Cantor, Reiss & Blasky, 1967-80, Max E. Greenberg, Cantor & Reiss, N.Y.C., 1980-88, Thelen, Marrin, Johnson & Bridges, N.Y.C., 1989-97, Thelen, Reid & Priest, 1997-2000; ret., 2003. Arbitrator Small Claims Ct., 1960—88; advisor Fed. Pub., Inc.; chmn. bd. AMT-Pacific, Israel, 2000—02; lectr. in field; cons. in field; rep. Japanese, Turkish, Israeli contractors internat. and doing bus. in Japan, Israel, Bahrain, Turkey, St. Croix, Puerto Rico, China, Rep. Korea, and Taiwan. Contbr. articles to profl. jours., chapters to books. Trustee Brownsville Boys Club and Alumni Assn.; gen. counsel Artist Fellowship, Inc. With USAAF, 1943—46. Fellow: Am. Coll. Constrn. Lawyers (founding mem.); mem.: IBA, ABA, N.Y. Bar Assn., Jacob K. Javits Conv. Ctr. Oper. Corp. (bd. dirs.), Mcpl. Assist. Corp. City of N.Y. (bd. dirs.), Am. Arbitrators Assn.

REISS, JOHN BARLOW, lawyer; b. London, Aug. 29, 1939; arrived in U.S., 1963; s. James Martin and Margaret Joan (Ping) R.; m. Mary Jean Maudsley, Aug. 6, 1967 (div. 1978); m. Kathleen Strouse, Aug. 2, 1979; 1 child, Juliette Blanche. BA with honors, Exeter U., Devon, Eng., 1961; AM, Washington U., St. Louis, 1966, PhD, 1971; JD, Temple U., 1977. Bar: Pa. 1977, N.J. 1977, U.S. Dist. Ct. N.J. 1977, D.C. 1980, U.S. Supreme Ct. 1981, U.S. Dist. Ct. D.C. 1982. Economist Commonwealth Econ. Com., London, 1962-63; asst. prof. Allegheny Coll., Meadville, Pa., 1967-71; assoc. prof. Stockton State Coll., Pomona, N.J., 1971-75; asst. health commr. State of N.J., Trenton, 1975-79; dir. office of health regulation U.S. Dept. HHS, Washington, 1979-81; assoc. Baker & Hostetler, Washington, 1981-82, Dechert Price & Rhoads, Phila., 1982-86, ptnr., 1986-93, asst. chair health law group, 1984-91, chmn. health law group, 1991-93; ptnr. Saul Ewing LLP, Phila., 1993—, chmn. health law dept., 1995—2002, chmn. health law practice group, 2002—. Mem. editl. bd. Topics in Hosp. Law, 1985-86, Hosp. Legal Forms Manual, 1985-2002, Jour. Health Care Tech., 1984-86; contbr. Hosp. Contracts Manual, 1983-2002; contbr. articles to profl. jours., chpts. to books. Bd. dirs. Gateway Sch. Little Children, Phila., 1986-99; bd. dirs. ECRI, Plymouth Meeting, Pa., 1994—, chmn. bd., 2001—; mem. bd. vestry All Saints Ch., Wynnewood, Pa., 1993, 96-2001. Pub. Health Svc. fellow, 1979-81, English Speaking Union fellow, 1963-66, Econ. Devel. Adminstr. fellow Washington U., 1966-67. Mem. Nat. Health Lawyers Assn., Phila. Bar Assn., Brit. Am. C. of C. of Greater Phila. (bd. dirs. 1991), Union League of Phila., Univ. Barge Club, Brit. Officers Club of Phila. (first v.p. 2003—). Avocations: gardening, house restoring, reading, sculling. Home: 415 Wister Rd Wynnewood PA 19096-1808 Office: Saul Ewing LLP 3800 Centre Sq W Philadelphia PA 19102 E-mail: jreiss@saul.com.

REISS, LENORE ANN, language educator, retired secondary school educator; b. Bklyn., Apr. 17, 1936; d. Morris and Alice Shestack; m. Edward Lawrence Reiss, Sept. 13, 1959 (dec. June 5, 2000); children: Stephanie Lynne, Jonathan David. BA cum laude, Boston U., 1957; student, Middlebury Coll., 1956, NYU, 1974—76, U. Miami, 1979. Tchr. Spanish and French Martin Van Buren HS, Queens Village, NY, 1957—59; pvt. tutor N.Y.C., 1960—77; pvt. sch. tchr. Studio on Eleventh St., N.Y.C., 1970—77; tchr. The Livingston Sch., N.Y.C., 1977—78, Chiaravalle Montessori Sch., Evanston, Ill., 1986—87; pvt. tutor Evanston, 1990—95; ret., 1995. Author: White-Robed Recluse: A Study of Emily Dickinson, 1993, Genius of Darkness: A Study of Edgar Allan Poe, 1994, The Good Lady of Nohant: A Study of George Sand, 1995; contbr. poems to jours., articles to profl. jours. Avocations: reading, music, dance, antiques, theater. Home: 2025 Sherman Ave Evanston IL 60201

REISS, PAUL JACOB, academic administrator; b. Lake Placid, NY, Aug. 10, 1930; s. Julian J. and Daisy M. (Smith) R.; m. Rosemary A. Donohue, June 25, 1955; children: Catherine, Paul, Gregory, Mark, Julia, David, Steven, Martha, John. BS, Holy Cross Coll., 1952; MA, Fordham U., 1954; PhD, Harvard U., 1960; LHD (hon.), Showa U., 1994; LLD (hon.), Middlebury Coll., 1996. Tutor Harvard U., 1954-57; instr., asst. prof. Marquette U., 1957-63, chmn. dept. sociology, 1961-63; asso. prof. sociology Fordham U., Bronx, N.Y., 1963-75, prof., 1976-85, chmn. dept. sociology and anthropology, 1964-68; dean Fordham U. (Liberal Arts Coll.), 1968-69, v.p. acad. affairs, 1969-75, exec. v.p., 1975-85; pres. St. Michael's Coll., Colchester, Vt., 1985-96, pres. emeritus, 1996—. Editor: Sociological Analysis: A Journal in the Sociology of Religion, 1961-68; contbr. articles to profl. jours. Chmn. bd. dir. Julian Reiss Found., Lake Placid, N.Y.; trustee Wadhams Hall Sem. Coll.; bd. dirs. Lake Placid Sinfonietta, Mercy Ulblein Health Found., chmn.; treas. Greater Burlington Indsl. Commn., Nat. Assn. Ind. Colls. and Univs., Assn. Cath. Colls. and Univs., Lake Placid Vis. Bur., St. Edmund's Retreat. Fellow Am. Sociol. Assn.; mem. Assn. for Sociology of Religion (pres.), Assn. Vt. Ind. Colls. (pres.), Vt. Higher Edn. Coun. (pres.), Vt. Bus. Roundtable, Vt. World Trade Office (chmn.). Democrat. Roman Catholic. Home: 10 Forest Brook Rd Lake Placid NY 12946

REISS, ROBERT FRANCIS, physician; b. Watertown, N.Y., Dec. 11, 1938; s. Ernest Paul and Elizabeth Munk (Clark) R.; m. Giovanna Dora Bassi, Apr. 18, 1964; children: Carroll, Christian, Mark, Dylan. AB, Syracuse U., 1959; MD, U. Bologna, Italy, 1965. Diplomate Am. Bd. Pathology (hematology, transfusion medicine). Dir. lab. hematology and blood bank State U. Hosp., Bklyn., 1975-77; asst. prof. pathology SUNY Downstate Med. Ctr., Bklyn., 1975-77; dir. Hudson Valley Blood Svc., Valhalla, N.Y., 1978-85; assoc. prof. pathology and medicine N.Y. Med. Coll., Valhalla, 1978-88; med. dir. N.Y. Blood Ctr., N.Y.C., 1985-88; dir. lab. hematology and transfusion medicine Columbia-Presbyn. Med. Ctr., N.Y.C., 1988-98; prof. clin. pathology and clin. medicine Columbia U. Coll. Physicians and Surgeons, N.Y.C., 1988—; v.p., chief med. officer N.Y. Blood Ctr., N.Y.C., 1998—2001. Chmn. steering com. Hudson Valley Blood Resources Assn., Valhalla, 1981-85; chief examiner blood banking N.Y.C. Dept. Health, 1980-86, mem. adv. com. on blood banking, 1988-90; mem. instnl. rev. bd. N.Y. Blood Ctr., N.Y.C., 1991-2001. Editor, co-author: Clinical Laboratory Medicine, 1992; contbr. more than 40 articles to med. jours., chpts. to books. Bd. mgrs. camping plus N.Y.C. Mission Soc., 1975-78; scout leader Boy Scouts Am., N.Y.C., 1975-80. Col. U.S. Army, 1966-69, USAR, 1988—. Fellow Assn. Clin. Scientists; mem. Am. Assn. Blood Banks (dist. advisor 1982-88, vice chair sect. on hematology and transfusion medicine, mem. editl. bd. Ann. Clin. Labs. Sci. 1999—), Coun. Hosp. Blood Bank Dirs. Greater N.Y. (bd. dirs. 1989-98), Am. Soc. Hematology. Avocations: travel, running, stamps. Office: NY Blood Ctr 310 E 67th St New York NY 10021-6273 Office Phone: 212-570-3142.

REISS, STEVEN, psychology educator; b. N.Y.C., Apr. 10, 1947; s. Benjamin A. and Margaret (Schmidt) R.; m. Maggi B. Reiss, Sept. 4, 1971; children: Michael, Ben AB magna cum laude, Dartmouth Coll., 1964; PhD in Psychology, Yale U., 1972. Registered psychologist, Ill. Prof. psychology U. Ill.-Chgo., 1972-91; prof. psychology and psychiatry Ohio State U., Columbus, 1991—, dir. Nisonger Ctr., 1991—. Dir. ISDD Mental Health Clinic, Chgo., 1980-91. Author: Who Am I: The 16 Basic Desires, 2000; editor: Psychophropic Medications, 1998; author psychol. tests: Reiss Screen, 1988, Anxiety Sensitivity Index, 1986. ARC Rsch. awardee, 1991, NADD Career awardee, 1998. Fellow APA, Am. Assn. Mental Retardation (bd. dirs. 1987, Svc. award 1987). Office: Ohio State Univ 1581 Dodd Dr Columbus OH 43210-1267 Office Phone: 614-292-2390. E-mail: reiss.7@osu.edu.

REISS, STEVEN ALAN, lawyer, law educator; b. NYC, Dec. 18, 1951; s. Louis and Ruth (Harrow) R.; m. Mary A. Mattingly; children: Alexandra Mattingly Reiss, Tyler Brennan Reiss. BA, Vassar Coll., 1973; JD, Stanford (Calif.) U., 1976. Bar: N.Y., D.C., Calif. Law clk. to John Minor Wisdom U.S. Ct. Appeals for 5th Cir., New Orleans, 1976-77; law clk. to justice William J. Brennan U.S Supreme Ct., Washington, 1977-78; assoc. Miller, Cassidy, Larroca & Lewin, Washington, 1978-80; vis. prof. Georgetown U. Law Ctr., Washington, 1981; asst. prof. Law Sch., NYU, 1981-83, assoc. prof., 1984-87, prof., 1987-91; ptnr. Weil, Gotshal & Manges, N.Y.C., 1990—. Editor-in-chief White Collar Crime Reporter, 1987-91, contbg. editor, 1991—. Trustee Vassar Coll. Poughkeepsie, N.Y., 1978-82; bd. dirs. NYU Cmty. Fund, 1984-87, Concert Artists Guild, 1991-94, Lyrics Chamber Music Soc., 2000—; gen. counsel Brennan Ctr. for Justice, 1996—; bd. trustees Vols. of Legal Svcs. Mem. N.Y. State Bar Assn., D.C. Bar Assn., Calif. Bar Assn., Assn. of Bar of City of N.Y. (fed. legis. com. 1981-87), 2d Jud. Conf. (reporter 1984—). Home: 25 E 86th St New York NY 10028-0553 Office: Weil Gotshal & Manges 767 5th Ave Fl Concl New York NY 10153-0119 E-mail: steven.riess@weil.com.

REISS, SUSAN MARIE, editor, writer; b. Washington, Sept. 14, 1963; m. Paul L. Roney Jr., May 25, 1991. BA in English Lit., U. Va., 1985; MA in English, George Mason U., 1989. Editl. asst. Water Pollution Control Fedn., Alexandria, Va., 1985-87; freelance writer, editor Arlington, Va., 1987-90; staff writer George Mason U., Fairfax, Va., 1988-90, Optical Soc. Am.,

Washington, 1990-91, news editor, 1991-93, mng. editor, 1993-96; editor On Campus With Women Assn. Am. Colls. and Univs., 1996—2000; freelance writer, editor Arlington, 1996—. Newsletter editor: Arlington County Tennis Assn., 1990-91, On Campus with Women, 1996-2000; contbr. articles to profl. jours. and mags. Mem. Nat. Press Club, Washington Ind. Writers, D.C. Sci. Writers Assn., N.Y. Acad. Scis., Sigma Tau Delta (founding mem. U. Va. chpt.). Avocations: tennis, piano, cross country skiing. Home and Office: 6814 30th Rd N Arlington VA 22213-1602

REISTER, RAYMOND ALEX, retired lawyer; b. Sioux City, Iowa, Dec. 22, 1929; s. Harold William and Anne (Eberhardt) R.; m. Ruth Elizabeth Alkema, Oct. 7, 1967 AB, Harvard U., 1952, LLB, 1955. Bar: N.Y. 1956, Minn. 1960. Assoc. Paul, Weiss, Rifkind, Wharton & Garrison, N.Y.C., 1955-56; ptnr. Dorsey & Whitney LLP, Mpls., 1959-92; ret., 1993. Instr. U. Minn. Extension Divsn., 1964-66. Editor (with Larry W. Johnson): Minnesota Probate Administration, 1968. Trustee Mpls. Soc. Fine Arts, 1981-87; mem. exec. coun. Minn. Hist. Soc., 1984-2002; bd. dirs. Mpls. Athenaeum, 1992—, pres., 1998-2001; bd. dirs. Minn. Humanities Commn., 1997—. 1st lt. U.S. Army, 1956-59. Mem. Minn. Bar Assn., Hennepin County Bar Assn. Home: 93 Groveland Ter Minneapolis MN 55403-1142 Office: Dorsey & Whitney LLP Ste 1500 50 South 6th Street Minneapolis MN 55402-1498

REISTER, RUTH ALKEMA, lawyer, finance company executive; b. Grand Rapids, Mich., May 30, 1936; d. Henry and Lena (Land) Alkema; m. Raymond A. Reister, Oct. 7, 1967. BA, U. Mich., 1958, JD, 1964; grad. Program in Bus. Adminstrn., Harvard U., 1959, postgrad. Program in Mgmt. Devel., 1976. Bar: Minn., Mich. 1964, U.S. Supreme Ct. 1976. Trust officer Northwestern Nat. Bank, Mpls., 1964-70; asst. counsel, asst. v.p., sec. Fed. Res. Bank, Mpls., 1970-81; asst. sec., bd. govs. Fed. Res. System, 1977; dep. under sec. U.S. Dept. Agr., Washington, 1981-83; pres. First Bank Systems Agrl. Credit Corp., Mpls., 1983-84; pres. Groveland Corp., Mpls., 1986—; dir. Herman Miller, Inc., Zealand, Mich., 1984—. Bd. dirs. United Way, ARC, Jones Harrison Home, Mpls.; bd. dirs., chair Gustavus Adolfus Coll.; chmn. Jones-Harrison Found. Mem. Harvard Bus. Sch. Club Minn., Minn. Women's Econ. Round Table (pres. 1980-81).

REITAN, DANIEL KINSETH, electrical and computer engineering educator; b. Duluth, Minn., Aug. 13, 1921; s. Conrad Ulfred and Joy Elizabeth R.; m. Marian Anne Stemme, July 18, 1946; children: Debra Leah, Danielle Karen. BSEE, N.D. State U., 1946; MSEE, U. Wis., 1949, PhD, 1952. Registered profl. engr., Wis. Control engr. GE, Schenectady, NY, 1946-48; transmission line engr. Gen. Telephone Co., Madison, Wis., 1949-50; mem. faculty Coll. Engring. U. Wis., Madison, 1952-85, prof. elec. and computer engring., 1962-85; cons. Energy Industries, 1985-95; dir. power sys. simulation lab. Coll. Engring. U. Wis., 1968-84, also dir. wind power rsch. Energy Ctr. Coll. Engring. Cons. Nat. Inst. Sci. and Tech. (formerly U.S. Nat. Bur. Stds.); dir. electric network calculator lab. Wis. Utilities, 1959-68. Author: Interstellar Space Travel at Near Light Speed, 1995, The Visual Appearance of Relativistically Moving Objects, 1999; contbr. articles to profl. jours.; patentee in field. Served with U.S. Army, World War II. Recipient Outstanding Tchr. award Polygon Engring. Council., Gov.'s citation for service to State of Wis. Fellow IEEE (Centennial medal and cert. for outstanding achievement 1984, Centennial medal and cert. dept. ECE U. Wis., 1991, IEEE power Engring., Computer Control Indsl. Applications and Edn. Soc.), Conf. Internat. des Grand Reseaux Electriques a Haute Tension, Am. Soc. Engring. Edn., Wis. Acad. Scis., Am. Wind Energy Assn., Sigma Xi, Tau Delta Pi, Tau Beta Pi, Eta Kappa Nu, Kappa Eta Kappa. Lutheran. Home: 1200 Harwood Dr Apt 322 Fargo ND 58104-6294 *I believe that in one's career professionalism and perseverance are key factors in success. In one's personal life, the family should be the center, but not the circumference, about which all activities revolve.*

REITAN, HAROLD THEODORE, management consultant; b. Max, N.D., Nov. 3, 1928; s. Walter Rudolph and Anna Helga (Glesne) R.; m. Margaret Lucille Bonsac, Dec. 29, 1954 (div.); children: Eric, Karen, Chris, Jon. BA, St. Olaf Coll., 1950; MA in Social Psychology, U. Fla., 1962, PhD, 1967. Commd. officer USAF, 1951, advanced through grades to col., 1971; comdr. USAF Spl. Treatment Ctr., Lackland, Tex., 1971-74, USAF Corrections and Rehab. Group, Lowry, Colo., 1974-76, USAF Tech. Tng. Wing, 1976-78; ret., 1978; mgr. health svcs. Coors Industries, Golden, Colo., 1978-84, mgr. tng. and orgnl. devel., 1984—89, cons. mgmt. assessment, tng. and devel., 1989—. Contbr. articles to profl. jours. Decorated D.F.C. with oak leaf cluster, Bronze Star, Legion of Merit with oak leaf cluster, Air medal with 5 oak leaf clusters. Mem. APA, Phi Kappa Phi. Republican. Lutheran. Home and Office: 116 S Nome St Aurora CO 80012-1242 Personal E-mail: htr1@earthlink.net.

REITAN, PAUL HARTMAN, geologist, educator; b. Kanawha, Iowa, Aug. 18, 1928; s. John Olsen and Anna (Meldahl) R.; m. Reidun Engebretsen, Sept. 28, 1962; children: Kirsten Berit, Eric Hartmann. AB (Salisbury fellow), U. Chgo., 1953; PhD (Fulbright fellow), U. Oslo, Norway, 1956. Instr. U. Ill., Chgo., 1955; geologist U.S. Geol. Survey, 1953-56; state geologist Geol. Survey of Norway, 1956-60; asst. prof. mineralogy Stanford U., 1960-66; mem. faculty SUNY, Buffalo, 1966-98, prof. dept. geology emeritus, dean, 1975-79. Cons. U. Calif.-Davis, Am. Geol. Inst.; guest scientist Centre for Geol. Sci., Acad. Sci., Warsaw, Poland, Geol. Survey Prague, Czechoslovakia., Geol. Survey, Norway, Nat. Geophys. Rsch. Inst. and Geol. Survey, India Author: (with Davis and Pestrong) Geology, 1976; contbr. articles to profl. jours. Served with U.S. Army, 1946-49. NATO sr. fellow in sci., 1972; G. Unger Vetlesen fellow, 1973; Fulbright sr. lectr., India, 1986; Norwegian Marshall Fund grantee, 1986, 93. Fellow Geol. Soc. Am., Mineral. Soc. Am., Soc. Econ. Geology, Geol. Soc. India; mem. AAAS, Internat. Assn. Geochemistry and Cosmochemistry, Royal Norwegian Soc. Scis. and Letters (fgn.), Norsk Geologisk Forening (life), Sigma Xi. Home: 120 Walton Dr Buffalo NY 14226-4556 Office: U Buffalo Dept Geology Buffalo NY 14260-3050 Office Phone: 716-645-6800 3988. E-mail: preitan@eng.buffalo.edu.

REITAN, RALPH MELDAHL, clinical neuropsychologist, former educator; b. Beresford, S.D., Aug. 29, 1922; s. John O. and Anna (Meldahl) Reitan; m. Lucille Ann Kirsch, Feb. 14, 1952 (dec. July 1985); children: Ellen, Jon, Ann, Richard, Erik. BA, Ctrl. YMCA Coll., Chgo., 1944; PhD, U. Chgo., 1950. Cert. in clin. psychology and clin. neuropsychology Am. Bd. Profl. Psychology. Instr. U. Chgo., 1948-51; asst. prof. Roosevelt U., Chgo., 1950-51; from asst. prof. to prof. Ind. U. Med. Sch., Indpls., 1951-70; prof. U. Wash., Seattle, 1970-77, U. Ariz., Tucson, 1977-86; pres. Reitan Neuropsychology Labs., Tucson, 1981—. Cons. NIH, Bethesda, Md., 1960-71, VA, Washington, 1955-84, NASA, Washington, 1964-66. Author: Traumatic Brain Injury, 1985, Neuropsychological Evaluation of Older Children, 1992, The Halstead-Reitan Neuropsychological Test Battery, 1993, Detection of Malingering and Invalid Test Results, 1998, Mild Head Injury: Intellectual, Cognitive and Emotional Consequences, 2000, also 15 others; contbr. articles to profl. jours. Trustee Easter Seal Rsch. Found., Chgo., 1974-83. With U.S. Army, 1942-43. Fellow APA, Nat. Acad. Neuropsychology; mem. Am. Neurol. Assn., Am. Acad. Neurology (affiliate), Coalition Clin. Neuropsychology Practitioners, Reitan Soc. Avocations: walking, bird watching. Home: 4831 N Via Serenidad Tucson AZ 85718-5715 Office: Reitan Neuropsychology Labs PO Box 66080 Tucson AZ 85728-6080 Office Phone: 520-299-5725. Personal E-mail: reitanlabs@aol.com.

REITEMEIER, RICHARD JOSEPH, physician; b. Pueblo, Colo., Jan. 2, 1923; s. Paul John and Ethel Regina (McCarthy) Reitemeier; m. Patricia Claire Mulligan, July 21, 1951; children: Mary Louise, Paul, Joseph, Susan, Robert, Patrick, Daniel. AB, U. Denver, 1944; MD, U. Colo., 1946; MS in Internal Medicine, U. Minn., 1954. Diplomate Am. Bd. Internal Medicine . Intern Corwin Hosp., Pueblo, 1946—47; resident Henry Ford Hosp., Detroit, 1949—50, Mayo Found., Rochester, Minn., 1950—53; cons. internal medicine and gastroenterology Mayo Clinic, Rochester, 1954—87; chmn. dept. internal medicine Mayo Clinic (Mayo Clinic and Mayo Med. Sch.), 1967—74, prof., 1971—; bd. govs. Mayo Clinic, 1970—74. Gov. Am. Bd. Internal Medicine, 1971—79, chmn., 1978—79, rep. to Federated Council Internal Medicine, 1977—80, 1983—84, accreditation council grad. med. edn., 1979—85, chmn., 1982—83; governing bd. Am. Bd. Med. Specialties, 1983—86; sci. and med. dir. Ludwig Inst. Cancer Rsch., 1987—88; cons. Kaiser Family Med. Found., 1989—90; med. dir. Phoenix Alliance Inc., 1990—93. Author (with C.G. Moertel): Advanced Gastrointestinal Cancer, Clinical Management and Chemotherapy, 1969; contbr. articles to profl. jours. Trustee Mayo Found., 1970—74, St. Mary's Hosp., Rochester, 1976—82. With U.S. Army, 1947—49. Recipient Alumni award, U. Colo. Sch. Medicine, Irving Cutter award, Phi Rho Sigma, 1986, Disting. Alumnus award, Mayo Found., 1997. Master: ACP (regent 1979—82, gov. for Minn. 1975—79, pres. 1983—84, Alfred Stengel Meml. award 1990); fellow: AMA, Nat. Bd. Med. Examiners (treas. 1987—89), Am. Assn. Study Liver Disease, Am. Assn. Cancer Rsch., Inst. Medicine, Coun. Med. Splty. Socs., Am. Soc. Clin. Oncology, Am. Fedn. Clin. Rsch., Am. Clin. and Climatol. Assn., Am. Gastroenterol. Assn.; mem.: Alpha Omega Alpha. Republican. Roman Catholic. Home: 707 12th Ave SW Rochester MN 55902-2027 Office: 200 1st Ave SW Rochester MN 55902-3129

REITEN, RICHARD G. natural gas industry executive; b. 1939; BA, U. Wash., 1962. With Simpson Timber Co., Seattle, 1962-64, St. Regis Paper Co., Tacoma, 1964-66, Hearin Products, Inc., Portland, Oreg., 1966-71, Di Giorgio Corp., San Francisco, 1971-79, pres. bldg. material group; with Nicoli Co., Portland, 1979-87; dir. Oreg. Econ. Devel. Dept., Salem, 1987-89; pres. Portland Gen. Corp., 1989-92, Portland Gen. Electric Co., 1992-95, pres., COO, 1996-97, pres., CEO, 1997—. Office: Northwest Natural Gas Co One Pacific Square 13th Fl 220 NW 2nd Ave Portland OR 97209-3943

REITER, GLENN MITCHELL, lawyer; b. N.Y.C., Feb. 1, 1951; s. Bernard Leon and Helene (Edson) R.; m. Marilyn Beckhorn, Sept. 5, 1976; children: Benjamin, Diana, Julie. BA, Yale U., 1973, JD, 1976. Bar: N.J. 1976, Pa. 1977, D.C. 1978, N.Y. 1979. Law clk. to judge U.S. Ct. Appeals, Phila., 1976-77; assoc. Schnader, Harrison, Segal & Lewis, Phila., 1977-78, Simpson Thacher & Bartlett LLP, N.Y.C., 1978-84, ptnr., 1984—, resident ptnr. London, 1986-90. Mem. Phi Beta Kappa.

REITER, JOSEPH HENRY, lawyer, retired judge; b. Phila., Mar. 21, 1929; s. Nicholas and Barbara (Hellmann) Reiter; m. Beverlee A. Bearman, Nov. 8, 1993. AB, Temple U., 1950, LLB, 1953. Bar: D.C. 1953, Pa. 1954. Atty. advisor U.S. Army, 1955—61; asst. U.S. atty. Ea. Dist. Pa., 1961—63, asst. U.S. atty. in charge of civil div., 1963—69; chief organized crime and racketeering strike force Western N.Y. State U.S. Dept. Justice, 1969—70, sr. trial atty. tax divsn., 1970—72, regional dir. office of drug abuse law enforcement, 1972—73; dep. atty. gen., dir. Drug Law Enforcement Office of Pa., 1973—77; ptnr. Stassen, Kostos and Mason, Phila., 1978—85, Kostos Reiter & Lamer, 1985—89; judge Armed Svcs. Bd. of Contract Appeals, Falls Church, Va., 1989—95; of counsel Kostos & Lamer, Phila., 1995—. Mem. adv. com. Joint State Commn. on Procurement; lectr. in field. Contbr. articles to profl. jours. With U.S. Army, 1953—55. Recipient Meritorious Svc. award, U.S. Atty. Gen. Clark, 1967, Spl. Commendation, Asst. U.S. Atty. Gen. Tax Divsn., 1969, Outstanding Performance award, U.S. Atty. Gen. Richardson, 1973. Mem.: ABA, Phila. Bar Assn., D.C. Bar Assn., Fed. Bar Assn., Pan Am. Assn. Phila., Vesper Club, Am. Legion. Office: Kostos & Lamer 1608 Walnut St Ste 1300 Philadelphia PA 19103-5407 Office Phone: 215-545-0570., 865-795-7927.

REITER, MICHAEL A. lawyer, educator; b. Pitts., Nov. 15, 1941; BS, U. Wis., 1963, MS, 1964, JD, 1967, PhD, 1969. Bar: Wis. 1967, Ill. 1975, U.S. Supreme Ct. 1975. Ptnr. Holleb & Coff, Chgo., 1987-99, Duane Morris LLC, Chgo., 1999—. Adj. prof. law Northwestern U., Chgo., 1977—99; mem. faculty Nat. Inst. Trial Advocacy, 1980—. Office: Duane Morris LLP 227 W Monroe St Ste 3400 Chicago IL 60606-5098

REITER, ROBERT EDWARD, banker; b. Kansas City, Mo., Dec. 27, 1943; s. Robert Vincent and Helen Margaret (Petrus) R.; m. Mary J. Darby, June 20, 1964; children: Mollie K., Jennifer M., Ellen R., Robert E. Jr. BA, Rockhurst Coll., 1964; JD, St. Louis U., 1967; LLM, U. Mo., Kansas City, 1969. Bar: Mo. 1967. Assoc. atty. Burke, Jackson & Millin, Kansas City, 1967-69; personal trust adminstr. City Nat. Bank and Trust Co., Kansas City, 1969-71; estate planning officer United Mo. Bank of Kansas City, 1971-73, v.p., 1973-80, sr. v.p., 1980-85; exec. v.p. UMB Bank, N.A., 1985—. Pres., corp. bd. Seton Ctr., Kansas City, 1992-95. Contbr. articles to profl. jours. Bd. of Counselors St. Joseph Health Ctr., Kansas City, 1977-85; pres. St. Joseph Health Ctr. Adv. Coun., Kansas City, 1985-86; treas., bd. trustees Endowment Trust Fund for Cath. Edn., 1989—; bd. regents Rockhurst U., 1999—, mem. planned giving coun., 1999—. Grantee St. Louis U. Sch. of Law, 1964-67. Mem. Mo. Bar Assn., Kansas City Bar Assn. (chmn. employee benefits com. 1989-90), Employee Benefit Inst. (adv. bd. 1986—, chmn. 1989), Inst. Cert. Bankers (cert. retirement svcs. profl. 1995—), Estate Planning Soc. Kansas City (pres. 1985-86), Serra Club of Kansas City (v.p. 1987-89). Home: 1024 W 70th St Kansas City MO 64113-2004 Office: UMB Bank NA 1010 Grand Blvd PO Box 419692 Kansas City MO 64141-6692

REITH, CARL JOSEPH, apparel industry executive; b. Peoria, Ill., Jan. 11, 1914; s. Joseph and May (Kolb) R.; m. Jennie S. Habbinga, Apr. 3, 1936; 1 child, Joyce Elaine. Grad. high sch. Office staff sales Peoria Creamery Co., Ill., 1932; with Kroger Co., 1934-60, successively asst. br. acct., office mgr., acct.; adminstr., coord. tng. and mgmt. devel. programing Kroger Co. (Gen. Offices), Cin.; gen. merchandising mgr. Kroger Co. (St. Louis br.), 1946-50; br. mgr. Kroger Co., Indpls., 1950-55, div. v.p. Cin., 1955-57, regional v.p., 1957-60; pres., chief exec. officer Colonial Stores, Inc., 1960-67; bd. dir., pres. Oxford Industries, 1967-78, now dir. Adv. bd. Salvation Army, Atlanta.; bd. dirs. Atlanta Coll. Art; trustee Robert Woodruff Art Ctr. Mem. Indiana Chain Store Council (pres., v.p. 1951-55), Ind. C. of C. (bd. 1954-55), Indpls. C. of C. (bd. 1950), Ga. C. of C. (indsl. devel. council), Atlanta C. of C. (v.p., bd. dir. 1964-67), Augusta (Ga.) Nat. Golf Club, Piedmont Driving Club, Capital City Club, Peachtree Golf Club, Masons, Shriners, Rotary. Home: 3747 Peachtree Rd NE Apt 1708 Atlanta GA 30319-1376 Office: Oxford Industries Inc 222 Piedmont Ave NE Atlanta GA 30308-3391

REITH, MAARTEN EDWARD A. neurochemist; b. Utrecht, The Netherlands, Dec. 29, 1946; arrived in U.S., 1978; s. Jan Franciscus and Katherina (Poelmann) R.; m. Irma Arauo, Apr. 26, 1980; 1 child, Catherina. BS, U. Utrecht, 1968, MS, 1971, PhD, 1975. Rsch. scientist Rudolf Magnus Inst. Pharmacology, Utrecht, 1971-74; sr. rsch. scientist Inst. Molecular Biology, Utrecht, 1974-78; rsch. scientist Ctr. Neurochemistry, N.Y.C., 1978-80, sr. rsch. scientist, 1980-91; assoc. prof. pharmacology Coll. Medicine U. Ill., Peoria, 1991-95, prof., 1995—. Adj. prof. biol. sci. Ill. State U., Normal, 1996—; consulting mem. study sect. Nat. Inst. Drug Abuse, Rockville, Md., 1987—; invited panelist Winter Conf. Brain Rsch., 1988, 91, 93-95, 97, 2001 Editor: Neurotransmitter Transporters, 1996, 2d edit., 2002; editor Cerebral Signal Transduction, From First to Fourth Messengers, 2000; mem. editl. bd. Jour. Neurosci. Methods, 2001—, European Jour. Pharmacology, 2002—. Rsch. grant, NIH, 1983—. Fellow European Brain Behavior Soc.; mem. Am. Soc. Neurochemistry, Am. Soc. Biochemistry and Molecular Biology, Internat. Soc. Neurochemistry, Soc. Neurosci. Achievements include first characterization of receptors for cocaine, first description of regulation of dopamine transport by arachidonic acid, elucidation of factors determining dopamine interaction with its transporter. Office: U Ill Coll Medicine 1 Illini Dr Peoria IL 61605-2576

REITMAN, IVAN, film director, producer; b. Komarmo, Czechoslovakia, Oct. 27, 1946; came to Can., 1951; s. Leslie and Clara R.; m. Genevieve Robert, Sept. 12, 1976; children: Jason, Catherine, Caroline. MusB, McMaster U., 1969. Judge FOCUS Nissan-Datsun, N.Y.C., 1981-83. Theatrical prodr.: The Magic show, 1974, The National Lampoon Show, 1975, Merlin, 1983 (also dir.); Films include: (dir., exec. prodr.) Cannibal Girls, 1973; (prodr.) They Came From Within (aka Shivers), 1975, Death Weekend (aka The House by the Lake), 1977, Blackout, 1978, National Lampoon's Animal House, 1978, Heavy Metal, 1981, Stop! Or My Mom Will Shoot, 1992, Space Jam, 1996, Private Parts, 1996, Father's Day, 1997, Six Days and Seven Nights, 1998, Doomsday Man, 1999, Evolution, 2001; (prodr., dir.) Foxy Lady, 1971, Meatballs, 1979, Stripes, 1981, Ghostbusters, 1984, Legal Eagles, 1986, Twins, 1988, Ghostbusters II, 1989, Kindergarten Cop, 1990, Dave, 1993, Junior, 1994; (exec. prodr.) Rabid, 1976, Spacehunter: Adventures in the Forbidden Zone, 1983, Big Shots, 1987, Casual Sex?, 1988, Feds, 1988, Beethoven, 1992, Beethoven's 2nd, 1993, Commandments, 1996, Road Trip, 2000, Killing Me Softly, 2002, Old School, 2003, Eurotrip, 2004; TV Series: (prodr., dir.) Delta House, 1978; TV film exec. prodr. The Late Shift, 1996, Fathers Day, 1997. Mem. Dirs. Guild Am. also: Bldg 489 100 University City Plz Universal City CA 91608-1002*

REITMAN, JERRY IRVING, advertising agency executive; b. Phila., Jan. 9, 1938; s. Benjamin and Ruth (Eisenberg) R.; m. Monica Birgitta Hall, Oct. 27, 1968; children: Jennifer Sharon, Sarah Beth. BS in Fin., Pa. State U., 1961. Exec. v.p., CEO Brit. Pubs., N.Y.C. and London, 1965-69; pres., pub. Acad. Media, Sherman Oaks, Calif., 1969-73; v.p. Pubs. Clearing House, Port Washington, N.Y., 1973-78; exec. v.p. Ogilvy & Mather, N.Y.C., 1978-81; with Scali, McCabe, Sloves, Inc., N.Y.C., 1981-86; pres. Scali, McCabe, Sloves Direct, N.Y.C.; chmn. bd. dirs. The Reitman Group, 1986; exec. v.p. The Leo Burnett Co., Chgo., 1986-96; pres., CEO, vice chair Internat. Data Response Corp., Chgo., 1996—. Dir. Scandinavian Airlines Sys. Pub./Distbn. Svcs.; mem. adv. bd. Ill. Dept. Trade and Tourism, 1988—; internat. awards chmn., bd. dirs. John Caples Internat., 1989—; mem. Internat. Direct Mktg. Symposium, Zürich, Switzerland. Author: A Common Sense Approach to Small Business, 1968, Beyond 2000: The Future of Direct Marketing, 1994; contbr. articles to profl. jours. Trustee Locust Valley Libr. Assn., N.Y., 1982—; exec. com. mem. Pub. Hall of Fame, 1987—; bd. govs. Children's Miracle Network, 1992—, vice chmn., chmn. bd. govs., 1998—, 1999-2001; bd. dirs. Children's Meml. Found. Telethon, The Direct Mktg. Ednl. Found., exec. dir., 1996—. Anderson scholar, 1960; recipient Key to City, New Orleans, 1959, Silver Apple award N.Y. Direct Mktg. Club, 1989, Ed Mayer award Ednl. Found., 1996, Charles S. Downs award, 1997. Fellow Psychiat. Re-Edn. Assn.; mem. Am. Mktg. Assn. (at-large mem., 2000, bd. dirs.), Direct Mktg. Assn. (bd. mem. ethics com. 1984), Creative Guild (dir. 1984), Internat. Direct Mktg. Assn. (bd. dirs. 1981-82), Publ. Hall of Fame (exec. com. 1988—), Direct Mktg. Club N.Y. (pres. 1983-84), Beta Gamma Sigma, Delta Sigma Pi. Avocations: tennis, old car restoration, classical woodworking. Home and Office: Callahan Group LLC 2204 N Leavitt St Chicago IL 60647-3204 E-mail: jireitman@aol.com.

REITMAN, ROBERT STANLEY, business consultant, nonprofit agency advisor; b. Fairmont, W.Va., Nov. 18, 1933; s. Isadore and Freda A. (Layman) R.; m. Sylvia K. Golden, Dec. 24, 1955; children: Scott Alan, Alayne Louise. BS in Acctg., W.Va. U., 1955; JD, Case Western Res. U., 1958. Bar: Ohio 1958. Mem. firm Burke, Haber & Berick, Cleve., 1958-60, ptnr., 1960-68; exec. v.p., vice chmn. Tranzonic Cos. (formerly AAV Cos.), Pepper Pike, Ohio, 1968-70, pres., vice-chmn., 1970-73, chief exec. officer, pres., vice chmn., 1973-82, pres., chmn., CEO, 1982-98, chmn. emeritus, bd. dirs., 1998—; prin. Riverbend Advisors, 1998—. Mem. bus. adv. com. Mandel Ctr. for non-profit Orgn. Case We. Res. U., 1995-99, vis. com. Weatherhead Sch. of Bus., 1995-2003, vis. com. Sch. of Law, 1998-2003, chmn. Dean's Nat. Adv. Com., Sch. of Law, 1997-98; mem. pvt. banking adv. bd. Key Bank, N.A., 1997--. Mem. Rep. fin. com., Cuyahoga County, 1968-78; mem. Com. for Econ. Growth for Israel, Cleve., 1977-80, pres., 1978-80; mem. adv. coun. Cleve. Mus. Nat. History, 1982-85, Cleve. Opera, 1977—; del. Coun. of Jewish Fedns., N.Y.C., 1981-97; gen. co-chmn. Jewish Welfare Fund, Cleve., 1975-78, 81-85, gen. vice chmn., 1985-89, gen. chmn., 1989-91; sect. and div. chmn., team capt. United Way Svcs., 1974-97, mem. del. assembly, 1976-85, trustee, 1977-83, 84-90, 91—2000, v.p., 1985-88, chmn. nominating. com., 1988-90, campaign chmn., 1993, chair fund raising planning com., 1994-97, chair bd. trustees, 1997-2000, life trustee, 2000—; mem. employment com. Jewish Vocat. Svc., Cleve., 1974-83; bd. dirs. Capital for Israel, Inc., N.Y.C., 1986-87; nat. vice chmn. United Jewish Appeal, 1987-92, nat. allocations chmn., 1987-90, trustee, 1988-94, chair retirement fund com., 1994-97; trustee B'nai B'rith Hillel Found., 1975-81, Cleve. Jewish News, 1976-79, Ideastream (pub. broadcasting), Cleve., 1976-99, vice chmn. 1986-90, chmn. bd., 1990-97, immediate past chair, 1997-99, chair emeritus, 1999—; trustee, pres. Bus. Volunteerism Coun., 1994-96, chmn. 1996-97; trustee Jewish Cmty. Fedn. Cleve., 1983-98, 1999-2003, treas., 1991-94, v.p., 1995-97, life trustee, 2003—, Jewish Edn. Ctr. of Cleve., 1993-96, Cleve. Zool. Soc., 1972—, pres., 1979-87, chmn., 1987-92, chmn. emeritus, 1992—, chmn. JDC-Brookdale Inst. of Gerontology and Human Devel. (Israel), 1995; trustee Am. Jewish Joint Distbn. Com., 1988-96, 97—, United Israel Appeal, 1987-94, Mt. Sinai Med. Ctr., Cleve., 1976-96, chmn., 1982-85; trustee Cleve. State U. Devel. Found., 1988—, Greater Cleve. Roundtable, 1991-2004; trustee The Wilds, 1995-99, adv. bd., 1999-2002, trustee The Mt. Sinai Health Care Foundation, 1995-2004, life trustee, 2004—, vice chair 1998-2001, chair, 2001-04; trustee Univ. Hosps. Health Sys., 1999-2004, Univ. Hosps. Cleve., 1999—; trustee, chair Heather Hill, Inc., 2001—; coun. mem. Village of Gates Mills, Ohio, 1997-2000, clk., 2000—. Mem. The 50 Club Cleve., Case We. Res. Univ. Sch. of Law Soc. Benchers, Am. Kennel Club (regional del. 1960-75), We. Res. Kennel Club (officer, trustee 1959-75), Beechmont Club (fin. com. 1972-80, house com. 1974), Pepper Pike Club, Union Club, Carambola Golf Club, Masons, Zeta Beta Tau, Tau Epsilon Rho. Avocations: golf, swimming, pure-bred dogs. Office: Riverbend Advisors 2087 Chagrin River Rd Gates Mills OH 44040-9740 Office Phone: 440-423-0792. Personal E-mail: rsrform@megsinet.net. Business E-Mail: rsrform@core.com.

REITMAN, SANFORD, radiologist; b. Newark, June 12, 1933; BS, Allegheny Coll., U. Pa., 1954; MS in Physiology and Biochemistry, Rutgers U., 1955; MD, U. Ala., 1959. Diplomate Am. Bd. Radiology. Rsch. fellow neuroanatomy Nat. Found., 1956-57; intern radiology Naval Hosp., Phila., 1959-60; resident radiology San Diego Naval Hosp., 1961-64; med. dir. radiology Harris Hosp. NW, Fort Worth; assoc. prof. biomed. engring. U. Tex.; physician group practice Radiology Assocs. Tarrant County, Fort Worth. Chief resident therapy and diagnosis, Regional Naval Med. Ctr., San Diego; chief of radiology Newport Naval Hosp., 1975-85; sr. cons. interventional radiology Meml. Hosp., R.I.; chmn. radiology Arlington Meml. Hosp., 1973-87, Harris Southwest Hosp., 1987-96. State bd. dirs. Am. Cancer Soc., 1972-74, dist. dir. 1972, pres. county chpt. 1970-71. NIH fellow, 1957-58. Fellow Royal Soc. Health; mem. Am. Coll. Radiology, Assn. Mil. Surgeons of the U.S., Am. Nuc. Soc., Biomed. Engring. Soc., Royal Coll. Surgeons (faculty radiologist), Radiol. Soc. N.Am., Am. Assn. Univ. Profs., Tex. Med. Assn., Tex. Radiol. Soc., New Eng. Roentgen Ray Soc., Ala. Acad. Sci. Office: Hidden Creek Ranch 2208 Farmer Rd Weatherford TX 76087-6964

REITMEISTER, NOEL WILLIAM, financial planner, investment advisor, insurance agent, writer; b. Bklyn., Aug. 12, 1938; s. Morris G. and Anna (Miller) Reitmeister; m. Elaine Schendelman, Sept. 16, 1961; children: Gregg Allen, Stephen Michael. Student, Alfred U., 1956-57; BA in Econs. and Polit. Sci., Queens Coll., CUNY, 1960; MBA in Psychology and Mgmt., Zicklin Sch. of Baruch Coll., CUNY, 1969; diploma, N.Y. Inst. Fin., 1969; diploma in fin. planning, Coll. Fin. Planning, Denver, 1974. CFP, Bd. of Stds. for Cert. Planners, 1974; LCSW; lic. in investments, commodities, options, life, accident and health ins., variable annuities, variable life, long term care, registered rep. N.Y. Stock Exch., Am. Stock Exch., Chgo. Stock Exch., Pacific Stock Exch., Boston Stock Exch., PBW Exch., Chgo. Bd. Trade, Chgo. Merc. Exch., Comex, NASD, Chgo. Options Exch., lic. investment broker N.Y., N.J., Mass., Fla., Ariz., Calif., Tex., Mich., Wis., Ill., Ind., Kans., Mo., Va., Ala., N.C., D.C., N. Mex., Okla., registered investment advisor agt. Asst. merchandise mgr. Bloomingdales, N.Y.C., 1962-63; sales and mktg. exec. Cosmair div. L'Oreal, Paris, 1963-67; project dir. advt. rsch. Toni Div. Gillette Co., 1967-68; account exec. duPont Walston, Chgo., Gary, Merrillville, Ind., 1969-71, br. coord., 1971-74; ptnr. Frances I. duPont & Co.; sr. fin. cons. A.G. Edwards & Sons Inc., Merrillville, 1974-79, v.p.-investments, 1979-99, trust specialist, 1992—, sr. v.p.-investments, 1999—. Ptnr. Ind. Investors, 1980-88, Nat. Property Investors, 1980-84, Petro Lewis, 1979-84, Can. Am. Oil, 1980-94, Rollingbrook Properties, 1983-, Nora Assocs., 1981-2000; vice chmn. bd. Menorah Credit Union, 1979-81, chmn. 1981-82, chmn., CEO, pres., 1982-83; owner Le Baron Comms., 1980-96; dir., prin. Arctic Exploration, Inc.; co-mng. ptnr. Filthy Rich Enterprises, 1980-90; owner Anglo Am. Prodns., 1987-98; conducted Roundtable at Advanced Conf. on Retirement Planning, Washington, 1986, also attended White House Briefing by Chief of

Pres.'s Coun. Econ. Advisors; lectr. in investments and fin. planning Inst. Continuing Edn., Purdue U., Calumet, 1976-92, adj. prof. fin. Sch. Mgmt., 1994-97; lectr. Purdue North Ctrl., Roosevelt U., Calumet Coll. of St. Joseph; adj. prof. fin. Sch. Bus., Ind. U. N.W.; adj. faculty Coll. for Fin. Planning, Denver, 1974-92; columnist The Star, 1984-86, Am. Med. News Jour., Post-Tribune, 1996—; fin. planning and retirement cons. BP-Amoco, 1974-94, LTV, 1982-92, Inland Steel, 1983-94, Ford Motor Co., 1987-91, C.B. Geigy Pharm., 1991-93; examiner in fin. planning, 1974-78; assoc. Bd. Examiners Cert. Fin. Planners, examination criteria com., 1999, hearings officer, 2000-02, com. to assign exam questions, bd. profl. rev., 2000. Author: Portfolios, Inc. "Key Objectives in Investments"; co-author text "Retirement Planning" for Coll. Fin. Planning; producer, host cable TV show Money Doctor, 1985-94 (ACE award nomination), PBS spl. "Market Crisis of October 1987"; contbr. articles on fin. planning and retirement to profl. jours. including Jour. Inst. Cert. Fin. Planning, Fin. Planning and Nursing mags., Post Tribune, The Times, Vidette Messenger, The Star, The Economist, Daily Southtown, Financial Services Weekly, N.Y. Times, Registered Rep. Mag., Merrillville Herald, Financial Planning News. Mem. exec. com., sec. Ill. Theatre Ctr., 1985-88; bd. dirs. South Suburban HELP, 1968-69, N.W. Ind. Pub. Broadcasting, 1986-90; trustee Temple Anshe Sholom, 1975-82, chmn. adult edn., 1977-82, chmn. house and grounds, 1977-78, co-chmn. social action com., 1979-82, Temple's Endowment Com., 1992-95, 96-2001, Rabbinical Selection Com., 1981-82; dir. Vis. Nurse Assn. NW Ind., 1992-98, 2000-02, mem. fin. com., 1992-98, 2000—, devel. com., chmn. by-laws com., exec. com., co-chmn., 1992-98, exec. com., 1998-2003; bd. dirs., mem. trustees com., fin. com.and mktg. com. Ill. Philharm. Orch., 2002—; dir. Drug and Alcohol Edn. Sheriff's Dept. Cook County, Ill., 1989-91; v.p., sec. S. Suburban Acad. Jewish Studies, 1979-82; local troop coord. Boy Scouts Am., 1977-78, vol. Richton Crossing Nursing Home; mem. Anti-Defamation League Cabinet, 1978-82; v.p. Young Rep. Club of Queens County, 1958-60; v.p. Chgo. B'nai B'rith Coun., Chai Unit, pres. (4 terms), parliamentarian (29 terms); co-founder, treas. SESSA; life mem. Volunteered Optometrists Serving Humanity. With USAR, 1960-65, active duty, 1960-62, mil. intellegence specialist, 1961-62, staff sgt., Ft. Dix, Ft. Devens, Ft. Hamilton, Ft. Drum; mem. diversity com. Ind. U. N.W. Decorated Order of William Tell (Switzerland); apptd. col. on staff Gov. of Ky., 1988; named Man of Yr., B'nai B'rith, 1986; recipient Excellence award Nat. Assn. Accts., 1985. Mem.: AAUP, Six Million Coun., Three Million Dollar Coun., Pres.'s Coun., Chmn.'s Coun., Ind. TV Prodrs. Assn., Chgo. Coun. on Fgn. Rels., Weisenthal Inst., Registry Fin. Planning Practitioners (chartered 1983—95), Fin. Plannig Assn., Internat. Soc. Registered Reps. (charter), Internat. Assn. Fin. Planners (v.p. Chgo. South chpt.), Mich. Assn. Fin. Planners, Chgo. Assn. Fin. Planners (charter 1973—78, pres. 1975), Internat. Assn. Registered Fin. Planners, Inst. Cert. Fin. Planners (pres. Illiana Soc. 1985—86, 1987—93, chmn. 1993—97, amb. 1997—, charter), Jerusalem Soc., Jewish War Vets, Flossmor Arts Coun., Yad Vashem Soc., Steppenwolf Theatre Soc., Am. Friends of the Technicon, Friends of Israel Defense Forces, Anti-Defamation League Cabinet, Queen Coll. Alumni Assn., Am. Legion, Stratford Shakespeare Soc., Ont. Can., Friends of Hebrew U. Jerusalem, Nat. Geog. Soc., Spertus Inst., Lyric Opera League, Friends of the Ill. Philharm., Art Inst. Chgo., Goodman Theater Prodn., Grant Park Symphony Soc., Smithsonian Soc., Chgo. Shakespeare Theatre Soc., Crest Club (Silver Crest award, Gold Crest award, Diamond Crest award), Idlewild Country Club, Tower Club (assoc.), Union League Club (assoc.), Boston Harvard Club (assoc.), Univ. Club (Chgo.) (assoc.), Alfred U. Alumni Assn., Baruch Coll. Alumni Assn., Century Club, Convenant Club, Homewood-Flossmoor Racquet and Fitness, Ancient Arabic Order of the Noble Mystic Shrine, VIP Club, Williams Club (N.Y.C.) (N.Y.C.), N.Y., Chgo. U. Club, Mariners Club, Neighbor Lodge, Scottish Rite of Chgo. (32d degree mason), Tau Delta Phi (social chmn. Queens Coll., co-pres., pledge master), Queen's Coll. Alumni Assn., Delta Omega Kappa (v.p. Alpha chpt. 1953, pres. Beta chpt. 1954—56, nat. pres. 1955—60), Zeta Beta Tau (pres. pledge class 1956—57, soc. chmn. 1956—57,), Alpha Epsilon Pi (chpt. v.p., pres. Queen Coll.). Home: 2246 Flossmoor Rd Flossmoor IL 60422-1612 Office: AG Edwards & Sons Inc 1477 E 83d Ave Merrillville IN 46410-6307 Personal E-mail: abba.12@netzero.com. Business E-Mail: reitmeistergroup@agedwards.com.

REITSEMA, HAROLD JAMES, aerospace engineer; b. Kalamazoo, Jan. 19, 1948; s. Robert Harold and Bernice Jean (Hoogsteen) R.; m. Mary Jo Gunnink, Aug. 6, 1970; children: Ellen Celeste, Laurie Jean. BA, Calvin Coll., 1972; PhD, N.Mex. State U., 1977. Rsch. assoc. U. Ariz., Tucson, 1977-79, sr. rsch. assoc., 1979-82, vis. scientist, 1987—; sr. mem. tech. staff Ball Aerospace, Boulder, Colo., 1982-85, prin. systems engr., 1985-88, program mgr., 1988-89, staff cons., 1989-96, dir., 1996—. Cons. Aerospace Tech., 1987—. Contbr. articles to profl. jours. including Astrophys. Jour., Aston. Jour., Nature, Sci., Icarus. Bd. dirs. EE Barnard Obs., Golden, Colo., 1984-91. Fellow AIAA (assoc., tech. com. chair 1991, Engr. of Yr. Colo. region 1990); mem. Am. Astron. Soc. (planetary sci. com. 1991-94), Internat. Astron. Union. Achievements include discovery of Larissa, fifth satellite of Neptune; co-discovery of Telesto, seventeenth satellite of Saturn; patents for Optically-coupled Shaft Angle Encoder. Home: 4795 Hancock Dr Boulder CO 80303-1103 Office: Ball Aerospace 1600 Commerce St Boulder CO 80301-2734 E-mail: hreitsema@ball.com.

REITZ, BRUCE ARNOLD, cardiac surgeon, educator; b. Seattle, Sept. 14, 1944; BS, Stanford U., 1966; MD, Yale U., 1970. Diplomate: Am. Bd. Surgery, Am. Bd. Thoracic Surgery. Intern Johns Hopkins Hosp., Balt., 1970-71, cardiac surgeon-in-charge, 1982-92; resident Stanford U. Hosp., (Calif.), 1971-72, 74-78; clin. assoc. Nat. Heart Lung Blood Inst., NIH, Bethesda, Md., 1972-74; asst. prof. Stanford U. Sch. Medicine, 1977-81, assoc. prof., 1981-82; prof. surgery Johns Hopkins U. Sch. Medicine, Balt., 1982-92; prof., chmn. Sch Medicine Stanford (Calif.) U., 1992—. Developer heart-lung transplant technique, 1981. Office: Stanford U Sch Medicine Dept Cardiothoracic Surgery Stanford CA 94305-5407 Office Phone: 650-725-4497. Business E-Mail: breitz@stanford.edu.

REITZ, CURTIS RANDALL, lawyer, educator; b. Reading, Pa. s. Lester S. and Magdalene A. (Crouse) R.; m. Virginia R. Patterson, Dec. 19, 1953 (div.); children— Kevin R., Joanne E., Whitney A.; m. Judith N. Renzulli, Sept. 18, 1983 BA, U. Pa., 1951, LL.B., 1956. Bar: Pa. 1957, U.S. Supreme Ct. 1959. Law clk. to Chief Justice Earl Warren U.S. Supreme Ct., 1956-57; mem. faculty law U. Pa., Phila., 1957—, asst. prof. law, 1957-60, assoc. prof., 1960-63, prof., 1963—, provost, v.p., 1971-73, Algernon Sydney Biddle prof. law, 1985—. Trustee Internat. House Ctr. Phila.; bd. mgrs. Glen Mills Schs., Pa. Served to 1st lt. U.S. Army, 1951-53 Life Mem. Am. Law Inst., Mem., Nat. Conf. Commrs. on Uniform State Laws, Order of Coif Office: U Pa Law Sch 3400 Chestnut St Philadelphia PA 19104-6204 E-mail: creitz@law.upenn.edu.

REITZ, DAN, state representative; b. Red Bud, Ill, Mar. 16, 1954; m. Joyce Reitz; children: Nathan, Nicholas, Natalie. HS Diploma, Steelville HS, 1972. Legis. dir. Peabody Coal Co., Ill.; elected rep., Demo. State Rep., dist. 116, Ill., 1997, 2002. Apptd. House of Representatives, 1997; Chair, Bd. of Commissioners Ill., 1993—94; Bd. of Commissioners, 1986—96; Chair, Bd. of Commissioners, 1989—90. Mem.: Ill. Assoc. of County Officials, Gov. Task Force on Workers' Compensation, Ill. County Bd. Assoc. (pres. 1996, v.p. 1993—95), Freeway Team (mem. 1989—), Scott Joint Use Comm. (chair, SW Ill.), Western Egyptian Econ. Opportunity Coun., SW Ill. Law Enforcement Commission Exec. Council, Randolph County Housing Authority, Randolph County Progress Comm., Welfare Svc. Committee on Pub. Aid, Tri-County Develop. Council (chair 1996—), Southwestern Ill. Planning Council Exec. Bd. (pres. 1996—97), Randolph County Farm Bureau, United Mine Workers Local 1820, St. Paul's Lutheran Ch. in Wine Hill. Democrat. Lutheran. Office: 200-9s Stratton Office Bldg Springfield IL 62706 Mailing: 128 A West Main Sparta IL 62286

REITZ, ROGER, state representative; b. St. Joseph, Mo., Nov. 11, 1932; m. Virginia Haas; 5 children. BS, Kans. State U.; MD, Kans. U. Diplomate Am. Bd. Internal Medicine. Physician; mem. Kans. Ho. of Reps., 2003—. Dir. USD #383 Found., Manhattan Cmty. Found.; sch. bd. USD #383, 1977—89; mem. Manhattan Mcpl. Band; city commr. Manhattan, 1997—; mayor City of Manhattan, 1999—2000; Sunday Sch. Tchr. Capt. U.S. Army. Mem.: Rotary. Republican. Methodist. Office: 174-W State Capitol 300 SW 10th Ave Topeka KS 66612 Home: 1332 Sharingbrook Manhattan KS 66503

REIZNER, GEORGE TERRY, medical educator; b. Sept. 9, 1954; BS, U. mich., 1976; MD, George Washington U., 1980. Asst. prof. U. Wis., Madison, 1986-91, assoc. prof., 1991-97, prof., 1997—, vice-chair dermatology, 2002—. Office: One South Park 7th Flr Madison WI 53715

REJ, ROBERT, biochemist; Dir. clin. chemistry N.Y. State Dept. Health, Albany, 1987—; asso. prof. biomedical scis. SUNY, Albany, 1985—. Internat. fellow Am. Assn. Clin. Chemistry, 1995. Office: NY State Dept Health Wadsworth Ctr Labs & Rsch PO Box 509 Albany NY 12201-0509

REJAI, MOSTAFA, political science educator; b. Tehran, Iran, Mar. 11, 1931; came to U.S., 1954; s. Taghi and Forough (Lashgari) R. AA, Pasadena City Coll., 1957; BA, Calif. State U., L.A., 1959, MS, 1961; PhD, UCLA, 1964. Teaching fellow UCLA, 1963-64; asst. prof. polit. sci. Miami U., Oxford, Ohio, 1964-67, assoc. prof., 1967-70, prof., 1970-83, Disting. prof., 1983—. Vis. scholar Ctr. for Internat. Affairs, Harvard U., 1972, Hoover Instn. on War, Revolution and Peace, Stanford U., 1973, Inst. Internat. Studies, Iran, 1974-75; vis. prof. Western Coll., Oxford, 1971, 72. Author: World Miltary Leaders: A Collective and Comparative Analysis, 1996, The Strategy of Political Revolution, 1973, The Comparative Study of Revolutionary Strategy, 1977, Comparative Political Ideologies, 1984; (with Kay Phillips) Leaders of Revolution, 1979, World Revolutionary Leaders, 1983, Loyalists and Revolutionaries: Political Leaders Compared, 1988, Political Ideologies: A Comparative Approach, 1991, 2d edit., 1995, Demythogizing an Elite: American Presidents in Empirical, Comparative, and Historical Perspectives, 1993, World Military Leaders: A Collective and Comparative Analysis, 1996, Leaders and Leadership: An Appraisal of Theory and Research, 1997, The Young George Washington in Psychobiographical Perspective, 2000, Concepts of Leadership in Western Political Thought, 2002; editor, contbr.: Democracy: The Contemporary Theories, 1967, Decline of Ideology?, 1971; editor: Mao Tse-Tung on Revolution and War, 1969, rev. edit., 1970; assoc. editor Jour. Polit. and Mil. Sociology, 1973—; contbr. articles to profl. jours., book chpts. Recipient Outstanding Teaching award Miami U., 1970. Mem. Am. Polit. Sci. Assn. (polit. psychology sect.), Am. Sociol. Assn. (polit. soc. sect.), Internat. Polit. Sci. Assn., Internat. Soc. Polit. Psychology, Internat. Studies Assn., Inter-Univ. Seminar on Armed Forces and Soc., Conf. for Study Polit. Thought, Midwest Polit. Sci. Assn., So. Polit. Sci. Assn., Western Polit. Sci. Assn., Pi Gamma Mu, Pi Sigma Alpha. Office: Miami U Dept of Political Science Oxford OH 45056

REJENT, MARIAN MAGDALEN, retired pediatrician; b. Toledo, Aug. 12, 1920; d. Casimir Stanley and Magdalen (Szymanowski) R. BS, Mary Manse Coll., 1943; MD, Marquette U., 1946; MPH, U. Mich., 1960. Diplomate Am. Bd. Pediatrics. Intern St. Vincent Med. Ctr., Toledo, 1946-47; resident communicable diseases City Hosp., Cleve., 1947-48; resident pediatrics Childrens Hosp., Akron, Ohio, 1948-50; pvt. practice Toledo, 1950-54; chief div. maternal child health Toledo Bd. Health, 1953-64; dir. pediatrics Maumee Valley Hosp., Toledo, 1964-69; assoc. prof. pediatrics Med. Coll. Ohio, Toledo, 1969-76; med. dir. State Crippled Childrens Program, Columbus, Ohio, 1976-78; attendant pediatrician St. Vincent Med. Ctr., Toledo, 1978-80, 87-99; chief pediatric svcs. Wake County Health Dept., Raleigh, N.C., 1980-87; ret. clin. prof. pediatrics Med. Coll. Ohio, 1998; ret., 1999. Exec. com. March of Dimes, 1988-92. Mem. AMA, APHA, Am. Acad. Pediatrics, Am. Med. Women's Assn., Ohio PHA, Ohio State Med. Assn., NW Ohio Pediatric Assn., Acad. Medicine Toledo, Alpha Omega Alpha. Republican. Roman Catholic. Avocations: travel, photography, painting. Home: The Woodlands Apt 401 4030 Indian Rd Toledo OH 43606

REKATE, ALBERT C. physician; b. Buffalo, June 12, 1916; s. Gustave E. and Fannie (Hummell) R.; m. Elizabeth Foster, June 12 1943 (dec. 1985); 1 child, Suzanne (Mrs. R. Willis Post); m. Linda Ann Holt, Aug. 1, 1992. MD, U. Buffalo, 1940. Diplomate Am. Bd. Internal Medicine. Intern E.J. Meyer Meml. Hosp., Buffalo, 1940-41, med. resident, 1941-44; asst. prof. medicine SUNY-Buffalo, 1954-61, assoc. prof., 1961-65, prof., 1965-86, prof. emeritus, 1986—; dir. rehab. medicine SUNY, Buffalo, 1965-72, acting dean Sch. Health Related Professions, 1965-66, assoc. dean, 1966-74, acting chmn. dept. rehab. medicine, 1972-75; assoc. dir. medicine E.J. Meyer Meml. Hosp., Buffalo, 1957-63, head dept. rehab. medicine, 1964-69, dir. primary rehab. center, 1965-69, acting head cardiology, 1966-69, dir., 1970-72. Bd. dirs. Buffalo Hearing and Speech Ctr., 1973-99; mem. adv. bd. Coastal Empire Mental Health Ctr., S.C., 1980-81, bd. dirs., 1981-93; mem. dean's adv. coun. SUNY-Buffalo Sch. Medicine and Biomed. Scis., 1995—, med. emeritus faculty group steering com., 2000—. Contbr. articles to profl. jours. Served with M.C. AUS, World War II. Mem. Am. Heart Assn., Western N.Y. Heart Assn. (pres. 1954-55), Assn. Am. Med. Colls., N.Y. State Heart Assembly, N.Y. Acad. Scis., Med. Union (pres. 1974-75), Buffalo Acad. Medicine (pres. 1969-70), Erie County Med. Soc., Med. Alumni Assn. U. Buffalo (pres. 1960-61), Beaufort-Jasper Mental Health Assn. (dir. 1980-86). Home and Office: 52 Hampton Hill Dr Williamsville NY 14221-5840 E-mail: lre1832886@aol.com.

REKAU, RICHARD ROBERT, architect; b. June 6, 1936; s. Robert Richard and Charlotte (Ryan) Rekau Altier; m. Carolyn Pritchett, Dec. 20, 1962; 1 child, Ryan Richard. BArch, BS, Ga. Tech. Inst., 1965. Registered arch., Ga., N.C., Ala., Fla., Md., S.C., Tenn.; cert. Nat. Coun. Archtl. Registration Bds. Project mgr. John Portman & Assocs., Atlanta, 1970-76; assoc. Herndon & Harris, Atlanta, 1976-77; v.p. Devel. Contractors, Inc., Atlanta, 1979-81; pres. Richard R. Rekau, Arch., P.C., Atlanta, 1977—. Pres. Rekau Properties, 1984—. Prin. works include Lanier Plaza, Gainesville, Ga. Corp. Plaza N.W., Atlanta, Pkwy. Village, Macon, Ga., Carrollton (Ga.) Crossroads Shopping Ctr., Tuxedo Park, Atlanta, Griffin (Ga.) Mall, Festival Ctr. Hilton Head, Perimeter Village, Atlanta, Tuxedo Park, Carrollton Crossroads, Festival Ctr. Indigo Run, Hilton Head, S.C., Park Centre Commons, Ocala, Fla., The Desoto, Savannah, Ga, Tenenbaum Residence, Kronowitz Residence, Savannah; two residential works featured in Savannah Tour of Homes. Mem. AIA, Am. Solar Energy Soc., Hist. Preservation Found. N.C., Nat. Trust Hist. Preservation, Ga. Tech. Alumni Assn., Ga. Canoeing Assn. Home: 1771 Beverly Woods Ct Atlanta GA 30341-1418 Office: Ste 1240 1000 Abernathy Rd NE Atlanta GA 30328-5653 Office Phone: 770-392-9091. Personal E-mail: richardrekau@aol.com.

REKERS, GEORGE ALAN, education educator, clinical psychologist; b. Waterloo, Iowa, July 11, 1948; s. Roger Arthur and Helen K Rekers; m. Sharon Lee Chapin, Aug. 26, 1972; children: Steven, Andrew, Matthew, Timothy, Mark. BA in psychology, Westmont Coll., 1969; PhD, U. Calif., L.A., 1972; ThD, U. South Africa, 1997; MBA, So. Wesleyan U., 2004. Rsch. fellow/vis. scholar Harvard U., 1972—73; clin. psychology intern Tufts U. Med. Ctr., Boston, 1973—74; asst. rsch. psychologist U. Calif., 1974—77; pres. and CEO (part time) Logos Rsch. Inst., Van Nuys, Calif., 1975—85; assoc. prof. and chief psychologist U. Fla., 1977—80; dept. head and prof. Kans. State U., 1980—85; prof. and chair., med. sch. faculty in psychology U. So. Carolina, 1985—. Bus. cons. and seminar leader 33 Dynamics Cons., LLC, Columbia, SC, 2003—; invited lectr. and cons. over 50 universities in Africa, Asia, Europe, Latin Am. and Mid. East, 1986—; chmn., bd. dirs. InterAct Internat. Inc., Columbia, SC, 1994—; invited cons. U.S. Sec. of Health Human Svcs., Wash., DC, 1989; invited expert to testimony U.S. Senate and House of Rep., 1983—91; invited cons. and rev. Office of the Gov. of SC, 1998—2001. Author: (book) Susan Smith: Victim or Murderer, 1996, There's Room at the Top: 33 Dynamics for Managerial Excellence, 2004; editor: (book) Family Building, 1985, Handbook of Child and Adolescent Sexual Problems, 1995; author: over 130 academic jour. articles and textbook chpts. Recipient Sigmund Freud award, Nat. Assn. for Rsch. and Therapy, 2000, Postdoctoral fellowship award, Found. for Rsch. in Psychiatry, Harvard U., 1972—73; Rsch. grants, Nat. Inst. Mental Health, 1973—80. Fellow: Am. Acad. Clin. Psychology; mem.: Univ. Studies Coun. (adv. bd. mem., chmn. 2001—), Nat. Register of Health Service Providers in Psychology. Avocations: piano, organ, charity. Office: Univ South Carolina Dept Neuropsychiatry 3555 Harden St E Ste 104A Columbia SC 29203 Office Phone: 803-434-4250. Business E-Mail: g@sc.edu.

RELCH, JOHN, banker, federal agency administrator; BS, So. Ill. U.; MBA, U. South Fla.; grad., La. State U. Sch. Banking. Pres., CEO Nat. Bank Sarasota, Fla., 1980—89; staff mem. Office US Senator Connie Mack, 1990—98, chief staff, 1998—2000; bd. mem. FDIC Bd. Dirs., 2001—, acting chmn., 2001, vice chmn., 2002—. Chmn. bd. dirs. Sarasota Family YMCA. Office: FDIC 500 17th St NW Washington DC 20429-9990

RELDAN, ROBERT RONALD, law educator, psychological consultant, poet; b. Bklyn., June 2, 1942; s. William and Marie (Garis) R.; m. Judith Feldman, Nov. 7, 1971 (div. June 1979); 1 child, Edward. BS, Fairleigh Dickinson U., 1965; MS (hon.), Park Coll., 1975; JD, LaSalle U., St. Louis, 1988. Sales mgr. Pistilli Ford, Oradell, N.J., 1967-69; owner Triple "R" Co., Tenafly, N.J., 1969-75; dir. Legal Ltd., Trenton, N.J., 1975—. Author of poetry. Facilitator in Alternative to Violence program, Trenton. Served with USN, 1965-67. Mem. Nat. Lawyers Guild, Toastmasters Internat. (v.p. Trenton chpt. 1987-88), Am. Entrepreneurs Assn., Aircraft Owners and Pilots Assn. Avocations: flying, skydiving, scuba diving, poetry. Office: ACSU 557463 Bag R Rahway NJ 07065

RELIAS, JOHN ALEXIS, lawyer; b. Chgo., Apr. 2, 1946; s. Alexis John and Marie Helen (Metos) R.; m. Linda Ann Pontious, Nov. 27, 1971; children: Anne, Alexandra. BA, Northwestern U., Evanston, 1968; LLB, Northwestern U., Chgo., 1972. Bar: Ill., 1972, U.S. Dist. Ct. (no. dist.) Ill. 1972, U.S. Ct. Appeals (9th cir.) 1981, U.S. Ct. Appeals (7th cir.) 1983, U.S. Supreme Ct. 1997. Assoc. Vedder, Price, Kaufman & Kammholz, Chgo., 1972-78, ptnr., 1979-94, Franczek, Sullivan, Mann, Crement, Hein & Relias, Chgo., 1994—. Mem. bd. edn. Wilmette (Ill.) Sch. Dist. 39, 1989-97, 2001—, pres., 1992-93, 1995-96. Mem. Nat. Assn. Sch. Attys., Ill. Assn. Sch. Attys., Order of the Coif, Phi Beta Kappa. Greek Orthodox. Home: 2500 Kenilworth Ave Wilmette IL 60091-1337 Office: Franczek Sulian Mann Crement Hein & Relias 300 S Wacker Dr Chicago IL 60606-6680

RELL, M. JODI, governor; b. Norfolk, Va., June 16, 1946; m. Lou Rell; children: Meredith, Michael. Student, Old Dominion U., Western Conn. State U.; LLD (hon.), Univ. of Hartford, 2001. Mem., dep. minority leader Conn. Ho. Reps., 1984-94; lt. gov. State of Conn., 1995—2004, gov., 2004—. Past vice chmn. Brookfield Rep. Town Com., appt. chair of the Hartford Econ. Devel. Adv. Group, (HEDAG), 1998; trustee YMCA Western Conn; played a key role in raising funds for the Conn. Firefighters Meml.; estab. the Lt. Gov.'s Comm. on State Mandate Reform, Lt. Gov.'s Conn. Treasures award. Named Melvin Jones Fellow, Lions Club Internat. Found., 2003; recipient Leadership award, Nat. Order of Women Legislators (NOWL), Impact award, Conn. Tech. Coun., 2001, First Kids 2001 Policy Leadership award, Conn. Voices for Children, Arnold Markle Public Service award. Mem. Nat. Order Women Legislators (past nat. pres., former v.p., treas., corr. sec.), Women Execs. in State Govt., Brookfield Rep. Women's Club (past pres.), Brookfield Bus. and Profl. Women's Club, Prison and Jail Overcrowding comm., Governor's Law Enforcement Coun., Yale Corp., State Finance Advisory Com. Republican. Office: Office Gov Exec Chambers 210 Capitol Ave Hartford CT 06106*

RELLA, FRANCIS JOHN, paramedic, writer; s. Concetta Rella; m. Tammy Bartunek, June 5, 1988; children: Rose Vincenza, Maria Concetta. MusM, U. of S.D., 1988. Lic. paramedic Nat. Registry of Emergency Med. Technicians. Actor Light Opera of Manhattan, N.Y.C., 1980—87; singer N.Y.C. Opera, N.Y.C., 1997—98; paramedic St. Vincent's Hosp., N.Y.C., 2000—. Author: (memoir) Manhattan Medics. Sgt. USMCR, 1978—97. Democrat. Eastern Orthodox. Personal E-mail: medicfrankie@yahoo.com.

RELLE, FERENC MATYAS, chemist; b. Gyor, Hungary, June 13, 1922; came to U.S., 1951, naturalized, 1956; s. Ferenc and Elizabeth (Netratics) R.; m. Gertrud B. Tubach, Oct. 9, 1946; children: Ferenc, Ava, Attila. BSChemE, MS, Jozsef Nador Poly. U., Budapest, Hungary, 1944. Lab. mgr. Karl Kohn Ltd. Co., Landshut, Germany, 1947-48; resettlement officer Internat. Refugee Orgn., Munich, 1948-51; chemist Farm Bur. Coop. Assn., Columbus, Ohio, 1951-56; indsl. engr. N.Am. Aviation, Inc., Columbus, 1956-57; rsch. chemist Keever Starch Co., Columbus, 1957-65, Ross Labs. divsn. Abbott Labs., Columbus, 1965-70, rsch. scientist, 1970-89; cons. in field. Congl. sci. counselor, 1971—81. Chmn. Columbus and Ctrl. Ohio UNWeek, 1963; pres. Berwick Manor Civic Assn., 1968; trustee Stelios Stelson Found., 1968-69; deacon Brookwood Presbyn. Ch., 1963-65, 92-93, trustee, 1990-91. Decorated knight St. Ladislaus Order. Mem. Am. Chem. Soc. (emeritus; alt. councilor 1973, chmn. long range planning com. Columbus sect. 1972-76, 78-80), Am. Assn. Cereal Chemists (life; chmn. Cin. sect. 1974-75), Ohio Acad. Sci., Arpad Acad. (gold medal mem.), Internat. Tech. Inst. (adv. dir. 1977-82), Nat. Intercollegiate Soccer Ofcls. Assn., Am. Hungarian Assn., Hungarian Cultural Assn. (pres. 1978-81), Ohio Soccer Ofcls. Assn., Columbus Mannerchor, Germania Singing and Sport Soc., Civitan (gov. Ohio dist. 1970-71, dist. treas. 1982-83, pres. Ea. Columbus 1963-64, 72-73, gen. sec. for Hungary 1991-92, Ea. European growth mgr. 1993-94, amb. at large 1994—, established 1st Civitan club in Hungary 1991, Ukraine, 1992, Slovakia 1994, Internat. Gov. of Yr. award 1971, Internat. Honor Key 1992, Internat. Found. fellow 2000, master club builder award 1992, various other awards), World Fedn. Hungarian Engrs. Home and Office: 3487 Roswell Dr Columbus OH 43227-3560

RELLER, L. BARTH, medical microbiologist, infectious diseases physician, educator; Prof. medicine and pathology Med. Ctr. Duke U., Durham, N.C. Recipient Becton Dickinson award in clin. microbiology Am. Soc. Microbiology, 1991, Sonnenwirth Meml. award, 1997. Office: Duke Univ Med Ct Box 3938 Durham NC 27710-0001

RELMAN, ARNOLD SEYMOUR, physician, educator, editor; b. N.Y.C., June 17, 1923; s. Simon and Rose (Mallach) Relman; m. Harriet Morse Vitkin, June 26, 1953; children: David Arnold, John Peter, Margaret Rose. AB, Cornell U., 1943; MD, Columbia U., 1946; LLD (hon.), U. Pa.; ScD (hon.), Med. Coll. Wis., Union U., Med. Coll. Ohio, CUNY; DMSc (hon.), Brown U.; DLH (hon.), SUNY; LittD (hon.), Temple U. Diplomate Am. Bd. Internal Medicine. House officer New Haven Hosp., Yale, 1946—49; NRC fellow Evans Meml., Mass. Meml. hosps., 1949—50; practice medicine, specializing in internal medicine Boston, 1950—68, Phila., 1968—77; asst. prof., prof. medicine Boston U. Sch. Medicine, 1950—68; dir. Boston U. Med. Services, Boston City Hosp., 1967—68; prof. medicine, chmn. dept. medicine U. Pa.; chief med. services Hosp. of U. Pa., 1968—77; editor New Eng. Jour. Medicine, Boston, 1977—91, editor emeritus, 1991—; sr. physician Brigham and Women's Hosp., Boston, 1977—; prof. medicine and social medicine Harvard Med. Sch., 1977—93, prof. medicine and social medicine emeritus, 1993—95, prof. emeritus, 1995—. Cons. NIH, USPHS; mem. bd. registration in medicine Commonwealth of Mass., 1995—2001. Editor: Jour. Clin. Investigation, 1962—67; editor: (with F.J. Ingelfinger and M. Finland) Controversy in Internal Medicine, Vol. 1, 1966, Controversy in Internal Medicine, Vol. 2, 1974; contbr. articles to profl. jours. Trustee Columbia U., 1990—96; bd. dirs. Hastings Ctr., 1981—83. Recipient Columbia Alumni Gold medal, 1980, Disting. Svc. award, Am. Coll. Cardiology, 1987, McGovern award, Cosmos Club Washington, 1991, John Peters award, Am. Soc. Nephrology, 1992, George Polk award in journalism, 2003. Master: ACP (John Phillips medal 1985); fellow: Am. Acad. Arts and Scis.; mem.: AMA, Am. Fedn. Clin. Rsch. (past pres.), Am. Soc. Clin. Investigation (past pres.), Inst. of Medicine of NAS (coun. 1979—82), Mass. Med. Soc., Am. Physiol. Soc., Assn. Am. Physicians (coun., pres. 1983—84, Kober medal 1993), Alpha Omega Alpha, Phi Beta Kappa (senator 1991—98). Office: Brigham and Women's Hosp Dept Medicine 181 Longwood Ave Fl 5 Boston MA 02115-5804

RELYEA, CARL MILLER, retired hydrologist; b. Claverack, N.Y., Dec. 29, 1912; s. Charles Miller Croswell and Edna (Pulver) R.; m. Harriet Watson, Sept. 6, 1946 (dec. Nov. 1982); children: Richard, Deborah, Cornelia. AB, Columbia Coll., 1935; MA, Columbia U., 1938; postgrad., MIT, 1943.

Organist, choirmaster Morrow Meml. Ch., Maplewood, N.J., 1937-41; meteorologist Air Corps, Pan Am., Weather Bur., Bermuda, 1946-48, Weather Bur., JFK Internat. Airport, N.Y., 1948-50; hydrologist Ohio River Forecast Ctr., Cin., 1950-65, hydrologist-in-charge, 1965-77; ret., 1977; dep. dir. Hamilton County Emergency Mgmt. Agy., Cin., 1979-2000. Contbr. articles to profl. jours. Organist Highland United Meth. Ch., Fort Thomas, Ky., 1962-99, now organist emeritus; clk. of vestry Grace Episcopal Ch., Cin. Capt. U.S. Army Air Corps, 1943-46. Recipient Pub. Svc. cert. Hamilton County Disaster Coun., Cin., 1990. Mem. Ret. Engrs. and Scientists Cin. (chmn. 1984-86), N.Y. Acad. Scis., Columbia U. Club N.Y., Downtown Kiwanis Club. Republican. Avocations: travel, music, organist, home maintenance. Home: 1346 Teakwood Ave Cincinnati OH 45224-2126

RELYEA, HAROLD CLARENCE, political scientist; b. Oneida, N.Y., Apr. 5, 1944; s. Clyde Frederick and Pauline Elizabeth R.; children: Jennifer L., Stephen F. AB, Drew U., 1966; PhD, American U., 1971. Specialist in Am. nat. govt. Congrl. Rsch. Svc. Libr. Congress, Washington, 1971—. Author: A Brief History of Emergency Powers in the United States, 1974, The Evolution and Organization of the Federal Intelligence Function: A Brief Overview 1776-1975, 1988, Silencing Silence: National Security Controls and Scientific Communication, 1994; co-author: Presidential Staffing-A Brief Overview, 1978, United States Government Information: Policies and Sources, 2002; editor, contbg. author: The Presidency and Information Policy, 1981, Striking a Balance: National Security and Scientific Freedom, 1985, The Executive Office of the President, 1997; co-editor, contbg. author: Freedom of Information Trends in the Information Age, 1983, United States Government Information Policies: Views and Perspectives, 1989; bd. editors Presdl. Studies Quar., 1979-99, Govt. Publs. Rev., 1981-83, Transnational Data Report, 1982-89, Jour. Media Law and Practice, 1982-95, Govt. Info. Quar., 1984-, Internat. Jour. E-Govt. Rsch., 2004-, Jour. E-Govt., 2004-; contbr. articles to profl. jours. Mem. adv. bd. Coll. Info. Studies, U. Md., 2004—. Named Expert's Expert on U.S. Freedom Info. Act, The Economist of London, 1981; recipient Exec. Bd. award for superior pub. svc. Am. Soc. Access Profls., 1983, The Best of 1983 award for essay selection Libr. Lit. 14, 1984, Blue Pencil award Nat. Assn. Govt. Communicators, 1984; named to Freedom of Info. Act Hall of Fame, Freedom Forum, 1996. Mem. Pi Sigma Alpha. Office: Libr Congress CRS 101 Independence Ave SE Washington DC 20540-7470

REMAR, ROBERT BOYLE, lawyer; b. Boston, Nov. 19, 1948; s. Samuel Roy and Elizabeth Mary (Boyle) R.; m. Victoria A. Greenhood, Nov. 11, 1979; children: Daniel A.G., William B.G. BA, U. Mass., 1970; JD, Boston Coll., 1974. Bar: Ga. 1974, Mass. 1975, U.S. Ct. Appeals (5th cir.) 1978, U.S. Ct. Appeals (11th cir.) 1981, U.S. Ct. Appeals (2d cir.) 1995, U.S. Supreme Ct. 1981. Staff atty. Ga. Legal Svcs. Program, Savannah, 1974-76, Western Mass. Legal Svcs., Greenfield, 1976-77; sr. staff atty. Ga. Legal Svcs. Program, Atlanta, 1977-82; ptnr. Remar & Graettinger, Atlanta, 1983-95, Kirwan, Parks, Chesin & Remar PC, Atlanta, 1993-96, Rogers & Hardin, Atlanta, 1996—. Bd. dirs., exec. com. ACLU, N.Y.C., pres. Ga. chpt., 1985-87, gen. counsel, 1980-83; hearing officer Ga. Pub. Svc. Commn., Atlanta, 1985-98; adj. prof. Ga. State U., Atlanta, 1984-98, spl. asst. atty. gen., 1990-2003; bd. experts Lawyers Alert, Boston, 1985-94. Mem. Ga. Energy Regulatory Reform Commn., Gov. of Ga., 1980-82, Ga. Consumer Adv. Bd., 1981-82, City Atl. Bd. Ethics, AAA Comml. Panel; pres. Ga. Consumer Ctr. Inc., 1988-91, bd. dirs., exec. com. Ga. Resource Ctr.; v.p. Ga Ctr. Law Pub. Inst., 1991-94. Fellow Am. Coll. Trial Lawyers; mem. ABA (chmn. individual rights access to civil justice com. 1988-99), Ga. Bar Assn. (chmn. individual rights sect. 1981-83, co-chmn. consumer rights and remedies com. 1979-83, chmn. death penalty re. com. 1993—, mem. legis. adv. com. 1994-97, mem. indigent def. com. 2000—), Atlanta Bar Assn., Lawyers Club Atlanta, Lamar Inn of Ct. (master of the bench). Democrat. Avocations: golf, gardening. Home: 1714 Meadowdale Ave NE Atlanta GA 30306-3114 Office: Rogers & Hardin Internat Tower Peachtree Ctr 229 Peachtree St NE Ste 2700 Atlanta GA 30303-1638 Office Phone: 404-522-4700. Business E-Mail: RBR@RH-LAW.COM.

REMBE, TONI, lawyer, director; b. Seattle, Apr. 23, 1936; d. Armin and Doris (McVay) R.; m. Arthur Rock, July 19, 1975. Cert. in French Studies, U. Geneva, 1956; LL.B., U. Wash., 1960; LLM in Taxation, NYU, 1961. Bar: N.Y., Wash., Calif. Assoc. Chadbourne, Parke, Whiteside & Wolff, N.Y.C., 1961-63, Pillsbury, Madison & Sutro, San Francisco, 1964-71, ptnr., 1971—. Bd dirs. Aegon N.V., The Netherlands, Potlatch Corp., Spokane, Wash., SBC Comms., Inc., San Antonio. Pres. VanLobenSels/RembeRock Charitable Found., San Francisco; trustee Am. Conservatory Theatre, San Francisco. Fellow Am. Bar Found.; mem. ABA, Am. Judicature Soc., State Bar Calif., Bar Assn. San Francisco, Commonwealth Club of Calif. Office: Pillsbury Winthrop LLP 50 Fremont St San Francisco CA 94105-2230

REMBER, JOHN V. literature educator; b. Sun Valley, Idaho, Oct. 22, 1950; s. Craig V. and Elizabeth L. Rember; m. Julie A. Mitchell, Aug. 17, 1996. BA cum laude, Harvard U., 1972; MFA, U. Mont., 1987. Tchr. Cmty. Sch., Sun Valley, 1974—83; prof. Coll. Idaho, Caldwell, Idaho, 1989—. Adv. bd. Fishtrap Writers Organ., Joseph, Oreg., 1991—; sr. fellow Gallatin Writers Inc., Bozeman, Mont., 1996—; contr. editor Skiing Mag., 1998—. Author: Coyote in the Mountains, 1989, Cheerleaders From Gomorrah, 1995, Traplines, 2003. Grantee, Idaho Commn. on the Arts, 1990. Democrat. Avocations: skiing, bicycling. Home: PO Box 195 Stanley ID 83278 Office: Coll of Idaho 2112 Cleveland Blvd Caldwell ID 83605

REMBOLT, JAMES EARL, lawyer; b. Nov. 13, 1943; s. Earl Lester and Dorothy Elouise (Mehring) Rembolt; m. Marilyn Sue Schmadeke, July 16, 1972; children: Tami Anne, Michelle Sue. BBA, U. Nebr., 1965; MA in Bus. Orgn. and Mgmt., 1967, JD with distinction, 1972. Bar: Nebr. 1972, U.S. Dist. Ct. Nebr. 1972, U.S. Tax Ct. 1978, U.S. Ct. Claims 1978. Pres. Nebr. Moot Ct. Bd., 1972; pilot Nebr. Air Nat. Guard, Lincoln, 1969-74; lectr. legal writing U. Nebr. Coll. Law, 1973-74; ptnr. Rembolt, Ludtke LLP, Lincoln, 1976—. Chmn. bd. trustees YWCA, Lincoln, 1982—83; mem., past pres. Lincoln/Lancaster Sr. Ctrs. Found., Inc., bd. dirs., 1988—90; mem., past chair bd. dirs. Madonna Found., Inc., 1989—91; trustee, past bd. dirs. U.Nebr. Found.; past bd. dirs., pres. Nebr. Continuing Legal Edn., Inc.; bd. elders Eastridge Presbyn. Ch., Lincoln, 1979—82. Fellow: ABA, Nebr. State Bar Found., Am. Coll. Trust and Estate Counsel; mem.: Lincoln Estate Planning Coun. (past pres.), Lincoln Probate Discussion Group (charter mem., exec. coun. ho. of dels.), Nebr. State Bar Assn. (pres. 2002—03, exec. coun., ho. of dels.), Lincoln Bar Assn., U. Nebr. Lincoln Coll. Bus. Adminstrn. Alumni Assn. (past pres.). Office: Rembolt Ludtke LLP 1201 Lincoln Mall Ste 102 Lincoln NE 68508-2839 Office Phone: 402-475-5100. E-mail: jrembolt@remlud.com.

REMBUSCH, JOSEPH JOHN, psychologist, management consulting company executive; b. Joliet, Ill., June 29, 1939; s. Joseph Earl and Agnes Cecilia (Heinen) R. AA, Joliet Jr. Coll., 1959; BS in Psychology, U. Ill., 1962; MA in Teaching, Rockford (Ill.) Coll., 1970; postgrad., No. Ill. U., 1961-66, 70-73, Western Colo. U., 1973-75, U. Chgo., 2002—. Registered psychologist, Ill. Sci. tchr. Crete-Monee Sch. Dist., Crete, Ill., 1963-64; clin. caseworker Ill. State Sch. Boys, St. Charles, 1964-65; dir. guidance Hiawatha Unit Dist. #426, Kirkland, Ill., 1966-69; registrar Kishwaukee Community Coll., Malta, Ill., 1969-81; spl. rep., dist. mgr., regional mgr. George S. May Internat., Park Ridge, Ill., 1982-86, 89-01, divisional sales mgr., 1986-89, coord. client svcs., 2001—02, maj. account exec., 2002—03; ret., 2003. Pvt. practice psychology DeKalb, Ill., 1971-80; cons. psychologist Ill. Div. Vocat. Rehab., DeKalb, 1971-79. Mem. Illini Great Dane Club, Delta Upsilon, Phi Delta Kappa. Republican. Roman Catholic. Home: 1616 Margaret Ln Dekalb IL 60115

REMEN, RACHEL NAOMI, pediatrician, integrative medicine physician; b. N.Y.C., Feb. 8, 1938; d. Isidore J. and Gladys Sara Remen. MD, Cornell U., 1962; PhD in Psychology (hon.), Calif. Inst. Integral Studies, San Francisco, 1996; PhD in Humane Letters (hon.), John F. Kennedy U., 1999; MA (hon.), Spertus Inst. Jewish Studies, Chgo., 2000. Intern N.Y. Hosp., N.Y.C., 1962-63, resident, 1963-65; fellow Stanford U. Sch. Medicine, Palo Alto, Calif., 1965-67, asst. prof. pediat., 1967-74, assoc. dir. pediat. clinic, 1974-77; clin. prof. family and cmty. medicine U. Calif. Sch. Medicine, San Francisco, 1996—; med. dir. Commonweal Cancer Help Program, Bolinas, Calif., 1985—; pvt. practice, 1981—; founding dir. Inst. Study of Health & Illness, 1992—. Author: Kitchen Table Wisdom, 1996, My Grandfather's Blessings, 2000; editor: (poetry book) Wounded Healers, 1995. Fellow Am. Acad. Pediats. Office: Commonweal PO Box 316 Bolinas CA 94924-0316

REMENAR, ROBERT J. automotive executive; BBA, Central Mich. U.; MBA, Walsh Coll. Assoc. adminstr. Gen. Motors, Warren, Mich., 1985—86; sr. adminstr. Saturn Corp., Troy, 1986—89, mgr. fin. Spring Hill, Tenn., 1989—91; mgr. Gen. Motors, Detroit, 1991—93, dir. corp. fin. analysts, 1993—94, dir. health care cost analysis, 1994—96; dir. compensation, policy devel., and employee rels. Gen. Motors North Am., 1996—98; dir. human resources Delphi Chassis Systems, Dayton, Ohio, 1998; dir. worldwide fin. Delphi Energy, Flint, Mich., 1998—99; worldwide fin. dir. Delphi Energy & Cassis Systems, 1999—2000, exec. dir. bus. lines, 2000—02; v.p., pres. Delphi steering sys. Delphi Corp., Saginaw, Mich., 2002—. Bd. dirs. Blue Cross/Blue Shield Mich. Office: Delphi Saginaw Steering Systems 3900 Holland Rd Saginaw MI 48601 also: Delphi Corp World Headquarters 5725 Delphi Dr Troy MI 48098-2815

REMEZ, SHEREEN G. government executive; M. Lee R. Johnson; 1 child: Erik. BA in Psychology and Communications, MA in Edn., Am. U; PhD, U. Md., 1981. Various positions U.S. Govt.; asst. chief info. officer GSA, 1996-97, chief info. officer. Office: GSA 1800 F St NW Rm 6122 Washington DC 20405-0001

REMICK, FORREST JEROME, JR., former university official; b. Lock Haven, Pa., Mar. 16, 1931; s. Forrest Jerome Sr. and Ruth Betsy (Saiers) R., m. Grace Louise Grove, June 7, 1953; children: Beth Ann Remick Gillio, Eric Forrest; m. Soon Ja Cho, Dec. 8, 1995. BSME, Pa. State U., 1955, MSME, 1958, PhD in ME, 1963; diploma, Oak Ridge (Tenn.) Sch. Reactor Tech., 1956. Engr. Bell Telephone Labs., Whippany, NJ, 1955—56; dir. nuclear reactor facility Pa. State U., University Park, 1959—65, dir. Inst. Sci. Engring., 1967—79, acting dir. Ctr. Air Environ. Studies, 1976—78, dir. intercoll. research programs, 1979—85, asst. v.p. research, grad. studies, 1979—84, assoc. v.p. research, 1985—89; dir. Curtiss Wright Nuclear Research Lab., Quehanna, Pa., 1960—65; chief tng. sect. dept. tech. assistance IAEA, Vienna, 1965—66. Mem. Nat. Nuclear Accrediting Bd., Inst. Nuclear Power Ops., Atlanta, mem. adv. coun., 1995—; mem. Sci. Adv. Com. Idaho Nat. Engring. Lab., Idaho Falls, 1984-89, Reactor Safety Adv. Com., Savannah River Lab., Aiken, S.C., 1986-89, chmn., 1989; mem. Adv. Com. on Reactor Safeguards, Washington, 1982, vice chmn., 1987-88, chmn., 1989; commr. U.S. Nuclear Regulatory Commn., 1989-94, cons., 1994—; bd. dirs. Pub. Svc. Enterprise Group, Pub. Svc. Electric and Gas; mem. adv. bd. Applied Rsch. Lab., Pa. State U., 1994—. Served to sgt. U.S. Army, 1951-52. Named Outstanding Engring. Alumnus, Pa. State U., 1993; recipient Thomas P. Hamrick award for contbns. to tng. of nuclear facility pers., 1995. Fellow Am. Nuclear Soc. (bd. dirs. 1995—, meml. lectr. award 1971, disting. speaker award 1983); mem. ASME, Am. Soc. Engring. Edn., Nuclear Accrediting Bd. Republican. Lutheran. Home and Office: Canterbury Crossing 439 Brandywine Dr State College PA 16801-7984

REMINE, WILLIAM HERVEY, JR., retired surgeon; b. Richmond, Va., Oct. 11, 1918; s. William Hervey and Mabel Inez (Walthall) ReM.; m. Doris Irene Grumbacher, June 9, 1943; children: William H., Stephen Gordon, Walter James, Gary Craig. BS in Biology, U. Richmond, 1940, D.Sc. (hon.), 1965; MD, Med. Coll. Va., Richmond, 1943; MS in Surgery, U. Minn., Mpls., 1952. Diplomate Am. Bd. Surgery. Intern Doctor's Hosp., Washington, 1944; fellow in surgery Mayo Clinic, Rochester, Minn., 1944-45, 47-52; instr. surgery Mayo Grad. Sch. Medicine, Rochester, Minn., 1954-59, asst. prof. surgery, 1959-65, assoc. prof. surgery, 1965-70, prof. surgery, 1970-83, prof. surgery emeritus, 1983—. Surg. cons. to surgeon gen. U.S. Army, 1965-75; surg. lectr., USSR, 1987, 89, Japan, 1988, 90, Egypt, 1990; lectr. Soviet-Am. seminars, USSR, 1987, 89. Sr. author: Cancer of the Stomach, 1964, Manual of Upper Gastro-intestinal Surgery, 1985; editor: Problems in General Surgery, Surgery of the Biliary Tract, 1986; mem. editorial bd. Rev. Surgery, 1965-75, Jour. Lancet, 1968-77; contbr. 200 articles to profl. jours. Served to capt. U.S. Army, 1945-47 Recipient St. Francis surg. award St. Francis Hosp., Pitts., 1976, Disting. Svc. award Alumni Council, U. Richmond, 1976, Dist. Alumnus award Mayo Found., 2000. Mem. ACS, AAAS, Am. Assn. History of Medicine, AMA, Am. Med. Writers Assn., Am. Soc. Colon and Rectal Surgeons, Soc. Surgery Alimentary Tract (v.p. 1983-84), Am. Surg. Assn., Assn. Mil. Surgeons U.S., Internat. Soc. Surgery, Digestive Disease Found., Priestley Soc. (pres. 1968-69), Central Assn. Physicians and Dentists (pres. 1972-73), Central Surg. Assn., Soc. Med. Cons. Armed Forces, Mayo Clinic Surg. Soc. (chmn. 1964-66), Soc. Head and Neck Surgeons, Soc. Surg. Oncology, So. Surg. Assn., Western Surg. Assn. (pres. 1979-80), Minn. State Med. Assn., Minn. Surg. Soc. (pres. 1966-67), Zumbro Valley Med. Soc., Sigma Xi; hon. mem. Colombian Coll. Surgeons, St. Paul Surg. Soc., Flint Surg. Soc., Venezuelan Surg. Soc., Colombian Soc. Gastroenterology, Dallas So. Clin. Soc., Ga. Surg. Soc., Soc. Postgrad. Surgeons Los Angeles County, Japanese Surg. Soc., Argentine Surg. Digestive Soc., Bassanese Surg. Assn. (Italy), Tex. Surg. Soc., Omicron Delta Kappa, Alpha Omega Alpha, Beta Beta Beta, Kappa Sigma (pres. 1939-40). Methodist. Avocations: hunting, fishing, golf, photography, boating, music. Home: Sawgrass Players Club 8212 Seven Mile Dr Ponte Vedra Beach FL 32082-3129

REMINGER, RICHARD THOMAS, lawyer, artist; b. Cleve., Apr. 3, 1931; s. Edwin Carl and Theresa Henrietta (Bookmyer) Reminger; m. Billie Carmen Greer, June 26, 1954; children: Susan Greer, Patricia Allison, Richard Thomas. AB, Case-Western Res. U., 1953; JD, Cleve. State U., 1957. Bar: Ohio 1957, Pa. 1978, U.S. Supreme Ct. 1961. Pers. and safety dir. Motor Express, Inc., Cleve., 1954-58; mng. ptnr. Reminger & Reminger Co., L.P.A., Cleve., 1958-90. Mem. nat. claims coun. adv. bd. Comml. Union Assurance Co., 1980—90; lectr. transp. law Fenn Coll., 1960—62; lectr. bus. law Case Western Res. U., 1962—64; lectr. products liability U. Wirtschaft at Schloss Gracht, Erfstadt-Liblar, Germany, 1990—91, Bar Assn. City of Hamburg, Germany, 1990; mem. faculty Nat. Inst. Trial Advocacy, 1992. Trustee Cerebral Palsy Assn., 1984—87, Andrew Sch., 1984—96, Meridia Huron Hosp., Cleve., 1978—96, Cleve. Sch. Blind, 1987—88, Intracoastal Health Sys., Palm Beach, Fla., 1992—2000; mem. joint com. Cleve. Acad. Medicine-Greater Cleve. Bar Assn.; v.p. Cleve. Zool. Soc., 1984—87. With AC USNR, 1950—58. Mem.: FBA, ABA (profl. responsiblity com. 1977—90, com. law and medicine), Palm Beach County Bar Assn., Internat. Ins. Law Soc., Am. Coll. Law and Medicine, Maritime Law Assn., Def. Rsch. Inst., Am. Judicature Soc., Ohio Assn. Civil Trial Attys., Soc. Ohio Hosp. Attys., Am. Soc. Hosp. Attys., Cleve. Assn. Civil Trial Attys., Transp. Lawyers Assn., Cleve. Bar Assn. (prof. liability com. 1977—90, chmn. med. legal com. 1978—79), Pa. Bar Assn., Ohio Bar Assn. (coun. dels. 1987—90, internat. law com. 1990—91), Internat. Bar Assn., Fedn. Ins. and Corp. Counsel, 8th Jud. Bar Assn. (life), Internat. Soc. Marine Painters (v.p.), Oil Painters Am., Soc. Four Arts, Cleve.-Marshall Law Alumni Assn. (hon. trustee 1980—), Univ. Club (N.Y.C.), Salmagundi Club (N.Y.C.), Rolling Rock Club (Pa.), Kirtland Country Club (Cleve.), Everglades Club (Fla.), Lost Tree Club (Fla.) (bd. govs. 1991—94), Hermit Club (Cleve.) (pres. 1973—75), Mayfield Country Club (Cleve.) (pres. 1980—82), Case Res. Athletic Club (life).

REMINGTON, DEBORAH WILLIAMS, artist; b. Haddonfield, N.J., June 25, 1935; d. Malcolm Van Dyke and Hazel Irwin (Stewart) R. BFA, San Francisco Art Inst., 1955. Adj. prof. art Cooper Union, N.Y.C., 1973—97, NYU, 1994—98; tchr. Nat. Acad. Design, N.Y.C., 2003—. One-woman shows include Dilexi Gallery, San Francisco, 1962, 63, 65, San Francisco Mus. Art, 1964, Bykert Gallery, N.Y.C., 1967, 69, 72, 74, Galerie Darthea Speyer, Paris, 1968, 71, 73, 92, Pyramid Gallery, Washington DC, 1973, 76, zola-Leiberman Gallery, Chgo., 1976, Hamilton Gallery, N.Y.C., 1977, Portland (Oreg.) Ctr. for Visual Arts, 1977, Michael Berger Gallery, Pitts., 1979, Mary Ryan Gallery, N.Y.C., 1982, Ramon Osuna Gallery, Washington D.C., 1983, Newport Harbor Art Mus., 1983, Oakland (Calif.) Mus., 1984, Jack Shainman Gallery, N.Y.C., 1987, Shoshana Wayne Gallery, L.A., 1988, Mitchell Algus Gallery, N.Y.C., 2001; group shows include Whitney Mus. Am. Art, N.Y.C., 1965, 67, 72, San Francisco Mus. Art, 1956, 60, 61, 63, 64, 65, Lausanne Mus., Switz., 1966, Fondation Maeght, St. Paul de Vence, France, 1968, Smithsonian Am. Art Mus., Washington, D.C., 1968, Art. Inst., Chgo., 1974, Inst. Contemporary Art, Boston, 1975, Nat. Gallery Modern Art, Lisbon, Portugal, 1981, Toledo Mus. Art, 1975, The 6 Gallery, 1954-57, Natsoulas Gallery, Davis, Calif., 1990, 1st Trienalle des Ameriques Maubeuge, France, 1993, Tamarind Inst. Retrospective, 2000, Worcester (Mass.) Art Mus., 2001, San Jose (Calif.) Mus. Art, 2002, numerous others; represented in permanent collections Whitney Mus. Am. Art, Smithsonian Am. Art Mus., Washington, Art Inst., Chgo., Centre d'Art et de Culture Georges Pompidou, Paris, Carnegie Mus., Pitts. Recipient Hassam and Speicher Purchase award Am. Acad. and Inst. Arts and Letters, 1988; NEA fellow, 1979-80; Tamarind Inst. fellow, 1973; Guggenheim fellow, 1984; Pollock-Krasner Found. grantee, 1999. Mem. NAD (Benjamin Altman prize for painting 178th Ann. Exhbn. 2003). Home: 309 W Broadway New York NY 10013-5325 Office Phone: 212-925-3037. E-mail: deborahremington@aol.com. *Be aware of yourself, aware of what makes you distinctive from others, and make those individual characteristics part of your work, whatever that may be. Read philosophy. Develop your own. This gives you ballast when the pendulum swings too far in one direction.*

REMINGTON, MARY, artist, author; b. Kansas City, Mo., Jan. 15, 1930; d. Edwin Jennings and Mary Pauline (Remington) Anderson; m. Robert Alan Smith, Dec. 14, 1957 (div. 1978); 1 child, Susanah Mara Smith. BA, Ottawa (Kans.) U., 1951; postgrad., U. Kans., 1951, Kansas City Art Inst. Artist animation dept. Walt Disney Prodns., Burbank, Calif., 1954-58; pvt. cartoonist Calif., 1977-97; humor and cartooning tchr. Mira Costa Coll. Extension course, Calif., 1997; tchr. So. Oreg. U., 1993. Freelance cartoonist, caricaturist, Calif., Oreg. Author: Long Ago Elf, 1968, Crocodiles Have Big Teeth All Day, 1970; one-woman show at Josephine County Main Libr., Grants Pass, Oreg., Adobe Gallery, San Diego County, Rogue Gallery, Medford, Oreg., Grants Pass Art Mus.; group exhibitions include Yosemite Mus. Gallery, Okla. Art Workshops 15th Nat. Exhbn., Tulsa, Wiseman Gallery, Grants Pass, others; artist for animated films Lady and the Tramp, Sleeping Beauty. Mem. Grants Pass Art Museum. Avocations: history, reading.

REMINI, LEAH, actress; b. Bklyn., June 15, 1970; m. Angelo Pagan, July 19, 2003. Appearances include (TV series) Living Dolls, 1989, Saved By The Bell, 1989, The Man in the Family, 1991, Getting Up and Going Home, 1992, King of Queens, 1999—, (voice) Gabriel Knight: Sins of the Fathers, 1994, (voice) Phantom 2040: The Ghost Who Walks, 1994, The First Time Out, 1995, Glory Daze, 1996, Fired Up, 1997, Follow Your Heart, 1998, also numerous guest appearances, including Cheers, 1982, Who's the Boss?, 1984, Evening Shade, 1990, Blossom, 1992, Diagnosis Murder, 1993, NYPD Blue, 1993, Friends, 1994; TV Movies: Legend of the Lost Tribe, 2002 (voice), Hooves of Fire, 1999 (voice); Films: Old School, 2003, Follow Your Heart, 1998. Office: Gold Marchak & Liedtke 3500 W Olive Ave Ste 1400 Burbank CA 91505-5512

REMINI, ROBERT VINCENT, historian; b. N.Y.C., July 17, 1921; s. William Francis and Lauretta (Tierney) R.; m. Ruth Theresa Kuhner, Oct. 9, 1948; children: Elizabeth Mary, Joan Marie, Robert William. BS, Fordham U., 1943; MA, Columbia U., 1947, PhD, 1951; LHD (hon.), Gov.'s State U., 1989; LittD (hon.), Ea. Ky. U., 1992, Fordham U., 1993, Columbia Coll. Chgo., 2000, So. Ill. U., 2004. Prof. History, emeritus prof. U. Ill. Chgo., 1965—, historian, 1997—. Vis. lectr. Columbia U., 1959-60. Author: Martin Van Buren and the Making of the Democratic Party, 1959, The Election of Andrew Jackson, 1963, Andrew Jackson, 1966, Andrew Jackson and the Bank War, 1968, The Revolutionary Age of Andrew Jackson, 1976 (award of merit Friends of Am. Writers), Andrew Jackson and the Course of American Empire, 1767-1821, 1977, Andrew Jackson and the Course of American Freedom, 1822-1832, vol. II, 1981 (George Washington medal of Honor, Freedoms Found.), Andrew Jackson and the Course of American Democracy, 1833-1845, vol. III, 1984 (Am. Book award for non-fiction 1984, Chgo. Found. for Lit. award 1985, English Speaking Union U.S. Ambassador of Honor award 1985); The Legacy of Andrew Jackson: Essays on Democracy, Indian Removal and Slavery, 1988, The Life of Andrew Jackson (abridgement of 3-vol. biography), 1988 (Carl Sandbury Lit. award for non-fiction 1989), The Jacksonian Era, 1989, Henry Clay: Statesman for the Union, 1991 (award for biography Soc. Midland Authors 1992), The Battle of New Orleans, 1999, Andrew Jackson and His Indian Wars, 2001, (Am. Hist. Assn. award for scholarly dist., 2001, Western Writers of Am. award, 2002, John Hope Franklin Hist. Maker award, Chgo. Hist. Soc., 2003), John Quincy Adams, 2002, Joseph Smith, 2002; co-author: We the People: A History of the United States, 1975, The Era of Good Feelings and the Age of Jackson, 1816-1841, 1979, The American People: A History, 1981, Andrew Jackson: A Bibliography, 1991; also articles, chpts. in books.; editor: The Decline of Aristocracy in the Politics of New York, 1965, The Presidency of Andrew Jackson, 1967, The Age of Jackson, 1972; spl. editor Am. history, Crowell-Collier Co., 1960-68, 72-73; mem editl. bd. Jour. Am. History, 1969-72; editl. cons. Papers of Andrew Jackson, 1972— . Served with USNR, 1943-46. Lt. USN, 1943—46. Recipient Encaenia award Fordham U., 1963; Silver Circle award U. Ill., Chgo., 1981, Univ. Scholar award, 1986; grantee Am. Coun. Learned Socs., 1964, Am. Philos. Soc., 1966, 80; Guggenheim fellow, 1978-79. Mem. Am. Hist. Assn. (council 1979-82), So. Hist. Assn., Orgn. Am. Historians. Roman Catholic. Home: 215 Ninth St Wilmette IL 60091 Office: Univ Ill at Chgo Office of Historian 815 W Van Buren Chicago IL 60607

REMLEY, THEODORE PHANT, JR., counseling educator, lawyer; b. Eustis, Fla., Feb. 7, 1947; s. Theodore Phant Sr. and Era Annie (Forehand) R. BA, U. Fla., 1969, EdS, 1971, PhD, 1980; JD, Catholic U., 1980. Bar: Va. 1981, Fla. 1982; lic. profl. counselor, Va., Miss., La. Exec. dir. Am. Counseling Assn., Alexandria, Va., 1990-94; prof. counseling U. New Orleans, 1994—. Contbr. articles to profl. jours., chpts. to books. Mem. Am. Counseling Assn., Am. Assn. State Counseling Bds. Democrat. Roman Catholic. Home: 3800 Camp St New Orleans LA 70115-2629 Office: Dept Edn Leadership Counseling & Founds Rm 348 U New Orleans New Orleans LA 70148-0001

REMLINGER, ROLF, music educator, composer; b. Detroit, Mar. 9, 1963; s. Florian and Hermina Remlinger; m. Annette C. Tischler, Apr. 1, 1989; children: Eric, Matthew. BA, Hiram Coll., 1985. Cert. tchr. Mich., Ohio. Tchr. music St. Fabian Elem. Sch., Farmington Hills, Mich., 1985—86; dir. marching band percussion sect. Midpark H.S., Middleburg Heights, Ohio, 1986—86; tchr. music, dir. choir Lincoln Elem. Sch., Youngstown, 1987—95; asst. orch. dir. Harding H.S., Marion, 1997—98; tchr. music, dir. choir Taft Mid. Sch., 1995—; transition team Marion City Schs., 2001—03. Tchr. drama tchr., dir. Youngstown Playhouse, Ohio, 1988—95; mem. theater tech. staff Interlochen Summer Arts Camp, Interlochen, Mich., 1984; tchr. youth theater drama Jewish Cmty. Ctr., Youngstown, 1991—94; percussionist Ohio Boy Choir, Cleve., 1985—89; vocal instr. Pleasent City Schools Theater Dept., Marion, 1996. Hockey Daze Hockey Comics, 1993; composer: (songs) Slow Day in City Traffic, 1986, Meadow Walk, 1986, Kyrie, 2001, Praise the Lord!, 2002, Salve Regina, 2002, Ave Regina Coelorum, 2002; contbr. articles to mags. Den leader Boy Scouts of Am., Delaware, 1996—, tiger cub coach, 2000—, merit badge counselor, 2002, instr. Pow Wow Columbus, 2003—; choir mem., composer and dir. St. Mary's Ch., 1997—, vacation bible sch. tchr., 1998—99. Recipient Bissel Meml. Music award, Hiram Coll., 1984, Profl. Svc. award, Youngstown State U., 1991, Tiger Cub Coach award, Boy Scouts of Am., 2002, Cub Scout Den Leader award, 2002; grantee, Ohio Theatre Alliance, 1990; scholar Hubbell scholar, Hiram Coll., 1984, 1985, Martin scholar, 1985. Mem.: PTA, NEA, Nat. Mid. Sch. Assn., Ohio Mid. Sch. Assn., Marion Edn. Assn., Ohio Edn. Assn., Music Educators Nat. Conf., Ohio Music Edn. Assn., Brigade of Am. Revolution, KC. Roman Catholic. Avocations: music, art, hockey, comic book collecting, collecting sports cards.

REMMEN, LAWRENCE P. city planner; b. Detroit Lakes, Minn., Oct. 21, 1958; s. Palmer H. and Lois D. (Brown) R.; m. Kellie R. Newton, June 21, 1980; children: Grant Newton, Cole Nicolai. BA in Geography and City Planning, Moorhead State U., 1981; M in Cmty. and Regional Planning, N.D. State U., 1983. Planning asst. City of Moorhead, 1980-83, cmty. devel. planner, 1983, planning dir., 1983-86; planning cons. Detroit Lakes, Minn., 1986-89; cmty. devel. dir. City of Henning, Minn., 1989-90, City of Detroit

Lakes, 1990—. Planning cons. Detroit Lakes, 1986-89; exec. dir. Becker Lakes Indsl. Devel. Corp., Detroit Lakes, 1990—. Den leader Boy Scouts of Am., Detroit Lakes, 1997—; ch. coun. First Luth. Ch., 1997—; pres. Geography Club, Moorhead State U., 1980-81. Mem. Am. Inst. Cert. Planners (Nat. Outstanding Planning Student award 1983), Am. Planning Assn., Minn. Planning Assn., Econ. Devel. Assn. of Minn., Mid-Am. Econ. Devel. Coun., Urban Land Inst. Republican. Lutheran. Avocations: music, history, refinishing antiques, snow sculpture, sailing. Office: City of Detroit Lakes 1025 Roosevelt Ave Detroit Lakes MN 56501-3637 Home: 272 Cherry Ridge Dr Detroit Lakes MN 56501-2127

REMNICK, DAVID J. journalist, editor; b. Hackensack, N.J., Oct. 29, 1958; s. Edward C. and Barbara (Seigel) Remnick; m. Esther B. Fein; children: Alexander, Noah, Natasha. BA, Princeton U., 1981. Reporter The Washington Post, 1982—88, Moscow (Russia) corr., 1988—92; staff writer The New Yorker, N.Y.C., 1992—98, editor, 1998—. Author: (book) Lenin's Tomb: The Last Days of the Soviet Empire, 1993 (Pulitzer Prize for gen. non-fiction, 1994, George Polk award, 1994), Resurrection, 1997, The Devil Problem (and other True Stories), 1997, King of the World: Muhammad Ali and the Rise of an American Hero, 1998. Recipient Livingston award, 1991, Helen Bernstein award, N.Y. Pub. Libr., 1994. Office: The New Yorker 4 Times Sq New York NY 10036-6561

REMPFER, DIETMAR, research scientist, consultant; b. Reutlingen, Germany, Mar. 7, 1962; s. Kurt and Doris Erika (Fäser) R. Dipl.-Ing. in Aerospace Engring., U. Stuttgart, Germany, 1988, Dr.-Ing. Mech. Engring. summa cum laude, 1991. Cons. Dornier Sys. GmbH, Friedrichshafen, Germany, 1987-88; rsch. asst. Inst. for Mechanics, Stuttgart, 1988-90; postdoctoral fellow dept. aerospace and mech. engring. U. Ariz., Tucson, 1992-93; rsch. asst. Inst. for Aerodyn. and Gasdynamics, Stuttgart, 1990-92, rsch. scientist, 1993—. Reviewer European Jour. Mechanics B/Fluids, 1992—, Physics of Fluids, 1995—; vis. assoc. prof. Sibley Sch. Mech. & Aerospace Engring. Cornell U., 1996-2001; assoc. prof. mech. materials and aerospace engring. Ill. Inst. Tech., 2001—. Contbr. articles to sci. jours. Recipient Hermann-Reissner award Hermann-Reissner-Stiftung, 1992; grantee Deutsche Forschungsgemeinschaft; fellow Studienstiftung des deutschen Volkes, 1989. Mem. Am. Phys. Soc., N.Y. Acad. Scis., Deutsche Gesellschaft für Luft- und Raumfahrt. Office: Ill Inst Tech 3110S State St Chicago IL 60616 Office Phone: 312-567-3189.

REMSHARD, JOHN W. insurance company executive; BS in Acctg. and English, MBA in Fin., LaSalle U.; degree, Dartmouth Coll. CPA. Acct. Touche Ross; v.p. Fin. Divsn. CIGNA Corp., 1978—95; sr. v.p. Audit Dept. HealthChoice, 1995—96; sr. v.p. WellChoice, N.Y., 1996—, CFO, 1996—. Office: WellChoice 11 West 42nd Street New York NY 10036

REMSING, DENNIS, advertising agency executive; Exec. v.p., gen. mgr. Rubin Postaer and Assocs., Santa Monica, Calif. Office: Rubin Postaer and Assocs 1333 2d St Santa Monica CA 90401

REMY-SCHUMACHER, TESS, music educator, musician; arrived in U.S., 1987; m. David M. Morris, Apr. 4, 2003. Student, Menuhin Music Sch., Gstaad, Switzerland, 1983; pvt. student of Jacqueline Du Pre and William Pleet, London, 1984—85; artist diploma, Musik Hochschule, Köln, Germany, 1987; MusM, U. So. Calif., L.A., 1989, D in Musical Arts, 1998; pvt. student of Lynn Harrell and Elenore Schoenfeld. Recording artist, concert cellist, 1978—; prin. cellist Rheinisches Kammer Orchester, Köln, 1990—91, Detmolder Kammer Orchester, Germany, 1991—98; faculty for cello James Cook U., Australia, 1992—98; asst. prof. U. Ctrl. Okla., Edmond, 1998—2003, assoc. prof., 2003—. Musician CD and Radio Recordings. Cmty. svc. vol. JCU, Australia, 1992—98, U. Ctrl. Okla., Edmond, 1998—; fundraiser United Way, Okla., 2002. Finalist, East and West Ashst Competition for Carnegie Hall, 1993; recipient first prize, Internat. Carlo Zecchi Competition, Rome, 1990. Mem.: Verein Deutscher Musikerzieter and Konzertierender Kunstler, Fulbright Assn. Avocations: scuba diving, hiking, literature. Home: Dürener Str 132 50931 Köln Germany Office: Univ Ctrl Okla Sch Music Box 179 100 N University Dr Edmond OK 73034 Office Phone: 405-974-5650.

REN, JIYU, library director; b. Pingyuan County, Shandong, China, Apr. 15, 1916; s. Zijiu and Guofang (Song) R.; m. Zhongyun Feng, Sept. 15, 1946; children: Ren Yuan, Ren Zhong. Student, Peking U., 1934-37; BA, Southwest Union U., Kun Ming, China, 1938; MA, Southwest Union U., 1939-42. Lectr. philosophy dept. Southwest Union U., 1946-49; assoc. prof. philosophy dept. Peking U., 1949-56, prof. philosophy dept., 1956-64; dir. Inst. for World Religion Study Chinese Acad. Social Scis., Beijing, 1964-87; dir. Nat. Libr. of China, Beijing, 1987—. Author: Re-Explanation of Philosophy, 1981; editor: History of Chinese Philosophy, vols. 1-4, 1963-79 (Nat. Excellent Textbook spl. prize 1987), Chinese History of Buddhism, Vols. 1-3, 1984, The Complete Collections of Buddhism, Vols. 106 (Zhung Hwa Da Zangjing), 1984-93, History of Chinese Taoism, 1990, rev. edit. 2001, Religion Dictionary, 1981, (100 books) The Historical Knowledge of Chinese Culture Series, 1998; co-editor: Abstracts of Classical Works of Daoism, 1991, Selected Essays of Ren Jiyu, 1991, Ren Jiyu's Essays on Philosophy and Religion, 1996, Relations Between God and Man, 1998, Great Religion Dictionary, 1998, Great Buddhism Dictionary, 2003; mem. editl. bd. Chinese Ency., philosophy vol., 1987. Rep. Nat. People's Congress 1980, 84, 88, 92. Mem. Chinese Religion Soc. (dir.), Chinese Soc. Philosophy History (pres.), Chinese Libr. Soc. (dir.), Chinese Inst. of Tibetan Buddhists. Mem. Communist Party of China. Home: Sanlihe Rd 100045 Beijing China Office: Nat Libr of China 33 Zhongguancun Nandajie 100081 Beijing China Office Phone: 86-10-8854-5072.

REN, XING JIAN, physician; b. Shanghai, June 27, 1961; s. Yun Feng Ren and Xin Yi Zhang; m. Bei Xie, June 27, 1990; 1 child, Oriana Leigh. MD, Shanghai First Med. Coll., 1984. Diplomate internal medicine and geriatric medicine Am. Bd. Internal Medicine. Resident in surgery Shanghai Ruhui Hosp., China, 1984-85; resident Ft. Wayne (Ind.) Med. Edn. Program, 1993-94; resident, intern in medicine Loyola U. of Chgo., Maywood, Ill., 1994-97; fellow in medicine Harvard Med. Sch., Boston, 1997-99; staff physician Scripps Clinic Found., La Jolla, Calif., 1999—; asst. clin. prof. medicine U. Calif. Sch. Medicine, 2003—. Co-author: Virology, 1986; contbr. articles to profl. jours. Fellow Harvard Med. Sch., 1998; recipient 1st prize Nat. Med. Student Competition for Knowledge of Med. Lit., 1983, grad. student scholarship U. N.C., Chapel Hill, scholarship Carolina Biotechnolgoy Ctr., others. Fellow ACP; mem. AMA, Mass. Med. Soc., Am. Geriatrics Soc., Fell. Am. Coll. Physician. Office Phone: 858-268-9500., 858-794-9284.

REN, YING, engineer; arrived in USA, 2001; s. Kean Ren and Yuee Bai; 1 child, Bob. BA Eng., Shanghai Jiao-tong Univ., Shanghai, 1986; MS, Imperial Coll., London, 1988, PhD, 1992. Project engr. Orbital Engine Co., Australia, 1998—2001; sr. project engr. Roush Industries, Livonia, Mich., 2001—. Contbr. articles to profl. jours. Scholar, Brit. Coun., 1988—92. Mem.: SAE, ASME. Achievements include research in System dynamics, modal analysis, structural dynamics, engine NVH.

RENARD, RONALD LEE, allergist; b. Chgo., July 31, 1949; s. Robert James and Dorothy Mae (Fruik) R.; m. Maureen Ann Gilmore, Aug. 5, 1972 (div. Mar. 1992); children: Jeffrey, Stephen, Justin, Leigh Ellen; m. Catherine L. Walker, Apr. 1, 1992; children: Morgan, Michal, Luke. 1 & 2 Degre de la Langue, U. de Montepellier, France, 1970; BS in French, U. San Francisco, 1971; MD, Creighton U., 1976. Dir. med. ICU, lt. U.S. Army Hosp., Ft. Leonard Wood, Md., 1980-81; dir. respiratory therapy, asst. chief allergy svc. Walter Reed Med. Ctr., Washington, 1981-84; staff allergist Chico (Calif.) Med. Group, 1984-86; allergist pvt. practice Redding, Calif., 1986—. Dir. ACLS program Enloe Hosp., Chico, 1988-91; bd. dirs. Am. Lung Assn. Calif., 1989-91, med. dir. asthma camp, Chico, Redding, 1986-95; asst. prof. medicine USPHS, Bethesda, Md., 1982-84; asst. prof. family medicine U. Calif. Davis Med. Sch., Redding, 1990-94; Shasta County Planning Commr., 1994-95. Contbr. articles to profl. jours. Fellow Am. Acad. Allergy & Immunology, Am. Coll. Allergists; mem. Alpha Omega Alpha Nat. Honor Med. Soc., Assn. Mil. Allergists, Calif. Thoracic Soc. Republican. Roman Catholic. Avocations: hunting, biking. Office: 2632 Edith Ave Ste B Redding CA 96001-3043 Office Phone: 530-246-2760. Home Fax: 530-246-8856. Personal E-mail: rlr@reddingallergy.com.

RENAU, DONALD IRWIN, lawyer; b. Louisville, Apr. 28, 1936; m. Scholl, Dec. 21, 1961. BA, Principia Coll., 1958; JD, U. Louisville, 1967. Bar: Ky. 1968, U.S. Ct. Appeals (6th cir.) 1968. Pvt. practice, Louisville, 1968—. Columnist Am. Agt. & Broker, 1997—. Bd. dirs. Salvation Army Adv. Bd., Louisville, 1990—; past pres. Lions club, 1966—. Avocation: horses. Office: PO Box 7669 Louisville KY 40257-0669 Office Phone: 502-893-2020. Personal E-mail: drenau@thepoint.net.

RENAUD, BERNADETTE MARIE ELISE, author; b. Ascot Corner, Que., Can., Apr. 18, 1945; d. Albert and Aline (Audet) R. Diploma, Présentation de Marie, Granby, Que., 1962-64. Librarian asst. Schs. of Waterloo, Que., 1964-67, tchr. primary schs., 1967-70; adminstrv. sec. Assn. Medi-Tech-Sci., Montreal, Que., 1972-76. Author: Emilie La Baignoire A Pattes, 1976 (Can. Coun. Children's Lit. prize, 1976, Assn. Advancement of Scis. and Technics of Documentation award, 1976), 2d edit., 2002, Le Chat de l'Oratoire, 1978, Emilie la baignoire á pattes album, 1978, La maison tête de pioche, 1979, La révolte de la courte pointe, 1979, La dépression de l'ordinateur, 1981, Une boîte Magique Très Embêtante, 1981, La grande question de Tomatelle, 1982, Comment on fait un livre?, 1983, The Cat in the Cathedral, 1983, The Computer Revolts, 1984, (book and movie) Bach et Bottine, 1986 (awards for movie, 19 awards across the world, transl. ino 8 langs., subtitled into 18 langs.), Bach and Broccoli, 1986, (short movie) Quand l'accent devient grave, 1989, (novels) Un Homme Comme Tant d'Autres, tome 1, 1992, tome, II, 1993, tome, III, 1994, Prix Germaine Guévremont, 1995, Gala des Arts du Bas-Richelieu (QC); dir., coord.: Ecrire pour la jeunesse, 1990; author: short stories, adaptations of 8 children's classics, 1977—79; dir., coord.: La quête de Kurweena, 1997, Le petit violon muet, 1997, Héritiers de l'éternité, 1998, Les Funambules D'un Temps Nouveau, 2001, Les Chemins d'Eve Tome I, 2002, Les Chemins d'Eve Tome II, 2002, Grand Prix du Livre de la Monteregie, 2001, 2002.

RENBAUM, BARRY JEFFREY, lawyer; b. Balt., Feb. 26, 1948; s. David and Leah (Cohen) R.; m. Carol Barbash, June 22, 1980. BS magna cum laude, Rider U., 1970; postgrad., NYU, 1973; JD, Georgetown U., 1973. Bar: Md. 1973, U.S. Dist. Ct. Md. 1998. Jud. clk. to Hon. John C. Eldridge, Md. Ct. Appeals, 1974-75; asst. pub. defender State of Md., 1975-79; exec. v.p., gen. counsel Custom Savs. Bank, Tmple Fin. Co., Balt., 1980-91; pvt. practice Glyndon, Md., 1991—. Mem. ATLA, Md. Bar Assn., Alpha Epsilon Zeta. Office: Brydonwood Glyndon MD 21071-0326 E-mail: brydonwood@earthlink.net.

RENCH, STEPHEN CHARLES, lawyer; b. Coffeyville, Kans., Oct. 11, 1930; s. Stephen and Gladys Mae (Carpenter) R.; m. Loraine Pennock, Oct. 11, 1966. BA in Econs., U. Kans., 1952; JD, Georgetown U., 1959. Bar: Colo. 1959, U.S. Dist. Ct. Colo. 1959, U.S. Ct. Appeals (10th cir.) 1961, U.S. Supreme Ct. 1979. Law clk to judge U.S. Ct. Appeals (10th cir.), Denver, 1959; law clk. to chief judge U.S. Dist. Ct. Colo., Denver, 1960-61; assoc. Tippit and Haskell, Denver, 1961-63; clk. Probate Ct., Denver, 1964-65; dep. state pub. defender Denver, 1966-74; tng. dir. Colo. State Pub. Defender System, Denver, 1974-77, tng. dir. as ind. contractor tng. seminars, 1980-82; pvt. practice Denver, 1977—. Mem. permanent lecturing faculty for summer sessions and seminars Nat. Coll. Criminal Def., Houston, 1974—, course dir., 1977; instr. trial tactics and strategy, evidence courses U. Denver Law Sch., 1979-91; lectr. in field throughout U.S. Author: Fingertip Law for Colorado Public Defenders, 1975, Strategy for Colorado Public Defenders, 1979, The Rench Book, Trial Tactics and Strategy, 1990, Courtbook, 1982, monthly columnist Trade Secrets of a Trial Lawyer, Washington Memo, 1977-78; contbr. articles to profl. jours. 1st lt. USAF, 1952-56. Mem. ABA, Colo. Trial Lawyers Assn., Colo. Criminal Def. Bar, Nat. Assn. Criminal Def. Lawyers, Nat. Legal Aid and Defenders Assn., Nat. Practice Inst., Assn. Trial Lawyers Am., Denver Bar Assn., Colo. Bar Assn. Office: 580 S Franklin St Denver CO 80209-4502 Office Phone: 303-777-0134.

RENDA, DOMINIC PHILLIP, airline executive; b. Steubenville, Ohio, Dec. 25, 1913; s. Joseph J. and Catherine (Roberta) R.; m. Delores E. Noland, July 12, 1980; children: Dominique Patricia, Dominic Phillip, Patrick Blake. BS in Bus. Adminstrn; JD, Ohio State U., 1938. Bar: Ohio 1938. Practice law, Steubenville, 1938-41; adminstrv. asst. to mem. Congress, 1941-42; with Western Air Lines, Inc., Los Angeles, 1946-68, asst. sec., 1947, v.p. legal, 1954-65, sr. v.p. legal, corp. sec., 1958-68; pres. Air Micronesia, Inc., Los Angeles, 1968-73; sr. v.p. internat. and pub. affairs Continental Air Lines, Inc., 1968-73; exec. v.p., dir., mem. exec. com. Western Air Lines, 1973-76, pres., mem. exec. and nominating coms., 1976-81, chief exec. officer, mem. mgmt. resources and compensation com., 1979-81, chmn. bd., 1981, emeritus chmn., 1982-85. Dir. Bank of Montreal, Calif.; Mem. bus. adminstrn. adv. council Coll. Adminstrv. Sci., Ohio State U., 1974-82; bd. councilors Sch. Internat. Relations, U. So. Calif., 1967-82 Trustee Peace Found., Ponape, Caroline Islands, 1976-84; chmn. devel. com. Marymount High Sch., 1977-82. Served to lt. comdr. USNR, 1942-46. Mem. Calif., Ohio state bars, ABA, Los Angeles County Bar Assn. (past trustee), Calif. C. of C. (dir.), Phi Alpha Delta (pres. Los Angeles 1965-66) Clubs: Los Angeles Chancery (pres. 1966-67), Morningside Country Club, Rancho Mirage.

RENDA, LARREE M. retail executive; Exec. v.p. retail ops., human resources, pub. affairs, labor and govtl. rels. Safeway, Inc., Pleasanton, Calif., 1999—, joined, 1974. Office: Safeway Inc 5918 Stoneridge Mall Rd Pleasanton CA 94588

RENDA, PATRICK BLAKE, investment company executive; b. Santa Monica, Calif., July 19, 1968; s. Dominic P. and Patricia Renda; m. Karen Suzanne Krieger, Nov. 28, 1998. BA, U. So. Calif., 1991. Prodn. mgr. NBC, Burbank, Calif., 1991-93; paralegal Fragomen, Del Rey, Bernsen & Loewy, Palo Alto, Calif., 1994-96; v.p., investment officer J&W Seligman & Co., Palo Alto, Calif., 1996—. Named among Best of Buyside 2000, Instl. Investor Mag. Mem.: Balboa Bay Club. Republican. Roman Catholic. Avocations: athletics, music, travel. Office: J&W Seligman & Co 101 University Ave Palo Alto CA 94301-1622 Fax: 650-330-1015. E-mail: rendap@jwseligman.com.

RENDA, ROSA A. special education educator; b. Jamaica, N.Y., Nov. 03; d. Liborio and Josephine (Finamore) Lombardo; m. Philip F. Renda, Mar. 30, 1980; children: Felicia-Anne, Philip Jr. BA, Molloy Coll., 1971; MEd, St. John's U., Jamaica, N.Y., 1973; postgrad., L.I. U., 1977. Tchr., asst. prin. St. Rose of Lima, Massapequa, NY, 1967—73, Acad. of St. Joseph, Brentwood, NY, 1973—79; tchr. Sewanhaka H.S., Brentwood, NY, 1979—81, Queen of the Rosary Acad., Amityville, NY, 1981—86, Blessed Trinity, Ocala, Fla., 1987—93, math. coord., 1993—94; S.E.D. tchr. Emerald Ctr., Ocala, Fla., 1994; tchr./children's supr. for the emotionally/mentally disturbed Marion Citrus Mental Health, Ocala, 1994—96; tchr. for autistic children Maplewood Sch., Ocala, 1996—97; tchr. math. Lake Weir H.S., 1997—99; tchr. North Marion Mid. Sch. for Emotionally Handicapped, Citra, Fla., 1999—2001; tchr. math. Webster Coll., Ocala, 2002—03, cmty. tech. and adult edn., 2003; tchr., NovaNet and GED Cmty. Tech. and Adult Edn., 2003—. Author: Teaching Metrics, 1975. Vol. Nassau County Rep. Club, Hempstead, N.Y., 1974-76. Mem. ASCD, NEA, Nat. Coun. Tchrs. Math., Nat. Cath. Edn. Assn., Marion Edn. Assn., Nassau/Suffolk Math. Tchrs., Women of the Moose, Columbiettes, K.C. Aux. Roman Catholic. Avocations: reading, swimming, gourmet cooking. Office: CTAE 1014 SW 7th Rd Ocala FL 34474 E-mail: 3637twofar85@aol.com.

RENDALL, DONALD JAMES, JR., lawyer; b. Phila., Jan. 31, 1956; s. Donald James and Mary (Hough) R.; m. Sandra Smallwood, July 28, 1979; children: Samuel, Katherine, Ann. AB summa cum laude, Dartmouth Coll., 1978; JD, Duke U., 1981. Bar: Ill. 1982, U.S. Dist. Ct. (no. dist.) Ill. 1983, U.S. Dist. Ct. Vt. 1984, Vt. 1985, U.S. Ct. Appeals (2d cir.) 1986. Law clk. to Hon. James S. Holden U.S. Dist. Ct. for Vt., Rutland, 1981-82; assoc. Jenner & Block, Chgo., 1982-84; asst. U.S. atty. U.S. Atty.'s Office for Dist. Vt., Rutland, 1984-87; assoc. Sheehey Furlong Rendall & Behm PC, Burlington, Vt., 1987, ptnr., 1988—; v.p. & gen. counsel Green Monster Power Corp., 2002—. Mem. ABA, Vt. Bar Assn.(pres. 2002-03), Chittenden County Bar Assn., Order of Coif, Phi Beta Kappa. Home: 51 Old Farm Rd South Burlington VT 05403-6804 Office: Green Mountain Power Corp 163 Acorn Ln Burlington VT 05446-6611 E-mail: rendall@greenmountainpower.bix.

RENDELL, EDWARD GENE, governor, former mayor, lawyer; b. N.Y.C., Jan. 5, 1944; s. Jesse T. and Emma (Sloat) R.; m. Marjorie Osterlund, July 10, 1971; 1 son, Jesse Thompson. BA in Polit. Sci., U. Pa., 1965; JD, Villanova U., 1968. Bar: Pa. 1968, U.S. Supreme Ct. 1981. Asst. dist. atty., chief homicide unit Office Dist. Atty., Phila., 1968-74; dep. spl. prosecutor Phila., 1976; dist. atty., 1978-86; mayor City of Phila., 1992—2000; gov. Commonwealth of Pa., Harrisburg, 2003—. Gen. chmn. Dem. Nat. Com., 1999—2000. 2d lt. USAR, 1968—74. Recipient Man of Yr. award VFW, 1980, Am. Cancer League, 1981, Disting. Pub. Svc. award Pa. County Detectives Assn., 1981. Mem. ABA, Pa. Dist. Attys. Assn. (legis. chmn. 1979—), Phila. Bar Assn., B'nai B'rith, United Jewish Orgns., Jewish War Vets. Democrat. Office: Governor's Office Rm 225 Main Capitol Bldg Harrisburg PA 17120

RENDELL, KENNETH WILLIAM, rare and historical documents dealer, consultant; b. Boston, May 12, 1943; s. Harry H. and Pauline (Walsh) R.; m. Diana J. Angelo, June 3, 1967 (div. 1985); children: Jeffrey H., Jason J. (dec.); m. Shirley L. McNerney, July 14, 1985; 1 child, Julia Louise. Student, Boston U., 1961-63. Pres. Kingston Galleries, Inc., Somerville, Mass., 1960-67, Kenneth W. Rendell, Inc., Newton, Mass., 1967—, Kenneth W. Rendell, Ltd., London, 1970—, Kenneth W. Rendell Gallery, Inc., N.Y.C., Tokyo, 1985—. Bd. dirs. John Wilson Autographs Ltd., London, 1961-75, Charles Ede Gallery Ltd., London, 1976-92; chmn. New England Antiquarian Booksellers Assn., 1975-77; pres. Internat. League Autograph and Manuscript Dealers, 1975-77; cons. numerous univ. librs., govtl. and media orgns. 0uthor: The Fundamentals of Autograph Collecting, 1976, Tax Appraisals of Manuscript Collections, 1983, Changing Concepts of Value and Rarity, 1985, The Hitler Diaries: Bad Forgeries But a Great Hoax, 1986, The Mormon Conman, Forger and Killer, 1987, Other People's Mail: 30 Years As a Dealer in Historical Documents, 1988, The One Hundred Americans Who Have Made America What it is Today, 1989, The Detection of Forged Historical Letters and Documents, 1990, With Weapons and Wits: Propaganda and Psychological Warfare in World War II, 1991, Forging History: The Detection of Fake Historical Letters and Documents, 1994, History Comes to Life, !995; co-editor: Autographs and Manuscripts: A Collector's Manual, 1978 (Outstanding Reference Book award ALA); contbr. numerous articles in field to mags. and profl. jours. Trustee D-Day Mus., New Orleans, 1998, Youth Enrichment Svcs., Boston, 1998, William J. Donovan Meml., N.Y., 1998. Recipient Dept. Justice award, 1991. Fellow Manuscript Soc. (bd. dirs. 1968-74, pres. 1972-74); mem. Assn. Internat. de Bibliophilie Paris, Art and Antique Dealers League Am., Inc., Grolier Club, Army and Navy Club, Am. Antiquarian Soc., Bohemian Club (San Francisco), Appalachian Mountain Club (trustee 2000). Avocation: ski racing. Office: Kenneth W Rendell Inc 46 Eliot St Natick MA 01760-6042 also: 989 Madison Ave New York NY 10021-1825

RENDELL, MARJORIE O. federal judge; b. 1947; m. Edward G. Rendell. BA, U. Pa., 1969; postgrad., Georgetown U., 1970—71; JD, Villanova U., 1973; LLD (hon.), Phila. Coll. Textile and Sci., 1992. Ptnr. Duane, Morris & Heckscher, Phila., 1972—93; judge U.S. Dist. Ct. (ea. dist.) Pa., 1994—97, U.S. Ct. Appeals (3d cir.), Phila., 1997—. Mem. Am. Jud. Soc., Fed. Judges Assn. Asst. to dir. ann. giving Dept. Devel. U. Pa., 1973—78; mem. adv. bd. Chestnut Hill Nat. Bank/East Falls Adv. Bd.; mem. alternative dispute resolution com. mediation divsn. Ea. Dist. Pa. Bankruptcy Conf.; active Acad. Vocal Arts, Market St. East Improvement Assn., Pa.'s Campaign for Choice, Phila. Friends Outward Bound; vice chair Ave. of Arts, Inc.; vice chair bd. trustees Vis. Nurse Assn. Greater Phila.; bd. mem. Alumni Trust, U. Penn. Mem.: ABA, Phila. Bar Found. (bd. dirs.), Phila. Bar Assn. (bd. dirs. young lawyers sect. 1973—78), Pa. Bar Assn., Am. Bankruptcy Inst., Internat. Women's Forum, Forum Exec. Women, Phi Beta Kappa. Office: US Courthouse 601 Market St Rm 21613 Philadelphia PA 19106-1715

RENDELL-BAKER, LESLIE, anesthesiologist, educator; b. St. Helens, Eng., Mar. 27, 1917; came to U.S., 1957, naturalized, 1963; s. Frank Nelder and Ada (Gill) Rendell-B.; m. Rosemary Carr Hogg, Aug. 17, 1946; children: Sheila Diane, Helen Rosemary, Frances Nelda. BS, MB, London U. Guys Hosp. Med. Sch., 1941. Diplomate: Am. Bd. Anesthesiology. Resident in anesthesiology Brit. Army of Rhine Hosps., 1945-46, Guy's Hosp., London, 1946-48; sr. asst. (assoc. prof.) anesthesiology Welsh Nat. Sch. Medicine, Cardiff, 1948-57; Fulbright asst. prof. anesthesiology U. Pitts., 1955-56; from asst. prof. to assoc. prof. Sch. Medicine Case Western Res. U., Cleve., 1957-62; dir. dept. anesthesiology Mt. Sinai Hosp., N.Y.C., 1962-79; prof., chmn. dept. anesthesiology Mt. Sinai Sch. Medicine, CUNY, 1966-79; prof. dept. anesthesiology Sch. Medicine Loma Linda (Calif.) U., 1979-97, prof. emeritus, 1998—. Chmn. sect. com. Z79 standards for anesthesia and respiratory equipment Am. Nat. Stds. Instn., 1962-68, vice chmn., 1969-81, mem. exec. com. med. devices stds. mgmt. bd., 1973-79, bd. dirs., 1976-79; chmn. classification panel on anesthesiology devices FDA, 1972-76 Author: (with W.W. Mushin) Principles of Thoracic Anesthesia, 1953, (with W.W. Mushin and Thompson) Automatic Ventilation of the Lungs, 3rd edit., 1980, The Origins of Thoracic Anesthesia, 1991, (with others) The Care of Anesthesia Equipment, 1992; editor: Problems with Anesthetic and Respiratory Therapy Equipment, 1982, The History and Evolution of Pediatric Anesthesia Equipment, 1992, Maintenance, Cleaning and Sterilization of Anesthetic Equipment, 1998, Future Directions in Anesthesia Apparatus, 1998. Served to capt. Royal Army Med. Corps, 1942-46. Fellow Royal Coll. Anaesthetists; fellow Royal Soc. Medicine, Assn. Anaesthetists Gt. Britain and Ireland; mem. Am. Soc. Anesthesiologists (chmn. com. equipment and standardization 1962-68), Am. Soc. for Testing and Materials (chmn. subcom. D10-34 1981-91), Assn. Advancement Med. Instrumentation, AAAS. Achievements include invention of baby endotracheal connector, pediatric face masks and equipment. Home: 630 Beauregard Crest Redlands CA 92373-5602 Office: Loma Linda U Sch Medicine Dept Anesthesiology 11234 Anderson St Loma Linda CA 92354-2804

RENDER, ARLENE, former ambassador; 2 adopted children. Joined Fgn. Svc., Dept. State, 1970, consular officer, 1971-73, Tehran, Iran, 1973-76, Genoa, Italy, 1976-78, polit. officer, 1978-79, internat. rels. officer AF/C, 1979-81, dep. chief of mission, 1981-84, consul-gen. Kingston, Jamaica, 1984-86, dep. chief of mission Accra, Ghana, 1986-89, mem. sr. seminar, 1989-90, amb. to The Gambia, 1990-93, dir. Office of Ctrl. African Affairs, 1993—96, amb. to Republic of Zambia, 1996-99, dir. So. African Affairs, 1996—99, U.S. amb., 2001—04. Achievements include speaks French and Italian.

RENDL-MARCUS, MILDRED, artist, economist; b. May 30, 1928; d. Julius and Agnes (Hokr) Rendl; m. Edward Marcus, Aug. 10, 1956. BS, NYU, 1948, MBA, 1950; PhD, Radcliffe Coll., 1954. Economist GE, 1953-56, Bigelow-Sanford Carpet Co., Inc., 1956-58; instr. econs. Hunter Coll. CUNY, 1959-60, Columbia U., 1960-61, rschr., 1961-63; sr. economist Nat. Indsl. Conf. Bd., 1963-66; asst. prof. Pace Coll., 1964-66; assoc. prof. Borough of Manhattan C. of C. CUNY, 1966-71, prof., 1972-85. Lectr. econs. CCNY, 1953-58; vis. prof. Fla. Internat. U., 1986; bd. dirs. N.Y.C. Coun. on Econ. Edn.; cons. in field. Exhibited group shows at in New Canaan Art Show, 1982-85, Am. Soc. Bus. and Behavioral Scis., 1990-96, New Cannan Soc. for Arts Ann., 1983, 85, New Canaan Arts, 1985, Silvermine Galleries, 1986, Stamford Art Assn., 1987, Phoenix Gallery, 1988, N.Y.C., Parkview Point Gallery, 1982-89, Miami Beach, Fla., 1982-89, Art Complex, New Canaan, Miami Beach, 1985—, Lever House, N.Y.C., 1990, Cork Gallery, Lincoln Ctr., N.Y.C., 1990, Women's Caucus for Art, San Antonio, 1990, Artist's Equity, Broome St. Gallery, N.Y.C., 1991, Greater Hartford Architecture Conservancy, 1991, N.H. Arts Ctr., 1997, Just Originals Art Web, Albuquerque, 1999, Ward-Nasse Gallery, N.Y.C., 2000—, Liliana Fine Art Gallery, Lenox, Mass., 2003—, Artists Gallery, Chelsea, N.Y.C., 2003, Nat. Assn. Women Artists, 2003—, 115-Yr. Anniversary Show, World Trade Ctr., N.Y.C., 2004; author (with E. Marcus) Investment and Development of Tropical Africa, 1959,

International Trade and Finance, 1965, Monetary and Banking Theory, 1965, Economics, 1969, Economic Progress and the Developing World, 1970, Economics, 1978, Fine Art with Many Equilibrium Prices, 1995; editor Women in the Arts Found. Newsletter, 1986-92; contbr. articles to profl. jours. Founder Rendl Fund for Slavic Art, Mus. of Modern Art, N.Y.C., 1999—, Harvard U. Art Mus. Fund for Slavic Art, Cambridge, 2000—, Harvard Mus. Natural History, Peabody Mus. Archeology and Ethnology, Rendl Fund for the Conservation of Slavic Artifacts, 2000—, Rendl Fund for the Conservation of the Ware Collection of Blaschka Glass Models of Plants, 2001—; mem. mus. coun. Harvard Mus. Natural History, 2001—. Recipient Merit award Manhattan Arts Internat., 1998, Excellence award 1998, Artist Showcase award Manhattan Arts Internat., 1999; Dean Bernice Brown Cronkhite fellow Radcliffe Coll., 1950-51, Anne Radcliffe Econ. Rsch. Sub-Sahara Africa fellow, 1958-59; fellow Gerontol. Assn. Mem. AAUW, Internat. Schumpeter Econs. Soc. (founding), Met. Econ. Assns. (sec. 1954-56), Indsl. Rels. Rsch. Assn., Women's Econ. Roundtable (program planning com.), N.Y.C. Women in Arts, Allied Social Sci. Assn. (artist 1994), NYU Grad. Sch. Bus. Adminstrn. Alumni (sec. 1956-58), Radcliffe Club, Women's City Club (art and landmarks com.).

RENDU, JEAN-MICHEL MARIE, mining executive; b. Tunis, Tunisia, Feb. 25, 1944; s. Paul C. and Solange M. (Krebs) R.; m. Karla M. Meyer, Aug. 18, 1973; children: Yannick P., Mikaël P. Ingénieur des Mines, Ecole des Mines St. Etienne, France, 1966; MS, Columbia U., 1968, D of Engring. Sci., 1971. Mgr. ops. rsch. Anglovaal, Johannesburg, 1972-76; assoc. prof. U. Wis., Madison, 1976-79; assoc. Golder Assocs., Denver, 1979-84; dir. tech. and sci. systems Newmont Mining Corp., Danbury, Conn., 1984-88; v.p. Newmont Gold Co., Denver, 1988-93, Newmont Mining Corp., Denver, 1993-2001; ind. cons. Denver, 2001—. Author: An Introduction to Geostatistical Methods of Mineral Evaluation, 1978, 81; contbr. tech. papers to profl. jours. Fellow South African Inst. of Mining and Metallurgy (corr. mem. of coun.), Australasian Inst. Mining and Metallurgy; mem. NAE, Soc. Mining, Metallurgy and Exploration (bd. dirs. 1998—, Jackling award 1994, Pres.'s citation 1993), Sigma Xi. Roman Catholic. E-mail: JMRendu@aol.com.

RENEAU, DANIEL D. academic administrator; Prof., head dept. biomed. engring. La. Tech. U., Ruston, 1973-80, v.p. acad. affairs, 1980-87, pres., 1987—. Office: LA Tech U Tech Station PO Box 3168 Ruston LA 71272-0001

RENEBERG, RICHARD (RICHEY RENEBERG), professional tennis player; b. Phoenix, Oct. 5, 1965; m. Marget Reneberg, Nov. 16, 1991. Student, SMU, 1985-87. Ranked 10th US Tennis Assn., 1991; ranked 8th, 1993; ranked 20th, 1996; ranked 55th, 1997; ranked 160th, 1999. Winner US Open Men's Double Title (with Jim Grabb), 1992, Australian Open Men's Doubles Title (with Jared Palmer), 1995; mem. US Davis Cup team, 1993, 94, 95, 97, 98. Named All-American NCAA, 1985, 86, 87; 8 U.S. Junior Titles, 2 Profl. Singles Titles. Address: Senior World Tennis Championships 1201 Bethlehem Pike Flourtown PA 19031*

RENEHAN, ROBERT FRANCIS XAVIER, Greek and Latin educator; b. Boston, Apr. 25, 1935; s. Francis Xavier and Ethel Mary (Sullivan) R.; m. Joan Lee Axtell-Damerow, Sept. 9, 1966; children— Martin, Sharon, Stephen, Judith, John. AB, Boston Coll., Chestnut Hill, Mass., 1956; A.M., Harvard, 1958, PhD, 1963. Instr. Greek and Latin U. Calif. at Berkeley, 1963-64; instr. Harvard U., 1964-65; asst. prof. Boston Coll., 1966-69, assoc. prof., 1969-71, prof., 1971-77, chmn. dept. classical studies, 1969-77; prof. Greek and Latin U. Calif. at Santa Barbara, 1976—, chmn. dept., 1984-88, 93-200. Author: Greek Textual Criticism, 1969, Leo Medicus, 1969, Greek Lexicographical Notes, 1975, 2d series, 1982, Studies in Greek Texts, 1975; assoc. editor Classical Philology, 1976—, Am. Jour. Philology, 1987-95; sr. mem. editl. bd. Classical Antiquity, 1980-87, Revised Supplement to Liddell-Scott-Jones Greek-English Lexicon, 1987-96; contbr. articles to profl. jours. Nat. Endowment for Humanities Sr. fellow, 1972-73 Mem. Am. Philol. Assn., Soc. for Ancient Medicine. Office: U Calif Dept Classics Santa Barbara CA 93106 Office Phone: 805-893-3254. E-mail: renehan@classics.ucsb.edu.

RENEKER, MAXINE HOHMAN, librarian; b. Chgo., Dec. 2, 1942; d. Roy Max and Helen Anna Christina (Anacker) Hohman; m. David Lee Reneker, June 20, 1964 (dec. Dec. 1979); children: Sarah Roeder, Amy Johannah, Benjamin Congdon. BA, Carleton Coll., 1964; MA, U. Chgo., 1970; DLS, Columbia U., 1992. Asst. reference libr. U. Chgo. Libraries, 1965-66; classics libr. U. Chgo. Libr., 1967-70, asst. head acquisitions, 1970-71, personnel libr., 1971-73; personnel/bus. libr. U. Colo. Libr., Boulder, 1978-80; asst. dir. sci. and engring. div. Columbia U., N.Y.C., 1981-85; assoc. dean of univ. librs. for pub. svcs. Ariz. State U. Libr., Tempe, 1985-89; dir. instrnl. and rsch. svcs. Stanford (Calif.) Univ. Librs., 1989-90; assoc. provost for libr. and info. resources Naval Postgrad. Sch., Monterey, Calif., 1993—. Acad. libr. mgmt. intern Coun. on Libr. Resources, 1980-81; chmn. univ. librs. sect. Assn. Coll. and Rsch. Librs., 1989-90. Contbr. articles to profl. jours. Rsch. grantee Coun. on Library Resources, Columbia U., 1970-71, fellow, 1990-92. Mem. ALA, Am. Soc. Info. Sci., Sherlockian Soc., Phi Beta Kappa, Beta Phi Mu. Home: 740 Dry Creek Rd Monterey CA 93940-4208 Office: Naval Postgrad Sch Dudley Knox Libr 411 Dyer Rd Monterey CA 93943-5198 Office Phone: 831-656-2343. Business E-Mail: mreneker@nps.edu.

RENFORD, EDWARD J. hospital administrator; b. July 16, 1943; married. AA, L.A. City Coll., 1969; BA, Calif. State U., 1971; MA, Pepperdine U., 1983. Asst. fiscal officer Martin Luther King Jr., Drew Med. Ctr., L.A., 1974-75, assoc. adminstr. fin. svcs., 1984-86, hosp. adminstr., 1990—; dir. fiscal svcs. LAC Harbor UCLA Med. Ctr., Torrance, Calif., 1975-77, asst. adminstr. fin., 1977-79, assoc. adminstr., 1979-82; asst. adminstr. Centinela Hosp. Med. Ctr., Inglewood, Calif., 1982-84; assoc. exec. dir. LAC Rancho Los Amigos Med. Ctr., Downey, Calif., 1986-89; chief staff Hosp. Adminstrn./Dept. Health Svcs., L.A., 1989-90; CEO, pres. Grady Meml Hosp, Atlanta. Recipient numerous awards. Home: PO Box 54221 Atlanta GA 30308-0221 Office: PO Box 189 Atlanta GA 30301-0189

RENFORTH, D. JOYCE, art educator, artist; d. George Glenn and Clara McDonnell (Geisler) Raths; m. Raymond Renforth (div.); children: Rae'Deana Lynn, Reefe Zane, Shawna Leeane, Renetta Dawn; m. Joseph Pritts, Aug. 1988 (dec.). Student, Ctrl. Mich. Coll., 1947—48; tchr. cert., U. Detroit, 1973, continuing cert., 1987. File clk. VA, Detroit, 1946—47; substitute tchr. Chippewa Valley, Royal Oak, Oak Park schs., Mich., 1948—49, 1955—56; art tchr. Clawson (Mich.) Sch. Dist., 1977—78; tchr. arts and crafts to sr. citizens Van Dyke Schs., Ukranian Village, Warren, Mich., 1987—88. Enumerator U.S. Census, Oakland County, Mich., 1980, Oakland County, 90. Author: (poetry) A Stroll Along Poetry Lane, Run-Away Keno; author, artist: board game License To Play. Mem. Women's Rights Orgn., 1970—85; election worker Hazel Park Election Com. Recipient Golden Poetry award, 1989, cert. of achievement, NY Pro/Am Song Jubilee. Mem.: Ongoing Mich. Artists Program. Democrat. Avocations: poetry, typing, knitting, writing. Home: 99 W Garfield Hazel Park MI 48030

RENFREW, ANDREW COLIN (LORD RENFREW OF KAIMSTHORN), archaeologist, academic administrator; b. July 25, 1937; s. Archibald and Helena Douglas (Savage) R.; m. Jane Margaret Ewbank, Apr. 21, 1965; children: Helena Margaret, Alban Robert, Magnus Archibald. BA, St. John's Coll., Cambridge U., 1962, MA, 1964, PhD, 1965, ScD, 1976. Lectr. archaeology U. Sheffield, 1965-72; prof. U. Southampton, 1972-81; Disney prof. archaeology Cambridge U., 1981—2004. Vis. lectr. UCLA, 1967; fellow St. John's Coll., 1981-86, hon. fellow 2004-; master Jesus Coll., Cambridge, 1986-97, fellow, 1997-; George Grant McCurdy lectr. Harvard U., 1977; Patten lectr. Ind. U., 1982; field excavations in Saliagos, 1961-64, Sitagroi, 1968-70, Quanterness, Orkney, 1972-74, Phylakopi, Melos, 1974-76. Author (with J. D. Evans): Excavations at Saliagos Near Antiparos, 1968 in Orkney, 1979; author: Problems in European Prehistory, 1979; author: (with J. M. Wagstaff) An Island Polity, 1982; author: Approaches to Social Archaeology, 1984, The Prehistory of Orkney, 1985, The Archaeology of Cult, 1985, Archaeology and Language, 1987; author: (with G. Daniel) The Idea of Prehistory, 1988; author: The Cycladic Spirit, 1991; author: (with P. Bahn) Archaeology, 1991; author: Loot, Legitimacy and Ownership: The Ethical Crisis in Archaeology, 2000, Figuring It Out, 2003; editor: The Explanation of Culture Change, 1973, British Prehistory, 1974, Transformations: Mathematical Approaches to Culture Change, 1979, Theory and Explanation in Archaeology, 1982; presenter (TV films) The Tree That Put the Clock Back, 1970, Islands Out of Time, 1973, Orkney Underground, 1974, Aphrodite's Other Island, 1977, Bronze Age Blast Off, 1978, Lost Kings of the Desert, 1980, The Emperor's Immortal Army, 1981, City of the Dead, 1982, Who Built Stonehenge, 1986. Trustee Brit. Mus., 1991-2001. With RAF, 1956-58. Recipient European Sci. Found. Latsis Prize, 2003, Rivers Meml. medal Royal Anthrop. Inst., 1979, Huxley Meml. medal, 1991; named Fgn. Assoc. NAS, 1996; elevated to peerage, 1991. Fellow Brit. Acad., Soc. Antiquaries London, Royal Soc. Edinburgh (hon.); mem. Athenaeum. Office: Dept Archaeology Downing St Cambridge CB2 3DZ England also: House of Lords London SW1A 0PW England

RENFREW, CHARLES BYRON, lawyer; b. Detroit, Oct. 31, 1928; s. Charles Warren and Louise (McGuire) R.; m. Susan Wheelock, June 28, 1952 (div. June 1984); children: Taylor Allison Ingham, Charles Robin, Todd Wheelock, James Bartlett; m. Barbara Jones Orser, Oct. 6, 1984; 5 stepchildren. AB, Princeton U., 1952; JD, U. Mich., 1956. Bar: Calif. 1956. Assoc. Pillsbury, Madison & Sutro, San Francisco, 1956-65, ptnr., 1965-72, 81-82; U.S. dist. judge No. Dist. Calif., San Francisco, 1972-80; dep. atty. gen. U.S. Washington, 1980-81; instr. U. Calif. Boalt Hall Sch. Law, 1977-80; v.p. law Chevron Corp. (formerly Standard Oil Co. Calif.), San Francisco, 1983-93, also bd. dirs.; ptnr. LeBoeuf, Lamb, Greene & McRae, San Francisco, 1994-97; pvt. practice San Francisco, 1998—. Mem. exec. com. 9th Cir. Jud. Conf., 1976-78, congl. liaison com. 9th Cir. Jud. Council, 1976-79, spl. com. to propose standards for admission to practice in fed. cts. U.S. Jud. Conf., 1976-79; chmn. spl. com. to study problems of discovery Fed. Jud. Ctr., 1978-79; mem. council on role of cts. U.S. Dept. Justice, 1978-83; mem. jud. panel Ctr. for Pub. Resources, 1981—; head U.S. del. to 6th UN Congress on Prevention of Crime and Treatment of Offenders, 1980; co-chmn. San Francisco Lawyers Com. for Urban Affairs, 1971-72, mem., 1983—; bd. dirs. Internat. Hospitality Ctr., 1961-74, pres., 1967-70; mem. adv. bd. Internat. Comparative Law Ctr., Southwestern Legal Found., 1983-93; trustee World Affairs Council No. Calif., 1984-87, 94—, Nat. Jud. Coll., 1985-91, Grace Cathedral, 1986-89. Contbr. articles to profl. jours. Bd. fellow Claremont U., 1986-94; bd. dirs. San Francisco Symphony Found., 1964-80, pres., 1971-72; bd. dirs. Coun. Civic Unity, 1962-73, pres., 1971-72; bd. dirs. Opportunity Through Ownership, 1969-72, Marin County Day Sch., 1972-74, No. Calif. Svc. League, 1975-76, Am. Petroleum Inst., 1984—, Nat. Crime Prevention Coun., 1982—; alumni trustee Princeton U., 1976-80; mem. vis. com. u. chgo. Law Sch., 1977-79, u.Mich. Law Sch., 1977-81; bd. visitors J. Reuben Clark Law Sch., Brigham Young U., 1981-83, Stanford Law Sch., 1983-86; trustee Town Sch. for Boys, 1972-80,pres. 1975-80; gov. San Fransciso Symphony Assn., 1974—; mem. nat. adv. bd. Ctr. for Nat. Policy, 1982—; bd. dirs. Nat. Coun. Crime and Deliquency, 1981-82,NAACP Legal Def. and Edn. Fund, 1982—; parish chancellor St. Luke's Episcopal Ch., 1968-71, sr. warden, 1974-76; mem. exec. coun. San Francisco Deanery, 1969-70; mem. diocesan coun. Episcopal Diocese of Calif., 1970; chmn. Diocesan Conv., 1977, 78, 79. Served with USN, 1946-48, 1st lt. U.S. Army, 1952-53. Fellow Am. Bar Found.; mem. ABA (coun. mem. sect. antitrust law 19778-82, vice c hmn. sect. antitrust law 1982-83), San Francisco Bar Assn. (past bd. dirs.), Assn. Gen. Counsel, State Bar Calif., Am. Judicature Soc., Am. Coll. Trial Lawyers (pres. 1995-96), Am. Law Inst., Coun. Fgn. Rels., Order of Coif, Phi Beta Kappa, Phi Delta Phi. Office: 710 Sansome St San Francisco CA 94111-1704 Office Phone: 415-397-3933.

RENFREW, MALCOLM MACKENZIE, chemist, educator; b. Spokane, Wash., Oct. 12, 1910; s. Earl Edgar and Elsie Pauline (MacKenzie) R.; m. Carol Joy Campbell, June 26, 1938. BS, U. Idaho, 1932, MS, 1934, D.Sc., 1976; PhD, U. Minn., 1938. Asst. physics U. Idaho, 1932-33, Asst. chemistry, 1933-35, U. Minn., 1935-37, duPont fellow, 1937-38; research chemist plastics dept. duPont Co., 1938-44, supr. process devel., 1944-46, supr. product devel., 1946-49; head chem. research dept., research labs. Gen. Mills, Inc., 1949-52, dir. chem. research, 1952-53, dir. chem. research and devel., 1953-54; dir. research and devel. Spencer Kellogg & Sons, Inc., 1954-58; phys. sci. div. head, prof. chemistry U. Idaho, 1959-73, prof., 1973-76, emeritus, 1976—; dir. U. Idaho (Coll. Chem. Cons. Service), 1969-76. On leave as sr. staff assoc. Adv. Coun. Coll. Chemistry, Stanford, 1967-68; mem. materials adv. bd. Nat. Rsch. Coun.; exec. v.p. Idaho Rsch. Found., 1977-78, patent dir., 1978-88. Editor: Safety in the Chemical Laboratory, Vol. IV, 1981, (with Peter Ashbrook), Safe Laboratories: Principles and Practices for Design and Remodeling, 1991; safety editor: Jour. Chem. Edn, 1977-91; Contbr. to tech. and trade publs. on plastics, coatings, safety, chem. edn. Recipient Excellence in Teaching award Chem. Mfrs. Assn., 1977, Outstanding Achievement award U. Minn., 1977; named to U. Idaho Hall of Fame, 1977, Idaho Hall of Fame, 1996. Fellow AAAS, Am. Inst. Chemists; mem. Am. Chem. Soc. (councilor 1948, 59, 67-89, chmn. paint varnish and plastics div. 1949, chmn. chem. mktg. and econs. div. 1958-59, chmn. chem. health and safety div. 1982, James Flack Norris award 1976, Chem. Health and Safety award 1985, Mosher award 1986), Am. Inst. Chem. Engrs., Soc. Chem. Industry, Phi Beta Kappa, Sigma Xi, Phi Kappa Phi, Sigma Pi Sigma, Phi Gamma Delta (disting. Fiji 1986). Presbyterian. Home: 1271 Walenta Dr Moscow ID 83843-2426 Office: U Idaho Coll Sci Dept Chemistry PO Box 442343 Moscow ID 83844-2343

RENFRO, BRAD, actor; b. Knoxville, Tenn., July 25, 1982; Actor: (films) The Client, 1994, The Cure, 1995, Tom and Huck, 1995, Sleepers, 1996, Telling Lies in America, 1997, Apt Pupil, 1998, 2 Little, 2 Late, 2000, Skipped Parts, 2000, Hershcel Hopper: New York Rabbit, 2000, Delilah, 2000, Happy Campers, 2001, Tart, 2001, Bully, 2001, Ghost World, 2001, Deuces Wild, 2002, American Girl, 2002, (voice): (TV series) Hercules, 1998; assoc. prodr.: Bully, 2001. Office: c/o United Talent Agy 9560 Wilshire Blvd Fl 5 Beverly Hills CA 90212-2400

RENFRO, WILLIAM LEONARD, futurist, lawyer, inventor, entrepreneur; b. West Palm Beach, Fla., Sept. 9, 1945; s. Ernest Leonard and Oine Warren (McAdams) R. BS in Physics, Rensselaer Poly. Inst., 1967, MS in Nuclear Engring., 1972; postgrad., Yale U., 1967-68; JD, U. Conn., 1972. Bar: Conn. 1973, U.S. Ct. Fed. Claims, Fed. Ct. Appeals (D.C. cir.). Physicist Compustion Engring., Windsor Locks, Conn., 1968-69; pvt. practice law, Hartford, Conn., 1973-74; sr. rsch. assoc. The Futures Group, Glastonbury, Conn., 1973-76; analyst futures rsch. Congl. Rsch. Svc., U.S. Congress, Washington, 1976-80; pres. Policy Analysis Co., Inc., Washington, 1980—. Vis. fellow Ark. Inst.; guest lectr. Georgetown U., Brookings Inst., Nat. War Coll.; adj. prof. George Washington U., Indsl. Coll. Armed Forces Nat. Def. U.; mem. nat. foresight network U.S. Congress. Author: (with others) The Futures Research Handbook, 1997, Anticipatory Democracy, 1978, The Public Affairs Handbook, 1983, The Legislative Role of Corporations, 1982, Applying Methods and Techniques of Futures Research, 1983, Future Research and the Straegic Planning Process, 1985, Non-Extrapolative Forecasting in Business, 1988, Futures Research Methodology: The UN Millennium Project, 1999; author: Issue Management in Stratetic Planning, 1993, Vision-2020, 1999; editor Futures Rsch. Quar. World Futures Soc., 1980-1991; issues mgmt. editor the Futurist, 1982—, Tech. Analysis and Strategic Mgmt. Mem. long range planning com. United Way; trustee World Tech. Found., Am. Friends of Romania, 2002—; lic. pastoral vis. lay eucharistic min. Wash. Diocese; Atlantic Coun, 2004—. Mem.: ABA, Washington Choral Ensemble (trustee 2004—), Russian Am. Student Exchange (chmn., founder), Georgetown Hist. Structures Preservation Soc. (chmn., co-founder), People to People Internat., Hartford County Bar Assn., Conn. Bar Assn., Internat. Pub. Rels. Assn., Assn. Former Intelligence Officers, World Futures Soc., Issues Mgmt. Assn. (bd. dirs. 1981—98, v.p. 1986—88, pres. 1988—96), Pub. Rels. Soc. Am., St. Andrews Soc., Clan Hamilton Soc., English Speaking Union (trustee, v.p. internat. programs Washington br.). Episcopalian. Achievements include U.S. and foreign patents.

RENFROE, W. DOUGLAS, musician, conductor, music educator; b. Anderson, Ind., Mar. 7, 1948; s. Walter D. and Mary M. Renfroe; m. Halina K. Gawel, May 26, 1990 (div. May 2001); m. Lorraine Murphy-Renfroe, Apr. 6, 2002; children: Brenna, Sean, James. B in Music Edn., Westminster Choir Coll., 1970; MusM, Cath. U. Am., 1974. Concert artist, tchr. Columbia Artist Mgmt. et al, Boston, 1974—88, N.Y.C., 1974—88, 1974—88; v.p. sales and mktg. Brand Svcs./Waste Mgmt., Chgo., 1988—94; concert artist, condr. ES Mgmt., Bristol, NH, 1994—98, Fantasia Mgmt., Sarasota, Fla., 1998—2001, SRO DOLOR, Inc., Ft. Myers, Fla., 2001—. Prof. Edison Coll., Ft. Myers, 1999—; consulting, clinician in field, 1972—; consulting and adv. bd. dir. Lowcountry Theatre, Beaufort, SC, 1976—88; mem. adv. bd. Literacy of Am., Columbia, SC, 1976—86. Author: The Art of German Lieder, 1979; contbr. articles to profl. jours. With USN, 1970—74. Named Outstanding Tchr. Yr., S.C. Bd. Edn., 1978, N.H. Bd. Edn., 1986; named to, Outstanding Young Men of Am., 1980. Mem.: Music Tchrs. Nat. Assn. (v.p. 1978—), Am. Legion (life), Rotary Club Internat. (v.p. 1995—2000). Avocations: reading, swimming, golf, travel. Home: 1448 S Brandywine Cir Fort Myers FL 33919 Office: SRO DOLOR Inc PO Box 826 Fort Myers FL 33919

RENGASWAMY, RAGHUNATHAN, chemical engineering researcher, educator; b. Madras, Tamilnadu, India, Aug. 15, 1969; s. Rengaswamy Srinivasan and Saroja Rengaswamy; m. Suchitra Veeravalli, June 28, 1998; children: Abhishek Raghunathan, Aadarsh Raghunathan. B in Tech., IIT Madras, India, 1990; PhD, Purdue U., West Lafayette, Ind., 1995. Sr. engr. Asea Brown Boveri, Bangalore, India, 1995; asst. prof. IIT Bombay, Mumbai, India, 1996—2000; vis. asst. prof. Purdue U., West Lafayette, Ind., 2001; assoc. prof. Clarkson U., Potsdam, NY, 2002—. Cons. Asea Brown Boveri, Bangalore, Karnataka, India, 1996—2002. Author: (20 peer reviewed articles) Chem. Engring. Jours., aiche conf. presentation. Recipient Young Engr. award, Indian NAE, 2000. Mem.: Am. Chem. Soc., AIChE. Achievements include invention of Qualitative trend analysis (QTA) technique while at Purdue University. Home: 401 Swan St Potsdam NY 13676 Office: Clarkson Univ Dept of Chem Engring Potsdam NY 13699-5705 Personal E-mail: raghu@clarkson.edu. E-mail: raghu@clarkson.edu.

RENGER, MARILYN HANSON, elementary school educator; b. Shelly, Idaho, July 17, 1949; d. Merril H. and Betty Jean (Hendricksen) Hanson; m. Robert Carl Renger, Sept. 11, 1971; children: Katherine, James. BA in History, U. Calif., Santa Barbara, 1971; postgrad., Calif. Luth. U., 1973-74. Tchr. Ventura (Calif.) Unified Schs., 1974-79, 85-98, asst. prin., 1998—. Cons. State of Calif., 1989-93. Recipient Disting. Tchr. K-12 award Nat. Coun. for Geog. Edn., 1992. Mem. Nat. Coun. Geographic Edn. (Nat. Disting. Teaching award 1992), Calif. Geographic Soc. (steering com. 1989-93, co-dir. summer inst. 1992), Nat. Coun. Social Studies. Office: Balboa Mid Sch 247 S Hill Rd Ventura CA 93003-4401

RENICK, JAMES CARMICHAEL, academic administrator, educator; b. Rockford, Ill., Dec. 8, 1948; s. Constance Renick; m. Peggy Renick; 1 child, Karinda. BA, Ctrl. State U., Ohio, 1970; MSW, Kans. U., 1972; PhD in public adminstrn., Fla. State U., 1980. Cmty. mental health counselor; asst. prof social work U. West Fla., 1975—81; assoc. prof. pub. adminstrn. U. South Fla., 1981—85, asst. to pres., 1983—85; asst. dean adminstrn. U. South Fla., Grad. Sch., 1985—88; founding edn. chair Exec. Fellows Prog. Inst. of Govt., U. South Fla., 1985—88, dir. pub. adminstrn. prog., 1988; assoc. provost & dir. Early Identification Prog. George Mason U., 1989—91, vice provost academic initiative & external affairs, 1991—93; chancellor U. Mich., Dearborn, 1993—99; prof polit. sci. NC A&T State U., 1999—, chancellor, 1999—. Cons. in edn. field nat. and internat.; mem. President's Bd. Adv. on Historically Black Coll. and Univ., NC Bd. of Sci. and Tech., Bus.-Higher Edn. Forum; bd. trustees JSTOR; bd. dirs. Microelectronics Ctr. of NC, Piedmont Triad Ctr. for Adv. Mfg., Piedmont Triad Partnership. Contbr. articles to profl. jours. Mem. James Lawrence Found., Parrin J. Mitchell Found.; mem. hon. edn. coun. Nat. Minority Military Mus. Found.; bd. dirs. Greater Greensboro C. of C; pres. Greensboro Merchants Assn. Named to Donald K. Anthony Achievement Hall of Fame, Ctrl. State U., Ohio, 1993; recipient President's Medallion, U. Mich., Exemplary Award for Pub. Service, Am. Assn. for Higher Edn. Black Caucus. Office: Office of the Chanceller NC A&T State U 1601 E Market St Greensboro NC 27411

RENICK, KYLE, artistic director; b. St. Louis, Apr. 24, 1948; s. Mark Allen and Annabelle (Myers) R. BA magna cum laude, Tufts U., 1970. Sr. fund acct. New Eng. Mchts. Nat. Bank, Boston, 1970-73; fund acct. Fidelity Mgmt. and Rsch. Corp., Boston, 1973; bus. mgr. Am. Pl. Theatre, N.Y.C., 1973-78; producing dir. WPA Theatre, N.Y.C., 1977-82, artistic dir., 1982—; pres. WPA Prodns., Inc., N.Y.C., 1987—. Trustee Alliance of Resident Theatres-N.Y., 1982-92; cons. N.Y. State Council on Arts, 1982-85, Nat. Endowment for Arts, 1986. Producer Steel Magnolias, 1987, The Lady in Question, 1989; contbr. articles to profl. publs. Recipient spl. award for outstanding achievement Drama Desk Assn., 1983. Mem.: Neue Bachgesellschaft, Nev. Hist. Soc., Film Music Soc., Wildlife Conservation Soc., The Packard Club, Phi Beta Kappa. Avocations: early music, record collecting, ghost town photography. Home: 2 Bethune St Apt 4B New York NY 10014-1862 Office: WPA Theatre 159 W 25th St # 301 New York NY 10001-7203 E-mail: wpatheatre@msn.com.

RENK, KIMBERLY DAWN, social sciences educator; m. Robert William Renk, June 29, 1991; 1 child, Kyle Matthew. BS, U. Ill., 1992; MA, Ill. State U., 1994; PhD, U. South Fla., 2000. Asst. prof. U. Ctrl. Fla., Orlando, 2000—. Svc. provider Nemours Children's Clin., Orlando, 2000—. Contbr. articles to profl. jours. Grantee, U. Ctrl. Fla., 2002; Gala endowment, Fla. Hosp., 2002—03. Mem.: APA, Southeastern Psychol. Assn. Office: U Ctrl Fla Dept Psychology 4000 Central Florida Blvd Orlando FL 32816

RENKA, ROBERT JOSEPH, computer science educator, consultant; b. Summit, NJ, Dec. 28, 1947; s. John and Elizabeth (Pierce) R. BA in Computer Sci., BS in Math., U. Tex., 1976, MA in Math., 1979, PhD in Computer Sci., 1981. Numerical analyst Oak Ridge (Tenn.) Nat. Lab., 1981-84; asst. prof. computer sci. U. North Tex., Denton, 1984-89, assoc. prof. computer sci., 1989-99, prof. computer sci., 1999—. Cons. in field. Contbr. articles to profl. jours. With USN, 1967-69, Vietnam. Rsch. grantee U. North Tex., 1984-89, NSF, 1990-93, Nat. Security Agy., 1999—. Mem. Assn. for Computing Machinery (algorithms editor 1988-94, editor-in-chief 1989-94), Soc. Indsl. and Applied Math. Avocations: racquetball, rock climbing. Home: 1700 Kendolph Dr Denton TX 76205-6931 Office: U North Tex Dept Computer Sci and Engring PO Box 311366 Denton TX 76203-1366 Office Phone: 940-565-2767.

RENKES, GREGG, state attorney general; m. Maureen Renkes; 2 children. BA, Vassar Coll.; MS, Yale U.; JD, U. Colo. Bar: Alaska 1987. Law clk., magistrate State Alaska Ct. Sys.; chief of staff, chief counsel to U.S. Senator Frank Murkowski; majority staff dir. U.S. Senate Com. on Energy and Natural Resources, 1995—98; pres. The Renkes Group, Ltd.; atty. gen. State of Alaska, Juneau, 2003—. Spkr. in field. Contbr. articles to profl. jours. Mem. Campaign to Re-elect Senator Frank Murkowski, 1992, 1998, Murkowski 2002 Alaska Gubernatorial Campaign; active Rep. Nat. Conv. Platform Com., 1996. Republican. Office: Diamond Courthouse PO Box 110300 Juneau AK 99811-0300

RENKIS, ALAN ILMARS, plastics formulating company executive; b. Preili, Latvia, Apr. 16, 1938; arrived in U.S., 1950, naturalized, 1958; s. Joseph and Malvine (Sturitis) R.; m. Inara Balodis, July 15, 1961; children: Martin Alan, Laura Alise. BSChemE, Pa. State U., 1960. Staff product devel. and tech. svc. divsn. Diamond Alkali Co., Painesville, Ohio, 1960-63; tech. dir. G.S. Plastics Co., Cleve., 1963; founder, pres. Thermoclad Co., Erie, Pa., 1963—, Riverside, Calif., 1972-80, Ocala, Fla., 1985—. Developer comml. PVC resins for formulating fluidized bed and electrostatic coating powders; formulations and compounding techniques. Mem. World Pres. Orgn., Soc. Plastic Engrs., Soc. Mfg. Engrs., Am. Latvian Assn., Erie Yacht Club, Kahkwa Club, Aviation Club, Sigma Pi, Fraternitas Met. Home: 214 Crystal Point Dr Erie PA 16505 Office: Thermoclad Co 361 W 11th St Erie PA 16501-1703 Business E-Mail: arenkis@thermoclad.com.

RENNA, CATHY, communications executive, activist; Grad., Adelphi U. Vol. Gay and Lesbian Alliance Against Defamation (GLAAD), NY, 1990, dir. regional media and cmty. rels., 1996—2001, news media dir., 2001—04; media rels. dir. Fenton Comm., NY, 2004—. Office: Fenton Comm 260 Fifth Ave Ninth Fl New York NY 10001 Office Phone: 212-584-5000 319. Office Fax: 212-584-5045. E-mail: crenna@fenton.com.

RENNE, PAUL F. retired food products executive; b. Pitts. BS in Acctg., St. Vincent Coll. CPA. With acctg. firm, 1965-73; fin. analyst H.J. Heinz Co., Pittsburgh, Pa., 1973-75, dir. fin. rels., 1975-81, v.p. fin. Heinz Can., 1981-84, corp. treas. Heinz World Hdqrs., 1984-86, v.p., treas., 1986-1996, v.p. fin., treas., 1989—, CFO, 1996—2001, sr. v.p. fin. to exec. v.p., 1997—2001, spl. advisor, fin., 2002.*

RENNER, ANDREW IHOR, surgeon; b. Buenos Aires, Aug. 1, 1951; came to U.S., 1956; s. Vladimir and Emelia R.; m. Cristina Sasyk, Apr. 17, 1982. MD, Albert Einstein Coll. Medicine, 1975. Diplomate Am. Bd. Surgery. Pvt. practice gen. surgery, Burbank, Calif. Chmn. dept. surgery St. Joseph Hosp., Burbank, 1995-97, vice chief of staff Providence St. Joseph Med. Ctr., Burbank, 2003-04, chief of staff, 2004-. Fellow ACS, Internat. Coll. Surgeons; mem. Am. Soc. Gen. Surgeons, L.A. Surg. Soc. Office: 2701 W Alameda Ave Ste 300 Burbank CA 91505-4408 Fax: 818-843-5283.

RENNER, MARGUERITE, history educator; b. San Antonio, Oct. 17, 1947; d. Robert Nelson and Paula Irene (Hess) R.; m. Robert Nelson; children: Tom, Chet. BA, U. Pitts., 1969, MA, 1971, PhD, 1981. Asst. prof. history Stephens Coll., Columbia, Mo., 1980-81, U. Tex., El Paso, 1983-84, U. Utah, Salt Lake City, 1984-85, Calif. State U., Northridge, 1985-89; prof. history Glendale (Calif.) Coll., 1989—. Pres. acad. senate Glendale Coll., 2002—03. Pres. Western Assn. Women Historians, 1992-94, UN Assn., Pasadena, 1999, Dem. Club, Pasadena, 1989-91; mem. Commn. on Status of Women, Pasadena, 1988-95, Huntington Women's Studies Seminar, San Marion, Calif., 1992-96. Named to Daus. of Honor, Phila. H.S. for Girls, 2000. Mem. Am. Hist. Assn., Coord. Coun. for Women in History (exec. dir. 1994-97). Avocations: gardening, carpentry, animal care. Office: Glendale Coll 1500 N Verdugo Rd Glendale CA 91208

RENNER, ROBERT GEORGE, federal judge; b. Nevis, Minn., Apr. 2, 1923; s. Henry J. and Beatrice M. (Fuller) R.; m. Catherine L. Clark, Nov. 12, 1949; children: Robert, Anne, Richard, David. BA, St. John's U., Collegeville, Minn., 1947; JD, Georgetown U., 1949. Bar: Minn. 1949. Pvt. practice, Walker, 1949-69; U.S. atty. Dist. of Minn., 1969-77, U.S. magistrate, 1977-80, U.S. dist. judge, 1980-92, assumed sr. status, 1992—. Mem. Minn. Ho. of Reps., 1957-69. Served with AUS, 1943-46. Mem. FBA. Roman Catholic. Office: US Dist Ct 748 US Courthouse 316 Robert St N Saint Paul MN 55101-1495

RENNERT, IRA LEON, manufacturing executive; b. 1934; BA, Bklyn. Coll., 1954; MBA, NYU, 1956. Credit analyst M. Lowenstein Corp., N.Y.C., 1956-57; salesman Underwood Corp., N.Y.C., 1957-58; registered rep. Francis I. Dupont & Co., N.Y.C., 1958-60; established I.L. Rennert & Co., Inc. (formerly Rubin, Rennert & Co., Inc.), N.Y.C., 1960-64; cons. N.Y.C., 1964-75; pres. Consolidated Sewing Machine Corp., N.Y.C., 1975—; pres., CEO, chmn. Renco Group, Inc., N.Y.C., 1980—; ceo WCI Steel Inc., Warren, Ohio, 1988—. Chmn. bd. Am. Gen. Corp., South Bend, Ind., 1992. Office: Renco Group 30 Rockefeller Plz New York NY 10112

RENNERT, OWEN MURRAY, pediatrician, geneticist, educator; b. N.Y.C., Aug. 8, 1938; s. David Rennert and Frieda (Weinsteiner) Sommer; m. Sandra Serota, Mar. 22, 1964; children: Laura, Rachel, Ian. BS, BA, U. Chgo., 1957, MD, 1961, MS in Biochemistry, 1963. Diplomate Am. Bd. Pediatrics, Am. Bd. Genetics, Am. Bd. Med. Genetics. Assoc. prof. pediatrics U. Fla. Coll. Medicine, Gainesville, 1968—70, assoc. prof. biochemistry, 1970—71, head instl. divsn. genetics, endocrinology and metabolism, 1970—78, prof. pediatrics, biochemistry and neurosci., 1971-78; prof. biochemistry, prof. and head dept. pediatrics U. Okla., Oklahoma City, 1977-88; chief pediatrics svc. and head genetics, sect. endocrinology and metabolism Okla. Children's Mem. Hosp., Oklahoma City, 1977-88; prof., chmn. dept. pediatrics Georgetown U. Sch. Medicine, Washington, 1988-98, prof. dept. biochemistry and molecular biology, 1995—98, prof. emeritus, 1998—2000; spl. asst. to dir. ctr. rsch. mothers and children Nat. Inst. Child Health Human Devel., NIH, Bethesda, Md., 1998—2000, dir. Ctr. Rsch. Mothers and Children, 2000, sci. dir. divsn. intramural rsch., 2000—. Co-author: Metabolism of Trace Metals in Man: Developmental Biology and Genetic Implications (2 vols.), 1984; assoc. editor: Molecular Clinical Medicine, 1999—; contbr. articles to profl. jours. Bd. dirs. Children's Med. Research, Oklahoma City, 1984-88. Served to sr. surgeon USPHS, 1964-66. Named Clin. Scientist of Yr., Am. Assn. Clin. Scientists, 1978. Mem. Am. Pediatric Soc., Am. Acad. Pediatrics, Soc. Pediatric Research, Am. Coll. Clin. Nutrition, Biochem. Soc., Am. Soc. Molecular Biology and Biochemistry, Am. Coll. Med. Genetics, Am. Soc. Human Genetics. Office: NICHD/NIH Divsn Intramural Rsch 31 Center Dr Bldg 31 Rm 2A46 Bethesda MD 20892-2425 Business E-Mail: rennerto@mail.nih.gov.

RENNERT, WOLFGANG PETER, pediatrician, educator; b. Koblenz, Germany, Oct. 14, 1956; s. Alfred Heinrich and Gertrud Rennert; m. Kedibone Letlaka-Rennert, Dec. 2, 1988; children: Lindiwe Claudia, Lwazi Enno. MD, Albert Ludwig U., Freiburg, Germany, 1982, D in Med. Sci., 1985; Diploma in Tropical Medicine and Hygiene, U. Witwatersrand, Johannesburg, South Africa, 1989. Diplomate Am. Bd. Pediat., German Bd. Family Practice. Sr. specialist in pediat. Chris Hani Baragwanath Hosp., Soweto, South Africa, 1996—2001; assoc. prof. pediat. Georgetown U., Washington, 2001—. Residency program dir. Georgetown U., Washington, 2002—. Grantee, Georgetown U., 2002. Achievements include research in HIV infection in children. Office: Georgetown U Hosp 3800 Reservoir Rd NW Washington DC 20057

RENNEY, TOM, professional hockey coach; m. Glenda Renney. Head coach Kamloops Blazers (WHL), 1991—93, Team Can., 1993—96, Vancouver Canucks (NHL), 1996—97; v.p. hockey Can. Nat. Team, 1998—99, head coach, v.p., 1999—2000; dir. player pers. N.Y. Rangers (NHL), 2000—02, asst. coach, v.p. player devel., 2003—04, head coach, v.p. player devel., 2004—. Head coach Team Canada, Lillehammer Olympic Games, 1992. Office: 2 Pennsylvania Plaza New York NY 10121*

RENNIE, I. DRUMMOND, periodical editor, medical educator; Dep. editor Jour. AMA; nephrologist Rush-Presbyn. St. Lukes Hosp. and Rush Med. Sch., Chgo., 1967-77; assoc. prof. medicine Harvard (Brigham and Women's Hosp.); dep. editor New England Jour. of Medicine. Adv. com. on scientific integrity to Pub. Health Svc.; adj. prof. of medicine U. Calif. San Francisco; co-dir. San Francisco Cochrane Ctr.; proposal rev. adv. team Nat. Sci. Found.; founder CONSORT, QUOROM coms. Contbr. numerous articles to profl. publs. Fellow ACP; mem. New World Assn. of Med. Editors (pres. coun. of biology editors, past pres., exec. bd.). Office: Inst for Health Policy Studies Adjunct Prof UCSF School of Medicine San Francisco CA 94118 E-mail: rennie@itsa.ucsf.edu.

RENNIE, MILBREY TOWER, television news producer; b. Milw., Aug. 19, 1946; d. William Roxburgh and Jean (Tower) R.; m. David Hendrickson Taylor, Jr., Sept. 15, 1973; children: Rennie, Milbrey. BA, Vassar Coll., 1968. Caseworker Sen. Charles Percy, Washington, 1968-69; campaign asst. to Re-elect Mayor John Lindsay, N.Y.C., 1969; rschr. ABC News, Washington, 1970-71; reporter, prodr. NPACT (PBS), Washington, 1971-75; exec. prodr. CBS News, N.Y.C., 1976—. Trustee Vassar Coll., Poughkeepsie, N.Y., 1989—, Miss Porter's Sch., Farmington, Conn., 1976-81, 93—, Nightingale Bamford Sch., 1994—; dir. OTR Lecture Series, FPA, N.Y.C., 1990—; mem. Counkilon Fgn. Rels. Luce scholar Henry Luce Found., Manila, 1975-76. Avocation: tennis. Office: CBS News Weekend News/Sunday News 524 W 57th St New York NY 10019-2924

RENNIE, PAUL STEVEN, research scientist; b. Toronto, Ont., Can., Feb. 9, 1946; m. Carol Andrews, 1968; 1 child, Jan. BSc, U. Western Ont., 1969; PhD in Biochemistry, U. Alta., Can., 1973. Rsch. assoc. U. Alta., 1975-76, asst. prof. medicine, 1976-79, assoc. prof., 1979; rsch. scientist B.C. Cancer Agy., Canada, 1979-92, dir. rsch., 1992-97; prof. surgery U. B.C., 1986—, dir. prostate rsch. lab., 1998—. Med. Rsch. Coun. rsch. fellow Imperial Cancer Rsch. Fund, 1973-75; rsch. scholar Nat. Cancer Inst. Can., 1976-79. Mem. Can. Soc. Clin. Investigation, Biochem. Soc., Endocrine Soc. Achievements include research on biochemical control of growth in androgen responsive organs and neoplasms; genetic markers in prostate cancer. Office: Prostate Ctr Jack Bell Rsch Ctr 2660 Oak St Vancouver BC Canada V6H 3Z6 E-mail: prennie@interchange.ubc.ca.

RENNINGER, MARY KAREN, librarian; b. Pitts., Apr. 30, 1945; d. Jack Burnell and Jane (Hammerly) Gunderman; m. Norman Christian Renninger, Sept. 3, 1965 (div. 1980); 1 child, David Christian. BA, U. Md., 1969, MA, 1972, M.L.S., 1975. Tchr. English West Carteret High Sch., Morehead City, N.C., 1969-70; instr. in English U. Md., College Park, 1970-72; head network services Nat. Libr. Svc., Libr. of Congress, Washington, 1974-78, asst. for network support, 1978-80; mem. fed. women's program com. Libr. of Congress, Washington, 1978-80; chief libr. divsn. Dept. Vets. Affairs, Washington, 1980-90; chief serial and govt. publs. divsn. Libr. of Congress, Washington, 1991—, mem. fed. libr. com., 1980-90, mem. exec. adv. bd., 1985-90. Mem. USBE pers. subcom., 1982-84; bd. regents Nat. Libr. of Medicine, 1986-90, mem. outreach panel, 1988-89; fed. libr. task force for 1990 White House Conf. on Librs., 1986-90; liaison to The White House Conf. Med. Libr. Assn., 1989-90. Recipient Meritorious Svc. award Libr. of Congress, 1974, Spl. Achievement award, 1976, Performance award VA, ann. 1982-89, Adminstr.'s Commendation, 1985, Spl. Contbn. award, 1986. Mem. ALA (Govt. Documents Roundtable), Libr. Tech. Assn., Med. Libr. Assn. (govt. rels. com. 1985—), D.C. Libr. Assn., Soc. Applied Learning Tech., Med. Interactive Videodisc Consortium, Govt. Documents Roundtable, Knowledge Utilization Soc., Nat. Multimedia Assn. Am., U.S. Tennis Assn., Phi Beta Kappa, Alpha Lambda Delta, Beta Phi Mu. Home: 840 College Pky Rockville MD 20850-1931 Office: Libr of Congress Ser and Govt Pub Divsn Lm 133 Washington DC 20540-0001 Office Phone: 202-707-5647. Business E-Mail: Kren@loc.gov.

RENO, JANET, former attorney general; b. Miami, Fla., July 21, 1938; d. Henry and Jane (Wood) R. AB in Chemistry, Cornell U., 1960; LL.B., Harvard U., 1963. Bar: Fla. 1963. Assoc. Brigham & Brigham, 1963-67; ptnr. Lewis & Reno, 1967-71; staff dir. judiciary com. Fla. Ho. of Reps., Tallahassee, 1971-72; cons. Fla. Senate Criminal Justice Com. for Revision Fla.'s Criminal Code, spring 1973; adminstrv. asst. state atty. 11th Jud. Circuit Fla., Miami, 1973-76, state atty., 1978-93; ptnr. Steel Hector and Davis, Miami, 1976-78; U.S. atty. gen. Dept. Justice, Washington, 1993-2001. Mem. jud. nominating commn. 11th Jud. Circuit Fla., 1976-78; chmn. Fla. Gov.'s Council for Prosecution Organized Crime, 1979-80. Recipient Women First award YWCA, 1993. National Women's Hall of Fame, 2000. Mem. ABA (Inst. Jud. Adminstrn. Juvenile Justice Standards Commn. 1973-76), Am. Law Inst., Am. Judicature Soc. (Herbert Harley award 1981), Dade County Bar Assn., Fla. Pros. Atty.'s Assn. (pres. 1984-86). Democrat. Address: 11200 N Kendall Dr Miami FL 33176-1108

RENO, JOHN F. foundation administrator; b. Peoria, Ill., June 15, 1939; s. John Henkle and Alice Hanna (Findley) R.; m. Suzanne McKnight, Apr. 18, 1964; children: David, Anne. AB, Dartmouth Coll., 1961; MBA, Northwestern U., 1963. Ptnr. G.H. Walker & Co., Boston, 1968-74; divsn. pres. Dynatech Cryomedical Co., Burlington, Mass., 1974-79; corp. v.p. Dynatech Corp., Burlington, 1979-82, group v.p., 1982-87, pres., COO, 1987-93, pres., CEO, 1993-99, chmn., 1996-99, Reno Family Found., Winchester, Mass., 1999—. Bd. dirs. Millipre Corp., Bedford, Mass. Trustee, chmn. Boston Mus. of Sci., 1992—; bd. dirs. CEOs for Fundamental Change in Edn., Cambridge, Mass.; dir. WGBH Pub. TV, 1999— Named Entrepreneur of Yr., Inc. mag., 1995. Avocations: painting, writing. Office: Reno Family Found 63 Shore Rd Ste 33 Winchester MA 01890-2828

RENO, JOSEPH HARRY, retired orthopedic surgeon; b. Allentown, Pa., Mar. 5, 1915; s. Harvey Luther and Olive May (Wilson) R.; m. Maude Olivia Mutchler, June 27, 1942; children: Joseph David, Sally Jo, Diana Jane, Deborah Marion. Student, Temple U., 1934-37, MD, 1941. Intern. Chester (Pa.) Hosp., 1941-42; resident Tex. Scottish Rite Hosp. for Crippled Children, Dallas, 1942-43, 44-45, Robert Packer Hosp., Sayre, Pa., 1943-44; assoc. Homer Stryker, M.D., Kalamazoo, 1945-46; pvt. practice Bethlehem, Pa., 1946-71, Flagstaff, Ariz., 1971-93; team physician Lehigh U., Bethlehem, 1946-70, No. Ariz. U., Flagstaff, 1971-77, Ariz. State U., Tempe, 1977-84. Chief surg. staff Flagstaff Hosp., 1975. Contbr. articles to profl. jours.; prodr. surg. films for Am. Acad. Ortho. Surgeons and others, 1952-70. Pres. Coconino County Easter Seal Soc., 1973; bd. dirs., med. advisor Ariz. Easter Seal Soc., 1974-84. Recipient Pioneer award Ariz. Med. Assn., 1981, Cert. of Appreciation, Pa. Dept. Health Crippled Children's Div., 1971; Dr. Joseph Reno Sports Medicine award named in honor, No. Ariz. State U. and Blue Cross Blue Shield, 1986. Fellow Am. Acad. Ortho. Surgeons, Am. Assn. for Surgery of Trauma, Am. Coll. Sports Med., Am. Coll. Surgeons (chmn. Lehigh Valley subcom. on trauma 1954-66, Ea. Pa. chpt. pres. 1969); mem. NRA, Am. Bd. Ortho. Surgery (cert., diplomate 1948), Coconino County Med. Soc. (pres. 1976), Western Ortho. Assn., Babcock Surg. Soc., Mason, Phi Chi, Alpha Tau Omega. Home: 405 Jacks Canyon Rd Apt 105 Sedona AZ 86351-7860

RENO, OTTIE WAYNE, former judge; b. Pike County, Ohio, Apr. 7, 1929; s. Eli Enos and Arbannah Belle (Jones) Reno; m. Janet Gay McCann, May 22, 1947; children: Jennifer Lynn, Lorna Victoria, Ottie Wayne II. A in Bus. Adminstrn., Franklin U., 1949; LLB, Franklin Law Sch., 1953; JD, Capital U., 1966; grad. Coll. Juvenile Justice, U. Nev., 1973. Bar: Ohio 1953. Practiced in Pike County; recorder Pike County, 1957-73, common pleas judge probate and juvenile divsn., 1973-79. Author: Story of Horseshoes, 1963, Pitching Championship Horseshoes, 1971; 2d rev. edit., 1975; author: The American Directory of Horseshoe Pitching, 1983, Ohio vs. Smith, Murder, 1990, Reno and Apsaalooka Survive Custer, 1996. Del. Dem. Nat. Conv., 1972, 1996; mem. Camp Creek precinct Dem. Ctrl. Com., 1956—72, 1983—90, 1999—2002; sec. Pike County Dem. Exec. Com., 1971—72, 1988—90; mem. Ohio Dem. Ctrl. Com., 1969—70; Dem. candidate 6th Ohio dist. U.S. Ho. of Reps., 1966; Dem. candidate 88th Ohio dist. Ohio Ho. of Reps., 1992; pres. Scioto Valley Local Sch. Dist., 1962—66. Named to Nat. Horseshoe Pitchers Hall of Fame, 1978; recipient Disting. Svc. award, Ohio Youth Commn., 1974, 6 Outstanding Jud. Svc. awards, Ohio Supreme Ct., 17 times Ala. horseshoe pitching champion. Mem.: Pike County Bar Assn., Nat. Coun.Juvenile Ct. Judges, Ohio Bar Assn., Am. Legion. Mem. Ch. Of Christ In Christian Union. Home: 148 Reno Rd Lucasville OH 45648-9580

RENO, ROGER, lawyer; b. Rockford, Ill., May 16, 1924; s. Guy B. and Hazel (Kinnear) R.; m. Janice Marie Odelius, May 17, 1952; children: Susan Marie, Sheri Jan Reno-Rudolph, Michael Guy. Student, Kenyon Coll., 1943-44, Yale U., 1944, U. Wis., 1946; AB, Carleton Coll., 1947; LL.B., Yale U., 1950. Bar: Ill. 1950. Practiced in Rockford, 1950; assoc. firm Reno, Zahm, Folgate, Lindberg & Powell, 1950-56, partner, 1956-84, of counsel, 1984—. Chmn. Amcore Fin. Inc., 1982-95; atty. Rockford Bd. Edn., 1955-64. Past pres., bd. dirs. Childrens Home Rockford; trustee Swedish-Am. Hosp. Assn., 1967-77, Keith Country Day Sch. Served to 1st lt. USAAF, 1943-46. Mem. ABA, Ill. Bar Assn., Winnebago County Bar Assn. (pres. 1979-80) Clubs: Forest Hills Country (Rockford). Republican. Methodist. Home: 2515 Chickadee Trl Rockford IL 61107 Office: Reno Zahm Folgate Lindberg & Powell Amcore Fin Plaza Rockford IL 61104 Fax: 815-961-7723.

RENO, RUSSELL RONALD, JR., lawyer; b. Gary, Ind., Nov. 28, 1933; s. Russell Ronald Sr. and Katherine Narcissus (White) R.; m. Mary Ellen Klock, Jan. 30, 1956; children: Mary Hall, Russell III, William, Elizabeth. AB, Haverford Coll., 1954; JD, U. Pa., 1957. Bar: Md. 1957, D.C. 1983. Assoc. Venable, Baetjer & Howard, Balt., 1958-66, ptnr., 1966—; asst. atty. gen. State of Md., Balt., 1962-64. Author: Maryland Real Estate Law-Practice, 1983. Bd. dirs. Balt. Choral Arts Soc., 1966—; trustee Goucher Coll., Balt., 1978-98, trustee emeritus, 1998—; chancellor Episcopal Diocese of Md., Balt., 1985—; bd. mgrs. Haverford Coll., 1990-2002. Fellow Am. Bar Found., Md. Bar Found.; mem. ABA, Md. State Bar Assn., Am. Coll. Real Estate Lawyers, Hamilton St. Club, Wednesday Law Club. Home: 706 W Joppa Rd Baltimore MD 21204-3810 Office: Venable Baetjer & Howard 2 Hopkins Plz Ste 2100 Baltimore MD 21201-2982 Office Phone: 410-244-7480. E-mail: rrreno@venable.com.

RENOUF, ANNE, technology commercialization financier; b. N.Y.C., Apr. 3, 1937; Diploma, Emma Willard Sch., 1954; student, Inst. World Affairs, 1957; AB magna cum laude, honors in Anthropology, Columbia U., 1959; MA, Yale U., 1962, PhD, 1966; JD with honors, Am. U., 1978; postgrad., Duke U. Asst. prof. U. N.C., Chapel Hill, 1966-71; sr. profl. cons. U.S. Govt., Washington, 1972-75; pvt. practice fin. cons. Washington, 1976—; vis. assoc. prof. George Washington U. Sch. Bus. Adminstrn., Washington, 1983-84; gen. ptnr., v.p. Tech. Mgmt. Corp., Montgomeryville, Pa., 1986-88; chmn. Pivot, Inc., 1988—90; founding prin. SaraTech Fin. Inc., 1990-92; pvt. practice, fin. cons. A.E. Rosica & Co., Inc., 2003—04. Founding dir., chmn. bd., CFO/bd. treas. Initiatives in Industry, Inc., 1996-02; corp. dir.; dir. fin. devel. Ctr. for Space and Advanced Tech., 1990; cons. The Brookings Instn., Washington, 1966, U.S. Dept. State, Washington, 1967, World Bank, 1992—; mem. Pres.'s Commn. Grad. Edn., 1967-68, Nat. Chamber Found. Task Force on Space Commercialization, Washington, 1983-86; vis. scholar Carnegie Endowment for Internat. Peace, N.Y.C., 1968-69; fellow U.S. Dept. State, EUR/RPE, 1967; northeastern dir. Va. Advanced Tech. Assn., 1984-88; fin. and tech. spkr.; mem. Coun. on Competitiveness, 1998—2003, Tech. Coun. Washington, 1998—; mem. Greater Washington Bd. Trade, The Potomac Conf., 1999—; mem. The World Bank, The Global Devel. Network, 1998—. Contbr. articles on tech. commercialization and fin. to profl. jours. Co-chair, charter mem. U.S./China Capital Cities Coun., Washington, 1985-95; advisor Greater Washington D.C. Bd. Trade, 1985-86, Internat. Red Cross, 1987-90; mem. Mayor's Adv. Coun. on Trade and Investment, 1987-91; mem. adv. coun. Ctr. for Internat. Bus. Edn. U. Alaska, Fairbanks, 1990-91, co-chmn. World Trade Day, 1989; bd. dirs. Nat. Symphony Orch., 1990-99, Greater Washington Met. Boys and Girls Clubs, 1992-2000; dir. Initiatives in Industry, Inc., 1996-02. Woodrow Wilson fellow, 1958, Bushnell fellow, Yale U., 1964, Hon. Officer-Faculty fellow U.S. Dept. State, 1967; recipient citation Washington D.C. Mayor's Office, 1986. Fellow Washington Acad. Scis.; mem. Am. Soc. Internat. Law, Internat. Forum U.S. C. of C., Internat. Energy Seminar-Johns Hopkins Sch. for Advanced Internat. Study, Corcoran Gallery of Art (nat. coun.), Washington Internat. Trade Assn., Assn. for Corp. Growth, Phi Beta Kappa. Office Phone: 202-965-3000.

RENOUF, EDDA, artist; b. Mexico City, June 17, 1943; d. Edward and Catharine Smith; m. Alain Middleton, Sept. 20, 1977; 1 child, Mélisande. BA, Sarah Lawrence Coll., 1965; M.F.A., Columbia U., 1971. One-woman shows include Yvon Lambert Gallery, Paris, 1972, 1974, 1976, 1978, 1980, 1982, 1984, 1993, Konrad Fischer Gallery, Düsseldorf, Germany, 1974, 1979, Blum-Helman Gallery, N.Y.C., 1978, 1980, 1982, 1985, 1987, 1989, U. Mich. Mus. Art, 1995, Elisabeth Kaufmann Gallery, Basel, Switzerland, 1994, 1996, Galerie Sollertis, Toulouse, France, 1994, 1996, 1998, Staatliche Kunsthalle Karlsruhe, Germany, 1997, Galerie Hubert Winter, Vienna, Austria, 1998, Galerie Liesbeth Lips, Rotterdam, 1998, 2001, Helman Gallery, N.Y.C., 2001—02, Joseph Helman Gallery, 2002, Nat. Mus. Women in the Arts, Washington, D.C., 2004, Brenau U. Galleries, Gainesville, Ga., 2004, exhibited in group shows at Mus. Modern Art, N.Y.C., 1973, 1990, 1998, Stedelijk Mus., Amsterdam, 1974, 8th Paris Biennale, 1973, Whitney Mus. Am. Art, N.Y.C., 1979, 1985, Centre Georges Pompidou, Paris, 1979, 2002, Met. Mus. Art, N.Y.C., 1982, Serpentine Gallery, 1984, Galerie Denise René, Paris, 1985, Tel Aviv Mus., 1986, 1998, Mus. Fridericianum, Kassel, Germany, 1988, Mus. d'Art Moderne de Lille, France, 1992, Bibliothèque Nationale, Paris, 1992, Nat. Gallery Art, Washington, 1993—94, Harvard U. Straus Gallery, 1996, Yokohama (Japan) Mus. Art, 1998, Yale U. Art Gallery, 1998, Cabinet des Estampes et des Dessins, Liege, Belgium, 1999, Brit. Mus., 2000, Corcoran Gallery, Washington, 2001, Neue Galerie, Graz, Austria, 2001—02, Ctr. Georges, Pompidon, Paris, 2002, Riva Yares Gallery, Santa Fe, N.Mex., 2004, Brit. Mus., London, 2004, Represented in permanent collections Mus. Modern Art, Whitney Mus. Am. Art, Met. Mus. Art, Centre Georges Pompidou, Paris, Chgo. Art Inst., Mus. of Contemporary Art, Chgo., Phila. Art Mus., Yale U. Art Gallery, Neuberger Mus., Australian Nat. Gallery, Cin. Mus. Art, St. Louis Art Mus., Tel Aviv Mus., La. Mus., Denmark, Walker Art Ctr., Washington, BibliotequeNationale Paris, Brit. Mus., London, Bklyn. Mus. Am. Art, Dallas Mus. Fine Art, Detroit Mus. Art, Mus. Contemporary Art, L.A., High Mus., Atlanta, Corcoran Gallery, Washington, Staatliche Kunsthalle, Karlsruhe, Nat. Gallery Art, Washington, Kunstmuseum Winterthur, Switzerland, Neue Galerie, Graz, Nat. Mus. of Women in the Arts, Washington, D.C. Nat. Endowment Arts grantee, 1976-77, Pollock-Krasner Found. Inc. grantee, 1990-91, Ctr. Nat. Arts Plastiques grantee, 1996. Address: 26 Juniper Meadow Rd Washington CT 06794 Office Phone: 860-868-9722.

RENOUF, HAROLD AUGUSTUS, retired transportation executive; b. Sandy Point, Nfld., Can., June 15, 1917; s. John Robert and Louisa Maud (LeRoux) R.; m. Janet Dorothy Munro, June 16, 1942; children: Janet Dorothy, Ann Louise Petley-Jones, John Robert, Susan Elizabeth Thompson. B.Commerce, Dalhousie U., 1938, LL.D. (hon.), 1981. N.S.C.A., Halifax, 1942 C.M.A., 1950. With H.R. Doane and Co., Halifax, N.S., Can., 1938-75, ptnr., 1942-75, ptnr. in charge New Glasgow, N.S., Can., 1947-62, ptnr. in charge mgmt. svcs. Halifax, 1963-67, chmn., 1967-75; bd. dirs. Associated Acctg. Firms Internat., N.Y.C., 1967-75; commr. Anti-Inflation Bd., Ottawa, Ont., 1975-77, chmn., 1977-79, Petroleum Monitoring Agy., Ottawa, 1980-82, VIA Rail Can. Inc., Montreal, Que., 1982-85; pres. Fundy Industries Ltd., Halifax, 1990-94; ret., 1996. Cons. to N.S. Provincial Mcpl. Fact-Finding Com., 1967-70; pres. Can. Inst. Chartered Accts., 1974-75. Contbr. articles to profl. publs. Chmn. adv. commn. Dalhousie U. Grad. Sch. Bus. Adminstrn., 1978-86. Recipient Queen's medal, Queen's Golden Jubilee medal, 2002, Commemorative medal for 125th anniversary of Can. Confedn., 1992; decorated officer Order of Can.; named to Acctg. Hall of Fame St. Mary's Univ., N.S., 1993. Fellow Inst. Chartered Accts. N.S. (pres. 1948); mem. Can. Inst. Chartered Accts. (pres. 1974-75), Can. Tax Found. (gov. 1969-71), Soc. Mgmt. Accts. N.S., Dalhousie U. Alumni Assn. (hon. chmn. 1987-89), Halifax Club, Saraguay Club (treas. 1972-75), Waegwaltic Club. Liberal. Mem. United Ch. Can. Avocations: boating, fishing. Home: 6369 Coburg Rd Apt 1605 Halifax NS Canada B3H 4J7

RENOUX, ANDRÉ, physicist, researcher; b. Courbevoie, France, Oct. 27, 1937; s. Robert and Jeanne (Noël) R.; divorced; children: Vincent, Nathalie. Lic. Sci., Faculty Scis. Paris, 1958, Dr 3rd cycle, 1961, Drs, 1965. Asst. Faculty Scis., Paris, 1959-61, master asst., 1961-66; prof. faculty of scis. U. Tunis, Tunisia, 1966—69, U. Brest, France, 1969-80; prof. U. Paris, 1980—2003, dir. lab. phys. aérosols et transfert des contaminations, 1980—, dir. DESS (3d cycle) sci. des aerosols-génie de l'Aérocontamination, 1981—2003, prof. emeritus, 2003—. Gen. conf. chmn. European Aerosol Conf., Blois, France, 1994; del. Internat. Coun. for Engring. and Tech., UNESCO, 2000—. Author: (with D. Boulaud, Lavoisier, Ed.) Les Aérosols, Physique et Métrologie, 1998; mem. editl. bd. Idojaras, 1979—, Pollution Atmosphérique, 1979-2003, Aerosol Sci. & Tech., 1992-2000, Revue Salles Propres, 2000-02; contbr. over 300 articles to profl. jours. Gen. sec. Syndicat d'initiative, Brest, 1973-77; mem. Cons. Com. Univs., France, 1973-77. Mem. AAAS, N.Y. Acad. Scis., Com. Regional Anti-Pollution Brest (pres. 1973-80), Soc. France for Nuclear Energy idFNE (pres. 1987-91), Am. Assn. Aerosol Rsch., Gesellschaft Aerosolforschung, Hungarian Meteorol. soc. (hon.), French Aerosol. Rsch. Assn. (pres. 1983-2000, hon. pres. 2000—), European Aerosol Assembly (co-founder, pres. 1998-2000), Office Professionnel de qualification des Entreprises de l'Ultrapropreté (pres. 1995—), Chevalier des Dames du vin et de la Table, Ordre de l'Écharpe. Avocations: tennis, opera, photography. Home: 11 Sq de L'eau Vive 94000 Créteil France Office: U Paris XII Lab Phys Aerosols Ave Gal de Gaulle 94000 Creteil France Office Phone: 33-6-84211880. E-mail: renoux.andre@numericable.fr.

RENSCHLER, CLIFFORD L. chemist; b. Evansvill, Ind., Sept. 20, 1955; s. Ervin Leroy and Vera Mae (Grabert) Renschler; m. Karen Leigh Brown, Aug. 19, 1978; children: Tyler Adam, Clinton William. BS in Chemistry, U. Evansville, 1977; PhD in Chemistry, U. Ill., 1981. Mem. tech. staff Sandia Nat. Labs., Albuquerque, 1981—89, dept. mgr., 1989—2001, dep. dir., 2001—. Organizer workshop on frontiers of engring. NAE, Orange County, Calif., 1999; bd. dirs. Exptl. Sta., Coll. of Engring., U. Mo., Columbia, 1997—98; mem. adv. bd. Nat. Ctr. for Mfg. Scis. Advanced Elect., 1996—99; adj. prof. chemistry U. N.Mex., Albuquerque; U.S. del. to U.S./Canada/Mexico trilateral Materials Workshop, Saltillo, Mexico, 1995. Contbr. tech. papers to profl. jours.; editor symposium procs. Various roles St. John's United Meth. Ch., Albuquerque. Mem.: Materials Rsch. Soc. (meeting chair 1996), Am. Chem. Soc. Republican. Achievements include 5 patents in field; development of tantomeric energy transfer dyes for enhanced scintillators; dyed photoresist for advanced lithography; carbon film technology used in smallest scale electrochemical characterizations. Avocations: mountain biking, cross country skiing. Office: Sandia Nat Labs MS 0134 Albuquerque NM 87185 E-mail: clrensc@sandia.gov.

RENSE, PAIGE, editor, publishing company executive; b. Iowa, May 04; m. Kenneth Noland, Apr. 10, 1924. Editor-in-chief Architectural Digest, L.A., 1970—. Appeared on (television) Good Morning Am., The Today Show, Entertainment Tonight. Named Woman of Yr., LA Times, 1976, to Interior Design Hall of Fame; recipient Pacifica award, So. Calif. Resources Coun., 1978, Editl. award, Dallas Market Ctr., 1978, Golden award, Chgo. Design Resources Coun., 1978, Agora award, 1982, Outstanding Profl. Incomms. award, 1982, Nat. Headliner award, Women in Comms., 1983, Muses, 1986, Woman of Internat. Accomplishment, 1991, Spirit of Achievement award, 1995, Pratt Inst. Founders award, 1997. Office: Archtl Digest The Conde Nast Publ Inc 6300 Wilshire Blvd Fl 11 Los Angeles CA 90048-5204

RENSHAW, AMANDA FRANCES, retired physicist, nuclear engineer; b. Wheelwright, Ky., Dec. 10, 1934; d. Taft and Mamie Nell (Russell) Wilson; divorced; children: Linda, Michael, Billy. BS in Physics, Antioch Coll., 1972; MS in Physics, U. Tenn., 1982, MS in Nuclear Engring., 1991. Rsch. asst. U. Mich., Ann Arbor, 1970-71; teaching asst. Antioch Coll., Yellow Springs, Ohio, 1971-72; physicist GE, Schenectady, N.Y., 1972-74, Union Carbide Corp., Oak Ridge, Tenn., 1974-79; rsch. assoc. Oak Ridge Nat. Lab., 1979-91, mgr. strategic planning, 1991-92, liaison for environ. scis., 1993-96; ret., 1996. Asst. to counselor for sci. and tech. Am. Embassy, Moscow, 1990; asst. to dir. nat. acid precipitation assessment program Office of Pres. U.S., 1993-94. Contbr. articles to profl. jours. Mem. AAUW, Am. Women in Sci., Am. Nuclear Soc. (Oak Ridge chpt.), Soc. Black Physicists. Avocations: reading, travel. Home: 1850 Cherokee Bluff Dr Knoxville TN 37920-2215

RENSLOW, CHARLES GEORGE, entrepreneur; b. Chgo., Ill., Aug. 26, 1929; Student, Wright U., Northwestern U. Pub. Kris Studio, 1950—79; owner GoldCoast Leather Bar, 1958—93; pub. Gay Life Newspaper, 1979—85; prodr. Internat. Mr. Leather, Inc., 1979—; owner Chgo. Eagle Leather Bar, 1997—. Pres. Leather Archives and Mus., 1994—. Charter mem. City Chgo. Gay/Lesbian Hall of Fame, 1991; participant Internat. Gay/Lesbian Assn. Conf., Austria, 1989; mem. Nat. Gay Task Force, 1981—88; founder Am. Found. AIDS Rsch., 2002—; mem. Nat. Trust Historic Preservation, 2002—; Nat. Orgn. Women, 2002—; mem. Dem. Nat. Com., 2002—; mem. adv. bd. (O'Brien) 43d Ward Dem. Party; mem. adv. bd. (Orbach) 46th Ward Dem. Party; organizer Second Harvest, 1st Dist. Wide Masonic Food Dr., 1997, Masonic Children's Home, Franzen Circus fundraiser, 1995; charitable fundraiser Gay Rights Nat. Lobby, 1979—85. Named Humanitarian of Yr., 1977, Pantheon Bus. Person of Yr., Leather Jour., 1996, Leather Man of Century, 2000; named to Hall of Fame, Gay Chgo. mag., 1982; recipient Chgo. Gay/lEsbian CC, Cmty. Svc. award, 1997, Lodge Builder's award, Hesperia Masonic Lodge AF & AM, 1999, award, Min. of Canadian Heritage, City of San Francisco, 1993, Cmty. Builder award, Masonary Lodge #411, 2004. Home: 4535 N Beacon Chicago IL 60640 Office: Renslow Family Enter 5015 N Clark St Chicago IL 60640 Fax: 773-878-5184. Office Phone: 773-878-6360. E-mail: chuck@chuckrenslow.com.

RENT, CLYDA STOKES, academic administrator; b. Jacksonville, Fla., Mar. 1, 1942; d. Clyde Parker Stokes Sr. and Edna Mae (Edwards) Shuemake; m. George Seymour Rent, Aug. 12, 1966; 1 child, Cason Rent Lynley. BA, Fla. State U., 1964, MA, 1966, PhD, 1968; LHD (hon.), Judson Coll., 1993. Asst. prof. Western Carolina U., Cullowhee, N.C., 1968-70, Queens Coll., Charlotte, N.C., 1972-74, dept. chair, 1974-78, dean Grad. Sch. and New Coll., 1979-84, v.p. for Grad. Sch. and New Coll., 1984-85, v.p. acad. affairs, 1985-87, v.p. cmty. affairs, 1987-89; pres. Miss. U. for Women, Columbus, 1989—. Mem. adv. bd. Nat. Women's Hall of Fame; cons. Coll. Eb. N.Y.C., 1983-89; sci. cons. N.C. Alcohol Rsch. Authority, Chapel Hill, 1976-89; bd. mem. So. Growth Policies Bd., 1992-94; adv. bd. Nat. Women's Hall of Fame, Trustmark Nat. Bank, 1991-97; rotating chair Miss. Instns. Higher Learning Pres. Coun., 1990-91; commn. govtl. rels. Am. Coun. Edn., 1990-93; mem. adv. bd. Entergy/Miss., 1994-97, Freedom Forum 1st Amendment Ctr., 1996-2001; mem. Miss. adv. bd. Trustmark Nat. Bank, 1991-97; mem. Mary Baker Eddy Adv. Group, 2000—; mem. Rhodes Scholar selection com. of Miss., 1996-98; mem. Free Sprit Awards selection com., 1996—; mem. ACE Commn. on Women in Higher Edn., 1999—. Mem. editl. bd. Planning for Higher Education, 1995; contbr. articles to profl. jours.; speeches pub. in Vital Speeches; mem. editl. bds. acad. jours. Trustee N.C. Performing Arts Ctr., Charlotte, 1988-89, Charlotte County Day Sch., 1987-89; bd. visitors Johnson C. Smith U., Charlotte, 1985-89; exec. com. bd. dirs. United Way Allocations and Rev., Charlotte, 1982-88; bd. advisors Charlotte Mecklenburg Hosp. Authority, 1985-89; bd. dirs. Jr. Achievement, Charlotte, 1983-89, Miss. Humanities Coun., Miss. Inst. Arts and Letters, Miss. Symphony, Miss. Econ. Coun.; chair Leadership Miss. and Collegiate Miss.; chmn. bd. dirs. Charlotte/Mecklenburg Arts and Sci. Coun., 1987-88; Danforth assoc. Danforth Found., St. Louis, 1976-88, Leadership Am., 1989; mem. golden triangle adv. bd. Bapt. Meml. Hosp., 1999—; pres. So. Univs. Conf., 1994-95; mem. commn. govt. rels. Am. Coun. Edn., 1990-93; mem. alumni bd. First United Meth. Ch., 1996—. Recipient Grad. Made Good award Fla. State U., 1990, medal of excellence Miss. U. for Women, 1995, Women Who Make a Difference award IWF, 2000; named Prof. of Yr., Queens Coll., 1979, One of 10 Most Admired Women Mgrs. in Am., Working Women mag., 1993, One of 1000 Women of the 90's, Mirabella mag., 1994; Ford Found. grantee, 1981; Paul Harris fellow, 1992; OWHE fellow, 1999—. Mem. Am. Assn. State Colls. and Univs. (bd. dirs. 1994-96, 99), Sociol. Soc., So. Assn. Colls. and Schs. (mem. commn. on colls. 1996-98), N.C. Assn. Colls. and Univs. (exec. com. 1988-89), N.C. Assn. Acad. Officers (sec.-treas. 1987-88), Soc. Internat. Bus. Fellows, Miss. Assn. Colls. (pres. 1992), Newcomen Soc. U.S., Internat. Women's Forum, Univ. Club, Rotary. Achievements include 1st female pres. of Miss. U. for Women (1st pub. coll. for women in Am.). Office: Miss State U Social Scis Rsch Ctr PO Box 5287 Mississippi State MS 39762

RENTER, LOIS IRENE HUTSON, librarian; b. Lowden, Iowa, Oct. 23, 1929; d. Thomas E. and Lulu Mae (Barlean) Hutson; m. Karl A. Renter, Jan. 3, 1948; children: Susan Elizabeth, Rebecca Jean, Karl Geoffrey. BA cum laude, Cornell Coll., 1965; MA, U. Iowa, 1968. Tchr. Spanish Mt. Vernon High Sch., 1965-67; head libr. Am. Coll. Testing Program, Iowa City, Iowa, 1968-89, ret., 1989. Vis. instr. U. Iowa Sch. Library Sci., 1972-82. Mem. Phi Beta Kappa. Methodist. Home: 1308 Brendel Hill Dr NW Cedar Rapids IA 52405-1566 E-mail: thisislois@mchsi.com.

RENTERIA, VICTOR MANUEL, secondary school educator; b. Ruidoso, New Mex., May 9, 1948; s. Victor and Ramona Sanchez Renteria. BSEE, Univ. Tex., El Paso, Tex., 1973, student MBA, 1979, MA Indsl. Engring., 1976. Cert. tchg. Tex. Teller El Paso Saving's & Loan, El Paso, Tex., 1975—77; Karate instr. El Paso Pks. & Rec., El Paso, Tex., 1977—92; prodn. & test tech. GUS Mfg., El Paso, Tex., 1977—82; prodn. & test supr. Rockwell Internat., El Paso, Tex., 1983—85; self employed El Paso, Tex., 1985—90; sub. tchr. El Paso Ind. Dist., El Paso, Tex., 1990—92, tchr. math H.S., 1993—. Mem. Tau Kappa Epsilon Alumni Assn., Inpls., 1976—, Univ. Tex. Alumni Assn., El Paso, 1976—; ptnr. U.S. Olympic Team, Colo. Springs, Colo., 1996—, Spl. Olympics, Colo. Springs, Colo., 1996—. Mem.: IEEE, Math. Assn. of Am., Nat. Coun. Tchrs. of Math. Achievements include 4th degree black belt. Avocations: weightlifting, jogging, record collector, rock and roll memorabilia collector. Office: Bowie H S 801 S San Marcial St El Paso TX 79905-4122

RENTON, HOLLINGS C. health products executive; BS Maths., Colo. State U.; MBA, U. Mich. Chmn., pres., CEO Onyx Pharms. Inc., Richmond, Calif., 1992—; pres., COO Chiron Corp., 1991—92, Cetus Corp., 1987—91. Office: Onyx Pharms 3031 Research Dr Richmond CA 94806

RENTOUMIS, ANN MASTROIANNI, psychotherapist; b. New Haven, Apr. 27, 1928; d. Luigi Mastroianni and Marion Dallas; m. George Rentoumis, June 27, 1959; children: Michael, Mary, Anne. BA in Psychology, Vassar Coll., 1949; postgrad., Boston U. Med. Sch., 1949-50; MS in Social Work, Columbia U., 1952. Diplomate Am. Bd. Social Work, Am. Psychotherapy Assn.; lic. cert. social worker; lic. marriage and family therapist. Child and adolescent therapist Bklyn. Psychiat., 1952-55; family therapist Community Svc. Soc., N.Y.C., 1955-58; psychotherapist Bleuler Psychotherapy Ctr., L.I., N.Y., 1958-60, Adolescent Psychiat. Clinic, Tex. Children's Hosp., Houston, 1975-76; pvt. practice Houston, 1976-77, Lauderdale Psychiat. Group, Ft. Lauderdale, Fla., 1978-90, Pompano Beach, Fla., 1990-93, Ft. Lauderdale, 1993—. Bd. dirs. Envirodyne, Inc. Pres. Pine Crest Sch. Mothers Club, 1985-86; v.p. Opera Soc., 1987-88, bd. mem., 1998—, parliamentarian 2000—; bd. govs., v.p. exec. bd. Fla. Philharm Orch., 1988-91, bd. dirs., 1990—; pres. Ft. Lauderdale Philharm. Soc., 1988-90. Recipient Golden Rule award J.C. Penney Co., 1990; named Woman of Yr., Am. Cancer Soc., 1989, Woman of Style and Substance, Ft. Lauderdale Philharm. Soc., 1998. Fellow Am. Psychotherapy Assn., Am. Orthopsychiat. Assn.; mem. Am. Assn. Marriage and Family Therapists, Am. Group Therapy Assn., Harbor Beach Surf Club (v.p. 1986-90). Avocations: piano, tennis, swimming. Home: 2200 S Ocean Ln Ph 6 Fort Lauderdale FL 33316-3836 Office: 1326 SE 3d Ave Fort Lauderdale FL 33316-1260

RENWICK, EDWARD S. lawyer; b. L.A., May 10, 1934; AB, Stanford U., 1956, LLB, 1958. Bar: Calif. 1959, U.S. Dist. Ct. (cen. dist.) Calif. 1959, U.S. Ct. Appeals (9th cir.) 1963, U.S. Dist. Ct. (so. dist.) Calif. 1973, U.S. Dist. Ct. (no. dist.) Calif. 1977, U.S. Dist. Ct. (ea. dist.) Calif. 1981, U.S. Supreme Ct. 1985. Ptnr. Hanna and Morton LLP, L.A. Mem., bd. vis. Stanford Law Sch., 1967-69; mem. environ. and natural resources adv. bd. Stanford Law Sch. bd. dirs. Calif. Supreme Ct. Hist. Soc. Fellow Am. Coll. Trial Lawyers, Am. Bar Found.; mem. ABA (mem. sect. on litigation, antitrust law, bus. law, chmn. sect. of nat. resources, energy and environ. law 1987-88, mem. at large coord. group energy law 1989-92, sect. rep. coord. group energy law 1995-97, Calif. del. legal com., interstate oil compact com.), Calif. Arboretum Assn. (trustee 1986-92), L.A. County Bar Assn. (chmn. natural resources law sect. 1974-75), The State Bar of Calif., Chancery Club (pres. 1992-93), Phi Delta Phi. Office: Hanna and Morton LLP 444 S Flower St Ste 1500 Los Angeles CA 90071-2922 E-mail: erenwick@hanmor.com.

RENWICK, GLENN M. insurance company executive; b. May 22, 1955; Chief info. officer Progressive Casualty Ins. Co., pres., chmn. bd. dirs., CEO, 2000—; CEO ins. ops. Progressive Corp., 2000, pres., CEO, 2001—. Office: Progressive Corp 6300 Wilson Mills Rd Cleveland OH 44143*

RENYI, THOMAS A. bank executive; b. 1946; BA, Rutgers U., 1967, MBA, 1968. With The Bank of N.Y., Inc., 1971—; pres., COO, dir. parent holding co., 1992—; vice chmn., dir. The Bank of N.Y., Inc., 1992-98, chmn., CEO, 1998—. With U.S. Army, 1968-70.

RENZ, CHRISTOPHER DAVID, priest; s. Charles William Renz. PhD, Northwestern U., Chgo., 1986; MA in Theology, Grad. Theol. Union, Berkeley, Calif., 1997; MDiv, Dominican Sch. of Philosophy and Theology, Berkeley, 1997. Pastoral assoc. U. of Oreg. Newman Ctr., Eugene, 1997—99; master of students Western Dominican Province, Oakland, Calif., 1999—. Adj. faculty prof. Dominican Sch. of Philosophy and Theology, Berkeley, Calif., 1999—. Editor: (acad. journal) Ruah: A Journal of Spiritual Poetry. Fellow Postdoctoral Rsch. fellow, NIH, 1988—89, Am. Heart Assn., 1987—88; scholar Domenica Rea scholar, Dominican Sch. of Philosophy and Theology, 1993. Mem.: The Acad. of Am. Poets, Nat. Assn. of Pastoral Musicians, Amnesty Internat. USA. Office: Dominican School of Philosophy & Theolog 2401 Ridge Rd Berkeley CA 94709 E-mail: cjrenzop@yahoo.com.

RENZAGLIA, KAREN A. biologist, educator; PhD, So. Ill. U. Vis. prof. dept. plant biology So. Ill. U., Carbondale. Recipient Edgar T. Wherry award Bot. Soc. Am., 1993, Michael Cichan award Bot. Soc. Am., 1999. Office: So Ill U Dept Plant Biology Mail Code 6509 Carbondale IL 62901-6509

RENZETTI, ATTILIO DAVID, JR., retired physician; b. N.Y.C., Nov. 11, 1920; s. Attilio and Anna (Accardi) R.; m. Mabel Lucille Woodruff, May 24, 1947; children: Patricia Ann, Laurence, Pamela Sorensen, David. AB, Columbia Coll., 1941, MD, 1944. Diplomate: Am. Bd. Internal Medicine (chmn. subsplty. bd. pulmonary disease 1970-72). Intern, resident Bellevue Hosp., N.Y.C., 1944-45, 47-49, 51-52, fellow cardiopulmonary physiology, 1949-51; asst. prof. medicine U. Utah, 1952-53, State U. N.Y., Syracuse, 1953-57; assoc. prof. SUNY, 1957-60; asst. prof. Johns Hopkins U., 1960-61; assoc. prof. U. Md., 1960-61, U. Utah, Salt Lake City, 1961-67, prof., 1967-90, emeritus, 1990—. Editorial bd.: Am. Rev. Respiratory Disease, 1964-67; Contbr. articles to med. jours. Pres. Utah TB and Health Assn., 1965-66; bd. dirs. Am. Lung Assn., 1965-74, 78-81. With M.C. AUS, 1945-47. Mem. Am. Thoracic Soc. (pres. 1975-76) Home and Office: 1801 London Plane Rd Salt Lake City UT 84124-3531

RENZI, RICK, congressman; b. Ft. Monmouth, N.J., June 11, 1958; m. Roberta Renzi; 12 children. BS, No. Ariz. U., 1980; JD, Cath. U., 2001. Small bus. owner; mem. U.S. Ho. Reps. from 1st Ariz. dist., 2003—. Republican. Office: 418 Cannon HOB Washington DC 20515-0301

REOCK, ERNEST C., JR., retired government services educator, academic director; b. Belleville, N.J., Oct. 13, 1924; s. Ernest C. and Helen Rutan (Evans) R.; m. Jeanne Elizabeth Thomason, Jan. 25, 1953; children: Michael, Thomas, Kathleen. BS, Swarthmore Coll., 1945; AB, Rutgers U., 1948, MA, 1950, PhD, 1959. Rsch. assoc. bur. govt. rsch. Rutgers U., New Brunswick, N.J., 1950-59, asst. prof., dir., 1960-63, assoc. prof., dir., 1963-68, prof., dir., 1968-92. Cons. N.J. Constnl. Conv., New Brunswick, 1966, N.J. State and Local Revenue and Expenditure Commns., 1986-88. Author: Handbook for New Jersey Assessors, 1962, School Budget Caps in New Jersey, 1981 (Govtl. Rsch. Assn. award, 1983), Unfinished Business: The New Jersey Constitutional Conv. of 1966, 2003; editor: New Jersey Legislative District Data Book, 1972—92. Chmn. Middlesex County Charter Study Commn., New Brunswick, 1973—74; cons. State Apportionment Commn., 1981, 1991, 2001, various mcpl. charter commns., 1965—2003. Lt. USN, 1943—46, lt. USN, 1951—53. Recipient Gov.'s award for Pub. Svc., 1997. Mem. Am. Soc. Pub. Adminstrn. (Pub. Adminstr. of Yr. 1982), Am. Ednl. Fin. Assn. Avocations: sailing, swimming. Home: 7 Kendall Rd Kendall Park NJ 08824-1010 Office: Rutgers U Ctr Govt Svcs 33 Livingston Ave New Brunswick NJ 08901-1900 Office Phone: 732-932-3640 633.

REPASS, RANDY, electrical company executive; Chmn., CEO West Marine, Watsonville, Calif. Office: West Marine PO Box 50050 500 Westridge Dr Watsonville CA 95077-5050

REPETTI, ANAMARIA, healthcare foundation executive; b. Pasadena, Calif., Oct. 8, 1962; d. Francis Joseph Repetti and Dextra Kay Sharples; m. Gregory Rel Schmitt, Oct. 27, 1990; children: Siena Louise, Maximilian Finn Clyde, Wyatt Francis Gregory. AB, U. Calif., Irvine, 1993. Cmty. rels. rep. U. So. Calif. Sch. Medicine, L.A., 1984-85, asst. editor periodicals, 1985-87; pub. rels. mgr. Huntingon Meml. Hosp., Pasadena, 1987-90; prin., cons. Repetti Comms., Pasadena, 1990-95; dir. pub. rels. ARC San Gabriel Valley, Pasadena, 1995-96; v.p., exec. dir. Palomar Pomerado Health Found., San Diego, 1996—. Cons. ARC, Pasadena, 1994-95, San Diego County Podiatric Med. Soc., 1997-2000, L.A. Soc. Ophthalmology, 1997—, Rsch. Study Club, 2000—. Mem. AAUW, NAFE, Assn. for Healthcare Philanthropy, Nat. Soc. Fundraising Execs. Republican. Roman Catholic. Avocations: running, kayaking, painting, horticulture, reading. Office: Palomar Pomerado Health Found 15255 Innovation Dr San Diego CA 92128 E-mail: axr5@pphs.org.

REPHAN, JACK, lawyer; b. Little Rock, Mar. 16, 1932; s. Henry and Mildred (Frank) R.; m. Arlene Clark, June 23, 1957; children: Amy Carol, James Clark. BS in Commerce, 1954; LLB, U. Va., 1959. Bar: Va. 1959, D.C. 1961. Assoc. Kanter & Kanter, Norfolk, Va., 1959-60; law clk. to Judge Sam E. Whitaker, U.S. Ct. Claims, Washington, 1960-62; assoc. Pierson, Ball & Dowd, Washington, 1962-64; ptnr. Danzansky, Dickey, Tydings, Quint & Gordon, Washington, 1964-77; mem. Braude, Margulies, Sacks & Rephan, Washington, 1977-87; ptnr. Porter, Wright, Morris & Arthur, Washington, 1987-88, Sadur, Pelland & Rubinstein, Washington, 1988-93; counsel Hofheimer Nusbaum P.C., Norfolk, Va., 1993-00; principal Rephan Lassiter PLC, Norfolk, 2001—. Mem. Nat. Panel Arbitrators Am. Arbitration Assn., Nat. Panel Mediators Am. Arbitration Assn., NASD Bd. Arbitrators; lectr. joint com. continuing legal edn. State Bar Va. Contbr. articles to legal jours. Pres. Patrick Henry PTA, Alexandria, Va., 1968-69, Linkhorn Bay Condominium Assn., 2000—; treas. John Adams Mid. Sch. PTA, Alexandria, 1970-71; pres. Seminary Ridge Citizens Assn., 1976-77; Dem. candidate for Alexandria City Com., 1969. 1st lt. AUS, 1955-57. Mem. ABA (chmn. subcom. on procurement of jud. remedies pub. contract sect. 1973-74), Va. Bar Assn. (govt. sect. constrn. law 1979-81, 99—, vice chmn. 1980-81, chmn. 1981-82), D.C. Bar Assn., Assoc. Gen. Contractors, Hampton Roads Utility and Heavy Contractors Assn. (gen. counsel), Cavalier Golf and Yacht Club, Kiwanis (pres. Landmark Club 1969). Jewish. Home: 1276 Laskin Rd Ste 402 Virginia Beach VA 23451-5272 Office: 500 E Main St Ste 1200 Norfolk VA 23510 Office Phone: 757-274-0045. Business E-Mail: jrephan@rephanlassiter.com.

REPINE, JOHN EDWARD, internist, educator; b. Rock Island, Ill., Dec. 26, 1944; married, 1969, 88; 6 children. BS, U. Wis., 1967; MD, U. Minn., 1971. Instr., then assoc. prof. internal medicine U. Minn., Mpls., 1974-79; asst. dir divsn. exptl. medicine Webb-Waring Inst. Biomedical Rsch., Denver, 1979-89; prof. medicine, pres. and dir. Webb-Waring Inst. Cancer, Aging & Antioxidant Rsch., Denver, 1989—; prof. medicine U. Colo., Denver, 1979—, James J. Waring prof. medicine, 1996—, prof. pediatrics, 1981-96. Mem. rsch. com., co-chmn. steering com. Aspen Lung Conf., 1980, chmn., 1981; assoc. dean for student advocacy Nat. Heart and Lung Inst., 1990—. Young Pulmonary Investigator grantee Nat. Heart & Lung Inst., 1974-75; recipient Basil O'Connor Starter Rsch. award Nat. Found. March of Dimes, 1975-77. Mem. AAAS, Am. Assn. Immunologists, Am. Soc. Clin. Investigation, Am. Heart Assn. (established investigator award 1976-81), Am. Thoracic Soc., Assn. Am. Physicians. Achievements include research in role of phagocytes and oxygen radicals in lung injury and host defense (ARDS). Office: Webb Waring Inst Cancer Aging & Antioxidant Rsch Box C322 4200 E 9th Ave Denver CO 80220-3706

REPLOGLE, DAVID ROBERT, publishing company executive; b. Chgo., Feb. 24, 1931; s. Homer Mock and Helen (Fluke) R.; m. Jeanne Lonnquist, Nov. 4, 1954; children: William T., Bruce R., Stewart D., James M., John B. AB, Dartmouth Coll., 1953; postgrad., Princeton U., 1957-58. V.p., gen. mgr. Doubleday & Co., Inc., N.Y.C., 1958-70; pres., chmn. bd. G. & C. Merriam Co., Springfield, Mass., 1970-75; pres. Praeger Publishers, N.Y.C., 1970-75; exec. v.p., dir. Houghton Mifflin Co., Boston, 1975-91; pres. DR&A Inc., Cohasset, Mass., 1992—; pres., publ. Hot House Press, Cohasset. Dir. L.I. Replogle Found., Chgo., 1982—; trustee South Shore Health and Ednl. Found, 2000—. Served to lt. USNR, 1953-57. Mem. Cohasset Golf Club, Plantation Golf and Country Club. Home: 84 Gammons Rd Cohasset MA 02025-1406 Office: David Replogle & Assocs 760 CJ Cushing Hwy Cohasset MA 02025-2124 E-mail: drreplogle@aol.com.

REPLOGLE, MICHAEL A. civil engineer, urban planner, environmentalist; b. Gt. Lakes, Ill., Dec. 28, 1953; s. Fred W. and Wilma E. (Furhman) R.; m. Linda Frazee Baker, June 6, 1986. BA in Sociology cum laude, BSE in Civil & Urban Engring. cum laude, MSE in Civil & Urban Engring., U. Pa., 1978. USPHS officer U.S. Indian Health Svc., Kayenta, Ariz., 1978; rsch. assoc. Pub. Tech. Inc., Washington, 1979-82; transp. coord. for Montgomery County Nat. Capital Park and Planning Commn., Silver Spring, Md., 1983-92; transp. dir. Environ. Def., Washington, 1992—. Cons. World Bank, U.S. Fed. Hwy. Adminstrn., 1990-92. Author: Bicycles and Public Transportation, 1983, Transportation Conformity and Demand Management, 1993; contbr. articles to profl. jours. Nat. coord., founder, Bikes Not Bombs Campaign, Washington, 1984-89; mem. steering com. Campaign for New Transp. Priorities, Washington, 1989-92, Surface Transp. Policy Project, 1995—; founder, treas. Clean Air and Transp., Washington, 2000—. Mem. Inst. for Transp. Devel. Policy (founder, pres. 1985-92, 2000—, bd. dirs. 1992-2000), ITDP Europe/SUSTRANS. Office: Environ Def 1875 Connecticut Ave NW Washington DC 20009-5728 E-mail: mreplogle@environmentaldefense.org.

REPLOGLE, ROBERT LEE, cardiovascular and thoracic surgeon; b. Ottumwa, Iowa, Sept. 30, 1931; s. Ralph Ruby and Edith Dorothy (Swartz) R.; m. Carol A. Heeschen, Aug. 24, 1958; children: Robert E., Jennifer Bremer, Edith Sheffer. MD cum laude, Harvard U., 1960; DSc (hon.), Cornell Coll., 1972. Diplomate Am. Bd. Surgery, Am. Bd. Thoracic Surgery, Am. Bd. Pediat. Surgery. Intern in surgery U. Minn. Hosp., 1960-61; asst. resident in surgery Peter Bent Brigham Hosp., Boston, 1961-63, Mass. Gen. Hosp., Boston, 1965-66; sr. resident in surgery Children's Hosp. Med. Ctr., Boston, 1966; asst. in surgery Children's Hosp. Med. Ctr. and Harvard Med. Sch., Boston, 1966-67; asst. prof. surgery Pritzker Sch. Medicine U. Chgo., 1967-70, assoc. prof. surgery and head, sect. pediat. surgery, 1970-73, prof. surgery and head, sect. pediat. surgery, 1973-74, prof. surgery and head, sect. cardiac surgery, 1973-80, prof. surgery, sect. cardiac surgery, 1973-90; med. dir. cardiac surgery unit Ingalls Meml. Hosp., 1989-98; chief divsn. cardiac surgery Columbus Hosp., Chgo., 1987-97; pres. CTS Net Inc., Chgo., 1998—. Vis. prof. Albany Med. Coll., 1974, Dalhousie Sch. of Medicine, Halifax, 1975, Walter Reed Army Med. Ctr., 1978, U. Miami Med. Sch., 1992, Philippine Heart Ctr. for Asia March, 1979, Health Inst. Japan, Tokyo, 1982, Creighton Med. Sch., 1988, Brooke Army Med. Ctr., 1993, U. Heidelberg, 1995, Kerkoff Clinic/Max Planct Inst., Bad Nanheim, Germany, 1995, German Heart Ctr., Munich, 1995, Peter Bent Brigham Hosp. Harvard Med. Sch., 1996; mem. surgery and bioengrig. study sect. HHS, NIH, 1979-83; mem. ad hoc adv. com. bypass angioplasty revascularization investigation, NIH, 1993-94; mem. subcom. on quality N.Y. State Dept. Health, 1989-96, mem. subcom. on resources and facilities, 1993—, mem. cardiac adv. com., 1989—; pres. Ctsnet.org, Inc., 1999—. Author: (with others) Microcirculation, Perfusion, and Transplantation of Organs, 1970, The Critically Ill Child, 1972, Surgical Clinics in North America, 1976, Biprosthetic Cardiac Valves, 1979, Year Book of Nuclear Medicine, 1981, among others; mem. editl. bd. Jour. Cardiac Surgery, 1982-99; contbr. more than 125 articles to profl. jours. With USN, 1951-54. Recipient Merit award Philippine Heart ctr. for Asia, Manila, 1985, Friendship award Shanghai Chest Hosp., 1987. Mem. AMA (diagnostic and therapeutic tech. assessment panel 1995—, ho. of dels. 1992—, joint rev. com. on ednl. programs for physicians assts. 1979-84), ACS (com. on allied health pers. 1979-84, chmn. 1983-84, com. on med. motion pictures 1979-85, com. on membership 1988—, residency rev. com. for thoracic surgery of the accreditation com. for grad. med. edn. 1992-95, 96—), Ill. State Med. Soc., Chgo. Med. Soc., Am. Surg. Assn., European Assn. for Cardiothoracic Surgery, Soc. for Acad. Surgery, Am. Heart Assn. (adv. com. cardiovasc. surgery 1968-71), Soc. Univ. Surgeons, Internat. Cardiovasc. Soc., Societe Internationale de Chirurgie (N.Am. chpt.), Am. Assn. for Thoracic Surgery (del. AMA 1992—, com. on soc. responsibility 1991—), Soc. Thoracic Surgeons (program com. 1978-81, chmn. 1981, com. on medico-legal affairs, chmn. 1985-88, ad hoc fin. adv. com. 1987-89, ad hoc exhibitors adv. com. 1988-89, ad hoc com. on social responsibility 1992-95, ad hoc database liaison com. 1993-94, database liaison com. 1994—, ad hoc com. on physician-specific mortality for cardiac surgery 1993-96, stds. and ethics com. 1984-88, treas. 1986-92, exec. com. 1986—, pres.-elect. 1995-96, pres. 1996-97, rep. to the coun. of med. specialty socs. 1990—, annals of thoracic surgery liaison com. 1992—, com. on grad. edn. in thoracic surgery 1992—, com. on major

issues in thoracic surgery 1993, chmn. 1994, 95, pres.-elect coun. med. splty. socs. 1997-98, pres. coun. med. specialty socs. 1998-99), Coun. of Med. Specialty Socs., German Cardiac Surgery Soc. (hon. mem.). Avocations: wine collecting, photography, travel. Address: CTS Net Inc 1160 E 56th St Chicago IL 60637-1541

REPP, JOAN MERCEDES, retired librarian; b. N.Y.C., Oct. 24, 1930; d. Paul Francis and Anna Crescentia (Stock) McIntyre; m. Victor E. Repp, Sept. 3, 1949; children: Anna, James. BS, State Tchrs. Coll., Oswego, N.Y., 1951; MEd, U. Md., 1954; AMLS, U. Mich., 1974. Cert. elem. educator. Tchr. Arlington County (Va.) Schs., 1951-57, Perrysburg (Ohio) Pub. Schs., 1968-69; from instr. English and libr. to head cataloging dept. Bowling Green (Ohio) State U., 1972-82, chmn. access svc., 1983-87, dir. access svcs., 1987-91; ret., 1991. Cons. State Libr. Ohio, Columbus, 1980—83, Ohionet Instrn. and Tng. Coun., 1983—87; workshop dir. N.W. Libr. Dist., North Ctrl. Libr. Consortium, Ohio Ednl. Libr. and Media Assn., Dade County Libr. Assn., 1984, 577 Foundation, Perrysburg, Ohio, 1998; mem. Ohio Libr. Info. Sys./Ohio Bd. Regents, 1988—91. Contbr. articles to profl. jours. Svc. unit dir. Girl Scouts Am., Toledo, 1963—67; mem. Environ. Health Coun. Ohio and Mich., 1964; cons. Ronald McDonald House, Toledo, 1987; docent Toledo Zoo, 1998—; trustee Maumee Sch. Found., 2000—, Victor E. Repp Charitable Trust, 2000—. Mem. AAUP, ALA, Acad. Libr. Assn. Ohio, Assn. Coll. and Rsch. Librs., Libr. Adminstrn. and Mgmt. Assn., Resources and Tech. Svcs. Assn., Mensa, Beta Phi Mu, Kappa Delta Pi.

REPP, RONALD STEWART, insurance company executive; b. Phila., Dec. 12, 1944; s. Carl George Jr. and Pauline Francis (Hunley) R.; m. Nancy Elaine Hannigan, Sept. 16, 1967; children: Christopher Robert, Justin Ronald. Grad. high sch., Pitts.; cert., Am. Coll., Bryn Mawr, Pa., 1973, Am. Inst., Malvern, Pa., 1977. CLU, CPCU, assoc. in risk mgmt. Adminstr. Liberty Mut. Ins. Group, Pitts., 1963-65, sales rep., 1967-70, sales supr., 1970-72, sales mgr., 1972-78; spl. agt. The Prudential, Pitts., 1966-67; account exec. Ind. Ins. Svc. Corp., Canton, Ohio, 1978-83, v.p., 1983-90, sr.v.p., 1990—. Mem. adv. bd. dirs. Silver Lake Estates. Contbr. articles to profl. jours. Staff sgt. U.S. Army, 1964-65. Mem. Soc. CPCUs, Soc. CLUs, Ind. Ins. Agts. Assn., Akron City Club (chmn. mem. com. 1992-94), Bay Point Yacht Club, Akron Cruising Club (commodore), Silver Lake Country Club. Lutheran. Avocations: sailing (coast guard captain, masters license). Home: 3103 Silver Lake Blvd Silver Lake OH 44224-3130 Office: Ind Ins Svc Corp 200 Market Ave N Ste 100 Canton OH 44702 E-mail: rrepp@schauergroup.com.

REPPERT, NANCY LUE, retired municipal official, legal consultant; b. Kansas City, Mo., June 17, 1933; d. James Everett and Iris R. (Moomey) Moore; m. James E. Cassidy, 1952 (div.); children: James E., II, Tracy C. Student, Ctrl. Mo. State U., 1951-52, U. Mo., Kansas City, 1971-75; cert. legal asst., Rockhurst Coll., Kansas City, 1980, cert. risk mgr., 1979. With Kansas City chpt. ARC, 1952-54, N. Ctrl. Region Boy Scouts Am., 1963-66, Clay County Health Dept., Liberty, Mo., 1966-71, city of Liberty, 1971-80; risk mgr. City of Dallas, 1982-83; dir. Dept. Risk Mgmt., Pinellas County, Fla., 1984-94; ind. legal cons. Cedar Rapids, Iowa, 1994—. Mem. faculty William Jewell Coll., Liberty, 1975-80; vis. prof., U. Kans., 1981; adj. prof. dept. polit. sci. masters program, U. South Fla., 1990; seminar leader, cons. in field. Author: Kids are People, Too, 1975, Pearls of Potentiality, 1980; also contbr. articles to publs. Lay min., United Meth. Ch., 1965—; dir. youth devel., Hillside United Meth. Ch., Liberty; co-chmn. youth dir. Collegiate United Meth. Ch. scouting coord. Palm Lake Christian Ch., Exec. Fellow U. South Fla., mem. Coun. Ministries; advancement chmn. Mid-Iowa Coun. Boy Scouts Am., membership chmn. White Rock Dist. Coun., health and safety chmn. West Ctrl. Fla. Coun., 1985—; scouting coord., chmn. youth dept., bd. dirs., pastor's cabinet, diaconate Palm Lake Christian Ch., 1987—; skipper Sea Explorer ship, 1986—; bd. dirs. Neighborly Sr. Svcs., Inc.; vol. sailing master, instr., Boys & Girls Clubs and Hawkeye Coun. Boy Scouts Am., Cedar Rapids. Recipient Order of Merit, Boy Scouts Am., 1979, Living Sculpture award, 1978, 79; Svc. award Rotary Internat., 1979; Internat. awrd of Merit/Leadership Excellence, IBA, 1992; Exec. fellow, U. South Fla., 1988. Mem. NAFE, Am. Mgmt. Assns., Internat. Platform Assn., Risk Mgrs. Soc., Pub. Risk & Ins. Mgmt. Assn., Am. Soc. Profl. & Exec. Women, Am. Film Inst., U.s. Naval Inst., Nat. Inst. Mcpl. Law Officers. Home: 257 38th Street Dr SE Apt 8 Cedar Rapids IA 52403-1116 E-mail: windsongsailor@netzero.com.

REPPERT, RICHARD LEVI, lawyer; b. Phila., Nov. 6, 1948; s. William Downing and Angela R. (Schmid) R.; m. Faith Simpson, Dec. 30, 1972 (div. Aug. 1992); 1 child, Richard Jacob; m. Jeanette T. deHaven, Apr. 10, 1994. BA, Lehigh U., 1970; JD, Villanova U., 1974. Bar: Ohio 1974, U.S. Dist. Ct. (no. dist.) Ohio 1974, Pa. 1993. Assoc. Thompson, Hine and Flory, Cleve., 1974-82, ptnr., 1982-89, Jones Day, Cleve., 1989—. Mem. ABA, Am. Coll. Real Estate Lawyers, Ohio State Bar Assn., Cleve. Bar Assn. Office: Jones Day North Point 901 Lakeside Ave Cleveland OH 44114-1190 E-mail: rreppert@jonesday.com.

REPPERT, STEVEN MARION, pediatrician, scientist, educator; b. Sioux City, Iowa, Sept. 4, 1946; s. Ray Fred and Norma Grace (Coppock) R.; m. Mary Alice Herman, Dec. 28, 1968; children: Jason Steven, Katherine Mary, Christina Marie. BS, U. Nebr., Lincoln, 1973; MD with distinction, U. Nebr., Omaha, 1973; MA (hon.), Harvard U., 1993. Diplomate Nat. Bd. Med. Examiners. Intern Mass. Gen. Hosp., Boston, 1973-74, resident in pediatrics, 1974-76, asst. in pediatrics, 1979-80, asst. pediatrician, 1980-85, dir .lab devel. chronobiology, 1983-2001, assoc. pediatrician, 1985-2000, pediatrician, 2000-2001. Clin. assoc. NIH, Bethesda, Md., 1976-79; instr. pediatrics Harvard Med. Sch., Boston, 1979-81, asst. prof., 1981-85, assoc. prof., 1985-93, prof., 1993—, Higgins family prof. neurosci., 2001—; vis. scientist Lab. Molecular Neurobiology, Mass. Gen. Hosp., 1989-90; prof., chair dept. neurobiology U. Mass. Med. Sch., 2001—. Editor: Development of Circadian Rhythmicity and Photoperiodism in Mammals, 1989; co-editor: Suprachiasmatic Nucleus: The Mind's Clock, 1991; mem. editl. bd. Neuron, 1997—; contbr. articles to sci. jours., chpt. to books. Mem. adv. com. Charles H. Hood Found., 1993-98. Recipient E. Mead Johnson award, 1989, NIH Merit award, 1992; Regents scholar U. nebr., 1971; Pfizer Labs. Med. scholar, 1971; Charles King Trust rsch. fellow, 1981-83; grantee NIH, 1981—, Nat. Found./March of Dimes, 1981-88. Mem. Am. Pediatric Soc., Am. Physiol. Soc., Am. Soc. for Clin. Investigation, Endocrine Soc., Soc. for Pediatric Rsch., Soc. for Neurosci., Soc. for Rsch. on Biol. Rhythms (adv. com.), Am. Heart Assn. (established investigator 1985-90), Lepidopterists Soc., Cambridge Entomol. Club, Alpha Omega Alpha. Democrat. Office: Mass Gen Hosp 32 Fruit St Boston MA 02114-2620

REQUENO, NESTOR DANILO, human services administrator; b. San Salvador, El Salvador, 1964; came to U.S., 1979; s. Humberto and Maria Elodia R.; m. Raquel, 1988. AA in Liberal Arts, East L.A. Coll., 1993; BS in Pub. Adminstrn. summa cum laude, Calif. State U., 1997, MPA, 2003. Real estate and retail entrepreneur/broker Bell, Calif., 1988—; social svcs. worker L.A. County Dept. Social Svcs., Rancho Dominguez, Calif., 1991-95, job developer, cons. South L.A. County, 1995-98, lead analyst City of Industry, Calif., 1998, strategic planner, 1999—2002; dir. intergovtl. and interagy. rels. City of Industry, Calif., 2002—03, adminstr. intergovtl. and interagy. rels., 2002—03, legis. cons., 2003—. Cons., mem. adv. bd. Super Job Fair Com., Carson, Calif., 1997-98; exec. dir. Transp. and Human Svc. Exec. Coun., 1999-2001. Author: Cash Assistance Program for Immigrants Implementation and Resource Guide, 1998 (Spl. Commendation award), speech and written testimony U.S. Ho. of Reps., 1998; author, designer: General Relief Opportuities for Work Program Interactive On-line Policy Manual: A "Killer App": to implement digital strategies and welfare-to-work best-practices for masses of users via L.A. County Info. Web. (Spl. Commendation award). Pub. rels. dir. 7th Day Adventist Spanish Ch., Huntington Park, Calif., 1986, missionary outreach dir., 1987; vol. U.S. Citizenship Action Network, L.A. County, 1996-98, City of L.A. Marathon, 1995-2000. Recipient The Pub. Social Svcs. Partnerships in Excellence award. Mem. Am. Soc. Pub. Adminstrn., L.A. County Hispanic Mgrs. Assn., Am. Inst. Certified Pub. Acct., Pub. Adminstrn. Alumni Soc. (adv. bd. 1997—), Pi Alpha Alpha, Phi Kappa Phi. Avocations: public speaking, volunteerism, fundraising, mentoring, hiking. Home: 1148 N Chicago St Apt 8 Los Angeles CA 90033-1471 Office: LA County Dept Pub Social Svcs 12860 Crossroads Pkwy S City Of Industry CA 91746-3411 Mailing: PO Box 86127 Los Angeles CA 90086-0127 E-mail: nrequeno@ladpss.org.

RESCH, CHARLOTTE SUSANNA, plastic surgeon; b. Charlottesville, Va., Sept. 24, 1957; d. Johann Heinrich and Eleonore Susanne (Stenzel) R.; m. John Arthur Niero, Jan. 31, 1990. Student, Dalhousie U., Halifax, Nova Scotia, Can., 1974-76; MD with distinction, Dalhousie U. Med. Sch., Halifax, Nova Scotia, Can., 1980. Diplomate Dalhousie U., Am. Bd. Plastic Surgery; licentiate Med. Coun. Can.; cert. Bd. Med. Quality Assurance Calif. Intern Ottawa Gen. Hosp., Ont., Can., 1980-81; gen. surgery resident Dalhousie U., Halifax, Nova Scotia, Can., 1981-85; plastic surgery resident Wayne State U., Detroit, 1985-87; pvt. practice San Francisco, 1988-89; pre-ptnr. Southern Calif. Permanente Physicians Group, Fontana, 1989-92, ptnr., 1992—. Contbr. articles to profl. jours. Fellow ACS; mem. Am. Soc. Plastic and Reconstructive Surgeons, Calif. Med. Soc., San Bernardino Med. Soc., Alpha Omega Alpha. Avocations: travel, skiing, bicycling, gardening, gourmet cooking. Office: Kaiser Found Hosp Dept Plastic Surgery 9985 Sierra Ave Fontana CA 92335-6720

RESCH, EDWARD J. corporate financial executive; BS, Lehigh U.; MBA, Rutgers U. Sr. positions Salomon Brothers Inc., Price Waterhouse, Procter & Gamble; CFO, capital markets group Donaldson, Lufkin & Jenrette, Inc., mng. dir., chief acctg. officer; mng. dir., CFO Pershing; exec. v.p., CFO State Street Corp., Boston, 2002—. Office: State Street Corp 225 Franklin St Boston MA 02110

RESCH, JOSEPH ANTHONY, neurologist; b. Milw., Apr. 29, 1914; s. Frank and Elizabeth (Zetsch) R.; m. Rose Catherine Ritz, May 25, 1939; children— Rose, Frank, Catherine. Student, Milw. State Tchrs. Coll., 1931-34; BS, U. Wis., Madison, 1936, MD, 1938. Intern St. Francis Hosp., LaCrosse, Wis., 1938-39; gen. practice medicine Holmen, Wis., 1939-40; med. fellow in neurology U. Minn., 1946-48, clin. instr. neurology, 1948-51, clin. asst. prof., 1951-55, clin. assoc. prof., 1955-62, assoc. prof., 1962-65, prof., 1965-84, prof. emeritus, 1984—, head dept. neurology, 1976-82, asst. v.p. health sci., 1970-79, prof. lab. medicine and pathology, 1979-84; practice medicine specializing in neurology Mpls., 1948-62. Contbr. articles and abstracts to profl. jours., chpts. to books. Served to lt. col. M.C. U.S. Army, 1940-46; col. Med. Res. 1946-53. Mem. Hennepin County Med. Soc., Minn. Med. Assn., AMA, Minn. Soc. Neurol. Scis., Am. Acad. Neurology, Am. Neurol. Assn., Am. Assn. Neuropathologists, Am. Clin. Neurophysiol. Soc., Am. Epilepsy Soc. Home: 1609 Pleasant St Apt 307 Lauderdale MN 55108

RESCH, MARY LOUISE, town agency administrator; b. David City, Nebr., Oct. 26, 1956; d. Ernest John and Mary Jean (Roelandts) Cermak. BS in Psychology, SUNY, Albany, 1984; MS in Counseling and Edn. with high honors, U. Wis., Platteville, 1986. Enlisted U.S. Army, 1974, advance through ranks to sgt., 1982, bomb disposal tech., 1977-79, bomb disposal instr. Indian Head, Md., 1979-80, resigned, 1985; instr., intern family advocacy Army Community Svc., U.S. Army, Ft. Belvoir, 1986; sr. counselor, child therapist Community Crisis and Referral Ctr., Inc., Waldorf, Md., 1986-87; adminstr. Walter Reed Army Med. Ctr. USDA Grad. Sch., Washington, 1987-88, contract mgr. Ft. Jackson, S.C., 1988-91; pres. Athena Cons., Columbia, S.C., 1991-93; dir. spl. programs Newberry (S.C.) Commn. on Alcohol and Drug Abuse, 1993-95; resource devel. coord. Cities in Schs.-SC, Inc., Columbia, 1995-97; exec. dir. S.C. Ctr. for Family Policy, Columbia, 1997—2001; pub. rels. dir. Xpress Group, Inc., 2001—02; resource devel. specialist Town of Lexington, SC, 2002—. Human svcs. cons., Washington, 1986-87; adj. instr. Coker Coll., Ft. Jackson, 1989-95. Active Govs. Juvenile Justice Adv. Coun., Govs. Substance Abuse Prevention Coun.; amb. Greater Lexington C. of C. Mem. S.C. Assn. Prevention Profls. and Advs., State Assn. Crime Prevention Officers, Nat. Contract Mgmt. Assn. (fellow, former pres., mentor). Republican. Lutheran. Avocations: needlepoint, racquetball, reading, bowling, jewelry making. Home: 312 Edgewater Ln West Columbia SC 29169-6957 Office: Town of Lexington 111 Maiden Lane Lexington SC 29072 Office Phone: 803-356-8238. E-mail: mresch@lexsc.com.

RESCH, RITA MARIE, music educator; b. Minot, N.D., Dec. 26, 1936; d. Clement Charles and Magdalena Marie (Zeltinger) Resch. BS in Edn., Minot State U., 1957; MM in Music Lit., Eastman Sch. Music, Rochester, N.Y., 1960; MA in English Lit., U. N.D., 1967; MFA in Voice, U. Iowa, 1973, DMA in Piano Chamber Music/Accompanying, 1974. Music tchr. (vocal) Biwabik Sch. Dist., Minn., 1957—58, S. Redford Twp., Detroit, 1958—59; instr. music Fontbonne Coll., St. Louis, 1960—63; asst. prof. music Wis. State U., Stevens Point, 1965—68, Ctrl. Mo. State U., Warrensburg, 1974—79, assoc. prof., 1979—89, full prof., 1989—. Adjudicator for vocal music Mo. State High Sch. Activities Assn., Columbia, Kans. State High Sch. Activities Assn., Topeka, other orgns., 1976—. Author (with Judith E. Carman, William K. Gaeddert, Gordon Myers): Art Song in the United States: An Annotated Bibliography, 1976, 2001. Assoc. organist Sacred Heart Cath. Ch., Warrensburg, 1980—. Mem.: Mo. Music Tchrs. Assn. (v.p. auditions 1995—98), Music Tchrs. Nat. Assn., Nat. Assn. Tchrs. Singing. Office: Ctrl Mo State U Dept Music Warrensburg MO 64093 E-mail: resch@cmsul.cmsu.edu.

RESCHER, NICHOLAS, philosopher, author, educator; b. Hagen, Westphalia, Germany, July 15, 1928; came to U.S., 1938, naturalized, 1944; s. Erwin Hans and Meta Anna (Landau) R.; m. Dorothy Henle, Feb. 10, 1968; children: Mark, Owen, Catherine; 1 child from previous marriage, Elizabeth. BS in Math., Queens Coll., 1949; PhD, Princeton U., 1951; LHD (hon.), Loyola U., Chgo., 1970, Lehigh U., 1993; Dr. honoris causa (hon.), U. Córdoba, Argentina, 1992, U. Constance, Germany, 1995; DS (hon.), CUNY, 1999; PhD (hon.), Fern U., Hagen, 2001. Instr. philosophy Princeton (N.J.) U., 1951-52; mathematician RAND Corp., 1954-56; assoc. prof. philosophy Lehigh U., Bethlehem, Pa., 1957-61; univ. prof. philosophy U. Pitts., 1961—, vice chmn. Ctr. for Philosophy of Sci., 1988. Trustee St. Edmunds Acad., Pitts., 1980-85; nonresident mem. Corpus Christi Coll., Oxford; disting. vis. lectr. Oxford, Salamanca, Munich, Konstanz; cons. in field. Author: The Coherence Theory of Truth, 1973, Methodological Pragmatism, 1977, Scientific Progress, 1978, The Limits of Science, 1985, Luck, 1995, Predicting the Future, 1997, Complexity, 1998, Nature and Understanding, 2000, Paradises, 2000, Philosophical Reasoning, 2001; exec. editor Am. Philos. Quar., 1961—; mem. editl. bd. 15 jours.; contbr. over 250 articles to profl. jours. Sec. gen. Internat. Union History and Philosophy of Sci., UNESCO, 1969-75. With USMC, 1952-54. Recipient Alexander von Humboldt Humanities prize, 1983; fellow Ford Found., 1959-60, Guggenheim Found., 1970-71. Mem. Am. Philos. Assn. (past pres.), Am. Cath. Philos. Assn. (past pres.), Am. Metaphys. Soc. (past pres.), Royal Asiatic Soc., G.W. Leibniz Soc. Am. (past pres.), C.S. Peirce Soc. (past pres.), Inst. Internat. de Philosophie, Academie Internat. de Philosophie des Scis., Acad. Europaea. Roman Catholic. Avocation: reading history and biography. Home: 5818 Aylesboro Ave Pittsburgh PA 15217-1446 Office: Univ of Pitts Dept Philosophy 1012 Cathedral Pittsburgh PA 15260 Business E-Mail: rescher@pitt.edu.

RESCHKE, MICHAEL W. real estate executive; b. Chgo., Nov. 29, 1955; s. Don J. and Vera R. (Helmer) R.; m. Kim P. Shaw, July 17, 1977; children: Michael W. Jr., Tiffanie G., Taylor N. BS summa cum laude with univ. honors, No. Ill. U., 1977; JD summa cum laude, U. Ill., 1980. Bar: Ill. 1980; CPA, Ill. Assoc. Winston & Strawn, Chgo., 1980-82; also chmn. bd. dirs. The Prime Group, Inc., Chgo., 1981—, pres., CEO, 1982—. Trustee Prime Retail, Inc., Prime Group Realty Trust. Mem. Chgo. Devel. Coun., 1987—. Mem. ABA, Ill. Bar Assn., Urban Land Inst., Chgo. Econ. Club, Real Estate Roundtable (dir.), Order of Coif, Phi Delta Phi, Beta Alpha Psi.

RESCHLY, DANIEL J. education educator, psychologist; b. Wayland, Iowa, Dec. 30, 1943; married; 3 children. BS, Iowa State U., 1966; MA, U. Iowa, 1968; PhD, U. Oreg., 1971. Lic. sch. psychologist Iowa, Oreg., Ariz.; nat. cert. sch. psychologist, cert. secondary edn. educator Iowa. Sch. psychologist Louisa County Schs., Wapello, Iowa, 1967—69; dir. summer head start program Louisa County, Iowa, 1969; sch. psychology intern Albina Youth Opportunity Ctr. and Portland (Oreg.) Pub. Schs., 1970—71; asst. prof. U. Ariz., Tucson, 1971—75; assoc. prof., prof., disting. prof., dir. Sch. Psychology Program Iowa State U., 1975—98, interim assoc. dean Coll. Edn., 1996—98, dir. Rsch. Inst. for Studies in Edn., 1996—98; prof. edn. and psychology, chair dept. spl. edn. Vanderbilt U., Nashville, 1998—. Presenter in field. Contbr. chapters to books, articles to profl. jours. Fellow: APA, Am. Psychol. Soc.; mem.: Tenn. Assn. Sch. Psychologists, Internat. Sch. Psychology Assn., Am. Assn. Applied and Preventive Psychology, Coun. for Exceptional Children, Am. Assn. on Mental Retardation, Am. Ednl. Rsch. Assn., Iowa Acad. Edn. (charter), Nat. Assn. Sch. Psychologists (pres., editor Sch. Psychology Rev., chair grad. program approval, Lifetime Achievement award, three Disting. Svc. awards). Office: Vanderbilt Univ Box 328 Peabody Coll Nashville TN 37203-5701

RESCIGNO, RICHARD JOSEPH, editor; b. N.Y.C., Apr. 13, 1946; s. Vincent James and Rose (Sofia) R.; m. Carol Sue Conyne, Apr. 22, 1978; children: Timothy, Daniel. BA in English Lit., Fairleigh Dickinson U., 1967; MS in Journalism, Columbia U., 1968. Reporter The Hudson Dispatch, Union City, N.J., 1967; reporter, copy editor The Bergen Record, Hackensack, N.J., 1971-75; reporter, copy editor, asst. city editor Newsday, Melville, N.Y., 1975-81; news editor, asst. mng. editor, mng. editor Barron's, The Dow Jones Bus. and Fin. Weekly, N.Y.C., 1981—, mng. editor, 1987—. With U.S. Army, 1968-70. Avocations: foreign languages, travel, sports. Office: Barron's 200 Liberty St New York NY 10281-1003

RESCOE, MICHAEL E. computer company executive; b. 1953; BA, Tulane U.; MBA, U. Tex. Sr. v.p. corp. fin. Kidder, Peabody & Co.; sr. mng. dir. Bear, Stearns & Co. Inc.; CFO, ENSERCH Corp., Dallas, until 1997; sr. v.p., CFO, PG&E Corp., San Francisco, from 1997; now v.p. fin. 3Com Corp., Santa Clara, Calif. Office: 3Com Corp PO Box 58145 Santa Clara CA 95052

RESCORLA, ROBERT ARTHUR, psychology educator; b. Pitts, May 9, 1940; s. Arthur R. and Mildred J. (Jenkins) Rescorla; m. Shirley Steele; children: Eric, Michael. BA, Swarthmore Coll., 1962; PhD, U. Pa., 1966; MA, Yale U., 1974. Successively asst. prof., assoc. prof., prof. Yale U., New Haven, 1966—80; prof. psychology U. Pa., Phila., 1981—, James Skinner prof. sci., 1986—2000, Christopher Browne disting. prof. psychology, 2000—, dean of coll. Sch. Arts and Scis., 1994—97. Author: Pavlovian Second-Order Conditioning, 1980; editor: Animal Learning and Behavior, 1995—97; contbr. articles to profl. jours. Recipient Ira Abrams Tchg. award, 1999. Mem.: AAAS (pres. sect. J., psychology 1988—89), NAS, APA (pres. divsn. 3 1985, Disting. Sci.Contbn. award 1986), Psychonomic Soc. (mem. governing bd. 1979—85, chmn. publ. bd. 1985—86), Ea. Psychol. Assn. (bd. dirs. 1983—86, pres. 1986—87), Soc. Exptl. Psychologists, Am. Psychol. Soc. (William James fellow). Office: U Pa Dept Psychology 3815 Walnut St Philadelphia PA 19104-3604

RESEK, ROBERT WILLIAM, economist; b. Berwyn, Ill., July 2, 1935; s. Ephraim Frederick and Ruth Elizabeth (Rummele) R.; m. Lois Doll, July 9, 1960; 1 child, Richard Alden. BA, U. Ill., 1957; AM, Harvard U., 1960, PhD, 1961. Vis. scholar MIT, Cambridge, 1967-68; asst. prof. econs. U. Ill., Urbana, 1961-65, assoc. prof., 1965-70, prof., 1970—; dir. Bur. Econ. and Bus. Rsch., 1977-89, acting v.p. for acad. affairs, 1987-89, v.p. for acad. affairs, 1989—94, v.p. emeritus, 1995—; prof. Inst. Govt. and Pub. Affairs, 1994—. Tchg. fellow Harvard U., 1959-61; vis. prof. U. Colo., 1967, 74, 75, 76, 82, Kyoto (Japan) U., 1976; cons. GM, 1964-66, U.S. Congress Joint Econ. Com., 1978-80, ABA, 1980-82; vis. scholar UCLA, 1994-95; co-dir. Midwest Economy: Issues and Policy, Midwest Govs. Conf., 1981; bd. dirs. Midwest U. Consortium Internat. Activities, 1989-94, v.p., 1991-94; mem. Ill. Gov.'s Econ. Policy Coun., 1999-2003. Co-author: Environmental Contamination by Lead and Other Heavy Metals--Synthesis and Modeling, 1978, Special Topics in Mathematics for Economists, 1976, A Comparative Cost Study of Staff Panel and Participating Attorney Panel Prepaid Legal Service Plans, 1981, Illinois Higher Education: Building the Economy, Shaping Society, 2000; editor: Illinois Economic Outlook, 1982-87, Illinois Economic Statistics, 1981, Economic Edge, 1996—; co-editor: The Midwest Economy: Issues and Policy, 1982, Frontiers of Business and Economic Research Management, 1983, Illinois Statistical Abstract, 1987, 2002, 03. Mem. exec. com. Assn. Univ. Bus. and Econ. Rsch., 1977-89, v.p., 1978-82, pres., 1982-83. Woodrow Wilson fellow, 1957; Social Sci. Rsch. Coun. grantee, 1964; NSF fellow, 1967-69, grantee, 1974-77; U.S. Dept. State scholar, Japan, 1976; grantee Ill. Bd. Higher Edn., 1998-99. Mem. Am. Statis. Assn., Econometric Soc., Beta Gamma Sigma, Phi Kappa Phi. Home: 201 E Holmes St Urbana IL 61801-6612 Office: Univ Ill 211 IGPA 1007 W Nevada St Urbana IL 61801-3812 Business E-Mail: resek@uiuc.edu.

RESENDE, MARCELO, economist, educator; b. Rio de Janeiro, Aug. 26, 1963; s. Eduardo de Mendonça e Silva and Edna Vieira de Resende. BA in Econs., State U. Rio de Janeiro, 1985, BS in Psychology, 1990; MSc in Econs., Pontifical Cath. U., Rio de Janeiro, 1989; MA in Econs., U. Pa., 1993; DPhil in Econs., Oxford (Eng.) U., 1997. Lectr. Pontifical Cath. U. Rio de Janeiro, 1987-89; asst. prof. econs. State U. Rio de Janeiro, 1990, Fed. U. Rio de Janeiro, 1990-98, assoc. prof., 1998—. Contbr. articles to profl. jours., including Oxford Econ. Papers, Bull. Econs. Rsch., Oxford Bull. Econs. and Stats., Rev. Indsl. Orgns., Info. Econs. and Policy. Scholar Brazilian Ministry Sci. and Tech., 1986-88, rsch. grants, 1998-2003; scholar Brazilian Ministry Edn., 1991-95; rsch. grantee Brazilian Ministry Planning, 1988. Mem. Brazilian Econometric Soc. Avocations: music concerts, movies, sports practice (soccer), theater. Office: Fed U Rio de Janeiro Inst Econs Av Pasteur 250 22290-240 Rio de Janeiro Brazil E-mail: mresende@ism.com.br., mresende@ie.ufrj.br.

RESHOTKO, ELI, aerospace engineer, educator; b. N.Y.C., Nov. 18, 1930; s. Max and Sarah (Kalisky) R.; m. Adina Venit, June 7, 1953; children: Deborah, Naomi, Miriam Ruth. BS, Cooper Union, 1950; MS, Cornell U., 1951; PhD, Calif. Inst. Tech., 1960. Aero. research engr. NASA-Lewis Flight Propulsion Lab., Cleve., 1951-56, head fluid mechanics sect., 1956-57; head high temperature plasma sect. NASA-Lewis Research Center, 1960-61, chief plasma physics br., 1961-64; asso. prof. engring. Case Inst. Tech., Cleve., 1964-66, dean, 1986-87; prof. engring. Case Western Res. U., Cleve., 1966-88, chmn. dept. fluid thermal and aerospace scis., 1970-76, chmn. dept. mech. and aerospace engring., 1976-79, Kent H. Smith prof. engring., 1989-98, Kent H. Smith prof. emeritus, 1999—. Susman vis. prof. dept. aero. engring. Technion-Israel Inst. Tech., Haifa, Israel, 1969-70; cons. United Technologies Research Ctr., Inst. Def. Analyses, Dynamics Tech. Inc., Micro Craft Tech., Martin-Marietta Corp., Rockwell Internat.; mem. adv. com. fluid dynamics NASA, 1961-64; mem. aero. adv. com. NASA, 1980-87, chmn. adv. subcom. on aerodynamics, 1983-85; chmn. U.S. Boundary Layer Transition Study Group, NASA/USAF, 1970—; U.S. mem. fluid dynamics panel AGARD-NATO, 1981-88; chmn. steering com. Symposium on Engring. Aspects Magneto-hydro-dynamics, 1966, Case-NASA Inst. for Computational Mechanics in Propulsion, 1985-92, USRA/NASA ICASE Sci. Coun., 1992; Joseph Wunsch lectr. Technion-Israel Inst. Tech., 1990. Contbr. articles to tech. jours. Chmn. bd. govs. Cleve. Coll. Jewish Studies, 1981-84; mem. bd. govs. Technion-Israel Inst. Tech., Haifa, Israel, 1999—; mem. NRC Air Force Sci. Tech. bd., 2000—. Guggenheim fellow Calif. Inst. Tech., 1957-59. Fellow ASME, AAAS, AIAA (Fluid and Plasma Dynamics award 1980, Dryden lectr. in rsch. 1994), Am. Phys. Soc. (vice-chmn. divsn. fluid dynamics 1998, chair-elect 1999, chair 2000, Otto Laporte award in fluid dynamics 1999), Am. Acad. Mechanics (pres. 1986-87); mem. NAE, AAUP, Ohio Sci. and Engring. Roundtable, Sigma Xi, Tau Beta Pi, Pi Tau Sigma. Office: Case Western Reserve Univ University Cir Cleveland OH 44106 Home: 1200 Humboldt St Apt 601 Denver CO 80218-2454

RESIKA, PAUL, artist; b. N.Y.C., Aug. 15, 1928; Student, Sol Wilson, N.Y.C., 1940-44, Hans Hofmann Sch., 1945-47, Venice, Italy, 1950-53. Adj. prof. art Cooper Union, 1966-78; instr. Art Students League, 1968-69; faculty Skowhegan Sch. Painting and Sculpture, 1973, 76; chmn. M.F.A. program Parsons Sch. Design, 1978-89. Dartmouth Coll. 1972 Artist in Residence. One-man shows include George Dix Gallery, N.Y.C., 1948, Peridot Gallery, 1965, 1967, 1968, 1969, 1970, Washburn Gallery, 1971, 1973, Hopkins Ctr.

Dartmouth Coll., 1972, Graham Gallery, 1976, 1979, 1981, 1983, 1985, Longpoint Gallery, Provincetown, Mass., 1979, 1981, 1989, 1992, 1995, 25-yr. survey Artists Choice Mus., 1985, Merideth Long Gallery, Houston, 1986, 1997, Walker-Kornbluth Gallery, Fair Lawn, N.J., 1986, 1995, 1997, Crane Kalman Gallery, London, 1986, Graham/Modern Gallery, 1987—88, 1990, Salander-O'Reilly Galleries, N.Y.C., 1993, 1994, 1995, Vered Gallery, East Hampton, N.Y., 1995, 2003, Gerald Peters Gallery, Santa Fe, 1996, Provincetown Art Assn. and Mus., 1997, Lori Bookstein Gallery, N.Y.C., 1998, 2001, Berta Walker Gallery, Provincetown, 1998, 2001, 2003, Lizan Tops Gallery, East Hampton, N.Y., 1998, Salander-O'Reilly Galleries, N.Y.C., 1999, 2001, 2002, Hackett Freedman, San Francisco, 1998, Hackett-Freedman, 1999, 2000, 2002, Metta Galleria, Madrid, 2000, Camino Real Gallery, Boca Raton, Fla., 2003, Berta Walker Gallery, Provincetown, Mass., 2004, Represented in permanent collections Nat. Mus. Am. Art, Washington, Muson-Williams-Proctor Inst. Mus. Art, Utica, N.Y., U. Nebr. Art Gallery, Indpls. Mus. Art, Chase Manhattan Bank, N.Y.C., Neuberger Mus., SUNY, Purchase, U. Wyo., Laramie, Met. Mus. Art, N.Y., Colby Coll., NAD, Owensboro (Ky.) Mus. Art, U. Ariz., William Benton Mus. Art, Hood Mus., Dartmouth Coll., Hanover, N.H., Tucson Mus. Art, Crackow Mus. Art, Poland, Parish Art Mus., Southampton, N.Y., Heckscher Mus., Huntington, N.Y., Mills Coll. Mus., Oakland, Calif., Meml. Art Gallery, Rochester, Whitney Mus., NYC, also pvt. collections. Recipient award Am. Acad. Arts and Letters, 1977; Altman prize NAD, 1982, 91, 97, 2003, Obrig prize, 1996; Louis Comfort Tiffany grantee, 1959, Ingram Merrill grantee, 1969; John Simon Guggenheim Meml. fellow, 1984. Mem. NAD, Am. Acad. Arts and Letters. Office: care Salander-O'Reilly Galleries 20 E 79th St New York NY 10021-0106

RESING, MARYLORETTO RACHEL, guidance counseling administrator, elementary school educator, pastoral counselor; b. Covington, Ky., Jan. 27, 1949; d. Raymond Anthony and Carole Mary (Glover) Seifert; m. John Joseph Resing, Sept. 6, 1969; children: Jayne Carole, Matthew Raymond-Albert, Markus John, Joseph Thomas. BA, Thomas More Coll., Crestview Hills, Ky., 1984; MEd, Xavier U., Cin., 1989; M of Religious Studies, Athenaeum, Cin., 1994. Cert. elem. tchr. Ky., elem. and secondary guidance counselor Ky., Nat. Cert. Counselor 2002. Tchr. St. Joseph Sch. Diocese of Covington, Crescent Springs, Ky., 1969-70, tchr. St. Cecelia Sch. Independence, Ky., 1984-85, tchr. Covington Cath. H.S. Park Hills, Ky., 1985-90, dir. religious edn. St. Therese Parish Southgate, Ky., 1990-95; guidance counselor Kenton County Sch., Erlanger, Ky., 1995-96; dir. religious edn. St. Agnes Parish Diocese of Covington, Park Hills, 1995-96; tchr., dir. alternative coop. edn. program Covington Ind. Sch., 1997-99; counselor Holmes Jr. H.S., 2000—. Mem. Covington Diocesan Family Life Bd., Erlanger, Ky., 1994-96; initiator, chair Religious Edn. Group, Erlanger, 1991-96. Contbr. to mag. and diocesan newspaper. Active Boy Scouts Am., Independence, Ky., 1983—; bd. dirs. YMCA, Independence, 1986-92; mem. Greater Cin. NCCJ, 1985-90; chair St. Cecilia Sch. Bd., Independence, 1985-89; mem. La Leche League No. Ky., 1970-80, leader, 1976-80; bd. dirs. Nat. Assn. Parish Coords. and Dirs. of Religious Edn., 1997. Mem.: Ky. Sch. Counselor Assn., Covington Edn. Assn., No. Ky. Counseling Assn. (v.p. 2002—03, pres.-elect 2002—03, pres 2004—), Am. Counseling Assn., Ky. Edn. Assn. (rep.), Dirs. of Religious Edn. Support Group, Phi Delta Kappa. Roman Catholic. Avocations: antiques, gardening, reading.

RESNECK, JACK SELWYN, JR., dermatologist, medical educator; b. 1974; MD, U. Calif., San Francisco. Resident in dermatology U. Calif., San Francisco; fellow Inst. Health Policy Studies, U. Calif., San Francisco; asst. prof. dermatology and health policy U. Calif., San Francisco. Recipient Clinical Career Devel. award in health care policy, Dermatology Found., 2003, 2004, Excellence in Medicine Leadership award, AMA Found., 2004. Mem.: AMA, Calif. Soc. Dermatology and Dermatologic Surgery. Office: 350 Parnassus Ave Ste 404 San Francisco CA 94117 Office Phone: 415-476-9350. Office Fax: 415-476-3686.

RESNECK-SANNES, HELEN, psychologist; b. Marion, Ind., Dec. 14, 1947; d. William and Charlotte Resneck; m. Larry David Sannes, June 20, 1976; children: Aaron Sannes, Myrrhia. PhD, U. Wis., Madison, 1974. Lic. psychologist Bd. of Med. Quality Assurance, 1975. Pvt. psychotherapy practice Helen Resneck-Sannes, Ph.D., Santa Cruz, Calif., 1977—; tchr. trainer Internat. Inst. for Bioenergetic Analysis, N.Y.C., 1997—. Asst. prof. Antioch Coll., Monterey, Calif., 1977—77; prof. U. Calif., Santa Cruz, 1989; presenter in field. Author: (memoir) Father's Rooms; contbr. articles to profl. jours. Recipient medal, Phi Kappa Phi Hon. Soc., 1969; Work study grant, Western Interstate Commn. for Higher Edn., 1968, fellowship, NIMH, 1970-1974, grant to establish a women's therapy ctr., Wis. Psychol. Assn., 1972. Mem.: APA, Monterey Bay Psychol. Assn., Calif. Psychol. Assn., Internat. Inst. for Bioenergetic Analysis (bd. of trustees 2002—03, co-editor jour. 2003). Avocations: jazz, African, and hip hop dancing, mountain biking, travel. Home and Office: 216 Suburbia Ave Santa Cruz CA 95062 Personal E-mail: helenrs@aol.com.

RESNICK, ADRIENNE JO, psychotherapist; b. N.Y.C., July 19, 1954; d. Martin and Molly Starkman; m. Paul Resnick, Sept. 30, 1978; 1 child, Elana. BA, NYU, 1975, MSW, 1981. Psychotherapist Stamford Child Guidance Clinic, Conn., 1981—83; group facilitator YWCA, White Plains, NY; psychotherapist pvt. practice, Sleepy Hollow, 1983—. Author: Sometimes I Feel Blue, 2002, Food Play, 2002. Recipient Founders Day award, NYU, N.Y.C., 1975. Mem.: NASW (diplomate), Acad. Cert. Social Workers, Soc. Clin. Social Work. Avocations: writing, travel, yoga. Office: 239 N Broadway Sleepy Hollow NY 10591

RESNICK, ALICE ROBIE, judge; b. Erie, Pa., Aug. 21, 1939; d. Adam Joseph and Alice Suzanne (Spizarny) Robie; m. Melvin L. Resnick, Mar. 20, 1970 PhB, Siena Heights Coll., 1961; JD, U. Detroit, 1964. Bar: Ohio 1964, Mich. 1965, U.S. Supreme Ct. 1970. Asst. county prosecutor Lucas County Prosecutor's Office, Toledo, 1964-75, trial atty., 1965-75; judge Toledo Mcpl. Ct., 1976-83, 6th Dist. Ct. Appeals, State of Ohio, Toledo, 1983-88; instr. U. Toledo, 1968-69; justice Ohio Supreme Ct., 1988—. Co-chairperson Ohio State Gender Fairness Task Force. Trustee Siena Heights Coll., Adrian, Mich., 1982—; organizer Crime Stopper Inc., Toledo, 1981—; mem. Mayor's Drug Coun.; bd. dirs. Guest House Inc. Mem. ABA, Toledo Bar Assn., Lucas County Bar Assn., Nat. Assn. Women Judges, Am. Judicature Soc., Toledo Women's Bar Assn., Ohio State Women's Bar Assn. (organizer), Toledo Mus. Art, Internat. Inst. Toledo. Roman Catholic. Home: 2407 Edgehill Rd Toledo OH 43615-2321 Office: Supreme Ct Office 30 E Broad St Fl 3 Columbus OH 43215

RESNICK, JEFFREY I. plastic surgeon; b. Jersey City, Mar. 2, 1954; s. Victor and Regina (Bristitz) R.; m. Michele Gail Zinger, July 12, 1981; children: Andrew Gregory, Daniel Zachary. BS, Yale U., 1975; MD, U. Pa., 1980. Diplomate Am. Bd. Surgery, Am. Bd. Plastic Surgery. Resident in surgery Mass. Gen. Hosp., Boston, 1980—85, resident in plastic surgery, 1985—87; asst. clin. prof. plastic surgery UCLA, 1987—, fellow in craniofacial surgery, 1987—88; full time asst. prof. clin. surgery U. So. Calif, Santa Monica, 1998—. Contbr. articles to profl. jours. Surgeon Interplast, Vietnam, Nepal. Mem. Am. Assn. Plastic Surgeons., Am. Soc. Plastic Surgeons, Am. Soc. Maxillofacial Surgeons, Am. Cleft Palate-Craniofacial Assn., Plastic Surgery Ednl. Found., Sigma Xi, Alpha Omega Alpha. Office: 1301 20th St Ste 470 Santa Monica CA 90404-2082

RESNICK, JEFFREY LANCE, federal magistrate judge; b. Bklyn., Mar. 5, 1943; s. Bernard and Selma (Monheit) R.; m. Margery O'Connor, May 27, 1990. BA, U. Conn., 1964; LLB, U. Conn., West Hartford, 1967. Bar: Conn. 1967, N.Y. 1968, U.S. V.I. 1968, D.C. 1979, U.S. Ct. Appeals (3d cir.) 1979. Assoc. Office of J.D. Marsh, Christiansted, St. Croix, V.I., 1967-69; asst. atty. gen. Dept. Law, Christiansted, 1969-73; ptnr. James & Resnick, Christiansted, 1973-89; magistrate judge U.S. Dist. Ct. V.I., Christiansted, 1989—. Active V.I. Bridge Team, 1971—. Jewish. Avocation: writing poetry and palindromes. Office: US District Court 3013 East Golden Rock Christiansted VI 00820-4256

RESNICK, LAUREN B. psychology educator; EdD in Rsch. in Instrn., Harvard U., 1962; doctorate (hon.), U. Geneva, 1991. With dept. psychology U. Pitts., 1966—; dir. Learning Rsch. & Devel. Ctr., U. Pitts., 1977—. Author, editor chpts. to books; contbr. articles to profl. jours. Trustee Nat. Ctn. Edn. and the Economy, Harvard U. Bd. of Overseers, Ednl. Testing Svc., Carnegie Found. for the Advancement of Teaching. Recipient Disting. Svc. medal Teacher's Coll., Columbia U., Oeuvre award for outstanding contbns. to the sci. of learning and instruction European Assn. for Rsch. on Learning and Instruction, 1999; fellow Ctr. Advanced Study in the Behavioral Scis., 1976-77; vis. fellow Nat. Inst. Edn., 1974-75. Fellow AAAS, Am. Psychol. Assn. (divsn. exptl. psychology, devel. psychology, ednl. psychology, exptl. analysis of behavior, past pres. divsn. ednl. psychology, Edward L. Thorndike award 1998); mem. Am. Ednl. Rsch. Assn. (past v.p. divsn. learning and instrn., pres. 1986-87, Disting. Contbns. in Edn. award), Nat. Acad. Edn. Office: U Pitts Learning Rsch Devel Ctr 3939 Ohara St Pittsburgh PA 15213

RESNICK, LYNDA, business executive; Co-owner, vice chmn. Franklin Mint; co-owner Roll Internat. Chmn. Teleflora. Chmn. mktg. com. Conservation Internat.; bd. dirs. Assn. for Cure of Cancer of the Prostate, CaP CURE, Milken Family Found.; mem. exec. com., trustee, chmn. acquisitions com. L.A. County Mus. Art; mem. com. on sculpture and decorative arts Met. Mus. Art; trustee Phila. Mus. Art. Recipient Gold Effie award, 1983; named one of Top 50 U.S. Women Bus. Owners, Working Women, #1 L.A.-based woman Bus. Owner, L.A. bus. Jour., one of top 100 U.S. art collectors Art & Antiques mag. Office: Roll Internat Corp 11444 W Olympic Blvd Los Angeles CA 90064-1549

RESNICK, MYRON J. retired insurance company executive, lawyer; b. Louisville, July 13, 1931; s. Harry C. and Sybil G. (Glick) R.; m. Alicia M. Ward, Dec. 16, 1967; children— Hugh, Clay, David BS in Econs., U. Pa., 1953; JD, U. Mich., 1956. Various positions Allstate Ins. Co., Northbrook, Ill., 1959-88, sr. v.p., treas. bd. dirs., 1959-95; chmn. bd. Federated Ins. Co. Ltd. (U.K.), Sale, Cheshire, Eng., 1979-81. Dir. Allstate Ins. Co. Ltd. (U.K.), Sale; pres. Allstate Investment Mgmt. Co.; mem. adj. faculty John Marshall Law Sch., Chgo., 1996-98. Mem. Chgo. exec. com. Anti-Defamation League, 1975—; bd. dirs. Chgo. Urban League, 1987-2001, St. Scholastica High Sch., Chgo., 1977-79; trustee George Williams Coll., Downers Grove, Ill., 1981-93, chmn. bd. trustees, 1991-93, trustee Aurora U., 1993—; bd. advisors Inst. Law and Econs. U. Pa., 1994—. With U.S. Army, 1956-58. Mem. ABA, Chgo. Bar Assn., Ill. Bar Assn., Assn. Life Ins. Counsel, Chgo. Mortgage Attys. Assn. (bd. dirs. 1965-75), Reform Club (London).

RESNICK, PAUL R. research chemist; b. N.Y.C., Apr. 7, 1934; married, 1966; 1 child. BA, Swarthmore Coll., 1955; PhD in Organic Chemistry, Cornell U., 1961. Fellow U. Calif., Berkeley, 1960-62; from chemist to sr. rsch. chemist E.I. DuPont De Nemours & Co., Inc., 1962-74, rsch. assoc., 1974-85, rsch. fellow, 1985-88, sr. rsch. fellow, 1988-91, DuPont fellow, 1991—. Recipient Dupont Lavoisier medal for tech. achievement, 1996. Mem. Am. Chem. Soc. (Award for Creative Work in Fluorine Chemistry 1995). Office: DuPont Fluoroproducts 22828 NC Highway 87 W Fayetteville NC 28306-7332

RESNICK, RHODA BRODOWSKY, psychotherapist; b. Mar. 22, 1930; d. Isador and Rose (Wasserman) Brodowsky; m. Jack H. Resnick, May 21, 1950; children: Steven E., Caryn B. BS, CCNY, 1951; MS, Queens Coll., 1973; postgrad., Hunter Coll. Tchr. N.Y.C. Bd. Edn., 1960—80, guidance counselor, 1980—; psychotherapist L.I. Cons. Ctr., 1973—77; pvt. practice psychotherapy, 1975—. Fellow, L.I. Inst. Mental Health, 1975. Mem.: PGA, United Fedn. Tchrs., Am. Pers. and Guidance Assn. Home: 340 E 64th St New York NY 10021-7503 E-mail: xrojac@hotmail.com.

RESNICK, ROBERT, physicist, researcher; b. Balt., Jan. 11, 1923; s. Abraham and Anna (Dubin) R.; m. Mildred Saltzman, Oct. 14, 1945; children— Trudy, Abby, Regina. AB, Johns Hopkins U., 1943, PhD (Pres.'s Fund scholar 1946-49), 1949. Physicist NACA, Cleve., 1944-46; asst. prof., assoc. prof. physics U. Pitts., 1949-56; assoc. prof., prof. physics Rensselaer Poly. Inst., Troy, N.Y., 1956-93; prof. emeritus, 1993—; chmn. interdisciplinary sci. curriculum Rensselaer Poly. Inst., Troy, N.Y., 1973-88, Edward P. Hamilton Disting. prof. sci., 1975-93; hon. research fellow Harvard U., 1964-65; Fulbright prof. Peru, 1971. Hon. vis. prof. Peoples Republic of China, 1981, 85; mem. Commn. on Coll. Physics, 1960-68; commencement speaker Rensselaer Poly. Inst., 1993; mem. U.S. adv. bd. Quantum Joint USSR/USA sci. mag., 1989-93. Author: A Manual for Laboratory Physics, 1954, (with D. Halliday) Physics, 1960, 3d edit., 1978, 4th edit., 1991, 5th edit., 2000, (with Halliday and Krane) extended version, 1986, 2d edit. extended version, 1991, 3rd edit., 2000, 5th edit., 2003, (with Halliday and Krane) Introduction to Special Relativity, 1968, (with R. Eisberg) Notes on Quantum Theory, 1968, Notes on Modern Physics, 1969, Quantum Physics of Atoms, Molecules, Solids, Nuclei and Particles, 1974, 2d edit., 1985, (with D. Halliday) Fundamentals of Physics, 1970, 5th edit., 1996, extended version, 1988, 2d edit., 1993, 3rd edit., 1996, 4th edit., 1999, (with J. Walker and D. Halliday) 6th edit., 2000, (with others) Student Study Guide for Physics, 1970, 6th edit., 2001, Basic Concepts in Relativity and Early Quantum Theory, 1972, 2d edit., 1985, Basic Concepts in Relativity, 1991; author: (with others) Sourcebook for Programmable Calculators, 1978, (with E. Derringh) Solutions to Physics Problems, 1980, 5th edit., 1996, (with K. Brownstein) Tests for Physics, 1987, (with J. Walker and D. Halliday) CD Physics, 1993, 3rd edit., 2000; books translated into numerous fgn. langs; So You Want to Write a Textbook, 1999 (video); mem. adv. bd., project staff: Physical Science for Non-Scientists, 1964-68, pub., 1968; co-dir.: Project Physics Demonstration Experiments, 1962-70; pub. project, 1970, Workshop on Apparatus for College Physics, 1964-65, 66, Videotapes in Physics Instruction, 1975-78; dir. Physics Demonstration and Laboratory Apparatus Workshop, 1960-61; adv. editor: John Wiley & Sons, Inc., 1967-89, Macmillan Pubs., 1990-94. Recipient Disting. Svc. citation Am. Assn. Physics Tchrs., 1967, Hans Christian Oersted medal, 1974; named to Hall of Fame, Balt. City Coll., 1989, Rensselaer Poly. Inst., 2003; Robert Resnick Ctr. for Physics established at Rensselaer Poly. Inst., 1993, Robert Resnick Ann. Sci. Lectr. series endowed, 1993. Fellow AAAS, Am. Phys. Soc.; mem. AAUP, Am. Assn. Physics Tchrs. (v.p. 1986, pres.-elect 1987, pres. 1988), Am. Soc. Engring. Edn., Am. Inst. Physics (governing bd. 1987-90, mem. coun. Ctr. for History of Physics 1997—), Philosophic Soc. South Fla. (exec. bd. 1997-2000), Textbook Author Assn. (coun. 1990-93), Phi Beta Kappa, Sigma Xi. Achievements include rsch. publs. in aerodynamics, nuclear physics, atomic physics, upper atmosphere physics, history of physics, physics edn. Home: 23221 L'Ermitage Cir Boca Raton FL 33433-7144

RESNICK, ROSALIND, multimedia executive; b. N.Y. BA, MA in Italian Renaissance History, Johns Hopkins U., 1981. Bus. reporter The Miami Herald, 1984-89; freelance writer various computer trade mags., 1990-95; pres., CEO NetCreations, Bklyn., 1995—. Co-author: The Internet Business Guide, 1995. Office: NetCreations 379 W Broadway Rm 202 New York NY 10012-5125

RESNICK, STEWART ALLEN, diversified company executive; b. Jersey City, Dec. 24, 1936; s. David and Yetta (Goldmaker) R.; children from previous marriage: Jeffrey Brian, Ilene Sue, William Jay; m. Lynda Rae Harris, Nov. 26, 1972; children: Jonathan Charles Sinay, Jason Daniel Sinay. BS, UCLA, 1959, LLB, 1962. Chmn., owner Roll Internat. Corp., L.A., 1958—; chmn. The Franklin Mint, Franklin Center, Pa., 1985—; chmn., owner Teleflora, L.A., Paramount Citrus Co., L.A., Paramount Farms, Inc., L.A. Bd. trustees Bard Coll., N.Y.C.; acquistions com. Nat. Gallery, Washington; co-chmn. mktg. dept., adv. bd., mem. Mgmt. Edn. Coun., The Wharton Sch., U. Pa. Avocation: health and fitness related activities. Office: The Franklin Mint Us Rt 1 Media PA 19091-0001

RESNIK, HARVEY LEWIS PAUL, psychiatrist; b. Buffalo, Apr. 6, 1930; s. Samuel andCelia (Greenberg) R.; m. Audrey Ruth Frey, Aug. 30, 1964 (dec. 1993); children: Rebecca Gabrielle, Henry Seth Maccabee, Jessica Ruth. BA magna cum laude, U. Buffalo, 1951; MD, Columbia, 1955; grad., Phila. Psychoanalytic Inst., 1967. Diplomate: Am. Bd. Psychiatry and Neurology. Intern Phila. Gen. Hosp., 1955-56, resident in surgery, 1956-57; resident in psychiatry Jackson Meml. Hosp., Miami, Fla., 1959-61; fellow U. Pa. Hosp., 1961-62, mem. staff, 1962-67; instr; Sch. Medicine, U. Pa., 1962-66; instr. med. hypnosis Sch. Medicine, U. Pa. (Grad. Sch. Medicine), 1963-65; clin. dir. psychiatry E. J. Meyer Meml. Hosp., Buffalo, 1967, dir. psychiatry, 1968; from assoc. prof. to prof., assoc. chair Sch. Medicine, SUNY at Buffalo, Buffalo, 1968—70; chief Nat. Center for Studies of Suicide Prevention, NIMH, 1969-74, chief mental health emergencies sect., 1974-76; with Reproductive Biology Rsch. Found., St. Louis, 1971; clin. prof. psychiatry and behavioral sci. Sch. Medicine, George Washington U., 1969—2002, prof. emeritus clin. psychiatry and behavioral scis., 2002—; dir. Human Behavior Found., 1975—; lectr. Sch. Medicine, Johns Hopkins, Balt., 1969-74; adj. lectr. Johns Hopkins U. Sch. Pub. Health, Balt., 1981-82. Prof. cmty. health Fed. City Coll., 1971-75; med. dir. Johns Hopkins U. Compulsive Gambling Ctr., 1981-83; med. dir. alcohol and substance abuse program U. Md., College Park, 1986-2000; vis. prof. Katholieke U., Leuven, Belgium, 1986-93; cons. to Sec.-Gen. Ministry of Health, Belgium, 1986-95, NATO fellow, 1986-87; cons. various hosps. and orgns., Medicare, Pa. Blue Shield, 1984-96, Trailblazer Health, 1996-99, Blue Cross/Blue Shield S.C., 1999; Sr. attending and chair-elect Dept. of Psychiatry, Suburban Hosp., Bethesda, MD (1976-) Author: Suicidal Behaviors: Diagnosis and Management, 1968, 2d edit., 1994, (with M. E. Wolfgang) Treatment of the Sexual Offender, 1971, Sexual Behaviors: Social, Clinical and Legal Aspects, 1972, (with B. Hathorne) Suicide Prevention in the Seventies, 1973, (with H.L. Ruben) Emergency Psychiatric Care, 1974, (with others) The Prediction of Suicide, 1974, Emergency and Disaster Management, 1976; (with J.L. Mitchell) Emergency Response to Crisis, 1981; Editor: Bull. Suicidology, 1969-74; Contbr. (with others) articles on hypnosis, sexual offenders, marriage and sexual dysfunction treatment, suicide, death and dying, emergency psychiatric care. Mem. Addictions Adv. Bd. Prince Georges County, 1980-85. Served to capt. USAF, 1957-59, ETO-Middle East; capt. USNR; ret. Decorated officer in the Order King Leopold, Belgium, 1990. Fellow Am. Coll. Mental Health Adminstrs. (life), Am. Coll. Psychiatrists (life), Am. Psychiat. Assn. (life); mem. Med-Chi of Md., Prince Georges County Med. Assn. (co-chair joint com. with Bar Assn. 1996-2001), Washington Psychiatry Soc., Am. Acad. Psychiatry and Law (suicidology com. 1998-2000), Phila. Psychoanalytic Soc., NIH Alumni Assn., Columbia U. Med. Alumni Assn. (bd. dirs. 1993-95), Cosmos Club (Washington), Phi Beta Kappa, Beta Sigma Rho (grand vice warden 1963). Jewish. Office: Resnik Psychiatric Lifeklok Human BE PO Box 656 College Park MD 20741-0656 Mailing: 4209 Bradley Ln Chevy Chase MD 20815-5234

RESNIK, LINDA ILENE, marketing and information executive, publisher, consultant, writer; b. Dallas, Oct. 26, 1950; d. Harold and Reatha (Gordon) R. BJ in Broadcast Journalism, U. Mo., 1971; MA in Journalism, U. North Tex., 1977, MBA in Mktg., 1980. News and documentary producer Sta. KDFW-TV, Dallas, 1971-73; mktg.-info. officer Dallas County C.C. Dist., 1973-79; dir. mktg. The Learning Channel, Washington, 1980-82; dir. Nat. Narrowcast Svc., Pub. Broadcasting Svc., Washington, 1982-85; exec. dir. Am. Soc. Info. Sci., Washington, 1985-89, White House Conf. on Libr. and Info. Svcs., Washington, 1990-91; cons., 1991—; mng. ptnr. FAQs Press, 1998—. Adv. com. ALA Library/Book Fellows Project; fellow Ctr. for Info. and Comm. Scis., Ball State U.; U.S. exec. com. U. of the World; mktg., tng. and telecomm. cons. to edml. assns., others Writer and editor college-level study guides; scriptwriter college credit TV courses. Youth activities coordinator YMCA, Dallas, 1975-78; spl. event organizer Am. Cancer Soc., Dallas, 1976-77; com. leader Goals for Dallas, 1978-80; co-chair Friends of the Troup (Tex.) Libr., 1996—; mem. com. Tyler Race for the Cure, 1999. Recipient Best TV Feature Story award AP, Tex., 1973. Mem. Am. Soc. Assn. Execs., Am. Soc. Info. Sci. (pub. bull. 1985-89), Women in Cable, Info. Inst., Am. Mktg. Assn. Avocations: travel, racquet sports, reading, theater. Office: PO Box 130115 Tyler TX 75713-0115 E-mail: LIResnik@FAQsPress.com.

RESNIK, ROBERT, medical educator; b. New Haven, Dec. 7, 1938; s. Nathan Alfred and Elsie (Hershman) R.; m. Lauren Brahms, Oct. 29, 1966; children: Andrew Scott, Jamie Layne. BA, Yale U., 1960; MD, Case Western Res. U., 1965. Intern in internal medicine Mt. Sinai Hosp., Cleve., 1965-66; resident in ob-gyn. Yale U. Sch. Medicine, 1966-70; asst. prof. Sch. Medicine U. Calif., San Diego, 1974-78, assoc. prof., 1978-82, prof. reproductive medicine, 1982—, chmn. dept., 1982-95, dean clin. affairs, 1988-90, dean admissions, 1995—2003. Cons. Nat. Heart, Lung and Blood Inst. NIH, Washington, 1987; mem. exec. com. Coun. Residency Edn. Ob-Gyn, Washington, 1988-94, residency rev. com., 1988-94. Editor: (textbook) Maternal-Fetal Medicine: Principles and Practice, 1984, 5th edit., 2004; contbr. numerous articles to profl. jours. Major U.S. Army, 1970-72. Rsch. grantee Nat. Found., NIH. Fellow: Royal Coll. Obstet. Gynecologists (ad eundem), N.W. Obstet. Gynecological Soc., Pacific Coast Obstet. and Gynecol. Soc., Am. Coll. Ob-Gyn. (vice chmn. obs. practice com. 1998—2000), New England Obstet. Gynecological Soc.; mem.: San Diego Gynecol. Soc. (pres. 1982), Am. Gynecologic and Obstet. Soc. (treas. 2003), Perinatal Rsch. Soc. (pres. 1985), Soc. Gynecologic Investigation (coun. 1983—88), Yale Club, Am. Gynecol. Club (pres. 2002—03). Office: UCSD Med Ctr 200 W Arbor Dr 8433 San Diego CA 92103-8433

RESO, ANTHONY, geologist, educator, earth resources economist; b. London, Eng., Aug. 10, 1931; arrived in U.S., 1940, naturalized, 1952; AB, Columbia Coll., N.Y.C., 1954; MA, Columbia U., 1955; postgrad., U. Cin., 1956-57; PhD, Rice U., 1960; postgrad., Grad. Sch. Bus. U. Houston, 1964-68. Instr. geology Queens Coll., Flushing, NY, 1954; geologist Atlantic Richfield Corp., Midland, Tex., 1955-56; asst. prof. geology and curator invertebrate paleontology Pratt Mus., Amherst (Mass.) Coll., 1959-62; staff rsch. geologist Tenneco Oil Co., Houston, 1962-86; geol. mgr. Peak Prodn. Co., Houston, 1986—, v.p., 1988—. Cons. in geol. rsch. Tenn. Gas and Oil Co., 1960—61; lectr. U. Houston, 1962—65; vis. prof. Rice U., 1980; mem. bd. advisers Gulf Univs. Rsch. Corp., Galveston, Tex., 1967—75, chmn., 1968—69. Contbr. articles to profl. jours. Grantee Rsch., Eastman Fund, 1962, NSF fellow, 1958—59. Fellow: AAAS, Geol. Soc. Am. (com. investments 1984—95, chmn. 1985—92, budget com. 1993—95, found. trustee 1999—, Rsch. grantee 1958, Disting. Svc. award 1996); mem.: English-Speaking Union U.S. (dir. Houston br. 1978—, v.p. 1982—88, mem. scholarship com. 1988—97, chmn. 1991—97, pres. 1997—98), Houston Geol. Soc. (v.p. 1973—75, pres. 1975—76, chmn. constn. revision com. 1981, Disting. Svc. award 1985), Tex. Acad. Sci., Am. Assn. Petroleum Geologists (life; com. convs. 1977—83, gen. chmn. nat. conv. 1979, chmn. 1980—83, com. investments 1982—88, chmn. com. group ins. 1986—88, treas. 1986—88, found. trustee assoc. 1991, Rsch. grantee 1958, 1959, Disting. Svc. award 1985), Paleontol. Rsch. Instn., SEPM Soc. for Sedimentary Geology (com. investments 1990—, chmn. 1992—95, treas. SEPM Found. 1997—2003, Disting. Svc. award 2003), Paleontol. Soc., Varsity C Club, Beta Theta Pi, Sigma Gamma Epsilon, Sigma Xi. Episcopalian. Home: 1805 Brun St Houston TX 77019-5712 Office: care Peak Prodn Co PO Box 130785 Houston TX 77219-0785 E-mail: aresogeo@swbell.net.

RESOR, PAMELA P. state legislator; b. Lincoln, Nebr., Feb. 26, 1942; d. Roland B. and Margaret L. (Flynn) Phillips; m. Griffith L. Resor III, July 6, 1963; children: Karen E. Resor Savage, Philip G., Kristen M. BA, Smith Coll., 1964. Exec. dir. Mass. Assn. Conservation Com., Belmont, 1986-88; mem. Mass. Ho. Reps., Boston, 1990-99, Mass. Senate, Boston, 1999—. Selectman Town of Acton, Mass., 1981-87. Mem. LWV (pres. 1978-80). Avocations: hiking, skiing. Office: Mass State Senate State House Rm 413-F Boston MA 02133

RESOR, STANLEY ROGERS, lawyer; b. N.Y.C., Dec. 5, 1917; s. Stanley Burnet and Helen (Lansdowne) R.; m. Jane Lawler Pillsbury, Apr. 4, 1942 (dec.); children: Stanley R., Charles P., John L., Edmund L., William B., Thomas S., James P.; m. Louise Mead Walker, May 1, 1999. BA, Yale U., 1939, LLB, 1946. Bar: NY 1947. Assoc., then ptnr. firm Debevoise & Plimpton, NYC, 1946-65, 71-73, 79-87, of counsel, 1988-90; undersec. Dept. Army, 1965, sec., 1965-71, amb. negotiations for Mut. and Balanced Force Reductions in Ctrl. Europe, 1973-78; undersec. for policy Dept. Def., 1978-79; ret. Fellow Yale Corp., 1979-86. Served to maj. AUS, 1942-45. Decorated

Silver Star, Bronze Star, Purple Heart; recipient George C. Marshall award Assn. US Army, 1974, Sylvanus Thayer award Assn. Graduates of US Mil. Acad., 1984. Mem. ABA, Assn. of Bar of City of NY (chmn. com. internat. arms control and security affairs 1983-86), Atlantic Coun., Arms Control Assn. (chmn. bd. 1994-2000), UN Assn. USA, Coun. Fgn. Rels., Lawyers Alliance for World Security, Internat. Inst. Strategic Studies. Republican. Episcopalian. Home: 809 Weed St New Canaan CT 06840-4023 Office: 1824 Phelps Pl NW #1804 Washington DC 20008 Office Phone: 202-462-8183. E-mail: srresor@aol.com.

RESS, CHARLES WILLIAM, management consultant; b. Columbus, Ohio, Aug. 6, 1933; s. George Leonard and Martha (Lake) R.; m. Virginia M. Beck, Aug. 28, 1954; children: Beverly Beck, Suzanne E., Charles W. Jr., Linda Perrins Foxworth, Jennifer Laurel Brulé. BS, Miami U., 1955; MA in Psychology, Rutgers U., 1969. Buyer The Higbee Co., Cleve., 1956-59; asst. to gen. mdse. mgr. The Halle Bros. Co., Cleve., 1959-64; research dir. The Associated Mdse. Corp., N.Y.C., 1964-73; v.p. Mgmt. Horizons, Columbus, 1973-76; founder, chmn. bd. C.W. Ress & Assoc., Inc., Columbus, 1976-90; gen. mgr. Levi Strauss & Co., Columbus, 1990-94, mgmt. cons., 1994—. Lectr. in field. Author: Future Trends in Retailing, 1983, Trans National Retailing, 1988, Retailing 2000, 1991; contbr. articles to profl. jours. Republican. Avocations: cooking, wine tasting. Office: 3860 Lyon Dr Columbus OH 43220-4907 Office Phone: 614-457-8885. E-mail: ressandress@wowway.com.

RESSEL, TERESA MULLETT, federal agency administrator; BS in Engring., MS in Engring., U. Del.; MBA, Rensselaer Poly. Inst., 1990. V.p., chief compliance officer Kaiser Found. Health Plan, Inc., Kaiser Found. Hosps., Inc.; prin. dep. asst. sec. for mgmt. and budget U.S. Dept. Treasury, Washington, 2001—02, asst. sec. for mgmt. and CFO, 2003—. Recipient Presdl. Citation for Outstanding Alumni Achievement, U. Del., 1996, Disting. Svc. award, Dept. Treasury, 2003. Office: US Dept of the Treasury 1500 Pennsylvania Ave NW Washington DC 20220

RESSLER, PARKE E(DWARD), lawyer, accountant; b. Lancaster, Pa., Aug. 21, 1916; s. Parke H. and Sadie (Weiser) R.; m. Margaret B. Tucker, June 3, 1944; children: Nancy Parke, Margaret Anne. BS, U. Pa., 1947; BBA, Baylor U., 1947, LLB, 1952, JD, 1969; MBA, U. Houston, 1949. Bar: Tex. 1952. Agt. Internal Revenue Svc., 1947-50; part time instr. Baylor U., 1950-65; law practice Waco, 1952—; assoc. firm Edwin P. Horner. Mem. AICPA, ABA, Tex. Soc. CPA, Tex. Bar Assn., McLennan County Bar Assn., Am. Assn. Atty.-CPAs, Ridgewood Country Club, Hedonia Club, Ridgewood Yacht Club, Baylor Bear Club, Rotary, Phi Alpha Delta, Delta Sigma Pi. Mem. Christian Ch. Home and Office: 2209 Arroyo Rd Waco TX 76710-1626

RESSLER, ROBERT, sculptor; b. Bklyn., June 25, 1954; s. Benjamin Seigfreid Ressler and Eleanore; m. Eileen Merwin, Sept. 1, 1988; children: Ben, Moriah & Elias T. BFA, Pratt Inst., 1977. Sculpture, NYC Public Works (Pollack-Krasner fellow, 1990). Artist grantee, Change Inc, Pollack-Krasner, NYFA, Riverside State Pk., 1990, 1993, 1994. Achievements include Commissions & Grants for Public Artworks. Home: 857 Kent Ave Brooklyn NY 11205 Office: Vermont Studio 1114 Rt 30 Bomoseen VT 05732 Personal E-mail: ressler1@aol.com.

REST, ANN H. state legislator; b. Apr. 24, 1942; 1 child. BA, Northwestern U.; MA, U. Chgo.; MAT, MPA, Harvard U.; MBT, U. Minn. Mem. Minn. Ho. of Reps. dist. 46A, St. Paul, 1985-2000, Minn. Senate from 46th dist., St. Paul, 2001—. Chmn. taxes com., rules and legis. adminstrv. com., mem. ways and means com.; CPA. Recipient Women of Achievement award North Hennepin Bus. and Profl. Women, 1988; named Legislator of Yr., Politics in Minn., 1990. Mem. Resources for Adoptive Parents, Libr. Found. of Hennepin County, YMCA. Democrat. Home: 7611 36th Ave N Apt 322 Minneapolis MN 55427-2085 Office: Minn State Senate 439 State Office Bldg Saint Paul MN 55155-0001

RESTANI, JANE A. federal judge; b. San Francisco, Feb. 27, 1948; d. Roy J. and Emilia C. Restani. BA, U. Calif., Berkeley, 1969; JD, U. Calif., Davis, 1973. Bar: Calif., 1973. Trial atty. U.S. Dept. Justice, Washington, 1973-76, asst. chief comml. litigation sect., 1976-80, dir. comml. litigation sect., 1980-83; judge U.S. Ct. Internat. Trade, N.Y.C., 1983—. Mem. Order of Coif. Office: US Ct Internat Trade 1 Federal Plz New York NY 10278-0001*

RESTIVO, JAMES JOHN, JR., lawyer; b. Pitts. s. James J. and Dorothy (Ardolino) R.; m. Gail Sharon Hackenburg, July 11, 1970; 4 children. BA in History, U. Pa., 1968; JD, Georgetown U., 1971. Bar: Pa. 1971, U.S. Dist. Ct. (we. and ea. dists.) Pa. 1971, U.S. Ct. Appeals (3d cir.) 1971, U.S. Supreme Ct. 1979. Ptnr. Reed Smith, Pitts., 1979—; head litig. dept. Reed, Smith, Shaw & McClay, Pitts., 1986-97. Mem. editl. staff Georgetown Law Rev., 1970-71. Bd. dirs. Rebuilding Together-Greater Pitts., Pitts. Regional Alliance. Fellow Am. Coll. Trial Lawyers; mem. Acad. Trial Lawyers Allegheny County, Allegheny County Bar Assn., Pa. Economy League (We. divsn.), Def. Rsch. Inst. Home: 209 Deer Meadow Dr Pittsburgh PA 15241-2253 Office: Reed Smith 435 6th Ave Ste 2 Pittsburgh PA 15219-1886 Office Phone: 412-288-3122. Business E-mail: jrestivo@reedsmith.com.

RESTON, ROCKY RUSSELL, anesthesiologist, engineer, educator; b. Cheyenne, Wyo., Sept. 8, 1962; s. Russell Turrefiel and Beverly Elaine Reston. BSEE, USAF Acad., 1984; PhD, Air Force Inst. Tech., 1993; MD, Uniformed Svcs. U. Health Scis, 1998. Cert. board cert. Am. Bd. of Anesthesiology, 2003. Commd. 2d lt. USAF, 1984, advanced through grades to maj., 1999; instrumentation engr. 4484th Test Squadron, Tyndall AFB, Fla., 1984-87; electronics device processing engr. Wright Labs., Wright Patterson AFB, Ohio, 1992-94; resident in internal medicine Wilford Hall Med. Ctr., Lackland AFB, Tex., 1998-99, resident in anesthesiology, 1999—2002; assoc. prof. tech. and mgmt. U. Md., College Park, 1996—; staff anesthesiologist Wright Patterson Med. Ctr., Ohio, 2002—03; chmn. anesthesia dept. Wright-Patterson Med. Ctr., Ohio, 2003—. Presenter in field. Contbr. articles to profl. jours.; patentee in field. Mem. IEEE, Am. Soc. Anesthesiologists, USAF Acad. Assn. Grads, Eta Kappa Nu (treas. 1988-89), Tau Beta Pi. Address: 2726 Greenridge Cir Beavercreek OH 45431 Office: 74 MDOS/SGOSA 4881 Sugar Maple Dr Wright Patterson Afb OH 45433 E-mail: Rocky_R@msn.com.

RESWICK, JAMES BIGELOW, former government official, rehabilitation engineer, educator, biomedical engineer; b. Ellwood City, Pa., Apr. 16, 1922; s. Maurice and Katherine (Parker) R.; children: James Bigelow, David Parker (dec.), Pamela Reswick; m. Irmtraud Orthlies Hoelzerkopf, Dec., 27, 1973. SBME, MIT, 1943, SM, 1948, ScD, 1952; DEng (hon.), Rose Poly. Inst., 1968. Asst. prof., then assoc. prof., head machine design and graphics div. MIT, 1948-59; Leonard Case prof. engring., dir. Engring. Design Ctr., Case Western Res. U., 1959-70; prof. biomed. engring. and orthopaedics U. So. Calif., also dir. of rsch. dept. orthopaedics, 1970-80; assoc. dir. tech. Nat. Inst. Handicapped Rsch., U.S. Dept. Edn.; dir. VA Rehab. R & D Evaluation Unit VA Med. Ctr., Washington, 1984-88; dir. rsch. scis. Nat. Inst. on Disability and Rehab. Rsch. U.S. Dept. Edn., Washington, 1989—94; ret., 1994; acting dir. Nat. Inst. Disability and Rehab. Rsch., Washington, 1989-91. Engring. cons. on automatic control, product devel., automation and bio-med. engring. Mem. com. prosthetics R & D Nat. Acad. Scis., 1962-; chmn. design and devel. com.; mem. bd. rev. Army R & D Office, 1965-; mem. applied physiology and biomed. engring. study sect. NIH, 1972-. Author: (with C.K. Taft) Introduction to Dynamic Systems, 1967; also articles.; Editor: (with F.T. Hambrecht) Functional Electrical Stimulation, 1977; series on engring. design, 1963-; inventor, patentee in field. Chmn. Mayor's Commn. for Urban Transp., Cleve., 1969. Served to lt. (j.g.) USNR, 1943-46, PTO. Decorated officer Yugoslav Flag with golden wreath medal (Yugoslavia), 1990; recipient Product Engring. Master Designer award, 1969, Isabelle and Leonard H. Goldenson award United Cerebral Palsy Assn., 1973; NSR sr. postdoctoral fellow Imperial Coll., London, 1957. Fellow IEEE, Am. Inst. Med. and Biological Engring. (founder); mem. ASME (honor award for best paper 1956, sr. mem.), Am. Soc. Engring. Edn., Instrument Soc. Am., Biomed. Engring. Soc. (sr. mem., pres. 1973, dir.), Am. Acad. Orthopedic Surgeons (assoc.), Inst. Medicine of NAS, NAE, Internat. Soc. Orthotics and Prosthetics, Orthopaedics Rsch. Soc., Rehab. Engring. Soc. N.Am. (founding pres.), Sigma XI. Home: 1834 Calf Mountain Rd Crozet VA 22932 E-mail: jimreswick@aol.com.

RETALLACK, GREGORY JOHN, geologist, educator; b. Hobart, Australia, Nov. 8, 1951; arrived in U.S., 1977; s. Kenneth John Retallack and Moira Wynn (Dean) Gollan; m. Diane Alice Retallack, May 31, 1981; children: Nicholas John, Jeremy Douglas. BA, Macquarie U., Sydney, 1973; BSc with honors, U. New Eng., 1974, PhD, 1978. Vis. asst. prof. No. Ill. U., DeKalb, 1977—78; vis. scholar Ind. U., Bloomington, 1978—81; asst. prof. U. Oreg., Eugene, 1981—86, assoc. prof., 1986—92, prof., 1992—. Author: Late Eocene and Oligocene Paleosols from Badlands National Park, South Dakota, 1983, Soils of the Past, 1990, 2d edit., 2001, Miocene Paleosols and Ape Habitats in Pakistan and Kenya, 1991, Colour Guide to Paleosols, 1997; contbr. articles to profl. jours. Grantee, NSF, 1979—, Wenner-Gren Found., 1983. Fellow: AAAS, Geol. Soc. Am.; mem.: Soc. Econ. Paleontologists and Mineralogists, Oreg. Acad. Sci. (pres. 1986), Paleontology Soc. (pres. Pacific sect. 1986), Bot. Soc. Am., Geol. Soc. Australia, Sigma Xi (pres. U. Oreg. chpt. 1983—84). Home: 2715 Elinor St Eugene OR 97403-2513 Office Phone: 541-346-4558.

RETHORE, BERNARD GABRIEL, retired manufacturing and mining company executive; b. May 22, 1941; s. Francis Joseph and Katharine Eunice (MacDwyer) Rethore; m. Marilyn Irene Watt, Dec. 1, 1962 (div. Apr. 2002); children: Bernard Michael, Tara Jean, Kevin Watt, Alexandra Marie, Rebecca Ann, Christopher Philip, Abigail Lyn. BA, Yale U., 1962; MBA, U. Pa., 1967. Assoc. McKinsey & Co., Inc., Washington, 1967—73, sr. assoc., 1973; v.p., gen. mgr. Greer div. Microdot, Inc., Darien, Conn., 1973—77, v.p. ops. connector group, 1977—78, pres. bus. devel. group, 1978—82, pres. fastening sys. and sealing devices groups, 1982—84; pres. Microdot Industries, Darien, Conn., 1984—87, pres., CEO, 1988; pres. Microdot Europe Ltd., Darien, Conn., 1984—88; sr. v.p. Phelps Dodge Corp., Phoenix, 1989—95; group exec. Phelps Dodge Industries, Phoenix, 1989—90, pres., 1990—95; pres., CEO, bd. dirs. BW/IP Internat., Inc., Long Beach, Calif., 1995—97, chmn., 1997; CEO, chmn. bd. dirs. Flowserve Corp., Dallas, 1997—2000, chmn. emeritus, 2000—; chmn. McDyre & Spendley, Ltd., 2000—. Bd. dirs. Maytag Corp., Belden, Inc., Dover Corp., Walter Industries, Inc.; cons. U.S. Govt., UN; mem. Thunderbird Global Bus. Coun., Garvin Sch. Internat. Mgmt., 1990—, chmn., 1991—94; mem. dean's adv. bd. Wharton Sch. Bus., U. Pa., 1972—80. Elected mem. bd. fin. Town of Westport, Conn., 1986-90; trustee Ballet Ariz., 1989-95, vice chmn., 1991-95; bd. dirs. Boys Hope of Phoenix, 1989-95; trustee Phoenix Country Day Sch., 1992-2003, Thunderbird, Garvin Sch. Internat. Mgmt., 1994—, vice chmn., 2004—. Served to capt., inf. AUS, 1962-65. Decorated Bronze Star. Mem. Nat. Assn. Mfrs. (bd. dirs. 1994-95, 96-99), Yale Club (N.Y.C.), Union League (Chgo.), Nat. Assn. Corp. Dirs. (blue ribbon com. on bd. role in strategic plan 2000), Gainey Ranch Club (Scottsdale, Ariz.). Home: 7010 East Avenida El Alba Paradise Valley AZ 85253 Office: McDyre & Spendley Ltd Ste 300 7702 E Doubletree Ranch Rd Scottsdale AZ 85258 Business E-mail: brethore@msltd.cc.

RETTIE, DWIGHT FAY, retired political science educator, writer; b. New Haven, Mar. 27, 1930; s. James Cardno and Lois (Morris) Rettie; m. Karen Ross, Aug. 4, 1984; children: Stuart, Catherine, Thomas, Jeffery. BA, Yale U., 1952; MA, U. Calif., Berkeley, 1955; cert. leadership tng., George Washington U., 1959; cert. def. mgmt. sys. course, U.S. Naval Postgrad. Sch., 1964. Various positions Dept. of Interior, Washington, 1957-65; program dir. Dept. Housing and Urban Devel., Washington, 1965-71; exec. dir. Nat. Recreation and Park Assn., Arlington, Va., 1971-75; exec. Nat. Park Svc., Washington, 1975-81, chief office policy devel., 1981-86; instr. Carteret C.C., Morehead City, N.C., 1995-98; vis. prof. East Carolina U., Greenville, NC, 1998—2001. Dir. Arlington Telecomm. Inc., Va., 1973-79; cons. Nat. Parks and Conservation Assn., 1995-96. Author: Our National Park System: Caring for America's Greatest Natural and Historic Treasures, 1995. Mem. nat. coun. Boy Scouts Am., 1958-62; chmn. Arlington County Pub. Utilities Commn., 1967-73; mem. U.S. Bd. Geographic Names, Washington, 1981-86; gov. bd. No. Va. Regional Park Authority, Fairfax, Va., 1973-81. Staff sgt. U.S. Army, 1952-54. Democrat. Mem. Unitarian Ch. Avocations: sailing, teaching, writing. Home: 415 Hardy Rd Newport NC 28570 Business E-Mail: tarwathie@clis.com.

RETTIG, TERRY, veterinarian, wildlife consultant, construction contractor; b. Houston, Jan. 30, 1947; s. William E. and Rose (Munves) R.; m. Helen Rettig, Mar. 12, 1996; 1 child, Bill; children from previous marriage: Michael Thomas, Jennifer Suzanne. BS in Zoology, Duke U., 1969, MAT in Sci., 1970; DVM, U. Ga., 1975; MBA honors in Constrn. Mgmt., Keller Grad. Sch., 2003. Resident veterinarian, mgr. animal health The Wildlife Preserve, Largo, Md., 1975-76; wildlife veterinarian dept. environ. conservation State of N.Y., Delmar, 1976-77; owner Atlanta Animal Hosp., 1976—2001; CEO Atlanta Svcs., P.C. Quality Home Builders, 1977—2002; pres. Am. Dream Constrn., Inc., 2002—. Sec., dir. Atlanta Pet Supply, Inc., 1983-89; cons. Six Flags Over Ga., Yellow River Game Ranch, Stone Mountain Park Animal Forest, Atlanta Zoo. Author: (with Murray Fowler) Zoo and Wild Animal Medicine (Aardvark award 1978), 1978, 2d edit., 1986 (Order of Kukukifuku award 1986); contbr. articles to profl. jours. Del. Dekalb County Republican Conv., 1983; mem. Roswell United Meth. Ch., Boy Scouts Am., 1954—, mem. troop coun., asst. scoutmaster, scout master, Philmont expedition leader, 1988, 89. Spl. scholar Cambridge U. Coll. Vet. Medicine, 1973-74, Honor Medal with Crossed Palms, 1995. Mem.: AVMA, Sys. Homebuilders Assn. Ga., Greater Atlanta Homebuilders Assn., Nat. Assn. Homebuilders, Am. Buffalo Assn., Soc. Aquatic Vet. Medicine, Internat. Wildlife Assn., Am. Animal Hosp. Assn., Am. Assn. Avian Vets., Am. Fedn. Aviculturists, Atlanta Zool. Soc., Nat. Wildlife Assn., Nat. Wildlife Health Found., Am. Assn. Zool. Parks and Aquaria, Am. Assn. Zoo Vets., Acad. Vet. Medicine, Dekalb Vet. Soc., Greater Atlanta Vet. Med. Assn., Ga. Vet. Med. Assn., Cousteau Soc. Methodist. Home and Office: Am Dream Constrn Inc 5035 Kimball Bridge Rd Alpharetta GA 30005-5649 Personal E-mail: AmericanDreamConstruction@comcast.net.

RETZ, WILLIAM ANDREW, retired naval officer; b. Blauvelt, N.Y., June 3, 1940; s. Andrew Macmillan and Katherine (Deyoe) R.; m. Julia Irene Patterson, Sept. 23, 1989; children: Andrew, Gregory, Mark, Alyse Reavis, Mark Rogers. Student, Tex. A&M U., 1957; BS in Mech. Engring., U. N.Mex., 1963; MS, George Washington U., 1970; grad., Naval War Coll., 1972. Commd. ensign USN, 1963, advanced through grades to rear adm., 1991, patrol officer river div. 511, 1968-69, flag sec. to comdr. Amphibious Group Two, 1972-74, exec. officer USS Ainsworth, 1974-76, commanding officer USS Stump, 1980-82, commodore Destroyer Squadron 22, 1985-87, dep. for ops. U.S. Cen. Command Tampa, Fla., 1987-90; comdr. Naval Base Pearl Harbor, 1992-94, Naval Surface Group Mid. Pacific, 1992-94; commanded and closed Naval Base Phila., 1994-95; ret. USN, 1995; v.p. govt. svcs. Aramark Corp., Phila., 1996-99; ind. cons., 1999; CEO Nofire Techs., Inc., 2000—03; exec. dir. Am. Competitiveness Inst., Phila., 2003—. Active Episcopal Ch., Media, Pa.; bd. dirs. Ind. Seaport Mus. Decorated Disting. Svc. medal, Legion of Merit, Def. Disting. Svc. medal, Meritorious Svc. medal, Bronze Star, Purple Heart. Mem. Surface Navy Assn. (bd. dirs.), Nat. Def. Indsl. Assn. (bd. dirs.), Navy League (bd. dirs.). Avocations: running, sailing. Office: Am Competitiveness Inst One Internat Plaza Ste 600 Philadelphia PA 19113 E-mail: retzw@comcast.net.

RETZEL, FRANK, music educator, composer; b. Detroit, Aug. 11, 1948; s. Ludwig William and Mildred Mary Retzel; m. Kathleen Ann Buhl, Aug. 9, 1975. MusB, Wayne State U., 1972, MusM, 1974; PhD, U. Chgo., 1978. Asst. prof. music, dir. electronic music studio Cath. U. Am., Washington, 1981—82; asst. prof. music Bklyn. Coll., 1983—84; assoc. prof. music NYU, 1984—89; prof. music Fordham U., N.Y.C., 1992—. Organist, choral and music dir. St. Barnabas Ch., N.Y.C., 1980—81, St. Elizabeth Ch., N.Y.C., 1985—92, Ch. of Mary's Nativity, N.Y.C., 1992—, others; dir. contemporary music ensemble Cath. U. Am., 1981—82, Bklyn. Coll., 1983—84; composer-in-residence Bennington Coll., Vt., 1984; dir. electronic music studio U. Chgo., 1981—82; dir. rsch. for Am. music New World Records, N.Y.C., 1984—85, 1987—88; spkr. in field. Composer: Schism I, 1975, Swamp Music, 1978 (League-ICSM award, 1979), One, 1978, Amber Glass, 1979—80, Anamnesis: The City of God, 1980, Line Drawings and Earthen Clay Figures, 1980, 1985, Canticles, 1981—83, Lumen, 1983, Movements, 1984 (1st prize New Music for Young Ensembles, 1987), Horae, 1986 (Pulitzer prize nominee, 1988), Chansonnier, 1983, Trinity, 1993, Daughter of Dawn, 1993, Tamarind, 1993—96, Summer Songs, 1996, Blue-Line Strophes, 1996, Portrait in Fantasy, 1997, Landscapes, 1998, 2002, Reflections, 2002, Duets, 2002, Night Neon: Images, 2003—04, numerous others; contbr. articles to profl. jours. Mem. com. for music edn. N.Y.C. Coun., 1998; mem. music commn. Diocese of Bklyn., 1993—99; bd. dirs. Am. New Music Consortium, 1984—86. Recipient Paul Paray award, Wayne State U., 1971, Harold Laugenslager award, 1973; fellow, Nat. Endowment for the Arts, 1980—81, Mellon Found., 1983—84; grantee, Meet the Composer, 1980—; Fulbright fellow, 1982—83. Mem.: BMI, L.I. Composers' Alliance, League of Composers-Internat. Soc. Contemporary Music (bd. dirs. 1983—, treas. 1984—85), Coll. Music Soc., Assn. for Promotion of New Music, Am. Musicol. Soc., Am. Music Ctr., Am. Guild Organists (new music com. for 1996 nat. conf.). Democrat. Roman Catholic. Avocations: reading, billiards, art museums, movies. Home: 84-49 168th St Jamaica NY 11432 Personal E-mail: frankretzel@aol.com.

RETZER, KENNETH ALBERT, mathematics professor, entrepreneur; b. Jacksonville, Ill., Nov. 6, 1933; s. Samuel Stark and Cora Edith (Martin) R.; m. Dorcas Anne Schroeder, Apr. 18, 1953 (dec. Aug. 4, 1990); children: Martin Wayne, Kent Arnold, Sheryl Kaye; m. Wei Dong, Feb. 14, 1991; 1 child, Roger Dong Retzer. AB, Ill. Coll., 1954; MEd, U. Ill., 1957, PhD, 1969. Cert. tchr., Ill., 1954-57; cert. sch. adminstrn., Ill., 1957—. Tchr. Saunemin (Ill.) Twp. High Sch., 1954-58, asst. supt., 1955-58; prof. math. Ill. State U., Normal, 1959-89, Abilene (Tex.) Christian U., 1989—97; v.p., bd. dirs. DR Global Enterprises, DBA Cafe China, DBA DR Gifts and Accessories, 1995—2000; v.p., bd. dir. WD Mgmt. LLC, DBA Gary's Pizza, 2002—. Asst. chmn. math. dept. Ill. State U., Normal, 1969-71; vis. prof. U. Ga., Athens, 1973, Tex. A&M U., College Station, 1984, U. Hawaii-Maui, Kahului, 1990, 91; cons. Arabian Am. Oil Co., Dhahran, Saudi Arabia, 1984, Ill. State Bd. Edn., Springfield, 1983-88; rsch. fellow U. Western Sydney, Australia, 1993; lectr. Zhejiang U., Hangzhou, China, Northwest Normal U., Lanzhou, China, Gansu Edn. U., Lanzhou, Lanzhou Normal U., Zhangye Normal U., China, summer 1994. Contbr. articles to profl. jours. in the U.S., Can., China. Mem. NEA, AAUP, Nat. Coun. Tchrs. Math., Sch. Sci. and Math. Assn., Math. Assn. Am., Rsch. Coun. on Diagnostic and Prescriptive Math., Ill. Coun. Tchrs. Math. (Max Beberman award 1988), Tex. Coun. Tchrs. Math., Big County Coun. Tchrs. Math., Ill. Assn. Higher Edn., Pi Mu Epsilon, Phi Delta Kappa. Mem. Church of Christ. Avocations: travel, photography, hiking, reading, Christian studies. Home: 31 Rue Maison St Abilene TX 79605-4710 E-mail: ken.retzer@math.acu.edu.

RETZER, MARY ELIZABETH HELM, retired librarian; b. Balt. d. Francis Leslie C. and Edna (Smith) Helm; m. William Raymond Retzer, June 28, 1945; children: Lesley Elizabeth, April Christine. BA, Western Md. Coll., 1940; MA, Columbia U., 1946; postgrad., George Washington U., 1941, Ind. U., 1952, U. Ill., 1958-59, Ill. State U., 1964-66, Bradley U.; PhD, Western Colo. U., 1972. Faculty Rockville (Md.) Bd. Edn., 1940-47, elem. supr., 1945-47; staff Peoria Pub. Libr., 1957-63, homebound libr., 1961-63; cons., organizer libr. Bergan High Sch., 1964-67; condr. libr. sci. course in reference Bradley U., 1966-83. Libr. Hines Elem. Sch., 1963-66, Roosevelt Jr. H.S., 1966-69; head media ctr. Manual H.S., Peoria, Ill., 1969-83. Instr. water safety courses ARC, 1938-93; pres. Entre Nous, 1949-51; pres. women's bd. Salvation Army, 1952-54; pres. Peoria Nursery Sch. Assn., 1953-54; mem. legis. action com. Ill. Congress PTA, 1955-56; mem. Crippled Children's Adv. Com., Peoria, 1957-60; active various community drives; women's adv. bd. Peoria Jr. Star, 1970-73; vol. Sarasota Internat. Airport, 1990-98. Mem. AAUW (life), NEA, ALA (life), Ill. Edn. Assn. (life), Peoria Edn. Assn. (life), Ill. Libr. Assn., Ill. Valley Librs. Assn. (pres. 1971-72), Ill. Assn. Media in Edn. (cert. com. 1973-80), Ill. Audiovisual Assn., Internat. Platform Assn., Order Ea. Star (life), Ill. State U. Adminstrs. Club, Willowknolls Country Club, Sarasota Yacht Club, Ladies Oriental Shrine. Republican. Presbyterian. Home: Unit 308 435 S Gulfstream Ave Sarasota FL 34236-6705

REUBEN, ALVIN BERNARD, communications and entertainment executive; b. Harrisburg, Pa., Aug. 11, 1940; s. Maurice and Lillian (Katzef) R.; m. Barbara Ann Harrison, Mar. 18, 1968; 1 dau., Mindee Jill. BS in Commerce, Rider U., 1962. Buyer Pomeroy's div. Allied Stores Corp., Harrisburg, 1962-67; sales rep. Random House, Inc., N.Y.C., 1967-74; dir. mktg. Ballantine Books, Inc. (div. Random House), N.Y.C., 1974-76; v.p. sales Simon & Schuster, N.Y.C., 1976-79, sr. v.p. sales Pocket Books div., 1979-81, sr. v.p. mktg., 1981-82, pres. ref. and promotional pub. group, 1982-83, exec. v.p. electronic pub. div., 1983-85; exec. v.p. Prentice Hall div. Simon & Schuster, 1985-86; sr. v.p. mktg., sales and distbn. Vestron, Inc., 1986-89; sr. v.p. St. Martin's Press, N.Y.C., 1989-91; sr. v.p. sales, mktg. Sony Music Video, N.Y.C., 1991-92; sr. v.p. spl. markets Sony Music, N.Y.C., 1992-95; sr.v.p. video and interactive sales and distbn. BMG Entertainment, 1995-97; pres. BMG Video, 1997-99. Instr. edn. in pub. program, grad. program SUNY. With USAFR, 1963-69. Mem. Tau Kappa Epsilon. Home and Office: 5 Tyler Ln Bluffton SC 29909-5028 Personal E-mail: alreubenschh@aol.com.

REUBEN, DON HAROLD, lawyer; b. Chgo., Sept. 13, 1928; s. Michael B. and Sally (Colucci) R.; m. Evelyn Long, Aug. 27, 1948 (div.); children: Hope Reuben Boland, Michael Barrett, Timothy Don, Jeffrey Long, Howard Ellis; m. Jeannette Hurley Haywood, Dec. 13, 1971; stepchildren: Harris Hurley Haywood, Edward Gregory Haywood. BS, Northwestern U., 1949, JD, 1952. Bar: Ill. 1952, Calif. 1996. With firm Kirkland & Ellis, Chgo., 1952-78, sr. ptnr., Reuben & Proctor, Chgo., 1978-86, Isham, Lincoln & Beale, Chgo., 1986-88; sr. counsel Winston & Strawn, Chgo., 1988-94; of counsel Altheimer & Gray, Chgo., 1994—2003, Kane, Carbonara & Mendoza, Ltd., Chgo., 2003—. Spl. asst. atty. gen. State of Ill., 1963—64, 1969, 84; gen. counsel Tribune Co., 1965—88, Chgo. Bears Football Club, 1965—88, Cath. Archdiocese of Chgo., 1975—78; counsel spl. session Ill. Ho. of Reps., 1964, for Ill. treas. for congl., state legis. and jud. reapportionment, 1963; spl. fed. ct. master, 1968—70; dir. Lake Shore Nat. Bank, 1973—93, Heitman Fin., 1993—98, News-Gazette, Champaign, 1997—99; mem. citizens adv. bd. to sheriff County of Cook, 1962—66, jury instrn. com., 1963—68; mem. rules com. Ill. Supreme Ct., 1963—73; past mem. pub. rels. com. Nat. Conf. State Trial Judges; mem. com. study caseflow mgmt. in law divsn. Cook County Cir. Ct., 1979—88; mem. adv. implementation com. U.S. Dist. Ct. No. Dist. Ill., 1981—82; mem. Chgo. Better Sch. Com., 1968—69, Chgo. Crime Commn., 1970—80; mem. supervisory panel Fed. Defender Program, 1971—78; sec. gen. counsel Palm Springs Air Mus., 1996—. Bd. dirs. Lincoln Pk. Zool. Soc., 1972—84; trustee Northwestern U., 1977—; mem. vis. com. U. Chgo. Law Sch., 1976—79; bd. dirs. Blood Bank of the Desert, 1999—2004, vice-chmn., 2003—04; chmn. gen. plan adv. com. City of Rancho Mirage, 1994—. Recipient Northwestern U. Law Sch. Alumni Achievement medal, 2002. Fellow: Am. Bar Found., Internat. Acad. Trial Lawyers; mem.: ABA (standing com. on fed. judiciary 1973—79, standing com. on jud. selection, tenure and compensation 1982—85), Desert Bar Assn., Calif. Bar Assn., Am. Arbitration Assn. (nat. panel arbitrators 1998—), Am. Coll. Trial Lawyers (Rule 23 com. 1975—82, judiciary com. 1987—91), Am. Law Inst., Chgo. Bar Assn. (chmn. subcom. propriety and regulation of contingent fees com. devel. 1966—69, subcom. on media liaison 1980—82, com. on profl. info. 1980—82), Ill. Bar Assn., Mission Hills Country Club, Casino Club, Mid-Am. Club, Com. of 25 Palm Springs, Chgo. Club, Tamarisk Country Club (hon.), Order of Coif, Beta Gamma Sigma, Beta Alpha Psi, Phi Eta Sigma. Office: 20 Jill Ter Rancho Mirage CA 92270-2635 Office Phone: 760-324-0619., 312-726-2322.

REUBEN, GLORIA, actress; b. Toronto, Ont., June 9, 1964; T.V. and movie actress; backup singer and dancer Tina Turner's World Tour, 2000. T.V. films include The Day They Came to Arrest the Book, 1986, Shadowhunter, 1993, Dead Air, 1994, Indiscreet, 1998, Sara, 1999, Deep in My Heart, 1999, Little John, 2002, Salem Witch Trials, 2002; film appearances include Immediate Family, 1989, Johnny's Girl, 1993, Timecop, 1994, Nick of Time, 1995, Macbeth in Manhattan, 1999, Bad Faith, 1999, Happy Here and Now, 2001; T.V. series include ER, 1995-99 (Emmy Best Supporting Actress nominee 1997, 98), The Agency, 2001-02; T.V. guest appearances in The Flash, 1990,

Silk Stalkings, 1991, Homicide: Life on the Street, 1993, others. Recipient SAG Awards, 1998, 99, Q Award, 1997, 98. Office: Gerson Saines Mgmt Ste 2303 250 W 57th St New York NY 10107-2399

REUBEN, LAWRENCE MARK, lawyer; b. Akron, Ohio, Apr. 5, 1948; s. Albert G. and Sara I. (Rifkin) R. Student, London Sch. Econs., 1969; BS, Ind. U., 1970; JD, Ind. U., Indpls., 1973. Bar: Ind. 1973, U.S. Dist. Ct. (so. dist.) Ind. 1973, U.S. Dist. Ct. (no. dist.) Ind. 1975, U.S. Ct. Appeals (7th cir.) 1975, U.S. Supreme Ct. 1976, U.S. Ct. Appeals (9th cir.) 1978, U.S. Ct. Appeals (D.C. cir.) 1994, U.S. Ct. Appeals (fed. cir.) 1999. Ptnr. Atlas, Hyatt & Reuben, Indpls., 1976-87, Atlas & Reuben, Indpls., 1987-90; chief counsel Ind. Dept. Ins., 1990-91; gen. counsel Ind. Dept. Transp., 1991-93; chief deputy Ind. Atty. Gen., Indpls., 1993-94; gen. counsel State Lottery Commn. Ind., Indpls., 1994-97; pvt. practice Indpls., 1997—. V.p. Ind. Civil Liberties Union, 1975-84; sec., bd. dirs. Indpls. Humane Soc., 1974-85; fellow Indpls. C. of C.-Lacey Leadership Program, 1982; sec., v.p., bd. dirs. Julian Ctr., Inc., 1983-89; mem. ch.-state commn. Nat. Jewish Community Relations Adv. Council, N.Y.C., 1982-89; bd. dirs. Indpls. Consumer Credit Counseling Bur., 1983-89; pres. Bur. Jewish Edn., 1984-86; parliamentarian Ind. State Dem. Party, 1985-86; mem. Indpls. Police Community Relations Rev. Com., 1983. Recipient Robert Risk award Ind. Civil Liberties Union, 1981, David M. Cook Meml. award Indpls. Jewish Community Rels. Coun., 1982; L.L. Goodman Leadership award, Jewish Fed. Indpls., 1989. Mem. Am. Trial Lawyers Assn., Ind. State Bar Assn., Indpls. Bar Assn. Office: Jefferson Plaza 1 Virginia Ave Ste 600 Indianapolis IN 46204-3671 E-mail: Lmreubenlaw@yahoo.com.

REUBER, GRANT LOUIS, banking insurance company executive; b. Mildmay, Ont., Can., Nov. 23, 1927; s. Jacob Daniel and Gertrude Catherine (Wahl) R.; m. Margaret Louise Julia Summerhayes, Oct. 21, 1951 (dec. Feb. 1998); children: Rebecca, Barbara, Mary. BA, U. Western Ont., 1950; AM, Harvard U., 1954, PhD, 1957; LLD (hon.), Wilfred Laurier U., 1983, Simon Fraser U., 1985, U. Western Ont., 1985, McMaster U., 1994; postgrad., Cambridge U., 1954-55. Mem. research dept. Bank Can., Ottawa, 1950-52; mem. Can. Dept. Finance, Ottawa, 1955-57; asst. prof. econ. U. Western Ont., London, 1957-59, assoc. prof., 1959-62, prof., head dept., 1963-69, 1963-69; mem. bd. govs. U. Western Ont., London, 1974-78, acad. v.p., provost, 1975-78, chancellor, 1988-92; sr. v.p., chief economist Bank of Montreal, Que., Can., 1978-79, exec. v.p., 1980 81, dep. chmn., dep. chief exec. officer, 1981-83, dir., mem. exec. com., 1981-89, pres., chief operating officer, 1983-87, dep. chmn., 1987-89; dep. minister fin. Can., 1979-80; chmn. Can. Deposit Ins. Corp., 1993-99; sr. adv., dir. Sussex Circle, 1999—. Staff mem. Royal Commn. Banking and Fin., Toronto, 1962—63; chmn. Ont. Econ. Coun., 1973—78; cons. Can. Internat. Devel. Agy., 1968—69; hon. rsch. assoc. in econs. Harvard U., 1968—69; cons. devel. ctr. OECD, 1969—73; lectr. U. Chgo. Sch. Bus., 1992—93. Author: Private Foreign Investment in Development, 1973, Canada's Political Economy, 1980; contbr. articles. Bd. dirs. Can. Merit Scholarship Found., 1994—2000; bd. govs. Royal Ont. Mus., 2000—02; chmn. Can. Ditchley Found., 1981—. Decorated officer Order of Can. Fellow: Royal Soc. Can. Office Phone: 416-867-3614.

REUBISH, GARY RICHARD, English language educator; b. Breckenridge, Minn., Jan. 6, 1946; s. Irving Earl and Genevieve Loretta (Miller) R. AA, N.D. State Coll. Sci., Wahpeton, 1969; BS, Valley City State Coll., 1971. Cert. tchr., N.D. Tchr. English Wolford (N.D.) Pub. Sch., 1971-72, Lake Benton (Minn.) Pub. Sch., 1972-76, Wahpeton (N.D.) Pub. Sch., 1976—. With USAF, 1965-71. Mem. NEA, N.D. Edn. Assn., Wahpeton Edn. Assn. Office: Wahpeton Mid Sch 1209 Loy Ave Wahpeton ND 58075-5038 Address: PO Box 181 Wahpeton ND 58074-0181

REULER, JACK, theater director; s. Robert Gordon and Betty Eva Reuler; 1 child, Taj Ruler. BA, Macalester Coll., 1975. Artistic dir. Mixed Blood Theatre Co., Mpls., 1976—. Office: Mixed Blood Theatre Co 1501 S 4th St Minneapolis MN 55454-1100

REUM, JAMES MICHAEL, lawyer; b. Oak Park, Ill., Nov. 1, 1946; s. Walter John and Lucy (Bellegay) R. BA cum laude, Harvard U., 1968, JD cum laude, 1972. Bar: N.Y. 1973, D.C. 1974, U.S. Dist. Ct. (so. dist.) N.Y. 1974, Ill. 1979, U.S. Dist. Ct. (no. dist.) Ill. 1982. Assoc. Davis Polk & Wardwell, N.Y.C., 1973-78; assoc. Minority Counsel Com. on Judiciary U.S. Ho. of Reps., Washington, 1974; ptnr. Hopkins & Sutter, Chgo., 1979-93, Winston & Strawn, Chgo., 1994—. Midwest advance rep. Nat. Reagan Bush Com., 1980; nominee commr. Securities and Exchange Comm., Pres. Bush, 1992; mem. G.W. Bush fin. com, 2000. Served to SP4 USAR, 1969-75. Recipient Harvard U. Honorary Nat. Scholarship, 1964-72. Mem. Monte Carlo Country Club (Monaco), Univ. Club (NYC), Racquet Club Chgo. Republican. Home: 12 E Scott St Chicago IL 60610-2320 Office: Winston & Strawn 35 W Wacker Dr Ste 4200 Chicago IL 60601-1695 Office Phone: 312-558-5644. E-mail: jreum@winston.com.

REUM, W. ROBERT, manufacturing executive; b. Oak Park, Ill., July 22, 1942; m. Sharon Milliken. BA, Yale U., 1964; JD, U. Mich., 1967; MBA, Harvard U., 1969. Dir. investment analysis City Investing Co., N.Y.C., 1969-72; v.p. corp fin. Mich. Nat. Corp., Bloomfield Hills, Mich., 1972-78; v.p., treas. White Motor Corp., Cleve., 1978-79; v.p. fin., CFO, Lamson & Sessions, Cleve., 1980-82, The Interlake Corp., Oak Brook, Ill., 1982-88, exec. v.p., 1988-90, chmn., pres., CEO, 1991-99, Amsted Industries Inc., Chgo., 2001—, also bd. dirs. Bd. dirs. Lindberg Corp. Contbr. articles to Harvard Bus. Rev. Bd. dirs. Morton Arboretum, Lisle, Ill.; trustee Elgin (Ill.) Acad. Mem. Chgo. Golf Club, Chgo. Club, Rolling Rock Club (Ligonier, Pa.). Office: AMSTED Industries Inc 205 N Michigan Ave 44th Fl Chicago IL 60601

REUTER, FRANK THEODORE, history educator; b. Kankakee, Ill., Mar. 18, 1926; s. Frank Theodore and Evelyn Marie (Scott) R.; m. Kathleen Ann Pester, June 16, 1951; children: Mark, Stephen, Christopher, Ann, Katherine. BS, U. Ill., 1950, MA, 1959, PhD, 1960. Instr. West Liberty (W. Va.) State Coll., 1960-62; asst. prof. Texas Christian U., Fort Worth, 1962-66, assoc. prof., 1966-71; prof. history Tex. Christian U., 1971-92; dean Texas Christian U. (Grad. Sch.), 1970-75, chmn. dept. history, 1980-83; prof. emeritus Tex. Christian U., 1992—. Vis. prof. Pázmány Péter Cath. U., Budapest, Hungary, 1999. Author: West Liberty State College: The First 125 Years, 1963, Catholic Influence on American Colonial Policies, 1898-1904, 1967, Trials and Triumphs: George Washington's Foreign Policy, 1983; co-author: Injured Honor: The Chesapeake-Leopard Affair, 1996. Served with USNR, 1944-46. U. Durham Rsch. fellow, 1991. Mem. Orgn. Am. Historians, Am. Hist. Assn., Soc. Historians Early Republic, Soc. Historians Am. Fgn. Relations, Phi Beta Kappa, Phi Alpha Theta. Roman Catholic. Home: 3617 Winifred Dr Fort Worth TX 76133-2126 Office: Tex Christian U Dept History Fort Worth TX 76129-0001 Office Phone: 817-257-7288. E-mail: rfkreuter@aol.com.

REUTER, HELEN HYDE, psychologist; b. McGehee, Ark. d. John Lloyd and Sallie Elizabeth (Holcomb) Hyde; m. George S. Reuter Jr.; children: Don N., M. Allan, K.L. BA, Westmar U., 1968; AM, U. S.D., 1969; PhD, Westgate U., 1976; LHD (hon.), Sioux Empire Coll.; LLD (hon.), St. John U., New Orleans; DD (hon.), Temple Bapt. Coll. Ordained So. Bapt. minister. Postmaster U.S. Post Office, College Heights, Ark.; sch. counselor various pub. sch. systems, Mo., Iowa; sch. psychologist Oak Park (Ill.) and River Forest High Sch.; v.p., sec. Internat. Assocs. for Christians, Holden, Mo. Cons. in field. Co-author: One Blood, 1964, 2d edit., 1988, Democracy and Quality Education, 1965, 2d edit., 1966. Named Mother of Yr., City of Monticello, 1960; cited as Psychologist of Yr., Internat. U., Lagos, Nigeria, 1992. Mem. P.E.O. (v.p.), Shakespeare Club (v.p.), Garden Club (v.p.). Democrat. Baptist. Avocations: travel, classical music. Home: 3100 Club Dr Apt 320 Lawrenceville GA 30044

REUTER, JAMES WILLIAM, lawyer; b. Bemidji, Minn., Sept. 30, 1948; s. John Renee and Monica (Dugas) R.; m. Patricia Carol Creelman, Mar. 30, 1968; children: Kristine, Suzanne, Natalee. BA, St. John's U., 1970; JD, William Mitchell Coll. Law, 1974. Bar: Minn. 1974, U.S. Dist. Minn. 1975, U.S. Ct. Appeals (8th cir.) 1985; cert. civil trial specialist. Editor West Pub. Co., St. Paul, 1970-73; assoc. Terpstra & Merrill, Mpls., 1974-77; ptnr. Barna, Guzy, Merrill, Hynes & Giancola, Ltd., Mpls., 1977-89, Lindquist & Vennum, Mpls., 1989—. Recipient Cert. award Nat. Inst. Trial Advocacy, 1978. Mem. ABA (torts and ins. practice, and civil litigation sects.), ATLA, Minn. Bar Assn. (civil litigation and computer sects.), Hennepin County Bar Assn. (ins. com.), Anoka County Bar Assn. (pres. 1981-82). Avocations: skiing, golf, reading. Office: Lindquist & Vennum 4200 IDS Ctr 80 S 8th St Ste 4200 Minneapolis MN 55402-2274 Office Phone: 612-371-3519.

REUTER, STEWART RALSTON, retired radiologist, lawyer, educator; b. Detroit, Feb. 14, 1934; s. Carl H. and Grace M. R.; m. Marianne (Ahfeldt), June 6, 1966. BA, Ohio Wesleyan U., 1955; MD, Case Western Res. U., 1959; JD, U. San Francisco, 1980. Diplomate: Am. Bd. Radiology, Am. Bd. Legal Medicine. Bar: Tex., 1981. Intern U. Calif., San Francisco, 1959—60, resident in radiology, 1960—63; instr. radiology Stanford U., Calif., 1963—64; asst. prof. U. Mich., Ann Arbor, 1966—69; assoc. prof. U. Calif., San Diego, 1969—72; prof. U. Mich., Ann Arbor, 1972—76, U. Calif., San Francisco and Davis, 1976—80; prof., chmn. dept. radiology Health Sci. Ctr., U. Tex., San Antonio, 1980—2001, prof. emeritus, 2001. Co-author: Gastrointestinal Radiology, 3d edit., 1986; mem. editorial bd. Am. Jour. Roentgenology, 1975-91, Iatrogenics, 1990-93; contbr. articles to profl. journals. Picker Fellow, 1964-66. Fellow: Soc. Interventional Radiologists (pres. 1978, Gold Medal 2004, Gold medal 2004), Am. Coll. Legal Medicine (bd. gov. 1985—91, 1992—94, sec. 1994, pres. elect 1995, pres. 1996), Am. Heart Assn., Am. Coll. Radiology (councillor 1996—99, fellow emeritus 2000); mem.: Am. Roentgen Ray Soc., Assn., Soc. Gastrointestinal Radiologists, Tex. Radiol. Assn. (trustee 1989—92, pres. 1994, trustee 1995—98, Gold medal 2000), Assn. Univ. Radiologists, Am. Bd. Legal Medicine, Tex. Bar Assn. Home: 3923 Morgans Creek San Antonio TX 78230-1945 Office: U Tex Health Sci Ctr Dept Radiology 7703 Floyd Curl Dr San Antonio TX 78284-6200 Business E-Mail: reuter@uthscsa.edu.

REUTER, VICTOR E. pathologist, educator; m. Maria del Mar Reuter; children: Glorimar, Maria Victoria. MD, U. Nat. Pedro Henriquez Urena, Santo Domingo, Dominican Republic, 1978. Diplomate Am. Bd. Pathology (Anatomic and Clinical). Clin. fellow anatomic pathology Am. Cancer Soc., 1983—84; chief fellow dept. pathology Meml. Sloan-Kettering Cancer Ctr., N.Y.C., 1984—85, attending pathologist, 1998—, mem. Meml. Hosp. for Allied Diseases, N.Y.C., 1998—; acting chief surg. pathology svc. Meml. Sloan-Kettering Cancer Ctr., N.Y.C., 2000—; prof. pathology Weill Med. Coll., Cornell U., N.Y.C., 2001—. Pres. med. staff Meml. Sloan-Kettering Cancer Ctr., N.Y.C., 2001—03, co-dir. pathology core, cancer ctr. support grant, 2001—; sci. adv. bd. Armed Forces Inst. Pathology, Dept. Def., Washington, 2000—04. Mem.: U.S. and Can. Acad. Pathology (chmn. edn. com. 1998—2003, coun. mem. 2003—). Office: Meml Sloan-Kettering Cancer Ctr Dept Pathology 1275 York Ave New York NY 10021 E-mail: reuterv@mskcc.org.

REUTER, WILLIAM CHARLES, historian, educator; b. Yosemite, Calif., Aug. 14, 1933; s. Charles Henry and Mildred Estelle Reuter; m. Ruth Susan Major, Aug. 10, 1985; m. Elaine Roggero Reuter, Nov. 4, 1954 (div. Dec. 1981); children: Jan Rubin, Barbara de Veer. AB with highest honors, U. Calif., Berkeley, 1955, MA, 1958, PhD, 1966. Tchr. Fontana H.S., Calif., 1956—61; prof. Calif. State U., Hayward, 1965—95, prof. emeritus, 1995—. Mem. adv. bd. Scholar-Osher Lifelong Learning Inst., Concord, Calif., 2001—. Contbr. articles to profl. jours. Mem.: Orgn. Am. Historians, Phi Beta Kappa. Democrat. Avocations: reading, walking, swimming. Home: 2 Commodore Dr # 175 Emeryville CA 94608

REUTHER, DAVID LOUIS, retired children's book publisher, writer; b. Detroit, Nov. 2, 1946; s. Roy Louis and Fania (Sonkin) R.; m. Margaret Alexander Miller, July 21, 1973; children: Katherine Anna, Jacob Alexander. BA with honors, U. Mich., 1968. Tchr. Lewis-Wadhams Sch., Westport, NY, 1969-71; asst. dir. Children's Book Coun., N.Y.C., 1971-73; editor children's books Macmillan Pub. Co., N.Y.C., 1973-76; sr. editor Four Winds Press-Scholastic Inc., N.Y.C., 1976-82; sr. v.p., pub. Morrow Jr. Books, N.Y.C., 1982-98; co-founder Baseball Ink, Inc., 1986-90; pub. Lothrop Lee & Shepard, N.Y.C., 1996-98, Beech Tree Books, N.Y.C., 1997-98; pres., pub. SeaStar Books, N.Y.C., 1999—2002, North-South Books, N.Y.C., 1999—2002. Chmn., bd. dirs. Children's Book Coun. Author: (with Roy Doty) Fun To Go, A Take-Along Activity Book, 1982, Save-the-Animals Activity Book, 1982, (with John Thorn and Pete Palmer) The Hidden Game of Baseball, 1984, Total Baseball, 1989, The Whole Baseball Catalog, 1990, Total Baseball II, 1991; editor: (with John Thorn) The Armchair Quarterback, 1982, The Armchair Aviator, 1983, The Armchair Mountaineer, 1984, The Armchair Book of Baseball, 1985, The Armchair Angler, 1986, The Armchair Book of Basesball II, 1987, The Armchair Traveler, 1988. Mem.: NSTA (children's book coun. joint com. 1982—85), ALA (co-chmn. children's book coun. joint com. 2000—02), Am. Bookseller Assn. (childrens book coun. joint com. 1990—93). Home: 271 Central Park W New York NY 10024-3020

REUTHER, RONALD THEODORE, museum director; b. Dec. 29, 1929; s. Frederick and Grace (Roehll) R.; m. Mary B. Howard, 1956; children: Catherine Virginia, Paul Douglas, Jon Frederick, Victoria Grace. BA, U. Calif., 1951, postgrad., 1953, U. Ariz., 1952. Mgr. Micke Grove Zoo, 1957-62; gen. curator Cleve. Zoo, 1958-62, asst. dir., 1964-66; dir. Indpls. Zoo, 1962-64, San Francisco Zoo, 1966-73; pres., exec. dir. Phila. Zoo, 1973-78; dir. corp. devel. Exploratorium, San Francisco, 1980-81; founder, pres. Western Aerospace Mus., Oakland, Calif., 1980—88, exec. dir., 1995-99; field rep. Bell & Howell Edn. Corp./DeVry Inst. Tech., 1983-88; exec. dir. Whale Ctr., Oakland, 1988-89; edn. cons. Sierra Acad. Aeronautics, Oakland, 1989-92; lectr. Golden State U., San Francisco, 1992. Co-founder Pt. Reyes Bird Obs., Calif., 1968-70; v.p. Del. Valley Mus. Coun., 1976-78. Author zoo guidebooks, Wings Over San Francisco Bay, 1997. Mem. exec. com. Greater Phila. Cultural Alliance, 1976-78; owner, moderator internet Amelia Earhart Rsch. Discussion Group, 2000-03. 1st lt. USAF, 1953-57; with USARNG, 1958-66; lt. col. USAR, 1966-81, ret. Mem. The Explorers Club (chmn. No. Calif. chpt. 1990-95), Tamalpais Conservation Club (life mem.), Aero Club No. Calif. (bd. dirs. 2004-), Ox-5 Pioneers (bd. govs. Golden Gate chpt. 1996—, editor newsletter). E-mail: reuther@comcast.net.

REUTHINGER, GEORGEANNE, special education educator; b. Laredo, Tex., Mar. 10, 1952; d. George and Maria Josefina (Elizondo) Ramon; m. David Lawrence Reuthinger, Apr. 5, 1952; 1 child, David L. Jr. AA in Music and Drama, Laredo Jr. Coll., 1972; BS in Speech and Drama Edn., Tex. A&I U., 1974, MS in Edn., 1978; postgrad., Tes. A&M Internat. U. Lic. speech therapist, Tex.; cert. speech therapist, ednl. diagnostician, profl. supervision. Speech and drama tchr. Laredo ISD Martin High Sch., 1974; supr., diagnostician spl. edn. program Laredo ISD Martin H.S., 1992-96, Cigarra H.S., Nixon H.S., 1998—; speech therapist Laredo ISD, 1974-78, ednl. diagnostician, 1978-92; sales assoc. Country Wide Real Estate, Laredo, 1997—; cons. in spl. edn. United Ind. and Laredo Ind. Sch. Dists., 1997-98. Founding mem., lead actress in bilingual theatrical touring co. Tex. A&I U., 1974. Active in fundraising for charities Women's City Club, Boy Scouts Am.; judge UIL Acad. & Fine Arts events, Spl. Olympics. Scholar Art League, 1970, Tex. A&I Alumni, 1972-74; recipient awards U.S. Army, 1973, USO Shows, 1973-74. Mem. Tex. Speech and Hearing Assn. (legis. network 1992-97), Coun. for Exceptional Children (lobbyist 1995, sec. Laredo chpt. 1975), Valley Coun. Adminstrs. and Suprs. in Spl. Edn., ASCD, Tex. Coun. Adminstrs. and Suprs. in Spl. Edn., Delta Kappa Gamma (sec. Alpha Nu chpt. 1977-78). Avocations: directing and acting in theatrical productions, singing in community choirs, special olympics volunteering and judging. Home: 206 Granada Dr Laredo TX 78041-2615 Office: Country Wide Real Estate 1303 Calle Del Norte Ste 6 Laredo TX 78041-6041 also: Laredo Ind Sch Dist 1702 Houston St Laredo TX 78040-4906

REUTIMAN, ROBERT WILLIAM, JR., lawyer; b. Mpls., June 4, 1944; s. Robert William and Elsbeth Bertha (Doering) R.; m. Virginia Lee Traxler, June 25, 1983; children: Robert James, Joseph Lee. BA magna cum laude, U. Minn., 1966, JD, 1969. Bar: Minn. 1969, U.S. Ct. Mil. Appeals 1969, U.S. Dist. Ct. Minn. 1973, U.S. Ct. Appeals (8th cir.) 1976, U.S. Tax. Ct. 1979. Mem. Armstrong, Phleger, Reutiman & Vinokour, Ltd., Wayzata, Minn., 1973-76; ptnr. Phleger & Reutiman, Wayzata, 1976-81; pvt. practice Wayzata, 1981—. Chmn. Spring Pk. Planning Commn., 1978; city ct. judge, Hopkins and Minnetonka, Minn. Capt. U.S. Army, 1969-73. Decorated Army Commendation medal. Mem. ABA, Minn. Bar Assn., Hennepin County Bar Assn., Phi Beta Kappa. Lutheran. Avocations: fishing, rose growing. Home: 11610 3rd Ave N Plymouth MN 55441-5919 Office: 305 Rice St E Wayzata MN 55391-1615 Office Phone: 952-473-7328. E-mail: billreutiman@lycos.com.

REUTTER, EBERHARD EDMUND, JR., education and law educator; b. Balt., May 28, 1924; s. Eberhard Edmund and Irene Louise (Loewer) R.; m. Bettie Marie Lytle, Aug. 16, 1947; 1 son, Mark Douglas. BA, Johns Hopkins U., 1944; MA, Columbia U., 1948, PhD, 1950. Dir., Tokyo Army Edn. Program Sch., 1945-47; head math. dept. Barnard Sch., N.Y.C., 1947-49; mem. faculty Tchrs. Coll., Columbia U., 1950—, prof., 1957-96, prof. emeritus, 1996—. Vis. prof. U. Alaska, 1960, 66, U. P.R., 1954, U. So. Calif., 1960; speaker, cons. Coordinator spl. edn. projects NAACP Legal Def. Fund, 1965-68 Author: The School Administrator and Subversive Activities, 1951, Schools and the Law, 5th edit., 1981, (with W.S. Elsbree) Staff Personnel in the Public Schools, 1954, (with R.R. Hamilton) Legal Aspects of School Board Operation, 1958, (with W.S. Elsbree) Principles of Staff Personnel Administration in Public Schools, 1959, (with L.O. Garber) The Yearbook of School Law, 1967, 68, 69, 70, Legal Aspects of Control of Student Activities by Public School Authorities, 1970, The Law of Public Education, 4th edit., 1994, The Courts and Student Conduct, 1975, The Supreme Court's Impact on Public Education, 1982; also articles, chpts. in books. Chmn. citizens adv. com. Emerson (N.J.) Bd. Edn., 1954-57. Served from pvt. to 1st lt. inf. AUS, 1943-46. Recipient Marion A. McGhehey award for outstanding service in field edn. law, 1986. Mem. NEA, AAUP, Nat. Orgn. Legal Problems of Edn. (pres. 1967), Am. Assn. Sch. Adminstrs., Am. Assn. Sch. Pers. Adminstrs., Internat. Pers. Mgmt. Assn., Phi Beta Kappa, Kappa Delta Pi, Phi Delta Kappa. Home: 316 Grand Blvd Emerson NJ 07630-1157 Office: Columbia Univ Tchrs Coll New York NY 10027

REVAK, FRANCIS CHARLES, priest, educator; b. Philadelphia, Pa., Jan. 28, 1914; s. Joseph J. and Emma E. Revak. BA, St. Charles Sem., Overbrook, PA, 1939; ME, Lehigh U., Bethlehem, PA, 1968; MA, St. Charles Sem., Overbrook, PA, 1974. Ordained Catholic Priest Diocese of Phila., 1940. Priest Parish Ministry, 1940—67; theology and lang. educator Allentown Ctrl. Cath. H.S., Allentown, Pa., 1967—2002. Moderator, chaplain Allentown Ctrl. Cath. H.S. Football Team, Allentown, Pa., 1990—90. Roman Catholic. Avocations: reading church, state and world news, walking, bicycling. Office: Allentown Central Catholic High School 301 N Fourth Street Allentown PA 18102-3098 E-mail: altlcchs@ptd.net.

REVANKAR, NAGESH SUBRAY, economics educator; b. Kumta, India, Aug. 2, 1936; came to U.S., 1963, naturalized, 1974; d. Subray Ganapat and Saraswati Babu Shet; m. Neena Shantaram Rajani Revankar, June 4, 1969; children: Usha, Rajeev. B.A. in Math., U. Poona (India), 1958, M.A. in Stats., 1960; M.A. in Econs., U. Wis., 1965, Ph.D., 1967. Lectr. stats. Vikram U., Ujjain, India, 1960-61; asst. prof. econs. SUNY-Buffalo, Amherst, 1967-72, assoc. prof., 1972-78, prof., 1978—; cons. migrant farm workers, Western N.Y., 1983, participant Migrant Enumeration Conf., Washington, 1983, chair, 1984, dir. grad. studies, 1999—. Contbr. articles to profl. jours. Mem. Am. Econ. Assn., Econometric Soc., Am. Statis. Assn. Office Phone: 716-645-2121 428. Business E-Mail: ecorevan@acsu.buffalo.edu.

REVEAL, ERNEST IRA, III, retired lawyer; b. Chgo., Oct. 19, 1948; s. Ernest Ira Jr. and Hazel (Holt) R.; m. Katherine Trennerry, Nov. 24, 1979; children: Genevieve, Adrienne, Danielle. BA, Cornell U., 1970; JD cum laude, U. Mich., 1973. Bar: Minn. 1973, U.S. Dist. Ct. Minn. 1973, U.S. Ct. Appeals (8th cir.) 1974, U.S. Dist. Ct. S.D. 1976, U.S. Ct. Claims 1976, U.S. Ct. Appeals (7th cir.) 1984, U.S. Dist. Ct. (ctrl. dist.) Calif. 1991, U.S. Ct. Appeals (9th cir.) 1991, U.S. Supreme Ct., 1991, U.S. Cir. Ct. Appeals (fed. Cir.)2001. Assoc. Robins, Kaplan, Miller & Ciresi, Mpls., 1973—79, ptnr., 1979—2002, mediator, arbitrator, 2003—. Author: Public Sector Labor Law, 1983. Mem. Civil Svc. Commn., St. Paul, 1976; bd. dirs. Nat. Leadership Coun.; vice chair regional adv. com. So. Calif. Pub. Radio. Mem. ABA, Minn. Bar Assn. (past chair labor law and employment law sect.), Calif. Bar Assn. (advisor and past exec. com. mem., antitrust and unfair competition sect.), Cornell Club of Minn. (past pres.), L.A. Theatre Works. Democrat. Presbyterian. Avocations: history, travel. Office Phone: 949-589-1276. E-mail: ernest.reveal@cox.net.

REVELEY, WALTER TAYLOR, III, dean; b. Churchville, Va., Jan. 6, 1943; s. Walter Taylor and Marie (Eason) R.; m. Helen Bond, Dec. 18, 1971; children: Walter Taylor, George Everett Bond, Nelson Martin Eason, Helen Lanier. AB, Princeton U., 1965; JD, U. Va., 1968. Bar: Va. 1970, D.C. 1976. Asst. prof. law U. Ala., 1968-69; law clk. to Justice Brennan U.S. Supreme Ct., Washington, 1969-70; fellow Woodrow Wilson Internat. Ctr. for Scholars, 1972-73; internat. affairs fellow Coun. on Fgn. Rels., N.Y.C., 1972-73; assoc. Hunton & Williams, Richmond, Va., 1970-76, ptnr., 1976-98, mng. ptnr., 1982-91, cons., 1998—; dean William and Mary Law Sch., 1998—. Lectr. Coll. William and Mary Law Sch., 1978-80; cons. in field. Author: War Powers of the President and Congress: Who Holds the Arrows and Olive Branch, 1981; mem. editl. bd. Va. Law Rev., 1966-68; contbr. articles to profl. jours. Trustee Princeton U., 1986-90, 91-2001, Presbyn. Ch. (U.S.A.) Found., 1991-97, Va. Hist. Soc., 1991-96, 2003—, Union Theol. Sem., 1992-2000, Andrew W. Mellon Found., 1994—, JSTOR, 1995—, Va. Mus. Fine Arts, 1995—, pres. 1996-99, St. Christopher's Sch., 1996-01, Carnegie Endowment for Internat. Peace, 1999—; bd. dirs. Fan Dist. Assn., Richmond, Inc., 1976-80, pres., 1979-80; bd. dirs. Richmond Symphony, 1980-92, pres., 1988-90, pres. symphony coun., 1994-99; bd. dirs. Presbyn. Outlook Found., 1985-2003, 2004-, pres., 1992-95; bd. dirs. Va. Mus. Found., 1990-99; elder Grace Covenant Presbyn. Ch.; bd. dirs. New Covenant Trust Co., 1997-99, Va. Found. Humanities, 2001-. Mem. ABA, Va. Bar Assn., D.C. Bar Assn., Am. Bar Found., Va. Bar Found., Princeton Assn. Va. (bd. dirs. 1981—, pres. 1983-85), Va. State Bar (edn. Lawyers sect. bd. govs. 1992—, chmn. 1992-95), Raven Soc., Phi Beta Kappa, Omicron Delta Kappa. Home: 2314 Monument Ave Richmond VA 23220-2604 Office: William and Mary Law Sch PO Box 8795 Williamsburg VA 23187-8795 E-mail: Taylor@wm.edu.

REVELLE, DONALD GENE, manufacturing and health care company executive, consultant; b. Cape Girardeau, Mo., July 16, 1930; s. Lewis W. and Dorothy R.; m. Jo M. Revelle, Aug. 1, 1954; children— Douglas, David, Daniel, Dianne BA, U. Mo., 1952; JD, U. Colo., 1957; grad., Harvard U. Bus. Sch., 1971. Dir. employee relations Westinghouse Corp., Pitts., 1957-65; asst. to v.p. Diebold Corp., 1966; v.p. human resources TRW Corp., Cleve., 1967-84; sr. v.p. human resources Black and Decker Co., Towson, Md., 1984-86; exec. v.p. corp. rels. Montefiore Acad. Med. Ctr., Bronx, 1987-98; pres., CEO Syzygy, Inc., 1998—. Univ. lectr.; cons. Duerba Ship, Blue Cross N.Y., Windsor Hosp., Salvation Army Contbr. articles to profl. jours. Mem. sch. bd. State of N.Y. Lt. USNR, 1952-54 Mem.: ABA (labor law com.), Human Resource Planning Soc., Fed. Bar Assn., Colo. Bar Assn., MBA Assn., Rotary. Methodist. Home and Office: Syzygy Inc 29903 Baywood Ln Wesley Chapel FL 33543-9744 Office Phone: 813-994-3403.

RE VELLE, JACK B(OYER), statistician, consultant; b. Rochester, NY, Aug. 2, 1935; s. Mark A. and Myril (Bubes) Re V.; m. Brenda Lorraine Newcombe, Aug. 2, 1968; 1 child, Karen Alyssa. BSChemE, Purdue U., 1957; MS in Indsl. Engring. and Mgmt., Okla. State U., 1965, PhD in Indsl. Engring. and Mgmt., 1970. Commd. 2d lt. USAF, 1957, advanced through grades to major, 1968, resigned, 1968; adminstrv. asst. Gen. Dynamics, Ft. Worth, 1970-71; cons. engr. Denver, 1971-72; chmn. decision scis. U. Nebr., Omaha, 1972-77; dean Chapman U. Sch. Bus. and Mgmt., Orange, Calif., 1977-79; sr. staff engr. McDonnell Douglas Space Systems, Huntington Beach, Calif., 1979-81; head mfg. tng. and devel. Hughes Aircraft Co., Fullerton, Calif., 1981-82, sr. statistician, 1982-86, corp. mgr. R & D LA, 1986-88, corp. chief statistician, 1988-93; leader continuous improvement Raytheon Missile Systems Co., Tucson, 1994-97; dir. Ctr. for Process Improvement GenCorp Aerojet, Azusa, Calif., 1998-99; consulting statistician Tustin, Calif., 1999—. Bd. examiners Malcolm Baldrige nat. quality award Nat. Inst. Stds. and Tech.,

U.S. Dept. Commerce, Washington, 1990, 93; judge Ariz. Quality Alliance, Phoenix, 1994-96, Rochester Inst. Tech.-USA Today Quality Cup Competition, 1994-2001, Def. Contract Mgmt. Command-Commdrs. Cup, 1995-2000; cons., presenter, lectr. in field. Author: Safety Training Methods, 1980, 2d edit., 1995, The Two-Day Statistician, 1986, The New Quality Technology, 1988, Policy Deployment, 1993, What Your Quality Guru Never Told You, 2000, Quality Essentials, 2004; (with others) Quest for Quality, 1986, Mechanical Engineers Handbook, 1986, 2d edit., 1998, 3d edit., 2005, Production Handbook, 1987, Handbook of Occupational Safety and Health, 1987, A Quality Revolution in Manufacturing, 1989, Quality Engineering Handbook, 1991; co-author: Quantitative Methods for Managerial Decisions, 1978, The Executive's Handbook on Quality Function Deployment, 1994, From Concept to Customer, 1995, The Quality Function Deployment Handbook, 1998, Manufacturing Handbook of Best Practices, 2001; (software) TQM ToolSchool, 1995, QFD/Pathway, 1998. Bd. dirs. Assn. for Quality and Participation, Cin., 1985-86; mem. adv. bd. dept. indsl. and mech. engring. Calif. Poly. State U., Pomona, 1985-2000; mem. adv. bd. dept. indsl. and sys. engring. Ohio U., Athens, 2000—. Recipient Disting. Econs. Devel. award Soc. Mfg. Engrs., 1990. Fellow Am. Soc. for Quality (co-chair total quality mgmt. com. 1990-92), Inst. Advancement Engring., Inst. Indsl. Engrs. (regional v.p. 1982-84, treas. 1992-93, sr. v.p. 1993-94); mem. Aerospace and Def. Divsn. (dir. 1997-99). Office: The Wizard of Odds A Consulting Statistician Re Velle Solutions LLC PO Box 10315 Santa Ana CA 92711-0315 Office Phone: 714-289-1664. Personal E-mail: cactus_statman@yahoo.com.

REVELOS, CONSTANTINE NICHOLAS, law educator, writer; b. Middletown, Ohio, Mar. 1, 1938; s. Nicholas George and Efrosine (Aredas) R. AB, Bowdoin Coll., 1961; JD, Duke U., 1965; LLM, U. Calif., Berkeley, 1971. Bar: Ohio 1965, Mich. 1975, U.S. dist. Ct. (so. dist.) Ohio 1967, U.S. Ct. Appeals (6th cir.) 1967, U.S. Supreme Ct. 1968. With sales-svc. dept. Armco Steel Corp., Middletown, 1961-62; asst. prof. law No. Ky. State U., Cin., 1965-67, assoc. prof., dean, 1968-70; prof. law Detroit Coll. Law, East Lansing, Mich., 1971—. Dir. King scholars program, 1996—; arbiter N.Y. Stock Exchange, 1981—, Am. Arbitration Assn; Ctrl. & Eastern European Law Initiative specialist and lectr. Faculty of Law, Babes/Bolyai U., Cluj, Romania, 1994-95; lectr., faculty of law, Vytautus Magnus Univ. Kaunas, Lithuania, 2000. Author: Michigan Business Organizations, 1985. Pres. Sts. Constantine & Helen Greek Orthodox Ch., Middletown, 1967-70; trustee, Annunciation Cathedral, Detroit, 1982-91. Mem. ABA, Ohio Bar Asns., Mich. Bar Assn., Am. Judicature Soc., Am. Arbitration Assn. (arbitrator), N.Y. Stock Exch. (arbitrator), Order Ahepa. Home: 1575 Mojave Ct Okemos MI 48864-3442 Office: Mich State U-DCL 353 Law College Bldg East Lansing MI 48824-1300 Office Phone: 517-432-6882. Business E-Mail: revelos@law.msu.edu.

REVENS, JOHN COSGROVE, JR., state legislator, lawyer; b. Providence, Jan. 29, 1947; s. John C. and Rita M. (Williams) R.; m. Susan L. Shaw, Aug. 31, 1974; children: Leigh Elizabeth, Marcie Greene, Emily May. AA, C.C. of RI, 1966; BA, Providence Coll., 1969; JD, Suffolk U., 1973. Bar: RI 1973. Mem. RI Ho. of Reps., Providence, 1968-74, sec. house steering com., 1971-74, mem. edn. and welfare com., 1968—78; pres. Revens, Revens & St. Pierre, Warwick, RI, 1977—; mem. RI Senate, Dist. 31, Providence, 1990—. Mem. RI Senate, 1974-89, 1991—, fin. svs., tech. and regulatory issues, mem. jud. and labor coms., 1974, chmn. jud. com., 1980-83, majority whip, 1977-80, Senate majority leader, 1983-89; Senate pres., pro tempore, 1993-95, 2001—; dir. New Eng. Bd. Higher Edn., 1975-83, chmn., 1977-81; chmn. RI Children's Code Commn., 1979-83; bd. dirs. C.C. of RI Found., Vols. of Warwick Schs., RI Acad. Decathlon Assn.; mem. Commn. on Jud. Tenure and Discipline, 1982-84, Family Ct. Bench Bar Com., 1980-82, Women and Infants Hosp. Corp., 1983—; commr. Uniform State Laws, 1982-84. Bd. dirs. Senate Presidents' Forum. Mem. RI Bar Assn., Kent County Bar Assn., Am. Arbitration Assn. (panel of arbitrators 1980-), State Legis. Leaders Found. (pres. senate forum, bd. dirs.), KC. Democrat. Roman Catholic. Office: 946 Centerville Rd Warwick RI 02886-4398

REVERDIN, BERNARD J. lawyer; b. Baden, Switzerland, June 21, 1919; came to U.S., 1948, naturalized, 1954; s. Jean and Germaine Reverdin; m. Marcelle Coicou Reverdin; children: Caroline Reverdin Flanagan, Brigitte, Nathalie. LLB, U. Geneva, 1942; postgrad., Harvard Law Sch., 1949. Bar: Switzerland 1945, N.Y. 1955. Atty., legal asst. Geneva Govt., 1945-48; assoc. Sullivan & Cromwell, N.Y.C., 1949-51; assoc., ptnr. Lovejoy, Wasson & Ashton, N.Y.C., 1951-84; ptnr., counsel Hunton & Williams, N.Y.C., 1984-88; ptnr. Eaton & Van Winkle, N.Y.C., 1988-97, sr. counsel intern, 1998—. Dir. subs. of European corps. Contbr. articles to profl. jours.; lectr. in field V. p., treas., bd. dirs. Friends of Cuttington Coll., Liberia; v.p. LCM Found. on European Affairs Inc., Found. for Self-Determination and Internat. Rels., Liechtenstein. Mem. N.Y. State Bar Assn. (chair com. internat. trust and estate 1988-90), Am. Fgn. Law Assn. (past pres.), Consular Law Soc. (past pres.), Internat. Law Assn., Union Internat. des Avocats, Swiss Soc. N.Y., German Am. Law Assn. Office: Eaton & Van Winkle 3 Park Ave Fl 16 New York NY 10016-5902

REVERE, VIRGINIA LEHR, clinical psychologist; b. Long Branch, NJ; d. Joseph and Essie Lehr; m. Robert B. Revere; children: Elspeth, Andrew, Lisa, Robert Jr. PhB, U. Chgo., 1949, MA, 1959, PhD, 1971. Lic. cons. clin. psychologist, Va. Intern, staff psychologist Ea. Mental Health Reception Ctr., Phila., 1959-61; instr. Trenton (N.J.) State Coll., 1962-63; psychologist Trenton State Hosp., 1964-65, Bucks County Psychiat. Ctr., Phila., 1965-67; assoc. prof. Mansfield (Pa.) State U., 1967-77; clin. rsch. psychologist St. Elizabeth Hosp., Washington, 1977-81, tng. psychology coord., 1981-83, psychologist, 1985-91; child psychologist Cmty. Mental Health Ctr., Washington, 1983-85; pvt. practice Alexandria, Va., 1980—. Cons., lectr. in field. Author: Applied Psychology for Criminal Justice Professionals, 1982; contbr. articles to profl. jours. Recipient Group Merit award St. Elizabeth's Hosp., 1983, Community Svc. award D.C. Psychol. Assn., 1978, Outstanding Educator award, 1972; traineeship NIH, USPHS, Chgo., 1963-65; fellow Family Svcs. Assn., 1958-59. Mem. APA, No. Va. Soc. Clin. Psychologists, Va. Acad. Clin. Psychologists. Office Phone: 703-780-4872. E-mail: rrevere923@aol.com.

REVES, JOSEPH GERALD, dean, anesthesiology educator; b. Charleston, S.C., Aug. 14, 1943; s. George Everett and Frances (Masterson) R.; m. Virginia Cathcart, Jan. 05, 1945; children: Virginia Masterson, Christine Frances, Elizabeth Cathcart. BA, Vanderbilt U., 1965; MD, Medical Coll. S.C., 1969; MS, U. Ala., Birmingham, 1973. Lic. anesthesiologist S.C., Ala., Md., N.C.; Diplomate Am. Coll. Anesthesiology, Am. Bd. Anesthesiology. Rsch. asst., dept. pharmacology Med. Coll. S.C., 1965, 66 (summers); intern U. Ala. Hosp. and Clinics, Birmingham, Ala., 1969-70, resident in anesthesiology, 1970-72; post-doctoral, dept. anesthesia and physiology U. Ala. Med. Sch., 1972; instr., dept anesthesiology U. Ala. Hosp. and Clinics, 1973; dept. tng. staff, anesthesiology Nat. Naval Med. Ctr., Bethesda, Md., 1973-75; clin. instr., dept. anesthesiology George Washington U. Sch. Med., Washington, 1973-75; assoc. prof., dept. anesthesiology U. Ala. Hosp. and Clinics, 1975-78; dir., div. anesthesiology rsch. U. Ala., 1977-84, prof. anesthesiology, 1978-84; clin. anesthesia coord. UAB Cardiac Transplant Program, Birmingham, 1982-84; prof. anesthesiology, dir. cardiothoracic anesthesia Duke U. Med. Ctr., Durham, NC, 1984-1991; dir. Duke Heart Ctr., Duke Med. Ctr., Durham, NC, 1987-97; interim chmn., dept. anesthesiology Duke U. Med. Ctr., 1990-91, prof. and chmn., dept. anesthesiology, 1991—2001; dean, v.p. for med. affairs Med. U. S.C. Coll. Medicine, Charleston, 2001—. Cons. Hoffman-LaRoche, Somatogen, Abbott/Oximetric. Contbr. to numerous profl. jours., refereed jours., chpts. in books, published scientific reviews, selected abstracts, editorials, films, audio visual presentations, letters, positions and background papers; author: Acute Revascularization of the Infracted Heart, 1987, Common Problems in Cardiac Anesthesia, 1987, Intravenous Anesthesia and Analgesia, 1988, Anesthesiology Clinics of North America, 1988, Anesthesia, 1990, International Anesthesiology Clinics, 1991; Cardiac Anesthesia, Privileges and Practice, 1994; editor: Anesthesia and Analgesia, 1984—, cardiovascular sect. editor 1991—; editorial bd. Society Cardiovascular Anesthesia Monograph Series (chmn. 1986-89), Current Opinion in Anaesthesia 1987—, American Antec Newsletter 1989—; co-editor in chief: Current Opinion in Anaesthesiology 1990—. Dir. Clairmont Ave Hist. Preservation Com. 1976-78; Am. Heart Assn. (Durham chpt. pres. 1988-90, com. mem. anesthesiology, radiology and surgery rsch. study com. 1988-91). Grantee NIH 1991—, Janssen Pharmaceutica 1991-93, Anaquest 1989-92, Diprivan Ednl. grant ICI Pharmaceuticals Group 1991-92. Fellow Am. Coll. Cardiology; mem. AMA, Durham County Medical Soc., Internat. Soc. on Oxygen Transport to Tissue, N.C. Soc. Anesthesiologist (edn. com. 1992—), N.C. State Medical Soc., Birmingham Vanderbilt Club (bd. dirs. 1975-80, 1st v.p. 1979, pres. 1980), Southern Med. Assn. (chmn. elect. anesthesiology sect. 1976-77, chmn. 1977-78, chmn. 1988-89), Southern Soc. Anesthesiologists (v.p. 1978-79, pres. elect 1979-80, pres. 1980-81), Soc. Cardiovascular Anesthesiologists (pres. 1979-80), Assn. Univ. Anesthetists (elected to mem. 1980), Assn. Cardiac Anesthesiologists (elected to mem. 1982, pres. 1990), Soc. for Neuroleptanalgesia (bd. dirs. 1988), U. Ala. Birmingham Nat. Alumni Soc. (dist. dir., bd. dirs. 1991-93), Internat. Anesthesia Rsch. Soc. (bd. Trustees 1992—), Am. Soc. Anesthesiologists (com. sub-specialty representation 1980—, subcommittee on clin. circulation 1992—, com. geriatric anesthesia 1992—), Sigma Xi, Alpha Omega Alpha. Achievements include research on effects of age on neurologic response to cardiopulmonary bypass; cerebral blood flow and metabolism during cardiac surgery; automated delivery system of intravenous anesthetic drugs; pathophysiology of cardiopulmonary bypass. Office: Med U SC PO Box 250617 96 Jonathan Lucas St Ste 601 Charleston SC 29425

REVESZ, AKOS GEORGE, physicist; b. Balassagyarmat, Hungary, July 25, 1927; came to U.S., 1959; s. Eugen and Ilona (Rachler) R.; m. Agnes Ernszt, June 1956 (div. May 1973); 1 child, Tom; m. Kinga M. Lutter, Jan. 10, 1975; 1 child, Paul. Diploma in engring., Tech. U., Budapest, Hungary, 1950, PhD, 1968. Rsch. asst. Tech. U., Budapest, 1947-48; rsch. engr. Iron and Steel Rsch. Inst., Budapest, 1950, Philips, Eindhoven, The Netherlands, 1957-59; rsch. engr., head dept. Tungsram, Budapest, 1951-53, 56; mem. tech. staff RCA Rsch. Lab., Princeton, N.J., 1959-69; sr. scientist Comsat Labs., Clarksburg, Md., 1969-83; ind. cons. Revesz Assocs., Bethesda, Md., 1984—. Co-author: Field-Effect Transistors, 1966; editor books in field; contbr. over 150 articles to profl. publs.; patentee in field. Mem. Electrochem. Soc. Avocations: reading, classical music, hiking, swimming. Home and Office: 7910 Park Overlook Dr Bethesda MD 20817-2719

REVESZ, RICHARD LUIS, law educator; b. Buenos Aires, May 9, 1958; BSE in Civil Engring. summa cum laude, Princeton U., 1979; MS, Mass. Inst. Tech., 1980; JD, Yale U., 1983. Bar: N.Y. 1986, D.C. 1986, U.S. Supreme Ct. 1989, U.S. Ct. Appeals (D.C. cir.) 1986, U.S. Dist. Ct. (so. dist.) N.Y. 1986. Jud. clerk for Chief Judge Wilfred Feinberg U.S. Ct. Appeals (2d cir.) N.Y., 1983-84; jud. clerk for Justice Thurgood Marshall U.S. Supreme Ct., 1984-85; asst. prof. NYU Law Sch., 1985-88, assoc. prof., 1988-90, prof., 1990—2001, Lawrence King prof. law, 2001—, dean, 2002—. Cons. superfund settlements Adminstrv. Conf. U.S., 1991-92, cons. nonacquiescence by agys., 1986-89; term mem. Coun. Fgn. Rels., 1989—; pro-bono rep. Natural Resources Def. Coun., 1987; cons. dept. tech. coop. for devel. UN, 1980-81. Contbr. articles to profl. jours. Cons. Carnegie Commn. Sci., Tech. and Govt., 1989-90. Recipient Exploratory Rsch. grant EPA, 1991—. Mem. ABA (vice chmn. com. jud. review sect. adminstrv. law 198898, chair, 1998—), Am. Law Inst. (mem.'s consultative group 1993—), N.Y. State Bar Assn. (chmn. com. adminstrv. law 1988-91, sec. com. second century 1986-88, mem. com. environ. law 1986-88), Phi Beta Kappa, Sigma Xi, Tau Beta Pi (prize winner). Office: NYU Sch Law Vanderbilt Hall 40 Washington Sq S Ste 406 New York NY 10012-1099

REVILLS, ISAIAH, minister; b. Moultrie, Ga., Aug. 23, 1931; s. William Mack and Irene Revills; m. Ullainee S. Sanders, June 4, 1955; 5 children. DD, LHD, United Christian Coll., Goldborg, N.C., 1995. Marriage counselor, Albany, Ga., 1969—; founder, pastor Evangelical Faith Vision Ministry, Inc., Albany, Ga., 1970—. Author: (book) The Unfolding Vision, 1996, God's Added Blessings, 1998. Mem. Complete Count Com., Albany, Ga., 2000. Avocations: travel, reading, golf, fishing. Home: 1618 Moultrie Rd Albany GA 31705 Office: Evangelical Faith Vision Ministry Inc 1506 S Slappey Blvd Albany GA 31701

REVOILE, CHARLES PATRICK, lawyer; b. Jan. 15, 1934; s. Charles Patrick and Olga Lydia (Zecca) R.; m. Sally Cole Gates, Nov. 8, 1963. BA, U. Md., 1957, LLB, 1960. Bar: Md. 1962, U.S. Dist. Ct. Md. 1962, U.S. Supreme Ct. 1970, U.S. Ct. Claims 1976, U.S. Ct. Appeals (fed. cir.) 1982. Legis. counsel Nat. Canners Assn., Washington, 1960-64; asst. counsel Deco Electronics Inc., Washington, 1964-67; divsn. counsel Westinghouse Electric, Leesburg, Va., 1967-71; v.p., gen. counsel Stanwick Corp., Arlington, Va., 1971-85; sr. v.p., gen. counsel, sec. CACI Internat. Inc., 1985-92, bd. dirs., 1992—, chmn. compensation com., 1995—, exec. com., 1999—, mem. investor rels. com., 2001—, mem. corp. governance com., 2003—. Mem. regional adv. coun. NASD, 1989-92; lectr., panelist, advisor. Active in Md. Ednl. Found., College Park, 1974-98; assoc. Nat. Symphony Orch., Washington, 1972-93, Smithsonian Instn., 1980-93, M Club Found., 1985-98; lawyer, lobbyist various non-profit orgns., Washington, 1984-98; mem. exec. com. ann. bus. campaign Gallaudet U., 1989-91; chmn. various coms. Kemper Open Championships, 1980-86; exec. com. 1995 USGA Sr. Open, 1997 USGA Open Championships; gen. counsel, mem. exec. com. 1995, 96, 97 Kemper Open Championship. Mem. Md. Bar Assn., Washington Corp. Counsels Assn., Am. Corp. Counsels Assn., Nat. Assn. Corp. Dirs., USGA, Mid. Atlantic Golf Assn. (exec. com. 1989-99, v.p., pres. 1998), Roger Howell Soc. U. Md. Sch. Law (charter), Congl. Country Club (com. chmn. 1966-92, bd. govs. 1987-93, Bethesda, Md.), Avondale Golf Club (Pymble, Australia), Ocean Forest Golf Club (Sea Island, Ga.), Sea Island Club (founder), Sea Island Srs. Golf Assn. (pres. 2003). Home: PO Box 31223 Sea Island GA 31561-1223

REW, LAWRENCE BOYD, lawyer; b. Eugene, Oreg., June 22, 1936; BA, Whitman Coll., 1958; JD, Willamette U., 1961. Bar: Oreg. 1961. Ptnr. Corey, Byler, Rew, Lorenzen & Hojem, LLP, Pendleton, Oreg., 1965—. Fellow Am. Bar Found.; mem. ABA, Oreg. State Bar Assn. (pres. 2000, Pub. Svc. award 1991, bd. bar examiners 1975-79, bd. govs. 1996-2000). Office: Corey Byler Rew Lorenzen & Hojem LLP PO Box 218 222 SE Dorion Ave Pendleton OR 97801-2553

REW, WILLIAM EDMUND, civil engineer; b. Corning, N.Y., Nov. 24, 1923; s. Robert James and Clara (Neal) R.; m. Jean Ella Ohls, Aug. 16, 1947 (dec.); children: Virginia Ann, Robert James, John Edward. BE, Yale U., 1954, M in Engring., 1955. Registered profl. engr., N.Y., Fla., Calif., Ill. Project engr. Texaco & Affiliate, USA and Saudi Arabia, 1955-62; sr. engr. Martin-Marietta Corp., Cape Kennedy, Fla., 1962-63, Chrysler Corp, Cape Kennedy, 1963-65, The Boeing Co., Cape Kennedy, 1965-70; project mgr. Brevard Engring. Co., Cape Canaveral, Fla., 1970-74; city engr. City of Vero Beach (Fla.), 1974-77; resident engr. Post, Buckley, Schuh & Jernigan, Miami, Fla., 1977-85; mgr. Keith & Schnars, P.A., West Palm Beach, Fla., 1985-90; pvt. practice consulting Lake Placid, Fla., 1990—. Active Rep. Party of Highlands County. 1st lt. U.S. Army, 1942-46, ATO. Scholar of 2d rank Yale U., 1953, grad. scholar, 1955. Fellow ASCE (chmn. Fla. ann conv. 1971, Engr. of Yr. 1974); mem. NSPE, Soc. Am. Mil. Engrs. (bd. dirs. 1982-83), Fla. Engring Soc. (chpt. pres. 1976), Yale Club, Browning Assn. Club. Episcopalian. Avocations: woodworking, reading. Home: 1425 S Washington Blvd NW Lake Placid FL 33852-4301 Office Phone: 863-465-3921. Home Fax: 863-465-3921.

REWAK, WILLIAM JOHN, former academic administrator, clergyman; b. Syracuse, N.Y., Dec. 22, 1933; s. William Alexander and Eldora Venetia (Carroll) R. BA, Gonzaga U., 1957, MA in English, 1958; MA in Theology, Regis Coll., Toronto, Ont., Can., 1965; PhD in English, U. Minn., 1970. Joined S.J., 1951, ordained priest Roman Cath. Ch., 1964. Tchr. English Bellarmine Coll. Prep. Sch., 1958-61; asst. prof. English Santa Clara (Calif.) U., 1970-71, pres., 1976-88; rector Jesuit Community, 1971-76; pres. Spring Hill Coll., Mobile, Ala., 1989-97; ret., 1997. Bd. dirs. Gulf Coast Broadcasting Inc., Badger-Stonewall Ins. Co., Marine Environ. Scis. Consortium. Contbr. articles to theol. and critical jours., poetry, short stories to lit. jours. Bd. dirs. Mobile Bay Area Partnership for Youth, Mercy Med. Ctr.; mem. Ala. Ind. Colls., Coun. for Advancement Pvt. Colls. in Ala.; bd. trustees Loyola U. New Orleans. Mem. MLA, Coll. English Assn., Bienville Club. Democrat. Home and Office: Spring Hill Coll Office of Pres 4000 Dauphin St Mobile AL 36608-1780

REWCASTLE, NEILL BARRY, neuropathology educator; b. Sunderland, Eng., Dec. 12, 1931; arrived in Can., 1955; s. William Alexander and Eva (Coapes) R.; m. Eleanor Elizabeth Barton Boyd, Sept. 27, 1958 (dec. Jan. 1999); 4 children. MB, ChB cum laude, U. St. Andrews, Scotland, 1955; MA, U. Toronto, 1962. Licentiate Med. Coun. Can., 1957; cert. in gen. pathology and neuropathology Royal Coll. Physicians, Can. Rotating intern U. Vancouver, Canada, 1955-56; resident in pathology Shaughnessy Hosp., Vancouver, 1956-57, U. Toronto, Canada, 1957-60, demonstrator dept. pathology, 1964-65, lectr., acting head divsn. neuropathology, 1965—69, assoc. prof., 1969-70, prof., head divsn. neuropathology, 1970—81; fellow Med. Rsch. Coun. Can., 1960-64; prof., head dept. pathology U. Calgary, Canada, 1981-91, prof., 1981-2000, prof. emeritus pathology, lab. medicine, clin. neuroscis., 2000—, mem. neurosci. rsch. group, 1982—2003; sr. pathologist Toronto Gen. Hosp., 1970—81. Dir. dept. histopathology Foothills Hosp., Calgary, 1981-91, pathologist, 1981—, cons. neuropathology, 1981—; spl. acad. adv. to dean faculty medicine U. Calgary, 1995-97; presenter in field. Contbr. over 145 articles to profl. jour., chpts. to books. Recipient Queen Elizabeth Silver Jubilee medal, 1977. Fellow: Royal Coll. Physicians (cert.); mem. Can. Assn. Neuropathologists (sec. 1965-69, pres. 1976-79). E-mail: rewcastb@telus.net.

REX, CHRISTOPHER DAVIS, classical musician; b. Orlando, Fla., Feb. 1, 1951; s. Charles Gordon Rex and Betty Helen (MacCauslin) Soubricas; m. Martha Anne Wilkins, Nov. 30, 1985; children: Caroline Bethea, Christopher Austell. MusB, Curtis Inst. of Music, Phila., 1972; postgrad., The Juilliard Sch., 1972-73, Atlanta Coll. Art, 1997—. Cellist Lyric Opera and Grand Opera, Phila., 1970-75, Phila. Orchestra, 1972-79, Georgian Chamber Players, Atlanta, 1984—; cello tchr. Gettsburg (Pa.) Coll., 1972-73, New Sch. of Music, Phila., 1969-74, Ga. State U., 1980-83; cellist, tchr. Eastern Music Festival, Greensboro, N.C., 1969-74; prin. cello Atlanta Symphony Orchestra, 1979—. Concert soloist Hillyer Internat. Inc., N.Y.C., 1984—; bd. dirs. Ga. Cello Soc., Inc., Atlanta, Georgian Chamber Players, Atlanta; acting prin. during Europe Tour Cello of N.Y. Philharm., 1988; premiered Double Concerto for Violin, Cello, and Orch. N.Y. Philharm., 1994. Recordings include The Muse and the Poet (with Boheslaw Martina Philharm. Orch.), 1998; editor: (mus. transcription) Pictures at an Exhibition (Moussorgsky), 1987. Recipient First prize Young Artist Competition Am. Fedn. of Music Clubs, 1979. Mem. Phila. Musical Soc., Atlanta Fedn. of Music. Presbyterian. Avocations: art, watercolor painting. Home: 3602 Hadden Hall Rd NW Atlanta GA 30327-2628 Office: Atlanta Symphony Orch Woodruff Arts Ctr Atlanta GA 30309

REX, LONNIE ROYCE, religious organization administrator; b. Caddo, Okla., May 11, 1928; s. Robert Lavern and Lennie Cordy (Gilcrease) R.; m. Betty Louise Sorrells, Apr. 8, 1949; children: Royce DeWayne, Patricia Louise, Debra Kaye. MusB, Oklahoma City U., 1950; DD (hon.), Am. Bible Inst., 1970; LLD (hon.), Wesley Synod, N.Y.C., 1999, Meth. Wesley Synod, Toledo, 1999; LittD, Wesley Synod, 2000. Advt. mgr. Oral Roberts Evang. Assn., Tulsa, 1955-57; bus. mgr. T.L. Osborn Found., Tulsa, 1957-69; gen. mgr. Christian Crusade, Tulsa, 1969-80; sec.-treas. David Livingstone Missionary Found., Tulsa, 1970-80, pres., 1980—. Dep. dir. gen. Internat. Biog. Assn.; bd. dirs. Intra-Ch. Pension Fund, Bethany, Okla.; spkr. internat. confs. Eng., Hungary, Korea, Singapore, Spain, N.Y.C., Congress of Arts and Comms., Oxford U., 1997; invited Pyongyang, North Korea to meet as an NGO with Peace Com. and med. aid, 1996, 97; participant peace conf. Carter Ctr. between North Korea and South Korea, 1997. Author: Never a Child, 1989. Mem. Internat. PHC Loan Fund; bd. dirs. Armand Hammer United World Coll. of Am. West, 1993—; bd. mem. Internat. Humanitarian Centre Russia, Moscow, 2000. Recipient Merit award Korea, 1975, Moran medal Republic of Korea, Humanitarian award Senator Hugh Scott, 1983, Svc. to Mankind award Internat. Biog. Congress, Spain, 1987, Internat. Lions Club award, UN award, medal Gen. Ground Forces USSR, 1990, World Humanitarian Leadership award by M. Susan Savage Mayor of Tulsa, 1998, Roseland Cook Bronze award David Livingstone Found., 1998; knighted in Moscow, 1993; Lonnie Royce Rex Day named in his honor by Gov. Keating of Okla., Jan. 24, 1998. Mem. Knights of Malta (Sword of Svc. 1996), Phi Beta Kappa. Home: 2437 E 73d Pl Tulsa OK 74136-5520 Office: St Matthews Pub Tulsa OK 74136-1010 *In my work among the starving in Ethiopia, I walked into a tent of over 100 mothers, lying on mats, who had given birth during the last three days. It was silent! Morbid silence! That haunting silence lives with me since that moment. I asked why? I was informed the babies did not have the strength to cry. I have given my life to "cry out" for those in need that did not have the strength to "cry".*

REX, WALTER EDWIN, III, humanities educator; b. Bryn Mawr, Pa., Jan. 31, 1927; s. Walter Edwin Jr. and Barbara (Clayton) R. AB, Harvard U., 1950, AM, 1951, PhD, 1956. Instr. Brown U., Providence, 1956-57, Harvard U., Cambridge, Mass., 1957-60; asst. prof. U. Calif., Berkeley, 1960-65, assoc. prof., 1965-72, prof., 1972-92, prof. emeritus, 1992—. Chair James L. Clifford prize com. Am. Soc. 18th Century Studies, 1997—98. Author: Essays on Pierre Bayle and Religious Controversy, 1965, The Attraction of the Contrary, 1987, Diderot's Counterpoints, 1998; collaborator multi-vol. book (7 vols.) Inventory of Diderot's Encyclopédie, 1971-72, 89; mem. editl. bd. Eighteenth-Century Studies, 1979-82, 89-92; asst. editor The French Rev., 1981-86; contbr. to books in field. Grantee Humanities Rsch. Inst., 1966-67, 73-74; Pres.'s fellow U. Calif., 1990-91. Mem. MLA, Am. Soc. 18th Century Studies (Clifford lectr. ann. meeting 2000), Soc. Francaise d'étude du 18 siècle, Arts Club (Berkeley), Kosmos Club (Berkeley). Democrat. Avocation: chamber music. Home: 287 Alvarado Rd Berkeley CA 94705-1512 E-mail: Tedrex@AOL.com.

REXNER, ROMULUS, publishing executive; b. Odessa, Russia, July 16, 1920; came to U.S., 1951; s. Richard Rexner and Nina Norvid; m. Elisabeth Unger, Aug. 22, 1964. BS in Econs. with hons., Univ. London, 1951. Founder, mgr. Pantheon Press, Gen. Enterprises, L.A., 1951-86, Honolulu, 1986—. Author: (book) Planetary Legion, 1961, 4th edit., 2001; pub.: periodical Cosmopolitan Contact, 1962—. Founder Planetary Legion for Peace, 1955. With Brit. Forces WWII. Achievements include patents in field. Office: Pantheon Press Gen Enterprises Planetary Legion PO Box 89300 Honolulu HI 96830-7300

REXROTH, NANCY LOUISE, photographer; b. Washington, June 27, 1946; d. John Augustus and Florence Bertha (Young) R. B.F.A., Am. U., 1969; M.F.A. in Photography, Ohio U., Athens, 1971. Asst. prof. photography Antioch Coll., Yellow Springs, Ohio, 1977-79, Wright State U., Dayton, Ohio, 1979-82. Author: Iowa, 1976, The Platinotype, 1977, 1976; exhibited photography at Weinstein Gallery, Mpls. Nat. Endowment Arts grantee, 1973; Ohio Arts Coun., 1981. Mem. Am. Massage Therapy Assn. Democrat. Home and Office: 2631 Cleinview Ave Cincinnati OH 45206-1810 E-mail: rexnex@cinci.rr.com.

REY, MARK E. federal agency administrator; b. Canton, Ohio; BS in Wildlife Mgmt., BS in Forestry, MS in Natural Resources Policy and Adminstrn., U. Mich. Staff asst. bur. land mgmt. U.S. Dept. of Interior's, 1974—75; various positions Am. Paper Inst./Nat. Forest Products Assn., 1976—84; v.p. pub. forestry programs Nat. Forest Products Assn., 1984—89; exec. dir. Am. Forest Resource Alliance, 1989—92; v.p. forest resources Am. Forest and Paper Assn., 1992—94; staff mem. U.S. Senate Com. on Energy and Natural Resources, 1995—2001; under sec. for natural resources and environ. USDA, Washington, 2001—. Office: USDA Natural Resources and Environ 1400 Independence Ave SW Washington DC 20250

REYELTS, PAUL C. chemical company executive; MBA, Harvard U. V.p. corp. fin. dept. Piper, Jaffray & Hopwood; sr. v.p. fin., CFO Valspar Corp., Mpls. Office: Valspar Corp 1101 Third St South Minneapolis MN 55415

REYES, ANNA MARIA, broadcast executive; b. Phoenix, Aug. 21, 1957; d. Perfecto C. and Esperanza (Del Castillo) R. BA in Fin., Ariz. State U., 1983. Radio-Tel. operators permit FCC; notary public, Ariz. Traffic/continuity dir. First Media Corp./KOPA AM and FM, Scottsdale, Ariz., 1978-81, music dir., air talent, 1981-83; bus. mgr., asst. sta. mgr. Cook Inlet Radio Ptnr. KSLX-FM and KOPA-AM, 1983-92; sta. contr., asst. gen. mgr. Jacor/Citicasters KSLX AM/FM, Phoenix, 1992-96; gen. mgr. Jacor Comm. KSLX AM/FM, Phoenix, 1997—. Interviewer KSLX FM/KOPA AM, Scottsdale, 1990. Co-author: INXS Newsletter, 1994. Spokeswoman campaign against radio for men format KSLX FM/KOPA AM, Scottsdale, 1988. Recipient Cert. for Announcing, City of Phoenix-Hello Phoenix, 1985, Bus. Mgr. award Corp. Chain Contest, Phoenix, 1990-92. Mem. AAUW, Am. Women in Radio and TV, Broadcast Cable Fin. Mgmt., Univ. Women London. Democrat. Roman Catholic. Avocations: european travel, ballet, reading, music. Home: 12340 W Elwood St Avondale AZ 85323-9618 Office: KSLX Radio FM/AM 4343 E Camelback Rd Ste 200 Phoenix AZ 85018-8306

REYES, ARTURO PACHECO, civilian military employee; b. Manila, Philippines, Nov. 30, 1951; s. Anastacio Cenon Reyes and Aurora Cruz Pacheco; m. Zenaida Tarlit Abon, Jan. 2, 1975 (div. July 1998); children: Michelle, Heila Leilani. MSc in adminstrn., Ctr. Mich. U., 1997; BSc in edn., Wayland Bapt. U., 1983; AA, U. of the City of Manila, 1971. Cert. nursing asst., 2002. Perm mem., sr. chief U.S. Naval Res., Washington, 1972—; U.S. civil svc. employee U.S. Civil Svc., 1993—2000; capt., pacific eagle U.S. Coast Guard, 2000; dep. clk. U.S. Dist. Ct., Honolulu, 1998; gen. vessel asst. U.S. Dept. of Commerce, 1997; clk. U.S. Census Bur., Honolulu, 2000; contracting ofcl. U.S. Dept. of Veterans Affairs, 1994. Records mgr. privacy act officer U.S. Dept. of the Army, 1994, chief of the boat U.S.N., 1991; adult correction officer Maui Cmty. Corrections Ctr., Hawaii, 1999. City coun. mem. candidate City and County of Honolulu, 1998; U.S. senate candidate U.S. Senate, Washington, 2000; gov. candidate State of Hawaii, 2002; U.S. congress candidate U.S. Congress, Washington, 2002—03. Mem.: Wayland Bapt. Assn., Sigma Iota Epsilon. Independent. Home: 94-1432 Kahuli St Waipahu HI 96797 Office: Friends of Reyes 94-1432 Kahuli St Waipahu HI 96797 Office Phone: 808-671-7450. E-mail: ap_reyes@msn.com.

REYES, J. CHRISTOPHER, food products distribution executive; Co-founder, CEO Reyes Holdings, Lake Forest, Ill., 1976—. Office: Reyes Holdings LLC 9500 W Bryn Mawr Ave Ste 700 Rosemont IN 60018 Office Fax: (847) 604-9972.

REYES, JOSE ANTONIO, SR., minister; b. Canovanas, P.R., May 24, 1940; s. Dionisio Reyes and Antonia (Rodriguez) R.; m. Olfa R. Martinez, May 30, 1964; 1 child, Jose A. BA in Edn., U. P.R., 1962; MA, Sch. Theology, Cleveland, Tenn., 1984; D Ministry, Logos Sch., 1985. Ordained to ministry Ch. of God of Prophecy, 1969. Youth dir. Ch. of God of Prophecy, Rio Piedras, P.R., 1956-58, pastor, 1963-68, mission rep. for Latin Am. Cleveland, Tenn., 1969-75, internat. radio speaker, 1969—, internat. asst. gen. overseer, 1981—. Pres. Hispanic Nat. Religious Broadcasting, Parsippany, 1985-88; v.p. Nat. Orgn. Advancement of Hispanic, 1983-86; com. mem. Hispanic Task Force of Am. Bible Soc., 1985-87; mem. Hispanic Commn., Nat. Assn. Evangelicals, Carol Stream, Ill., 1988—; exec. com. Nat. Religious Broadcasters, 1990-93, bd. dirs., 1990—; founding mem. Alliance Nat. Evang. Ministries, 1993—; pres. ref. com. Latin Am. Christian Comm., 1992—; mem. exec. com. Washington for Jesus, 199—; founding mem. Israel Christian adv. coun., 1996. Author: The Hispanics in USA - A Challenge, An Opportunity for the Church, 1984; author 10 Bible Study Guides on books of the Bible, 1985-90. Recipient Excellence in Hispanic Program Producer award Nat. Religious Broadcasters, 1988, Excellence in Ministry award Internat. Ministry Com., 1990. Mem. Spanish Voice of Salvation Sponsorship Club (pres.). Republican. Home: 13670 Hawk Lake Dr Orlando FL 32837-8094 *Equalling our Lord is an impossible task, but imitating Him is our supreme duty.*

REYES, JOSE OCTAVIO, food products executive; BSChE, U. Autónoma de Mex.; MBA, Inst. Tech. Superior Studies, Monterrey, Mex. Devel. mgr., strategic planning mgr., corp. devel. asst. dir., mktg. asst. dir. Mex. Divsn. The Coca-Cola Co., 1980—87, region mktg. dir., 1987, brand mgr. Diet Coke and Sprite, 1987—90, divsn. mktg. mgr., 1990—93, mktg. and ops. v.p., dep. divsn. pres. Mex. divsn., 1993—96, pres. North Latin Am. Divsn., 1996—2002, pres., COO Coca-Cola Latin Am., corp. exec. v.p., 2002—. Office: The Coca-Cola Co PO Box 1734 Atlanta GA 30301

REYES, LUZVIMINDA CANUTO, social welfare administrator; arrived in U.S., 1977; d. Feliciano Rivero Canuto and Serena Dizon Delos Santos; m. Manuel Tibi Reyes, Jan. 13, 1977; children: Rachelle Ann Canuto Reyes, Elvin Lee Canuto Reyes. BS in Foods and Nutrition, De Ocampo Coll., Manila, 1977; Cert. in Mortgage Banking, Calif. State U., Hayward, 1991, MPA, 2000. Cert. tchr. Calif. Mgr., owner M and L Sports/Trades, Union City, Calif., 1985—2000; part-time tchr. Unified Sch. Dist., Fremont, Calif., 1991—2000; mortgage cons. Western Fin. Mortgage and Cmty. Funding, San Jose, 1992—95; med. outreach worker Alameda County Social Svc. Agy., Oakland, Calif., 1994—; founder, adminstrv. dir. Youth Embracing Luv, Fremont, 1999—. Author: Changing Time, Charnging Organization, 2003, YEL Newsletter, 1999—. Cmty. coord. Marriage Encounter of No. Calif., San Leandro, 2003—; spiritual formation dir. Third Order Lay Carmelite, 2000—. Recipient Commendation award, State of Calif., Letter of Recognition, Office of V.P. of the U.S., Commendation award, FAHAP, Calif., Cert. of Recognition, Alameda County Passing the Torch Mentor Program, Life Long Learning award, Alameda County Social Svcs. Agy. Mem.: Toastmasters. Avocations: reading, travel, dance. Home and Office: PO Box 3050 Union City CA 94584

REYES, M. JUDE, food products distribution executive; Bachelor's in economics, Wofford College, NC. Principal Reyes Holdings LLC, Lake Forest, Ill. Bd. mem., officer Premium Distributors, Va., bd. mem., DC, Chicago Beverage Sys., Harbor Distributing, Zema Foods, Martin Brower Co.; bd. dirs. Building One Svcs. Corp., Nat. Rehabilitation Hosp. Mem.: Miller Brewing Company Distributors Adv. Panel, VA Beer Wholesalers Assn., Nat. Beer Wholesalers Assn., Young President's Orgn. Office: Reyes Holdings 225 E Deerpath Rd Lake Forest IL 60045 Office Fax: (847) 604-9972.

REYES, MARCIA STYGLES, medical technologist; b. Winchester, Mass., July 15, 1950; d. Bernard Francis and Eleanore Cecilia (Nicgorska) Stygles; m. Carlos Reyes, Aug. 5, 1978. BS in Med. Tech., Merrimack Coll., North Andover, Mass., 1972; MS in Health Scis., SUNY, Buffalo, 1977. Sr. med. technologist Symmes Hosp., Arlington, Mass., 1970-73; sr. microbiologist and serologist Mt. Auburn Hosp., Cambridge, Mass., 1973-75; asst. prof., clin. coord. Quinnipiac Coll., Hamden, Conn., 1976-81; lab. supr. Canberra Clin. Labs., Meriden, Conn., 1981-86, Hill Health Ctr., New Haven, 1984—, clin. lab. mgr., dir., 1995—. Cons. in med. tech. mgmt., allied health edn.; cons. F.Q.H.C. Lab. Devel./Implementation. Adv. bd. to bd. dirs. Sawyer Schs.; adv. bd. New Haven Adult Edn. Programs. Mem. Am. Soc. Clin. Pathologists, Am. Soc. Med. Tech., Conn. Soc. Med. Tech. (Spkr. awards, bd. dirs. 1996—), Am. Soc. Microbiology, Am. Soc. Allied Health Profls. Home: 199 Dover St New Haven CT 06513-4818 E-mail: msrmt@comcast.net., msrmt@msn.com.

REYES, MARIA ELENA, academic program director; b. Eagle Pass, Tex. d. Jorge Vargas and María Claudia (Cardona) R.; div.; children: Paul David, Benjamin, Jenny, Matthew. BA in Sociology and English cum laude, Pan-Am. U., 1973; MA in Secondary Edn., Sul Ross U., 1988; PhD in Curriculum and Instrn., U. Tex., 1991. Part-time Spanish tutor lang. lab. U. Tex., Austin, 1968-70; state caseworker Tex. Welfare Dept., Pharr, 1971-75; tchr. English Eagle Pass H.S., 1978-88; supr. student tchrs. English edn. dept. U. Tex., Austin, 1988-90, rsch.-tchg. asst. to prof. emeritus Don Americo Paredes, 1990-91, cons. Grad. Sch., 1991-92, project dir. Hispanic Mother-Dau. Program, 1992—. Vol. United Farm Workers, McAllen, Tex., 1970-73; intern in urban studies, Pan Am. U., 1971-72; rsch. asst. focus group series U. Tex. Sch. Nursing, 1990; developer Lang. Arts IV Course Eagle Pass H.S., 1986, mgr. migrant tutoring program; advisor, bd. dirs. SMART Student Orgn., U. Tex., Austin, cons. Mex. Am. Health Professions Orgn., pres. Chicana/o Grad. Students Assn., minority recruiter, mem. adv. bd. Ctr. for Mex.-Am. Studies; trainer Family Math program; presenter in field. Author: The 1995 Guide to the Top 25 Colleges for Hispanics, 1995; contbr. articles to Hispanic Mag. Mem. KLRU Cmty. Bd., 1995-96, 4-H Acrospace Task Force, Mendez Mid. Sch. PTA; bd. dirs. Found. for Women's Resources Conf., Austin; head Bilingual Students' Support Group Martin Jr. H.S. PTA; vol. tutoring program Bedichek Mid. Sch. Recipient Nat. Hispanic Achievement award, 1995, cert. appreciation Eagle Pass H.S. Student Coun., 1985; rsch. fellow U. Tex. at Austin Ctr. for Mex.-Am. Studies, 1991, Title VII fellow, 1990-91, Univ. Grad. fellow, 1988-91, Urban Studies fellow Pan Am. U., 1973. Mem. ASCD, AAUW (adv. panel, Internat. Fellowship Awards Panel 1995—), Am. Assn. Higher Edn., Exec. Women in Tex. Govt., Expanding Your Horizons (Austin chpt.), Hispanic Assn. Colls. and Univs., U. Tex. Latina Women's Caucus, Tex. Assn. Chicanos in Edn., Kappa Delta Pi (v.p. U. Tex., Austin), Phi Kappa Phi.

REYES, RAUL GREGORIO, surgeon; b. Tegucigalpa, Morazan, Honduras, June 18, 1928; came to U.S., 1939; s. Julio Gregorio and Mercedes Ofelia (Mazzoni) Reyes-Zelaya; m. Mildred Dane Smith, 1951 (dec. May 1990); children: Tyra, Kimberly; stepchildren: Javier, Christian; m. Blanca Lidia Milla, Apr. 2, 1993. BS, Georgetown U., 1945; MD, George Washington U., 1950. Diplomate Nat. Bd. Med. Examiners, Am. Bd. Surgery. Intern Charity Hosp., New Orleans, 1950-51; resident Emergency Hosp./George Washington U., Washington, 1951, Charity Hosp., New Orleans, 1952-55; chief thoracic surgery San Felipe Hosp., Tegucigalpa, 1955-56; assoc. to ptnr. Browne-McHardy Clinic, New Orleans, 1955-60, 60 73; med. dir. New Orleans Indsl. Clinic, 1956-58; chief of surgery and orthopedics Lallie Kemp Regional Hosp., Independence, La., 1987-89, med. dirs., 1988-89; owner, pres. Raul G. Reyes, A Med. Corp., New Orleans, 1973—. Owner, pres. Internat. Maritime Med. Svcs., New Orleans, 1978—, Catracho Enterprises, New Orleans, 1975—, Phys. Therapy Svcs. of New Orleans, 1975—; faculty La. State Univ. Sch. Medicine, 1953—, others. Inventor in field; contbr. articles to profl. jours. Chmn. Rep. Hispanic Assembly, New Orleans, 1983; pre-cand. Nat. Party, Honduras, 1985; founder Literacy Ctrs. of Honduras, 1991; presdl. candidate Christian Dem. Party of Honduras, 1994. Named to Hon. Consul of Honduras, Hon. Citizen, City of New Orleans. Mem. ACS, AMA, So. Med. Assn., La. State Med. Soc., Orleans Parish Med. Soc., Colegio Medico de Honduras. Roman Catholic. Avocations: tennis, reading, writing, social progs. Office: PO Box 15379 New Orleans LA 70175-5379

REYES, REYNERIS, dancer; Student, Escuela Vocacional de Arte Raúl Sánchez, Pinar del Rio, Cuban Nat. Ballet Sch. Mem. Cuban Nat. Ballet, 1993—99; soloist Royal Winnipeg Ballet, 1999—. Dancer toured U.S., Spain, France, Switzerland and Columbia, 1998—99. Dancer (ballets) Swan Lake, Cuban Nat. Ballet, Cinderella, Giselle, Don Quixote, Coppélia, La Fille Mal Gardée, Les Sylphides, Romeo and Juliet, Royal Winnipeg Ballet, Cherry Pink and Apple Blossom White, Dracula, Butterfly, Giselle. Office: Royal Winnipeg Ballet 380 Graham Ave Winnipeg MB Canada R3C 4K2

REYES, SARAH, state representative; b. Fresno, Calif. Grad., Fresno City Coll., Calif. State U. Field reporter, news anchor KSEE TV-24, Fresno; field reporter KCRA TV-3, Sacramento; asst. to chancellor State Ctr. C.C. Dist.; mem. Calif. Assembly, 1998—. Bd. dirs. KVPT Channel 18, Radio Bilingue. Elector U.S. Electoral Coll., 1996; bd. dirs. Barrios Unidos Gang Prevention Program; Fresno/Madera Area Agy. Aging; bd. dirs. Rape Counseling Svcs. Fresno. Mem.: Hispanic C. of C. (past pres., founding chair Latina conf.). Democrat. Office: PO Box 942849 Rm 5136 Sacramento CA 94249-0001 Address: 2550 Mariposa Mall STe 5031 Fresno CA 93721

REYES, SILVESTRE, congressman; b. Canutillo, Texas, Nov. 10, 1944; m. Carolina Gaytan; children: Monica, Rebecca, Silvestre Jr. AA, El Paso C. C., 1977; student, U. Tex. Mem. 105th-108th Congress from 16th Tex. Dist., 1997—; asst. regional commr. U.S. Immigration and Naturalization Svc., chief, 1984-95, mem. nat. security and vet. affairs coms. Democrat.

REYES-CUBIDES, WILLIAM, language educator, researcher, writer; b. Bogotá, Colombia, Dec. 21, 1969; arrived in U.S., 1992; s. Alvaro Reyes and Patricia Cubides. BA, Nat. Pedagogical U., Bogota, 1990; MA in Applied Linguistics, Nat. U., Bogota, 1992; postgrad. in PhD program, Boston Coll., 1999—. Fgn. langs. lectr. Goucher Coll., Towson, Md., 1995—96, Towson U., Towson, Md., 1996—99; Romance langs. tchg. fellow Boston Coll., Chestnut Hill, Mass., 1999—. Editor-in-chief Romance Rev., Boston, 2000—02; conf. dir. Internat. Congress on Romance Studies, Boston, 2000—02. Scriptwriter: pedagogic video Impresiones, 2002. Dir. Colombia's March for Peace, Boston, 1999. Grantee U.S. Dept. Edn., Boston, 2003. Fellow: Internat. Alliance of Tchr.-Scholars; mem.: MLA, L.Am. Studies Assn., Romance Langs. Grad. Assn. (pres. Boston chpt. 2002—04). Office: Boston Coll 140 Commonwealth Ave Chestnut Hill MA 02467 E-mail: reyescub@bc.edu.

REYES HEROLES, JESUS, former Mexican government official; b. Tuxpan, Veracruz, Mex., Apr. 3, 1921; s. Jesus Reyes Martinez and Juana Heroles Lombera; m. Gloria Gonzalez Garza, May 8, 1951; children: Jesus, Federico. LL.B. with special honors, Nat. Autonomous U. Mex., 1944; postgrad., U. Buenos Aires and La Plata, Colegio Libre de Estudios Superiores de Buenos Aires, 1945; honoris causa doctorate, Alcalá de Henares U., Madrid, 1981. Assessor Dept. Labor and Social Planning, Mexico City, 1944; substitute pres. special group no. 1 Fedl. Bd. Reconciliation and Arbitration, Mexico City, 1946; sec. gen. Mexican Book Inst., 1949-53; assessor Office of Pres., Mexico City, 1952-58; chief economic studies Mexican Nat. Railroads, Mexico City, 1953-58; tech. subdir. gen. Mexican Inst. Social Security, Mexico City, 1958-64; dir. gen. Petroleos Mexicanos, Mexico City, 1964-70, Diesel Nacional (S.A.), Constructora Nacional de Carros de Ferrocarril (S.A.), Siderurgica Nacional (S.A.), Mexico City, 1970-72, Mexican Inst. Social Security, 1975-76; Sec. Interior (Fed. Govt.) Mexico City, 1976-79; full-time investigator Nat. Autonomous U., Mexico City, 1979-82; Sec. Edn. Mex. Govt., Mexico City, 1982-96, min. energy, 1996-97; amb. to Am. Mexican Government, Washinton, DC, 1997—2001. Various professorial positions, colls. in, Mex., 1944-67; pres. Interamerican Center for Studies in Social Security; bd. dirs. Fondo para la Historia de las Ideas Revolucionarias de Mex.; Various positions in the Partido Revolucionario Institucional (PRI), 1939-60; rep. XLV legis. Congreso de la Union; pres. Nat. Exec. Com. PRI. Author: various studies in politics, economics, including El Liberalismo Mexicano (3 volumes), 1957, 58, 61. Hon. mem. Spanish Royal Acad. Hist.; mem. Mex. Acad. Hist., Mex. Soc. Geography and Statistics, College Lawyers.; Partido Revolucionario Institucional. Office: Embassy of Mexico 1911 Pennsylvania Ave NW Washington DC 20006

REYMAN, JONATHAN ERIC, archaeologist, anthropologist, researcher; b. Greenwich, Conn., July 31, 1943; s. Solon Aaron and Ethel Jeanette (Pearlman) R.; 1 child, Mika Ranjit Mini. BA, Ind. U., 1965; PhD, So. Ill. U., 1971. Instr. anthropology So. Ill. U., Carbondale, 1969—70, postdoctoral rsch. assoc., 1971—72; asst. prof. anthropology Ill. State U., Normal, 1972—77, assoc. prof., 1977—82, prof., 1982—91; rsch. assoc. in anthropology Ill. State Mus., Springfield, 1993—2004, curator Anthropology Dept., 2004—. Rsch. collaborator Nat. Park Svc., Mesa Verde Nat. Park, Colo., 1975-76; founder, operator Feather Distbn. Project, Springfield, 1982—; vis. prof. anthropology U. Ill., Urbna, 1994, 95; mem. peer rev. panel tchg. with tech. NEH, Washington, 1996. Editor: Rediscovering Our Past: Essays on the History of American Archaeology, 1992, The Gran Chichimeca: Essays on the Archaeology and Ethnohistory of Northern Mesoamerica, 1995; contbr. over 140 articles and revs. to profl. jours., also chpts. to books. NDEA Title IV grad. fellow So. Ill. U., 1966-69; sr. rsch. grantee NSF, 1973-78, 87-88, rsch. grantee Wenner-Gren Found. for Anthrop. Rsch., 1980. Fellow Am. Anthrop. Assn., Soc. Profl. Archeologists (tchg. cert. panel 1989-93, chmn. com. on pub. land use, 1978-79), Soc. for Applied Anthropology (co-chmn. Am. Indian issues com. 1997-2000), Coun. for Mus. Anthropology, Soc. for Am. Archaeology (history of archaeology com. 1987-89), Sigma Xi, Phi Kappa Phi. Avocations: travel, cooking, reading, music. Home: 1220 Larchmont Dr Springfield IL 62704-2110 Office: Ill State Mus Rsch and Collections Ctr 1011 E Ash St Springfield IL 62703-3535 E-mail: reyman@museum.state.il.us.

REYNA, BENIGNO G. federal agency administrator; BS in Criminal Justice, U. Tex., Brownsville; grad., FBI Nat. Acad. Joined Brownsville (Tex.) Police Dept., 1976, various positions including comdr. profl. stds. and emergency mgmt. coord., chief of police; mem. Tex. Commn. on Law Enforcement Officer Stds. and Edn., 1997—2000, presiding officer, 2000—01; dir. U.S. Marshals Svc. U.S. Dept. Justice, Arlington, Va., 2001—. Instr. criminal justice U. Tex., Brownsville; regional law enforcement tech. expert Counter Drug Tech. Assessment Ctr., 1998—2001; law enforcement advisor to law enforcement coordinating com. U.S. Attys. Office, So. Dist. Tex. Recipient Disting. Alumnus award, Tex. Southmost Coll., 2002. Mem.: Internat. Assn. Chiefs Police. Office: US Marshals Service Washington DC 20530-0001

REYNA, CLAUDIO, professional soccer player; b. Springfield, N.J., July 20, 1973; Student, U. Va. Midfielder Bayer Leverkusen (German Bundesliga), 1994—98, U.S. Nat. Soccer Team, Chgo., 1998—. Mem. 1994 World Cup Team. Named Freshman of Yr., Soccer Am., 1991, Player of Yr., 1992, 1993, 3-time first-team All-Am., Nat. Soccer Coaches Assn. Am.; recipient Player of Yr. award, Mo. Athletic Club, 1992, 1993. Office: US Soccer Fedn 1801 S Prairie Ave Chicago IL 60616-1319

REYNIK, ROBERT JOHN, materials scientist, research and education administrator; b. Bayonne, N.J., Dec. 25, 1932; m. Georgiana M. Walker, Apr. 12, 1959; children: Michael, Christopher, Jonathan, Katherine, Steven, Kevin. BS in Math. and Physics, U. Detroit, 1956; MSEE, U. Cin., 1960, PhD in Phys. Chemistry, 1963. Rsch. assoc. Sch. Metall. Engring. U. Pa., Phila., 1963-64, asst. prof., 1964-67; assoc. prof. Drexel U., Phila., 1967-70, assoc. dir. engring. materials program NSF, Washington, 1970-71, dir. engring. materials program, 1971-74, dir. metallurgy program, 1974-82, head metallurgy, polymers, ceramics and electronic materials, 1983-90, head office spl. programs in materials, 1990-94, sr. staff scientist divsn. materials rsch. Arlington, Va., 1994-96; exec. sec. and cognizant program dir. US-USSR Internat. Agreement in Sci. and Tech., Washington, 1974-79; NSF liaison rep. Nat. Materials Adv. Bd., Washington, 1985-94; math. and phys. sci. directorate coord. Integration of Rsch. and Edn., 1996-97; sr. scientist Office of Sci. and Tech. Infrastructure, 1997-98, sr. staff scientist divsn. materials rsch., 1998-99, grantsmanship cons. and estate planning advisor, 1999—. Dir. electrometallurgy and materials, corrosion, program US-USSR internat. agreement sci. and tech., 1974-80; mem. First U.S. Metall. Del. People's Republic China, 1978; vis. prof. materials sci. and engring. U. Pa., 1982-83; tech. coord. Sci. & Tech. Ctrs. in Materials Sci. & Engring., 1990-94; co-chair Fed. Coord. Coun. for Sci., Engring. and Tech. joint com. edn. and tng. Office of Sci. and Tech. Policy, 1992-93; co-chair task group edn. and tng. Aeronautics Materials and mfg. Techs. Working Groups Nat. Sci. and Tech. coun., Office of Vice Pres. of U.S., 1994; tech. mgr. rsch. grants mfg. devel. and mfg. Tech. Reinvestment Project, Fed. Govt., 1994-96; cons. in field. Fellow Am. Soc. Materials Internat. (mem.-at-large materials sci. coun. 1990-96, mem.-at-large materials sci. tech. sector coun. 1993-96, fed. affairs com. 1996—, gold medal selection com.); mem. AAAS, AIME (chmn. govt. pub. affairs com. 1994-96), Am. Chem. Soc., Am. Assn. Engring. Socs. (honors and awards com.), The Metals, Minerals and Materials Soc. (mem. and chmn. tech. coms., Leadership award 2004), Materials Rsch. Soc., Sigma Xi (past chpt. pres., exec. counselor), Tau Beta Pi. Fax: 856-428-2186. Office Phone: 856-428-4336. E-mail: r.reynik@worldnet.att.net.

REYNOLDS, ALBERT BARNETT, nuclear engineer, educator; b. Lebanon, Tenn., Feb. 1, 1931; s. George Lazenby and Marion (Barnett) R.; m. Helen Buck, Sept. 6, 1954; children— Albert Jr., Charlotte, Marion Student, U. of South, 1948-51; S.B. in Physics, MIT, 1953, S.M. in Nuclear Engring., 1955, Sc.D. in Chem. Engring., 1959. Physicist-mgr. Gen. Electric Co., San Jose, Calif., 1959-68; prof. nuclear engring. U. Va., Charlottesville, 1968-96, chmn. dept. nuclear engring. and engring. physics, 1991-92, prof. emeritus, 1996—. Cons. NRC, Washington, 1970-84, U.S. Dept. Energy, 1987-89; fields of rsch. include liquid metal reactor safety, electric cable aging. Author: Bluebells and Nuclear Energy, 1996; co-author: Fast Breeder Reactors, 1981; contbr. numerous articles to profl. jours. Fellow Am. Nuclear Soc. (exec. com. div. nuclear reactor safety 1980-83, chair Va. sect. 1986-87); mem. ASME, IEEE, Am. Soc. Engring. Edn., Sigma Xi, Tau Beta Pi Home: 2600 Barracks Rd Apt 449 Charlottesville VA 22901-3132 E-mail: hareyn@aol.com.

REYNOLDS, ANNETTE, secondary school educator; Master degree, Ind. U., 1973. 7th and 8th grade physical edn. health tchr. Grissom Mid. Sch., Mishawaka, Ind.; 10th-12th grades physical edn. tchr. Penn HS, Mishawaka, Ind., Tipton HS, Ind.; 9th-12th grades physical edn. tchr. Northridge HS, Middlebury, Ind.; 10th-12th grades dance tchr., gymnastics coach, cheerleader sponsor Richardson HS, Tex. Vol. Iron Kids Triathalon, Am. Heart Assn. Mem. Nat. Assn. Student Activity Advisors, Richardson Edn. Assn., Delta Kappa Gamma (chmn., dir. Flip For Sight fundraiser). Home: 9554 Atherton Dr Dallas TX 75243-6134

REYNOLDS, BARBARA C. mental health educator, academic dean, retired; b. Syracuse, N.Y. d. Robert J. Clark; m. George L. Reynolds, June 9, 1962 (dec.); children: George L. III, Katherine C.; m. George Barnard, Apr. 17, 2004. BSN, Syracuse U., 1952; MPH, U. Minn., 1968, PhD, 1990. Asst. prof. U. Cin., 1968-75; ind. human resources cons. Cin., 1975-76; asst. prof. sch. pub. health U. Minn., 1976-82; asst. prof. Vanderbilt U., Nashville, 1986-90, N.Y. Med. Ctr. Sch. Nursing, 1964—69, Coll. Mt. St. Joseph, 1973—75; dean sch. nursing Tenn. Tech. U., Cookeville, 1991-98. Bd. dirs. Tenn. Health Care Campaign 2002—. Contbr. articles to profl. jours. Mem. Leadership Putnam Alumni Assn. (pres. 1995-96), Rotary (Cookeville chpt., bd. dirs.), Sigma Theta Tau, Phi Kappa Phi. Home: 1750 Heathrow Dr Cookeville TN 03850

REYNOLDS, BARBARA E. mathematics professor; d. George A. and Charlotte E. (Davison) R. AB, St. Louis U., 1971; MS in Math. and Edn., U. of South Fla., 1975; PhD in Math., St. Louis U., 1979. Joined Sisters of the Divine Savior, 1979. Computer operator, sci. programmer, statis. cons. St. Louis U., Yalem Computer Ctr., St. Louis, 1967—72; tchr. corps intern Dowdell Jr. H.S., Tampa, Fla., 1972—73; math. tchr. secondary schs. Peace Corps, Ghana, 1973—75; grad. tchg. fellow St. Louis U., St. Louis, 1975—79, internat. student advisor, 1976—79; prof. math. and computer sci. Cardinal Stritch U., Milw., 1979—. Mem. Clavius Group, 1985—; participant calculus project Purdue U., summer, 1991, curriculum reform undergrad. math., 1992-93, Inst. Retng. Computer Sci., Clarkson U., 1986-87. Author, editor: book Cooperative Learning in Undergraduate Mathematics: Issues that Matter & Strategies that Work, 2001; co-author (with Nancy Baxter Hastings): (textbook) Workshop Calculus with Graphing Calculators, 1999; editor: (anthology of readings) Readings in Cooperative Learning for Undergraduate Mathematics, 1997; author: (textbook) Precalculus, Concepts & Computers, 1996, (book) A Practical Guide to Cooperative Learning in Collegiate Mathematics, 1995. Mem. Sisters of the Divine Savior, Milw., 1979. Mem. Math. Assn. Am., Nat. Coun. Tchrs. Math., Wis. Math. Coun., Assn. Women in Math. Roman Catholic. Avocations: reading, swimming, biking, sewing, photography. Office: Cardinal Stritch U 6801 N Yates Rd Milwaukee WI 53217 E-mail: breynolds@stritch.edu.

REYNOLDS, BENEDICT MICHAEL, surgeon; b. N.Y.C., Sept. 12, 1925; s. Benedict and Delia (Coan) R.; m. Alice Marie Hodnett, May 3, 1952; children: Benedict, John, Ann Marie, Mary Alice, Daniel. Student, Columbia U., 1942-43, U. Rochester, 1943-44; MD, NYU, 1948. Diplomate: Am. Bd. Surgery, Pan Am. Med. Assn. Intern Bellevue Med. Center, N.Y.C., 1948-49, surg. resident, 1951-55; asst. in surgery N.Y. U., N.Y.C., 1953-55; instr. surgery Albert Einstein Coll. Medicine, Bronx, N.Y., 1955-56, asst. prof. surgery, 1956-58, clin. asst. prof., 1958-71, vis. prof. surgery, 1977; prof. surgery N.Y. Med. Coll., N.Y.C., 1971—; practice medicine specializing in surgery Bronx, 1955—; dir. surgery Misericordia Hosp. Med. Center, Bronx, 1962-83, Fordham Hosp., 1964-76; chmn. dept. surgery Lincoln Hosp., Bronx, 1976-82. Attending surgeon Met. Hosp., N.Y.C., 1972—; cons. Community Gen. Hosp. of Sullivan County, 1972—; dir. dept. surgery N.Y. Westchester Square Med. Ctr., Bronx, 1994—. Contbr. articles in field to med. jours. Served with USN, 1943-45, 49-51. Fellow N.Y. Acad. Medicine, A.C.S.; mem. AMA, N.Y. State Med. Soc., N.Y. Acad. Sci., Soc. Surgery Alimentary Tract,

N.Y. and Bklyn. Regional Chpt. on Trauma, Internat. Soc. Lymphology, N.Y. Surg. Soc., Am. Gastroent. Assn. Roman Catholic. Home: 55 Roundtop Rd Yonkers NY 10710-2327 Office: 1578 Williamsbridge Rd Bronx NY 10461-6265

REYNOLDS, BILLIE ILES, insurance agent; b. Oakland, Calif., Mar. 26, 1929; d. Walter F. and Frances Olive (Blakesley) Iles; m. William V. Reynolds, June 23, 1950; children: Gilbert, Wendy Lee Bryant, Cynthia Lea Waple, Christy Dirren. Registered fin. rep., fin. counselor, pension and retirement specialist, investment advisor. Ptnr. Reynolds Advt. Agy., 1963-70; asst. exec. dir. Nat. Sch. Transp. Assn., Springfield, Va., 1964-76, exec. dir., 1976-83, Ariz. Landscape Contractors Assn., 1984-86. Registered life and health ins. agt. Freelance writer scripts for radio, TV, newspapers, nat. mags., 1953-70; author: Planning is the Key: Basics of Financial Understanding for Beginners, 1984. Methodist. E-mail: azreynolds@juno.com. *Freedom must also be balanced with responsibility...and truth.*

REYNOLDS, CALVIN, management consultant, business educator; b. N.Y.C., Oct. 2, 1928; s. Charles Edward and Edna (Klockgeter) R.; m. Mary Virginia Gregg, May 4, 1985; children from a previous marriage: Dwight, Neal J. BS in Bus., Columbia U., 1952, MS in Bus., 1959. Dir. ops. Europe Uniroyal Internat., Geneva, 1956—67; v.p. Nat. Fgn. Trade Coun., N.Y.C., 1967—74; sr. v.p. Orgn. Resources Counselors, N.Y.C., 1975—92, sr. counselor Ossining, 1993—2001, ret., 2001; pres. Calvin Reynolds and Assocs., Ossining, NY, 1993—. Author: Guide to Global Compensation and Benefits, 2001; contbr. articles to profl. jours. Wharton Sch. U. Pa. sr. fellow, 1993-94. Republican. Congregationalist. Avocations: golf, music, reading. Home and Office: Calvin Reynolds & Assocs 52 Underhill Rd Ossining NY 10562-5118 E-mail: calreynolds@verizon.net.

REYNOLDS, CHARLES PATRICK, pediatric oncologist, researcher; b. El Paso, Tex., Aug. 8, 1952; s. Charles Albert and Lallah Elizabeth (Munro) R.; m. Debra Dawn Adams, Feb. 3, 1979; children: Amy Elizabeth, Jennifer Ann. BA in Biology, U. Tex., 1974; MD, U. Tex. Southwestern Med. Sch., Dallas, 1979; PhD, U. Tex., 1979. Lic. Tex., Calif., Ga. Postdoctoral fellow U. Tex. Southwestern Med. Sch., Dallas, 1979-80; pediatric intern Nat. Naval Med. Ctr., Bethesda, Md., 1980-81; battalion surg. Third Marine Div., Okinawa, Japan, 1981-82; rsch. med. officer Naval Med. Rsch. Inst., Bethesda, 1982-87; asst. prof. UCLA, 1987-89; assoc. prof. U. So. Calif., L.A., 1989-2000, prof., 2000—; head devel. therapeutics sect. divsn. hematology-oncology Children's Hosp. L.A., L.A., 1993—; co-dir. develpmental therapeutics program U. So. Calif. Norris Comprehensive Cancer Ctr., 2000—; dir. devel. therapeutics program U. So. Calif.-Children's Hosp. L.A. Inst. for Pediat. Clin. Rsch., 2003—. Dir. Neuroblastoma Marrow Purging Lab. Childrens Cancer Group, L.A., 1988-99; team physician U.S. Shooting Team, 1991—; dir. neuroblastoma purging lab. Children's Oncology Group, L.A., 2000—; mem. FDA Pediat. Subcom. of Oncologic Drug Adv. Com., 2000—. Patentee in field; contbr. articles to profl. jours. Mem. 1992 USA Olympic Shooting Team, Barcelona, Spain. Grantee Nat. Cancer Inst. Mem. Am. Soc. Clin. Oncology, Am. Assn. Cancer Rsch., Soc. Analytical Cytology, AAAS, Children's Oncology Group, Internat. Soc. for Pediat. Oncology. Roman Catholic. Avocations: filmmaking, guitar playing. Office: Childrens Hosp LA Divsn Hematology Oncology PO Box 54700 Los Angeles CA 90054-0700

REYNOLDS, CHRISTOPHER JOHN, lawyer; b. Mpls., Aug. 1, 1947; s. Jack Elton and Virginia Mary (Foley) R.; m. Margaret Ann Weekes, June 21, 1969; 1 child, Rowan Foley. BA, U. Santa Clara, 1969; JD, Am. U., 1972. Bar: D.C. 1973, Md. 1992, U.S. Dist. Ct. D.C. 1974, U.S. Ct. Appeals (D.C. cir.) 1974, U.S. Supreme Ct. 1977. Atty., advisor Rev. Bd. FCC, Washington, 1972-74; assoc. Dempsey & Koplovitz, Washington, 1974-78, ptnr., 1978-88, Peper, Martin, Jensen, Maichel & Hetlage, Washington, St. Louis, others, 1988-92; atty. Law Offices of Christopher J. Reynolds, Prince Frederick, Md., 1992-94; shareholder Reynolds and Manning, P.A., Prince Frederick, 1995—. Mem. Calvert County Econ. Devel. Commn., 1994—, chmn., 1997-2000; bd. dirs. Calvert County Christmas in April, 1995-97; bd. dirs. Calvert County United Way, 2003—, vice chmn., 2004—; mem. core svc. agy. adv. bd. Calvert County Health Dept., 1996-98; mem. adv. bd. Entrepreneur and Leadership Ctr., Coll. So. Md., 2000-03; bd. govs. So. Md. Higher Edn. Ctr., 2002—; mem. Econ. Devel. Authority for Calvert County, Md., 1997-2000, 2003—. Fellow Md. Bar Found.; mem. ABA, AHA (Calvert County bd. dirs. 1994-97), Fed. Comms. Bar Assn., Md. Bar Assn., D.C. Bar Assn., Calvert County Bar Assn. (pres. 2001-02), Calvert County C. of C. (pres. 2000-01), So. Md. Econ. Devel. Assn. (bd. dirs. 1999-2001), Barristers Club, John Carroll Soc. (Washington). Democrat. Roman Catholic. Office: Reynolds & Manning PA PO Box 2809 260 Merrimac Ct Prince Frederick MD 20678-4110 Office Phone: 410-535-9220. E-mail: calvertlawyer@comcast.net.

REYNOLDS, CLARK WINTON, economist, educator; b. Chgo., Mar. 13, 1934; m. Nydia O'Connor Viales; children: Rebecca, C. Winton III, Matthew, Camila. AB, Claremont (Calif.) Men's Coll., 1956; student, MIT, 1956-57, 58; student divinity sch., Harvard U., 1957-58; MA, U. Calif., Berkeley, 1961, PhD in Econs., 1962. Asst. prof. Occidental Coll., L.A., 1961-62; from asst. to assoc. prof. dept. edn. and econ. growth Yale U., New Haven, 1962-67; sr. fellow The Brookings Inst., Washington, 1975-76; prof. econs., prin. investigator, founding dir. Americas program Stanford (Calif.) U., prof. emeritus econs., 1996—. Vis. prof. Nat. U. Mex., Chapingo, 1966, El Colegio de Mex., Mexico City, 1964, 65, 79, Hopkins-Nanjing Ctr. for Chinese and Am. Studies, Nanjing, China, 1999-2002, China Europe Internat. Bus. Sch., Shanghai, 2002, 03; vis. lectr. in econs. Stockholm U. Econs., 1968; fellow St. Antony's Coll., Oxford, 1975; vis. rsch. scholar Internat. Inst. for Applied Systems Analysis, Laxenburg, Austria, 1978; Fulbright chair in internat. econs. U. Viterbo, Italy, 2001. Author: The Mexican Economy, 1970; co-author: Essays on the Chilean Economy, 1965, (with C. Tello) U.S.-Mexican Relations: Economic and Social Aspects, Las Relaciones Mexico Estados Unidos, 1983, Dynamics of North American Trade, 1991, North American Labor Market Interdependence, 1992, Open Regionalism in the Andes, 1996. Dir. Monticello West Found., 1980-2003. Woodrow Wilson Found. fellow, 1956-57, Rockefeller Found. fellow, 1957-58, Doherty Found. fellow, 1960-61, Inst. Internat. Studies fellow Stanford U., 1990-2000; grantee Social Sci. Rsch. Coun., Ford Found., Hewlett Found., Rockefeller Found., Mellon Found., MacArthur Found., Tinker Found. Mem. Am. Econ. Assn.

REYNOLDS, DEBBIE (MARY FRANCES REYNOLDS), actress; b. El Paso, Tex., Apr. 1, 1932; m. Eddie Fisher, Sept. 26, 1955 (div. 1959); children— Carrie, Todd; m. Harry Karl, Nov., 1960 (div. 1973); m. Richard Hamlett (div. May 1996). Active high sch. plays; screen debut Daughter of Rosie O'Grady; motion pictures include: June Bride, 1948, The Daughter of Rosie O'Grady, 1950, Three Little Words, 1950, Two Weeks With Love, 1950, Mr. Imperium, 1951, Singin' in the Rain, 1952, Skirts Ahoy!, 1952, I Love Melvin, 1953, The Affairs of Dobie Gillis, 1953, Give a Girl a Break, 1953, Susan Slept Here, 1954, Athena, 1954, Hit the Deck, 1955, The Tender Trap, 1955, The Catered Affair, 1956, Bundle of Joy, 1956, Tammy and the Bachelor, 1957, This Happy Feeling, 1958, The Mating Game, 1959, Say One for Me, 1959, It Started With a Kiss, 1959, The Gazebo, 1959, The Rat Race, 1960, Pepe, 1960, The Pleasure of His Company, 1961, The Second Time Around, 1961, How the West Was Won, 1962, My Six Loves, 1963, Mary, Mary, 1963, The Unsinkable Molly Brown, 1964, Goodbye Charlie, 1964, The Singing Nun, 1966, Divorce American Style, 1967, How Sweet It Is!, 1968, What's the Matter with Helen?, 1971, Charlotte's Web, (voice only) 1973, That's Entertainment!, 1974, The Bodyguard, 1992, Heaven and Earth, 1993, (with Albert Brooks) Mother, 1996, That's Entertainment III, 1994, In & Out, 1996, In and Out, 1997, Zack and Reba, 1998; star TV program The Debbie Reynolds Show, 1969; star Broadway show Irene, 1973-74, Annie Get Your Gun, Los Angeles, San Francisco, 1977, Woman of the Year, 1984, The Unsinkable Molly Brown, 1989-90 (nat. tour); author: If I Knew Then, 1963, Debbie-My Life, 1988; creator exercise video Do It Debbie's Way, 1984; recurring role (TV series) Will and Grace; actress (TV movies) Perry Mason, 1989, Battling for Babies, 1991, Halloweentown, 1998, The Christmas Wish, 1998, A Gift of Love, 1999 (Emmy nominee), Virtual Mom, 1999, These Old Broads, 2001, Return to Halloweentown, 2001, Connie and Carla, 2003. Named Miss Burbank, 1948 Office: Debbie Reynolds Studios care Margie Duncan 6514 Lankershim Blvd North Hollywood CA 91606-2409

REYNOLDS, DON WILLIAM, geologist; b. Centerburg, Ohio, Apr. 6, 1926; s. Loren William and Charlotte Lones (Hunt) R.; m. Betty Jeannette Spears, Sept. 4, 1953; children: Don William Jr., Richard Allen (dec.), Brenda Gay. BS, Ohio State U., 1952. Registered profl. geologist, Calif., 1970-2000. Mgr. Geochem. Engring., Inc., Midland, Tex., 1950-52; geologist Union Oil Co. Calif., Midland, 1953-66, dist. exploration geologist Anchorage, 1966-68, area geologist Bakersfield, Calif., 1968-76, dis. devel. geologist Ventura, Calif., 1976-86, dis. devel. geologist mid-continent divsn. Oklahoma City, 1986-89, regional mgr. mid-continent devel., 1989-90, advisor geology, 1990-92. Gen. ptnr. Reynolds Farm, 1979—; sec. ASF Inc., IFP Inc., Austin, 1989—; chmn. bd. Future Petroleum Corp., 1992-98, bd. dirs., 2001-2004. Pres. Park Stockdale Civic Assn., Bakersfield, 1970, Clearpoint Homeowner's Assn., Ventura, 1980-86; chmn. Kern County Freeway Com. Bakersfield, 1970-73. Served with USAF, 1944-45. Mem. Am. Assn. Petroleum Geologists, West Tex. Geol. Soc. (sec. 1965-66), Kans.-Okla. Oil and Gas Assn. (nomenclature com. 1987-92), San Joaquin Geol. Soc. (treas. 1974-75), Am. Assn. Petroleum Geologists (sec. Pacific sect. 1975-76). Republican. Methodist. Home: 5009 Reynolds Rd Centerburg OH 43011 E-mail: Don_Wm_Reynolds@compuserve.com.

REYNOLDS, DONALD MARTIN, art historian, foundation administrator, educator; b. Kansas City, Mo., Jan. 11, 1931; s. James Martin and Mary Helen (Hughes) Reynolds; m. Nancy Zlobik, June 5, 1970. Student, Amarillo Coll., 1949-51; BA, Assumption Sem., San Antonio, 1955, Columbia U., 1968, MA, 1970, PhD, 1975. Announcer Sta. KGNC Radio/TV, Amarillo, Tex., 1949-51; account exec. Monte Rosenwald & Assocs., Amarillo, 1957-59; copy writer, account rep., account supr. J. Walter Thompson, N.Y.C., C.Am., 1959-61; mgr. Ctrl. Am., Young & Rubicam Advt., N.Y.C., Panama, 1961-62; advt. mgr., mktg. dir. Colgate-Palmolive Co. Western Hemisphere Divsn., 1962-64; founder, dir. Image, Internat. Mktg. Agy., N.Y.C., 1964-66; mus. educator in charge Dept. Pub. Edn. Met. Mus. Art, 1977-79; curator pks. Dept. Pks. and Recreation, N.Y.C., 1986-88; founder, coord. Ann. Symposium Pub. Monuments, N.Y.C., 1991—; founder, dir. Monuments Conservancy, Inc., N.Y.C., 1992—. Adj. prof. art history Columbia U., NYC, 1970—, Fairfield (Conn.) U., 1981—; adj. asst. prof. Hunter Coll., 1972—81; asst. prof. Coll. Mt. St. Vincent, 1973—77, Manhattan Coll., 1973—77; cons. Corps of Discovery monument Kemper Found., Kansas City, Mo., 2000; designer sculpture program Our Mother of Africa Chapel, Nat. Shrine of the Immaculate Conception, Nat. Black Cath. Congress, Washington, 2001. Author: (book) The Ideal Sculpture of Hiram Powers, 1977, The Architecture of New York City: Histories and Views of Important Structures, Sites, and Symbols, 1984, The Architecture of New York City: Histories and Views of Important Structures, Sites, and Symbols, rev. edit., 1994, Nineteenth-Century Art, 1985, Manhattan Architecture, 1988, Monuments and Masterpieces: Histories and Views of Public Sculpture in New York City, 1988, Nineteenth Century Architecture, 1992, Masters of American Sculpture, The Figurative Tradition from American Renaissance to the Millennium, 1993; editor, compiler: book The Impact of Non-European Civilizations on the Art of the West: Selected Lectures of Rudolf Wittkower, 1989; co-author: MacMillan Ency. Archs., 1982. With U.S. Army, 1952—61. Mem.: Authors Guild, Coll. Art Assn., Nat. Sculpture Soc. Office: PO Box 608 New York NY 10003

REYNOLDS, EDGAR L. telecommunications industry executive; b. Ala. BS in Elec. Engring., Auburn U.; MBA, U. Ala. Pres. BellSouth Wireless, Inc., BellSouth Mobility DCS, Am. Cellular Comm. Corp., BellSouth Mobility; pres., network opers. Cingular Wireless, Atlanta, 2001—. Office: Cingular Wireless Glenridge Highlands Two 5655 Glenridge Connector Atlanta GA 30342*

REYNOLDS, EDWIN CLINTON, JR., engineering manager; b. Olney, Ill., Mar. 4, 1939; s. Edwin Clinton and Alberta Elizabeth (Wilson) R.; m. Wanda Faye Wesson, June 19, 1965; children: Courtney Rae, Gregory Clinton. BSME, U. Okla., 1962, M of Mech. Engring, 1969. Registered profl. engr., Okla. Assoc. engr. LTV Aerospace Corp., Dallas, 1962-63; propulsion design engr. Gen. Dynamics Corp., Ft. Worth, 1963-64; aerospace engr. Oklahoma City Air Logistics Ctr., Tinker AFB, Okla., 1965-75, dep. chief engine test br., 1975-80, chief prodn. engring. test sect., 1980-81, br. chief prodn. engring. br., 1981—. Contbr. tech. papers to profl. jours. and confs. Mem. membership com., treas. Putnam City Sch. PTA, Oklahoma City; mem. planning com. Boy Scouts Am., Oklahoma City. Recipient Fed. Engr. of the Year Awd., 1994, Nat. Soc. Profl. Engr. Mem. NSPE (Fed. Engr. of Yr. 1994), ASME (program treas.), Okla. Soc. Profl. Engrs. (sec., treas., Young Engr. of Yr. 1973, Engr. of Yr. 1980, Engr. in Mgmt. 1987), Air Force Assn., Tinker Soc. Profl. Engrs., Tinker Mgmt. Assn. Baptist. Avocations: tennis, golf, model airplanes. Home: 6507 NW 96th St Oklahoma City OK 73162-7408 Office: Oklahoma City Air Log Ctr LPPN Tinker AFB Oklahoma City OK 73145

REYNOLDS, EDWIN WILFRED, JR., retired secondary education educator; b. Englewood, N.J., Mar. 23, 1937; s. Edwin W. and Ellen H. (Hueber) R.; m. Sharon Policastro, Feb. 12, 1983. BA cum laude, Fairleigh Dickinson U, 1961, MAT magna cum laude, 1966; postgrad., NYU, 1964-65, Seton Hall U., 1970-71, Montclair State Coll., 1972-73. Cert. social studies tchr., supr., tchr. psychology, N.J. Supr. installation Western Electric Co., N.Y.C., 1961-65; tchr. social studies Teaneck (N.J.) High Sch., 1965-92, chmn. dept. social studies, 1968-71; supr. social studies Teaneck Secondary Schs., 1971-80, supr. grades K-12, 1980-92, supr. bus. edn. grades 7-12, 1984-92, ret., 1992. Pres. bd. dirs. Global Learning, Inc., 1992-97; sr. state cons. in Holocaust Edn., N.J.; curriculum coord. Ctr. for Holocaust/Genocide Studies, Ramapo Coll.; guest lectr. Kean Coll.; coord. M.A.T. program Fairleigh Dickinson U., 1969-71; mem. planning com. N.E. Regional Social Studies Conf., mem. steering com. Mid-Atlantic Conf.; mem. N.J. Dept. Edn. Social Studies Adv. Com., N.J. Gov.'s Adv. Coun. for Holocaust Edn. in the Pub. Schs.; cons. world history Scott Foresman Pub. Co. Author curriculum devel. and learning guides, 1973-92; co-editor: Holocaust and Genocide: A Search for Conscience. V.p., newsletter editor Pike County Hist. Soc.; elder Presbyn. Ch. U.S. With USN, 1955-57. Recipient Human Rights Award Temple Beth Tikvah, 1985, Brotherhood Award B'nai B'rith No. and Pascack Valleys, 1986, Daniel Roselle Lectr. award Mid. States Coun. for Social Studies, 1988. Mem. ASCD, Nat. Coun. for Social Studies (former bd. dirs.), N.J. Coun. for Social Studies (bd. dirs., past pres.), Greater Bergen County (N.J.) Coun. for Social Studies (bd. dirs., past pres.), Nat. Social Studies Suprs. Assn. (bd. dirs., past pres.), Assn. Ednl. Suprs. (bd. dirs., past pres.), Am. Hist. Assn., Pike County Hist. Soc. (pres. 1998-99), Phi Delta Kappa, Phi Omega Epsilon. Home: PO Box 626 Milford PA 18337-0626

REYNOLDS, ERNEST WEST, retired internist, educator; b. Bristow, Okla., May 11, 1920; s. Ernest West and Florence (Brown) R. BS, U. Okla., 1942, MD, 1946, MS, 1952. Diplomate: Am. Bd. Internal Medicine. Intern Boston City Hosp., 1946-47; resident Grady Meml. Hosp., Atlanta, 1949-50; practice medicine Tulsa, Okla., 1953-54; prof. medicine U Mich., 1965-72; prof. medicine, dir. cardiology U. Wis., 1972-90, prof. emeritus, 1991—. Dir. Kellogg Found. Comprehensive Coronary Care Project, 1967-72; chmn. NIH Cardiovascular Study Sect. A, 1972-73 Mem. editorial bd.: Am. Heart Jour; Contbr. articles to profl. jours. Served to capt. AUS, 1947-49. Mem. Am. Heart Assn. (fellow coun. clin. cardiology), Ctrl. Soc. Clin. Rsch. Home: 17 Red Maple Trl Madison WI 53717-1515 Personal E-mail: ernest_reynolds@yahoo.com. *In the academic environment, research oriented toward the solution of human problems is more productive in career advancement than the pursuit of applications of new technology. In the private sector applied research which solves real problems rather than copies or improves existing technology is met with surprising sales success and few failures.*

REYNOLDS, FRANK MILLER, retired government administrator; b. Tulsa, Jan. 8, 1917; s. Frank Miller and Grace (Shields) R.; m. Barbara G. MacWilliams, Dec. 7, 1946; children: Susan G., Ellen M., Frank M. AB, LL.B., U. Okla., 1939; LL.M., George Washington U., 1942; BS, Georgetown Sch. Fgn. Service, 1946. Bar: Okla. 1940. Mem. firm Flippo & Reynolds, Tulsa, 1940; elec. engr. Bur. Ships, Dept. of Navy, 1942-43; with Office Gen. Counsel, Dept. of Navy, 1946; chief negotiator, dep. dir. contract div. Office Naval Research, 1947-54; dep. dir., dir. resources div. Office Asst. Sec. Def., 1954-57; asst. sec. Inst. for Defense Analyses, 1957-61; sec., treas. Logistics Management Inst., Washington, 1961-65, v.p., 1966-76; dir. adminstrv. affairs Uniformed Services U. Health Scis., Bethesda, Md., 1976-78, dir. resource mgmt., 1978-82, exec. sec. bd. regents, 1978-83; dir. patient relations Sibley Meml. Hosp., 1983-84, cons., 1984-87. Professorial lectr. mgmt. research George Washington U. Sch. Engring., 1956—; cons. Nat. Exec. Service Corps., United Srs. Health Coop., 1984— . Served with radio divsn. Naval Research Lab., 1944-46. Mem. Okla. Bar Assn., Congl. Country Club, Delta Upsilon. Home: 415 Russell Ave Apt 113 Gaithersburg MD 20877-2845 E-mail: frank17r@comcast.net.

REYNOLDS, FREDRIC G. broadcasting company executive; b. Miami, Fla. married; 4 children. BBA in Fin., U. Miami, 1972. CPA. Tax cons., staff auditor Touche Ross & Co., from 1972, prin.; v.p. fin. Burger King Internat. divsn. Pillsbury Co.; various positions to sr. v.p. and CFO Frito-Lay unit PepsiCo Foods Internat., 1981-94, CFO KFC, Pepsi-Cola Internat., Pizza Hut units; exec. v.p., CFO, Westinghouse Elec. Corp., 1994-96; CFO, CBS Inc., N.Y.C., 1996—; exec. v.p., CFO, CBS Corp., N.Y.C., 1997-2000; exec. v.p., CFO Viacomm, N.Y.C., 2000—. Office: Viacomm 1515 Broadway New York NY 10036

REYNOLDS, GEORGE ANTHONY, JR., engineering executive; b. Columbia, S.C., May 5, 1961; s., George Anthony and Flora Mae (La Coste) R.; m. Katherine Alison Albea, Apr. 14, 1984; children: Amanda Kate, William Anthony. BSME, Clemson U., 1983; postgrad., U. Ala., Huntsville, 1985. Design engr. Motorola, Plantation, Fla., 1983-85; sr. engr. Chrysler, Huntsville, Ala., 1985-88; prin. engr. NCR, Liberty, S.C., 1988-91, project leader, 1991-94; mgr. mech. engring. Sensormatic Electronics, Boca Raton, Fla., 1994-96, dir. product engring., 1996-98, dir. active products, 1998-2000, v.p. hard tag and product line engring., 2000—02; v.p. electronic article surveillance Tyco Internat., Boca Raton, Fla., 2002, v.p. radio frequency identification, 2002—. Mem. editl. quality audit panel Electronic Packaging & Prodn. Mag., N.Y.C., 1992. Advisor Clemson U. Mech. Engring. Endowment Fund; elder, mem. ednl. dir. search com., chair Christian edn. com., nominating com., chair stewardship campaign 1st Presbyn. Ch., Delray Beach, Fla.; pres. Seagate Neighborhood Assn., 1996-97; team mgr. Caloosa Park Girls Fast Pitch Softball Assn. Finalist S. Fla. Up and Comers award, 1997. Mem. ASME (life), NRA (life; Legion of Honor), S.E. Pro/Engr. User Group (pres. 1992-93), S. Fla. Clemson Alumni Club, Nature Conservancy, Nat. Wildlife Fedn., Ducks Unltd., Fla. Sheriff's Assn. (life), Fla. Wildlife Fedn., Billfish Found., Tau Beta Pi, Phi Kappa Phi, Alpha Tau Omega (alumni adv. bd. Eta Pi chpt. 1993-94). Republican. Presbyterian. Avocations: tennis, genealogy, hunting, fishing. Office: Sensormatic Electronic Corp 951 Yamato Rd Boca Raton FL 33431-4425 Home: 2580 Greenbriar Dr Delray Beach FL 33445-7169

REYNOLDS, GERALD, federal agency administrator; Grad., CUNY York Coll., Boston U. Atty. Schatz & Schatz, Ribicoff & Kotkin, Conn.; legal analyst Ctr. Equal Opportunity; pres. Ctr. New Black Leadership; sr. regulatory counsel Kansas City Power and Light Co.; asst. sec. civil rights Dept. Edn., Washington, 2001—. Mem. editl. bd.: Am. Jour. Law and Medicine. Office: Dept Edn Office Civil Rights 400 Maryland Ave SW Washington DC 20202-1100

REYNOLDS, GLENN FRANKLIN, medicinal research scientist; b. Rahway, N.J., July 16, 1944; s. Frank Vanderbilt and Estelle (Ohlott) R.; m. Marianne DelliSanti, Nov. 25, 1967; children William Matthew, David Glenn, Wendy Joy. Student, Rutgers U., 1962-63, Union Coll., 1963-65; BS in Chemistry, Phila. Coll. Pharmacy and Sci., 1967. Rsch. scientist Merck & Co., Rahway, 1967-70, staff chemist, 1970-77, rsch. chemist, 1977-86, sr. rsch. assoc., 1991—. Merck recruiter Fairleigh Dickinson U., 1980, Howard U., 1980, U. N.C., 1981, Rutgers U., 1985. Inventor Proscar; contbr. articles to profl. jours.; patentee in field. Named Inventor of Yr. Intellectual Property Owners, 1993. Mem. Am. Chem. Soc., Masons (Lafayette lodge #27). Presbyterian. Avocations: computer science, biking, skiing, reading. Home: 252 Edgewood Ave Westfield NJ 07090-3918 Office: Merck & Co Inc PO Box 2000 126 E Lincoln Ave # 121267C Rahway NJ 07065-4687

REYNOLDS, HAROLD CRAIG, professional baseball player; b. Eugene, Oreg., Nov. 26, 1960; Student, San Diego State U., Canada Coll., Redwood City, Calif., Calif. State U., Long Beach. Infielder Seattle Mariners, 1983-92; with Balt. Orioles, 1993, Calif. Angels, 1994; broadcaster, analyst ESPN, Bristol, Conn., 1996—. Mem. Am. League All-Star Team, 1987-88. Office: care ESPN Corp Headqtrs Baseball Tonight ESPN Plaza 935 Bristol St Bristol CT 06010 Address: ESPN 605 3rd Ave Fl 8 New York NY 10158-0899

REYNOLDS, HARRAH (H.) ROBERT, conductor, artistic director; b. Canton, Ohio, Apr. 10, 1934; BMus in Edn., U. Mich., 1956, MMus in Performance, 1958. Dir. univ. bands, dir. divsn. instrumental studies Sch. Music, U. Mich. Condr. Detroit Chamber Winds and Strings; guest condr., clinician numerous univs. and confs.; lectr., condr. internat. confs. World Assn. of Symphonic Bands and Ensembles, Norway, Belgium, Eng., The Netherlands; master condr., tchr. Europaisches Seminar fur Dirigenten von Blasorchestern, Bundesakademie, Trossingen, Germany, Austrian Wind Band Condrs. Assn.; condr. Royal Danish Band, Copenhagen, Carnegie Hall, Lincoln Ctr., N.Y.C., Orch. Hall, Chgo., Kennedy Ctr., Washington, Powell Symphony Hall, St. Louis, Acad. Music, Phila.; condr. premiers La Scala Opera, Milan, concerts at Maggio Musicale, Florence, Italy, Tonhalle, Zurich, Switzerland, Concergebouw, Amsterdam, The Netherlands; condr. recs. for Koch Internat., Pro Arte, Caprice, Deutsche Grammophon; mem. nat. awards panel ASCAP. Mem. Coll. Band Dirs. Nat. Assn. (past pres.), Big Ten Band Dirs.' Assn. (past pres.). E-mail: hrr@umich.edu.

REYNOLDS, HELEN ELIZABETH, management services consultant; b. Minerva, NY, Aug. 30, 1925; d. Henry James and Margurite Catherine (Gallagher) McNally; m. Theodore Laurence Reynolds, Feb. 27, 1948; children: Laurence McBride, David Scott, William Herbert. BA, SUNY, Albany, 1967; MA, Union Coll., Schenectady, N.Y., 1971. Grad. Realtors Inst., NY. Owner, mgr. Schafer Studio, Schenectady, 1970-73; co-owner, v.p. Reynolds Chalmers Inc., Schenectady, 1971-97; program coord. Schenectady County, 1980-81; adminstr. Wellspring House of Albany, 1981-94; pres. HR Mgmt. Cons., Port Charlotte, Fla., 1994—2002. Cons., examiner NY State Civil Service, Albany, 1971-81; adv. council SBA, Washington, 1978-80. Planning bd. Town of Niskayuna, NY, 1977-81, town councilwoman, 1986-94; co-chair Great N.E. Festival on the Mohawk River, 1989-90; bd. dirs. HAVEN, Schenectady YWCA; mem. NY State Commn. on The Capital Region, 1994-98, Acad. of Women of Achievement, Schenectady, 1994; pres. Photo Arts Group of Charlotte County, 1998-2003, Buena Vista Property Owners Assn., Port Charlotte, Fla., 1998-2003. Named Woman Vision, 1986-87, Today's Woman, 1987, Schenectady YWCA. Mem. Antique and Classic Boat Soc. (bd. dir. 1974-89, Disting. Svc. award 1979, Founders award 1989), Assn. Adminstrs. Ind. Housing (pres. 1986-88, 92-94), Zonta (pres. 1981-82), Adirondack Mus., Antique Boat Mus., Lake George Antique Boat & Auto Mus. (bd. dir.), Charlotte Symphony League (v.p.), Union Coll. Alumni Assn., Charlotte Harbor Yacht Club, Charlotte County Art Guild. Avocations: photography, reading, golf, skiing, canoeing. Home and Office: 104 Leland St SW Port Charlotte FL 33952-9131

REYNOLDS, HERBERT HAL, university administrator; b. Frankston, Tex., Mar. 20, 1930; s. Herbert Joseph and Ava Nell (Taylor) R.; m. Joy Myrla Copeland, June 17, 1950; children: Kevin Hal, Kent Andrew, Rhonda Sheryl. BS, Trinity U., 1952; MS, Baylor U., 1958, PhD, 1961; ScD (hon.), Seinan Gakuin U., Japan, 1990, Baylor Coll. Dentistry, 1993; PhD (hon.), Yonok Coll., Thailand, 2000. Entered USAF, 1948, advanced through grades to col., 1966; with Aeromed. Lab., Alamogordo, N.Mex., 1961—68, Air Force Human Resources Lab., San Antonio, 1968; ret., 1968; exec. v.p. Baylor U., Waco,

Tex., 1969—81, pres., 1981—95, chancellor, 1995—2000, pres. emeritus, 2000—. Vis. fellow, scholar Cambridge U., 1994-97. Contbr. articles to profl. jours. Mem.: Sigma Xi, Phi Beta Kappa, Omicron Delta Kappa, Alpha Chi. Office: Baylor U Office of Pres Emeritus Waco TX 76798 Office Phone: 254-710-1311. E-mail: president_emeritus@baylor.edu.

REYNOLDS, HERBERT YOUNG, physician, internist; b. Richmond, Va., Aug. 20, 1939; s. George Audney and Pearle Maupin (Young) R.; m. Anne Browning Leavell, July 11, 1964; children: Nancy, George, William Stuart. BA in English, U. Va., 1961, MD, 1965; MA (hon.), Yale U., 1979. Diplomate Am. Bd. Internal Medicine, Am. Bd. Allergy and Immunology. Intern The NY Hosp., Cornell Med. Ctr., NYC, 1965-66, asst. physician, fellow in medicine, 1966-67; clin. assoc., lab. clin. investigation Nat. Inst. Allergy, Infectious Diseases, NIH, Bethesda, Md., 1967-70, chief clin. assoc., lab. clin. investigation, 1968-69; chief resident, instr. medicine U. Hosp. U. Wash., Seattle, 1970-71; sr. investigator, lab. clin. investigation Nat. Inst. Allergy, Infectious Diseases, NIH, Bethesda, 1971-76; assoc. prof. internal medicine, head pulmonary div. Sch. Medicine Yale U., New Haven, 1976-79, prof., 1979—88; J. Lloyd Huck prof. medicine, chmn. dept. Pa. State U., Milton S. Hershey Med. Ctr., 1988—2002; assoc. chmn. divsn. medicine Pa. State Geisinger Health Sys., 1997-2000, chief medicine ops. Hershey Med. Ctr. Region, 1997-2000; med. officer Lung Biology and Disease program, divsn. lung diseases NHLBI/NIH, Bethesda, 2002—; prof. medicine emeritus Pa. State U. Coll. Medicine, 2002—. Adj. prof. medicine Uniformed Svcs. U. Health Scis., Bethesda, 2003—; mem. exec. com. Coll. Medicine Pa. State U.-Hershey Med. Ctr., 1988-2002, exec. bd. U. Hosp., 1988-2002, fin. bd. acad. enrichment fun, 1988-95, dean's adv. com., 1988-97, diversity task force, 1995-2002, physicians faculty practice plan exec. com. 1996-97, human resources team leader, 2000 02; dept. chair rep. Milton S. Hershey Med. Ctr. Bd., 2000-2002; cons. in infectious diseases Nat. Naval Med. Ctr. NIH, Bethesda, 1971-76, clin. rsch. com., 1971-76, chmn., 1974-76, pulmonary disease adv. com. divsn. of lung diseases NHLBI, 1978-82, sci. counselors bd., 1984-88, data and safety monitoring bd. registry of patients with deficiency of Alpha-1 Antitrypsin, 1989-96. Mem. editl. bd. Lung, 1978—, Am. Jour. Medicine, 1979-89, Jour. Clin. Investigation, 1980-86, Am. Rev. Respiratory Diseases, 1980-87, Jour. Applied Physiology, 1981-89, Resident Physician, 1981-95; contbr. over 285 articles to profl. jours. Parent com. Troop 1 Boy Scouts Am., Madison, 1979-82; bd. dirs. Neighborhood Music Sch., Guilford, Conn., 1978-87, Music at Gretna, 1994-2002; bd. dirs. Harrisburg Symphony, 1996-2000, active All Saints Episc. Ch., Hershey; pulmonary infections com. Cystic Fibrosis Found., Bethesda, 1980-86; mem. coun. sci. advisors Parker B. Francis Found., Kansas City, Kans., 1983-87; internat. com. World Orgn. for Sarcoidosis and other Granulomatous Disorders, 1987-95; bd. dirs., mem. coun. Am. Lung Assn., 1989-93, bd. govs. 1990-93, com. mem., 1990-93; coach Guilford Soccer League, 1985-88; vol. Mercy Health Clinic, Germantown, Md., 2003—. Surgeon USPHS, 1967-70. John Edward Nobel fellow, 1961-65; named Outstanding Med. Specialist in USA, Town and Country Mag., 1989, 97, The Best Med. Specialists, Town & Country mag., 1995, One of 400 Best Doctors in U.S. Good Housekeeping Mag., 1991. Fellow ACP (coun. subsplty. socs. 1989-00, gov. Pa. Eastern Region 1, 2000-02), Am. Coll. Chest Physicians (program com. 1978-84), Infectious Disease Soc. Am., Coll. Physicians Phila.; mem. Am. Thoracic Soc. (sec.-treas. 1987-88, bd. dirs. 1989-93, v.p. 1988 89, pres. 1991-92), Am. Soc. Clin. Investigation, Assn. Am. Physicians, Am. Assn. Immunologists, Am. Fedn. Clin. Rsch., Am. Clin. and Climatological Assoc. (v.p. 2001-02, pres. 2002-03), Acad. Medicine Wash., Interurban Clin. Club (emeritus 1989), Country Club of Hershey, Farmington Country Club, Raven Soc., Phi Beta Kappa, Alpha Omega Alpha, Omicron Delta Kappa. Republican. Avocations: tennis, violin. Home: 226 E Caracas Ave Hershey PA 17033-1309 Office: NHLBI/NIH Divsn Lung Diseases 6701 Rockledge Dr Rm 10112 Bethesda MD 20892-7952 Business E-Mail: reynoldh@nhlbi.nih.gov.

REYNOLDS, JAMES, management consultant; s. Richard James and Esther (Nikander) R.; m. Joanne M.J. BA in Econs., NYU, 1965, postgrad., 1965-66. Cons. to pres. Rothrock, Reynolds & Reynolds Inc., N.Y.C., 1966-70; sr. v.p. health, med. div. Booz, Allen & Hamilton, N.Y.C., 1970-80; pres. Reynolds & Co. (mgmt. cons.), San Francisco, N.Y.C., Washington, 1981—. Developer Turning Clin. Quality into Competitive Advantage, ACHE, 2002; bd. dirs. Booz, Allen & Hamilton, 1977-79; chmn. bd. J.X. Reynolds Fine Arts, Ltd., 1979—; bd. dirs. Health Center Mgmt. Inst.; lectr. Harvard Sch. Pub. Health; faculty mem. Am. Coll. of Healthcare Execs.; bd. dirs. Health Ctr. Mgmt. Inst., Richmond, Va., 1977; mem. health adv. bd. Hunter Coll., 1980—. Editorial bd. Physicians Fin. News. Recipient NYU Founders award, 1965 Mem. Am. Pub. Health Assn., Am. Mgmt. Assn., Assn. Am. Med. Colls., Am. Hosp. Assn., Hosp. Mgmt. Systems Soc., Hosp. Fin. Mgmt. Assn., Asia Soc., China Inst., Phi Beta Kappa, Guggenheim Mus., Mus. Modern Art, Met. Mus. Art, Met. Opera Guild (N.Y.C.) Episcopalian. Home and Office: Reynolds & Co 333 E 51st St New York NY 10022-6702 also: 2500 3 Mile Run Rd Perkasie PA 18944-2020 Office Phone: 212-826-1818. E-mail: jreynolds@jxreynolds.com.

REYNOLDS, JAMES, JR., finance company executive; BA in Polit. Sci., U. Wis., LaCrosse; MBA in Fin., Northwestern U., 1982. Asst. v.p. Smith Barney; dir. Merrill Lynch, Chgo.; founder, chmn., CEO Loop Capital Markets LLC, Chgo., 1997—. Bd. mem. Ill. Econ. Devel. Bd., Lincoln Acad. Ill., Chgo. State U., U. Chgo. Hosp., Chgo. Zool. Soc., Youth Leadership Found., ETA Theatre, City Year, Chgo. Pub. Edn. Fund, Chgo. Summer Bus. Inst. Mem.: Alliance Bus. Leaders and Entrepreneurs (pres.), Chgo. Urban League (treas.). Office: Loop Capital Markets LLC Ste 1600 200 W Jackson Blvd Chicago IL 60606*

REYNOLDS, JAMES FRANCIS, JR., physician; b. St. Albans, Vt., June 20, 1947; s. James F. Sr. and Eleanor (Paquette) R.; married; children: Matthew, Katelyn, Aaron. BS, U.S. Mil. Acad., West Point, N.Y., 1969; MD, U. Louisville, 1978. Diplomate Am. Bd. Pediatrics, Am. Bd. Med. Genetics. Commd. U.S. Army, 1969, advanced through grades to brig. gen., 2003; pediatrics resident U. Va., Charlottesville, 1978-81, genetics fellow, 1981-83; clin. geneticist dept. med. genetics Shodair Hosp., Helena, Mont., 1983—. Assoc. editor Am. Jour. Med. Genetics, 1983-95; editor various books on med. genetics; contbr. articles to profl. jours. Mem. health profl. adv. com. Mont. March of Dimes, 1987—; mem. Mont. Coun. for Maternal and Child Health, 1987—. Fellow Am. Acad. Pediatrics, Am. Coll. Med. Genetics; mem. Am. Soc. Human Genetics. Avocations: hiking, skiing, stained glass craft. Office: Shodair Hosp PO Box 5539 Helena MT 59604-5539

REYNOLDS, JEAN EDWARDS, publishing executive; b. Saginaw, Mich., Dec. 11, 1941; d. F. Perry and Kathrine (Edwards) R.; m. Cary Wellington, Sept. 10, 1975 (div. 1982); children, Bradley, Abigail, Benjamin; m. Jon Haddon, Nov. 8, 1997. BA, Wells Coll., 1963; postgrad., CCNY, 1965-67. Asst. editor, sr. editor trade book div. Prentice-Hall, Englewood Cliffs, N.J., 1963-66, dir. children's books, 1966-69, McCall Pub. Co., N.Y.C., 1969-71; sr. v.p., editorial dir. Franklin Watts Inc., N.Y.C., 1971-75; pres. Pet Projects Inc., Ridgefield, Conn., 1975-81; editor in chief young people's publs. Grolier Inc., Danbury, Conn., 1981-89; founder, pub., exec. v.p. The Millbrook Press, Brookfield, Conn., 1989—. Bd. dirs. Wellington Leisure Products, Atlanta, Kiper Enterprises, Oswego, N.Y., Graduate Inst., New Haven, Conn., Jewish Fedn. Greater Danbury; chairperson Conn. Ctr. for the Book, 1991-94. Mem. Bd. of Govs. for Higher Edn., State of Conn., 2004—; mem. Bd. of Govs. for Higher Edn. State of Conn., 2004—; pres. Jewish Fedn. Greater Danbury, 1991—93, 2003—; bd. dirs. Jewish Home for the Elderly, Fairfield, Conn., 1989—90, 1999, Book Industry Study Group, 1991—98, The Wooster Sch., Danbury, Conn., 1992—, chair headmaster search, 2002—; bd. dirs. Temple Shearith Israel, Ridgefield, Conn., 1994—97, chair Kehila campaign, 2002; bd. dirs. The Children's Book Coun., 1996—2000, vice chair, 1997—98, chair, 1998—99; bd. dirs. The Learning Collaborative, 2000—02. Mem. ALA, Children's Book Coun., Mensa. Jewish. Avocations: skiing, sailing, needlecrafts. Home: 33 Corntassle Rd Danbury CT 06811-3208 Office: The Millbrook Press Inc 2 Old New Milford Rd Brookfield CT 06804-2426

REYNOLDS, JERRY OWEN, sports team executive; b. French Lick, Ind., Jan. 29, 1944; Student, Vincennes U., Oakland City Coll., Ind. U., Ind. State U. Coach Rockhurst Coll., Kansas City, Mo., 1975—84, Pittsburg (Kans.) State U., 1984—85; asst. coach Sacramento Kings, 1985—88, head coach, 1988—89, dir. player personnel, 1989—92, gen. mgr., 1992—94; gen. mgr, v.p. Sacramento Monarchs, (WNBA), 1998—. Office: Sacramento Monarchs 1 Sports Pkwy Sacramento CA 95834-2300

REYNOLDS, JOHN FRANCIS, insurance company executive; b. Escanaba, Mich., Mar. 29, 1921; s. Edward Peter and Lillian (Harris) R.; m. Dorothy Gustafson, May 1, 1946; children; Lois, Margaret, Michael. BS, Mich. State U., 1942. Claims and assoc. surety mgr. Hartford Ins. Co., Escanaba, Mich. and Chgo., 1946-55; asst. v.p., bond mgr. Wolverine Ins. Co., Battle Creek, Mich., 1955-64, v.p. underwriting, 1964-69; Midwest zone underwriting mgr. Transamerica Ins. Co. (Wolverine Ins. Co.), Battle Creek, Mich., 1969-74; pres., gen. mgr. Can. Surety Co. subs. Transamerica Ins. Co., Toronto, Ont., Canada, 1974-75; v.p. midwestern zone mgr. Transamerica Ins. Group, Battle Creek, Mich., 1975-83, pres., chief operating officer Los Angeles, 1983-84, chmn., chief exec. officer, 1984-85; apptd. spl. dep. ins. commr., dep. conservator Cadillac Inc. Co., 1989. Pres. Underwriting Exec. Council Midwest, 1967; dir. Underwriters Adjustment Bur., Toronto, 1974, Underwriters Labs. of Canada, Montreal, 1974; chmn. Mich. Assn. Ins. Cos., Lansing, 1976, Mich. Basic Property Ins. Assn., Detroit, 1973. Commr. City of Battle Creek, 1967-69; dir. Urban League, Battle Creek, 1969, 70, dir. Mich. Ins. Fedn., Lansing, 1975-83. Served to sgt. U.S. Army, 1942-45; New Guinea Roman Catholic. Avocations: golf, fishing. Home: 14037 N Cameo Dr Sun City AZ 85351-2903

REYNOLDS, JOHN R. hospital executive; Joined Hosp. for Special Surgery, NYC, 1985, CFO, 1985—97, co-CEO, 1997—99, pres., CEO, 1999—. Office: Hosp for Special Surgery 535 East 70th St New York NY 10021 Office Phone: 212-606-1000.

REYNOLDS, JONATHAN FRANKLIN, printing company executive; b. Abilene, Tex., June 16, 1951; s. Joe Leslie and Joyce Marie Reynolds; m. Janet Gay Shubert, July 23, 1969; children: Jon Anthony, Jennifer Leslie. BA, Trinity U., 1970—74. Mcse Microsoft, 2000, Mcp+I Microsoft, 2000, Net+ New Horizons, 2000; Lrep Tex., 1986. Chief info. officer/quality assurance mgr. Gazlay Graphics, San Antonio, 1989—95; chief info. officer Clarke Printing, San Antonio, 1995—2000; nat. dir. ecommerce Mail-Well Corp., Englewood, Colo., 2000—02; CEO Hilltop Computer Svcs., Kerrville, Tex., 2002—. Nat. procurement cons. AOL/Time Warner, NYC, 1999—2002; nat. implementation mgr. PrintCafe, Pitts., 1999—2002; nat. sales IT cons. Mail-Well, Englewood, 2000—02; nat. implementation mgr. SalesLogix, Phoenix, 2001—02. Mem. Nat. Assn. Realtors, San Antonio, 1986—88; dir. Computer Specialties, San Antonio, 1989—95, Hilltop Computer Svcs., Kerrville, Tex., 2002—03. Recipient GRACOL Keynote Presentation, GRACOL, 2001. Libertarian. Meth. Achievements include first to design, implementation and support of internat. CRM/SFA sys; nat. implemetation and support internat. Ecommerce sys; internat. cons. and implementation internat. ERP sys. Avocations: Harley Davidson motorcycles, hunting, travel. Personal E-mail: jonrey@ktc.com.

REYNOLDS, JOSEPH PATRICK, chemical engineering educator, consultant; b. N.Y.C., May 19, 1935; s. Patrick Joseph Reynolds and Ann Marie Brady; m. Barbara Geary, Apr. 22, 1974; children: Megan, Marybeth. BA in Chemistry, Cath. U. Am., 1957; PhD in Chem. Engring., Rensselaer Poly. Inst., 1964. Mem. chem. engring. faculty Manhattan Coll., Bronx, N.Y., 1964—, chmn. dept. chem. engring., 1975-83, prof. chem. engring., 1976—. Cons. U.S. Dept. Justice, Washington, 1993-94, 97-00, U.S. EPA, Raleigh, N.C., 1996-97. Co-author: Introduction to Hazardous Waste Incineration, 1987, 2d edit., 2000, Hazardous Waste Incineration Calculations and Software, 1991, Handbook of Chemical and Environmental Engineering Calculation, 2002; contbr. over 50 articles to profl. jours. and conf. procs. Mem. AIChE (bd. dirs. local sect. 1997-03), Air and Waste Mgmt. Assn., Sigma Xi (past pres. Manhattan Coll. chpt.). Democrat. Roman Catholic. Avocations: skiing, jogging, travel. Office: Manhattan Coll Chem Engring Dept Manhattan Coll Pkwy Bronx NY 10471 Office Phone: 718-862-7187. E-mail: joseph.reynolds@manhattan.edu.

REYNOLDS, LEO THOMAS, electronics company executive; b. Mpls., May 24, 1945; s. Donald Charles and Elizabeth (Graham) R.; m. Betty Gail Herrington, Aug. 8, 1966 (div. 1978); children: William, Nathan; m. Diana Frances Boyd, Feb. 26, 1982 (div. 1990); children: Jeffrey, Daniel; m. Sandra Kay Sonne, Feb. 26, 1994; stepchildren: Troy, Tyler. BSEE, U. Iowa, 1972; postgrad. in bus., Mankato State U., 1972-74. Registered profl. engr., S.D. Mech. draftsman John Deere Co., Dubuque, Iowa, 1970-71; engring. supr. 3M Co., New Ulm, Minn., 1972-76; supt. Litton Microwave, Sioux Falls, S.D., 1976-80; founder, pres., CEO Electronic Systems, Inc., Sioux Falls, 1980—. Apptd. 21st Century Workforce Commn., 1998. Editor Transit mag., 1972. Bd. dirs., exec. com. Sioux Falls Devel. Found., 1989-97, chmn. bd. dirs., 1996; svc. team chmn. Sioux Exploring Coun., 1992-96; bd.d irs. Vols. Am. S.D. Mem. NSPE, 21st Century Workforce Commn., Surface Mount Tech. Assn., IPC (sec.-treas., bd. dirs.). Republican. Avocations: reading, sailing, motorcycling, o gauge model railroading. Office: Electronic Systems Inc 600 E 50th St PO Box 5013 Sioux Falls SD 57117-5013

REYNOLDS, LEWIS DAYTON, pastor; b. Charleston, W.Va., July 26, 1937; s. James Shelby and Sybil Catherine (Lanham) R.; m. Ann Kathryn Combs, Aug. 25, 1962; children: John Mark, Daniel Adam. BBA, Marshall U., 1959; BTh, Aurora U., 1961; MDiv, Evang. Theol. Sem., Naperville, Ill., 1962. Ordained to ministry Advent Christian Ch., 1962. Pastor Mendota (Ill.) Advent Christian Ch., Mendota, Ill., 1961-64, Clendenin (W.Va.) Advent Christian Ch., Clendenin, W.Va., 1964-72, New Covenant Fellowship, Penfield, N.Y., 1972-89; gen. overseer Elim Fellowship, Lima, N.Y., 1989-97; sr. pastor Faith Christian Fellowship, Clarksburg, W.Va., 1997—2002, Charismatic Episcopal Ch. of the Transfiguration, Sterling, Va., 2002—; dir. Appalachian Highlands mission, eastern province Charismatic Episcopal Ch., 2003—. Mem. Phi Eta Sigma. Republican. Personal E-mail: ldaytonr@charter.net.

REYNOLDS, LLOYD GEORGE, economist, educator; b. Wainwright, Alberta, Can., Dec. 22, 1910; came to U.S., 1934, naturalized, 1940; s. George F. and Dorothy (Carl) R.; m. Mary F. Trackett, June 12, 1937; children: Anne Reynolds Skinner, Priscilla Reynolds Roosevelt, Bruce Lloyd. AB, U. Alberta, 1931, LL.D., 1958; A.M., McGill U., 1933; PhD, Harvard, 1936. Instr. econs. Harvard, 1936-39; asso. polit. economy Johns Hopkins, 1939-41, asso. prof., 1941-45; asso. prof. econs. Yale, 1945-47, prof. econs., 1947-52, Sterling prof. econs., 1952-81, chmn. dept. econs., 1951-59; prof. emeritus, 1981—; dir Econ. Growth Center, 1961-67; vis. fellow All Souls Coll., Oxford, 1967-68. Mem. adv. bd. Pakistan Inst. Devel. Econs., 1965-73; cons. to Social Sci. Research Center, U. P.R., 1951-65; dir. Nat. Bureau Econ. Research, 1958-81; Research dir. labor studies 20th Century Fund, 1940-43; research sec., com. on employment Social Sci. Research Council, 1941-42; co-chmn. appeals com. N.W.L.B., 1943-45; cons. Bur. of Budget, 1945-47; Guggenheim fellow, 1954-55, 1966-67; dir. program in econs. and bus. adminstrn. Ford Found., 1955-57 Author: The British Immigrant in Canada, 1935, Control of Competition in Canada, 1940, Labor and National Defense, 1941, An Index to Trade Union Publications, 1945, Labor Economics and Labor Relations, 1949, The Structure of Labor Markets, 1951, The Evolution of Wage Structure, 1956, Economics: A General Introduction, 1963, Wages, Productivity and Industrialization in Puerto Rico, 1965, The Three Worlds of Economics, 1971, Agriculture in Development Theory, 1975, Image and Reality in Economic Development, 1977, The American Economy in Perspective, 1981, Economic Growth in the Third World, 1850 1980, 1985, contbr. articles to profl. jours. Fellow Am. Acad. Arts and Scis.; mem. Indsl. Rls. Rsch. Assn. (pres. 1955), Am. Econ. Assn. (v.p. 1959, exec. com. 1952-54), Am. Acad. Polit. Sci., Am. Stats. Assn., Phi Beta Kappa. Clubs: Graduates (New Haven) (pres. 1961-64); Harvard (Boston); Century (N.Y.C.); Cosmos (Washington). Home: 4000 Cathedral Ave NW Washington DC 20016-5249 Office: Yale University Economics Dept New Haven CT 06520

REYNOLDS, MARGARET ANN, minister, educator; b. York, Nebr., Dec. 9, 1920; d. Emmett and Nora Estelle (Jacobs) Osborn; m. John Milton Reynolds, June 27, 1948; children: Matthew Osborn (dec.), Jonathan Mark. BA, U. Nebr., 1942; MA, Columbia U., 1947; MDiv, Union Theol. Sem., 1948. Cert. tchr., Calif.; ordained to ministry Disciples of Christ, 1948. Dir. Christian edn. Plymouth Congl. Ch., Ft. Wayne, Ind., 1942-43; nat. sec. Forerunners Fellowship of Reconciliation, N.Y.C., 1943-45; dir. youth campaign Japan Internat. Christian U., N.Y.C., 1949-50; county dir. Retarded and Handicapped Ctr., San Bernardino, Calif., 1966-67; tchr. McKinley Sch., Colton, Calif., 1967-78; assoc. min. Laguna Beach, Calif., 1979-83; min. emerita Neighborhood Congl. Ch., Laguna Beach, 1983—. Moderator N.J. Assn. Congl. Christian Chs., 1954-56, Kern Assn. United Ch. of Christ, Bakersfield, Calif., 1963-64; bd. dirs. Pacific S.W. Conf. on Christian World Missions, 1989-99; del. Oslo World Christian Youth Conf., N.Y.C., 1946-47; mem. planning com., historian Ea. Assn. United Ch. of Christ, 1995—. Author: Handbook for Retarded and Handicapped of San Bernardino County, 1967, (novels) Peg's Charms, 1999. Mem. AAUW, So. Calif. Campanology Club (chaplain 1995—, past pres.), Nat. Mus. Women in Arts (charter), Am. Bell Assn. Internat., McKinley Sch. PTA (life). Democrat. Avocations: reading, painting, collecting bells and eggs, swimming, travel. Home: 627 Leyden Ln # 202 Claremont CA 91711-4236 E-mail: Belleggs@aol.com.

REYNOLDS, MARSHALL TRUMAN, printing company executive; b. Logan, W.Va., Feb. 21, 1937; s. Douglas Vernon and Dorothy Lee (Dingess) R.; m. Shirley Ann Earwood, Mar. 24, 1968; children: Jack Marine, Douglas Vernon. Student, Marshall U., 1956-58. Sales mgr. Chapman Printing Co., Huntington, W.Va., 1960-61, gen. mgr., 1961-64, pres., gen. mgr. Huntington, Parkersburg and Charleston, W.Va., Lexington, Ky., 1964—. Chmn. bd. McCorkle Machine & Engring., Huntington, KYOWVA Corrugated Container, Huntington, Stationers, Inc., Huntington, Charleston, Radisson Hotel, Huntington, Huntington Indsl. Corp., Champion Industries Inc., Am. Babbit Bearing Inc.; bd. dirs. Guyan Machinery, Huntington, United Huntington Industries, Persinger Supply Co., Prichard, W.Va., First Guaranty Bank, Hammond, La., Banc One WV Corp., Charleston, W.Va. Bd. dirs. W.Va. Roundtable, Huntington, 1989—, W. Va. Bus. Found., Huntington, 1989—, Boys and Girls Club, Huntington, 1989—, Huntington United Way, 1989—, mem. Gov.'s Task Force on Children, Youth and Families, 1989—; guest lectr. various high schs. on free enterprise. Named Outstanding Small Businessman of Yr., Huntington Jaycees, 1983, Business Man of Yr. Jaycess, 1988. Mem. Huntington C. of C., Western Star Lodge (Guyandotte, W.Va.). Republican. Baptist. Avocation: raising cattle. Home: 1130 13th St Huntington WV 25701-3632 Office: Chapman Printing Co 2450 1st Ave Huntington WV 25703-1218

REYNOLDS, NANCY REMICK, writer, researcher, editor; b. San Antonio, July 15, 1938; d. Donald Worthington and Edith (Remick) R.; m. Brian Rushton, June 25, 1983; 1 child, Ehren T. Park. Student, Sch. Am. Ballet, 1951, student, 1953—61, Juilliard Sch. Music, 1957, Martha Graham Sch. Contemporary Dance, NYC, 1959, U. Sorbonne, Paris, 1962; BA in Art History, Columbia U., 1965; postgrad., Goethe Inst., Prien, 1972, U. Chgo. and Sarah Lawrence Coll., 1974—77. Dancer NYC Ballet, 1956-61; editor Praeger Pubs., NYC, 1965-71; dir. rsch. book Choreography by George Balanchine: A Catalogue of Works, 1979-82 (pub. 1983); dir. rsch. pub. TV spl. Balanchine, NY, 1983-84; assoc. editor Internat. Ency. of Dance, 1998; dir. rsch. The George Balanchine Found., NYC, 1994—. Co-pub. Twentieth-Century Dance in Slides, 1978-93. Author: Repertory in Review: Forty Years of the New York City Ballet, 1977 (De la Torre Bueno prize 1977), The Dance Catalog: A Complete Guide to Today's World of Dance, 1979, co-author: In Performance, 1980, Dance Classics, 1991 (rec. for teen age NY Pub. Libr.), No Fixed Points: Dance in the Twentieth Century, 2003; editor: Movement and Metaphor: Four Centuries of Ballet (Lincoln Kirstein), 1970, Dance as a Theatre Art: Source Readings in Dance History from 1581 to the Present (Selma Jeanne Cohen), 1974, School of Classical Dance (V. Kostrovitskaya and A. Pisarev), 1978; contbr. (book) Ballet: Bias and Belief, "Three Pamphlets Collected" and Other Dance Writings of Lincoln Kirstein, 1983, also numerous articles and revs. to Dancing Times, Ballet News, Playbill, ArtsLine, Dancemag., Town & Country, Connoisseur, NY Times, Ency. Britannica., Ency. of NYC, others. Ford Found. Travel and Study grantee, 1974; Mary Duke Biddle Found. grantee, 1990. Mem. Dance Critics Assn. (pres. 1986-87), Soc. Dance History Scholars, Soc. for Dance Rsch., Am. Soc. for Theatre Rsch., European Assn. Dance Historians, Internat. Fedn. for Theatre Rsch. in affiliation with Societe Internat. des Bibliotheques et Musees des Arts du Spectacle, Phi Beta Kappa. Home: 9 Prospect Park W Brooklyn NY 11215-1758

REYNOLDS, PAUL DAVIDSON, social sciences educator; b. Mattoon, Ill., Mar. 5, 1938; s. John Tom and Barbara Barteldes Reynolds; m. Anne-Marie T. Lair, Aug. 5, 1963; children: Christopher Mosdale, Nicole. BS in Engring., U. of Kans., 1960; MBA, Stanford U., 1964, MA in Psychology, 1966, PhD, 1969. Asst. prof. of sociology U. of Calif., Riverside, 1968—70; asst. to full prof. of sociology U. of Minn., Mpls., 1970—90; Coleman fFund. chairholder in entrepreneurial studies Marquette U., Milw., 1990—95; Paul T. Babson chairholder in entrepreneurial studies Babson Coll., Wellesley, Mass., 1995—99; prof. of entrepreneurship London Bus. Sch., London, 1999—. Author: (monograph) Ethical Dilemmas and Social Science Research, (introductory text) A Primer in Theory Construction; editor: (conference proceedings) Frontiers of Entrepreneurship Research.; contbr. articles to profl. jours. Co-chair of state platform com. Dem. Farmer Labor Polit. Party, Minn., 1986—88. 1st lt. Ordnance Corps U.S. Army, 1963—64. Recipient Internat. Award for Entrepreneurship and Small Bus. Rsch., Swedish Bus. Devel. Agy. & Swedish Found. for Small Bus. Rsch., 2004. Achievements include research in Coordinated design and implementation of US Panel Study of Entrepreneurial Dynamics (PSED). Home: 67 Gilson Rd Scituate MA 02066 Personal E-mail: pauldreynolds@earthlink.net.

REYNOLDS, PETER JAMES, physicist; b. N.Y.C., Nov. 19, 1949; s. Rudolph and Lydia Mary (Schanzer) R.; m. Louise Perini, Aug. 7, 1982. AB in Physics, U. Calif., Berkeley, 1971; PhD, MIT, 1979. Rsch. assoc., lectr. Boston U., 1978, asst. rsch. prof., 1979-83; mem. sci. staff Nat. Resource for Computation in Chemistry Lawrence Berkeley Lab., U. Calif., 1980-81, mem. rsch. staff materials and chem. scis. divsn., 1982-88; vis. scientist NEC Fundamental Rsch. Lab., Kawasaki, Japan, 1986; vis. rsch. chemist U. Calif., Berkeley, 1988; adj. assoc. prof. dept. chemistry San Francisco State U., 1988-91; program mgr. Office Naval Rsch., 1988—2003, Army Rsch. Office, 2003—, assoc. dir. head physics, 2004—. Vis. scientist Inst. for Theoretical Physics, Santa Barbara, 1994; rsch. prof. Georgetown U., Washington, 1996—; lectr. and rschr. in field of statis., chem. and computational physics and Monte Carlo Methods; program mgr. atomic and molecular physics, laser cooling and trapping, Bose-Einstein condensates, quantum degenaracy, quantum coherence and control, atom lasers, quantum computing. Editor: On Clusters and Clustering: From Atoms to Fractals, 1993; co-author: Monte Carlo Methods in Ab Initio Quantum Chemistry, 1994; contbr. articles to profl. jours., also rev. articles, book chpts. NATO lectr., NSF fellow, 1971-74, IBM fellow, 1975; Lawrence Berkeley Lab. grantee, 1982-83. Fellow Am. Phys. Soc. (chmn. membership com. 1998, nominating com. Divsn. Computational Physics and Forum on Physics and Soc. 1996-97, exec. com. Divsn. Computational Physics 1992-96, 2002—); mem. Materials Rsch. Soc., Optical Soc. Am., N.Y. Acad. Scis., Phi Beta Kappa, Sigma Xi. Office: ONR ARO Phys PO Box 12211 Research Triangle Park NC 27709

REYNOLDS, R. JOHN, academic administrator, educator; b. Milw., Dec. 3, 1936; s. Edward R. and Elizabeth (Wickenhauser) R.; m. Carol G. Lucas, Dec. 15, 1956; children: John D., Katherine A. BEd, U. Wis., Whitewater, 1961; MA, No. Mich. U., 1967; PhD, So. Ill. U., 1971. Bus. instr. Green Bay (Wis.) Tech. Inst., 1964-65; dir. vocat. tng. No. Mich. U., Marquette, 1965-68; v.p. Tech. Edn. Corp., St. Louis, 1968-69, prof., 1969-71; acting dean, chmn dept. So. Ill. U., Carbondale, 1969-71, 74-80, 81-82; assoc. acad. dean N.H. Coll., Manchester, 1971-74; head. bus. and econs. dept. Lake Superior State U., Sault Ste. Marie, Mich., 1981-82; pres. Nat. Coll., Rapid City, S.D., 1982-84, Huron (S.D.) U., 1984-93, Tri-State U., Angola, Ind., 1993—. Cons. in field.

Contbr. articles to profl. jours. Pres. Dakotaland Mus., Huron, 1986-91. Named Researcher of Yr. Ill. Bus. Edn. Assn., 1971. Office: Tri State Univ 1 University Ave Angola IN 46703-1764

REYNOLDS, RICHARD CLYDE, internist, educator; b. Saugerties, N.Y., Sept. 2, 1929; s. Thomas Watson and Myrtle Edith (Myer) R.; m. Mary Jane Beck, July 7, 1954; children— Karen Sue, Stephanie Ann, Wayne Thomas. BSc, Rutgers U., 1949; MD, Johns Hopkins U., 1953; DSc (hon.), Hahnemann U., 1988, N.Y. Med. Coll., 1992, Uniformed Svcs. U. Health Sci., 1995, U. Medicine and Dentistry N.J., 1997, SUNY Downstate Med. Ctr. Coll. Medicine, 2000. Diplomate Am. Bd. Internal Medicine. Intern Johns Hopkins Hosp., Balt., 1953-54, asst. resident, 1954-55, 57-58, fellow in infectious disease, 1958-59; practice medicine specializing in internal medicine Frederick, Md., 1959-68; mem. faculty U. Fla. Coll. Medicine, 1968-78, prof. medicine, prof., chmn. dept. community health and family medicine, 1970-78; prof. medicine, prof. environ. and community medicine, dean U. Medicine and Dentistry N.J., Robert Wood Johnson Med. Sch., 1978-87; sr. v.p. acad. affairs U. Medicine and Dentistry N.J., 1984-87; exec. v.p. Robert Wood Johnson Found., 1987-96; mem. faculty U. Fla. Coll. Medicine, Gainesville, 1997—. Mem. Liaison Com. on Med. Edn., 1982-87. Co-author: The Health of a Rural County: Perspectives and Problems, 1976, Patient Wishes and Physician Obligations, 1978; co-editor: On Doctoring: Stories, Poems, Essays, 1991, 3d edit., 2001; contbr. articles to med. publs. Sr. asst. surgeon USPHS, 1955-57. Mem. ACP, AMA. Office: U Fla Coll Medicine PO Box 100277 Gainesville FL 32610-0277 E-mail: rreyn63922@aol.com.

REYNOLDS, ROBERT, artist, educator; b. San Luis Obispo, Calif., Mar. 7, 1936; s. Agee Grady and Viola Elizabeth (Curran) R.; m. Sharon Ardelle Bodley, June 17, 1962 (div. 1979); children: Robert Scott, Richard Lance, Jill Elizabeth; m. Patricia Lee Smith, Oct. 5, 1981. BPA with honors, Art Ctr. Coll. Design, L.A., 1963; MA, Calif. Poly. U., 1970. Artist Creative Arts Studio, San Luis Obispo, 1955-56; free-lance artist/illustrator L.A., San Luis Obispo, 1957—; staff artist Calif. Poly. U., San Luis Obispo, 1964—, assoc. prof. architecture, 1970-75, prof. art & design, 1980-81, dept. chair art & design, 1984-86, acting head dept. art, 1983-84. Artist Ford Times mag., Dearborn, Mich., 1971-79; instr. Cuesta Coll., San Luis Obispo, 1972-76; artist, tchr., co-founder High Sierra Watercolor Workshop, 1975—, Asilomar Watercolor Workshop, Pacific Grove, Calif., 1980-83; free-lance illustrator for variousi studios, Calif., 1972—; painting instr. Robert Reynolds Workshop, high Sierra, 1973-2002; resident dir. London Study Program Calif. Poly. U., London, 1986, 91; art. acquisitions com. mem. Calif. Poly. State U., 1997—, performing arts adv. com., 1995—, London Study Program Com., 1986—. Over 50 one-man shows including San Luis Obispo Art Ctr., 1975, Calif. State U. Hdqrs./Gallery, 1979, Allan Hancock Coll., Santa Maria, Calif., 1981, Olive Tree Gallery, Santa Maria, 1983, Johnson Gallery, 1998, 99, 2000, 01, 02, Harbinger Gallery, 1998, 99, 02; group shows include Calif. Survey Drawing and Watercolor, Humboldt, 1982, U. Gallery, Calif. Poly. State U., 1985; represented in permanent collections at City of Stockton, Calif., City of San Luis Obispo, Santa Barbara Mus. Natural history, Calif. Stat eU. and CSU Collection, Long Beach, Mid-State Fair Assn., also numerous pvt. collections; works include design of San Luis Obispo bicentennial symbol and coin, design of ofcl. seal County of San Luis Obispo, ofcl. painting 1984 Mozart Festival, San Luis Obispo; designer U.S. Commemorative Postcard Stamp, 1987; author: Painting Nature's Peaceful Places, 1993; executed mural Mus. Nat. History, Calif., 1983; commd. to do poser for Morro Bay Nat. Estuary Program, 2001; subject of books and articles. Mem. San Luis Obispo Design and Rev. Bd., 1970-73; chmn. San Luis Obispo Glad Design Competition, 1973. With USNR, 1955-63. Recipient Disting. Teaching award Calif. Poly. State U., 1986, Pres. Art award, 1993, Bronze award Nat. Painting Competition Artist mag., 1996, finalist 1999, 2000, Gold medal Art Inst. Calif., 1994; Purchase prize IronStone Vineyards Nat Art Competition, 1999; named Calif. Ctrl. Coast Wine Classic Commemorative Artist, 2002. Mem. San Luis Obispo Art Assn. (past pres. 1970-71), Ctrl. Coast Watercolor Soc. (co-founder 1978, pres. 1980-81). Achievements include being invited artist for participation in the Florence Biennale Internat. Art Exhbn., Italy, 2003; solo art exhbn. at the Elverhoj Mus. of Art and History, Solvang, Calif. 2004; poster artist for the 2004 Annual Bear Valley Music Festival, Calif.; bio and work featured in the Cental Coast Mag., 2004; artwork now featured in over 15 art books in the US and England. E-mail: rgreynolds@charter.net.

REYNOLDS, ROBERT A., JR., electric distributor executive; Degree in bus., Stonehill Coll., 1972. Joined Graybar Electric Co., St. Louis, 1972, various mgmt. positions, v.p. commn./data divsn., 1991, pres., CEO, 2000—, chmn., 2001—. Office: Graybar Electric 34 N Meramec Ave Saint Louis MO 63105

REYNOLDS, ROBERT HARRISON, retired export company executive; b. Mpls., Sept. 6, 1913; s. Clarence H. and Helen (Doyle) R.; m. Gladys Marie Gaster, Apr. 7, 1934 (dec.); 1 child, Shirley Anne Reynolds Potestio (dec.); m. Viola E. Shimel, June 26, 1982. Export sales mgr., rolled products sales mgr. Colo. Fule & Iron Corp., Denver, 1938-46; pres. Rocky Mountain Export Co., Inc., Denver, 1941-93. Mem.: Denver Club (life). Home: 13850 E Marina Dr Aurora CO 80014-5509 Office: 12331 E Cornell Ave Aurora CO 80014-3323

REYNOLDS, ROBERT HUGH, lawyer; b. St. Louis, Jan. 3, 1937; s. Leslie A. and Rebecca (McWaters) R.; m. Carol Jemison, Apr. 8, 1961; children: Stephen H., Cynthia C., Laura M. BA, Yale U., 1958; JD, Harvard U., 1964. Assoc. Barnes & Thornburg, Indpls., 1964-70, ptnr., 1970—, chmn. bus. dept., 1983-91; chmn. internat. practice group, 1992—; vice-chmn. TerraLex, 1996—2003, chmn., 2003—. Co-chmn., editor Comml. Real Estate Financing for Ind. Attys., 1968; vice-chmn., co-editor Advising Ind. Businesses, 1974; chmn., editor Counseling Ind. Businesses, 1981, The Purchase and Sale of a Business, 1987. Bd. dirs. Crossroads Am. Coun. Boy Scouts Am., v.p., 1971—75, pres., 1987—89, v.p. Area 4 Ctrl. Region, 1989—92, pres., 1992—93, pres. Ctrl. Region, 1993—96, nat. exec. bd., 1993—; bd. dirs. Family Svc. Assn. Indpls., 1974—81, pres., 1978—80; bd. dirs. Family Svc. Am., 1979—88, Greater Indpls. Fgn. Trade Zone, 1987—2000, Indpls. Conv. and Visitors Assn., 1989—2000, Indpls. Econ. Devel. Corp., 1983—99, Greater Indpls. Progress Com., 1986—2000, exec. com., vice chmn.; hon. trustee Children's Mus. Indpls., trustee, 1988—96, chmn., 1992—94; bd. dirs. Indpls. Downtown Inc., chmn., 1996—99; bd. govs. Legacy Fund, 1992—, vice chmn., 2000—03, chmn., 2004—; bd. dirs. Noyes Meml. Found., pres., 2004—; bd. dirs. Japan-Am. Soc. Ind., pres., 1994—, Ctrl. Ind. Cmty. Found., 2003—, Indpls. Symphony Orch. Found., 2004—. Named Hon. Consul Gen. of Japan, 1999—; recipient Silver Buffalo award, Boy Scouts Am., Charles L. Whistler award, Greater Indpls. Progress Com. Fellow Ind. Bar Found., Indpls. Bar Found.; mem. ABA, Ind. Bar Assn. (chmn. corp., banking and bus. law sect. 1981-82, chmn. internat. sect. 1994-96), Internat. Bar Assn., Indpls. Bar Assn., Greater Indpls. C. of C. (bd. dirs., sec. 2000—), Econ. Club Indpls. (bd. dirs.). Clubs: Univ., Skyline (Indpls.). Lodges: Kiwanis. Republican. Office: Barnes & Thornburg LLP 11 S Meridian St Indianapolis IN 46204-3535 Office Phone: 317-231-7227. Business E-Mail: robert.reynolds@btlaw.com.

REYNOLDS, ROBERT JOEL, economist, consultant; b. Indpls., May 13, 1944; s. Joel Burr and Betty (Schimpf) R.; m. Lucinda Margaret Lewis, May 27, 1979; children: Joel, Sarah. BSBA in Fin., Northwestern U., 1965, PhD in Econs., 1970. Asst. prof. econs. U. Idaho, Moscow, 1969-73, assoc. prof., 1973-75; asst. dir, sr. economist econ. policy office Dept. Justice, Washington, 1973-81; sr. economist, v.p. ICF Inc., Washington, 1981-87, sr. v.p., 1987-91; exec. v.p., prin. Econsult Corp., Washington, 1991-96; chmn., exec. v.p. Econsult of D.C., Inc., Washington, 1997; chmn. Competition Econs., Inc., Washington, 1997—2004; prin. Brattle Group, 2004—, 2004—. Vis. assoc. prof. U. Calif., Berkeley, 1976-77, Cornell U., Ithaca, N.Y., 1981. Reviewer: NSF, Rand Jour. of Econs., Internat. Econ. Rev., Internat. Jour. Indsl. Orgn., Jour. Indsl. Econs., Am. Econ. Rev.; mem. editorial bd. Managerial and Decision Econs.; contbr. numerous papers to profl. jours. Recipient Dow Jones award Wall St. Jour., 1965; AT&T grantee, 1971-72, Brookings Instl. grantee, 1968-69; NDEA fellow, 1965-69. Mem. AAAS, IEEE (computer sect.), SIAM, Am. Math. Assn., Am. Econ. Assn., Econometric Soc., Royal Econ. Soc., Am. Statis. Assn., European Assn. for Rsch. in Indsl. Econs., Soc. for the Promotion of Econ. Theory, Math. Assn. Am. Congregationalist. Home: PO Box 59712 Potomac MD 20859-9712 Office: Competition Econs Inc 4800 Montgomery Ln Bethesda MD 20814 Office Phone: 202-955-5050. Personal E-mail: rjrcei@aol.com. E-mail: bob.reynolds@brattle.com.

REYNOLDS, ROGER LEE, composer, educator; b. Detroit, July 18, 1934; s. George Arthur and Katherine Adelaide (Butler) Reynolds; m. Karen Jeanne Hill, Apr. 11, 1964; children: Erika Lynn, Wendy Claire. BSE in Physics, U. Mich., 1957, MusB in Music Lit., 1960, MusM in Composition, 1961. Assoc. prof. U. Calif. San Diego, La Jolla, 1969—73, founding dir. Ctr. Music Expt. and Related Rsch., 1972—77, prof., 1973—; George Miller prof. U. Ill., 1971—. Vis. prof. Yale U., New Haven, 1981; sr. rsch. fellow ISAM Bklyn. Coll., 1985; Valentine prof. Amherst (Mass.) Coll., 1988; Rothschild composer in residence Peabody Conservatory of Music, 1992—93; pub. Peters Music Pubs.; mgr. Graham Hayter, Contemporary Music Promotions. Author: MIND MODELS: New Forms of Musical Experience, 1975, A Searcher's Path: A Composer's Ways, 1987, A Jostled Silence: Contemporary Japanese Musical Thought, 1992—93, Form and Method: Composing Music, 2002; first Dolby Digital 5.1 DVD release of custom-designed, multichannel classical compositions: WATERSHED, Mode Records, 1998; contbr. numerous articles and revs. to profl. jours. Mem. bd. govs. Inst. Current World Affairs; co-founder ONCE festivals, 1960; bd. dirs. Am. Music Ctr., Meet the Composer; bd. dirs. Fromm Found. Harvard U. Named sr. fellow, Inst. Studies in Am. Music, 1985, fellow, Inst. Current World Affairs, Rockefeller Found., Guggenheim Found., Fulbright scholar; recipient Koussevitzky Internat. Rec. Award, 1970, Nat. Inst. Arts and Letters award, 1971, NEA awards, 1975, 1978, 1979, 1986, Pulitzer prize for music, 1989. Office: U Calif San Diego Dept Music 0326 La Jolla CA 92093 Office Phone: 858-534-3230. E-mail: ping@rogerreynolds.com.

REYNOLDS, ROSINA WIDDOWSON, actress, theater director; d. Robert and Rosina Alicia Widdowson; m. Michael Henry Reynolds, Apr. 1, 1977; 1 child, Katie Rose. Student, New Coll. of Speech and Drama, London, 1967—70. Actor, dir., San Diego, 1978—. Artistic dir. Chequamegon Children's Theatre, Cable, Wis., 1987—, Actors Alliance of San Diego, 1994—2002, Gaslamp Quarter Theatre, San Diego, 1994—95; tchr. San Diego State U., 2001—02. Author, actor, prodr.: stage play An Evening with Eleanor (Critic's Pick, San Diego Union-Tribune, 2000); author: (screenplay) Riley's Bones. Bd. dirs. Actors Alliance of San Diego, 2002—04. Recipient Best Actress award, San Diego Theatre Critic's Cir., 1988, Patte' award for outstanding performance, KPBS, 1998, 2001, 2002, Patte' award for outstanding direction, 2001, 2002, Craig Noel award for best direction, San Diego Critics Cir., 2002. Mem.: SAG (assoc.), Actors Equity Assn. (assoc.). Labor. Avocations: hiking, swimming, skiing, reading, travel. Home: 6515 High Knoll Rd San Diego CA 92111 Personal E-mail: rosina@rreynolds.com.

REYNOLDS, SALLIE BLACKBURN, artist, civic volunteer, federal employee; b. Kansas City, Mo., Feb. 9, 1940; d. Anton and Sallie Churchill (Blackburn) Zajic; m. Jeffrey Calhoun Loker, Mar. 25, 1959 (div. May 1965); children: Toni Lynne Loker, Michael David Loker, Kathryn Lee Loker Simpson; m. Everett Lee Reynolds, Mar. 29, 1969 (dec. Sept. 1992). Student, William Jewell Coll., 1959, BA magna cum laude, 1977; student, U. Mo., Kansas City, 1966-67, Kansas City Art Inst., 1966-70; Cert., Famous Artists Sch., 1965. Cert. tchr., Mo. From clk. to sec. Hdqrs. Strategic Air Command, Offutt AFB, Omaha, 1960-62; sec., wage and hr. law enforcement asst., wage-hr. divsn. U.S. Dept. of Labor, Kansas City, 1963-68, exec. sec. to regional manpower adminstr., 1968-71, spl. asst. to regional exec. com., 1971-72, mgmt. asst. Office of Regional Dir., 1972-73; co-owner Claycomo Skelly Svc. Sta. & Garage, 1970—78; from. clk. to sec. air carrier dist. office FAA, Kansas City, 1978-81; from clk. typist procurement and contracts divsn. to sec. regional pers. officer Bur. of Reclamation, U.S. Dept. of Interior, Boulder City, Nev., 1982—84; editl. asst. divsn. of planning Bur. of Reclamation, Boulder City, 1984-86; substitute tchr.; owner, operator B-Bar-L Wandering Star Ranch (registered angus and horses, beefalo, various real estate), Stover, Kansas City, Osage beach, Versailles, Mo., 1989—. Editor newsletter Laurie Fine Art, 1989-90; designer historic landmark plaque Clay County, Mo.; designer hist. painting for annual Dogwood Festival pageants Camden County, Mo., 1994. Ofcl. commr., sec., corr. Clay County (Mo.) Bicentennial Commn., 1974-76; mem. Ozark Brush and Palette, Inc., Camdenton, Mo., 1987—, editor newsletter, 1988-89; v.p., sec., life mem. Clay County Hist. Soc., 1972—, active Nat. Wildlife Fedn. Recipient 1st Pl. award Nat. Soc. DAR Am. Heritage Contest in oil/acrylic painting, 1990, 3d pl., 1991, 1st pl. gold award 1992, 1st pl. award profl. photography Laurie Fine Art Show, 1991; named one of Top 50 Profl. Artists, Mo. State Fair, 1992. Mem. Nat. Soc. DAR (pub. rels. chmn., rec. sec., archives chmn., corr. sec. Niangua chpt. Camdenton 1987—, Eldon Mo. chpt. 1999), Nat. Oil and Acrylic Painters Soc., Phi Epsilon of Phi Beta Kappa, Versailles Saddle Club, Mo. Paint Horse Club (sec. 1998). Presbyterian. Avocations: horses, art, history, cats, needlecrafts, music, photography. Home and Office: B-Bar-L Wandering Star Ranch 23688 S 135 Hwy Stover MO 65078

REYNOLDS, SCOTT WALTON, academic administrator; b. Summit, N.J., July 15, 1941; s. Clark Leonard and Shirley (Hill) R.; m. Margaret Ann Johnson, July 5, 1969; children: Jane, Amy, David. BA, Trinity Coll., Hartford, Conn., 1963; MBA, Harvard U., 1965. Mng. dir. corp. staff Bankers Trust Co., N.Y.C., 1967-94; asst. to the pres. St. Peter's Coll., Jersey City, 1994-96, Trinity Coll., Hartford, Conn., 1996-98, sec., 1998—. Chmn. fund campaign Montclair (N.J.) ARC, 1974; chmn. bus. and fraternal group Montclair Bicentennial Com., 1976; bd. fellows Trinity Coll., 1982-88, trustee, 1992-96, sec., exec. com., 1993-96. 1st lt. U.S. Army, 1965-67. Recipient 150th Anniversary award Trinity Coll., 1978, Alumni medal for Excellence, 1988, Pres.' Leadership medal, 1993. Mem. Montclair Jaycees (treas. 1973), Trinity Coll. Alumni Assn. N.Y. (pres. 1972-73) Clubs: Harvard (N.Y.C.). Episcopalian. Office: Trinity Coll Office of Pres 300 Summit St Hartford CT 06106-3100 Office Phone: 860-297-2093. E-mail: Scott.Reynolds@mail.trincoll.edu.

REYNOLDS, SHERI, writer; b. Conway, SC, 1967; BA in English, Davidson Coll., 1989; MFA in creative writing, Va. Commonwealth U., 1992. Adj. instr. English Va. Commonwealth U., Richmond, 1992—. Author: Bitterroot Landing, 1994, The Rapture of Canaan, 1996, A Gracious Plenty, 1997. Office: VCU Dept English 900 Park Ave Hibbs Bldg 306 PO Box 842005 Richmond VA 23284-2005

REYNOLDS, STEPHEN CURTIS, hospital administrator; b. Little Rock, May 1, 1946; married. BA, Ark. State U., 1968; MA, Washington U., 1972. Adminstrv. resident Baptist Meml. Health Care System, Memphis, 1971-72, adminstrv. asst., 1972-75, asst. v.p., 1975-80, v.p., 1980-86, sr. v.p., 1986-89, exec. v.p., 1992, Baptist Meml. Hosp., Memphis, 1990-92, pres., 1992—. With Armed Forces, 1968-70. Mem. Tenn. Hosp. Assn. (chmn., 1989-90, bd. dirs. 1986-91). Home: 461 Princeton Wood Cv Memphis TN 38117-1907 Office: Bapt Meml Hosp 350 N Humphreys Blvd Memphis TN 38120

REYNOLDS, THOMAS M. congressman; b. Springville, NY, Sept. 3, 1950; m. Donna Reynolds; 4 children. Student, Kent (Ohio) State U. Pres. T.M. Reynolds Ins. Agy.; rep. Dist. 147 N.Y. State Assembly, 1988-98, ranking rep. mem. housing com., mem. banking com., mem. corrections com.; mem. U.S. Congress from 26th N.Y. dist., 1999—; mem. rules com., adminstrn. com.; dep. majority whip in Ho. Leadership. Exec. asst. N.Y. State Assemblyman Ronald Tillis; councilman Town of Concord, N.Y., 1974-82; clk. Erie County Legis.; legis. asst. to minority Rep. leader, 1987. Mem. NRA, Southtowns Walleye Assn., Masons. Republican. Office: Ho of Reps 332 Cannon HOB Washington DC 20515-3226 also: 500 Essjay Rd # 260 Williamsville NY 14221

REYNOLDS, VALRAE, museum curator; b. San Francisco, Dec. 18, 1944; d. Ralph Stanley and Valberta May (Eversole) R.; m. Richard Lee Huffman, Sept. 14, 1974; children: Elizabeth Anne, Margaret Lee. BA in Fine Arts with honors, U. Calif., Davis, 1966; MA, NYU, 1969. Asst. curator Asian collections Newark Mus., 1969-70, curator Asian collections, 1970—2002, sr. curator Asian collections, 2003—. Cons. SITES Exhbn., 1988; adj. prof. art history Columbia U., 1996; lectr., presenter in field. Author: From the Sacred Realm, Treasures of Tibetan Art from the Newark Museum, 1999; editor: Newark Mus. Quar., 1976, Tibetan Jour., 1976, Asia Soc., 1977, Arts of Asia, 1989, Explore Tibet, 1992; contbr. over 36 articles and revs. to profl. jours.; prodr. multimedia prodns. in field. Grantee NEA, NEH, 1972-74, 82-83, 85-86, 88-91, 89-92, 99, 2003, J. Paul Getty grantee, 1986, 89-91, Travel grantee Asian Cultural Coun., 1989, NEA grantee, 2003-04, Wallace Found. grantee, 2003-04, Freeman Found. grantee, 2003-04. Office: Newark Mus 49 Washington St Newark NJ 07102

REYNOLDS, WILLIAM BRADFORD, lawyer; b. Bridgeport, Conn., June 21, 1942; s. William Glasgow and Nancy Bradford (DuPont) R.; m. Marguerite Lynn Morgan, June 27, 1964 (div. Feb. 1987); children: William Bradford Jr., Melissa Morgan, Kristina DuPont, Wendy Riker; m. Clare Alice Conroy, Aug. 29, 1987 (div. June 2000); 1 child, Linda Matisan; m. Barbara Lynn Wooster, July 15, 2000; children: Courtney Enright, Brooke Ashley. BA, Yale U., 1964; LLB, Vanderbilt U., 1967. Bar: N.Y. 1968, D.C. 1973, U.S. Supreme Ct. 1971. Assoc. Sullivan and Cromwell, N.Y.C., 1967-70; asst. to Solicitor Gen. U.S. Dept. Justice, Washington, 1970-73; ptnr. Shaw, Pittman, Potts & Trowbridge, Washington, 1973-81; asst. atty. gen. Civil Rights div. U.S. Dept. Justice, Washington, 1981-88, counselor to Atty. Gen., 1987-88; ptnr. Ross & Hardies, 1989-91, Dickstein, Shapiro & Morin, 1991-94, Collier, Shannon, Rill & Scott, 1994-2000, Howrey Simon Arnold & White, Washington, 2000—. Chmn. Archtl. Transp. Barriers Compliance Bd., 1982-84. Editor-in-chief Vanderbilt Law Rev., 1966. Disting. scholar Free Congress Found., 1989-93, Disting. fellow Nat. Legal Ctr. for Pub. Interest, Washington, 1989-90. Mem. ABA, Fed. Bar Assn., D.C. Bar Assn., Order of Coif. Republican. Episcopalian. Office Phone: 202-383-6912. E-mail: reynoldsw@howrey.com.

REYNOLDS, WILLIAM FRANCIS, mathematics professor; b. Boston, Jan. 31, 1930; s. William Leo and Grace Regina (Devlin) R.; m. Pauline Jane Fitzgerald, Aug. 5, 1962; children: Nancy Elizabeth, Jane Anele. AB summa cum laude, Holy Cross Coll., 1950; A.M., Harvard, 1951, PhD, 1954. Instr. Holy Cross Coll., Worcester, Mass., 1954-55; instr. Mass. Inst. Tech., Cambridge, 1955-57; asst. prof. math. Tufts U., Medford, Mass., 1957-60, assoc. prof., 1960-67, prof., 1967-98, Walker prof. math., 1970-98, prof. emeritus, 1998—. Contbr. articles to math. jours. Mem. Am. Math. Soc. Achievements include research on modular and projective representations of finite groups. Home: 3 Preble Gardens Rd Belmont MA 02478-3460 E-mail: wfr@post.harvard.edu.

REYNOLDS, WILLIAM LEROY, lawyer, educator; b. Balt., July 26, 1945; s. Austin Leroy and Doris (Hill) R.; m. Theodora Hoe, Sept. 3, 1966; children: William, Megan, Sarah AB, Dartmouth Coll., 1967; JD, Harvard U., 1970. Bar: Md. 1972, U.S. Supreme Ct. 1975. Clk. to judge U.S. Dist. Ct. Md., 1970-71; asst. prof. law U. Md., 1971-74, assoc. prof., 1974-77, prof., 1977—; of counsel PiperRudnick LLP, Balt., 1992—. Bd. dirs. Md. Jud. Inst. Author: Judicial Process in a Nutshell, 1980, 3d edit., 2002, Understanding the Conflict of Laws, 1984, 3d edit., 2002, Cases and Materials on Conflict of Laws, 1990, 2d edit., 2003. Mem. Am. Law Inst., Md. State Bar Assn., Am. Judicature Soc. Clubs: Serjeants' Inn, Wranglers (Balt.); St. Regis Yacht (Paul Smiths, N.Y.), Hamilton St. Office: U Md Sch Law 500 W Baltimore St Baltimore MD 21201-1701 Business E-Mail: wreynolds@law.umaryland.edu.

REYNOLDS, W(YNETKA) ANN, academic administrator, educator; b. Coffeyville, Kans., Nov. 3, 1937; d. John Ethelbert and Glennie (Beanland) King; m. Thomas H. Kirschbaum; children— Rachel Rebecca, Rex King. BS in Biology-Chemistry, Kans. State Tchrs. Coll., Emporia, 1958; MS in Zoology, U. Iowa, Iowa City, 1960, PhD, 1962; DSc (hon.), Ind. State U., Evansville, 1980; LHD (hon.), McKendree Coll., 1984, U. N.C., Charlotte, 1988, U. Judaism, L.A., 1989, U. Nebr., Kearney, 1992; DSc (hon.), Ball State U., Muncie, Ind., 1985, Emporia (Kans.) State U., 1987; PhD (hon.), Fu Jen Cath. U., Republic of China, 1987; LHD (hon.), U. Nebr., Kearney, 1992, Colgate U., 1993; LHD, No. Mich. U., 1995. Asst. prof. biology Ball State U., Muncie, Ind., 1962-65; asst. prof. anatomy U. Ill. Coll. Medicine, Chgo., 1965-68, assoc. prof. anatomy, 1968-73, rsch. prof. ob-gyn, 1973—, prof. anatomy, 1973—, acting assoc. dean acad. affairs Coll. Medicine, 1977, assoc. vice chancellor, dean grad. coll., 1977-79; provost, v.p. for acad. affairs, prof. ob-gyn. and anatomy Ohio State U., Columbus, 1979-82; chancellor Calif. State Univ. system, Long Beach, 1982-90, prof. biology, 1982-90; chancellor CUNY, 1990-97; pres. U. Ala., Birmingham, 1997—2002. Bd. dirs. Abbott Labs., Maytag, Owens-Corning, Humana, Inc., News-Gasette, Champaign, Ill.; clin. prof. ob-gyn. UCLA, 1985-90; mem. Nat. Rsch. Coun. Com. Undergrad Sci. Edn., 1993-97; co-chair Fed. Task Force on Women, Minorities and Handicapped in Sci. and Tech., 1987-90, Pacesetter Program Reform for Secondary Sch. Coll. Bd., 1992-96. Contbr. chpts. to books, articles to profl. jours; assoc. editor Am. Biology Tchr., 1964-67. Active activities involving edn. and the arts; nat. adv. bd. Inst. Am. Indian Arts, 1992-97; bd. dirs. Lincoln Ctr. Inst., 1993—; trustee Internat. Life Scis. Inst.-Nutrition Found., 1987-2001, Southwest Mus. Recipient Disting. Alumni award Kans. State Tchrs. Coll., 1972, Calif. Gov.'s Award for the Arts for an Outstanding Individual in Arts in Edn., 1989, Prize award Cen. Assn. Obstetricians and Gynecologists, 1968; NSF Predoctoral fellow, 1958-62, Woodrow Wilson Hon. fellow, 1958. Fellow ACOG; mem. AAAS, Perinatal Rsch. Soc., Soc. Gynecol. Investigation (sec./treas. 1980-83, pres. 1992-93), Nat. Assn. Systems Heads (pres. 1987-88), Sigma Xi. Office: Ctr for Cmty Outreach Devel Univ Ala 933 19th St S Birmingham AL 35294-2041

REYNOLDSON, WALTER WARD, retired judge, lawyer; b. St. Edward, Nebr., May 17, 1920; s. Walter Scorer and Mabel Matilda (Sallach) Reynoldson; m. Janet Aline Mills, Dec. 24, 1942 (dec. 1986); children: Vicki, Robert; m. Patricia A. Frey, June 3, 1989. BA, State Tchrs. Coll., 1942; JD, U. Iowa, 1948; LLD (hon.), Simpson Coll., 1983, Drake U., 1987. Bar: Iowa 1948. Justice Iowa Supreme Ct., 1971-78, chief justice, 1978-87, sr. judge, 1989-93; of counsel Reynoldson Law Firm, Osceola, Iowa, 1993—. County atty. Clark County, Iowa, 1953—57; adj. prof. law Drake U., 1989—93. Co-author: (book) Trial Handbook, 1969. Pres. Nat. Ctr. State Cts.; trustee Drake U., 1987—2000. With USNR, 1942—46. Recipient Osceola Cmty. Svc. award, 1968. Fellow: Am. Bar Found.; mem.: Am. Coll. Trial Lawyers, Conf. Chief Justices (pres. 1984—85), Acad. Trial Lawyers, Am. Judicatrue Soc. (bd. dirs. 1983—87, Herbert Harley award 1990), Iowa Bar Assn. (chmn. com. legal edn. and admission to bar 1964—71). Office: Reynoldson Law Firm 200 W Jefferson St Osceola IA 50213-1206 Office Phone: 641-342-2157.

REZA, ALI HAJMOHAMMAD, cardiologist; b. Tehran, Iran, Apr. 14, 1957; came to U.S., 1988; s. Tayeb Hajmohammad and Fakhri (Mohajer) R.; m. Elizabeth Gheisari; children: Tara, Arteen. MD, Nat. U. Iran, Tehran, 1982. Diplomate Am. Bd. Internal Medicine, Am. Cardiovasc., Am. Bd. Interventional Cardiology; bd. cert. nuclear cardiology. Rsch. in pathology Rush Med. Sch., Chgo., 1988-89; resident in internal medicine SUNY, Buffalo, 1989-93, fellow in nephrology, 1992-93; fellow in cardiology Tulane U., New Orleans, 1993-96; pvt. practice, Chalmette, La., 1996—; pvt. practice Oschner Cardiovascular Inst., 2001—. Mem. ACP, AMA, Am. Coll. Cardiology. Moslem. Home: 1804 Octavia St New Orleans LA 70115 Office: 5701 Deerpark Blvd New Orleans LA 70127

REZA, YASMINA, author, playwright; Author: (plays) Conversations After A Burial, 1987 (Moliere award for best author, SACD New Talent award, Johnson Found. award), Winter Crossing, 1990 (Moliere award for best fringe prodn., 1990), The Unexpected Man, Art, 1995 (Moliere award for best author, Olivier award, Evening Standard award, Tony award), (novels) Hammerklavier, 1997, (translator) (Kafka) Metamorphosis (Moliere award for best translation); screenwriter (TV films) See You Tomorrow, Kunst, 1997, (films) Le Pique-nique de Lula Kreutz, 2000. Address: 83 Rue du Cherche diMidi 75006 Paris France

REZANKA, THOMAS W. lawyer; b. Plainfield, NJ, Mar. 3, 1954; s. William L. and Helen G. Rezanka; m. Karen T. Rezanka, May 21, 1977. BA, Montclair State U., Upper Montclair, N.J., 1976; JD, Stetson U., 1980. Bar: Fla. 1980, U.S. Ct. Appeals (5th and llth cirs.) 1980. Pvt. practice, Palm Harbor, Fla., 1980—. Presenter Joint Conf. on Law and Aging, Washington, 1995. Columnist Tropical Breeze, 1995-2001, Countryside Cougar, East Lake Eagle, Palm Harbor Panther, 1995—, Dunedin Highlander, 2001—. Mem. adv. com. Countryside H.S., Clearwater, Fla., 1998-99; bd. dirs. Tampa Bay Area Planned Giving Coun., Tampa, 2001. Mem. ABA, Nat. Acad. Elder Law Atty., Fla. Bar Assn. (former mem. legis. drafting com. real property, probate and trust law sect.) exec. coun. elder law sect. 1995-99, faculty counseling your Fla. client seminar for out-of-state atty. 1999, faculty elder law bd. cert. rev. course 1998, editor The Advocate newsletter 1996-97), Clearwater Bar Assn. (estate planning columnist 1996-97, 2000-01, probate, guardianship and trust practice com.), Pinellas County Estate Planning Coun. (bd. dir. 1995-99). Office: 2672 Westlake Rd Palm Harbor FL 34684

REZEK, FRANCISCO, judge, former supreme court justice, educator; b. Cristina, Brazil, Jan. 18, 1944; s. Elias and Baget Rezek; m. Myreia de Palma Castro, Jan. 14, 1971; children: Adriana, Veronica, Francisco, João Paulo. LLB, U. Minas Gerais, Belo Horizonte, 1966; LLD, U. Paris, 1970; diploma in law, Oxford (Eng.) U., 1979. Atty. Rep. of Brazil, 1972-79, dep. atty. gen., 1979-83, justice Supreme Ct., 1983—90, 1992—97; fgn. min. Dept. State, Brasilia, 1990-92; dean faculty of law U. Brasilia, 1978-79; judge Intl. Ct. of Justice (the Hague), Brussels, Netherlands, 1997—. Chief justice at the High Electoral Ct., Brasilia, 1989. Author: Law of Treaties, 1984, International Law, 1989, 4th edit., 1994. Recipient Grand Cross Orders of Brazil, Argentina, Chile, Colombia, Lebanon, Tunisia, Korea, Portugal, Spain, and Italy, 1986-92. Roman Catholic. Office: Internat Ct of Justice Peace Palace 2517 KJ The Hague Netherlands

REZELMAN, DAVID ALAN, historian, educator; b. Anchorage, Apr. 20, 1973; s. James Alan and Karen Nigh Rezelman. BS in Computer Sci., U. Fla., Gainesville, 1995, BA in History. Exec. coord. Temple U. Ctr. for the Study of Force and Diplomacy, Phila., 1997—98; instr. history Gainesville Coll., Ga., 1998—99, Temple U., Phila., 2000—01; Glenn T. Seaborg fellow in nuc. history History Divsn., Dept. of Energy, Washington, 2001—02; instr. history Norfolk Acad., Va., 2003—. Participant NEH Summer Inst.: New Sources and Findings on Cold War Internat. History, Washington, 1999, West Point Summer Seminar in Mil. History, 2000; doctoral candidate Temple U., Phila., 1995—. Contbr. website, articles to ency. and reference works, book reviews and conference papers. Conwell Fellow, Temple U., 1995—98, 1999—2000. Mem.: Soc. for the History of Tech., Soc. for Mil. History, Soc. for Historians of Am. Fgn. Rels., Orgn. of Am. Historians, Phi Beta Kappa. Personal E-mail: dave@rezelman.org.

REZIN, ANDREW ANTHONY, academic administrator, educator; b. Cleve., May 25, 1950; s. Andrew Frank and Josephine (Rozinka) R.; m. Michele Elizabeth Rezin, Mar. 31, 1973; children: Jennifer, Jonathan, Jessica, Jordan. BA in Mktg., Kent State U., 1972; MA in Vocat. Edn., Ohio State U., 1993, PhD in Edn., 1998. Dist. mgr. Chrysler Corp., Centerline, Mich., 1976—81; svc. dir. Bob Caldwell Chrysler-Plymouth, Columbus, Ohio, 1981—86; ops. mgr. Spitzer Columbus, 1986—87; svc. dir. David Hobbs BMW, Columbus, 1987—88; svc. mgr. Dennis Pontiac, Columbus, 1988—93; dept. chair automotive tech. Columbus State C.C., 1993—99, adminstr. automotive and applied tech., 1999—. Mem. adv. bd. Southwestern Career Acad., Grove City, Ohio, 1997—, Northwest Career Ctr., Dublin, Ohio, 1997—; editl bd., Acad. Leadership Jour., 2001—. Contbr. articles to profl. jours. Chmn. Westerville Baha'i Assembly, Westerville, Ohio, 1995-2004, leadership inst. Columbus State C.C., 2002—; bd. dir. Ctrl. Ohio CleanFuels Coalition, 2003—. Mem. Westerville C. of C. (edn. com. 2003—), Phi Kappa Phi, Omicron Tau Theta (past pres.). Office: Columbus State Cmty Coll 550 E Spring St Columbus OH 43215-1722 Office Phone: 614-287-5303. Business E-Mail: arezin@cscc.edu.

REZIN, JOYCE JUNE, pediatric nurse practitioner; b. Kalamazoo, Apr. 29, 1936; d. Stephen Palc and Alexandra Kwiatkowski Salerno; m. Joseph Gerald Rezin, Feb. 15, 1958; children: Michael, William, Valerie. BSN, San Diego State U., 1971; MS, U. LaVerne, 1991. Cert. pediatric nurse practitioner; RN, Calif. Staff nurse med./surg. St. Vincent's Hosp., L.A., 1957-58; staff nurse surgery City of Hope Med. Ctr., Duarte, Calif., 1958-59; sch. nurse Sweetwater Union H.S. Dist., Chula Vista, Calif., 1973-84, San Diego Unified Sch. Dist., 1984—. Guest lectr. San Diego State U. Sch. Pub. Health, 1994, 95, 96, 97. Vol. nurse Otay Cmty. Clinic, Chula Vista, 1978-79; CPR instr., ARC, Chula Vista, 1977-81, 95, 96, 97, 98, 99, 2000; sch. nurse governance team mem. San Diego Unified Sch. Dist., 1991-94, 98-2000; bd. dirs. Adult Protective Svcs., Inc., San Diego, 1995-96, 97, 98, 99, 2000; mem. outdoor phys. activities com. San Diego Unified Sch. Dist., 1998-2000; NAPNAP liaison to AAP com. on early childhood and dependent care, 1998-2000. Named Woman of Achievement, Southland Bus. and Profl. Woman's Club, 1987. Fellow Nat. Assn. Pediatric Nurse Assocs. and Practitioners (bd. dirs. San Diego chpt. 1984-85, 95—, vol. liaison to Healthy Child Care Am. Campaign 1996-97, 98, 99, 2000, vol. adv. task force Healthy Child Care Calif. 1997, liaison com. on early chilodhood, adoption and dependent care 1998-2000, co-chair child care spl. interest group 1998-2000); mem. Calif. Sch. Nurse Orgn. (bd. dirs. San Diego/Imperial counties chpt. 1981-86, pres. elect 2000—), Nat. Assn. Sch. Nurses. Roman Catholic. Avocations: travel, reading. Home: 10747 Viacha Dr San Diego CA 92124-3418 Office: San Diego City Schs Early Childhood Edn Program 2441 Cardinal Ln IMC San Diego CA 92123

REZKALLA, LAURENCE, internist; b. Asyut, Egypt, Mar. 9, 1958; arrived in U.S., 1990; s. Lamie Rezkalla Rophael and Eniat William Basaly; m. Evette Wadie Kamel, Apr. 15, 1990; children: Paul, Peter, John, Mary. ND, Asyut Med. Sch., 1982; ob-gyn. specialist, Ain Shams Med. Sch., Cairo, 1988. Cert. Am. Bd. Internal Medicine. Intern Asyut U. Hosp., 1983—84; med. mil. svcs. Egyptian Army, 1984—86; ob-gyn resident El-Iman Gen. Hosp, Asyut, 1986—88; ob-gyn. physician Oasis Gen. Hosp., El-Wahat El-Bahria, Egypt, 1989, Sahelsleem (Egypt) Hosp., 1989—91; internal medicine resident Kingsbrook Jewish Med. Ctr., Bklyn., 1995—98; physician St. Barnabas's Hosp., East Elmhurst, NY, 1998—2000, Woodull Hosp., Bklyn., 1999—, N.Y. Meth. Hosp., 2002—, Victory Meml. Hosp., 2004—. Pres. Bay Ridge Med. Svcs., Bklyn., 2001—; mem. exec. com. Kingsbrook Hosp., 1996—2003. Author: (book) 10 Cases of Ob/Gyn, 1988. Leader youth meetings Salvation Soc., Asyut, 1973—81; founder Arab 2000 Inc., Bklyn., 1997—2000; ptnr. Internat. Resource Ctr., Johannesburg, 1997—2000. Scholar Full scholar, Egyptian Govt., Asyut U., 1976. Mem.: ACP, AMA, Egyptian Med. Syndicate, Com. of Internal Residents (del. 1996—97). Avocations: travel, reading, painting. Home: 124 86th St Brooklyn NY 11209 Office: Bay Rige Med Svcs 124 86th St Brooklyn NY 11209 Office Phone: 718-921-1977.

REZNECK, DANIEL ALBERT, lawyer; b. Troy, NY, Apr. 26, 1935; s. Samuel and Elizabeth (Fishburne) R.; m. Beverly Ann Macht, Mar. 7, 1971; children: Jonathan Noah, Abigail Rebecca. BA, Harvard U., 1956, JD, 1959. Bar: N.Y. 1959, D.C. 1961. Rsch. asst. Harvard U. Law Sch., Cambridge, Mass., 1959-60; law clk. to Justice William J. Brennan U.S. Supreme Ct., Washington, 1960-61; asst. U.S. atty. Dept. Justice, Washington, 1961-64; assoc. Arnold & Porter, Washington, 1964-68, ptnr., 1969-95; gen. counsel D.C. Fin. Responsibility and Mgmt. Assistance Authority, Washington, 1995—2001, D.C. Office of the Corp. Counsel, 2001—04; asst. atty. gen. Dist. of Columbia, 2004—. Adj. prof. law Georgetown U., Washington, 1963—; mem. D.C. Commn. on Jud. Disabilities and Tenure, 1979-86, D.C. Bd. Profl. Responsibility, 1994-2000; trustee D.C. Pub. Defender Svc., 1981-87. Contbr. articles to profl. jours. Named Young Lawyer of Yr. for D.C., 1971. Fellow Am. Coll. Trial Lawyers, Am. Bar Found.; mem. ABA, D.C. Bar (pres. 1975-76, pres. Bar Found. 1994-97), Bar Assn. D.C., Asst. U.S. Attys. Assn. Jewish. Avocations: American history, reading, writing. Home: 2852 Albemarle St NW Washington DC 20008-1036 Office: DC office Atty Gen 441 4th St NW 6th Fl S Washington DC 20001 Office Phone: 202-724-5691. Business E-Mail: daniel.rezneck@dc.gov.

REZNICK, RICHARD HOWARD, pediatrician; b. Chgo., Oct. 31, 1939; s. Louis and Mae Reznick; m. Barbara Ann Glantz, June 20, 1965; children: Steven L., Alicia T., Scott M., Stacey R. BS, U. Ill., 1961; MD, Loyola U., Chgo., 1965. Diplomate Am. Bd. Pediatrics. Resident in pediat. Michael Reese Hosp., Chgo., 1966-68; pediatrician USAF, Homestead AFB, Fla., 1968-70; pediatrician pvt. practice Winnetka, Ill., 1970—71, Scottsdale, Ariz., 1971—. Pres. med. staff Phoenix Children's Hosp., 1990-93, bd. dirs. 1990-94. Capt. USAF, 1968-70. Fellow Am. Acad. Pediatrics (treas. Ariz. chpt. 1982-84); mem. AMA, Ariz. Med. Assn., Phoenix Pediatric Soc. (treas. 1976-77), Maricopa County Med. Soc. Avocations: aerobics, bicycling, gardening, classical music, collecting stamps. Office: Papago Buttes Pediatric Ctr 8573 E San Alberto Ste E100 Scottsdale AZ 85258-4318 Office Phone: 480-778-1732.

REZNICK, STEVEN MICHAEL, orthopedic surgeon, educator; b. Washington, 1954; 3 children. BS, U. Md., 1975; MD, George Washington U., 1979; MBA, Columbia U., 2000. Diplomate Am. Bd. Orthopedic Surgery. Resident in gen. surgery George Washington U., 1979-81; resident in orthop. surgery U. Mich., Ann Arbor, 1981-84; clin. instr. orthopedic surgery UCLA Sch. Medicine, 1988-94. Sr. aviation med. examiner FAA, 1985-87; talk show host KGIL-Radio, L.A., 1987-90. Mem. Calif. Rep. Party, Calif. Rep. Assembly, bd. dirs. Palm Springs chpt., 1996-98. Fellow Internat. Coll. Surgeons, Am. Coll. Surgeons, Am. Acad. Orthopedic Surgeons, Beta Gamma Sigma Honor Soc. Avocation: commercial pilot. Home: PO Box 101 Somers NY 10589 E-mail: smr50@columbia.edu.

REZNIK, ALAN A. petroleum engineering educator; b. Pitts., Sept. 25, 1939; s. Lawrence S. and Rose R.; m. Marion Bergstein, Sept. 8, 1963; children: Amy Jean, Robert I.S. BS, U. Pitts., 1963, MS, 1964, PhD, 1971. Research scientist Continental Oil Co., Ponca City, Okla., 1964-66; instr. chem. and petroleum engring. dept. U. Pitts., 1966-67; instr. dept. civil engring. Technion-Israel Inst. Tech., Haifa, 1967-68; sr. research assoc. Calgon Corp., Pitts., 1969; engring. supr. U.S. Bur. Mines, Pitts., 1973-75; assoc. prof. chem. and petroleum engring. U. Pitts., 1975—, dir. petroleum engring. program, 1981-92; cons. and lectr. in field. Assoc. editor Jour. Petroleum Sci. and Engring., 1986-93 . Contbr. articles to profl. jours. Recipient Continental Oil Co. fellowship, 1961, Socony Mobil Internat. fellowship, 1962, U. Pitts. Outstanding Sr. award, 1963; U.S. Dept. Energy grantee, 1976-78, Gulf Oil Found. grantee, 1979, U.S. Dept. Energy grantee, 1978-79, 80-82, 85-86. Mem. Soc. Petroleum Engrs. of AIME, Am. Chem. Soc. (sec.-treas. 1975-76), Sigma Xi, Sigma Tau, Sigma Gamma Epsilon. Achievements include research in flow in porous media enhanced petroleum recovery and methane production from coals, tensor analysis. Office: U Pitts Chem & Petroleum Engring Dept 1249 Benedum Hall Pittsburgh PA 15261-2212

REZNIK, SANDRA EVE, physician, consultant; b. Newark, N.J., May 2, 1962; d. Frank and Renee Breitbarth; m. Edward J. Reznik, Sept. 6, 1987; children: Samantha Jill, Sabrina Mae. AB, Harvard U., Cambridge, Mass., 1980—84; MD, PhD, Mt. Sinai Sch. Medicine, N.Y.C., 1984—91. Diplomate Nat. Bd. Med. Examiners U. State of NY Edn. Dept., 1992. Resident in anatomic pathology N.Y. Hosp., Cornell U. Med. Coll., N.Y.C., 1991—94; Arthur Purdy Stout Soc. fellow in surg. pathology Montefiore Med. Ctr., Albert Einstein Coll. Medicine, Bronx, NY, 1996—97, fellow in placental and perinatal pathology, 1997—98; attending physician in pathology Montefiore Med. Ctr., Bronx, NY, 1998—; asst. prof., pathology Albert Einstein Coll. Medicine, Bronx, NY, 1998—, asst. prof., obstetrics and gynecology and women's health. Grantee, Nat. Inst. Child Health and Human Devel., 1998—2003. Avocations: ice skating, cooking, travel. Home: 7 Dante St Larchmont NY 10538-1608 Office: Albert Einstein Coll Medicine 1300 Morris Park Ave - Forch 2nd Fl Bronx NY 10461 E-mail: sreznik@aecom.yu.edu.

REZNIKOV, VLADIMIR LVOVICH, historian, playwright; b. Donetzk, Ukraine, May 26, 1937; s. Lev Davidovich Reznikov and Sofia Semyonovna Baskina; m. Natalya Klueva, Nov. 4, 1994; children: Lev, Michael, Sonya. MS in History, Moscow State Pedagogic U., 1962; PhD in History, Russain Acad. Scis., 1972; MS in screen play writing (hon.), State Inst. Cinematography, Moscow, 1973. Sci. editor Oriental Book Publishers, Moscow, 1962—69; dept. editor Asia and Africa Today, Moscow, 1977—81; sr. rsch. fellow Inst. Oriental Studies of Russian Acad. of Scis., Moscow, 1969—97, 1981—97; freelance playwright scholar of art history, 1997—. Author: (screen play) Encounter, 1971, Forgive me, Vietnam, 1971, Personal Case, 1971, Nature and Society, 1980, Voice of the Centuries, 1975, Use of Isotope Control Devices in Automatization of Production Processes, 1975, (book) Policy of Caeser's Germany in Oceania, 1975; editor: India - Country and People (Hon. Diploma Geog. Soc. of USSR, 1973). Mem.: Journalist Soc. of Russia. Personal E-mail: natalya.klueva@ttu.edu.

RGUZMAN, JOSE JAVIER, aeronautical engineer; b. Bayamon, Pr, Oct. 27, 1970; s. Jose Dolores Guzman and Nydia Margarita Rivera; m. Natalia Ramirez, May 12, 2001. BSEngr. in Aero/Astronautical Engring., Purdue U., West Lafayette, Ind., 1993, MS in Aero/Astronautical Engring., 1995, PhD in Aero/Astronautical Engring., 2001. Astrodynamics specialist, mission analyst a.i. solutions, Inc., Lanham, Md., 2001—; sr. tech. staff mem. Johns Hopkins U. Applied Physics Lab, 2004—. Astrodynamics specailist sr. staff John Hopkins Univ. Contbr. articles. Recipient Indsl. Roundtable Leadership Award, Purdue U., 1991, Triana Project Group Achievement award, NASA Goddard Space Flight Ctr., 2002; award, Nat. Hispanic Scholarship Fund, 1991, scholar, McDonnell Douglas Found., 1992, Grad. Student Rschrs. Program fellowship, NASA Goddard Space Flight Ctr., 1996-1999. Mem.: AIAA (assoc.; evolution of flight chair 2002—03, sec. 2003—04, mem. astrodynamics tech. com. 2004—), Planetary Soc., Am. Astronautical Soc. (assoc.).

RHAMES, VING (IRVING), actor; b. N.Y.C., May 12, 1961; Appeared in films Stop! Or My Mom Will Shoot, 1992, The People Under the Stairs, 1992, Dave, 1993, The Saint of Fort Washington, 1993, Bound By Honor Blood In Blood Out, 1993, Pulp Fiction, 1994, Drop Squad, 1994, Kiss of Death, 1995, Ed McBain's 87th Precinct, 1995, Deadly Whispers, 1995, Mission: Impossible, 1996, Striptease, 1996, Con Air, 1997, Rosewood, 1997, Dangerous Ground, 1997, Don King: Only in America, 1997 (Golden Globe for best performance by an actor in a mini-series or motion picture made for TV 1998), The Split, 1998, Out of Sight, 1998, Doctor Doolittle, 1998, Entrapment, 1999, Bringing Out the Dead, 1999, Mission Impossible II, 2000, Baby Boy, 2001, Sins of the Father, 2002, Lilo & Stitch (voice only), 2002, Dark Blue, 2002, Undisputed, 2002, Dawn of the Dead, 2004. Office: William Morris Agy 151 S El Camino Dr Beverly Hills CA 90212-2775

RHEAD, WILLIAM JAMES, biochemical geneticist; b. Feb. 20, 1946; s. Wallace Max and Marie Jeanne (Muller) R.; m. Deborah Elizabeth Sheppard, July 15, 1972 (div. Apr. 1997); children: Paul Joseph, Evan James, Jack; m. Pamela Finberg, Jan. 11, 1998. BA with highest honors, U. Calif., San Diego, 1968, MD, 1974, PhD, 1975; MPh, Yale U., 1969. Diplomate Am. Bd. Human Genetics, Am. Bd. Pediats. Intern and resident in pediats. U. N.C., Chapel Hill, 1975-77; fellow in human genetics and pediats. Yale U. Sch. Medicine, 1977-79; asst. prof. pediats. U. Iowa Coll. Medicine, 1979-84, assoc. prof. pediats., 1984-89, prof. pediats., 1989-2000; prof., sect. chief med. genetics Med. Coll. Wis., Milw., 2000—. Bd. dirs. Assn. for Glycogen Storage Disease, 1984. Recipient Noel Raine award Soc. Study of Inborn Errors of Metabolism, 1983. Fellow Am. Acad. Pediats.; mem. Am. Soc. Human Genetics, Soc. Inherited Metabolic Disease, Soc. Pediat. Rsch., Soc. Study Inborn Errors of Metablism. Democrat. Avocations: bicycling, skiing, travel, gardening. Home: 12605 W Grove Ter Elm Grove WI 53122-1976 Office: Med Coll Wis Med Genetics/Pediats PO Box 1997 Milwaukee WI 53201-1997 Fax: (414) 266-1616. E-mail: wrhead@mcw.edu.

RHEAMS, ANNIE ELIZABETH, education educator; b. Lake Providence, La. d. Curtis Kleinpeter Sr. and Annie Augusta (Webb) Kleinpeter; 1 child, Darryl Jemall Rheams. BA, Grambling (La.) U., 1971; MS, Ala. A&M U., 1975; PhD, U. Wis., Milw., 1989. Cert. tchr. in exceptional edn., adminstrn. Tchr. Ala. A&M U., Normal, 1971-79, adminstr., 1977-79; acad. specialist U. Wis., Milw., 1979-82, Parkside, 1982-84; tchr. diagnostician, adminstr. Milw. Schs., 1984-89; asst. prof. dept. edn. Marquette U., Milw., 1989-96; asst. prin. North Divsn. H.S., Milw., 1996—, Marshall H.S., Milw., 1997—99, tchr. exceptional edn. cognitively disabled, consumer math., 1999—, adminstr., asst. prin., 1999. Career counselor Madison County Career Counseling Svcs., Huntsville, 1975; adj. prof. Oakwood (Ala.) SDA Coll., 1975-78; tchr. Gateway to Engring. Program, Milw., 1984-88; cons. pub. schs./Wee Care Day Care, Milw., 1992-96; condr. workshops in field. Author: P.A.C.E.: A Thematic Approach to Developing Essential Experiences, 1996. Voter registrar/poll watcher NAACP, Lake Providence, 1966; v.p. Work for Wis., Inc., Milw., 1993-94, Messmer H.S. Bd., Milw., 1990-94; com. chmn. Citizen's Rev. Bd., Milw., 1980-82, Met. Milw. Alliance Black Sch. Educators, 1994-95. Assoc. fellow Ctr. for Great Plains Studies, U. Nebr.-Lincoln, 1995; named Outstanding Tchr. Educator, Am. Assn. for Coll. Tchr. Educators Directory, 1995. Mem. Zonta Internat., Alpha Kappa Alpha, Phi Delta Kappa. Avocations: tennis, sewing, ceramics, horseback riding, biking. Home: PO Box 90681 Milwaukee WI 53209-0611 Fax: 414-902-8315. E-mail: rheams@mailandnews.com.

RHEE, SORAH, biomedical engineer; b. Oberhausen, Germany, Aug. 6, 1972; arrived in U.S., 2000; MSc, Aachen (Germany) U. Tech., 1997; PhD, Freiburg (Germany) U., 2000. Rsch. asst. Nat. Rsch. Lab., Karlsruhe, Germany, 1997—2000; rsch. fellow Osaka (Japan) U., 1998; postdoctoral fellow Pa. State U., University Park, 2000—02, rsch. assoc., 2002—03; exec. dir. Fraunhofer-IBMT Tech. Ctr., Hialeah, Fla., 2003—. Editor-in-chief NIH Resource Ctr. for Ultrasonic Transducer Tech., University Park, Pa., 2000—02. Monbusho scholar, Japanese Ministry of Sci., 2000. Mem.: IEEE Ultrasonics, Ferroelectronics and Frequency Control Soc. (web editor 2001—03, publicity chair 2001—03), Am. Ceramics Soc. Office: Fraunhoter-IBMT Tech Ctr 601 W 20th St Hialeah FL 33010 E-mail: dr.rhee@hunyar.net.

RHEIN, ARTHUR, emergency medical technician; V.p. mktg. Harvey Electronics, 1983—86; sr. v.p. mktg. Pioneer, 1986; from v.p. mktg. to pres., CEO Agilysys, Inc., Mayfield Heights, Ohio, 1986—2002, pres., 2002—, CEO, 2002—, chmn. bd., 2003—. Office: Agilysys Inc 6065 Parkland Blvd Mayfield Heights OH 44124*

RHEIN, DAVE, newspaper editor; b. Chgo., Ill., Mar. 9, 1949; BE, Drake U., 1970. Deputy mng. editor Des Moines Register, 1995-99, asst. metro editor, 1999—. Office: Des Moines Register 715 Locust St Des Moines IA 50309-3767

RHEIN, JOHN HANCOCK WILLING, III, publishing executive; b. Richmond, Va., Aug. 8, 1931; s. John Hancock Willing Jr. and Margaret (Packard) R.; m. Phyllis Betz, June 13, 1953; children: Susan Rhein Dubowski, Deborah B., John Hancock Willing IV. BA, Hobart Coll., 1953. With rsch. dept. Benton & Bowles Advt., N.Y.C., 1957; sales mgmt. asst. to pub. Forbes Mag., N.Y.C., 1957-71; sr. v.p., assoc. pub. Fin. Mag., N.Y.C., 1971-73, Fin. World Mag., N.Y.C., 1973-81; pres. Nat. Bus. Confs., N.Y.C., 1975-81; sr. v.p. dir. sales and mktg. Sat. Rev. Mag., N.Y.C., 1980-81, View Mag., N.Y.C., 1980-81; pub. Equities Mag. (formerly OTC Rev.), N.Y.C., 1981-93, Emeritus Equities Mag., 1993—; pres., CEO Am. Depository Receipt Assn., 1993—. Pub. ADR Investor & Global Securities Almanac, CapitalistForum.com, 2000—03; chmn. bd. W.R. Keegan Corp., Focus the Nat. H.S. News Mag., 1994—; pres. The Investor Intelligence Group, Garden City, NY, 1981—; dir. Top Tier Writers, Inc., 2000—03; mng. dir. Hill Ho. Pub., 2003—, Creative Resources Adv. and Pub. Rels., 1995—. Office: Investor Intelligence Group 96 10th St Garden City NY 11530-1560 Personal E-mail: John_Rhein3@yahoo.com.

RHEIN, TIMOTHY J. retired transportation company executive; b. 1941; BS, U. Santa Clara, 1962. Mil. contract and revenue analyst Am. Pres. Lines Ltd., Oakland, Calif., 1967-71, sr. analyst, 1971-72, mgr. mktg. planning, 1972-73, dir. traffic systems and adminstrn., 1973-75, dir. mktg. adminstrn., 1975-76, dir. worldwide sales, 1976-78, v.p. N.Am., 1978-80, v.p. traffic, 1980-84, sr. v.p., 1984-87, pres., also chief oper. officer, 1987-90; pres., chief exec. officer APL Ltd., Oakland, Calif., 1990-2000, retired, 2000. With U.S. Army, 1962-67. Office: APL Ltd 1111 Broadway Fl 25 Oakland CA 94607-4036

RHEINFRANK, SALLY LYMAN, volunteer; b. Boston, Mar. 23, 1941; d. J. Robert and Charlotte Cox (Litchfield) Lyman; m. Lamson Rheinfrank, Jr., June 15, 1963; children: Caroline Adams, Virginia Lamson, Emily Lyman, Lydia Spitzer. BA, Vassar Coll., 1963. Asst. to dir. admissions Oberlin Coll., 1963; substitute tchr. jr. and sr. high schs., Michigan City, Ind., 1963-65; arts program aid Western Mo. Mental Health Ctr., Kansas City, 1965-67; with Am. Field Svc., 1966—73; regional coord. area bd. dirs. Ams. Abroad Program, 1975. Sec. Mo. Rep. Theatre, 1987—91, mem. exec. com., fin. com., planning and devel. com., chair capital campaign, 1990—93; bd. dirs. parents guild St. Paul's Episcopal Parish Day Sch., 1970—79, co-chmn. sch. capital campaign, 1978—79, mem., v.p. bd. trustees, chmn. scholarship fund, 1975—81; mem. admissions com. Sunset Hill Sch., 1977—78, chmn., exec. bd. mem. parents assn., 1978—79, mem. student svcs. com., 1979—80, sec. parents assn., 1980—81, mem. parents awareness com., 1980—81; bd. trustees, mem. various coms. Pembroke Hill Sch., 1986—93; curriculum chair Pembroke Hills Sch., 1987—88, devel. chair, 1989—91, exec., v.p. bd., 1989—93, mem. exec. com. new head, 1990; mem. bd. trustees Vassar Coll., 1987—99, chair acad. affairs com., 1989—99, mem. nominating com., bldg. and grounds com., devel. com., exec. com., personel com., 1989—99, nat. co-chair 8200 capital campaign, 1993—96, co-chair leadership gifts for 40th reunion, 2001—02. Mem. Rockhill Homes Assn. (bd. dirs.), Neebish Pioneer Assn. (pres., bd. dirs. 1982—), Mo. Repertory Theatre, Inc. (sec. 1984-87, bd. trustees 1980—, mem. various coms.), Friends of Chamber Music (bd. dirs., v.p. 1983—), Met. Performing Arts Found. (bd. dirs. 1984—), Vassar Club Kansas City (v.p. 1968-70, pres. 1970-72, alumni admissions rep. 1976-83, scholarship project chmn. 1984—). Episcopalian. Avocations: reading, gardening, art, travel, sports.

RHEINS, CARL JEFFREY, historian, director; b. Cin., Sept. 17, 1945; s. Joseph Melvin and Gertrude (Mandell) R.; m. Brenda Dale Gevertz, July 8, 1979; children: Jason Gabriel, Jaclyn Gail. BS with distinction, U. Wis., 1967; MA, SUNY, Albany, 1970; PhD, SUNY, Stony Brook, 1978. Lectr. Judaic studies SUNY, Stony Brook, 1974-78, asst. to provost, 1978-80, 81-86; dir. acad. affairs Nat. Found. Jewish Culture, N.Y.C., 1980-81; asst. dean Adelphi U., Garden City, N.Y., 1986-87, assoc. dean, 1987, exec. asst. to pres., 1987-90, dean student life and devel., 1990-92, v.p. student life and devel., 1992-97, v.p. external affairs and comty. rels., 1997—99; exec. dir., CEO Yivo Inst. for Jewish Rsch., N.Y.C., 1999—. Bd. dirs. Coalition on Higher Edn., Jewish Community Rels. Coun., N.Y.C.; Delegate (NGO) Vilinius Internat. Forum on Holocaust-Era Looted Cultural Assets, 2000. Contbg. author: Yearbook of the Leo Baeck Inst., 1978, 80, 81; co-editor: Jewish Almanac, 1980 (dual main selection Jewish Book Club Am. 1981). Mem. nat. governing coun. Am. Jewish Congress, N.Y.C., 1986-87, 1st v.p. Suffolk County, N.Y., 1985-87; bd. govs. L.I. region Am. Jewish Com., N.Y., 1984-85; judge Nat. Jewish Book Awards, 1993, 94. Summer fellow NEH, 1987. Mem. Garden City C. of C. (bd. dirs. 1997—99), Phi Kappa Phi, Phi Alpha Theta, Alpha Epsilon Pi. Home: 424 West End Ave New York NY 10024 Office: YIVO Institute 15 W 16th St New York NY 10011-6301

RHEINSTEIN, PETER HOWARD, healthcare company executive, consultant, physician, lawyer; b. Cleve., Sept. 7, 1943; s. Franz Joseph Rheinstein and Hede Henrietta (Neheimer) Rheinstein Lerner; m. Miriam Ruth Weissman, Feb. 22, 1969; 1 child, Jason Edward. BA with high honors, Mich. State U., 1963, MS, 1964; MD, Johns Hopkins U., 1967; JD, U. Md., 1973. Bar: Md. 1973, D.C. 1980, U.S. Supreme Ct. 2000; diplomate Am. Bd. Family Practice; cert. added qualifications in geriatric medicine. Intern USPHS Hosp., San Francisco, 1967-68, resident in internal medicine Balt., 1968-70; instr. internal medicine U. Md., Balt., 1970-73; med. dir. extended care facilities CHC Corp., Balt., 1972-74; dir. drug advt. and labeling divsn. FDA, Rockville, Md., 1974-82, acting dep. dir. Office Drugs, 1982-83, acting dir. Office Drugs, 1983-84, dir. Office Drug Stds., 1984-90, dir. medicine staff Office Health Affairs, 1990-99; sr. v.p. for med. and clin. affairs Cell Works, Inc., Balt.,

1999—2004. Bd. dirs. Marnac, Inc., Dallas; chmn. Com. on Advanced Sci. Edn., 1978-86, Rsch. in Human Subjects Com., 1990-92; adj. prof. forensic medicine George Washington U., 1974-76; WHO cons. on drug regulation Nat. Inst. for Control Pharm. and Biol. Products, China, 1981-90; advisor on essential drugs WHO, 1985-90; FDA del. to U.S. Pharmacopeial Conv., 1985-90, coord. com. for assessment and transfer of tech. NIH, 1990-99, mem. health care fin. adminstrn. tech. adv. com., 1990-98, Nat. Adv. Coun. on Healthcare Policy, Rsch. and Evaluation, 1990-99, Healthy People 2000/2010 Steering Com., 1990-99, CDC and Prevention Task Force on Cmty. Preventive Svcs., 1996-99, Nat. Task Force on CME Industry/Provider Collaboration, 1992—, ann. meeting chmn., 2003, US Adopted Names Coun. Review Board, 2004-; cons. in legal medicine and regulatory affairs, 1999—. Co-author: (with others) Human Organ Transplantation, 1987; spl. editl. advisor Good Housekeeping Guide to Medicine and Drugs, 1977-80; mem. editl. bd. Legal Aspects Med. Practice, 1981-89, Drug Info. Jour., 1982-86, 91-95; pub. Discovery Medicine, 2001-; contbr. articles to profl. jours. V.p. Intercultural Friends Found., 1998—. Recipient Commendable Svc. award, FDA, 1981, Group award of merit, 1983, 1988, Group Commendable Svc. award, 1989, 1992—93, 1995, 1999, Commr.'s Spl. citation, 1993; NIH Nat. Cancer Inst. SBIR grant, 2001. Fellow: Am. Acad. Family Physicians, Am. Coll. Legal Medicine (bd. govs. 1983—93, chmn. fin. com. 1985—88, chmn. publs. com. 1988—93, chmn. fin. com. 1990—91, jud. coun. 1993—95, treas., Pres.'s awards 1985, 1986, 1989—91, 1993, Gold medal 2003); mem.: APHA, AMA (life; ho. of dels. 2002—), ABA, US Adopted Names Review Bd., Soc. Indsl. and Applied Math., Math. Assn. Am., Md. Bar Assn., Johns Hopkins Med. and Surg. Assn., Balt. City Med. Soc., Md. State Med. Soc., Fed. Bar Assn. (chmn. food and drug com. 1976—79, Disting. Svc. award 1977), Drug Info. Assn. (bd. dirs. 1982—90, pres. 1984—85, v.p. 1986—87, pres. 1988—89, chmn. ann. meeting 1991, steering com. Ams. 1991—, chmn. ann. meeting 1994, Outstanding Svc. award 1990), Am. Bd. Legal Medicine (treas. 2003—), Am. Acad. Pharm. Phys. (trustee 1999—2003, pres. Washington-Balt. chpt. 1999—2003, v.p. AMA rels. 1999—), FDA Alumni Assn., U. Md. Alumni Assn. (life), Mensa (life), Fed. Exec. Inst. Alumni Assn. (life), Mich. State U. Honors Coll. Alumni Assn. (bd. dirs. 1998—2001, pres. 2000—01), Mich. State U. Alumni Assn. (life), Johns Hopkins U. Alumni Assn. (life), Chartwell Golf and Country Club, Delta Theta Phi. Avocations: boating, electronics, physical fitness, real estate investments. Home: 621 Holly Ridge Rd Severna Park MD 21146-3520 Office Phone: 410-647-9500. E-mail: phr@jhu.edu.

RHEINTGEN, LAURA DALE, research center official; b. Takoma Park, Md., July 13, 1962; d. Robert William and Ethel Frances (Snyder) Schiedel. BA in Internat. Studies and German, W.Va. U., 1984; MA in Internat. Affairs, Am. U., 1988. Rsch. asst. Brookings Instn., Washington, 1986; staff cons. Birch & Davis Assocs., Inc., Silver Spring, Md., 1988-89; devel. analyst Ctr. for Strategic and Internat. Studies, Washington, 1989-92, mgr. devel. rsch. and records, 1992-93, asst. dir. devel., 1994-95, dir. found. rels., 1995-97; assoc. dir. devel. Aspen Inst., Washington, 1997-98; devel. assoc. Nat. Acad. Scis., Washington, 1998-99, devel. officer, 1999; devel. dir. Am. Inst. Contemporary German Studies, Johns Hopkins U., Washington, 1999—. Mem. Women in Internat. Security Studies, German Lang. Soc. Office: Am Inst Contemporary German Studies Johns Hopkins U 1400 16th St NW Ste 420 Washington DC 20036-2216

RHETT, HASKELL EMERY SMITH, educator; b. Evanston, Ill., Aug. 29, 1936; s. Haskell Smith and Eunice Campbell (Emery) R.; m. Roberta Teel Oliver, Sept. 9, 1961 (div. 1973); children: Kathryn Emery, Cecily Coffin; m. Anita Leone, May 30, 1983 (div. 1993); m. Janet Lee Rollings, Nov. 15, 1997. Diploma, Gov. Dummer Acad., 1954; AB, Hamilton Coll., 1958; MA, Cornell U., 1967, PhD, 1968. Asst. to the pres. Hamilton Coll., Clinton, N.Y., 1961-64; rsch. asst. Cornell U., Ithaca, N.Y., 1964-66; rsch. assoc. U. London, 1966-67; dir. program devel. Ednl. Testing Svc., Princeton, N.J., 1967-73; asst. chancellor N.J. Dept. Higher Edn., Trenton, 1973-85; v.p. The Coll. Bd., N.Y.C., 1985-90; pres. The Woodrow Wilson Nat. Fellowship Found., Princeton, 1990-97, pres. emeritus, 1997—. Author: Going to College in New Jersey, 1978; contbg. author: Government's Role in Supporting College Savings, 1990. Commr. N.J. Pub. Broadcasting Authority, Trenton, 1983-85; mem. Nat. Task Force on Student Aid Problems, Washington, 1974-75; mem. Gov.'s Adv. Panel on Higher Edn. Restructuring, State of N.J., 1994; trustee Dominican U. of Calif., San Rafael, Calif., 1990-99, 2001—, William Alexander Procter Found., 1998-2002; del. Dem. Nat. Conv., Miami, 1972; sr. warden Trinity Episcopal Ch., Princeton, 1988-92, vestryman, 1979-82, 87-88, 2001—04; dep. Gen. Conv., Detroit, 1988, Phoenix, 1991; mem. standing com. Episcopal Diocese of N.J., 1992-97; trustee The Coll. of N.J., 1992-97, vice-chmn., 1995-97, chmn., 1997; trustee Gov. Dummer Acad., Mass., 1993—, Heartland Edn. Comty., Ohio, 1992-97, Forums Inst. for Pub. Policy, N.J., 1999—, treas., 2000—; bd. dirs. Reach the World, Inc., N.Y.C., 1998-2000, Trenton After Sch. Program, 2001—04. Lt. USNR, 1958—61, Heavy Attack Squadron 5 (VAH-5), USS Forrestal. Nat. Def. fellow U.S. Govt., 1966-67, Eliot-Winant fellow Brit.-Am. Assocs., 1982, Harvard U. fellow, 1985, faculty fellow Wilson Coll., Princeton U., 1993-97. Mem. Nat. Assn. State Scholarship and Grant Programs (pres. 1976-78), Princeton Officers Soc., English-Speaking Union, Springdale Golf Club. Avocations: travel, tennis, golf, sailing, classic automobiles. Home: 80 Province Line Rd Skillman NJ 08558-1102 E-mail: hrhett@patmedia.net.

RHETTS, PAUL FISHER, publishing executive; b. Washington, Mar. 26, 1946; s. Charles Edward and Ruth (Fisher) R.; m. JoAnn Rhodes, Aug. 26, 1968 (div. Dec. 1979); children: Joanna Katherine, Alexandra Copeland; m. Barbe J. Awalt, Mar. 13, 1982. BA, Bucknell U., 1968; student Pub. Adminstrn. MS program, U. So. Calif., 1975-77. Pub. affairs producer Sta. WMAL-TV, Washington, 1969-70, Md. Pub. TV, Owings Mills, 1970-73; asst. supt. Balt. City Pub. Schs., 1973-74; publs. cons. Community Coll. Balt., 1975-78; pub. info. officer Howard County Schs., Ellicott City, Md., 1976-86; pres. Laser Pub. and Design, Md. and N.Mex., 1986-95; sr. ptnr. LPD Press, 1995—. Trainer Pagemaker Desktop Pub. Software, 1986-94; mem. adj. faculty Loyola Coll., Balt., 1978-80; bd. dirs. UNM Cancer Ctr., Maxwell Mus. of Anthropology. Author: Finding Out How People Feel, 1984, Charlie Carrillo: Tradition & Soul, 1994; pub. Tradición Revista: The Jour. of Contemporary and Traditional Spanish Colonial Arts and Culture, 1995—, The Regis Santos: Thirty Years of Collecting, 1966-96, 1997, Our Saints Among Us: 400 Years of New Mexican Devotional Art, 1997, Seeds of Struggle: Harvest of Faith, 1998, Portfolio of Spanish Colonial Design in New Mexico, 2001, Nicholas Herrera: Visiones de mi Corazon, 2003. Mem. exec. bd. Family Life Ctr., Columbia, Md., 1980-86, Humanities Inst., Columbia, 1978-82, Columbia Archives, 1984-86. Recipient award San Francisco Internat. Film Festival, 1971, Broadcasting award Ohio State U., 1972, Community Svc. Merit award So. Ednl. Communications Assn., 1973, Nat. Community Svc. award Corp. for Pub. Broadcasting, 1973, Publ. award of Excellence, 1986. Mem. Nat. Sch. Pub. Rels. Assn. (state coord. 1978-83, pres. Chesapeake chpt. 1981-82, 86-87, exec. bd., 1976-90, chmn. nat. conv. planning com., treas. N.Mex. chpt. 1991-92, Blue Ribbon award 1982, 87, Gold Medallion award 1985-92, Mariner award 1990, Pres. award 1991), Pub. Rels. Soc. Am. (treas. N.Mex. soc. 1991-92, Conquistador award 1991, 93, 94, 95, pres. elect 1993, pres. 1994, Nat. Pres.'s Citation for Leadership 1994), Am. Profl. Graphic Artists Assn., N.Mex. Book Assn., Columbia Bus. Exch., Ednl. Press Assn., Desktop Pub. Assn., C. of C. (bd. dirs.). Democrat. Episcopalian. Home: 925 Salamanca St NW Albuquerque NM 87107-5647 Office Phone: 505-344-9382. E-mail: info@nmsantos.com.

RHIEW, FRANCIS CHANGNAM, radiologist, physician; b. Korea, Dec. 3, 1938; came to U.S., 1967, naturalized, 1977; s. Byung Kyun and In Sil (Lee) R.; m. Kay Kyungja Chang, June 11, 1967; children: Richard C., Elizabeth. BS, Seoul Nat. U., 1960, MD, 1964. Cert. Am. Bd. Nuclear Medicine. Intern St. Mary's Hosp., Waterbury, Conn., 1967-68; resident in radiology and nuclear medicine L.I.U.-Queens Hosp. Ctr., N.Y., 1968-71; instr. radiology W. Va. U. Sch. Medicine, Morgantown, 1971-73; mem. staff Mercy Hosp. and Moses Taylor Hosp. Scranton, Pa., 1973—; also dir. nuclear medicine; clin. instr. Temple U., 1987—. Pres. Radiol. Consultants, Inc., 1984—, F.C.R. Co. Chmn., CEO Francis and Kay Rhiew Charitable Found. With M.C., Korean Army, 1964-67. Recipient Minister of Health and Welfare award, 1963. Mem. AMA, Soc. Nuclear Medicine, Radiol. Soc. N.Am., Am. Coll. Nuclear Medicine, Am. Coll. Radiology, Am. Inst. Ultra Sound, Country Club Scranton, Pres.'s Club U. Scranton, Elks. Home: 14 Lakeside Dr Clarks Summit PA 18411-9419 Office: 746 Jefferson Ave Scranton PA 18510-1624

RHIM, JOHNG SIK, physician, educator, medical researcher; b. Kwang Ju, Korea, July 24, 1930; came to U.S., 1958; s. Hac Woon and Moo Duc (Choi) R.; m. Mary Margaret Lytle, Aug. 24, 1930; children: Jonathan, Christopher, Peter, Andrew, Michael, Kathleen. MD, Seoul (Korea) Nat. U., 1957. Intern Seoul Nat. U. Hosp., 1958; rsch. fellow Children's Hosp. Rsch. Found., Cin., 1958-60, Baylor U. Coll. Medicine, Houston, 1961; rsch. assoc. Grad. Sch. Pub. Health, U. Pitts., 1962, La. State U. Acad. Medicine, New Orleans, 1962-64; vis. scientist Nat. Inst. Allergy and Infectious Diseases, NIH, Bethesda, Md., 1964-66; project dir. cancer rsch. Microbiol. Assocs., Bethesda, Md., 1966-78; sr. investigator Nat. Cancer Inst., NIH, Bethesda, 1978-98; assoc. dir., prof. surgery Ctr. Prostate Disease Rsch., Uniformed Svcs. U. of the Health Sci., Bethesda, 1999—; rsch. prof. dept. surgery Uniformed Svcs. U. Health Scis., Bethesda, 2000—. Adj. prof. Georgetown U. Med. Ctr., Washington, 1988—. Editor: Neoplastic Transformation in Human Cell Culture, 1991, 1995, 1999, 2003; mem. editl. bd.: Internat. Jour. Oncology Prostate Cancer and Prostate Disease, Cancer Therapy; contbr. articles to profl. jours., chapters to books. Mem. AAAS, AMA, Am. Assn. Cancer Rsch., Am. Soc. Virology, Soc. Exptl. Biology and Medicine, Internat. Assn. Leukemia Rsch. Achievements include patents for in field. Home: 11455 S Glen Rd Potomac MD 20854-1851 Office: CPDR Dept Surgery Uniformed Svcs Univ Health 4301 Jones Bridge Rd Bethesda MD 20814-4712 Office Phone: 301-319-8223. Business E-Mail: jrhim@pdr.org.

RHIND, JAMES THOMAS, lawyer; b. Chgo., July 21, 1922; s. John Gray and Eleanor (Bradley) R.; m. Laura Haney Campbell, Apr. 19, 1958; children: Constance Rhind Robey, James Campbell, David Scott. Student, Hamilton Coll., 1940-42; AB cum laude, Ohio State U., 1944; LL.B. cum laude, Harvard U., 1950. Bar: Ill. bar 1950. Japanese translator U.S. War Dept., Tokyo, 1946-47; congl. liaison Fgn. Operations Adminstrn., Washington, 1954; atty. Bell, Boyd & Lloyd, Chgo., 1950-53, 55—, ptnr., 1958-92, chmn. exec. com., 1979—90, of counsel, 1993—. Bd. dirs. Kewaunee Scientific Corp., Statesville, NC. Commr. Gen. Assembly United Presbyn. Ch., 1963; life trustee Ravinia Festival Assn., Hamilton Coll., Clinton, N.Y., U. Chgo.; Northwestern Univ. Assocs.; chmn. Cook County Young Republican Orgn., 1957; Ill. Young Rep. nat. committeeman, 1957-58; v.p., mem. bd. govs. United Rep. Fund Ill., 1965-84; pres. Ill. Childrens Home and Aid Soc., 1971-73, life trustee; bd. dirs. E.J. Dalton Youth Center, 1966- 69; governing mem. Chgo. Symphony Orch., Chgo.; mem. Ill. Arts Council, 1971-75; mem. exec. com. div. Met. Mission and Ch. Extension Bd., Chgo. Presbytery, 1966-68; trustee Presbyn. Homes, W. Clement and Jessie V. Stone Found., U. Chgo. Hosps. Served with M.I. AUS, 1943-46. Mem. ABA, Ill. Bar Assn., Chgo. Bar Assn. (bd. mgrs. 1967-69), Fed. Bar Assn., Chgo. Coun. on Fgn. Rels., Japan Am. Soc. Chgo., Lawyers Club Chgo., Phi Beta Kappa, Sigma Phi. Clubs: Chicago, Glen View (Ill.), Commercial (Chgo.), Mid-Day Club (Chgo.), Economic (Chgo.). Home: 830 Normandy Ln Glenview IL 60025-3210 Office: Bell Boyd & Lloyd 3 First National Pla 70 W Madison St Ste 3200 Chicago IL 60602-4244 Office Phone: 312-372-1121. E-mail: jrhind@bellboyd.com.

RHINE, JOHN E. lawyer; b. Eldorado, Ill., Nov. 12, 1952; s. R.L. and Iris Faye (Harlow) R.; children: Oliver Sampson, Tison Hausser, Julia Eva. BA, So. Ill. U., 1974; JD magna cum laude, U. Ill., 1977. Bar: Ill. 1977, U.S. Dist. Ct. (so. dist.) Ill. 1979, U.S. Ct. Appeals (7th cir.) 1985. Law clk. to justice Ill. Supreme Ct., Springfield, 1977-78; pvt. practice law Mt. Carmel, Ill., 1978-79; ptnr. Rhine, Ernest & Vargo, Mt. Carmel, 1979—. Bd. dirs. Koester Cos., Nat. Land & Mineral Co., Inc., Starlight TV Corp., chmn., 1989-94; vis. prof. law Moscow State Inst. Internat. Rels., 1993, 95. Adv. coun. mineral lands mgmt. U. Evansville (Ind.), 1984-88; active Mt. Carmel Planning Commn., 1986-88; del. Moscow Conf. on Law and Econs., 1990; bd. dirs. Voices Ill. Children, 1990—, chmn. bd. dirs., 1993-96. Mem. Ill. Bar Assn. (mineral law subcom. 1984, law office econs. sect. coun. 1986-93, chmn. 1991-92, mineral law sect. coun. 1993—), Wabash Valley Coll. Found. (trustee, 2002—). Presbyterian. Office: Rhine Ernest & Vargo 631 N Market St Mount Carmel IL 62863-1458 Office Phone: 618-262-8611.

RHINEHARDT, PETER KEVIN, elementary school educator, writer, artist; b. Dover, NH, Feb. 26, 1966; s. Carl Allen and Elizabeth Ann Rhinehardt; divorced; children: Nathaniel, Sadie. BA, U. So. Maine, 1993. Tchr. MSAD 72, Fryberg, Maine, 1995—97, MSAD 61, Bridgeton, Maine, 1997—98; asst. tchr. Falmouth (Maine) Schs., 1998—2000; tchr. Portland (Maine) Pub. Schs., 2000—. Home: 16 Westlawn Rd Portland ME 04103 Office: West Sch 57 Douglass St Portland ME 04102

RHINESMITH, STEPHEN HEADLEY, management consultant; b. Mineola, N.Y., Dec. 13, 1942; s. Homer Kern and Winifred Headley (Long) Rhinesmith; m. Kathleen Alys Law, Aug. 28, 1965; children: Christopher Law, Colin Headley. BA (Baker scholar), Wesleyan U., 1965; M in Pub. and Internat. Affairs, (Heinz fellow), U. Pitts., 1966, PhD (NDEA fellow), 1972. Dir. internat. svcs. McBer and Co., Cambridge, Mass., 1969-71; pres. AFS Intercultural Programs, N.Y.C., 1972-80, 87-89, Holland Am. Cruises, N.Y.C., 1980-82, Moran, Stahl, Boyer, N.Y.C., 1982-84, Rhinesmith & Assocs. Inc., West Chatham, Mass., 1984—; ptnr. CDR Internat., 1998—, Mercer Delta Con., 2004—. Named amb., coord. Pres.'s U.S.-Soviet Exch. Initiative, 1986—87; chmn. dept. orgnl. sociology Moscow State U., 1991—96. Author: (book) Bring Home the World: A Management Guide to Community Leaders of International Programs, 1975, 1985, A Manager's Guide to Globalization: Six Skills for Success in a Changing World, 2d edit., 1996. Mem.: ASTD (chair 1994), Met. Club (Washington). Home and Office: PO Box 1645 West Chatham MA 02669-1645 Office Phone: 503-223-5678. E-mail: SHRglobal@aol.com.

RHOAD, RICHARD E. healthcare executive; s. John E. and Florice F. Rhoad; m. Marlaine J. Walker; children: Scott R., Bradley R., Nicholas W. BS, Ind. U.; MBA, U. Notre Dame. Cert. mem. Am. Coll. Med. Practice Execs., 1995, diplomate Am. Coll. Healthcare Execs., 1995. Sales mgmt. Xerox Corp., Los Angeles, Calif., 1971—82; exec. v.p. and gen. mgr. North Am. Van Lines, Fort Wayne, Ind., 1982—91; healthcare exec. mgmt. Allied Profl. Services, LLC, 1991—2001; ceo Ft. Wayne Orthopaedics, Fort Wayne, Ind., 2001—. Dir. Luth. Hosp., Fort Wayne, Ind. Author: (refereed literature) Strategic Approach to the Income Statement (award Inst. Mgmt. Accts., 2002); contbr. articles Mgmt. Acctg. Quar. Trustee U. St. Francis; coun. mem. Trinity English Luth. Ch.; bd. mem. Early Childhood Alliance, Anthony Wayne Svcs. Mem.: Gulf Harbour Yact & Country Club (corr.), Ft. Wayne Country Club (corr.). R-Conservative. Lutheran. Office: Fort Wayne Orthopaedics 7601 W Jefferson Blvd Fort Wayne IN 46804 E-mail: rrhoad@fwortho.com.

RHOADES, DONALD SCOTT, zoo and botanical park curator, biology professor; b. Madison, Wis., Aug. 15, 1950; s. Albert Leonard and Rosemary Agnes (Patterson) R.; m. Beverly Lynn Grey (div.); children: Aaron Douglas, Amy Cherie; m. Cheryl Jean McCulloch, Mar. 21, 1986; children: Ryan Alexander MacDonald, Amelia Lee MacDonald. BS, No. Ariz. U., 1972, MS, 1976; D of Arts, Idaho State U., 1980. Lectr. in biology Idaho State U., Pocatello, 1978; educator San Diego Zoo, 1980-83; curator of edn. Kansas City Zoo, 1983-87; curator edn. Riverbanks Zoo and Garden, Columbia, 1987—; adj. asst. prof. U. S.C., Columbia, 1992—. Contbr. essays to Riverbanks Mag., 1987—. Mem. exec. bd. Midlands Improving Math. and Sci., Columbia, 1993—; co-founder AMAZE, 1988. Fellow Am. Zoo and Aquarium Assn. (profl., mem. edn. com. 1990-92, studbook keeper for hawk-headed parrot 1993—); mem. Am. Assn. Bot. Gardens and Arboreta, Internat. Assn. Zoo Educators, Explorers Club. Office: Riverbanks Zool Park Bot Garden 500 Wildlife Pkwy Columbia SC 29210-8093 Home: 511 S Chester St Gastonia NC 28052-4021 E-mail: drhoades@riverbanks.org.

RHOADES, JOHN SKYLSTEAD, SR., federal judge; b. 1925; m. Carmel Rhoades; children: Mark, John, Matthew, Peter, Christopher. AB, Stanford U., 1948; JD, U. Calif., Hastings, 1951. Prosecuting atty. City of San Diego, 1955-56, dep. city atty., 1956-57; pvt. practice San Diego, 1957-60; ptnr. Rhoades, Hollywood & Neil, San Diego, 1960-85; judge U.S. Dist. Ct. (so. dist.) Calif., San Diego, 1985—. With USN, 1943-46. Office: US Dist Ct 940 Front St San Diego CA 92101-8994

RHOADES, KITTY, state legislator; b. Hudson, Wis., Apr. 7, 1951; m. Frank Rhoades; 3 children. BA, U. Wis., River Falls, 1973; MA, Ill. State U., 1978. Exec. dir. Hudson C. of C., 1991—96; pres. Suburban C. of C., 1996—; sml. bus. owner; classroom tchr.; mem. Wis. State Assembly, Madison, 1998—, chair aging and long-term care com., mem. colls. and univs. com., mem. edn. com., mem. fin. instns. com., mem. joint legis. coun. Mem. U. Wis. River Falls Alumni Found.; mem. pres.'s adv. coun. Century Coll.; mem. pastoral coun. St. Patrick's Ch.; bd. dirs. Minn. C. of C. Exec. Assn., United Way. Mem.: Rotary. Republican. Roman Catholic. Office: State Capitol Bldg Rm 321 E PO Box 8953 Madison WI 53708-8953 Address: 708 4th St Hudson WI 54016

RHOADES, M. STEPHEN, career officer; m. Vivian Rhoades; children: Whitney, Jessica, Hunter, Taylor. B in Engring., U. Fla., 1973, M in Engring., 1980; grad., U.S. Army Command Coll., Indsl. Coll. Armed Forces, Nat. Def. U. Commd. U.S. Army Corps Engrs., 1973, advanced through grades to col., platoon leader, bn. staff officer, co. comdr., TUSEG area engr., with hdqrs. USAREUR, exec. officer 39th Engr. Bn., brigade ops. officer 136th Engr. Brigade, brigade exec. officer 136th Engr. Brigade, comdr. 3d Engr. Bn., 24th Inf. Divsn., with dept. Army Staff, Office Chief Engrs., comdr. Engr. Brigade, 1st Inf. Divsn., chief of staff U.S. Army Engr. Ctr., 1997—99; CEO The Board of Commissioners of the Metropolitan District Commission, 2003—.

RHOADES, MARGARET, health care association executive; MA, Wellesley Coll.; PhD, Georgetown U. Rsch. analyst U.S. Dept. State Bur. Intelligence and Rsch., 1962-67; assoc. prodr. documentaries NBC News, 1971-77; asst. commr. pub. affairs U.S. Office Edn.; assoc. commr. pub. affairs Social Security Adminstrn.; pub. affairs dir. Brookings Instn., 1981-86; exec. dir. Nat. Leadership Commn., 1986-90, Nat. Coalition on Health Care, 1990—. Office: Nat Coalition on Health Care 1200 G St NW Ste 760 Washington DC 20005-3814 E-mail: info@nchc.org.

RHOADES, RODNEY ALLEN, physiologist, educator; b. Greenville, Ohio, Jan. 5, 1939; s. John H. and Floris L. Rhoades; m. Judith Ann Brown, Aug. 6, 1961; children: Annelisa, Kirsten. BS, Miami U., 1961; MS, 1963; PhD, Ohio State U., 1966. Asst. prof. Pa. State U., State College, 1966-72, assoc. prof., 1972-75; rsch. scientist NIH, Bethesda, Md., 1975-76; prof. Ind. U. Sch. Medicine, Indpls., 1976-81, 81—, chmn., 1981—2003. Dir. Indpls. Ctr. for Advanced Rsch. Author: Physiology, 1984; contbr. articles to profl. jours. Fellow NASA, 1964-66; recipient Rsch. Career Devel. award NIH, 1975-80. Mem. Am. Physiol. Soc, AHA, Am. Thoracic Soc., Biophysics Soc., Sigma Xi. Home: 1768 Spruce Dr Carmel IN 46033-9025 Office: Ind U Sch Medicine 635 Barnhill Dr Indianapolis IN 46202-5126

RHOADES DUMLER, KELLY J. medical educator; d. Irving Dale and Thora Rhoades; m. Jeffrey Dumler, July 24, 1993; 1 child, Allison Louise. BA, Ctrl. Mich. U., 1985; MS, Mich. State U., 1987, PhD, 1994. Dir. bereavement GranCare Hospice, Livonia, Mich., 1996—98; assoc. prof., chair dept. hospice edn. Madonna U., 1995—. Avocations: photography, writing, calligraphy. Office: Madonna U 36600 Schoolcraft Rd Livonia MI 48150 E-mail: krhoades@madonna.edu.

RHOADS, GEORGE GRANT, medical epidemiologist; b. Phila., Feb. 11, 1940; s. Jonathan Evans and Teresa (Folin) R.; m. Frances Ann Secker, June 5, 1965; children: Thomas C., James E. MD, Harvard U., 1965; MPH, U. Hawaii, 1970. Intern Hosp. of U. Pa., Phila., 1965-66, resident in internal medicine, 1966-68; resident in preventive medicine U. Hawaii Sch. Pub. Health, 1968-71; epidemiologist Japan-Hawaii Cancer Study, Honolulu, 1974-75; assoc. prof. U. Hawaii, Honolulu, 1974-79, chair dept. pub. health sci., 1978-81, dir. gen. preventive medicine, 1978-81, prof. pub. health, 1979-82; chief epidemiology br. Nat. Inst. Child Health and Human Devel./NIH, Bethesda, Md., 1982-89; prof., dir. grad program in pub. health U. Medicine and Dentistry N.J.-Robert Wood Johnson Med. Sch., Piscataway, 1989-2000; assoc. dean UMDNJ Sch. Pub. Health, 2000—. Contbr. more than 180 articles on the epidemiology of non-infectious diseases to profl. jours. Recipient Dirs. award NIH, 1987, EEO award NICHD, 1984. Fellow Am. Coll. Physicians; mem. Am. Epidemiol. Soc. Mem. Soc. Of Friends. Achievements include research on the protective effect of high density Lipoprotein in the blood against development of heart attacks. Office: Environ and Occupl Health Scis Inst 170 Freinghuysen Rd Piscataway NJ 08854

RHOADS, GERALDINE EMELINE, editor, consultant; b. Phila., Jan. 29, 1914; d. Lawrence Dry and Alice Fegley (Rice) R. AB, Bryn Mawr Coll., 1935. Publicity asst. Bryn Mawr (Pa.) Coll., 1935-37; asst. Internat. Students House, Phila., 1937-39; mng. editor The Woman mag., N.Y.C., 1939-42; editor Life Story mag., 1942-45, Today's Woman mag., N.Y.C., 1945-52, Today's Family Mag., N.Y.C., 1952-53; lectr. Columbia U., 1954-56; assoc. editor Readers Digest, 1954-55; producer NBC, 1955-56; assoc. editor Ladies Home Jour., 1956-62, mng. editor, 1962-63; exec. editor McCall's mag., 1963-66; editor Woman's Day mag., 1966-82, editorial dir., 1982-84, Woman's Day Resource Center, 1984-89; v.p. Woman's Day mag., 1972—84, CBS Consumer Publs., 1977-84; cons. Woman's Day, N.Y.C., 1989-91. Editorial cons., dir. Nat. Mag. Awards, 1991-94. Author: (with others) Woman's Day Help Book, 1988. Mem. journalism awards com. James Beard Found., 1993-2001. Recipient award for profl. achievement Diet Workshop Internat., 1977; Elizabeth Cutter Morrow award YWCA Salute to Women in Bus., 1977; Recipient Econ. Equity award Women's Equity Action League, 1982; March of Dimes Women Editor's citation, 1982 Mem.: Women's Forum (bd. dirs. 1985—87), Advt. Women in N.Y. (bd. govs. 1983—85, 2d v.p. 1985—87, 1st v.p. 1987—89, bd. dirs. 1989—90, Pres.'s award 1987), N.Y. Women in Comm. (Matrix award 1975), Am. Soc. Mag. Editors (chmn. exec. com. 1971—73), Fashion Group (bd. govs. 1977—79, 1987—88, chmn. bd. govs. 1978—80, treas. bd. govs. 1983—85, bd. dirs. Found. 1980—81), Nat. Press Club (dir.), Bryn Mawr Coll. Alumni Assn. (bd. dirs. 1989—94), Turtle Bay Assn. (bd. dirs. 1989—92), Literacy Vols. of N.Y.C. (bd. dirs. 1986—93), YWCA Acad. Women Achievers, Bryn Mawr Club of N.Y.C. (bd. dirs. 1994—2000), Women's City Club of N.Y. (bd. dirs. 1996—, chair comm. 2001—). Home: 185 W End Ave Apt 21A New York NY 10023-5548 Office Phone: 212-873-6288. Personal E-mail: rhoadsge@aol.com.

RHOADS, JAMES BERTON, archivist, former government official, consultant, educator; b. Sioux City, Iowa, Sept. 17, 1928; s. James Harrison and Mary (Keenan) R.; m. S. Angela Handy, Aug. 12, 1947; children: Cynthia Patrice Neven, James Berton, Marcia Marie MacKellar. Student, Southwestern Jr. Coll., 1946-47, Union Coll., Lincoln, Neb., 1947-48; BA, U. Calif.-Berkeley, 1950, MA, 1952; PhD, Am. U., 1965. With GSA-Nat. Archives and Records Service, Washington, 1952-79, asst. archivist for civil archives, 1965, dept. archivist U.S., 1966-68, archivist U.S., 1968-79; chmn. Nat. Archives Trust Fund Bd., 1968-79; chmn. adminstrv. com. Fed. Register, 1968-79; chmn. Nat. Hist. Publs. and Records Commn., 1968-79; mem. Fed. Council on Arts and Humanities, 1970-79; pres. Rhoads Assos. Internat., 1980-84; dir. grad. program in archives and records mgmt. Western Wash. U., Bellingham, 1984-94, prof. history, 1987-94, dir. Ctr. for Pacific N.W. studies, 1994-97; prof. emeritus, 1994—. Trustee Woodrow Wilson Internat. Center for Scholars, 1969-79; v.p. Intergovtl. Coun. UNESCO Info. Program, 1977-79; mem. adv. bd. Wash. State Hist. Records, 1990-97. Recipient Meritorious and Disting. Service awards GSA, 1966, 68, 79 Fellow Soc. Am. Archivists (pres. 1974-75); mem. Internat. Coun. Archives (pres. 1976-79), Am. Antiquarian Soc., Am. Coun. Learned Socs. (com. Soviet-Am. archival coop. 1986-91), Mass. Hist. Soc. (corr.), Wash. State Hist. Soc. (trustee 1986-95), Acad. Cert. Archivists (pres. 1992-94).

RHOADS, MICHAEL DENNIS, sales executive; b. Vinton, Iowa, June 25, 1949; s. Lloyd and Marilyn Mae (Appleton) Rhoads. BS in Indsl. Edn., Iowa State U., 1973; MBA, York Coll. of Pa., 1984. Order detailer, sales rep. Fisher Controls Inc., Marshalltown, Iowa, 1973-75; inside sales engr. Proconex, King

of Prussia, Pa., 1975-79, outside sales engr. York, Pa., 1979-85, br. mgr., 1985-87, v.p. process instrumentaion sales King of Prussia, Pa., 1987-90, v.p., sales mgr., 1990—, sr. v.p., 1992—. Instr. Continuing Adult Edn., Marshalltown, 1973—75. Youth group leader Meth. Ch., Center Square, Pa., 1977—79. With USN, 1968—70, Vietnam. Mem.: VFW, Instrument Soc. Am. (v.p. 1984—86, pres. 1986—87, Best Sect. Pres. award 1987, Old Shoe award 1990), Am. Legion. Lutheran. Avocations: woodworking, carpentry, hunting, boating, sailing. Home: 205 Claremont Ln Downingtown PA 19335-1563 Office: Proconex 101 Enterprise Dr Royersford PA 19468 Office Phone: 610-495-1835. Personal E-mail: mrhoads835@aol.com.

RHOADS, PAUL KELLY, lawyer; b. La Grange, Ill., Sept. 4, 1940; s. Herbert Graves and Mary Margaret (Gurrie) R.; m. Katheryn Virginia Reissaus, Sept. 14, 1963; children: Elizabeth S. R. Saline, Katheryn B.R. Meek, Julia C. Rhoads Brenneman. BA, Washington & Lee U., 1962; JD, Loyola U., Chgo., 1967. Bar: Ill. 1967, U.S. Dist. Ct. (no. dist.) Ill. 1967, U.S. Tax Ct. 1980. Trust officer 1st Nat. Bank Chgo., 1963-69; with Schiff Hardin & Waite, Chgo., 1969-98, ptnr., 1973-98; sole practitioner Western Springs, Ill., 1999—. Author: Starting a Private Foundation, 1993, Managing a Private Foundation, 1997; contbr. articles to profl. jours. and chpts. to books. Trustee Ill. Inst. Tech., 1985-95, Western Springs (Ill.) Hist. Soc., 1983-92, Philanthropy Roundtable, Washington, 1992-2000; bd. dirs. Cyrus Tang Scholarship Found., 1984-91, McKay Enterprises, Chgo., 1981-2002; bd. overseers Ill. Inst. Tech. Chgo.-Kent Coll. Law, 1985-95; pres., bd. dirs. Grover Hermann Found., Chgo., 1984—; sec., bd. dirs. Western Springs Svc. Club, 1976-86; sec. Vandivort Properties, Inc., Cape Girardeau, Mo., 1990-2002; mem. adv. com. estate, tax and fin. planning Loyola U., 1986 92; adv. com. Thomas A. Roe Inst. for Econ. Policy Studies, Heritage Found., 1989—. Fellow Am. Coll. Trust and Estate Coun.; mem. Ill. State Bar Assn., Chgo. Bar Assn., Portage Lake Yacht Club (Onekama, Mich.) (commodore 1988, bd. dirs. 1985-89), Heathlands Golf Club (Onekama). Republican. Avocations: sailing, golf, tennis. Office: 1000 Hillgrove Ave Western Springs IL 60558-1420 E-mail: paulkrhoads@ameritech.net.

RHOADS, REBECCA R. electronics executive; BS, MS, Calif. Poly. U.; MA in Bus. Mgmt., UCLA. With Gen. Dynamics, 1979—96; v.p. IT, electronics systems Raytheon Co., Lexington, Mass., 1997—2001, v.p., chief info. officer, 2001—. Office: Raytheon Co 141 Spring St Lexington MA 02421

RHOADS, ROBERT K. lawyer, retail executive; b. 1954; BA, U. Ark, 1976, JD, 1980. Bar: Ark. 1980. Asst. gen. counsel Wal-Mart Stores Inc., Bentonville, Ark., 1980-85, gen. counsel, sec., 1985-88, sr. v.p., gen. counsel, sec., 1988—2002. Office: Hall Estill Hardwick Gable Golden & Nelson PC One East Center St Fayetteville AR 72701

RHOADS, STEVEN ERIC, political science educator; b. Abington, Pa., May 12, 1939; s. John Reginald and Barbara Ann (Dugan) Rhoads; m. Diana Cabanis Akers, May 17, 1944; children: Christopher, Nicholas, John. BA, Princeton U., 1961; MPA, Cornell U., 1965, PhD, 1972. Mem. staff Office Mgmt. and Budget, Washington, 1965—66; asst. prof. dept. politics U. Va., Charlottesville, 1970—76, assoc. prof., 1977—86, prof., 1986—. Author: Policy Analysis in the Federal Aviation Administration, 1974, Valuing Life: Public Policy Dilemmas, 1980, The Economist's View of the World: Government, Markets and Public Policy, 1985, Incomparable Worth: Pay Equity Meets the Market, 1993, Taking Sex Differences Seriously, 2004; contbr. articles to profl. jours. Lt. (j.g.) USN, 1961—63. Fellow, Slkoan NEH, Inst. Ednl. Affairs, Bradley Found., Olin Found. Mem.: Assn. Pub. Policy and Mgmt., Am. Polit. Sci. Assn. Home: 3190 Dundee Rd Earlysville VA 22936-9621 Office: U Va Dept Politics Cabell Hall 232 Charlottesville VA 22903 Office Phone: 434-924-7866.

RHODA, JANICE TUCKER, writer, educator, musician; b. Lynn, Mass., Mar. 24, 1955; d. Robert Samuel and Cecilia Mary Ann (DiTroia) Tucker; m. David Michael Cleary, Jan. 21, 2001. BMus, New Eng. Conservatory of Music, Boston, 1989; Suzuki Tchr. Tng., Ithaca (N.Y.) Coll., 1980—81. Pvt. violin tchr., 1975—; violin tchr. Wakefield Pub. Schs., 1979—80, Newton Pub. Schs., 1979—81, All-Newton Music Sch., 1980—84, McGill U., 1982, 1983, Boston Ctr. for Adult Edn., 1992—95, 1997—98, New Eng. Conservatory of Music, Boston, 2000, Cambridge Ctr. for Adult Edn., Mass., 2003—; dir., tchr. Suzuki program Longy Sch. Music, Cambridge, Mass., 1980—87, Brookline Music Sch., Mass., 1992—94; clinician The ABCs of Strings, 1998—, Royal Conservatory Music, Toronto, 2004, Vancouver (Can.) Acad. Music, 2004. Author: (book series) The ABCs of Strings; concertmistress North-Eastern Dist. Orch., 1972—73, Mass. All-State Orch., 1972. Mem.: Nat. Assn. for Music Edn., Am. String Tchrs. Assn., Suzuki Assn. of Ams., Mu Phi Epsilon. Office: The ABCs of Strings PO Box 400428 Cambridge MA 02140 Personal E-mail: abcsofstrings@comcast.net.

RHODE, ALFRED SHIMON, business consultant, finance educator; b. Vienna, July 31, 1928; came to U.S., 1940, naturalized, 1949; s. Aron and Olga (Schwarz) Rothkirch; m. Phyllis Mazur, Dec. 28, 1959; children: Yael, Tamar, Yvette, Liane. BCE, CUNY, 1950; MEA, George Washington U., 1959; PhD, Am. U., 1973. Registered profl. engr., Md. Engr. Bur. of Reclamation, Sacramento, 1950—52; various engring. positions U.S. Govt., 1954—63; head logistics rsch. Navy Supply Sys. Command, Washington, 1963—68; head support forces, manpower and logistics br. Navy Program Planning Office, Washington, 1968—75; sr. v.p. nat. security analysis and warfare support group Info. Spectrum, Inc., Arlington, Va., 1976—89, cons., 1989—92; professorial lectr. George Washington U., Washington, 1969—75; adj. faculty Sch. Mgmt. George Mason U., Fairfax, Va., 1990—2002; adj. faculty Sch. Bus. Adminstrn. Georgetown U., Washington, 1998—. Exec. dir. Montgomery County Retail Security and Loss Prevention Assn. Contbr. articles to profl. jours. Capt. USAF, 1952-54. Congl. fellow, 1962. Fellow Mil. Ops. Rsch. Soc. (1st v.p., dir.); mem. Inst. Ops. Rsch. and Mgmt. Scis. (chmn. mil. applications sect.), Washington Inst. for Ops. Rsch. and the Mgmt. Scis. Home: 8305 Fox Run Potomac MD 20854-2576 E-mail: arhode@comcast.net.

RHODE, DEBORAH LYNN, law educator; b. Jan. 29, 1952; BA, Yale U., 1974, JD, 1977. Bar: D.C. 1977, Calif. 1981. Law clk. to judge U.S. Ct. Appeals (2d cir.), N.Y.C., 1977-78; law clk. to Hon. Justice Thurgood Marshall U.S. Supreme Ct., D.C., 1978-79; asst. prof. law Stanford (Calif.) U., 1979-82, assoc. prof., 1982-85, prof., 1985—; dir. Inst. for Rsch. on Women and Gender, 1986-90, Keck Ctr. of Legal Ethics and The Legal Profession, 1994—2003; sr. counsel jud. com. Ho. of Reps., Washington, 1998. Trustee Yale U., 1983-89; pres. Assn. Am. Law Schs., 1998; Ernest W. McFarland prof. Stanford Law Sch., 1997—; sr. counsel com. on the jud. U.S. Ho. of Reps., 1998; dir. Stanford Ctr. on Ethics. Author: Justice and Gender, 1989, (with Geoffrey Hazard) the Legal Profession: Responsibility and Regulation, 3d edit., 1993, (with Annette Lawson) The Politics of Pregnancy: Adolescent Sexuality and Public Policy, 1993, (with David Luban) Legal Ethics, 2001, (with Barbara Allen Babcock, Ann E. Freedman, Susan Deller Ross, Wendy Webster Williams, Rhonda Copelon, and Nadine H. Taub) Sex Discrimination and the Law, 1997, Speaking of Sex, 1997, Professional Responsibility: Ethics by the Pervasive Method, 1998, In the Interests of Justice, 2000 (with Geoffrey Hazard, Jr.) Professional Responsibility and Regulation, 2002; editor: Theoretical Perspectives on Sexual Difference, 1990, Ethics in Practice, 2000, The Difference Difference Makes: Women and Leadership, 2002, Access to Justice, 2004; contbr. articles to profl. jours. Mem.: ABA (chmn. commn. on women 2000—02). Office: Stanford U Law Sch Crown Quadrangle Stanford CA 94305

RHODE, EDWARD ALBERT, veterinary medicine educator, veterinary cardiologist; b. Amsterdam, N.Y., July 25, 1926; s. Edward A. and Katherine (Webb) R.; m. Dolores Bangert, 1955; children: David E., Peter R., Paul W., Robert M., Catherine E. DVM, Cornell U., 1947. Diplomate Am. Coll. Veterinary Internal Medicine. Prof. emeritus vet. medicine U. Calif., Davis, 1964—, chmn. dept. vet. medicine, 1968-71; assoc. dean instrn. U. Calif. Sch. Vet. Medicine, Davis, 1971-81, dean, 1982-91. Mem. AAAS, Nat. Acad. Practices, Am. Coll. Vet. Internal Medicine, Am. Vet. Medicine Assn., Basic Sci. Coun., Am. Heart Assn., Am. Acad. Vet. Cardiology, Am. Physiol. Soc., Calif. Vet. Medicine Assn. Office: U Calif Sch Vet Med Davis CA 95616

RHODE, KIM, Olympic athlete; b. El Monte, CA, July 16; Recipient Bronze medal in women's skeet 1994 USASNC, bronze medal women's double trap 1995 Seoul World Cup, team Gold medal skeet, team Bronze medal double trap 1995 World Shotgun Championships, Gold medal women's double trap 1995 U.S. Olympic Festival, Gold medal women's double trap Olympic Games, Atlanta, 1996; winner Doubletrap Champion USA Shooting Nat. Championships, 1997.Spokewoman for WPRO 7 Guncleaner & Snake Oil. Mem. Safari Club Internat., Women's Sports Shooting Found. Avocations: skiing, hunting.

RHODES, ALAN CHARLES, minister; b. Plattsburgh, N.Y., July 25, 1951; s. Charles Oliver and Lillian Mary (Cromie) R.; m. Holly C. Craver, June 14, 1975 (div. June 1987); m. Nancy Lichtenhan, June 18, 1988. BA, Lycoming Coll., Williamsport, Pa., 1973; MDiv, Boston U., 1976; DMin, Bangor (Maine) Theol. Sem., 1997. Ordained to ministry United Meth. Ch. as deacon, 1974, as elder, 1977. Assoc. pastor Shenendehowa United Meth. Ch., Clifton Park, N.Y., 1976-79; pastor Ft. Plain (N.Y.) and Freysbush United Meth. Chs., 1979-83, St. Paul's United Meth. Ch., Castleton-on-Hudson, N.Y., 1983-87, Grace United Meth. Ch., Ravena, N.Y., 1987-98, North Main St. United Meth. Ch., Gloversville, NY, 1998—2002, Mechanicville (N.Y.) United Meth. Ch., 2002—. Trustee Troy Ann. Conf., 1993—, mem. bd. ordained ministry Troy Conf., 1996-2004, bd. dirs. Captain Youth and Family Svcs., Inc. Founder, former co-chair R.C.S. Task Force Against Domestic Violence; chair Fulton County Domestic Violence Task Force, 1998—2002; mem. Gloversville Ethics Bd., 2000—02; mem., v.p. Gloversville Coun. Chs., 1998—2002; bd. dirs. Mechanicville (N.Y.) Cmty. Ctr. Mem.: Rotary Club (pres. Champlain Canal 2004—). Republican. Home: 148 S 2d Ave Mechanicville NY 12118-2200 Office: Mechanicville United Meth Ch 7 N Main St PO Box 429 Mechanicville NY 12118-2200 E-mail: anrhodes@telenet.net.

RHODES, ALICE GRAHAM, lawyer; b. Phila., June 15, 1941; d. Peter Graham III and Fannie Isadora (Bennett) Graham; m. Charles Milton Rhodes, Oct. 14, 1971 (div. Apr. 21, 1997); children: Helen, Carla, Shauna. BS, East Stroudsburg U. Pa., 1962; MS, U. Pa., 1966, LLB, 1969, JD, 1970, cert. program exec. adminstrn. Bar: N.Y. 1970, U.S. Dist. Ct. (so. and ea. dists.) N.Y. 1971, U.S. Ct. Appeals (2d cir.) 1971, Ky. 1983, U.S. Dist. Ct. (ea. dist.) Ky. 1985. Staff atty. Harlem Assertion Rights, Mobilization for Youth Office Econ. Opportunity, N.Y.C., 1969-70, coord. Cmty. Action Legal Svcs., 1970-72; assoc. dir. in charge of civil representation HUD Model Cities Cmty. Law Offices, N.Y.C., 1972-73; resource assoc. Commn. on Edn. & Employoment of Women, N.C. Dept. Adminstrn., Raleigh, 1975; mgr. policies and procedures Div. for Youth, N.C. Dept. Human Resources, Raleigh, 1976; in-house counsel, petroleum transactional atty. Ashland, Inc. (formerly Ashland Oil, Inc.), 1980-82; corp. atty. core group Ashland, Inc., 1985-87, 88-91; mem. Ashland City Commn. Human Rights, 1993-99; mem. bd. regents Ea. Ky. U., 1994-2001; exec. bd., chmn. internal affairs com., academic affairs, 1997-98; asst. county atty. Jefferson County, 1999—2000. Mem. Property Valuation Appeals Commn., 1994; cons. pub. mem. selection and performance stds. review bd. Fgn. Svc., U.S. Dept. State, 1995, Fgn. Agrl. Svc. USDA, 1997; prison program planner, cons. N.Y. City Dept. Corrections, 1971; lectr. N.Y.C. Corrections Acad., Riker's, 1971; lectr. juvenile justice N.C. Law Enforcement Acad., Salemburg, 1976. Mem. usher bd. New Hope Bapt. Ch., Ashland, 1980-94; bd. dirs. YWCA Ashland, 1983-84, Ashland Heritage Pk. Commn., 1983-85; bd. dirs., budget com. United Way, Greenup County, Ky., Ashland, 1988-92; driver Meals on Wheels, 1983-91; vol. Am. Heart Assn., 1982-91; bd. dirs. Our Lady of Bellefonte Hosp. Found. Franciscan Sisters of the Poor, Ky. Health System, 1996-99; mem. adv. com. task force post secondary edn. Gov. of Ky.; bd. dirs. exec. com. Boyd County Dem. Women, 1996-2000; mem. presdl. search com. Ea. Ky. U., 1997-98, Ky. Gov.'s Conf. on Postsecondady Edn., 1999. Recipient Cmty. Svc. award Queens Community Corp., N.Y.C., 1972, Ashland C.C., 1986, Cmty. Svc. award NAACP, Ky.; NSF fellow, 1964, 65,; faculty friends of Penn scholar U. Pa., 1966-69, Reginald Heber Smith postgrad. fellow cmty. law, 1969-71; named to Hon. Order of Ky. Cols., 1989. Fellow Ky. Bar Found.; mem. AAUW (bd. dirs. Phila. chpt. 1963-65), Nat. Bar Assn., N.Y. Bar, Ky. Bar Assn. (mem. edn. law, corp. house counsel, law sects.), Pilot Club (exec. bd. Ashland 1983), Links, Inc., Penn Club, Assn. Gov. Bds. Colls. and Univs., Pyramid Club of Phila. Democrat. Avocations: interior decorating, sports, dance, gourmet cooking, gardening. Home: PO Box 12408 Philadelphia PA 19151 Address: 658 N 65th St Philadelphia PA 19151

RHODES, ALLEN FRANKLIN, engineering executive; b. Estherville, Iowa, Oct. 3, 1924; m. Carol Haisler, 1962; children: James Fleming, Stephen Haisler. BSME, Villanova U., 1947; ML, U. Houston, 1950. Reg. profl. engr., Tex. Asst. dir. engring. adminstrn. Hughes Tool Co., Houston, 1947-52; pres. McEvoy Co., Houston, 1952-63; v.p. engring. & rsch. Rockwell Mfg. Co., Pitts., 1963-70; v.p. corp. planning & devel. ACF Industries, N.Y.C., 1971-73; pres., CEO McEvoy Oilfield Equipment Co., Houston, 1974-79; exec. v.p., CEO Goldrus Marine Drilling, Houston, 1979-82; pres., CEO Warren Oilfield Svc., Houston, 1981-82, Anglo Energy, N.Y.C., 1983-86, Grippper Inc., Houston, 1987-90; v.p., CFO Hydrotech Sys. Inc., Houston, 1991; cons. Allen F. Rhodes, Bus. Advisor & Consulting Engr., Houston, 1991—, Silver Fox Advisors, 1986—. Chmn. Com. Dept. Transp. Gas Pipelin Safety Std., 1969-73; dir. Keystone Internat., 1980-97, Triten Corp., 1980—, Rawson-Koenig, 1986-98, S.W. Rsch. Inst., 1989—, Tex. Microsystem, 1989-92, Houston Humane Soc., 1999—; adj. prof. mech. engring. U. Houston, 2001-. Dir. T&B Lehman Animal Shelter, Inc., 2002—. Recipient Charles Russ Richards Meml. award, 1987, Howard Conley medal Am. Nat. Std. Inst., 1980. Fellow ASME (past pres., Robert Henry Thurston award 1978), Inst. Mech. Engrs. (Gt. Britain); mem. Nat. Acad. Engring., Soc. Petroleum Engrs., Am. Petroleum Inst. Home and Office: 8720 Memorial Dr Houston TX 77024-7011

RHODES, ANNE GREGORY (PANNY RHODES), state legislator; b. Durham, N.C., July 30, 1942; m. James Thomas Rhodes; children: James Thomas Jr., Anne Gregory. AB in Math., Duke U., 1963. Mem. Va. State Legis., 1992—, mem. appropriations com., mem. health welfare & insts. com., mem. sci. & tech. com. Angler B. Duke scholar. Republican. Episcopalian. Office: Gen Assembly Bldg PO Box 406 Richmond VA 23218-0406

RHODES, ARTHUR DELANO, benefits administrator; b. Philadelphia, Miss., Nov. 26, 1960; s. A.D. and Mary (McNair) R.; m. Angela Marie Jolly, May 21, 1988. AA, Miss. Delta Jr. Coll., Moorhead, 1980; BA in Polit. Sci., Millsaps Coll., 1982; JD, U. Miss., 1985. Bar: Miss. 1985, U.S. Dist. Ct. (no. and so. dist.) Miss. 1985. Intern asst. dist. atty. Dist. Atty's Office, Hernando, Miss., 1985; counsel Child Support Unit, Dept. of Human Svcs., Brookhaven, Miss., 1985-87; assoc. Prewitt & Bradley, Jackson, Miss., 1987-88; chief of staff Congressman Mike Parker, Washington, 1988-98; pres., CEO The Benefits Bd., Inc., Cleveland, Tenn., 1999—. Republican. Mem. Ch. of God. Avocations: travel, reading. Home: 2014 Woodchase Way NE Cleveland TN 37311-1461 Office: The Benefits Bd PO Box 4608 Cleveland TN 37320-4608 Office Phone: 423-478-7131.

RHODES, BETTY FLEMING, rehabilitation services professional, nurse; b. Franklin, Pa., Nov. 28, 1920; d. John and Twyla Odella (Callen) Fleming; m. Donald Muir Cain, Dec. 31, 1952 (div.); m. Lee Chester Rhodes, June 23, 1962 (dec. Apr. 1997). RN, Allegheny Gen. Hosp., Pitts., 1942. Lic. phys. therapist, Pa. Phys. therapist Office of D.T. Watson, Pitts., 1947, Ky. Soc. for Crippled Children, Louisville, 1947-51, St. Anthony Hosp., Louisville, 1953-78. Nurse U.S. Army, 1943-45; capt. Army Nurse Corps, 1951-52. Decorated Bronze Star. Mem. Am. Phys Therapy Assn. (pres. Ky. chpt.). Roman Catholic. Home: Providence Retirement Home 4915 Charleston Rd Apt 312 New Albany IN 47150

RHODES, DAISY CHUN, writer, researcher, oral historian; b. Kahuku, Hawaii, Nov. 16, 1933; d. Pyung Chan Chun and Shin Ai Park; children: Joseph, Carmella, Thomas Francese. BA in Creative Writing, Eckerd Coll., 1995. Info. specialist Reconstrn. Devel. Corp., Washington, 1970; specialist indigent funding George Washington U. Hosp., Washington, 1971-74; mgr. hosp. assistance Alexandria (Va.) Hosp., 1975-79; asst. editor Employee Futures Rsch., Luray, Va., 1980-84; editor Inside Negotiations, Rochester, N.Y., 1985-87, Educators Negotiating Svc., New Port Richey, Fla., 1987-89; novelist, writer New Port Richey, 1989-95; rschr., oral historian Honolulu, 1994; writer Colorado Springs, 1995—; rschr., cons. Donna Ladd, Writer, Colorado Springs, 1996. Rschr., cons. Donna Ladd, Writer, Colorado Springs, 1996; presenter Asian Studies Conf., Honolulu; presenter scholarly and abstract Korean Picture Brides We. Asian Studies Conf., Boulder, Colo., 1997; lectr. Ctr. for Korean Studies U. Hawaii, 1998. Author: Forever Long-Never End, 1990, Wahaiawa Red Dirt, 1991, At Crossroads of Inspiration, 1993, Shirley Temple Feet, 1993, Remembering the Fallen, 1994, Passages to Paradise: Early Korean Immigrant Narratives from Hawaii, 1998; author: (play) I Know About Olympus, 1993; author: Eye of the Dragon, 1994 (finalist Hemingway 1st Novel Competition, 1994); author: (scholarly and abstract) How Oral History of the First Koreans in America Advances Archival Research, 1996; author: My Father's Voice, Echoes Upon Echoes, 2002, A Place of Noise, 2003. Pres. Colorado Springs Friends of Aquatics, 1997—; bd. dirs. All Souls Unitarian Ch.; mem. adv. bd. City of Colorado Springs Pks. and Recreation, 2004—. Recipient Work Study award for profls., Rotary Internat. Found., South Korea, 1998—99. Mem.: Korean Am. Women's Soc. Greater Washington (pres. 1983 84, bd. dirs., Commendation), Korea Soc., Assn. for Asian Studies, West Pasco Kiwanis (pres. 1990—92). Home: 1912 Eastlake Blvd # 502 Colorado Springs CO 80910 E-mail: dyschun@msn.com.

RHODES, DAMIAN, professional hockey player; b. St. Paul, May 28, 1969; Goaltender Toronto Maple Leafs, 1990—96, New York Islanders, 1996, Ottawa Senators, 1996—99, Atlanta Thrashers, 1999—. Mem. St. John's Leads Am. Hockey League, 1992—93. Avocations: music, golf. Office: Atlanta Thrashers 1 Cnn Ctr NW # 13S Atlanta GA 30303-2762

RHODES, DAVID J. academic administrator; Pres. Sch. Visual Arts, 1978—. Office: Sch Visual Arts Office of Pres 209 E 23rd St New York NY 10010-3994

RHODES, DONALD ROBERT, musicologist, retired electrical engineer; b. Detroit, Dec. 31, 1923; s. Donald Eber and Edna Mae (Fulmer) R.; children: Joyce R. Holbert, Jane E., Roger C., Diane R. Herran. BEE, Ohio State U., 1945, MEE, 1948, PhD, 1953. Research assoc. Ohio State U., Columbus, 1945-54; research engr. Cornell Aero. Lab., Buffalo, 1954-57; head basic research dept. Radiation, Inc., Orlando, Fla., 1957-61, sr. scientist Melbourne, Fla., 1961-66; Univ. prof. N.C. State U., Raleigh, 1966-94, univ. prof. emeritus, 1994—. Author: Introduction to Monopulse, 1959, 2d edit., 1980, Synthesis of Planar Antenna Sources, 1974, A Reactance Theorem, 1977. Co-founder Central Fla. Community Orch., Winter Park, 1961, pres., 1961-62. Recipient Benjamin G. Lamme medal Ohio State U., 1975; Eminent Engr. award Tau Beta Pi, 1976; named to N.C. State U. Acad. Outstanding Tchrs., 1980. Fellow AAAS, IEEE (John T. Bolljahn award 1963, pres. Antennas and Propagation Soc. 1969); mem. Am. Musicological Soc. Home: Apt 101 625 Centennial Pkwy Raleigh NC 27606-3255 Office: PO Box 7911 Raleigh NC 27695-7911

RHODES, DORIS CHANEY, freelance/self-employed secondary school educator; b. Ft. Worth, Sept. 10, 1942; d. R. C. and Louis (Churchill) Chaney; m. Larry Williams, Jan. 19, 1969 (div. 1975); m. King Rhodes, 1981. BS, Bishop Coll., 1968; MS, Calif. State U., Hayward, 1975. Cert. tchr. Tex., Calif. Tchr. Dallas Ind. Sch., 1968—69, Kansas City (Kans.) Schs., 1969—70; project dir., counsellor Oakland (Calif.) Sch. Dist., 1974—75, tchr., resource, 1970—73, sch. adminstr., 1975—80; owner Opportunities Unltd., Plano, Tex., 1980—. Bd. dirs. Boys and Girls Club, Collin County, Tex., 1998, Goodwill Industries, Oakland, 1978. Recipient Excellence in Field of Bus. award, Dallas Met. Bus. and Profl. Womens Club, 1982. Avocations: reading, writing, art, music, travel. Office: Opportunities Unltd Ste 267-153 1900 Preston Rd Plano TX 75093

RHODES, DOROTHY LEE, public health service officer; b. N.Y.C., Aug. 19, 1947; d. Samuel James and Oralee Rhodes. Studied, Fordham U., Bronx, 1967. Pub. health advisor Dept. Health and Welfare, N.Y.C., 1992—. Office: Dept Health & Welfare 125 Worth St New York NY 10013

RHODES, EDWARD JOSEPH, national security specialist, political scientist; b. Elmhurst, Ill., Oct. 1, 1959; s. Charles Harker, Jr. and Mae Ellen (Svoboda) Rhodes; m. Anne Catherine Case, Oct. 18, 1986 (div. June 1996); m. Kadri Kallikorm, Dec. 29, 2002. AB, Harvard U., 1980; MPA, Princeton U., 1982, PhD, 1985. Fellow Princeton (N.J.) U., 1980—84; peace studies fellow Cornell U., Ithaca, 1984; arms control fellow Stanford U., 1984—85; Hubert H. Humphrey fellow U.S. Arms Control and Disarmament Agy., 1984—85; Paul-Henri Spaak fellow, fellow Ford program Harvard U., Cambridge, Mass., 1985—86; fellow Rutgers U., New Brunswick, 1986—88, asst. prof. polit. sci., 1986—92, assoc. prof. polit. sci., 1992—, dir. Ctr. Global Security and Democracy, 1997—2003, dean social/behavioral sciences, 2003—. Assoc. Ctr. Internat. Affairs Harvard U., Cambridge, Mass., 1988—89; vis. scholar Charles Warren Ctr. Studies in Am. History, 1989—90; fellow office chief naval opers. USN, Washington, 1996—97; mem. U.S. State Dept. Adv. Com. on Hist. Diplomatic Documentation, 2003—. Author: Power and Madness: The Logic of Nuclear Coercion, 1989; co-author: Presence, Prevention, and Persuasion: A Historical Analysis of Military Force and Political Influence; editor: International Relations, 1992, 1998, 2003; co-editor: The Politics of Strategic Adjustment: Ideas, Institutions, and Interests, 1999, Global Politics in a Changing World, 2000, 2002; assoc. editor: Security Studies, 2003—, mem. edit. bd.: Internat. Studies Quarterly, 1999—, Defense Analysis, 2000—; contbr. articles to profl. jours. Pew fellow, 1990, Fulbright fellow U. Latvia, 2000-2001. Mem.: Internat. Inst. Strategic Studies, U.S. Naval Inst., Internat. Studies Assn. Avocations: travel, outdoor sports. Office: Rutgers U Office of Dean of Faculty Arts and Scis 77 hamilton St New Brunswick NJ 08901-1248 Office Phone: 732-932-8435. Business E-Mail: rhodese@rci.rutgers.edu.

RHODES, ERIC FOSTER, employee relations consultant, writer; b. Luray, Va., Feb. 5, 1927; s. Wallace Keith and Bertha (Foster) R.; m. Barbara Ellen Henson, Oct. 19, 1946; children: Roxanne Jane, Laurel Lee; m. Lorraine Endresen, July 29, 1972; m. Daisy Chun, May 31, 1980 AA, George Washington U., 1949, AB, 1950, MA, 1952, EdD, 1967. Tchr. high sch., Arlington, Va., 1950-52; counselor Washington Lee High Sch., Arlington, Va., 1952-53, dir. publs., 1953-54, chmn. dept. English, 1954-55; exec. sec. Arlington Edn. Assn., Arlington, Va., 1952-53, Montgomery County (Md.) Edn. Assn., Rockville, Md., 1955-57; lectr. edn. George Washington U., Washington, 1955-60, 65-70; salary cons. NEA, Washington, 1957-58, asst. dir. membership div., 1958-60; dir. N.Y. regional office, N.Y.C., 1960-64; ednl. cons. Ednl. Rsch. Svcs., White Plains, N.Y., 1964-65; pres. Ednl. Svc. Bur., Inc., Arlington, Va., 1965-72, chmn. bd., 1972-80; pres. Negotiations Consultation Svcs., Inc., Arlington, 1969-80, Eastern States Advt. Inc., Arlington, 1970-79, EFR Corp., Arlington, 1972-90; exec. dir. Assn. Negotiators and Contract Adminstrs., 1981-89; area coord. U.S. Legal Protection Co., 1989-95; pres. Employee Futures Rsch., Colorado Springs, Colo., 1980—, Waterfront Only Real Estate, New Port Richey, Fla., 1988-92, Inst. for Negotiations Tng., New Port Richey, 1989-95, Asset Protection Co., 1991—; asst. supt. for adminstrn. Brighton Schs., Rochester, N.Y., 1983-88; owner Frederick Foster Galleries, Arlington, 1974-80. Cons. Va. Dept. Community Colls., Richmond, 1965-77; vice chancellor Va. Community Coll. System, 1970-71; employee rels. ofcl. City of Orlando, 1980-83; lectr. edn. Frostburg (Md.) State Coll., 1967 Author: Negotiating Salaries, 41 Ways to Cut Budget Costs, Making Good Things Happen Through Negotiation; editor: Inside Negotiations, Wages and Benefits, Employers' Negotiating Service. Mem. Civil Rights Commn., Franklin Twp., N.J., 1962-64; mem. Sr. victim assistance team Colorado Springs Police Dept., 1997—; mem. Franklin Twp. Bd. Edn., 1964-65; mem. adv. bd. Keep Am. Beautiful, 1964-75, nat. chmn., 1968; bd. dirs., v.p. Unitarian-Universalist Ch., Tarpon Springs, Fla., 1990-95, pres., 1994-95;

treas. Friends of Aquatics, 2001—. With U.S. Army, 1945-47. Mem. Am. Assn. Sch. Adminstrs., Internat. Assn. Sch. Bus. Officials, NEA, Edn. Press Assn., Nat. Assn. Ednl. Negotiators (exec. dir. 1971-81), Am. Arbitration Assn. (labor arbitrator), Indsl. Rels. Rsch. Assn., United C. of C. of Pasco County (sec., treas. 1989-90, exec. dir. 1990-91), Am. Legion, Fed. Schoolmen's Club, N.Y. Schoolmen's Club, Lions (v.p. N.Y.C. club 1964-65), Kiwanis (pres. West Pasco club 1991-93), Order of St. John of Jerusalem, Phi Delta Kappa (chpt. pres. 1959-60). Home: 5547 Richey Dr New Port Richey FL 34652 Office: PO Box 1178 New Port Richey FL 34656 E-mail: ericrhodes@netzero.com.

RHODES, FRANK HAROLD TREVOR, academic administrator, geologist; b. Warwickshire, Eng., Oct. 29, 1926; came to U.S., 1968, naturalized, 1976; s. Harold Cecil and Gladys (Ford) R.; m. Rosa Carlson, Aug. 16, 1952; children: Jennifer, Catherine, Penelope, Deborah. BSc, U. Birmingham, 1948, PhD, 1950, DSc, 1963; LLD (hon.), Wooster Coll., 1976, Nazareth Coll. Rochester, 1979, Skidmore Coll., 1989, U. Mich., 1990, Clemson U., 1991, Dartmouth Coll., 1993, U. Birmingham, Eng., 1999, Fla. Internat. U., 2000, Trinity Coll., U. Dublin, 2001; LHD (hon.), Colgate U., 1980, Johns Hopkins U., 1982, Wagner Coll., 1982, Hope Coll., 1982, Rensselaer Poly Inst., 1982, LeMoyne Coll., 1984, Pace U., 1986, Alaska Pacific U., 1987, Hamilton Coll., 1987, SUNY, 1992, Canisius Coll., 1994, Ithaca Coll., 1995, Fla. Atlantic U., 1996, Coll. St. Rose, 2002; DSc (hon.), U. Wales, Eng., 1981, Fla. Atlantic U., 1996, Bucknell U., 1985, U. Ill., 1986, Reed Coll., 1988, Elmira Coll., 1989, U. Southampton, Eng., 1989, U. Sydney, Australia, 1995, U. Durham, Eng., 1995, Millsaps Coll., 1996; DLitt (hon.), U. Nev., 1982; EdD (hon.), Ohio State U., 1992; D Univ. (hon.), U. Stirling, Eng., 1994; LHD (hon.), U. NC, 2003. Post-doctoral fellow, Fulbright scholar U. Ill., 1950-51, vis. lectr. geology, summers 1951, 52; lectr. geology U. Durham, 1951-54; asst. prof. U. Ill., 1954-55, assoc. prof., 1955-56; dir. U. Ill. Field Sta., Wyo., 1956; prof. geology, head geology dept. U. Wales, Swansea, 1956-68, dean faculty of sci., 1967-68; prof. geology and mineralogy Coll. Lit., Sci. and Arts, U. Mich., 1968-77, dean, 1971-74, v.p. for acad. affairs, 1974-77; pres., prof. geology Cornell U., Ithaca, N.Y., 1977-95, pres emeritus, 1995—. Gurley lectr. Cornell U., 1960; Bownocker lectr. Ohio State U., 1966; Case lectr. U. Mich., 1976; Jefferson lectr. U. Calif., Berkeley, 1996-98; dir. NSF, Am. Geol. Inst., summer field inst., 1963; Australian vice-chancellors' visitor to Australian univs., 1964; vis. fellow Clare Hall, Cambridge, 1982; Bye fellow Robinson Coll., Cambridge, 1986-87; Am. Fulbright Disting. fellow, Kuwait, 1987, scholar in residence, Bellagio study and conf. ctr., 1995. Author: The Evolution of Life, 1962, 2d edit., 1976, Fossils, 1963, Geology, 1972, Evolution, 1974, Language of the Earth, 1981, Creation of the Future: The Role of the American University, 2001; author numerous articles and monographs on sci. and edn.; editor, contbr.: Successful Fund Raising for Higher Edn., 1997. Trustee Carnegie Found. for Advancement Tchg., 1978-86, vice chmn., 1983-85, chmn. 1985-86; trustee The Freedom Forum, 1983-93, Com. for Econ. Devel., 1984-93; prin. Washington Adv. Group, 1997—; bd. dirs. KMI Continental, Inc., 1985-86, Tompkins County Trust Co., 1984-98, Gen. Electric Co., 1984-2002, NBC, 1986-2002, H. John Heinz III Ctr. Sci., Econs. & Environ., 1996-98, Am. Coun. on Edn., 1983-88, vice chair, 1985-86, chair, 1986-88, The Johnson Found., 2000—, Atlantic Philanthropies, 1995—, chmn., 2000—; bd. dirs. Goldman Sachs Found., 2000—; bd. overseers Meml. Sloan-Kettering Cancer Ctr., 1979-91, Koç U., Turkey, 1996—; chmn. adv. bd. Freedom Forum Media Studies Ctr., 1984-93; mem. Nat. Sci. Bd., 1987-98, chair, 1994-96, Internat. Exec. Svc. Corps Coun., 1984-95; v.p. Dyson Charitable Trust, 1996-98; bd. mem. The Johnson Found., 2000—. Recipient Clark Kerr medal U. Calif., Berkeley, 1995, Reginald Wilson Diversity Leadership award Am. Coun. Edn., 2003; Sr. Vis. Rsch. fellow NSF, 1965-66; scholar U. Calif., Berkeley, 1995. Fellow Am. Acad. Arts and Scis., Geol. Soc. London (council 1963-66, Bigsby medal 1967); mem. Am. Philos. Soc. (pres. 1999—), Palaeontol. Assn. (v.p. 1963-68), Brit. Assn. Advancement Sci., Geol. Soc. Am., Am. Assn. Petroleum Geologists, Soc. Econ. Paleontologists and Mineralogists, Phi Beta Kappa (hon.) Office: Cornell U Office of President Emeritus 3104 Snee Hall Ithaca NY 14853-1504

RHODES, JIM, human resources professional; V.p. human resources and compliance Publix Supermarkets, Lakeland, Fla. Office: Publix Supermarkets 1936 George Jenkins Blvd Lakeland FL 33815-3760

RHODES, JOEL PAUL, social studies educator; b. Pittsburg, Kans., Feb. 11, 1967; s. Ralph James and Judith Kathryn Rhodes; m. Jeanie Lorena Rhodes, Aug. 2, 2003; children: Alex K Bess, Olivia C Bess, Ella Holley. BSE, U. Kans., Lawrence, 1989; MA, U. Mo., Kansas City, 1995, PhD, 2000. Asst. prof. S.E. Mo. State, Cape Girardeau, Mo., 2001—. Author: The Voice of Violence: Performative Violence in the Vietnam Era. Bd. dir. Mo. Alliance for Hist. Preservation, Columbia, 2002—, The Stars and Stripes Mus. and Libr., Bloomfield, Mo., 2002—. U. Mo. Kans. City Sch. of Grad. Studies Disting. Dissertation Fellowship, 1999, Arthur Mag Grad. Fellowship, Edward Swinney Trust of Greater Kans. City Cmty. Found., 1998. Office: SE Mo State Univ Ms 2960 Cape Girardeau MO 63701 E-mail: jrhodes@semo.edu.

RHODES, KARREN, public information officer; b. Calif., 1947; married; 2 children. Diploma in Journalism, U. Utah, 1984. Journalist, Salt Lake City, 1983—85, UPI, Cheyenne, Wyo., 1985—86, Green River (Wyo.) Star, 1986—88; pub. info. officer Nev. Dept. Employment Security, Carson City, 1989—94, Nev. Dept. Employment, Tng. and Rehab., Carson City, 1994—. Trustee Carson Access Found., Carson City, 1996—2001. Recipient Vol. of Yr. award, State of Utah Gov.'s Office, Salt Lake City, 1984, Best of Nat. Collegiate Photography award, 1984. Mem.: Soc. Profl. Journalists. Avocations: photography, graphic design, writing, travel, mentoring.

RHODES, LAWRENCE, artistic director; b. Mt. Hope, W.Va., Nov. 24, 1939; Studied with Violette Armand. Joined Ballet Russe de Monte Carlo, 1958-60; from dancer to prin. dancer Joffrey Ballet, N.Y.C., 1960-64; prin. dancer Harkness Ballet, 1964-68, dir., prin. dancer, 1968-70; tchr. dance dept. NYU, 1978—, prin. ballet tchr., 1981—, chmn. dance dept., 1981-91; ballet master, choreographer, tchr., artistic dir. Les Grands Ballets Canadiens, Montreal, 1989-99; dir. dance divsn. The Juilliard Sch., 2002—. Guest artist Het Nationale Ballet, Amsterdam, 1970—71, Pa. Ballet, 1971—76, Feld Ballet, N.Y.C., 1973—75; free-lance master ballet tchr., coach. Danced with Makarova, Hayden and Fracci, danced for Butler, Joffrey, Ailey, Lubovitch, Harkarvy, Nault, Van Dantzig and Mac Donald, featured dancer (TV films) A Dancer's Vocabulary, PBS's Dance Am. series, CBS's Camera Three. Office Phone: 212-799-5000 x 255. E-mail: llrhodes@worldnet.att.net.

RHODES, LINDA JANE, psychiatrist; b. San Antonio, May 23, 1950; d. George Vernon and Lucy Agnes (O'Dowd) R. BA, Trinity U., 1972; MD, U. Tex. Med. Br., 1975. Diplomate Am. Bd. Pediat.; bd. certified, Am. Bd. Psychiatry and Neurology. Resident in pediat. U. Tex. Med. Br., Galveston, 1975-78; fellow in ambulatory pediat. U. Tex. Health Sci. Ctr., Houston, 1978-80, asst. prof. psychiatry San Antonio, 1995—, resident in psychiatry, 1990-92, child and adolescent psychiatrist, fellow in biol. psychiatry, 1992-95; pediatrician Kelsey Seybold Clinic, P.A., Houston, 1980-95. Pediat. rep. Tex. Lay Midwifery Bd. Tex. Dept. Health, Austin, 1994-95. Active San Antonio Conservation Soc., San Antonio Herb Soc., Nat. Trust for Hist. Preservation, San Antonio Mus. Assn., Trinity U. Assocs., 1992-95, Witte Mus. Assn.; patron McNay Art Inst.; bd. dirs. Tex. Found. for Psychiatric Edn. & Rsch., 1997—, sec., 1998-99, treas., 1999-2004. Fellow Am. Acad. Pediat.; mem. Am. Psychiat. Assn., Am. Acad. Child and Adolescent Psychiatry (gifts and endowments com.), Ambulatory Pediat. Assn., Tex. Pediat. Soc., Tex. Soc. Psychiat. Physicians, Tex. Acad. Child and Adolescent Psychiatry, Am. Med. Women's Assn., Am. Soc. Clin. Psychopharmacology, Tex. Med. Assn. (com. on child and adolescent health), AMA, Bexar County Psychiat. Soc. (sec. 2000-2001, pres. 2002-2003, past pres. 2003-2004). Office: U Tex Health Sci Ctr-SA Dept Psych/Mail Code 7792 7703 Floyd Curl Dr San Antonio TX 78229-3900

RHODES, LINDA L. medical transcriptionist, medical assistant; b. Jackson, Miss., Dec. 19, 1957; d. Clifton E. and Minnie H. Rhodes. AS in Med. Asst., Phillips Coll., 1995; BA in English, Millsaps Coll., 1980. Cert. med. asst. Am. Assn. Med. Assts. (Ill.). Registered bond clk. Deposit Guaranty Nat. Bank, Jackson, 1981-87; med. asst. Family Health Care, Brandon, Miss., 1995-96; med. transcriptionist Mid-South Transcription, Jackson, 1996—. Mem. Phi Theta Kappa. Avocations: pets, reading. Home: 714 Country Place Dr Jackson MS 39208 Office: Mid-South Transcription 1765-A Lelia Dr Jackson MS 39216 E-mail: cer29cer28@juno.com.

RHODES, PAMELA, state representative; m. David; 1 child, Ryan. BSEE. State rep. State of Colo., 2002—, mem. bus. affairs and labor com., mem. info. and tech. com., mem. joint com. on legis. audit. Mem.: MOPS, North Suburban Rep. Forum. Republican. Avocations: reading, travel. Address: 13271 Clermont Cir Denver CO 80241 Office: State Capitol #205 200 E Colfax Ave Denver CO 80203 E-mail: pam.rhodes.house@state.co.us.

RHODES, PETER EDWARD, label company executive; b. Rochester, N.Y., Sept. 25, 1942; s. Robert A. and Anne (Ward) R.; m. Cassandra Durkee, May 26, 1962 (div. Sept. 1991); children: Tamara, Amy, Brian; m. Nancy Lewis, Aug. 16, 2002. BS, Rochester Inst. Tech., 1964, MBA, 1970. With Touche Ross & Co., Rochester, 1962-69, sr. auditor, to 1969; with Xerox Co., Rochester, 1969, Fay's Drug Co., Inc., Liverpool, N.Y., 1970-87, exec. v.p., 1974-87, also dir.; pres. Syracuse Label Co., Inc., Liverpool, 1987—2002, 2002—, also bd. dirs. Dir. Byrne Dairy Inc. Mem.: AICPA, NY State Soc. CPAs, Bellevue Country Club.

RHODES, RAYMOND EARL, professional sports team executive; b. Mexia, Tex., Oct. 20, 1950; Student, Tex. Christian. Asst. def. backs coach San Francisco 49ers/NFL, 1981-82, def. backs coach, 1982-91; def. coord. Green Bay Packers NFL, 1992-93, San Francisco 49ers/NFL, 1994, asst. def. backs coach, 1981-82, def. backs coach, 1982-91; def. coord. Green Bay Packers NFL, 1992-93, San Francisco 49ers/NFL, 1994; head coach Phila. Eagles, 1995-99, Green Bay Packers, 1999-2000; defensive coord. Washington Redskins, 2000—. Named Named NFL Coach of the Yr., The Sporting News, 1995.

RHODES, RHONDA LYNN, business educator; b. Cottonwood, Ariz., Dec. 9, 1951; d. Thomas Pierce and Merry Lynn (Tissaw) R.; m. Randall E. Hanna, May 26, 1978. B in bus. edn., Northern Ariz. Univ., 1973, M in bus. edn., 1977; PhD in bus. adminstrn., Ariz. State Univ., 1983. Bus. tchr. Prescott (Ariz.) H.S., 1973-77; bus. instr. Yavapai Cmty. Coll., Prescott, Ariz., 1977-78; lectr. Calif. State Polytech. Univ., Pomona, Calif., 1978-80; western reg. dir. Wiley Office Systems Seminars Wiley Publ. Co., N.Y., 1980-82; mgr., mktg. dir. Info Ctr., Inc., Prescott, 1982-85; trainer/systems analyst RR Cons., Hermosa Beach, Calif., 1982—. Dir. grad. bus. programs Calif. State Polytech. Univ., 1988-97, prof. tech. and ops. mgmt., 1985—; cons. Calif. Inst. Local Gov., Claremont; adv. bd. Prescott Coll. Co-author: Office Systems, 1990; contbr. articles to profl. jours. Named Rodeo Queen Prescott Frontier Days Rodeo, 1970. Mem. Nat. Assn. Female Execs., Am. Quarter Horse Assn., Golden Key Hon. Soc., Delta Pi Epsilon. Avocations: training quarter horses, team roping. Office: Calif State Polytech Univ 3801 W Temple Ave Pomona CA 91768-2557 Fax: 520-639-4282. E-mail: rrhodes@csupomona.edu.

RHODES, RICHARD (LEE), writer; b. Kansas City, Kans., July 4, 1937; s. Arthur and Georgia Saphronia (Collier) R.; children: Timothy James, Katherine Hampton; m. Ginger Kay Untrif, Oct. 3, 1993. BA cum laude, Yale U., 1959; LHD (hon.), Westminster Coll., Fulton, Mo., 1988. Author: The Inland Ground, 1970, The Last Safari, 1970, The Ungodly, 1973, The Ozarks, 1974, Holy Secrets, 1978, Looking for America, 1979, Sons of Earth, 1981, The Making of the Atomic Bomb, 1987, Farm, 1989, A Hole in the World, 1990, Making Love, 1992, Nuclear Renewal, 1993, How to Write, 1995, Dark Sun, 1995, (with Ginger Rhodes) Trying to Get Some Dignity, 1996, Deadly Feasts, 1997, Visions of Technology, 1998, Why They Kill, 1999, Masters of Death, 2002, John James Audubon, 2004. Trustee Andrew Drumm Inst., Independence, Mo., 1991—. Recipient Nat. Book Critics Cir. award for nonfiction, Nat. Book award for nonfiction, 1987, Pulitzer prize, 1988; Guggenheim fellow, 1974-75, fellow Nat. Endowment for Arts, 1978-79, Ford Found., 1981-83, Sloan Found., 1985, 89, 91, 92, 2002-, MacArthur Found., 1990-91. Office: c/o Janklow & Nesbit Assoc 445 Park Ave New York NY 10022-2606

RHODES, SAMUEL, violist, educator; b. Long Beach, N.Y., Feb. 13, 1941; s. Bernard and Martha (Ephraim) R.; m. Hiroko Yajima, Dec. 30, 1968; children— Amy, Harumi. BA, Queen's Coll., CUNY, 1963; M.F.A., Princeton U., 1967; D.F.A. (hon.), Mich. State U., 1984; MusD (hon.), Jacksonville U., 1986, San Francisco Conservatory, 1996. Mem. faculty Juilliard Sch., N.Y.C., 1969—, Mich. State U., East Lansing, 1977-85, SUNY-Purchase, 1982-86; violist Marlboro Festival, 1960-68, 78-81, 91—, Galimir String Quartet, 1961-68, Juilliard String Quartet, 1969—; mem. faculty Tanglewood Music Ctr., 1988—. Office: Juilliard Sch Music Lincoln Ctr New York NY 10023

RHODES, SAMUEL EARL, writer; b. Dallas, Tex., Jan. 20, 1953; s. Sanford and Pearline Rhodes; 1 child, Cameron. BS in Rehab. Sci., U. of Tex., Dallas, 1992. Facility mgr. St. Jude Chapel, Dallas; office pers. Jenkens-Gilchrist P.C., Dallas. Author: (book) Native American Rhymes, The People of the Far North, 2004. Independent. Roman Catholic. Achievements include creating the website www.nativeamericanrhymes.com, where children can learn about Native Am. history. Avocations: reading, writing, working with children. Office: Rhodes Educational Publications 222 East Sixth Street Dallas TX 75203 Office Phone: 214-742-2508. Business E-Mail: historyrhymes@earthlink.net.

RHODES, STEPHEN MICHAEL, poultry company executive; b. Harrisonburg, Va., Mar. 12, 1949; s. Trovilla Geil and Ogretta (Dove) R.; m. Judy Ann Higgs, June 19, 1971; children: Jeremy, Meridith. AA, Shenandoah Coll., 1969; BA in Biology, Madison Coll., 1971. Mgr. quality control Rocco Farm Foods, Inc., Edinburg, Va., 1971-95, wastewater/environ. mgr., 1996—. V.p., bd. dirs. Plains Youth Baseball League, Va., 1989-91, coach 1984-90; coach pony league, 1991; 1st lt., pres. Broadway Emergency Squad, 1971-77; chmn. coun. on Ministries Sunset Dr. United Meth. Ch., Broadway, 1991, 94-96, 99—, vice chmn., 1997-98; mem. PPR com., 1994-95; coach Timberville Midget League Football, 1985-89; bd. dirs. Community Pk. Bd., Broadway, 1984-86; mem. Rockingham County Recreation Commn., 1990-97; pres. Broadway H.S. Athletic Booster Club, 1994-96, v.p., 1996-97. Mem. Va. Poultry Industry Lab. (chmn. bd. dirs. 1983, 87), Southeastern Poultry and Egg Fedn. (sci. adv. com. 1983-91). Avocations: hunting, fishing, swimming. Home: 199 3rd St Broadway VA 22815-9511 Office: Rocco Farm Foods Inc 19992 Senedo Rd Edinburg VA 22824-3172

RHODES, THOMAS WILLARD, lawyer; b. Lynchburg, Va., Mar. 9, 1946; s. Howard W. and Ruth R.; m. Ann Bloodworth, May 31, 1975; children: Mildred, Andrew. AB, Davidson (N.C.) Coll., 1968; JD, U. Va., 1971. Bar: Ga. 1971. Assoc. Smith, Gambrell & Russell and predecessor firms, Atlanta, 1971-76, ptnr., 1976—. Dir., pres. Atlanta Vol. Lawyers Found., 1984-89; dir. Fed. Defender Program, Atlanta, 1988-92, 2003—, pres., 1991-92. Contbr. articles to profl. jours.; editor: Nonprofit News. Capt. USAR, 1968—72. Recipient Heiner award, Atlanta Vol. Lawyers Found., 1989. Fellow Am. Law Inst.; mem. Ga. Bar Assn. (past chmn. antitrust law sect.), ABA. Office: Smith Gambrell & Russell Promenade II 1230 Peachtree St NE Ste 3100 Atlanta GA 30309-3592

RHODES, WILLIAM REGINALD, banker; b. N.Y.C., Aug. 15, 1935; s. Edward R. and Elsie Rhodes; divorced; 1 child, Elizabeth. BA in History, Brown U., 1957. From sr. officer internat. banking group-L.Am. and Caribbean to vice-chmn. Citibank, NA, NYC, 1977—2001; sr. vice chmn. Citibank, 2001—03, Citigroup, 1999—; chmn. Citicorp and Citibank, NA, NYC, 2003—. First vice chmn. Inst. Internat. Fin.; mem. Met. Mus. Bus. Com., U.S.-Russia Bus. Coun.; past chmn. adv. com. Export-Import Bank of US; past chmn. U.S. sect. Venezuela-U.S. Bus. Coun.; founding mem. U.S. Nat. Adv. Coun. to the Internat. Mgmt. Ctr., Budapest; active U.S.-Egyptian Pres. Coun.; bd. dirs. ConocoPhillips, Pvt. Export Funding Corp. Chmn. Northfield-Mt. Hermon Sch., Hong Kong-U.S. Bus. Coun.; bd. dirs. NY and Presbyn. Hosp.; bd. overseers Watson Inst. for Internat. Studies; active Lincoln Ctr. Corporate Leadership Com.; bd. dirs. Africa-Am. Inst.; vice chmn. bd. Nat. Com. on U.S.-China Rels.; hon. chmn., Sister City Program of City of NY. Decorated comdr. and grand officer Nat. Order of the So. Cross (Brazil); officer Legion of Honor (France); Orden de Mayo (Argentina); officer Order Francisco Miranda 1st and 3rd classes, Order Merito en el Trabajo 1st class (Venezuela); Order of Diplomatic Svc., Heung-In medal, Korea; recipient Am.'s award, 1997, African Bus. Devel. award African Am. Inst., 1998, Banker's Lifetime Achievment award Arab Bankers Assn. N.Am., 1999, Stephen P. Duggan award for Internat. Understanding, Inst. for Internat. Edn., 1999, William I. Spencer award NY Blood Ctr., 1999. Mem. Americas Soc. (chmn. bd. dirs.), Coun. of Ams. (chmn. bd. dirs.), Bankers Assn. Fin. and Trade (past pres., Banker of Yr. award 2004), Coun. Fgn. Rels., Venezuelan-Am. C. of C. (past pres.), Fgn. Policy Assn. (bd. dirs.). Avocations: reading history, jogging, swimming, archeology. Office: Citigroup Inc 399 Park Ave New York NY 10043-0001

RHODES, YORKE E(DWARD), organic chemist, educator; b. Elizabeth, N.J., Mar. 25, 1936; s. Yorke Edward and Helen (Pyper) R.; m. Mechthilde Weggenmann, May 24, 1975; children: Yorke Edward III, Christopher A., Matthias Raabe, Timothy A. BS, U. Del., 1957, MS, 1959; PhD, U. Ill., 1963. Chemist Thiokol Chem. Corp., Elkton, Md., 1959; lectr. Yale U., New Haven, 1964-65; asst. prof. chemistry NYU, N.Y.C., 1965-71, assoc. prof., 1971—, asst. dean Coll. Arts and Sci., 1987-89, dir. NYU-Stevens dual degree program in sci. and engring., 1988-2000. Vis. prof. U. Freiburg, Germany, 1972-73, Tech. U. Munich, 1977, Harvard U., 2001; vis. prof. astrophysics U. Grenoble, France, 1987; Humboldt vis. prof. Tech. U. Munich, 1978; Dept. State sci. exch. visitor Zagreb, Yugoslavia, and Prague, Czechoslovakia, 1977. Contbr. articles to sci. jours. Committeeman Englewood Dem. Com., 1968-72. NIH fellow Yale U., 1964-65, NASA summer faculty fellow Jet Propulsion Lab., Pasadena, Calif., 1980, 81; recipient Humboldt award, 1978. Mem.: Phi Lambda Upsilon, Planetary Soc., Royal Soc. Chemistry, Am. Chem. Soc. (vice-chmn. N.Y. sect. 1997, chmn. 1998, councilor 1998—, chair nat. local sect. activities com. 2002—), Sigma Xi. Avocations: opera, photography, travel, gardening, railroads. Office: NYU Dept Chemistry 100 Washington Sq E New York NY 10003-6688 Business E-Mail: yorke.rhodes@nyu.edu.

RHODIN, JOHANNES ARNE GÖSTA, medical educator; b. Lund, Sweden, Sept. 30, 1922; s. Johannes and Alma Rhodin; m. Gunvor Thorstenson, Aug. 9, 1947 (div. July 1, 1980); children: Anders, Erik; m. Judith Rae Laurent, May 21, 1994. BA, Hvitfeldtska Gymnasium, Göteborg, Sweden, 1942; MD, Karolinska Inst., Stockholm, 1950; PhD in Anatomy, Karolinska Inst., 1954. Lic. gen. med. practitioner Sweden. Prof. anatomy NYU, 1958—64; chmn. dept. anatomy N.Y. Med. Coll., Valhalla, 1964—74, U. Mich., Ann Arbor, 1974—77, Karolinska Inst., 1977—79, U. South Fla., Tampa, 1979—98, prof. anatomy, 1998—. Mem. Nobel Assembly, Karolinska Inst., 1977—79; mem. adv. panel Edn. Commn. for Fgn. Med. Grads., Washington, 1995—97. Author: An Atlas of Ultrastructure, 1964, Histology: A Text and Atlas, 1974, An Atlas of Histology, 1975. Served with Swedish Army, 1942—43. Recipient Landis Rsch. award, Microcirculatory Soc. of USA, 1970, Freshman Class Outstanding Instruct., 1996, Most Outstanding Pre-Clin. Prof., 1997, USF Prof. Excellence Award, 1998. Mem.: Tampa Yacht and Country Club. Home: 5101 Tollbridge Ct Tampa FL 33647 Office: Dept Anatomy Coll Medicine U South Fla 12901 Bruce B Downs Blvd Tampa FL 33612

RHODY, RONALD EDWARD, banker, communications executive; b. Frankfort, Ky., Jan. 27, 1932; s. James B. and Mary M. (Clark) R.; m. Patricia Schupp, Apr. 23, 1955; children: Leslie K., Mary M., Virginia K., Ronald C. Student, Georgetown (Ky.) Coll., 1950-52, U. Ky., 1953-55. Pub. rels. dir. Kaiser Aluminum & Chem. Corp., Ravenswood, W.Va., 1959-62, N.Y.C., 1962-67, corp. v.p. Oakland, Calif., 1967-83; sr. v.p. corp comm. Bank of Am. NT&SA, San Francisco, 1983—, exec. v.p., 1992-94; CEO Rhody, Inc., 1994—. Author: The CEO's Playbook, 1999; contbr. articles to profl. jours. Founding chmn. adv. bd. San Francisco Acad.; mem. Global Pub. Affairs Inst., N.Y.C. Named Pub. Rels. Profl. of Yr., Pub. Rels. News, 1981; recipient Hall of Fame award Page Soc., 1997. Mem. Pub. Rels. Soc. Am. (accredited, pres.'s adv. coun. Rex Harlow award), Internat. Assn. Bus. Communicators (Gold Quill award 1980), Pub. Rels. Roundtable San Francisco (mem. bd. govs., awards 1980, 85). Home: 2725 Pontiac Dr Walnut Creek CA 94598-4437 Office: Rhody Inc 2725 Pontiac Dr Walnut Creek CA 94598-4437 E-mail: ron.rhody@att.net.

RHONE, DOUGLAS PIERCE, pathologist, educator; b. Bloomsburg, Pa., Mar. 27, 1940; s. Wilbur Clayton and Marian Faye (Shaffer) R.; m. Leta Daiva Budelskis, Sept. 27, 1969; children: Jennifer Ann, Todd Brader. BS, Ill. Benedictine U., 1965; MD, MS in Pathology, U. Ill., 1969. Diplomate Am. Bd. Pathology. Attending pathologist Ill. Masonic Med. Ctr., Chgo., 1976, chmn. dept. pathology, 1976—, dir. residency pathology, 1976—90; asst. prof. pathology U. Ill. Coll. Medicine, Chgo., 1976—80, assoc. prof. pathology, 1980—98; prof. pathology, 1998—; dir. residency pathology U. Ill. Met. Hosps., Chgo., 1990—; assoc. dir. med. affairs Ill. Masonic Med. Ctr., Chgo., 1992—95; pres. Ill. Masonic Med. Ctr. Pathologists, S.C., Chgo., 1977—, Lab. Cons., Ltd., Chgo., 1977—2001. Contbr. articles to profl. jours. Maj. U.S. Army, 1974-76. Recipient Raymond B. Allen award U. Ill. Coll. Medicine, 1979, 80, 95, 97, 98, 2000, C. Thomas Bombeck award, 1991, 2002. Fellow: Coll. Am. Pathologists, Am. Soc. Clin. Pathologists (Sheard-Sanford Rsch. award 1969); mem.: Ill. Soc. Pathologists, Chgo. Pathology Soc., Alpha Omega Alpha. Roman Catholic. Avocations: antiquities, gardening, painting, classical music and opera, russian history and culture. Home: 222 S Spring Ave La Grange IL 60525-2243 Office: Ill Masonic Med Ctr Dept Pathology 836 W Wellington Ave Chicago IL 60657-9224 Office Phone: 773-296-7900. E-mail: doug.rhone@advocatehealth.com.

RHONE, SYLVIA MARIE MILLER, recording industry executive; b. Phila., Mar. 11, 1952; BS in Econs.(hon.), U. Pa., 1974; Degree (hon.), Adelphi U., LHD (hon.), 1996. Comml. lending trainee Bankers Trust Co., N.Y.C.; sec. Buddha Records, 1974, nat. promotion coord., Bareback Records; regional promotions mgr. ABC Records, 1976—78, Ariola Records, 1978—79; N.E. regional promotions mgr./special markets Elektra Records, 1980—83, dir. mktg./special markets, 1983—85; dir. nat. black music promotion Atlantic Records, N.Y.C., 1985—88, v.p., gen. mgr. black music ops., 1988—88, sr. v.p., gen. mgr. black music ops., 1988—90; CEO, co-pres. EastWest Records America, N.Y.C., 1990—91; chmn., CEO EastWest/Atco Records, 1991—94; chair/CEO Elektra Entertainment, N.Y.C., 1994—2004. Mem., bd. dirs. Alvin Ailey Am. Dance Theatre, The RIAA, Rock n' Roll Hall of Fame, Jazz at Lincoln Ctr., R&B Found., Studio Mus. of Harlem; bd. dirs. NARAS. Alumni trustee U. Pa., 2001—. Recipient Whitney M. Young Svc. Award, Boy Scouts of Am., 1992, New Music Seminar Joel Webber Prize for Excellence in Music and Bus. award, 1993, Sony Soul of Am. Music Excellence Award, 1993, Legacy Life Mem. award, Nat. Coun. of Negro Women, 1995, Urban Network Exec. Yr. Award, 1995, Herbert H. Wright award, Nat. Assn. Market Developers, 1995, Studio Mus. Corp. award, 1996, Creative Spirit Award, Black Alumni of Pratt Inst., Echo Awards, Trumpet Awards, Turner Broadcasting, 2004. Achievements include became 1st African American and first woman chairman and CEO of a major record company, 1994.*

RHOTEN, JULIANA THERESA, retired principal; d. Julius Joseph and Gladys Maude (Grant) Bastian; m. Marion Rhoten, Aug. 7, 1956 (dec.); 1 child, Don Carlos. BA, Hunter Coll., 1954, MS, 1956; EdS, U. Wis., Milw., 1977. Tchr. elem. schs., Milw., 1957—65; reading specialist, 1965—71; adminstr., 1971—80; prin. Ninth St. Sch., Milw., 1980—83, Parkview Sch., Milw., 1983—90; ret. Bd. dirs. Eisenhower Ctr., 1994—. Mem.: ASCD, Adminstrs. and Suprs. Coun., Nat. Coun. Tchrs. English, Nat. Assn. Elem. Sch. Prins., Internat. Reading Assn., Phi Delta Kappa, Alpha Kappa Alpha. Home: 7222 N 99th St Milwaukee WI 53224-3802

RHOTEN, KENNETH D. writer; b. Hammond, Ind., Dec. 28, 1950; s. James Edward and Helen Louise (Wasson) R.; m. Virginia Haynie (div.); m. Linda Robin Damron (div.); m. Josephine Meese (dec.). Grad. H.S., New Carlisle, Ind. Draftsman Hahn, Inc., Evansville, Ind., 1973-75; laborer Inland Steel

Works, Ind., 1975; draftsman N.W. Ind. Regional Planning Com., Highland, 1975-76; draftsman, artist graphic sys. divsn. Rockwell Internat., Cicero, Ill., 1977-78; designer Roper Outdoor Products (in cooperation with Espo Engring.), Bradley, Ill., 1978-79; draftsman Fedders Corp., Effingham, Ill., 1982-83. Author, editor: Dark Twist of Fate, 1995, 3d edit., 2003, Dark Twist of Fate and Other Works, 1999; author: A Voice From Beyond, 1999, The Complete Works of Kenneth D. Rhoten, 1999; composer pub. songs; patentee automatic brewing apparatus, 1984. Candidate state rep. State of Ill.-Rep. Party, 1986. Achievements include successful redevelopment of the Edison storage cell, and development of new secondary cell, deduced mechanism of Bessler's wheel and constructed model; development of mechanical advantage gravity motors. Home: PO Box 225 Stoy IL 62464-0225

RHOTON, ALBERT LOREN, JR., neurological surgery educator; b. Nov. 18, 1932; s. Albert Loren and Hazel Arnette (Van Cleve) R.; m. Joyce L. Moldenhauer, June 23, 1957; children: Eric L., Albert J., Alice S., Laural A. BS, Ohio State U., 1954; MD cum laude, Washington U., St. Louis, 1959. Diplomate Am. Bd. Neurol. Surgery (bd dirs. 1985-91, vice-chmn. 1991). Intern Columbia Presbyn. Med. Ctr., N.Y.C., 1959; resident in neurol. surgery Barnes Hosp., St. Louis, 1961-65; cons. neurol. surgery Mayo Clinic, Rochester, Minn., 1965-72; chief divsn. neurol. surgery U. Fla., Gainesville, 1972-80, R.D. Keene prof., 1980—, chmn. dept. neurol. surgery, 1980-2000, chmn. emeritus, 2000—. Developer microsurg. tng. ctr.; lectr. in field. Author: The Orbit and Sellar Region: Microsurgical Anatomy and Operative Approaches, 1996, Cranial Anatomy and Surgical Approaches, 2003, Millenium issue Neurosurgery, 25th Anniversary issue; designed more than 200 microsurgery instruments; mem. editl. bd. Neurosurgery, Jour. Microsurgery, Surg. Neurology, Jour. Fla. Med. Assn., Am. Jour. Otology, Skull Base Surgery; contbr. articles to profl. jours. Bd. dirs. Neurosurgery Edn. and Rsch. Found. Recipient Disting. Faculty award, U. Fla., 1981, Alumni Achievement award, Washington U. Sch. Medicine, 1985, Jones award for outstanding spl. med. exhibit of yr., Am. Assn. med. Illustrators, 1969, Jameison medal, Neurosurg. soc. Australasia, 1997, Outstanding Achievement award, World Congress of Skull Base Surgery, 2000, medal of honor, World Fedn. Neurosurg. Socs., 2001, medal, Neurosurg. Soc. Am., 2001, endowed professorship named in his honor, U. Fla., Lifetime Achievement award, Wall of Fame Honoree, Honorary Alumnus award, 2001, medal of honor, Neurosurg. Soc. of Am., 2001, Bucy award, U. Chgo., 2002; grantee NIH, VA, Am. Heart Assn. Mem. ACS (bd. govs. 1978-84), AMA (Billings Bronze medal 1969), Congress Neurol. Surgeons (pres. 1978, honored guest 1993), Nat. Found. Brain Rsch. (bd. dirs. 1990-94), Nat. Coalition for Rsch. in Neurol. Disorders (bd. dirs. 1990-94), Neurol. Soc. Am. (medal 2001), Internat. Congress Meningiomas (hon. pres. 2000), Neurosurg. Soc. Brazil (hon.), Neurosurg. Soc. Japan (hon., Honored guest 2002), Neurosurg. Soc. Mex. (hon.), Neurosurg. Soc. Can. (hon.), Neurosurg. Soc. Uruguay (hon.), Neurosurg. Soc. Venezuela (hon.), Neurosurg. Soc. Turkey (hon.), Neurosurg. Soc. Tex. (hon.), Neurosurg. Soc. Okla. (hon.), Neurosurg. Soc. Wis. (hon.), Neurosurg. Soc. Ga. (hon.), Neurosurg. Soc. Rocky Mountain (hon.), Neurosurg. Soc. China (hon.), Neurosurg Soc. Argentina (hon.), Latin Am. Neurosurg. Soc. (hon.), Fla. Neurosurg. Soc. (pres. 1978), Am. Assn. Neurol. Surgeons (chmn. vascular sect., treas. 1983-86, v.p. 1987-88, pres. 1989-90, exec. com. 1993, Cushing medal 1998), Soc. Neurol. Surgeons (treas. 1975-81, pres. 1993), So. Neurol. Soc. (v.p. 1976), Alachua County Med. Soc. (exec. com. 1978), Fla. Med. Assn., Am. Surg. Assn., Soc. Univ. Neurosurgeons, Am. Heart Assn. (stroke coun., Outstanding Achievement award 1971), N.Am. Skull Base Soc. (pres. 1993-94, honored guest 2001), Am. Acad. Neurol. Surgery, Acoustic Neuroma Assn. (med. adv. bd. 1983-2000, chmn. 1992-2001, chmn. emeritus 2001—), Trigeminal Neurol. Assn. (med. advisor bd. 1992—), Hemifacial Spasm Assn. (med. adv. bd. 2002--), Internat. Interdisciplinary Congress on Craniofacial and Skull Base Surgery (pres. 1996-97), Internat. Soc. Neurosurg. Tech. and Instrument Invention (pres. 1997—), Japanese Skull Base Soc. (hon. pres. 2000), Internat. Soc. for Microsurgery Anatomy (hon. pres. 2002). Home: 2505 NW 22d Ave Gainesville FL 32605-3819 Office: U Fla Dept Neurosurgery PO Box 100265 100 S Newell Dr Gainesville FL 32610

RHYNE, JAMES JENNINGS, condensed matter physicist; b. Oklahoma City, Nov. 14, 1938; s. Jennings Jefferson and Clyde Margaret (Russell) R.; m. Susan Margaret Watson, May 26, 1990; children: Nancy Marie, Edward Paxton. BS in Physics, U. Okla., 1959; MS in Physics, U. Ill., 1961; PhD in Physics, Iowa State U., 1965. Rsch. scientist Naval Ordnance Lab., White Oak, Md., 1965-75; rsch. physicist Nat. Inst. of Stds. and Tech., Gaithersburg, Md., 1975-90; prof. physics U. Mo., Columbia, 1991—2003, dir. Rsch. Reactor Ctr., 1991-96; dep. group leader Lujan Ctr., Los Alamos Nat. Lab., 2003—. Assoc. editor Jour. of Magnetism and Mag. Materials, 1990—; editl. bd. Jour. Applied Physics, 1986-89; co-editor procs. Fellow: Neutron Scattering Soc. Am. (pres. 1999—2002), Am. Phys. Soc. Office Phone: 505-665-0071. E-mail: rhyne@lanl.gov.

RHYNE, SIDNEY WHITE, lawyer; b. Charlotte, N.C., Apr. 2, 1931; s. Sidney White and Ruth (Dry) R.; m. Rosemarie Kennedy, July 11, 1959; children: Patricia Ruth, Kendall Sidney, Randall Sylvanus. AB, Roanoke Coll., 1952; LLB, U. Pa., 1955; LLM, Georgetown U., 1961. Bar: Pa. 1955, D.C. 1957, U.S. Supreme Ct. 1959, Md. 1987. Assoc. Rhyne, Mullin, Connor and Rhyne, Washington, 1957-60; mem. Mullin, Rhyne, Emmons and Topel, Washington, 1961-97; individual practice law Washington, 1997—. Lectr. law ctr. Georgetown U., Washington, 1964-70. Pres. Legal Aid Soc. of D.C., 1976-78, trustee, 1968-80, pres. coun., 1991—; trustee Luth. Theol. Sem. at Phila., 1988-93, pres. coun., 1993—. With U.S. Army, 1955-57. Prettyman fellow Georgetown U., 1960-61. Fellow Am. Bar Found. (life); mem. ABA (mem. house delegates 1972-73, 75, 76-78, 98-2001), Bar Assn. D.C. (bd. dirs. 1969-73, 92-94, 98-2002, trustee Found., v.p. 1990-91, presdl. award 2000-2001), Fed. Comm. Bar Assn. (mem. exec. com. 1988-96, treas. 1991-92, Disting. Svc. award 1992, pres. 1994-95). Republican. Lutheran. Office: 3250 Arcadia Pl NW Washington DC 20015-2330 Office Phone: 202-244-6248. E-mail: swrhyne@abanet.org.

RHYNEDANCE, HAROLD DEXTER, JR., lawyer, consultant; b. New Haven, Conn., Feb. 13, 1922; s. Harold Dexter and Gladys (Evans) R.; m. Barbara Ann Hall (dec.); 1 child, Harold Dexter III; m. Ruth Cosline Hakanson. BA, Cornell U., 1943, JD, 1949; grad., U.S. Army Command and Gen. Staff Coll., 1961, U.S. Army War Coll., 1970. Bar: N.Y. 1949, D.C. 1956, U.S. Tax Ct. 1950, U.S. Ct. Mil. Appeals 1954, U.S. Supreme Ct. 1954, U.S. Ct. Appeals (D.C. cir.) 1956, (2d cir.) 1963, (3rd cir.) 1963, (4th cir.) 1973, (5th cir.) 1968, (7th cir.) 1973, (9th cir.) 1964, U.S. Temporary Emergency Ct. Appeals 1975, U.S. Dist. Ct. D.C. 1956, U.S. Dist. Ct. (so. and ea. dist.) N.Y. 1963. Pvt. practice, Buffalo, Eggertsville, N.Y., 1949-50; examiner/gen. atty. ICC, Washington, 1950-51; atty.-advisor Subversive Activities Control Bd., Washington, 1951-52; trial atty., spl. asst. to atty. gen., asst. U.S. atty. U.S. Dept. Justice, Washington, 1953-62; sr. trial atty., asst. gen. counsel, gen. counsel FTC, Washington, 1962-73; counsel Howrey & Simon, Washington, 1973-76; mng. atty., asst. gen. counsel, corp. counsel Washington Gas Light Co., 1977-87; counsel Conner & Wetterhahn, 1987-90; cons. Fairview, N.C., 1990—. Exec. sec. adv. coun. on rules of practice and procedures FTC; mem. Jud. Conf. (D.C. Cir.), 1967—; chmn. legal and regulatory subcom. Solar Energy Com., Am. Gas Assn., Washington, 1978-84; lectr. George Washington U. Law Ctr., 1974; faculty moderator Def. Strategy Seminar Nat. War Coll., 1973; participant spl. programs Indsl. Coll. of Armed Forces, 1962, 69, Armed Forces Staff Coll., 1964. V.p. bd. dirs. Peninsula Symphony Assn., Palos Verdes Peninsula, Calif., 1989-94; bd. dirs. Help-The-Homeless-Help-Themselves, Inc., Palos Verdes Peninsula, 1991-93. 1st lt. U.S. Army, 1943-46, PTO; col. AUS, 1982—. Mem.: ABA, Selden Soc. (London), Cornell Lawyers Club D.C. (pres. 1959—61), Washington Met. Area Corp. Counsel Assn. (bd. dirs. 1981—84), Bar Assn. of D.C., D.C. Bar Assn., Fed. Bar Assn., Cornell Alumni Assn., Leadership Asheville Forum, Res. Officers Assn. (life), U.S. Army War Coll. Alumni Assn. (life), Mil. Officers Assn. of Am., Res., Order Carabao, Downtown Club Asheville (past pres.), Scottish Soc., Montreat (N.C.), Biltmore Forest Country Club (Asheville, N.C.), Am. Legion (life), Phi Delta Phi, Sigma Chi. Republican. Episcopalian. Home and Office: Eagles View 286 Sugar Hollow Rd Fairview NC 28730-9559

RIAL, MARTHA, photographer; Grad., Art Inst. Pitts.; postgrad., Ohio U. Staff photographer Jour. Newspapers, Alexandria, Va., Ft. Pierce (Fla.) Tribune, Pitts. Post-Gazette, 1994—. Recipient Recognition award, Pitts. chpt. Women in Comm., Press Club Western Pa., Pitts. Slack Media Fedn., Pulitzer prize. Office: C/O Pitts Post-Gazette Blade Comms 34 Blvd Of The Allies Pittsburgh PA 15222-1204

RIASANOVSKY, NICHOLAS VALENTINE, retired historian, educator; b. Harbin, China, Dec. 21, 1923; arrived in U.S., 1938, naturalized, 1943; m. Arlene Ruth Schlegel, Feb. 15, 1955; children: John, Nicholas, Maria. BA, U. Oreg., 1942; AM, Harvard U., 1947; DPhil, Oxford (Eng.) U., 1949. Mem. faculty U. Iowa, 1949-57, U. Calif., Berkeley, 1957—, prof. history, 1961—, Sidney Hellman Ehrman prof. European history, 1969—2003, ret., 2003. Vis. rsch. prof. USSR Acad. Scis., Moscow, 1969, Moscow and Leningrad, 1974, 79. Author: Russia and the West in the Teaching of the Slavophiles: A Study of Romantic Ideology, 1952, Nicholas I and Official Nationality in Russia, 1825-1855, 1959, A History of Russia, 1963, 6th edit., 1999, The Teaching of Charles Fourier, 1969, A Parting of Ways: Government and the Educated Public in Russia, 1801-1855, 1976, The Image of Peter the Great in Russian History and Thought, 1985, The Emergence of Romanticism, 1992, Collected Writings 1947-94, 1993; co-editor: California Slavic Studies, 1960—; editl. bd. Russian rev., Zarubezhnaia Periodicheskaia Pechat' na Russkom Iazyke, Simvol; contbr. articles to profl. jours. Trustee Nat. Coun. Soviet and East European Rsch., 1978—82; mem. Kennan Inst. Acad. Coun., 1986—89. 2d lt. AUS, 1943—46. Decorated Bronze Star; recipient Silver medal Commonwealth Club Calif., 1964; Rhodes scholar, 1947-49; Fulbright grantee, 1954-55, 74, 79; Guggenheim fellow, 1969; sr. fellow NEH, 1975; Fulbright sr. scholar, sr. fellow Ctr. Advanced Studies in Behavioral Scis., 1984-85; sr. fellow Woodrow Wilson Internat. Ctr. for Scholars, 1989-90. Mem. Am. Assn. Advancement Slavic Studies (pres. 1973-76, Disting. Contbr. award 1993), Am. Hist. Assn. (award for Scholarly Distinction 1995), Am. Acad. Arts and Scis.

RIBA, SHIRLEY, artist; d. Arthur Roy and Idell Carolina Riba. BFA, Calif. Coll. of Arts & Crafts, Oakland, 1977. Sales/dept. display Gumps Oriental Antique Dept., San Francisco, 1979—90; owner Artriba, Laporte, Colo., 1995—. Exhibitions include Corcoran Sch. Art, Washington, D.C., 1977—78, Calif. Coll. of Arts & Crafts, San Francisco, 1977, E.B. Crocker Kingsley, Sacramento, 1979, Gump's Gallery, San Francisco, 1979—90, 1981, 1986, mural, After Parrish, 2002. Home: PO Box 800 Laporte CO 80535

RIBAC, CATALINO TAGATAC, retired accountant; b. Batac, The Philippines, Apr. 30, 1934; came to U.S., 1969; s. Felixberto and Gerarda (Tagatac) R.; m. Adelaida Obando, Dec. 26, 1964; 1 child, Maria-Elma Ribac-Horton. BS in Acctg., Adamson U., Manila, 1967. CPA, Calif. Janitor Ker & Co., Ltd., Manila, 1957-59, messenger, 1960-61, bill collector, 1961-62, acctg. clk., 1963-64, internal auditor, 1965-69; acct. Belinkoff & Co., L.A., 1969-75; ptnr. Berlinkoff & Co., L.A., 1976-2001; ret., 2001. Mem. AICPA, Calif. Soc. CPAs. Republican. Roman Catholic. Avocations: gardening, playing acoustic guitar, travel. Home: 4941 Herperia Ave Encino CA 91316 E-mail: linor34b@netzero.net.

RIBARY, URS, neuroscientist, researcher, educator; b. Lucerne, Switzerland, Nov. 24, 1955; came to U.S., 1988; s. Max and Hilde (Brunner) Ribary; m. Evelyne Dahinden, July 11, 1986; 1 child, Samanta R. MS, U. Tech., Zurich, Switzerland, 1981, DSc, 1985. Rsch. asst. prof. NYU Med. Ctr., N.Y.C., 1988-93, dir. ctr. for neuromagnetism, 1989—, assoc. prof., 1993—. Vis. asst. prof. Simon Fraser U., Can., 1986-88. Cons. (Time Life series) The Brain, 1990; contbr. articles to profl. jours. Co-founder, chmn. Samanta S. Ribary Found. Inc. Mem. AAAS, Am. Soc. Neurosci., N.Y. Acad. Scis., European Neurosci. Assn., Soc. Cognitive Neuroscience. Achievements include work on using functional brain imaging techniques, to study quantal sequences of coherent thalamo-cortical activity in humans during normal cognitive processing, and its alterations in neurological and neuropsychiatric patients. Office: Dept Physiology and Neurosci NYU Med Ctr 550 1st Ave New York NY 10016-6402 E-mail: urs.ribary@med.nyu.edu.

RIBBLE, JOHN CHARLES, medical educator; b. Paris, Tex., July 26, 1931; s. Elbert Alfred and Dorothy (Pyeatt) R.; m. Anne Blythe Hoerner; 1 stepchild Helen Blythe Strate Kielty. MD, U. Tex., 1955. Diplomate Am. Bd. Internal Medicine. Asst. prof. medicine Cornell U., N.Y.C., 1962-66, assoc. prof. pediatrics, 1966-78, assoc. dean, 1974-78, Med. Sch., U. Tex., Houston, 1978-86, dean, 1986-95; vis. scholar The Health Inst. New Eng. Med. Ctr., Boston, 1995-96; prof. medicine U. Tex., Houston, 1996—. Mem. Nat. Adv. Coun. Gen. Med. Scis. NIH, Bethesda, Md., 1988-91. Episcopalian. Home: 6200 Willers Way Houston TX 77057-2808 Office: U Tex Med Sch 6431 Fannin St Houston TX 77030-1501 E-mail: jribble@houston.rr.com.

RIBBLE, RONALD GEORGE, retired psychologist, educator, writer; b. West Reading, Pa., May 7, 1937; s. Jeremiah George and Mildred Sarah (Folk) Ribble; m. Catalina Valenzuela Torres, Sept. 30, 1961; children: Christina, Timothy, Kenneth. BSEE cum laude, U. Mo., 1968, MSEE, 1969, MA, 1985, PhD, 1986. Bd. cert. forensic examiner, diplomate Am. Bd. Psychol. Spltys., Am. Coll. Forensic Examiners; cert. in homeland security. Enlisted man USAF, 1956-60, advance through grades to lt. col., 1976; rsch. dir. Coping Resources, Inc., Columbia, Mo., 1986; pres., co-owner Towers and Rushing Ltd. (Pubs. and Psychol. Cons., Troubadour 1997-2001), San Antonio, 1986—; referral devel. Laughlin Pavilion Psychiat. Hosp., Kirksville, Mo., 1987; program dir. Psychiat. Insts. of Am., Iowa Falls, Iowa, 1987-88; lead psychotherapist Gasconade County Counseling Ctr., Hermann, Mo., 1988; sr. lectr. U. Tex., San Antonio, 1989—2002; lectr. Trinity U., San Antonio, 1995-96; assessment clinician Afton Oaks Psychiat. Hosp., San Antonio, 1989-91; ret. from tchg., 2002. Faculty cons. Edn. Testing Svc., 1997; psychologist Olmos Psychol. Svcs., Inc., San Antonio, 1991—93; vol. assessor Holmgreen Children's Shelter, San Antonio, 1992—93; founder Ruth Bohn Weissman Scholarship in Creative Writing U. Tex., San Antonio, 1994; cosponor Lyric Recovery Festival, Carnegie Hall, 2000; condr. seminars, revs. for maj. publs. *Since his USAF retirement in 1981, Dr. Ribble has signficantly broadened his educational background, knowledge, experience, and constructive involvement in the fields of behavioral analysis, education, literary arts, and international relations. As a consequence, he has been recognized by several organizations as a meaningful contributor to the understanding of complex human relations and endeavors. He is one of a very small percentage of university faculty members across America to be continuously recognized over an eight-year period by dean's list students as the one teacher who had the single greatest influence on their academic career and/or their personal life. Besides his on-going leadership roles in the WPDF and The Jefferson Council, Dr. Ribble is active as a behavioral consultant in Special Security matters.* Author: (book) Apples, Weeds, and Doggie Poo, 1995, Dont' Eat the Snake!; contbr. essays to psychol. refernce books, poetry to anthologies periodicals, lyrics to popular music; interviewer: celebrities in performing and lit. arts, 1995—, columnist: Feelings, 1993—97; pub. access TV appearances, 1991—. Founding cabinet mem. World Peace and Diplomacy Forum; vol. announcer pub. radio sta., Colombia, 1993; vol. Cath. Family and Children's Svc., San Antonio, 1989—91; chpt. advisor Rational Recovery Program for Alcoholics, San Antonio, 1991—92; mem. Pres. Leadership Cir., 1994—2002; contbg. mem. Dem. Nat. Com., 1983—, Presdl. Congl. Task Force, 1994; del. Boone County (Mo.) Dem. Conv., 1984. Recipient Roberts Meml. prize in Poetry, 1995, DaVinci Diamond award, 2004, Internat. Peace prize, United Cultural Conv., U.S.A., 2002, Am. medal Hon., 2004. Master: APA; fellow: Am. Coll. Forensic Examiners; mem.: ACLU, Acad. Polit. Sci., Soc. for the Psychol. Study of Social Issues, The Jefferson Coun. (founder, dir. 2002), Physicians for Social Responsibility (leadership cir.), So. Poverty Law Ctr. (leadership coun. for tchg. tolerance), Soc. Profl. Journalists, Interfaith Alliance, Mil. Officers Assn., Air Force Assn., Internat. Platform Assn. (Poetry award 1995). Deist. Avocations: running and fitness, poetry, singing, public speaking. Home: 14023 N Hills Village Dr San Antonio TX 78249-2534 also: Towers and Rushing Ltd San Antonio TX 78249 Office Phone: 210-690-5557. E-mail: rgrib@stic.net.

RIBEAU, SIDNEY A. academic administrator; M in Interpersonal Comm., U. Ill., 1973, D in Interpersonal Comm., 1979. Prof. comm. studies Calif. State U., L.A., 1976, chair Pan African studies dept., 1987; dean Coll. Liberal Arts Calif. Poly., San Luis Obispo, 1990, v.p. for acad. affairs Pomona, 1992; pres. Bowling Green (Ohio) U., 1995—. Bd. dirs. The Andersons Inc., Maumee, Ohio; lectr., spkr. and presenter in field. Co-author: African American Communication: Ethnic Identity and Cultural Interpretations, 1994 (Disting. Scholarship award Speech Comm. Assn.); contbr. papers to scholarly jours. Mem. Ohio Bd. Regent's Higher Edn. Funding Commn., Am. Coun. on Edn.'s Leadership and Instnl. Change Commn., Higher Edn. Bus. Coun., Urban League Toledo; bd. dirs. Toledo Symphony Orch. Mem. Bowling Green C. of C., Toledo C. of C. Office: Bowling Green State U Bowling Green OH 43403-0001

RIBEIRO, LUCIA C. language educator; d. Americo and Marina Adelaide (De Andrade) Ribeiro. BA in Bus. Adminstrn., Kennesaw State U., Ga., 1982, BA in Spanish, 1985; MA in Spanish Lit., Ga. State U., Atlanta, 1992; PhD in Higher Edn. Adminstrn., U. So. Miss., Hattiesburg, 2003. Dir., fgn. lang. resource ctr. Kennesaw State U., Ga., program dir., critical lang. Mem. Ga. Partnership for Excellence in Edn., Atlanta, 2002—03. Mem.: Gamma Beta Phi, Sigma Delta Phi. Home: 688 Coventry Township Ln Marietta GA 30062 Office: Kennesaw State Univ 1000 Chastain Rd Kennesaw GA 30144 Business E-Mail: lribeiro@kennesaw.edu.

RICAPITO, JOSEPH VIRGIL (GIUSEPPE RICAPITO), Spanish, Italian and comparative literature educator; b. Giovinazzo, Bari, Italy, Oct. 30, 1933; came to U.S., 1933; s. Frank and Filomena (Cervone) R.; m. Carolyn Sue Kitchen, Apr. 7, 1958; children: Frank Peyton, Maria Avadna. BA, CUNY, Bklyn., 1955; MA, U. Iowa, 1956; PhD in Romance Langs., U. Calif., L.A., 1966. From instr. to asst. prof. Pomona Coll., Claremont, Calif., 1962-70; from assoc. prof. to prof. Ind. U., Bloomington, Ind., 1970-80; prof. La. State U., Baton Rouge, 1980—, chmn. dept., 1980-85, Joseph Yenni disting. prof. Italian studies, 1999. Author: Bibliografia Razonada y anotada, 1980; editor: La Vida de Laz de Tormes, 1976; translator: Dialogue of Mercury and Charon, 1986, Cervantes's Novelas ejemplares: Between History and Creativity, 1996. Pres. Greater Baton Rouge Am.-Italian Assn., 1984-85. With U.S. Army, 1957-59. Grantee NEH, 1981; named Knight Order of Merit, Republic of Italy, 1988, Knight Order of Queen Isabel, Govt. of Spain, 1990; named Disting. Rsch. Master La. State U., 2001, Cervantes Lectr., Fordham U., 2004. Mem. MLA, Renaissance Soc. Am., Am. Comparative Lit. Assn., Am. Assn. Tchrs. Spanish and Portuguese, Cervantes Soc. Am. Avocations: music, photography, films. Office: La State U 309 Hodges Hall Baton Rouge LA 70803-0001 E-mail: ricapito@lsu.edu.

RICARD, JOHN H. bishop, educator; b. Baton Rouge, Feb. 29, 1940; s. Maceo and Albanie (St. Amant) R. BA, St. Joseph Sem., 1962, MA, 1968; MS, Tulane U., 1970. Ordained priest Roman Cath. Ch., 1968. Pastor Holy Redeemer Ch., Washington, 1972—75, Holy Comforter Ch., Washington, 1975—84; ordained titular bishop of Rucuma, 1984; aux. bishop Balt., 1984—97; assoc. prof. Cath. U. Am., Washington, 1973—; bishop of Pensacola-Tallahassee Fla., 1997—. Mem. priest's senate Archdiocese of Washington, 1974—, mem. sch. bd., 1976—. Pres. Cath. Relief Svcs. USCC, 1995—; mem. Pontifical Coun., COR UNUM, 1996—; Chmn. Com. on Social Devel. and World Peace, Domestic Social Devel., 1992—95. Mem.: Secretariat of Black Caths. Office: PO Drawer 17329 Pensacola FL 32522-7329

RICARDO-CAMPBELL, RITA, economist, educator; b. Boston, Mar. 16, 1920; d. David and Elizabeth (Jones) Ricardo; m. Wesley Glenn Campbell, Sept. 15, 1946; children: Barbara Lee, Diane Rita, Nancy Elizabeth. BS, Simmons Coll., 1941; MA, Harvard U., 1945, PhD, 1946. Instr. Harvard U., Cambridge, Mass., 1946—48; asst. prof. Tufts U., Medford, Mass., 1948—51; labor economist U.S. Wage Stabilization Bd., 1951—53; economist Ways and Means Com. U.S. Ho. of Reps., 1954; economist, 1957—60; prof. San Jose (Calif.) State U., 1960—61; sr. fellow Hoover Instn. on War, Revolution, and Peace, Stanford, Calif., 1968—95, sr. fellow emerita, 1995—. Lectr. health Stanford U. Med. Sch., 1973—78; bd. dirs. Watkins-Johnson Co., Palo Alto, Calif., Gillette Co., Boston; mgmt. bd. Samaritan Med. Ctr., San Jose. Author: Voluntary Health Insurance in the U.S., 1960, Economics of Health and Public Policy, 1971, Food Safety Regulation: Use and Limitations of Cost-Benefit Analysis, 1974, Drug Lag: Federal Government Decision Making, 1976, Social Security: Promise and Reality, 1977, The Economics and Politics of Health, 1982, 2d edit., 1985, Resisting Hostile Takerovers: The Gillette Company, 1997; co-editor: Below-Replacement Fertility in Industrial Societies, 1987, Issues in Contemporary Retirement, 1988; contbr. articles to profl. jours. Commr. Western Interstate Commn. for Higher Edn. Calif., 1967-75, chmn., 1970-71; mem. Pres. Nixon's Adv. Coun. on Status of Women, 1969-76; mem. task force on taxation Pres.'s Coun. on Environ. Quality, 1970-72; mem. Pres.'s Com. Health Svcs. Industry, 1971-73, FDA Nat. Adv. Drug Com., 1972-75; mem. Pres. Reagan's Econ. Policy Adv. Bd., 1981-90, Pres. Reagan's Nat. Coun. on Humanities, 1982-89, Pres. Reagan's Nat. Medal of Sci. com., 1988-91, Pres. Bush's Nat. Medal of Sci. com., 1991-94; bd. dirs. Ind. Colls. No. Calif., 1971-87; mem. com. assessment of safety, benefits, risks Citizens Commn. Sci., Law and Food, Rockefeller U., 1973-75; mem. adv. com. Ctr. Health Policy Rsch., Am. Enterprise Inst. Pub. Policy Rsch., Washington, 1974-80; mem. adv. coun. on social security Quadrennial Health and Human Svcs., 1974-75; bd. dirs. Simmons Coll. Corp., Boston, 1975-80; mem. adv. coun. bd. assocs. Stanford Librs., 1975-78; mem. coun. SRI Internat., Menlo Park, Calif., 1977-90. Mem. Am. Econ. Assn., Mont Pelerin Soc. (bd. dirs. 1988-92, v.p. 1992-94), Harvard Grad. Soc. (coun. 1991-94), Phi Beta Kappa. Home: 26915 Alejandro Dr Los Altos Hills CA 94022-1932 Office: Stanford U Hoover Instn Stanford CA 94305-6010 Office Phone: 650-723-2074.

RICART, FRED, automotive company executive; Owner Ricart Automotive, Columbus, Ohio. Office: Ricart Automotive Rte 33 and Hamilton Rd Columbus OH 43227-1342

RICART, GLENN, Internet company executive; b. Wheeling, W.Va., Aug. 1, 1949; s. Donald Glenn and Elizabeth Ricart; m. Patricia M. Guenther, Oct. 26, 1974; children: Brendon Guenther, Genevieve Guenther. BS, Case We. Res. U., 1971, MS in Computing and Info. Scis., 1973; PhD in Computer Sci., U. Md., 1980. Head, DEC-10 systems NIH, Bethesda, Md., 1971-82; prin. investigator SURAnet, College Park, Md., 1984-94; dir., Computer Sci. Ctr. U. Md., College Park, Md., 1982-93; asst. vice chancellor U. Md. Sys., Adelphi, Md., 1990-93; program mgr. Def. Advanced Rsch. Projects Agy., Fairfax, Va., 1993-95; sr. v.p., chief tech. officer Novell, Provo, Utah, 1995-99; founder, exec. v.p., chief tech. officer CenterBeam, Santa Clara, Calif., 1999—. Bd. dirs. Nat. Assn. State Univs. and Land Grant Colls., Washington, 1993—94, CACI, Inc., Arlington, Va., 1998—2002. Asst. scoutmaster Boy Scouts Am., Salt Lake City, 1995—99; asst. leader Girl Scouts U.S., Bethesda, 1990—2002; ruling elder 1st Presbyn. Ch., Salt Lake City, 1998—2001; coach Odyssey of the Mind, 1995—99; co-chair Blue Ribbon Panel Netcentricity, 1999—2000. Environ. health officer USPHS, 1971—78. Mem.: Internet Soc. (bd. dirs. 2002—), Assn. Computing Machinery, IEEE Computer Soc., Phi Kappa Phi, Tau Beta Pi. Presbyterian. Achievements include patents in field. Avocation: American Coaster Enthusiasts. Office: Pricewaterhouse Coopers 10 Almaden Blvd Ste 1600 San Jose CA 95113

RICART, RHETT C. retail automotive executive; b. 1956; Grad., Ohio State U., 1977. Prin. Ricart Ford, Groveport, Ohio, 1977—, pres., CEO, 1988—; ceo Ricart Automotive, Columbus, Ohio. Office: Ricart Automotive PO Box 27130 Columbus OH 43227-0130 also: Ricart Automotive 4255 S Hamilton Rd Groveport OH 43125-9332

RICCARDI, VINCENT MICHAEL, pediatrician, researcher, educator, entrepreneur; b. Bklyn., Oct. 14, 1940; s. Gabriel John and Frances Mary (Novak) R.; m. Susan Leona Bogda, July 27, 1967; children: Angela M., Ursula M., Mikah F. AB, UCLA, 1962; MD, Georgetown U., 1966; MBA, U. LaVerne, 1993. Intern, resident in medicine U. Pitts., 1966-68; fellow in genetics Harvard Med. Sch., Boston, 1968-70, 72; asst. prof. medicine U.

Colo. Med. Ctr., Denver, 1973-75; assoc. prof. medicine, pediatrics Med. Coll. Wis., Milw., 1975-77; prof. medicine, pediatrics Baylor Coll. Medicine, Houston, 1977-90; med. dir. The Genetics Inst., Pasadena, Calif., 1990-92; clin. prof. pediatrics UCLA, 1991—; founder, CEO Am. Med. Consumers, La Crescenta, 1992. Dir. The Neurofibromatosis Inst., La Crescenta, Calif., 1985—. Author: Genetic Approach to Human Disease, 1977, Communication and Counseling in Health Care, 1983, Neurofibromatosis, 1986, rev. edit., 1992, 99. Maj. U.S. Army, 1970-71. Fellow ACP, AAAS, Am. Coll. Med. Genetics; mem. Am. Soc. Human Genetics, Am. Coll. Physician Execs. Avocations: writing poetry and screenplays, acting in movies. Office: Am Med Consumers 5415 Briggs Ave La Crescenta CA 91214-2205 Office Phone: 818-957-3508. Business E-Mail: riccardi@medcomsumer.com.

RICCARDS, MICHAEL PATRICK, academic administrator; b. Hillside, N.J., Oct. 2, 1944; s. Patrick and Margaret (Finelli) Riccards; m. Barbara Dunlop, June 6, 1970; children: Patrick, Catherine, Abigail. BA, Rutgers U., 1966, MA, 1967, MPhil, 1969, PhD, 1970. Spl. asst. to chancellor Dept. Higher Edn., Trenton, NJ, 1969-70; from asst. prof. to assoc. prof. SUNY, Buffalo, 1970-77; dean U. Mass., Boston, 1977-82; provost Hunter Coll. CUNY, NY, 1982—83, prof., 1982-86; pres. St. John's Coll., Santa Fe, 1986-89, Shepherd Coll., Shepherdstown, W.Va., 1989-95, Fitchburg (Mass.) State Coll., 1995—2002; pub. policy scholar-in-residence Coll. Bd., Washington, 2002—. Mem. joint commn. tchr. preparation, 1999—2000. Author: (book) The Making of the American Citizenry, 1973, A Republic, If You Can Keep It, 1987, The Ferocious Engine of Democracy, 2 vols., 1995, 2002, Vicars of Christ, 1998, The Presidency and the Middle Kingdom, 2000, The Odes of DiMaggio, 2001, The Papacy and the Early Christendom, 2003; co-editor: Relfections on American Political Thought, 1973. Chmn. N.Mex. Endowment Humanities, 1989; trustee Albuquerque Acad.; mem. Coun. Humanities W.Va., Nat. Skills Stds. Bd., 1993—98; mem. nat. adv. com. Ctr. Study Presidency, 1987—89. Fulbright fellow, 1973, Huntington Libr. fellow, 1974, NEH fellow, Princeton U., 1976—77. Home: 3319 14th St NE Washington DC 20017 Office: Coll Bd 1233 20th St NW Washington DC 20036

RICCI, CHRISTINA, actress; b. Santa Monica, Calif., Feb. 12, 1980; Appeared in films Mermaids, 1990, The Hard Way, 1991, The Addams Family, 1991, The Cemetery Club, 1993, Addams Family Values, 1993, Casper, 1995, Now and Then, 1995, Gold Diggers: The Secret of Bear Mountain, 1995, Bastard Out of Carolina, 1996, The Last of the High Kings, 1996, That Darn Cat, 1996, Ice Storm, 1997, Little Red Riding Hood, 1997, Souvenir (voice) 1998, Pecker, 1999, I Woke Up Early When I Died, 1998, Fear and Loathing in Las Vegas, 1998, Desert Blue, 1998, Buffalo 66, 1998, The Opposite of Sex, 1998, Small Soldiers (voice only), 1998, Souvenir (voice only), 1998, 200 Cigarettes, 1999, No Vacancy, 1999, Sleepy Hollow, 1999, Bless the Child, 2000, The Man Who Cried, 2000, All Over the Guy, 2001, Prozac Nation (also co-prod.), 2001, The Laramie Project, 2002, Pumpkin (also prod.), 2002, Miranda, 2002, The Gathering, 2002, Anything Else, 2003, I Love Your Work, 2003, Monster, 2003; TV appearances include H.E.L.P., 1990, The Simpsons (voice only), 1996, Ally McBeal, 2002, Malcolm in the Middle, 2002. Office: ICM 8942 Wilshire Blvd Beverly Hills CA 90211-1934

RICCI, ROBERT RONALD, manufacturing executive; b. N.Y.C., Jan. 11, 1945; s. George and Mary Pauline (Barbieri) R.; m. Sandra Piccione, Jan. 18, 1948; children: Jason, Sean. AAS, S.I. Community Coll., 1972; BBA, Bernard Baruch Coll., 1974, MBA, 1976. Sales mgr. G.A.F. Photo, Elizabeth, N.J., 1974-76; v.p. Photo Drive Thru, Pennsauken, N.J., 1976-80; head nat. accounts Berkey Photo, Phila., 1980-85; dir. nat. account sales Qualex, Inc., Durham, N.C., 1988-92, v.p. sales east, 1993-95; v.p. new acct. devel. sales National, 1995-99; sr. v.p. sales and mktg. Kodak Processing Labs, 1999—; ptnr. and exec. v.p. AAA Imaging and Supplies, Inc., 2002—. Pres. Sanjasean, Inc., Marlton, N.J., 1978-86. Served with USN, 1966-70. Mem. Photo Mktg. Assn. Republican. Roman Catholic. Avocations: photography, carpentry, computers. Home: 30766 La Brise Laguna Niguel CA 92677-5525

RICCI, RUGGIERO, violinist, educator; b. San Francisco, July 24, 1918; s. Pietro Ricci and Emma Bacigalupi; m. Ruth Rink, 1942; m. Valma Rodriguez, 1957; m. Julia Whitehurst Clemenceau, 1978; 5 children. Pupil, Louis Persinger, Mischel Piastro, Paul Stassevitch, Georg Kulenkampff. Began career as child prodigy, San Francisco, 1928; N.Y. debut Manhattan Symphony, 1929; tchr. Mozarteum Conservatory, Salzburg, Austria; 1st European tour, 1932; specializes in violin solo; introduced Ginastera, von Einem and Veerhoff violin concerti; U.S. premiere Paganini, 6th violin concerto; prof. music Ind. U., 1971-74, Juilliard Sch., 1974-79, U. Mich., Ann Arbor, 1982-87; prof. Mozarteum, Salzburg, Austria, 1989—. Tchr. masterclasses, Berlin. Recordings include The GreatViolinist Series, The Making of a Legend, Vols. 3, 4, Portrait of an Artist, Vol. 4, Vol. 6, Ruggiero Ricci, Virtuoso Recital, over 500 others; performer over 5,000 concerts; author: Left Hand Violin Technique. Served with USAAF, 1942-45. Decorated Knight Order of Merit Italy. Mem. Royal Acad. Music (hon.) Achievements include making first complete recording of Paganini's Caprices. Office: Intermusica Stephen Lumsden 16 Duncan Terr London N1 8B2 England also: Albany Music Distrs Inc 915 Broadway Albany NY 12207-1326 also: c/o John Gingrich Mgmt Inc PO Box 1515 New York NY 10023-9462

RICCIARDI, J.P. professional sports team executive; m. Diane Ricciardi; 2 children. Baseball coach minor league N.Y. Yankees, 1982—84, Milw. (Minn.) Brewers, 1985; from scout to dir. player pers. Oakland (Calif.) Athletics, 1986—99, dir. player pers., 1999—2001; sr. v.p. Toronto (Can.) Blue Jays, 2001—, gen. mgr., 2001—. Office: 1 Blue Jays Way Ste 3200 Toronto ON Canada M5V 1J1*

RICCIARDI, SALVATORE, wholesale distribution executive; Pres., CEO Purity Wholesale Grocers, Boca Raton, Fla. Office: Purity Wholesale Grocers Ste 100 5400 Broken Sound Blvd NW Boca Raton FL 33487-3511

RICCIARDONE, FRANCIS J. ambassador; b. Boston; m. Marie Dunn Ricciardone; 2 children. BA summa cum laude, Dartmouth Coll., 1973. Tchr., Iran, 1976—78; with U.S. Fgn. Svc., 1978—, with Bur. Intelligence and Rsch., sr. mgmt. positions under dir. gen., chief civilian observer unit Multinational Force and Observers in Egype Sinai Desert, polit. advisor to U.S. and Turkish commanding gens. Operation Provide Comfort, dep. chief of mission and charge d'affaires, 1995—99; spl. coord. for transition of Iraq US Dept. State, Washington, 1999—2001, U.S. amb. to Philippines and Palau Manilla, 2002—. Office: 8600 Manila Pl Washington DC 20521-8600 also: Am Embassy 1201 Roxas Blvd Ermita Manila Philippines

RICCIO, FRANK JOSEPH, lawyer, educator; b. Somerville, Mass. BS, Boston Coll., 1973; JD, Suffolk U., 1985; D of Dental Medicine, Boston Coll., 1986. Bar: Mass. 1985, U.S. Dist. Ct. Mass. 1986, U.S. Ct. Appeals (1st cir.) 1986. Dentist, Lowell, Mass., 1977-83, Metheun, Mass., 1983-84; assoc. Sugarman & Sugarman, Boston, 1985-87; pvt. practice Braintree, Mass., 1987. Clin. instr. oral medicine Harvard U., Boston, 1995—. Dental extern USPHS, 1976. Mem. Am. Assn. Trial Attys., Nat. Bd. Trial Attys. (cert. civil trial specialist), Mass. Bar Assn., Mass. Acad. Trial Attys., Million Dollar Advocates Forum. Office: Law Offices of Frank J Riccio PC 25 Braintree Hill Park Ste 208 Braintree MA 02184-8702 E-mail: fjriccio@socialaw.com.

RICCITIELLO, JOHN S. former interactive software/gaming executive, venture capitalist; Pres., CEO Wilson Sporting Goods Co.; pres., CEO bakery divsn. Sara Lee Corp.; pres., COO Electronic Arts, Redwood City, Calif., 1997—2004; co-founder Elevation Partners, Menlo Park, Calif., 2004—.

RICE, ADRIAN CLIFFORD, adult education educator; b. Harlow, Essex, United Kingdom, Nov. 15, 1970; s. Michael John and Maureen Rosalind Rice. BS in Math., U. Coll. London, 1989—92; MS in History, Philosophy of Sci.and Math., King's Coll. London, 1992—93; PhD in History of Math., Middlesex U., London, 1994—97. Lectr. in math. Middlesex U., London, 1995—98; vis. asst. prof., math. U. of Va., Charlottesville, 1998—99; asst. prof., math. Randolph-Macon Coll., Ashland, 1999—. Coun. mem. Brit. Soc. for the History of Math., 1994—99, Can. Soc. for the History and Philosophy of Math., 2002—. Co-editor (with Karen Hunger Parshall) (book) Math. Unbound: The Evolution of an Internat. Math. Rsch. Cmty., 1800-1945. Mem.: London Math. Soc., Am. Math. Soc., Can. Soc. for the History and Philosophy of Math., Brit. Soc. for the History of Math. Office: Department of Mathematics Randolph-Macon College Ashland VA 23005-5505 E-mail: arice4@rmc.edu.

RICE, ANNE, writer; b. New Orleans, Oct. 14, 1941; d. Howard and Katherine (Allen) O'Brien; m. Stan Rice, Oct. 14, 1961 (dec.); children: Michele (dec.), Christopher. Student, Tex. Woman's U., 1959-60; BA, San Francisco State Coll., 1964, MA, 1971. Author: Interview with the Vampire, 1976, The Feast of all Saints, 1980, Cry to Heaven, 1982, The Vampire Lestat, 1985, The Queen of the Damned, 1988, The Mummy or Ramses the Damned, 1989, The Witching Hour, 1990 (TV series, 2002), Tale of the Body Thief, 1992, Lasher, 1993, Taltos, 1994, Memnoch the Devil, 1995, Servant of the Bones, 1996, Violin, 1998, The Vampire Armand, 1998, Pandora: New Tales of the Vampires, 1998, Vittorio the Vampire, 1999, Merrick, 2000, Blood and Gold, 2001, The Master of Rampling Gate, 2002, Blackwood Farm, 2002, Blood Canticle, 2003; (as A.N. Roquelaure) The Claiming of Sleeping Beauty, 1983, Beauty's Punishment, 1984, Beauty's Release: The Continued Erotic Adventures of Sleeping Beauty, 1985 (as Anne Rampling) Exit to Eden, 1985, Belinda, 1986; screenwriter: Interview with a Vampire, 1994. Office: care Alfred A Knopf Inc 201 E 50th St New York NY 10022-7703*

RICE, ARTHER MAE, dietician; d. Arthur Leroy and Novella M. Winford; m. James O. Rice, Apr. 17, 1960; children: Anthony George, Michael Christopher. BS, A&T State U., Greensboro, NC, 1963. Registered dietician U. Del., 1964, cert. Women in Mgmt. Immaculate U., 1980. Dir. dietetics Rush Hosp., Malverna, Pa., 1964; asst. hosp. adminstr. Metropolital Hosp., Springfield, Pa., 1981; regional dietician Am. Medicorp, Bala Cynwyd, Pa., 1982; cons. dietician nursing schs. and ctrs. Springfield, Pa., 1984; dir. dietetics Tri-County Hosp., Springfield, Pa., 1984—98, Metropolital Hosp., 1998. Pres. Food Svc. Dirs., Phila.; com. mem. Am. Dietetic Assn., Pa. Dietetic Assn. Author: (books) God in Waiting, vol. 1, 1984, God in Waiting, vol. 2, 1998. Pres. Triad Rowan Continentals, 2003; mem. Del. Area Continentals, 1999, 2004. Recipient Pa. Gov. award, Sojourner truth award, Bus. and Profl. Women's Clubs, Inc., Pres. award, Hosp. Ford Dirs. Episcopalian. Avocations: writing, reading. Home: 202 Kirk Rd Greensboro NC 27455

RICE, CHARLES EDWARD, bank executive; b. Chattanooga, Tenn., Aug. 4, 1936; s. Charles Edward and Louise (Goodson) R.; m. Dianne Tauscher; children: Danny, Celeste, Michelle. BBA, U. Miami, 1958; MBA, Rollins Coll., Winter Park, Fla., 1964; grad., Advanced Mgmt. Program, Harvard U., 1975. Vice pres., then pres. Barnett Bank, Winter Park, 1965-71; exec. v.p. Barnett Banks Fla., Inc., Jacksonville, 1971-73, pres., from 1973; CEO Nationsbank, Jacksonville, 1979-98, now also chmn., bd. dirs., until 1998; vice chmn. corp. devel. Bank of Am., Jacksonville, 1998—. Bd. dirs. Sprint Corp., CSX Corp. Trustee Univ. of Miami, Rollins Coll. Office: Bank of Am FL 9-001-42-01 50 N Laura St Jacksonville FL 32202-3664

RICE, CHARLES LANE, surgical educator; b. Atlanta, May 22, 1945; s. Marion Jennings and Molly Black (Moore) R.; m. Lynn Carol Inscoe, Dec. 27, 1968 (div. 1976); m. Judith Josephine Bousha, July 9, 1977; children: Aaron Nicholas, Patrick Marion. AB, U. Ga., 1964; MD, Med. Coll. Ga., 1968. Commd. ensign USN, 1966, advanced through grades to comdr., 1976, ret., 1977; intern Bowman Gray Sch. Medicine, Winston-Salem, N.C., 1968-69; resident Nat. Naval Med. Ctr., Bethesda, Md., 1969-73; asst. prof. surgery U. Chgo., 1977-80, assoc. prof. surgery, 1980-84; dir. intensive care unit Michael Reese Hosp., Chgo., 1977-84; prof., vice chmn. dept. surgery U. Wash., Seattle, 1985-92; surgeon-in-chief Harborview Med. Ctr., Seattle, 1985-92; Dr. Lee Hudson- Robert R. Penn prof., chmn., divsn. gen. surgery U. Tex. Southwestern Med. Ctr., Dallas, 1992-93; prof. surgery U. Ill., Chgo., 1993—, prof. physiology and biophysics, 1996—, vice dean Coll. Medicine, 1994-99, vice chancellor health affairs, 1999—. Robert Wood Johnson Health Policy fellow, 1991-92; legis. asst. to U.S. senator Tom Daschle, 1991-92. Assoc. editor Jour. of Surg. Rsch., 1983-90; contbr. articles to profl. jours. Rep. Accrediting Coun. Grad. Med. Edn., chair elect, 2001—02, chair, 2002—. Capt. USNR, 1989—2003. Decorated Legion of Merit. Fellow ACS (gov. 1992-98, vice chmn. com. on trauma 1992-93), Am. Surg. Assn., Am. Assn. for Surgery of Trauma (com. chair 1989-91); mem. Soc. Univ. Surgeons, Am. Physiol. Soc., Shock Soc. (pres. 1991-92). Democrat. Episcopalian. Office: U Ill at Chgo V Chancellor Health Affairs 914 S Wood St Rm 101 Chicago IL 60612-7337 E-mail: clrice@uic.edu.

RICE, CHARLES M. virologist, educator; BS in Zoology, U. Calif., Davis, 1974; PhD in Biochemistry, Calif. Inst. Tech., 1981. Postdoctoral rsch. fellow Calif. Inst. Tech., 1981—85; asst. prof. Washington U. Sch. Medicine, prof. dept. molecular microbiology, 1995; head lab. virology and infectious disease Rockefeller U., N.Y.C., 2000—, Maurice R. and Corinne P. Greenberg chair virology, 2000—. Achievements include research in molecular genetics; virology. Office: Rockefeller U 1230 York Ave New York NY 10021

RICE, CLARE I. electronics company executive; b. Rice Lake, Wis., Nov. 3, 1918; s. Chris Nilson and Ingeborg (Haug) R.; m. Virginia M. Bateman; children: Karen Rice, Carol Rice Brannon, David Alan; m. Barbara Carlson Denniston, 2002. BSEE, U. Wis., 1943; BS in Law, St. Paul Coll. Law, 1950; DEngring, Rose-Hulman Inst. Tech., 1979. Registered profl. engr., Minn., D.C. Supr. aircraft radio engring. Northwest Airlines, Inc., Mpls., 1946-51; staff engr. Aero. Radio, Inc., Washington, 1951-53; aviation sales mgr., gen. mgr. Bendix Avionics Divsn., Balt., 1953-62; pres. Sunbeam Electronics, Inc., Ft. Lauderdale, Fla., 1962-66; v.p. Nova U., Ft. Lauderdale, 1966-68; asst. v.p., v.p., sr. v.p. Collins Radio Co., pres. Collins Avionics group Rockwell Internat. Corp., Cedar Rapids, Iowa, 1968-83. Dir. Rockwell-Collins Internat., Inc., Dallas. Chmn. United Way, Cedar Rapids, 1973-74; trustee Coe Coll., 1979-83, Hoover Presdl. Libr.; eminent fellow Wisdom Hall of Fame; bd. dirs. St. Luke's Hosp., 1976-82, Mchts. Nat. Bank, 1977-83; chmn. Mcpl. Airport Commn., Cedar Rapids, 1980-84; charter mem. Aviation Hall of Fame; capt. Hon. Dep. Sheriffs Assn., 1987—; pres. Sales and Mktg. Execs. Balt., 1960-61, Cmty. Assn. Bernardo Heights, 1988-91; dir. Rancho Bernardo Cmty. Found. Lt. comdr. USNR, 1943-46. Recipient Disting. Svc. citation U. Wis., 1979, 84; Pioneer award Milw. Sch. Engring., 1981. Sr. mem. IEEE; mem. Iowa Mfrs. Assn. (bd. dirs. 1975-81), Gen. Aviation Mfrs. Assn. (dir. 1970-81, chmn. 1979), U. Wis. Alumni Assn. (chmn. 1981-82, pres. 1980-81, Disting. Svc. award 1984). Clubs: Wings (N.Y.C.); Nat. Aviation (Washington); Rancho Bernardo Heights Country. Lodges: Royal Order of Jesters (dir. 1979). Republican. Presbyterian. Home: The Remington Club 16925 Hierba Dr # 219 San Diego CA 92128

RICE, CONDOLEEZZA, national security advisor; b. Birmingham, Ala., Nov. 14, 1954; BA cum laude, U. Denver, 1974, PhD, 1981; MA, U. Notre Dame, 1975; PhD (hon.), Morehouse Coll., 1991, U. Ala., 1994, U. Notre Dame, 1995, Miss. Coll. Sch. of Law, 2003, U. Louisville, 2004. Asst. prof. dept. polit. sci. to assoc. prof. Stanford (Calif.) U., 1981-93, prof., 1993—99, provost, 1993-99; spl. asst. to dir. of the Joint Chiefs of Staff U.S. Dept. Def., Washington, 1986; spl. asst. to U.S. President Nat. Security Affairs, 1989-91; dir. to sr. dir. Soviet and East European Affairs, 1989—91; sr. fellow Hoover Inst., Stanford, Calif., 1991—93; asst. to the Pres. for Nat. Security Affairs Nat. Security Council, Washington, 2001—. Cons. ABC News, Washington; mem. spl. advisory panel to comdr. and chief strategic air commd.; mem. gov. ind. advisory redistricting the state of Calif.; mem. U.S. Delegation to 2+4 Talks on German Unification. Author: Uncertain Allegiance; The Soviet Union and the Czechoslovak Army, 1984; co-author (with Alexander Dallin): The Gorbachev Era, 1986; co-author: (with Philip Zelikow) Germany Unified and Europe Transformed, 1995. Recipient Sch. of Humanities and Sciences Dean's award for disting. teaching, Stanford U., 1993, Walter J. Gores award for excellence in teaching, Stanford U., 1984. Mem. Coun. Fgn. Rels. Republican. Office: The White House National Security Council 1600 Pennsylvania Ave Washington DC 20500*

RICE, DALE R. education educator; b. New Castle, Pa., Aug. 6, 1948; s. Paul Richard and Charlotte Mae Rice; m. Judy B. Rice, Aug. 6, 1984; children: Brandon Dale, Kristen Leigh, Courtney Alletta; m. Luann Moser Rice, June 10, 1972 (div. Nov. 4, 1983). BS, Penn State, State College, PA, 1966—70, MEd, 1970—73; PhD, Ohio State, Columbus, OH, 1974—77. Educator Bethel Pk. City Schools, Bethel Park, Pa., 1970—74; rsch. asst. Ohio State U., Columbus, Ohio, 1974—77; lectr. East Carolina U., Greenville, NC, 1977—80; asst. prof. U. of So. Ala., Mobile, Ala., 1980—86; assoc. prof. Auburn U., Auburn, Ala., 1986—89; educator Gwinnett County Schools, Lawrenceville, Ga., 1989—. Article reviewer Sch. Sci. & Math Jour., 1980—88; ednl. cons. Ednl. Jour., 1987—89. Author: (book) Life Science, Earth Science, Energy from Fossil Fuels. Avocation: landscaping. Personal E-mail: dale.rice@att.net.

RICE, DAVID LEE, university president emeritus; b. New Market, Ind., Apr. 1, 1929; s. Elmer J. and Katie (Tate) R.; m. Betty Jane Fordice, Sept. 10, 1950; children: Patricia Denise Rice Dawson, Michael Alan. BS, Purdue U., 1951, MS, 1956, PhD, 1958; degree (hon.), U. Evansville, 1994, U. So. Ind., 1995; LHD, U. Evansville, 1994; LLD, U. So. Ind., 1995. Dir. prof. research Ball State U., Muncie, Ind., 1958-66; v.p. Coop. Ednl. Research Lab., Inc., Indpls., 1965-67; research coordinator, bur. research HEW, Washington; dean campus Ind. State U., Evansville, 1967-71, pres. campus, 1971-85; pres. U. So. Ind., Evansville, 1985-94, pres. emeritus, 1994—. Adminstrv. asst. Gov.'s Com. on Post High Sch. Orgn. Contbr. articles to profl. jours. Past mem. State Citizens Adv. Bd. Title XX Social Security Act; bd. dirs., past pres. bd. commrs. Evansville Housing Auth.; pres. Leadership Evansville, 1978-79; bd. dirs., past pres. S.W. Ind. Pub. TV, 1972—; chair Indian Pub. Broadcasting Sts., 1990-93; bd. dirs. Villages Inc.; mem. Buffalo Trace Coun. Boy Scouts Am., 1963—, New Harmony Commn., 1989-94; chair So. Ind. Rural Devel. Project., Inc.; bd. trustees Rapp Granary-Owen Found.; bd. dirs. So. Ind. Higher Edn. Inc., U. So. Ind. Found. With inf. U.S. Army, 1951-53. Decorated Bronze Star, Combat Infantryman's Badge; recipient Svc. to Others award Salvation Army, 1974, Citizen of Yr. award Westside Civitan Club, 1972, Boss of Yr. award Am. Bus. Women's Assn., 1976, Disting. Citizen of Yr. award Ivy Tech State Coll., 1994; David L. Rice Libr./U. So. Ind. named in his honor, 1994. Mem. DAR (medal of honor for cmty. svc. 1998), Am. Assn. Higher Edn., Am. Ednl. Rsch. Assn., Am. Assn. State Colls. and Univs., Nat. Soc. Study Edn., Met. Evansville C. of C. (dir.), Evansville Kennel Club, Rotary (civic award Evansville club 1985, life), Alpha Kappa Psi, Alpha Zeta, Phi Delta Kappa. Methodist. Home: 1223 S Main St New Harmony IN 47631 Office: Neef Lesueur House 404 Church St New Harmony IN 47631

RICE, DAVID PRESTON, minister; b. Parkersburg, W.Va., July 7, 1953; s. Ernest Granville Rice and Mary Alice Lee; m. Dorothy Lee Tehas, Sept. 18, 1976; 1 child, Nathan Granville. BS, U. Tex., San Antonio, 1978; M of Divinity, Christian Bible Coll. and Sem., 1993, D of Divinity, 1996. Cert. trainer Evangelist Explosion, Tex. Pastor, ch. planter Benjamin Ave. Bapt. Ch., Grand Rapids, Mich., 1986-88; assoc. pastor Columbia Ave. Bapt. Ch., Pontiac, Mich., 1988-90, Bell Shoals Bapt. Ch., Brandon, Fla., 1990-93; sr. pastor Belmont Bapt. Ch., Tampa, Fla., 1993-97; assoc. dir. Sunday sch. dept. Fla. Bapt. Conv., Jacksonville, 1997-99; sr. pastor Ancient City Bapt. Ch., Augustine, Fla., 1999—. Nat. ch. growth cons. So. Bapt. Conv., Nashville, 1991—. Author: (implementation strategy) FAITH Sunday School Evangelism Strategy, 1998. Sgt. 1st class U.S. Army, 1972-85, Vietnam. Mem. So. Bapt. Religious Educators Assn., Fla. Bapt. Religious Educators. Southern Baptist Convention. Avocations: golf, horticulture, collecting miniature lighthouses. Office: Ancient City Bapt Ch 27 Sevilla St Saint Augustine FL 32084-3550

RICE, DENIS TIMLIN, lawyer; b. Milw., July 11, 1932; s. Cyrus Francis and Kathleen (Timlin) R.; children: James Connelly, Tracy Ellen. AB, Princeton U., 1954; JD, U. Mich., 1959. Bar: Calif. 1960. Practiced in, San Francisco, 1959—; assoc. firm Pillsbury, Madison & Sutro, 1959-61, Howard & Prim, 1961-63; prin. firm Howard, Rice, Nemerovski, Canady, Falk & Rabkin, 1964—. Bd. dirs. Gensler & Assocs., Inc., Anabas, Inc.; chmn., mng. com. San Francisco Inst. Fin. Svcs., 1983—92. Councilman, City of Tiburon, Calif., 1968-72, mayor, 1970-72; dir. Marin County Transit Dist., 1970-72, 77-81, chmn., 1979-81; supr. Marin County, 1977-81, chmn., 1979-80; commr. Marin Housing Authority, 1977-81; mem. San Francisco Bay Conservation and Devel. Commn., 1977-83; bd. dirs. Planning and Conservation League, 1981—, Marin Symphony, 1984-92, Marin Theatre Co., 1987-97, Marin Conservation League, 1995-2000, Digital Village Found., 1995—, pres., 1997—; mem. Met. Transp. Commn., 1980-83; mem. bd. visitors U. Mich. Law Sch. 1st lt. AUS, 1955-57. Recipient Freedom Found. medal, 1956 Fellow Am. Bar Found.; mem. ABA (fed. regulation of securities com., chair Asia-Pacific Bus. Law Com., chmn. subcom. on internat. venture law), State Bar Calif. (editor 1978-80, vice chair sect. bus. law 1978-80, chair com. adminstrn. justice 1997-98, chair com. cyberspace law 1997-2001), San Francisco Bar Assn., Am. Judicature Soc., Computer Law Assn. (bd. dirs.), Am. Internat. Property Law Assn., South End Rowing Club, Tiburon Peninsula Club, Pacific Union Club, Olympic Club, Order of Coif, Phi Beta Kappa, Phi Delta Phi. Office: 3 Embarcadero Ctr Ste 700 San Francisco CA 94111-4003 Office Phone: 415-434-1600. Personal E-mail: drice@hrice.com.

RICE, DONALD B. biotechnology company executive; Asst. dir. Office of Mgmt. and Budget The White House, Washington; pres., CEO The RAND Corp., 1972—89; sec. Air Force U.S. Dept. Def., Washington, 1989—93; pres., COO, dir. Teledyne, Inc., 1993—96; pres., CEO, dir. UroGenesys, Inc., 1997—; dir. Scios, Inc., Sunnyvale, Calif., 1997—, chmn. bd., 1998—. Bd. dirs. Wells Fargo & Co., Vulcan Materials Co., Unocal Corp., Amgen, Inc. Office: 6500 Paseo Padre PKWY Fremont CA 94555-3658

RICE, DONALD BLESSING, business executive, former secretary of air force; b. Frederick, Md., June 4, 1939; s. Donald Blessing and Mary Celia (Santangelo) R.; m. Susan Fitzgerald, Aug. 25, 1962; children: Donald Blessing III, Joseph John, Matthew Fitzgerald. BSChemE, U. Notre Dame, 1961, DEng (hon.), 1975; MS in Indsl. Adminstrn., Purdue U., 1962, PhD in Mgmt. and Econs., 1965, D (hon.) in Mgmt., 1985; LLD (hon.), Pepperdine U., 1989; LHD (hon.), West Coast U., 1993; D in Pub. Policy (hon.), Rand Grad. Sch., 1995. Dir. cost analysis Office Sec. Def., Washington, 1967-69, dep. asst. sec. def. resource analysis, 1969-70; asst. dir. Office Mgmt. and Budget, Exec. Office Pres., 1970-72; pres., CEO The Rand Corp., Calif., 1972-89; sec. USAF, 1989-93; pres., COO Teledyne, Inc., L.A., 1993-96; chmn. Scios, Inc., Sunnyvale, Calif., 1998—2003; chmn., pres., CEO Agensys, Inc., Santa Monica, Calif., 1996—. Bd. dirs. Vulcan Materials Co., Wells Fargo & Co., GKN Aerospace Transparency Sys., Unocal Corp., Amgen Inc.; mem. nat. adv. com. oceans and atmosphere Dept. Commerce, 1972-75; mem. Nat. Sci. Bd., 1974-86; mem. adv. coun. Coll. Engring., U. Notre Dame, 1974-88; chmn. Nat. Commn. Supplies and Shortages, 1975-77; mem. adv. panel Office Tech. Assessment, 1976-79; mem. Def. Sci. Bd., 1977-83, sr. cons., 1984-88; dir. for sec. def. and Pres. Def. Resource Mgmt. Study, 1977-79; mem. U.S. Commn. Nat. Security/21st Century, 1998-2001; trustee RAND, 2001-, chmn. grad. sch. bd. govs., 1999—. Author articles. Served to capt. AUS, 1965-67. Recipient Sec. Def. Meritorious Civilian Svc. medal, 1970, Def. Exceptional Civilian Svc. medal, 1993, Forrestal award, 1992; Ford Found. fellow, 1962-65. Fellow AAAS, Nat. Acad. of Pub. Adminstrn.; mem. Inst. Mgmt. Scis. (past pres.), Tau Beta Pi. Office: Agensys Inc 1545 17th St Santa Monica CA 90404 E-mail: drice@agensys.com.

RICE, DONALD SANDS, lawyer, entrepreneur; b. Bronxville, NY, Mar. 25, 1940; s. Anton Henry and Lydia Phipps (Sands) R.; m. Edgenie Higgins, Aug. 27, 1966; children: Alice Higgins, Edgenie Rice Thomas. AB magna cum laude, Harvard U., 1961, LLB/JD cum laude, 1964; LLM in Taxation, NYU, 1965. Bar: NY 1964, US Ct. Claims 1965, US Supreme Ct. 1981. Law clk. judge US Ct. Claims, 1965-67; assoc. Barrett, Smith, Schapiro & Simon, NYC, 1967-71; ptnr. Barrett, Smith, Schapiro & Armstrong, NYC, 1971-86; vice chmn. bd. Bowery Savs. Bank, NYC, 1986-88; ptnr. Chadbourne & Parke, NYC, 1988-96; mng. dir., prin. Ravitch Rice & Co. LLC, NYC, 1996—; ptnr. Rice & Ravitch LLP, NYC, 1996—. Bd. dirs. B-Line, LLC, Yaddo, 1982—2004, chmn., 1987—2003; lectr. Nat. Assn. Real Estate Investment Trusts, Bank Adminstrs. Inst., Bank Tax Inst., 1971—86; co-chmn.

Russian-Am. Banking Law Working Group, 1991—99; v.p., treas., bd. dirs. Soviet Bus. Comml. Law Edn. Found., 1991—96; vol. lectr. Fin. Svcs. Vol. Corps Mongolian Bank Tng. Program, 1993, Georgetown Internat. Law Inst., NYU Sch. Continuing Edn., Russian Trade Fair-US Dept. Commerce, 1994; mem. nat. com. Am. fgn. policy study group dels. to China, Taiwan, 96, 2000, 01; roundtable US China Policy Cross-Strait Rels., 1996—; mem. real estate adv. bd. NY State Comptr., 1987—93; bd. advisors Am.-Russian Investment Forum, 1999—2002. Contbr. articles to profl. jours. Trustee Nat. Com. Am. Fgn. Policy, 1994—, sr. v.p., 1996—; trustee Chapin Sch., 1980—91, v.p., 1989—91; trustee Marimed Found., 1984—97, Hackley Sch., 1974—81, St. Philip's Episcopal Ch., Mattapoisett, Mass., 1987—; pres. Quadequina Co./Mattapoisett Casino, 2001—04; mem. adv. bd. Shorenstein Ctr. onf Press, Politics and Pub. Policy, JFK Sch. Govt., Harvard U., 2003—; bd. dirs. African Med. Rsch. Found., 1978—2002. Mem. ABA, Coun. Fgn. Rels., NY State Bar Assn., Assn. Bar City NY, Century Assn., Harvard Club NY, NY Yacht Club, Bay Club, Mattapoisett Casino. Home: 1120 Fifth Ave New York NY 10128-0144 Office: Ravitch Rice & Co LLC 610 5th Ave Rm 420 New York NY 10020-2403 Office Phone: 212-218-7880. E-mail: ravricellc@aol.com.

RICE, DOROTHY PECHMAN (MRS. JOHN DONALD RICE), medical economist; b. Bklyn., June 11, 1922; d. Gershon and Lena (Schiff) Pechman; m. John Donald Rice, Apr. 3, 1943; children: Kenneth D., Donald B., Thomas H. Student, Bklyn. Coll., 1938—39; BA, U. Wis., 1941; DSc (hon.), Coll. Medicine and Dentistry N.J., 1979. With hosp., and med. facilities USPHS, Washington, 1960—61; med. econs. studies Social Security Adminstrn., 1962—63; health econs. br. Community Health Svc., USPHS, 1964—65; chief health ins. rsch. br. Social Security Adminstrn., 1966—72, dep. asst. commr. for rsch. and statistics, 1972—75; dir. Nat. Ctr. for Health Stats., Rockville, Md., 1976—82; prof. Inst. Health & Aging U. Calif., San Francisco, 1982—94, prof. emeritus, 1994—. Developer, mgr. nationwide health info. svcs.; expert on aging, health care costs, disability, and cost-of-illness. Contbr. articles to profl. jours. Recipient Social Security Adminstrn. citation, 1968, Disting. Svc. medal, HEW, 1974, Jack C. Massey Found. award, 1978, UCSF medal, 2002. Fellow: Am. Statis. Assn.; mem.: LWV, APHA (domestic award for excellence 1978, Sedgwick Meml. medal 1988), Assn. Health Svc. Rsch. (President's award 1988), Inst. Medicine. Home: 13895 Campus Dr Oakland CA 94605-3831 Office: U Calif Sch Nursing Calif San Francisco CA 94143-0646 Office Phone: 415-476-2771.

RICE, DOUGLAS M. music educator; b. St. Louis, Sept. 17, 1976; s. G. Duane and Janet F. Rice; m. Cassandrea Rice, June 15, 2002. BS in Edn., Southwest Mo. State, 2000. Band dir. Mt. Grove (Mo.) R-3 Schs., 2000—01, Union (Mo.) R-X1 Schs., 2001—. Mem.: Mo. Band Masters Assn., Music Educators Nat. Conf., St. Louis Wind Symphony. Office: Union R-X1 Sch Dist PO Box 440 Union MO 63084 Office Phone: 636-583-2513. E-mail: dougrice@union.k12.mo.us.

RICE, EDWARD PERRY, secondary school educator; b. Brookline, Mass., Oct. 18, 1947; s. Albert and Ruthe Irene Rice; m. Cheryl Rose Leavitt, June 30, 1974 (div. Apr. 2000); 1 child, Meisha. BA, Northeastern U., 1971; MS in Edn., U. So. Maine, 1975. Instr. Journalism dept. U. Maine, Orono, 1987—89; asst. prof. comm. studies Doane Coll., Crete, Nebr., 1989—93; editor Winchester (Mass.) Town Crier, 1994—96; mng. editor Penobscot Bay Press, Stonington, Maine, 1997—98; English tchr. Katahdin H.S., Sherman Station, Maine, 1998—99; English tchr., cross country coach Forest Hills H.S., Jackman, Maine, 1999—2001; meeting facilitator Amicus, Bangor, Maine, 2002—; adj. instr. Ea. Maine Cmty. Coll., 2003—. Theater critic Portland Press Herald/Maine Sunday Telegram, 1972—77; theater/film critic Maine Pub. Broadcasting-Radio, Orono, 1980—84; theatre critic Maine Times, Topsham, 1984—89. Author: Baseball's First Indian, Louis Sockalexis: Penobscot Legend, Cleveland Indian, 2003. With U.S. Army Nat. Guard and USAR, 1971—93. Decorated Keith L. Ware award, 1st Pl. Dept. of Army, Thomas Jefferson award, 2d Pl. Dept. of Def.; recipient Cmty. Support award of 2002, Cancer Care of Maine, 2002; Eugene O'Neill fellow, Nat. Com. for the Performing Arts, 1976. Independent. Jewish. Achievements include founded and organized for over 20 years the annual Terry Fox 5-K Run in Bangor, Maine; co-founder Angel Fund, supporting rsch. efforts to find a cure for Lou Gehrig's disease. Avocations: art, baseball history, reading, running, golf. Home: Apt 3 64 Mill St Orono ME 04473

RICE, FRANCES MAE, physician; b. Oakland, Calif., Apr. 19, 1931; d. George Henry and Clara Evelyn (Youngman) Rice. AB in Psychology cum laude, U. Calif., Berkeley, 1953, MPH in Epidemiology, 1964; MD, U. Calif., San Francisco, 1957. Intern U. Calif. Hosp., San Francisco, 1957-58; pediatric resident U. Calif., San Francisco, 1959-61; pediatric and family physician HMO, Hanford, Calif., 1974-75; clin. pediatrician Kern County Health Dept., Bakersfield, Calif., 1975-76, physician, 1989, Kern Med. Group, Inc., Bakersfield, 1976-83; pvt. practice Shafter, Calif., 1983-89; physician Mercy Medicenter, Bakersfield, 1990-91, K.C.E.O.C. Family Health Clinic, Bakersfield, 1993-98, Berkeley Women's Health Ctr., 1999—. USPHS fellow, 1963—64. Fellow: Royal Soc. Medicine; mem.: N.Y. Acad. Sci. Avocations: music, hiking. Home: 6103 Majestic Ave Oakland CA 94605

RICE, FUHRMAN D. (RUNT RICE), retired paper company executive; b. June 12, 1927; s. Robert Fulton and Carie Ann (Whitaker) R.; m. Marie Mayben, 1967; 1 child, Kathleen Ann. Forest ranger Ala. Forestry Commn., Marshall County, 1951-74; procurement agent Paperboard Divsn. Mead Corp., Stevenson, Ala., 1974-91. Pres. Grant Conservation Club, 1964-73; chmn. Marshall County Rep. Exec. Com., Ala., 1995-99; bd. dirs. Ala. Wildlife Fedn., 1961-77 (Conservationist of Yr. 1970); mem. Boy Scouts of Am. (Dist. Scouters award 1964, Silver Beaver award 1974); v.p. soc. Ala. Retirees, Guntersville, 1999, Alder Springs Cmty. Assn., Marshall County, 1999, 2003; mem. Alder Springs Vol. Fire Dept. Home: 5050 Hustleville Rd Albertville AL 35951-4747 E-mail: runt@hiwaay.net.

RICE, GARY RUSSELL, special education educator; b. Franklin, Pa., Oct. 11, 1951; s. Robert Russell and Della Elizabeth Rice. Grad. cum laude, Cleve. State U., 1973. Cert. polit. sci. tchr., learning disabilities, behavioral disorders, Ohio. Substitute tchr. Lakewood, Rocky River, Westlake (Ohio) Schs., 1973-77; instr. West Side Inst. Tech., Cleve., 1977-78; spl. edn. tchr. Parma (Ohio) City Sch. Dist., 1978—. Learning disabilities tutor, Lakewood, 1974-75; guitar cons. Rock and Roll Hall of Fame and Mus., Cleve. Asst. scoutmaster, leader Boy Scouts Am., Cleve.; former Sunday sch. tchr. local chs., Lakewood; spkr. to various groups on Exceptional Children, the Holocaust and Native Americans; charter mem. U.S. Holocaust Meml. Mus. Recipient Outstanding Spl. Educator award Parma PTA Spl. Edn. com., 1985, Thanks to Tchrs. award Sta. TV-8 WJW, Cleve., 1994, dist. award of merit Boy Scouts Am., 1997. Mem. Parma Edn. Assn., Cleve. Fedn. Musicians, DeMolay (active Legion of Honor 1996), Masons, Shriners. Avocations: music, photography.

RICE, GLEN ANTHONY, professional basketball player; b. Flint, Mich., May 28, 1967; Grad., U. Mich., 1989. Player Miami Heat, 1989—95, Charlotte Hornets, 1995—99, L.A. Lakers, 1999—. Named NBA All Star, 1996, 1997, capt., Miami Heat, 1994; named to NBA All-Rookie Second Team, 1990, All-NBA Second Team, 1996—97, All-NBA Third Team, 1997—98; recipient MVP award, Miami Heat, 1993—94, 1994—95, All Star MVP award, 1997. Office: Houston Rockets Rockets 2 Greenway Plz Ste 400 Clutch City TX 77046-3865

RICE, HERBERT WILLIAMS, SR., dean; b. Montgomery, Ala., Aug. 7, 1952; s. Herbert William and Nancy Mason Rice; m. Ansley C. Rice, Sept. 9, 1978; children: Herbert William Rice, Jr., Matthew Callaway. BA magna cum laude, Huntingdon Coll., 1974; MA in English, Auburn U., 1978; PhD in English, U. Ga., 1993. Social worker State Ala., Phenix City, Ala.; instr. English Andrew Coll., Cuthbert, Ga., 1983—86; asst. prof. English Shorter Coll., Rome, Ga., 1986—93, assoc. prof. English, 1993—2001, prof. English, 2001—, dean Sch. Liberal Arts, 2001—. Cons. Apollo Group, Phoenix, 1995—; presenter in field. Author: Toni Morrison and the American Tradition: A Rhetorical Reading, 1996, Ralph Ellison and the Politics of The Novel, 2003; contbr. articles to profl. jours. Avocations: woodworking, running, reading.

RICE, J. ANDREW, management consultant, tree farmer; b. Cleveland, Tex., July 24, 1953; s. Jakie Andrew and Neva (Richardson) R.; m. Susan Elaine Black, July 29, 1977; children: Faith Ann, Joy Elizabeth, Jakie Weldon, Luke Andrew. BA in Psychology cum laude, Baylor U., 1975; MA in Pub. Mgmt., U. Houston, 1979. Tchr. Tarkington Ind. Sch. Dist., Cleveland, Tex., 1975-76, La Marque (Tex.) Ind. Sch. Dist., 1976-77; jobs coord. Galveston (Tex.) County, 1977-78; adminstrv. asst. City of La Marque, 1978-80; cons. Community Mgmt. Svcs., Houston, 1980-82; owner, cons. Pub. Mgmt., Cleveland, 1982-92; pres. Pub. Mgmt., Inc., Cleve., 1992—. Min. of music Rural Shade Bapt. Ch.; pres. Tarkington Comty. Devel. Assn.; pres. Rice Richardson Found. Mem.: Tarkington Hist. Soc., Cleveland C. of C. (chmn.), Tex. Forestry Assn., World Future Soc., Omicron Delta Kappa. Office: Pub Mgmt PO Box 1827 Cleveland TX 77328-1827

RICE, JAMES ROBERT, engineering scientist, geophysicist; b. Frederick, Md., Dec. 3, 1940; s. Donald Blessing and Mary Celia (Santangelo) R.; m. Renata Dmowska, Feb. 28, 1981; children by previous marriage: Douglas, Jonathan. BS, Lehigh U., 1962, Sc.M., 1963, PhD, 1964; DSc (hon.), Northwestern U., Evanston, Ill., 1996, Brown U., 1997. Postdoctoral fellow Brown U., Providence, 1964-65, asst. prof. engring., 1965-68, assoc. prof., 1968-70, prof., 1970-81, Ballou prof. theoretical and applied mechanics, 1973-81; McKay prof. engring. sci. and geophysics Harvard U., Cambridge, Mass., 1981—. Recipient awards for sci. publs. ASME, awards for sci. publs. ASTM, awards for sci. publs. U.S. Nat. Com. Rock Mechanics, Timoshenko medal Am. Soc of Mechanical Engineers, 1994, Francis J. Clamer medal Franklin Institute, 1996, Arpad L. Nadai award, 1996. Fellow ASME, AAAS; mem. NAS, NAE, ASCE, Am. Geophys. Union, Fgn. Mem. Royal Soc. Achievements include research contbns. to solid mechanics, materials sci. and geophysics. Office: Harvard U Divsn Engring Applied Sci Cambridge MA 02138

RICE, JERRY LEE, professional football player; b. Starkville, Miss., Oct. 13, 1962; m. Jackie Rice; children: Jaqui, Jerry Jr. Student, Miss. State Valley U. Football player San Francisco 49ers, 1985—2000, Oakland Raiders, 2001—. Named Sports Illustrated Player of Yr., 1986, 1990, MVP, NFL, 1987, Sporting News NFL Player of Yr., 1987, 1990, MVP, Super Bowl XXIII, 1989, AP/NFL/Sports Illustrated Offensive Player of Yr., 1993, MVP, Blue-Gray Game; named to Sporting News Coll. All-Am. team, 1984, Sporting News All-Pro team, 1986—92, Pro Bowl team, 1986—96, 1995; recipient Pro Bowl MVP, 1995. Achievements include holder of NFL career records for most touchdown receptions (131); most touchdowns (139); most consecutive games with one or more touchdowns (13), 1987; NFL single-season record for most touchdown receptions (22), 1987; shares NFL single-game record for most touchdown receptions (5), 1990. Office: Oakland Raiders 1220 Harbor Bay Pkwy Alameda CA 94502

RICE, JERRY MERCER, biochemist, consultant, pathologist; b. Washington, Oct. 3, 1940; s. John Earle Rice and Leona (Mercer) Greiner; m. Mary Jane Janocha, Jan. 10, 1978; children: Stacey Lynn, Stephen Mark. BA, Wesleyan U., 1962; PhD, Harvard U., 1966. Commd. officer USPHS, 1966, ret., 1996; rsch. scientist Nat Cancer Inst., Bethesda, Md., 1966-81, chief Lab. of Comparative Carcinogenesis Frederick, Md., 1981-94, 96, assoc. dir. Frederick Cancer Rsch. and Devel. Ctr., 1994-95, acting dir. divsn. cancer etiology, 1994-95, ret., 1996; sr. scientist WHO, 1996—2002, ret., 2002; chief unit of carcinogen identification and evaluation Internat. Agy. for Rsch. on Cancer, Lyons, France, 1996—2002, cons. in toxicology, 2003—; Disting. prof. dept. oncology Georgetown U., Washington, 2003—. Editor: Perinatal Carcinogenesis, 1979; co-editor: Organ and Species Specificity in Chemical Carcinogenesis, 1983, Perinatal and Multigeneration Carcinogenesis, 1989, The Use of Short and Medium Term Tests for Carcinogens and Data on Genetic Effects in Carcinogenic Hazard Evaluation, 1999, Species Differences in Thyroid, Kidney and Urinary Bladder Carcinogenesis, 1999, Mech. of Carcinogenesis-contributions of molecular epidemiology, 2004,; contbr. rsch. articles and revs. in mechanisms of chem. carcinogenesis to profl. jours.; dir. emeritus IARC monographs on the evaluation of carcinogenic risks to humans. Mem. Soc. Toxicology, European Assn. Cancer Rsch., Am. Assn. Cancer Rsch., Phi Beta Kappa, Sigma Xi. Avocations: viticulture, tropical orchids. Home: 3213 Coquelin Ter Bethesda MD 20815-4840 Personal E-mail: jmricewas@aol.com. Business E-Mail: jr332@georgetown.edu.

RICE, JIM, state supreme court justice; b. Ramore Air Force Base, Ont., Canada, Nov. 15, 1957; (parents Am. citizens); BA in Polit. Sci., Mont. State U., 1979; JD U. Mont., 1982. Pub. defender Lewis and Clark County; ptnr. Jackson & Rice, Helena, Mont., 1985—2001; assoc. justice Mont. Supreme Ct., 2001—. Mem. Mont. Ho. Reps., 1989—95, ho. majority whip, 1993. Office: Justice Bldg Rm 323 PO Box 203003 Helena MT 59620-3003

RICE, JOHN D. agricultural products supplier; Pres. food oils divsn. Archer Daniels Midland Co., Decatur, Ill., 1996—2000, v.p., 1993—99, group v.p., pres. N.Am. oilseed processing divsn., 1999—2000, sr. v.p. corn processing and food specialties, 2000—. Office: Archer Daniels Midland Co 4666 Faries Pkwy Decatur IL 62526

RICE, JOHN G. diversified technology and services executive; BA in Econs., Hamilton Coll. Mem. fin. mgmt. program GE, 1978-81, mem. corp. audit staff, 1981-84; mgr. materials GE Appliances, 1984-86, mgr. quality control prodn. engring. and materials ops., 1986-87; pres. GEM Products, Inc., Garden Grove, Calif., 1987-90; gen. mgr. material resources GE Appliances, 1990-92; pres., COO Camco, Inc., Can., 1992-94; head corp. audit staff GE, 1994-95; pres. GE Plastics Pacific, Singapore, 1995-97; pres., CEO GE Transp. Sys., Erie, Pa., 1997—2000, GE Energy, 2000—. Chmn. U.S. Energy Assn. Office: GE 3135 Easton Tpke Fairfield CT 06431-0002

RICE, JOHN THOMAS, architecture educator; b. New London, Conn., Feb. 4, 1931; s. Clarence Benjamin and Emily (Gudal) R. BS in Engring., U. Conn., 1952; MSME, Newark Coll. Engring., 1954; D.Sc. in Engring., Columbia U., 1962. Registered profl. engr., N.Y. Test equipment designer propeller div. Curitss-Wright Corp., Caldwell, N.J., 1952-54; stress analyst Wright Aeronautical div. Curtiss-Wright Corp., Woodridge, N.J., 1954-59; chief structural mechanics Gen. Dynamics/Electric Boat, Groton, Conn., 1962-64; asst. prof. mech. engring. Pratt Inst., Bklyn., 1964-66, assoc. prof., 1966-74, prof., 1974—, chmn. dept. mech. engring., 1981-90. Mem. ASME (chmn. mech. engring. dept. heads com. region II 1987-89, chmn. profl. devel. region II 1989-93, mem. exec. com. met. sect. 1990—, vice chmn. 1991-92, chmn. 1992-93, sec. region II 1993-96, treas. met. sect. 1999—), Pi Tau Sigma, Tau Beta Pi. Office: Pratt Inst Dept of Architecture 200 Willoughby Ave Brooklyn NY 11205-3899

RICE, JON RICHARD, managed care administrator, physician; b. Grand Forks, N.D., July 10, 1946; s. Harry Frazer and Marian (Lund) R.; m. Roberta Jane Lindbergh, June 7, 1969; children: Kristen, Jennifer. BA, U. N.D., 1969, BS, 1970; MD, U. Tex., San Antonio, 1972; MS in Health Adminstrn., U. Colo., 1991. Intern U.S. Naval Hosp., San Diego, 1972-73; resident U. N.D. Sch. Medicine, Minot, 1975-77; physician Valley Med., Grand Forks, 1977-93; state health officer N.D. Dept. Health, Bismarck, 1993-97; dir. managed care Blue Cross Blue Shield of N.D., Fargo, 1997—. Contbg. author: Pilots, Personality and Performance. Lt. USN, 1972-75. Recipient Outstanding Vol. award Dakota Heart Assn., 1989, YMCA, 1992, Outstanding Health Care Provider Grand Forks C. of C., 1992, Award of Excellence N.D. Hosp. Assn., 1995. Mem. AMA, Am. Acad. Family Physicians, Am. Coll. Physician Execs., Alpha Omega Alpha. Office: Blue Cross Blue Shield ND 4510 13th Ave S Fargo ND 58121-0002 E-mail: jon_rice_1999@yahoo.com., jon.rice@noridian.com.

RICE, JOSEPH ALBERT, retired bank executive; b. Cranford, NJ, Oct. 11, 1924; s. Louis A. and Elizabeth J. (Michael) R.; m. Katharine Wolfe, Sept. 11, 1948; children: Walter, Carol, Philip, Alan. B in Aero. Engring., Rensselear Poly. Inst., 1948; M in Indsl. Engring., NYU, 1952, MA, 1968. With Grumman Aircraft Engring. Corp., 1948-53, IBM, NYC, 1953-65, mgr. ops., real estate, constrn. divsns., 1963-65; dep. group exec. N.Am. comml. telecom. group, pres. telecom. divsn. ITT, NYC, 1965-67; sr. v.p. Irving Trust Co., NYC, 1967-69, exec. v.p., 1969-72, sr. exec. v.p., 1972-73, vice chmn., 1973-74, pres., 1974-83, chmn., 1984-88, ret., 1988. Exec. v.p. Irving Bank Corp., 1971-74, vice chmn., 1974-75, pres., 1975-83, chmn. bd., CEO, 1984-88. Chmn., trustee John Simon Guggenheim Meml. Found.; trustee Blanton-Peale Inst., vice chmn., trustee Hist. Hudson Valley. Mem. Coun. Fgn. Rels., NY Acad. Scis., Univ. Club, Links, Sky Club.

RICE, JOY KATHARINE, psychologist, educational policy studies and women's studies educator; b. Oak Park, Ill., Mar. 26, 1939; d. Joseph Theodore and Margaret Sophia (Bednarik) Straka; m. David Gordon Rice, Sept. 1, 1962; children: Scott Alan, Andrew David. BFA with high honors, U. Ill., 1960; MS, U. Wis., 1962, MS, 1964, PhD, 1967. Lic. clin. psychologist. USPHS predoctoral fellow dept. psychiatry Med. Sch. U. Wis., Madison, 1964-65, asst. dir. Counseling Ctr., 1966-74, dir. Office Continuing Edn. Svcs., 1972-78, prof. ednl. policy studies and women's studies, 1974-95, clin. prof. psychiatry, 1995—; pvt. practice psychology Psychiat. Svcs., S.C., Madison, 1967—. Mem. State Wis. Ednl. Approval Bd., Madison, 1972-73; mem. Adult Edn. Commn., U.S. Office Career Edn., Washington, 1978. Author: Living Through Divorce, A Developmental Approach to Divorce Therapy, 1985, 2d edit., 1989; edit. bd. Lifelong Learning, 1979-86; cons. editor Psychology of Women Quar., 1986-88, assoc. editor, 1989-94; cons. editor Handbook of Adult and Continuing Education, 1989, Encyclopedia of Women and Gender, 2001; contbr. articles to profl. jours. Knapp fellow U. Wis.-Madison, 1960-62, tchg. fellow, 1962-63; recipient Disting. Achievement award Ednl. Press Assn. Am., 1992. Fellow APA (exec. bd. psychology of women divsn. 1994—, internat. psychology divsn. 1998—, chair internat. com. for women 2000-02, exec. bd. 1998—, Disting. Leadership award 2000-02); mem. Nat. Assn. Women in Edn. (editl. bd. jour. 1984-88, cons. editor Initiatives 1988-91), Internat. Coun. Psychologists (sec. 2000—, bd. dirs. 2003—), Am. Assn. Continuing and Adult Edn. (meritorious svc. award 1978-80, 82), TEMPO Internat. (bd. dirs., sec. 2000-2003), Big Bros. Big Sisters of Dane County (pres. 2002, bd. dirs. 1995—), Rotary Internat., Phi Delta Kappa. Avocations: interior design, collecting art, gardening, travel. Home: 4230 Waban Hl Madison WI 53711-3711 Office: 2727 Marshall Ct Madison WI 53705-2255

RICE, JULIAN CASAVANT, lawyer; b. Miami, Fla., Dec. 31, 1923; s. Sylvan J. and Maybelle (Casavant) R.; m. Dorothy Mae Haynes, Feb. 14, 1958; children— Scott B., Craig M. (dec.), Julianne C., Linda D., Janette M. Student, U. San Francisco, 1941-43; JD cum laude, Gonzaga U., 1950. Bar: Wash. 1950, Alaska 1959, U.S. Tax Ct. 1988. Pvt. practice law, Spokane, 1950-56, Fairbanks, Alaska, 1959—; prin. Law Office Julian C. Rice (and predecessor firms), Fairbanks, 1959, Salcha, Alaska, 1999. Founder, gen. counsel Mt. McKinley Mut. Savs. Bank, Fairbanks, 1965-99, chmn. bd., 1979-80; v.p., bd. dirs., gen. counsel Skimmers, Inc., Anchorage, 1966-67; gen. counsel Alaska Carriers Assn., Anchorage, 1960-71, Alaska Transp. Conf., 1960-67. Mayor City of Fairbanks, 1970-72. Served to maj. USNG and USAR, 1943-58. Decorated Bronze Star, Combat Infantryman's Badge. Fellow Am. Bar Found. (life); mem. ABA, Wash. State Bar Assn. (50-Yr. mem. award 2000), Alaska Bar Assn., Transp. Lawyers Assn., Alternative Dispute Resolution Com., Am. Arbitration Assn. (mem. transp. comml., transp. panel), Spokane Exch. Club (pres. 1956). Home and Office: 10104 Salcha Dr Salcha AK 99714-9624 E-mail: j.c.rice@att.net.

RICE, KENNER CRALLE, medicinal chemist; b. Rocky Mount, Va., May 14, 1940; s. Kenner Cralle Jr. and Annie Grace Rice. BS, Va. Mil. Inst., 1961; PhD, Ga. Inst. Tech., 1966. Sr. scientist Ciba-Geigy Corp., Summit, 1969—72; sr. staff fellow NIH, Bethesda, Md., 1972—76, rsch. chemist, 1977—86; chief sect. drug design and synthesis Nat. Inst. Diabetes, Digestive and Kidney Diseases, Bethesda, Md., 1987—88; chief lab. medicinal chemistry NIDDK, NIH, Bethesda, Md., 1989—. Adj. prof. pharmacology U. Md., Balt., 1985—; mem. Fed. Sr. Exec. Svc., Bethesda, 1989—98, Fed. Sr. Biomed. Rsch. Svc., 1998—; affiliate prof. Va. Commonwealth U., Richmond, 1995—; vis. prof. pharmacology U. Ill., Peoria, 1995—; adj. prof. medicinal chemistry Comprehensive Drug Rsch. Ctr. U. Miami, 1995—. Author (with others): Pharmacological Reviews, 1987; editor: NIDA Research Monograph 96, 1990; contbr. more than 500 rsch. papers to profl. jours. Capt. U.S. Army, 1966—68. Recipient Internat. Sato Meml. award, Japanese Pharm. Soc., 1983, Rsch. Achievement award, Am. Pharm. Assn., 1987, Hillebrand prize, Chem. Soc. Washington, 1986, Divsn. Medicinal Chemistry award, Am. Chem. Soc., 1996, Rsch. Achievement award, Am. Assn. Pharm. Scientists, 1998, Chem. Pioneer award, Am. Inst. Chemists, 2000, Nathan B. Eddy award, Coll. Problems of Drug Dependence, 2001. Fellow: Coll. on Problems of Drug Dependence (bd. dirs. 1988—92, 1997—2001); mem.: Am. Coll. Neuropsychopharmacology, Cosmos Club. Achievements include 42 patents in organic chemical synthesis and pharmacology of drugs of abuse; development of NIH opiate total synthesis as first practical synthesis of opium alkaloids and derivatives as narcotics and narcotic antagonists. Office: NIH NIDDK Lab Medicinal Chemistry Bldg 8 Rm B1-23 Bethesda MD 20892

RICE, LESTER, electronics company executive; b. Detroit, Feb. 23, 1927; s. Carvel Lester and Irene R.; m. Barbara Helen Winston, June 27, 1957; children— Scott W., Jody I., Jeffrey C., Judy A., Timohty D. BSE.E., U. Mich., 1951. Gen. sales mgr. Westinghouse Semicondr. Div., Youngwood, Pa., 1951-68; pres. Airco Speer Elec. div. Airco Inc., Bradford, Pa., 1968-80; vice chmn., dir. KOA Speer Electronics, Inc., Bradford, 1980-98; chmn. KOA Europe GMBH, 1998—. Bd. dirs. DeFond No. Am. Inc.; chmn. bd. Lester Rice, Inc., Bradford, 1980—. Adv. bd. U. Pitts. With USN, 1945-46. Mem. IEEE, Electronics Industries Assn. (bd. govs.), Am. Legion, Masons. Republican. Home: 2 Vista Avenue Ext Bradford PA 16701-2759 Office: PO Box 547 Bradford PA 16701-0547

RICE, LINDA JOHNSON, publishing executive; b. Chicgo, Mar. 22, 1958; d. John J. and Eunice Johnson; m. Andre Rice, 1984. BA Journalism, Univ. Southern Calif., L.A., 1980; MBA, Northwestern Univ., Evanston, Ill., 1987. With Johnson Pub. Co., 1980—, past v.p. and asst. to pub., COO, 1987—2002; pres. Johnson Pub. Co., Inc., Chgo., 1987—, CEO, 2002—; pres. Fashion Fair Cosmetics, Ill., 1987—. Office: Johnson Pub Co Inc 820 S Michigan Ave Chicago IL 60605-2191

RICE, LOIS DICKSON, former computer company executive; b. Portland, Maine, Feb. 28, 1933; d. David A. and Mary D. Dickson; m. Alfred B. Fitt, Jan. 7, 1978 (dec. 1992); children: Susan, John Rice. AB magna cum laude, Radcliffe Coll., 1954; postgrad. (Woodrow Wilson fellow), Columbia U., 1954-55; LLD (hon.), Brown U., 1981, Bowdoin Coll., 1984. Dir. counseling services Nat. Scholarship Service and Fund for Negro Students, N.Y.C., 1955-59; with The Coll. Bd., N.Y.C. and Washington, 1959-81, v.p. Washington, 1973-81; sr. v.p. govt. affairs Control Data Corp., 1981-91. Guest scholar The Brookings Inst., Washington, 1991—; bd. dirs. McGraw Hill, Inc., 1987—2003, Internat. Multifoods, 1991—2003, UNUM/Provident Corp., 1992—2003; overseer Tuck Sch. Mgmt. Dartmouth Coll., 1990—94; mem. Pres.'s Fgn. Intelligence Adv. Bd., 1993—2001; trustee George Washington U., 1992—98, co-chair Mgmt. Leadership for Tomorrow, 1994—; trustee CNA Corp. Pub. Agenda Found., Harry Frank Guggenheim Found. Contbr. articles on edn. to profl. publs.; editor: Student Loans: Problems and Policy Alternatives, 1977. Mem. adv. bd. to dir. NSF, 1981—89, chair, 1986—89; mem. Gov.'s Commn. on Future of Postssecondary Edn. in N.Y. State, 1976—77, Carnegie Coun. on Higher Edn., 1975—80; trustee Radcliffe Coll., 1969—75, Stephens Coll., Mo., 1976—78, Beauvoir Sch., Washington, 1970—76, Children's TV Workshop, 1970—73; bd. dirs. Potomac Inst., 1977—92, German Marshall Fund, 1984—94, Joint Ctr. Polit. and Econ. Studies, 1991—94, Reading is Fundamental, 1991—. Recipient Disting. Service award HEW, 1977 Mem. Cosmos Club, Phi Beta Kappa. Episcopalian. Home: 2332 Massachusetts Ave NW Washington DC 20008 Office: The Brookings Instn 1775 Massachusetts Ave NW Washington DC 20036-2103

RICE, LUANNE, writer; b. 1955; B of humane letters, Conn. Coll., 1977, degree (hon.), 2002. Author: Angels All Over Town, 1985, Crazy in Love, 1988, Stone Heart, 1990, Secrets of Paris, 1991, Blue Moon, 1994, Home Fires, 1996, Cloud Nine, 2000, Follow The Stars Home, 2001, Firefly Beach, 2001, Dream Country, 2002, Summer Light, 2002, True Blue, 2002, Safe Harbor, 2003, The Secret Hour, 2003, The Perfect Summer, 2003, Dance With Me, 2004. Office: c/o Jane Rotrosen Agency 318 E 51st St New York NY 10022

RICE, LYNDA LU, elementary school educator, writer; b. San Antonio, July 21, 1944; d. James Franklin Perry and Sarah Wren Medlock; m. Robert Roland Rice, Sept. 5, 1964; children: Kelly Wren, Tami Elaine. BA in elem edn. and lang. arts, U. Houston, 1974. Cert. GATE N.J. Writing Tng., tchr. Tex., 1974. 6th grade reading, social studies tchr. Pearland (Tex.) I. Sch. Dist., 1975—87; 4th grade tchr. Pasadena (Tex.) I. Sch. Dist., 1990, 5th grade liberal arts tchr., 1990—97, 7th grade Tex. History, 1997—2000, hons. English tchr., 1997—99. Student activities comm. ch. Pearland (Tex.) I. Sch. Dist., 1980, grade level chair, dept. chair, 1980—90; student coun. sponsor Pasadena (Tex.) I. Sch. Dist., 1990, academic games coach, 1997—2000. Author: History in Review, 2002, 6th grade reading curriculum; co-author: (presentation prod.) History in Review, Teaming Through the Gulf of Mexico. Pres. Fedn. of A&M Mother's Club, Pasadena, Tex., 1980, corr. sec. Coll. Station, Tex., 1990; campus adv. Assn. of Tex. Prof. Educators, Pasadena, Tex., 1990; elder Presbyterian Ch., Pasadena, Tex., 1990—. Republican. Presbyterian. Avocations: reading, camping, travel, church. Home and Office: Presentation Prodns 11006 Sagemorgan Dr Houston TX 77089 Office Phone: 281-481-3451. Home Fax: 281-481-3451.

RICE, MARTIN, education educator; BS, Pa. State U., 1984, PhD, 1996; MS, Western Mich. U., 1987. Assoc. prof. Med. Coll. of Ohio, Toledo, 1997—. Achievements include research in Motor control and learning in occupl. therapy. Office Phone: 419-383-4713. Office Fax: 419-383-5880. E-mail: mrice@mco.edu.

RICE, MARY ESTHER, biologist; b. Washington, Aug. 3, 1926; d. Daniel Gibbons and Florence Catharine (Pyles) R. AB, Drew U., 1947; MA, Oberlin Coll., 1949; PhD, U. Wash., 1966. Instr. biology Drew U., Madison, N.J., 1949-50; rsch. assoc. Columbia U., N.Y.C., 1950-53; rsch. asst. NIH, Bethesda, Md., 1953-61; curator invertebrate zoology and dir. Smithsonian Marine Sta., Smithsonian Instn., Washington, 1966—2002, sr. rsch. scientist emeritus, 2002—. Mem. adv. panel on systematic biology NSF, Washington, 1977-78; mem. com. on marine invertebrates Nat. Acad. Sci., 1976-81; mem. overseers com. on biology Harvard U., Cambridge, Mass., 1982-88. Assoc. editor Jour. Morphology, Ann Arbor, Mich., 1985-91, Invertebrate Biology, 1995—; editor: (with M. Todorovic) Biology of Sipuncula and Echiura, 1975, 2nd vol., 1976, (with F.S. Chia) Settlement and Metamorphosis of Marine Invertebrate Larvae, 1978, (with F.W. Harrison) Microscopic Anatomy of Invertebrates, Vol. 12, 1993; contbr. articles to profl. jours. Recipient Drew U. Alumni Achievement award in sci., 1980. Fellow AAAS; mem. Am. Soc. Zoologists (pres. 1979), Am. Microscopical Soc. (pres. 1999), Phi Beta Kappa. Office: Smithsonian Marine Sta 701 Seaway Dr Fort Pierce FL 34949-3140

RICE, NANCY E. judge; b. Denver, June 2, 1950; 1 child. BA cum laude, Tufts U., 1972; JD, U. Utah, 1975. Law clerk U.S. Dist. Ct. of Colo., 1975-76, dep. state pub. defender, appellate divn., 1976-77; asst. U.S. atty. Dist. of Colo., 1977-87; dep. chief civil divn. U.S. Attorney's Office, 1985-88; judge Denver Dist. Ct., 1988-98; apptd. judge Colo. Supreme Ct., 1998—. Contbr. articles to profl. jours. Mem. Denver Bar Assn., Colo. Bar Assn. (bd. govs. 1990-92, exec. coun., 1991-92), Women's Bar Assn., Rhone-Brackett Inn of Ct. (master 1993-97), Women Judges Assn. (co-chair nat. conf. 1990). Office: Colo Supreme Ct Colo State Jud Bldg 2 E 14th Ave Fl 4 Denver CO 80203-2115

RICE, NORMAN B. bank executive, former mayor; b. Denver, May 4, 1943; m. Constance Rice; 1 child, Mian. BA in Comm., MPA, U. Wash. Past mgr. corp. contbns. and soc. policy Rainier Nat. Bank; past dir. govt. svcs. Puget Sound Coun. Govts.; past asst. dir. Seattle Urban League; past reporter KIXI Radio; past editor, writer KOMO TV; with govt. City of Seattle, 1978—, city councilman, 1978-89, mayor, 1990-97; pres., chief exec. officer Fed. Home Loan Bank of Seattle, 1999—. Pres. U.S. Conf. of Mayors, 1995; bd. dirs. Safeco Corp. Office: Fed Home Loan Bank 1501 4th Ave Ste 1900 Seattle WA 98101-1693

RICE, PATRICIA JANE, journalist; b. St. Louis, Oct. 20, 1942; d. Canice T. and Jane Elizabeth Tobin) R. BA, Maryville Coll., 1964; postgrad., St. Louis U., 1965, 66. Copywriter Wohl Co., St. Louis, 1964-67; free-lance journalist Paris, 1967; copywriter D'Arcy Adut. Co., St. Louis, 1968; feature writer, columnist St. Louis Post, 1969-94, religion writer, 1994—2004, South reporter, 2004—. Moderator Rutgers U./Eagleton Ctr. Women in Politics Conf., 1980, 82, 84; lectr. in field. Author: City House, 1968, The Eclectic Shopper, 1973; co-author: In the Running: The New Political Woman, 1981. V.p. The St. Louis Forum, 1997—; bd. dirs. Leadership St. Louis, 1985-90. Recipient Quest award Mo. Press Women's, 1998; Knight Ctr. fellow, U. Md., College Park, 1996. Mem. Journalism Found. Met. St. Louis (pres. 1984-91), St. Louis Newspaper Guild (treas. 1977-87), Soc. Profl. Journalists. Avocations: gardening, skiing. Office: St Louis Post 900 N Tucker Blvd Saint Louis MO 63101-1069

RICE, PATRICIA OPPENHEIM LEVIN, special education educator, consultant; b. Detroit, Apr. 5, 1932; d. Royal A. and Elsa (Freeman) Oppenheim; m. Charles L. Levin, Feb. 21, 1956 (div. Dec. 1981); children: Arthur David, Amy Ragen, Fredrick Stuart; m. Howard T. Rice, Dec. 16, 1990 (div. Apr. 1994). AB in History, U. Mich., 1954, PhD, 1981; MEd, Marygrove Coll., 1973. Cert. elem. tchr., Mich. Tchr. reading and learning disabled, cons., Detroit Pub. Schs., 1967-76; assoc. prof., coord. spl. edn., Marygrove Coll., 1976-86; adj. prof. Oakland U., 1987-90, U. Miami, 1989-95; edn. curriculum cons. Lady Elizabeth Sch., Jávea (Alicante) Spain, 1988-91; v.p. Machpelah Non-profit Cemetary Bd., Ferndale, Mich., 1978-87, co-pres., 1987—; adv. bd. Eton Acad., Birmingham, Mich., 1991-93; workshop presenter Dade City Schs., 1992-97; presenter in field. Mem. Mich. regional bd. ORT, 1965-68; mil. affairs and youth svcs. S.E. Mich. chpt. ARC Bd., 1973-79; v.p. exec. bd. Women's Aux. Children's Hosp. Mich., 1968-73; bd. dirs. women's com. United Cmty. Svcs., 1968-73; judge Dade County Schs. for Tchr. Grants, 1996—; bd. dirs. Detroit Grand Opera Assn., 1970-75; com. chair morning of music benefits Detroit Symphony Orch.; torch drive area chmn. United Found., 1967-70; benefactor Fla. Grand Opera, 1990-2001, grand benefactor, 2002—, guild exec. bd., 1992-, v.p., 1998-99, co-pres. 2000-02, chair, found. bd. dirs., 2000-01; guild exec. bd. Miami City Ballet, 1996-2000, Choreographers Cir., 1990-; chair Lincoln Rd. Walk, 1996, co-chair All Star Luncheon, 1996, Ball Com., 1992; active Diabetes Rsch. Inst. & Found. Love & Hope Com., Fla. Concert Assn. Cresendo Soc., 1993-97, Villa Maria Angel, 1996—, v.p. angel bd. 1998—, found. bd. dirs. 2000—; v.p. Miami Children's Hosp., 2004—; panel judge Dada County Cultural Affairs Coun., 2002-2004. Mem. NAACP (life), Navy League, Greater Miami Social Register, Citizens Interested in the Arts (charter, grant chair, exec. bd. 1997—), Williams Island Club, Turnberry Isle Golf Club (signature), Miami Shores Country Club, Surf Club, Phi Delta Kappa, Pi Lambda Theta.

RICE, PAUL JACKSON, lawyer, educator; b. East St. Louis, Ill., July 15, 1938; s. Ray Jackson and Mary Margaret (Campbell) Rice; m. Carole Jeanne Valentine, June 6, 1959; children: Rebecca Jeanne Ross, Melissa Ann Hansen, Paul Jackson Jr. BA, U. Mo., 1960, JD, 1962; LLM, Northwestern U., 1970; student, Command and Gen. Staff Coll., 1974-75, Army War Coll., 1982-83. Bar: Mo. 1962, Ill. 1969, U.S. Dist. Ct. (no. dist.) Ill. 1970, U.S. Supreme Ct. 1972, U.S. Ct. Appeals (DC cir.) 1991, DC 1993, U.S. Dist. Ct. DC 2000. Commd. 1st lt. U.S. Army, 1962, advanced through grades to col., 1980; asst. judge advocate 4th Armored Div., Goeppingen, Germany, 1966-69; dep. staff judge advocate 1st Cavalry Div., Vietnam, 1970-71; inst., prof. Judge Adv. Gen. Sch., Charlottesville, Va., 1971-74, commdt., dean, 1985-88; br. chief Gen. Law Br., Pentagon, 1975-78; chief adminstrv. law div. Office Judge Adv. Gen., Pentagon, Washington, 1978-79; staff judge adv. 1st Inf. Div., Ft. Riley, Kans., 1979-82, V Corps U.S. Army, Frankfurt, Germany, 1983-85, USACAC, Ft. Leavenworth, Kans., 1989-90; faculty Indsl. Coll. Armed Forces, 1988-89; chief counsel Nat. Hwy. Traffic Safety Adminstrn., Washington, 1990-93; ptnr. Arent Fox, Washington, 1993—. Contbr. articles to profl. jours. Recipient Granted Legal Svc. award, State of Hessen, Germany, 1985, cert. of merit, U. Mo. Alumni Assn., 1987. Mem.: Ctr. Law and Nat. Security, Mo. Bar Assn., Lion Tamers, Phi Delta Phi. Methodist. Avocations: writing, reading, golf. Home: 7835 Vervain Ct Springfield VA 22152-3107 Office: Arent Fox 1050 Connecticut Ave NW Washington DC 20036-5339 E-mail: ricepj@arentfox.com.

RICE, PEGGY A. librarian; d. Jasper Frank and Vivian Louise Watkins; m. Dennis R. Rice, Apr. 30, 1966; children: Dennis Jr., Steven, Brian, Kari. AA in Data Processing, Paducah CC, Ky., 1989. Student asst. Paducah CC, Ky.; libr. asst. Bennet Acad., Lisle, Ill.; head, circulation Itasca Cmty. Libr., Ill. Chair, sec. DuPage Libr. Sys. Circulation, Geneva, 2000—02; sec. LINC Task Force Circulation, St. Charles, Ill., 2002—03, Laconi Circulation Sect., Ill., 2003. Office: Itasca Cmty Libr 500 W Irving Pk Rd Itasca IL 60143

RICE, REGINA KELLY, marketing executive; b. Yonkers, N.Y., July 11, 1955; d. Howard Adrian and Lucy Virginia (Butler) Kelly; m. Mark Christopher Rice, Sept. 11, 1981; children: Amanda Kelly, Jaime Brannen. BS in Community Nutrition, Cornell U., 1978. Account exec. J. Walter Thompson Co., N.Y.C., 1978-79; sr. account exec. Ketchum, MacLeod & Grove, N.Y.C., 1979-80; supr. Burson Marstellar, Hong Kong, 1981-83; v.p., dep. dir. food and beverage unit, creative dir. N.Y. office Hill and Knowlton, N.Y.C., 1983-91; mktg. cons. Rice & Rohr, N.Y.C., 1991-93; sr. v.p., dir. consumer mktg. practice Manning, Selvage & Lee, N.Y.C., 1993-97, sr. v.p. global tng. dir., 1999—; chief inspiration officer, dir. corp. devel. Internat. Pub. Rels. Assn., 1999-2001. Writer Fast and Healthy Mag., 1991-2000. Mem. Pub. Rels. Soc. Am. Roman Catholic. Avocation: collecting Provence pottery. Home: 31 Wrangler Ln Bell Canyon CA 91307 Office: Manning Selvage & Lee 6500 Wilshire Blvd Los Angeles CA 90048-4920 Office Phone: 323-866-6023.

RICE, RICHARD CAMPBELL, retired state official, retired army officer; b. Atchison, Kans., Dec. 11, 1933; s. Olive Campbell and Ruby Thelma (Rose) R.; m. Donna Marie Lincoln, Aug. 4, 1956; children: Robert Alden, Holly Elizabeth. BS in History, Kans. State Univ., 1955; MA in Social Studies, Eastern Mich. Univ., 1965; grad., U.S. Army Command and Gen. Staff Coll., 1968, U.S. Army War Coll., 1977; attended, FBI Nat. Exec. Inst., 1990; grad. prog. for sr. execs., state and local govt., Harvard Univ., 1985. Commd. 2nd lt. U.S. Army, 1955; advanced through grades to col., 1976; with Joints Chief of Staff, Washington, D.C., 1975-76; fac. U.S. Army War Coll., Carlisle Barracks, PA, 1977-79; chief of staff Hdqrs. 3rd ROTC Region, Ft. Riley, KS, 1982-83; ret., 1983; dir. Mo. State Emerg. Mgmt. Agy., Jefferson City, 1983-85, Mo. Dept. Pub. Safety, Jefferson City, 1985-93. Trustee Mo. State Employees Retirement System, 1990-93; bd. visitors Nat. Emergency Mgmt. Inst., 1991-92. Grad. Leadership, Mo., 1991; mem. Coordinating Coun. Health Edn., Mo.'s Chldrn. and Adolescents, Mo. Jail and Prison Overcrowding Task Force, Gov.'s Domestic Violence Task Force, Gov.'s Commn. on Crime, Gov.'s Adv. Coun. on Driving While Intoxicated, Mo. Children's Svcs. Commn., Blur Ribbon Commn. on Svcs. to Youth, Campaign to Protect Our Children; mem. policy com. Mo. Youth Initiative; chmn. Gov.'s Cabinet Coun. for Justice Adminstrn., Mo. Statistical Analysis Ctr. adv. bd. adv. bd. Mo. Criminal Hist. Records; mem. Boone County Mo Bd. of Jail Vis., 2003—; bd. dirs. Mo. Law Enforcement Meml. Found., Gt. Rivers coun. Boy Scouts Am. (James E. West fellow), 1993—; bd. dirs. Mid-Mo. chpt. Alzheimer's Assn., 2002–; peer rev. cons. Nat. Inst. of Justice; chmn. Alliance for Uniform Hazmat Transp. Procedures, 1991-93. Decorated Legion of Merit, Bronze Star (3), Meritorious Svc. Medal (4), Air medal (2), Joint Svc. Commendation medal, Army Commendation medal (2); Republic of Vietnam Cross of Gallantry with Silver Star; recipient Conspicuous Svc. medal State of Mo., Silver Beaver award Boy Scouts Am.; James E. West fellow. Mem. Nat. Eagle Scout Assn., Assn. U.S. Army, Soc. First Divsn., Am. Legion, VFW, Disabled Am. Vets., AMVETS, Mil. Order of World Wars, Nat. Soc., SAR, Mil. Officers Assn. Am., Nat. Criminal Justice Assn. (bd. dirs. 1987-93), Rotary (Paul Harris fell.), Mo. Symphony Soc., St. Andrews Soc., Theta Xi. Republican. Avocation: sailing.

RICE, RICHARD LEE, retired architect; b. Raleigh, N.C., May 4, 1919; s. Robert Edward Lee and Grace Lucille (Betts) R.; m. Cora Belle Stegall, Apr. 12, 1946; children— Richard Lee, Westwood Carter, David Sinclair. BS in Archtl. Engring., N.C. State U., 1941; grad., U.S. Army Command and Gen. Staff Coll., 1961. Assoc. Cooper-Shumaker, Architects, Raleigh, 1946-47; prin. Richard L. Rice, Architects, Raleigh, 1947-48; assoc. Cooper, Haskins & Rice and predecessor firm, Raleigh, 1948-52, ptnr., 1953-54, Haskins & Rice, Architects, Raleigh, 1954-85; prin. Haskins, Rice, Savage & Pearce, Architects, 1985-91, pres., 1985-91. V.p. N.C. Design Found., 1973; pres. N.C. Archtl. Found., 1975; mem. Raleigh Arts Commn., 1978-82, Raleigh Hist. Properties Commn., 1990-92, Raleigh Hist. Dists. Commn., 1991-92. Archtl. works include renovations, Raleigh Meml. Auditorium, 1964, 78, 91 (SE Regional AIA award of merit 1964), Auditorium, 4 high schs. and 13 elem. schs., Raleigh Civic Ctr., stack addition Wilson Libr. U. N.C., Chapel Hill, 1977, Reidsville, N.C. Jr. High Sch.; assoc. architect Raleigh Radisson Hotel, 1980, One Hanover Sq. Office Bldg., 1985, Two Hannover Sq. Office Bldg., 1990, additions and renovations to Raleigh Meml. Auditorium, 1989, 3 indsl. plants, 7 bldgs., Wake Tech. C.C., 50 chs. Pres. Wake County (N.C.) Hist. Soc., 1973-74; mem. N.C. Gov.'s Com. for Facilities for Physically Handicapped, 1970-73; arbitrator Am. Arbitration Assn. With inf. and C.E. U.S. Army, 1941-46, ETO; col. USAR; ret. Decorated Silver Star; Legion of Merit; Bronze Star; Purple Heart. Fellow AIA (pres. N.C. chpt. 1970, Disting. Svc. award N.C. chpt. 1975); mem. Raleigh Council Architects (pres. 1950), Nat. Trust for Hist. Preservation, N.C. State Art Soc., Ret. Officers Assn. U.S. (pres. Triangle chpt. 1983), N.C. State U. Gen. Alumni Assn. (pres., chmn. bd. 1960-61, pres. Class 1941, 1986-91), Carolina Country Club, Lions, Torch Club (pres. 1982-83), Phi Eta Sigma, Phi Kappa Phi. Democrat. Baptist.

RICE, RICK BLACKBURN, computer programmer, systems analyst; b. Louisville, Sept. 17, 1954; s. Blackburn M. and Alice Jane (Walker) R.; m. Peijuan Miao, June 23, 1989; children: Richard J., Franklin W. BA in Psychology, U. Mich., 1978; MS in Computer Systems Mgmt., U. Md., 1997. Mem. computing staff Hughes Aircraft Co., El Segundo, Calif., 1980-84; programmer, analyst Candle Corp., L.A., 1984-86; sr. programmer, analyst Computer Assocs., L.A., 1986-88; fgn. expert Shaanxi Inst. Fin. and Econs., Xi'an, People's Republic of China, 1989-90; sr. programmer, analyst Disclosure, Inc., Bethesda, Md., 1988-96; info. sys. specialist IBM, Gaithersburg, Md., 1996—97; sr. programmer analyst Sci. Applications Internat. Corp., Falls Church, Va., 1998—2003. Avocation: sinology. Home: 7610 Maple Ave Apt 302 Takoma Park MD 20912-5523 E-mail: rick_rice@hotmail.com.

RICE, ROBERT ARNOT, school administrator; b. San Francisco, Apr. 4, 1911; s. Abraham Lincoln and Mary Eugenia (Arnot) R.; m. Frances Von Dorsten, Aug. 15, 1936 (dec. sept. 1986); m. Esther Roossink, July 11, 1989. BA, U. Calif., Berkeley, 1934, MA, 1947; postgrad., Columbia U., 1948. Various ednl. positions, 1935-61; supr. sci. and math. Berkeley Unified Sch. Dist., 1961-64; adminstr. NSF Summer Insts. for Sci. Tchr., U. Calif., Berkeley, 1957-65; dir. On Target Sch., Berkeley Unified Sch. Dist., 1971-73; coord. pub. programs Lawrence Hall of Sci., 1964-70; work experience edn. coord. Berkeley Unified Sch. Dist., 1973-75; exec. dir. Calif. Sci. Tchr. Assn., 1964-90; dir. No. Calif.-Western Nev. Jr. Sci. and Humanities Symposium, 1962-93. Cons. Berkeley Unified Sch. Dist., 1964-70; bd. dirs. San Francisco Bay Area Sci. Fair, 1960—; mem. steering com. Chem. Study, 1960-75; coord. Industry Initiatives for Sci. and Math. Edn. Program, 1985-86; dir. Industry Initiatives for Sci. and Math. Edn. Acad., 1987; mem. Internat. Sci. and Engring. Fair Coun., Sci. Svc., Inc., 1959-68; dir. 18th Internat. Sci. and Engring. Fair, San Francisco, 1967; exec. dir. San Francisco Bay Area Sci. Fair, 1954-59; resource cons. Calif. Farm Bur. Fedn.-Youth Power Conf., Asilomar, 1966; judging chair Nat. Jr. Sci. and Humanities Symposium, 1993-97. Contbr. articles to profl. publs. Bd. dirs. Calif. Heart Assn., 1966-71, Alameda County Heart Assn., 1966-71; mem. Cen. Calif. Sci. Com., 1965-70; mem. rsch. com. Alameda County TB and Health Assn., 1965-69, mem. adv. com., 1965-69. Named to Berkeley H.S. Hall of Fame, 1994; recipient Benjamin Ide Wheeler medal, 1985, San Francisco Bay Area Sci. Fair award, Calif. Acad. Sci., 1970, Armed Forces Chem. Assn. award for outstanding chemistry tchr. in San Francisco Bay Area, 1965, Robert Rice award, No. Calif. JSHS Competition, 1996, 50-yr. award for starting the San Francisco Bay Area Sci. Fair, 2003. Mem. NEA, Nat. Sci. Tchrs. Assn. (pres. 1960-61, region VIII dir. 1955-57, Calif. state dir. 1949-56, mem. chemistry com. 1956-60, Disting. Svc. to Sci. Edn. award 1986), No. Calif. Com. on Problem Solving in Sci., Calif. Sci. Tchrs. Assn. (pres. no. sect. 1949-50, Disting. Svc. to Sci. Tchg. award 1981, Lifetime Achievement award 1999), Calif. Tchrs. Assn., N.C. Sci. Specialists, Berkeley Kiwanis Club, Phi Delta Kappa (pres. Lambda chpt. 1942-43). Office: U Calif Berkeley Lawrence Hall Of Sci Berkeley CA 94720-0001

RICE, RONALD JAMES, hospital administrator; b. Springfield, Mo., Feb. 5, 1944; s. Glen Elwood and Alice Jeanett (Robinson) R. BSBA, Cen. Mo. State U., 1966, MABA, 1969, Specialist, 1972. Lic. nursing home adminstr.; lic. risk mgr. Unit mgr. Bapt. Med. Ctr., Kansas City, Mo., 1970-71; dir. unit mgmt. Ind. Health Ctr., Independence, Mo., 1971-72; adminstrv. officer Meth. Hosp., Jacksonville, Fla., 1972-73, dir. personnel, 1973-74; assoc. adminstr. Humana Hosp. Orange Park (Fla.), 1974-77; adminstr. Cathedral Rehab. Hosp., Jacksonville, 1977-79, Marion County Gen. Hosp., Hamilton, Ala., 1979-80, Nassau Gen. Hosp., Fernandina Beach, Fla., 1980-85, Reception Med. Ctr., Lake Butler, Fla., 1985-91; regional adminstr. health svcs. Dept. Corrections, Gainesville, Fla., 1991—. Cons. Clay Meml. Hosp., Green Cove Springs, Fla., 1976-77, Allied Health Care, Jacksonville, 1989. Mem. Polit. Action Com., Fla. Hosp. Assn., 1990, Coun. on Crime and Delinquency, Gainesville, 1990, Human Resources Com., Orlando, 1991; active Orange Park Presbyn. Ch. With U.S. Army, 1967-69. Decorated Army Commendation medal. Fellow Am. Coll. Health Care Execs.; mem. Am. acad. Med. Adminstrs., Am. Coll. Health Care Adminstrs., Am. Soc. Personnel Adminstrs., Fla. Hosp. Assn., Rotary (pres. 1984-86). Democrat. Avocations: boating, auto collecting model, antique juke box collecting, reading. Home: 1744 Horton Dr Orange Park FL 32073-2757

RICE, STANLEY ARTHUR, biology professor; b. Cushing, Okla., May 30, 1957; s. Arthur John and Nina Irene (Hicks) R.; m. Althea Lisette Clarkston, June 9, 1984; 1 child, Anita. BA, U. Calif., Santa Barbara, 1979; PhD, U. Ill., 1987. Vis. teaching specialist U. Ill., Urbana, 1986-87; asst. prof. The King's Coll., Briarcliff Manor, N.Y., 1987-90; vis. faculty Sarah Lawrence Coll., Bronxville, N.Y., 1989-90; asst. prof. Huntington (Ind.) Coll., 1990-93, S.W. State U., Marshall, Minn., 1993-98, S.E. Okla. State U., Durant, 1998—2003, assoc. prof., 2003—. Vis. faculty mem. Wheaton (Ill.) Coll. Sci. Sta., 1993—, Taylor U., Upland, Ind., 1993. Contbr. articles to Am. Biol. Tchr., Jour. Coll. Sci. Tchg., Oecologia, Perspectives on Sci. and Christian Faith, Nat. Ctr. for Sci. Edn. Reports, Jour. Entomol. Sci. Predoctoral fellowship NSF, Univ. Ill., 1980. Mem. Ecol. Soc. Am., British Ecol. Soc., Bot. Soc. Am., Am. Sci. Affiliation, Am. Biol. Tchrs. Office: Dept Biol Sci SE Okla State Univ Durant OK 74701 E-mail: srice@sosu.edu.

RICE, STEPHEN GARY, medical educator, pediatrician, sports medicine physician; b. Bklyn., Dec. 21, 1945; s. Abraham S. and Anne (Shelling) R.; m. Hilary Jo Turett, May 10, 1987; children: Adam, Bryan. AB, Columbia Coll., 1967; MD, PhD, NYU, 1974; MPH, U. Wash., 1983. Diplomate in pediat. and sports medicine Am. Bd. Pediat. Intern, resident Children's Hosp. and U. Wash., Seattle, 1974-77; faculty mem. sports medicine U. Wash., Seattle, 1977-96; program dir. primary care sports medicine fellowship Jersey Shore Univ. Med. Ctr., Neptune, NJ, 1996—; clin. assoc. prof. pediat. Robert Wood Johnson Med. Sch. U. Medicine and Dentistry N.J., New Brunswick, 1999—. Developer, dir. Athletic Health Care Sys., 1978—; cons. in field. Author: Athletic Health Care System, 1988. Team physician U. Wash., 1977-81. Fellow Am. Acad. Pediat. (chmn. sports medicine com. N.J. chpt. 1999—, chmn. govt. affairs com. N.J. chpt. 2000-03, sec.-editor N.J. chpt. 2002-04, treas. N.J. chpt. 2004—, sports medicine and fitness com. 2003—), Am. Coll. Sports Medicine (sec. Greater N.Y. regional chpt. 1997-2002, chmn. health and sci. policy com., 2000—, chmn. liaison com. 2002-04); mem. AAHPERD, Nat. Strength and Conditioning Assn., Am. Med. Soc. Sports Medicine, Med. Soc. N.J. Avocations: sports, cooking, gardening, gilbert & sullivan, chess. Home: 6 Wildflower Ct Manalapan NJ 07726-2861 Office: Jersey Shore Univ Med Ctr Dept Pediat PO Box 397 Neptune NJ 07754-0397 Office Phone: 732-776-2384. Business E-Mail: srice@meridianhealth.com.

RICE, STUART ALAN, chemist, educator; b. N.Y.C., Jan. 6, 1932; s. Harry L. and Helen (Rayfield) Rice; m. Marian Ruth Coopersmith, June 1, 1952 (dec. June 1994); children: Barbara, Janet; m. Ruth O'Brien, Sept. 27, 1997; 1 child, David Lawrence. BS, Bklyn. Coll., 1952; MA, Harvard, 1954, PhD, 1955. Jr. fellow Harvard, 1955—57; faculty U. Chgo., 1957—60, prof. chemistry, 1960—69, Louis Block prof. phys. scis., 1969—77, chmn. dept. chemistry, 1971—76, Frank P. Hixon disting. service prof., 1977—, dean phys. scis. div., 1981—95, dir. Inst. Study Metals, 1957—59; Newton Abraham prof. Oxford U., 1999—2000. Mem. Nat. Sci. Bd., 1980—86. Author: Polyelectrolyte Solutions, 1961, Statistical Mechanics of Simple Liquids, 1965, Physical Chemistry, 1980, 2d edit., 2000, Optical Control of Molecular Dynamics, 2000; contbr. articles to profl. jours. Named Falk-Plautt lectr., Columbia U., 1964, Riley lectr., Notre Dame U., 1964, U. lectr. chemistry, U. Western Ont., 1970, Seaver lectr., U. So. Calif., 1972, Noyes lectr., U. Tex., 1975, Foster lectr., SUNY, 1976, Frank T. Gucker lectr., Ind. U., 1976, Fairchild lectr., Calif. Inst. Tech., 1979, Baker lectr., Cornell U., 1985—86, Centenary lectr., Royal Soc. Chemistry, 1986—87, Nat. lectr., Phi Beta Kappa, 1994—95, Kennedy lectr., Washington U., 2002, Noyes lectr., U. Oreg., 2002; recipient Centennial medal, Harvard U., 1997, Nat. Medal of Sci., 1999, Hirschfelder award for Theoretical Chemistry, 2002; fellow, Guggenheim, 1960—61, Sr. Postdoctoral fellow, NSF, 1965—66, USPHS Spl. Postdoctoral fellow, U. Copenhagen, 1970—71. Fellow: Royal Irish Acad. Scis., Am. Philos. Soc.; mem.: AAAS, Danish Acad. Sci. and Letters, N.Y. Acad. Scis. (A. Cressy Morrison prize 1955), Faraday Soc. (Marlowe medal 1963), Am. Phys. Soc., Am. Acad. Sci. (Hirschfelder award for theoret. chemistry 2002, Willis Lamb medal 2004), Nat. Acad. Sci., Am. Chem. Soc. (Pure Chemistry award 1963, Leo Hendrik Baekland award 1971, Peter Debye award 1985, Hildebrand award 1987). Office Phone: 773-702-7199. Business E-Mail: s-rice@uchicago.edu.

RICE, SUE ANN, dean, industrial and organizational psychologist; b. Ponca City, Okla., Sept. 17, 1934; d. Alfred and Helen (Revard) R. BS in Edn., U. Okla., 1956; MA, Cath. U., 1979, PhD, 1988. Ensign USN, 1956, advanced through grades to comdr., 1973; ednl. svcs. officer 9th Naval Dist., Great Lakes, Ill., 1956-58; adminstr., asst. staff, comdr. in-chief Pacific Fleet, Honolulu, 1958-61; head edn. div. Naval Air Sta., Lemoore, Calif., 1961-63; instr., acad. dir. Women Officers' Sch., Newport, R.I., 1963-66; head. tng. div. Naval Command Systems Support Activity, Washington, 1966-70; head, ops. support sec. staff, comdr.-in-chief Lant, Norfolk, Va., 1970-74; sr. U.S. rep. NATO, subgroup 5 orgn. JCS, Washington, 1974-77; ret. USN, 1977; head vocation office Archdiocese of Washington, 1977-78; cons. Notre Dame Inst., Arlington, Va., 1989-97, dean of students, 1990-95. Lectr. Cath. U. Am., Washington, 1983-84; bd. dirs. Villa Cortona Apostolic Ctr., Bethesda, 1984-94. Tech. reviewer Personnel Administration, 1964; editor (newsletter) Vocation News, 1978. Conoco scholarship Continental Oil Co., 1952-56; recipient Meritorious Svc. medal Pres. of U.S., 1977, rsch. grant Cath. U., Sigma Xi, 1986. Mem.: Lay Women's Assn. (internat. v.p., internat. mem. fin. com., nat. v.p.), Cath. War Vets. (nat. membership task force com., nat. youth act com., vets. affairs com.), Gamma Phi Beta, Kappa Delta Pi. Roman Catholic. Avocations: travel, music, gardening, woodworking. Home: PO Box 2742 Ponca City OK 74602-2742

RICE, SUSAN F. fundraising consultant; b. Chgo., Dec. 10, 1939; BA, St. Mary's Coll., 1961; MPA, UCLA, 1976; EdD, Pepperdine U., 1986. Pres. YWCA, Santa Monica, Calif., 1978, League of Women Voters Calif., San Francisco, 1979-81; sr. fundraising profl. adminstr., instr. Santa Monica (Calif.) Coll., 1978-81; dir. govtl. rels. UCLA Alumni Assn., 1981-82; dir. devel. UCLA Grad. Sch. Mgmt., 1982-89; dep. dir. mktg. and devel., dir.

major gifts Spl. Olympics Internat., Washington, 1989-90; v.p. devel. Bus. Exec. Nat. Security, Washington, 1991-92; pres., CEO Greater L.A. Zoo Assn., 1992-96; prin. SFR Consulting, L.A., 1996—. Co-author: Women, Money and Political Clout in Women as Donors, Woman as Philanthropists, 1994, Fund Raising in Crisis Mode in Advancing Philanthropy, 1997. Bd. dirs. St. Mary's Coll. Alumnae Assn., Notre Dame, Ind., 1982-84, Santa Monica Coll. Assocs., 1984-94, Internat. Human Rights Law Group, 1990-92; trustee, chair pers. compensation com. L.A. Mus. Nat. History Found., 1982-89; treas. Women's Commn. Refugee Women, 1990-96; vice chmn. pers. commn. Santa Monica Coll. Dist., 1985-89. Recipient Disting. Alumna award St. Mary's Coll., 1986, Humanitarian award, NCCJ-L.A., 1995. Mem. Nat. Soc. Fundraising Execs. (bd. dirs. 1995-97, v.p. Greater L.A. chpt.).

RICE, SIR TIMOTHY MILES BINDON, lyricist; b. Amersham, Eng., Nov. 10, 1944; s. Hugh Gordon and Joan Odette (Bawden) Rice; m. Jane McIntosh, Aug. 19, 1974; children: Eva Jane Florence, Donald Alexander Hugh. Student, Lancing Coll., Sussex, 1958—62. Solicitor's articled clk. Pettit & Westlake, London, 1963—66; mgmt. trainee E.M.I. Records Manchester Sq., London, 1966—68; record prodr. Norrie Paramor Orgn., London, 1968—69; ind. writer, record producer London, 1969—; broadcaster BBC Radio and TV, Ind. TV, England, 1973—. Founder, dir. GRRR Books, 1978—, Pavilion Books, 1981—. Host (TV) Friday Night Saturday Morning, Musical Triangles, Disco; lyricist for: Marvin Hamlisch, Rick Wakeman, Vangelis, Paul McCartney, Mike Batt, Francis Lai, John Barry, Freddie Mercury, Richard Kerr, Graham Gouldman, lyricist stage musicals (with music by Andrew Lloyd Weber: Joseph and the Amazing Technicolor Dreamcoat, 1968, Joseph and the Amazing Technicolor Dreamcoat, rev., 1973 (Tony award nominations best book of musical and best original score, 1982, Grammy award nomination best cast show album, 1982), Jesus Christ Superstar, 1970 (Grammy award nomination album of the year, 1971, Tony award nomination best original score, 1972), lyricist: Evita, 1976, rev., 1978 (Tony awards best book of musical and best original score, 1980, Grammy award best cast show album, 1980), lyricist: Cricket, 1986, lyricist with music by Stephen Oliver: Blondel, 1983, lyricist with music by Benny Andersson and Björn Ulvaeus: Chess, 1984, rev., 1986, lyricist with music by Michel Berger: Tycoon, 1992, lyricist with music by Alan Menken: Beauty and the Beast, 1994, lyricist for film musicals (with music by Menken): Aladdin, 1992, lyricist for film musicals (with music by Elton John): The Lion King, 1994, lyricist for songs (from Aladdin, with Menken): A Whole New World, 1992 (Academy award best original song, 1992, Grammy award song of the year, 1993), lyricist for songs from The Lion King with John: Can You Feel the Love Tonight, 1994 (Academy award best original song, 1994), Circle of Life, 1994 (Academy award nomination best original song, 1994), Hakuna Matata, 1994 (Academy award nomination best original song, 1994); prodr.: (stage musical) Anything Goes, 1989; author: Heartaches Cricketers' Almanack (yearly), 1975—; author: (with others) The Guiness Book of British Hit Singles, 1977, The Guiness Book of Hits of the Seventies, 1980, Treasures of Lord's, 1989; editor: Lord Taverners Sticky Wicket Book, 1980. Chmn. Stars Orgn. for Spastics, 1983—85, Shaftesbury Ave. Centenary Com., 1984—86, Found. for Sport and the Arts, 1991—; pres. Lord's Taverners, 1988—90. Recipient 10 Ivor Novello awards. Mem.: Garrick, Saints and Sinners Club, Heartaches Cricket Club, Marylebone Cricket Club. Address: 31 The Terrace London SW13 ONR England

RICE, TROY, retail executive; m. Diane Rice; 3 children. BBA in Fin., Kennesaw State U. From assoc. mgr. to store mgr. Midsouth divsn. (now Ea. divsn.) Home Depot, Inc., Atlanta, 1990—94, dist. mgr., 1994—99, regional v.p. ops. S.W. divsn., 1999—2001, divsn. pres. N.W. ops., 2001—02, sr. v.p. ops., 2002—. Office: Home Depot Inc 2455 Paces Ferry Rd NW Atlanta GA 30339-4024

RICE, WALTER HERBERT, federal judge; b. Pitts., May 27, 1937; s. Harry D. and Elizabeth L. (Braemer) R.; m. Bonnie Rice; children: Michael, Hilary, Harry, Courtney Elizabeth. BA, Northwestern U., 1958; JD, MBA, Columbia U., 1962; LLD (hon.), U. Dayton, 1991; DHL (hon.), Wright State U., 2000. Bar: Ohio 1963. Asst. county prosecutor, Montgomery County, Ohio, 1964-66; assoc. Gallon & Miller, Dayton, Ohio, 1966-69; 1st asst. Montgomery County Prosecutor's Office, 1969; judge Dayton Mcpl. Ct., 1970-71, Montgomery County Ct. Common Pleas, 1971-80, U.S. Dist. Ct. (so. dist.) Ohio, 1980-95, chief judge, 1996—. Adj. prof. U. Dayton Law Sch., 1976—, bd. visitors, 1976—; chmn. Montgomery County Supervisory Council on Crime and Deliquency, 1972-74; vice chmn. bd. dirs. Pretrial Release, Inc., 1975-79 Author papers in field. Pres. Dayton Area Coun. on Alcoholism and Drug Abuse, 1971-73; chmn. bd. trustees Stillwater Health Ctr., Dayton, 1976-79, Family Svc. Assn. Dayton, 1978-80; chmn. RTA in 2000 Com., 2003 Com. Designed To Bring Nat. Park to Dayton To Honor Wright Bros. and Birth of Aviation; chmn. Martin Luther King Jr. Meml. Com., Dayton Aviation Heritage Commn.; trustee Montgomery County Vol. Lawyers Project, Miami Valley Cultural Alliance, Barbara Jordan Com. Racial Justice; co-chmn., Dayton Dialogue on Race Rels.; former bd. mem. Sinclair C.C., U.S. Air & Trade Show. Recipient Excellent Jud. Service award Ohio Supreme Ct., 1976, 77, Outstanding Jud. Service award, 1973, 74, 76, Man of Yr. award Disting. Service Awards Council, Dayton, 1977, Outstanding Jurist in Ohio award Ohio Acad. Trial Lawyers, 1986, Pub. Ofcl. of Yr. award Ohio region of Nat. Assn. Social Workers, 1992, Humanitarian award NCCJ, 1993, City Mgr.'s Cmty. Svc. award City of Dayton, 1994, Paul Laurence Dunbar Humanitarian award, 1996, Pres.' award NAACP, 1996, greater Dayton Peace Bridge (civil rights) Hall of Fame, Mark of Excellence award Nat. Forum Black Pub. Adminstrs., 2001, Conservation Svc. award U.S. Dept. of the Interior, 2002. Mem. Dayton Bar Assn., Fed. Judges Assn., Carl D. Kessler Inn of Ct. (founder, former chmn.).

RICE, WILLIAM EDWARD, journalist; b. Albany, N.Y., July 26, 1938; s. Harry Edward, Jr. and Elizabeth (Lally) R.; m. Carol Timmon, June 3, 1978 (div.); m. Jill Van Cleave, Aug. 20, 1983. BA in History, U. Va., 1960; MS with honors, Columbia U., 1963. Reporter, editorial writer, critic Washington Post, 1963-69; student LeCordon Bleu, Paris, 1969-70; dir. L'Ecole de Cuisine, Bethesda, Md., 1971-72; freelance writer, restaurant critic Washingtonian Mag., 1971-72; exec. food editor Washington Post, 1972-80; editor-in-chief Food and Wine Mag., N.Y.C., 1980-85; food and wine columnist Chgo. Tribune, 1986—2003. Dining In columnist Gentlemen's Quarterly, 1987-89; chmn. restaurant awards com.James Beard Found., 1993-2003. Author: Feasts of Wine and Food, 1986, Steak Lovers Cookbook, 1997; editor: (with others) Where to Eat in America, 1978, 2d edit., 1980, 3d edit., 1987. Served with USN, 1960-62. Recipient Vesta award as outstanding newspaper food editor, 1979, Ordre du Merite Agricole (France), 1983 Home: 655 W Buena Ave Chicago IL 60613-2201 E-mail: wricechicago@yahoo.com.

RICE, WILLIAM PHIPPS, finance company executive; b. Bronxville, NY, Mar. 27, 1944; s. Anton Henry Jr. and Lydia Phipps (Sands) R.; m. Lynn Lucas Rice, May 21, 1972; children: William Phipps Jr., Paige Sands Rice. BA cum laude, Kenyon Coll., 1966. Analyst Spencer Trask & Co., N.Y.C., 1960-67; v.p., portfolio mgr. Endowment Mgmt. and Rsch. Corp., Boston, 1969-77, Ft. Hill Investors Mgmt. Corp., Boston, 1977-83; pres., founder Anchor Capital Advisors Inc., Boston, 1983—, Anchor/Russell Capital Advisors, Boston, 1989—. Trustee Mass. Bible Soc., Boston, 1985-89, Albert O. Wilson Found., Inc., 1998—, U.S.S. Constn. Mus., 2002—; trustee of donations Episcopal Ch. Diocese of Mass., Boston, 1989—; trustee, v.p. Duxbury Rural and Hist. Soc. With U.S. Army, 1967-69. Mem. Assn. for Investment Mgmt. and Rsch., Assn. Investment Mgmt. Sales Execs., Boston Security Analysts Soc., Boston C. of C., N.Y. Yacht Club, Duxbury Yacht Club, Ocean Reef Club, Boston Coll. Club, Harvard Club. Avocations: skiing, boating, woodworking. Home: PO Box 1599 Duxbury MA 02331-1599 Office: Anchor Capital Advisors Inc One Post Office Sq Boston MA 02109-2106

RICE, WINSTON EDWARD, lawyer; b. Shreveport, La., Feb. 22, 1946; s. Winston Churchill and Margaret (Coughlin) R.; m. Barbara Reily Gay, Apr. 16, 1977; 1 child, Andrew Hynes; children by previous marriage: Winston Hobson, Christian MacTaggart. Student, Centenary Coll. La., 1967; JD, La. State U., 1971. Bar: La. 1971, Colo. 1990, Tex. 1992. Cons. geologist, Gulfport, Miss., 1968-70; ptnr. Phelps, Dunbar, New Orleans, 1971-88; sr. ptnr. Rice, Fowler, New Orleans, Houston, Miami, Fla., London and Bogota, 1988-2000; gen. mgr. Winston Edw. Rice LLC, Covington, La., 2000—. Instr. law La. State U., Baton Rouge, 1970-71. Assoc. editor La. Law Rev., 1970-71. Mem.: Trucking Industry Def. Assn., Ctr. Transp. Law and Policy, Soc. Ins. Trainers and Educators, Assn. Average Adjusters (U.K.), Assn. Average Adjusters U.S., Maritime Law Assn. U.S. (chmn. subcom. on offshore exploration and devel. 1985—88, vice chmn. com. internat. law of the sea 1988—91, chmn. 1991—95, membership sec. 1998—2002), Com. Maritime Internat. (titulary mem.), Fedn. Ins. and Corp. Counsel, La. Assn. Def. Counsel, New Orleans Assn. Def. Counsel, Can. Transp. Lawyers Assn., New Orleans Bar Assn., Tex. State Bar, Colo. State Bar Assn., La. Bar Assn., Stratford Club, Boston Club, Mariners Club (treas. 1974—75, 1978—79, sec. 1975—76, v.p. 1976—77, pres. 1977—78), Kappa Alpha, Phi Kappa Phi, Phi Delta Phi, Order of Coif. Republican. Episcopalian. Office: 527 E Boston St Ste 201 Covington LA 70433 Office Phone: 504-893-8949.

RICE-SEE, LYNN, music educator; b. Pine Bluff, Ark., Feb. 28, 1955; d. Owen Reed and Frankie Shults Rice; m. David Ralph See, July 15, 1989. MusB in Piano Performance, Peabody Inst. of the City of Balt., 1973—77; MusM, The Juilliard Sch., 1977—79; D of Musical Arts, U. of So. Calif., 1979—81. Asst. prof. William Carey Coll., Hattiesburg, Miss., 1981—83; pianist/coach Opera Ho., Münster, Germany, 1985—86, Essen, Germany, 1986—87; faculty Manhattan Sch. of Music Prep. Divsn., N.Y.C., 1987—89; prof. of piano East Tenn. State U., Johnson City, 1989—. Author: (article) Schubert's Wonderful Dances, Clavier Mag.; musician: (piano recital) Carnegie Recital Hall, (piano soloist) Schumann Piano Concerto, Janacek Phil harm. Orch. Recipient 5th prize, Career Award competition, Nat. Soc. of Arts & Letters, 1981, Ala. & So. Young Artist, Nat. Fedn. of Music Clubs, 1979, Miss. Young Artist, Fedn. of Music Clubs, 1981. Mem.: Music Teachers Nat. Assn., Pi Kappa Lambda (theta alpha chpt. pres. 1997—2003). Office: East Tenn State U Box 70661 Dept of Music Johnson City TN 37614 Personal E-mail: lricesee@alum.juilliard.edu. E-mail: ricesee@etsu.edu.

RICH, ADRIENNE, writer; b. Balt., May 16, 1929; d. Arnold Rice and Helen Elizabeth (Jones) R.; m. Alfred H. Conrad (dec. 1970); children: David, Paul, Jacob. AB, Radcliffe Coll., 1951; LittD (hon.), Wheaton Coll., 1967, Smith Coll., 1979, Brandeis U., 1987, Coll. Wooster, Ohio, 1988, CCNY, Harvard U., 1990, Swarthmore Coll., 1992. Tchr. workshop YM-WHA Poetry Ctr., N.Y.C., 1966-67; vis. lectr. Swarthmore Coll., 1967-69; adj. prof. writing divsn. Columbia U., 1967-69; lectr. CCNY, 1968-70, instr., 1970-71, asst. prof. English, 1971-72, 74-75; Fannie Hurst vis. prof. creative lit. Brandeis U., 1972-73; prof. English Douglass Coll., Rutgers U., 1976-79; Clark lectr., disting. vis. prof. Scripps Coll., 1983-84; A.D. White prof.-at-large Cornell U., 1981-87; disting. vis. prof. San Jose State U., 1984-85; prof. English and feminist studies Stanford U., 1986-93. Marjorie Kovler vis. lectr. U. Chgo., 1989. Author: Collected Early Poems, 1950-1970, 1993, Diving into the Wreck, 1973, The Dream of a Common Language, 1978, A Wild Patience Has Taken Me This Far, 1981, Your Native Land, Your Life, 1986, Time's Power, 1989, An Atlas of the Difficult World, 1991, Dark Fields of the Republic, 1995, Midnight Salvage, 1999, Fox, 2001, The Fact of a Doorframe: Selected Poems 1950-2001, 2002, The School Among the Ruins, 2004; (prose) Of Woman Born: Motherhood as Experience and Institution, 1976, 10th anniversary edit., 1986, On Lies, Secrets and Silence, 1979, Blood, Bread and Poetry, 1986, What Is Found There: Notebooks on Poetry and Politics, 1993, 2d edit., 2003, Arts of the Possible: Essays and Conversations, 2001; editor: Muriel Rukeyser, Selected Poems, 2004. Mem. nat. adv. bd. Nat. Writers Union, Rosenberg Fund for Children. Recipient Yale Series of Younger Poets award, 1951, Nat. Inst. Arts and Letters award in poetry, 1961, Eunice Tietjens Meml. prize, 1968, Shelley Meml. award, 1971, Nat. Book award, 1974, Fund for Human Dignity award Nat. Gay Task Force, 1981, Ruth Lilly Poetry prize, 1986, Brandeis U. Creative Arts medal for Poetry, 1987, Nat. Poetry Assn. award, 1989, Elmer Holmes Bobst award arts and letters NYU, 1989, MacArthur fellowship, 1994-99, Dorothea Tanning award Acad. Am. Poets, 1996, others; chancellor Acad. Am. Poets, 1999-2001, Lannan Found. Lifetime Achievement award, 1999, Bollingen prize, 2003, Nat. Found. Jewish Culture award, 2003, others. Mem. PEN, Nat. Writers Union. Office: care W W Norton Co 500 5th Ave New York NY 10110-0002

RICH, ALAN, music critic, editor, author; b. Boston, June 17, 1924; s. Edward and Helen (Hirshberg) R. AB, Harvard, 1945; MA, U. Calif-Berkeley, 1952. Alfred Hertz Meml. Traveling fellow in music, Vienna, Austria, 1952-53; Asst. music critic Boston Herald, 1944-45, N.Y. Sun, 1947-48; contbr. Am. Record Guide, 1947-61, Saturday Rev., 1952-53, Mus. Am., 1955-61, Mus. Quar., 1957-58; tchr. music U. Calif. at Berkeley, 1950-58; program and music dir. Pacifica Found., FM radio, 1953-61; asst. music critic N.Y. Times, 1961-63; chief music critic, editor N.Y. Herald Tribune, 1963-66; music critic, editor N.Y. World Jour. Tribune, 1966-67; contbg. editor Time mag., 1967-68; music and drama critic, arts editor N.Y. mag., 1968-81, contbg. editor, 1981-83; music critic, arts editor Calif. (formerly New West mag.), 1979-83, contbg. editor, 1983-85; gen. editor Newsweek mag., N.Y.C., 1983-87; music critic L.A. Herald Examiner, 1987-89, L.A. Daily News, 1989-92, L.A. Weekly, 1992—. Tchr. New Sch. for Social Rsch., 1972-75, 77-79, U. So. Calif. Sch. Journalism, 1980-82, Calif. Inst. Art, 1982-94, UCLA, 1990-91; artist-in-residence Davis Ctr. for Performing Arts CUNY, 1975-76. Author: Careers and Opportunities in Music, 1964, Music: Mirror of the Arts, 1969, Listeners Guides to Classical Music, Opera, Jazz, 3 vols., 1980, The Lincoln Center Story, 1984, Play-by-Play: Bach, Mozart, Beethoven, Tchaikovsky, 4 vols., 1995, American Pioneers, 1995; author: (interactive CD-ROM computer programs): Schubert's Trout Quintet, 1991, So I've Heard: Bach and Before, 1992, So I've Heard: The Classical Ideal, 1993, So I've Heard: Beethoven and Beyond, 1993; contbr. articles to entertainment mags. Recipient Deems Taylor award ASCAP, 1970, 73, 74 Mem. Music Critics Circle N.Y. (sec. 1961-63, chmn. 1963-64), N.Y. Drama Critics Circle, Am. Theatre Critics Assn., Music Critics Assn., PEN. Home: 2925 Greenfield Ave Los Angeles CA 90064-4019 E-mail: KV467@comcast.net.

RICH, ALBERT CLARK, solar energy manufacturing executive; b. Wolfeboro, N.H., Feb. 8, 1950; s. Nelson Barnard and Alberta Louise (Pigon) R.; m. Patricia Ann Murphy, July 16, 1973 (div. Aug. 1975); m. Susan Maura McGee, Jan. 26, 1985; children: Ashley, Katherine, Clark, Thomas. BA in Polit. Sci. and Research Processes, Principia Coll., 1979; cert., Solar Energy Research Inst., Golden, Colo., 1981. Owner Antique Classic Auto Restoration, Ft. Lauderdale, Fla., 1975-77, AC-Rich & Sun, Herndon, Va., 1979—; pres., CEO AnuPower Corp. Founder., pres. Am. Solar Network Ltd., 1989—; pres. Suncorps Inc., Watertown, Mass., 1980-82, Cambridge Alt. Power Co., 1982-83; dist. mgr. Sears/Am. Solar King, Herndon, 1983-85; bd dirs. Monegon Solar, Washington br., 1984; cons. NEEIC, Boston, 1982; chmn. Sec. Energy, Boston, 1983; speaker New Eng. Solar Energy Assn. MIT, Cambridge and Boston, 1983; chmn. solar thermal div. New Eng. Solar Energy Assn., Bay chpt., Boston, 1982-83; contractor White House Pagent of Peace Exhibit. Developer heat cell, heliophase, solar storage tank; inventor, patentee Solar "Skylite" water heater, "Fireball 2001", "Megamatt." Organizer Earth Day, Boston, 1982-83, Sec. of Energy, Boston, 1983, founder ACR Solar Internat., 1997, SolarRoof.com, 1998. Mem. Sacramento Solar Energy Industries Assn. (DOE energy innovation award 1992, DOE energy related inventions program grantee 1994). Avocations: automobile restoration, squash, woodcraft. Four patents granted, including Modular Firebar 2001 solar system, Megamat solar system, 1999. Home and Office: ACR Solar Internat 5840 Gibbons Dr Carmichael CA 95608-6903

RICH, ALEXANDER, molecular biologist, educator; b. Hartford, Conn., Nov. 15, 1924; s. Max and Bella (Shub) R.; m. Jane Erving King, July 5, 1952; children: Benjamin, Josiah, Rebecca, Jessica. AB magna cum laude in Biochem. Scis, Harvard U., 1947, MD cum laude, 1949; Dr. (hon.), Fed. U. Rio de Janeiro, 1981; PhD honoris causa, Weizmann Inst. Sci., Rehovot, Israel, 1992; DSc (hon.), Eidgenössische Technische Hochschule, Zurich, Switzerland, 1993, Freie U., Berlin, 1996. Rsch. fellow Gates and Crellin Labs., Calif. Inst. Tech., Pasadena, 1949-54; chief sect. phys. chemistry NIMH, Bethesda, Md., 1954-58; vis. scientist Cavendish Lab., Cambridge (Eng.) U., 1955-56; assoc. prof. biophysics MIT, Cambridge, 1958-61, prof. biohpysics, 1961—, William Thompson Sedgwick prof. biophysics, 1974—. Mem. AAAS (coun. mem. 1967-71), com. career devel. awards NIH, 1964-67, postdoctoral fellowship bd., 1955-58; mem. com. exobiology space sci. bd. NAS, 1964-65, adv. bd., acad. forum, 1975-82, nominating com., 1980, exec. com. of council, 1985-88; mem. U.S. nat. com. Internat. Orgn. Pure Applied Biophysics, 1965-67; vis. com. biology dept. Yale U., 1963, Weizmann Inst. Sci., 1965-66, co-chmn. sci. and adv. com. 1987-91; life scis. com. NASA, 1970-75, lunar planetary missions bd., 1968-70; biology team Viking Mars Mission, 1969-80; mem. corp. Marine Biol. Lab., Woods Hole, Mass., 1965-77, 87—; sci. rev. com. Howard Hughes Med. Inst., Miami, Fla., 1978-90; vis. com. biology div. Oak Ridge Nat. Lab., 1972-76; chmn. com. on USSR and Ea. Europe Exch. Bd. NAS, 1973-76; mem. Internat. Rsch. and Exchs. Bd. Am. Coun. Learned Socs., N.Y.C., 1973-76, panel judges N.Y. Acad. Sci. ann. book award for children's sci. books, N.Y.C., 1973-90; chmn. nominating com. Am. Acad. Arts and Sci., 1974-77; sci. adv. bd. Stanford Synchrotron Radiation Project, 1976-80, Mass. Gen. Hosp., Boston, 1978-83; mem. U.S. Nat. Sci. Bd., 1976-82; bd. govs. Weizmann Inst. Sci., 1976—; rsch. com. Med. Found., Boston, 1976-80; mem. U.S.-USSR Joint Commn. on Sci. and Tech., Dept. State, Washington, 1977-82; sr. cons. Office of Sci. and Tech. Policy, Exec. Office of Pres., Washington, 1977-81; mem. council Pugwash Confs. on Sci. and World Affairs, Geneva, 1977-82; chmn. basic rsch. com. Nat. Sci. Bd., Washington, 1978-82; mem. U.S. Nat. Com. for Internat. Union for Pure and Applied Biophysics, NAS, 1979-83; bd. dirs. Med. Found., Boston, 1981-90; vis. com. divsn. med. sci. Harvard U., 1981-87; mem. govt.-univ.-industry rsch. round table, 1984-87; chmn. sci. adv. com. dept. molecular biology Mass. Gen. Hosp., Boston, 1983-87; governing bd. NRC, 1985-88; nat. adv. com. Pew Scholars program Pew Meml. Trust, 1986-88; com. on USSR and Eastern Europe Nat. Rsch. Council, Washington, 1986-92; external adv. com. Ctr. for Human Genome Studies, Los Alamos Nat. Lab., N.Mex., 1989-97, Nat. Critical Techs. Panel, Office of Sci. & Tech. Policy, Exec. Office of Pres., Washington, 1990-91; vis. com. NASA Ctr. Exobiology, La Jolla, Calif., 1992-95; vis. prof. Coll. France, Paris, 1987. Editor: (with Norman Davidson) Structural Chemistry and Molecular Biology, 1968; mem. editl. bd. Biophys. Jour, 1961-63, Currents Modern Biology, 1966-72, Science, 1963-69, Analytical Biochemistry, 1969-81, Bio-Systems, 1973-86, Molecular Biology Reports, 1974-85, Procs. NAS, 1973-78, Jour. Molecular and Applied Genetics, 1980-84, DNA, 1981-89, EMBO Jour., 1988-90, Jour. Biotech., 1987—, Genomics, 1987—, Proteins, Structure, Function and Genetics, 1986-91, Jour. Molecular Evolution, 1983—, Springer Series on Molecular Biology, 1980-88; mem. editl. adv. bd. Jour. Molecular Biology, 1959-66, Accounts of Chemical Research, 1980-82, Jour. Biomolecular Structure and Dynamics, 1983—, PAABS Revista, 1972-77, Biopolymers, 1963-74, Jour. of Molecular Evolution, 1983-94, others; contbr. over 500 articles to profl. jours. With USN, 1943-46. Fairchild disting. scholar Calif. Inst. Tech., Pasadena, 1976; recipient Skylab Achievement award NASA, 1974, Theodore von Karmin award Viking Mars Mission, 1976, Presdl. award N.Y. Acad. Scis., 1977, Jabotinsky medal Jabotinsky Found., 1980, James R. Killian Faculty Achievement award MIT, 1980, Lewis S. Rosenstiel Basic Biomed. Rsch. award Brandeis U., 1983, Nat. medal Sci. NSF, 1995, Merck award Am. Soc. Biochemistry and Molecular Biology, Washington, 1998, Bower award Franklin Inst., 2000, Proctor prize Sigma Xi, 2001, Passano award, Passano Found., 2002; NRC fellow, 1949-51; Guggenheim Found. fellow, 1963; mem. Pontifical Acad. Scis. The Vatican, 1978. Fellow AAAS; mem. NAS (chmn. biotech., program, com. on scholarly comm. with China 1986-93, exec. com. 1985-88, com. on sci. comm. and nat. security 1982), Am. Chem. Soc. (exec. com. divsn. biol. chemistry 1962, Linus Pauling award 1995), Biophys. Soc. (coun. 1960-69), Am. Soc. Biol. Chemists, Am. Crystallographic Soc., Internat. Soc. for Study of Origin of Life (fgn.), French Acad. Scis., Russian Acad. Scis. (fgn., Lomonosov Large Gold medal 2002), European Molecular Biology Orgn. (assoc.), Japanese Biochem. Soc. (hon.), Physicians for Social Responsibility (nat. adv. bd. 1983—), Am. Philos. Soc., Inst. of Medicine (sr.), Phi Beta Kappa, Alpha Omega Alpha. Office: MIT Dept Biology 77 Mass Ave Rm 68-233 Cambridge MA 02139-4307

RICH, ANDREA LOUISE, museum administrator; BA, UCLA, 1965, MA, 1966, PhD, 1968. Asst. prof. comms. studies UCLA, L.A., 1976, asst. dir. office learning resources, 1976, acting dir. Media Ctr., 1977, dir. office of instructional devel., 1978-80, asst. vice chancellor office of instructional devel., 1980-86, asst. exec. vice chancellor, 1986-87, vice chancellor acad. adminstrn., 1987-91, exec. vice chancellor, 1991-95; pres., CEO L.A. County Mus. of Art, L.A., 1995—, pres., Wallis Annenberg dir., 2003—. Office: L A County Mus Art 5905 Wilshire Blvd Los Angeles CA 90036-4597*

RICH, BRADFORD WHITMAN, insurance executive; b. Winchester, Mass., May 11, 1947; m. Linda Lee Beebe, May 31, 1969; children: Heather, Eric. AB with honors, Denison U., 1969; JD with honors, George Washington U., 1972. Bar: Va. 1972, Pa. 1978. Staff asst., domestic council U.S. Govt., White House, 1971-73; staff judge adv. USAF, Washington, Tucson, 1973-77; assoc. gen. counsel, v.p. litigation counsel, pres. INAPRO Ins. Co. of N. Am., Phila., 1977-83; pres. Albany Ins. Co., Princeton, NJ, 1983-86, Atlas Ins. Co., Princeton, NJ, 1983-86, Talbot Bird & Co, Inc., Princeton, NJ, 1983-86; sr. v.p. Crum & Forster Corp., Morristown, NJ, 1987—91; gen. counsel Ace Ins. Co., Hamilton, 1991—95; exec. v.p. USAA, San Antonio, sec., gen. counsel, 1995—. Bd. dirs. Talbot, Bird & Co., Inc., N.Y.C.; lectr. legal profl., ins. orgns. Served to capt. USAF, 1973-77. Mem. ABA, Internat. Assn. Ins. Counsel, Fedn. Ins. Counsel, Va. Bar Assn., Pa. Bar Assn. Republican. Presbyterian. Office: United Svcs Auto Assn 9800 Fredericksburg Rd San Antonio TX 78288-0001

RICH, CLAYTON, retired academic administrator, educator; b. N.Y.C., May 21, 1924; s. Clayton Eugene and Leonore (Elliot) R.; m. Mary Bell Hodgkinson, Dec. 19, 1953 (div. May 1974); 1 son, Clayton Greig; m. Rosalind Morgan-Jones, Apr. 6, 1987. Grad., Putney Sch., 1942; student, Swarthmore Coll., 1942-44; MD, Cornell U., 1948. Diplomate Am. Bd. Internal Medicine. Intern Albany (N.Y.) Hosp., 1948-49, asst. resident, 1950-51; research asst. Cornell U. Med. Coll., 1949-50; asst. Rockefeller U., 1953-58, asst. prof., 1958-60; asst. prof. medicine U. Wash. Sch. Medicine, 1960-62, assoc. prof., 1962-67, prof., 1967-71, assoc. dean, 1968-71; chief radioisotope service VA Hosp., Seattle, 1960-70, assoc. chief staff, 1962-71, chief staff, 1968-70; v.p. med. affairs, dean Sch. Medicine; prof. medicine Stanford U., 1971-79, Carl and Elizabeth Naumann prof., 1977-79; chief staff Stanford U. Hosp., 1971-77, chief exec. officer, 1977-79. Sr. scholar Inst. Medicine, Nat. Acad. Sci., Washington, 1979-80; Mem. gen. medicine B study sect. NIH, 1969-73, chmn., 1972-73; mem. spl. med. adv. group VA, 1977-81; provost U. Okla. Health Scis. Ctr., Oklahoma City, 1980-92—, v.p. for healh scis., 1983-92; also exec. dean, prof. U. Okla. Coll. Medicine, 1980-83, emeritus Regents prof. and provost U. Okla., 1993—. Editorial bd.: Calcified Tissue Research, 1966-72, Clin. Orthopedics, 1967-72, Jour. Clin. Endocrinology and Metabolism, 1971-72; Contbr. numerous articles to med. jours. Bd. dirs. Children's Hosp. at Stanford, Stanford U. Hosp., 1974-79; chmn. Gordon Research Conf. Chemistry, Physiology and Structure of Bones and Teeth, 1967; bd. dirs. Okla. Med. Research Found.; bd. dirs. Leadership Oklahoma City, 1981-92, v.p., 1985-92; bd. dirs. Okla. Blood Inst., 1982-92, Oklahoma City chpt. ARC, 1983-92. Lt. USNR, 1951-53. Fellow ACP, AAAS; mem. Assn. Am. Physicians, Western Assn. Physicians, Am. Soc. Mineral and Bone Research (adv. bd. 1977-80), Am. Soc. Clin. Investigation, Assn. Am. Med. Colls. (exec. council 1975-79), Inst. of Medicine, Western Soc. Clin. Research (v.p. 1967-68), Endocrine Soc., Assn. Acad. Health Ctrs. (bd. dirs. 1984-88, chmn. 1987-88), Sigma Xi, Alpha Omega Alpha. Office: 13450 64th Ter NE Kirkland WA 98034-1656 Personal E-mail: claytrich@aol.com.

RICH, DANIEL, provost; B in Polit. Sci., Bklyn. Coll.; M in Pub. Adminstrn. and Internat. Affairs, U. Pitts.; PhD in Polit. Sci., MIT. Dean Coll. Urban Affairs and Pub. Policy U. Del., Newark, 1971—97, former dean Coll. Human Resources, Edn. and Pub. Policy, provost. Hon. vis. prof. U. Strathclyde, Scotland, 1970—; sr. rsch. assoc. Ctr. for Energy and Environ. Policy U. Del. Author: 13 books; contbr. articles to profl. jours. Active Del. Ctr. for Edn. Tech., Wilmington Cmty. Devel. Partnership, Del. C. of C. Fellow: AAAS. Office: U Del Office of the Provost 129 Hullihen Hall Newark DE 19716-1001

RICH, DANIEL HULBERT, chemistry professor; b. Fairmont, Minn., Dec. 12, 1942; married, 1964; 2 children. BS, U. Minn., 1964; PhD in Organic Chemistry, Cornell U., 1968. Rsch. assoc. organic chemist Cornell U., 1968; rsch. chemist Dow Chem. Co., 1968-69; rsch. assoc., organic chemist Stanford U., 1969-70; asst. prof. pharm. chemistry U. Wis., Madison, 1970-75, assoc. prof., 1975-81, prof. dept. medical chemistry, 1981—, prof. dept. organic chemistry, 1988—, Ralph F. Hirschmann prof. medicinal and organic chemistry, 1994—. Cons. biorganic natural product study sect., NIH, 1981-85, chmn., 1985. Recipient H.I. Romnes award, 1980, Vincent du Vigneaud award, 1990, Hitchings award for innovative methods in drug design, 1992, Alexander von Humboldt award, 1993, E. Volwiler award Am. Assn. Colls. Pharmacy, 1995, Outstanding Achievement award U. Minn., 2004; fellow NIH, 1968. Fellow AAAS, Am. Chem. Soc. (Ralph F. Hirschmann award in peptide chemistry 1993, divsn. medicinal chemistry award 1991, A.C. Cope scholar 1999), Am. Assn. Pharm. Sci. (rsch. achievement award 1992), Am. Assn. Coll. Pharmacy (Volwiler award 1995). Am. Peptide Soc. (R.B. Merrifield award 1999). Achievements include research in synthesis in peptides and hormones, inhibition of peptide receptors and proteases, characterization, synthesis and mechanisms of action of peptide natural products. Office: U Wis Dept Med Chemistry 7109 Rennebohm Hall 777 Highland Ave Madison WI 53705-2222

RICH, DAVID BARRY, financial executive, accountant, entertainer, publishing executive; b. Bronx, NY, July 3, 1952; s. Steven and Gizella (Kornfeld) R.; m. Biverly Hayag, Dec. 6, 1995; 1 child, Suzanne Stephanie. BS in Health Adminstrn., Ithaca Coll., 1976; postgrad. in acctg., Bryant and Stratton Coll., Buffalo, 1977. Office mgr. Rubin Gorewitz, CPA, N.Y.C., 1977-78; auditor State of Ariz., Phoenix, 1979-83; internal auditor City of Phoenix, 1983-84; sales use tax auditor City of Mesa (Ariz.), 1984-98; pub. Technology TnT, 2003—. Pres. Clovis Acctg. Inc., Mesa, 1980-94; rep. H.D. Vest Investment Inc., Irving, Tex., 1984-94; owner D.B. Rich Enterprises Import/Export Internet Sales, Chandler, 1992—; stage name Barry Rich, Stand-up Comedy, 1994—. Treas., bd. dirs. Missing Mutts Inc., Tempe, Ariz., 1986-88. With USAF, 1971-76. Fellow Nat. Assn. Tax Preparers; mem. Toastmasters (treas. Mesa 1986-87), Phi Beta Kappa. Office Phone: 602-741-6640. Business E-Mail: d.rich@technologytnt.com. *The world is one big neighborhood and we are all neighbors. If we will survive as a planet we must work together as friends. We must treat all people as our equals.*

RICH, DONNA L. school system administrator; b. Elmira, N.Y., Sept. 24, 1955; d. Thomas Alexis Markert and Martha Jean Glessing; m. Joseph Edward Rich, May 25, 1998; 1 child, Janell Theresa; m. Jurt Fredrick Straub (div.); children: Michaela Joy Straub, Christine Noelle Straub. BE, SUNY, Fredonia, N.Y., 1977; ME, Coll. St. Rose, Albany, N.Y., 1980. Cert. adv. study SUNY, New Paltz, N.Y., 1993, permanent in adminstrn., spl. edn., elem. edn., music N.Y. Spl. edn. tchr. Catskill Ctrl. Sch., Catskill, NY, 1988—93; prin. Taconic Hills Ctrl. Sch., Crayville, NY, 1993—2003, reading for results coord., 2003—. Adult edn. tchr. Taconic Hills Ctrl. Sch., Craryville, NY, 2004—, Columbia Greene Cmty. Coll., Hudson, NY, 2001—03. Family literacy adv. Taconic Hills Ctrl. Sch., 2003—; bd. mem. Stay and Play Kids, Inc., Hillsdale, NY, 1993—96. Mem.: Internat. Reading Assn., Phi Delta Kappa. Republican. Christian. Avocations: piano, music, travel, water sports. Home: 275 Soller Heights Rd Ghent NY 12075

RICH, DOROTHY KOVITZ, writer, educational administrator; BA in Journalism and Psychology, Wayne U.; MA, Columbia U.; EdD, Catholic U. Founder, pres. The Home and Sch. Inst., Inc., Washington, 1964—. Adv. coun. Nat. Health Edn. Consortium; adv. com. Ctr. for Workplace Prep. and Quality Edn., U.S. C. of C.; mem. readiness to learn task force U.S. Dept. Edn., urban edn. team Coun. Gt. City Schs.; legislative nat. initiatives including work on Family/Sch. Partnership Act, 1989, Improving America's Edn. Act, 1994; formulator New Partnerships for Student Achievement program, 1987; creator MegaSkills Edn. Ctr. The Home and Sch. Inst. Inc., 1990; designer MegaSkills Leader Tng. for Parent Workshops, 1988, MegaSkills Essentials for the Classroom, 1991, Learning and Working program for sch.-to-work initiatives, 1996, Career Megaskills, 1999, New MegaSkills Bond Tchr./Parent Partnership, 1994, Career MegaSkills materials and tng., 1998, Adult MegaSkills for Profl. Growth, 1999, MegaSkills Behavior Mgmt. Kit, 2002; developer NEA/MegaSkills nat. mentor tng. initiative, 2000—, MegaSkills for the Job, 2002, Adult MegaSkills and MegaSkills for Teachers, 2002., MegaSkills for Teachers Video Programs, 2003. Author: MegaSkills in School in Life: The Best Gift You Can Give Your Child, 1988, rev. edit., 1992, What Do We Say? What Do We Do? Vital Solutions for Children's Educationsl Success, 1997, MegaSkills, 3d edit., 1997, 18 tng. books, MegaSkills: Building Children's Achievement for the Information Age, new and expanced edit., 1998, Improving Student Teaching through MegaSkills; TV appearances include The Learning Channel, NBC Today Show, Good Morning Am.; subject of videos nat. ednl. programs in Thailand, Singapore and China: Families and Schools: Teaming for Success, Survival Guide for Today's Parents. Recipient Am. Woman Leader award, Citation U.S. Dept. Edn., Nat. Gov.'s Assn., Alumni Achievement award in edn. Cath. U., 1992, Golden Apple award for MegaSkills Tchrs. Coll., Columbia U., 1996; grantee John D. and Catherine T. MacArthur Found.; named Washingtonian of Yr., ADv. Bd. of McNeil-Lehrer NewsHour, 2004. Mem. Nat. Press Club. Office: MegaSkills Edn Ctr Home and Sch Inst Inc 1500 Massachusetts Ave NW Washington DC 20005-1821 Business E-Mail: edstaff@megaskillshsi.org.

RICH, FRANK HART, newscaster; b. Washington, June 2, 1949; s. Frank Hart Rich and Helene Bernice (Aaronson) Fisher; m. Alexandra Rachelle Witchel, 1991; children from previous marriage: Nathaniel Howard, Simon Hart. BA in Am. History and Lit. with honors, Harvard U., 1971. Co-editor Richmond (Va.) Mercury, 1972-73; sr. editor, film critic New Times mag., N.Y.C., 1973-75; film critic N.Y. Post, N.Y.C., 1975-77; film and TV critic Time mag., N.Y.C., 1977-80; chief drama critic N.Y. Times, N.Y.C., 1980-93; columnist N.Y. Times Sunday Mag., N.Y.C., 1993; Op-Ed columnist N.Y. Times, N.Y.C., 1994—2003, assoc. editor, columnist, 2003—. Author: (with others) The Theatre Art of Boris Aronson, 1987, Hot Seat: Theater Criticism for the New York Times 1980-93, 1998, Ghost Light, 2000. Assoc. fellow Jonathan Edwards Coll., Yale U., 1998—. Office: The NY Times 229 W 43rd St New York NY 10036-3959

RICH, FREDERIC CARL, lawyer; b. Elizabeth City, N.C., 1956; AB, Princeton U., 1977; JD, U. Va., 1981. Ptnr., head global project fin. group Sullivan & Cromwell, N.Y.C., 1981—; pres. Scenic Hudson Land Trust, Inc.; dir. Lila Acheson and DeWitt Wallace Fund Hudson Highlands, Hudson River Found., Scenic Hudson Inc. Keasby fellow King's Coll., Cambridge, Eng., 1978. Office: Sullivan & Cromwell 125 Broad St Fl 28 New York NY 10004-2489*

RICH, HARRY EARL, corporate financial executive; b. Wichita, Kans., Mar. 5, 1940; s. Hubert E. and Lorene (Sadler) R.; m. Elfreda Elizabeth Babcock, Aug. 8, 1964; children: Lisa G., Carey E., Ashley H. BA, Harvard U., 1962, MBA, 1968. Pres. instrumentation divsn. Baxter Travenol, Deerfield, Ill., 1977-78; group v.p. Mallinckrodt, Inc., St. Louis, 1978-83; sr. v.p., chief fin. officer Brown Group, Inc., St. Louis, 1983-88, exec. v.p., chief fin. officer, 1988-00, also bd. dirs. Bd. dirs. Gen. Am. Capital Co. divsn. GenAm. Bd. dirs. Repertory Theatre, 1984-90, 1998—, pres. bd. dirs.,1988-90; treas., v.p. Fair Found., 1985-88; bd. trustees Mary Inst., 1986-90, Mary Inst./St. Louis Country Day Sch., 1990-97, chmn., 1995-97. Lt. USN, 1962-66. Avocations: tennis, jogging, sailing. Home: 101 Fair Oaks Saint Louis MO 63124-1579 Office: Brown Shoe Co Inc 8300 Maryland Ave Saint Louis MO 63105-3693

RICH, JEFFREY A. computer company executive; BA, U. Mich., 1982. Asst. v.p. Interfirst Bank Dallas, 1982-86; v.p. Citibank, 1986-89; sr. v.p., CFO Affiliated Computer Svcs., Inc., Dallas, 1989-95, pres., COO, 1995—, CEO, 1999—. Office: Affiliated Computer Svcs 2828 N Haskell Dallas TX 75204

RICH, JOHN MARTIN, humanities educator, researcher; b. Tuscaloosa, Ala., Dec. 14, 1931; s. Emanuel Morris and Bertha (Rose) R.; m. Martha Elaine Schur, June 6, 1955 (div. June 1966); children— Jeffrey Brian, Suzanne Elon; m. Joyce Ann Stegemoller, Aug. 28, 1967 (div. Mar. 1985); m. Audrey Faye Arnold, Aug. 1, 1987. BA, U. Ala., 1954, MA, 1955; PhD, Ohio State U., 1958. Grad. asst. Ohio State U., Columbus, 1955, asst. instr. edn., 1956-58; asst. prof. edn. U. Tenn.-Martin, 1958-60; assoc. prof. edn. Coll. SUNY-Oneonta, 1960-61; from asst. prof. to assoc. prof. Iowa State U., Ames, 1961-66; assoc. prof. social and philos. studies U. Ky., Lexington, 1966-69; prof. cultural founds. edn. U. Tex., Austin, 1969-96, prof. emeritus, 1996—, chmn. dept. cultural founds. edn., 1969-75. Vis. lectr. Nat. Kaohsiung (Taiwan) Normal U., 1993. Author: (books) Education and Human Values, 1968, Humanistic Foundations of Education, 1971, Portuguese translation, 1975, Korean translation, 1985, Challenge and Response, 1974, New Directions in Educational Policy, 1974, Discipline and Authority in School and Family, 1982, Professional Ethics in Education, 1984, Innovative School Discipline, 1985, Foundations of Education, 1992; co-author: Theories of Moral Development, 1985 (named an Outstanding Book of 1985-86 Choice mag.), 2d edit., 1994, Korean translation, 1999, Helping and Intervention, 1988, Competition in Education, 1992, The Success Ethic, Education, and the American Dream, 1996, Korean translation, 1998; editor: Readings in the Philosophy of Education, 1966, 2d edit., 1972, Conflict and Decision, 1972, Innovations in Education, 6th edit., 1992; co-editor, editl. adv. bd. Ednl. Studies, 1970-74, 77-80, 89-91; bd. contbg. editors Rev. Edn., 1977-85; editl. bd. Focus on Learning, 1980-84, Educational Foundations, 1985-91; bd. cons. Jour. Rsch. and Devel. in Edn., 1982-96, Ednl. Theory, 1991-95; contbr. articles to profl. jours., U.S., Can., Eng., Australia. Recipient Faculty Research Assignment award Univ. Research Inst., Austin, Tex., 1983-84; vis. scholar U. London, 1977; Univ. Research Inst. grantee, 1981-82, 84-85 Mem. North Central Philosophy of Edn. Soc. (pres. 1966-67), Ohio Valley Philosophy of Edn. Soc. (pres. 1967-68), Philosophy of Edn. Soc. (exec. bd. 1967-68, 80-82, Cert. Significant Svc.), Am. Ednl. Studies Assn. (exec. council 1972-74, pres. 1975-76) Home: 1801 Lavaca St Apt 8M Austin TX 78701-1312 Office: U Tex Edn Bldg 406 Austin TX 78712

RICH, JOSEPH JOHN, accountant; b. Detroit, Sept. 5, 1944; s. John H. and Edna R. (Swallow) R.; m. Carolyn A. Atkinson, Nov. 3, 1962 (div. Dec. 19, 1983); children: Marcella, Loren; m. Darlene E. Kornfehl, Aug. 2, 1985 (div. Sept. 20, 2000). A in Ins. Law, Am. Edn. Inst., 1974; A of Commerce, Alpena Community Coll., 1975. Accredited bus. acct. Pres. Tax Svcs., Inc., Portland, Mich., 1965—2002; claim specialist State Farm Ins., Marshall, Mich., 1966-80; owner Someplace Else Travel Ctr., Portland, 1990—2002, The Expresso Experience, 1995-2001, Benefit Mgmt. Corp., Portland, 1996—2002; pres. JR Cons., Inc., Portland, 2002—. Author: Insurance Guide for Theatres, 1977, Accounting for Non-Profit Theatres, 1976. Chmn. Ionia (Mich.) County Commn., 1986-90. Named one of Outstanding Young Men in Am., 1981. Mem. Portland Civic Club, Ind. Accts. Assn. of Mich., Comdrs. Club of Lansing. Republican. Avocations: theater, travel. Office: JR Cons Inc 202 W Bridge St Portland MI 48875 E-mail: joerich@cablespeed.com.

RICH, JOSEPH WILLIAM, engineering educator, consultant; b. New Orleans, Aug. 6, 1937; s. William Edward and Hortense Maud (Martinez) R.; m. Beatrice Mae Jewell, July 9, 1960; children: Grant Jewell, Anne Elizabeth. BSME, Carnegie Inst. Tech., 1959; MAE, U. Va., 1961; M.A., Princeton U., 1963, PhD, 1965. Aero. engr. Calspan Corp., Buffalo, 1965-71, prin. engr., 1971-82, mgr. laser physics and chemistry program, 1982-86; adj. prof. elec. engring. SUNY-Buffalo, 1983-86; vis. prof. mech. engring. Carnegie-Mellon U., Pitts., 1985; prof. mech. engring. Ohio State U., 1986—, Ralph W. Kurtz prof. mech. engring, 1996—. Contbr. articles to profl. jours. Patentee in field. Mem. Com. on Ednl. Goals, East Aurora (N.Y.) pub. schs., 1982-83. Panelist Joint U.S.-Japan Seminar on Molecular Energy Transfer, U.S. Nat. Acad. Scis., 1976; Guggenheim Found. fellow, 1961-65, Fulbright sr. fellow Ecole Centrale Paris, 1988. Fellow AIAA (assoc.); mem. Am. Phys. soc., AAAS, Sigma Xi. Democrat. Office: Ohio State U Dept Mech Engring 206 W 18th Ave Columbus OH 43210-1189 Business E-Mail: rich.2@osu.edu.

RICH, LAURIE M. federal official, educator; b. Dallas, Tex. Grad., U. N. Tex., Denton. Tchr. Dallas Pub. H.S.; spl. asst. and sr. legis. asst. Sen. Phil Gramm, Washington, 1985—93; acting adminstrv. asst. Sen, Kay Bailey Hutcison, Washington, 1993—95; exec. dir. Tex. Office of State-Fed. Rels., Dallas, 1995—2001; asst. sec. for intergovt. and interagy. affairs U.S. Dept. Edn., Washington, 2001—. Dir. of coalitions Bush/Quayle Campaign, Washington, 1992. Office: US Dept Edn 400 Maryland Ave SW Washington DC 20202

RICH, LAWRENCE VINCENT, manufacturing and engineering company executive; b. Ambridge, Pa., May 23, 1951; s. Frank Joseph and Letizia Mary (Giammatteo) R.; m. Frances Ann Banks, July 8, 1977; children: Alison, Amy. BS in Chemistry, Pa. State U., 1974; postgrad., U. Pitts., 1975-76. Cert. in combustion tech.; pres. ALFA Industries, Inc., bd. dirs., exec. bd. dirs.; cons. Hal Roach Cos., Birmingham, Ala. Project engr. Bricmont and Assocs., McMurray, Pa., 1977-81; corp. combustion engr. Wheeling-Pitts. Steel Corp., Wheeling, W.Va., 1981-85; mgr. steel sales and furnace tech. N.Am. Mfg. Co., Cleve., 1985—. Exec. bd. dirs. A-PAC Sys., Pitts.; cons. Weirton (W.Va.) Steel Co., 1992. Mem., coach Soccer Assn., Moon Twp., Pa., 1997; mem. fin. and planning bd. and cluster reorgn. bd. St. Catherine's Ch., Wireton, Pa., 1997; mem. Crimewatch Orgn., Moon Twp., 1997; mem. adv. com. Internat. Airport, Pitts., 1992. Mem. Am. Iron and Steel Engrs. (Recognition award 1987, 89, 92, 93, 96), Iron and Steel Soc. of AIME (Recognition award 1990), Steel Mfrs. Assn. (co. rep.), Materials Enging. Soc., KC (3d degree), Chanticlear Swimming Club (bd. dirs.). Republican. Roman Catholic. Avocations: racquetball, squash, swimming, working with computers. Home: 2006 Broad Hill Farms Rd Coraopolis PA 15108-9008 Office: NAm Mfg Co 4455 E 71st St Cleveland OH 44105-5601

RICH, LESLEY MOSHER, artist; b. Chgo., May 12, 1944; d. Robert Gollnick and Lillian Schmelzle; m. Keith Rich, July 6, 1995. Student, U. Ill., 1962-66, Inst. Allende, San Miguel de Allende, Mex., 1976-78. Cons., artist Med. Imaging Sys., Chgo., 1990-93; art instr., 1993—. One-woman shows include Palette & Chisel, Chgo., 1995 (Best Show of Yr. 1995), Gallery North, New Buffalo, Mich., 1995, 98, Birchstone, Egg Harbor, Wis., 1996, 1997; exhibited in group show at China Art Mus., Beijing, 1996, Dinan, France, 2003, Bozeman, 2003, 2004, Taos 2004, Atlanta 2004. Artist Art for Inner City, Chgo., 1988-89, Arusha (Tanzania) Women's Devel. Ctr., 1996. Recipient award of excellence, Oil Painters of Am., 1994, Wichita Art Mus., 1994, Arts for Parks, 1996, 1998, Alta Prima Internat., 1999—2003, Am. Impressionist Soc., 2001, Hilton Head Nat., 2002, Salon Internat., 2003, 2004, Exposition Chateau-Musee de Dinan, 2003, OPA Nat., 2003, Biennale Internazionale dell' Arte Contemporanea, Italy. Mem. Palette & Chisel (Harriet Bitterly award 1994, award of excellence 1994), Am. Artists Profl. League, Pacific Art League, Allied Artists, Alla Prima Internat. Home: 4225 Park Blvd Palo Alto CA 94306-4144 E-mail: lesley@lesleyrich.com.

RICH, MARVIN P. health association executive; Formerly with CalFed Bank, Carter Hawley Hale Stores, Inc., Dart Industry; former exec. v.p., fin. and info. svcs. Wellpoint Health Networks/Blue Cross of Calif.; exec. v.p. strategic planning, fin. and adminstrn. K-Mart, Troy, Mich., 1994-98; CEO, exec. v.p. Oxford Health, Norwalk, Conn., 1998—99; pres., CEO CareInsight, 2000; pres. WebMD, Elmwood Park, NJ, 2000—01; exec. v.p., fin. and ops. Health Net, Inc., Woodland Hills, Calif., 2002—. Office: Health Net, Inc 21650 Oxnard St Woodland Hills CA 91367

RICH, MICHAEL DAVID, research corporation executive, lawyer; b. LA, Jan. 23, 1953; s. Ben Robert and Faye (Mayer) R.; m. Debra Paige Granfield, Jan. 12, 1980; children: Matthew, William. AB, U. Calif., Berkeley, 1973; JD, UCLA, 1976. Bar: Calif., 1976. Extern law clk. to judge U.S. Dist. Ct., Boston, 1975; staff mem. RAND, Santa Monica, Calif., 1976-85, dir. resource mgmt. program, 1980-85, dep. v.p., 1986, v.p. nat. security rsch. and dir. Nat. Def. Rsch. Inst., 1986-93, sr. v.p., 1993-95, exec. v.p., 1995—. Chmn. bd. dirs. Coun. for Aid to Edn., 1996—; co-chmn. bd. overseers Rand-Qatar Policy Inst., 2003—; chmn. bd. trustees Internat. Inst. Strategic Studies-U.S., 2004—. Author numerous classified and unclassified reports and articles. Bd. dirs. WISE Sr. Svcs.; mem. bd. councillors UCLA Found., 2000—; fin. oversight com., Santa Monica-Malibu Unified Sch. Dist., 2000—; bd. advisers Santa Monica-UCLA Med. Ctr.; chmn. bd. trustees The Comm. Inst., 2003—. Mem. Coun. Fgn. Rels., Internat. Inst. Strategic Studies (governing coun., chmn. bd. dirs.). Office: RAND PO Box 2138 1776 Main St Santa Monica CA 90407-2138 Office Phone: 310-451-6934. E-mail: mrich@rand.org.

RICH, MICHAEL JOSEPH, lawyer; b. N.Y.C., June 19, 1945; s. Jesse and Phyllis (Sternfeld) R.; m. Linda Christine Kubis, July 19, 1969; children: David Lawrence, Lisa Diane. BA, Gettysburg Coll., 1967; JD, Am. U., 1972. Bar: Del. 1973, U.S. Dist. Ct. Del. 1973, U.S. Supreme Ct., 1976, Pa., 1981. Law clk. Del. Supreme Ct., Georgetown, 1972-73; assoc. Tunnell & Raysor, Georgetown, 1973-76; ptnr. Dunlap, Holland & Rich, P.A., Georgetown, 1976-80; gen. counsel Pearlette Fashions, Inc., Lebanon, Pa., 1981-83; assoc. Morris, Nichols, Arsht & Tunnell, Georgetown, 1983-86; ptnr., 1987-91, Twilley, Street, Rich Braverman & Hindman, P.A., Dover, Del., 1991-95; state solicitor, 1995-2001; dep. atty. gen., 2001—. Mem. Bd. Bar Examiners, Del., 1986-97, chmn., 1996-97;minority counsel Del. Ho. of Reps., Dover, 1977-79; mem. Del. Gov's Magistrate Commn., 1980, 83-86; sec. Del. Gov's. Jud. Nominating Commn., 1986-89. Bd. dirs. People's Place II, Inc., Milford, Del., 1973-77; pres. Bi-County United Way, Inc., Milford, 1977-78; mem. Partnership Greater Milford Commn., 1987-89, Friends Milford Library. Served to 1st lt. U.S. Army, 1967-69, Vietnam. Dean's fellow Am. U., 1971-72. Mem. ABA, Am. Judicature Soc., Del. Bar Assn. (pres. 1990-91), Sussex County Bar Assn. (pres. 1987-89). Republican. Office Phone: 302-739-4251. Business E-Mail: michael.rich@state.de.us.

RICH, NORMAN MINNER, surgeon; b. Ray, Ariz., Jan. 13, 1934; s. George and Leona LuVerne Minner R.; m. Ann Lois Rich, June 20, 1959; children: Suzanne, Alison, David, Bethany. BA, Stanford U., 1956, MD, 1960, Cath. U., Santiago, Chile, 1977; MD (honoris causa), Mayab U., 2000. Diplomate Am. Bd. Surgery, Med. Care Catastrophes; cert. ATLS instr. Rotating intern Tripler Gen. Hosp., Honolulu, 1960-61; gen. surgery resident Letterman Gen. Hosp., San Francisco, 1961-65; chief surg. svc. 2d Surg. Hosp., Fort Bragg, N.C., and Rep. of Vietnam, 1965-66; chief vascular surgery svc. Walter Reed Army Med. Ctr., Washington, 1967-78, dir., vascular fellowship program, 1967-78; vascular rsch. coord. Armed Forces Inst. of Pathology, Edgewood Arsenal, Md., 1966-76; cons. in vascular surgery The Surgeon Gen. of the Army, Washington, 1970-82; chmn. dept. of surgery USUHS, Bethesda, Md., 1977—2002, prof. surgery, 1976—, mil. medicine, 1983—. Leonard Heaton and David Packard Prof., 1999—; lectr. in field worldwide, including Scudder Oration/Am. Coll. Surgeons, Mitchiner Meml. Lectr./Royal Army Med. Coll.; Emile Holman lectr. Stanford U.; cons. to nat. and internat. activities and mem. govt./specialty socs. Author/co-author books in field, including: (with Frank C. Spencer) Vascular Trauma, 1978; mem. 10 editl. bds. jours. in field. Decorated Legion of Merit, Bronze Star, Meritorious Svc. award, Vietnam medals, Medaille D'Honneur, France, others; recipient J.E. Wallace Sterling Lifetime Alumni Achievement award Stanford Med. Alumni Assn., 1999, Carol Johns medal Uniformed Svcs. U. Health Scis., 2003. Fellow ACS (Surgeons award for service to safety 2003), Am. Surg. Assn.; mem. Am. Assn. Surgery for Trauma, Am. Soc. for Vascular Surgery, Apothecaries of London, Am. Venous Forum, Assn. Acad. Surgery, Mexican Acad. Surg., French Surg. Assn., Chesapeake Vascular Soc., Ea. Vascular Soc., Halsted Soc., Hellenic Surg. Soc., Internat. Soc. for Cardiovascular Surgery, Soc. of Univ. Surgeons, Soc. for Vascular Surgery, So. Assn. for Vascular Surgery, So. Surg. Assn., Royal Belgian Soc. of Surgery (assoc.), Royal Australian Coll. Surgeons (vascular sect.), German Surg. Soc. (hon.), Alpha Omega Alpha, numerous others. E-mail: nrich@usuhs.mil.

RICH, NORMAN S. food service executive; From mem. staff to pres., CEO Weis Markets, Sunbury, Pa., 1964—2002, pres., 2002—, CEO, 2002—. Dir. Food Mktg. Inst.; bd. trustees Evang. Cmty. Hosp.; bd. dirs. Weis Markets. Office: Weis Markets 1000 S Second St Sunbury PA 17801*

RICH, PHILIP DEWEY, publishing executive; b. Nashua, N.H., Feb. 1, 1940; s. John Parker and Olive Frances (Hussey) R.; m. Leslie Ann Burke, June 14, 1974 (div. 1982). AB magna cum laude, Harvard U., 1961; MA, NYU, 1962; postgrad., Princeton U., 1962. Editor Houghton Mifflin Co., Boston, 1964-73; asst. mng. editor UpCountry Mag. Berkshire Eagle, Pittsfield, Mass., 1976-77; editor Book Creations Inc., Canaan, N.Y., 1977-80, editor-in-chief, 1980-91, v.p., exec. editor, 1991-92; cons. editor Berkshire Ho. Publs., Lee, Mass., 1992-93, mng. editor, 1993-96, mng. editor and prodn. editor, 1996-99, editl. dir., prodn. dir., 1999—2003; editl. cons. Pittsfield, Mass., 2003—. Office: 18 Boylston St Pittsfield MA 01201-6748 Office Phone: 413-443-1737. Personal E-mail: prich@bcn.net.

RICH, R(OBERT) BRUCE, lawyer; b. N.Y.C., Oct. 28, 1949; s. John J. and Sylvia (Berkenblit) R.; m. Melissa Jo Saxe; children— Megan, Alexander. A.B., Dartmouth Coll., 1970; J.D., U. Pa., 1973. Bar: N.Y. 1974, U.S. Dist. Ct. (so. and ea. dists.) N.Y. 1974, U.S. Ct. Appeals (2d cir.) 1980, U.S. Supreme Ct. 1980, U.S. Ct. Appeals (D.C. cir.) 1985. Assoc. firm Weil, Gotshal & Manges, N.Y.C., 1973-81, ptnr., 1981-. Mem. bd. overseers U. Pa. Law Sch., 2002-, bd. dirs. Expeditionary Leaning Outward Bound, 2002-, Appleseed Found., 2003-. Contbg. author: Cultivating the Wasteland: Can Cable Put the Vision Back in TV?, 1983, The International Libel Handbook, 1995. Contbr. articles to profl. jours.; co-editor: Business and Legal Guide to Online-Internet Law, 1997. Mem. ABA (antitrust law sect., forum com. on communications law), Assn. Bar City N.Y. (com. on trade regulation 1982-85, communications law com. 1985-88), Phi Beta Kappa. Office: Weil Gotshal & Manges 767 5th Ave Fl Conc1 New York NY 10153-0119

RICH, ROBERT E., SR., frozen foods company executive; b. 1941; married. Grad., U. Buffalo, 1935; DHL (hon.), D'Youville Coll.; LLD (hon.), U. Buffalo. Owner, operator Wilber Farms Dairy (later named Jones-Rich Milk Co.), 0935; founder, chmn. bd. dirs. Rich Products Corp., Buffalo, 1944—. Chmn. bd. dirs. Rich Kwality Foods, Ltd., Pune, India, Rich Products South Africa, Rich Products Can., Ltd., Rich-SeaPak Corp., St. Simons Island, Ga., Rich Holdings Corp., Buffalo, Palm Beach Nat. Golf and Country Club. War food adminstr., Mich., 1945. Named to, Nat. Frozen Food Industry Hall of Fame; recipient Svc. to Mankind award, WNY chpt. Leukemia Soc. Am., Founder award, Frozen Food Industry, Spl. Svc. citation, Internat. Food Svc. Exec. Assn., Exemplary Citizenship award, Theodore Roosevelt Inaugural Site Found., Disting. Svc. award, U. Buffalo, Niagara Frontier Businessman of Yr. award, Bus. Adminstrn. Alumni, Herbert Hoover award, Food Distbrs. Internat. Office: Rich Products Corp 1 W Ferry St Buffalo NY 14213-1701*

RICH, ROBERT EDWARD, lawyer; b. Corbin, Ky., Feb. 4, 1944; s. Edward Bluch and Marjorie Brooks (Wentworth) R.; m. Janet Sue Shearer, May 14, 1966; children: Susan M., Christopher R., David E., Sarah M. AB, U. Ky., 1966; JD, Harvard U., 1969. Bar: Ohio 1970. Jud. clk. U.S. Ct. Appeals for 6th Cir., Louisville, 1969-70; assoc. Taft, Stettinius & Hollister, Cin., 1970, ptnr., 1978—. Pres. Lighthouse Youth Svcs., Inc., Cin., 1985, Ky. YMCA Youth Assn., Frankfort, 2001; mem. exec. bd. Ky. Hist. Soc.; pres. Cin. Bar Found., 1991. Mem. ABA, Cin. Bar Assn. Republican. Presbyterian. Home: 215 Hilltop Ln Wyoming OH 45215-4121 Office: 1800 US Bank Tower 425 Walnut St Cincinnati OH 45202-3923 Office Phone: 513-357-9355.

RICH, ROBERT F. law and political science educator; married; 3 children. BA in Govt. with honors, Oberlin Coll., 1971; student, Free U. of Berlin, 1971-72; MA in Polit. Scis., U. Chgo., 1973, PhD in Polit. Scis., 1975. Project dir., asst. rsch. scientist Ctr. for Rsch. on Utilization Sci. Knowledge, Inst. Social Rsch., U. Mich., lectr. dept. polit. sci., 1975-76; asst. prof. politics and pub. affairs Princeton U., 1976-82, coord. domestic and urban policy field Woodrow Wilson Sch., 1976-82; assoc. prof. polit. sci., pub. policy and mgmt. Sch. Urban and Pub. Affairs, Carnegie-Mellon U., 1982-86; prof. polit. sci. law, health resources mgmt., med. humanities and social svcs., cmty. health, prof. Inst. Environ. Studies U. Ill., Urbana, 1986—2003, dir. Inst. Govt. and Publ. Affairs, 1986-97, acting head med. humanities and social scis. program Urbana-Champaign, 1988-90, prof. law and polit. sci., health resources mgmt., 1996—, prof. law; fellow Johns Hopkins U. Ctr. for Study of Am. Govt., Washington, 1993-95; Mercator prof. Humboldt U., Berlin, 2002—03. Cons. U.S. Dept. Health and Human Svcs., Carnegie-Mellon U., 1986—, MacArthur

Found., NIMH, 1988-89, Food, Drug and Law Inst., HHS, 1989, Am. Career Soc., 1996-97; disting. lectr. German Marshall Fund, Hamburg, Germany, 1997. Author: Social Science Information and Public Policy Making: The Interaction Between Bureaucratic Politics and the Use of Survey Data, 1981; co-author: Government Information Management: A Counter-Report of the Commission on Federal Paperwork, 1980; editor: Translating Evaluation into Policy, 1979, The Knowledge Cycle, 1981, Knowledge, Creation, Diffusion, Utilization, 1979-88, 88-91; co-editor: Competitive Approaches to Health Policy Reform, 1993, Health Policy, Federalism and the Role of the American States, 1996; assoc. editor Society, 1984-88, Evaluation Rev., 1985-89; mem. editl. bd. Policy Studies Rev. Series, 1980-83, Evaluation and Change, 1979-82, Law and Human Behavior, 1983-87; contbr. articles to profl. jours., book chpts. Recipient Emil Limbach Teaching award Carnegie-Mellon U., Sch. Urban and Pub. Affairs, 1985; fellow German Acad. Exch. Program, Fed. Republic Germany, 1971-72, Nat. Opinion Rsch. Ctr. fellow, 1972-73, German Govt. fellow, 1974, Russel Sage Found. Rsch. fellow, 1974-75; vis. scholar Hastings Ctr. for Society, Ethics and Life Scis., 1982. Mem. APA (task force on victims of crime and violence 1982-84), Soc. for Traumatic Stress Studies (bd. dirs. 1980—), World Fedn. for Mental Health (chmn. com. on mental health needs of victims 1985—, vice chmn. 1981-83, Robert F. Rich rsch. ann. award established in his honor, sci. com. on mental health needs of victims 1983), Howard R. Davis Soc. for Knowledge Utilization and Planned Change (pres. 1986-89), Polit. Sci. 400, Policy Studies Assn. (Aaron Wildausky award 1994), Phi Beta Kappa, Sigma Xi, Phi Kappa Phi. Office: U Ill Inst Govt & Pub Affairs 1007 W Nevada St # 204 Urbana IL 61801-3812 also: 815 W Van Buren St Chicago IL 60607-3506 Office Phone: 217-244-8550. Business E-Mail: rrich@law.uluc.edu.

RICH, ROBERT REGIER, immunology educator, physician; b. Newton, Kans., Mar. 7, 1941; s. Eldon Stahly and Margaret Joy (Regier) R.; m. Susan Jepsen Solliday, Mar. 22, 1974; children from previous marriage: Kenneth Eldon, Cathryn Louise; 1 stepchild, Lynn Solliday Todorov. AB, Oberlin Coll., 1962; MD, U. Kans., 1966. Diplomate Am. Bd. Internal Medicine (bd. dirs. 1990-93); Am. Bd. Allergy and Immunology (bd. dirs. 1987-93, chmn. 1991); cert. spl. qualification Diagnostic Lab. Immunology. Intern, resident in internal medicine U. Wash., Seattle, 1966-68; clin. asso., chief clin. asso., sr. staff fellow NIH, Bethesda, Md., 1968-71; research asso. Harvard Med. Sch., Boston, 1971-73; asst. in medicine Peter Bent Brigham Hosp., 1972-73; asst. prof., assoc. prof. microbiology, immunology and internal medicine Baylor Coll. Medicine, Houston, 1973-78, prof., 1978-95, Disting. Svc. prof., 1995—2002, head immunology sect., 1978-98, chief clin. immunology, 1979-91, v.p., dean rsch., 1990-98; exec. assoc. dean, prof. medicine & microbiology/immunology Emory U. Sch. Medicine, 1998—. Investigator Howard Hughes Med. Inst., Bethesda, Md., 1977-91; mem. immunobiology study sect. NIH, 1977-81; mem. transplantation biology and immunology com. Nat. Inst. Allergy and Infectious Disease, 1982-86, chmn., 1984-86; mem. nat. ctr. grants com. Arthritis Found., 1983-86, chmn., 1984-86, nat. rsch. com., 1984-89, chmn., 1986-89, ho. of dels., 1985-91, Blue Ribbon com. on rsch. 2000-01; mem. rsch. adv. com. Nat. Multiple Sclerosis Soc., 1989-94, chmn., 1993-94; adv. panel on rsch. Assn. Am. Med. Coll., 1990—, shared responsibility advocacy com., 1997-98; chmn. ctrs. working group Nat. Inst. Arthritis Musculoskeletal Skin Diseases, 1996-97; mem nat. human rsch. protections adv. com., dept. health and human svcs., 2000-02. Assoc. editor: Jour. Immunology, 1978-82, sect. editor, 1991-96, deputy editor, 1997-2002, editor-in-chief, 2003--; assoc. editor: Jour. Infectious Diseases, 1984-88; adv. editor: Jour. Exptl. Medicine, 1980-84; mem. editl. bd. Jour. Clin. Immunology, 1989-96, Clin. and Exptl. Immunology, 1995—; editor-in-chief Clin. Immunology: Principles and Practice, 1996, 2d edit., 2001; contbr. articles to profl. jours. Served with USPHS, 1968-70. Recipient Research Career Devel. award NIH, 1975-77, Merit award NIH, 1987. Fellow ACP, Am. Acad. Allergy, Asthma, and Immunology (chmn. basic and clin. immunology interest sect. 1992-93, chmn. profl. edn. coun. 1996-98, v.p. 2001-2002), Infectious Diseases Soc. Am.; mem. AMA, AAAS, Am. Bd. Internal Medicine (diplomate, bd. dirs. 1990-93), Am. Bd. Allergy and Immunology (diplomate, bd. dirs. 1987-93), Assn. Am. Physicians, Am. Soc. Clin. Investigation, Am. Assn. Immunologists (chmn. pub. affairs com. 1994-2000, Disting. Svc. award 1999), Am. Assn. Investigative Pathology, Am. Soc. Microbiologists, Am. Fedn. Med. Rsch., Am. Clin. Climatological Assn. (councillor 2001-), Fedn. of Am. Socs. for Exptl. Biology (bd. dirs. 1998-2003, pres. and chmn. bd. dirs. 2001-02), Clin. Immunology Soc. (coun. 1990-96, pres. 1995), Nat. Assn. Biomedical Rsch. (bd. dirs. 2002-), Assn. for Assessment and Accreditation of Lab. Animal Care Internat. (bd. trustees 2003—), Alpha Omega Alpha, Sigma Xi. Office: Emory U Sch Medicine 1440 Clifton Rd NE Atlanta GA 30322-1053

RICH, ROBERT STEPHEN, lawyer; b. NYC, Apr. 30, 1938; s. Maurice H. and Natalie (Priess) R.; m. Myra N. Lakoff, May 31, 1964; children: David, Rebecca, Sarah. AB, Cornell U., 1959; JD, Yale U., 1963. Bar: N.Y. 1964, Colo. 1973, U.S. Tax Ct. 1966, U.S. Supreme Ct. 1967, U.S. Ct. Claims 1968, U.S. Dist. Ct. (so. dist.) N.Y. 1965, U.S. Dist. Ct. (ea. dist.) N.Y. 1965, U.S. Dist. Ct. Colo. 1980, U.S. Ct. Appeals (10th cir.) 1978; conseil juridique, Paris, 1968. Assoc. Shearman & Sterling, N.Y.C., Paris, London, 1963-72; ptnr. Davis, Graham & Stubbs, Denver, 1973—. Adj. faculty U. Denver Law Sch., 1977—; mem. adv. bd. U. Denver Ann. Tax Inst., 1985—, global bus. and culture divsn., U. Denver, 1992—, Denver World Affairs Coun., 1993—; mem. Colo. Internat. Trade Coun., 1985—; mem. Rocky Mt. Dist. Export Coun., US Dept. Commerce, 1993—; tax adv. com. US Senator Hank Brown; bd. dirs. Clos du Val Wine Co. Ltd., Danskin Cattle Co., Ouray Ranch, Areti Wines, Ltd., Taltarni Vineyards, Christy Sports, others. Contbr. articles to profl. jours. Actor, musician N.Y. Shakespeare Festival, 1960; sponsor Am. Tax Policy Inst., 1991—; adv. bd. Middle Park Land Trust, Granby, Colo., 2003—; pres. So. Boulder Park Ecol. Assn., 1999—; sec. Bhutan Found., Citizens for Arts to Zoo; bd. dirs. Alliance Francaise, 1977—, Copper Valley Assn., Denver Internat. Film Festival, 1978—79, Anschutz Family Found.; trustee, sec. Denver Art Mus., 1982—; pres., bd. dirs. Ouray Ranch, Granby, Colo., 2001—; bd. dirs. Aspen Music Festival and Sch., 2004—. Capt. U.S. Army, 1959—60. Fellow Am. Coll. Tax. Coun. (bd. regents 10th cir. 1992—), Soc. Fellows Aspen Inst.; mem. ABA, Internat. Bar Assn., Colo. Bar Assn., NY State Bar Assn., Assn. Bar City of NY, Asia-Pacific Lawyers Assn., Union Internat. des Avocats, Internat. Fiscal Assn. (pres. Rocky Mt. br. 1992—, US regional v.p. 1988—), Japan-Am. Soc. Colo. (bd. dirs. 1989—, pres. 1991-93), Confrerie des Chevaliers du Tastevin, Rocky Mt. Wine and Food Soc., Meadowood Club, Denver Club, City Club Denver, Mile High Club, Cactus Club Denver, Yale Club, Denver Tennis Club. Office: Cherry Creek Sta PO Box 61429 Denver CO 80206-8429 also: Antelope Co 555 17th St Ste 2400 Denver CO 80202-3941 Office Phone: 303-299-1230. Business E-Mail: robertrich@aya.yale.edu.

RICH, RUTHANNE, musician, educator; b. Salisbury, N.C., Dec. 20, 1941; d. Arthur Lowndes and Helen (Wall) Rich; m. Frederick B. Humphrey. MusB, Fla. State U., 1963; MusM, Peabody Conservatory of Music, 1964; diplôme de Virtuosité, Schola Cantorum, Paris, 1966; MusD, U. Rochester, 1973. Piano soloist various symphony orchs., 1957—, Europe, 1964—; artist-in-residence Mercer U., Macon, Ga., 1966-68; asst. prof. Lawrence U., Appleton, Wis., 1968-69; assoc. prof. Valdosta State U., Ga., 1971-73; prof. piano Kansas City (Mo.) Conservatory Music, 1974—2000, prof. emerita, 2000—; piano soloist Asia, 1977—. Contbr. articles to profl. jours. Del. Edgar Snow Found., China, 1981, 84, Sister City, Macon, Ga.; with Kaohsiung, Taiwan, 1979. Recipient First Prize Nat. Biennial Contest Nat. Fedn. Music Clubs, 1961, Nat. Marie Morrissey Keith award Nat. Fedn. Music Clubs, 1962; Fulbright scholar, 1964-65; Hariett Hale Woolley Grant Found. des Etats-Unis, 1965-66. Mem. Music Tchrs. Nat. Assn., Mo. Music Tchrs. Assn. (v.p. 1975-78), Internat. Guild of Piano Tchrs. (Gold medal for Best Rec.). Avocations: Karate, environmental issues. Home: 6537 Valley Rd Kansas City MO 64113-1822

RICH, WILLIAM E. biotechnology executive; BS in Chemistry, Carson Newman Coll.; PhD, U. N.C.; postgrad., Duke U. Mem. mktg., sales, R&D depts., sr. v.p. Dionex Corp., 1975—90; pres. BioSepra, 1991—94; sr. v.p. Sepracor, Inc., 1991—94; pres., CEO, bd. dirs. Ciphergen Biosystems, Inc., Fremont, Calif., 1994—. Office: Ciphergen Biosystems Inc 6611 Dumbarton Cir Fremont CA 94555

RICH, WILLIS FRANK, JR., banker; b. Ft. Dodge, Iowa, July 26, 1919; s. Willis Frank and Agnes Reed (Paterson) R.; m. Jo Ann Rockwell, Apr. 12, 1947; children: Ronald Rockwell, Roxanne, Andrew Paterson. BA, Princeton U., 1941. Credit analyst Northwestern Nat. Bank, Mpls., 1947-52, asst. cashier, 1952-55, asst. v.p., 1955, v.p., 1955-57; pres. N.W. Nat. Bank, Bloomington-Richfield, Minn., 1952-58, v.p., cashier, 1957-60, v.p. div. A, 1960-68, sr. v.p. nat. and internat. divs., 1968-73, exec. v.p., 1973-81, vice chmn. bd. dirs., chief credit officer, 1981-84; fin. cons., 1984—. Dir. Advance Acceptance Corp., 1985-2000. Pres. Viking coun. Boy Scouts Am., 1970-71, trustee found., 1971-86; mem. exec. bd. Minn. Cmty. Rsch. Coun., 1969-77; dir. Minn. Zoo, 1987-95; trustee St. Martin's Found., 1986-90; vestry mem. St. Martin's-By-The-Lake Ch. With AUS, 1941-46. Decorated Bronze Star. Mem. Robert Morris Assocs. (nat. pres. 1977-78), Mpls. Suburban Gyro Club. Clubs: Woodhill, Swan Lake Country. Episcopalian. Home: 378 Waycliffe N Wayzata MN 55391-1390

RICHARD, ALISON FETTES, anthropology educator; b. Great Britain, Mar. 1, 1948; BA, Cambridge U., 1969; PhD, London U., 1973, U. Peking, 2004. Asst. prof. anthropology Yale U., New Haven, 1972-76, assoc. prof. anthropology, 1976-85, prof. anthropology, 1985—2003, provost, 1994—2002, Franklin Muzzy Crosby prof., 1998—2002, prof. emeritus, 2003—; vice-chancellor Univ., Cambridge, 2003—. Dir. Yale Peabody Mus. Natural History, 1990-94. Bd. dir. Yale-New Haven Health Svc., 1994-2002, World Wildlife Fund, 1995-2004. Mem. Am. Primatological Soc., Am. Assn. Phys. Anthropologists, Am. Anthrop. Assn., Brit. Ecol. Soc., Primate Soc. Gt. Britain, Zool. Soc. London, Cambridge Philosophical Soc. Office: Office of the Vice Chancellor Univ of Cambridge The Old Schools CB2 1TN Cambridge England Office Phone: 44 1223 332290. E-mail: v-c@admin.cam.ac.uk.

RICHARD, EDWARD H. manufacturing company executive, former municipal government official; b. Mar. 15, 1937; s. Henry and Ida Richard. BA, Antioch Coll., 1959. Pres., chmn., bd. dirs. Magnetics Internat. Inc., Maple Heights, Ohio, 1967-86; exec. v.p. Stearns Magnetics S.A., Brussels, Belgium, 1974-77; prin. Edward H. Richard & Assocs., Cleve., 1967-96; pres., treas. David Round & Son, Inc., Cleve. Chmn. Cleve. dist. adv. council Small Bus. Adminstrn., 1975-79; former mem. nat. adv. council Dept. Treasury; cons. and advisor in field; del. world trade fairs. Former trustee Regional Econ. Devel. Coun., Met. Cleve. Jobs. Coun., Cleve. Devel. Found., Cleve. BBB; former trustee Hiram House, Antioch U., former treas., 1972-77; N.E. Ohio Regional Sewer Dist., Greater Cleve. Domed Stadium Corp., Greater Cleve. Conv. and Visitor Bur.; former trustee, vice-chmn. Cleve. Ctr. Econ. Edn.; former pres. Bratenahl Condominium Assn.; mem., chmn. fin. com. Bratenahl Bd. Edn., 1971-75; trustee, chair nominating com., chair investment/endowment com. La Jolla Playhouse; chair bd. Mainly Mozart Festival, 1998—; mem. fin. com. San Diego Mus Art; chair bd. orch. rels. com., mem. fin. com., trustee San Diego Symphony Orch.

RICHARD, ELLEN, theater executive; b. Bridgeport, Conn., Dec. 12, 1957; d. Laurent and Anne (Markham) R. Bus. mgr. Atlas Scenic Studio, Bridgeport, 1977-82; theater mgr. Stamford (Conn.) Ctr. for Arts, 1980-83; bus. mgr. Westport (Conn.) Country Playhouse, 1982-84; gen. mgr. Roundabout Theatre Co. Inc., N.Y.C., 1983—. Mng. dir. Broadway plays including A View From the Bridge, 1997-98 (Tony award Revival of a Play 1998), Cabaret, 1998-2004 (Tony award Revival of a Musical 1998), The Deep Blue Sea, 1998, Side Man, 1998-99 (Tony award Best Play 1999), Little Me, 1998-1999, Death of a Salesman, 1999, The Lion in Winter, 1999, The Rainmaker, 1999-2000, Uncle Vanya, 2000, The Man Who Came to Dinner, 2000, Betrayal, 2000-01, Design for Living, 2001, Major Barbara, 2001, The Women, 2001-02, An Almost Holy Picture, 2002, The Crucible, 2002, The Man Who Had All the Luck, 2002, An Evening with Mario Cantone, 2002, The Boys from Syracuse, 2002, Tartuffe, 2003, A Day in the Death of Joe Egg, 2003, As Long As We Both Shall Laugh, 2003, Nine, 2003 (Tony award Best Revival of a Musical, 2003), The Look of Love, 2003, "MASTER HAROLD"...and the boys, 2003, Big River, 2003, The Caretaker, 2003-04, Twentieth Century, 2004, Assassins, 2004. Mem. N.Y. Cycling Club. Republican. Avocations: bicycling, skiing, sailing. Office: Roundabout Theatre Co 231 W 39th St Ste 1200 New York NY 10018-3109

RICHARD, JAMES THOMAS, retired psychologist, educator; b. Phila., Dec. 18, 1937; s. Elwood and Anna F. (McCall) R.; m. Ruth Mary D. Guiniven, May 5, 1962; children: Marianne, James Jr., Susan, Barbara, Jeannine. BA, LaSalle U., 1960; EdM, Temple U., 1963, EdD, 1968. Lic. psychologist, Pa. Tchr., counselor Cardinal Dougherty H.S., Phila., 1960-62; dir. student affairs Temple U. C.C., Phila., 1962-67; prof. psychology Bucks County C.C., Newtown, Pa., 1967-2000; ret., 2000; prof. emeritus, 2000—. Pres., psychologist Newtown Psychol. Ctr., 1972—. Author: Not Too High, Not Too Low: Stress Management for Professional Baseball Players and Their Fans, 1991. Sgt. Pa. Nat. Guard, 1956-65. Fellow Pa. Psychol. Assn., Phila. Soc. Clin. Psychologists;; mem. APA. Roman Catholic. Avocations: golf, photography, finance. Office: Newtown Psychol Ctr 660 Newtown Yardley Rd Ste 102 Newtown PA 18940-1759 Office Phone: 215-968-5378. E-mail: DRJRichard@aol.com.

RICHARD, JEAN-FRANCOIS, education educator, consultant; b. Uccle, Belgium, Feb. 10, 1943; s. Marcel Richard and Anne De Brouwer; m. Colette Dubois, Sept. 2, 1967; children: Oliver M., Tanguy C. PhD in Econs., Cath. U. of Louvain, Belgium, 1973. Lic. Physics Cath. U. of Louvain (Belgium), 1965. Vis. lectr. London Sch. of Econs., 1973—74; assoc. prof. Cath. U. of Louvain, Belgium, 1973—78, prof., 1978—88; vis. Belgian prof. U. of London, London, 1984—85; prof. Duke U., Durham, NC, 1988—91, U. of Pitts., 1991—98; univ. prof. U. Pitts., 1998—. Assoc. editor Econometrica, Evanston, Ill., 1979—84; asst. editor Rev. of Econ. Studies, Oxford, England, 1982—85; rsch. dir. Ctr. for Ops. Rsch. & Econometrics, Louvain-la-Neuve, Belgium, 1983—86; assoc. editor Jour. of Econometrics, Amsterdam, Netherlands, 1990—93; chmn. dept. of econs. U. of Pitts., 2000—. Author: Posterior And Predictive Densities For Simultaneous Equation Models, 1973, Bayesian inference in dynamic econometric models, 1999; contbr. articles to profl. jours. Pres. Royal Automobile Club Jr., Brussels, 1964—66; cub scout leader Brussels, 1958—61. Instr. Royal Cadet Sch., 1962—63, Brussel, Belgium. Recipient Chevalier, Ordre de Leopold (Belgium), 1989, Marschack Lectr., Econometric Soc., 1999, Auger lectr., Societe Canadienne d'economie, 1999; grantee Rsch. Grants, NSF, 1987—, Rsch. Grant, Pew Charitable Trust, 1988—90, Ford Found., 1989—91; W. Hallam Tuck Fellow, Belgian Am. Ednl. Found., 1968. Fellow: Econometric Soc.; mem.: Am. Statis. Assn. Roman Catholic. Achievements include research in weak exogeneity, encompassing, importance sampling, empirical auction models, Monte Carlo simulation, constrained strategic equilibrium, GDP forecasting. Avocations: model train collecting, stamp collecting/philately, jogging, bicycling, skying. Home: 4107 Bigelow Blvd Pittsburgh PA 15213-1407 Office: Pitts U WWPH Bouquet St Pittsburgh PA 15260 Office Phone: 1-412-648-1750. Office Fax: 1-412-648-7038. Personal E-mail: fantin+@pitt.edu.

RICHARD, OLIVER, III, (RICK RICHARD), energy company executive; b. Lake Charles, La., Oct. 11, 1952; s. Oliver Gonzard and Mary Jean (Turvey) R.; m. Donna Margaret Guzman, July 6, 1974; 1 child, David Turvey. BA, La. State U., 1974, JD, 1977; MLT, Georgetown U., 1981. Bar: La. 1977, U.S. Dist. Ct. (ea., we. and mid. dists.) La., 1977, U.S. Supreme Ct. 1981. Assoc. Sanders, Downing, Kean & Cazedessus, Baton Rouge, 1977; legis. asst. to U.S. Senator J. Bennett Johnston, Washington, 1977-81; ptnr. Hayes Durio & Richard, Lafayette, La., 1981-82; mem. FERC, Washington, 1982-85; v.p., gen. counsel Tenngasco Corp. divsn. Tenneco, 1985-87; v.p. regulatory and competitive analysis Enron Corp., 1987-88; pres., CEO No. Natural Gas Co., 1989-91; chmn. bd. dirs., CEO, pres. N.J. Resources Corp., 1995; chmn. bd. dirs., pres., CEO Columbia Energy Group, Inc., Reston, Va., 1995—. Mem. Interstate Pipeline Assn. (chmn., dir. exec. com.), Nat. Petroleum Coun. (chmn.), Am. Gas Assn. (chmn., bd. dirs.), Omicron Delta Kappa. Democrat. Roman Catholic. Office: Columbia Energy Group 200 Civic Center Dr Columbus OH 43215-4157

RICHARD, ROBERT CARTER, psychologist; b. Waterloo, Iowa, Apr. 4, 1938; s. Quentin Leroy and Adeline Pauline (Halverson) R.; m. Shirley Ruth Jones, Aug. 25, 1962 (div. Mar. 1999); children: David, John; m. Jacqueline J. Mendes, Feb. 19, 2000. BA Wheaton (Ill.) Coll., 1960; BD, Fuller Theol. Sem., 1963, PhD, 1973; STM, Andover Newton Theol. Sch., 1964. Ordained to ministry Am. Bapt. Conv., 1963; lic. psychologist, Calif. Pastor Peninsula Bapt. Ch., Gig Harbor, Wash., 1965-68; marriage and family counselor Glendale (Calif.) Family Svc., 1970-71; psychol. asst. Oakland and Pleasant Hill, Calif., 1972-71; psychologist Rafa Counseling Ctr., Pleasant Hill, 1974—. Mem. faculty John F. Kennedy U., Orinda, Calif., 1975-78; adj. faculty mem. New Coll., Berkeley, Calif, 1986; co-founder, bd. dirs. New Directions Counseling Ctr., 1974-81; rschr. assertiveness tng., lay counselor tng., psychotherapy and religious experience, treatment of adults abused as children. Author: (with Deacon Anderson) The Way Back: A Christian's Journey to Mental Wholeness, 1989; contbr. articles to profl. publs. Recipient Integration of Psychology and Theology award, 1973. Mem.: APA, Christian Assn. Psychol. Studies, Contra Costa Psychol. Assn. (past pres.), Calif. Psychol. Assn. Republican. Baptist. Office: Rafa Counseling Ctr 101 Gregory Ln Ste 33 Pleasant Hill CA 94523-4915 Office Phone: 925-827-9876. E-mail: robertcrichard@cs.com.

RICHARD, ROBERT MAX, cardiologist; b. Harmon, Okla., Sept. 11, 1926; s. Rolla Roy and Edith Belle (Drake) R.; m. Betty Ann Heavin, Aug. 14, 1948; 1 child, Robert Max. PhD in biochemistry, U. Wis., 1952; MD, U. Okla., 1961; postgrad., U. So. Calif., 1962-67. Physician specialist in internal medicine L.A. County, 1967-90, Motion Picture and TV Hosp., Woodland Hills, Calif., 1967-69; cardiology specialist Rancho Los Amigos Hosp.-U. So. Calif., Downey, 1969-72; assoc. prof. medicine, sect. cardiology U. So. Calif., L.A., 1973-90; cardiology specialist, dir. So. Calif. Heart Inst., Newport Beach, Laguna Beach, Calif., 1991—; staff cardiologist U. So. Calif. Diagnostic Ctr., Norris Cancer Hosp.-U. So. Calif., Doheny Eye Inst.-U. So. Calif., Univ. Hosp.-U. So. Calif. Author: Electrocardiography, 1980, Electrocardiology-Vector Cardiology, 1999, Holtre Monitoring and Exercise Stress Testing, 2001. With USN, 1945-46. Fellow Am. Coll. Cardiology (Outstanding Young Cardiologist 1975, Honoree plaque Dr. George Griffith Meml. Libr. 1975, Heart House Outstanding Cardiology 50th Anniversary 1999); mem. AMA (Master of Profession award 1993), AHA, Am. Soc. Internal Medicine, Oil Prodr. Soc. Okla., Phi Kappa Phi, Phi Lambda Upsilon, Sigma Xi. Republican. Presbyterian. Office: 522 Emerald Bay Laguna Beach CA 92651-1270

RICHARD, SUSAN MATHIS, communications executive, screenwriter; b. Detroit, June 21, 1949; d. Robert Louis and Maybelle Ann (Kromm) Engel; m. Paul Carl Mathis, May 12, 1973 (div. 1982); m. Robert Stephen Richard, Oct. 26, 1985. BA, U. Mich., 1971. Cert. tchr., Mich. Tchr. Carl Brablec High Sch., Roseville, Mich., 1971-73; anchorperson, producer Sta. WNCC-Cable TV, East Lansing, Mich., 1973-76; press asst. Ford-Dole Presdl. Campaign, Washington, 1976; TV and radio reporter Cox Communications, Washington, 1977-81; dep. dir. media rels. White House, Washington, 1981-84, spl. asst. to Pres., dir. media rels., 1985-87; mgr. pub. rels. Walt Disney World, Lake Buena Vista, Fla., 1987-88; v.p. industry communications Nat. Cable TV Assn., Washington, 1989; dep. assoc. adminstr. for pub. affairs NASA, Washington, 1990-93; v.p. Dittus Comm., Washington, 1998-2000; mgr. press rels. INTEL, Washington, 2000—. Mem. exec. com. Radio-TV Corrs. Galleries, Washington, 1978-81. Dir. promotions Action for Children's TV, East Lansing, 1975; mem. Strategic Planning Adv. Coun. of the Orange County (Fla.) Pub. Schs., 1988; communications dir. Bush-Quayle Fla. Campaign, 1988. Named Outstanding Young Working Woman, Lansing C. of C., 1975, Outstanding Working Woman, Washington Woman mag., 1985. Mem. AAUW (bd. dirs. Lansing chpt. 1974), Am. Soc. Assn. Execs. (Pub. Rels. trophy 1994), Radio-TV News Dirs. Assn., Fla. Youth and Family Svcs. Network (bd. dirs. 1988), Acad. TV Arts and Scis. (pub. rels. com. 1989), Women in Aerospace, Women in Wireless, Women in Film and Video, Washington Women in Pub. Rels., U. Mich. Alumni Assn. (bd. dirs. 1983-85), Gamma Phi Beta Alumnae Assn. Episcopalian.

RICHARDI, RALPH LEONARD, airline executive; b. Jersey City, Oct. 10, 1947; s. Nicholas Frank and Genevieve (Miele) R.; m. Cathy A. Himmelberger, Apr. 11, 1981. BS in Indsl. Mgmt., Fairleigh Dickinson U., 1969, MBA, 1976; cert. advanced mgmt. program, Harvard U., Boston, 1991. Indsl. engr. Ford Motor Co., Mahwah, N.J., 1969-72, Chase Manhattan Bank, N.Y.C., 1974-76, Am. Airlines, Dallas-Ft. Worth, 1976-80, dir. indsl. engring., 1980-83, dir. quality of work life, 1983-85, asst. v.p. labor rels., 1985-87, gen. mgr. reservations L.A., 1987-88, gen. mgr. San Francisco Airport, 1988-89, v.p. Dallas-Ft. Worth Airport, 1989-95; pres. Simmons Airlines/Am. Eagle, 1995—. Vice chmn. fund drives United Way, Dallas-Ft. Worth Airport, 1989-91. Avocation: golf. Address: 6103 Mimosa Ln Dallas TX 75230-5041 Office: Am Airlines Inc PO Box 619616 Dallas TX 75261-9616

RICHARDS, ALAN EDWARD, lawyer; b. Chgo., Mar. 7, 1949; s. Robert E. and Ann R. (Ekhart) R.; m. Meridee G. Johnson, June 13, 1970; children: Kate Elizabeth, Zachary Stephen. B.A., Carthage Coll., Kenosha, Wis., 1970; J.D., Marquette U., 1976. Bar: Wis. 1976, Ill. 1977, U.S. Dist. Ct. (no. dist.) Ill. 1977. Ptnr. Richards & Ralph, Chartered, Libertyville, Ill., 1977-87, Richards, Ralph & Schwab Chartered, Vernon Hills, Ill., 1987- . Editor Marquette U. Law Rev., 1975-76. Mem. ABA, Ill. Bar Assn., Lake County Bar Assn. Office: Richards Ralph & Schwab Chartered 175 E Hawthorne Pkwy Vernon Hills IL 60061-1463 E-mail: arichards@rrs-chartered.com.

RICHARDS, ANN, actress, educator, poet; b. Sydney; came to U.S., 1942; d. Mortimer Delaforce and Marion Bradshaw (Dive) Richards; m. Edmond J. Angelo, Feb. 4, 1949 (dec. Mar. 1983); children: Christopher E., Mark R., Juliet M.; m. Paul M. Kramer, Feb. 14, 1987 (dec. Aug. 1996). Student, Stotts Coll., 1936-37, Studio Sch. of Drama, 1936-38. Actress Cinesound Studio, Australia, 1936-42, Metro-Goldwyn Mayer, 1942-45, Hall Wallis-Paramount, 1945-47, R.K.O., 1947, Eagle-Lion Studios, 1947-48, Edmond Angelo Prodns., 1953, Anthony Buckley Prodns., Australia, 1995. Poetry reader with Robert Pinsky's nat. program Lib. of Congress Bicentennial Project, 1999. Author: The Grieving Senses, 1971, Odyssey for Edmond, 1996, New Poems-Old Themes, 1997; contbr. poetry to anthology Poetry From the Art, 1999; actress films including An American Romance, Love Letters, The Searching Wind, Badman's Territory, Sorry, Wrong Number, Lost Honeymoon, Breakdown, Don't Call Me Girlie, Celluloid Heroes, 1994-95; appearances TV program, film, and tape maker Australia, Time Life Assocs., 1977. Vice pres. Tchr. Rememberance Day Found., 1952—; internat. chmn. Apple of Gold Edn. awards, 1953—. Recipient meritorious svc. citation Govs. of Great Britain, U.S., New Zealand, Australia, 1939-46, Star Pattern award Inst. Profl. Direction, 1951, Cert. of Appreciation award Literacy is Reading Program, 1997, Edward Dean Mus., 1996. Mem. AAUW, Nat. Mus. Women in Arts, San Gorgonio Poets Soc., San Gorgonio Artists Soc., Zeta Phi Eta (v.p. nat. coun. 1970-73).

RICHARDS, ANN WILLIS, former governor; b. Lakeview, Tex., Sept. 1, 1933; d. Cecil and Ona Willis; children: Cecile, Daniel, Clark, Ellen. BA, Baylor U., 1954; postgrad., U. Tex., 1954-55. Cert. tchr. Tex. Tchr. Austin Ind. Sch. Dist., Tex.; mgr. Sarah Weddington Campaign, Austin, Tex., 1972, adminstrv. asst., 1973-74; county commr. Travis County, Austin, 1976-82; treas. State of Tex., Austin, 1983-91, gov., 1991-95; sr. advisor Verner, Liipfert, Bernhard, McPherson & Hand, Austin, 1995—; with Pub. Strategies Inc., Austin, 2001—. Chair Dem. Nat. Conv. 1992; Austin Transp. Study, Tex., 1977-82, Capital Indsl. Devel. Corp., Austin, Tex., 1980-81, Spl. Commn. Delivery Human Services in Tex., 1979-81; Dem. com. Southern Governor's Assn. Travis County Dem. com. Author (with Peter Knobler): Straight From the Heart, 1989. Com. mem. strategic planning Dem. Nat. Com., 1983; keynote speaker Dem. Nat. Conv., 1988. Named Woman of Yr. Tex. Women's Polit. Caucus, 1981, 83. Mem. Nat. Govs. Assn. Democrat. Office: Public Strategies Inc 98 San Jacinto Ste 900 Austin TX 78701

RICHARDS, BERNARD, investment company executive; b. N.Y.C., July 12, 1927; s. Charles and Sadie (Rubin) R.; m. Arlene Kaye, Dec. 23, 1948; children: Carol Leslie, Patricia Ellen, Lori Gale. BBA, Baruch Coll., 1949. CPA, N.Y. Acct. Eisner & Lubin, N.Y.C., 1949-53, S.D. Leidesdorf, N.Y.C.,

1953-56; from contr. to treas. to v.p. fin. to pres. Slattery Group Inc., N.Y.C., 1956-87; pres. Slattery Investors Corp., N.Y.C., 1988—; chmn. bd. dirs. Slattery Assocs., Inc., N.Y.C., 1968-87. Trustee Temple Sinai, Roslyn, N.Y., 1987-89; bd. dirs. Variety Boys Club, Queens, N.Y., 1972-96; bd. dirs. N.Y.C. Indsl. Devel. Bd., 1973-76; bd. dirs. Baruch Coll. Fund, N.Y.C., 1975—, pres., 1996-98. Recipient Heavy Constrn. award United Jewish Appeal, 1980, Pres.'s medal Baruch Coll., 1989; named Oustanding Alumnus of Yr. Baruch Coll., 1979, Man of Yr. United Jewish Appeal, 1980, March of Dimes, 1983, Man of Yr. Baruch Coll. Fund, 1972; Wood fellow Baruch Coll., 1979. Mem. AICPA, N.Y. State Soc. CPAs, Moles, Beavers (bd. dirs. 1982-96), Shelter Rock Tennis Club. Republican. Jewish. Avocations: tennis, travel, bicycling, swimming, hiking. Home: 18 Applegreen Dr Old Westbury NY 11568-1203 Office: Slattery Investors Corp 1 Hollow Ln Ste 311 New Hyde Park NY 11042-1215

RICHARDS, BRAD, professional hockey player; b. Murray Harbour, Prince Edward Island, May 2, 1980; Player Rimouski Oceanic (QMJHL), 1998—2000, Tampa Bay Lightning, 2000—. Player Team Can., World Championships, 2001; mem. Team Can., World Cup of Hockey, 2004. Named to, NHL All-Rookie Team, 2000; recipient Conn Smythe Trophy, 2004, Lady Byng Trophy, 2004. Achievements include member of Stanley Cup Champion Tampa Bay Lightning, 2004; mem. World Cup Champion Team Can., 2004. Office: c/o Tampa Bay Lightning 401 Channelside Dr Tampa FL 33602*

RICHARDS, CAROL ANN RUBRIGHT, editor, columnist; b. Buffalo, Sept. 24, 1944; d. Jesse Bailey and Emma Amanda (Fisher) Rubright; m. Clay F. Richards, Aug. 12, 1967; children: Elizabeth Amanda, Rebecca Diana. BA, Syracuse U., 1966. Reporter Rochester (N.Y.) Times-Union, 1966; legis. corr. Gannett News Svc., Albany, N.Y., 1967-73, White House corr. Washington, 1974-76, regional/nat. editor, 1979-84; founding editor USA Today, Arlington, Va., 1982, mem. editl. bd., 1985-87; dep. editor editl. page Newsday, Melville, N.Y., 1987—. Pres. Washington Press Club, 1981-82. Mem.: Women's Press Club N.Y. (named to Hall of Honor 2003), Nat. Press Club. Home: 352 Scudder Ave Northport NY 11768-3021 Office: Newsday 235 Pinelawn Rd Melville NY 11747-4250 Office Phone: 631-843-2912.

RICHARDS, CRAIG M. wholesale distribution executive; b. 1950; BA, Brigham Young Univ., 1975. Audit staff Arthur Andersen & Co., 1975-77; dir. fin. reporting Marriott Corp., 1978-86; dir. fin. analysis, v.p. project finance Bear Stearns, N.Y., 1986-92; CEO Baker & Taylor, 1992—2001.

RICHARDS, DAVID ALAN, lawyer; b. Dayton, Ohio, Sept. 21, 1945; s. Charles Vernon and Betty Ann (Macher) R.; m. Marianne Catherine Del Monaco, June 26, 1971; children: Christopher, Courtney. BA summa cum laude, Yale U., 1967, JD, 1972; MA, Cambridge (Eng.) U., 1969. Bar: N.Y. 1973. Assoc. Paul, Weiss, Rifkind, Wharton & Garrison, N.Y.C., 1972-77, Coudert Bros., N.Y.C., 1977-80, ptnr., 1981-82; ptnr., head real estate group Sidley & Austin, N.Y.C., 1983-2000; ptnr. McCarter & English, N.Y.C., 2001—, mng. ptnr. N.Y. office, 2002—. Gov. Anglo-Am. Real Property Inst. U.S./U.K., 1983-88, chair, 1993; mem. Chgo. Title N.Y. Realty Adv. Bd., 1992—. Co-editor: Kipling and His First Publisher, 2001; co-author: The Commercial Office Lease Handbook, 2003; contbr. articles to profl. jours. Trustee Scarsdale Pub. Libr., 1984-89, pres., 1988-89; co-chair N.Y. Lawyers for Clinton/Gore, 1996. Fellow Am. Bar Found.; mem. ABA (real property, probate and trust sect., coun. 1982-88, chair 1991-92), Am. Coll. Real Estate Lawyers (gov. 1987-93), Assn. of Bar of City of N.Y. (real property com. 1978-80, 84-87), Kipling Soc. (N.Am. rep.), Assn. Fellows of Morgan Libr., Shenorock Shore Club (Rye, N.Y.), The Grolier Club (N.Y.C., coun. 2003—), Yale Club (N.Y.C.), Yale Libr. Assoc. (trustee 2003—). Democrat. Home: 18 Forest Ln Scarsdale NY 10583-6464 Office: McCarter & English 245 Park Ave Fl 27 New York NY 10167 Office Phone: 212-609-6817. E-mail: darichards21@aol.com., drichards@mccarter.com.

RICHARDS, DAVID GLEYRE, German language educator; b. July 27, 1935; s. Oliver L. and Lilian Marie (Powell) R.; m. Annegret Horn, Sept. 3, 1959 (div. 1992); 1 child, Stephanie Suzanne; m. Friederike Hensler, Oct. 11, 1997. BA, U. Utah, 1960, MA, 1961; PhD, U. Calif., Berkeley, 1968. Asst. prof. German SUNY, Buffalo, 1968-74, assoc. prof., 1974-84, prof., 1984-99, prof. emeritus, 1999—. Author: Georg Buchners Woyzeck, 1975, George Buchner and the Birth of the Modern Drama, 1976, The Hero's Quest for the Self: An Archetypal Approach to Hesse's Demian and other Novels, 1987; editor: (with H. Schulte) Crisis and Culture in Post-Enlightenment Germany: Essays in Honor of Peter Heller, 1993, Exploring the Divided Self: Hermann Hesse's Steppenwolf and its Critics, 1996, Georg Buchner's Woyzeck: A History of Its Criticism, 2001. SUNY grantee, 1973; NEH grantee, 1977-78, Fulbright Commn. grantee, 1980. Rsch. Found. of SUNY fellow, 1982. Democrat. Avocation: photography. E-mail: dgrich@nc.rr.com.

RICHARDS, DENISE, actress; b. Downers Grove, Ill., Feb. 17, 1971; m. Charlie Sheen; 1 child. Former model. Actor: (films) Loaded Weapon 1, 1993, Nowhere, 1997, Starship Troopers, 1997, Wild Things, 1998, Lookin' Italian, 1998, Drop Dead Gorgeous, 1999, The World is Not Enough, 1999, Tail Lights Fade Away, 1999, Valentine, 2001, Good Advice, 2001, Empire, 2002, Undercover Brother, 2002, The Third Wheel, 2002, You Stupid Man, 2002, Love Actually, 2003, Scary Movie 3, 2003; (TV films) 919 5th Avenue, 1995, In the Blink of an Eye, 1996, Pier 66, 1996, (guest appearances): (TV series) Spin City, Melrose Place. Office: 722 Elvira Ave #A Redondo Beach CA 90277

RICHARDS, DUSTY, writer; b. Chgo., Nov. 11, 1937; s. John C. and Jeave Richards; m. Patricia A. Richards, June 5, 1961; children: Anna Barnes, Rhonda Albright. BS in agrl., Ariz. State U., 1960. Tchr., Ark., 1960—61, 1962—63; mgr. Tyson Food, Springsdale, Ark., 1963—94; T.V. anchor Agrl. Direct, Fayettville, Ark., 1987—94; auctioneer, 1960—; rodeo announcer, 1963—; writer, 1980—. Dir. bd. Ozark Elec. Corp., Fayettville, Ark., 1983—. Author: Two Trails to Rosa, 1984, Marshal Lockhart and The Tomboy, 1984, Bountyman and Doe, 1985, The Lawless Land, 2000, Servant of the Law, 2000, Rancher's Law, 2001, The Natural, 2002 (Fiction Book of Yr., Okla. Writer's, 2003), The Abilene Trail, 2003, Dances Wild, 2004, Waltzing with Tumbleweed, 2004. Committeman Rodeo of Ozark, Springdale, Ark., 1976—; bd. dirs. Western Writers of Am., 1990—93. Sgt. USAAF, 1960—68. Named to Ark. Writers Hall of Fall, 2004. Mem.: Ozark Writers League (bd. mem., past pres.). Avocation: trout fishing. Home: PO Box 6460 Springdale AR 72766 Office Phone: 479-751-7246.

RICHARDS, EARL FREDERICK, electrical engineer, educator; b. Detroit, Mar. 11, 1923; s. Earl Frederick Richards and Esther Branning; m. Marjorie Phyllis Holt, Jan. 12, 1946; 2 children. BSEE, Wayne State U., 1951; MSEE, Mo. Sch. of Mines and Metallurgy, Rolla, 1961; PhD, U. Mo., 1971. Registered engr., Mo., Mich. Elec. engr. Electronic Control Corp., Detroit, 1951—52, Pa. Salt Mfg. Co., Wyandotte, Mich., 1952—53; chief elec. engr. Revere Copper and Brass, Detroit, 1954—58; prof. elec. engring. U. Mo.-Rolla, 1958—92, prof. emeritus, 1992—. Cons. in field. Author: (book) Handbook of Small Electric Motors, 2000; contbr. articles to profl. jours. and publs. With Office of strategic Svcs. U.S. Army, 1942—46. Named to Hall of Fame, Sml. Motors Mfrs. Assn., 1995. Mem.: Eta Kappa nu, Sigma Xi. Avocation: antiques, woodworking, reading. Office Phone: 573-341-4516.

RICHARDS, FEMI SOYINKA, lawyer; b. Pontiac, Mich., Aug. 29, 1971; s. Josephus and Laura Richards; m. Nettie Mahone, Mar. 23, 2002. Master of Pub. Policy, Harvard U., Cambridge, MA, 1997—99; JD, U. of Conn. Sch. of Law, Hartford, CT, 1994—97; BA, U. of Mass. - Amherst, Amherst, MA, 1989—94. Connecticut Bar: Conn. 1997, District of Columbia Bar: DC 2002. Assoc. Holland & Knight, LLP, Washington, 2001—; sr. policy analyst Ct. Services and Offender Supervision Agy. for the DC, Washington, 1999—2001. Contbr. journal . Multiculturalism and the Democratic State: Three Frameworks for Social Equity. Public Integrity. Spring 2000. Volume 2. Number 2, journal . Sports and the Socialization of Women. Five College Journal of Law and Society. Spring 1993. Volume 1. Number 2. Recipient Outstanding Performance Award, Ct. Services and Offender Supervision Agy., 2000, Manuel C. Carballo Meml. Prize, John F. Kennedy Sch. of Govt., Harvard U., 1999, Cali Excellence for the Future Award, U. of Conn. Sch. of Law, 1997, Round Robin Moot Ct. Competition Best Brief, Nova Southeastern U. Sch. of Law, 1997, Best Oral Adv., Alva P. Loiselle Moot Ct. Competition, U. of Conn. Sch. of Law, 1995, Academic Achievement Award, U. of Mass., Black Student Union, 1993. Mem.: Acad. of Polit. Sci. (assoc.), ASPA (assoc.), Conn. Bar Assn. (assoc.), DC Bar Assn. (assoc.), ABA (assoc.), Harvard Club of Wash., DC (assoc.). D-Liberal. Avocations: basketball, travel. Home: 98 East Wayne Avenue Silver Spring MD 20901 Office: Holland & Knight LLP 2099 Pennsylvania Avenue NW Washington DC 20006 Personal E-mail: frichards_mpp99@post.harvard.edu. E-mail: fsrichar@hklaw.com.

RICHARDS, FREDERIC MIDDLEBROOK, biochemist, educator; b. N.Y.C., Aug. 19, 1925; s. George and Marianna Richards; m. Heidi Clarke, 1948 (div. 1955); children: Sarah, Ruth Gray; m. Sarah Wheatland, 1959; 1 child, George Huntington. BS, MIT, 1948; PhD, Harvard U., 1952; DSc (hon.), U. New Haven, 1982. Rsch. fellow in phys. chemistry Harvard Med. Sch., Cambridge, Mass., 1952-53; NRC postdoctoral fellow Carlsberg Lab., Denmark, 1954; NSF fellow Cambridge U., Eng., 1955; asst. prof. biochemistry Yale U., New Haven, Conn., 1955-59, assoc. prof., 1959-62, prof., 1963-89, Henry Ford II prof. molecular biophysics, 1967-89, Sterling prof. molecular biophysics, 1989-91, Sterling prof. emeritus, 1991—, chmn. dept. molecular biology and biophysics, 1963-67, chmn. dept. molecular biophysics and biochemistry, 1969-73. Dir. Jane Coffin Childs Meml. Fund Med. Rsch., 1976-91, bd. dirs., 1997—; mem. Nat. Adv. Rsch. & Resources Coun., 1983-87; mem. corp. Woods Hole Oceanographic Inst., 1977-83, 84-90; mem. bd. advisors Whitney Marine Lab., 1979-84, Purdue U. Magnetic Resonance Lab., 1980-84, Biology divsn. Argonne Nat. Lab., 1982-84, Brookhaven Nat. Lab., Nat. Synchrotron Light Source; mem. sci. adv. bd. structural biology Howard Hughes Med. Inst., 1988-89, adv. bd., 1989-92; mem. sci. adv. bd. Donaghue Found. Med. Rsch., 1991-92, external adv. bd. U. Ill. Beckman Inst., 1994-99. Mem. editorial bd. Jour. Biol. Chemistry, 1963-69, 82-84, Jour. Molecular Biology, 1973-75, Advances in Protein Chemistry, 1963—; contbr. articles on protein and enzyme chemistry. Sgt. U.S. Army, 1944-46. Recipient Pfizer-Paul Lewis award in enzyme chemistry, 1965, Kai Linderstrom-Lang prize in protein chemistry, 1978, Sci. medal State of Conn., 1995; Guggenheim fellow, 1967-68. Fellow AAAS, Am. Acad. Arts and Scis. (mem. coun. 1998—); mem. NAS, Am. Philos. Soc., Am. Soc. Biochemistry and Molecular Biology (Merck award 1988), Protein Soc. (Stein and Moore award 1988), Internat. Union Pure and Applied Biophysics (mem. coun. 1975-81), Am. Soc. Biol. Chemists (pres. 1979-80), Biophys. Soc. (pres. 1972-73), Am. Chem. Soc., Am. Crystallographic Assn., Conn. Acad. Sci. and Engring. Avocations: sailing, hiking trail maintenance. Home: 69 Andrews Rd Guilford CT 06437-3715 Office: Yale U Dept Molecular Biophysics PO Box 208114 New Haven CT 06520-8114

RICHARDS, FREDERICK FRANCIS, JR., manufacturing executive, consultant; b. Payette, Idaho, Jan. 28, 1936; s. Frederick Francis and Dorothy Lucille (Taylor) R.; m. DeAnne Aden, Aug. 10, 1958; children: Frederick Francis III, Craig, Jeffrey. BS in Indsl. Engring., So. Meth. U., 1959; MBA, Harvard U., 1961. Indsl. engr. Collins Radio Inc., 1955-59; rsch. asst. Harvard U., 1961-62; fin. analyst H.F. Linder & William T. Golden, N.Y.C., 1962-65; pres., CEO Adrich Corp. and subs., Dallas, 1965—; exec. v.p. FSE Corp., Plano, Tex., 1990—91; pres. Resource Locators Inc., Dallas, 1992—95. Exec. v.p. FSE Corp., Plano, Tex., 1991-92; v.p. and prin. Capital Alliance Corp., Dallas, 1985-91; v.p. GTex., Inc., Dallas, 1986-87; pres. Work Lite Dist., Dallas, 1990-95, AR Assocs., internat. mgmt. cons., Dallas, 1972—2002; dir. Dallas Pub. Inc., 1982-84, Aden-Richards Inc., 1979—. Author papers in field; bus. columnist. Mem. ASTM, Am. Inst. Indsl. Engrs. (sr.), Assn. for Tech. Analysis, Airplane Owners and Pilots Assn., Am. Soc. Indsl. Security, Internat. Assn. Chiefs Police, Nat. Pilots Assn., Exptl. Aircraft Assn., Harvard Club (N.Y.C.), The Tech. Club of Dallas. Home and Office: 3 Cumberland Pl Richardson TX 75080-4926 E-mail: ffr@adrich.com.

RICHARDS, GALE LEE, communications educator; b. Long Run, W.Va., July 31, 1918; s. Robert Amaziah and Edna Jane (Scott) R.; m. Barbara Lee Neely, Apr. 19, 1944; children: Robin Lee, Wendell Scott, Jeffrey Marshall. BA (Pixley scholar), U. Akron, O., 1940; MA (C.S. Knight Meml. scholar), U. Ia., 1942, PhD, 1950. Instr. speech U. Akron, 1941-42; asst. prof. speech Drake U., 1947-48; asst. prof. English U. Nev., 1948-52; asst. prof. speech U. Wash., 1952-58; assoc. prof. speech U. So. Calif., 1958-65; prof. communication Ariz. State U., Tempe, 1965—, chmn. dept. speech and theatre, 1965-73. Pub. relations cons. Red Feather campaign United Fund, Los Angeles, 1955-58; mgmt. and tng. cons. various profl. and comml. orgns., 1955— Cons. editor: Western Speech, 1957-61, 62-65, 69-72, Jour. of Communication, 1961-67; Contbr. articles profl. jours. Bd. dirs. Phoenix Little Theatre. Served to lt. USNR, 1942-45, PTO. Recipient Distinguished Alumni award Radio Sta. WSUI, 1942 Mem. We. States Communication Assn. (adminstrv. coun., legis. coun., chair commn. on Am. Parliamentary procedure, 1988, emeritus 1991), Internat. Communication Assn. (adminstrv. coun.), Am. Inst. Parliamentarians, Western States Communication Assn. (2d v.p. 1956, 71, pres. Execs. club 1975, Disting. Svc. award 1989), Ariz. Communication and Drama Assn. (pres. 1967, editor jour. 1984-87), Blue Key, Phi Kappa Phi, Delta Sigma Rho. Democrat. Presbyterian. Home: 614 E Bishop Dr Tempe AZ 85282-2325 E-mail: galeri@imap3.asu.edu.

RICHARDS, GEORGE ALVAREZ, psychiatrist, educator; b. La Paz, Bolivia, May 11, 1934; came to U.S., 1952; s. John Joseph and Matilde (Alvarez) R.; m. LaClaire Lissetta Jones, July 26, 1958; children: Leslie Rosario Richards-Yellen, Lia Mercedes Richards Palmiter. BA, Hastings Coll., 1957; MD, U. Autonoma Guadalajara, Jalisco, Mex., 1970. Lic. physician, S.D. Lang. asst. Hastings (Nebr.) Coll., 1953-57; nursing asst. Hastings State Hosp., 1952-57; tchr. lang. and sci. Knoxville (Iowa) Pub. Sch., 1960-65; rotating intern Regina (Sask., Can.) Gen. Hosp., 1970-71; gen. med. officer Dept. Vets. Affairs, Knoxville, 1974; resident psychiatrist Mental Health Inst., Cherokee, Iowa, 1974-77; acting chief, adminstrv. chief, staff psychiatrist Royal C. Johnson Vets. Meml. Hosp., Sioux Falls, S.D., 1977—; asst. prof. psychiatry U. S.D. Sch. Medicine, Sioux Falls, 1977—. Mem. planning and health coms. Multi-Cultural Ctr., Sioux Falls, 1996—; mem. NAACP, Sioux Falls, 1980—. Recipient Exemplary Psychiatrist award Nat. Alliance for Mentally Ill, 1996—. Fellow Interam. Coll. Physicians and Surgeons; mem. AMA (Hispanic Physicians), Am. Psychiat. Assn. (Nancy C. A. Roeske, MD, Cert. of Excellence 1998), S.D. State Med. Assn., S.D. Psychiat. Assn., 7th Dist. Med. Assn. Avocations: languages, mentoring, music, reading, jogging. Office: Royal C Johnson Vets Meml Hosp 2501 W 22d St Sioux Falls SD 57117

RICHARDS, GERALD THOMAS, lawyer, consultant, educator, writer; b. Monrovia, Calif., Mar. 17, 1933; s. Louis Jacquelyn Richards and Inez Vivian (Richardson) Hall; children: Patricia M. Richards Grauf, Laura J., Dag Hammarskjold; m. Mary Lou Richards, Dec. 27, 1986. BS magna cum laude, Lafayette Coll., 1957; MS, Purdue U., 1963; JD, Golden Gate U., 1976. Bar: Calif. 1976, U.S. Dist. Ct. (no. dist.) Calif. 1977, U.S. Patent Office 1981, U.S. Ct. Appeals (9th cir.) 1984, U.S. Supreme Ct. 1984. From computational physicist to asst. lab. counsel Lawrence Livermore Nat. Lab., Calif., 1967—84, asst. lab. counsel, 1984—93; sole practice Livermore, Calif., 1976-78, Oceanside, Calif., 1994-97; emeritus atty. pro bono participant Calif. State Bar, 1998—; staff atty. Contra Costa Sr. Legal Svcs., Concord, 1998—. Constrn. law instr. Contrs. State License Schs., Van Nuys, Calif., 1998; mem. exec. com., policy advisor Fed. Lab. Consortium for Tech. Transfer, 1980-88; panelist, del. White House Conf. on Productivity, Washington, 1983; del. Nat. Conf. on Tech. and Aging, Wingspread, Wis., 1981. Author: (novel) Jimmy, 2003. Commr. Housing Authority, City of Livermore, 1977, vice chair, 1978, chair, 1979; mem. Bd of Adminstrn. Appeals, City of Antioch, Calif., 2003-; pres. Housing Choices, Inc., Livermore, 1980-84; bd. dirs. Valley Vol. Ctr., Pleasanton, Calif., 1983, pres., 1984-86; mem. staff Calif. Boys' State Am. Legion, 1996—. Served to maj. U.S. Army, 1959-67. Recipient Engring. award GE, 1956. Mem. ABA, Calif. State Bar (conv. alt. del. 1990-92, del. 2000, mem. com. on sr. lawyers 2002—), Alameda County Bar Assn., Contra Costa County Bar Assn., Ea. Alameda County Bar Assn. (sec. 1978, bd. dirs. 1991-92, chair lawyers referral com. 1992-93), Santa Barbara County Bar Assn., San Diego County Bar Assn., Bar Assn. No. San Diego County, San Francisco Bar Assn., Phi Beta Kappa, Tau Beta Pi, Sigma Pi Sigma. Home: 3400 Richmond Pkwy Apt 1007 Richmond CA 94806-5215 E-mail: hesiod@calbears.com.

RICHARDS, HERBERT EAST, minister emeritus, commentator; b. Hazleton, Pa. s. Herbert E. and Mabel Richards; m. Lois Marcey, Jan. 1, 1942; children: Herbert Charles, Marcey Lynn, Robyn Lois, Fredrick East, Mark Allen. AB, Dickinson Coll., 1941; BD, Drew U., 1944; MA, Columbia, 1944; DD, Coll. of Idaho, 1953; postgrad., Union Theol. Sem., 1941-48, Bucknell U., 1943-44. Accredited news reporter Nat. Assn. Broadcasters. Ordained to ministry Methodist Ch., 1944; pastor in Boiling Springs, Pa., 1937-40, West Chester, Pa., 1940-41, Basking Ridge, N.J., 1941-47; mem. faculty Drew U. and Theol. Sem., 1944-51, assoc. prof. homiletics and Christian criticism, chmn. dept., asst. dean, 1947-51; spl. lectr. religion Howard U., 1947; minister 1st Meth. Cathedral, Boise, Idaho, 1951-69, 1st United Meth. Ch., Eugene, Oreg., 1969-78, Tabor Heights United Meth. Ch., Portland, Oreg., 1978-86, minister emeritus, 1986—. Weekly radio broadcaster Sta. KBOI, Sta. KIDO, 1941—; weekly TV broadcaster CBS, 1945—, ABC, 1969—, NBC, 1973; pres. Inspiration, Inc., TV Found., 1965—, TV Ecology, 1973; producer Life TV series ABC, 1974-85, PBS TV, 1968-85, also BBC, Eng., Suise Romande, Geneva; chmn. Idaho bd. ministerial tng. Meth. Conf., 1954-60, TV, Radio and Film Commn., 1954-62, Oreg. Coun. Public Broadcasting, 1973; del. Idaho Conf. Meth. Gen. Conf., 1956, Jurisdictional Conf., 1956, World Meth. Coun., 1957, 81, World Meth. Conf., 1981, mem. Gen. Conf., 1956-60, Jurisdictional Conf., 1956, 60; meml. chaplain Idaho Supreme Ct., 1960; chaplain Idaho Senate, 1960-68; mem. Task Force on TV and Ch., 1983 Author: In Time of Need, 1986, Faith and the Pursuit of Healing, 1996; contbr. articles to religious publs.; composer: oratorios Prophet Unwilling, 1966, Meet Martin Luther, 1968, Dear Jesus Boy, 1973. Mem. Commn. on Centennial Celebration for Idaho, 1962-63; committeeman Boy Scouts Am.; bd. dirs. Eugene chpt. ARC, 1954-73; trustee Willamette U., Cascade Manor Homes; adv. bd. Medic-Alert Found. Recipient Alumni citation in religious edn. Dickinson Coll., 1948, Golden Plate award Am. Acad. Achievement, 1965, Jason Lee Mass Media TV award, 1983, Disting. Citizen award Idaho Statesman Newspaper, 1964, Disting. Alumnus award Drew U., 1965, disting. Eagle award Boy Scouts Am.; named Clergyman of Yr., Religious Heritage Am., 1964. Mem. AAUP, CAP (chaplain Idaho wing, lt. col.), Am. Acad. Achievement (bd. govs. 1967—), Am. Found. Religion and Psychiatry (charter gov.), Idaho Found. Medicine and Biology (charter), Greater Boise Ministerial Assn. (pres.), Eugene Ministerial Assn. (pres. 1978), Masons (33 degree, editor Pike's Peak Albert That Is), Shriners, Elks, Rotary (editor Key and Cog, pres. dist. 510 Pioneer Club), Kappa Sigma (Grand Master of Beta Pi). Home: 10172 SE 99th Dr Portland OR 97266-7227 *When a person presses his face against the window pane of life, he becomes as a child waiting for his father's return; simple, trusting and infinitely wiser. In our present time of growth/conflict, such a face-pressing is essential to get us safely from where we are to where we ought to be.*

RICHARDS, JAY CLAUDE, commercial photographer, news service executive, historian; b. Glen Ridge, N.J., Apr. 6, 1954; s. Jacob Tilghman and Joan Louise (Walsh) Richards. Student, Tenn. Wesleyan Coll., Athens, 1972-73. Various positions armed security work, 1973-75; reporter, photographer Press Publs.: The News, Belvidere, N.J., 1977-98; pres. J.C. Richards Assocs., Harmony Twp., N.J., 1980—; owner Poor Richards' Brit. Gun Shop, Harmony Twp., 1976—; freelance ct. reporter The Morning Call, Allentown, Pa., 1986—; reporter The Knowlton News, 1998—2002, NorthWarren News, 2002—04. Photography judge Warren County 4-H, Belvidere, 1990—; press officer Warren County Office Emergency Mgmt, Belvidere, 1989—98; news corresp WRNJ-News, 1991—, NJN Pubs, The News, 2001—02. Author: Penn, Patriots and the Pequest: The History of Pre-Victorian Belvidere, 1716-1845, 1995, Flames Along the Delaware, 1996 (NJ Frontier Guard's Book Award, 1997), Bugles, Battles and Belvidere: Warren County, N.J. in the Civil War, 1997, Officers and Men of Warren County, N.J. Civil War, 1998, More Bugles, Battles and Belvidere: Warren County, N.J. in the Civil War Letters to Home, 1999, Following the Hand of Franklin: Warren County, N.J. and the Search for the North Pole, 2000, Warren, Warriors & The World: Warren County, New Jersey In the Plains Indians Wars & The Spanish-American War 1865-1902, 2002, 1903 Flood Centennial Souvenier Book, 2003; contbr. art work Hackettstown, NJ "Billy Yank" Civil War Monument, 2001. Mem Hazardous Materials Adv Coun, Warren County, NJ, 1989—98, Joint Emergency Mgmt Coun, Belvidere/White Township, NJ, 1989—98, Warren County Arts Adv Coun, Warren County War Mem Comt, 1997—98; trustee Warren County War Mem Corp, 1999—; consult Harmony NJ Hist Preservation Comn, 2000—; mem Warren County Purple Heart Monument Construction Comt, 2000; mem. Statue of Liberty - Ellis Island Found.; participant foriegn policy leadership George Washington Univ., 1999, 2003; Civil War monument project Hackettstown, NJ, 2001; mem. Glamour Photographers Internat., 2003—04. Named Hon Mem, Boy Scout Troop 141, Belvidere, 1993; recipient Outstanding Community Serv Award, Am Legion Post 131, 1994. Mem.: Nat Indian War Asn, Oxford NJ Hist Soc, US Naval Inst, Sr Army Res Comdrs Asn, Res Officers Asn US, Soc Profl Journalists, Nat Press Photographers Asn, NRA, Forks of the Del. Hist. Arms Soc., Frederick A. Cook Soc., Sigma Delta Chi. Episcopalian. Avocations: collecting Richards of Sheffield pocket knives and tools, gourmet cooking, gardening, herbal medicine, restoring WWI Austro-Hungarian canteens and harnesses. Home and Office: 3110 Belvidere Rd Phillipsburg NJ 08865-9515 E-mail: jayrichards@enter.net.

RICHARDS, JERRY LEE, academic administrator, religious educator; b. Lawrenceville, Ill., Nov. 4, 1939; s. Russell O. and Elvessa A. (Goodman) R.; m. Lee Ann, Apr. 25, 1986; children: Mark, Renee, Teresa, Angela. BA, Lycoming Coll., 1965; BD, Evang. Congregational Sch. Theology, 1967; MDiv, Garrett Theol. Sem., 1968; D in Ministry, St. Paul Sch. Theology, 1975. Ordained to ministry Meth. Ch., 1968. Pastor chs., Pa., 1960-65, 1965-70; mem. faculty Iowa Wesleyan U., Mt Pleasant, 1970-85, prof. religion, dir. responsible social involvement Mt. Pleasant, 1975-85, v.p. for acad. affairs, 1975-82, pres., 1982-85; dir. gift planning U. Wis., Eau Claire, 1985—. Pres. Mental Health Inst. Aux., Mt. Pleasant, 1976. Mem. Phi Alpha Theta Office: U Wis Office of Devel 215 Schofield Hall Eau Claire WI 54702-4004

RICHARDS, JODY, state legislator, journalism educator, small business owner; b. Columbia, Ky., Feb. 20, 1939; m. Neva Richards; 1 child, Roger. BA in English, Ky. Wesleyan Coll., Owensboro; MA in Journalism, U. Mo., 1962. Mem. faculty in journalism Western Ky. U., from 1962; owner Superior Books, Bowling Green, Ky.; mem. Ky. Ho. of Reps., 1976—, speaker, 1995—; vice chair So. Legislative Conf., 1998—. Mem. adv. bd. dirs. Republic Savs. Bank. Pres. bd. dirs. So. Ky. Fair; bd. dirs. Bowling Green Girls Club, United Way, Warren County (Ky.) Drug Abuse Task Force. Recipient Disting. Svc. award Nat. Art Edn. Assn., 1992. Mem. Bowling Green C. of C., Bowling Green Noon Rotary Club. Office: Ky Ho of Reps State Capitol Rm 309 Frankfort KY 40601

RICHARDS, JOHN DALE, social worker, educator, counselor; s. Guy Edward and Margaret Jane (Gray) Richards; m. Susan McCallister, June 23, 1990. PhD, Ohio U., 1996—2000. Lic. profl. counselor W.Va. Bd. Examiners Counseling, 2003. Family and marriage counselor Family Svc. Kanawha Valley, Charleston, W.Va., 1988—93; assoc. prof., chair W.Va. State Coll., Institute, 1993—. Cons. in field, Charleston, W.Va., 1998—; cons. Gov.'s Cabinet on Families and Children, Charleston, 1995, Human Resource Mgmt. Co., Charleston, 1995. Editor: (textbook) Origins: Texts for Inquiry; author: (book) Coping with Grief, 1995; co-author: The Family Education Experience, 1995; author: (poetry book) Uncreated Light, 1995. Pres. bd. dirs. Dreikurs Family Edn. Ctr., Charleston, 1995; mem. adv. bd. Glenwood Family Resource Ctr., Charleston, 1995; treas. Assn. Study Esotericism, East Lansing, Mich., 2002—03. Recipient Dr. W.E.B. Dubois award, Alpha Kappa Delta, 1995; grantee Fulbright-Hays Rsch. Grant, U.S. Dept. Edn., 2002. Mem.: W.Va. Sociol. Assn. (v.p. 1995—96), W.Va. Soc. Adlerian Psychology (pres. 1995—96, Dr. Manford A. Sonstegard award 1995), Am. Sociol. Assn., Masons, Grand Lodge W.Va. A.F. & A.M. (corr.; grand chaplain 1998—99).

Democrat. Avocations: writing music, poetry, collecting rocks, woodworking, archaeology. Home: 1211 Strawberry Rd Saint Albans WV 25177 Office: West Virginia State College 312 Hill Hall Institute WV 25112 Personal E-mail: jrichards@citynet.net

RICHARDS, JOHN RAY, emergency physician, educator; BA, U. Calif., Berkeley, 1989; MD, U. Calif., Davis, 1993. Cert. Am. Bd. Emergency Medicine. Prof. U. Calif.-Davis Sch. Medicine, 1996—. Author: (book) Management of Office Emergencies, 1999; contbr. articles to profl. jours. Recipient Outstanding Rsch. award Am. Acad. Emergency Medicine; rsch. fellow Alpha Omega Alpha, 1991. Fellow Am. Acad. Emergency Medicine; mem. Soc. Acad. Emergency Medicine (Excellence in Emergency Medicine award 1993). Office: Emergency Medicine 2315 Stockton Blvd Sacramento CA 95817-2201 Fax: (916) 734-7950. E-mail: jrrichards@ucdavis.edu.

RICHARDS, JOHN THOMAS, JR., lawyer; b. Pitts., Aug. 11, 1930; s. John Thomas and Hannah B. (Williams) Richards; m. Rosemary Brennen, June 27, 1953; children: John Thomas III, Veronica A. Arnstein, Charles B., Lynn Ellen. BBA, Ohio State U., 1953; JD, Duquesne U., 1959. Bar: Pa. 1960, U.S. Dist. Ct. (we. dist.) Pa. 1960, U.S. Supreme Ct. 1965. Assoc. McMonigle-Vesely, Pitts., 1959—65; pvt. practice Pitts., 1965—68; ptnr. Richards & Kelly, Pitts., 1968—. Pres. Stone Lodge Inc., Pitts., 1982—97. 1st. lt. U.S. Army, 1953—55. Mem.: Allegheny County Bar Assn. (officer, real estate coun. 1980—), Wildwood County Club Pitts. (bd. dirs., sec., counsel 1971—80). Republican. Baptist. Home: 4193 Rothschild Ct Allison Park PA 15101-2868 Office: Richards & Kelly LLP 16020 Perry Hwy Warrendale PA 15086

RICHARDS, JOSEPH EDWARD, artist; b. Des Moines, Oct. 10, 1921; s. Earl L. and Ivanore M. (Shelledy) R.; m. Elizabeth Anne Morrow, Mar. 23, 1943. Student, Am. Acad. Art, Chgo., 1946-49, Pa. Acad. Fine Arts, 1950-52. Exhbns. include: Butler Inst. Am. Art, Youngstown, Ohio, 1976, 77, 78, 81, 2001, Tex. Fine Arts Assn./Laguna Gloria Art Mus., Austin, Tex., 1977, NAD, N.Y.C., 1978, Silvermine Guild Artists, New Canaan, Conn., 1978, 79, Pa. Acad. Fine Arts, Phila., 1978, 80, 94, Va. Mus., Richmond, 1979, O.K. Harris Gallery, N.Y.C., 1982, 89, 92, 94, 1998-2002, O.K. Harris West Gallery, Scottsdale, Ariz., 1981, 82, Robert Kidd Galleries, Birmingham, Mich. 1984, Soghor, Leonard & Assocs. Gallery, N.Y.C., 1985, O.K. Harris South, Miami, Fla., 1986, Butler Inst. Am. Art, Youngstown, 1987, Tortue Gallery, Santa Monica, Calif., 1988, Art Expo, Tokyo, 1990, Art Now Gallery, Gothenburg, Sweden, 1990, Louis Stern Gallery, Beverly Hills, Calif., 1991, Bobbitt Visual Arts Ctr., Albion (Mich.) Coll., 1991, Survey of Am. Realism, Seoul, Korea, 1996, OK Harris, N.Y.C., 1998; represented in pvt. and corp. collections in U.S., Can., Europe. Recipient Disting. Artists award Va. Mus. Fine Art, 1979. Fellow Pa. Acad. Fine Arts. Home: PO Box 374 Hillsdale NY 12529-0374

RICHARDS, KEITH, musician; b. Dartford, Kent, Eng., Dec. 18, 1943; s. Bert and Doris Richards; m. Anita Pallenberg; children: Marlon, Angela; m. Patti Hansen, Dec. 18, 1983; children: Theodora, Alexandra. Student, Sidcup Art Sch. Recording artist on label Mindless Records. Lead & rhythm guitarist, vocalist Rolling Stones, 1962—, films include Sympathy for the Devil, Gimme Shelter, 1970, Ladies and Gentlemen, the Rolling Stones, 1974, Let's Spend the Night Together, 1983, The Magic Years, Vol. 1, 1989, 25X5: The Continuing Adventures of the Rolling Stones, 1989, At the Max, 1991, Rolling Stones: Voodoo Lounge, 1994, The History of Rock 'N' Roll, Vol. 7, 1995, The Rolling Stones Rock 'N' Roll Circus, 1996, Can't You Hear the Wind Howl? The Life & Music of Robert Johnson, 1997, Rolling Stones: Bridges to Babylon Tour, 1997—98, Forty Licks Tour, 2002—03, film mus. dir. (with Chuck Berry, Eric Clapton and friends) Hail! Hail! Rock & Roll, 1987; composer (with Mick Jagger): numerous songs and ablums, 1964; including (albums) The Rolling Stones, Now!, 1964, Aftermath, 1966, Flowers, 1967, Beggars Banquet, 1968, Let It Bleed, 1969, Sticky Fingers, 1971, Hot Rocks, Exile on Main Street, 1972, Goat's Head Soup, 1973, It's Only Rock and Roll, 1974, Metamorphosis, 1975, Black and Blue, 1976, Some Girls, Emotional Rescue, 1980, Tattoo You, 1981, Still Life, 1982, Under Cover, 1983, Dirty Work, 1986, Steel Wheels, 1989, Flashpoint, 1991, Voodoo Lounge, 1994 (Grammy award Best Rock Album, 1994), Stripped, 1995, Bridges to Babylon, 1997, No Security, 1999, 40 Licks, 2002, songs Wild Horses, Angie, Start Me Up, Honky Tonk Woman, Jumpin' Jack Flash, (I Can't Get No) Satisfaction, Before They Make Me Run, Miss You, Happy, Shattered, Paint It Black, Waiting On a Friend, Ruby Tuesday, You Can't Always Get What You Want, Brown Sugar, Tumbling Dice, Faraway Eyes, Mixed Emotions, Rock and a Hard Place, Highwire, Love is Strong, Anybody Seen My Baby; prodr.: Wingless Angels, 1997, (soundtrack album) Hail! Hail! Rock 'N Roll, 1987; solo albums Talk Is Cheap, 1988, Keith Richards & The X-Pensive Winos Live At The Hollywood Palladium, Dec. 15, 1988, 1991, Main Offender, 1992. Named to Rock and Roll Hall of Fame, 1989; recipient Living Legend award Internat. Rock, Knight Comdr. of Brit. Empire, 2003. Address: care Raindrop Svcs 1776 Broadway New York NY 10019-2002

RICHARDS, LACLAIRE LISSETTA JONES (MRS. GEORGE A. RICHARDS), social worker; b. Pine Bluff, Ark. d. Artie William and Geraldine (Adams) Jones; m. George Alvarez Richards, July 26, 1958; children: Leslie Rosario, Lia Mercedes. BA, Nat. Coll. Christian Workers, 1953; MSW, U. Kans., 1956; postgrad, Columbia U., 1960. Diplomate Clin. Social Work, Am. Bd. of Examiners in Clin. Social Work, Nat. Assn. Social Workers; cert. gerontologist. Psychiat., supr., tchg., cmty. orgn., adminstrv., cons. Hastings Regional Ctr., Ingleside, Nebr., 1956-60; supr., cons., adminstrv. VA Hosp., Knoxville, Iowa, 1960-74; field instr. for grad. students U. Mo., 1969-74, 78-90, com. chmn., 1969-70; sr. social worker Mental Health Inst., Cherokee, Iowa, 1974-77; adj. asst. prof. dept. social behavior U. S.D., Cherokee, Iowa, 1974-77, instr. dept. psychiat., 1988-96, Augustina Coll., 1981-86; outpatient social worker VA Med. and Regional Office Ctr., Sioux Falls, S.D., 1978-96, med., surg. and intensive care social worker, 1992-96, 1990-92, sur. and intermediate care social worker, 1992-96, EEO counselor. EEO counselor. Mem. Knoxville Juvenile adv. com., 1963-65, 68-70, sec., 1965-66, chmn., 1966-68; sec. Urban Renewal Citizens' adv. com., Knoxville, 1966-68; mem. United Meth. Ch. task force Expt. Styles Ministry and Leadership, 1973-74, adult choir, ch. and society com.; counselor Knoxville Youth Line program; sec. exec. com. Vis. Nurse Assn., 1979-80; canvasser cmty. fund drs., Knoxville; active Cherokee Civil Rights Commn.; bd. dirs., pub. rels., devel. and program devel. cons. YWCA, 1983-85; bd. dirs. Family Svc. Agy., 1989-90, Food Svcs. Ctr., Inc., 1992-96; active SD Symphonic Choir, 1991—, Youth-At-Risk Task Force and Multicultural Ctr. Advocate; deaconess 1st Evang. Free Ch., 1999-2004. Named S.D. Social Worker of Yr., 1983. Mem. NAACP (chmn. edn. com. 1983-85), AAUW (sec. Hastings chpt. 1958-60), Nat. Assn. Social Workers (co-chmn. Nebr. chpt. profl. standards com. 1958-59), Acad. Cert. Social Workers, S.D. Assn. Social Workers (chmn. minority affairs com., v.p. S.E. region 1980, pres. 1980-82, exec. com. 1985-84, mem. social policy and action com.), Nebr. Assn. Social Workers (chmn. 1958-59), Seventh Dist. S.D. Med. Soc. Aux., Coalition on Aging., Nat. Assn. Social Workers (qualified clin. social worker 1991—), Methodist (Sunday Sch. tchr. adult divsn.; mem. commn. on edn.; mem. Core com. for adult edn.; mem. Adult Choir; mem. Social Concerns Work Area). Home: 1701 E Ponderosa Dr Sioux Falls SD 57103-5019

RICHARDS, LEONARD MARTIN, investment executive, consultant; b. Phila., June 4, 1935; s. Leonard Martin and Marion Clara (Lang) R.; m. Phyllis Janelle Mowrey, Aug. 26, 1961 (div. Aug. 1978); children: Lisa, David Reed. BS, Pa. State U., 1957; MBA, U. Pa., 1963; MTh, Universal Sem., 1996, ThD, 2000. Asst. to sr. ptnr. Van Cleef, Jordan & Wood, N.Y.C., 1963-68; v.p., portfolio mgr. Bernstein-Macaulay, Inc., N.Y.C., 1968-72; ptnr. G. H. Walker, Laird Co., N.Y.C., 1972-74; v.p., trust officer, mgr. instnl. funds group Republic Bank N.A., Dallas, 1974-77; v.p., sr. investment officer, mem. exec. com. Variable Annuity Life Ins. Co., Houston, 1977-88; v.p., sr. investment officer Am. Gen. Series Portfolio Co., 1985-88; pres. L.M. Richards & Co., Houston, 1982—, also bd. dirs.; mem. adv. bd. Trinity Life Ctr., Houston, 1996-2000. Pres., bd. dirs. Sand Dollar, Inc., Houston, 1985—96; trustee Post Oak Sch., Houston, 1997—99, Universal Sem., 1997—2000, pres., 2001—; mem., bd. dir. Capital Institutional Services, Dallas, 1991—99; bd. dirs. Houston Chorale, 1988—90; mng. dir. The Enhancement Inst., Houston, 2003—. Capt. U.S. Army, 1957—65. Mem. Assn. Investment Mgmt. and Rsch., Houston Soc. Fin. Analysts, Wharton Club (Houston), Houstonian Club. Republican. Avocations: skiing, travel, scuba. Home: 9023 Briar Forest Dr Houston TX 77024-7220 Office: LM Richards & Co 4600 Post Oak Place Dr Ste 301 Houston TX 77027-9727 Office Phone: 713-961-5243. E-mail: lrichards1@sbcglobal.net.

RICHARDS, LLOYD GEORGE, theatrical director, university administrator; b. Toronto, Ont., Can. came to U.S., 1923; s. Albert George and Rose Isabelle (Coote) R.; m. Barbara Davenport, Oct. 11, 1957; children: Scott, Thomas. Grad., Wayne U., 1944. Head actor tng. NYU Sch. Arts, N.Y.C., 1966-72; artistic dir. Nat. Playwrights Conf., Eugene O'Neill Meml. Theatre Ctr., Waterford, Conn., 1969—; prof. theatre and cinema Hunter Coll., N.Y.C., 1972-79; dean Yale U. Sch. Drama, New Haven, 1979-91; artistic dir Yale Repertory Theatre, New Haven, 1979-91. Prof. emeritus Sch. Drama, 1991—; artistic dir. Yale Repertory Theater, 1979-91; pres. Theater Devel. Fund; head actor tng. Sch. Arts NYU, 1966-72; lectr., cons. in field; bd. dirs. Theatre Comm. Group, U.S. Bicentennial World Theatre Festival; mem. various profl. adv. groups, task forces; mem. playwrights selection com. Rockefeller Found.; mem. new Am. plays program com. Ford Found.; mem. com. on profl. theater tng. Nat. Endowment Arts. Actor on radio, TV and theater, 1943—; including Broadway plays The Egghead, 1957, Freight, 1956; disc jockey, Detroit; dir. for: radio, TV, film and theater, including Broadway plays A Raisin in the Sun, 1958, The Long Dream, 1960, The Moon Besieged, 1962, I Had a Ball, 1964, The Yearling, 1966, Paul Robeson, 1977-78, Ma Rainey's Black Bottom, 1984, Fences, 1987 (Tony award 1987), Joe Turner's Come and Gone, 1986, The Piano Lesson, 1990, Two Trains Running, 1992, 7 Guitars, 1996; and TV prodns. include: segment of Roots: The Next Generation, 1979, Bill Moyers' Jour, 1979, Robeson, 1979, Hallmark Piano Lesson 95. Served with USAAF, 1943-44. Recipient Pioneer award Audience Devel. Co., 1986-87, Frederick Douglas award, 1986-87, Golden Plate award, 1987, Nat. Medal of Arts, 1993, Mr. Abbott award, 1996; Hoffman Eminent scholar Fla. State U., 1997. Mem. Soc. Stage Dirs. and Choreographers (pres.), Actors Equity Assn., AFTRA, Dirs. Guild Am. Office: 18 W 95th St New York NY 10025-6708

RICHARDS, MARTA ALISON, lawyer; b. Mar. 15, 1952; d. Howard Jay and Mary Dean (Nix) Richards; m. Richard Peter Massony, June 16, 1979 (div. Apr. 1988); 1 child, Richard Peter Massony Jr. Student, Vassar Coll., 1969-70; AB cum laude, Princeton U., 1973; JD, George Washington U., 1976. Bar: La. 1976, U.S. Dist. Ct. (ea. dist.) La. 1976, U.S. Ct. Appeals (5th cir.) 1981, U.S. Supreme Ct. 1988, U.S. Dist. Ct. (mid. dist.) La. 1991. Assoc. Phelps, Dunbar, Marks, Claverie & Sims, New Orleans, 1976-77; assoc. counsel Hibernia Nat. Bank, New Orleans, 1978; assoc. Singer, Hutner, Levine, Seeman & Stuart, New Orleans, 1978-80, Jones, Walker, Waechter, Poltevent, Carrere & Denegre, New Orleans, 1980-84; ptnr. Montgomery, Barnett, Brown, Read, Hammond & Mintz, 1984-86, Montgomery, Richards & Ballin, 1986-89, Gelpi, Sullivan, Carroll and Laborde, 1989; gen. counsel Maison Blanche Inc., Baton Rouge, 1990-92, La. State Bond Commn., 1992-97; pvt. practice, cons., 1998—. Lectr. paralegal inst. U. New Orleans, 1984-89, adj. prof., 1989; of counsel Sanford & Assocs. Law Firm, 2004—. Contbr. articles to legal jours. Treas. alumni coun. Princeton U., 1979 81. Mem. ABA, La. State Bar Assn., New Orleans Bar Assn., Baton Rouge Bar Assn., Nat. Assn. Bond Lawyers, Princeton Alumni Assn. New Orleans (pres. 1982-86), Princeton Alumni Assn. Baton Rouge (pres. 2002—). Episcopalian. Home: 4075 S Ramsey Dr Baton Rouge LA 70808-1653 Office: 5800 One Perkins Pl Ste 5F Baton Rouge LA 70808 Office Phone: 225-761-9600.

RICHARDS, MARTIN, theatrical producer; m. Mary Lea Johnson (dec.). Co-founder Prodr. Circle, 1976—. Prodr. plays including Chicago (11 Tony nominations Best Musical London and L.A.), The Norman Conquests (Outer Critics Circle award), On the Twentieth Century (5 Tony awards), Sweeney Todd (8 Tony awards including Best Musical), Crimes of the Heart (Pulitzer prize), Foxfire, La Cage aux Folles (6 Tony awards including Best Musical), Grand Hotel (5 Tony awards), The Will Rogers Follies (6 Tony awards including Best Musical), Sally Marr... and Her Escorts, Dylan (Obie award), March of the Falsettos (Outer Critics Circle award Best Musical), Mayor, The Best of Friends, 1971, The Life, films include The Boys From Brazil, 1978, The Shining, 1980, Fort Apache the Bronx, 1981, Chicago, 2002 (Best Picture Academy award, 2003). Trustee Trust for Cultural Resources of City of N.Y. Office: Prodrs Circle 200 W 57th St Ste 1403 New York NY 10019-3211

RICHARDS, MARTY GROVER, foundation administrator, director; b. Spartanburg, SC, July 14, 1962; s. Joseph Defoe and Anne Ellen (Chastain) R. BA, Wofford Coll., 1984; MA, Ohio State U., 1986. Chmn. dept. polit. sci. Spartanburg Meth. Coll., 1987-89; assoc. prof. U. S.C., Spartanburg, 1989-92; campaign mgr. Hartnett for U.S. Senate, Greenville, S.C., 1992-94; found. dir. Spartanburg Tech. Coll., 1994—. Pres.-elect Spartanburg Music Guild, 1997, pres., 1998; publicity chmn. A Dickens of a Christmas Festival, Spartanburg, 1997—2000, chmn., 2001—02, Bill Drake Christmas Music Festival, Spartanburg, 1996—, Spartanburg County Tennis Assn., Spartanburg, 1987—95; com. mem. Arts in Edn. Arts Partnership of Greater Spartanburg; mem. Mayor's Adv. Group, City of Spartanburg, 2001—; mem. bd. commrs. Spartanburg Meml. Auditorium, 2004—; bd. dirs. Spartanburg Little Theater, 1995—2002, pres., 1999—2001; bd. dirs. Arts Partnership Greater Spartanburg, 1998—2001, Mobile Meals of Spartanburg, 1986—94, Habitat for Humanity, 1988—92, Team Spartanburg, Spartanburg C. of C., 2000—, Ballet Spartanburg, 2001—02, Miss S.C. Found., 2004—, Mt. Moriah Found., 2001—, Spartanburg Events and Festivals, 2002—. Mem. S.C. Nat. Soc. Fund Raising Execs. (pres. Piedmont chpt. 1997-98). Presbyterian. Avocations: tennis, music, theater, reading, ohio state sports. Office: Spartanburg Tech Coll Found PO Box 4386 Spartanburg SC 29305-4386 Office Phone: 864-591-3814. Business E-Mail: richardsm@stcsc.edu.

RICHARDS, NORMAN BLANCHARD, lawyer; b. Melrose, Mass., May 27, 1924; s. Henry Edward and Annie Jane (Blanchard) R.; m. Diane Maionchi, July 9, 1977; children— Terri, Jeffrey. BS, Bowdoin Coll., 1945; JD, Stanford U., 1951. Bar: Calif. bar 1951. Mem. firm McCutchen Doyle Brown & Enersen, San Francisco, 1951—, partner, 1960—. Mem. faculty Tulane Admiralty Law Inst., Hastings Coll. Advocacy. Bd. visitors Stanford Law Sch. With USN, 1943-46. Fellow Am. Coll. Trial Lawyers; mem. ABA, Calif. State Bar, San Francisco Bar Assn., Maritime Law Assn. U.S. Home: 85 Platt Ave Sausalito CA 94965-1897 Office: Bingham McCutchen 3 Embarcadero Ctr San Francisco CA 94111-4003 Office Phone: 415-393-2030.

RICHARDS, PAUL GRANSTON, geophysics educator, seismologist; b. Cirencester, Eng., Mar. 31, 1943; came to U.S., 1965; s. Albert George and Kathleen Margaret (Harding) R.; m. Jody Margaret Porterfield, June 1, 1968; children: Mark, Jessica, Gillian. BA, Cambridge (Eng.) U., 1965; MS, Calif. Inst. Tech., Pasadena, 1966, PhD, 1970. Prof. geol. scis. Columbia U., N.Y.C., 1971—, chmn. dept. geol. scis., 1980-83. Co-author: Quantitative Seismology, 2 vols., 1980, 2nd edit., 2002. Guggenheim Found. fellow, 1977-78, MacArthur Found. fellow, 1981-86. Fellow Royal Astron. Soc.; mem. Am. Geophys. Union (Macelwane award 1976), Coun. Fgn. Rels. Episcopalian. Office: Lamont-Doherty Earth Obs 61 Rte 9W Palisades NY 10964 E-mail: richards@ldeo.columbia.edu.

RICHARDS, PAUL LINFORD, physics educator, researcher; b. Ithaca, N.Y., June 4, 1934; s. Lorenzo Adolph and Zilla (Linford) R.; m. Audrey Jarratt, Aug. 24, 1965; children: Elizabeth Anne, Mary-Ann. AB, Harvard U., 1956; PhD, U. Calif., Berkeley, 1960. Postdoctoral fellow U. Cambridge (Eng.), 1959-60; mem. tech. staff Bell Telephone Labs., Murray Hill, N.J., 1960-66; prof. physics U. Calif., Berkeley, 1966—. Faculty sr. scientist Lawrence Berkeley Lab., 1966-2001; advisor NASA, 1975-92, 98-2000; hon. prof. Miller Inst. Rsch. in Phys. Scis., Berkeley, 1969-70, 87-88, 2001; vis. prof. Ecole Normale Superieure, Paris, 1984, 92; vis. astronomer Paris Obs., 1984. Contbr. over 350 articles to profl. jours. Guggenheim Meml. Found. fellow, Cambridge, Eng., 1973-74; named Calif. Scientist of Yr. Mus. Sci., L.A., 1981; recipient sr. scientist award Alexander von Humboldt Found., Stuttgart, Fed. Republic Germany, 1982, Button medal, 1997; Berkeley Faculty Rsch. lectr. 1991. Mem. NAS; fellow Am. Phys. Soc. (Isakson prize 2000), Am. Acad. Arts and Scis. Avocations: vineyardist, wine making.

RICHARDS, ROBERT CHARLES, management consultant; b. Portland, Oreg., Jan. 18, 1939; s. Charles Robert and Mildred Marie (Merrill) R.; m. Marilyn Cornelia Poole, Sept. 1, 1961 (dec.); children: Kristin Elizabeth (dec.), Jeffrey Robert. BA, Lewis and Clark Coll., 1961. Tng. officer, mgr. edn. dept. U.S. Bancorp, Portland, Oreg., 1965-74; mgr. orgn. devel. Coors Container Co., Golden, Colo., 1974-77; mgmt. cons., mgr. western office Cons. Assocs. Internat., Inc., Lakewood, Colo., 1977-84; mgmt cons., pres. Cons. Network, Lakewood, 1985—; pres., CEO Epoch Prodns., 1986—; exec. v.p., sec.-treas. A Pretty Woman, Inc., Lakewood, Colo., 1994—; instr. Portland State U., 1972-73, U. Oreg., Portland Extension, 1973-74, Portland C.C., 1971-74; adj. faculty Bryant Coll. Ctr. for Mgmt. Devel., Smithfield, R.I., 1979—; mgmt. cons.; seminar leader; devel. cons. Martin Marietta Space Systems Co., 1989-91, Martin Marrietta Astronautics Group, 1991-92, Inst. Integrated Product/Process Design and Devel., 1993—, founder, chmn.; bd. dir., sec. Sr. Mgmt. Programs, Inc., 1971-73, pres., 1973-74. Author tng. materials; contbr. articles to profl. publs. Mem. adv. com. C.C. of Denver, scholarship and employment com. Portland State U. Found.; adj. faculty USMC Svc. Support Schs., Camp Lejeune, N.C. With USMCR, 1961-64; col. Res., 1966-92, Persian Gulf, 1990-91. Mem. Am. Soc. Tng. and Devel. (bd. dirs. chpt. 1976, v.p. 1977, bd. dirs. Oreg. chpt. 1972, pres. 1971, bd. dirs. Western region 1971-72), World Futures Soc., Planning Execs. Inst., Rocky Mountain Orgn. Devel. Network, Marine Corps Res. Officers Assn. (pres. Mile High chpt.), Marine Corps Meml. Assn. (sec.). Home and Office: 12265 SW Lanewood St Portland OR 97225-5825

RICHARDS, ROY, JR., wire and cable manufacturing company executive. Chmn., CEO, dir. Southwire Co., Carrollton, Ga., 1989—. Office: Southwire Co Inc PO Box 1000 Carrollton GA 30119-1000

RICHARDS, RUTH, psychiatrist, educational psychologist; b. Lincoln, Nebr. d. Dexter N. and Ruth (Fulton) R. BS with honors, Stanford U., 1965; MA, U. Calif., Berkeley, 1969, PhD, 1971; MD, Harvard Med. Sch., Boston, 1980. Diplomate Am. Bd. Psychiatry and Neurology; lic. psychologist, Mass.; cert. secondary edn. educator in physics, math, art, Calif. Asst. prof. ednl. psychology Boston U. Sch. Edn., 1971-75; lectr. in psychology dept. psychiatry Harvard Med. Sch., Boston, 1978—, fellow, instr., asst. clin. prof. psychiatry, 1981-94; assoc. attending psychiatrist, rsch. affiliate, various appointments McLean Hosp., Belmont, Mass., 1978—; assoc. clin. prof. U. Calif., San Francisco, 1994—; prof. psychology Saybrook Grad. Sch., San Francisco, 1995—, faculty co-chair, 1996-98; chair Consciousness and Spirituality, 1999-2000. Mem. exec. adv. bd. Ency. of Creativity, 1996-99; adv. bd. Manic-Depressive Illness Found., 1989—. Mem. editl. bd. Creativity Rsch. Jour., 1992—, Jour. Humanistic Psychology, 1996—; co-editor: Eminent Creativity, Everyday Creativity and Health, 1997; contbr. numerous articles to profl. jours. and chpts. to books. Mem. adv. panel biol. application program, Office of Technol. Assessment, U.S. Congress, 1987-88; dir. women's leadership project in adult edn., Boston U., 1974-75, others. Sr. asst. surgeon USPHS, 1980-81. Mem. APA, Soc. Chaos Theory in Psychology and the Life Scis., Psychologists for Social Responsibility. Avocations: visual art, creative writing, photography, physics.

RICHARDS, STANFORD HARVEY, advertising agency executive, design studio executive; b. Phila., Nov. 8, 1932; s. Jack and Ruth (Stein) R.; m. Betty Jo Pugh, July 12, 1957; children— Grant Leonard, Bradford Craig Student, Pratt Inst., 1950-53. Creative dir. Bloom Advt., Dallas, 1954-55; owner Stan Richards & Assocs., Dallas, 1955-75; owner, pres. The Richards Group, Inc., Dallas, 1975—; also bd. dirs. Instr. E. Tex. State U., Commerce, 1976-77; assoc. bd. mem. Cox Sch. Bus., So. Meth. U., Dallas, 1980-84, 88—. Author: Hobo Signs, 1965 Trustee Dallas Symphony, 1978, Dallas Ballet, 1978; bd. dirs. Episcopal Sch., Dallas, 1981—, Dallas Arboretum, 1984-86, The Sci. Pl., 1987-90; mem. Dallas Citizens Council, adv. council Salvation Army Adult Rehab. Ctr., 1986—, adv. bd. Dallas County Salvation Army, 1987—; exec. com. United Way, 1990—; bd. dirs. YMCA, 1990—. Named Top Creative, AdWeek, Entrepreneur of Yr., Inc Mag.; named one of All Wall Street Jours. Giants of our Time; recipient Alumni Achievement award, Pratt Inst., Bklyn., 1985, Reddick award, U. Tex. Mem.: Aerobic Activity Ctr. Avocations: deep sea fishing, running, skiing. Office: The Richards Group 8750 N Central Expy Ste 1200 Dallas TX 75231-6436

RICHARDS, STEVEN GEORGE, lawyer; b. Milw., Aug. 19, 1960; s. Joseph and Bessie A. Richards; m. LaNor L. Burgermeister, Feb. 17, 2000; children: Jessica, Michelle, Leilani, Gabrielle, Christian. AAS, Gateway Tech. Coll., Kenosha, WIs., 1985; BS in Applied Sci. and Tech., Thomas Edison State Coll., 1991; JD, John Marshall Law Sch., 1999. Bar: Wis. 2001, U.S. Dist. Ct. (ea. dist.) Wis. 2002, U.S. Dist. Ct. (we. dist.) Wis. 2003, Wis. 2003. Clk. William A. Pangman, Waukesha, Wis., 1994—98; intern Wis. State Ct. Appeals, Dist. I, Milw., 1995; clk. Robin Shellow, Milw., 1995—97; pvt. practice Van Dyne, Wis., 2001—03; of counsel Anderegg & Mutschler, Fond Du Lac, Wis. Assigned counsel Wis. State Pub. Defender. Mem. Wis. Coalition Against the Death Penalty; mem. fed. defender panel U.S. Dist. Ct. (ea. dist.) Wis., Green Bay. Mem.: Internat. Criminal Def. Attys. Assn., Calif. Def. Attys. for Criminal Justice, Wis. Assn. Criminal Def. Lawyers, Nat. Assn. Criminal Def. Lawyers. Serbian Orthodox. Avocations: fishing, golf. Home and Office: PO Box 8 127 Main St Casco WI 54205 Office Phone: 920-837-2653. Personal E-mail: sgrlaw@yahoo.com.

RICHARDS, SUSAN R. management consultant; b. Madison, Ind., Aug. 30, 1948; d. Chester Burns and Martha (Mefford) Goins; m. Kim E. Richards, Sept. 6, 1967 (div. 1969); 1 child, Natalie S. Richards. Student, Ind. U.-Purdue U., Indpls., 1970-72. Co-owner, pres. Baker Bros. Sales & Rentals, Indpls., 1976-87; owner, chmn. Party Concepts, Indpls., 1982-87; asst. dir., adminstr. L.A. Land Co., 1989-90; mgmt. cons. to small bus. cos., Malibu, Woodland Hills, Calif., 1990—. Inner city boys basketball coach, Indpls., 1977; tchr. Profl. Women Entrepreneurs, Indpls., 1980-81, Indpls. chpt. Exec. Women's Network, 1983; mem. Tri Valley Spl. Olympics, 1992—. Mem. Actors and Others for Animals. Republican. Roman Catholic. Avocations: tennis, polo.

RICHARDS, SUZANNE V. lawyer; b. Columbia, S.C., Sept. 7, 1927; d. Raymond E. and Elise C. (Gray) R. AB, George Washington U., 1948, JD with distinction, 1957, LLM, 1959. Bar: D.C. 1958. Sole practice, Washington, 1974—. Lectr. in family and probate law; mem. D.C. Jud. Conf., 1975—2004. Bd. dirs. Coun. for Ct. Excellence. Recipient John Bell Larner award George Washington U., 1958; named Woman Lawyer of Yr., Women's Bar Assn. D.C., 1977. Mem. ABA (ho. of dels. 1988-90), Bar Assn. D.C. (pres. 1989-90, named Lawyer of Yr. 2002), Women's Bar Assn. (pres. 1977-78), Trial Lawyers Assn. of D.C. (bd. govs. 1978-82, 85-2001, treas. 1982-85), D.C. Bar, Fed. Bar Assn. Home: 530 N St SW Washington DC 20024-4546 Office: PO Box 65466 Washington DC 20035-5466 Office Phone: 202-554-5829.

RICHARDS, THOMAS H. lawyer, arbitrator; b. Exeter, N.H., May 29, 1942; s. Frank F. and Ella (Higgins) R.; m. Barbara M. Blackmer, Mar. 23, 1975; children: Daniel, Matthew. BA cum laude, U. N.H., 1964; JD, NYU, 1967. Bar: N.H. 1967, U.S. Dist. Ct. N.H., U.S. Ct. Appeals (1st cir., D.C. cir.) 1987. Assoc. to v.p. Sheehan Phinney Bass & Green, Manchester, N.H., 1967-68, 70-99, ret., 1999, of counsel. Mem. N.H. Jud. Coun., Concord, 1988-90; mem. long range planning com. N.H. Supreme Ct., 1989-90, mem. profl. conduct com., 1989-90. Capt. 25th inf. divsn., U.S. Army, 1968-69. Root-Tilden fellow. Fellow Am. Bar Found., Am. Coll. Trial Lawyers, Internat. Soc. Barristers, N.H. Bar Found. (chmn. 1991-92); mem. Manchester Bar Assn. (bd. govs. 1975-80), New Eng. Bar Assn. (bd. govs. 1989-92), N.H. Bar Assn. (bd. govs. 1985-87, pres. 1989-90), Nat. Conf. Bar Pres., Phi Beta Kappa. Avocations: carpentry, collecting and restoring antique tools. Home: 164 Browns Hill Rd Sunapee NH 03782 Office: Sheehan Phinney Bass & Green 1000 Elm St Manchester NH 03101-1800

RICHARDS, VARGRAVE A. lieutenant governor; b. Santurce, P.R., Sept. 15, 1950; s. Ansel, and Beulah Anduze R.; 1 child, Renee. High School Teacher; mem. V.I. Senate, 1995—2003, senate pres., 1999—2000; lt. gov. V.I., 2003—. Democrat. Office: Office Lt Gov 1131 Kings St Ste 101 Christiansted VI 00820 also: #18 Kongens Gade St Thomas VI 00802

RICHARDS, VINCENT PHILIP HASLEWOOD, retired librarian; b. Sutton Bonington, Nottinghamshire, Eng., Aug. 1, 1933; arrived in Can., 1956, naturalized, 1961; s. Philip Haslewood and Alice Hilda (Moore) R.; m. Ann Beardshall, Apr. 3, 1961; children: Mark, Christopher, Erika. ALA, Ealing Coll., London, 1954; BLS with distinction, U. Okla., 1966. Cert. profl. libr., B.C. Joined Third Order Mt. Carmel, Roman Cath. Ch., 1976; with Brentford and Chiswick Pub. Librs., London, 1949-56; asst. librarian B.C. (Can.) Pub. Libr. Commn., Dawson Creek, 1956-57; asst. dir. Fraser Valley Regional Libr., Abbotsford, 1957-67; chief librarian Red Deer Coll., Canada, 1967-77; dir. librs. Edmonton (Alta.) Pub. Libr., Edmonton, 1977-89; libr. and book industry cons. Victoria, Canada, 1990—. Pres. Faculty Assn. Red Deer Coll., 1971-72, bd. govs., 1972-73. Contbr. articles to profl. jours. V.p. Jeunesses Musicales, Red Deer, 1969-70; bd. dirs. Red Deer TV Authority, 1975-76, Alta. Found. Lit. Arts, 1984-86. Served with Royal Army Ednl. Corps, 1951-53. Home and Office: 105 1049 Costin Ave Victoria BC Canada V9B 2T4 E-mail: grandann@hotmail.com. *Dedication to public service, in spite of its frustrating aspects, diversity of experience, people and places, and the avoidance of overspecialization are great contributors to an enjoyable working life.*

RICHARDS, VIRGINIA (GINNIE), social worker; b. Danville, Ill. d. Leon Jarod and Emma Storll; 1 child, Ronald. BA in Philosophy, Northwestern U., 1977; MA in Social Svc., U. Chgo., 1981; PhD, Kensington U., 1996. LCSW Fla. Counselor Sertoma, Chgo., 1983—88, cmty. social svc. mgr., 1988—90; psychiat. social worker Desert Cmty. Mental Health Ctr., Indio, Calif., 1991—93; pvt. practice Daytona, Fla., 1999—. Home and Office: 524 Brown Pelican Dr Daytona Beach FL 32119-8776

RICHARDS, VIRGINIA M. psychologist; Asst. prof. psychology U. Pa., Phila., grad. group mem. psychology, biomed. engring. and neurosci. Contbr. chpts. to books and articles to profl. jours. Recipient Troland Rsch. award NAS, 1998. Office: Univ Pa Dept Psychology 3815 Walnut St Philadelphia PA 19104 E-mail: richards@cattell.psych.upenn.edu.

RICHARDS, WALTER DUBOIS, artist, illustrator; b. Penfield, Ohio, Sept. 18, 1907; s. Ralph DuBois and Ruby Mildred (Smith) R.; m. Glenora Case, June 20, 1931; children: Timothy, Henry Tracy. Grad., Cleve. Sch. Art, 1930. With Sundblom Studios, Chgo., 1930-31, Tranquillini Studios, Cleve., 1931-36, Charles E. Cooper Studios, N.Y.C., 1936-50; freelance artist, 1950—. Executed paintings and illustrations for leading indsl. corps., nat. mags.; designed: U.S. postage stamps including Frederick Douglas 25 cent stamp; block of 4 stamps on beautification of Am.; Am. bald eagle-Mus. Natural History with commemorative; Cape Hatteras Nat. Parks Centennial block of four stamps; Paul Lawrence Dunbar Am. Poets commemorative; block of 4 stamps on Am. trees, 1978, blocks of 4 stamps on Am. architecture, 1979-82; co-designer anti-pollution block of four stamps; James Hoban stamp, 1981, Timberline Lodge 50th Anniversary U.S. commerorative stamp, 1987; exhibited, Cleve. Mus. Art, Art Inst., Chgo., Met. Mus., N.Y.C., Pa. Acad. Fine Arts, Bklyn. Mus., N.A.D., Whitney Mus., 200 Years Watercolor Painting, Met. Mus., 1966, 200 Years Am. Illustration, N.Y. Hist. Soc., 1976; represented in permanent collection, Whitney Mus., New Britain Mus. Am. Art, Cleve. Mus. Art, William A. Farnsworth Library and Art Mus., West Point Mus., Worcester (Mass.) Art Mus., Yale U. Art Gallery-New Haven, Conn., Smithsonian, Washington, D.C. Bd. dirs. Rowayton Art Center, Historic New Orleans Collection, 1989. Recipient highest award in lithography Cleve. Mus. Art, ann. 1935-38; Spl. Honor USAF, 1964; ann. Environ. Improvement award, 1983; named to Rocky River (Ohio) High Sch. Hall of Fame, 1991. Mem. Am. Watercolor Soc. (2d v.p. 1965-67), Conn. Watercolor Soc., NAD, Soc. of Illustrators, Fairfield Watercolor Group (pres., founder), Westport Artists. Address: 87 Oak St New Canaan CT 06840-5840

RICHARDS, WESLEY JON, newscaster, writer, producer; b. N.Y.C., Apr. 9, 1942; s. Mark and Pearl R. Richards; m. Carole A. Louis, June 8, 1962; children: Wesley, Julie, Lynn, Charles. Student, Hofstra U., 1959-62; MA, Antioch U., 1990. Radio personality Sta. WFYI, Mineola, N.Y., 1965, Sta. WGBB, Freeport, N.Y., 1966-70; editor AP, N.Y.C., 1971-74; radio personality Sta. WHLI, Hempstead, N.Y., 1974-76, Sta. WRFM, N.Y.C., 1976-86; broadcaster NBC Radio Network, N.Y.C., 1987-89; newscaster Sta. WYNY, N.Y.C., 1989-90, Sta. WOR, N.Y.C., 1990-92; writer, prodr. NBC News, 1992—2000; radio host Bloomberg News, 2000—. Freelance entertainer, 1955—; correspondent ABC Radio Network, N.Y.C., 1975, 90. Writer numerous essays, poems and songs, 1960—. Mem. AFTRA, Writers Guild Am., Broadcast Pioneers, Nat. Assn. Broadcast Employees and Technicians.

RICHARDS-BARNARD, SANDRA L. control systems engineer, computer graphics consultant; b. Houston, Oct. 18, 1948; d. Earl Douglas and Joleta (Phillips) Lively; m. Daniel R. Barnard (dec.); children: Jamie Raquel Richards, Laurie Joanna Richards Nichols, Micah Waverly Barnard. Student, San Jacinto Coll., 1966-68; BS in Chemistry and Math., Sam Houston State U., 1970; MBA, Houston Bapt. U., 1987; post-Baccalaureate, U. St. Thomas, 2000, 01, Tex. A&M U., 2000. INTEL cert. Chemist Sorbotec, Inc., Houston, 1971-72, Champion Papers, Inc., Pasadena, Tex., 1974-75, Core Labs., Inc., Houston, 1981-82; account rep. Foxboro Co., Houston, 1982-88; sr. control systems engring. technologist SIP (Parsons) Engring. Inc., Houston, 1989-90; sr. control sys. engr., control sys. supr. Bechtel, 1990-93; moon rock chemist at Lunar Receiving Lab. Johnson Space Ctr., Brown & Root-Northrup, Houston, 1970-71; salesman Tex. Real Estate Commn., 1972—; staff chem. cons. HL&P Reliant Energy, 1993-95; owner Richards & Assocs., Houston, 1995—. Tchr. bus. comm. and info. sys. Pasadena Ind. Sch. Dist., 1999—; mem. Act for Eight Community TV, Cousteau Soc. Charter mem. Nat./State Leadership Tng. Inst. on Gifted and Talented, Ventura, Calif., 1979—; mem. Houston Mus. Natural Sci., Houston Contemporary Arts Mus.; ann. rep. Nat. Engrs. Week, Bechtel, sci. fair judge. Sam Houston State U. undergrad. rsch. fellow in organic chemistry, 1969-70; grantee Job Shadowing, 2000; recipient Pedagogy award PISD, 2000. Mem. Soc. Women Engrs., Nat. Assn. Corrosion Engrs., Am. Chem. Soc., Instrument Soc. Am. (sr., bd. dirs. standards and practices com. 1987, standards and practices com. liaison), Nat. Mus. for Women in the Arts (charter), Christian Women's Club. E-mail: s4andra@yahoo.com.

RICHARDS-KORTUM, REBECCA RAE, biomedical engineering educator; b. Grand Island, Nebr., Apr. 14, 1964; d. Larry Alan and Linda Mae (Hohnstein) Richards; m. Philip Ted Kortum, May 12, 1985; children: Alexander Scott, Maxwell James, Zachary Alan. BS, U. Nebr., 1985; MS, MIT, 1987, PhD, 1990. Prof., chair engring. U. Tex., Austin, 1990—. Named Presdl. Young Investigator NSF, Washington, 1991; NSF presdl. faculty fellow, Washington, 1992; recipient Career Achievement award Assn. Advancement Med. Instrumentation, 1992, Dow Outstanding Young Faculty awd., Am. Soc. for Engineering Education, 1992. Mem. AAAS, Am. Soc. Engring. Edn. (Outstanding Young Faculty award 1992), Optical Soc. Am., Am. Soc. Photobiology. Achievements include research in photochemistry, photobiology, applied optics and bioengring. Office: U Texas Depart Biomed Engineering 1 U StationC0800 Austin TX 78712-0238

RICHARDSON, ALBERT EDWARD, chemistry educator, consultant, researcher; b. Lovelock, Nev., Feb. 4, 1929; s. James Harold and Mary Lorraine Richardson; m. Shirley Arlene Richardson, June 10, 1959 (dec. Apr. 1997); children: Anne Ikard, John (dec.), Stephen; stepchildren: Corinne Jameson, Elisabeth Anderson, David Beckman, Margaret Chambers. BS in Chemistry, U. Nev., 1950; PhD, Iowa State U., 1956. Accredited profl. chemist Am. Inst. Chemists. Rsch. chemist Ames (Iowa) Lab. of the Atomic Energy Commn., 1950—55; asst. prof. chemistry N.Mex. State U., Las Cruces, 1955—60, radiation safety officer, 1957—75, assoc. prof. chemistry, 1960—91, assoc. prof. emeritus, 1991—. Vis. scientist N.Mex. secondary schs., 1960—91; vis. prof. chemistry Adams State Coll., Alamosa, Colo., 1963; summer rschr. Ames Lab. Atomic Energy Commn., 1964, Lawrence Livermore (Calif.) Nat. Lab., 1979; cons. White Sands (N.Mex.) Missile Range, 1965—71, contractor, 1973—74, chemist, 1981—82, 1984—92; vis. staff mem. Los Alamos (N.Mex.) Nat. Labs., 1975—80; summer faculty Sandia Nat. Lab., Albuquerque, 1983; owner, mgr. Timberline Bed and Breakfast, Cedaredge, Colo., 1992—98. Contbr. over 20 articles to profl. jours. Mem. founding cabinet The World Peace and Diplomacy Forum, 2003—; bus. mgr. Coll. Cmty. Chorus, Las Cruces, 1956—57; pres. U. Park Toastmaster's Club, Las Cruces, 1961; dir. Southwestern N.Mex. Regional Sci. Fair, Las Cruces, 1967—68; vol. reading aide to elem. schs. Las Cruces, 2000—. Rsch. grantee NASA, 1966, Equipment grantee Atomic Energy Commn., 1968; postdoctoral rsch. fellow Atomic Energy Commn., 1968-69. Mem. Am. Chem. Soc. (chmn. so. N.Mex. sect. 1962, chmn. Rio Grande Valley sect. 1977), World Peace and Diplomacy Forum (charter), Sigma Xi, Phi Kappa Phi (pres. N.Mex. State U. chpt. 1972-73), Phi Lambda Upsilon, Sigma Pi Sigma. Democrat. Avocations: photography, collecting coins and CD's, travel, gardening, cultural activities. Home: 1185 Villita Loop Las Cruces NM 88007 E-mail: aerinlc@earthlink.net.

RICHARDSON, ALLISON, financial services company official; Grad. in acctg., Fordham U.; MBA in Fin., NYU, 1999. Mgr. assurance and adv. bus. svcs. Ernst & Young, Cleve. Former mentor Adlain Stevenson H.S., N.Y.C.; coord. co. vols. Coun. Fashion Designers Am.-Vogue Initiative/NYC AIDS Fund; counselor to young profls. Recipient Black Achiever in Industry award Harlem YMCA. Mem. Beta Alpha Psi. Office: Ernst & Young LLP 925 Euclid Ave Ste 1300 Cleveland OH 44115-1476

RICHARDSON, ANN BISHOP, foundation executive, lawyer; b. New Rochelle, N.Y., Dec. 15, 1940; d. Erwin Julius and Mary Frances (Stuart) Heilemann; children: Timothy William, Lynn Patricia, Melanie Elizabeth. BA summa cum laude, Georgetown U., 1977; JD, George Washington U., 1984; cert., Oxford (Eng.) U., 1986. Bar: Md. 1988, D.C. 1989. Student counselor Amideast, Beirut, 1967-68, program specialist, 1970-73; adminstrv. asst. UN Devel. Program, Yaounde, Cameroon, 1968-70; adminstrv. mgr. Antioch Sch. Law, Washington, 1977-79; chief adminstrv. officer for internat. ops. Peace Corps, Washington, 1980-84; dir. adminstrn. and fin. African Devel. Found., Washington, 1984-87; atty. Karr and McLain, Washington, 1987-92; v.p., gen. counsel Time Dollar, Inc., Washington, 1992-98; adj. prof. law D.C. Sch. Law, Washington, 1994-98, prof., acad. dean, 1998—. Bd. dirs. Bur. Rehab., Inc. Active Neighbors, Inc., Washington, 1976—, Time Dollar, Inc. Recipient Spl. Achievement award Peace Corps, 1981, 82, African Devel. Found., 1986. Mem. ABA, ACLU, D.C. Bar Assn., Am. Women Univ. Grads., Soc. for Internat. Devel., Phi Beta Kappa. Office: DC Sch Law 4200 Connecticut Ave NW Washington DC 20008-1122

RICHARDSON, ARTEMAS P(ARTRIDGE), retired landscape architect; b. Phila., May 24, 1918; s. Eugene Stanley and Jessica (Ripple) R.; m. Frederica McAfee, Sept. 2, 1945; children: Steven, David, Ann, Vida, Stanley. BA in Fine Arts, Williams Coll., 1940; student, Pa. State U., 1940-42; BS in Landscape Architecture, Iowa State U., 1947. Registered landscape architect, Conn., Fla., Md., Mass., Miss., N.Y., Ohio, R.I., Tenn. Asst. landscape architect McCloud & Scatchard, Lilitz, Pa., 1947-48, Olmsted Bros., Brookline, Mass., 1949-50, ptnr., 1950-61, Olmsted Assocs., Brookline, 1961-64, pres, treas., 1964-80; owner The Olmsted Office, Fremont, N.H., 1980-2000; ret. Lectr. Harvard U., Cambridge, 1961; mem., chair Bd. Registration Landscape Architects, Mass., 1968-77. Illustrator: Trees for Every Purpose, 1980. Mem., chair Planning Bd., Needham, Mass., 1956-62, Conservation Commn., Fremont, 1982-2000, chair, 1984-2000; mem. N.H. Gov.'s Task Force on Community Trees, Concord, 1989-91; mem., chair Exeter River Local Adv. Com., 1995-2001. Lt. USNR, 1942-46, ETO. Named Outstanding Mcpl. Vol., N.H. Mcpl. Assn., 1993. Fellow Am. Soc. Landscape Architects, Boston Soc. Landscape Architects (pres. 1952-56); mem. N.H. Landscape Assn. (bd. dirs. 1984-87), Granite State Landscape Architects (vice chair 1990-91), Herb Soc. Am. (life), Scarab, Rotary (pres. local club 1965-66, dist. trustee 1968-69, dist. gov. 1970-71, bd. dirs. R.I. 1978-80), Delta Phi, Tau Sigma Delta, Pi Gamma Alpha. Avocations: photography, woodworking, gardening. Home: Langdon Pl 17 Hampton Rd Apt 106 Exeter NH 03833-4822 E-mail: aprich@ttlc.net.

RICHARDSON, ARTHUR WILHELM, lawyer; b. Glendale, Calif., Apr. 3, 1963; s. Douglas Fielding and Leni (Tempelaar-Lietz) R.; m. Noriko Satake, Nov. 14, 1998. Student, London Sch. Econs., 1983; AB, Occidental Coll., 1985; JD, Harvard U., 1988. Bar: Calif. 1989, Ohio 2002. Assoc. Morgan, Lewis and Bockius, L.A., 1988—90; staff lawyer U.S. SEC, L.A., 1990—92, br. chief, 1992—96, sr. counsel, 1996—2001; of counsel Arter and Hadden, Columbus, Ohio, 2002—03. Mem. ABA, Calif. Bar Assn., L.A. County Bar Assn., Harvard/Radcliffe Club So. Calif., Town Hall Calif., L.A. World Affairs Coun., Sierra Club, Phi Beta Kappa. Presbyterian. Home: Apt 107 11663 Kiowa Avenue Los Angeles CA 90049

RICHARDSON, BARBARA HULL, state legislator, social worker; b. Danville, Pa., Sept. 30, 1922; d. Robert Alonzo and Clara Lucille (Woodruff) H.; widowed; children: Barbara Follansbee, Lawrence, Christine, Lovel Pratt. BA, Bryn Mawr Coll., 1944; MSW, Smith Coll. School for Social Work, 1973. Social worker child and family svcs. divsn. children and youth svcs. HHS, Keene, N.H., 1969-71, administr. child and family svcs. Concord, N.H., 1975-88, supr. policy writers, 1988-91; mem. N.H. Ho. Reps., Concord, 1992—. Trustee Meeting Sch., 1980—; bd. dirs. Cheshire Housing Trust, 1986-93; adv. bd. Casey Family Svcs. N.H., 1990—; vol. Hospice Monadnock Region, 1991—; mem. community coun. Luth. Social Svcs. New England, 1993—; bd. dirs. Keene Day Care Ctr. Democrat. Home: 101 Morgan Rd Richmond NH 03470-4909 Office: NH Ho of Reps State Capitol Concord NH 03301

RICHARDSON, BECKY D. state representative; b. Chester, SC, Mar. 1, 1943; d. Hiram Ross Davis and Sara Grant McDill; m. J. R. Richardson, July 10, 1999; children: William Layman, James Brennan. BA, Limeston Coll., 1965. Mem. SC Ho. of Reps., 1991—, chmn. ho. ethics com. Pres. United Way, Fort Mill, 1990, campaign chmn., 1989; recycling chmn. Fort Mill, 1988—; women's adv. bd. Piedmont Med. Ctr., 1989—92; solid wste task force York County, 1990—92; chmn. Red Ribbon Week for Drug-Free Am., 1990—2001; adv. bd. Leap Ahead, 1991—99; hon. adv. bd. Teen Challenge, toast of yr., 1993; mem. City Coun., Fort Mill., 1988; pres. women of ch. Unity Presbyn., 1988—90; bd. dirs. Downtown Revitalization Commn., 1988—, Police Athletic League, 1990—92, Fort Mill Mus., 1990—94, Fort Mill Rescue Squad, Tri-County Sisterhelp, 1992—96, Teen Connection, 1996—98. Named Legis. of Yr., SC Wildlife Fedn., 1997, Sierra Club, 1998, SC Optometrist Assn., 1997; recipient Legis. award, Victims' Adv., 1996. Mem.: Fort Mill Area C. of C. (bd. dirs. 1988—91). Republican. Office: State Capitol 519 B Blatt Bldg Columbia SC 29211

RICHARDSON, BETTY H. lawyer, former prosecutor; b. Oct. 3, 1953; BA, U. Idaho, 1976; JD, Hastings Coll. Law, 1982. Staff aid U.S. Senator Frank Church, 1976-77; tchg. asst. Hastings Coll. Law, 1980-82, 1980-82; legal rsch. asst. criminal divsn. San Francisco Superior Ct., 1982-84; jud. law clk. Chamber of Idaho Supreme Ct. Justice Robert C. Huntley Jr., 1984-86; atty. U.S. Dept. Justice, Boise, Idaho, 1993-2001, Richardson & O'Leary, Eagle, Idaho, 2001—; jud. law clk. Chamber of Chief U.S. Dist. Ct. Judge B. Lynn Winmill, Idaho, 2003—. Instr. Boise State U., 1987, 89; mem. U.S. Atty. Gen.'s Adv. Com. subcoms. on environ., civil rights and native Am. issues, others, 1993-2001; mem. hon. adv. bd. for Crime Victims Amendment in Idaho, 1994; mem. Dist. of Idaho Judges and Lawyer Reps. com., gender fairness com., Civil Justice Reform Act com. and criminal adv. com., 1993-2001; Dem. nominee Dist 1 Idaho, U.S. Ho. of Reps., 2003; adj. prof. constnl. law Boise State U., 2004; program planner Idaho State Bar and Law Found., 2004—. Mem. Idaho Indsl. Commn., 1991-93, chmn., 1993; mem. adv. bd. Family and Workplace Consortium, 1995-2001; mem. Assistance League of Boise, 2001—; bd. dirs. Tony Patino Fellowship. Recipient Harold E. Hughes Exceptional Svc. award Nat. Rural Inst. on Alcohol and Drug Abuse, 1999; Tony Patino fellow Hastings Coll. Law, 1982. Mem. Idaho Bar Assn. (governing coun. govt. and pub. sectors lawyers sect. 1999-2001, Pro Bono Svc. award 1988), Idaho Women Lawyers, Assistance League Boise, YMCA, City Club Boise. Office: Richardson & O'Leary 99 E State St Eagle ID 83616

RICHARDSON, BRUCE ALAN, academic administrator; b. Iowa City, Iowa, May 2, 1947; s. George Barnes and Margaret Jean (Horn) Richardson. BA in English, UCLA, 1972, MA in English, 1978, PhD of English, 1983. Asst. dir. Writing Programs UCLA, 1982—83, lectr. Comparative Lit., 1983; asst. prof., assoc. prof. U. Wyo., Casper, Laramie, 1984—. Assoc. dean U. Wyo., Laramie, 1997—2001, dir., 2000—01; pres. Nicolaysen Art Mus., Casper, 2002—03, bd. dirs., 1997—2003, Wyo. Humanities Coun., Laramie, 1996—2000; v.p. Artcore, Casper, 1994—; cons. Star Ln. Sch., Casper, 1991—, Natrona County Pub. Libr., Casper, 2001—. Contbr. articles to profl. jours. Democrat. Avocation: geyser gazing. Office: Univ Wyoming 125 College Dr Casper WY 82601

RICHARDSON, CAMPBELL, retired lawyer; b. Woodland, Calif., June 18, 1930; s. George Arthur and Mary (Hall) R.; m. Patricia Packwood, Sept. 3, 1957 (dec. Oct. 1971); children: Catherine, Sarah, Thomas; m. Carol Tamblyn, June 1975 (div. Dec. 1977); m. Susan J. Lienhart, May 3, 1980; 1 child, Laura. AB, Dartmouth Coll., 1952; JD, NYU, 1955. Bar: Oreg. 1955, U.S. Dist. Ct. Oreg. 1957. Ptnr. Stoel Rives LLP, Portland, 1964-2000; ret., 2000—. Co-author: Contemporary Trust and Will Forms for Oregon Attorneys, 2003, and for Idaho Attorneys, 2001; contbr. articles to profl. jours. Mem. Portland/Metro Govt. Boundary Commn., 1976; mem. Oreg. Adv. Com. to U.S. Commn. on Civil Rights, 1976-84; bd. dirs. Ctr. for Urban Edn., Portland, 1980-84, Dorchester Conf., Inc., 1982, Oreg. Zoo Found., 1993-2003; chmn. planned giving com. St. Vincent Med. Found., 1988-98; mem. planned giving coun. Oreg. Health Scis. Found., 1994-2003; trustee Met. Family Svc. Found., 1990-98; bd. dirs. Elders in Action, Portland, 2000-. Served with U.S. Army, 1955-57. Mem. ABA, Oreg. Bar Assn., Multnomah County Bar Assn., Estate Planning Coun. Portland (pres. 1978), Am. Coll. Trust and Estate Counsel, City Club, Multnomah Athletic Club (Portland). Republican. Home: 1500 SW 5th Ave Unit 1701 Portland OR 97201-5430 Office: Stoel Rives LLP 900 SW 5th Ave Ste 2300 Portland OR 97204-1229 Office Phone: 503-294-9337. E-mail: crichardson@stoel.com.

RICHARDSON, CHARLES CLIFTON, biochemist, educator; b. Wilson, NC, May 7, 1935; s. Barney Clifton and Florence Elizabeth (Barefoot) R.; m. Ute Ingrid Hanssum, July 29, 1961; children: Thomas Clifton, Matthew Wilfrid BSM., Duke U., 1959, MD, 1960; A.M. (hon.), Harvard U., 1967. Intern dept. medicine Duke U., Durham, N.C., 1960-61; postdoctoral fellow dept. biochemistry Stanford U. Med. Sch., Calif., 1961-63; asst. prof. biol. chemistry Harvard Med. Sch., Boston, 1964-67, assoc. prof., 1967-69, prof. biol. chemistry, 1969—, chmn. dept. biol. chemistry, 1978-87, Edward S. Wood prof., 1979—. Physiol. chemistry study sect. NIH, 1970-74; mem. Fachbeirat of Max-Planck Inst. für Moleculare Genetik, Berlin, Fed. Republic Germany, 1980-89; sci. adv. com. U.S. Biochem. Corp., Cleve., 1983-93, Genetics Inst., Cambridge, Mass., 1986-99, NYCOMED-Amersham, U.K., 1998-2000; mem. Nat. Bd. Med. Examiners, 1973-76; nucleic acids and protein adv. com., Am. Cancer Soc. Inst., 1975-78; vis. com. Boston Biomed. Rsch. Found., 1985—; assoc. Helicon Found., San Diego, 1983-2000; sci. adv. bd. Amersham Life Sci. Inc., 1994-98. Assoc. editor: Ann. Rev. Biochemistry, 1973-82, editor, 1983-2003; mem. editl. bd. Jour. Biol. Chemistry, 1968-73, 84-88, Jour. Molecular Biology, 1976-79. Recipient Career Devel. award NIH, 1967-76, Merit award, 1986. Fellow Am. Acad. Arts and Scis., Inst. of Medicine; mem. Nat. Acad. Scis., Am. Chem. Soc. (Eli Lilly Co. biol. chem. award 1968), Am. Soc. Biol. Chemists (mem. nominating com. 1974-75, 1983-84), Am. Cancer Soc. (coun. for rsch. and clin. investigation 1989-92), Am. Soc. Biochemistry and Molecular Biology (Merck award in biochemistry and molecular biology 1996). Business E-Mail: ccr@hms.harvard.edu.

RICHARDSON, DANA ROLAND, technology consultant; b. Mason City, Iowa, Jan. 11, 1945; s. Dana Roland Richardson and Louise Marion (Duke) Sarles; m. Sandra Anderson, June 12, 1966; children: Patricia Nan, Dana Roland, Jr. BS, UCLA, 1966, MBA, 1967. CPA, Calif., N.Y. Staff acct. Arthur Young, L.A., 1967-72, mgr., 1972-76, prin. N.Y.C., 1976-78; ptnr. Ernst & Young, N.Y.C., 1978-94; founder, ptnr. Dream Street Prodns., New Canaan, Conn., 1994—2002; pres. Richardson Media & Tech. LLC, 2003—. Author: A Manager's Guide to Computer Timesharing, 1975, Audit and Control of Information Systems, 1987. Staff sgt. Reserves USANG, 1967-73. Named one of Techology 100 Top 100 Achievers in Techn. in Am., Tech. Mag., 1982; recipient Nat. Videographer award, Nat. Videography Assn., 1998, 1999, Telly award, 1999. Mem. AICPA, Calif. Soc. CPA's. Republican. Episcopalian. Avocations: boating, fishing, music, videography, multimedia. Office: Richardson Media & Tech LLC 24 Blueberry Ln Canton CT 06019 Home: 24 Blueberry Ln Canton CT 06019-4503 Business E-Mail: rick@richardon-media-tech.com.

RICHARDSON, DAVID WALTHALL, cardiologist, educator, consultant; b. Nanking, China, Mar. 22, 1925; s. Donald William and Virginia (McIlwaine) R.; m. Frances Lee Wingfield, June 12, 1948; children: Donald, Sarah, David. BS, Davidson Coll., 1947; MD, Harvard U., 1951. Diplomate Am. Bd. Internal Medicine, Am. Bd. Cardiology. Intern, resident Yale New Haven Hosp., 1951-53; resident, fellow Med. Coll. Va., Richmond, 1953-56, assoc. prof. to prof. medicine, 1962-95, prof. emeritus, 1995—. Chmn. divsn. cardiology, 1972-87; interim chmn. dept. medicine, 1973-74; chief cardiology, assoc. chief staff for rsch. VA Hosp., Richmond, 1956-61, dir. cardiology tng. program, 1990-95; vis. scientist Oxford U., Eng., 1961-62; vis. prof. U. Milan, Italy, 1972-73. Contbr. articles to profl. jours. Moderator Hanover Presybery, Presbyn. Ch. U.S., Richmond, 1970; chmn. events com., NHLBI Cardiac Arrhythmia Suppression Trial, 1983-92, NHLBI Anti-Arrhythmics versus Implantable Defibrillators Trial, 1993-97. Served with USN, 1944-46. Fellow Am. Coll. Cardiology (gov. VA 1970-72), Am. Heart Assn. (coun. clin. cardiology and high blood pressure rsch.); mem. Am. Soc. Clin. Investigation, Am. Clin. and Climatol. Assn. Home: 5501 Queensbury Rd Richmond VA 23226-2121 Office Phone: 804-288-2302. Personal E-mail: davidwrl@comcast.net.

RICHARDSON, DENNIS MICHAEL, lawyer, educator; b. L.A., July 30, 1949; s. Ralph Lee and Eva Catherine (McGuire) R.; 1 child from previous marriage, Scott Randol; m. Catherine Jean Coyl, July 27, 1973; children: Jennifer Eve, Valerie Jean, Rachel Catherine, Nicole Marie, Mary Rose, Marie Christina, Laura Michelle, Alyssa Rose. BA, Brigham Young U., 1976, JD, 1979. Bar: Oreg. 1979. Owner Dennis Richardson & Assocs., P.C., Central Point, Oreg., 1979—; pvt. practice law Central Point, Oreg., 1979—; CEO IMPEX U.S. Corp., 1999—; state leg. Oreg. House of Reps., 2003—. Guest lectr. in field. Contbr. articles to profl. jours. Bd. dirs. Oreg. Lung Assn., 1980, Shakespearean Festival, Ashland, 1981, Jackson County Legal Services, 1982; chmn. GOP Oreg. 2d. Congl. Dist., 1996-2000, treas. GOP Oreg. Exec. Com., 1996-2002; councilman Ctrl. Point City, 2001-2002. Served as helicopter pilot U.S. Army, 1969-71, Vietnam. Decorated Vietnamese Cross Gallantry. Republican. Office: Dennis Richardson & Assocs PC 55 S 5th St Central Point OR 97502-2474 E-mail: rep.dennisrichardson@state.or.us.

RICHARDSON, DENNISE MARIE, physician assistant; b. Patuxent River, Md., July 16, 1944; d. Hershel Elroy and Suzanne Marie (Ahern) R.; m. Richard Harold Browne, Aug. 10, 1970. BS, Lamar U., 1966, U. Tex., 1995; MS, Okla. State U., 1970, PhD, 1973. Cert. physician asst. Rsch. technician MD Anderson Hosp., Houston, 1967-68; fellow U. Tex., Dallas, 1974-75, rsch. assoc., 1978-93; rsch. immunologist Wadley Insts., Dallas, 1975-76; physician asst. Lakewood Med. Ctr., Dallas, 1996-97, Lewis Group, Dallas, 1997-98; pediat. physician asst. George Monroe, MD, Dallas, 1998—. Fellow Am. Assn. Physician Assts.; mem. People to People Internat., Tex. Acad. Physician Assts., Alzheimer Assn. (group leader), Dallas Com. Fgn. Visitors, Dallas Camera Club (sec.), Beta Beta Beta, Phi Sigma. Republican. Avocations: photography, canoeing, writing. Home: 12045 Inwood Rd Dallas TX 75244-8016

RICHARDSON, DOT (DOROTHY GAY), softball player, physician; b. Orlando, Fla., Sept. 22, 1961; married. Student, Western Ill. U.; BS Kinesiology, UCLA; M in Exercise, Adelphi U.; MD, U. Louisville; PhD (hon.), Western Ill. U., 2003. Mem., captain US Olympic Softball Team; resident in orthopedic surg. U. Calif. Med. Ctr.; med. dir. USA Triathlon Nat. Tng. Ctr., Clermont, Fla., 2001—. Recipient Gold medal Pan. Am. Games, 1979, 87, 95,

ISF Women's World Championship, 1986, 94, South Pacific Classic, 1994, Superball Classic, 1995, Atlanta Olympics, 1996, Sydney Olympics, 2000; Rev Linda award, Flo Hyman award, 2002; named All-Am. Am. Softball Assn., MVP Am. Softball Assn. Major Fast Pitch Nat. Championship, Player of 1980s NCAA. Office: Amateur Softball Assn 2801 NE 50th St Oklahoma City OK 73111-7203 also: Exec Dir USAT Nat Tng Ctr 1099 Citrus Tower Blvd Clermont FL 34711

RICHARDSON, EARL STANFORD, university president; b. Westover, Md., Sept. 25, 1943; m. Sheila Bunting; 1 child, Eric. BA, U. Md., Eastern Shore, 1965; MA, U. Pa., 1973, EdD, 1976. Lectr. edn. dept. U. Md., Eastern Shore, 1975-82, acting dir. admissions, 1971-72, dir. career planning and placement, 1974-75, exec. asst. to chancellor, 1975-82; grad. asst. U. Pa., Phila., 1973-74; asst. to pres., Cen. Adminstrn. U. Md., Adelphi, 1982-84; pres. Morgan State U., Balt., 1984—. Mem. segmental adv. com. Md. State Bd. Higher Edn., 1984—. Mem. Policy Com. Greater Balt., 1982—; bd. dirs. Goldseker Found., Balt., 1985—, Balt. Symphony Orch., 1984—. Ford Found. fellow, 1972, Kellogg Found. fellow, 1980. Mem. Phi Kappa Phi. Office: Morgan State U 1700 E Cold Spring Ln Baltimore MD 21251-0002

RICHARDSON, EDWARD R. school system administrator; b. Pensacola, Fla., Jan. 24, 1939; s. Edward H. and Doria (Parker) R.; m. Nell C.; children: Merit Lynn Richardson Smith, Laura Leigh. BS, Auburn U., 1962, MEd, 1967, EdD, 1972. Sci. tchr. Montgomery Pub. Schs., Montgomery, Ala., 1962-64, prin., 1967-70, Andalusia High Sch., Andalusia, Ala., 1972-80; asst. prof. Auburn U., Montgomery, 1980-82; supt. Auburn City Schs., Auburn, Ala., 1982-95, state of Ala., Montgomery, 1995—. Bd. mem. So. Regional Edn. Bd., Atlanta, 1989—; co-dir. Ala. Mgmt. Inst. Sch. Leaders, Montgomery, 1980-82. Ednl. advisor Gov. Guy Hunt, Montgomery, 1987—; active Landmarks Found., Montgomery, 1968-69. Named Supt. of Yr., State PTA, Montgomery, 1986-87, Educator of Yr., Andalusia Jaycees, 1973-74. Mem. Ala. Assn. Secondary Sch. Adminstrs. (pres. 1978-79), Ala. Assn. Sch. Adminstrs. (pres. 1986-87), Rotary (Auburn chpt. pres. 1987-88), Capitol Lions Club (pres. 1968-69), Phi Delta Kappa (Auburn U. chpt. pres. 1971-72). Republican. Methodist. Avocations: tennis, reading, gardening. Office: Ala Dept of Edn 50 Ridley St Rm 5114 PO Box 302101 Montgomery AL 36130-2101

RICHARDSON, ELAINA, foundation administrator, former magazine editor; MA, U. Edinburgh, Scotland, 1982; MLitt, Oxford (Eng.) U., 1984. Writer, editor Stills mag., 1984-86; freelance writer, 1986-88; mng. editor In Fashion, 1988; reporter, writer N.Y. Post, 1989; features editor Mirabella mag., 1990-93; mng. editor Elle mag., N.Y.C., 1993-96, dep. editor, editor-in-chief, 1996-00; pres. Yaddo, Saratoga Springs, New York, 2000—. Contbr. to BBC radio program Kaleidoscope, and to various newspapers and mags., including Washington Post, Seventeen, New Women, N.Y., View, Travel and Leisure, and Nat. Pub. Radio. Office: Corp of Yaddo PO Box 395 Saratoga Springs NY 12866-0395

RICHARDSON, ELAINE, state legislator; Student, Bryant Coll., Pima Coll.; U. Ariz.; D (hon.), Tucson U. Comml. real estate broker, Ariz.; small bus. owner; mem. Ariz. Senate, Dist. 11, Phoenix, 1996—. Mem. West Univ. Neighborhood Assn., real estate rev. com. on Edn. Initiatives; precinct com. person legis. dist. #11, Ariz.; mem. adv. bd. Emergency Med. Svcs. for Children, U. Ariz. Health Scis. Ctr.; bd. dirs., community substance abuse adv. coun. Altar Valley Sch. Dist.; del. Jt. Protocol Session, Ariz.-Mex. Commn.; bd. mem. La Frontera Ctr., Inc.; regional dir. Nat. Order of Women Legislators. Recipient Women on the Move award, 1997. Mem. Dems. of Greater Tucson, Ariz. Women's Polit. Caucus, Nat. Conf. of State Legislatures (vice chair energy and transp. com.), Toastmasters, Plateau Club, Sierra Club.

RICHARDSON, ELIZABETH HALL, retired ecologist; b. Waltham, Mass., June 5, 1937; d. Livingston and Elizabeth (Blodgett) Hall; m. (div.); children: Elisabeth F. Richardson, Anne K. Richardson. AB, Radcliffe Coll., 1959; MPA, U. So. Calif., 1975; MBA, U. Denver, 1986. Asst. biology tchr. Presbyn. Ladies Coll., Pymble, NSW, Australia, 1959; tchr. drama Middlesex Sch., Concord, Mass., 1961-62; adminstrv. asst. Gov. Richard D. Lamm, Denver, 1975-76; coord. govt. affairs Rocky Mountain Energy Co., Lakewood, Colo., 1977-79; exec. dir. Thorne Ecol. Inst., Boulder, Colo., 1981-82; rsch. asst. Boettcher & Co., Denver, 1988-89; land protection specialist Colo. Open Lands, Lakewood, 1991—2002. Sec. Colo. Coalition of Land Trusts, Golden, 1992—. Sec. Simon's Rock Coll. of Bard, 1989—; active N.Mex. Land Conservation Collaborative, 2002—. Mem. ASPA, Rocky Mountain Women's Inst. (chair 1982-97). Democrat. Home: 2400 S Jackson St Denver CO 80210-5637

RICHARDSON, EMILIE WHITE, manufacturing company executive, investment company executive, lecturer; b. Chattanooga, July 08; d. Emmett and Mildred Evelyn (Harbin) White; 1 child, Julie Richardson Milunic. BA, Wheaton Coll. With Christy Mfg. Co., Inc., Fayetteville, N.C., Ft. Lauderdale, Fla., 1952—, sec., 1956-66, v.p., 1967-74, exec. v.p., 1975-79, pres., CEO, 1980—. V.p. E. White Investment Co., 1968-83, pres., 1983—; cons. Aerostatic Industries, 1979—; v.p. Gannon Corp., 1981—; cons. govt. contacts and offshore mfg., 1981—; lectr., spkr. in field. V.p. pub. rels. Ft. Lauderdale Symphony Soc., 1974-76, v.p. membership, 1976-77, adv. bd., 1978—; active Atlantic Found., Ft. Lauderdale Mus. Art, Beaux Arts, Freedoms Found.; mem. East Broward Women's Rep. Club, 1968—, Americanism chmn., 1971-72. Mem. Internat. Platform Assn., Nat. Spkrs. Assn., Fla. Spkrs. Assn., Toastmasters, Coral Ridge Yacht Club. Methodist. Home: 1531 NE 51st St Fort Lauderdale FL 33334-5709 Office: 3311 Fort Bragg Rd Fayetteville NC 28303-4763 Personal E-mail: emilier@mindspring.com.

RICHARDSON, EVERETT VERN, hydraulic engineer, educator, administrator, consultant; b. Scottsbluff, Nebr., Jan. 5, 1924; s. Thomas Otis and Jean Marie (Everett) R.; m. Billie Ann Kleckner, June 23, 1948; children: Gail Lee, Thomas Everett, Jerry Ray. BS, Colo. State U., 1949, MS, 1960, PhD, 1965. Registered profl. engr., Colo. Hydraulic engr. U.S. Geol. Survey, Wyo., 1949-52, 1953-56, rsch. hydraulic engr., 1956-63, project chief, 1963-68; adminstr. Engring. Rsch. Ctr. Colo. State U., Ft. Collins, 1968—88, dir. Egypt water use project, 1977-84, prof. in charge of hydraulic program, 1982-88, dir. hydraulic lab. Engring. Rsch. Ctr., 1982-88, prof. emeritus, 1988—, dir. Egypt irrigation improvement project, 1985-90; dir. Egypt Water Rsch. Ctr. Project, Ft. Collins, 1988-89; sr. assoc. Ayers Assocs. Inc. (formerly Resource Cons./Engr., Inc.), Ft. Collins, 1989—. Dir. Consortium for Internat. Devel., Tucson, 1972-87; developer stream stability and scour at hwy. bridges course for State Dept. Transps. for NHI, FHWA; investigator for NTSB 1987 I-90 bridge failure, NY, 1997, railroad bridge failure, Ariz., CALTRAN 1995 I-5 bridge failure; cons. in field; lectr. in field. Sr. author: Highways in the River Environment: Hydraulic and Environmental Considerations, FHWA, 1975, 1990, Evaluating Scour at Bridge, FHWA, 1991, 1993, 1995, 2001, FHWA Hydr. Design Series No. 6: River Engineering for Highway Encroachments, 2001; contbr. papers TRB 9th Internat. Bridge Mgmt. Conf., 2003, to Engring. and Civil Engring. Handbook, 1995, Handbook of Fluid Dynamics and Fluid Machinery, 1996, Water Resources-Environmental Planning, Management and Development, 1996, articles to profl. jours., chapters to books. Mem. Ft. Collins Water Bd., 1969-84; mem. NY State Bridge Safety Assurance Task Force, 1988-91. Decorated Bronze Star, Purple Heart, Combat Infantry Badge; U.S. Govt. fellow MIT, 1962-63. Fellow: ASCE (chair task com., bridge scour rsch. 1990—96, vice chair 1997—2002, editor Compendium of Stream Stability and Scour Papers 1991—98, J.S. Stevens award 1961, hydraulics divsn. task com. excellence award 1993, Hans Albert Einstein award 1996); mem.: Internat. Congress for Irrigation and Drainage (bd. dirs.), Sigma Xi, Sigma Tau, Chi Epsilon. Home: 824 Gregory Rd Fort Collins CO 80524-1504 Office: Ayres Assocs PO Box 270460 Fort Collins CO 80527-0460 Office Phone: 970-223-5556.

RICHARDSON, F. C. academic administrator; b. Memphis, Sept. 22, 1936; m. Bernice Tanner. AB in Biology, Rust Coll., 1960; MS in Biology, Atlanta U., 1964; PhD in Botany, U. Calif., Santa Barbara, 1967. Asst. prof. botany Ind. U. N.W., Gary, 1967-71, assoc. prof., 1971-82, prof., 1982-84, chair dept. biology, 1971-72, chair div. arts and scis., 1972-84; prof. Jackson (Miss.) State U., 1984-85, v.p. for acad. affairs, 1984-85, Moorhead (Minn.) State U., 1985-89; prof. SUNY Coll. at Buffalo, 1989, pres., 1989-96; chancellor Ind. U.-S.E., New Albany, 1996—. Cons., evaluator North Ctrl. Assn., 1987-89; mem. commn. on elem. schs. Mid. States Assn., 1990—; mem. Commn. on Minorities in Higher Edn., Am. Coun. on Edn.; mem. task force on outcomes and accountability Coun. on Postsecondary Edn., 1991—. Mem. editorial bd. Negro Ednl. Rev., 1977—, exec. editor, 1981—; contbr. numerous articles to profl. jours. Mem. fellowship selection com. for Martin Luther King, Jr. Fellowship Program, Woodrow Wilson Nat. Fellowship Found., Chgo., 1969-74; bd. dirs. Lake County Assn. for Retarded Citizens, 1969-75; chair Ind. U. N.W./Community Adv. Bd. for Spl. Svcs., 1970-74; mem. Gary Air Pollution Control Adv. Bd., 1970-84, chair; chair steering com. for creation of Gary Neighborhood Svcs., Inc., 1970-71, bd. dirs., 1971-84; mem. N.W. Ind. Clean Air Coordinating Com., N.W. Ind., 1970-73, Comprehensive Health Planning Coun., 1971-75, Com. on Sci. and Tech. R&D, State of Minn., 1987, Moorhead Chamber Edn. Task Force, 1987-88; mem. Gary Bd. Health, 1972-82, sec., 1976-79, pres., 1979-82; bd. dirs. Meth. Hosps., Gary, 1973-84, Med. Ctr. of Gary, Inc., 1975-81, Greater Buffalo Devel. Found., 1989—, Buffalo Soc. Natural Scis., 1989—, Western N.Y. Tech. Devel. Ctr., Inc., 1991—, Buffalo Fine Arts Acad., 1991—; mem. Lake area planning and allocation com. United Way, 1981-83, chair Lake area campaign exec. group, 1982-83, bd. dirs. United Way Buffalo and Erie County, 1990—; mem. local organizing com. World Univ. Games 1993, 1989—; mem. bd. govs. NCCJ of Western N.Y., 1989—. Univ. scholar Atlanta U., 1962-64; fellow NSF, 1966, U. Calif., 1967-68. Mem. Am. Inst. Biol. Scis., Bot. Soc. Am., Internat. Soc. Plant Morphologists, Am. Assn. State Colls. and Univs. (SCAN team 1986).

RICHARDSON, GRACE ELIZABETH, consumer products company executive; b. Salem, Mass., Nov. 22, 1938; d. George and Julia (Sheridan) R.; m. Ralph B. Henderson, Mar. 3, 1979. BS, Simmons Coll., 1960; MS, Cornell U., 1962; MBA, NYU, 1981. Textile technologist Harris Rsch. Lab., Washington, 1962-65; instr. Simmons Coll., Boston, 1965-66; dir. consumer edn. materials J.C. Penney, N.Y.C., 1966-73; dir. residential conservation Con Edison, N.Y.C., 1974-81; dir. consumer affairs Chesebrough-Ponds, Greenwich, Conn., 1981-85; v.p. global consumer affairs Colgate Palmolive, N.Y.C., 1985—. Chair Simmons Coll. Leadership Coun., 1993—97; mem. com. Juilliard Sch., 1996—; bd. dirs. SOCAP, 1996—99, Nat. Coalition Consumer Edn., 1983—93; mem. Cornell U. Coun., chair pub. rels. com., 1988—97; bd. mem. UNIFEM, 2002—. Named Nat. Bus. Home Economist of Yr., Home Economists in Bus., 1979. Mem. Women's Forum, Cornell Club N.Y.C. (bd. dirs. 1989—). Home: 180 E 79th St New York NY 10021-0437 Office: Colgate Palmolive Co 300 Park Ave Fl 8 New York NY 10022-7499

RICHARDSON, HERBERT HEATH, mechanical engineer, educator, institute director; b. Lynn, Mass., Sept. 24, 1930; s. Walter Blake and Isabel Emily (Heath) R.; m. Barbara Ellsworth, Oct. 6, 1973. SB, SM with honors, MIT, 1955, ScD, 1958. Registered profl. engr., Mass., Tex. Research asst., research engr. Dynamic Analysis and Control Lab. MIT, 1953-57, instr. Dept. Mech. Engring., 1957-58, mem. faculty, 1958-84, prof. mech. engring., 1968-85, head dept., 1974-82, assoc. dean engring., 1982-81; Disting. prof. engring. Tex. A&M U., 1984—; Regents prof. Tex. A&M U. System, College Station, 1993—; dean, vice chancellor engring. Tex. A&M U. Sys., 1984-85; dep. chancellor, dean, dir. Tex. Engring. Expt. Sta. Tex. A&M U., 1985-91; chancellor Tex. A&M U. System, College Station, 1991-93, assoc. vice chancellor engring., 1993—, assoc. dean engring., 1993—; dir. Tex. Trans. Inst., Tex. A&M Univ. Sys., 1993—. With Ballistics Rsch. Lab. Abderdeen Proving Ground, Md., 1958; chief scientist U.S. Dept. Transp., 1970-72; bd. dirs. Foster-Miller Inc., Mass., Ten X Inc., Tex. Utilities Co.; chmn. adv. com. for engring. NSF, 1987-89, adv. com. basic energy scis. U.S. Dept. Energy, 1987-91. Author: Introduction to System Dynamics, 1971; contbr. articles to profl. publs. Trustee S.W. Rsch. Inst. Officer U.S. Army, 1968. Recipient medal Am. Ordnance Assn., 1953, Gold medal Pi Tau Sigma, 1963, Meritorious Service award and medal Dept. Transp., 1972. Fellow AAAS, ASME (Moody award fluid engring. divsn. 1970, Centennial medallion 1983, Rufus Oldenberger medal 1984, Meritorious Svc. medal 1986, Disting. Svc. award 1986, hon. mem. 1987); mem. NAS (assoc.), NAE (coun. 1986-92, com. on engring. edn.), Am. Soc. Engring. Edn. (Disting. Svc. medal 1993, Lamme award 1997), N.Y. Acad. Sci., Inst. Transp. Engrs., Nat. Rsch. Coun. (gov. bd. 1986-92, chmn. transp. rsch. bd. 1988-89), Nat. Acads. (nat. assoc., life), Sigma Xi, Tau Beta Pi. Office: Tex A&M U Sys MS 3135 College Station TX 77843-0001

RICHARDSON, IAN WILLIAM, actor; b. Edinburgh, Scotland, Apr. 7, 1934; s. John and Margaret R.; m. Maroussia Frank, Feb. 2, 1961; children: Jeremy, Miles. Diploma in Acting and Teaching, Royal Scottish Acad. Music and Drama, D in Drama, 1999. Actor Royal Shakespeare Co., Stratford on Avon and London, 1960-75, Shaw Festival Theatre, Niagara, Ont., Can., 1977. Appeared in plays including My Fair Lady, Broadway, 1976-77, The Miser, 1995, The Magistrate, 1997-98, The Seven Ages of Man, 1999, The Hollow Crown, 2002-04; films and TV plays include Tinker, Tailor, Soldier, Spy, Private Shulz, The Sign of Four, The Hound of the Baskervilles, Phantom of the Opera, 1990, The Gravy Train, 1990, House of Cards, 1991, The Gravy Train Goes East, 1991, To Play the King, 1993, Foreign Affairs Remember, Savage Play, 1994, The Final Cut, 1995; films include Brazil, Whoops!, Apocalypse, The Fourth Protocol, Cry Freedom, The Fifth Province, 1996, Dark City, 1998, From Hell, 2000; TV programs includes Star Quality, Porterhouse Blue, The Winslow Boy, 1989, An Ungentlemanly Act, 1992, Catherine the Great (miniseries), 1994, Gormenghast, 1999, (miniseries) Magician's House, 1999, Murder Rooms, 1999, Murder Rooms II, 2000, Strange, BBC TV, 2001, 03, (ITV) Miss Marple, 2004; author prefaces to Shakespearean works. Recipient CBE award, 1989, BAFTA award, 1991, award Royal TV Soc., 1991. Fellow Royal Scottish Acad. Music and Drama; mem. Brit. Actors Equity, Actors Equity, Screen Actors Guild, Garrick Club (London), Players Club (N.Y.C.). Office: care Diamond Mgmt 31 Percy St London W1T 2DD England E-mail: maroussia@maroussia.freeserve.co.uk.

RICHARDSON, J. WILLIAM, hotel executive; Acting pres. Interstate Hotels Corp., Pitts., 1999—, vice chmn., CFO, 1999—. Office: Interstate Hotels Corp Foster-Plaza Ten 680 Andersen Dr Pittsburgh PA 15220-2700

RICHARDSON, JAMES, computer company executive; married; 2 children. B in Mktg. and Fin., Queens U., Kingston, Ont., Can. Formerly with Unisys; with Cisco Systems, Inc., 1990—, v.p. intercontinental ops., 1992—94, v.p. N.Am. ops., 1995—96, pres., Europe, Mid. East and Africa ops., 1996—99, sr. v.p. Enterprise Line of Bus., sr. v.p., chief mktg. officer, 2001—. Avocations: hockey, skiing, sailing. Office: Cisco Systems Inc 170 W Tasman Dr San Jose CA 95134

RICHARDSON, JAMES DAVID, surgeon; b. Morehead, Ky., 1945; MD, U. Ky., 1970. Diplomate Am. Bd. Surgeons, Am. Bd. Vascular Surgery, Am. Bd. Thoracic Surgery, Am. Bd. SCC. Intern U. Ky. Med. Ctr., Lexington, 1970, resident, 1971-72, U. Tex., San Antonio, 1972-76; surgeon Norton Hosp., Louisville, 1977—; prof. surgery U. Louisville, 1979—; pres. Am. Bd. Surgery, 1998-99. Fellow ACS (bd. regents); mem. AMA, Am. Assn. Surgery of Trauma, Soc. Surgery Alimentary Tract, Alpha Omega Alpha. Office: U Louisville Dept Surgery 550 S Jackson St Louisville KY 40202-1622

RICHARDSON, JASON ANTHONEY, professional basketball player; b. Jan. 20, 1981; Student, U. Mich. Profl. basketball player Golden State Warriors, Oakland, Calif., 2001—. Named to NBA All-Rookie First Team, 2002. Achievements include member of NCAA championship team, 2000; won NBA Slam Dunk Contest, 2002, 2003. Office: Golden State Warriors 1011 Broadway Oakland CA 94607*

RICHARDSON, JOHN, retired international relations executive; b. Boston, Feb. 4, 1921; s. John and Hope (Hemenway) R.; m. Thelma Ingram, Jan. 19, 1945; children: Eva Teleki, Teren de Cossy, Hope Gravelly, Catherine Munch, Hetty L AB, Harvard U., 1943, JD, 1949. Bar: NY 1949. Assoc. Sullivan & Cromwell, NYC, 1949-55; with Paine, Webber, Jackson & Curtis, NYC, 1955-69, gen. ptnr., 1958-61, ltd. ptnr., 1961-69; pres., chief exec. officer Free Europe, Inc. (Radio Free Europe), 1961-68; asst. sec. for ednl. and cultural affairs Dept. State, 1969-77, also acting asst. sec. state for pub. affairs, 1971-73; exec. dir. for social policy Ctr. for Strategic and Internat. Studies; rsch. prof. internat. comm. Sch. Fgn. Svc., Georgetown U., Washington, 1977-78; pres., chief exec. officer Youth for Understanding, Inc., 1978-86, bd. dirs., 1986-98; counselor US Inst. of Peace, 1987-90. Spl. advisor Aspen Inst. Humanistic Studies, 1977—80. Founder Polish Med. Aid Project, 1957—61; co-founder, chmn. bd. Am. Com. to Aid Poland, 1989—95; pres. Internat. Rescue Com., 1960—61, bd. dirs., 1958—61, 1978—; chmn. Am. Coun. for UN U., 1977—87, Consortium for Internat. Citizens Exch., 1980—84, Delphi Internat., 1995—99, bd. dirs., 1999—2001; chmn., bd. dirs. Nat. Endowment for Democracy, 1984—88, bd. dirs., 1991—92, chmn. emeritus, 1992—; bd. dirs. Freedom House, 1963—69, pres., 1977—84; mem. Coun. Fgn. Rels., 1957—; Citizens Commn. on S.E. Asian Refugees, 1978—85; bd. dirs. Fgn. Policy Assn., 1958—68, 1977—86, Japan-US Friendship Commn., 1976—77; chmn. NYC Met. Mission United Ch. of Christ, 1966—69; bd. dirs. Kennedy Ctr. for the Performing Arts, 1970—77, Inter-Am. Found., 1970—77, East-West Ctr., 1975—77, Am. Forum for Global Edn., 1977—, Social Sci. Found., U. Denver, 1992—, World Learning, 2001—, Meridian House Internat., 1978—83, Atlantic Coun. U.S., 1982—84, Fgn. Student Svc. Coun., 1978—82, Coun. for Advancement of Citizenship, 1991—96, Coun. for Cmty. of Democracies, 1996—, pres., 1999—2001, pres. emeritus, 2001—. With paratroops USAR, WWII. Decorated Bronze Star with v device, Japan Order of the Sacred Treasure, Gold and Silver Star; Germany Order of Merit, Commdr.'s Cross, Poland Order of Merit, Knight Cross. Home: 9707 Old Georgetown Rd Apt 1104 Bethesda MD 20814-1746

RICHARDSON, JOHN CARROLL, lawyer, tax legislative consultant; b. Mobile, Ala., May 3, 1932; s. Robert Felder and Louise (Simmons) R.; m. Cicely Tomlinson, July 27, 1961; children: Nancy Louise, Robert Felder III, Leslie. BA, Tulane U., 1954; LLB cum laude, Harvard U., 1960. Bar: Colo. 1960, N.Y. 1965, D.C. 1972. Assoc. Holland & Hart, Denver, 1960-64; legal v.p. Hoover Worldwide Corp., N.Y.C., 1964-69; v.p., gen. counsel Continental Investment Corp., Boston, 1969; dep. tax legis. counsel U.S. Dept. Treasury, Washington, 1970-71, tax legis. counsel, 1972-73; ptnr. Brown, Wood, Ivey, Mitchell & Petty, N.Y.C., 1973-79, LeBoeuf, Lamb, Leiby & MacRae, N.Y.C., 1979-88, Morgan, Lewis & Bockius, N.Y.C., 1988-93; ret., 1993. Tax legis. cons., Orford, N.H., 1993—; adj. prof. Law Sch. Fordham U., 1990-94. Served to lt. comdr. USN, 1954-58. Mem. ABA (chmn. com. adminstrv. practice tax sect. 1984-86), N.Y. State Bar Assn. (exec. com. tax sect. 1975-84), D.C. Bar Assn., Am. Coll. Tax Counsel, N.Y. Athletic Club, Royal Automobile Club. Office Phone: 603-353-4608.

RICHARDSON, JOHN DAVID, physicist; b. Middlesbrough, Cleveland, United Kingdom, Nov. 17, 1968; s. Bridget Dolly Egan and David William Richardson; m. Susan Bowyer, July 14, 1997; 1 child, Megan. BS with honors, Liverpool U., 1991, PhD, 1995. Sr. rsch. assoc. U. Liverpool, England, 1995—96. Fellow, Particle Physics and Astronomy Rsch. Coun., England, 1996, U. Liverpool, 1996—97. Office: Lawrence Berkeley Lab 1 Cyclotron Rd Berkeley CA 94720 Home: 115 Northcreek Cir Walnut Creek CA 94598-1314 Personal E-mail: john.richardson@cern.ch. E-mail: john.richardson@cern.ch.

RICHARDSON, JOHN VINSON, JR., library and information science educator; b. Columbus, Ohio, Dec. 27, 1949; s. John Vinson Sr. and Hope Irene (Smith) R.; m. Nancy Lee Brown, Aug. 22, 1971. BA, Ohio State U., 1971; MLS, Peabody Coll., 1972; PhD, Ind. U., 1978. Asst. prof. UCLA, 1978-83, assoc. prof., 1983-98, editor The Libr. Quar., 1994—2003, prof., 1998—, assoc. dean grad. divsn., 2002—, mem. editl. bd., The Libr. Quar., 2004—. Faculty coord. UCLA-St. Petersburg State Acad. of Culture Exch. Program, 1996—; fellow advanced rsch. Inst. U. Ill., 1991; pres. Info. Transfer, Inglewood, Calif., 1988—; vis. fellow Charles Sturt U. NSW Australia, 1990; vis. scholar ALISE Russia Project, St. Petersburg and Moscow, 1996; vis. disting. scholar OCLC Inc., Dublin, Ohio, 1996-97; presidential scholar, Libr. Sys. & Svcs., LLC, 2002—03; chmn. Calif. Pacific Ann. Conf. Com. on Archives and History, 1992-96; Henderson lectr. U. N.C., Chapel Hill, 1997; mem. UCLA Privilege and Tenure, 1999-2000, chair, 2000-02. Author: Spirit of Inquiry, 1982, Gospel of Scholarship, 1992, Knowledge-based Systems for General Reference Work, 1995, Understanding Reference Transactions, 2002; mem. editl. bd. Ref. Svcs. Rev., Ann Arbor, Mich., 1991—, Jour. Govt. Info., Oxford, Eng., 1975—, Index to Current Urban Documents, Westport, Conn., 1987—, U. Calif. Press Catalogues and Bibliographies series, 1994-97, The Libr. Quarterly, 2003—. Mem. UCLA Grad. Coun., 1992-96, chair, 1995-96; mem. U. Calif. systemwide coord. com. on grad. affairs, 1993-96; pres. Wesley Found., L.A., 1981-87; lay del. Cal-Pac Conf. United Meth. Ch., 1985, 86, 92-96, chair conf. commn. on archives and history, 1992—96. Rsch. grantee Coun. on Libr. Resources, 1985, 90, Assn. Libr. and Info. Sci. Educators rsch. grantee, 1984, 87, 98, Online Computer Libr. Ctr. Libr. and Info. Sci. rsch. grantee, 1999; Harold Lancour scholar Beta Phi Mu, 1986, 99, Kaliper Sr. scholar U. Mich., 1998-99, Presdl. scholar Libr. Systems and Svcs. LLC, 2002—03; recipient Louise Maxwell award Ind. U. Alumni Assn., 1995. Mem. ALA (Justin Winsor prize 1990, Ref. and Adult Svcs. divsn. Outstanding Paper award 1992), AAAS, Assn. Libr. and Info. Sci. Educators (rsch. paper prize 1986, 91, rsch. grants 1984, 87, 98), Am. Soc. for Info. Sci. (Best Info. Sci. book 1995), Am. Assn. Adv. Slavic Studies, Sigma Xi. Democrat. Avocations: wine tasting,reading, internat. travel, lilac point Siamese. Office: UCLA GSE&IS DIS Campus Box 951520 Los Angeles CA 90095-1520 E-mail: jrichard@ucla.edu. *By our common action, we can bend the flow of history.*

RICHARDSON, JOSEPH BLANCET, retired science educator, educational consultant; b. Louisville, Nov. 12, 1936; m. Mary Irene Murphy, Dec. 27, 1960; children: Pamela, Joseph Blancet Jr., John, Karen. BSCE, The Citadel, 1958; BA in Zoology with high honors, Rutgers U., 1973, PhD in Zoology, 1979; MS in Anatomy, N.Y. Med. Coll., 1975; cert. in work life ministry, Immaculate Conception Sem., 2001. Ordained deacon Roman Cath. Ch., 1995. Design engr. Ky. Hwy. Dept., 1958-59; tech. rep. Shell Oil Co., Balt., 1968-72; asst. prof. biology Ramapo Coll., Mahwah, NJ, 1976-80, from program coord. biology to dir. campus planning, 1979-86; pres. Richardson Recreational Svcs., Inc., Kinnelon, NJ, 1981-88, Whitehall Assocs., Inc., Kinnelon, 1986—. Dir. recreational water testing programs Kinnelon Environ. Commn., 1977—82; trustee Kinnelon Bd. Edn., 1989—94; pres. Morris County Ednl. Svcs. Commn., 1991—92; edn. coun. Diocese of Paterson, 2004—; deacon Our Lady of Mt. Carmel Roman Cath. Ch., Boonton, NJ, 2001; coord. Work Life Ministry Diocese of Paterson, NJ, 1997—; bd. dirs. St. Ephrem Found., Inc., 1998—2004. Capt. U.S. Army, 1959—68, Vietnam. Mem.: Coun. Ednl. Facilities Planners, N.Y. Acad. Sci., Soc. Am. Mil. Engrs., N.J. Assn. Sch. Bus. Ofcls., N.J. Assn. Sch. Bus. Adminstrs., N.J. Sch. Bds. Assn., N.Y. Med. Coll. Alumni Assn., Rutgers U. Alumni Assn., Citadel Alumni Assn., Sigma Xi. Republican. Home and Office: 65 Fayson Lake Rd Kinnelon NJ 07405-7823 E-mail: whitehall6@msn.com.

RICHARDSON, JOSEPH HILL, physician, medical educator; b. Rensselaer, Ind., June 16, 1928; s. William Clark and Vera (Hill) R.; m. Joan Grace Meininger, July 8, 1950; children: Lois N., Ellen M., James K. MS in Medicine, Northwestern U., 1950, MD, 1953. Diplomate Am. Bd. Internal Medicine. Intern U.S. Naval Hosp., Great Lakes, Ill., 1953-54; physician internal medicine, hematology pvt. practice, Marion, Ind., 1959-67, Ft. Wayne, Ind., 1967—. Assoc. clin. prof. medicine Ind. U. Sch. Medicine, 1993—; founding mem. The Reviewing Physician Group, 2001—. Contbr. articles to profl. jours. Fellow in medicine Cleve. Clinic, 1956-59. Fellow ACP, AAAS; mem. AMA, Masons. Home and Office: 8726 Fortuna Way Fort Wayne IN 46815-5725 Office Phone: 260-485-1391.

RICHARDSON, JUDY MCEWEN, education administrator, consultant, cartoonist; b. Appleton, Wis., June 3, 1947; d. John Mitchell and Isabel Annette (Ruble) McEwen; m. Larry Leroy Richardson, Mar. 19, 1972 (div. Oct. 1983). BA in English, Stanford U., 1968, MA in Edn., 1969; PhD in Higher Edn., U. Wash., 1975. Dir. ednl. rsch. St. Olaf Coll., Northfield, Minn., 1975-79; evaluation specialist Northwest Regional Ednl. Laboratory, Portland,

1980-82; legis. rsch. analyst Ariz. State Sen., Phoenix, 1982-87; dir. sch. fin. Ariz. Dept. Edn., Phoenix, 1987-92, assoc. supt., 1992-94; edn1. cons. Scottsdale, Ariz., 1994-96; exec. dir. Ariz. State Bd. for Sch. Capital Facilities, Phoenix, 1996-98; sch. fin. cons. Peacock, Hislop, Staley & Given, Phoenix, 1998—2002, Stone & Youngberg, Phoenix, 2002—. Cartoonist for the Ariz. Capitol Times, 1995-96. Office: Stone & Youngberg LLC 2555 E Camelback Rd Ste 280 Phoenix AZ 85016 E-mail: jrichardson@syllc.com.

RICHARDSON, JULIE G. investment company executive; BA, Univ. Wis. at Madison, 1985; PhD, Stanford Univ. Graduate Sch. of Bus. Mng. dir. Merrill Lynch, 1986—98; vice chmn., co-chair JP Morgan Chase & Co., NYSE, 1998—2003; mng. dir. Providence Equity Prtnrs., Providence, 2003—. Office: Providence Equity Ptnrs 50 Kennedy Plaza, 18th Flr Providence RI 02903

RICHARDSON, KATHY KREAG, state legislator; Ed., Purdue U. Clk. Hamilton County Circuit Ct., 1984-91; mem. from 29th dist. Ind. State Ho. of Reps., 1992—. Mem. cts. and criminal code com., judiciary com., local govt., cityies and towns, county and twp. com., election and apportionment com., family and children com. Mem. Hamilton County Bd. Election Surps. Mem. Assn. Clks. Circuit Cts., Assn. Ind. Counties, Noblesville C. of C. (bd. dirs.), Noblesville H.S. Alumni Assn. (sec.), Kiwanis, Soroptimist, Republican Woman, Hamilton County Hist. Soc. Home: 1363 Grant St Noblesville IN 46060-1925 Office: Ind Ho of Reps State Capitol Indianapolis IN 46204

RICHARDSON, KELLY CHRISTOPHER, literature and language educator, writer; b. Decatur, Ga., Feb. 11, 1973; s. Alan Lee and Janet Ann Richardson; m. Elizabeth Shea Turner, Dec. 29, 2001; 1 child, Jacob Christopher. BA in English, Ga. State U., 2000, MA in Edn., 2001; PhD in Ednl. Policy and Leadership, Berne U. and Internat. Grad. Sch., St. Kitts, West Indies, 2004. Cert. help desk profl. Support Techs., Ga., 1999; T5 tchr. Ga. Profl. Standards Commn., 2001. Distbn. specialist DeKalb Med. Ctr., Decatur, Ga., 1992—94; tech. support specialist DeKalb County Sch. Sys., Decatur, Ga., 1994—99; cert. help desk profl. Support Techs., Inc., Atlanta, 1999—2000; English tchr. Gwinnett County Sch. Sys., Lilburn, Ga., 2000—01, Fulton County Sch. Sys., Atlanta, 2001—; owner Richardson Inspired Interactive, Alpharetta, Ga., 2003—. Mentor DeKalb County Sch. Sys., Decatur, Ga., 1994—99, coach, Atlanta, 1994—2000; mentor Gwinnett County Sch. Sys., Lilburn, Ga., 2000—01; sch. improvement plan com. Fulton County Sch. Sys., Atlanta, 2001—02, coach, mentor, nat. honor soc. selection com., 2001—04; copywriter/cons. Richardson Inspired Interactive, Alpharetta, Ga., 2003—04. Contbr. Milton H.S. Sch. Improvement Plan. Appointed to, West Point Mil. Acad. Mem.: Ga. Coun. Tchrs. of English, Nat. Coun. Tchrs. of English, Profl. Assn. of Ga. Educators, Pi Lambda Theta. Office Phone: 678-859-2960. Personal E-mail: kellyrichardson@bellsouth.net.

RICHARDSON, LAWRENCE, JR., Latin language educator, archeologist; b. Altoona, Pa., Dec. 2, 1920; widower. BA, Yale U., 1942, PhD in Classics, 1952. Instr. classics Yale U., New Haven, 1946-47, instr. to assoc. prof., 1955-66; prof. Duke U., Durham, N.C., 1966-78, James B. Duke prof. Latin, 1978-91, prof. emeritus, 1991—. Field archeologist Am. Acad. Rome, 1952-55, Mellon prof., 1980-81; mem. Inst. Advanced Study, 1967-68. Author: Pompeii: An Architectural History, 1988, A New Topographical Dictionary of Ancient Rome, 1992, A Catalog of Identifiable Figure Painters of Ancient Pompeii, Herculaneum and Stabiae, 2000; contbr. articles to profl. jours. Guggenheim fellow, 1958-59; Am. Council Learned Socs. fellow, 1967-68, 72-73; NEH fellow, 1979-80 Mem. German Archeol. Inst. (corr.), Am. Philol. Assn., Archeol. Inst. Am. Office: Duke U West Campus Dept Classical Studies Durham NC 27708 Office Phone: 919-684-3779. E-mail: classics@duke.edu.

RICHARDSON, MARGARET MILNER, former accounting firm executive, lawyer; b. Waco, Tex., May 14, 1943; d. James W. and Margaret Wiebusch Milner; m. John L. Richardson, July 22, 1967; 1 child, Margaret Lawrence. AB in Polit. Sci., Vassar Coll., 1965; JD with honors, George Washington U., 1968. Bar: Va. 1968, D.C. 1968, U.S. Dist. Ct. D.C. 1968, U.S. Ct. Appeals (4th, 5th, D.C. and Fed. cirs.) 1968, U.S. Claims Ct. 1969, U.S. Tax Ct. 1970, U.S. Supreme Ct. 1971. Clk. U.S. Ct. Claims, Washington; with Office Chief Counsel IRS, Washington, 1969-77; with Sutherland, Asbill and Brennan, Washington, 1977-80, ptnr., 1980-93; commr. IRS, Washington, 1993-97; ptnr. Ernst & Young, Washington, 1997—2003. Mem. commr.'s adv. group IRS, 1988-90, chair, 1990; bd. advisors George Washington Law Sch.; mem. D.C. Bar Commn. on Multidisciplinary Practice, Presdl. Commn. on Holocaust Assets; bd. dirs. Legg Mason, Inc. Contbr. articles to profl. jours. Assisted Clinton 1992 primary and gen. election campaign; served as team leader Justice Dept./Civil Rights Cluster during Presdl. Transition; mem. bd. Nat. Mus. Women in Arts, Mayor's Transition Team, 1998, Women's Campaign Fund, Nat. Cathedral Sch., Hosp. for Sick Children; trustee Eurasia Found., USA for UNHCR, Woodrow Wilson Coun., U.S.-Russia Bus. Coun., 1999-2003. Mem. ABA, D.C. Bar Assn. (tax sect.), Va. State Bar, Fed. Bar Assn. (com. taxation), Fin. Women's Assn. N.Y., Washington Women's Forum, Internat. Alliance, U.S. Russia Bus. Coun., Woodrow Wilson Ctr. Avocations: travel, antiques, needlepoint, gardening. Office Phone: 202-667-6617. Personal E-mail: margaretrichardson@yahoo.com.

RICHARDSON, MIRANDA, actress; b. Lancashire, Eng., Mar. 3, 1958; Studied, Drama Program Bristol. Stage performances include Moving, All My Sons, Who's Afraid of Virginia Woolf, The Life of Einstein, A Lie of the Mind, Edmond, Insignificance, Aunt Dan & Lemon, The Changeling, Mountain Language, Educating Rita, The Maids, The Designated Mourner, Ella Jenks; actor(TV appearances): The Hard Word, Sorrel and Son, A Woman of Substance, Underworld, Death of the Heart, The Scold's Bridle, 1998, Merlin, 1998, Alice, 1999,: (TV series) Black Adder II & III, Sweet as You Are; (TV miniseries) Die Kinder, The James Bond Story, 1999, (voice): The Miracle Maker, 2000,: (films) Dance with a Stranger, 1985, The Innocent, 1986, Empire of the Sun, 1987, Eat the Rich, 1987, Twisted Obsession, 1990, The Bachelor, 1991, Enchanted April, 1992 (Golden Globe award), Damage, 1992 (B.A.F.T.A. award for Best Supporting Actress), The Crying Game, 1992 (B.A.F.T.A. award for best supporting actress), Fatherland, HBO, 1994 (Golden Globe award), Tom & Viv, 1994 (Acad. award nominee for best actress, 1995), La Nuit et Le Moment, 1994, Kansas City, 1996, The Evening Star, 1996, Swann, 1996, Saint-Ex, 1997, The Apostle, 1997, The Designated Mourner, 1997, All for Love, 1998, Jacob Two Two and the Hooded Fang, 1998, Sleepy Hollow, 1999, Blackadder Back and Forth, 1999, Get Carter, 2000, Spider, 2001, The Hours, 2001, Rage on Placid Lake, 2002, The Lost Prince, 2002, Chicken Run, 2000, Snow White, 2000, The Actors, 2002, Waw-Waw, 2002, Falling Angels, 2003, The Prince and Me, 2003, Phantom of the Opera, 2003, Churchill The Hollywood Years, 2003, Wan-Waid, 2004, Harry Potter, 2004. Address: c/o Harriet Robinson 76 Oxford St London W1D 1BS England

RICHARDSON, NATASHA JANE, actress; b. May 11, 1963; d. Tony Richardson and Vanessa Redgrave; m. Liam Neeson, July 3, 1994; children: Micheal Richard Antonio, Daniel Jack. Trained, Ctrl. Sch. Speech and Drama. Acting debut on stage at Leeds (Eng.) Playhouse, 1983; appearances include (plays) A Midsummer's Night Dream, Hamlet, 1985, The Seagull, 1985, High Society, 1987, Anna Christie, 1993, (Tony award nominee 1993, Drama Desk award), Cabaret, 1998 (Tony award, Drama Desk award, Outer Critics award), Closer (Broadway, 1999); (TV) In the Secret State, 1984, Sherlock Holmes, The Copper Beaches, 1984, Ghosts, 1986, Suddenly Last Summer, 1992, Hostages, 1993, Zelda, 1993, (Cable Ace nomination), Haven, 2001; (films) Gothic, 1987, A Month in the Country, 1987, Patty Hearst, 1988, Fat Man and Little Boy, 1989, The Handmaid's Tale, 1990, The Comfort of Strangers, 1991, The Favor, The Watch and the Very Big Fish, 1992, Past Midnight, Widow's Peak, 1994, (Best Actress Karlovy Vary), Nell, 1995, The Parent Trap, 1998, Blowdry, 2001, Wakin Up in Reno, 2001, Maid in Manhattan, 2002. Recipient Most Promising Newcomer award Plays & Players, 1986; named Best Actress by London Theatre Critics, Plays & Players, 1990, Evening Standard Best Actress, 1990; Tony Award, actress in a musical, Cabaret, 1999.

RICHARDSON, PATRICIA, actress; b. Bethesda, Md., Feb. 23, 1951; d. Laurence Baxter and Elizabeth (Howard) R.; m. Raymond Baker, June 20, 1982; children: Henry, Roxanne, Joseph. BFA, So. Meth. U., 1972. Appearences include (Broadway) Gypsy, Loose Ends, The Wake of Jamie Foster; (off-Broadway) The Collected Works of Billy the Kid, The Frequency, Vanities, The Coroner's Plot, Hooters, Company, Fables for Friends, The Miss Firecracker Contest, Cruise Control; (regional theatre) King Lear, The Killing of Sister George, Relatively Speaking, The Importance of Being Earnest, Of Mice and Men, The Philadelphia Story, Room Service, Fifth of July, About Face; (nat. tours) Gypsy, Vanities; (films) Gas, 1972, You Better Watch Out, Lost Angels, 1988, In Country, 1988, Ulee's Gold, 1997; (TV) Double Trouble, 1984, Eisenhower & Lutz, 1988, FM, 1989-90, Home Improvement, 1991-99 (Lead Actress in a Comedy Series Emmy award nominee, 1994, Golden Globe award nominee, 1993, 94), Sophie and the Moonhanger, 1995, Undue Influence, 1996, Viva Las Nowhere, 2000. Office: William Morris Agy care Jonathon Howard 151 S El Camino Dr Beverly Hills CA 90212-2775

RICHARDSON, PATRICK WILLIAM, lawyer; b. Huntsville, Ala., Oct. 5, 1925; s. Schuyler Harris and Suzane Agnes (Smith) R.; m. Martha Alice Holliman, Dec. 23, 1949; m. Mary McAlpine Moore, Oct. 9, 1970; children: Schuyler Harris, III, James Holiman. BS, U. Ala., 1946, JD, 1948, LLD (hon.), 1976. Bar: Ala. 1948, U.S. Ct. Appeals (5th cir.) 1955, U.S. Supreme Ct. 1957, U.S. Ct. Appeals (11th cir.) 1981. Ptnr. Bell Richardson LLP, Huntsville, 1948—; dep. atty. gen. State of Ala., 1996—. Spl. cir. solicitor 23d Cir. Ala., 1951. Bd. dirs. U. Ala. Huntsville Found., 1962—, pres., 1962-74. Fellow Am. Coll. Trial Lawyers; mem. Ala. State Bar (pres. 1969-70), Huntsville-Madison County Bar Assn. (pres. 1966-67), Ala. Law Inst. (council), Am. Coll. Mortgage Attys. (regent 1975-77), Rotary. Republican. Methodist. Office: 116 Jefferson St S Huntsville AL 35801-4818 E-mail: pwr@bellrich.com.

RICHARDSON, PAUL, publishing executive; BA in Accountancy with honors, Stirling U., Scotland, 1982. Audit asst. Finnie & Co., London, 1983-87; tax mgr. Touche Ross Chartered Accts., London, 1987-89; tax planning mgr. Reed Elsevier plc, London, 1989-92; Luxembourg br. dir. Reed Stanspak BV, 1992-93; dep. mng. dir. Elsevier S.A., Switzerland, 1993-95; sr. v.p. fin., group treas. Reed Elsevier plc, N.Y.C., 1995—. Office: Reed Elsevier Inc 125 Park Ave 23rd Fl New York NY 10017 E-mail: paul.richardson@reed-elsevier.com.

RICHARDSON, RALPH C. dean; BS, Kans. State U., 1969, DVM, 1970. Intern Purdue U.; resident small animal internal medicine dept. U. Mo., Columbia, 1973; asst. prof. medicine dept. small animal clinics Purdue U., West Lafayette, Ind., 1976, assoc. prof. medicine dept. small animal clinics, 1980, prof. internal medicine and comparative oncology, 1984—98, head dept., 1987—98; dean Kans. State U. Coll. Vet. Medicine, Manhattan, 1998—. Capt. Vet. Corps U.S. Army. Named Paws Vet. of Yr., Ind. Divsn. Am. Cancer Soc., 1996. Mem.: Am. Assn. Vet. Clinicians, Am. Assn. Vet. Med. Colls., Am. Animal Hosp. Assn., Am. Coll. Vet. Internal Medicine (diplomate internal medicine, diplomate oncology), Am. Vet. Medicine Assn. Office: Kans State U Coll Vet Medicine 101 Trotter Hall Manhattan KS 66506-5601

RICHARDSON, RICHARD JUDSON, retired political science educator; b. Poplar Bluff, Mo., Feb. 16, 1935; s. Jewell Judson and Naomi Fern (Watson) R.; m. Sammie Sue Cullum, Dec. 29, 1961; children: Jon Mark, Anna Cecile, Ellen Elizabeth, Megan Leigh. BS, Harding Coll., 1957; cert., U. Dublin, 1958; MA, Tulane U., 1961, PhD, 1967. Instr. Tulane U., 1962—65; 67asst. prof. polit. sci. Western Mich. U., Kalamazoo, 1965, assoc. prof., 1967—69; vis. assoc. prof. U. Hawaii, 1967—68; from asso. prof. to v.p. acad. affairs U. N.C., Chapel Hill, 1969—91, assoc. v.p. acad. affairs univ. gen. adminstrn., 1991—92. Adj. prof. Duke U., Durham, 1972-74; provost, vice chancellor acad. affairs U. N.C., 1995-2000; cons. in field. Author: (with Kenneth Vines) The Politics of Federal Courts, 1971, (with Darlene Walker) People and the Police, 1973, (with Marian Irish, James Prothro) The Politics of American Democracy, 1981. Del. County Dem. Conv., 1972, 83; vice chmn. Dem. Party Precinct, 1983-85; chmn. bldg. fund YMCA, 1976; chmn. Carolina Challenge for endowment U. N.C., Chapel Hill, 1979-80; chmn. U. N.C. Bicentennial Observance, 1991-94; chmn. United Way, 1983, pres., 1985; pres. PTA County Coun., 1984. Recipient Edward S. Corwin award Am. Polit. Sci. Assn., 1967, Tanner Disting. Teaching award U. N.C., 1972, Univ. award for Outstanding Teaching, 1981, Thomas Jefferson award, 1987, James Johnston Disting. Tchg. award, 1993, Alumni Faculty Disting. Svc. award, 1994, Disting. Eagle Scout award Boy Scouts Am., 1998, Laura Thomas award, 1999, C. Knox Massey award, 2000, Disting. Svc. medal U. N.C. Alumni Assn., 2001; named life regent Boy Scouts Am., 1998; Edgar Stern fellow, 1959-61; NEH grantee, 1970. Mem. N.C. Polit. Sci. Assn. (pres. 1978-79), Am. Polit. Sci. Assn., So. Polit. Sci. Assn., ACLU (bd. dirs. local chpt. 1985-88, state bd. dirs. 1988-89), Order of Janus, Order of the Long Leaf Pine, Order of Golden Fleece, Order of the Grail. Home: 234 Terrells Creek Ln Pittsboro NC 27312-5145

RICHARDSON, ROBERT ALLEN, retired lawyer, educator; b. Cleve., Feb. 15, 1939; s. Allen B. and Margaret C. (Thomas) R.; m. Carolyn Eck Richardson, Dec. 9, 1968. BA, Ohio Wesleyan U., 1961; LLB, Harvard U., 1964. Bar: Ohio 1964, Hawaii 1990. Ptnr. Caffee, Halter & Griswold, Cleve., 1968-89; counsel Mancini, Rowland & Welch (formerly Case & Lynch), Maui, Hawaii, 1990—2001; lectr., affirmative action officer, atty., exec. com. Maui (Hawaii) C.C., 1989—2001; ret., 2001. Chmn. gov. fin. dept., chmn. cmty. svc. com., mem. oper. com. Caffee, Halter & Griswold; past lectr. Sch. Law Cleve. State U.; counsel Maui C. of C., Kahului, 1994-98. Pres. trustee Big Bros., Big Sisters of Maui, 1990-94; v.p., trustee, pres. Ka Hole A Ke Ole Homeless Resource Ctr., 1990—; trustee Maui Acad. Performing Arts, 1990-97, Maul Counseling Svc., 1990-96, Kapalua Music Festival, Friends of Children Advocate Ctr., Legal Aid Soc. Hawaii, pres., 1998-88; v.p., trustee, chmn. devel. com. Cleve. Playhouse, 1984-89; trustee, mem. exec. com., program chmn. Cleve. Coun. World Affairs, 1970-89; past model UN chmn. Cleve. Com. on Fgn. Rels.; trustee, mem. exec. com., budget chmn. Neighborhood Ctrs. Assn., 1980-89; trustee Maui Symphony, 1995-98, v.p., 1999—. Recipient T.S. Shinn award Maui C. of C., 2000. Mem. Rotary Club of Maui, Maui Country Club, Roufant Club (adv.), Cleve. Skating Club. Home: 1365 Lower Kula Rd Kula HI 96790-9724

RICHARDSON, ROBERT COLEMAN, physics educator, researcher; b. Washington, June 26, 1937; s. Robert Franklin and Lois (Price) R.; m. Betty Marilyn McCarthy, Sept. 2, 1962; children: Jennifer, Pamela. BS in Physics, Va. Poly. Inst. and State U., 1958, MS, 1960; PhD in Physics, Duke U., 1966. Research assoc. Cornell U., Ithaca, NY, 1966-67, asst. prof., 1968-71, assoc. prof., 1972-74, prof., 1975—86, Floyd R. Newman prof. physics, 1987—, dir., Lab. of Atomic and Solid State Physics, 1990—97, vice provost for rsch., 1998—. Chmn. Internat. Union Pure and Applied Physics Commn. (C-5), 1981-84; mem. bd. assessment Nat. Bur. Standards, 1983—; vis. scientist Bell Labs., Murray Hill, N.J., 1984; mem. Internat. Space Station Mgmt. and Cost Evaluation Task Force, NASA, 2001-; trustee Duke U., 1997—, exec. com. bd. trustees, 2001—; bd. dirs. Brookhaven Sci. Assocs. Author: College Physics, 2003; mem. editorial bd. Jour. of Low Temperature Physics, 1984—. Served to 2d lt. U.S. Army, 1959-60. Guggenheim fellow 1975-76, 82-83; recipient Simon Meml. prize Brit. Phys. Soc., 1976; co-recipient Nobel prize in physics, 1996. Fellow AAAS (bd. dirs. 2000—), Am. Phys. Soc. (Oliver E. Buckley prize 1981), Am. Philos. Soc; mem. NAS, Nat. Sci. Bd. (exec. com. 2000—). Achievements include research in experimental low temperature physics, especially the properties of liquids and solids at sub-millikelvin temperatures. Avocations: photography, gardening. Office: Cornell U Lab of Atomic and Solid Physics 529A Clark Hall Ithaca NY 14853-2501

RICHARDSON, ROBERT DALE, JR., English language educator; b. Milw., June 14, 1934; s. Robert Dale and Lucy Baldwin (Marsh) R.; m. Elizabeth Hall, Nov. 7, 1959 (div. 1987); m. Annie Dillard, Dec. 10, 1988; children: Elisabeth, Anne, Rose. AB magna cum laude in English, Harvard U., 1956, PhD in English Lit., 1961; DHL (hon.), Meadville-Lombard Theol. Sch., 2003. Instr. English Harvard U., Cambridge, Mass., 1961-63; asst. prof. English U. Denver, 1963-68, assoc. prof., 1968-72, prof., 1972-87, Lawrence C. Phipps prof. humanities, 1979-82, chmn. dept., 1968-73, pres. Univ. senate, 1972-73, assoc. dean grad. studies, 1975-76; prof. English, U. Colo., Boulder, 1987; vis. prof. letters Wesleyan U., Middletown, Conn., 1989-94. Vis. prof. Harvard U., summer 1976, CUNY, 1978, Sichuan U., 1983, U. N.C., Chapel Hill, 2002; vis. fellow Huntington Libr., 1973-74; vis. instr. Yale U., 1988; bd. dirs. David R. Godine Pub., Key West Literary Seminar. Author: Literature and Film, 1969, Henry Thoreau: A Life of the Mind, 1986 (Melcher award, 1986), Emerson: The Mind on Fire, 1995 (Parkman prize, 1995, Melcher award, 1995, Washington Irving award, 1995), Myth and Literature in the American Renaissance, 1978; author: (with Burton Feldman) The Rise of Modern Mythology 1680-1860, 1972; author: (with Allen Mandelbaum) Three Centuries of American Poetry, 1999. Trustee Meadville-Lombard Theol. Sch., 1981-87. Guggenheim fellow, 1990; recipient Acad. award in lit. Am. Acad. of Arts and Letters, 1998. Fellow Nat. Humanities Ctr.; mem. Soc. Am. Hist., Soc. Eighteenth Century Studies, Melville Soc., Author's Guild, Thoreau Soc., Emerson Soc., Assn. Lit. Scholars and Critics. Democrat. Unitarian Universalist. E-mail: rrchardson@aol.com.

RICHARDSON, R(OSS) FRED(ERICK), insurance executive; b. Renfrew, Ont., Can., Feb. 4, 1928; came to U.S., 1980; s. Garfield Newton and Grace Mary (MacLean) R.; m. Betty Blanche Betts, Feb. 4, 1972; children by previous marriage— Sheri Joan, Robert John, Paul Frederick. BA in Math. and Physics with honors, Queens U., 1950. Actuarial asst. Empire Life Ins. Co., Kingston, Ont., Can., 1950-55; sec. Maritime Life Ins. Co., Halifax, N.S., Can., 1955-59, dir. sales, 1959-65, chief exec. officer, 1967-72; mng. dir., chief exec. officer Abbey Life Ins. Co., U.K., 1972-80; group gen. mgr. Hartford Europe Group, 1975-80; sr. v.p., dir. worldwide life ins. ops. Hartford Ins. Group, Conn., 1980-83, dir. worldwide life ins. ops., 1983-88; pres., COO, Hartford Life Cos., 1983-88; pvt. ins. cons., Boca Raton, Fla., 1988; pres., CEO, Crown Life Ins. Co., 1988-93; cons. INSCE, Boca Raton, 1993—. Fellow Soc. Actuaries, Can. Inst. Actuaries. Home and Office: 300 SE 5th Ave Apt 1090 Boca Raton FL 33432-6093 Office Phone: 561-417-9390. E-mail: richard_f@bellsouth.net.

RICHARDSON, RUDY JAMES, toxicology and neurosciences educator; b. May 13, 1945; BS magna cum laude, Wichita State U., 1967; Sc.M., Harvard U., 1973, Sc.D., 1974. Diplomate Am. Bd. Toxicology. Rsch. geochemist Columbia U., N.Y.C., summer 1966; NASA trainee SUNY, Stony Brook, 1967-70; rsch. biochemist Med. Research Council, Carshalton, England, 1974-75; asst. prof. U. Mich., Ann Arbor, 1975-79, assoc. prof., 1979-84, prof. toxicology, 1984—, assoc. prof. neurotoxicology neurology dept., 1987—, Dow prof. toxicology, 1998—, acting dir. toxicology program, 1993, dir., 1994-99, dir. toxicology tng. program, 2003—. Vis. scientist Warner-Lambert Co., Ann Arbor, 1982-83; vis. prof. U. Padua, Italy, 1991; cons. NAS, Washington, 1978-79, 84, Office Tech. Assessment U.S. Congress, 1988-90, Nat. Toxic Substance Disease Registry, 1990—; mem. sci. adv. panel on neurotoxicology EPA, 1987-89; chmn. work group on neurotoxicity guidelines Orgn. for Econ. Coop. and Devel., 1990, Nat. Inst. Orgnl. Safety and Health, 1990, 94; mem. acute cholinesterase risk assessement expert panel Internat. Life Scis. Inst., 1996; mem. steering com., working group Risk Sci. Inst., 1997; presenter sci. adv. panel U.S. EPA, 1998-99, WHO, Geneva, 1998; chair expert panel on dichlorvos neurotoxicity and cholinesterase inhibition SRA Internat., Washington, 1998-99, guest panel mem. Mich. Environ. Sci. Bd., 2003—; invited spkr. in field. Mem. editorial bd. Neurotoxicology, 1980—, Toxicology and Indsl. Health, 1986—, Toxicology and Applied Pharmacology, 1989-97, Jour. Toxicology and Environ. Health, 1997—; contbr. articles to profl. jours., chpts. to books. Mem. Mich. Lupus Found., Ann Arbor, 1979—. Grantee NIH, 1977-86, 95—, EPA, 1977-86, U.S. Civilian R & D Found., 1996—, U.S. Army Rsch. Office, 2002—. Mem. AAAS, Am. Coll. Toxicology, Soc. Toxicology (pres. neurotoxicology sect. 1987-88, councillor 1988-89, co-recipient Best Paper award 2003), Soc. for Neurosci., Am. Diabetes Assn., Am. Chem. Soc., Internat. Soc. Neurochemistry, Internat. Brain Rsch. Orgn. Achievements include co-discoverer (with B.R. Dudek) of lymphocyte neuropathy target esterase (NTE); development of lymphocyte NTE as biomarker of exposure to neuropathic organophosphates; refinement of NTE assay for use in neurotoxicity testing; use of protein mass spectrometry in mechanistic toxicology and sensor development. Office: U Mich Toxicology Program M 7525 Sph # 2 Ann Arbor MI 48109 E-mail: rjrich@umich.edu.

RICHARDSON, SALLY KEADLE, health care administrator; b. Mar. 2, 1933; d. Okey P. and Viola Miriam (Graybeal) Keadle; m. Don Rule Richardson, Dec. 15, 1961; children: Miriam Paige, Ruth Evan. AB, Vassar Coll., 1954. Regional pub. info. rep. Columbia Gas Sys., Charleston, W.Va., 1958-62; dir. Children's Mus., Charleston, 1963; coord. space-related sci. project Kanawha County Schs., Charleston, 1967-68; vol. dir. Rockefeller for Gov. Campaign, Charleston, 1972, program dir., 1976, 80; dir. admissions W.Va. Wesleyan Coll., Buckhannon, 1974-75; spl. asst. Office of Gov. State of W.Va., 1977, dep. commr. dept. welfare, 1978-79, dep. dir. dept. health, 1979-83; chmn. W.Va. Health Care Cost Rev. Authority, Charleston, 1983-85. Health care cons., Charleston, 1985-89; dir. W.Va. Pub. Employees Ins. Agy., Charleston, 1989-93; vice-chmn. W.Va. Health Care Planning Task Force, 1992-93; mem. White House Health Care Reform Task Force, Washington, 1993; dir. Medicaid Bur., Health Care Financing Adminstrn., U.S. DHHS, Balt., 1993-96; acting dep. adminstr. HCFA, U.S. DHHS, Washington, 1996-97; dir. HCFA Ctr. for Medicaid and State Ops., 1997-99; mem. U.S. DHHS Governing Coun. on Children and Youth, 1993-97, co-chmn. U.S. DHHS Children's Health Initiative, 1997-99; co-chmn. U.S. DHHS Home and Cmty. Based Svcs. Task Force, 1996-99; mem. U.S. DHHS Pub. Health Coun.'s D.C. Task Force, 1994-99; mem. Nat. Adv. Com. on Rural Health, DHHS, 2000-04; bd. dirs. Moline Healthcare, Inc. W.Va. rep. Task Force on So. Children, So. Growth Policies Bd., 1978-79; co-chmn. exec. com. W.Va. Internat. Yr. of Child, 1979; staff mem. Com. on Human Resources Nat. Gov. Assn., 1983-85; bd. trustees U. Charleston, 1994-; bd. dirs. Children's Home Soc., Charleston, 1999—. Mem. Acad. Health, Nat. Rural Health Assn. Democrat. Office: WVa U Inst Health Policy Rsch 3110 Maccorkle Ave SE Rm 3015 Charleston WV 25304-1210

RICHARDSON, SHIRLEY MAXINE, editor; b. Rising Sun, Ind., May 3, 1931; d. William Fenton and Mary (Phillips) Keith; m. Arthur Lee Richardson, Feb. 11, 1950; children: Mary Jane Hunt, JoDee Mayfield, Steven Lee Richardson. Pers. mgr. Mayhill Pubs., Knightstown, Ind., 1967-87, prodn. mgr., 1975-87, editor, 1967-87; info. staff, assoc. editor Ind. Farm Bur., Inc., 1987-89, dir. info. and pub. rels., 1989-94; genealogy editor AntiqueWeek, 1996-2001; exec. editor Knightstown Banner, 2001—. Avocations: travel, reading, boating, quilting. Home: 366 E Carey St Knightstown IN 46148-1208 Office: 24 N Washington St Knightstown IN 46148-1242 Office Phone: 765-345-2292.

RICHARDSON, STEPHEN GILES, biotechnology company executive; b. Mpls., Sept. 17, 1951; s. Richard Giles and Constance Bernice (Krieg) R. BA cum laude, Wartburg Coll., 1972; MS, U. Iowa, 1974, PhD, 1981; postdoctoral, Duke U., 1982-84. Cert. mgmt. profl. Project Mgmt. Inst. Ter. mgr. Wyeth Labs., Phila., 1974-76; rsch. asst. U. Iowa, Iowa City, 1976-82; rsch. assoc. Duke, Durham, N.C., 1982-84; scientist Becton Dickinson Rsch. Ctr., Research Triangle Park, N.C., 1984-86; devel. group leader Dade Diagnostics divsn. Baxter Healthcare, Miami, Fla., 1986; rsch. group leader Organon Teknika Corp divsn., Akzo Nobel N.V, Durham, N.C., 1987-89, R & D sect. head, internat. R & D area mgr., 1989-90, program mgr., 1990-94, assoc. dir., head product devel., 1994-96, project mgmt. dir., microbiology bus. area R & D, 1997—2001; program dir. global mktg. and strategic devel. bioMerieux, Inc., Durham, NC, 2001—. Contbr. articles to profl. jours.; patentee in field; bd. readers IVD Technology Mag. Co-founder Libertarian Party Minn., Mpls., 1972, del. nat. conv., 1998; exec. sec. Iowa Coun. to Repeal Conscription, Waterloo, 1971. Mem. Am. Soc. for Microbiology, Am. Chem. Soc., Am. Assn. for Clin. Chemistry, Royal Soc. Chemistry (U.K.), N.Y. Acad. Scis., Electronic Frontier Found., Sigma Xi. Achievements include discovery of transient neutral heteroaryl radicals as viable organic synthetic intermediates, such as, to halopurine nucleosides; MDA-180 hemostasis analyzer system, BacT/ALERT 3D blood culture system family. Office: bioMerieux Inc 100 Rodolphe St Durham NC 27712-9402 E-mail: BTA3D@aol.com.

RICHARDSON, THADDEUS MAURICE, funeral director; b. Amite, La., June 21, 1965; s. Samuel Richardson, Dorothy (Johnson) Richardson. FSC, Commonwealth Coll., 1985; GSC, So. U., 1986; NC, Southeaster La. U., 1997. Dir. Richardson Funeral Home, Hammond, La., 1985—. Author: How To Get the Strong Man in Marriage, 2000. Bd. dirs. La. State Bd. Funeral Dirs., New Orleans; city coun. bd. State of La., Baton Rouge, 1996—2000; v.p. L.M.A.B.C., Baton Rouge, 1998—2000; pres. L.E.T.A., Greensburg, La., 1995—96, P.D.A., Amite, 2000—; bd. dirs. Health Care, Independence, La., S.E.F.A., Covington, La., R.F.C., Amite. Mem.: Progressive Citizens (pres. 2001, Star award 2002), Mt. Nebo Grand Lodge (Master 1994). Democrat. Avocations: farming, fishing, football, hunting, racing. Home: 411 E Palmetto St Amite LA 70422 Office: Richardson Funeral Home 1601 W Thomas St Hammond LA 70404

RICHARDSON, THOMAS HAMPTON, design consulting engineer; b. St. Louis, Nov. 25, 1941; s. Claude Hampton and Pearl Lily (Burks) R.; m. Lois Louise Atteberry June 8, 1963; children: Shelley Ann, David Hampton, Stephanie Lynn. BTEE, Wash. U., St. Louis, 1974. Registered profl. engr., Mo., Ill., Ind., Kans., Iowa, Fla., Ky., Miss. Elec. project designer Fruco Engrs. Inc., St. Louis, 1967-68; mgr., mech./elec. engr. MBA Engrs. Inc., St. Louis, 1968-74, Kenneth Balk and Assoc., St. Louis, 1974-76; instr. elec. engring. Wash. U., St. Louis, 1976; v.p., chief engr. John F. Steffen Assoc., St. Louis, 1976-79; prin. ptnr. Keeler, Webb and Richardson, St. Louis, 1979-94; pres./owner The Richardson Engring. Group, St. Louis, 1979—. Contbr. articles to profl. jours. Recipient Internat. Lighting Design award Illuminating Engr. Soc. St. Louis 1985, Edwin F. Guth award of Merit Illuminating Engr. Soc. N.Am. 1986. Mem. NSPE, ASHRAE, Illuminating Engring. Soc. (past pres.), Soc. for Mktg. Profl. Svcs. (v.p.), Mo. Soc. Profl. Engrs. (govt. rels. com.), Engr's Club St Louis, Nat. Fire Protection Assn., Green Turtle Bay Yacht Club, Grand Lake Yacht Club, Ky. Lake Club, U.S. Coast Guard Aux. Avocations: sailing, fiction writing, painting, photography. Office: The Richardson Engring 7227 Devonshire Ave Saint Louis MO 63119-3419

RICHARDSON, TOM (EDWARD THOMPSON RICHARDSON), artist; b. Upper Darby, Pa, Aug. 12, 1948; s. Edward Thompson and Elizabeth Catherine (Fredericks) R.; m. Margaret Reed Colvin, July 1, 1972; 1 child, Edward Thompson III. BFA, U. Pa., 1974, MFA, 1975. Scenic artist San Francisco Opera Assn., 1979-84, San Francisco Ballet Assn., 1982-84; scenic designer music dept. Stanford U., Calif., 1980-84; scenic designer San Jose Opera Assn., Calif., 1985; lead scenic artist FM Prodn., Brisbane, Calif., 1984-87, artist-in-charge, 1987-93. Scenic artist: (films) James and the Giant Peach; Down Periscope; Phenomenon; A Smile Like Yours; Rainmaker; Flubber; What Dreams May Come; The Horse Whisperer; Mumford; Bicentennial Man; Invisible Circus; A Woman on Top; Boys and Girls; Bartleby; Sweet November; Forty Days and Forty Nights; High Crimes; The Matrix Reloaded; Revolutions; Twisted; The Assassination of Richard Nixon; Bee Season; (TV series) Nash Bridges; Partners. Mem. Internat. Alliance Theatrical Stage Employees (Bay area bus. rep. 1984-88, Bay area field rep. 2000—, pres. 1998—). Home: 87 Roosevelt Cir Palo Alto CA 94306-4219

RICHARDSON, VANESSA, education educator; b. Camp Lejeune, N.C., Aug. 31, 1960; d. Matthew and Margaret Ethel (Cox) R. Cert. in traffic mgmt., U.S. Army Transp. Sch., Ft. Eustis, Va., 1985; BS in Urban and Regional Planning, East Carolina U., 1988; MS in Safety and Driver Edn., N.C. Agrl. and Tech. State U., 1990, MS in Reading Edn., 1992; PhD, U. N.C., Greensboro, 1998. Cert. G grad. level tchr., N.C. Planning intern Pitt County Econ. Devel. Commn., Greenville, N.C., summer 1987; grad. intern in transp. planning City of Greensboro, 1989; transp. adminstrn. mgmt. clk. USMCR, Greensboro, 1985-90; planning/grants coord. City of Fayetteville, N.C., 1990-91; rsch. asst. Sch. Bus. and Econs. N.C. Agrl. and Tech. State U., Greensboro, 1988, grad. asst. Sch. Tech., 1989-90, tutor coord., 1991-92, instr. Upward Bound program, 1992-93, instr., tech. assoc., 1992-94; grad. tchg. asst. U. N.C., Greensboro, 1993-97; cmty. rels. coord. Sch. Tech., N.C. A&T State U, Greensboro, 1997—. Co-author: New Teacher Handbook for Trade and Industrial Educators, 1993, Research on Teaming: Insights from Selected Studies; also author articles. Vol. Greater Greensboro Cities in Schs., 1991-92; coord. Fayetteville Area Sys. Transit campaign United Way. With USMCR. Mem. NEA, ASCD, N.C. Assn. Educators, Internat. Reading Assn., Soc. Tech. Comm., Assn. Grad. Students (v.p.), Am. Planning Assn., N.C. Pub. Transp. Assn., N.C. Driver and Traffic Safety Edn. Assn., Gamma Theta Upsilon, Epsilon Pi Tau, Delta Nu Alpha. Avocations: physical fitness, health, travel. Home: 1504 Cedar Ln Kinston NC 28501-5844

RICHARDSON, WALTER JOHN, architect; b. Long Beach, Calif., Nov. 14, 1926; s. Walter Francis and Ava Elizabeth (Brown) R.; m. Marilyn Joyce Brown, June 26, 1949 (div. 1982); children: Mark Steven, Glenn Stewart; m. Mary Sue Sutton, Dec. 4, 1982. Student, UCLA, 1944—45, Long Beach City Coll., 1946; BA, U. Calif., Berkeley, 1950. Registered arch., Ala., Ariz., Calif., Colo., Fla., Hawaii, Ill., Kans., Md., Mass., Nev., N.J., N.Y., Okla., Oreg., Tex., Utah, Vt., Va., Wash. Draftsman Wurster, Bernardi, Emmons, San Francisco, 1950-51, Skidmore, Owings & Merrill, San Francisco, 1951; designer Hugh Gibbs Arch., Long Beach, 1952-58; ptnr. Thomas & Richardson Archs., Long Beach, Costa Mesa, 1958-70; pres. Walter Richardson Assocs. Archs., Newport Beach, Calif., 1970-74; chmn. bd. Richardson, Nagy, Martin Archs. and Planners, Newport Beach, 1974—. Co-author: The Architect and the Shelter Industry, 1975. Chmn. Planning Commn., City of Orange, Calif., 1967-68. With USAF, 1945. Recipient over 200 Gold Nugget Design awards Pacific Coast Builders Conf., San Francisco, 1969-96, 12 Builders Choice Design awards Builder Mag.; named Arch. of Yr. Profl. Builder mag., 1986. Fellow AIA (pres. Orange County chpt. 1970, chmn. nat. housing com. 1976, 77 design awards); mem. Nat. Assn. Home Builders, Nat. Coun. Archtl. Registration Bds., Urban Land Inst., Alpha Tau Omega. Republican. Avocations: photography, downhill skiing, travel. Office: RNM Archs Planners 4611 Teller Ave Ste 100 Newport Beach CA 92660-2104 Office Phone: 949-752-1800.

RICHARDSON, WILLIAM BERKLEY, lawyer, b. Parkersburg, W.Va., Jan. 2, 1923; s. William Berkley and Jane Butcher (Carle) R.; m. Edythe Ourbacker, Feb. 2, 1951; children— William B., Jane Richardson McCabe. B.A. in Bus. Adminstrn., Va. Poly. Inst. and State U., 1947; LL.B., W.Va. U., 1951. Bar: W.Va., U.S. Dist. Ct. (no. dist.) W.Va., U.S. Dist. Ct. (so. dist.) W.Va., U.S. Ct. Claims Practice, Parkersburg, W.Va., 1951—; ptnr. Richardson & Richardson, 1977— . Bd. dirs. W.Va. Jaycees; chmn. Wood County (W.Va.) Democratic Party. Served to 1st lt. U.S. Army; World War II. Mem. Wood County Bar (past pres.), W.Va. Bar. Baptist. Clubs: Masons, Elks. Address: PO Box 266-Richardson PO Box 325- Parkersburg WV 26102-0325

RICHARDSON, WILLIAM BLAINE, governor; b. Pasadena, Calif., Nov. 15, 1947; m. Barbara Flavin, 1972. BA, Tufts U., Medford, Mass., 1970; MA, Fletcher Sch. Law and Diplomacy, 1971. Mem. staff U.S. Ho. of Reps., 1971-72, Dept. State, 1973-75; mem. staff fgn. relations com. U.S. Senate, 1975-78; exec. dir. N. Mex. State Democratic Com., 1978, Bernalillo County Democratic Com., 1978; businessman Santa Fe, N. Mex., 1978-82; mem. 98th-103rd Congresses from 3rd N.Mex. dist., Washington, 1982-96; democratic chief dep. majority whip 103d Congress; permanent US rep. UN, 1997-98; sec. U.S. Dept. Energy, Washington, 1998-2001; sr. mng. dir. Kissinger McLarty, Washington, 2001—02; gov. State of N. Mex., Santa Fe, 2003—. Ranking minority mem. Resources Com. on Nat. Pks., Forests and Lands; mem. Select Com. on intelligence, Helsinki Commn.; adj. prof. pub. policy Harvard U., 2001; cons. Salomon Smith Barney Vice chair Dem. Nat. Com.; active Big Bros.-Big Sisters, Santa Fe. Mem. Santa Fe Hispanic C. of C., Santa Fe C. of C., Council Fgn. Relations, NATO 2000 Bd., Congl. Hispanic Caucus, Am. G.I. Forum Office: Office of the Gov State Capitol Rm 400 Santa Fe NM 87501

RICHARDSON-MELECH, JOYCE SUZANNE, music educator, singer; b. Perth Amboy, N.J., Nov. 15, 1957; d. Herbert Nathaniel and Fannie Elaine (Franklin) Richardson; m. Gerald Melech, July 28, 1990. MusB, Westminster Choir Coll., 1979, MusM, 1981; postgrad., Rutgers U., 1999—. Cert. music tchr. N.J., supr. N.J. Musical play dir. Perth Amboy H.S., 1989-92, asst. band dir., 1984-94; music tchr. Perth Amboy Bd. Edn., 1981—, gifted and talented music tchr., 1992-96; vocal soloist N.Y.C. Vocal soloist N.Y. Philharm. and Westminster Symphonic Choir, 1977, United Moravian Ch., N.Y.C., 1980-81, Ctrl. Jersey Concert Orch., Perth Amboy, 1994-96; mezzo-soprano soloist in The Messiah, John Hus Moravian Ch., Bklyn., 1998; master tchrs. collaborative with N.J. Symphony Orch., 2000-01, 03. Contbg. author: Teacher's Resource Book, 2000, 2001, 2003; actor: Perth Amboy Adult Cmty. Theatre; illustrator: The Peacock of Half-Way Tree: A Caribbean Fable, 2004. Participant Perth Amboy Adult Cmty. Theatre, 1983. Recipient award for excellence in tchg., NJ Symphony Orch., 2000, 2001, 2003. Mem. NAACP, Am. Fedn. Tchrs., Am. Fedn. Musicians (local 204-373), Music Educators Nat. Conf., Internat. Platform Assn., Am. Mus. Natural History (assoc.), Alliance for Arts Edn. N.J., Ctrl. Jersey Music Educators, N.J. Music Educators Assn., Alpha Phi Omega. Democrat. Mem. African Meth. Episcopal Zion Ch. Avocations: needlepoint, cross-stitch, knitting, sewing, crocheting. Home: 148 Carson Ct Somerset NJ 08873-4790 Office: Samuel Shull Sch 380 Hall Ave Perth Amboy NJ 08861-3205 Office Phone: 732-376-6060 26662. Business E-Mail: joycrichardson@paps.net.

RICHART, DOUGLAS STEPHEN, retired chemist; b. Harrisburg, Pa., June 6, 1931; s. Howard Winans and M. M. Richart; m. Joan J. Lombardo, Apr. 19, 1986; children: Deborah, Sandra, Stephen, Catherine. BS in Chemistry, Franklin and Marshall Coll., Lancaster, Pa., 1954. Rsch. chemist Union Carbide Corp., Bound Brook, N.J., 1954-60; group leader R&D, Polymer Corp., Reading, Pa., 1960-65, mgr. R&D coatings, 1965-86; mgr. R&D chem. divsn. Morton Internat. Powder Coating, Reading, Pa., 1986-89, sr. scientist, 1989-94; pres. coating powder cons. D.S. Richart Assocs., Reading, Pa., 1994—2002, ret., 2002. Author: in field; patentee powder coatings. Named to Powder Coating Inst. Hall of Fame, 2003. Mem. AAAS, Am. Chem. Soc., Soc. Plastics Engrs., Nat. Assn. Corrosion Engrs., The Powder Coating Inst. Republican. Personal E-mail: dsrichart@aol.com.

RICHELSON, PAUL WILLIAM, curator; b. Montpelier, Idaho, Sept. 27, 1939; s. Paul Newton and June (Quayle) R. BA, Yale U., 1961; MFA, Princeton U., 1967, PhD, 1974. Asst. prof. Lawrence U., Appleton, Wis., 1970-77, U. Denver, 1977-84; asst. dir., curator Trisolini Gallery of Ohio U., Athens, 1984-87; chief curator Grand Rapids (Mich.) Mus., 1987-91; curator of Am. art Mobile Mus. Art, Mobile, Ala., 1991-97, asst. dir., chief curator, 1997—. Author: (book) Studies in the Personal Imagery Collection of 20th Prints Ohio University, 1985, (catalogue) The Golden Age 19th Century Prints by David Roberts, 1988, Lee Loring: A Southern Sophisticate, 1992, Modernism and American Painting of the 1930s, 1993, ThirtySomething, 1994, Alabama Impact: Contemporary Artists with Alabama Ties, 1995, Louise Lyons Heustis (1865-1951): A Retrospective, 1995, The French Connection: Jean Simon Chaudron Returns To Mobile, 1996, John Roderick Dempster MacKenzie (1865-1941): A Retrospective, 1997, Celebrating the Creative Spirit, 1998, Contemporary Southeastern Furniture, 1998, Coming Home: American Paintings, 1930-1950, from the Schoen Collection, 2003. Lt. (j.g.) USN, 1961-63. Recipient Elizabeth B. Gould Rsch. award Mobile Hist. Devel. Commn., 1997; Fulbright-Hays fellow to Italy, 1967-69; Mus. Purchase Plan grantee Nat. Endowment for the Arts, 1991; grantee Mus. Loan Network, 2002. Mem. Southeastern Museums Conf. Home: 6427 Grelot Rd Apt 405 Mobile AL 36695 2630 Office: Mobile Museum of Art 4850 Museum Dr Mobile AL 36608-1917 Fax: 251-208-5201. E-mail: prichelson@mobilemuseumofart.com.

RICHENBURG, ROBERT BARTLETT, artist, retired art educator; b. Boston, July 14, 1917; s. Frederick Henry and Spray (Bartlett) R.; m. Libby Chic Peltyn, Nov. 11, 1942 (dec. 1977); 1 child, Ronald P.; m. Margaret Kerr, Feb. 9, 1980; stepchildren: William Blakeley Kerr, David Garrett Kerr, Margaret Frances Kerr. Student, Boston U., George Washington U., Corcoran Sch. Art, Art Students League N.Y., Ozenfant Sch. Fine Arts, Hans Hofmann Sch. Art. Tchr. painting Schrivenham Am. U., Eng., 1945; instr. Coll. City N.Y., 1947-52, Cooper Union, 1954-55; instr., dir. Bklyn.-Queens Central YMCA, 1947-51; instr. NYU, 1960-61, Pratt Inst., Bklyn., 1951-64; assoc. prof. art Cornell U., Ithaca, N.Y., 1964-67; prof. art Hunter Coll., N.Y.C., 1967-70, Aruba (Netherlands Antiles) Research Center, 1970, Ithaca Coll., 1970-83, mem. council on arts. Panelist in field. One-man shows include Hendler Gallery, Phila., NY Artists Gallery, Tibor DeNagy Gallery, Hansa Gallery, NY, Dwan Gallery, LA, Santa Barbara Mus. (Calif.), Dayton Art Inst., Dana Arts Center Colgate U., Ithaca Coll. Mus. Art, Grad. Sch. Bus. Cornell U., Rose Art Mus., Brandeis U., U. Art Gallery, Staller Ctr., SUNY Stonybrook, Pollock-Krasner House and Study Ctr., East Hampton, N., Arlene Bujese Gallery, East Hampton, Guild Hall Mus., East Hampton, MB Modern Gallery, NY, 2001, Thomas McCormick Gallery, Chgo., 2002, David Findlay Jr. Fine Arts, NY, 2003-04 others; exhibited in group shows at Mus. Modern Art, Solomon Guggenheim Mus., NYC, Chrysler Art Mus., Yale Art Gallery, Whitney Mus., NYC, Univ. Art Mus., Austin, Tex., Balt. Mus., Cocoran Mus. Art, Washington, Bklyn. Mus., Knox Albright Mus., Buffalo, Larry Aldrich Mus., Seattle Art Mus., Boston Mus. Fine Arts, others; represented in permanent collections Mus. Modern Art, Whitney Mus., Hirschorn Mus., Inst. Valenciano de Arte Moderno, Valencia, Spain, Phila. Mus. Art, Pasadena Mus. Fine Art, U. Art Mus. U. Calif., Berkeley, U. Tex. Art Mus., Austin, Zimmerli Art Mus. Rutgers U., Rose Art Mus. Brandeis U., Coll. William and Mary, Chrysler Mus. Art, Hofstra U. Mus., Johnson Mus. Cornell U., Ithaca Coll. Mus., Parrish Mus. Art, Southampton, Guild Hall Mus., East Hampton, Heckscher Mus. Art, Huntington, NY, others. Served with AUS, 1942-45. Mem. Am. Assn. U. Profs., Coll. Art Assn., Internat. Platform Assn., Art Students League N.Y. (life) Clubs: (N.Y.C.).

RICHENS, MURIEL WHITTAKER, marriage and family therapist, educator; b. Prineville, Oreg. d. John Reginald and Victoria Cecilia (Pascale) Whittaker; children: Karen, John, Candice, Stephanie, Rebecca. BS, Oreg. State U.; MA, San Francisco State U., 1962; postgrad., U. Calif., Berkeley, 1967-69, U. Birmingham, Eng., 1973, U. Soria, Spain, 1981. Lic. sch. adminstr., tchr. 7-12, pupil pers. specialist, Calif.; lic. marriage and family therapist, Calif. Tchr. Springfield (Oreg.) High Sch.; instr. San Francisco State U.; instr., counselor Coll. San Mateo, Calif., San Mateo High Sch. Dist., 1963-86; therapist AIDS Health Project U. Calif., San Francisco, 1988—; marriage and family therapist, pvt. practice San Mateo. Guest West German-European Acad. seminar, Berlin, 1975. Lifeguard, ARC. Postgrad. student Ctr. for Human Communications, Los Gatos, Calif., 1974, U. P.R., 1977, U. Guadalajara (Mex.), 1978, U. Durango (Mex.), 1980, U. Guanajuato (Mex.) 1982. Mem. U. Calif. Berkeley Alumni Assn., Am. Contract Bridge League (Diamond Life Master, cert. instr., cert. dir.), Women in Comm., Computer-Using Educators, Commonwealth Club, Pi Lambda Theta, Delta Pi Epsilon. Republican. Roman Catholic. Home and Office: 1112 SW Chestnut Dr Portland OR 97219-2169

RICHERSON, HAL BATES, physician, internist, allergist, immunologist, educator; b. Phoenix, Feb. 16, 1929; s. George Edward and Eva Louise (Steere) R.; m. Julia Suzanne Bradley (dec. 1996), Sept. 5, 1953; children: Anne, George, Miriam, Julia, Susan. BS with distinction, U. Ariz., 1950; MD, Northwestern U., 1954. Diplomate Am. Bd. Internal Medicine, Am. Bd. Allergy and Immunology, Bd. Diagnostic Lab. Immunology; lic. physician, Iowa. Intern Kansas City (Mo.) Gen. Hosp., 1954-55; resident in pathology St. Luke's Hosp., Kansas City, 1955-56; trainee in neuropsychiatry Brooke Army Hosp., San Antonio, 1956; resident in medicine U. Iowa Hosps., Iowa City, 1961-64, fellow in allergy and immunology, 1964-66; fellow in immunology Mass. Gen. Hosp., Boston, 1968-69; instr. internal medicine U. Iowa Coll. Medicine, Iowa City, 1964-66, asst. prof., 1966-70, assoc. prof., 1970-74, prof., 1974-98, prof. emeritus, 1998—; acting dir. divsn. allergy/applied immunology U. Iowa Hosps. and Clinics, Iowa City, 1970-72, dir. allergy and clin. immunology sect., 1972-78, dir. divsn. allergy and immunology, 1978-91; gen. practice, asst. to Gen. Surgeon Ukiah, Calif., 1958; gen. practice medicine Holbrook, Ariz., 1958-61. Vis. lectr. medicine Harvard U. Sch. Medicine, Boston, 1968-69; vis. prof., rsch. scientist U. London and Brompton Hosp., 1984; prin. investigator Nat. Heart, Lung and Blood Inst., 1971-94, mem. pulmonary diseases adv. com., 1983-87; prin. investigator Nat. Inst. Allergy and Infectious Diseases, 1983-94; dir. Nat. Inst. Allergy and Infectious Diseases' Asthma and Allergic Diseases Ctr., U. Iowa, 1983-94; mem. VA Merit Rev. Bd. in Respiration, 1981-84; mem. com. NIH Gen. Clin. Rsch. Ctrs., 1989-93; mem. rev. reserve NIH, 1993-98; mem. bd. sci. advisors Merck Inst., 1990-94; presenter lectures, seminars, continuing edn. courses; mem. numerous univ., coll. and hosp. coms., 1970—; cons. Merck Manual, 1982, 87, 92, 96-97. Contbr. numerous articles and revs. to profl. jours., chpts. to books; reviewer Sci., Jour. Immunology, Jour. Allergy and Clin. Immunology, Am. Rev. Respiratory Disease, New Eng. Jour. Medicine, Ann. Internal Medicine. Served to capt. U.S. Army, 1956-58. NIH fellow 1968-69. Fellow ACP (Laureate award 1996), Am. Acad. Allergy Asthma & Immunology (Disting. Clinician award 1998); mem. AMA (mem. residency and rev. com. for allergy and immunology; mem. accreditation coun. for grad. med. edn. 1980-85, vice-chmn. 1984-85), AAAS, Iowa Med. Soc., Iowa Thoracic Soc. (chmn. program com. 1964-65, 69-71, pres. 1972-73, mem. exec. com. 1972-74), Am. Thoracic Soc. (bd. dirs. 1981-82, councilor assembly on allergy and immunology 1980-81, mem. nominating com. 1988-90), Iowa Clin. Med. Soc., Am. Fedn. Clin. Rsch., Am. Assn. Immunologists, Ctrl. Soc. Clin. Rsch. (chmn. sect. on allergy-immunology 1980-81, mem. coun. 1981-84), Alpha Omega Alpha. Avocations: reading, trombonist, swimming, scuba diving. Home: 331 Lucon Dr Iowa City IA 52246-3300 Office: U Iowa Health Care Dept Internal Medicine 200 Hawkins Dr Iowa City IA 52242-1009 Office Phone: 319-356-2117. Personal E-mail: richersonh@mchsi.com. Business E-Mail: hal-richerson@uiowa.edu.

RICHERT, JOHN ROLIN, neuroimmunologist, educator; b. Boston, June 9, 1945; s. Daniel Arnold and Esther (Beamer) Richert; m. Nancy Dembeck, July 5, 1969. BA, Cornell U., 1966; MD, U. Rochester, 1970. Diplomate Am. Bd. Med. Examiners, Am. Bd. Psychiatry and Neurology. Intern, resident in medicine Strong Mcml. Hosp. U. Rochester, NY, 1970-72; resident in neurology Mayo Clinic, Rochester, Minn., 1974-77; fellow Nat. Multiple Sclerosis Soc. NIH, Bethesda, Md., 1977-80; rsch. asst. prof. neurology Georgetown U. Med. Ctr., Washington, 1980-83, asst. prof. neurology, 1983-89, assoc. prof. neurology, 1989-93, prof. neurology, 1993—, prof., chair dept. microbiology and immunology, 1997—. Mem. physician adv. bd. Biogen Inc., Cambridge, Mass., 1994-2000; cons. Immunex, Inc., Seattle, 1998-2000; bd. dirs. Georgetown U. Hosp., Washington; external adv. com. VA Multiple Sclerosis Ctr. of Excellence, U. Md. Multiple Sclerosis Ctr., Balt.; sci. adv. bd. TolerGenics, Inc., Rockville, Md.; cons. Health Sci. Ctr. for Continuing Med. Edn., NY, 2003. Mem. editl. bd.: NeuroRx. Mem. immunol. scis. study sect. NIH, 1989, mem. mental health AIDS and immunology rsch. study sect., 1992, mem. neurol. disorders program project com., 2003, Brain Disorders and Clin. Neuroscience spl. emphasis panel. Maj. USAF, 1972-74. Fellow Am. Acad. Neurology; mem. Internat. Soc. Neuroimmunology, Nat. Multiple Sclerosis Soc. (med. adv. bd. 1988-91, 93-96, profl. adv. com. 1988—, sci. peer rev. com. 1993-98), Am. Neurol. Assn., Am. Assn. Immunologists, Assn. Med. Sch. Microbiology and Immunology Chairs (pub. policy com. 2002-, chair 2004-), Am. Soc. for Biochemistry and Molecular Biology, Am. Soc. for Exptl. Neurotherapeutics, Alpha Omega Alpha. Avocations: tennis, golf, skiing. Office: Georgetown U Med Ctr 3900 Reservoir Rd NW Washington DC 20057 Office Phone: 202-687-1513. Business E-Mail: richertj@georgetown.edu.

RICHESON, HUGH ANTHONY, JR., lawyer; b. Aberdeen, Md., Apr. 22, 1947; s. Hugh Anthony Sr. and Mary Evelyn (Burford) R.; m. Melissa Anne Baum, Apr. 4, 1970; children: Hugh Anthony III, Heidi E., Holly K., Hagin G., Herald Joshua. BBA, U. Richmond, 1969; JD, U. Fla., 1973; student, St. Catherine's Coll., Oxford U., Eng., summer 1973. Bar: Fla. 1974, U.S. Dist. Ct. (mid. dist.) Fla. 1975, U.S. Supreme Ct. 1992. Assoc. Bryant, Dickens, Rumph, Franson & Miller, Jacksonville, Fla., 1974—76, ptnr., 1977; sole practice Orange Park, Fla., 1977—82; ptnr. Smith, Hallowes & Richeson, Orange Park, 1982—83; sole practice Palm Harbor, Fla., 1984—98; of counsel Carey Leisure & Battle, Clearwater, Fla., 1998—. Author: Legally Yours, 2002. Pres. Full Gospel Bus. Men's Fellowship Internat., Orange Park, 1983-84, Palm Harbor, 1985-92, field rep., 1987—. Mem. Fla. Coun. Bar Assn. Pres. (life), Gideons Internat., Phi Delta Phi, Sigma Phi Epsilon. Republican. Methodist.

RICHESON, JAMES G., JR., dentist; m. Nancy Richeson; 1 child, Suzanne. DDS, Georgetown U. Dentist, Washington. Recipient Disting. Svc. award, Georgetown Dental Alumni, 2003. Fellow: Pierre Fauchard Acad., Am. Coll. Dentists, Acad. Gen. Dentistry (pres.-elect 2001—02, pres. 2002—03, v.p., treas., bd. trustee, budget and fin. com., regional dir., Found. bd. dirs.); mem.: ADA (alt. del. 2001—), DC Dental Soc. (The Sterling V. Meade award 2004), DC Acad. Gen. Dentistry (past pres.), Georgetown U. Alumni Club of Met. Washington (past pres.). Office: 4400 Jenifer St NW Ste 340 Washington DC 20015-2113 Office Phone: 202-364-5246.

RICHEY, ELLEN, credit card company executive; BA summa cum laude, Harvard U.; JD, Stanford U. Law clk. Hon. Lewis F. Powell, Jr. U.S. Supreme Ct.; law clk. Hon. Charles B. Renfrew U.S. Dist. Ct. (no. dist.); ptnr. Farella, Braun & Martel, San Francisco, 1980—94; from gen. counsel, sec. Providian Fin. Corp., San Francisco, 1995—, exec. v.p., 1997—99, vice chmn. Enterprise Risk Mgmt., 1999—. Office: Providian Financial Corp 201 Mission Street Lobby San Francisco CA 94105

RICHEY, KIMBERLY KAY, singer, actress, composer; b. Zanesville, Ohio, Dec. 1, 1956; Student, Western Ky. U., Bowling Green, 1975-79; BS in Environ. Edn., Ohio U., 1980-82. With Mercury Nashville, 1994—; composer Nobody Wins, Those Words We Said, Believe Me Baby I Lied; rec. artist Kim Richey, 1995, Bitter Sweet, 1997, Glimmer, 1999; opener, headliner various shows. Recipient Grammy nomination, 1996. Office: Mercury Records Ste 300 54 Music Sq E Nashville TN 37203-4386

RICHEY, RUSSELL E. university dean; b. Asheville, N.C., Oct. 19, 1941; m. Merle Bradley Umstead, Aug. 28, 1965; children: William McMurry, Elizabeth Umstead. BA with with high honors, Wesleyan U., 1963; BD, Union Theol. Sem., 1966; MA, Princeton U., 1968, PhD, 1970. From instr. to prof. ch. history Drew U., 1969-86, asst. to pres., 1978-81; assoc. dean acad. programs Duke U., 1986-2000, rsch. prof. ch. history Div. Sch., 1986-92, prof. ch. history, 1992-2000; dean Candler Sch. Theology Emory U., Atlanta, 2000—. Mem. editl. adv. bd. Quar. Rev., Christian History, Jour. So. Religion, Ch. History, editor, 2000; pres. Wesley Wks. Editl. Project. Co-editor: American Civil Religion, 1974, 2d edit., 1990, Rethinking Methodist History, 1985, Perspectives on American Methodism: Interpretive Essays, 1993, The People(s) Called Methodist: Forms and Reforms of Their Life, 1998, Doctrines and Discipline, 1999; editor, co-author: Denominationalism, 1977, Ecumenical and Interreligious Perspectives: Globalizaion in Theological Education, 1992, Episcopacy in the Methodist Tradition, 2004; co-author, co-editor: Reimagining Denominationalism, 1994; author: Early American Methodism, 1991, The Methodist Conference in America: A History, 1996; co-author: The Methodists, 1998, The Methodist Experience in America, 2000, Esiscopay in the Methodist Tradition; co-author, primary co-editor: Questions for the Twenty-First Century Church, 1999. Mem. Am. Soc. Ch. History (mem. coun. 1976-78, 95-97), Am. Acad. Religion, Hist. Soc. United Meth. Ch., Atlanta Theol. Assn. (pres.). Home: 1198 Oakdale Rd Atlanta GA 30307 Office: Emory U Candler Sch Theology Atlanta GA 30322

RICHEY, SCOTT H, language educator; b. Mesa, Ariz., Feb. 3, 1954; s. Milford G and Doreen O Richey; m. Susan L Watts, Aug. 2, 1979; children: Brandon J, Ryan M, Kara L, Sheri A, Michael S, Catherine D. BA, Brigham Young U., 1972—90, MA, 1990—93; PhD, Ind. U., 1992—2002. Prof. of spanish Buena Vista U., Storm Lake, Iowa, 1998—, So. Utah U., 1996—98; v.p. Richey Cable Inc., St. Johns, Ariz., 1977—87. Dept. head Buena Vista U., 1999—. Bd. of directors and later pres. C. of C., Springerville, Ariz., 1984—87. Mem.: MLA, Iowa World Languages Assn. Avocation: wooden boat building. Home: 421 Otsego St Storm Lake IA 50588 Office: Buena Vista University 610 West 4th St Storm Lake IA 50588 E-mail: richey@bvu.edu.

RICHEY, VAN L. steel company executive; Pres., CEO Am. Cast Iron Pipe Co., Birmingham, Ala. Address: Am Cast Iron Pipe Co 1501 31st Ave N Birmingham AL 35207-4101

RICHIE, JEROME PAUL, surgeon, educator; b. San Antonio, 1944; MD, U. Tex., 1969. Surg. intern UCLA, 1969—70, resident in gen. surgery, 1970—71, resident in urology, 1971—75, lectr. surg. urology, 1974—75; asst. clin. prof. U. Calif., San Diego, 1975—77; asst. prof. urology Harvard U., 1977—80, assoc. prof., 1980—86, prof., 1986—, Elliott C. Cutler prof. surgery, 1987—, chmn. program in urology, 1987—. Chief urol. Brigham and Women's Hosp., Boston, 1977—; cons. Dana Farber Cancer Ctr., Boston, 1977—. Lt. comdr. M.C. USN, 1975—77. Mem.: ACS, Am. Surg. Assn., Am. Soc. (Clin.) Oncology, Assn. Acad. Surgery, Am. Urol. Assn., Am. Assn. Gerito-Urinary Surgeons. Office: Brigham & Womens Hosp 45 Francis St # 3 Boston MA 02115-6105 E-mail: jrichie@parnters.org.

RICHIE, LIONEL B., JR., singer, songwriter, producer; b. Tuskegee, Ala., June 20, 1949; s. Lionel and Alberta Richie; m. Brenda Harvey, 1975 (div.); 1 child, Nicole; m. Diane Alexander, 1996; children: Miles, Sofia. BS in Econs., Tuskegee U., 1971, MusD (hon.), 1985, Boston Coll., 1986. Pres. Brockman Music, L.A. Mem. group The Mystics (name changed to The Commodores), 1969-81; writer, producer songs for Commodores including: Easy, Three Times a Lady (Am. Music award 1979, People's Choice award for best song 1979), Still (People's Choice award for best song 1980), Sail On, Lady (Nat. Music Pubs. award 1980, 81, People's Choice award for best composer 1981); songwriter, producer album for Kenny Rogers; albums (with The Commodores) include Midnight Magic, Machine Gun, Movin' On, Commodores, Caught in the Act, Hot on the Tracks, Natural High, Heroes, (solo albums) Lionel Richie, 1982, Can't Slow Down, 1983 (Grammy award Album of Yr. 1985), Dancing on the Ceiling, 1986, Back to Front, 1992, Louder Than Words, 1996, Truly-The Love Songs, 1997, Time, 1998, Renaissance, 2001 (Grammy nomination for Angel); prodr., composer: (songs) Truly (Grammy award 1982, 2 Am. Music awards 1983, People's Choice award Best Song, 1983), All Night Long (Nat. Music Pubs. award 1984, 3 Black Gold awards 1984, Am. Music award 1984, Hello (2 Am. Music awards 1985), Say You, Say Me (ASCAP Pop award 1987, Am. Music award 1987, Oscar award Best Song 1986, Golden Globe award Best Song 1986), Dancing on the Ceiling (3 Am. Music awards 1987), (duet with Diana Ross) Endless Love (Grammy award 1982, 2 Am. Music awards 1982, Am. Movie award 1982, Rojo award Gold Status in Hong Kong 1982, People's Choice award Best Song 1982), (sung by Kenny Rogers) Lady, (with Michael Jackson) We Are The World, 1985 (Grammy awards Best Song, Record of Yr. 1986, People's Choice award Best Song 1986); actor (film) The Preacher's Wife, 1996. Recipient Best Young Artist in Film award, 1980, 2 NAACP image awards, 1983, Favorite Male Vocalist Pop/Rock award Am. Music Acad., 1987, Favorite Male Vocalist Soul/R&B award Am. Music Acad., 1987, Lifetime Achievement award San Remo Festival, Italy, 1996, Lifetime Achievement award World Music Awards; inductee Ala. Music Hall of Fame, 1997; named Man of Yr. Children's Diabetes Found., 1984, Alumnus of Yr. United Negro Coll. Fund, 1984, Favorite Male Singer People mag. Readers Poll, 1985, Entertainer of Yr., NAACP, 1987. Mem. ASCAP (Writer of Yr. 1984, 85, 86, Pub. of Yr. 1985).

RICHIE, NICOLE, television personality; b. Sept. 21, 1981; d. Lionel and Brenda Harvey Richie. Co-star: (TV series) The Simple Life, 2003—04; The Simple Life 2: Road Trip, 2004—; guest appearance Punk'd, 2003; Mad TV, 2004; Rock Me Baby, 2004; Six Feet Under, 2004.*

RICHIE, ROBERT DOUGLAS, not-for-profit executive; b. Washington, Sept. 25, 1962; s. David Arthur and Catherine Richie; m. Cynthia R. Terrell, Apr. 6, 1964; children: Savanna, Lucas, Rebecca. BA, Haverford Coll., 1987. Media rels. profl. Christic Inst., Washington, 1987-89; rschr. Jolene Unsoeld for Congress, Olympia, Wash., 1990-92; exec. dir. Ctr. for Voting and Democracy, Washington & Takoma Park, Md., 1992—. Coord., newsletter editor S.P.E.E.C.H., Olympia, Wash., 1990—91; mem. adv. bd. Ctr. Collaborative Democracy, N.Y.C., 1999—. Co-author: (book) Reflecting All of Us, 1999, Whose Vote Counts, 2001; contbr. articles to profl. jours.; mem. editl. adv. bd.: Representation, 1997—. Bd. dirs. Citizens in Charge, Va., 2001—. Office: Ctr for Voting and Democracy 6930 Carroll Ave Ste 610 Takoma Park MD 20912-4466 E-mail: rr@fairvote.org.

RICHIE, RODNEY CHARLES, critical care and pulmonary medicine physician; b. Big Springs, Tex., Aug. 17, 1946; s. Howard Mouzon and Gloria (Hollingshead) R.; m. Sara Lee Dilley, July 13, 1968; children: Megan Kathryn, Paul Nathan. BA in Chemistry, So. Meth. U., 1968; MD cum laude, Baylor Coll., 1972. Diplomate in Internal Medicine, Pulmonary, Crit. Care and Ins. Medicine. Resident in medicine Baylor Affiliated Hosps., Houston, 1973-75, chief med. resident, 1975, fellow in pulmonary medicine, 1976-77; pres. Waco (Tex.) Lung Assocs., 1977—2004; assoc. clin. prof. cmty. medicine Heart of Tex. Cmty. Health Ctr./U. Tex. S.W. Med. Sch., 2004—. Med. dir. Tex. Life Ins., Waco, 1985—, Cmty. Hospice of Waco, 1996—, EMSI, Waco, Tex., 1997—. Chmn. med. staff Hillcrest Bapt. Med. Ctr., Waco, 1993; chmn. bd. dirs. GH Pape Found., Waco, 1993. Fellow: ACP, Am. Coll. Chest Physicians; mem.: AMA, Am. Thoracic Soc., Am. Acad. Internal Medicine (del. to AMA), Tex. Club Internists. Episcopalian. Avocations: skiing, writing, reading. Home: 3509 Lake Heights Dr Waco TX 76708-1005 Office: Waco Med Group 2911 Herring Ave Ste 212 Waco TX 76708-3244 Office Phone: 254-755-4444. E-mail: rcrichie@earthlink.net.

RICHMAN, ALAN, magazine editor; b. Bronx, N.Y., Nov. 12, 1939; s. Louis and Sonia (Carity) R.; m. Kelli Shor, June 21, 1964; children: Lincoln Seth Shor, Matthew Mackenzie Shor. BA, Hunter Coll., 1960. Reporter Leader-Observer, N.Y.C., 1960-61; asst. editor Modern Tire Dealer, N.Y.C., 1962-64; assoc. editor ASTA Travel News, N.Y.C., 1964-65; pub. rels. rep. M.J. Jacobs, Inc., N.Y.C., 1965-66; mng. editor Modern Floor Coverings, N.Y.C., 1966-68; editor Bank Systems & Equipment, N.Y.C., 1968-79, Health Care Product News, N.Y.C., 1976; from assoc. pub. to pub. Bank Systems & Equipment, N.Y.C., 1969-79; editorial dir. Nat. Jeweler, N.Y.C., 1979-81; editor Health Foods Bus.; editorial dir. Army/Navy Store and Outdoor Merchandiser, 1981-88, The Pet Dealer, 1983-88; editor Cabinet Mfg. and Fabricating KBC Publs., 1988-94. Program dir. Cabinet Mfg. Fair, 1989-94; adj. faculty NYU, 1989—, Brookdale C.C., 1992—, Bergen County C.C., 1994—. Exec. editor: Kitchen and Bath Design News, 1992-93; editor-in-chief Wood Digest, PTN Pub. Co., 1992-94; editor: Whole Foods, 1994—; author: Czechoslovakia in Pictures, 1969, A Book on the Chair, 1968. With AUS, 1961-62. Recipient Jesse H. Neal certificate merit Am. Bus. Press, 1973. Mem. Internat. Platform Assn.

RICHMAN, ANTHONY E. textile rental industry association executive; b. Dec. 13, 1941; s. Irving M. and Helen V. (Muchnic) R.; Judy Harriet Richman, Dec. 19, 1964; children: Lisa Michele, Jennifer Beth. BS, U. So. Calif., 1964. With Reliable Textile Rental Svcs., L.A., 1964—; svc. mgr., 1969; sales and svc. mgr., 1970-73; plant mgr., 1973-75; gen. mgr., bd. dirs., 1975-78; v.p., sec.-treas., 1975-82; exec. v.p., CEO, 1982-84; pres., CEO, 1984—. Bd. dirs. Guild for Children, 1979—, Valley Guild for Cystic Fibrosis, 1974—, Cystic Fibrosis Found. of L.A. and Orange Counties, 1989—; pres. Textile Rental/Svc. Assn. Am., 1993-95; exec. dir. Western Textile Svcs. Assn., Studio City, Calif., 1996—. Office: Western Textile Svcs Assn 12400 Ventura Blvd Ste 213 Studio City CA 91604-2409

RICHMAN, DAVID PAUL, neurologist, educator, researcher; b. Boston, June 9, 1943; s. Harry S. and Anne (Goodkin) R.; m. Carol Mae von Bastian, Aug. 31, 1969; children: Sarah Ann, Jacob Charles. AB, Princeton U., 1965; MD, Johns Hopkins U., 1969. Diplomate Am. Bd. Psychiatry and Neurology. Intern, then asst. resident in medicine Albert Einstein Coll. Medicine, N.Y.C., 1969-71; resident in neurology Mass. Gen. Hosp., Boston, 1971-73, chief resident, 1973-74; instr. neurology Harvard U. Med. Sch., Boston, 1975-76; assoc. prof. neurology U. Chgo., 1976-80, assoc. prof., 1981-85, prof., 1985-91, Straus prof. neurol. Scis., 1988-91; prof. neurology U. Calif., Davis, 1991—, chmn. dept., 1991-97. Mem. com. Nat. Inst. Aging, NIH, 1984-85, mem. immunogical scis. study sect., 1986-90. Mem. AAAS, Am. Assn. Immunologists, Am. Acad. Neurology, Am. Neurol. Assn., Phi Beta Kappa, Sigma Xi. Office: U Calif Davis Dept Neurology 1515 Newton Ct Davis CA 95616-4859 Office Phone: 530-752-5013. E-mail: dprichman@ucdavis.edu.

RICHMAN, DOUGLAS DANIEL, medical virologist, educator, internist; b. N.Y.C., Feb. 15, 1943; s. Daniel Powell and Louise Kohnstamm (Woolf) R.; m. Eva Acquino, June 21, 1965; children: Sara, Matthew. AB cum laude, Dartmouth Coll., 1965; MD, Stanford U., 1970. Diplomate Am. Bd. Internal Medicine, Am. Bd. Infectious Diseases, Am. Bd. Med. Examiners. Intern Stanford (Calif.) Med. Sch., 1970-71, resident, 1971-72; rsch. assoc. LID/NIAID NIH, Bethesda, Md., 1972-75; fellow Beth Israel and Children's Hosps., Harvard Med. Ctr., Boston, 1975-76; asst. prof. depts. pathology and medicine U. Calif., San Diego, 1976-82, assoc. prof., 1982-88, prof., 1988—, Florence Seeley Riford chair in AIDS rsch., 2004—. Vis. prof. Hubei Med. Coll., Wuhan, People's Republic of China, 1987, Tokyo Med. and Dental U., Kumamoto U. Sch. Medicine, Inst. for Virus Rsch. at Kyoto U., St. Marianna U., Tokyo, Inst. Med. Rsch., Tokyo, Fukishima Prefecture Med. Sch., Japan, 1990; vis. fellow Clare Hall, U. Cambridge, 1984-85; mem. U. Calif. Pres.'s Cancer Rsch. Coord. Com., 1984-89, NIH AIDS Rsch. Rev. Com., 1987-90; cons. FDA Ctr. for Drugs and Biologics, 1986-89; dir. U. Calif.-San Diego Ctr. for AIDS Rsch., AIDS Rsch. Inst. Co-editor: Clin. Virology, —; mem. editl. bd.: Antimicrobial Agts. and Chemotherapy, 1987—, Jour. of AIDS, 1988—, Antiviral Agts., 1988—, AIDS, 1990—, AIDS Alert, 1990—, Antiviral Drug Resistance, 1996—, Virology, 1997—, others; contbr. more than 490 articles to profl. jours. Recipient Lowell Rantz award in infectious diseases, 1970, AMA Physicians Recognition award, 1976, 79, 82, 85, 88, William S. Middleton award Dept VA, 2002; John Simon Guggenheim fellow, 1984. Fellow: ACP, AAAS, Western Assn. Physicians, Am. Assn. Physicians, Infectious Diseases Soc. Am.; mem.: Am. Clin. and Climatologic Assn., VA Soc. for Physicians in Infectious Diseases, Internat. AIDS Soc., Internat. Soc. Antiviral Rsch., Am. Soc. for Virology, Am. Fedn. for Clin. Rsch., Am. Soc. for Microbiology. Office: U Calif San Diego Dept Pathology & Medicine 9500 Gilman Dr La Jolla CA 92093-0679

RICHMAN, HAROLD ALAN, social welfare policy educator; b. Chgo., May 15, 1937; s. Leon H. and Rebecca (Klieman) R.; m. Marlene M. Forland, Apr. 25, 1965; children: Andrew, Robert. AB, Harvard U., 1959; MA, U. Chgo., 1961, PhD, 1969. Asst. prof., dir. Ctr. for Study Welfare Policy, Sch. Social Svc., U. Chgo., 1967-69, dean, prof. social welfare policy, 1969-78, Hermon Dunlap Smith prof., 1978—, dir. of ctr., 1978-81, dir. Children's Policy Rsch. Project, 1978-84, dir. Chapin Hall Ctr. for Children, 1985—2002, faculty assoc. Chapin Hall Ctr. for Children, 2002—, chmn. univ. com. on pub. policy studies, 1974-77. Chmn. Univ. Lab. Schs., 1985-88; cons. to gov. State of Ill., Edna McConnell Clark Found., 1984-95, Lilly Endowment, 1987-90, Ford Found., 1987-89; co-chair Aspen Roundtable on Cmty. Change, 1993—. Chmn. editl. bd. Social Svcs. Rev., 1970-79; contbr. articles to profl. jours. Bd. dirs. Chgo. Com. Fgn. and Domestic Policy, 1969-78, S.E. Chgo. Commn., 1970—, Jewish Fedn. Met. Chgo., 1970-75, Ill. Facilities Fund, 1989-94, Welfare Coun. Met. Chgo., 1970-72, Erikson Inst. Early Childhood Edn., 1972-79, Nat. Urban Coalition, 1975-86, Family Focus, 1980-89, Jewish Coun. Urban Affairs, 1982-87, Ctr. for Study Social Policy, 1983-92, chmn., 2003—; bd. dirs. Nat. Family Resource Coalition, 1990-93, Pub./Pvt. Ventures, 1992-98, Benton Found., 1994-2004; bd. dirs. Israel Ctr. on Children, chmn., 1995-2004; bd. dirs. Info. and Rsch Ctr., Amman, Jordan, 2001—, Michael Reese Health Trust, 2002—, bd. dirs. U. Capetown Childen's Inst., dep. chair, 2002—; mem. adv bd. John Gardner Ctr., Stanford U., 2003—; bd. dirs. Brookdale Inst., Jerusalem, 2004—. White House fellow, Washington, 1965-66; recipient Disting. Svc. citation U.S. Dept. Health, Edn. & Welfare, 1970, Quantrell award U. Chgo., 1990. Mem. White House Fellows Assn. (v.p. 1976-77), Am. Pub. Welfare Assn. (bd. dirs. 1989-92). Home: 5715 S Dorchester Ave Chicago IL 60637-1726 Office: U Chgo Chapin Hall Ctr for Children 1313 E 60th St Chicago IL 60637-2830 Office Phone: 773-256-5176. Business E-Mail: hrichman@chapinhall.org.

RICHMAN, JOAN M. lawyer; b. Chgo., Dec. 15, 1965; Diploma in Internat. Bus., The Netherlands Sch. Bus., 1989; B of Commerce with distinction, McGill U., 1988; JD, Georgetown U., 1992. Bar: Ill. 1992. Summer assoc. Baker & McKenzie, Chgo., 1991, assoc., 1992—99, ptnr., 1999—. Office: Baker and McKenzie One Prudential Plz 130 E Randolph Dr Chicago IL 60601

RICHMAN, JOSEPH HERBERT, retired public health services official; b. Balt., Aug. 13, 1941; s. Samuel and Beatrice R. BS, Howard U., 1962, MD, 1966; MPH, Johns Hopkins U., 1974. Intern Maimonides Med. Ctr., Bklyn., 1966-67; resident in pediat. Sinai Hosp. of Balt., 1967-69; chief sch. health P.G. Health Dept. of Md., Cheverly, Md., 1972-75; dir. area health svcs. Montgomery County Health Dept., Bethesda, Md., 1975-82; county chief pub. health physician State of Del., Dover, 1982-99; ret., 2000. Capt. USAF, 1969—71. Recipient Outstanding Svc. award, Delaware Health and Soc. Svc., 1999. Fellow Am. Acad. Pediatrics (emeritus), Am. Coll. Preventive Medicine; mem. AMA, Masons, Amity Club D.C., Phi Beta Kappa. Democrat. Jewish. Avocations: golf, photography. Home: 4485 Sedgwick St NW Washington DC 20016-2713 Personal E-mail: joefortsedgwick@aol.com.

RICHMAN, KEITH STUART, state representative; married; 2 children. Student, U. Calif., Davis; MD, MA in Pub. Health Adminstrn., UCLA. Chair bd. dirs. Lakeside HealthCare, Inc.; mem. Calif. Assembly, 2000—. Commr. City Redevelopment Agy., LA; mem. Sun Valley Rotary Found.; chair task force intercollegiate athletics Calif. State U., Northridge; past chair Valley Cmty. Clinic, adv. bd. Mem.: Am. Diabetes Assn. (chpt. founding pres.), Rotary. Republican. Office: PO Box 942849 Rm 5128 Sacramento CA 94249 Address: 10727 White Oak Ave Ste 124 Granada Hills CA 91344

RICHMAN, LIBBIE I. writer; b. Landsberg, Germany, Apr. 19, 1946; arrived in US, 1949; d. Henry and Rachel Fox; m. Ross A. Richman, Nov. 21, 1965; children: Marc, Steven. Purchasing agent Office Supply Co., Detroit, 1973—80; investigator rschr. Equifax Corp., Southfield, Mich., 1981—88. Author: (novels) Let It Be Me, 2003, Sincerely, 2002, five volumes of poetry and lyrics, children's books. Contbr./supporter Holocaust Meml. Fund. Recipient Recognition Awards, Hollywood Poets Soc./Calif.; Famous Poets Soc.; Illiad Press; World of Poetry, 2nd place winner, poem A Child Is A Person, Poetic Justice competition. Mem.: Romance Writers of Am. Democrat. Jewish. Achievements include receiving letters from Pres. Ronald Reagan, Barbara Bush, George Bush, Doris Day, Red Skelton, Hilary Rodham Clinton, Elie Weisel and others in politics and entertainment in regards to my writing. Avocations: writing, reading, painting.

RICHMAN, MARC HERBERT, forensic engineer, educator; b. Boston, Oct. 14, 1936; s. Samuel and Janet (Gordon) R.; m. Ann Raeshel Yoffa, Aug. 31, 1963. BS, MIT, 1957, ScD, 1963; MA, Brown U., 1967. Registered profl. engr., Conn., Mass., R.I.; cert. forensic examiner. Cons. engr., 1957—; engr. shipbldg. div. Bethlehem Steel Corp., Quincy, Mass., 1957; instr. metallurgy MIT, Cambridge, 1957-60, research asst. dept. metallurgy, 1960-63; instr. metallurgy div. univ. extension Commonwealth of Mass., 1958-62; asst. prof. engring. Brown U., Providence, 1963-67, assoc. prof., 1967-70, prof., 1970-98, dir. central electron microscopy facility Materials Research program, 1971-86, dir. undergrad. program in engring., 1991-98; prof. emeritus, 1998—; pres. Ednl. Aids of Newton Inc., Providence, 1968-71, Marc H. Richman Inc., Providence, 1981—. Guest scientist Franklin Inst., Phila., 1959; vis. prof. U. R.I., Kingston, 1970-71; biophysicist dept. medicine Miriam Hosp., Providence, 1974-87; biogengr. dept. orthopaedics R.I. Hosp., 1979-93; prof. emeritus Brown U., Providence, 1998—. Author: Introduction to Science of Metals, 1967; also articles; editor Soviet Physics: Crystallography, 1970-94; mem. editl. adv. bd. Materials Characterization, 1970—. Jour. Forensic Engring., 1985-88. Served to maj. Ordnance Corps, U.S. Army, 1963. Recipient Engr. of Yr. award R.I. Soc. Profl. Engrs., 1993. Fellow Nat. Acad. Forensic Engrs. (cert.), Am. Coll. Forensic Examiners (cert.), Am. Inst. Chemists, Inst. Materials (U.K.); mem. ASCE, AIME, NSPE, ASEE (Outstanding Young Faculty award 1969), NAFE (bd. cert. diplomate in forensic engring.), Am. Acad. Forensic Scis., Am. Soc. Metals (sec.-treas. 1965-68, chmn. R.I. chpt. 1968-69, Albert Sauveur Meml. award 1968, 69), Providence Engring. Soc. (pres. 1991-92, Freeman award for engring. achievement 1989), B'nai B'rith, Sigma Xi, Tau Beta Pi. Home: 291 Cole Ave Providence RI 02906-3452 Office: One Richmond Sq Providence RI 02906 Office Phone: 401-751-9656. E-mail: MHRichman@aol.com.

RICHMAN, MARTIN FRANKLIN, lawyer; b. Newark, Feb. 23, 1930; s. Samuel L. and Betty E. (Goldstein) R.; stepson Doris (Bloom) R.; m. Florence E. Reif, May 6, 1962; children— Judith, Andrew. BA magna cum laude, St. Lawrence U., 1950; LL.B. magna cum laude, Harvard U., 1953. Bar: N.Y. 1953. Law clk. to Judge Calvert Magruder and Chief Justice Earl Warren, 1955-57; assoc., mem. firm Lord Day & Lord, Barrett Smith (and predecessors), N.Y.C., 1957-66, 69-94; of counsel Kirkpatrick & Lockhart, LLP, N.Y.C., 1994—; dep. asst. atty. gen. Office Legal Counsel, Dept. Justice, Washington, 1966-69. Public mem. Adminstrv. Conf. U.S., 1970-76; bd. dirs. Community Action for Legal Services, 1977-80 Trustee St. Lawrence U., 1979-95, trustee emeritus, 1995—, vice chmn. bd., 1988-95; bd. dirs. Friends of Law Libr. of Congress, 1992-99. Recipient Alumni citation St. Lawrence U., 1972 Fellow Am. Bar Found., N.Y. Bar Found.; mem. ABA (chmn. sect. adminstrv. law 1983-84), N.Y. State Bar Assn. (ho. of dels. 1981-84), Assn. of Bar of City of N.Y. (sec. and mem. exec. com. 1976-79, chmn. com. fed. legislation 1972-75, com. lawyer's pro bono obligations 1977-81), Am. Law Inst. Office: Kirkpatrick & Lockhart LLP 599 Lexington Ave New York NY 10022-6030 Business E-Mail: mrichman@kl.com.

RICHMAN, PAUL, semiconductor industry executive, educator; b. N.Y.C., Nov. 17, 1942; s. Harry and Molly (Armel) Richman; m. Ellen Margaret Kleiman, July 3, 1966; children: Lee Stuart, Alyson Michelle, Daniel Noah. BSEE, MIT, 1963; MSEE, Columbia U., 1964. V.p. R & D Standard Microsystems Corp., Hauppauge, N.Y., 1971-76, pres., 1976-81, pres., chief exec. officer, 1981-83, pres., chmn. bd., chief exec. officer, 1983-2000; co-founder Toyo Microsystems Corp., Tokyo, 1987—. Pres Consortium Technology Licensing Ltd, Nissequogue, NY, 1994—99, chmn bd dirs, CEO, 1999—; vis prof elec eng SUNY, Stony Brook, 1976—85; mem vis comt elec eng and computer sci dept MIT, 1996—; adj. prof. elec. engring. CUNY, 1973—75. Author: (book) Characteristics and Operation of MOS Field Effect Devices, 1967, MOS Field Effect Transistors and Integrated Circuits, 1974. Named one of 30 Most Important Contributors in the World to Devel Integrated Circuit Technology, Elec Eng Times/Elec Buyer's News/VLSI Sys Design, 1988; recipient Ann Award Achievement in Electronics, Electronics Mag, 1978. Fellow: IEEE (Award for Outstanding Technical Achievement 1980, Third Millennium Medal 2000). Achievements include invention of COPLAMOS technology. E-mail: paul.richman@smsc.com., paul_consortium@verizon.net.

RICHMAN, PETER, electronics executive; b. N.Y.C., Nov. 7, 1927; s. Emil H. and Janet (Seidler) R.; m. Vivian Hoffman, July 29, 1951; children: Meredith, Jeremy. BS, MIT, 1946; MS, NYU, 1953. Asst. chief engr. Reeves Instrument Corp., Garden City, N.Y., 1948-58; chief engr. Epsco, Inc., Cambridge, Mass., 1959-60; v.p., co-founder Rotek Instrument Corp., Watertown, Mass., 1960-64; v.p. Weston-Rotek, Lexington, Mass., 1964-67; cons. electronics engr. Lexington, 1967—. Bd. dirs. Thermo Voltek Corp, Thermo Sentron Corp.; founder, pres. KeyTek Instrument Corp., 1975-93; mem. NRC/NAS/Nat. Acad. Engring. Evaluation Panel for electricity divsn. Nat. Bur. Standards; mem. sci. adv. groups for several indsl. and sci. orgns. Patentee in precision electronic instrumentation; pioneer in precision dc and audio-frequency measurements, surge electrostatic discharge generation and electrostatic discharge measurements; author: The Insider's Guide to Growing a Small Business, 1996; contbr. articles to profl. jours. Mem. bd. overseers Boston Mus. Sci. Fellow IEEE; mem. Electromagnetics Acad., Instrument Soc. Am. (sr.), Sigma Xi, Tau Beta Pi.

RICHMAN, PETER MARK, actor, painter, writer, producer; b. Phila., Apr. 16, 1927; s. Benjamin and Yetta Dora (Peck) R.; m. Theodora Helen Landess, May 10, 1953; children: Howard Bennett, Kelly Allyn, Lucas Dion, Orien, Roger Lloyd. BS in Pharmacy, U. of the Scis., 1951; student of Lee Strasberg, N.Y.C., 1952-54; mem., Actors' Studio, N.Y.C., 1954—. Registered pharmacist, Pa., N.Y. Appeared in little theater, Phila., 1946-51, on stage radio and in live TV, Phila., N.Y.C., and Los Angeles, 1948-65, including Have I Got a Girl for You (pre-Broadway tryout), Biltmore Theater, L.A., 1963, The Deputy, Ctr. Theater Group, L.A., 1965; appeared at Grove Theater, Nuangola, Pa., 1952, Westchester Playhouse, 1953, Drury Lane, Chicago, 1957, Strand, N.J., 1957, Capri, 1959, Ogonquit (Maine) Playhouse, 1955-62, Matunuck, R.I., 1955, Falmouth, Mass., 1953-55, Westport, Conn., 1955, Harrison, Maine, 1962, Dennis, Mass., 1955-62, Phila. Playhouse in the Park, 1962-63; Broadway plays include End as a Man, 1953, Hatful of Rain,Broadway and Nat. Tour, 1956-57, Masquerade, 1959; off-Broadway plays include End as a Man, 1953, The Dybbuk, 1954, The Zoo Story (400 performances), 1960-61; Rainmaker, Private Lives, Angel Street, Arms and the Man, Rose Tattoo, Liliom, Funny Girl, Owl and the Pussycat, Hold Me, Equus, Night of the Iguana, Blithe Spirit, Twelve Angry Men, Henry Fonda Theatre, L.A., 1985, Babes in Toyland, Calif. Mus. Theater, 1988, Ray Bradbury's Next in Line, L.A., 1992, and numerous others; writer, performer (one man show) 4 Faces, L.A., 1995, N.Y.C., 1996, The Actors Studio, N.Y.C., 1996, and others; motion pictures include Friendly Persuasion, 1956, The Strange One, 1956, Black Orchid, 1958, The Dark Intruder, 1965, Agent for HARM, 1965, For Singles Only, 1967, Judgement Day (formerly The Third Hand), 1988, Friday the 13th, Part 8 (Jason Takes Manhattan), 1989, Naked Gun 2 1/2 (The Smell of Fear), 1991, Pool Hall Junkies, 2003; prodr., writer, actor 4 Faces (film), 2000; appeared on TV series as Nick Cain in Cain's Hundred, 1961-62, as David in David Chapter III for CBC, 1966, as Duke Page in series Longstreet, 1971-72, as Reverend Snow in series Three's Company, 1978-79, as Andrew Laird in series Dynasty, 1981-84, as Channing Capwell in series Santa Barbara, 1984, voice of God series Heroes of the Bible, 1979, voice of the Phantom in animated series Defenders of the Earth, 1986, as Madros in Berlin series My Secret Summer (formerly Mystery of the Keys), 1991; guest star over 500 TV shows, including Hotel, Dallas, Hart to Hart, Fantasy Island, Murder She Wrote, Nothing Sacred, Three's Company, Knight Rider, Star Trek: The Next Generation, Matlock, Beverly Hills 90210, others; starred in TV movies House on Greenapple Road, 1968, McCloud, 1969, Yuma, 1970, Nightmare at 43 Hillcrest (Wide World of Entertainment), 1974, Mallory, 1975, The Islander, 1978, Greatest Heroes of the Bible, 1979, Blind Ambition, 1979, The PSI Factor, 1981, Dynasty, 1981, Dempsey, 1983, City Killer, 1984, Bonanza, The Next Generation, 1988; one-man shows (paintings) Am. Masters Gallery, L.A., 1967, Orlando Gallery, L.A., 1966, McKenzie Gallery, L.A., 1969, 73, Hopkins Gallery, L.A., 1971, Goldfield Gallery, L.A., 1979, Galerie des Stars, L.A., 1988, Crocker Mus., Sacramento, 1967, Parkhurst Gallery, Seal Beach, Calif., 1991, 1996 March thru July, inaugural exhibition of the Henley Gallery Chapman U., Orange, Calif. (a 30 yr. retrospective, A life in Art); group shows include Bednarz Gallery, L.A., 1968, Dohan Gallery, L.A., 1966, Celebrity Art Exhibits, 55-city tour, 1964-65; represented in permanent collections U.S. and abroad; playwright: Heavy, Heavy What Hangs Over?, 1971, A Medal for Murray, 1991, 4 Faces, 1995 (Commendation award Prism Film Festival, 2002); dir. plays Apple of His Eye, 1954, Glass Menagerie, 1954; author: (novels) Hollander's Deal, 2000, (stories) The Rebirth of Ira Masters, 2001; featured in book Actor as Artists, 1992, Guide to Artists in Southern California, 1994. Trustee Motion Picture and TV Fund. Served with USN, 1945-46. Recipient silver medallion Motion Picture TV Fund, 1990, Sybil Brand Humanitarian award Jeffrey Found., 1990, Spl. award, 1997, Drama-Logue critics performance award for 4 Faces, 1996, Golden Halo Eagle award, So. Calif. Motion Picture Coun., 1997. Mem. SAG, AFTRA, Actors Equity Assn., Assn. Can. TV and Radio Artists, Acad. Motion Picture Arts and Scis., Acad. TV Arts and Scis. Office: 4 Faces Prodns 19528 Ventura Blvd Ste 385 Tarzana CA 91356 Office Phone: 818-623-6476. Personal E-mail: pmri@petermarkrichman.com. *I have always been grateful to be able to work in more than one medium. In a way they are all related, each solidifying and nurturing the other. I have a strong belief in God...and spiritual values. This, along with my marriage, children, and family life, has helped me enormously to express my own individuality as an artist.*

RICHMAN, PHYLLIS CHASANOW, newspaper critic; b. Washington, Mar. 21, 1939; d. Abraham and Helen (Lieberman) C.; m. Alvin Richman, June 5, 1960 (div. 1984); children— Joseph, Matthew, Libby BA, Brandeis U., 1961; postgrad., U. Pa., 1961-63, Purdue U., 1966-70. Exec. food editor Washington Post, 1980-88, food critic, 1976—. Author: Barter, 1976, Best Restaurants, 1980, 82, 85, 89, The Washington Post Dining Guide, 1996, 98, The Butter Did It, 1997, Murder on the Gravey Train, 1999. Mem. Washington

Ind. Writers (adv. bd.), James Beard Restaurant Awards (exec. com.). Home: 2118 O St NW Washington DC 20037-1007 Office: Washington Post 1150 15th St NW Washington DC 20071-0002

RICHMAN, STEPHEN CHARLES, lawyer; b. Nov. 13, 1943; s. Abraham and Sylvia (Weissman) Richman; m. Dinah Ellenberg, Aug. 25, 1968; children: Alex, Marni. BS in Bus. Adminstrn., SUNY, Buffalo, 1965; JD, George Washington U., 1968. Bar: D.C. 1968, Pa. 1972, N.Y. 1983. Field atty. NLRB, 1969—72; assoc. Wilderman, Markowitz & Kirschner, 1972—73; assoc. then ptnr. Markowitz & Kirschner, 1973—79; ptnr. Markowitz & Richman, Phila., 1979—. Lectr. Temple U. Sch. Law; former instr. Pa. State U. Mem.: ABA, Phila. Bar Assn., Pa. Bar Assn. (chmn. labor and employment law sect.). Office Phone: 215-875-3114.

RICHMAN, STEPHEN ERIK, lawyer; b. Austin, Tex., Mar. 10, 1945; s. Allen A. and Erika (Zimmerman) R.; m. Frances Ellen Sharpe, Aug. 29, 1971; children: Joshua Eric, Wendy Michelle. BA magna cum laude, Amherst Coll., 1967; JD cum laude, Harvard U., 1970. Bar: Wis. 1972. Assoc. Webster Sheffield, N.Y.C., 1970-72, Quarles & Brady, Milw., 1972-78, ptnr., 1978—. Pres. Milw. Youth Symphony Orch., 1985-87, Milw. Jewish Fedn., 1996-98; chmn. Milw. Symphony Orch., 2000-2002; bd. dirs. Jewish Cmty. Found., Milw., 1992—; chmn. steering com. Milw. Youth Arts Ctr., 2003—. Mem. ABA, Nat. Assn. Bond Lawyers, State Bar Wis., Phi Beta Kappa. Home: 709 E Carlisle Ave Milwaukee WI 53217-4835 Office: Quarles & Brady 411 E Wisconsin Ave Ste 2550 Milwaukee WI 53202-4497 Office Phone: 414-277-5683.

RICHMAN, STEPHEN I. lawyer; b. Washington, Pa., Mar. 26, 1933; m. Audrey May Grfsky. BS, Northwestern U., 1954; JD, U. Pa., 1957. Bar: Pa. 1958, U.S. Dist. Ct. (we. dist.) Pa. Assoc. McCune Greenlee & Richman, 1960—63, Greenlee Richman Derrico & Posa, 1963—84; ptnr. Richman, Smith Law Firm, PA, Washington, 1985—. Lectr. U. South Fla. Sch. Medicine, Mine Safe Internat. Chamber of Mines of We. Australia, W.Va. U. Med. Ctr. Grand Rounds, Am. Coll. Chest Physicians, Pa. Thoracic Soc., Am. Thoracic Soc., The Energy Bur., Coll. Am. Pathologists, Allegheny County Health Dept., APHA, Internat. Assn. Ind. Accident Bds. and Commns., Indsl. Health Found., Nat. Coun. Self-Insurers Assn., Am. Iron and Steel Inst., Can. Thoracic Soc., I.L.O./N.I.O.S.H., Univs. Associated for Rsch. and Edn. in Pathology, Am. Ceramics Soc., Nat. Sand Assn.; mem. adv. com. U.S. Dist. ct. We. Dist. Pa., 1994—. Author: Meaning of Impairment and Disability, Chest, 1980, Legal Aspects for the Pathologist, in Pathology of Occupational and Environmental Lung Disease, 1988, A Review of the Medical and Legal Definitions of Related Impairment and Disability, Report to the Department of Labor and the Congress, 1986, Medicolegal Aspects of Asbestos for Pathologists, Arch. Pathology and Laboratory Medicine, 1983, Legal Aspects of Occupational and Environmental Disease, Human Pathology, 1993, Impairment and Disability in Pneunoconiosis, State of the Art Reviews in Occupational Medicine-The Mining Industry, 1993, House Bills 2103 and 885; co-author: Act 44 and 57 amending Pa. Workmen's Compensation act. Mem. legal com. Indsl. Health Found., Pitts.; bd. dirs. Pitts. Opera Soc., Pitts. Jewish Fedn., 1994—97; dir. Jewish Family and Children's Svc., Pitts., 1995—2001. Mem.: ATLA, ABA (former vice chair workers compensation and employers liability law com, toxic and hazardous substance and environ. law com., lectr.), Pa. Chamber Bus. and Industry (worker's compensation com., chmn. subcom. on legis. drafting, lectr.), Pa. Bar Assn. (former coun. worker's compensation sect., contbr. bar assn. quar. 1992, 1993). Home: 820 E Beau St Washington PA 15301-2906 Office: Washington Trust Bldg Ste 200 Washington PA 15301 Office Phone: 724-222-5100.

RICHMOND, ALICE ELENOR, lawyer; b. N.Y.C. d. Louis A. and Estelle (Muraskin) R.; m. David L. Rosenbloom, July 26, 1981; 1 child, Elizabeth Lara. BA magna cum laude, Cornell U., 1968; JD, Harvard U., 1972; grad. Owners and Pres.'s Mgmt. Program, Harvard U., Harvard Bus. Sch., 2001; DLH (hon.), North Adams State U., 1987. Bar: Mass. 1973, U.S. Dist. Ct. Mass. 1975, U.S. Ct. Appeals (1st cir.) 1982, U.S. Supreme Ct. 1985. Law clk. to justices Superior Ct., Boston, 1972-73; asst. dist. atty. Office of Dist. Atty., Boston, 1973-76; spl. asst. atty. gen. Office of Atty. Gen., Boston, 1975-77; asst. prof. New Eng. Sch. of Law, Boston, 1976-78; assoc. Lappin, Rosen, Boston, 1978-81; ptnr. Hemenway & Barnes, Boston, 1982-92, Deutsch, Williams, Boston, 1993-95, Richmond, Pauly & Ault, Boston, 1996—2002; prin. Richmond & Assocs., Boston, 2002—. Asst. team leader, faculty Trial Advocacy Course, 1978—82; examiner Mass. Bd. Bar Examiners, Boston, 1983—; trustee Mass. Continuing Legal Edn., Inc., Boston, 1985—96, Boston, 1998—; treas. Nat. Conf. Bar Examiners, 1995—, chmn., 2003—04; v.p., bd. dirs. Am. Bar Ins., Inc., 1996—. Author (2 chpts.) Rape Crisis Intervention Handbook, 1976; contbr. articles to profl. jours. Mem. Pres. Adv. Com on the Arts, 1995—99; bd. overseers Handel & Haydn Soc., 1985—94, bd. govs., 1994—2002, v.p., 1996—2002; mem. Boston 2000 Millennium Commn., 1997—98; sec., dir. Boston 2000, Inc., 1998—2001; mem., pres. Coun. of Cornell Women, Cornell U. Coun.; trustee Red Auerbach Youth Found., Fund for Justice and Edn., 1998—2002; mem. adv. bd. Ctrl. and Ea. European Law Initiative, 1997—2002; mem. Angell Meml. Hosp. Coun. of Fellows, 2001—. Named one of Outstanding Young Leaders Boston Jaycees, 1982; Sloan Found. Urban fellow, N.Y.C., 1969 Fellow: Am. Coll. Trial Lawyers; mem.: NOW, Legal Def. and Edn. Fund (trustee 1995—2002, sec. 1998—2002), ABA (ho. of dels. 1980—, vice chmn. com. on rules and calendar 1986—88, bd. govs. 2002—), Latin Am. Legal Initiatives Coun., Mass. Bar Found. (pres. 1988—91), Mass. Bar Assn. (pres. 1986—87), Am. Law Inst., Boston Club, Harvard Club. Office: Richmond & Assocs 39 Brimmer St Boston MA 02108 Office Phone: 617-523-8187. Business E-Mail: arichmond@rpalaw.com.

RICHMOND, ANTHONY HENRY, sociologist, emeritus educator; b. Ilford, Essex, Eng., June 8, 1925; s. Henry James and Ellen Bertha R.; m. Freda Williams, Mar. 29, 1952; 1 dau., Glenys Catriona Richmond Troth. BSc in Econs., London Sch. Econs., 1949; MA, U. Liverpool (Eng.), 1951; PhD, U. London, 1965. Rsch. officer U. Liverpool, 1949-51; lectr. dept. social study U. Edinburgh, Scotland, 1952-63; reader in sociology Bristol (Eng.) Coll. Sci. and Tech., 1963-65; prof. sociology York U., Toronto, Ont., Can., 1965-89, prof. emeritus, sr. scholar, 1989—; dir. York U. (Inst. Behavioral Rsch.), 1979-82. Social rsch. cons.; vis. prof. Australian Nat. U., Canberra, 1971, 77, St. Antony's Coll., Oxford, Eng., 1984-85. Author: Colour Prejudice in Britain, 1954, 2d edit., 1971, The Colour Problem: A Study of Racial Relations in Britain, Africa and the West Indies, 1955, rev. edit., 1961, Post-War Immigrants in Canada, 1967, (with others) Immigrant Integration and Urban Renewal in Toronto, 1973, Migration and Race Relations in an English City, 1973, (with W. E. Kalbach) Factors in the Adjustment of Immigrants and Their Descendants, 1980, Immigration and Ethnic Conflict, 1988, Caribbean Immigrants: A Demoeconomic Analysis, 1989, Global Apartheid: Refugees, Racism and the New World Order, 1994; editor: Readings in Race and Ethnic Relations, 1972, (with D. Kubat) Internal Migration: The New World and the Third World, 1976; contbr. chpts. to books, articles to profl. jours. Recipient research grants and scholarships. Fellow Royal Soc. Can.; mem. Can. Sociology and Anthropology Assn. (Outstanding Contbrn. award 2001), Can. Population Soc. Mem. Soc. Of Friends. Avocations: classical music, photography.

RICHMOND, DAVID WALKER, lawyer; b. Silver Hill, W.Va., Apr. 20, 1914; s. David Walker and Louise (Finlaw) Richmond; m. Gladys Evelyn Mallard, Dec. 19, 1936; children: David Walker, Nancy L. LLB, George Washington U., 1937. Bar: DC 1936, Ill. 1946, Md. 1950. Ptnr. Miller & Chevalier, Washington. Lectr. fed. taxation. Contbr. articles to profl .jours. Served to lt. comdr. USNR, 1942—46. Decorated Bronze Star; recipient Disting. Alumni Achievement award, George Washington U., 1976. Fellow: Am. Coll. Tax Counsel, Am. Bar Found.; mem.: ABA (chmn. taxation sect. 1955—57, ho. of dels. 1958—60), Am. Law Inst., Lawyers Club Washington, Masons. Republican. Methodist. Home: 7979 S Tamiami Trl Apt S359 Sarasota FL 34231-6819 Office: 655 15th St NW Washington DC 20005-5701

RICHMOND, DIANA, lawyer; b. Milw., July 5, 1946; d. Lee and Laurel Jean (Bohlmann) Schultz; 1 child, Kavana. BA, U. Chgo., 1967; JD with highest honors, Golden Gate U., 1973. Bar: Calif. 1973, U.S. Dist. Ct. (no. dist.) Calif. 1973. Assoc. Stern, Stotter & O'Brien, San Francisco, 1973—77; sole practice San Francisco, 1977—80, 1983—2001; ptnr. Sideman & Bancroft, LLP, San Francisco, 2001—. Chmn. exec. com. family law sect. Calif. State Bar, 1984-85. Editor: California Marital Termination Settlements, 1988; editl. cons. Calif. Family Law Practice, 1984—; cons. editor: California Family Law Practice and Procedure II, 1995—. Recipient Outstanding Alumna award, Golden Gate U. Sch. Law, 1985, Golden Gate U., 1990. Fellow Am. Acad. Matrimonial Lawyers (pres. No. Calif. chpt. 1988-89, C. Rick Chamberlin award No. Calif. chpt. 2000), Bar Assn. San Francisco (bd. dirs. 1983-84, cert. of merit 1977), Barrister Club San Francisco. Democrat. Office: Sideman & Bancroft LLP 8th Fl One Embarcadero Ctr San Francisco CA 94111 Office Phone: 415-392-1960. E-mail: drichmond@sideman.com.

RICHMOND, EERO, composer, music librarian; b. Tacoma, Wash., Jan. 5, 1938; s. Orin August and Esther Maija (Johnson) R. BA in Music, U. Wash., 1961, MLS, 1966. Music libr. N.Y.C. Pub. Libr., 1966-68, head music cataloger, 1969-80; dir. info. svcs. Am. Music Ctr., N.Y.C., 1982-93, head music cataloger, 1994-95, coord. info. svcs., 1995-99. Pianist Slavic Arts Ensemble, N.Y.C., 1985—, Inoue Chamber Ensemble, N.Y.C., 1993—. Composer musical works performed throughout U.S., Europe, South Am., Japan; contbr. articles to profl. jours. Mem. ASCAP, Internat. Soc. for Contemporary Music (v.p. 1986-90), Sibelius Soc. (v.p. 1985—), Phi Mu Alpha Sinfonia, Beta Phi Mu. Democrat. Lutheran. Avocations: travel (especially berlin), reading. Home: 152 Kent St Brooklyn NY 11222-2142 Office Phone: 718-389-6030. E-mail: kafka333@aol.com.

RICHMOND, GAIL LEVIN, law educator; b. Gary, Ind., Jan. 9, 1946; d. Herbert Irving and Sylvia Esther (Given) Levin; children: Henry, Amy. AB, U. Mich., 1966, MBA, 1967; JD, Duke U., 1971. Bar: Ohio 1971, U.S. Claims Ct. 1986, U.S. Ct. Mil. Appeals, 1994; CPA, Ill. Acct. Arthur Andersen & Co., Chgo., 1967-68; assoc. Jones, Day, Cleve., 1971-72; asst. prof. Capital U. Law Sch., Columbus, Ohio, 1972-73, U. N.C. Law Sch., Chapel Hill, 1973-78; vis. asst. prof. U. Tex. Law Sch., Austin, 1977-78, Nova U. Law Ctr., Ft. Lauderdale, Fla., 1979-80, assoc. prof., 1980-81, assoc. prof., assoc. dean, 1981-85, prof., assoc. dean., 1985-93, 95—, prof., acting dean, 1993-95. Author: Federal Tax Research, 6th edit., 2002; co-author: Tax Planning for Lifetime and Testamentary Dispositions, 1997; contbr. articles to profl. jours. Pres. Greater Ft. Lauderdale Tax Coun., 1987-88; trustee Law Sch. Admission Coun., 1994-99, chair audit com., 1991-93, chair svcs. and programs com., 1997-99. Mem. ABA (chair commn. on individual income, tax sect. 2001-03, chair AMT Task Force, tax sect. 2003-2004, chair adj. com., legal edn. sect. 2002-), Am. Assn. Atty.-CPAs (dir. Fla. chpt. 1992-98), Assn. Am. Law Schs. (mem. audit com. 1992, chair sect. adminstrn. of law schs. 1996, pres. S.E. chpt. 1993-94, sec. S.E. chpt. 1995-2002), Broward County Women Lawyers Assn., S.E. Assn. Law Schs. (pres. 2002-03). Democrat. Jewish. Avocation: reading. Office: Nova Southeastern U Shepard Broad Law Ctr 3305 College Ave Fort Lauderdale FL 33314-7721

RICHMOND, HAROLD NICHOLAS, lawyer; b. Elizabeth, N.J., Apr. 5, 1935; s. Benjamin I. and Eleanor (Turbowitz) R.; m. Elaine Zemel, June 16, 1957 (div. Nov. 1972); children: Bonnie J. Ross, Michele Weinfeld; m. Marilyn A. Wenrich, Aug. 26, 1973; children: Eric L., Kacy L. BA, Tulane U., 1957; LLB, NYU, 1961, LLM in Taxation, 1965. Estate tax examiner IRS, Newark, 1963-65; tax mgr. Puder & Puder/Touche Ross & Co., CPAs, Newark, 1965-73; ptnr. Sodowick Richmond & Crecca, Newark, 1973-84; prin. Harold N. Richmond, West Orange, N.J., 1984-86; ptnr. Wallerstein Hauptman & Richmond, West Orange, 1986-91, Hauptman & Richmond, West Orange, 1992—. With U.S. Army, 1959-60. Mem. ABA (tax sect. closely held bus. com., real property and probate sect.), N.J. Bar Assn. (tax, real property and probate sects.), Essex County Bar Assn. (chmn. tax com. 1989, real property and probate sect.). Avocations: running, tennis. Office: Hauptman & Richmond 100 Executive Dr Ste 330 West Orange NJ 07052-3309 Office Phone: 973-731-1100. E-mail: hnr@hrlawfirm.com.

RICHMOND, JAMES ELLIS, retired restaurant company executive; b. Chgo., Feb. 16, 1938; s. Kenneth E. and Irene M. (Anderson) R.; m. Karen Ann Ryder, Oct. 6, 1956; children: Scott, Brian, Ann, Susan. BBA, Case Western Res. U., 1960. CPA, Ohio. Sr. auditor Ernst & Ernst, Cleve., 1960-64; treas. Cook United, Inc., Cleve., 1964-75, Fairmont Foods Co., Houston, 1975-80, v.p. ops., 1980-82; v.p., treas. U-tote-M, Inc., 1982-84; mktg. exec. Circle K Convenience Stores, 1984-86; v.p. Consol. Products, Inc., Indpls., 1986-2000; ret. Lutheran. Home: 331 Wild Turkey Blvd Boerne TX 78006- E-mail: jkrich@gvtc.com.

RICHMOND, JAMES GLIDDEN, lawyer; b. Sacramento, Feb. 20, 1944; s. James Gibbs and Martha Ellen (Glidden) R.; m. Lois Marie Bennett, Oct. 22, 1988; 1 child, Mark R. BS in Mgmt., Ind. U., 1966, postgrad., 1966-69, JD, 1969. Bar: Ind. 1969, Ill. 1991, U.S. Dist. Ct. (no. dist.) Ind. 1971, U.S. Dist. Ct. (so. dist.) Ind., 1969, U.S. Ct. Appeals (7th cir.) 1975, U.S. Tax Ct. 1980. Spl. agent FBI, 1970-74; spl. agent Criminal Investigation Divsn. IRS, 1974-76; asst. U.S. atty. no. dist. U.S. Atty. Office, Ind., 1976-80; assoc. Galvin, Stalmack & Kirschner, Hammond, Ind., 1980-81; pvt. practice Highland, Ind., 1981-83; ptnr. Goodman, Ball & Van Bokkelen, Highland, Ind., 1983-85; U.S. atty. no. dist. State of Ind., Hammond, 1985-91; spl. counsel to dep. atty. gen. of the U.S. U.S. Dept. Justice, Washington, 1990-91; mng. ptnr. Ungaretti and Harris, Chgo., 1991-92, ptnr., 1995—2002; exec. v.p., gen. counsel Nat. Health Labs., 1992-95; shareholder Greenberg Traurig, Chgo., 2002—. Practitioner in residence Ind. U. Sch. Law, Bloomington, 1989. Minority counsel senate republicans October Surprise Hearings, 1992. Fellow Am. Coll. Trial Lawyers. Republican. Avocation: fly fishing. Office: Greenberg Traurig 77 W Wacker Dr Ste 2500 Chicago IL 60601

RICHMOND, JONATHAN Y. public health administration officer; b. Norwalk, Conn., Feb. 10, 1941; BA in Zoology, U. Conn., 1962, MS in Genetics, 1964; PhD in Genetics, Hahnemann U., 1967. Post-doctoral resident rsch. fellow Plum Island Animal Disease Ctr., Greenport, N.Y., 1967-69; rsch. microbiologist Plum Island Animal Disease Ctr., USDA, ARS, Greenport, 1969-79; biol. safety officer Plum Island Animal Disease Ctr., USDA, Greenport, 1979-83; chief safety ops. sect. Occupl. Safety and Health br., Divsn. Safety NIH, Bethesda, Md., 1983-90; dir. WHO Collaborating Ctr. Applied Biosafety and Tng., Ctrs. for Disease Control, Atlanta, 1990—2002, Office Health and Safety, Ctrs. for Disease Control and Prevention, Atlanta, 1990—2002; CEO Jonathan Richmond and Assocs., Inc., Southport, NC, 2002—. Mem. planning com. ann. NIH Rsch. Safety Symposia, 1983—84, 1988; chairperson Ctrs. for Disease Control Nat. Symposium on Biosafety, 1992, 94, 96, 98, 2000, 02; coord. Pub. Health Merit Badge Sem., 1993, 95; internat. cons. lab. design projects, 1993—; internat. cons. Project RETRO-CI, Abidjan, Ivory Coast, Africa, 1994—, Kemri, Kenya, 1996—, Plasma-derived Hepatitis B Vaccine Project, Bulandshar, Uttar Pradesh, India, 1994, Viral Diagnostic Lab., Toronto, 1995; cons. WHO. Editor: Biosafety in Microbiological and Biomedical Laboratories, 4th edit., 1999, Primary Containment of Biohazards: Selection and Use of Biological Safety Cabinets, 2d edit., 2001, Designing a Modern Microbiol./Biomed. Lab., 1998, Anthology of Biosafety Vols. I, II, III, IV, V, VI, VII; contbr. articles to profl. jours. Fellow: Am. Acad. Microbiology; mem.: Am. Soc. Microbiology (coord. biosafety workshops 1986—94, mem. lab. safety com. 1993—95), Am. Biol. Safety Assn. (steering com. 1979—81, exec. coun. 1985—88, pres. 1986—87, ann. cong. chairperson 1988, pres. Chesapeake Area chpt. 1989—90, Everett Hanal Jr. Meml. award 1995, Arnold G. Wedum Disting. Achievement award 1999). Office: Jonathan Richmond & Assocs 927 E Leonard St Southport NC 28461

RICHMOND, JULIUS BENJAMIN, retired pediatrician, health policy educator; b. Chgo., Sept. 26, 1916; s. Jacob and Anna (Dayno) Richmond; m. Rhee Chidekel, June 3, 1937 (dec. Oct. 9, 1985); children: Barry J., Charles Allen; m. Jean Rabow, Jan. 11, 1987; 1 child, Dale Keith (dec.). BS, U. Ill., 1937, MS, MD, 1939; DSc (hon.), Ind. U., 1978, Rush-Presbyn.-St. Luke Med. Ctr., 1978, U. Ill., 1979, Georgetown U., 1980, SUNY, Syracuse, 1986, U. Ariz., 1991; DMS (hon.), Med. Coll. Pa., 1980; D in Pub. Svc. (hon.), Nat. Coll. Edn., Evanston, Ill., 1980; DHL (hon.), Tufts U., 1986; DMS (hon.), Yale U., 1999; DEd (hon.), Wheelock Coll., 2000; DSci, Harvard U., 2002. Intern Cook County Hosp., Chgo., 1939—41, resident, 1941—42, 1946, Mcpl. Contagious Disease Hosp., Chgo., 1941; faculty U. Ill. Med. Sch., Chgo., 1946—53, prof. pediat., 1950—53; dir. Inst. Juvenile Rsch., Chgo., 1952—53; prof., chmn. dept. pediatrics Coll. Medicine, SUNY at Syracuse, 1953—65, dean med. faculty, chmn. dept. pediatrics, 1965—70; prof. child psychiatry and human devel., prof., chmn. dept. preventive and social medicine Harvard Med. Sch., 1971—77, prof. health policy, 1981—88, dir. divsn. health policy rsch. and edn., 1983—88, prof. health policy emeritus, 1988—; also faculty Harvard Sch. Pub. Health. Psychiatrist-in-chief Children's Hosp. Med. Ctr., Boston, 1971—77, adv. on child health policy, 1981—; dir. Judge Baker Children's Ctr., Boston, 1971—77; asst. sec. health and surgeon gen. HHS, 1977—81; mem. Pres.'s Commn. on Mental Health, 1977. Author: Pediatric Diagnosis, 1962, Currents in American Medicine, 1969. Nat. dir. Project Head Start; dir. Office Health Affairs, OEO, 1965—66. Flight surgeon U.S. Army Air Force, 1942—46. Recipient Agnes Bruce Greig Sch. award, 1966, Parents Mag. award, 1966, Disting. Svc. award, Office Econ. Opportunity, 1967, Family Health Mag. award, 1977, Myrdal award, Assn. for Evaluation Rsch., 1977, award for disting. sci. contbn., Soc. for Rsch. in Child Devel., 1979, Dolly Madison award, Inst. on Clin. Infants Programs, 1979, Pub. Health Disting. Svc. award, HEW, 1980, Illini Achievement award, U. Ill. Alumni Assn., 1982, Cmty. Svc. awrad, Health Planning Coun. Greater Boston, 1985, Lemuel Shattuck award, Mass. Pub. Health Assn., 1985, 1st Ann. Ronald McDonald Children's Charities award for Outstanding Contbns. to Child Health and Welfare, 1986, David E. Rogers award, Assn. Am. Med. Colls., 1997, A.L. Ellis award, Children's Home Soc. Fla., 1997, John Stearns award, N.Y. Acad. Medicine, 1999. Fellow: Am. Psychiat. Assn. (disting.), Am. Orthopsychiat. Assn. (Ittleson award 1994); mem.: APHA (Martha May Eliot award 1970, Sedgwick medal 1992), AMA (AMA-ERF award in health edn. 1988), Am. Psychosomatic Soc., Soc. Pediatric Rsch., Am. Acad. Child Psychiatry (hon.), New Eng. Coun. Child Psychiatry (assoc.), Am. Acad. Pediat. (C. Anderson Aldrich award 1966, ann. award sect. on cmty. pediat. 1977, Outstanding Contbn. award sect. cmty. pediat. 1978, Job Lewis Smith award 2000), Am. Pediatric Soc. (John Howland award 1990), Inst. Medicine of NAS (1st ann. Gustav O. Lienhard award 1986, McDermott medal 2022), Phi Eta Sigma, Alpha Omega Alpha, Sigma Xi.

RICHMOND, LYLE L. judge; LLB, Yale U., 1955. Dep. dist. atty., San Diego, 1959—64; pvt. practice, 1964—70; atty. gen., 1975—78; adminstr., legal mgr. Samoa Packing Co., Pago Pago, 1989—91; assoc. justice High Ct., Pago Pago, 1991—; legal counselor to American Samoa govs. Peter T. Coleman and A. P. Lutali, 1978—89; head legal divsn. atty.'s gen. office, 1973—75; dist. atty. Truk/Ponape dists., 1970—73. Capt. USNR. Office: Courthouse PO Box 309 Pago Pago AS 96799

RICHMOND, MARILYN SUSAN, lawyer; b. Bethesda, Md., Oct. 19, 1949; d. Carl Hutchins Jr. and Elizabeth Adeline (Saeger) R. BA with honors, U. Fla., 1971; JD, Georgetown U., 1974. Bar: Md. 1974, D.C. 1975. Atty. Office of Gen. Counsel, FTC, Washington, 1974-77, antitrust atty. Bur. of Competition, 1977-81; counsel, consumer subcom. of com. on commerce, sci. and transp. U.S. Senate, Washington, 1981-85; assoc. Heron, Burchette, Ruckert & Rothwell, Washington, 1985-87, ptnr., 1987-90; dep. asst. sec. for govtl. affairs U.S. Dept. Transp., Washington, 1990-91, acting asst. sec. for govtl. affairs, 1991-92; cons. Raffaelli, Spees, Springer & Smith, Washington, 1993-94; asst. exec. dir. govt. rels. APA Practice Orgn., 1995—. Lectr. Brookings Instn. Ctr. for Pub. Policy Edn., Washington, 1985-88. Active Lawyers for Bush-Quayle, Washington, 1988. Mem. ABA (antitrust, adminstrv. law sect., vice chair transp. industry com. antitrust sect. 1992-99). Republican. Methodist. Avocations: horseback riding, tennis. Home: Apt 601 2725 Connecticut Ave NW Washington DC 20008-5305

RICHMOND, MARSHA LEIGH, science historian; b. Muskogee, Okla., Oct. 1, 1950; d. William Eugene and Eldora Pearl (Hyde) R.; m. Joe Harris Lunn, Oct. 4, 1980; children: Sarah Elizabeth Lunn, Laura Patricia Lunn. BS, U. Okla., 1972; PhD, Ind. U., 1986. Editor Charles Darwin Corr., Cambridge, Eng., 1987-93; asst. prof. Wayne State U., Detroit, 1994—. Editl. advisor Corr. of Charles Darwin, Cambridge, 1993—. Mem. editl. bd.: NTM, Internat. Jour. History and Ethics of Natural Scis., Tech. and Medicine, History and Philosophy of the Life Scis., 2003—, Jour. of the History of Biology, 2004—; contbr. articles to profl. jours. Grantee NSF, 1992-95. Mem. Internat. Soc. for History, Philosophy and Social Studies of Biology, Brit. Soc. for History of Sci., History of Sci. Soc. Home: 1950 Coronada St Ann Arbor MI 48103-5014 Office: Wayne State U Interdisciplinary Studies 5700 Cass Ave Detroit MI 48202-3629 Office Phone: 313-577-6499. Business E-Mail: marsha.richmond@wayne.edu.

RICHMOND, MITCHELL JAMES, professional basketball player; b. Ft. Lauderdale, Fla., June 30, 1965; m. Juli Richmond; children: Phillip Mitchell, Jerin Mikell. B in Social Sci., Kans.State U., 1988. Guard Golden State Warriors, 1988—91, Sacramento Kings, 1991—98, Washington Wizards, 1998—2001; player L.A. Lakers, El Segundo, Calif., 2002—. Established Solid As A Rock Scholarship Found., Ft. Lauderdale, Fla., 1992; hon. bd. dir. NCPCA. Named Rookie of the Yr., 1989, Rookie of the Month 3 times, Dec., Jan., March, NBA Player of the Week, March 25, 1991; named to NBA All-Star team, 1993, 1994, 1995; recipient Spl. Friend award, NCPCA. Avocations: bowling, video games. Office: 555 N Nash St El Segundo CA 90245

RICHMOND, RAY S(AM), journalist; b. Whittier, Calif., Oct. 19, 1957; s. Henry and Terri C. (Epstein) R.; m. Beth Lyn Trachman, Oct. 2, 1983 (div. Feb. 1993); children: Joshua Adam, Gabrielle Reneé; m. Heidi Merle Lieberman, May 28, 1994; 1 child, Dylan Jake. B, Calif. State U., Northridge, 1980. Feature writer L.A. Daily News, Woodland Hills, Calif., 1978-85; segment prodr. Merv Griffin Show, Hollywood, Calif., 1985-86; television writer L.A. Herald Examiner, 1986-87; television critic Orange County Reigster, Santa Ana, Calif., 1987-92, L.A. Daily News, 1992-96; television reporter Daily Variety, L.A., 1996—. Co-author: Unofficial Olympic Guide, 1984; editor: The Simpsons: A Complete Guide to our Favorite Family, 1997. Vol. AIDS Project L.A., 1993-94. Mem. Television Critics Assn. Democrat. Jewish. Avocations: exercise, reading, family, television, travel. Home: 1010 Hammond St Apt 302 West Hollywood CA 90069-3851 Office: Daily Variety 5700 Wilshire Blvd Ste 120 Los Angeles CA 90036-5804

RICHMOND, RICHARD THOMAS, journalist; b. Parma, Ohio, May 16, 1933; s. Arthur James and Frances Marie (Visosky) R.; m. Charlotte Jean Schwoebel, Dec. 19, 1933; children: Kris Elaine, Leigh Alison, Paul Evan. AB, Washington U., St. Louis, 1961. Bur. mgr. UPI News Pictures, St. Louis, 1957-62; from asst. picture editor to editor color sect. Post-Dispatch, St. Louis, 1962-80, columnist, 1971—2002, editor calendar sect., 1983-94, asst. entertainment editor, 1995-96, prodn. coord. Get Out Mag. Clayton, Mo., 1996—2000; v.p. Golden Royal Enterprises, St. Louis, 1976-78; pres. Oroquest Press, St. Louis, 1977-80; dir. U.S. Mortgage & Investment Corp., Hilton Head Island, NC, 1977-81; pres. Magalar Mining, Texarkana, Ark., 1979-83. Co-author: Treasure Under Your Feet, 1974, In the Wake of the Golden Galleons, 1976, Diabetes: The Facts That Will Let You Regain Control of Your Life, 1986; editor: You Can Be Rich By Thursday, 1997, Male Homemaker's Handbook, 1997. Bd. dirs. Coll. Fine Arts and Comm. U. Mo., St. Louis, 2003—. Avocation: undersea treasure hunting. Home: 307 Lebanon Ave Belleville IL 62220-4126

RICHMOND, ROCSAN, television and video producer, director, publicist, actress, dancer, inventor, teacher; b. Chgo., Jan. 30; d. Alphonso and Annie Lou (Combest) R.; divorced; 1 child, Tina S. Student, Wilson Jr. Coll., 1963, 2d City Theatre, Chgo., 1969, Alice Liddel Theatre, 1970; cert. fingerprint classifier, L.A. City Coll., 1996. Lic. 3d class radio/tel. operator FCC. Vegetarian editor Aware mag., Chgo., 1977—78; investigative reporter, film critic Chgo. Metro News, 1975—81; prodr., talk show host Sta. WSSD, Chgo., 1980—81; dir. pub. rels. IRMCO Corp., Chgo., 1981—82; dir. pub. rels., newsletter editor Hollywood (Calif.) Reporter, 1985—86; exec. prodr. Donald Descendent's Prodns., Hollywood, 1983—, Future News, TV show,

1983—86; pres. Richmond Estates; tchr. TV prodn. Profl. Bus. Acad., Hollywood, 1998—2000; founder & pres. Richmond Acad. Fine Manners, 2000—. Jehovah'S Witness. Achievements include invention of invisible drapery tieback. Office: PO Box 665 Los Angeles CA 90078-0665 Personal E-mail: roscanr@aol.com.

RICHMOND, SAMUEL BERNARD, management educator; b. Boston, Oct. 14, 1919; s. David E. and Freda (Braman) R.; m. Evelyn Ruth Kravitz, Nov. 26, 1944; children: Phyllis Gail, Douglas Emerson, Clifford Owen. AB cum laude, Harvard U., 1940; MBA, Columbia U., 1948, PhD, 1951. Mem. faculty Columbia U., 1946-76, assoc. prof., 1957-60, prof. econ. and statistics, 1960-76; assoc. dean Grad. Sch. Bus. Columbia U., 1971-72, acting dean, 1972-73; dean prof. mgmt. Owen Grad. Sch. Mgmt. Vanderbilt U., Nashville, 1976—86, Ralph Owen prof. mgmt., 1984—88, Ralph Owen prof. mgmt. emeritus, dean emeritus, 1988—, adj. prof., 1988—96. Vis. prof. U. Sherbrooke, Que., 1967, U. Buenos Aires, Argentina, 1964, 65, Case Inst. Tech., Cleve., 1958-59, Fordham U., N.Y.C., 1952-53; dir. IMS Internat. Inc., N.Y.C., 1978-88, 1st Am. Corp., Nashville, 1981-86, Winners Corp., Nashville, 1983-89, Corbin Ltd., N.Y.C., 1970-85, Ingram Industries Inc., Nashville, 1981-92; cons. to maj. comml., ednl., profl. and govtl. orgns. Author: Operations Research for Management Decisions, 1968, Statistical Analysis, 1957, 2d edit., 1964, 3d edit., 1997, Regulation and Competition in Air Transportation, 1961; talk show host Nashville Bus. Edit., WDCN-TV, 1984-86. Trustee Ramapo Coll., N.J., 1975-76; bd. dirs. Jewish Fedn. Nashville and Mid. Tenn., Temple Ohabai Shalom, Nashville; trustee Endowment Fund Jewish Fedn. Nashville and Mid. Tenn. 1st lt. USAAF, 1943-45. Recipient Honor award CAB, 1971, Alumni award for outstanding svc. Grad. Sch. Bus., Columbia U., 1973 Mem. Am. Statis. Assn. (chmn. adv. com. rsch. to CAB 1966-74, dir. 1965-67), Am. Econ. Assn., Inst. Mgmt. Sci., Ops. Rsch. Soc. Am., Beta Gamma Sigma. Home: 5404 Camelot Rd Brentwood TN 37027-4113 Office: Vanderbilt U Owen Grad Sch Mgmt Nashville TN 37203 E-mail: samuel.b.richmond@vanderbilt.edu.

RICHTER, BURTON, physicist, educator; b. N.Y.C., Mar. 22, 1931; s. Abraham and Fanny (Pollack) Richter; m. Laurose Becker, July 1, 1960; children: Elizabeth, Matthew. BS, MIT, 1952, PhD, 1956; laurea honoris causa in physics, U. Pisa, 2001. Research assoc. Stanford U., 1956—60, asst. prof. physics, 1960—63, assoc. prof., 1963—67, prof., 1967—, Paul Pigott prof. phys. sci., 1980—, tech. dir. Linear Accelerator Ctr., 1982—84, dir. Linear Accelerator Ctr., 1984—99; dir. emeritus, 1999—. Cons., sec. energy adv. bd. NSF; sec. Energy Adv. Bd.; bd. dirs. Varian Med. Systems, AREVA Enterprises, Inc., Litel Instruments; Astor vis. lectr. Oxford U., 2000; Loeb lectr. Harvard U., 1974; DeShalit lectr. Weizmann Inst., 1975; pres. Internat. Union of Pure and Applied Physics, 1997. Contbr. over 300 articles to profl. publs. Recipient E.O. Lawrence medal, Dept. Energy, 1976, Nobel prize in Physics, 1976. Fellow: AAAS, Am. Acad. Arts and Scis., Am. Phys. Soc. (pres. 1994); mem.: NAS, Nat. Rsch. Coun. (mem. bd. physics and astronomy, chair 2003—), Internat. Coun. Sci. (mem. exec. bd.), Regents Mercersbury Acad. (hon.), Nat. Climate Change Assessment (PCAST rev. panel), Acceleration Transmutation Nuc. Waste (chair NERAC subcom.), Am. Phil. Soc. (bd. dirs.). Achievements include research in elementary particle physics. Office: SLAC 2575 Sand Hill Rd Menlo Park CA 94025

RICHTER, DONALD PAUL, lawyer; b. New Britain, Conn., Feb. 15, 1924; s. Paul John and Helen (Racoske) R.; m. Jane Frances Gumpright, Aug. 10, 1946; children: Christopher Dean, Cynthia Louise. AB, Bates Coll., 1947; LL.B., Yale U., 1950. Bar: N.Y. 1951, Conn. 1953. Assoc. Winthrop, Stimson, Putnam & Roberts, N.Y.C., 1950-52; ptnr. Murtha, Cullina, Richter and Pinney, Hartford, Conn., 1954-94; counsel Murtha Cullina LLP, Hartford, Conn., 1994—. Trustee Bates Coll., 1962-94, Manchester (Conn.) Meml. Hosp., 1963-94, Hartford Sem., 1973-85; trustee Suffield Acad., 1974—, pres., 1982-89; bd. dirs. Met. YMCA Greater Hartford, 1970-94, pres., 1976-81, trustee, 1994—; mem. nat. coun. YMCA, 1978-82; bd. dirs. Church Homes, 1967-81; trustee, v.p., Silver Bay Assn., 1971-96. With USNR, 1943-46. Fellow Am. Coll. Trust and Estate Counsel; mem. ABA, Conn. Bar Assn., Univ. Club, Hartford Club, 20th Century Club, Rotary (Paul Harris fellow 1996), Phi Beta Kappa, Delta Sigma Rho. Congregationalist. Home: 140 Boulder Rd Manchester CT 06040-4508 Office: Murtha Cullina LLP City Place I 185 Asylum St Hartford CT 06103-3469 Office Phone: 860-240-6000.

RICHTER, GLENN, manufacturing executive; BBA, George Washington U.; MBA, Duke U. Various exec. level positions with Frito-Lay Co., McKinsey and Co.; pres., CEO Specialty Foods Corp., 1994—97; sr. v.p., corp. contr. Dade Behring, Deerfield, Ill., 1997-99, CFO, 1998—99; exec. v.p., CFO St. Paul Companies Inc., 1997—2000; v.p., controller Sears Roebuck, Hoffman Estates, Ill., 2000—02, senior v.p., CFO, 2002—. Office: Sears Roebuck 3333 Beverly Rd Schaumburg IL 60179

RICHTER, HANS JÜRGEN, technologist, researcher; b. Cologne, Germany, Feb. 14, 1960; arrived in U.S., 1995; ME, Rheinisch Westfälische Technische Hochschule, Aachen, Germany, 1984, PhD in Engring., 1989. Rschr. BASF Ctrl. Rsch., Ludwigshafen, Germany, 1989—95; technologist Seagate, Fremont, Calif., 1995—. Insic strategy team INSIC, San Diego, 1999—. Contbr. chapters to books, articles to encys., to profl. jours. Recipient Friedrich Wilhelm prize, RWTH Aachen, 1989, Best lectr., NATO Summer Sch., 1993, Outstanding tech. contbns. award, Seagate Tech., 2000. Mem.: IEEE (mem. editl. bd. IEE TRansition Magnetics 1996—, chair tech. com. Magnetic Soc. 1999—). Achievements include invention of One Trade Secret; patents in field; patents pending in field. Office: Seagate 47010 Kato Rd Fremont CA 94538 Office Phone: 510-353-4988. Business E-Mail: hans.j.richter@seagate.com.

RICHTER, HARVENA, retired english literature and creative writing teacher, writer; b. Reading, Pa., Mar. 13, 1919; d. Conrad Michael and Harvena Maria (Achenbach) R. BA, U. N.Mex., 1938; MA, NYU, 1955, PhD, 1967. Advt. copyrighter Saks 5th Ave., N.Y.C., 1942-43, R.H. Macy, N.Y.C., 1944-46; copy chief Elizabeth Arden, N.Y.C., 1946-47; advt. dir. I. Miller, N.Y.C., 1947-48; European corr. various newspapers, 1948-49; lectr. NYU, N.Y.C., 1952-66, U. N.Mex., 1969-89. Author: The Human Shore, 1959, Virginia Woolf: The Inward Voyage, 1970, Writing to Survive: The Private Notebooks of Conrad Richter, 1988, The Yaddo Elegies and Other Poems, 1995, Green Girls, Poems Early and Late, 1996, The Innocent Island, 1999, Frozen Light, the Crystal Poems, 2002, The Golden Fountains, Sources of Energy and Life, 2002, Passage to Teheran, 2004; contbr. poetry to The New Yorker, Chelsea, New Letters, others; short stories to Sat. Eve. Post, New Am., Blue Mesa Rev.; essays to Atlantic, Modern Fiction Studies, C.S. Monitor, others. AAUW fellow, 1964-65; grantee Yaddo, 1963-64, MacDowell Colony, 1965-66, Wurlitzer Found., Taos, N.Mex., 1968, 73-75, Va. Ctr. for Creative Arts, 1983, 85, Ragdale Found., 1990. Mem. Author's Guild, Virginia Woolf Soc., Kappa Kappa Gamma. Avocation: gardening. Home and Office: 1932 Candelaria Rd NW Albuquerque NM 87107

RICHTER, JUDITH ANNE, pharmacology educator; b. Wilmington, Del., Mar. 4, 1942; d. Henry John and Dorothy Madelyn (Schroeder) R. BA, U. Colo., 1964; PhD, Stanford U., 1969. Postdoctoral fellow Cambridge (Eng.) U., 1969-70, U. London, 1970-71; asst. prof. pharmacology Sch. Medicine Ind. U., Indpls., 1971-78, assoc. prof. pharmacology and neurobiology, 1978-84, prof., 1984—. Vis. assoc. prof. U. Ariz. Health Sci. Ctr., Tucson, 1983; mem. biomed. rsch. rev. com. Nat. Inst. on Drug Abuse, 1983-87. Mem. editl. bd. Jour. Neurochemistry, 1982-87; contbr. numerous articles to sci. jours. Scholar Boettcher Found., 1960-64; fellow Wellcome Trust, 1969-71. Mem. AAAS, Am. Soc. for Pharmacology and Exptl. Therapeutics (exec. com. neuropharmacology div. 1989-91), Am. Soc. for Neurochemistry, Internat. Soc. for Neurochemistry, Soc. for Neurosci., Women in Neurosci., Assn. Women in Sci., Phi Beta Kappa, Sigma Xi. Achievements include research in neuropharmacology, especially barbiturates, neurobiology of mutant mice and dopaminergic systems, and regulation of sensory neuron glutamate release. Office: Ind U Sch Medicine 635 Barnhill Dr Indianapolis IN 46202-5126 Office Phone: 317-274-7593. Business E-Mail: jrichter@iupui.edu.

RICHTER, JULIA MAUREEN, music educator, musician; b. Patchogue, N.Y., May 23, 1969; d. Paul James and Crystal Mae Richter. MusB, Portland State U., 1992; MusM, U. North Tex., 1994. Piccolo Irving Symphony Orch., Tex., 1994—97; prin. flute Vancouver Symphony Orch., Wash., 1997—99; piccolo Columbia Symphony Orch., Portland, 1997—99, Elgin Symphony Orch., Ill., 1999—; instr. flute Elgin C.C., 2001—. Adj. instr. music application Elgin C.C., 2001—; prin. flute Curs Internat. de Musica Safonia Orch., Menorca, Spain, 1996. Musician (flutist): (albums) Songs for Funerals and Healing, 1992. Mem.: Chgo. Flute Club (bd. dirs., corr. sec. 2002—), Greater Portland Flute Soc. (bd. dirs. 1991—92). Avocations: running, reading. Home: 2119 N Stave St #1R Chicago IL 60647

RICHTER, PETER CHRISTIAN, lawyer; b. Opava, Czechoslovakia, June 13, 1944; came to U.S., 1951; s. Hanus and Alzbeta (Kindlarova) R.; m. Leslie Diane Rousseau, Nov. 25, 1967; children: Timothy Jason, Lindsey Berta. BS, U. Oreg., 1967, JD, 1971. Bar: Oreg. 1971, U.S. Dist. Ct. 1972, U.S. Ct. Appeals (9th cir.) 1972, U.S. Supreme Ct. 1983. Assoc. Veatch, Lovett & Stiner, Portland, Oreg., 1971-73; ptnr. Miller Nash LLP, Portland, 1978—. Adj. prof. law trial advocacy Northwestern Sch. of Law, Lewis and Clark Coll., Portland, 1986—; pro tempore judge Multnomah County Cir. Ct., Portland, 1985—1998, Oreg. State Bar Trial Advocacy Seminars, 1988—; trial advocacy coll. planner, instr. Oreg. State Bar, 1998—. Author: (handbook) Oregon State Bar, 1987, 88, 89; co-author: (chpt. in book) Oregon State Bar Damage Manual, 1985, 90; editor, program planner Sales: The Oregon Experience, 1989. Trustee, bd. dirs. Parry Ctr. for Children, Portland, 1990; former bd. dir. Boy Scouts of Am., Columbia Pacific Coun., Portland, Nat. Conf. Christians and Jews, Portland, 1983; bd. advisers Pacific Crest Outward Bound, 2000. With Oreg. Army N.G., 1967-75. Recipient Cert. of Appreciation Northwestern Sch. of Law, 1990; named one of ten Best Litigators in Oreg, Nat. Bar Jour. Fellow Am. Bar Found.; mem. ABA (trial techniques com.), Fed. Bar Assn. (Oreg. chpt.), Am. Bd. Trial Advocates (advocate), Internat. Assn. of Def. Counsel, Oreg. Bar Assn. (lectr. trial advocacy seminars 1988—, mem. jud. adminstn. com, bus. lit. sec. exec. comm.), Multnomah Bar Assn. (former bd dirs.), Oreg. Assn. Def. Counsel (cert. of appreciation 1987, 89) Inns of Ct., Multnomah Athletic Club (trustee, pres.), Arlington Club. Avocations: squash, tennis, skiing, golf, reading, motorcycling riding. Office: Miller Nash LLP 111 SW 5th Ave Ste 3500 Portland OR 97204-3699 E-mail: peter.richter@millernash.com.

RICHTER, RICHARD PAUL, academic administrator; b. Bryn Mawr, Pa., Mar. 6, 1931; s. Manuel DeWitt and Emma Margaret (Theilacker) R.; m. Margot Denithorne, Sept. 5, 1953; children: Karen Lee, Kurt Richard. BA, Ursinus Coll., 1953, LLD (hon.), 1976; MA, U. Pa., 1957; cert., Inst. Ednl. Mgmt., Harvard U., 1974; DHL (hon.), Tohoku Gakuin U., Sendai, Japan, 1986, Muhlenberg Coll., 1989. Editor Provident Mut. Life Ins. Co., Phila., 1956-58; supr. employee communications Phila. Gas Works divsn. UGI Corp., 1958-65; alumni dir. Ursinus Coll., Collegeville, Pa., 1965-67, asst. to pres., 1967-69, v.p. adminstrv. affairs, 1969-76, pres., 1976-94; pres. emeritus, 1995—; instr. in English Ursinus Coll., Collegeville, Pa., 1965-73, asst. prof. English, 1973-86, prof. of coll. Collegville, Pa., 1986-94. Chmn. Commn. for Ind. Colls. and U. Pa., 1984, Found. for Ind. Colls. of Pa., Harrisburg, 1985; past chmn. Coun. for Higher Edn. United Ch. of Christ. Contbr. articles, poems to various publs. Recipient Gold Quill award Am. Assn. Indsl. Editors, 1964, Lindback award for excellence in tchg. Ursinus Coll., 1973, Silver Beaver award Boy Scouts Am., 1985, Muhlenberg Leadership award Hist. Soc. Trappe, Pa., 1994, Francis J. Michelini award for outstanding svc. Assn. Ind. Colls. and Univs. of Pa., 1996, Arthur V. Ciervo award Coll. and Univ. Pub. Rels. Assn. of Pa., 1996. Mem. Pa. Assn. Colls. and Univs. (bd. dirs.), Phi Beta Kappa. Home: 236 6th Ave Collegeville PA 19426-2510 Office: Ursinus Coll PO Box 1000 Collegeville PA 19426-1000 Business E-Mail: rrichter@ursinus.edu.

RICHTER, ROBERT C. automotive executive; V.p.- admin. Dana Corp., Toledo, 1997—98, v.p.- fin. and admin., 1998—99, v.p., CFO, 1999—; chmn. Dana Credit Corp., 2002—. Office: Dana Corp PO Box 1000 4500 Dorr St Toledo OH 43697

RICHTER, STEPHEN C. real estate company executive; BBA in Acctg., Sam Houston U. CPA AICPA. Acct. BDO Siedman; from acctg. supr. to sr. v.p., CFO Weingarten Realty Investors, Houston, 1980—2000, sr. v.p., 2000—, CFO, 2000—. Mem.: Nat. Assn. Real Estate Cos. (officer, bd. dir.), Nat. Assn. Real Estate Investment Trusts (co-chmn. acctg. com., co-chmn. ins. com.). Office: Weingartne Realty Investors PO Box 924133 Houston TX 77292-4133*

RICHTERS, ARNIS, medical educator, researcher; b. Sauka, Latvia, Sept. 23, 1928; arrived in U.S., 1950; s. Arturs and Alma Richters; m. Valda Zalmans, June 2, 1951; 1 child. BS, U. Ariz., 1957, MS, 1959; PhD, U. So. Calif., L.A., 1967. Instr. pathology U. So. Calif., L.A., 1968—70, asst. prof. pathology, 1970—75, assoc. prof. pathology, 1975—91, prof. pathology, 1991—2003, emeritus prof. pathology, 2003—. Cons. U. Latvia, Riga, 1994—; mem. breast cancer task force NCI, Bethesda, Md., 1972—75; Fulbright sci. and environ. rschr. Fulbright Assn., Washington, 1995—. Author: (films) The Embattled Cell, 1968 (Gold medal, The Coun. on Internat. Non-Theatrical Events, 1968); contbr. over 77 articles to profl. jours. Cpl. U.S. Army, 1951—53. Scholar Fulbright scholar, CIES, Washington, 1994. Mem.: So. Calif. Soc. Electron Microscopy (pres. 1984—85), Tissue Culture Assn. (pres. Calif. br. 1978—79). Avocations: golf, cooking, photography. Home: 2205 Tall Pine Dr Duarte CA 91010 Office: Univ Southern Calif 1840 N Soto St EDM-130 Los Angeles CA 90089

RICHTMAN, JACK, French language educator; b. N.Y.C., Mar. 15, 1927; s. Fred and Rose (Blumenfeld) R. BA, Bklyn. Coll., 1959; MA, Columbia U., 1961, PhD, 1969. Prof. French studies SUNY, Albany, 1962-95, prof. emeritus, 1995—. Assoc. dean Coll. of Humanities SUNY, Albany, 1992-94. Author: Adrienne Lecouvreur: The Actress and the Age, 1971; contbr. articles to profl. jours. Fulbright fellow Fulbright Commn., 1961-62. Mem. MLA (editor Lesbian and Gay Studies Newsletter, 1999—), Les Amis de Jean Ccteau (Am. corr. 2002--). Home: 484 W 43d St Apt 44G New York NY 10036

RICHTOL, HERBERT HAROLD, science foundation consultant; b. Bklyn., Aug. 13, 1932; s. Israil and Pearl (Boshnack) R.; m. Iris Gloria Klar, Aug. 11, 1956; children: Nancy Anne, Susan Gail, Elise Carol, Michael Bruce. BS, St. Lawrence U., 1954; PhD, NYU, 1961. Instr. Queens (N.Y.) Coll., 1960-61; chemistry prof. Rensselaer Poly. Inst., Troy, N.Y., 1961-85, dean undergrad. coll., 1985-94; program dir. Divsn. Undergrad. Edn. NSF, Arlington, Va., 1994-99, cons., 1999—. Contbr. articles to profl. jours. Bd. dirs. Temple Beth El, Troy, 1980-85. Served with U.S. Army, 1954-56. Mem. Am. Chem. Soc., AAAS, Am. Assn. Higher Edn., Woodrow Wilson Soc., Sigma Xi. Democrat. Jewish. Avocations: theater, squash. Home: 850 N Randolph St Arlington VA 22203-4000 Office: NSF/Nat Sci Found Divsn Undergrad Edn 4201 Wilson Blvd Room 835 Arlington VA 22230-0001

RICK, NEWTON MARCUS, literature and language professor, classicist; b. St. Louis, May 8, 1949; m. Evangeline Vlanton Newton, Aug. 20, 1972; children: JoAnna, Olympia, Elias. BA, Washington U., St. Louis, 1971; MA, U. Mich., Ann Arbor, 1972; attended, Am. Acad, Rome, Italy, 1973; PhD classical studies, U. Mich., Ann Arbor, 1975. Asst. prof. classics Kent State U., Kent, Ohio, 1975—80; assoc. prof., 1980—89, prof., 1989—, chmn., dept. of modern and classical languages, 1991—; vis. asst. prof Coll. Yr. in Athens, Greece, 1977. Translator: (book) 3 X 11 Tristichs by Yannis Ritsos, 1991; author: (articles) Greek, Roman, Byzantine Studios, Am. Jour. Philology, Classical Jour., Syllecta Classica, Classical Philology, 1977—. Recipient E. Constantiuides Memorial Translation Award, Modern Greek Studies Assn., 2002. Mem.: Am. Lit. Translators Assn., Classical Assn. of Middle West & South (exec. com. 1975—). Greek Orthodox. Home: 1106 Oakwood Dr Kent OH 44240 Office: Dept Modern & Classical Language Studies Kent State U Kent OH 44242

RICKABAUGH, VICKI, horse farm owner, mayor; b. Phila., June 22, 1951; d. William C. and Marilyn Kirschner; m. Charles David Rickabaugh Jr., Sept. 15, 1973; children: Gloria, George, Peggy, Marc. AA, Brookdale C.C., 1981; BS in Edn., Monmouth U., 1972. RN, N.J., state cert. EMT, N.J.; cert. elem. tchr., N.J. Owner, instr. Blue Spruce Horse Farm Dressage Ctr., Jackson, N.J., 1972—; dep. mayor Jackson Twp. (N.J.) Com., 1996, 99, mayor, 1997-98; owner, instr. Blue Spruce Farm Dressage Ctr. Founder, dressage advisor East Coast Regional Dressage Assn., Medford, N.J., 1993—; lectr. in field. Author: (book) Horse Riding for Beginners, 1985; author: (lecture series) Trace and Equine Circle of Needs, 1982—; contbr. articles on dressage and horses to East Coast Regional Dressage Assn. newsletter, 1994—. Bd. dirs. Jackson Twp. Bd. of Edn., 1991-94, v.p., 1992; Rep. committeewoman Ocean County (N.J.) Rep. Orgn., 1995—; committeewoman Jackson Twp. Com., 1996; founder, mem. Jackson Coun. for Arts, 1998—, Tourism and Bus. Coun., Jackson, 1997-99; EMT Jackson Twp. 1st Aid Squad, 1989-95; mem. Jackson Twp. Mcpl. Alliance for Prevention of Alcohol and Drug Abuse, 1995-99. Recipient Proclamation to Mayor Rickabaugh, N.J. Gov. Christine Todd Whitman, N.J. Exec. Dept., Trenton, 1997, Senate and Gen. Assembly Joint Legis. Resolution for disting. svc. State of N.J., 1997, Svc. award Jackson Coun. for Arts, 1998. Mem. Am. Horse Show Assn. (life), U.S. Dressage Fedn. ("L" judge), Ea. States Dressage and Combined Tng. Assn. (life), Pathfinders (founder). Republican. Avocations: horses, tennis, sailing. Home: 5 Stanley Pl Jackson NJ 08527-4454 Fax: 732-833-0255. E-mail: v.rickabaugh@usa.net.

RICKARD, DAVID B. food company executive; b. Oneida, N.Y., 1946; BS, Cornell U., 1969; MBA, Harvard U., 1971. From internat. acct. to fin. control mgr. U.S. mktg. S.C. Johnson Wax, Inc., 1971-74; with Gen. Foods Corp., fin. dir. internat.; dir. investor rels. Kraft Gen. Foods; v.p. fin. and strategy Kraft USA; sr. v.p., CFO Grand Metropolitan, 1991-94, group contr., 1994-95; fin. dir. Internat. Distillers and Vintners, Ltd., 1995-96; exec. v.p. Internat. Distillers and Vintners-Americas, 1996-97; sr. v.p., CFO RJR Nabisco, N.Y.C., 1997-99; CFO CVS Corp., Woonsocket, RI, 1999—. Office: CVS Corp 1 CVS Dr Woonsocket RI 02895

RICKARD, LISA ANN, lawyer; b. Englewood, N.J., Oct. 22, 1955; d. Joseph Mitchell and Ann Marie (Samen) Moore; m. J. Scott Rickard, June 18, 1977; children: Jack Taylor, Justin Moore. BA in Govt. and French, Lafayette Coll., 1977; JD, Am. U., 1982. Legis. asst. Bank of Am., Washington, 1977-78; spl. asst. and press asst. to Sen. Richard Stone, Washington, 1978-80; legis. asst. to Sen. Frank Murkowski, Washington, 1981; assoc. and ptnr. Akin, Gump, Strauss, Haver & Feld, Washington, 1982-93; v.p. federal affairs Ryder System, Inc., Washington, 1993-97, sr. v.p. govt. affairs, 1997—. Mem., corp. adv. coun. Women's Rsch. and Edn. Inst., Washington, 1991—. Polit. fundraiser various fed. dem. candidates. Diplome D'Etudes Francaises Cours Moyen, Deuxieme Degres, U. Strasbourg, France, 1976. Mem. D.C. Bar Assn. Episcopalian. Avocation: travel. Home: 10112 Darmuid Green Dr Potomac MD 20854-4852 Office: Ryder System Inc 3600 NW 82nd Ave Miami FL 33166-6623

RICKARD, MARGARET LYNN, retired library director; b. Detroit, July 31, 1944; d. Frank Mathias and Betty Louise (Lee) Sieger; m. Cyriac Thannikary, Nov. 13, 1965 (div. Feb. 1973); 1 child, Luke Anthony Thannikary; m. Marcos T. Perez, Mar. 1973 (dec. Oct. 1973); m. Lui Gotti, Dec. 23, 1984 (dec. Aug. 1997); m. William A. Rickard, Aug. 22, 1998. AB, U. Detroit, 1968; MLS, Pratt Inst., 1969; postgrad., NYU, 1976-77. Cert. libr. N.Y. Sr. libr. Queens Pub. Libr., Jamaica, NY, 1969-77; libr. dir. El Centro (Calif.) Pub. Libr., 1977-99; ret., 1999. Vice chmn., chmn. Serra Coop. Libr. Sys., San Diego, 1980—82, libr. cons., 1998—; county libr./cons. Imperial County Free Libr., 1993—99. Pres. Hist. Site Found., El Centro, 1988—99, 1992, sec., 1989, trustee, 1989—99, v.p., 1991—92; mem. Downton El Centro Assn., mem. arches bus. improvement dist.; mem. comm. and arts task force Imperial County Arts Coun.; coord. arts and culture com. City of El Centro Strategic Plan; fin. sec. St. Elizabeth Luth. Ch., El Centro, 1988. Recipient Disting. Svc. award, El Dorado County ACSA, 2004, El Dorado County Disting. Employee Svc. award, ACSA, 2004; Title IIB fellow, Pratt Inst., 1968—69. Mem.: AAUW (v.p. El Centro 1988), ALA, Calif. County Librs. Assn., Calif. Libr. Assn., Toastmasters, El Centro C. of C., Women of Moose (sr. regent El Centro 1988—89, ednl. advancment chmn. 1999—2000), Soroptomists (life; v.p. El Centro 1978, corr. sec. 1990—91, 1st v.p. 1991—92, pres. 1992—93, 2d v.p. 1995—96, 1998—99, rec. sec. 1997—98). Democrat. Lutheran. Home and Office: 6169 Terrace Dr PO Box 232 Pollock Pines CA 95726

RICKARD, RUTH DAVID, retired history and political science educator; b. Fed. Republic Germany, Feb. 20, 1926; came to U.S., 1940; d. Carl and Alice (Koch) David; m. Robert M. Yaffe, Oct. 1949 (dec. 1959); children: David, Steven; m. Norman G. Rickard, June 1968 (dec. 1988); 1 stepson, Douglas. BS cum laude, Northwestern U., 1947, MA, 1948. Law editor Commerce Clearing House, Chgo., 1948; instr. history U. Ill., Chgo., 1949-51, instr. extension program Waukegan, 1960-67; instr. history Waukegan Schs., 1960-69; original faculty, prof. western civilization, polit. sci. Coll. of Lake County, Grayslake, Ill., 1969-92. Mem. Inter-Univ. Seminar on Armed Forces and Soc.; mem. Hospitality Info. Svc. for Diplomatic Residents and Families affiliate Meridian Internat. Ctr.; spkr. in field. Author: History of College of Lake County, 1987 (honored by city of Waukegan 1987), (poem) I Lost My Wings, 1989, Au Revoir from Emeritusdom, 1993, Where are the Safety Zones, 1994; contbg. author: History of National Press Club: Reliable Sources, 1997; contbr. articles to profl. jours. Mem. Econ. Devel. Com., Waukegan, 1992-93; working with homeless through Samaritans of Greater Washington area, 2000—. Scholar Freedoms Found. Am. Legion, Valley Forge, Pa., 1967. Mem. AAUW (pres. Waukegan chpt. 1955-57, scholarship named for her 1985, program co-chair McLean chpt. 1997-2000), LWV (charter, v.p. Waukegan chpt.), Nat. Press Club D.C., Northwestern U. Alumni Washington (bd. dirs.). Avocations: writing, travel, lecturing, reading, theater.

RICKEL, ANNETTE URSO, psychology and psychiatry researcher, educator; b. Phila. d. Ralph Francis and Marguerite (Calcaterra) Urso; 1 child, John Ralph Rickel. BA, Mich. State U., 1969; PhD, MD, U. Mich., 1972. Lic. psychologist, Mich. Faculty early childhood edn. Merrill-Palmer Inst., Detroit, 1967-69; adj. faculty U. Mich., Ann Arbor, 1969-75; asst. dir. N.E. Guidance Ctr., Detroit, 1972-75; asst. prof. psychology Wayne State U., Detroit, 1975-81; vis. assoc. prof. Columbia U., N.Y.C., 1982-83; assoc. prof. psychology Wayne State U., 1981-87, asst. provost, 1989-91, prof. psychology, 1987-95; Am. Coun. on Edn. fellow Princeton and Rutgers Univs., 1990-91. AAAS and APA Congl. Sci. fellow on Senate Fin. Subcom. on Health and Pres.'s Nat. Health Care Reform Task Force, 1992—93; clin. prof. dept. psychiatry Georgetown U., Washington, 1995—2000; program officer The Rockefeller Found., 2000—03; pres. The Annette Urso Rickel Found., 2003—. Cons. editor Jour. of Cmty. Psychology, Jour. Primary Prevention; co-author: Social and Psychological Problems of Women, 1984, Preventing Maladjustment..., 1987; author: Teenage Pregnancy and Parenting, 1989, Keeping Children From Harm's Way, 1997, Understanding Managed Care, 2000; contbr. articles to profl. jours Mem. Pres.'s Task Force on Nat. Health Care Reform, 1993; bd. dirs. Children's Ctr. of Wayne County, Mich., 1989—, The Epilepsy Ctr. of Mich., 1984-92, Nat. Symphony Orch., 1997—, Reading is Fundamental, 2000—, Chamber Music Soc. of Lincoln Ctr., 2002—, Soc. Meml. Sloan Kettering Cancer Ctr., The Kellogg Found., 1996-97, The John D. and Catherine T. MacArthur Found., 1998-99. Grantee NIMH, 1976-86, Eloise and Richard Webber Found., 1977-80, McGregor Fund, 1977-78, 82, David M. Whitney Fund, 1982, Katherine Tuck Fund, 1985-90, NIH, 2000; recipient Career Devel. Chair award, 1985-86. Fellow APA (div. pres. 1984-85); mem. Internat. Women's Forum, Soc. for Rsch. in Child Devel., Soc. for Rsch. in Child and Adolescent Psychopathology, Internat. Assn. of Applied Psychologists, Sigma Xi, Psi Chi. Roman Catholic. Office Phone: 212-659-7760. Personal E-mail: rickelau@aol.com.

RICKELS, KARL, psychiatrist, educator; b. Wilhelmshaven, Germany, Aug. 17, 1924; came to U.S., 1954, naturalized, 1960; s. Karl E. and Stephanie (Roehrhoff) R.; m. Rosalind Wilson, June 27, 1964; children: Laurence Arthur, PhD, Stephen W., Michael R. MD, U. Muenster, 1951. Intern Dortmund (Germany) City Hosp., 1951-52; postgrad. tng. U. Erlangen, U. Frankfurt, City Hosp. Kassel, 1952-54; resident in psychiatry Mental Health Inst., Cherokee,

Iowa, 1954-55, Hosp. U. Pa., Phila., 1955-57; from instr. to assoc. prof. U. Pa., Phila., 1957-69, prof. psychiatry, 1969—, prof. pharmacology, 1976-98, Stuart and Emily B.H. Mudd prof. human behavior, 1977—, chief mood and anxiety disorders program, 1964—, chmn. com. on studies involving human beings, 1985-98. Chief psychiatry Phila. Gen. Hosp., 1975-77. Editor, author 9 books; contbr. over 550 articles to profl. publs. Fellow Am. Coll. Neuropsychopharmacology (life; charter), Am. Soc. Clin. Psychopharmacology, Am. Psychiat. Assn. (life), Coll. Physicians Phila., Collegium Internat. Neuro-Psychopharmacologicum; mem. Psychiat. Rsch. Soc., European Coll. Neuropsychopharmacology (corr.). Home: 1324 Youngsford Rd Gladwyne PA 19035 Office: U Pa Dept Psychiatry Ste 670 3535 Market St Philadelphia PA 19104-3515 Office Phone: 215-746-6417. Business E-Mail: krickels@mail.med.upenn.edu.

RICKER, JON, retail executive; V.p. corp. sys. devel. Fed. Express; v.p., CIO BellSouth, Ltd., Inc., Columbus, Ohio, 1996—99; pres., CEO, cIO Ltd. Tech. Svcs., Columbus, 1999—. Office: Ltd Brands Three Ltd Pkwy Columbus OH 43230

RICKERD, DONALD SHERIDAN, foundation executive; b. Smiths Falls, Ontario, Canada, Nov. 8, 1931; s. Harry M. and Evaline Mildred (Sheridan) R.; m. Julie (Rekai), Dec. 14, 1968; one child, Christopher. Attended, St. Andrews U., Scotland, 1951-52; BA, Queen's U., Can., 1953; BA Rotary Found. fellow, Balliol Coll., Oxford U., Eng., 1955; MA, Oxford U., Eng., 1963; LLD, Queen's U., Can., 1985; DCL, Mount Allison U., Can., 1985; LLD, Trent U., Can., 1986; LLB, York U., Can., 1991. Bar: Ont. 1959; apptd. Queen's Counsel, 1978. Assoc. Fasken & Calvin, Toronto, 1957-61; registrar, lectr. history, asst. prof. law Faculty of Adminstrv. Studies York U., Toronto, 1961-68; pres. Donner Can. Found., Toronto, 1968-89, W.H. Donner Found., Inc., N.Y.C., 1971-87, Max Bell Found., Toronto, 1989-97, Zavikon Found., 1997—. Former chmn. bd. dir. Draeger Can. Ltd., Canada; former bd. dir. ICWI Found., Kingston, Jamaica; assoc. dir. Asian Bus. and Mgmt. Studies Program, Toronto-York U. Mem. Royal Commn. concerning activities Royal Can. Mounted Police, 1977—81; trustee, vice chmn. bd. trustees Queen's U., 1989—2001; former chmn. Coun. Ont. Coll. Art., Toronto; past chmn. Ctrl. Hosp., 1993—96; former bd. govs. Upper Can. Coll., Toronto; former mem. bd. regents Mt. Allison U.; former chair, pres. Wellesley Ctrl. Health Corp., Toronto. Decorated Order of Can. Mem.: Bd. Trade Met. Toronto (former pres.), U. Club Toronto. E-mail: drickerd@yorku.ca.

RICKERT, JANET E. medical/surgical nurse; b. Chgo., Sept. 18, 1959; d. Donald Paul and Yvonne H. (Davis) Mattz; m. Mark Donald Rickert, July 24, 1982; 1 child, Russ Edward. Student, Trinity Christian Coll., 1978—79; nursing diploma, Evang. Sch. Nursing, 1981; student, St. Xaviers Coll., 1988. RN Ill., cert. ob-gyn. RN labor and delivery Christ Hosp., Oaklawn, Ill., 1981—82, Hinsdale (Ill.) Hosp., 1982—99. Author: Russ & The Apple Tree Surprise, 1999, Russ & The Firehouse, 2000, Russ & The Almost Perfect Day, 2001. Mem.: NADS.

RICKERT, JEANNE MARTIN M. lawyer; b. Cambridge, Mass., May 13, 1953; d. Robert Torrence and Margaret (Mutchler) Martin; m. Scott Edwin Rickert, Aug. 19, 1978. BA, Cornell U., 1975; JD, Case Western U., 1978. Bar: Ohio 1980, U.S. Dist. Ct. (no. dist.) Ohio 1980. Law clk. to presiding justice U.S. Dist. Ct. Ohio, Akron, 1978-80; assoc. Jones, Day, Reavis & Pogue, Cleve., 1980-86; ptnr. Jones & Day, Cleve., 1987—. Author: The Limited Liability Company in Ohio: 1994 Senate Bill 74, with Commentary and Practice Pointers, 1994. Mem. Ohio State Bar Assn. (corp. law com. 1985—). Office: Jones Day Reavis & Pogue N Point 901 Lakeside Ave E Cleveland OH 44114-1190

RICKERT, JONATHAN BRADLEY, retired foreign service officer; b. Washington, July 23, 1937; s. Van Dusen and Margaret Eleanor (Bradley) R.; m. Ulla Gerd Margareta Granstrand, June 20, 1969; children: Ulla Margaret, Jonathan Bernt. AB cum laude, Princeton U, 1959; diploma Russian lang., U.S. Army Lang. Sch., 1962; student, Harvard U., 1976-77; MA, George Washington U., 1982. Rotational jr. officer Exec. Sec. State Dept., 1963-65; consular officer Embassy, London, 1965-66, staff aide to amb., polit. officer Moscow, 1966-68; exchanges officer Office Soviet and Eastern European Exchanges State Dept., 1969-70, with Romanian Lang. Tng. FSI, 1971; consular officer Embassy Bucharest, 1971-73, polit. officer, 1973-74; spl. asst. to U.S. Rep. U.S. Delegation MBFR, Vienna, 1974-76; polit./labor officer Embassy Port of Spain, 1977-80; desk officer Trinidad, Guyana, Suriname, acting dep. dir. Office Caribbean Affairs State Dept., 1980-82, desk officer Romania, Office Eastern European and Yugoslav Affairs, 1982-84, with Bulgarian Lang. Tng., 1984-85; dep. chief mission Embassy Sofia, 1985-88; chief European Assignments divsn. State Dept., 1988-90; legis. asst. to Sen Bob Packwood, 1990-91; dep. chief mission Embassy Bucharest, 1991-95; dir. Office of N. Cen. European Affairs State Dept., 1995-98, program officer Office of the Coord. for U.S. Assistance to Europe and Eurasia, 1998; bd. dirs. Project on Ethnic Rels., Princeton, N.J., 1999. With U.S. Army, 1961-62. Mem. Am. Fgn. Svc. Assn. Episcopalian. E-mail: rickertjb@state.gov.

RICKERT, ROBERT RICHARD, pathologist, educator; b. Harrisburg, Pa., Oct. 19, 1936; s. Alton G. and Henrietta (Gey) R.; m. Sonja Murray Hansen, Aug. 26, 1961; children: Kristin, Robin, Anne. AB, U. Mich., 1958; MD, John Hopkins U., 1962. Diplomat Am. Bd. of Pathology. Intern Yale-New Haven (Conn.) Med. Ctr., 1962-63, resident in pathology, 1963-64, 66-67; rsch. assoc. Atomic Bomb Casulty Commn., Hiroshima, Japan, 1964-66; asst. prof. pathology Yale U. Sch. Med., New Haven, 1966-70; attending pathologist Yale New Haven Med. Ctr., 1968-70; dir. surg. pathology U. Med. and Dentistry N.J.-N.J. Med. Sch., Newark, 1970-73, assoc. prof. pathology, 1970-73; clin. prof. pathology U. of Med. and Dentistry N.J.-N.J. Med. Sch., Newark, 1985—; co-chmn. dept. pathology St. Barnabas Med. Ctr., Livingston, N.J., 1973-2000, chmn. dept. pathology, 2000—. Adj. assoc. prof. pathology Columbia U. Coll. Physicians & Surgeons, N.Y.C., 1974-89. Contbr. chpts. to med. textbooks and articles to profl. jours. Chmn. med. com. Am. Cancer Soc., N.J., 1989-91, v.p. 1991-93, pres. elect 1993-94, pres. 1995-97 (Physician of Yr., N.J. Divsn., 1998), chief med. officer, bd. dirs. Ea. divsn., 1998-2000. Recipient honoree, ACS Coaches vs. Cancer Classic, 2003. Fellow Coll. Am. Pathologists (vice-chmn., internat. regional commr. commn. on lab. accreditation, Pathologist of Yr. 2001), Am. Soc. Clin. Pathologists, U.S.-Can. Acad. Pathology; mem. AMA, N.J. Soc. Pathologists (pres. 1980-82), Gastrointestinal Pathology Soc. (pres. 1988-89), Med. Soc. N.J., Acad. Medicine N.J. (trustee 1988—, treas. 1994-95, v.p. 1995-97, pres. 1998), Am. Soc. Cytopathology, Short Hills Club, Phi Beta Kappa, Alpha Omega Alpha. Republican. Congregationalist. Avocations: antiques, wine collecting, art. Office: St Barnabas Med Ctr Dept Pathology Livingston NJ 07039

RICKETSON, GEORGE MANNING, III, retired surgeon; b. Atlanta, Ga., 1937; MD, U. Fla., 1966. Diplomate Am. Bd. Surgery. Intern Behtesda Naval Hosp, Md., 1966-67; resident in surgery USN Hosp., Portsmouth, Va., 1967-71; pvt. practice Sacred Heart Hosp., Pensacola, Fla.; pvt. practice, group partnership McMahon Ricketson Stockamp, Pensacola, Fla.; ret., 2001. Fellow ACS; mem. AMA, Southeastern Surg. Congress, So. Med. Assn. Office: McMahon Ricketson Stockamp 5014 Barranca Lora Pensacola FL 32514 Personal E-mail: gricketson@att.net.

RICKETSON, MICHAEL E. financial company executive; Exec. v.p., CFO Central and So. Holding Co., 1993-97, Premier Bancshares Inc., Atlanta, 1998—. Office: Premier Bancshares Inc 950 E Paces Ferry Rd NE Atlanta GA 30326-1180

RICKETT, CAROLYN KAYE MASTER, artist, criminologist; b. Ft. Worth, Apr. 24, 1941; d. Lester Buford and Dorothy Minerva (Whittington) Master; m. David Franklin Rickett, May 3, 1981; 1 child, Julia Beth Allen. BFA, Tex. Christian U., 1993; MFA, Tex. Woman's U., 1997; M in Criminology, U. Tex., Arlington, 2001, postgrad. in Econs., 2002—. Artist, owner StarMaster Graphic Design and Fine Art, Ft. Worth, 1988—; represented by Downstairs Gallery, Dallas, Kincannon Fine Arts Gallery. Presenter in field. Represented in permanent collections Jasper Mus., Nat. Women's Caucus Arts Archives, also pvt. collections, one-woman shows include Jasper Mus., Alta., Can., 1994, Downstairs Gallery, Jasper, 1994, Del Bello Gallery, Toronto, Ont., Can., 1996, exhibitions include Tex. Christian U., Ft. Worth, 1991, Greater Denton Coun. Arts., Tex., 1994—96, Tex. Christian U., 1995, 1997, UN 4th Conf. Women, Beijing, 1995, Bass Mus., Miami Broward C.C., Davie, Fla., 1996, San Jacinto Coll., Houston, 1996, Aisling Studio, Durango, Colo. 1996, U. Tex., Arlington, 1998, World Trade Ctr., Dallas, 1998, (traveling show) Beijing and Beyong, N.Y., 1998—2000, others. Grantee, Tex. Christian U., 1990—93; scholar, 1991—93, Ray and Bertha Lakey Meml., 1994—96. Mem.: Am. Soc. Crime, Tex. Art Educators Assn., Nat. Trust for Hist. Preservation, Mus. Women in Arts, Am. Soc. Criminology, Am. Criminal Justice Scis. Home: 5816 Broadway Ave Fort Worth TX 76117-3305

RICKETTS, JAMES F. treasurer; BSBA, Ohio State U., 1969, MBA, 1973. Various treasury and controller positions Ford Motor Cor.; corp. v.p., treas. Ingram Micro Inc, Santa Ana, Calif., 1996—. Bd. dirs. Mission Aviation Fellowship, PACTEC. With U.S. Army, 1970—71. Office: Ingram Micro Inc 1600 E St Andrew Pl PO Box 25125 Santa Ana CA 92799

RICKETTS, VIRGINIA LEE, historian, researcher; b. Jamestown, Kans., Jan. 12, 1925; d. Roy Earl Eastman and Alma Anna Hunter; m. Clair Keith Ricketts, June 3, 1944; children: Keith Alan, Dennis Lee, Donald Gene. Grad. H.S., Filer, Idaho. Clk. dist. ct., auditor, recorder Jerome County, Idaho, 1972-79; pvt. practice historian, rschr. Jerome, 1979—. Mem. Idaho State Hist. Records Adv. Bd., Boise, 1976-2002; pres. Idaho Assn. Recorders and Clks., 1977-78; cons. Idaho State Supreme Ct., Boise, 1979-81; tour dir., instr. Coll. So. Idaho, Twin Falls, 1984-97; mem. Bur. Land Mgmt. Adv. Bd., Shoshone, Idaho, 1989-95, Upper Snake River Ecosystem Adv. Bd., Idaho, 1995-98; Internat. Toastmistress communicator, 1988; lectr. in field. Author: The History of the North Side-The First 75 Years, 1982, Greater Twin Falls Historical Guide, 1988, A History of the Middle Snake River, 1996, Then and Now in Southern Idaho, 1998. Organizer Friends St. Stricker Ranch, Inc., Twin Falls, 1984. Recipient Cert. of Commendation, Am. Assn. for State and Local History, 1984, Cert. of Resolution of Appreciation, Idaho State Bd. Edn., 1998; named Idaho Disting. Citizen, Idaho Statesmen, 1988, Centennial Citizen, Citizens of Jerome County Idaho, 1990. Mem. Idaho State Hist. Soc. (trustee 1987-99, chairperson bd. trustees 1991-98), Oreg. Calif. Trails Assn. (organizer Idaho chpt. 1984, treas. Idaho chpt. 1985-99), Jerome County Hist. Soc., Inc. (co-organizer 1984, former pres., curator 1985-2004), Idaho Assn. of Mus. (Outstanding Svc. award 1998), Soroptomist Internat. of Am. (Woman of Distinction 1999), PEO (chpt. E Idaho, historian 1987-98). Republican. Presbyterian. Avocations: needlecrafts, gardening, sports, family activities. Home: 516 E 300 S Jerome ID 83338-6747

RICKEY, HORACE B., JR., retired engineer; b. New Orleans, July 2, 1924; s. Horace Bushnell Rickey and Marjorie Bouvier; m. Jewel Katherine Seybold, Aug. 15, 1947 (dec. Dec. 1984); children: Sharon Jewel, Marjorie Anna, Priscilla Gail; m. Maude Elizabeth Dudley, Nov. 30, 1985 (div. Apr. 1995). BSCE, U. Wyo., 1947, BS in Archtl. Engring., 1948. Registered profl. engr., La.; lic. profl. surveyor, realtor, ins. agt., La. CAO Horace B. Rickey Constrn. Co., Lafayette, La., 1948—67; pvt. practice engring. Horace B. Rickey Jr. PE, Lafayette, 1948-89; pres. S.W. Materials, Lafayette, 1956-78, S.W. Homes, Lafayette, 1963-78, Buck Enterprises, Albuquerque, 1978-86; real estate agt. Lafayette, 1986-92; dir. pub. works City of Lafayette, 1992; project engr. Lafayette Consol. Govt., 1993-98; ret., 1998. V.p. Union Fed. S&L, Lafayette, 1960-85; sec., treas., CAO Motor Logdes of Lafayette, 1966-86; operating dir. Computers for Bus. Mgmt., Lafayette, 1970-86; pres., CAO Buck Enterprises Motel, Albuquerque, 1978-86. Scoutmaster, cubmaster Boy Scouts Am., New Orleans, 1942-43; v.p. Bayou coun. Girl Scouts U.S., Lafayette, 1961-65, pres., 1965-69; bd. dirs. Hunter-Jumper Assn., La., 1971, Southwestern La. Inst. Assn., Lafayette, 1969-72, Salvation Army, Lafayette, 1960-62; chmn. constrn. divsn. United Fund, Lafayette, 1968, campaign chmn., 1969, pres., 1970; bd. dirs. Lafayette C. of C., 1960-62, 69-71, v.p., 1961; chmn. Citizen's Adv. Com. for City and Parish under Interstate Act, Lafayette, 1960-62; chmn. Rep. Parish Exec. Com., Lafayette, 1953-65; sec. Rep. State Ctrl. Com., La., 1955-65; deacon First Presbyn. Ch., Lafayette, 1958-62, ruling elder, 1962-74. Sgt. AUS, 1943-46, ETO. Recipient Thanks Badge, Bayou Coun. Girl Scouts U.S., 1969, Outstanding Svcs. to Arts award, La. Arts Coun., 1971, Expert Tapiestier award, Acadian Weavers, 1978. Avocations: flat loom weaving, Goblein tapestry weaving, genealogy. Home: 129 Betts ST Lafayette LA 70503

RICKIN, SHEILA ANNE, personnel professional; b. N.Y.C., Oct. 13, 1945; d. Louis and Ethel (Schmukler) Bernstein; BA, CCNY, 1966; postgrad. NYU; MBA, Pace U., 1988. Rsch. asst. pre-baccalureate program CCNY, 1966-68; placement counselor Elaine Revell, Inc., N.Y.C., 1968; adminstr. assoc. to CEO Parenthood Fedn. of Am., N.Y.C., 1969-74; pers. mgr. Family Circle Mag./N.Y. Times Mag. Group, 1974-87; sr. human resources rep., Drexel Burnham Lambert, 1987-88; asst. v.p., dir. pers. and adminstrn. Oppenheimer Mgmt. Corp. div. Mass Mut. Ins. Co., 1989-93; assoc. human resources mgr. AVSC Internat., N.Y.C., 1994-96; cons. human resources, 1993-96; dir. human resources WNYC Found., 1996-97; mgr. human resources and internal cons. C&S Sys./N.Y. Times Co., N.Y.C., 1997—. Mem. APHA, ASTD (security industry group 1987-93), Am. Compensation Assn., Human Resources Soc., Soc. Human Resources Mgmt. (employee rels./diversity com.), Internat. Found. Benefits, Am. Mgmt. Assn., N.Y. Human Resources Planners, N.Y. Pers. Mgrs. Assn. (program com.), Mag. Pubs. Assn. (pers. com. 1978-87). Office: C&S Sys/NY Times Co 1111 Marcus Ave Ste M21 Lake Success NY 11042

RICKLEFS, DALE LYNNE, library director; b. Chgo., July 29, 1953; d. Glenn Harley and Eleanor Clara Rogers; 1 child, Reyhan. BA, Ill. Wesleyan U., 1974; MLS, U. Tex., 1977. Libr. Radian Corp., Austin, Tex., 1975—80; libr. dir. City of Round Rock, Tex., 1980—. Mem. ex officio Friends Round Rock Pub. Libr., Round Rock, 1983—, Round Rock Pub. Libr. Found., Round Rock, 1991—. Pres. Round Rock Rotary Club, Round Rock, 2000—01, Bus. and Profl. Women's Club, Round Rock, 1983—84; pres United Way Greater Williamson Co., Round Rock, 2003—; mem. bd. dirs. Round Rock Cmty. Choir, 1998—2003; pres. Main St. Quilt Guild, 2002—03; boy scout dist. cub trainer Boy Scouts of Am. Tomahawk Dist., Austin-Georgetown, Tex., 1991—92. Recipient Dist. Cubscouter of Yr., Boy Scouts Am. Tomahawk Dist., Texas, 1992. Mem.: ALA, Texas Mun. League Libr. Dir.'s Divsn. (pres. 1988—89), Tex. Libr. Assn. (chmn. dist. 3 1984—85). Avocations: quilting, machine embroidery, old house renovations, painting. Office: City Round Rock Pub Libr 216 E Main St Round Rock TX 78664 Business E-Mail: dale@round-rock.tx.us.

RICKLEFS, ROGER ULRICH, retired newspaper editor; b. San Rafael, Calif., July 26, 1940; s. Robert U. and Marian (Markarian) R. BA, Harvard U., 1961. With Wall Street Jour., 1964—, Paris bur. chief, 1983-86, nat. corr., 1986-89, dep. news editor, 1989-90, enterprise editor, 1990-97, Can. editor, 1997-2001; ret., 2001. Editor: The Mind of Robert Louis Stevenson, 1963. 1st lt. U.S. Army, 1962-64. E-mail: ricklefs@att.net.

RICKLES, DONALD JAY, comedian, actor; b. L.I., N.Y., May 8, 1926; s. Max S. and Etta (Feldman) R.; m. Barbara Sklar, Mar. 14, 1965; children: Mindy Beth, Lawrence Corey. Grad., Am. Acad. Dramatic Arts, N.Y.C. Appeared in TV shows The Don Rickles Show, 1971-72, C.P.O. Sharkey, 1976-77, Foul-Ups, Bleeps and Blunders, 1984, Daddy Dearest, 1993; appeared in movies Run Silent, Run Deep, 1958, The Rat Race, 1960, Kelly's Heroes, 1992, Casino, 1995, Toy Story, 1995, Quest for Camelot, 1998, Toy Story 2, 1999, others; appeared as comedian at Stardust Hotel, Las Vegas, Nev., Harrah's Club, Reno and Lake Tahoe, Nev., Resorts Atlantic City, numerous other nightclubs; numerous appearances TV variety shows; rec. albums include Don Rickles Speaks and Hello Dummy. Served with USN, 1943-45. Named Entertainer of Yr. Friars Club, 1974; awarded star on Hollywood Walk of Fame, 2000. Office: care Shefrin Co 808 S Ridgeley Dr Los Angeles CA 90036-4727 Office Phone: 323-931-8200.

RICKMAN, DAN SCOTT, economics professor; s. Jerry Dean and Shirley Rickman; m. Rebecca Jean Kossan, Dec. 1, 1989; children: Shane Daniel, Rachel Rebecca. BS, U. of Wyo., 1980, MPA, 1982, PhD, 1987. Rsch. dir. REMI, Amherst, Mass., 1988—91; asst. prof. of econs. U. of Nev., 1991—93; univ. prof. of econ. devel. Ga. So. U., Statesboro, Ga., 1993—96; chairholder in regional econ. analysis Okla. State U., Stillwater, Okla., 1996—. Assoc. dir. Ctr. for Bus. and Econ. Rsch., Las Vegas, 1991—93. Editor: The Review of Regional Studies. Mem.: So. Regional Sci. Assn., N.Am. Regional Sci. Assn., Am. Econ. Assn. Office: Okla State U 338 Coll Bus Stillwater OK 74078 E-mail: rdan@okstate.edu.

RICKS, DAVID ARTEL, business educator, editor; b. Washington, July 21, 1942; s. Artel and Focha (Black) R. BS, Brigham Young U., 1966; MBA, Ind. U., 1968, PhD, 1970. Asst. prof. Ohio State U., 1970-75, assoc. prof., 1975-81; prof. internat. bus. U. S.C., Columbia, 1981-92; v.p. acad. affairs Thunderbird-the Am. Grad. Sch. Internat. mgmt., 1992-94, disting. prof., 1992-99, U. Mo., St. Louis, 1999—2002, curators' prof., 2002—. Author books, articles in field, including Directory of Foreign Manufactures in the U.S. (Best Reference Book 1974 ALA, 1975); editor Kent Pub. Co., Boston, 1978—; editor-in-chief Jour. of Internat. Bus. Studies, 1984-92, Jour. Internat. Mgmt., 1994-97. Mem. Acad. internat. Bus. (treas. 1981-82), Acad. Mgmt. (chmn. internat. divsn. 1988-89). Home: 7445 Byron Pl Clayton MO 63105-2967 Office: 8001 Natural Bridge Rd Saint Louis MO 63121-4401

RICKS, JOHN ADDISON, III, history professor; b. Charlotte, NC, Aug. 18, 1939; s. John Addison Jr. and Mamye Snow (Turner) R.; m. Nancy Elaine Ricks, Apr. 23 1966; children: Elizabeth Anne, John Addison IV. BA, Davidson Coll., 1961; MA, Tulane U., 1963; PhD, U. N.C., 1974. Instr. history Montreat- Anderson Coll., NC, 1966-68; from instr. to prof. Valdosta State U., Ga., 1968-88; prof. history, chmn. social sci. edn., bus. adminstrn. div. Mid. Ga. Coll., Cochran, 1988—2003. Contbr. articles to jour., newspapers. Pres. Friends of the Libr., Cochran, 1989-90; clk. of session, elder First Presbyn. Ch., Eastman, 1990-93; 1998-2001, scoutmaster Boy Scouts Am., Valdosta, 1982-84; mem. Valdosta Bd. Edn., 1976-80. 1st lt. US Army, 1963-65. Fulbright Found. grantee, 1992, 97. Mem. So. Assn. Coll. and Sch. (mem. vis. team 1990), So. Assn. Secondary Sch. and Coll. (mem. vis. team 1979), Ga. Assn. Historians (pres. 1994-95), Cochran C. of C., Rotary (pres. 1993-94, Rotarian of Yr. 1997, Paul Harris fellow 2001), Kiwanis (pres. 1980-82, Kiwanian of Yr. 1979). Democrat. Presbyterian. Avocations: piano, weight-lifting, nordic track exercise, reading, chess. Home: 712 Beech St Cochran GA 31014 Office: Cochran Better Hometown Inc 318 Second St Cochran GA 31014 Office Phone: 478-934-0017. E-mail: jricks39@yahoo.com.

RICKS, JOYCIA CAMILLA, retired lawyer; b. Atlanta, Feb. 17, 1949; d. George Palmer and Johnnie Mae (Ricks) Redd. BBA, Albany State Coll., 1971; MS, Ga. State U., 1977; JD, Woodrow Wilson Coll. Law, Atlanta, 1979, LLM, 1987. Bar: Ga. 1979, US Dist. Ct. (no. dist.) Ga. 1979, US Ct. Appeals (5th cir.) 1979. Acctg. clk. Gulf Oil Corp., Atlanta, 1971; clk. EEOC, Atlanta, 1971-73, paralegal specialist, 1973-79, investigator, 1979-91, supervisory investigator, 1992-2000; complaints mgr. CDC, Atlanta, 2000—03; gen. counsel Albany State Coll. Alumni Assn., 1986-90. Mem. NAACP, Atlanta, 1983—. Recipient Presdl. citation award Equal Opportunity in Higher Edn., Washington, 1981, Spl. Achievement award EEOC, Atlanta, 1982-84, 86-89, Employee of Yr., Atlanta Dist. Office, 1997; Woman of the Yr.: Tara chpt. 1985, 1991, Atlanta Peach Chpt., 2003. Mem. ABA, Atlanta Bar Assn., Ga. Assn. Black Women Attys., Albany State Coll. Alumni Assn. (pres. Atlanta chpt. 1983-85, gen. counsel 1986-90), ATLA, Ga. State U. Alumni Assn., Woodrow Wilson Coll. Law Alumni Assn., Women of the Ch. Presbyn. (hon. life), Am. Bus. Women's Assn. (Woman of Yr., Tara chpt. 1985, 91), Spreading Oak Cmty. Club. Democrat. Presbyterian.

RICO, MARIA L. publishing executive; b. San Luis Potosi, Mex., Mar. 9, 1954; arrived in U.S., 1974; d. Florentino A. Rico and Conception Muñoz; children from previous marriage: Robertha C. Medina, Francisco J. Medina, Earl A. Medina. Student, Inst. Tech., Guadalajara, Mex.; cert. nurse asst., Assn. Ho., Chgo.; student, City Wide Coll., Chgo.; cert., Wright Coll. Humboldt Park Vocat., Chgo. Grant writing bd. mem. Near N.W. Neighborhood Network, Chgo., 1995—97; cert. nurse asst. Lakeview Rehab. Ctr., Chgo., 1997—2000; mail clk. Desplaines (Ill.) Pub. Co., 2000—03, mechanic, mgr., 2003—. Recipient Vol. award, Christopher Columbus Sch., 1992, cert. of merit, A.N. Pritzker Sch., Chgo., 1995, cert. of achievement, Innovation & Reform in Edn., 1997. Avocations: dance, poetry, music. Home: 4620 W Waveland Chicago IL 60641

RICO, SUZANNE, newscaster; BA in mass comm., UCLA; MA in broadcast comm., San Francisco State U. Reporter WLS-TV, Chicago, KABC, Los Angeles; anchor, reporter NBC, San Diego, 2000—02; co-anchor, CBS 2 News at 5, 6 and 11pm KCBS, Los Angeles, 2002—. Reporter Olympic Winter Games, Salt Lake City. Contbr. & mem. Muscular Dystrophy Assn.; mem. Los Angeles Mentoring Connection. Office: CBS 2 News 6121 Sunset Blvd Los Angeles CA 90028

RICO-GUTIERREZ, LUIS F. architecture educator; BArch, ITESM, 1986; grad. degree in modular design, Rafael Leoz Found., 1988; M in Bldg. Performance, Carnegie Mellon U., 1997. Jr. designer Rafael Leoz Found., Madrid, 1988—90, projects mgr., 1990—91, mgr. arch. dept., 1991—92; ind. CAD cons. Madrid, 1992—93; prof. ITESM, Queretaro, 1993—96; asst. prof. Carnegie Mellon U. Sch. Arch., Pitts., 1996—, assoc. dean Coll. Fine Arts, 1996—, assoc. head, 1996—. Recipient Nationwide award for ednl. innovation, Borrego Dorado ITESM, Mexico, 1997, Andrew Heiskell award for tech. enhanced learning in internat. edn., Inst. for Internat. Edn., 2003. Office: Carnegie Mellon Univ Sch Arch CFA 201 201 College Fine Arts Pittsburgh PA 15213*

RICORD, KATHY, diversified financial services company executive; Grad., Denison U.; degree in City and Regional Planning and Bus. Adminstrn., Ohio State U. With Nationwide Mutual Ins. Co., 1986—, asst. to CEO, 1997—99, sr. v.p. mktg. and strategy, 2002—03, exec. v.p., chief mktg. officer, 2003—. Office: Nationwide Mutual Ins Co One Nationwide Plaza Columbus OH 43215-2220

RICORDI, CAMILLO, surgeon, transplant and diabetes researcher; b. N.Y.C., Apr. 1, 1957; m. Valerie A. Grace, Aug. 8, 1986; children: M. Caterina, Eliana G., Carlo A. MD, U. Milan (Italy) Sch. Medicine, 1982. Trainee in gen. surgery San Raffaele Inst., Milan, 1982-85; NIH trainee Washington U. Sch. Medicine, St. Louis, 1985-88; attending surgeon San Raffaele Inst., Milan, 1988-89; asst. prof. to assoc. prof. surgery U. Pitts., Pa., 1989-93; prof. surgery and medicine, pathology, microbiology and immunology, chief divsn. cellular transpl. Diabetes Rsch. Inst., U. Miami, Fla., 1993—, sci. dir., chief acad. officer, 1996—, Stacy Joy Goodman chair in Diabetes Rsch., 1998—. Reviewer of applications for grants Can. and Am. Diabetes Assns., Juvenile Diabetes Found., NIH; chmn. First and Third Internat. Congresses of Cell Transplant Soc., Pitts., 1992, Miami, 1996, 5th Internat. Congress on Pancreas and Islet Transplantation, Miami, 1995, others; mem. editl. bd. Transplantation, Cell Transplantation, Transplantation Procs., Jour. Tissue Engring. Editor: Pancreatic Islet Cell Transplantation, 1992, Methods in Cell Transplantaion, 1995; co-editor-in-chief Cell Transplantation, Graft; contbr. numerous chpts. to books and articles to jours. including Immunology Today, Jour. Clin. Investigation, New Eng. Jour. Medicine, Hepatology, Diabetes, Transplantation, Endocrinology, Procs. NAS, USA, Am. Jour. Physiology, Surgery, Nature, Nature Genetics, Lancet. Grantee Juvenile Diabetes Found. Internat., 1988—, NIH, 1993—; recipient NIH trainee award, 1986-88, Nessim Habif World prize of surgery, 2001. Mem. AAAS, Cell Transplant Soc. (founder, pres. 1992-94), Am. Soc. Transplant Surgeons, Internat. Pancreas and Islet Transplant Assn. (v.p. 1979-99, pres. 1999—), The Transplantation Soc., Am. Diabetes Assn. (Rsch. award 1996, Outstanding Achievement award 2002), Am. Fedn. Clin. Rsch., Nat. Diabetes Coalition (co-founder 1994—, chmn. 1997—). Achievements include patent for Automated Method for Cell Separation. Office: U Miami Diabetes Rsch Inst PO Box 016310 Miami FL 33101-6310

RICOTTA, JOHN JOSEPH, vascular surgeon, educator; b. Buffalo, N.Y., Sept. 13, 1949; s. Joseph J. and Joan (Tarantino) R.; m. Gloria DeSantis, July 25, 1970; children: Joseph, Genna, Lise. BA, Yale Coll., 1969; MD, Johns Hopkins U., 1973. Diplomate Am. Bd. Surgery with spl. certification in vascular surgery. Intern, resident Johns Hopkins Hosp., 1973-79; instr. surgery Johns Hopkins U., Balt., 1979-80; asst. prof. surgery U. Rochester, N.Y., 1980-85, assoc. prof. surgery, 1985-88; prof. surgery, dir. vascular surgery SUNY, Buffalo, 1988-97, prof., chmn. dept. surgery Stony Brook, 1997—. Fellow ACS; mem. Soc. Vascular Surgery, Soc. Univ. Surgeons, Ctrl. Surg. Assn., Ea. Vascular Soc. (recorder 1992—, sec. 1996—, pres. 2001), Soc. Clin. Vascular Surgery (pres. 2001), Am. Surg. Assn.,Am. Assn. Vascular Surgery. Office: U Med Ctr Hsc T 19 Rm 020 Stony Brook NY 11794-0001 E-mail: JRicotta@notes.cc.sunysb.edu.

RIDDER, LINDA GAYLE, librarian; b. Chgo., Apr. 17, 1949; d. Gale Eugene and Yvonne Lucille (Marcotte) A.; m. George Larry Ridder, Mar. 29, 1970; 1 child, Michael Eric. BA English, St. Mary's U., 1971; MS Libr. Sci., Our Lady of the Lake U., 1977. Cert. media specialist; profl. libr.; provisional cert. secondary English and social studies, Tex. Tchr. fourth grade St. Thomas More Cath. Sch., San Antonio, Tex., 1971-72; tchr. English/dept. coord. Sam Rayburn Mid. Sch., San Antonio, 1972-77; libr. media specialist Gregorio Esparza Elem., San Antonio, 1977-85, H.B. Zachry Mid. Sch., San Antonio, 1985—. Mem. Sch. Leadership Team, 1985—, Sch. Adv. Team, 1994—, recording sec.; mem. Northside Dist. Comm. Network Com., 1996—, Zachry Tech. Task Force Com., 1996—. Author Middle School Integrated Curriculum Guide of Library Skills, 1991; dir. accreditation reports, 1979, 84. Mem. St. Luke's Cath. Ch., San Antonio, 1975—. Mem. Nat. Reading Assn., Tex. Libr. Assn., Phi Delta Kappa. Home: 4607 Lightning Ln San Antonio TX 78238-2907 Office: HB Zachry Mid Sch 9410 Timber Path San Antonio TX 78250-4921

RIDDER, PAUL ANTHONY, newspaper executive; b. Duluth, Minn., Sept. 22, 1940; s. Bernard H. and Jane (Delano) Ridder; m. Constance Louise Meach, Nov. 6, 1960; children: Katherine Lee Pennoyer, Linda Jane, Susan Delano Cobb, Paul Anthony Jr. BA in Econs., U. Mich., 1962. With Aberdeen (S.D.) Am. News, 1962—63; With Pasadena (Calif.) Star News, 1963—64; with San Jose (Calif.) Mercury News, 1964—86, bus. mgr., 1968—75, gen. mgr., 1975—77, pub., 1977—86, pres., 1979—86, Knight-Ridder Newspaper Divsn., Miami, Fla., 1989—; pres., chmn., CEO Knight-Ridder, Miami, 1995—, also bd. dirs. Bd. dirs. Seattle Times, Knight-Ridder, Inc.; adv. bd. Stanford U. Grad. Sch. Bus. Bd. trustees Santa Clara U. Named Calif. Pub. of Yr., 1983, Newspaper Exec. of Yr., Ad Week, 1991. Mem.: San Francisco Golf Club, Pine Valley Golf Club, Cypress Point Club.

RIDDER, PETER B. publishing executive; b. Duluth, Minn. Former pub. St. Paul (Minn.) Pioneer Press, 1992—97; pub. Charlotte Observer, 1997—. Founding sponsor Leadership Long Beach, Calif. Office: Charlotte Observer PO Box 32188 Charlotte NC 28232-2188

RIDDERHEIM, MARY MARGARET, psychotherapist; b. Chillicothe, Ohio, Mar. 13, 1946; d. Marion Othello and Esther Marie (Justice) Park; m. Denson Coy Pate, Jr., Dec. 19, 1965 (dec. Mar., 1990); children: Elizabeth Jewel, Mary Kathryn, Melissa Fay; m. David Sigfreid Ridderheim, Jr., Oct 19, 1991; stepchildren: Cheryl, Carla, Katie, Kris, David, Joe. BS in Psychology, W. Tex. A&M, Canyon, 1988; MS in Psychology, St. Francis Coll., Fort Wayne, Ind., 1991; postgrad studies in Psychology, Adler Sch. Profl. Psychology, Chgo., 1992-96. Lic. mental health counselor, Fort Wayne, Ind., 1996—; therapist Barry and Barry, Fort Wayne, 1996-98; ind. contractor therapist Luth. Social Svcs., Fort Wayne, 1998—2002. Program dir. After Sch. Activities Forest Hills Sch. Dist., Cin., 1972-74, New Richmond Exempted Sch. Dist., 1973-75; initiator Young Authors Program, New Richmond Sch. Dist., 1976; outpatient svcs. counselor Charter Beacon Hosp., Fort Wayne, 1994-95. Mem. APA, Am. Counseling Assn., Am. Assn. Christian Counselors, Stepfamily Assn. Am. (pres. Ind. chpt.), Ind. Counselors Assn., Alcohol and Drug Abuse, No. Am. Soc. Adlerian Psychology. Home and Office: 12117 Chesterbrook Ct Fort Wayne IN 46845-1965

RIDDICK, DANIEL HOWISON, obstetrics and gynecology educator, priest; b. Lynchburg, Va., Dec. 12, 1941; s. Joseph Henry and Nancy Eloise (Gordon) R.; m. Louisa McIntosh Spruill, June 9, 1963; children: Ellen, Daniel. BA, Duke U., 1963, MD, 1967, PhD in Physiology, 1969. Diplomate Am. Bd. Ob-Gyn, Am. Bd. Reproductive Endocrinology; ordained priest Episc. Ch., 1969. Asst. prof. physiology Duke U., Durham, N.C., 1973-74; asst. prof. ob-gyn U. Conn. Sch. Medicine, Farmington, 1974-76, dir. reproductive endocrinology and infertility, 1974-85, assoc. prof. ob-gyn, 1976-81, prof. ob-gyn, 1981-85; prof., chmn. ob-gyn dept. U. Vt., Burlington, 1985-97, assoc. dean grad. med. edn., 1987-88. Editor: Reproductive Endocrinology in Clinical Practice, 1987; editor: (with others) Pathology of Infertility, 1987. Mem. ACOG, Am. Fertility Soc. (pres. 1992-93), Am. Gynecol. and Obstet. Soc. Avocation: sheep-raising. Home: 680 Mayo Rd Huntington VT 05462-9410 Office: Fletcher Allen Health Care Dept of Obstetrics & Gynecology 111 Colchester Ave Burlington VT 05401-1416

RIDDICK, FRANK ADAMS, JR., physician, health care administrator; b. Memphis, June 14, 1929; s. Frank Adams and Falba (Crawford) Riddick; m. Mary Belle Alston, June 15, 1952; children: Laura Elizabeth Dufresne, Frank Adams III, John Alston. BA cum laude, Vanderbilt U., 1951, MD, 1954. Diplomate Am. Bd. Internal Medicine. Intern Barnes Hosp., St. Louis, 1954—55, resident in medicine, 1957—60; fellow in metabolic diseases Washington U., St. Louis, 1960—61; staff Ochsner Clinic (Ochsner Found. Hosp.), New Orleans, 1961—, head sect. endocrinology and metabolic disease, 1976—83, asst. med. dir., 1968—72, assoc. med. dir., 1972—75, med. dir., 1975—92; CEO Alton Ochsner Med. Found., New Orleans, 1992—2001; CEO emeritus Ochsner Clinic Found., 2001—. Bd. govs. Am. Bd. Internal Medicine, 1973—80; clin. prof. Tulane U., New Orleans, 1977—; trustee Alton Ochsner Med. Found., 1973—, CEO, 1991—; chmn. bd. Ochsner Health Plan, 1983—92; pres. Orleans Svc. Corp., 1976—80, South La. Med. Assocs., New Orleans, 1978—; dir. Brent House Corp., New Orleans, 1980—; chmn. Accreditation Coun. on Grad. Med. Edn., 1986—87, v.p. nat. resident matching program, 1986—90, mem. accreditation coun. on med. edn., 1988—90. Bd. govs. Isidore Newman Sch., New Orleans, 1987—93; trustee St. Martin's Protestant Episc. Sch., Metairie, La., 1970—84. Recipient Tchg. award, Alton Ochsner Med. Found., 1969, Disting. Alumnus award, Castle Heights Mil. Acad., 1979, Physician Exec. award, Am. Coll. Med. Group Adminstrs., 1984, Disting. Alumnus award, Vanderbilt U. Sch. Medicine, 1988. Master: ACP; fellow: Am. Coll. Physician Execs. (pres. 1987—88); mem.: NAS Inst. Medicine, AMA (ho. dels. 1971—92, chmn. coun. on med. edn. 1983—85, coun. on jud. and ethical affairs 1995—2002, chair 2001—02, Disting. Service award 2003), Am. Group Practice Assn. (pres. 1992—94), Soc. Med. Adminstrs. (pres. 1995—), Am. Diabetes Assn., Endocrine Soc., Am. Soc. Internal Medicine (trustee 1970—76, Disting. Internist award), Cosmos Club, New Orleans Country Club, Boston Club. Home: 1923 Octavia St New Orleans LA 70115-5651 Office: Ochsner Clinic 1516 Jefferson Hwy New Orleans LA 70121-2429 Office Phone: 504-842-4019. Business E-Mail: friddick@ochsner.org.

RIDDICK, WINSTON WADE, SR., lawyer; b. Crowley, La., Feb. 11, 1941; s. Hebert Hobson and Elizabeth (Wade) R.; m. Patricia Ann Turner, Dec. 25, 1961;1 child, Winston Wade. BA, U. Southwestern La., 1962; MA, U. N.C., 1963; PhD, Columbia U., 1965; JD, La. State U., 1973. Bar: La. 1974, U.S. Dist. Ct. (so., mid. and we. dists.) La., U.S. Ct. Appeals (5th cir.), U.S. Supreme Court. Asst. prof. gov., dir. Inst. Gov. Rsch. La. State U., Baton Rouge, 1966-67; dir. La. Higher Edn. Facilities Commn., Baton Rouge, 1967-72; exec. asst. state supt. La. Dept. Edn., Baton Rouge, 1972-73; law ptnr. Riddick & Riddick, Baton Rouge, 1973—; asst. commr., gen. counsel La. Dept. Agr., Baton Rouge, 1981-82. Cons. Riddick & Assoc., Baton Rouge, 1973—; part-time law faculty mem. So. Univ. Law Ctr., Baton Rouge, 1974-95; assoc. prof., 1995-99, prof. law, 1999—, exec. asst. atty. gen. State of La., 1987-91. Spl. asst. to Gov. John J. McKeithen on Nat. Ctr. for Edn. in Politics Fellowship, 1966-67; state campaign mgr. Gillis W. Long for Gov., Baton Rouge, 1971; mem. East Baton Rouge Parish Dem. Exec. Com., 1981-84. Mem. La. Trial Lawyers Assn. (bd. govs. 1978-80), real estate investor and property mgr., 1975—. Presbyterian. Office: Riddick & Assocs Inc 1563 Oakley Dr Baton Rouge LA 70806-8622 Business E-Mail: wriddick@sulc.edu.

RIDDIFORD, LYNN MOORHEAD, zoologist, educator; b. Knoxville, Tenn., Oct. 18, 1936; d. James Eli and Virginia Amalia (Berry) Moorhead; m. Alan William Riddiford, June 20, 1959 (div. Jan. 1966); m. James William Truman, July 28, 1970. AB magna cum laude, Radcliffe Coll., 1958; PhD, Cornell U., 1961. Rsch. fellow in biology Harvard U., Cambridge, Mass., 1961-63, 65-66, asst. prof. biology, 1966-71, assoc. prof., 1971-73; instr. biology Wellesley (Mass.) Coll., 1963-65; assoc. prof. zoology U. Wash., Seattle, 1973—75, prof. biology, 1975—2003. Mem. study sect. tropical medicine and parasitology NIH, Bethesda, Md., 1974—78, 1997; mem. Competitive Grants panel USDA, Arlington, Va., 1979, 89, 95; mem. regulatory biology panel NSF, Washington, 1984—88, Washington, 2001; mem. governing coun. Internat. Ctr. for Insect Physiology and Ecology, 1985—91, chmn. program com., 1989—91; chmn. adv. com. SeriBiotech, Bangalore, India, 1989; mem. biol. adv. com. NSF, 1992—95. Contbr. articles to profl. jours. Bd. dirs. Entomol. Found., 1998—2001, Whitney Lab., 2000—04. Recipient Gregor J. Mendel award, Czech Republic Acad. Scis., 1998; fellow, NSF, 1958—63, John S. Guggenheim Found., 1979—80, NIH, 1986—87; grantee, NSF, 1964—, NIH, 1975—, Rockefeller Found., 1970—79, USDA, 1978—82, 1989—. Fellow: AAAS, Entomol. Soc. Am. (Recognition award in insect physiology, biochemistry and toxicology), Royal Entomol. Soc., Am. Acad. Arts and Sci.; mem.: Soc. Devel. Biology, Am. Soc. Cell Biology, Am. Soc. Biochem. and Molecular Biology, Soc. Integrative and Comparative Biology (pres. 1991). Methodist. Home: 16324 51st Ave SE Bothell WA 98012-6138 Office: U Wash Dept Biology PO Box 351800 Seattle WA 98195-1800 E-mail: lmr@u.washington.edu.

RIDDLE, CHARLES ADDISON, III, district attorney, former state legislator; b. Marksville, La., June 8, 1955; s. Charles Addison Jr. and Alma Rita (Gremillion) R.; m. Margaret Susan Noone, Mar. 24, 1978; children: Charles Addison IV, John H., Michael J. BA, La. State U., 1976, JD, 1980. Bar: La. 1980, U.S. Dist. Ct. (mid. and we. dists.) La. 1983, U.S. Ct. Appeals (5th cir.) 1988, U.S. Supreme Ct. 1991, U.S. Ct. Vets. Appeals 1994. Assoc. Riddle & Bennett, Marksville, 1980; pvt. practice Marksville, 1981—; mem. La. Ho. of Reps., Baton Rouge, 1992—2003; reelected La. House of Reps., Baton Rouge, 1995—99, 1999—2003; dist. atty. Avoyelles Parish 12th Jud. Dist., 2003—. Elected La. State Dem. Cen. com., Avoyelles Parish, 1983-87, Parish Exec. Demo. Com. 1987-91. Mem. Avoyelles Bar Assn. (pres. 1987-88), Bunkie Rotary (bd. dirs.), Marksville Lions, Marksville C. of C. (pres. 1988-92). Office: PO Box 608 208 E Mark St Marksville LA 71351-2416 Office Phone: 318-253-4551. Personal E-mail: criddle777@aol.com.

RIDDLE, JARED MATTHEW, English educator, actor; b. Gary, Ind., July 3, 1969; adopted s. Lee Jay and Sandie Lee Jewett; s. Gerald Ellis and Wava Marie Riddle; life ptnr. Brian Michael Stevens, Aug. 15, 1998. BA, Ind. U., 1994; postgrad. in English, Purdue U. Pineapple picker Maui (Hawaii) Pineapple Co., 1985; shoe salesman Kaplan Shoe, Merrillville, Ind., 1987-88; missionary LDS Ch., Tampa, Fla., 1988-90; artistic dir. Bulldog Enterprises, Hobart, Ind., 1994-96; adj. faculty Ivy Tech. State Coll., East Chicago, Ind., 1996-2000, instr. English, 2000—; dir. Success by Six Preschool, Gary Housing Authority, 2001—. Adj. faculty Vincennes U., 2002—. Actor Joseph and the Amazing Technicolor Dreamcoat, 1995, 2001, Jesus Christ Superstar, 1996, 2001, 2002, Elvis the Musical, 1999, Little Shop of Horrors, 1998, Brigadoon, 1999. Mem. ASCD, at. Coun. Tchrs. English, Alpha Psi Omega (pres. 1993-94, Outstanding Sr. in Theatre 1994). Democrat. Unitarian-Universalist. Avocations: Shakespeare, movies, theories of Foucault & Deleuze. Office: Ivy Tech State Coll 410 E Columbus Dr East Chicago IN 46312 E-mail: naoslives@aol.com., jriddle@ivytech.edu.

RIDDLE, MARK ALAN, child psychiatrist; b. Huntingburg, Ind., Feb. 18, 1948; s. James G. and Louise (Burgdorf) R.; m. Clarine Carol Nardi, Aug. 15, 1971; children: Carl, Julia. BA, Ind. U., 1970, MS, 1973, MD, 1977. Intern in pediatrics Ind. U. Med. Ctr., Indpls., 1977-78; resident in psychiatry Sch. Medicine Yale U., New Haven, 1978-81; fellow in child psychiatry Yale Child Study Ctr., New Haven, 1981-83; asst. prof. child psychiatry Sch. Medicine Yale U., New Haven, 1983-89, assoc. prof. child psychiatry, 1989-93; dir. divsn. child and adolescent psychiatry Johns Hopkins Med. Inst., 1993—. Mem. pediatrics panel U.S. Pharmacopea, 1995-2000. Assoc. editor Jour. Child and Adolescent Psychopharmacology, 1992—; editor Pediatric Psychopharmacology I & II, 1995; contbr. over 100 articles to profl. jours. Mem. med. com. Tourette Syndrome Assn., 1989-98. Mem. Am. Acad. Child and Adolescent Psychiatry (coun. mem. 1999—). E-mail: mriddle@jhmi.edu.

RIDDLE, MATTHEW C(ASEY), physician, educator; b. Portland, Oreg., Dec. 9, 1938; s. Matthew Casey and Katharine Hope (Kerr) Riddle; m. Diane M. Karl, 1994; children from previous marriage: Matthew Casey III, Ann E., James K., Sarah A. BA in English magna cum laude, Yale U., 1960; MD, Harvard U., 1964. Diplomate Am. Bd. Internal Medicine. Resident in medicine Rush-Presbyn. St. Luke Hosp., Chgo., 1964—66, 1968, fellow endocrinology, 1969—71, U. Wash., Seattle, 1971—73; asst. prof. medicine Oreg. Health Scis. U., Portland, 1973-82, assoc. prof. medicine, 1982-96, head diabetes sect., 1975—, prof. medicine, 1996—. Mem. editl. bd.: Diabetes Care, Diabetes Therapeutics and Tech., Jour. Clin. Entocrinology and Metabolism; contbr. articles to profl. jours. Capt. U.S. Army, 1966-68, Vietnam. Mem. Am. Diabetes Assn. (bd. dirs., pres., chmn. bd. Oreg. affiliate), Am. Fedn. Clin. Rsch., Endocrine Soc., Am. Assn. Clin. Endocrinologists. Office: Oreg Health and Sci U L-345 3181 SW Sam Jackson Park Rd Portland OR 97239-3098

RIDDLE, MICHAEL LEE, lawyer; b. Oct. 7, 1946; s. Joy Lee and Francis Irene (Brandes) R.; m. Suzan Ellen Shaw, May 25, 1969 (div.); m. Carol Jackson, Aug. 13, 1977; 1 child, Robert Andrew. BA, Tex. Tech U., 1969, JD with honors, 1972. Bar: Tex. 1972, U.S. Dist. Ct. (no. dist.) Tex. 1972, U.S. Ct. Appeals (5th cir.) Tex. 1972. Assoc. Geary Brice Barron & Stahl, Dallas, 1972-75; ptnr. Baker Glast Riddle Tuttle & Elliott, Dallas, 1975-80; ptnr., mng. ptnr. Middleburg, Riddle & Gianna, 1980—; chmn., CEO MRG Document Techs., 2000—. Bd. dirs. Dallas Opera. Bd. dirs. U.S.A. Film Festival, pres., 1984-86, North Tex. Pub. Broadcasting, 1992-97; chmn., bd. dirs. Provident Bancorp Tex., 1987-90. Mem. ABA, Tex. Bar Assn., Dallas Bar Assn., Coll. of State Bar of Tex., Lakewood Country Club, Crescent Club. Democrat. Lutheran. Office: 717 N Harwood Ste 2400 Dallas TX 75201 Office Phone: 214-220-6300. Personal E-mail: mriddle@midrid.com.

RIDDLE, THAD (TAD) W., III, music educator, webmaster; b. Greenville, S.C., May 1, 1954; s. Thad W. Riddle Jr. and Glenn Bolt Riddle; m. Andrea Lamar Franks, Nov. 11, 1953; children: Heather Riddle Henderson, Melissa. BA, Lander U., 1979. Cert. instrumental music edn. grades K-12 SC. Dept. Edn., 1979. Band dir. Pickens County Sch. Dist. - Liberty H.S. and Dacusville Jr. High, Easley, SC, 1979—81, Abbeville (S.C.) Sch. Dist. #60, 1982—86; band dir. music appreciation/jazz Sch. Dist. Greenville (S.C.) County - Southside H.S., 1986—88; ins. sales Liberty Life Ins. Co., Greenville, 1988—89; bus. owner Riddle's Office and Sch. Supplies, Greenville, 1989—91; band dir. Sch. Dist. Greenville County - Carolina H.S. and Tanglewood Mid. Sch., 1990—95; music tchr., sch. webmaster Sch. Dist. Greenville County - Brushy Creek Elem. Sch., 1995—. Performer, dir. various organs.- concert bands, big bands, orchestras, theatre, Greenville, 1970—; choir dir. Westminster Presbyn. Ch., Greenwood, 1982—86; handbell dir. Taylors (S.C.) First Bapt. Ch., 1992—; music tech. cons. MacMillan/McGraw-Hill Pub., Atlanta, 1997—; sch. webmaster Sch. Dist. Greenville County - Brushy Creek Elem. Sch., 1999—; performer Palmetto Posaunon trombone ensemble, 2000—; music tech. cons. Named Outstanding Young Men Am., 1983; Making Music With Art grantee, Brushy Creek Elem. PTA, 2001—02. Mem.: Am. Orff-Schulwerk Assn. (newsletter editor local chpt. 1996—98), Music Educators Nat. Conf., Phi Mu Alpha Sinfonia (rec. sec. 1974—75). Avocations: reading, walking, listening to music, computers. Home: 408 Cherokee Dr Greenville SC 29615 Office: Brushy Creek Elem Sch 1344 Brushy Creek Rd Taylors SC Personal E-mail: triddle902@aol.com. E-mail: tbnmusic@msn.com.

RIDDLE, VERYL LEE, lawyer; b. Campbell, Mo., Dec. 6, 1921; s. Elvis Lloyd and Etter Whitehead (Wood) R.; m. Mary J. Riggs, Jan. 15, 1941 (div. 1967); children— Kay, Jo, Janet, Veryl Lee, Jr.; m. Janet Lewis, Nov. 24, 1985. Student, Southeast Mo. U., 1939-41; student, U. Buffalo, 1942, 45-46; JD, Washington U., St. Louis, 1948. Bar: Mo. 1948, U.S. Dist. Ct. (ea. and we. dists.) Mo. 1949, U.S. Ct. Appeals (8th cir.) 1949, U.S. Supreme Ct. 1969, U.S. Ct. Appeals (7th cir.) 1970, U.S. Ct. Appeals (5th cir.) 1974, U.S. Ct. Appeals (3d cir.) 1975. Agt. U.S. Dept. Justice, N.Y., Ohio, Tex., Mex., 1942-43; U.S. atty. Eastern Dist. Mo. Dept. Justice, St. Louis, 1967-69; ptnr. Riddle, Baker & O'Herin, Malden, Mo., 1948-67; sr. ptnr. Bryan Cave, St. Louis, 1969—. Pros. atty. Dunklin County, Mo., 1950-53; chmn. merit selection panel for U.S. Magistrate, St. Louis, 1983-84 Del., Nat. Democratic Conv., Chgo., 1956, Los Angeles, 1960. With U.S. Army, 1943-45, European Theatre, Military Intelligence. Recipient Disting. Alumni award Washington U. Sch. Law, 1993. Fellow Am. Coll. Trial Lawyers, Internat. Acad. Trial Lawyers; mem. Acad. Mo. Squires. Clubs: Bellerive Country, Noonday, Round Table (St. Louis). Baptist. Office: Bryan Cave 211 N Broadway Saint Louis MO 63102-2733 E-mail: verylriddle@bryancavellp.com.

RIDDLE, WESLEY ALLEN, army officer, writer; b. Houston, Apr. 19, 1961; s. Walter Abige Riddle and Gloria Texane (Longnecker) Riddle-Roe; m. Maria Aida Albesa, Dec. 21, 1985; stepchildren: Catalina Louise Oates, Danilo Albesa Calabia. BS cum laud, U.S. Mil. Acad., 1983; MPhil in Modern History with distinction, Oxford (Eng.) U., 1993. Commd. U.S. Army, 1983, advanced through grades to lt. col., 2000, platoon leader, battery exec. officer 1-62 ADA (C/V), 1984-87; asst. S-3 Plans, S-4 and Battery Comdr. 2-43 ADA (Patriot) Hanau, Germany, 1988-91; battery comdr. B/2-43 ADA Gulf War SWA, 1991; asst. prof. history U.S. Mil. Acad., West Point, N.Y., 1993-96; Theater Missile Def. evaluation officer Air Def. Directorate Operational Test and Evaluation Command, Alexandria, Va., 1996-98; exec. officer 2-6 ADA, Ft. Bliss, Tex., 1998-99; chief AD br., requirements divsn. DCD, Ft. Bliss, 1999-2000; air def. readiness br. chief (OMC-K) USASATMO, Ft. Bragg, N.C., 2000—. Chmn. Am. Civility Project, 1996-99. Mem. adv. bd. The Social Critic mag., 1996-99; U.S. corr. Fragments Mag., 1998—; contbr. chpts. to books; columnist Belton Jour., 2000—. Founder, pres. Northbrook Teenage Reps., Houston, 1975-79; youth advisor State of Tex. to Citizens for the Republic, 1978-79; page, Rep. Nat. Conv., Kansas City, Mo., 1976. Decorated Bronze Star; Salvatori fellow Heritage Found., Washington, 1996-99; Nat. Humanities Inst. fellow, 1997—. Mem. VFW, Am. Legion, Mil. Order of Saint Barbara, Phi Kappa Phi, Phi Alpha Theta. Republican. Christian Scientist. Avocations: music, poetry, weightlifting, running, water sports.

RIDDOCH, HILDA JOHNSON, accountant; b. Salt Lake City, July 25, 1923; d. John and Ivy Alma (Wallis) Johnson; m. Leland Asa Riddoch, Nov. 22, 1942 (dec.); children: Ivy Lee (dec.), Leland Mark. Vocal student, Ben Henry Smith, Seattle; student, Art Instrn. Schs. Sales clk., marking room and sec. dist. office Sears, Seattle, 1940-42; with billing dept., receptionist C.M. Lovsted & Co., Inc., Seattle, 1942-51; acct., exec. sec. Viking Equipment Co., Inc., Seattle, 1951-54; acct., office mgr. Charles Waynor Collection Agy., Seattle, 1955-57, Argus Mag., Seattle, 1962-67; acct. Law Offices Krutch, Lindell, Donnelly, Dempsey & Lageschulte, Seattle, 1967-72, Law Offices Sindell, Haley, Estep, et al, Seattle, 1972-77; co-founder, acct. Bus. Svc., Inc. and Diversified Design & Mktg., Fed. Way, Auburn & Orting, Wash., 1975-96; co-founder L & H Advt. and Distbg. Co., Wash., 1992-96. Sec.-treas., dir. Jim Evans Realty Inc., Seattle, 1973-87; agt. Wise Island Water Co., P.U.D., Wise Island, B.C., 1973-88, Estate Executrix, Seattle, 1987-96; exec. sec., acct. Cougar Mountain Assn. Ltd. Partnership, 1964-78. Author: Ticking Time on a Metronome, 1989-90, Beloved Miss Ivy, 1996-97, Siegfield, Earth Angel; writer, dir. hist. video Presidents of Relief Society Thru Ages; writer epic poetry; writer, dir. teenager activation video, 1984; pub., editor Extended Family Newsletter, 1983-96. Dir. speech and drama LDS Ch., 1983-88; ward pres. young women's orgn.; mem. ward and stake choirs, 1963-85; stake genealogy libr., Fed. Way, 1983-85; ward and stake newsletter editor various areas, West Seattle, Seattle, Renton, Auburn, Wash., 1950-90; 1st counselor in presidency, tchr. various courses Ladies' Relief Soc. Orgn., 1965-96; co-dir., organizer 1st Silver Saints Group, 1990-92; interviewer LDS Ch. Employment Svcs., 1992-93; co-resident mgr. Mountain View Estates, Orting, Wash., 1994-96. Recipient Letter of Recognition Howard W. Hunter, Pres. LDS Ch. Mem. NAFE. Avocations: needlecrafts, painting, writing, singing, speech and drama. Home: 464 Lariat Cir Idaho Falls ID 83404-7173

RIDE, SALLY KRISTEN, physics educator, scientist, former astronaut; b. L.A., May 26, 1951; d. Dale Burdell and Carol Joyce (Anderson) R.; m. Steven Alan Hawley, July 26, 1982 (div.). BA in English, BS in Physics, Stanford U., 1973, PhD in Physics, 1978. Teaching asst. Stanford U., Palo Alto, Calif., researcher dept. physics; astronaut candidate, trainee NASA, 1978-79, astronaut, 1979-87, on-orbit capsule communicator STS-2 mission Johnson Space Ctr., on-orbit capsule communicator STS-3 mission, mission specialist STS-7, 1983, mission specialist STS-41G, 1984; sci. fellow Stanford (Calif.) U., 1987-89; dir. Calif. Space Inst. of U. Calif. San Diego, La Jolla, 1989-96, pres. space com., 1999-2000; prof. Physics U. Calif. San Diego, La Jolla, 1989—; pres., CEO Imaginary Lines, Inc., 2001—. Mem. Presdl. Commn. on Space Shuttle, 1986, Presdl. Com. of Advisors on Sci. and Tech., 1994—. Author: (with Susan Okie) To Space and Back, 1986, (with T.O'Shaughnessy) Voyager: An Adventure to the Edge of the Solar System, 1992, The Third Planet: Exploring the Earth From Space, 1994, The Mystery of Mars, 1999, Exploring our Solar System, 2003. Achievements include becoming the first American woman to orbit Earth when she flew aboard Space Shuttle Challenger in 1983. Office: U Calif San Diego Calif Space Inst 0426 La Jolla CA 92093-0426

RIDELL, CAROL ANNE, reporter; married. BA, Tufts U.; MS in Jooournalism, Northwestern U., Evanston, Ill. Reporter WMAQ-TV, Chgo., 1989—92; reporter, host, anchor New York 1 News, N.Y.C., 1992—96; reporter education and children specialist NewsChannel4 NBC, N.Y. C., 1996—. Named N.Y. Cub Reporter of Yr., N.Y. Press Club, 1993, runner -up for Gold Typewrier award; recipient Outstanding Hard News story award, N.Y. State Broadcasters, 2001, Nat. award, Edn. Writers Assn. . Office: NBC 30 Rockefeller Plz New York NY 10112

RIDEN, MICHAEL DAVID, nuclear engineer; b. Maryville, Tenn., July 2, 1947; s. William Walter and Grace Ella (Elrod) R.; m. Perry Dene Thyberg, Mar. 28, 1970; children: Chad Michael, Kirk David, Eric Wesley. Cert. nuclear weapons specialist, Lowry Tng. Ctr., Denver, 1968; cert. nuclear weapons technician, Gen. Electric Co. Tng. Program, King of Prussia, Pa., 1969; BS, U. Tenn., Knoxville, 1974. Cert. regional judge, Duck Town, Tenn., 1995. Asst. engr. Duke Power Co. Oconee Nuclear Sta., Seneca, S.C., 1974-78; reactor insp. Nuclear Regulatory Commn., Glen Ellyn, Ill., 1978-79; gen. mgr. Chgo. Barra Corp. Am., Inc., Wheaton, Ill., 1979-82; reg. mgr. Watpro, Inc., Orland Park, Ill., 1982-83; pres. ETs, Glen Ellyn, 1983-87; engring. assurance engr. TVA Watts Bar Nuc. Plant, Spring City, Tenn., 1987-88, Sequoyah Nuc. Plant, Soddy-Daisy, Tenn., 1988-89; supervising engr. United Energy Svcs. Corp., Palo Verde Nuc. Power Plant, Wintersburg, Ariz., 1989-90; nuc. engr. Sigma Sci. Browns Ferry Nuc. Plant, Athens, Ala., 1990-93; lead auditor SECORE Svcs. Inc., Trans-Alaska Pipeline, Anchorage, 1994; plant ops. and betterment I&C cons. engr. Raytheon Engrs. and Constructors Inc. TVA Watts Bar Nuclear, Spring City, Tenn., 1994-95; cons. nuc. engr. Sci. Applications Internat. Corp. TVA Sequoyah Nuclear Plant, Soddy-Daisy, Tenn., 1995-96; sports staff mem. Atlanta com. Olympic Games, Cherokee Nat. Forest, Tenn., 1996; cons. nuc. engring. environ. qualification Cooper Nuc. Station, Brownville, Nebr., 1996-97; sys. engring. mentor Duke Engring. & Svc. Resources, Inc., Two Rivers, Wis., 1997-98; maintenance commitment project mgr. Cook Nuc. Plant Cook Nuc. Plant, Duke Engring. & Svcs. Resources, Inc., Sun Tech. Svcs., Inc. and S&L, Bridgman, Mich., 1998-2001; agt. Ednl. Tng. Svcs., Riceville, Tenn., 2000—; elec. supt. Newberg, Perini, Stone and Webster, Braceville, Ill., 2001—02. Re-entry system evaluation team mem. minuteman III missile USAF, Minot, N.D., 1969-71. Deacon Presbyn. Ch. U.S., Seneca, 1976-77; lay spkr. United Meth. Ch. Holston Conf., 1991-2001. Sgt. USAF, 1967-71. Recipient Outstanding Achievement in Poetry During the 20th Century award Internat. Libr. of Poetry, 2000. Mem. Am. Nuclear Soc. Sovereign American.

RIDENHOUR, CORY TODD, association executive, consultant, accountant; b. Peoria, Ill., July 22; s. Terrance James and Patricia Ann Ridenhour. BA in Acctg. and Bus., Westminster Coll., Fulton, Mo., 1992. Exec. asst. to state auditor Mo. State Auditor's Office, Jefferson City, 1992—97; exec. dir., CEO Mo. Forest Products Assn., Jefferson City, 1997—. V.p. Mo. Forest Heritage Ctr., Jefferson City, 1997—; sec./treas. Mo. Tree Farm Sys., Jefferson City, 1997—; sec. Mo. Wood Industry Ins. Trust, Kansas City, 1998—; pres. Mo. Forest Found., Jefferson City, 2001—, Jefferson City, 2001—; nat. pres. Nat. Coun. Forestry Assn. Execs., 2003—. State chmn. Mo. Fedn. Young Reps., Jefferson City, Mo., 1995—97; elder First Presbyn. Ch., 2000—03, bd. deacons, 1997—99. Mem.: Mo. Soc. Assn. Execs., Rotary (Jefferson City treas. 2001—02, sec. 2002—03, v.p. 2003—), Delta Tau Delta (divsn. v.p. 1999—). Republican. Presbyterian. Home: 901 Tanya Lynn Dr Jefferson City MO 65109 Office: Mo Forest Products Assn 611 E Capitol Ave Ste 1 Jefferson City MO 65101

RIDENOUR, AMY MORITZ, research center administrator; b. Pitts., Nov. 9, 1959; d. Karl Berkoben and Carol Lee (Riley) M. B or Econs., U. Md., 1981. Exec. dir. Nat. Ctr. for Pub. Policy Rsch., Washington, 1982-88, trustee, 1986—; pres. The Nat. Ctr. for Pub. Policy Research, Washington, 1988—; formerly host Scoop!, Nat. Empowerment Television, Washington; nationally sundicated columnist UPI and Knight-Ridder Tribune, 1998—. Chmn. Liberty Inst., Washngton. Assoc. pub. Cath. Study Coun. Bull.; editor Nat. Policy Watch Jour., Liberation Bull.; exec. editor Liberty Letter; contbr. articles to Policy Rev. and other profl. jours. Regional coord. Reagan-Bush Nat. Campaign, Washington, 1980; bd. dirs., v.p. Internat. Youth Yr. Commn. for U.S., 1985; chmn. Md. Fedn. Coll. Rep. Clubs, 1978-80. Mem. Accuracy in Academia (adv. bd.). Lutheran. Avocations: skiing, books, history. Office: Nat Ctr for Pub Policy Rsch 777 N Capitol St NE Ste 803 Washington DC 20002-4294

RIDENOUR, JOEY, medical association administrator, operations research specialist; BSc in Nursing, Ariz. State U.; MN, U. Phoenix. RN Ariz. COO Maricopa Health Sys., Phoenix, 1975—95; exec. dir. Ariz. State Bd. Nursing, 1995—98; pres. Nat. Coun. State Bds. of Nursing, Chgo., 1998; exec dir Ariz State bd of nursing. Pres. Ariz. State Bd. Nursing, Phoenix, 1986—89, 1994—95; adj. faculty Ariz. State U. Recipient Disting. Achievement award, Am. Soc. Pub. Adminstrn., Ariz. State U. Coll. Nursing, U. Phoenix; fellow, Wharton. Office: Boards of Nursing Natl Coun of State 111 E Wacker Dr Ste 2900 Chicago IL 60601-4277

RIDEOUT, PATRICIA IRENE, operatic, oratorio and concert singer; b. St. John, N.B., Can., Mar. 16, 1931; d. Eric Aubrey and Florence May (Chase) R.; m. Rolf Edmund Dissmann, Sept. 3, 1955 (dec. 1975); m. Leonard R. Rosenberg, May 25, 1987. Ed., U. Toronto Opera Sch., Royal Conservatory Music, 1952-55. Tchr. voice Queen's U., Kingston, Ont., 1980-86, Royal Conservatory Music, Toronto, 1980-91. Singer Can. Opera Co., Toronto, 1954-85; leading roles in operas, Stratford, Ont., Vancouver, B.C., Guelph, Ont., 1956-85, CBC, 1958-90. Mem. Actors Equity Assn., Assn. Radio and TV Artists, Toronto Heliconian Club. Unitarian Universalist. E-mail: prosenberg@intown.net.

RIDEOUT, WALTER BATES, English educator; b. Lee, Maine, Oct. 21, 1917; s. Walter John and Helen Ruth (Brickett) R.; m. Jeanette Lee Drisko, Aug. 2, 1947; children: Linda Carolyn, Richard Bates, David John. AB, Colby Coll., 1938; MA, Harvard U., 1939, PhD, 1950. Teaching fellow English Harvard U., 1946-49, asst. prof., summer 1954, prof., summer 1969; from instr. to assoc. prof. English Northwestern U., Evanston, Ill., 1949-63, dir. program Bell System execs., 1957-58, 59-61; prof. English U. Wis., Madison, 1963—, Harry Hayden Clark prof. English, 1972—, chmn. dept., 1965-68, sr. vis. prof. Inst. Research in Humanities, 1968-69. Vis. prof. U. Hawaii, summer 1977; Disting. lectr. English Kyoto Am. Studies Summer Seminar, Kyoto, Japan, 1981 Author: The Radical Novel in the United States, 1900-1954, 1956; editor: (with Howard Mumford Jones) Letters of Sherwood Anderson, 1953, (with James K. Robinson) A College Book of Modern Verse, 1958, A College Book of Modern Fiction, 1961, The Experience of Prose, 1960, I. Donnelly-Caesar's Column, 1960, (with G.W. Allen and J.K. Robinson) American Poetry, 1965, Sherwood Anderson: Collection of Critical Essays, 1974. Recipient MidAm. award Soc. for Study of Midwestern Lit., Mich. State U., 1983, Outstanding Educator award, 1993; fellow Newberry Libr., 1951, Guggenheim fellow, 1957; Fulbright grantee to Kyoto, 1981. Mem. ACLU, MLA (mem. nat. exec. council 1970-73), Phi Beta Kappa. Home: Brookline Apts 7707 N Brookline Dr Apt 220 Madison WI 53719-3532 Office: Dept English U Wis 600 N Park St Madison WI 53706-1403

RIDER, JAMES LINCOLN, lawyer; b. Newburgh, N.Y., Feb. 11, 1942; s. Meyer J. Rider and Marion (Weinberg) Levin; m. Eleanor Yazbeck, Nov. 5, 1977; children: Jordan E., Michael J. BA, Lafayette Coll., Easton, Pa., 1963; JD, Fordham U., 1966. Bar: N.Y. 1966, D.C. 1971, U.S. Ct. Appeals (D.C. cir.) 1971, U.S. Dist. Ct. D.C. 1971, Va. 1972, U.S. Dist. Ct. (ea. dist.) Va. 1972, U.S. Ct. Appeals (4th cir.) 1972, U.S. Dist. Ct. Md. 1973, U.S. Supreme Ct. 1975, U.S. Ct. Appeals (8th cir.) 1976. Ptnr. Margolius, Mallios & Rider, LLP, Washington, 1971—. Capt. U.S. Army, 1967-71. Decorated Disting. Svc. medal. Fellow Am. Acad. Matrimonial Lawyers; mem. D.C. Bar, Va. Bar Assn., Assn. Trial Lawyers Am. Office: Margolius Mallios & Rider LLP 1828 L St NW Ste 500 Washington DC 20036-5127

RIDER, KATHERINE LOVETA THOMPSON, clinical social worker; b. Roswell, N.Mex., Apr. 18, 1945; d. Donald and Setta Loveta (Jones) Thompson; m. Kent Morrison Rider, June 8, 1968; children: Tracy Lyn, Courtney Elizabeth, Kelley Michelle. BA, U. Tex., 1967, MSSW, 1969. LCSW, Tex.; cert. group psychotherapist. Social worker adult mental health staff Austin-Travis County Mental Health-Mental Retardation Ctr., 1969-77; cons. Model Cities Project, Austin, Tex., 1971-72, cmty. orgn. specialist alcohol-related svcs., 1974-76; clin. field faculty Sch. Social Work, U. Tex., Austin, 1977-81; pvt. practice social work, 1977—. Clin. staff mental health dept. Austin Regional Clinic, 1982—84; mem. homemaker svcs. bd. Child and Family Svc. Austin, 1970—75; adj. prof. St. Edward's U., 1983—91; adj. faculty Sch. Social Work U. Tex., Austin, 1999—2001. Pres. L.L. Campbell Elem. Sch. PTA, 1984—86; mem. Austin Family Mediation Assn. Bd., 1985—87; pres. Brykerwoods Elem. Sch. PTA, 1987—88, Austin H.S., 1988—89; v.p., trustee Austin Ind. Sch. Dist., 1992—94, pres., 1994—2002; adminstrv. v.p. Austin City Coun. PTAs, 1986—88, pres., 1991—92; mem. Austin Travis County MHMR Bd., 1989—99, First Bapt. Day Sch. Bd., Austin, 1980—82. Mem.: NASW (dir. Tex. chpt. 1980—84), Austin Women's Forum, Tex. Soc. Clin. Social Work (chair govtl. affairs 2000—, pres. 2003—), Settlement Club, Tau Beta Sigma. Baptist. Home: 3221 Clearview Dr Austin TX 78703-2753 Office: 3724 Jefferson St Ste 206 Austin TX 78731-6221

RIDER, KATHLEEN MARY, dietician; b. Bronx, N.Y., Mar. 21, 1953; d. William Anthony and Elizabeth Catherine (Gavin) Browne; m. David York Rider, Oct. 15, 1983; children: Kathleen M., Colleen M., David Y., Elizabeth A., Erin M. AAS, Maria Coll., 1976; BS, Empire State Coll., 1978; M of Profl. Studies, SUNY, New Paltz, 1982; cert. alternative & complimentary health, Marist Coll., 1999. Cert. dietitian/nutritionist, N.Y. Food svc. dir./dietitian Lovely Hill Nursing Home, Pawling, N.Y., 1979-81; adminstrv. dietitian Hudson River Psychiat. Ctr., Poughkeepsie, N.Y., 1981-82; cmty. svc. dietitian Wassaic (N.Y.) Developmental Ctr., 1982-83; ind. cons. dietitian, 1981—. Cons. Hudson Haven Health Care Ctr., Bapt. Home, Hospice Inc., Greystone Inc., Mountainview Nursing Ctr., Assn. for Retarded Citizens, Dutchess Ulster and Orange Counties, Home Care, Alcohol Rehab. Ctr., various other orgns.; advisor Mid Hudson Food Svc. Mgrs. Assn., Poughkeepsie. Vol. nutrition educator area parochial schs., Dutchess County, 1996; instr. religious edn. St. Peter's Ch., Poughkeepsie, 1981-84; team mem. engaged encounter Cath. Engaged Encounter, Dutchess County, 1986-89. Soroptomist scholar, Schenectady, N.Y., 1976. Fellow Am. Dietetic Assn., del. 1999, Flora Wishart Davies Meml. award for Outstanding Caregiver 1994, Outstanding Svc. award); mem. Am. Assn. Diabetes Educators, N.Y. State Dietetic Assn. (state profl. recruitment coord. 1976—, scholar 1976), Mid Hudson Dietetic Assn. (pres. 1992-94). Democrat. Home and Office: 13 Edna Dr Hyde Park NY 12538-2939

RIDER, NEAL J. food wholesale executive; BS in Acctg., U. Mont.; MBA, U. Utah. CFO Am. Stores Co., Salt Lake City; CFO, exec. v.p. Regal Cinemas Inc., Fleming Cos., Inc., Oklahoma City, 2000—. Office: 6301 Waterford Blvd Oklahoma City OK 73118-1157

RIDGE, DAVY-JO STRIBLING, school librarian; b. Westminster, S.C., Jan. 16, 1932; d. David Waren and Thelma Josephine (Braselton) Stribling; m. George Ross Ridge, June 9, 1956 (div. Dec. 1964). BA, Queens Coll., 1954; MLN, Emory U., 1955. Catalog libr. U. Ga., Athens, 1955—56; head ref. libr. Dekalb Regional Libr., Decatur, Ga., 1956—64; ref. libr. U. S.C., Columbia, 1965—66, head ref. dept., 1967—74, asst. dir. libr., 1975—76, assoc. dir. libr., 1977—88, ret., 1988. Author: A Load of Gratitude: Audubon and South Carolina, 1985, A South Carolina Family in Wartime, 2003. Mem.: S.C. Libr. Assn. (chmn. legis. & pub.), S.C. Libr. Soc. (life), Thomas Cooper Libr. Soc. (life), S.E. Libr. Assn. (life; chmn. constrn. & bylaws 1980—84). Episcopialian. Avocations: gardening, reading, cats.

RIDGE, ROBERT A. oil industry executive; b. Walsenburg, Ohio, 1948; BS in Chem. and Petroleum Refining Engring., Colo. Sch. Mines, 1971. Process sect. supr. Sweeney Refinery Phillips 66 Co., 1978, mgr. planning and budgeting, 1978—92, mgr., 1994, v.p. health safety and environ., 2001—02; v.p. health, safety and environ. Conoco Phillips, Houston, 2002—. Liaison Colo. Sch. Mines. Mem.. Am. Petroleum Inst. (mem. operation practices com.), Tes. Inst. for Advancement of Chem. Tech. (bd. dirs.). Office: ConocoPhllips 600 N Dairy Ashford Rd PO Box 2197 Houston TX 77252-2197

RIDGE, THOMAS JOSEPH (TOM RIDGE), secretary of homeland security; b. Munhall, Pa., Aug. 26, 1945; s. Thomas Regis Ridge and Laura A. Sudimack; m. Michele Moore, 1979, children, Lesley & Tommy. BA in govt. studies, Harvard U., 1967; JD, Dickinson Sch. Law, Carlisle, Pa., 1972. Bar: Pa. 1972. Pvt. practice, Erie, Pa., 1972-82; asst. dist. atty. Erie County, Pa., 1979-82; mem. 98th-103rd Congresses from Pa. 21st dist., Washington, 1983-1995; mem. Banking, Fin., Urban Affairs com., subcoms. Econ. Growth and Credit Formation, Housing and Community mem. banking, Devel., Veteran's Affairs com.; gov. State of Pa., 1995—2001; dir. U.S. Dept. Homeland Security, Washington, 2001—02, sec., 2003—. Staff Sergeant, U.S. Army, 1968-70, Vietnam; Awarded a Bronze Star for Bravery. Republican. Office: Office Homeland Security 3801 Nebraska Ave NW Washington DC 20016

RIDGEWAY, JAMES FOWLER, journalist; b. Auburn, N.Y., Nov. 1, 1936; s. George L. and Florence (Fowler) Ridgeway; m. Patricia Carol Dodge, Nov. 1966; 1 child, David Andrew. AB, Princeton U., 1959. Assoc. editor New Republic, Washington, 1962-68, contbg. editor, 1968-70; editor Hard Times, 1968-70, Elements, 1974-78; assoc. editor Ramparts, 1970-75; assoc. fellow Inst. for Policy Studies, 1973-77; mem. Pub. Resource Center, 1977—; staff writer Village Voice, 1973—. Author: (book) The Closed Corporation, 1969, Politics of Ecology, 1970, The Last Play, 1973, New Energy, 1975; author: (with Alexander Cockburn) Smoke, 1978; author: Political Ecology, 1979, Energy-Efficient Community Planning, 1979, Who Owns the Earth, 1980, Powering Civilization, 1983, Blood in the Face, 1991, The March to War, 1991; author: (with Jean Casella) To Cast a Cold Eye, 1991; author: The Haiti Files, 1994; author: (with Jasmika Udovicki) Yugoslavia's Ethnic Nightmare, 1995; author: (with Sylvia Plachy) Red Light, 1996; author: (with Jeffrey St. Clair) Environmental Bad Guys, 1999; author: (with Kevin Rafferty, Fran K. Kerandren) Who Wants to Be President; prodr., dir. (with Anne Bohlen, Kevin Rafferty): (films) Blood in the Face, 1990; prodr., dir. (with Kevin Rafferty) Feed, 1992; cons. prodr. Awful Truth, 1999; author: It's All For Sale, 2004. With N.G. U.S. Army, 1959. Home: 3103 Macomb St NW Washington DC 20008-3325 E-mail: jridgew@yahoo.com.

RIDGEWAY, LUANN, state legislator; m. Richard Ridgeway. Student, Am. U., 1977; BA in History and Polit. Sci., Westminster Coll., 1978; student, Oxford (Eng.) U., 1978; JD, U. Mo., 1981. Mem. Mo. State Ho. of Reps. Dist. 35, 1992—. Mem. criminal law com., judiciary com., urban affairs com., chldn., youth and families com., civil and administrv. law com., joint com. on administrv. rules. Mem. Mo. Bar Assn. Home: 19405 Platte County Line Rd Smithville MO 64089-8798 Office: Mo Ho of Reps State Capitol Building Jefferson City MO 65101-1556

RIDGWAY, DELISSA ANNE, lawyer; b. Kirksville, Mo., June 28, 1955; d. Kenneth Driggs and Margaret Anne (Warner) R. BA, U. Mo., 1975, postgrad., 1976; JD, Northeastern U., 1979. Bar: D.C. Ct. Appeals 1979, U.S Dist. Ct. D.C. 1980, U.S. Ct. Appeals (D.C. cir.) 1980, U.S. Supreme Ct. 1983, U.S. Ct. Appeals (1st cir.) 1988. Law clk. to presiding justice U.S. Dist. Ct. D.C., Washington, 1979; assoc. Shaw, Pittman, Potts & Trowbridge, Washington, 1979-88, counsel, 1988—. Lectr. nuclear and environ. law to various orgns. Mem. Women's Legal Def. Fund. Hardin-Craig fellow U. Mo., Columbia, 1974. Mem. ABA, Women's Bar Assn. (sec. 1989-90), Fed. Bar Assn. (chair adminstrv. law sect. com. agy. adjudication 1985-89, chair adminstrv. law sect. com. regulatory reform 1984-85). Roman Catholic. Office: Shaw Pittman Potts & Trowbridge 2300 N St NW Fl 5 Washington DC 20037-1172

RIDGWAY, JAMES MASTIN, retired government official; b. Sedalia, Mo., Mar. 14, 1917; s. Amelius Biddle and Maude Anna (Brandt) R.; m. Lillian Belle Shaneyfelt, May 25, 1941; children: Duressa, Richard (dec.), Cheryl. BSBA, U. Mo., 1939, MA, 1940; PhD, U. Chgo., 1953. Tchr. High Schs., Mo., Kans., 1940-44, prin., 1944-45; instr. Southwest & Ctrl. Mo. State U., Springfield, Warrensburg, Mo., 1945-47; chmn. dept. edn. Carroll Coll., Waukesha, Wis., 1949-55; instr. dept. head Nat. Civil Def. Coll., Battle Creek, Mich., 1955-62, dir., 1958-62; deputy asst. dir. tng. & edn. Office Civil Def., Def. Civil Preparedness Agy., Washington, 1963-73; edn. advisor DCPA/DOD and FEMA, Washington, 1973—80. Cons. in field. Contbr. articles to profl. jours. Mem. Am. Strategic Def. Assn., Internat. Assn. Emergency Mgrs., Am. Soc. Profl. Emergency Planners, Heritage Found. Avocation: stamp collecting/philately.

RIDGWAY, MARCELLA DAVIES, veterinarian; b. Sewickley, Pa., Dec. 24, 1957; d. Willis Eugene and Martha Ann (Davies) R. BS, Pa. State U., 1979; VMD, U. Pa., 1983; MS, U. Ill., 1997. Diplomate Am. Coll. Vet. Internal Medicine. Intern U. Ill., Urbana, 1983-84, resident in small animal internal medicine, 1984-87; small animal vet. Vet. Cons. Svcs., Savoy, Ill., 1987-97; clin. asst. prof. small animal vet. medicine U. Ill., Urbana, 1997—. Contbr. articles to profl. jours. Mem. Am. Vet. Med. Assn., Acad. Vet. Clinicians, Ea. Ill. Vet. Med. Assn. (pres. 2000-2001), Heartland Pathways (bd. dirs.), Savoy Prairie Soc. (pres. 1989—), Grand Prairie Friends (bd. dirs. 1993-96), Sangamon Valley Conservancy (bd. dirs. 1995—). Avocations: prairie conservation activities, hiking, canine collectibles, running, dog obedience training. Office: U Ill Vet Med Teaching Hosp 1008 W Hazelwood Dr Urbana IL 61802-4714 Home: 808 Indigo Savoy IL 61874

RIDGWAY, ROZANNE LEJEANNE, retired diplomat; b. St. Paul, Aug. 22, 1935; d. H. Clay and Ethel Rozanne (Cote) R.; m. Theodore E. Deming. BA, Hamline U., 1957, LLD (hon.), 1978, George Washington U., 1986, Elizabethtown Coll., 1990, U. Helsinki, 1992; LLD in Pub. Svc. (hon.), Coll. of William and Mary, 1994; DHL (hon.), Hood Coll., 1994; LLD (hon.), Albright Coll.; DHL in Pub. Adminstrn. (hon.), The Citadel, 2003; DHL (hon.), Ill. Coll., 2003. Career diplomat U.S. Fgn. Svc., 1957-89, amb. at large for oceans and fisheries, 1975-77; amb. to Finland, 1977-80; counselor of Dept. State, 1980-81, spl. asst. to sec. state, 1981, amb. to German Dem. Republic, 1982-85, asst. sec. state Europe and Can., 1985-89; pres. Atlantic Coun. U.S., 1989-92, co-chmn., 1993-96; chmn. Baltic-Am. Enterprise Fund, Washington, 1994—. Bd. dirs. 3M Corp., Emerson Electric Co., The Boeing Corp., Sara Lee Corp., Manpower, Inc., Nat. Geog. Soc., New Perspective Fund. Trustee Hamline U.; bd. dirs. Ctr. for Naval Analyses. Decorated Grand Cross Order of the Lion (Finland); recipient Profl. awards Dept. State, Presdl. Disting. Performance awards, Joseph C. Wilson Internat. Rels. Achievement award, 1982, Sharansky award Union Couns. Soviet Jewry, 1989, U.S. Presdl. Citizens medal, 1989; named Person of Yr. Nat. Fisheries Inst., 1977, Knight Comdr., Order of Merit, Germany; inducted into Nat. Women's Hall of Fame, 1998. Fellow Nat. Acad. Pub. Adminstrn.; mem. Am. Acad. Diplomacy, Met. Club, Army-Navy Country Club. Fax: 703-527-3862.

RIDINGS, DOROTHY SATTES, association executive; b. Charleston, W.Va., Sept. 26, 1939; d. Frederick L. and Katharine E. (Backus) Sattes; m. Donald Jerome Ridings, Sept. 8, 1962 (dec. June 1997); children: Donald Jerome Jr., Matthew Lyle. Student, Randolph-Macon Woman's Coll., 1957-59; BSJ, Northwestern U., 1961; MA, U. N.C., 1968; D.Pub. Svc. (hon.), U. Louisville, 1985; LHD (hon.), Spalding U., 1986; LLD (hon.), U. Charleston, 1999. Reporter Charlotte Observer, N.C., 1961-66; instr. U. N.C. Sch. Journalism, 1966-68; freelance writer Louisville, 1968-77; news editor Ky. Bus. Ledger, Louisville, 1977-80, editor, 1980-83; communications cons., editor, 1983-86; mgmt. assoc. Knight-Ridder Inc., Charlotte, N.C., 1986-88; pres., pub. The Bradenton (Fla.) Herald, 1988-96; pres., CEO, Coun. on Founds., Washington, 1996—. Adj. prof. U. Louisville, 1982-83; v.p. Nat. Mcpl. League, 1985-86; bd. dirs. com. on Constl. Sys., Nat. Com. Against Discrimination in Housing, 1982-87, Com. for Study of Am. Electorate, 1982—; bd. dirs. Ind. Sector, 1983-88, 92-97; mem. exec. com. Leadership Conf. Civil Rights, 1982-86; mem. Accrediting Coun. on Edn. in Journalism and Mass Comm., 2000—. Pres. LWV U.S., 1982-86, 1st v.p., 1980-82, human resources dir., 1976-80, chair edn. fund, 1982-86, 1st vice chair, 1980-82, trustee, 1976-80, pres. Louisville/Jefferson County, 1974-76, bd. dirs., 1969-76; chmn., bd. dirs. Nat. Civic League, 2000—; trustee Louisville Presbyn. Theol. Sem., 1992—, chmn., 2000—; trustee Ford Found., 1989-96, Manatee C.C., 1992-96; bd. dirs. Benton Found., 1989-96, Fla. Press Assn., 1994-96, Leadership Ky., 1984-87, Leadership Louisville, 1983-86, Louisville YWCA, 1978-80, Jr. League Louisville, 1972-74; mem. ABA Accreditation Com., 1987-93, ABA coun. legal edn. and admissions to bar, 1997-2003, Gov.'s Coun. Ednl. Reform, 1984-85; chair Prichard Com. Acad. Excellence, 1985-86; mem. Gov.'s Commn. Full Equality, 1982-83; mem. state adv. coun. U.S. Commn. Civil Rights, 1975-79; mem. steering com. Task Force for Peaceful Desegregation, 1974-75; elder 2d Presbyn. Ch., 1972-75, 78-81; mem. adv. coun. on ch. and soc. United Presbyn. Ch. in USA, 1978-84; mem. bd. visitors U. N.C., 1993-96; mem. Nat. Commn. on Presdl. Debates, 1997—. Recipient Northwestern U. award of merit, 1994, Disting. Alumna award U. N.C., 1995, Leadership award Nat. Assn. Cmty. Leadership Orgns., 1986, Alumnae Achievement award Randolph-Macon Woman's Coll., 1985, Disting. Citizen award Nat. Mcpl. League, 1983; inducted into Northwestern U. Medill Sch. Journalism Hall of Fame, 1996, U. N.C. Journalism Hall of Fame, 1997. Office: Council on Foundations 1828 L St NW Washington DC 20036-5104

RIDINGTON, CANDACE ELIZABETH, writer, educator; b. Camden, N.J., July 25, 1941; d. William Robbins and Edith Ursula (Farr) Ridington; m. Jack Lebowitz, June 1998. BA, Drew U., 1963; MA, Ind. U., 1964, McDaniel Coll., 1976. Asst. prof. Susquehanna U., 1964—73; tchr. St. Augustine Sch. for Deaf, Fla., 1976—78; lectr. U. Ala., Birmingham, 1978—96. Author: (novel) Rubicon, 1998. Mem.: Emily Dickinson Internat. Soc., Am. Recorder Soc. Unitarian. Avocations: recorder, public speaking, drama.

RIDKER, PAUL M. cardiologist, medical educator; b. St. Louis, Oct. 2, 1959; BS, Brown U., 1981; MD, Harvard U., 1986, MPH, 1992. Assoc. prof. medicine Harvard U., Boston; dir. Ctr. for Cardiovascular Disease Prevention Brigham and Women's Hosp., Boston; cons. cardiologist So. Jamaica Plain Health Ctr., Boston. Simon Dack vis. prof. Mt. Sinai Med. Ctr., 2000. Recipient Doris Duke Disting. Clin. Scientist award, 2000, Linus Pauling Lecture and 2000 Prevention award, Am. Coll. for Advancement in Medicine, 2000, SmithKline Beecham Faculty Devel. award, 1997—99, Clinician Scientist award, Am. Heart Assn., 1992—97. Fellow: Am. Coll. Cardiology; mem.: Am. Soc. of Clin. Investigation, Am. Epidemiol. Soc. Office: Harvard Univ Sch Medicine Brigham & Womens Hosp 75 Francis St Boston MA 02115*

RIDLEN, SAMUEL FRANKLIN, agriculture educator; b. Marion, Ill., Apr. 24, 1916; s. Will and Leoma Josephine (Sneed) R.; m. Helen Louise Camp, Apr. 17, 1946; children: Judith Elaine, Barbara Jo, Mark Ellis. BS, U. Ill., 1940; MS, Mich. State U., 1957. Agr. instr. Westville (Ill.) Twp. High Sch., 1940-43; gen. mgr. Honegger Breeder Hatchery, Forrest, Ill., 1953-56; assoc. prof. poultry sci. U. Conn., Storrs, 1957-58; from asst. prof. to prof. poultry extension U. Ill., Urbana-Champaign, 1946-86, prof. emeritus poultry extension, 1986—, asst. head dept. animal scis., 1978-86. Author: An Idea and An Ideal-Nabor House Fraternity 1939-1989, 1989; poultry editorial cons. Successful Farming, Wonderful World Ency., 1960; poultry editor Am. Farm Youth, 1949-53, Ill. Feed Folks, 1949-53. Founding mem., charter mem. Nabor House Frat. Recipient Superior Svc. award U.S. Dept. Agr., 1982, Paul A. Funk Recognition award Coll. Agr., U. Ill., 1983, numerous others. Fellow Poultry Sci. Assn.; mem. World's Poultry Sci. Assn., Ill. State Turkey Growers Assn., Ill. Poultry Industry Coun., Ill Egg Market Devel. Coun. (adv. mem.), Ill. Animal Industry Coun., Coun. for Agr. Sci. and Tech., Ill. Alumni Assn. (life), DAV (life), Alpha Tau Alpha, Epsilon Sigma Phi, Gamma Sigma Delta (pres. 1982-83). Home: 1901 Lakeside Dr Unit C Champaign IL 61821-5997

RIDLEY, BETTY ANN, religous educator, lay worker; b. St. Louis, Oct. 19, 1926; d. Rupert Alexis and Virginia Regina (Weikel) Steber; m. Fred A. Ridley, Jr., Sept. 8, 1948; children: Linda Drue, Clay Kent. BA, Scripps Coll., Claremont, Calif., 1948. Christian Sci. practitioner, Oklahoma City, 1973—. Tchr. Christian Sci., 1983—; mem. Christian Sci. Bd. Lectureship, 1980-85. Trustee Daystar Found.; mem. The First Ch. of Christ Scientist, Boston, Fifth Ch. of Christ Scientist, Oklahoma City. Mem. Jr. League Am. Home: 2933 Lansdowne Ln Oklahoma City OK 73120-4343 Office: Suite 100-G 3000 United Founders Blvd Oklahoma City OK 73112 E-mail: BARidley@aol.com.

RIDLEY, CLARENCE HAVERTY, retail executive; b. Atlanta, June 3, 1942; s. Frank Morris Jr. and Clare (Haverty) R.; m. Eleanor Horsey, Aug. 22, 1969; children: Augusta Morgan, Clare Haverty. BA, Yale U., 1964; MBA, Harvard U., 1966; JD, U. Va., 1971. Bar: Ga. 1971. Ptnr. King & Spalding, Atlanta, 1977—2000, chmn., policy com., 1995—97; chmn. bd. Haverty Furniture Cos., Inc., 2001—. Bd. dirs. Carvel Corp., Crawford & Co., Inc.; bd. trustees STI Classic Funds and Variable Trusts, 2001—. Co-author: Computer Software Agreements, 1987, 3d edit., 2003; exec. editor Va. Law Rev., 1970-71. Chmn., bd. trustees St. Joseph's Health Sys., 2003—; founding trustee Atlanta Girls Sch., 2000-2003; chmn., bd. visitors Emory U., 1999-2000; dir. Atlanta Ballet Co., 1993-2003; bd. councilors Carter Ctr., 2000-2001; mem. Atlanta bd. Am. Red Cross, 2002—. Lt. U.S. Army, 1967—68, Korea. Mem.: Atlanta Rotary Club. Roman Catholic. Home: 2982 Habersham Rd NW Atlanta GA 30305-2854 Office: Haverty Furniture Companies Inc 780 Johnson Ferry Rd Atlanta GA 30342

RIDLEY, KEITH ALEXANDER, IV, funeral director; b. Petersburg, Va., Jan. 7, 1968; s. Janice Ridley Harkins. BA, U. D.C., 1987; MBA, Am. U., 1992. Funeral svc. asst. James M. Wilkerson Funeral Establishment, Va., 1977-89; pres., gen. mgr. Ridley Funeral Establishment, Washingtno, 1991—. Bd. dirs. Kate B. Moorefield Scholarship, 1993—, Moorefield Found., 1993—, Greater S.W. Hosp., Washington, 1995—; vice chmn. Dem. Bus. Coun. Mem. NAACP, Alpha Phi Alpha, Pi Sigma Eta. Democrat. Baptist. Avocations: reading, travel, classical studies, history, writing. Office: Ridley Funeral Establishment Inc 131 Mississippi Ave SE Washington DC 20032-6162

RIDLEY, STANLEY EUGENE, clinical psychologist, consultant; b. Atlanta, Aug. 9, 1950; s. Young Walter and Bessie M. (Jones) R.; children: Mark B., Jason. BA in French and Human Rels., Domincan Coll., 1972; MS in Clin.-Cmty. Psychology, Howard U., 1975, PhD in Clin. Psychology, 1981.

Lic. psychologist. Clin. instr. child devel. and psychiatry George Washington U. Med. Sch., Washington, 1981-89; dir. clin. psychology grad. program Howard U., Washington, 1984-90; clin. psychologist, cons. Ridley and Assocs., Washington and Lanham, Md., 1983—; grad. assoc. prof. psychology Howard U., Washington, 1987-91; rsch. cons. Hogan and Hartson Attys. at Law, Washington, 1988-90; assessment, tng. and rsch. cons. Carter Goble Assocs. Inc., Washington, 1988-92; dir. mental health unit Correctional Med. Svcs., Arlington, Va., 1994-97; sr. assoc. tng. and orgn. Resolution Dynamics Inc., Washington, 1994—. Vis. assoc. prof. George Mason U., Fairfax, Va., 1992-94; cons. St. Luke Inst., Suitland, Md., 1991-94; cons., trainer Nuclear Regulatory Commn., Rockville, Md., 1995—, IRS, Washington, 1995—; distbr. Carlson Learning Co., Mpls., 1996—. Author (book chpt.) Ethnic Minority, 1991; contbr. articles to profl. jours. Bus. champion Archbishop Carroll H.S., Washington, 1996-99; mem. mental health adv. bd. D.C. Pub. Schs. Head Start, 1997—. Mem. APA, ASTD, Am. Coll. Forensic Examiners, Orgn. Devel. Network, Am. Bd. Psychol. Spltys., Soc. Indsl. and Orgnl. Psychology, Beta Kappa Chi, Alpha Mu Gamma. Avocations: roller skating, tennis, bowling, golf, developing quotable sayings. Home and Office: Ridley & Assocs 4360 Varnum Pl NE Washington DC 20017-2101

RIDLOFF, RICHARD, real estate investment advisor, lawyer, consultant; b. N.Y.C., July 18, 1948; s. Sol and Daisey (Metz) R.; m. Caren Sara Berger, Mar. 27, 1977; children: Michael Joshua, Daniel Joseph. BA cum laude, Queens Coll., 1969; JD, Cornell U., 1972. Bar: N.Y. 1973. Assoc. counsel MONY, N.Y.C., 1972-79; sr. v.p., gen. counsel, sec. MONY Real Estate Investors, N.Y.C., 1979-85; v.p. investments MONY Fin. Svcs., N.Y.C., 1985-87; pres. MONY Realty Ptnrs. Inc., Glen Point, N.J., 1985-91; v.p. for investment mgmt. MONY Real Estate Investment Mgmt., N.Y.C., 1988-91; exec. v.p. Tibor Pivko and Co., Clifton, N.J., 1991-94; pres., dir. Growth & Income Inc., 1993-94; spl. projects dir. Kimco Realty Corp., 1995-96; pres. The Richardson Co., 1996—. Mem. adv. commn. on real property ins. to Calif. Sen. Com. on Ins. Claims and Corps., 1986-92; adv. com. N.Y. chpt. Nat. Assn. Corp. Real Estate Execs., 1990. Author: A Practical Guide to Construction Lending, 1985; editor Real Estate Financing Newsletter, 1980-85; contbr. articles to profl. jours. Mem. secondary sch. interviewing com. Cornell U., Ithaca, NY, 1981—; treas. Lansman Housing Corp., 2000—02; chmn. fed. legis. com. Nat. Assn. Real Estate Investment Trusts; trustee Jericho Jewish Ctr., 2002—. Mem.: Oakwood-Princeton Park Civic Assn., N.Y. Bar Assn., Alpha Epsilon Pi, Pi Sigma Alpha, Omicron Delta Epsilon. E-mail: ricar77@hotmail.com.

RIDOLFI, DOROTHY PORTER BOULDEN, nurse, real estate broker; b. SI, NY, Jan. 24, 1937; d. David Porter and Helen Marie (McCloskey) Boulden; m. Edward Benjamin Ridolfi, Aug. 16, 1958; children: Edward Brian, Judyann Nixon, Jacqueline Ryan. RN, St. Francis Hosp., 1957; student, Seton Hall U., 1958, Mercer CC, 1974, student, 1984, Thomas Edison Coll., 1979—84. Cert. coronary and critical care nurse; real estate cert. South Jersey Sch. Profl. Bus., 1976, lic. real estate instr. NJ, broker NJ, sales person NJ. Owner Stay 'N Play Day Camp, 1963—65; nurse Princeton (NJ) Med. Ctr., 1972—73; pres., broker Ridolfi Realty Inc., Trenton, NJ, 1977—91; nurse Hamilton (NJ) Hosp., 1982—85; instr. real estate Mercer County CC and Career Devel. Sch. Corr. sec. Hist. Soc., Hightstown, NJ, 1971—72; bd. dirs. Campfire Girls and Boys, 1984; committeewoman Burlington County Dem. Com., Willingboro, NJ, 1966—67, Mercer County Dem. Com., East Windsor, NJ, 1969—72. Mem.: Mercer County Multiple Listing, Nat. Assn. Realtors, Nat. Fedn. Ind. Bus. (PAC chmn. 1989), NJ Assn. Realtors (bd. dirs., v.p. 5th dist. 1989, Make Am. Better award 1982), Mercer County Bd. Realtors (bd. dirs. 1981—83, treas., v.p., pres. 1988—), Soroptomist Club, Mercer County C. of C. Democrat. Roman Catholic. Office: Gloria Nilson Realtors GMAC Real Estate 1970 Rt 33 Hamilton Square NJ 08690 Office Phone: 609-890-0007 ext. 115.

RIDOLFI, PATRICK MURPHY, music educator, tenor; b. San Francisco, Calif., July 29, 1954; s. Joseph Oreste Ridolfi and Lillian Ruth Scott; m. Margie Gayatin, May 22, 1993; 1 child, Justin Robert; m. Barbara Ridolfi, Sept. 20, 1980 (dec. Nov. 6, 1989); 1 child, Joseph Patrick. BA, U. of Calif. at Santa Barbara, Santa Barbara, CA, 1977; BM, Calif. State U. at Northridge, Northridge, CA, 1987. Elem. tchr. LA Unified Sch. Dist., Los Angeles, Calif., 1991—2003; free-lance operatic tenor LA Opera, LA Master Chorale, Long Beach Opera, Carnegie Hall, Roger Wagner Chorale, Los Angeles, Calif., 1981—; elem. music tchr. LA Unified Sch. Dist., Los Angeles, Calif., 1995—. Grantee ELSA Grant, Fed. Arts Grant, 1999, 2000. Mem.: UTLA, MENC. Avocations: swimming, snorkeling, travel.

RIDOUX, DENISE C. director, educator; d. James Richard and Elizabeth Correia; m. Serge Henri Jr. Ridoux, Mar. 10, 2003; children: Austin, Shane. B of Music Edn., Shenandoah U., 1990; M of Music Edn., Coll. NJ, 1995. Band dir. East Windsor (NJ) Regional Sch. Dist., 1990—98, Colts Neck (NJ) Twp. Schs., 1998—. Pep band dir. Monmouth U., West Long Branch, NJ, 1998—2001, adj. prof., 1998—2001. Mem.: NJ Music Educators Assn., NJ Edn. Assn., Am. Fedn. Musicians. Office: Cedar Dr Sch 73 Cedar Dr Colts Neck NJ 07722

RIECK, WILLIAM ALBERT, education educator, academic administrator; b. Hackensack, N.J., Jan. 15, 1942; s. William Emanual and Grace Adeline (Bormann) R.; m. Judith Ann Klindt, Apr. 18, 1965; children: Melissa, William Albert Jr. BA, Jersey City State Coll., 1963; MA, Montclair (N.J.) State Coll., 1966; DEd, Loyola U., Chgo., 1976. Asst. prof. Trenton State Coll., NJ, 1966-69; area mgr. Dupont Chem., Chgo., 1969-72; chemistry tchr. Lockport H.S., 1972-74; asst. prin. Oak Forest H.S., Ill., 1974-75; prin. Evanston Twp. H.S., Ill., 1975-76, Rock Island H.S., Ill., 1975-77, Fallsburg H.S., NY, 1977-80, Hicksville H.S., NY, 1980-90, Nottingham H.S., Trenton, 1982-90; prof. edn./dir. tchr. cadet corps U. La., Lafayette, 1991—, prof., dir. grad. studies edn., 1991—. Contbr. articles to profl. jours. Mem. Hamilton (N.J.) Say No to Drugs Com., 1987—, Hamilton Citizens for Edn., 1989—; advisor DeMolay chpt., Hamilton Sq., N.J., 1987—; trustee First Presbyn. Ch., Levittown, N.Y., 1981-84. Recipient Disting. Alumnu award Jersey City State Coll., 1983, Citation, N.J. Gen. Assembly, 1983, Cert. of Appreciation, N.Y. Congress Parents and Tchrs., 1982; NSF grantee, 1968, 1994-95. Mem. Nat. Assn. Secondary Sch. Prins. (Svc. award 1989), N.J. Prins. and Suprs. Assn. (exec. coun. 1985—, Svc. award 1989), Assn. for Supervision and Curriculum Devel., Mercer County Prins. and Suprs. Assn. (sec. 1988—), Masons, Shriners (youth com. chmn. 1975-80). Presbyterian. Home: 108 Shadowbrush Bnd Lafayette LA 70506-7852 Office: U La Foster Hall 221 PO Box 42051 Lafayette LA 70504-0001 E-mail: wrieck@louisiana.edu.

RIECKEN, HENRY WILLIAM, psychologist, research director; b. Bklyn., Nov. 11, 1917; s. Henry William and Lilian Antoinette (Nieber) R.; m. Frances Ruth Manson, Aug. 7, 1955; children— Mary Susan, Gilson, Anne AB, Harvard U., 1939, PhD, 1950. Social sci. analyst Dept. Agr., 1941-46; lectr. social psychology, research assoc. clin. psychology Harvard U., 1949-54; assoc. prof. then prof., sr. mem. lab. research social relations U. Minn., 1954-58; program dir. social sci. research NSF, Washington, 1958-59; head Office Social Sci., Washington, 1959-60, asst. dir. social scis., 1960-64, assoc. dir. sci. edn., 1964-66; v.p. Social Sci. Research Council, N.Y.C., 1966-69, pres., 1969-71; prof. behavioral scis. U. Pa., Phila., 1972-85, prof. emeritus, 1985—; assoc. dir. for planning Nat. Library Medicine, Bethesda, Md., 1985-87. Fellow Ctr. Advanced Study Behavioral Scis., Stanford, Calif., 1971-72; Paterson Meml. lectr. U. Minn., 1970; Jensen lectr. Duke U., 1973; mem. adv. com. to dir. NIH, 1966-70, chmn. internat. ctrs. com., 1968-73; pres. Am. Psychol. Found., 1971-73; vice chmn., chmn. com. nat. needs for biomed. and behavioral rsch. pers. NRC, 1975-80; report rev. com. Nat. Acad. Scis., 1982-99; adj. prof. psychiatry U. Tex. Med. Br., 1988—2002. Author: The Volunteer Work Camp, 1952, When Prophecy Fails, 1956, Social Experimentation, 1974, Experimental Testing of Public Policy, 1976; contbr. articles to profl. jours. Bd. dirs. Found. Child Devel. (formerly Assn. Aid Crippled Children), N.Y., 1962-2003; trustee W.T. Grant Found., N.Y., 1979-96. Served with USAAC, 1943-45. Fellow APA (Harold M. Hildreth award 1971), Am. Acad. Arts and Scis.; mem. Am. Assn. Pub. Opinion Rsch., Sociol. Rsch. Assn. (pres. 1966), Nat. Acad. Scis., Inst. Medicine, Harvard Club (N.Y.C.), Cosmos Club (Washington).

RIEDEL, ALAN ELLIS, retired manufacturing company executive, lawyer; b. Bellaire, Ohio, June 28, 1930; s. Emil George and Alberta (Shafer) R.; m. Ruby P. Tignor, June 21, 1953; children: Ralph A., Amy L., John T. AB magna cum laude, Ohio U., 1952, LLD (hon.), 1994; JD, Case Western Res. U., 1955; grad., Advanced Mgmt. Program, Harvard, 1971. Bar: Ohio 1955, Tex. 1968. Assoc. Squire, Sanders & Dempsey, Cleve., 1955-60; from gen. counsel to sec. Cooper Industries Inc. (formerly Cooper Bessemer Co.), Mt. Vernon, Ohio, 1960-68; from sec. to v.p. indsl. rels. Cooper Industries Inc., Mt. Vernon, Ohio, 1963-73; from sr. v.p. adminstrn. to vice chmn. Cooper Industries, Inc., Houston, 1973-94. Dir. Factory Mut. Ins., 1999-2000; bd. dirs. Belden Inc., St. Louis, 1993-2000, Gardner Denver Inc., Quincy, Ill., 1994-2000, chmn. bd. dirs., 1994-98; of counsel Squire, Sanders & Dempsey, Houston, 1994—. Past chmn. bd. dirs. Jr. Achievement of S.E. Tex.; trustee, past chmn. bd. trustees Ohio U. Endowment Found. Mem. Order of Coif, Phi Beta Kappa, Omicron Delta Kappa, Delta Tau Delta. Home: Bunker Hill Village 4 Heritage Ct Houston TX 77024 E-mail: aeriedel@swbell.net.

RIEDEL, BERNARD EDWARD, retired pharmaceutical sciences educator; b. Provost, Alta., Can., Sept. 25, 1919; s. Martin and Naomi E. (Klingaman) R.; m. Julia C. McClurg, Mar. 5, 1944 (dec. Mar. 1992); children: Gail Lynne, Dwain Edward, Barry Robert; m. Della Williams, Sept. 2, 2000. BS in Pharmacy, U. Alta., Edmonton, 1943, MS in Pharmacology, 1949, DSc (hon.), 1990; PhD in Biochemistry, U. Western Ont., 1953. Lectr., asst. prof. Faculty of Pharmacy U. Alta., Edmonton, 1946-49, asst. prof. then assoc. prof., 1953-58, prof., 1959-67, exec. asst. to v.p., 1961-67; dean, prof. Faculty Pharm. Scis. U. B.C., Vancouver, Canada, 1967-84, coord. Health Scis. Centre, 1977-84. Mem. sci. adv. com. Health Rsch. Found. of B.C., 1991-95. Contbr. numerous articles on pharmacology to profl. jours. Elder Ryerson United Ch.; mem. exec. bd. Boy Scouts Can., Edmonton Region, Alta.; mem. Cancer Control Agy. of B.C., trustee 1979-86, v.p., 1984, pres. 1985-86; bd. dirs. B.C. Lung Assn., 1988-2000, v.p., 1989, pres., 1990-91; chmn., bd. dirs. B.C. Organ Transplant Soc., 1986-89, hon. bd. dirs., 2000. Wing comdr. RCAF, 1943-46, 49-67. Decorated mem. Order of Can.; recipient Gold medal in Pharmacy, 1943; Centennial medal, 1967, 75th Anniversary medal U. B.C., 1990; Can Forces decoration, 1965; Commemorative medal for 125th Anniversary of the Confedn. of Can., 1992, Spl. Svcs. award Assn. Faculties of Pharmacy of Can., 2001, Queen Elizabeth II Golden Jubilee medal, 2002. Mem. Alta. Pharm. Assn. (hon. life), Can. Pharm. Assn. (hon. life), Assn. of Faculties of Pharmacy of Can. (hon. life, chmn. 1959, 69, Spl. Svc. award 2001), Can. Biochem. Soc., Pharmacol. Soc. Can., Can. Assn. of Univ. Tchrs., Can. Soc. Hosp. Pharmacists, B.C. Coll. Pharmacists (hon. life), U. B.C. Profs. Emeriti Divsn. Alumni Assn. (pres. 1993-95). Home: 8394 Angus Dr Vancouver BC Canada V6P 5L2 E-mail: briedel@interchange.ubc.ca.

RIEDEL, BUNNIE, not-for-profit organization executive; m. Daniel M. Gartland; 2 children. Formerly founder, exec. dir. Religious Coalition for Reproductive Choice of So. Calif.; formerly nat. field dir. Ams. United for Separation of Ch. and State; exec. dir. Alliance for Cmty. Media, Washington, 1998—. Spkr. in field. Author: (booklets) Faith and Freedom: Church/State Separation in Our Time, Reflections on Religious Liberty, A Matter of Conscience; contbr. articles to jour., mags., textbooks; appearances on numerous TV and radio programs. Recipient award, V.p. Al Gore, 1999, Recognition for Leadership award, Calif. State Senate. Mem.: Phi Kappa Phi. Office: Alliance for Cmty Media 666 11th St NW Washington DC 20001-4542

RIEDER, CONLY LEROY, cell biologist, consultant; b. Orange, Calif., Nov. 2, 1950; s. Alvin Ray Rieder and Margaret Morgan; m. Susan Nowogrodzki, Aug. 11, 1979; children: Leila E., Rachel M. BS, U. of Calif., Irvine, 1972; MS, U. of Oreg., 1972, PhD, 1977. Prof. Dept. Biomed. Scis., SUNY, Albany, NY, 1984—2002, Albany Med. Coll., NY, 1988—; sr. rsch. scientist, lab. chief Molecular Medicine, Wadsworth Ctr., Albany, NY, 1998—. Cons. Health Rsch. Inc., Albany, NY, 2001—. Author (editor): (book) Proceedings of the Microscopy Society of America, 1993, Mitosis and Meiosis, 2001; assoc. editor Cell Motility and the Cytoskeleton, mem. editl. bd. (sci. jours.) Protoplasma, Chromosoma, Jour. Cell Biology, Animal Biology;, author over 150 rsch. papers on cell biology. Bd. mem. Capital Dist. Physicians Health Plan, Albany, NY, 1985—87; treas. East Greenbush Edn. Found., NY, 1999—2002. Recipient Merit award, NIH, 1984—, Commrs. Recognition award, NY State Dept. of Health, 2001, Photographic prizes, Olympus and Zeiss, varioius years. Mem.: N.Y. Acad. of Scis., Microscopy Soc. of Am. (bd. dirs. 1993—96), Am. Soc. for Cell Biology. Achievements include research in Chromosomes attach to the spindle and how progression through mitosis is controlled. Avocations: photography, fishing, travel, skiing. Home: 261 Elliot Rd East Greenbush NY 12061 Office: Wadsworth Ctr NYS Dept Health Empire State Plz Albany NY 12201-0509 Office Phone: 518-474-6774. Personal E-mail: conlyrieder@hotmail.com. Business E-Mail: rieder@wadsworth.org.

RIEDINGER, EDWARD ANTHONY (TED RIEDINGER), international educator, Brazilianist; b. Cin., Mar. 26, 1944; s. Charles Anthony and Ida Gertrude (Winter) R. Student, Latin Sch. Indpls., 1962; BA cum laude, Butler U., 1967; MA, U. Chgo., 1969, PhD, 1978; MLIS, U. Calif., Berkeley, 1989; postgrad., Harvard U., 1969, U. Oxford, 1970, U. Cambridge, 1986. Pvt. sec. to ex-Pres. Brazil Juscelino Kubitschek, 1972-76; asst. prof. Pontifical Cath. U., Rio de Janeiro, 1976-77, U. Ams., Puebla, Mex., 1978; ednl. adv. officer Fulbright Commn. U.S. Consulate, Rio de Janeiro, 1979-88; founder Overseas Ednl. Advisers Profl. Edn. Group Nat. Assn. for Fgn. Student Affairs, 1985, Latin Am. rep., 1988; acting bibliographer L.Am., Spain, Portugal U. Calif., Berkeley, 1990; lectr. Brazilian history San Francisco State U., 1990; prof., head Latin Am. Libr. Ohio State U., 1991—. Mem. organizing exec. com. Brazilian Studies Assn., 1993, sec., 1994-96; founder, adminstr. Overseas Ednl. Advisers Profl. Net, 1992-95; cons. on Brazil and internat. ednl. advising for U.S. and internat. orgns. and agys.; adj. prof. dept. history, dept. Spanish and Portuguese, Ohio State U.; adj. prof. Ohio U., Athens, 1998—; cons. in field. Author: Brief View of American Literature, 1976, Como se faz Uu Presidente, a campanha de J.K., 1988, Procs. of 1st BRASA conf., 1994, Procs. of 2d BRASA conf., 1995, Turned on Advising, 1995, Where in the World to Learn, 1995, Bibliography of Rise of West, 2002; contbr. more than 200 articles to profl. and scholarly jours. and reference books; mem. editl. bd. Phi Beta Delta Internat. Rev., 1992-96, Manguinhos, 1994—. Ford Found. fellow, 1968-72; travel grantee NEH, 1992, OSU/Tinker Found. field rsch. grantee 1992, 96; Fulbright-Hays scholar, 1996, Fulbright Sr. Specialist, 2001-06; recipient commendations Brazilian Army Corps of Engrs., 1982, U.S. Info. Svc., 1984, Brazilian War Coll., 1985, Fulbright Commn., 1988, 2001—, U.S. amb. to Brazil, 1988, Berkeley City Commons, 1990, Instituto Brasil-Estados Unidos, Rio de Janeiro, 1995. Office: Ohio State U Librs 1858 Neil Ave Rm 312 Columbus OH 43210 E-mail: riedinger.4@osu.edu.

RIEDL, JOHN ORTH, university dean; b. Milw., Dec. 9, 1937; s. John O. and Clare C. (Quirk) R.; m. Mary Lucille Priestap, Feb. 4, 1961; children: John T., Ann E., James W., Steven E., Daniel J. BS in Math. magna cum laude, Marquette U., Milw., 1958; MS in Math., U. Notre Dame, 1960, PhD in Math., 1963; postgrad., Northwestern U., 1963. Asst. prof. math. Ohio State U., Columbus, 1966-70, assoc. prof., 1970—2003, asst. dean Coll. Math. and Phys. Sci., 1969-74, assoc. dean, 1974-87, acting dean, 1984-86, spl. asst. to provost, 1987—2003, dean, dir. Mansfield (Ohio) Campus, 1988—2003, exec. dean regional campus, 1988—2003, assoc. prof. emeritus, 2003—. Panelist sci. edn. NSF, 1980-91; cons. Ohio Dept. Edn., 1989, Ohio bd. regents subsidy cons., 1991, 95, 97, 99, 2001, 03; bd. dirs. Richland County Univ. and Coll. Access Network, 2002—. Pres., v.p. exec. com. Univ. Cmty. Assn., Columbus, 1970-78; mem. edn. commn. St. Peter's Schs., Mansfield, 1989-95; trustee Rehab. Svc. N. Ctrl. Ohio, Mansfield, 1990-99, v.p., 1993-94, pres., 1995-97; pres. Ohio Assn. Regional Campuses, 1993-94; co-chair capital campaign St. Peter's Schs., 1998. NSF grad. fellow, 1960, 61, 62; recipient Faculty Svc. award Nat. U. Continuing Edn. Assn., 1988, Creative Programming award, 1988. Mem. Math. Assn. Am. (chair com. on minicourse 1981-87), Downs Am. Chestnut Found. of Ohio (bd. dirs. 2001-04), Rotary Internat. (bd. dirs., pres.-elect, pres.) C. of C. (bd. dirs.). Democrat. Roman Catholic. Avocations: fishing, woodworking, gardening. Home: 745 Clifton Blvd Mansfield OH 44907-2284 Office: Ohio State U 1680 University Dr Mansfield OH 44906-1547 E-mail: riedl.1@osu.edu.

RIEDLINGER, STEPHEN C. federal judge; b. 1950; BA, La. State U., 1971, JD, 1977. Bar: La. 1977, U.S. Dist. Ct. (ea. dist.) La. 1979, U.S. Dist. Ct. (mid. dist.) 1978, U.S. Ct. Appeals (5th cir.) 1983. Law clk. U.S. Dist. Ct. La., 1977-78; pvt. practice Baton Rouge, 1978-86; magistrate judge U.S. Dist. Ct. (mid. dist.) La., Baton Rouge, 1986—. With USNR, 1971-77. Office: Russell B Long Fed Bldg & Courthouse 777 Florida St Ste 260 Baton Rouge LA 70801-1717 Fax: 225-389-3501., 225-389-3585. Office Phone: 225-389-3584.

RIEDMAN, JAMES ROBERT, insurance company executive; b. Rochester, N.Y., May 4, 1959; s. John Robert and Eileen (Kiefer) R.; m. Carron Herrmann, Nov. 5, 1988. BA, U. Notre Dame, 1981; MBA, U. Wis., 1982. Dir. corp. planning Balboa Ins. Group, Newport Beach, Calif., 1983-84; exec. sr. v.p. TFS&C subs. Transam. Ins. Group, L.A., 1984-87; prin. Riedman Corp., Rochester, 1987—. Bd. dirs. Niagara Exch. Corp., Gordon S. Black, Inc., Rochester. Bd. dirs. Otiena Coun. Boy Scouts Am., 1988—, St. Ann's Home, 1988—. Republican. Roman Catholic. Avocation: sailing. Office: Daniel Green Co 1 Main St Dolgeville NY 13329

RIEDTHALER, WILLIAM ALLEN, risk management professional; b. Cleve., May 13, 1948; s. Robert Wilbert and Jean Margaret (Trojanowski) R.; m. Janet Louise Clark, Nov. 10, 1973; children: Jennifer Margaret, Valerie Gretchen. AS in Law Enforcement, Cuyahoga C.C., 1968; BA in Pub. Safety Adminstrn., BA in Criminal Justice Studies, Kent State, 1974; EMBA in Healthcare, Baldwin-Wallace Coll., 2000. Cert. instr. and peace officer; cert. tchr., Ohio, Fla., Tex., Mich.; accredited healthcare fraud investigator. Police cadet Cleve. Police Dept., 1967-69, patrolman, 1969-74, detective, 1974-81, sgt. police, 1981-84; assoc. security advisor Cleve. Electric Illuminating Co., 1984-87, investigator, 1987-90; security advisor Centerior Energy Corp., Cleve., 1990-93, supr. claims Independence, 1993-96, mgr. risk mgmt., 1996-98; dir. spl. risk programs N.Am. Benefits Network, Inc., Rocky River, Ohio, 1998—2003; dir. mktg. and audit investigations Watermark Audit Group, Cleve., 2003—. Instr. gambling and vice Case Western Res. U., Cleve., 1979—90, Cleve. Police Acad., Cleve., 1974—, Ohio Peace Officers Tng. Acad., 1976—2004, Cuyahoga County Sheriffs Officers Acad., Cleve., 1981—98, Shaker Heights (Ohio) Police Acad., 1990—98; facilitator Tiffin U. Criminal Justice Program, 2002—. Author: An Enforcement Guide to Carnival Games Gambling and Fraud, 1981, An Enforcement Guide to Monetary Operated Gambling Devices or Slot Machines, 2002; contbr. articles to profl. jours. Spl. dep. sheriff Cuyahoga County Sheriff's Office, Cleve., 1985—2004; past pres. Metrop. Crime Bur; trustee, 2d v.p. Metrop. Crime Clinic, 2d v.p., 2002—; trustee, 2d v.p. Cleve. Crime Clinic, 1999—2003; bd. govs. Nat. Healthcare Antifraud Assn., 1999—2003. Recipient Patrolman of Yr. award Cleve. Exchange Club, 1979. Mem. Am. Soc. Indsl. Security, Met. Crime Clinic (v.p. 1992-93, 2001—, pres. 1994-95), German Am. Police Assn., Fraternal Order of Police, Cleve. Claims Assn. Republican. Avocations: photography, hiking, swimming. Home: 8525 Olde Eight Rd # 4 Northfield OH 44067 Office: Watermark Audit Group 20325 Center Ridge Rd Ste 330 Rocky River OH 44116 Office Phone: 440-333-4113. Personal E-mail: larsonegames@yahoo.com. Business E-Mail: briedthaler@watermarkaudit.com., wriedthaler@enforcementguide.com.

RIEDY, MARK JOSEPH, finance educator; b. Aurora, Ill., July 9, 1942; s. Paul Bernard and Kathryn Veronica R.; m. Erin Jeanne Lynch, Aug. 29, 1964; children: Jennifer Erin, John Mark. BA in Econs. maxima cum laude, Loras Coll., 1964; MBA, Washington U., St. Louis, 1966; PhD, U. Mich., 1971. Asst. prof. bus. adminstrn. U. Colo., Boulder, 1969-71; sr. staff economist Council of Econ. Advisers, Washington, 1971-72; spl. asst. to chmn. Fed. Home Loan Bank Bd., Washington, 1972; v.p., dir. research PMI Investment Corp., San Francisco, 1973; v.p., chief economist Fed. Home Loan Bank of San Francisco, 1973-77; exec. v.p., chief operating officer Mortgage Bankers Assn. of Am., Washington, 1978-84; pres., chief operating officer Fed. Nat. Mortgage Assn., Washington, 1985-86, cons., 1986-87; pres., chief operating officer J.E. Robert Cos., Alexandria, Va., 1987-88; pres., chief exec. officer Nat. Coun. Community Bankers, Washington, 1988-92, also bd. dirs.; prof. real estate fin. U. San Diego, 1993—, dir. Burnham-Moores Ctr. Real Estate, 1993—. Mem. adv. coun. Credit Rsch. Ctr., Purdue U., 1981-82; bd. dirs. Fed. Nat. Mortgage Assn., Continental Savs. Bank, AccuBanc Mortgage Corp., Pan Pacific Retail Properties, Inc., Am. Residential Investment Trust, Noble Broadcast Group, Drayton Ins. Cos., Perpetual Savs. Bank, Ctr. for Fin. Studies; bd. dirs., Neighborhood Bancorp; mem. San Diego Mayor's Renaissance Commn. Bd. dirs. St. Vincent De Paul Village; Lambda Alpha Internat. Woodrow Wilson scholar, 1964; Nat. Def. scholar, 1964-66; U.S. Steel Found. fellow, 1966-68; Robert G. Rodkey Found. fellow, 1966-69; Earhart Found. fellow, 1968-69 Mem. Am. Econ. Assn., Am. Fin. Assn., Nat. Assn. Bus. Economists, Am. Soc. Assn. Execs., Urban Land Inst. Office: U San Diego Sch Bus Adminstrn 5998 Alcala Park San Diego CA 92110-2492 Office Phone: 619-260-4872. Business E-Mail: mriedy@sandiego.edu.

RIEFLER, DONALD BROWN, financial consultant; b. Washington, Nov. 10, 1927; s. Winfield W. and Dorothy (Brown) R.; m. Patricia Hawley, Oct. 12, 1957; children: Duncan, Linda, Barbara. BA, Amherst Coll., 1949. With J.P. Morgan & Co. Inc., N.Y.C., 1952-91; v.p. Morgan Guaranty Trust Co. of N.Y., 1962-68, sr. v.p., 1968-77, chmn. sources and uses of funds com., 1977—88, chmn. market risk com., 1989—91; fin. mkts. cons., 1991—. With U.S. Army, 1950-52. Mem. John's Island Club, Riomar Country Club, Quail Valley River Club, Birchwood Farms Club, Harbor Point Club. Home: 512 Bay Dr Vero Beach FL 32963-2107

RIEGEL, BYRON WILLIAM, ophthalmologist; b. Evanston, Ill., Jan. 19, 1938; s. Byron and Belle Mae (Huot) Riegel; m. Marilyn Hills, May 18, 1968; children: Marc William, Ryan Marie, Andrea Elizabeth. BS, Stanford U., 1960; MD, Cornell U., 1964. Diplomate Am Bd Ophthalmology, Nat Bd Med Examiners. Intern King County Hosp., Seattle, 1964-65; asst. resident in surgery U. Wash., Seattle, 1965; resident in ophthalmology U. Fla., Fla., 1968-71; pvt. practice medicine specializing in ophthalmology Sierra Eye Med. Group, Inc., Visalia, Calif., 1972—. Mem staff Kaweah Delta Dist Hosp, chief staff, 1978—79, bd dirs, asst secy, 1983—90; asst med dir Sierra Ambulatory Surg Ctr, Visalia, Calif., 2000—. Flight surgeon USN, 1966—68. Co-recipient Fight-for-Sight Citation for rsch. in retinal dystrophy, 1970. Fellow: ACS, Am. Acad. Ophthalmology; mem.: Internat. Pacoemulsification and Cataract Methodology Soc., Am. Soc. Cataract and Refractive Surgery, Calif. Acad. Ophthalmology (v.p. 3d party liaison 1994—96, dir. 1996—98), Tulare County Med Asn, Calif. Med. Assn. (del. 1978—79), Rotary (Visalia). Roman Catholic. Home: 3027 Keogh Ct Visalia CA 93291-4228 Office: 2830 W Main St Visalia CA 93291-4331 Office Phone: 559-636-1000. Personal E-mail: briegel@pacbell.net. Business E-Mail: briegel@sierraeye.com.

RIEGEL, KURT WETHERHOLD, environmental protection executive; b. Lexington, Va., Feb. 28, 1939; s. Oscar Wetherhold and Jane Cordelia (Butterworth) R.; children: Tatiana Suzanne, Samuel Brent Oscar, Eden Sonja Jane. BA, Johns Hopkins U., 1961; PhD, U. Md., 1966; PMD, Harvard U., 1977. Asst. prof. astronomy UCLA, 1966-74; prof. astronomy U. Calif. Extension, Los Angeles, 1968-74; mgr. energy conservation program Fed. Energy Adminstrn., Washington, 1974-75; chief tech. and consumer products energy conservation Dept. Energy, Washington, 1975-78, dir. consumer products divsn., conservation and solar energy, 1978-79; assoc. dir. environ. engring. and tech. EPA, 1979-82; head Astronomy Ctrs. NSF, 1982-89; dir. Environ. Protection Office USN, 1989-94, dir. environ. tech., 1994—2001. Adj. prof. George Washington U., 1995, Johns Hopkins U., 2001—; vis. prof. Washington & Lee U., 1993; cons. Aerospace Corp., El Segundo, Calif., 1967-70, Rand Corp., Santa Monica, Calif., 1973-74; vis. fellow U. Leiden, Netherlands, 1972-73; mem. Casualty Council Underwriters Labs., Nat. Radio Astron. Observatory Users Com., 1968-74; chair gov.'s environ. edn. adv. commn. colls. and univs., Va., 2000-2003. Contbr. articles to profl. jours. Mem. AAAS, Am. Phys. Soc., Sierra Club, Audubon Soc., Internat. Radio Sci. Union, Am. Astron. Soc., Internat. Astron. Union, Assn. of Scientists and Engrs. Home: 171 Gulchleigh Ln Glasgow VA 24555-2266 E-mail: riegel.kurt@apl.jhu.edu.

RIEGER, MITCHELL SHERIDAN, lawyer; b. Chgo., Sept. 5, 1922; s. Louis and Evelyn (Sampson) R.; m. Rena White Abelmann, May 17, 1949 (div. 1957); 1 child, Karen Gross Cooper; m. Nancy Horner, May 30, 1961 (div. 1972); stepchildren: Jill Levi, Linda Hanan, Susan Perlstein, James Geoffrey Felsenthal; m. Pearl Handelsman, June 10, 1973; stepchildren: Steven Newman, Mary Ann Malarkey, Nancy Halbeck. AB, Northwestern U., 1944; JD, Harvard U., 1949. Bar: Ill. 1950, U.S. Dist. Ct. (no. dist.) Ill. 1950, U.S. Supreme Ct. 1953, U.S. Ct. Mil. Appeals 1953, U.S. Ct. Appeals (7th cir.) 1954. Legal asst. Rieger & Rieger, Chgo., 1949-50, assoc., 1950-54; asst. U.S. atty. No. Dist Ill., Chgo., 1954-60, 1st asst., 1958-60; assoc. gen. counsel SEC, Washington, 1960-61; ptnr. Schiff Hardin & Waite, Chgo., 1961—, sr. counsel, 1998—. Instr. John Marshall Law Sch. Chgo., 1952-54. Contbr. articles to profl. jours. Active Chgo. Crime Commn., bd. dirs., 1998—; pres. Park View Home for Aged, 1969-71; Rep. precinct committeeman, Highland Park, Ill., 1964-68; bd. dirs. Spertus Mus. Judaica, 1987-91, vis. com., 1991—. Served to lt. (j.g.) USNR, 1943-46, PTO. Fellow Am. Coll. Trial Lawyers; mem. ABA, FBA (pres. Chgo. chpt. 1959-60, nat. v.p. 1960-61), Chgo. Bar Assn., Ill. Bar Assn., Am. Judicature Soc., 7th Circuit Bar Assn., Standard Club, Lawyers Club Chgo., Vail Racquet Club, Phi Beta Kappa. Jewish. Avocations: photography, skiing, sailing. Office: SchiffHardin LLP 6600 Sears Tower Chicago IL 60606 E-mail: mrieger@schiffhardin.com., msheridanr@aol.com.

RIEGLER, GUENTER, federal agency administrator; m. Sandra Riegler; 2 children. Degree, Vienna Inst. Tech., 1964; PhD, U. Md., 1969. Postdoctoral fellow Calif. Inst. Tech., 1969—71; group supr. space sci. group Bendix Aerospace, 1971—75; mem. tech. staff Jet Propulsion Lab., 1975—87; detailee from Jet Propulsion Lab. NASA, Washington, 1987—95, chief scientist rsch. divsn. Office Space Sci., 1995—99, exec. dir. sci. Office Space Sci., 1999—. Office: NASA Hdqrs Mail Code S 300 E St SW Washington DC 20546

RIEGSECKER, MARVIN DEAN, pharmacist, state senator; b. Goshen, Ind., July 5, 1937; s. Levi and Mayme (Kauffman) R.; m. Norma Jane Shrock, Aug. 3, 1958; children: Steven Scott, Michael Dean. BA in Pharmacy, U. Colo., 1967. Pharmacist Parkside Pharmacy, Goshen, Ind., 1967-73; pharmacist, mgr. Hooks Drugs, Inc., Goshen, 1973-94; coroner Elkhart County, Goshen, 1977-84; mem. Ind. Senate from 12th dist., Indpls., 1988—; pharmacist Walgreens, Goshen, 1994-96, Meijer, Goshen, 1998—. Bus. affairs cons. Goshen Health Sys., 1997-98. Rep. commr. Elkhart County, 1985-88; bd. commrs. pres., 1987-88; past adv. bd. dirs. Oaklawn Hosp.; past chmn. Michiana Area Coun. of Govts. Mem. Ind. Pharm. Assn. Republican. Mennonite. Avocation: jogging. Home: 1814 Kentfield Way Goshen IN 46526-5610 Office: Ind Senate Statehouse 200 W Washington St Indianapolis IN 46204-2728

RIEHECKY, JANET ELLEN, writer; b. Waukegan, Ill., Mar. 5, 1953; d. Roland Wayne and Patricia Helen (Anderson) Polsgrove; m. John Jay Riehecky, Aug. 2, 1975; 1 child, Patrick William. BA summa cum laude, Ill. Wesleyan U., 1975; MA in Comm., Ill. State U., 1978; MA in English, Northwestern U., 1983. Tchr. English Blue Mound (Ill.) H.S., 1977-80, West Chicago (Ill.) H.S., 1984-86; editor Child's World Pub. Co., Elgin, Ill., 1987-90; freelance writer Elgin, 1990—. Author: Dinosaur series, 24 vols., 1988, UFOs, 1989, Saving the Forests, 1990, Irish Americans, 1995, The Mystery of the Missing Money, 1996, The Mystery of the UFO, 1996, Stegosaurus, 1998, Triceratops, 1998, Tyrannosaurus, 1998, Velociroptor, 1998, A Ticket to China, 1999, Greece, Sweden, 2000, George Lucas, 2001, The Emancipation Proclamation, 2002, The Osage Nation, 2002, The Cree Nation, 2002, Indonesia, 2002, The Plymouth Colony, 2002, The Settling of Jamestown, 2002, The Settling of St. Augustine, 2002, The Siege of the Alamo, 2002, Benjamin Franklin, 2003, Daniel Boone, 2003, The Wampanoag, 2003, Ulysses S. Grant, 2004. Nat. dir. Kids Love a Mystery, 1999-2004. Recipient Summit award for best children's nonfiction Soc. Midland Authors, 1988. Mem. Soc. Am. Magicians, Soc. Children's Book Writers and Illustrators, Mystery Writers of Am. (midwest bd. dirs. 2000-04), Sisters in Crime, Phi Kappa Phi. Democrat. Baptist. Avocations: reading, hiking, dinosaur hunting. Office Phone: 847-695-9781. Personal E-mail: jr@janetriehecky.com.

RIEHL, JANE ELLEN, education educator; b. New Albany, Ind., Oct. 17, 1942; d. Henry Gabbart Jr. and Mary Elizabeth Willham; m. Richard Emil Riehl, June 15, 1968; 1 child, Mary Ellen. BA in Elem. Edn., U. Evansville, 1964; MS, Ind. U., Bloomington, 1966; postgrad., Spalding U., 1979, Ind. U. S.E., New Albany, 1991—2002. Cert. 1-8 and kindergarten tchr., Ind.; lic. profl. elem adminstrn., reading minor kindergarten tchr., Ind. Elem. tchr. Clarksville (Ind.) Cmty. Sch., 1964-68, 70-75, 81-82, tchr. kindergarten, 1975-81; elem. tchr. Chapelwood Sch. Wayne Twp., Indpls., 1968-70; lectr. edn. Ind. U. S.E., 1988-97, dir. tchg. and rsch. project, 1990-91, 92-93, dir. field and career placement, cert./lic. grad advisor, 1998, coord. elem./spl. edn. field and career placement, license and grad. advisor, 1998—. Cons. Riehl Assocs., Jeffersonville, Ind., 1995—. Co-author: An Integrated Language Arts Teacher Education Program, 1990, The Reading Professor, 1992, Multimedia: HyperStudio and Language Education, 1996, Technology: Hypermedia and Communications, 1997, others; author procs. Parent vol. Girl Scouts U.S.A., Jeffersonville, 1988-95; mem. adminstrtv. bd. Wall Street United Meth. Ch., Jeffersonville, 1993-95; mem. women's health adv. coun. Clark Meml. Hosp., Jeffersonville, 1995—; bd. dirs. Clark Meml. Hosp. Found., vice chair, 1999, chair 2000, sec. 2002-03; team mem. People to People Citizen Amb. Program, 1993, 95, 96; chair internat. bylaws Altrusa Internat., Inc., 2001—. Named Young Career Woman of Yr. Bus. and Profl. Women New Albany and Dist. 13 Ind., 1966; tchg. and rsch. grantee Ind. U. S.E., 1990, 94, 95, 96, 97, 2000; recipient Disting. Tchg. award Ind. U. S.E., 1997, Tchg. Excellence Recognition award, 1997. Mem. Nat. Coun. Tchrs. English, Profs. Reading Tchr. Edn., Ind. State Med. Assn. Alliance (v.p. so. area 1999-2000), Clark County Med. Soc. Alliance (pres.-elect 1997-98, pres. 1998-99), Altrusa Internat. Inc. (internat. bd. 1993-95, dist. gov. 1993-95, svc. award 1995), Phi Delta Kappa (v.p. 1991-92, pres. 1997—, svc. award 1991), Kappa Kappa Kappa (pres. Jeffersonville 1975-76, 90-91, Outstanding Mem. award 1987). Avocations: travel, reading, crafts, decorating. Home: 1610 Fox Run Trl Jeffersonville IN 47130-8204 Office: Ind U SE 4201 Grant Line Rd New Albany IN 47150-2158

RIEHLE, B. HUDSON, trade association executive; b. Cin., Sept. 10, 1953; s. Robert Arthur Riehle and Lois W. Hudson; m. Eileen Patricia Betit, Aug. 2, 1986; children: B. Hudson Jr., Bradley Patrick. BA, Skidmore Coll., 1975; MBA, U. Pa., 1986. Rsch. cons. Avmark, Inc., Washington, 1976-78; rsch. analyst Airline Pilots Assn., Washington, 1978-81, supr. econ. analysis, 1981-84; rsch. mgr. Nat. Restaurant Assn., Washington, 1986-91, sr. rsch. mgr., 1991-95, dir. rsch., 1995-97, sr. dir. rsch., 1997-99, v.p. rsch. & info. svcs., 1999-2000, sr. v.p. rsch. and info. svcs., 2000—; bd. dirs. Alexandria Econ. Devel. Partnership, 2002—04. Bus. rsch. adv. coun. Bureau of Labor Stats., 2003—. Editor: Comml. Airline Fleets, 1976—78, Restaurant Industry Ops. Report, 1986—; contbr. Airline Pilot, 1978—84, Restaurants USA, 1986-2002. Mem., bd. dirs., 1st v.p. Fairlington Meadows, Arlington, 1990—92. Mem.: Alexandria Conv. and Visitors Assn. (vice chmn. bd. govs. 2001—02, chmn. bd. govs. 2002—04, treas. 2004—). Avocations: geology, cross country skiing, photography. Home: 2431 Davis Ave Alexandria VA 22302-3209 Office: Nat Restaurant Assn 1200 17th St NW Ste 700 Washington DC 20036-3006

RIEHLE, HELEN S. state senator; b. Somerville, N.J., May 5, 1950; m. Theodore M. Riehle III; children: Augusta, Emily, Sarah. BS, U. Vt., 1972. Tchr. social studies, South Burlington, Vt.; mem. Vt. Ho. of Reps., 1983-92; mem. dist. 6 Vt. State Senate, 1993—. Bd. dirs. Elizabeth Lund Home; co-chmn. Ward County Rep. Com. Trustee U. Vt., Montpelier, 1985-91; bd. govs. Med. Ctr. Vt. Named Outstanding Conservative Woman Legislator Renaissance mag., 1987. Republican. Congregationalist. Office: Vt House of Reps Office of House Mems Montpelier VT 05602

RIEHLE, ROBERT ARTHUR, JR., medical director, surgeon; b. San Diego, Oct. 24, 1947; s. Robert Arthur and Lois (Wulfkoetter) R.; children: Christopher, Kyra. BA, Yale U., 1969; MD, Columbia U., 1973. Intern Columbia Presbyn. Hosp., 1973-74, resident, 1974-77, N.Y. Hosp., Cornell, N.Y.C., 1977-80, assoc. prof. surgery, 1980-90; med. dir. Albany (N.Y.) Meml. Hosp., 1990-94, Blue Shield Northeastern N.Y., Albany, 1994-97, Prudential Healthcare, Charlotte, N.C., 1997-98, Cigna Healthcare, Charlotte, NC, 1998-2000; chief med. officer Spartanburg Regional Healthcare Sys., 2000—. E-mail: rriehle@srhs.com.

RIEKE, FORREST NEILL, lawyer; b. Portland, Oreg., May 26, 1942; s. Forrest Eugene and Mary Neill (Whitelaw) R.; m. Madonna Bernardi, Apr. 2, 1966; children: Mary Jane, Forrest Ermelindo. AB in Polit. Sci., Stanford U., 1968; JD, Willamette U., 1971. Bar: Oreg. 1971, U.S. Dist. Ct. Oreg. 1974, U.S. Ct. Appeals (9th cir.) 1975, U.S. Supreme Ct. 1977. Sr. dep. dist. atty. Multnomah County, Portland, 1971-76; ptnr. Rieke & Savage P.C., Portland, 1977—2003; owner Forrest Rieke and Assocs., Zigzag, Oreg., 2004—. Instr. Oreg. State Police Acad., Ft. Rilea, 1979-2001 Contbr. editor Williamette U. Law Rev., 1971. Pres., bd. dirs. Council Great City Schs., Washington, 1985-93; trustee Emanuel Hosp. Found., 1987-93; bd. dirs. Portland Pub. Schs., 1978-93. Mem. ABA, Oreg. Bar Assn. (indigent accused def. com., chmn. law related edn. com. 1985, bd. dirs. criminal law sect. 1979-84, mem. pub. info. com. 1987-90, ho. dels. 1995-98), Nat. Criminal Def. Lawyers Assn., Oreg. Criminal Def. Lawyers Assn., Multnomah Athletic. Presbyterian. Avocations: skiing, reading, coaching youth sports. Home: PO Box 266 Zigzag OR 97049 Office: Forrest Rieke and assocs PO Box 245 Zigzag OR 97049 E-mail: jrieke@gte.net.

RIEKE, RONALD ALFRED, computer company executive; b. Rugby, ND, Aug. 16, 1951; s. Lawrence Allen Rieke and Emma Marie (Lord) Cooper; m. Madelyn E. Owens, May 2, 1987; children: Ronald Alexander, Sara Emma, Ren William. AS, ND State U., 1971; BS, U. ND, 1973; MA, Webster U., St. Louis, 1976; DSc, Buxton U., 2003. Operator Lystads, Inc., Kansas City, Kans., 1972-74; sales rep. Parke-Davis Co., St. Louis, 1974-76; with bio-med. engring. and sales Gen. Electric Corp., Tulsa, 1976-78; mgr., sales engr. Digital Equipment Corp., Houston, 1978-85; pres. R.A.R.E. Systems, Inc., Houston, 1985—. Bd. dirs. TechSmith Corp., Dallas, Bosque County Emergency Med. Svcs., Inc., Cookoff, Inc. Mem.: Lions (v.p. Meridian chpt. 2004—). Republican. Mem. Christian Ch. (Ch. of Christ). Avocations: Karate, computer technology. Office: RARE Systems Inc 1790 W Sam Houston Pkwy N Houston TX 77043-3113 Home: PO Box 645 Meridian TX 76665-0645 E-mail: ron@rare.com.

RIEKE, WILLIAM OLIVER, foundation director, medical educator, former university president; b. Odessa, Wash., Apr. 26, 1931; s. Henry William and Hutoka S. (Smith) R.; m. Joanne Elynor Schief, Aug. 22, 1954; children: Susan Ruth, Stephen Harold, Marcus Henry. BA summa cum laude, Pacific Luth. U., 1953; MD with honors, U. Wash., 1958. Instr. anatomy U. Wash. Sch. Medicine, Seattle, 1958, asst. prof., 1961-64, adminstrv. officer, 1963-66, assoc. prof., 1964-66; prof., head dept. anatomy Coll. Medicine U. Iowa, Iowa City, 1966-71; dean protem Coll. Medicine U. Iowa (Coll. Medicine), 1969-70, chmn. exec. com., 1969-70; vice chancellor for health affairs, prof. anatomy U. Kans. Med. Center, Kansas City, 1971-73, exec. vice chancellor, prof. anatomy, 1973-75; affiliate prof. biol. structure U. Wash. Sch. Medicine, Seattle, 1975-96; pres. Pacific Lutheran U., Parkland, Wash., 1975-92; pres. emeritus, 1992—; exec. dir. Ben B. Cheney Found., 1992—. Mem. interdisciplinary gen. basic sci. test com. Nat. Bd. Med. Examiners, 1968-72, chmn. anatomy test com., 1972-75, mem. at large, 1975-79; spl. cons. NIH, 1970-72; mem. adv. com. Inst. Medicine, Nat. Acad. Scis., 1974-76; mem. Commn. on Colls., NW Assn. Schs. and Colls., 1979-84 Editor: Procs. 3d Ann. Leucocyte Culture Conf, 1969; editorial bd.: Am. Jour. Anatomy, 1968-71. Bd. dirs. Luth. Ednl. Council N. Am., 1980-83, pres., 1982-83; chmn. Wash. Friends Higher Edn., 1983-91. Named one of Most Effective Coll. or Univ. Pres., Bowling Green State U. Rsch. Study, 1986, Disting. Alumnus Pacific Luth. U., 1970, Disting. Alumnus Pi Kappa Delta, 1977, Disting. Alumnus U. of Washington Med. Alumni, 1989; decorated Knight First Class Royal Norwegian Order of Merit, 1989; named to Cashmere H.S. Wall of Fame, 1995. Lutheran (mem. ch. council 1967-70). Home: 13905 18th Ave S Tacoma WA 98444-1006 Office: Ben B Cheney Found 1201 Pacific Ave Ste 1600 Tacoma WA 98402-4379 E-mail: cheneyfndn@aol.com.

RIEL, PAULINE, association executive; married; 1 child. BSc in Edn., Ohio U.; MA, Ohio State U. adv. com. Special Standards for Minimum Wages U.S. Dept. Labor; delegate Nat. Rep. Conventions. Second v.p. Nat. Fedn. Rep. Women, Alexandria, Va. GOP chmn.; founding mem. MORCO Water Co., Inc. Named Ohio's first Outstanding Bus. and Profl. Women Mem. of Yr., 1982, Morrow County Outstanding Cmty. Leader Bicentennial Com.; inducted into Ohio Women's Hall of Fame, 1993. Office: Nat Fedn Republican Women 124 N Alfred St Alexandria VA 22314-3011 Fax: 703-548-9836. E-mail: nfrw@worldweb.net.

RIELLY, JOHN EDWARD, educational association administrator; b. Rapid City, SD, Dec. 28, 1932; s. Thomas J. and Mary A. (Dowd) R.; m. Elizabeth Downs, Dec. 28, 1957 (marriage annulled 1976); children: Mary Ellen, Catherine Ann, Thomas Patrick, John Downs; m. Irene Diedrich, Aug. 1, 1987. BA, St. John's U., Collegeville, Minn., 1954; postgrad. (Fulbright scholar), London Sch. Econs. and Polit. Sci., 1955-56; PhD, Harvard U., 1961. Faculty dept. govt. Harvard U., 1958-61; with Alliance for Progress programs Dept. State, Washington, 1961-62; fgn. policy asst. to Sen. then Vice Pres. Hubert Humphrey, Washington, 1963-69; cons. office European and internat. affairs Ford Found., N.Y.C., 1969-70; sr. fellow Overseas Devel. Council, Washington, 1970-71; exec. dir. Chgo. Council on Fgn. Relations, 1971-74, pres., 1974—2001. Adj. prof. Northwestern U., 2001—; vis. prof. Grad. Sch. Internat. Rels. U. Calif., San Diego, 2003-; cons. NSC; adv. bd. Grad. Sch. Arts and Scis., Harvard U.; bd. dirs. Am. Coun. on Germany, Nat. Com. on U.S.-China Rels., China Coun. of Asia Soc., Am. Ditchley Found., Trilateral Commn., commn. on U.S.-Brazilian Rels.; past pres. Nat. Coun. Cmty. World Affairs Orgns. Contbr. articles to profl. jours.; editor: American Public Opinion and U.S. Foreign Policy, 1975, 2d edit., 1979, 83, 87, 91, 95, 99; editl. bd. Fgn. Policy Quar., 1974—. Former trustee St. John's U. Recipient Legion d'Honneur, France, Distinguished Service Cross, Germany, Commendatore of the Italian Republic, Bernardo O'Higgins Award, Chile, The Golden Decoration, Austria, European Friendship Award, European Union, Order of Leopold (Belgium). Mem. Am. Polit. Sci. Assn., Council on Fgn. Relations, N.Y.C. Home: 2021 Kenilworth Ave Wilmette IL 60091-1519 Office: Sidley & Austin One First National Plz Chicago IL 60603

RIELY, JOHN CABELL, English educator, art historian, consultant; b. Phila., Aug. 27, 1945; s. James Evans and Marianne Augusta (Gateson) R.; m. Elizabeth Dumesnil Gawthrop, Aug. 23, 1969 (separated 2001); children: Christopher Cabell, Andrew Carrington. AB cum laude, Harvard Coll., 1967; MA, U. Pa., 1968, PhD, 1971. Assoc. rsch. editor Yale Edn. of Horace Walpole's Correspondence, New Haven, 1971-79; lectr. English Yale U., New Haven, 1973-77; asst. prof. English Columbia U., N.Y.C., 1979-80; vis. prof. English U. Minn., Mpls., 1980-81; from asst. to assoc. prof. English Boston U., 1981—. Adv. bd. Age of Johnson AMS Press, 1987—90, Studies in 18th-Century Culture Johns Hopkins U. Press, 1986—. Author: The Age of Horace Walpole in Caricature, 1973, Rowlandson Drawings from the Paul Mellon Collection, 1977, Henry William Bunbury (1750-1811), 1983; co-author: Gainsborough and Rowlandson, 1990; editor: Horace Walpole's Misc Corresp, 3 vols., 1980; cons.-reviewer Choice, 1983-92; contbr. articles to profl. jours; curator internat. exhbns. including English Caricature 1620 to the Present, 1984-85. Fellow Am. Coun. Learned Socs., 1972, Huntington Libr., 1973, Yale Ctr. for Brit. Art, 1982-83, Swann Found. for Caricature and Cartoon, 1984, NEH, 1988-89, Boston Pub. Libr., 1995-96. Fellow Soc. Antiquaries London, Royal Soc. Arts; mem. Commanderie de Bordeaux Boston (prévot), Am. Soc. 18th Century Studies (organizer symposia and seminars, chmn.), Coll. Art Assn., Historians British Art, Boston Athenaeum, The Johnsonians (U.S.), Johnson Club (U.K.), Walpole Soc. (U.K.), St. Botolph Club, Club of Odd Vols. (v.p. 1995-96), Signet Soc. Harvard U., Elizabethan Club Yale U. Democrat. Episcopalian. Avocations: reading, book and art collecting, wine and food, mountain climbing, racquet sports. Home: 33 Hammond Pond Pkwy Chestnut Hill MA 02467 Office: Boston Univ Dept English 236 Bay State Rd Boston MA 02215-1403 Personal E-mail: jriely@comcast.net.

RIEMENSCHNEIDER, ALBERT LOUIS, retired engineering educator; b. Cody, Nebr., May 18, 1936; s. Albert L. and Agnes E. (Schilling) R.; m. Norma Mae Geisler, June 24, 1962 (dec.); children: Richard L., David F., Barbara J.; m. Sandra Ann Pryor, Feb. 14, 1998; stepchildren: Neil G. Pryor Jr., Phillip R. Pryor, Lorin L. Pryor. BSEE, S.D. Sch. Mines and Tech., 1959, MSEE, 1962; PhD, U. Wyo., 1969. Registered profl. engr., S.D., Fla., Nev. Engr. Sperry Utah Corp., Salt Lake City, 1959-60; design engr. Dakota Steel & Supply Co., Rapid City, S.D., 1960-61; instr. U. Wyo., Laramie, 1961-67; chief engr. Dunham Assocs., Rapid City, 1974-80; grad. tchg. asst. S.D. Sch. Mines and Tech., Rapid City, 1961-62, asst. prof., 1967-73, assoc. prof., 1973-74, 80-84, prof., dept. head, 1983-95, prof., 1995-98, prof. emeritus, 1998—. Cons. ALR Engring., RE/SPEC, Inc., Rapid City, 1987—90, HC Galloways, Black Hawk, SD, 1999—; adj. prof. We. Nebr. C.C., Alliance, 2002—. Mem. IEEE, NSPE, Am. Soc. Engring. Edn., Elks. Democrat. Episcopalian. Avocations: electronics, computers, hunting, fishing. Home and Office: ALR Engring 1204 Cheyenne Ave Alliance NE 69301-2529

RIEMKE, RICHARD ALLAN, mechanical engineer; b. Vallejo, Calif., Oct. 11, 1944; s. Allan Frederick and Frances Jewell (O'Brien) R. BA in Physiology, U. Calif., Berkeley, 1967, MA in Physiology, 1971, PhD in Engring. Sci., 1977. Postdoctoral fellow U. So. Calif., Los Angeles, 1977-78; rsch. engr. Del Mar Avionics, Irvine, Calif., 1979; staff fellow NIH, Bethesda, Md., 1980; cons. engr. Idaho Nat. Engring. and Environ. Lab., Idaho Falls, 1980—. With USAR, 1969—75. Mem. AAAS, ANS, Am. Soc. Mech. Engrs., Biomed. Engring. Soc., Soc. Computer Simulation, Soc. Math. Biology, Soc. Engring. Sci., Order of Golden Bear, Alpha Sigma Phi. Republican. Roman Catholic. Avocations: swimming, surfing. Home: 1727 Grandview Dr # 4 Idaho Falls ID 83402-5016 Office: Bechtel BWXT Idaho Idaho Nat Engring Envir Lab Idaho Falls ID 83415-3890

RIENDEAU, THERESA FRANCES, rehabilitation nurse; b. Revere, Mass., June 12, 1953; d. Samuel and Eleanor M (Rizzo) Spinazzola, m. Armand D. Riendeau, Dec. 31, 1994; children: James, Richard, Mark Russo. Diploma, New Eng. Bapt. Hosp. Sch., Boston, 1975. Reiki practioner. Charge nurse VA Med. Ctr., West Roxbury, Mass., 1975-80; asst. nurse mgr. Braintree (Mass.) Hosp., 1981-90; supr. nursing Randolph (Mass.) Crossings Nursing Ctr., 1990—93; utilization rev. coord., home health aide/homemaker educator Alternative Care Med. Svcs., Salem, NH, 1990—98; rehab. nurse Vis. Nurse Assocs. Inc., Dedham, Mass., 1993—94, VNA Homecare, Andover, Mass., 1994—95; unit mgr., restorative coord., staff developer Greenery Extended Care Ctr., North Andover, Mass., 1998—2001; clin. practice leader Spaulding Rehab. Hosp., Boston, 2001—. Mem. Assn. Rehab. Nurses. Home: 35 Wheeler St Dracut MA 01826-4219 Office: 125 Nashua St Boston MA 02114 E-mail: tfrrncrrn@aol.com.

RIENDL, ROBIN WENDY, financial consultant; b. Madison, Wis., Feb. 8, 1966; d. Jim McCaslin and Dean Naomi Brown; m. Paul Alex Riendl, Feb. 4, 1994. B in Natural Resources Mgmt., U. Alaska, Fairbanks, 1988; MBA, U. Alaska, 1991. Field investigator Harding Lawson Assocs., Anchorage, 1988—89; rsch. asst. U. Alaska, Fairbanks, 1989; planner Fairbanks N. Star Borough, 1989—90; forestry tech. Environ. Rsch. Inst., 1989—90; environ. analyst State of Alaska Dept. Transportation, Anchorage, 1992—96; fin. advisor Morgan Stanley, 1996—2002, Smith Barney, 2002—. Recipient Outstanding Young Woman of Am., 1997. Mem.: Fin. Planning Assn., Zonta Internat., U. Alaska Fairbanks Alumni Assn. Avocations: martial arts, skiing. Office: Smith Barney 2550 Denali St 17th Fl Anchorage AK 99503

RIENNER, LYNNE CAROL, publishing executive; b. Pitts., Aug. 3, 1945; d. David and Molly (Rice) R. BA, U. Pa., 1967. Exec. v.p., assoc. publisher, editorial dir. Westview Press Inc., Boulder, Colo., 1975-84; pub., owner Lynne Rienner Pub. Inc., Boulder, Colo., 1984—. Pub. cons. various orgns.; lectr. U. Denver Pub. Inst., 1981-84, 93—; panelist nat. meetings Bd. dirs. Boulder Breast Cancer Coalition, 1993-95. Mem. Assn. Am. Pubs. (bd. dirs. 1992-96, 99—, exec. coun. of profl. and scholarly pub. divsn. 1996—). Office: Lynne Rienner Pub Inc 1800 30th St Ste 314 Boulder CO 80301-1026

RIENZO, ROBERT JAMES, radiologist; b. Jersey City, N.J., July 27, 1949; s. James Joseph and Marie Nicoletta (Bernardo) R.; m. Janice Meyer, Apr. 8, 1972 (div. Dec. 1991); 1 child, Michael Robert; m. Catherine Elizabeth Rafferty, Jan. 11, 1992; 1 child, Robert Francis. AB, Cornell U., 1971; MD, N.Y. Med. Coll., 1975. Diplomate Am. Bd. Radiology, Am. Bd. Nuclear Medicine. Resident St. Vincent's Hosp., N.Y.C., 1975-80; staff physician Jefferson Hosp., Pitts., 1980-81, Allentown (Pa.) Hosp., Lehigh Valley Hosp., Pa., 1981—; dir. divsn. nuclear medicine Lehigh Valley Hosp., Allentown, Pa., 1998—. Contbr. articles to profl. jours. Mem. Exch. Club Western LeHigh, Emmaus, Pa., 1983—. Mem. AMA (Physicians Recognition award 1986—), Soc. Nuclear Medicine, Am. Coll. Radiology. Avocations: skiing, racquetball, golf. Office: Med Imaging Lehigh Valley 1251 S Cedar Crest Blvd Allentown PA 18103-6205

RIEPE, DALE MAURICE, philosopher, writer, illustrator, educator, Asian art dealer; b. Tacoma, June 22, 1918; s. Rol and Martha (Johnson) R.; m. Charleine Williams, 1948; children: Kathrine Leigh Riepe Herschlag, Dorothy Lorraine. BA, U. Wash., 1944; MA, U. Mich., 1946, PhD, 1954; postgrad. (Rockefeller-Watamull-McInerny fellow), U. Hawaii, Banaras and Madras, India, Tokyo and Waseda, Japan, 1949; diploma, Universidad de la Habana, 1997. Instr. philosophy Carleton Coll., 1948-51; asst. prof. U. S.D., 1952-54; assoc. prof. U. N.D., 1954-59, prof., 1959-62, chmn. dept., 1954-62; prof., chmn. C.W. Post Coll., 1962-63; prof. philosophy SUNY, Buffalo, 1963—; chmn. dept. social scis., assoc. dean SUNY Grad. Sch., 1964—. Instr. marine electricity Naval Tng. Program, Seattle, 1943-45; mem. nat. screening bd. South Asia, Fulbright Selection, 1968-70, Asia, 1970-72; chmn. Fulbright Selection Com. for Asia, 1972, 82; vis. Fulbright lectr. Tokyo U., 1957-58; vis. lectr. Western Wash. U., 1961, Delhi U., 1967; docent Albright-Knox Art Gallery; cons. Ctr. for Sci., Tech. and Devel., Council of Sci. adn Indsl. Rsch., Govt. India, 1978—, Inst. Fang Studies, 1987—, Can. Ednl. Coun.; del. Cuban-N.Am. Philosophy Conf., Cuban Inst. Social Sci., 1982, Fang Centennial, Taiwan Nat. U., Taipeh, 1987, Hungarian-Am. Philos. Conf., Budapest, 1988; sports columnist The Town Crier; vis. scholar Andhra U., 1996; lectr. in field. Author: The Naturalistic Tradition in Indian Thought, 1961, The Philosophy of India and its Impact on American Thought, 1970, Indian Philosophy Since Independence, 1979, The Owl Flies by Day, 1979, Asian Philosophy Today, 1981, Objectivity and Subjectivism in the Philosophy of Science, 1985, Philosophy and Revolutionary Theory, 1986, also articles in field.; editor: Phenomenology and Natural Existence, 1973, Philosophy and Political Economy; co-editor: The Structure of Philosophy, 1966, Contributions of American Sankritists in the Spread of Indian Philosophy in the United States, 1967, Radical Currents in Contemporary Philosophy, 1970, Reflections on Revolution, 1971, Philosophy at the Barricade, 1971, Contemporary East European Philosophy, 1971, Essays in East-West Dialogue, 1973, Explorations in Philosophy and Society, 1978; illustrator The Quick and the Dead, 1948; editorial com. Chinese Studies in History, 1970—, Chinese Studies in Philosophy, 1970—; publs. bd. Conf. for Asian Affairs; Editor various series.; editl. bd. Philos. Currents and Revolutionary World, 1972-86, Soviet Studies in Philosophy, 1979-87, Marxist Dimensions, 1987—, Active ACLU; mem. com. overseers Chung-an U., Korea; bd. dirs. Evergreen Coll. Cmty. Orgn., 1988—; bd. dirs. Friends of Evergreen Coll. Libr., 1992—; active Henry Gallery, Frye Gallery, Palm Springs Desert Mus., Seattle Art Mus., Phila. Mus. Art; mem. Capital Mus. and Art Soc., Wash. State Hist. Soc.; mem. libr. bd. Evergreen Coll.; founder Ars Asiatica. Fulbright scholar India, 1951-52; Fulbright lectr. U. Tokyo, 1957-58; U. Mich. fellow, 1945-48, Carnegie Corp. fellow Asian Studies, 1960-61, Am. Inst. Indian Studies Rsch. fellow, 1966-67; grantee 4th East-West Philosophers Conf., 1964, Penrose fund Am. Philos. Soc., 1963; SUNY Research Found., 1965-67, 69, 72-73, Bulgarian Acad. Sci., 1975, London Sch. Oriental and African Studies, 1971. Fellow Royal Asiatic Soc., Far Eastern Inst. (Tokyo); mem. AAAS, Internat. Hegel-

Vereinigung, Conf. Asian Affairs (sec. 1995), Am. Oriental Soc., Am. Philos. Soc., Indian Inst. Psychology, Philosophy and Psychical Rsch. (hon. adviser), Soc. for Am. Philosophy (chmn. 1960), Am. Inst. Indian Studies (trustee 1965-66), Soc. for Creative Ethics (sec.), Am. Archaeol. Soc., Am. Assn. Asian Studies, Am. Math. Soc., Am. Aesthetics Soc., Internat. Soc. Aesthetics, Am. Soc. Comparative and Asian Philosophy, N.Y. Acad. Scis., Asiatic Soc. (Calcutta), Soc. for Philos. Study Dialectical Materialism (founding sec.-treas. 1962—), Chinese Acad. Social Sci., Soc. for Philos. Study Marxism (publs. sec. 1973-86), Union Am. and Japanese Profls. Against Nuclear Omnicide (treas. U.S. sec. 1978—), Internat. House of Japan, Internat. Philosophers for Prevention Nuclear Omnicide, United Univ. Profs. of SUNY-Buffalo (v.p.), Kokusai Bunka Shinkokai, N.Y. Acad. Scis., Union Concerned Scientists, Nat. Geog. Soc., Olympia Philosophy Club (co-founder 1988—), Tumwater Golf, Alpha Pi Zeta. Office: SUNY 605 Baldy Hall Buffalo NY 14260-1000

RIEPE, JAMES SELLERS, investment company executive; b. Bryn Mawr, Pa., June 25, 1943; s. Henry Brunt and Marjorie (Sellers) R.; m. Gail Nelms Petty, Sept. 14, 1968; children: Christina, James, Jr. BS, Wharton Sch., U. Pa., 1965, MBA, 1967. Mem. audit staff Coopers & Lybrand, C.P.A.s, Phila., 1967-69; asst. to pres. Wellington Mgmt. Co., Phila., 1969-72, v.p., 1972-75; exec. v.p. Vanguard Group, Inc., Valley Forge, Pa., 1975-82, dir., 1979-82; vice chmn., mem. mgmt. com. T. Rowe Price Group, Inc., Balt., 1982—; chmn. T. Rowe Price Investment Svcs., 1982—, TRP Trust Co., 1982—, TRP Retirement Plan Svcs., 1982—. Bd. dirs. Balt. Equitable Soc., NASDAQ Stock Market, Inc. Trustee, former chmn. Balt. Mus. Art; trustee U. Pa., chmn. bd. trustees, 1999—. Mem. Investment Co. Inst. (gov.), Greenspring Valley Hunt Club, Caves Valley Golf Club. Office: T Rowe Price Group Inc 100 E Pratt St Baltimore MD 21202-1090

RIERSON, ROBERT LEAK, retired broadcasting executive, television writer; b. Walnut Cove, N.C., Sept. 5, 1927; s. Sanders C. and Anna (Cox) R.; m. Barbara Eugenia McLeod, Sept. 23, 1950 (dec. Feb. 1988); children: Barbara Elaine, Richard Troy; m. Rosemary L. McCampbell, Apr. 20, 1997. Student, Duke U., 1945-46, Davidson Coll., 1946-47; BS in Speech cum laude, Northwestern U., 1948. Program dir., program ops. mgr. WBT Radio and WBTV, Charlotte, N.C., 1948-66; program mgr. WJBK-TV, Detroit, 1966-69, WTOP-TV, Washington, 1969-71; dir. broadcasting WCBS-TV, N.Y.C., 1971-73; pres. Rierson Broadcast Consultants, N.Y.C., 1973-75; program exec. Grey Advt., N.Y.C., 1975-77; v.p., dir. programming Dancer-Fitzgerald-Sample, N.Y.C., 1977-80; exec. producer Corinthian Prodns., N.Y.C., 1980-82; dir. news programming CNN TV, Atlanta, 1982-96; ret., 1996. Producer-creator TV show ABCs of Democracy, 1965; producer, writer TV show George Washington's Mt. Vernon, 1970; creator, writer TV series 24 Days of Christmas, 1978, 21 Days of America, 1979. Bd. dirs. Mich. Coun. Chs., Detroit, 1968-69, ARC, Charlotte, 1960-62; 1st v.p. Charlotte Oratorio Singers, 1960-66. Lt. USNR, 1952-54. Recipient Edn. award Charlotte Jr. Woman's Club, 1961, George Washington Honor medal Freedoms Found., 1970; named Young Man of Yr., 1960. Mem. Nat. Assn. Radio-TV Program Execs. (charter, bd. dirs.), Radio-TV News Dirs. Assn., Order Long Leaf Pine (hon. N.C. award). Republican. Mem. Moravian Episcopal Ch. Avocations: reading, travel, movies.

RIES, CHARLES P. ambassador; b. 1951; BA, MA, Johns Hopkins U. Dep. asst. U.S. Trade Rep. for N.Am. Affairs Office of the U.S. Trade Rep., Washington, 1990—92; min. counselor for econs. affairs U.S. Mission to the Euorpean Union, Brussels, 1992—96, U.S. Embassy, London, 1996—2000; prin. dept. asst. sec. of state for European and Euroasian affairs Dept. of State, Washington, 2000—04, U.S. amb. to Greece, 2004—.*

RIES, EDWARD RICHARD, petroleum geologist, consultant; b. Freeman, S.D., Sept. 18, 1918; s. August and Mary F. (Graber) R.; m. Amelia D. Capshaw, Jan. 24, 1949 (div. Oct. 1956); children: Rosemary Melinda, Victoria Elise; m. Maria Wipfler, June 12m 1964. AB magna cum laude, U. S.D., 1941; MS, U. Okla., 1943, PhD, 1951; postgrad., Harvard U., 1946-47, Harvard, 1946-47. Asst. geologist Geol. Survey S.D., White River area, 1941; geophys. interpreter Robert Ray Inc., Western Okla., Okla., 1942; jr. geologist Carter Oil Co., Mont., Wyo, 1943-44; geologist Standard Vacuum Oil Co., Mont., Wyo., Colo., India, 1944-49, sr. geologist Asam, Tripura, Bangladesh, India, 1951-53; sr. regional geologist N.Y. Standard Vacuum Petroleum, Maatschappij, N.Y., Indonesia, 1953-59, geol. advisor Far East and Africa White Plains, N.Y., 1959-62, Oceania, Mobile Petroleum Co., N.Y.C., 1962-65; geol. advisor Europe, Far East Mobil Oil Corp., N.Y.C., 1965-71, sr. regional explorationist Far East, Australia, New Zealand, 1971-73, sr. regional explorationist Asia-Pacific, Dallas, 1973-76, sr. geol. advisor Rsch. Geology, 1976-79; assoc. geol. advisor Geology-Geophysics, Dallas, 1979-82; sr. geol. cons., 1982-83. Ind. internat. petroleum geol. cons. Europe, Africa, Sino-Soviet and S.E. Asia, 1986—; grad. asst., teaching fellow U. Okla., 1941-43, Harvard, 1946-47. Contbr. numerous domestic and internat. proprietary and pub. hydrocarbon generation and reserve evaluations, reports and profl. papers. With AUS, 1944-46. Warden-Humble fellow, U. Okla., 1951. Mem. AAAS, Am. Inst. Econ. Rsch., Am. Assn. Petroleum Geologists (assoc. editor 1978-83, 50 Yr. Mem. Svc. award 1993, 60 Yr. Mem. Svc. award 2003), Geol. Soc. Am., Am. Geol. Inst., Nat. Wildlife Fedn., Nat. Audubon Soc., N.Y. Acad. Scis., Soc. Exploration Geophysicists, Wilderness Soc., Am. Legion, Harvard Club (Dallas), Phi Beta Kappa, Sigma Xi, Sigma Gamma Epsilon. Republican. Mennonite. Home and Office: 6009 Royal Crest Dr Dallas TX 75230-3434

RIES, WILLIAM CAMPBELL, lawyer; b. Pitts., Apr. 8, 1948; s. F. William and Dorothy (Campbell) R.; m. Mallory Burns, Oct. 26, 1968; children: William Sheehan, Sean David. AB, Cath. U. Am., 1970; JD, Duquesne U., 1974; cert. Grad. Sch. Indsl. Adminstrn., Carnegie Mellon U., 1980. Bar: Pa. 1974, U.S. Dist. Ct. (we. dist.) Pa. 1974, U.S. Supreme Ct. 1979. Atty., then mng. counsel trust and investment svc. Mellon Bank, N.A., Pitts., 1974-90; ptnr. Dickie, McCamey and Chilcote, Pitts., 1990-98; mem. Sweeney, Metz, Fox, McGrann & Schermer, LLC, 1998-2001; shareholder Tucker Arensberg, 2001—. Mem. adv. com. decedents' estates and trust law Pa. Joint State Govt. Commn., 1981—; adj. prof. Duquesne U., 1984—. Author: The Regulation of Investment Management and Fiduciary Services West, 1997. Pres. McCandless Twp. Civic Assn., Pitts., 1981—, McCandless Town Coun., chair pub. safety com., vice chair fin com.; sec. McCandless Indsl. Devel. Auth.; liaison McCandless zoning hearing bd. Fellow Am. Bar Found.; mem. ABA (chmn. fiduciary svcs. subcom.), Pa. Bar Assn., Allegheny County Bar Assn., Pitts. Estate Planning Coun., Am. Bankers Assn. (co-chmn. nat. conf. lawyers and corp. fiduciaries, chmn. trust counsel com.), Pa. Bankers Assn. (trust com., trust legis. com.), Rivers Club, Treesdale Golf and Country Club. Republican. Avocations: golf, sailing, cross country skiing, exercise. Home: 9602 Fawn Ln Allison Park PA 15101-1737 E-mail: wries@tuckerlaw.com.

RIESENBECK, RONALD, supermarket executive; CFO Save Mart Supermarkets, Modesto, Calif. Office: Save Mart Supermarkets PO Box 4278 Modesto CA 95352-4278

RIESENBERGER, JOHN RICHARD, science administrator; b. NYC, Sept. 25, 1948; s. Richard Raymond and Marie Teresa (Long) R.; m. Patricia Ann Casey, Nov. 23, 1974; children: Christine, Jennifer. BS in Econs. and Bus., Hofstra U., 1970, MBA in Mgmt., 1975; cert. internat. sr. mgmt. program, Harvard U., 1989. Customer svc. supr. Chase Manhattan Bank, 1970-72; gen. sales rep. various regions Upjohn Co., Bklyn., 1972-75, sales rep., sales mgr. various locations, N.Y., 1976-81, profl. tng. and devel. officer Kalamazoo, 1981-83, dir. Chgo. sales area, 1983-87; v.p., group mgr. Upjohn Co. of Can., Toronto, Ont., 1987-89; exec. dir., worldwide med. scis. liaison Upjohn Co., Kalamazoo, 1989-92, exec. dir. worldwide strategic mktg., 1992-95; exec. dir. corp. info. tech. Pharmacia & Upjohn, Inc., Kalamazoo, 1995, v.p. bus. info., 1996-97; v.p. global bus. mgmt. Pharmacia & Upjohn Inc., Bridgewater, N.J., 1998-99; pharm. cons., 1999—; exec.-in-residence Mich. State U., 2000—; pres. Consilium Ptnrs. Inc., 2000—; exec. v.p. Shaw Sci. Ptnrs., Atlanta, 2000—. Chmn. industry adv. bd. dirs. SEI Ctr. Advanced Studies in Mgmt., Wharton Sch., U. Pa.; mem. Global Adv. bd. Am. Mktg. Assn., 1999; mem. edtl. review bd. Jour. Internat. Mktg.; Ciber adv. bd. Mich. State U. Author: (with Robert T. Moran) The Global Challenge: Building the New Worldwide Enterprise, 1994, Global Business Strategies for the Year 2000, 1995. Mem. ciber adv. bd. Mich. State U. Mem. Am. Mgmt. Assn., Am. Mktg. Assn., Strategic Mgmt. Soc., Pharm. Rsch. Mfrs. Am. (chmn. mktg. practices com.), The Planning Fom, Internat. Soc. for Strategic Planning and Mgmt., Harvard Bus. Sch. Club, Pharm. Bus. Intelligence and Rsch. Group, European Pharm. Market Rsch. Assn., Harvard Bus. Sch. Health Industry Alumni Assn. Avocation: golf. Home: 42 Independence Dr Basking Ridge NJ 07920-3815

RIESER, JOSEPH A., JR., lawyer; b. Pitts., Aug. 28, 1947; s. Joseph Alexander and Ruth Margaret (Piper) R.; m. Susan Jean Irving, Feb. 28, 1976; 1 child, Alexander H.I. AB, Princeton U., 1969; JD, MPP, Harvard U., 1974. Bar: Pa. 1974, D.C. 1976, U.S. Supreme Ct. 1979. Assoc. Reed Smith LLP, Pitts. and Washington, 1974-82, ptnr. Washington, 1983—2003; mem. Arent Fox PLLC, Washington, 2003—. Mem. D.C. Office of Tax and Revenue Adv. Group, 1997-2001. Chmn. nat. alumni assn. Kennedy Sch. Govt., Cambridge, Mass., 1979-82; bd. dirs. Harvard U. Alumni Assn., 1982-84; gen. counsel 1984 Dem. Nat. Conv., Washington, 1983-84; gen. counsel Nat. Dem. Party, Washington, 1985-89; spl. counsel Clinton/Gore '92, Inc.; mem. Clinton-Gore 1992 Presdl. Transition Team. Mem. D.C. Bar (chmn. bus. related taxes com. 1989-92, tax policy steering com., chmn. D.C. Bar Nat. Fed. Tax Inst. 1991, 92, 2000, chmn. state and local taxes com. 1994-97, tax sect. steering com. 1997-2003, co-chair tax sect. 1998-2001), Ctr. for Nat. Policy Bd. Advisors, Harvard-Yale-Princeton Pitts. Club, Cosmos Club. Presbyterian. Home: 3517 Davis St NW Washington DC 20007-1426 Office: Arent Fox PLLC 1050 Connecticut Ave NW Washington DC 20036 Office Phone: 202-857-8964.

RIESS, GORDON SANDERSON, management consultant; b. Thessaloniki, Greece, Feb. 25, 1928; came to U.S., 1932; s. Lewis William and Dorothy Onward Riess; m. Priscilla Rich, June 2, 1951; children: Mark C., Kimberly A., Blake G. AB with highest honors, Whitman Coll., 1949; MBA cum laude, Harvard U., 1951. Cert. mgmt. cons.; registered profl. cons.; accredited profl. cons. With Ford Internat. Div., N.Y.C., 1951-53; asst. fin. mgr. Ford Motor Co., Mid. East, Alexandria, Egypt, 1953-57; gen. sales mgr. Ford Motor Co., Rome, Italy, 1957-60; regional fin. mgr. Ford Motor Co., Scandinavia, Copenhagen, Denmark, 1960-62; gen. mgr. Ford Motor Co., European, Brussels, Belgium, 1962-67; v.p. Internat. Paper Co., Zurich, Switzerland, 1967-71; exec. v.p. Cinema Internat. Corp., London, 1971-75; chmn., pres. Stewart-Riess Labs. Inc., Tarzana, Calif., 1976-83; pres., CEO Intercontinental Enterprises Ltd., Beverly Hills, Calif., 1983—. Chmn. Vis. Nurse Found., L.A., 1985-87; bd. dirs., chmn. Vis. Nurse Assn., L.A., 1976-97; bd. dirs. Beverly Found., Pasadena, Calif., 1990-97; vice-chmn. of bd. Witman Coll., Walla Walla, Wash., 1985-96. Author: Confessions of a Corporate Centurion--Tales of International Adventures, 2000, From Communism to Capitalism, 2001; inventor/patentee pre-fillable hypodermic syringe. Chmn. Inter-Community Sch. Zurich, 1968-71; trustee Am. Sch. London, 1972-75; vice chmn. Krafterliner Mfgs. Assn., Zurich, 1968-71; bd. dirs. Vols. in Tech. Assistance, Arlington, Va., 1986-93; bd. overseers Muhlenberg Coll., 1993—; internat. bd. Czechoslovak Mgmt. Ctr., 1992—. Sgt. U.S. Army, 1946-47. R.H. Macy scholar, Harvard Bus. Sch., 1949. Mem. Am. Assn. Profl. Cons., Am. Cons. League, Asia Acad. Mgmt., Hollywood Radio & Television Soc., Inst. Mgmt. Cons., Lic. Execs. Soc. Avocations: skiing, scuba diving. Office: Intercontinental Ent Ltd # 3194 256 S Robertson Blvd Beverly Hills CA 90211-2898 Personal E-mail: gsr@mindspring.com.

RIESS, STEVEN ALLAN, historian, educator; b. N.Y.C., Aug. 26, 1947; s. Herman and Cecelie (Finder) R.; m. Tobi Ellen Epstein. BA, NYU, 1968; MA, U. Chgo., 1969; PhD, U. Chgo., 1974. Vis. asst. prof. history SUNY, Brockport, 1974-75; lectr. in social scis. U. Mich., Dearborn, 1975-76; from asst. prof. to prof. Northeastern Ill. U., Chgo., 1976—. Coord. MA in Social Sci. Northeastern Ill. U., 1982-91; co-dir. NEH Seminar for Coll. Tchrs., "Sport and Am. Culture." Author: Sport in Industrial America, 1850-1920, 1995 (Outstanding Acad. Book 1995), City Games: The Evolution of American Urban Society and the Rise of Sports (Outstanding Acad. Book 1990), 1989, Touching Base: Professional Baseball and American Culture in the Progressive Era, 1980; editor Sport and Entertainment Series for Syracuse U. Press, Sports and the American Law, 1999 (Outstanding Acad. Book 1999); editor Jour. Sport History, 1985-93; assoc. editor Am. Nat. Biography, 1990—; contbr. articles to profl. jours. Organizer Chgo. Seminar on Sport and Culture. NEH fellow, 1983-84; recipient Webb-Smith Essay prize U. Tex. Arlington, 1989. Mem. Am. Hist. Assn., Orgn. Am. Historians, North Am. Soc. for Sport History, Soc. Am. Baseball Rsch. Democrat. Jewish. Avocations: stamp collecting/philately, baseball card collecting. Office: Northeastern Ill U 5500 N Saint Louis Ave Chicago IL 60625-4679

RIESZ, PETER CHARLES, marketing educator, consultant; b. Orange, N.J., Apr. 30, 1937; s. Kolman and Ellen (Wachs) R.; m. Elizabeth Strider Dunkman, Dec. 28, 1968; children: Sarah Kathleen BS, Rutgers Coll., 1958; MBA, Columbia U., 1963, PhD, 1971. From asst. prof. to assoc. prof. U. Iowa, Iowa City, 1968-80, prof. mktg., 1980—, chmn. dept. mktg., 1981-87, Williams prof. tchg., 1994-97. Vis. prof. Boston U., 1974-75, Duke U., Durham, N.C., 1984-85; guest prof. Meiji U., Japan, summer 2004; cons. in field. Contbr. articles to profl. jours. Recipient Teaching Excellence award HON Industries, 1989; named MBA Prof. of Yr., 1990; Old Gold fellow U. Iowa, 1972. Mem. Am. Chem. Soc., Am. Mktg. Assn. Democrat. Presbyterian. Avocation: photography. Home: 2411 Tudor Dr Iowa City IA 52245-3638 Office: U Iowa Dept Mktg Tippie Coll Bus Adminstrn Iowa City IA 52242 Office Phone: 319-335-0937. Business E-Mail: peter-riesz@uiowa.edu.

RIEW, K. DANIEL, cervical spine surgeon; b. Seoul, Republic of Korea, July 28, 1958; arrived in U.S., 1966; s. C. Keith and H. Kim Riew; m. Mary Kahng, Sept. 12, 1992. MD, Case Western Res. U., 1984. Diplomate Am. Bd. of Orthopaedic Surgery. Asst. attending physician, instr. medicine Cornell U. Med. Ctr., N.Y.C., 1987—89; resident gen. surgery Beth Israel Med. Ctr., N.Y.C., 1989—90; resident orthop. surgery George Washington U. Hosp., Washington, 1990—94; fellow spine surgery U. Hosps. Cleve./Case We. Res. U.; asst. prof. Washington U. Sch. Medicine, St. Louis, 1995—2001, assoc. prof. dept. orthop. surgery, 2002—, chief cervical spine surgery. Contbr. articles to profl. jours. (Cervical Spine Rsch. Soc. Outanding Basic Sci. Rsch. award, 2000, Mayfield award for basic sci. Am. Assn. of Neurol. Surgeons, 2000, North Am. Spine Soc. Outstanding Paper award, 2000, Russell S. Hibbs Basic Sci. award Scoliosis Rsch. Soc., 2000). Recipient C. Richard Bowman award, N.Y. Hosp., Cornell Med. Ctr., 1987, Caring Spirit award, Barnes-Jewish Hosp., 2001; grantee, Orthopaedic Rsch. and Edn. Found., 2002—05. Fellow: Am. Acad. Orthop. Surgeons; mem.: Mo. State Orthop. Assn., Mid. Am. Orthop. Assn., Am. Orthop. Assn., Scoliosis Rsch. Soc., Orthop. Rsch. Soc., N.Am. Spine Soc. (CME com. and surg. care com. 2000), Cervical Spine Rsch. Soc. (clin. outcomes com. 2001). Avocations: skiing, golf. Office: Washington U Sch of Medicine ste 11300 One Barnes-Jewish Hosp Plz Saint Louis MO 63110 Office Phone: 314-747-2565.

RIFE, DOUGLAS M. publishing executive; BA, Iowa State U., 1982, MA, 1994. Artist Perfection Form Co., Des Moines, 1977—84, social studies editl. dir., 1984—88; cons. Des Moines, 1989—89; exec. editor Simon & Schuster Co., Parsippany, NJ, 1990—97; v.p. of devel. Frank Schaffer Publs., Torrance, Calif., 1997—2001; pres., pub. Corwin Press, Thousand Oaks, Calif., 2001—. Author: (book) A Family History Handbook, 1985, Declaration of Independence: History Speaks, 1997, Bill of Rights: History Speaks, 1997, Gettysburg Address: History Speaks, 1997, Pledge of Allegiance: History Speaks, 1998, Preamble to the U.S. Constitution: History Speaks, 1998, Star Spangled Banner, The: History Speaks, 1998, History in the Headlines: Sinking of the Maine, 1999, History in the Headlines: The Louisiana Purchase, 1999, History in the Headlines: Gold Rush!, 1999, History in the Headlines: The Day Lincoln Was Shot, 1999, Pilgrims, History in the Headlines: Nixon Resigns, 2000, History in the Headlines: Stock Market Crash, 2000, History in the Headlines: Man Walks on the Moon, 2000, History in the Headlines: March on Washington, 2001, Chief Joseph Surrenders: History Speaks, 2002, Emancipation Proclamation: History Speaks, 2002, Seneca Falls Declaration of Sentiments and Resolutions: History Speaks, 2002, Research & Writing: Activities That Explore Family History, 2002, (poster) My Family History. Mem.: ASCD, Nat. Assn. Elem. Sch. Prins., Nat. Staff Devel. Coun. Office: Corwin Press 2455 Teller Rd Thousand Oaks CA 91320 Office Phone: 805-499-9734.

RIFE, ELIZABETH, musician, music educator; b. Zebulon, Ga., Feb. 23, 1938; d. Jack and Ouida Dorothy (Walker) Bridges; m. Robert M. Hill, June 25, 1959 (div.); 1 child, Dorothy Hill Bremer; m. C. David Rife, Feb. 15, 1986. BS in Music Edn., Ga. State Coll. and U., 1959; postgrad., Ga. State U., 1976-81, Vanderbilt U., 1977-79. Music tchr., Marietta, Ga., 1959—; choir master, organist Holy Trinity Luth. Ch., Marietta, 1966-79. Pres., chmn. bd. Assist, Inc., Marietta, 1982-84. Guest columnist Marietta Daily Jour., 1980-84, Horizons mag., 1997. Dir. WSB-TV Call for Action, Atlanta, 1980—82; spkr. Foster Children Program, Marietta, 1980—83, United Way, 1982—83; sec. bd. dirs. Help for Hispanics, 2002; conducted seminars, workshops on hunger ch. and civic groups, Atlanta, 1981—; concert coord. Musica Sacra Atlanta, 2003; mem. steering com. Presbyn. Answer to Hunger, 1991—. Mem. Music Tchrs. Nat. Assn., Music Educators Nat. Assn., Ga. Music Educators Conf. (adjudicator piano competition 1967—), Cobb County Music Tchrs. Assn., Sigma Alpha Iota. Presbyterian. Avocations: running, reading, travel, fashion consulting, tutoring. Home: 1296 Poplar Pointe SE Smyrna GA 30082-2213

RIFENBURGH, RICHARD PHILIP, investment company executive; b. Syracuse, NY, Mar. 3, 1932; s. Russell D. and Edna (MacKenzie) R.; m. Doris Anita Hohn, June 24, 1950; children: David, Susan, Robert. Student, Wayne State U. With Mohawk Data Scis. Corp., Herkimer, N.Y., 1964-74, pres., 1970-74, chmn., 1974, Moval Mgmt. Corp., Herkimer, 1968—; CEO, GCA Corp., Andover, Mass., 1986-87; gen. ptnr. Hambrecht and Quist Venture Ptnrs., 1987-90; chmn. Miniscribe Corp., Longmont, Colo., 1988-91, Ironstone Group Inc., 1988-91, St. G Crystal Ltd., Jeannette, Pa., 1985—; vice-chmn. Paradise Music and Entertainment Inc., 2000—03. Bd. dirs. Verance Corp.; chmn. Tristar Corp., 1992—2002. With USAF, 1951-55. Address: Moval Mgmt Corp PMB 133 2637 E Atlantic Blvd Pompano Beach FL 33062-4939 Personal E-mail: dickrif@aol.com.

RIFFEE, STEPHEN, corporate financial executive; BS in Commerce, U. Va. Asst. v.p. Burlington No. Railroad Nat. Transp. Practice KPMG Peat Marwick; v.p. fin., chief acctg. officer Marriott Internat., Inc., 1996—99; sr. v.p., contr., treas. CarrAmerica Realty Corp., Washington, 1999—2002, CFO, 2002—, mem. oper. and investment coms. Office: CarrAmerica Realty Corp Ste 500 1850 K St Washington DC 20006*

RIFFENBURGH, GERRYE H. artist, educator; b. Richmond, VA, June 30, 1929; d. Herman Harvey and Mary (Beryl) Harlow; m. Robert Harry Riffenburgh, Nov. 22, 1952; children: Robin, Scott, Marc, Karen, Douglas. BS, Coll. William and Mary, 1951, MS, 1955; BA summa cum laude, San Diego State U., 1979. Freelance artist, San Diego, 1968—73, Pembrokeshire, Wales, 1974—77; artist and instruct. San Diego Adult Coll., 1978—81; freelance artist The Hague, Netherlands, 1982—86, La Spezia, Italy, 1986—89, San Diego, 1990—. Rep. exhibitor Cosmopolitan Fine Arts Gallery, La Jolla, Calif., 2001—, Courtyard Gallery, Rancho Santa Fe, Calif., 2001—. Author: (article on color choice) Jour. of Gen. Psychol.; over 45 juried exhibitions, Europe, U.S. Vol. Coastal Planning Coun., San Diego, 1971—73; leader Girl Scouts, San Diego, 1968—74, Girl Guides, Pembrokeshire, Wales, 1974—77; vol. polit. groups, San Diego, 1978—81; fund raiser vol. COTA, San Diego, 1978—82. Named hon. mention, Nat. Annual Galleon Exhibit/London, 1975, Hon. mention, Associazione Artisti Versiliese /Italy, 1989; recipient First Pl., Pembrokeshire artists assoc./UK, 1974, Third Pl., Congressgebouw /Netherlands, 1984, Cenacolo Buttini /Italy, 1988, First Pl., Maurice Braun Meml. Plein Air Exhbn. /CA, 2000, selected Gold Medal Exhbn., Calif. Art Club/Calif., 2002, Salon d'Automne/Pasadena, Calif., 2002, Third Pl., Offtrack Gallery/Leucadia, Calif., 2002, Chas Schultz award, Am. Impressionist Soc./Fla., 2002, Second Pl., Municipal Art Gallery/Escondido, Calif., 2003, Spl. Merit, Calif. Art Club/Calif., 2001. Mem.: Am. Soc. Marine Artists (juried artist mem.), Artists' Guild, San Diego Mus. of Art, Oil Painters of Am., Plein Air Painters Assn. of San Diego (founder), Am. Impressionists Soc., Laguna Plein Air Painters Assn., Market St. Studio, San Diego Portrait Soc. (bd. dirs. 1995—96), San Diego Art Inst., La Jolla Art Assn. (life; tres., bd. dirs. 1996—2001), Calif. Art Club (juried artist mem.). Avocations: photography, piano, walking, tennis, yoga. Home: 3069 Award Row San Diego CA 92122-2231

RIFFENBURGH, ROBERT HARRY, biostatistician, researcher; b. Christiansburg, Va., June 19, 1931; s. Harry Buchholz and Ada Swallow Riffenburgh; m. Gerrye Harlow, Nov. 22, 1952; children: Robin, Scott, Marc, Karen, Douglas. B.S., Coll. of William and Mary, Richmond VA, 1951, M.S., 1953; Ph.D., Va. Poly. Inst., Blacksburg VA, 1957. Asst. prof. of math. Va. Poly. Inst., Blacksburg, Va., 1955—57, U. of Hawaii, Honolulu, 1957—61; prof. and head, stats. dept. U. of Conn., Storrs, Conn., 1962—70; prof. stats. San Diego State U., 1968—74, 1979—82, 1990—93; head, biomedical program Naval Undersea Ctr., San Diego, 1970—73; scientist Naval Facility, Brawdy, Wales, 1974—77; math. statistician Naval Ocean Systems Ctr., San Diego, 1977—82; leader, naval ops. rsch. NATO SHAPE Tech. Centre, The Hague, Netherlands, 1982—86; head, ops. rsch. NATO SACLANT Undersea Rsch. Centre, La Spezia, Italy, 1986—90; chief of biostatistics Naval Med. Ctr. San Diego, San Diego, 1991—. Pres. and ceo Gen. Systems Analysis Co., Storrs, Conn., 1963—70. Author: (scientific book) Statistics in Medicine, (scientific articles) 130 Articles In Journals In The Fields Of Statistics, Medicine, Oceangraphy, Fisheries, Sociology, Psychology, Cybernetics, Operations Research, Education, and Engineering. Capt. (navy)(nato equivalent) NATO, 1982—89, Europe. Recipient Membership, Sigma Xi (hon. sci.), 1956, Phi Kappa Phi (hon. scholastic), 1956, Fellow, San Diego Biomedical Symposium, 1974, Royal Statis. Soc., 1998, Am. Statis. Assn., 2000, Navy Commendation Medal, Naval Med. Ctr. San Diego, 1996; fellow Predoctoral Fellowship, NIH, 1954-1956. Mem.: Internat. Biometrics Soc., Am. Stats. Assoc., Royal Statis. Soc. (life), Phi Kappa Phi (hon.), Sigma Xi (hon.). Office Phone: 619-532-9414.

RIFFKIN, MITCHELL SANFORD, lawyer; b. Providence, Dec. 30, 1944; s. Ira and Rose (Kirshenbaum) R. BA, U. R.I., 1966; JD, Boston U., 1969. Bar: R.I. 1969, U.S. Dist. Ct. R.I. 1970, U.S. Ct. Appeals (1st cir.) 1980. Pros. atty. City of Warwick, R.I., 1971-72, mcpl. judge, 1980-93; magistrate bail commr. Kent County, R.I., 1973-99. Chmn. Fed. Block Grant Allocation Subcom., Warwick, 1976-99; chmn. Group Home Placement for Mentally Retarded, Warwick, 1976-93; chmn. Mayor's Fin. Adv. Commn., Warwick, 1985-93. Named One of Outstanding Young Men of Yr., U.S. Jaycees, 1976. Fellow Pi Sigma Alpha (past pres.); mem. ABA (arbitrator), R.I. Bar Assn. (ho. of dels., chmn. ethics com. 1982-86), R.I. Audubon Soc., U.S. Power Squadron. Lodges: B'nai B'rith (bd. govs. 1978), Masons. Democrat. Jewish. Home: 259 Merrymount Dr Warwick RI 02888-5524 Office: 631 Jefferson Blvd Warwick RI 02886-1318

RIFKIN, ARNOLD, film company executive; b. Bklyn. m. Rita George; two children. BA, U. Cin. Founder Rifkin-David, 1974-80; merged to form Rifkin/David/Kimble/Parseghian, 1980-81, DHKPR, 1981-84; head motion picture dept. Triad Artists, Inc., 1984-92, founding ptnr.; exec. v.p., worldwide head motion picture divsn. William Morris Agy., Beverly Hills, Calif., 1992-96; pres. William Morris Talent and Lit. Agy., Beverly Hills, Calif., 1996-2000; CEO Cheyenne Enterprises, LLC, Santa Monica, Calif., 2000—. Bd. dirs. Am. Cinematheque; faculty, co-chair UCLA Sch. Theatre, Film & TV; lecturer Yale Law Sch., Harvard Sch. Bus., 2002-. Bd. councillors U. So. Calif. Office: Cheyenne Enterprises 406 Wilshire Blvd Santa Monica CA 90401-1410*

RIFKIN, BARRY R. dean, dental educator, researcher; b. Trenton, N.J., Mar. 30, 1940; s. Samuel H. and Ida M. Rifkin; m. Harriet Smith, Mar. 1960 (div. Sept. 1981); children: Avery, Carl; m. Linda Ruth Rosenberg, Nov. 1993; 1 child, Hannah. BS, Ohio State U., 1961; MS, U. Ill., 1964; DDS, Temple U., 1968; PhD, U. Rochester, 1974. Andrew Mellon fellow U. Rochester Med. Ctr., 1974; assoc. pathologist Strong Meml. Hosp., 1974—80; assoc. prof. NYU, NYC, 1980—84, chmn. dept. oral medicine, 1980—87, prof., 1984—91, chmn. dept. oral medicine and pathology, 1987—91, head divsn. basic scis., 1991—98, prof. emeritus, 1998—; prof. oral biology and pathology, dean SUNY Stony Brook Health Sciences Ctr. Sch. Dental Medicine, 1998—. Rschr. in field. Sr. editor Biology and Physiology of the Osteoclast, 1992; mem. editl. bd.: Jour. Dental Rsch.; contbr. articles and abstracts to

profl. jours. Fellow: Am. Coll. Dentists; mem.: AAAS, Am. Soc. Bone and Mineral Rsch., Internat. Assn. Dental Rsch., Am. Soc. Cell Biology, N.Y. Acad. Scis., Am. Assn. Oral Biologists (pres. 1992—93), Sigma Xi, Omicron Kappa Upsilon. Office: Stony Brook Univ Sch Dental Medicine 160 Rockland Hall Stony Brook NY 11794-8700*

RIFKIN, LEONARD, metals company executive; b. N.Y.C., Apr. 10, 1931; s. Irving W. and May (Goldin) Rifkin; m. Norma Jean Smith, Aug. 22, 1954 (dec. Jan. 1983); children: Daniel Mark, Richard Sheldon, Martin Stuart; m. Ariel Kalisky, Jan. 14, 1984. BS, Ind. U., Bloomington, 1952. Pres., CEO Omni Source Corp., Ft. Wayne, Ind., 1960—98, chmn., CEO, 1998—. Bd. dirs. Steel Dynamics, Butler, Ind., Qualitech Steel, Indpls. With U.S. Army, 1956—58. Office: Omni Source Corp 1610 N Calhoun St Fort Wayne IN 46808-2762

RIFKIN, STEPHEN, nephrologist; s. Morris and May Rifkin; children: Steven, Laura. AB, U. Rochester, 1963, MD, 1967. Diplomate Am. Bd. of Internal Medicine, 1972. Pvt. practice nephrology, Tampa, Fla., 1980—; assoc. prof. medicine U. South Fla. Coll. Medicine, Tampa, 1999—. Chief of staff Tampa Gen. Hosp., 1988—90, chief of nephrology sect., 2002—; pres. Fla. End Stage Renal Disease Network #7, Tampa, 1990—92, mem., bd. of directors, 1999—. Capt. U. S. Army, 1969—71. Recipient Exemplary Practice award for nephrology, Nat. Kidney Found. of Fla., 1996. Fellow: ACP; mem.: Am. Soc. of Internal Medicine, Fla. Soc. of Nephrology, Am. Soc. of Nephrology. Avocations: tennis, travel. Office: Stephen I Rifkin MD PA 2403 West Azeele St Tampa FL 33609-3317 Office Phone: 813-254-4272.

RIFKIND, ARLEEN B. pharmacologist, researcher, educator; b. N.Y.C., June 29, 1938; d. Michael C. and Regina (Gotlieb) Brenner; m. Robert S. Rifkind, Dec. 24, 1961; children: Amy, Nina. BA, Bryn Mawr Coll., 1960; MD, NYU, 1964. Intern Bellevue Hosp., N.Y.C., 1964-65, resident, 1965; clin. assoc. Endocrine br. Nat. Cancer Inst., 1965-68; rsch. assoc., asst. resident physician Rockefeller U., 1968-71; asst. prof. medicine Cornell U. Med. Coll., N.Y.C., 1971-82, assoc. prof. medicine, 1983—, asst. prof. pharmacology, 1973-78, assoc. prof., 1978-82, prof., 1983—, chmn. Gen. Faculty Coun., 1984-86. Mem. Nat. Inst. Environ. Health Scis. Rev. Com., 1981-85, chmn., 1985-86; mem. toxicology study sect. NIH, 1989-91, chmn., 1991-93; bd. sci. counselors USPHS Agy. for Toxic Substances and Disease Registry, 1991-95; adv. com. FDA, Spl. Studies Relating to the Possible Long-Term Health Effects of Phenoxy Herbicides and Contaminents, 1995-99; external adv. bd. Environ. Health Scis. Ctr., Wayne State U., 1999—. Assoc. editor Drug Metabolism and Disposition, 1997—; mem. editl. bd. Toxicology and Applied Pharmacology, 1996-2002, Biochem. Pharmacology, 1996—2003; contbr. articles to profl. jours. Chair Friends of the Libr., Jewish Theol. Sem. Am., 1984-86; trustee Dalton Sch., 1986-92; mem. Environ. Health and Safety Coun., Am. Health Found., 1990—; bd. govs. Am. Jewish Com., 1999—; bd. dirs. N.Y. chpt. Am. Jewish Com., 2001-. Recipient Andrew W. Mellon Tchr.-Scientist award, 1976-78; USPHS spl. fellow, 1968-72. Mem. AAAS, Internat. Soc. Study Xenobiotics, Am. Soc. Clin. Investigation, Am. Soc. Pharmacology and Exptl. Therapeutics, Endocrine Soc., Soc. Toxicology. Office: Cornell U Med Coll Dept Pharmacology 1300 York Ave New York NY 10021-4805 E-mail: arifkind@med.cornell.edu.

RIFKIND, RICHARD ALLEN, physician; b. N.Y.C., Oct. 26, 1930; s. Simon H. and Adele (Singer) R.; B.S., Yale U., 1951; M.D., Columbia U., 1955; m. Carole Lewis, June 24, 1956; children— Barbara, Nancy. Intern. Presbyn. Hosp. N.Y.C., 1955-56, resident, 1957-61, dir. hematology, 1972-81; asst. prof. dept. medicine Columbia U., 1963-67, asso. prof., 1967-70, prof., 1970-81, dir. comprehensive Cancer Center, 1980-81, chmn. dept. genetics, 1980-81; dir. Grad. Sch. Meml. Sloan-Kettering Cancer Center, N.Y.C., 1981-2000, chmn. Sloan-Kettering Inst., 1983—2000, chmn. emeritus, 2000-. Served to capt. M.C., USAF, 1957-59. Diplomate Am. Bd. Internal Medicine. Mem. Am. Soc. Clin. Investigation, Am. Assn. Physicians, Am. Soc. Hematology. Democrat. Jewish. Contbr. articles in field.

RIFKIND, ROBERT S. lawyer; b. N.Y.C., Aug. 31, 1936; s. Simon H. and Adele (Singer) R.; m. Arleen Brenner, Dec. 24, 1961; children: Amy, Nina. BA, Yale U., 1958; JD, Harvard U., 1961; LHD (hon.), Jewish Theol. Sem. Am., 1998. Bar: N.Y. 1961, U.S. Supreme Ct. 1965. Asst. to solicitor gen. Dept. Justice, 1965-68; assoc. firm Cravath, Swaine & Moore LLP, N.Y.C., 1962-65, 68-70, ptnr., 1971—2001, sr. counsel, 2002—. Trustee Dalton Sch., N.Y.C., 1975-83, hon. trustee, 1983—, pres., 1977-79; trustee Brandeis U., 1998—, The Loomis Inst., 1987-95, Citizens Budget Commn.; bd. dirs. Charles H. Revson Found., 1991—, chmn., 1997-2003; bd. dirs. Jewish Theol. Sem. Am., 1983—, Jerusalem Found., 1998-, Leo Baeck Inst., 1999—, Benjamin N. Cardozo Sch. Law, 1984-89; pres. Am. Jewish Com., 1994-98; chmn., adminstr. coun., Jacob Blaustein Inst. Advancement of Human Rights, 1999-. Fellow Am. Coll. Trial Lawyers, Am. Bar Found.; mem. ABA, Coun. Fgn. Rels., Am. Law Inst., Assn. of Bar of City of N.Y., The Century Assn., Phi Beta Kappa. Democrat. Office: Cravath Swaine & Moore LLP Worldwide Pla 825 8th Ave Fl 38 New York NY 10019-7475 Office Phone: 212-474-1450. Business E-Mail: rrifkind@cravath.com.

RIGALI, JUSTIN F. archbishop; b. L.A., Apr. 19, 1935; s. Henry Alphonsus and Frances Irene (White) Rigali. B in Sacred Theology, Cath. U. Am., 1961; Lic. in Canon Law, Gregorian U., Rome, 1963, D in Canon Law, 1964; LHD (hon.), St. Louis U., 1995. Ordained priest Roman Cath. Ch., 1961, ordained bishop 1985, elevated to cardinal 2003. Served at Apostolic Nunciature, Madagascar, 1966—70; named Papal Chamberlain to Pope Paul VI, 1967; titular archbishop of Bolsena, 1985—94; sec. Congregation for Bishops Holy See, Vatican City, 1989—94, sec. Coll. of Cardinals, 1990—94; archbishop Archdiocese of St. Louis, St. Louis, 1994—2003, Archdiocese of Philadelphia, Pa., 2003—; dir. English-lang. sect. Vatican Secretariat of State. Pres. Pontifical Ecclesiastical Acad., 1985—89. Office: Archdiocese of Philadelphia 222 N 17th St Philadelphia PA 19103

RIGAUD, EDWIN JOSEPH, museum administrator; b. New Orleans, June 25, 1943; m. Carole Rigaud; children: Simone, Edwin, Eric. BS in Chemistry, Xavier U., Louisiana, 1965; MA in Biochemistry, U. Cincinnati, Ohio, 1972; LHD (hon.), Saint Joseph Coll., N. Kentucky U. Joined Proctor & Gamble, 1966, v.p., gen. mgr. food and beverage products, 1993—95; v.p. govt. relations Procter & Gamble, 1995—2001; exec. dir. Nat. Underground Railroad Freedom Ctr., Cincinnati, 1996—2001, pres., 2001—. Trustee emeritus Nat. Conference for Community & Justice, Cincinnati; trustee Greater Cincinnati 2012 Olympics Selection Com.; mem. Ohio Bicentennial Commn.; co-chair, bd. mem. marketing com. Greater Cincinnati 2000 Commn.; bd. mem. Amistad Rsch. Ctr., Tulane U. Bd mem. Cincinnati Children's Hospital Med. Ctr., Greater Cincinnati's Nat. Conference of Christians & Jews, Greater Cincinnati Literacy Task Force, Internat. Youth Inst., Cincinnati Museum of Nat. History. Recipient Annual YMCA Black Achiever award, 1980. Office: Nat Underground Railroad Freedom Ctr 50 E Freedom Way Cincinnati OH 45202*

RIGBY, PAUL CRISPIN, artist, cartoonist; b. Melbourne, Australia, Oct. 25, 1924; came to U.S., 1977; s. James Samuel and Violet Irene (Wood) R.; m. Marlene Anne Cockburn, Nov. 16, 1956; children: Nicole, Pia, Peter, Paul, Danielle. Student, Brighton Tech. Sch., Australia, Art Schs., Victoria, Victoria Nat. Gallery, Australia. Free lance artist, 1940-42; illustrator West Australian News, Ltd., 1948-52; editorial cartoonist Daily News Australia, 1952-69; daily cartoonist London Sun and News of the World, 1969-74; editorial cartoonist New York Post, 1977—84, 1993—2000, New York Daily News, 1984-93. Illustrator numerous books; represented in exhbns. of painting in, Australia, Europe and U.S.A.; Contbr. work to numerous publs., U.S., Europe, Asia. With Royal Australian Air Force, 1942-46. Decorated Order of Australia, knight comdr. Order of St. John, Knights of Malta; recipient Walkley award Australia, 1960, 61, 63, 66, 69; N.Y. Press Club award for art, 1981, 83, Page One award for excellence in journalism Newspaper Guild, 1982, 83, 84, 85. Mem.: Rolls Royce Owners, Royal Freshwater Bay Yacht; Friars (N.Y.C.), Players (N.Y.C.). Mem. Ch. Of Eng. Home: 119 Monterey Point Dr Palm Beach Gardens FL 33418 E-mail: rigbyateastend@aol.com.

RIGBY, PERRY GARDNER, medical center administrator, educator, former university dean, physician; b. East Liverpool, Ohio, July 1, 1932; s. Perry Lawrence and Lucille Ellen (Orin) R.; m. Joan E. Worthington, June 16, 1957; children: Martha, Peter, Thomas, Matthew. BS summa cum laude, Mt. Union Coll., 1953, D.Sc. hon., 1976; MD, Western Res. U., 1957. Diplomate: Am. Bd. Internal Medicine. Intern in medicine U. Va. Hosp., Charlottesville, 1957-58, asst. resident in medicine, 1958-60; research fellow in hematology Mass. Meml. Hosp., Boston, 1960-62; clin. asst. in medicine Boston City Hosp., 1961-62; research assoc. in medicine Mass. Meml. Hosp., Boston U. Med. Ctr., 1961-62; asst. prof. internal medicine and anatomy U. Nebr., Omaha, 1964-66, assoc. prof. internal medicine and anatomy, 1966-69, prof. internal medicine, 1969-78, prof. anatomy, 1969-74, prof. med. edn., 1973-74, head sect. hematology Eugene C. Eppley Inst. for Research in Cancer and Allied Diseases, 1964-68, dir. hematology div., 1968-74, asst. dean for curriculum Coll. Medicine, 1971-72, assoc. dean for acad. affairs, 1972-74, dir. office ednl. services, 1972-74, acting assoc. dean for allied health professions, 1973-74, vice chmn. dept. med. and ednl. adminstrn., 1974, dean, 1974-78, chmn. dept. med. and ednl. adminstrn., 1974; prof. internal medicine La. State U., Shreveport, 1978—, assoc. dean acad. affairs Sch. Medicine, 1978-81, acting dean, 1981-82, dean, 1982-85, chancellor, 1985-94, dir. Health Care Systems, 1994—, mem. clin. bd. Univ. Hosp., 1978-94, chmn. clin. bd., 1981-85, program dir. biomed. research support grant program, 1980-81; chmn. dean's com. VA Hosp., 1978-85; mem. courtesy staff Immanuel Med. Ctr.; bd. dirs. Health Planning Council of Midlands, Omaha, 1976-78; cons. WHO, Kabul, Afghanistan, 1976. Bd. dirs. Fontenelle Forest, Omaha, 1976-78; bd. dirs. River Cities High Tech. Group, Shreveport, 1982-85. Served as capt. M.C. U.S. Army, 1962-64. Markle scholar, 1965 Fellow ACP; mem. Am. Fedn. Clin. Research (councillor 1971), AMA (del.), Am. Soc. Hematology, N.Y. Acad. Scis., Am. Assn. Med. Colls. (council of deans of Midwest-Gt. Plains 1974-78, chmn. Midwest-Gt. Plains 1976), Am. Assn. Cancer Research, AAAS, Am. Heart Assn., Central Soc. Clin. Research, Internat. Soc. Hematology, Health Edn. Media Assn., Am. Assn. Physicians' Assts., So. Soc. Clin. Investigation, Shreveport C. of C. (dir. 1982-85), Sigma Xi, Alpha Omega Alpha, Phi Rho Sigma Office: La State U Med Ctr Resource Ctr 433 Bolivar St New Orleans LA 70112-2223

RIGG, CAROL MARGARET ELIZABETH RUTH, calligrapher, graphics designer, art educator; b. Pitts., Dec. 14, 1928; d. Carl Hazlett and Ruth Standish (Massey) Rigg. BA, Fla. State U., 1951; MA, Presbyn. Sch. Christian Edn., 1955; MFA, Chgo. Art Inst., 1963. Art. dir. bd. publs. Fla. State U., Tallahassee, 1950-53; art editor motive mag., Nashville, 1954-65; artist-in-residence Fla. Presbyn. Coll., St. Petersburg, 1965-66; prof. visual arts Eckerd Coll., St. Petersburg, 1967-93, prof. emerita, 1999—. Founder Possum Press, St. Petersburg, 1969; lectr. Princeton Div. Sch., 1972; vis. art lectr. Harvard Div. Sch., 1982. Exhibitions include in more than 60 solo art shows; calligraphy featured on two CBS-TV shows, 1969, 1971; one-woman shows include calligraphy Cultural Olympics, Seoul, Republic of Korea, 1987; author: (book) Calligraphy of the Americas, 1977-95. Pres. Nashville Artists Guild, 1960—62. Fulbright grantee, 1972. Mem.: Am. Calligraphic Arts Assn., Fla. Artist Group, Fla. Gulfcoast Soc. Scribes (founder, pres. 1976—78). Mem. Soc. Of Friends. Office: Eckerd Coll PO Box 12560 Saint Petersburg FL 33733-2560

RIGG, CHARLES ANDREW, retired pediatrician; b. Hamilton, Victoria, Australia, Oct. 18, 1926; arrived in U.S., 1963; s. Arthur Oscar and Mary Eileen (Wingrove) Rigg. B in Medicine, Surgery with honors, Sydney U., 1951. Registrar, professorial unit Children's Hosp., Sydney, Australia, 1954-56; registrar pediat. unit St. Mary's Hosp. Med. Sch., London, 1956, 58; from sr. resident to chief resident Children's Hosp., Boston, 1957, fellow in adolescent medicine, 1963-64, staff adolescent medicine, 1964-65; chief dept. adolescent medicine Children's Nat. Med. Ctr., Washington, 1967-80; asst. prof. pediat. Georgetown U. Med. Sch., 1965-67; from asst. prof. to assoc. prof. child health George Washington U. Med. Sch., 1967-80; chief dept. adolescent medicine Boston City Hosp., 1981-83; assoc. prof. pediatrics Sch. Medicine Boston U., 1981-83; med. dir. Outer Cape Health, Provincetown, Mass., 1983-88; pediatrician, med. dir. Medicenter Five, Harwich, Mass., 1988-95, pediatrician, 1995-97, May Ctr. Child Devel., Chatham, Mass., 1990—, Harwich Town Pub. Sch. System, 1997—; ret., 2004. Cons. Nat. Naval Med. Ctr., Bethesda, Md., 1973—80, Walter Reed Army Med. Ctr., Washington, 1973—80; courtesy staff medicine Children's Hosp., Boston, 1983—; vis. prof. Philippine Pediat. Soc., 1978, 9th Congress Brazilian Med. Assn., 1979, 16th Internat. Congress Pediat., Barcelona, 1980. Editor: Adolescent Medicine Present and Future Concepts, 1980; contbr. articles to profl. jours. Mem. Mus. Fine Arts, Boston, Shakespeare Libr., Washington, Nat. Trust Hist. Preservation, Nat. Trust Australia, Tasmania, Royal Oak Soc. Maj. M.C. Royal Australian Army, 1951—60, lt. col. USAR, 1985—91. Model Tng. Program Adolescent Medicine grantee, Maternal and Child Health Svcs.-U.S. Govt., 1967—80, Comprehensive health Svcs. Adolescent Ctr. grantee, Mass. Dept. Pub. Health, 1981—83. Fellow: Royal Australasian Coll. Physicians, Am. Headache Soc., Royal Soc. Medicine, Am. Acad. Pediatrics (life); mem.: Soc. Adolescent Medicine (Washington, DC chpt. pres. 1974—76, New Eng. chpt. pres. 1982—84, charter, treas., chmn., legis. com.), Folger Shakespeare Libr., City Tavern Club (Washington), Royal Sydney Golf Club. Episcopalian. Avocations: historic preservation, gardening, theater, music, walking.

RIGG, DAME DIANA, actress; b. Doncaster, Yorkshire, Eng., July 20, 1938; d. Louis and Beryl (Helliwell) R.; m. Menahem Gueffen, July 6, 1973 (div. Sept. 1976); m. Archibald Hugh Stirling, Mar. 25, 1981 (div. Apr. 1993); 1 child, Rachael Atlanta. Grad., Fulneck Girls' Sch., Pudsey, Yorkshire; student, Royal Acad. Dramatic Art, London; D (hon.), Stirling U., Eng., 1988, Leeds U., 1992, Southbank U., 1996. Prof. of theater studies Oxford U., 1998—. Stage debut as Natella Abashwilli in The Caucasian Chalk Circle, Theatre Royal, York, Eng., 1957; joined Royal Shakespeare Co., Stratford-on-Avon, 1959, debut as Andromache in Troilus and Cressida, 1960; London debut as Philippe Trincant in The Devils, London, 1961; numerous repertory appearances; joined Nat. Theatre, 1972; appeared in Jumpers, Macbeth, 1972, The Misanthrope, 1973, Pygmalion, 1974, Phaedra Britannica, 1975, Night and Day, 1978, Colette, 1982, Heartbreak House, 1983, Little Eyolf, 1985, Antony and Cleopatra, 1985, Wildlife, 1986, Follies, 1987, Love Letters, 1990, All for Love, 1991, Putting It Together, 1992, Berlin Bertie, 1992, Medea, 1992 (Tony award, Broadway prod., 1994, Eve. Standard award, Variety Club award), Mother Courage and Her Children, 1995, Who's Afraid of Virginia Wolf, 1996, Humble Boy, 2001; film appearances include A Midsummer Night's Dream, The Assassination Bureau, On Her Majesty's Secret Service, Julius Caesar, The Hospital, Theatre of Blood, A Little Night Music, The Great Muppet Caper, Evil Under the Sun, A Good Man in Africa, Parting Shots, 1998; co-starred as Emma Peel in Brit. TV miniseries: Charles II: The Power and the Passion, 2003. TV series The Avengers, 1965-67; star TV series Diana, 1973-74; numerous TV movies including This House of Brede, 1975, Hedda Gabler, 1981, Little Eyolf, 1982, Witness for the Prosecution, 1982, King Lear, 1983, Bleak House, 1984, A Hazard of Hearts, 1987, Worst Witch, 1987, Unexplained Laughter, 1989, Mother Love (Broadcasting Guild Award, BAFTA), 1989, Genghis Cohn, 1994, Zoya, 1995, The Haunting of Helen Walker, 1995, Moll Flanders, 1996, Samson and Delilah, 1996, Rebecca, 1997 (Emmy award, 1997); host PBS series Mystery, 1989—, Mrs. Bradley Mysteries, 1999—, In the Beginning, 2000, The American, 2000, Victoria & Albert, 2001; author: No Turn Unstoned, 1982, U.S. edit., 1983, So To The Land, 1994. Decorated comdr. Brit. Empire; created dame, 1994; recipient Tony award nomination as best actress in Abelard and Heloise and The Misanthrope; Plays and Players award for Phaedra Britannica and Night and Day; Variety Club Gt. Britain award for best actress for Evil Under the Sun; Brit. Acad. Film and TV Arts award for best TV actress in Mother Love, 1989, Award for Women in TV & Film, 2001. Mem. United Brit. Artists (co-founder, dir. 1982—). Address: c/o Lionel Larner Ltd 119 W 57th St New York NY 10019-2303*

RIGGENBACH, JEFF, journalist; b. Highland Park, Mich., Jan. 12, 1947; s. Frank Riggenbach and Dorothy Jane Miller; m. Suzanne Hoy Riggenbach, Mar. 10, 1996; m. Leslee J. Newman, Sept. 5, 1976 (div. 1989); m. Patricia Streeter, Mar. 29, 1967 (div. 1973); children: Max Rigman, Blaine Streeter. BS in Liberal Studies, Excelsior Coll. (formerly Regents Coll.); MA in humanities, Calif. State U., 2004. Anchor/newswriter KNUZ Radio, Houston, 1967—72; anchor/book critic/cultural affairs reporter KFWB All News Radio, LA, 1972—78; editor The Castalian (mag.), LA, 1972—74; instr. (journalism) Pierce Coll., LA, 1977—78; freelance writer L.A. Times, 1977—86; reporter, prod. Pub. Affairs Broadcast Group, Los Angeles, 1977—79; exec. editor The Libertarian Rev., San Francisco, 1978—82; exec. prodr., Byline Cato Inst., Washington, 1979—90; contbg. editor Inquiry mag., Washington, 1982—85; freelance writer San Jose (Calif.) Mercury News, 1983—88, U.S.A. Today, 1983—95; editl. writer Oakland Tribune, Calif., 1984—85; contbg editor Reason mag., LA, 1984—90; editl. writer/columnist Orange County Register, Santa Ana, Calif., 1985—87; daily economics commentator CNN Radio, Atlanta, 1985—87; prodr./program host KFAC Classical Radio, LA, 1987—89; mng. editor Pacific Bus. Rev., San Francisco, 1992—93; prodr./program host KKHI Classical Radio, San Francisco, 1993—94; instr. (liberal arts) Acad. of Art Coll., San Francisco, 1996—2000; contbg. editor Liberty mag., Port Townsend, Wash., 2001—. Co-founder, vice chair Free Press Assn., Columbus, Ohio, 1983—87. Author: (book) In Praise of Decadence. Mem.: Orgn. of Am. Historians. Home: 633 Post Street #337 San Francisco CA 94109 Personal E-mail: jriggenbach@bigfoot.com.

RIGGIN, DONALD L. health science association administrator; With, Arthritis Found., 1965—, v.p. southwest area, 1979-85, sr. v.p. ops., 1985-88, exec. v.p., COO, 1988-90, pres., 1990—2001; exec. council, CTE Associates, NY, 2001—. Fellow Am. Soc. Assn. Execs. (cert. assn. exec., bd. dirs., Key award, 1998); mem. Ga. Soc. Assn. Execs. (past chmn. GSAE Found., Alan R. Johnson Leadership award, 1994-95, Clifford M. Clarke award, 1998). Office: Changing Our World Inc CTE Assocs GrayBar Bldg 420 Lexington Ave Ste 2320 New York NY 10170

RIGGIO, LEONARD, book publishing executive; b. 1941; Mdse. mgr. NYU Bookstore, N.Y.C., 1962—65; pres., CEO, bd. dirs. Barnes & Noble Bookstores, Inc., 1965—86; chmn. bd., CEO, pres., treas. Barnes & Noble Inc., N.Y.C., 1986—; chmn. bd., prin. beneficial owner Software Etc. Stores, Inc., Mpls., MBS Textbook Exch. Inc., Columbia, Mo. Office: Barnes & Noble Inc 4th Fl 122 5th Ave Fl 4 New York NY 10011-5605 Address: MBS Textbook Exchange Inc 2711 W Ash St Columbia MO 65203-4613

RIGGIO, NICHOLAS JOSEPH, SR., lawyer; b. St. Louis, Oct. 1, 1930; s. Joseph and Anna (Trapani) R.; m. Etta G. Riggio, Nov. 6, 1954; children: Nicholas Jr., Michael John, Joy Ann. BS, St. Louis U., 1953; LLB, Washington U., 1959, JD, 1968. Pvt. practice, St. Louis, 1959—. Co-founder Hill 2000 Orgn., St. Louis, 2000. Inducted into St. Louis Soccer Hall of Fame, 1985. Office: 5149 Daggett Ave Saint Louis MO 63110-3039

RIGGIO, STEPHEN, book store chain executive; married; 3 children. BA in Anthropology, Bklyn. Coll., 1974. Buying, mktg. areas Barnes & Noble Bookstores, Inc., N.Y.C., 1974-78, gen. mdse. mgr., 1978-81, head direct mail bus., 1981-86, exec. v.p. merchandising, 1986-90, exec. v.p., chief oper. officer, 1990—97; vice-chmn. Barnes & Noble, Inc., 1997—; vice-chmn. and acting CEO barnesandnoble.com, 2000—02; CEO Barnes & Noble, Inc., 2002—. Originator Children With Special Needs collection books about and for children with learning disabilities. Bd. dirs. N.Y. chpt. Assn. Help Retarded Children. Office: Barnes & Noble, Inc 122 5th Ave New York NY 10011-5605

RIGGLE, PATRICIA CAROL, special education educator; b. Gallipolis, Ohio, May 28, 1965; d. Pat and Freadith Fay Price; m. Richard Allan Riggle; children: Alana, Emily. BS, U. Rio Grande, 1989. Sub. tchr. Gallia County Local Schs., Gallipolis, Ohio, 1989—92, Gallipolis City Schs., Gallipolis, Ohio, 1989—92; tchr. Wellston City Sch., Wellston, Ohio, 1992—; child care provider Rio Grande Child Devel. Ctr., Rio Grande, Ohio, 1992—93. Vol. asst. dir. drama club Wellston H.S., Wellston, Ohio, 1998—; career assessment adv. com. Gallia-Jackson-Vinton Joint Vocats. Sch. Dist., Rio Grande, Ohio, 2001—. Youth Sunday sch. tchr. Okey Chapel, Scottown, Ohio, 1985—2000. Mem.: NEA, Wellston Tchrs. Assn., Ohio Edn. Assn. Avocations: camping, travel, crafts. Home: 4767 Hannan Trace Rd Patriot OH 45658

RIGGS, ARTHUR D. health facility administrator, research scientist; b. Modesto, Calif., Aug. 8, 1939; s. John Arlis and Nelly Laura Riggs; m. Jane Merill, June 12, 1960; children: Karen, Lynelle, Derrick. AB, U. Calif., Riverside, 1961; PhD, Calif. Inst. Tech., 1966. Assoc. prof. City of Hope Nat. Med. Ctr., Duarte, Calif., 1969—74, prof., 1974—83, chmn. divsn. biology, 1981—87; founding dean City of Hope Grad. Sch., Duarte, 1994—98; CEO, dir. Beckman Rsch. Inst. City of Hope, Duarte, 2000—. Contbr. articles to profl. jours. Recipient Rsch. award, Juvenile Diabetes Found., 1979, Disting. Alumni award, U. Calif., Riverside, 1988. Achievements include first human protein produced in bacteria; first man-designed and man-made gene; discovery of new type of genetics. Avocations: hiking, kayaking, mountain biking. Office: Beckman Rsch Inst City of Hope 1450 E Duarte Rd Duarte CA 91010

RIGGS, ARTHUR JORDY, retired lawyer; b. Nyack, N.Y., Apr. 3, 1916; s. Oscar H. and Adele (Jordy) R.; m. Virginia Holloway, Oct. 15, 1942 (dec.); children: Arthur James (dec.), Emily Adele Riggs Freeman, Keith Holloway, George Bennett; m. Priscilla McCormack, Jan. 16, 1993. AB, Princeton U., 1937; LLB, Harvard U., 1940. Bar: Mass. 1940, Tex. 1943; cert. specialist in labor law. Assoc. Warner, Stackpole, Stetson & Bradlee, Boston, 1940-41; staff mem. Solicitors Office U.S. Dept. Labor, Washington, Dallas, 1941-42; mem. Johnson, Bromberg, Leeds & Riggs, Dallas, 1949-81; of counsel Geary & Spencer, Dallas, 1981-91. Mem. ABA, State Bar Tex., Phi Beta Kappa. Avocations: maya archeology, history, photography. Home and Office: 2110 Antibes Dr Carrollton TX 75006-4326

RIGGS, DONALD EUGENE, librarian, university official; b. Middlebourne, W.Va., May 11, 1942; m. Jane Vasbinder, Sept. 25, 1964; children: Janna Jennifer, Krista Dyonis. BA, Glenville State Coll., 1964; MA, W.Va. U., 1966; MLS, U. Pitts., 1968; EdD, Va. Poly. Inst. and State U., 1975. Head libr., tchr. sci. Warwood (W.Va.) H.S., 1964-65; head libr., audiovisual dir. Wheeling (W.Va.) H.S., 1965-67; sci. and econs. libr. California State Coll. of Pa., 1968-70; dir. libr. and learning ctr. Bluefield State Coll., 1970-72; dir. librs. and media svcs. Bluefield State Coll., Concord Coll., Greenbrier C.C., and So. campus W.Va. Coll. of Grad. Studies, 1972-76; dir. librs. U. Colo., Denver, Met. State Coll., and C.C. of Denver- Auraria Campus, 1976-79; univ. libr. Ariz. State U., 1979-88, dean univ. librs., 1988-90; prof. info. and libr. sci., dean univ. libr. U. Mich., Ann Arbor, 1991-97; prof., v.p. for info. svcs., univ. libr. Nova Southeastern U., Ft. Lauderdale, Fla., 1997—. Adj. prof. Calif. State Coll., 1968-70, W.Va. U., 1970-72, U. Colo., 1977-79, U. Ariz., 1985, Emporia State U., 1996—, U. South Fla., 1997—; fed. rels. coord. Am. and W.Va. Libr. Assns., 1970-75; chmn. bd. dirs. Ctrl. Colo. Libr. Sys., 1976-79; chmn. Colo. Coun. Acad. Librs., 1977-78; mem. exec. bd. Colo. Alliance Rsch. Librs., 1978-79; cons. to librs.; fgn. assignments in Xi'an, China, 1988, Guadalajara, Mex., 1990, Budapest, Hungary, 1991, 95, Hong Kong, 1992, 94, San Juan, P.R., 1993, Melbourne, Australia, 1994, Eupatory, Republic Crimea, Ukraine, 1995, London, 1996, Prague, Czech Republic, 1996, Beijing, China, 1996, 98, Pretoria, South Africa, 1996, others; del. Users Coun. Online Computer Libr. Ctr., Dublin, Ohio, 1987-91, pres.-elect, 1990-91, chair artificial intelligence and expert systems nat. group, 1987-88; bd. govs. Rsch. Librs. Group, Inc., Mountain View, Calif., 1991-92; vice chmn. mgmt. com. William L. Clements Libr., 1991-97. Editor: W.Va. Librs., 1973-75, Libr. Hi Tech, 1993-96, Coll. & Rsch. Librs., 1996-2002; founding editor: Libr. Adminstrn. and Mgmt., 1987-89; assoc. editor: Southeastern Libr., 1973-75; contbg. editor: Libraries in the Political Process, 1980, Options for the 80's, 1982, Library and Information Technology: At the Crossroads, 1984; contbg. author, editor: Library Leadership: Visualizing the Future, 1982; author: Strategic Planning for Library Managers, 1984, (with Helen Gothberg) Time Management in Academic Libraries, 1986, (with Gordon Sabine) Libraries in the 90's: What the Leaders Expect, 1988, Creativity, Innovation and Entrepreneurship in Libraries, 1989, Library Communication: The Language of Leadership, 1991, (with Rao Aluri) Expert Systems in Libraries, 1990, Cultural Diversity in Libraries, 1994; editl. bd. Am. Librs., 1987-89, Jour. Libr. Adminstrn., 1987-97, Coll. and Rsch. Librs., 1990-96, Coll. and Rsch. Librs. News,

1996-2002. Trustee Mesa (Ariz.) Pub. Libr., 1980-86, chmn., 1985-86; mem. Ariz. State Libr. Adv. Coun., 1981-84; bd. dirs. Documentation Abstracts, Inc., 1986-90. Recipient Alumnus of Yr. award Glenville State Coll., 1992; named Outstanding Young Educator, Ohio County Schs., 1966; Coun. on Libr. Resources grantee, 1985; sr. fellow UCLA, 1989. Mem. ALA (councilor-at-large 1982-86, 89-93, chmn. coun.'s resolutions com. 1985-86, pub. com. 1988-92, Hugh Atkinson award 1991), Ariz. Libr. Assn. (pres. coll. and univ. divsn. 1981-82, pres. 1983-84, Spl. Svc. award 1986, Disting. Svc. award 1990), Colo. Libr. Assn. (pres. 1978-79), W.Va. Libr. Assn. (pres. 1975-76), Assn. Coll. and Rsch. Librs. (pres. Tri-State chpt. 1972-74, pres. Ariz. chpt. 1981-82), So. Libr. Assn. (chmn. coll. and univ. sect. 1982-83), Assn. Rsch. Librs. (100th meeting planning com. 1982, mgmt. of rsch. libr. resources com. 1990-93, rsch. collections com. 1993-96), AMIGOS Bibliograph Coun. (trustee 1986-90, chmn. bd. trustees 1988-89), Libr. Adminstrn. and Mgmt. Assn. (bd. dirs. 1987-89, pres.-elect 1993-94, pres. 1994-95), Libr. Info. and Tech. Assn. (bd. dirs. 1989-93), Ctr. for Rsch. Librs. (councilor 1979-97), Fla. Libr. Assn. (chair leadership devel. com. 2003-2004), Mountain Plains Libr. Assn. (bd. dirs. 1987-90, pres.-elect 1990-91), S.E. Fla. Libr. Info. Network (exec. com., bd. dirs. 1997—, pres. 1998-99), Beta Phi Mu, Chi Beta Phi, Phi Delta Kappa, Phi Kappa Phi. Office: Nova Southeastern U Alvin Sherman Libr Rsch & Info Tech Ctr Ray Ferrero Jr Blvd Fort Lauderdale FL 33314-7721 Business E-Mail: driggs@nsu.nova.edu.

RIGGS, FRED WARREN, political science educator; b. Kuling, China, July 3, 1917; (parents Am. citizens); s. Charles H. and Grace (Frederick) R.; m. Clara-Louise Mather, June 5, 1943; children: Gwendolyn, Ronald (dec.). Student, U. Nanking, China, 1934-35; BA, U. Ill., 1938; MA, Fletcher Sch. Law and Diplomacy, 1941; PhD, Columbia U., 1948. Lectr. CUNY, 1947-48; rsch. assoc. Fgn. Policy Assn., 1948-51; asst. dir. Pub. Adminstrn. Clearing House, N.Y.C., 1951-55; Arthur F. Bentley prof. govt. Ind. U., 1956-67; dir. Social Sci. Rsch. Inst. U. Hawaii, 1970-73, prof. polit. sci., 1967-87, prof. emeritus, 1987—. Vis. asst. prof. Yale U., 1955-56; vis. lectr. Nat. Officials Tng. Inst., Korea, 1956; vis. prof. U. Philippines, 1958-59, MIT, 1965-66, CUNY, 1974-75; vis. scholar Inst. Soc. Studies, The Hague, 1972; sr. specialist East-West Ctr. U. Hawaii, 1962-63. Author: Pressures on Congress: A Study of the Repeal of Chinese Exclusion, 1950, reprinted, 1973, Formosa under Chinese Nationalist Rule, 1952, reprinted, 1972, The Ecology of Public Administration, 1961 (pub. in Portuguese, 1964), Administration in Developing Countries: The Theory of Prismatic Society, 1964 (pub. in Korean, 1966, Portuguese, 1968), Thailand: The Modernization of a Bureaucratic Polity, 1966, Organization Theory and International Development, 1969, Administrative Reform and Political Responsiveness: A Theory of Dynamic Balancing, 1971, Prismatic Society Revisited, 1973 (pub. in Korean, 1987), Applied Prismatics, 1978, (with Daya Krishna) Development Debate, 1987; author: (with others) Contemporary Political Systems: Classifications and Typologies, 1990, Handbook of Comparative and Development Public Administration, 1991, Terminology: Applications in Interdisciplinary Communication, 1993, Parliamentary vs. Presidential Government, 1993, Public Administration in the Global Village, 1994, Comparing Nations: Concepts, Strategies, Substance, 1994, Handbook of Bureaucracy, 1994, Standardizing and Harmonizing Terminology, 1995, Korea in the Era of Post-Development and Globalization, 1996, Designs for Democratic Stability, 1997, Modernity and Bureaucracy, 1997, Presidentialism vs. Parliamentarism, 1998, Public Administration in America, 1998, The Modernity of Ethnic Identity and Conflict, 1998, Impeachment vs. Harassment, 1999; Ethnic Diversity, Nationalism and Constitutional Democracy, 2000, The Para-Modern Context of Ethnic Nationalism, 2000, Globalization, Ethnic Diversity and Nationalism, 2002, Globalization and Faith, 2002, Electronic Nomenclators, 2002, A Comparativist's Sojourn, 2003, American Myth as Global Model, 2004; co-author, editor: Frontiers of Development Administration, 1971, Tower of Babel: On the Definition and Analysis of Concepts in the Social Sciences, 1975. Dir. INTERCOCTA project Internat. Social Sci. Coun., 1970-93; chair UNESCO com. INTERCONCEPT project, 1977-79; chair Comm. on Conceptual and Terminological Analysis (COCTA), Internat. Polit. Sci. Assn., Internat. Sociol. Assn. and Internat. Social Sci. Coun., 1973-79; co-chair N.AM. roundtable on cooperation Social Sci. Info. Mpls., 1979; chair lexicographic terminology com. Dictionary Soc. N.Am., 1983-86; co-chair Com. on Viable Constitutionalism (COVICO), 1993—. Decorated Order of White Elephant, King of Thailand, 1986; fellow com. comparative politics Social Sci. Rsch. Coun., 1957-58, Ctr. Advanced Study in Behavioral Scis., 1966-67; honoree Eastern Regional Orgn. Pub. Adminstrn. Conf., 1983. Mem. Am. Soc. for Pub. Adminstrn. (chair comparative adminstrn. group 1960-71, Dwight Waldo award 1991), Am. Polit. Sci. Assn., Internat. Studies Assn. (chair comparative interdisciplinary studies sect. 1970-74, v.p. 1970-71, co-chair ethnicity, nationalism and migration sect. 1994-95), Internat. Polit. Sci. Assn., Internat. Sociol. Assn., Assn. Asian Studies (chair com. rsch. materials S.E. Asia 1969-73), Soc. for Comparative Rsch. (co-founder 1994—). Home: 3920 Lurline Dr Honolulu HI 96816-4006 Office: U Hawaii Political Science Dept 2424 Maile Way Honolulu HI 96822-2223 E-mail: fredr@hawaii.edu.

RIGGS, HENRY EARLE, academic administrator, engineering educator; b. Chgo., Feb. 25, 1935; s. Joseph Agnew and Gretchen (Walser) Riggs; m. Gayle Carson, May 17, 1958; children: Elizabeth, Peter, Catharine. BS, Stanford U., 1957; MBA, Harvard U., 1960. Indsl. economist SRI Internat., Menlo Park, Calif., 1960—63; v.p. Icore Industries, Sunnyvale, Calif., 1963—67, pres., 1967—70; v.p. fin. Measurex Corp., Cupertino, Calif., 1970—74; prof. engrng. mgmt. Stanford U., Calif., 1974—88, Ford prof., 1986—88, Ford prof. emeritus, 1990, v.p. for devel., 1983—88; pres. Harvey Mudd Coll., Claremont, Calif., 1988—97, pres. emeritus, 1997; pres. Keck Grad. Inst., Claremont, 1997—2003, trustee, pres. emeritus, 2003—. Bd. dirs. Capital Rsch. Group. Author: Accounting: A Survey, 1981, Managing High-Tech Companies, 1983, Financial and Economic Analysis, 1994, 2d edit., 2004; contbr. articles to profl. jours. Recipient Gores Tchg. award, Stanford U., 1980; scholar Baker scholarship, Harvard Bus. Sch., 1959. Mem.: Stanford U. Alumni Assn. (bd. dirs. 1990—94, chmn. 1993), Sunset Club, Calif. Club, Tau Beta Pi, Phi Beta Kappa. Congregationalist. Office: Keck Grad Inst 535 Watson Dr Claremont CA 91711-4817 Home: 24 Peter Coutts Circle Stanford CA 94305 E-mail: henry_riggs@kgi.edu.

RIGGS, JACK EDWARD, neurologist, educator; b. Toledo, Oct. 6, 1949; s. Paul Henson and Bertha Jean (Terry) R.; m. Christine Marie Gunther, Sept. 18, 1978; children: Allison, Kevin, Lauren, Todd. BA, BS, U. Toledo, 1972; MD, U. Rochester, 1976. Diplomate Am. Bd. Internal Medicine. Diplomate Am. Bd. Neurology and Psychiatry. Asst. prof. neurology W.Va. U., Morgantown, W.Va., 1981-84, assoc. prof. neurology, 1984-87, prof. neurology, 1987—. Contbr. over 200 articles to profl. jours. Fellow Am. Acad. Neurology; mem. Am. Neurol. Assn. Avocations: astronomy, history, biology, evolution. Home: 298 Lakeview Dr Morgantown WV 26508-9254 Office: WVa U Dept Neurology PO Box 9180 Morgantown WV 26506-9180 Office Phone: 304-293-2341. Business E-Mail: jriggs@wvu.edu.

RIGGS, JACK TIMOTHY, emergency physician, former state lieutenant governor; b. Coeur d'Alene, Idaho, Oct. 1, 1954; BS summa cum laude, U. Idaho, 1976; MD, U. Wash., 1980. Diplomate Am. Bd. Emergency Medicine. Intern Deaconess Med. Ctr., Spokane, Wash., 1980-81; mem. Idaho Senate, Dist. 4, Boise, 1996-2000; owner North Idaho Immediate Car Ctrs., 1985—; lt. gov. State of Idaho, 2001—03. Fellow Am. Coll. Emergency Physicians; mem. AMA, Am. Coll. Physician Execs., Idaho Med. Assn., Am. Coll. Occupl. and Environ. Medicine. Address: 927 E Polston Post Falls ID 83854

RIGGS, JEANETTE TEMPLETON, civic worker; b. Little Rock, Mar. 13, 1933; d. Donald M. and Fay (Templeton) Brewer; student Little Rock U., 1950-51, Tex. Coll. for Women, 1951-52; B.S., U. Ark., 1955; m. Byron Lawrence Riggs, June 1955; children— Byron Kent, Ann Templeton. Founder, Rochester (Minn.) Ballet Guild, 1970, pres., 1974; mem. establishing bd., exec. bd. Rochester Arts Council, 1972, producer, dir. T.S. Elliot's The Rock, 1970; founder, performer So. Minn. Ballet Co., 1974; sponsor Nat. Ballet Cos., Rochester, 1970-75; exec. bd. for restoration 1875 Pattern Book House, Rochester Heritage Assn., 1975-77; exec. bd. Savino Ballet Nat., 1975-78; founder, exec. bd. Citizens Action Com., 1977-79; asso., commentator Women, Cable TV Program for Women, Rochester, 1979; mem. Mayor's Com. on Drug Abuse, 1979-80; mem. Olmsted County Steering Com. for George Bush, 1979-80, a founder, mem. exec. bd. Olmsted County Republican Women's Orgn., 1979—, mem. Olmsted County Rep. Central Com., 1979—, exec. bd. issues com., 1979-80. Home: 432 10th Ave SW Rochester MN 55902-2911

RIGGS, JOHN M. army officer; b. Mo., Dec. 2, 1946; BA in Polit. Sci., Tarkio Coll.; MA in Pers. Mgmt. and Adminstrn., Ctrl. Mich. U.; postgrad., Harvard U. Commd. 2d lt. U.S. Army, advanced through grades to maj. gen.; served overseas in Korea, Belgium, Vietnam, Germany; asst. divsn. comdr.; dep. comdg. gen. U.S. Army Aviation Sch., Ft. Rucker, Ala.; asst. dep. chief staff for ops. and plans Hdqs. Dept. Army, Washington, 1997-99; comdg. gen. 1st U.S. Army, Forest Park, Ga., 1999—. Decorated DSM, Legion of Merit with 3 oak leaf clusters, DFC, Bronze Star medal, others; Nat. Security fellow. Office: 1st US Army 4705 Wheeler Dr Forest Park GA 30297-5000

RIGGS, LEW, foundation executive; b. Indpls., Apr. 1, 1937; s. Frank Lloyd Riggs and Marie Loretta (Shaner) Ellis; m. Christine Marie Stiemke, Dec. 2, 2000. BS in Bus. Adminstrn., U. Ariz., 1961, EdD, 1976; MBA, George Washington U., 1964. Mktg. adminstr. TRW Systems, L.A., 1964-67; assn. exec. Electric League Ariz., Phoenix, 1967-68; pub. affairs adminstr. Ariz. Regional Med. program Coll. of Medicine, U. Ariz., Tucson, 1968-73; dir. community affairs Tucson Med. Ctr., 1973-82; dir. pub. rels. Good Samaritan Med. Ctr., Phoenix, 1982-85; pres. The Lew Riggs Co., Phoenix, 1985-88; chief exec. officer Tucson Osteo. Med. Found., Tucson, 1988—. Adj. prof. U. Ariz. Coll. Edn., Tucson, mem. internat. adv. bd., 1996-99, pres., 2000; cons. to hosps. and physicians in group practice nationally; presenter in field. Editor: Public Relations Handbook, 1982; co-author booklets; contbr. articles to profl. jours. Chmn. pub. rels. Nat. Arthritis Found., Atlanta, 1985-87; participant Ariz. Strategic Planning and Econ. Devel., 1991-92. Lt. col. USAFR, 1987. Recipient IABC gold quill award, Silver Anvil award Pub. Rels. Soc. Am., Golden Mike award Am. Legion Aux., MacEachern citation Acad. Hosp. Pub. Rels., Pres.'s citation Pub. Rels. Soc. Mem. Pub. Rels. Soc. Am. (trustee 1999—), Nat. Assn. Osteo. Founds. (pres. 1991-93), Student Osteo. Med. Assn. (found. bd. dirs. 1990—), Soc. Assn. Execs. (bd. dirs. 1995—), Rotary. Republican. Presbyterian. Home: 4566 E Camino De Oro Tucson AZ 85718-4475 Office: Tucson Osteo Med Found 4280 N Campbell Ave Ste 200 Tucson AZ 85718-6594 E-mail: lriggs@tomf.org.

RIGGS, LORRIN ANDREWS, psychologist, educator; b. Harput, Turkey, June 11, 1912; parents Am. citizens; s. Ernest Wilson and Alice (Shepard) R.; m. Doris Robinson, 1937 (dec.); children: Douglas Rikert, Dwight Alan; m. Caroline Cressman, 1994. AB, Dartmouth Coll., 1933; MA, Clark U., 1934, PhD, 1936; DSc, Brown U., 2001. NRC fellow biol. scis. U. Pa., 1936-37; instr. U. Vt., 1937-38, 39-41; with Brown U., 1938-39, 41—, from asst. to assoc. prof., 1938-51, prof., 1951—, L. Herbert Ballou prof., 1960-68, E.J. Marston Univ. prof., 1968-77, prof. emeritus, 1977—; Guggenheim fellow U. Cambridge, 1971-72. Author sci. articles on vision, physiol. psychology. Recipient Kenneth Craik award Cambridge U., 1979, Prentice medal Am. Acad. Optometry, 1973 Mem. AAAS (chmn., v.p. sect. 1 1964), APA (div. pres. 1962-63, Disting. Sci. Contn. award 1974), Eastern Psychol. Assn. (pres. 1975-76), Optical Soc. Am. (Tillyer medal 1969, Ives medal 1982), Nat. Acad. Scis., Am. Physiol. Soc., Internat. Brain Rsch. Orgn., Soc. for Neurosci., Soc. Exptl. Psychologists (Howard Crosby Warren medal 1957), Assn. Rsch. in Vision and Ophthalmology (pres. 1977, Friedenwald award 1966), Am. Acad. Arts and Scis., Am. Psychol. Soc. (William James fellow 1989), Sigma Xi (chpt. pres. 1962-64). Home: Kendal at Hanover # 104 80 Lyme Rd Hanover NH 03755-1225 Personal E-mail: clriggs@bigplanet.com.

RIGGS, LOUIS, lawyer, columnist; s. Ronald and Louise Riggs; m. Anne Jameson, Aug. 15, 1987; children: Meredith, Thomas. BA, Westminster Coll., 1983; JD, U. Mo., 1990. Mng. ptnr. Dempsey, Dempsey, Riggs & Moellring, P.C., Hannibal, Mo., 1995—2003; owner RPGS, Inc., 1997—; on-air host KHBL-FM; online columnist louisriggs.com, 2002—; atty. pvt. practice, 2003—; on-air host KHMO-AM, Hannibal, Mo., 2003—. Author: (history) 50th Anniversary History of Missouri Boys' State. Pres. Missourians Against Methamphetamines, Hannibal, 2003—04; 6th ward committeeman Marion County Rep. Ctrl. Com., 2004—04; chair, endowment com. Holy Family Parent & Sch. Orgn., 2003—04; adv. Hannibal Area C. of C., 2003—04, Hannibal Nutrition Ctr., 2003—04; v.p. Hannibal Main St. Program, 1995—98; chmn. Hannibal Nutrition Ctr., 1991—92; secretary-treasurer 10th Jud. Circuit Bar Assn., 1990—91. Recipient Peoples Choice award, Favorite Columnist, Hannibal Courier-Post, 2001, 2002. Mem.: Adams County Bar Assn., 10th Jud. Circuit Bar Assn., Ill. State Bar Assn., Mo. Bar Assn., Hannibal Rotary Club. Conservative. Baptist. Avocations: family outings, writing, running, reading. Home: 308 Magnolia Avenue Hannibal MO 63401 Office: Louis Riggs LLC 201 North 3rd Street Suite 205 Hannibal MO 63401

RIGGS, MICHAEL DAVID, writer, editor; b. Frankfort, Ky., Apr. 30, 1951; s. Homer David and Helen Marion (Webber) R.; m. Elizabeth Susan Borman, Apr. 24, 1983; children: David B., William B. AB, Washington U., 1973. Chief trader Thomte & Co., Boston, 1975-77; tech. writer Saddlebrook Corp., Cambridge, Mass., 1977-79; assoc. editor Mini-Micro Systems Mag., Boston, 1979-80; editor High Fidelity Mag., N.Y.C., 1980-89; exec. editor Stereo Review Mag., N.Y.C., 1989-95; editor-in-chief Audio Mag., N.Y.C., 1995-2000; ind. technology writer, editor, cons. Westfield, N.J., 2000—. Author: Understanding Audio and Video, 1989; sr. contbg. editor: Sound and Vision Mag., 2001—04, sr. editor:, 2004—. Mem. Audio Engrng. Soc., Boston Audio Soc. E-mail: michael@riggsnet.com.

RIGGS, R. WILLIAM, judge; Grad., Portland State U., 1961; JD, U. Oreg., 1968. Atty. Willner Bennett & Leonard, 1968—78; judge circuit ct. 4th Jud. Dist., 1978—88; judge Oreg. Ct. of Appeals, 1988—98, Oreg. Supreme Ct., 1998—. Active mem. Cmty. Law Project; founder Integra Corp. Capt. USNR. Office: Supreme Ct Bldg 1163 State St Salem OR 97310-0260 E-mail: r.william.riggs@ojd.state.or.us.

RIGGS, ROBERT DALE, plant pathology and nematology educator, researcher; b. Pocahontas, Ark., June 15, 1932; s. Rosa MacDowell and Grace (Million) R.; m. Jennie Lee Willis, June 6, 1954; children: Rebecca Dawn, Deborah Lee, Robert Dale Jr., James Michael. BS in Agr., U. Ark., 1954, MS in Plant Pathology, 1956; PhD in Plant Pathology, N.C. State U., 1958. Grad. asst. U. Ark., Fayetteville, 1954—55, asst. prof., 1958—62, assoc. prof., 1962—68, prof., 1968—92, 1992—; grad. asst. N.C. State U., Raleigh, 1955—58. Chair of faculty Coll. Agrl., Food and Life Scis., 1999. Editor: Nematology in the Southern United States, 1982; co-editor: Biology and Management of the Soybean Cyst Nematode, 1992; contbr. articles to profl. jours.; inventor fungal control of nematodes. Recipient John W. White award Coll. Agr. and Home Econs., 1989, Honor award for Rsch. in Environ. Protection USDA, 1994, Outstanding Rschr. award Ark. Agrl. Extension Specialists, 2000, Spitze Land Grant Univ. Faculty award, 2001, Meritorious Svc. award United Soybean Bd., 2002. Fellow Soc. of Nematologists (v.p. 1991-92, pres.-elect 1992-93, pres. 1993-94, editor-in-chief jour. 1987-90), Am. Phytopath. Soc. (Outstanding plant pathologist in so. region 1994); mem. So. Soybean Disease Workers (Disting. Svc. award 1987), U. Ark. Alumni Assn. (Dist. Faculty Achievement award 1993), Orgn. of Nematologists of Tropical Am., Sigma Xi, Gamma Sigma Delta. Democrat. Baptist. Home: 1840 Woolsey Ave Fayetteville AR 72703-2557 Office: U Ark 217 Plant Sci Fayetteville AR 72701 E-mail: rdriggs@mail.uark.edu.

RIGGS, RORY B. pharmaceutical executive; b. Orange, N.J., May 5, 1953; d. Thomas Jeffries and Virginia (Griggs) R. BA, Middlebury Coll.; MBA, Columbia U. Mng. dir. PaineWebber, Inc.; CEO RF&P Corp.; mng. dir. Pharma Ptnrs. LLC; pres. Biomatrix Inc., Ridgefield, N.J., 1995—. Bd. dirs. Biomatrix, Inc. 1990—; bd. mem. Fibrogen Corp., Spartan Corp., Pharma Ptnrs, LLC. Mem. Young Pres. Orgn. Office: Biomatrix Inc 65 Railroad Ave Ste 3 Ridgefield NJ 07657-2176

RIGGS, SCOTT, race car driver; Racecar driver PPC Racing. Named champion, So. Nat. Speedway; recipient 5th pl., NASCAR Craftsman Truck Series, 2001. Office: PPC Racing Team 177 Knob Hill Rd Mooresville NC 28117

RIGGS, SONYA WOICINSKI, elementary school educator; b. Newhall, Calif., Oct. 9, 1935; d. Jack Lewis Woicinski and Mittie Mozelle (Bennett) Gillett; m. Eugene Garland Riggs, Dec. 21, 1956; children: Georgia Ann, Madeline Sue, Dana Eugene. BS in Elem. Edn., U. Tex., 1970; MEd in Reading Edn., S.W. Tex. State U., 1980. Cert. elem. tchr., Tex.; cert. reading specialist K-12. Sec. state govts., Nebr./Tex., 1955-57; piano instr. Elgin, Tex., 1961-66; tchr. 1st grade Elgin Elem. Sch., Elgin, 1967-69, tchr. Music 3rd/4th grades, 1971-72, tchr. 4th grade, 1972-73; pres. El Tesoro internacionale, 1973-74; sec. region office Planned Parenthood/World Population, Austin, 1975-76; tchr. 8th-12th grades Giddings (Tex.) State Sch., 1976-78; tchr. 4th/5th grades Thorndale (Tex.) Ind. Sch. Dist., 1979-80; tchr. remedial reading Brazosport Ind. Sch. Dist., Freeport, Tex., 1980-81; tchr. 6th grade reading and chpt. I Bastrop (Tex.) Mid. Sch., 1981-94, Bastrop Intermediate, 1994-99. Developer Enrichment Ctr., Bastrop Intermediate, 1995—2000, Cedar Creek Elem. Enrichment, 2000—01; mem. 12th ann. Highlights Found. Writers Workshop at Chautauqua Instn., NY, 1996; adj. instr. reading Austin C.C., 2000—; Level III master Reiki practitioner, animal communicator; puppy cons. Contbr. articles to Shih Tzu Reporter, 1993 French Bulldog Ann., French Bullytin, Boston Quar., Golden Retriever World, Frenchie Forum 2003; contbr. poetry to anthologies Garden of Life, 1996, Best Poems of 1996, Of Sunshine and Daydreams, 1996, A View from Afar, 1997. Mem. Elgin Band Boosters, 1970-83, sec., 1976. Mem. Assn. Tex. Profl. Educators (campus rep. 1996-97, state del. 1997, sec. 1997-98), Austin Kennel Club (bd. dirs. 1990-91, 95-97, sec. 1996-97, v.p. 2003—), Am. Shih Tzu Club (edn. and rescue com. mem. south ctrl. regional hearing com.), French Bulldog Club Am. (rescue com.), Mission City Ring Stewards Assn., Internat. Soc. Poets, Tex. Writers League, Greater Austin Doberman Pinscher Club. Avocations: exhibiting dogs to Am. Kennel Club confirmation and obedience championships, poetry, playing piano, painting, drawing.

RIGGS, SUSAN DUNNAGAN, music educator, musician; b. Winston Salem, NC, Feb. 19, 1962; d. Phillip Arvin and Barbara Moorefield Dunnagan. BA in Psychology, U. of N.C. at Greensboro, 1980—84, MusB in Piano Performance, 1990—94. Contract musician Musician's Booking Agy., Raleigh, NC, 1998—; composer, musician Silent Resonance Band, Raleigh, 2000—; tchr. Raleigh Music Acad., NC, 2002—; self employed musician The Triangle area. Composer (singer, artist, musician): (music cd) Dream Come True, Classical Lunacy. Mem.: Raleigh Music Teacher's Assn., Music Teacher's Nat. Assn., Am. Modeler's Assn. Democrat. Home: 104 Bridle Trail Youngsville NC 27596 Office: Riggsmusic PO Box 658 Youngsville NC 27596 Office Phone: 919-556-0218. E-mail: susan@riggsmusic.com.

RIGGSBY, DUTCHIE SELLERS, education educator; b. Montgomery, Ala., Oct. 26, 1940; d. Malcolm Sellers and Marcelia Sellers Dickman; m. Ernest Duward Riggsby, Aug. 25, 1962; 1 child, Lyn. BS, Troy (Ala.) State Coll., 1962, MS, 1965; postgrad., George Peabody Coll., 1963; EdD, Auburn U., 1972. Cert. tchr., Ala., Ga.; cert. libr., Ga. Tchr. Montgomery Pub. Schs., 1962-63, Troy City Schs., 1963-67; instr. Auburn (Ala.) U., 1968-69; asst. prof. Columbus (Ga.) Coll., 1972-77, assoc. prof., 1978-83, prof., 1983—; coord. Instrnl. Tech. Sch. Edn., 1996-97; program coord. Ednl. Founds., 2001—. Vis. prof. U. P.R., Rio Piedras, 1972—73; leader various workshops, 1989, 1993—; sorfware reviewer NSTA; chmn. publicity Ga. Ednl. Tech. Conf., 1997—, bd. dirs., 1998—; bridal cons. Hist. Moments, Inc., 1998—2001, v.p., 1998—2001; chair scholarship com. Ga. Ednl. Consortium, 1999—. Contbr. more than 90 articles on state, regional, nat., and internat. programs to profl. jours., 1968—. Active Internal Aerospace Edn. CAP, Maxwell AFB, 1980-90; dir. Air and Space Camp for Kids, 1990-98. Recipient STAR Tchr. award NSTA, 1968; named to Lee H.S. Hall of Fame, Montgomery, 1997. Mem. Assn. for Ednl. Comms. and Tech. (non-periodical publs. com. 1994-99, awards com. 1994-96, chair meml. awards com. 1996-99), Nat. Congress on Aviation and Space Edn. (dir. spl. promotions 1986-90), World Aerospace Edn. Orgn. (v.p. for the Ams. 1996-98, pres. for the Ams. 1998—, pres. 1999—), Ga. Assn. Instrnl. Tech. (bd. dirs. 1982-84), Phi Delta Kappa (pres. Chattahochee Valley chpt. 1986-87, Svc. award 1989, Svc. Key award 1993). Baptist. Avocations: photography, mining for gemstones. Office: Columbus State U Coll Edn 4225 University Ave Columbus GA 31907-5679 Office Phone: 706-565-7802.

RIGGSBY, ERNEST DUWARD, science educator, educational consultant; b. Nashville, June 12, 1925; s. James Thomas and Anna Pearl (Turner) Riggsby; m. Dutchie Sellers Riggsby, Aug. 25, 1964; 1 child, Lyn-Dee. BS, Tenn. Polytech. Inst., 1948; BA, George Peabody Coll. Tchrs., 1952, BA, 1953, MA, 1956, EdS, 1961, EdD, 1964. Vis. grad. prof. U. P.R., Rio Piedras, George Peabody Coll., 1963-64; prof. Auburn (Ala.) U., Troy (Ala.) State U., Columbus (Ga.) Coll.; pres. Ednl. Developers, Inc., Columbus. Vis. grad. prof. George Peabody Coll., 1963—64; vis. lectr. Fla. Inst. Tech., 1967—77. Contbr. articles to profl. jours. Col. USAF, 1944—85. Named to Aerospace Edn. Hall of Fame, 1982. Fellow: AAAS; mem.: World Aerospace Edn. Assn. (v.p. for Ams.), Nat. Sci. Tchrs. Assn. Office: Columbus State U Columbus GA 31907-5645

RIGHTER, DALE A. state senator; b. Mattoon, Ill., Aug. 23, 1966; m. Teresa Righter; children: Jonathan, Benjamin. BA, Eastern Ill. Univ., 1988; JD, St. Louis Univ. Sch. of Law, 1991. State Senator US Senate, Dist. 55, Ill., 2002—; Counsel Atty. Komada & Geisler Atty. of Law, 1997—; pros. atty. State Appellate Prosecutors Office, Ill., 1992—97. Rep. House of Rep., Dist. 106, Ill., 1997—2002; committeeman Rep. precinct, Celes County, Ill., 1997—; mem. Fin. Inst. Comm.; spokesperson Health & Human Svc., trans. Mem.: Mattoon Ducks Unlimited, 1992-present, Elks Club, 1992-present, Exch. Club of Mattoon, 1992-present, CHOICE of Mattoon, 1992-present. Republican. Christian. Office: Capitol M103E Capitol Bldg Springfield IL 62706 Home and Office: Dist 105 North Tenth St Mattoon IL 61938

RIGHTER, WALTER CAMERON, bishop; b. Phila., Oct. 23, 1923; s. Richard and Dorothy Mae (Bottomley) R.; m. Nancy Ruth DeGroot, Aug. 22, 1992; children: Richard, Rebecca. BA, U. Pitts., 1948; MDiv, Berkeley Div. Sch., New Haven, 1951, DD, 1972; DCL, Iowa Wesleyan U., 1982; DD, Seabury Western Sem., 1984. Ordained priest Episcopal Ch., 1951, consecrated bishop, 1972; lay missioner St. Michael's Ch., Rector, Pa., 1947-48; priest-in-charge All Saints Ch., Aliquippa, Pa., 1951-54, St. Luke's, Georgetown, Pa., 1952-54; rector Ch. of Good Shepherd, Nashua, N.H., 1954-71; bishop Diocese of Iowa, Des Moines, 1972-89; asst. bishop Dio. of Newark, 1989-91; interim rector St. Elizabeth's, Ridgewood, N.J., 1991; assisting bishop Diocese of Mass., 2000—. Mem. exec. coun. Protestant Episcopal Ch. U.S.A., 1979-85; spl. adv. NH Cursillo, 1994-96; interim rector Emmanuel, Rockford, Ill., 1989. Author: A Pilgrim's Way, 1998. Mem. N.H. com. White House Conf. on Youth, 1962, Regional Crime Commn., Hillsboro County, N.H., 1969-71; trustee Nashua Libr., 1968-71, Seabury Western Sem., 1986-89; founding trustee The Morris Fund, Des Moines; planning com. Town of Alstead, N.H., 1993-96. Fellow Coll. Preachers, Washington Cathedral. Episcopalian. E-mail: Walter.Righter@verizon.com.

RIGHTS, GRAHAM HENRY, retired minister; b. Winston-Salem, N.C., Jan. 14, 1935; s. Douglas LeTell and Cecil Leona (Burton) R.; m. Sybil Critz Strupe, Sept. 7, 1963; children: Susan Elizabeth, John Graham. BA, U. N.C., 1956; BD, Yale U., 1959; postgrad., Moravian Theol. Sem., 1959-60, DHL (hon.), 1997; postgrad., U. Edinburgh, Scotland, 1965-66; DD (hon.), Wofford Coll., 1989. Ordained to ministry Moravian Ch., 1960. Pastor Union Ch., Managua, Nicaragua, 1960-63, Managua Moravian Ch., 1960-65, Mayodan (N.C.) Moravian Ch., 1966-72, Messiah Moravian Ch., Winston-Salem, 1972-81; exec. dir. Bd. World Mission Moravian Ch., Bethlehem, Pa., 1981-83, pres. exec. bd. so. province Winston-Salem, 1983-95, pres. exec. bd. world-wide, 1991-94; pastor First Moravian Ch., Greensboro, N.C., 1995-

2000; ret. Bd. dirs. Crisis Control Ministry, Forsyth County, 1976-, Ecumenical Inst., 1995-, Moravian Music Found., 1996-. Mem. N.C. Soc. Mayflower Descendants (elder 2000—). Mem. Moravian Ch. Home: 553 Steeple View Ct Winston Salem NC 27101-5850

RIGNEY, JAMES OLIVER, JR., (ROBERT JORDAN, CHANG LUNG, REAGAN O'NEAL, JACKSON O'REILLY), writer; b. Charleston, S.C., Oct. 17, 1948; s. James Oliver and Eva May (Grooms) Rigney; m. Harriet Stoney Popham, Mar. 28, 1981; 1 child, William Popham McDougal. BS, The Citadel, 1974. Nuc. engr. U.S. Civil Svc., 1974—78. Author: Conan the Invincible, 1982, Conan the Defender, 1982, Conan the Triumphant, 1983, Conana the Unconquered, 1983, Conana the Destroyer, 1984, Conana the Magnificent, 1984, Conan the Victorious, 1985, The Eye of the World, 1990, The Great Hunt, 1990, The Dragon Reborn, 1991, The Shadow Rising, 1992, The Fires of Heaven, 1993, Lord of Chaos, 1994, A Crown of Swords, 1996, The Path of Daggars, 1998, Winter's Heart, 2000, Crossroads of Twighlight, 2003, New Spring, 2004. Office: Elena Stokes Dir Publicity Tor Books 175 5th Ave New York NY 10010*

RIGNEY, JANE, copy editor, writer; b. Flushing, N.Y., Dec. 4, 1948; d. William John and Janet (Teesink) R. BA in English, U. Ill., 1972. Dance critic, night copy desk chief N.Y. Tribune, N.Y.C., 1983—85; copy editor TIME Mag., N.Y.C., 1988—. Pub. rels. cons. The Juilliard Sch., N.Y.C., 1977-82; freelance writer Dance Mag., 1982—, Am. Banker, 1988-95, freelance copy editor, 1988-95, N.Y. Daily News, N.Y.C., 1984-90; freelance editor, writer Am. Health, N.Y.C., 1990-93. Editor: Dance Horizons, 1978-85. Freedom writer Amnesty Internat., N.Y.C., 1980—; vol. spl. projects Sch. Am. Ballet, N.Y.C., 1988—. Mem.: N.Y. Deadline Club, NY Press Club, Editl. Freelancers Assn., The Newspaper Guild, Women in Comm., U. Ill. Alumni Club NY. Democrat. Roman Catholic. Avocations: swimming, crocheting, reading, travel, theater. Office: TIME Mag Time & Life Bldg 1271 Ave of Americas New York NY 10020 E-mail: jane_rigney@timemagazine.com.

RIGOLOSI, ELAINE LA MONICA, lawyer, educator, consultant; b. Astoria, N.Y., Oct. 12, 1944; d. Richard Anthony La Monica and Caroline La Monica; m. Robert Salvatore Rigolosi, June 15, 1997. BS, Columbia Union Coll., Takoma Park, Md., 1964; MN, U. Fla., 1967; EdD, U. Mass., 1975; JD, Benjamin N. Cardozo Sch. Law, N.Y.C., 1993. Bar: N.J. 1994, N.Y. 1994, D.C. 1995; RN, N.Y. Chair dept. nursing edn. Tchrs. Coll., Columbia U., N.Y.C., 1988-91, prof. nursing edn., 1982-96, acting chair dept. nursing edn., 1994-96, prof. dept. orgn. and leadership, 1996—, dir. Inst. Rsch. in Nursing, 1981—; health care mgmt. cons. in pvt. practice, N.Y.C., 1974—. Bd. dirs. Hooper Holmes, Inc., Basking Ridge, N.J., 1989—; cons. Delaware Valley Transplant Program, Phila., 1998, U. Tenn. Coll. Pharmacy, Memphis, 1995-98. Author: The Nursing Process: A Humanistic Approach, 1979 (Am. Jour. Nursing Book of Yr. 1979), Management in Health Care, 1994. Dept. HHS grantee, 1977-80, 80-83. Fellow Am. Acad. Nursing; mem. ABA, Assn. Bar City N.Y. (com. on health law 1994-97), Am. Health Lawyers Assn., Am. Assn. Nurse Attys., Am. Coll. Legal Medicine, Sigma Theta Tau. Avocations: tennis, skiing, needlepoint, interior design. Home: 158 Summit Dr Paramus NJ 07652-1312 Office: Tchrs Coll Columbia U 525 W 120th St New York NY 10027-6625

RIGOLOT, FRANÇOIS, French literature educator, literary critic; b. Chateau-du-Loir, Sarthe, France, May 21, 1939; s. Paul and Madeleine (Overnoy) R.; m. Carol Nolan, Sept. 5, 1970; children— Sophie, Stephanie. Diplôme, Hautes Etudes Commerciales, Paris, 1961; MA in Econs., Northwestern U., 1963; PhD in French, U. Wis.-Madison, 1969. Asst. prof. U. Mich, Ann Arbor, 1969-74; bicentennial preceptor Princeton U., N.J., 1974-77, assoc. prof. dept. romance langs. and lits., 1977-79, prof., 1979-81, Meredith Howland Pyne prof. French lit., chmn. dept., 1984-91, 96-99, 2001—02, chair Renaissance studies, 1993—2004. Prof. French Middlebury (Vt.) Coll., 1973; dir. NEH seminar for coll. tchrs., Princeton, 1981, 84, 86, 88, 90; vis. prof. Johns Hopkins U., 1981; vis. mem. Inst. for Advanced Study, Princeton, 1982-83, 1999-2000; dir. seminar The Folger Inst., Washington, 1987; prof. Inst. d'Etudes Françaises, Avignon, 1989, 95; ofcl. lectr. Alliance Française, 1994-95. Author: Les Langages de Rabelais, 1972, reprint, 1996, Poétique et Onomastique, 1977, Le Texte de la Renaissance, 1982 (Gilbert Chinard Lit. prize 1984), Les Métamorphoses de Montaigne, 1988, Louise Labé ou La Renaissance au féminin, 1997; editor: Complete Works of Louise Labé, 1986, Jour. de Voyage of Montaigne, 1992, Sainte-Beuve, Causeries sur Montaigne, 2003; co-editor: A New History of French Literature, 1989 (MLA James Russell Lowell prize 1990), De la Littérature Française, 1993; collaborator: Sémantique de La Poèsie, 1979, L'Erreur de la Renaissance, 2002, Poesie et Renaissance, 2003. Decorated officier des Palmes Academiques, chevalier Nat. Order of Merit (France); recipient Médaille de la ville de Bordeaux, Médaille de la ville de Tours, 1992, Howard T. Behrman award for Disting. Achievement in the Humanities, 1993; NEH fellow, 1979-80, Guggenheim Found. fellow, 1982-83. Mem. Acad. Literary Studies, Am. Assn. Tchrs. French, Renaissance Soc. Am., MLA, Assn. Internat. des Etudes Françaises. Home: 13 Constitution Hill Princeton NJ 08540 Office: Princeton U East Pyne Dept French and Italian Princeton NJ 08544-5264 E-mail: rigolot@princeton.edu.

RIGSBEE, DAVID E. poet, educator; b. Durham, NC, Apr. 1, 1949; s. Earl Hickman and Geneva (Odom) R.; m. Doris Francine Low, Oct. 7, 1978 (div. July 1984); m. Jill Bullitt, July 28, 1995; 1 child, Makaiya. BA, U. N.C., Chapel Hill, 1971; MA, Johns Hopkins U., 1972, Hollins Coll., 1991; PhD, U. Va., 1995. English instr. Hamilton Coll., Clinton, NY, 1972-76, U. NC, Greensboro, NC, 1978-82, La. State U., Baton Rouge, 1982-86, Va. Tech., Blacksburg, 1987-92; prof. English, chair dept. lang. and lit. Mt. Olive Coll., NC, 1995—. Vis. assoc. prof. St. Andrews Coll., Laurinburg, N.C., 1986-87; vis. prof., dir. creative writing Hamilton Coll., Clinton, N.Y., 1992-95; dir. St. Andrews Press, Laurinburg, 1986-87; cons. Ardis Pubs., Ann Arbor, Mich., 1974-77. Author: (poetry) A Skeptic's Notebook: Longer Poems, 1997, Scenes on an Obelisk, 2000, Greatest Hits: 1975-2000; The Disolving Island, 2003, Sonnets to Hamlet, 2004; co-editor: Invited Guest: An Anthology of Twentieth Century So. Poetry, 2001; (criticism) Styles of Ruin: Joseph Brodsky and the Postmodernist Elegy, 1999, (nonfiction) Trailers, 1996. Fellow NEH, 1999, creative Writing fellow NEA, 1985, Artist's fellow Va. Commn. on the Arts, 1993; Am. Acad. in Rome vis. fellow, 1999; recipient prize Acad. Am. Poets, 1992, Vachel Lindsey Poetry prize Willow Springs Lit. mag., 1994. Mem. MLA, Poetry Soc. Am. Democrat. Episcopalian. Avocations: opera, art, photography. Home: 315 Oakwood Ave Raleigh NC 27601-1062 Office: Mount Olive Coll 634 Henderson St Mount Olive NC 28365-1263

RIGSBY, LINDA FLORY, lawyer; b. Topeka, Kans., Dec. 16, 1946; d. Alden E. and Lolita M. Flory; m. Michael L. Rigsby, Aug. 14, 1963; children: Michael L. Jr., Elisabeth A. MusB, Va. Commonwealth U., 1969; JD, U. Richmond, 1981. Bar: Va. 1981, D.C. 1988. Assoc. McGuire, Woods, Battle & Boothe, Richmond, Va., 1981-85; dep. gen. counsel and corp. sec. Crestar Fin. Corp., Richmond, 1985-99, gen. counsel, 1999-2000; mng. atty. Sun Trust Banks Inc., 2000—. Recipient Disting. Svc. award U. Richmond, 1987; named Vol. of Yr. U. Richmond, 1986, Woman of Achievement, Met. Richmond Women's Bar, 1995. Mem. Va. Bar Assn. (exec. com. 1993-96), Richmond Bar Assn. (bd. dirs. 1992-95), Va. Bankers Assn. (chair legal affairs 1992-95), U. Richmond Estate Planning Coun. (chmn. 1990-92). Roman Catholic. Avocations: music, gardening. Home: 163 W Square Pl Richmond VA 23233-6157 Office: SunTrust Bank 919 E Main St Richmond VA 23219-4625

RIGTRUP, KENNETH, state judge, arbitrator, mediator; b. Burley, Idaho, Mar. 13, 1936; s. Robert Peter and Bessie Viola (Price) R.; m. Susanne Joan Remund, May 15, 1964; children: Mark Robert, Michael James, Scott Kenneth, Melissa Ann, Jennifer Marie. BS in Acctg., U. Utah, 1960, JD, 1962. Bar: Utah 1962; U.S. Dist. Ct. Utah, 1962. Clk. Utah Supreme Ct., Salt Lake City, 1962; ptnr. Rigtrup & Hadley, Salt Lake City, 1962-68; pvt. practice, Salt Lake City, 1968-72, admin. law judge Indsl. Commn., Salt Lake City, 1972-77; mem. Pub. Svc. Commn., Salt Lake City, 1977-80; judge 3d Dist. Ct., Salt Lake City, 1980-97; active sr. judge Utah Cts., Salt Lake City, 1997—. Chmn. Bd. Sr. Judges, 1998-99; mem. adv. com. on rules of juvenile procedure Utah Supreme Ct., Salt Lake City, 1993-95. Copy and rsch. editor Utah Law Rev., 1961-62. Chmn. Utah White House Conf. on Handicapped Individuals, Salt Lake City, 1976—77; mem. Citizens Evaluation and Selection Com. to Rev. Pvt. Non-profit Orgn. Applications for Urban Mass Transit Authority Grants, 1975—77; dir., chair Utah Assistive Tech. Found., 1991—; mem. Utah Gov.'s Com. on Employment of Handicapped, 1976—80, vice chmn. and acting chmn., 1977—80. Recipient Disting. Svc. award Utah Rehab. Counseling Assn., Salt Lake City, 1976-77; Nat. Citation award Nat. Rehab. counseling Assn., 1977; Maurice Warshaw Golden Key award, Utah Gov.'s Com. on Employment of Handicapped, 1975. Mem. ABA, ATLA, Utah Bar Assn. (exec. com. family sect. 1980-90, lawyers helping lawyers com., alt. dispute resolution com.), Nat. Ass. Regulatory Utility Commns. (water com. 1977-78, gas com. 1978-80), Am. Judicature Soc., Utah Coun. on Conflicts Resolution. Republican. Mem. Lds Ch. Home: 1961 Millbrook Rd Salt Lake City UT 84106-3853 Office: Arbitration/Mediation Svcs 3098 Highland Dr Ste 399 Salt Lake City UT 84106-6004

RIIS, THOMAS LAURENCE, music educator; b. Concord, N.H., Oct. 6, 1950; s. Laurence Johannes and Ruth (Norquist) Riis. BA, Oberlin Coll., Ohio, 1973; MA, U. Mich., 1976, PhD, 1981. Instr. U. Mich., Interlochen, 1980—81, 1988; asst. prof. U. Ga., Athens, 1981—87, assoc. prof., 1987—92; prof. music U. Colo., Boulder, 1992—, Joseph Negler Endowed Chair in music, 2002—. Sr. fellow, vis. prof. Bklyn. Coll./CUNY, 1987; Endowed chair music U. Ala., Tuscaloosa, 1997; disting. vis. prof. Colo. Coll., Colorado Springs, 2001; dir. Am. Music Rsch. Ctr., Boulder, 1992—; guest choir dir. First Congl. Ch., Boulder and Erfurt, Germany, 1996—97; co-founder Renaissance choir Voix Fortes Claires, Athens, Ga., 1986. Author: (book) Just Before Jazz, 1989 (ASCAP Deems Taylor award 1995), The Music and Scripts of In Dahomey; editor-in-chief Am. Music Rsch. Ctr. Jour., 1993—. Resource counselor Boulder County AIDS Project, Boulder, 1997—. Mem.: Soc. for Am. Music (bd. trustees 1978—80), Am. Musicol. Soc. United Ch. Of Christ. Avocations: bicycling, hiking. Office: Univ of Colorado-Boulder 301 UCB Boulder CO 80309

RIKER, WILLIAM KAY, pharmacologist, educator; b. N.Y.C., Aug. 31, 1925; s. Walter Franklin and Eleanore Louise (Scafard) R.; m. Carmela Louise DePamphilis, Dec. 21, 1947 (dec. 1981); children: Eleanor Louise, Gainor, Victoria; m. Leena Mela, Aug. 13, 1983. BA, Columbia U., 1949; MD, Cornell U., 1953. Intern 2d Cornell med. div., Bellevue Hosp., 1953-54; practice medicine, specializing in pharmacology Phila., 1954-69, Portland, Oreg., 1969—. Instr., asst. prof. dept. pharmacology U. Pa. Sch. Medicine, 1954-61; spl. fellow dept. physiology U. Utah Sch. Medicine, 1961-64; assoc. prof., prof., chmn. dept. pharmacology Woman's Med. Coll., Phila., 1964-69; prof., chmn. dept. pharmacology U. Oreg. Sch. Medicine, U. Oreg. Health Scis. Center, 1969-91, prof., 1991-98, prof. emeritus, 1998—, asst. dean. for admissions, 1986-89; mem. neurol. disorders program project com. NIH, 1975-79. Editor: Jour. Pharmacology and Exptl. Therapeutics, 1969-72; contbr. articles to biomed. jours. Served with USNR, 1943-46. Recipient Christian R. and Mary F. Lindback Found. award for disting. teaching, 1968; Pa. Plan scholar, 1957-61; Nat. Inst. Neurol. Diseases and Blindness spl. fellow, 1961-64; USPHS-NIH research grantee, 1958-83 Mem. Am. Soc. Pharmacology and Exptl. Therapeutics (sec.-treas. 1978-81, pres. 1985-86), Western Pharmacol. Soc. (pres. 1976), Japanese Pharmacol. Soc., Assn. Med. Sch. Pharmacologists (sec. 1976-78), Epilepsy Assn. Am., Pharm. Mfrs. Assn. Found. (chmn. pharmacology-morphology adv. com., sci. adv. com. 1976-92), Cosmos Club. E-mail: bileena@SpiritOne.com.

RIKLI, DONALD CARL, lawyer; b. Highland, Ill., June 16, 1927; s. Carl and Gertrude Louise (Stoecklin) R.; m. Joan Tate, Oct. 10, 1953; children: Kristine, David. AB, Ill. Coll., 1951; JD, U. Ill., 1953. Bar: Ill. 1953, U.S. Dist. Ct. (so. dist.) Ill. 1961, U.S. Ct. Appeals (7th cir.) 1968, U.S. Supreme Ct. 1974. Pvt. practice law, Highland, 1953-97. Atty. City of Highland, 1956-59; lectr. in field. Author: The Illinois Probate System, 1974, 75, 77, 78; bd. editors Illinois Real Property I, 1966, 71, Lawyers World, 1970-72, Law Notes, 1981-83, The Compleat Lawyer, 1985-87; contbr. over 60 articles to profl. jours. Mem. consistory United Ch. of Christ, 1960-62, 93-95. With U.S. Army, 1945-47. Fellow Am. Coll. Trust and Estate Counsel, Ill. Bar Found., Am. Bar Found.; mem. ABA (sec. chairperson gen. practice sect. 1990-91, Ho. of Dels. 1991-93, mem. coun. gen. practice sect. 1981-93, Sole Practitioner of Yr. 1990, posthumous Donald C. Rikli Solo Lifetime Achievement award gen. practice, solo practice and small firms sect.), Ill. Bar Assn. (chmn. Bill of Rights com. 1967-68, coun. estate planning probate and trust sect. 1976-81, sec. 1980-81), Madison County Bar Assn. (pres. 1966-67), Am. Acad. Estate Planning Attys. (bd. govs. 1994-95). Address: PO Box 366 Edwardsville IL 62025-0366

RIKLIS, MESHULAM, manufacturing and retail executive; b. Turkey, Dec. 2, 1923; came to U.S., 1947, naturalized, 1955; s. Pinhas and Betty (Guberer) R.; children: Simona Riklis Ackerman, Marcia Riklis Hirschfeld, Ira Doron, Kady Zadora Riklis, Kristofer Riklis. Student, U. Mexico, 1947; BA, Ohio State U., 1950, MBA, 1968. Co-dir. youth activities and mil. tng. Hertzlia High Sch., Tel-Aviv, 1942; tchr. Hebrew Talmud Torah Sch., Mpls., 1951; research dept. Piper, Jaffray & Hopwood, 1951-53, sales rep., 1953-56; vice chmn. McCrory Corp., N.Y.C., 1960-69, vice chmn. exec. com., from 1970, chmn., 1975-85, dir., former pres.; with Rapid-Am. Corp., N.Y.C., 1956—, chmn., 1956—, pres., chief exec. officer, 1957-73, chmn., chief exec. officer, 1973-76, chmn., pres., chief exec. officer, 1976—; E-II Holdins, 1988-90. Served Brit. 8th Army, 1942-46. Mem. Pi Mu Epsilon. Jewish.

RIKON, MICHAEL, lawyer; b. Bklyn., Feb. 2, 1945; s. Charles and Ruth (Shapiro) R.; m. Leslie Sharon Rein, Feb. 11, 1968; children: Carrie Rachel, Joshua Howard. BS, NY Inst. Tech., 1966; JD, Bklyn. Law Sch., 1969; LLM, NYU, 1974. Bar: NY 1970, U.S. Dist. Ct. (so. and ea. dists.) NY 1971, U.S. Ct. Appeals (2d cir.) 1972, U.S. Supreme Ct. 1973, U.S. Ct. Appeals (5th and 11th cirs.) 1981. Asst. corp. counsel City of NY, 1969-73; law clk. NY State Ct. Claims, 1973-80; ptnr. Rudick and rikon, P.C., NYC, 1980-88; pvt. practice NYC, 1988-94; ptnr. Goldstein, Goldstein and Rikon, P.C., NYC, 1994—. Contbr. articles to profl. jours. Pres. Village Greens Residents Assn., 1978-79; chmn. bd. Arden Heights Jewish Ctr., S.I., NY, 1976-77; pres. North Shore Rep. Club., 1977; mem. cmty. bd. S.I. Borough Pres., 1977. Fellow Am. Bar Found.; mem. ABA (chair com. Condemnation) NY State Bar Assn. (spl. com. of condemnation law), Suffolk County Bar Assn., NY County lawyers Assn. (chair condemnation com.), Assn. Bar City of NY (condemnation com.), Mt. Vernon Bar Assn., Owners Counsel Am. (dir.). Republican. Jewish. Avocations: collecting stamps, photography, collecting miniature soldiers. Home: 133 Avondale Rd Ridgewood NJ 07450-1301 Office: 80 Pine St New York NY 10005-1702 Office Phone: 212-422-4000.

RIKOSKI, RICHARD ANTHONY, engineering executive, electrical engineer; b. Kingston, Pa., Aug. 13, 1941; s. Stanley George and Nellie (Gober) R.; m. Giannina Batchelor Petrullo, Dec. 18, 1971 (div. 1979); children: Richard James, Jennifer Anne; m. Carol Westbrook. BEE, U. Detroit, 1964; MSEE, Carnegie Inst. Tech., 1965; PhD, Carnegie-Mellon U., 1968; postdoctoral fellow, Case-Western Res. U./NASA, 1971. Registered profl. engr., Ill., Mass., Pa. Engr. 1st communication satellite systems Internat. Tel. & Tel., Nutley, N.J., 1961-64; engr. Titan II ICBM program Gen. Motors, Milw., 1964; trainee NASA, 1964-67; instr. Carnegie-Mellon U., Pitts., 1966-68; asst. prof. U. Pa., Phila., 1968-74; assoc. prof., dir. hybrid microelectronics lab., chmn. ednl. TV com. IIT, Chgo., 1974-80, chmn. ednl. TV com., 1974-80; rsch. engr. nuclear effects IIT Rsch. Inst., Chgo., 1974-75; pres. Tech. Analysis Corp., Chgo., 1980—. Engr. color TV colorimetry Hazeltine Rsch., Chgo., 1969; engr. Metroliner rail car/roadbed ride quality dynamics analysis U.S. Dept. Transp., ENSCO, Inc., Springfield, Va., 1970; pres. Tech. Analysis Corp., Chgo., 1978-91; contractor analysis of color TV receiver safety hazards U.S. Consumer Product Safety Commn., 1977, analysis heating effect in aluminum wire Beverly Hills Supper Club Fire, Covington, Ky., 1978; engr. GFCI patent infringement study 3M Corp., St. Paul, 1979-81; elec. systems analyst Coca-Cola Corp., Atlanta, 1983-91; fire investigator McDonald's Corp., Oak Brook, Ill., 1987-90; engring. analyst telephone switching ctrs. ATT, Chgo., 1990-91; expert witness numerous other govtl. and corp. procs.; evaluator Accreditation bd. Engring. and Tech., 2000—. Author: Hybrid Microelectronic Circuits, 1973; editor: Hybrid Microelectronic Technology, 1973; contbr. articles to profl. jours. Officer Planning Commn., Beverly Shores, Ind., 1987-93, trustee town coun., 1992—, police liason 1993-96, dir. emergency mgmt., 1998, coun. pres., 1999-2000; mem. Chgo. Coun. Fgn. Rels., USAF SAC Comdrs. Disting. Program; adv. coun. Nat. Park Svc. Ind. Dunes Nat. Lake Shore, 1993—. NASA fellow, 1964-67, 70. Mem. IEEE (sr. ednl. activities bd. N.Y.C. 1970-74, USAB career devel. com. 1972-74, editor Soundings 1973-75, Cassette Colloquia 1973-74, del. Popov Soc. Tech. Exch. USSR, mgr. Dial Access Tech. Edn. program 1972), Assn. for Media Based Continuing Engring. Edn. (bd. dirs.), Nat. Fire Protection Assn., Sigma Xi, Tau Beta Pi, Eta Kappa Nu. Republican. Avocations: sailing, travel. Home: One E Lakefront Dr Beverly Shores IN 46301-0444 Office: Tech Analysis Corp 1032 W Diversey Pkwy Chicago IL 60614-1317 E-mail: rikoski@technicalanalysiscorp.com.

RIKVOLD, PER ARNE, physics researcher and educator; b. Hadsel, Norway, Oct. 4, 1948; arrived in U.S., 1980; s. Per and Inger-Johanne (Corneliussen) R.; m. Paulette Alice Bond, Apr. 10, 1993. BS, U. Oslo, 1971, MS in Physics, 1976; cert. Japanese lang., Osaka (Japan) U. Fgn. Studies, 1977; PhD in Physics, Temple U., 1983. Rsch. assoc. dept. physics U. Oslo, 1978-81; rsch. assoc. dept. mech. engring. SUNY, Stony Brook, N.Y., 1983-85; sr. rsch. chemist ARCO Chem. Co., Newtown Square, Pa., 1985-87; assoc. prof. physics Fla. State U., Tallahassee, 1987-92, prof. physics, 1992—2004, James G. Skofronick prof. physics, 2004—. Vis. scientist Kyushu U., Fukuoka, Japan, 1979, U. Geneva, Switzerland, 1981-82, Inst. Solid State Physics, Jülich, Germany, 1982; vis. rsch. IBM, Bergen, Norway, 1987, 88, U. Colo., Boulder, 1997, U. Tex., Austin, 1999, Va. Poly. Inst. and State U., 2002; cons. Pony Industries, Malvern, Pa., 1987; vis. scholar Temple U., Phila., 1986-87, Tohwa Inst. Sci., Japan, 1991, Kyushu (Japan) U., 1991, Kyoto (Japan) U., 1993, 96, 98, 2001, McGill U., Montreal, Que., Can., 1995; vis. rsch. prof. Miss. State U., 2003. Contbr. numerous articles to profl. jours. and books. Rsch. grantee Petroleum Rsch. Fund, 1988-91, NSF, 1991—; grad. rsch. fellow Japanese Ministry Edn., 1976-78, Norwegian Rsch. coun., 1981-83, Japan Found. Ctr. for Global Partnership Sci. fellow, 1996. Fellow: Am. Phys. Soc.; mem.: AAAS, European Phys. Soc., Norwegian Acad. Sci. and Letters, Norwegian Phys. Soc., Electrochem. Soc., Materials Rsch. Soc., Sigma Xi. Democrat. Achievements include theoretical and computational research in statistical and condensed-matter physics and complex-systems theory, with applications to materials science, electrochemistry, engineering, computer science and evolutionary biology. Office: Fla State U Physics Dept Tallahassee FL 32306 Office Phone: 850-644-6011. E-mail: rikvold@csit.fsu.edu.

RILEY, B. GRESHAM, college president; b. Jackson, Miss., June 27, 1938; married; 2 children. BA, Baylor U., 1960; MA, Yale U., 1963, PhD, 1965. Asst. instr. philosophy Yale U., 1963-64; from asst. prof. to assoc. prof. New Coll., 1965-75, acting provost, 1972-73, provost, 1973-75; prof. philosophy, dean faculty arts and sci. U. Richmond, 1975-81; pres. Colo. Coll., Colorado Springs, 1981—. Younger scholar fellow Nat. Found. Arts and Humanities, 1968-69; vis. fellow Ctr. Advanced Studies Behavior Sci Stanford U., 1968-69; cons. Nat. Endowment for Humanities, 1971—; mem. adv. bd. Project Gen. Edn. Models, 1978-81. Contbr. articles to profl. jours. Trustee Keystone (Colo.) Ctr., 1989—; bd. dirs. Ind. Coll. Fund of Colo., 1981—, Ind. Higher Edn. Colo., 1989—; chmn. selection com. Colo. Rhodes Scholarship, 1981-85; pres. bd. trustees, campaign chmn. Pikes Peak United Way, 1988; trustee Keystone (Colo.) Ctr., 1989—, Nat. Assn. Ind. Colls. and Univs., 1989—. Mem. Nat. Assn. Ind. Colls. and Univs. (chair task force on nat. and community svc. 1988-89, mem. commn. on financing higher edn. 1988-89, trustee 1989—), Am. Philos. Assn., CS Peirce Soc., Soc. Values Higher Edn., Assn. Am. Colls. (oversight com., project on redefining the meaning and purpose of Baccalaureate degrees 1981-85), Commn. on Women in Higher Edn., Am. Coun. on Edn., North Cen. Assn. Assn. (cons., evaluator 1984—), Assoc. Colls. Midwest (bd. dirs. 1981—). Address: 156 N 3rd St Philadelphia PA 19106-1814

RILEY, CARROLL LAVERN, anthropology educator; b. Summersville, Mo., Apr. 18, 1923; s. Benjamin F. and Minnie B. (Smith) R.; m. Brent Robinson Locke, Mar. 25, 1948; children: Benjamin Locke, Victoria Smith Evans, Cynthia Winningham AB, U. N.Mex., 1948, PhD, 1952; MA, UCLA, 1950. Instr. U. Colo., Boulder, 1953-54; asst. prof. U. N.C., Chapel Hill, 1954-55, So. Ill. U., Carbondale, 1955-60, assoc. prof., 1960-67, prof., 1967-86, Disting. prof., 1986-87, Disting. prof. emeritus, 1987—, chmn. dept., 1979-82, dir. mus., 1972-74; rsch. assoc. lab. anthropology Mus. N.Mex., 1987—. Rsch. collaborator Smithsonian Instn., 1988—; adj. prof. N.Mex. Highlands U., 1989—. Author: The Origins of Civilization, 1969, The Frontier People, 1982, expanded edit., 1987, Rio del Norte, 1995, Bandelier, 1996, The Kachina and Cross, 1999, 2003; editor: American Historical Anthropology, 1967, Man Across the Sea, 1971, Southwestern Journals of Adolph F. Bandelier, 4 vols., 1966, 70, 75, 84, Across the Chichimec Sea, 1978, A Zuni Life, 1998, The Casas Grandes World, 1999, others; contbr. numerous articles to profl. jours. Served in USAAF, 1942-45 Decorated 4 battle stars; grantee Social Sci. Rsch. Coun., NIH, Am. Philos. Soc., Am. Council Learned Socs., NEH, others. Home and Office: 1106 6th St Las Vegas NM 87701 E-mail: criley@newmexico.com.

RILEY, DANIEL JOSEPH, lawyer, educator; b. Amarillo, Tex., Jan. 14, 1947; s. Roy Weldon and Joette Aline (Winger) R.; m. Glenda Joy Hoel, Apr. 15, 1947; children: Carla Annette, Ragan Patrick. BA cum laude, U. Tex., 1969, JD summa cum laude, 1971. Bar: Tex. 1971, U.S. Ct. Fed. Claims 1974, U.S. Supreme Ct. 1979, U.S. Ct. Appeals (fed. cir.) 1982, D.C. 1999. Ptnr. Baker Bolts LLP, Washington, 1993—. Adj. prof. grad. sch. U. Dallas, 1983-94. Assoc. editor U. Tex. Law Rev., 1970. Mem. constitution rev. com. State of Tex., Austin, 1978. Mem. ABA (uniform state procurement code com. 1980), Nat. Contract Mgmt. Assn. (bd. advisors), Tex. Bar Found., Tex. Bar Assn., Dallas Bar Assn., Order of Coif, Phi Beta Kappa. Republican. Home: 712 W Braddock Rd Alexandria VA 22302-3601 Office: Baker Bolts LLP 1299 Pennsylvania Ave NW Washington DC 20004-2400

RILEY, DAVID JOSEPH, medical educator; b. N.Y.C., Sept. 6, 1942; s. Edwin Glover and Gertrude (Pfanner) R.; m. Katherine Elizabeth Moran, June 9, 1969; children: Meredith Ann, Gavin Douglas. BA, Johns Hopkins U., 1964; MD, U. Md., 1968. Diplomate Am. Bd. Internal Medicine; cert. Am. Bd. Pulmonary Disease. Intern Balt. City Hosps., 1968-69, resident, 1969-70; fellow in pulmonary disease U. Pa., 1970-72; resident Johns Hopkins Hosp., Balt., 1972-73; asst. prof. Robert W. Johnson Med. Sch. U. Medicine and Dentistry N.J., New Brunswick, N.J., 1972-76; assoc. prof. Robert Wood Johnson Med. Sch., New Brunswick, N.J., 1976-86, prof. medicine, 1986—. Adj. prof. physiology and biophysics Robert W. Johnson Med. Sch., 1990—; mem. grad. faculty Rutgers U., 1986—. Contbr. articles to profl. jours. With U.S. Army N.G., 1966-70. Recipient Osler Humanitarian award Am. Lung Assn., N.J., 1998. Mem. Am. Thoracic Soc. (chmn. cell moelcular biology assembly 1993-94, pres. ea. sect. 1988-90, bd. mem. 1993-94). Democrat. Episcopalian. Office: Robert Wood Johnson Med Sch 675 Hoes Ln Piscataway NJ 08854-5627

RILEY, DAVID RICHARD, management consultant, retired military officer; b. Spokane, Wash., Mar. 28, 1940; s. Lee James and Louise Elizabeth (Duncan) R.; m. Anna Maria Formigoni, July 6, 1963; children: David Scott, Michelle Andrea. BS in Naval Sci., USN Acad., 1963; MS in Applied Math., USN Post Grad. Sch., 1972; postgrad., Armed Forces Staff Coll., 1975. Navy ops. mgmt. specialist, Navy aerospace engring. specialist, Navy material specialist, Navy weapon sys. mgmt. specialist. Ensign USN, 1963, advanced through grades to capt., 1984, antisubmarine warfare/antisubmarine rocket officer, 1963-65, pilot trainee Pensacola, Fla., 1965-67, designated naval pilot San Diego, 1967, with antisubmarine/antiair warfare, 1967-74, maintenace officer, 1976-78, officer in charge Nerna Naples, Italy, 1978-81; exec. officer Naval Aviation Depot, Alameda, Calif., 1981-84, comdg. officer Pensacola, 1987-90; aviation depot program mgr. Navairsyscom Hdqrs., Washington, 1984-87; ret., 1990; cons. bus. planning and organizational devel., internat. commerce, 1990-94; pres., COO Speco Corp., Springfield, Ohio, 1994-95; pres. David Riley Assocs., Inc., 1998—. Mem. Assn. Naval Aviation, Ret.

Officers Assn., Am. Legion, Naval Helicopter Assn. Republican. Presbyterian. Avocation: golf. Home and Office: David Riley Assocs Inc 115 Eastwick Ct Dayton OH 45440-3647 E-mail: dra-inc@earthlink.net.

RILEY, DYANNE, music professor; b. San Diego, Feb. 16, 1944; d. Ralph Ellis Schrock and Coral Jean Clark; m. Michael Arthur Riley; children: Michael Timothy, AnnaMarie, David Patrick, Keri Jo, Suzanne. BA with distinction in music, San Diego State U.; MusM, Brigham Young U. Tchr. Mt. Miguel High Sch.; grad. asst. Brigham Young U., Provo; lectr. Utah Valley State Coll., asst. prof. Vocal specialist Chorale on Temple Sq., Salt Lake City, 2003. Singer: Mormon Tabernacle Choir, 1995—. Recipient Adj. faculty of Yr., Utah Valley State Col., 1998—99, 2002—03. Mem.: Soc. Music Theory, Am. Choral Dirs. Assn., Nat. Assn. Tchrs. Singing. Avocations: harp, quilting, outdoor activities. Home: 4323 N Imperial Way Provo UT 84604 Office: Utah Valley State Coll 800 W Univ Pky Orem UT 84058 E-mail: rileydy@uvsc.edu.

RILEY, HAROLD JOHN, JR., manufacturing executive; b. Syracuse, N.Y., Nov. 13, 1940; s. Harold John and Esther Emma (Denmark) R.; m. Diane Marie Slattery, June 15, 1963; children— Beth Ann, Thomas, Patrick BS in Indsl. Engring., Syracuse U., 1961; postgrad., Harvard Bus. Sch., 1985. Mfg. tng. program Gen. Elec. Co., various locations, 1961-63; various mfg. assignments Crouse-Hinds Co., Syracuse, 1963-74; gen. mgr. Midwest Elec., Chgo., 1974-77; v.p., gen. mgr. Crouse Hinds Distbn. Equipment Div., Earlysville, VA., 1977-79; v.p. Crouse-Hinds Co., Syracuse, 1979-82; exec. v.p. Cooper Industries Inc., Houston, 1982-92, pres., chief oper. officer, 1992-95, pres., 1995—2004, CEO, 1995—, chmn., 1996—, also bd. dirs. Bd. dirs. Wyman-Gordon Co., North Grafton, Mass. Bd. dirs. Jr. Achievement Southeast Tex., Houston Ctrl., Houston Symphony, The Greater Houston Partnership, The Houston Forum, The Mus. Fine Arts, Houston, Jr. Achievement, Inc. Mem. Mfrs. Alliance for Productivity Improvement, The Bus. Roundtable, Houston Club, Lakeside Country Club, Farmington Country Club. Republican. Roman Catholic. Home: 3669 Chevy Chase Dr Houston TX 77019-3009 Office: Cooper Industries Inc PO Box 4446 Houston TX 77210-4446*

RILEY, HARRIS DEWITT, JR., pediatrician, medical educator; b. Clarksdale, Miss., Nov. 12, 1924; s. Harris DeWitt and Louise (Allen) R.; m. Margaret Barry, Sept. 16, 1950; children: Steven Allen, Mark Barry, Margaret Ruth. BA, Vanderbilt U., 1945, MD, 1948. Intern Balt. City Hosps., Johns Hopkins Hosp., 1948-49; resident in pediatrics Babies and Children's Hosp., Case Western Res. U., Cleve., 1949-50, Vanderbilt U. Hosp., 1950-51; instr., fellow in pediatrics and infectious diseases Vanderbilt U. Med. Sch., 1953-57; prof. pediatrics, chmn. dept. U. Okla. Med. Sch., 1958—; med. dir. Children's Meml. Hosp., 1972—; disting. prof. pediatrics U. Okla., 1976; prof. pediatrics Vanderbilt U. Sch. of Medicine, Nashville, 1991—. Served as capt. M.C. USAF, 1951-53. Office: Vanderbilt Children Hosp Vanderbilt U Med Ctr Nashville TN 37232-0001 E-mail: harris.riley@mcmail.vanderbilt.edu.

RILEY, HELENE MARIA KASTINGER, Germanist; b. Vienna, Mar. 11, 1939; came to U.S., 1959; d. Josef and Helene (Friedl) Kastinger; m. Edward R. Riley, Nov. 6, 1957 (div. May 1970); children: India Helene, John Edward, Jesse Dale, Michael Rutledge; m. Darius G. Ornston, May 11, 1983. Grad., bus. coll., Vienna, 1955; BA in Music, North Tex. State U., 1970; MA in Germanics, Rice U., 1973, PhD in Germanics, 1975. Teaching asst. Rice U., Houston, 1971-75; asst. prof. German Yale U., New Haven, Conn., 1975-78, head summer lang. inst., 1979-81, assoc. prof., 1979-85; chmn. Dept. Fgn. Langs. Wash. State U., Pullman, 1981-82; head Dept. Langs. Clemson (S.C.) U., 1985-86, prof., 1985-95, Alumni Disting. prof., 1996—. Guest prof. Middlebury (Vt.) Coll., 1976; speaker in field. Author: Achim von Arnim, 1979, Virginia Woolf, 1983, Clemens Brentano, 1985, Die Weibliche Muse, 1986, Max Weber, 1991, Hildegard von Bingen, 1997, John Adam Treutlen: The European Heritage of Georgia's First Governor, 1999, Clemson University, 2002; producer, dir. traveling exhibit Cultural Contbns. of German-speaking Settlers in S.C., 1996—; others; contbr. numerous articles to profl. jours. Recipient German-Am. Friendship award Consul Gen. of the German Fed. Republic, 1989; grantee Griswold Found., 1975-76, 78, S.C. Dept. Edn., 1986, NEH, 1986, Provost's award Clemson U., 1989, 96, Hilles Fund, 1976, 79, 82, S.C. Humanities Coun., 1996; NDEA fellow, 1972, 73, Rice fellow, 1971, 74, Morse fellow, 1977-78, Deutscher Akademischer Austausch-Dienst fellow, 1979, Yale U. sr. faculty fellow, 1981-82, Holland Fund fellow, 1982, Deutsche Forschungsgemeinschaft fellow, 1982, Mesda fellow, 1993. Fellow Davenport Coll., Yale U.; mem. AAUP (v.p. 1987-88, pres. 1988-89), MLA, Am. Assn. Tchrs. German, So. Comparative Lit. Assn., others. Democrat. Avocations: reading, writing, sports, needlecraft, painting. Office: Clemson U Dept Langs 717 Strode Twr Clemson SC 29634-0001 E-mail: rhelene@clemson.edu.

RILEY, HENRY CHARLES, banker; b. Newton, Massachusetts, Mar. 23, 1932; s. Charles Matthew and Marion Anna (Armstrong) R.; m. Patricia Ann (Buchanan), Mar. 3, 1962; children: Lauren Elizabeth, Carolyn Ann, Julie Louise. BA, Yale U., 1954; MBA, Boston Coll., 1965. With Bay Bank Harvard Trust Co., Cambridge, Mass., 1958—89, treas., sec., 1967—70, sr. v.p., sec., 1972—82, exec. v.p., 1982—87; mng. dir. cmty. banking Bay Bank Systems Inc., Waltham, Mass., 1987—90; exec. v.p., dir. cmty. banking Bay Bank Boston, 1990—92; exec. v.p. Bay Bank Systems, Inc., Waltham, Mass., 1992—97. Mem. pvt. banking adv. com. fleet Boston, Sarasota, Fla., 2000—. Trustee, treas. Longy Sch. Music, 1970-92; bd. dir. Richard Warren Surg. Rsch. and Ednl. Fund Inc., 1984—; bd. dir., pres. Cambridge Econ. Devel. Corp., 1982-87; corporator, past asst. treas. Mt. Auburn Hosp.; mem. exec. bd. Gettysburg Coll. Parents Assn.; treas. St. John's Episcopal Ch., sr. warden, Westwood, Mass., 1982-85; mem. St. Paul's Cathedral chpt., Boston, 1990-93. Served in USNR, 1956-57. Mem. Am. Bankers Assn. (chmn. 1991-92, exec. com. br. adminstrv. divsn. 1992, chmn. nat. retail banking conf. 1990), Nat. Br. Adminstr. Roundtable, Boston Coll. Sch. Mgmt. Alumni Assn. (past dir., pres.), Harvard Sq. Bus. Assn. (past dir.), Cambridge C. of C. (past dir., past treas., v.p. 1975-87), Rotary (club dir. 1976-80, pres. 1979-80), Yale Club (Boston), Yale Club of the Suncoast (Sarasota, Fla., bd. dir. 2001, v.p., 2004-), Harvard Club (Boston), Dennis Yacht Club (mem. bd. gov., treas. 1993-94), The Meadows Country Club (Sarasota, Fla.), Ivy League Club (Sarasota, Fla.). Episcopalian. Home: 33 York Way Westwood MA 02090-2633 also: PO Box 1192 240 New Boston Rd Dennis MA 02638-2121 also: 5284 Huntingwood Ct Sarasota FL 34235-5600

RILEY, J. MICHAEL, energy executive; Sr. v.p., CFO AGL Resources Inc., Atlanta. Office: PO Box 4569 Atlanta GA 30302-4569

RILEY, JACK, actor, writer; b. Cleve., Dec. 30, 1935; s. John A. and Agnes C. (Corrigan) R.; m. Ginger Lawrence, May 18, 1975; children: Jamie, Bryan. BS in English, John Carroll U., 1961. Mem. Rolling Along of 1960, Dept. Army Travelling Show; co-host: Baxter & Riley, Sta.-WERE, Cleve., 1961-65; numerous TV appearances, including: as Mr. Carlin on Bob Newhart Show, CBS-TV, 1972-78; Occasional Wife, 1966, Mary Tyler Moore, 1972, Barney Miller, 1979, Diff'rent Strokes, 1979, Hart to Hart, 1980, Love Boat, 1984, Night Court, 1985-91, St. Elsewhere, 1986, Evening Shade, 1992, Family Matters, 1993, Married with Children, 1994, Coach, 1996, The Drew Carey Show, 1996, Seinfeld, 1997, Working, 1998, Son of the Beach, 1999-2002, Lucky, 2003, numerous appearances on Tonight Show with Jay Leno, 1997-99; appeared in feature films including Catch-22, 1969, McCabe and Mrs. Miller, 1970, Long Goodbye, 1972, Calif. Split, 1974, World's Greatest Lover, 1978, High Anxiety, 1978, Butch and Sundance: The Early Years, 1979, History of the World, Part I, 1981, Frances, 1983, To Be or Not To Be, 1983, Finders Keepers, 1984, Spaceballs, 1987, Rented Lips, 1987, Gleaming the Cube, 1988, The Player, 1992, T-Rex, 1995, (voice) The Rugrat's Movie, 1998, Boogie Nights, 1997, Rugrats in Paris, 2000, Rugrats Go Wild, 2003; plays West Coast premier of Small Craft Warnings, 1975, Los Angeles revival of 12 Angry Men, 1985, Zeitgeist, 1990, House of Blue Leaves, at Cleve. Playhouse and tour Ea. Europe, 1993, The Odd Couple, Beck Ctr., Cleve., 1999, Do I Hear a Waltz? at Pasadena playhouse, 2001; TV writer: Don Rickles Show, 1968, Mort Sahl Show, 19667; writer commls. for, Blore & Richman Inc., Los Angeles, 1966-84; numerous radio commls. and TV voice-overs, Rugrats (cartoon series), 1993. Served with U.S. Army, 1958—61. Named to, Ohio Broadcasters' Hall of Fame, 2002. Mem.: AFTRA, Acad. TV Arts and Scis., Acad. Motion Picture Arts and Scis., Writers Guild Am., Actor's Equity, Screen Actors Guild. Office: c/o Ho Reps 400 S Beverly Dr Beverly Hills CA 90212-4424

RILEY, JAMES CLIFFORD, military career officer; b. Montecello, Calif., Nov. 13, 1946; m. Linda Jean Axtater. BS, U. Nebr., 1971; MA, Webster U., 1978; grad., Command and Gen. Staff Coll., 1980, U.S. Army War Coll., 1987. Drafted U.S. Army, 1965, commd. 2d lt., 1966, advanced through grades to lt. gen., 1999, co. comdr., S4 and Battalion Maintenance Officer 1st Bn., 6th Inf., 1st Armored Divsn., 1972-75, dep. G3 1st Armored Divsn., exec. officer 1st Bn., 52d Inf., S3, 3d Brigade, 1981-83, comdr. 2d Bn., 7th Cavalry, 1st Cavalry Divsn. Ft. Hood, Tex., 1983-86, G3 and chief of staff 2d Armored Divsn. (forward) Garlstedt, Germany, 1987-89, comdr. 3d Brigade, 3d Infantry Divsn. Aschaffenburg, Germany, 1989-90, with 1st Armored Divsn., 1990-91, chief European divsn., J-5, the Joint Staff, Joint Chiefs of Staff rep. for European security matters, 1992-94, asst. divsn. comdr. for support, 1st Armored Divsn. Hanau, Germany, 1994-95, chief U.S. Mil. Tng. Mission, 1995-97, comdr. 3d Inf. Divsn. (Mechanized), 1997-99. Decorated Def. Disting. Svc. medal, Disting. Svc. medal, Def. Superior Svc. medal, Legion of Merit with oak leaf cluster, Bronze Star medal with oak leaf cluster, Meritorious Svc. medal with four oak leaf clusters, Army Commendation medal. Home and Office: 1 Scott Fort Leavenworth KS 66027

RILEY, JAMES KEVIN, lawyer; b. Nyack, N.Y., July 21, 1945; s. Charles A. and Mary Lenihan R.; m. Joan Leavy Riley, Oct. 4, 1969; children: Carolyn, Tara, Sean. AB, Fordham Coll., 1967; JD, Rutgers U., 1970. Bar: N.Y. 1971, N.J. 1983, U.S. Supreme Ct. 1984; cert. fin. planner., estate planner. Asst. dist. atty. Rockland County, New City, NY, 1973-74; ptnr. Amend & Amend, N.Y.C., 1974-78, O'Connell & Riley, Pearl River, NY, 1978—. Pub., pres. 1099 Express Software, 1099 Express Ltd., Pearl River, 1987-97; adj. prof. estate planning Pace Univ., White Plains, N.Y.; atty. Town of Orangetown. Bd. dirs. United Way of Rockland County, N.Y., 1974-80, Rockland Family Shelter for Victims of Domestic Violence, 1981-85, Literacy Vols. Rockland County, 1989—; chmn. bd. dirs. New Hope Manor, Barryville, N.Y., 1985-88. Mem. ABA, Am. Soc. Hosp. Attys., Nat. Coun. Sch. Dist. Attys., N.Y. State Bar Assn. (ho. of dels. 1988-92, 2002—), Rockland County Bar Assn. (bd. dirs. 1986—, pres. 1997-98), Internat. Platform Assn., Rotary Club of Pearl River (pres. 1999—). Democrat. Roman Catholic. Home: 145 Franklin Ave Pearl River NY 10965-2510 Office: O'Connell & Riley 144 E Central Ave Pearl River NY 10965 also: 103 Chestnut Ridge Rd Montvale NJ 07645

RILEY, JOHN FREDERICK, lawyer; b. Salisbury, N.C., Oct. 18, 1938; s. John Horace and Beatrice (Williams) R.; m. Jan Colby, June 20, 1965; children: John Michael, Jennifer Lynn, Julia Grace. BA, Wake Forest U., 1960; JD, U. N.C., 1967. Bar: N.C. 1967. Law clk. to presiding justice N.C. Supreme Ct., Raleigh, 1967-68; assoc. Leroy, Wells, Shaw & Hornthal, Elizabeth City, N.C., 1968-70; ptnr. Leroy, Wells, Shaw, Hornthal & Riley, Elizabeth City, N.C., 1970-85, Hornthal, Riley, Ellis & Maland, Elizabeth City, N.C., 1985-2001, of counsel, 2001—. Chmn. adv. bd. Salvation Army, Elizabeth City, 1976-77; trustee Elizabeth City State U., 1981-86. Hankins scholar Wake Forest U., Winston-Salem, N.C., 1956. Mem. ABA, N.C. Bar Assn. (bd. dirs. real property sect. 1979-83), N.C. Land Title Assn., Elizabeth City Bar Assn. (pres. 1973-74), 1st Jud. Dist. Bar Assn. (pres. 1985-86), Rotary, Pine Lakes Country. Democrat. Methodist. Avocations: golf, tennis, boating. Home: 101 Inlet Dr Elizabeth City NC 27909-3225 Office: Hornthal Riley Ellis & Maland 301 E Main St # 220 Elizabeth City NC 27909-4425 E-mail: friley@hrem.com.

RILEY, JUDITH MERKLE, writer, educator; b. Brunswick, Maine, Jan. 14, 1942; d. Theodore Charles Merkle and Helene Antonia Suarez; m. W. Parkes Riley (div.); children: Elizabeth, Marlow. BA, U. Calif., Berkeley, 1962, PhD, 1974; MA, Harvard U., 1964. Intelligence analyst Dept. of Def., Washington, 1965—66; tchg. asst., acting instr., lectr. U. Calif., Berkeley, 1967—70; vis. asst. prof., asst. prof. U. Oreg., Eugene, 1971—82; assoc. prof. Claremont (Calif.) McKenna Coll./Claremont Grad. Sch., 1982—. Author: (non-fiction) Management and Ideology, 1980, (novels) A Vision of Light, 1989, In Pursuit of the Green Lion, 1990, The Oracle Glass, 1993, The Water-Devil, 1995, The Serpent Garden, 1997, The Master of All Desires, 1999 (Libr. Jour. 100 Best of 1999). Recipient Career Achievement award, Romantic Times, 1999. Fellow: Brit. Inst. Homeopathy (Di Hom 1998); mem.: Am. Soc. Pub. Adminstrn., Am. Polit. Sci. Assn., Novelists, Inc., Pen USA West, Nat. Ctr. Homeopathy, Phi Beta Kappa. Democrat. Episcopalian. Avocations: homeopathy, painting, stained glass, choral singing. Office: Claremont McKenna Coll Dept Govt 850 Columbia Ave Claremont CA 91711 Office Phone: 909-607-2996. E-mail: jmerkle@mckenna.edu.

RILEY, KENNETH JEROME, athletic director; b. Bartow, Fla., Aug. 6, 1947; m. Barbara Moore, May 3, 1969; children: Kimberly, Kenneth II, Kenisha. BS in Health, Physical Edn. & Recreation, Fla. A&M U., 1969; MS in Ednl. Adminstrn. Suprv., U. North Fla. Cornerback Cin. Bengals, 1969-84; asst. coach Green Bay (Wis.) Packers, 1984-85; football coach Fla. A&M U., Tallahassee, 1986-93, dir. athletics, 1994—. Mem. NFL's Player's Coun. Named to Fla. A&M U. Sports Hall Fame, Tallahassee Sports Hall Fame, Fla. Sports Hall Fame, Bartow County Sports Hall Fame, Polk County Sports Hall Fame. Avocations: fishing, reading. Office: Fla A&M U Martin Luther King Jr Blvd Tallahassee FL 32307

RILEY, MARY JANE, computer scientist; b. Raleigh, N.C., May 26, 1946; d. Charles William and Geraldine Lucile (Adams) Hampton; m. William Walter Schubert, Dec. 30, 1967 (div. June 1979); children: Kristen, Stephen, Betsy, Kathryn; stepchildren: Lee, Scott; m. Jim Riley, Oct. 17, 1998. BA in Math., Park Coll., 1967. Cert. IBM exec. project mgr. Programmer U. Mo. Med. Ctr., Columbia, 1968-72, City and County of Denver, 1979-80; sr. sys. programmer Citicorp Person to Person, Denver, 1980-82; sys. support rep. Software AG, NA, Denver, 1982-83; prin. info. sysm. specialist Idaho Nat. Engring. Lab., EG&G, Idaho Falls, 1983-89; adv. svcs. specialist IBM Profl. Svcs., Albuquerque, 1989-91; field mgr. IBM Svc., Boulder, Colo., 1991-93; project mgr. IBM Global Svcs., Denver, 1993-99; exec. project mgr. IBM Global Svcs. Healthcare, 1999—2002; delivery project exec. IBM Global AMS, Boulder, Colo., 2002—03, N.Y.C., 2003—. Presenter career workshop for girls No. Colo. U., Greeley, 1993. Leader Girl Scout Am., Pocatello, Idaho, Columbia, Mo., 1969-79, Idaho Falls, 1986-89, cluster leader, Rigby, Idaho, 1988-89; active Albuquerque Civic Chorus, 1990-91, Luth. Ch. Coun., 1994-96; bd. dirs. LWV, Pocatello, 1977-79, 84-85, pres., 1978-79; bd. dirs. Luth. Ch. Women, Pocatello, 1978-79; youth advisor Luth. Ch., Idaho Falls, 1984-89; tchr. Sunday sch. local ch., Albuquerque, 1990-91; youth com. chair local ch., Boulder, Colo., 1994-96; tchr. 7th and 8th grade Sunday sch., 1993-96, mem. ch. choir, 1995-96; mem. Denver Art Mus., Denver Nat. History Mus. Mem. AAUW. Episcopalian. Avocations: youth work, reading, choir, photography, swimming. Home: 6581 S Cook Way Littleton CO 80121-3605

RILEY, MATILDA WHITE (MRS. JOHN W. RILEY JR.), sociologist; b. Boston, Apr. 19, 1911; d. Percival and Mary (Cliff) White; m. John Winchell Riley, Jr., June 19, 1931; children: John Winchell III, Lucy Ellen Riley Sallick. BA, Radcliffe Coll., 1931, MA, 1937, DSc (hon.), 1994; DSc, Bowdoin Coll., 1972; LHD (hon.), Rutgers U., 1983, SUNY, Albany, 1997. Rsch. asst. Harvard U., Cambridge, Mass., 1932; v.p. Market Rsch. Co. Am., 1938-49; chief cons. economist WPB, 1941; rsch. specialist Rutgers U., 1950, prof., 1951-73, dir. sociology lab., chmn. dept. sociology and anthropology, 1959-73, emeritus prof., 1973—; Daniel B. Fayerweather prof. polit. econ. and sociology Bowdoin Coll., Brunswick, Maine, 1974-78, prof. emeritus, 1978—, hon. rsch. prof. Assoc. dir. Nat. Inst. on Aging, 1979-91, sr. social scientist, 1991-98, scientist emeritus, Nat. Inst. of Health, 1998—; mem. faculty Harvard U., summer 1955; staff assoc., dir. aging and society Russell Sage Found., 1964-73, staff sociologist, 1974-77; chmn. com. on life course Social Sci. Rsch. Coun., 1977-80; sr. rsch. assoc. Ctr. for Social Scis., Columbia U., 1978-80; adv. bd. Carnegie Aging Soc. Project, 1985-87; mem. Commn. on Coll. Retirement, 1982-86; vis. prof. NYU, 1954-61; cons. Nat. Coun. on Aging, Acad. Ednl. Devel.; mem. study group NIH, 1971-79, Social Sci. Rsch. Coun. Com. on Middle Years, 1973-77; chmn. NIH Task Force on Health and Behavior, 1986-91; cons. WHO, 1987—; Winkelman lectr. U. Mich., 1984, Selo lectr. U. No. Calif., 1987, Boettner lectr. Am. Coll., 1990, Claude Pepper lectr. Fla. State U., 1993, Disting. lectr. Southwestern Social Scis. Assn., 1990, U. N.C., 1997; Standing lectr. SUNY, 1992, Inaugural lectr. Cornell U., 1992; lectr. Internat. Inst. of Sociology, Plenary, 1993, Inter-Univ. Consortium Pol. and Social Rsch., U. Mich., 1993, Duke U., 1993; adv. bd. Internat. Encyclopedia of the Social and Behavioral Sciences, 2000. Author: (with P. White) Gliding and Soaring, (with Riley and Toby) Sociological Studies in Scale Analysis, 1954, Sociological Research, vols. I, II, 1964, (with others) Aging and Society, vol. I, 1968, vol. II, 1969, vol. III, 1972, (with Nelson) Sociological Observation, 1974, Aging from Birth to Death: Interdisciplinary Perspectives, 1979, (with Merton) Sociological Traditions from Generation to Generation, 1980, (with Abeles and Teitelbaum) Aging from Birth to Death: Sociotemporal Perspectives, 1982, (with Hess and Bond) Aging in Society, 1983; editor: (with M. Ory and D. Zablotsky) AIDS in an Aging Society: What We Need to Know, 1989; co-editor: Perspectives in Behavioral Medicine: The Aging Dimension, 1987, (with J. W. Riley) The Quality of Aging, 1989, The Annuals, 1989; mem. editl. com. Ann. Rev. Sociology, 1978-81, Social Change and the Life Course, vol. 1, Social Structures and Human Lives, (with B. Huber and B. Hess) Sociological Lives, vol. II, 1988, (with R. Kahn and Anne Foner) Structural Lag, 1994; contbr. chpts. to books, articles to profl. jours. Former trustee The Big Sisters Assn. Recipient Lindback Rsch. award Rutgers U., 1970, Social Sci. award Andrus Gerontology Ctr., U. So. Calif., 1972, Radcliffe Alumnae award, 1982, Commonwealth award 1984, Kesten Lecture award U. So. Calif., 1987, Sci. Achievement award Washington Acad. Scis., 1989, Disting. Sci. award, 1989, Disting. Creative award Gerontol. Soc. Am., 1990, Presdl. Meritorious award, 1990, Stuart Rice award D.C. Columbia Sociol. Soc., 1992, Kent award Gerontol. Soc. Am., 1992; fellow Advanced Study in Behavioral Scis., 1978-79; Matilda White Riley award in rsch. and methodology established in her honor Rutgers U., 1977; Matilda White Riley prize established Bowdoin Coll., 1987; Matilda White Riley House dedicated Bowdoin Coll., 1996. Fellow AAAS (chmn. sect. on social and econ. scis. 1977-78); mem. NAS, Inst. Medicine of NAS (sr.), Acad. Behavioral Medicine Rsch., Am. Sociol. Assn. (exec. officer 1949-60, v.p. 1973-74, pres. 1986, 91, chmn. sect. on sociology of aging 1989, Disting. Scholar in Aging 1988, Career award 1992), Am. Assn. Public Opinion Rsch. (sec.-treas. 1949-51, Disting. Svc. award 1983), Eastern Sociol. Soc. (v.p. 1968-69, pres. 1977-78, Disting. Career award 1986), Soc. for Study Social Biology (bd. dirs. 1986-92), Am. Acad. Arts and Scis., D.C. Sociol. Soc. (co-pres. 1983-84), Sociol. Rsch. Assn., Internat. Orgn. Study Human Devel., Am. Philos. Soc. (membership lectr. 1987), Phi Beta Kappa, Phi Beta Kappa Assocs. Home: 22 Monument Ln Brunswick ME 04011-8106 Office: Bowdoin Coll Brunswick ME 04011 E-mail: rileym@suscom-maine.net.*

RILEY, MICHAEL ROBERT, marketing and business development executive; b. Wisconsin Rapids, Wis., Apr. 17, 1938; s. Robert William and Anne Bates (Clark) R.; m. Judith Wood, Aug. 12, 1961; children: David T., Christopher W. BS, Hampton U., 1974; MS, Indsl. Coll. of Armed Forces, Washington, 1975; MPA, Golden Gate U., 1976, MBA, 1977. Commd. 2d lt. USAF, 1958, advanced through grades to lt. col., 1977, ret., 1979; mktg. exec. McDonnell Douglas Corp., St. Louis, 1979-90; pres. MRR Assocs., St. Louis, 1990—. Cons. Regional Commerce and Growth Assn., St. Louis, 1980-85, 90—. Pres. trustees Lake of the Woods Subdiv., St. Louis, 1980-85; pres. bd. dirs. St. Louis Chamber Chorus, 1986-88; mem. St. Louis Ambassadors, 1990—. Decorated D.F.C. with 2 oakleaf cluster, Bronze Star, Air medal with 23 oakleaf clusters; named Swimmer of the Yr., U.S. Amateur Athletic Union/NCAA, Portland, Oreg., 1956; recipient USAF Navigator Wings, Harlingen, Tex., 1959, USAF Pilot Wings, Chandler, Ariz., 1964, USN Wings, Beeville, Tex., 1971. Mem. Air Force Assn., Assn. Naval Aviation, Am. Mgmt. Assn., Internat. City Mgrs. Assn., Army Aviation Assn. Am., Am. Helicopter Soc., Navy League, River Rats. Avocations: sailing, golf, flying. Office: MRR Assocs 5846 Mango Dr Saint Louis MO 63129-2243

RILEY, NANCY C. state legislator; b. Tulsa, Okla., June 20, 1958; m. Jerry A. Riley; children: Dan, Robin, Patrick stepchildren: Steve, Phil. Student, Okla. Christian U., 1976-79; BSE, UCT Langston, 1985. Tchr. Tulsa Pub. Schs., 1986—; mem. Okla. Senate from 37th dist., Oklahoma City, 2001—. Active PTA, Berryhill Hoover, S.W. Tulsa Chamber, Sand Springs Chamber, Bixby Chamber, Green Country Campfire Adv. Coun., Interagency Coun. Early Childhood Intervention, Okla. Fedn. Rep. Women, Okla. First Ladies, Tulsa Rep. Men's Club, After Five Rep. Women's Club, Tchr. Recruitment Con. for Minorities. Mem. Tulsa Classroom Tchrs. Assn. (del. 1986-2000), Rolling Oaks Homeowners Assn. (past pres. 1999-2000), Delta Kappa Gamma (sec. 1994-97). Republican. Mailing: State Capitol Bldg Rm 528A 2300 N Lincoln Blvd Oklahoma City OK 73105 E-mail: Rileyn@lsb.state.ok.us.

RILEY, PAMELA JANERICO, artist; b. Winchester, Mass., Aug. 27, 1970; children: Samuel Adrian Jenkins, James Mark Jenkins. Student, So. Maine Tech. Coll. Ordained to ministry Universal Life Ch., Calif. Data entry clk. Orlando Pub. Libr., 1999. Vol. Caring Unltd., Sanford, Biddeford, Maine, 1999; parent St. Louis Childcare Devel. Svcs., 1999; crime watcher Forest Green Apt. Complex, York County, 1999. Home: PO Box 1984 Biddeford ME 04005-1984

RILEY, PATRICK JAMES, former professional basketball coach; b. Rome, N.Y., Mar. 20, 1945; s. Leon R.; m. Chris Riley; children: James Patrick, Elisabeth. Grad., U. Ky., 1967. Guard San Diego Rockets, 1967-70, L.A. Lakers, 1970-75, asst. coach, 1979-81, head coach, 1981-90, N.Y. Knicks, 1991-95; guard Phoenix Suns, 1975-76; broadcaster L.A. Lakers games Sta. KLAC and Sta. KHJ-TV, 1977-79, NBC Sports, 1990-91; player NBA Championship Team, 1972, coach, 1982, 85, 87, 88; head coach Miami (Fla.) Heat, 1995—2003. Author: The Winner Within: A Life Plan for Team Players, 1993. Named NBA Coach of Yr., 1990, 93, 97 Achievements include being a holder of NBA record most playoff wins (137).

RILEY, RICHARD WILSON, lawyer, former federal official; b. Greenville, S.C., Jan. 2, 1933; s. Edward Patterson and Martha Elizabeth (Dixon) Riley; m. Ann Osteen Yarborough, Aug. 23, 1957; children: Richard Wilson, Anne Y., Hubert D., Theodore D. BA, Furman U., 1954; JD, U. S.C., 1959. Bar: S.C. 1960. Ptnr. Riley & Riley, Greenville, 1959—78, Nelson, Mullins, Riley & Scarborough, Greenville and Columbia, 1987—93, Greenville, 2001—; gov. State of S.C., 1979—87; sec. U.S. Dept. Edn., Washington, 1993—2001; disting. univ. prof. U. S.C., Columbia, 2001—; disting. prof. govt., politics, and pub. policy Furman U., 2001—. Spl. asst. to subcom. U.S. Senate Jud. Com., 1960; mem. S.C. Ho. of Reps., 1963—66, S.C. Senate senate form Greenville-Laurens Dist., 1966—76; sr. adv. and chair Richard W. Riley Inst. Govt., Politics and Pub. Leadership, Furman U., 2001—; bd. dirs. Sylvan Learning Sys., Inc., 2001—, Sylvan Internat. U., 2001—, ACT (Am. Coll. Testing Program), 2002—, Pub. Broadcasting Svc. (PBS); bd. trustees Knowledge Works Found., 2001—. Lt. (j.g.) USNR, 1954—56. Recipient Dist. Svc. award, Coun. Chief State Sch. Officers, 1994, James Bryant Conant award, Edn. Comm. of the States, 1995, T.H. Bell award for outstanding edn. advocacy, Com. for Edn. Funding, 1996, Dist. Svc. award, Am. Coun. on Edn., 1998; disting. sr. fellow, NAFSA: Assn. Internat. Educators, Wash., D.C. Mem.: Greenville Bar Assn., S.C. Bar Assn., Furman U. Alumni Assn. (pres. 1968—69), Rotary, Phi Beta Kappa. Office: Nelson Mullins Riley & Scarborough Poinsett Plaza Ste 900 104 S Main St Greenville SC 29601 E-mail: rwr@nmrs.com.*

RILEY, ROBERT, governor; b. Ashland, Ala., Oct. 3, 1944; m. Patsy Adams; children: Rob, Jenice, Minda, Krisalyn. Degree in bus. administrn., U. Ala. Past poultry and egg bus. co-owner, Ala.; past owner automobile dealership, Ala.; owner trucking co., Ala.; past owner grocery store and local pharmacy, Ala.; mem. Ho. of Reps. from 3d Ala. dist., 1996—2002, asst. whip, mem. house armed svcs. com., mem. house banking and fin. svcs. com., mem. house agr. com., house-senate conferee on FY 1998 Def. Authorization bill, 1997, mem. ho. agrl. com.; gov. State of Ala., 2003—. Past chmn. fin. com. Clay

County Hosp.; mem. First Baptist Ch., men's Sunday sch. tchr., past chmn. bd. trustees; pres., Ala. State Bd. Edn, 2003-. Mem. Masons, Shriners, Jaycees (past pres. Ashland chpt.). Office: Office of the Gov State Capitol 600 Dexter Ave Montgomery AL 36130

RILEY, ROBERT BARTLETT, landscape architect; b. Chgo., Jan. 28, 1931; s. Robert James and Ruth (Collins) R.; m. Nancy Rebecca Mills, Oct. 5, 1956; children: Rebecca Hill, Kimber Bartlett. PhB, U. Chgo., 1949; BArch, MIT, 1954. Chief designer Kea, Shaw, Grimm & Crichton, Hyattsville, Md., 1959-64; prin. partner Robert B. Riley (A.I.A.), Albuquerque, 1964-70; campus planner, asso. prof. architecture, dir. Center Environ. Research and Devel., U. N.Mex., 1966-70; prof. landscape architecture and architecture U. Ill., Urbana-Champaign, 1970—, head dept. landscape architecture, 1970-85, dir. PhD program, 1999—; vis. prof. Harvard U., 1996-97; prof. emeritus, dir. joint PhD program U. Ill., 1997—. Sr. fellow landscape architecture studies Dumbarton Oaks/Harvard U., 1992—, chmn. fellows, 1996—; mem. rev. panel landscape architects Fed. Civil Service-Nat. Endowment Arts. Assoc. editor Landscape mag., 1967-70; editor Landscape Jour., 1987—. Served with USAF, 1954-58. Nell Norris fellow U. Melbourne, Australia, 1977; project fellow Nat. Endowment Arts, 1985 Fellow Am. Soc. Landscape Architects (Nat. Honor award 1979); mem. Coun. of Educators in Landscape Architecture, pres. 1984-85, chmn. bd. dirs. 1985-86, Outstanding Educator award 1992, Pres.'s award 1994, chmn. editl. adv. bd. Landscape Architecture 1996-99), AIA (Design award Md. 1962, N.Mex. 1968, Environ. Svc. award N.Mex. 1970), Environ. Design Rsch. Assn. (chmn. bd. 1990-91, Career award 2003), Phi Beta Epsilon. Unitarian Universalist. Office: Univ Ill 101 Temple Buell Hall 611 E Lorado Taft Dr Champaign IL 61820-6921 Home: 407 E George Huff Dr Urbana IL 61801-6703 Business E-Mail: rbriley@uiuc.edu.

RILEY, ROBERT SHEAN, writer, publishing executive, retired army officer; b. West Point, Ky., Oct. 16, 1929; s. Niram Brooks and Nan Estelle (Shean) R.; m. Matsuko Uechi, Mar. 24, 1955; children: Elizabeth Mae, Robert Jr. BS in Engring., U.S. Mil. Acad., 1952; MPA, U. Okla., 1974; M in Internat. Affairs, Columbia U., 1975. Commd. 2d lt. U.S. Army, 1952, advanced through grades to col.; writer, pub. Lawton, Okla., 1978—. Author: History of Shumate Family, 1992, Our European Origins, 1992, History O'Ferrall-Shaen Family, 1994, History of Ditto Families, 1996, The Colonial Riley Families of the Tidewater Frontier, 1999, Marc Hardouin (Mark Hardin) and Descendants, 2003. Decorated Bronze Star medal with 3 oak leaf clusters, Air medal, Joint Svc. Commendation medal, Meritorious Svc. medal with 1 oak leaf clusters, Army Commendation medal. Mem. Mil. Order of World Wars, West Point Soc. Methodist. E-mail: rsriley29@sbcglobal.net.

RILEY, ROCHELLE ROSALIND, writer; b. Detroit, May 6, 1967; d. James Paul and Prenzetta Jenice (Beckford) Riley; m. Sidney Wilson, Aug. 28, 1998; children: Michael Clark, Kayla Wilson, Krista Wilson. AA in langs., Oakland C.C., Mich., 1987; diploma in paralegal, Lawton U., Mich., 2004. Cert. therapeutic massage Mich., 1999. Author, 1984—; writer, prodr., dir. Continental Cablevision, Mich., 1985—89; geriatric nurse, 1991—99. Natural healing cons., 1998—. Author: (book) Memoirs of Nate Garfinkel, Holocause Survivor, 1983, How to Make love to your Child, 1991, Elephant the Ant, 1999—, (movie) Joanna, 1986; author: (prodr.) The Exchange, 1987; editor: (mag.) Disting. Singles, 1990—92. Avocations: volunteering, bicycling, reading. Office: JW Promotions 25545 Lahser Rd Southfield MI 48034 Office Phone: 248-355-3814.

RILEY, RONALD JIM, industrial engineer, consultant; b. Flint, Mich., June 10, 1950; s. Jack Robert and Rose Alice (Millard) R.; m. Laura Jean Gill, June 23, 1979; children: Meghan Kathleen, Caitlin Rose. Student, C.S. Mott C.C., Flint, 1969-70. Asst. mgr., salesman Howat Electronics, Flint, 1968-70; proprietor Customtronics, Flint, 1970-74; engr. med. equipment Werby Labs., Flint, 1974-76; plant engr. Cara Corp., Detroit, 1976-78; indsl. controls engr. Atlas Techs., Fenton, Mich., 1978-84; engr., mgr. J.N. Fauver Co. subs. Sun Oil, Madison Heights, Mich., 1984-90; inventor Riley Cons., Inc., Grand Blanc, Mich., 1990—. Founder, exec. dir. InventorEd, Inc., 1996—. Contbr. articles to profl. jours.; patentee in field. Mem. Union of Concerned Scientists, Action on Smoking and Health, Pub. Citizen, Profl. Inventors Alliance (pres. 1996—), Alliance for Am. Innovation Inc. (pres. adv. bd. 1996-2002), Intellectual Property Creators (adv. bd. 1995-2000), Student Coalition for Handling Intellectual Property. Avocations: horticulture, carpentry, solar and renewable energy, education. Office: Riley Cons, Inc 1323 W Cook Rd Grand Blanc MI 48439-9364 E-mail: rjriley@rjriley.com.

RILEY, RUTH ELLEN, professional basketball player; b. Macy, Ind. d. Sharon Riley. B in psychology in Psychology, U. Notre Dame, 2001. Basketball player North Miami High Sch., U. Notre Dame, Miami Sol, WNBA, 2001—03, Detroit Shock, WNBA, 2003—. Mem. USA Select Team, 1998, USA Basketball Women's Sr. Nat. Team, 2004; mem., NCAA Divsn. 1 Nat. Championship Team U. Notre Dame, 2001; mem., WNBA championship team Detroit Shock, 2003; mem. US Women's Basketball Team, Athens Olympic Games, Greece, 2004. Named Big East Female Scholar-Athlete of Yr. award, 2001, Most Outstanding Player, Final Four, 2001, Naismith and AP Coll Player of Yr., 2001, Most Valuable Player, WNBA Finals, 2003; named to Verizon Women's Basketball Academic All-American first team, 2000, 2001; recipient Silver medal, World U. Games, 1999. Achievements include No. 5 overall pick by the Miami Sol in the 2001 WNBA draft; only Norte Dame player to have reached 2,000 points and 1,000 rebounds. Office: USA Basketball 5465 Mark Dabling Blvd Colorado Springs CO 80918-3842*

RILEY, SUSAN JEAN, retail executive; b. N.Y.C., Apr. 6, 1958; d. Donald E. and Regina A. (Alt) R.; m. Clive D. Conley, June 22, 1985 (dec. 1994); 1 child, Emily Claire. BS, Rochester Inst. Tech., 1981; MBA, Pace U., 1987. CPA, N.Y. Acct. Goldstein & Viele, Rochester, N.Y., 1979-81; auditor Arthur Andersen & Co., Rochester, 1981-82; internal auditor Bristol Myers Squibb, N.Y.C., 1982-83, sr. fin. analyst, 1983-84, mgr. finance, 1984-85, mgr. treas. ops., 1985-87; internat. fin. mgr. Tambrands Inc., Lake Success, N.Y., 1987-90, dir. fin. White Plains, N.Y., 1990-92, v.p. fin. Ams. divsn., 1992-94, v.p. corp. fin., 1994-95, CFO, 1995—97; sr. v.p., CFO Dial Corp., 1997—2000; CFO Mt. Sinai Med. Ctr., NY, 2002—04, Abercrombie & Fitch Co., 2004—. Named Fin. Exec. of Yr. Inst. Mgmt. Accts., 1995, one of Acad. of Women Achievers YWCA of N.Y., 1994. Mem. Fin. Execs. Inst. Avocations: youth soccer coach, needlepoint, collecting doll house furniture. Office: Abercrombie & Fitch 6301 Fitch Path New Albany OH 43054*

RILEY, THOMAS JOSEPH, anthropologist, educational administrator; b. Portland, Maine, Nov. 2, 1943; s. Joseph Gerard and Virginia C. (Cunningham) R.; m. Karma Jean Ibsen, July 10, 1967 (div. 1985); children: Kirsten, Katharine, Erin; m. Carol Ann, Nov. 21, 1989; 1 child, Julia Wade. BA, Boston Coll., 1965; MA, U. Hawaii, 1970, PhD, 1973. Asst. prof. NYU, 1972-74; from asst. prof. to prof. anthropology U. Ill., Urbana, 1974-96, assoc. dean Grad. Coll., 1983-86, head dept. anthropology, 1986-93, chmn. univ. senate coun., 1995-96; dean Coll. Arts, Humanities/Social Scis., prof. anthropology N.D. State U., Fargo, 1996—; dir. N.D. Inst. for Regional Studies, 1996—. Acad. adv. bd. SALT Ctr., Portland, 1980-96. Co-author: Prehistoric Agriculture, 1972; mem. editl. bd. Ency. of World Cultures, 1993-96, Ency. of Cultural Anthropology, 1994-95, Encyclopedia of World Prehistory, 1996-2001; contbr. over 100 articles to profl. jours. Chmn. bd. Devel. Svcs. Ctr., Champaign, 1986-89, Human Rels. Area Files at Yale U., 1995-96, v.p. 1996; sec. bd. C-U Independence, Champaign, 1987-96; bd. dirs. Disabled Citizens Found., Champaign, 1988-96, Ill. Assn. Retarded Citizens, Chgo., 1988-94, Champaign County Mental Health Bd., 1993-96, Prairie Pub. Broadcasting, 1999-, Plains Art Mus., Fargo, vice-chmn., 2001-; bd. dirs. N.D. State Hist. Soc. Found., 2001-, Ill. State Hist. Sites Adv. Coun., 1986-89, United Way Cass-Clay, 2001-. Fellow, NSF, 1978—79; grantee, 1978—99. Mem. AAAS, Am. Assn. State and Local History, Am. Anthropology Assn., Ill. Archeol. Survey, Soc. Am. Archaeology, Soc. Archeol. Scis. (treas. 1982-83), Sigma Xi (chpt. v.p. 1987-88, chpt. pres. 1988-91). Roman Catholic. Home: 1108 42nd Ave N Fargo ND 58102-5318 also: 155 Beach Ave Kennebunk ME 04043-7625 Office: ND State U 221 Minard Hall Fargo ND 58105 Office Phone: 701-231-8338. E-mail: thomas.riley@ndsu.nodak.edu.

RILEY, TOM JOSEPH, lawyer; b. Cedar Rapids, Iowa, Jan. 9, 1929; s. Joseph Wendell and Edna (Kyle) R.; m. Nancy Evans, Jan. 21, 1952; children: Pamela Chang, Peter, Lisa Thirnbeck, Martha Brown, Sara Riley, Heather Mescher. BA, U. Iowa, 1950, JD, 1952. Bar: Iowa 1952, U.S. Dist. Ct. (no. dist.) Iowa 1952, U.S. Ct. Appeals (8th cir.) 1960, U.S. Ct. Appeals (7th cir.) 1977, U.S. Ct. Appeals (9th cir.) 1996, U.S. Supreme Ct. 1966. Assoc. Simmons, Perrine, Allbright & Ellwood, Cedar Rapids, 1952-60, ptnr., 1960-80; pres. Tom Riley Law Firm, P.C., Cedar Rapids, 1980—. Adj. prof. trial advocacy Coll. Law, U. Iowa, Iowa City, 1979. Author: Proving Punitive Damages, 1981, The Price of a Life, 1986, Trial Handbook for Iowa Lawyers (Civil), 1997, Iowa Practice: Civil Litigation Handbook, 2000-01. Mem. Iowa Ho. of Reps., 1960-64, Iowa Senate, 1965-74. First lt. USAF, 1952-54. Named Outstanding Freshman Legislator, Des Moines Press and Radio Club, 1961. Fellow Iowa Acad. Trial Lawyers (bd. govs. 1982-91); mem. Iowa Trial Lawyers Assn. (bd. govs. 2000-2002), Cedar Rapids Country Club. Democrat. Presbyterian. Avocations: tennis, sailing, downhill skiing. Home: 5300 Lakeside Rd Rural Route Marion IA 52302 Office: 4040 1st Ave NE Cedar Rapids IA 52402-3143 Office Phone: 319-363-4040. Business E-Mail: rtom@trlf.com.

RILEY, VICTOR J., JR., financial services company executive; b. Buffalo, Aug. 29, 1931; s. Victor J. and Gwenevieve Riley; m. Marilyn A. Felrath, Aug. 8, 1954; children: Victor J. III, Karen, Patricia, Kevin, Shawn, Mary Katherine BA in Econs., U. Notre Dame; LLD, Coll. St. Rose, 1983. With trust div. 1st Nat. Bank Miami, Fla., 1955-62; mgr. Miami office Bowles, Andrews & Towne, 1962-64; trust officer Nat. Comml. Bank (now Key Bank N.A.), Albany, N.Y., 1964-73; pres., chief exec. officer KeyCorp (formerly Key Banks Inc.), Albany, 1973-96, chmn. emeritus, 1996—; ret., 1996. Also dir.; chmn. bd. Key Bank N.A., Albany, 1984—, Ctr. Econ. Growth; dir. Albany Med. Ctr., Interstate Banking Commn. for State of N.Y., 1986—. Hon. chmn. Capital Dist. Cerebral Palsy Telethon, Albany, 1981-87; bd. dirs. Pop Warner Football League; chmn. various fund raising drives. Served with U.S. Army, 1953-55. Apptd. civilian aide to Sec. Army, 1985—. Decorated Knight of Malta Mem. N.Y. State Bankers Assn. (long-range planning com.), Interstate Banking Com. State N.Y. Republican. Roman Catholic. Avocations: travel, fishing, cooking. Home: PO Box 2414 Cody WY 82414-2414 Office: KeyCorp 1130 Sheridan Ave Cody WY 82414-3647

RILEY, WILLIAM, corporate executive, writer, conservationist; b. Indpls., June 30, 1931; s. Leo Michael and Edna (Wilhelm) R.; m. Laura Etz, Apr. 20, 1957. AB, U. Notre Dame, 1952; LLB, Yale U., 1955. V.p., dir., chmn. Ivy Corp., Atlanta, 1960-80; CEO, chmn. Moore-Handley, Inc., Birmingham, Ala., 1981—. Bd. dirs. Fabco-Air, Inc., Gainesville, Fla. Author: (with Laura Riley) Guide to the National Wildlife Refuges, 1979 (Pulitzer prize nominee), 2d edit., 1993, Lifetime Conservation award Nat. Audubon Soc., 2000. Trustee The Raptor Trust, Basking Ridge, N.J., 1980-2000; bd. dirs. Nat. Wildlife Refuge Assn., Potomac, Md., 1985-94, Hawk Mountain Sanctuary Assn., Kempton, Pa., 1989-98, Nat. Audubon Soc., N.Y.C., 1990-94; chmn. exec. com. Everglades Fdn., 1997—. With U.S. Army, 1957-58. Recipient Conservationist of Yr. award Everglades Coalition, 2001. Mem.: Explorers Club of N.Y.C., Met. Club of N.Y.C. Office: 767 Fifth Ave 44th Floor New York NY 10153

RILEY, WILLIAM JAY, federal judge; b. Lincoln, Nebr., Mar. 11, 1947; s. Don Paul and Marian Frances (Munn) R.; m. Norma Jean Mason, Dec. 27, 1965; children: Brian, Kevin, Erin. BA, U. Nebr., 1969, JD with distinction, 1972. Bar: Nebr. 1972, U.S. Dist. Ct. Nebr. 1972, U.S. Ct. Appeals (8th cir.) 1974; cert. civil trial specialist Nat. Bd. Trial Advocacy. Law clk. U.S. Ct. Appeals (8th cir.), Omaha, 1972-73; assoc. Fitzgerald, Schorr Law Firm, P.C., LLO, Omaha, 1973-79; shareholder Fitzgerald, Schorr Law Firm, Omaha, 1979—2001; US Circuit Judge 8th Circuit Ct. Appeals, 2001—. Adj. prof. trial practice Creighton U. Coll. Law, Omaha, 1991—; chmn. fed. practice com. Fed. Ct., 1992-94. Scoutmaster Boy Scouts Am., Omaha, 1979—89, scout membership chair Mid. Am. coun., 1995—98, trustee, 2001—. Recipient Silver Beaver award Boy Scouts Am., 1991. Fellow Am. Coll. Trial Lawyers (chair state com. 1997-99), Nebr. State Bar Found.; mem. Am. Bd. Trial Advs. (Nebr. chpt. pres. 2000), Nebr. State Bar Assn. (chmn. ethics com. 1996-98, ho. of dels. 1998—, profl. com. 2002—), Omaha Bar Assn. (treas. 1997-98, pres. 2000-01), Robert M. Spire Inns of Ct. (master 1994—, counselor 1997-98), Order of Coif, Phi Beta Kappa. Republican. Methodist. Avocations: reading, hiking, bicycling. Office: Roman L Hruska US Courthouse 111 S 18th Plaza Ste 4303 Omaha NE 68102-1325

RILL, JAMES FRANKLIN, lawyer; b. Evanston, Ill., Mar. 4, 1933; s. John Columbus and Frances Eleanor (Hill) R.; m. Mary Elizabeth Laws, June 14, 1957; children: James Franklin, Roderick M. AB cum laude, Dartmouth Coll., 1954; LLB, Harvard, 1959. Bar: D.C. bar 1959. Legis. asst. Congressman James P. S. Devereux, Washington, 1952; pvt. practice Washington, 1959-89; assoc. Steadman, Collier & Shannon, 1959-63; ptnr. Collier, Shannon & Rill, 1963-69, Collier, Shannon, Rill & Scott, 1969-89; asst. atty. gen., antitrust div. U.S. Dept. Justice, Washington, 1989-92; ptnr. Collier, Shannon, Rill & Scott, Washington, 1992-2000; co-chair internat. competition policy adv. com. U.S. Dept. Justice, 1997-2000; ptnr. Howrey Simon Arnold & White LLP, Washington, 2000—. Pub. mem. Adminstrv. Conf. of U.S., 1992-94; coun. prin. Coun. for Excellence in Govt.; mem., advisor panel Office of Tech. Assessment of Multinat. Firms and U.S. Tech. Base. Contbr. articles to profl. jours. Trustee emeritus Bullis Sch., Potomac, Md. Served to 1st lt. arty. AUS, 1954-56. Fellow: Am. Bar Found.; mem.: ABA (antitrust law sect., past chmn.), DC Bar Assn., Loudoun Valley Club, Met. Club, Phi Delta Theta. Home: 7305 Masters Dr Potomac MD 20854-3850 Office: Howrey Simon Arnold & White, LLP Rm 621 1299 Pennsylvania Ave NW Washington DC 20004-2402

RILLING, DAVID CARL, surgeon; b. Phila., Oct. 10, 1940; s. Carl Adam and Elizabeth Barbara (Young) R.; m. Karina Sturman, Mar. 25, 1972; children: Jonathan David, Alexander Valentine, Claudia Carla. BS with honors in Biology, Dickinson Coll., Carlisle, pa., 1962; MD, Hahnemann U., 1966. Diplomate Am. Bd. Surgery. Intern Hosp. of U. Pa., Phila., 1966-67; resident Abington (Pa.) Meml. Hosp., 1967-68, 70-73; surgeon Pennridge Surg Assocs., Sellersville, Pa., 1973—. Active staff Grand View Hosp., Sellersville, Pa., chmn. dept. surgery, 1985-89, pres. med. staff, 1995. Lt. col. U.S. Army, 1968-70, Vietnam, USARMC. Decorated Bronze Star medal, Nat. Def. Svc. medal, Vietnam Svc. medal. Fellow Am. Coll. Surgeons; mem. AMA, Soc. Clin. Vascular Surgery, Pa. Med. Soc., Bucks County Med. Soc., Vietnam Vascular Registry. Avocations: paleontology, tennis, skiing. Office: Pennridge Surg Assocs 670 Lawn Ave Sellersville PA 18960-1571

RILLING, JOHN ROBERT, history professor; b. Wausau, Wis., Apr. 28, 1932; s. John Peter and Esther Laura (Wright) R.; m. Joanne Marilyn McCrory, Dec. 21, 1953; children: Geoffrey Alan, Andrew Peter. BA summa cum laude, U. Minn., 1953; AM, Harvard U., 1957, PhD, 1959. Asst. prof. history U. Richmond, Va., 1959-62, assoc. prof. history, 1962-68, prof. history, 1968-99, prof. English history emeritus, 1999—, chmn. dept. history, 1977-83, Westhampton Coll., 1965-71. Pres. Faculty Senate of Va., 1975-77. Contbr. articles to profl. jours. Elder, Ginter Park Presbyn. Ch., 1973-83. Served with U.S. Army, 1953-55. Recipient U. Richmond Disting. Educator award, 1975, 76, 77, 80, 87, Prof. of Yr. finalist Coun. for Advancement and Support of Edn., 1981. Woodrow Wilson fellow, 1955-59; Harvard U. travelling fellow, 1958; Coolidge fellow, 1955-56; Folger Libr. fellow, 1960. Mem. Am. Hist. Assn., Econ. History Soc., Agecroft Assn. (bd. dirs.), Conf. Brit. Studies, Phi Beta Kappa, Omicron Delta Kappa (Prof. of Yr. 1995). Avocations: hiking, bicycling, enology. Home: 1507 Wilmington Ave Richmond VA 23227-4429 Office: U Richmond Dept History Richmond VA 23173 Business E-Mail: jrilling@richmond.edu.

RIMA, INGRID HAHNE, economics professor; b. Fed. Republic of Germany; d. Max F. and Hertha G. (Grunsfeld) Hahne; m. Philip W. Rima; children: David, Eric. BA with honors, CUNY, 1945; MA, U. Pa., 1946, PhD, 1951. Prof. econs. Temple U., Phila., 1967—. Author: Development of Economic Analysis, 1967, 6th edit., 2000, Labor Markets Wages and Employment, 1981, The Joan Robinson Legacy, 1991, The Political Economy of Global Restructuring, Vol. I, Production and Organization, Vol. II, Trade and Finance, 1993, Measurement, Quantification and Economic Analysis, 1994, Labor Markets in a Global Economy, 1996. Fulbright Disting. Lectr. Lingnan U., China, 2000. Fellow Ea. Econ. Assn.; mem. Am. Econ. Assn., History of Econs. Soc. (pres. 1993-4), Phi Beta Kappa. Office: Temple U Broad & Montgomery Ave Philadelphia PA 19122

RIMBACH, EVANGELINE LOIS, retired music educator; b. Portland, Oreg., June 28, 1932; d. Raymond Walter and Viola Clara (Gaebler) Rimbach. BA, Valparaiso (Ind.) U., 1954; MMus, Eastman Sch. Music, Rochester, N.Y., 1956; PhD, Eastman Sch. Music, 1967; student, Pacific Luth. U., Parkland, Wash., 1950-52. Vocal music instr. Goodwin Jr. High Sch., Redwood City, Calif., 1956-57; music instr. Calif. Concordia Coll., Oakland, Calif., 1957-62; prof. music Concordia U., River Forest, Ill., 1964-97, chmn. dept., 1989-97; ret., 1997. Contbg. editor: Church Music, 1965—80; editor: (book) Johann Kuhnau: Magnificat, 1980, (cantata) Johann Kuhnau: Lobe den Herrn, 1993; contbr. (essays) Hymnal Supplement '98 Handbook, Keywords in Church Music, 2004; contbr. articles to profl. jours. Bd. dirs. Civic Symphony of Oak Park-River Forest, 1974-80, concert com. chmn., 1976-78, prog. annotator, 1976-80; mem. choir Grace Luth. Ch., River Forest, 1964-97. AAUW postdoctoral fellow, 1969-70; DAAD grantee, Munich, 1980; recipient Rose of Honor award, Sigma Alpha Iota, 1987. Mem. Am. Musicol. Soc., Assn. Luth. Ch. Musicians (editor newsletter 1998—), Sigma Alpha Iota (Rose of Dedication award 1997). Republican. Lutheran. Avocations: travel, cooking, needlecrafts. Home: Apt L-206 12121 Admiralty Way Everett WA 98204-7507 Fax: 425-265-0837.

RIMEL, IRA WESLEY, writer, US Navy supply officer, real estate specialist, real estate appraiser, real estate broker; b. Wibaux, Mont., Jan. 10, 1921; s. Ira Dice and Hazel Barbara (Webber) Rimel; m. Mary Mackinlay, Dec. 13, 1943 (div.); children: Patricia, Valerie, Linda, David, Glenn. Basic sci./engring, Mont. Sch. Mines, 1943—44; BA in mgmt./acctg., U. Wash., 1943—47; Navy supply, acctg. grad., Harvard Grad. Sch. Bus., 1945—46; nat. security, econ., Indust. Coll. Armed Forces, 1965. Tech. writer Military Manuals Co., Renton, Wash., 1952—55; indsl. agent No. Pacific Railway, Seattle, 1955—58; right of way agent/supr. Mont. Hwy. Dept., Helena, 1958—65; right of way agent Lane County, Eugene, Oreg., 1965—86; columnist Fishing & Hunting News, Seattle, 1992—95; freelance writer, 1956—2003. Ensign, reserve, supply, disbursing, acctg. officer U.S. Navy Naval Prison, Norfolk, Va., 1946; LTJG supply officer liaison U.S. Navy, Republic of Korea, 1950—51. Author: (short stories) Dynamic Tension, 1990 (First Prize, 1990), Lucky Man, 2002 (Best of Show/Class, 2002), Winter Travel, 2002 (First Prize, 2002). Adj., publicity officer/comdr. Disabled Am. Vet., Renton, Wash., 1952—58, Wash. publicity officer Seattle, 1953—58; lifetime mem. VFW, Marcola, Oreg., 1960—2003. Lt. jr. grade USN, 1942—46, WWII, Korea, lt. jr. grade USN, 1950—51, WWII, Japan, selected for V-12 Coll. Prog. USN. Named rep. to Rep. Korea, Yokosuka, Japan, Celebration of Commissioning Frigates to Korea, U.S. Navy, 1950; recipient cert., Mont. Sports Outdoors, Missoula, 1959, Author "Lady Gets Her Buck", 1959. Mem.: DAV. Avocations: hunting, fishing, boating, horseback riding, gardening.

RIMEL, REBECCA WEBSTER, foundation administrator; BS, U. Va., 1973; MBA, James Madison U., 1983. Head nurse, emergency dept. U. Va. Hosp., Charlottesville, 1973-74, coord. med. out-patient dept., 1974-75, nurse practitioner dept. neurosurgery, 1975-77, instr. in neurosurgery, 1975-80, asst. prof., 1981-83; program mgr. health Pew Charitable Trusts, Phila., 1983-84; asst. v.p. Glenmede Trust Co., Pew Charitable Trusts, Phila., 1984-85; v.p. for programs Pew Charitable Trusts, Phila., 1985-88, exec. dir., 1988-94, pres., 1994—. Mem. Coun. on Founds., Washington; prin. investigator dept. neurosurgery U. Va., 1981—83; adv. com. Boxing U.S. Olympics, 1983—86; adv. coun. Nat. Inst. of Neurol. Disorders and Strokes, 1988—91, bd. dirs., Thomas Jefferson Meml. Found., Deutsche Banc Flag Investors Fund. Contbr. chpts. in books, articles and abstracts to profl. jours. Recipient Disting. Nursing Alumni award, U. Va., 1988; fellow Kellogg Nat. fellow, 1992. Mem.: APHA, ANA, Va. State Nurses Assn. (membership and credentials com. 1982—86), Emergency Dept. Nurses Assn., Am. Assn. Neurosurg. Nurses, Am. Acad. Nursing.

RIMER, BARBARA K. health facility administrator, educator; b. Wilkes Barre, Pa., Jan. 14, 1949; married. BA in English, U. Mich., 1970, MPH in Med. Care Adminstrn. and Health Edn., 1973; PhD in Health Edn., Johns Hopkins Sch. of Hygiene and Public Health, 1981. Instr. Wayne State U. Sch. Medicine, Detroit, 1973-75; program dir. Nat. Cancer Inst., Bethesda, Md., 1975-77; intervention coord. Johns Hopkins Oncology Ctr., Balt., 1977-79; rsch. assoc. Johns Hopkins Sch. Hygiene and Public Health, Balt., 1977-79; sr. health educator Fox Chase Cancer Ctr., Phila., 1981-87, dir. health comms. rsch., 1981-87, dir. behavioral rsch., 1987-91, dir. population sci. for behavioral rsch., 1990-91; dir. cancer prevention, detection and ctrl. rsch. Duke Comprehensive Cancer Ctr., Durham, NC, 1991-97; sr. fellow Aging Ctr. Duke U. Med. Ctr., Durham, NC, 1991-97, assoc. prof. in cmty. and family medicine, 1991-93, prof. cmty. and family medicine, 1993-97; acting dep. dir. Duke Comprehensive Cancer Ctr., Durham, NC, 1995-96; dir. cancer ctrl. and population scis. Nat. Cancer Inst., Rockville, Md., 1997—2002; prof., Dept. Health Behavior & Health Edn. UNC, Chapel Hill, 2003—, dep. dir., population sciences, Lineberger Cancer Ctr., 2003—. Adj. assoc. prof. dept. health behavior and health edn. U. N.C. Sch. of Public Health, Chapel Hill, NC, 1992-97; adj. mem. Fox Chase Cancer Ctr., Phila., 1992-97; preceptor, lectr. Temple U., 1993-91; guest lectr. Duke U. Med. Ctr., 1991-97, U. N.C. Sch. Public Health, 1991-93; Judith P. Schlager vis. prof. Dana-Farber Cancer Inst., 1995; disting. vis. lectr. Harvard U., 1998; mem. institutional review bd. Fox Chase Cancer Ctr., 1983-88, vice chair, 1988-91; proposal review, site visitor Nat. Cancer Inst., 1985-95; chairperson tech. advisory com. Am. Lung Assn., 1987; external advisory com. Vermont Regional Cancer Ctr., 1988-89; advisory com. Brown U., U. R.I. Cancer Prevention Rsch. unit, 1988-95; mem. Am. Assn. Retired Persons task force on smoking, 1989-91, Health Promotion adv. bd. Wesley Found., 1990-91, program com. annual mtg. Am. Soc. Preventive Oncology, 1990-93, chair, 1993 mtg., expert adv. com. AMC Cancer Rsch. Ctr./Ctrs. for Disease Ctrl. Coop. Agreement, 1991, adult edn. subcom. and tobacco materials review group Am. Cancer Soc., 1991; mem. Nat. Task Force on Breast Cancer Ctrl. Am. Cancer Soc., 1992, chair Nat. and State (NC) Task Force on Breast Cancer Ctrl., 1992; mem. Pub. Edn. subcom. on Adult Edn. Am. Cancer Soc., 1992; mem. adv. bd. Office of Cancer Comms., NCI, 1992; mem. Clin. Cancer com. Duke U. Med. Ctr., 1992-95; mem. Cancer Ctrs.' Support com. NCI, 1993-94, Recruitment and Adherence com. Office of Women's Health NIH, 1993, Report com. Internat. Workshop on Screening for breast cancer NCI, 1993, Detection and Treatment subcom. on Breast Cancer Am. Cancer Soc., 1993, 94, Nominating com. Soc. Behavioral Medicine, 1993-96, adv. com. on cancer coordination and ctrl. State of NC, 1993-97; invited participant and com. chair Frontiers of Behavioral Medicine mtg., Chantilly, Va., 1993; invited co-chair Sec. Shalala's Mtg. to develop nat. strategic plan for breast cancer, Bethesda, Md., 1993; chair, mem. Nat. Cancer Adv. Bd. (presdl. appointment), 1994-97; bd. dirs. Am. Family Life Assurance Corp., 1995—; fellowship selection com. Am. Assn. Cancer Rsch., 1996; mem. exec. com. Acad. Behavioral Medicine Rsch., 1998, Charles S. Mott Selection com. of Gen. Motors Cancer Rsch. Found., 1999, Inst. Medicine com. effective health comm. and behavior change strategies for diverse populations, 2000. Editor: special cancer issue Health Education Research, 1998-89; editl. bd. Health Education Quarterly, 1985-87, guest editl. bd. 1983; editl. bd. Jour. of Compliance in Health Care, 1989-90, Health Edn. Rsch., 1990-98, Cancer Prevention, Epidemiology and Biomarkers, 1990—, Patient Edn. and Counseling, 1994—, Breast Diseases, 1998—, Cancer Causes and Control, 1998—, Effective Clin. Practice, 2000—; assoc. editor: Preventive Medicine, 1990—; reviewer Am. Jour. Preventive Medicine, Am. Jour. Public Health, Annals of Internal Medicine, Health Edn. Quarterly, Health Services Research, Jour. of Am. Med. Assn., Jour. Nat. Cancer Inst., Milbank Quarterly, Women's Health, 1986—; contbr. numerous articles, papers to profl. pubs. Fellow Johns Hopkins Sch. of Hygiene and Public Health, 1979-81, Soc. of Behavioral Medicine, 1997; recipient Mayhew Derryberry award Am. Public Health Assn., 1992, Best Visual Presentation of Session award Soc. of Behavioral Medicine, San Diego, 1995, Citation award

Soc. Behavioral Medicine, 1996, Disting. Achievement award Am. Soc. Preventive Oncology, 1997, Herbert J. Block Leadership award Ohio State U., 1997, John P. McGovern award in Health Promotion U. Tex. Sch. Public Health, 1999.

RIMER, JOHN THOMAS, foreign language educator, academic administrator, writer, translator; b. Pitts., Mar. 2, 1933; s. John T. and Naomi (Bowser) R.; m. Laurence E. Mus., Apr. 18, 1964; children: John, Mark. BA, Princeton U., 1954; MA, Columbia U., 1969, PhD, 1971. Asst. cultural officer USIA, Laos, Japan; then dir. Am. Cultural Ctr. Kobe, Japan, 1958-67; assoc. prof., then prof. Japanese lang. and lit. Washington U., St. Louis, 1973-83, chmn. dept. Chinese and Japanese, 1973-83; chief Asian div. Library of Congress, Washington, 1983-86; chmn. Hebrew and East Asian langs. and lits. U. Maryland, College Park, 1986-91; chmn. East Asian langs. and lit. U. Pitts., 1991—. Mem. Am. adv. bd. Japan Found., 1984- Author: Toward a Modern Japanese Theatre, 1974, Traditions in Modern Japanese Fiction, 1978; translator: stories Mori Ogai, 2 vols., 1977, Mask and Sword: Two Plays for the Contemporary Japanese Theatre, 1980, On the No Drama, 1983, Pilgrimages, 1988, A Reader's Guide to Japanese Literature, 1988; editor: Multiple Meanings, 1987; editor, contbr.: Culture and Identity, Japanese Intellectuals during the Interwar Years, 1990, Shisendo, 1991, Youth and Other Stories by Mori Ogai, 1994, Kyoto Encounters, 1995, A Hidden Fire: Russian and Japanese Cultural Encounters, 1868-1929, 1995, The Blue-eyed Tarōkaja: Essays by Donald Keene, 1996, Nara Encounters, 1997, The Voyage of Japanese Theatre: Theatre Criticism of Senda Akihiko, 1997, Poems to Sing: The Wakan Rōeishū, 1997, (with Marlene J. Mayo) War, Occupation, and Creativity: Japan and East Asia 1920-1960, 2001, Collected Writings of J. Thomas Rimer, 2004. Served with U.S. Army, 1955-58. NEH fellow France, 1976-77; NEH grantee, 1979-81; recipient Order of the Sacred Treasure award Japanese Govt., 1997. Mem. Social Sci. Research Council (joint com. on Japan studies 1979-83) Episcopalian. Home: 1400 N Negley Ave Pittsburgh PA 15206-1118 Office: U Pitts Dept East Asian Langs and Lits 1501 CL Pittsburgh PA 15260 Office Phone: 412-624-5568.

RIMES, LEANN, country music singer; b. Jackson, Miss., Aug. 28, 1982; Singer: (albums) Blue, 1996, Unchained Melody: The Early Years, 1997, You Light Up My Life: Inspirational Songs, 1997, Sittin' on Top of the World, 1998, LeAnn Rimes, 1999, I Need You, 2001, Twisted Angel, 2002; writer: (TV films) Holiday in Your Heart, 1997; guest appearance: (TV series) American Dreams, 2003; (films) Coyote Ugly, 2000; author: (children's books) Jag, 2003. Nominated Best Country Singer award Country Music Assn., 1996; recipient Grammy award (2), 1997, Best New Artist, 1997, Acad. of Country Music award (3), 1997; named Billboard Artist of Yr., 1997. Office: care Curb Records 3907 W Alameda Ave 2d Fl Burbank CA 91505-4332

RIMLER, ANITA A. secretary of state; Campaign aide, legis. asst. former Del. Rob James, 1975; asst. Atty. Gen. Mary Sue Terry, 1985—91; dir. fin. ops. Terry for Gov. campaign, 1993, Robb for Senate campaign, 1994, Warner's U.S. Senate campaign, 1996; sr. advisor, dir. fin. ops. Warner for Gov. campaign; Sec. of State State of Va., 2002—. Democrat. Office: Office Sec Commonwealth 830 E Main St 14th Fl Richmond VA 23219 Business E-Mail: socmail@gov.state.va.us.*

RIMOIN, DAVID LAWRENCE, medical geneticist; b. Montreal, Nov. 9, 1936; s. Michael and Fay (Lecker) Rimoin; m. Mary Ann Singleton, 1962 (div. 1979); 1 child, Anne; m. Ann Piilani Garber, July 27, 1980; children: Michael, Lauren. BSc, McGill U., Montreal, 1957, MSc, MD, CM, 1961; PhD, Johns Hopkins U., 1967; LHD (hon.), Finch U., 1997. Asst. prof. medicine, pediat. Washington U., St. Louis, 1967—70; assoc. prof. UCLA, 1970—73, prof., 1973—, chief med. genetics, Harbor-UCLA Med. Ctr., 1970—86; chair dept. pediat., dir. Med. Genetics and Birth Defects Ctr. Cedars-Sinai Med. Ctr., L.A., 1986—2004, Steven Spielberg chair, 1989—, dir. Med. Genetics Inst., 2004—. Chmn. coun. Med. Genetics Orgn., 1993. Co-author: Principles and Practice of Medical Genetics, 1983, 1990, 1996, 2002; contbr. articles to profl. jours., chapters to books. Recipient E. Mead Johnson award, Am. Acad. Pediat., 1976, Col. Harland Saunders award, March of Dimes, 1997, Pioneer in Medicine award, Cedars Sinai Med. Ctr., 2001. Fellow: Am. Coll. Med. Genetics (pres. 1991—96, bd. dirs. 1996—2000), AAAS, ACP; mem.: Inst. of Medicine, Assn. Am. Physicians, Am. Pediat. Soc., Am. Soc. Human Genetics (pres. 1984), Am. Bd. Med. Genetics (pres. 1979—83), Western Soc. Pediat. Rsch. (pres. 1995, Ross Outstanding Young Investigator award 1976), Western Soc. Clin. Rsch. (pres. 1978,), Am. Fedn. Clin. Rsch. (sec.-treas. 1972—75), Am. Coll. Med. Genetics Found. (pres. 1999—2002, bd. dirs. 2002—), Johns Hopkins Soc. Scholars. Office: Cedars Sinai Med Ctr 8700 Beverly Blvd Los Angeles CA 90048-1865 Office Phone: 310-423-4461. Business E-Mail: david.rimoin@cshs.org.

RIMPEL, AUGUSTE EUGENE, JR., management and technical consulting executive; b. St. Thomas, V.I., Aug. 25, 1939; s. Auguste Eugene and Leah Eudora (Harris) R. B.A. magna cum laude, Inter-Am. U. P.R., 1957; M.S. in Ch.E., M.I.T., 1961; Ph.D., Carnegie Inst. Tech., 1964; M.B.A., Columbia U., 1964-65; m. Maria Czernetski, Sept. 23, 1966; children: Nicole, Christopher. Research chem. engr. Am. Cyanamid Co., Stamford, Conn., 1961-62; with Arthur D. Little, Inc., Cambridge, Mass., 1965-75, sr. staff mem., 1973-75; commr. of commerce, spl. advisor to gov. for econ. affairs Govt. U.S. V.I., St. Thomas, 1975-78; mem. corp. spl. staff Arthur D. Little, Inc., Cambridge, 1978-81, also v.p. Arthur D. Little Internat., Inc.; v.p. Booz-Allen and Hamilton, Inc., 1981-83; v.p., ptnr., Price Waterhouse, 1983-98, ptnr. Price Waterhouse Coopers, 1998—. sr. partner Boston Global Partners, 2001-; Bd. dirs. Caribbean/Lat. Am. Action, 1979-; chair, bd. dirs. U. V.I., 1997—; mem. subcoms. on internat. econ. devel. U.S. C. of C., 1980-83; bd. dirs. travel adv. bd. U.S. Dept. Commerce, 1977-78; pres. Caribbean Tourism Assn., 1977-78; bd. dirs., mem. exec. com. Caribbean Tourism Research Center, 1976-78. Mem. Am. Inst. Chem. Engrs., Am. Chem. Soc., Am. Inst. Chemists, Soc. Internat. Devel., Sigma Xi. Office: Ste 400 283 Franklin St Boston MA 02103-1195 E-mail: arimpel@aol.com.

RIMSZA, SKIP, former mayor; b. Chgo. m. Kim Gill; children: Brian, Jenny, Alexander, Taylor, Nicole. Mem. Phoenix City Coun., 1990-94; vice mayor City of Phoenix, 1993, mayor, 1994—2003. Former pres. Bd. Realtors. Mem. several cmty. bds.

RINAKER, SAMUEL MAYO, JR., retired utilities executive; b. Chgo., Sept. 29, 1922; s. Samuel Mayo and Marjorie (Horton) R.; m. Alice Benthey, Dec. 17, 1949 (div. 1974); children: Elizabeth Cherry, Samuel M. III, Laura Frazier, Mary Clark. Student, UCLA, 1941-42. Farmer, Nebr. and Ill., 1946-49; exec. sec. to atty. gen. Olympia, Wash., 1949-52; news dir. Sta. KTNT-TV, Tacoma, Wash., 1952-57, Sta. KIRO-TV, Seattle, 1957-60; assoc. news dir., news anchor Sta. KGTV, San Diego, 1960-75; dir. pub. policy San Diego Gas & Electric Co., 1976-84. Bd. dirs. 1st Nat. Bank, Beatrice, Neb., 1976-93. Maj. U.S. Army Air Corps, 1942-46, ETO. Mem. Rotary (bd. dirs. 1965-67), La Jolla Beach Tennis Club. Republican. Presbyterian. Avocation: golf. Home: 5935 Rutgers Rd La Jolla CA 92037-7834 E-mail: smr11@san.rr.com.

RINALDINI, LUIS EMILIO, investment banker; b. Cambridge, Eng., July 29, 1953; came to U.S., 1964; s. Luis Maria and Fanny Josefina (Lopez) R.; m. Elaine Nash McHugh, June 22, 1974 (div. 1987); m. Julie Sayre Short, Aug. 1, 1987. BSE, Princeton U., 1974; MBA, Harvard U., 1980. Architect Johnson Burgee Architects, N.Y.C., 1974-78; assoc. Lazard Freres & Co. LLC, N.Y.C., 1980-85, mng. dir., 1986—. Mem. Piping Rock Club (Locust Valley, N.Y.), Meadowbrook Club (Jericho, N.Y.), Lyford Cay Club (Bahamas), Raquet and Tennis Club (N.Y.C.). Home: 151 Post Rd Old Westbury NY 11568-1712 Office: Lazard Freres & Co LLC 30 Rockefeller Plz Fl 59 New York NY 10112-5900

RINAMAN, JAMES CURTIS, JR., lawyer; b. Miami, Fla., Feb. 8, 1935; s. James Curtis and Ruth Marie (Rader) R.; m. Gloria Margaret Kaspar; children: James, Mark, Christine, Karen BA, U. Fla., 1955, JD, 1960. Bar: Fla. 1960, U.S. Dist. Ct. (so. dist.) Fla. 1960, U.S. Ct. Appeals (5th cir.) 1960, U.S. Supreme Ct. 1963, U.S. Dist. Ct. (mid. dist.) Fla. 1967, U.S. Dist. Ct. (no. dist.) Fla. 1981, U.S. Ct. Appeals (11th cir.) 1981, U.S. Ct. Claims 1991, U.S. Ct. Mil. Appeals 1994; cert. civil trial lawyer Fla. Bar. With Marks, Gray, Conroy & Gibbs, P.A., Jacksonville, Fla., 1960—. Gen. counsel Fla. Bd. Architecture, 1965-79, City of Jacksonville, 1970-71, Jacksonville C. of C., 1973-76, 90; adj. prof. Coll. Architecture, U. Fla., 1975-90; dir. gen. The Southern Acad. Letters, Arts and Scis., 1997—. Pres. Jacksonville Cmty. Coun. Inc., 1985. Leadership Jacksonville, Inc., 1987; mem. Jacksonville Transp. Authority, 1971-80, Jacksonville Base Realignment and Closure Commn., 1993-95. Jacksonville Cecil Field Devel. Commn., 1994-96; chmn. N.E. Fla. chpt. ARC, 1996. With U.S. Army, 1955-57, Fla. NG, 1957-92. ret. brig. gen., 1992. Named to U. Fla. Hall of Fame. Fellow Am. Coll. Trial Lawyers, Am. Bar Found., Fla. Bar Found. (bd. dirs. 1982-87, 88, Disting. Svc. award 1983, 86, Medal of Honor 1988); mem. ABA (ho. of dels. 1982-86), Jacksonville Bar Assn. (pres. 1972-73, Lawyer of Yr. 1994), The Fla. Bar (pres. 1982-83), Def. Rsch. Inst. (so. regional v.p. 1980-83, bd. dirs. 1976-78, 83-87), Am. Judicature Soc. (Herbert Harley award 1987), Fla. Coun. Bar Pres. (Outstanding Past Pres. award 1989), Lawyers for Civil Justice (pres. 1989-91, chmn. bd. dirs. 1991-94), Vol. Lawyers Resource Ctr. of Fla., (pres. 1984-89, chmn. bd. dirs. 1989-93), So. Conf. of Bar, Nat. Conf. of Bar, Assn. Def. Trial Attys. (internat. pres. 1976-77), Internat. Assn. Def. Counsel, Jacksonville Assn. Def. Counsel, Fla. Defense Lawyers Assn. (pres. 1973), Fla. C. of C., Jacksonville C. of C. (chmn. 1994), Meninak Civic Club (pres. 1986), Jacksonville Commodores League, The Army War Coll. Alumni Assn. (life), Fla. Blue Key, San Jose Country Club, River Club, Phi Gamma Delta (bd. trustees ednl. found. 1995—), Phi Alpha Delta. Republican. Methodist. Office: Marks Gray Conroy & Gibbs 1200 Riverplace Blvd Ste 800 Jacksonville FL 32207-1805 also: PO Box 447 Jacksonville FL 32201-0447 E-mail: jrinaman@marksgray.com.

RINCHIUSO, DIANA LYNN, academic administrator; b. Louisiana, Mo., Jan. 31, 1949; d. Mary Lou Palmer; m. Angelo Patrick Rinchiuso, June 17, 1972; children: Raegan Janel, Ryan Patrick. BS in Edn., Ill. State U., 1967—71; MS in Edn., U. of Mo., 1973—75. Cert. special edn. tchr. Ill. State Bd. Edn., 1971. Physically handicapped tchr. Quincy Pub. Schools, Ill., 1971—76; cmty. tutor coodinator John Wood C.C., Quincy, 1986—88; adult edn. tchr. Quincy Pub. Schools, 1988—93, Decatur Pub. Schools, Ill., 1993—96; adult edn. dir. Richland C.C., Decatur, 1996—. Committe mem. Westminster Presbyn. Ch., Decatur, Ill., 1993—2003. Mem.: Parent Tchr. Assn. (v.p. 1983—84), United Meth. Women (pres. 1980—81), Beta sigma (sec. 2002—03). Avocations: travel, sewing, gardening, stained glass crafts. Home: 464 Bayshore Dr Decatur IL 62521 Office: Richland C C One Coll Pk Decatur IL 62521 E-mail: drinchiu@richland.edu.

RINDEN, DAVID LEE, clergyman; b. Lake Mills, Iowa, Aug. 1, 1941; s. Oscar Henry and Iva (Stensrud) R.; m. Gracia Elizabeth Carlson, Sept. 11, 1966; children: Jonathan, Elizabeth, Amy. BA, Moorhead State U., 1964; diploma, Luth. Brethren Sem., 1966; postgrad., Seattle Pacific U., 1973. Ordained to ministry Luth. Ch., 1967. Pastor Bethesda Luth. Ch., Eau Claire, Wis., 1968-72, Maple Pk. Luth. Ch., Lynnwood, Wash., 1972-79; v.p. Ch. of the Luth. Brethren of Am., Fergus Falls, Minn., 1991—; editor Faith & Fellowship, Fergus Falls, Minn., 1979-2000; exec. dir. Faith and Fellowship Press Ch. of the Luth. Brethren of Am., Fergus Falls, 1979-2000; pastor Gethsemane Lutheran Ch., Rochester, Minn., 2000—. Chmn. com. on commitment Ch. of Luth. Brethren, Fergus Falls, 1981-82, com. on role of women in ch., 1984-86, chmn. com. on 90th anniversary, chmn. bd. publs., 1986-78. Editor: Explanation of Luther's Small Catechism, 1988; author: Biblical Foundations, 1981. Founding com. JAIL, Inc., Fergus Falls, 1991; pres. bd. dirs. Fergus Falls Fed. Community Credit Union, 1987-2000. Mem. Fergus Falls Ministerial Assn. (sec. 1989-90, v.p. 1991-92, pres. 1992-93), Kiwanis (pres. 1994-95, lt. gov. 1996-97). Home: 1925 Century Valley Rd NE Rochester MN 55906-7705 Office: Gethsemane Lutheran Ch 2204 22d St NW Rochester MN 55901 E-mail: rinden@att.net.

RINDER, LAWRENCE R. curator; Curator 20th-century art & contemporary projects Berkeley Art Museum; found. dir. Wattis Inst. Calif. Coll. of Arts, San Francisco; curator contemporary art Whitney Museum of Am. Art, NYC, 2000—04, adjunct curator, 2004—; dean grad. studies California Coll. of Arts, San Francisco, 2004—. Office: California Coll of Arts 1111 Eighth St San Francisco CA 94107-2247*

RINDFUSS, RONALD RICHARD, sociology educator; b. Buffalo, Dec. 11, 1946; married Aug. 1968; 2 children. BA, Fordham U., 1968; PhD, Princeton U., 1974. Rsch. asst. Nat. Fertility Study, Office Population Rsch., Princeton U., 1971-73; rsch. assoc. Ctr. Demography and Ecology U. Wis., Madison, 1973-76; asst. prof. sociology U. N.C., Chapel Hill, 1976-79, assoc. prof., 1979-84, prof. sociology, 1984-2000, Robert Paul Ziff Disting. prof., 2000—; dir. Carolina Population Ctr., Chapel Hill, 1992-97. Cons. in field Contbr. numerous articles to profl. jours.; assoc. editor Social Forces, 1976—; cons. editor Am. Jour. Sociology, 1977-80; contbg. editor Sociol Biology, 1974; referee for numerous jours. Recipient NIH traineeship, 1968—71, 1st place Erdas award for best sci. paper on remote sensing, 2000. Fellow: AAAS (mem. nominating com. sect. K 2001—); mem.: Sociol. Rsch. Assn., Coun. on Family Rsch., So. Sociol. Soc., So. Regional Demographic Group, Nat. Coun. on Family Rels., Internat. Union for Sci. Study Population, Population Assn. Am. (pres. 1991, Mindel C. Sheps award com. 1990, bd. dirs. 1984—87), Am. Sociol. Assn. (chmn. sociology of population sect. 1989—90, publs. com. 1983—84). Office: Carolina Population Ctr CB # 8120 University Sq 123 W Franklin St Chapel Hill NC 27516-2524 E-mail: Ron_Rindfuss@unc.edu.

RINDONE, JOSEPH PATRICK, clinical pharmacist, educator; b. Santa Fe, Oct. 4, 1954; s. Guido Salvatore and Elizabeth Ann (Murphy) R.; m. Diane Marie Rollins, June 23, 1991; children: Jacqueline, Alexandra. BS, U. Nebr., 1977; PharmD, Creighton U., 1978. Lic. pharmacist, Nebr., Calif. Staff pharmacist Bergan Mercy Hosp., Omaha, 1978, Phoenix (Ariz.) VA Med. Ctr., 1978-81, clin. resident, 1981; clin. pharmacist Tucson VA Med. Ctr., 1982-93; assoc. prof. U. Ariz., Tucson, 1982—; clin. pharmacist Prescott (Ariz.) VA Med. Ctr., 1993—, rsch. coord., 1994—. Author: Therapeutic Monitoring of Antibiotics, 1991; contbr. articles to Arch. Internal Medicine, Pharmacotherapy, Clin. Therapeutics, Am. Jour. Cardiology, Am. Jour. Therapeutics, Chest, West Jour. Medicine, Am. Jour. Health Sys. Pharm., Fereral Practioner, Jour. AMA. Regents scholar U. Nebr., 1976. Avocations: sports, photography, bridge, astronomy. E-mail: JosephRindone@med.va.gov.

RINEHART, AMY HUTCHINSON, publishing executive, consultant; b. Mpls., Apr. 4, 1958; d. Charles Smith and Elizabeth Hall Hutchinson; m. Frederick Roberts Rinehart, June 28, 2003; children: Kay Elizabeth Sorrells, Brian Daniel Sorrells, Alexander V., C.C. BFA, Colo. State U., Fort Collins, 1981. Mktg. coord. Fins & Feathers Pub. Co., Mpls., 1982—83; assoc. media dir. Fitzgerald Advt., New Orleans, 1984—86; dir. of media rsch. WWL-TV, New Orleans, 1986—87; dir. mail supr. The C.S. Monitor, Boston, 1987—88; pub. dir. Geosci. Press, Tucson, 1991—94; mng. editor Roberts Rinehart Pubs., Niwot, Colo., 1994—96, U. Press of Colo., Boulder, 1996—97; editor/assoc. pub. VeloPress, Boulder, Colo., 1997—. Pres. Moonlight Pub. LLC, Lafayette, Colo., 1987—. Mem.: Publishers Assn. of the West (life; bd. of directors 2000—04). Home: 2528 Lexington St Lafayette CO 80026 Office: VeloPress 1830 N 55th St Boulder CO 80301 Personal E-mail: moonlightpubllc@msn.com. E-mail: velopress@7dogs.com.

RINEHART, JAMES FORREST, international relations professor; b. Kansas City, Mo., Dec. 1, 1950; s. Kenneth Perry and Eleanor Louise (Lane) R.; m. Betty Keller, Feb. 3, 1973; children: Erica Christine, Andrew James. BA, U. Fla., 1972; M of Social Sci., Syracuse U., 1991, PhD, 1993. Vis. prof. internat. rels. U. Tenn., Chattanooga, 1993-95; dir., prof. grad. program in internat. rels. U.S. Army John F. Kennedy Spl. Warfare Sch. Troy State U., 1995—, lectr. regional studies program, 1996—. Author: Revolution and the Millennium: China, Mexico and Iran, 1997; contbr. articles to profl. jours. Mem. Coun. on Peace Rsch. in History, 1992-94; founding mem. Mediation Svcs. Task Force for Chattanooga, 1991-95; active Program on Analysis and Resolution of Conflict, Syracuse U., 1991-93; bd. dirs. Ulster Project Chattanooga, 1993-94. Capt. USAR, 1972-80. Recipient Cert. of Achievement U.S. Army JFK Spl. Warfare Ctr. and Sch., 1996. Mem. Am. Polit. Sci. Assn., Internat. Studies Assn, Soc. for Scientific Study of Religion, Internat. Soc. Polit. Psychology, Am. Radio Relay League, Pinewild Country Club, Phi Gamma Delta, Fla. Blue Key Soc. Democrat. Presbyterian. Home: 201 Hampton Ave Troy AL 36081-4045

RINEHART, JOHN MCLAIN, composer, education educator; b. Pitts., Pa., Mar. 17, 1937; s. John McLain and Emilie Anna (Dierker) Rinehart; m. Joyce Reynolds; children: John, Guy, Nina, Mary, Pattie, Carla. AB, Kent State U., 1959; MusM, Cleve. Inst. Music, 1961; PhD, Ohio State U., 1970; studied at, Yale U., 1959—60, Case Western Res. U., 1963—67. Piano faculty Cleve. Inst. Music, 1960—63, head of composition, 1984—87; prof. of music Heidelberg Coll., Tiffin, 1963—75, Ctrl. Wash. U., Ellensburg, Wash., 1975—78, Shenandoah Conservatory, Winchester, Va., 1978—82, Oberlin Coll., 1982—83, Wilkes U., Wilkes Barre, 1987—90; chmn. of music dept. Antioch Coll., Yellow Springs, Ohio, 1990—. Co-chair region III Am. Soc. of U. Composers, 1979—82; founding mem./bd. trustees Res. Musica Am., Balt., 1980—82. Composer: of more than 40 compositions. Recipient Ind. Symphony Orch. award, Ind. Symphony; Yaddo Colony Fellow, Yaddo, 1983, Oberlin Rsch. grant, Oberlin Coll., 1982. Mem.: Cleveland Composers Guild. Office: Antioch Coll 795 Livermore Yellow Springs OH 45387 Home: 1610 Ironwood Dr Fairborn OH 45324-3416

RINEHART, NEIL, financial consultant; b. Mt. Ayr, Iowa, May 9, 1951; s. Park and Joan Rinehart; m. Sheila Kay Funderburgh, Sept. 3, 1977; children: Allison Rinehart Billodeau, Matthew. MBA, U. of Iowa, 1970—75. Fin. cons. E.F. Hutton, Dallas, 1977—90; sr. v.p. - investments Smith Barney, Inc., Plano, Tex., 1990—2004; sr. v.p. investments and sr. portfolio mgr. UBS Financial Svc., Dallas, 2004—. Sr. portfolio mgr. Smith Barney, Inc., Plano, Tex., 1999—2004. Author: (book) It's All The Same Game: The Sports Fan's Guide to Success in the Stock Market, 2003. Mem.: Assn. of Authors and Publishers, U. of Iowa Alumni Assn. Avocations: sports, sports psychology, travel. Office: UBS Fin Svc 5080 Spectrum Dr Ste 1000-W Addison TX 75001 Office Phone: 972-450-4367. Personal E-mail: nrtexas@comcast.net. E-mail: neil.rinehart@ubs.com.

RINELLA, BARBARA, book dramatist; b. Rochester, Minn., Aug. 18, 1943; d. George Donald and Agnes Dorothy (van Oostenbrugge) Albers; m. Richard Anthony Rinella, Mar. 22, 1969; children: Richard A. Jr., Anne Albers. AB, Duke U., 1965; MA, U. Mich., 1966. Asst. editor Putman Pub. Co., Chgo., 1966, 67; English tchr. Needham (Mass.) H.S., 1966-67, New Trier H.S., Northfield, Ill., 1967-73; rschr. Mademoiselle mag., Chgo., 1973-78; book reviewer, dramatist Chgo. area, 1979—. Developer creative writing program Joseph Sears Sch., Kenilworth, Ill., 1979-90; guidebook editor Lincoln Park Zoo, Chgo., 1970-75. Mem. drama dept. adv. bd. Duke U., Durham, N.C., 1994-97, mem. alumni governing bd., 1995-99, chmn. alumni admissions coun., 1994—, interviewer, 1979—; mem. sch. bd. New Trier H.S., 1993-97; vol. United Way/Crusade of Mercy, Chgo., 1979-90, chmn. spl. gifts, 1979-80; coach Wilmette (Ill.) Girls Softball, 1988-89; coach, commn., Kenilworth Little League Baseball, 1982-83; vol. Joseph Sears Sch., 1979-90; troop leader, mem. adv. com. local coun. Boy Scouts Am.; variety show coord. local coun. Girl Scouts U.S.A.; chmn. Upward Bound tutoring project, Chgo., 1975; mem. Guild Bd. Lyric Opera, 1974-81; benefit chmn. Mental Health Assn. Chgo., 1982. Recipient Outstanding Vol. award, Duke U., 1988, Woman of Distinction in the Arts award, Girl Scouts U.S., 1997, Best Lectr. rating, Crystal Cruises, 1998—2004, Breast Cancer Heroine award, BMW Ultimate Drive for the Cure, 1999, Visions of Hope award, AstraZeneca, 2003. Avocations: tennis, paddle tennis, travel, reading, writing.

RINER, RONALD NATHAN, cardiologist, business consultant; b. Mar. 7, 1949; AB, Princeton U., 1970; MD, Cornell U., NYC, 1974. Diplomate Am. Bd. Internal Medicine, Am. Bd. Cardiovasc. Disease. Resident in internal medicine NY Hosp., Meml. Sloan-Kettering, Hosp. for Spl. Surgery, NYC, 1974-76; resident in cardiology Mayo Grad. Sch. Medicine, Rochester, Minn., 1976-79; program dir. internal medicine St. Mary's Health Ctr., St. Louis, 1979-82, chmn. dept. internal medicine, 1980-82; pvt. practice St. Louis, 1979-95. Asst. prof. medicine, Washington U. Med. Ctr., 1985-88, pres. Riner Group, Inc., 1980—, Riner Heart Group, Inc., 1980-95; sr. advisor pharm. divsn. BioMed Sys., St. Louis, 1984-95; prof. St. Louis U.; corp. dir. quality affairs SSM Health Care Sys., 1989-91; chmn. Mo. State Med. Assn. Commn. on Med. Econs., 3rd Party Medicine and Govt. Rels., 1990-92; v.p. clin. svcs. Daus. Charity Nat. Health Sys., 1991-95; bd. dirs. Alleghany Health Sys., Tampa, Fla., 1991-96, chmn. bd. dirs., 1994-96; bd. dirs. Horizon/CMS Healthcare, 1996-98, Seton Inst. for Internat. Devel., San Francisco, 1995-97, Seton Inst. for Internat. Devel., San Francisco, 1995-97, Liferate Sys., Inc., 1997-99, Assn. for Corp. Growth, 1998-2001, Mathew Dickey Acad., St. Louis, 1998-2001. Editor practice mgmt. and econs. sect. Jour. Invasive Cardiology, 1996—. Adv. bd. Washington U. Health Policy Inst., 2004. Fellow Inst. for Advanced Study in Internat. Bus., Washington U., 1991. Fellow ACP, Am. Coll. Cardiology, Am. Acad. Med. Dirs.; mem. AAAS, NY Acad. Scis. (life), Mo. Soc. Internal Medicine (coun.), Gov. Rel. Com., Am. Acad. Physician Execs., Mayo Alumni Assns., Am. Cons. League, Am. Mgmt. Assn., Cornell U. Alumni Assn., Princeton Alumni Assn., Princeton U. Club (bd. dirs. 2000—). Office: The Riner Group Inc 1034 S Brentwood Blvd Ste 1640 Saint Louis MO 63117-1216 Office Phone: 314-727-7098.

RINES, JOHN RANDOLPH, investment banker; b. Balt., Aug. 3, 1947; s. John William and Betty (Singer) R.; m. Peggy J. Daugaard, Sept. 19, 1969 (dec. 1978); m. Katherine M. Duff, Nov. 29, 1980; children: Jacqueline D., Eleanor W. BS in Econs., Colo. State U., 1970; MBA, U. Va., 1977. With GM, 1970-75, 77—, fin. analyst, 1977-78, dir. product programs, 1978-80, asst. to pres., 1980-81, gen. dir. fin., 1981-82, exec. dir. Sao Paulo, Brazil, 1982-84, dir. fin. Buick/Oldsmobile/Cadillac group Flint, Mich., 1984-85, gen. mgr. motors holding div. and GM auction Detroit, 1985-91, gen. mgr. parts ops., 1991—; pres. GM Acceptance Corp., Detroit, 1992-97; exec. v.p. Citicorp, Global Markets, 1997-2000; ptnr. Carday.com., N.Y.C., 2000—; pres. Sand Bros. Ltd., 2001—. Trustee Arts Found. Mich., Detroit. Mem. Grosse Pointe (Mich.) Club, Old Club (Harsen's Island), Birmingham Athletic Club. Office: Sands Bros 90 Park Ave New York NY 10016 E-mail: jrines@sandsbros.com.

RINES, ROBERT HARVEY, lawyer, educator, composer; b. Boston, Aug. 30, 1922; s. David and Lucy (Sandberg) R.; m. Carol Williamson, Dec. 29, 1972 (dec. 1993); 1 son, Justice Christopher; children by previous marriage: Robert Louis, Suzi Kay Ann; m. Joanne Hayes, June 2, 1996; 1 stepchild, Laura Ellen Hayes. BS in Physics, MIT, 1942; JD, Georgetown U., 1947; PhD, Nat. Chiao Tung U., 1972; DJ (hon.), New Eng. Coll. Law, 1974; DSc (hon.), Notre Dame Coll., 1994; LLD (hon.), Franklin Pierce U., 2004. Bar: Mass. 1947, D.C. 1947, N.H. 1974, Va. 1983, U.S. Supreme Ct., FCC, Tax Ct., U.S. and Can. patent offices; Registered profl. engr., Mass. Asst. examiner U.S. Patent Office, 1946; partner Rines & Rines, Boston, NH, 1947—; pres., founder, chmn. emeritus Franklin Pierce Law Center, 1973-97. Pres. Jura Corp., 1996—; bd. dirs. Megapulse, Inc., Nat. Inventors Hall of Fame Found., 1997-99, Lord Corp., New Eng. Fish Farming Enterprises-D.E. Salmon Inc., 1983-99, Acad. Applied Sci.-Project Orbis Bangladesh and Singapore Opthamology Programs and Loch Ness Rsch. Program, 1972—, Seagull Tech., Inc., New Eng. Aquarium, 1973-75, Albavision Ltd. U.K., Promotion of Am. Chinese Tech., Knox Mt. Licensors Inc., Ctr. Broadcasting Corp. of N.H., Accelerated Genomics Inc.; Gordon McKay lectr. patent law Harvard, 1956-58; lectr. inventions and innovation MIT, 1962—; commerce tech. adv. bd. Dept. Commerce, 1963-67, nat. inventors coun., 1963-67, 81—; mem. N.H. Gov.'s Crime Study Com., 1976-78; trustee Mass. Eye and Ear Infirmary, 2001—. Author: A Study of Current World-Wide Sources of Electronic and Other Invention and Innovation; Computer Jurisprudence: Create or Perish--The Case for Patents and Inventions; patentee in field of radar and sonar, fish farming and plant nutrients; composer music for on and off broadway prodns. including Drums Under the Windows (S. O'Casy, P. Shyre), Different, Long Voyage Home, Whitman Portrait, Blasts and Bravos (H.L. Menken), Hizzoner the Mayor (Emmy winning tv prodn.), 1-800-Save Me and Friendly Acquaintances (Jack Betts), Bob's Dream, Lincoln Ctr., 1999, Life at MIT suite, (films) Search at Loch Ness, Irish Eyes, 2002. Campaign chmn. United Fund, Belmont Mass., 1960; mem. adv. bd. Harvard-MIT Biomed. Engring. Ctr.,

1976-80; bd. dirs. Allor Found. Capt. AUS, 1942-46, Brevet Col., 1994, U.S. Army Signal Corps. Named to Nat. Inventors Hall of Fame, 1994, Wall of Fame U.S. Army Signal Corps, 1994; recipient Inventions citation Pres. Carter and U.S. Dept. Commerce, 1980, N.H. High Tech. Entrepreneur award, 1989, Beyond Peace award, 1989, Disting. Svc. award Bangladesh, 1990, 96, honors Town of Inverness, Scotland, 2003, Dinsdale award Soc. Sci. Exploration, 2004, Disting. Lifetime award Boston Patent Law Assn., 2004; Robert H. Rines Bldg. dedication at Franklin Pierce Law Ctr., 1993, Distance Learning Ctr. Bldg. dedication MIT, 1997. Fellow Internat. Soc. Cryptozoology; mem. IEEE (sr.), AAAS, ABA, Acad. Applied Sci. (pres., founder, Medal of Honor 1989), Am. Patent Law Assn. (Disting. Lifetime Achievement award Boston chpt. 2004), Sci. Rsch. Soc. Am., Aircraft Owners and Pilots Assn., Nat. Acad. Engring. (patent com. 1969-80, cons. to exec. officer 1979-80), Explorers Club, Harvard Club, Chemists Club, MIT Faculty Club, Nat. Lawyers Club, Capitol Hill Club, Highland Club, Commonwealth Club, Sigma Xi. Unitarian Universalist. Home: 13 Spaulding St Concord NH 03301-2571

RINEY, HAL PATRICK, advertising executive; b. Seattle, Wash., July 17, 1932; s. Hal Patrick and Inez Marie R.; children: Benjamin Kennedy, Samantha Elizabeth. BA, U. Wash., Seattle, 1954. From art dir./writer to v.p., creative dir. BBDO, Inc., San Francisco, 1956-72; exec. v.p., creative dir. Botsford Ketchum, San Francisco, 1972-76; sr. v.p., mng. dir., creative dir. Ogilvy & Mather, San Francisco, 1976-81; exec. v.p. Ogilvy & Mather West, 1981-86; chmn., CEO, Hal Riney & Ptnrs., Inc., San Francisco, 1986-98; chmn. emeritus Publicis & Hal Riney, San Francisco, 1998—. Recipient 5 Lion d'Or du Cannes awards, 19 Clio awards, 15 Addy awards, Grand Prix du Cannes; named to Creative Hall of Fame, Advt. Hall of Fame. Mem. Am. Assn. Advt. Agys., San Francisco Soc. Communicating Arts, Wild Goose Club. Home: 3022 Washington St San Francisco CA 94115 Office: Publicis & Hal Riney 2001 The Embarcadero San Francisco CA 94133-5200

RING, ALICE RUTH BISHOP, retired preventive medicine physician; b. Ft. Collins, Oct. 11, 1931; d. Ernest Otto and Mary Frances Bishop; m. Wallace Harold Ring, July 26, 1956 (div. 1969); children: Rebecca, Eric, Mark; m. Robert Charles Diefenbach, Sept. 10, 1977. BS, Colo. State U., 1953; MD, U. Colo., 1956; MPH, U. Calif., Berkeley, 1971. Diplomate Am. Bd. Preventive Medicine. Physician cons. Utah State Divsn. Health, Salt Lake City, 1960—65; med. dir., project head start Salt Lake City Cmty. Action Program, 1965—70; resident Utah State Divsn. Health, 1969—71; asst. assoc. regional health dir. USPHS, San Francisco, 1971—75, med. cons. Atlanta, 1975—77, dir. primary care, 1977—84; dir. divsn. diabetes control Ctrs. Disease Control, Atlanta, 1984—88; dir. WHO Collabor Ctr., Atlanta, 1986—91; dir. preventive medicine residency Ctrs. Disease Control, Atlanta, 1988—93; exec. dir. Am. Bd. Preventive Medicine, 1993—98. Trustee Am. Bd. Preventive Medicine, 1990—92; lectr. Emory U. Sch. Pub. Health, 1988—94; bd. dirs. Redwood Coast Med. Svcs., v.p., 1994—2004; mem. adv. com. Shamli Hospice, Gualala, Calif.; mem. adv. coun. Sonoma County Area Agy. on Aging, Santa Rosa, Calif., 2001—; bd. dirs. Alliance for Rural Cmty Health, Calif. Co-author: Clinical Diabetes, 1991; author: History of the American Board of Preventive Medicine, 2002. Bd. dirs. Diabetes Assn. Atlanta, 1985—90. Recipient Disting. Svc. award, Am. Bd. Med. Splties, 2004. Fellow: Am. Coll. Preventive Medicine (bd. dirs. 1990—94, Spl. Recognition award 1998); mem.: AMA (grad. med. edn. adv. com. 1993—97), Am. Bd. Med. Specialists (Disting. Svc. award 2004), Am. Acad. Pediat., Assn. Tchrs. Preventive Medicine (steering com. environ. commons 2004—). Office: PO Box 364 Gualala CA 95445-0364 Office Phone: 707-785-2015. Business E-Mail: ard@mcn.org.

RING, ALVIN MANUEL, pathologist, educator; s. Julius and Helen (Krolik) R.; m. Cynthia Joan Jacobson, Sept. 29, 1963; children— Jeffrey, Melinda, Heather. BS, Wayne State U., 1954; MD, U. Mich., 1958. Intern Mt. Carmel Hosp., Detroit, 1958-59; resident in pathology Michael Reese Hosp., Chgo., 1960-62; asst. pathologist Kings County Hosp., Bklyn., 1962-63; assoc. pathologist El Camino Hosp., Mountain View, Calif., 1963-65; chief pathologist, dir. labs. St. Elizabeth's Hosp., Chgo., 1965-72, Holy Cross Hosp., Chgo., 1972-87, Silver Cross Hosp., Joliet, Ill., 1990—. Instr. SUNY, 1962-63, Stanford U., 1963-65; asst. prof. pathology U. Ill., Chgo., 1966-69, assoc. prof., 1969-78, prof., 1978—; adj. clin. prof. No. Ill. U., 1981-87; adj. prof. med. edn. U. Ill. Coll. Medicine, 1988—; chmn. histotech. Nat. Accrediting Agy. for Clin. Lab Scis., 1977-81; mem. spl. adv. com. Health Manpower, 1966-71; pres. Spear Computer Users Group, 1981-82; mem. adv. com. Mid-Am. chpt. ARC, 1979-85; pres. Pathology and Lab Cons., Inc., 1985—; adj. prof., med. dir. Med. Tech., Moraine Valley C.C., 1994—; originator, coord. pathology, med. decision-making courses Nat. Ctr. for Advanced Med. Edn., 1981—, others; co-coord. computer courses Midwest Clin. Conf., 2000—. Author: Laboratory Correlation Manual, 1968, 82, 86, Laboratory Assistant Examination Review Book, 1971, Review Book in Pathology, Anatomic, 1986, Review Book in Pathology, Clinical, 1986; mem. editorial bd. Lab. Medicine, 1975-87; contbr. articles to med. jours. Fellow Coll. Am. Pathology (insp. 1973—, ins. com. 2002-), Am. Soc. Clin. Pathology; mem. AMA, Ill. Med. Soc., Chgo. Med. Soc. (alt. councilor 1980-85, mem. adv. com. on health care delivery), Ill. Pathol. Soc. (trustee 1997—), Chgo. Pathol. Soc. (censor 1980-88, exec. com. 1985-89, program. com. 1987—), Am. Assn. Blood Banks, Assn. Brain Tumor Rsch. (cons.), Exec. Svc. Corps (exec. cons. 1988—), Phi Lambda Kappa (chpt. pres.). Home: 100 Graymoor Ln Olympia Fields IL 60461-1213 Office: Silver Cross Hosp 1200 Maple Rd Joliet IL 60432-1497

RING, GERALD J. real estate developer, insurance executive; b. Madison, Wis., Oct. 6, 1928; s. John George and Mabel Sarah (Rau) R.; m. Armella Marie Dohm, Aug. 20, 1949; children: Michael J., James J., Joseph W. Student public schs., Madison. With Sub-Zero Freezer Co., Madison, 1948-70, mfr.'s rep., 1954-70; founder, chmn. bd. Parkwood Hills Corp., Madison, from 1965; founder, pres. Park Towne Devel. Corp., Madison, from 1969, Ring Devel. Co., 1992—. Bd. dirs. CUNA Mut. Ins. Soc., CUNA Mut. Ins. Group, CUNA Mut. Investment Corp., CUDIS Ins. Soc., all Madison, 1968-98, exec. com., 1973-83, chmn. bd., 1979-81; bd. dirs. CUMIS Ins. Soc., mem. exec. com., 1973-83, chmn. bd., 1977-79; bd. dirs. CMCI Corp., mem. exec. com., 1974-83, chmn. bd., 1981-83; treas. CUNADATA Corp., 1974-81; bd. dirs. Wis. Credit Union League, 1958-79, pres., 1965-67; mem. Wis. Credit Union Rev. Bd., 1967-83, chmn., 1973-76, 82-83; bd. dirs. CUNA Credit Union Nat. Assn., Inc., 1964-81, League Life Ins. Co., League Gen. Ins. Co., Southfield, Mich., CUNA Mut. Fin. Svcs. Corp., Century Ins. Co. Am., Waverly., Iowa. Chmn. Greater Madison C. of C., 1980, bd. dirs., 1976-89, v.p. econ. devel., 1983-85, v.p. govtl. affairs, 1985-89, mem. capital fund raising com., 1983—, chmn. 1983-86; mem. Mayor's Emergency Housing Com., 1984-85; chmn. fin. com. St. Patrick's Congregation, 1983-89; bd. dirs. Cath. Charities of Madison, 1995—, pres., 1996-99; bd. dirs. Future Madison Housing Fund, 1997—. Served with USMC, 1951-53. Mem. Aircraft Owners and Pilots Assn. Lodges: Rotary. (bd. dirs. 1981-83). Roman Catholic. Home: 607 Farwell Dr Madison WI 53704-6029 Office: 402 S Gammon Rd Madison WI 53719-1002

RING, HERBERT EVERETT, management executive; b. Norwich, Conn., Dec. 19, 1925; s. Herbert Everett and Catherine (Riordan) R.; m. Marilyn Elizabeth Dursin, May 21, 1955 (dec. Jan. 1994); children: Nancy Marie, Herbert Everett. BA, Ind. No. U., 1971, MBA, 1973; AMP, Harvard U., 1981. V.p. ops. Ogden Foods, Inc., Toledo, 1963-74, sr. v.p. Boston, 1974-75; v.p. concessions SportSvc. Corp., Buffalo, 1976-78, sr. v.p., 1978-80, pres., 1980-83, bd. dir.; pres. Universal Mgmt. Concept Counseling, Sylvania, Ohio, 1983—2003; prin. Hysen Group II, Livonia, Mich., 1991-95. Counselor L.A. Olympic Concessions Food Svc., 1984, Phila. Meml. Stadium, 1985, Del. North Cos. Internat. London Eng., 1985-86, Chgo. Stadium Corp., 1989-92, Buffalo Sabres N.Y., 1992, Fine Host Inc. Greenwich Ct., 1993, Delaware North of Australia Ltd., 1994, Temp DNC Health Support Ltd., Wellington, New Zealand, 1995, Fanfare Enterprises, 1997, Geneva Lakes Kennel Club, Delavan, Wis., 1997, St. Francis Health Care Ctr., Greenspring, Ohio, 1998, Detroit Opera House, 2000; bd. dirs. Greenfield Restaurant Co., Inc., Letheby and Christopher Ltd., Reading, Berkshire, Eng., Air Terminal Svcs., Inc., The Aud Club, Inc., Bluegrass Turf Svc., Inc., Concession Suppliers, Inc., Cosel Drive-In Theatre, Inc., G&H Sports Concessions, Inc., Hazel Park Parking, Inc. Mem. Toledo Mus. Art., 1985-92. Sgt. Air Corps U.S. Army, 1944-46, ETO, USAF, 1950-51. Mem.: N.W. Ohio Restaurant Assn. (bd. dirs. 1990—93), Internat. Assn. Auditorium Mgrs., Am. Culinary Fedn. Inc. Roman Catholic. Home and Office: 5540 Radcliffe Rd Sylvania OH 43560-3740

RING, JAMES EDWARD PATRICK, mortgage banking consulting executive; b. Washington, Feb. 12, 1940; s. Edward Patrick and Eleanor Elizabeth R.; m. Kathleen Murphy, Aug. 10, 1979; children: Christopher James, Daniel Edward Patrick. Student, Holy Cross Coll., Worcester, Md., 1958-59; BSEE, U.S. Naval Acad., 1963; MBA in Fin., Wharton Sch. Bus., U. Pa., 1972. Lic. securities broker, comml. pilot. Fin. analyst Exec. Office of the President, Washington, 1972-74; sr. budget analyst Bd. Govs. Fed. Res. System, Washington, 1974-77; dir. fin. planning Fed. Home Loan Mortgage Ins., Washington, 1977-83; dir. mktg. Ticor Mortgage Ins., Falls Church, Va., 1983-84, G.E. Mortgage Ins., Mc Lean, Va., 1985-86; sr. v.p. First Chesapeake Mortgage, Beltsville, Md., 1986-88; v.p. G.E. Capital Mortgage Corp., McLean, 1988-94; cons. Mortgage Dynamics, McLean, 1994—2001; sr. mortgage analyst Fed. Housing Fin. Bd., 2001—. Vol. Big Bros. Am., Washington, 1973-81; pres. U.S. Naval Acad. Class of 1963 Found., 1983-2000. Lt. USN, 1963-69. Mem. Wharton Club (Washington), U.S. Naval Acad. Alumni Assn., Army-Navy Country Club. Republican. Roman Catholic. Home: 1716 Stonebridge Rd Alexandria VA 22304-1039 Office: 1777 F St NW Washington DC 20006

RING, JAMES WALTER, physics educator; b. Worcester, NY, Feb. 24, 1929; s. Carlyle Conwell and Lois (Tooley) R.; m. Agnes Elizabeth Muir, July 18, 1959; 1 son, Andrew James. AB, Hamilton Coll., 1951; PhD (Root fellow), U. Rochester, 1958. Asst. prof. physics Hamilton Coll., Clinton, NY, 1957—62, assoc. prof., 1962—69, prof., 1969—75, Winslow prof., 1975—2003, chmn. dept. physics, 1968—80, 1987—88, 1991—92, radiation safety officer, 1964—84, engring. liaison officer, 1969—2002, prof. emeritus, 2003—. Attached physicist Atomic Energy Rsch. Establishment, Harwell, Eng., 1965-66; vis. physicist Phys. Chemistry Lab., Oxford (Eng.) U., 1973; vis. fellow Ctr. for Energy and Environ. Studies, Princeton U., 1981; vis. scientist Lab. for Heating and Air Conditioning, Danish Tech. U., Copenhagen, 1987. Contbr. articles to profl. jour. and books in physics, chemistry, solar energy, environ. sci., health physics, archaeology, and engring. Recipient prize Acad. Edn./Devel., 1980; NSF grantee, 1959-66; NSF sci. faculty fellow, 1965-66 Mem. AAUP (chpt. pres. 1987-92); Am. Phys. Soc., Am. Assn. Physics Tchrs., Phi Beta Kappa, Sigma Xi. Achievements include solar house design and testing; indoor air studies in radon dangers and thermal comfort; study of the use of solar energy by the Romans during the Roman Empire; analysis of experimental evidence for the validity of continuous spontaneous localization theory as an alternative to standard quantum mechanics; detection of Pb210 gamma radiation to establish geochronology for sediment core samples taken in antarctic peninsula bay and straits; to study global warming. Office: Hamilton Coll Dept Physics Clinton NY 13323 Office Phone: 315-859-4366.

RING, LUCILE WILEY, lawyer; b. Kearney, Nebr., Jan. 2, 1920; d. Myrtie Mercer and Alice (Cowell) W.; m. John Robert Ring, Mar. 28, 1948; children: John Raymond, James Wiley, Thomas Eric. AB, U. Nebr., Kearney, 1944; JD, Washington U., 1946. Bar: Mo. 1946, U.S. Dist. Ct. (ea. dist.) Mo. 1947, U.S. Ct. Appeals (8th cir.) 1972. Atty.-adviser, chief legal group adjudications br. Army Fin. Ctr., St. Louis, 1946-52; exec. dir. lawyer referral svcs. St. Louis Bar, 1960-70; pvt. practice St. Louis, 1960-2000; staff law clk. U.S. Ct. Appeals (8th cir.), St. Louis, 1970-72; exec. dir. St. Louis Com. on Cts., 1972-85. Legal advisor Mo. State Anat. Bd., 1965-95; adj. prof. adminstrv. law Webster Coll., Webster Groves, Mo., 1977-78; mem. Mo. Profl. Liability Rev. Bd., State of Mo., 1977-79. Author, editor: Guide to Community Services - Who Do I Talk To, 1974, 75, 76-79, St. Louis Court Directories, 1972, 73, 74, 75, Felony Procedures in St. Louis Courts, 1975; author: Breaking Barriers: The St. Louis Legacy of Women in Law 1869-1969, 1996; author (series): Women Lawyers in St. Louis History, 1996, Women Breaking Barriers, 1998; contbr. articles to profl. jours. Mem. Mo. Mental Health Authority, 1964-65; bd. dirs., v.p. Drug and Substance Abuse Coun., met. St. Louis, 1976-83; mem. adv. coun. St. Louis Agy. on Tng. and Employment, 1976-83; mem. Mayor's Jud. Reform Subcom., St. Louis, 1974-76. Recipient letter of commendation Office of Chief of Fin., U.S. Army, 1952, Outstanding Alumni award, U. Nebr., Kearney, 1994; Washington U. Sch. Law scholar, 1944—46, 1st Mo. woman nominated for Mo. Ct. Appeals, St. Louis Dist., Mo. Appellate Commn., 1972, 1st woman nominated judgeship Mo. Non-Partisan Ct. Plan, 1972. Mem. Bar Assn. Met. St. Louis (v.p. 1975-76), Legal Svcs. Ea. Mo., Inc. (v.p. 1978-79, dir.), Legal Aid Soc. St. Louis City and County (bd. dirs. 1977-78), HUD Women and Housing Commn. (commr. 1975), Women's Bar Assn. (treas. St. Louis chpt. 1949-50), Mo. Assn. Women Lawyers (treas. 1959-60, pres. 1960-61), Washington U. Dental Faculty Wives (pres. 1972-74), Mortar Board, Pi Kappa Delta, Sigma Tau Delta. Methodist. Home and Office: 2041 Reservoir Loop Rd Selah WA 98942-9616

RING, NANCY GAIL, writer; b. Irvington, N.J., Dec. 24, 1956; d. Frank and Dorothy (Kasoff) R.; m. Eric Mark Kaplan, Aug. 1, 1993. Student, Sch. of Mus. of Fine Arts, Boston, 1975-76; BFA, Syracuse U., 1978. Food history columnist, feature food article contbr. N.J. Star Ledger, Newark, 1998—2004. Author, illustrator: Walking on Walnuts, 1996; art exhibited Women Figure, 1990; muralist with pvt. commns., 2000—. Recipient Drawing award Barbara Chase Burke, 1978; fellow Mid-Atlantic Arts Found., 1988, N.Y. Found. for Arts, 1987, Montalvo Ctr. for Arts, 1987. Avocations: baking, cooking, exercise, travel, reading.

RING, RENEE ETHELINE, lawyer; b. Frankfurt, Germany, May 29, 1950; arrived in U.S., 1950; d. Vincent Martin and Etheline Bergetta (Schoolmeesters) R.; m. Paul J. Zofnass, June 24, 1982; children: Jessica Renee, Rebecca Anne. BA, Catholic U. Am., 1972; JD, U. Va., 1976. Bar: N.Y. 1977. Assoc. Whitman & Ransom, N.Y.C., 1976-83, Carro, Spanbock, Fass, Geller, Kaster & Cuiffo, N.Y.C., 1983-86, ptnr., 1986, Finley Kumble Wagner et. al., N.Y.C., 1987; of counsel Kaye, Scholer, Fierman, Hays & Handler, N.Y.C., 1988; ptnr. Kaye, Scholer, Fierman, Hays & Handler, LLP, N.Y.C., 1989-97, Hunton & Williams, N.Y.C., 1997—2002. Trustee The Spence Sch., 2001—02; advisor WestWind Found., 2001—; mem. exec. com. Lawyers for Clinton, Washington, 1991—92; team capt. Clinton Transition Team, Washington, 1992—93; mem. Nat. Lawyers Coun. Dem. Nat. Com., 1993—98; trustee The Clinton Legal Expense Trust, 1998—2002, Pound Ridge Land Conservancy, 2003—, Queens Bot. Garden Soc., 2003—; mem. Alumni Coun. U. Va. Sch. of Law, 1997—, 2d v.p., 2000—01, 1st v.p., 2001—03, pres., 2003—. Mem. ABA, N.Y. Women's Bar Assn. Democrat. Roman Catholic.

RING, RONALD HERMAN, lawyer; b. Flint, Mich., Nov. 30, 1938; s. Herman and Lydia (Miller) R.; m. Joan Kay Whitener, Aug. 5, 1966. AB, U. Mich., 1961, LLB, 1964. Bar: Mich. 1964, U.S. Dist. Ct. (ea. dist.) Mich. 1966. Assoc. Beagle, Benton & Hicks, Flint, 1964-69; ptnr. Beagle & Ring, Flint, 1970-80, Beagle, Ring & Beagle, Flint, 1980-85, Ring, Beagle & Busch, Flint, 1985-93, Ronald H. Ring, P.C., Flint, 1993-95; pvt. practice Flint, 1991—. Mem. meml. com. Crossroads Village, Flint, 1981; pres. Family Service Agy., Genesee County, Mich., 1986. Mem. ABA, Assn. Trial Lawyers Am., Mich. Bar Assn. (delivery of legal service com. 1986, med. malpractice panel 1986), Genesee County Bar Assn. (pres. 1980-81, bd. dirs. 1979-82, cir. ct. mediation panel 1986). Clubs: Ostego Ski (Gaylord, Mich.). Avocations: skiing, sailing. Office: 7993 Bussa Ln Rapid City MI 49676-9203 Office Phone: 616-264-5549. E-mail: ronhring@cs.com.

RING, TERRY WILLIAM, company executive, environmentalist; b. Lewiston, Idaho, Nov. 11, 1955; s. Robert L. and Irene M. (Sullivan) R. BA, Boise State U., 1979. Pres. Silver Creek Outfitters, Inc., Ketchum, Idaho, 1980—. Bd. dirs. Idaho Nature Conservancy, Ketchum, 1982—, chmn., 1986-2; bd. dirs. The Peregrine Fund, Boise, Idaho, 1994—. Mem. Nature Conservancy (Oak Leaf Awd. 1993) Home: PO Box 1096 Sun Valley ID 83353-1096

RING, TWYLA L. state legislator, newspaper editor; b. Sept. 15, 1937; m. Ardell Ring; 4 children. Student, Cambridge C.C. Mem. Minn. Senate from 18th dist., St. Paul, 1999 . Home: 8500 285th Ave NE North Branch MN 55056-6406 Office: Capitol 75 Constitution Ave Saint Paul MN 55155-1601

RINGEL, DEAN, lawyer; b. N.Y.C., Dec. 12, 1947; m. Ronnie Sussman, Aug. 24, 1969; children: Marion, Alicia. BA, Columbia Coll., 1967; JD, Yale U., 1971. Bar: N.Y. 1972, U.S. Ct. Appeals (6th cir.) 1972, U.S. Ct. Appeals (2d and D.C. cirs.) 1974, U.S. Supreme Ct. 1976, U.S. Ct. Appeals (10th cir.) 1982, U.S. Ct. Appeals (11th cir.) 1997, U.S. Ct. Appeals (9th cir.) 2000. Law clk. to Judge Anthony J. Celebrezze U.S. Ct. Appeals (6th cir.), 1971—72; assoc. Cahill Gordon & Reindel, N.Y.C., 1972—79; ptnr. Cahill, Gordon & Reindel, N.Y.C., 1979—. Mem.: ABA (vice chmn. com. on freedom of speech and press 1978—79), Pub. Edn. Assn. (trustee, sec. 1997—2000, trustee CEI-PEA 2000—), Assn. Bar City NY (commn. comm., fed. litigation, antitrust and trade regulation), NY State Bar (chmn. antitrust litigation com., sect. comml. and fed. litigation 1994—96, co-chmn. fed. judiciary com. 1997—2001, co-chair newsgathering com. Media Law Resource Ctr. 2001—, media law com.). Office: Cahill Gordon & Reindel 80 Pine St 17th Fl New York NY 10005-1790

RINGEL, ROBERT LEWIS, university administrator; b. N.Y.C., Jan. 27, 1937; s. Benjamin Seymour and Beatrice (Salis) R.; m. Estelle Neuman, Jan. 18, 1959; children— Stuart Alan, Mark Joseph. BA, Bklyn. Coll., 1959; MS, Purdue U., 1960, PhD, 1962. cert. speech pathologist. Rsch. scientist, laryngeal rsch. lab. Ctr. Health Scis., UCLA, 1962-64; asst. prof. communication disorders U. Wis., 1964 66; from mem. faculty to provost Purdue U., 1966—91, provost, 1991—2001, prof. audiology and speech sci., Donald S. Powers disting. univ. adminstr., 2001—. Vis. prof. Inst. Neurology and Nat. Hosps. Coll. Speech Scis., U. London, 1985; cons. NIH, NEH, Bur. Edn. Handicapped of U.S. Office Edn.; bd. dirs. Indpls. Ctr. for Advanced Rsch., 1988-92; hon. prof. Coll. of Computer Scis. and Mgmt., Rzeszów, Poland, 2000—; bd. dir., faculty adv. Hillel Found. Purdue U., 2000-. Author sci. articles; contbr. to monographs and textbooks; cons. editor Chapman & Hall, London. Bd. dirs. Lafayette Home Hosp., 1978-87, Lafayette Symphony Orch., 1983-85. Recipient Rsch. Career Devel. award Nat. Inst. Dental Rsch., 1967-70, Award for highest merit for sci. article Jour. Speech and Hearing Rsch., 1979, Disting. Alumnus award Bklyn. Coll., 1985; Para-Rabbi fellow Hebrew Union Coll., 2001—; Robert L. Ringerl Art Gallery at Purdue U. named in his honor. Fellow Am. Speech and Hearing Assn. (v.p. Found. 1990—, honors 1998); mem. Nat. Assn. State Univs. and Land Grant Colls. (exec. com. 1988-91, rsch. policy and grad. edn., exec. com. coun. on acad. affairs 1991-2001, com. on instnl. coop., exec. com. provosts instn. coop. com. 1991-2001), Sigma Xi (v.p. 1986—). Office: Purdue Univ Audiology & Speech Sci 1353 Heavilon Hall G-12B West Lafayette IN 47907-1353 Home: 208 Rosebank Ln West Lafayette IN 47906-8613

RINGEL, SHOSHANA, psychotherapist, educator; b. Nahariya, Israel, Mar. 9, 1951; arrived in U.S.A., 1970; d. Asher and Chana Schonfeld; m. Roy J. Ringel, Nov. 7, 1992; children: Gvanit, Godare. BA, Hunter Coll., N.Y., 1982, MSW, 1984; PhD, Smith Coll., Mass., 2001. LCSW Md. Dept. of Health and Mental Hygiene, 2002. Asst. prof. U. No. Iowa, Cedar Falls, Iowa, 1999—2000, We. Mich. U., Kalamazoo, 2000—02, U. Md., Balt., 2002—. Editor: Psychoanalytic Social Work Jour., 2003—; mem. editl. bd.: Clin. Social work Jour., 2003—; contbr. articles to profl. jours. Mem. Coun. Social Work Edn., 2000—. Fellow, Am. Psychoanalytic Assn., 2002—03. Mem.: Nat. Assn. Social Work. Avocations: swimming, yoga, art, reading, meditation. Home: 5 Suntop Ct 301 Baltimore MD 21209 Office: Univ Md 525 W Redwood St Baltimore MD 21201

RINGENBACH, PAUL THOMAS, historian, consultant; b. N.Y.C., Jan. 9, 1936; s. Paul and Helen A. (Lynch) Ringenbach; m. Sally J. Evans, Aug. 29, 1959; children: Kathleen L., Paul J., Daniel P., Edward T. BA in History, Lehigh U., 1957, MA in History, 1959; PhD in History, U. Conn., 1970. Commd. USAF, 1957, advanced through grades to col., 1958—86, ret., 1986; asst. v.p. USAA, San Antonio, 1987—97; cons., 1998—. Cons. Arnold Shapiro Prodns., Santa Monica, Calif., 1998. Author: Tramps and Reformers 1873-1916, 1973, USAA: A Tradition of Service, 1997; co-author: The Battle for An Loc, 1973, 1993. Vice chmn. Bexar County Hist. Commn., San Antonio, 1998—; bd. dirs., adv. bd. Los Campadres, San Antonio, 1990—; bd. dirs. San Antonio Pub. Libr. Found., 1988—96. Mem.: Orgn. Am. Historians, Sigma Nu. Roman Catholic. Avocations: fishing, gardening. Home: 3913 Arroyo Seco Schertz TX 78154 E-mail: Ringpault@aol.com.

RINGER, JAMES MILTON, lawyer; b. Orlando, Fla., July 9, 1943; s. Robert T. and Jessie M. (Rowe) R.; m. Jaquelyn Hope, Apr. 10, 1965; children: Carolyn Hope, James Matthew. AB, Ohio U., 1965; JD, Cornell U., 1968. Bar: N.Y. 1968, U.S. Dist. Ct. (no. dist.) N.Y. 1968, U.S. Dist. Ct. (so. and ea. dists.) N.Y. 1972, U.S. Ct. Appeals (2d cir.) 1972, U.S. Ct. Claims 1976, U.S. Dist. Ct. (we. dist.) N.Y. 1978, U.S. Ct. Appeals (4th cir.) 1981, U.S. Ct. Appeals (9th cir.) 1983. Assoc. Clifford Chance U.S., LLP, N.Y.C., 1968-78, ptnr., 1978—. Instr. bus. law U. Alaska, 1970-71. Editor Cornell Law Rev., 1967-68. Served to lt. JAGC, USNR, 1969-72. Republican. Episcopalian. Office: Clifford Chance US LLP 200 Park Ave Fl 8E New York NY 10166-0899 Office Phone: 212-878-8340. E-mail: james.ringer@cliffordchance.com.

RINGER, JENNIFER, dancer; b. New Bern, N.C. m. James Fayette, July 2000. Student, Wash. Sch. Ballet, Sch. Am. Ballet; BA in English, Fordham U., 1997. Apprentice N.Y.C. Ballet, 1989—90, mem. corps de ballet, 1990—95, soloist, 1995—2000, prin., 2000—. Dancer (ballets) Brahms-Schoenberg Quartet, Divertimento No. 15, A Midsummer Nights Dream, The Nutcracker, Gershwin Concerto, Mozart Serenade, The Sleeping Beauty, Swan Lake, Tributary, I Have My Own Room, Correlazione, 1994, Prism, 2000, Appalachia Waltz, 2000, Morgen, Huoah, The Beethoven Seventh. Office: NYC Ballet NY State Theatre 20 Lincoln Ctr Plz New York NY 10023-6913

RINGGOLD, FAITH, artist; b. N.Y.C., Oct. 8, 1930; BS, CCNY, 1955, MA, 1959; DFA (hon.), Moore Coll. Art, Phila., 1986, Coll. Wooster, Ohio, 1987, Mass. Coll. Art, Boston, 1991, CCNY of CUNY, 1991, Russell Sage Coll., Troy, N.Y., 1996, Parsons Sch. Design, 1996; DSc (hon.), Brockport (N.Y.) State U., 1992, Calif. Coll. Arts and Crafts, Oakland, 1993; DHL (hon.), Malloy Coll., 1997; DHL (hon.), U. Chicago Art Inst., 2001; DFA (hon.), Mary Grove Coll., 2000, William Patterson U., 2001, Chgo. Art Inst., 2001, Marymount Coll., 1999. Art tchr. N.Y. Pub. Schs., 1955-73; lectr. Bank St. Coll. Grad. Sch., N.Y.C., 1970-80; prof. art U. Calif., San Diego, 1984—2002, prof. emeritus, 2002—, ret., 2002. Solo exhbns. include Bernice Steinbaum Gallery, 1991, ACA, 2000, Spectrum Gallery, N.Y.C., 1967, 70 10 year retrospective, Studio Mus. in Harlem, N.Y.C., 1984, Bernice Steinbaum Gallerym N.Y.C., 1987-88, Balt. Mus., Deland (Fla.) Mus., Faith Ringgold 25 Yr. Survey Fine Arts Mus. L.I., Hempstead, 1990-93, Textile Mus., Washington, 1993, Children's Mus. of Manhattan, N.Y.C., 1993-95, Hewlett-Woodmere Pub. Libr., Hewlett, N.Y., 1993-94, St. Louis Art Mus., 1994, Athenaeum, La Jolla, Calif., 1995, A.C.A. Gallery, N.Y.C., 1995, 98, Ind. U. of Pa., 1995, Bowling Green State U., Ind., 1996, New Mus. Contemporary Art, N.Y.C., 1998; exhibited in group shows at Harlem Cultural Coun., N.Y.C., 1966, Meml. Exhibit for MLK, Mus. Modern Art N.Y.C., 1968, Chase Manhattan Bank Collection, Martha Jackson Gallery, N.Y.C., 1970, Am. Women Artists, Gedok, Kunstalle, Hamburg, Ger., 1972, Jubliee, Boston Mus. Fine Arts, 1975, Major Contemporary Women Artists, Suzanne Gross Gallery, Phila., 1984, Committed to Print Mus. Modern Art, N.Y.C., 1988, The Art of Black Am. in Japan, Terada Warehouse, Tokyo, Made in the USA, Art in the 50s and 60s U. Calif. Berkeley Art Mus., Craft Today Poetry of the Physical, Am. Craft Mus., N.Y.C., Portraits and Homage to Mothers Hecksher Mus. Huntington, 1987, N.J. State Mus., Trenton, 1992-94, Fukui Fine Art Mus., Fuki, Japan, 1992, Takushima Modern Art Mus., Japan, 1993, Otani Meml. Art Mus., Japan, 1993, Salina Art Atr., Kans., 1993, Bruce Watkins Ctr. Kansas City, Mo., 1993, Barton County C.C., Great Bend, Kans., 1993, Del. State Coll. Arts Ctr. Gallery, Dover, 1993-94, Roswell Mus. and Art Ctr., N.Mex., 1994, Aknaton Gallery, Cairo, Alexandria, Egypt, Exit Art, N.Y.C., 1994, New Mus. Contemporary Art, N.Y.C., 1996, Spellman Coll. Mus., Atlanta, 1996, Whitney Mus., N.Y.C., 1996, Centre Georges Pompidou, Paris, 1997, Mus.

Art, Ft. Lauderdale, Fla., 1997, N.J. Ctr. Arts, Summit, N.J., 1997, Trout Gallery Dickenson Coll., Carlisle, Pa., numerous others; represented in collections at Chase Manhattan Bank, N.Y.C., Philip Morris Collection, N.Y.C., Children's Mus., Bklyn., Newark Mus., The Women's House of Detention, Rikers Island, N.Y., The Studio Mus., N.Y.C., High Mus., Atlanta, Guggenheim Mus., Met. Mus. Art, Boston Mus. Fine Arts, MOMA, AARP, Washington, Am. Craft Mus., N.Y.C., Clark Mus., Williamstown, Mass., ARCO Chem., Phila., Coca-Cola, Atlanta, Ft. Wayne Mus. Fine Art, Ind., Harold Washington Libr. Ctr., Chgo., Lang Comm. Corp., Coll., Phila. Mus. Art, Pub. Art Pub. Schs., P.S. 22, Bklyn., Spenser Mus. Lawr., Kans., St. Louis Mus. Art, Balt. Mus., Nat. Mus., Washington, Woman's Mus., Washington, Eugenio Maria de Hostos C.C., N.Y.C., MTA 125th St. IRT subway sta. installation, N.Y.C., numerous others; author: Tar Beach, 1991, Aunt Harriet's Underground Railroad in the Sky, 1992 (Picture Book award 1993, Best Children's Book of Yr. 1993), Dinner at Aunt Connie's House, 1993 (Reading Magic award 1993), We Flew Over the Bridge: Memoirs of Faith Ringgold, 1995, Talking to Faith Ringgold, 1995, Bonjour Lonnie, 1996, My Dream of Martin Luther King, Jr., 1996, The Invisible Princess, 1999, If a Bus Could Talk: The Story of Rosa Parks, 1999, Counting to Tar Beach, 1999, Cassie's Colorful Day with Daddy, 1999, Cassie's Word Quilt, 2000; author: (video prodn.) Goodnight Moon: and Other Sleepy Time Tales, Tar Beach, 2000; contbr. articles to profl. jours. Recipient AAUW travel award to Africa, 1976; John Simon Guggenheim Meml. Found. Fellowship (painting), 1987, N.Y. Found. for Arts award (painting), 1988, Nat. Endowment Arts award (sculpture), 1978, (painting) 1989, La Napoule Found. award (painting in So. of France), 1990, Video and Software award Calif. children's book, 1991, Parent's Choice Gold award, 1991, Artist award Studio Mus., Harlem, 1991, Artist of Yr. award Sch. Art League N.Y., 1991, Coretta Scott King award for illustration, 1992, Dist. Artist award Nat. Coun. Art Adminstrs., 1992, award, 1993, Arts Internat. award (travel to Morocco), 1992, Honors award for outstanding achievement in the visual arts Woman's Caucus Arts, N.Y., 1994, Towsend Harris medal City Coll. Alumni Assn., 1995, N.J. Artist of Yr. award N.J. Ctr. Visual Arts, 1997, 31st NAACP Image award, 1999. Home: PO Box 429 Englewood NJ 07631-0429 Office: ACA Gallery 529 W 20th St Fl 5 New York NY 10011-2800 E-mail: any1canfly@aol.com.

RINGKAMP, STEPHEN H. lawyer, educator; b. St. Louis, Nov. 14, 1949; s. Aloysius G. and Melba Ann (Finke) Ringkamp; m. Patricia Sue Fuse, July 5, 1971; children: Christa, Angela, Laura, Stephen M., Kara. BSEE, St. Louis U., 1971, JD cum laude, 1974. Bar: Mo. 1974, U.S. Dist. Ct. (ea. dist.) Mo. 1974, U.S. Ct. Appeals (8th cir.) 1974, U.S. Supreme Ct. 1990. Law clk. 22d Jud. Cir. Mo., St. Louis, 1974-75; mng. prin. The Hullverson Law Firm, St. Louis, 1976—. Chmn., mem. com. on civil instrns. Mo. Supreme Ct., 1981—; adj. prof. law St. Louis U., 1983—; mem. faculty Mo. Jud. Coll., 1993-2003; lectr. legal seminars. Contbr. articles to legal jours. Recipient Trial Lawyer award Mo. Bar Found. 1983, Smithson award for Excellence, 1996. Mem. ABA, ATLA, Mo. Bar Assn. (vice chmn. civil practice com. 1983-84), Mo. Assn. Trial Attys. (pres. 1991), Bar Assn. Met. St. Louis, Lawyers Assn. St. Louis. Office: The Hullverson Law Firm 1010 Market St Ste 1550 Saint Louis MO 63101-2091 Office Phone: 314-421-2313. E-mail: sringkamp@hullverson.com.

RINGLE, BRETT ADELBERT, lawyer, petroleum company executive; b. Berkeley, Calif., Mar. 17, 1951; s. Forrest A. and Elizabeth V. (Darnall) R.; m. Sue Kinslow, May 26, 1973. BA, U. Tex., 1973, JD, 1976. Bar: Tex. 1976, U.S. Dist. Ct. (no. dist.) Tex. 1976, U.S. Supreme Ct. 1980, U.S. Ct. Appeals (5th cir.) 1984. Ptnr. Shank, Irwin & Conant, Dallas, 1976-86, Jones, Day, Reavis & Pogue, Dallas, 1986-96; v.p. Hunt Petroleum Corp., Dallas, 1996—. Adj. prof. law So. Meth. U., Dallas, 1983. Author: (with J.W. Moore and H.I. Bendix) Moore's Federal Practice, 2d edit., Vol. 12, 1980, Vol. 13, 1981, (with J.W. Moore) Vol. 1A, 1982, Vol. 1A Part 2, 1989. Mem. Dallas Bar Assn. Home: 3514 Gillon Ave Dallas TX 75205-3220 Office: Hunt Petroleum Corp 5000 Thanksgiving Tower 1601 Elm St Dallas TX 75201 Office Phone: 214-922-1004. Business E-Mail: bar@huntpetroleum.com.

RINGLEE, ROBERT JAMES, consulting engineering executive; b. Sacramento, Apr. 23, 1926; s. Francis and Marie N. R.; m. Helen Laura Carleton, Aug. 27, 1949; children— Sarah N., Jane C., Robert K. BSEE, U. Wash., 1946, MSEE, 1948; PhD in Mechanics, Rensselaer Poly. Inst., 1964. Registered profl. engr., N.Y. With advanced engrng. program Gen. Electric Co., 1948-51, advanced devel. engr., power transformer dept., 1951-55, supr. power transformer design, 1955-60, sr. analytical engr., 1960-65, mgr. system and equipment reliability, 1965-69; prin. engr. dir. Power Technologies, Inc., Schenectady, 1969-86, prin cons., 1986-93; TAG assoc. Power Techs., Inc., 1993-94, assoc. cons., 1994-98. Contbr. articles to profl. publs.; patentee in field. Mem. Schalmont Bd. Edn., 1966-70, pres., 1968-69. Served with USNR, 1944-46. Recipient Managerial award Gen. Electric Co., 1953 Fellow IEEE (3 prize paper awards), AAAS; mem. Internat. Conf. on High Voltage Power Systems (expert advisor, Attwood Assoc.), Adirondack Mountain Club (pres. 1990-93, acting exec. dir. 1994). Democrat. Unitarian Universalist. Home and Office: 315 Juniper Dr Schenectady NY 12306-1705 E-mail: robert.ringlee@verizon.net.

RINGLER, JAMES M. cookware company executive; b. 1945; BS, U. Buffalo, 1967, MBA, 1968. Mgr., cons. Arthur Andersen & Co., 1968-76; v.p. appliance group Tappan Co., Mansfield, Ohio, 1976-78, gen. v.p., mgr. appliance div., 1978-87, pres., COO, 1987-90, also bd. dirs., 1987-90; exec. v.p. Premark Internat., Inc., Deerfield, Ill., 1990-92, pres., COO, 1992-96, pres., CEO, 1996—, chmn., 1997—; vice chmn. Ill. Tool Works, Inc., Glenview, 1999—. Office: Premark Internat Inc 3600 W Lake Ave Glenview IL 60025-1215 also: Ill Tool Works Inc 3600 W Lake Ave Glenview IL 60025-1215

RINGO, SHIRLEY G. state representative; b. Ft. Collins, Colo., Oct. 29, 1940; m. John Ringo; children: Shawn, Stacy, Shelley. BA, Wash. State U., 1962, MAT, 1965. Math. instr. Edmunds C.C., 1969, Madison Jr. H.S., 1962—68, 1969—71, Wash. State U., 1974—76, Moscow Sch. Dist., 1976—2000; state rep. dist. 6B Idaho Ho. of Reps., Boise, 2002—, mem. commerce and human resources, edn., and transp. and def. coms. Chair Latah County Dems., 1992—96, 2000—02; candidate Idaho Ho. of Reps. Dist 5B, 1999—2000. Mem.: NEA, Nat. Coun. Tchrs. Math., Moscow Edn. Assn. (pres. 1976—2000), Idaho Edn. Assn. (pres. region II 1984—86), Am. Assn. Ret. Persons (bd. dirs. 2001—). Democrat. Methodist. Office: State Capitol PO Box 83720 Boise ID 83720-0081

RINGPFEIL, FRAZISKA, dermatologist; b. Sept. 13, 1967; MD, 1992. Diplomate Am. Bd. Dermatology. Pvt. practice dermatology, Phila. Mem.: Am. Acad. Dermatology (Young Investigators award 2001). Home: 1215 Sandringham Rd Bala Cynwyd PA 19004-2024

RINGWALD, MOLLY, actress; b. Sacramento, Feb. 18, 1968; d. Bob and Adele Ringwald. Grad. high sch., Los Angeles. Actress: (stage prodns.) The Glass Harp, 1973, Annie, 1977, Cabaret, 2001, Enchanted April, 2004 (feature films) Tempest, 1982, Spacehunter: Adventures in the Forbidden Zone, 1983, Sixteen Candles, 1984, The Breakfast Club, 1985, Pretty in Pink, 1986, The Pick-Up Artist, 1987, For Keeps, 1988, Betsy's Wedding, 1990, Seven Sunday, 1994, Office Killer, 1996, Kimberly, 1999, Requiem For Murder, 1999, Teaching Mrs. Tingle, 1999, Cut, 2000, In the Weeds, 2000, Ring of Fire, 2000, Not Another Teen Movie, 2001, The Tulse Luper Suitcases: The Moab Story, 2003; (TV movies) Packin' It In, 1983, P.K. and the Kid, Something to Live For: The Alison Gertz Story, 1992, Twice Upon a Time, 1998, Since You've Been Gone, 1998, The Big Time, 2002; (TV mini-series) The Stand, 1994; regular (TV series) The Facts of Life, 1979-80, Townies, 1996; guest-star: (TV shows) Diff'rent Strokes, The Merv Griffin Show; (Album) Molly Sings, 1974. Office: William Morris Agy 151 S El Camino Dr Beverly Hills CA 90212-2775*

RINI, JOEL, language educator, linguist; b. Cleve., Dec. 4, 1957; s. Joseph Charles and Virginia Ann Rini; m. Pamela Jean De Vries; children: Christopher Michael, Marcus Joel. PhD, U. Mich., Ann Arbor, 1982—87; BS in Ed., Kent State U., 1981. Asst. prof., Spanish linguistics U. Va., 1987—93, assoc. prof., Spanish linguistics, 1993—2000, prof., Spanish linguistics, 2000—. Chmn. of spanish, italian & portuguese U. Va., Charlottesville, 1998—. Author: (books) Motives for Linguistic Change in the Formation of the Spanish Object Pronouns, 1992, Exploring the Role of Morphology in the Evolution of Spanish, 1999; contbr. articles to profl. jours. Home: 1039 Hayrake Ln Charlottesville VA 22903 Office: Univ Virginia 115 Wilson Hall Charlottesville VA 22904 Office Phone: 434-924-4657. Personal E-mail: jrini@adelphia.net. E-mail: jr6b@virginia.edu.

RINK, CHRISTOPHER LEE, information technology consultant, photographer; b. Fullerton, Calif., May 20, 1952; s. Wesley Winfred and Doreen (Warman) R.; children: Christopher Lee, David E., Caroline S. BS in Acctg., No. Ill. U., 1974, MBA, 1976. Teaching asst. No. Ill. U., Dekalb, 1974-76; region acct. Hewlett-Packard Co., Chgo., 1976-77, systems programmer, 1977-80; pres. Amity Systems Assocs., Elmhurst, Ill., 1978-81; programming mgr. Hewlett-Packard Co., Chgo., 1980-81, systems engr., 1981-84, response ctr. engr. Atlanta, 1984-86, info. tech. mgr., 1986-90, info. tech. cons., 1990-2000. Established response ctr. info. tech. dept. Hewlett-Packard, Atlanta, 1986, tech. dir., 1990, established info. tech. resource mgmt. group, established corp.-wide remote ref. sys., designer corp-wide network printing strategy; project mgr. New Ams. Data Ctr., AMS Sys. Co. split project, AMS server Y2K project mgr.; tech. directory AMS network back up; tech. cons. AMS server consol. project, high availability cons. e-commerce solutions. Author (manual) Stock Market Analysis System, 1976; designer Hewlett-Packard centralized call mgmt. sys., e-commerce solutions arch., 1990, corp-wide performance mgmt. sys./Webmaster America's Info. Tech., corp-wide server capacity planning sys., AMS server backup strategy, AMS info. tech. intranet, AMS info. tech. co. split project; author computer programs. Coord. Ptnrs. in Edn. Cobb County, Atlanta, 1987-89. Mem. Inforum INner Cir., Interex, Computer Measurement Group. Avocations: personal computers, photography, tennis. Home: 3409 Bonaire Xing Marietta GA 30066-4789 Office: Hewlett Packard Co 20 Perimeter Summit Blvd NE Atlanta GA 30319-1417 E-mail: chris_rink@chp.com.

RINK, LAWRENCE DONALD, cardiologist; b. Indpls., Oct. 14, 1940; s. Joe Donald and Mary Ellen (Rand) R.; m. Eleanor Jane Zimmerly, Aug. 10, 1963; children: Scott, Virginia. BS, DePauw U., 1962; MD, Ind. U., 1966. Diplomate Am. Bd. Internal Medicine, Am. Bd. Cardiology, Critical Care Medicine. Clin. asst. prof. Ind. U. Med. Sch., Indpls., 1973-79, clin. assoc. prof., 1979-85, clin. prof. medicine, 1985—; cardiologist IMA, Inc., Bloomington, Ind., 1974—; med. dir. Ind. U. Human Performance Lab., 1994—; dir. cardiac rehab. Bloomington Hosp., 1976—, dir. cardiology, 1983—; CEO, chmn. bd. dirs. IMA Inc., 1995—. Physician Ind. U. Basketball Team, 1979—; dir. med. edn. Bloomington Hosp., 1976—; med. dir. Track and Field Pan Am. Games, 1987; U.S. Olympic Physician Olympic Sports Festival, 1989, World Univ. Games, 1990, Olympic Games, Barcelona, 1992, World Univ. Games, Daegu, Korea, 2993, Fukuoka, Japan, 1995, Korea, 1997, Majorca, Spain, 1999, Beijing, 2001; N.Am. continent rep. Fed. Internat. Student Univ. Sports, v.p., 2001—, pres. med. commn. Bd. dirs. J.O. Ritchie Soc., Ind. U. Med. Sch. Bd. dirs., dean's coun. Ind. U. Med. Sch., 1992—. Recipient Quality of Life award Major Bloomington, 1978; named Most Outstanding Flight Surgeon, USN, 1968, Most Outstanding Alumnus, Ind. U. Med. Sch., 1998. Fellow Am. Coll. Cardiology, Am. Heart Assn. (Coivitae award 2003), Am. Soc. Critical Care, Am. Coll. Sports Medicine; mem. AMA, Ind. U. Med. Alumnae Assn. (pres. 1986-87, exec. alumna coun.). Avocations: reading, writing, golf, tennis. Office: IMA Inc 550 Landmark Ave Bloomington IN 47403 Office Phone: 812-331-3407.

RINK, WESLEY WINFRED, retired bank executive; b. Hickory, N.C., June 14, 1922; s. Dewey Lee and Mabel E. (Yount) R.; m. Patricia A. Jones, Aug. 19, 2000; children from previous marriage: Rebecca S., Christopher L. BS in Accountancy, U. Ill., 1947, MS, 1948. Acct., Glidden Co., Chgo., 1948-58; adminstrv. mgr. Central Soya Co., Chgo., 1958-65; v.p., comptroller State Nat. Bank, Evanston, Ill., 1965-71; exec. v.p., dir. Pioneer Trust & Savs. Bank, Chgo., 1971-76; corp. v.p. Exchange Bancorp., Inc., Tampa, 1977-82; sr. v.p. NCNB Nat. Bank Fla., Tampa, 1982-86; fin cons. Temple Terrace, Fla., 1986-2001; ret., 2001. Served to capt. USAAF, 1942-46. Home: 11402 Robles Del Rio Pl Temple Terrace FL 33617-3819

RINKENBERGER, RICHARD KRUG, physical scientist, geologist, consultant; b. Gridley, Ill., May 15, 1933; s. Burl E. and Olive J. (Krug) R.; m. Marilyn Ruth Ratliff, Feb. 19, 1960; children: Janice L., Ginger R., Rebekah P. BA in Geology, U. Colo., 1959. Dir. prospecting Grubstake Assn., Sask., Can., 1958-59; engr. Martin-Marietta Aerospace Co., Denver, 1960-75; geologist U.S. Geol. Survey, Denver, 1975; geologist remote sensing U.S. Mine Safety and Health Adminstrn., Denver, 1975-79; pres., exploration geologist Banner Set, Ltd., Denver, 1980-84; pres., cons. geologist R.K. Rinkenberger & Assocs., Aurora, Colo., 1979-87; phys. scientist U.S. Dept. Energy, Germantown, Md., 1987-97; cons. geologist, rsch. geologist Denver, Rockville, Md., 1988—. Educator prospecting Denver Sch. Prospecting, 1968-71, U. Colo., Denver, Boulder, 1970-75; rsch. geochemist Heritage Chem. Co., Englewood, 1984-86; prospecting researcher, gold and silver prospector R.K. Rinkenberger & Assocs., 1965—. Contbr. articles to profl. publs. Mem. parent adv. bd, supt. of schs. Westminster, Colo., 1982-83. Grantee Saskatchewan (Can.) Dept. Mineral Resources, 1958, 59, U.S. Geol. Survey (remote sensing), 1978. Mem. Denver Mining Club, Sigma Gamma Epsilon. Mem. Ch. of the Nazarene. Achievements include geological theory and experimentation, research on animal and plant killing mechanisms responsible for dinosaur extinction and other mass plant and animal extinctions. Office: 12183 Monaco Dr Brighton CO 80602-9603

RINKER, MARIANNE MARIE, rehabilitation nurse; b. Milford, Del., Aug. 5, 1960; d. James Warren and Ann Marie (Vissman) Graham. LPN, Parkview Hosp., Nashville, 1982; BSN, Vanderbilt U., Nashville, 1988. CRRN. Staff nurse West Side Hosp., Nashville, 1982-85; primary nurse Vanderbilt Med. Ctr., Nashville, 1986-89; head trauma coord. Georgetown Pinnacle Rehab., Louisville, 1989-91; clin. mgr. rehab. svcs. Alliant Health Svcs., Louisville, 1991-92; dir. rehab. nursing Healthsouth Med. Ctr., Richmond, Va., 1992-94; program cons. Rehabcare Group, Inc., St. Louis, 1994-98, dir. clin. edn., 1998—. Facilitator Ky. Head Injury Assn., Louisville, 1989-91; surveyor Commn. on Accreditation of Rehab. Facilities, 1997—. Counselor cmty. educator Vanderbilt AIDS Project, Nashville, 1987-88. Mem. Assn. Rehab. Nurses (adminstrv. mgmt. group 1994—). Avocations: music, literature, swimming, running. Home: 21546 Flanders St Farmington Hills MI 48335-5338

RINKER, RUBY STEWART, foundation administrator; b. Dayton, Ohio, June 11, 1936; d. Encle Stewart and Addie (Hamilton) Stewart-Smith; children: William Bertram Klawonn, Elizabeth Lynn Dennis, William Stewart-Bradley Klawonn. Human relations counselor Palm Beach County Sch. System, West Palm Beach, Fla., 1974-84; adminstrv. asst. Bohmfalk Estate, Palm Beach, Fla., N.Y.C, Newport, R.I., 1984—; pres., CEO Ruby S. Rinker Co., Inc., Palm Beach. Hon. counselor U.S. Naval Acad., U.S. Air Force Acad.; mem. exec. bd. Intercoastal Health Care Sys. Trustee Bohmfalk Charitable Found., Crystal Cathedral Ministries; bd. dirs. Crystal Cathedral Ministries Internat. Bd., Vatican Mus.; mem. adv. bd. Drug Free Am. Mem. Phi Delta Kappa. Home: 561 Island Dr Palm Beach FL 33480-4746 Office: 225 Peruvian Ave Palm Beach FL 33480-4672

RINNE, AUSTIN DEAN, retired insurance company executive; b. Aug. 14, 1919; s. Hermann Henry and Marie (Knudsen) R.; m. Martha Jo Runyan, Dec. 29, 1941; children: Erik Knudsen, Barbara Jane Rivera. Student, Ind. U., 1938-40; grad. ins. mktg., Purdue U., 1947. Spl. agt. Northwestern Mut. Life, Indpls., 1946-56, dist. agt., 1956-58, gen. agt. Dallas, 1958-84, gen. agt. emeritus, 1984—. Bd. dirs., v.p. English Speaking Union, Dallas, 1972, Dallas Opera, 1984—, Indianapolis Philarmonic Orch., 2001— (hon.), Taca Bd., Dallas Cultural Arts Assn. Capt. USAF, 1941-45, ETO. Decorated Purple Heart, Air Medal with cluster, POW medal, Presdl. unit citation Happy Warriors WWII Combat pilots, 8th Air Force Assn., 1995; recipient Trail Boss award S.W. Gen. Agts. and Mgrs. Assn., 1993. Mem. Dallas Estate Planning Coun. (pres. 1965-66), Dallas Assn. Life Underwriters (bd. dirs. 1960-63, Hall of Fame 1989), Million Dollar Roundtable (life), Dallas Knife and Fork (pres., bd. dirs. 1986—), Mil. Order World Wars, English-Speaking Union (dir., v.p. Dallas chpt. 1972—), Dallas Coun. on World Affairs, Dallas Sales and Mktg. Execs. (bd. dirs. 1970-73), Am. Legion Dallas (comdr. met. post 1967), VFW, Sertoma (pres. Dallas chpt. 1967-68, mem. found. bd. 1975—, Sertoman of Yr. 1990), Phi Kappa Psi Alumni Assn. (pres. 1951-52), Ind. U. Alumni Assn. (pres. Dallas/Ft. Worth 1968-69), Phi Kappa Psi (exec. coun. 1972-76, endowment bd. 1989—, Dallas sales and mktg. chpt. bd. 1969-72), Park City Club, Dallas Country Club, Northshore Club. Republican. Methodist. Home: 4311 Bordeaux Ave Dallas TX 75205-3719 Office: 3102 Oak Lawn Ave Ste 650 Dallas TX 75219-6400 Fax: (214) 521-4760.

RINO, BARBARA ELIZABETH, music educator, musician; b. Lincoln, Nebr., Jan. 14, 1945; d. Howard Gillette and Elizabeth Lucille Cook; m. Louis Stanislaus Rino, Dec. 22, 1974; 1 child, John Gaspare. MusB (with distinction), Nebr. Wesleyan U., 1966; violin study, Harold Wippler, Denver, Colo., 1974—77. Lic. tchr. Colo., 1967. Violinist Lincoln Symphony Orch., Lincoln, Nebr., 1962—66; music educator Denver Pub. Sch., Denver, 1966—68; orch. dir. Adams County Sch. Dist. 50, Westminster, Colo., 1969—78, Adams County Sch. Dist. 12 Five Star Schs., Thornton, Colo., 1988—2001; pvt. studio tchr. self employed, Westminster, Colo., 1971—; concertmaster Brico Symphony Orch., Denver, 1972—74; dir. orch. Denver Youth Musicians Inc., 1973—77, 1984—89; free lance violinist Denver Musicians Assn., Denver, 1973—95; orch. clinician, adj. Solo and Group Competitions Youth Orch. Chair Auditions, Colo., 1973—; concertmaster Rocky Mountain Chamber Orch., 1985—87. Conductor: Colo. Music Educators State Conf., 1972, 1975; musician: Disneyland and Universal Studios, Kennedy Arts Ctr., 1976, Expo '86; author (curriculm): Dist. Orch. grades 6-12, 1990. Music activities Westminister United Meth. Ch., Colo., 1980—. Mem.: Music Tchrs'. Nat. Assn., Am. String Tchrs. Assn. (Colo. Outstanding Tchr. of the Yr. 2003), Music Educators Nat. Conf., Phi Kappa Phi, Kappa Delta Pi. Meth. Achievements include pvt. violin and viola students consistently chosen to participate in Colo. All State HS Orch., Western States honor Orch., Denver Young Artist Orch., MTNA divsn., Nat. solo competitions.

RINSCH, MARYANN ELIZABETH, occupational therapist; b. L.A., Aug. 8, 1939; d. Harry William and Thora Analine (Langlie) Hitchcock; m. Charles Emil Rinsch, June 18, 1964; children: Christopher, Daniel, Carl. BS, U. Minn., 1961. Registered occupational therapist Calif., lic. Calif., 2003. Staff occupational therapist Hastings (Minn.) State Hosp., 1961-62, Neuropsychiat. Inst., L.A., 1962-64; staff and sr. occupational therapist Calif. Children's Svcs., L.A., 1964-66, head occupational therapist, 1966-68; researcher A. Jean Ayres, U. So. Calif., L.A., 1968-69; pvt. practice neurodevel. and sensory integraton Tarzana, Calif., 1969-74; pediat. occupational therapist neurodevel. & sensory integration St. Johns Hosp., Santa Monica, Calif., 1991-95; pvt. practice, cons. Santa Monica-Malibu Unified Sch. Dist., 1994-2001; pvt. practice, 2001—. Mem. alliance bd. Natural History Mus., L.A. County, 1983—, pres., 1998-99; cub scouts den mother Boy Souts Am., Sherman Oaks, Calif., 1986-88, advancement chair Boy Scout Troop 474, 1989-92; mem. Vol. League San Fernando Valley, Van Nuys, Calif., 1985-93; trustee Viewpoint Sch., Calabasas, Calif., 1987-90; bd. dirs. Valley Women's Ctr., 1990-91. Mem. Am. Occupational Therapy Assn., Calif. Occupational Therapy Assn. Home: 19849 Greenbriar Dr Tarzana CA 91356-5428

RINSKY, ARTHUR C. lawyer; b. Cin., July 10, 1944; AB with honors, U. Cin., 1966; JD cum laude, U. Mich., 1969; LLM in Taxation, NYU, 1974. Bar: Fla. 1969, Calif. 1975, U.S. Tax Ct. 1974; cert. tax specialist. Ptr. Gray, Cary, Ware & Freidenrich, LLP, Palo Alto, Calif., 1975—. Mem. ABA, State Bar Calif., Phi Beta Kappa, Phi Eta Sigma. Office: Gray Cary Ware & Freidenrich LLP 400 Hamilton Ave Palo Alto CA 94301-1833

RINSKY, JUDITH SUE LYNN, foundation administrator, educator consultant; b. Sept. 12, 1941; d. Allan A. and Sophie (Schwartz) Lynn; m. Joel C. Rinsky, Jan. 29, 1963; children: Heidi Mae Schnapp, Heather Star Maxon, Jason Wayne. BA in Home Econs., Montclair State U., 1963. Tchr. home econs. Florence Ave. Sch., Irvington, NJ, 1963—66; substitute tchr. Millburn-Short Hills Sch. Sys., Millburn Twp., NJ, 1978—82, Millburn-Short Hills Sch. Sys., Millburn Twp., 1990—98; sr. citizen coord. Millburn-Short Hills Sch. Sys., Millburn Twp., 1982—87; coord. respite care Essex County Divsn. on Aging, East Orange, NJ, 1988—90; pvt. practice educator Short Hills, NJ, 1990—98; tchr. basic skills Millburn H.S., 1998—. Bd. mem. adv. com. gerontology Seton Hall U., 1984—90; coord. Mayor's Adv. Bd. Sr. Citizens, Millburn-Short Hills, 1982—87; home instrn. Millburn-Short Hills Sch. Sys., 1997—98; tchr. adv. Millburn H.S. Interart Club, 2000—. Pres. Deerfield Sch. PTA, 1979-80, Millburn H.S. PTA, 1983-85; co-chmn. dinner dance Charles T. King Student Loan Fund, 1981; active Handicapped Access Study Com., 1983-85; bd. dirs. Coun. on Health and Human Svcs., 1985-90, 94-97; acting dir. B'nai Israel Nursery Sch., 1994. Mem. Lake Naomi Assn. (chmn. sailing com. 1981), N.J. Home Econs. Assn., Am. Home Econs. Assn., Rotary (hon., pres. Millburn-Short Hills club 1992-93, bd. dirs. 1992-2000, advisor Millburn interact club 1987-98, 2000-04, chmn. internat. interact dist. 7470 1993-95, advisor 1995-98). Home and Office: 87 Sullivan Dr West Orange NJ 07052-2262 Office Phone: 973-376-3600. Personal E-mail: jsr_07041@yahoo.com. Business E-Mail: rinsky@millburn.org.

RINSLAND, ROLAND DELANO, retired university official; s. Charles henry and Lottie Rinsland. AB with distinction, Va. State U.; AM, profl. diploma, EdD, Columbia U. Asst. to dean of men Va. State Coll., Petersburg; asst. purchasing agt. Glyco Products Co., Inc., N.Y.C.; asst. office registrar Tchrs. Coll. Columbia U., N.Y.C., tchr. cert. advisor, registrar, 1966-71, asst. dean student affairs, registrar, dir. doctoral studies, 1971-95; ret., 1995. Mem. Tchrs. Coll. Devel. Coun.; rep., presenter degrees Tchrs. Coll., Japan, 1989, 91, 93, 94. 1st lt. AUS, 1954-56. Mem. AAAS, NEA (Leah B. Sykes award for life mem.), Am. Coll. Pers. Assn., Nat. Soc. Study Edn., Am. Edni. Rsch. Assn., Assn. Collegiate Registrars and Admission Officers (inter-assn. rep. to state edn. depts. tchr. cert. 1973-74, mem. com. orgn. and adminstrn. registrars activities 1973, 74-76), Assn. Records Execs. and Adminstrs. (charter mem., by-laws and program chmn. 1969), Am. Acad. Polit. and Social Sci., Am. Assn. Higher Edn., Assn. Instl. Rsch., Internat. Assn. Applied Psychology, Soc. Applied Anthropology, Am. Assn. Counseling and Devel., Assn. Study Higher Edn., Mid. States Assn. Collegiate Registrars and Officers of Admission, N.Y. State Pers. and Guidance Assn., N.Y. Acad. Scis., Scabbard and Blade, Kappa Phi Kappa, Kappa Delta Pi, Phi Delta Kappa (emeritus).

RINTAMAKI, JOHN M. automotive executive; BBA, U. Mich., 1964, JD, 1967. Bar: Mich. 1968, Pa. 1973. Sr. atty. internat. Ford Motor Co., 1978-84, assoc. counsel corp. and financings, 1984-86, asst. sec., assoc. counsel, 1986-92, sec., asst. gen. counsel, 1993-98, v.p., gen. counsel, sec., 1999-00, chief staff, 2000—. Office: Ford Motor Co One American Rd Dearborn MI 48126-1899

RINTELMAN, DONALD BRIAN, lawyer; b. Madison, Wis., May 25, 1955; s. Donald Carl Rintelman and Eugenie Elizabeth Kroll; m. Ann Marie Gall, Aug. 2, 1980; children: Katherine Ann, Brian James. BA, U. Wis., 1976; JD, U. Mich., 1980. Bar: Wis. 1980, U.S. Dist. Ct. (ea. dist.) Wis. 1980, U.S. Dist. Ct. (we. dist.) Wis. 1984. Assoc. Whyte & Hirschboeck, S.C., Milw., 1980-86, shareholder, 1986—; mng. dir. Whyte Hirschboeck Dudek, S.C., Milw., 1994—. Chmn. comml. practice group Am. Law Firm Assn. Internat., L.A., 1998-2001. Bd. dirs. Ozaukee County United Way Allocations, Mequon, Wis., 1986-88; pres.-elect Greater Cedarburg (Wis.) Cmty. Found., Inc., 2002—, Cedarburg Booster Club, Inc., 2003—; treas. Cedarburg Cmty. Scholarship Fund, 1991-93; coun. pres. Advent Luth. Ch., Cedarburg, 1996-97. Fellow Am. Coll. Investment Counsel; mem. ABA, Wis. Bar Assn., Milw. Bar Assn. Republican. Avocations: travel, golf, enjoying children's soccer, swimming. Home: N108W7365 Balfour St Cedarburg WI 53012-3248 Office: Whyte Hirschboeck Dudek SC 111 E Wisconsin Ave Ste 2100 Milwaukee WI 53202-4861 Office Phone: 414-978-5506.

RIOPELLE, ARTHUR JEAN, psychologist; b. Thorp, Wis., Apr. 22, 1920; s. Wilfred Gaspar and Ann Marie (Schroeder) R.; m. Mary Jane Astell, May 2, 1942; children— Mary Ann, James Michael, Jean Elizabeth. BS, U. Wis., 1941, MS, 1948, PhD, 1950. Asst. prof., then assoc. prof. Emory U., 1950-57; dir. psychology div. U.S. Army Med. Research Lab., Ft. Knox, Ky., 1957-59; dir. Yerkes Labs. Primate Biology, Orange Park, Fla., 1959-62, Delta Regional Primate Research Ctr., Covington, La., 1962-71; prof. psychology La. State U., Baton Rouge, 1972—, Boyd prof., 1977-89, Boyd prof. emeritus, 1989—. Mem. NRC panel on manganese, Com. on Med. and Biol. Effects of Environ. Pollutants Editor Jour. Gen. Psychology, 1978-95; asst. editor Animal Behavior, 1962-65; cons. editor Jour. Genetic Psychology and Genetic Psychology Monograph, 1978-95; contbr. chpts. to books. La. Bd. Examiners of Psychologists, 1972-75; mem. panel on Air Force tng. Nat. Acad. Sci.-NRC, 1955-56; primate research study sect. Am. Inst. Biol. Scis.-NASA, 1959-63; chmn. sub-com. on man Lunar Receiving Lab. Study, 1970-71; chmn. U.S.-Japan Conf. Primate Research, 1963-64; chmn. sub-com. primate standards Inst. Lab. Animal Resources, NRC, 1964-69. Served with USAAF, 1942-46, ETO. Mem. Am. Psychol. Assn., Am. Physiol. Soc., So. Soc. Philosophy and Psychology, Internat. Primatological Soc., AAAS, Psychonomic Soc., Southeastern Psychol. Assn., Sigma Xi, Phi Kappa Phi, Sigma Chi. Home: 9710 Highland Rd Baton Rouge LA 70810-4031 Office: La State U Dept Psychology Baton Rouge LA 70803-0001

RIORDAN, CORNELIUS, sociology educator, writer, consultant; b. Worcester, Mass., May 29, 1940; s. Cornelius H. and Mary J. Riordan; m. Arline K. Riordan; children: Julie, Kate. BS in Edn., Fitchburg (Mass.) State Coll., 1962; MA in Sociology, Clark U., 1970; PhD in Sociology, Syracuse (N.Y.) U., 1975. Prof. sociology Providence Coll., 1972—; postdoctoral fellow The Johns Hopkins U., Balt., 1979-81. Cons. Childreach, USA, Warwick, R.I., 1993-2002, Regional Lab. at Brown U., Providence, 1997-98, NSF, 2000-02; expert witness cases involving single-sex schooling, 1989-2000; project dir. U.S. Dept. Edn. funded study on single-sex schs: characteristics and effects, 2004—. Author: Girls and Boys in School: Together or Separate, 1990, Equality and Achievement, 2d edit., 2004; contbr. articles to profl. jours. Vol. U.S. Peace Corps, Kerman, Iran, 1963-65; dir. Encampment for Citizenship, N.Y.C., 1965-69. Mem. Am. Sociol. Assn. (coun. 1990-92), Am. Ednl. Rsch. Assn. (grantee 1992-93, 2000-2002). Office: Dept Sociology Providence Coll River & Eaton Sts Providence RI 02918

RIORDAN, GEORGE NICKERSON, investment banker; b. Patchogue, N.Y., May 16, 1933; s. E. Arthur and Constance E. (Whelden) R.; m. Ann Wiggins, Jan. 4, 1958; children— Susan M., Peter G. BS, Cornell U., 1955; MBA, Harvard U., 1960. Vice-pres. Lehman Bros., N.Y.C., 1960-71; mng. dir. Blyth Eastman Paine Webber, Los Angeles and N.Y.C., 1971-81, Prudential-Bache Securities, Los Angeles, 1981-88, Bear Stearns & Co., Inc., L.A., 1988-89, Dean Witter Reynolds Inc., 1989-91. Chmn. bd. MSC Software, Inc., 1997-99; bd. dirs. MSC Software, Inc., L.A. Served to capt. USAF, 1955-57 Mem. Calif. Club, Quoque Field Club (L.I., N.Y.), Athenaeum Club, Valley Hunt Club (Pasadena, Calif.). Office: 815 Colorado Blvd Ste 104 Los Angeles CA 90041-1720 E-mail: george.riordan@mscsoftware.com.

RIORDAN, JAMES QUENTIN, retired company executive; b. Bklyn., June 17, 1927; s. James A. and Ruth M. (Boomer) R.; m. Gloria H. Carlson, June 23, 1951; children: Harris, Susan, James, Ruth. BA, Bklyn. Coll., 1945; LLB, Columbia U., 1949. Bar: N.Y. 1951, U.S. Supreme Ct 1954. Atty. Winthrop, Stimson, Putnam & Roberts, N.Y.C., 1949-51; mem. staff Ways and Means sub-com., Washington, 1951-52; atty. tax div. Justice Dept., Washington, 1952-55; atty. Chadbourne, Parke, Whiteside & Wolff, N.Y.C., 1955-57; various positions to vice chmn., chief fin. officer Mobil Corp., 1957-89; pres. Bekaert Corp., 1989-92; chmn. Quentin Ptnrs. Co., 1996—. Bd. dirs. Com. Econ. Devel., Tax Foun., Inc.; trustee Bklyn. Mus. Mem. Rembrandt Club (N.Y.C.), Blind Brook Club, Sailfish Point (Fla.), Stockbridge Club. Office: 851 Johnson Ave Stuart FL 34994 Office Phone: 772-220-4127.

RIORDAN, JOHN THOMAS, trade association executive; b. Newark, June 5, 1937; s. Daniel Francis and Kathleen May (Hanan) R.; m. Mary Theresa Fleming, Sept. 19, 1966; children: Sheila, Patrick, Aidan, Meghan, Brendan, Caitlin. BA, Montclair St. Coll., 1959; MA, Laval U., Que., Can., 1963; postgrad., Harvard U., 1980. Tchr. Princeton (N.J.) Pub. Schs., 1959-64; instr. SUNY, Cortland, 1965; editor McGraw-Hill Book Co., St. Louis, 1966; assoc. examiner Ednl. Testing Svc., Princeton, 1967-68; mgr. Houghton Mifflin Co., Boston, 1968-73, editl. dir., 1973-74; v.p. Hougton Mifflin Co., Boston, 1974-75, dir., 1975, sr. v.p., 1975-81; dir. programs Internat. Coun. Shopping Ctrs., N.Y.C., 1982-83, gen. mgr., 1983-85, exec. v.p., 1986-96, pres., CEO, 1997—. Cons., leader Experiment in Internat. Living, Brattleboro, Vt., 1961-64; mem. adv. bd. Sch. Internat. Tng., Brattleboro, 1971-79, Real Estate Ctr. U. Pa., 1991—, Ctr. for Real Estate MIT, 1992—; mem. fin. adv. bd. City of Georgetown, Mass., 1972-75; trustee The Pike Sch., Andover, Mass., 1973-76; bd. trustees Travel Bus. Roundtable; mem. adv. bd. Baruch Coll., adv. bd. MIT ctr. for real estate, adv. bd. U Pa. real estate ctr. Mem. Assn. Am. Pubs. (bd. dirs. 1978-80), Am. Soc. Assn. Execs. Office: Internat Council Shopping Ctrs 665 5th Ave New York NY 10022-5305

RIORDAN, MICHAEL C. hospital administrator; b. N.J., 1959; BA in liberal arts and English, Columbia U., 1980, MA in edn. and psychology, 1981; M in health sys., Ga. Inst. Tech., 1986. Various positions Crawford Long Hosp., Atlanta; COO Emory U. Hosp. Sys., 1995—2000; exec. v.p. and COO U. Chgo. Hosps., 2000—01, pres. and CEO, 2001—. With USMC, 1981—85. Office: U Chgo Hosps and Health Sys 5841 S Maryland Ave Chicago IL 60637*

RIOS, EVELYN DEERWESTER, columnist, musician, artist, writer; b. Payne, Ohio, June 25, 1916; d. Jay Russell and Flossie Edith (Fell) Deerwester; m. Edwin Tietjen Rios, Sept. 19, 1942 (dec. Feb. 1987); children: Jane Evelyn, Linda Sue Rios Stahlman. BA with honors, San Jose State U., 1964, MA, 1968. Cert. elem., secondary tchr. Calif. Lectr. in music San Jose (Calif.) State U., 1969-75; from bilingual cons. to assoc. editor Ednl. Factors, Inc., San Jose, 1969-76, mgr. field rsch., 1977-78; writer, editor Calif. MediCorps Program, 1978-85; contbg. editor, illustrator Cmty. Family Mag., Wimberly, Tex., 1983-85; columnist The Springer, Dripping Springs, Tex., 1985-90. Author, illustrator, health instr. textbooks elem. schs., 1980—82. Author: (book) The Best of It Seems To Me, 2002. Chmn. Dripping Springs Planning and Zoning Commn., 1991—93; music dir. Cambrian Park (Calif.) Meth. Ch., 1961—64; choir dir. Bethel Luth. Ch., Cupertino, Calif., 1965—66, 1968—83; dir. music St. Aban's Ch., Bogota, Colombia; organist Holy Spirit Episcopal Ch., Dripping Springs, 1987—94. Mem.: Am. Guild Organists (dean 1963—64), Phi Kappa Phi (pres. San Jose chpt. 1973—74). Avocations: weaving, stitching, painting. Home and Office: 5700 Maya Ln Atascadero CA 93422-2552

RIOS, JO MARIE, political science educator; b. San Antonio; d. Joseph and Guadalupe S. Rios MA, St. Mary's U., San Antonio, 1989, U. Okla., 1994, PhD in Polit. Sci., 1995. Asst. prof. pub. adminstrn. U. Ctrl. Fla., Orlando, 1996-99; asst. prof. polit. sci. and pub. adminstrn. Tex. A&M U., Corpus Christi, 1999—. Vis. instr. pub. adminstrn. U. Tex., San Antonio, 1995-96. Mem. Am. Soc. Pub. Adminstrs., Am. Polit. Sci. Assn., Southwest Polit. Sci. Assn., Policy Studies Orgn., Pi Alpha Alpha. Office: Tex A&M U 6300 Ocean Dr Corpus Christi TX 78412 Home: 4442 Aspen Grove DR Corpus Christi TX 78413-5023 Fax: 361-825-6098. E-mail: jo.m.rios@att.net., jrios@falcon.tamucc.edu.

RIOUX, PIERRE AUGUST, psychiatrist; b. Hartford, Conn., Sept. 2, 1953; s. Berchmans and Mary (Sauter) R. BA, Concordia Coll., 1975; MD, U. N.D., 1981. Diplomate Am. Bd. Psychiatry and Neurology. Intern U. Mich., 1981-82, resident, 1982-85; asst. prof. dept. psychiatry Emory U., Atlanta, 1985-86; attending physician VA Med. Ctr., Atlanta, 1985-86; staff physician UniMed Med. Ctr., Minot, N.D., 1986-87, med. dir. adult partial hospitalization program, 1988-98, dir. behavioral health svcs., 1990—2001; med. dir. North Ctrl. Human Svc. Ctr., Minot, 1987-98; med. dir. stress unit Austin Med. Ctr., 2001—; med. dir. behavioral health Mayo Health Sys., Austin; instr. Mayo Med. Sch., 2003—. Cons. North Ctrl. Human Svc. Ctr., 1986—2001; mem. chem. dependency unit UniMed Med. Ctr, 1986—; mem. adv. bd. UniMed Med. Ctr., 1998—2001; clin. prof. neurosci. U. N.D. Sch. Medicine, 1986—96; mem. family practice residence adv. bd. com. U. N.D., 1987—95; physician advisor N.D. Health Care Rev., Inc., 1987—2001; dir. psychiat. svcs. Dakota Boys Ranch, Minot, 1990—94; med. dir. Rural Mental Health Consortium, 1999—2001; instr. Mayo Med. Sch., 2003—. Bd. Am. Coll. of Heraldry, 2003; comsumer rsch. coun. America's Top Psychiatrists, 2002—. Recipient Nat. Alliance for the Mentally Ill Exemplary Psychiatrist award, 1993, Top Psychiatrists in Am. award Consumers Rsch. Coun. Am., 2003. Fellow Am. Coll. Forensic Examiners (life); mem. AMA, Am. Psychiat. Assn. (pres. N.D. dist. br. 1993-96, dep. rep. area IV coun. 1993-98, mem. psychiat. svcs. achievement awards bd. 1996-97, chmn. 1998, fellowship award 1996, disting. fellowship award 2003), Assn. Am. Physicians and Surgeons, Am. Soc. Clin. Psychopharmacology, N.D. Psychiat. Assn. (dist. br. exec. coun. 1997-2001), N.D. Med. Assn. (mem. commn. on socio-econ. affairs 1997-2001), Internat. Soc. for Philos. Enquiry (pres.). Avocation: art. Office: PO Box 188 Austin MN 55912-0188

RIOUX, SCOTT PAUL, music educator; b. Hartford, Conn., Nov. 25, 1963; s. Louis Thomas and Angela Antoinette Rioux. MusB, Hartt Sch. Music, W. Hartford, Conn., 1986; MusM, U.Conn., Storrs, 1990. Music Education pre-K to 12 Conn., 1986, cert. music edn.pre-K-12 Conn., 1986. Music tchr. Pub. Schools, Glastonbury, Conn., 1987—99; choral dir. Wethersfield H.S., Conn., 1999—. Choir dir. Roman Cath. Ch., Windsor, Conn., 1997—. Musician: (performance, directing) Many Concerts, Competitions (2 Choirs 1st Pl., Festivals of Music, Williamsburg, VA, 2003). Mem.: Am. Choral Directors Assn. (assoc.). Home: 19 Allspice Ln Glastonbury CT 06033 Office: Wethersfield HS 411 Wolcott Hill Rd Wethersfield CT 06109 Office Phone: 860-571-8292. E-mail: srioux hx1@cox.net.

RIPA, KELLY MARIA, television personality; b. Stratford, N.J., Oct. 2, 1970; d. Joseph and Esther Ripa; m. Mark Consuelos, 1996; children: Michael Joseph, Lola Grace, Joaquin Antonio. Student, Camden (N.J.) C.C. Co-host Live with Regis and Kelly, N.Y., 2001—. Dancer (TV series) Dance Party USA, 1986; actor: (TV series) All My Children, 1990—2002 (Soap Opera Digest award, 1996, 1998, 2000, 3 Daytime Emmy nominations); (films) Marvin's Room, 1996, The Stand-In, 1999 (Best Actress award N.Y. Internat. Ind. Film and Video Festival, 1999), It's a Very Merry Muppet Christmas Movie, 2002, Cheaper by the Dozen, 2003; (TV films) Someone to Love, 2001; voice: (films) Kim Possible: A Stitch in Time, 2003; Batman: Mystery of the Batwoman, 2003; actor: (TV series) Hope & Faith, 2003—. Nominee Outstanding Talkshow Host award, Daytime Emmy; named one of 25 Most Intriguing People, People Mag., 2001, Top 20 Entertainers of Yr., E! Entertainment. Office: Live with Regis and Kelly 7 Lincoln Sq New York NY 10023*

RIPKEN, CALVIN EDWIN, JR., (CAL RIPKEN), retired professional baseball player; b. Havre de Grace, Md., Aug. 24, 1960; Player minor league teams, Bluefield, Miami, Charlotte, Rochester, 1978—81; player Balt. Orioles, 1978—2001. Named Am. League MVP, 1983, 1991, MLB All-Star Game MVP, 1983, 2001; named to All-Star Team, Am. League, 1983—2001, MLB All-Century Team, 1999; recipient Rookie of Yr. award, 1982, Golden Glove award, 1991—92. Achievements include being a holder of the major league record for consecutive games played; breaking Lou Gehrig's record of 2131 consecutive games played, 1995; maj. league record home runs by shortstop; highest single season fielding percentage (.996), 1990; most consecutive errorless games at shortstop (95); led Am. League in Runs (121), Hits (211), 1983.*

RIPLEY, ROBERT, actor, writer; s. Robert C. and Elizabeth P. Ripley. BA, Moores Sch. Music, U. Houston, 1992; MFA, Carnegie Mellon U., 2003. Music tchr. Ft. Bend Ind. Sch. Dist., Sugar Land, Tex., 1988—95; writer Los Angeles, Calif., 1995—; film devel. CW Productions, Los Angeles, Calif., 2003. Prodr. Summer New Play Festival, Pittsburgh, 2003—04. Writer (play) Among Cannibals (Runner Up, Maxim Mazumdar prize for new plays, 2002), The Game (Bay Area New Play Festival Finalist, 2002), Reciprocity (ACTF 10 Minute Play Competition Winner, 2001), The Game (Chesterfield Writer's Project Semi-Finalist, 2002), (screenplay) Clock Without Hands (Chesterfield Semi-Finalist, 2002). Mentor AIDS Project, Los Angeles, Calif., 1999—2001. Grantee Shubert Playwriting Fellowship. Mem.: Dramatists Guild (assoc.), AFTRA (assoc.), SAG (assoc.). Independent. Agnostic. Avocations: travel, languages, theater, art. Personal E-mail: rbripley@earthlink.net.

RIPLEY, STUART MCKINNON, real estate consultant; b. July 28, 1930; s. Rob Roy and Nina Pearl (Young) R.; m. Marilyn Haerr MacDiarmid, Dec. 28, 1964; children: Jill, Bruce, Kent. BA, U. Redlands, 1952; MBA, U. Calif., Berkeley, 1959. V.p., dir. J.H. Hedrick & Co., Santa Barbara/San Diego, 1958-63; v.p. mktg. Cavanaugh Devel. Co., San Gabriel, Calif., 1963-65; v.p. mktg. dir. Calabasas Park, Bechtel Corp., Calabasas, Calif., 1967-69; v.p. mktg. Avco Cmty. Developers, Inc., La Jolla, Calif., 1969-74; mktg. dir. U.S. Home Corp., Fla. Divsn., Clearwater, 1974-75; pres., dir. Howard's Camper Country, Inc., National City, Calif., 1975-77; v.p., mktg. dir. Valcas Internat. Corp., San Diego, 1976-77, pres., 1977-79, Stuart M. Ripley, Inc., 1977-79, Sunview Realty, Inc., Watt Industries Co., Santa Monica, Calif., 1979-80; owner Everett Stunz Co., Ltd., La Jolla, 1981—. Exec. v.p. Harriman-Ripley Co., Fallbrook, Calif.; avocado/floraculture rancher, subdivider, Fallbrook, 1978—; lectr. UCLA, 1961; pres. Century 21 Coastal, Century 21 Bajamar, Baja Calif., Mex., 1994-97. Lt. comdr. USNR, 1952-55, ret. U. Redlands fellow, 1960—. Mem. Nat. Assn. Homebuilders, Sales and Mktg. Coun., Sales and Mktg. Execs., Elks, Pi Chi. Republican. Episcopalian. Home: 2085 Via Ladeta La Jolla CA 92037-6905 Office: 7624 Girard Ave La Jolla CA 92037-4420 Office Phone: 858-459-3305. Personal E-mail: sturip@aol.com.

RIPPE, LYNN E. contract administrator; b. Superior, Nebr., Dec. 27, 1947; children: Douglas E., Christopher C. BA in Econs., Kansas State U., 1969; MBA, So. Ill. U., Edwardsville, 1977. Contract specialist, contracting officer Naval Constrn. Bn. Ctr., Port Hueneme, Calif., 1989-93; sr. contract adminstr. U. Calif. Lawrence Livermore (Calif.) Nat. Lab., 1993-98; computing scis. subcontracts mgr. U. Calif. Lawrence Berkeley Nat. Lab., 1998—. Mem. Nat. Contract Mgmt. Assn. (v.p. Tri Valley chpt. 1995-96, pres. 1996-97, nat. dir. 1997-98, 2000-01, nat. v.p. 2001-03). Republican. Roman Catholic. Home: 3478 FM 1670 Belton TX 76513 Office: U Calif Lawrence Berkeley Nat Lab M-50B One Cyclotron Rd Berkeley CA 94720 E-mail: lerippe@nersc.gov.

RIPPERT, ERIC THEODORE, oral and maxillofacial surgeon; b. Ft. Devens, Mass., Feb. 22, 1942; s. Jacob Kopf and Kathleen (Faughnan) R.; m. Mary Ellen Dormer, Nov. 25, 1965; children: Thomas, Kathleen. AB, Holy Cross Coll., 1964; DMD, U. Pa., 1968. Diplomate Am. Bd. Oral and Maxillofacial Surgery. Intern Phila. Gen. Hosp., 1968-69, resident, 1973-76; dental officer U.S. Navy, 1965-95; asst. prof. oral and maxillofacial surgery U. Nebr., Lincoln, 1996-99; asst. prof. U. Pitts., 1999-2000; assoc. prof. Med. Coll. Va., Richmond, 2000—02; assoc. prof., dir. residency tng., oral and maxillofacial surgery Med. Coll. Ga., Augusta, Ga., 2002—. Clin. asst. prof. Med. Coll. Va., Richmond, 1979-81; adj. assoc. prof. Temple U., Phila., 1984-87; asst. prof. U. Calif., San Francisco, 1991-93. Fellow Am. Assn. Oral and Maxillofacial Surgeons, Internat. Coll. Dentists; mem. Varsity Club Coll. Holy Cross, Delta Sigma Delta. Republican. Roman Catholic. Avocations: tennis, skiing, speech and dialogue, writing. Office: Dept Oral and Maxillofacial Surg Med Coll Ga Sch of Dentistry Augusta GA 30912 E-mail: erippert@mail.mcg.edu.

RIPPETEAU, BRUCE ESTES, archaeologist, administrator; BA, U. Nebr., 1968; MA, U. Ariz., 1970; PhD, Case Western Res. U., 1973. Registered prof. archaeologist. Faculty SUNY, Oneonta, 1973-76; state archaeologist State Mus. Colo., Denver, 1976-80; v.p. archaeology svcs. A.C. Nielsen subs. Powers Elevation, Denver, 1980-83; pres., owner The Rippeteau Co., Denver, 1974-84; dir. S.C. Inst. Archaeology and Anthropology, U. S.C., Columbia, 1984—2003, rsch. prof., 1984—2004; ret., 2004—. Mem. adv. coun. Pub. Lands Inst., Natural Resources Def. Coun., 1979—; mem. com. on engring. responsibility Am. Soc. Civil Engrs., 1979-93; spkr. in field; adj. prof. U. Denver, 1976-80, U. Colo., 1977-80. Editor-in-chief Southwestern Lore, 1976-78; contbg. editor Am. Archaeology, 1981-90; contbr. numerous articles to profl. pubs. Mem. Hist. Commn. Bd., Historic Camden, S.C., 1984—; founding mem. S.C. Quincentennial Commn., Palmetto Trust for Hist. Preservation, 1990-98; pres. Crimestoppers of the Midlands, 1993; mem. adv. bd. S.C. Heritage Trust, 1984-2000, chmn. 1990-92; mem. Richland County Airport Commn., 1997—, vice chmn., 2000—. Fellow AAAS; mem. Soc. Am. Archaeology (sec. 1992-95, chair bylaws com. 1997-2003, Presdl. Citation award 1995), Soc. Profl. Archaeologists, Loblolly Soc., Nature Conservancy, Archaeology Soc. S.C. (bd. dirs. 1984-2000, Outstanding Svc. award 1989, 99), Explorers Club (pres. Greater Piedmont chpt. 1991-92), Rotary (bd. dirs. Columbia 1998-, pres. 2003-04), Sigma Xi, Richland Co. Airport Commn. (vice chair 2000-03, mem. new terminal com. 2003-), Celebrate Freedom Found. (co-founder 1997, corp. sec. 1997-). Office: U SC SC Inst Archaeology 1321 Pendleton St Columbia SC 29201-3715 E-mail: rippeteau@sc.edu., bruce rippeteau@sc.rr.com.

RIPPETEAU, DARREL DOWNING, retired architect; b. Clay Center, Nebr., Jan. 14, 1917; s. Claude LaVerne and Eva (Downing) R.; m. Donna Doris Hiatt, Jan. 8, 1939 (dec. 1988); children: Bruce Estes, Darrel Downing, Jane Upson Heffron; m. Joyce Spencer, May 18, 1991. BA in Architecture, U. Nebr., 1941. Staff architect FHA, Omaha, 1941-42; project mgr., mng. ptnr. Sargent-Webster-Crenshaw & Folley, Archs. and Engrs., Watertown, Buffalo, Syracuse, N.Y., Burlington, Vt, Bangor, Maine, 1946-81; treas., dir. Empire Forest System, Albany, N.Y., 1984-89; ret., 1990. Bd. dirs. Archtl. Corp. Atlanta, Key Bank No. N.Y., Watertown, Assn. Island Recreational Corp.; commr. N.Y. State Coun. Architecture, 1975-85; mem. N.Y. State Forest Practice Bd., 1980-2000, chmn., 1994-98; nat. adv. bd. mem. Remington Art Mus., Ogdensburg, N.Y., 1983-95. Prin. works include Justice Bldg, Albany, N.Y. State Office Bldg Watertown, Toomey Abbott Towers Syracuse, State U. N.Y. Cortland, U.S. P.O. Facility Syracuse. Mem. nat. fin. com. Rep. Party, 1971-73; bd. trustees The Antique Boat Mus., Clayton, N.Y., 1973-99, Glenn Curtiss Mus., Hammondsport, N.Y. Maj. U.S. Army, 1942-46; lt. col. Corps of Engrs. retired, 1977. Recipient North Country citation St. Lawrence U., Canton, N.Y., 1971; Sears-Roebuck scholar, 1936-37; U. Nebr. Dept. Architecture grantee, 1940-41; Nebr. master U. Nebr., 1971; Disting. Alumni award Coll. of Architecture Alumni Assn., U. Nebr., 1996. Fellow AIA (nat. dir. 1969-73, trustee AIA Found. 1970-73); mem. Greater Watertown C. of C. (past pres.), N.Y. State Assn. Indsl. Devel. Agys. (past v.p.), N.Y. State Assn. Architects (pres. 1968-69, polit. action com. 1980-98, James Kideney award 1987), Bldg. Rsch. Inst., Res. Officers Assn. (past pres.), Am. Tree Farm Assn., Jefferson County Hist. Soc. (dir. 1974-78), OX-5 Aviation Pioneers (chpt. pres.), Assn. U.S. Army (chpt. pres. 1985-86). Republican. Presbyterian. Home: 1011 NW 3rd Ave Delray Beach FL 33444-2938

RIPPLE, KENNETH FRANCIS, federal judge; b. Pitts., May 19, 1943; s. Raymond John and Rita (Holden) Ripple; m. Mary Andrea DeWeese, July 27, 1968; children: Gregory, Raymond, Christopher. AB, Fordham U., 1965; JD, U. Va., 1968; LLM, George Washington U., 1972, LLD (hon.), 1992. Bar: Va. 1968, N.Y. 1969, U.S. Supreme Ct. 1972, U.S. Supreme Ct. 1972, D.C. 1976, Ind. 1984, U.S. Ct. Appeals (7th cir.), U.S. Ct. Mil. Appeals, U.S. Dist. Ct. (no. dist.) Ind. Atty. IBM Corp., Armonk, NY, 1968; legal officer U.S. Supreme Ct., Washington, 1972—73, spl. asst. to chief justice Warren E. Burger, 1973—77; prof. law U. Notre Dame, 1977—; judge U.S. Ct. Appeals (7th cir.), South Bend, 1985—. Reporter Appellate Rules Com., Washington, 1978—85; commn. on mil. justice U.S. Dept. Def., Washington, 1984—85; cons. Supreme Ct. Ala., 1983, Calif. Bd. Bar Examiners, 1981, Anglo-Am. Jud. Exch., 1977; adv. com. Bill of Rights to Bicentennial Constn. Commn., 1989; adv. com. on appellate rules Jud. Conf. U.S., 1985—90, chmn., 1990—93; chmn. adv. com. on appellate judge edn. Fed. Jud. Ctr., 1996—2003; mem. adminstrn. Office of U.S. Cts.; mem. jud. conf. adminstrv. office U.S. Cts. Com., 2003—. Author: Constitutional Litigation, 1984. With JAGC USN, 1968—72. Mem.: ABA, Judiacil Conf. Comm. on the Adminstrv. office of the U.S. Courts, Am. Law Inst., Phi Beta Kappa. Office: US Ct of Appeals 208 US Courthouse 204 S Main St South Bend IN 46601-2122 also: Fed Bldg 219 S Dearborn St Ste 2660 Chicago IL 60604-1803

RIPPLE, ROCHELLE POYOUROW, educational administrator, educator; b. N.Y.C., Apr. 23, 1936; d. Gerald G. and Hortense (Philips) Bernheimer; m. Julian D. Ripple, Mar. 15, 1985; children: Mitchell, Jill, David. AAS, Fashion Inst. Tech., 1955, Pace U., BPS, 1974; MEd, Temple U., 1977, EdD, 1990. Cert. tchr. handicapped, Pa.; cert. prin., sch. supt., Wyo. Fashion designer Skampalon, Inc., N.Y.C., 1955-60; tchr. fashion design Pleasantville (N.Y.) Cottage Sch., 1969-74; spl. edn. tchr. Horsham Clinic, Ambler and Phila., Pa., 1974-78; fed. project dir. Montgomery County Intermediate Unit, Norristown, Pa., 1978-80; exec. dir. N.E. Wyo. Bd. Coop. Ednl. Svcs., Gillette, Wyo., 1980-86; tchg. assoc. Temple U., Phila., 1986-88; dir. vocat.-tech. edn. Ulster County BOCES, New Paltz, 1988-90; prof. ednl. adminstrn. Columbus (Ga.) State U., 1990—. Contbr. articles to profl. jours. Pres. Yorktown (N.Y.) Cmty. Rels. Coun., 1967-70; mem. adv. bd. Sheridan (Wyo.) Coll. Pace U. Trustee scholar, 1973; named Woman of Yr., Beta Sigma Phi, 1982. Mem. LWV, ASCD, Coun. for Exceptional Children, Am. Assn. Sch. Adminstrs., Assn. Retarded Citizens, Assn. Severely Handicapped, Phi Delta Kappa. Home: 612 Rudgate Rd Columbus GA 31904-2927 Office: Columbus State Univ Dept Edn Columbus GA 31907-5645

RIPPLINGER, GEORGE RAYMOND, JR., lawyer; b. East St. Louis, Ill., Apr. 19, 1945; s. George Raymond and Virginia Lee (Toupnot) R. AB, U. Ill., 1967, JD, 1970. Bar: Ill. 1970, U.S. Dist. Ct. (so. dist.) Ill. 1970, U.S. Ct. Appeals (7th cir.) 1970, U.S. Dist. Ct. (ctrl. dist.) Ill. 1972, U.S. Tax Ct. 1971, U.S. Claims Ct. 1973, U.S. Ct. Mil. Appeals 1985, U.S. Supreme Ct. 1973, U.S. Ct. Internat. Trade 1973, U.S. Dist. Ct. (ea. dist.) Mo. 1977, U.S. Ct. Appeals (8th cir.) 1977. Assoc. Meyer & Meyer, Belleville and Greenville, Ill., 1970-72; assoc. Meyer & Kaucher, 1972—73; sole practice Belleville, 1974; ptnr. Ripplinger & Walsh, Clayton, Mo., 1974-76, Ripplinger, Dixon & Johnston, Belleville, Ill., St. Louis, Scott AFB, and Bellvue, Neb., 1976-94; prin. George Ripplinger & Assoc., Belleville, 1994—. Bd. visitors Coll. of Law U. Ill., 1979-86, pres., 1983-84; chmn. Southwestern Ill. chpt. ACLU, 1971-74, 76-80; mem. exec. com. Sierra Club, 1981-85. Col. USAR, 1970-2001. Fellow Am. Bar Found., Ill. Bar Found. (bd. dirs. 1988-2004, treas. 1998-2004); mem. ABA (ho. of dels. 1989-93, 95-99, chmn. workers compensation com. 1985-88, divsn. dir. 1988-89, 95-99, mem. coun. 1989-93, 99-2003, sec. 1999-2000, vice-chmn. 2000-2001, chmn. 2001-02, gen. practice/solo and small firm sect.), ATLA, Lawyers Trust Fund Ill. (bd. dirs. 1988-94), Ill. Bar Assn. (bd. govs. 1981-83, 87-93, sec. 1991-92), St. Clair County Bar Assn., Bar Assn. Met. St. Louis, Mo. Bar Assn., Ill. Trial Lawyers Assn. (bd. advs. 1993—), Land of Lincoln Legal Assistance Found. (bd. dirs. 1982-88, vice-chmn. 1987-88), Res. Officers Assn. Democrat. Office: George Ripplinger & Assoc 2215 W Main St Belleville IL 62226-6668 Office Phone: 618-234-2440., 800-733-8333. Business E-Mail: george@ripplingerlaw.com.

RIS, HANS, zoologist, educator; b. Bern, Switzerland, June 15, 1914; came to U.S., 1938, naturalized, 1945; s. August and Martha (Egger) R.; m. Hania Wislicka, Dec. 26, 1947 (div. 1971); children: Christopher Robert, Annette Margo; m. Theron Caldwell, July 14, 1980. Diploma high sch. teaching, U. Bern, 1936; PhD, Columbia, 1942. Lectr. zoology Columbia U., 1942; Seessel fellow in zoology Yale U., 1942; instr. biology Johns Hopkins U., 1942-44; asst. Rockefeller Inst., N.Y.C., 1944-46, assoc., 1946-49; assoc. prof. zoology U. Wis., Madison, 1949-53, prof., 1953-84, prof. emeritus, 1984—. Hon. prof. Peking U., Beijing, 1995—. Fellow AAAS, Am. Acad. Arts and Scis.; mem. Nat. Acad. Scis., Electron Microscopy Soc. Am. (Disting. Investigator award 1983), Am. Soc. for Cell Biology (E.B. Wilson award 1993). Achievements include research on mechanisms of nuclear division, chromosome structure, nuclear envelope, cell ultrastructure, electron microscopy. Office: U Wis Zoology Rsch 1117 W Johnson St Madison WI 53706-1705 E-mail: hris@facstaff.wisc.edu.

RIS, HOWARD CLINTON, JR., nonprofit public policy organization administrator; b. Rockville Centre, N.Y. BA in Math., Duke U., 1970, postgrad., 1972; M in Landscape Architecture, SUNY, Syracuse, 1974. Sr.

assoc. Roy Mann Assocs., Inc., Cambridge, Mass., 1974-76; sr. planner Mass. Office Coastal Zone Mgmt., Boston, 1976-78; program mgr. New Eng. River Basins Commn., Boston, 1980-81; dep. dir. Union Concerned Scientists, Inc., Cambridge, 1981-84, exec. dir., 1984—2001, pres., 2001—03. Founding dir. Profls. Coalition for Nuc. Arms Control, Internat. Network Engrs. and Scientists for Global Responsibility. Mem. Energy and Transp. Task Force, Pres. Clinton's Coun. on Sustainable Devel.; mem. adv. bd. Inst. for Transp. Studies U. Calif., Davis; bd. dirs. Keystone Ctr. Mem. Environ. Media Assn. (adv. bd.).

RIS, WILLIAM KRAKOW, JR., lawyer; b. Denver, Oct. 27, 1947; s. William K. and Patty (Nash) R.; m. Adrienne Wolf, June 14, 1970; children: Dylan, Ethan. BA, Northwestern U., 1969; MA, Johns Hopkins U., 1971; JD, U. Denver, 1974; LLM, Georgetown U., 1978. Bar: Colo., 1975, D.C., 1977, U.S. Supreme Ct., 1978. Trial atty. Civil Aeronautics Bd., Washington, 1975-78; counsel Senate Commerce Com., Washington, 1978-83; sr. v.p. The Wexler Group, Washington, 1983-96; v.p. govt. affairs Am. Airlines, Washington, 1996—. Contbr. articles to profl. jours. Home: 5219 Moorland Ln Bethesda MD 20814-6119 Office: Am Airlines 1101 17th St NW Washington DC 20036-4704

RISBERG, ERICA LYNN, archivist, film producer; b. New Milford, Conn., Feb. 17, 1969; d. Roland Eric and Linda Ann Risberg. BA, Western Conn. State U., 1991, MA, 1996; postgrad., U. Maine, 2000—. Underwriter Gt. Western Mortgage Corp., Southport, Conn., 1994—96; adminstrv. asst. Duke Engring. and Svcs., Inc., Portland, Maine, 1997—2000; sound archivist Maine Folklife Ctr., Orono, Maine, 2001—03; asst. prodr. Edge Pictures, Bangor, Maine, 2002—; rsch. asst. Maine Atlas Project, 2003—04; radio announcer Maine Pub. Radio, 2003—; prodr. 3leggedog Productions, 2003—04. Cons. Old Town (Maine) Hist. Soc., 2002—03, Bangor Mus. and Ctr. for History, 2001—02. Prodr., writer, narrator (audio documentary) Community in Maine: Life During the Great Depression. Reader Maine Audio Info. and Reading Svcs., Brewer, 2000—02; candidate for state senate Maine Rep. Party, Portland, 1998; sec. Cumberland County Rep. Party, Portland, 1998—99. Recipient Gold award, Girl Scouts of Am., 1987. Mem.: Maine Hist. Soc., Orgn. Am. Historians, Oral History Assn., Am. Hist. Assn., Phi Alpha Theta. Avocations: swimming, hiking, writing, filmmaking, music. Office: Maine Folklife Ctr/U Maine 5773 S Stevens Hall Orono ME 04469-5773 also: Maine Pub Radio 65 Texas Ave Bangor ME 04401 Personal E-mail: elrisberg@msn.com. E-mail: erica_risberg@umit.maine.edu.

RISCH, FRANK A. oil industry executive; BBA, Pa. State U., 1964; M Indusl. Adminstrn., Carnegie Mellon U. Treas. Exxon Chem. Co., 1984, v.p. fin. and corp. affairs, mem. exec. com., 1986; various positions fin., planning and mktg. Exxon Mobil, London, Athens, Seattle, fin. analyst dept. treas., 1966, mgr. corp. fin., 1980, exec. asst. to chmn., 1990, asst. controller, 1992, asst. treas., 2002—, v.p., treas., 1999—. Mem. bd. dirs., exec. com. Dallas-CASA; mem. exec. com. Dallas Meml. Ctr. Holocaust Studies. Mem.: Carnegie Mellon U. Grad. Sch. Indusl. Adminstrn. (co-chmn. coun. on fin.), Am. Petroleum Inst., Fin. Execs. Inst. Office: Exxon Mobil 5959 Las Colinas Blvd Irving TX 75039-2298

RISCH, JAMES E. lieutenant governor, former state legislator, lawyer; b. Milw., May 3, 1943; s. Elroy A. and Helen B. (Levi) R.; m. Vicki L. Choborda, June 8, 1968; children: James E., Jason S., Jordan D. BS in Forestry, U. Idaho, 1965, JD, 1968. Dep. pros. atty. Ada County, Idaho, 1968-69, chief dep. pros. atty., 1969-70, pros. atty., 1971-75; mem. Idaho Senate, Dist. 18, Boise, 1974—88, 1995—2002; majority leader Idaho Senate, 1977—82, 1997—2002, pres. pro tem, 1983-88; ind. counsel to Gov. of Idaho, 1996; ptnr. Risch Goss & Insinger, Boise, Idaho, 1975—; lt. gov. State of Idaho, Idaho, 2003—. Prof. law Boise State U., 1972-75. Bd. dirs. Nat. Dist. Attys. Assn., 1973, Idaho Co., 1992-94, State Legis. Leaders Found., 2002—; chmn. bd. dirs. Am. Trailer Mfg. Co., 1995—; pres. Idaho Pros. Attys., 1970-74; chmn. George Bush Presdl. Campaign, Idaho, 1988; gen. counsel Idaho Rep. Party, 1991-2002. Mem. ABA, Idaho Bar Assn., Boise Bar Assn., Ducks Unlimited, Nat. Rifle Assn., Nat. Cattlemans Assn., Idaho Cattlemans Assn., Am. Angus Assn., Idaho Angus Assn., Am. Legis. Exch. Coun., Boise Valley Angus Assn., Phi Delta Theta, Xi Sigma Pi Republican. Roman Catholic. Avocations: hunting, fishing, skiing. Home: 5400 S Cole Rd Boise ID 83709-6401 Office: Risch Goss & Insinger 407 W Jefferson St Boise ID 83702-6012 Office Phone: 208-345-9974.

RISDON, MICHAEL PAUL, manufacturing executive; b. Hamburg, Iowa, Feb. 24, 1946; s. Paul A. and Vesta Mae (Melton) R.; m. Ann Lorraine Grandowski, June 4, 1966; children: Anita Ann, Carter Paul. BS, Iowa State U., 1967, U. Ky., 1968; MBA, U. Pitts., 1971. Sr. acct. Ernst & Young, Indpls., 1971-75; audit supr. Ashland (Ky.) Oil, Inc., 1975—77; v.p. fin. and sys. Diesel ReCon Co., Memphis, 1982-86; budget analyst Cummins Engine Co., Columbus, Ind., 1969-70, mgr. corp. audit, 1977-78, dir. corp. and EDP audit, 1978-82, dir. fin. and planning power sys. group, 1987-88; v.p. Cummins Power Generation, Columbus, 1989; v.p. fin., CFO Metal Powder Products Co., Inc., Indpls., 1989-99; pres. MPM LLC, Carmel, Ind., 1998-99; pres., CEO The Cumbernauld Group, 1999—; exec. v.p., chief adminstrv. officer PiezoTech, LLC, Indpls., 1999—2003. V.p. Columbus Child Care Ctr., 1981-82; vol. Big Sisters Ctrl. Ind., 1994-98. Mem. AICPA, Ind. CPA Soc., Metal Powder Industry Fedn. (fin. com. 1991-98, chmn. 1994-98), APMI Internat., Fin. Execs. Internat. (sec. 1997-98, v.p. 1998, pres. 1999), Inst. Mgmt. Accts. (nat. bd. dirs. 1981-87, v.p. 1985), Kiwanis (v.p. Columbus 1981). Roman Catholic. Avocations: bicycling, hiking, spectator sports, motor sports. Office: The Cumbernauld Group 9801 Fall Creek Rd # 404 Indianapolis IN 46256-4802

RISHEL, JAMES BURTON, manufacturing executive, director; b. Omaha, Apr. 27, 1920; s. James Blaine and Elizabeth Helen (Kerr) R.; m. Alice Jane Snyder, June 30, 1945; children: James Richard, Sara Jane Rishel Fields. BSME, U. Nebr., 1946. Profl. engr., Ohio. Pres. Corp. Equipment Co., Cin., 1962-82; chmn. bd. Systecon Inc., Cin., 1982-2000; cons. Pumping Solutions LLC, 2000—. Author: The Water Management Manual, 1994, HVAC Pump Handbook, 1996, Water Pumps and Pumping Systems, 2002; patentee hydraulic systems; contbr. numerous articles to profl. jours. Capt. USAF, 1942-46, 51-52. Fellow ASHRAE. Avocations: philanthropy, walking. Home: 7570 Thumbelina Ln Cincinnati OH 45242-4937 Office Phone: 513-791-3474. Business E-Mail: jbrishel@fuse.net.

RISHEL, RICHARD CLINTON, retired bank executive; b. Oreland, Pa., June 7, 1943; S. Herbert Beale and Evelyn (Lauer) R.; m. Carol Staub, Apr. 3, 1965; children: Christian Daniel, Peter James. BA, Pa. State U., 1965; postgrad., Drexel Inst. Tech., 1965-66. Credit analyst 1st Pa. Banking & Trust Co., Phila., 1965-69; comml. lending officer Nat. Bank of Chester County, West Chester, Pa., 1969; asst. v.p. Continental Bank of Norristown, Pa., 1969-70, sec., 1970-71, v.p., 1971-73, sr. v.p., chief fin. officer, 1973-75, exec. v.p., chief fin. officer, 1975-81, vice chmn., 1981-83, pres., chief adminstrv. officer, 1984-89, also dir.; pres., chief exec. officer Continental Bank, Continental Bancorp, 1990-92; vice chmn. bd. Continental Bank, 1981-84; pres. parent co. Continental Bancorp., 1981-92; dir. Barnett Inst. U. North Fla., 1993-94; sec. of banking Commonwealth of Pa., 1995-99; ret., 1999.

RISI, LOUIS JAMES, JR., business executive; b. Highland Park, Ill., July 2, 1937; s. Louis J. and Ann E. Risi; m. Mary Jean Anson, Jan. 15, 1958; children: Steven, Janet, Andrew. BS, Bradley U.; MBA, U. Chgo. Pres. and CEO, bd. dirs., mem. exec. com. Norin Corp., Miami, Fla., 1969-81; exec. com. dir. Maple Leaf Mills Ltd., Toronto, Can., 1970-81, Corp. Foods, Inc., 1970-81; chmn. bd. dirs. Louis Sherry, Inc., 1976-81; chmn. bd., chief exec. officer Nat. Investors Fire & Casualty Co., 1975-77; exec. com. dir. Investors Equity Life Ins. Co. of Hawaii, 1970-75; pres., dir. The Abbey, Lake Geneva, 1970-75; exec. com., dir. Upper Lakes Shipping, Ltd., Toronto, Can., 1970-76; pres., dir. The Pioneer, Lake Oshkosh, 1971-76; exec. com., dir. Port Weller and St. Lawrence Dry Dock, Ltd., St. Catharines, Can., 1971-76; pres., dir. Homosassa Springs, Fla., 1971-78, Ivan Tors Films Inc., Culver City, Calif., 1971-78, Ivan Tors Studios Inc., Miami, Fla., 1976-80; exec. com. dir. Midland Nat. Bank, 1976-80; pres., dir. Norris Grain Co., 1980-82; chmn. bd., CEO CTC Corp., 1981-83. Exec. com. Nat. Investors Life Ins. Co., 1970-77; chmn. bd., pres. Victory Industries, Inc.; chmn. bd. dirs. Red Wing Co., Oklawaha Farms, Inc., Assured Security Co.; dir. Breckinridge Group; exec. v.p. Ft. Worth Red Wings Hockey Club, Inc., 1975-78, Detroit Red Wings Hockey Club, Inc., 1976-82, Adirondack Red Wings Hockey Club, Inc., 1976-82; bd. govs. Nat. Hockey League, 1976-82; bd. dirs. Chgo. Rock Island and Pacific R.R.; exec. com. AfriAir Corp., 1972-79, Southeastern Airlines, Inc., 1972-78; exec. com., bd. dirs. Peter Bowden Drilling Ltd., Bankmgrs. Corp.; U.S. rep. Grain negotiations with USSR; U.S. rep. Feedstuffs negotiations with China; adv. coun. Am. Stock Exch.; mem. Agrl. Processors Liaison com. FTC; adv. bd. Nat. Millers Assn.; bd. govs. Internat. Hockey League, 1978-82, Am. Hockey League, 1975-79; pres., chmn. bd. dirs. Kinnard Body Works, Inc., 1970-73. Trustee Fairchild Tropical Garden, Miami, Fla. Lt. comdr. USN, 1959—66. Mem. Ocean Reef Yacht Club (Key Largo, Fla.), Santa Rosa (Calif.) Country Club, Riviera Country Club (Coral Gables, Fla.), Lake Toxaway Country Club (Lake Toxaway, NC), Coral Reef Yacht Club (Miami, Fla.), Anabelle's Club (London), St. James Club (London). Home: 10915 Lakeside Dr Coral Gables FL 33156-4209 Office: 9200 S Dadeland Blvd Miami FL 33156-2715

RISIN, JACK See BUTCHER, JACK

RISINGER, C. FREDERICK, social studies educator; b. Paducah, Ky., July 15, 1939; s. Charles Morris and Mary Neal (Barfield) R.; m. Margaret M. Marker, July 4, 1994; children: Donna Lyne, Alyson, Laura, John. BS in Edn., So. Ill. U., 1961; MA in History, No. Ill. U., 1968. Newscaster, disc jockey WMOK Radio, Metropolis, Ill., 1955-61; tchr., adminstr., coach Lake Park H.S., Roselle, Ill., 1962-73; coord. sch. social studies Ind. U., Bloomington, 1973-86, assoc. dir. social studies devel. ctr., 1986-90, dir. nat. clearinghouse for U.S.-Japan studies, 1990—, assoc. dir. tchr. edn., 1995-97, dir. profl. devel., sch. svcs. and summer sessions, 1997—. Mem. adv. bd. Learning Mag., Boston, 1988—; pres. Nat. Coun. for the Social Studies, 1990-91. Co-author: America! America!, 1974, America's Past and Promise, 1997, Creating America, 2000, Scott Foresman Social Studies K-6 Series, 2003; editor jour. News and Notes on the Social Sciences, 1973-86. Pres. Social Studies Suprs. Assn., Washington, 1985-86; exec. dir. Ind. Coun. for Social Studies, Bloomington, 1975-87. Recipient numerous pub. and pvt. ednl. grants; named Tchr. of Yr. DuPage County Edn. Assn., 1973. Mem. ASCD, Nat. Coun. for Social Studies, Ind. Assn. Historians, Phi Delta Kappa. Democrat. Home: 7039 E State Rd 45 Bloomington IN 47408-9580 E-mail: risinger@indiana.edu.

RISJORD, MARK WINDEN, humanities educator; b. Charlottesville, Va., July 14, 1960; s. Norman Kurt and Constance Winter Risjord; m. Barbara Carol Jacobsen, Aug. 4, 1984; children: Andrea Constance, Hannah Marie. PhD, U. N.C., 1984—90. Asst. prof., dept. philosophy Mich. State U., East Lansing, 1990—93; assoc. prof., dept. philosophy Emory U., Atlanta, 1993—. Associated faculty, Woodruff sch. of nursing Emory U., 1999—. Author: (book) Woodcutters and Witchcraft. Office: Philosophy Dept Emory Univ Atlanta GA 30322

RISK, RICHARD ROBERT, health care executive; b. Chgo., Sept. 15, 1946; s. Clement Albert and Mary Catherine (Clarke) R.; m. Rebecca Ann Sandquist, Jan. 11, 1969 (div. Sept. 1984); children: Michael, Daniel, Laura; m. Louise L. Lawson, Dec. 1, 1984; stepchildren: Carrie Lawson, Valerie Lawson. BS in Econs., U. Ill., 1968; MBA in Health Adminstrn., U. Chgo., 1971. Asst. adminstr. U. Ill. Hosp., Chgo., 1969-72, Ctrl. DuPage Hosp., Winfield, Ill., 1972-74; mgmt. cons., v.p. Tribrook Group, Inc., Oak Brook, Ill., 1974-81; v.p. cons. svcs. Parkside Med. Svcs., Park Ridge, Ill., 1981-83; prin. health and med. divsn. Booz, Allen, & Hamilton, Inc., Chgo., 1983-84; exec. v.p. EHS Health Care, Oak Brook, 1984-92, pres., CEO, 1992-95, Advocate Health Care, Oak Brook, 1995—. Bd. dirs. Landauer Corp.; mem. faculty Healthcare Fin. Mgmt. Assn., 1978-86, Am. Assn. Hosps. Cons., 1978-84; bd. dirs., mem. ad hoc ins. com., fin. com. Premier; lectr. grad. program social scis. No. Ill. U., 1982-88; lectr., adv. bd. multi-hosp. system study Kellogg Sch. Health Mgmt. Program Northwestern U., 1985—; lectr. Grad. Program in Health Adminstrn. U. Chgo., 1982-94. Mem. access com. Gov.'s Task Force on Health Reform, 1992-94; mem. chancellor's adv. bd. U. Ill. at Chgo.; chair South Cook county region United Way. Fellow Am. Assn. Hosp. Cons. (bd. dirs., treas., chmn. govt. rels. com., chmn. membership task force, liaison Nat. Coun. Cmty. Hosps.); mem. Am. Hosp. Assn. (chair healthcare systems sect.), Ill. Hosp. Assn. (chmn. coun. on health fin., mem. strategic plan com., bd. dirs., treas.), U. Chgo. Hosp. Adminstrn. Alumni Assn. (pres. exec. com. alumni coun., chmn. 50th ann. com.), Chgo. Health Policy Rsch. Coun. Home: 801 Clinton Pl River Forest IL 60305-1501 Office: Advocate Health Care 2025 Windsor Dr Oak Brook IL 60523-1586

RISKE, WILLIAM KENNETH, producer, cultural services consultant; b. Lamont, Alta., Can., May 9, 1949; s. Norman Elmer and Clara Jeanette (Krause) R.; m. Barbara Elizabeth Malcolm, Apr. 28, 1973; children: Elizabeth Nicola, William Norman Malcolm. BFA, U. Alta., 1969. Stage mgr. Royal Winnipeg Ballet, Man., Can., 1971-73, prodn. stage mgr., 1973-76, prodn. mgr., 1976-77, assoc. gen. mgr., 1978-79, gen. mgr., 1979-92, cultural svcs. cons., 1992—; assoc. prodr., gen. mgr. Cirque Du Soleil-Mystère, 1994-96; gen. mgr. Cirque du Soleil U.S., Inc., 1996—2003. Mem. Assn. Cultural Execs. Home: 227 Deer Crossing Way Henderson NV 89012-2289 E-mail: wriske@LVDI.net.

RISKEN, JARED CLEVELAND, physician; b. Oakland, Calif., Dec. 13, 1947; s. Maurice Forrest and Virginia (Cleveland) R.; m. Gloria Leona Hanger, Jan. 11, 1969; children: Douglas Jared, Sarah Julianne. BA in Anthropology and Biology, Loma Linda U., 1973; MD, Am. U., 1979. Resident in family practice Luth. Med. Ctr., St. Louis, 1980-81; med. dir. Alpha Therapeutics, St. Louis, 1981-85; indsl. medicine-safety engr. Torno America, Cortez, Colo., 1989-91, OJB Engring., Apple Valley, Calif., 1990-92; with U. Ill. Sch. Medicine, Champaign, 1992—. Active cmty. and ch. activities. Mem. Am. Profl. Practice Assn., Nat. Assn. Residents and Interns, Physicians for Social Responsibility, Christian Med. Dental Soc. Office: 2617 Willoughby Rd Champaign IL 61822-7567 E-mail: jrisken@uiuc.edu.

RISKIN, VICTORIA, former trade association administrator; d. Robert Riskin and Fay Wray; m. David Rintels. Pres. Writers Guild Am., West, 2001—04. Author: (TV films) My Antonia, 1995; prodr.: (TV films) The Last Best Year, 1990, A Town Torn Apart, 1992, World War II: When Lions Roared, 1994, The Member of the Wedding, 1997.*

RISKO, VICTORIA J. language educator; BS, U. Pitts., 1966; MS, W.Va. U., 1969, EdD, 1971; postgrad., U. London, 1975. Fellow Learning Disabilities Inst. W.Va. U., 1969—70; tchr. Johnstown (Pa.) Pub. Sch. Sys., 1967—68; tchr. remedial reading Johnstown (Pa.) Pub. Sch. Dist., 1967; instr. home econs. W.Va. U., 1968—69, instr., supr. reading clinic, 1969; rschr.-tchr. Robert F. Kennedy Youth Ctr., Morgantown, W.Va., 1969—70; tchr.-cons. inservice edn. of tchrs. Belair-Manchester Schs. of Mandeville, Jamaica, 1974—75; instr., asst. prof., assoc. prof., dir. reading clinic programs, mem. grad. faculty SUNY, Fredonia, 1970—75; rsch. scientist Learning Tech. Ctr., mem. faculty interdisciplinary team Child Study Ctr., Kennedy Ctr. Peabody Coll., Vanderbilt U., Nashville, 1978—89, assoc. prof., 1975—94, prof. lang. and learning, 1994—. Vis. prof. reading W.Va. U., 1971. Recipient Disting. Svc. and Leadership award, Coll. Reading Assn., 1995, Disting. Rsch. in Tchr.'s Edn. award, Assn. Tchr. Educators Conf., 1992. Office: Vanderbilt U Peabody Coll Box 330 Nashville TN 37203

RISKOWSKI, GERALD LEE, engineering educator; b. Loup City, Nebr., Feb. 26, 1952; s. Stanley George and Rose Marie (Eurek) R.; m. Janet Ann Riskowski, June 19, 1976; 1 child, Ryan Lee. BS in Agrl. Engring., U. Nebr., 1974, MS in Agrl. Engring., 1976; PhD in Agrl. Engring., Iowa State U., 1986. Registered profl. engr., Ill., Iowa, Wis. Design engr. Lesters Bldgs., Lester Prairie, Minn., 1976-77; product engr. Wick Bldg. Systems, Mazomanie, Wis., 1977-80; instr. Iowa State U., Ames, 1980-86; prof. dept. agrl. engring. U. Ill., Urbana, 1986—2001; prof., head biol. and agrl. engring. dept. Tex. A&M U., College Station, 2002—. Swine facilities cons. Am. Tech. Products, Savoy, Ill., 1997-2002; pres. Internat. Air Technologies, Savoy, 1994-2003. Author: Designing Facilities for Pesticide and Fertilizer Containment, 1991 (Am. Soc. Agrl. Engrs. Blue Ribbon 1992); editor: Swine Housing and Equipment Handbook, 1983 (Am. Soc. Agrl. Engrs. Blue Ribbon 1984), Livestock Waste Facilities, 1985, Farm Buildings Wiring Handbook, 1986 (Am. Soc. Agrl. Engrs. Blue Ribbon 1987). Named to Rural Builders Hall of Fame, 1998. Mem. ASHRAE (TC.2 Handbook chair 1993-2000), Am. Soc. Agrl. Engrs. (S&E program chair, stds. chair, Henry Giese award 2001). Office: Tex A&M U 2117 TAMU College Station TX 77843-2117 E-mail: riskowski@tamu.edu.

RISLEY, DAVID MILO, controller; b. Davenport, Iowa, Dec. 3, 1944; s. Ernest and Emma (Remke) R.; m. Karen Ann McConkey, Aug. 26, 1967; children: Kristen Anne, Matthew Christopher. BBA in Acctg., U. Iowa, 1966; MBA in Fin., Loyola U., Chgo., 1970. CPA, Ill. Staff auditor Authur Young & Co., Chgo., 1970-76; dir. internal audit Trans. Union Corp., Lincolnshire, Ill., 1976-79, group controller, 1979-81; v.p., controller Heizer Corp., Chgo., 1981-84; corp. controller Trinova Corp., Maumee, Ohio, 1984—. Trustee Knox Presbyn. Ch., Naperville, Ill., 1976-84, Toledo Hearing and speech ctr., Ohio, 1988—; bd. dirs. Toledo Opera, 1989—; instr. Jr. Achievement, Toledo, 1985—. Served as 1st lt. U.S. Army, 1966-69, Vietnam. Mem. AICPA, Ohio Soc. of CPAs, Fin. Exec. Inst., Nat. Assn. Accts. Clubs: Inverness Golf (Toledo). Republican. Methodist. Home: 2710 Derby Rd Toledo OH 43615-2144 Office: Trinova Corp 1705 Indian Wood Cir Maumee OH 43537-4097

RISLEY, GREGORY BYRON, furniture company executive, interior designer; b. Vincennes, Ind., Feb. 2, 1949; s. Jack Byron and Elizabeth Louise (Rockwell) R.; children: Christopher Byron, Timothy Neal. BS, Oakland City (Ind.) Coll., 1973; postgrad., Butler U., 1973-74, Oxford Worcester Coll. Pres. Risley Furniture & Design, Bicknell, Ind., 1974—, Risley Enterprises Inc., Bicknell, Ind., 1979—. Co-author: Preview IV The Home Furnishings Store. Pres. Better Bicknell Club, 197l; coach Pee Wee League, Bicknell, 1975-77; leader cub pack Boy Scouts Am., Bicknell, 1977; chmn. Queen Pageant, Bicknell, 1978-85. Mem. Nat. Home Furnishings Assn. (chmn. nat. execs. 1978-80), Am. Contract Bridge League (life master, unit sec. 1986-88, v.p. 1989, pres. 1991-92, bd. dirs. unit 193, 1993-95), Bicknell Mchts. Assn., Interior Design Soc. (outstanding rm. design award 1980), Knox County Assn. Retarded Citizens, French Club, Masons, Scottish Rite, Old Town Players (charter), Elks (past exalted ruler Bicknell 1976-77). Avocations: bridge, golf, reading. Office: 114 S Main St Bicknell IN 47512-2626 Office Phone: 812-735-2016. Business E-Mail: rizzzz2@aol.com.

RISLEY, ROD ALAN, education association executive; b. Hutchinson, Kans., Oct. 17, 1954; s. Ralph Edward and Patricia Ann (Gaulding) R. AA, San Jacinto Coll., 1975; BBA, Sam Houston State U., 1982; AA (hon.), Austin (Tex.) C.C., 1991; MBA, Millsap Coll., 1995; PhD (hon.), Highpoint U., 1996, Mt. Ida Coll., 1996, Landmark Coll., 2003; postgrad., Miss. State U., 2003. Dir. alumni affairs Phi Theta Kappa, 1976-82; assoc. dir. Phi Theta Kappa Internat. Hdqrs., Jackson, Miss., 1982-85, exec. dir., 1985—. Grant reviewer NSF, C.C. Humanities Assn., NEH; mem. adv. bd. Horne CPA Group. Judge Truman Scholarship Found., 1993, 94, Coca-Cola Scholars Found., 2001-04, USA Today's All-USA Acad. Team for High Schs., 2003-04, Jack Kent Cooke Found., 2004, Nat. Assn. C.C. Tchr. Edn. Program. Named one of Outstanding Young Men Am., 1982, 83, 84, 85, 86, 87, 88, 89, Top Bus. Leaders Miss., 1994, Disting. Alumnus, San Jacinto Coll., 1997; Mid South Found. C.C. fellow, 2001. Mem. Assn. Coll. Honor Soc. (stds. and definitions com.), Am. Assn. of Cmty. Colls. (commr. coun. for acad., student and cmty. devel., grant reviewer, Disting. Alumnus award 1996), Phi Theta Kappa (sec., pub. jour.), Phi Kappa Phi. Episcopalian. Office: Phi Theta Kappa Soc PO Box 13729 Jackson MS 39236-3729 Office Phone: 601-984-3518.

RISLEY, TODD ROBERT, psychologist, educator; b. Palmer, Alaska, Sept. 8, 1937; s. Robert and Eva Lou (Todd) R.; 1 child, Todd Michael; m. Cheryl Thomas, Mar. 30, 1996. AB with distinction in Psychology, San Diego State Coll., 1960; MS, U. Wash., 1963, PhD, 1966. Asst. prof. psychology Fla. State U., Tallahassee, 1964-65; rsch. assoc. Bur. Child Rsch., U. Kans., Lawrence, 1965-77, sr. scientist, 1977—2003, emeritus, 2003—, asst. prof. dept. human devel., 1967-69, assoc. prof., 1969-73, prof., 1973-84; prof. psychology U. Alaska, Anchorage, 1982—2003, prof. emeritus, 2003—. Pres. Ctr. for Applied Behavior Analysis, 1970-82; dir. Johnny Cake Child Study Ctr., Mansfield, Ark., 1973-74; vis. prof. U. Auckland (N.Z.), 1978; acting dir. Western Carolina Ctr., Morgantown, N.C., 1981; dir. Alaska Div. Mental Health and Devel. Disabilities, 1988-91; cons. in field to numerous orgns. and instns. Co-author: The Infant Center, 1977, Shopping with Children: Advice for parents, 1978, The Toddler Center, 1979, Meaningful Differences, 1995, The Social World of Children, 1999; editor: Jour. Applied Behavior Analysis, 1971-74; mng. editor: Behavior Therapy, The Behavior Therapist, Behavioral Asessment, 1977-80; assoc. editor: Jour. Positive Behavior Support, 1998--; mem. editl. bds. of numerous profl. jours.; contbr. revs. and numerous articles. Co-chmn. Fla. task force on use of behavioral procedures in state programs for retarded, 1974—; mem. resident abuse investigating com. div. retardation Fla. Dept. Health and Rehab. Services, 1972—; mem. adv. com. Social Research Inst., U. Utah, 1977—; mem. Alaska Gov.'s Council on Handicapped and Gifted, 1983-88, NIH Mental Retardation Research Com., 1987-88, Alaska Mental Health Bd., 1988. Grantee NIMH, 1971-72, 72-73; rsch. grantee Nat. Ctr. Health Services, 1976-79; grantee Nat. Inst. Edn., 1973, NIH, 1967-86; grantee U.S. Dept. Edn., 1997-2002. Fellow APA (coun. of reps. 1982-85, pres. div. 25, 1989, Edgar Doll award 2000), Am. Psychol. Soc.; mem. AAAS, Am. Assn. Mental Deficiency (Rsch. award 2000), Assn. Advancement of Behavior Therapy (dir. 1975-80, pres. 1976-77, chmn. profl. rev. com. 1977—, series editor Readings in Behavior Therapy 1977—), Soc. Behavioral Medicine, Assn. Behavior Analysis, Sigma Xi. Office Phone: 907-745-4360. Business E-Mail: risley@alaska.net.

RISLEY, TOM, aerospace transportation executive; BBA in Acctg., U. Tex., Arlington. With aerospace and def. ops. LTV Corp., Dallas, 1968—79, programs control mgr. for advanced devel. programs, 1980—88, mgr. for program controls, mil. aircraft divsn., 1987—89, dir. program controls, bus. ops., 1989—92, dir. cost, schedule and configuration controls, Vought Aircraft Divsn., 1992; dir. Empennage Integrated Product Team Northrop Grumman, Comml. Aircraft Divsn., v.p. Empennage and Control Surfaces Programs; v.p., integrated product team leader Northrop Grumman, Boeing Comml. Programs; COO, corp. sr. v.p. Northrup Grumman, Vought Aircraft Industries, Inc., 1999—2000, COO, corp. exec. v.p., 2000—02, pres., CEO, bd. dirs., 2002—. Exec. bd. March of Dimes North Tex.; adv. bd. North Tex. Food Bank. Mem.: Aerospace Industries Assn. (bd. govs. and exec. com.). Office: Vought Aircraft Industries PO Box 655907 Dallas TX u7526-5907

RISMAN, MICHAEL, lawyer, business executive, securities company executive, real estate developer; b. Everett, Mass., Apr. 2, 1938; s. Morris Charles and Doris (Rosenbaum) R.; m. Rebecca R. Fuchs, Mar. 23, 1974; 1 stepchild, Ian Carlton Murray; children: Matthew Craig, Deborah Risman Kyle, Jared Evan. BA, U. Mich., 1960; LLB, Georgetown U., 1964. Bar: D.C. 1964. Staff mem. Democratic Nat. Com., Washington, 1964; atty. U.S. Fgn. Claims Settlement Commn., Washington, 1964-66, SEC, Washington, 1966-67; counsel Seaboard Planning Corp., Beverly Hills, Calif., 1967-72, pres., 1970-72; v.p. Seaboard Corp., Beverly Hills, 1970-72; sec. B.C. Morton Realty Trust, 1967-71; with Arlington Investments Corp., Santa Monica, Calif., 1979-86; founder The Quincey Group, 1986; owner, pres. Armstrong Kitchens, San Francisco, 1988-90; sr. v.p. AFC Am. Housing Corp., L.A., Calif., 1991-97; mng. dir. Hollingsworth & Lord, L.A., 1997—; ptnr. Dorama, L.L.C., 2002—. Bd. dir. Competitive Capital Fund, Income Fund Boston, Inc., Admiralty Fund. Home: 1133 Centinela Ave Santa Monica CA 90403-2316

RISNER, ANITA JANE, vocational school educator; b. Durant, Okla., Nov. 10, 1946; d. Forrest W. and Jane J. (Nelms) Carter; m. Curt Risner, Jan. 21, 1968; children: Patrick, Brandon. AS, Eastern Okla. Jr. Coll., 1967; BS, Okla. State U., 1971; MEd, Northeastern State U., 1981. Hospitality careers tchr. Pryor (Okla.) Pub. Schs., 1971-73, N.E. Area Vo-Tech, Pryor, 1973-75; child devel. tchr. Tulsa Tech. Ctr., 1976-81, counselor, 1981-89; staff devel. specialist Okla. Dept. of Vo-Tech Edn., Stillwater, Okla., 1989-94; instrnl.

coord. Indian Capital Area Vo-Tech Sch., Muskogee, Okla., 1994—; regional career devel. specialist Okla. Dept. Vocat. Tech. Edn., 1994-97; asst. supt. Tri-County Tech. Ctr., Bartlesville, Okla., 1997-99, dep. supt., 1999—. Advisor Vocat. Student Orgns., Tulsa, 1976 89; career adv. com. mem. Bixby (Okla.) Pub. Schs., 1992—; participant Craftmanship 2000 program, Tulsa; presenter in local, state, nat. confs. Editor: (curriculum guide) Integrating Career Days, 1992, Integrating OK Career Search, 1993; editor (newsletter) Classworks, 1995. Mem. ASCD, Am. Vocat. Assn. (Region IV Outstanding Vocat. Educator of Yr. 1994, Outstanding Vocat. Educator of Yr. award 1995), Okla. Vocat. Assn. (Educator of Yr.-Guidance 1993), Okla. Assn. for Supervision and Curriculum Devel., Phi Delta Kappa. Democrat. Avocations: reading, flower gardening. Address: 1729 Melrose Dr Bartlesville OK 74006-7025 Office: Tri-County Tech Ctr 6101 Nowata Rd Bartlesville OK 74006-6029

RISNER, RAY D. computer company executive; V.p. fin. adminstrn. RJR Nabisco, 1987-89; vice chmn. RJM Group, Inc., 1989—; exec. v.p. So. Elecs. Corp., 1995; pres, chief oper. officer SED Corp., Tucker, Ga., 1995—. Bd. dirs. So. Elecs. Corp.; cons. in field. Office: SED Internat Holdings Inc 4916 N Royal Atlanta Dr Tucker GA 30084-8605 Office Phone: 770 491 962.

RISOM, JENS, furniture designer, manufacturing executive; b. Copenhagen, May 8, 1916; came to U.S., 1939; naturalized, 1944; s. Sven J. and Inger Risom; m. Iben Haderup, Dec. 12, 1939 (dec. Jan. 1977); children: Helen Ann, Peggy Ann, Thomas Christian, Sven Christian; m. Henny Panduro, May 12, 1979. Student, Krebs, Denmark, 1922 27, St. Annae, 1927-32, Niels Brock Bus. Coll., 1932-34, Sch. for Arts and Indust., Denmark, 1935-38; DFA (hon.), R.I. Sch. Design, 2003. With design and decorating divsn. Nordiska Kompanet, Stockholm, Inge Westin, Stockholm, 1934-35, Ernst Kühn, Arch., Copenhagen and N.Y.C., 1937-38; with Dan Cooper, Inc., N.Y., 1939-41; freelance furniture designer, 1941-46; founder, pres. Jens Risom Design Inc., 1946-71; pres. Jens Risom Design, Inc. (became subs. Dictaphone Corp. 1971); v.p. Dictaphone Corp., 1971-73; pres. Design Control, New Canaan, Conn., 1973—. Cons. design, mktg., space planning. Trustee RISD, New Canaan Libr., Indsl. Design Soc. Am. With U.S. Army, 1943-45, ETO. Decorated Danish Knight's Cross (Denmark); recipient awards Archtl. League, Am. Inst. Internat. Design, Lifetime Achievement award Bklyn. Mus. Art, 1994, numerous Danish and Am. design awards. Home and Office: 24 Parade Hill Ln New Canaan CT 06840-4119 also: PO Box 596 Block Island RI 02807-0596 Home Fax: 203-966-6144.

RISS, ERIC, psychologist; m. Miriam Barbara Schoen; children: Arthur, Suzanne, Wendy. BA, Bklyn. Coll., 1950; PhD, NYU, 1958. Diplomate Am. Bd. Psychotherapy. Pvt. practice psychotherapy, family therapy and marriage counseling, N.Y.C., 1952; sr. psychologist N.Y.C. Diagnostic Ctr., 1954-57; with Marriage and Family Life Inst., N.Y.C., 1956-92, cons., 1956-58, dir. pub. edn., 1960-73, chmn. bd. dirs., 1961-73, dir., 1973-92; mem. attending staff, supr. psychotherapy and family therapy Payne Whitney Psychiat. Clinic, N.Y. Hosp., N.Y.C., 1971-78; clin. instr. psychology and psychiatry Cornell U. Med. Coll., 1971-72, clin. asst. prof., 1973-78; dir. Inst. for Exploration of Marriage, 1976-84; chief psychologist Artists, Writers and Performers Psychotherapy Ctr., 1978-92. Sr. psychologist N.Y.C. Diagnostic Center, 1954-57; with Marriage and Family Life Inst., N.Y.C., 1956-92; cons., 1956-58, dir. pub. edn., 1960-73, chmn. bd. dirs., 1961-73, dir., 1973-92; mem. attending staff, supr. psychotherapy and family therapy Payne Whitney Psychiat. Clinic, N.Y. Hosp., N.Y.C., 1971-78; clin. instr. psychology and psychiatry Cornell U. Med. Coll., 1971-72, clin. asst. prof., 1973-78; dir. Inst. for Exploration of Marriage, 1976-84; chief psychologist Artists, Writers and Performers Psychotherapy Center, 1978-92; lectr. Bklyn. Coll., 1955-62; cons. Fordham Hosp., 1956-68; psychotherapist N.Y. Neuropsychiat. Center, 1958-60; psychotherapist Community Guidance Service, N.Y.C., 1958-61; founder, head Natural Psychotherapy Internat., 1999—; webmaster www.naturalpsychotherapy.com. Contbr. numerous articles to profl. jours. Mem. APA, N.Y. State Psychol. Assn. (chair colleague assistance program 2000—), Am. Acad. Psychotherapy, N.Y. State Marriage, Family and Child Counseling Assn. (pres. 1971-72), Acad. Family Psychology. Office: 174 E 73rd St New York NY 10021-4352 Office Phone: 212-988-4700. E-mail: eriss@naturalpsychotherapy.com., eriss@npsy.com.

RISS, MURRAY, photographer, educator; b. Stryj, Poland, Feb. 6, 1940; came to U.S., 1951, naturalized, 1958; s. Elias and Dora (Feit) R.; m. Karen Mason; children: Shanna, Adya. Student, CCNY, 1958-63; BA, Cooper Union, 1966; M.F.A., R.I. Sch. Design, 1968. Prof., chmn. dept photography Memphis Acad. Arts, 1969-84; lectr. film and photography Southwestern U., Memphis, 1972-82; artist-in-residence U. Syracuse, N.Y., 1980, U. Haifa, Israel, 1976 One man shows include Art Inst., Chgo, 1971, Mpls. Inst. Fine Arts, 1971, U. Rochester, N.Y., 1975, Photographers Gallery, London, 1977, Afterimage Gallery, Dallas, 1979, Visual Studies Workshop, Rochester, 1980, Hampshire (Mass.) Coll., 1981, Loomis Inst., Conn., 1984; group shows include Mus. Modern Art, N.Y.C., 1970, 71, New Orleans Mus. Art, 1975, Nexus Gallery, Atlanta, 1981, Askew Nixon Gallery; touring show So. Arts Fedn., 1985-86; conceived, organized, dir. Southern Eye, Southern Mind, A Photographic Inquiry, Memphis, 1981; illustrator: History of Memphis Architecture until 1900, 1983, Guide to Mud Island, 1989; curator, dir. Emerging Southern Photographers, Memphis Coll. Art Gallery, 1992, Memphis Brooks Mus. Art, 1994. Nat. Endowment for Arts fellow, 1979 Mem. Soc. Photographic Edn. Home: 1306 Harbert Ave Memphis TN 38104-4514 Office: Murray Riss Photography 516 S Main St Memphis TN 38103-4443 Personal E-mail: mur3435ris@aol.com. *Had I designed the events and outcomes of my life I would not have done as well as my fate has done for me.*

RISS, RICHARD MICHAEL, research economist, church history educator; b. Rochester, N.Y., May 22, 1952; s. Walter and Barbara Ann (Johnson) R.; m. Kathryn Janet Grieser, Mar. 3, 1979. BA, U. Rochester, 1974; MCS, Regent Coll., Vancouver, B.C., Can., 1979; MA, Trinity Evang. Div. Sch., Deerfield, Ill., 1988; MPhil, Drew U., 2002. Instr. ch. history Christian Life Coll., Mt. Prospect, Ill., 1980-83; data base mgr. Systems and Mgmt. Infor. Svcs. 1st Chgo. Corp., 1980-85; rsch. assoc. to chief economist Prudential Securities, N.Y.C., 1988-91, C.J. Lawrence/Deutsche Bank Securities Corp., N.Y.C., 1991-96; assoc. prof. ch. history Somerset Christian Coll., 1989—. Author: The Evidence for the Resurrection of Jesus Christ, 1977, Latter Rain, 1987, A Survey of Twentieth Century Revival Movements in North America, 1988, A History of the Worldwide Awakening, 1992-95, 1995, A Defense of the Revival, 1996, Images of Revival, 1997; also articles to New International Dictionary of Pentecostal and Charismatic Movements, Ency. Hanoverian Eng. and The Library of Christian Worship. Mem. Soc. for Pentecostal Studies, Conf. on Faith and History, Evang. Theol. Soc., Soc. Christian Philosophers, Am. Soc. Ch. History, Wesleyan Theol. Soc. Avocation: playing violin. Home: 290 River Rd Apt M-1 Piscataway NJ 08854-7516

RISS, ROBERT BAILEY, real estate investor; b. Salida, Colo., May 27, 1927; s. Richard Roland and Louise (Roberts) R.; married; children: Edward Stayton, G. Leslie, Laura Bailey, Juliana Warren. BSBA, U. Kans., 1949. Pres. Riss Internat. Corp., Kansas City, Mo., 1950-80, chmn. bd., 1964-86; founder, chmn. bd., pres. Republic Industries, Inc., Kansas City, Mo., 1969-86; chmn. bd. Grandview Bank and Trust Co., 1969-86, Commonwealth Gen. Ins. Co., 1986-93. Chmn. bd. dirs., exec. com. Heart of Am. Fire and Casualty Co.; chmn. bd. dirs. Comml. Equipment Co. Vice chmn. bd. trustees Kansas U. Endowment Assn., 1980-89. Recipient Silver Beaver award Kansas City Area coun. Boy Scouts Am., 1972; Disting. Svc. citation U. Kans., 1976; Fred Ellsworth medal U. Kans., 1979; named Most Outstanding Young Man in Mo. U.S. Jr. C. of C., 1956 Mem. Kans. U. Alumni Assn. (nat. pres. 1969-70), Sigma Nu. Episcopalian.

RISSANEN, JORMA JOHANNES, computer scientist; b. Pielisjarvi, Finland, Oct. 20, 1932; came to the U.S., 1964; m. Riitta T. Åberg, Nov. 6, 1956; children: Juhani, Natasha. PhD, Finland Inst. Tech., 1960. With Helsinki Inst. Info. Tech., 2003—. Assoc. editor: Jour. Control and Info.; contbr. articles to profl. jours.; patentee in field:. Recipient Outstanding Innovation award, IBM Rsch. divsn., 1980, Best Paper award, Automatica, 1982, Infithy Group, 1986, R.W. Hamming medal, 1993, Golden Jubilee award for tech. innovation, 1998. Fellow: IEEE (info. theory soc.), Helsinki Inst. Info. Tech. Home: 140 Teresita Way Los Gatos CA 95032-6517

RISSE, GUENTER BERNHARD, physician, historian, educator; b. Buenos Aires, Apr. 28, 1932; s. Francisco B. and Kaete A. R.; m. Alexandra G. Paradzinski, Oct. 14, 1961; children— Heidi, Monica, Alisa. MD, U. Buenos Aires, 1958; PhD, U. Chgo., 1971. Intern Mercy Hosp., Buffalo, 1958-59; resident in medicine Henry Ford Hosp., Detroit, 1960-61, Mt. Carmel Hosp., Columbus, Ohio, 1962-63; asst. dept. medicine U. Chgo., 1963-67; asst. prof. dept. history of medicine U. Minn., 1969-71; asso. prof. dept. history of medicine and dept. history of sci. U. Wis., Madison, 1971-76, prof., 1976-85, chmn. dept. history of medicine, 1971-77; prof. dept. history health scis. U. Calif., San Francisco, 1985-99, prof. dept. anthropology, history and social medicine, 1999-2001, prof. emeritus, 2001—, dept. chair, 1985—99; affiliate prof. dept med. history and ethics Univ. Wash. Sch. of Medicine, Seattle, 2002—. Mem. project com. Ctr. for Photog. Images in Medicine and Health Care. Author: Paleopathology of Ancient Egypt, 1964, Hospital Life in Enlightenment Scotland, 1986, Mending Bodies—Saving Souls: A History of Hospitals, 1999; editor: Modern China and Traditional Chinese Medicine, 1973, History of Physiology, 1973, Medicine Without Doctors, 1977, AIDS and the Historian, 1991, Culture, Knowledge and Healing, Historical Perspectives of Homeopathic Medicine in Europe and North America, 1998; mem. editl. bd. Jour. History of Medicine, 1971-74, 90-93, Clio Medica, 1973-88, Bull. History of Medicine, 1980-94, Medizinhistorisches Jour., 1981 , Med. History, 1989-95, NTM Internat. Jour. of History, Ethics, Medicine, 1992—, History of Philos. Life Scis., 1993—, Asclepio, 1995—, Health and History, 1998—. Served with Argentine Armed Forces, 1955. Recipient NIH grants, 1971-73, 82-84, WHO grant, 1979, named Logan Campbell Disting. Lectr., New Zealand, 1994, Karl Sudhoff Meml. Lectr., Germany, 2000. Mem. Am. Assn. History of Medicine (pres. 1988-90, William H. Welch medal 1988), History Sci. Soc., Deutsche Gesellschaft fur Geschichte der Medizin, European Assn. History of Medicine and Health, Internat. Network for History of Pub. Health, Mex. Soc. History and Philosophy of Medicine, Peruvian Assn. Med. Ethnology and History, Brit. Soc. for Social History of Medicine, Argentine Ateneo de Historia de la Medicina, AIDS History Group (co-chair 1988-94), Internat. Network for History of Hosps. (convenor 1995—), Bay Area Med. Hist. Club (pres. 1994-96). Home: 933 NW Richmond Beach Rd Shoreline WA 98177-3219 E-mail: profgrisse@comcast.net.

RISSER, FRED A. state legislator; b. Madison, Wis., May 5, 1927; married; 3 children. BA, U. Oreg., LLB, 1952. Bar: Wis. Sole practice, Madison, 1952—; mem. Wis. Senate from 26th dist., Madison, 1962—; asst. minority leader Wis. State Senate, 1965-67, minority leader, 1967-75, pres. pro tem, 1975-79, pres., 1979-93, asst. minority leader, 1993-96, pres., 1996—. Mem. Wis. State Assembley, 1956-62; del. Democratic Conv., 1960, 64; presdl. elector-chmn. Wis. Electoral Coll., 1964; vice chmn. Bldg. Commn., Wis. Democrat. also: 5008 Risser Rd Madison WI 53705-1365 Office: Madison Office State Capitol Rm 220 S PO Box 7882 Madison WI 53707-7882 E-mail: sen.risser@legis.state.wi.us.

RISSER, HILARY S. secondary school educator; d. Richard and Jean Smith; m. Scott D. Risser, June 3, 2000. BS, BA, So. Meth. U., 2000, MS, 2001. Tchg. asst. So. Meth. U., Dallas, 1998—2002; math. tchr. Plano (Tex.) Ind. Sch. Dist., 2002—. Recipient Betty McKnight Spears Award, So. Meth. U. Math dept., 2001; Nat. Merit Scholar, 1996. Mem.: Tex. Forensics Assn., Tex. Speech Communicators Assn., Am. Math. Soc., SIAM, Tau Beta Pi, Nat. Forensics League, Gamma Phi Beta (rec. sec., area reference chair, Dallas alumnae webdesigner 1997—2003). Avocations: Tae Kwon Do, quilting, needlepoint.

RISSER, JAMES VAULX, JR., journalist, educator; b. Lincoln, Nebr., May 8, 1938; s. James Vaulx and Ella Caroline (Schacht) R.; m. Sandra Elizabeth Laaker, June 10, 1961; children: David James, John Daniel. BA, U. Nebr., 1959, cert. in journalism, 1964; JD, U. San Francisco, 1962. Bar: Nebr. 1962. Pvt. practice law, Lincoln, 1962-64; reporter Des Moines Register and Tribune, 1964-85, Washington corr., 1969-85, bur. chief, 1976-85; dir. John S. Knight fellowships for profl. journalists, prof. communication Stanford U., 1985-2000. Lectr. Wells Coll., 1981; mem. com. on agrl. edn. in secondary schs. Nat. Acad. Scis., 1985-88. Trustee Reuter Found., 1989-2000, Am. Conservatory Theater, 2000-2003, Oreg. Shakespear Fest., 2003—, Jefferson Pub. Radio, 2003—; mem. Pulitzer Prize Bd., 1990-99; mem. journalism adv. com. Knight Found., 2000—. Profl. Journalism fellow Stanford U., 1973-74; recipient award for disting. reporting public affairs Am. Polit. Sci. Assn., 1969; Thomas L. Stokes award for environ. reporting Washington Journalism Center, 1971, 79; Pulitzer prize for nat. reporting, 1976, 79; Worth Bingham Found. prize for investigative reporting, 1976; Raymond Clapper Meml. Assn. award for Washington reporting, 1976, 78; Edward J. Meeman award for Conservation Reporting, 1985. Mem. Soc. Environ. Journalists, Soc. Profl. Journalists (Disting. Svc. award 1976), Investigative Reporters and Editors Assn., Com. Concerned Journalists, Gridiron Club. Clubs: Gridiron. Home: 71 Water St # 206 Ashland OR 97520 E-mail: jimrisser@earthlink.net.

RISSER, PAUL GILLAN, academic administrator, botanist; b. Blackwell, Okla., Sept. 14, 1939; s. Paul Crane and Jean (McCluskey) R.; children: David, Mark, Stephen, Scott. BA, Grinnell Coll., 1961; MS in Botany, U. Wis., 1965, PhD in Botany and Soils, 1967. From asst. prof. to prof. botany U. Okla., 1967-81, also asst. dir. biol. sta., chmn. dept. botany and microbiology, 1977-81; dir. Okla. Biol. Survey, 1971-77; chief Ill. Natural History Survey, 1981-86; program dir., ecosystem studies NSF; provost and v.p. acad. affairs U. N.Mex., 1989-92; former pres. Miami U., Oxford, Ohio; pres. Oreg. State U., 1996—2002; chancellor Okla. Sys. Higher Edn., 2003—. Author: (with Kathy Cornelison) Man and the Biosphere, 1979, (with others) The True Prairie Ecosystem, 1981; research, numerous publs. in field. Trustee Pioneer Multi-County Library Bd. Mem. Am. Acad. Arts and Scis., Ecol. Soc. Am. (pres.), Brit. Ecol. Soc., Soc. Range Mgmt., Southwestern Assn. Naturalists (pres.), Am. Inst. Biol. Sci. (pres.), Torrey Bot. Club. Presbyterian. Address: OK State Regents Higher Edn Off Chancellor 655 Rsch Pky Ste 200 Oklahoma City OK 73104

RISSETTO, HARRY A. lawyer; b. Dec. 1, 1943; AB, Fairfield U., 1965; JD, Georgetown U., 1968. Bar: N.Y. 1969, D.C. 1970. Law clk. to Hon. John J. Sirica U.S. Dist. Ct. D.C., 1968-69; law clk. to Chief Justice Warren E. Burger U.S. Supreme Ct., 1969-70; ptnr. Morgan, Lewis & Bockius, Washington. Adj. prof. Law Ctr., Georgetown U., 1986-89. Mem. ABA (co-chmn. railway labor act com. sect. of labor and employment law 1987-89). Office: Morgan Lewis & Bockius 1111 Pennsylvania Ave NW Washington DC 20004 Office Phone: 202-739-5130. Business E-Mail: hrissetto@morganlewis.com.

RISSMAN, BURTON RICHARD, lawyer; b. Chgo., Nov. 13, 1927; s. Louis and Eva (Lyons) R.; m. Francine Greenberg, June 15, 1952; children: Lawrence E., Thomas W., Michael P. BS, U. Ill., 1947, JD, 1951; LLM, NYU, 1952. Bar: Ill. 1951, U.S. Dist. Ct. (no. dist.) Ill. 1954, U.S. Ct. Appeals (7th cir.) 1978, U.S. Supreme Ct. 1982. Assoc. Schiff, Hardin & Waite, Chgo., 1953-59, ptnr., 1959—2003, mem. mgmt. com., 1984-92, chmn. mgmt. com., 1986-90; ret., 2003. Mem. faculty Practicing Law Inst. Bd. editor U. Ill. Law Forum, 1949-51; contbr. articles to profl. jours. 1st lt. JAGC USAF, 1952—53. Food Law fellow, 1951. Mem. ABA, Ill. Bar Assn., Chgo. Bar Assn., Chgo. Coun. Lawyers, Carlton Club.

RISTAU, MARK MOODY, lawyer, petroleum consultant; b. Warren, Pa., Mar. 21, 1944; s. Harold J. and Eleanor K. (Moody) Ristau. BA, Pa. Mil. Coll., 1966, Widner Coll., 1966; JD, Case Western Res. U., 1969. Bar: Pa. 1970, D.C. 1972, U.S. Supreme Ct. 1973, N.Y. 1982. Pvt. practice, Warren, Pa., 1970—85, Warren and Vancouver, Canada, 1976—85, Jamestown, NY, 1982—85; sr. ptnr. Ristau & McKeirnan, Warren, 1986—2002; sr. dir. Pa. Allied Oil Prodrs., 1972—78; atty. Pa. Field Prodrs., 1981—85; ptnr. SAR Devel., 1984—91, Slagle Almendinger & Ristau, 1983—89. Counsel United Refining Co., Pennbank, Enhanced Oil Recovery, Consol. Svcs., 1982—84; chmn. bd. Comml. Svc. Corp., U.S. interim trustee, 1979—88, bankruptcy trustee, 1988—98; CEO Silicon Electro-physics Corp., Inc., 1988—91, Phoenix Materials Corp., Inc., 1988—91; dirs. Warren Industries, Inc., 1991—94; bd. dirs. Petrex, Inc., A & A Metal Fabricating; U.S. counsel Brazilian Promotions, Inc. of Brazilian Govt., 1981—85; v.p. Daytona Apts., Inc., Daytona Beach, Fla.; case reporter Legal Intelligencer, 1972—79; CEO Warren Industries, Inc., 2003—. Contbr. articles to profl. jours. Sec. Daytona Devel. League; mem. Warren County Bd. Pub. Assistance, 1970—71, chmn., 1971—72; mem. Broward County (Fla.) Devel. League, 1981—83, Fla. Profl. Recruitment Assn., 1980—83. Recipient Tate Meml. award, 1981, Sambas award, 1981. Mem.: ATLA, Warren County Bar Assn. (past pres.), Am. Arbitration Assn., Conewango (Warren), Ipanema (Brazil), Eagles (life). Home and Office: PO Box 885 Warren PA 16365-0885 E-mail: ristaulaw@penn.com.

RISTER, GENE ARNOLD, humanities educator; b. Merkel, Tex., Apr. 18, 1943; s. Jettie William and Mary Evelyn (Scott) R.; m. Janet Kathleen Ledermann, Jan. 21, 1967. BA summa cum laude, McMurry U., 1965; MA, Tex. Christian U., 1966; PhD, U. Wis., 1972; postgrad., U. Ariz., 1990, No. Ariz. U., 1990. Prof., divsn. chmn. McMurry U., Abilene, Tex., 1970-81, East Ctrl. U., Ada, Okla., 1981-83; prof. dept. humanities, divsn. chmn. Maricopa C.C., Phoenix, 1983—. Adj. prof. No. Ariz. U., Phoenix, 1994—; del. Nat. Inst. Higher Edn. for Mex.-Ams., Albuquerque, 1975. Author: (poems) Canticles I, 2002, Canticles II, 2003, Canticles III, 2004; book reviewer Tex. Rev., 1985; illustrator Tex. Rev. and Tex. Anthology, 1979-82; contbr. articles to profl. jours.; contbr. numerous poems to jours., anthologies. Regional cons. Human Rels. Coun., Midland; moderator, dir. West Tex. Coun. Govts.; mem. Tex. Com. for Humanities and Pub. Policy, 1975-81; ECU rep. Intertribal Coun., Five Nations, Sulphur, Okla., 1981; co-sponsor Tex. Reading Cir. Consortium of Univs., 1977-79. Recipient Faculty Recognition award Consortium for C.C. Devel., 1996; named Innovator of the Yr. Maricopa CCD/League for Innovation, 1988, Outstanding Faculty Employee award Maricopa C.C. Dist., 1985, 89, 92; NDEA Title VI fellow, 1965-67, Am. Grad. Sch. Internat. Mgmt. fellow, 1995, East-West Ctr. fellow, 1994, Japan Found. fellow, 1995; U.S. Dept. Edn. Title VIA grantee, 1996-98. Mem. C.C. Humanities Assn. (Ariz. state rep. to nat. bd. 1992). Democrat. Baptist. Avocations: archaeology, art and art history, cinema, music, travel. Home: 14407 N 60th St Scottsdale AZ 85254-5540 Office: Paradise Valley Cmty Coll 18401 N 32nd St Phoenix AZ 85032-1210 Office Phone: 602-787-6575. E-mail: gene.rister@pvmail.maricopa.edu.

RISTICH, MIODRAG, psychiatrist; b. Belgrade, Yugoslavia, July 19, 1938; arrived in US, 1967; s. Teodosije and Gordana (Isailovic) Ristich; m. Yvonne Muriel Cunliffe, May 6, 1967; children: Katharine Alexandra, Elizabeth Victoria. MD, U. Belgrade, 1962. Resident psychiatry Manhattan Psychiat. Ctr., NYU, 1980-83; med. dir. Cambridge (Minn.) State Hosp., 1967-72; dir. Willowbrook State Sch., Staten Island, NY, 1972-74; med. dir. DeWitt Rehab. Nursing Ctr., NYC, 1976—; clin. asst. prof. psychiatry NYU Med. Sch., 1996—. Pvt. practice psychiatry, NYC, 1973—. Mem.: AMA, Royal Coll. Psychiatrists, Am. Assn. Geriatric Psychiatry, Am. Psychiat. Assn. Republican. Avocation: tennis. Home: 37 Sunrise Ln Upper Saddle River NJ 07458-1631 Office: 201 E 79th St Apt 7J New York NY 10021-0833 Office Phone: 212-737-6990. E-mail: mristich@yahoo.com.

RISTOW, BRUNNO, plastic surgeon; b. Brusque, Brazil, Oct. 18, 1940; s. Arno and Ally Odette (von Bruettner) Ristow; m. Urannia Carrasquilla Gutierrez, Nov. 10, 1979; children from previous marriage: Christian Kilian, Trevor Roland. Student, Coll. Sinodal, Brazil, 1956—57; MD magna cum laude, U. Brazil, 1966. Diplomate Am. Bd. Plastic and Reconstructive Surgery. Intern in surgery Hosp. dos Estrangeiros, Rio de Janeiro, 1965, Hosp. Estuadual Miguel Couto, Brazil, 1965—66, Instituto Aposentadoria Pensao Comerciarios Hosp. for Gen. Surgery, 1966; resident in plastic and reconstructive surgery Dr. Ivo PItanguy Hosp. Santa Casa de Misericordia, Rio de Janeiro, 1967; fellow Inst. Reconstructive Plastic Surgery NYU Med. Ctr., N.Y.C., 1967—68, jr. resident, 1971—72, sr. and chief resident, 1972—73; practice medicine specializing in plastic surgery Rio de Janeiro, 1967, N.Y.C., 1968—73, San Francisco, 1973—; asst. surgeon NY Hosp., Cornell Med. Ctr., N.Y.C., 1968—71. Clin. instr. surgery NYU Sch. Medicine, 1972—73; chmn. plastic and reconstructive surgery divsn. Presbyn. Hosp., Pacific Med. Ctr., San Francisco, 1974—92, chmn. emeritus, 1992—. Contbg. author: Cancer of the Hand, 1975, Current Therapy in Plastic and Reconstructive Surgery, 1988, Male Aesthetic Surgery, 1989, How They Do It: Procedures in Plastic and Reconstructive Surgery, 1990, Middle Crus: The Missing Link in Alar Cratilage Anatomy, 1991, Surgical Technology International, 1992, Aesthetic Plastic Surgery, 1993, Mastery of Surgery: Plastic and Reconstructive Surgery, 1993, Reoperative Aesthetic Plastic Surgery of the Face and Breast, 1994; contbr. articles on plastic surgery to profl. publs. With M.C. Brazilian Army Res., 1959—70. Decorated knight Venerable Order of St. Hubertus, Knight Order St. John of Jerusalem; fellow in surgery, Cornell Med. Sch., 1968—71. Fellow: ACS, Internat.Coll. Surgeons; mem.: AMA (Physician's Recognition award 1971—83), San Francisco Med. Assn., Calif. Med. Assn., Calif. Soc. Plastic Surgeons, Internat. Soc. Aesthetic Plastic Surgeons, Am. Soc. Plastic and Reconstructive Surgeons, Am. Soc. Aesthetic Plastic Surgery (chmn. edn.), San Francisco Olympic Club. Republican. Mem. Evangelical Lutheran Ch. Office: Calif Pacific Med Ctr 2100 Webster St Ste 501 San Francisco CA 94115-2373 Office Phone: 415-202-1507. Personal E-mail: info@brunnoristow.com.

RISTOW, GAIL ROSS, art educator, paralegal, children's rights advocate; b. Carmel, Calif., Oct. 18, 1949; d. Kenneth E. and Lula Mae (Craft) Ross; m. Steven Craig Ristow, Sept. 15, 1971. BS in Biochemistry, Calif. Polytech State U., San Luis Obispo, 1972; MEd, Ariz. State U., 1980. Cert. tchr., Calif. Asst. instr. Calif. State Polytech U., Pomona, 1972; grad. asst. Calif. Polytech State U., Pomona, 1973-74; tchr. Mt. Carmel High Sch., L.A., 1974-76, Cartwright Sch. Dist., Phoenix, 1976-80; pres., owner Handmade With Love, Bay City, Tex., 1984-88; tchr. art Aiken, S.C., 1989-96. Tchr. Community Edn., Bay City, 1986-88, Palacios, Tex., 1987. Sec. Chukker Creek Homeowners, Aiken, S.C., 1989-96; mem. S.C. Foster Care Rev. Bd., 1991-96; vol. tchr. elem. schs., Korea. Mem. AAUW, Am. Chem. Soc., Nat. Soc. Tole and Decorative Painters, Aiken Newcomer's Club (sec. 1989-91), Aiken Lioness Club (pres. 1991-94), Aiken Lions Club, Alpha Delta Kappa (v.p. 1986-87). Avocations: painting, woodworking, sewing, reading, children's rights advocacy. Home: 396 Lombardy Ln Richland WA 99352

RISTOW, GEORGE EDWARD, neurologist, educator; b. Albion, Mich., Dec. 15, 1943; s. George Julius and Margaret (Beattie) R.; 1 child, George Andrew Martin. BA, Albion Coll., 1965; DO, Coll. Osteo. Medicine/Surgery, Des Moines, 1969. Diplomate Am. Bd. Psychiatry and Neurology. Intern Garden City Hosp., 1969-70; resident Wayne State U., 1970-74; fellow U. Newcastle Upon Tyne, 1974-75; asst. prof. dept. neurology Wayne State U., Detroit, 1975-77; assoc. prof. Mich. State U., East Lansing, 1977-83, prof., 1983-84, 95—, prof., chmn., 1984-95, prof. emeritus, 2001—. Fellow Am. Acad. Neurology, Royal Soc. Medicine; mem. AMA, Am. Osteo. Assn., Pan Am. Med. Assn., World Fedn. Neurology, Am. Coll. Neuropsychiatrists (sr.). Home: 2070 Riverwood Dr Okemos MI 48864-2814 Office Phone: 517-374-7600. E-mail: ristowge@aol.com.

RISUKHIN, VLADIMIR NIKOLAYEVICH, aeronautical engineer, educator; b. Verkhnyaya Pokrovka, Ukraine, Dec. 26, 1946; arrived in U.S., 2001; s. Nikolay Ostapovich Risukhin and Nina Josephovna (Linevich) Risukhina; m. Tatyana Vasilyevna Chernysh, July 12, 1969; children: Dmitry, Ekaterina. BS in Radio Comm., Coll. Elec. Comm., 1965; BS in Flight Ops., Coll. Civil Aviation, 1968; MS in Aeronautical Engring., Acad. Civil Aviation, 1974, PhD in Aeronautical Engring., 1988. Radio tech. Airport, Lugansk, Ukraine, 1964—65; pilot Regoinal Adminstrn. Civil Aviation, Yakutsk, 1968—77; flight ops. mgr. Ctrl. Adminstrn. Internat. Airline, Moscow, 1977—83; flight tng. mgr. Min. Aviation Industry, 1983—90; sr. instr. pilot Aeroflot-Russian Airlines, 1990—2002; assoc. prof. Coll. Aviation, Western Mich. U., Battle Creek, 2002—. Cons. Internat. Air Transp. Assn., Montreal, 2000—. Author:

Controlling Pilot Error: Automation, 2001. Mem.: Univ. Aviation Assn. (assoc.). Avocations: photography, tennis. Office: Coll Aviation Western Mich U 237 N Helmer Rd Battle Creek MI 49015 E-mail: vladimir.risukhin@wmich.edu.

RITA, ROBERT, state representative; b. Springfield, Ill., Oct. 2, 1969; 1 child, Ashley. AA, Moraine Valley Comm. Coll., 1999; attending, Gov. State Univ. Heavy equipment op. Cook County Hwy. Dept., Ill., 1989—; Op. Engr. Local 150, 1989—; State Rep. House of Rep., Dist. 28, 2003—. Trustee Calumet Twp., Ill., 1997—; dir. Township Officials of Ill., Ill., 2001—. Mem.: Ins. Comm., Gaming Comm., Consumer Protection Comm., Computer Tech. Comm., Appropriations - pub. safety, Ill. Twp. Officials (dir.), Cook County Twp. Officials (former exec. bd. chmn. 1997—), Am. Liberties Soc. (Dei Lucani 1995—). Democrat. Roman Catholic. Mailing: Capitol 247-E Stratton Office Bldg Springfield IL 62706 Office: District 13543 Cicero Ave Crestwood IL 60445

RITACCO, PATSY RICHARD, sales executive; b. Newark, Aug. 27, 1956; s. Michael Patsy and Adelaide (Caruso) Ritacco; m. Linda La Falce, Nov. 5, 1978; children: Michael A., Patsy Richard Jr. B in History, William Paterson Coll., 1978. Notary pub. N.J. Tchr. Belleville (N.J.) HS, 1978-82; bd. pneumatics Robert Tool, Saddle Brook, NJ, 1983-94; dist. sales mgr. Std. Abrasives, Simi Valley, Calif., 1994—. Concert promotion dir. edn. groups 50s and 60s Bklyn. Bridge, Coasters, 1980—; scholar bd. Unico Nat., Nutley, NJ, 1995—, treas., 1998—99, v.p., 2000—; guest lectr. in field. Contbr. poetry to anthologies; contbg. writer: Italian Tribune. Fellow bdlgs. and grounds pub. rels. Christ Ch. Sch. Bd., 1985—88; chmn. com. Nutley Hall of Fame, 2002—; chmn. Ferraro Found., 2004; assoc. mem. Mus. Natural History. Named in Greatest Poets and Poems of the 20th Century, 1999; recipient Editor's Choice award "Riddle of the Rose", Internat. Libr. of Poetry, Color of Heart, 2000, Poetry's Elite: The Best Poets, 2000, Unican of the Yr. award, Nutley chpt. Unico Nat., 2002, Poetry's Elite: The Best Poet, 2001, 2002, Outstanding Achievement award, Ferraro Found., 2003, Cmty. Svc. award, 2003, Parable of Time Editor's Choice award, 2003, Poetry's Elite: The Best Poet, 2003. Mem.: Internat. Soc. Poets, Platers Assn. (contbg.), Soc. Engrs. (contbg.), Am. Softball Assn. (assoc.). Roman Catholic. Avocations: reading, cooking, music, sports. Office: Standard Abrasives 4201 Guardian St Simi Valley CA 93063-3372 Office Phone: 800-423-5444. E-mail: BaBiBard@aol.com.

RITCH, KATHLEEN, diversified company executive; b. Harbor Beach, Mich., Jan. 23, 1943; d. Eunice (Spry) R. BA, Mich. State U., 1965; student, Katharine Gibbs Sch., 1965—66. Exec. sec., adminstrv. asst. to pres. Katy Industries, Inc., N.Y.C., 1969-70; exec. sec., adminstrv. asst. to chmn. Kobrand Corp., N.Y.C., 1970-72; adminstrv. to chmn. and pres. Ogden Corp., N.Y.C., 1972-74, asst. sec., adminstr. office svcs., asst. to chmn., 1974-81, corp. sec., adminsr. office svcs., 1981-84, v.p., corp. sec., adminstr. office svcs., 1984-92, v.p. corp. sec., 1992-2000; freelance executive NYC, 2000—. Co-owner Unell Mfg. Co., Port Hope, Mich., 1966-87. Bd. dir. Young Concert Artists, Inc. Mem. Am. Soc. Corp. Secs. Home: 500 E 77th St New York NY 10162-0025

RITCH, ROBERT HARRY, ophthalmologist, educator; b. New Haven, May 14, 1942; s. Edward Lewis and Minerva (Grosberg) R. BA cum laude, Harvard U., 1965, MA, 1967; postgrad., Rice U., 1967—68; MD, Albert Einstein Coll. Medicine, 1972. Diplomate Am. Bd. Ophthalmology, Am. Bd. Laser Surgery. Intern St. Vincent's Med. Ctr., NYC, 1972-73; resident in ophthalmology Mt. Sinai Sch. Medicine, NYC, 1973-75, chief resident, 1975-76, Heed Ophthalmic Found. fellow, 1976-77, NIH-Nat. Rsch. Svc. fellow, 1976-78, asst. clin. ophthalmologist, 1976-77, instr., 1977-78, asst. prof., 1978-80, assoc. prof., 1980-82; attending ophthalmologist Beth Israel Med. Ctr., NYC, 1978—. Cons. ophthalmologist VA Hosp., Bronx, 1978-82, Manhattan Eye, Ear & Throat Hosp., 1989—; dir. glaucoma svc. Elmhurst Hosp., 1978-82, acting dir. dept. ophthalmology, 1979-82, chief glaucoma svc. NY Eye and Ear Infirmary, NYC, 1983—, surgeon dir., 1991—; prof. clin. ophthalmology NY Med. Coll., Valhalla, 1983—; Arthur Bedell Meml. lectr. Wills Eye Hosp., Phila., 1995; John Edwin Brown Meml. lectr. Ohio State U., Columbus, 1996; Schoenburg Meml. lectr. Ill. Eye and Ear Infirmary, Chgo., 1996; Schlaegel lectr. U. Ind., Indpls., 1996; Gerasimos Frenimopoulos Meml. lectr. Duke U., 1997, Joseph M. Bryan Meml. lectr., 1997; Roger P. Mason Meml. lectr. Howard U., 1997; Abraham S. Ticho lectr., Jerusalem, 1998; Anagnostakis-Trantus lectr., Athens, 1998; Sanford Gifford Meml. lectr., Chgo., 1998, Annie Wong lectr. Chinese U., Hong Kong, 1999, Arthur Lim lectr., Hong Kong, 2001, Am. Glaucoma Soc. Subspecialty Day lectr., Am. Acad. Ophthalmology, New Orleans, 2001, King Khaled Meml. Lctr, Riyadh, 2003; Chew Sek-Jin Meml. lectr., Hong Kong, 2003, Irving Leopold Meml. lectr., Irvine, Calif, 2004; program chmn. East Coast Glaucoma Symposium, NY, 2000; cons. Sukhumvit Hosp., Bangkok, Thailand, 1994—; pres. Internat. Eye Cons., Ltd., 1995—, NY Glaucoma Rsch. Inst., 1996; adj. sr. scientist Singapore Eye Rsch. Inst., 1997; mem. adv. bd. Dr.-to Dr., Berkeley, Calif., 1995—; sec., treas., chmn. sci. adv. bd. Glaucoma Found., 1984—, med. dir., chmn., grant rev. com.; med. dir. Children's Right to Sight, prin. investigator Collaborative Initial Glaucoma Treatment Study, 1993-2003; mem. adv. bd. Sturge-Weber Found., 1996: mem. glaucoma adv. com. Nat. Soc. to Prevent Blindness, 1986—; organizing chmn. Bangkok Ophthal. Cong., 1985-93, Optic Nerve Rescue & Restoration Think Tank, NY, 1994-2003, First Internat. Think Tank on Exfoliation Syndrome, New York, 1999, Myanmar Internat. Ophthal. Congress, 1997, 99, 2003; internat. sci. com. Internat. Congress of Ophthalmology, Sydney, Australia, 2002; sci. organizing com. mem. 4th Internat. Glaucoma Cong., Barcelona, Spain, 2003; external assessor U. Malaya, 1988-96; cons. Tun Hussein Onn Nat. Eye Hosp., Kuala Lumpur, Malaysia, 1996—; internat. adv. bd. 4th Internat. Symposium of Ophthalmology, Shantou, China, 2002; mem. steering com. Assn. Internat. Glaucoma Soc., 2002—; internat. advisor Tianjin Med. Ctr., China, 2002—; hon. pres. Chinese Internat. Glaucoma Congress, Beijing, 2004. Author: (with M.B. Shields) The Secondary Glaucomas, 1982; (with M.B. Shields and T. Krupin) the Glaucomas, 1988, 2d edit., 1996, (with R. Caronia) Classic Papers in Glaucoma, 2000; spl. sect. editor Jour. Glaucoma, 1991-98; mem. editl. bd. Sightsaving, 1981-86, Ophthalmic Laser Therapy, 1984-88, Ophthalmic Resident, 1992-95, Ophthalmic Surgery and Lasers, 1995—, Microsurgery, 1994—, Ophthalmology Times, 1996-2001, Jour. Glaucoma, 1998—, Internat. Glaucoma Rev., 1999—; contbg. editor Ophthalmic Practice, 1993—; contbr. to films on laser therapy, over 900 articles and abstracts in field. Bd. dirs. Dooley Found./Intermed. U.S.A., 1991—, UN, Southeastern Nigeria Eye Care Outreach Coll. Med. Scis. U. Calabar, Nigeria, 1996—; vol. Devel. Coun., 1991-93; chmn. bd. dirs. I-Med. Devel Corp., 1991-94; sci. adv. bd. Singapore Eye Rsch. Inst.; bd. govs. Internat. Soc. for Imaging of the Eye, 2002—; adv. com. Internat. Coun. Ophthalmology, 2002—. Hon. scholar Harvard U., 1965; NSF fellow Harvard U., 1966-67, Harvard traveling fellow Rice U., 1967-68; recipient Acad. Investigator award NIH, 1978-81, Disting. Svc. award Internat. Ctr. NY 1981, Exec. Dirs. award, 1985, Founders award Nat. Exhibits by Blind Artists, 1985, Gold medal of Merit and Honor Greek Glaucoma Soc., 1998, Ophthalmology Times Achievement in Ophthalmology award, 1998, Louis Rudin award for rsch. in glaucoma, 1999, Jesse H. Neal award for editl. achievement, 2000; spl. honoree Helen Keller Found., 2000, spl. honoree Glaucoma Found, 2000; decorated comdr. Grace Sovereign Order of Orthodox Knights Hospitaller of St. John of Jerusalem. Fellow Am. Acad. Ophthalmology (edn. distbn. subcom. 1994-97, book/jour. link subcom. 1994-97, distbn. adv. subcom. 1997-2000, chmn. subcom., 2001—, Honor award, 1985, sr. honor award 1995), Heed Ophthalmic Found. (ophthalmologist of Yr. 1996), Am. Ophthalmol. Soc. (program com. 2002—), NY Acad. Medicine, Royal Coll. Ophthalmologists (U.K.), ACS, Internat. Coll. Surgeons, Am. Soc. Laser Surgery Medicine (chmn. ophthalmology sect. 1991-92, moderator and program chmn. joint sci. symposium on glaucoma 1991), NY Acad. Medicine (sec. sect. on ophthalmology 1991-92, chmn. 1993-94, Charles May Meml. Lectr. 1991, bd. trustees 2003—); mem. AMA, AAAS, NY State Med. Soc., NY County Med. Soc., Assn. Rsch. in Vision and Ophthalmology (program com., glaucoma sect. 1991-93, program chmn. 1993-94, internat. com. 2003—, bd. trustees 2003—), Am. Assn. Ophthalmology, Ophthal. Soc. U.K., Internat. Assn. Ocular surgeons, Internat. Congress Ophthalmology (glaucoma com. 1994—), NY Intra-Ocular Lens Implant Soc., Manhattan Ophthal. Soc., Assn. Internat. Glaucoma Soc., Internat. Soc. Eye Rsch., Soc. Clin. Trials, Pan-Pacific Anterior Segment Soc. (v.p. 1985-88), Internat. Coun. Ophthalmology (adv. com.), NY Acad. Sci., Ophthalmic Laser Surgery Soc. (sec.-treas. 1982-98, 2000-, pres. 1998-2000), NY Soc. Clin. Ophthalmology (rec. sec. 1988-90, program chmn. 1990-91, pres. 1991-92), NY Glaucoma Rsch. Inst. (pres. 1996—), Am. Soc. Cell Biology, Am. Telemed Assn., Internat. Soc. On-Line Ophthalmologists (mem. orgn. com., chmn. glaucoma sect. 1995—), Internat. Fedn. Cell Biologists, Philippine Soc. Ophthalmology (hon.), Thailand Ophthal. Soc. (hon.), Italian Assn. for Study of Glaucoma (hon.), La.-Miss. Ophthal. and Otolarygol. Soc. (hon.), Can. Implant Soc. (hon). Home: 455 E 57th St # 14D New York NY 10022-3065 Office: NY Eye and Ear Infirmary 310 E 14th St New York NY 10003-4201 Office Phone: 212-673-5140. E-mail: ritchmd@earthlink.net.

RITCHEY, CAMILLA COLLETT, real estate executive; b. Ft. Worth, Tex., July 30, 1945; d. Edwin White and Camilla Collett Ritchey; m. Roy Marsden Adell, May 14, 1972; children: Alexander, Leila. BA, Trinity U., 1967, MA, 1971. Pres. Lezander Partnership, San Antonio; pres./founder Brigher Sky Found., 1998—; mgr. and gen. ptnr. Cibolo Creek Ranch, 1999—, co-mgr. Cibolo Creek Bed and Breakfast.

RITCHEY, KENNETH WILLIAM, administrator; b. Washington, June 7, 1947; s. Conrad Monroe and Katherine Costance (Sheris) (dec. 2004) R.; m. Nancy Jayne Kirk, Aug. 22, 1970; children: Kirk Damon, Erin Kathryn (dec. Apr. 1988). BS in Edn., Shippensburg U., 1969; MEd in Spl. Edn., U. Va., 1972; MS in Ednl. Adminstrn., U. Dayton, 1980; grad. sr. execs. in state & local govt. program, Harvard U., 1992. Spl. edn. tchr. Shippensburg (Pa.) Area Sch. Dist., 1969-71; head cross country and track coach Shippensburg U., 1970-74; master tchr., coord. work experience program Lincoln Intermediate Unit, New Oxford, Pa., 1971-76; adult edn. tchr. Franklin County Prison, Chambersburg, Pa., 1972-76; asst. supt. mgmt. svcs. Montgomery County Bd. Mental Retardation & Devel. Disabilities, Dayton, Ohio, 1977-83, supt. bd., 1983-99; dir. Ohio Dept. Mental Retardation and Devel. Disabilities, Columbus, 1999—; mem. Gov.'s Cabinet. Mem. part-time faculty edn. dept. U. Dayton, 1983-97; mem., vice-chair cmty. and mil. adv. com. ARC, 1986-95, needs and priorities com. Human Svcs. Levy Coun., 1982-84, 87-99; trustee Ohio Polit. Action Com., Brighter Tomorrow Found., 1990-2000, County Corp., 1992-98, Leadership Dayton, 1991. Former editor statewide newsletter for tchrs. and profls. in Work Experience. Vol. mem. cmty. and agys. resources coun. United Way, 1986—98; v.p. HelpLink Bd., pres.; mem. Gov.'s Vision Com., Ill., 1997—2000; bd. dirs. Ohio Pub. Images, Inc., past pres. Recipient Harold Hilty Humanitarian award, United Cerebral Palsy Rehab. Svcs., 1994, Robert Weaver Disting. Svc. award, Montgomery County Bd. Mental Retardation and Devel. Disabilities, 1999, Svc. award, Profl. Assn. on Retardation, 2002. Mem.: Ohio Self Determination Assn. (Catalyst award 2003), Nat. Assn. State Dirs. Developmental Disabilities Svcs. (mem. nat. policy work group 2002, bd. trustees 2004), Supts. Assn. (exec. com.), Ohio Supts. County Bds. Mental Retardation (v.p., pres.), Am. Assn. Mental Retardation, Phi Beta Kappa. Democrat. Methodist. Home: 7660 Turtle Creek Dr Dayton OH 45414-1756 Office: 1810 Sullivant Ave Columbus OH 43222-1055 E-mail: k1ritchey@aol.com.

RITCHEY, PATRICK WILLIAM, lawyer; b. Pitts., July 9, 1949; s. Joseph Frank and Patricia Ann (Giovengo) R. BA, Haverford Coll., 1971; JD, Yale U., 1974. Bar: U.S. Dist. Ct. (we. dist.) Pa. 1974, U.S. Ct. Appeals (3d. cir.) 1976, U.S. Supreme Ct. 1980, U.S. Ct. Appeals (4th cir.) 1981, U.S. Ct. Appeals (6th cir.) 1982, U.S. Dist. Ct. (ea. dist.) Wis. 1987, U.S. Ct. Appeals (7th cir.) 1991, U.S. Ct. Appeals (D.C. cir.) 1993, U.S. Ct. Appeals (8th cir.) 1993. Assoc. Reed Smith Shaw & McClay, Pitts., 1974-82, ptnr., 1982—. Mem. Pitts. Personnel Assn., Pitts., 1982—, U.S. Dist. Ct. Rules Task Force, Pitts., 1988. Bd. dirs. Pitts. Opera. Mem. Fed. Bar Assn. (labor and employment sect.), Allegheny County Bar Assn. (labor law and fed. ct. sects.), Harvard-Yale-Princeton Club, Duquesne Club. Office: Reed Smith LLP James H Reed Bldg 435 6th Ave Ste 2 Pittsburgh PA 15219-1886

RITCHEY, SAMUEL DONLEY, JR., retired retail store executive; b. Derry Twp., Pa., July 16, 1933; s. Samuel Donley and Florence Catherine (Litsch) R.; m. Sharon Marie Anderson, Apr. 6, 1956; children: Michael Donley, Tamara Louise, Shawn Christopher. BS, San Diego State U., 1955, MS, 1963; postgrad., Stanford U., 1964. With Lucky Stores Inc., 1951-61, 64-86, pres., chief operating officer, 1978-80, pres., chief exec. officer, 1980-81, chmn., chief exec. officer, 1981-85, chmn. bd., 1981-86. Bd. dirs. SBC Comms. The McClatchey Co., De La Salle Inst., John Muir/Mt. Diablo Health Sys.; grad. mgr. San Diego State U., 1961-63; lectr. in field; past chmn. Calif. Power Exchange, mem. adv. coun. Grad. Sch. Bus., Stanford U. Sloan Found. fellow. Mem. Mex. Am. Legal Def. and Edn. Fund, Western Assn. Food Chains (bd. dirs., pres.), Food Mktg. Inst. (bd. dirs., vice chmn.), Sloan Alumni Assn. (adv. bd., pres.).

RITCHIE, ALBERT, lawyer; b. Charlottesville, Va., Sept. 29, 1939; s. John and Sarah Dunlop (Wallace) R.; m. Jennie Wayland, Apr. 29, 1967; children: John, Mary. BA, Yale U., 1961; LLB, U. Va., 1964. Bar: Ill. 1964, Tenn. 2000. Assoc. Sidley & Austin, Chgo., 1964-71, ptnr., 1972-99, ret., 1999. Bd. dirs. Erie Neighborhood House, Chgo., 1978-88; bd. dirs. United Charities of Chgo., 1979-90; trustee U. Va. Law Sch. Found., 1997-99. Capt. U.S. Army, 1965-67. Mem. ABA, Am. Coll. Real Estate Lawyers, Chgo. Legal Aid Soc., Legal Club Chgo. (pres. 1986-87), U. Va. Law Sch. Alumni Assn. (v.p. 1989-93, pres. 1993-95), Cherokee Country Club, Hillsboro Club, Indian Hill Club. Episcopalian. Home: 436 Boxwood Sq Knoxville TN 37919-6627 E-mail: ritchiea@bellsouth.net.

RITCHIE, ALEXANDER BUCHAN, lawyer; b. Detroit, Apr. 19, 1923; s. Alexander Stevenson and Margaret (May) R.; m. Sheila Spellacy, June 1998; 1 child, Barbara Ritchie Drolshagen. BA, Wayne State U., 1947, JD, 1949. Bar: Mich. 1949. Pvt. practice, Detroit, 1949-52, 84—; asst. gen. counsel, asst. v.p. Maccabees Mutual Life Ins. Co., Detroit, 1952-65, v.p., sec., gen. counsel Southfield, Mich., 1977-84; sec., house counsel Wayne Nat. Life Ins. Co., Detroit, 1966-67; ptnr. Fenton, Nederlander, Dodge & Ritchie, Detroit, 1967-77. Spl. asst. atty. gen. State Mich., 1974-77. Bd. mem. Detroit Bd. Edn., 1971-77, Detroit Ctrl. Bd. Edn., 1971-73; bd. Police Commrs., Detroit, 1974-77; bd. dirs. Doctor's Hosp., Detroit, 1974-89. With U.S. Army, 1943-46. Recipient Key to the City of Detroit, Mayor Coleman Young, 1977. Mem. Mich. State Bar Assn. Avocations: reading, golf, theater, gourmet. Home: 29255 Laurel Woods Dr Apt 201 Southfield MI 48034-4647

RITCHIE, ALLEN W. insurance company executive; Degree, U. Ala. Ptnr. Arthur Andersen & Co., Atlanta; from CFO to pres. Fin. and Adminstrv. Group AGCO Corp., 1991—96, pres. Fin. and Adminstrv. Group, 1996—97; exec. v.p., CFO, COO Per-Se Technologies, 1998, pres., CEO, 1998—2000; exec. v.p. Protective Life Corp., Birmingham, Ala., 2001—, CFO, 2001—. Office: Protective Life Corp 2801 Hwy 280 S Birmingham AL 35223*

RITCHIE, ANNE, educational administrator; b. Grants Pass, Oreg., July 1, 1944; d. William Riley Jr. and Allie Brown (Clark) R.; m. Charles James Cooper, Sept. 4, 1968 (div. 1985); children: Holly Anne, Wendy Nicole. BA in Edn. with honors, Calif. State U., Sacramento, 1981. Cert. elem. tchr., Calif. CEO El Rancho Schs., Inc., Carmichael, Calif., 1981—. Citizen amb. del. People to People Internat., Russia, Lithuania, Hungary, 1993, China, 1994. Active Crocker Art Mus.; mem. Rep. Senatorial Inner Circle, Washington, 1999. Mem. AAUW, Nat. Assn. Edn. for Young Children, Profl. Assn. Childhood Educators, Nat. Child Care Assn. Episcopalian. Avocations: travel, skiing, reading.

RITCHIE, CHARLES MICHAEL, education educator, consultant; b. CHarollette, N.C., Jan. 20, 1954; s. William Ray Ritchie and Nancy Ritche; m. Carolyn Guess Johnson; children: Michael, Thomas, Joseph. BS, Clemson Univ., Clemson, N.C., 1976; MBA, Augusta State Univ., Augusta, Ga., 1984; PhD, Univ. S.C., Colimbia, S.C., 1993; grad., Gradute Sch. of Banking, So. La. State Univ., 1989. Assoc. prof. Univ. S.C., Aiken, SC, S.C. State Univ., Orangebury, SC; v.p. Citizen So. Nat. Bank, Augusta, Ga. Prin. ptnr. Moore-Rotiche Group, Columbia, Ohio. Contbr. articles pub. to profl. jour. Recipient Eagle Scout, 1969. Mem.: So. Mgmt. Assn., Acad. Mgmt. Lutheran. Avocation: music. Office: Univ SC 471 Univ Pkwy Aiken SC 29801

RITCHIE, DANIEL LEE, academic administrator; b. Springfield, Ill., Sept. 19, 1931; s. Daniel Felix and Jessie Dee (Binney) R. BA, Harvard U., 1954, MBA, 1956. Exec. v.p., CFO MCA, Inc., LA, 1962—70; pres. Archon Pure Products Co., Los Angeles, 1970-73; exec. v.p. Westinghouse Electric Corp., Pitts., 1975-78; pres. corp. staff and strategic planning Westinghouse Broadcasting Co., 1978-79, pres., chief exec. officer, 1979-81, chmn., chief exec. officer, Westinghouse Broadcasting & Cable, Inc., 1981-87; owner Rancho Cielo, Montecito, Calif., 1977—; chancellor U. Denver, 1989—. With U.S. Army, 1956-58. Office: U Denver Office of Chancellor University Park Denver CO 80208-0001 E-mail: dritchie@du.edu.

RITCHIE, DENNIS M. software engineer; b. Bronxville, N.Y., Sept. 9, 1941; B, Harvard U., PhD, 1968. With Bell Labs/Lucent Techs., Murray Hill, NJ, 1967—, head sys. software rsch. dept. Computing Scis. Rsch. Ctr. Recipient award, Assn. Computing Machinery, 1974, Turing award, 1983, Emmanuel Piore award, IEEE, 1982, Hamming medal, 1990, award, Assn. Computing Machinery Software Systems, 1982, C&C Found. award of, NEC, 1989, U.S. Nat. Medal of Tech., 1999. Mem.: U.S. Nat. Acad. Engring. Achievements include development of UNIX Operating System in 1969; C Programming Language; exploration of distributed operating systems, languages and routing/switching hardware. Office: Bell Labs Lucent Techs 600 Mountain Ave Rm 2c-517 Murray Hill NJ 07974-2008

RITCHIE, DONALD A. historian; b. N.Y.C., N.Y., Dec. 23, 1945; s. Arthur V. and Jeannette M. Ritchie; m. Anne G. Campbell, June 18, 1988; children: Jennifer Reid, Andrea Campbell. BA, CCNY, 1967; MA, U. Md., 1969, PhD, 1975. Instr. U. Coll., U. of Md., Coll. Pk., 1974—76; assoc. historian U.S. Senate Hist. Office, Washington, 1976—; adj. asst. prof. Cornell in Wash. Program, 1990—2000. Author: James M. Landis: Dean of the Regulators, 1980, Press Gallery: Congress and the Washington Correspondents, 1991 (OAH Richard W. Leopold prize, 1992), Am. Journalists, 1997 (N.Y. Pub. Librs. best books for teen readers, 1999), Doing Oral History, 2003, (reference book) The Oxford Guide to the United States Govt., 2001, (textbook) The Am. Vision, 2003. Cpl. USMC, 1967—69. Recipient Forrest C. Pogue award, Oral History in the Mid-Atlantic Region, 1984, Henry Adams prize, Soc. for History in the Fed. Govt., 1992; grantee Rsch. Grant, Eleanor Roosevelt Inst., 1974. Mem.: Nat. Coun. on Pub. History (nominating com. 1992—95), Soc. for History in the Fed. Govt. (coun. mem. 1989—91), Orgn. of Am. Historians (nominating bd. 1985—87), Am. Hist. Assn. (coun. mem. 1992—96), Oral History Assn. (pres. 1986—87), Arts and Humanities Alumni Assn., U. of Md. (pres. 2002—04). Office: Senate Hist Office US Senate Washington DC 20510 E-mail: don_ritchie@sec.senate.gov.

RITCHIE, FRAN A. interior designer, small business owner; b. Nov. 23, 1940; d. Homer C. and Margaret H. (Simmons) Kyle; m. Byron D. Ritchie, Dec. 23, 1959. Grad. Seminole H.S.; student interior design (hon.), La Salle Extension U., Chgo., 1987. Lic. interior designer New Mex. Designer and sales staff Miller-Waldrop Furniture, Hobbs, N.Mex., 1967—, mgr., buyer, 1976—; part owner, designer Eileen's Bed, Bath & Kitchen, Hobbs, 1976—2002. Co-owner, Chapparal Racing Farm, 1985; leader seminars and h.s. programs on design. Mem.: Am. Soc. Interior Design (assoc.), Am. Bus.Women's Assn. (Woman of Yr. 1970), Hobbs C. of C. (bd. dirs. 1983—86, pres. 1987—88, chair southeasterm chambers legis. tour), Beta Sigma Phi (Outstanding mem. 1999). Home: 620 E Luna Dr Hobbs NM 88240-4016 Office: 100 W Bender Blvd Hobbs NM 88240-2232 Office Phone: 505-392-6508.

RITCHIE, GARRY HARLAN, television broadcast executive; b. Earling, W.Va., Aug. 18, 1938; s. Edgar Harlan and Elsie Pearl (Meador) R.; m. Nancy Lee Gladwell, June 14, 1958; children: Arthur Harlan, Michael Lee. Student, U. Charleston, 1956-60; student, Baldwin-Wallace Coll., 1965; BA, Thomas Edison State Coll., 1979. Engr., reporter Sta. WTIP Radio, Charleston, W.Va., 1956—60; sta. mgr. Sta. WRON Radio, Ronceverte, W.Va., 1960—63; reporter, newscaster Stas. WDOK AM & FM Radio, Cleve., 1963—65, Sta. WHK AM & FM Radio, Cleve., 1965—67; reporter, assignment editor Scripps-Howard Broadcasting Co., Sta. WEWS-TV, Cleve., 1967—69, from news dir. to sta. mgr., 1969—82; cable news mgr. corp. office Scripps-Howard Broadcasting Co., Westport, Conn., 1982—83; asst. gen. mgr. Scripps-Howard Broadcasting Co., Sta. WCPO-TV, Cin., 1983—84; v.p., gen. mgr. Diversified Communications, Sta. WCJB-TV, Gainesville, Fla., 1984—86, Diversified Communications, Sta. WYOU-TV, Scranton, Pa., 1986—91; pres. broadcast divsn. Diversified Communications, Portland, Maine, 1991—93; v.p., gen. mgr. Gateway Comms., Inc., Sta. WOWK-TV, Huntington, W.Va., 1993—96, v.p. community affairs, 1996—99; pres. Mus. Radio and Tech., Huntington, W.Va., 2000—02. Bd. dirs. Hippodrome Theatre, Gainesville, 1985-86, Vol. Ctr. Alachua County, Gainesville, 1985-86, Crimetrac Gainesville, Fla., 1985-86, Police Adv. Commn., Gainesville, 1985-86, Barnett Bank Alachua County, Gainesville, 1986, Scranton chpt. ARC, 1988-91, Better Bus. Bur. N.E. Pa., Scranton, 1988-91, United Way Lackawanna County, Scranton, 1989-91, Cabell Huntington (W.Va.) Hosp. Found., 1995-2003, Mus. of Radio and TV Tech., 2004—; bd. dirs., v.p. Girls Club Alachua County, Gainesville, 1985-86; mem. adv. bd. Scranton Area Found., 1989-91; trustee Keystone Jr. Coll. Laplume, Pa., 1991-92; trustee Huntington Mus. Art, 1996-99, v.p., 1998-99, gen. chmn. ann. fund campaign, 1998; trustee Tri-State Amateur Radio Assn., Huntington, 1998—, v.p., 1999-2000, pres., 2000-02. Recipient 5 Emmy awards Cleve. chpt. NATAS, 1973-80, Mel Burka Outstanding Broadcaster of W.Va. award, W.Va. Assn. Broadcasters, 1999. Mem. Nat. Assn. Broadcasters, Nat. Assn. TV Programming Execs., W.Va. Broadcasters Assn. (bd. dirs. 1995-99), Pa. Assn. Broadcasters (bd. dirs. 1989-91), Greater Scranton C. of C. (bd. dirs. 1987-90), Downtown Scranton Bus. Ass. (bd. dirs. 1989-91), Rotary (Scranton, bd. dirs. 1989-91), Rotary (Huntington, Wva.), Huntington Area C. of C. (bd. dirs. 1995-99, vice-chmn. 1996-98). Republican. Methodist. Avocations: amateur radio, astronomy, computers, reading. Home and Office: 19 Pinecrest Dr Huntington WV 25705-3439 E-mail: W8oi@arrl.net.

RITCHIE, J. MURDOCH, pharmacologist, educator; b. Aberdeen, Scotland, June 10, 1925; came to U.S. 1956; s. Alexander Farquharson and Agnes Jane (Bremner) R.; m. Brenda Rachel Bigland; children: Alasdair J., A. Jocelyn. BSc, Aberdeen (Scotland) U., 1944, U. Coll. London, 1949, PhD, 1952, DSc, 1960; MA, Yale U., 1968; DSc, Aberdeen U., 1987. Lectr. physiology U. Coll. London, 1949-51; sci. staff Nat. Inst. Med. Rsch., London, 1951-55; asst. prof. to prof. Albert Einstein Coll. Medicine, N.Y.C., 1954-63, prof. pharmacology, 1963-68; prof. and chmn. pharmacology Yale U., New Haven, 1968-74, dir. biol. scis., 1975-78, prof. pharmacology, 1968—. Contbr. articles to profl. jours.; editor sci. books and jours. Fellow Royal Soc., Univ. Coll. London, Inst. Physics London. Home: 47 Deepwood Dr Hamden CT 06517-3414 Office: Yale Univ Sch Medicine 333 Cedar St New Haven CT 06510-3206 E-mail: murdoch.ritchie@yale.edu.

RITCHIE, JAMES L. cardiologist; BA, Yale U., 1963. Chief divsn. of cardiology U. Wash. Sch. Medicine. Recipient Disting. Achievement award Am. Heart Assn., 1996. Office: U Wash Sch Medicine Box 356422 1959 NE Pacific St Seattle WA 98195-0001

RITCHIE, RICHARD LEE, media company executive; b. Grand Rapids, Mich., July 20, 1946; s. Robert George and Gertrude (Dryer) R.; m. Marlene Barton, Nov. 16, 1969; children: Gabrielle Gay, Steven Barton. BA, Mich. State U., 1968, MBA, 1972; P.MD, Harvard U., 1982. C.P.A., Mich. Sr. acct. Peat, Marwick, Mitchell & Co., Detroit, 1968-69, 72-74; mgr. corp. acctg. Grand Trunk Western R.R., Detroit, 1974-76, treas., 1976-79, asst. v.p., treas., 1980-83; v.p., treas. James River Corp., Richmond, Va., 1984-86; sr. v.p. fin., chief fin. officer Harte Hanks Communications, San Antonio, 1987-96; exec. v.p., CFO Big Flower Holdings, Inc., N.Y.C., 1997-2000. Prof. Oakland

Community Coll., Farmington, Mich. Served with AUS, 1969-71. Mem. AICPA, Mich. Assn. CPAs, Am. Acctg. Assn., Beta Alpha Psi, Beta Gamma Sigma. Jewish. Office: Bice Mercato 551 Madison Ave #1601 New York NY 10022-3261

RITCHIE, ROBERT OLIVER, materials science educator; b. Plymouth, Devon, Eng., Jan. 2, 1948; came to U.S., 1974; s. Kenneth Ian and Kathleen Joyce (Sims) R.; m. Connie Olesen (div. 1978); 1 child, James Oliver; m. HaiYing Song, 1991; 1 child, Duncan Soong. BA with honors, U. Cambridge, Eng., 1969, MA, PhD, 1973, ScD, 1990. Cert. engr., U.K. Goldsmith's rsch. fellow Churchill Coll. U. Cambridge, 1972-74; Miller fellow in basic rsch. sci. U. Calif., Berkeley, 1974-76; assoc. prof. mech. engring. MIT, Cambridge, 1977-81; prof. U. Calif., Berkeley, 1981—; dep. dir. Materials Scis. Divsn. Lawrence Berkeley Nat. Lab., Cambridge, 1990-94, dir. Ctr. for Advanced Materials, 1987-95, head Structural Materials Dept., Materials Scis. Divsn., 1995—. Cons. Alcan, Allison, Applied Materials, Boeing, Chevron, Cordis, Exxon, GE, GM, Grumman, Guidant, Instron, Northrop, Rockwell, Westinghouse, Baxter, Carbomedics, Med. Inc., Shiley, St. Jude Med.; Van Horn Disting. lectr. Case Western U., 1997. Editor: 17 books; contbr. more than 450 articles to profl. jours. Recipient Curtis W. McGraw Rsch. award Am. Soc. Engring. Educators, 1987, Rosenhain medal Inst. Materials London, 1992, G.R. Irwin medal ASTM, 1985, Mathewson gold medal TMS-AME, 1985, Van Horn Disting. Lectr. award Case Western Res. U., 1997; named one of Top 100 Scientists, Sci. Digest mag., 1984. Fellow: Royal Acad. Engring. (London), Minerals, Materials and Metals Soc. (Mathewson Gold medal 1985, Disting. Structural Materials Scientist/Engr. award 1996), Internat. Congress on Fracture (pres. 1997—2001), Am. Soc. Metals Internat., Inst. Materials (London); mem.: NAE, ASME (NADAI medal 2004), Am. Ceramic Soc., Materials Rsch. Soc. Avocations: skiing, hiking, antiques, orchids. Home: 590 Grizzly Peak Blvd Berkeley CA 94708-1238 Office: U Calif Dept Materials Sci and Engring Berkeley CA 94720-1760 Office Phone: 510-486-5798. Business E-Mail: roritchie@lbl.gov.

RITCHIE, WALLACE PARKS, JR., retired surgeon, educator; b. St. Paul, Nov. 4, 1935; s. Wallace Parks and Alice Ransome (Otis) R.; m. Barbara Carey Jewell, Aug. 10, 1960; children: Stephanie, David, Jessica. BA, Yale U., 1957; MD, Johns Hopkins U., 1961; PhD, U. Minn., 1971. Diplomate Am. Bd. Surgery. Intern, resident in surgery Yale U., New Haven, 1961-63; resident in surgery U. Minn. Hosps., Mpls., 1963-69, instr. in surgery, 1969-70; from asst. prof. to prof. surgery U. Va. Sch. Medicine, Charlottesville, 1973-83; prof., chmn. dept. surgery Temple U. Sch. Medicine, Phila., 1983-93; exec. dir. Am. Bd. Surgery, Phila., 1994—2002; ret. Editor textbook: Essentials of Surgery, 1994; contbr. over 160 sci. articles to profl. jours. Lt. col. M.C., U.S. Army, 1970-73. USPHS grantee, 1974-85. Office: Am Bd Surgery Inc 1617 John F Kennedy Blvd Philadelphia PA 19103-1821 Office Phone: 215-568-4000. E-mail: wallace.ritchie@verizon.net.

RITCHIE-DUNHAM, JAMES LOOMIS, academic administrator, researcher; married. PhD, U. of Tex., Austin, TX, 1996—2002. Engr. Conoco, Inc, New Orleans, 1990—93; prof. Inst. Tech. Autonomo de Mex., Mex. City, 1993—96; pres. Inst. for Strategic Clarity, Wilton, NH, 1996—. Vis. scholar MIT, Cambridge, Mass., 2003—. Trustee Soc. for Orgnl. Learning, Boston, Mass., 2002—04; v.p. Pine Hill Waldorf Sch., Wilton, NH, 2002—. Office: Institute for Strategic Clarity 540 Abbot Hill Rd Wilton NH 03086 E-mail: jimrd@instituteforstrategicclarity.org.

RITCHIE-RAMIREZ, JUDY, small business owner, artist; b. Merced, Calif., Jan. 13, 1948; d. Heber G. and Jewell D. Foster; m. Ronald Ramirez, Nov. 18, 1949; m. James R. Ritchie, Apr. 27, 1938 (div. Feb. 10, 1999); m. James E. Sutherland, Mar. 30, 1946 (div. Feb. 12, 1971); children: Jamie R. Ritchie, James H. Ritchie. Collector Associates Credit Card, Pleasanton, Calif., 1984—89; supervision Associated Credit Card, Irving, Tex., 1989—2000, CitiGroup, Irving, Tex., 2000—02; owner My Sister's Attic, Atwater, Calif., 2002—03, Charms Galore, Lewisville, Tex., 2003—03, My Sis's Attic, Irving, Tex., 2003—. Exhibition, Boquet of Flowers, Hercules, Castle on A Hill;, author numerous poems. Democrat. Southern Babtist. Office: My Sis's Attic 2320 Rock Island Rd Irving TX 75060 Office Phone: 214-762-1465. Personal E-mail: mysissattic@lycos.com.

RITCHIN, BARBARA SUE, educational administrator, consultant; b. N.Y.C., Mar. 7, 1940; d. Harry and Miriam Rosalyn (Schoenberg) R. BS in Spl. Edn., SUNY, Buffalo, 1961; MS in Ednl. Guidance, CCNY, 1969; diploma in ednl. supervision-adminstrn., Fordham U., 1982, PhD in Urban Edn., 1990; postgrad., Harvard U., 1991, 96. Cert. tchr., spl. edn. tchr., counselor, adminstr., N.Y. Tchr. spl. edn. East Elem. Sch., Long Beach, N.Y., 1962-68; asst. prof. N.Y.C. Community Coll., Bklyn., 1970-76; ednl. cons. N.Y.C., 1976-92; dir. bus. programs N.Y.C. Tech. Coll., Bklyn., 1981-87; exec. dir. continuing edn. programs Queens Coll. CUNY, Flushing, NY, 1988—2004; prin. Programs Distinction LLC, 2004. Bd. dirs. Foresight Sch., S.I., N.Y., 1986-92; cons. N.Y. Telephone Co., N.Y.C., 1988-92; chair subcom. on community outreach Queens Coll. Presdl. Com. on Multiculturalism. Co-author: Teachers Learn Metrics, 1981. Pres. bd. dirs. Greenwich Village Orch., 1991; mem. admissions and rules mem. 401 E. 74 Corp., N.Y.C., 1990-92, sec. bd. dirs., 1997—. Named Disting. Woman of Yr. Queens Women's Ctr., 1989. Mem. Continuing Edn. Assn. N.Y. (pres. 1995-96, regional chair 1990-91, membership chair 1988-90), UN Assn. N.Y. (bd. dirs.), Assn. Continuing Higher Edn. (sec.-treas. 1991-92), Phi Delta Kappa, Kappa Delta Pi. Avocations: collecting depression glass, british detective novels, needlepoint, quilting. Office Phone: 212-988-6172. E-mail: prodistinction@aol.com.

RITCHINGS, FRANCES ANNE, priest; b. Balt., June 26, 1946; d. Edward Peyton and Frances Evangeline (Beegle) R. BA in Edn., English, Salisbury (Md.) State U., 1968; MA in English, U. Va., 1970; MS in Libr. Sci., Cath. U., Washington, 1975; MDiv, Episc. Div. Sch., Cambridge, Mass., 1987. Ordained priest, 1988. Instr. Germanna C.C., Locust Grove, Va., 1970-74; ref. libr. Libr. of Congress, Washington, 1975-79, supervisory libr., congl. rsch., 1979-84; assoc. rector St. Stephen's Ch., Providence, 1987-89, St. Thomas Ch., Ft. Washington, Pa., 1989-93; founding pastor Ch. of the Holy Spirit, Harleysville, Pa., 1993—2001; cons. Bear Resources, LLC, 2002—. Chair liturgical commn. Diocese of Pa., 1998-2001. Painter icon, 1994—; contbr. poems to Windchimes, 2000. Recipient Salmon Wheaton prize Episc. Div. Sch., 1987; DuPont fellow, 1970, S.S.U. Achievement Key, 1967, 68. Mem. Soc. of St. Margaret (assoc.), Fellowship of St. John the Evangelist (assoc.), Network of Bibl. Storytellers, Assn. of Anglican Musicians, Associated Parishes, Ecclesiol. Soc., Foodways Alliance, Slow Food, Beta Phi Mu, Phi Alpha Theta, Alpha Psi Omega.

RITSCHER, LEE A, literature educator; b. Murfreesboro, Tenn., July 12, 1961; d. Ralph Wright (Stepfather) and Ann Kay McDonald; m. Paul Brian Ritscher, Oct. 27, 1984; children: Laurel Ann, Carol Elizabeth. BA, Tenn. State U., 1991—95; MA, U. of Notre Dame, 1995—97; PhD in Lit., U. of Calif. Santa Cruz, 1997—. Tchg. asst., dept. of lit. U. of Calif., Santa Cruz, 1997—. Mem. Colloquium Com., Dept. of Lit., Santa Cruz, 1999—2000; com. mem. Coordinating Com. on Grad. Affairs, Oakland, 2000—01, Grad. Student Commons Governance Bd., Santa Cruz, 2000—03, V.P. of Academic Affairs Search Com., Nashville, Campus Welfare Com., Santa Cruz, 2001—, Campus Ombudsman Search Com., Santa Cruz, 2001, Career Ctr. Grad. Student Advisor Search Com., Santa Cruz, 2002. Rep. Grad. Student Assn., Santa Cruz, 1998—99, external v.p., 1999—2000, pres., 2000—03. Fellow Grad. Student Summer Fellowship, UCSC Grad. Divsn., 2001, Doctoral Student Tchg. Sabbatical, 2002; grantee Travel Grant, UCSC Inst. for Humanities Rsch., 1999, UCSC Dept. of Lit., 1999, UCSC Inst. for Humanities Rsch., 2000, UCSC Dept. of Lit., 2000, 2002. Mem.: Women of Color and Conflict Study Group, Bay Area Pre- and Early Modern Studies Group, MLA, Phi Kappa Phi (life). Home: 702 Koshland Way Santa Cruz CA 95064 Office: UCSC Dept of Lit 1156 High St Santa Cruz CA 95064 Personal E-mail: lritscher@aol.com. E-mail: ritscher@cats.ucsc.edu.

RITSON, SCOTT CAMPBELL, management consultant; b. New London, Conn., July 20, 1945; s. Ian Douglas and Ann Breyer (Maxwell) R.; m. Dianne Kischitz, May 16, 1966 (div. Oct. 1977); children: Mark Douglas (dec.), Carrie Stewart; m. Donna Dianne Nietschmann, Feb. 25, 1978; 1 child, Evan Ray-Bernard. Student, U. Vt., 1963-65. Field engrs. asst. Gilbane Bldg. Co., Providence, 1966-67; project control engr. Olin Corp., Stamford, Conn., 1967-73; v.p. Reed Corp., Roxbury, Conn., 1973-76; pres. Ritson & Assocs., Lake Forest, Ill., 1976—; sr. project engr. Abbott Labs., North Chicago, Ill., 1990-95. Pres., treas. Axeman Island, Ltd., Gananoque, Ont., Can., 1990—, v.p., 1979-90, dir., 1981-90; pres. Ritson, Ryan Inc., Gurnee, Ill., 1983-86; sr. program mgr. Project Leadership Group, Inc., Libertyville, Ill., 2001—. Charter mem. Congrl. Adv. Com., Washington, 1982. Can. nat. sailfish champion, 1961. Mem. Internat. Assn. Profl. Planners and Schedulers (charter mem.), Chgo. Yacht Club, Lake Forest Yacht Club. Home: 1084 Old Colony Rd Lake Forest IL 60045-3898 Office: Unit 2 14045 Petronella Dr Libertyville IL 60048-9699 Office Phone: 847-996-6962.

RITT, ROGER MERRILL, lawyer; b. N.Y.C., Mar. 26, 1950; m. Mimi Santini, Aug. 25, 1974; children: Evan Samuel, David Martin. BA, U. Pa., 1972; JD, Boston U., 1975, LLM, 1976. Bar: Mass. 1977, Pa. 1975, U.S. Tax Ct. Sr. ptnr. Hale and Dorr, Boston, 1984—. Adj. prof. grad. tax program Boston U., 1979-92; panelist Am. Law Inst., Mass. Continuing Legal Edn., World Trade Inst., NYU Inst. on Fed. Taxation; mem. exec. com. Fed. Tax Inst. New Eng. Treas. Found. for Tax Edn. Mem. ABA (tax sect.), Boston Bar Assn. Office: Hale and Dorr 60 State St Boston MA 02109-1816

RITTEL, KATHLEEN ANN, former school system administrator, middle school educator; d. William Michael and Ann Marilyn; m. Donald Russell Rittel; 1 child, Sophia Anndrina Maria. BA in English and Edn., Queens Coll., 1972, MS in Edn., 1977; postgrad., SUNY, Albany, 1978, Brigham Young U., 1978, McPherson Coll., 1978; PD in Adminstrn. and Supervision, St. John's U., Jamaica, NY, 1982; postgrad., Adelphi U., 1983, U. Mont., 1986, U. N.Mex., 1999, L.I. U., 2000, Coll. St. Rose, 2000, Ind. Wesleyan U., 2003, Endicott Coll., 2003. Cert. tchr., adminstr., supr., N.Y. Tchr. Elijah Clark Jr. H.S., South Bronx, NY, 1972-75, Intermediate Sch. 291, Bklyn., 1975; tchr., dean, asst. prin. Jean Nuzzi Jr. H.S., Queens Village, 1975-83; asst. prin. William Cowper Intermediate Sch., Maspeth, 1983-93; adminstr.-in-charge I.S. 73 Annex, Elmhurst, 1994—97, 51st Ave. Annex for P.S. 7 and P.S. 71, 1997-99; adminstr.-in charge 51st Ave. Annex for P.S. 7 and I.S. 5, 1999; tchr. Jericho Mid. Sch., 2003—. Doctoral fellow Hofstra U., 1990. Mem. Nat. Coun. Tchrs. English, Internat. Reading Assn. Roman Catholic. Avocations: playing piano, roller skating, ice skating, dance, travel. Personal E-mail: superprofessor1@yahoo.com.

RITTENHOUSE, NANCY CAROL, elementary school educator; b. Humeston, Iowa, May 26, 1941; d. Myrl Matthews and Opal L. (McCartney) Hixson; m. J. Kent Rittenhouse, Dec. 18, 1960 (div. Mar. 1984); children: Brenda L. Carroll, J. Aaron, Timothy K. Grad., Kirksville State Tchrs. Coll., 1960; student, St. Mary of the Plains Coll., 1984-87; degree in elem. edn., Ft. Hays State Coll., 1989. Cert. tchr., Kans. Reading instr. Sacred Heart Sch., Dodge City, Kans., 1984; elem. tchr. Miller Sch., Dodge City, Kans., 1985-86, Washington Sch., Hays, 1987; city-county recreation dir. Sherman County, Goodland, 1988; elem. tchr. Northside Sch., Larned, 1989-90; with Great Bend (Kans.) Tribune. Artist numerous paintings; author poetry. Mem. Menninger Found., Topeka, 1984—; hon. mem. Boy Scouts Am., 1978; camp instr. Spl. Olympics Blind Found., Junction City, Kans., 1985-90, Dodge City, 1984; leader Girl Scouts USA, 1975-77. Recipient Hon. award Spl. Olympics, 1984, 1st pl. poetry award, 1990, watercolor award, 1990, oils award, 1988, pen and ink award, 1984. Mem. AAAS, Nat. Trust for Hist. Preservation, Nat. Geog. Soc., Planetary Soc., Smithsonian Assn., MIT. Republican. Avocations: painting, drawing, walking, swimming, writing prose. Home: PO Box 1872 Great Bend KS 67530-1872 Office: Great Bend Tribune 2012 Forest Ave Great Bend KS 67530-4014

RITTER, ALFRED FRANCIS, JR., retired communications executive; b. Norfolk, Va., Dec. 31, 1946; s. Alfred Francis Ritter and Lucile Grey Woodward; m. Caroline Buchanan O'Keefe, Aug. 10, 1968; children: Alfred F. III, Caroline O'Donnell. BA, Coll. of William and Mary, 1968. CPA Va. Staff acct. Goodman & Co. CPAs, Norfolk, Va., 1971-76; corp. contr. Landmark Comm., Norfolk, 1976-78, v.p., contr., 1978, v.p. fin., 1978, TeleCable Corp., Norfolk, 1983-89, exec. v.p., 1989-96, Landmark Comm., Inc., Norfolk, 1996—2001; ret., 2001. Trustee Norfolk Acad., 1991—, pres. bd. trustees, 1998—. Lt. USN, 1968—71. Mem.: Bayville Golf Club (pres. 1995—98). Episcopalian.

RITTER, ANN L. lawyer; b. N.Y.C., May 20, 1933; d. Joseph and Grace (Goodman) R. BA, Hunter Coll., 1954; JD, N.Y. Law Sch., 1970; postgrad. Law Sch., NYU, 1971-72. Bar: N.Y. 1971, U.S. Ct. Appeals (2d cir.) 1975, U.S. Supreme Ct. 1975. Writer, 1954-70; editor, 1955-66; tchr., 1966-70; atty. Am. Soc. Composers, Authors and Pubs., N.Y.C., 1971-72, Greater N.Y. Ins. Co., N.Y.C., 1973-74; sr. ptnr. Brenhouse & Ritter, N.Y.C., 1974-78; sole practice N.Y.C., 1978—. Editor N.Y. Immigration News, 1975-76. Mem. ABA, Am. Immigration Lawyers Assn. (treas. 1983-84, sec. 1984-85, vice-chair 1985-86, chair 1986-87, chair program com. 1989-90, chair spkrs. bur. 1989-90, chair media liaison 1989-90), N.Y. State Bar Assn., N.Y. County Lawyers Assn., Assn. Trial Lawyers Am., N.Y. State Trial Lawyers Assn., N.Y.C. Bar Assn., Watergate East Assn. (v.p., asst. treas. 1990—). Democrat. Jewish. Home: 47 E 87th St New York NY 10128-1005 Office: 420 Madison Ave Rm 1200 New York NY 10017-1171

RITTER, C. DOWD, diversified financial services company executive; b. Birmingham; m. Susan; 2 children. BA, Birmingham-Southern Coll., 1969; grad., Sch. Banking of South, L.S.U. With AmSouth Bancorporation and AmSouth Bank, Birmingham, Ala., 1969—, exec. v.p., 1980-88, sr. exec. v.p., 1988-93, vice chmn. bd., 1993-94, pres., COO, 1994-96, chmn., pres., CEO, 1996—. Bd. dirs. AmSouth Bancorporation, AmSouth Bank, Ala. Power Co., Bus. Coun. ala., Econ. Devel. Partnership Ala. (chmn. 1998), Region 2020 Inc. Bd. trustees Birmingham Mus. Art, Birmingham-Southern Coll., Leadership Birmingham, adv. bd. Birmingham Crime Commn., Juvenile Diabetes Found., bd. visitors U. ala. Coll. Commerce and Bus. Adminstrn., campaign co-chmn. Am. Cancer Soc. Five Points South Ctr. and Hope Lodge, campaign steering com. YWCA Birmingham, pres's. coun. U. Ala., campaign chmn. United Way Central Ala., 1993. Named Ala. Outstanding Young Banker 1984. Mem. Ala. Young Bankers (past pres.), Birmingham Festival Arts (past pres.). Office: Amsouth Bancorporation 1900 6th Ave N Birmingham AL 35203-2610

RITTER, DALE WILLIAM, obstetrician, gynecologist; b. Jersey Shore, Pa., June 17, 1919; s. Lyman W. and Weltha B. (Packard) Ritter; m. Winnie Mae Bryant, Nov. 13, 1976; children: Eric, Lyman, Michael, Gwendolyn, Daniel. AB, UCLA, 1942; MD, U. So. Calif., 1946. Diplomate Am. Bd. Obstetrics and Gynecology. Intern Los Angeles County Hosp., L.A., 1945-46, resident, 1948-52, admitting room resident, 1948-52; pvt. practice Chico, Calif., 1952-98; founder, mem. staff, past chmn. bd. dirs. Chico Cmty. Meml. Hosp. Guest lectr. Chico State Coll., 1956—; mem. staff Enole Hosp., Chico, 1952—, Glenn Gen. Hosp., Willows, Calif., 1953-98, Gridley Meml. Hosp., Calif., 1953-80; spl. cons. obs. Calif. Dept. Pub. Health, No. Calif., 1958-70. Contbr. articles to profl. jours. Bd. dirs. No. dist. Children's Home Soc., Chico, 1954-70. Served with AUS, 1943-45, M.C., AUS, 1946-48. Recipient Pro-Life award Calif. KC; Paul Harris fellow Rotary Internat., 1989. Fellow ACS, Am. Coll. Ob-Gyn; mem. AMA, AAAS, SAR, Calif. Med. Assn., Internat. Soc. Hypnosis, Am. Soc. Clin. Hypnosis, Am. Fertility Soc., Pacific Coast Fertility Soc., Assn. Am. Physicians and Surgeons, Pvt. Drs. Am., Butte-Glenn County Med. Soc. (past pres.), Am. Cancer Soc. (past bd. dirs. Butte County), Christian Med. Soc., Am. Assn. Pro-life Obstetricians and Gynecologists, Butte Glenn County Tumor Bd., Anthrop. Assn. Am., Archaeol. Inst. Am., Soc. Calif. Archaeology, Oreg. Archaeology Soc., Archeol. Survey Assn., Southwestern Anthrop. Soc., Am. Rock Art Rsch. Assn. (Pioneer award), Calif. Hist. Soc., Calif. Oreg. Trails Assn., Australian Rock Art Rsch. Assn., Internat. Assn. for Study of Prehistoric and Ethnologic Religions, Fretted Instrument Guild Am. (dir. Banjo Kats 'n Jammers), North Valley Banjo Band, Am. Philatelic Soc., Am. Horse Coun., Peruvian Paso Horse Registry of N.Am., Assn. Owners Breeders Peruvian Paso Horses, Gideon Soc., Am. Legion, Am. Vets. WWII, Rotary (Paul Harris fellow), Gideons Internat., Phi Chi, Lambda Sigma, Zeta Beta Sigma. Republican. Home: PMB 156 975 East Ave Chico CA 95926-1308

RITTER, DANIEL BENJAMIN, lawyer; b. Wilmington, Del., Apr. 6, 1937; s. David Moore and Bernice Elizabeth (Carlson) R.; m. Shirley F. Sether, Jan. 29, 1971 (dec. Jan. 1998); 1 child, Roxane Elise. AB with honors, U. Chgo., 1957; LLB, U. Wash., 1963. Bar: Wash. 1963, U.S. Dist. Ct. (we. dist.) Wash. 1963, U.S. Tax Ct. 1965, U.S. Ct. Appeals (9th cir.) 1963. Assoc. Davis, Wright Tremaine LLP (formerly Davis, Wright and Jones), 1963-69, ptnr., 1969—. Lectr. Bar Rev. Assocs. Wash., Seattle, 1964-86; chmn. internat. dept. Davis, Wright and Jones, Seattle, 1984-85, chmn. banking dept., 1986-89. Casenote editor U. Wash. Law Rev., 1962-63; editor-in-chief, contbg. author Washington Revised Article 9 Deskbook, 2003; contbg. author: Washington Commercial Law Desk Book, 1982, rev. edit., 1987, Washington Community Property Desk Book, 1977. Trustee Cathedral Assoc., Seattle, 1980-86; legal counsel Wash. State Reps., Bellevue, 1983-92; bd. dirs. U. Chgo. Club Puget Sound, Seattle, 1982-95, pres., 1984-86; bd. dirs. Am. Lung Assn. Wash., Seattle, 1983-92; mem. vis. com. U. Wash. Law Sch., 1984-88; trustee U. Wash. Law Sch. Found., 1989-92; chmn. alumni rels. coun. U. Chgo., 1986-88; mem. statute law com. State of Wash., 1978-87; bd. dirs. Seattle Camerata, 1991-93; bd. dirs. Early Music Guild, Seattle, 1993-96. Mem. ABA (bus. law sect.), Wash. State Bar Assn. (chmn. bus. law sect. 1988-89, uniform comml. code com. 1980—, chmn. 1980-86, chmn. internat. law com. 1979-81, jud. recommendations com. 1991-93), Seattle-King County Bar Assn. (chmn. internat. and comparative law sect. 1980-82), Rainier Club, Order of Coif. Republican. Lutheran. Avocations: reading, theater, early music. Home: 907 Warren Ave N Apt 202 Seattle WA 98109-5635 Office: Davis Wright Tremaine 2600 Century Sq 1501 4th Ave Seattle WA 98101-1688 Office Phone: 206-628-7751. Business E-Mail: danritter@dwt.com.

RITTER, DEBORAH ELIZABETH, anesthesiologist, educator; b. Phila., May 16, 1947; d. Charles William and Elizabeth Angeline (Coffman) R. BA, Susquehanna U., 1968; MS, U. Pa., 1969; MD, Med. Coll. Pa., 1973. Diplomate Am. Bd. Anesthesiology (assoc. examiner oral bds. 1990, 92). Intern Thomas Jefferson Univ. Hosp., Phila., 1973-74, resident in anesthesia, 1974-76, clin. fellow in anesthesiology, 1976-77; affiliate resident in anesthesia Children's Hosp. Pa., Phila., 1975; assoc. in anesthesiology Frankford Hosp., Phila., 1977-78; clin. instr. anesthesiology Med. Coll. Pa., Phila., 1977-78, Thomas Jefferson U., 1978-80, clin. asst. prof., 1980-86, clin. assoc. prof., 1986—, vice chmn. dept. anesthesiology, 1985—. Contbr. articles to profl. jours. Named Top Doc, Phila. Mag., 1994, 96. Mem. AMA, Am. Women's Med. Assn., Am. Soc. Anesthesiologists, Internat. Anesthesia Rsch. Soc., Soc. Edn. Anesthesia, Assn. Anesthesia Clin. Dirs. Lutheran. Avocations: gardening, music, history, wilderness preservation, american indian culture. Office: Thomas Jefferson U Dept Anesthesiology 111 S 11th St Ste 8490G Philadelphia PA 19107-5084

RITTER, DONALD LAWRENCE, environmental policy institute executive; b. N.Y.C., Oct. 21, 1940; s. Frank and Ruth R.; m. Edith Duerksen; children: Jason, Kristina. BSMetE, Lehigh U., 1961; MS in Phys. Metallurgy, MIT, 1963, ScD, 1966. Mem. faculty Calif. State Poly. U., also contract cons. Gen. Dynamics Co., 1968-69; mem. faculty dept. metallurgy and materials scis., asst. to v.p. for research Lehigh U., 1969-76; mgr. research program devel., 1976-79; mem. 96th-102d congresses from 15th Pa dist., 1979-93; scientist, chmn., pres. Nat. Environ. Policy Inst., Washington, 1994—. Mem. energy and commerce com. and subcoms. telecommunications and fin.; ranking minority mem. transp. and hazardous materials; mem. sci., space and tech. com. and ranking subcoms. environment and tech. and competitiveness; chmn. house Rep. task force on tech. and policy; co-chair Cngl. High Tech. Caucus; ranking minority mem. house Commn. on Security and Cooperation in Europe (Helsinki Commn.), mem. 1980-93; co-chmn. ad hoc com. on Baltic states and Ukraine; treas. Congl. steel caucus; mem. Congl. textile and apparel caucus; mem. environ. and energy study conf.; sci. echange fellow U.S. Nat. Acad. Scis.-Soviet Acad. Sci., Baikov Inst., Moscow, 1966-67. Contbr. articles to environmental sci., engring. and quality jours. Recipient award for disting. pub. svc. IEEE, 1990. Fellow Am. Inst. Chemists (honor scroll award); mem. NSPE, Am. Soc. for Metals (disting. life), Sigma Xi, Tau Beta Pi, Pi Mu Epsilon. Unitarian Universalist. Office: Nat Environ Policy Inst 1401 K St NW Ste M103 Washington DC 20005-3452

RITTER, ELISE DAWN, therapist, clinical social worker, writer, artist, artist; b. Balt., Aug. 14, 1952; d. Nelson Fred and Marjorie Jean (Corke) Ritter; m. Philip Anthony Gibson, Apr. 7, 1979 (div. Feb. 1990); 1 child, Christopher Ritter Gibson; m. Victor Wayne Clough, Jr., Mar. 3, 1990; stepchildren: Wesley T., Lindsay, Sharon. Student, Austro-Am. Inst., Vienna, Austria, 1973; BS, U. Kans., 1974; M Psychiatric Social Work, Va. Commonwealth U., 1998. LCSW. Rschr. impeachment inquiry staff U.S. Ho. of Reps., Washington, 1974; rschr. APA, Washington, 1975; editor prodn. The New Republic Mag., Washington, 1976-77; copy editor Time-Life Books, Alexandria, Va., 1977-79, assoc. editor, 1979-83, adminstrv. editor, 1983-87, asst. dir. editl. resources, 1988-90; dir. editl. resources Time Warner, Time-Life Books, Alexandria, 1990-94; pvt. practice therapist, 2000—. With Arlingtonians Ministering to Emergency Needs-AMEN, 1995; vol. Mental Health Program, Visiting Nurse Assn., 1996, Women's Ctr., Vienna, Va., 1997-99, PsychologyNetwork.com, 2000—, DiscoveryHealth.com, 2002-03. Mem.: Rappahannock Art League Studio Gallery. Office Phone: 703-731-5744.

RITTER, ELZA K. music educator; b. Moscow, Apr. 27, 1964; arrived in U.S., 1999, permanent resident, 2003; d. Radic Kmassanou and Olija Kmassanoua; m. Steven A. Ritter, Mar. 31, 1999; 1 child, Tim. MusB, Music Coll., Moscow, Russia, 1982—99; MusM, The Russian Acad., Moscow, Russia, 1983—89. Opera coach Nat. Inst. of Theatrical Art, Moscow, 1982—99; piano inst. pvt. practice, 1982—, No. Va. Cmty. Coll., Sterling, Va., 1999—2003; pres. The Russian Music Acad. of Am., Reston, Va., 2003—. Performed as concert master Bolshio Theater, 1999—. Mem.: Music Tchr. Nat. Assn. (assoc.). Buddhist. Home: 11407 Fieldstone Ln Reston VA 20191 Office: The Russian Music Acad of America PO Box 710083 Oak Hill VA 20171

RITTER, HAL, newspaper editor; Mng. editor money sect. USA Today, Arlington, Va., 1985-95, mng. editor news, 1995—2004. Office: USA Today 7950 Jones Branch Dr Mc Lean VA 22108-0001

RITTER, JACK CHARLES, mathematician, computer graphics designer; b. Hokkaido, Japan, Apr. 4, 1948; arrived in U.S., 1949; s. James William Ritter and Maureen Ruth Gutenkunst; m. Barrie Jane Jacobs, Sept. 5, 1973. Student, Princeton U., 1966—68; BA in Philosophy, U. Wis., 1970, MS in Computer Sci., 1973. Software engr. Nat. Cash Register, San Diego, 1974—78; video game designer Atari Games, Sunnyvale, Calif., 1981—83; 2D graphics engr. Versatec-Xerox, Santa Clara, Calif., 1984—88; 3D programmer-artist SGI Graphics, Mountain View, Calif., 1989—93; 3D hardware mktg. nVidia, Sunnyvale, 1995—96; PC video game programmer Accolade Games, San Jose, Calif., 1997—2000. Author: Graphics Gems, Vol. 1 & 2, 1990. Mem. Homicide Rsch. Working Group, Chgo., 2000—; vol. City of Racchi, Sacred Valley, Peru, 2000—. Mem.: The Manly Club (Hartland, Wis.). Achievements include design of prototype for computer controlled electronic dog trainer; Infogramme's Ecstacy Graphics Engine used in game Slave Zero; design and programming of a software image synthesizer Rat Racer. Avocations: teaching, website development, artificial intelligence, writing. E-mail: jack@you2peru.com.

RITTER, JEFFREY BLAKE, lawyer, consultant; b. Iowa City, Iowa, Sept. 13, 1954; s. Charles Clifford and Patricia Ann (Wise) R.; children: Jordan, Chelsea. BA, MA, Ohio State U., 1976; JD, Duke U., 1979. Bar: Ky. 1979, D.C. 1980, Ohio 1983. Assoc. Barnett & Alagia, Louisville, 1979-82, Schwartz, Kelm, Warren & Rubenstein, Columbus, Ohio, 1982-90; of counsel Vorys, Sater, Seymour & Pease, Columbus, 1991-94; U.S. legal adviser for facilitation UN Working Party, Geneva, 1990-96; dir. ECLIPS, Columbus,

1994-98, Document Authentication Sys., Inc., Balt., 1998-99; counsel Kirkpatrick & Lockhart, Washington, 1999-2000, ptnr., 2000—. Chair Adv. Group on Internat. Trade, Columbus, 1990. Mem. ABA (chair sect. of bus. law com. on cyberspace law, 1995-98, reporter, subcom. on scope of uniform comml. code 1990-91). Democrat. Avocations: bicycling, jazz, poetry. Office: 1800 Massachusetts Ave NW Washington DC 20036-1806 E-mail: jritter@kl.com.

RITTER, JOHN C. manufacturing executive; CFO Howmet Corp., Greenwich, Conn. Office: Howmet Corp 475 Steamboat Rd Ste 1 Greenwich CT 06830-1960

RITTER, MADELIENE, practical nurse, surgical technologist; b. Camden, N.J., Feb. 11, 1954; m. James W. Ritter. Degree in practical nursing, Ocean County Vocat. Tech. Sch., 1975. Cert. surgical technologist; lic. practical nurse. Staff nurse Cmty. Meml. Hosp., Toms River, NJ, 1975—77, staff nurse/pacu, 1979—85; office nurse Stafford Orthopedics, Manahawkin, NJ, 1985—98; oper. rm. nurse Cmty. Med. Ctr., Toms River, NJ, 1998—2000, So. Ocean County Hosp., Manahawkin, NJ, 1999—, 1999—. Mem. Am. Cancer Soc. Relay for Life, Manahawkin, NJ, 2001, co-captain. Leader Ocean County Girl Scouts, Toms River, NJ, 1982—98; lifetime mem. Girl Scouts of Am.; mem. Barnegat First Aid Squad, Barnegat, NJ; co-leader internat. travel Switzerland/Mex. troops Ocean County Girl Scout Coun., Toms River, NJ. Mem.: Assn. Surg. Technologists, Nat. Assn. Practical Nurse Edn. and Svc.

RITTER, ROBERT FORCIER, lawyer; b. St. Louis, Apr. 7, 1943; s. Tom Marshall and Jane Elizabeth (Forcier) R.; m. Karen Gray, Dec. 28, 1966; children: Allison Gray Campione, Laura Thompson Capstick, Elisabeth Forcier Schoenecker. BA, U. Kans., 1965; JD, St. Louis U., 1968. Bar: Mo. 1968, U.S. Dist. Ct. (ea. and we. dists.) Mo. 1968. U.S. Ct. Mil. Appeals 1972, U.S. Supreme Ct. 1972, U.S. Ct. Appeals (8th cir.) 1980, U.S. Dist. Ct. (so. dist.) Ill. 1982. Assoc. Gray & Sommers, St. Louis, 1968-71; ptnr. Gray Ritter & Graham, P.C., St. Louis, 1974—; chmn., pres. Gray & Ritter, St. Louis, 1983—. Adv. com. 22nd cir. Supreme Ct., 1985—92; mem. Supreme Ct. com. civil jury instrns., 1988—2003; adv. com. U.S. Dist. Ct., 1993—95; mem. exec. planning com. Mo. Inst. for Justice, 2002—; mem. nat. adv. bd. Ctr. for Perinatal Medicine and Law, U. Calif., Davis, 2002—; lectr. in field. Contbr. articles to profl. jours. Mem. nat. adv. bd. Ctr. for Perinatal Medicine and Law, U. Calif., Davis, 2002—; bd. dirs. Cystic Fibrosis Found., Gateway chpt., pres., 1991; mem. exec. planning com. Mo. Inst. Justice, 2002—. Recipient Law Week award, Bur. Nat. Affairs, 1968, award of merit, Nat. Conf. Met. Cts., 1995, Lawyers Assn. award of honor, 2003. Fellow: Internat. Acad. Trial Lawyers, Am. Coll. Trial Lawyers, Internat. Soc. Barristers (bd. govs. 1994); mem.: Mo. Assn. Trial Attys. (bd. govs. 1984—), Lawyers Assn. St. Louis (exec. com. 1976—81, pres. 1977—78, award of honor 2003, 2003), Mo. Bar Found. (outstanding trial lawyer award 1978), Mo. Bar Assn. (coun. practice and procedure com. 1972—, coun. tort law com. 1982—, bd. govs. 1984—91, fin. com. 1984—91), Bar Assn. Met. St. Louis (chmn. trial sect. 1978—79, exec. com. 1980—82, chmn. bench bar conf. 1983, award merit 1976, award achievement 1982), Am. Bd. Trial Advocates (advocate), Assn. Trial Lawyers Am., Am. Judicature Soc., ABA, Windsor Club (founding mem.), Roaring Fork Club, Red Stick Golf Club (founding mem.), Racquet Club (bd. govs. 1988—93, pres. 1991—92), John's Is. Club (bd. dirs. 1998—), Bellerive Country Club, Noonday Club. Presbyterian. Home: 11 Gem Island Dr Vero Beach FL 32963 Office: Gray Ritter & Graham PC 701 Market St Fl 8 Saint Louis MO 63101-1850 E-mail: rritter@grgpc.com.

RITTER, ROBERT T. diversified company executive; BBA in Acctg., Coll. William and Mary, 1973. Various fin. positions Am. Cyanamid Co.; CFP WLR Foods, Inc.; v.p., CFO The Pittston Co., Glen Allen, Va., 1998—. Mem. AICPAs. Office: The Pittston Co 1801 Bayberry Ct PO Box 18100 Richmond VA 23226

RITTER, STACY JOY, state legislator, lawyer; b. Washington, June 8, 1960; BA, Rollins Coll., 1982; JD, Nova U., 1985. Bar: Fla. 1985. Mem. Fla. Ho. of Reps., 1996—; mem. regulated svcs. com., 1996-97; mem. civil justice and claims com., 1996-97. Editor Shalom mag. Vice chmn. Coral Springs Civic, Cultural and Ednl. Found., State Pub. Affairs, 1995-96, pres. 1993-95; mem. Cmty. Info. Coun.; mem. leadership Coral Springs Inaugural Class, 1993. Mem. Nat. Coun. Jewish Women (life), Kappa Alpha Theta, Phi Alpha Delta. Democrat. Jewish. Avocations: reading, travel, pilates. Office: Ste 200 3200 N University Dr Coral Springs FL 33065-4100 E-mail: ritter.stacy@myfloridahouse.com.

RITTER, WILLIAM FREDERICK, civil and agricultural engineering educator; b. Stratford, Ont., Can., Mar. 25, 1942; came to U.S., 1966. s. John Louis and Norma Willehmine (Foerster) R.; m. Carol-Anne Gertrude Turner, June 25, 1966; children: John WIlliam, Amy Lynn. BSA, U. Guelph, Ont., 1965; BAS, U. Toronto, 1966; MS, Iowa State U., 1968, PhD, 1971. Rsch. assoc. Iowa State U., Ames, 1966-71; asst. prof. U. Del., Newark, 1971-77, assoc. prof., 1977-82, prof., 1982—, dept. chair, 1992—98, 2003—; owner Ritter Engring., Elkton, Md., 1990—. Sr. engr. Environ. Cons. Internat., Rehoboth Beach, Del., 1991-94. Editor: Irrigation and Drainage Conf. Procs., 1991, Jour. Irrigation and Drainage Engrs., 2001—; contbr. more than 290 articles to profl. jours. and tech. reports. Pres. Newark Day Nursery, 1984-86. Recipient Superior Achievement award U.S. EPA, Phila., 1979; Salzberg fellow U. Del., 1987. Fellow ASCE (editor Jour. Irrigation and Drainage Engring. 2001—, News Corr. award 1997, Outstanding Svc. award 1993, Svc. to Divsn. award 1997, Civil Egr. of Yr. award 1999, Royce J. Tipton award, 2004), Am. Soc. Agrl. Engrs. (Young Engr. of Yr. 1981, Country Side Engring. award 1988, Disting. Svc. award, 2003); mem. (life)Am. Water Works Assn., Water Environment Fedn., Am. Acad. Environ. Engrs. (diplomate). Lutheran. Home: 63 Papermill Rd Elkton MD 21921-3518 Office: U Del Newark DE 19717 Office Phone: 302-831-2468. E-mail: williamritter@udel.edu.

RITTEREISER, FREDERICK J. technology company executive; Spl. cons. Booz-Allen and Hamilton, Inc.; pres. Sherwood Group, Troster Singer, Instinet; chmn. bd., CEO Ashton Tech. Group, Inc.; co-founder Universal Trading Techs. Corp., Gomez Advisors, Inc. Mem. Nat. Assn. Securities Dealers, Inc. Office: The Ashton Tech Group 1900 Market St Ste 701 Philadelphia PA 19103-3514 Fax: 215-636-3560.

RITTERHOUSE, KATHY LEE, librarian; b. Hutchinson, Kans., May 24, 1952; d. Fayne Lee and Elizabeth Rose (Tener) R.; m. Michael Raymond Demmitt, July 8, 1972 (div. Apr. 1990). BA in English, Kans. State U., 1974; MLS, U. Okla., 1979. Circulation libr. Grand Prairie (Tex.) Meml. Libr., 1979-80. libr. dir., 1980—. Bd. dirs. Grand Prairie Arts Coun., 1980-2000, pres., 1989. Recipient Women in History award, 1999; named Pub. Svc. Employee of Yr. Grand Prairie C. of C., 1989. Mem.: ALA (intellectual freedom com. 1998—2001), Tex. Libr. Assn. (Tex./SIRS Intellectual Freedom award 1993), Metro Rotary Club (bd. dirs. 1992—99, pres. 2003—04, dist. new generations chair 2001—04), Beta Phi MU. Office: Grand Prairie Meml Libr 901 Conover Dr Grand Prairie TX 75051-1521 E-mail: ritterh@gptx.org.

RITTERSEISER, ROBERT, investment company executive; Pres., CEO Grunthal & Co Inc., N.Y.C. Office: Grunthal & Co Inc 1 Liberty Plz Fl Conc New York NY 10006-1404

RITTERSKAMP, DOUGLAS DOLVIN, lawyer; b. St. Louis, July 7, 1948; s. James Johnstone Jr. and Linn M. (Dolvin) R.; m. Linda S. Vansant, Mar. 23, 1974; 1 child, Tammy. AB, Washington U., 1970, JD, 1973; LLM in Taxation, NYU, 1978. Bar: N.Y. 1974, Mo. 1979. Assoc. Patterson, Belknap, Webb & Tyler, N.Y.C., 1974-78; jr. ptnr. Bryan Cave LLP (and predecessors), St. Louis, 1978-82; ptnr. Bryan Cave LLP, St. Louis, 1983—. Trustee Scottish Rite Clinic for Childhood Lang. Disorders of St. Louis, Inc., 1987-97, St. Louis Mission and Ch. Ext. Soc., United Meth. Ch., 1987-97, Mo. United Meth. Found., 1994—2003, pres., 2000—03; trustee The Coll. Sch., 1995-2001. Capt. USAR, 1970-79. Mem. ABA (employee benefits com. sect. taxation 1987-91, 96—), Bar Assn. Met. St. Louis (steering com. employee benefits 1989—), Masons (32d degree, knight comdr. ct. of honor), Shriners. Methodist. Home: 5223 Sutherland Ave Saint Louis MO 63109-2338

RITVO, EDWARD ROSS, psychiatrist; b. Boston, June 1, 1930; s. Max Ritvo; m. Riva Golan, Sept. 11, 1989; children: Deborah, Eva, Anne, Matthew, Victoria, Skylre, Max. BA, Harvard U., 1951; MD, Boston U. Sch. Medicine, 1955. Diplomate Am. Bd. Psychiatry and Neurology, Am. Bd. Child Psychiatry. Prof. UCLA Sch. Medicine, 1963—. Author 4 books; contbr. over 150 articles to profl. jours. Capt. U.S. Army, 1959-61. Recipient Blanche F. Ittleson award Am. Psychiat. Assn., 1990. Mem. Nat. Soc. for Autistic Children, Profl. Adv. Bd. (chmn.). Office: UCLA Sch Medicine Dept Psychiatry 760 Westwood Plz Los Angeles CA 90095-8353

RITVO, ROGER ALAN, vice chancellor, health management-policy educator; b. Cambridge, Mass., Aug. 12, 1944; s. Meyer and Miriam R.S. (Meyers) R.; m. Lynn Lieberman; children: Roberta, Eric. BA, Western Res. U., 1967; MBA, George Washington U., 1970; PhD, Case Western Res. U., 1976. Asst. adminstr. N.Y. Mental Health System, 1968-70; asst. prof., asst. dean Sch. Applied Social Scis. Case Western Res. U., Cleve., 1976-79, assoc. prof., 1981-83; assoc. prof., founding dir. Grad. Program in Health Adminstrn. Cleve. State U., 1983-87; prof. health mgmt. and policy, dean Sch. Health and Human Svcs. U. N.H., Durham, 1987-97; sr. health policy analyst to sec. DHHS, Washington, 1980-81; vice chancellor acad. and student affairs Auburn U. Montgomery, Ala., 1997—. Vis. rsch. scholar WHO, Copenhagen, 1978; vis. prof. Am. U., Washington, 1980-81, U. W.I., 1993; chair Ala. Coun. Chief Acad. Officers, 1998-2000; vis. scholar U. Sheffield, Eng., 1985; cons. to numerous orgns. on profit and non-profit strategic planning. Editor, author 7 books, including Managing in the Age of Change, 1994, Improving Governing Board Effectiveness, 1996, Sisters in Sorrow Voices of Care in the Holocaust, 1998, Ethical Governance in Health Care, 2004; mem. cmty. editl. bd. Montgomery Advertiser newspaper, 1999; contbr. articles to profl. jours. Trustee Hosp. Sisters of Charity, Cleve., 1980-85, Greater Seacoast United Way, 1991-93; chmn. health care adv. com. Ohio Senate, 1983-85; bd. mem. Fairmount Temple, Beachwood, Ohio, 1980-85; trustee Leadership Seacoast, 1991-93, bd. dirs., 1992-95; bd. dirs. N.H. chpt. United Way, 1992-95, Higher Edn. Leadership Partnership, 1998-2000; chair higher edn. divsn. United Way, Montgomery, Ala., 2004. Recipient Outstanding Adminstr. award, 1992, Cert. of Merit U. N.H. Pres.'s Commn. on Women, 1994; Govt. fellow Am. Coun. Edn., 1980-81. Mem. Nat. Tng. Labs. Inst. (bd. dirs. 1981-85, 92-96), Cert. Cons. Internat., Jewish Philatelic, Hist. Soc. N.Y.C. Avocations: collecting flat irons and masks, philatelist, white water rafting. Office: Auburn U Montgomery 7300 University Dr Montgomery AL 36117-3596

RITZ, DAVID M. photographic retail company executive; Various positions Ritz Camera, Beltsville, Md., 1969-74, mgmt. positions to pres., 1974—, pres., chmn., CEO now; chmn. Ritz Interactive, Irvine, Calif. Office: Ritz Camera 6711 Ritz Way Beltsville MD 20705-1318 also: Ritz Interactive 2010 Main St Ste 400 Irvine CA 92614

RITZ, GERRY, member of parliament; Mem. House of Commons, Ottawa, Canada. Can. Alliance Caucus. Office: House of Commons Ottawa ON K1A 0A6 Canada Address: 1322-100th St North Battleford SK S9A 0V8 Canada E-mail: ritz.g@parl.gc.ca., ritz@canadianalliance.ca.

RIVARA, FREDERICK PETER, pediatrician, educator; b. Far Rockaway, N.Y., May 17, 1949; s. Frederick P. and Mary Lillian (Caparelli) R.; m. J'May Bertrand, May 17, 1975; children: Matthew, Maggie. BA, Holy Cross Coll., 1970; MD, U. Pa., 1974; MPH, U. Wash., 1980. Diplomate Am. Bd. Pediatrics. Intern Children's Hosp. and Med. Ctr., Boston, 1974-75, resident, 1975-76, Seattle, 1978-80; RWJ clin. scholar U. Wash., Seattle, 1978-80, assoc. prof. pediatrics, 1984-89, prof. pediatrics, head divsn. gen. pediatrics, 1990—; mem. staff Nat. Health Svc. Corps, Hazard, Ky., 1976-78; asst. prof. pediatrics U. Tenn., Memphis, 1981-84. Editor Archives of Pedatrics and Adolescent Medicine. Fellow Am. Acad. Pediatrics; mem. Ambulatory Pediatrics Assn., Internat. Assn. Child, Adolescent and Injury Prevention (pres. 1993-2000). Office: Harborview Med Ctr 325 9th Ave PO Box 359960 Seattle WA 98195-9960

RIVARD, JEROME G. engineering executive; b. Hudson, Wis., Nov. 21, 1932; BSME, U. Wis., 1955. Dir. engring. Bendix, 1962-76; chief engr. Ford Motor Co., 1976-86; vice pres., group exec. Bendix Electronics Group, 1986—88; pres. Global Tech. & Bus. Devel., Harrison Twp., Mich., 1988—. Fellow IEEE, Soc. Automotive Engrs.; mem. NAE. Acheivements include research in the application of electronics to automotive systems. Office: 29401 S Seaway Ct Harrison Township MI 48045

RIVARD, ROBERT, editor; b. Nov. 17, 1952; m. Monika Maeckle, Sept. 19, 1981; children: Nicolas, Alex. BA in Polit. Sci., U. Tex., San Antonio, 1996; postgrad., Northwestern U., 1996. Sportswriter Brownsville Herald, 1977-78; news reporter Corpus Christi (Tex.) Caller, 1978-79; reporter Dallas Times Herald, 1979-81, Ctrl. Am. bur. chief, 1981-83, Newsweek, 1983-85, sr. editor, chief corrs., 1985-90; dep. mng. editor San Antonio Light, 1990-93; mng. editor Express News, San Antonio, 1993-97, editor, sr. v.p., 1997—. Named Editor's and Pub.'s Editor of Yr., 2000. Mem.: Soc. Profl. Journalists (Disting. Svc. award 1982). Office: San Antonio Express-News PO Box 2171 San Antonio TX 78297-2171

RIVAS, FERNANDO, composer; b. Habana, Cuba, Mar. 16, 1952; s. Raimundo Rivas and Justa Martinez Suarez; m. Maria Deluca Rivas, Feb. 2003; m. Ellen Garcia, July 10, 1976 (div. Sept. 1998). MusB, Juliard Sch., 1973—77. Bd. mem. Chamber Music Soc. of Charleston, 2003—. Composer: (songs) Elmopalooza (grammy award, 1998). Recipient Princess Grace award, Princess Grace Found. ASCAP, 1987. Mem.: MENC, ASCAP. Democrat. Cath. Avocation: writing. Home and Office: P O Box 80847 Charleston SC 29416 Business E-Mail: rivas2750@comcast.net.

RIVENBARK, JAN MEREDITH, business consultant; b. Spartanburg, S.C., Feb. 22, 1950; s. George Meredith and Audrey Isabel (Frady) R.; m. Barbara N. Newton, Sept. 25, 1976; children: Abigail, Justin, Patrick. BS in Math., Duke U., 1972; postgrad., Ga. State U., 1980. Mgmt. trainee Citizens & So. Nat. Bank, Atlanta, 1972, br. mgr., 1974, employee rels. mgr., 1975-77, v.p. compensaton, benefits, payroll and data mgmt., 1977-80; mgr. pers. 1st Tenn. Bank, Memphis, 1980-81; dir. compensation and benefits Hanes group Consol. Foods Corp. (now Sara Lee Corp.), Winston-Salem, N.C., 1981-83, exec. dir. compensation and benefits Chgo., 1983-84; exec. dir. internat. staff Sara Lee Corp., Chgo., 1985, exec. dir. corp. planning, 1985-87, sr. v.p. PYA/Monarch divsn. Greenville, S.C., 1987-89; pres. JP Foodsvc., Hanover, Md., 1989-92; COO PCA Internat., Inc., Charlotte, N.C., 1992-97; pres., COO Starboard Inc., Charlotte, 1997-2000; pres. Fresher-than-Fresh, Inc., Charlotte, 1998-2000; pres., CEO The Rivenbark Group, 2000—. Mem. Alpha Tau Omega. Republican. Home and Office: 4107 Foxcroft Rd Charlotte NC 28211-3760 E-mail: jan@rivenbark.com.

RIVERA, CHERYL A. state representative, lawyer; BA, Northeastern Univ.; JD, Western New Eng. Sch. of Law. State rep., Mass., 1999—; atty. Chairperson Sprinfield Pk. Commn., 1988—2000; com. Springfield Planning Bd., 1999—2000, Mass. Dem. State, 1999—, Energy, Govt. Regulations, House Long Term Debt and Capital Expenditures; mem. Mass. Womens Causus; co-founder, mem. Latino Caucus. Mem.: Mass. Assn. of Hispanic Atty., Hampden County Bar Assn. Democrat. Office: State Ho Rm 540 Boston MA 02133

RIVERA, CHITA (CONCHITA DEL RIVERO), actress, singer, dancer; b. Washington, Jan. 23, 1933; d. Pedro Julio Figuerva del Rivero; m. Anthony Mordente. Student, Am. Sch. Ballet, N.Y.C. Broadway debut: Call Me Madam, 1952; appeared on stage in: Guys and Dolls, Can-Can, Seventh Heaven, Mister Wonderful, West Side Story, Father's Day, Bye Bye Birdie, Three Penny Opera, Flower Drum Song, Zorba, Sweet Charity, Born Yesterday, Jacques Brel is Alive and Well and Living in Paris, Sondheim-A Musical Tribute, Kiss Me Kate, Ivanhoe, Chicago, Bring Back Birdie, Merlin, Jerry's Girls, 1985, The Rink, 1984 (Tony award 1984), Can-Can, 1988, Kiss of the Spider Woman (Tony award, Best Actress in a musical), 1993; performs in cabarets and nightclubs around world; starred in: film Sweet Charity, 1969; numerous TV appearances include Kojak and the Marcus Nelson Murders, 1973, The New Dick Van Dyke Show, 1973-74, Kennedy Ctr. Tonight-Broadway to Washington!, Pippin, 1982, The Mayflower Madam, 1987, Sammy Davis Jr.'s 60th Birthday Celebration, 1990, Ira Gershwin at 100: A Celebration at Carnegie Hall, 1997, Venecia, 2001, Anything Goes, 2000, The Visit, 2001. Recipient Best Actress, Outer Critics Circle award, 1993, Drama League award, Spider Woman, 1993, Ellis Island Medal of Honor, 2000, Best Leading Actress in a Musical, Tony award. Mem. AFTRA, SAG, Actors Equity Assn. Office: William Morris Agy c/o Samuel Liff 1325 Ave of the Ams New York NY 10019

RIVERA, GERALDO, television personality, journalist; b. N.Y.C., July 4, 1943; s. Cruz Allen and Lillian (Friedman) R.; m. Sheri Rivera (div. 1984); m. C.C. Dyer, 1987 (div. 2002); children: Gabriel, Cruz, Isabella, Simone. BS, U. Ariz., 1965; JD, Bklyn. Law Sch., 1969; postgrad., U. Pa., 1969, Sch. Journalism, Columbia U., 1970. Bar: N.Y. 1970. Mem. anti-poverty neighborhood law firms Harlem Assertion of Rights and Community Action for Legal Svcs., N.Y.C., 1968-70; with Eyewitness News, WABC-TV, N.Y.C., 1970-75; reporter Good Morning America program ABC-TV, 1973-76, corr., host Good Night America program, 1975-77, corr., sr. producer 20/20 Newsmag., 1978-85; host syndicated talk show The Geraldo Rivera show, N.Y.C., 1987-98; host investigative show on cable CNBC Rivera Live, N.Y.C., 1994—2001; host nightly news show on cable CNBC Upfront Tonight, NJ, 1998—2000; spl. corr. Fox News Channel, 2001—; host weekend show on cable At Large with Geraldo Rivera; contbr. Fox newsmag. The Pulse. Author: Willowbrook, 1972, Island of Contrasts, 1974, Miguel, 1972, A Special Kind of Courage, 1976, Exposing Myself, 1991; host numerous syndicated TV spls.; film appearances: The Bonfire of the Vanities, 1990; television movie: Perry Mason: The Case of the Reckless Romeo. Recipient 7 Emmy awards, Peabody award, Kennedy Journalism award, 1973, 75, numerous others; named Broadcaster of Yr. N.Y. State AP, 1971, 72, 74; Smith fellow U. Pa., 1969. Jewish. Office: Fox News Channel 1211 Ave of Ams New York NY 10036

RIVERA, JOSE, poet, security firm executive; b. Winona, Minn., Jan. 3, 1955; m. Maria Teresa Canete, June 8, 2000. BA, Winona State U., 1977; Cert. in Internat. Bus., U. San Diego, 1993. Author: Macrossan Street, 1998, Cat Of Nine Tails, 1998, Nightshades, 1999, Vagabond Heart, 1999, The Healing Art Of Poetic Qigong, 2000, Little Buddha, 2002, Haiku Honeysuckle, 2003, On Poetry, 2003, Renegade Lover, 2003, River of Dreams, 2004. Recipient President's Award For Lit. Excellence, The Nat. Authors Registry, 1997, 1998, 2001. Mem.: World Congress Poets (life).

RIVERA, LIONEL, mayor; b. El Paso, Tex. B in Microbiology, Tex. Tech. U.; MBA, Jacksonville State U. V.p. investments UBS. Mem. Colorado Springs (Colo.) City Coun., 1997—2001; vice mayor City of Colorado Springs, 2001—03, mayor, 2003—; founder, past pres. Colorado Springs Hispanic C. of C.; trustee United Way; mem. exec. com., co-chair The Springs Cmty. Action Plan; mentor Big Bros.-Big Sisters. Capt. U.S. Army. Mem.: Colorado Springs C. of C. Office: PO Box 1575 Colorado Springs CO 80901 Office Phone: 719-385-5986. Office Fax: 719-385-5495. E-mail: lrivera@ci.colospgs.co.us.

RIVERA, MARIANO, professional baseball player; b. Panama City, Panama, Nov. 29, 1969; Baseball player N.Y. Yankees, 1995—. Named World Series MVP, 1999, ALCS MVP, 2003; named to Am. League All-Star Team, 1997, 1999—2002, 2004; recipient Am. League Rolaids Relief Award, 1999, 2001. Achievements include mem. of World Series Champions New York Yankees, 1996, 1998, 1999, 2000; led Am. League in saves (45), 1999, (50), 2001. Office: New York Yankees Yankee Stadium East 161St and River Ave Bronx NY 10451*

RIVERA, MAXIMIANO MARQUEZ, academic administrator, writer; b. Mindoro, The Philippines, Aug. 24, 1946; arrived in U.S., 1991; s. Maximiano Corea Rivera, Sr. and Rosita Marquez Rivera; m. Roela Victoria Rivera, Oct. 5, 1974; children: Paul Christian, Paul John, Norman Vincent Paul. BS, U. of the East, Manila, 1967, BS in Biosci., 1969, BS in Edn., 1970, MEd, 1974; diploma in aquaculture, M of Aquaculture, U. Philippines, Iloilo, 1985; profl. diploma, Centro Escolar U., Manila, 1979, D of Edn., 1980. Cert. sci./technol. specialist. Supervising tchr. Secondary Sch. U. of the East, Manila, 1969—70, coll. prof., 1971—81; rschr., sta. head S.E. Asian Fisheries, Iloilo, 1982—85; gen. mgr., rschr. Seahorse Aquaculture, Mindoro, 1986—87; exec. asst. Dept. Edn., Pasig, 1988—92; v.p., prof. Makati (Philippines) U., 1993—96; NSE program coord. Tenn. State U., Nashville, 1997—. Cons. Seoul Art Theol. Sch., Korea and the Philippines, 1994—95; adj. faculty Vol. State C.C., Gallatin, Tenn., 1997—98; faculty honors program Tenn. State U., Nashville, 1998—. Author: (book) Thesis/Dissertation Writing, 1999; co-author: Practical Guide to Thesis and Dissertation, 1996; contbr. articles to profl. jours. Election coord., supr. Commn. on Election, Makati U., 1993—95. Named Outstanding Father, Devel. of Filipino Youth Inc., 1998; recipient Man of Yr. award, New Life Family Devel. Coun., 1994, Golden medal of honor, Philippine Exptl. Ednl. Rsch. Soc. Inc., 1995, Profl. Achievement award, Media for Devel. and Progress Inc., 1995, Golden Record Achievement award in field of edn., Asian Inst. Humanitarian Devel., 1995, Dr. Jose Rizal Immortal award, Philippine Exptl. Ednl. Rsch. Soc. Inc., 1994, Golden Leadership award for outstanding educator, Social Action and Civic Movement Inc., 1994, Golden Scroll of Honor award, New Life on Family Devel. and Youth Coun. Inc., 1997, scholarships, Japan Internat. Coop. Agy., SEAFDEC, AQD, State of Israel, Fund for Assistance to Pvt. Edn., U. of the East, Coun. Internat. Ednl. Exch., travel grant, TSU; fellow, Exxon Mobil. Mem.: So. Regional Honors Coun., Am. Soc. for Pub. Adminstrn., Philippine Geog. Soc. (life), Philippine Soc. for Microbiology (life; bus. mgr. 1980—), Philippine Assn. for Advancement of Sci. (life), Biology Tchrs. Assn., Inc. (life; bd. dirs., Outstanding Svc. award 1991), Phi Kappa Phi (scholarship chair 1999—). Achievements include patents for anti-pimples formula; massaging device. Avocations: reading, sitar, gardening. Office: Tenn State U Honors Program 3500 John A Merritt Blvd Nashville TN 37209 Office Phone: 615-963-5612. E-mail: mrivera@tnstate.edu.

RIVERA, RHONDA RAE, law professor, legal scholary lawyer, artibrator; b. Phila., Mar. 9, 1938; d. Preston Robert and Katherine Lowe (MacSorley) Rieley; 1 child, Robert Preston. BA cum laude, Douglass Coll., 1959; MPA, Syracuse U., 1960; JD magna cum laude, Wayne State U., 1967; cert. in urban econs., MIT, 1972. Bar: Mich. 1968, Ohio 1976, Ariz. 1995, N.Mex., 2002, U.S. Dist. Ct. (so. dist.) Ohio 1977. Asst. prof. law Ohio State U. Law Sch., Columbus, 1976-78, assoc. prof. law, 1978-81, prof. law, 1982-95, prof. emeritus, 1995, assoc. dean, 1982-86, dir. 2d Yr. Legal Writing Program, 1983-87. Vis. prof. law, U. Ariz., 1995-99; labor arbitrator Fed. Mediation and Conciliation Svcs., 1986—, U.S. Postal Svc., Am. Postal Workers Union, 1995—. Author: (with D.J. Whaley) Problems and Materials on Sales, 1983; contbr. articles and revs. to legal and bus. jours. Mem. fin. com. LWV, 1971-74; lay reader St. Stephen's Episcopal Ch., Columbus, 1976-95, St. Michael and All Angels Episcopal Ch., 2001—; mem. Ctrl. Ohio Diocesan Coun., 1980-81, chancery judge So. diocese Ohio, 1982-90; active Boy Scouts Am., 1976-80, Columbus Com. for Battered Women, 1979-80; pres. Stonewall Union, Columbus, 1983-84, bd. dirs. and clk., 1981-88; founder Integrity Ctrl. Ohio, 1983; bd. dirs. Ohio Women Ind., 1980-82, treas., 1981-82; bd. dirs. Franklin County Legal Aid Soc., Columbus, 1983-85. Recipient Susan B. Anthony award Woman Law Students Assn. U. Mich., 1976, Evelyn Hooker Rsch. award Gay Acad. Union, 1984, Dir.'s award Ohio Dept. Health for AIDS work, 1988, Woman of Achievement award YWCA, 1989. Mem. ABA (adv. bd. sect. individual rights and responsibilities 1979-80), ACLU, Nat. Acad. Arbitrators (labor arbitrator 1990-), NOW (Legal Achievement award Legal Def. and Edn. fund 1986, Uppity Woman of Yr. Ann Arbor chpt. 1975), AAUP, Am. Assn. Law Schs. (chmn. women in legal edn. sect. 1979-80, sect. exec. com. 1980-82, chmn. gay and lesbian legal issues sect. 1982-83), Soc. Am. Law Tchrs. (exec. com. of bd. govs. 1979-81, bd. govs. 1978-95, pres.

1984-86), Nat. Lawyers Guild, Ohio Human Rights Bar Assn. (founder 1988, pres. 1989-91, bd. trustees 1991-95), Gay and Lesbian Lawyers of N.Mex., Women Lawyers N.Mex., N.Mex. Basic Rights. Home and Office: 10218 Prescott Ct NW Albuquerque NM 87114-4519 Personal E-mail: rrivera38@comcast.net.

RIVERA, RICHARD EDWIN, former restaurant chain executive; b. Jan. 6, 1947; m. Leslie Suzanne Pliner, Nov. 18, 1984. BA, Washington & Lee U., 1968. Credit analyst Nat. Bank Commerce, Dallas, 1970-71; from mgmt. trainee to exec. v.p., dir. Steak and Ale Restaurants of Am., Dallas, 1971-80; pres. restaurant div. El Chico Corp., 1980-82; exec. v.p., chief operating officer T.J. Applebee's and Taco Villa Mexican Restaurant, Dallas, 1982-87; exec. v.p. ops. TGI Friday's Inc., Dallas, 1987-88, pres., CEO, 1988-94, RARE Hosp. Internat., Inc., Atlanta, 1994-97, Chart House Restaurants, Inc., 1997; pres. Red Lobster Restaurants, Orlando, Fla., 1997—2002, 2003—04; vice-chmn. Darden Restaurants, Inc., Orlando, Fla., 2002; interim pres. Bahama Breeze Restaurants, 2002—03; pres., COO Darden Restaurants, Inc., 2003—04.

RIVERA, SHAWNA COLLEEN, small business owner; b. San Diego, Feb. 28, 1940; d. Eric Anthony and Meghan Eileen (Rowan) Thomas; m. Jose Mariano Rivera, Sept. 22, 1966; children: Julio, Manuela, Miguel. BA, Indiana U., Bloomington, 1962; MA, U. Texas, 1966. Store mgr. Woolworth, Inc., Houston, 1970—74; v.p. human resources K-Mart, Clinton, Iowa, 1975—90; founder, owner Meriks Bobbleheads & Collectibles, West Union, 1991—. Protestant. Avocations: acting, keyboards, pinochle. Office: Meriks Bobbleheads & Collectibles 317 Water St West Union IA 52175 1511

RIVERA CARRERA, NORBERTO CARDINAL, archbishop; b. Tepehuanes, Mexico, June 6, 1942; Ordained priest Roman Cath. Ch., 1966, elevated to Cardinal Roman Cath. Ch., 1998. Bishop, Tehuacan, Puebla, Mexico, 1985—95; archbishop primate Mexico City, 1995—. Office: Apartado Postal 24-433 06700 Mexico City Mexico

RIVERA-DOMINGUEZ, ALBERTO, chemistry educator, mechanical engineer; b. Vega Baja, P.R., June 17, 1958; s. Angel Rivera-Delgado and Concepcion Dominguez-Suarez; m. Elli Reyes-Grote, Jan. 6, 1985; 1 child, Albert Vincent Rivera-Reyes. BSME magna cum laude, U. P.R., 1981; MSME, La. Tech. U., 1990. Engr. Boeing Comml. A/P Co., Seattle, 1981-82; lectr. U. P.R., Mayaguez, P.R., 1983-84, asst. to the assoc. dean of engring., 1984; tchg. asst. La. Tech. U., Ruston, 1985-86; mech. engr. U.S. Army, Fort Buchannan/San Juan, P.R., 1987-90, USN/AFWTF, Ceiba, P.R., 1990-91; gen. engr. USN - NUWC, Newport, R.I., 1991-95; engr. Breeze-Eastern, Union, NJ, 1995—2001; tchr. h.s. math NJ, 2001—. Lectr. U. P.R., 1983-84. Contbr. articles to profl. jours. Recipient tuition award MIT, Cambridge, Mass., 1982-84, Panam. Surety Assn. scholarship La. Tech. U., Ruston, 1986. Mem. ASME, NSPE, Am. Soc. for Composites, NJ Edn. Assn., Colegio de Ingenieros Y Agrimensores de P.R. Achievements include rsch. on viscoelastic characterization of composite materials; theoretical rsch. findings include: co-established the prin. of virtual equillibrium state of viscoelasticity; devel. a generalized predictive creep response formulation suitable for composite materials; developed algorithm and techniques for reliability prediction of assembled products; applied finite-difference modeling to simulate the performance of mechanically-assembled products. Home: PO Box 868 Matawan NJ 07747-1370

RIVERA PEREZ, EFRAIN E. state supreme court justice; b. Mayaguez, P.R., July 15, 1951; s. Efrain Padilla Rivera and Irene Perez Camacho; m. Border Mariluz; 1 child, Mariela Mariluz. B in Adminstrn. of Cos., U. Enclosure Mayaguez, 1971; JD, Pontifica Cath. U. Ponce Sch. Right, Ponce, P.R., 1975. Dist. judge Judicial Region Mayaguez, 1983—84, superior judge, 1984—85; pvt. practice law Maguayez, 1985—92; chmn. U. Enclosure Mayaguez U. P.R., 1986—92; adviser judicial subjects, dir. office judicial appts.; dir. office of commn. Judicial Reformation; temp. sec. justice, 1993—95; judge Ct. Cir. Appeals, 1995—2000; assoc. justice Supreme Ct. of P.R., 2000—. Office: PO Box 902 2392 San Juan PR 00902-2392

RIVERA-VALDÉS, SONIA, humanities educator; b. LaHabana, Cuba, Aug. 8, 1937; arrived in U.S., 1966; d. Enrique Rivera Fernandez and Angela Valdés; m. Mario Picayo (div.); children: Mario Picayo, Jesús Picayo, José Picayo. PhD in Spanish, CUNY, 1989. Spanish instr. Benedict Sch., 1970—72, 1974—76, Humacao, PR, 1973—74, P.R. Inst. Psychiatry, Hato Rey, 1975—76; asst. instr. grad. tchg. Kent State U., Ohio, 1976—77; Spanish tutor CUNY, 1978—81; instr. modern lang. Coll. New Rochelle, NY, 1979—80; adj. instr. modern lang. CUNY, 1980—81, instr. romance lang., 1981—82, 1981—92, adj. instr. fgn. lang., 1985—88, adj. asst. prof., 1990—96, substitute asst. prof., 1996—97, assoc. prof. fgn. lang., coord. ethnic studies, 1998—; instr. modern lang. Coll. New helle, 1982—83; adj. instr. dept. humanities Fordham U., 1985—88. Lit. panelist various arts couns. Author: Cinco ventanas del mismo lado, 1997, The Forbidden Stories of Marta Veneranda, 1998, Las historias prohibidas de Marta Veneranda, 2000, Historias de mujeres grandes y chiquitas, 2003; contbr. articles to profl. jours. Pres. Latino Artists Roundtable, N.Y.C., 1999—; bd. dirs. CUNY European Exchange Program, 1994—, Dominican Studies Assn. Recipient Lit. award, Premio Casa de las Américas for Hispanic Lit. in U.S., 1997; grantee Caribbean Exch. Travel grantee, CUNY, 1996, Ford Found. grantee, 1980, 1978—80. Home: 226 E 2d St Apt 4A New York NY 10009

RIVERO, MARILYN ELAINE KEITH, state legislator; b. Burlington, Vt., Aug. 22, 1942; d. Kenneth Charles and Irene (Haskell) Keith; m. Victor Paul Rivero, Sr., 1966; children: Lina, Mita, Victor Jr., Amy, Nicholas. BS, U. Vt., 1964, MS, 1988; postgrad., Middlebury Coll., 1973, St. Michaels Coll., 1986. Vol. Peace Corps., 1964-66; mem. Vt. Ho. of Reps., 1991—; mem. health and welfare com., 1991—. Recipient Beyond War award. Mem. ANA, Vt. Nurses Assn., Returned Peace Corps. Vol., Am. Assn. Retired People. Roman Catholic. Home: PO Box 37 Milton VT 05468-0037

RIVERS, ALMA FAYE, secondary school educator; b. Marion, N.C., Oct. 13, 1949; d. Arthur Henry and Lena (Deyton) Letterman; m. Charles Edwin Rivers, June 29, 1980. BA, Mars Hill Coll., 1971; MEd, W. Ga. Coll., 1978. Tchr., choral dir. W. Fannin H.S., Blue Ridge, Ga., 1971-76, W. Fannin Jr. H.S., Blue Ridge, 1976-80; tchr. Truett-McConnell Coll., Young Harris, Ga., 1975-76, 78-80, Sprayberry H.S., Marietta, Ga., 1980—. Student tchr. supr. State of Ga., 1988—, tchr. mentoring program, 1990—; tchr., cons. Kennesaw (Ga.) State U., 1995—; presenter workshops, confs., and confs. on 19th century women's lit. and multiculture lit. Mem. Standing Peachtree NA, Atlanta, 1994—; vol. PGA Tournament. NEH fellow, 1995. Mem. Nat. Coun. Tchrs. English, Ga. Coun. Tchrs. English, Thomas Wolfe Soc., Cooking Club of Am., Alpha Delta Kappa. Methodist. Avocations: golf, piano, literature, travel, book collecting. Office: Sprayberry High Sch 2525 Sandy Plains Rd Marietta GA 30066-5799

RIVERS, BEVERLY D. former district secretary; b. 1965; JD U. Ala. Sch. Law; BS in bus. mgmt., Oakwood Coll., Huntsville, Ala. Sec. D.C.; spl. asst. CFO; chief legis. asst. State Senator Henry L. Marsh, Richmond, Va.; atty. Hill Tucker Firm, Marsh Firm; acting sec. of didt. Washington, D.C., 1999, sec. of the dist., 1999—2003. Mem.: Nat. Forum Black Pub. Adminstr., Wash. Bar Assn., Ala. Bar Assn., D.C. Bar Assn.*

RIVERS, CHERYL P. state legislator; b. Rutland, Vt. m. Richard H. Rivers; 1 child. Student, U. Vt., Burlington; BS, Castleton State Coll., 1978. Mem., Windsor County Vt. Senate, Montpelier, 1991—; owner River Echo Morgans. Office: Vt State House State Capitol Montpelier VT 05602

RIVERS, GLENN ANTON (DOC RIVERS), professional basketball coach; b. Maywood, Ill., Oct. 13, 1961; m. Kris Rivers, 1987. Student, Marquette U., 1980-83. Player Atlanta Hawks, 1983-91, Los Angeles Clippers, 1991-92, New York Knicks, 1992-94, San Antonio Spurs, 1994-96; sports analyst Turner Sports, 1996-1999; head coach Orlando Magic, 1999—2003, Boston Celtics, 2004—. Mem. NBA All-Star Team, 1988; recipient Coach of Yr. award, 1999-2000. Office: c/o Boston Celtics 151 Merrimac St Boston MA 02114*

RIVERS, JOAN, entertainer; b. N.Y.C., June 8, 1937; d. Meyer C. Molinsky; m. Edgar Rosenberg, July 15, 1965 (dec.); 1 child, Melissa. BA, Barnard Coll., 1958. Formerly fashion coordinator Bond Clothing Stores. Debut entertaining, 1960; mem. From Second City, 1961-62; TV debut Tonight Show, 1965; Las Vegas debut, 1969; nat. syndicated columnist Chgo. Tribune, 1973-76; creator: CBS TV series Husbands and Wives, 1976-77; host: Emmy Awards, 1983; guest hostess: Tonight Show, 1983-86; hostess The Late Show Starring Joan Rivers, 1986-87, Hollywood Squares, 1987, (morning talk show) Joan Rivers (Daytime Emmy award 1990), 1989-93, Can We Shop? Home Shopping Network, 1994, (radio) The Joan Rivers Show, 1997—, E! Pre-awards Show, 1995—; originator, screenwriter TV movie The Girl Most Likely To, ABC, 1973; other TV movies include: How to Murder A Millionaire, 1990, Jackie Collins' Lady Boss, 1992, Tears and Laughter: The Joan and Melissa Rivers Story, 1994; cable TV spl. Joan Rivers and Friends Salute Heidi Abromowitz, 1985; film appearances include The Swimmer, 1968, Uncle Sam, The Muppets Take Manhattan, 1984; co-author, dir.: (films) Rabbit Test, 1978 (also acted), Spaceballs, 1987, Serial Mom, 1994; actress: theatre prodn. Broadway Bound, 1988, Sally Marr...and her escorts, 1994; recs. include: comedy album What Becomes a Semi-Legend Most, 1983; author: Having a Baby Can be a Scream, 1974, The Life and Hard Times of Heidi Abromowitz, 1984, (autobiography with Richard Meryman) Enter Talking, 1986, (with Richard Meryman), Still Talking, 1991, From Mother to Daughter: Thoughts and Advice on Life, Love and Marriage, 1998, Don't Count the Candle, Just Keep the Fire Lit, 1999; debuted on Broadway (play) Broadway Bound, 1988, creator Seminar You Deserve To Be happy, 1995. Nat. chmn. Cystic Fibrosis, 1982—, benefit performer for AIDS, 1984. Recipient Cleo awards for commls., 1976, 82, Jimmy award for best comedian, 1981; named Hadassah Woman of Yr., 1983, Harvard Hasty Pudding Soc. Woman of Yr., 1984. Mem. Phi Beta Kappa. Office: William Morris Agy 151 S El Camino Dr Beverly Hills CA 90212-2775 also: JR Worldwide 150 E 58th St New York NY 10155-0002

RIVERS, JULIE ELAINE, concert pianist, composer, recording industry executive; b. Ft. Worth; d. Theodore and Astrid (Ojerholm) Moberg; m. James C. Rivers (div.); children: David Aaron, James Arthur. MusB magna cum laude, U. North Tex., 1966. Concert pianist, 1960—; rec. artist, 1994—; pres. EarthStar Recs./Pubns. LLC, Topeka, 1996—. Premier Season com. Topeka Performing Arts Ctr., 1990. Rec. albums include Tidings of Joy, 1995, Spinning Gold: The Piano Music of Eugenie Rocherolle, 1995; pianist, composer: One Starry Night, 1996, The Kiss of the Sun, 1998, Romancing the Piano, 1998, Christmastide, 1999, As Far As the Heart Can See, 2003. Recipient Disting. Guest Artist award Zonta Internat., Topeka, 1989; fellow in composition Kans. Arts Commn., 1998. Mem. ASCAP (award 1997-2004), Kans. Music Tchrs. Assn. (composition chmn. 1993-95), Topeka Music Tchrs. Assn. (pres. 1973-74), Northeast Kans. Music. Tchrs. Assn. (pres. 1994-95), Nat. League Am. Pen Women (Nat. Composition award 1992, 98, 2002, Kans. Federated Music Club Composer of the Yr., 2003), Nat. Guild Piano Tchrs., Nonosa Honor Soc., Mortar Bd. Office: EarthStar Rec/Pubns PO Box 4462 Topeka KS 66604-0462 E-mail: julie@earthstarrecordings.com.

RIVERS, KENNETH JAY, retired judicial administrator, consultant; b. N.Y.C., Feb. 13, 1938; s. Alexander Maximillian and Albertina Ray (Gay) R.; m. Leah B. Files, Sept. 21, 1957 (div.); children: Londa Denise, Nancy Laura, Terrie Ruth, Kenneth J. Jr. AAS in Criminal Justice, BS in Criminal Justice, St. Francis Coll., Bklyn., 1978; MPA, L.I. Univ., 1981. Correction officer N.Y.C. Dept. Correction, 1965-69; ct. officer N.Y. State Unified Ct. System, N.Y.C., 1969-71, asst. ct. clk., 1971-73, sr. ct. clk., 1973-85, assoc. ct. clk., 1985-88, prin. ct. clk., 1988-90, dep. chief clk., 1991-93; ret., 1993. Tng. instr. N.Y. State Unified Ct. System, N.Y.C., 1985—, pers. assessor, 1985—; lectr. John Jay Coll. NYU, N.Y.C., 1987. Author: Juvenile Crime Survey, 1982, New York State Jury Selection, 1984. Bd. dirs. Parkway Consumers Med. Coun., Bklyn., 1983—, Cen. Bklyn. Tenant's Rights, 1988—. Recipient Leadership award Tribune Soc., N.Y. State Cts., 1987, Svc. award, 1988, Cert. of Merit award Fedn. Afro-Am. Civil Svc. Orgns., 1987. Mem. ASPA, Internat. Pers. Mgmt. Assn., Acad. Polit. Sci., Conf. Minority Pub. Adminstrs., Masons. Democrat. Methodist. Avocation: jazz musician. E-mail: kchiefclerk@aol.com.

RIVERS, LYNN N. former congresswoman; b. Augres, Mich., Dec. 19, 1956; 2 children. BA, U. Mich., 1987; JD, Wayne State U., 1992. Mem. sch. bd. City of Ann Arbor, Mich., 1984-92; mem. Mich. House of Reps., 1992-94. U.S. Congress from 13th Mich. dist., 1994—2002; mem. edn. and workforce com., sci. com., 1994. Mem.: Nat. Adv. Bd., Univ. Mich. Depression Center, 2003-. Democrat.

RIVERS, PATRICK A. education educator, researcher; b. Oct. 18, 1958; s. Cosmas and Amma Rivers; m. Mary Alice Patton, May 3, 1983; 1 child, Patrick Cosmas. PhD, U. Ala., 1997; MBA in Fin., Investment, & Banking, U. Wis., Madison, 1988; cert., Maguire Energy Inst., 2000. Faculty devel. fellow U. Ala., Birmingham, 1993—97; rsch. fellow RAND Corp., Santa Monica, Calif., 1997—98; clin. prof. U. Ariz., Tucson, 1998—; prof. Ariz. State U., Tempe, 1998—; prof., dir. So. Ill. U., 2004—. Recipient Nat. Rsch. Svc. award, Agy. for Health Rch. and Quality, 1997—98; scholar Most Published scholar, U. Ala., 1996—97. Fellow: Am. Coll. Health Care Execs.; mem.: Strategic Mgmt. Soc., Acad. Mgmt. Office: Ariz State Univ PO Box 874506 Tempe AZ 85287-4506 Home: 2215 B Nichole Ln Marion IL 62959 Business E-Mail: patrick.rivers@asu.edu.

RIVERS, RICHARD ROBINSON, lawyer; b. Dallas, June 9, 1942; s. Stewart Robinson and Madge (Fiske) R.; children: Laura Ellen, Jonathan Stewart. BA, Tulane U., 1964; JD, Cath. U. Am., 1974; MA, Johns Hopkins U., 2003. Bar: D.C. 1974. Writer Bauerlein, Inc., New Orleans, 1965-68; staff asst. Office of House Majority Whip, Washington, 1968-70, Office of House Majority Leader, Washington, 1971—72; internat. trade counsel Com. on Fin. U.S. Senate, Washington, 1973-77; gen. counsel Office Spl. Trade Rep., Washington, 1977-79; ptnr. Akin, Gump, Strauss, Hauer & Feld, Washington, 1979-96. Instr. Dalian (Peoples Republic of China) Inst. Tech., 1986. Trustee Am. Indian Coll. Fund. Mem. ABA, D.C. Bar Assn., Coun. Fgn. Rels., Met. Club City of Washington. Democrat. Episcopalian. Home: 4809 V St NW Washington DC 20007

RIVERS, ROBERT ALFRED, microwave company executive; b. Phillipston, Mass., Sept. 5, 1923; s. Frank Allen and Marie Ange (Pelchat) R.; m. Priscilla Bradford, Oct. 8, 1944; children: Lucy Marie, Rosalind Dolley, Robert Bradford. BSEE, MIT, 1953. Registered profl. engr., N.H. Flight radio officer Pan Am. Airways, various locations, 1942-50; design engr. Gen. Electronic Labs., Boston, 1953-54; pres. Aircom, Inc., various cities, 1954—. Editor Tech. Employment and Engring. Manpower Newsletter, 1989—; contbr. articles to profl. jours. Inventor wideband cavity resonator; designer over 1300 microwave components, portable and desktop microcomputer systems. Fellow IEEE (bd. dirs. 1975-76, mem. numerous coms. and bds., ethics rev. panel 1982-88, Centennial medal 1984, U.S. Activities Bd. citation of hon., Haraban Pratt award, 1997); mem. IEEE Microwave Theory and Techs. Soc. (pres. 1974, mem. numerous coms., chmn. Boston chpt. 1958-59, digest editor 1967), Eta Kappa Nu, Tau Beta Pi. Republican. Avocations: gardening, travel, reading. Office: Aircom Inc 334 E Main St Orange MA 01364

RIVERS, WILGA MARIE, foreign language educator; b. Melbourne, Australia, Apr. 13, 1919; arrived in U.S., 1970, d. Harry and Nina Diamond (Burston) R. BA, U. Melbourne, 1939, diploma in Edn., 1940, MA, 1948; Licence es L., U. Montpellier, France, 1952; PhD, U. Ill., 1962; MA (hon.), Harvard U., 1974; PhD of Langs. (hon.), Middlebury Coll., 1989. H.S. tchr., Victoria, Australia, 1940-48; asst. in English lang., 1949-52; tchr. prep. schs., 1953-58; asst. prof. French No. Ill. U., DeKalb, 1963-64; assoc. prof. Monash U., Australia, 1964-69; vis. prof. Columbia U., 1970-71; prof. French U. Ill., Urbana-Champaign, 1971-74; prof. Romance langs. and lit., coord. lang. instrn. Harvard U., 1974-89, prof. emerita, 1989—. Cons. NEH, Ford Found., Rockefeller Found., others; lectr 44 countries and throughout U.S., mem. adv. bd. Modern Lang. Ctr., Ont. Inst. for Studies in Edn., Nat. Fgn. Lang. Ctr., Lang. Acquire Rsch. Ctr., San Diego. Author: The Psychologist and the Foreign-Language Teacher, 1964, Teaching Foreign-Language Skills, 1968, 2d edit., 1981, Speaking in Many Tongues, 1972, 3d edit., 1983, A Practical Guide to the Teaching of French, 1975, 2d edit., 1988,3rd edit., 2001 (on Web), Opportunities for Careers in Foreign Languages, 1993; co-author: A Practical Guide to the Teaching of German, 1975, 2d edit., 1988, A Practical Guide to the Teaching of Spanish, 1976, 2d edit., 1988, 3rd edit., 2003 (on Web), A Practical Guide to the Teaching of English as a Second or Foreign Language, 1978, Communicating Naturally in a Second Language, 1983, Teaching Hebrew: A Practical Guide, 1989, others; editor, contbr. Interactive Language Teaching, 1978, Teaching Languages in College: Curriculum and Content, 1992, Down Under/Up Top: Creating a Life, 2004; writing translated into 11 langs.; editl. bd. Studies in Second Language Acquisition, Applied Linguistics, Language Learning, Mosaic, System; adv. com. Can. Modern Lang. Rev.; contbr. articles to profl. jours. Decorated chevalier des Palmes Académiques; recipient Disting. Fgn. Lang. Leadership award N.Y. State Assn. Fgn. Lang. Tchrs., 1974, Disting. Alumni award U. Ill., 1999, Dean's Disting. Svc. award Harvard Continuing Edn., 2004. Mem. MLA, Am. Assn. Applied Linguistics (charter pres.), Am. Coun. on Tchg. Fgn. Langs. (Florence Steiner award 1977, Anthony Papalia award 1988), Mass. Fgn. Lang. Assn. (Disting. Svc. award 1983), Tchrs. of English to Spkrs. of other Langs., Am. Assn. Tchrs. French, Linguistic Soc. Am., Am. Assn. Univ. Suprs. and Coords. Fgn. Lang. Programs Northeast Conf. (Nelson Brooks award 1983), Internat. Assn. Applied Psycholinguistics (v.p. 1983-89), Japan Assn. Coll. English Tchrs. (hon.), Am. Assn. Tchrs. German (hon.), Internat. Assn. Lang. Labs. (hon.). Episcopalian. Home and Office: 84 Garfield St Watertown MA 02472-4916

RIVERS BAKER, DAWN, writer, publisher, consultant; b. Phila., Apr. 3, 1959; d. David Dean and Gwendolyn Regina Rivers; m. Aubrey B. Baker III, Mar. 21, 1984; children: A. David, Regina, Kimberly, Richard. Student, Princeton U., 1977-1979, Columbia U., 1980-1981. Editor-in-chief The MicroEnterprise Jour., Sidney, NY, 1999—; owner, CEO, Wahmpreneur Pub., Inc., Sidney, 2000—. Small bus. cons. Career-Intelligence.com., Rowayton, Conn., 2000—. Author: (novel) The Rise of the Phoenix, 1999, E-commerce for the Unfunded, 2001, Financial Management 101, 2003. Recipient Small Bus. Journalist of Yr., U.S. Small Bus. Adminstrn., Syracuse, 2003. Mem. NAFE, Soc. Profl. Journalists, Online News Assn., Women Impacting Pub. Policy, Nat. Small Bus. Assn. Office: Wahmpreneur Pub Inc PO Box 41 Sidney NY 13838 Office Phone: 607-428-0521. E-mail: editor@wahmpreneur.com., dawn@wahmpreneur.com.

RIVES, JACK L. military officer; BA in Polit. Sci., U. Ga., 1974, JD, 1976; postgrad., Squadron Officer Sch., 1982, Air Command and Staff Coll., 1983, Nat. Security Mgmt., 1985, Naval War Coll., 1993. Commd. 2d lt. USAF, 1974, advanced through grades to maj. gen., 2002; asst. staff judge advocate Griffiss AFB, NY, 1977; area def. counsel, 1977—78; dep. staff judge advocate Kunsan AB, Republic of Korea, 1978—79; asst. staff judge advocate Hellenikon AB, Greece, 1979—81; cir. def. counsel Pacific Cir., Clark AB, Philippines, 1981—83; judge advocate air staff tng. officer The Pentagon, Washington, 1983—84; staff judge advocate Plattsburgh AFB, NY, 1984—86; chief officer br., judge advocate profl. devel. divsn. Office of Judge Advocate Gen., Washington, 1986—90; appellate judge USAF Ct. Mil. Rev., Bolling AFB, DC, 1990—93; dep. legal counsel Chmn. Joint Chiefs of Staff, Washington, 1993—95; commandant Air Force Judge Advocate Gen. Sch., Maxwell AFB, Ala., 1995—98; chief AF Exec. Issues Team Office of Sec. of Air Force, Washington, 1998—2000; staff judge advocate Hdqrs. Air Combat Command, Langley AFB, Va., 2000—02; dep. judge advocate gen. Hdqrs. USAF, Washington, 2002—. Decorated Legion of Merit with oak leaf cluster. Office: USAF Pentagon Washington DC 20330

RIVES, STANLEY GENE, university president emeritus; b. Decatur, Ill., Sept. 27, 1930; s. James A. and Frances (Bunker) R.; m. Sandra Lou Belt, Dec. 28, 1957; children: Jacqueline Ann, Joseph Alan. BS, Ill. State U., 1952, MS, 1955; PhD, Northwestern U., 1963; EdD (hon.), Lincoln Coll., 1998. Instr. W.Va. U., 1955-56, Northwestern U., 1956-58; prof. Ill. State U., Normal, 1958-80, Am. Coun. on Edn. Fellows Program, 1969-70, assoc. dean faculties, 1970-72, dean undergrad. instrn., 1972-80, assoc. provost, 1976-80, acting provost, 1979-80; provost, v.p. acad. affairs, prof. Eastern Ill. U., Charleston, 1981-83, pres., 1983-92, pres. emeritus, 1992—. Vis. prof. U. Hawaii, 1963-64 Author: (with Donald Klopf) Individual Speaking Contests: Preparation for Participation, 1967, (with Gene Budig) Academic Quicksand: Trends and Issues in Higher Education, 1973, (with others) Academic Innovation: Faculty and Instructional Development at Illinois State University, 1979, The Fundamentals of Oral Interpretation, 1981; contbr. articles to profl. jours. Bd. dirs. Ill. State Univs. Retirement System, 1992—, treas., 1995-2001, pres., 2001—; Ea. Ill. Univ. Found., 1993-98, also pres., 1996-98, East Ctrl. Ill. Devel. Corp., 1983-92, Charleston Area Econ. Devel. Found., 1986-92, Coles Together, 1988-92; mem. pres. commn. NCAA, 1986-91; trustee Nat. Debate Tournament, 1967-75. With U.S. Army, 1952-54. Recipient Alumni Achievement award Ill. State U., 1998, Co. of Edn. Hall of Fame. Mem. Am. Assn. State Colls. and Univs., Ill. State C. of C. (bd. dirs. 1990-92), Charleston C. of C. (bd. dirs. 1985-88), Theta Alpha Phi, Phi Kappa Delta, Pu Gamma Mu, Alpha Phi Omega, Alpha Zeta, Sigma Phi Epsilon (hon.). Home: 2231 Andover Pl Charleston IL 61920-3807 Personal E-mail: srives@consolidated.net.

RIVES, TERRY EDWARD, public health service officer, researcher, epidemiologist; b. Cleburne, Tex., Jan. 31, 1947; s. T. E. and Lora Earline Rives; m. Najiba Sayeed Rives, May 6, 2001; children: Lori, Justin. BS, LeTourneau U., Longview, Tex., 1992, MPH, 1994; DPH, U. Tex. Health Svcs. Ctr., Houston, 1996. Cert. Am. Coll. of Epidemiology. Epidemiologist Tex. Children's Hosp., Houston, 1993—97; rsch. scientist M.D. Anderson Cancer Ctr., Houston, 1997; chief epidemiologist City of Ft. Worth, 1998—99; dir. inst. rsch. U. Tex., Brownsville, 1999—2000; dir. assessment and biostatistical svcs. U. Tex. Health Svcs. Ctr., Houston, 2000—. Health assessor UN High Command Refugees, Peshawar, Pakistan, 2001, Peshawar, 02. With USAF, 1966—69, Vietnam. Mem.: Am. Pub. Health Assn., Am. Coll. Epidemiology. Office: Univ of Texas Health Svcs Ctr 7000 Fannin M60 Houston TX 77030 Business E-Mail: terry.e.rives@uth.tmc.edu.

RIVET, DIANA WITTMER, lawyer, developer; b. Auburn, N.Y., Apr. 28, 1931; d. George Wittmer and Anne (Jenkins) Wittmer Hauswirth; m. Paul Henry Rivet, Oct. 24, 1952; children: Gail, Robin, Leslie, Heather, Clayton, Eric. BA, Keuka Coll., 1951; JD, Bklyn. Law Sch., 1956. Bar: N.Y. 1956, U.S. Dist. Ct. (ea. and so. dists.) N.Y. 1975; cert. organic NOFA, 2001. Sole practice, Orangeburg, NY, 1957—2000; farmer Danny's Backyard Organic Farm, Orangeburg, 2000—. County atty. Rockland County (N.Y.), 1974-77; asst. to legis. chmn. Rockland County, 1978-79; counsel, adminstr. Indsl. Devel. Agy., Rockland County, 1980-91, Rockland Econ. Devel. Corp., 1981-90; counsel, exec. dir. Pvt. IndustryCoun. Rockland county, 1980-90; pres., CEO Environ. Mgmt. Ltd., Orangeburg, 1980-98; mem. air mgmt. adv. com. N.Y. State Dept. Environ. Conservation 1984-92, Orangetown Planning Bd., 1993-2000, master plan com., 2000-03. Pres. Rockland County coun. Girl Scouts U.S., 1981-84; chmn. Rockland County United Way, 1996-97, mem. campaign com., 1983-84, 88-89, 93, sec., 1997-99, bd. dirs., 1988-94, 95-2004; mem. Leadership Rockland, 1991-94. Recipient Cmty. Svc. award Keuka Coll., 1965, Disting. Svc. award Town of Orangetown, 1970, Disting. Svc. award Rockland County, 1989, Econ. Devel. award Rockland Econ. Devel. Corp., 1990; named Businessperson of Yr. Jour. News, Rockland County, 1982. Mem. ABA, N.Y. State Bar Assn. (mcpl. law sect. exec. com. 1976-83, environ. law sect. exec. com. 1974-86), Rockland County Bar Assn. (chair environ. law com. 1994-96), Rockland Bus. Assn. (bd. dirs. 1981-97, small bus. adv. com. 1998, gov. affairs com. 1998-2004), Rockland Computer Users' Group (bd. dirs. 1998-99). Democrat. Mem. Religious Soc. of Friends. Home: 1 Lester Dr Orangeburg NY 10962-2316 Office Phone: 845-359-1515. Personal E-mail: ydanny@fcc.net.

RIVET, JEANNINE M. health plan administrator; BS in Nursing, Boston Coll.; MPH, Boston U. Sch. Public Health. From v.p. health svc. ops. to CEO United HealthCare, Minnetonka, Minn., 1990-98, CEO health plans, 1998—2000; exec. v.p. Unitedhealth Group, 2000—. Office: United Health-Care Group 300 United HealthCare Group Ctr 9900 Bren Rd E Minnetonka MN 55343-9664

RIVETTE, FRANCIS ROBERT, lawyer; b. Syracuse, N.Y., May 1, 1952; s. Francis Patrick and Barbara Parker (Smith) R.; m. Judith A. La Manna, 1993. BA, Allegheny Coll., 1974; JD, Syracuse U., 1977. Bar: N.Y. 1978, D.C. 1980, U.S. Dist. Ct. (no. dist.) N.Y. 1978, U.S. Supreme Ct. 1993. Ptnr. Rivette & Rivette P.C., Syracuse, 1978—; corp. counsel Nicom Techs., Inc., 1995—, Group 52, Inc., 2002—. Corp. counsel Fangand Enterprises Ltd., 1978—; co-founder Apex Racing. Mem. ATLA, N.Y. State Trial Lawyers Assn., Syracuse Corvette Club (pres. 1985-86), Sportscar Vintage Racing Assn., Nat. Corvette Restorers Soc. (nat. judge, 1985, 88, 95, 97), Historic Sportscar Racing Ltd., Phi Delta Phi, Phi Gamma Mu. Republican. Home: 200 Old Liverpool Rd Liverpool NY 13088-6354 Office: Rivette & Rivette PC 224 Harrison St Ste 306 Syracuse NY 13202-3067 Office Phone: 315-478-1122. Business E-Mail: frr-rr@accucom.net.

RIVETTI, ANDREW FRANCIS, language educator, department chairman; b. Greenville, Ohio, June 19, 1970; s. Louie F., II and Nan H. Rivetti; m. Veronica Urbina, May 11, 1996; children: Diego F., Gabriela I. BA, Wright State U., Dayton, Ohio, 1993; MA, Miami U., Oxford, Ohio, 2000. Instr. English (ESL) Tronwell, S.A., Santiago, Chile, 1993—95; instr., translator Fundes Multimedia, Santiago, 1995—96; graphic designer/layout tech. Suburban Newspapers Dayton, 1996—98; instr. Spanish Miami U., Oxford, 1998—2000; instr. Spanish, dir. fgn. lang. dept. Three Rivers C., Poplar Bluff, Mo., 2000—. Recipient Irvin Essay award, Faculty of Miami U., 1999. Roman Catholic. Avocations: classical music, cooking, basketball. Office: Three Rivers Cmty Coll 2080 Three Rivers Blvd Poplar Bluff MO 63901 Office Phone: 573-840-9639. Business E-Mail: arivetti@trcc.edu.

RIVIERE, JIM EDMOND, pharmacologist, educator, toxicologist; b. New Bedford, Mass., Mar. 3, 1953; s. Raymond R. Riviere and Gertrude E. Pelletier-Riviere; m. Nancy Ann Monteiro-Riviere, May 31, 1976; children: Christopher, Brian, Jessica. BS, MS, Boston Coll., 1976; DVM, PhD, Purdue U., 1980. Lic. to practice vet. medicine; diplomate Am. Bd. Forensic Examiners, Am. Bd. Forensic Medicine. From asst. prof. to assoc. prof. N.C. State U., Raleigh, 1981-88, prof., 1988-92, Burroughs-Wellcome disting. prof. pharmacology, 1992—, dir. Ctr. Chem. Toxicology Rsch. and Pharmacokinetics, 1989—. Cons. for govt. and pharm. cos.; mem. com. on revision U.S. Pharmacopeia, 1995—; mem. sci. bd. FDA. Author/editor 9 books; author over 375 rsch. manuscripts; holder 5 patents in field. Recipient Ebert prize Am. Pharm. Assn., 1991, Outstanding Rsch. award N.C. State U. Alumni Assn., 1993, Disting. Alumni award Purdue U., 1991, Harvey Wiley medal, 1997, FDA Commrs. Spl. citation, 1997, O. Max Gardner award U. N.C. Sys., 1999, numerous rsch. grants. Fellow Am. Acad. Vet. Pharmacology and Therapeutics (editor 1989-92, 99—, First Rsch. award 1998); mem. Am. Assn. Pharm. Scientist, Soc. Toxicology, Am. Vet. Med. Assn., Am. Coll. Forensic Examiners, Inst. Medicine Nat. Acads. Office: NC State U 4700 Hillsborough St Raleigh NC 27606-1428 Business E-Mail: Jim_Riviere@ncsu.edu.

RIVIN, ARTHUR UDELL, medical educator; b. Sioux City, Iowa, June 30, 1923; s. Hyman and Bella (Woolf) R.; m. Frieda Riekes; children: Kenneth, Carol, Laurie. BS, U. Nebr., 1943, MD, 1946. Diplomate Am. Bd. Internal Medicine. Intern Michael Reese Hosp., Chgo., 1946-47; resident VA Wadsworth Hosp., L.A., 1949-51; clin. instr. medicine UCLA, L.A., 1952-56, asst. clin. prof. medicine, 1956-66, assoc. clin. prof. medicine, 1967—, clin. prof. medicine, 1976—, prof. emeritus, 2004—. Chmn. UniHealth Am. Bioethics Com., 1994-96, Santa Monica/West L.A. Clin. Rsch. Coop., 1992-96, Ctr. for Humane and Ethical Med. Care, founder, chmn.; lectr. in field. Contbr. articles to profl. jours. Pres. Calif. Health Decisions, L.A., 1987-92, bd. dirs., 1991-94. Cardiology fellow UCLA, 1952, Nat. Endowment Humanities fellow, Washington, 1977. Fellow Am. Coll. Physicians, Am. Coll. Cardiology; mem. AMA, Am. Heart Assn., L.A. Med. Assn., L.A. Heart Assn., Assn. Hosp. Med. Educators, Phi Beta Kappa, Alpha Omega Alpha. also: Santa Monica UCLA Hosp 1250 16th St Santa Monica CA 90404-1249 Business E-Mail: arivin@mednet.ucla.edu.

RIVKIND, PERRY ABBOT, federal railroad agency administrator; b. Boston, Jan. 22, 1930; s. Samuel Alexander and Mae Edna (Polisnor) R.; m. Dolores Russo; children: Robert Douglas, Valerie Jean; m. Kathleen Marie Lysher, Aug. 14, 1989. AA, Miami (Fla.) Community Coll., 1963; BA, Fla. State U., 1965; MA, Fla. Atlantic U., 1966; postgrad., Nat. War Coll., Washington, 1981. Comml. charter pilot, 1956-58; police officer Met. Police Dept., Miami, 1958-61; chief investigator Dade County State Atty. Office, Miami, 1961-67; prof., dir. dept. Cen. Piedmont Coll., Charlotte, N.C., 1967-68; asst. dir. Fed. Bur. Narcotics, Washington, 1968-74; asst. adminstr. Law Enforcement Assistance Adminstrn., Washington, 1974-81; assoc. commr. U.S. Immigration and Naturalization Svc., Washington, 1981-84, dist. dir. Miami, 1984-88; safety mgr. Miami Herald Pub. Co., 1988-89; dep. adminstr. Fed. R.R. Adminstrn., Washington, 1989—. Chmn. com. on tng. Pres.'s Coun. on Drug Abuse, Washington, 1971-74, chmn. com. on rsch. Working Group on Terrorism Nat. Security Coun., Washington, 1978-81. With U.S. Army, 1951-53. Perry A. Rivkind Day established in his honor City of Miami/Dade County/City of Miami Beach, 1985-89. Republican. Avocations: boating, hunting, fishing, motorcycling, camping.

RIVLIN, ALICE MITCHELL, federal agency administrator, economist; b. Phila., Mar. 4, 1931; d. Allan C. G. and Georgianna (Fales) Mitchell; m. Lewis Allen Rivlin, 1955 (div. 1977); children: Catherine Amy, Allan Mitchell, Douglas Gray; m. Sidney Graham Winter, 1989. BA, Bryn Mawr Coll., 1952; MA, Radcliffe Coll., 1955, PhD, 1958; LLD (hon.), U. Mich., 1975, U. Md., 1975; DSc (hon.), U. Ind., 1976; LLD (hon.), Yale U., 1984; DSc (hon.), N.J. Inst. Tech., 1998; LLD (hon.), U. Dist. of Columbia, 1999, Harvard U., 2001. Mem. staff Brookings Instn., Washington, 1957-66, 69-75, 83-93; dir. econ. studies Brookings Instn., 1983-87; dir. Congl. Budget Office, 1975-83; prof. pub. policy George Mason U., 1992—93; dep. dir. U.S. Office Mgmt. and Budget, 1993-94, dir., 1994-96; vice chmn., bd. governors Fed. Res. Sys., Washington, 1996-99; chair Fin. Assistance and Mgmt. Authority, 1998—2001; sr. fellow, econ. studies program Brookings Instn., Washington, 1999—; Henry J. Cohen prof. New Sch. U., 2001—; co-dir. Greater Wash. Rsch. Program, Brookings Instn., 2001—. Dep. asst. sec. program coordination HEW, Washington, 1966-68, asst. sec. planning and evaluation, 1968-69; mem. Staff Adv. Commn. on Intergovtl. Rels., 1961-62. Author: The Role of the Federal Governemnt in Financing Higher Education, 1961, (with others) Microanalysis of Socioeconomic Systems, 1961, Systematic Thinking for Social Action, 1971, (with others) Economic Choices 1987, 1986, (with others The Swedish Economy, 1987, (with others) Caring for the Disabled Elderly: Who Will Pay?, 1988, Reviving the American Dream, 1992, The Economic Payoff from the Internet Revolution (co-edited with Robert E. Litan), 2001, Beyond the Dot.Coms: The Economic Promise of the Internet (with Robert E. Litan), 2001. MacArthur fellow, 1983-87, Elliot J. Richardson prize for excellence in pub. svc., 2002, Barnard medal of distinction, Barnard Coll., 2002. Mem. Am. Econ. Assn. (nat. pres. 1986), Nat. Acad. Pub. Administrn., Nat. Acad. of Social Insurance, Coun. on Fgn. Rels., Office: Brookings Instn 1755 Massachusetts Ave Washington DC 20036

RIVLIN, BENJAMIN, political science educator; b. Bklyn., July 10, 1921; s. Moses and Esther (Ribnick) R.; m. Leanne Green, July 9, 1957; 1 child, Marc Alexander. BA, Bklyn. Coll., 1942; MA, Harvard U., 1947, PhD, 1949. With OSS, 1943-45; teaching fellow Harvard U., 1948; mem. trusteeship dept. UN Secretariat, 1948, 50, 52; research assoc. Hoover Commn., 1948; mem. faculty Bklyn. Coll. of CUNY, 1949-75, prof. polit. sci., 1962-70, chmn. dept., 1966-70; mem. Grad. Sch. faculty CUNY, 1970-85, exec. officer polit. sci. Ph.D. program, 1970-75, dean research and univ. programs Grad. Sch. and Univ. Center, 1975-78, prof. emeritus, 1985—, dir. Ralph Bunche Inst. on UN, 1984—91, dir. emeritus, 1991—. Vis. lectr. Johns Hopkins Sch. Advanced Internat. Studies, 1956; vis. prof. African and Middle East Insts., Columbia U., 1963-68; co-chair RalphBunche Centenary Commemoration com., 2001—. Author: The United Nations and The Italian Colonies, 1950, Self-Determination and Dependent Areas, 1955, (with J.S. Szyliowicz) The Contemporary Middle East: Tradition and Innovation, 1965, Ralph Bunche: The Man and His Times, 1990, (with Leon Gordenker) The Challenging Role of the UN Secretary-General, 1993; also articles. Served with AUS, 1942-45. Grantee Social Sci. Research Council, 1951, 54, 64; Fulbright scholar France and N. Africa, 1956-57 Fellow Middle East Studies Assn.; mem. Internat. Studies Assn. (pres. Middle Atlantic region 1978-80), Am. Polit. Sci. Assn., Acad. Coun. on UN System (vice chair 1990-91). Office: CUNY Grad Ctr 365 5th Ave New York NY 10016-4334 Office Phone: 212-817-2100. E-mail: brivlin@gc.cuny.edu.

RIVLIN, RACHEL, lawyer; b. Bangor, Maine, Sept. 1, 1945; d. Lawrence and A. Sara (Rich) Lait. BA, U. Maine, 1965; MA, U. Louisville, 1968; JD, Boston Coll., 1977. Bar: Mass. 1977, U.S. Dist. Ct. Mass. 1978, U.S. Ct. Appeals (1st cir.) 1983, U.S. Supreme Ct. 1985. Audiologist Boston City Hosp., 1969-72; dir. audiology Beth Israel Hosp., Boston, 1972-74; atty. Legal Sys. Devel., Boston, 1977-78, Liberty Mut. Ins., Boston, 1978-82; counsel, sec. Lexington Ins. Co., Boston, 1982-85, v.p., assoc. gen. counsel, sec., 1985—. Mem. civil rights com. Anti-Defamation League, Boston, 1982—; bd. dirs. DanceArt, Inc., Boston, 1985—92. Mem.: ABA (vice chmn. pub. rels. 1981—84, excess surplus lines and reins com. 1983—, internat. ins. law com. 1983—, nat. inst. insurer insolvency 1986, nat. inst. reins collections and insolvency 1988, chmn. 1988—89, nat. inst. insurer insolvency 1989, vice chmn. com. pub. regulation of ins. 1997—, vice chmn. 1997—, task force ins. and corp. counsel interests and involvement 1999—2003), Boston Bar Assn. (chmn. corp. counsel com. 1987, steering com. corp. bus. law and fin. sect. 1987—89, edn. com. 1987—89, chmn. ins. law com. 1987—90, nominating com. 1988, dinner dance com. 1989, edn. com. 1990—91, chmn. ins. com. 1990—, ethics com. 1993—, dinner dance com. 1994, multi-disciplinary practice task force 2000—02, comprehensive revision Mass. corp. law 2000—, coun., 1983-86 2002—), Boston Coll. Law Sch. Alumni Assn. (ann. fund com. 1981—89, chmn. telethon com. 1989—94, nominating com. 1990, search com. for dean 1993, search com. for law sch. fund dir. 1993, leadership gifts exec. com. 1994—98, search com. for dir. instl. advancement 1995, reunion com. 2002, Father James Malley award 1996). Home: 122 Lincoln St Newton MA 02461-1528 Office: Lexington Ins Co 100 Summer St 18th Fl Boston MA 02109 Office Phone: 617-330-8436. Business E-Mail: rachel.rivlin@aig.com.

RIVLIN, RICHARD SAUL, physiologist, educator; b. Forest Hills, N.Y., May 15, 1934; s. Harry Nathaniel and Eugenie (Graciany) R.; m. Barbara Melinda Pogul, Aug. 28, 1960 (div.); children: Kenneth Stewart, Claire Phyllis; m. Rita Klausner, Feb. 29, 1976; children: Michelle Elizabeth, Daniel Elliott. AB cum laude in Biochem. Scis., Harvard U., 1955, MD cum laude, 1959. Diplomate Am. Bd. Internal Medicine. Intern Bellevue Hosp., N.Y.C., 1959-60; asst. resident in medicine Johns Hopkins U. Hosp., Balt., 1960-61, asst. resident, 1963-64; clin. assoc. endocrinology br. Nat. Cancer Inst., NIH, Bethesda, Md., 1961-63; fellow dept. physiol. chemistry, medicine Johns Hopkins U. Sch. Medicine, Balt., 1964-66, lectr. clin. medicine, 1965-66; attending physician med. service Balt. City Hosps., 1964-66; assoc. in medicine Columbia U. Coll. Physicians and Surgeons, N.Y.C., 1966-67, asst. prof. medicine, 1967-71, assoc. prof. medicine, 1971-79; mem. Inst. Human Nutrition, 1972-79; chief endocrinology, asst. physician Francis Delafield Hosp., N.Y.C., 1966-75; asst. physician Presbyterian Hosp., N.Y.C., 1966-73, assoc. attending physician, 1973-79; chief nutrition service Meml. Sloan-Kettering Cancer Ctr., N.Y.C., 1979-90; prof. medicine Cornell U. Med. Coll., 1979—; chief div. nutrition dept. medicine N.Y. Hosp. -Cornell Med. Center, 1979—2001; NIH Nutrition Study Sec., 2000—02; vis. prof. Creighton U., 1974, U. Guadalajara (Mexico), 1974, N.J. Coll. Medicine and East Orange VA Hosp., Newark Med. Sch., N.J., 1974, 1976, 1983; Upjohn vis. prof. in nutrition Med. Coll. Ga., 1976; vis. prof. Syracuse U., 1980; Nat. Dairy Coun. vis. prof. in nutrition U. Mich., Ann Arbor, 1982; vis. prof. Washington U.-Jewish Hosp., St. Louis, 1983; external examiner in physiology Calcutta U., India; prin. investigator clin. nutrition rsch. unit Meml. Sloan-Kettering Cancer Ctr. and Inst. Cancer Preention, N.Y.C., 1980—; sr. v.p. med. affairs, Naylor-Dana chair in nutrition Inst. Cancer Prevention, N.Y.C., 2001—; vis. prof. UCLA, 2000, Emory U., 2002, Purdue U., 2002. Rsch. program oversight com. Am. Inst. Cancer Rsch., 1995—; Sydenstricker lectr. Med. Coll. Ga., 1989. Editor: Riboflavin, 1975; referee numerous profl. jours.; contbr. articles to profl. jours. Served with USPHS, 1961-63. Recipient Grace A. Goldsmith Lectre award Am. Coll. Nutrition, 1981, Lifetime Achievement award, 2001. Fellow ACP, AAAS; mem. Am. Soc. Clin. Nutrition (v.p. 1992-93, pres. 1993-94), Am. Fedn. Clin. Rsch., Endocrine Soc., Am. Thyroid Assn., Am. Physiol. Soc., Am. Soc. Clin. Investigation, Am. Inst. Nutrition, Soc. Exptl. Biology and Medicine. Home: 30 Farragut Rd Scarsdale NY 10583-7206 Office Phone: 212-551-2516. Office Fax: 212-687-2339. Business E-Mail: rrivlin@ifcp.us.

RIZER, MAGGIE, model; b. Watertown, NY, Jan. 9, 1978; Model Elite Modeling Agy.; appeared in ads for Calvin Klein, Versace, the Gap. Actor(guest appearances): (TV series) Sex and the City, The Victoria's Secret Fashion Show, 2001, America's Top Model, 2003. Office: Elite Premier 111 E 22nd St New York NY 10010

RIZKALLAH, MORRIS Z. translator; b. Cairo, Nov. 24, 1945; arrived in U.S., 1975; s. Zachari Rizkallah and Hanem Morcos Ghabbour; m. Nadia Elkes Girgis, Aug. 20, 1947; children: Matta, Mouhab, Christine. BS in Mech. Engring., Helwan U., Cairo, 1967; MS in Engring. Mgmt., Fla. Inst. Tech., 1981. Mech. engr. U.S. Army Armament R&D Command, Dover, NJ, 1979—85; translator Dept. Justice, N.Y.C., 1999—. With U.S. Army, 1975—78.

RIZOWY, CARLOS GUILLERMO, lawyer, educator, political analyst; b. Sarandi Grande, Uruguay, Mar. 5, 1949; arrived in U.S., 1973, naturalized, 1981; s. Gerszon and Eva (Visnia) R.; m. Charlotte Gordon, Mar. 14, 1976; children: Brian Isaac, Yael Deborah, Michal Evie. BA, Hebrew U., Jerusalem, 1971; MA, U. Chgo., 1975, PhD, 1981; JD, Chgo. Kent Coll. Law, Ill. Inst. Tech., 1983. Bar: Ill. 1983, U.S. Dist. Ct. (no. dist.) Ill. 1983, U.S. Ct. Appeals (7th cir.) 1983. Asst. prof. polit. sci. Roosevelt U., Chgo., 1982-89, chmn. dept. polit. sci., 1983-86, dir. internat. studies program, 1986-89; mng. ptnr. Ray, Rizowy & Fleischer, Chgo., 1983-90; ptnr. corp. law dept. Gottlieb and Schwartz, 1990-92; ptnr. Levenfeld, Eisenberg, Janger, Glassberg, Samotny & Halper, 1993-94; of counsel Sonnenschein, Nath & Rosenthal, 1994—2004; internat. bus. cons., 2004—. Hon. consul of Uruguay, Chgo., 1994—; adj. assoc. prof. Spertus Coll. Judaica, Chgo., 1984—; weekly polit. analyst on Mid. East, internat. law and fgn. policy, resource specialist Sta. WBEZ Pub. Radio and BBC L.Am.; mem. panel of arbitrators of Mediation and Arbitration Ctr., Internat. Arbitration Ct. for Mercosur Bolsa de Comercio, Uruguay, 1999—; gen. counsel Assn. Iberoamerican Consuls, 2003-; internat. bus. cons., 2004-. Author: Avoiding Premises Liability Suits by Improving Security, 1991, Middle East Security: Five Areas to Watch, 1997, Latin American Business Cultures, 2004. V.p., resource specialist to exec. com. Orgn. Children of Holocaust Survivors, Chgo., 1982; pres. Assn. Children Holocaust Survivors, 1986-91; pres. bd. dirs. Soviet Jewry Legal Advocacy Ctr., 1986-88; rsch. com. Nat. Strategy Forum, bd. dirs. UN Assn. U.S., 1985-89; mem. cmty. rels. com. Jewish Fedn. Met. Chgo., 1983-84; mem. adv. bd., chmn. internat. affairs commn. Am. Jewish Congress, Chgo., 1983-85, chmn. subcom. for Israel, 1986-88; mem. Nat. Spkrs. Bur. United Jewish Appeal, Nat. Spkrs. Bur. Devel. Corp. for Israel; spkr. to CEOs The Exec. Com., 1980-; mem. adv. bd. Chgo. Action for Soviet Jewry, 1983-85; bd. dirs. Am. Friends of Hebrew U., Chgo., 1984-86, Florence Heller Jewish Cmty. Ctr., 1986-88; mem. human rights com. Anti-Defamation League, 1986, bd. dirs., 1989—; bd. dirs. Bd. Jewish Edn., 1989-91, Hispanic Coalition for Jobs, 1991-94; chmn. univ. educators divsn. Jewish United Fund, 1988-90; mem. consular corp. adv. bd. Internat. Vis. Ctr. Chgo., 1995—, com. fgn. affairs Chgo. Coun. Fgn. Rels., 1994—. Scholar Hebrew U., 1967-72, U. Chgo., 1972-78, Hillman Found., 1978, Peter Volid Found., 1980; recipient Globalist award Heritage Internat. Trade Assn., 1997. Mem. ATLA, ABA (chmn. bus. com. 1993-95), Assn. Ibero-Am. Consuls of Chgo., Ill. State Bar Assn., Chgo. Bar Assn. (internat. trade com.), Latin Am. Bar Assn., Nat. Hispanic Bar Assn., Am. Immigration Lawyers Assn., Am. Polit. Sci. Assn., Am. Judicature Soc., Exec. Club Chgo., Internat. Platform Assn., Wexner Heritage Found., Am. Forum, Latin Am. C. of C. (bd. dirs. 1991—, gen. counsel 1992—), Anshe Emet Congregation, Masons. Office: Sonnenschein Nath & Rosenthal 8000 Sears Tower Chicago IL 60606 E-mail: crizowy@hotmail.com.

RIZZETTA, CAROLYN TERESA, musical instrument, sound recording entrepreneur; b. Chgo., June 22, 1942; d. Frank Thomas and Teresa Margaret (Sylvester) Peter; m. Samuel Charles Rizzetta, Apr. 23, 1966. Student, Art Inst. Chgo., 1961-63; BA, Rosary Coll., 1964, MLS, 1965. Reference librarian Art Dept. Chgo. Pub. Library, 1965; freelance illustrator Macmillan Pub. Co., N.Y.C., 1966; registrar, cataloger Kalamazoo (Mich.) Pub. Mus., 1967; asst. librarian Def. Nuclear Agy., Washington, 1968-69; serials cataloger Library of Congress, Washington, 1970-73, with intern, 1971-72; head of serials U. Va., Charlottesville, 1974-77; musical instrument maker Valley Head, W.Va., 1978-83; bus. mgr. Rizzetta Music, Inwood, W.Va., 1984—. Illustrator Invertebrate Zoology, 1969. Mem. Am. Craft Council, Guild of Am. Luthiers. Avocations: photography, gardening, hiking. Home and Office: Rizzetta Music PO Box 530 Inwood WV 25428-0530

RIZZI, JOSEPH VITO, banker; b. Berwyn, Ill., Dec. 5, 1949; s. Joseph and Mary Catherine (Mancini) R.; m. Candace Kunz, June 24, 1972; children: Jennifer, Joseph, Sammantha. BS in Commerce summa cum laude, DePaul U., 1971; MBA, U. Chgo., 1973; JD magna cum laude, U. Notre Dame, 1976. Bar: Ill. 1976. Law clk. to judge U.S. Dist. Ct. (no. dist.) Ill., 1976—77; exec. v.p. T.B.R. Enterprises, Inc., Downers Grove, Ill., 1977—83; mng. dir., exec. v.p. ABN AMRO, N.Y.C., 1983—. Mem. Delta Epsilon Sigma. Roman Catholic. Home: 287 Bartram Rd Riverside IL 60546-1886 Office: Gustav Mahlerlaan 10 HQ 2040 ABN/Amro Bank 1082 PP Amsterdam Netherlands Office Phone: 31-20-629-0396. E-mail: joe.rizzi@abnamro.com.

RIZZO, JAMES, editor; b. Tulsa, Nov. 1, 1957; s. Vincent Joseph Rizzo and Bonnie Merceri; m. Candace Darlene Flynn, Aug. 5, 1978. Asst. mgr. wholesale parts dept. Hoffman Enterprises, East Hartford, Conn., 1986—95; editor Rod & Custom Mag. Primedia, Anaheim, Calif., 1995—. Product devel./mktg. cons. Flor Techs., Garden Grove, Calif., 2003—. Associate editor: Street & Custom Rodding Illustrated. Active mem. ASPCA, 1999—2004. Recipient Superior Svc. Award, BBB, 1994. Mem.: Rd. Agts. (corr.). Republican. Southern Baptist. Avocations: custom automotive fabrication, automotve paint & body work, metal working, sculpturing. Office: Primedia 2400 E Katella Ave 11th Floor Anaheim CA 92806

RIZZO, JOYCE A. environmental services executive; CEO Leak-X Environ Corp, 1990—. Office: Lexicon Environmental PO Box 2470 West Chester PA 19380-0301

RIZZO, RAYMOND S. advertising executive; Chmn. Clarion Mktg. and Comm., Inc., Greenwich, Conn. Office: Clarion Mktg & Comm Inc 5 Greenwich Office Park Greenwich CT 06831-5128

RIZZO, RONALD STEPHEN, lawyer; b. Kenosha, Wis., July 15, 1941; s. Frank Emmanuel and Rosalie (Lo Cicero); m. Mary Rizzo; children: Ronald Stephen Jr., Michael Robert. BA, St. Norbert Coll., 1963; JD, Georgetown U., 1965, LLM in Taxation, 1966. Bar: Wis. 1965, Calif. 1967, Ill. 1999. Assoc. Kindel & Anderson, L.A., 1966-71, ptnr., 1971-86, Jones & Day, L.A., 1986—93, Chgo., 1993—. Bd. dirs. Guy LoCicero & Son Inc., Kenosha, Oaks Country Club Enterprises, Bristol, Wis. Contbg. editor ERISA Litigation Reporter, 1994-99; mem. internat. adv. editl. bd. Jour. Pensions Mgmt. and Mktg. Schulte zur Hausen fellow Inst. Internat. and Fgn. Trade Law, Georgetown U., 1966. Fellow Am. Coll. Tax Counsel, Am. Coll. Employee Benefits Counsel (charter); mem. ABA (chmn. com. on employee benefits sect. on taxation 1988-89, vice chair com. on govt. submissions 1995-99), Los Angeles County Bar Assn. (chmn. com. on employee benefits sect. on taxation 1977-79, exec. com. 1977-78, 90-92), State Bar Calif. (co-chmn. com. on employee benefits sect. on taxation 1980), West Pension Conf. (steering com. L.A. chpt. 1980-83). Avocations: reading, golf, travel. Home: 1040 N Lake Shore Dr #19C Chicago IL 60611-6164 Office: Jones Day 77 W Wacker Ste 3500 Chicago IL 60601-1692 Business E-Mail: rsrizzo@jonesday.com.

RIZZUTO, LEANDRO PETER, consumer products company executive; b. N.Y.C., Apr. 10, 1938; s. Julian and Josephine (Rizzo) Rizzuto; children: Leandro P. Rizzuto Jr., Denis, Rita. Student, St. Johns U. Pres., chmn. bd. Conair Corp., Edison, N.J., 1959—. Bd. dirs. St. Jude's Children's Hosp., Memphis. Named Humanitarian of Yr., Cabrini Hosp., 1985; recipient Man of Yr. award, Boys Town of Italy, 1980, Achievement award, Italian Legions of Merit, 1983; fellow faculty, U. Bridgeport, 1984. Mem.: Columbus Club N.Y.C. Roman Catholic. Office: Conair Corp 1 Cummings Point Rd Stamford CT 06902-7901

RIZZUTO, RICHARD PETER, entrepreneur; s. Richard S. and Theresa A. Rizzuto; m. Alexis C. Koch, Apr. 30, 2004. BS, Rider U., Lawrenceville, NJ, 1996. Owner, CEO R.P. Rizzuto Enterprises, New Vernon, NJ, 1997—2000; sr. ptnr. RPR Mktg. Solutions, NYC, 2001—. Hon. co-chmn. Nat. Rep. Congress Com., 2003. Recipient Nat. Leadership award, Nat. Rep. Com., 2003. Mem.: Advt. Club NY, Exec. Assn. NJ. Avocations: skiing, skydiving, wine tasting. Office: RPR Mktg Solutions 22 W 21st Ste 801 New York NY 10010 Office Phone: 212-352-9090 3. Fax: 212-352-9099. E-mail: rick@RPRmarketingsolutions.com.

ROACH, JAMES CLARK, government official; b. Charleston, W. Va., Sept. 29, 1943; m. Susan Roelke Roach, June 27, 1970; children: Edward J., Andrew A. BA in Social Studies and History, W. Va. Wesleyan Coll., 1965; MA in Am. History, W. Va. U. Historian Harpers Ferry (W. Va.) Nat. Hist. Pk., 1967-68, 70-72; chief interpretation resource mgmt. Ft. Frederica Nat. Monument, St. Simons Island, Ga., 1972-74; asst. chief interpretation visitor svcs. Colonial Nat. Hist. Pk., Yorktown, Va., asst. chief interpretation, visitor svc. Jamestown, Va.; chief interpretation visitor svcs. Gettysburg (Pa.) Nat. Mil. Pk., Eisenhower Nat. Hist. Site, 1981-94; site mgr. Eisenhower Nat. Hist. Site, 1995—2001; sch.-to-work coord. Adams County Bus. Edn. Partnership, Gettysburg, Pa., 2001—. Sec. Gettysburg Peace Celebration Commn. Inc. (former bd. dirs.); sec. Tri-County Econ. Edn. Found. With U.S. Army, 1968-70, Vietnam. Recipient Freeman Tilden award Mid-Atlantic Region Interpreter of Yr., 1984, Ea. Superior Performance award Nat. Park and Monument Assn., 1985, Spl. Events award GETT Travel Coun. award, 1986, 87. Mem. Assn. Nat. Pk. Rangers, Lincoln Fellowship Pa. (sec., past pres.), Adams County Torch Club (past pres.), Rotary (bd. dirs. Gettysburg club). Lutheran. Avocations: gardening, reading, fishing, stamp collecting/philately. Home: 84 Knoxlyn Orrtanna Rd Gettysburg PA 17325-7215 Office: Adams County Bus Edn Partnership 18 Carlisle St Ste 203 Gettysburg PA 17325 E-mail: jsroach@cvn.net.

ROACH, JAMES RICHARD, university president; b. Lynn, Mass., July 29, 1932; married. BS in Edn. cum laude, Boston Coll., 1957; postgrad., St. John's Coll., Brighton, Mass., 1963; certificat d'etude, U. Geneva, Switzerland, 1969; PhD in World Religions, Boston U., 1972; postgrad., Harvard U. Inst. Ednl. Mgmt., summer 1978. Tchr. Annotto Bay Coll., Jamaica, West Indies, 1957-58, Coll. Ctr., Salem State Coll., 1965-69; tchr. grad. sch. St. John's and Boston Univs., 1970-72; tchr. divsn. grad. studies Salem State Coll., 1972-73, North Adams State Coll., 1974-75, tchr. dept. philosophy, 1973-76, dir. acad. counseling svcs., 1973-76, acad. dean, 1976-78, v.p. acad. affairs, 1978-86, acting pres., 1984; interim vice chancellor acad. affairs Mass. Bd. Regents, 1980-81; pres. U.Maine, Presque Isle, 1986-92, Western Conn. State U., Danbury, 1992—. Bd. dirs. Savs. Bank Danbury; state rep. Am. Assn. State Colls. and Univs., chair com. acad. affairs, 1991-92, mem. task force on bldg. polit. support, 1991-92; chmn. reaccreditation vis. com. Castleton (Vt.) State Coll., 1991; mem Trustee Task Force on Rsch. and Grad. Edn.; mem. State of Maine Legislature's Spl. Commn. to Study and Evaluate the Status of Edn. Reform in Maine, 1990; mem. Univ. Sys./State Govt. Partnership Policy Group, 1989—, Mass.Bd. Regents Design Team for Collective Bargaining,

1983, Gov.'s Edn. Task Force, 1982-86, Mass. Bd. Regents Adv. Task Force on Program Rev., 1982-86; mem. Mass. State Coll. Sys. Task Force for Devel. Skills, 1977, Task Force for Profl. Devel., 1978, Pers. Mgmt. Adv. Com., 1979; dir. Maine Devel. Found., 1989-92; pres. Maine Higher Edn.Coun., 1989-92; chmn. bd. dirs. Maine Rsch. and Productivity Ctr., 1988-92; coord.-tchr. Monroe Ednl. Release Program, 1973-77; chmn. Mass. State Coll. Ad Hoc Com., 1979; corporator North Adams State Coll. Found., 1981-86; dir. acad. program evaluation project North Adams State Coll., 1977-82; cons. Wang Inst. Grad. Studies, 1983; state rep. Am. Assn. State Colls. and Univs. Acad. Affairs Resource Ctr. Assocs., 1982-86; presenter papers, spkr. various orgns. and confs. Bd. trustees United Way of No. Fairfield County, Inc.; mem. exec. bd. dirs. No. Maine Regional Planning Commn./Econ. Devel. Dist., 1987—; bd. dirs. Maine/Loring Assn., 1986—; bd. dirs. Croissant Club No. Berkshire County, 1984-86. With USN, 1952-53. Mem. Danbury C. of C. (bd. dirs.), Am. Acad. Religion, Am. Assn. Higher Edn.,Am. Assn. Colls. Tchr. Edn., Assn. Am. Colls., Internat. Assn. Univ. Pres., Pi Lamba Theta. Home: 177 Lake Pl S Danbury CT 06810-7264 Office: Western Conn State Univ 181 White St Danbury CT 06810-6826

ROACH, JAMES ROBERT, retired political science educator; b. Rock Rapids, Iowa, Aug. 25, 1922; s. Paul Ramsey and Doris (Kline) R. BA, U. Iowa, 1943; AM, Harvard U., 1948, PhD, 1950. Mem. faculty, adminstrn. U. Tex., Austin, 1949—, prof. govt., 1965-95, prof. emeritus, 1995—, dir. spl. programs, 1965-69, vice provost, dean interdisciplinary programs, 1971-72, dean divsn. gen. and comparative studies, 1972-74; counselor for cultural affairs Am. embassy, New Delhi, 1974-78. Fulbright vis. lectr. polit. sci. Rajasthan U., India, 1961-62; mem. Bd. Fgn. Scholarships, 1965-74, chmn., 1969-71; mem. U.S. Commn. for UNESCO, 1966-69. With USNR, 1943-46. Fulbright rsch. grantee, Australia, 1951-52, Ford Found. fgn. fellow, India, 1956-57. Mem. Assn. Asian Studies, Phi Beta Kappa, Kappa Tau Alpha, Sigma Delta Chi, Phi Kappa Psi. Democrat. Congregationalist. Home: 8604 Dorotha Ct Austin TX 78759-8113 Office: U Tex Dept Govt Austin TX 78712-1087

ROACH, JOHN D. building products company executive; b. West Palm Beach, Fla., Dec. 3, 1943; s. Benjamin Browning and Margaret (York) R.; m. Pam Flebbe, Dec. 29, 1967 (div. Aug. 1981); children: Vanessa, Alexandra; m. Elizabeth Louise Phillips, Aug. 28, 1982; children: Bruce Phillips, Bryce Phillips, Brian Phillips. BS in Indsl. Mgmt., MIT, 1965; MBA, Stanford U., 1967. Dir. mgmt. acctg. and info. systems Ventura div. Northrop Corp., Thousand Oaks, Calif., 1967-70; co-founder, mgr. Northrop Venture Capital, Century City, Calif., 1970-71; v.p., dir. Boston Consulting Group, Boston and Menlo Park, Calif., 1971-80; v.p., world-wide strategic mgmt. practice mng. officer Booz, Allen, Hamilton, Houston, 1980—83, San Francisco, 1980—83; vice chmn., mng. dir. Braxton Assocs., Houston, 1983-87; sr. v.p., chief fin. officer Manville Corp., Denver, 1987-88, exec. v.p. ops., 1988-91; pres. Manville Bldg. Products Group, Denver, 1988-90, Manville Mining and Minerals Group, Denver, 1990-91, Celite Corp., Denver, 1990-91; chmn., pres., chief exec. officer Fibreboard Corp., Walnut Creek, Calif., 1991—96; chmn., pres., CEO Stonegate Resources, Dallas, 1997—2001, Builders First-Source, Inc., Dallas, 1998—2001; chmn., CEO Stonegate Internat., Dallas, 2001—; bd. dirs. PMI Group, 1997—; chmn. Unidare U.S., Muskogee, Okla., 2002—. Bd. dirs. Kaiser Aluminum, 2002—, URS Corp., 2003—, Mat. Scis., 2003—, NCI Bldg. Systems, Wash. Internat., Am. Stock Exch., Thompson PBE, Magma Power, Fibreboard Corp., Builders First Source. Author: Strategic Management Handbook, 1983. Bd. dirs. Opera Colo., Denver, 1987-91, Bay Area Coun., San Francisco, 1991-96, Dallas Symphony, 1996-03, mem. exec. com., 1996-03; bd. trustees Alta Bates Med. Ctr.; mem. exec. com. San Francisco Opera Assn. Mem.: MIT Alumni Club, Stanford Grad. Sch. Bus. Club, Dallas Country Club, Cordillera Country Club (Colo.), Beaver Creek (Colo.) Country Club, Red Sky Golf Club (Wolcott, Colo.), Preston Trail Golf Club (Dallas), Cherry Hills Country Club (Englewood, Colo.). Avocations: skiing, hunting, golf. Home: 4278 Bordeaux Ave Dallas TX 75205-3718 Office: Stonegate Internat 100 Crescent Ct 7th Fl Dallas TX 75201

ROACH, JOHN HENDEE, JR., bank executive, investment banker, financial service executive; b. N.Y.C., Oct. 24, 1941; s. John Hendee and Julia (Casey) R.; m. Joan Hayden Muchmore, Sept. 23, 1972; children: Hayden, Cameron, John, Lauriston, Schuyler. BA, Washington and Jefferson Coll., 1964; postgrad., Aspen Inst., 1987, Harvard U., 1989. With Chem. Bank, N.Y.C., 1968-71, sr. v.p. corp. bank, 1972-87, mng. dir. corp. fin., 1987-92, ret., 1992; sr. mng. dir., vice chmn. The Geneva Cos., N.Y.C., 1992-94; sr. mng. dir., client mgmt. and mktg. Am. Internat. Group, N.Y.C., 1994-97; sr. mng. dir. Reliance Nat., N.Y.C., 1998-99, JP Morgan Pvt. Bank, Greenwich, Conn., 2000—01, Jamison Prince Asset Mgmt., 2003—. Bd. dirs. Strategic Capital Resources Inc., Boca Raton, Fla., PrivaTechnologies, Arlington, Va., MBAs 4 N.Y.C. Capt. U.S. Army, 1964-66. Mem. Round Hill Club. Republican. Roman Catholic. Home: 16 Oakwood Ln Greenwich CT 06830-3909 Office: 530 Fifth Ave New York NY 10036 Office Phone: 212-944-7153. E-mail: jhr.jr@att.net.

ROACH, JOHN VINSON, II, retail company executive; b. Stamford, Tex., Nov. 22, 1938; s. John V. and Agnes M. (Hanson) R.; m. Barbara Jean Wiggin, Mar. 31, 1960; children: Amy, Lori. BA in Physics and Math., Tex. Christian U., 1961, MBA, 1965. V.p. Radio Shack, 1972-75, Radio Shack Mfg., 1975-78; exec. v.p. Radio Shack, 1978-80; gen. mgr. data processing Tandy Corp., Ft. Worth, 1967-73, pres., from 1980, CEO, from 1981, chmn., 1982-99. Chmn. bd. Justin Ind., 1999—2001. Bd. dirs. Van Cliburn Found.; chmn. bd. Tex. Christian U. Mem. Ft. Worth Club, City Club, Colonial Country Club. Office: River Crest Country Club 400 Throck Morton Ste 480 Fort Worth TX 76102-2819

ROACH, KATHLEEN LYNN, lawyer; b. Santa Monica, Calif., Nov. 6, 1962; d. William Russell and Margaret Rose (Balogh) R. AB, U. Calif., Berkeley, 1982; JD, U. Chgo., 1985. Bar: Ill. 1985, Calif. 1988, U.S. Dist. Ct. (no. dist.) Ill. 1985, U.S. Dist Ct. (ea. dist.) Calif. 1988, U.S. Ct. Appeals (7th cir.) 1985. Assoc. Sidley & Austin, Chgo., 1985-93, ptnr., 1993—. Bd. dirs. AIDS Legal Coun., Chgo., 1990—; bd. govs. Chgo. Coun. of Lawyers, 1992—. Office: Sidley & Austin 1 S First National Plz Chicago IL 60603-2000

ROACH, KEVIN JOSEPH, set designer; b. Alton, Ill., July 4, 1955; s. John Thomas and Carol Irene (Roy) Roach. BFA, Boston U., 1978. Freelance set designer, Boston, 1985—85; prodn. asst. Am. Repertory Theatre, Cambridge, Mass., 1981—84; set designer Cir. Repertory Lab, N.Y.C., 1986—92, 52d St. Project, N.Y.C., NY, 1988—, Tubes Blue Man Group, 1991, Fire Zone @ Rockefeller Plz., 2000, Marionette Theatre in Ctrl. Pk., 1998—. Student Lester Polakov's Studio and Forum for Stage Design, 1986—88; theatre constrn. and tech. ops. Boston Shakespeare Co., Boston, 1978; debut set designer and cons. Cir, Repertory Lab, N.Y.C., 1992. Co-author: 57 Pick-Up: The Replication Manual of the 52d St. Project, 1994; contbg. author: City Streets: N.Y.C., 2002. Mem.: Internat. Assn. Stage and Tech. Employees Local 52. Avocations: tai chi, hiking, swimming, snorkeling, white water rafting. Home: 162 Bergen St Brooklyn NY 11217 Office Phone: 917-609-2572. E-mail: kjoro2003@yahoo.com.

ROACH, MARGARET, editor-in-chief; Editor., mgr. N.Y. Times; garden columnist Newsday Newspapers; creative developer Martha Stewart Living Omnimedia, 1995; gardening editor Martha Stewart Living; mgr. devel. and execution marthastewart.com; editor-in-chief Martha Stewart Living, N.Y.C., 2001—. Author: A Way to Garden, 1998 (Garden Writers Assn. Am. Best Book, 1998). Office: Martha Stewart Living Omni Advt New York NY 10036

ROACH, MARGOT RUTH, retired biophysicist, educator; b. Moncton, N.B., Can., Dec. 24, 1934; d. Robert Dickson and Katherine (McMillan) R.; m. Franklyn St. Aubyn House, Dec. 20, 1994 (wid. Feb. 2000). B.Sc. in Math. and Physics with honors, U. N.B., Fredericton, Can., 1955; MD, C.M. cum laude, McGill U., Montreal, Can., 1959; PhD in Biophysics, U. Western Ont., Can., 1963; D.Sc. (hon.), U. N.B., St. John, Can., 1981. Jr. intern Victoria Hosp., London, Ont., Can., 1959-60, fellow in cardiology, 1962-63, asst. resident in medicine, 1963-64, Toronto Gen. Hosp., 1964-65; mem. faculty, dept. biophysics U. Western Ont., London, Ont., Can., 1965—, head dept. biophysics, 1970-78, prof., 1971-98, asst. prof. medicine, 1965-72, assoc. prof., 1972-78, prof., 1978-98, prof. emeritus Biophysics & Med., 1998. Mem. staff dept. medicine Victoria Hosp., 1967-72, U. Hosp., London, 1972-98; Commonwealth vis. sci., dept. applied math. theoretical physics Cambridge U., 1975; vis. sci. Bioengring. Inst., Chonqing U., People's Republic of China, 1991; mem. bioengring. grants com. Med. Rsch. Coun. Can., 1993-96; cons. and lectr. in field. Mem. editl. bd.: Imprints. Active civic orgns. and coms. including Univ. Rsch. Coun., 1976-79; mem. interview bd. London Conf. of United Ch., 1967-90; steward United Ch. of Can., 1967-73, elder, 1973-82, mem. com. on ministry vocations, 2004—, mem. imprints editl. bd., 2004—, chair unified bd. Tatamagouche Pastoral Charge, 2001—; chmn. stewardship devel. com. Colborne St. United Ch., 1990-93. Recipient A. Wilmer Duff prize in physics U. N.B., 1955, Cushing prize in pediatrics, 1959, Ciba Found. award for research in aging, 1959, Teaching award Faculty of Medicine U. Western Ont., 1990, Dean's award, 1997, Women of Distinction award YWCA, 1997; Med. Research Council fellow U. Western Ont., 1960-62, Arthur Guyton award Internat. Soc. Cardiovascular Medicine and Sci., 1997; numerous other fellowships and grants in medicine. Fellow Royal Coll. Physicians (Can.), Am. Coll. Cardiology (Young Investigator's award 1963); mem. Can. Physiol. Soc., Can. Cardiovascular Soc. (off council), Can. Clin. Investigation Soc. (council 1980-84), Can. Biophys. Soc., Can. Soc. Internal Medicine. Address: RR #1 104 Sea Shore Dr Tatamagouche NS Canada B0K 1V0 E-mail: mroach@pchg.net.

ROACH, MAUREEN S. primary school educator; Bachelors Degree, Boston U.; Masters Degree, U. Mass. Primary sch. educator Lyndon Pilot Sch., West Roxbury, Mass. Presenter Nat. Bd. Insts. Mem.: Nat. Bd. for Profl. Tchg. Stds. (bd. mem.). Avocations: cross country skiing, reading. Office: Patrick Lydon School 20 Mount Vernon St West Roxbury MA 02132-2809

ROACH, PAM, state legislator; m. Jim Roach; 5 children. BA in History, Brigham Young U., 1970. Mem. Wash. Legislature, Olympia, 1990—, mem. econ. devel. fin. authority com., mem. energy, tech., and telecom. com., mem. jud. com., mem. waysn and means com., mem. sentencing guidelines commn., mem. joint com. on pension policy, mem. statute law com. Guardian mem. Boy Scouts Am.; bd. dirs. Auburn Food Bank; past mem. Gov.'s Juvenile Issues Task Force; mem. local coun. Boy Scouts Am.; past mem. adv. com. Soos Creek Cmty. Plan Tech., Maple Valley Cmty. Summit. Mem. Am. Legis. Exch. Coun., Nat. Conf. State Legislatures, Auburn C. of C. Republican. Office: 202 Irving Newhouse Ofc Olympia WA 98504-0001

ROACH, RALPH LEE, human services and rehabilitation consultant; b. Silver Spring, Md., Mar. 27, 1957; s. William A. and Mary B. (Collins) R.; m. Susan Diane Schirmacher, Aug. 17, 1985. BA, Messiah Coll., 1982; MS, Shippensburg U., 1985; postgrad., Kennedy-We. U., 1992—. Cert. rehab. counselor. Inventory controller Messiah Coll., Grantham, Pa., 1977-85; therapist, crisis interviewer Stevens Mental Health, Carlisle, Pa., 1983-86; psychotherapist, teenline counselor Holy Spirit Cmty. Mental Health Inst., Camp Hill, Pa., 1986—; presentor, cons. Lebanon (Pa.) Valley Coll., 1986; vocat. tng. mgr. Ctr. for Indsl. Tng., Mechanicsburg, Pa., 1985-87; program mgr. living unltd. program U. Hosp. Rehab./Children Pa. U. Hosp. Milton S. Hershey Med. Ctr., Hershey, Pa., 1987-92; corp. officer, clin. dir. Avalon Affiliates Rehab. Consultants, Inc. (now MRW, Inc.), Duncannon, Pa., 1993-95, MRW, Inc., 1995-97; behavior specialist and mobile therapist United Staffing Svcs./Edgewater Psychiat. Ctr., 1998-99; teenline counselor Holy Spirti Hosp./E. Pennsboro H.S., Camp Hill, Pa., 1999—. Faculty instr. dept. psychology Elizabethtown Coll., 1987; presenter at profl. confs. Edn. dir. Cumberland Valley Ch., Dillsburg, Pa., 1980-83; presentor Gov.'s Com. on Handicapped, Harrisburg, Pa., 1986; presentor various state/nat. confs. on vocat. rehab., Harrisburg, 1986—. Mem. ACA, Am. Acad. Rehab. Medicine, Pa. Specialists in Group Work, Pa. Crisis Intervention Assn., Pa. Assn. Rehab. Facilities, Keystone State Head Injury Found. Presbyterian. Avocations: boating, fishing, black powder hunting, gardening, civil war history and curio collecting. Office: Holy Spirit Hosp 503 N 21st St Camp Hill PA 17011-2288 Home: 325 S Sporting Hill Rd Mechanicsburg PA 17050-3062 E-mail: rroach@057yahoo.com.

ROACH, WESLEY LINVILLE, lawyer, insurance executive; b. Norlina, N.C., Oct. 8, 1931; s. Joseph Franklin and Florence G. (Sink) R.; m. Mary Jon Gerald, Aug. 13, 1955; children: Gerald, Mary Virginia. BS, Wake Forest U., 1953, JD, 1955. Bar: N.C. 1955. With Pilot Life Ins. Co., Greensboro, N.C., 1958-86, also bd. dirs.; sr. v.p., gen. counsel Jefferson-Pilot Life Ins. Co., Greensboro, 1986-88; sec. Great Ea. Lif. Ins. Co., 1975-85; of counsel Smith, Anderson, Blount, Dorsett, Mitchell & Jernigan, Attys. at Law, Raleigh, N.C., 1988—. Former chmn. bd. dirs. N.C. Life and Accident and Health Ins. Guaranty Assn., Va. Life, Accident and Health Guaranty Assn., S.C. Life, Accident and Health Guaranty Assn.; sec. JP Investment Mgmt. Co., Jefferson-Pilot Equity Sales, Inc., Spl. Services Agy., Inc., 1974-84; mem. exec. com., bd. dirs. N.C. Ins. Edn. Found., 1978—; trustee In-Home Care, Inc., 1999—, chmn., 2001. Mem. fin. com. Greensboro United Fund, 1964-65; mem. fin. com. Greensboro 1st Bapt. Ch., 1963-66, 83-86, chmn., 1983-85, chmn. bd. deacons, 1974-76, 80-81; nat. chmn. alumni coun. coll. fund Wake Forest U., 1971-76, pres. nat. alumni coun., 1975-76, trustee univ., 1978-82, emeritus trustee, 1999—; trustee So. Bapt. Theol. Sem., Louisville, 1973-84; trustee Bapt. Retirement Homes N.C., Inc., 1992-2000, chmn., 1993-94, emeritus trustee, 2001-; trustee In Home Care, Inc., 1997—, chmn., 2001; trustee Bapt. Retirement Homes Found. 2001-. With USNR, 1955-58. Mem. ABA, N.C. Bar Assn., Raleigh Bar Assn., Assn. Life Ins. Counsel (bd. govs. 1984-88), Greensboro C. of C. (chmn. nat. legis. com. 1973—), Nat. Orgn. Life Guaranty Assn. (bd. dirs. 1982-87). Democrat. Home: PO Box 1690 601 Selma Rd Wendell NC 27591-8648 Office: 2500 First Union Capitol Ctr PO Box 2611 Raleigh NC 27602-2611 Office Phone: 919-821-6630.

ROACHE, PATRICK MICHAEL, JR., management consultant; b. Elizabeth, N.J., Oct. 8, 1946; s. Patrick Michael and Rose Marie (Remite) R. BS, St. Peter's Coll., 1969. Adminstrv. aide to a state assemblyman N.J. Assembly, N.J., 1969-71; supr. acctg. Dept. Pub. Works Newark, Newark, 1971-78, asst. to dir. pub. works, 1978-79, mgr. div. motors, 1979-84; mgmt. specialist Dept. Gen. Svcs., Newark, 1985-86, 2002; pvt. practice as mgmt. and fin. cons. Brick, N.J., 1986—. Mem. Lions (treas. 1983-86, pres. 1988-89). Republican. Roman Catholic. Home and Office: 170 Binnacle Rd Brick NJ 08723-6704 E-mail: proache@hotmail.com., proache@haywardnet.com.

ROADARMEL, STANLEY BRUCE, civilian military employee; b. Albion, NY, May 5, 1937; s. Kenneth A. and Catherine Louise (Bobel) R.; m. Carole Ann Hayes, Nov. 26, 1959; children: Karen Marie, Oscar Pacific, Ann Catherine, William Hayes. Student, Purdue U., 1956—58; BA, Syracuse U., 1962; grad., Squadron Officer Sch., 1965, Air Command Staff Coll., 1976, Indsl. Coll. Armed Forces, 1976; postgrad., Golden Gate U., 1976—78. Commd. 2d lt. USAF, 1962, advanced through grades to maj.; adminstrv., security and recruiting ops. officer Air Tng. Command, Tex. and W.Va., 1962-69; chief field maintenance Titan II ICBM Strategic Air Command, Davis Monthan AFB, Ariz., 1969-71, chief Hq SAC's 3901st Titan II maintenance evaluation team Vandenberg AFB, Calif., 1971-74, logistics staff officer, 1974-77, contract specialist, 1977-82, U.S. Air Forces Europe, Adana, Turkey, 1980-81; ret. USAF, 1982; launch complex constrn. contract negotiator, adminstr. NASA/USAF Space Shuttle Program, Lompoc, Calif., 1983-89, USAF Titan IV Space Booster, Vandenberg AFB, 1991-92; constrn. and maj. svcs. contract negotiator, adminstr. 30th Contracting Squadron USAF Space Command, Vandenberg AFB, 1992-2001; ret. active fed. svc., 2001. With Ctrl. Coast Profls., Mut. Profl. Counseling/Placement, Santa Maria, Calif., 1990-91. Author manual: Man Lifting Crane Operations, 1976 (Air Force Commendation award 1977); revision officer Air Force Manual 66-1 Maintenance Management, 1976 (Air Force Commendation award 1977); contbr. Strategic Air Command Manual 66-12 ICBM Maintenance Mgmt. Spkr. World Orgn. Ovulation Method, Calif., 1987—; pro life advocate, activist Am. Life League, Nat. Right to Life, 1980—; vol. Rep. Party, 1992—; marriage preparation instr. Cath. Archdiocese of LA, Santa Maria, 1995—; life mem. Holy Family Inst., Soc. St. Paul. Mem. NRA, Nat. Contract Mgmt. Assn., Air Force Assn. (life), Mil. Officers Assn. Am. (life), Disabled Am. Vets. (life), Assn. Air Force Missileers (life), Am. Legion, Couple to Couple League, The Heritage Found., Exptl. Aircraft Assn. Avocations: aviation, music, marksmanship, travel, literature. Home and Office: 4532 Glines Ave Santa Maria CA 93455-4313 Personal E-mail: csroadarmel@earthlink.net.

ROADEN, ARLISS LLOYD, retired higher education executive director, former university president; b. Bark Camp, Ky., Sept. 27, 1930; s. Johnie Samuel and Ethel Nora (Killian) R.; m. Mary Etta Mitchell, Sept. 1, 1951; children: Janice Arletta Roaden Skelton, Sharon Kay Roaden Vogt. Grad., Cumberland Coll., 1949; AB, Carson Newman Coll., 1951; MS, U. Tenn., 1958, EdD, 1961; PhD (hon.), Cumberland Coll., 1986; DLitt (hon.), Tusculum Coll., 1992. With Oak Ridge Inst. Nuclear Studies, 1957-59, Auburn U., 1961-62; mem. faculty Ohio State U., 1962-74, prof. edn., 1967-74, acting dean Coll. Edn., 1968-70, vice provost for research, dean Grad. Sch., 1970-74; pres. Tenn. Tech. U., 1974-85, pres. emeritus, 1985—; dir. Tenn. Higher Edn. Commn., Nashville, 1985-95, exec. dir. emeritus, 1995—. Summer vis. prof. Marshall U., 1961, U. So. Calif., 1964, Ind. U., 1967; cons. ednl. instns., 1961—; pres. Tenn. Coll. Assn., 1978; chmn. sci. and tech. com. Am. Assn. State Colls. and Univs., 1980; chmn. task force on program and instl. assessment State Higher Edn. Exec. Officers', 1987, pres. 1993-94, chmn. coun. postsecondary accreditation liaison com., 1986-88, exec. com., 1988-95, pres. elect 1992-93; mem. exec. bd. trustees Southern Assn. Colls. and Schs., 1986—, chair communications com., 1990—, mem. task force, 1990—; mem. Southern Regional Edn. Bd., 1985—, chmn. procedures com. for reviewing bylaw changes and revisions, 1988-89; mem. exec. com., state rep., treas., chair Internal Audit Com., 1990-91, Edn. Commn. States, 1987-90; mem. Tenn. Econ. Cabinet Coun., 1988—, chmn.m 1988-91, bd. dirs. 1988—, Fgn. Lang. Inst.; treas., chair Internal Audit Com., 1990-91; mem. Performance Standards in Vocat.-Tech. Edn. Working Group, U.S. Dept. Edn., 1990. Co-author: The Research Assistantship: Recommendations for Colleges and Universities, 1975, Cultures of the States: A Handbook on the Effectiveness of State Governments, 2003; editor: Problems of School Men in Depressed Urban Areas, 1967; contbr. articles to profl. jours. State chmn. Tenn. Cancer Soc. Crusade, 1986-88, bd. dirs., 1987—; mem. exec. bd., commr. Mid. Tenn. coun. Boy Scouts Am., 1987-88, mem. nat. coun., 1988—, chmn. scouts membership rels. com.; mem. Phi Delta Kappa Found., 1965—, past chmn. bd. govs., mem. futures and diamond jubilee coms., 1989—; chmn. Blue Ribbon Com. To Respond to Edn. Goals, 1990; bd. dirs. Nat. Project 714, 1986—, pres.-elect, 1987-88, chmn., 1988-89; pres. alumni assn. bd. Cumberland Coll., 1987-88, chmn. devel. bd., 1994—; adult Sunday sch. tchr. Woodmont Bapt. Ch., chmn. pers. com., 1989—, chmn. deacons, ch. moderator, 1998-99. With U.S. Army, 1951-53. Rsch.grantee Phi Delta Kappa Internat., 1968; named Disting. Alumnus Cumberland Coll., 1970; recipient Disting. Alumni and Faculty Centennial medallion Coll. Edn., 1970, Disting. Service award Coun. Grad. Students, 1974, both Ohio State U.; recipient Silver Beaver award Boy Scouts Am.; named Rotarian of Yr., 1984; Eagle Scout honoree Middle Tenn. Coun. Boy Scouts Am., 1989, others. Fellow Oxford Soc. Scholars; mem. AAAS, Am. Assn. Higher Edn., Acad. Polit. and Social Scis., Am. Ednl. Rsch. Assn. (chmn. publs. com. 1979-80), Nat. Soc. Study Edn., Nat. Assn. State Colls. and Land Grant Univs., Lions (bd. dirs. Nashville 1988-90, pres. 1991-92, zone chmn. 1992-93, dist. gov. 1996), Rotary (bd. dirs.), Order of Lion and Eagle, Phi Kappa Phi, Phi Delta Kappa (Disting. Svc. award Ohio State U. chpt. 1974), Kappa Phi Kappa, Kappa Delta Pi. Baptist.

ROADS, CURTIS, music educator, composer; b. Cleve., May 9, 1951; BA summa cum laude, U. Calif., San Diego, 1977; PhD, U. Paris, 1999. Editor, assoc. editor Computer Music Jour., MIT Press, Cambridge, Mass., 1978-2000; rsch. assoc. MIT, Cambridge, 1980-87; lectr. Harvard U., Cambridge, 1989, U. Paris 8, 1994-95; dir. pedagogy Les Ateliers UPIC, Paris, 1993-96; prof. U. Calif., Santa Barbara, 1996—, assoc. prof. media arts and tech., 2002—. Vis. prof. Oberlin (Ohio) Conservatory, 1991. Author: Foundations of Computer Music, 1985, The Music Machine, 1987, The Computer Music Tutorial, 1996, Field electronic music, 1981, Clang-Tint, 1994, Half-life, 1999, Tenth Vortex, 2000, Eleventh Vortex, 2001, Sculptor, 2002, Microsound, 2002; co-inventor Creatovox synthesizer. Office: Univ Calif Media Arts and Tech 3431 South Hall Santa Barbara CA 93106-6065 Business E-Mail: clang@create.ucsb.edu.

ROADY, ELSTON EDWARD (STEVE), political scientist, educator; b. Kane, Ill., Apr. 9, 1920; s. Thomas Golman Sr. and Lela Leone (Williams) Roady; m. Barbara Louise Elder, Dec. 27, 1945; children: Elizabeth Ellen Lines, Stephen Elston, Christopher Sr. BS, Ill. State U., 1942; MA, U. Ill., 1947, PhD, 1951. Instr. in polit. sci. Fla. State U., Tallahassee, 1947—49, asst. prof., 1951—54, assoc. prof., 1954—58, prof., 1959—84, prof. emeritus, 1984—. Exec. dir. Fla. Ctr. for Edn. in Politics, Tallahassee, 1957—77; cons. on election laws. Author: USA-USSR, Two Worlds in Conflict, 1958; co-author: Florida Votes, 1965, rev. edit., 1972; editor: (bull.) Politics in Fla., 1957—67. Treas. Tallahassee Jr. Mus., 1952; pres. Friends of Libr., Tallahassee, 1947—54. Col. (ret.) USAF. Named Disting. Alumni, Ill. State U., 1986. Mem.: Lions (treas. Tallahassee club 1988—91), Masons. Democrat. Methodist. Achievements include research in model campaign contributions and expenditures law. Avocation: stamp collecting/philately. Home: 1916 W Indian Head Dr Tallahassee FL 32301-5860

ROAF, ANDREE LAYTON, judge; b. Mar. 31, 1941; m. Clifton G. Roaf; 4 children. BS in Zoology, Mich. State U., 1962; JD with high honors, U. Ark., 1978; LLD (hon.), Mich. State U., 1996. Bar: Ark. 1978. Bacteriologist Mich. Dept. Health, Lansing, 1963—65; rsch. biologist FDA, Washington, 1965—69; staff asst. Pine Bluff (Ark.) Urban Renewal Agy., 1971—75; biologist Nat. Ctr. for Toxicological Rsch., Jefferson, Ark., 1978—79; assoc. Walker, Roaf, Campbell, Ivory & Dunklin, Little Rock, 1979—86, ptnr., 1986—95; assoc. justice Ark. Supreme Ct., Little Rock, 1995—96; appellate judge Ark. Ct. Appeals, 1997—. Editor: Ark. Law Rev. Mem. PTA bd. Forest Park Elem. Sch., 1972—74, 34th Ave. Sch., 1974—76, 1980—83, Southeast Jr. High, 1976—77; mem. ad hoc com. for voter registration Jefferson County, 1972—73; bd. trustees Southeast Ark. Arts and Scis. Ctr., 1972—75, sec., 1974—75, Pine Bluff OIC Bd., 1972—78, Pine Bluff Police-Cmty. Rels Task Force, 1973; mem. Jefferson County Com. on Black Adoptions, 1973—75, chmn., 1974—75; mem. Ark. Code of Ethics Commn., 1987, Friends of Sta. KRLE-FM, 1982—88, 1990—94, pres., 1985—86; trustee Winthrop Rockefeller Found., 1990—94; mem. Jefferson County Dem. Com., 1980—82; mem. vestry Grace Episcopal Ch., 1995—; bd. dirs. Ark. Coun. on Human Rels., 1972—73, Ark. for Arts, 1983, Ark. Student Loan Authority, 1977—81, Vocals, 1989—. Named Gayle Pettus Pontz outstanding Ark. woman lawyer, 1996; named to Ark. Black Hall of Fame, 1996; recipient disting. alumni award, Mich. State U., 1996. Mem.: ABA, W. Harold Flowers Law Soc., Jefferson County Bar Assn., Pulaski County Bar Assn. (chmn. hist. com. 1986—87), Ark. Bar Assn. (chmn. youth edn. com. 1979—80). Office: Justice Bldg 625 Marshall St Ste 1230 Little Rock AR 72201-1052

ROAF, WILLIAM LAYTON, professional football player; b. Pine Bluff, Ark., Apr. 18, 1970; s. Clifton George and Andree Yvonne (Layton) R. B.A. in Sociology, Louisiana Tech. Tackle New Orleans Saints, 1993—2001, Kansas City Chiefs, 2002—. Named to NFL Pro-Bowl, 1994—2000, 2002—03, 1990's All-Decade Team, Pro Football Hall of Fame. Episcopal. Office: One Arrowhead Dr Kansas City MO 64129

ROALOFS, LINDA A. language educator; b. Cin., Sept. 4, 1943; d. Stanley Randolph and Inis Frances (Prater) Brown; m. Roger Leonard Roalfs, Sept. 19, 1964; children: Scott, Christine, Karen, Eric, Katherine. BS in Edn., Ohio U., 1964; MS in Edn., U. Louisville, 1980. Tchr. English Parma City Schs., Ohio, 1964—65, St. Augustine Acad., Lakewood, 1967—71, St. Jerome, Fairdale, Ky., 1977—78, St. Martha, Louisville, 1978—83, Mercy Acad., 1983—99, Ky. Country Day, 2000—02. Chair fundraising com. Highview United Ministries, Louisville, 1999—2003; sec. RLS Enterprises (dba Papa John's Pizza), 1987—2003. Contbr. articles to newspapers. Grantee, Ky Shakespeare Festival, 1994—95. Avocations: scrapbooks, reading, travel, gardening.

ROAN, FORREST CALVIN, JR., lawyer; b. Waco, Tex., Dec. 18, 1944; s. Forrest Calvin and Lucille Elizabeth (McKinney) R.; m. Vickie Joan Howard, Feb. 15, 1969 (div. Dec. 1983); children: Amy Katherine, Jennifer Louise; m. Leslie D. Hampton Roan, Jan. 2, 1999. BBA, U. Tex., Austin, 1973, JD, 1976. Bar: Tex. 1976, U.S. Dist. Ct. (we. dist.) Tex. 1977, U.S. Dist. Ct. (so. dist.) Tex. 1998, U.S. Ct. Appeals (5th cir.) 1977, U.S. Supreme Ct. 1979, U.S. Ct. Appeals (11th cir.) 1981, U.S. Ct. Appeals (fed. cir.) 1998, U.S. Ct. Internat. Trade, 1998. Prin. Roan & Assocs., Austin, 1969-71; counsel, com. dir. Tex. Ho. of Reps., 1972-75; assoc. Heath, Davis & McCalla, Austin, 1975-78; prin. Roan & Gullahorn, P.C., Austin, 1978-85, Roan & Autrey (formerly Roan & Simpson), P.C., 1986-99; sr. ptnr. Cantey, Hanger, Roan & Autrey, 1999—2003; shareholder Winstead, Sechrest & Minick, P.C., Austin, 2003—. Bd. dirs. Lawyers Credit Union, chmn., 1982-83; bd. dirs. pub. law sect. State Bar Tex., 1980-84; trustee, Safeplace Found.; mem. Chancellor's Coun., U. Tex.; life mem. Mensa. With Tex. Army N.G., 1966-74. Fellow Tex. Bar Found., Travis County Bar Found. (founding fellow); mem. ABA, Tex. Assn. Def. Counsel, Tex. Assn. Bank Counsel, Def. Rsch. Inst., Travis County Bar Assn., Tex.-Mex. Bar Assn., Knights of the Symphony (Lord Chancellor 2003-04), Tex. Lyceum Assn. (v.p., bd. dirs. 1980-87), Austin C. of C., Austin Club, Headliners Club, Masons, Shriners (Parsons Masonic master 1976-77). Methodist. Office: Winstead Sechrest & Minick PC 401 Congress Ste 2100 Austin TX 78701 Office Phone: 512-370-2999. E-mail: froam@winstead.com.

ROARK, BARBARA ANN, librarian; b. Evanston, Ill., July 24, 1958; d. Edward B. and Ann H. Rowe; m. Paul E. Roark, Sept. 18, 1982; children: Sarah, John. BA in History, U. Ky., 1981, MLS, 1982. Dir. Hopkins County Madisonville (Ky.) Pub. Libr., 1983-85; ops. mgr. Wurzburg Inc., Nashville, 1985-91; dir. Spies Pub. Libr., Menominee, Mich., 1991-98, Franklin (Wis.) Pub. Libr., 1998—. V.p. adv. coun. Mid-Peninsula Libr. Coop., Mich., 1993-95, sec. adv. coun., 1991-93; chair tech. adv. com. Milwaukee County Federated Libr. Sys., 2001—. Grant writer Title II, 1994, Title I, 1995. Treas. Franklin Area Jr. Woman's Club. Recipient Cert. of Excellence Libr. of Mich., 1995, Cert. of Appreciation Menominee Area C. of C., 1998. Mem. ALA, Wis. Libr. Assn. (pers. and profl. concerns com. 1999—, Muriel Fuller award 2002), Spies Pub. Libr. Found., PEO, Order Ea. Star, U. Ky. Alumni Assn., Franklin Area Jr. Women's Club (treas. 1999—), Kiwanis (pres. Milw. suburban S.W. chpt. 2002—), Zeta Tau Alpha. Methodist. Avocations: golf, reading, cross stitching, travel. Office: Franklin Public Library 9151 W Loomis Rd Franklin WI 53132-9630 Office Phone: 414-425-8214. E-mail: barbara.roark@mcfls.org.

ROARK, JIMMY LEE, lawyer; b. Hazard, Ky., Dec. 5, 1948; s. John and Emma Lou (Fowler) R.; m. Deborah Louise McIntyre, July 6, 1983. BBA, Morehead State U., 1973; JD, U. Ky., 1977. Bar: Ky. 1977, US Dist. Ct. (ea. and we. dists.) Ky. 1979, US Ct. Appeals (6th cir.) 1979. Ptnr. Cook & Roark, Whitesburg, Ky., 1977—80; asst. county atty. Letcher County, 1978—80; ptnr. Barret, Haynes, May, Carter & Roark P.S.C., Hazard, 1980—2004, J.L. Roark & Assocs. PSC, Hazard, 2004—. Served with US Army, 1970-72. Mem. ABA, Assn. Trial Lawyers Am., Ky. Bar Assn., Ky. Acad. Trial Attys., Perry County Bar Assn. Office: JL Roark & Assocs PSC PO Box 898 272 E Main St Hazard KY 41702 Office Phone: 606-435-0712.

ROARK, ROBERT CAMERON, insurance broker; b. San Diego, Jan. 11, 1931; s. Alfred T. and Virginia J. Roark; m. Lois J. Maynard, July 19, 1952; children: Cynthia, Susan, Kellie, Robert. BA, San Diego State U., 1954. Life underwriter Mass. Mut. Life, San Diego, 1955-57; supr. John Hancock Mut., San Diego, 1957-59; gen. agt., mgr. Am. Mut. Life Ins., San Diego, 1959-65; regional v.p. Northwestern Life Ins., Seattle, 1965-68; broker, owner Roark Ins., San Juan Capistrano, Calif., 1968—. Author: Good News Letter, 1991—. Divsn. capt. USCG Aux., 1990, flotilla comdr., 1987, vice capt., 1989, publs. officer, 1997. Mem. Mission Hills Homeowners Assn. (pres. 1970-73, bd. mem. 1991-92), Lions Internat. (zone chmn. 1972, club pres. 1971).

ROARK, SHEILA B. writer; b. N.Y.C., N.Y., Dec. 17, 1946; d. Harry and Mary Galvin; m. V. Gail Roark, Feb. 10, 1988; children: Cyndee Lee Rule, Teri Patricia Tramuto, Meri Elaine Rule. Writing course, Tarrant County Jr. Coll., 1998. Model, actress, NY; writer, 1972—. Contest judge various poetry contests. Model (featured on mag. covers); actor: (Broadway plays) A Clearing in the Woods, (TV commls.); author: (book of poetry) Words Say So Much, Vol. I and II; contbr. poetry to anthologies. Avocations: reading, gourmet cooking, travel, bowling. Home: PO Box 1392 Euless TX 76039 E-mail: SBRoark@ev1.net.

ROATH, STEPHEN D. retired pharmaceutical company executive; b. 1941; With Long's Drug Stores Corp., 1964—2002, exec. v.p. store ops., 1988-91, pres., CEO, 1991—2001, retired, 2002. Mem.: bd. dirs., Calif. Symphony.

ROAZEN, PAUL, writer; b. Boston, Aug. 14, 1936; s. Julius and Anna (Lebow) R.; divorced; children: Jules, Daniel. BA, Harvard U., 1958, PhD, 1965. Instr. dept. govt. Harvard U., Cambridge, Mass., 1965-68, asst. prof., 1968-71; assoc. prof. social and polit. sci. York U., Toronto, Ont., Can., 1971-74, prof., 1974-95; ret., 1995. Author: Freud: Political and Social Thought, 1968, Brother Animal: The Story of Freud and Tausk, 1969, Freud and His Followers, 1975, Erik H, Erikson, 1976, Helene Deutsch, 1985, Encountering Freud: The Politics and Histories of Psychoanalysis, 1990, Meeting Freud's Family, 1993, How Freud Worked: First Hand Accounts of Patients, 1995, Canada's King: An Essay in Political Psychology, 1998, Political Theory and the Psychology of the Unconscious, 2000, Oedipus in Britain: Edward Glover and the Struggle Over Klein, 2000, The Historiography of Psychoanalysis, 2001, The Trauma of Freud: Controversies in Psychoanalysis, 2002, Cultural Foundations of Political Psychology, 2003, On the Freud Watch: Public Memoirs, 2003, Oedipus in Italy: Edoardo Weiss and the House that Freud Built, 2004. Fellow Royal Soc. Can.; mem. Phi Beta Kappa. Home: 73 Prince St Cambridge MA 02139-4413

ROBAK, JENNIE, state legislator; b. Surprise, Nebr., May 4, 1932; m. Cleo F. Robak; children: Karen, Kim, Frank, Kurt, Tony, Andrea. With Fed. Emergency Mgmt. Agy., Kansas City, Mo.; owner, operator RKR Foods, Inc.; mem. Nebr. Senate from 22d dist., Lincoln, 1988—. Trustee Jr. Achievement Columbus; bd. dirs. Platte County Red Cross; den mother Boy Scouts Am. Col. Nebr. Army N.G. Recipient Breaking Rule of Thumb award Nebr. Domestic Violence and Sexual Assault Coalition, 1989, Communicaiton and Leadership award Toastmasters Internat., 1992; named Woman of Distinction Soroptomist Internat. Colubmus, 1990. Mem. VFW Aux., Nat. Orgn. Vol. Leaders, Cath. Daus., Mrs. Jaycees, Kiwanis, Eagles Aux. Office: Rm 1118 State Capitol Lincoln NE 68509

ROBAK, KIM M. academic administrator, lawyer; b. Columbus, Nebr., Oct. 4, 1955; m. William J. Mueller; children: Katherine, Claire. BA with distinction, U. Nebr., 1977, JD with highest distinction, 1985. Tchr. Lincoln Pub. Schs., Nebr., 1978—82; clerk Cline Williams Wright Johnson & Oldfather, 1983; summer assoc. Cooley Godward Castro Huddleson & Tatum, San Francisco, 1984, Steptoe & Johnson, Washington, 1985; ptnr. Rembolt Ludtke Parker & Berger, Lincoln, 1985—91; legal counsel Gov. E. Benjamin Nelson/State of Nebr., 1991—92, chief of staff, 1992—93; lt. gov. State of Nebr., 1993—98; v.p. external affairs, corp. sec. U. Nebr., 1999—. Chair Prairie Fire Internat. Symposium on Edn., 1986. Program com. Leadership Lincoln, 1987—90; chair program com. Leadership Lincoln Alumni Assn., 1987, selection com., 1990; mem. Toll Fellowship Program, 1995; chair Nat. Conf. Lt. Govs., 1996; hon. chair Daffodil Day Campaign An, Cancer Soc.; hon chair Walktoberfest Am. Diabetes Assn.; hon. chair Prevent Blindness Campaign, Nebr.; hon. mem. Red Ribbon Campaign Mothers Against Drunk Driving, 1994—95; active Groundwater Found., 1997, Medicaid Managed Care Commn., 1993—; bd. dirs. Nebr. Health Sys., 1997—, Nat. Found. Women Legislators Found., 1997—98; chair Nebr. Info. Tech. Commn., 1997—98; hon. Christmas chair Salvation Army, 1997; cert. program chair Nat. Order Women Legislators, 1997; bd. dirs. Doane Coll., 1997—, Lincoln Pub. Sch. Found., 1998—, Martin Luther Home Bd., 1999—; mem. Lincoln Partnership for Econ. Devel. Bd., 2000—, Martin Luther Home Soc., 1999—2001, Dem. Gen. Counsel, Nebr., 1985—92; bd. dirs. women's ministries First Congl. Ch., 1988—91, trustee, 1991—99, asst. moderator, 1999—; trustee Plymouth Congl. Ch., 1998—. Named Notable Woman, First Plymouth Congl. Ch.'s Bd. Women's Ministries, 1996; fellow, Leadership Lincoln, 1986—87. Mem.: ABA (steering com. 1997—), Lincoln Bar Assn., Nebr. State Bar Assn. (ethics com. 1987—92, vice chair com. pub. rels. 1988—92, chari com. yellow pages advt. 1988, ho. of dels. 1988—95), Nat. Inst. Trial Advocaty, Alzheimers Assn. (hon. chair Lincoln-Greater Nebr. chpt. 1996—98), Updowntowners, Order of Coif, U. Nebr. Coll. Alumni Assn. (bd. dirs. 1986—89). Office: 3835 Holdrege St PO Box 830745 Lincoln NE 68583-0745 Business E-Mail: Krobak@nebraska.edu.

ROBALINO, BENJAMIN DAVID, cardiologist; b. Peru, Jan. 7, 1957; MD, Cayetano Heredia U., 1982. Diplomate Am. Bd. Internal Medicine, Cardiovascular Disease, Interventional Cardiology. Intern, resident Jackson Meml. Hosp.-U. Miami, Fla., 1983-86; fellow cardiology Cleve. Clinic Found., 1986-91; chief cardiologist McAllen (Tex.) Med. Ctr., 1994-95; dir. catheterization lab. Mc Allen Heart Hosp., 1998—2002; cardiologist McAllen, 1991—. Cardiologist Rio Grande (Tex.) Regional Hosp., Mission (Tex.) Hosp., Edinburg (Tex.) Hosp., McAllen Heart Hosp. Mem. AMC, AMA, Am. Coll. Cardiology, Tex. Med. Assn., Tex. Med. Found., Soc. for Cardiac Angiography and Interventions. Office: 500 E Ridge Rd Ste 101 Mcallen TX 78503-1508 Office Phone: 956-686-5226. E-mail: bdrobalino@hotmail.com.

ROBART, JAMES LOUIS, federal judge, lawyer; b. Seattle, Sept. 2, 1947; m. Mari C. Jalbing, Nov. 15, 1980. AB, Whitman Coll., 1969; JD, Georgetown U., 1973. Bar: Wash. 1973, U.S. Dist. Ct. (we. dist.) Wash. 1973, U.S. Supreme Ct. 1977, U.S. Ct. Appeals (9th cir.) 1978, U.S. Dist. Ct. (ea. dist.) Wash. 1981, Alaska 1985, U.S. Dist. Ct. Alaska 1985, U.S. Ct. Appeals (fed. cir.) 1985. Assoc. Lane Powell Moss Miller LLP, Seattle, 1973—79, ptnr., 1980—90, Lane Powell Spears Lubersky LLP, 1990—98; co-mng. ptnr. Lane Powel Spears Lubersky, 1998—2002, mng. ptnr., 2003—04; judge US Dist. Ct. (we. dist.) Wash., 2004—. Trustee Children's Home Soc., 1991-92, Seattle Children's Home, pres., 1984; bd. overseers Whitman Coll., 1988-2000; trustee Whihman Coll., 2000—. Mem. Fed. Cir. Bar Assn. (trustee 1985-88).

ROBB, CHARLES SPITTAL, former senator, former governor, lawyer, educator; b. Phoenix, Ariz., June 26, 1939; s. James Spittal and Francis Howard (Wooley) R.; m. Lynda Bird Johnson, Dec. 9, 1967; children: Lucinda Desha, Catherine Lewis, Jennifer Wickliffe. BBA, U. Wis., 1961; JD, U. Va., 1973. Bar: Va. 1973, U.S. Supreme Ct. 1976. Law clk. to Hon. John D. Butzner 4th U.S. Ct. Appeals, 1973—74; atty. Williams & Connolly, 1974-77; lt. gov. State of Va., 1978—82, gov., 1982—86; ptnr. Hunton & Williams, 1986—88; U.S. Senator from Va., 1989—2001; disting. prof. law and pub. policy George Mason U., 2001—. Former mem. armed svcs. com., intelligence com., senate Dem. policy com., senate Dem. tech. and comm. com., subcom. on readiness, subcom. on seapower, subcom. on strategic forces Com. on Fin., subcom. on internat. trade, subcom. on social security and family policy, subcom. on taxation and IRS oversight Select Com. on Intelligence, Joint Econ. Com., Dem. Policy Com.; chmn. Nat. Conf. Lt. Govs., 1979-80, Am. Coun. Young Polit. Leaders Dels. to Peoples Republic of China, 1979, edn. Commn. of the States, 1985; vis. prof. pub. affairs George Mason U., spring 1987. Chmn. Jobs for Am.'s Grads. Inc., 1985-90, Dem. Leadership Coun., 1986-88; gov. Atlantic Inst. for Internat. Affairs, 1987. With USMC 1961-70. Active duty USMC, 1961—70. Decorated Bronze Star, Vietnam Service medal with 4 Stars; Vietnamese Cross of Gallantry with Silver Star; recipient Raven award, 1973, Seven Soc. award U. Va. Mem. ABA, Va. Bar Assn., So. Govs. Assn. (chmn.), Dem. Govs. Assn. (chmn.), Coalition for Dem. Majority, Res. Officers Assn., USMC Res. Officers Assn., U.Fa. La. Alumni Assn. (bd. dirs. 1974-85), Am. Legion, Raven Soc., Navy League U.S., Coun. on Fgn. Rels., Omicron Delta Kappa. Democrat. Episcopalian. Office: George Mason U Sch Law 3301 N Fairfax Dr Rm 409 Arlington VA 22201-4498

ROBB, CURTIS, air transportation executive; B in Physics, Emporia State U. With Citicorp Credit Svcs., IBM; sr. v.p., chief tech. officer Delta Tech., Inc., 2000—02, pres., CEO, 2002—; sr. v.p., chief info. officer Delta Air Lines, Inc., Atlanta, 2002—. With USAF. Office: Delta Air Lines Inc Hartsfield Atlanta Internat Airport 1030 Delta Blvd Atlanta GA 30320-6001

ROBB, GARY CHARLES, lawyer; b. Kansas City, Mo., May 17, 1955; m. Anita Candace Porte, Apr. 30, 1983. BA with distinction, U. Mo., Kansas City, 1977, MA in Econs., 1978; JD cum laude, U. Mich., 1981. Bar: Ill. 1981, U.S. Dist. Ct. (no. dist.) Ill. 1981, Mo. 1982, U.S. Dist. Ct. (we. dist.) Mo. 1982, U.S. Ct. Appeals (8th cir.) 1982. Assoc. Mayer, Brown & Platt, Chgo., 1981—82, Shughart, Thomson & Kilroy, Kansas City, Mo., 1982—84; ptnr. Robb & Robb, Kansas City, Mo., 1984—. Adj. prof. law U. Mo., Kansas City; lectr., program chmn. Nat. Conf. on Products Liability Law, Chgo., 1983, lectr., 84. Contbg. author: Tort Law, Missouri Bar Handbook, 1982, Products Liability, 1984; editor: U. Mich. Jour. Law Reform, 1980—81; contbg. editor: Products Liability, 1983; mem. bd. editors: Products Liability Newsletter, 1982—, mem. bd. experts: Lawyers Alert Newsmag.; contbr. articles. Mem.: ATLA (tort and aviation sects.), ABA (tort and ins. practice 1981—, trial evidence com. 1981—, sect. litigation, products, liability and consumer law com., chmn. future programs and projects subcom.), Lawyers Assn. Kansas City, Mo. Bar Assn. (fed. practice com.), Kansas City Bar Assn., Mo. Assn. Trial Attys. (bd. govs. 1993—, pres. elect), Univ. Mo.-Kansas City Alumni Assn. (chmn. career planning com.), Pi Sigma Alpha (pres. 1977—78), Omicron Delta Epsilon, Phi Kappa Phi. Republican. Office: 1200 Main St Ste 3900 Kansas City MO 64105-2100

ROBB, GEOFFREY LAWRENCE, plastic surgeon; b. El Paso, Tex., May 28, 1946; s. Giles Anthony and Mary Jo (Lawrence) R.; m. Cathy Jean Cross, May 31, 1974; children: Tiffany, Kimberly, Courtney, Carly, Melaney, Mary. BS, U. Miami, 1969, MD, 1974. Diplomate Am. Bd. Otolaryngology. Commd. ensign USNR, 1970-92; advanced through grades to capt., 1989; resident in otalaryngology, mem. staff US Naval Hosp., San Diego, 1974-79, otolaryngologist Orlando, Fla., 1979-83; plastic surgeon USN Sponsorship at U. Pitts., 1983-85, microvascular surgeon, 1985; plastic surgeon U.S. Naval Hosp., Portsmouth, Va., 1985-88; ret., 1992; chief plastic surgery U.S. Naval Hosp., Portsmouth, Va., 1988-92; vice chmn. plastic surgery M.D. Anderson Cancer Ctr., Houston, 1992-97, chmn. plastic surgery, 1997—, dep. chmn. divsn. surgery, 1994—, dir. postgrad. med. edn., 1992—, med. dir. plastic surgery clinic, 1992—, assoc. med. dir. skin cancer ctr., 1996. Contbg. author: Reconstructive Plastic Surgery for Cancer, 1995, Endoscopic Plastic Surgery, 1995, Advanced Skin Cancer of Head and Neck, 1995; contbr. articles to profl. jours. Fellow ACS, Am. Soc. Plastic Reconstructive Surgeons, Am. Soc. Reconstructive Microsurgeons, Am. Assn. Plastic Surgeons; mem. Internat. Soc. Reconstructive Microsurgery, Tex. Soc. Plastic Surgeons, Houston Soc. Plastic Surgeons, KC. Avocations: physical fitness, weightlifting, tennis, running. Office: MD Anderson Cancer Ctr 1515 Holcombe Blvd # 443 Houston TX 77030-4009 E-mail: grobb@mdanderson.org.

ROBB, JAMES ALEXANDER, lawyer; b. Huntingdon, Que., Can., May 3, 1930; s. Alexander George and Irma Mary (Martin) R.; m. Katherine Ann Teare, June 26, 1960; children: Laura, John, Andrew. BA, McGill U., 1951, B.C.L., 1954; postgrad., U. Montreal, 1961-63. Bar: Que. 1955, queen's counsel 1970. Lectr. comml. law and taxation Sir George Williams U., 1958-60; ptnr., Stikeman Elliott LLP and predecessor firm Stikeman, Elliott, Tamaki, Mercier & Robb, Montreal, 1967—2002, sr. counsel, 2003—. Bd. dirs. Itochu Can. Ltd., Majorich Investments Inc., YKK Can. Inc., NGK Spark Plugs Can. Ltd., KSH Solutions Inc., KSH Constrn. Inc., Vancana Inc.; chmn. Western Fin. Group Inc.; pres. Que-Japan Bus. Forum, 1993—95. Mem. Protestant Sch. Bd. Greater Montreal, 1971-75; chmn. bd. trustees Martlet Found., 1967-69; v.p. Que. Liberal Party, 1976-79; mem. adv. com. McGill Ctr. for Study of Regulated Industries; bd. dirs. Montreal Mus. Fine Arts, 1987-90; bd. govs. McGill U., 1991-95. Mem.: Consumers Assn. Can. (past chmn. regulated industries program), Bar Que. (chmn. multidisciplinary com. 1998—2001), McGill Alumni Assn. (pres. 1996—98), Hillside Tennis Club, Royal Montreal Curling Club (pres. 1999—2000), Kanawaki Golf Club (Que.), Univ. Club, Can. Club Montreal (pres. 1990—91). Home: 9 Renfrew Ave Westmount QC Canada H3Y 2X3 Office: 1155 Renè Lèvesque Blvd W 40th Fl Montreal QC Canada H3B 3V2 E-mail: jrobb@stikeman.com.

ROBB, JAMES ARTHUR, pathologist; b. Pueblo, Colo., Nov. 13, 1938; s. William Arthur and Mary Ann (Hutchinson) R.; m. Carla May Felte, June 16, 1962; 4 children. BA, U. Colo., 1960, postgrad., 1960-61, MD, 1965. Diplomate Am. Bd. Anat. and Clin. Pathology, Am. Bd. Dermatopathology, Am. Bd. Cytopathology. Intern then resident in anatomic pathology Yale U., New Haven, 1965-68; research assoc. NIH, Bethesda, Md., 1969-71; asst. prof. pathology U. Calif., San Diego, 1971-75, assoc. prof., 1975-78; staff pathologist Scripps Clinic, La Jolla, Calif., 1978-81, vice chmn. pathology, 1981-90; assoc. dir. pathology, dept. pathology Cedars Med. Ctr., Miami, 1990—2000, dir., anatomic & molecular pathology, 1990—2000; med. dir. Integrated Regional Labs. Fla., 2000—; v.p. med. affairs MDS Diagnostic Svcs., 2003—. Assoc. adj. prof. U. Calif., San Diego, 1978—84, adj. prof., 1984—90. Contbr. articles to profl. jours. Treas. San Diego Jr. Theatre, 1981. Served with USPHS, 1962-80. Grantee NIH, Am. Cancer Soc. Mem. AMA, AAAS, Am. Soc. Cell Biology, Am. Assn. Pathologists, Fla. Med. Assn., South Fla. Soc. Pathology, Broward County Med. Assn., Internat. Soc. Dermatopathology, Internat. Acad. Cytology, Am. Soc. Dermatopathology, Internat. Acad. Pathology, Am. Soc. Virology, Alpha Omega Alpha, Sigma Tau, Sigma Pi Sigma. Office: Integrated Regional Labs Fla 5361 NW 33rd Ave Fort Lauderdale FL 33309 Office Phone: 954-777-0018.

ROBB, JAMES B. utilities executive; B in Chem. Engring. with distinction, Purdue U.; MBA in Mktg., U. Pa. Process engr. Chevron Corp.; ptnr. McKinsey & Co., San Francisco, Seattle; sr. v.p. performance mgmt. Reliant Resources, Inc., Houston, 2002—. Office: Reliant Enegy Exec Offices PO Box 2286 Houston TX 77252-2286

ROBB, JAMES WILLIS, Romance languages educator; b. Jamaica, N.Y., June 27, 1918; s. Stewart Everts and Clara Johanna (Mohrmann) R.; m. Cecilia Uribe-Noguera, 1972. Student, Inst. de Touraine, Sorbonne, 1937-38; BA cum laude, Colgate U., 1939; postgrad., U. Nacional de Mex., 1948; MA, Middlebury Coll., 1950; PhD, Cath. U. Am., 1958. Instr. romance langs. Norwich U., 1946-50; from asst. prof. to prof. romance langs. George Washington U., Washington, 1950-88, prof. emeritus, 1988—. Corr. mem. Academia Mexicana de la Lengua, 1998. Author: El Estilo de Alfonso Reyes, 1965, 78, Repertorio Bibliográfico de Alfonso Reyes, 1974, Prosa y Poesía de Alfonso Reyes, 1975, 84, Estudios sobre Alfonso Reyes, 1976, Por los Caminos de Alfonso Reyes, 1981, Imágenes de América en Alfonso Reyes y en Germán Arciniegas, 1990, Más Páginas Sobre Alfonso Reyes, 1996-97; contbr. articles to profl. jours. With USNR, 1942—44, Brazil, with USNR, 1944—46, PTO. Recipient Alfonso Reyes Internat. Lit. prize, 1978; Lit. Diploma of Merit, State of Nuevo León and City of Monterrey, Mex., 1979; OAS grantee, 1964; Am. Philos. Soc. grantee, 1977 Mem. MLA, Internat. Assn. Ibero-Am. Lit., Am. Assn. Tchrs. Spanish and Portuguese, Assn. Colombianistas, Phi Beta Kappa. Office: George Washington U Romance Langs Dept Washington DC 20052-0001

ROBB, JOHN WESLEY, religion educator; b. Los Angeles, Dec. 1, 1919; s. Edgar Milton and Alta (Boger) R.; m. Ethel Edna Tosh, June 13, 1942; children: Lydia Joan Robb Durbin, Judith Nadine Robb Eggerman. AB, Greenville Coll., 1941; Th.M., U. So. Calif., 1945, PhD, 1952; L.H.D., Hebrew Union Coll.-Jewish Inst. Religion, 1977. Asst. prof. philosophy and religion Dickinson Coll., Pa., 1948-51; fellow Fund for Advancement Edn., 1951-52; asso. prof. U. So. Calif., L.A., 1954-62, chmn. dept. religion, 1954-67, assoc. dean humanities Coll. Letters, Arts and Scis., 1963-68, Leonard K. Firestone prof., 1974-75, prof., 1962-87, prof. emeritus, 1987—, prof. Sch. Medicine, 1981-87; coun. mem. Inst. of Lab. Animal Resources Nat. Acad. Scis. Nat. Rsch. Coun., 1986-93. Vis. disting. prof. USAF Med. Ctr., Wilford Hall, Tex., 1985; mem. rev. com. NIH Guide for the Care and Use of Lab. Animals, NRC, NAS, 1993-96; advisor/tutor Med. Quality Assurance Commn., Dept. Health, State of Wash., 1994-2001; mem. ethics com. Swedish Med. Ctr., N.W. Hosp., Seattle, 1992-2002; adj. prof. bioethics Sch. Medicine, U. So. Calif., 1989-91, adj. prof. emeritus, 1991—. Author: Inquiry Into Faith, 1960; co-editor: Readings in Religious Philosophy: The Reverent Skeptic, 1979. Served as lt. (j.g.) USNR, 1945-47; to lt. 1952-54. Recipient award for excellence in tchg. U. So. Calif., 1960, 74, Dart award for acad. innovation, 1970, Raubenheimer Disting. Faculty award divsn. humanities, 1980, Robert Fenton Craig award Blue Key, 1980, Outstanding Faculty award Student Senate, 1981, Disting. Emeritus award, 1995, Educator of Yr. award Swedish Med. Ctr., Providence, Seattle, 2002. Fellow Soc. for Values in Higher Edn.; mem. Am. Acad. Religion (v.p. 1966, pres. 1967), Am. Philos. Assn., AAUP (v.p. Calif. Conf. 1977, pres. 1978-79), Phi Beta Kappa (hon.), Phi Kappa Phi, Phi Chi Phi. United Methodist. Home: 8001 Sand Point Way NE Apt C35 Seattle WA 98115-6356

ROBB, LYNDA JOHNSON, writer; b. Washington, Mar. 19, 1944; d. Lyndon Baines and Claudia Alta (Taylor) Johnson; m. Charles Spittal Robb, Dec. 9, 1967; children: Lucinda Desha, Catherine Lewis, Jennifer Wickliffe. BA with honors, U. Tex., 1966. Writer McCall's Mag., 1966-68; contbg. editor Ladies Home Jour., 1968-80; lectr., bd. dirs. Reading Is Fundamental, 1968—, Lyndon B. Johnson Family Found., 1969-95. Past mem. Va. State Coun. on Infant Mortality, Va. Maternal & Child Health Coun.; mem. Nat. Commn. to Prevent Infant Mortality, 1987-93; chmn. Pres.'s Adv. Com. for Women, 1979-81; pres. bd. dirs. Nat. Home Libr. Found., Ford Theatre; chmn. Va. Women's Cultural History Project, 1982-85; chmn. Reading is Fundamental, 1996-2001. Mem. Zeta Tau Alpha. Office: Reading is Fundamental Ste 400 1825 Connecticut Ave NW Washington DC 20009-5708

ROBB, ROBERT, biotechnology company executive; BS in Environ. Biology, MS in Parasitology/Microbiology, U. Utah. Founder InMedica Devel. Corp.; dir. bus. devel. BCM Technologies, Inc., a subsidiary of Baylor Coll. Medicine; dir. tech. mgmt. office U. Mich., Ann Arbor, Mich.; pres., co-founder BioVentures West, San Diego; pres., CEO, dir. Quorex Pharms., Inc., Carlsbad, Calif. Office: Quorex Pharmaceuticals Inc 1890 Rutherford Rd #200 Carlsbad CA 92008

ROBB, WALTER LEE, retired electric company executive, management company executive; b. Harrisburg, Pa., Apr. 25, 1928; s. George A. and Ruth (Scantlin) R.; m. Anne Gruver, Feb. 27, 1954; children: Richard, Steven, Lindsey. BS, Pa. State U., 1948; MS, U. Ill., 1950, PhD, 1951; DEng (hon.), Milw. Sch. Engring., 1994, Worcester Poly. Inst., 1988. With GE, 1951-93, mgr. R & D dept. silicone products, 1966-68, venture mgr. med. devel. ops. Schenectady, N.Y., 1968-71, sr. v.p., group exec. med. sys. group Milw., 1973-86, sr. v.p. corp. R & D Schenectady, 1986-93; pres. Vantage Mgmt., Schenectady, N.Y., 1993—. Bd. dirs. Celgene Corp., Mech. Tech., Inc.; chmn. Capital Dist. Sports, Inc. Recipient Nat. Tech. medal, 1993, Indsl. Rsch. Inst. medal, 1994. Mem. NAE, Am. Philos. Soc. Achievements include patentee in field of membranes and gas separation; research in diagnostic imaging equipment. Home: 1358 Ruffner Rd Niskayuna NY 12309-2500 Office: Vantage Mgmt 3000 Troy-Schenectady Rd Schenectady NY 12309-1643 Office Phone: 518-782-0050. Business E-Mail: waltrobb@nycap.rr.com.

ROBBINS, ALLEN BISHOP, physics educator; b. New Brunswick, N.J., Mar. 31, 1930; s. William Rei and Helen Grace (Bishop) R.; m. Shirley Mae Gernert, June 14, 1952 (div. 1978); children: Catherine Jean, Marilyn Elizabeth, Carol Ann, Melanie Barbara; m. Alice Harriet Ayars, Jan. 1, 1979. Student, Oberlin Coll., 1948—49; BS, Rutgers U., 1952; MS, Yale U., 1953, PhD, 1956. Rsch. fellow U. Birmingham (Eng.), 1957-58, lectr., 1960-61; instr. physics Rutgers U., New Brunswick, 1956-57, asst. prof. physics, 1957-60, assoc. prof., 1960-68, prof., 1968-97, prof. emeritus, 1997—, chmn. dept. physics and astronomy, 1979-95. Contbr. articles on nuc. physics to profl. jours. Recipient Lindbach Christian and Mary F. Lindbach Found., Rutgers U., 1975. Fellow Am. Phys. Soc.; mem. Am. Assn. Physics Tchrs., AAAS, Phi Beta Kappa, Sigma Xi. Office: Rutgers U Dept Physics and Astronomy 136 Frelinghuysen Rd Piscataway NJ 08854-8019 Personal E-mail: allenbobbins@aol.com.

ROBBINS, ANDREW CHARLES, sound recording engineer, music producer; b. LA, Dec. 14, 1968; s. David Bennett and Walborg Robbins; m. Sandy Hyon-Shil Kim, Nov. 26, 1994; 1 child, Noah Myeong-Soo. MusB magna cum laude, Calif. State U., Dominguez Hills, 1991. Engr.'s apprentice, intern Aspen (Colo.) Music Festival, 1991; staff engr., prodr. Vision Studios, Houston, 1992—93; freelance audio engr., prodr. Houston, 1993—96; sr. audio engr. Premiere Conferencing, Colorado Springs, Colo., 1996—2002; owner Audio-File Solutions, Colorado Springs, 2002—. Mem.: Audio Engrng. Soc. Avocations: fly fishing, tennis, photography. Office Phone: 719-477-9600. Office Fax: 719-477-9602. Business E-Mail: andy.robbins@adelphia.net.

ROBBINS, ANNE FRANCIS See REAGAN, NANCY DAVIS

ROBBINS, AUDREY, county official; b. Chgo., Mar. 1, 1932; d. Philip I. and Manya Lehr; children: Dana Merfeld, Cindy Buss. BA, DePaul U., 1993. Mfrs. rep. Museum Reprodns. - Marwall Industries, N.Y.C., 1969—79; asst. to chief counsel Arthur Andersen & Co., Chgo., 1979—98; mem. staff Office of Chief Judge, Cook County Cir. Ct., Chgo., 1999—. Author: Goldblatt's Galloping Gourmets, 1974 (Tribune award, 74). Vol. intensive care infants Northwestern Meml. Hosp., Chgo., 1979—80; vol. Art Inst. Chgo., 1984—86; touring docent Terra Mus. Am. Art, 1999—; bd. dirs., sec., pres. Nathan & Francis Goldblatt Soc. for Cancer Rsch., 1955—83. Mem.: Golden Key (life). Avocations: art history, watercolors, cooking. Home: 910 N Lake Shore Dr # 718 Chicago IL 60611 Office: Cir Ct Cook County 50 W Washington Chicago IL 60602 Business E-Mail: arobbin@cookcountygov.com.

ROBBINS, BRENDA JEAN, music therapist; Music therapist Leon County Sch. Dist., Tallahassee. Mem. Coun. Exceptional Children (Hug award 1995). Office: Leon County Sch Dist 2757 W Pensacola St Tallahassee FL 32304-2907

ROBBINS, CARRIE F(ISHBEIN), costume designer, educator; d. Sidney W. and Bettye A. (Berman) Fishbein; m. Richard D. Robbins, Feb. 15, 1969. BS, BA, Pa. State U., 1964; MFA, Yale Drama Sch., 1967. Over 30 Broadway shows, NYC, 1968-2001, White Christmas, 2004, A Class Act at the Ambassador Theatre, 2001—, Grease (Tony nomination best costumes), Over Here (Tony nomination best costumes), Secret Affairs of Mildred Wilde, Yentl, Cyrano, Iceman Cometh, Octette Bridge Club, Look to the Lillies, Sweet Bird of Youth, Agnes of God, Boys of Winter, The First, Frankenstein, Shadow Box, Samson et Dalila, San Francisco Opera, 1980, LA Opera, 1999, Houston Grand Opera, 2002, Rigoletto, Russlan et Ludmilla, Taverner, Bernstein's Mass, Opera Co. Boston, 1975-76, 86, 89, Hamburg State Opera (W.Ger.), 1979, Washington Opera Soc., 1975, designed for NY Shakespeare Festival, Jules Irving's Lincoln Ctr. Repertory Theatre, Tyrone Guthrie Theatre, Mpls. (including Hamlet, Julius Caesar and Three Penny Opera), Mark Taper Forum, LA (including The Tempest with Anthony Hopkins, Fashion Inst. Tech. Surface Design award, Flea in Her Ear (Dramalogue Critics award), The Wedding Banquet, Seattle and Taiway, 2003, Williamstown, Chelsea Theatre Ctr., Bklyn., John Houseman's City Ctr. Acting Co., Juilliard Sch., NYC, WNET and cable TV, off-broadway theatres, NYC including Promenade Theatre, It's Only a Play, Big Potato, Women's Project's Exact Center of the Universe, Two-Headed, Westport Country Playhouse's Bench in the Sun, Arclite Theatre Tennessee Williams Remembered, Paper Mill Playhouse Rags; designer sets and costumes Tallulah Hallelujah; tchr. Henry Le Tang Profl. Sch. Tap Dance, 1989-91; vis. guest lectr. costume design U. Ill., UCLA, Oberlin Coll., Pa. State U., others; master tchr. costume design NYU; costume designer: (TV) Saturday Night Live-NBC, 1985-86, The Rita Show; (TV film) In the Spirit, 1987; designer apparel Rainbow Room, Rockefeller Ctr., 1987-97, Aurora Grill, 1988, Empress Ct., Caesar's Palace, Las Vegas, 1988, Windows on the World Restaurant Complex, 1996 (Image of Yr. award Nat. Assn. Uniform Mfrs. and Distbrs. 1997); regional theatres including Berkshire Theatre, Mass., Toys in the Attic, Fla. Stage It's Only a Play, Arena Stage, Washington, M. Butterfly, 2004. One-woman show Cen. Falls Gallery, N.Y.C., 1980; exhibited in group shows at Cooper Hewitt Mus., Pa. State U., Wright-Hepburn Gallery, N.Y.C., Scottsdale, Ariz., Salmagundi Club, 1983, 84; illustrations and calligraphy pub. ann. calendar Soc. of Scribes competition, Ms. mag.; original costume work photographed in books; Costume Design, 1983, Fabric Painting and Dying for the Theatre, 1982; original drawing reproduced Time-Life Series: The Ency. of Collectibles; profiled in Costume Design-Techniques of Modern Masters, 1996, Contemporary Designers, 1990, 97; designer loft conversions, comml. lobby space, studios, others; contbr. articles Stage Directions Mag.; illustrator: Who Was Wolfgang Amadeus Mozart?, 2003; contbr. to profl. jours. Named Disting. Alumna, Pa. State U., 1979; recipient Antoinette Perry nominations for Best Costumes for a Broadway Show, 1971-72, 73-74, Drama Desk award, Am. Theatre Wing, N.Y.C., 1971, 72, Maharam award for design, Joseph Maharam Found., N.Y.C., 1975, nomination, 1984, Juror's Choice award for surface design, Fashion Inst. of Tech., 1980, Dramalogue Critics' award for Outstanding Achievement in Theatre Costume Design, L.A., 1982, Silver Medal, 6th Triennial of Theatre Design, Novisad, Yugoslavia, 1981, Diplome L'Honneur, 1990, Audelco nomination, 1990, Henry Hewes nomination, 1999, League N.Y. Theatres, N.Y.C., 1971-72, 73-74. Mem. League Profl. Theatre Tng. Programs (steering com.), League Profl. Theatre Women (bd. dirs. 2001—, Designing Woman of Yr. 2004), Graphic Artists Guild, Soc. Scribes, Am. Soc. Interior Designers, United Scenic Artists Local 829; adv. com. The Costume Collection of Theatre Devel. Fund. Home and Office: 11 W 30th St 15th Fl New York NY 10001 E-mail: crobb10001@aol.com.

ROBBINS, CORNELIUS (CORNELIUS VAN VORSE), educational administration educator; b. Wilmington, Del., Nov. 2, 1931; s. Cornelius V. and Irene (Tatman) R.; m. Janet Porter, Aug. 1953; children: Eva Robbins Burke, Susan Robbins, Laurel Robbins, Melissa Robbins Beegle. BA in Polit. Sci, U. Del., 1953, MEd in Social Scis, 1961; EdD in Ednl. Adminstrn, U. Pa., 1964. Asst. mgr. Robbins & Clark Hardware, 1953-57; mem. faculty U. Del., 1957-58; tchr. Marshallton (Del.) Sch. Dist., 1958-60, Mt. Pleasant (Del.) Sch. Dist., 1960-62; asst. to dir. sch. study councils U. Pa., 1962-64; dean instrn. Ocean County Coll., 1965-67; dean of coll. C/C. of Delaware County, Pa., 1967-69; sr. assoc., coll. div. dir. McManis Assocs., Washington, 1969-70; pres. Genesee C.C., 1970-75; assoc. chancellor for community colls. SUNY, 1975-85; acting pres. Potsdam State Coll. (N.Y.), 1982-83; pres. Cobleskill (N.Y.) Coll. Agr. & Tech., 1985-92; prof. edn. adminstrn. SUNY, Albany, N.Y., 1992—. Cons. Middle States Assn. Colls.; area liaison officer U.S. Mil. Acad., 1971-75; chmn. SUNY West Pres.'s Council and mem. Chancellor's Council, 1973-91. Contbr. articles to profl. publs. Served with U.S. Army, 1954-56; maj. USAR ret. Recipient Outstanding Educator's award N.Y. State Assn. Jr. Colls., 1975, Disting. Svc. award Faculty Coun. Community Colls., 1988. Mem. Am. Assn. Higher Edn., State Dirs. of Community Colls. Assn., Phi Delta Kappa. Office: SUNY Albany Ed 332 Albany NY 12222-0001 E-mail: crobbins@uamail.albany.edu.

ROBBINS, DOREN GURSTEIN, poet, educator, artist; b. L.A., Aug. 20, 1949; s. Ralph and Florence R.; m. Linda Drand Mazak Janakos; 1 child, Samantha. MFA, U. Iowa, 1993. Instr. English Umpqua C.C., Roseburg, Oreg., 1993-95, Linfield Coll., McMinnville, Oreg., 1994-95; instr. creative writing U. Iowa, Iowa City, 1991-93; English instr. East Los Angeles Coll., Monterey Park, Calif., 1997—; instr. creative writing, poetry U. Calif., L.A., 1996-99; English instr. Santa Monica (Calif.) Coll., 1998—; instr. advanced creative wiritng Mount Saint Mary's Coll., L.A., 2001—. Author: (poetry) Driving Face Down, 2001 (Blue Lynx prize 2001), The Donkey's Tale, 1998 (The Villon prize 1998), Sympathetic Manifesto, 1988 (Emma Goldman award 1988), Seducation of the Groom, 1982, Dignity in Naples and North Hollywood, 1996. Poet, artist Salvadoran Med. Relief Fund, Salinas, Calif., 1984-85; poet-activist Ctrl. Am. Refugee Com., L.A., 1984-86; poetry organizer Amnesty Internat., L.A., 1980. Recipient Anna Davidson Roseberg award Judah Magnes Mus., Commendation prize Chester H. Jones Found., 1993, 96, 97; poetry fellowship Oreg. Literary Arts, L.A. County Mus. of Art, 1999, The Loft Found., 1985. Jewish. Avocations: contemplation, travel, walking. Home: 4161 Alla Rd Los Angeles CA 90066 Office: Foothill Coll care Lang Arts 12345 El Monte Rd Los Altos Hills CA 94022-4599 E-mail: pantagruli@aol.com., robbinsdoren@foothill.edu.

ROBBINS, DOROTHY ANN, librarian; b. Altha, Fla., Dec. 2, 1939; d. Robert C. and Pauline Johnson; m. Richard N. Robbins, Jan. 16, 1960; children: Cynthia R. Peacock, Pamela T., LeAnne M. Lusk. AA, Gulf Coast C.C., Panama City, 1959. With Bay County Pub. Libr., Panama City, Fla., 1959—, libr. clk., bookmobile clk., br. mgr., circulation supr., literacy dir., pub. svcs. supr. Adv. bd. Literacy Vols. of Bay County, Panama City, 1982-2003; troop leader Girl Scouts of the Apalachee Bend, Panama City, 1972-75. Mem. Greater Panama City Dog Fanciers (sec. 1988-2003), S.E. Bullmastiff Assn. (b. dirs., pres. 1991-2003), Am. Bullmastiff Assn., United Daus. of the Confederacy. Democrat. Baptist. Avocations: showing bullmastiffs, reading, antiques, crafts, gardening. Home: 435 S Palo Alto Ave Panama City FL 32401-3954 Office: Bay County Pub Libr 25 W Government St Panama City FL 32401-2743

ROBBINS, ELEANORA IBERALL, biogeologist, researcher; b. Washington, July 20, 1942; d. Arthur Saul and Helene Iberall; m. Charles Brian Robbins, June 18, 1972. BS, Ohio State U., 1964; MS, U. Ariz., 1972; PhD, Pa, State U., 1982. Geologist U.S. Geol. Survey, Reston, Va., 1969—2001; adj. faculty dept. geology San Diego State U., 2001—. Dir. Explorer's Club, San Diego, 2001—. Peace corps vol. Tanzania Geol. Survey, Dodoma, Tanzania; defender Huntley Meadows Pk., Alexandria, Va. Recipient Point of Light, U.S. Dept. Interior, 1989, The Secretary's Stewardship award Edn., 1993, Woman of Distinction, Soroptiminst Internat., 1998, Timis Eneken, Greek Aerospace Med. Assn. and Space Rsch., 2000; fellow, NSF, 1978—79. Mem.: AAUW, Assn. Women Geoscientists (vice chmn. 1984—86), Am. Soc. Surface Mining and Reclamation, Am. Assn. Stratigraphic Palynologists (bd. dirs. 1989—91), Soc. Wetland Scientists, Am. Indian Sci. and Engrng. Soc. Democrat. Jewish. Achievements include patents for Ozonation of acid mine water. Avocations: teaching outdoors science, Native American students. Home: 11017 Via Merida La Mesa CA 91941 Office: San Diego State U Dept Geol 5500 Campanile Dr MC 1020 San Diego CA 92182-1020 Personal E-mail: norrierobbins@cox.net.

ROBBINS, EMMALEE ELIZABETH, fine arts director, speech and theater coach, choreographer, writer; b. Kingstree, SC, Mar. 29, 1941; d. Thomas Earl and Elizabeth Eloise (Payne) Gaddy; m. Alicia Rhett Howard; m. Christopher Michael Robbins; children: Alicia Rhett Howard, Christopher Michael. BA in speech and drama, Columbia Coll., 1963; MFA in theatre, U. of NC at Greensboro, 1977. Cert. teaching 1965. Dance instr. Columbia Coll., 1961—63; dir., christian youth activities Kingstree Meth. Ch., 1962; dir., christian edn. Main St. Meth. Ch., Columbia, SC, 1963—64; dir., prod., choreographer Charleston County Playhouse, Summer Playhouse and St. Andrew's Parish H.S., 1969—72; tchg. asst. U. NC, 1972—74; T.V. hostess Today's Woman on CBS, 1972—74; dir., prod., choreographer Charleston County Playhouse, Summer Playhouse and St. Andrew's Parish H.S., 1974—79; tchr. Charleston Southern U., 1969—70; T.V. guest, choreographer ABC, 1977; theatre dir. Town Theatre, Columbia, SC, 1979—97; instr. Newberry Coll., Newberry, SC, 1979—80; dir. Young Town Players and Young People's Theatre, 1985—97; tchr. Buckley Sch. of Pub. Speaking, Camden, SC, 1998—. Vol., tchg. character edn. Lugoff Elem. Sch., Camden, SC, 2002—03; vol. tchg. character edn. Carolina Care Plan, 2003. Recipient Career Achievement award, Columbia Coll., 1990. Mem.: SC Theater's Assn., Daughters of Am. Colonists. Republican. Christian Luth. Avocations: ballroom dancing, travel, reading, writing, pilates. Home: 30 Royal Gate Columbia SC 29223 Office Phone: 803-736-1555. E-mail: eer_productions@msn.com.

ROBBINS, HARVEY ARNOLD, textile company executive; b. N.Y.C., Apr. 29, 1922; s. Ira B. and Mildred (Lowy) R.; m. Carolyn Edith Goldsmith, June 8, 1947; children: Margaret Ann (Mrs. Lew Enker), James Andrew. Student, U. Mich., 1940-42, Cornell U., 1943, Columbia U., 1945. V.p. Silberstein-Goldsmith, N.Y.C., 1946-50, North Advt., Chgo., 1950-59, M. Lowenstein & Sons, Inc., N.Y.C., also pres. Wamsutta/Pacific Domestic divsn., 1959-69; pres. Burlington Domestics divsn. Burlington Industries, 1969-73; v.p. United Mchts. & Mfrs., 1973-78, PRF Corp., 1978-80; exec. v.p. Whisper Soft Mills, N.Y.C., 1980-84; dir. product devel. Springs Industries, 1984-85, textile cons., 1985—. Bd. dir. Ednl. Found. for Fashion Industries; corp. mem. Lesley Coll., Cambridge, Mass. With U.S. Army, 1942-45. Deocrated Purple Heart, Combat Inf. badge. Mem. Am. Mgmt. Assn., Am. Arbitration Assn., Textile Distbrs. Assn., U. Mich. Alumni Club. Home and Office: 35 Brook Rd Valley Stream NY 11581-2401

ROBBINS, HENRY ZANE, public relations and marketing executive; b. Winston-Salem, N.C., Jan. 17, 1930; s. Romulus Mayfield and Vera Ethel (Daniel) R.; m. Barbara Anne Brown, Jan. 19, 1955; children: Zane Scott, Jill Stewart, Gail Ruth. AB, U. N.C., 1952; student, Emory U., 1952. Reporter Atlanta Constn., 1952; exhibit specialist Gen. Electric Co., Schenectady, 1952, employee relations specialist Cin., 1955, editor Schenectady, 1955, account supr. Winston-Salem, 1956-58, group supr. Schenectady, 1958-60; v.p., gen. mgr. Burson-Marsteller, Pitts. and Chgo., 1960-70, sr. v.p., 1970; pres., chief exec. officer SL&H-Robbins Inc., Chgo., 1970-72; also dir.; pres., chief exec. officer Beveridge Kraus Robbins & Manning, Chgo., 1973-75; also dir.; pres., dir., chief exec. officer Beveridge and Robbins Inc., Chgo., 1975-77; pres., chief exec. officer Financial Advt. of Ill., Inc., Chgo.; mng. dir. Sports Mgmt. Group, Chgo., 1975-77; dir. communications Arthur Andersen & Co., Chgo. and Geneva, Switzerland, 1977-81, dir. mktg. support services, 1981-89, dir. mktg. and comms., 1989-91; mem. Worldwide Alpha Group, 1991-96, exec. dir. global 1000 program, 1995—2000; prin. Arthur Andersen & Co., 1980—2000; cons. Exec. Svc. Corps, 2004—. Mem. journalism adv. com. Harper Coll., Palatine, Ill., exec. svc. corp.; dir. Evanston Environ. Assn.; mem. Ladd Arboretum Commn., Evanston, Ill.; pub. rels. com. Chgo. Met. Crusade Mercy; mem. Nat. Task Force on Environment; cons. sec. Dept. Health, Edn. and Welfare, 1970; chmn. pub. rels. com. Honor Am. Day Com., 1970. Author: Vision of Grandeur, 1988, Globalizing the Enterprise, 2000, Tradition of Excellence, 2001; contbr. articles to profl. jours. Counselor Council of Mojave, 1972-74; gen. chmn. Chgo. Children's Classic Golf Tournament, 1974-77; chmn. Chgo. fin. com. Am.'s Freedom Train, 1976; chmn. fund devel. com. Presbytery of Chgo., 1977-83, maj. mission fund, 1977-79; dist. commr. Boy Scouts Am., 1976-79, chmn. Wildcat dist., 1980-83; mem. exec. bd. N.E. Ill. council, 1980-85; mem. Republican Citizens Com. Ill., 1960-61, Allegheny County (Pa.) Rep. Com., 1962-65; Trustee Roycemore Sch., Evanston, 1971-74; trustee, v.p. devel. Child and Family Services Chgo.; bd. dirs. Fellowship of Christian Athletes, U. N.C. Alumni Ill., Stockbrokers Assn. Chgo.; chmn. devel. com. Potawotamie Dist., 2000, chmn. fin. com., 2001; bd. dirs. Evanston Environ. Ctr., Ladd Arboretum, North Shore Nature Ctr. Served to 1st lt. AUS, 1952-54. Elected to N.C. Pub. Rels. Hall of Fame, 1994. Mem. Pub. Relations Soc. Am., Nat. Investor Relations Inst., Midwest Travel Writers Assn., Chgo. Ednl. TV Assn., Pub. Relations Counselors Roundtable, Am. Mgmt. Assn., Environ. Writers Assn. Am., Optimist Internat., Chgo. Assn. Commerce and Industry, Art Inst. Chgo., Univ. Club, Sunset Ridge Country Club, Optimist Club, Chi Psi. Republican. Presbyterian. Home: 2759 Broadway Ave Evanston IL 60201-1556

ROBBINS, HULDA DORNBLATT, artist, printmaker; b. Atlanta, Oct. 19, 1910; d. Adolph Benno and Lina (Rosenthal) Dornblatt. Student, Phila. Mus's. Sch. Indsl. Art, 1928-29, Prussian Acad., Berlin, 1929-31, Barnes Found., Merion, Pa., 1939. Poster designer and maker ITE Circuit Breaker Co. Inc., Phila., 1944; instr. serigraphy Nat. Serigraph Soc. Sch., N.Y.C., 1953-60; instr. creative painting Atlantic County Jewish Community Centers, Margate and Atlantic City, N.J., 1960-67. Represented by WIlliam P. Carl, Fine Prints, Boston, The Picture Store, Boston. One-man shows, Lehigh U. Art Galleries, 1933, ACA Galleries, Phila., 1939, 8th St. Gallery, N.Y.C., 1941, Serigraph Gallery, N.Y.C., 1947, Atlantic City Art Center, 1961, 71, numerous group shows, 2d Nat. Print ann. Bklyn. Mus., Carnegie Inst., Library of Congress, LaNapoule Art Found., Am. Graphic Contemporary Art; represented in permanent collections, including, Met. Mus. Art, N.Y.C., Mus. Modern Art, N.Y.C., Bibliotheque Nationale, Smithsonian Instn., Art Mus. Ont., Can., Victoria and Albert Mus., London, U.S. embassies abroad, Lehigh U., Princeton (N.J.) Print Club. Recipient Purchase prize Prints for Children, Mus. Modern Art, N.Y.C., 1941; prize 2d Portrait of Am. Competition, 1945; 2d prize Paintings by Printmakers, 1948 Mem. Am. Color Print Soc., Print Club, Graphics Soc., Serigraph Soc. (mem. founding group, charter sec., Ninth Ann. prize 1948, 49) Home and Office: 16 S Buffalo Ave Ventnor City NJ 08406 2635 Office Phone: 609-823-7314. *To cherish and express living through devotion to art.*

ROBBINS, IRA PAUL, law educator; b. Bklyn., Jan. 2, 1949; AB, U. Pa., 1970; JD, Harvard U., 1973. Bar: N.Y. 1974, U.S. Ct. Appeals (2d cir.) 1975, D.C. 1984. Law clk. to presiding justice U.S. Ct. Appeals (2d cir.), N.Y.C., 1973-75; assoc. prof. law, dir. Kans. Defender Project U. Kans., Lawrence, 1975-79; prof. law and justice Am. U., Washington, 1979—. Vis. prof. law Georgetown U. Law Ctr., Washington, 1982, 90; cons. Nat. Inst. Corrections, Washington, 1983—, Fed. Jud. Ctr., Washington, 1983—, also acting dir. Continuing Edn. and Tng. Div. Fed. Jud. Ctr., 1986; bd. dirs. D.C. Prisoners Legal Svcs. Inc.; cons. editor The Am. Univ. Press, Jour. Criminal Law & Criminology, Judicature, Fed. Probation, Justice Quar., Justice System Jour., State-Fed. Jud. Observer; cons. criminal rules com. judicial Conf. of the U.S., 2001—. Author: Comparative Postconviction Remedies, 1980, Judicial Sabbaticals, 1987, The Legal Dimensions of Private Incarceration, 1988, Toward a More Just and Effective System of Review in State Death Penalty Cases, 1990, Habeas Corpus Checklists, 2005; editor, contbr.: Prisoners' Rights Sourcebook, 1980; editor, contbr. The Law and Processes of Post-Conviction Remedies, 1982; editor, contbr.: Prisoners and the Law, 2005; contbr. articles to profl. jours. Ethel and Raymond F. Rice scholar, 1978, Pauline Ruyle Moore scholar, 1980, 90, Barnard T. Welsh scholar, 1982—; Supreme Ct. fellow, 1985-86; named one of Outstanding Young Men Am., U.S. Jaycees, 1982, Recipient of Chief Judge John R. Brown Award for Jud. Scholarship and Edn., 1998. Mem. ABA (reporter study on pvt. prisons 1986-88, cons. 1986-90, task force on death penalty habeas corpus 1988-90), Am. Law Inst., Assn. Am. Law Schs. (exec. coun. criminal justice sect. 1983-89), Internat. Assn. Penal Law, Am. Judicature Soc. (nat. coun. crime and delinquency 1997—), Phi Beta Kappa. Office: Am U Washington Coll Law 4801 Massachusetts Ave NW Washington DC 20016-8001

ROBBINS, JACK WINTON, lawyer; b. Flemington, Mo., Nov. 1, 1919; s. Winnie and Opal (Pitts) R.; m. Hilda Haynes, Feb. 2, 1946; children: Randel Bliss Brodrique, Mark Haynes Robbins. BS, U. North Tex., 1941; JD, Columbia U., 1943. Bar: N.Y. 1944, Pa. 1956, U.S. Supreme Ct. 1953. Law clk. N.Y. Ct. of Appeals, Albany, 1943-44; assoc. atty. Cravath, Swaine & Moore, N.Y.C., 1944-53; prosecutor Nuremberg (Germany) War Crimes Trials, 1946-48; counsel Pitcairn Trust Co., Jenkintown, Pa., 1953—. Bd. dirs. Upper Dublin Twp. Sch. Bd., Ft. Washington, Pa., 1960-73, Ursinus Coll., Collegeville, Pa., 1984—. Mem. ABA, Pa. Bar Assn., Phila. Bar Assn. Republican. Methodist. Home: 3500 West Chester Pike Newtown Square PA 19073- Office: Pitcairn Trust Co 165 Township Line Rd Jenkintown PA 19046-3531

ROBBINS, JAMES O. communications executive; BS in Am. studies, Univ. Pa.; MBA, Harvard Univ. Mng. editor WBZ-TV News, Boston, 1969-72; mgmt. position Continental Cablevision, 1972-79, Montachusett Cable Television, 1972-79; v.p., gen. mgr. Viacom Cablevision, Long Island, N.Y., 1979-83; pres., CEO Cox Communications, Inc., 1983—. Bd. dirs. NCR Corp., Teleport Communications, Inc., TeleWest. Treas., bd. dirs. Nat. Cable Television Assn., exec. com. Cable Satellite Pub. Affairs Network; v.p. Cable in Classroom; trustee Westminster Sch., Atlanta. Office: Cox Communications Inc 1400 Lake Hearn Dr NE Atlanta GA 30319-1464

ROBBINS, JEFFREY HOWARD, media consultant, research writer, educator; b. N.Y.C., Mar. 29, 1941; s. Stanley Samuel and Miriam (Cooper) R.; m. Marsha Sue Rimler, Nov. 3, 1984 (div. Dec. 1996); 1 child, Nina Camille. BSME, Carnegie Mellon U., 1962; MS in Physics, U. N.Mex., 1966, ABD in Physics, 1967; postgrad., U. Calif., Berkeley and L.A., 1963-64. Summer rsch. assoc. Linde Co., Tonawanda, NY, 1961; rsch. engr. N.Am. Aviation (Rockwell), Downey, Calif., 1962—64; summer rsch. assoc. Los Alamos Nat. Lab., N.Mex., 1965; sr. engr. Radio Engring. Labs., L.I., NY, 1968—70; engring. cons. PRD Electronics, Syosset, NY, 1972—73; sr. cons. Bendix Corp., Teterboro, NJ, 1974—76; sr. engr. Giordano Assocs., Franklin Lakes, NJ, 1977—81; sr. applications engr. Racal-Redak, Mahwah, NJ, 1981—83; tech. media cons. Allied Signal Corp., Teterboro, 1983—92, U.S. Army, Picatinny Arsenal, NJ, 1992; tech. cons. Ford Motor Co., Lansdale, Pa., 1992—98, Visteon Automotive Electronics, Markham, Canada, 1998; adj. prof. Rutgers U., New Brunswick, NJ, 2002—. Cons. Tyco Internat., Clark, N.J., 1998-2002; tech. cons., rsch. writer media literacy programs Packer Collegiate Inst., Bklyn., N.Y.C., 1992-93, On TV, Inc., N.Y.C., 1992; initiator, moderator Media Literacy Forum, 1995; evening sch. instr. New Sch. for Social Rsch., N.Y.C., 1979-85; presenter in field. Author: On Balance and Higher Education, 1970; contbr. articles to profl. jours. Organizer, co-moderator Future Impact of Artificial Intelligence, Robotics Forum, 1984. Recipient 1st prize for essay The World and I Mag., 1990; nominee Grawemeyer award in Edn., 1988; NDEA fellow, 1966-67, others; feature essay premier issue Plain mag., 1994. Mem. IEEE (presenter Internat. Symposium in Tech. and Soc. 1993, 96, 98, Internat. Soc. Sys. Scis. Conf. 1993, 95, 97, 99, 2000, 02, initiator, moderator, media literacy forum Packer Collegiate Inst. 1995, presenter World Order Conf., Toronto 1999, 2001), N.Y. Acad. Scis., Sigma Xi, Phi Kappa Phi, Pi Tau Sigma. Home and Office: PO Box 335 Long Beach NY 11561-0335 E-mail: jhrobbins@erols.com.

ROBBINS, JEFFREY W. theologian, philosopher; b. Baton Rouge, Apr. 12, 1972; s. William H. and Mary Ann Robbins; m. Noelle Robbins Vahanian. BA, Baylor U., 1994; MDiv, Tex. Christian U., 1997; MPhil, Syracuse U., 1999, PhD, 2001. Lectr. theology St. Bonaventure (N.Y.) U., 2001—02; asst. prof. religion and philosophy Lebanon Valley Coll., Annville, Pa., 2002—. Author: Between Faith and Thought: An Essay on the Ontotheological Condition, 2003, In Search of a Non-Dogmatic Theology, 2004; editor: Contemporary Religious Thought; assoc. editor: Jour. Cultural and Religious Theory, 2002—. Fellow: Internat. Inst. Hermeneutics (assoc.); mem.: Soc. Phenomenology and Existential Philosophy, Am. Acad. Religion. Democrat. Avocations: tennis, travel. Office: Lebanon Valley Coll 101 N College Ave Annville PA 17003 Office Phone: 717-867-6720. Personal E-mail: robbins@lvc.edu. E-mail: robbins@lvc.edu.

ROBBINS, JENNIFER KAY, journalist; b. Cin., Nov. 10, 1962; d. Douglas Jay and Paula Jane (Wyatt) R.; m. Steven M. Hanger, Apr. 5, 1996; children: Cheyenne, Winston. A in Acctg., MacArthur State U., 1983; BS in Mass Comm., Auburn U., 1998. Acct. Small Bus. Svc., Montgomery, Ala., 1983-85, Computer Bus. Svcs., New Orleans, 1985-88, Ala. Assn. Realtors, Montgomery, 1990-93; owner, acct. Affordable Acctg., Montgomery, 1993-95; editor-in-chief AUMnibus, Montgomery, 1995-98; mng. editor Butler County News, Greenville, Ala., 1998-99; editor The Luverne (Ala.) Jour., 1999—. Founder, chairperson People Against Vetoing Edn., Montgomery, 1997; mem. PTA, Tallassee, Ala., 1995—; mem. leadership coun. Auburn U., 1997—. Recipient Emerging 30 award Montgomery Area C. of C., 1995, 3rd pl. news photography spot Coll. Press Assn., 1998. Mem. Soc. Profl. Journalists, Omicron Delta Kappa. Avocations: writing short stories, reading.

ROBBINS, JERRY HAL, educational administration educator; b. DeQueen, Ark., Feb. 28, 1939; s. James Hal and Barbara I. (Rogers) R. BA in Math, Hendrix Coll., 1960; M.Ed., U. Ark., 1963, Ed.D., 1966. Tchr. math. and music Clinton (Ark.) pub. schs., 1960-61; prin. Adrian (Mo.) High Sch., 1961-63; exec. sec. Ark. Sch. Study Council, Fayetteville, 1963-65; mem. faculty U. Miss., University, 1965-74, prof. ednl. adminstrn., 1970-74, chmn. dept. ednl. adminstrn., 1970-74; dean Coll. Edn., U. Ark., Little Rock, 1974-79; asso. v.p. for acad. affairs Ga. State U., Atlanta, 1979-84, dean Coll. Edn., 1984-90, prof. ednl. adminstrn., 1990-91; dean. Coll. Edn. Ea. Mich. U., Ypsilanti, 1991—2004. Co-author: (with S. B. Williams Jr.) Student Activities in the Innovative School, 1969, School Custodian's Handbook, 1970, Administrator's Manual of School Plant Administration, 1970. Mem. NEA, Am. Assn. Sch. Adminstrs., Am. Assn. Colls. Tchr. Edn. (dir. 1979-82, 2000—), Nat. Assn. Secondary Sch. Prins., So. Regional Council Ednl. Adminstrn. (pres. 1970-71), Tchr. Edn. Coun. State Colls. and Univs. (pres. 1998-99), Phi Delta Kappa, Kappa Delta Pi (v.p. chpt. devel. 1978-80, pres. elect 1980-82, pres.

1982-84, past pres. 1984-86) Mem. United Meth. Ch. Home and Office: 3384 Bent Trail Dr Ann Arbor MI 48108-9316 Office: Ea Mich U 310 Porter Bldg Ypsilanti MI 48197 E-mail: jerry.robbins@emich.edu.

ROBBINS, JOHN BENNETT, medical researcher; b. Bklyn., Dec. 1, 1932; BA, NYU, 1956, MD, 1959, U. Goteborg, Sweden, 1976. Intern, resident Children's Med. Svc. Mass. Gen. Hosp., Boston, 1959—60; rsch. fellow dept. pediat. U. Fla., 1961—64; guest scientist dept. chem. immunology Weizmann Inst. Sci., Rehovot, Israel, 1965—66; asst. prof. pediat. and microbiology U. Fla., Gainesville, 1964—67; from asst. prof. to assoc. prof. pediat. Albert Einstein Coll. Medicine, 1967—70; clin. dir. Nat. Inst. Child Health and Human Devel. NIH, 1970—72; chief devel. immunology br. NIH, 1971—74; dir. divsn. bacterial products FDA, 1974—83; chief lab. devel. and molecular immunity Nat. Inst. Child Health and Human Devel. NIH, 1983—. Henry Bale Meml. lectr. Nat. Inst. Biol. Stds. and Control, 1979; Erwin Neter Meml. lectr. U. Buffalo, 1984; Henry L. Barnett lectr. Albert Einstein Coll. Medicine, 1985; Maxwell Finland lectr. Infectious Disease Soc. Am., 1989; Louis Weinstein lectr. Tufts U., 1989. Recipient E. Mead Johnson award, Am. Acad. Pediat., 1975, Albert Lasker Clin. Med. Rsch. award, Albert and Mary Lasker Found., 1996. Fellow: Am. Acad. Microbiology; mem.: Nat. Acad. Svc., Nat. Inst. Medicine, Am. Assn. Immunologists, Assn. Am. Physicians, Am. Soc. Clin. Investigation, Soc. Infectious Disease, Soc. Pediatric Rsch., Inst. Medicine of NAS. Achievements include development of first effective typhoid fever vaccine for children. Office: Nat Inst of Child Hlth & Hum Devel 9000 Rockville Pike Rm 424 Bethesda MD 20892-0001*

ROBBINS, JOHN CLAPP, management consultant; b. Cleveland, Jan. 22, 1921; s. John Clapp and Esther Turner (Holland) R.; m. Louise Severance Nash, Jan. 10, 1951 (div. Oct. 1974); children: Anne Millikin, Julia Severance, John Nash; m. Beatrice Blair, Aug. 2, 1975 (dec. July 1994); m. Sylvia Hordosch, Dec. 20, 2000. AB, Harvard U., 1942. Copy boy, reporter, writer, promotion editor Cleve. Press, 1946-57; exec. internat. div. Mobil Oil Corp., N.Y.C., Istanbul, 1957-70; chief exec. officer Planned Parenthood/World Population, N.Y.C., 1970-75; prin. mgmt. cons. Stanford Research Inst., 1976-83; v.p. GPA Inc., N.Y.C., 1983—; pres. John Robbins Assocs. Spl. fin. cons. Internat. Helsinki Fedn., Vienna, Parkinson Disease Found., N.Y.C., Alan Guttmacher Inst., N.Y.C. Author: Too Many Asians, 1959. Bd. dirs., pres. Am. Hosp. Istanbul; trea. Harvard Libr. in N.Y.C. Capt. AUS, 1942-45. Decorated Bronze Star, Purple Heart; Reid fellow, 1953 Mem. Internat. Planned Parenthood Fedn. London, N.Y. State Rep. Pro-Choice Alliance. Unitarian Universalist. Home and Office: 115 E 87th St New York NY 10128-1136 Office Phone: 212-369-9800. E-mail: johnrobbin@aol.com.

ROBBINS, KELLY, professional golfer; b. Mt. Pleasant, Mich., Sept. 29, 1969; d. Steve and Margie R. BA, U. Tulsa. Mem. Ladies Pro Golf Assn., 1991—. Mem. U.S. Solheim Cup, 1994, 96, 98, 2000, 02, 03. Achievements include 9 Career LPGA victories. Avocations: fishing, tennis, swimming, basketball. Office: c/o Ladies Pro Golf Assn 100 International Golf Dr Daytona Beach FL 32124-1082

ROBBINS, LARRY A. finance company executive; b. Dallas, Tex., Oct. 8, 1956; m. Kimberly Robbins; 2 children. B in Polit. Sci., U. Tex., Arlington, 1978. CIO Thrivent Fin. for Luths., Mpls., 2002—; joined Southwestern Life Ins. Co., Dallas, 1978, Perot Sys. Corp., Dallas, 1990. Active Cross View Luth. Ch., Edina, Minn. Office: Thrivent Fin for Lutherans 625 4th Ave South Minneapolis MN 55415

ROBBINS, MARY, concert pianist; b. Shelby, N.C., Feb. 14, 1950; d. Clyde Hugh and Hazel Marguerite (Lovett) Robbins; m. Carl Brockman, Jan. 16, 1983. Student, Converse Coll., Spartanburg, S.C., 1968-71; BMusic, U. Tex., 1973, MMusic, 1975, D Musical Arts, 1992. Concert coord. Austin (Tex.) Virtuosi, 1980-82; piano clinician Alfred Music Pub., Van Nuys, Cailf., 1991-94; pianist various chamber org., Austin, 1976-91; pvt. piano instr. for adults and children Austin, 1971—; tchg. asst., instr. piano U. Tex., Austin, 1971-75; founder, prin. pianist A. Mozart Fest, Austin, 1991—, artistic dir., 1991—. Accompanist U. Tex., Austin, 1971-84; invited lectr. Mozart Internat. Bicentennial Congress, Salzburg, Austria, 1991. Composer music and cadenzas following Mozart's style for his piano concertos, 1989—; composer, performer CD, A. Mozart Fest, 1998, CD with Austrian pianist Paul Badura-Skoda, 2002. Presenter, Music Tchr. Nat. Assoc. Conf., 2003. (Presenter of session on stylistic issues of interpretation in Mozart). Vol. music class tchr. First English Luth. Ch., Austin, 1992; founder combined groups Classical Music Consortium, Austin, 1997. Grantee Tex. Commn. on Arts, 1991, 93, City of Austin, 1992—. Mem. Austin Dist. Music Tchrs. Assn. (v.p. 1997-98, chair adult programs 1997—, chair festivals 1997-98, Pre-Coll. Tchr. of Yr. 1998), Mu Phi Epsilon. Lutheran. Avocations: cooking, entertaining, dance, outdoor sports, visual arts. Home: 2600 La Ronde St Austin TX 78731-5924

ROBBINS, NANCY LOUISE See MANN, NANCY LOUISE

ROBBINS, NANCY SLINKER, volunteer; b. New Kensington, Pa., Jan. 28, 1923; d. Charles Morris and Nancy Grace (Moore) Slinker; m. James Bingham Murray, Aug. 1, 1946 (div. 1959); m. Daniel Harvey Robbins, Nov. 21, 1964; children: Nancy Caroline, Christina Chapman. BA, Westminster Coll., 1945; grad., U. Pitts., 1946. Cert. tchr. Pa. Tchr. Lower Burrell Sch., New Kensington, 1945-48; asst. buyer Gimbel's, Pitts., 1951-53, buyer, 1953-57, La Salle's, Toledo, 1957-61, Sibley's, Rochester, N.Y., 1961-66. Editor: Fan Fare, 1980-81. Pres. bd. Woman's Edn. and Indsl. Union, Rochester, 1973-76, Women's Coalition for Downtown, Rochester, 1982-84; pres. bd. Ronald McDonald House, Rochester, 1986-90, adminstr. grants program, 1996—; chmn. Pub. TV Auction, Rochester, 1980. Recipient Jefferson award Am. Inst. Pub. Svc., 1988, Forman Flair award for outstanding volunteerism, 1990, DeWitt Clinton awrd for pub. svc. Masons, 1989. Avocations: antique collecting, travel, cooking. Home: 35 Schoolhouse Ln Rochester NY 14618-3231 E-mail: nandan0035@aol.com.

ROBBINS, NORMAN NELSON, lawyer; b. Detroit, Sept. 27, 1919; s. Charles and Eva (Gold) R.; m. Pamela Anne Eldred, April 22, 1946; children: Susan, Aimee. LLB, JD, Wayne State U., 1943. Bar: Mich. 1943. Pvt. practice, Birmingham, Mich., 1943—. Chmn. Mich. Bd. for Marriage Counselors, 1971-75; lectr. Inst. Continuing Legal Edn. Editor Mich. Family Law Jour., 1974—; mem. editorial bd. Am. Jour. Family Law; co-editor: Michigan Family Law, 2 vols., 1988; contbr. 600 articles to legal publs. Chmn. Wayne County unit Am. Cancer Soc., Detroit, 1971-76, Mich. Dept. Vets. Trust Fund, 1977-78. Capt. USMCR, 1943-46, PTO. Recipient Gov.'s award State of Mich., Cert. of Appreciation, Gov. of Mich., Cert. of Recognition, Detroit Common Coun. award Mich. Assn. Marriage Counselors, Lifetime Achievement award Mich. Family Law Sect. Mem. ABA (mem. family law coun. 1993-95, sr. editor ABA Family Adv. 1991—), Mich. Bar Assn. (chmn. family law sect. 1974-75), Oakland County Bar Assn., Am. Acad. Matrimonial Lawyers (pres. Mich. chpt. 1982), Am. Legion (judge adv. Mich. dept. 1968-69, comdr. Detroit chpt. 1970-71). Office: 7802 Lakeside Blvd Apt 723 Boca Raton FL 33434-6282

ROBBINS, OREM OLFORD, insurance company executive; b. Mpls., Feb. 5, 1915; s. Douglas Ford and Grace (Rorem) R.; m. Annette Strand Scherer, May 17, 1992; children: Ford M., Ross S., Gail R. Tomei, Cynthia R. Rothbard. BBA with distinction, U. Minn., 1936; BS in Law, William Mitchell Coll. Law, 1946, JD, 1948. Comml. rep. NW Bell Telephone Co., Mpls., 1936-48; dep. dir. U.S. Treas. Dept., Mpls., 1948-49; sales rep. Conn. Gen. Life Ins. Co., Mpls., 1949-56; founder, chmn. Security Life Ins. Co. Am., Mpls., 1956—. Bd. dirs., past pres. Family and Children's Svcs., Mpls., 1968—; bd. govs., past chmn. Meth. Hosp., Mpls., 1960-90; past treas., bd. dirs. Goodwill/Easter Seals, St. Paul, 1958-68, 75-88; life trustee Hamline U., St. Paul, 1979—, chmn. bd. trustees, 1990-91. Col. U.S. Army, 1941-46. Decorated Legion of Merit; recipient Outstanding Achievement award U. Minn., 2001. Fellow Life Mgmt. Assn.; mem. Am. Soc. CLU (pres. Mpls. chpt. 1959), Health Underwriters Assn., Chartered Fin. Cons., Am. Legion, Skylight Club (Mpls.), Hole in the Wall Golf Club, Naples Yacht Club, Mpls. Club, Officer's Club, Masons. Republican. Methodist. Office: Security Life Ins Co Am 10901 Red Circle Dr Minnetonka MN 55343-9304 Office Phone: 952-544-2121. E-mail: oorobbins@securitylife.com.

ROBBINS, RACHEL F. lawyer; b. Trenton, N.J., Oct. 30, 1950; BA, Wellesley Coll., 1972; JD, NYU, 1976. Bar: N.Y. 1977. Mng. dir., gen. counsel J.P. Morgan & Co., Inc., N.Y.C., 1981—. Mng. editor Ann. Survey Am. Law. Mem. ABA, Assn. of the Bar of the City of N.Y., N.Y. State Bar Assn., Order of the Coif. Office: JP Morgan & Co Inc 60 Wall St New York NY 10260-0001 E-mail: robbins_rachel@jpmorgan.com.

ROBBINS, RAY C. retired manufacturing executive; b. Syracuse, N.Y., Sept. 15, 1920; s. Frederick and Mary Elizabeth (Field) R.; children: Sandra Robbins Jannetta, Ray Charles Jr., Eric L. With Lennox Internat. Inc. (formerly Lennox Furnace Co.), 1940-48; asst sales mgr. Lennox Industries Inc. (formerly Lennox Furnace Co.), Syracuse, 1948-52; gen. mgr. new factory and sales office, Lennox Industries, Inc. (formerly Lennox Furnace Co.), Toronto, Ont., Can., 1952-67; dir. Lennox Can. and Timeplan Fin. Co. Ltd., 1953-65; pres. Lennox Can., 1965-69; exec. v.p. Lennox-Worldwide, 1969-70, pres., CEO, 1970-77; chmn. bd. Lennox Can., 1976-92; chmn. bd., chief exec. officer Lennox Industries Inc., 1977-80, chmn. bd., 1980-91, chmn. emeritus, 1991—. Bd. dirs. Lennox Internat., First Interstate of Iowa, Inc., Hawkeye Security Ins. Co., Des Moines, Fin. Security Group, Inc., Des Moines, Q-Dot, Garland, Tex.; pres., founder, bd. dirs. Exec. Inst., Inc., Dallas, 1983—; bd. advisor Internat. Exec. Svc. Corp., 1993—. Bd. dirs. Metro Toronto Big Bros., 1964-69, Queensway Gen. Hosp., 1957-69, Texx Found., 1979-81, Bus. Industry Polit. Action Com.; bd. govs., mem. exec. com. Iowa Coll. Found., 1975-78; v.p., mem. exec. bd. Mid-Iowa County Boy Scouts Am., 1972-78; mem. Pres.' Phys. Fitness Council, from 1979; exec. bd. Circle 10 council Boy Scouts Am., from 1979; mem. Dallas Citizens Council; bd. of govs. Nat. Women's Econ. Alliance Found.; bd. dirs. North Tex. Commn.; fellow Legacy for Pub. Opinion, 2001—. Served with AUS, 1942-45, PTO. Mem. ASHRAE (life), Am. Refrigeration Inst. (bd. dirs. 1973-74, 78, life from 1979, v.p. 1975-76, chmn. 1977), NAM (bd. dirs. 1974-75, dir. at large 1976, dir. State of Iowa 1977-78, dir. State of Tex. 1979-92), Nat. Mgmt. Assn. (exec. adv. com. 1979-92), Gas Appliance Mfrs. Assn. (past bd. dirs.), Can. Gas Assn. (pres.), Can. Mfg. Assn. (chmn. Toronto dist.), U.S. C. of C. (Can.-U.S. sect.), Bus.-Industry Polit. Action Com. (bd. dirs. 1991). Clubs: Park Cen., Landmark Athletic, Cooper Fitness Ctr. (Dallas); Canyon Creek Country (Richardson, Tex.).

ROBBINS, ROBERT B. lawyer; b. Canton, Ohio, Aug. 31, 1951; s. Nathan H. and Evelyn (Cohen) R.; m. Melinda Abbot Street, Oct. 18, 1981; children: Julia Bates, Katherine Melinda, Caroline Rachel, Eli Street. AB magna cum laude, Cornell U., 1972; JD cum laude, Harvard U., 1975. Bar: D.C. 1975. Ptnr. Shaw Pittman LLP, Washington, 1976—, also chmn. corp. securities group. Chmn. D.C. Bar Commn. on Broker-Dealer Regulation, 1985-90; co-chmn. Ann. Course Study on Pvt. Placements and Regulation D, Am. Law Inst.-ABA, 1992—. Mem. D.C. Bar (steering com., sect. corp., fin. and securities law 1991-94, chmn. 1993-94). Office: Shaw Pittman LLP 2300 N St NW Washington DC 20037-1172 Office Phone: 202-663-8000. E-mail: robert.robbins@shawpittman.com.

ROBBINS, ROBERT CLAYTON, surgeon; b. Laurel, Miss., Nov. 20, 1957; MD, U. Miss., 1983. Cert. cardiothoracic surgery Am. Bd. Thoracic Surgery, gen. surgery Am. Bd. Surgery. Intern U. Miss. Med. Ctr., 1983—84, resident, 1984—88; fellow Stanford U., 1989—91, asst. prof. then assoc. prof., 1993—; dir. Inst. Cardiovasc. Medicine, 2004—. Mem.: Western Thoracic Surgical Assn., Am. Assn. Thoracic Surgery, Cardiothoracic Surgery Network. Office: Falk Cardiovasc Rsch Ctr 300 Pasteur Dr CVRB MC 5407 Stanford CA 94305

ROBBINS, ROBERT MARVIN, accountant; b. Warren, Ohio, Aug. 2, 1924; s. Edward and May (Rubenson) R.; m. Phyllis Ann Dillon, Sept. 29, 1951; children: Michael C., Pat D., Robert J., Susan Jo Burkey. BSBA, Ohio State U., 1948; postgrad., NYU, 1972, 76, 79. CPA, Ohio. Sr. acct. Albert F. Turrell & Assocs. CPAs, Warren, Ohio, 1948-52; comptroller Harts Jewelry Stores, Ohio, 1952-54; pvt. practice Warren, 1954-59; mng. ptnr. Griffith & Robbins, CPAs, Warren, 1959-65; owner R.M. Robbins & Assocs., CPAs, Warren, 1966-82; pres., mgr. R.M. Robbins & Assocs., Inc., Warren, 1982-98; retired. Sec. and acctg. cons. Ohio-Ont. Clean Fuels, Inc., Warren, 1986-90; area owner, franchisee Red Barn Restaurants, Omaha, 1968-72. Treas. Planned Parenthood, Youngstown, Ohio, 1970s; acct. Sisters of Humility of Mary, Villa Maria, Pa., 1978-83. Sgt. U.S. Army armored div., 1943-45, ETO. Mem. Am. Inst. CPAs, (mem. tax div. subcoms.), ACUTE, Ohio Soc. CPAs, Rotary, Exchange Club (treas. Warren chpt. 1968-73), Squaw Creek Country Club (past bd. dirs.), Elks, Buckeye Club (Warren), Ohio State U. Pres. Club. Avocations: flying, golf, history of american revolution and civil war. Home: 376 Wainwood Dr SE Warren OH 44484-4650

ROBBINS, STEPHEN J. M. lawyer; b. Seattle, Apr. 13, 1942; s. Robert Mads and Aneita Elberta (West) R.; m. Nina Winifred Tanner, Aug. 11, 1967; children: Sarah E.T., Alicia S.T. AB, UCLA, 1964; JD, Yale U., 1971. Bar: D.C. 1973, U.S. Dist. Ct. D.C. 1973, U.S. Ct. Appeals (D.C. cir.) 1973, U.S. Ct. Appeals (3d cir.) 1973, U.S. Dist. Ct. (ea. and no. dists.) Calif. 1982, U.S. Dist. Ct. (cen. dist.) Calif. 1983, Supreme Ct. of Republic of Palau, 1994. Pres. U.S. Nat. Student Assn., Washington, 1964-65; dir. scheduling McGovern for Pres., Washington, 1971-72; assoc. Steptoe & Johnson, Washington, 1972-75; chief counsel spl. inquiry on food prices, com. on nutrition and human needs U.S. Senate, Washington, 1975; v.p., gen. counsel Straight Arrow Pubs., San Francisco, 1975-77; dep. dist. atty. City and County of San Francisco, 1977-78; regional counsel U.S. SBA, San Francisco, 1978-80; spl. counsel Warner-Amex Cable Communications, Sacramento, 1981-82; ptnr. McDonough, Holland and Allen, Sacramento, 1982-84; v.p. Straight Arrow Pubs., N.Y.C., 1984-86; gen. legal counsel Govt. State of Koror, Rep. of Palau, Western Caroline Islands, 1994-95; pvt. practice law, 1986—. Adj. prof. govt. Calif. State U., Sacramento, 1999—. Staff sgt. U.S. Army, 1966-68. Mem. ABA (sect. urban, state and local govt. sect. real property, probate and trust law, sect. natural resources energy, environ. law, forum com. on affordable housing and cmty. devel.), D.C. Bar, State Bar of Calif., Urban Land Inst., Am. Hist. Assn., Supreme Ct. Hist. Soc., Acad. Polit. Sci., Chamber Music Soc. of Sacramento, Oreg. Shakespeare Festival, Shaw Island Hist. Soc. Democrat. Unitarian. Avocations: theater, art, hiking. Office: 2150 3rd Ave Sacramento CA 95818-3102

ROBBINS, SUSAN PAULA, social work educator; b. Bklyn., Aug. 15, 1948; d. Harold Jess and Rose (Bernstein) R. AA, Manhattan C.C., 1972; BA summa cum laude, Hamline U., 1974; MSW, U. Minn., 1976; PhD, Tulane U., 1979. Adj. instr. dept. sociology and social work Augsburg Coll., Mpls., 1975-76; part-time instr. women's studies program U. Minn., Mpls., 1976; rsch. and grant cons. Seminole Tribe of Fla., Hollywood, 1978-79, child and adolescent caseworker, program planning cons., 1979-80; coord. criminal justice/corrections program St. Mary's Dominican Coll., New Orleans, 1979-80; asst. prof. social work New Orleans Consortium, 1978-80, U. Houston, 1980-86, assoc. prof., 1986—, assoc. dean acad. affairs, 1998-2000. Cons. ABA Multi Door Program, Houston, Cmty. Svc. Option Program, Houston; mediator Dispute Resolution Ctrs., Houston, 1982—; trainer Tex. Dept. Protective Svcs. Tng. Inst., 1995—. Author (with others): Encyclopedia of Social Work, Social Workers' Desk Reference; contbr. articles and book chpts. to profl. jours. Women's Club of Mpls. fellow, 1975, Nat. Inst. of Mental Health fellow, 1976-78; recipient Nat. Faculty Excellence award Univ. Continuing Edn. Assn., 1998. Mem. NASW, Coun. on Social Work Edn., Social Welfare Action Alliance, Assn. for Cmty. Orgn. and Social Adminstrn., So. Sociol. Soc., Phi Kappa Phi (sec. Houston chpt. 1984—). Democrat. Jewish. Office: Univ Houston 4800 Calhoun Rd Houston TX 77204-4013 E-mail: srobbins@uh.edu.

ROBBINS, THOMAS EUGENE, writer; b. Blowing Rock, N.C., 1936; m. Terrie Hemingway (div.); m. Alexa d'Avalon, 1995; 1 child, Fleetwood Starr. Student, Washington and Lee U., 1954-56, U. Wash., 1963; degree in social sci., Va. Commonwealth U., 1959. Former copy editor Richmond (Va.) Times-Dispatch, Seattle Post-Intelligencer; art critic Seattle Times. Author: Guy Anderson, 1965, Another Roadside Attraction, 1971, Even Cowgirls Get the Blues, 1976 (Best Am. Short Story 1977), Still Life with Woodpecker, 1980, Jitterbug Perfume, 1984, Skinny Legs and All, 1990, Half Asleep in Frog Pajamas, 1994, Fierce Invalids Home from Hot Climates, 2000. With USAF. Named one of 100 Best Writers of 20th Century, Writer's Digest. Office: PO Box 338 La Conner WA 98257-0338

ROBBINS, THOMAS LANDAU, humanities researcher; b. N.Y.C., Oct. 13, 1943; s. Manuel Lee and Elly (Landau) R. AB, Harvard U., 1965; MA, U. N.C., 1968, PhD in Sociology, 1973. Instr., asst. prof. Queens Coll., 1971-78; instr. Cen. Mich. U., 1982-83; NIMH postdoctoral trainee in sociology Yale U., New Haven, 1979-81; sr. rsch. assoc. Santa Barbara (Calif.) Ctr. for Humanistic Studies, 1990—. Author: Cults, Converts and Charisma, 1988; co-editor: In Gods We Trust, 1981, 2d edit., 1990, Cults, Culture and the Law, 1985, Church-State Relations, 1987, Millennium, Messiahs and Mayhem, 1997, Misunderstanding Cults; assoc. editor Sociol. Analysis, 1984-90; edtl. cons. Nova Religio, 1997—; contbr. articles to various publs.; edtl. cons. Nova Religio. Mem. Soc. for the Sci. Study of Religion (exec. coun. 1988-91), Assn. for the Sociology Religion, (exec. coun. 1985-87), Am. Sociol. Assn., Soc. for the Study of Social Problems. Meher Baba. Home and Office: 427 4th St SW Apt 8A Rochester MN 55902-3226 *I am becoming concerned these days about threats to freedom of religion in the United States and Europe.*

ROBBINS, TIMOTHY (FRANCIS), director, actor; b. West Covina, Calif., Oct. 16, 1958; life ptnr. Susan Sarandon; children: John Henry, Miles 1 stepchild, Eva Maria. BA, UCLA, 1981. Founder, artistic dir. The Actor's Gang, 1981—. Actor: (films) No Small Affair, 1984, Toy Soldiers, 1984, Fraternity Vacation, 1985, The Sure Thing, 1985, Howard the Duck, 1986, Top Gun, 1986, Five Corners, 1987, Bill Durham, 1988, Tapeheads, 1989, Eric The Viking, 1989, Miss Firecracker, 1989, Cadillac Man, 1990, Twister, 1990, Jacob's Ladder, 1990, Jungle Fever, 1991, The Player, 1992 (Best Actor award Cannes Film Festival 1992), Short Cuts, 1993, The Hudsucker Proxy, 1994, The Shawshank Redemption, 1994, Ready to Wear (Prêt-à-Porter), 1994, I.Q., 1994, Nothing to Lose, 1997, Arlington Road, 1999, Austin Powers: The Spy Who Shagged Me, 1999, Mission to Mars, 2000, High Fidelity, 2000, Antitrust, 2001, Human Nature, 2001, The Truth About Charlie, 2002, The Day My God Died (voice), 2003, Mystic River, 2003 (Golden Globe for best supporting actor in a drama, 2004, Screen Actors Guild Award for best supporting actor, 2004, Acad. Award for best supporting actor in a drama, 2004), Code 46, 2003, (TV movies) Quarterback Princess, 1983, Malice in Wonderland, 1985; actor, dir., writer, composer: Bob Roberts, 1992; dir., writer, prodr.: Dead Man Walking, 1995 (Golden Globe nomination for best dir. of film 1996, Acad. Award nomination for best dir. 1996), The Cradle Will Rock, 1999; exec. prodr., The Typewriter, the Rifle, and the Movie Camera, 1994, The Spectre of Hope, 2000; dir. (plays) Ubu Roi (L.A. Weekly Dir. award), A Midsummer's Night Dream, Methuselam, the Eternal Bourgeois, The Good Woman of Setzuan (L.A. Drama Critics Circle nominee), and others, (TV series) Queen's Supreme, 2003; co-writer: (plays) Alagazam...After the Dog Wars, Violence: The Misadventures of Spike Spangle, Farmer, Carnage, a Comedy, Embedded, and others. Recipient Tribute to Ind. Vision Award, Sundance Film Festival, 1997. Office: ICM c/o Elaine Goldsmith Thomas 40 W 57th St New York NY 10019*

ROBBINS-WILF, MARCIA, educational consultant; b. Newark, Mar. 22, 1949; d. Saul and Ruth (Fern) Robbins; 1 child, Orin. Student, Emerson Coll., 1967-69, Seton Hall U., 1969, Fairleigh Dickinson U., 1970; BA, George Washington U., 1971; MA, NYU, 1975; postgrad., St. Peter's Coll., Jersey City, 1979, Fordham U., 1980; MS, Yeshiva U., 1981, EdD, 1986; postgrad., Monmouth Coll., 1986. Cert. elem. tchr., N.Y., N.J., reading specialist, N.J., prin., supr., N.J., adminstr., supr., N.Y. Tchr. Sleepy Hollow Elem. Sch., Falls Church, Va., 1971-72, Yeshiva Konvitz, N.Y.C., 1972-73; intern Wee Folk Nursery Sch., Short Hills, N.J., 1978-81, dir. day camp, 1980-81, tchr., dir., owner, 1980-81; adj. prof. reading Seton Hall U., South Orange, N.J., 1987, Middlesex County Coll., Edison, N.J., 1987-88; asst. adj. prof. L.I. U., Bklyn., 1988, Pace U., N.Y.C., 1988—. Ednl. cons. Cranford High Sch., 1988; presenter numerous workshops; founding bd. dirs. Stern Coll. Women Yeshiva U., N.Y.C., 1987; adj. vis. lectr. Rutgers U., New Brunswick, N.J., 1988. Chairperson Jewish Book Festival, YM-YWHA, West Orange, N.J., 1986-87, mem. early childhood com., 1986—, bd. dirs., 1986—; vice chairperson dinner com. Nat. Leadership Conf. Christians and Jews, 1986; mem. Hadassah, Valerie Children's Fund, Women's League Conservative Judaism, City of Hope; assoc. bd. bus. and women's profl. divsn. United Jewish Appeal, 1979; vol. reader Goddard Riverside Day Care Ctr., N.Y.C., 1973; friend N.Y.C. Pub. Libr., 1980—; life friend Millburn (N.J.) Pub. Libr.; pres. Seton-Essex Reading Coun., 1991-94. Co-recipient Am. Heritage award, Essex County, 1985; recipient Award Appreciation City of Hope, 1984, Profl. Improvement awards Seton-Essex Reading Council, 1984-86, Cert. Attendance award Seton-Essex Reading Council, 1987. Mem. N.Y. Acad. Scis. (life), N.J. Council Tchrs. English, Nat. Council Tchrs. English, Am. Ednl. Research Assn., Coll. Reading Assn. (life), Assn. Supervision and Curriculun Devel., N.Y. State Reading Assn. (council Manhattan), N.J. Reading Assn. (council Seton-Essex), Internat. Reading Assn., Nat. Assn. for Edn. of Young Children (life N.J. chpt., Kenyon group), Nat. Council Jewish Women (vice chairperson membership com. evening br. N.Y. sect. 1974-75), George Washington U. Alumni Club, Emerson Coll. Alumni Club, NYU Alumni Club, Phi Delta Kappa (life), Kappa Gamma Chi (historian). Clubs: Greenbrook Country (Caldwell, N.J.); George Washington Univ. Avocations: reading, theater. Home: 242 Hartshorn Dr Short Hills NJ 07078-1914 E-mail: dr.mrw349@aol.com.

ROBBOY, STANLEY J. pathologist, educator; b. Cleve., Jan. 5, 1941; s. John and Sarah (Shapiro) R.; m. Anita Wyzanski, July 21, 1968 (div. 1981); children: Elizabeth, Caroline; m. Marion Meyer, June 14, 1990. Student, U. Mich., 1958-61, MD, 1965. Diplomate Am. Bd. Pathology, Am. Bd. Med. Mgmt. Intern Mt. Sinai Hosp, Cleve., 1965-66; resident to chief in pathology Mass. Gen. Hosp., 1966-70, asst. in pathology, 1972-73, asst. pathologist, 1973-76, assoc. pathologist, 1976-84; resident in pathology Boston Hosp. for Women, 1970; instr. Tufts Med. Sch., 1968-69; asst. prof. pathology Harvard Med. Sch., Boston, 1972-76, assoc. prof., 1976-84; prof. pathology U. Medicine and Dentistry N.J.-N.J. Med. Sch., Newark, 1984—92, chmn. dept., 1984-89, prof. ob-gyn, 1990—92, pathologist-in-chief, 1984-89, dir. faculty practice service, 1985-89; prof., v. chmn. dept. pathology Duke U., 1992—. Cons. pathologist St. Joseph Hosp., Paterson, N.J., 1985—92, St. Barnabas Hosp., Livingston, N.J., 1985—92, Beth Israel Hosp., Newark, 1985—92, VA Med. Ctr., Durham, 1992-; pathologist (DES) Clear-Cell Adenocarcinoma Registry, 1972-83; pathologist, prin. investigator Nat. Collaborative Diethylstilbestrol project, 1974-82; vis. scientist New Eng. Primate Ctr., 1973-84; vis. prof. U. Shiraz Med. Sch., Iran, 1976; commr. N.J. Commn. on Cancer Research, 1987-92; sr. advisor East Asia Cons. Group, Boston, Los Angeles and Tokyo, 1984-85; reference panel for diagnostic and therapeutic tech. AMA, 1982—99; mem. nat. med. com. Planned Parenthood Fedn. Am., 1990-93, vice chmn. com. on oncology, 1993; mem. steering com. Nat. Cancer Inst., 1995—; bd. dirs. Pamet Sys. Inc. Mem. editorial bd. Human Pathology, 1980-90, Cervix and the Low Female Genital Tract, 1983-94, Internat. Jour. Gynecologic Pathology, 1985-; editor: Pathology of the Female Reproductive Tract, 2002; book rev. editor, Informatics in Pathology, 1985-88, Pathology Rsch. and Practice, 1990--, Gynecologic Oncology, 1997--, InsSight, 1998--; contbr. articles to profl. jours. Trustee Am. Pathology Found., 1984-86. Served to maj. U.S. Army, 1970-72. Recipient Jr. Faculty award Am. Cancer Soc., 1972-75, Found. prize Am. Coll. Ob-Gyn, 1975; Pardee fellow U. Mich., 1961, Lederle Lab. fellow, 1962, Eliza Howell fellow, 1964, Ford Found. fellow, 1964-65; clin. fellow Am. Cancer Soc., 1967-68. Fellow Am. Soc. Clin. Pathologists (chmn. pathology telecommunications network com. 1983, task force on computers 1980-83, council on med. informatics 1983-84, planning and scope com. 1983-84, co-chmn. pathology communication network 1983-87, coun. anatomic pathology, 1995-2001, future directions, 1995-98), Coll. Am. Pathologists (alt. Mass. del. to house dels. 1981-84, co-chmn. pathology communication network 1983-85, alt. N.J. del. to house dels. 1985-92, exec. com. and advisor nomenclature and classification of disease 1975-80, editorial bd. Systematized Nomenclature Medicine 1976-80,

gov. 1999--, mem. reimbursement com., 1992-94, profl. and econ. affairs com., 1995-97, outcomes com., 1999-2000, vice chmn. coun. on pub. affairs 1999-, coun. of govt. prof. affairs, 2000—, credentials com., 2000—, spokesperson, 2001—, performance measurement com., 2002—), Soc. Gynecologic Oncologists Assocs.; mem. Arthur Purdy Stout Soc. Surg. Pathology (membership com. 1980-86, treas. 1993-2001, pres.-elect 2001-03, pres. 2003—), Internat. Acad. Cytology, Internat. Acad. Pathology (edn. com. 1979-83), Internat. Soc. Gynecologic Pathologists (chmn. membership com. 1982-84), Mass. Soc. Pathology (3d party relations 1978-84, chmn. computer com. 1981-84), N.C. Med. Soc., N.C. Soc. Pathology, N.J. Med. Soc., N.J. Soc. Pathology (edn. and profl. relations Coms. 1984-92, exec. com. 1985-92), Chapel Hill Kehilla (co-pres. 2004—). Jewish. Office: Duke U Med Ctr PO Box 3712 Durham NC 27710-0001 Office Phone: 919-684-3656. E-mail: stanley.robboy@duke.edu.

ROBE, THURLOW RICHARD, engineering educator, dean; b. Petersburg, Ohio, Jan. 25, 1934; s. Thrulow Scott and Mary Alice (McKibben) R.; m. Eleanora C. Komyati, Aug. 27, 1955; children: Julia, Kevin, Stephen, Edward. BSC.E., Ohio U., 1955, MS in Mech. Engring., 1962; PhD in Applied Mechanics, Stanford U., 1966. Engr. Gen. Electric Co., Niles, Ohio, Cleve., Erie, Pa., Evendale,Ohio, 1954-60; instr. Ohio U., Athens, 1960-63; asst. prof to prof., assoc. dean U. Ky., Lexington, 1965-80; dean Ohio U., Athens, 1980-96, Cruse W. Moss prof. Engring. Edn., 1992-96, dir. Innovation Ctr. Authority, 1983-96; dean emeritus, Moss prof. emeritus Russ Coll. Engring. and Tech., Ohio U., Athens, 1996—; pres., chmn. bd. Q.E.D. Assocs., Inc., Lexington, 1975-83. Trustee Engring. Found. Ohio, 1988-94; bd. govs. Edison Materials Tech. Ctr., 1987-96; dir. T. Richard and Eleanora K. Robe Leadership Inst., Ohio U., 1997—. Contbr. articles to profl. jours.; patentee trailer hitch. Bd. dirs. Athens County Cmty. Redevel. Corp., 1980-86; treas. South Lexington Little League, 1976-80; vice chmn. Thoroughbred dist., Boy Scouts Am., 1975-77; pres. Tates Creek H.S. PTA, Lexington, 1975-76; bd. dirs. U. Ky. Athletics Ass.n, 1975-80; trustee Ohio U. Found. Bd. Trustees, 1998—. Maj. USAF Res., 1955-85. Recipient Alumni medal of merit Ohio U., 1993; named Am. Coun. on Edn. Adminstrn. fellow, 1970-71, Ohio U. Alumnus of Yr., 1996, inductee Acad. Disting. Grads., Russ Coll. Engring. & Tech., 2001. Mem. ASME, NSPE (Profl. Engring. in Edn. exec. bd., ctrl. region vice-chmn. 1987-89), Am. Soc. Engring. Edn. (Outstanding Contbn. in Rsch. award 1966), Athens Reading Club, Athens Symposiarchs, Rotary, Sigma Xi, Tau Beta Pi, Omicron Delta Kappa, Alpha Lambda Delta. Office: Russ Coll Engring & Tech Ohio U Athens OH 45701 E-mail: robe@ohio.edu.

ROBECK, MILDRED COEN, education educator, writer; b. Walum, ND, July 29, 1915; d. Archie Blain and Mary Henrietta (Hoffman) Coen; m. Martin Julius Robeck, Jr., June 2, 1936; children: Martin Jay Robeck, Donna Jayne Robeck Thompson, Bruce Wayne Robeck. BS, U. Wash., 1950, MEd, 1954, PhD, 1958. Ordnance foreman Sherman Williams, U.S. Navy, Bremerton, Wash., 1942-45; demonstration tchr. Seattle Pub. Schs., 1946-57; reading clinic dir. U. Calif., Santa Barbara, 1957-64; rsch. cons. State Dept. Edn., Sacramento, Calif., 1964-67; prof., head early childhood edn. U. Oreg., Eugene, Oreg., 1967-86; vis. scholar West Australia Inst. Tech., Perth, 1985; v.p. acad. affairs U. Santa Barbara, Calif., 1987-95. Vis. prof. Victoria Coll., B.C. Can., summer 1958, Dalhousie U., Halifax, 1964; trainer evaluator U.S. Office of Edn. Head Start, Follow Thru, 1967-72; cons., evaluator Native Am. Edn. Programs, Sioux, Navajo, 1967-81; cons. on gifted Oreg. Task Force on Talented and Gifted, Salem, 1974-76; evaluator Early Childhood Edn., Bi-Ling. program, Petroleum and Minerology, Dhahran, Saudi Arabia, 1985. Author: Materials KELP: Kgn. Evaluation Learning Pot, 1967, Infants and Children, 1978, Psychology of Reading, 1990, Oscar: His Story, 1997, 2nd edit., 2000; contbr. articles to profl. jours. Evaluation cons. Rosenburg Found. Project, Santa Barbara, 1966-67; faculty advisor Pi Lambda Theta, Eugene, Oreg, 1969-74; guest columnist Oreg. Assn. Gifted and Talented, Salem, Oreg., 1979-81; editorial review bd. ERQ, U.S. Calif., L.A., 1981-91. Recipient Nat. Dairy award 4-H Clubs, Wis., 1934, NYA and U. Wis. scholar, Madison, 1934-35, Faculty Rsch. grant U. Calif., Santa Barbara, 1958-64, NDEA fellow Retraining U.S. Office Edn., U. Oreg., 1967-70. Mem. APA, Am. Ednl. Rsch. Assn., Internat. Reading Assn., Phi Beta Kappa, Pi Lambda Theta. Democrat. Avocations: dyslexia research, historical research, duplicate bridge, writing. Home: 95999 Highway 101 S Yachats OR 97498-9714 Office Phone: 541-547-3967. E-mail: mrobeck@casco.net.

ROBEK, MARY FRANCES, business education educator; b. Superior, Wis., Jan. 30, 1927; d. Stephen and Mary (Hervert) R. BE, U. Wis., 1948; MA, Northwestern U., 1951; MBA, U. Mich., 1962, PhD, 1967. Tchr. Bergland (Mich.) High Sch., 1948, Tony (Wis.) High Sch., 1948-50, Sch. Vocat. and Adult Edn., Superior, 1950-58; prof. bus. edn. and office tech. Ea. Mich. U., Ypsilanti, 1958-93; instr. Jazyckova Gymnasium, Banská, Slovakia, 1994. Author: Information and Records Management, 1995. Assn. of Records Mgrs. and Adminstrs. fellow, 1992. Mem. Assn. Records Mgrs. and Adminstrs. (life), Inst. Cert. Mgrs. (pres. 1980-81, Emmett Leahy award 2000), Cath. Daus. Am., Delta Pi Epsilon, Delta Kappa Gamma, Pi Lambda Theta. Republican. Roman Catholic. Home: 515 Clough Ave Superior WI 54880 Personal E-mail: RobekMary@aol.com. *Opportunity to do creative and innovative things without infringing on the rights of others is limited only by priorities set considering people and technology.*

ROBEL, LAUREN, law educator; b. Dec. 1953; BA, Auburn U., 1978; JD, Ind. U., 1983. Bar: US Supreme Ct., Ind., Ill. Law clk. to Hon. Jesse Eschbach, U.S. Ct. Appeals (7th cir.), 1983—85; dean, Val Nolan prof. law Ind. U. Sch. Law, Bloomington. Vis. faculty U. Panthenon-Assas, Paris; reporter rules com. U.S. Dist. Ct. (so. dist.) Ind.; mem. rules com. Ind. Supreme Ct. Contbr. articles to profl. jours.; author: Les États des Noires: Federalisme et question raciale aux États-unis, 2000. Mem.: Ind. State Bar Women (Law Recognition award), Ind. Bar Found. (Pro Bono Publico award), Order of Coif. Office: Ind Univ Sch Law 211 S Indiana Ave Bloomington IN 47405

ROBELOT, JANE, anchor; b. Greenville, S.C., Oct. 9, 1960; married; 1 child. BA in Econs., Clemson U. News and sports dir., reporter WCCP-AM Radio, Clemson, SC; anchor, reporter WSPA-TV, CBS affiliate, Spartanburg, SC, 1983—90; gen. assignment reporter WCAU-TV, Phila., 1990—92, co-anchor 6:00 PM news, 1991—92, co-anchor 11:00 PM news, 1992—95; co-anchor CBS Morning News, N.Y.C., 1995; news reader This Morning CBS News, N.Y.C., 1995—96, co-anchor This Morning, 1996—99, co-anchor CBS Atlanta News, 1999—. Office: WGCL TV 46 Meredith Corp 425 14th St NW Atlanta GA 30318-7965

ROBENALT, JOHN ALTON, lawyer; b. Ottawa, Ohio, May 2, 1922; s. Alton Ray and Kathryn (Straman) R.; m. Margaret Morgan Durbin, Aug. 25, 1951 (dec. July 1990); children: John F., William A., James D., Robert M., Mary K., Margaret E., Thomas D.; m. Nancy Leech Kidder, Sept. 21, 1991. BA, Miami U., 1943; LL.B., JD, Ohio State U., 1948. Bar: Ohio 1948. Asst. atty. gen., Ohio, 1949-51; practice in, 1951-59; acting municipal judge Lima Municipal Ct., 1955-59; partner Robenalt, Daley, Balyeat & Balyeat, 1959-82; ptnr. Robenalt, Kendall & Robenalt, 1983-85, Robenalt, Kendall, Rodabaugh & Staley, 1985-92, Robenalt & Robenalt, 1993—. Chmn. Lima March of Dimes, 1957-58; Bd. dirs. Lima Civic Center, pres., 1971-72; bd. dirs. Lima Rotating Fund; trustee Allen County Regional Transit Authority, Lima, pres., 1975— . Served with AUS, 1943-45. Mem. ABA, Ohio Bar Assn., Allen County Bar Assn. (pres. 1969-70), Am. Legion, Lima Automobile Club (bd. dirs., pres. 1975-82), Shawnee Country Club (pres. 1968-70), Ohio Automobile Club (trustee 1982-2002, chmn. 1995-97), Elks (bd. trustees 1991-97), Rotary, Delta Tau Delta, Phi Delta Phi. Home: 1755 Shawnee Rd Apt 700 Lima OH 45805-3857 Office Phone: 419-229-0054.

ROBERGE, M. SHEILA, state legislator; b. Manchester, N.H. 2 children. Ed., St. Anselm's Coll. Mem. Dist. 19 N.H. Senate, Concord, 1985—. Chmn. Manchester, N.H., Rep. com., 1979-80; del., Rep. Nat. Conv., 1980, 84; Rep. nat. committeewoman from N.H.; vice-chmn., Rep. Nat. Com., 1980-88. Roman Catholic. Address: Senate House 107 N Main St Rm 312 Concord NH 03301-4951

ROBERSON, BRUCE HEERDT, lawyer; b. Wilmington, Del., Mar. 7, 1941; s. A. L. and Virginia Amelia (Heerdt) R.; m. Mary E. Abrams; children: Cheryl Anne, David B., Douglas M. BS cum laude, Washington and Lee U., 1963; JD, U. Va., 1966. Bar: Va. 1966, Del. 1966, Fla. 1969. Assoc. Morris, Nichols, Arsht & Tunnell, Wilmington, 1966-67; assoc. Holland & Knight, Tampa, Fla., 1969-74; ptnr. Holland & Knight LLP, Tampa, Fla., 1975—. Contbg. editor Pratt's Banking and Lending Institution Forms, 1992—. Capt. U.S. Army, 1967-69 Decorated Bronze Star. Fellow Am. Bar Found. (life), Fla. Bar Found.(life); mem. ABA (bus. law sect. com. on consumer fin. svcs. 1976—, banking law com. 1980—, savs. instns. com. 1989-96), Am. Judicature Soc., Fla. Bar Assn. (corp. banking and bus. law sect. exec. coun. 1978-86, chmn. banking law com. 1982-84), Del. Bar Assn., Va. Bar Assn., Hillsborough County Bar Assn., Univ. Club, Tampa Yacht and Country Club, Lambda Chi Alpha. Republican. Methodist. Office: Holland & Knight LLP PO Box 1288 Tampa FL 33601-1288 Office Phone: 813-227-8500. Business E-Mail: bruce.roberson@hklaw.com.

ROBERSON, DEBORAH KAY, secondary school educator; b. Crane, Tex., Jan. 15, 1955; d. David B. and Virginia L. (King) Cole; m. Larry M. Roberson; children: Justin, Jenai, Julie. BS in Secondary Edn., Coll. S.W., 1981; MA in Sch. Adminstrn., Sul Ross State U., 1991. Cert. biology and history tchr., mid-mgmt. cert., supt. cert., Tex., biology and history tchr., secondary prin., supt., Okla. Sci. and social studies tchr. Andrews (Tex.) Ind. Sch. Dist., 1987-95; forum tchr. gifted social studies program, social studies dept. chair Ctrl. Mid. Sch., Broken Arrow, Okla., 1995—99; asst. prin. Ctrl. Middle Sch., Broken Arrow, Okla., 1999—2001; sci. tchr. 6th grade Jamison Mid. Sch., Pearland, Tex., 2001—02; asst. prin. Alvin Jr. HS, 2002—04, prin., 2004—. 7th grade history curriculum com. Andrews Ind. Sch. Dist., 1988, outdoor classroom com., 1989-90, chair sci. curriculum com., 1989-90, chair health curriculum com., 1990-91, Tex. pub. schs. open house com., 1989-90, 92-93, dist. textbook com., 1990-91; secondary edn. rep. Ptnrs. in Parliament, Berlin, 1993; site-based com. Broken Arrow Pub. Schs., 1995—, B.A.S.I.S. com., 1995—, nat. history day coord. Ctrl. Middle Sch., 1995, geography bee coord., 1995—, tech. com., 1996—, discipline com., 1996, remediation com., 1996—, Tools for Tomorrow Conf. com., 1996—, others; state geography com. Okla. State Dept. Edn., 1997. Prodr., dir.: Real History Radio, Broken Arrow Hist. Soc., 1997. Livestock leader Andrews County 4-H Program, 1985-89; vol. Am. Heart Assn., Andrews, 1988; vol., team mother Little League, Andrews, 1990; vol., treas. Mustang Booster Club, Andrews, 1993-95. Recipient Appreciation awards Mustang Booster Club, 1993, 94, VFW Ladies Aux. Post 10887 award, Broken Arrow, 1996—, Tchr. of Today award Masons, Broken Arrow, 1997, Nat. History Day Outstanding Tchr. award Tulsa C.C., 1997, Best Mannered Tchr. award Nat. Jr. Cotillion, 1999; Tchr. Program scholar Fulbright Meml. Fund, Japan, 1998. Mem. AAUW, Nat. Assn. Secondary Sch. Prins., Nat. Staff Devel. Coun., Assn. Tex. Profl. Educators (pres. local unit 1992-93, mem. resolutions com. 1994-95, Appreciation award 1993, sec. region 1993-94, v.p. region 1994-95), ASCD, Tex. Assn. Supervision and Curriculum Devel., Tex. Network for Continuous Quality Improvement, Nat. Coun. Social Studies, Okla. Assn. Supervision and Curriculum Devel., Okla. Alliance Geographic Edn., Okla. Assn. Secondary Sch. Prins., Coop. Orgn. Okla. Secondary Adminstrs., Redskins Booster Club (sec. 1996-97). Avocations: meeting people, travel, golf, rafting, hiking. Office: Alvin Jr HS 2301 W South St Alvin TX 77511 Home: 9402 Sunperch Ct Pearland TX 77584-2886

ROBERSON, DORIS JEAN HEROLD, retired social worker; b. N.Y.C., Oct. 15, 1924; d. Albert and Rosalind (Lowenstein) Herold; m. Lloyd Willis Roberson, Aug. 31, 1949; children: Lynn, Patricia, Katherine, Irene. BA cum laude, Mount Holyoke Coll., 1945; MSW, Fordham U., 1947. Cert. social worker, N.Y. Social worker Children's Aid Soc., N.Y.C., 1947-52, Yonkers (N.Y.) Pub. Schs., 1966-89; ret., 1989. Mem. NASW, Acad. Cert. Social Workers, N.Y. State Sch. Social Workers Assn., Phi Beta Kappa. Home: 145 Hoover Rd Yonkers NY 10710-3408

ROBERSON, JAMES O. foundation executive; m. Rita Quinn; children: Melanie Merrill, Sharyl Shatz, James Jr., Trisha, Joel. AB in Journalism, Baylor U., 1956; student Indsl. Devel. Inst., U. Okla.; student Inst. Orgnl. Mgmt., U. Houston. Cert. econ. developer. Dir. info. West Tex. C. of C., Abilene, 1956-59; area devel. mgr. Mo.-Kans.-Tex. R.R., 1959-63; exec. dir. Albuquerque Indsl. Devel. Svc., 1963-65; dir. N.Mex. Dept. Devel., Santa Fe, 1965-69; mgr. Forward Metro Denver, 1969-72; dir. R.I. Dept. Econ. Devel., Providence, 1972-77; v.p., dir. new bus. devel. Howard Rsch. and Devel. Corp. subs. Rouse Co., Columbia, Md., 1977-79; sec. Md. Dept. Econ. and Community Devel., Annapolis, 1979-83; pres. Louisville C. of C., 1983-88; pres., CEO Rsch. Triangle Found. N.C., 1988—. Chmn. bd. dirs. Charlotte br. Fed. Res. Bank Richmond; cons., speaker in field. Editor West Tex. Today mag., 1956-59. Trustee, vice chmn. Wake Tech. C.C.; bd. dirs. N.C. Biotech. Ctr. Fellow Am. Econ. Devel. Coun. (past chmn.); mem. Indsl. Devel. Rsch. Coun., Nat. Assn. State Devel. Agys. (past pres.), Assn. Univ. Related Rsch. Parks (pres.).

ROBERSON, JESSIE HILL, federal agency administrator; Grad., U. Tenn. Nuc. reactor ops. mgr. DuPont, 1982—87; sys. engr. Ga. Power Co., 1987—89; project engring. dir., asst. mgr. environ. restoration Savannah River Site, U.S. Dept. Energy, 1989—96; mgr. Rocky Flats Field Office Dept. Energy, Colo., 1996—99, asst. sec. environ. mgmt., 2001—. Mem. Def. Nuc. Facilities Safety Bd., 2000—01. Named Nat. Black Engr. of Yr. for profl. achievement in govt. Office: Dept Energy Environ Mgmt 1000 Independence Ave SW Washington DC 20585-0001

ROBERSON, NATHAN RUSSELL, physicist, researcher; b. Robersonville, N.C., Dec. 13, 1930; s. Nathan Russell and Myrtle (Taylor) R.; m. Ruth Haislip, June 19, 1954; children: David Wintner, Michael Taylor, Mary Russell. BS, U. N.C., 1954, MS, 1955; PhD, Johns Hopkins U., 1960. Jr. instr. Johns Hopkins U., Balt., 1955-60; research assoc. Princeton (N.J.) U., 1960-63; asst. prof. physics Duke U., Durham, N.C., 1963-68, assoc. prof., 1968-74, prof., 1974-98, prof. emeritus, 1998—. Instrumentation subcom. Nuclear Sci. Adv. Com., 1982-85; mem. energy sci. network steering com. Dept. Energy, 1987-90, nuclear physics panel on computer networks, 1988-90, dep. dir. Triangle U. Nuclear Lab., 1990-92; dir. Triangle Univs. Nuclear Lab., 1992-96, assoc. dir., 1996-98. Contbr. articles to profl. jours. Treas. N.C. Council Chs., 1974-79. Fellow AAAS, Am. Phys. Soc.; mem. IEEE, Phi Beta Kappa. Presbyterian. Home: 38 Stoneridge Pl Durham NC 27705 Office: Duke U Dept Physics Durham NC 27708 Personal E-mail: russell-roberson@nc.rr.com.

ROBERSON, PATT FOSTER, mass communications educator; b. Middletown, N.Y., Dec. 3, 1934; d. Gilbert Charles and Mildred Elizabeth (O'Neal) Foster; m. Murray Ralph Roberson Jr., May 10, 1963 (dec. 1968). AA, Canal Zone Jr. Coll., 1954; BA in Journalism, La. State U., 1957, MA in Journalism, 1973; MA in Media, So. U., Baton Rouge, 1981; PhD in Mass Communication, U. So. Miss., 1985. Exec. sec. Lionel H. Abshire and Assocs., AIA, Architects, Baton Rouge, 1958-60, Murrell and Callari, AIA, Architects, Baton Rouge, 1960-63; bus. mgr. So. Rev. La. State U., Baton Rouge, 1963-69; free-lance researcher, ind. contractor Baton Rouge, 1969-74; rep. dept. info. State of La., Baton Rouge, 1974-75; asst. prof. mass. comm. So. U., 1976-86, assoc. prof. mass comm., 1986-93, prof. mass comm., 1993-96, prof. emeritus, 1996—. Printed program, advt., & editl. cons. Baton Rouge performing arts org., 1971-; reviewer Random House Pubs., N.Y.C., 1981; profl. devel. intern Baton Rouge Morning Advocate, 1991, Baker Observer, 1991-92; reporter-photographer Canal Record, Seminole, Fla., 1967—; biographer of Edward Livermore Burlingame, John H. Johnson, Daniel Kimball Whitaker, (book) American mag. journalists series, Dictionary Literary Biography, Detroit, 1986-87; tutor Operation Upgrade, 1978-82; vol. reporter, photographer, proofreader The Platinum Record, Baton Rouge, 1996-99; cons. in field. Co-editor: La. State U. cookbook Tiger Bait, 1976; biographer Frank E. Gannett in Biographical Dictionary of American Journalism, 1987; freelance writer/editl. cons.; editl. bd. Am. Journalism, 1986-87; reviewer Longman Publs. 1991-92; contbr. articles to profl. jours. Mem. poll commn. East Baton Rouge Parish Govt., 1978-95; pres. Our Lady Lake Regional Med. Ctr., 1971-72; bd. dirs. Dist. Atty.'s Rape Crisis Commn., 1976-79, Plan Govt. Study Commn., 1973-76, Selective Svc. System Bd. 8, Baton Rouge, 1986-98, 2002—; docent Greater Baton Rouge Zoo, 1974-77, 2002-; vol. ARC, 1989-99, Capital Area Ct.-Apptd. Spl. Adv., 1997-99; mem. East Baton Rouge Parish Commn. on Govtl. Ethics, 1992-93, Cajun Clickers Computer Club, 1997-; council appointee Baker Strategic Planning Com., 2003-; mayoral appointee Baker Mobile Home Rev. Bd., 1990—; v.p. Baker Hist. and Cultural Found., 1990-93; bd. mem. Baker Heritage Mus., 1993-; mem. Baker Interclub Coun., 1990-91, Baker Civic Pride, 2004-; organizer human-animal therapy svc. Baker Manor Nursing Home, 1994; mem. 1st class Citizens Basic Police Tng. Acad., Baton Rouge Police Dept., 1994; chairpub. rels., bd. dirs. Panama Canal Mus., 1998-2001. Mem. AAUP (sec.-treas. La. conf. 1988-89, sec. 1992-93, chmn. pub. rels. 1994-95), Assn. Edn. Journalism and Mass Comm., Am. Newspapers Pubs. Assn. (nat. coop. com. on edn. in journalism 1989-92), Women in Comm. (pres. Baton Rouge chpt. 1982, nat. judge Clarion awards 1987), Pub. Rels. Assn. La., La. State U. Journalism Alumni Assn. (pres. 1977), Soc. Profl. Journalists (pres. S.E. La. chpt. 1982), Am. Journalism Historians Assn., Oral History Assn., La. State U. Alumni Assn. (pres. East Baton Rouge Parish chpt. 1978-80), Popular Culture Assn., Investigative Reporters and Editors Assn., Baker C. of C., Toasmasters (adminstrv. v.p. Baton Rouge 1977), Pilot Club of Baker. Home: 2801 Allen Ct Baker LA 70714-2253

ROBERSON, ROBERT S. investment company executive; b. Mt. Kisco, N.Y., 1942; m. Barbara Drane, 1967; children: Elizabeth de V., Merritt B., Barbara D. BS, NYU, 1964; MBA, Coll. William and Mary, 1973. Various positions in fin. and bldg. industries, 1964-67; mem. N.Y. Produce Exchange, 1965-66; with Weaver Bros., Inc., Newport News, Va., 1967—, now pres., dir. Bd. dirs. First Peninsula Bank & Trust Co., Hampton, Va., 1977-78. Former dir. Peninsula Unit Am. Cancer Soc., Newport News; former dir. Heritage Coun. Girl Scouts U.S.A., Hampton; former trustee Newport News Pub. Libr., former trustee Va. Living Mus., Newport News; former trustee, chmn. com. on devel. Hampton Roads Acad., Newport News; former mem. bd. visitors to George Washington's Mt. Vernon Nat. Shrine; hon. dep. chief N.Y.C. Fire Dept.; trustee, pres., chief curator Golf Mus., Newport News;trustee, sec. Va. War Mus. Found., Newport News; former mem. bd. visitors, mem. exec. com., chmn. com. on devel. and alumni affairs Coll. William and Mary, Williamsburg, Va.; former mem. bd. visitors, mem. exec. com. Richard Bland Coll., Petersburg, Va. Decorated officer Order of St. John (England). Mem. Newcomen Soc. of the U.S., Hon. Fire Officers Assn., U.S. Golf Assn. (former nat. com. mem. mus. & libr.), Gen. Soc. Colonial Wars, St. Nicholas Soc. of the City N.Y., Colonial Order Acorn, Sovereign Mil. Order of the Temple of Jerusalem (comdr.), Squadron A Assn., Pilgrims of the U.S./U.K., Union Club, The Brook, Church Club (N.Y.C.), Southampton Club (N.Y.), Cypher Soc. of William and Mary, James River Country Club, Hampton Roads German Club (past pres.), Hampton Roads Assembly, The Hundred Club (Newport News, Va.), N.Y. Yacht Club, Fishers Island Yacht Club (N.Y.), Rotary Internat. (Paul Harris fellow), Blue Key, Delta Sigma Pi. Republican. Episcopalian. Home: PO Box 3 Williamsburg VA 23187-0003

ROBERT, ELISABETH B. toy company executive; b. N.Y.C. children. Catie, Ruthie. Grad., Phillips Acad., 1973; BA in French, Middlebury Coll., 1978; M in Bus., u. Vt., 1984. Asst. to pres. Vt. Gas Systems, 1984-88, exec., 1988-89; campaign mgr. Vt. Gubernatorial Campaign, 1989-90; with computer tech. firm, 1990-95; CRO The Vt. Teddy Bear Co., Shelburne, 1995-97, pres., CEO, 1997—. Bd. dirs. Com. on Temporary Shelter, Vt. Gov.'s Commn. on Women; basketball coach Mater Christi Sch., Burlington, Vt., 1996—. Office: Vt Teddy Bear Co Inc 6655 Shelburne Rd Shelburne VT 05482-6500

ROBERT, KENNETH J. aviation administrator; Dir. aviation Bradley Internat. Airport, Windsor Locks, Conn., aviation adminstr. Office: Bur Aviation and Ports 2800 Berlin Tpke Newington CT 06111-4113 also: PO Box 317546 Newington CT 06131-7546

ROBERT, NICHOLAS JAMES, hematolgist, oncologist; b. Quebec City, Can., Nov. 3, 1948; came to U.S., 1976; s. Francois and Marie F. (Chauveau) R.; m. Katherine F. Box, July 8, 1972; children: Katherine, Michael. BSc, McGill U., 1970, MD, 1974. Diplomate Am. Bd. Internal Medicine, Am. Bd. Anatomic Pathology, Am. Bd. Med. Oncology, Am. Bd. Hematology, Am. Bd. Med. Examiners. Intern, resident in medicine Royal Victoria Hosp., Montreal, 1974-76; resident in anatomic pathology Mass. Gen. Hosp., Boston, 1976-78, chief resident anatomic pathology, 1978-79; fellow in hematology Brigham and Women's Hosp., Boston, 1979-80; fellow in med. oncology Dana Farber Cancer Inst., Boston, 1980-81; clin. fellow in pathology/medicine Harvard Med. Sch., Boston, 1977-81; asst. prof. medicine U. Conn. Health Ctr., 1981-84; asst. prof. medicine, pathology, radiation oncology Tufts U. Sch. Medicine, 1984-91. Reviewer Am. Jour. Hematology, Breast Cancer Rsch. & Treatment, Breast Disease, J.A.M.A., Jour. Clin. Oncology, Jour. Oncology, New England Jour. Medicine; contbr. articles to profl. jours. Grantee Am. Cancer Soc., numerous others. Mem. Am. Cancer Soc. (profl. edn. com. 1982-83, co-chmn. student health care profl. com. 1988-90, editl. bd. 1989-90, bd. dirs. 1989-91), Am. Soc. Clin. Oncology. Office: Ste 400 8503 Arlington Blvd Fairfax VA 22031-4629

ROBERT, STEPHEN, academic administrator; b. Haverhill, Mass., June 13, 1940; s. Samuel R.; m. Catherine Price; children: Tracey Alexandra, Elisabeth Amory. AB with honors, Brown U., 1962; postgrad., London Sch. Econs., 1962-63, Columbia Bus. Sch., 1963-65. Co-chmn., CEO Faulkner Dawkins and Sullivan, 1965-67; v.p. Oppenheimer Funds, N.Y.C., 1968-76, chief portfolio mgr., 1969-76; gen. ptnr. Oppenheimer & Co., Inc., N.Y.C., 1970-82, dir. research, 1976-78, pres., 1979-83, chmn., chief exec. officer, 1983-97; chancellor Brown U., Providence. Dir. NacRe Corp. Bd. dirs., chmn. fin. com. Wiltwyck Sch., 1968-78; bd. dirs. Joffrey Ballet, 1981—; trustee The Dalton Sch., 1984—, Brown U., 1984—. Mem.: Harmonie (N.Y.C.). Office: Brown Univ Presidents Office Box 1860 Providence RI 02912-1860

ROBERTS, ALAN SILVERMAN, orthopedic surgeon; b. Apr. 20, 1939; s. Joseph William and Fannie (Margolies) S.; children: Michael Eric, Daniel Ian. BA, Conn. Wesleyan U., 1960; MD, Jefferson Med. Coll., 1966. Rotating intern Lankenau Hosp., Phila., 1966-67; resident in orthoaedics Tulane U. Med. Coll., 1967-71; pvt. practice specializing in orthopaedics and hand surgery L.A., 1971—. Mem. clin. faculty UCLA Med. Coll., 1971-76. Contbr. articles to profl. jours. With AUS, 1961. Riordan Hand fellow, 1969, Boyes Hand fellow, 1971. Mem. AMA, ACS, Am. Acad. Orthopaedic Surgeons, Calif. Med. Assn., L.A. County Med. Assn., Western Orthopaedic Assn., Riordan Hand Soc. Republican. Jewish. Office Phone: 323-939-3700.

ROBERTS, ALBERT DEE, internist; b. Ft. Worth, Mar. 7, 1930; s. Albert D. and Irene Burnett (Lewis) R.; m. Diane Truett, Dec. 22, 1952; children: Truett, Hillary. BS, So. Meth. U., 1951; MD, U. Tex. Southwestern, Dallas, 1954. Diplomate Am. Bd. Internal Medicine, Am. Bd. Nephrology. Pvt. practice, Dallas, 1960-75, 88-91; assoc. dean, prof. medicine U. Tex. Southwestern, 1975-88, prof. medicine, 1991—, Hartman prof. medicine, 1995—. Mem. ACP (master, gov. 1977-81, regent 1981-87, vice chair 1986-87), AMA, Am. Soc. Nephrology, Internat. Soc. Nephrology, Tex. Med Assn., Dallas County Med. Assn. Avocations: reading, music, tennis, travel. E-mail: albertroberts@utsouthwester.edu.

ROBERTS, ARCHIBALD EDWARD, retired career officer, writer; b. Cheboygan, Mich., Mar. 21, 1915; s. Archibald Lancaster and Madeline Ruth (Smith) R.; m. Florence Snure, Sept. 25, 1940 (div. Feb. 1950); children: Michael James, John Douglas; m. 2d, Doris Elfriede White, June 23, 1951; children: Guy Archer, Charles Lancaster, Christopher Corwin. Grad., Command and Gen. Staff Coll., 1952; student, U.S. Armed Forces Inst., 1953, U. Md., 1958. Enlisted U.S. Army, 1939, advanced through grades to lt. col., 1960; served in Far East Command, 1942, 53-55, ETO, 1943-45, 57-60; tech. info. officer Office Surgeon Gen., Dept. Army, Washington, 1950, Ft. Campbell, Ky., 1952-53, info. officer Camp Chicamauga, Japan, Ft. Bragg, N.C., Ft. Campbell, 1953-56, 1956-57, Ft. Benning, Ga., Wurzburg, Germany, 1957-58; spl. projects officer U.S. Army, Augsburg, Germany, 1959-60, U.S. Army Info. Office, N.Y.C., 1960-61; writer program precipitating Senate Armed Svcs. Hearings, 1962; ret., 1965. Mgr., salesman Nu-Enamel Stores, Asheville, N.C.,

1937-38; co-owner, dir. Roberts & Roberts Advt. Agy., Denver, 1946-49. Author: Rakkasan, 1955, Screaming Eagles, 1956, The Marne Division, 1957, Victory Denied, 1966, The Anatomy of a Revolution, 1968, Peace: By the Wonderful People Who Brought You Korea and Viet Nam, 1972, The Republic: Decline and Future Promise, 1975, The Crisis of Federal Regionalism: A Solution, 1976, Emerging Struggle for State Sovereignty, 1979, How To Organize for Survival, 1982, The Most Secret Science, 1984; also numerous pamphlets and articles. Pres. Found. for Edn., Scholarship, Patriotism and Americanism, Inc.; founder, nat. bd. dirs. Com. To Restore Constn., Inc., 1965—. Recipient Merit award Am. Acad. Pub. Affairs, 1967, Good Citizenship medal SARa, 1968, Liberty award Congress of Freedom, 1969, Man of Yr. awards Women for Constl. Govt., 1970, Wis. Legis. and Rsch. Com., 1971; medal of merit Am. Legion, 1972, Spkr. of Yr. award We, The People, 1973, spl. tribute State of Mich., 1979; Arch Roberts Week named in his honor City of Danville, Ill., 1974. Mem.: SAR, Sons Am. Colonists, Airborne Assn., Res. Officers Assn. Home: 2218 W Prospect PO Box 986 Fort Collins CO 80522-0986 E-mail: comminc@webaccess.net.

ROBERTS, BERT C., JR., telecommunications company executive; b. 1942; married. BS, Johns Hopkins U., 1965. Project dir., mgr. Westinghouse Electric Corp., 1960-69; dir. Leasco Response Inc., 1969-72; with MCI Communications Corp., Washington, 1972—, v.p., 1974-76, sr. v.p., 1976-83, pres., 1983-85; chief operating officer MCI Telecommunications Corp., Washington, 1985-91, chief exec. officer, 1991-94; chmn. World Comm. Inc., Washington, 1992—2002. Office: World Comm Inc 500 Clinton Center Dr Clinton MS 39056

ROBERTS, BILL GLEN, retired fire chief, investor, consultant; b. Deport, Tex., June 2, 1938; s. Samuel Westbrook and Ann Lee (Rhodes) R.; m. Ramona Ryall, June 1, 1963 (dec. Nov. 1988); 1 child, Renee Ann; m. Johana R. Caines, Oct. 14, 2000. Student, So. Meth. U., 1968, North Tex. State U., 1974; grad. paramedic course, U. Tex. Southwestern Med. Sch., 1974; grad. Exec. Program for Fire Service, Tex. A&M U., 1978; AAS, El Centro Jr. Coll., Dallas, 1980; grad. exec. fire officer program, Nat. Fire Acad., 1989. With Dallas Fire Dept., 1958-82, lt., 1964-67, capt., 1967-71, div. fire chief, 1971-79, asst. fire chief, 1979-83; fire chief Austin (Tex.) Fire Dept., 1983-94. Tech. bd. dirs. Found. Fire Safety, Washington, 1982-85; adj. faculty Nat. Fire Acad., 1981-86; aft. State Life of Indpls., Dallas, 1962; owner Personnel Testing Lab., Dallas, 1963; real estate salesman Dale Copus Realtor, Dallas, 1963-66; salesman intercommunications equipment Chandler Sound, Dallas, 1966-67; field engr. IBM Corp., Dallas, 1968; cons. U. Tenn., 1974, Ga. Inst. Tech., 1974, Tex. Dept. Health Resources, 1973-78, Rand Corp., Washington, Mission Rsch., Santa Barbara, Calif., Macro Author: EMS Dallas, 1978; (with others) Anesthesia for Surgery Trauma, 1976, EMS Measures to Improve Care, 1980; contbr. articles to periodicals. Com. chmn. Dallas Jaycees, 1962-65; mem. task force Am. Heart Assn., Austin, 1973-83; bd. dirs. Brackenridge Hosp., 1989, Rehab. Hosp. Austin, 1992-94, Austin Police Pensions Bd., 1989, Capitol Area coun. Boy Scouts Am., 1989-92. Recipient John Stemmons Service award Dallas Fire Dept., 1979; Internat. Assn. Fire Chiefs scholar, 1967. Mem. Internat. Assn. Fire Chiefs, Am. Heart Assn., North Tex. Coun. of Govts. (regional emergency svc. adv. coun. 1973-79), Found. Fire Safety (tech. bd. dirs. 1982-85), Tex. Assn. Realtors, Rotary. Methodist. Home: 192 Hunter's Ridge Rd Canton NC 28716 E-mail: bglenrob@aol.com.

ROBERTS, BRIAN L. communications executive; b. Phila., June 28, 1959; s. Ralph J. and Suzanne F. Roberts; m. Aileen Kennedy, Dec. 28, 1985; children: Sarah, Tucker, Amanda. Bachelor, U. Pa., 1981. V.p. ops. Comcast Cable Communications, Inc., Phila., 1985-86; exec. v.p. Comcast Corp., 1986-92, pres., 1992—97, CEO, 1997—. Bd. dirs. The Bank of N.Y.; bd. trustees Simon Wiesenthal Ctr.; founding co-chair Phila. 2000; dir., exec. com. CableLabs. Vice chmn. The Walter Katz Found. Mem. Nat. Cable and Telecom. Assn. (chmn. 1995-96, treas., bd. dirs., exec. com.). Avocation: squash (All-American, silver medal with U.S. team 1981, 85 and 97). Office: Comcast Corp Fl 35 East Twr 1500 Market St Fl 33 Philadelphia PA 19102-2100*

ROBERTS, BRIAN WAYNE, middle school educator, minister; b. Owensboro, Ky., Dec. 2, 1974; s. Clyde Wayne and Donna Lynn Roberts; m. Jenny Rebecca Westerfield. ThM, Luther Rice Sem., Lithonia, Ga., 2001. Ordained minister Green Brier Baptist, Utica, Ky., 1997; cert. tchr. Pastor New Life Bapt. Ch., Hawesville, Ky., 1997—2002, Sorgho (Ky.) Bapt. Ch., 2002—. Faculty sponsor Christian Student Fellowship, Owensboro, 1998—. Author: (study guide) God's Apocalypse: According to John, 1996. Student counselor Daviess/McLean Bapt. Assn., 1993—98, Ky. Wesleyan Meth. Workers, 1993—98. Recipient Elizabeth Munday Cmty. Svc. award, Ky. Wesleyan Coll., 1997. Mem.: Christian Educators Assn. Internat. R-Consevative. Avocation: University of Kentucky basketball. Home: 7030 Jack Hinton Rd Philpot KY 42366 Office: Daviess County Mid Sch 1415 E Fourth St Owensboro KY 42303

ROBERTS, BURTON BENNETT, lawyer, retired judge; b. N.Y.C., July 25, 1922; s. Alfred S. and Cecelia (Schanfein) R.; m. Gerhild Ukryn. BA, NYU, 1943, LL.M., 1953; LL.B., Cornell U., 1949. Bar: N.Y. 1949. Asst. dist. atty., New York County, 1949-66; chief asst. dist. atty. Bronx County, Bronx, N.Y., 1966-68, acting dist. atty., 1968-69, dist. atty., 1969-72; justice Supreme Ct. State N.Y., 1973-98, adminstrv. judge criminal br. Bronx County 12th Jud. Dist., 1984-98, adminstrv. judge civil br. Bronx County 12th Dist., 1988-98; ret., 1998; counsel Fischbein, Badillo, Wagner & Harding, 1999—. Pres. Bronx div. Hebrew Home for Aged, 1967-72. With U.S. Army, 1943-45. Decorated Purple Heart, Bronze Star with oak leaf cluster. Mem. Assn. Bar City N.Y., Am. Bar Assn., N.Y. Bar Assn., Bronx County Bar Assn., N.Y. State Dist. Attys. Assn. (pres. 1971-72) Jewish (exec. bd. temple). Home: 215 E 68th St Apt 19A New York NY 10021-5727 Office: Fischbein Badillo et al 909 3rd Ave New York NY 10022-4731 Office Phone: 212-453-3968. E-mail: broberts@fbwhlaw.com.

ROBERTS, CARL GEOFFREY, lawyer; b. Boston, June 17, 1948; s. Simon Matthew and Ruth (Gorfinkle) Roberts; m. Sharon Ash, Mar. 24, 1979 (div. June 19, 2002); 1 child, Dennis; m. Susan Busch, Dec. 28, 2002. BA, Harvard U., 1970; JD, U. Pa., 1974. Bar: Pa. 1974, U.S. Dist. Ct. (ea. dist.) Pa. 1974, U.S. Ct. Appeals (3d cir.) 1978, U.S. Supreme Ct. 1980, U.S. Ct. Claims 1980, U.S. Dist. Ct. (mid. dist.) Pa. 1986. Law clk. U.S. Dist. Ct. (ea. dist.) Pa., Phila., 1974-76; assoc. Dilworth, Paxson, Kalish & Kauffman, Phila., 1978-82, ptnr., 1982-92, Ballard, Spahr, Andrews & Ingersoll, Phila., 1992—. Bd. dirs. Phila. Chamber Ensemble, sec., 1977-92, pres., 1992-95; mem. Hillel com. U. Pa., 1999—, chair 2001—; bd. dirs. Hillel of Greater Phila., 2000—. Mem.: ABA (law practice mgmt. sect. sec. 2002—03, vice chmn. 2003—04, chmn.-elect 2004—). Office: Ballard Spahr Andrews & Ingersoll 1735 Market St Fl 51 Philadelphia PA 19103-7599 Office Phone: 215-864-8120. E-mail: cgroberts@ballardspahr.com.

ROBERTS, CAROLYN C. former hospital administrator; b. Parkersburg, W.Va., Dec. 4, 1938; married. M, Northeastern U., 1981. Various positions, 1962-75; dir. clin. administrn. svcs. Sidney Farber Cancer Inst., Boston, 1975-82; pres., CEO Copley Health Sys., Morrisville, Vt., 1982—. Author books; contbr. articles to profl. jours. Recipient cmty. svc. awards. Fellow Am. Acad. Med. Administrs.; mem. Am. Hosp. Assn. (bd. dirs., chmn., del., trustee), Am. Soc. Healthcare Risk Mgmt. (coms.), Vt. Hosp. Assn. (coms., trustee). Home: RR 1 Box 3290 Hyde Park VT 05655-9759 Office: Copley Health Sys RR 3 Box 760 Morrisville VT 05661-9209

ROBERTS, CECIL EDWARD, JR., labor union administrator; b. Oct. 31, 1946; s. Cecil E. and Evelyn R.; m. Carolyn Sue Stewart; children: Kyle Edward, Melissa Dawn. Student, Beckley Jr. Coll.; grad., W.Va. Technical Coll., 1987. Gen. laborer Carbon Fuels Mine, Winifred, W.Va., 1971-77; v.p. dist. 17 United Mine Workers of Am., 1977-82, v.p., 1982-95, pres., 1995—. Mem. Com. Employer Support Vet. Employment, 1985, 86; pres. Nat. Coun. Holmes Safety Assn., 1985—; mem. W.Va. Employment Opportunities and Econ. Devel. Commn. Past bd. dirs. Blue Cross and Blue Shield So. W.Va., Cabin Creek (W.Va.) Clinic, past mem. adv. com. Black Lung Program; gen. v.p. Nat. Coun. Sr. Citizens; mem. adv. bd. W.Va. U. Inst. Labor Studies and Rsch., 1996—. With U.S. Army, 1966-67, Vietnam. Recipient Martin Luther King award Rainbow Coalition, Citizen Action award, Midwest Acad. award. Mem. Am. Legion, Vietnam Vets. of Am. Office: United Mine Workers of Am Internat Union 8315 Lee Hwy Fairfax VA 22031-2215*

ROBERTS, CELIA ANN, librarian; b. Bangor, Maine, Feb. 6, 1935; d. William Lewis and Ruey Pearl (Logan) Roberts. AA, U. Hartford, 1957, BA, 1961; postgrad., So. Conn. State Coll., 1963—. With catalog, acquisition and circulation depts. U. Hartford Libr., 1956-65; libr. Simsbury Free Libr., Simsbury, Conn., 1965-69; reference libr. Simsbury Pub. Libr., 1969—. Tchr. ballet, 1965—66; tchr. genealogy, 1977—; ballet mistress Ballet Soc. Conn., Inc., 1968—70; with corps de ballet Conn. Opera Assn., 1963—64; active in prodns. Simsbury Light Opera Assn., 1964—69. Contbr. articles to profl. jours. Vol. Family History Ctr., 1970—. Mem.: DAR (Abigail Phelps chpt.), AAUW (past pres. Greater Hartford br.), ALA, Simsbury Hist. Soc., Conn. Libr. Assn., Denison Soc., Inc., Daus. of Scotia, Simsbury Geneal. and Hist. Rsch. Libr., Chateauguay Valley Hist. Soc., New Brunswick Geneal. Soc., Conn. Hist. Soc., Dance Masters Am. (Conn. Dance Tchrs. Club chpt.), Soc. Mayflower Descs. Conn., Conn. Soc. Genealogists (registrar Hartford 1983), Pro Dance, New Eng. Historic Geneal. Soc., Ont. Geneal. Soc. Unitarian Universalist. Office: Simsbury Public Libr 725 Hopmeadow St Simsbury CT 06070-2243 E-mail: croberts@simsbury.lib.ct.us.

ROBERTS, CHARLES PATRICK (PAT ROBERTS), senator; b. Topeka, Kans., Apr. 20, 1936; m. Franki Fann, 1969; children: David, Ashleigh, Anne-Wesley. BS, Kans. State U., 1958. Pub. Litchfield Park, Ariz., 1962-67; adminstrv. asst. to U.S. Senator Frank Carlson, U.S. Senate, Washington, 1967-68; adminstrv. asst. to U.S. Congressman Keith Sebelius U.S. Ho. of Reps., Washington, 1968-80; mem. 97th to 104th Congresses from Kans. 1st Dist., Washington, 1980-96, U.S. Senate from Kans., Washington, 1997—; mem. agr., nutrition and forestry com.; mem. armed svcs. com.; chmn. intelligence com.; mem. ethics com. Served with USMC, 1958-62. Republican. Office: US Senate 109 Hart Senate Off Bldg Washington DC 20510-1605

ROBERTS, CHRIS, strategy and finance educator, researcher; b. New Castle, Pa., July 16, 1954; s. Samuel Bruce and Jan Roberts, Della V. Roberts (Stepmother), Sheldon S. Smith (Stepfather). BS in Mgmt., U. Utah, 1975, BS in Fin., 1981; MBA, U. Phoenix, Salt Lake City, 1986; PhD in Mgmt., U. Mass., 1995. Supr. Holiday Inns Reservation Ctr., Memphis, Utah, 1972—78; product mgr. Mountain Bell/Qwest Comms., Salt Lake City, 1978—89; assoc. prof. Isenberg Sch. Mgmt. U. Mass., Amherst, 1993—, assoc. dept. head dept. Isenberg Sch. Mgmt., 2001—. Contbr. articles to profl. jours.; editor: Jour. Hospitality and Tourism Edn. Mem.: Acad. Mgmt., Strategic Mgmt. Soc., Coun. Hotel, Restaurant & Instnl. Edn. (chair symposium com. 1998—2002, Outstanding Peer Reviewer 1999), Beta Gamma Sigma. Avocations: contract bridge, international travel. Home: PO Box 521895 Salt Lake City UT 84152-1895 Office: U Mass Flint 206 90 Campus Center Way Amherst MA 01003-9247 Personal E-mail: q@qutah.com. Business E-Mail: q@ht.umass.edu.

ROBERTS, CORINNE BOGGS (COKIE ROBERTS), correspondent, news analyst; b. New Orleans, Dec. 27, 1943; d. Thomas Hale and Corinne Morrison (Claiborne) Boggs; m. Steven V. Roberts, Sept. 10, 1966; children: Lee Harriss, Rebecca Boggs. BA in Polit. Sci., Wellesley Coll., 1964; hon. degrees, Amherst Coll., Columbia Coll., Loyola U. of the South, Manhattanville Coll., Gonzaga U., Boston Coll., Hood Coll., Chestnut Hill Coll., Miss. Women's U., Notre Dame U. Md., Xavier U., St. Louis U., Duke U. Assoc. prodr., host Altman Prodns., Washington, 1964—66, prodr. L.A., 1969—72; reporter, editor Cowles Comm., N.Y.C., 1967; prodr. Sta. WNEW-TV, N.Y.C., 1968, Sta. KNBC-TV, L.A., 1972—74; reporter CBS News, Athens, Greece, 1974—77; corr. Nat. Pub. Radio, Washington, 1977—, MacNeil/Lehrer Newshour, Washington, 1984—88; spl. Washington corr. ABC News, Washington, 1988—92; interviewer, commentator This Week With David Brinkley, Washington, 1992—96; co-anchor This Week, 1996—2002; chief congrl. analyst ABC News, 1998—. Lectr. in field. Co-host weekly pub. TV program on Congress The Lawmakers, 1981—84, prodr., host pub. affairs program Sta. WRC-TV, Washington; prodr.: Sta. KNBC-TV Serendipity (award for excellence in local programming, Emmy nomination for children's programming); author: We Are Our Mother's Daughters, 1998, Founding Mothers: The Women Who Raised Our Nation, 2004; contbr. articles to newspapers, mags. Bd. dis. Dirksen Ctr., Pekin, Ill., 1988—95; bd. dirs. Fgn. Students Svc. Ctr., Washington, 1990—, Manhattanville Coll., Purchase, NY, 1991—99, Children's Inn at NIH, Bethesda, Md., 1992—. Recipient Broadcast award, Nat. Orgn. Working Women, 1984, Everett McKinley Dirksen disting. reporting of Congress, 1987, Weintal award, Georgetown U., 1988, Corp. Pub. Broadcasting award, 1988, Edward R. Murrow award, Corp. Pub. Broadcasting, 1990, Broadcast award, Nat. Women's Polit. Caucus, 1990, David Brinkley Comm. award, 1991, Mother of Yr. award, Nat. Mother's Day Com., 1992, Emmy award news and documentary, 1992. Mem.: Radio-TV Corrs. Assn. (pres. 1981—82, bd. dirs. 1980—94), U.S. Capitol Hist. Soc. Roman Catholic.*

ROBERTS, CURTIS CREED, minister, writer; b. Lenox, Ga., Nov. 20, 1920; s. Walter C. Roberts and LeeAnnie Goodwin; m. Pauline Powell Roberts (dec.); children: Don Wayne, Marcus Carroll, Randy Curtis. BA, Valdosta (Ga.) State Coll., 1967. Co-owner Roberts Furniture Co., Lenox, Ga., 1947—58, Bradenton, Fla., 1958—60; pastor United Meth. Ch., Ga., 1963—2001; bookkeeper Roberts Property Mgmt., Tifton, Ga., 1988—. Co-author: (book) The Leesburg Methodist Story, 1974; author: More Precious Than Gold, 2002. Ordained elder United Meth. Ch., 1970. Sgt. U.S. Army, 1942—45. Decorated EAMET Svc. medal U.S. Army, Am. Theatre Ribbon, World War II Victory medal. Methodist. Avocation: art. Home: 2440 Madison Dr Tifton GA 31793 Office: Roberts Property Mgmt 1015 E 12th St Tifton GA

ROBERTS, DAVID, airport executive; Dir. Indpls. Internat. Airport. Office: Indpls Internat Airport Indpls Airport Authority 2500 S High School Rd Indianapolis IN 46241-4943

ROBERTS, DAVID GLEN, prospector, investor; b. Plainview, Tex., Feb. 8, 1952; s. Doris Glen and Anna Grace (Mathis) R. Student, Tex. A&M U., 1970-71, Dallas Bapt. Coll., 1971-75; BA in Comm., U. Tex. Permian Basin, 1987. Lic. minister Bapt. Ch.; cert. profl. landman. Profl. stuntman, actor, 1972-76; mgr. Channel 100, Midland, Tex., 1976-78; owner D.G. Roberts Land Mgmt., Midland, Tex., 1978—, Diamond Developers Fire and Enviro-Safety Co.; regional mktg. dir. Nochar Inc.-Region 11, Midland, Tex., 1990-96; pub., owner Basin Voice newspaper. Cons. EPA, Indpls., 1991—. Appeared in film Giovanni & Ben, 1974, Drive In, 1976; theatre appearance at Globe Theatre, Odessa, Tex., 1975, Shakespeare in the Park, Dallas, 1976. Past chair Midland County Libertarian Party; past mem. exec. com. Dist. 31 Tex. Libertarian Party; organizer Sons of Liberty, Midland, 1990—. Mem. Am. Assn. Petroleum-Landmen, Five Aces, NRA, Tex. State Rifle Assn., Permian Basin Landman's Assn., N.O.R.M.L. Libertarian. Avocations: golf, motorcycling, hiking, shooting, photography. Office: Diamond Developers 3105 Barkley Ave Midland TX 79701-6215 E-mail: davy.roberts@bodywise.net.

ROBERTS, DAVID LOWELL, journalist, educator; b. Lusk, Wyo., Jan. 12, 1954; s. Leslie James and LaVerne Elizabeth (Johns) R. BA, U. Ariz., 1979; MA, U. Nebr., 1997. Founder, editor, publisher Medicine Bow (Wyo.) Post, 1977-88; journalism instr. U. Wyo., Laramie, 1987-92; adviser U. Wyo. Student Publs., Laramie, 1987-92; gen. mgr. Student Media Corp U No. Colo., Greeley, 1995-98; founder, publisher Hanna Herald, Wyo., 1979-80; asst. prof. mass comm. Missouri Valley Coll., Marshall, Mo., 2001—. Exch. reporter The Washington Post, 1982; freelance reporter Casper (Wyo.) Star-Tribune, 1978-83, various publs.; freelancer, 1977—. Co-author: (book) The Wyoming Almanac, 1988, 90, 94, 96, 2001; author: (book) Sage Street, 1991; columnist Sage Street, 1989-92. Chmn. Medicine Bow Film Commn., 1984; treas. Friends of the Medicine Bow Mus., 1984-88; pres. Medicine Bow Area C. of C., 1984; dir. Habitat for Humanity of Albany County, Laramie, 1991-92. Recipient Nat. Newspaper Assn. awards, over 40 Wyo. Press. Assn. awards, Five Editorial awards U. Wyo., Citizen of Yr. award People of Medicine Bow, 1986, Student Publs. awards U. Wyo., 1990, 92. Mem. Friends of Medicine Bow Mus. Mem. Green Party. Methodist. Avocations: writing, golf, visiting museums, photography. Business E-Mail: robertsd@moval.edu.

ROBERTS, DELMAR LEE, editor; b. Raleigh, N.C., Apr. 9, 1933; s. James Delmer and Nellie Brockelbank (Tyson) R. BS in Textile Mgmt., NC State U., 1956; postgrad., Inst. Polit. Studies, U. Paris, 1963; MA in Journalism, U. SC, 1974. Product devel. engr. U.S. Rubber Co. (Uniroyal), Winnsboro, SC, 1959—63; process improvement engr. Allied Chem. Co., Irmo, S.C., 1965-67; assoc. editor S.C. History Illustrated Mag., Columbia, 1970; editor-in-chief, editl. v.p. Sandlapper-The Mag. of S.C., Columbia, 1968-74; mng. editor, art dir. Legal Econs. mag. of the ABA, Chgo., 1975-89, Law Practice Mgmt. mag. of the ABA, Chgo., 1990-2000, editor emeritus, 2000—. Editor: The Best of Legal Economics, 1979; freelance editor and/or designer of over 35 books. Active World Affairs Coun. Columbia, 1997-; 1st v.p. English-Speaking Union, 1996-97, pres. 1997-2003, bd. dirs. 2003-. With U.S. Army, 1956-58. Hon. fellow Coll. of Law Practice Mgmt., Golden, Colo., 1995—. Mem. Soc. Profl. Journalists, Capital City Club (Columbia), Phi Kappa Tau, Kappa Tau Alpha. Avocations: european travel, turkish carpet/kilim collecting, antique collecting.

ROBERTS, DENISE (DENISE ROBERTS HURLIN), dancer; Studied dance with Ilene Danek; BFA in dance, SUNY, Purchase. Dancer Paul Taylor Dance Co., N.Y.C., 1989—95. Dancer with Hannah Kahn, Kevin Wynn, Douglas Wright; founding mem., toured with David Parsons Co.; faculty mem. SUNY, The Juilliard Sch., 1989-90; co-founder (with Hernando Cortez), Dancers Responding to AIDS, 1991-; panelist, Arts Alive Grants Com. of Westchester, NY, Broadyway Cares/Equity Fights AIDS Nat. Grants prog. Named Outstanding performer by Joan Acocella, 1994. Office: Dancers Responding to AIDS 165 W 46th St 1300 New York NY 10036

ROBERTS, DENNIS WILLIAM, association executive; b. Chgo., Jan. 7, 1943; s. William Owen and Florence Harriet (Denman) R. BA in Journalism, U. N.Mex., 1968; MA in Legal Studies, Antioch U., 1982; MA, St. John's Coll., 1984. Gen. assignment reporter Albuquerque Pub. Co., 1964, sports writer, 1960-64, advt. and display salesman, 1967-68; dir. info. N.Mex. bldg. br. Asso. Gen. Contractors Am., Albuquerque, 1968-79, asst. exec. dir., 1979-82, dir., 1982—. Adj. prof. civil engring. U. N.Mex., 2004. Active United Way, Albuquerque, 1969-78; chmn. Albuquerque Crime Prevention Coun., 1982; bd. dirs. Rio Grande chpt. ARC, 1992-95, Albuquerque Lit. Coun., 1998-2004; cmty. adv. coun., Albuquerque (N.Mex.) Jobs Corps. Recipient Pub. Rels. Achievement award Assoc. Gen. Contractors Am., 1975, 78. Mem. N.Mex. Pub. Rels. Conf. (chmn. 1975, 82-83), Pub. Rels. Soc. Am. (accredited, pres. N.Mex. chpt. 1981, chmn. S.W. dist. 1984, chmn. sect. 1988), Constrn. Specifications Inst. (Outstanding Industry Mem. 1974, Outstanding Com. Chmn. 1978), Am. Soc. Safety Engrs., Toastmasters Club (dist. gov. 1977-78, Disting. Dist. award 1978, Toastmaster of Yr. 1979-80), Masons, Shriners, Sigma Delta Chi (pres. N.Mex. chpt. 1969). Republican. Lutheran. Home: Apt 21 1410 Girard NE Albuquerque NM 87106 Office: Assn Gen Contractors 1615 University Blvd NE Albuquerque NM 87102-1717 Office Phone: 505-842-1462. Business E-Mail: dennisr@agc.nm.org. *Personal philosophy: Set your priorities in life, then your goals. In pursuing your goals, visualize their accomplishment. Be persistent, and you will accomplish what you set out to accomplish. Learn to be fair to others and empathetic.*

ROBERTS, DONALD ALBERT, advertising, public relations, marketing and media consultant; b. Boston, Dec. 17, 1935; s. Albert Arthur and Linette Violette (Ouelette) R.; m. Gabrielle Dorothy St. Laurent, Apr. 20, 1957; children: Lynne Dianne, Tammy Denise. Student, U. Maine, 1987-88, 97-99. Program mgr., dir. sports Sta. WIMA-TV, Lima, Ohio, 1965-68; v.p., gen. mgr. Sta. WABK/WKME, Gardiner, Maine, 1968-74; pres., owner Sta. WRDO, Augusta, Maine, 1974-77; cons. group gen. mgr. Valley Communications, Bangor, Maine, 1977-78; pres., owner Roberts Advt. Agy., Augusta, 1977-78; v.p., gen. mgr. Sta. WLOB AM/FM, Portland, Maine, 1978-80, Sta. WKCG/WFAU, Augusta, 1980-83; pres., owner Roberts & Co., Augusta, 1983—; exec. v.p. mktg., programming and advt. sales State Cable TV Corp., Augusta, 1983-92; cons. gen. mgr. Capital Weekly Newspaper, Augusta, 1993—. Cons. New Eng. Ziebart Dealers Assn., 1982—; cons. gen. mgr. Capital Weekly Newspaper, Augusta, Maine, 1994—. Contbr. articles to profl. jours. Pres. Auburn (Maine) City Coun., 1957-60; chmn. Jefferson-Jackson Dinner, Rockland, Maine, 1959, Preserve Augusta Neighborhood Assn., 1989—; del. Dem. State Conv., Bangor, 1980; city councilor-at-large of Augusta, 1990-94; mem. Augusta City Charter Commn., 1997-98; del. Maine Rep. Conv., 1996, 98, 2000. Named Maine Sportscaster of Yr. Nat. Sportscasters Assn., 1962, 63; recipient Tiger award Maine Broadcasting System, 1965. Mem. So. Kennebec Valley Realtors Assn., Cable Advt. Bur., Cable TV Adminstrs. and Marketers, Ohio Sportscasters Assn. (co-founder 1965), Maine Assn. Broadcasters (bd. dirs.), Kennebec Valley C. of C. (bd. dirs.). Avocations: politics, reading, golf. Home and Office: 44 Longwood Ave Augusta ME 04330-4131

ROBERTS, DONALD FRANK, JR., communications educator; b. Seattle, Mar. 30, 1939; s. Donald Frank Sr. and Ruth Amalia (Geiger) R.; m. Karlene Hahn, 1963 (div. 1981): 1 child, Donald Brett; m. Wendy G. Roberts, Aug. 26, 1983; stepchildren: Richard L., David L., Katherine M. AB, Columbia U., 1961; MA, U. Calif., Berkeley, 1963; PhD, Stanford U., 1968. Instr., dept. English U. Hawaii, Honolulu, 1963-64; asst. dir. ednl. svc. bur. The Wall Street Jour., Princeton, N.J., 1964-65; asst. prof., rsch. assoc. dept. Comm., Inst. Comm. Rsch. Stanford (Calif.) U., 1970-76, assoc. prof., 1976-84, prof. Comm., 1984—, dir. Inst. Comm. Rsch., 1985-90, chmn. dept. Comm., 1990-96, Thomas More Storke Prof., 1991—. Cons. NIMH, 1970—71, Rand Corp., 1972—74, Sta. KQED-TV, 1975—77, Far West Lab. Ednl. Rsch. and Devel., 1978—79, FTC, 1978—80, Westinghouse Broadcasting, 1983—86, Soc. Nutrition Edn., 1984—86, The Disney Channel, 1986—87, WHO, 1988—89, SRI Internat., 1988—89, Carnegie Coun. Adolescence, 1989—90, NBC, 1992, Ctr. Disease Control, 1992, Children Now, 1992—, Software Pubs. Assn., 1994, Nickelodeon, 1994, JP Kids, 1995—97, MGM Animation, 1996—98, DIC Entertainment, 1997—, Planet Lingo, 1997—2001, Sunbow Entertainment, 1999—2000, ABC/Disney TV Animation, 2000—02, Disney Online, 2000—02, Nelvana, Ltd., 2000—01; bd. advisors Media Scope, 1992—94; proposal reviewer NIMH, NSF, U.S. Agy. Internat. Devel., Can. Coun., John and Mary R. Markle Found., W.T. Grant Found.; spkr. numerous seminars, confs., symposia. Co-author: Process and Effects of Mass Communication, 1971, Television and Human Behavior, 1978, It's not ONLY Rock and Roll, 1998, Kids and Media at the New Millennium, 1999, Kids and Media in America, 2004; mem. editl. bd. Jour. Broadcasting, 1980—88, Pub. Opinion Quarterly, 1981—86, Communicare, 1986—, editl. reviewer Commn. Rsch., —, Comm. Monograph, Comm. Yearbook, Human Comm. Rsch., Jour. Comm., Jour. Quarterly, Child Devel., Jour. Applied Psychology, Jour. Ednl. Psychology, Psychology Bull., Jour. Adolescent Health; contbr. articles, chapters to books. Fellow Human Scis. Rsch. Coun., Pretoria. South Africa, 1985, 1987, Fullbright Teaching fellow Inst. for Unterrichtstechnologie Und Medienpadagogic, Austria, 1987. Mem. APA, Internat. Comm. Assn., Assn. Edn. in Journalism and Mass Comm., Soc. Rsch. Child Devel., Soc. Personality and Soc. Psychology. Office: Stanford U Dept Comm McClatchy Hall Stanford CA 94305-2050 Office Phone: 650-723-0780. E-mail: droberts@stanford.edu.

ROBERTS, DONALD JOHN, economics and business educator, consultant; b. Winnipeg, Man., Can., Feb. 11, 1945; came to U.S., 1967; s. Donald Victor and Margaret Mabel R.; m. Kathleen Eleanor Taylor, Aug. 26, 1967. BA with honors, U. Man., 1967; PhD, U. Minn., 1972. Instr. dept. managerial econs. and decision scis. J.L. Kellogg Grad. Sch. Mgmt., Northwestern U., Evanston, Ill., 1971—72, asst. prof., 1972—74; assoc. prof. J. L. Kellogg Grad. Sch. Mgmt., Northwestern U., Evanston, Ill., 1974—77; prof. J.L. Kellogg Grad. Sch. Mgmt., Northwestern U., Evanston, Ill., 1977—80, Grad. Sch. Bus., Stanford (Calif.) U., 1980, Jonathan B. Lovelace prof., 1980—2001, assoc.

dean, dir. rsch., 1987—90, dir. exec. program in strategy and orgn., 1992—, dir. global mgmt. program, 1994—, sr. assoc. dean, 2000—, John H. Scully prof., 2001—; co-dir. Ctr. for Global Bus. and the Economy, 2003. Prof. (by courtesy) dept. econs. Stanford U., 1986—; vis. rsch. faculty U. Catholique de Louvain, Belgium, 1974-75; inaugural Clarendon lectr. mgmt. studies Oxford U., 1997; cons. bus., econs. and antitrust, 1976—; vis. fellow All Souls Coll., Oxford U., 1995, Nuffield Coll., Oxford U., 1999-00; vis. acad. fellow in leadership and orgn. McKinsey & Co., London, 1999-00. Author The Modern Firm: Organizational Design for Performance and Growth, 2004; co-author: Economics, Organization and Management, 1992; assoc. editor Jour. Econ. Theory, 1977-92, Econometrica, 1985-87, Games and Economics Behavior, 1988-; mem. editl. bd. Am. Econ. Rev., 1991-95, Jour. Econs. and Mgmt. Strategy, 1991-98, Orgns. and Markets Abstracts, 1996-; contbr. articles to profl. jours. NSF grantee, 1973-93; rsch. fellow Ctr. Ops. Rsch. and Econometrics, Heverlee, Belgium, 1974, fellow Ctr. for Advanced Study in the Behavioral Scis., 1991-92. Fellow Econometric Soc. (coun. 1994-96); mem. Am. Econ. Assn., Beta Gamma Sigma. Home: 835 Santa Fe Ave Stanford CA 94305-1022 E-mail: roberts_john@gsb.stanford.edu.

ROBERTS, DONALD MUNIER, retired banker, trust company executive; b. Paterson, N.J., Aug. 3, 1935; s. Edward and Dorothy (Munier) R.; m. Sally D. Ingram, Sept. 6, 1958 (dec. Feb. 1978); 1 dau., Sarah M.; m. Mary Ayer Gordon, June 23, 1978; children: Edward (dec.), John, Martha. BS, Yale U., 1957; MBA, NYU, 1961. Exec. v.p., 1979-90; vice chmn., treas. U.S. Trust Co. N.Y., N.Y.C., 1990-95; retired, 1995. Bd. dirs. York (Pa.) Internat. Corp., Burlington Resources, Inc. Mem. N.Y. Road Runners Club Inc. (bd. dirs., past chmn.), Tau Beta Pi. Clubs: Links (N.Y.C.). Republican. Home: 10 Gracie Sq New York NY 10028-8031 Office: 18th Fl 645 Fifth Ave New York NY 10022-5910

ROBERTS, DONALD WILSON, pathologist, consultant; b. Phoenix, Jan. 20, 1933; s. Alpha Wilson and Rubye Clotilde (Finklea) R.; m. Mae Astrid Strand, June 17, 1959; children: Marc Donald, Sara Judith Roberts Roundy. BS, Brigham Young U., 1957; MS, Iowa State U., 1959; PhD, U. Calif., Berkeley, 1964. Postdoctoral Swiss Fed. Inst. Tech., Zurich, 1964-65; insect pathologist Boyce Thompson Inst. for Plant Rsch., Ithaca, N.Y., 1965-96; insect pathologist, res. prof. dept. biology Utah State U., Logan, 1997—. Cons. WHO, Kaduna, Nigeria, 1974, 76, Empresa Brasileira de Pesquisa Agropecuraria, Brasilia, Brazil, 1978, 79, 80, 94, 96; mem. sci. adv. bd. EcoSci. Corp., Worcester, Mass., 1990-95; project reviewer UN Devel. Program, Africa and South Am., 1993-96, USAID Africa, 1991-96; adj. prof. dept. entomology Cornell U., Ithaca, N.Y., 1993—, adj. prof. dept. plant pathology, 1994-99. Editor: (3 books) Diseases of Medically Important Arthropods, 1977, 80, 83, Invasion Processes of Fungi, 1983, Biotechnology in Pest Control, 1989; contbr. over 200 articles to profl. jours. Recipient Fulbright Sr. Rsch. scholarship Fulbright Found., Australia, 1985; named Family of Yr., Utah State U. Internat. Students, 1999. Mem. Soc. for Invertebrate Pathology (hon. 1998, founding mem., pres. 1988-90, Founder's Lectr. 1996, Svc. to Brazilian Insect Pathology award 2002), Entomol. Soc. Am. (Ea. br., Ciba-Geigy Recognition award 1985, 86, L.O. Howard Disting. Achievement award 1989), Am. Soc. Microbiology, Mycol. Soc. Am., Brazilian Entomol. Soc. (hon., recognition award 1996). Avocation: ballroom and swing dance. Office: Utah State U Dept Biology Logan UT 84322-5305 Office Phone: 435-797-0049. E-mail: dwroberts@biology.usu.edu.

ROBERTS, DORIS, actress; b. St. Louis, Nov. 4, 1930; d. Larry and Ann (Meltzer) R.; m. Michael E. Cannata, June 21, 1950; 1 child, Michael R.; m. William Goyen, Nov. 10, 1963 (dec.) Student, NYU, 1950-51; studies with, Sanford Meisner, Neighborhood Playhouse, N.Y.C., 1952-53, Lee Strasberg, Actors' Studio, 1956. Ind. stage, screen and TV actress, 1953—. Profl. stage debut, Ann Arbor, Mich., 1953; appeared in summer stock Chatham, Mass., 1955; Broadway debut in The Time of Your Life, 1955; other Broadway and off-Broadway appearances include The Desk Set, 1955, The American Dream, 1961, The Death of Bessie Smith, 1961, The Office, 1965, The Color of Darkness, 1963, Marathon 33, 1963, Secret Affair of Mildred Wilde, 1972, Last of the Red Hot Lovers, 1969-71, Bad Habits, 1973 (Outer Circle Critics award 1974), Cheaters, 1976, Fairie Tale Theatre, 1985, The Fig Tree, 1987, It's Only a Play, 1992, Bye Bye Birdie, 2004; movie debut Something Wild, 1961, film appearances include: Barefoot in the Park, 1968, No Way to Treat a Lady, 1973, A Lovely Way to Die, 1969, Honeymoon Killers, 1969, A New Leaf, 1970, Such Good Friends, 1971, Little Murders, 1971, Heartbreak Kid, 1972, Hester Street, 1975, The Taking of Pelham, One, Two, Three, 1974, The Rose, 1979, Good Luck, Miss Wyckoff, 1979, Rabbit Test, 1979, Ordinary Hero, 1986, #1 with a Bullet, 1987, For Better or for Worse-Street Law, 1988, National Lampoon's Xmas Vacation, 1989, Used People, 1992, The Night We Never Met, Momma Mia, 1994, Walking to Waldheim, 1995, The Grass Harp, 1995, A Fish in the Bathtub, 1997, My Giant, 1998, All Over the Guy, 2001, Dickie Roberts-Child Star, 2003, Lucky 13, I Can See You.Com; TV debut on Studio One, 1958, Mary Hartman, Mary Hartman, 1975, Mary Tyler Moore Hour, 1976, Soap, 1978-79, Angie, 1979-80, Remington Steele, 1984-88, Lily Tomlin Comedy Hour, Barney Miller, Alice, Full House, Perfect Strangers, Sunday Dinner, A Family Man, The Fig Tree (PBS), 1987, (TV films) The Story Teller, 1979, Ruby and Oswald, 1978, It Happened One Christmas, 1978, Jennifer: A Woman's Story, 1979, The Diary of Anne Frank, 1982, A Letter to Three Wives, Blind Faith, 1989, A Mom For Christmas, 1990, The Sunset Gang, 1990, Crossroads, 1993, Dream On, 1993, The Boys, 1993, A Time To Heal, 1994, A Thousand Men and a Baby, 1997, One True Love, 2000, Sons of Miseltoe, 2001, A Time to Remember (Hallmark channel) 2003, Raising Waylon, (CBS) 2003. TV series appearances include St. Elsewhere, 1982 (Emmy award best sup. actress drama) Murder She Wrote, 1990, Step By Step, 1994, Burk's Law, 1994, Walker Texas Ranger, 1995, High Society, 1996, Everybody Loves Raymond, 1996- (Amer. Comedy award, 1999, Emmy award best sup. actress comedy, 2001, 02, 03, nom., 04, Gracie Allen award, 2004). Mem. SAG (Ensemble award 2002), AFTRA, Actors Equity Assn., Dirs. Guild Am.

ROBERTS, DORIS EMMA, epidemiologist, consultant, public health nurse; b. Toledo, Dec. 28, 1915; d. Frederic Constable and Emma Selina (Reader) Roberts. Diploma, Peter Bent Brigham Sch. Nursing, Boston, 1938; BS, Geneva Coll., Beaver Falls, Pa., 1944; MPH, U. Minn., 1958; PhD, U. N.C., 1967. RN Mass. Staff nurse Vis. Nurse Assn., New Haven, 1938—40; sr. nurse Neighborhood House, Millburn, NJ, 1942—45; supr. Tb Baltimore County Dept. Health, Towson, Md., 1945—46; Tb cons. Md. State Dept. Health, Balt., 1946—50; cons., chief nurse Tb program USPHS, Washington, 1950—57, cons. divsn. nursing, 1958—63; chief nursing practice br. Health Resources Adminstrn., HEW, Bethesda, Md., 1966—75; adj. prof. U. N.C. Sch. Pub. Health, 1975—92. Cons. WHO, 1961—82. Contbr. articles to profl. jours. Capt. commn. corps USPHS, 1945—75. Recipient Disting. Alumna award, Geneva Coll., 1971, Disting. Svc. award, USPHS, 1971, Outstanding Achievement award, U. Minn., 1983. Fellow: APHA (v.p. 1978—79, Disting. Svc. award Pub. Health Nursing sect. 1975, Sedgwick Meml. medal 1979), Am. Acad. Nursing (hon.); mem.: Inst. Medicine of NAS, Sigma Theta Tau, Delta Omega. Democrat. Episcopalian. Avocations: needlepoint, gardening, reading, ch. vol. work. Home: 9707 Old Georgetown Rd Apt 1112 Bethesda MD 20814-1746

ROBERTS, DOROTHY HYMAN, accessory company executive; b. N.Y.C., Dec. 6, 1928; d. Edgar C. and Theresa M. (Marks) Hyman; m. Paul M. Roberts, June 18, 1950 (dec.); children: Lynn, Steven; m. Paul M. Cohen. BA, Conn. Coll., 1950. With Echo Design Group Inc. (formerly Echo Scarfs Inc.), N.Y.C., 1950—, pres., 1978—, chmn., CEO. Mem. The Fashion Group. Office: The Echo Design Grp 10 E 40th St New York NY 10016-0200

ROBERTS, DWIGHT LOREN, engineering consultant, writer; b. San Diego, June 3, 1949; s. James Albert and Cleva Lorraine (Conn) R.; B.A., U. San Diego, 1976, M.A., 1979; m. Phyllis Ann Adair, Mar. 29, 1969; children: Aimee Renee, Michael Loren, Daniel Alexandr. Engring. aide Benton Engring. Inc., San Diego, 1968-73; pres. Robert's Tech. Research Co., also subs. Marine Technique Ltd., San Diego, 1973-76; pres. Research Technique Internat., 1978—; freelance writer, 1979—; owner Agrl. Analysis, 1985-88; constrn. mgr. Homestead Land Devel. Corp., 1988-92; sr. engr. cons. Morrison Knudson, 1992-95; sr. soils analyst Geotechnics, Inc., 1995-98; offsite field supt. coastal divsn. Kaufman and Broad, 1998—. Served with U.S. Army, 1969 71. Mem. ASTM, AAAS, Nat. Inst. Sci., N.Y. Acad. Scis., Nat. Inst. Cert. in Engring. Techs., Soil and Found. Engr. Assn., Phi Alpha Theta. Baptist. Author: Geological Exploration of Alaska, 1898-1924, Alfred Hulse Brooks, Alaskan Trailblazer, Papaveraceae of the World, Demarchism, Arid Regions Gardening, Visions of Dame Kind: Dreams, Imagination and Reality, Antal's Theory of the Solar System, Science Fair-A Teacher's Manual, Common Ground: Similarities of the World Religions, Black Sheep-Scientific Discoveries From the Fringe, After Manhattan, The Christofilos Effect; and others; contbr. articles to profl. jours. Office: 3111 E Victoria Dr Alpine CA 91901-3679 *Personal philosophy: Honesty and ethical behavior at all times. Trueness of being throughout my life. Love of my wife and children makes my life worth living and is always a light when there is darkness. God watches over my shoulder.*

ROBERTS, E. F. lawyer, educator; b. 1930; m. Alice A. Dunn, July 4, 1955; children: Martha, Ernest III, Michael, Marianne. BA, Northeastern U., Boston, 1952; LL.B., Boston Coll., 1954. Bar: Mass. 1954. Asst. prof. law Villanova U., Pa., 1957-59, assoc. prof. law, 1959-60, prof. law, 1960-64, Cornell U., Ithaca, N.Y., 1964-96, Edwin H. Woodruff prof. law, emeritus prof., 1996. Vis. prof. Nottingham U., Eng., 1962-63, Harvard U., 1983; mem. edn. panel Environ. Law Reporter, 1971-80; cons. in field. Author: Public Regulation of Title Insurance, 1960, Land Use Planning, 2d edit., 1975, Law and the Preservation of Agricultural Land, 1982, (with Strong et al) McCormick on Evidence, 5th edit., 1999. Mem. Am. Law Inst. (life). Office: Cornell U Sch Law Ithaca NY 14853 Office Phone: 607-257-6298. E-mail: e-f-roberts@law.mail.cornell.edu.

ROBERTS, EDWARD BAER, technology management educator; b. Chelsea, Mass., Nov. 18, 1935; s. Nathan and Edna (Podradchik) Roberts; m. Nancy Helen Rosenthal, July 14, 1959; children: Valerie Jo Friedman, Mitchell Jonathan, Andrea Lynne. BSEE, MSEE, MIT, 1958, MS in Mgmt., 1960, PhD in Econs., 1962. Founding mem. system dynamics program MIT, 1958-84, instr., 1959-61, asst. prof., 1961-65, assoc. prof., 1965-70, prof., 1970—, David Sarnoff prof. mgmt. of tech., 1974—, assoc. dir. research program on mgmt. of sci. and tech., 1963-73, chmn. tech. and health mgmt. group, 1973-88, chmn. mgmt. of tech. and innovation, 1988-99, founder, chmn. ctr. for entrepreneurship, 1992—94, 1997—, co-dir. internat. ctr. rsch. mgmt. tech., 1993-2000, dir. mgmt. of tech. program, 1980-89, co-chmn., 1989-99, chmn. mgmt. tech. innovation and entrepreneurship, 1999—2003. Co-founder, dir. Med. Info. Tech., Inc., Westwood, Mass., 1969—; co-founder, gen. ptnr. Zero Stage Capital Group, 1981—99; co-founder, dir. SOHU.com, Inc., Beijing, 1996—; bd. dirs. Advanced Magnetics, Inc., Cambridge, Pegasystems, Inc., Cambridge, PR Restaurants, LLC, Andover, Mass. Author: (book) The Dynamics of Research and Development, 1964, Systems Simulation for Regional Analysis, 1969, The Persistent Poppy, 1975, The Dynamics of Human Service Delivery, 1976, Entrepreneurs in High Technology, 1991; prin. author, editor: book Managerial Applications of System Dynamics, 1978; editor (with others): Biomedical Innovation, 1981; editor: Generating Tech nological Innovation, 1987, Innovation, 2002; mem. editl. bd. IEEE Trans. on Engring. Mgmt., Indsl. Mktg. Mgmt., Jour. Engring. and Tech. Mgmt., Jour. Product Innovation Mgmt., Sloan Mgmt. Rev., Tech. Forecasting and Social Change, Internat. Jour. Entrepreneurship and Innovation, Internat. Jour. Product Devel., Internat. Jour. Tech. Mgmt. Mem.: IEEE, Tau Kappa Alpha, Eta Kappa Nu, Tau Beta Pi, Sigma Xi. Home: 300 Boylston St Apt 1102 Boston MA 02116-3940 Office: MIT 50 Memorial Dr Cambridge MA 02142-1347 Office Phone: 617-253-4934. Business E-Mail: eroberts@mit.edu.

ROBERTS, EDWARD GRAHAM, librarian; s. Samuel Noble and Frances Johnson (Boykin) R.; m. Anna Jean Walker, Nov. 12, 1949; children: Galer Walker, Edward Graham, John Boykin. BA, U. South, 1943; BA in Library Sci., Emory U., 1948; PhD, U. Va., 1950. Curator manuscripts Duke U., Durham, N.C., 1948-52; dir. libraries (Drake U.), Des Moines, 1952-56; dir. Southeastern Interlibrary Research Facility, Atlanta, 1956-59; asst. prof. info. sci. Ga. Inst. Tech., Atlanta, 1963-66, assoc. prof., 1966-69, prof., 1969-73, assoc. dir. libraries, 1966-71, dir. libraries, 1971-84, dir. emeritus, 1984—. Chmn. info bank com. Ga. Tech. Service Program, Atlanta, 1965-67; mem. exec. bd. Southeastern Library Network, Atlanta, 1973-74; library cons. So. Regional Edn. Bd., Atlanta, 1958-59 Compiler, editor: Southeastern Supplement to the Union List of Serials, 1959; author: Literature of Science and Engineering, 1966, 2d edit.,1969. Served with U.S. Army, 1942-43. Mem. ALA, Southeastern Library Assn., Ga. Library Assn. Democrat. Episcopalian. Home: 1639 Adelia Pl NE Atlanta GA 30329-3807

ROBERTS, EDWIN ALBERT, JR., newspaper editor, journalist; b. Weehawken, N.J., Nov. 14, 1932; s. Edwin Albert and Agnes Rita (Seuferling) R.; m. Barbara Anne Collins, June 14, 1958; children: Elizabeth Adams, Leslie Carol, Amy Barbara, Jacqueline Harding. Student, Coll. William and Mary, 1952-53, NYU, evenings 1955-58; AA in Coll. & Cmty. Svc., St. Petersburg Jr. Coll., 1994. Reporter N.J. Courier, Toms River, 1953-54, Asbury Park (N.J.) Press, 1954-57; reporter Wall Street Jour., N.Y.C., 1957, editorial writer, 1957-63; news editor Nat. Observer, Silver Spring, Md., 1963-68, columnist, 1968-77; editorial writer, columnist Detroit News, 1977-78, editorial page editor, 1978-83; editor editorial page Tampa Tribune, 1983—. Author: Elections, 1964, 1964, Latin America, 1965, The Smut Rakers, 1966, Russia Today, 1967; Editor anthology: America Outdoors, 1965. Recipient Disting. Reporting Bus. award U. Mo., 1969; Pulitzer prize for distinguished commentary, 1974 Mem. Am. Soc. Newspaper Editors, Nat. Conf. Editorial Writers Office: 202 S Parker St Tampa FL 33606-2308

ROBERTS, ELIZABETH H. state legislator; b. Washington, Apr. 17, 1957; m. Thomas H. Roberts; children: Kathleen, Nora. BA, Brown U., 1978; MBA, Boston U., 1984. Mem. R.I. Senate, Dist. 11, Providence, 1996—. Mem. fin. com. R.I. State Senate, health, edn. and welfare com. Mem. bd. dirs. Childrens Mus. R.I., Southside Cmty. Land Trust. Democrat. Office: RI State Senate State House Providence RI 02903 E-mail: sen-roberts@rilin.state.ri.us.

ROBERTS, ERNST EDWARD, marketing consultant; b. Wheeling, W.Va., Dec. 19, 1926; s. Charles Emmitt and Virginia Mae (Stephenson) R.; m. Donna Clare Davis, Dec. 27, 1949; children: Ernst Edward II, Carol Lee Roberts Gaydac. BS, U.S. Mil. Acad., 1949; MBA, Xavier U., Cin., 1954; MS in Mech. Engring., U. So. Calif., 1957; grad. with distinction, Air War Coll., 1970. Commd. 2nd lt. U.S. Army, 1949, advanced through grades to brig. gen., 1971, served as officer in combat, 1950-52; prof. mil. sci. Xavier U., 1952-54; mgmt. asst. to asst. comdt. U.S. Army Air Def. Sch., Fort Bliss, Tex., 1957-60; admissions officer U.S. Mil. Acad., West Point, NY, 1961-62, asst. to supt. (pres.), 1962-64, dir. admissions, 1964-65; comdg. officer 3d Missile Bn., 71st Arty., Fed. Republic of Germany, 1965-67; staff officer Gen. Staff U.S. Army, Washington, 1968-70; commdg. officer NATO Air Def. Arty. Group, Germany, 1970-71; commdg. gen. 38th Air Def. Arty. Brigade, Korea, 1971-72; asst. comdt. U.S. Army Air Def. Sch. and Ctr., Fort Bliss, 1972-74; ret. U.S. Army, 1974; v.p. bldg. and property mgr. El Paso (Tex.) Nat. Bank and Corp., 1974-79, sr. v.p., dir. pers. and tng., 1979-83, exec. v.p., dir. mktg., 1983-92; mktg. cons., 1992—. Mem. exec. mgmt. com. Tex. Commerce Bank, El Paso, 1983-92; vis. lectr. mktg. Webster U. Mem. bd. advisors SBA; mem. mayor's Citizens Com. on Police Dept. Matters, El Paso; mem. Task Force to Evaluate Mgmt. of Sheriff's Dept.; head bond-issue campaign, El Paso; adv. dir. Armed Svcs. YMCA, past pres.; adv. dir. nat. bd. dirs. Armed Svcs. YMCA, El Paso Cmty. Found.; past pres. U. Tex.-El Paso Eldorados; mem. bd. dirs., trustee Found. Lighthouse for Blind; chmn. adv. bd. dirs. El Paso Bus. Com. for Arts; chmn. capital fund drive com. Rio Grande Girl Scouts Am., Plz. Theatre-Plz. Park Restoration bd.; past mem. campaign cabinet United Way El Paso County; chmn. Capital Fund Drive, Air Def. Arty. Mus., Ft. Bliss; bd. dirs. City of El Paso, mem. steering com. Safe 2000; bd. dirs. Crimestoppers of El Paso. Decorated D.S.M., Legion of Merit, Silver Star, Meritorious Svc. medal; recipient Pro Eclesio Et Pontifice, Vatican, 1971; Conquistator award City of El Paso, Liberty Bell award Legal Cmty. El Paso, 1988. Mem. Am. Inst. Banking, Assn. U.S. Army (Gen. Army Omar N. Bradley chpt.), El Paso C. of C. (mem. armed forces com., chmn. spl. task force to evaluate chamber mgmt.), Mil. Order World Wars (chpt. chmn. citizen of yr. award 1996-2001), U.S. Army Air Def. Arty. Assn. (past pres., named Disting. Korean War Vet. 2004), El Paso Club (past pres., bd. dirs.), Rotary (past pres.). Republican. Roman Catholic. Home: 8212 Antero Pl El Paso TX 79904-2401

ROBERTS, FRANCIS STONE, advertising executive; b. Scranton, Pa., Aug. 15, 1944; s. Gordon Link and Eleanor Swartz (Stone) R.; m. Julie Ann Dolan; children: Francis Stone, Link McGregor. BA, Grove City (Pa.) Coll., 1966; A.M.P., U. Chgo., 1984. With media dept., then account exec. Compton Advt. Inc., N.Y.C., 1966-69; account exec. Tatham-Laird & Kudner Advt., N.Y.C., 1969-70; account supr., v.p. SSC&B Advt. Inc., N.Y.C., 1970-78, sr. v.p., mgmt. supr., 1994; group exec. v.p. SSC&B: Lintas Advt. Worldwide, 1987-89; COO, pres. Lintas, N.Y., 1990-94; mem. policy and ops. coms., chmn. strategy rev. bd. Lintas N.Y.; also dir. Lintas N.Y. and U.S.A.; CEO, chmn. The CEO-Gotham Grp., N.Y.C., 1994-95; chmn., CEO Gotham Inc., N.Y.C., 1995—2004; mng. dir. Gotham Ltd., London, 1996—2004; CEO, pres. Carlson & Pontnews, N.Y.C., 2004—. Mem. bd. dirs. Am. Assn. Advertising Agencies, Am. Advertising Fedn., The Ad Coun.; bd. trustees Pro Ad PAC. Alumni coun. Grove City Coll., 1999—. Mem. William Penn Charter Alumni Assn. (pres. N.Y. chpt. 1984-88), Ad Club N.Y., The Union League N.Y. Clubs: New Canaan Field, New Canaan Winter, New Canaan Country. Republican. Presbyterian. Home: 28 Landing Dr Dobbs Ferry NY 10522 Office: Carlson & Pontnews 437 Madison New York NY 10022 E-mail: stoner@gothaminc.com.

ROBERTS, FRED STEPHEN, mathematician, educator; b. N.Y.C., June 19, 1943; s. Louis and Frances (Lindner) R.; m. Helen Miriam Marcus, June 25, 1972; children: Sarah, David. AB, Dartmouth Coll., 1964; MS, Stanford U., 1967, PhD, 1968. Postdoctoral fellow U. Pa., Phila., 1968; with staff The RAND Corp., Santa Monica, Calif., 1968-71; fellow Inst. for Advanced Study, Princeton, N.J., 1971-72; assoc. prof. math. Rutgers U., New Brunswick, N.J., 1972-76, prof. math., 1976-81, prof. II mathematics, 1981—, dir. Ctr. for Ops. Rsch., 1982-83, assoc. dir. Ctr. for Discrete Math. and Theoretical Computer Sci., 1989-92, dir. Ctr. for Discrete Math. and Theoretical Computer Sci., 1992-93, 96—. Cons. Orgn. for Econ. Cooperation and Develop., Paris, 1972-73, The RAND Corp., 1972-73, Constrn. Engring. Rsch. Lab., Champaign, Ill., 1974, Social Engring. Tech., Westwood, Calif., 1975, Inst. for Gas Tech., Chgo., 1979-82; vis. prof. ops. rsch. Cornell U., Ithaca, N.Y., 1979-80; vis. scientist AT&T Bell Labs., Murray Hill, N.J., 1986-88; Robert G. Stone vis. prof. Northeastern U., Boston, 1990-95. Author: Discrete Mathematical Models with Applications to Social, Biological and Environmental Problems, 1976 (transl. into Russian, 1986), Graph Theory and its Applications to Problems of Society, 1978, Measurement Theory with Applications to Decisonmaking, Utility, and the Social Sciences, 1979, Applied Combinatorics, 1984; editor 14 books in field, 12 jours. in field; contbr. over 140 articles to profl. jours. Recipient outstanding math. lectr. award U. New Haven, 1983, Univ. Rsch. Initiative award Dept. Def., 1989-93, Disting. Svc. prize Assn. Computing Machinery, 1999; named Carl N. Jacobs lectr. by U. Wis. at Stevens Pt., 1975, Sigma Xi lectr. by Swarthmore Coll., 1976; Daniel Webster nat. scholar Dartmouth Coll., 1961-64; rsch. grantee NSF, 1972-79, 83—, USAF Office Sci. Rsch., 1979-83, 85-96, Office of Naval Rsch., 1993—, Nat. Security Agy., 1995—, Def. Advanced Rsch. Projects Agy., 1996—, Alfred P. Sloan Found., 1999—, AT&T Found., 2000—; Woodrow Wilson Found. fellow, 1964-65. Mem. Am. Math. Soc., Math. Assn., Am., Ops. Rsch. Soc. Am., Soc. for Indsl. and Applied Math. (sec. 1977-81, v.p. 1984-87), Conf. Bd. Math. Scis. (lectr. rsch. conf. 1977, mem. coun. 1981-82), Consortium for Math. and its Applications (mem. coun. 1980-86), Societal Inst. for the Math. Scis. (bd. dirs. 1983-92, sec. 1987-92), Soc. for Math. Psychology, Classification Soc. N.Am. Office: DIMACS Ctr for Discrete Math 96 Frelinghuysen Rd Piscataway NJ 08854-8018 E-mail: froberts@dimacs.rutgers.edu.

ROBERTS, GEORGE BERNARD, JR., management and government relations consultant, former state legislator; b. Andover, Mass., June 13, 1939; s. George Bernard and Helene F. (Eversen) R.; m. Margaret Fay Edmunds, Aug. 26, 1967; children: Abigail Emerson, Jessica Swift. BS, U. N.H., 1964, M.P.A., 1967. Ptnr. Roberts Real Estate Assocs., Gilmanton, N.H., 1966—; mem. N.H. Ho. of Reps., 1967-80, majority leader, 1971-74, speaker, 1975-76, 77-78, 79-80; pres. Policy Mgmt. Assocs., Concord, N.H., 1980—. Pres. and treas. Concord, Concord Coach Soc. Del. Nat. Rep. Conv., 1972-76; mem. N.H. Constl. Conv., 1974, 84, N.H. Rep. Party Fin. Com.; pres. Nat. Conf. State Legislatures, 1979-80; chmn. exec. com. 1st Congl. Soc. Gilmanton. Mem. Nat. Rep. Legislators Assn. (founding, past pres.), Masons, Shriners, Scottish Rite, Historic Dist. Commn. Gilmanton, Sigma Alpha Epsilon. Republican. Office: Concord Policy Mgmt Assocs 4 Park St Ste 100 Concord NH 03301-6313

ROBERTS, GEORGE J. information technology executive; Grad., U. Wis. Regional mgr. north ctrl. region Oracle Corp., Redwood City, Calif., 1990, group v.p. ctrl. sales divsn., 1990—97, sr. v.p. Bus. Online Application hosting initiative, 1997—98, sr. v.p. N.Am. sales, 1998—99, exec. v.p. N.Am. sales, 1999—2003. Bd. dirs. Informance Internat., Northbrook, Ill., 2004—.

ROBERTS, GEORGE P. computer company executive; Chmn., CEO P-Com, Campbell, Calif. Office: P Com 3175 Winchester Blvd Campbell CA 95008-6557

ROBERTS, GEORGE R. investment banking company executive; married; 3 children. Grad., Claremont McKenna Coll.; JD, U. Calif. Hastings Law Sch., San Francisco, 1969. Joined corp. fin. dept. to partner Bear Stearns & Co., New York, 1969—79; founding sr. ptnr. Kohlberg, Kravis, Roberts, San Francisco, 1976—. Dir. Accel-KKR, Safeway, Inc., DPL, Inc., KinderCare Learning Centers, Inc., Owens-Illinois, Inc. and PRIMEDIA Inc. Bd. San Francisco Symphony, San Francisco Ballet, Fine Arts Mus., San Francisco, Claremont McKenna Coll. Achievements include historic billion dollar buyout of Wometco Companies in 1984; $25 billion RJR Nabisco buyout in 1989. Office: Kohlberg Kravis Roberts & Co 2800 Sand Hill Rd Ste 200 Menlo Park CA 94025-7055

ROBERTS, HAROLD ROSS, medical educator, hematologist; b. Four Oaks, N.C., Jan. 4, 1930; s. Walter Lee and Matilda Alicia (Daughtry) R.; m. Marilyn Claassen; children— Eric Michael, John Claassen BS, U. N.C., 1952, MD, 1955. Research assoc. U. N.C., Chapel Hill, 1961-62, instr. medicine, 1962-64, asst. prof., 1964-67, assoc. prof., 1967-70, prof., 1970—, chief hematology, 1968-77, dir. Hemophilia Treatment Ctr., 1977-80, dir. Ctr. for Thrombosis and Hemostasis, 1978—, co-chief hematology and oncology, 1979-81, chief hematology, 1981—. Vis. prof. U. Aarhus, Denmark, 1973-74; dir. clin. coagulation lab. N.C. Meml. Hosp., Chapel Hill, 1977— Assoc. editor Thrombosis & Hemostasis, 1975-81; editor Hemostasis, 1975-83; mem. editorial bd. Blood, 1976-82, assoc. editor, 1983—; contbr. articles to profl. jours. Chmn. Orange County Bd. Adjustment, N.C. Recipient Disting. Career award Temple U. Health Sci. Ctr., Stockholm, 1983 Fellow ACP; mem. Assn. Am. Physicians, Am. Soc. for Clin. Investigation, AMA, Internat. Soc. on Thrombosis and Hemostasis Anglican. Avocations: arborist; ornithology; philosophy. Home: 2502 Jones Ferry Rd Chapel Hill NC 27516-9369 Office: U NC Chapel Hill Sch Medicine Ctr Thrombosis & Hemostasis Campus Box 7015 Chapel Hill NC 27514

ROBERTS, HARRY MORRIS, JR., lawyer; b. Dallas, June 10, 1938; s. Harry Morris and La Frances (Reilly) R.; m. Nancy Beth Johnson, Mar. 7, 1964; children: Richard Whitfield, Elizabeth Lee. BBA, So. Meth. U., 1960; LLB, Harvard U., 1963. Bar: Tex. 1963, U.S. Dist. Ct. (no. dist.) Tex. 1964, U.S. Ct. Appeals (5th cir.) 1972, U.S. Supreme Ct. 1971. Assoc. Thompson & Knight, Dallas, 1963-69, ptnr., 1970-75, sr. ptnr., 1975—. Lawyer; chmn. real estate, probate and trust law sect. State Bar Tex., 1984-85; vis. scholar U. Tex. Law Sch., 1986. Contbr. articles to profl. jours. Trustee Shelter Ministries of Dallas, 1982—, chmn. bd. trustees, 1992-95, 2004—. Mem. ABA, Dallas Bar Assn. (chmn. real estate sect. 1981), Am. Bar Found., Tex. Bar Found., Dallas Bar Found., Am. Coll. Real Estate Lawyers, Tex. Coll. Real Estate Attys.

(vice-chmn., bd. dirs. 1990-93), Salesmanship Club (Dallas), Dallas Country Club. Episcopalian. Office: Thompson & Knight 1700 Pacific Ave Ste 3300 Dallas TX 75201-4693 E-mail: robertsh@tklaw.com.

ROBERTS, JAMES ALLEN, urologist; b. Beach, N.D., May 31, 1934; s. Earl Fernando and Maria Ellen Roberts; m. Hilda Peachy Roberts, Nov. 29, 1986; children from previous marriage: Jennifer Lou Roberts Walsh, Mary Ellen Roberts Wargo, Thomas Jay. MD, U. Chgo., 1959. Diplomate: Am. Bd. Urology. Intern U. Chgo. Sch. Medicine, 1959-60, resident in urology, 1961-65; from mem. faculty to prof. Tulane U. Med. Sch., New Orleans, 1971-99, prof. urology, 1999—, assoc. chmn., 1986—99; sr. research scientist, head dept. urology Tulane Regional Primate Research Center, Covington, 1972-99; prof. emeritus, 1999—; fellow Fogarty Sr. Internat. NIH, 1984. Mem. editorial bd. Am. Jour. Kidney Diseases and Urol. Rsch.; contbr. articles to profl. jours. Bd. dirs. Highland Park Hosp., 1985-87. With USN, 1965—67. Recipient grants NIH, Original Rsch. award Southern Med. Assn., 1990, Cert. Achievement Am. Urological Assn., 1997; Fulbright Sr. scholar, 1999-2000. Fellow ACS; mem. St. Tammany Parish Med. Soc. (pres. 1979), Soc. Rsch. on Calculous Kinetics, La. Urol. Soc., Am. Urol. Assn., Soc. Univ. Urologists, Nat. Kidney Found., Soc. Exptl. Biology and Medicine, Nat. Inst. Health (SAT study sect. 1995-99), Sigma Xi. Office: 285 Roberts Dr Hendersonville NC 28739-9457 Personal E-mail: jrhr285@mchsi.com.

ROBERTS, JAMES CARL, communications executive, engineer; b. Orlando, Fla., May 6, 1953; s. James Ira and Avis Jean (Marg) R.; m. Lynne K. Lovvorn, Sept. 29, 1980; children: William D, Christine N., Jameson S., Michael B. BSEE, U. Miss., 1974; MBA, Newport (Calif.) U., 1988, DBA, 1992. Registered profl. engr., Kans. Pres. Accent Communications, Lakeland, Fla., 1977-80; engrng. mgr. Motorola Corp., Foster City, Claif., 1980-83; regional mgr. MCI, Washington, 1983-84; dir. McCaw Communications, Denver, 1984-86; pres., chief exec. officer Communications Group Internat., Denver, 1986-97; chief exec. officer Metro Page of Fla., Boca Raton, 1988-97, Metrotek Ariz., Phoenix, 1988-97; founder, pres. VDC Corp., Greenwich, Conn., 1997-98; CEO, bd. chmn. Telecom. Wireless Corp., 1998—. Chief operating br. Tri-Pro, Denver, 1988-97, CGI, Inc., Denver, 1986-97, Metro, Inc., Ft. Meyers, Fla., 1988-97, CGI, Denver, 1992-97, Albania, 1992-97; bd. dirs. Malta Cellular, Valeta; chmn., gen. dir. CGI-MT of Serbia, Yugoslavia, 1990-92; gen. dirs., chmn. Serbia Cellular, 1989-92. Author: Cellular for Malta, 1987. Staff sgt. USAF, 1969-77. Mem. Cellular Telephone Industry Assn., Telocator, Colo. Arabian Assn., Intercircle, Internat. Arabian Assn., Met. Club, St. James Club. Republican. Baptist. Office: VDC 75 Holly Hill Ln Greenwich CT 06830-6098 also: 2628 Martin Ave Lakeland FL 33803

ROBERTS, JAMES E. civil engineer; b. Jameson, Mo., Nov. 24, 1930; BS, U. Calif. Berkeley, 1953; MS, U. So. Calif., 1966. Registered profl. engr., Calif. Mgr. bridge design sect. Calif. Dept. Transp., 1968-72, chief engr. equipment divsn., 1976—81, from project dir. to chief dep. dir. ops. and engrng., 1981—2001; with Imbsen and Assocs., Sacramento, 2001—. Fellow ASCE (Constrn. Mgmt. award 1996); mem. Nat. Acad. Engring., Am. Concrete Inst., Am. Welding Soc., Am. Assn. State Hwy. & Transp. Ofcls. Home: 1960 Tudor Ct Carmichael CA 95608-5742 Office: Imbsen and ASsocs 9912 Business Park Dr Ste 130 Sacramento CA 95827-0001

ROBERTS, JAMES HAROLD, III, lawyer; b. Omaha, Aug. 11, 1949; s. James Harold Jr. and Evelyn Doris (Young) R.; m. Marilyn Novak, June 29, 1974; children: Jessica Noël, Meredith Caitlin. BA, U. Notre Dame, 1971; JD, St. Louis U., 1974. Bar: Iowa 1974, U.S. Ct. Mil. Appeals 1974, U.S. Supreme Ct. 1979, D.C. 1981. Govt. contract atty. U.S. Gen. Acctg. Office, Washington, 1978-83, U.S. Dept. Treasury, Washington, 1983-88; pvt. practice Van Scoyoc Kelly PLLC, Washington, 1988—. Editor St. Louis U. law rev., 1973-74. Lt. col. JAGC, U.S. Army, 1974-78, USAR/NG, 1978-99. Mem. ABA (pub. contract law sect.), D.C. Bar Assn., Fed. Bar Assn. Roman Catholic. Home: 308 N Monroe St Arlington VA 22201-1736 Office: Van Scoyoc Kelly PLLC 101 Constitution Ave NW Ste 675E Washington DC 20001-1737 Office Phone: 202-898-1898. Business E-Mail: jroberts@vsklaw.com.

ROBERTS, JAMES LEWIS, medical sciences educator; b. Lima, Peru, Oct. 23, 1951; U.S. citizen; s. David and Mary (Fuller) R.; m. Mariann Blum, Mar. 7, 1986. BS, Colo. State U., 1973; PhD, U. Oreg., 1977. Fellow U. Calif., San Francisco, 1977-79; asst. prof. Columbia U., N.Y.C., 1979-86, assoc. prof., 1986; dir., prof. Mt. Sinai Sch. Medicine, N.Y.C., 1986—2001; prof. U. Tex., San Antonio, 2001—. Cons. Calif. Biotech., Mountain View, Calif., 1986-88, NIH, Bethesda, Md., 1979—. NIH Rsch. grantee, 1979—, NSF Rsch. grantee, 1981-84, 95-99, Mellon Found. Rsch. grantee, 1980-84. Mem. AAAS, Soc. for Neurosci., Endocrine Soc., Internat. Endocrine Soc., N.Y. Acad. Scis., Am. Soc. Biochemists and Molecular Biologists. Achievements include research in biosynthesis and regulation of the ACTH endorphin and gonadotropin releasing hormone precursor, glucocorticoid and estrogen regulation of gene expression, gene structure. Office: U Tex Health Sci Ctr Dept Pharmacology, MC6205 7703 Floyd Curl Dr San Antonio TX 78229-3900 E-mail: robertsjl0@uthscsa.edu.

ROBERTS, JAMES MCGREGOR, retired professional association executive; b. Moncton, N.B., Can., Nov. 24, 1923; came to U.S., 1949, naturalized, 1956; s. Roland M. and Edith M. (Shields) R.; m. Thelma E. Williams, May 6, 1944; 1 dau., Jana M. B.Commerce, U. Toronto, Ont., Can., 1949. Auditor Citizens Bank, Los Angeles, 1949-54; auditor Acad. Motion Picture Arts and Scis., Hollywood, Calif., 1954—, controller, 1956-71, exec. dir., 1971-89, exec. sec. acad. found., 1971-89, exec. cons., 1989-92, 1990-93; ret., 1994. Served as pilot Royal Can. Air Force, World War II. Home: 4968 Lerkas Way Oceanside CA 92056-7428 E-mail: jmr-ter@cox.net.

ROBERTS, JAMES OWEN, financial planning executive, consultant; b. Madison, Wis., Aug. 19, 1930; s. John William and Sada (Buckmaster) R.; m. Georgianna Timmons, Jan. 30, 1954; children: Stephen, Susan, Ellen, Timmons. BS, Ohio State U., 1952; MBA, Case Western Res. U., 1970. With Owens-Ill., Inc., Toledo, 1952-71, food divsn. mgr. N.Y.C., 1963-66, br. mgr. Cleve., 1966-71; mgr. corp. fin. Stone & Webster Securities Corp., Cleve., 1971-74; from regional dir. to pres. Mgmt. Planning, Inc., Cleve., 1976-96, chmn., 1996—. Lectr. valuation and bus. ownership succession. Contbr. articles to profl. jours. Trustee Applewood Ctrs. Found., 1996—, Soc. for the Blind, Cleve., 1983—86, Ohio Motorists Assn., 1985—94, chmn., 1990—92; pres. Childrens Svcs., Inc., 1986—88; trustee Great Lakes Theatre, co-chmn., 1998—2001; elder Fairmount Presbyn. Ch. 1st lt. USAF, 1952—54. Mem. Cleve. Skating Club, Nassau Club, Huron Yacht Club. Republican. Avocations: sailing, skiing, hiking, photography. Home: 12411 Fairhill Rd Cleveland OH 44120 Office: Mgmt Planning Inc 545 Hanna Bldg Cleveland OH 44115 also: 101 Poor Farm Rd Princeton NJ 08540-1941 Office Phone: 216-861-1555. Business E-Mail: jroberts@mpival.com.

ROBERTS, JANICE, marketing professional; Honors degree in Econs. Dir. mktg. and bus. devel. BICC Techs. Group BICC PLC, 1989, pres. BICC Comm., mng. dir. Data Networking, 1989; v.p., gen. mgr. 3Com Corp., Santa Clara, Calif., Eng., 1992, sr. v.p. bus. devel., pres. 3Com Vemtures. Mem. Chartered Inst. Mktg. Office: 3Com 5400 Bayfront Plz PO Box 58145 Santa Clara CA 95052-8145

ROBERTS, JEAN REED, lawyer; b. Dec. 19, 1939; AB in Journalism, U. N.C., 1966; JD, Ariz. State U., 1973. Bar: Ariz. 1974. Pvt. practice Jean Reed Roberts P.C., Scottsdale, Ariz., 1975—; with Fin. Health Advisors, Scottsdale Healthcare. Judge pro tem Superior Ct., Maricopa County, Ariz., 1979-92; judge pro tem Ariz. Ct. Appeals, 1995-99; chmn., adv. endowment bd. City of Scottsdale, Ariz., 1994-98; past pres. Charter 100 of Phoenix. Recipient Dorothy Wiley award YWCA Maricopa County, 1999. Mem. AAUW, Ariz. Bar Assn., Ariz. Women's Town Hall, Scottsdale Bar Assn. Office: 8669 E San Alberto Dr Ste 101 Scottsdale AZ 85258-4309 E-mail: jean.roberts@azbar.org.

ROBERTS, JEANNE ADDISON, retired literature educator; b. Washington; d. John West and Sue Fisher (Nichols) Addison; m. Markley Roberts, Feb. 19, 1966; children: Addison Cary Steed Masengill, Ellen Carraway Masengill Coster. AB, Agnes Scott Coll., 1946; MA, U. Pa., 1947; PhD, U. Va., 1964. Instr. Mary Washington Coll., 1947-48; instr., chmn. English Fairfax Hall Jr. Coll., 1950-51; tchr. Am. U. Assn. Lang. Center, Bangkok, Thailand, 1952-56; instr. Beirut (Lebanon) Coll. for Women, 1956-57, asst. prof., 1957-60, chmn. English dept., 1957-60; instr. lit. Am. U., Washington, 1960-62, asst. prof., 1962-65, asso. prof., 1965-68, prof., 1968-93. Dean faculties Am. U., 1974; lectr. Howard U., 1971-72; seminar prof. Folger Shakespeare Libr. Inst. for Renaissance and 18th Century Studies, 1974; dir. NEH Summer Inst. for HS Tchrs. on Teaching Shakespeare, Folger Shakespeare Libr., 1984-86; dir. NEH summer inst. Va. Commonwealth U. 1995-96 Writings By and About Women in The English Renaissance; group leader inst. Learning in Retirement, Am. U., 1999-2004. Author: Shakespeare's English Comedy: The Merry Wives of Windsor in Context, 1979, The Shakespearean Wild: Geography, Genus and Gender, 1991; editor: (with James G. McManaway) A Selective Bibliography of Shakespeare: Editions, Textual Studies, Commentary, 1975; (with Peggy O'Brien) Shakespeare Set Free, vol. 1, 1993, vol. 2, 1994, vol. 3, 1995, (with Georgianna Ziegler) Shakespeare's Unruly Women, 1997; contbr. articles to profl. jours. Danforth Tchr. grantee, 1962-63; Folger Sr. fellow, 1969-70, 88. Mem. MLA (chmn. Shakespeare div. 1981-82), Renaissance Soc. Am., Milton Soc., Shakespeare Assn. Am. (trustee 1978-81, 87-89, pres. 1986-87), AAUP (pres. Am. U. chpt. 1966-67), Southeastern Renaissance Conf. (pres. 1981-82), Phi Beta Kappa, Mortar Board, Phi Kappa Phi. Episcopalian. Home: 4931 Albemarle St NW Washington DC 20016-4359

ROBERTS, JERRY, newspaper editor; Polit. editor city desk San Francisco Chronicle, editl. pg. editor, 1995-98, mng. editor, 1998—2002; exec. editor Santa Barbara News-Press, 2002—. Office: Santa Barbara News-Press 715 Anacapa St Santa Barbara CA 93101 Mailing: PO Box 1359 Santa Barbara CA 93102 E-mail: jroberts@newspress.com.

ROBERTS, JO ANN WOODEN, school system administrator; b. Chgo., June 24, 1948; d. Tilmon and Annie Mae (Wardlaw) Wooden; m. Edward Allen Roberts Sr. (div.); children: Edward Allen Jr., Hillary Ann. BS, Wayne State U., 1970, MS, 1971; PhD, Northwestern U., 1977. Speech, lang. pathologist Chgo. Bd. Edn., 1971—78, adminstr., 1987—88; project dir. Ednl. Testing Svc., Evanston, Ill., 1976—77; instr. Chgo City C.C., 1976—77; exec. dir. Nat. Speech Lang. and Hearing Assn., Chgo., 1984—86; dir. spl. svcs. Rock Island (Ill.) Pub. Schs., 1988—90; supt. Muskegon Hts. (Mich.) Pub. Schs., 1990—93; dep. supr. Chgo. Pub. Schs., 1993—96; supt. of schs. Hazel Crest (Ill.) Sch. Dist. #152 1/2, 1996—98; cons. Chgo. Pub. Schs., 1998—2000, dep. accountability svcs., 1999—, InterVention officer, 2000—01, chief troubleshooter, 2001—. Hon. guest lectr. Gov.'s State U., U. Pk., Ill., 1983—86; cons. in field. Author: Learning to Talk, 1974. Trustee Muskegon County Libr. Bd., 1990, Mercy Hosp. Bd., Muskegon, 1990, St. Mark's Sch. Bd. Dirs., Southborough, Mass., 1989, United Way Bd., Muskegon, 1990; mem. Mich. State Bd. Edn. Systematic Initiative in Math and Sci., 1991, Gov. John Engler Mich. 2000 Task Force, 1991, Chpt. II Adv. Commn., 1991. Recipient Leadership award Boy Scouts Am., 1990; named finalist Outstanding Young Working Women, Glamour Mag., 1984, Outstanding Educator, Blacks in Govt., 1990. Mem. Am. Assn. Sch. Adminstrs., Nat. Alliance Black Sch. Educators, Mich. Assn. Sch. Adminstrs., Assn. Supervision & Curriculum Devel., Phi Delta Kappa. Avocations: creative writing, peotry, modern dance, theater, drawing. Address: Chgo Pub Schs 125 S Clark St Chicago IL 60603-5200

ROBERTS, JOHN, news anchor; b. Toronto, Ont., Nov. 15, 1956; Student, U. Toronto. Various reporting positions; co-anchor Can. A.M., CBS Morning News, 1992, Sta. WCBS-TV, N.Y.C., 1994; anchor CBS Evening News Sunday, N.Y.C., 1995—; corr. N.E. bur. CBS News, N.Y.C. Office: c/o Evening News Saturday Edition 524 W 57th St New York NY 10019-2902

ROBERTS, JOHN CHARLES, law educator; b. Aberdeen, S.D., Feb. 29, 1940; s. Jacob John Schmitt and Leona (Blethen) Blake; m. Kathleen Kelly (div. 1985); children: Katherine, John Charles Jr.; m. Lynn Dale Friedman, Dec. 22, 1985; 1 child, Emily Sara. BS, Northwestern U., 1961; LL.B., Yale U., 1968. Bar: U.S. Dist. Ct. D.C. 1969, Mich. 1981. Assoc. Covington & Burling, Washington, 1968-71; assoc. dean, lectr. Yale U. Law Sch., New Haven, 1971-77; gen. counsel U.S. Senate Com. on Armed Services, 1977-80; adj. prof. law Washington Coll. Law, Am. U., 1978-80; dean, prof. law Wayne State U. Law Sch., Detroit, 1980-86; prof., dean Law Sch. DePaul U., Chgo., 1986-96, v.p. for univ. advancement, 1996-97, prof. law, 1997—. Mem. exec. com. Inst. for Continuing Legal Edn., Chgo., 1988-91. Mem. adv. com. Mich. Psychiat. Soc., 1980-86; bd. dirs. Constl. Rights Found., 1992-96. Lt. USN, 1961-65. Mem. ABA, Assn. Am. Law Schs. (mem. exec. com., chmn. sect. instn. advancement 1987-88, chmn., sec. adminstrn. law schs. 1993-94), Order of Coif. Democrat. Avocation: collecting modern first editions. Office: DePaul U Coll Law 25 E Jackson Blvd Chicago IL 60604-2289 Office Phone: 312-362-8776.

ROBERTS, JOHN D. chemist, educator; b. L.A., June 8, 1918; s. Allen Andrew and Flora (Dombrowski) Roberts; m. Edith Mary Johnson, July 11, 1942; children: Anne Christine, Donald William, John Paul, Allen Walter. AB, UCLA, 1941, PhD, 1944; D in Natural Scis. (hon.), U. Munich, 1962; DSc (hon.), Temple U., 1964, Notre Dame U., 1993, U. Wales, 1993, Scripps Rsch. Inst., 1996. Instr. chemistry UCLA, 1944—45; NRC fellow chemistry Harvard U., 1945—46, instr. chemistry, 1946, MIT, 1946, asst. prof., 1947—50, assoc. prof., 1950—52; vis. prof. Ohio State U., 1952, Stanford U., 1973—74; prof. organic chemistry Calif. Inst. Tech., 1953—72, inst. prof. chemistry, 1972—88, inst. prof. chemistry emeritus, lectr., 1988—, dean of faculty, v.p., provost, 1980—83, lectr., 1988—, chmn. divsn. chemistry and chem. engring., 1963—68, acting chmn., 1972—73. Bd. dirs. Huntington Med. Rsch. Insts., 1984—99, Organic Syntheses Inc.; Robert Noyce vis. prof. sci. Grinnell Coll., 2001. Author: Basic Organic Chemistry Part I, 1955, Nuclear Magnetic Resonance, 1958, Spin-Spin Splitting in High-Resolution Nuclear Magnetic Resonance Spectra, 1961, Molecular Orbital Calculations, 1961; author: (with M.C. Caserio) Basic Principles of Organic Chemistry, 1964, 2d edit., 1977, Modern Organic Chemistry, 1967; author: (with R. Stewart and M.C. Caserio) Organic Chemistry-Methane To Macromolecules, 1971; author: At The Right Place at the Right Time, 1990, ABCs of FT-NMR, 2000; contbg. editor: McGraw-Hill Series in Advanced Chemistry, 1957—60; editor: Organic Syntheses, Vol. 41, 1961; Spectroscopy, mem. editl. bd.: Organic Magnetic Resonance in Chemistry, Asymmetry, Tetrahedron Computer Methodology. Trustee L.S.B. Leakey Found., 1983—92; bd. dirs. Coleman Chamber Music Assn.; adv. com. Calif. Competitive Tech., 1989—92. Co-recipient Robert A. Welch award, 1990; named Hon. Alumnus, Calif. Inst. Tech., 1990, SURF dedicatee, 1992; named one of Most Influential Chemists of Last 75 yrs., Chem. and Engring. News, 1998; recipient Alumni Profl. Achievement award, UCLA, 1967, Nichols medal, 1972, Tolman medal, 1975, Michelson-Morley award, 1976, Norris award, 1978, Pauling award, 1980, Theodore Wm. Richards medal, 1982, Willard Gibbs Gold medal, 1983, Golden Plate award, Am. Acad. Achievement, 1983, Priestley medal, 1987, Madison Marshall award, 1989, Nat. Medal Sci., NSF, 1990, Glenn T. Seaborg medal, 1991, Award in nuclear magnetic resource, 1991, Svc. to Chemistry award, 1991, History Maker award, Pasadena Hist. Soc., 1994; fellow, Guggenheim, 1952—53, 1955—56. Mem.: AAAS (councillor 1992—95), NAS (councillor 1980—83, com. on sci. and engring. pub. policy 1983—87, Chem. Scis. award 1999), Am. Acad. Arts and Scis., Am. Philos. Soc. (coun. mem. 1983—86), Am. Chem. Soc. (chmn. organic chemistry divsn. 1956—57, Auburn-Kosolapoff award 2003, award pure chemistry 1954, Harrison Howe award 1957, Roger Adams award in organic chemistry 1967, Arthur C. Cope award 1994, Chem. Pioneer award 1994, Nakanishi prize 2001, Auburn-Kosolapoff award 2003), Phi Lambda Upsilon, Phi Lambda Upsilon, Sigma Xi. Office: Calif Inst Tech Crellin Lab Pasadena CA 91125-0001

ROBERTS, JOHN DERHAM, lawyer; b. Orlando, Fla., Nov. 1, 1942; s. Junius P. and Mary E. Roberts; m. Malinda K. Swineford, June 11, 1965; 1 child, Kimberlyn Amanda. Cert., Richmond (Va.) Bus. Coll., 1960; BS, Hampden-Sydney (Va.) Coll., 1964; LLB, Washington & Lee U., 1968. Bar: Va. 1968, Fla. 1969, U.S. Supreme Ct. 1969, U.S. Ct. Customs and Patent Appeals 1970, U.S. Tax Ct. 1970, U.S. Ct. Appeals (5th cir.) 1970, U.S. Ct. Appeals (9th cir.) 1974, U.S. Supreme Ct. 1969. Law clk. U.S. Dist. Ct., Jacksonville, Fla., 1968-69; assoc. Phillips, Kendrick, Gearhart & Aylor, Arlington, Va., 1969-70; asst. U.S. Atty. mid. dist. Fla. U.S. Dept. Justice, Jacksonville, 1970-74, Dist. of Alaska, Anchorage, 1974-77, U.S. magistrate judge, 1977—. Bd. dirs. Teen Challenge Alaska, Anchorage, 1984-93; chmn. Eagle Scout Rev. Bd., 1993—; bd. dirs. Alaska Youth for Christ, 1993-96; govs.'s Prayer Breakfast Com., 1994—, vice-chair, 1998—. Recipient Citizenship award DAR, Anchorage, 1984, plaque, U.S. Navy, Citizen Day, Adak, Alaska, 1980. Mem. ABA, Nat. Conf. Spl. Ct. Judges (exec. bd. 1985-92), 9th Cir. Conf. Magistrates (exec. bd. 1982-85, chmn. 1984-85), Alaska Bar Assn., Anchorage Bar Assn., Chi Phi, Psi Chi, Phi Alpha Delta. Republican. Office: US Magistrate Judge 222 W 7th Ave Unit 46 Anchorage AK 99513-7504 Office Phone: 907-677-6255.

ROBERTS, JOHN DOUGLAS, veterinarian, educator; b. Jefferson, Iowa, July 29, 1950; s. Carl and Georgia Elizabeth Roberts; m. Marie Elaine Nelson, May 24, 1974 (div. Aug. 1975); m. Beverly Theresa Malek, Jan. 26, 1978; children: Amy, Nicholas, Lee. DVM, Iowa State U., 1974; PhD, N.C. State U., 1998. Animal practitioner Britt Vet. Clinic, Iowa, 1974—79; owner Prairie Vet. Assocs., Oelwein, 1979—92; mgr. vet. svcs. Seaboard Farms, Buyman, Okla., 1995—99; asst. prof. N.C. State U., Raleigh, 1999—. Mem. ext. engagement com. N.C. State U., 2000—, mem. admissions com, 1999—2003; mem. nat. park coun. edn. Nat. Park Coun., Des Moines, 2003—. Grantee, N.C. State U., 2000, N.C. Park Coun., 2001, 2002. Mem.: N.C. Vet Med. Assn., Am. Assn. Ext. Vets., Am. Assn. Swine Vet., Alpha Zeta. Roman Catholic. Avocations: motocross, martial arts. Home: 411 Satinwood Dr Apex NC 27502 Office: NC State U Coll Vet Medicine 4700 Hillsborough St Raleigh NC 27606 E-mail: j_roberts@ncsu.edu.

ROBERTS, JOHN GLOVER, JR., federal judge; b. Buffalo, Jan. 27, 1955; s. John Glover and Rosemary (Podrasky) R. AB summa cum laude, Harvard U., 1976, JD magna cum laude, 1979. Bar: D.C. 1981, U.S. Ct. Appeals (fed. cir.) 1982, U.S. Ct. Appeals (D.C., 5th, 9th cirs.) 1988, U.S. Ct. Appeals (3d, 7th, and 10th cirs.) 1996, U.S. Ct. Claims 1982, U.S. Supreme Ct. 1987. Law clk. to Hon. Henry Friendly U.S. Ct. Appeals 2d cir., N.Y.C., 1979-80; law clk. to Justice William H. Rehnquist U.S. Supreme Ct., Washington, 1980-81; spl. asst. to U.S. atty. gen. Dept. Justice, Washington, 1981-82; assoc. counsel to Pres. U.S., Washington, 1982-86; assoc. Hogan & Hartson, Washington, 1986-87, ptnr., 1988—89; dep. solicitor gen. U.S. Dept. Justice, Washington, 1989-93; ptnr. Hogan & Hartson, Washington, 1993—2003; judge U.S. Ct. of Appeals (D.C. cir.), 2003—. Editor: Harvard Law Rev., 1977-79 Mem. Am. Law Inst., Am. Acad. Appellate Lawyers, Phi Beta Kappa. Republican. Office: 333 Constitution Ave NW Washington DC 20001

ROBERTS, JOHN J. accounting firm executive; b. 1945; With Coopers & Lybrand, 1967—, ptnr., 1974—, dep. chmn., 1991—, chief oper. officer, 1994-98; global mng. ptnr. PricewaterhouseCoopers, 1998—. Office: PricewaterhouseCoopers 1301 Avenue Of The Americas New York NY 10019-6022

ROBERTS, JUDITH MARIE, librarian, educator; b. Bluefield, W.Va., Aug. 5, 1939; d. Charles Bowen Lowder and Frances Marie (Bourne) Lowder Alberts; m. Craig Currence Johnson, July 1, 1957 (div. 1962); 1 child, Craig Jr.; m. Milton Rinehart Roberts, Aug. 13, 1966 (div. 1987). BS, Concord State Tchrs. Coll., 1965. Libr. Cape Henlopen Sch. Dist., Lewes, Del., 1965—91; with Lily's Gift Shop, St. Petersburg, Fla., 1991—. Pres. Friends of Lewes Pub. Libr., 1986—90; chmn. exhibits Govs. Conf. Librs. and Info. Svcs., Dover, Del., 1978; mem. Gov.'s State Libr. Adv. Coun., 1987—91. Mem.: NEA, ALA, Del. Learning Resources Assn. (pres. 1976—77), Del. Library Assn. (pres. 1982—83), Sussex Help Orgn. for Resources Exch. (pres. 1984—85), Del. State Edn. Assn. Methodist. Office Phone: 727-867-7974. Business E-Mail: judyoffice2003@yahoo.com. E-mail: roberts-jud@aol.com.

ROBERTS, JULIA FIONA, actress; b. Smyrna, Ga., Oct. 28, 1967; d. Betty and Walter Roberts; m. Lyle Lovett, Jun. 27, 1993 (div. 1995); m. Daniel Moder, July 4, 2002. Film appearances include Blood Red, 1986, Satisfaction, 1987, Mystic Pizza, 1988, Steel Magnolias, 1989 (Acad. Award nominee, Golden Globe award), Pretty Woman, 1990 (Acad. Award nominee, Golden Globe Award), Flatliners, 1990, Sleeping With the Enemy, 1991, Hook, 1991, Dying Young, 1991, The Player, 1992, The Pelican Brief, 1993, I Love Trouble, 1994, Ready to Wear (Prêt-à-Porter), 1994, Something To Talk About, 1995, Mary Reilly, 1996, Everybody Says I Love You, 1996, Michael Collins, 1996, My Best Friend's Wedding, 1997, Conspiracy Theory, 1997, Stepmom, 1998, Notting Hill, 1999, Runaway Bride, 1999, Erin Brokovich, 2000 (Acad. award for Best Actress), The Mexican, 2001, America's Sweethearts, 2001, Ocean's Eleven, 2001, Full Frontal, 2002, Confessions of a Dangerous Mind, 2002, Mona Lisa Smile, 2003; TV appearances include: AFI's 100 Years...100 Movies, 1998, In the Wild, 1998; TV movies include Baja Oklahoma, 1988 Named Female Star of the Yr., Nat. Assn. Theatre Owners, 1991; recipient People's Choice awards Favorite Motion Picture Actress, 1991, 98, Favorite Comedy/Dramatic Motion Picture Actress, 1992, Favorite Dramatic Motion Picture Actres, 1994; recipient Woman of Yr. award Hasty Pudding Theatricals, 1997, Spl. award Internat. Star of Yr., ShoWest Conv., 1998. Office: c/o Kevin Huvane Creative Artists Agency 9830 Wilshire Blvd Beverly Hills CA 90212-1825*

ROBERTS, KATHLEEN JOY DOTY, secondary school educator; b. Jamaica, N.Y., Apr. 19, 1951; d. Alfred Arthur and Helen Caroline (Sohl) Doty; m. Robert Louis Roberts, Nov. 24, 1974; children: Robert Louis, Michael Sean, Kathleen Meagan. BA in Edn., CUNY, 1972, MS in Spl. Edn., 1974; cert. advanced study in ednl. adminstrn., Hofstra U., 1982; Ednl. Specialist, Nova Southeastern U., 2003, PhD Computing Tech. in Edn., 2004. Cert. sch. adminstrn., tchr. math., N.Y.; cert. N.Y. Dept. Mental Hygiene; lic. spl. edn. supr., ednl. adminstr., N.Y. Tchr. health conservation Woodside (N.Y.) Jr. H.S., 1973-77; coord. spl. edn. dept. Ridgewood (N.Y.) Jr. H.S., 1977-81; adminstrv. asst., health, compliance and mainstream coord. Grover Cleveland H.S., Ridgewood, 1981—, also coord. transition linkage, resource tchr. mentor, 1981—. Grant writer. Author: Closed Circuit TV and Other Devices for the Partially Sighted, 1971, Nat. Soc. Colonial Daughters of the Seventeenth Century Lineage Book (Centennial Remembrance edit.), 1999; contbr. articles to profl. jours. Legis. chmn. Fairfield Jr. and Sr. H.S. PTA and Massapequa coun., 1987-92. Mem.: ACM, DAR, NEA, Internat. Soc. Tech. in Edn., N.Y. State Tchrs. Assn., Colonial Dames of the XVII Century, Colonial Daus. of the XVII Century (pres. 1985—91, nat. chmn. hist. activities com. 1988—91, registrar, historian Founders chpt. 1991—94, nat. councillor, publicity chmn. 1991—94, centennial com. 1994—96, registrar gen. nat. soc. 1997—2000, pres. 2000—), Pilgrim Edward Doty Soc. Republican. Home: 52 Hicksville Rd Massapequa NY 11758-5843 Office: Grover Cleveland HS 2127 Himrod St Flushing NY 11385-1299

ROBERTS, KATHLEEN MARY, retired school system administrator; b. Syracuse, N.Y., Apr. 15, 1947; d. Casimer and Lorrayne Arletta (Molloy) Piegdon; m. James C. Roberts, June 29, 1968 (div. Sept. 1988). BA, Cen. State U., Edmond, Okla., 1968, MEd, 1971; PhD, U. Okla., 1977. Cert. tchr., prin., supt., Okla.; cert. supt., N.Y. Tchr. Putnam City Schs., Oklahoma City, 1960-72; reading specialist Moore (Okla.) Pub. Schs., 1973-74, Crooked Oak Pub. Schs., Oklahoma City, 1974-77, 1990-95; rsch. assoc. Oklahoma City Pub. Schs., 1977-80; supt. Okla. Dept. Corrections, Oklahoma City, 1980-86, Healdton (Okla.) Pub. Schs., 1986-90; supr. Crooked Oak Schs., Oklahoma City, 1990—95; supt. Piedmont (Okla.) Pub. Schs., 1995-98, ret., 1998; registered investment advisor McDonald & Assocs., 1998—. Contbr. articles to profl. publs. Bd. dirs. United Meth. Prism Ministry, Oklahoma City, 1986—, Children's Shelter, Ardmore, Okla., 1989-90; mem. State Vocat. Edn. Coun., Oklahoma City, 1980-85. Recipient citation Okla. State Senate, 1986. Mem. ASCD, Internat. Reading Assn., Am. Assn. Sch. Adminstrs., Okla. Assn. Sch. Adminstrs., Piedmont C. of C. (v.p. 1997—), Phi Delta Kappa, Alpha Chi, Kappa Delta Phi. Democrat. Roman Catholic. Avocations: furniture refinishing, reading, gardening.

ROBERTS, KENNETH LEWIS, investor, lawyer, foundation administrator; b. Dungannon, Va., Dec. 12, 1932; s. Clarence Eugene and Katherine (Osborne) R.; m. Anne Foster Cook, Sept. 10, 1955 (dec. Dec. 5, 1999); children— Kenneth L., Patrick Hagan Foster; m. Delphine Oman Sloan, July 20, 2002. BA, Vanderbilt U., 1954, LLB, 1959. Bar: Tenn. Assoc. prof. law Vanderbilt U., 1959-60; assoc. Waller, Lansden & Dortch, Nashville, 1960-66; exec. v.p. Commerce Union Bank, Nashville, 1966-71; pres., CEO, dir. Cen. Nat. Bank, Richmond, Va., 1971-76; pres., CEO First Am. Nat. Bank, Nashville, 1976-90; dir. First Am. Corp., Nashville, 1976-90, vice-chmn., 1976-77, pres., CEO, 1977-79, chmn., CEO, 1979-90; pres., exec. dir. FRIST Found., Nashville, 1991—. Past pres. Cen. Nat. Corp. Trustee Vanderbilt U.; bd. dirs. Leadership Nashville, Country Music Found. Lt. Chem. Corps, AUS, 1955-57. Mem. ABA, Tenn. Bar Assn., Nashville Bar Assn., Nashville C. of C., Belle Meade Country Club, Univ. Club, Ponte Vedra (Fla.) Inn & Club. Office: FRIST Found 3319 W End Ave Ste 900 Nashville TN 37203-6827

ROBERTS, KEVIN, advertising executive; b. Lancaster, Eng. m. Ro Roberts; children: Ben, Rebecca, Dan. D(hon.), Waikato U., Hamilton, New Zealand, 1998. With Mary Quant, London, Gillette, Procter & Gamble; CEO Pepsi-Cola Middle East; with Lion Breweries, New Zealand and Australia; CEO Worldwide Saatchi & Saatchi, now part of Publicis Groupe SA, N.Y.C., 1997—. Sr. fellow U. Waikato; CEO in residence Judge Inst. Mgmt., Cambridge U.; mem. Global Bus. Policy Coun. A.T. Kearney; mem. judging panel Fast Co.'s "Fast 50" Competition. Bd. mem. New Zealand Rugby Football Union; coach, mentor Turn Your Life Around Trust, Auckland, New Zealand. Office: Saatchi & Saatchi 375 Hudson St New York NY 10014-3520 Address: U Waikato Mgmt Sch Pvt Bag 3105 Hamilton New Zealand

ROBERTS, KEVIN JOHN, ideas company executive, b. Lancaster, Eng., Oct. 20, 1949; s. John and Jean (Lambert) R.; m. Barbara Beckett; 1 child, Nicola Jane; m. Rowena Jean Honeywill, Dec. 31, 1974; children: Ben, Rebecca, Daniel. Brand mgr. Gillette Co., London, 1972-74; group mktg. mgr. Procter & Gamble, Geneva, 1975-82; v.p. Pepsico, Nicosia, Cyprus, 1982-86; pres., CEO Pepsi Cola Can., Toronto, Ont., 1987-89; COO Lion Nathan, Auckland, New Zealand, 1990-96; CEO Worldwide Saatchi & Saatchi, N.Y.C., 1997—. Sr. fellow Waikato Mgmt. Sch., U. Waikato, New Zealand. Co-author: Peak Performance: Business Lessons from the World's Best Sporting Organizations, 2000. Trustee Team New Zealand, Turn Your Life Around Trust, Auckland. Avocations: rugby, tennis, art, travel, music. Office: Saatchi & Saatchi 375 Hudson St New York NY 10014-3658

ROBERTS, KRISTIE, researcher; b. Atlanta, Dec. 1, 1970; d. Joe Charles and Brucie May Roberts. BA, Fort Valley State Coll., 1993; MPA, Albany State Coll., 1995; postgrad., Jackson State U., 1998—. Field dir. Flint River Girl Scout Coun., Albany, Ga., 1995-96, dir. membership svcs., 1996-97, fund devel. mgr., 1997-98; dir. 2000 Friends Mentoring Program Albany/Dougherty Cmty. Partnership for Edn., 1998; rschr. Jackson (Miss.) State U., 1998—. Contbr. articles to profl. jours. Regent's Opportunity scholar Albany State Coll., 1995, Departmental Tuition scholar Dept. Pub. Policy, Jackson State U., 1998-2001, African-Am. Leadership Program scholar U. Md., 1999—. Mem. Am. Soc. Pub. Adminstrs., Conf. Minority Pub. Adminstrs., PPAD Student Assn. (v.p. 1998-99), PPAD Toastmasters Internat. (pres. 1998—, Leadership award 2001), Public Policy Adminstrn. Avocations: reading, travel, bowling, singing. Office: Jackson State Univ Box 18 3825 Ridgewood Rd Jackson MS 39211 Fax: 601-432-6322. E-mail: kroberts1201@yahoo.com.

ROBERTS, LARRY SPURGEON, biological science educator, zoologist; b. Texon, Tex., June 30, 1935; s. E. Fowler and Frances Wray (Huggins) R.; m. Maria Elek, Feb. 7, 1962; children: Gregory Lorinc, Bruce Tibor, Teresa Margit, Eric Miklos. BS, So. Meth. U., 1956; MS (NSF fellow), U. Ill., 1958; DSc, Johns Hopkins U., 1961. Cert. scuba instr. Nat. Assn. Underwater Instrs. From asst. prof. to prof. zoology U. Mass., Amherst, 1963-79; prof. biol. scis. Tex. Tech U., Lubbock, 1979-90, chmn. dept., 1979-84. Adj. prof. biol. scis. U. Miami, 1990-99, Fla. Internat. U., 1990-93, 99—. Author: (with others) Foundations of Parasitology, 1977, 7th edit., 2005, Integrated Principles of Zoology, 1979, 12th edit., 2005, Biology of Animals, 1982, 7th edit., 1998, The Underwater World of Sport Diving, 1991, Animal Diversity, 3d edit., 2003. Mem. Amherst Dem. Town Com., 1968-79, vice chmn., 1972-76; mem. Amherst Town Meeting, 1966-76; mem. Amherst Zoning Bd. Appeals, 1972-75, vice chmn., 1972-75; recorder West Tex. Dems., 1985-86; mem. Dade County Dem. Exec. Com., 1991—. NIH postdoctoral trainee, 1961-63; NIH fellow, 1969-70; recipient Disting. Service cert. Mass. Tchrs. Assn., 1979 Mem. AAAS, ACLU (vice chmn. Hampshire County chpt. 1966-68, bd. dirs. Lubbock chpt. 1985-89, vice chmn. 1988-89, bd. dirs. Miami, Fla. chpt. 1991—, 1st v.p. 1998-2000, treas. 2000—, Fla. State bd. dirs.), Am. Soc. Parasitologists (Henry Baldwin Ward medal 1971, council mem. at large 1980-83, v.p. 1984-85, 96-97, pres. 1998-99), Am. Micros. Soc. (v.p. 1974-75, exec. com. 1978-81), Mass. Soc. Profs. (pres. 1977-78), Soc. Protozoologists, Am. Soc. Tropical Medicine and Hygiene, Southwestern Assn. Parasitologists (v.p. 1982, pres. 1983), Southeastern Soc. Parasitologists (pres. elect 1993, pres. 1994), Internat. Soc. Reef Studies, Crustacean Soc., Am. Acad. Underwater Scis., Sigma Xi. Home: 27700 SW 164th Ave Homestead FL 33031-2846 E-mail: Lroberts1@compuserve.com.

ROBERTS, LAWRENCE GILMAN, telecommunications company executive; b. Dec. 21, 1937; s. Elliott John and Elizabeth (Gilman) R.; m. June Ellen Stuller, 1959 (div. 1973); children: Paul, Kenny. BS, MIT, 1959, MS, 1960, PhD, 1963. Dir. info. proc. Advanced Rsch. Projects Agy. U.S. Dept. Def., Arlington, Va., 1969-73; pres., CEO, GTE Telenet Corp., Vienna, Va., 1973-82; pres. DHL, Redwood City, Calif., 1982-83; chmn., CEO, NetExpress, Inc., Foster City, Calif., 1983-93; pres. ATM Systems, Santa Clara, Calif., 1993-98; founder, chief tech. officer Caspian Networks, San Jose, Calif., 1998—2004; founder, CEO Anagran Inc., Woodside, Calif., 2004—. Recipient L.M. Ericsson award for comms., 1981, Prince of Asturias award, 2002. Mem.: AAAS, IEEE (W. Wallace McDowell award 1992, Internet award 2000), NAE (Draper award 2001), Assn. Computing Machinery (SIGCOM award 1998), Am. Fedn. Info. Processing, IEEE Computer Soc., Sigma Xi. Personal E-mail: lroberts@packet.cc.

ROBERTS, LEIGH MILTON, psychiatrist; b. Jacksonville, Ill., June 9, 1925; s. Victor Harold and Ruby Harriet (Kelsey) R.; m. Marilyn Edith Kadow, 1946 (dec. 1995); m. Ellen Rabenhorst, 2003; children: David, Carol Troxell, Paul, Nancy Mills. BS, U. Ill., 1945, MD, 1947. Diplomate Am. Bd. Psychiatry and Neurology. Intern St. Francis Hosp., Peoria, Ill., 1947-48; gen. practice medicine Macomb, Ill., 1948-50; resident in psychiatry U. Wis. Hosps., Madison, 1953-56; staff psychiatrist Mendota (Wis.) State Hosp., 1956-58; mem. faculty U. Wis. Med. Sch., Madison, 1959-89, prof. psychiatry, 1971-89, acting chmn. dept., 1972-75. Cons. in psychiatry, 1989-; mem. spl. rev. bd. Wis. Parole Bd. Sex Crimes Law, 1962-88, forensic cons., 1988—; mem. Dane County Devel. Disabilities Bd., 1962-66, Wis. Planning Com. Mental Health, 1963-65, Wis. Planning Com. Health, 1969-71, Wis. Planning Com. Vocat. Rehab., 1966-68, Wis. Planning Com. Health Centers, 1967-71, Wis. Mental Health Adv. Com., 1973-78; bd. dirs. Methodist Hosp., Madison, Dane County Rehab. House, Dane County Assn. Mental Health; cons. in field. Editor: Community Psychiatry, 1966, Comprehensive Mental Health, 1968; contbr. articles profl. jours. Pres. Wis. Coun. Chs., 1976-78; bd. dirs. Madison Campus Ministry, St. Benedict Center; trustee North Central Coll., Naperville, Ill. Served with USNR, 1943-45, 50-53. Decorated Bronze Stars, Purple Heart. Fellow Am. Psychiat. Assn. (trustee 1981-84), Wis. Psychiat. Assn. (pres. 1967) Methodist. Home and Office: 33 S Midvale Blvd Madison WI 53705 *Life is a precious gift whose journey is molded and shaped by cumulative experiences and relationships. Religious belief and practice which provides future-oriented hope, disciplined accountability and living service are balanced by professional psychiatric vistas on the uniqueness and worth of each human person.*

ROBERTS, LEONARD H. retail executive; b. Chgo., Feb. 19, 1949; s. Jack and Goldie (Solomon) R.; m. Laurie Susan Osser, Aug. 20, 1967; children: Dawn, Adina, Melissa. BS in Chemistry and Mktg., U. Ill., 1971; JD, DePaul U., 1974. Food scientist Armour Foods, Chgo., 1968-71, Cen. Soya, Chgo., 1971-74; govt. lobbyist Ralston Purina Co., St. Louis, 1974-76, dir. mktg., 1976-78, mng. dir. Raltech Madison, Wis., 1978-81, v.p. food service ops. St. Louis, 1981-85; pres., chief exec. officer Arby's Inc., Atlanta, 1985-89; chmn. bd., chief exec. officer Shoney's Inc., 1989-93; pres. Radio Shack, Fort Worth, Tex., 1993—99, Tandy Corp., Fort Worth, 1996—99; chmn., pres. and CEO Radioshack Corp., Fort Worth, 1999—. Bd. dirs. Ghirardelli Chocolate Co., Tandy Corp. Holder numerous patents on Soya protein research. Active United Way Met. Tarrant County, 1994, Nat. Crime Prevention Coun., 1994, Clark U. Students in Free Enterprise, Girl Scouts U.S., Harris Meth. Bd.; mem. exec. com. Fort Worth Symphony. Recipient Pvt. Sector Initiative award Office Pres. of U.S., Washington, 1987, Disting. Achievement award B'nai B'rith, Restaurant Bus. Leadership award, 1991, Golden Plate award Nations Restaurant News, 1991, Wall St. Bronze Critics award, 1992. Mem. ABA, Ill. Bar Assn. Home: 3516 Briarhaven Rd Fort Worth TX 76109-3128 Office: RadioShack 100 Throckmorton St Ste 1800 Fort Worth TX 76102-2800

ROBERTS, LEONARD ROBERT, English language educator, poet; b. Cohoes, N.Y., Mar. 13, 1947; s. Raymond Richard and Margery Elizabeth (Trudeau) R.; m. Denise Geiger, Nov. 12, 1972 (div. June 1978); m. Nancy Jean Crane, Dec. 31, 1981; 1 child, Joshua Roberts; stepchildren: Tamara Day, Bradford Day. BA in English, Siena Coll., Loudonville, N.Y., 1970; MA in English, U. Dayton, 1972; PhD in English, Lehigh U., 1975. Prof. English Northampton C.C., Bethlehem, Pa., 1974—. Vis. prof. poetry Lafayette Coll., Easton, Pa., 1983-85; Fulbright lectr. Janus Pannonious U., Pécs, Hungary, 1988-89, U. Turku, Finland, 1994; judge numerous poetry competitions; condr. workshops and readings in poetry. Author: Cohoes Theater, 1980, From the Dark, 1984, Sweet Ones (Great Lakes & Prairies award 1988), Black Wings, 1989, Learning About the Heart (Silverfish Rev. Ann. chapbook competition winner 1992), Dangerous Angels, 1993, The Million Branches: Selected Poems and Interview, 1993, Counting the Black Angels, 1994, The Trouble-Making Finch, 1998, The Silent Singer: New and Selected Poems, 2001; contbr. poetry to jours. including Am. Poetry Rev., Antaeus, Antioch Rev., Boston Rev., Calif. Quar., Ga. Rev., Ind. Rev., Mass. Rev., Mich. Quar. Rev., Poetry Australia, Paris Rev.; translator: (books) The Selected Poems of Sándor Csoóri, 1992, Call to Me in My Mother Tongue, 1990, Selected Poems of Sándor Csoóri, 1989, Before and After the Fall: New Poems by Sandor Csoori, 2004; translator articles in jours. With USCGR, 1968-74. Recipient Nat. Poetry Series award, 1988, Pa. Coun. on the Arts Writing awards in poetry, 1981, 86-87, 89, 91, 00, Soros Found. Transl. awards for Hungarian transl., 1989-90, 92, 97, Nat. Endowment for Arts Writing awards in poetry, 1984, 89, John Simon Guggenheim Meml. award, 1990-91, Pushcart Prize XVI Best of the Small Presses award for Gift Shop in Pecs, 1991, Witter-Bynner Transl. award, 1991-92, others, Nat. Faculty award in fine arts Am. Assn. Cmty. and Jr. Colls., 1987, Internat. Award for tchg. excellence Coll. Leadership program of Internat. Conf. on Excellence, Austin, Tex., 1989, Prof. Joseph A. Buff award for Alumni of the Yr., Career Achievement, Siena Coll., 1991, Disting. Alumni of Yr. award Lehigh U., 1993, Translation award NEH, 1999, Nat. Endowment fellowship for Coll. Tchrs. and Scholars, 1999. Mem. MLA, Poetry Soc. Am., Poets and Writers, Pa. Coun. on the Arts (adv. bd. 1990—). Democrat. Roman Catholic. Avocations: basketball, swimming, house re-building. Home: 2443 Wassergass Rd Hellertown PA 18055-2111 Office: Northampton CC Dept English Bethlehem PA 18020

ROBERTS, LIA, investor, political organization worker; b. Bucharest, Romania, 1949; arrived in U.S., 1979, naturalized, 1982; married; 1 child. Degree in Geology and Geotechnical Engring., U. Bucharest. Prin., owner, Las Vegas, 1979—93; pvt. investor, 1993—; chmn. Nev. Rep. Party, Las Vegas, 2003—. Mailing: Nevada Republicatn Party Chmn 8625 W Sahara Ave Las Vegas NV 89117*

ROBERTS, LINDA, truck transportation services company executive; With Profit Freight Sys.; co-founder Profl. Sales Group Ltd., sales and mktg. co., 1990, Profl. Transp. Group, Ltd., 1990; with Truck, Net, Inc., 1991, Timely Transp., Inc., 1992, Rapid Transit, Inc., 1995; pres. Profl. Transp. Group, Ltd., Inc., Newport Beach, Calif., 1997—.

ROBERTS, LORIN WATSON, botanist, educator; b. Clarksdale, Mo., June 28, 1923; s. Lorin Cornelius and Irene (Watson) Roberts; m. Florence Ruth Greathouse, July 10, 1967; children: Michael Hamlin, Daniel Hamlin, Margaret Susan. BA, U. Mo., 1948, MA, 1950; PhD in Botany, U. Mo.-Columbia, 1952. Asst. prof., then assoc. prof. botany Agnes Scott Coll., Decaur, Ga., 1952-57; vis. asst. prof. Emory U., 1952-55; mem. faculty U. Idaho, 1957—, prof. botany, 1967-91, prof. botany emeritus, 1991—; Fulbright research prof. Kyoto (Japan) U., 1967-68; research fellow U. Bari, Italy, 1968; Cabot fellow Harvard, 1974; Fulbright teaching fellow North-Eastern Hill U., Shillong, Meghalaya, India, 1977; Fulbright sr. scholar and fellow Australian Nat. U., Canberra, 1980; sr. researcher U. London, 1984; pres. botany sect. 1st Internat. Congress Histochemistry and Cytochemistry, Paris, 1960; Alexander von Humboldt vis. fellow Australian Nat. U., 1992. Author: Cytodifferentiation in Plants, 1976; author: (with J. H. Dodds) Experiments in Plant Tissue Culture, 1982, 3d edit., 1995; author: (with P. B. Gahan and R. Aloni) Vascular Differentiation and Plant Growth Regulators, 1988; contbr. articles to profl. jours. With USAAF, 1943—46. Decorated chevalier de l'Ordre du Merit Agricole France; Alexander von Humboldt fellow, 1992. Fellow: AAAS; mem.: Idaho Acad. Scis., Am. Inst. Biol. Scis., Internat. Assn. Plant Tissue Culture, Am. Soc. Plant Physiologists, Bot. Soc. Am., N.W. Sci. Assn. (pres. 1970—71), Sigma Xi, Phi Sigma, Phi Kappa Phi. Home (Winter): 920 Mabelle St Moscow ID 83843-3834

ROBERTS, LOUISE NISBET, philosopher, educator; b. Lexington, Ky., Apr. 21, 1919; d. Benjamin and Helen L. Nisbet; m. Warren Roberts, June 14, 1952 (dec.); children: Helen Ward Roberts Hill, Valeria Lamar Roberts Emmett. AB, U. Ky., 1942, MA, 1944; PhD, Columbia U., 1952. Instr. philosophy Fairfax Hall, Waynesboro, Va., 1943—44, Fairmount Casements, Ormond Beach, Fla., 1944—45; mem. faculty Newcomb Coll., Tulane U., 1948—, prof. philosophy, 1969—85, dept. head, prof. emeritus, 1985—. Contbr. articles to profl. jours. Univ. scholar, 1945-46. Mem. AAUW (fellow 1947-48, pres. New Orleans chpt. 1986-88), DAR (vice regent New Orleans chpt. 1987-90, 2002-03), So. Soc. Philosophy and Psychology, Phi Beta Kappa (pres. 1956-57), Delta Delta Delta (fellow 1946-47). Democrat. Episcopalian. Office: Tulane U Dept Philosophy New Orleans LA 70118

ROBERTS, LYNN NOVAK, government employee; b. Dayton, Ohio, Sept. 17, 1941; d. George Vincent and Marjorie Alice Novak; children: Janet Lynn Geier-Moriarty, Rosalie Catherine Geier. BA in English cum laude, U. Ala., 1978. Level III cert. U.S. Army Acquisition Corps. Sec. pvt. sector, 1965-72; contract specialist Dept. of Def., Redstone Arsenal, Ala., 1972—. Author of poetry, articles and short stories. Bd. dirs. Humane Soc., Huntsville, Ala., 1993-94; active animal rescue. Mem. Dog Writers' Assn. Am. (judge 1994). Democrat. Avocations: hiking, camping, reading, boating, research on current novels. Home: 87 Stoney Brook Dr Union Grove AL 35175 E-mail: lynn.roberts@redstone.army.mil.

ROBERTS, M. WESLEY, musician, educator; b. Plant City, Fla., 1953; s. Maynard and Jewel Faye Roberts; m. Sida Roberts, 1978; children: Emmanuelle, Gabrielle. BA, U. of South Fla., Tampa, 1974; MCM, New Orleans Baptist Theol. Sem., 1976; DMA, So. Bapt. Theol. Sem., Louisville, 1981; post grad., Ariz. State U., 1980, Alliance Français Bibliotheque National, Paris, 1990—91, Acad. de France, Rome, 1993. Instr. music So. Bapt. Theol. Sem., Louisville, 1978—79, 1980—82; asst. prof. of music Grand Canyon U., Phoenix, 1979—80; faculty French Piano Inst., Paris, 1994, 1996; prof. of music Campbellsville U., Ky., 1982—. Organist Calvin Presbyn. Ch., Louisville, 2003—, First Bapt. Ch., Somerset, Ky., 1992—99. Musician: (premieres of works by) Hans Osleck, Johan van Kempen, Tom Johnson, James Moore, internat. performer; contbr. articles to profl. jours. Mem.: Ctrl. Ky. Music Tchrs. Assn. (founder and pres. 1983—86, 1991—97), Ky. Music Tchrs. Assn. (pres. 1986—88, sec. 1984—86), Ky. Arts Series (pres. 2000—). Avocation: gardening. Office: Campbellsville Univ Box 1282 1 Univ Dr Campbellsville KY 42718 Office Phone: 270-789-5287.

ROBERTS, MARGARET HAROLD, editor, publisher; b. Aug. 18, 1928; AB, U. Chattanooga, 1950. Editor, pub. series Award Winning Art, 1960-70, New Woman mag., Palm Beach, Fla., 1971-84; editor, pub. BONKERS mag., 1992—2001. Author: juvenile book series Daddy is a Doctor, 1965.

ROBERTS, MARIE DYER, retired computer systems specialist; b. Statesboro, Ga., Feb. 19, 1943; d. Byron and Martha (Evans) Dyer; m. Hugh V. Roberts, Jr., Oct. 6, 1973 (dec. 2001). BS, U. Ga., 1966; student, Am. U., 1972. Cert. sys. profl.; cert. in data processing. Mathematician, computer specialist U.S. Naval Oceanographic Office, Washington, 1966-73; sys. analyst, programmer Sperry Microwave Electronics, Clearwater, Fla., 1973-75; data processing mgr., asst. bus. mgr. Trenam, Simmons, Kemker et al, Tampa, Fla., 1975-77; mathematician, computer specialist U.S. Army C.E., Savannah, Ga., 1977-81, 83-85, Frankfurt, West Germany, 1981-83; ops. rsch. analyst U.S. Army Constrn. Rsch. Lab., Champaign, Ill., 1985-87; data base adminstr., computer sys. programmer South Pacific divsn. U.S. Army C.E., San Francisco, 1987-93; computer specialist, IDEF repository coord. Functional Process Improvement Expertise/Def. Info. Sys. Agy, Arlington, Va., 1993-95; computer specialist Ctrl. Integration Def. Info. Sys. Agy., MacDill AFB, Fla., 1995—, ret., 2001. Instr. computer scis. City Coll. of Chgo. in Frankfurt, 1982-83. Author: Harris Computer Users Manual, 1983. Recipient Sustained Superior Performance award Dept. Army, 1983, 2 Nat. Peformance Rev. Hammer awards V.P. Al Gore, 1996, DISA Dirs.'s award for Project of Yr., 1999. Mem. Assn. Info. Tech. Profls., U. Ga. Alumni Assn., Sigma Kappa. Personal E-mail: hurob@juno.com.

ROBERTS, MARK SCOTT, lawyer; b. Fullerton, Calif. s. Emil Seidel and Theda (Wymer) R. BA in Theater, Pepperdine U., 1975; JD, Western State U., 1978; cert. civil trial advocacy program, U. Calif., San Francisco, 1985; cert. program of instrn. for lawyers, Harvard U., 1990. Bar: Calif. 1980, U.S. Dist. Ct. (cen. dist.) Calif. 1980, U.S. Supreme Ct. 1989, U.S. Ct. Mil. Appeals 1989, U.S. Tax Ct. 1990. Prin. Mark Roberts & Assocs., Fullerton, Calif., 1980—. Instr. bus. law Biola U., La Mirada, Calif., 1980-84; judge pro tem Orange County Superior Ct., Santa Ana, 1989—; adj. prof. wills and trusts Trinity Law Sch., Santa Ana, 2000—. Co-author: Legacy-Plan, Protect and Preserve Your Estate, 1996, Generations Planning Your Legacy, 1999. Mem. Calif. State Bar Assn., Orange County Bar Assn. (charter), Nat. Network Estate Planning Attys., Soc. Cert. Sr. Advisors. Office: 1440 N Harbor Blvd Ste 900 Fullerton CA 92835-4122 Office Phone: 714-449-3353. Personal E-mail: mroberts@marksroberts.com.

ROBERTS, MARKLEY, economist, educator; b. Shanghai, Sept. 3, 1930; s. Donald and Frances Charlotte (Markley) R.; m. Jeanne Addison, Feb. 19, 1966; children: Addison, Ellen. AB, Princeton U., 1951; MA, Am. U., 1960, PhD, 1970. Reporter Washington Star newspaper, 1952-57; legis. asst. Office of Senator Hubert Humphrey of Minn., Washington, 1957-62; legis. asst., economist AFL-CIO, Washington, 1962-96, asst. dir. econ. rsch. dept., 1989-96. Bd. dirs., vice-chmn. Econ. Edn. Found. for Clergy, 1972-80; chmn. labor rsch. adv. coun. Bur. Labor Stats. Dept. Labor, 1972-96; adj. prof. econs. U. Md., 1966—, George Washington U., 1972-96; bd. dirs., chair Inst. Learning in Retirement, 2002—. Contbr. numerous articles on labor and econ. affairs, tech., productivity to various publs.; author monographs in field. Mem. D.C. Dem. Ctrl. Com., 1964-68; ward III coord. Washington Mayor Walter Washington, 1974-78; bd. dirs. Laymen's Nat. Bible Com. Inc., N.Y.C., 1972-82. Mem. UN Assn. (bd. dirs., labor chair nat. capitol area chpt. 1995—), Am. Econ. Assn., Indsl. Rels. Rsch. Assn. (exec. bd. 1975-77), Am. Polit. Sci. Assn., Nat. Acad. Social Ins., Assn. Evolutionary Econs., Am. Statis. Assn., Nat. Consumers League (bd. dirs. 1991-99), Newspaper Guild, Ams. for Dem. Action (exec. bd. 1992—), Social Dems. USA. Democrat. Episcopalian. Home: 4931 Albemarle St NW Washington DC 20016-4359

ROBERTS, MARY BELLE, clinical social worker; b. Sept. 27, 1923; d. Joseph Gill and Inez Wilson (Garvey) Roberts. BS, U. Mich., 1948, MSW, 1950. LCSW Fla., cert. social worker Md. Instr. dept. psychiatry U. Ala. Med. Coll., 1950—53; psychiat. social worker divsn. mental hygiene Ala. Dept. Pub. Health, 1950—52, acting dir., dir., 1952—53; sr. psychiat. social worker bur. mental health divsn. cmty. svc. Pa. Dept. Welfare, 1954—55; cons. psychiat. social work cmty. svc. br. NIMH, USPHS, HEW, 1955—64; pvt. practice, 1964—68; caseworker Family Svc., Miami, Fla., 1968—70, Family and Childrens Svc., Miami, 1971—75; casework cons. United Family and Children Svcs., Miami, 1975—85; clin. social worker Family Counseling Svcs., Miami, 1985—90; pvt. practice, 1990—; clin. social worker Apogee, Inc., 1994—96. Home: 8126 SW 105th Pl Ocala FL 34481-9132

ROBERTS, MARY LOIS, music educator; b. Kalamazoo, Mich., Feb. 12, 1934; d. Gerben Zichterman and Anna G. Booden; children: Kathleen, Kerry. BA, Grand Canyon U., 1963. Cert. tchr. Ariz., Ill. 4th grade tchr. Bible Chapel Christian Sch., Phoenix, 1963, 2d and 3d grade tchr., 1963—64; 1st grade tchr. Maple Sch. Elem. Sch., Des Plaines, Ill., 1965, 2d grade tchr., 1965—66; substitute tchr. Goshen (Ind.) Pub. Schs., 1980—82; music tchr. Roberts Studio, 1982—. Accompanist H.S. choir Goshen H.S., 1983—89; organist 8th St. Mennonite Ch., 1991—92, St. James Episcopal Ch., Goshen, 1992—. With USAF, 1953—55. Mem.: Music Tchrs. Nat. Assn., Goshen/Elkhart Music Tchrs. Assn. (pres. 2001—03). Avocations: swimming, travel. Home: 215 E Douglas Goshen IN 46526

ROBERTS, MELVILLE PARKER, neurosurgeon, neuroanatomist, educator; b. Phila., Oct. 15, 1931; s. Melville Parker and Marguerite Louise (Reimann) R.; m. Sigrid Marianne Magnusson, Mar. 27, 1954; children: Melville Parker III, Julia Pell, Erik Emerson. BS, Washington and Lee U., 1953; MD, Yale U., 1957. Diplomate: Am. Bd. Neurol. Surgery. Intern Yale Med. Ctr., 1957, neurosurgical resident, 1958-60, 62-64, Am. Cancer Soc. fellow in neurosurgery, 1962-64, instr., 1964; asst. prof. surgery Sch. Medicine U. Va., Charlottesville, 1965-69; practice medicine specializing in neurol. surgery Hartford, Conn., 1970-1998; mem. staff Hartford Hosp.; asst. prof. surgery Sch. Medicine U. Conn., Farmington, 1970-71, assoc. prof., 1972-75, assoc. prof. neurology, 1974-77, chmn. divsn. neurosurgery, 1971-84, prof. surgery, 1975—, acting chmn. dept. neurology, 1973-77, acting chmn. dept. surgery, 1974-77, William Beecher Scoville prof. neurosurgery, 1976-98, prof. emeritus, 1998—. James Hudson Brown rsch. fellow Yale U., 1957. Author: Atlas of the Human Brain in Section, 1970, 2d edit., 1987, The Brain Atlas, 1998; mem. editl. bd.: Conn. Medicine, 1973-98; contbr. articles to profl. jours. Capt. MC, US Army, 1960-61. Fellow Royal Soc. Medicine (London); mem. Am. Assn. Neurol. Surgeons, Soc. Neurol. Surgeons, Congress Neurol. Surgeons (bd. dirs. joint spinal sect. with Am. Assn. Neurol. Surgeons, chmn. ann. meeting 1987, sci. program chmn. ann. meeting 1988), Assn. for Rsch. in Nervous and Mental Diseases, New Eng. Neurosurgical Soc. (bd. dirs. 1976-79, pres. 1989-91), Soc. Brit. Neurol. Surgeons, Rsch. Soc. Neurol. Surgeons, Soc. Rsch. into Hydrocephalus and Spina Bifida, Conn. Acad. Arts and Sci., Vereingung Schweizer Neurochirurgen, Mory's Asns., Graduate Club, Beaumont Med. Club (pres. 1988, New Haven, Conn.), Sloane Club, Naval Club (London). Episcopalian. Home: 15 The Courtyard 70B Hampton Rd Teddington England TW11 OJF Address: 48 Hickory Dr South Glastonbury CT 06073-3212 E-mail: melvilleroberts@aol.com.

ROBERTS, MICHAEL J. food products executive; b. Chgo., Oct. 20, 1950; m. Maureen Long; children: Lauren, Lindsey, Michelle. BA in Sociology, Loyola U. Asst. v.p., district mgr., McDonald's LA region McDonald's Corp., 1989—90; v.p., supply chain mgmt. McDonald's Corp, 1990—95; regional v.p., Chgo. north region McDonald's Corp., 1995—96, v.p., field ops.; pres. West div. McDonald's USA, pres., 2001—04, CEO, 2004—. Adv. dir. McDonald's Corp. Office: McDonalds USA 1 McDonalds Plaza Oak Brook IL 60523

ROBERTS, NANCY, computer educator; b. Boston, Jan. 25, 1938; d. Harold and Annette (Zion) Rosenthal; m. Edward B. Roberts, June 14, 1959; children: Valerie Friedman, Mitchell, Andrea. AB, Boston U., 1959, MEd, 1961, EdD, 1975. Elem. tchr. Sharon (Mass.) Pub. Schs., 1959-63; asst. prof. Lesley U., Cambridge, Mass., 1975-79, assoc. prof., 1980-83, prof., 1983—99, dir. grad. programs in tech. in edn., 1980—99, dir. Project Bridge, 1987-92, dir. divsn.

tchg., learning and leadership, 2001—04; dir. Ctr. for Math., Sci. and Tech. in Edn., Cambridge, Mass., 1990-91. Rsch. assoc. MIT, Cambridge, 1976-79;mem. nat. steering com. Nat. Edn. Computing Conf., Eugene, Oreg., 1979-96, co-chmn. nat. conf., 1989, vice chmn. steering com., 1991-95. Author: Dynamics of Human Service Delivery, 1976, Practical Guide to Computers in Education, 1982, Computers in Teaching Mathematics, 1983, Introduction to Computer Simulation, 1983 (J.W. Forrester award 1983), Integrating Computers into the Elementary and Middle School, 1987, Computers and the Social Studies, 1988, Integrating Telecommunications into Education, 1990, Computer Modeling and Simulation in Science and Mathematics Education, 1999; mem. editl. bd. Jour. Ednl. Computing, 1983—, Jour. Rsch. in Sci. Teaching; editor Computers in Edn. book series, 1984-89. Mem. Computer Policy Com., Boston, 1982-84, mem. adv. bd. Electronic Learning, 1989-91; bd. dirs. Computers for Kids, Cambridge, 1983-85; mem. State Ednl. Tech. Adv. Coun., 1990-93, bd. mem. Boston Ctr. Adult Education, 2000-, Citizens for Charter Schs., 1997-. Grantee NSF, 1985-96, DOE, 1994—. Mem. System Dynamics Soc. (bd. dirs. policy com. 1987-89). Republican. Jewish. Home: 300 Boylston St Apt 1102 Boston MA 02116-3940 Office: Lesley Coll 29 Everett St Cambridge MA 02138-2702 Office Phone: 617-349-8419.

ROBERTS, NANCY COHEN, art dealer, marketing professional; b. Washington, Oct. 12; d. Norman G. and Roberta B. Cohen; m. Marc R. Roberts, Aug. 22, 1985; 2 children. BA, U. Pa., Phila., 1976; MBA, NYU, 1982. Actress, 1976—80; exec. tng. program Bloomingdales, 1980—82; advt. salesperson Hearst Corp., N.Y.C., 1982—84; dir. pub. rels./mktg. Karastan, N.Y.C., 1984—86; CEO Nancy C. Roberts Inc., Loveed Corp., N.Y.C., 1987—. Bd. dirs. Manhattan Theatre Club, N.Y.C., Children's Mus. Manhattan, N.Y.C., Auction Live, Washington. Active ann. fundraiser Chapin Sch., N.Y.C.; active capital campaign Riverdale Country Sch., N.Y.C., 1995—2001; grade rep. Edward R. and Rosalind Roberts Found., N.Y.C. Mem.: Breakers Country Club, Club Colette, Army Navy Club, Vassar Club. Office: Nancy C Roberts Inc Loveed Corp 575 Madison Ave New York NY 10022

ROBERTS, NORA, writer; b. Silver Spring, Md., 1950; m. Bruce Wilder, 1985. Author: Promise Me Tomorrow, 1984, Hot Ice, 1987, Sacred Sins, 1987, Brazen Virtue, 1988, Sweet Revenge, 1989, Public Secrets, 1990, Genuine Lies, 1991, Carnal Innocence, 1992, Divine Evil, 1992, Honest Illusions, 1992, reprint, 1993, Private Scandals, 1993, Hidden Riches, 1994, Born in Fire, 1994, Born in Ice, 1995, True Betrayals, 1995, reprint, 1996, Born in Shame, 1996, Daring to Dream, 1996, Montana Sky, 1996, reprint, 1997, Holding the Dream, 1997, Finding the Dream, 1997, Sanctuary, 1997, Rising Tides, 1998, Once Upon a Castle, 1998, Homeport, 1998, Sea Swept, 1998, The Reef, 1998, Inner Harbor, 1999, Jewels of the Sun, 1999, River's End, 1999, Heart of the Sea, 2000, Tears of the Moon, 2000, Carolina Moon, 2001, Heaven and Earth, 2001, The Villa, 2002, Three Fates, 2002, Chesapeake Blue, 2002, Key of Knowledge, 2003, Key of Light, 2003, Once Upon a Midnight, 2003, Birthright, 2003, Blue Dahlia, 2004, Once Upon a Moon, 2004, Northern Lights, 2004, A Little Fate, 2004, Key of Valor, 2004; (under pseudonym J.D. Robb) Naked in Death, 1995, Glory in Death, 1995, Immortal in Death, 1996, Rapture in Death, 1996, Ceremony in Death, 1997, Vengeance in Death, 1997, Holiday in Death, 1998, Loyalty in Death, 1999, Conspiracy in Death, 1999, Judgment in Death, 2000, Witness in Death, 2000, Betrayal in Death, 2001, Seduction in Death, 2001, Interlude in Death, 2001, Purity in Death, 2002, Reunion in Death, 2002, Imitation in Death, 2003, Portrait in Death, 2003, Visions in Death, 2004; author numerous category romances for Silhouette. Recipient Lifetime Achievement award Waldenbooks. Mem. Romance Writers Am. (charter, mem. Washington chpt., inductee Hall of Fame, Centennial award, Lifetime Achievement award 1997), Mystery Writers Am., Sisters in Crime, The Crime League of Am., Novelists, Inc. Office: GP Putnams Sons 375 Hudson St New York NY 10014-3658

ROBERTS, ORAL (GRANVILLE ORAL ROBERTS), clergyman; b. nr. Ada, Okla., Jan. 24, 1918; s. Ellis Melvin and Claudius Priscilla (Irwin) R.; m. Evelyn Lutman, Dec. 25, 1938; children: Rebecca Ann (dec.), Ronald David (dec.), Richard Lee, Roberta Jean. Student, Okla. Bapt. U., 1942-44, Phillips U., 1945-47; LLD (hon.), Centenary Coll., 1975; MDiv, Oral Roberts U., 1981; DD, Internat. Ch. Foursquare, 1988. Ordained to ministry Pentecostal Holiness Ch., 1936, United Meth. Ch., 1968. Evangelist, 1936-41; pastor, 1941, Shawnee, Okla., 1942-45, Toccoa, Ga., 1946, Enid, Okla., 1947; began worldwide evangelistic ministry thru crusades, radio, TV, printed page, 1947; founder Oral Roberts Evangelistic Assn., Inc., Tulsa, 1948, Univ. Village Retirement Center, 1970, City of Faith Med./Research Ctr., 1981, Healing Outreach Ctr., 1986; founder, pub. Miracles Now mag., Your Daily Guide; founder, pres. Oral Roberts U., Tulsa, 1963-93, chancellor, 1993—. Founding chmn. Internat. Charismatic Bible Ministries, 1986. Author over 122 books including: If You Need Healing, Do These Things, 1947, God is a Good God, 1960, If I Were You, 1967, Miracle of Seed-Faith, 1970, The Miracle Book, 1972, A Daily Guide to Miracles, 1975, 3 Most Important Steps to Your Better Health and Miracle Living, 1976, How to Get Through Your Struggles, 1977, Don't Give Up, 1980, Your Road to Recovery, 1986, Attack Your Lack, 1985, How to Resist the Devil and His Demons, 1989, Fear Not!, 1989, A Prayer Cover Over Your Life, 1990, Is God Your Source?, 1992, Unleashing the Power of Praying in the Spirit, 1993, (autobiography) Expect a Miracle, My Life and Ministry, 1995, A Thousand Times More!, 1997, Don't Park Here!, 1997, Keys to Success, 1998, Seed-Faith 2000, 1999, Still Doing the Impossible, 2002; also numerous tracts, brochures, Bible commentaries. Recipient Outstanding Am. Indian of Yr. award Am. Indian Expn., 1963; inducted into Okla. Hall of Fame, 1972; named Oklahoman of Yr., Am. Broadcasters Assn., 197, One of 50 Most Influential Oklahomans, Okla. Today mag., 2000. Mem.: Rotary. Methodist. Office: Oral Roberts U 7777 S Lewis Ave Tulsa OK 74171-0001

ROBERTS, PAMELA J. lawyer; BA in Econs., U. Calif., Berkeley, 1977; JD, Southwestern U., 1980. Cert.: Supreme Ct. S.C. (mediator) 1997, bar: S.C., Ga., Calif., U.S. Dist. Ct. S.C., U.S. Dist. Ct. (no. and mid. dists.) Ga., U.S. Dist. Ct. (no. dist.) Calif., U.S. Ct. Appeals (4th, 9th and 11th cirs.), U.S. Supreme Ct. Ptnr. Nelson, Mullins, Riley & Scarborough LLP, Colubmia, SC. Instr. Harvard Law Sch., 1999; mediation instr. U.S. Dept. Justice Advocacy Ctr.; presenter in field. Chairwoman bd. trustees EdVenture Children's Mus.; mem. adv. bd. Trinity Housing Corp.; bd. dirs. YWCA of the Midlands. Fellow: S.C. Bar Found., Am. Bar Found.; mem.: ABA (bd. govs. 2002—, former mem. Commn. on Women in the Profession, former mem. Commn. on Opportunities for Minorities in the Profession, chairwoman young lawyers divsn., mem. nominating com., mem. spl. com. on governance), U.S. Fourth Cir. Jud. Conf., Richland County Bar Assn., S.C. Women Lawyers Assn. (bd. dirs., pres. 1999—2001), S.C. Bar (bd. govs., ho. dels.), Nat. Bar Assn., Am. Judicature Soc., Phi Alpha Delta. Office: 3rd Fl 1330 Lady St PO Box 11070 Columbia SC 29211

ROBERTS, PATRICIA LEE, education educator; b. Coffeyville, Kans. d. Philip Lee Brighton and Lois Ethel Wortham; m. James E. Roberts, Oct. 5, 1953; children: James Michael, Jill Frances. BA, Calif. State U., Fresno, 1953, MA, 1964; EdD, U. Pacific, 1975. Lifetime tchg. diploma; sch. adminstrn. cert. Prof. edn. Calif. State U., Sacramento, 1969—. Cons. in field. Author (textbooks): Alphabet: A Handbook of ABC Books and Book Extensions for the Elementary Classroom, 2d edit., 1994, Integrating Language Arts and Social Studies for Kindergarten and Primary Children, 1996, Literature-Based History Activities for Children, Grades 4-8, 1997, Taking Humor Seriously in Children's Literature, 1997, Multicultural Friendship Stories and Activities for Children Ages 5-14, 1997, Language Arts and Environmental Awareness, 1998, Literature-Based History Activities for Children, Grades 1-3, 1998, Family Values Through Children's Literature, Grades K-3, 1999, A Resource Guide for Elementary School Teaching, 6th edit., 2000, Family Values Through Children's Literature, Grades 4-6, 2003, A Guide for Developing an Interdisciplinary Thematic Unit, 3d edit., 2003. Named Disting. Alumnae of Yr., U. Pacific, 1975-76. Mem. Internat. Reading Assn., Nat. Coun. Rsch. on English.

ROBERTS, PATRICIA LEE, small business owner, consultant; b. Tuscaloosa, Ala., Feb. 13, 1942; d. Felton H. and Floy Robin Lee; m. Tom David, July 27, 1993; m. Ralph Myron Roberts (div.); children: Sharon DeeAnne Aizer, Frances Lee Revere. BA Elem. Edn., Univ. Ala., Tuscaloosa, Ala., 1968; BA Social Work, Univ. W. Fla., Pensacola, Fla., 1975; MA, Troy State, Mobile, Ala., 1977. Loan officer First Am. Bank, Pensacola, Fla., 1970—74; social worker CETA, Pensacola, Fla., 1974—78; tchr. Returning Women U. West Fla., Pensacola, Fla., 1974—78; ct. appt. receiver Ct. Sys., Pensacola, Fla., 1989—91; owner, mgr. golf course, Pensacola, Fla., 1985—91; owner constrn. cleaning co., Pensacola, Fla., 1978—2004; cons., counselor. Adv. bd. Coun. on Aging, Pensacola, Fla., Am. Red Cross, Pensacola, Fla., United Way, Pensacola, Fla. Com. chmn. Am. Red Cross; com. mem. Jaycess, Lions Club. Recipient Outstanding Svcs., Jaycees, Cancer Soc., numerous awards to contrb. to cmty. and social svc. activities. Mem.: Home Bldg. Assn. of W. Fla., Pensacola Beach Yacht Club. Achievements include patents pending in field. Avocations: boating, skiing, golf, walking, beach. Office Phone: 850-932-0087.

ROBERTS, PAUL, chef; Master sommelier Cafe Annie, Houston. Recipient Krug Cup. Achievements include being the only Master Sommelier in the State of Tex. and 1 of only 50 in country; becoming the first person in six years to pass the very intense Master Sommelier's test. Office: 1728 Post Oak Blvd Houston TX 77001

ROBERTS, PAUL C. paper company executive; CFO, treas. Schweitzer Mauduit Internat. Inc., Alpharetta, Ga., 1995—. Office: Schweitzer Mauduit Internat Inc 100 N Point Ctr E Ste 600 Alpharetta GA 30022-8263

ROBERTS, PAUL CRAIG, III, economics educator, author, columnist; b. Atlanta, Apr. 3, 1939; s. Paul Craig and Ellen Lamar (Dryman) R.; m. Becky B. Bickerstaff, 1959 (div. 1968); m. Linda Jane Fisher, July 3, 1969 (div. 1994); children: Becky Ellen, Stephanie Bradford, Pendaran Struan Sherman. BS, Ga. Inst. Tech., 1961; postgrad., U. Calif., Berkeley, 1962—63, Merton Coll., Oxford (Eng.) U., 1964—65; PhD, U. Va., 1967. Asst. prof. econs. Va. Poly. Inst., 1965-69; assoc. prof. U. N.Mex., 1969-71; rsch. fellow Hoover Instn., Stanford U., 1971-77, sr. rsch. fellow, 1978—2004; mem. U.S. Congl. Staff, 1975-78; asst. sec. of treasury for econ. policy Dept. Treasury, Washington, 1981-82; William E. Simon prof. polit. economy Georgetown U. Ctr. for Strategic and Internat. Studies, Washington, 1982-93; chmn. Inst. for Polit. Economy, 1985—, John M. Olin fellow, 1994—2004; rsch. fellow Ind. Inst., 1990—. Disting. adj. scholar Ctr. Strategic and Internat. Studies, Washington, 1993-96; adj. scholar Cato Inst., 1987-93, disting. fellow, 1993-96; assoc. editor, columnist Wall St. Jour., N.Y.C., 1978-80; columnist Bus. Week, 1983-98, Fin. Post, Can., 1988-89, Liberation, Paris, 1988-89, Erfolg, Fed. Rep. of Germany, 1988, Washington Times, 1988—, San Diego Union, 1988-92, Le Figaro, Paris, 1992-96, Investors Bus. Daily, 1998—; nationally syndicated columnist Scripps Howard News Svc., 1989-97, Creators Syndicate, 1997—; contbr. editor Nat. Rev., 1993-2003, Reason Mag., 1993-95, World Trade mag., 1997-98; mem. Pres.-elect Reagan's Task Force on Tax Policy, 1980; dir. Value Line Investment Funds, N.Y.C., A. Schulman, Akron, Ohio; cons. Morgan Guaranty Trust Co., Lazard Freres Asset Mgmt., 1983-97; pres. Econ. & Communication Svcs. Inc.; cons. Dept. Commerce, 1983, Dept. Def., 1983-84; mem. adv. bd. Marvin and Palmer, 1986-96, Am. studies program Harding U.; mem. ad. com. Ctr. for the Am. Founding; mem. Wright Investors' Svc. Internat. Bd. Econ. and Invesmtent Advisors; bd. dirs. Com. on Present Danger; trustee Intercollegiate Studies Inst., Com. on Developing Am. Capitalism; mem. selection com. Frank E. Seidman disting. award in Polit. Economy; pres. Inlet Beach Water Co., 2000—. Author: Alienation and the Soviet Economy, 1971, new edit., 1990, Marx's Theory of Exchange, 1973, new edit., 1983, The Supply-Side Revolution: An Insider's Account of Policymaking in Washington, 1984, The Cost of Corporate Capital in the U.S. and Japan, 1985, Meltdown: Inside the Soviet Economy, 1990, The New Color Line: How Quotas and Privilege Destroy Democracy, 1995; The Capitalist Revolution in Latin America, Oxford U. Press, 1997, The Tyranny of Good Intentions, 2000, Chile: Dos Visiones-la Era Allende-Pinochet, 2000; mem. editl. bd. Modern Age, Intercollegiate Rev.; contbg. editor Harper's Mag. Drafted original Kemp-Roth Bill, 1976. Recipient Meritorious Svc. award Dept. Treasury, 1982, Pub. Svc. award GSA, 1991, Warren Brookes award for Excellence in Journalism, 1992; Am. Philos. Soc. grantee, 1968; named to Chevalier de la Légion d'Honneur, 1987, Gridiron Secret Soc., U. Ga.; Earhart fellow U. Va., 1966-67, Nat. Chamber Found. fellow, 1984-85. Mem. Mont Pelerin Soc., Beethoven Soc., Am. Soc. French Legion of Honor, U.S. C. of C. (taxation com.), Polanyi Soc. Home and Office: 169 Pompano St Panama City FL 32413-7245 E-mail: pcroberts@postmark.net.

ROBERTS, PAUL DALE, state agency administrator, writer; b. Fresno, Calif., Jan. 17, 1955; s. Paul Marceau and Rosemarie Roberts; divorced; 1 child, Jason Randall Porter. AA, Sacramento City Coll., 1977; diploma in pvt. investigations, Ctrl. Investigation & Security, 1984, Office asst. I, Dept. Benefit Payments, Sacramento, Calif., 1976-77; firefighter Calif. Divsn. Forestry, Colfax, 1977; key data operator Dept. Justice, Sacramento, 1977-78; intelligence analyst, spl. forces instr. U.S. Army Mil. Intelligence, Seoul, Korea, 1979-84; office asst. 1 Calif. State Lottery Commn., 1987-89; law libr. Employment Devel. Dept., Sacramento, 1989-92; office asst. II, Calif. Dept. Health Svcs., Sacramento, 1992-98, chief cert. support, 1992-93; supervising program technician II Dept. Cmty. Svcs. and Devel., State Calif., Sacramento, 1998-2000; divsn. supr. polit. reform Sec. of State, Sacramento, 2000—. Office asst I, Calif. Lottery Commn., 1987-89; disaster courier dept. social svcs. Gov.'s Office of Emergency Svcs., L.A., 1994. Author: Organization of D.E.A.T.H. (Destroy Evildoers and Teach Harmony), 1984, The Cosmic Bleeder, 1991, Madam Zara, Vampiress, 1993, People's Comic Book Newsletter, 1996, The Legendary Dark Silhouette, 1997, Vacationing in Dublin, Ireland and Newry, Northern Ireland, 1997, (comic book) The Legendary Dark Silhouette, 1997, Jazma Universe Online!, 1998, Jazma League of Justice, 1999, Jazma Man/Jazma Girl, 2000, My Adventures in Brazil, 2001, My Adventures in Thailand/Burma, 2003, My Adventures in Moscow, Russia, 2004. Sgt. U.S. Army Mil. Police, 1973-76. Democrat. Roman Catholic. Avocations: private pilot, tennis, photography, hot air balloon/glider riding, sky diving. Home: 5606 Moonlight Way Elk Grove CA 95758-6837 Office: 1500 11th St Rm 495 Sacramento CA 95814 Office Phone: 916-653-8504. Business E-Mail: jazmapika@cs.com.

ROBERTS, PAUL FRANKLIN, II, financial executive; b. Laredo, Tex., Apr. 16, 1949; s. Paul Franklin and Bernice Clevenger (Alworth) R.; m. Martha Diane Dow, Dec. 19, 1970; children: Averi Alison, Briana Alane, Paul Franklin III. BS in Math. cum laude, S.W. Tex. State U., 1970; M of Pub. Fin. Mgmt., The Am. U., 1983; postgrad., George Mason U., 1989-95. Team leader U.S. Army Communications Command, Fort Huachuca, Ariz., 1975-77; dep. comptroller U.S. Army Combined Arms Ctr., Fort Leavenworth, Kans., 1977-79; tech. dir. Comptroller of Army, Pentagon, Washington, 1981-82, dir. mgmt.engring., 1982-84; supr. program analyst U.S. Army Material Command, Alexandria, 1982-84, chief productivity mgmt. div., 1985-89; dir. resource mgmt. U.S. Army Devel. & Employment Agy., Fort Lewis, Wash., 1984-85; chief productivity improvement div. Asst. Sec. of Def., Pentagon, Washington, 1989-90; dir. investment Asst. Sec. of Army, Pentagon, Washington, 1990-95, dir. bus. resources, 1995-98; CFO, chief adminstrv. officer NOAA, Dept. Commerce, Washington, 1998—2000, Nat. Tech. Info. Svc., Dept. Commerce, Washington, 2000—. Mem. sr. exec. svc. Fed. Civil Svc., 1990—. Author: (study) Functional Army Manpower Evaluation, 1981. Dist. scout commr. Cochise dist. Boy Scouts Am., 1975—77, asst. scoutmaster George Washington dist., 1998—2000, asst. dist. commr. Tomahawk dist., cubmaster George Washington Dist., 1995—98; bd. dirs. Marriage Encounter/United Meth. Ch., 1986—88, jurisdictional exec. couple, 1986—88, state exec. couple, 1981—84. Recipient Eagle Scout award, 1962. Mem.: Ctr. for Study of Presidency, Am. Assn. Program and Budget Analysts, Am. Soc. for Pub. Adminstrn., Sr. Exec. Assn., Delta Tau Delta. Methodist. Avocations: golf, basketball, baseball card collecting. Home: 8011 Lake Pleasant Dr Springfield VA 22153-3005 Office: 5285 Port Royal Rd Springfield VA 22161-0001 E-mail: proberts@ntis.gov.

ROBERTS, PHILIP JOHN, history educator, editor; b. Lusk, Wyo., July 8, 1948; s. Leslie J. and LaVerne Elizabeth (Johns) R. BA, U. Wyo., 1973, JD, 1977; PhD, U. Wash., 1990. Bar: Wyo. 1977. Editor Lake Powell Chronicle, Page, Ariz., 1972-73; pvt. practice in law Carbon and Laramie County, Wyo., 1977-84; historian Wyo. State Hist. Dept., Cheyenne, 1979-84; editor Annals of Wyo., Cheyenne, 1980-84, 95—; owner, pub. Capitol Times, Cheyenne, 1982-84; co-editor Wyo. History Jour., 1995-96; editor, 1996-97; owner, pub. Skyline West Press, Seattle, 1985-90; prof. history U. Wyo., Laramie, 1990—; law liaison ABA_CEELI, Baku, Azerbaijan, 2004—. Indexer Osborne-McGraw-Hill, Berkeley, 1988-95; guest lectr. media law, Dubai, United Arab Emirates, 1996, Cairo, 2001; mem. editl. bd. Annals of Wyo., 1990-95; legal edn. cons., curriculum specialist ABA-CEELI, Baku, Azergaijan, 2004. Author: Wyoming Almanac, 1989 (pub. annually), Buffalo Bones: Stories from Wyoming's Past, 1979, 82, 84, Readings in Wyoming History, 1994, 96, 2000, Penny for the Governor, A Dollar for Uncle Sam: The Politics of Taxation in Washington, 2002; contbr. articles to profl. jours. Cand. for gov. of Wyo., 1998; chmn. Albany County Dem. Party, 1999-2001, 2003-04; pres. Albany County Hist. Soc., 2000-02; mem. Albany County Hist. Preservation Commn., 2000—; bd. mem. Laramie Plains Mus., 2000-2004. With USMC, 1970-72. Mem. Wyo. State Hist. Soc. (life), Wyo. State Bar, Am. Bar Assn., Pacific N.W. Historians' Guild, 9th Judicial Cir. Hist. Soc., Western History Assn., Am. Hist. Assn., Orgn. of Am. Historians, Albany County Hist. Soc. (pres. 2000-02). Business E-Mail: philr@uwyo.edu. E-mail: philwyo@yahoo.com.

ROBERTS, PRISCILLA WARREN, artist; b. Montclair, N.J., June 13, 1916; d. Charles Asaph and Florence (Berry) R. Student, Art Students League, 1937-39, Nat. Acad., 1939-43. Represented in permanent collections Met. Mus., Cin. Art Mus., Canton (Ohio) Art Inst., Westmoreland County Mus. Art, Pa., IBM, Dallas Mus., Walker Art Ctr., Mpls., Butler Inst., Youngstown, Ohio, Nat. Mus. Am. Art, Washington, Nat. Mus. Women in the Arts, Washington. Recipient Proctor prize, 1947, popular prize Corcoran Biennial, 1947, prize Westmoreland County Mus., 3d prize Carnegie Internat., Pitts., 1950, Nat. Mus. Women in Arts, Washington, Snite Mus., U. Notre Dame, Ind. Mem. Nat. Acad. Design (Hallgarten prize 1945), Allied Artists Am. (Zabriskie prize 1944, 46), Catherine Lorillard Wolfe Assn. (hon.). Address: PO Box 716 Georgetown CT 06829-0716

ROBERTS, R. MICHAEL, animal scientist, biochemist, educator; b. U.K., 1941; BA in Botany, PhD in Plant Physiology and Biochemistry, Oxford U.; doctorate (hon.), U. Liege, Belgium, 1998. Prof. animal scis. and biochemistry U. Mo., Columbia, 1985—, curators' prof., 1996—. Vice-chmn. Gordon Conf. on Mammalian Genital Tract Plymouth State Coll., 1986; chmn. Gordon Conf. on Reproductive Tract Biology Brewster Acad., 1988; fgn. specialist Nat. Inst. Animal Industry, Japan, 1998; chief scientist Nat. Rsch. Initiative Competitive Grants Program/Coop. State Rsch., Edn., Extension Svc./USDA, 1998—2000. Contbr. articles to profl. jours. Named Disting. Scientist, USDA, 1992; recipient Rsch. award, Soc. for Study of Reproduction, 1990, Merit award, NIH, 1990—2000, Milstein award, Internat. Soc. Interferon and Cytokine Rsch., 1995, Alexander von Humboldt award for agr., 1996, Wolf prize in agr., 2003. Mem.: NAS. Office: Animal Sciences U Missouri-Columbia 158 Animal Sciences Center Columbia MO 65211

ROBERTS, RALPH JOEL, telecommunications executive, cable broadcast executive; b. N.Y.C., Mar. 13, 1920; s. Robert and Sara (Wahl) Roberts; m. Suzanne Fleisher, Aug. 23, 1942; children: Catherine, Lisa, Ralph Jr., Brian, Douglas. BS in Econs., U. Pa., 1941; LHD (hon.), Holy Family Coll., 1994; HHD (hon.), Arcadia U., 2004. Account exec. Aitken Kynett Advt., Phila., 1946-48; v.p. Muzak Corp., N.Y.C., 1948-50; pres., chief exec. officer Pioneer Industries, Inc., Darby, Pa., 1950-61; pres. Internat. Equity Corp., Bala Cynwyd, Pa., 1961-83; chmn. bd., Comcast Corp., Phila., 1969—; chmn., chief exec. officer Sural Corp. (merger with Internat. Equity Corp. 1983); chmn. Comcast Corp., Phila. Trustee, chmn. conflict interest com. Albert Einstein Med. Ctr.; bd. dirs. Phila. Electric Co., Phila. Nat. Bank, Corestates, Penn Medicine; bd. trustees U. Pa. Health Sys., 2002. Bd. dirs. regional NCCJ; trustee Brandywine Mus. and Conservancy, charter mem. World Bus. Coun.; past mem. mentor program and Benjamin Franklin assocs. U. Pa.; bd. dirs. Phila. Orch., 1993; past v.p. Family Svc. Phila.; past bd. dirs., mem. budget and fees com. State Coll. and Univ. Dirs.; mem. re-regulation and legis. affairs coms. Nat. Cable TV Assn.; past mem. Gov.'s Rev. of Govt. Mgmt., Inc. Lt. USNR, 1942-45. Reipient Americanism award Anti-Defamation League of B'nai B'rith, Brotherhood award NCCJ, 1989, award for outstanding svc. to cable TV industry Walter Kaitz Found., 1990, Acres of Diamonds Entrepreneurioal Excellence award Entrepreneurial Inst. Temple U., 1991, Disting. Vanguard award for leadership Nat. Cable TV Assn., 1993, Golden Plate award Am. Acad. Achievement, 1994, PAL award Police Athletic League Phila., 1995, Edward Powell award for cmty. svc. City of Phila., 1995, Joseph P. Wharton award U. Pa., 1995, Whitney M. Young Jr. Leadership award Urban League Phila., 1997, Disting. Cmty. Leadership award Operation Understanding, 1997, Cable TV Hall of Fame award, 2000, Mensa Achievement award, 2000, Heroes of Liberty award Liberty Mus., 2000, William Penn award Greater Phila. C. of C., 2002, Am. Horizon award for Visionary Leadership, Media Inst., Washington, 2002, Humanitarian award United Jewish Appeal Fedn. of NY, 2003, Trustee award NATAS, 2003; named to Broadcasting and Cable Hall of Fame, 1993. Avocations: tennis, travel. Home: Sural Farm 505 Fairview Rd East Fallowfield PA 19320-4451 Office: Comcast Corp 1500 Market St Philadelphia PA 19102-4782

ROBERTS, RAY CROUSE, JR., retired economics educator; b. Burlington, N.C., Jan. 8, 1929; s. Ray Crouse and Bessie (Cloniger) R.; m. Alice Suzanne Molnar, June 24, 1952; children: David, Rebecca, Eric, Mark. AB, Duke U., 1950; MS, U. N.C., 1957, PhD, 1961. Indsl. engr. Glen Raven Cotton Mills, N.C., 1952-54; asst. prof., assoc. prof., prof. econs. Old Dominion Coll., Norfolk, Va., 1956-67, chmn. dept. econs., 1962-67; vis. assoc. prof. econs. Duke U., 1964-65; dean Sch. Bus. Adminstrn., Winthrop Coll., Rock Hill, S.C., 1967-69; Frederick W. Symmes prof. econs. Furman U., Greenville, S.C., 1969-95, chmn. dept. econs., 1969-73, 85-88, 1993-94, acting v.p. for acad. affairs, dean, 1994-95; ret., 1995—. Served to 1st lt. USMCR, 1950-52; col. Res. ret. Mem. Am. Arbitration Assn. (nat. labor panel). Democrat. Methodist.

ROBERTS, RICHARD, mechanical engineering educator; b. Atlantic City, N.J., Feb. 16, 1938; s. Harold and Marion (Hofman) R.; m. Rochelle S. Perelman, Oct. 2, 1960; children: Lori, Lisa, Scott. BSME, Drexel U., 1961; MSME, Lehigh U., 1962, PhD in Mech. Engring., 1964. Asst. prof. mech. engring. Lehigh U., Bethlehem, Pa., 1964-68, assoc. prof., 1968-75, prof., 1975—. Editor: Proceedings of the Thirteenth Nat. Symposium on Fracture Mechanics, 1980, ASME PVP Division's Design Handbook, Materials and Fabrication, Vol. III. Recipient W. Sparagen award Am. Welding Soc., 1972, Adams Meml. award, 1981. Home: 317 Bierys Bridge Rd Bethlehem PA 18017-1142 Office: Lehigh Univ MSE/200 W Packer Bethlehem PA 18015

ROBERTS, RICHARD C., III, lawyer; b. Jackson, Miss., Mar. 18, 1951; BA, U. Miss., 1973, JD with distinction, 1976. Bar: Miss. 1976, U.S. Dist. Ct. (no. and so. dists.) Miss. 1976, U.S. Ct. Appeals (5th cir.) 1976, U.S. Ct. Appeals (11th cir.) 1981, U.S. Supreme Ct. 1989. Pvt. practice, Jackson, Miss. Mem.: ABA (sect. on family law, gen. practice, solo and small firm practice), Nat. Lawyer's Assn., Bar Assn. 5th Fed. Cir., Miss. Bar (chmn. solo and small firm practitioner's task force 1993—94, exec. com. family law sect. 1994—95, chmn. 1996, bd. bar commrs. 1996—99, nominating com. 1998—99, bench-bar liaison standing com. 2001—, sect. litigation and gen. practice, labor and employment, pres. 2003—04), Hinds County Bar Assn. (bd. dirs. 1990—96, sec.-treas. 1992—93, pres. 1994—95, chmn. long range planning com. 1995—97), Fed. Bar Assn. (pres. Miss. chpt. 1987—88, nat. coun. 1988, jud. liaison for U.S. Dist. Cts.-So. Dist. Miss. 1989), Am. Inss of Ct., Phi Kappa Phi. Office: Richard C Roberts III PO Box 55882 814 N President St Jackson MS 39296-5882

ROBERTS, RICHARD GUY, physician, educator; b. Beaver Dam, Wis., Mar. 21, 1953; m. Laura Roberts; 4 children. BS in Philosophy, JD, U. Wis. Madison; MD, George Washington U. Sch. Medicine, 1980. Diplomate Am.

Bd. Family Practice. Resident family practice UCLA/Santa Monica Hosp., 1980—83; family physician U. Wis. Med. Sch. Hosp., Madison, 1983—. Family physician Bellevue (Wis.) Family Med. Clinic, 1983—; attending physician St. Mary's Hosp. and Med. Ctr., Madison, 1987—; prof. U. Wis. Med. Sch., Madison, 1994—. Chair Working Party on Quality in Family Medicine World Orgn. Family Doctors; founder CHILDSAFE Found. Fellow: Am. Coll. Legal Medicine, Am. Acad. Family Physicians (pres.-elect 1999—2000, pres. 2000—01, bd. dirs., task force on quality assessment, chair commn. on clin. policies, legislation and govtl. affairs commn., health care svcs. commn., bd. chair 2002—); mem.: AMA, NRHA, State Med. Soc. Wis. (pres.), Wis. Acad. Family Physicians (pres.). Office: Univ Wis Dept Family Medicine 777 S Mills St Madison WI 53715-1849

ROBERTS, RICHARD JOHN, molecular biologist, consultant, research director; b. Derby, Eng., Sept. 6, 1943; came to U.S., 1969; s. John Walter and Edna Wilhelmina (Allsop) R.; m. Elizabeth Dyson, Aug. 21, 1965 (dec.); children: Alison, Andrew; m. Jean E. Tagliabue, Feb. 14, 1986; children: Christopher, Amanda. BS, Sheffield (Eng.) U., 1965, PhD, 1968. Rsch. fellow Harvard U., Cambridge, Mass., 1969-70, rsch. assoc., 1971-72; sr. staff investigator Cold Spring Harbor Lab., N.Y., 1972-87, asst. dir., 1987-92; cons. New Eng. Biolabs, Beverly, Mass., 1974-92, rsch. dir., 1992—; sci. adv. bd. Genex, Rockville, Md., 1977-85, Molecular Tool, Balt., 1994—. Contbr. articles to profl. jours. Recipient Nobel prize in physiology or medicine, Nobel Found., 1993. John Simon Guggenheim Found. fellow, 1979. Fellow Royal Soc.; mem. Am. Soc. Microbiology, Am. Soc. Biol. Chemists. Office: New Eng Biolabs 32 Tozer Rd Beverly MA 01915-5599*

ROBERTS, RICHARD N. psychologist; AB in Govt., Columbia U., 1968; MSW, U. Hawaii, 1974, PhD in Psychology, 1977. Asst. prof. dept. psychology U. N.C., Greensboro, 1978-82; dir. pre-kindergarten ednl. program Ctr. Devel. Early Edn. Kamehameha Schs., Honolulu, 1983-89; assoc. prof. dept. psychology Utah State U., Logan, 1989—, co-dir. Early Intervention Rsch. Inst., 1989—, dir. rsch. and evaluation Ctr. for Persons with Disabilities, 1989—. Cons. to Hawaii State Hosp., 1977, Hawaii Job Corps, 1977, USAF, 1976, others. Editor: Coming home to preschool: The sociocultural context of early education, 1993; author monograph and workbook; contbr. chpts. to books, articles to profl. jours.; presenter in field. Served as lt. USN, 1968-72. Recipient numerous grants. Mem. APA, APHA, Utah Pub. Health Assn., Assn. Maternal and Child Health Programs, Soc. for Rsch. in Child Devel., Coun. for Exceptional Children. Office: Utah State U Early Intervention Rsch Logan UT 84322-0001

ROBERTS, ROBERT, engineering organization executive, think-tank executive; Pres. Syracuse Rsch. Corp., Syracuse, N.Y. Office: Syracuse Rsch Corp 6225 Running Ridge Rd North Syracuse NY 13212-2510

ROBERTS, ROBERT WINSTON, social work educator, dean; b. Balt., July 23, 1932; s. Kelmer Swan Roberts and Lettie Mae (Collins) Johnston; m. Helen Elizabeth Perpich, Mar. 4, 1964 (div. Aug. 1997); life ptnr. Paul Edwards. BA with high honors, San Francisco State U., 1957; MSW, U. Calif., Berkeley, 1959; D in Social Welfare, Columbia U., 1970. Caseworker Edgewood Protestant Orphanage, San Francisco, 1959-62, Jewish Family Service, San Francisco, 1962-63; research assoc. U. Calif., Berkeley, 1963-65; research analyst Family Service Assn. Am., N.Y.C., 1965-69; asst. prof. U. Chgo., 1967-70; prof. U. So. Calif., Los Angeles, 1970-90, dean sch. social work, 1980-88, dean emeritus, prof. emeritus, 1990—. Vis. prof. Western Australia Inst. Tech. (now Curtin U.), Perth, 1976-77, Chinese U. Hong Kong and U. Hong Kong, 1980; cons. Crittenton Services, Los Angeles, 1970-72, James Weldon Johnson Community Ctr., N.Y., 1966-67; bd. dirs. El Centro, Los Angeles. Editor: The Unwed Mother, 1966; co-editor: Theories of Social Casework, 1970, Child Caring: Social Policy and the Institution, 1973, Theories of Social Work with Groups, 1976, Theory and Practice of Community Social Work, 1980; editorial bd. Social Work Jour.; contbr. articles to profl. jours. Staff sgt. USAF, 1950-54; sgt. 1st class USAR, 1956-59. Fellow NIMH, 1957-58, 65-67, Crown Zellerbach Found., 1958-59; recipient Outstanding Educator award Los Amigos de la Humanidad, 1979; named Disting. Assoc., Nat. Acad. Practice in Social Work, 1985. Mem. ACLU, NASW (chmn. social action com. 1960-61), Coun. on Social Work Edn. (bd. dirs. 1970-73, del. to assembly 1971-72, commn. minority groups 1972-73). Avocations: cooking, reading, travel, photography. Office: U So Calif Montgomery Ross Fisher Rm 21 Los Angeles CA 90089-0001

ROBERTS, ROBIN, sportscaster; b. Nov. 23, 1960; BA in Comms. cum laude, Southeastern La. U., 1983. Sports dir. WHMD/WFPR Radio, Hammond, La., 1980-83; spl. assignment sports reporter KSLU-FM, 1982; sports anchor, reporter WDAM-TV, Hattiesburg, Miss., 1983-84, WLOX-TV, Biloxi, Miss., 1984-86, WSMV-TV, Nashville, 1986-88, WAGA-TV, Atlanta, 1988-89; with WVEE-FM, Atlanta; host. Sunday SportsDay, contbr. NFL Prime Time, reporter, interviewer ESPN, Bristol, Conn., 1990-95, host, anchor SportsCenter, host In the SportsLight, 1995—; host Wide World of Sports ABC, 1995—. Apptd. adv. bd. Women's Sports Found., 1991; spkr. charity, civic functions. Recipient DAR T.V. Award of Merit, 1990, Women at Work Broadcast Journalism award, 1992, Excellence in Sports Journalism award Broadcast Media Northeastern U. Ctr. Study of Sport in Society and Sch. Journalism, 1993; inducted to Hall of Fame Women's Inst. Sport and Edn. Found., 1994. Office: ESPN Inc Comms Dept ESPN Plz 935 Middle St Bristol CT 06010-1099

ROBERTS, RUSSELL L. artist; BA in English Lit., Vassar Coll.; diploma, Sch. Mus. Fine Arts; MFA in Painting, Boston U. Exhibitions include include NYU Washington Sq. East Gallery, N.Y.C., 1990, Muscarelle Mus., Coll. William and Mary, 1990, 1994, Charles River Mus. of Industry, Mass., 1991, South Shore Art Ctr., 1992, 1993, Boston U. Art Gallery, 1995, Mus. Fine Arts, Boston, 1996, Horn Gallery at Babson Coll., Mass., others. Grantee Charles Cummings Meml. Travel grantee, Sch. Mus. Fine Arts, Boston, 1996; scholar Clarissa Bartlett scholar, 1996; Guggenheim fellow in painting, 1997—98.

ROBERTS, SAMUEL SMITH, television news executive; b. Port Chester, N.Y., Feb. 8, 1936; s. Robert M. and Lillian (Smith) R.; m. Harriet Rubin, July 27, 1975; children: Rachel, David; children by previous marriage: Nancy, Pamela. BS, Northwestern U., 1957. With UPI, N.Y.C., 1961, Capital Cities Broadcasting, Providence, 1962, CBS News, 1962-95; sr. prodr. CBS Evening News, N.Y.C., 1978-81, nat. editor, 1982-84, fgn. editor, 1984-87; exec. prodr. CBS News Prodns., 1992-95, 20th Century, 1994-95; pres. Roberts Media Internat., N.Y.C., 1995-96; v.p., gen. mgr. TV programming Electronic Media Co., N.Y. Times, 1996-99; Frances L. Wolfson chair U. Miami, Coral Gables, Fla., 1999—. Served to lt. USN, 1957-61. Office: U Miami Sch Comm PO Box 248127 Coral Gables FL 33124-8127

ROBERTS, SANDRA, editor; b. Humboldt, Tenn., July 22, 1951; d. Harold and Margaret (Headrick) R.; m. Parker W. Duncan Jr., Aug. 11, 1990. Student, Tex. Christian U., 1969-70; BS, U. Tenn., 1972; MLS, Peabody Coll. Libr. The Tennessean, Nashville, 1975-82, editorial writer, 1982-87, editorial editor, 1987—. Pres. Women's Polit. Caucus, Nashville, 1982. Recipient John Hancock award John Hancock Co., 1983, Freedom award Tenn. Trial Lawyers Assn., 1988. Mem. Am. Soc. Newspaper Editors, Nat. Conf. Editorial Writers, Sigma Delta Chi (Nat. Headliner award 1982). Mem. Christian Ch. Office: The Tennessean 1100 Broadway Nashville TN 37203-3134

ROBERTS, SANDRA BROWN, realty company executive; b. Boston, May 26, 1939; d. Frederick Thomas and Christine (Peyton) Brown; m. Joseph Peter Roberts Aug. 26, 1962 (div. May 1984); children: Christine, Joseph, Paul. BA, Boston Coll., 1981. Lic. real estate broker, Mass. Owner, mgr. real estate, Wellesley, Mass., 1963—; pres. Riverview Realty, Wellesley, 1970—; comml. realtor Boston, 1974—. Cons. Berkshire Hathaway, New Bedford, Mass., 1983-87; asst. to pres. BHR, Inc., New Bedford, 1988-2000. Founder, pres., bd. dirs. Friends of Ft. Washington, Inc.; active Friends of Boston Ballet, 1983—. Mem. DAR (Boston Tea Party chpt. regent 1983-84, 84-85), Navy League U.S., New Eng. Hist. Geneal. Soc., Boston Coll. Club (bd. dirs.), Order of Crown of Charlemagne (life), Order of Lafayette). Republican. Roman Catholic. Home and Office: 52 Kenilworth Rd Wellesley MA 02482-7428 Office: Friends Ft Washington Inc 1 Post Office Sq Ste 310 Boston MA 02109-2106

ROBERTS, SHAUNA S. editor, writer; b. Dayton, Ohio, Sept. 17, 1956; d. Edward Arthur and Janice Colleen (Bowser) Roberts; m. David A. Malueg, July 17, 1982. BA, U. Pa., 1977; MA, Northwestern U., 1979, PhD, 1984. Editor Guide to Biotechnology Products and Instruments AAAS, Washington, 1986—89; writer Jour. NIH Rsch., Washington, 1989—90; freelance sci. and med. writer New Orleans, 1990—. Author: The Commonsense Guide to Weight Loss for People with Diabetes, 1998 (hon. mention Am. Med. Writers Assn., Bronze award Nat. Health Info. Awards, 1999). Named to Beavercreek H.S. Alumni Assn. Hall of Fame, 2001. Mem.: Coun. Sci. Editors, Am. Med. Writers Assn., Nat. Assn. Sci. Writers. Avocations: playing recorder, playing harp, baking bread. Office: 66 Versailles Blvd New Orleans LA 70125-3551 E-mail: shaunaroberts@nasw.org.

ROBERTS, SIDNEY, biological chemist; b. Boston, Mar. 11, 1918; s. Samuel Richard and Elizabeth (Gilbert) R.; m. Clara Marian Szego, Sept. 14, 1943. BS, MIT, 1939; postgrad., Harvard U., 1939-41; MS, U. Minn., 1942, PhD, 1943. Instr. physiology U. Minn. Med. Sch., 1943-44, George Washington U. Med. Sch., 1944-45; rsch. assoc. Worcester Found. Exptl. Biology, Shrewsbury, Mass., 1945-47; asst. prof. physiol. chemistry Yale U. Med. Sch., 1947-48; mem. faculty U. Calif. Med. Sch., Los Angeles, 1948—, prof. biol. chemistry, 1957—; chmn. acad. senate UCLA, 1989-90; mem. adv. panel regulatory biology NSF, 1955-57, adv. panel metabolic biology, 1957-59; mem. metabolism study sect. NIH, 1960-63; basic sci. study sect. Los Angeles County Heart Assn., 1958-63. Cons. VA Hosp., Long Beach, Calif., 1951-55, Los Angeles, 1958-62, Pew Fin. Biomed. Scholar Program, 1992-; air conservation tech. adv. com. Los Angeles County Lung Assn., 1972-76 Author articles, revs.; editor med. jours. Served to 2d lt. AUS, 1944-48. MIT Nat. Entrance scholar, 1935; Guggenheim fellow, 1957-58. Fellow AAAS; mem. Am. Physiol. Soc., Endocrine Soc. (v.p. 1968-69, Ciba award 1953), Brit. Biochem. Soc., Soc. Neurosci., Am. Chem. Soc. (exec. com. div. biol. chemistry 1956-59), Am. Soc. Biol. Chemists, Am. Soc. Neurochemistry, Internat. Soc. Neurochemistry, Phi Beta Kappa, Sigma Xi (pres. UCLA chpt. 1959-60). Home: 1371 Marinette Rd Pacific Palisades CA 90272-2627 Office: UCLA Sch Med Dept Biol Chemistry Los Angeles CA 90095-1737 Office Phone: 310-825-6997. Business E-Mail: sr@ucla.edu.

ROBERTS, STANLEY DWAYNE, physician, medical educator; b. Edmonton, Alta., Can., Sept. 17, 1959; came to U.S., 1994; s. Stan and Margaret Rosslyn (Rye) R.; m. Debra Elizabeth Bell, Aug. 20, 1981; children: Matthew, Brent, Michelle, Jared, Bradley. BSc with honors, U. Alta., Edmonton, 1980, BSc in Psychology with distinction, 1981, MD, 1985; grad., IHC Inst., 1999. Diplomate in family practice and sports medicine Am. Bd. Family Practice; cert. Family Medicine and Emergency Medicine, Coll. Family Physicians of Can. Resident in family medicine U. Alta., 1985-87; resident in physical rehab. and sports medicine McMaster U., Hamilton, Ont., Can., 1987-88, resident in emergency medicine, 1988-89, asst. prof. family and emergency medicine, 1989-94; med. dir., internat. med. cons. Med. Emergency, Inc., Toronto, Ont., Can., 1990-94; chief emergency svcs. Queensway Gen. Hosp., Toronto, Ont., Can., 1992-94; employee health physician, family physician Norman (Okla.) Regional Hosp., 1994-95; family physician Bigstone Cree Indian Reserve, Alberta, 1995—96; pvt. practice Provo, Utah, 1996-97; faculty physician Utah Valley Family Practice Residency, Provo, 1997—2003; emergency physician Utah Valley Regional Med. Ctr., Provo, 1997—; assoc. team physician Brigham Young U., 1999—2002. Med. dir. Redcliff Ascent Wilderness Behavioral Reclamation Program Youth, 2000—; moderator, planner Telemedicine Can./USA Broadcasts, 1990—98; team doctor World Cup Speed Skating, 1999; dir. Utah Valley Sports Medicine Fellowship, 1999—2003; site physician 2002 Winter Olympics and Paralympics/Ice Hockey, Sledge Hockey; developer internat. tng. program for physicians, Nepal, 2000, Western Samoa, 01, Fiji, 01; cons. Global Emergency Medicine Support; cons. devel. plan emergency svcs., Malaysia, 1990—92, Thailand, 1990—92; lectr. in field. Contbr. articles to profl. jours.; guest radio talk shows; developer internat. tng. program in emergency medicine: Art in EM = Advanced Resuscitation Training in Emergency Medicine. Chmn. coms. life support Heart and Stroke Found. (Can.) Ont., 1991-93; scoutmaster Boy Scouts Am., Kaysville, Utah, 1995, Orem, Utah, 1998-99. Recipient Achievement award for internat. distinction in music Govt. Alberta, 1976, Disting. Lectr. award Thailand and Asia Coll. Surgeons, 1993. Mem. AMA, Am. Acad. Family Physicians, Utah Med. Assn., Coll. Family Physicians (Can.), Am. Coll. Sports Medicine. Mem. Lds Ch. Avocations: mountain biking, photography, family enrichment. Office: 155 N 400 W B6 Orem UT 84057 Office Phone: 801-224-1300. Business E-Mail: uvdrober@ihc.com.

ROBERTS, SUSAN STURGEON, art educator, writer; b. Aurora, Colo., Aug. 15, 1953; d. Thomas James Sturgeon, Lela Selby Nagle; m. Eugene Arden Roberts. BS, Calif. State Poly. U., 1978. Tchr. Redlands Unified Sch. Dist., Calif., 1978—80; needle arts tchr. Grants Pass, Oreg., 1974—. Double knits designer Western Textile MIll., Ontario, Calif., 1978. Author: (book) The Complete Needlepoint Guide 400+ Needlepoint Stitches, 2000; sculpture, Stitchin Suzi and Three Ply, 1998. Mem.: Embroiderer's Guild Am. Inc. (asst. editor 1973—76, program dir. 2001—03), Am. Needlepoint Guild Inc. Office: 450 Genverna Glen Grants Pass OR 97527-9570 Home Fax: 541-471-0917; Office Fax: 541-471-0917. Business E-Mail: susanroberts15@hotmail.com.

ROBERTS, SUZANNE CATHERINE, artist; b. San Antonio, Oct. 27, 1953; d. Thomas Simons and Marceline Margaret (Conrady) Garrett; m. Ted Blake Roberts, May 22, 1976; 1 child, Elizabeth. BS in Radio-TV-Film, U. Tex., 1975, B of Journalism, 1977; MA in Interdisciplinary Studies, Corpus Christi (Tex.) State U., 1982, MS in Gen. Counseling, 1989; MA in Polit. Sci., S.W. Tex. State U., 1995. News announcer Sta. KIXL Radio, Austin, Tex., 1976, Sta. KSIX Radio, Corpus Christi, 1977-78; news anchor Sta. KZTV-TV, Corpus Christi, 1979, news reporter, 1977-80; news announcer, reporter Sta. KRYS-AM-FM, Corpus Christi, 1983-87; freelance reporter United Press Internat., Austin, 1989-94, Tex. State Network, Austin, 1995-97, Des Moines, 1997-2000; artist, 1998—.

ROBERTS, TERI ALANE, accountant, educator, civic activist; b. Mission Hills, Calif., Oct. 25, 1963; d. Alan Lewis and Barbara Ann (Taylor) R. BA in Speech Comm., Calif. State U., Northridge, 1990, BA in Polit. Sci. with honors, 1993, MA in Polit. Sci., 1997, MA in History Progress. Peer educator on rape Discovering Alternatives to Today's Encounters, Northridge, 1996-97; dir. Save the Animals Fund, Pasadena, Calif., 1997. Vol. Ga. Mercer for City Coun., Encino, Calif., 1997; mem. planning com., presenter at workshop Ending Violence Against Women Conf., Northridge, 1997; mem. planning com. Rainbow Sisters Project, L.A., 1999. Recipient Commendation for Rainbow Sisters Project, L.A. County, 1999. Mem. Polit. Sci. Club Calif. State U. (dir. fundraising 1992-93, dir. graduation com. 1992-93), Student Speech Comm. Assn. Calif. State U. (dir. social activities 1987-88), Delta Sigma (life). Democrat. Avocations: reading, dance, church activities. Home: 8545 Balboa Blvd Apt 250 Northridge CA 91325-3531 E-mail: teriroberts@socal.rr.com.

ROBERTS, THEODORE HARRIS, banker; b. Gillett, Ark., May 14, 1929; s. Edward and Gertrude (Harris) R.; m. Elisabeth Law, July 17, 1953; children: Susan, William(dec.), Julia. BA in Govt., Northwestern State U., 1949; MA in Polit. Sci., Okla. State U., 1950; postgrad., U. Chgo. Grad. Sch. Bus., 1956. With Harris Trust and Savs. Bank, Chgo., 1953-82; exec. v.p., sec., treas. Harris Bank and Harris Bankcorp Inc., 1971-82, dir., exec. com., 1975-82; pres. Fed. Res. Bank St. Louis, 1983-85; chmn. bd., chief exec. officer Talman Home Fed. Savs. & Loan, Chgo., 1985-92; pres. LaSalle Nat. Corp., 1992-95, retired. Sr. cons. ABN AMRO, 1995—. Mem. Chgo. Club, Comml. Club Chgo., Econ. Club Chgo., Exmoor Country Club (Highland Park, Ill.). Office: 135 S La Salle St Ste 260 Chicago IL 60603-4500

ROBERTS, THOMAS ALBA, lawyer; b. Ft. Wayne, Ind., Sept. 7, 1946; s. Jack and Elizabeth (Wallace) R.; m. Mary Alice Buckley, Aug. 11, 1973; children: Kaitrin M., John A., Kara B. BA, Georgetown U., 1969, JD, 1972. Bar: N.Y. 1973, U.S. Dist. Ct. (so. dist.) N.Y. 1973, U.S. Ct. Appeals (2d cir.) 1973, Tex. 1976, U.S. Supreme Ct. 1977, U.S. Dist. Ct. (so. dist.) Tex. 1978, U.S. Ct. Appeals (5th and 11th cirs.) 1982. Assoc. Winthrop, Stimson, Putnam & Roberts, N.Y.C., 1972-76; ptnr. Moore & Peterson, Dallas, 1976-89, mng. ptnr., 1980-88; ptnr. Johnson & Gibbs, Dallas, 1989-92; sr. ptnr. Weil, Gotshal & Manges, Dallas, N.Y.C., 1992—. Chmn. Internat. Corp. Practice Group, 1997—2001, chmn. corp. dept., 2001—, mem. mgmt. com., 1997—; adj. prof. law So. Meth. U., Dallas, 1977—78; lectr. in field. Lectr. in field. Mem. fin. com. St. Rita Ch., Dallas, 1983—88; mem. Ch. of the Resurrection; mem. fin. com. Our Lady of the Lord, Rockwall, Tex., 1995—98; bd. dirs. Make-A-Wish Found. Met. N.Y., 1998—, Make-A-Wish of Am., 2002—. Mem. ABA, Tex. Bar Assn., Dallas Bar Assn., Assn. of Bar of City of N.Y. Roman Catholic. Avocations: skiing, golf, literature. Home: 133 Grandview Ave Rye NY 10580-2030 E-mail: thomas.roberts@weil.com.

ROBERTS, THOMAS GEORGE, retired physicist; b. Ft. Smith, Ark., Apr. 27, 1929; s. Thomas Lawrence and Emma Lee (Stanley) R.; m. Alice Anne Harbin, Nov. 14, 1958 (dec. 1994); children: Lawrence Dewey, Regina Anne; foster child, Marcia Roberts Dale; m. Betty Howard McElyea, July 28, 1995. AA, Armstrong Coll., 1953; BS, U. Ga., 1956, MS, 1957; PhD, N.C. State U., 1967. Rsch. physicist U.S. Army Missile Command, Huntsville, Ala., 1958-85; cons. industry and govt. agys., 1970—, SAIC, Huntsville, Ala., 1997-2001; owner Technoco, Huntsville, 1985-96. Contbr. articles to profl. jours.; patentee in field. Sgt. USAF, 1948-52. Fellow Am. Optical Soc.; mem. Am. Phys. Soc., IEEE, Huntsville Optical Soc. Am. (pres. 1980, 92), Toastmaster Internat. (pres. 1963). Episcopalian. Achievements include research in laser physics, optics, particle beams and instrumentation; diagnostic devices and techniques development.

ROBERTS, THOMAS HEYM, city and regional planner, consultant; b. Cleve., Jan. 28, 1928; s. Burke Brockway and Charlotte (Heym) R.; m. Jacquelyn Kline, June 4, 1950; children: Judith, Mark, Holly, Tod. BSCE, Case Inst. Tech., 1950; M of Regional Planning, U. N.C., 1952. Planning asst. City Planning Commn., Cleve., 1950, sr. planner Youngstown, Ohio, 1952-54, County Planning Bd., Charleston County, S.C., 1954-56; various positions to planning dir. Atlanta Region Metro. Planning Commn., Atlanta, 1956-66; dir. of planning Metro. Washington Coun. Govts., 1966-69; exec. dir. Am. Inst. Cert. Planners, Washington, 1969-72; dir. of planning Atlanta Regional Commn., 1972-78; pres. Thomas H. Roberts and Assocs., Atlanta, 1978—. Contbg. author: Lincoln Institute of Land Policy, 1985, 86, Land Development Control Law, 1986, The Practice of State and Regional Planning, 1986, Urban Planning, 1988. Fellow Am. Inst. Cert. Planners; mem. Am. Planning Assn. (bd. dirs. 1974-77, v.p. 1977-78, pres. 1978). Unitarian-Universalist. Avocations: quartet singing, vocal arranging, guitar. Home and Office: 4241 Smithsonia Ct Tucker GA 30084-2627

ROBERTS, THOMASENE BLOUNT, entrepreneur; b. Americus, Ga., Sept. 5, 1943; d. Thomas Watson and Mary Elizabeth (Smith) Blount; m. Henry Lee Roberts, Apr. 24, 1970 (div. 1991); 1 child, Asha Maia. Student, Fisk U., 1960-63; BA, Morris Brown Coll., 1965; MA, Atlanta U., 1970, postgrad., 1979-82, Clark Atlanta U. Social worker Gate City Day Nursery Assn., Atlanta, 1965-66; ticket agt. Delta Air Lines, Inc., Atlanta, 1966-68; clk. accounts payable Kraft Foods, Inc., Decatur, Ga., 1968; cons. family svcs. Atlanta Housing Authority, 1970-72, supr. family svcs., 1972-73, mgr. family relocation, 1974-79; grad. rsch. asst. Sch. Edn. Atlanta U., 1979-82; city coun. asst. City of Atlanta, 1984-88, rsch. asst. Dept. Pub. Safety, 1988; dir. govtl. rels. Morris Brown Coll., Atlanta, 1988-93; owner TBR Ent., Atlanta, 1993—2002; adminstrv. analyst human svcs. City of Atlanta, 1995-97, adminstrv. analyst, prin. dept. adminstrv. svcs., 1997; owner Dream Catcher Events, Inc., 1997—; psychol. svcs. specialist City of Atlanta, 1998—2002. Researcher/intern Project Focus Teen Mother Program, Atlanta, 1981-82; moderator Nat. Black Women's Health Project, Atlanta, 1985; workshop leader Assn. Human Resources Mgrs., Atlanta, 1989; pres.'s rep. U. Ctr. Devel. Corp., Inc., 1989-93; cons. entrepreneur devel. workshop Morris Brown Coll. Chairperson Ida Prather YWCA Cmty. Bd., Atlanta, 1985-90; bd. dirs. YWCA Met. Atlanta, 1986-90, Met. Atlanta Coalition 100 Black Women, 1988-90, 92-2001, sec., mem. bd. dirs., 1994-96, 1st v.p., 1997-2000; trustee Hammonds House Mus., 1995-2001; active fund dr. com. Jomandi Prodn., 1988-89; v.p. maj. gifts com. Camp Best Friends, City of Atlanta, 1989; mem. Multi-Cultural Leadership Group, Gov.'s Coun. on Developmental Disabilities, 1990; bd. dirs. Atlanta Black/Jewish Coalition, 1997-2000; apptd. mem. Atlanta Sister Cities Commn.; presenter, cons. Youth Motivation Task Force, 1998-2001. Mem. Atlanta-Trinidad/Tobago Exch. (sec., treas. 1983-89, Pt. of Spain cert. 1986), Nat. Polit. Congress Black Women (corr. sec. 1989-90), Nat. Assn. for Equal Opportunity Higher Edn. (coll. liaison 1988-93), Coun. for Advancement-Support of Edn., Info. Forum, Atlanta Urban League, Inc., Nat. Assn. for Equal Opportunity in Higher Edn. (Disting. Alumni award 1991), Nat. Soc. Fund-Raising Execs. (cert. 1992), Nat. Soc. Fund-Raising Execs. Leadership Inst., Friends of Morehouse Sch. Medicine, Assn. Bridal Cons., Internat. Spl. Events Soc. (v.p. programs 2001-02), Atlanta Bus. League, Delta Sigma Theta (pub. rels. asst. 1986-89). Avocations: dance, theater, music, film, art, fine dining. Home and Office: 1817 King Charles Rd SW Atlanta GA 30331-4909 Fax: 404-344-0378.

ROBERTS, TIFFANY MARIE, former soccer player; b. Petaluma, Calif., May 5, 1977; BA in Comm. Studies, U. N.C., 1998. Mem. U.S. Women's Nat. Soccer Team, 1994—; including CONCAFAF Qualifying Championship Montreal, 1994; 3d place FIFA Women's World Cup, 1995; gold medal U.S. Olympic Team, 1996; mem. Under-20 Nat. Team 1997 Nordic Cup, Denmark; mem. Tri Valley Team, San Ramon, Calif.; profl. soccer player Carolina Courage, 2001—03. Named 1994 Calif. H.S. Player of Yr., Most Valuable Player, Far Western Regional, 1993, World Cup Champion, 1999. Achievements include member U. N.C. NCAA national championship teams, 1996, 97. Office: US Soccer Fedn 1801-1811 S Prairie Ave Chicago IL 60616

ROBERTS, TONY (DAVID ANTHONY ROBERTS), actor; b. N.Y.C., Oct. 22, 1939; s. Kenneth and Norma R.; 1 child, Nicole. BS, Northwestern U., 1961. Movie debut in The Million Dollar Duck, 1971; other film appearances include Star Spangled Girl, 1971, Play It Again, Sam, 1972, Serpico, 1974, The Taking of Pelham, One Two Three, 1974, Annie Hall, 1977, Lovers Like Us, 1977, Just Tell Me What You Want, Stardust Memories, 1980, A Midsummer Nights Sex Comedy, 1982, Question of Honor, 1982, Packin' It In, 1983, Amityville IIID, 1983, Hannah and her Sisters, 1986, 18 Again!, 1988, Popcorn, 1990, Switch, 1991; TV movies The Lindbergh Kidnapping Case, 1976, Girls in the Office, 1979, If Things Were Different, 1980, A Question of Honor, 1982, Our Sons, 1992, Not in My Family, 1993, The American Clock, 1993, Perry Mason: The Case of the Jealous Jokester, 1995; regular on TV series The Edge of Night, 1963-65, Rosetti and Ryan, 1977, The Four Seasons, 1986, The Lucy Arnaz Show, 1987, The Thorns, 1989; other TV appearances include The Way They Were, 1980; Broadway debut in Something about a Soldier, 1962; toured with nat. co. of Come Blow Your Horn, 1962; other Broadway stage appearances Take Her, She's Mine, 1964, Never Too Late, Barefoot in the Park, The Last Analysis, 1964, Don't Drink the Water, 1966, How Now, Dow Jones, 1967 (nominated for Tony award), Play It Again, Sam, 1969 (nominated for Tony award), Promises, Promises, 1971, Sugar, 1972, Absurd Person Singular, 1974, Murder at the Howard Johnson's, 1979, They're Playing Our Song, 1981, Doubles, 1985, Arsenic and Old Lace, 1986, Jerome Robbins Broadway, 1990, The Seagull, 1992, Tale of the Allergist's Wife, 2002; London debut in Promises, Promises, 1969 (London Critics Poll award as Best Actor in Musical), 1974; appeared in: Darkroom, Yale Repertory Theatre, New Haven, Hamlet, Otterbein Coll. (Ohio) Winter Drama Festival, 1975, Taming of the Shrew, Atlanta, 1978, Let 'Em Eat Cake, Berkshire Theatre Festival, Serenading Louis, Acad. Festival Theatre; The Seagull, Saratoga Performance Arts Festival, 1985, Who's Afraid of Virginia Woolf, 1986, (voice) audio books The Short Forever, 2002, Leadership, 2002. Served in U.S. Army. Mem. SAG (bd. dirs. 1990—, v.p. of NY div.,2001-), Actors Equity Assn. (governing coun. 1968-74) Office: Innovative Artists 1505 10th Ave Santa Monica CA 90401

ROBERTS, VICTORIA LYNN P. antique expert; b. N.Y.C., Sept. 15, 1953; d. Edgar Alan Parmer and Nina Joyce (Ash) Gross; m. George E. Roberts, Dec. 1, 1978 (div. 1985); 1 child, Joshua Henry. BA in Polit. Sci., Am. govt., const. law, Yale U., 1998; MBA, Fairfield U., 1999. Pres. High Gear Creative Svcs., Savannah, Ga., 1979-81; v.p. Rossignol Modeling Agy., N.Y.C., 1981-82; mgr., dir. Parc Monceau Antiques, Westport, Conn., 1982-85; pres., owner, CEO Victoria & Cie LLC, Custom Furniture Mfg., Norwalk, Conn., 1985—; pres., owner L.L.C. Custon Furniture Mfg. Antiques tchr. Sacred Heart U., Fairfield, Conn., 1988, 89, Norwalk Community Coll., 1989; antique lectr. various hist. socs., Conn., 1989-90; speaker in antiques field; antique expert seminars to interior designers, Norwalk, 1989; creator, sole contbr. spls. on antiques CNBC TV, 1989, 90. Antiques editor Brooks Community Newspaper, Westport, 1989-91; contbr. Antiques Mag., 1991—. Mem. Appraisers Assn. Am. (sr.), Coll. Arts Assn., Yale Club (N.Y.C. admissions com. mem.), Alpha Sigma Lambda. Avocations: scenic photography, bicycling, history, rose gardening. Office: Stamford Industrial Park Canal Street Stamford CT 06902 E-mail: victoria@victoriacie.com.

ROBERTS, VIRGIL PATRICK, lawyer, business executive; b. Ventura, Calif., Jan. 4, 1947; s. Julius and Emma D. (Haley) R.; m. Brenda Cecilia Banks, Nov. 10, 1979; children: Gisele Simone, Hayley Tasha. AA, Ventura Coll., 1966; BA, UCLA, 1968; JD, Harvard U., 1972. Bar: Calif. 1972. Assoc. Pacht, Ross, Warne Bernhardt & Sears, L.A., 1972-76; ptnr. Manning, Reynolds & Roberts, L.A., 1976-79, Manning & Roberts, 1980-81; mng. ptnr. Bobbitt & Roberts, 1995—; exec. v.p., gen. counsel Solar Records, L.A., 1981—; pres. Dick Griffey Prodns., L.A., 1982—, Solar Records, 1988—; judge pro tem L.A., Beverly Hills Mcpl. Cts., 1975—. Bd. dirs. Broadway Fed. Bank. Past bd. dirs. L.A. Black Leadership Coalition, L.A. Mus. African Am. Art, Beverly Hills Bar Assn., L.A. Legal Aid Found.; bd. dirs. Coro Found., 1984-90, L.A. Ednl. Alliance for Restructuring Now, Cmty. Build; bd. dirs. Calif. Cmty. Found., 1991—, chmn. bd., 1999—; past pres. Beverly Hills Bar Scholarship Found.; commr. Calif. Commn. for Tchr. Credentialing, 1980-83; chmn. L.A. Ednl. Partnership, 1989—, v.p. 1983-89; vice-chmn. Nat. Pub. Edn. Fund Network; chmn. bd. dirs. L.A. Annenberg Met. Project; trustee Com. Econ. Devel., 1991—, Occidental Coll., Marlborough Sch.; mem. bd. councillors UCLA. Recipient NAACP Legal Def. Fund Equal Justice award, 1988, Rose award U. So. Calif., 1998. Mem. Recording Industry Assn. Am., Black Entertainment and Sports Lawyers (treas., bd. dirs. 1982—). Lead atty. for NAACP in Crawford vs. Bd. Edn. desegregation case, L.A., 1979-80. Address: 4820 Vista De Oro Ave Los Angeles CA 90043-1611 Office: Bobbitt & Roberts 6100 Center Dr Ste 910 Los Angeles CA 90404 Office Phone: 310-645-4100. Business E-Mail: vroberts@bobroblaw.com.

ROBERTS, WALTER HERBERT BEATTY, anatomist, educator; b. Field, B.C., Can., Jan. 24, 1915; came to U.S., 1956, naturalized, 1965; s. Walter McWilliam and Sarah Caroline (Orr) R.; m. Olive Louise O'Neal, Sept. 1, 1937; children: Gayle, Sharon, David. MD, Coll. Med. Evangelists (later Loma Linda U.), 1939. Intern St. Paul's Hosp., Vancouver, Canada, 1938-40; med. dir. Rest Haven Hosp. Sanitarium and Hosp., Sidney, Vancouver Island, Canada, 1940-53; post doctoral tng. White Meml. Hosp., L.A., 1946-47, Edinburgh (Scotland) Hosp., 1953-55; instr. in anatomy Loma Linda U., 1955-58, asst. prof. anatomy, 1959-62, assoc. prof., 1962-70, prof., 1971—, chmn. dept. anatomy, 1974-81, prof. emeritus. Mem. Alpha Omega Alpha. Adventist. Home: 11366 Campus St Loma Linda CA 92354-3302 Office: Loma Linda Univ Dept Path & Human Anatomy Divsn Human Anatomy Loma Linda CA 92350-0001 Office Phone: 909-558-7602.

ROBERTS, WALTER RONALD, political science educator, former government official; b. Waltendorf, Austria, Aug. 26, 1916; arrived in U.S., 1939, naturalized, 1944; s. Ignatius and Elizabeth (Diamant) R.; m. Gisela K. Schmarak, Aug. 22, 1939; children: William M., Charles E., Lawrence H. MLitt, Cambridge (Eng.) U., 1940, PhD, 1980. Rsch. asst. Harvard U. Law Sch., 1940-42; writer, editor Voice of Am., 1942-49; press officer U.S. del. to Austrian Treaty talks, 1949, 55; fgn. affairs officer Dept. State, 1950-53; dep. asst. dir. USIA, 1954-60; counselor of embassy for pub. affairs Am. Embassy, Belgrade, Yugoslavia, 1960-66; diplomat-in-residence Brown U., Providence, 1966-67; counselor U.S. Mission to Internat. Orgns., Geneva, 1967-69; dep. assoc. dir. USIA, Washington, 1969-71, assoc. dir., 1971-74; dir. diplomatic studies Ctr. Strategic and Internat. Studies Georgetown U., Washington, 1974-75; exec. dir. Bd. Internat. Broadcasting, Washington, 1975-85; diplomat-in-residence George Washington U., Washington, 1986-96. Author: Tito, Mihailovic and the Allies, 1941-45, 73, paperback, 1987, (with Terry L. Deibel) Culture and Information: Two Foreign Policy Functions, 1976; contbr. articles to profl. pubs. Apptd. mem. U.S. Adv. Commn. on Pub. Diplomacy, 1991-97, sr. advisor, 1998-2003; bd. dirs. Salzburg Seminar, 1993-97, Coun. Sr. Fellows, 1998—, Oxford and Cambridge com., 1975-, Pub. Diplomacy Coun., 1996—; bd. dirs. Pub. Diplomacy Inst., George Washington U., 2001—. Recipient Disting. Honor award USIA, 1974. Mem. Washington Inst. Fgn. Affairs, Coun. Fgn. Rels., Oxford-Cambridge Com., USIA Alumni Assn. (bd. dirs. 1995-98), Met. Club. Home: 4449 Sedgwick St NW Washington DC 20016-2713

ROBERTS, WILBUR EUGENE, dental educator, research scientist, wine importer; b. Lubbock, Tex., Nov. 16, 1942; s. Wilbur Eugene Roberts and Elva Etna (Chance) Turnwall; m. Cheryl Ann Jones, June 6, 1967; children: Jeffery Alan, Carrie Jean. DDS, Creighton U., 1967; PhD in Anatomy, U. Utah, 1969; cert. in orthodontics, U. Conn., 1974; DHC in Medicine (hon.), Lille (France) U., 1996. Diplomate Am. Bd. Orthodontics. Rsch. fellow U. Utah, Salt Lake City, 1967—69; postdoctoral fellow U. Conn., Farmington, 1971—74; from asst. prof. to prof. dentistry U. Pacific, San Francisco, 1974—88; prof. chmn. dept. orthodontics Ind. U., Indpls., 1988—93, chmn. dept. oral and facial devel., 1993—97, prof. physiology and biophysics Sch. Medicine, 1988—2000, dir. grad. orthodontics program Sch. Dentistry, 1988—, head orthodontics sect., 1997—; mem. steering com. Biomechs. and Biomaterials Rsch. Ctr. Ind. U.-Purdue U., Indpls., 1990—96; NRC sr. rsch. assoc. NASA Ames Rsch. Ctr., Moffett Field, Calif., 1982—83; Jarabak prof. orthodontics Ind. U., Indpls., 2001—; CEO, sec.-treas. VinElite Imports, Inc., Indpls., 1999—. Dir. Bone Rsch. Lab. U. Pacific, 1980—88, dir. Oral Devel. Clinic, 1980—86, Dr. Fred West Meml. lectr., 1989, 97; rsch. cons. Neodontics Corp., Laguna Nigel, Calif., 1982—85, Denar Corp., Anaheim, Calif., 1985—87, Nobelpharma AG, Goteborg, Sweden, 1988, Dental Implant Clin. Rsch. Group, Ann Arbor, Mich., 1991—, Align Tech., Mountain View, Calif., Oral Medicine and Biology Study sect. NIH, 1992—96, Rsch. Coun. ADA, 1992; accreditation cons. in orthodontics ADA Coun. on Dental Accreditation, 1996—; task force on faculty recruitment Am. Assn. of Orthodontics, 1998—; adj. prof. mech. engring. Purdue U., Indpls., 1990—; assoc. prof. implantology, maxillofacial surgery U. Lille, France, 1987—; guest prof. U. Western Ont., Canada, 1987; Dr. George Grieve Meml. lectr. Can. Dental Assn., 1993; mem. internat. affairs com. Ind. U.-Purdue U., Indpls., 1995—; sci. cons. Align Tech. Corp.; U.S. importer Mud House Wine Co. Ltd., Marlborough, New Zealand, Oakridge Vineyards, Ltd., Australia, Rymill Wines, Coonawarra, Australia; ptnr. Vinters of Zuperb Zinfandel, Paso Robles, Calif.; owner Roberts' Renner Rd. and Castle Vineyards, New Zealand; keynote lectr. Moyers Symposium, U. Mich., 2004. Contbr. sci. articles to profl. jours. Rep. campaign worker, Contra Costa County, Calif., 1980-82; ch. sch. supt. San Ramon Valley Meth. Ch., Alamo, Calif., 1979-81; adult ministries council San Ramon Valley Meth. Ch., Danville, Calif., 1984-86; sci. cons. St. Isadore Sch. and San Ramon Valley High Sch., Danville, 1978-86; chmn. bldg. com. Sunrise at Geist United Meth. Ch., Indpls.; mem. planning bd. Vols. in Medicine, Indpls., 2000-2001. Lt. comdr. USN, 1969-71, Vietnam. Decorated Navy Commendation medal; named Eminent scholar, Okla. U., 1995; recipient Cosmos Achievement award, NASA, 1981, 1988, 1992, medal, City of Paris, 1989, City of Rouen, France, 1991, Rsch. award, Ind. U. Sch. Dentistry, 1993, Gold Medallion award, U. of Pacific Sch. Dentistry, 2001, Isaac Lew award, Am. Acad. Implant Dentistry, 2002, Jarabak award, Am. Assn. Orthodontists, 2003. Fellow: Am. Coll. Dentists, Internat. Coll. Dentists; mem.: Pacific Dental Rsch. Found. (pres. 1976—80), Am. Assn. Dental Rsch., Med. Dental Guild Calif. (pres. 1982—83, Gold Key award 1985), Conf. of the Co. of Wine Tasters of Normandy (pres. Ind. med. chpt. 1992—97, Master of the Cave 1997—2001, Baron of Honor 1999, Master of Embassies 2001—), Omicron Kappa Upsilon. Avocations: fishing, skiing, enology. Home: 8260 Skipjack Dr Indianapolis IN 46236-8429 Office: Ind U Sch Dentistry Sch Dentistry Sect Orthodontics 1121 W Michigan St Indianapolis IN 46202-5211 E-mail: werobert@iupui.edu.

ROBERTS, WILLIAM B. lawyer, business executive; b. Detroit, Aug. 23, 1939; s. Edwin Stuart and Marjorie Jean (Wardle) R.; m. Cathleen Anne Thompson, Sept. 1, 1962; children: Bradford William, Brent William, Katrina Marjorie. BA, Mich. State U., 1961; JD with distinction, U. Mich., 1963; China law diploma, U. East Asia, Macau, 1989. Bar: Mo. 1964, Fla. 1983, U.S. Dist. Ct. (ea. dist.) Mo. 1964, U.S. Dist. Ct. (mid. dist.) Fla. 1993. Mem. firm Thompson & Mitchell, St. Louis, 1963-67; atty. Monsanto Co., 1967-70; sr. exec. v.p. adminstrn., sec., gen. counsel Chromalloy Am. Corp. (successor Segua Corp. N.Y.), St. Louis, 1970-78, exec. v.p.-adminstrn., gen. counsel, sec. Clayton, Mo., 1978-82; pvt. practice law, 1983-87; mng. ptnr. Roberts and Nordahl, St. Louis and Naples, Fla., 1988-89, Law Offices of William B. Roberts, St. Louis and Naples, 1989-90, Darrow & Roberts, P.A., Naples, 1992-93; pres., mng. dir. Law Offices of William B. Roberts, Naples, 1994—, Kansas City, Mo., 1999—. Pres., mng. dir. The Fairborne Group, Ltd., St. Louis and Naples, 1988-91, William B. Roberts & Assocs. Co., Merger and Acquisitions Specialists, 1982—; mem. exam. com. of policyowners Northwestern Mut. Life Ins. Co., Milw., 1978; del. to U.S.-China Joint Session on Trade Investment and Econ. Law, Beijing, 1987; sports rep. Steve Carlton, St. Louis Cardinals, Phila. Phillies baseball clubs, 1987-89; pres., CEO Tropical Tracks, Inc., Naples, 1994—. Mem. ABA, Fed. Bar Assn. (Mid. Dist. Fla.), Mo. Bar Assn., St. Louis Bar Assn. (chmn. antitrust sect. 1973), Fla. Bar Assn., Collier County Bar Assn., Delta Theta Phi. Methodist. Home: 133 Crestview Terr Lake Placid FL 33852 Also: 321 NE Landings Dr Lees Summit MO 64064-1586

ROBERTS, WILLIAM D. broadcast executive; b. Drummondville, Que., Can. BA, Trent U., Peterborough, Ont., 1973; MBA, St. Mary's U., Halifax, N.S., 1976; MA, Sorbonne, Paris, 1977; Diploma in Broadcast Mgmt., U. Notre Dame, Ind. Sr. policy analyst CRTC, Ottawa, Ont., 1980-84; sr. v.p. Can. Assn. of Broadcasters, Ottawa, 1984-89; sr. dir. gen. TV Ontario, Toronto, 1989-96; sec. gen. N.Am. Nat. Broadcasters Assn., Toronto, 1996—. V.p. Couchiching Inst. for Pub. Affairs, Toronto, 1993—; fellow Calumet Coll., York U., Toronto, 1996—, Massey Coll., U. Toronto, 1997—. Avocations: Karate, scuba diving. Office: North American National Broadcasters Assn NABA PO Box 500 Sta A Toronto ON Canada M5W 1E6

ROBERTS, WILLIAM EVERETT, lawyer; b. Pierre, S.D., May 12, 1926; s. Everett David and Bonnie (Martin) R.; m. Cynthia Cline, July 18, 1953; children: Catherine C. Roberts-Martin, Laura M., Nancy F., David H. BS, U. Minn., 1947; LLB, Yale U., 1950. Bar: Ind. 1950, U.S. Supreme Ct. 1964. Employee, ptnr. Duck and Neighbours, Indpls., 1950-58; ptnr. Cadick, Burns, Duck & Neighbours, Indpls., 1958-60, Roberts, Ryder, Rogers & Scism, Indpls., 1960-85, Barnes & Thornburg, Indpls., 1986-93, of counsel, 1994—. Pres., bd. dirs. Park-Tudor Sch., Indpls., 1982-83; elder Second Presbyn. Ch., Indpls., 1962—; trustee Indpls. Mus. Art, 1978—; pres. New Hope of Ind., Indpls., 1986-87. Fellow Am. Bar Found.; mem. ABA, Ind. Bar Assn., Indpls. Bar Assn., Rotary, Meridian Hills Country Club (pres. 1983-84). Republican. Home: 10466 Spring Highland Dr Indianapolis IN 46290-1101 Office: Barnes & Thornburg 11 S Meridian St Ste 1313 Indianapolis IN 46204-3535 Office Phone: 317-231-7520.

ROBERTS-BURKE, BERYL D. state legislator, lawyer; b. Columbia, S.C., Aug. 26, 1958; BS, Fla. State U., 1980, JD, 1987; student, Oxford U., Eng., 1981. Bar: Fla. Mem. Fla. Ho. of Reps., 1992—; mem. gen. govt. appropriations com., 1996-97; mem. rules, resolutions and ethics com., 1996-97, 97—. Del. Dem. Nat. Conv., 1988; mem. African-Am. Coun. Christian Clergy; bd. dirs. Concerned African Women, Kids, Miami River of Life. Recipient African-Am. Achievers award 1994, Carter G. Woodson award Postal Employees of United Cmty. Outreach Assn., Up and Comers in Govt. award, 1994; named Citizen of Yr., Miami Chpt. Nat. Black Nurses Assn., 1994. Mem. NAACP, Nat. Bar Assn. (Women Lawyers' divsn.), Dade County Black Lawyer's Assn., Coalition 100 Black Women, Continental Socs., C. of C. (N. Dade and Miami-Dade), Kiwanis, King of Clubs Greater Miami Inc., Omicron Delta Kappa, Alpha Phi Alpha (Beta Lambda chpt.), Delta Sigma Theta, Phi Delta Phi. Democrat. Avocations: reading, playing computer games, studying bible, sewing. Office: Fla Capitol 402 S Monroe St Rm 1402 Tallahassee FL 32399-6526 also: 7900 NE 2nd Ave Ste 705 Miami FL 33138-4424 E-mail: roberts.beryl@leg.state.fl.us.

ROBERTS-DEMPSEY, PATRICIA E. secondary school educator; Tchr. Challenger High Sch., Spanaway, Wash., 1969—. Recipient Wash. State Tchr. of Yr. award, 1991-91. Office: Challenger HS 18020 B St E Spanaway WA 98387-8316

ROBERTS-MAMONE, LISA A. lawyer; BA magna cum laude, Grove City Coll., 1985; JD magna cum laude, Case Wester Res. U., 1988. Bar: Ohio 1988. With Jones Day, Cleve., 1988—, ptnr., 2000—. Trustee The Estate Planning Coun. of Cleve., The Laub Found.; mem. Estate Planning Discussion Group, Cleve.; mem. estate adv. coun. U. Hosps. Cleve. Mem.: Cleve. Bar Assn. (estate planning, probate and trust law sect.), Ohio State Bar Assn. (estate planning, trust and probate sect.). Office: Jones Day North Point 901 Lakeside Ave Cleveland OH 44114-1190

ROBERTSON, A. HAEWORTH, actuary, benefit consultant, foundation executive; b. Oklahoma City, May 10, 1930; s. Albert Haeworth and Bonnie Tennessee (Duckett) R.; m. Mary Adeline Kissee, Feb. 3, 1952 (div. July 1979); children— Valerie Lynn, Alan Haeworth, Mary Kathryn. BA in Math., U. Okla., 1951; MA in Actuarial Sci., U. Mich., 1953. Actuary Wyatt Co., Washington and Dallas, 1955-58; actuary Bowles, Andrews & Towne, Dallas, 1958-60; v.p., actuary W. Alfred Hayes & Co., St. Louis, 1960-63; pres. First Am. Security Life Ins. Co. Mo., St. Louis, 1964-68; pvt. practice internat. cons. actuary Barbados and Ghana, 1969-72; sr. actuary ILO, Geneva, Switzerland, 1973-75; chief actuary U.S. Social Security Adminstrn., Balt., 1975-78; mng. dir. William M. Mercer, Inc., Washington, 1978-88; pvt. practice, internat. cons., actuary Washington, Kuwait, Turkey, Guyana, Zimbabwe, China, The Philippines, 1988—. Chmn. Retirement Bd. Actuaries, Dept. Def., 1984-95; mem. Edn. Benefits Bd. Actuaries, 1985-95; pres., founder Retirement Policy Inst. Inc., 1986—. Author: The Coming Revolution in Social Security, 1981, Social Security: What Every Taxpayer Should Know, 1992, The Big Lie: What Every Baby Boomer Should Know About Social Security and Medicare, 1997. Served to 2d lt. USAF, 1953-55 Recipient Commrs. citation, Social Security Adminstrn., Washington, 1976, Arthur J. Altmeyer award, HEW, Washington, 1978, Disting. Alumni award, Ctrl. H.S., Oklahoma City, 1997. Fellow Soc. Actuaries (bd. govs. 1979-81, v.p. 1985-87), Conf. Cons. Actuaries; mem. Am. Acad. Actuaries (Robert J. Myers Pub. Svc. award 2004), Internat. Actuarial Assn., Internat. Assn. Cons. Actuaries, U.K. Inst. Actuaries (assoc.), Cosmos Club, Phi Beta Kappa, Phi Eta Sigma, Phi Kappa Sigma. Republican. Methodist.

ROBERTSON, ABEL L., JR., pathologist; b. St. Andrews, Argentina, July 21, 1926; came to U.S., 1952, naturalized, 1957; s. Abel Alfred Lazzarini and Margaret Theresa G. (Anderson) R.; m. Irene Kirmayr Mauch, Dec. 26, 1958; children: Margaret Anne, Abel Martin, Andrew Duncan, Malcolm Alexander. BS, Coll. D.F. Sarmiento, Buenos Aires, Argentina, 1946; MD suma cum laude, U. Buenos Aires, 1951; PhD, Cornell U., 1959. Fellow tissue culture div. Inst. Histology and Embryology, Sch. Medicine Inst. Histology and Embryology, 1947-49; surg. intern Hosp. Ramos Mejia, Buenos Aires, 1948-50; fellow in tissue culture research Ministry of Health, Buenos Aires, 1950-51; resident Hosp. Nacional de Clinicas, Buenos Aires, 1950-51; head blood vessel bank and organ transplants Research Ctr. Ministry of Health, Buenos Aires, 1951-53; fellow dept. surgery and pathology Sch. Medicine Cornell U., N.Y.C., 1953-55; asst. vis. surgery U. Hosp. N.Y., N.Y.C., 1955-60; asst. prof. research surgery Postgrad. Med. Sch. NYU, N.Y.C., 1955-56; asst. vis. surgeon Bellevue Hosp., N.Y.C., 1955-60; assoc. prof. research surgery NYU, 1956-60, assoc. prof. pathology Sch. Medicine and Postgrad Med. Sch., 1960-63; staff mem. div. research Cleve. Clinic Found., 1963-73, prof. research, 1972-73; assoc. clin. prof. pathology Case Western Res. U. Sch. Medicine, Cleve., 1968-72, prof. pathology, 1973-82, dir. interdisciplinary cardiovascular research, 1975-82; exec. head dept. pathology Coll. Medicine, U. Ill., Chgo., 1982-88; prof. pathology Coll. Medicine U. Ill., 1982-93, prof. emeritus, 1993—; vis. prof. emeritus cardiovascular med. Core Analysis Lab., Stanford U. Coll. Medicine, 1995—, cardiac pathologist, 2000—. Rsch. fellow N.Y. Soc. Cardiovasc. Surgery, 1957-58; mem. rsch. study subcom. of heart com. N.E. Ohio Regional Med. Program, 1969—. Mem. internat. editorial bd.: Atherosclerosis, Jour. Exptl. and Molecular Pathology, 1964—, Lab. Investigation, 1989—, Acta Pathologica Japonica, 1991—; contbr. articles to profl. jours. Recipient Rsch. Devel. award NIH, 1961-63; recipient Disting. Alumnus award, Grad. Sch. Med. Sci., Cornell U., 2003. Fellow AAAS, Am. Coll. Cardiology, Am. Coll. Clin. Pharmacology, Am. Heart Assn. (established investigator 1956-61, nominating com. coun. on arteriosclerosis 1972), Royal Microscopical Soc., Royal Soc. Promotion Health (Gt. Britain), Am. Geriat. Soc., N.Y. Acad. Scis., Cleve. Med. Library Assn.; mem. AMA, AAUP, Am. Soc. for Investigative Pathology, Am. Inst. Biol. Scis., Am. Judicature Soc., Am. Soc. Cell Biology, Am. Soc. Pathologists, Am. Soc. Nephrology, Assn. Am. Physicians and Surgeons, Assn. Computing Machinery, Electron Microscopy Soc. Am., Assn. Pathology Chmn., Internat. Acad. Pathology, Soc. Cardiovasc. Pathology, Internat. Cardiovasc. Soc., Internat. Soc. Cardiology (sci. council on arteriosclerosis and ischemic heart disease), Internat. Fed. on Genetic Engring. and Biotechnology, Internat. Soc. for Heart Rsch., Internat. Soc. Nephrology, Internat. Soc. Stereology, Pan Am. Med. Assn. (life, councillor in angiology 1966), Ill. Registry Anatomical Pathology (treas. 1985-87), Chgo. Pathology Soc., Reticuloendothelial Soc. Leucocyte Biology, Soc. Cryobiology, Tissue Culture Assn., Ohio Soc. Pathologists, Electron Microscopy Soc. Northeastern Ohio (pres., trustee 11966-68), Heart Assn. Northeastern Ohio, N.Y. Soc. Cardiovasc. Surgery, N.Y. Soc. Electron Microscopists, Cuyahoga County Med. Soc., Cleve. Soc. Pathologists, The Oxygen Soc., Sigma Xi. Home: PO Box 3125 340 5th Ave Half Moon Bay CA 94019-3125 Personal E-mail: abelrobertsonmd@yahoo.com.

ROBERTSON, ANDREW, dancer; b. Carleton Place, Ontario, Can. Student, Nat. Ballet Sch., Toronto, Royal Winnipeg Ballet Sch. With Royal Winnipeg Ballet; mem. corps de ballet N.Y.C. Ballet, 1992—98, 2000—; with Am. Ballet Theatre, 1998—2000. Dancer (ballets) Chaconne, A Midsummer Nights Dream, The Nutcracker, Prodigal Son, Tschaikovsky Ste No. 3, Symphonic Dances, Concerti Armonici, West Side Story Ste., Variations Sérieuses. Office: NYC Ballet NY State Theatre 20 Lincoln Ctr Plz New York NY 10023-6913

ROBERTSON, ANDREW, advertising executive; b. Zimbabwe; Degree in econ., London U. Joined as media planner Ogilvy & Mather, London, 1982, account mgr., bd. dirs., 1986—89, mgmt. supr., new bus. dir., 1989; group account dir. J. Walter Thompson, London, 1989—90; CEO WCRS, London, 1990—95; mng. dir. Abbott Mead Vickers BBDO, London, 1995—99; CEO, pres. BBDO N. Am., NYC, 2001—04; pres. BBDO Worldwide, NYC, 2002—04, CEO, pres., 2004—. Office: BBDO Worldwide Inc 1285 Ave of the Americas New York NY 10019-6028

ROBERTSON, ANDREW WHITMORE, historian; b. Boston, June 19, 1951; s. Eugene Corley and Olivia Cooney Robertson; m. Wendy Lynn Wall, Mar. 17, 1962; children: Laura Joyce, Thaddeus Daniel Wall. PhD, Oxford U., Eng., 1987. Assoc. prof. history Grad. Ctr. and Lehman Coll., N.Y.C., 1998—. Vis. prof. history Calif. Inst. of Tech., Pasadena, 1993—96; O'Connor vis. prof. Am. Instns. Colgate U., 2003—04; vis. prof. history UCLA, 1996—98. Lectr. N.Y. Speakers in the Humanities, N.Y.C., 1999—2003. Mem.: Am. Antiquarian Soc. Episcopalian. Achievements include research in 1st Democratization Project, 1787-1824. Office: Grad Ctr CUNY 365 Fifth Aven New York NY

ROBERTSON, ARMAND JAMES, II, judge; b. San Diego, Sept. 23, 1937; s. Armand James and Muriel H. R.; m. Marion Sperry, Aug. 11, 1962; children: Armand James, Laura Marie. A.M. in Econs, Stanford U., 1960; LL.B., Harvard U., 1965. Bar: Calif. 1966. Law clk. to Charles M. Merrill, U.S. Ct. Appeals (9th cir.), 1965-66; assoc. firm Howard, Prim, Rice, Nemerovski, Canady & Pollak, San Francisco, 1966-71, ptnr., 1971-77; dir. Howard, Rice, Nemerovski, Canady, Robertson & Falk (P.C.), San Francisco, 1977-95; judge of the Superior Ct. City and County of San Francisco, 1995—. Bd. dirs. St. Francis Found., 1996—, chmn., 1999—. Lt. (j.g.) USN, 1960-62. Mem. Am. Law Inst., ABA (antitrust sect.), CPR Inst. for Dispute Resolution, Phi Beta Kappa. Home: Edgewood Ave San Francisco CA 94117-3713 Office: San Francisco Superior Ct 400 Mcallister St Rm 210 San Francisco CA 94102-4512

ROBERTSON, BEVERLY CARRUTH, retired steel company executive; b. Texarkana, Ark., May 16, 1922; s. Glenn C. Robertson (dec.); m. Ruth Mulcare, Oct. 31, 1945 (dec. Oct. 1993); children: Glenn J., Beverly R. Dodds, Rebecca A. Robertson Deans; m. Charlotte Doty Lawler, June 2, 1995. In sales Nat. Supply Co., Laurel, Miss., 1941-51; purchasing agt. Kirby Petroleum Co., Houston, 1951-54; exec. v.p. mktg. Lone Star Steel Co., Dallas, 1954-85, exec. v.p., 1985-86; pres., dir., chief exec. officer LSSCO Trading Corp., 1985-86; owner BSEER Enterprises, Dallas, 1986—; ptnr. Clayton Equipment Co., Dallas, 1992-97, retired, 1997—. Chmn. Sir Alec Inc., 1985-94; cons. Pipeco, Inc., Houston, 1986-88; exec. v.p. mktg. and procurement Nat. Pipe and Tube Co., Houston, 1988-89; pres., CEO Tex. Am. Pipe & Supply Co., Inc., Dallas, 1989—; cons. Ipsco Steel, Inc., Camanche, Iowa, 1991-92. Served to capt. USAF, 1943-46, ETO. Named Supplier of Yr. Petroleum Industry Buyers group Nat. Assn. Purchasing Mgmt., 1982 Mem. Dallas Country Club, Dallas Petroleum Club. Republican. Episcopalian. Home: PO Box 12688 Dallas TX 75225-0688

ROBERTSON, CHARLES JAMES, museum director emeritus; b. Houston, Sept. 12, 1934; s. Charles James and Felide Corinne (O'Brien) R. BA, U. Va., Charlottesville, 1956; MA, Harvard U., 1958; student, U. London Courtauld Inst., 1960; JD, George Washington U., 1964. Atty. Dow, Lohnes & Albertson, Washington, 1964-69; adminstr. Richard H. Chamberlain, M.D. & Assoc., Phila., 1969-75; assoc. dir. N.C. Mus. Art, Raleigh, 1975-77; deputy dir. Smithsonian Am. Art Mus., Washington, 1977—2001. Treas., exec. com. Am. Assn. Mus., Washington, 1982-84; mem. adv. com. Octagon House Mus., Washington, 1989-97, chmn. 1993-96; bd. dirs. Victorian Soc. in Am., Phila., 1990—, v.p., 1994-2000; mem. Hist. Preservation Rev. Bd. of the Dist. of Columbia, 1992-2004; bd. regents Am. Archtl. Found., Washington, 1993-96; trustee Cosmos Club Historic Preservation Found., Washington, 1993—, treas., 1999—2003. Contbr. articles to profl. jours. Pres. Dupont Circle Conservancy, Washington, 1978-92; v.p., bd. mem., Dupont Circle Citizens Assn. Washington, 1980-83, 86. Recipient Rumrill fellowship Harvard U., Cambridge, Mass., 1956-57. Mem. Cosmos Club, Phi Beta Kappa, Phi Pi Theta, Delta Theta Phi.

ROBERTSON, DAVID, physician, scientist, educator; b. Sylvia, Tenn., May 23, 1947; s. David Herlie and Lucille Luther (Bowen) R.; m. Rose Marie Stevens, Oct. 30, 1976; 1 child, Rose. BA, Vanderbilt U., 1969, MD, 1973. Diplomate Am. Bd. Internal. Medicine, Am. Bd. Clin. Pharmacology. Intern Johns Hopkins U., Balt., 1973-74, asst. resident, 1974-75, asst. chief svc. in medicine, 1977-78; fellow in clin. pharmacology Vanderbilt U., Nashville, 1975-77, asst. prof. medicine and pharmacology, 1978-82, assoc. prof., 1982-86, prof., 1986—, prof. neurology, 1991—, Elton Yates prof. autonomic disorders, 1998—, dir. clin. rsch. ctr., 1987—; dir. Ctr. Space Physiology and Medicine, 1989—, Med. Sci. Tng. Program, 1993—2003; mem. staff Vanderbilt Hosp., Burroughs Wellcome scholar in clin. pharmacology, 1985-91. Author: (with B.M. Greene and G.J. Taylor) Problems in Internal Medicine, 1980, (with C.R. Smith) Manual of Clinical Pharmacology, 1981, (with Italo Biaggioni) Disorders of the Autonomic Nervous System, 1995, (with Italo Biaggioni, Geoffrey Burnstock and Phillip A. Low) Primer on the Autonomic Nervous System, 1996, 2d edit., 2004; editor-in-chief: Drug Therapy, 1991-94; assoc. editor, Jour. Pharmacol. Exptl. Therapy, 1998—; mem. editl. bd. Am. Jour. Medicine, Autonomic Neuroscience, Clin. Pharm. and Therapeutics, Clin. Autonomic Rsch., Am. Jour. Med. Sci., Current Topics in Pharmacology.

Logan Clendening fellow, Reykjavik, Iceland, 1969; Adolph-Morsbach grantee Bonn, Germany, 1968; recipient Rsch. Career Devel. award NIH, 1981, Grant W. Liddle award for leadership in rsch., 1991; recipient Tchg. award Nat. Program Dir.'s Assn., 2003. Fellow Am. Heart Assn. Coun. Hypertension and Circulation, ACP (tchg. and rsch. scholar 1978-81), Am. Autonomic Soc. (pres. 1992-94); mem. Am. Acad. Neurology, Soc. Neurosci., Am. Inst. Aeronautics and Astronautics, U.S. Pharmacopeial Conv., Nat. Bd. Med. Examinars, Aerospace Med. Assn. (space sta. sci. and applications com.), NASA (microgravity human rsch. com.), FDA Consortium Rare Disorders, Rare Disorder Network, Am. Fedn. Med. Rsch., Am. Soc. Clin. Investigation, Assn. Am. Physicians, Assn. Patient-Oriented Rsch. (bd. dirs., pres.), So. Soc. Clin. Investigation, Am. Soc. Clin. Pharmacology and Therapeutics, Phi Beta Kappa, Alpha Omega Alpha (hon., bd. dirs. 1995—. William Darby award 2000). Baptist. Home: 4003 Newman Pl Nashville TN 37204-4308 Office: Vanderbilt U Clin Rsch Ctr 21st Ave S Nashville TN 37232-2195 Office Phone: 615-343-6499.

ROBERTSON, DAVID, conductor; b. Santa Monica, Calif. Student in French horn and composition, Royal Acad. Music. Resident condr. Jerusalem Symphony Orch., 1985—87; music dir. Ensemble Interconteporain, Paris, 1992—2000; musical dir. Orchestre Nat. de Lyon, France, 2000—; artistic dir. Lyon Auditorium, 2000. Guest condr. Minn. Orch., 2001, Phila. Orch., 2001, Chgo. Symphony, 2001, Boston Symphony, 2001, San Francisco Symphony, 2001, NDR Symphony Orch. Hamburg, Germany, 2001, Royal Concertgebouw Orch., 2001, Orch. del Maggio Musicale Fiorentino, 2001, London Symphony Orch., BBC Symphony, Halle Orch., Bayerisches Staatorchester, Munich, Berlin Staatskapelle, La Scala Philharm., Boston Symphony, Chgo. Orch., NY Philharm., L.A. Philharm., many others. Active outreach programs Ensemble Intercontemporain, Orchestre Nat. de Lyon, Paris Conservatory, Juilliard Sch., Tanglewood, Aspen Music Festival. Named Condr. of Yr., Musical Am., 2000; recipient Seaver/Nat. Endowment for Arts Condr. award, 1997. Office: 82 rue de Bonnel 69431 Lyon France Office Fax: 33 4 78 60 13 08.

ROBERTSON, DAVID ALLAN, JR., English educator; b. Chgo., July 30, 1915; s. David Allan Robertson and Anne Victoria Knobel; m. Beridge Ruth Leigh Mallory, June 18, 1940 (dec. Sept. 1953); children: Anne (Mrs. Robert Acheson Spencer), Susan, Allan; m. Victoria Adams Bryer, Oct. 10, 1964 (div. June 1988); children: Struan, Isabel, Samuel; m. Harriet Cooper Frothingham, Dec. 21, 1991. AB, Princeton U., 1936, MA, 1939, PhD, 1940. Instr. English, Barnard Coll. Columbia U., N.Y.C., 1940-42, 45-47, asst. prof., 1947-50, assoc. prof., 1950-56, prof., 1956-68, McIntosh prof., 1968-86, prof. emeritus, 1986—, chmn. dept., 1956-59, 64-67, 1975-77. Mem. commn. on English Coll. Entrance Exam Bd., 1959-64; mem. adv. bd. Victorian Studies, 1959-66, 75-87; mem. adv. coun. dept. English, Princeton U., 1970-92, chmn., 1977-82, libr., 1973-76, mem. dept. art and archaeology, 1974-85, chmn., 1977-82. Author: George Mallory, 1969, reprinted, 1999, Sir Charles Eastlake and the Victorian Art World, 1978, North of India, 1999; contbr. articles and revs. to profl. jours. Mem. coun. Friends of Princeton U. Libr., 1976—, chmn., 1991-95. Lt. comdr. USNR, 1942—, ret. Henry fellow Trinity Coll., Cambridge U., 1937-38, Howard Found. fellow, 1953-54. Mem. MLA, English Inst. (asst. sec. 1946, sec. 1947-48, editor English Inst. Essays 1946-48), Century Assn., Am. Alpine Club (co-editor jour. 1947-52), Nassau Club. Home: 75 Arreton Rd Princeton NJ 08540

ROBERTSON, DONNA VIRGINIA, architect, educator, dean; b. Richmond, Va., Feb. 26, 1952; d. Charles Henry and Florence (Givens) R.; m. Robert M. McAnulty, May 24, 1986; 1 child, Robertson. Cert. theater arts studies, Webster Coll., St. Louis, 1972; BA, Stanford U., 1974; MArch, U. Va., 1978. Registered arch., N.Y. Asst. prof. Harvard U., Cambridge, Mass., 1983-84; asst. prof. Barnard Coll. Columbia U., N.Y.C., 1984-92; dean Sch. Arch. Tulane U., New Orleans, 1992-96; dean Coll. Arch. Ill. Inst. Tech., Chgo., 1996—; ptnr. Robertson McAnulty Archs., Chgo., 1986—; owner Donna V. Robertson Archs., N.Y.C., 1982-86; sr. designer Kohn Pedersen Fox Archs., N.Y.C., 1980-82, Mitchell Giurgola Archs., N.Y.C., 1979-80. Adj. asst. prof. Barnard Coll., Columbia U., N.Y., 1982-83, dir. arch. program, fall 1985-92; vis. critic in design Harvard U., Cambridge, fall 1990, U. Va., Charlottesville, fall 1991; organizer, panelist Arch. and Lit. Symposium, N.Y.C., 1985; jury chair Am. Collegiate Schs. Arch., Boston, 1996; mem. bd. dirs. Nat. Archtl. Accrediting Bd., 2000—. Prin. arch. Fishback residence, New Orleans, Sunkel residence, New Orleans, Pisar residence, N.Y.C., Dachs residence, N.Y.C.; pres. Nat. Archtl. Accrediting Bd., 2002—. Mem. AIA (juror annual design hons. awards 1996, educators and practitioners network), Chgo. Network-Internat. Women's Forum, Raven Soc., Arts Club (Chgo.), Phi Beta Kappa. Office: Ill Inst Tech 3360 S State St Chicago IL 60616 E-mail: robertson@iit.edu.

ROBERTSON, EDDIE B. biologist, educator; b. Grayling, Mich., Apr. 29, 1947; s. Thomas E. and Ruth Mersereau Robertson; m. Sylvia Rutledge, June 21, 1969; children: Charity Robertson Bracewell, Nathan Rutledge. BS, Alma Coll., 1965—69; MS, U. of Minn., 1969—72, PhD, 1972—75. Palynologist Robertson Rsch. (N.A.) Ltd., Calgary, Canada, 1974—76, Mobil Oil Co., Dallas, 1976—77, Robertson Rsch., Houston, 1977—80, Phillips Petroleum Co., Bartlesville, Okla., 1980—86; prof. of biology Reinhardt Coll., Waleska, Ga., 1986—. Lay leader, united Meth. men Waleska United Meth. Ch., Waleska, Ga., 1986—2003. Mem.: Bot. Soc. of Am., Am. Assn. of Stratigraphic Palynologists (councilor 2002—03). Office: Reinhardt Coll 7300 Reinhardt Coll Cir Waleska GA 30183 E-mail: ebr@reinhardt.edu.

ROBERTSON, EDWARD NEIL, dentist; b. Rumford, Maine, Mar. 3, 1950; s. Edward Norris and Edith Louise (Kirk) Robertson; m. Susan E. Valentine, July 24, 2004; 1 child, Olivia; children: Christie Portia, Juliet Melissa(dec.), Jenni Celia, Edward Noah, Jessica Edith. BS in Biology, Antioch Coll., Yellow Springs, Ohio, 1973; MS in Epidemiology, Ohio State U., 1977; DDS, Case Western Res. U., 1983. Faculty adv. to med. students Ohio State U., Columbus, 1975-77; rsch. cons. Ohio Dept. Health, Columbus, 1976-77; rsch. assoc. UCLA, 1977; epidemiologic/statis. cons. L.A., 1977; medic J & L Steel Corp., Cleve., 1979-84; pvt. practice Cleveland Heights, Ohio, 1983-94, Lyndhurst, Ohio, 1995-2000. Mem. adj. faculty Cuyahoga C.C., Cleve., 1986-88; assoc. prof. Sch. Dentistry Case Western Res. U., 1991-96; asst. prof. Case Western Res. U. Sch. Dentistry, Cleve., 1997—; pvt. contractor Indian Health Svc. Dental Clinic, Pine Ridge, S.D., 1999-2000; clin. instr. U. Md. Dental Sch., 1999-00. Pres. Robertson Family Assn. of N.Am., 1986-88. Recipient numerous rsch. grants. Mem.: ADA, Greater Cleve. Dental Soc., Ohio Dental Assn., Acad. Gen. Dentistry, Midwest Pain Soc., Acad. Laser Surgery, U.S. Dental Inst., Am. Chronic Pain Assn., Ohio Acad. Gen. Dentistry, Am. Pain Soc., Am. Acad. Pain Mgmt. Avocations: soccer, cross country skiing, camping, canoeing, sailing. Office: 24755 Chagrin Blvd Ste 145 Beachwood OH 44122-5692 Office Phone: 216-468-0041. E-mail: dentalned@aol.com.

ROBERTSON, EDWIN DAVID, lawyer; b. Roanoke, Va., July 5, 1946; s. Edwin Traylor and Norma Burns (Bowles) R.; m. Anne Littelle Ferratt, Sept. 7, 1968, 1 child, Thomas Therit. BA with honors, U. Va., 1968, LLB, 1971. Bar: N.Y. 1972, U.S. Ct. Appeals (2d cir.) 1972, U.S. Dist. Ct. (ea. and so. dists.) N.Y. 1973, U.S. Supreme Ct. 1975, U.S. Dist. Ct. (ea. dist.) Mich. 1986. Assoc. Cadwalader, Wickersham & Taft, N.Y.C., 1972-80, ptnr., 1980—. Bd. dirs. Early Music Found. N.Y.C., 1983-99, chmn., 1993-99; bd. dirs. Oratorio Soc. of N.Y.C., 1988—, sec., 1991—. 1st lt. USAF, 1971-72. Echols scholar. Mem. ABA (ho. of dels. 2004—), Fed. Bar Coun., N.Y. County Lawyers Assn. (chmn. bankruptcy com. 1983-87, chmn. fin. com., bd. dirs. 1985-88, 95-99, 2000—, investment com. 1992—, exec. com. 1996—, treas. 2001-2002, v.p. 2002-2004, pres.-elect 2004—), N.Y. State Bar Assn. (ho. of dels. 2001-2004, nominatng com. 2002-), Assn. Bar City N.Y., Soc. Colonial Wars, Jefferson Soc., Echols Scholar, judge, Ct. of Review, Order of Coif, Phi Beta Kappa, Phi Kappa Psi. Republican. Episcopalian. Home: 315 E 72nd St New York NY 10021-4625 Office: Cadwalader Wickersham & Taft 100 Maiden Ln New York NY 10038-4818 Office Phone: 212-504-6000. E-mail: darob@cwt.com.

ROBERTSON, EDWIN OSCAR, banker; b. Speedwell, Tenn., May 28, 1923; s. John M. and Etta (Mayes) R.; m. Althea Maxine Moyers, June 3, 1948 (dec. Nov. 1970); children: Edwin Glenn, Craig Eric; m. Sarah Alice Parkman, Nov. 16, 1974. BS in Agr., U. Tenn., 1950, LLD (hon.), Lincoln Meml. U., 1984. Supr. vets. farm tng. County of Claiborne, Tazewell, Tenn., 1950-52; agr. rep. Citizens Bank, New Tazewell, Tenn., 1952; v.p., agr. rep. Nat. Bank, Middlesboro, Ky., 1953-57; chmn. bd., chief exec. officer Comml. Bancgroup, Inc., Harrogate, Tenn., 1976—; pres., chief exec. officer Comml. Bank, Middlesboro, 1958—, chmn., CEO Harrogate, 1988—. Chmn. bd. Comml. Bank, Harrogate, 1976—, chmn., CEO, 1988—; mem. Govt. Task Force on Banking, Ky., 1983; trustee Lincoln Meml. U., Harrogate, 1974—; bd. dirs. Cumberland Devel. Corp., Middlesboro. Gov. Ruritan Nat. Tenn. Dist., 1954-55; bd. dirs. Middlesboro Indsl. Commn., 1962—, Ky. C. of C., 1983-84. With USAF, 1943-45. Mem. Rotary. Republican. Baptist. Avocations: farming, horseback riding. Home: PO Box 100 Harrogate TN 37752-0100

ROBERTSON, HORACE BASCOMB, JR., retired law educator; b. Charlotte, N.C., Nov. 13, 1923; s. Horace Bascomb and Ruth (Montgomery) R.; m. Patricia Lavell, Aug. 11, 1947; children— Mark L., James D. BS, U.S. Naval Acad., 1945; JD, Georgetown U., 1953; MS, George Washington U., 1968. Commd. ensign U.S. Navy, 1945, advanced through grades to rear adm., 1972; line officer, 1945-55; law specialist, 1955-68; spl. counsel to sec. Navy, Washington, 1964-67, judge adv., 1968-76; spl. counsel to chief naval ops. Washington, 1970-72; dep. judge adv. gen. Navy Dept., Washington, 1972-75, judge adv. gen., 1975-76; prof. law Duke U., 1976-89, sr. assoc. dean, 1986-89, ret., 1990; Chas H. Stockton chair of internat. law Naval War Coll., Newport, R.I., 1991-92. Decorated D.S.M. Mem. ABA, Am. Soc. Internat. Law. Home: 9 Silver Maple Ct Durham NC 27705-5642 Office: Duke U Sch Law Durham NC 27708 Office Phone: 919-613-7038. Business E-Mail: hbr@law.duke.edu.

ROBERTSON, HUGH DUFF, lawyer; b. Grosse Pointe, Mich., Mar. 14, 1957; s. Hugh Robertson and Louise (Grey) Bollinger; m. Mercedes Dano, May 3, 1997. BBA in Fin., U. Wis., Whitewater, 1978; JD, Whittier Coll., 1982. Bar: Calif. 1983, U.S. Tax Ct. 1984, U.S. Supreme Court, 1999. Pres., CEO, A. Morgan Maree Jr. & Assocs., Inc., L.A., 1979—. Mem. ABA (forum com. on entertainment 1982—), State Calif., L.A. County Bar Assn., Beverly Hills Bar Assn., Acad. TV Arts and Scis., Am. Film Inst., Phi Alpha Delta. Republican. Episcopalian. Avocations: sports, swimming. Office: A Morgan Maree Jr & Assocs 1125 Gayley Ave Los Angeles CA 90024-3403

ROBERTSON, HUGH DUNBAR, biomedical researcher, consultant; b. Boston, June 12, 1943; s. Randal McGavock and Florence French (Dunbar) R.; m. Janet Abernathy, July 6, 1968; children: Andrew Dunbar, Michael Henry. BA in Life Scis., Harvard U., 1964; PhD in Genetics, Rockefeller U., 1969. Whitney postdoctoral fellow MRC Lab. of Molecular Biology, Cambridge, Eng., 1969-72; asst. prof. genetics Rockefeller U., N.Y.C., 1972-78, assoc. prof. genetics, 1978-88; assoc. prof. biochemistry Med. Coll. Cornell U., N.Y.C., 1989-97, prof. biochemistry Med. Coll., 1997—. Chair sci. adv. bd. Enzo BioChem, Inc., N.Y.C., 1981-87; co-founder, chair sci. adv. bd. Innovir Labs., Inc., N.Y.C., 1989-98; organizer Cold Spring Harbor (N.Y.) RNA meeting, 1983, 84, 86, 93; cons. in field. Mem. editl. bd. Virology, 1982-88, RNA Jour., 1995-99; contbr. more than 115 articles to profl. jours. on RNA rsch. Patentee ribozyme compositions and methods. Bd. dirs. Christodora Charitable Found., N.Y.C., 1984—, v.p., 1995-96; mem. Canterbury Choral Soc., N.Y.C., 1973—, bd. chair, 1989-95, pres., 1988-89. Recipient Rsch. Excellence award McKnight Found., 1983; grantee NIH, 1979—, NSF, 1973-91, USDA, 1978-84, N.Y. State, 1993—, Am. Cancer Soc., 1978-82—. Mem. Am. Soc. Virology (founding mem., 1982—, admission com. 1982-88), RNA Soc. (founding mem. 1993—), Appalachian Mountain Club, Mass. Audubon Soc. Democrat. Episcopalian. Achievements include discovery of first two RNA processing enzymes; replication mode for viroid-like pathogens, including that causing human hepatitis delta; hepatitis C translation start signals. Avocations: choral singing, hiking near country home in Berkshire County, Mass., research on RNA evolution. Home: 430 E 63rd St New York NY 10021-7918 Office: Cornell U Weill Med Coll Dept Biochemistry 1300 York Ave New York NY 10021-4805 E-mail: hdrober@mail.med.cornell.edu.

ROBERTSON, J. MARTIN, lawyer; b. Danville, Ill., Apr. 30, 1952; s. Calloway Middleton and Barbara (Holland) R. AB in Polit. Sci., Miami U., Oxford, Ohio, 1974; JD, U. Cin., 1978; postgrad., Ohio State U., 1978-79. Bar: Ohio 1978, U.S. Dist. Ct. (so. dist.) Ohio 1980, U.S. Dist. Ct. (no. dist.) Calif. 1984, Calif. 1989, U.S. Dist. Ct. (so. dist.) Calif. 1989, U.S. Dist. Ct. (ea. and ctrl. dists.) Calif. 1992, U.S. Ct. Appeals (9th cir.) 1992, U.S. Dist. Ct. (no. dist.) Tex. 1998, U.S. Ct. Appeals (5th cir.) 1998, Tex. 1999, Alaska 2001, U.S. Dist. Ct. Alaska 2002. Atty. Southeastern Ohio Legal Services, Chillicothe and Steubenville, 1979-80; staff atty., asst. dist. counsel Dept. of the Army, C.E. Office of Counsel, Huntington, W.Va. and Jacksonville, Fla., 1980-83; asst. atty. gen. State of Ohio, Columbus, 1983-84; trial atty., sr. trial atty. Dept. of Navy Office of Gen. Counsel, Washington and San Francisco, 1984-92; sr. assoc. mem. Ware & Freidenrich, Palo Alto, Calif., 1992—93; ptnr. mem. Gray, Cary, Ware & Freidenrich, Palo Alto, 1994-97, ptnr. San Francisco, 1997—2003; mem. Robertson Law Firm, Sausalito, Calif., 2003—. Mem. ABA (natural resources law sect.), Bar Assn. San Francisco (environment and water law sect.). Office: Robertson Law Firm 1001 Bridgeway #515 Sausalito CA 94965 E-mail: jmr@mrobertsonlaw.com.

ROBERTSON, JACK CLARK, accounting educator; b. Marlin, Tex., Apr. 27, 1943; s. Rupert Cook and Lois Lucille (Rose) R.; m. Caroline Susan Hughes, Oct. 23, 1965; children: Sara Ellen, Elizabeth Hughes. Student, Rice U., 1961-63; BBA with honors, U. Tex., Austin, 1965, M in Profl. Acctg., 1967; PhD, U. N.C., 1970. CPA, Tex. Tax acct. Humble Oil and Refining Co., Houston, 1964-65; auditor Peat, Marwick, Mitchell & Co., Houston, 1965-66; acct. Wade, Barton, Marsh CPAs, Austin, Tex., 1966-67; from asst. prof. to prof. emeritus U. Tex., Austin, 1970—2003, prof. emeritus, 2003—. Acad. assoc. Coopers & Lybrand, N.Y.C., 1975-76; acad. fellow U.S. Securities and Exchange Commn. Office of the Chief Acct., Washington, 1982-83; Erskine fellow U. Canterbury, Christchurch, New Zealand, 1988; tng. the trainers instr. Vilnius, Lithuania, 1993; lectr. in field. Contbr. articles to profl. jours. Lay reader St. Matthews Episcopal Ch., Austin, 1972-75, mem. vestry, 1973-75, 77-79, 84-86, treas., 1974-75, 77-96, chmn. bldg. fund, 1976-87, chmn. everymen. canvass, 1980, sr. warden, 1986; del. Diocese of Tex. Coun., 1993-95; Trompetista El Grupo Valor Latino, 2000—, lector laico, 2000—03, Miembro comite del obispo Iglesia San Francisco de Asis, 2000—03, treas., 2002-03; trustee Austin Chamber Music Ctr., 2003—. Mem. AICPA, Am. Acctg. Assn. (sec.-treas. auditing sect. 1976-77, v.p. auditing sect. 1977-78, pres. auditing sect. 1978-79, chmn. auditing stds. com. 1980-81, chmn. SEC liaison com. 1983-84, historian auditing sect. 1999-2001), Tex. Soc. CPAs (vice-chmn., profl. ethics com. 1986-94, 95-97, Presdl. citation 1994), Assn. Cert. Fraud Examiners (regent emeritus, cert.), Phi Kappa Phi, Beta Gamma Sigma, Beta Alpha Psi. E-mail: jcrobertson@austin.rr.com.

ROBERTSON, JAMES, judge; b. Cleve., May 18, 1938; s. Frederick Irving and Doris Mary (Byars) R.; m. Berit Selma Persson, Sept. 19, 1959; children: Stephen Irving, Catherine Anne, Peter Arvid. AB, Princeton U., 1959; LLB, George Washington U., 1965. Bar: D.C. 1966, U.S. Supreme Ct. 1969. Assoc. Wilmer, Cutler & Pickering, Washington, 1965-69, ptnr., 1973-94; U.S. dist. judge D.C., 1994—; chief counsel Lawyers Com. for Civil Rights Under Law, Jackson, Miss., 1969-70, dir. Washington, 1970-72, co-chmn., 1985-87. Co-chmn. D.C. Lawyers Com. for Civil Rights Under Law, Washington, 1982-84; mem. com. on grievances U.S. Dist. Ct., 1988-92, vice chmn., 1989-92; bd. dirs. South Africa Legal Svcs. and Edn. Project, Inc., 1987-01, pres., 1989-94; bd. dirs. D.C. Prisoners Legal Svcs., Inc., 1992-94. Editor in chief George Washington Law Rev., 1964-65. Lt. USN, 1959-64. Fellow Am. Coll. Trial Lawyers, Am. Bar Found.; mem. ABA, D.C. Bar (bd. govs. 1986-93, pres.-elect 1990-92, pres. 1991-92), Am. Law Inst. Home: 3318 N St NW Washington DC 20007-2807 Office: US Courthouse Rm 6315 333 Constitution Ave NW Washington DC 20001-2854

ROBERTSON, JAMES MUELLER, civil engineer, educator; b. Champaign, Ill., Apr. 18, 1916; s. William Spence and Gertrude (Mueller) R.; m. Margaret Dillinger, Oct. 23, 1943; children: Bruce D., Alan S. BSCE, U. Ill., 1938; MS, U. Iowa, 1940, PhD, 1941. Asst. physicist U.S. Navy Dept., Taylor Model Basin, 1941-42; mem. engring. faculty, dir. Water Tunnel Pa. State U., 1942-54; rsch. engr. Douglas Aircraft, Santa Monica, Calif., 1944-45; prof. theoretical and applied mechanics U. Ill., Urbana, 1954-82, acting head dept., 1982, prof. emeritus, 1982—. Cons. U.S. Army, various indsl. orgns., 1957-73; vis. lectr. hydraulic engring. Kans. State U., 1967; course instr. TAPPI, 1969; lectr. U. Tenn. Space Inst., 1973; vis. prof. civil engring. Colo. State U., 1974; adj. prof. mech. engring. Naval Postgrad. Sch., 1984; bd. dirs. Internat. Mgmt. and Engring. Ltd., Colo., Terabyte, Inc., Boulder, Colo. Author: Hydrodynamics in Theory and Application, 1965; contbr. numerous articles to profl. publs. Sec., v.p., pres. Summit County Sr. Citizens, Frisco, Colo., 1983-97; sec. Skylin Six Area Agy. on Aging Coun., Frisco, 1986-95, chair, 1995-96; bd. dirs. Breckenridge (Colo.) Music Inst., 1984-95, sec., 1989-93, mem. adv. coun., 1995-2002. Recipient Alumni Honor award, Coll. Engring., 1989. Fellow ASCE (life, Hilgard prize 1955), ASME (life); mem. Sigma Xi, Phi Eta Sigma, Chi Epsilon, Tau Beta Pi, Phi Kappa Phi. Achievements include co-design of hydrodynamics research water tunnel at Pennsylvania State University. Home: 14091 E Marina Dr Apt 202 Aurora CO 80014-3712

ROBERTSON, JAMES THOMAS, neurosurgeon; b. McComb, Miss., Apr. 5, 1931; s. Clyde Aubrey and Catherine Roberta (Darville) R.; m. Valeria Ann Brower, Nov. 26, 1952; children: James T. Jr., Elizabeth, Catherine, Clay, Roberta, Daniel. BS, Southwestern U., 1951; MD, U. Tenn., 1954. Diplomat Am. Bd. Neurol. Surgeons, 1962. Intern Bapt. Meml. Hosp., Memphis, 1955; resident U. Tenn., Memphis, 1956-59, Peter Bent Brigham & Children's Hosp., Boston, 1959-60; chief neurosurgery Travis AFB, Fairfield, Calif., 1960-63; asst. chief nuerosurgery Lackland AFB, San Antonio, 1963-64; assoc. physician Semmes Murphey Clinic, Memphis, 1964-65; asst. prof. neurosurgery U. Tenn., 1964-69, assoc. prof., 1969-73, prof., chmn. dept. neurosurgery, 1973—98, prof., 1998—. Chmn. dept. neurosurgery U. Tenn., Memphis, 1973-97. Editor: Subarachnoid Hemorrhage and Cerebroscacular Vasopasm, 1975; contbr. articles to mags. Vice chair Rep. Party, Shelby County, Memphis, 1989-90, treas., DeSoto County, Miss., 1993; pres. Shelby County chpt. Am. Heart Assn., 1996, chmn. stroke coun., 1992-94. Capt. USNR, 1982-98. Recipient Disting. Alumni award U. Tenn., 1990, Rhodes Coll., 1994. Fellow Am. Coll. Surgeons (bd. govs. 1987-92); mem. Am. Assn. Neurol. Surgeons (pres. 1990-91), Congress Neurol. Surgeons (pres. 1975), Am. Acad. Neurol. Surgery (pres. 1988), Soc. Univ. Neurosrugeons (pres. 1965). Presbyterian. Avocations: gardening, fly fishing. Home: 8570 Jones Rd Olive Branch MS 38654-9001 Office: U Tenn 847 Monroe Ave # 427 Memphis TN 38103-4901 Office Phone: 901-448-6375. Personal E-mail: jrober52@aol.com.

ROBERTSON, JAMES WOOLSEY, lawyer; b. Ft. Sam Houston, Tex., Aug. 6, 1942; s. Robert Charles Lee and Marjorie Evelyn (Woolsey) R.; 1 child, William Angus; m. Laura Ann Koons, Apr. 24, 1993. BBA, U. Tex., 1966, JD, 1967. Bar: Tex.; cert. real estate law specialist. Ptnr. Locke Liddell & Sapp L.L.P., Houston, 1971—, chmn. fin. com., 1985-90, chmn. banking and real estate sect., 1992-98. Chancellor Episcopal Ch. Holy Spirit, Houston, 1984-92, trustee, 1984-87; bd. dirs., sec., chmn.-elect Lighthouse for the Blind, Houston, 1998—. Lt. comdr. USCGR, 1968-71. Mem. State Bar Tex., Houston Bar Assn., Houston Real Estate Lawyers Coun. Republican. Avocations: golf, fly fishing, skiing, hunting. Office: 600 Travis St Ste 3200 Houston TX 77002-3095

ROBERTSON, JERRY EARL, retired manufacturing company executive; b. Detroit, Oct. 25, 1932; s. Earl Howard and Nellie (Wright) R.; m. Joanne Alice Wesner, Sept. 3, 1955; children: Scott Clark, Lisa Kay, Stuart Todd. BS, Miami U., Oxford, Ohio, 1954; MS, U. Mich., 1956, PhD, 1959. With Minn. Mining & Mfg. Co., St. Paul, 1963-94, tech. dir. med. products div., 1973-74, dept. mgr. surg. products dept., 1974-75, gen. mgr. surg. products div., 1975-79, div. v.p. surg. products div., 1979-80, group v.p. health care products and services, 1980-84, exec. v.p. life scis. sector, 1984-86, exec. v.p. life scis. sector and corp. svcs., 1986-94; ret., 1994. Bd. dirs. Coherent, Inc., Choice Hotels Internat., Steris Corp. Bd. reference MAP Internat., Brunswick, Ga., 1986-94; bd. dirs. Project HOPE, 1988-98, Manor Care Inc., 1989-98, Cardinal Health Distbn., Inc., 1991-99. Mem. Pharm. Mfrs. Assn. (bd. dirs. 1984-89), Health Industry Mfrs. Assn. (bd. dirs. 1982-91, chmn. 1990-91). Unitarian Universalist. Office: Minn World Trade Ctr 30 7th St E Ste 3050 Saint Paul MN 55101-4921

ROBERTSON, JOEL THOMAS, railroad executive; b. Milo, Maine, Aug. 30, 1947; s. Paul Russell Robertson and Denice Luella Stevens; m. Bonita Louise Hosford, July 29, 1966 (div. Nov. 1968); m. Patricia Rae Willinski, Mar. 14, 1970 (div. May 1990); children: Jason Thomas, April Dawn Robertson Bishop; m. Marie Paulette Melvin, Dec. 31, 1994; 1 child, Stuart Spencer Stratton. BS, W.Va. State U., 1982; MS, Marshall U., 1986. Cert. safety mgr. World Safety Orgn., 85. Agt. Bangor (Maine) & Aroosook R.R., 1966—70, Can. Pacific Rwy., St. John, 1970—80; hazardous materials inspector Fed. RR Adminstrn., Washington, 1980—2001, hazardous materials specialist, 2001—02; ptnr. Robertson & Assocs., LLC, 2002—; regulatory specialist Am. Honda Co. Inc., 2004—. Transp. cons. Union Carbide Corp., Danbury, Conn., 1989—90; expert witness/accident investigator Collins, Collins & Dinardo, Buffalo, 1989—; bus. devel. cons. Brothers Coal Cons., Charleston, W.Va., 1989—90, TransMar Inc., Spokane, Wash., 1994, Coal Tech. Corp., Bristol, Va., 1989—97; appearance on nat. news program ABC Wide World News Tonight, 1985; interviewed by Tass Soviet News Agy., 89; owner Guest Nat. Soc. of Profl. Engrs., Nat. Press Club, Washington, 1989; founder, devel. dir. Stuart Spencer Stratton Meml. Found., unit of Nat. Heritage Found., 2002—; regional sci. fair judge and scholarship founder for environ. scis. INTEL N.W., 2000—; adj. tech. faculty Marshall U., Transp. Safety Inst., 1987—; adv, U.S. Senate Murray U.S. Dept. State, Volpentest Hammer Tng. Inst., Transportation Safety Security, Richland, Wash.; leader, organizer Multi-Agy. Internat. Transp. Safety-Security Strike Force, 2000; internat. trade and devel. cons. Govt. Cameroon, West Africa; loaned exec. Combined Fed. Campaign, 2001—02; assoc. Oreg. Fed. Bd., 2001—02; mem. exec. potential program USDA Grad. Sch. Leadership, 2002; internat. lectr. and citizen amb. China Assn. of Sci. and Tech., 1989; acting regional adminstr., acting staff dir. U.S. Hazardous Materials, 1994—2002. Contbr. articles to profl. publs. Organizer, master of ceremonies First Joint Chem. Industry/Rwy. Safety Symposium, W.Va., 1985, Celebration of Engring. Career Day, Huntington, W.Va., 1989; sci. advisor Bush White House Space Coun., Washington, 1989. Recipient Commendation, Gov. of W.Va., 1985, Superior Achievement award, U.S. DOT-FRA. Mem.: Am. Soc. Metals, Am. Inst. Hygiene Assn., Soc. Mechanical Engrs., AIChE, Am. Soc. Quality Control, Am. Soc. Safety Engrs., Am. Soc. Profl. Engrs. (exec. affiliate 1983—89), Engrs. Club of Huntington (pres. 1987—88), Kiwanis (pres. West Huntington chpt. 1989—90). Republican. Mem. Lds Ch. Avocations: fundraising activities, event organizing, photography, travel, writing. Address: 16505 A SE 1st St Ste 285 Vancouver WA 98684 Home: 32154 E Punkin Center Rd Hermiston OR 97838-7510 Office Phone: 360-873-2329. E-mail: joel@safety.specialist.com.

ROBERTSON, JOHN ARCHIBALD LAW, nuclear scientist; b. Dundee, Scotland, July 4, 1925; s. John Carr and Ellen (Law) R.; m. Betty-Jean Moffatt, June 26, 1954; children: Ean Stuart, Clare Deborah, Fiona Heather. BA, Cambridge (Eng.) U., 1950, MA, 1953. Sci. officer UK Atomic Energy Authority, Harwell, England, 1950-57; rsch. officer Atomic Energy Can. Ltd., Chalk River, Ont., Canada, 1957-63, head reactor materials br., 1963-70, dir. fuels and materials div., 1970-75, asst. to v.p., 1975-82; dir. program planning Atomic Energy Can. Ltd. (Rsch. Co. Head Office), 1982-85; cons., 1985—. Mem. Atomic Energy Control Bd.'s Adv. Com. on Nuc. Safety, 1988-97. Author: Irradiation Effects in Nuclear Fuels, 1969, Decide the Nuclear Issues for Yourself: Nuclear Need Not Be Unclear, 2000; editor: Jour. Nuclear Materials, 1967-71. Served to capt., Royal Engrs. Brit. and Indian armies, 1943-47. Recipient W.B. Lewis medal Can. Nuc. Assn., 1987, W.J. Kroll Zirconium medal W.J. Kroll Inst. for Extractive Metallurgy, 1993. Fellow Royal Soc. Can. Office Phone: 613-584-2765. E-mail: jalrober@magma.ca.

ROBERTSON, JOSEPH E., JR., ophthalmologist, educator; b. Jackson County, Ind., July 24, 1952; s. Joseph E. and Virginia Faye (Baxter) R.; children: Kathryn Faye, Charles Joseph. BS cum laude, Yale U., 1974; MD, Ind. U., 1978; MBA, U. Oreg., 1997. Diplomate Am. Bd. Ophthalmology. Intern Bapt. Med. Ctr., Birmingham, Ala., 1978-79; resident Oreg. Health Sci. U., Portland, 1979-82; pvt. practice Vancouver, Wash., 1982-83; fellow Oreg. Health Sci. U./Devers Hosp./Good Samaritan Hosp., Portland, 1983-84; vitreous surgery fellow Steve Charles, M.D., Memphis, 1984-85; asst. prof. Oreg. Health Sci. U., Portland, 1985-92, assoc. prof., 1992-97, prof., chmn. dept. ophthalmology, 1997—, interim dean, 2001—02, dean Sch. Medicine, 2003—. Contbr. articles to profl. jours., chpts. to books; editor videotapes. Apptd. mem. Oreg. Commn. for the Blind, 1988-94. Mem. Am. Acad. Ophthalmology (Oreg. rep. to coun. 1992-95, COVE com. 1988-93, skills transfer adv. com. 1994-98, nat. chair and state coord. Diabetes 2000), Oreg. Acad. Ophthalmology (pres. 1990-91), Univ. Med. Group (exec. com. 1997—, v.p. 1998—), Oreg. Med. Assn. Democrat. Presbyterian. Avocations: skiing, windsurfing, snowboarding, hiking, jogging. Office: Casey Eye Inst OHSU 3375 SW Terwilliger Blvd Portland OR 97239

ROBERTSON, JOSEPH EDMOND, grain processing company executive; b. Brownstown, Ind., Feb. 16, 1918; s. Roscoe Melvin and Edith Penina (Shields) R.; m. Virginia Faye Baxter, Nov. 23, 1941; 1 son, Joseph Edmond, Jr. *Wife Virginia Baxter, BS Kansas State University, Kentucky Colonel, and she is a member of Traveler's Century and Circumnavigator's Clubs. She provided many of the notes Joe Robertson used in writing On Kilroy's Trail, published and released October, 1998. Son Joe Jr, BS Yale 1974, MD Indiana University 1978, MBA University of Oregon, 1997. He is Dean of the Medical School and director of Casey Eye Institute at Oregon Health Science University, Portland Oregon. Grandchildren, Katie, 20, is enrolled in Dartmouth, and Charles Joseph, 18, attends St.Paul School.* BS, postgrad., Kans. State U., 1940. Cereal chemist Ewing Mill Co., 1940-43, flour milling engr., 1946-50, feed nutritionist, 1951-59; v.p., sec. Robertson Corp., Brownstown, Ind., 1960-80, pres., 1980-97, chmn., 1997—. Author: On Kilroy's Trail, 1998. Mem. Kans. State U. Varsity Basketball Team, 1937-40; pres. Jackson County (Ind.) Welfare Bd., 1948-52; mem. Ind. Port Commn., 1986-91; mem. Ind. Gov.'s Coun. of Sagamores of the Wabash. Served with USAAF, 1943-45. Named to Hon. Order Ky. Cols.; recipient Brownstown (Ind.) First Lifetime Achievement award, 1999. Mem. Hardwood Plywood Mfrs. Assn. (v.p. affiliate div. 1971-73, 87-88, internat. lectr. forest products industry 1973-97), Am. Assn. Cereal Chemists, Assn. Operative Millers, Am. Legion, Brownstown C. of C. (dir. All Am. city program 1955), Kans. State U. Alumni Assn. (life), Blue Key, Phi Delta Theta, Phi Kappa Phi, Alpha Mu. Clubs: Internat. Travelers Century (L.A.), Circumnavigators Club (N.Y.C.), Elks. Presbyterian. Home: Lake and Forest Club 1268 E Lake Shore Dr PO Box A Brownstown IN 47220 Office: 200 N Front St Brownstown IN 47220-1040 E-mail: robmark@glux.com.

ROBERTSON, KENNETH CARL, music educator; b. Bethany, Mo., Oct. 14, 1963; s. Hal Dean and IRetha Robertson. MusB Edn., MusB Performance, Drake U., 1986; MusM, Conservatory of Music, Kansas City, Mo., 1988. Cert. Orff- Schulwerk Music Specialist 1999. Organist 1st Christian Ch., Pattonsburg, Mo., 1976—82, Glen Echo Christian Ch., Des Moines, 1982—86, Congl. United Ch. Of Christ, Prairie Village, Kans., 1986—89; organist/choirmaster St. Charles Ch., Gladstone, Mo., 1989—91; organist Pk. Christian Ch., Kansas City, Mo., 1991—99; music tchr. North Kans. City Schs., Kansas City, 1993—. Soloist Drake U. Choir, Des Moines, 1982—86; dance accompanist Alvin Ailey Dance Co., Kansas City, Mo., 1987—87. Singer: (recording) Handel's Messiah, 1983, (radio live performance) Three French Songs - Bernstein, 1984. Recipient Ctrl. Iowa 1st Pl. Music, Yamah Corp. Competition, 1979, 5 #1 music ratings, State of Mo., 1978—82. Mem.: Music Educators Nat. Conf., Am. Orff-Schulwerk Assn. Office: Gracemor Elem Sch 5125 N Sycamore Kansas City MO 64119 Personal E-mail: kcrmusic@aol.com. E-mail: krobert1@nkcsd.

ROBERTSON, LAVERNE, minister; MS, Nova Southeastern U., 1995. Pastor Mansion Ave. Triumphant Bapt. Ch., Richmond, Va., 2001—04. Singer: (songs) Freedom Day Has Come. Gospel music writer and performer, Richmond, 1980—99. Named 3rd runner up, Miss Black Richmond Pageant. Office: Mansion Ave Triumphant Baptist Ch 1801 Mansion Ave Richmond VA 23224 Office Phone: 804-232-6046. Personal E-mail: www.laverroberts@aol.com.

ROBERTSON, LAWRENCE MARSHALL, JR., neurosurgeon; b. Denver, Feb. 4, 1932; s. Lawrence M. and Mildred Eleanor (Blackwood) R.; m. Joan T. White, May 13, 1958 (div. Oct. 1973); children: Colette M., Michele E., Laurienne J., Lawrence M. III; m. Lee Ann Crawford, Sept. 24, 1982; one child, William M. BA, U. Colo., 1954; MD, U. Colo., Denver, 1957; postgrad., U. Denver, 1981-85. Diplomate Am. Bd. Med.-Legal Analysis in Medicine and Surgery, Am. Bd. Clin. Neurol. Surgery, Am. Bd. Forensic Medicine. Intern Kings County Hosp., Bklyn., 1957-58; resident in gen. surgery St. Joseph Hosp., Denver, 1958-59; resident in neurology U. Colo., Denver, 1959-60; resident in neurosurgery Boston City Hosp., 1960-64; fellow in neurosurgery Lahey Clinic, Boston, 1963; practice medicine specializing in neurosurgery Denver, 1964—. Contbr. articles on malpractice to legal jours. Capt. USNR, 1979-83, 85. Recipient Continuing Edn. Cert., Am. Assn. Neurol. Surgeons and Cong. Neurol. Surgeons, 1976, 1980-83, Physicians Recognition award AMA 1976-79, 80-83, 84-87. Fellow Internat. Coll. Surgeons, Royal Coll. Surgeons; mem. AAAS, ACS, AMA, Colo. Neurosurg. Soc., N.Y. Acad. Scis., Naval Res. Assn., U.S. Naval Inst., Interurban Neurosurg. Soc., Rocky Mountain Traumatologic Soc., Phi Alpha Delta. Office: Colo Neurosurgery PC 1635 Gilpin St Denver CO 80218-1632

ROBERTSON, LEON H. management consultant, educator; b. Atlanta; s. Grady Joseph and Pearline (Chandler) R. BS in Indsl. Mgmt., Ga. Inst. Tech., 1957, MS, 1959; postgrad., U. Okla.-Norman, 1958, U. Mich., 1961; PhD in Bus. Adminstrn., Ga. State U., 1968. Mgr. mgmt. cons. divsn. Arthur Andersen & Co., Atlanta, 1960-65; prof. bus. adminstrn. Ga. State U., 1965-75; corp. v.p. Tex. Gas Corp., Owensboro, Ky., 1975-78, sr. v.p., 1982-83; chmn., CEO Am. Carriers, Inc., Overland Park, Kans., 1978-88; chmn. bd. dirs. Midwest Coast Transport, Overland Park, 1988-89; prof. mgmt., dir. divsn. bus. adminstrn. U. Mo., Kansas City, 1990-96, prof. Internat. Acad. Programs, 1996-98, dir. Ctr. for Internat. Bus., 1999—. Office: Univ of Mo-Kansas City Henry W Bloch Sch Bus & Pub Admn 5110 Cherry St Kansas City MO 64110-2426

ROBERTSON, LINDA F. educational adminstrator; b. Powell, Wyo., July 15, 1946; d. Lee and Dorothy W. (Schweighart) Brunk; m. Darrell G. Robertson II, July 2, 1965; 1 child, Michelle. BA in elem. edn., U. Wyo., 1968; MA in edn. adminstrn., U. Akron, 1978; postgrad., Kent State U. Cert. supt., elem. prin., secondary prin., Ohio. Elem. prin. Aurora (Ohio) City Schs., asst. supt., high sch. prin.; dir. Ctr. for Internat. and Intercultural Edn., Kent State U. Named Ohio Prin. of Yr., 1992. Mem.: Kappa Delta Pi, Phi Delta Kappa. Home: 8220 Timber Trl Chagrin Falls OH 44023-5071 E-mail: lfrobert@kent.edu.

ROBERTSON, MARK ALLEN, lawyer; b. San Antonio, May 6, 1963; s. David Hearne and Margie Louise (McCleskey) R. BA, So. Meth. U., 1985; JD, Columbia U., 1989. Ptnr. Fulbright & Jaworski, L.L.P., Houston, 1989-2001, N.Y.C., 2001—. Editor (contbg.): 2002 ABA Antitrust Discovery Handbook; prodr.: (plays) Glass Bottom Cadillac, 1995. Bd. dirs. Houston Black Tie Dinner, Inc., 1997-2001; class fundraising chair So. Meth. U., Dallas, 1995—; mem. adminstrv. bd. St. Paul's United Meth. Ch., Houston, 1991-97. Mem. ABA, NY Bar Assn., D.C. Bar Assn., Tex. Bar Assn., Houston Bar Assn. (chair antitrust and trade regulation sect. 1998-99), Pi Kappa Alpha (regional pres. 1997—, Advisor of Yr. Internat. Chpt. 1995), So. Meth. U. N.Y.C. Alumni (exec. com. 2002—), N.Y.C. Bar Chorus. Avocations: travel, singing, golf. Office: Fulbright & Jaworski LLP 666 Fifth Ave New York NY 10103-3198

ROBERTSON, MARTHA RAPPAPORT, state legislator, consultant; b. Boston, Sept. 14, 1952; d. Jerome Lyle and Nancy (Vahey) Rappaport; divorced; 1 child, Colby. BA, Franklin & Marshall Coll., 1974; MBA, U. Pa., 1976. Mktg. and new bus. devel. exec. Gen. Mills, Inc., Mpls., 1976-91; mem. Minn. Senate from 45th dist., St. Paul, 1993—. Republican. Office: State of Minn 141 State Office Bldg Saint Paul MN 55155-0001

ROBERTSON, MARY LOUISE, archivist, art historian; b. L.A., May 19, 1945; d. Snell and Dorothy (Tregoning) R. BA, UCLA, 1966, MA, 1968, PhD, 1975. Teaching asst. dept. history UCLA, 1967-70; acting instr. UCLA Extension, 1973-74; acting instr. dept. history Pepperdine U., L.A., 1970, Calif. State U., Northridge, 1972-73; asst. curator manuscripts Huntington Libr., San Marino, Calif., 1975, assoc. curator, 1977, chief curator, 1979—. Adj. prof. English Claremont Grad. Sch., 1994. Author: Guide to British Historical Manuscripts in the Huntington Library, 1982; co-author, editor: Guide to American Historical Manuscripts in the Huntington Library, 1979; co-editor: State, Sovereigns & Society in Early Modern England, 1998; contbr. articles on Tudor history to profl. jours. Mabel Wilson Richards dissertation fellow, 1970-72. Mem. Am. Hist. Assn., Soc. Calif. Archivists, N.Am. Conf. on Brit. Studies, Pacific Coast Conf. on Brit. Studies (treas. 1986-88, pres. 1988-90), Phi Beta Kappa. Office: Huntington Libr 1151 Oxford Rd San Marino CA 91108-1299

ROBERTSON, MICHAEL, Internet company executive; B in Cognitive Sci., U. Calif. San Diego. Founder MR Mac Software, 1994—95, Media Minds, Inc., 1995—96; founder, pres. The Z Co., 1996; founder, CEO, chmn. MP3.com, San Diego, 1998—2001; founder, CEO Linspire, Inc., San Diego, 2001—; CEO SIPphone, 2003—. Cons. San Diego Super Computer Ctr.; cons. in field. Founder Robertson Educational Empowerment Found. (REEF), San Diego, 2002—. Named one of 100 most influential individuals in the music industry BAM Mag. Achievements include established Filez and Websitez. Office: Linspire 9333 Genesee Ave 3rd Fl San Diego CA 92121*

ROBERTSON, MICHAEL SWING, minister; b. Boston, July 20, 1935; s. Charles Stuart and Elizabeth (Swing) R.; m. Margaret Filoon, Sept. 17, 1960 (dec. Oct. 1996); children: Michael Swing, Ashlee Whipple, Christopher Filoon, Andrew Stuart; m. Emily Erickson, Feb. 22, 1998. AB, Harvard U., 1957, grad. Advanced Mgmt. Program, 1979. With Robertson Factories, Inc., 1957-80, exec. v.p., 1968-73, pres., 1973-79, chmn. bd., 1979-80; dir. Robertson-Swing Co., 1980—; pres. The Berkley Co. Inc., 1981-90, Reactions Inc., 1985-90; treas. Falmouth Marine Inc., 1981-88; pres., treas. Orchard Computer Inc., 1984-91, chmn., treas., 1991-93; exec. sec. Nat. Assn. Congl. Christian Chs., Oak Creek, Wis., 1991-97; minister Pilgrim Congl. Ch., Taunton, Mass., 2000—02; ch. coord. Cmty. Faith Alliance, Milw., 1997-2000; exec. dir. Cmty. Village, Ltd., 1998-2000, 2003—; pastor Pilgrim Congrl. Ch., Taunton, 2001—02, Urban Ministry Cmty. Bapt. Ch., Milw., 2003, Union Congl. Ch., Braintree, Mass., 2004—. V.p. adv. coun. Coll. of Bus. and Industry, Southeastern Mass. U., North Dartmouth, Mass., 1979-91; selectman, Town of Berkley, Mass., 1974-80, chmn. 1979-80; mem. Pres.'s Adv. Com. for Trade Negotiations, 1983-86; bd. dirs. Mass. Easter Seal Soc., 1977-91, pres. 1982-83; bd. dirs. Nat. Easter Seal Soc., 1985-91, Wis. Easter Seal Soc., 1994-95; chmn. Berkley Rep. Town com., 1977-91; Rep. nominee U.S. Senate from Mass., 1976, nominee for Mass. state auditor, 1982; co-chmn. Mass Reagan for Pres. Com., 1980; Bristol County coord. Reagan/Bush campaign; co-chmn. Mass. Dole for Pres. Commn., 1987; chmn. Southeastern Mass. campaign Harvard Coll., 1981; chmn. Friends of Harvard Track, 1986-91; trustee Barnstable County Hosp., 1985-90, chmn., 1988. Mem. Harvard Varsity Club, Falmouth Yacht Club, Harvard Club of Boston. Congregationalist. Home: 7 Swing Lane Falmouth MA 02540 Office: 74 Commercial St Braintree MA 02184 Office Phone: 781-843-1333. E-mail: miker@cape.com. *Accept responsibility with enthusiasm and gratitude. Our individual freedom is unmatched in history, compelling us to remain true to our heritage and our God.*

ROBERTSON, OSCAR PALMER (BIG O ROBERTSON), chemical company executive, former professional basketball player; b. Charlotte, Tenn., Nov. 24, 1938; BBBA, U. Cin., 1960. Player U.S. Olympic Basketball Team, 1960; basketball player Cin. Royals, 1960-70, Milw. Bucks, 1970-74; founder, pres., CEO, Orchem, Inc., Cin., 1981-1996, Orpack-Stone Corp., Herrin, Ill., 1990—, Orflex Ltd., Cin., 1995—, ORDMS, Marlton, N.J., 1997—. Player NBA Championship Team, 1971. Named Sporting News Coll. Player of Yr., 1958, 59, 60, Sporting News All-Star Fitrst Team, 1958, 59, 60, NBA Rookie of Yr., 1961, All NBA First Team, 1961-69; player NBA All Star Games, 1961-72; named MVP, NBA, 1964, M VP in NBA All-Star Games, 1961, 64, 69; named to NBA 35th Anniversary All-Star Team, 1980; elected to Naismith Meml. Basketball Hall of Fame, 1979 Office: Orchem Corp 4293 Mulhauser Rd Fairfield OH 45014-5450

ROBERTSON, PAUL FRANCIS, mathematician, educator; b. Galveston, Tex., Aug. 23, 1953; s. Gilfred and Wilda Robertson; m. Ana Cecilia Moreno, May 17, 1988 (div. Nov. 1993); m. Cynthia Arnet Gilford, June 3, 1978 (div. Dec. 1980); children: Chiquita Monique, Paul Alexander, Andrea Celeste. BA in Math. magna cum laude, Tex. So. U., 1975. Cert. tchr. Tex., 1997. Data processing instr. Houston C.C. Sys., 1981; math./ computer literacy tchr. Galveston Ind. Sch. Dist., Tex., 1997—99; math. instr. Galveston Coll., Tex., 1999; math./ instrnl. tech. tchr. Galveston Cath. Sch., Tex., 1999—. Instrnl. tech. chairperson Galveston Cath. Sch., Tex., 2001—. Author (chairperson): (technical writing) Galveston Cath. Sch. Instrnl. Tech. Plan. Recipient Unsung Hero award, Galveston County - The Daily News, 2002, Cert. of Appreciation, Communities in Schs. Galveston, Inc., 2002, Cert. for Outstanding Support, Big Bros. Big Sisters of Gulf Coast, 2002; Four Yr. Acad. Scholarship award, The Moody Found., 1971. Mem.: Tex. Computer Edn. Assn. (corr.), Tex. Coun. Tchrs. of Math. (corr.). D-Conservative. Catholic. Avocations: reading, tutoring, volunteering. Office: Galveston Cath Sch 2601 Ursuline Ave Galveston TX 77550

ROBERTSON, PETER JAMES, oil company executive; b. Edinburgh, Scotland, Jan. 31, 1947; came to U.S., 1969; s. James Donald and Evelyn Patricia (McNaughton) R.; m. Candace Povey, Dec. 29, 1971; children: James Darrell, Nicole Povey, Emily Jemma. BS in Mech. Engring., Edinburgh U., 1969; MBA, U. Pa., 1971. Refinery engr. Union Oil Co. of Calif., Chgo., 1971-72; mcht. banker Noble Grossart Ltd., Edinburgh, 1972-73; fin. analyst Standard Oil Co. of Calif. (Chevron), San Francisco, 1973-78, audit mgr. Europe London, 1978-80; comptr. Chevron Oil Europe, London, 1980-83; asst. comptr. Chevron U.S.A., Inc., San Francisco, 1983-86, comptr., 1987-89, v.p. fin., 1989-91; asst. comptr. Chevron Corp., San Francisco, 1986-87; pres. Warren Petroleum Co., Tulsa, 1991—94; exec. V.P. Chevron U.S.A., 1996—97, pres., 1997—2000; VP Chevron Corp., 1997—2000; pres. Chevron Overseas Petroleum Co., San Ramon, Calif., 2000—02; vice chmn. bd. dir. Chevron/Texaco Corp., 2002—. Bd. dirs. Okla. chpt. The Nature Conservancy, Tulsa area United Way, Indian Nations coun. Boy Scouts Am., Tulsa. Recipient Thouron award Thouron Scholarship Found., U. Pa., 1969-71. Mem. Met. Tulsa C. of C., U.S. Hispanic C. of C. (sr. exec. adv. com. 1990-92), Midcontinent Oil and Gas Assn. Avocations: travel, map collecting (antique), skiing. Office: Chevron/Texaco 6001 Bollinger Canyon Rd San Ramon CA 94583-2324

ROBERTSON, RICHARD EARL, physical chemist, educator; b. Long Beach, Calif., Nov. 12, 1933; s. Earl Austin and A. Isobel (Roberts) R.; m. Joyce W. Conger, Sept. 4, 1955 (div. 1972); children: Christopher, Jill; m. Patricia L. Richmond, Apr. 20, 1974. BA, Occidental Coll., L.A., 1955; student, UCLA, 1955-56; PhD, Calif. Inst. Tech., 1960. Phys. chemist rsch. lab. GE, Schenectady, N.Y., 1960-70; staff scientist Ford Motor Co., Dearborn, Mich., 1970-86; prof. materials sci. and engring. U. Mich., Ann Arbor, 1986—, dir. Macromolecular Sci. and Engring. Ctr., 1995—2000. Contbr. articles to profl. jours. Postdoctoral fellow Washington U., St. Louis, 1959-60. Fellow Am. Phys. Soc.; mem. Am. Chem. Soc., Sigma Xi. Office: U Mich Dept Materials Sci Eng Ann Arbor MI 48109-2136 E-mail: rer@umich.edu.

ROBERTSON, RICHARD ROBERT, grain milling executive; b. Seymour, Ind., Aug. 20, 1934; s. Richard Shields Robertson and Cora DeAlba; m. Ruth Ann Horstman, June 25, 1957; children: Richard Andrew, Susan Lynn. BS in Grain Milling, Kans. State U., Manhattan, 1956. Flour miller The Robertson Corp., Brownstown, Ind., 1979-89, v.p., 1989-97, pres., 1997-98, also bd. dirs. Bd. dirs. Engineerd Wood Rsch. Found., Tacoma, 1990-98. Author: A History of the American Roller Mills. Bd. dirs. Meml. Hosp. Found., Seymour, 1982—2002. Col. USAF, 1956—79. Mem. Assn. Operative Millers, Presbyn. Coun. for Chaplains and Military Personnel, Elks. Presbyterian. Avocations: birding, antique phonographs, historic grist mills. Office: Robertson Corp 1015 E North Shore Dr Brownstown IN 47220-0301

ROBERTSON, RICHARD STUART, insurance holding company executive; b. Spokane, Wash., June 14, 1942; s. Stuart A. and Marjory (Moch) R.; m. Trudy Ann Prendergast, July 31, 1976; children: Thomas Stuart, Richard Andrew. BS, Calif. Inst. Tech., 1963. Chief reinsurance actuary Lincoln Nat. Life Ins. Co., Ft. Wayne, Ind., 1963-74; sr. v.p., chief fin. officer Lincoln Nat. Corp., Ft. Wayne, 1974-86, exec. v.p., CFO, 1986-92, exec. v.p., corp. risk officer, 1992-98; sr. v.p. Lincoln Nat. Reassurance Co., 1999—. Bd. dirs. Lincoln Re S.A., Lincoln China, Kyoei Lincoln Reins. Svc. Co., Linsco Reins. Co.; chmn. Actuarial Stds. Bd., 1996-97. Fellow Soc. Actuaries (pres. 1985-86); mem. Am. Acad. Actuaries (v.p. 1980-81, pres. elect 1998, pres. 1999). Episcopalian. Home: 12618 Aboite Center Rd Fort Wayne IN 46814-9725 Fax: 219-455-1036. E-mail: rrobertson@lnc.com.

ROBERTSON, RICHARD TRAFTON, entertainment company executive; b. Tacoma Park, Md., Aug. 23, 1945; s. Collins Trafton and Sigrid (Bergman) R.; m. Beverly Wise, Dec. 20, 1969 (div. Jan. 1984). BS, Va. Commonwealth U., 1967. Field rep. D. Van Nostrand Pub. Co., Princeton, N.J., 1968-69; account exec., sales mgr. NBC, Washington, San Francisco, Cleve. and N.Y.C., 1969-73; account exec., v.p. sports mktg. CBS TV Network, Chgo. and N.Y.C., 1973-78; exec. v.p., v.p. mktg. Office of Pres., Lorimar Telepictures, Culver City, Calif., 1978—; now pres. domestic TV distbn. Warner Bros., Burbank. Mem.: Bel-Air (Calif.) Country; Monterrey Country (Palm Desert, Calif). Lutheran. Avocations: golf, skiing, tennis. Office: Warner Bros Domestic TV Distbn 4001 W Olive Ave Burbank CA 91505-4272

ROBERTSON, ROBERT GRAHAM HAMISH, physicist; b. Ottawa, Ont., Can., Oct. 3, 1943; came to U.S., 1971; s. Hugh Douglas and Alice Madeleine (Bell) R.; m. Peggy Lynn Dyer, July 4, 1980; 1 child, Ian. BA, MA, Oxford (Eng.) U., 1965; PhD, McMaster U., Hamilton, Ont., 1971. Rsch. assoc. Mich. State U., East Lansing, 1971-72, asst. rsch. prof., 1972-73, asst. prof., 1973-78, assoc. prof., 1978-81, prof., 1981-82; mem. staff Los Alamos (N.Mex.) Nat. Lab., 1981—, fellow, 1988—; prof. U. Washington, Seattle, 1994—; sci. dir. Ctr. for Exptl. Nuc. Physics and Astrophysics, 2000—. Rsch. assoc. Princeton (NJ) U., 1975-76; vis. scientist Argonne (Ill.) Nat. Lab., 1979, Chalk River (Ont., Can.) Nuc. Lab., 1980. Contbr. over 60 articles to profl. jours. Alfred P. Sloan Found. fellow Mich. State U., 1976; Trevelyan scholar Eng., 1962-65, NRC scholar McMaster U., 1965-69, Oriel Coll. scholar, 1962-65. Fellow Am. Phys. Soc. (chair divsn. nuclear physics 2000, Tom W. Bonner prize 1997), Inst. Physics of Eng., Am. Acad. Arts and Scis.; mem. NAS, Can. Assn. Physicists. Achievements include first observation of nuclear isobaric quintet; development of technique for precise measurement of neutrino mass; determination of Lithium-6 synthesis in early universe; demonstration of neutrino mass, oscillations with Sudbury Neutrino Obs. Office: Dept Physics U Washington Seattle WA 98195-1560 Office Phone: 206-616-2745. E-mail: rghr@u.washington.edu.

ROBERTSON, ROSE MARIE, cardiologist, educator; b. Detroit, May 15, 1945; d. Joseph Michael and Rose Marie (Pink) Stevens; m. David Robertson, Oct. 31, 1978; 1 child, Rose Marie. BA, Manhattanville Coll., 1966; MD, Harvard Med. Sch., 1970. Diplomate Nat. Bd. Medicine, 1971, Am. Bd. Internal Medicine, 1974, Cardiovascular Medicine, 1975. Intern in medicine Mass. Gen. Hosp., Boston, 1970-71, resident in medicine, 1970-72; fellow in cardiovasc. medicine Johns Hopkins Med. Sch., Balt., 1973-75, asst. prof. medicine, 1972-78, Vanderbilt U. Med. Ctr., Nashville, 1975-82, assoc. prof. medicine, 1982-89, dir. cardiovasc. tng. program, 1990—2000, assoc. dir. cardiology, 1987—, prof. medicine, 1989—. Mem. adv. bd. Robert Wood Johnson Found., 1990-; mem. cardiovasc. study sect. NIH, Bethesda, Md., 1993-97; invited spkr., lectr. Contbr. articles to profl. jours., chpts. to books. Fellow Am. Coll. Cardiology, Am. Heart Assn. (pres. 2000-01, chief scientific officer 2003-), European Soc. Cardiology; mem. Am. Soc. Echocardiography, Am. Fedn. for Clin. Rsch., Am. Soc. Clin. Investigation, Am. Clin. and Climatol. Assn., Assn. Univ. Cardiologists. Home: 4003 Newman Pl Nashville TN 37204-4308 Office: 7272 Greenville Ave Danville TX 75240 E-mail: rmr@heart.org.

ROBERTSON, RUTH, artist, art gallery owner; m. John Foster Robertson, July 10, 1970. BFA, Va. Commonwealth U., 1973. Art instr. Fairfax County (Va.) Pub. Schools, 1973—77, Bishop O'Connell H.S., Arlington, Va., 1991—98; gallery owner Dist. West Fine Art, Leesburg, Va., 2001—04, Ruth Robertson Fine Art, 2004—. Freelance curator, Washington, 1998—; instr. MIS program Va. Commonwealth U., 2004—. One-woman shows include Into The Looking Glass, 1994, Touchstone Gallery, D.C. Arts Ctr., 1996, D.C. Arts Ctr., 1999, Mus. Contemporary Art, Washington, 1997, 1999, 2000, Hub Galleries, Pa. State U., Art Sites 96, Entre Luces y Sombras, Havana, Cuba, 2003, Bell Atlantic Gallery, 1993, Reston Art Gallery, 1994, Washington Ctr for Photography, 1994. Recipient Presdl. citation, Governor's Sch. for Visual And Performing Arts, U. Richmond, 1994, Outstanding Educator award, Phila. Coll. of Textiles and Scis., 1995. Office: Dist West Fine Art 3 1/2 South King St Leesburg VA 20175

ROBERTSON, SAMUEL HARRY, III, transportation safety research engineer, educator; b. Phoenix, Oct. 2, 1934; s. Samuel Harry and Doris Bryle (Duffield) R.; m. Nancy Jean Bradford, 1954 (div. 1989); children: David Lyle, Pamela Louise; m. Linda Faye O'Neill, 1999. BS, Ariz. State U., 1956; D in Aviation Tech. (hon.), Embry-Riddle Aero. U., 1972. Registered profl. engr.; cert. comml. pilot--fixed wing, rotary wing, glider and balloon. Chief hazards divsn. Aviation Safety Engring. and Rsch., Phoenix, 1960-70; pres. Robertson Rsch. Engrs., 1960-70; rsch. prof., dir. Safety Ctr. Coll. Engring. and Applied Scis., Ariz State U., Tempe, 1970-79; pres. Robertson Rsch. Inc., 1970-86, Robertson Aviation Inc., 1977-86, Internat. Ctr. for Safety Edn., 1982-96; pres., CEO Robertson Rsch. Group, Inc., Tempe, 1986—, Robertson Aviation, LLC, Tempe, 1995—. Airplane design and accident investigator, 1961—; instr. aircrash investigation Internat. Ctr. Safety Edn., 1960—, inst. aerospace safety U. So. Calif., 1962-70, Armed Forces Inst. Pathology, 1970-90, Dept. Transp. Safety Inst., 1970-89; pres. Pine Springs Ranch, Inc. 1976—; adv. bd. Rio Salado Bank, Tempe, 1985-94; mem. adv. coun. Ctr. Aerospace Safety Edn., Embry-Riddle Aero. U., Daytona Beach, Fla., 1986—, trustee, 1992—; pres. Devil Dog Rsch., Inc., 1990—, Robertson Land & Cattle Inc., 1990—; comml. pilot, 1957—. Contbr. over 85 articles to profl. jours.; patentee applying plastic to paper, fuel system safety check valves, crash resitant fuel system, safety aircraft seats; holder FAA STC's various fuel systems, fuel system components; designer, developer, mfr. crash resistant fuel systems for airplanes, helicopters, championship racing cars. Pilot USAF, 1956-60, Ariz. Army NG 1960-61, 70-74, Ariz. Air NG, 1961-69. Recipient Contbns. Automotive Racing Safety award CNA, 1976, Adm. Luis De Florez Internat. Flying Safety award, 1969, Cert. Commendation Nat. Safety Coun., 1969, Gen. W. Spruance award for safety edn., SAFE Soc., 1982; holder Nat. Speed Record for one class of drag racing car, 1955-62, 5 nat. records for flying model aircraft, 1950-56; named to Ariz. Aviation Hall of Fame, 1996, OX5 Aviation Pioneers Hall of Fame, 1996, U.S. Army Aviation Hall of Fame, 2001, Army Aviation Assn. Am. Hall of Fame, 2001. Mem. AIAA, Internat. Soc. Air Safety Investigators (Jerome Lederer Aircraft Accident Investigation award, 1981), Aerospace Med. Assn., Exptl. Aircraft Assn., Soc. Automotive Engrs., Soc. Exptl. Test Pilots, Am. Helicopter Soc., Nat. Fire Protection Assn., Aircraft Owners and Pilots Assn., U.S. Automobile Club (tech. com.). Home: Pine Springs Ranch PO Box 58 Williams AZ 86046 Office: 1024 E Vista Del Cerro Dr Tempe AZ 85281-5709

ROBERTSON, SAMUEL LUTHER, JR., special education educator, therapist, researcher; b. Houston, Apr. 28, 1940; s. Sam L. and Portia Louise (Burns) R.; children: Samuel Luther IV, Sean Lee (dec.), Ryan William, Susan Elizabeth (dec.), Henry Philmore. BS, McMurry U., 1969; MA, Hardin-Simmons U., 1973; PhD, U. Tex., 1993. Cert. tchr., adminstr., counselor, prevention specialist, Tex.; lic. chem. dependency counselor, lic. clin. mental health counselor, advanced addiction counselor., Tex. Instr., coach, athletic dir. Tex. and La. schs., 1969-94; social worker, supr. Children's Protective Svcs., Abilene, Tex., 1978-79; instr., adminstr. Harlandale Sch. Dist., San Antonio, 1980-84, 87-90; adminstr. night sch. Harlandale Ind. Sch. Dist., San Antonio, 1988-89; instr. Edgewood Ind. Sch. Dist., San Antonio, 1985-87; developer, instr., integrated unit program San Antonio, 1990—; CEO The Educative Inst., San Antonio, 1992—. CEO Educative Therapeutic Processes, 1972—; co-founder, dir. Inst. Organizational Personal Devel.; adj. prof. San Antonio Coll.; lectr. U. Tex. at San Antonio. Author: (play) The Challenged, 1965, Dream Poems, 1998; (poem) Trains in the Night, 1969; (screenplay) Tom & Jane, 2000; dir. (film) Tom & Jane, 2003. State co-chmn. Youth for Kennedy-Johnson, Tex., 1960; mem. W. Tex. Dem. Steering Com., Abilene, 1962-63; founding dir. Way Off Broadway Cmty. Theater, Eagle Pass, Tex., 1971-72; founding bd. dirs. Battered Women's Shelter, Abilene, 1978-79; v.p. bd. dirs. Mental Health Assn., San Antonio, 1980-83, bd. dirs Palmer Drug Abuse Program, San Antonio, 1985-87; pres., bd. dir. Alcoholic Rehab. Ctr., 1985-86, 1987-92; vice-chmn. Civilian and Mil. Addictive Programs, San Antonio, 1991-92; author, implementer Cmty. Vitalization Program, 1994—; mem. vestry St. George Episcopal Ch., mem. sch. bd., St. George Sch.1999—02; mem. standards chair Tex. Certification Bd. of Addiction Profls.; chmn. 1999—01. Named Tchr. of Yr. Southside Ind. Sch. Dist., San Antonio, 1970-71, Harlandale Alternative Ctr., San Antonio, 1987-88; Vol. of Yr., Mental Health Assn., San Antonio, 1982, Alcoholic Rehab. Ctr., San Antonio, 1992-93. Mem. ACA, NEA, Am. Mental Health Counseling Assn., Tex. State Tchrs. Assn., Am. Ednl. Rsch. Assn., Am. Assn. Sch. Adminstrs. Internat. Consortium Reciprocity Commn. Nat. Alcoholism and Drug Abuse Counselors, N.Mex. Mental Health Counselors Assn., N.Mex. Profl. Counselors Assn., Phi Kappa Phi, Kappa Delta Pi. Episcopalian. Avocations: reading, writing, travel, theater, sports. Office: Educative Therapeutic Processes 339 E Hildebrand Ave San Antonio TX 78212-2412 *I have participated in my life, my family's life, and my community's life in a responsible fashion through the Grace of God.*

ROBERTSON, SANDRA DEE (GRAEN), tax director; b. Denver, Nov. 7, 1953; d. Fredrick Philip Arthur Graen and Dorothea Stone (Bell) Kohler; m. Charles E. Robertson Jr., Aug. 4, 1973 (Jan. 1985); 1 child, Daniel Philip. BS in Bus. cum laude, U. Colo., 1980. CPA, Colo., Ga. Staff acct. Brock, Cordle & Assocs., CPA's, Boulder, Colo., 1980-82; corp. tax acct. Storage Tech. Corp., Louisville, Colo., 1983-87; state tax supr. RJR Nabisco, Inc., Atlanta, 1987-89; mgr. Ernst & Young CPA's, Atlanta, 1989-91; dir. state and local taxes Equifax Inc., Atlanta, 1991-94; dir. state and local tax Ga. Pacific Corp., Atlanta, 1994—2003; exec. dir. Robertson Consulting, Internat., CPAs, LLC, 2003—. Bd. dirs. Com. on State Taxation. Served with U.S. Army, 1972-75. Mem. AICPA, Toastmasters, Beta Gamma Sigma. Democrat. Avocations: russian language and history, cajun and zydeco music and dance, reading. Home: 450 Rock Springs Rd NE Atlanta GA 30324-5102 E-mail: wiseoldbird2@yahoo.com.

ROBERTSON, STERLING CLIFTON, music educator, pianist; b. Tientsin, Tiangjin, China, Jan. 22, 1928; arrived in U.S., 1932; s. Sterling Clifton and Mary Letitia (Grimes) Robertson. Student, Tex. Christian U., 1945—47, U. Tex., 1948—50, Julliard Sch. Music, N.Y.C., 1952—53, Columbia U., 1952—53, Royaumont-12th Century Monastery-Libr. and Found. Artists; grad., Ft. Worth Conservatory Music, 1945. Tchr. piano, N.Y.C., 1950—70, San Antonio, 1970—. Staff pianist Four Seasons Hotels, San Antonio, Hyatt Regency, San Antonio, Wyndham-St. Anthony, San Antonio; concert pianist Carnegie Hall, 1961, 63, Royal Danish Ballet, Royal Danish Ballet, Columbia Artist, 1961, Boston Music Ctr. (Music Circus), Ted Shawn's Jacob's Pillow. Grantee grantee for piano study with George Copeland, Fairfield Found. and William Hale Harkness/Rebekah Harkness, 1952—53. Democrat. Avocations: theater, film, art. Mailing: 314 Bryn Mawr Dr San Antonio TX 78209 Office Phone: 210-826-3376.

ROBERTSON, STEWART, conductor; b. Glasgow, Scotland; m. Meryl Owen; children: Keren, Niel. Attended, Royal Scottish Acad. of Music; studied with, Hans Swarowsky & Otmar Sultner. Past music dir., prin. condr. Santa Fe (N.Mex.) Symphony; music dir. Glimmerglass Summer Opera Festival, 1988—, Inland Empire Symphony Orchestra, San Bernardino, Calif.; music dir., prin. condr. San Bernardino Symphony Orchestra, 1989—2001. Guest condr. BBC Scottish Symphony, Ukraine State Philharmonic, Buenos Aires Philharmonic, Lille Festival, Fla. Philharmonic, Louisville Orchestra, Chgo. Lyric, N.Y.C. Opera, Cologne, Zurich, Scottish Opera, recordings Verdi-EMI. Office: Glimmerglass Opera 7300 State Hwy 80 PO Box 191 Cooperstown NY 13326*

ROBERTSON, TED ZANDERSON, judge; b. San Antonio, Sept. 28, 1921; s. Irion Randolf and Aurelia (Zanderson) R.; m. Margie Gardner. Student, Tex. A&I, 1940-42; LL.B., St. Mary's U., San Antonio, 1949. Bar: Tex. 1949. Chief civil dept. Dist. Atty.'s Office, Dallas County, Tex., 1960-65; judge Probate Ct. 2, Dallas County, 1965-69, Juvenile Ct. 2, Dallas County, 1969-75, 95th Dist. Ct., Dallas County, 1975-76, Ct. Civil Appeals, 5th Supreme Jud. Dist., Dallas, 1976-82, Supreme Ct. Tex., Austin, 1982; of counsel Frank Branson P.C., Dallas, 1989—. Guest lectr. So. Meth. U., Dallas, Dallas County Juvenile Bd., Tex. Coll. of the Judiciary, 1970-82 Active Dallas Assn. for Retarded Children; active Dallas County Commn. on Alcoholism, Dallas County Mental Health Assn. Served as yeoman USCG, 1942-46. Recipient Golden Gavel St. Mary's U., San Antonio, 1979; named Outstanding Alumnus St. Mary's U., 1981. Mem. Am. Judicature Soc., Tex. Bar Assn., Dallas Bar Assn., Dallas County Juvenile Bd. Lodges: Masons; Lions. Democrat. Methodist. Home: 6233 Highgate Ln Dallas TX 75214-2157 Office: Frank Branson 4514 Cole Ave Ste 1800 Dallas TX 75205-4185

ROBERTSON, THOMAS L. health facility administrator; b. June 23, 1943; AA, Nat. Bus. Coll., 1965; postgrad., St. Louis U., 1971-74. CPA Anderson and Reed, Roanoke, Va.; with Carilion Health System, 1969—, pres., ceo, 1986—, also bd. dirs. Chmn. bd. dirs. SunHealth Corp.; bd. dirs. Roanoke Electric Steel, Roanoke Gas Co., Shenandoah Life Ins. Co., 1st Union Corp. Va., Roanoke Valley Devel. Corp., Ctr. In The Sq. Chmn. Roanoke Valley Bus. Coun., Renew Roanoke; co-chmn. The New Century Coun.; bd. dirs. Va. Found. Ind. Colls., Roanoke Coll. Mem. Am. Hosp. Assn. (mem. ho. dels., mem. regional policy bd.), Va. Hosp. Assn. (bd. dirs., past chmn.), Roanoke Area Hosp. Coun. (past pres.), Hosp. Fin. Mgmt. Assn. (past pres. Va. chpt.), Roanoke Valley C. of C. (former pres.), Jaycees (past pres.), Roanoke Country Club (former pres.). Office: Carilion Health System PO Box 13727 Roanoke VA 24036-3727

ROBERTSON, THOMAS SINCLAIR, dean, marketing educator; b. Scotland, Nov. 16, 1942; s. Thomas C. and Ann Gorman (Mundie) R.; m. Diana S. Conway, June 18, 1966; children: Brian, Ashley, Alexandra BA, Wayne State U., Detroit, 1963; MA, PhD, Northwestern U., 1966. Asst. prof. mktg. UCLA, 1966-68, Harvard U., 1968-71; prof. mktg. Wharton Sch., U. Pa., 1971, chmn. mktg. dept., 1978-84, assoc. dean, 1984—88, London Bus. Sch., 1994-98; dean Goizueta Bus. Sch. Emory U., Atlanta, 1998—. Bd. dirs. Profit Recovery Group. Author: Innovative Behavior and Communication, 1971, Televised Medicine Advertising and Children, 1979, Consumer Behavior, 1984, Handbook of Consumer Behavior, 1991. Grantee NSF NIH. Mem. Am. Mktg. Assn., Assn. Consumer Rsch., Cherokee Town Club, Commerce Club. Republican. Office: 1300 Clifton Rd NE Atlanta GA 30322-2710

ROBERTSON, TIMOTHY JOEL, statistician, educator; b. Denver, Oct. 4, 1937; s. Flavel P. and Helen C. (Oliver) Girdner; m. Joan K. Slater, Aug. 18, 1959; children— Kelly, Jana, Doug, Mike BA in Math., U. Mo., 1959, MS in Math., 1961, PhD in Stats., 1966. Asst. prof. Cornell Coll., Mt. Vernon, Iowa, 1961-63; prof. stats. U. Iowa, Iowa City, 1965—2004, prof. emeritus, 2004—. Vis. prof. U. N.C., Chapel Hill, 1974-75, U. Calif.-Davis, 1983-84; Eugene Lukacs Disting. vis. prof. Bowling Green State U., 1991-92; vis. lectr. Com. Pres. Statis. Soc., 1971-74. Author: (with F.T. Wright and R.L. Dykstra) Order Restricted Statistical Inference; assoc. editor Am. Math. Monthly, 1977-81; mem. editl. bd. Comms. in Stats., 1981-92; assoc. editor Jour. Am. Statis. Assn., 1990-96; contbr. numerous articles to profl. jours. Recipient Collegiate Teaching award U. Iowa, 1990. Fellow Am. Statis. Assn. (council 1974-75), Inst. Math. Stats., Internat. Statis. Inst.; mem. Math. Assn. Am., Sigma Xi, Sierra Club Democrat. Avocations: canoeing, camping, bicycling, walking. Home: 673 Garfield Rd West Branch IA 52358-8574 Office: University of Iowa Dept Stats/Actuarial Sci Iowa City IA 52242 Office Phone: 319-335-2019.

ROBERTSON, TIMOTHY N. state legislator, retired real estate agent; b. Brattleboro, Vt., June 6, 1932; m. Elsie H. Robertson; 3 children. BA, Hobart Coll., 1958. Mem. N.H. Ho. of Reps. (dist. 18), Concord, 1994—; mem. transp. com. N.H. Ho. of Reps., Concord, 1994—, mem. exec. depts. and adminstrv. com.; ret. Active YMCA, Salvation Army; mem. RISE program Keene (N.H.) Unitarian Universalist Ch. Mem. Lions. Address: 185 Daniels Hill Rd Keene NH 03431-5704

ROBERTSON, VALERIA BROWER, state legislator, land developer; b. Memphis, Nov. 17, 1932; m. James T. Robertson. Grad. h.s.; student, coll. Mem. Miss. Ho. of Reps., 1996—; mem. constn., county affairs, pub. bldgs. coms.; mem. pub. health com. Commr. DeSoto Election; mem. DeSoto Econ. Coun., Shelby County Equalization; mem. exec. com. Tenn. Rep. Mem. DeSoto and Miss. Fedn. Rep. Women, C. of C. (Olive Branch and Hernando). Republican. Presbyterian. Home: 8570 Jones Rd Olive Branch MS 38654-9001 Office: State Capitol Bldg PO Box 1018 Jackson MS 39215-1018

ROBERTSON, WILLIAM ABBOTT, arbitrator, mediator, lawyer; b. San Francisco, Apr. 7, 1947; s. William Abbott Jr. and Roxana D. Robertson; children: Sara W., Claire S. BA, U. Calif., Davis, 1969; JD, U. Pacific, 1980. Bar: Calif. 1980, U.S. Dist. Ct. (no. and ea. dists.) 1981, U.S. Ct. Appeals (9th cir.) 1981. Atty. Rodeno & Robertson, Napa, Calif., 1984-94, Robertson Law Office, Napa, 1994-95; pvt. practice mediation and arbitration, Cotati, Calif., 1995—. Judge pro tem Napa Consol. Cts., 1982-96; assigned arbitrator Napa and Solano County Superior Cts., 1984-96. Avocations: ranching, quarter horses. Office: Robertson Mediation Office PO Box 550 Cotati CA 94931-0550

ROBERTSON, WILLIAM L. environmental services executive; BSBA in Econs., U. Tenn.; MS in Mgmt., MPA, Ga. State U.; JD, U. Tenn. Sr. positions U.S. Dept. Def., including U.S. Army Corps of Engrs.; assoc. chief engrs. Strategic Initiatives; pres. pvt. environ. tech. found.; founder OneSoft Corp.; advisor corps. and municipalities on bus. opportunities in the environment and tech. sectors; chmn., CEO Weston Solutions, Inc., West Chester, Pa., 1997—, chmn. bd., 1997—99. Office: Weston Solutions Inc PO Box 2653 1400 Weston Way West Chester PA 19380*

ROBERTSON, WILLIAM OSBORNE, physician; b. N.Y.C., Nov. 24, 1925; s. William Osborne and Barbara Konvalinka (Bennett) R.; m. Barbara Foster Simpson, Feb. 23, 1952; children: Kathy, Lynn, Kerry, Douglas, Andrew. BA, U. Rochester, 1946, MD, 1949. Intern Strong Meml. Hosp., Rochester, N.Y., 1949-51, resident, 1951-52, Grace New Haven Hosp., 1954-56; acting med. dir. Ross Labs., Columbus, Ohio, 1956-59; mem. faculty Ohio State Coll. Medicine, 1956-63, assoc. prof. pediatrics, 1961-63; mem. faculty dept. pediatrics U. Wash., Seattle, 1963—, prof., 1972—, assoc. dean, 1967-72, med. dir., 1963-67, acting chmn. dept. pediatrics, 1972-73, 80-84, head div. ambulatory pediatrics, 1975-77, 78-79; dir. med. edn. div. Children's Orthopedic Hosp., 1971-90, med. dir., poison control ctr., 1971—. Mem. staffs Children's, Harborview, Univ. hosps.; mem. advisory com., chmn. Wash. Alaska Regional Med. Program; bd. dirs. Wash. Med. Edn. and Research Found., 1968-73 Contbr. articles to profl. publs. Served with USNR, 1943-45, 52-54. Mem. Am. Acad. Pediatrics (chmn. edn. com. 1971-73, med. liability com. 1985-90, chmn. task force on quality assurance 1988-92), Am. Clin. Acad. Toxicology, King County Med. Soc. (pres. 1971-72), Wash. State Med. Assn. (pres. 1975-76), Am. Assn. Poison Control Ctrs. (pres. 1988-90), Phi Beta Kappa, Alpha Omega Alpha, Am. Coll. Med. Toxicology. Home: 18724 40th Pl NE Seattle WA 98155-2806 Office: U Wash Sch Medicine PO Box 5371C Seattle WA 98195-0001 Office Phone: 206-517-2356. Business E-Mail: robertso@wapc.org.

ROBERTSON, WILLIAM WITHERS, lawyer; b. Morristown, N.J., Nov. 3, 1941; s. Thomas Withers and Jessie (Swain) R.; m. Elizabeth Jeanne Robertson; children: Barbara Ellen Richmond, William Withers, Jr., Jessie Swain Wilt. BA, Rutgers U., 1964, LL.B., 1967. Bar: N.J. 1968. Law sec. to judge Superior Ct. N.J., 1967-68; asst. U.S. atty., 1972-76; 1st asst. U.S. atty., 1978-80; U.S. atty. Dist. N.J., 1980-81; chief Newark Organized Crime Strike Force, 1976-78; ptnr. Hannoch Weisman, Roseland, NJ, 1981-99, Robertson, Freilich, Bruno & Cohen, LLC, Newark, 1999—. Mng. editor: Rutgers Law Rev., 1966—67. Trustee Rutgers U., 1984-88. Served to capt. JAGC USAR, 1968-72. Mem. Nat. Assn. Former U.S. Attys. (bd. dirs. 1990-93, pres. 2002-2003), Rutgers U. Law Sch. Alumni Assn. (pres. 1990-91), Rutgers U. Alumni Fedn. (pres. 1981-83). Office: Robertson Freilich Et Al 4th Fl 1 Riverfront Plz Newark NJ 07102-5401 Office Phone: 973-848-2100. E-mail: wrobertson@rfbclaw.com.

ROBERTSON, WILLIAM WRIGHT, JR., orthopedist, educator; b. Mayfield, Ky., Dec. 26, 1946; m. Karel Virginia Dierks, Jan. 26, 1974. BA, Rhodes Coll., 1968; MD, Vanderbilt U., 1972; MBA, Geo Washington U., 2000. Intern U. Calif., San Diego, 1972-73, resident in orthop. surgery, 1975-76, Vanderbilt U., Nashville, 1976-79; asst. prof. orthop. Tex. Tech U., Lubbock, 1979-86; assoc. prof. U. Pa., Phila., 1986-90; prof. orthop. surgery George Washington U., Washington, 1990-2000; chmn. pediat. orthop. Children's Nat. Med. Ctr., Washington, 1990-99. Field rep. accreditation coun. grad. med. edn. Fellow Am. Acad. Orthop. Surgeons, Am. Orthop. Assn., Pediat. Orthop. Soc. (bd. dirs. 1993-96—). Avocations: gardening, music. Office: Accreditation Coun Grad Med Edn 515 N State St Chicago IL 60610 Business E-Mail: wrobertson@acgme.org.

ROBERTSON, WYNDHAM GAY, university official, journalist; b. Salisbury, N.C., Sept. 25, 1937; d. Julian Hart and Blanche Williamson (Spencer) R. AB in Econs., Hollins Coll., Roanoke, Va., 1958. Rsch. asst. Standard Oil Co., N.Y.C., 1958-61; rschr. Fortune Mag., N.Y.C., 1961-67, assoc. editor, 1968-74, bd. of editors, 1974-81, asst. mng. editor, 1981-86; bus. editor Time Mag., N.Y.C., 1982-83; v.p. comm. U. N.C., Chapel Hill, 1986-96. Bd. dirs. Media Gen. Inc. Contbr. numerous articles to Fortune Mag. Trustee Thomas S. Kenan Inst. for the Arts, U. NC Health Care Sys., Hollins U. Recipient Gerald M. Loeb Achievement award, U. of Conn., 1972. Mem. Phi Beta Kappa. Episcopalian.

ROBFOGEL, SUSAN SALITAN, lawyer; b. Rochester, N.Y., Apr. 4, 1943; d. Victor and Janet (Rosenthal) Salitan; m. Nathan Joshua Robfogel, July 12, 1965; children: Jacob Morris, Samuel Salitan. BA cum laude, Smith Coll., 1964; JD, Cornell U., 1967. Bar: N.Y.1967, U.S. Dist. Ct. (we. dist.) 1968, U.S. Ct. Appeals (2d cir.) 1971, U.S. Supreme Ct. 1971, U.S. Dist. Ct. (no. dist.) 1974, D.C. 1982. From asst. corp. counsel to sr. asst. corp. counsel City of Rochester, N.Y., 1967-70; assoc. Harris, Beach & Wilcox, Rochester, 1970-75; ptnr. Harris, Beach, Wilcox, Rubin & Levey, Rochester, 1975-85, Nixon, Peabody, LLP, Rochester and N.Y.C., 1985—; bd. mem. Office of Compliance, Washington, 1999—. Panel mem., Fed. Svc. Impasses Panel, Washington, 1983-94; mem., past chair Data Protection Rev. Bd., Albany, N.Y., 1984—. Mem. trustees vis. com. U. Rochester Med. Sch., 1990; mem. mgmt. adv. panel SUNY, 1990. Recipient Brockport Coll. Found. Community award, 1989. Fellow Am. Bar Found., N.Y. State Bar Found., Coll. Labor and Employment Lawyers; mem. ABA, N.Y. State Bar Assn., Washington D.C. Bar Assn., Monroe County Bar Assn. (Rodenbeck award 1988). Home: 1090 Park Ave Rochester NY 14610-1728 Office: Nixon Peabody LLP PO Box 1051 Rochester NY 14603-1051 also: 437 Madison Ave New York NY 10022-7001 Office Phone: 585-263 1586., 212-940-3116. Business E-Mail: srobfogel@nixonpeabody.com.

ROBIE, CLARENCE W. electric company executive; Pres. B & S Electric Supply Co., Atlanta, 1979—. Mem. Greater Atlanta Electric League. Office: B&S Electric Supply Co PO Box 44769 Atlanta GA 30336-5769

ROBIE, JOAN, elementary school principal; Prin. Monteith Elem. Sch., Grosse Pointe, Mich., 1989—. Recipient Elem. Sch. Recognition award U.S. Dept. Edn., 1989-90 Office: Monteith Elem Sch 1275 Cook Rd Grosse Pointe Woods MI 48236-2511

ROBILLARD, DONALD F., JR., gas and oil industry executive; Sr. v.p., CFO Hunt Consolidated, Dallas. Office: Hunt Consolidated Fountain Pl 1445 Ross Ave Dallas TX 75202 Office Fax: (214) 978-8888.

ROBILLARD, JEAN EUGENE, dean, educator; b. Montreal, 1943; m. Renee Robillard. BA, U. Montreal, 1964, MD, 1968. Pediat. residency Saint Justine Hosp., Montreal, 1969—72; pediat. nephrology fellowship UCLA Med. Ctr., Los Angeles, 1972—73, U. Iowa Med. Ctr., Iowa City, 1973—74; asst. prof., dept. pediat. U. Montreal Coll. Med., 1975—76; asst. prof. Dept. Pediat., Coll. Med., U. Iowa, 1974—75, 1976—78, assoc. prof., 1978—82, dir. nephrology div., 1976—96, prof., 1982—96, vice chmn.; chief pediat. U. Mich., Ann Arbor, 1996—2003; physician-in-chief C.S. Mott Children's Hosp., 1996—2003; dean Roy J. and Lucille A. Carver Coll Medicine, U. Iowa, 2003—. Editl. bd. Jour. Pediat., 2001—; bd. dirs. Am. Bd. Pediat., 2001—. Author of over 220 sci. papers. Recipient Disting. Alumni Award for Achievement, U. Iowa, 2002. Fellow: Coun. for High Blood Pressure Rsch., Am. Heart Assn., Royal Coll. Physicians & Surgeons; mem.: Assn. Med. Sch. Pediat. Dept. Chairs, Inc., Am. Soc. Transplant Physicians, The Perinatal Rsch. Soc., Soc. for Gynecologic Investigation, Am. Physiol. Soc., Am. Assn. for Advancement Sci. (fellow 1999), Am. Soc. Pediat. Nephrology (pres. 1994—95), Soc. Pediat. Rsch., Am. Heart Assn., Am. Soc. Nephrology, Internat. Soc. Nephrology, Internat. Pediat. Nephrology Assn., Midwest Soc. Pediat. Rsch. (Founder's Award 2002), Am. Acad. Pediat., Am Pediat. Soc. Office: Roy J & Lucille A Carver Coll Med 200 CMAB Iowa City IA 52242

ROBILLARD, JEAN JULES, engineering educator, researcher; b. Enguinegatte, France, Mar. 28, 1924; s. Jules Auguste and Augustine Marie (Delaroziere) R. MS, U. de Lille, France, 1945; DSc, Sorbonne U., Paris, 1947. Rsch. engr. L.M. Ericsson, Stockholm; cons. Gen. Dynamics, Rochester, N.Y.; staff scientist Motorola, Scottsdale, Ariz.; lab. rsch. scientist CBS, N.Y.C.; prof. rsch. scientist U. N.Mex., Las Cruces; prof., dir. materials sci. lab. U. Tex., El Paso. Dir. Cue Inc. (D. Nokia) Newton Upper Falls, Mass.; cons. Ricoh Co., Tokyo, Tektronix, Beaverton, Oreg., Fuji Photo Film, Tokyo. Author, editor: Industrial Applications of Holography, 1988, Nonlinear Optical Materials, 1991, Optical Data Processing and Holography, 1992, Non-Silver Photographic Processes, 1973. Recipient awards CRCM, 1993, IMIQ, 1997. Mem. SPSE (Charles Ives award 1964), SPIE, SID. Roman Catholic.

ROBILLARD, LUCIENNE, Canadian government official; b. Montreal, Canada, June 16, 1945; BA, Coll. Basile-Moreau, 1965; MA in Social Work, U. Montreal, 1967; Diploma in Adminstrn., École des hautes études commerciales, Montreal, 1983, MBA, 1986. Social worker, clin. practitioner Maisonneuve-Rosemont Hosp.; appt. min. of labour and fed. campaigns Que., 1995-96; sr. adminstr. Centre de svcs. sociaux Richelieu; youth leader in a kibbutz Israel, 1969-72; apptd. pub. curator City of Quebec, Canada, 1986-89; elected mem. Quebec Nat. Assembly for Chambly, 1989; apptd. min. cultural affairs, 1989-90; apptd. min. higher edn. and science, 1990-92; apptd. min. of edn., 1992-93; min. edn. and science, 1993-94; min. health and social svcs., 1994-95; minister of labor, minister responsible for fed. campaign, 1995; elected mem. parliament Saint-Henri-Westmount, 1995—; min. citizenship and immigration, 1996-99; re-elected to parliament Westmount-Ville-Marie, 1997—; pres. Treas. Bd., 1999—2003; min. infrastructure. Govt. of Canada, 1999—2003, min. industry, 2003—; min. responsible for econ. devel. agy. of Canada for the regions of Quebec, 2003—. Pres. Treasury Bd., Min. responsible for intrastructure; mem. Corp. professionelle des travailleurs sociaux de Québec, 1967—; mem. editl. com. (book) Le travail social et la santé au Québec, 1984-86, departmental study com. psychiatric svcs., Montreal region, 1984-85; pres. Commn. adminstrv. des svcs. de santé mentale of the Conseil régional de la Montérégie, 1983-86, Association des praticiens de service social en milieu de santé du Québec, 1984-86; cons. mental health dossier Rochon Commn., 1986, Mem. editl. com. Le Travail Social et la Santé du Québec, 1985. Mem. Corp Professionelle des Travailleurs Sociaux du Que. Office: 140 O'Connor St East Tower 9th Fl Ottawa ON Canada K1A OR5 also: Industry Canada 11th Fl East Tower CD Howe Bldg 235 Queen St K1A 0H5 Ottawa ON Canada

ROBIN, HOWARD W. biotechnology company executive; BS Acctg. & Fin., Fairleigh Dickinson U., 1974. Sr. assoc. Arthur Andersen & Co.; dir. bus. planning & devel. Berlex Labs., Inc., 1984—87, v.p. fin. and bus. devel., CFO, 1987—91, corp. v.p., gen. mgr., 1991—2001; CEO, pres., dir. Ribozyme Pharms., Boulder, Colo., 2001—. Office: Ribozyme Pharms 2950 Wilderness Pl Boulder CO 80301

ROBIN, KENNETH HOWARD, lawyer; b. Phila., Feb. 28, 1947; s. Leon and Ethel (Pastor) R.; m. Linda Beth Gelberd, Jan. 8, 1983. BS, Pa. State U., 1968; JD, Temple U., 1972. Bar: Pa 1972. Sr. atty. FRS Bd. Govs., Washington, 1972-77; asst. v.p. Citibank N.A., N.Y.C., 1977-80, assoc. gen. counsel, 1980-85, gen. counsel Latin Am. banking group, 1985—. Mem. ABA, N.Y. State Bar Assn. Office: Citibank NA 399 Park Ave New York NY 10022-4699

ROBIN, THEODORE TYDINGS, JR., lawyer, engineer, consultant; b. New Orleans, Aug. 29, 1939; s. Theodore Tydings and Hazel (Corbin) R.; m. Helen Jones, June 8, 1963; children: Corbin, Curry, Ted, Phil. BME, Ga. Inst. Tech., 1961, MS in Nuc. Engring., 1963, PhD, 1967; LLB, Blackstone Sch. Law, 1979. Bar: Calif. 1980, U.S. Patent and Trademark Office 1982; registered profl. engr., Ala., Calif. Rsch. engr. Oak Ridge (Tenn.) Nat. Lab., 1967; asst. prof. radiology and physics Emory U., Atlanta, 1968-69; project engr. Atomic Internat. divsn. N.Am. Rockwell, Canoga park, Calif., 1970-72; engr. mgmt, engring. divsn. So. Co. Svcs., Birmingham, Ala., 1972-83, mgr. nuc. support and quality assurance, 1989-90, mgr. quality assurance and resources, 1991-92; mgr. Hatch Design Configuration, 1993-94; program mgr. pooled inventory mgmt. program So. Electric Internat., Birmingham, 1984-88, bd. dirs. polit. action com., 1985-87; dir. nuc. stds., radiation safety officer, sr. patent counsel, prin. nuc. engring., cons. Theragenics Corp., Atlanta, 1996—. Mem. ABA, ASME (mem. nuc. quality assurance subcom. on stds. coordinating and radioactive waste 1991-99), Am. Assn. Physicists Medicine (legal info./risk mgmt. subcom. 2000—, mem. TG No6 Dose Equivalence in Br. Therapy 2001—), Am. Nuc. Soc. (chmn. Birmingham sect. 1987-88, nuc. power plant stds. com. 1989-94), Ga. Tech. Alumni Assn. (trustee 1997-2000), Rotary (pres. Shades Valley club 1987-88, chmn. dist. 6860 internat. youth exch. com. 1989-90, dist. gov. 6860 1994-95, tech. task force zone 30 coord. 2000-01), Sigma Xi. Achievements include research on power plant performance and reliability and effect of coal quality, space radiation effects on human cells, radiation safety, med. physics, boiling heat transfer, nuclear reactor safety, multi-utility contracting, reliability economics, risk analysis, benchmarking and total quality management; patent law. Home and Office: 4524 Pine Mountain Rd Birmingham AL 35213-1828 Office Phone: 205-870-7268. E-mail: robinty@mindspring.com.

ROBINETT, BETTY WALLACE, linguist, educator; b. Detroit, June 23, 1919; d. Henry Guy and Beulah (Reid) Wallace; m. Ralph F. Robinett, Apr. 10, 1952 (dec. div. 1960); 1 child, Richard Wallace. BA, Wayne State U., 1940; MA, U. Mich., 1941, PhD, 1951. Instr., adminstrv. asst. English Lang. Inst., U. Mich., Ann Arbor, 1945-50; cons. Dept. Edn., San Juan, P.R., 1950-51, 52-57; lectr. English, U. Mich., 1951-52, 55-56; asso. prof. English InterAm. U., San

German, P.R., 1957-59; asst. prof. English and linguistics Ball State U., Muncie, Ind., 1959-63, assoc. prof. English and linguistics, 1963-67, prof., 1967-68; prof. dept. linguistics U. Minn., Mpls., 1968-88, dir. program in English as a second lang., 1968-80, acting asst. v.p. acad. affairs, 1979-80, asst. v.p. acad. affairs, 1980-84, assoc. v.p. acad. affairs, 1984-88, prof. emerita, 1988, Morse alumni disting. tchg. prof. emerita, 1996; chmn. Univ. Senate Consultative Com., 1977-78. Vis. prof. Pa. State U., 1994-95; chmn. adv. panel on English tchg. USIA, 1988-93. Author: (with C.H. Prator) Manual of American English Pronunciation, 1972, 4th edit., 1985, Teaching English to Speakers of Other Languages, Substance and Technique, 1978, (with J. Schachter) Second Language Learning: Contrastive Analysis, Error Analysis and Related Aspects, 1983, (with Virginia F. Allen) Easy Latin Crossword Puzzles: Quid Pro Quo, 1999, Easy French Crossword Puzzles: Le mot Juste, 2002; editor Tesol Quar., 1967-72. Internat. Programs travel grantee, 1972, 77; recipient Morse-Amoco award for Excellence in Teaching, 1977 Mem. Tchrs. English to Speakers of Other Langs. (pres. 1974, James Alatis Svc. award 1990), Assn. Tchrs. ESL (chmn. 1976-77), Am. Assn. Applied Linguistics (v.p., pres. 1980-82), Linguistic Soc. Am. (life). Home: 1936 Park Forest Ave State College PA 16803-1329 E-mail: brobin4049@aol.com.

ROBINETTE, JOSEPH ALLEN, theater educator, playwright; b. Rockwood, Tenn., Feb. 8, 1939; s. Paul Henry and Willie Merle (Ghormley) R.; m. Helen Marie Seitz; children: John, Anne, Michael, Christopher, Andrew. BA, Carson-Newman Coll., 1960; MA, So. Ill. U., 1966, PhD, 1972. Tchr. Bearden H.S., Knoxville, Tenn., 1962-63; instr. Arkansas City (Kans.) Jr. Coll., 1963-64, U. Hawaii, Hilo, 1968-69, So. Ill. U., Carbondale, 1965-68, 69-71; prof. theatre arts Rowan U., Glassboro, N.J., 1971—. Author 49 pub. plays and musicals; authorized dramatizer Charlotte's Web, Stuart Little, The Lion, The Witch and the Wardrobe, The Paper Chase, A Rose for Emily, others. Founding mem. Opera for Youth, 1978—. Recipient ASCAP awards, 1975—; recipient Charlotte Chorpanning cup for outstanding writing of children's plays, Children's Theatre Assn. Am., 1976. Mem. Am. Alliance for Theatre in Edn. Home: PO Box 11 Richwood NJ 08074-0011 Office: Rowan U 201 Mullica Hill Rd Glassboro NJ 08028-1702 Business E-Mail: robinettej@rowan.edu.

ROBINO, DAVID J. computer company executive; b. Ft. Collins, Colo., Nov. 16, 1959; BS, Graceland Coll.; MS in Indsl. Rels., Iowa State U. With Maytag Co., Iowa, Pepsi-Cola., N.Y. and Ind., AC Nielsen, sr. v.p. internat. bus., 1993; v.p. bus. markets divsn. AT&T; with Gateway, Inc., San Diego, 1998—, vice chmn., 2000—. Bd. dirs. San Diego Regional Econ. Devel. Corp. Bd. dirs. San Diego Sci. and Tech. Commn., U. Calif. San Diego Found.; chmn. bd. trustees Graceland U., Lamoni, Iowa; exec. com. bd. dirs. Iowa Coll. Found. Office: Gateway Inc 14303 Gateway Pl Poway CA 92064-7140

ROBINOWITZ, MAX, pathologist, consultant; b. Washington, Aug. 11, 1936; s. William and Stella (Chaikin) R.; m. Carolyn Landeck Bauer, June 10, 1962; children: Mark, David L. BS, Georgetown U., 1957, MD, 1961. Med. intern Barnes Hosp., St. Louis, 1961-62, asst. resident, Internal Medicine, 1962-63; resident in pathology Mt. Sinai Hosp., N.Y.C., 1963-67; asst. chief clin. pathology Walter Reed Army Med. Ctr., Washington D.C., 1968-69; asst. pathologist Armed Forces Inst. of Pathology, Washington D.C., 1969-70; pathologist Mt. Sinai Med. Ctr., Miami Beach, Fla., 1970-72; asst. prof. pathology U. Miami, 1970-72; asst. prof. pathology, Sch. of Medicine Georgetown U., Washington D.C., 1972-75; pathologist Armed Forces Inst. of Pathology, 1976-90. Sr. med. officer Office In Vitro Diagnostic Device Evaluation Safety, CDRH, FDA, Rockville, Md., 1990—; clin. prof. pathology USPHS, Bethesda, Md., 1980—; clin. assoc. pathology Georgetown U. Med. Sch., Washington, 1976—. Maj. U.S. Army, 1967-69. Mem. AACC, AOA, USCAP, CAP, ASCP, AMA. Office: FDA HFZ-440 2098 Gaither Rd Rockville MD 20850-4017

ROBINS, BETTY DASHEW, antiques and arts dealer; b. N.Y.C., Feb. 14, 1923; d. Leon and Esther (Turits) Dashew; m. Arthur Joseph Robins, Sept. 26, 1948; children: Lisa Dale, Michael Lee. BA, NYU, 1952. Field staff Pearl Buck Open Door, N.Y.C., 1944-45; dir. MacArthur House, San Francisco, 1945-47, Georgetown House, Washington, 1948-50; asst. curator S. Asian Collection Mus. of Art and Archaeology, U. Mo., Columbia, 1967-68; owner BDR Assocs. Arts and Antiques, Columbia, 1976—. Founding mem., 1st pres. Columbia Art League, 1959-61; gen. chmn. 1st Tenn. Artist Craftsman Fair, Nashville, 1971-72; bd. mem. Mus. Assocs., Mus. Art and Archaeology, U. Mo., 1975-85, Boone County Hist. Soc., 2001—; mem. S. Asian studies com., 1976-85; coord. Festival of India, 1985-86, Festival of China, 1986-87, Peace Through the Arts, 1987-88, yr.-long programs commemorating 50th anniversary India independence, Columbia, 1997; mem. profl. visual arts adv. com. Mo. Arts Coun., 1980-82; cons. Denver Art Mus., 1991-92; advisor India Arts exhibit U. Mo. Mus. Art and Archaeology, 1997; organizer gallery exhibits, such as carved coconut Scrapers of Malaysia, India, Indonesia, Nat. Inst. of Pub. Adminstrn., Kuala Lumpur, 1989, Traditional Arts of India and U.S.A., U. Mo., 1989, Healing Imagery of Malaysia and U.S.A., U. Mo., 1991, Decorative Arts India, Stephens Coll., 1998, Storytelling through the Everyday Art of Mo. and India, Boone County Hist. Mus., 1998. Co-author: Everyday Art of India, 1968; contbr. articles to profl. jours. Bd. dirs. PAST (hist. preservation of Mo.), 1978-79. Named Woman of the Yr., Women in Comms., 1977-78, Vol. of Yr., Vol. Action Coun., 1983; recipient Quiet Hero award Columbia Pub. Schs., 1998. Home: 2316 Woodridge Rd Columbia MO 65203-1550

ROBINS, CLIVE JUSTIN, psychology educator, researcher, psychotherapist; b. London, Apr. 5, 1953; came to U.S., 1975; s. Thomas Justin and Doris May (Yardley) R.; m. Melissa Kathleen Doyle, May 6, 1978; children: Justin, Alexander, Daniel. B.Sc., U. Sussex, Brighton, Eng., 1974; M.A., Stanford U., 1978; Ph.D., SUNY-Stony Brook, 1982. Lic. psychologist, N.Y., N.C. Asst. prof. psychology NYU, N.Y.C., 1982-87; assoc. prof. psychiatry Duke U. Med. Ctr., 1987—; instr., supr. Inst. Behavior Therapy, N.Y.C., 1983-87; pvt. practice psychology, N.Y.C., 1984-87. Contbr. chpt., articles to profl. publs., 1974—. Rsch. Challenge Fund grantee NYU, 1984, NIMH grantee, 1986. Mem. Am. Psychol. Assn., Assn. Advancement Behavior Therapy, Soc for Rsch. in Psychopathology, Soc. Exploration Psychotherapy Integration. Avocations: tennis; jogging; cinema. Home: 28 E Bayberry Ct Durham NC 27713-9438 Office: Duke U Med Ctr Dept Psychiatry PO Box 3362 Durham NC 27702-3362

ROBINS, H(ENRY) IAN, medical oncologist; b. N.Y.C., Feb. 17, 1945; s. Edwin and Matilda (Morgenstern) R. AB in Biology, Boston U., 1966, AM in Biochemistry, 1968, PhD in Molecular Biology, 1971, MD, 1976. Diplomate Am. Bd. Internal Medicine, Am. Bd. Med. Oncology, Am. Bd. Forensic Medicine, Am. Bd. Forensic Examiners. Intern in internal medicine Univ. Hosps., Madison, Wis., 1976-77, resident in internal medicine, 1977-79; fellow in clin. oncology Wis. Clin. Cancer Ctr., Madison, 1979-81, fellow in rsch. oncology, 1981-82; instr. dept. human oncology, dept. medicine Dept. Human Oncology, Dept. Medicine U. Wis. Sch. Medicine, Madison, 1982-83, asst. prof., 1983-86, assoc. prof., 1986—; chief sect. med. oncology, dir. U. Wis. Sch. Medicine, Madison, 1990-95, prof. dept. human oncology, medicine and neurology, 1992—. Chmn. Systemic Hyperthermia Oncology Working Group. Contbr. numerous articles to profl. jours.; reviewer numerous sci. jours. including Biochem. Pharmacology, Internat. Jour. Radiation Biology, Jour. Clin. Oncology, New Eng. Jour. Medicine, others. Mem. N.Y. Acad. Scis., AAAS, ACP, Internat. Clin. Hyperthermia Soc., Radiation Rsch. Soc., N.am. Hyperthermia Group, Oncology Group, Am. Fedn. clin. Rsch., Ea. Coop. Oncology Group, European Soc. Hyperthermic Oncology, Vet. Cancer Soc., Transplantation Soc., Collaborative Ocular Melanoma Study Group, N.Am. Brain Tumor Consortium, Am. Soc. Clin. Hypnosis, Minn. Soc. Clin. Hypnosis, Sigma Xi. Office: Clin Sci Ctr K4/662 U Wis Sch Med 600 Highland Ave Madison WI 53792-0001

ROBINS, JAMES DOW, counselor; b. Athens, Ga., Oct. 17, 1952; s. Gerald Burns and Fay Ann Robins; m. Sharon Eileen Parker, Apr. 12, 1974 (div. 1976). BA in Psychology, SUNY, Albany, 1981; BA in Comm. cum laude, Tex. A&M U., 1981, MA in Secondary Edn., 1982; ABA, cert. legal asst., Southwestern Paralegal Inst., 1984; MS in Guidance and Counseling, Tex. A&M U., 1993. Bar: Tex., 1985; cert. counselor, psychologist, English and speech tchr., legal asst., Tex. Program dir. University City, Inc., Athens, 1971-73; sta. mgr. Bethany Broadcasting, Houston, 1973-76; program coord. for radio and TV, Tex. A&I U., Kingsville, 1977-82; dir. pub. rels. Kleberg Meml. Hosp., Kingsville, 1983-84; legal asst., cons. Kleberg, Dyer, Redford & Weil, Corpus Christi, Tex., 1984-86; tchr. English lit. Brownsville (Tex.) Ind. Sch. Dist., 1986-90; dir. testing and assessment, dir. suicide intervention Kingsville Ind. Sch. Dist., Kingsville, 1993—, counselor, 1993—. Cons. Conner Mus., Kingsville, 1981-82. Author: The School Counselor: A Profession in Transition, 1993; contbr. articles to various publs. Recipient Disting. Svc. award for Excellence in Broadcasting, Tex. A&M, 1980-81. Mem. ACA (profl.), Tex. Counseling Assn., Mensa, The Blues Found. (internat. voting mem.), State Bar of Tex. (legal asst. div. 1985), Am. Counseling Assn., Tex. Counselors Assn., Tex. Sch. Counselors Assn., Tex. Assn. for Humanistic Edn. and Devel., Tex. Assn. for Multi-Cultural Counseling and Devel., Am. Assn. Assessment in Counseling, World Wildlife Fedn., Gulf Coast Counseling Assn., Gulf Coast Assn. for Counseling and Devel., The Blues Found., Phi Delta Kappa, Alpha Chi. Methodist. Avocations: writing, guitar, computers. Home: 515 University Blvd Kingsville TX 78363-4242 E-mail: jrobins@intcomm.net.

ROBINS, JOEL, import/export company executive; Pres. Robbins Trading Co., Chgo., 1983—. Office: Robbins Trading Co Ste 760 8700 W Bryn Mawr Ave # 7ths Chicago IL 60631-3512

ROBINS, JUDY ROSELYN, interior designer; b. Cleve., Sept. 2, 1948; d. Stanley and Esther (Resnick) Waxman; m. Kenneth Michael Robins, Sept. 26, 1971. AAS, Fashion Inst. Tech.; BS, NYU, 1970, MA, 1972. Fabric coord. Celanese Corp., N.Y.C., 1970—71; merchandiser Bayly Corp., Denver, 1973—74; instr. Metro State Coll., Denver, 1977—81; self-employed interior designer Denver, 1975—. Mem. bd. Waxman Industries. Mem. steering com. Denver Art Mus., trustee, 1986—96, collections com., devel. com.; founding mem. Young Women's Leadership Cabinet United Jewish Appeal, 1977—82, Nat. Jewish Ctr. Bd., 1984—87, Nat. Women's Bd., 1984—; v.p. Mizel Mus. Judaica; bd. dirs. Nat. Found. for Jewish Culture; bd. govs. Nat. Jewish Ctr. for Immunology and Respiratory Medicine; mem. steering com. Alliance Contemporary Art; women's bd. Nat. Jewish Hosp., 1978—80, bd. dirs., 1984—88; bd. dirs. congregation Jewish Family and Children's Svc. Colo., Colo., 1975—83, Anti-Defamation League, 1987—90; bd. dirs., v.p. leadership Allied Jewish Fedn., assoc. campaign chmn., 1985, gen. chmn., 1987—88. Recipient Young Leadership award, Allied Jewish Fedn., 1977, Afkey award, Denver Art Mus., 1995. Mem.: United Jewish Appeal (nat. women's divsn. exec. com. 1985—98, nat.-vice chair 1990—98). Address: 2165 E Alameda Ave Denver CO 80209-2710 E-mail: kennyrobin@aol.com.

ROBINS, LEE NELKEN, medical educator; b. New Orleans, Aug. 29, 1922; d. Abe and Leona (Reiman) Nelken; m. Eli Robins, Feb. 22, 1946 (dec. Dec. 1994); children: Paul, James, Thomas, Nicholas; m. Hugh Chaplin, Aug. 5, 1998. Student, Newcomb Coll., 1938-40; BA, Radcliffe Coll., 1942, MA, 1943; PhD, Harvard U., 1951. Mem. faculty Washington U., St. Louis, 1954—, prof. sociology in psychiatry, 1968-91, prof. sociology, 1969-91, prof. social sci. and social sci. in psychiatry, 1991-2000, prof. emeritus, 2001—. Past mem. Nat. Adv. Coun. on Drug Abuse; past mem. task panels Pres.'s Commn. on Mental Health; mem. expert adv. panel on mental health WHO; Salmon lectr. N.Y. Acad. Medicine, 1983; Cutter lectr. Harvard U., 1997. Author: Deviant Children Grown Up, 1966; editor 11 books; mem. editl. bd. Psychol. Medicine, Jour. Studies on Alcohol, Social Psychiatry and Psychiatric Epidemiology, Epidemiol. e Psichiat. Sociale; contbr. articles to profl. jours. Recipient Rsch. Scientist award USPHS, 1970-90, Pacesetter Rsch. award Nat. Inst. Drug Abuse, 1978, Radcliffe Coll. Grad. Soc. medal, 1979, Sutherland award Am. Soc. Criminology, 1991, Nathan B. Eddy award Com. on Problems of Drug Dependence, 1993, Spl. Presdl. Commendation Am. Psychiat. Assn., 1999, Am. Acad. Arts and Scis., 1999, Commendation and Appreciation award Harvard Inst. Psychiat. Epidemiology and Genetics, 2000, Disting. Sci. Devel. award Soc. Rsch. in Child Devel., 2003; rsch. grantee NIMH, Nat. Inst. on Drug Abuse, Nat. Inst. on Alcohol Abuse and Alcoholism. Fellow Am. Coll. Epidemiology, Royal Coll. Psychiatrists (hon.), Am. Soc. Psychiatrists (hon.), Soc. Study of Addiction (hon.); mem. APHA (Rema Lapouse award 1979, Lifetime Achievement award sect. on alcohol and drug abuse 1994), Internat. Fedn. Psychiat. Epidemiology (com.1992-2002), World Psychiat. Assn. (sect. com. on epidemiology and cmty. psychiatry, 1985-2002, co-chmn. sect. on rsch. instruments in psychiatry), Soc. Life History Rsch. in Psychopathology, Am. Coll. Neuropsychopharmacology, Inst. Medicine, Am. Psychopath. Assn. (pres. 1987-88, Paul Hoch award 1978). Office: Washington U Med Sch Dept Psychiatry Saint Louis MO 63110

ROBINS, MARJORIE MCCARTHY (MRS. GEORGE KENNETH ROBINS), civic worker; b. Oct. 4, 1914; d. Eugene Ross and Louise (Roblee) McCarthy; m. George Kenneth Robins, Nov. 9, 1940; children: Carol Robins Von Arx, G. Stephen, Barbara A. Robins Foorman. Mem. Mo. Libr. Commn., 1937-38; bd. dirs. St. Louis Jr. League, 1945-46, Occupational Therapy Workshop St. Louis, 1941-46, pres., 1945-46; bd. dirs. Ladue Chapel Nursery Sch., 1957-64, pres. bd., 1963-64; past regional chmn. United Fund; past mem. St. Louis Met. Youth Commn., St. Louis Health and Welfare Coun.; bd. dirs. Internat. Inst. St. Louis, 1966-72, 76-92, sec., 1968, v.p., 1981; bd. dirs. Mental Health Assn. St. Louis, 1963-70, Washington U. Child Guidance and Evaluation Clinic, 1968-78, Cen. Inst. for Deaf, 1970—, v.p., 1975-76, pres., 1976-78; bd. dirs. Met. St. Louis YWCA, 1954-74, pres. bd., 1960-63, trustee, 1977—; nat. bd. YWCA, 1967-79, nat. v.p., 1973-76; vol. tchr. remedial reading clinic St. Louis City Schs., 1968-71; trustee John Burroughs Sch., 1960-63, John Burroughs Found., 1965-80, Roblee Found., 1972—, Nat. YWCA Retirement Fund, 1979-88; bd. dirs. Gambrill Gardens United Meth. Retirement Home, 1979-85, Thompson Retreat and Conf. Center, 1981-87, Springboard to Learning Inc., 1980-98, v.p., 1980-90; tutor I Have A Dream Found., 1995-98. Mem. Archaeol. Inst. Am. (bd. dirs. 1993-95, 97-00, treas. St. Louis chpt. 1985-87, 93-95), Vassar Club (sec. and pres. 1939-40), Wednesday Club (dir. 1968-70, 77-81, 93-95), St. Louis. Home: 1 McKnight Pl Apt 265 Saint Louis MO 63124

ROBINS, MARTIN B. lawyer; b. Chgo., Oct. 20, 1956; s. Sam I. and June (Tikulski) R.; m. Elizabeth Bangs Eaton, May 28, 1993. BS summa cum laude, U. Pa., 1977; JD cum laude, Harvard U., 1980. Bar: Ill. 1980, U.S. Dist. Ct. (no. dist.) Ill. 1980. Assoc. Sonnenschein Carlin Nath & Rosenthal, Chgo., 1980-83, Gottlieb & Schwartz, Chgo., 1983-85; v.p., gen. counsel, sec. IDC Svcs., Inc., Chgo., 1985-89; sr. v.p., gen. counsel Meridian Leasing Corp., Deerfield, Ill., 1990-99; ptnr. Law Office Martin B. Robins, Buffalo Grove, Ill., 1999—. Cons. in field. Author: Equipment Leasing-Matthew Bender Monograph, 2000, Cyberfinance: Financing the E-Business, 2001; contbr. articles to profl. jours. Bd. mem. Barrington Youth Svcs., Ill.; comml. arbitrator CLE Programs. Mem. ABA (panelist) 2003-2004, Chgo. Bar Assn. Avocations: participatory athletics, reading, gardening, cooking. Office: 1110 Lake Cook Rd #355 Buffalo Grove IL 60089 Office Phone: 847-229-8710. E-mail: mrobins@mr-laws.com.

ROBINS, MITCHELL JAMES, management consultant; b. Detroit, May 23, 1956; s. Melvin M. Robins and Judith (Bell) Martin; m. Amy Elizabeth Green, July 2, 1978; children: Alexander Philip, Sean Lewis, Emily Dinah. BBA, U. Mich., 1977; postgrad., U. Detroit, Oakland U. CPA, Mich., Fla., Ind., Nev., Calif. Exec. mgr. GM; founder, mng. ptnr., CEO Robins-Assocs., CPAs and Cons., Southfield, Mich., 1981—, founder, mng. ptnr. La Jolla, Calif., 1980—; founder, mgr., ptnr. Lumedics, Ltd., La Jolla, Calif., Paris. Bd. dirs. Campus Distbn., Inc., Ann Arbor, Mich., Internat. Med.-Dental Hypnotherapy Assn., LumeDics Ltd., San Diego; mem. Restaurant Bus. Research Adv. Panel, N.Y.C. Mem. steering com. Rep. 300 Com. of Mich., Oakland County, zoning bd. appeals City of Farmington Hills, Rep. Senatorial Inner Circle; mem. Carmel Valley Planning Bd., 1997. Named Nat. Rep. Congl. Com. Businessman of the Yr., 1999. Mem. AICPA, ABA, Mich. Assn. CPA's, Mich. Soc. Planning Ofcls., Assn. MBA Execs., U. Mich. Alumni Assn., Internat. Platform Assn. Clubs: Economic (Detroit), Detroit Athletic, Heritage Hills Country, Skyline. Republican. Avocations: golf, tennis, history, politics, travel. Home: 12885 Ralston Cir San Diego CA 92130-2447 Fax: 858-551-1215. E-mail: mrobinsooo@usa.net.

ROBINS, NORMAN ALAN, strategic planning consultant, former steel company executive; b. Chgo., Nov. 19, 1934; s. Irving and Sylvia (Robbin) Robins; m. Sandra Ross, June 10, 1956; children: Lawrence Richard, Sherry Lynn. BSChemE, MIT, 1955, MSChemE, 1956; PhD in Math., Ill. Inst. Tech., 1972. Asst. mgr. process sys. and controls Inland Steel Co., East Chicago, Ind., 1962—67, assoc. mgr. process sys. and controls, 1967—72, dir. process rsch., 1972—77, v.p. rsch., 1977—84, v.p. technol. assessment, 1984—86, v.p. strategic planning, 1986—91; ret., 1991; ind. cons. in strategic planning, 1991—. Mem. bd. edn. Homewood-Flossmoor HS, Ill., 1974—77. Mem.: AIChE, Assn. Iron and Steel Tech. (Nat. Open Hearth Conf. award 1972).

ROBINS, ROBERT SIDWAR, political science educator, administrator; b. Spangler, Pa., Apr. 20, 1938; s. Sydney and Katherine (Sidwar) R.; m. Marjorie McGann, Nov. 25, 1959; children: Anthony P., Nicholas A. BA, U. Pitts., 1959; MA, Duke U., 1961, PhD, 1963. Prof. polit. sci. Tulane U., New Orleans, 1965—, chmn. dept. polit. sci., 1979-90, dep. provost, 1991-98. Acad. visitor Inst. Commonwealth Studies, U. London, 1969-70, 78-79, mem. 1987-88; sr. assoc. mem. St. Antony's Coll., Oxford, Eng., 1972-73; vis. scholar Hastings Ctr., 1982; vis. scientist Tavistock Clinic, London, 1987-88. Author: Political Institutionalization and the Integration of Elites, 1976 (Carnegie Commn. report) Legislative Attitudes Toward Higher Education in Louisiana, 1968, Psychopathology and Political Leadership, 1977, Disease and Political Leadership, 1990; co-author: When Illness Strikes the Leader, Political Paranoia; contbr. articles to profl. publs. Vice chmn. Elections Integrity Commn., State of La., 1981-82. Recipient Excellence in Tchg. award Tulane U., 1978; Fulbright scholar, 1961-62. Mem. Am. Polit. Sci. Assn., Internat. Soc. Polit. Psychology, New Orleans Fgn. Rels. Assn. (bd. dirs.) Avocations: carpentry, gardening. Home: 64 Pond Rd Stamford CT 06902

ROBINSON, ADELBERT CARL, lawyer, judge; b. Shawnee, Okla., Dec. 13, 1926; s. William H. and Mayme (Forston) R.; m. Paula Kay Settles, Apr. 16, 1988; children from previous marriage: William, James, Schuyler, Donald, David, Nancy, Lauri. Student, Okla. Bapt. U., 1944-47; JD, Okla. U., 1950. Bar: Okla. 1950. Pvt. practice, Muskogee, Okla., 1956-97; with legal dept. Phillips Petroleum Co., 1950-51; adjuster U.S. Fidelity & Guaranty Co., 1951-54, atty., adjuster-in-charge, 1954-56; ptnr. Fite & Robinson, 1956-62, Fite, Robinson & Summers, 1963-70, Robinson & Summers, 1970-72, Robinson, Summers & Locke, 1972-76, Robinson, Locke & Gage, 1976-80, Robinson, Locke, Gage & Fite, 1980-83, Robinson, Locke, Gage, Fite & Williams, Muskogee, 1983-95, Robinson, Gage, Fite & Williams, Muskogee, 1995-97. Police judge City of Muskogee, 1963—64, mcpl. judge, 1964—70; prin. justice 84Temp. Divsn. 36 Okla. Ct. Appeals, 1981—84, spl. dist. judge, 1997—; pres., dir. Wall St. Bldg. Corp., 1969—78, Three Forks Devel. Corp., 1968—77, Rolo Leasing Inc., 1971—97, Suroya II Inc.1, 1977—99; mng. ptnr. RLG Ritz, 1980—97; ptnr. First City Real Estate Partnership, 1985—94; dir. First City Bank, Tulsa, Okla., 1985—92; del. to U.S./China Jt. Session on Trade, Investment and Econ. Law, Beijing, 1987; dir. First Bankshares of Muskogee, 1980—95, First of Muskogee Corp., 1980—95; adv. dir. First Nat. Bank and Trust Co. of Muskogee, 1978—95. Chmn. Muskogee County (Okla.) Law Day, 1963, Muskogee Area Redevel. Authority, 1963, Muskogee County chpt. Am. Cancer Soc., 1956; pres., bd. dirs. United Way of Muskogee Inc., 1980-88, v.p., 1982, pres., 1983; bd. dirs. Muskogee Cmty. Concert Assn., Muskogee Tourist Info. Bur., 1964-68; bd. dirs., gen. counsel United Cerebral Palsy Eastern Okla., 1964-68; trustee Connors Devel. Found., Connors Coll., 1981-99, chmn., 1987-89; active Muskogee Housing Authority, 1992-95. With inf. AUS, 1945-46. Mem. ABA, Okla. Bar Assn. (chmn. uniform laws com. 1970-72, chmn. profl. coop. com. 1965-69, past regional chmn. grievance com.), Muskogee County Bar Assn. (pres. 1971, mem. exec. coun. 1971-74), Okla. Assn. Def. Counsel (dir. 1970-74), Okla. Assn. Mcpl. Judges (dir. 1968-70), Muskogee c. of C., Delta Theta Phi., Rotary (pres. 1971-72). Methodist. Office: Muskogee County Courthouse PO Box 1350 Muskogee OK 74402-1350 Home: 3405 Park Pl N Muskogee OK 74403-1815

ROBINSON, AGNES CLAFLIN, educational administrator; b. N.Y.C., Oct. 2, 1918; d. Crittenden Hull and Agnes Sanger (Claflin) Adams; m. Albert Lewis Robinson (div.); children: Nicholas Adams, John Claflin, Hugh Wesley, James Allen, Lewis Stewart. AB, Barnard Coll., 1941; MS, NYU, 1949. Tech. asst. BEll Telephone Labs., Whippany, N.J., 1943-44; v.p. Family Service Assn., Morristown, N.J., 1946-48; bd. dirs. Adult and Child Guidance Clinic, San Jose, Calif., 1955-58; v.p. Palo Alto (Calif.) Mental Health Soc., 1959-63; pres. PTA, Palo Alto, 1961-63; trustee Palo Alto Unified Sch. Dist., 1963-73, pres., 1965-67. Chmn. Drug Abuse Bd., Palo Alto, 1971-74; mem. adv. bd. Nairobi Day Schs., East Palo Alto, 1969-72; mem. adv. bd. Child Care Now, 1972-73; mem. Calif. Post-Secondary Edn. Commn., 1974-80, chmn., 1978-80; advisor to pub. affairs com. YWCA, 1974-2002; mem. Mid-Peninsula Com. for Integrated Edn., 1974-80; bd. dirs. Addiction Research Found., 1974-78, pres., 1974-77; bd. dirs. Mid-Peninsula Learning Ctr. 1980-83; pres. New Ways to Work, 1976-79; mem. spl. legis. com. Calif. Student Fin. Aid Study Group, 1979; mem. Palo Alto Human Rels. Commn., 1981-82; bd. govs. Calif. Cmty. Colls., 1982—, pres., 1986-87; mem. accreditation coms. Western Assn. Schs. and Colls., 1989-97; co-chair Palo Alto com. Study Circles for Racial Understanding, 1998-2002. Author: (with Ruth McAneny Loud) New York, New York! A Knickerbocker Holiday for You and Your Children, 1946. Mem. NAACP (life), PTA (life), Sierra Club (life), Radcliffe Club of Mid-Peninsula. Democrat. Home: 1765 Fulton St Palo Alto CA 94303-2943 E-mail: acr1765@aol.com.

ROBINSON, ALEXANDER JACOB, clinical psychologist; b. St. John, Kans., Nov. 7, 1920; s. Oscar Frank and Lydia May (Beitler) R.; m. Elsie Louise Riggs, July 29, 1942; children: Madelyn K., Alicia A., David J., Charles A., Paul S., Marietta J., Stephen N. BA in Psychology, MS in Clin. Psychology, Ft. Hays (Kans.) State U., 1942; postgrad., U. Ill., 1942-44. Cert. psychologist, sch. psychologist. Chief psychologist Larned (Kans.) State Hosp., 1948-53, with employee selection, outpatient services, 1953-55; sch. psychologist County Schs., Modesto, Calif., 1955-61, Pratt (Kans.) Jr. Coll., 1961-66; fed. grantee, writer assoc. dir. Exemplary Federally Funded Program for Spl. Edn., Pratt, 1966-70; dir. spl. edn., researcher Stafford County Schs., St. John, 1970-81, ret., 1981. Supr. testing and data Incidence of Exceptional Children in Kansas, Kans. State U., Ft. Hays, 1946; writer, asst. dir. Best Exemplary Federally Funded Program on Spl. Edn., Pratt, 1966-70; fed. grantee, researcher, writer, study dir. Edn. for the High-Performance Child, St. John, 1970—, Psychogenesis of the Sociopathic Personality, a longitudinal study. Minister, The Ch. of Jesus Christ. Served to 2d lt. U.S. Army, 1944-46, PTO. Mem. N.Y. Acad. Scis., Libr. of Congress. Lodges: Lions (program chmn. St. John 1974-76). Achievements include research on normal children with a learning disability and their specific developmental requirement. Home and Office: 202 Grandview St Saint John KS 67576-2100

ROBINSON, ALICE JEAN MCDONNELL, retired drama and speech educator; b. St. Joseph, Mo., Nov. 17, 1922; d. John Francis and Della M. (Mavity) McDonnell; m. James Eugene Robinson, Apr. 21, 1956 (dec. 1983). BA, U. Kans., 1944, MA, 1947; PhD, Stanford U., 1965. Tchr. Garden City (Kans.) High Sch., 1944-46; asst. prof. Emporia (Kans.) State U., 1947-52; dir. live programs Sta. KTVH-TV, Hutchinson-Wichita, Kans., 1953-55; assoc. prof. drama and speech U. Md. Baltimore County, Balt., 1966-99, rsch. theatre history. Author: The American Theatre: A History in Slides, 1992, Betty Comden and Adolph Green: A Bio-Bibliography, 1993; co-editor: Notable Women in the American Theatre, 1989; appeared in plays, including Landscape, 1983, Tartuffe, 1985, Rockaby, 1990. Mem. Am. Soc. Theatre Rsch., Assn. Theatre Higher Edn., Phi Beta Kappa. Republican. Avocations: travel, reading, acting, directing. Home: 111 N Main St Caldwell KS 67022-1535

ROBINSON, ANN, state representative; b. Aberdeen, Wash., Oct. 9, 1947; m. Marvin Robinson. AAS, Casper Coll., 1987, AA, 1991. Engring., regulatory technician Oil and Gas Industry, 1979—86; paralegal Confidential Adoption Intermediary, 1991—; state rep. dist. 58 Wyo. State Legis., Cheyenne, 1997—. Mem. Edn. com. Wyo. State Legis., Cheyenne, mem. Labor, Health and Social Svcs.; editor Wyo. State Dem. Newspaper The Spokesman, 1979—81. Vol. Concerned Citizens for Quality Nursing Home Care. Mem.: DAR, Nat. Fedn.

Paralegal Assns., Wyo. Old-Time Fiddlers Assn., Casper Antique and Collectors Club. Democrat. Home: 1923 Grass Creek Rd Casper WY 82601 Office: Capitol Bldg Wyo State Legis Cheyenne WY 82002

ROBINSON, ANNETTE, councilwoman; married; six children. Dist. dir. Office of Congresswoman Majorie Owens; coord., liaison Comptr. Harrison J. Goldin; councilwoman Dist. 36 N.Y.C. Coun., Bklyn., 1992—. Mem. NAACP, Vanguard Ind. Dem. Assn. (exec. com.), Coalition for Cmty. Empowerment (exec. mem.), Knights and Ladies of Peter Claver Ladies Aux., South African Sisters Against Aparteid, African Am. Clergy and Elected Ofcls. Office: Rm 417 1360 Fulton St Ste 417 Brooklyn NY 11216-2600

ROBINSON, ANTHONY CHRISTOPHER, novelist, educator; b. Biskupitz, Germany, Mar. 10, 1931; came to U.S., 1931; s. Henry Morton and Gertrude (Ludwig) R.; m. Mary Chika, Nov. 16, 1957 (dec. Mar. 1976); children: Jennifer Eve, Henry David; m. Tatiana Padwa, Feb. 14, 1998. BA, Columbia Coll., N.Y.C., 1953; MA cum laude, Columbia U., 1960; grad., Phillips Acad., Andover, Mass., 1949. Prof. English, dir. creative writing SUNY, New Paltz, 1964-2000, prof. English emeritus, 2000—. Vis. prof. U. Paris, 1971-72. Author: A Departure From the Rules, 1960 (Bread Loaf fellow 1960), The Easy Way, 1963, Home Again, Home Again, 1969, The Whole Truth, 1990, The Member-Guest, 1991. Lt. USNR, 1953-56. Democrat. Roman Catholic. Avocations: golf, fly fishing, golf club making, hiking. Home: 153 Huguenot St New Paltz NY 12561 E-mail: robinsoa@newpaltz.edu.

ROBINSON, ARTHUR HOWARD, geography educator; b. Montreal, Que., Can., Jan. 5, 1915; s. James Howard and Elizabeth (Peavey) R.; m. Mary Elizabeth Coffin, Dec. 23, 1938 (dec. Jan. 1992); children: Stephen Michael, Patricia Anne; m. Martha Elizabeth Rodabaugh Phillips, Feb. 6, 1993. BA, Miami U., Oxford, Ohio, 1936, LittD, 1966; MA, U. Wis., 1938; PhD in Geography, Ohio State U., 1947, DSc (hon.), 1984. Sec. to mem. Ohio Bd. Liquor Control, 1936; asst. geography U. Wis., 1936-38, Ohio State U., 1938-41; chief map div. OSS, 1941-46; mem. faculty U. Wis., 1945—, prof. geography, 1951-80, prof. emeritus, 1980—, chmn. dept., 1954-58, 66-68, Lawrence Martin prof. cartography, 1967—; dir. Univ. Cartographic Lab., 1966-73; hon. cons. cartography Library of Congress, 1974-80. Chief map officer U.S. Delegation Quebec and Cairo confs., World War II, pres. Internat. Cartographic Assn., 1972-76 Author: Look of Maps, 1952, Early Thematic Mapping in the History of Cartography, 1982; co-author: Elements of Geography, 4th edit., 1957, Elements of Cartography, 6th edit., 1995, Fundamentals of Physical Geography, 3rd edit., 1977, The Nature of Maps, 1976; co-editor: Cartographical Innovations, 1987; editor Am. Cartographer, 1974-76; also articles; designer Robinson map projection, 1963. Served to maj. AUS, 1944-45. Decorated Legion of Merit; recipient Carl Mannerfelt medal Internat. Cartographic Assn., 1981, Helen Culver Gold Medal Geog. Soc. Chgo., 1983, John Oliver LaGorce medal Nat. Geog. Soc., 1988, Silver medal Brit. Cartographic Soc., 1991; Guggenheim rsch. fellow, 1964, 78. Fellow Brit. Cartog. Assn.; mem. Can. Cartog. Assn., Assn. Am. Geographers (coun. 1960-65, pres. 1963), Am. Congress Surveying and Mapping (hon.; chmn. cartography divsn. 1971), Am. Geog. Soc. (life, O.M. Miller medal). Home: 7707 N Brookline Dr Apt 302 Madison WI 53719-3526 E-mail: ahrobins@facstaff.wisc.edu.

ROBINSON, BARBARA PAUL, lawyer; b. Oct. 19, 1941; d. Leo and Pauline G. Paul; m. Charles Raskob Robinson, June 11, 1965; children: Charles Paul, Torrance Webster. AB magna cum laude, Bryn Mawr Coll., 1962; LLB, Yale U., 1965, Order of the Coif. Bar: N.Y. 1966, U.S. Dist. Ct. (so. and ea. dists.) N.Y. 1975, U.S. Tax Ct. 1972, U.S. Ct. Appeals (2d cir.) 1974. Assoc. Debevoise & Plimpton (formerly Debevoise, Plimpton, Lyons & Gates), N.Y.C., 1966-75, ptnr., 1976—; commr. Mayor's Commn. on Women's Issues, 2003—. Mem. adv. bd. Practicing Law Inst.; bd. dirs. Am. Arbitration Assn., 1987—2003. Mem. bd. editors: Chase Jour., 1997—2001; contbr. articles to profl. jours. Mem. adv. coun., bd. vis. CUNY Law Sch., Queens, 1984—90; active Coun. on Fgn. Rels.; trustee Trinity Sch., 1982—86, pres., 1986—88; bd. dirs. Found. for Child Devel., 1989—2000, 2001—, chmn., 1991—2000; bd. dirs., treas. Catalyst, 1993—; bd. dirs. Fund for Modern Cts., 1990—2003, Wave Hill, 1994—, Garden Conservancy, 1996—2002, Lawyers Com. for Civil Rights Under Law, 1997—2003, William Nelson Cromwell Found., 1993—, Irish Legal Rsch. Found. Inc., 1996—, Citizens Union Found. Inc., 1996—2004; trustee Bryn Mawr Coll., 2000—. Recipient Laura Parsons Pratt award, 1996. Fellow Am. Coll. Trust and Estate Counsel, Am. Bar Found., N.Y. Bar Found.; mem. ABA (commn. on women in profession 1999-2002), N.Y. State Bar Assn. (vice chmn. com. on trust adminstrn., trusts and estates law sect. 1977-81, ho. of dels. 1984-87, 90-92, pres. 1994-96, com. ann. award 1993-94), Assn. of Bar of City of N.Y. (chmn. com. on trusts, estates and surrogates cts. 1981-84, judiciary com. 1981-84, coun. on jud. adminstrn. 1982-84, chair nominating com. 1984-85, 99-, exec. com. 1986-91, chair 1989-90, v.p. 1990-91, chair com. on children 1993-94, com. on long-range planning 1991-94, co-chair coun. on childen 1997-99), Assn. of Bar of City of N.Y. Fund Inc. (bd. dirs. 2000-03, pres. 1994-96), Women's Forum, Yale Coun., Yale Law Sch. Assn. N.Y. (devel. bd., exec. com. 1981-85, pres. 1988-93), The Century Assn., Yale Club, Washington Club. Office: Debevoise & Plimpton 919 Third Ave New York NY 10022 E-mail: bprobinson@debevoise.com.

ROBINSON, BARRY E. financial company executive; Vice chmn., Ernst & Young LLP, N.Y.C. Office: Ernst & Young LLP 787 7th Ave Fl 14 New York NY 10019-6085

ROBINSON, BARRY R. lawyer; b. Dover, Ohio, Dec. 8, 1946; AB, Princeton U., 1969; JD cum laude, Ohio State U., 1972. Bar: Ohio 1972. Ptnr. Baker & Hostetler, Columbus, Ohio. Fellow Am. Coll. Trust and Estate Counsel; mem. ABA, Ohio State Bar Assn., Columbus Bar Assn. Office: Baker & Hostetler Capital Sq 65 E State St Ste 2100 Columbus OH 43215-4260

ROBINSON, BERNARD PAHL, retired thoracic surgeon, educator; b. N.Y.C., Apr. 12, 1919; s. Nathaniel and Augusta (Strauss) R.; m. Gloria Joyce Rehfuss, Oct. 3, 1943; children: Lawrence, Andrew. BS, NYU, 1938; MD, L.I. Coll. Medicine, 1942. Diplomate Am. Bd. Surgery, Am. Bd. Thoracic Surgery. Intern Mount Sinai Hosp., N.Y.C., 1942-43, resident in surgery, 1946-47, Beth Israel Hosp., Boston, 1948-49; resident in thoracic surgery VA Hosp, Castle Point, N.Y., 1949-50; assoc. attending surgeon Mt. Sinai Hosp., N.Y.C., 1956—; asst. clin. prof. surgery Mt. Sinai Sch. Medicine, N.Y.C., 1968—. Capt. U.S. Army, 1943-46. Fellow Am. Coll. Surgeons, Am. Coll. Chest Physicians; mem. N.Y. Soc. for Thoracic Surgery. Jewish. Avocations: sailing, golf, photography, travel. Home: 4601 Henry Hudson Pkwy W Bronx NY 10471-3800

ROBINSON, BOB LEO, retired international investment service executive; b. Franklin, Tenn., Sept. 9, 1933; s. W.A. and Cornelia Irene (Lampley) R.; m. Carolyn Overton, Dec. 18, 1955; children: Richard Glenn, Leigh Ann, Elizabeth Lynne. BS in Indsl. Mgmt, Tenn. Tech. U., 1955. Cert. property mgr. Quality control engr. Gates Rubber Co., Nashville, 1960; tech. rep. Home Ins. Co., 1961-65; civilian staff adminstrv. asst. Dept. Army, Nashville, 1965; exec. asst. to pres. Sullivan's Dept. Stores, Nashville, 1966-69; dir. engring. and devel. Venture Out in Am., Knoxville, Tenn., 1969; v.p., then exec. v.p. Hosp. Corp. Am., Nashville, 1970-79; pres., chief exec. officer Real Estate Group Inc., Nashville, 1974—, Fidelity Title Co., Nashville, 1974-83; now ret. Pres. Internat. Bus. and Investment Services, Orlando, 1978—; gen. partner Union Sq. Ltd., Jacksonville, Fla., 1973-79; dir. Am. Travel Service, World Health Cons.; chmn. bd. emeritus Arnold Palmer Devel. Co., Orlando, Fla., 1988—; past vice chmn. bd. dirs., chief exec. officer Clin. Diagnostic Systems, Inc., Orlando, 1988-89; past vice chmn. Space Rail Corp., Orlando, 1991; speaker patriotic Christian events. Mem. Mayor Nashville Blue Ribbon Com., 1975-77; commr. City of Brentwood, Tenn., 1969-71, vice mayor, 1969-71, mayor, 1971, mem. planning commn., 1970-71; bd. dirs. Goodwill Industries Ctrl. Fla., exec. com., chmn. ops. com.; chmn. bldg. fund St. Cecilia Acad., Nashville, 1978; vice chmn. Audubon council Boy Scouts Am., 1968; founder Tenn. Tech. ROTC Gen.'s Cup Scholarship Found., 1986; aide U.S. Com. for Normandy Meml. Mus., Caen, France, 1987—; parachutist Israeli Def. Forces, 1989, Royal Thai Spl. Warfare Command, 1990; campaign dir. Drage for County Chmn., Orange County, Fla., 1990; bd. dirs. Camp Blanding Mus. Found., 1995—, Camp Blanding Mus. and Hist. Assocs. Inc., 1996—, chmn. new mus. bldg. com., 1997—. Served as officer, master army aviator, parachutist, U.S. Army, 1955-60, USAR, 1960-83; maj. gen. (brevet) USAR, 1990. Decorated Army Commendation medal, Meritorious Service medal; recipient numerous public service awards; named to Tenn. Tech. ROTC Hall of Fame, 1988. Mem. Internat. Inst. Hosp. Cons., Inst. Real Estate Mgmt., Army Aviation Assn. Am., Res. Officers Assn., Internat. Assn. Airborne Vets., 82d Airborne Divsn. Assn. Republican. Baptist.

ROBINSON, BROOKS CALBERT, JR., former professional baseball player, TV commentator, business consultant; b. Little Rock, May 18, 1937; s. Brooks Calbert and Ethel (Denker) R.; m. Constance Louise Butcher, Oct. 8, 1960; children— Brooks David, Christopher Leslie, Michael Patrick, Diana Agnes. Student, U. Little Rock, 1956-57. Profl. baseball player Balt. Orioles, 1955-77; sports commentator for Baltimore Oriole Games Sta. WMAR-TV, Balt., 1978-90; spl. asst. mktg. dept. Crown Central Petroleum Corp., 1979—; v.p. Personal Mgmt. Assocs., 1979—. Selected Most Valuable Oriole, 1960, 62, 64, 71; named Am. League's Most Valuable Player, 1964, Most Valuable Player in Major League All-Star game at St. Louis, 1966; Most Valuable Player, 1970 World Series; recipient Hickock Athlete of Yr. award, 1970; Balt. Decade award, 1970; mem. World Series Championship Team, 1965, 70; named to Baseball Hall of Fame, Cooperstown, N.Y. Office: Crown Ctrl PO Box 1168 Petroleum Corp/Dept Mktg 1 N Charles St Ste 1168 Baltimore MD 21201-3740

ROBINSON, BRUCE BUTLER, physicist; b. Chester, Pa., Oct. 13, 1933; s. George Senior and Dorothy Conerly (Butler) R.; m. Dorothy Ross, June 4, 1960; children: Douglas Ross, Christopher Scott. BS in Physics, Drexel U., 1956; PhD in Physics, Princeton U., 1961; MBA, Rider U., 1977. Rsch. assoc. U. Calif., San Diego, 1961-63; rsch. scientist RCA David Sarnoff Lab., RCA, Princeton, N.J., 1963-73; exec. dir., mem. commerce tech. adv. bd. U.S. Dept. Commerce, Washington, 1973-75; dir. policy integration, dir. coal and synfuels policy U.S. Dept. Energy, Washington, 1975-81; sr. science advisor to v.p. rsch. Exxon Rsch. and Engring. Co., Linden, N.J., 1981-84; dep. dir. Office Naval Rsch., Arlington, 1984-87, dir. rsch., 1987-94, dep. dir. sci. and tech., 1994-96, assoc. tech. dir. for sci. and tech., 1996—. Prin. author nat. energy policy plan U.S. Dept. Energy, 1981; U.S. rep. to internat. energy agy., govt. expert group on tech., Paris, 1979-81; mem. internat. team to rev. R&D programs Dutch Ministry Econs. and Fin., The Hague, The Netherlands, 1979; presenter sci. lectures. Contbr. articles to sci. jours. NSF fellow Princeton U., 1956-58, NSF internat. summer fellow, Varenna, Italy, 1962; recipient Meritorious Presdl. Rank award Pres. of U.S., 1989, Disting. Civilian Svc. medal Sec. of the Navy, 1997. Mem. IEEE, Am. Phys. Soc., The Oceanography Soc. (founding).

ROBINSON, CHARLES PAUL, nuclear physicist, diplomat, business executive; b. Detroit, Oct. 9, 1941; s. Edward Leonard and Mary Opal (Edmondson) R.; m. Barbara Thomas Woodard; children by previous marriage: Paula S., Colin C. BS in Physics, Christian Bros. U., 1963; PhD in Physics, Fla. State U., 1967. Mem. nuclear test staff Los Alamos (N.Mex.) Nat. Lab., 1967-69, chief test operator, 1969-70, mem. advanced concepts staff, 1971-72, assoc. div. leader, lasers, 1972-76, div. leader, 1976-79, assoc. dir., 1980-85; sr. v.p., bd. dirs. Ebasco Services Inc. subs. Enserch Corp., N.Y.C., 1985-88; ambass. to nuclear testing talks U.S. Dept. State, Geneva, 1988-90; v.p. Sandia Nat. Labs., Albuquerque, 1990-95, pres., 1995—. Instr. U. N.Mex., Los Alamos, 1974-76; mem. sci. adv. group Def. Nuclear Agy., Washington, 1981-86; mem. nat. security bd. Los Alamos Nat. Lab., 1985-88; chmn. Presdl. Tech. Adv. Bd., 1991; mem. U.S. Strategic Command Adv. Bd. Pres. Student Concerts Inc., Los Alamos, 1972-74; exec. bd. Boy Scouts of N.Mex. Recipient Outstanding Pub. Svc. medal Joint Chiefs of Staff, 1996. Mem. Am. Phys. Soc., Am. Nuclear Soc., NAE. Avocation: choral singing. Office: Sandia Nat Labs PO Box 5800 Mail Stop 0101 Albuquerque NM 87185-0100

ROBINSON, CHARLOTTE HILL, artist; b. San Antonio, Nov. 28, 1924; d. Lucius Davis and Charlotte (Moore) Hill; m. Floyd I. Robinson, Mar. 1943; children: Floyd I. Jr., Lawrence H., Elizabeth H. Student, Incarnate Word Coll., 1943-45, NYU, 1947-48, Corcoran Sch. Art, 1951-52. Painting instr. Art League No. Va., Alexandria, 1967-75. Condr. Art World Seminar Washington Women's Art Ctr., 1975-80, drawing workshop Smithsonian Instn. Resident Assocs. Program, Washington, 1977; program dir. Nat. Women's Caucus for Art, 1979; project coord., exhbn. curator The Artist and the Quilt, nat. mus. traveling exhbn., 1983-86; vis. artist S.W. Craft Ctr., San Antonio, 1983-85; lectr. WFUV 90 FM, Fordham U., N.Y.C., 1990, San Antonio Art Inst., 1991, Nat. Mus. for Women in Arts, Washington, 1991, Iowa State U., Ames, 1991; panelist Nat. Mus. Women in Arts, 1997, Woman and the Arts, Douglass Coll./Rutgers U., 1998, Washington Women's Caucus for Art at the Millenium Art Ctr., 2001. Editor: The Artist & The Quilt, 1983; one-person shows include Thames Sic. Ctr., New London, Conn., 1991, Brunner Gallery & Mus., Iowa State U., 1991, 92, San Antonio Art. Inst., 1991, Fordham U., 1991, de Andino Fine Arts, Washington, 1992, Masur Mus. Art, Monroe, La., 1993, 96, 2001, Lee Hansley Art Gallery, Raleigh, N.C., 1993, 97, 2001, Sol Del Rio, San Antonio, 1995, 97-98, 1812 Artic Gallery, Virginia Beach, Va., 1995, Savannah Coll. Art and Design, 1997, Duke U. Sch. Law, 1998, No. Va. C.C., 1999, McLean Project for the Arts, 2002, Southwest Sch. Art & Craft, San Antonio, 2003; exhibited in group shows at Franklin Square and Watkins Gallery, Washington, 1992, Rutgers U., New Brunswick, N.J., 1992, 96, 98, Brody's Gallery, Washington, 1992, Lee Hansley Art Gallery, Raleigh, 1993, 96, 98-2001, 02, 03, Emerson Gallery, McLean, 1993, 95, 99, No. Va. C.C., 1994, 99, Harvard U., 1996, Ceres Gallery, N.Y.C., 1999-2000, Millennium Art Ctr., Washington, 2001, Am. Ctr. Physics, 2003. Trustee Bronx (N.Y.) Mus., 1977; bd. dirs. Washington Women's Art Ctr., 1977, New Art Examiner, 1985-86; nat. bd. dirs. Women's Caucus for Art, 1983-84. Recipient Concourse award Corcoran Sch. Art, 1952; Telfair Acad. Art scholar, Savannah, Ga., 1959; Nat. Endowment for Arts grantee, 1977-81; fellow Va. Ctr. for Creative Arts, Sweet Briar, Va., 1985. Address: Lee Hansley Gallery 225 Glenwood Ave Raleigh NC 27603

ROBINSON, CHRISTINE MARIE, mathematics educator; b. Savannah, Ga. d. Aaron Sr. and Lucille (Jones) Williams; m. Amos Robinson, Aug. 2, 1953; children: Michael Anthony, Pamela Michele. BS in Math. magna cum laude, Savannah State U., 1951; MA, U. Mich., 1965. Instr. in math. Chatham County Bd. of Instruction, Savannah, 1951-64, Duval County Bd. of Instruction, Jacksonville, Fla., 1964-71, master and resource tchr., 1971-76; prof. math. Fla. C.C., Jacksonville, 1976-99, ret., 1999. Mem. faculty task force Fla. Dept. Edn./Fla. Assn. C.C., Tallahassee, 1979-81; on-site coord. Fla. Devel. Edn. Assn. Conv., Jacksonville, 1986; chmn. Fla. C.C. EA/EO Com., Jacksonville, 1988, 89. Mem. YWCA, Jacksonville, 1989—; vol. driver Wheels for Cancer-AKA Sorority, Jacksonville, 1986; chmn. United Way, Jacksonville, 1987. Recipient Outstanding Faculty Mem. award Fla. Community Coll., 1987, Teaching Excellence award U. Tex., 1988; scholar U. Mich., U. Ill.; grantee NSF. Mem. Am. Math. Assn. Two-Yr. Colls., Fla. Devel. Edn. Assn. (bd. dirs. Jacksonville chpt. 1983-86), Fla. Assn. C.C., Math. Assn. Am., So. Assn. Colls. and Schs. (Fla. com.), LWV, Alpha Kappa Alpha. Democrat. Roman Catholic. Avocations: reading, piano, dance, bicycling. Home: 7426 Simms Dr Jacksonville FL 32209-1023

ROBINSON, CLEO PARKER, artistic director; Degree in Dance Edn. Psychology, Denver U., DFA (hon.), 1991. Founder, exec. artistic dir., choreographer Cleo Parker Robinson Dance, Denver. Mem. dance, expansion arts and inter-arts panels NEA; bd. dirs. Denver Ctr. Performing Arts; tchr. in workshops. Co-creator (documentary) African-Americans at Festae, Run Sister Run, (film) Black Women in the Arts, (music video) Borderline. Apptd. Nat. Coun. on Arts, 1999. Recipient Thelma Hill Ctr. for the Performing Arts award, 1986; Choreography fellow NEA; named one of Colo. 100, 1992; named to Blacks in Colo. Hall of Fame, 1994. Mem. Internat. Assn. Blacks in Dance (2nd v.p.). Office: Cleo Parker Robinson Dance 119 Parker Ave W Denver CO 80205

ROBINSON, CRYSTAL, professional basketball player; b. Atoka, Okla., Jan. 22, 1974; d. Billy and Nancy Robinson. Grad., S.E. Okla. State, 1996. Forward, WNBA New York Liberty, N.Y.C., 1999—. Named MVP, U.S. Sports Festival, 1993; named to Nat. Assoc. of Intercollegiate Athletics Hall of Fame, 2003; recipient ABL Rookie of the Yr. award, 1996—97.

ROBINSON, DANIEL BARUCH, retired banker; b. Hamilton, Ont., Can., Dec. 4, 1937; s. David A. and Zelda (Frank) R.; m. Marta A. Calero, May 7, 1960; children— Allegra, Robert B.Commerce, McMaster U., Hamilton, Ont., 1960; postgrad., U. Mich., 1969, Harvard U., 1971, Pontif Universidade Católica do Rio de Janeiro, 1979, Georgetown U., 1994, 96. Chartered acct. Vice pres. fin. Comsur, La Paz, Bolivia, 1971-72; fin. dir. Light Servicos, Rio de Janeiro, 1972-78; sr. fin. analyst The World Bank, Washington, 1978-79; v.p. fin. Jari Florestal, Rio de Janeiro, 1979-80, Manalta Coal, Calgary, Alta, Can, 1981-82; exec.v.p. Atomic Energy Can. Ltd., Mississauga, Ont., 1983-85; rep. Interam. Devel. Bank, Barbados, 1985-89, 1989-99. Pres. Canadian Club, Rio de Janeiro, 1974-75 Recipient Highest Standing prize Chartered Accts. Assn., 1961; Price, Waterhouse and Co. scholar, 1959 Mem. Inst. Chartered Accts. Ont., Canadian Inst. Chartered Accts., Fin. Execs. Inst. Clubs: Rio de Janeiro Yacht, Jockey Club do Rio de Janeiro, Itanhangá Golf (Rio de Janeiro), Sandy Ln. Property Owners Assn. (Barbados). Avocations: reading, translating from spanish and portuguese to english. Home: 352 Bay St S Hamilton ON Canada L8P 3J9 E-mail: drobinson11@cogeco.ca.

ROBINSON, DANIEL N. psychology and philosophy educator; b. N.Y., Mar 9, 1937; s. Henry S. and Margaret R.; children: Tracey, Kimberly; m. Francine Malasko, 1967. BA, Colgate U., 1958; MA, Hofstra U., 1960; PhD, CUNY, 1965. Rsch. psychologist, electronics rsch. labs. Columbia U., 1960-65, asst. dir. sci. honors program, 1964-68, sr. rsch. psychologist, electronics rsch. labs., 1965-68, asst. dir. of life scis. electronics rsch. labs., 1967-68; asst. prof. dept. psychology Amherst Coll., 1968-70, assoc. prof., 1970-71; dir. grad. program dept. psychology Georgetown Univ., 1981-83, chmn. dept. psychology, 1973-76, 85-91, assoc. prof., 1971-74, prof., 1974—, adj. prof. philosophy, 1996—, disting. rsch. prof. and prof. psychology, 1998—2001, disting. prof. emeritus, 2002—. Vis. lectr. psychology Princeton U., 1965 68; vis. prof. Folger Shakespeare Inst., 1977; vis. sr. mem. Linacre Coll., vis. lectr. philosophy Oxford (Eng.) U., 1991—, faculty fellow, 1999—, philos. faculty, 2002—; vis. prof. Princeton U., 2001; adj. prof. Columbia U., 2002—; cons. NIH, 1967-70, NSF, 1965-75, PBS, 1978-84, 1985-88, MacArthur Found., 1985, Atty. Gen's. Task Force on Crime, 1980, HHS, NIH, 1988. Author: Psychology: A Study of Its Origins and Principles, 1972, The Enlightened Machine: An Anlytical Introduction to Neuropsychology, 1973, 80, Psychology: Traditions and Perspectives, 1976, An Intellectual History of Psychology, 1976, The Mind Unfolded: Essay's on Psychology's Historic Texts, 1978, Systems of Modern Psychology: A Critical Sketch, 1979, Psychology and Law: Can Justice Survive the Social Sciences?, 1980, An Intellectual History of Psychology-Revised Edition, 1981, 3rd edit., 1995, Toward A Science of Human Nature: Essays on the Psychologies of Hegel, Mill, Wundt, and James, 1982, Philosophy of Psychology, 1985, Aristotle's Psychology, 1989, (with William R. Uttal) Foundations of Psychobiology, 1983, (with Sir John Eccles) The Wonder of Being Human: Our Mind and Our Brain, 1984; editor Heredity and Achievement, 1970, Readings in the Origins and Principles of Psychology, 1972, Significant Contributions to the History of Psychology, 1977-78, Annals of Theoretical Psychology, 1990, Social Discourse and Moral Judgment, 1992, Wild Beasts and Idle Humours: Legal Insanity from Antiquity to the Present, 1996; editor Jour. Theoretical and Philosophical Psychology, 1997-2002; contbr. chpts. to books, reference books, articles to profl. jours. Recipient Inst. for Advanced Study in the Humanities fellow, U. Edinburgh, 1986-87; Pres's. medal Colgate U., 1986, Pub. Svc. award Gen. Svcs. Adminstrn., 1986. Fellow APA (past pres. divsns. 24 and 26, Lifetime Achievement award Divsn. History of Psychology 2001, Disting. Contbn. award Divsn. Theoretical and Philos. Psychology 2001), Brit. Psychol. Soc.; mem. Sigma Xi, Psi Chi. Home: 300 E Main St Middletown MD 21769 Office: Columbia U Dept Psychology New York NY 10027 Business E-Mail: dan.robinson@philosophy.ox.ac.uk.

ROBINSON, DAVID BRADFORD, scientific writer, poet; b. Richmond, Va., Apr. 14, 1937; s. Albert Lewis and Martha Ellen (Lovern) R. BS, U. Miami, 1959, MS, 1961; D of Jurisprudence, Calif. Ctrl. U., 1961, MA, 1994; AA, Miami-Dade C.C., 1970; DSc, Northwestern Coll., 1978, PhD, 1979, MA, 1994. Author: Characteristics of Cesium, 1978, Collected Poems, 1987. Founder Ronald Reagan Rep. Ctr., Washington; exhibitor Statue of Liberty, Port of NY, 1986; mem. Heritage Found., 1989; sustaining sponsor Ronald Reagan Presdl. Found., 1987; charter mem. Ronald Reagan Trust; charter mem. Honor Roll Rep. Presdl. Task Force, 1990, life mem., 1989, Commemorative Honor Roll, 1991; mem. Nat. Rep. Senatorial Com. with Presdl. Commn., 1992; founding sponsor, founding mem. Space Life Sta., 1989; spkrs. citizen task force Inaugural Mem. Cert. of Honor; life mem. Rep. Nat. Com. Recipient 2d pl. Amateur Trophy, Capablanca Chess Club, 1964, Presdl. Sports award bicycling, 1976, Presdl. Achievement award Rep. Nat. Com., 1982, Cert. Good Standing Rep. Presdl. Task Force, 1982-85, Presdl. Merit medal, 1982, Appreciation cert. Sen. Paula Hawkins, 1986, Golden Poet Trophy award World of Poetry, 1987, Silver Anniversary Album, Nat. Geog. Soc., 1990, Pres. Ronald Reagan Appreciation cert., 1988, Pres. Bush Congl. Victory Squadron Recognition cert., 1989, Affidavit of Life Membership, Cert. from Rep. Nat. Com., Bush Inaugural/Freedom medal, 1989, World Time-Capsule cert., 1990, Am. in Space medal, 1990, Cert. of Appreciation, Nat. Rep. Congl. Com., 1990, Pegasus Time Capsule plaque, 1991, Congl. Merit cert. Nat. Rep. Congl. Com., 1992, Battle of Normandy Found. Appreciation award, 1993, Presdl. Legion of Merit medal, 1993, Congl. Order of Liberty award, 1993, Appreciation cert. Sen. Kay Bailey Hutchinson, 1993, Rep. Presdl. award, 1994, Albert Einstein medal Brit. Bur. Degree Promotion, 1994, Cert. of Appreciation, The Golden Heart Club, Mil. Order of Purple Heart Svc. Found., Congl. Order of Freedom, 1995, Cert. of Meritorious Svc. Rep. Party Planning Com., 1996, Cert. Appreciation World War II Meml., 1997, Chmn.'s Honor Roll cert., Rep. Nat. Com., 1997, Eisenhower Commn., 1997, Caesar medal Trinity Broadcasting Network, 1998, Cert. Recognition Rep. Nat. Com., 1999, Jubilee Yr. Blessing Cert. His Holiness John Paul II/Missionary Assn. Mary Immaculate, 1999, Cert. of Appreciation Concerns of Police Survivors, 2000, Cert. of Appreciation Rep. Nat. Com., 2000, Cert. Appreciation, Planetary Soc., 2001. Mem. Am. Air Mus. (Brit., founder 1991), Battle of Normandy Meml. Mus. (charter 1988), Sigma Xi, Russian Club, Phi Theta Kappa. Avocation: chess.

ROBINSON, DAVID BROOKS, retired naval officer; b. Alexandria, La., Oct. 26, 1939; s. Donald and Marion (Holloman) R.; m. Gene Kirkpatrick, Aug. 1, 1964; children: Kirk, David. Student, Tex. A&M U., 1958—59; BS, U.S. Naval Acad., 1963; MS in Physics, Naval Postgrad. Sch., Monterey, Calif., 1969. Commd. ensign USN, 1963, advanced through grades to vice adm., 1993; commdg. officer USS Canon and USS Ready, Guam, 1969-71; adminstrv. aide to Chmn. Joint Chiefs Staff, Washington, 1971-74; commdg. officer USS Luce, Mayport, Fla., 1976-78; surface comdr. assignment officer. and dir. fiscal mgmt. and procedural control divsn. Naval Mil. Pers. Command, 1979-81; mem. Fgn. Svc. Inst. Exec. Seminar, Washington, 1982; commdg. officer USS Richmond K. Turner, Charleston, SC, 1983-84; chief of staff, comdr. Naval Surface Force, Atlantic Fleet, Norfolk, Va., 1984; exec. asst. and sr. aide to vice chief Naval Ops., Washington, 1985, dir. Manpower and Tng. divsn., 1986, dir. Surface Warfare divsn., 1987-88; comdr. cruiser destroyer group 8, 1988-89; vice dir. and subsequently dir. operational plans and inter-operability directorate Joint Staff, Washington, 1989-91; dep., chief of staff to comdr. U.S. Pacific Fleet, 1991-93, comdr. naval surface force, 1993-96; ret. USN, 1996. Decorated Navy Cross, Def. D.S.M., D.S.M., Legion of Merit with 4 gold stars, Bronze Star, Purple Heart. Mem. Optimists (pres. Oakton, Va. 1986-87). Methodist. Avocations: golf, bicycling, stamp collecting/philately, reading.

ROBINSON, DAVID CLINTON, reporter; b. Goffstown, N.H., Nov. 5, 1963; s. Clinton and Barbara Lee (Ploss) R.; m. Karen Ruth Eckhardt, July 3, 1992; children: Laura Lee, Lindsay Lee, Clinton Nelson. AB, Syracuse U.,

1985. Reporter The Buffalo News, 1985—. Bd. dirs. ToyTown USA Found., 1998—. Mem. Buffalo Newspaper Guild (exec. com. 1989-98, vice chmn. 1991-92). Office: The Buffalo News 1 News Plz Buffalo NY 14203-2994

ROBINSON, DAVID E. pharmaceuticals executive; b. 1949;, Macquarie U., Sydney, Australia, 1974; BA in Hist. and Polit. Sci., MBA, U. New South Wales, Australia. With Abbott Labs., 1974-84, Adria Labs., Dublin, Ohio, 1984-87; COO Erbamont, Milan, Italy, 1987-89; pvt. practice, cons., 1989-91; pres., CEO Ligand Pharmaceuticals, 1991—. Office: Ligand Pharmaceuticals Inc 9393 Towne Centre Dr San Diego CA 92121-3070

ROBINSON, DAVID MASON, cell physiologist; b. July 7, 1932; came to U.S., 1969, naturalized, 1979. s. Thomas Leon Mason and Mabel (Orr) R.; m. Jean Marcia Smith, Sept. 10, 1965; children: Jane Leonie Mason, Simon Henry Mason; m. Christine Parfitt, July 1998. BSc with 1st class honors, U. Durham, 1955, PhD, 1958; BM, BChir, Oxford (Eng.) U., 1964. Mem. sci. staff Namulonge Rsch. Sta., Kampala, Uganda, 1959-61; rsch. officer, tutor Hope Dept. Zoology Oxford (Eng.) U., 1961-63; mem. sci. staff, biophysics group Med. Rsch. Coun., Radiobiol. Rsch. Unit, Harwell, Eng., 1963-66; prin. sci. officer, head cell biology Microbiol. Rsch. Establishment, Porton, Eng., 1966-69; asst. rsch. dir., head cell biology ARC Blood Rsch. Lab., Bethesda, Md., 1969-73; prof. biology, assoc. mem. Vincent Lombardi Cancer Rsch. Ctr., Georgetown U., Washington, 1974-80; prin. sci. officer, head cell biology Microbiol. Rsch. Establishment, Porton, Eng., 1966-69; asst. rsch. dir., head cell biology ARC Blood Rsch. Lab., Bethesda, Md., 1969-73; prof. biology, assoc. mem. Vincent Lombardi Cancer Rsch. Ctr., Georgetown U., Washington, 1974-80, adj. prof. anatomy and cell biology Sch. Medicine, 1982-90; adj. prof. liberal studies Georgetown U., Washington, 1980—. Assoc. dir. sci. programs, divsn. heart and vascular disease Nat. Heart, Lung and Blood Inst., NIH, Bethesda, Md., 1980-94, acting dir., 1993, dir. vascular rsch. program, 1994-2001, dep. dir. divsn. heart and vascular diseases, 2000—; mem. faculty biology and genetics NIH Grad. Sch., 1981-86; mem. faculty Brookings Inst., 1994-99, Nat. Def. U., 1995-1998. Author: (with G. A. Jamieson) Mammalian Cell Membranes, 5 vols., 1973-76; contbr. articles to profl. jours. Capt. 1st Royal Green Jackets, 43d and 52d, Brit. Ter. Army, 1062-65. Recipient Vicennial medal Georgetown U., 1992; named Disting. Vis. Prof. of Yr., Baylor Coll. Medicine, 1997, Presdl. Lectr., Am. Venous Forum, 1998; Philip Buckle Meml. scholar U. Durham, 1958, Empire Cotton Growing Corp. postgrad. scholar, 1957. Mem.: Am. Soc. Cell Biology, Soc. Cryobiology (sec. 1975), Soc. Complex Carbohydrates, Biophys. Soc., Royal Green Jackets Assn., Sigma Xi (pres. Georgetown chpt. 1978), Alpha Sigma Nu (hon.). Democrat. Episcopalian. Home: Stoneleigh Cottage PO Box 2164 Shepherdstown WV 25443-2164 Office: NIH Rm 9158 MSC 7940 Two Rockledge Ctr Bethesda MD 20892-7956 E-mail: dr14j@nih.gov.

ROBINSON, DAVID MAURICE, professional basketball player; b. Key West, Fla., Aug. 6, 1965; Grad., U.S. Naval Acad., 1987. Commd. ensign USN, 1987; with San Antonio Spurs, 1989—. Mem. U.S. Olympic Basketball Team, 1988, 92, 96, NBA Champions, 1999. Named Coll. Player of Yr., Sporting News, 1987, NBA Rookie of Yr., 1990, NBA Defensive Player of Yr., 1992, Most Valuable Player, 1994—95, Season Most Valuable Player, 1995; named to All-Am. 1st team, Sporting News, 1986, 1987, All-NBA 1st team, 1991; recipient Naismith award, 1987, Wooden award, 1987, IBM award, 1990, 1991, 1994, Schick Pivotal Player award, 1990, 1991, All-NBA 1st team, 1992, All-Star team, 1990—94. Achievements include being a holder of NCAA divsn. 1 single season record most block shots per game (5.91), 1986; being holder of NCAA divsn. 1 single record most blocked shots in 1 game (14), 1986; holding NBA career record most blocked shots per game (3.65). Office: care San Antonio Spurs 100 Montana St San Antonio TX 78203-1033

ROBINSON, DAVID MILTON, microbiologist; b. Findlay, Ohio, Nov. 22, 1935; s. John Milton Robinson and Josephine Alice Dulgar; m. Linda Ellen Hoy, June 29, 1958; children: Pamela, Diane, Greg. DVM, Ohio State U., 1959; MS, U. Md., 1965, PhD, 1968. Diplomate Am. Coll. Vet. Microbiologists. Prin. investigator Inst. for Med. Rsch., Kuala Lumpur, Malaysia, 1972—76; mgr. Hazardous Disease Lab. Walter Reed Army Inst. Rsch., Washington, 1976—81; mgr. Vet. Medicine Naval Med. Rsch. Unit, Cairo, 1981—83; program mgr., Biologics U.S. Army Med. Material Devel., Frederick, Md., 1983—87; dir. Infectious Disease Rsch. U.S. Army Med. Rsch. and Material Command, Frederick, 1987—91; dep. dir. Walter Reed Army Inst. Rsch., Washington, 1991—93; v.p. vaccine techs. Battelle Meml. Inst., Columbus, Ohio, 1993—. Contbr. articles to profl. jours. Col. U.S. Army, 1962—92. Decorated Disting. Svc. Medal U.S. Army, Legion of Merit, Bronze Star Medal. Fellow: Am. Acad. Microbiology. Avocations: reading, travel, coin collecting/numismatics. Home: 2044 Beverly Rd Columbus OH 43221-4208 Office: Battelle Meml Inst 505 King Ave Columbus OH 43201

ROBINSON, DAVID ZAV, non-profit agency consultant; b. Montreal, Que., Can., Sept. 29, 1927; s. Benjamin and Antonia (Seiden) R.; m. Nan Senior, Sept. 6, 1954; children: Marc, Eric. AB, Harvard U., 1946, AM, 1947, PhD, 1950. Asst. dir. rsch. Baird-Atomic Inc., Cambridge, Mass., 1949-59, 60-61; sci. liaison officer Office Naval Rsch., London, 1959-60; sci. advisor staff Office of Pres., Washington, 1961-67; v.p. acad. affairs NYU, 1967-70; v.p. Carnegie Corp. N.Y., N.Y.C., 1970-80, exec. v.p., 1981-85, exec. v.p., treas., 1986-88; exec. dir. Carnegie Commn. on Sci Tech. and Govt., 1988-97; cons., 1997—. Dir. Urban Research Corp., Chgo., 1968-75; cons. Congressional Office of Tech. Assessment, 1975-78; mem. com. women in sci. NRC, 1975-82, chair com. on tchr. testing, 1999-2000; mem. vis. com. dept. chemistry Harvard U., 1977-83; physics dept. Princeton U., 1970-76 Mem. N.Y. Energy Rsch. and Devel. Authority, 1971-77; trustee CUNY, 1976-81, Amideast, 1983-88, Citizen Union Found., 1985-, Inst. Schs. of the Future, 1986-, N.C. Sch. Sci. and Math., 1989-97, Santa Fe Inst., 1987-2004, Prep for Prep, 1989-98. Mem. AAAS, Optical Soc. Am., Coun. on Fgn. Rels., Am. Contract Bridge League, Fedn. Am. Scientists Coun., Bar Assn. of City of NY (commn. on future of CUNY 1999-2000), Harvard Club (NYC).

ROBINSON, DAVIS ROWLAND, lawyer, arbitrator; b. N.Y.C., July 11, 1940; s. Thomas Porter and Cynthia (Davis) R.; m. Suzanne Walker, June 11, 1966; children: Christopher Champlin II, Gracyn Walker. BA magna cum laude, Yale U., 1961; LLB cum laude, Harvard U., 1967. Bar: N.Y. 1968, D.C. 1971, U.S. Supreme Ct. 1972. Fgn. svc. officer U.S. Dept. State, Washington, 1961-69; assoc. Sullivan & Cromwell, N.Y.C., 1969-71; assoc., then ptnr. Leva, Hawes, Symington, Martin and Oppenheimer, Washington, 1971-81; the legal adviser U.S. Dept. State, Washington, 1981-85; ptnr. Pillsbury, Madison & Sutro, Washington, 1985-88, Le Boeuf, Lamb, Greene & MacRae LLP, Washington, 1988—2002, ret., 2002—; mng. dir. Richard C. Breeder & Co., LLC, 2003—. Dir. Mid. East Policy Coun., Washington, 1999—. Pres. Harvard Legal Aid Bur., 1966-67. Mem. Assn. of Bar of City of N.Y., Am. Law Inst. (adviser fgn. rels. law of U.S.), Am. Soc. Internat. Law, Internat. Centre for Settlement of Investment Disputes (U.S. panel, 2002-), Coun. on Fgn. Rels., Phi Beta Kappa. Office: Le Boeuf Lamb Greene & MacRae LLP 1875 Connecticut Ave NW Washington DC 20009-5728 Office Phone: 202-986-8049. Business E-Mail: drrobins@llgm.com.

ROBINSON, DONALD PETER, musician, retired electrical engineer; b. Phila., Jan. 27, 1928; s. Warren Frederick and Marcella Theresa (Derry) R.; m. Beatrice Graves, Sept. 22, 1951 (dec.); children: Donald, Stephen, Sharon Robinson-Byrd, Michael; m. Mary Katherine Robertson, June 9, 1990. A.A., Temple U. Sch. Tech., 1956. Sr. engr./technician Gen. Electric Co., Utica, N.Y., 1956-89, ret., 1989; organist emeritus St. Joseph-St. Patrick's Ch., Utica, 1983—; minister music/organist St. Paul's Baptist Ch., Utica, 1961-88; organist Utica Council K.C., 1969—; organist/choir dir. 4th degree assembly Central N.Y. dist. K.C., 1985—; producer, host Organ Loft radio program WLFH, Little Falls, N.Y., 1962-90; pipe organ cons. Served with AUS, 1948-54. Mem. Am. Guild Organists (past dean central N.Y. chpt.), Am. Theatre Organ Soc., Nat. Assn. R.R. Passengers (bd. dirs.), K.C. (past faithful navigator 4th degree assembly). Roman Catholic. Home: 715 Garfield Ave Rockford IL 61103-6023

ROBINSON, DONALD WARREN, retired art educator, artist; b. New Bedford, Mass., Sept. 18, 1932; s. Warren Fowler and Mary Irene (Johnson) R.; m. Dolores Carol Lee, July 9, 1955; 1 child, Richard Allen. BFA, U. Ga., 1953; MFA, Columbia U., 1954; EdD, Rutgers U., 1983. Instr. art Wagner Coll., summer 1953, Gettysburg (Pa.) Coll., 1954-55; tchr., head dept. art elem. and secondary schs. Edison Twp., N.J., 1957-67; vice prin. John Adams Jr. H.S., Edison, 1967-73; prin. M.L. King Sch., Edison, 1973-86, H. Hoover Mid. Sch., Edison, 1986-90; pvt. cons. in field. Workshop leader N.Y.C. Tchrs., S.I. Mus., N.Y., 1961-63. Works exhibited in Va., N.J., Md., Pa., N.Y. and Ga. Elder, Presbyn. Ch. Served with USN, 1955-57. Mem. John Dewey Soc., Art Students League N.Y. (life), Guild of Creative Art (exhibiting mem.), Art Alliance, NJ Am. Artist Profl. League, N.J. Prins. and Suprs. Assn., Printmaking Coun. N.J., Phi Kappa Phi, Kappa Delta Pi, Phi Delta Kappa. Home: 55 Frost Ave W Edison NJ 08820-3157 E-mail: dwrobbie29@aol.com.

ROBINSON, DOROTHY K. lawyer; b. New Haven, Feb. 18, 1951; children: Julia Robinson Bouwsma, Alexandra Toby Bouwsma. BA in Econs. with honors, Swarthmore Coll., 1972; JD, U. Calif., Berkeley, 1975; MA (hon.), Yale U., 1987. Bar: Calif. 1975, N.Y. 1976, Conn. 1981, U.S. Ct. Appeals (2d cir.) 1975, U.S. Dist. Ct. (so. dist.) N.Y. 1981. Assoc. Hughes Hubbard & Reed, N.Y.C., 1975-78; asst. gen. counsel Yale U., New Haven, 1978-79, assoc. gen. counsel, 1979-84, dep. gen. counsel, 1984-86, gen. counsel, 1986—95, dir. fed. rels., 1986-88, acting sec., 1993, v.p., gen. counsel, 1995—. Mem. Calif. Law Rev., 1973-75. Trustee Hopkins Grammar Day Prospect Hill Sch., New Haven, 1983-88, sec., 1986-88; trustee Wenner-Gren Found. Anthrop. Rsch., 1991-2003; bd. dirs. Cold Spring Sch., New Haven, 1990-95; mem. adv. bd. Conn. Mental Health Ctr., New Haven, 1979-89; bd. dirs. Nat. Assn. Ind. Coll. and Univs., 1995-98; mem. alumni coun. Swarthmore Coll., 1999-2002. Fellow Ezra Stiles Coll. Yale U., Am. Bar Found.; mem. ABA, Nat. Assn. Coll. and Univ. Attys. (bd. dirs. 1987-90), Conn. Bar Assn., Calif. Bar Assn., Assn. Bar City N.Y., Phi Beta Kappa. Office: Yale U Office of Gen Counsel PO Box 208255 New Haven CT 06520-8255

ROBINSON, DOROTHY MARIE, theater producer, director, actress; b. Beaver Falls, Pa., June 19, 1935; d. Delbert Lee Robinson and Dorothy Caroline Schmidt. Student, Pitts. (Pa.) Playhouse Sch. Theatre, 1956—58, Columbia U., 1988, Hollywood (Calif.) Film Inst., 1994, Nashville (Tenn.) Tech., 1996. Actor Nat. Tour Gypsy, 1961—62; actor, dir. Barter Theatre, Abingdon, Va., 1968—92; prin., owner Nashville (Tenn.) Pub. Theatre, 1988—. Music prodr. Audible Advt. & FSO, N.Y., 1964, 81; artistic dir. Lifework Prodns., Nashville, 1988—95; tchr. Tenn. Performing Arts Ctr., Nashville, 1988—. Actor: (plays) numerous others; author: (screenplays) Shapeshift, 1999, Alternate Routes, 1999 (Screenplay award, 2002); prodr., dir.: (films) Alternate Routes, 2002; author: (book) Quality Control Checklist, 2000, (plays) One-Acts About Choices, 1990, 1991; prodr.: (comml.) RC Cola, 1980 (nominated Clio award, 1980). Mem.: Assn. Ind. Video and Filmmakers, Soc. Stage Dirs. and Choreographers, Actors Equity Assn. Democrat. Avocations: sculpture, architecture.

ROBINSON, DOUGLAS, computer company executive; BBA, St. Michael's Coll.; M in Fin., Babson Coll. Acct. exec. Fred S. James & Co.; comml. underwriter Liberty Mutual Ins. Co.; CFO Cullinet Software; from v.p. fin. to sr. v.p. fin. Computer Assoc. Internat., Islandia, NY, 1989—2003, sr. v.p., interim CFO, 2003—. Office: Computer Assoc Internat One Computer Assoc Plz Islandia NY 11749

ROBINSON, E. GLENN, lawyer; b. Charleston, W.Va., Jan. 1, 1924; s. Elmer George and Eva Elena (Rexrode) Robinson; m. Emma Lou Legg, Dec. 23, 1947; children: Richard G., Martha L., William E., Ann K. BSc, Ohio State U., 1948; JD, W.Va. U., 1950. Bar: W.Va. 1950, U.S. Ct. Appeals (4th cir.) 1953, U.S. Ct. Appeals (3d cir.) 1980, U.S. Supreme Ct. 1982. Ptnr. Shannon & Robinson, Charleston, 1950—52, Love, Wise, Robinson & Woodroe, Charleston, 1952—83, Robinson & McElwee, Charleston, 1983—91, of counsel, 1991—. Served with AUS, 1942—45. Fellow: Am. Coll. Trial Lawyers, Am. Bar Found.; mem.: Am. Bd. Trial Advocates, Kanawha County Bar Assn. (pres. 1968—69), W.Va. Bar Assn. (pres. 1982—83), W.Va. State Bar (pres. 1972—73), Rotary. Republican. Home: 507 Superior Ave Charleston WV 25303-2024 Office: 400 Fifth Third Ctr 700 Virginia St E Charleston WV 25301 Office Phone: 304-347-8334. Business E-Mail: egr@ramlaw.com.

ROBINSON, EARL JAMES, academic administrator, information systems and statistics educator, consultant; b. Wilmington, Del., Apr. 15, 1949; s. Harry and Minerva Ruth (James) R.; m. Karen Frances Smith, July 5, 1980; children: Ruth Frances, Sarah Rebecca. AB, Davidson Coll., 1971; MS, Bucknell U., 1973; PhD, U. Ga., 1977. Asst. prof. U. Ga., Athens, 1977-78, St. Mary's U., Halifax, N.S., Can., 1978-81, assoc. prof., 1981-84, chmn. dept., 1981-84; assoc. prof., chmn. St. Joseph's U., Phila., 1984-91; dean, prof. Coll. Bus. Minot (N.D.) State U., 1991-94; exec. v.p. acad. affairs, dean faculty, prof. Briar Cliff Coll., Sioux City, Iowa, 1994-98; pres., prof. Lees-McRae Coll., Banner Elk, N.C., 1998—. Cons. Mgmt. Rsch. Assocs., Halifax, 1978-84; pres., cons. Robinson & Assocs., Phila., 1984-91, Minot, N.D., 1991-94, Sioux City, Iowa, 1991-98, Banner Elk, 1998—. Contbr. numerous articles to profl. jours. Recipient Golden M award St. Mary's U., 1981; grantee St. Joseph's U., 1985, St. Mary's U., 1982, Ashland Oil Corp., 1973, FAA, 1977, NSF, 1978. Mem.: AAUP, Am. Assn. Higher Edn., Sigma Phi Epsilon (social chmn. 1969—70, chpt. counselor 1988—91, nat. coms. 1996), Sigma Xi. Episcopalian. Avocations: choral music, flying. Home: PO Box 1856 Banner Elk NC 28604-1856 Office: Lees-McRae Coll PO Box 128 Banner Elk NC 28604-0128 Office Phone: 828-898-8785. Business E-Mail: robinson@lmc.edu.

ROBINSON, EDDIE GAY, college football coach; m. Doris Robinson; children: Lillian Rose, Eddie Jr. BA, Leland Coll., 1940; MS, U. Iowa; LLD (hon.), La. Tech. Coach football Grambling U., La., 1941—97, v.p. athletics, asst. v.p. univ. rels., sr. advisor to pres. for instnl. advancement, 1998—. Head coach East-West Shrine Game, 1977. Recipient Horatio Alger award, Nat. Football Found. award, NAACP award, VFW award, Bear Bryant award, Liberty Bowl award, others, Spl. Commendations from Pres. Ronald Reagan, Nat. Collegiate Athletic Assn., U.S. Congress, State of La., B'nai B'rith; holds record of most college football victories. Mem. Nat. Assn. Sports & Phys. Edn., Nat. Assn. Intercollegiate Athletics, Southwestern Athletic Conf., La. Sports Hall of Fame, Pop Warner, Sugar Bowl, Black Coll. Achievements include winning 10 nat. Black coll. football championships. Office: Grambling State Univ Pres's Office PO Box 607 Grambling LA 71245-0607*

ROBINSON, EDNA EARLE, real estate company executive; b. Mt. Vernon, Tex., Dec. 21, 1938; d. Thomas Colquitt and Myrtle Lee (McGill) Lindsey; m. Raymond Roy Robinson, Jr., June 3, 1960; 1 child, Randall Ray. BA, Baylor U., 1960. Cert. profl. sec. Office mgr., sec. Blanchard, Walker, O'Quin & Roberts, Shreveport, La., 1963-76; v.p. Shreveport Pub. LLC, 1976-2000, Snap One, Inc., Shreveport, 1983—2002, Snap Two, Inc., Shreveport, 1985—2002, Beaird Properties, LLC, Shreveport, 2000—. Sec.-treas. Charles T. Beaird Found., Shreveport, 1976—; pres. Shreveport Single Rm. Occupancy, Inc., 1995-99; bd. dirs. Shreveport-Bossier Svc. Connection, 2001-02. Mem. Shreveport C. of C. (leadership coun. 1987—), River Cities Network (treas. 1996-99, v.p. 2000—, pres. 2001), Profl. Secs. Internat. (treas., sec., v.p., pres. Pelican chpt. 1971-90), Cert. Profl. Sec. Acad., Cert. Profl. Secs. of La. (charter). Baptist. Avocations: reading, boating, travel. Home: 533 Hunters Run Bossier City LA 71111-8171 Office: Beaird Properties LLC 330 Marshall St Ste 1112 Shreveport LA 71101-3015 E-mail: ednalrobinson@aol.com.

ROBINSON, EDWARD LEE, retired physics educator, consultant; b. Clanton, Ala., Nov. 6, 1933; s. Alonzo Lee and Ollie Sarah (Mims) R.; m. Shirley Anne Burnett (div. Sept. 1972); children: Edward Lee Jr., James Allan, Paul David; m. Linda G. Moon, 1990. AB with honors, Samford U., 1954; MS, Purdue U., 1958, PhD, 1962. Dir. Cyclotron Lab. Samford U., Birmingham, Ala., 1961-67, asst. prof. physics, chmn. dept., 1961-62, assoc. prof., chmn. dept., 1962-66, prof., chmn. dept., 1966-67; assoc. prof. U. Ala., Birmingham, 1967-77, co-radiation safety officer, 1967-85, dir. Van de Graaff Accelerator Lab., 1970-91, acting chmn. dept., 1973-74, prof. physics, 1977-91, adj. prof. forensic sci., 1983-91, cons. in applied physics and accident reconstrn., 1991—; prin., owner Robinson & Assocs., LLC, 1998—. Cons. Hayes Internat. Corp., Birmingham, 1963-68, So. Rsch. Inst., Birmingham, 1968-69; rschr. Oak Ridge (Tenn.) Nat. Lab., 1968, 74-75, 82, U. Md., College Park, 1966, 67; bd. overseers Samford U., 1999—; adv. com. to dean Howard Coll. of Arts and Scis. of Samford U., 2002—. Active Birmingham YMCA; mem. at large nat. coun., chmn. sci. adv. com. for explorer scouting Boy Scouts Am., 1999—2002. Mem. Am. Phys. Soc., Soc. Automotive Engrs., AAAS, Ala. Acad. Sci. (life, v.p. 1964-65), Tex. Assn. Accident Reconstrn. Specialists (bd. dirs. 1999-2003), numerous other nat. and internat. profl. assns. Baptist. Achievements include discovery, co-discovery of six radioisotopes. Home: 233 Oakmont Rd Birmingham AL 35244-3264 Office Phone: 205-408-1692. E-mail: elrobinson@charter.net.

ROBINSON, EDWARD NORWOOD, lawyer; b. Roseboro, N.C., June 18, 1925; s. Edward Croswell and Lolita (Underwood) R.; m. Pauline L. Gray, Mar. 22, 1952; children: Edward Norwood Jr., James Gray, Michael Lindsay, Mark Alvin. BS in Engring., U.S. Mil. Acad., 1945; JD, Duke U., 1952. Bar: NC 1952. Atty. Robinson & Lawing, L.L.P., Winston-Salem, NC, 1959—. N.C. Civilian Aide to Sec. of Army, 1994-2001; apptd. to 5th Dist. U.S. Acad. Selection Bd.; mem. ethics com. Bowman Gray Sch. Medicine; bd. visitors Duke U. Sch. Law, Wake Forest U. Sch. Law, Duke Divinity Sch.; lectr. in field. Co-editor Duke Law Jour. Past pres. Winston-Salem Rotary Club; past campaign chmn. United Way; past pres. C. of C.; past pres. local chpt. ARC; past dir. Winston-Salem Housing Found.; mem. Centenary United Meth. Ch., Winston-Salem, tchr. Chapel class, chmn. bd. stewards; past chmn. Winston-Salem Dist. United Meth. Ch., Ch. Ext.; past dir., campaign chmn. Triad United Meth. Home. 1st Lt. U.S. Army, 1942-49. Recipient Charles L. Rhyne award Duke U. Law Alumni, 1997; named to Best Lawyers in Am. Fellow Am. Coll. Trial Lawyers; mem. ABA (antitrust and litig. sects.), U.S. 4th Cir. Jud. Conf. (life), N.C. Bar Assn. (past dir.), Forsyth County Bar Assn. (past pres.), Pvt. Adjudication Ctr. Duke U. (past chmn. bd.), U.S. Mil. Acad. Assn. Grads. (bd. trustees emeritus), Order of the Coif, Joseph Branch Inns of Ct., Am. Inns of Ct. Avocations: golf, travel. Office: Robinson and Lawing LLP 370 Knollwood St Ste 600 Winston Salem NC 27103-1830 E-mail: nrobinson@robinson-lawing.com.

ROBINSON, EDWARD T., III, lawyer; b. Glen Cove, N.Y., May 23, 1932; s. Edward Jr. and Helen (Rahilly) R.; m. Lynn Simmons; children: Edward IV, Wendy, Christopher, Jeffrey, Lesley, Michael. AB, Holy Cross Coll., 1954; JD, Georgetown U., 1960. Bar: N.Y. 1961, U.S. Ct. Appeals (2d cir.) 1966. Counsel Royal-Globe Ins. Co., Mineola, N.Y., 1960-64; pvt. practice, Oyster Bay, N.Y., 1964-70, 91-2000; ptnr. Robinson & Cincotta, Oyster Bay, 1970-85, Robinson & Lynch, Oyster Bay, 1985-91; counsel Cammarata & Cronin LLP, Oyster Bay, 2000—. Mem. adv. bd. Chgo. Title Ins. Co., N.Y.C., 1982-2000, Fleet Bank, 1989-95, United Cerebral Palsy, 1980—; mem. Nassau County Commn. on Govt. Revision, 1993—; mem. County Exec. Blue Ribbon Panel on Criminal Justice; mem. exec. coun. N.Y. State Conf. Bar Leaders, 1986-90; counsel Oyster Bay-East Norwich Ctrl. Sch. Dist., 1966-2000; mem. N.Y. State grievance com. 10th Jud. Dist., 1995—. Mem. Nassau County Traffic and Parking Violations Bur.; pres. Holy Cross Coll. Club, L.I., 1989-90; trustee Nassau County coun. Boy Scouts Am.; chmn. Forget-Me-Not Ball, United Cerebral Palsy. Recipient Community Svc. award Nassau County coun. Boy Scouts Am.; named Man of Yr. United Cerebral Palsy, Nassau County, 1979. Mem. N.Y. State Bar Assn. (del., v.p. 1992-95, mem. ho. of dels. 1995—), Nassau County Bar Assn. (pres. 1986-87), Oyster Bay C. of C. (pres. 1976-79), Meadowbrook Golf Club, Country Club La Romana (Dominican Republic). Republican. Roman Catholic. Avocations: golf, tennis, jazz music. Home: 60 Calvin Ave Syosset NY 11791-2106 Office: 34 Audrey Ave Unit 3 Oyster Bay NY 11771-1595

ROBINSON, ELLA D. state agency administrator; b. Ky. Bank examiner Dept. Fin. Insts., 1977—84, dir. thrift insts., 1984—93, dir. divsn. supervision, 1993—96, dep. commr., 1996—99, acting commr., 1997—98, 1999, commr., 1999—. Mem. Ky. State Treas. Commn. on Personal Savs. and Investment; chmn. Fin. Insts. Bd.; vice chmn. Dist. II Conf. State Bank Suprs., mem. nom. com., 2002—, mem. planning com.; team mem. PSC Ann. Rev. Mem.: Nat. Assn. Consumer Credit Adminstrs. (past bd. mem.), Nat. Assn. State Credit Union Suprs. (bd. mem. 1985—95, past pres., vice chmn. performance standards com.). Office: 1025 Capital Ctr Dr Frankfort KY 40601

ROBINSON, ENDERS ANTHONY, geophysicist, educator, writer; b. Boston, Mar. 18, 1930; s. Edward Arthur and Doris Gertrude (Goodale) Robinson; m. Eva Arborelius, Sept. 9, 1962 (div. 1973); children: Anna, Erik Arthur, Karin; m. Joyce McPeake, Aug. 8, 1992. BS in Math., MIT, 1950, MS in Econs., 1952, PhD in Geophysics, 1954. Dir. geophys. analysis group MIT, Cambridge, Mass., 1952-54, instr. math., 1955-56; geophysicist Gulf Oil Corp., Pitts., 1954-55; petroleum economist Standard Oil Co. N.J., N.Y.C., 1956-57; asst. prof. stats. Mich. State U., East Lansing, 1958; asst. prof. math. U. Wis., Madison, 1958-61, assoc. prof. math. (with tenure), 1961-62; dep. prof. stats. Uppsala (Sweden) U., 1960-64; v.p., dir. Digicon Inc., Houston, 1965-70; pres. Robinson Rsch. Inc., Houston, 1970-82; vis. prof. theoretical and applied mechanics Cornell U., Ithaca, NY, 1981-82; McMan prof. geophysics U. Tulsa, 1983-93; Maurice Ewing and J.L. Worzel prof. geophysics Columbia U., N.Y.C., 1993—2000, prof. emeritus, 2000—. Author: (book) Seismic Inversion and Deconvolution, Dual Sensor Technology, 1999, 31 other books on sci., tech. and history; editor: Internat. Jour. Imaging Sys. & Tech., 1988—; mem. editl. bd.: Multidimensional Sys. and Signal Processing, An Internat. Jour., 1990—. 2d lt. U.S. Army, 1950—51. Recipient Donald G. Fink Prize award, IEEE, 1984, Achievement award, Thayer Acad. Alumni, 1997, Alexander von Humboldt Rsch. award for sr. U.S. scientists, 1999. Fellow: European Acad. Scis.; mem.: Nat. Rsch. Coun. (com. undiscovered oil and gas resources), Nat. Acad. Engring. (petroleum and mining sect.), Soc. Exploration Geophysicists (hon. Classic Paper award 1953, 1957, Best Paper award 1964, Reginald Fessenden medal 1969, father of deconvolution 1983, Best Paper award 2001, Maurice Ewing Gold medal 2001), European Assn. Geoscientists and Engrs. (Conrad Schlumberger award 1969), Renaissance Inst. Washington, N.Y. Athletic Club, MIT Club N.Y. Office: Trump Place 160 Riverside Blvd #6U New York NY 10069-0705 Business E-Mail: ear11@columbia.eduu.

ROBINSON, FARREL RICHARD, pathologist, toxicologist; b. Wellington, Kans., Mar. 23, 1927; s. Farrel Otis and Norine (Sloan) R.; m. Mimi Agatha Hathaway, June 5, 1949; children— Farrel Richard, Kelly S., E. Scott, Brian A. BS, Kans. State U., 1950, D.V.M., MS, 1958; PhD, Tex. A&M U., 1965. Diplomate: Am. Coll. Vet. Pathologists, Am. Bd. Vet. Toxicology (v.p. 1971-74, pres. 1976-79). Served with USN, 1945-46; commd. 2d lt. USAF, 1951, advanced through grades to lt. col., 1971; vet. pathologist Aerospace Med. Research Labs., Wright-Patterson AFB, Ohio, 1958-68; chief Vet. Pathology div. Armed Forces Inst. Pathology, Washington, 1968-74; ret., 1974; scientist assoc. Univs. Associated for Research and Edn. in Pathology, Inc., 1972-74; asst. clin. prof. pathology George Washington U. Sch. Medicine, 1972-74; instr. NIH Grad. Program, 1973-74; prof. toxicology-pathology Sch. Vet. Medicine, Purdue U., 1974-93; dir. Animal Disease Diagnostic Lab., 1978-85, head dept. vet. sci., 1978-85, head dept. vet. microbiology, pathology and pub. health, 1986-88, chief toxicology service, 1984-93; emeritus, 1993. Cons. vet. pathology USAF surg. gen. and asst. surg. gen. for vet. services, 1970-74 Mem. editorial bd. Human and Vet. Toxicology, 1976— . Contbr. sci. articles to profl. jours. Decorated USAF Commendation medal, Meritorious Service medal; recipient Aerospace Med. Research Labs. Scientist of Year award, 1967 Mem. AVMA, Am. Bd. Vet. Toxicology, Am. Coll. Vet. Pathology, Am. Assn. Vet. Lab. Diagnosticians (bd. govs.1980-85, v.p. 1986, pres. 1987), Wildlife Disease Assn., Conf. Rsch. Workers in Animal Disease, Soc. Toxicology, U.S. Animal Health Assn., Sigma Xi, Phi Kappa Phi, Alpha Zeta, Phi Zeta. Democrat. Methodist. Home and Office: 201 W 600 N West Lafayette IN 47906-9727 Business E-Mail: robinsfr@purdue.edu.

ROBINSON, FLORINE SAMANTHA, marketing executive; b. Massies Mill, Va., Feb. 4, 1935; d. John Daniel and Fannie Belle (Smith) Jackson; m. Frederick Robinson (div. 1973); children: Katherine, Theresa, Freda. BS, Morgan State U., 1976; postgrad., U. Balt., 1977-81, Liberty U., 1987. Writer, reporter Phila. Independent News, 1961-63; freelance writer, editor Balt.,

1963-71; asst. mng. editor Williams & Wilkins Pubs. Inc., Balt, 1971-76; mktg. rep., then mktg. mgr. NCR Corp., Balt., 1977-93; assoc. minister, trustee Christian Unity Temple, Balt., 1976—; pres. ABCOM, Inc., Balt., 1993—. Bd. dirs. Armstrong & Bratcher, Inc., Balt. Editor: Stedman's Medical Dictionary, 1972; contbr. articles to profl. jours. Active PTA, Balt., 1963-65; bd. dirs. Howard Pk. Civic Assn., Balt., 1967—, pres. 1991—; leader, cons. Girl Scouts USA, 1970-73. Recipient Excellence in Rsch. award Psi Chi, 1976, Citizen citation Mayor of Balt. Mem. NAFE, Mid-Atlantic Food Dealers Assn., Am. Soc. Notaries, Internat. Platform Assn., Edelweiss Club, Order of Eastern Star. Democrat. Avocation: piano. Home: 3126 Howard Park Ave Baltimore MD 21207-6715

ROBINSON, FRED COLSON, English language educator; b. Birmingham, Ala., Sept. 23, 1930; s. Emmett Colson and Morwenna Hope (Bennett) R.; m. Helen Caroline Wild, June 21, 1959; children: Lisa Karen, Eric Wild. BA, Birmingham So. Coll., 1953; MA, U. N.C., 1954, PhD, 1961; DLitt (hon.), Williams Coll., 1985; MA (hon.), Yale U., 1989. Instr. Stanford (Calif.) U., 1960-61, asst. prof., 1961-65, assoc. prof., 1967-71, prof. English philology, 1971-72; asst. prof. Cornell U., Ithaca, N.Y., 1965-66, assoc. prof., 1966-67; prof. Yale U., New Haven, 1972-83, Douglas Tracy Smith prof., 1983—2000, prof. emeritus, 2000—, chmn. medieval studies, 1975-78, 80. Vis. prof. Harvard U., Cambridge, Mass., 1983; pub. com. Medieval Acad. Monographs, Cambridge, 1987-90. Author: Old English Literature: Select Bibliography, 1970, Beowulf and the Appositive Style, 1985, The Tomb of Beowulf, 1993, The Editing of Old English, 1994; co-author: A Bibliography...on Old English Literature, 1980, Old English Verse Texts from Many Sources: A Comprehensive Collection, 1991, A Guide to Old English, 6th edit., 2001, Beowulf: An Edition with Relevant Shorter Texts, 1998; editor Old English Newsletter, 1966-73, Early English MSS in Facsimile, 1971-2002, Jour. English Linguistics, 1971—, Anglo-Saxon England, 1972—, Anglistica, 1981—; contbr. over 90 articles to profl. jours. Trustee Yale Univ. Libr. Assocs., New Haven, 1986-89, 91-95, 97-2000, 03—. With U.S. Army, 1954-56. Recipient Disting. Vis. Scholar award U. Ala., 1999; fellow Guggenheim Found., 1974-75, Am. Coun. Learned Socs., 1968-69, Inst. Social and Econs. Rsch., Rhodes U., 1978, Japan Soc. for Promotion Sci., 1989; grantee NEH, 1976, 79, 81, 85, Am. Philos. Soc., 1973, 85; named Professore solo per ricerca Univ. di Roma "La Sapienza", 2000. Fellow AAAS, Medieval Acad. Am. (pres. 1983-84, Haskins medal 1984), Brit. Acad. (corr., Sir Israel Gollancz prize 1997), Meddeleeue-verenigung van Suidelike Afrika (corr.); mem. Finnish Acad. of Sci. and Letters (fgn. mem.), New Eng. Medieval Conf. (pres. 1982-83), Conn. Acad. Arts and Scis. (pres. 1980-85), Internat. Soc. Anglo-Saxonists (elected hon.), Elizabethan Club (bd. govs. 1986-88, v.p. 1989-90, pres. 1990-92), Manuscript Club (v.p. New Haven chpt. 1990-92), Phi Beta Kappa. Episcopalian. Office: Yale Univ Dept English New Haven CT 06520

ROBINSON, GAIL PATRICIA, retired mental health counselor; b. Medford, Oreg., Dec. 31, 1936; d. Ivan T. and Evelyn H. (Hamilton) Skyrman; m. Douglas L. Smith; children: Shauna J., James D. BS in Edn., Oreg. State U., 1958, PhD in Counseling, 1978; MS in Counseling, Western Oreg. State Coll., 1974. Tchr. Monterey (Calif.) Pub. Schs., 1958-59, Corvallis (Oreg.) Pub. Schs., 1959-62, 69-75, counselor, 1977-81; pvt. practice Corvallis, 1977-95. Vol. therapist Children's Svcs. divsn., Linn and Benton Counties, 1982-83; asst. prof. Western Oreg. State coll., 1977, counselor, 1982-83; mem. grad. faculty Oreg. State U., Corvallis, 1978-95; presenter workshops, lectr. in field. Contbr. articles to profl. jours. Mem. Benton County Mental Helath Citizens Adv. Bd., 1979-85, chair, 1982-83; trustee WCTU Children's Farm Home, 1978-84, chair child welfare com., 1982-83, pres., 1984; mem. Old Mill Sch. Adv. Bd., 1979-85, chair, 1979-81; bd. dirs. Cmty. Outreach, 1979-83; mem. Benton Com. for Prevention of Child Abuse, 1979-85, v.p., 1982; mem. Oreg. Bd. Lic. Profl. Counselors and Therapists, 1989-95, chair, 1989-90. Mem. ACA (govt. rels. com. 1988-91, professionalization com. 1988-92, pres. 1996-97), Am. Mental Health Counselors Assn. (chair consumer and pub. rels. com. 1988-91, bd. dirs. Western region 1989-91, chair strategic planning com. 1994-95, pres. 1992-93), Oreg. Counseling Assn. (chair licensure liaison com. 1985-91, exec. bd. 1985-88, steering com. 1986-87, register editorial com. 1985-86, Disting. Svc. award 1985, 87, Leona Tyler award 1989), Oreg. Mental Health Counselors Assn. Personal E-mail: robinsgp@comcast.net.

ROBINSON, GARRY LEWIN, television news executive; b. Kansas City, Mo., Oct. 26, 1951; s. Calvin Luin and Reba Kathleen (Owen) R.; m. Linda Sue Payton, Oct. 21, 1973 (div. 1982); children: Penny Lynn, Larry Calvin II, Jeff Noel. BS, Ark. State U., 1981. Cert. tech. Dynatech Newstar and AP Newscenter Computer Sys. Various positions Sta. KAWW-AM-FM, Heber Springs, Ark., 1969-76, dir. news, ops., 1978; asst. news dir. Sta. KARV-AM, Russellville, Ark., 1976-78; ops. mgr., news dir. Sta. KCON-AM, Conway, Ark., 1978-79; asst. news dir. Sta. KTVE-TV, El Dorado, Ark., 1979-81; mging. producer Sta. KAIT-TV, Jonesboro, Ark., 1981-84; newscast producer Sta. KOLD-TV, Tucson, 1984-85; newscast producer, now news ops. mgr. Sta. KSLA-TV, Shreveport, La., 1984—, exec. prodr., 10 PM prodr., newsroom computer sys. mgr., 1985—, exec. producer, computer system mgr., 1985—, new opers. mgr. Bd. dirs. North Ark. Fire Dist., Russellville, 1977; bd. advisors City Cable TV Commn., Conway, 1978; chmn. drama div. Conway Regional Arts Commn., 1977-78; advisor Explorer Scouts, Shreveport, 1987. Recipient numerous reporter awards Ark. AP, Little Rock, 1969-84, Radio Documentary award Am. Assn. Women in Radio and TV, Little Rock, 1978, various TV news awards La., Tex., Ark., AP Broadcasters Assn., 1985-90. Mem. Radio TV News Dirs. Assn. (Edward R. Murrow award 1987), Sigma Delta Chi (North La. chpt.) (bd. dirs. 1987). Clubs: Phi Eta Sigma (pres. 1970-71). Democrat. Baptist. Avocations: reading, writing, guitar, computers, outdoor sports. Home: 5063 Town North Dr Shreveport LA 71107-2843 Office: Sta KSLA-TV 1812 Fairfield Ave Shreveport LA 71101-4431 Office Phone: 318-677-6714. E-mail: garry@garryrobinson.com.

ROBINSON, GENE EZIA, biologist, educator; b. Buffalo, N.Y., Jan. 9, 1955; s. Jack and Sonja (Rubin) R.; m. Julia O. Robinson, Aug. 29, 1982; children: Aaron, Daniel, Sol. BS, Cornell U., 1977, MS, 1982, PhD, 1986. Postdoctoral assoc. Ohio State U., Columbus, 1986-89; asst. prof. biology U. Ill., Urbana, 1989-93, assoc. prof. biology, 1993-98, prof. biology, 1998—. Fulbright Sr. Rsch. fellow, Hebrew U., 1995-96. Fellow AAAS; mem. Animal Behavior Soc., Entomol. Soc. Am., Internat. Soc. Neuroethology, Soc. Neurosci., Internat. Union Study of Social Insects, Sigma Xi. Achievements include discovery of hormone, neural and genetic factors that regulate behavioral plasticity and division of labor in honeybee colonies. Office: U Ill Entomology Dept 505 S Goodwin Ave Urbana IL 61801-3707

ROBINSON, HARLOW LOOMIS, language educator, historian, writer; b. Bristol, Conn., Sept. 20, 1950; s. Raymond Loomis and Katherine Chaffee Robinson; life ptnr. Robert Frank Holley. BA magna cum laude, Yale U., 1972; MA, PhD, U. Calif., Berkeley, 1980. Prof. Russian SUNY, Albany, 1980—96; prof. modern langs. and history Northeastern U., Boston, 1996—. Presenter in field. Author: (biography) Sergei Prokofiev: A Biography, 1987, 1988, 2002, The Last Impresario: The Life, Times and Legacy of Sol Hurok, 1994 (Albany, NY, Pub. Libr., Author of the Yr., 1994); translator (editor): (translation) Selected Letters of Sergei Prokofiev, 1998; contbr. articles to profl. jours. Editl. bd. Northeastern U. Press, Boston, 2002—03; bd. mem. Citizen Exch. Coun., N.Y.C., 1988—94, Troy (N.Y.) Savs. Bank Music Hall, 1992—95. Fellow Grad. Student Rsch. in Eng. and France, Fulbright-Hayes, 1978—79, Grad. Student rsch. in USSR, IREX/Fulbright, 1979—80; Nat. Def. Fgn. Lang. fellow, 1973—75, Faculty Rsch. fellow, Am. Coun. Learned Socs., 1985, Sr. Scholar Rsch. fellow, Fulbright-Hayes/IREX in USSR, 1991—92, travel fellow for Czech Republic, Whiting Found., 2002, Sr. Rsch. grantee, NEH, 1988, Soviet Scholars Travel grantee, Soros Found., 1991, Short-Term Rsch. grantee, Kennan Inst., 1993. Mem.: MLA, Am. Assn. for the Advancement Slavic Studies, Authors Guild, Am. Assn. Tchrs. Slavic and East European Langs. (assoc.; v.p. 2001—03), Phi Beta Kappa. Avocations: travel, swimming, singing, piano. E-mail: h.robinson@neu.edu.

ROBINSON, HAROLD OSCAR, clergyman, educator; b. Trenton, N.J., Apr. 21, 1943; s. Oscar Alexander and Emma (Gale) R.; m. Alice Louise Steele, Sept. 21, 1991; children: Kheesa L., Harold Oscar. BA, Rutgers U., 1973, MEd, 1974; MDiv, Hood Theol. Sem., Salisbury, N.C., 1998. Ordained deacon A.M.E. Zion Ch., 1989, elder, 1991. Pastor Jonesboro (Tenn.) A.M.E. Zion Ch., 1989-90, Brown Hill A.M.E. Zion Ch., Locust, N.C., 1990-94; 1st resident missionary, presiding elder African Meth. Episcopal Zion Ch. South Africa, 1994-96; assoc. min. Little Rock A.M.E. Zion Ch., Charlotte, N.C., 1996-2000; prof. humanities Shaw U., Kannapolis, N.C., 1997-2001; tchr. social studies A.L. Brown H.S., Kannapolis, 1999-2001. Chmn. diversity task force Cabarrus County Schs., Concord, N.C., 1997-99; asst. prof. Essex County Coll., Newark, 1975-79; mgr. safety, security and law enforcement N.J. Job Corps Ctr., Edison, 1978-83. Editor: A History of African Americans in Cabarrus County, N.C., 1992 (book awrd 1993); book editor A.M.E. Zion Quar. Rev., 1989-98. Nat. Boy Scout dir. A.M.E. Zion Ch., Charlotte, 1994-2000; grad. Challenge Greensboro Clas I, 1989, Leadership Cabarrus, 1994; del. Dem. Nat. Conv., N.Y.C., 1980. Recipient Heritage award Livingstone Coll., Salisbury, N.C., 1997; named to Hon. Order Ky. Cols., 1994; named lt. col., aide-de-camp State of Tenn., 1994. Mem. NAACP (pres. 1991-93), Phi Beta Sigma. Avocations: camping, reading, collecting african american art. Home: 3735 Rock Hill Church Rd Concord NC 28027-6688

ROBINSON, HELEN MARGARET, emergency physician, internist; b. Atlanta, 1950; d. Richard Martin and Frances (Gibbs) Robinson; m. John Michael O'Farrell, July 24, 1974 (div. Dec. 1991); children: John R., Kevin D., William R. BA, Emory U., 1972; MD, Med. Coll. Ga., 1976. Diplomate Am. Bd. Emergency Medicine, Am. Bd. Internal Medicine. Intern Ga. Bapt. Hosp., Atlanta, 1976-77, resident in internal medicine, 1977-79; emergency physician Huntsville (Ala.) Hosp., 1985—, vice chmn. dept. emergency medicine, 1994—2000, chmn. dept. emergency medicine, 2001—. Fellow Am. Coll. Emergency Physicians; mem. AMA, Med. Assn. State of Ala., Madison County Med. Soc. Office: Huntsville Hospital 101 Sivley Rd SW Huntsville AL 35801-4470

ROBINSON, HENRY WARD, meteorologist; b. Schoharie, N.Y., June 30, 1940; s. Frank Locklyn and Esther (Lawyer) R.; m. Muriel Scott, Aug. 15, 1964; children: Katherine, Heather, David. BS, SUNY, Oneonta, 1964; MS, Pa. State U., 1970. Tchg. asst. Pa. State U., State College, 1968-72; instr. Upsala Coll., East Orange, N.J., 1973-75; analyst Computer Sci. Corp., Silver Spring, Md., 1975-78; meteorologist Nat. Wether Svc. NOAA, Silver Spring, 1978—. Adj. prof. Montgomery Coll., Germantown, Md., 1983—; mentor NASA Goddard Space Flight Ctr. Ea. Region Remote Sensing Applications Ctr.; vis. instr. NSF program Notre Dame U., South Bend, Ind.; data stream instr., adv. Am. Meteorol. Data Stream Project. Contbr. numerous articles to profl. jours.; writer, coord., dir., editor tng. videos. Mem. Am. Meteorol. Soc. (bd. sch. and popular meteorol. and oceanographic edn., contbg. editor operational terms Glossary of Meteorology, bd. women and minorities), Am. Geophys. Union. Home: 19622 Enterprise Way Montgomery Village MD 20886

ROBINSON, HERBERT HENRY, III, educator, psychotherapist; b. Leavenworth, Wash., Mar. 31, 1933; s. Herbert Henry II and Alberta (Sperber) R.; m. Georgia Murial Jones, Nov. 24, 1954 (div. 1974); children: Cheri Dean Asbury, David Keith, Peri Elizabeth Layton, Tanda Rene Graff, Gaila Daire. Grad. of Theology, Bapt. Bible Coll., 1959; BA in Philosophy/Greek, Whitworth Coll., 1968; MA in Coll. Teaching, Ea. Wash. U., 1976; PhD, Gonzaga U., 2002. Cert. psychotherapist, perpetrator treatment program supervision; nat. bd. cert. counselor. Choir dir. Twin City Bapt. Temple, Mishawaka, Ind., 1959-61; min. Inland Empire Bapt. Ch., Spokane, Wash., 1961-73; tchr. philosophy Spokane C.C., 1969-72; dir. Alternatives to Violence, Women in Crisis, Fairbanks, Alaska, 1985-87; tchr. pub. rels. U. Alaska, Fairbanks, 1986-87; dir. Alternatives to Violence Men Inc., Juneau, 1988-89; tchr. leadership mgmt. U. Alaska S.E., Juneau, 1988-89; min. Sci. of Mind Ctr., Sandpoint, Idaho, 1989-92; dir., therapist Tapio Counseling Ctr., Spokane, 1991—; cert. psychotherapist, supr. perpetrator treatment program Wash. Cons. Lilac Blind/Alpha Inc./Marshall Coll., Spokane, 1975-85, Alaska Placer Mining Co., Fairbanks, 1987; tchr. Spokane Falls C.C., Spokane, 1979-85; seminar, presenter Human Resource Devel., Spokane and Seattle, Wash., Pa., 1980; guest trainer United Way/Kellogg Found. Inst. for Volunteerism, Spokane, 1983. 1st trombone San Diego Marine Band, 1953-56, Spokane Symphony, 1961; bd. dirs. Tanani Learning Ctr., Fairbanks, 1987; mem. consensus bldg. team Sci. of Mind Ctr., Sandpoint, 1989-92. Cpl. USMC, 1953-56. Mem. ACA, Assn. for Humanistic Edn. and Devel., Assn. for Religious Values in Counseling, Internat. Assn. Addictions and Offender Counselors, Internat. Assn. Marriage and Family Counselors, Am. Assn. Profl. Hypnotherapists, Masterson Inst. Office: Tapio Counseling 5325 E Sprague Ave Spokane WA 99212-0820 Office Phone: 509-534-5028. E-mail: peace@herb-robinson.com.

ROBINSON, HOWARD ARTHUR, JR., minister; s. Howard Arthur Sr. and Mary Hairston Robinson; children: Dionne Carol, Angela Marie, Howard Arthur III. MDiv, Morehouse Sch. of Religion / Interdenominational Theol. Ctr., Atlanta, 1976. Cert. advanced marriage and family therapy Puget Sound Counseling Ctr., 1979, ordained as Bishop Full Gospel Bapt. Ch. Fellowship Internat., 2000. Pres. Berean Kingdom Ctr., Renton, Wash., 1995—2002; adj. prof. N.W. Coll. Assemblies God, Kirkland, 1999—2001; provost Sunday sch. curriculum Full Gospel Bapt. Ch. Fellowship, Seattle, 1999—2003, auxilliary bishop New Orleans, 2000—03, bishop for Wash. and Oreg. Seattle, 2000—03; pres. Berean Acad. Christian Devel., Renton, 1995—; pres. and chief apostle Agape Christian Fellowship Internat., Seattle, 2002—; pres. Howard A. Robinson, Jr. Ministries, Kent, 2002—. Pres. Black United Clergy for Action Pacific N.W., Seattle, 1995—2000; moderator Macedonia Dist. Bapt. Assn.; pres. pastors conf. Nat. Bapt. Conv. Am., Inc., v.p. congress of christian workers, Shreveport, La., 1998—99; sec. Gen. Bapt. Conv. N.W., Portland, Oreg. Author: Changing the 21st Century Ch., 2003. Adv. bd. mem. Wells Fargo Bank, Seattle, 1995—96, First Interstate Bank, Seattle. Maj. USAF, 1967—90. Decorated Am. Spirit Honor Medal U. S. Army, Trainee of the Cycle; M. L. King scholar, Coun. Chs. Seattle Wash., 1974—76. Avocations: swimming, travel, photography. Office: Agape Christian Fellowship International P O Box # 58009 Tukwila WA 98138 Office Phone: 425-255-4562.

ROBINSON, HUGH R. retired marketing executive; b. Syracuse, N.Y., Sept. 18, 1922; s. Frank J. and Gladys (Hunt) R.; m. Evelyn De Mattia, Nov. 24, 1949; children: Susan, Hugh R., Patrice. BS, Syracuse U., 1949. Dist. mgr. Syracuse China, 1949-59; with Royal Worcester Porcelain Co., N.Y.C., 1959-77, v.p. sales, 1971-75, pres., 1975-76, Royal Worcester Spode, Inc., 1977, Lance Internat., N.Y.C., 1977-84; v.p., dir. Caithness Glass Inc., N.Y.C., 1980-84; v.p. sales and mktg. Weil Ceramics & Glass Inc., 1985-86, CEO, exec. v.p., 1986-88; CEO LLadro U.S.A. Inc., 1988-91; v.p. Lladro Realty, Inc., 1988-94, Lladro Galleries, Inc., 1988-94; retired, 1994. Advisor Lladro Group, Valencia, Spain, 1991-97; cons. in giftware industry. Served with USAAF, 1942-46. Mem. Alumni Assn. Syracuse U. Home: 3433 57th Ave DRW Bradenton FL 34210

ROBINSON, IRWIN JAY, lawyer; b. Bay City, Mich., Oct. 8, 1928; s. Robert R. and Anne (Kaplan) R.; m. Janet Binder, July 7, 1957; children: Elizabeth Binder Schubiner, Jonathan Meyer, Eve Kimberly Wiener. AB, U. Mich., 1950; JD, Columbia U., 1953. Bar: N.Y. 1956. Assoc. Breed Abbott & Morgan, N.Y.C., 1955-58; asst. to ptnrs. Dreyfus & Co., N.Y.C., 1958-59; assoc. Greenbaum Wolff & Ernst, N.Y.C., 1959-65, ptnr., 1966-76; sr. ptnr. Rosenman & Colin, N.Y.C., 1976-90; of counsel Pryor, Cashman, Sherman & Flynn, 1990-92; sr. ptnr. Phillips, Nizer, Benjamin, Krim & Ballon, N.Y.C., 1992-99; pvt. practice N.Y.C., 1999—. Treas. Saarsteel, Inc., Whitestone, N.Y., 1970—. Bd. dirs. Henry St. Settlement, N.Y.C., 1960-85, Jewish Cmty. Ctr. Assn. N.Am., N.Y.C., 1967-94, mem. adv. bd., 1998—; bd. dirs. Heart Rsch. Found., 1989-94, pres., 1991-93. Mem. ABA, N.Y. State Bar Assn., Assn. Bar City of N.Y., Internat. Bar Assn., Thai-Am. C. of C. (founder, bd. dirs. 1992-95, pres. 1992-95), Vietnam-Am. C. of C. (founder, bd. dirs. 1992-95, pres. 1992-95), Philippine-Am. C. of C. (bd. dirs. 1960-98), Sunningdale Country Club, The Desert Mountain Club. Jewish. Home: 290 West End Ave New York NY 10023 Office: care Kramer Levin Naftalis & Frankel 919 3d Ave 40th Fl New York NY 10022-3902 Office Phone: 212-715-7656. E-mail: ijrjbr@aol.com.

ROBINSON, J. MACK, communications executive; Chmn. Gulf Capital Corp; owner, chmn. Atlantic Am. Corp., Atlanta, 1974—. Office: Gray Communications Systems Inc 126 N Washington St Albany GA 31701

ROBINSON, JACK ALBERT, retail executive; b. Detroit, Feb. 26, 1930; s. Julius and Fannie (Aizkowitz) Robinson; m. Aviva Freedman, Dec. 21, 1952; children: Shelby, Beth, Abigail. B in Pharmacy, Wayne State U., 1952. Founder, chief exec. officer, chmn. bd. Perry Drug Stores, Inc., Pontiac, Mich., 1957-95; founder, chmn., pres. JAR Group LLC, Bloomfield, Mich., 1996—. Chmn. Wayne State U. Fund, Detroit, 1986, Concerned Citizens for Arts Mich., 1990, 1991—; chmn. ann. fund Detroit Symphony Orch.; bd. dirs. United Way Pontiac, Mich., 1986, United Found. Detroit, 1986, Pontiac Area Urban League, Cmty. Found., S.E. Mich., Detroit Svc. Group, Save Orch. Hall, Inc., Cranbrook Inst. Sci., Jewish Fedn. Apts., Wetzman Inst. Sci., Holocaust Meml. Ctr., Harper-Grace Hosp., Detroit; past dir. Pontiac Symphony, Boys Club, Detroit Osteo. Hosp.; pres. United Jewish Found. Met. Detroit, 1992, Greater Detroit Interfaith Round Table NCCJ, 1994—95, co-chmn., 1992; pres. Jewish Fedn. Met. Detroit, 1992—94. Named Entrepreneur of the Yr., Harvard Bus. Sch., Detroit, 1982; recipient Disting. Alumni award, Wayne State U. Coll. Pharmacy, 1975, Eleanor Roosevelt Humanities award, State of Israel, 1978, Youth Svcs. Am. Tradition award, B'nai B'rith, 1982, Gt. Am. Traditions award, 1991, Disting. Alumni award, Wayne State U., 1985, Corp. Leadership award, 1985, Tree of Life award, Jewish Nat. Fund, 1985, Disting. Citizen award, Pontiac Boy Scouts Am., 1985, Brotherhood award, Booker T. Washington Bus. Assn., 1986, Humanitarian award, March of Dimes, 1987, Variety Club, 1988, award, Weizmann Rsch. Inst., 1987, Fred M. Butzel award, Jewish Fedn. Met. Detroit, 1991, Cmty. Svc. award, Am. Arabic and Jewish Friends, 1995, Outstanding Philanthropic award, Nat. Soc. Fundraising Execs., 1999, Mich. Hall of Fame award in Real Estate and Retailing, Internat. Coun. Shopping Ctrs., 2001, Gov.'s Arts award Spl. Recognition, 2003. Mem.: Econ. Club (bd. dirs. Detroit chpt.), Am. Found. for Pharm. Edn. (bd. dirs.), Am. Pharm. Assn., Nat. Assn. Chain Drug Stores (chmn. 1987, Lifetime Achievement award 1995, Robert B. Begley award 1995). Avocations: skiing, jogging, photography, classical music, glass collecting. Office: JAR Group LLC Ste 330 38500 N Woodward Ave Bloomfield Hills MI 48304-2961

ROBINSON, JACK FAY, clergyman; b. Wilmington, Mass., Mar. 7, 1914; s. Thomas P. and Ethel Lincoln (Fay) Robinson; m. Eleanor Jean Smith, Sept. 1, 1937 (dec. 1966); 1 child, Alice Virginia Dungey; m. Lois Henze, July 16, 1968; stepchildren: Susan Bentley, Cynthia Berkeley, Charles Henze. AB, Mont. State U., 1936; BD, Crozer Theol. Sem., 1939; AM, U. Chgo., 1949, postgrad., 1950-52. Ordained to ministry Bapt. Ch., 1939, Congl. Ch., 1945. Min. Bethany Ch., American Falls, Idaho, 1939—41, 1st Ch., Council Grove, Kans., 1944—49, United Ch., Chebanse, Ill., 1949—52, 1st Ch., Argo, Ill., 1954—58, Congl. Ch., St. Charles, Ill., 1958—64; assoc. min. Plymouth Congl. Ch., Lansing, Mich., 1964—66; tchr. Chgo. Pub. Schs., 1966—68; min. Waveland Ave. Congl. Ch., Chgo., 1967—79; interim pastor Chgo. Met. Assn. Interim pastor United Ch. of Christ, 1979, First Congl. Ch., Des Plaines, Ill., 1979, Bethany United Ch., Chgo., 1980, Eden United Ch. of Christ, Chgo., 1983-84, St. Nicolai Ch., Chgo., 1984, Grace United Ch. of Christ, Chgo., 1985-86, Christ Ch. of Chgo., 1987, First Congl., Evanston, Ill., 1987-88, First Congl. Ch., Brookfield, Ill., 1988-89, Steger, Ill., 1990-91, Berwyn, Ill., 1992, Immanual United Ch. of Christ, Streamwood, Ill., 1993, Immanuel United Ch. of Christ, Bartlett, 1994; assoc. pastor, calling min. of visitation People's Ch., Chgo., 1990-93; hist. cons. Bell & Howell Co., Chgo., 1981-82; coord. Inst. Cont. Learning Roosevelt U., 1998—. Author: The Growth of the Bible, 1969, From A Mission to a Church, 1976, Bell & Howell Company: A 75 Year History, 1982; co-author: Harza: 65 Years, 1986, History of the Illinois Conference, United Church of Christ, 1990, Forward Through the Ages 1852-2002, 2002. Assoc. Hyde Park dept. Chgo. YMCA, 1942-44, U. Chgo. Libr., 1952-54; chmn. com. evangelism Kans. Congl. Christian Conf., 1947-48; city chmn. Layman's Missionary Movement, 1946-49; trustee Congl. and Christian Conf. Ill., v.p., 1963-64; mem. exec. coun. Chgo. Met. Assn. United Ch. of Christ, 1968-70, sec. ch. and ministry com., 1982-88; mem. gen. bd. Ch. Fedn. Greater Chgo., 1969-71; mem. Libr. Bd. Coun. Grove, 1945-49; dean Northside Mission Coun. United Ch. of Christ, 1975-77, sec. pers. com. Ill. Conf. United Ch. of Christ, 1986-88; bd. dirs. Tri-Village United Way, 1996-2003; coord. Inst. Continued Learning Roosevelt U., Schaumburg, Ill., 1998—. Mem. Chgo. Coun. Fgn. Rels. Recipient Pres.' award Congl. Christian Hist. Soc. Home: 321 E Morse Ave Bartlett IL 60103-4168

ROBINSON, JAMES ALFRED, retired educator; b. Phila., May 13, 1939; s. James Alfred Sr. and Evelyn (Perry) R.; children: James, John, Marce Balais; m. Gladys Acaba, Mar. 9, 1996. BS, Cheyney (Pa.) U., 1961; postgrad., Temple U., 1966—68, Goddard Coll., 1989—90, C.C. Phila., 1989. Mid. sch. tchr. Phila. Pub. Sch. Sys., 1962-95. Chmn. J.A. Robinson Assocs. Video Prodn. Cons., Phila., 1988—; instr. ednl. media Temple U., 1988-90; video prodn. cons. In Search of History: The Underground Railroad, History channel, 1999; video documentaries include Linda Creed Concert, Mayoral Race: Phila., 1985, Duality, Bicentennial Celebration. Media arts fellow Mid-Atlantic region Pitts. Filmmakers NEA, Pa. Coun. for Arts, 1993. Mem. HTML Writers Guild. Baptist. Avocations: photography, music, tennis.

ROBINSON, JAMES ARTHUR, policy scientist; b. Blackwell, Okla., June 9, 1932; s. William L. and Ethel Bell (Hicks) R.; children: Adelaide, Luke. AB, George Washington U., 1954, DPS (hon.), 1977; MA, U. Okla., 1955; PhD, Northwestern U., 1957. Congl. fellow Am. Polit. Sci. Assn., 1957-58; Instr. polit. sci. Northwestern U., 1958-59, asst. prof., 1959-62, assoc. prof., 1962-64; prof. polit. sci. Ohio State U., Columbus, 1964-71; dir. Mershon Center, 1967-70, v.p. acad. affairs, provost, 1969-71; pres., prof. polit. sci. Macalester Coll., St. Paul, 1971-74; pres. U. West Fla., Pensacola, 1974-88, pres. emeritus, 1988—, Regents prof., 1988—2002. Author: (with R. C. Snyder) National and International Decision Making, 1961, Congress and Foreign Policy Making, rev. edit, 1967, House Rules Committee, 1963, (with J. Baum) Party Primaries in Taiwan, 1999, (with D. Brown and E. Moon) Appraising Steps in Democratization: Elections in Taiwan, 1986-2000, 2000. Mem.: Cosmos (Washington).

ROBINSON, JAMES D., III, finance company executive, investor; b. Atlanta, Nov. 19, 1935; m. Bettye Bradley (div.); 2 children; m. Linda Gosden, 1984; 2 children. BS, Ga. Inst. Tech., 1957; MBA, Harvard U., 1961. Officer various depts. Morgan Guaranty Trust Co. of N.Y., N.Y.C., 1961-66, asst. v.p., staff asst. to chmn. bd. and pres., 1967-68; gen. ptnr. White, Weld & Co., 1968-70; exec. v.p. Am. Express Co., N.Y.C., 1970-75, pres., dir., 1975-77, chmn. bd. dirs., CEO, 1977-93. Pres., CEO Am. Express Internat. Banking Corp., 1970-73; chair Am. Express Credit Corp., 1973-75; co-founder, gen. ptnr. RRE Ventures, 1994—; chmn., CEO RRE Investors LLC; bd. dirs. Coca Cola Co., Bristol-Myers Squibb Co., Novell, Inc., First Data Corp.; former co-chair Bus. Roundtable. Author: Inflation Overkill, 1994, Full Steam Ahead, 2000. Active Bus. Coun., Coun. on Fgn. Rels., U.S. Japan Bus. Coun., Dean's Adv. Coun. Roberto C. Goizueta Sch. Bus. Emory U., Exec. Adv. Bd., Ivan Allen Coll.; hon. co-chair bd. Meml. Sloan-Kettering Cancer Ctr., former chair bds. of overseers and mgrs. Meml. Sloan-Kettering Cancer Ctr.; hon. mem. The Brookings Instn.; mem. bd. dirs. Nat. Acad. Found.; mem. Pres.' Cir. The Asia Soc.; bd. dirs., chair emeritus Partnership of N.Y.C., Inc.; chair emeritus World Travel & Tourism Coun.; former chair Internat. Trade and Investment Task Force of the Bus. Roundtable, former chair svcs. policy adv. com.; former chmn. adv. com. on trade and policy negotiations United Way of Am.; former mem. Coun. on Competitiveness; former trustee Alfred P. Sloan Found., Coun. on Econ. Devel.; mem. Dewitt Wallace Found. Lt. USNR, 1957-59. Mem. Japan Soc. (bd. dirs.), Econ. Club (N.Y.C.). Office: RRE Ventures 126 E 56th St Fl 22 New York NY 10022-3613

ROBINSON, JAMES LEROY, architect, educator, developer; b. July 12, 1940; s. Willie LeRoy and Ruby Nell Robinson; m. Martha Robinson; children: James LeRoy II, Kerstin Gunilla, Maria Theresa Narvaez, Jasmin Marisol, Ruby Nell, Kenneth Arne. BArch, So. U., 1964; MCP, Pratt Inst., 1972. Arch. Pt. of N.Y. Authority, 1964; arch., store planner W.T. Grant, 1964; with Herbst & Rusciano, AIA, 1965; arch. Carson, Lundin & Shaw, N.Y.C., 1966, Kennerly, Slomanson & Smith, N.Y.C., 1967-69, arch.-on-bus., 1969;

pres. Robinson Archs., P.C., N.Y.C., 1969—. V.p. J&K Constrn. Cons., Inc.; vis. prof. CUNY; adj. prof. Pratt Inst. Prin. works include Stuyvesant Heights Christian Ch., David Chavis House, Fulton Ct. Houses, Sinclair Houses, Hamilton Heights Terr., Eliot Graham Houses, Sojourner Truth Houses, Nehemiah Plan, Casas Theresa, N.Y.C. Postal Data Ctr., Mt. Carmel Bapt. Ch., Consol. Edison Collection Ctr., Jasmin Houses, CityHomes CD&E, The Promenade, Gore Residence & Tse Residence. Bd. dirs. Boys Club Am. With U.S. Army, 1966. Decorated knight Order of St. John, Knight of Malta; recipient AIA Design award, 1976; Martin Luther King fellow Pratt Inst., 1972. Mem. Am. Arbitrators Assn. (arbitrator). Democrat. Address: 55C DeLancey St New York NY 10002-2804 Office Phone: 212-966-7828. Personal E-mail: jackrabbit85@hotmail.com.

ROBINSON, JAMES W. fire captain; b. Calif. m. Erika Robinson. MPA, Kennedy Sch. of Govt., Harvard U., Cambridge, MA, 2000—01; Fire Protection Adminstrn./ Pub. Adminstrn., Calif. State U. LA, Los Angeles, 1996—99. Exec. projects LA County Fire Dept., Los Angeles, Calif., 2001—, engr., 1998—2004, firefighter, 1992—98. Mem. Inst. of Supply Mgmt., Los Angeles, Calif., 2002—; bd. mem. LA County Fire Fighters Assoc., Los Angeles, Calif., 2001—. Interviewer and evaluator Harvard U. Schools Com., Los Angeles, Calif., 2002—. Recipient Alumni Achievement Award, Calif. State U. LA, 2000, Commendation, LA County Bd. of Supervisors, 2000, Magna Cum Laude, Calif. State U. LA, 1999; fellow Robert Wilmers State and Local Govt. Pub. Svc. Fellow, Kennedy Sch. of Govt., Harvard U., 2000-2001. Mem.: Harvard-Radcliffe Club of So. Calif. Avocations: reading, golf, travel. Office: LA County Fire Dept 1320 N Eastern Ave Los Angeles CA 90063 E-mail: jrobinso@lacofd.org.

ROBINSON, JANET L. publishing executive; BA cum laude in English, Salve Regina Coll., 1972; diploma in Exec. Edn., Dartmouth U., 1996; DBA (hon.), Salve Regina U., 1998. Tchr., reading specialist, 1972—83; account exec., Tennis Mag. The N.Y. Times Co., 1983—85, nat. resort and travel mgr., Golf Digest/Tennis, 1985—87, advt. dir., Tennis Mag., 1987—90, v.p. advt. sales and mktg., The Women's Mag. Group, 1990—92, group sr. v.p., advt. sales and mktg., The Women's Mag. Group, 1992—93, v.p., dir. advt., 1994, sr. v.p. advt., 1995, pres., gen. mgr., N.Y. Times newspaper, 1996—, sr. v.p. newspaper ops., 2001—04, exec. v.p., COO, 2004—. Cons. Dept. Edn., Mass., 1977—83. Mem. Literacy Vols. N.Y.; mem. adv. bd. Salve Regina Coll. Named Outstanding Newspaper Exec., Frohlinger's Mktg. Report, 1994. Mem.: Women in Comm., Advt. Women N.Y., Advt. Club N.Y. Office: NY Times 229 W 43rd St New York NY 10036-3959*

ROBINSON, JAY (JAY THURSTON ROBINSON), artist; b. Detroit, Aug. 1, 1915; s. Carter Boston and Marie Rose (Steger) R.; m. Dorothy June Whipple, Sept. 15, 1937 (dec. 1968); children: Theodore Carter, Thomas Whipple, James Jay; m. Anne Frances Helen Posch, Nov. 5, 1970 (dec. 1999). BA, Yale U., 1937; MFA, Cranbrook Acad. Art, 1943. One-man shows include, Guggenheim Mus. Non-Objective Painting, N.Y.C., 1947, Milch Galleries, N.Y.C., 1948, 51, 53, 54, 55, 56, J.B. Speed Art Mus., Louisville, 1953, Dayton Art Inst., 1953, Phila. Art Alliance, 1957, Monede Gallery, N.Y.C., 1961, 62, Raymond Burr Galleries, Beverly Hills, Calif., 1963, xxth Century West Gallery, N.Y.C., 1968, E. Kuhlik Gallery, N.Y.C., 1971, New Canaan Soc. for Arts, 1983, Broome St. Gallery, N.Y.C., 1994, group shows include, Guggenheim Mus., 1947, 49, Carnegie Inst., Pitts., 1949, Des Moines Art Center, 1950, Butler Inst., Youngstown, Ohio, 1953, also Audubon Artists, N.Y.C., Corcoran Gallery, Washington, Mich. Artists, Detroit, NAD, N.Y.C., Pa. Acad., Phila., Provincetown (Mass.) Annual, Va. Biennial, Richmond; represented in permanent collections, including, Detroit Inst. Art, Houston Mus. Fine Art, Witte Meml. Mus., San Antonio, Philbrook Art Center, Tulsa; Berea Coll., Goucher Coll., Fisk U.; represented also in corp. collections, including, IBM; Republic Steel Co., Bristol-Myers Squibb, portrait painter, designer china and textiles; illustrator: Seventeenth Summer (Maureen Daly), 1948, The New York Guide Book, 1964; contbr. illustrations to other books. Served with OSS, 1943; Served with USN, 1943-46. Louis Comfort Tiffany Found. award, 1950; various purchase awards Am. Acad. Arts and Letters, 1951-64; Outstanding Alumnus award Detroit Country Day Sch., 1966 Home: 305 E Landing Williamsburg VA 23185-8254 *I have always been drawn to the theme of Man in His Environment. By extension to our own, I love jazz music, many of whose players I have painted; classic cars; Japanese gardens; good company and active social life. Travel enables me to see what others have done and are doing.*

ROBINSON, JOE SAM, neurosurgeon, educator; b. Atlanta, Ga., July 21, 1945; s. Joe Sam and Nell (Mixon) R.; m. Elizabeth Ann Moate, Apr. 3, 1982; children: Joe Sam III, Edward Richard, Thomas McRae. AB cum laude, Harvard Coll., 1967; MD, U. Va., 1971; MS, Northwestern U., 1975. Surg. intern Emory U., 1971-72, resident in surgery, 1972-73; resident in neurosurgery Northwestern U., 1973-78; instr. U. Ill., 1978-79, Yale U., 1979-81; pres. Ga. Neurosurg. Inst. P.A., Macon, 1981—. Prof., chief neurosurgery Mercer U. Sch. Medicine, Macon, 1986; chief surgery Med. Ctr. Ctrl. Ga., Macon, 1989—, vice chmn. surgery, 1991-97, chmn. dept. surgery, 1996—; vis. neurosurgeon China, 1992, Konaus Acad. Neurosurgery Inst., Lithuania, 1992; clin. prof. Med. Coll. Ga., 2002. Lt. col. USANG, 1972-95. Fellow Internat. Coll. Surgeons (vice regent 1983-93); mem. Am. Assn. Neurol. Surgeons, Congress Neurol. Surgeons, AAAS, Ga. Neurosurg. Soc., Alpha Omega Alpha. Republican. Methodist. Office: Ga Neurosurg Inst PA 840 Pine St Ste 880 Macon GA 31201-7525 Office Phone: 912-743-7092. E-mail: teriwyn@hotmail.com.

ROBINSON, JOEL D. manufacturing executive; 3 children. Dir. Body-in-White assemble Chrysler; dir. vehicle assembly Am. Motors; Ford personnel devel. program Ford Motor Co.; dir. mfg. planning Am. Axle & Mfg., Detroit, 1994, dir. GMT800 program, exec. dir. mfg., v.p. mfg., exec. v.p., COO, 1998—2001, pres., COO, 2001—. Office: Am Axle and Mfg 1840 Holbrook Detroit MI 48212-3488

ROBINSON, JOHN ALAN, logic and computer science educator; b. Halifax, Eng., Mar. 9, 1930; came to U.S., 1952; naturalized citizen, 1990. s. Harry and Clara (Pilkington) R.; m. Gwen Groves, Dec. 18, 1954; children: Alan Groves, Hugh Parke Custis, Gwen Owen. BA in Classics with honours, Corpus Christi Coll., Cambridge (Eng.) U., 1952; MA, 1955; MA in Philosophy, U. Ore., 1953; MA, Princeton U., 1955, PhD, 1956; D in Applied Sci. honoris causa, U. Leuven, 1988; D in Philosophy honoris causa, U. Uppsala, 1994; D in Informatics honoris causa, U. Politechnica, Madrid, 2003. Operations research analyst E.I. du Pont de Nemours & Co., Inc., 1956-60; post-doctoral research fellow U. Pitts., 1960-61; mem. faculty Rice U., 1961-67, prof. philosophy, 1964-65, prof. computer sci. and philosophy, 1965-66, prof. computer sci., 1966-67; disting. prof. logic and computer sci. Syracuse U., 1967-84, Univ. prof., 1984-92, univ. prof. emeritus, 1993—. Cons. in applied math. divsn. Argonne Nat. Lab., 1961-67, Stanford Linear Acceleration Ctr., 1966-68; vis. rsch. fellow Australian Nat. U., 1989; Fujitsu vis. prof. U. Tokyo, 1991-92. Author: Logic: Form and Function, 1979; founder, editor-in-chief Jour. Logic Programming, 1984-86; contbr. articles to profl. jours. Served with RAF, 1948-49. Recipient Sr. U.S. Scientists prize Humboldt Found., 1995, Herbrand award, 1996; Guggenheim Found. fellow, 1967-68; hon. rsch. fellow U. Edinburgh, 1967—. Fellow Am. Assn. for Artificial Intelligence; mem. Kokusai Bunka Kaikan (Tokyo). Home and Office: PO Box 988 Northampton MA 01601-0988

ROBINSON, JOHN BECKWITH, development management consultant; b. Portland, Oreg., May 23, 1922; s. Jewell King and Arvilla Agnes (Beckwith) R.; m. Dilys Walters, Sept. 8, 1945; children— John Gwilym, David Gwyn. BA, U. Oreg., 1944; postgrad., U. Shrivenham, Eng., 1945, U. Oxford, 1946, Am. U., 1947. Staff U.S. Bur. Budget, 1947—48; sr. program and budget officer UNESCO, 1948—51; mem. staff U.S. Bur. Budget, 1951—52; chief personnel policy Mut. Security Agy., Washington, 1952-54, program officer Guatemala, 1954-59, planning officer, latter acting asst. dep. dir. for program and planning AID, 1959-61; dep. U.S. rep. devel. assistance com. OECD, 1961-64, asst. dir. devel. policy, 1964-68; dep. dir. North Coast Affairs, AID, State Dept., Washington, 1969-71; dep. mission dir. U.S. Econ. Aid Program, Colombia, 1971-73, mission dir. Dominican Republic, 1973-76, mission dir. Honduras, 1976—79; privatization adviser Gov. of Costa Rica, 1986-88; prin. assoc. J.B. Robinson & Assocs. (devel. mgmt. cons.), 1979—. Mem. faculty, fellow Harvard U., 1968-69; cons. NATO, 1951, UN, 1959 Served to 1st lt., inf. AUS, 1943-46, ETO. Mem. Oriental Club (London), DACOR BACON House (Washington), Minchinhampton Probus Club (pres. 1983-84). Episcopalian. Address: Anglezarke The Hithe Rodborough Common Stroud GL5 5BN Gloucestershire England also: 2323 SW Park Pl Portland OR 97205 *Summary: always do more than what is asked for the task at hand. The extra effort always leads to unexpected opportunities for career advancement. Helping others to realize their potential has its own rewards and their success helps to realize your own hopes and aspirations, and improve your own quality of life and satisfaction in a life well-spent. Never underestimate the contribution of your wife and family.*

ROBINSON, JOHN BEINECKE, writer; s. John Rowland and Barbara G. Robinson; m. Elizabeth Foster Stout, July 28, 2003; children: Rowland, Geneva Morley, Duncan Morley, Nicolas. AB, Harvard U., 1991; MFA, Brown U., 1995. Author: Kilimanjaro Burning, 1998, The Sapphire Sea, 2003. Fellow, Inst. Current World Affairs, Hanover, N.H., 1996—98. Address: 1 Longfellow Sq Portland ME 04101

ROBINSON, JOHN BOWERS, JR., retired bank holding company executive; b. Laconia, N.H., Oct. 9, 1946; s. John Bowers and Lee (Osborn) R.; m. Jane Frances Moore, Aug. 31, 1968; children: John Paul, Claire Frances, David Moore, Leanne Elizabeth, Gregory Joseph, Peter August. BA, Fairfield U., 1968; MBA, Adelphi U., 1977. V.p., asst. to pres. Hempstead Bank, N.Y., 1977-79, exec. v.p., 1979-81, pres., 1981-82; v.p. planning Norstar Bancorp, Inc., Albany, N.Y., 1982-84, exec. v.p., 1984-87, pres., 1987-88; mng. dir. govt. banking FleetBoston Fin. (formerly Fleet Fin. Group), Albany, 1988—2002. Mem. Albany Med. Ctr., 1989—. Pres. bd. trustees Doane Stuart Sch., Albany, N.Y., 1996—. Mem. Ft. Orange Club, Schuyler Meadows Club. Home: 90 Ridge Rd Rensselaer NY 12144-4306 E-mail: john_b_robinson@fleet.com.

ROBINSON, JOHN LAURENCE, academic administrator, writer; b. Danville, Ky., May 3, 1952; s. Wendell Alfred and Evelyn Louise Robinson; m. Barbara Jo Wasson, May 26, 1973; children: Michael, Joshua. BA in Broadcasting, Ea. Ky. U., 1974. Life ins. agt. various cos., Cin., 1977—84; mng. gen. agt. Pension Plus, Cin., 1984—2003; dir. admissions Southwestern Coll. Bus., Cin., 2003—. Author: (novels) Sock Monkey Blues, 2001, Until the Last Dog Dies, 2004. Avocations: travel, movies, music, reading. E-mail: sockmonkey123@juno.com.

ROBINSON, JOHN LEWIS, geography educator; b. Leamington, Ont., Can., July 9, 1918; s. William John and Emily Laverne (Dunphy) R.; m. Josephine Rowan, Oct. 14, 1944; children: David, Jo-Anne, Patricia. BA, Western Ont. U., 1940; MA, Syracuse U., 1942; PhD, Clark U., 1946; LLD (hon.), Western Ont. U., 1984; DSc (hon.), U. B.C., 1994. Geographer N.W.T. Adminstrn., Ottawa, Ont., 1943-46; prof., head dept. geography U. B.C., Vancouver, 1946-68, prof. geography, 1968-85, prof. emeritus, 1985—. Author 14 books on aspects of regional geography of Can., including British Columbia: 100 Years of Geographical Change, 1973, Themes in the Regional Geography of Canada, 1983, 2d edit., 1989; contbr. articles to profl. jours. Recipient citation of merit Assn. Am. Geographers, 1966; Massey medal Canadian Geog. Soc., 1971 Mem. Canadian Assn. Geographers (pres. 1956, citation for service to profession 1976) Office: U BC Dept Geography Vancouver BC Canada V6T 1Z2

ROBINSON, JOHN MINOR, lawyer, retired business executive; b. Uniontown, Pa., Mar. 18, 1910; s. John M. and Martha (Downs) R. AB, Harvard U., 1932, LL.B, 1935. Bar: Calif. 1936. Assoc. firm Macdonald & Pettit, 1935-41; partner firm Musick, Peeler & Garrett, 1947-77; v.p., sec. Consol. Western Steel div. U.S. Steel Corp. (and predecessors), 1941-57. Mem. Calif. Club (past pres. L.A.), Pacific Union Club (San Francisco), Cypress Point Club (Pebble Beach, Calif.), Royal and Ancient Golf Club of St. Andrews (Fife, Scotland). Office: 9500 Center St #38 Carmel CA 93923-8552

ROBINSON, JOHN VICTOR, lawyer; b. Harare, Zimbabwe, July 9, 1958; s. Denis Antony Beck and Elizabeth Jill R. BA, Rhodes U., Grahamstown, South Africa, 1983; MA, Oxford (Eng.) U., 1985; JD, U. Richmond (Va.), 1986. Bar: Va. Assoc. atty. Hunton & Williams, Richmond, Va., 1986-89, McSweeney, Burtch & Crump, Richmond, 1989-93, Cantor, Arkema & Edmonds, P.C., Richmond, 1993-97; pvt. practice Richmond, 1997—. Past mem. regional com. Nat. Trial Competition, Richmond; apptd. adminstrv. hearing officer Va. Supreme Ct.; adj. asst. prof. Law U. Richmond Sch. Law. Rhodes scholar Oxford U., 1983-85. Mem. ABA, Va. Bar Assn., Bar Assn. City of Richmond. Office: 7102 Three Cropt Road Richmond VA 23226-3615

ROBINSON, JOHN WILLIAM, IV, lawyer; b. Atlanta, Apr. 29, 1950; s. J. William III and Elizabeth (Smith) R.; m. Ellen Showalter, Dec. 28, 1976; children: William, Anna. BA with honors, Washington & Lee U., 1972; JD, U. Ga., 1975. Bar: Fla., Ga., U.S. Dist. Ct. (no., so. and mid. dists.) Fla., U.S. Ct. Mil. Appeals, U.S. Ct. Appeals (5th and 11th cirs.), U.S. Supreme Ct.; cert. labor & employment law, civil trial and bus. litigation lawyer, Fla., Nat. Bd. Trial Advocacy. Trial atty. Nat. Labor Rels. Bd., New Orleans, 1975-76; trial def. counsel 8th infantry U.S. Army, Mainz, Germany, 1977-78, trial counsel 8th infantry, 1979; law clerk, commr. Ct. Mil. Review, Washington, 1980; atty. Fowler, White, Boggs & Banker, PA, Tampa, Fla., 1980—, head labor and employment law dept., 1993—, dir., 1998—, sec./treas., 2001—. Mem. faculty U. Md., 1977-79; arbitrator U.S. Dist. Ct. (mid. dist.) Fla. Editor-in-chief: Employment & Labor Relations Law, 1991-95; editor: Developing Labor Law, 1982—, Model Jury Instructions for Employment Litigation, 1994—; editor: Employment Litigation Handbook, 1998. Chmn. Tampa Bay Internat. Trade Coun., 1990-91, Rough Riders Dist. Boy Scouts Am., 1990; legal counsel Drug Free Workplace Task Force, 1999-00, Greater Tampa C. of C., 1996, gen. counsel, bd. dirs., 1999—. Capt. U.S. Army, 1976-80. Named one of Best Lawyers in Am. for labor and employment law. Mem.: ABA (chmn. employment and labor rels. com. 1993—96, divsn. dir. 1996—2000, mem. coun. 2000—03, chmn. com. on multijurisdictional practice 2000—, litigation sect., task force on electronic discovery 2003—04), Hillsborough County Bar Assn. Trial Lawyers (bd. dirs. 1996—, chmn. 2003—), Am. Inn of Ct. (pres., dir. and master barrister, trustee Am. Inns of Ct. Found.), Washington & Lee U. Bd. (pres. nat. alumni bd. 1990—91, trustee 1995—), Fla. Bar Assn. (chmn. labor and employment law sect. 1992—93), Rotary (pres. Tampa Bay chpt.). Avocations: tennis, history. Office: Fowler White Boggs Banker PA 501 E Kennedy Blvd Tampa FL 33602-5237

ROBINSON, JOYCE MCPEAKE, administrator; b. Newark, July 28, 1941; d. Salvatore and Wilhelmina (Cervetto) Guinta; m. John David McPeake, June 15, 1963 (div. Aug. 1974); children: John Paul, David Samuel; m. Enders Anthony Robinson, Aug. 8, 1992. BA in English, Tufts U., 1962; MA in English, Boston U., 1965, EdD, 1979. Asst. to dean women & dept. adminstrn. Boston U., 1962-63, 65-67; reading specialist Hingham (Mass.) Pub. Schs., 1963-64; reading and learning specialist Manter Hall Sch., Cambridge, Mass., 1964-67; reporter Patriot Ledger, Quincy, Mass., 1967-69; dir. Christ Luth. Sch., Scituate, Mass., 1971-74; prin. and reading specialist Scituate Pub. Schs., 1974-80; chair English, dir. reading programs St. Andrew's Sch., Boca Raton, Fla., 1980-88; chair English, learning specialist Broadwater Acad., Exmore, Va., 1988-89; dir. learning resources, English Fountain Valley Sch., Colorado Springs, Colo., 1989-91; asst. prin. Islamic Saudi Acad., Alexandria, Va., 1991-93; chair English Masters Sch., Dobbs Ferry, N.Y., 1993-94; head QUEST program Dwight Sch., N.Y.C., 1994—96, head of sch., 1996—. Adj. prof. Nova U., Ft. Lauderdale, Fla., 1984-88, St. Thomas U., Miami, Fla., 1987-88; sch. evaluator Fla. Coun. Ind. Schs., 1985-88; cons. in field. Author: Teaching Study Skills, 1987, Wordworks, 1990; contbr. (poetry) Rhyme and Reason, 1987; editor: How to Double Your Child's Grades in School, 1997; contbr.: Fostering Creativity in Children, K-8, 2000. Coord. Am. Inst. Fgn. Study, Boston, 1987; parent agt. Hamilton Coll. Parents Fund, Clinton, N.Y., 1986—; mem. town adv. com. Scituate Town Com., 1975-80. Mem. Nat. Coun. Tchrs. English, Am. Acad. Poets, Nat. Assn. Ind. Schs., Fla. Coun. Librs., Ea. Ednl. Rsch. Assn. (membership chair 1993-95), Internat. Reading Assn., Coun. Exceptional Children, Modern Lang. Assn., Hemingway Soc., Am. Assn. Ednl. Rsch. (bd. mem. 1996—), Nat. Acad. Ednl. Rsch. Home: 8 Dorothy Lucey Dr Newburyport MA 01950 Office: Dwight Sch 291 Central Park W New York NY 10024-3002 E-mail: jrobinson@dwight.edu.

ROBINSON, JULIE ANN, judge; b. 1957; BS, U. Kans., 1978, JD, 1981. Bar: Kans. 1981. Asst. U.S. atty. for dist. Kans. U.S. Dept. Justice, Kansas City, Kans., 1983-94, sr. litigation counsel, 1991-94; law clk. to hon. Benjamin E. Franklin, U.S. Bankruptcy Ct. for Dist. Kans., Kansas City, Kans., 1981-83, bankruptcy judge, 1994—2001; judge bankruptcy appellate panel U.S. Ct. Appeals (10th cir.), Topeka, 1996—2001. Instr. trial practice U. Kans. Sch. Law, 1989-90. Fellow Am. Bar Found.; mem. ABA, Kans. Bar Assn., Kans. Inn of Ct. Office: US Dist Ct 405 US Courthouse 444 SE Quincy Topeka KS 66683

ROBINSON, JUNE KERSWELL, dermatologist, educator; b. Phila., Jan. 26, 1950; d. George and Helen S. (Kerswell) R.; m. William T. Barker, Jan. 31, 1981. BA cum laude, U. Pa., 1970; MD, U. Md., 1974. Diplomate Am. Bd. Dermatology, Nat. Bd. Med. Examiners, Am. Bd. Mohs Micrographic Surgery and Cutaneous Oncology. Intern Greater Balt. Med. Ctr., Hanover, NH, 1974, resident in medicine, 1974-75; resident in dermatology Dartmouth-Hitchcock Med. Ctr., Hanover, 1975-78, chief resident, clin. instr., 1977-78, instr. in dermatology, 1978; fellow Mohs; chemosurgery and dermatologic surgery NYU Skin and Cancer Clinic, N.Y.C., 1978-79; instr. in dermatology NYU, N.Y.C., 1979; asst. prof. dermatology Northwestern U. Med. Sch., Chgo., 1979, asst. prof. surgery, 1980-85, assoc. prof. dermatology and surgery, 1985-91, prof. dermatology and surgery, 1991-98; prof. medicine and pathology, dir. divsn. dermatology Cardinal Bernardin Cancer Ctr., Loyola U. Med. Ctr., 1998—2004, program leader skin cancer clin. program, 1998—2004; prof. medicine Med. Sch. Dartmouth U., 2004—, chief Dermatology Sect. Hitchcock Med. Ctr., 2004—. Mem. consensus devel. conf. NIH, 1992; mem. panel on use of sunscreens Internat. Agy. for Rsch. on Cancer, WHO, 2000; lectr. in field. Author: Fundamentals of Skin Biopsy, 1985, also audiovisual materials; editor: (textbooks) Atlas of Cutaneous Surgery, 1996, Cutaneous Medicine and Surgery: An Integrated Program in Dermatology, 1996; mem. editl. bd. Archives of Dermatology, 1988-97; sect. editor The Cutting Edge: Challenges in Med. and Surg. Therapeutics, 1989-97, editor, 2004—; contbg. editor Jour. Dermatol. Surgery and Oncology, 1985-88; mem. editl. com. 18th World Congress of Dermatology, 1982; contbr. numerous articles, abstracts to profl. publs., chpts. to books. Bd. dirs. Northwestern Med. Faculty Found., 1982-84, chmn. com. on benefits and leaves, 1984, nominating com. 1988. Grantee Nat. Cancer Inst., 1985-91, 2004—, Am. Cancer Soc., 1986-89, Skin Cancer Found., 1984-85, Dermatology Found., 1981-83, Northwestern U. Biomed. Rsch., 1981, Syntex, 1984. Fellow: Am. Coll. Chemosurgery (chmn. sci. program ann. meeting 1983, chmn. publs. com. 1986—87, chmn. task force on ednl. needs 1989—90, co-editor bull. 1984—87); mem.: Chgo. Dermatol. Soc., Women's Dermatol. Soc. (pres. 1990—92, Wilma Bergeld, MD Visionary and Leadership award 2002), Soc. Investigative Dermatology, Am. Soc. Dermatol. Surgery (pres. 1994—95), Dermatology Found. (trustee 1995—98), Am. Acad. Dermatology (asst. sec.-treas. 1995—98, sec.-treas. 1998—2001, bd. dirs. 1993—95, Stephen Rothman Lectr. award 1992, Presdl. citation 1992, 2000), Am. Dermatol. Assn., Am. Cancer Soc. (pres. Ill. divsn. 1996—98). Home: 132 E Delaware Pl Apt 5806 Chicago IL 60611-4951

ROBINSON, KAREN VAJDA, dietician; BS in Home Econs., Montclair State Coll., 1980; MS in Health Scis./Dietetics, James Madison U., 1992. Cert. food svc. sanitation mgr., N.J. 1984. Dietitian Roosevelt Hosp., Edison, N.J., 1980-85; asst. mgr. UVA (U. Va.) Dining Svcs., Charlottesville, 1985-86; temp. sales sec., mem. banquet prep. staff Boar's Head Inn, Charlottesville, 1986-88; head diet counselor Diet Ctr., Charlottesville, 1986-90; dietetic intern VA Med. Ctr., Hampton, Va., 1991; pub. health nutritionist Cen. Shenandoah Health Dist., Waynesboro (Va.) Health Dept., 1993-97. Grad. dietetic intern mentor, 1993—97; cons. dietitian Hebrew Hosp. Home, Bronx, NY, 1998; food svc. mgr. Sodexho Marriott Svcs., Morningside House Nursing Home, Bronx, 1998—99; clin. dietitian Yonkers (NY) Gen. Hosp., 1999—2001; cmty. svcs. instr. Westchester C.C., Valhalla, NY, 2001; inpatient/out patient dietitian Park Care Pavilion (formerly Yonkers Gen. Hosp.), 2001—; clin. dietitian St. John's Riverside Hosp., Yonkers, 2002—. Contbr. articles to local newspapers. Mem. Charlottesville Health Promotion Coalition, 1993-97. Mem.: Westchester Rockland Dietetic Assn. (health fairs chair 1998—2001, scholarship com. 2000, pub. rels. co-chair 2000—01, sec. 2001—05, chmn. nominating com. 2003—04, grantee 2000), Va. Dietetic Assn. (exec. bd. 1996—97), Blue Ridge Dietetics Assn. (nat. nutrition month coord. 1993—95, editor newsletter 1993—96, mem. exec. bd. 1993—97, pres.-elect 1995—96, scholarship com. 1996, pres. 1996—97), Va. Pub. Health Assn. (sec. 1995, awards chair 1996—97), Dietitians in Nutrition Support, Gerontol. Nutritionists Practice Group, Cons. Dietitians in Health Care Facilities, Am. Assn. Family and Consumer Scis. (cert.), Am. Dietetic Assn. (registered). Home: 10-02 Hunter Ln Ossining NY 10562 Office Phone: 914-964-4216.

ROBINSON, KAYNE B. lobbyist, former political organization officer; m. Donna R. Robinson. B, Drake U. With Des Moines Police Dept.; dep. Iowa chmn. Dole Presdl. campaign, 1988; Iowa chmn. Gramm Presdl. campaign, 1996; chmn. Iowa Rep. Party, 1999—2001. With USMC. Named Police Officer of the Yr. Iowa Assn. Women Police. Mem. NRA (1st v.p.), 1997-2003, (pres.), 2003-. Office: NRA 11250 Waples Mill Rd Fairfax VA 22030

ROBINSON, KEITH, newspaper editor; Bur. chief AP, Indpls., 2000—. Office: 251 N Illinois St Ste 1600 Indianapolis IN 46204-1943

ROBINSON, KENNETH CHARLES, management educator; b. Macon, Ga. s. Charles William Robinson and Joyce R. Sorrow. BBA, U. Ga., 1984, MBA, 1991, PhD, 1995. Gen. mgr., CFO Shoe Shack, Inc., Macon, 1984-90, controller, buyer, 1990-91, mgmt. advisor, 1991-94; grad. tchg. asst. U. Ga., Athens, 1991-95; lectr. U. Wollongong, NSW, Australia, 1995-96; assoc. prof. strategy & entrepreneurship Kennesaw (Ga.) State U., 1996—. Mem. rels. com. Greater Macon C. of C., 1988—90, vice chmn. small bus. coun., 1989—90. Recipient Heizer Best Doctoral Dissertation award, Entrepreneurship Divsn., Acad. Mgmt., 1996, Mescon/Coles Best Empirical Paper award, Acad. Mgmt., 1999, Best Paper award, Entrepreneurship/Ethics Track, So. Mgmt. Assn., 2001; fellow Kauffman Ctr. Entrepreneurial Leadership, 1994, Comer fellow, U. Ga., 1994. Mem.: Strategic Mgmt. Soc., U.S. Assn. Small Bus. and Entrepreneurship (Runner-Up award 1999), Acad. Mgmt. (mem. exec. com. entrepreneurship divsn. 1996—, chair awards com. 1998—). Presbyterian. Avocations: travel, skiing, scuba diving, hiking. Home: 2953 Lookout Pl NE Atlanta GA 30305 Office: Kennesaw State U Coles Coll Bus 1000 Chastain Rd NW #0404 Kennesaw GA 30144-5591 Fax: 770-423-6606.

ROBINSON, KENNETH JOHN, emergency medicine physician; b. Hanover, N.H., Mar. 17, 1964; s. Kenneth J. and Lilla F. (Finizio) R. BS in Biochemistry cum laude, U. Vt., 1986; MD, U. Pitts., 1991. Bd. cert. in emergency medicine, 1995. Intern, resident Geisinger Med. Ctr., Danville, Pa., 1991-94; staff Hartford (Conn.) Hosp., 1994—, John Dempsey Hosp., Farmington, Conn., 1994—; asst. prof. dept. traumatology and emergency medicine U. Conn. Sch. Medicine, Farmington. Med. dir., co-program dir., LIFE STAR Helicopter program Hartford Hosp.; presenter and spkr. in field. Mem. AMA, Am. Coll. Emergency Physicians, Air Med. Physician's Assn. (chair membership com. 1996—, trustee 1998—), Nat. Assn. Emergency Medical Svcs. Physicians, Wilderness Med. Soc. Office: Hartford Hosp 80 Seymour St Hartford CT 06102-8000

ROBINSON, KENNETH PATRICK, lawyer, electronics company executive; b. Hackensack, NJ, Dec. 12, 1933; s. William Casper and Margaret Agnes (McGuire) r.; m. Catherine Esther Lund, Aug. 26, 1961; children: James, Susan. BS in Elec. Engring., Rutgers U., 1955; JD, NYU, 1962. Bar: N.Y. 1962, U.S. Ct. Appeals (fed. cir.) 1990. With Hazeltine Corp., Greenlawn, N.Y., 1955-88, patent counsel, 1966-69, gen. counsel, 1969-88, sec., 1971-88; v.p. Hazeltine Rsch. Inc., Chgo., 1966-88; of counsel Brumbaugh, Graves,

Donohue & Raymond, N.Y.C., 1989-92; prin. Kenneth P. Robinson, Huntington, N.Y., 1992—. Dir. Hazeltine Ltd., London, 1973-80; dir. Imlac Corp., Needham, Mass., 1978-83. Served to 1st lt. USAF, 1955-57. Mem. ABA, IEEE, Am. Intellectual Law Assn., Licensing Execs. Soc. Roman Catholic. Home: 137 Darrow Ln Greenlawn NY 11740-2923 Office: 474 New York Ave Huntington NY 11743-3542

ROBINSON, KIM STANLEY, science fiction author; b. Waukegan, Ill., Mar. 23, 1952; m. Lisa Howell; 2 children. BS, U. Calif., San Diego, PhD in English and Am. Lit., 1982; MS, Boston U. Author: (book series) Mars (Red Mars 1992, Green Mars 1993, Blue Mars 1995), Orange County (The Wild Shore 1984, The Gold Coast 1988, Pacific Edge 1990), (novels) Icehenge, 1984, The Memory of Whiteness, 1985, Escape from Kathmandu, 1989, A Short, Sharp Shock, 1990, Antarctica, 1998, The Years of Rice & Salt, 2002, (collections) The Planet on the Table, 1986, Escape From Kathmandu, 1990, Remaking History, 1991, The Martians, 1999, (anthologies) Future Primitive: The New Ecotopias, 1994, (non-fiction series) Studies in Speculative Fiction, 1984; author numerous short fiction, essays and articles. Recipient World Fantasy award, 1984, John W. Campbell Meml. award, 1991, Nebula award, 1987, 93, Locus Poll award, 1985, 91, 94, 97, Hugo award, 1994, 97, SF Chronicle award, 1984, 92, Brit. Sci. Fiction award, 1993. Avocations: mountain trekking, swimming. Office: c/o Random House Inc Bantam Books 1540 Broadway New York NY 10036-4039

ROBINSON, LARRY CLARK, professional hockey coach; b. Winchester, Ont., Can., June 2, 1951; m. Jeannette; children: Jeffery, Rachelle. Player Montreal Canadians, 1971—89, Los Angeles Kings, 1989—92; asst. coach New Jersey Devils, 1993—95, asst. coach , 1999—2000; head coach L.A Kings, 1995—99, New Jersey Devils, 2000—02, spl. assignment coach, 2002—. Player Team Canada, 1976, 81, 84. Received 9 Stanley Cups including Year 2003, Norris trophy (NHL best defenseman) 1977, 1980, Conne Smythe trophy (playoff MVP) 1978, Avocations: polo, boating.

ROBINSON, LAURIE OVERBY, former assistant attorney general; b. Washington, July 7, 1946; d. Kermit and Ethel Esther (Schlasinger) Overby; m. Craig Baab, Oct. 22, 1977 (div. 1991); 1 child, Teddy Baab; m. Sheldon Krantz, Dec. 8, 1991. BA in Polit. Sci. magna cum laude, Brown U., 1968. Desk editor Cmty. News Svc., N.Y.C., 1968-71; asst. staff dir. sect. criminal justice ABA, Washington, 1972-74, dir. sect. criminal justice, 1979-93, assoc. dep. atty. gen. U.S. Dept. Justice, Washington, 1993-94, asst. atty. gen. Office Justice Programs, 1994-2000; sr. fellow program on crime policy U. Pa. Jerry Lee Ctr. Criminology, 2000—, exec. dir. Forum Crime & Justice; dir. Master of Sci. in Criminology program U. Pa., 2004—. Mem. ex-officio, bd. regents Nat. Coll. Dist. Attys., Houston, 1979—93; adv. bd. Fed. Sentencing Reporter, N.Y.C., 1990—; chair Nat. Forum Criminal Justice, Washington, 1991—93; bd. dirs. Nat. Ctr. Victims of Crime. Adv. bd. George Mason U. Adminstrn. of Justice Adv. Program.; Clinton transition com. Dept. Justice, 1992; trustee Vera Inst. Justice, 2001—; bd. dirs. Police Found. Mem.: ABA, Phi Beta Kappa. Democrat. Business E-Mail: robinsol@sas.upenn.edu. E-mail: laurieorob@aol.com.

ROBINSON, LEONARD HARRISON, JR., international government consultant, business executive; b. Winston-Salem, N.C., Apr. 21, 1943; s. Leonard Harrison and Winnie Cornelia (Thomas) R.; children: Kimberly Michelle, Rani Craft. NSF cert., Bennett Coll., Greensboro, N.C., 1959; BA, Ohio State U., 1964; postgrad., SUNY, Binghamton, 1966-67, Am. U., 1982-89, Harvard U., 1991; LLD (hon.), Shaw U., Raleigh, N.C., 1983; LHD (hon.), Huston-Tillotson Coll., 1991. Vol. Peace Corps., Bihar, India, 1964-66; assoc. dir. for India Peace Corps, Madras, 1967-70; dir. recruitment Peace Corps., Washington, 1970-71; dir. inner-city programs EPA, Washington, 1971-72; dir. mgmt. Family Planning Internat. Assistance, N.Y.C., 1972-74, Africa dir. Accra, Ghana and Nairobi, Kenya, 1974-77; task force dir. U.S. Ho. Reps., Washington, 1977-78; dir. population Africa AID, Washington, 1978-79; dir. Internat. Devel. Ctr. Battelle Inst., Washington, 1979-83; dep. asst. sec., sr. exec. svc. Dept. State, Washington, 1983-85; pres. African Devel. Found., Washington, 1985-90; dep. asst. sec. state, sr. exec. svc. Dept. State, Washington, 1990-93; vice chmn., COO Washington Strategic Consulting Group, Inc., Washington, 1993-97; founder, pres. LHR Internat. Group, Inc., Washington, 1997—; exec. v.p., then pres. and CEO Nat. Summit on Africa Secretariat, Washington, 1997—. Cons. area studies U. Mo. Peace Corps, summer 1966; mgmt. analyst ATAC, Washington, 1971; mem. U.S. presdl. del. to Dakar, Senegal, 1987, to Malawi, Mozambique, and Uganda, Sept. 1988, to Mali, Uganda, and Kenya, Dec. 1988, v.p.'s visit to Africa, 1991; hon. consul Govt. Sao Tome and Principe, 1996—. Author: monographs Assessment and Analysis of Population Attitudes in Tanzania, 1981, Analyze African Official Attitudes Concerning U.S. Population Assistance in Lesotho, Tanzania, Senegal and Togo, 1981. Adviser Population Resource Ctr., N.Y.C., 1978-82; adviser internat. program for health and tng., U. N.C., Chapel Hill, 1980-84; vice-chmn. New Directions Task Force Rep. Party, Montgomery County (Md.), 1982-83; adv. coun. Nat. Coun. Returned Peace Corps Vols., 1987—; bd. dirs. Washington Ballet, 1982-85, 86-91, v.p. bd. dirs. 1988-90; bd. dirs. Friends of Smithsonian Mus. African Art, Washington, 1982-84, Coalition for Equitable Representation in Govt., Montgomery County, Montgomery County Bd. Soc. Svcs., 1986-89, Joint Agrl. Consultative Corp., 1985-86, Alan Gutmacher Inst., 1992-96, Friends of the U. of Natal, South Africa, 1995—. Decorated commandeur de l'Ordre National du Niger, 1989; recipient Africare Disting. Svc. award, 1990, Key to the City of Greensboro, N.C., 1991, Christian D. Maxwell Disting. Svc. award Liberian Com. for Relief, Resettlement and Reconstruction, 1993; hon. counsel for the Govt. of Sao Tome and Principe, Ctrl. Africa; sr. fellow U. Mass. John W. McCormack Inst. Mem. Soc. Internat. Devel. (dir. 1982), Am. Pub. Health Assn. (sec. population sect. 1979-81), Coun. on Fgn. Rels., C. of C. of D.C. (dir. 1979-82), Metro Club Washington, Kappa Alpha Psi, Sigma Pi Phi. Office: Nat Summit on Africa Secretariat Enos Cosby Internat House 1218 16th St NW Washington DC 20036-3202 *Human life is precious and extraordinary. I have strived to live to the fullest, by being productive, impact-oriented, and successful in contributing to the improvement of people's lives. This quest has brought me happiness and fulfillment.*

ROBINSON, LESTER W. airport executive; B in Bus. Adminstrn., Mich. State U., 1973. CPA. With Coopers & Lybrand; CFO 1st Independence Corp., Detroit, 1980-83, pres., CEO, 1989-91; auditor gen. Wayne County, Detroit, 1988-89, dept. dir. airports fin. & adminstrn. dept. airports, 1991-93, CFO dept. budget, 1993-95, dir. dept. airports, 2000—; corp. fin. rep. 1st Mich. Corp., 1995-2000. Office: Dept Aviation Detroit Met Airport Williams Rogell Dr Detroit MI 48242

ROBINSON, LINDA GOSDEN, communications executive; b. LA, Jan. 10, 1953; d. Freeman Fisher and Jane Elizabeth (Stoneham) Gosden; m. Stephen M. Dart (div. June 1977); m. James Dixon Robinson III. Student, UCLA, 1970-72; BA summa cum laude in Psychology, U. So. Calif., 1978. Dep. press sec. Reagan Presdl. Campaign, LA, 1979; press sec., dir. pub. relations Rep. Nat. Com., Washington, 1979-80; dir. pub. affairs US Dept. Transp., Washington, 1981-83; ptnr. pub. and govt. affairs Heron, Burchette, Ruckert & Rothwell, Washington, 1983; dep. to spl. envoy Office of the Pres., NYC, 1985; sr. v.p. corp. affairs Warner Amex Cable Communications, NYC, 1983-86; chmn. Robinson Lerer & Montgomery, LLC, NYC, 1986—, CEO, 1986—2002. Bd. dirs. Revlon Group, Inc., NYC; dir. BlackRock, Inc., NYC, Rainbow Media Enterprises, Jericho, NY. Del. Rep. Nat. Conv., 1985; trustee NYU Sch. Medicine Found. Bd., vice chair; trustee NYU Hosp. Ctr.; bd. dirs. Lustgarten Found. Pancreatic Rsch. Mem.: Phi Beta Kappa. Avocations: tennis, horseback riding.

ROBINSON, LINDA SCHULTZ, art educator, artist; b. Oakland, Calif., Mar. 15, 1949; d. James Richie Schultz and Dorothy Louise Koster-Schultz; m. Steven R. Robinson, Aug. 10, 1980; children: Laura Anne, Chelsea Marie, Emily Louise. AA in Art, Mauna Olu Coll., 1970; BA in Criminal Justice, Calif. State U., Sacramento, 1979. Cert.: Calif. (paralegal). Legal typist U.S. Govt., Concord, Calif., 1975—79; paralegal Alternative Legal Choices, Pleasant Hill, Calif., 1985—87; spl. edn. para-profl. Acad. Sch. Dist., Colorado Springs, Colo., 1995—96; pvt. art instr. to spl. needs individuals Colorado Springs, 1999—. Art therapist Meml. Hosp., Colorado Springs, 2001—. Exhibitions include Colorado Springs Art Guild, 2001. Bd. dirs. Interfaith Hospitality Network, Colorado Springs, 1995—99; vol. art tchr. Acad. Dist. 20 Schs., Colorado Springs, 2001—. Avocations: guitar, reading, crafts.

ROBINSON, LOGAN GILMORE, lawyer; b. Cin., Ohio, Dec. 26, 1949; s. Landon Graves and Alis (Rule) R.; m. Edrie Baker Sowell, Sept. 22, 1983; children: Leyland G., Landon G., Linden G., Lane G. BA, Cornell U., 1972; JD, Harvard U., 1976; Cert. Competence in German, Goethe Inst., Freiburg, Germany, 1978. Bar: Ohio 1977, N.Y. 1979, Mich. 1989, U.S. Ct. Internat. Trade 1983. Rsch. faculty Leningrad State U., Russia, 1976-77; research officer U. Leiden, The Netherlands, 1977-78; assoc. Wender, Murase & White, NYC, 1978-81, Coudert Bros., NYC, 1981-83; sr. counsel TRW Inc., Cleve., 1983-87; asst. gen. counsel Chrysler Corp., Detroit, 1987—96; sec., v.p., gen. counsel ITT Automotive, Auburn Hills, Mich., 1996—98; v.p., gen. counsel Delphi Corp., 1998—. Mem. adv. com. Ctr. for Russian and East European Studies, U. Mich. Author: An American in Leningrad, 1982, paperback, 1984, Evil Star, 1986, paperback, 1987. Mem. Internat. Bar Assn. (vice chmn. corp. counsel com.), Mich. State Bar (former chmn. internat. sect.), German Am. C. of C. of Mich. (bd. dirs.), Coun. for U.S. and Italy, Phi Beta Kappa. Office: Delphi Corp World Headquarters 5725 Delphi Dr Troy MI 48098-2815

ROBINSON, LOIS HART, retired public relations executive; b. Freeport, Ill., Aug. 9, 1927; d. Seril N. and Cora (Stabenow) Hart; m. Noel M. Henze, Nov. 15, 1947 (div. 1964); children: Susan Bentley, Cynthia Berkeley, Charles Henze; m. Jack Fay Robinson, July 16, 1968; stepdau.: Alice Dungey. Student, Oakton C.C., 1976-77, Northwestern U., 1977-81. Med. sec. Freeport Meml. Hosp., 1945-47; sec. No. Ill. Corp., 1947-49; adminstrv. asst. to supt. schs. Cmty. Sch. Dist. 303, St. Charles, Ill., 1962-68; exec. sec. Bell & Howell Co., Chgo., 1969-73, supr. corp. rels., 1973-79, mgr. corp. comm., 1979-85, mgr. corp. comm. svcss., 1985-88; pres., dir. Bell & Howell Found., 1983-88; freelance writer Evanston, Ill., 1989-91. Bd. dirs. Evanston Ecumenical Action Coun., 1991-93, Tri-Village United Way, 1996-97, Friends of Judson Coll., 1998-2003, Friends Bartlett Libr., 1997-2002. Recipient Effie award Am. Mktg. Assn., 1983. Mem. United Ch. of Christ. Home: 321 E Morse Ave Bartlett IL 60103-4168

ROBINSON, LYNDA HICKOX, artist; b. Bakersfield, Calif., June 26, 1932; d. George Philip and Naida (Hathaway) Hickox; m. Arthur C. Robinson; children: Jill, Scott. BA, U. Calif., Berkeley, 1953; MA, Mills Coll., 1957. 1st v.p. San Francisco Women Artists, 1985-86, pres., 1986-87; chair gen. meeting East Bay Women Artists, Montclair, Calif., 1994—2004. Invited artist Glasgow Scotland City of Culture Exhbn., 1990. Dancer, tchr. dance, 1957-82; photographer, 1982-89, painter, 1990—; exhbns. include San Francisco Women Artists Gallery, 1992-94, Kaiser Cmty. Gallery, 1992-03, Alta Bates Cmty. Gallery, 1994-02, Valley Art Ctr. Gallery, 1992-02, Royal Ground Gallery, 1994-04, LIndsay Dinkx Brown Gallery, 2003; represented in permanent collections Fuji Vending, Dr. Louise Annand MacFarquar, Prof. and Mrs. Fred Casmir; contbr. artworks to jours. and mags. Recipient Tchg. fellowship Mills Coll., 1954, Francis Coen cash award, 1993. Mem. Phi Beta Kappa.

ROBINSON, MALCOLM S. lawyer; b. Chgo. JD, U. Kans., 1975. Bar: Ill., Tex. With law dept. SCOR Reinsurance Co., Dallas, 1979—84, v.p., gen. counsel, corp. sec.; co-founder, ptnr. Robinson & Hoskins, LLP, Dallas, 1984—. Immediate past chmn. Dallas Conv. and Visitors Bur., 1998—2000; past chmn. Greater Dallas Crime Commn.; past chmn. bd. trustees State Bar Tex. Ins. Trust; mem. Dallas Together Forum, past co-chair So. Sector Initiative; past mem. bd. North Tex. Commn. Mem.: Dallas Black C. of C. (chmn. 1990—92, bd. dirs., gen. counsel), Nat. Bar Assn. (pres. 2002—03), Salesmanship Club Dallas. Office: Robinson & Hoskins LLP Bank of Am Oak Cliff Tower 400 Zang Blvd Ste 600 Dallas TX 75208

ROBINSON, MARGUERITE STERN, anthropologist, educator, consultant; b. N.Y.C., Oct. 11, 1935; d. Philip Van Doren and Lillian (Diamond) Stern; m. Allan Richard Robinson, June 12, 1955; children: Sarah Penelope, Perrine, Laura Ondine. BA, Radcliffe Coll., 1956; PhD, Harvard U., 1965. Assoc. scholar Radcliffe Inst. for Advanced Studies, Cambridge, Mass., 1964-65; asst. prof. anthology Brandeis U., 1965-72, assoc. prof., 1972-78, prof., 1978-85, dean Coll. Arts and Scis., 1973-75; assoc. fellow Inst. Internat. Devel. Harvard U., Cambridge, 1978-80, fellow Inst. Internat. Devel., 1980-85, inst. fellow Inst. Internat. Devel., 1985-2000, inst. fellow emeritus Inst. Internat. Devel., 2000—; dir. Cultural Survival Inc., 1981-99, Am. Inst. Indian Studies, Chgo., 1977—, chmn., 1983-84. Cons. Ministry of Fin., Govt. of Indonesia, Jakarta, 1979-92, USAID, 1992-98, Banco Solidario, Bolivia, 1993-95, Bank Rakyat Indonesia, 1994-98, World Bank, 1994-95, Bank Danamon Indonesia, 1995-96, Office of the Comptroller of the Currency, 1996-99, UNESCO, 1997, World Bank, 1997-2004, Bank of Tanzania, 1997, Microfin. Tng. Program Econs. Inst., Boulder, Colo., 1995-2004, Dept. for Internat. Devel., U.K., 2000-03, Women's World Banking, 2000-02, Govt. of Mex., 2002-03, Shorebank Adv. Svcs., Chgo., 2002, USAID, 2002-04, German Tech. Coop., 2003-04, Bangladesh Rural Advancement Com., 2003, Dept. Internat. Devel., England, 2003, India, 2003, Deutsche Gesellschaft fur Technische Zusammen Arbeit (German Tech. Corp.), Indonesia, 2003, Uganda, 2004, USAID, Uganda, 2002-04, others. Author: Political Structure in a Changing Sinhalese Village, 1975, Local Politics: The Law of the Fishes, 1988, Pembiayaan Pertanian Pedesaan, 1993, The Microfinance Revolution, Vol. 1: Sustainable Finance for the Poor, 2001, Vol. 2: Lessons from Indonesia, 2002; contbg. author: Cambridge Papers in Social Anthropology 3, 1962, Cambridge Papers in Social Anthropology 5, 1968, Enterprises for the Recycling and Composting of Municipal Solid Waste, 1993, The New World of Microenterprise Finance, 1994, New Perspectives on Financing Small Business in Developing Countries, 1995, Assisting Development in a Changing World, 1997, Agricultural Development in the Third World, 1998, Strategic Issues in Microfinance, 1998, Microfinance: Conversations with the Experts, 1999; contbr. articles to profl. jours. Mem. internat. coun. advisors Calmeadow Found., 1996-2000; pres. The Greatest Gift Corp. Fellow NIH, 1964-65; grantee NSF, 1966-70, Ford Found., 1972-74, 79, Calmeadow Found., 1994; fellow Indo-Am. Fellowship Program-Indo-U.S. Subcommn. on Edn. and Culture, 1976-77, Am. Inst. Indian Studies, 1976-77; grantee Calmeadow Found., 1994. Fellow Am. Anthrop. Assn., Soc. Bunting Inst. Fellows; mem. Assn. Asian Studies, India Internat. Centre.

ROBINSON, MARIETTA S. lawyer; BA, U. Mich., 1973; JD, UCLA, 1978. Bar: Calif. 1978, Mich. 1979, U.S. Dist. Ct. (ea. dist.) Mich. 1979, U.S. Ct. Appeals (6th cir.) 1983, U.S. Supreme Ct. 1989. Data processing mktg. rep. IBM Corp., Flint, Mich., 1973-75; assoc. The Bank of Bermuda Legal Dept., Hamilton, 1978-79; from assoc. to ptnr. Dickinson, Wright, Moon, VanDusen & Freeman, Detroit, 1979-94; ptnr. Sommers, Schwartz, Silver & Schwartz, P.C., Southfield, Mich., 1985-89; owner Law Offices of Marietta S. Robinson, Detroit, 1989—. Dem. nominee for Mich. Supreme Ct., 2000; adj. prof. U. Detroit Sch. of Law, 1982-83, Wayne State U., Detroit, 1983-84; lectr. in field. Contbr. articles to profl. jours. Trustee Dalkon Shield Claimants Trust, 1989-97; appointee Gov. James Blanchard, State of Mich. Bldg. Authority, 1985-89, State Bar Mich./Mich. State Med. Soc. Coalition, 1993—; appointee Transition Team of Wayne County Exec. Robert Ficano, 2002; bd. dirs. Mich. Women's Found., 2003—. Named one of ten Mich. Lawyers of Yr., Lawyers Weekly, 2000. Fellow ABA, Internat. Soc. Barristers (bd. govs.), Am. Bar Found., Mich. State Bar Found.; mem. State Bar Mich., State Bar Calif., ATLA, Mich. Trial Lawyers Assn., Women Lawyers Mich., Am. Bd. of Trial Advocates, Detroit Bar Assn., Oakland Bar Assn., U.S. Ct. Appeals (6th cir.) Jud. Conf. (life). Office: 185 Oakland Ave Ste 260 Birmingham MI 48009 E-mail: mrobin6510@aol.com.

ROBINSON, MARK ALLEN, music educator; b. Nashville, Aug. 21, 1964; s. Ronald D. and Ann T. Robinson; m. Robin M. Hayes, Aug. 6, 1988; 1 child, Kyle Walker. B in Music Edn., Mid. Tenn. State U., 1988. Cert. career level I tchr. Tenn. State Dept. of Edn. Dir. of bands Mid. Tenn. Christian Sch., Murfreesboro, 1988—90; asst. dir. of band, dir. of bands Ripley (Tenn.) H.S., 1990—93; dir. of bands Barfield and Christiana Schs., Murfreesboro, 1993—2003, Christiana Middle Sch., 2003—. Audio ministry leader North Blvd. Ch. of Christ, Murfreesboro, 2002—. Mem.: Mid. Tenn. Sch. Band and Orch. Assn., Tenn. Music Edn. Assn., Music Educators Nat. Conf., Phi Mu Alpha. Republican. Avocations: antiques, jazz, travel, computers. Office Phone: 615-904-3885. Personal E-mail: mrjaz@comcast.net.

ROBINSON, MARK LEIGHTON, oil company executive, petroleum geologist, horse farm owner; b. San Bernardino, Calif., Aug. 4, 1927; s. Ernest Guy and Florence Iola)Lemmon) R.; m. Jean Marie Ries, Feb. 8, 1954; children: Francis Willis, Mark Ries, Paul Leighton. AB cum laude in Geology, Princeton U., 1950; postgrad., Stanford U., 1950-51. Geologist Shell Oil Co., Billings, Mont., Rapid City, S.D., Denver, Midland, Tex., dist. geologist Roswell, N.Mex., 1957-60, divsn. mgr., 1961-63, Jackson, Miss., 1964-65, Bakersfield, Calif., 1967-68, mgr. exploration econs. N.Y.C., 1969; ctrl. office staff BIPM (Royal Dutch Shell Oil Co.), The Hague, The Netherlands, 1966; pres., chmn. bd. dirs. Robinson Resource Devel. Co., Inc., Roswell, 1970—. Chmn., pres. Como Petroleum Corp., Roswell, 1994—. Campaign chmn. Chaves County Rep. Com., Roswell, 1962; mem. alumni schs. com. Princeton U., 1980—; vestry St. Andrew's Episcopal Ch., Roswell, N.Mex., 1999-2002. With USNR, 1945-46. Mem. Assn. Petroleum Geologists, Stanford U. Earth Scientists Assn., Yellowstone Bighorn Rsch. Assn., Am. Horse Show Assn., SAR, Sigma Xi. Episcopalian. Achievements include discovery of Lake Como oil field, Miss., 1971, McNeal oil field, Miss., 1973, North Deer Creek gas field, Mont., 1983, Bloomfield East oil field, Mont., 1986, West Cat Claw Draw gas field, N.Mex., 1997, Southeast Cemetary Gas Field, N Mex., 2000. Home: 1308 S Sunset Ave Roswell NM 88203-9346 Office: Como Petroleum Corp PO Box 1227 Roswell NM 88202-1227

ROBINSON, MARSHALL ALAN, economics educator, foundation executive; b. Berkeley, Calif., Feb. 16, 1922; s. Webster Richard and Evelyn (Casey) R.; m. Ynid Douglas Rankin, June 5, 1944 (div. 1973); children: Joan Douglas, Margaret Elaine, Richard Webster; m. Flavia Derossi, Oct. 1974. AB, U. Calif.-Berkeley, 1943; MA, Ohio State U., 1948, PhD, 1950. Instr. econs. Ohio State U., 1948-50; asst. prof. econs. Tulane U., 1951-53; research asso. Nat. Bur. Econ. Research, 1951-52; asst. prof. econs. Dartmouth Coll., 1953-55; sr. staff mem., asst. to pres. Brookings Instn., 1955-60; prof. econs., dean Grad. Sch. Bus., U. Pitts., 1960-63; dir. econ. devel. and adminstrn. program Ford Found., 1964-67, program officer in charge higher edn. and research, 1967-71, dep. v.p. edn. and research, 1971-73, v.p. resources and environ., 1973-79; pres. Russell Sage Found., N.Y.C., 1979-86; vis. prof. Grad. Sch. CUNY, 1986-89; fellow Inst. Social and Policy Studies Yale U., 1989-91; v.p. Daniele Agostino Found., 1992—. Author: An Introduction to Economic Reasoning, 1956, 5th edit., 1981, The National Debt Ceiling, 1959. Bd. dirs. Belgium-Am. Ednl. Found., 1981-96; trustee Antioch U., 1987-90. Served to 1st lt. USMCR, 1943-45, PTO. Decorated Royal Order of Leopold, Belgium. Mem. Am. Econs. Assn., N.Y. Sci. Policy Assn., Coun. on Fgn. Rels., Century Assn., Alpha Delta Phi.

ROBINSON, MARTIN (MARTY ROBINSON), television and radio broadcaster, media consultant; b. Chgo., Sept. 7, 1932; s. Edward Emmanuel Robinson and Florence Ruth (Cohen) Mayer; m. Mary Alice Wellingham, May 31, 1959; children: Paul Edward, Jill Marie. Broadcaster, host Stas. WAAF, WGN and WNIB, Chgo., 1956-58, Sta. WFMT, Chgo., 1958-93, Sta. WTTW-TV, Chgo., 1971-99. Speaker, concert narrator; lectr. Lyric Opera Chgo.; media cons. J. Walter Thompson, Hill & Knowlton, Burson Marsteller, Newell & Matthews, 1973—. Host, narrator programs (Peabody award, 15 Emmy awards, 8 Ohio State awards, Chgo. and San Francisco Film Festival Gold medals); prodr., host nationally syndicated opera program The First Fifty Years, 1967-93. Served with USN, 1950-53. Recipient Emmy awards, 1977, 78. Avocations: biking, weight training, the internet. Office: 5 Lynnbrook Dr Prospect Heights IL 60070-1022 E-mail: martyrob@comcast.net.

ROBINSON, MARY, former United Nations official; b. Ballina, County Mayo, Ireland, May 21, 1944; d. Aubrey Bourke and Tessa O'Donnell; m. Nicholas Robinson; children: Tessa, William, Aubrey. MA, Dublin U., Trinity Coll., Ireland, 1967; Barrister, King's Inns, Ireland, 1967, Mid. Temple, 1973; LLM, Harvard U., 1968; DCL, Oxford U.; LLD (hon.), Basle U., Brown U., Cambridge U., Columbia U., Coventry U., Dublin U., Fordham U., Harvard U., Kyung-Hee U., Seoul, Katholieke U., Leuven, Liverpool U., London U., Melbourne U., U. Montpellier U., Nat. U. Ireland, Nat. U. Mongolia, Nat. U. Wales, U. Poznan, Queen's U., Belfast, St. Andrews U., Toronto U., Uppsala U., Yale U.; D Internat. Law (hon.), U. Costa Rica; Dr., Essex U.; PhD (hon.), Dublin City U.; DPS (hon.), Northeastern U.; DSc (hon.), Humaines U. Kennes, A Schweitzer U. Berne. Reid prof. constitutional and criminal law Trinity Coll., Dublin, 1969-75; lectr. in European Cmty. law Trinity Coll., Dublin, 1975-90; senator Irish Parliament, 1969-89; pres. Ireland, 1990-97; high commr. for human rights UN, 1997—2002; hon. pres. Oxfam Internat., 2002—. Mem. Dublin City Coun., 1979-83; chancellor Dublin U., 1998—. Mem. Editorial Bd. Irish Current Law Statutes Annotated, 1984-90; adv. bd. Common Market Law Rev., 1976-90. Pres. Cherish, 1973-90; mem. Internatl. Commn. Jurists, 1987-90. Recipient Marisa Bellisario prize, Italy, CARE Humanitarian award, 1993, Internat. Human Rights award Internat. League of Human Rights, N.Y., Liberal Internat. prize for freedom, New Zealand Suffrage Centennial medal, Berkeley medal U. Calif., Medal of Honour, U. Coimbra, Portugal, Ordem dos Advogados, Portugal, Gold Medal of Honour, U. Salamanca, Spain, U. Chile, Global Leadership award UN Assn., Freedom prize Max Schmidheiny Found., Switzerland, UNIFEM award Noel Found., U.S., Collar of Hussein Bin Ali, Hashemite Kingdom of Jordan, North South prize Coun. of Europe, 1997, F.D. Roosevelt Four Freedoms medal, 1998, Dag Hammerskjold Medal, 1998, Erasmus prize, Govt. The Netherlands, 1999, Fulbright prize, 1999, Indira Gandhi Peace prize, 2000, Sydney Peace Prize, 2002; named to Internat. Hall of Fame, Internat. Women's Forum, USA. Fellow Instn. Engrs. of Ireland (hon.), Royal Coll. Physicians Ireland (hon.), Royal Coll. Psychiatrists London (hon.), Royal Coll. Surgeons, Ireland (hon.), Royal Coll. Obstetricians and Gynecologists London; mem. Royal Irish Acad., Am. Philos. Soc. Office: Oxfam International Ste 20 266 Banbury Rd OX2 7DL Oxford England E-mail: secrt.hchr@unog.ch.

ROBINSON, MARY LOU, federal judge; b. Dodge City, Kans., Aug. 25, 1926; d. Gerald J. and Frances Strueber; m. A.J. Robinson, Aug. 28, 1949; 3 children. BA, U. Tex., 1948, LL.B., 1950. Bar: Tex. 1949. Ptnr. Robinson & Robinson, Amarillo, 1950-55; judge County Ct. at Law, Potter County, Tex., 1955-59, (108th Dist. Ct.), Amarillo, 1961-73; assoc. justice Ct. of Civil Appeals for 7th Supreme Jud. Dist. of Tex., Amarillo, 1973-77, chief justice, 1977-79; U.S. dist. judge No. Dist. Tex., Amarillo, 1979—. Named Woman of Year Tex. Fedn. Bus. and Profl. Women, 1973. Mem. Nat. Assn. Women Lawyers, ABA, Tex. Bar Assn. (Outstanding 50-Yr. Lawyer award 2002), Amarillo Bar Assn., Delta Kappa Gamma. Presbyterian. Office: US Dist Ct Rm 226 205 E 5th Ave # F13248 Amarillo TX 79101-1559

ROBINSON, MARY REID, mathematics professor; d. Clifford M. and Louise K. Reid; m. Leonard B. Robinson, 1967; children: Christy, Thomas. PhD, U. N.Mex, 2003. Assoc. prof. of math. U. of N.Mex. - Valencia Campus, Los Lunas, 1991—. Chair math. and stats. dept. U. of N. Mex. - Valencia Campus, Los Lunas, 1999—, faculty pres., 1996—97. Mem.: N.Mex Math. Assn. of Two-Year Colls. (pres. 1994—96), Am. Math. Assn. of Two-Year Colls. (S.W. v.p. 2001—03, Tchg. Excellence award 2001), Math. Assn. of Am. (mem. two-year coll. com. 1997—2003). Office: U NMex - Valencia Campus 280 La Entrada Los Lunas NM 87031 Personal E-mail: maryrobn@unm.edu. E-mail: maryrobn@unm.edu.

ROBINSON, MAUREEN LORETTA, retired elementary school educator; b. NYC, May 17, 1945; d. Arthur Vincent and Paula (Dillon) R.; m. Derish Michael Wolff, Feb. 13, 1992. BA in English, Wagner Coll., 1967; MS, CUNY, 1970; LHD (hon.), Wagner Coll., 2003. Cert. tchr. secondary sch. English, K-12 reading, N.Y. Tchr. English Curtis H.S., S.I., N.Y., 1968-95, coord. student activities, 1985-94. Vis. lectr. Coll. of S.I., 1982; guest lectr. NYU, 1991, Pace U., N.Y.C., 1993; dir. Soc. de Management de Projets Internat., Paris, 1996—. Class agt. Wagner Coll., 1995—; pub chair Bernardsville Garden Club, 1995—97; trustee Somerset Hills Edn. Found., 1996—97; pub. chair Friends of the Bernardsville Libr., 1996—2002; pres. Bernardsville

Garden Club, 1997—99; elected mem. Somerset Hills Bd. Edn., Bernardsville, NJ, 1997—2003; trustee Wagner Coll., 1998—; sec. Bernardsville Garden Club, 1999—2001; v.p. Somerset County Ednl. Svcs. Commn., Raritan, 2000—02; pub chair Bernardsville Garden Club, 2001—03; vice chair Wagner Coll., 2001—03; pres. Somerset County Ednl. Svcs. Commn., Raritan, 2002—03; bd. dirs. Clarence Dillon Pub. Libr., 2002—03; sec. Friends for a Greener Bernardsville Inc., 2003—; nominations chair Bernardsville Garden Club, 2004—; bd. dirs. Friends of the Bernardsville Libr., Bernardsville Garden Club. Staff sgt. USAR, 1979—85. Recipient Human Rels. award Greater N.Y. Region of NCCJ, 1994, Army Achievement medal Dept. of Army, 1983, Bernardsville Vol. of Yr. award, 2003, Outstanding Comty. vol. award Borough Coun. and Mayor Bernardsville, 2003. Mem. AAUW, Wagner Coll. Nat. Alumni Assn. (1st v.p. 1999-2001, mem. at large 2000—), Friends of the Shelter. Avocations: reading, gardening, skiing, cooking, travel. Home: 160 Jockey Hollow Rd Bernardsville NJ 07924-1312

ROBINSON, MAURICE RICHARD, JR., publishing executive; b. Pitts., May 15, 1937; s. Maurice Richard and Florence (Liddell) R.; m. Helen V. Benham, Oct. 18, 1986; children: John Benham, Maurice. BA in English magna cum laude, Harvard U., 1959; postgrad., St. Catharines Coll., Cambridge U., 1959-60, Columbia U., 1959-61. Tchr. English, Evanston Twp. (Ill.) H.S., 1960-62; asst. editor Lit. Cavalcade, Scholastic Inc., N.Y.C., 1962-63; editor Scholastic lit. units Scholastic Inc., 1963-64; founder, editor Scope mag., 1964, editorial dir. English, 1967-71, pub. sch. divsn., 1971-74; pres. Scholastic Corp., 1974—, CEO, 1975—, chmn. bd., 1982—. Named Corp. Citizen of Yr., Robin Hood Found., 1999, The Creative Coalition, 2000, Publisher of Yr., UJA Fedn., N.Y., 2000; recipient EdPress Hall of Fame award, Assn. Ednl. Publrs., Cleveland E. Dodge medal, Tchrs. Coll. Columbia U., Best Friend award, LA's BEST After Sch. Enrichment Program, For the Love of Reading award, UJA-Fedn., Spotlight award, Creative Coalition, British Am. Bus. award, Partners for Children award. Mem. Nat. Coun. Tchrs. English, Nat. Assn. Bilingual Edn. (Corp. Citizen of Yr. 1996), Assn. Am. Pubs. (bd. dirs. 1989—, exec. com., chmn. 1996-98, LMP Publ. of Yr. 1998), Century Assn., Pubs. Lunch Club, University Club (N.Y.C.), Phi Beta Kappa. Office: Scholastic Inc 555 Broadway New York NY 10012-3919 E-mail: drobinson@scholastic.com.

ROBINSON, MICHAEL HILL, retired zoological park director, biologist; b. Preston, Eng., Jan. 7, 1929; came to U.S. 1984; s. Samuel and Ethel (Hill) R.; m. Barbara Cragg Robinson, May 19, 1955 (divorced). BS, U. Wales, U.K., 1963; DPhil, U. Oxford, Eng., 1966; DSc (hon.), U. Westminster, Eng., 2000. Tchr. sci. U.K. Secondary Schs., 1953-60; sr. sci. master Camborne Grammar Sch., 1958-60; biologist Smith. Tropical Research Inst., Panama, 1966-71; vis. lectr. U. Pa., Phila., 1969; reader in biology New U. Ulster, No. Ireland, 1971; biologist Smithsonian Tropical Research Inst., Panama, 1971-84, asst. dir., 1980, acting dir., 1980-81, dep. dir., 1981-84; dir. Nat. Zool. Park, Washington, 1984—2000; sr. scientist emeritus Smithsonian Tropical Rsch. Inst., 1999—. Contbr. articles to profl. jours. Mem.: Soc. for Study of Animal Behavior. Address: 8291 SW Bent Oak Ct Stuart FL 34997

ROBINSON, MICHAEL R. aeronautical engineer; Dir. bus. devel. The Boeing Co. (formerly Rockwell Internat. Corp.), Seal Beach, Calif. Co-originator and first program manager of the X-31 enhanced maneuverability fighter demonstrator and originator of the international team to conduct the program. Recipient DGLR Team award in recognition of exceptional achievements in the field of Aeronautics, 1996. Fellow Am. Inst. Aeronautics & Astronautics (aircraft design award 1994). Office: The Boeing Co Mail Stop SB74 2201 Seal Beach Blvd Seal Beach CA 90740 E-mail: michael.r.robinson2@boeing.com.

ROBINSON, NADINE CAROLINE, artist; b. London, Oct. 16, 1968; arrived in U.S., 1975; d. Lambert Gilbert and Carol St. Monica (Howell) Robinson. BFA, SUNY, Stony Brook, 1995; MFA, NYU, 1997. Artist-in-residence World Views Lower Manhattan Cultural Coun., N.Y.C., 1999, Studio-Mus. in Harlem, N.Y.C., 2000, Smack-Mellon Studio, Bklyn., 2002; artist Caren Golden Fine Art, N.Y.C., 2003. Panel mem. Nat. Assn. Artist Orgn., N.Y.C., 2000; panelist Studio Mus. Harlem, N.Y.C., 2001; Hazmat lectr. NYU, N.Y.C., 2001; panelist-artist forum Andy Warhol Mus., Pitts., Phila., 2001. Merit scholar, NYU, 1995—97, Emerging Artist fellow, N.Y. Cmty. Trust, 2002. Avocations: English horsemanship, travel. Home: 4627 Murdock Ave Bronx NY 10466

ROBINSON, NAN SENIOR, not-for-profit organization consultant; b. Salt Lake City, Jan. 11, 1932; d. Clair Marcil Senior and Lillian (Worlton) Senior Davis; m. David Zav Robinson; Sept. 6, 1954; children: Marc S. Robinson, Eric S. Robinson. BA with hons., Mills Coll., 1952; MA, Harvard U., 1953. Spl. asst. to undersec. Dept. Housing and Urban Devel., Washington, 1966-69; asst. to the pres. U. Mass. Statewide System, Boston, 1970-73, v.p. for planning, 1973-78; dep. commr. Conn. Bd. Higher Edn., Hartford, 1978-81; v.p. adminstrn. The Rockefeller Found., N.Y.C., 1981-90; ret., 1990. Mem. governing coun. Rockefeller Archive Ctr., Pocantico Hills, N.Y., 1986-89; com. mem. Coun. on Founds. N.Y. Regional Assn. Grantmakers, 1985-89; mem. nat. advisory panel on governance Carnegie Found. for the Advancement of Teaching, Princeton, N.J., 1980-82. Trustee, chmn. fin. com. Inst. for Current World Affairs, Hanover, N.H., 1987-90; trustee Calif. Sch. Profl. Psychology, San Francisco, 1985-96; vice chair bd. dirs. Fed. to Preserve the Greenwich Village Waterfront, 1996-99, bd. dirs., 1996—. Recipient Centennial award Am. Assn. U. Women Hartford Br., 1981; named Woman of Yr. Hartford YWCA, 1980; named to Centennial Honor List of 100 Women Barnard Coll., 1989. Mem. Soc. for Coll. and U. Planning (com. chmn. 1985-86, nominating com. 1980-85, regional rep. 1975-77), Phi Beta Kappa. Home: 622 Greenwich St Apt 5B New York NY 10014-3305

ROBINSON, NANCY NOWAKOWSKI, academic administrator; b. Pitts., Nov. 2, 1945; d. Theodore Joseph Nowakowski and Martha Radick; 1 child, David A. BA cum laude, U. Pitts., 1983, MA, 2000. Founding mem. bd. dirs., treas. Extrasolar Planetary Found., Pitts., 1980—97; mem. adv. com. Nazareth Housing Svcs., 1995—; assoc. Sisters of the Holy Family of Nazareth, Pitts., 1998—; pres. City of God Found., Pitts., 2000—02, bd. dirs. Chaplain and diversity advisor divsn. 7, 8th eastern region U.S. Coast Guard Aux., 2003. Recipient Sister Noel Kernan award, Seton Hill Coll., 1999, Weiner Israel Heritage Nationality Rms. award, U. Pitts., 1999; Dorot Found. grantee for study in Israel, 1999, Pax Christi grantee, Pax Christi, 1999. Mem.: Soc. Bibl. Lit., Am. Acad. Religion, Golden Key. Roman Catholic. Avocations: Jewish/Catholic relations, history, music, travel, outdoors. Business E-Mail: nancy1@pitt.edu.

ROBINSON, NAOMI JEAN, educational training systems educator; b. Storm Lake, Iowa, Oct. 10, 1951; d. Wendell and Norma (Wright) Robinson. BA, Buena Vista Coll., 1973; MAEd., George Washington U., 1978. Tchr. elem. sch., Storm Lake, Iowa, 1973—75; edn. specialist intern US Army, Ft. Monroe, Va., 1976—78, edn. and test specialist Ft. Eustis, Va., 1978—79; tng. systems analyst U.S. Army, White Sands Missile Range, N.Mex., 1979—82; tng. effectiveness analysis study coord. US Army, White Sands Missile Range, 1983—85, analyst ops. rsch. and tng. systems, 1985—87, edn. specialist, dir. tng. tech. field Advanced Concepts Team Ft. Huachuca, Ariz., 1987—88, edn. specialist, dir. tng. lab. for Tng. Devel. and Analysis Directorate, NJ N.G. High Tech Tng. Ctr. Ft. Dix, NJ, 1988—90, program mgr., COR Tng. Devel. and Analysis Directorate for TRADOC tng. mission support contract, 1990—94, chief spl. projects team, 1990—91, acting divsn. chief tng. rsch and studies divsn., 1992—96; chief TRADOC tng. Mission Support Contract Br., Ft. Monroe, 1991—94; chmn. Tng. Devel. Revitalization Joint Task Force Pentagon, Washington, 1994—96; dir. ops. support divsn. and exec. officer tng. devel. analysis activity Ft. Monroe, Va., 1996—97; asst. dep. chief of staff Tng. Hdqs. 5th Army, Ft. Sam Houston, Tex., 1997—2000; chief ADCST and Chief Resource Support Div., 2000—02; asst. dep. chief of staff G3-TNG, HQ Fifth Army, 2002—04; dep. chief of staff Homeland Security Def., 2004—. Author: Guidelines for Development of Skill Qualification Tests, 1977, Standard Operating Procedure for TRADOC Training Mission Support Contract, 1991, 1992. V.p. Young Reps., 1972—73. Mem.: NAFE, Iowa Edn. Assn., Human Factors Soc., Federally Employed Women (1st v.p. chpt. 1982—83, 1984—85), Bus. and Profl. Women Club. Republican. Presbyterian. Home: 13999 Old Blanco Rd Apt 3311 San Antonio TX 78216-7790 Office: Hdqs Fifth US Army Ste 146 Bldg 16 Rm 110 1400 E Grayson St Fort Sam Houston TX 78234-7000 Business E-Mail: naomi.j.robinson@us.army.mil.

ROBINSON, NATHANIEL DAVID, JR., physician, consultant; b. Kansas City, Mar. 6, 1941; s. Nathaniel David Robinson and Dorothy Mae McLaughlin; m. Joanne Marie Kaleida, July 7, 1979; children: Donelle, Nathaniel David Robinson III. BSEE, U. RI, 1963; MD, U. Bologna, Italy, 1975. Cert. bd. cert. ins. medicine. Intern Roger Williams Gen. Hosp., Brown U., Providence, 1975—76; resident St. Francis Hosp. and Med. Ctr., U. Conn., Hartford, 1976—77, Hamot Med. Ctr., Erie, Pa., 1977—79, Mt. Sinai Med. Ctr., Miami Beach, Fla., 1981—82; med. officer USPHS Hosp., Seattle, 1979—81, VA, Nashville, 1982—85; med. cons. State of Tenn., Nashville, 1983—95, 2004—; med. dir. CNA, Nashville, 1985—95, v.p., med. dir., 1997—2004; med. cons. State of Ind., Indpls., 1995—97; asst. med. dir. Am. United Life, Indpls., 1995—97. Contbr. articles to profl. jours. Mem.: IEEE, AMA, Fla. Med. Assn., Midwest Med. Dirs. Assn., So. Med. Assn., Providence Engrng. Soc., Nashville Acad. Medicine, Tenn. Med. Assn., Am. Acad. Ins. Medicine, Am. Radio Relay League. Avocation: amateur radio. E-mail: k1ant@ieee.org., 3djrob@bellsouth.net.

ROBINSON, NEIL, materials engineer, consultant; b. Lowestoft, Eng., Nov. 20, 1946; s. Harold Robinson and Lilian May Handford. BA with honors, Cambridge U., Eng., 1968, MA, 1972; PhD, UCLA, 1973. Metallurgist GKN Group, Birmingham, England, 1968—70; rsch. engr. UCLA, 1971—73; rsch. scientist Imperial Coll., U. London, 1973—75; prin. inspector Nuc. Installations Inspectorate, London, 1975—79; vis. expert lectr. Khonkaen U., Thailand, 1979—80; prin. Failure Analysis Assocs., Menlo Park, Calif., 1981—94; pvt. practice San Carlos, Calif., 1994—. Contbg. author Fracture Toughness & Slow-Stable Cracking, 1974, Prospects of Fracture Mechanics, 1974, Human Factors Perspectives on Warnings, 1994. Dir. The Sequoia Club, Redwood City, Calif., 2002—; mem. People for the Am. Way, Washington, 1990—, Human Rights Campaign, Washington, 1990—. Recipient Certificate of Recognition, NASA, 1984. Master: Am. Contract Bridge (life); mem.: Am. Soc. of Mech. Engr., Human Factors and Ergonomics Soc., Am. Soc. for Metals, Rolls-Royce League Owners Club (chmn., N. Calif. 1999—2000, Rolls-Royce of Am. trophy 1999). Avocations: tennis, bridge, classic cars. Home and Office: 24 Quail Ln San Carlos CA 94070 Office Phone: 650-594-9340.

ROBINSON, NEIL CIBLEY, JR., lawyer; b. Columbia, S.C., Oct. 25, 1942; s. Neil C. and Ernestine (Carns) R.; m. Judith Ann Hunter, Sept. 4, 1971 (div. Nov. 1979); 1 child, Hunter Leigh; m. Vicki Elizabeth Kornahrens, Mar. 2, 1985; children: Neil C. III, Taylor Elizabeth. BS in Indsl. Mgmt., Clemson U., 1966; JD, U. S.C., 1973. Bar: S.C. 1974, U.S. Ct. Appeals (4th cir.) 1974, U.S. Dist. Ct. S.C. 1976. Asst. to dean U. S.C. Law Sch., Columbia, 1973-74; law clk. to Hon. Charles E. Jr. Simons Jr. U.S. Dist. Ct. S.C., Aiken, 1974-76; assoc. Grimball & Cabaniss, Charleston, S.C., 1976-78; ptnr. Grimball, Cabaniss, Vaughan & Robinson, Charleston, 1978-84; ptnr., pres. Robinson, Wall & Hastie, P.A., Charleston, 1984-91; ptnr., exec. com. Nexsen, Pruet, Jacobs, Pollard & Robinson, Charleston, 1991—2003; mem. exec. com. Nexsen Pruet, LLC, 2004—. Permanent mem. 4th Cir. Jud. Conf., 1982—; pres. Coastal Properties Inst., Charleston, 1981—. Co-founder, chmn. Charleston Planning Project Pub. Edn., 1996; pres. Clemson Advancement Found., 2003—, Southeastern Wildlife Expn. Found., 2003—; mem. Gov. Sanford's Quality of Life Task Force, 2003; bd. dirs Charleston Edn. Found., Clemson U. Humanities Found., 2000—03, Charleston Edn. Network, chmn. bd. dirs, 2000—; edn. adv. bd. Coll. of Charleston; bd. dirs. Clemson U. Found., 2003—; pres. Southeastern Wildlife Expn. Found., 2003—, bd. dirs., 1987—; pres. Southeastern Wildlife Expn., 1994—99; bd. dirs. Charleston Maritime Festival, 1993—99, pres., 1994—98; bd. dirs. Parklands Found. of Charleston County, pres.; bd. dirs. S.C. Tourism Com., Columbia, 1991—99. Cpl. USMCR, 1960—66. Recipient Order of Palmetto, Gov. David Beasley, S.C., 1996. Mem. ABA, Urban Land Inst. (recreational devel. coun.), S.C. Bar Assn., Fed. Bar Assn., S.C. Def. Trial Lawyers Assn. (pres.), Hibernian Soc. (mgmt. com. 1984—, sec. 1998-2000, chmn. 2000-2002, v.p. 2002-04, pres. 2004-), Kiawah Club, Haig Point Club, Country Club of Charleston, Carolina Yacht Club, Phi Delta Phi. Presbyn. Avocations: golf, boating. Home: PO Box 121 Charleston SC 29402-0121 Office: Nexsen Pruet LLC 205 King St Ste 400 Charleston SC 29401 Office Phone: 843-577-9440. Business E-Mail: nrobinson@npjp.com.

ROBINSON, NICHOLAS ADAMS, lawyer, educator; b. NYC, Jan. 20, 1945; s. Albert Lewis and Agnes Claflin (Adams) R.; m. Shelley Miner, Jan. 5, 1969; children: Cynthia M., Lucy A. BA cum laude, Brown U., 1967; JD cum laude, Columbia U., 1970. Bar: N.Y. 1971, U.S. Dist. Ct. (so. and ea. dists.) N.Y. 1972, U.S. Supreme Ct. 1974, U.S. Ct. Appeals (2d and 7th cirs.) 1972. Law clk. to U.S. dist. judge So. Dist. Ct., N.Y., 1970-72; assoc. Marshall, Bratter, Greene, Allison & Tucker, N.Y.C., 1972-78, counsel, 1978-82; assoc. prof. Pace U. Sch. Law, White Plains, N.Y., 1978-81, prof., 1981-99, Gilbert and Sarah Kerlin Disting. prof. environ. law, 1999—; counsel Winer, Neuburger & Sive, N.Y.C., 1982-83; dep. commr., gen. counsel N.Y. State Dept. Environ. Conservation, Albany, 1983-85; counsel Sive, Paget & Reisel, 1985-92, Sidley & Austin, N.Y., London, 1992-96; legal advisor Internat. Union Conservation of Nature and Natural Resources, 1996—2004. Co-dir. Ctr. for Environ. Legal Studies, Pace U., 1982—; dir. IUCN Acad. Environ. Law, 2003—; del. U.S.A. environ. law meetings with USSR, 1974-92; chmn. Environ. Adv. Bd. to Gov. Mario Cuomo, 1985-94. Contbr. articles to profl. jours. Nat. bd. dirs. UN Assn. U.S.A., 1966-76, 79-84, U.S. Com. for UNICEF, 1970-80, World Environment Ctr., 1981—, chmn., 1993-96; bd. dirs. Westchester County Soil and Water Conservation Dist., 1976-83; chmn. N.Y. State Freshwater Wetlands Appeals Bd., 1976-83; chmn. planning bd. Village of Sleepy Hollow, N.Y., 1999—; bd. edn. Union Free Sch. Dist., Tarrytown, 1981-83, 85. Recipient N.Y. State Gov.'s Citation for Hist. Preservation, 1983, Eliz Haub prize in environ. law Free U., Brussels, 1992, Nat. Environ. Quality award Natural Resources Coun. Am., 2002. Fellow Am. Bar Found.; mem. Internat. Coun. Environ. Law (gov. 1993—), Commn. Environ. Law (chmn. 1996-2004), Am. Soc. Internat. Law, ABA, ALI, N.Y. State Bar Assn. (chmn. environ. law sect. 1979-80, Environ. Law award 1981), Assn. Am. Law Schs. (chair sect. on postgrad. legal edn. 1999-2000, chair sect. environ. law 1987-88), Assn. Bar City N.Y. (chmn. environ. law com. 1977-78, internat. law com. 1985-88, internat. environ. law com. 1990-92, Russian law com. 1992-95), Westchester County Bar Assn., Sierra Club (nat. bd. dirs. 1979-83), Phi Beta Kappa. Democrat. Unitarian Universalist. Home: 258 Kelbourne Ave Sleepy Hollow NY 10591-1322 Office: Pace U Sch Law 78 N Broadway White Plains NY 10603-3710 Office Phone: 914-422-4244. E-mail: nrobinson@law.pace.edu.

ROBINSON, PAMELA GAYLE, writer; b. Glasgow, Ky., Oct. 29, 1958; d. Harvey Herbert and Estelle Jaggers Huff; m. James Allen Robinson, July 14, 1989; children: Todd Allen, Jamie Paul, Jessica Meilan. MPhil, Drew U., Madison, NJ, 1980—84; BA, English, Ky. Wesleyan Coll., Owensboro, 1976—80. Adj. instr., English U. of So. Ind., Evansville, 1993—2004. Correspondent (feature stories) Mount Vernon Democrat, reviewer (book reviews) Charisma Magazine, Prism Magazine, Presbyns. Today. Mem. Evangelicals for Social Action, Wynnewood, Pa., 2004—04; jail min. St. Matthew Cath. Ch., Mt. Vernon, Ind., 2003—04. Recipient Cum Laude Grad., Ky. Wesleyan Coll., 1980. Mem.: Nat. Coun. of Teachers of English. D-Conservative. Roman Catholic. Avocations: writing, reading, fishing, travel. Home: 317 Lawrence Drive Mount Vernon IN 47620-1246 Office Phone: 812-425-8147. Personal E-mail: pamelawrite@sbcglobal.net.

ROBINSON, PAUL ARNOLD, historian, educator, writer; b. San Diego, Oct. 1, 1940; s. Joseph Cook and Beryl Marie (Lippincott) R.; m. Ute Brosche, Aug. 3, 1964 (div. Aug. 1967); 1 child, Susan Marie; life ptnr. Stephen Dunatov. BA, Yale U., 1962; postgrad., Free U. Berlin, 1962-63; PhD, Harvard U., 1968. Asst. prof. history Stanford U. (Calif.), 1967-73, assoc. prof., 1973-80, prof. history, 1980—. Richard W. Lyman prof. in the humanities, 1994—. Author: The Freudian Left, 1969, The Modernization of Sex, 1976, Opera and Ideas: From Mozart to Strauss, 1985, Freud and His Critics, 1993, Ludwig van Beethoven: Fidelio, 1996, Gay Lives: Homosexual Autobiography from John Addington Symonds to Paul Monette, 1999, Opera, Sex, and Other Vital Matters, 2002; editor: Social Thought in America and Europe, 1970; contbg. editor The New Republic, 1979-85. Guggenheim fellow, 1970-71, Stanford Humanities Ctr. fellow, 1984-85, 96-97, Inst. for Advanced Study fellow, 1990-91, Ctr. for Advanced Study in the Behavioral Scis. fellow, 2002-03. Mem. Am. Acad. Arts and Scis., Am. Hist. Assn. Home: 671 Santa Ynez St Stanford CA 94305-8542 Office: Stanford Univ Dept History Stanford CA 94305 E-mail: paulr@stanford.edu.

ROBINSON, PETER J. dean, periodontal educator, pathologist; b. St. Louis, May 31, 1941; s. Hamilton Burrows-Greaves and Katherine (Long) R.; m. Letticia Schumacher, July 18, 1964; children: Elizabeth Haskins Vance, Emily Hamilton. BA, Drake U., Des Moines, 1963; DDS, U. Mo., Kansas City, 1966; PhD, U. Pa., Phila., 1972. Dental intern U.S. Army, Washington, 1966-67; asst. prof. U. Pa., Phila., 1973-75; prof., chmn. periodontics Northwestern U., Chgo., 1975-88, chmn. stomatology, 1988-97; dean, prof. periodontology U. Conn. Sch. Dental Medicine, 1997—. Co-author: Transplantation for Dental Specialties, 1980. Pres. Dist. 38 Sch. Bd., Kenilworth, Ill., 1985-87. Capt. U.S. Army, 1966-69. Recipient Procter & Gamble Guest Scientist award Am. Dental Assn. Rsch. Inst., Chgo., 1983, Fogarty award NIH, Washington, 1984. Mem. ADA (sr. scientist Rsch. Inst.), Internat. Assn. Dental Rsch. (pres. periodontal rsch. group 1990-92), Midwest Soc. Periodontology (pres. 1986-87), Ill. Soc. Periodontology (pres. 1985-86). Achievements include patent on Northwestern periodontal probe. Office: U Conn Sch Dental Medicine 263 Farmington Ave Farmington CT 06030*

ROBINSON, PREZELL RUSSELL, academic administrator; b. Batesburg, SC, Aug. 25, 1922; s. Clarence and Annie (Folks) R.; m. Lulu Harris, Apr. 9, 1950; 1 dau. AB in Econs. and Social Sci., St. Augustine's Coll., 1946, hon. degree; MA in Sociology and Econs., Cornell U., 1951, Ed.D. in Sociology-Ednl. Adminstrn., 1956; D.C.L. (hon.), U. of the South, 1970; L.H.D., hon. degree, Cuttington U. Coll., Monrovia, Liberia; L.H.D., Voorhees Coll., 1981, hon. degree; L.H.D., Episcopal Theol. Sem., 1982; LL.D. (hon.), Bishop Coll., 1979; D.C.L., Columbia U., 1980, hon. degree; DHL (hon.), Kenyon Coll., 1988; hon. degree, Va. Theology Sem., Alexandria, Barton Coll., Campbell U., N.C. State U., Shaw U. Tchr. social sci., French Bettis Jr. Coll., Trenton, S.C., 1946-48; sucessively registrar, tchr., acting prin. high sch., acting dean jr. coll., instr., dir. adult edn. Voorhees Jr. Coll., Denmark, S.C., 1948-56; prof. sociology, dean coll. St. Augustine's Coll., Raleigh, N.C., 1956-64, exec. dean, 1964-66, acting pres., 1966-67, pres., 1967-95, pres. emeritus, 1995—. Pres. United Negro Coll. Fund, Inc., 1978-81, Nat. Assn. Equal Opportunity Higher Edn., 1981-84, N.C. Assn. Coll. & U., Cooperating Raleigh Colls., 1981, 86—; bd. dirs. Learning Inst. N.C.; scholar-in-residence Nairobi (Kenya) U., 1973; vis. lectr. Dept. State del. to African nations, 1971, 73, 78; dir. Wachovia Bank & Trust Co.; vice chmn. N.C. State Bd. Edn., mem., 1973-99, vice-chmn., 1994-99. Contbr. articles to profl. publs. Exec. com. N.C. Edn. Com. on Tchr. Edn.; active N.C. Bd. Edn.; chmn. bd. Assn. Episcopal Colls.; mem. Mayor's Community Relations Com.; vice-chmn. Wake County divsn. Occoneechee coun. Boy Scouts Am., 1959-67; chmn. Wake Occoneechee coun., 1963-66, exec. com., 1965—; vice-chmn. Wake County chpt. ARC; chmn. edn. divsn. United Fund of Raleigh, budget com., 1965—; exec. com. Wake County Libraries.; trustee Voorhees Coll. Fulbright fellow to India, 1965; appointed US alt. rep. or public mem. amb. Gen. Assembly UN, by Pres. George Bush, 1992, by Pres. Clinton, 1996. Served with AUS, 1942. Recipient Distinguished Alumni award Voorhees Coll., 1967, Silver Anniversary award N.C. Community System, 1989; decorated Star of Africia Liberia; recipient numerous service awards and citations; named one of the most effective coll. pres.s in U.S. Coun. for Advancement and Support of Edn., Washington, 1986; Univ. fellow Cornell U., 1954, rsch. fellow, 1955-56; Fulbright fellow, 1965. Mem. AAAS, Nat. Assn. Collegiate Deans and Registrars, Am. Acad. Polit. and Social Sci., Am. Sociol. Soc., N.C. Sociol. Soc. (exec. com.), Ctrl. Intercollegiate Athletic Assn. (exec. com.), N.C. Assn. Ind. Colls. and Univs. (dir.), Raleigh C. of C. (A.E. Finley Disting. Svc. award 1989), So. Sociol. Assn., Am. Acad. Polit. Sci., N.C. Lit. and Hist. Soc., N.C. Hist. Soc., Delta Mu Delta, Phi Delta Kappa, Phi Kappa Phi, Alpha Kappa Mu, Phi Beta Lambda. Protestant Episcopalian (lay reader). Home: 821 Glascock St Raleigh NC 27604-2317 Office: St Augustine's Coll 1315 Oakwood Ave Raleigh NC 27610-2247

ROBINSON, RAYMOND EDWIN, conductor, music educator, writer; b. San Jose, Calif., Dec. 26, 1932; s. Elam Edwin and Zula Mai (Hatley) R.; m. Ruth Aleen Chamberlain, Mar. 12, 1954; children: Cynthia Rae, Greg Edwin, David L., Brent Steven, Jeffrey Vernon. BA, San Jose State U., 1956; MMus, Ind. U., 1958, D in Mus. Edn., 1969; LHD, Westminster Choir Coll., 1987; postdoctoral study, Jagiellonian U., Poland, 1995, Cambridge U., 1987—89, postdoctoral study, 2002—03. Instr. music Ind. U., Bloomington, 1958-59; music critic Portland Reporter, 1962-63, Balt. Evening Sun, 1964-68, Palm Beach (Fla.) Post, 1991—, Palm Beach Daily News, 2003; founder, tchr. seminar for music adminstrs., 1972—; chmn. divsn. fine arts Cascade Coll., Portland, Oreg., 1959-63; dean Peabody Inst., Balt., 1963-69; pres. Westminster Choir Coll., Princeton, N.J., 1969-87; vis. fellow Wolfson Coll. U. Cambridge, England, 1987—89, 2002—03; disting. prof. choral studies, choral condr. Palm Beach Atlantic U., West Palm Beach, Fla., 1989—; pres. Prestige Publs., Inc., 1978—; prof. Sch. Ch. Music Knox Theol. Sem., Ft. Lauderdale, Fla., 1989—; vis. prof. U. Miami, 2001—. Choral condr. Palm Beach C.C., Lake Worth, Fla., 1992-93; condr.-in-residence, dir. music First Presbyn. Ch., West Palm Beach, 1989-97; dir. music Coral Ridge Presbyn. Ch., Ft. Lauderdale, Fla., 1997—, music dir. Palm Beach Symphony Orch., 2004—; chief guest choral condr. Palm Beach Opera, 1990—; interim condr. Choral Soc. Palm Beaches, 1992; condr. Ray Robinson Chorale, 1994—, Cambridge (Eng.) U., Cambridge, Eng., 1987-89, 2002-03, Kiev, Ukraine, 1997, Budapest, 1997, Cracow, 2002, Coral Ridge Presbyn. Ch., 1997; vis. prof. U. Miami, Fla., 2001-2002. Author: The Choral Experience, 1976, Choral Music, 1978; Krzysztof Penderecki, A Guide to His Works, 1983, A Study of the Penderecki St. Luke Passion, 1983, John Finley Williamson: A Centennial Appreciation, 1987; co-author: German Diction for the Choral Singer, 1992, A Bach Tribute: Bach Essays in Honor of William H. Scheide, 1993; co-author, editor: Studies in Penderecki, 1998, 2003; editor: Labyrinth of Time: Five Addresses for the End of the Millenium, 1998, Postcards from Cambridge, 2004; editor The Choral Tradition Series, Hinshaw Music Inc., 1978—. Bd. dirs. Balt. Symphony Orch., 1967-69, Am. Boy Choir Sch., 1970-73, N.Y. Choral Soc., 1972—, Palm Beach Atlantic U. choral series Hinshaw Music Inc., 1990—; bd. dirs. Palm Beach County Coun. Arts, chmn. profl. artists com., mem. task force for master plan, 1990-92; mem. cultural plan com. Palm Beach County Cultural Coun., 1992—; mem. task force for edn. Fla. Philharm. Orch., 1994-95; mem. art in pub. places com. West Palm Beach, Fla. 2004—. Recipient Disting. Alumni Merit award Ind. U., 1975, Disting. Alumni award Sch. Music Ind. U., 1973, Disting. Alumni award San Jose State U., 1990. Mem. Coll. Music Soc. (life), Am. Choral Dirs. Assn. (life, chmn. rsch. and publs. com. 1986—), Internat. Heinrich Schütz Soc. (chmn. Am. sect. 1984-87), Univ. Club N.Y., Nassau Club Princeton, Govs. Club West Palm Beach. Presbyterian. Home: 2413 Medina Way West Palm Beach FL 33401-8019 Office Phone: 561-803-2416. E-mail: Ray_Robinson@pba.edu.

ROBINSON, RICHARD, publishing company executive; b. 1937; married. Grad., Harvard U., 1959. Tchr. Evanston Twp. High Sch., Ill., 1960-62; v.p. Scholastic Inc., N.Y.C., 1971-74, pres., 1974—, now also chmn., chief exec. officer, dir. Office: Scholastic Inc 555 Broadway New York NY 10012-3919

ROBINSON, RICHARD ALLEN, JR., human resources development trainer, consultant; b. Ellensburg, Wash., Aug. 21, 1936; s. Richard Allen and Rosa Adele (Oswald) R.; m. R. Elaine Whitham, Sept. 8, 1956; children: Sharon E. Robinson Losey, Richard Allen, René L. Rivera. BA, U. Wash., 1958; postgrad., U.S. Army Command and Gen. Staff Coll., 1969-70; MA, U. Mo., 1971. Commd. 2d lt. U.S. Army, 1958, advanced through grades to lt. col., 1972, various infantry assignments including command, 1958-72, R&D assignments including dep. dir. test of behavioral sci., 1975-77, ret., 1979; chief office orgn. and employee devel. Wash. Dept. Social and Health Svcs.,

Olympia, 1979—2003; pvt. practice orgn. and mgmt. devel. cons./trainer, 1979—2002. Contbg. author: Games Trainers Play, vol. II, 1983. Decorated Legion of Merit with oak leaf cluster, Bronze Star. Personal E-mail: robbyr013@comcast.net.

ROBINSON, RICHARD FRANCIS, genealogist, personal historian, writer; b. Passaic, N.J., June 13, 1941; s. Francis Ward and Evelyn (Burnett) R.; m. Brenda Kay Moore, Feb. 6, 1970; 1 child, Kelly. Student, Coll. of William & Mary, 1959-60; BA in Journalism, Mich. State U., 1964; student, Nat. Geneaol. Soc. course, 2000. Cert. genealogical rsch. specialist 2002. Reporter, columnist North Jersey Herald News, Passaic, 1964-67; med. writer, reporter The Oakland Press, Pontiac, Mich., 1967-75; staff reporter Nat. Enquirer, Lantana, Fla., 1975-79; staff writer Hank Meyer Assocs., Miami, Fla., 1987-88; pres. Dick Robinson Co., Delray Beach, Fla., 1979—2003; prin., owner Legacy Scribe His. Svcs., Delray Beach, 2002—. Co-author: GeneWeaver Users Manual for Version 1.0, Clooz Version 1.2 Users Manual, 2000; editor: Foot and Leg Function, 1988—90; contbr. numerous articles to publs. including Geneal. Computing: Quar. Jour. and Everton's Family History Mag. Delegate Mich. State Rep. Conv., Detroit, 1970; mem. exec. bd. Mich. Fedn. Young Reps., 1970; mem. website com. Bd. for Certification of Genealogists. Recipient First Pl. award AP, 1973. Mem.: Nat. Assn. Sci. Writers, Am. Med. Writers Assn. (bd. dirs. 1984—85, chmn. trade book awards com. 1986, founding pres. Fla. chpt. 1983—84, pres. 1986—88), Passaic County (N.J.) Hist. Soc. (legislation chair), Writers and Editors, Geneal. Soc. N.J., Fedn. Geneal. Socs. (Fla. state liaison), Assn. Profl. Genealogists (info. officer 2003—, pres. Fla. chpt. 2004—), Nat. Geneal. Soc. (records preservation and access com.), N.Y. Geneal. and Biog. Soc., Fla. State Geneal. Soc. (legis. chmn. 2002—), Internat. Soc. Family History, Delray Beach Tennis Ctr. Avocations: tennis, computers, genealogy. Home and Office: 250 S Ocean Blvd Unit 252 Delray Beach FL 33483-6752 E-mail: dickrobinson@legacyscribe.com. *To succeed at anything in life, honestly believe you can do it well-and you will.*

ROBINSON, RICHARD GARY, management consultant, accountant; b. Oakland, Calif., Aug. 17, 1931; s. William Albert and Inez Wilhelmina (Zetterblad) R.; m. Rosemary Elsen, June 18, 1955 (dec. Dec. 1963); m. Lorraine Mary Deshaies, Nov. 13, 1965 (dec. Feb. 1984); children: Elisabeth Claudine (dec.), Christopher Paul. BBA, U. Minn., 1955; grad., Indsl. Coll. Armed Forces, 1972; M in Internat. Mgmt., Am. Grad. Sch. Internat. Mgmt., 1980; ABD in Internat. Econs., U. Denver. CPA, Colo., N.Mex.; cert. mgmt. cons. Commd. 2d lt. USAF, 1955, advanced through grades to maj., dir. radar ops. tactical air warfare, comdr. strategic missile operation and maintenance functions, project mgr., dir. mgmt. info. sys. Dept. Def. activities; ret., 1976; pvt. practice, 1976—; mng. ptnr. A-Action Acctg. & Tax Profls., Colorado Springs, Colo., 1994-96, Santa Fe Bus. Solutions, LLC, 1999—; pres. Bus. Devel. Specialists, Santa Fe, N.Mex., 1980—. Cons. People to People Project Assist to Baltic States Govts. on Trade and Econ. Legis.; dir., CFO Unique Equipment Co.; bd. dirs. United Air Freight Ltd.; CFO, bd. dirs. U.S. Gaming Fin. Corp.; adv. bd. Pegasus Learning Co., Inc.; adj. faculty Embry Riddle Aero. U., Luke AFB, Ariz.; faculty U. Phoenix; adj. prof. econs. and internat. bus. Regis U., Colorado Springs; U. So. Colo., Coll. of Santa Fe. Bus. adv. coun. Colo. Internat. Trade Office; bd. dirs. Santa Fe Family YMCA. Decorated Meritorious Svc. medal with oak leaf cluster, AF Commendtion medal with 2 oak leaf clusters. Mem. Colorado Springs Estate Planning Coun., Estate Planning Coun. Santa Fe, Internat. Bus. Assn. of the Rockies (past pres.), Colo. Springs World Affairs Coun. (bd. dirs.), Am. Mktg. Assn., Armed Forces Comm. and Electronics Assn., Am. Mgmt. Assn., Nat. Assn. Accts., Inst. Mgmt. Cons., Assn. Polit. Risk Analysts, N.Am. Soc. Corp. Planning. Lutheran. Home: HC 75 Box 15 24 Camino Caballos Lamy NM 87540-9623 Office: 5 Caliente Rd Bldg 1A Santa Fe NM 87508-8162 Office Phone: 505-466-2830. E-mail: rgrcpa@attglobal.net.

ROBINSON, RICHARD M. technical communication specialist; b. Bklyn., Nov. 28, 1934; s. Allen and Syd (Bell) R.; m. Rochelle Wolf, Dec. 25, 1967; children: Michelle P., Steven E. BS in Physics, Rensselaer Poly. Inst., Troy, N.Y., 1956, MS in Tech. Comm., 1959. Assoc. engr. Convair-Astronautics, San Diego, 1956-57; tech. writer Raytheon, Andover, Mass., 1957-58; pubs. engr. Hazeltine Electronics, Little Neck, N.Y., 1959-61; sr. pubs. engr. Sperry Gyroscope, Great Neck, N.Y., 1961-68; mgr. editl. svcs. Grumman Corp., Bethpage, N.Y., 1968-94; tech. comm. specialist/cons. Setauket, N.Y., 1995—. Adj. faculty Suffolk County C.C. Contbr. articles to profl. jours. Mem. IEEE (life sr., conf. chmn. 1989, tech. activities bd. 1992-93, Profl. Com. Soc. adminstrv. com. 1977-97, Profl. Com. Soc. pres. 1992-93, referee papers Trans. on Profl. Comm., Alfred N. Goldsmith award 1983, 3d Millennium medal 2000), Soc. Tech. Comms. (sr. mem.), Miramar Ski Club (pres. 1966-67), Amateur Ski Instrs. Assn. (cert. instr.). Home and Office: 10 Penelope Dr Setauket NY 11733-2010 E-mail: r.robinson@ieee.org.

ROBINSON, ROBERT EARL, chemicals executive; b. Covington, Ky., Aug. 3, 1927; s. Adolph Earl and Frances Elizabeth (Rouse) Robinson; m. Myrtle Caroline Tonne, June 10, 1951; children: Linda Ann, Carol Eileen Robinson Cranford, Timothy John. AB, Berea Coll., 1949; MS, Purdue U., 1951, PhD, 1953; postgrad., U. Cin., 1962-64. Project leader U.S. Indsl. Chems., Cin., 1953-64; group leader Stauffer Chem. Co., Weston, Mich., 1964-65; rsch. dir. Cardinal Chem. Co., Columbia, SC, 1965-66; exec. v.p. Lindau Chems. Inc., Columbia, 1966-86, pres., 1986—. Dir. Richland Land Devel. Co., Columbia. Contbr. articles to profl. jours. Fundraiser Am. Cancer Soc., Columbia, 1991; bd. dirs. S.C. Philharm. Orch., 1993—99, 2000—, Palmetto Opera, 1999—. With U.S. Army, 1946—47. Fellow: Am. Inst. Chemists; mem.: AAAS, N.Y. Acad. Scis., Am. Chem. Soc. (chair divsn. small chem. bus. 1993, 1998), Mensa, Sherlock Holmes Soc. London, Baker St. Irregulars. Achievements include patents in field. Avocations: sherlock holmes, computer science, serious music. Home: 6117 Lakeshore Dr Columbia SC 29206-4331 Office: Lindau Chems Inc 731 Rosewood Dr Columbia SC 29201-4633 Office Phone: 803-799-6863.

ROBINSON, ROBERT GEORGE, psychiatry educator; b. Pitts., May 22, 1945; s. Robert Campbell and Rosetta M. (Martindale) R.; m. Gretchen Priscilla Smith, Jan. 5, 1974; children: Christopher, Jonathan. BS in Engring. Physics, Cornell U., 1967, MD, 1971. Intern Montefiore Hosp. and Albert Einstein Med. Ctr., 1971-72; resident Cornell U., White Plains, N.Y., 1972-73; rsch. assoc. NIMH, Washington, 1973-75; resident Johns Hopkins U., 1975-77, asst. prof. to assoc. prof., 1977-85, prof., 1985—; prof., head of dept. U. Iowa Coll. Medicine, Iowa City, 1990—, Paul W. Penningroth prof., 1996—. Mem. editorial bds. Jour. Neuropsychiatry & Clinical Neurosciences, Int. Jour. Psychiatry in Medicine, Psychiatry, J. Nervous and Mental Diseases. Author: The Clinical Neuropsychiatry of Stroke, 1998; editor: Depression and Coexisting Disease, 1989, Depression in Neurologic Disease, 1993; mem. editl. bd. Jour. Neuropsychiatry and Clin. Neuroscis., Internat. Jour. Psychiatry in Medicine, Psychiatry, Jour. Nervous and Mental Diseases; contbr. more than 300 articles and chpts. to publs. Rsch. Scientist award, NIMH, 1989; Mellon fellow Johns Hopkins U., 1977; recipient Rsch. prize Am. Psychiat. Assn., 1999, Acad. Pscyosomatic Medicine, 1999. Fellow APA, Am. Coll. Neuropsychopharmacology, Soc. for Neurosci.; mem. AAAS, Soc. Biol. Psychiatry, Johns Hopkins Soc. Scholars, Am. Neuropsychiat. Assn. (pres., 1998-99). Office: U Iowa Coll Med 200 Hawkins Dr Iowa City IA 52242-1009 E-mail: robert-robinson@uiowa.edu.

ROBINSON, ROBERT L. former financial service company executive, lawyer; b. Ridgeway, Va., Feb. 22, 1936; s. Gerald L. and Annie (McBride) R.; m. Audrey M. Allen, July 30, 1960; children: Robert, Diane, Kelly. BA, Va. State Coll., 1957; LL.B., Harvard U., 1960; MBA, U. Conn., 1976. Bar: N.Y. 1961, Pa. 1978. Atty. N.Y. Central Ry. Co., N.Y.C., 1960-63; asst. gen. counsel Crane Co., N.Y.C., 1963-71; counsel Xerox Corp., Stamford, Conn., 1971-77; v.p., asst. gen. counsel and sec. INA Corp., Phila., 1977-82; sr. v.p., gen. counsel investment group CIGNA Corp., Bloomfield, Conn., 1982-84, sr. v.p., asst. gen. counsel, corp. sec., 1984-87, sr. v.p., gen. counsel property & casualty group Phila., 1987-88, sr. v.p., chief counsel litigation and ins., 1988-2000; ret., 2000. Dir. Phila. Reinsurance Corp., Am. Arbitration Assn., CPR Inst. for Dispute Resolution. Served to lt. U.S. Army, 1957. Mem. ABA, Pa. Bar Assn., Westchester-Fairfield Corp. Counsel Assn. (founder, bd. dirs. pres. 1976-77), Great Oak Yacht Cub, Harvard Club (N.Y.C.), Merion Cricket Club, Phila. Club., Phila. Cricket Club. Republican. Office: 451 Moreno Rd Wynnewood PA 19096 E-mail: rakr@erols.com.

ROBINSON, ROBIN, newscaster; b. Chgo. m. Terrence Brantley, 1986 (div. 1989). B, San Diego State U., 1980. Reporter KGTV, San Diego, 1979—81; consumer reporter CBS affiliate, Denver, 1981—84; reporter WBBM-TV, Chgo., 1984—87; co-anchor Fox News at 9 WFLD-TV, Chgo., 1987—. Co-recipient Emmy awards. Office: WFLD-TV 205 N Mich Ave Chicago IL 60601

ROBINSON, ROGER, actor, director; b. Seattle, Wash., May 2, 1940; s. Roger and Naomi Letitia Robinson; children: Kia Koutsialis, Dana Davis. Actor: (Broadway prodns.) Drowning Crow, Seven Guitars (Tony award nomination, Outer Critics Cir. award, Drama League award, Image award), The Iceman Cometh, Amen Corner - The Musical, Ain't Supposed to Die a Natural Death, The Miser, Does a Tiger Wear a Necktie?, Talent 64, (off-Broadway prodns.) Of Mice and Men, The Middle of Nowhere, Sty Farm, To Die for Havana; (films) Vig, Bunzy's Last Call, Meteor, Willie Dynamite, It's My Turn, The Lonely Guy, Believe in Me, Who's the Man, Real Estate, Brother to Brother, 2004; (TV series) ER, NYPD Blue, Law & Order, Homocide Life on the Streets, The Hoop Life, The Education of Max Bickford, NY Undercover, The Cosby Show; (films) On the One. Fellow: Fox Found. (hon. Fox Found. Study Grant 2000). Achievements include film and television acting credits. Office: Terri Kelly & Associates # 809 1443 Washington St Pasadena CA 91104

ROBINSON, RONALD ALAN, manufacturing executive; b. Louisville, Mar. 23, 1952; s. J. Kenneth and Juanita M. (Crosier) R.; m. Joan Parker, 1986; children: Rex, Jay. BS, GA Inst. Tech., 1974; MBA, Harvard U., 1978. Staff engr., asst. to exec. v.p. ops. Dual Drilling Co., Wichita Falls, Tex., 1978-80; v.p. Dreco, Inc., Houston, 1980-84, pres., dir. subs. Triflo Industries Internat., Inc.; pres., COO Ramteck Sys., Inc., 1984-87; chmn., CEO Denver Techs. Inc., 1988-95; pres. Svedala Industries, Inc., 1996-99; pres., CEO Alamo Group Inc., Seguin, Tex., 1999—. Recipient Optimist Internat. Citizenship award, 1970; Gardiner Symonds fellow, 1977. Mem. Harvard Alumni Assn. Home: 18 Pourtales Colorado Springs CO 80906 Office: Alamo Group Inc 1502 E Walnut St Seguin TX 78155-5202

ROBINSON, RONALD GENE, military contract negotiator, educator; b. Detroit, June 13, 1952; s. John Henry and Linnie (Mattingly) R.; m. Cheryl Lee Robinson, Aug. 27, 1982 (div. July 2000); children: Ronald Jr., Lindee Marie, Ryan John; m. Dee Robinson, May 6, 2001. AA, Schoolcraft Coll., 1972; B in Gen. Studies, U. Mich., 1974; MA, Western Mich. U., 1977. Cert. govt. contracting level III. Prof. polit. sci. Schoolcraft Coll., Livonia, Mich., 1976—; contract negotiator U.S. Army, Warren, Mich., 1981—. Pres. R&B Advt. Agy., Warren, 1996-98. Author: Judicial Character, 1977; columnist The County Line, Warren, 1990-97, The Warren Examiner, 1996-97. Candidate Warren City Coun., 1991, nominee, 1995, 2003; chmn. Hartsig Pk. Homeowners Assn., Warren, 1990-97; precinct del. Livonia Rep. Party, 1974-81; mem. Oakland County Young Reps., 2000—; bd. dirs. Warren-Centerline Right to Life, 1991—. Mem. So. Polit. Sci. Assn. Avocations: swimming, travel, dance, playing stratego, playing pool. Personal E-mail: rgr11897@aol.com.

ROBINSON, RONALD MICHAEL, financial executive, financial consultant; b. N.Y.C., May 1, 1942; s. Arthur John and Matilda (Siegel) R.; m. Mary Jane Reemelin, Feb. 25, 1972; children: Scott Edward, Elizabeth Drew. BS, Ohio State U., 1964; MBA, U. Pa., 1966. CPA, Pa. Fin. mgr. Am. Airlines, Inc., N.Y.C., 1969-72; mgmt. cons. Coopers & Lybrand, Phila., 1973-75; pres. Robinson Assocs., Inc., Paoli, Pa., 1975-81; dir. fin. and adminstrn., chief fin. officer Presbyn. Homes, Inc., Camp Hill, Pa., 1982-99. Bd. dirs. Healthamerica, Mems. First Fed. Credit Union, Continuing Care Rx, Presbyn. Apts., Cumberland Crossings. Mem. Carlisle (Pa.) Borough Coun., 1988-92. Home: 1214 Georgetown Circle Carlisle PA 17013-3548 Office: PO Box 908 Carlisle PA 11701 Fax: (717) 258-8727. E-mail: robinsonr@mindspring.com.

ROBINSON, RUSSELL F. foundation administrator; b. El Paso, Tex., Jan. 30, 1956; s. Richard Robinson and Ruth Rosenberg; m. Marci Morgan; children: Sam, Alyssa. BS in Social Work, U. Tex., 1976. Asst. v.p. United Jewish Appeal, Tex., 1987—94, v.p. campaign, 1994—96; CEO Jewish Nat. Fund, N.Y.C., 1996—. Office: Jewish Nat Fund 42 E 69th St New York NY 10021 Office Fax: 212-879-585-2088. E-mail: rrobinson@jnf.org.

ROBINSON, RUSSELL M. manufacturing executive; Chmn. Caraustar Industries Inc., Auftell, Ga. Office: PO Box 115 Austell GA 30168-0115

ROBINSON, RUSSELL MARABLE, II, lawyer; b. Charlotte, N.C., Mar. 13, 1932; s. John Moseley and Camilla Croom (Rodman) R.; m. Sally Gossett Dalton, Sept. 4, 1953; children: Camilla, Russell III, Sally. Student, Princeton U., 1950-52; LLB, Duke U., 1956. Bar: N.C. 1956, U.S. Dist. Ct. (ea., mid. and we. dists.) N.C. 1956, U.S. Ct. Appeals (4th cir.) 1960. From assoc. to ptnr. Lassiter, Moore & Van Allen, Charlotte, 1956-60; ptnr. Robinson, Bradshaw & Hinson P.A., Charlotte, 1960—. Author: Robinson on North Carolina Corporation Law, 7th edit., 2002. Gen. Counsel Morehead Found., Chapel Hill, N.C., 1965—; chmn. The Duke Endowment, 2002-. Fellow Am. Bar Found.; mem. ABA, Am. Law Inst., N.C. Bar Assn., Order of Coif, Phi Beta Kappa. Episcopalian. Home: 3829 Bonwood Dr Charlotte NC 28211-1752 Office: Robinson Bradshaw & Hinson 1900 E Independence Blvd Charlotte NC 28205-6117 Office Phone: 704-377-8311. Business E-Mail: rrobinson@rbh.com.

ROBINSON, SALLY SHOEMAKER, lay associate; b. N.Y.C., Dec. 31, 1931; d. Samuel M. and Helen Dominick Smith S.; m. James Courtland Robinson, Dec. 31, 1931; children: Samuel Shoemaker, W. Courtland, A. Alexander, Ellen Whitridge Robinson Mihalski. BA cum laude, Bryn Mawr Coll., 1953; postgrad. studies, Yonsei U. Lang. Inst., Korea, 1960-62, Children's Theatre Assn., 1964; MA, Towson State U., 1974. Ordained elder Brown Meml. Presbyn. Ch., 1985. Commd. missionary to Korea United Presbyn. Ch., 1959-71; dir. Brown Meml. Tutorial Program, 1974-84; exec. dir. Episcopal Social Ministries Diocese of Md., Balt., 1984-97; canon for social ministry Episcopal Diocese of Md., Balt., 1985-96. Met. chmn. 10th Decade Campaign Bryn Mawr Coll.,, 1974-76, nat. chmn. Centennial Campaign. 1980-85, trustee, 1985—; trustee Am. Bible Soc., 1988—, v.p., 1993—, chmn. bd., 1996-2001; chmn. global bd. United Bible Socs., 2001—; trustee United Bd. for Christian Higher Edn. in Asia, 1990-95; trustee emeritus Bryn Mawr Coll., 1997—. Home: 10522 Burnside Farm Rd Stevenson MD 21153-2024 Office: Brown Meml Ch 1316 Park Ave Baltimore MD 21217-4185

ROBINSON, SALLY WINSTON, artist; b. Detroit, Nov. 2, 1924; d. Harry Lewis and Lydia (Kahn) Winston; m. Eliot F. Robinson, June 28, 1949; children: Peter Eliot, Lydia Winston, Sarah Mitchell, Suzanne Finley. BA, Bennington Coll., 1947; postgrad., Cranbrook Acad. Art, 1949; grad., Sch. Social Work, Wayne U., 1948, MA, 1972; MFA, Wayne State U., 1973. Psychol. tester Detroit Bd. Edn., 1944; psychol. counselor and tester YMCA, N.Y.C., 1946; social caseworker Family Svc., Pontiac, Mich., 1947; instr. printmaking Wayne State U., Detroit, 1973—. Tchr. children's art Detroit Inst. Art, 1949-50, now artistic advisor, bd. dirs. drawing and pring orgn. One-woman shows include, U. Mich., 1973, Wayne State U., 1974, Klein-Vogel Gallery, 1974, Rina Gallery, 1976, Park McCullough House, Vt., 1976, Williams Coll., 1976, Arnold Klein Gallery, 1977, exhibited in group shows, Bennington Coll., Cranbrook Mus., Detroit Inst. Art, Detroit Artists Market, Soc. Women Painters, Soc. Arts and Crafts, Bloomfield Art Assn., Flint Left Bank Gallery, Balough Gallery, Detroit Soc. Woman Painters, U. Mich., U. Ind., U. Wis., U. Pitts., Toledo Mus., Krannert Mus., Represented in permanent collections, Detroit, N.Y.C., Birmingham, Bloomfield Hills. Bd. dirs. Planned Parenthood, 1951—, mem. exec. bd., 1963—; bd. dirs. PTA, 1956-60, Roeper City and Country Sch., U. Mich. Mus. Art, 1978; trustee Putnam Hosp. Med. Rsch. Inst., 1978; mem. Gov.'s Commn. Art in State Bldgs., 1978-79; mem. art and devel. coms. So. Vt. Art Ctr., 1987-88; mem. vol. com. Marie Selby Gardens; patron Graphic Art Studio, U. So. Fla., Tampa; patron, benefactor Clark Mus., Williamstown, Mass. Fellow: Williams Coll. Mus. Art (mem. visiting com.); mem.: Bloomfield Art Assn. (program co-chmn. 1956), Birmingham Soc. Women Painters (pres. 1974—76), Detroit Soc. Women Painters, Detroit Artists Market (dir. 1956—, hon. bd. mem.), Founders Soc. Detroit Inst. Art, Bennington Coll. Alumnae Assn. (regional co-chmn. 1954), Cosmopolitan Club (N.Y.C.), Founders Garden Club (Sarasota, Fla.), Garden Club Am. (bd. dirs.), Oaks Club (Fla.), Women's City Club (coord. art shows Detroit 1950), Village Women's Club (Birmingham, Mich.). Unitarian Universalist. Home: 209 Hills Point Rd Charlotte VT 05445-9698 also: 840 N Casey Key Rd Osprey FL 34229-9779

ROBINSON, SCHARN, lawyer, author, researcher; b. Albany, N.Y., Jan. 5, 1968; d. David McKinley and N. Ruth Penn R. BA, Union Coll., 1990; Phd, U. Mich., 1995; JD, U. Calif., Berkeley, 1998. Assoc. O'Melveny & Myers LLP, Washington, 1998—2001, Paul, Hastings Janofsky & Walker LLP, 2001—. Polit. sci. vis. prof. Union Coll., Schenectady, N.Y., 1995, SUNY, Albany, 1995, U. of the West Indies, Barbados, 1996; sociology vis. prof. St. Mary's of Calif., Moraga, Calif., 1998, U. Calif. Berkeley Ext., 1998. Vol. Berkeley Cmty. Law Ctr., 1996, San Francisco Coalition on Homelessness, San Francisco, 1996. Scholar Harry S. Truman Found., Stanley Becker scholar; fellow NSF; named to Acad. Hall of Fame City of Schenectady, 2000; recipient Bailey prize. Mem. ABA, Am. Polit. Sci. Assn. (fellow), Nat. Bar Assn., Phi Sigma Alpha. Avocations: tennis, jazz, kickboxing. Home: 4708 Queens Grove St White Plains MD 20695

ROBINSON, SHANE V. computer company executive; BS, MS, Univ. Utah. With Apple Computer Co., 1988, v.p. gen .mgr., 1994—95; exec. v.p. AT&T, 1995—97, pres. design productivity group, 1997—99, pres. internet tech., 1999—2000; sr. v.p., chief tech. officer Compaq Computer Co., 2000—02; exec. v.p. chief strategy and tech. officer Hewlett-Packard Co., Palo Alto, Calif., 2002—. Office: Hewlett-Packard Co 3000 Hanover St Palo Alto CA 94304

ROBINSON, SHARON BETH, health science association administrator; b. Balt., Sept. 28, 1959; BS, Towson State U., 1981; MS, Johns Hopkins U., 1986. Exec. asst. Congress of Neurol. Surgeons, Balt., 1983-86; office adminstr. Md. Inst. Emergency Med. Svcs., Balt., 1986-87; coord. spl. projects U. Md. Med. Systems, Balt., 1986-88; adminstr. Am. Bd. Med. Genetics, Bethesda, Md., 1988—, Am. Coll. Med. Genetics, Bethesda, 1992-98, Am. Bd. Genetic Counseling, Bethesda, 1993—. Mem. Catonsville Community Coll. Alumni Assn. (bd. dirs. 1984-89, sec. 1986, v.p. 1987, pres. 1988). Office: ABMG/ABGC 9650 Rockville Pike Bethesda MD 20814-3998 E-mail: srobinson@genetics.faseb.org.

ROBINSON, SHARON PORTER, professional society administrator; b. Louisville; B in Edn., English and Psychology, U. Ky., 1966, M in Edn., Curriculum and Instrn., 1976, D in Ednl. Adminstrn. and Supervision, 1979. Tchr., Lexington, Ky., U.S. AFB, Bitburg, Germany; assoc. dir. Jefferson County Edn. Consortium, Ky., late 1970's; dir. instrn. and profl. devel. NEA, 1980-89, dir. R & D arm Nat. Ctr. Innovation, 1989-93; asst. sec. ednl. rsch. and improvement U.S. Dept. Edn., 1993—96; v.p. State and Fed. Regulations EPS, Washington, 1997—98, sr. v.p., COO, 1998—. Cons. Nat. Bd. Profl. Teaching Standards; head tchr. edn. initiative Nat. Ctr. Innovation. Office: EPS 1800 K St NW Washington DC 20006

ROBINSON, SHAWNA, race car driver; b. Des Moines, Nov. 30, 1964; 2 children. Big-rig tractor driver Great Am. Truck Racing Tour, 1980; racecar driver Huffman Racing, 1991. Named winner, Dash Race, 1988, Most Popular Driver, 1988, Rookie of the Yr., 1988, winner, Talladega Pole award, 2000; recipient 3d pl., Goody's Dash Series, 1988, 4th pl., Bondo/Mar-Hyde Series Race, 1999, 2d pl., First Plus Fin. 200, 1999. Office: c/o BAM Racing 11881 Vance Davis Dr Charlotte NC 28269

ROBINSON, SIDNEY K. architecture educator; BArch, Columbia U., 1967; PhD in Arch., U. Mich., 1973. Dir. Inst. for Arch. and the Humanities; assoc. prof., dir. grad. studies Sch. Arch. U. Ill., Chgo. Author: Inquiry into the Picturesque, 1991; co-author: The Continuous Present of Organic Architecture, 1991. Office: Univ Ill Chgo Sch Arch Dept Code 2-2405 3100 A&A MC 030 845 W Harrison Chicago IL 60607-7024*

ROBINSON, STEPHEN A. music educator, musician; b. Port Chester, N.Y., Aug. 16, 1953; s. Edward G. and Marie Robinson; m. Patrece Shehan Robinson, May 31, 1980; children: Anthony, Nicolas, Alexander, Benjamin. MusB, Fla. State U., 1979, MusM, 1981, D.Mus., 1987; postgrad., Yale U., 1979—80. Grad. tchg. asst. Yale U., New Haven, 1979—80, Fla. State U., Tallahassee, 1980—83; adj. prof. guitar Valencia Coll., Orlando, Fla., 1984, Rollins Coll., Winter Park, Fla., 1984; prof. music Stetson U., Deland, Fla., 1983—; artistic dir. Stetson Internat. Guitar Workshop, Deland, 1991—. Adv. bd. Guitar Found. Am., L.A., 1998—; artistic dir. Lakeside Records, Deland, 1995—; classical guitarist throughout U.S., Can., Europe. Performer (CD) Al Christmas Feeling, 2000, Grand Solos, 1998, Under the Influence - An American Record and Stephen Robinson, 1994. Recipient Solo Recitalist award, Nat. Endowment for the Arts, 1985, 1989, 1989; fellow Fulbright fellow, Fulbright Found., 1992—93. Mem.: Pi Kappa Lambda, Phi Kappa Phi. Democrat. Roman Catholic. Avocations: boating, fishing. Office: Stetson Univ Sch Music 421 N Woodland Blvd Unit 8399 Deland FL 32723

ROBINSON, STEPHEN MICHAEL, applied mathematician, educator; b. Columbus, Ohio, Apr. 12, 1942; s. Arthur Howard and Mary Elizabeth (Coffin) R.; m. Chong-Suk Han, May 10, 1968; children: Diana Marie, James Andrew. BA, U. Wis., 1962, PhD, 1971; MS, NYU, 1963; Diploma, U.S. Army War Coll., 1986; Dr. honoris causa, Univ. Zürich, 1996. Adminstr. U. Wis., Madison, 1969-72, asst. prof., 1972-75, assoc. prof., 1975-79, prof. indsl. engring. and computer scis., 1979—, chmn. dept. indsl. engring., 1981-84. Cons. to various agys. Dept. Def., 1971—. Editor: Math. of Ops. Rsch., 1981-86, assoc. editor, 1975-80, Jour. Ops. Rsch., 1974-86, Math. Programming, 1986-91; mem. bd. editors Annals Ops. Rsch., 1984-99, Set-Valued Analysis, 1992-99, Jour. Convex Analysis, 1994—2002; adv. editor Math. of Ops. Rsch., 1987—, Ops. Rsch. Letters, 2002-; mem. editl. bd. Springer Series in Ops. Rsch., 1996—; contbr. numerous articles to profl. jours. Trustee Village of Shorewood Hills, Wis., 1974-76, mem. fin. com., 1973-87; bd. on math. scis. and their applications NRC, 2001—, bd. overseers Simon's Rock Coll., Great Barrington, Mass., 1991-2002. Served to capt. U.S. Army, 1963—69, Korea, Vietnam, col. AUS, ret. Decorated Legion of Merit, Bronze star, Air medal, Army Commendation medal with 2 oak leaf clusters; recipient John K. Walker Jr. award Mil. Ops. Rsch. Soc., 2001. Mem. Inst. for Ops. Rsch. and Mgmt. Scis. (mem. Ops. Rsch. Soc. Am. coun. 1991-94, sec. 2000-03), Inst. Indsl. Engrs., Soc. Indsl. and Applied Math., Math. Programming Soc. (mem.-at-large of coun. 1991-94, George B. Dantzig prize 1997), Madison Club. Home: 1014 University Bay Dr Madison WI 53705-2251 Office: U Wis Dept Indsl Engring 1513 University Ave Madison WI 53706-1572 Office Phone: 608-263-6862. E-mail: smrobins@wisc.edu.

ROBINSON, SUE L(EWIS), federal judge; b. 1952; BA with highest honors, U. Del., 1974; JD, U. Pa., 1978. Assoc. Potter, Anderson & Corron, Wilmington, Del., 1978-83; asst. U.S. atty. U.S. Attys. Office, 1983-88; U.S. magistrate judge U.S. Dist. Ct. (Del. dist.), 1988-91, dist. judge, 1991—. Mem. Del. State Bar Assn. (sec. 1986-87). Office: US Dist Ct J Caleb Boggs Fed Bldg 844 N King St Lockbox 31 Wilmington DE 19801-3519

ROBINSON, SUSAN MITTLEMAN, data processing executive; b. Bklyn., Nov. 18, 1941; d. Samuel and Ida (Priest) Mittleman; m. Sheldon N. Robinson, June 5, 1962; children: Edward Bruce, Nancy Michelle, Jonathan Scott, Karen Barbara, Judith Lynn. AAS in Computer Sci., BCC, Lincroft, N.J., 1981; BBA, CUNY, 1962; MS in Computer Sci., Fairleigh Dickinson U., 1983; postgrad., Seton Hall U., 1983-85. Engr. asst. United Technologies, East Hartford, Conn., 1962-64; programmer, sys. analyst Litton Industries (Sweda), Pine Brook, N.J., 1981-83; asst. prof. data processing Mercer Coll., West Windsor, N.J.,

1983-85; adj. instr. data processing Brookdale C.C., Lincroft, N.J., 1983—; coord. MIS N.J. Dept. Health and Sr. Svcs., Trenton, 1985—, NT LAN adminstr., 1994—, world wide web webmaster; med. data set liaison N.J. Dept. Health and Sr. Svcs. and HCFA, 1996—. Outsource cons. Medicare/Medicaid, Trenton, 1989—; cons. Health Care Fin. Authority, Balt., 1995—. Author (reference material) Info-Henco, 1987, Automated Survey Processing Environment Users Training Manual, 1993; developer computerized sys. to help patients and their family select a nursing home. Exec. bd. Temple Beth Am, Parsippany, N.J., 1972-80. Mem. SAS Users Group, N.J. DOH Prime Users Group. Avocations: knitting, puzzle-solving, travel. Office: NJ Dept Health and Sr Svcs PO Box 367 Trenton NJ 08625-0367

ROBINSON, THOMAS CHRISTOPHER, academic administrator, educator; b. Buffalo, Oct. 16, 1944; s. Christopher Sidney and Eleanor Florence (Martin) R.; m. Helen Dare Tew, June 21, 1986; children: Diane Dunn, Kristen Elizabeth, Molly Lindsay, Norman Ashley. BA, SUNY, Buffalo, 1966, EdM, 1968, PhD, 1971; grad. mgmt. devel. program, Harvard U., 1989. Admissions officer, office of admissions and records SUNY, Buffalo, 1966-72, assoc. dean Sch. Health Related Professions, 1975-78; asst. dir. Erie County Lab., Buffalo, 1972-75; assoc. dean Coll. Allied Health Professions, U. Ky., Lexington, 1978-84, dean Coll. Health Scis., 1984—. Cons. MDS Labs., Hamilton, Ont., Can., 1973-75, Joint U.S.-Arabian Commn. on Econ. Cooperation, 1986-87, West Sussex Inst. Higher Edn., Bogner Regis, U.K., 1987, U. Wis. Sys. Ctrs. of Excellence Program, 1988, Pub. Health Svc. Health Resources Adminstrn., 1983, 90-91; mem. exec. com. Nat. Practitioner Data Bank, 1992-94, cons. 1994-95; hon. mem. faculty Khabarovsk (Russia) Med. Inst., 1996; bd. dirs. Health Ky. Contbr. articles to profl. jours. Mem. Health Sys. Agy. Coun., Buffalo, 1977-78, Western N.Y. Hemophilia Soc. Bd. Buffalo, 1977-78, Lexington-Fayette County Bd. Health, Lexington, 1987-91, program excellence project Ohio Bd. Regents, United Way of Bluegrass Healthcare Devel. Bd., 1991; mem. La. Bd. Regents, 1995, Univ. Wolverhampton fellow, U.K. With N.Y. Army N.G., 1968-74. Recipient Svc. award Jour. Allied Health, 1986. Mem. Assn. Schs. Allied Health Professions (bd. dirs. 1985-87, Svc. award 1987, Fellow award 1988, pres. 1991-94, past pres. 1994-95, Outstanding Member award 1995), Ky. Allied Health Consortium (bd. dirs. 1985-93, chair 1995-96), So. Assn. Allied Health Deans (sec. 1986-88, chmn. 1988-90), Assn. Schs. Allied Health Professions (pres. 1991-94), Ky. Hosp. Assn., Ky. Assn. Healthcare Facilities, Lexington C. of C., Sigma Phi Epsilon. Avocations: golf, travel, geneology, gardening. Home: 620 Centennial Ln Lexington KY 40502-2770 Office: U Ky Coll Health Scis CTW Bldg 900 S Limestone Rm 123-D Lexington KY 40536-0200 Office Phone: 859-323-1100. Business E-Mail: tcrobi01@uky.edu.

ROBINSON, V. GENE (THE RIGHT REVEREND V. GENE ROBINSON), bishop; life ptnr. Mark Andrew; children: Jamee, Ella. BA in Am. Studies and History, U. South, 1969; MDiv, Gen. Theol. Sem., 1973. Curate Christ Ch., Ridgewood, NJ, 1973—75, youth ministries coord. Province 1, 1978—85; exec. sec. Episc. Province New England, 1983—2003; canon to the ordinary Episc. Diocese N.H., 1988—2003, bishop coadjutor, 2003—04, Bishop Diocesan, 2004—. Bd. trustees Gen. Theol. Sem., 2001—; co-owner, dir. Girl's Summer Camp and Horse Farm, 1975—78; founding dir. Sign of the Dove Retreat Ctr., Temple, NH; mem. Nat. Youth Ministries Devel. Team. Founder Concord Outright. Avocations: cooking, gardening, music, running. Office: Episcopal Diocese of NH 63 Green St Concord NH 03301-4243 Office Phone: 603-224-1914.

ROBINSON, VIANEI LOPEZ, lawyer; b. Houston, Mar. 6, 1969; d. David Tiburcio and Romelia Gloria (Guerra) Lopez. AB in Psychology cum laude, Princeton U., 1988; JD, U. Tex., 1991. Bar: Tex. 1991; mediator's cert. Assoc. Bracewell & Patterson LLP, Houston, 1991-94, Wagstaff Law Firm, Abilene, Tex., 1994-97; owner Robinson Law Firm, Abilene, 1997—. Contbr. articles to profl. jours., chpts. to School Law in Texas, A Practical Guide, 1996, Texas Employment Law, 1998; weekly wine columnist, Abilene Reporter News. Bd. dirs., sec. Historic Paramount Theatre, 2003, bd. dirs. Ctr. for Contemporary Arts, pres., 2000, sec., 2001; mem. adv. bd., Day Nursery of Abilene. Presdl. scholar, Nat. Merit scholar, Nat. Hispanic scholar, 1985, Vinson & Elkins scholar U. Tex. Sch. Law, Austin, 1988-91. Fellow Tex. Bar Found.; mem. ABA, State Bar Tex. (minority dir. 2000-05, various coms.), Coll. of the State Bar of Tex. (bd. dirs. 2000-01), Tex. Young Lawyers Assn. (bd. dirs. 1994-97), Abilene Bar Assn., Abilene Young Lawyers Assn., Big Country Soc. for Human Resource Mgmt. (pres. 1999). Avocations: theater and dance, fine art, food and wine. Home: 2410 Wyndham Ct Abilene TX 79606-4370 Office: Robinson Law Firm First Nat Bank Tower 400 Pine St Ste 1070 Abilene TX 79601-5173 Fax: 915-677-6044. Business E-Mail: vlr@robinsonlawfirm.com.

ROBINSON, W. LEE, lawyer; b. Rome, Ga., Sept. 24, 1943; m. Irene Scales, 1966; children: Christine, Jacquelyn. BS, Ga. Inst. Tech.; MBA, JD, Mercer U., 1985. With Robinson Hardware Store, Macon, Ga., 1954-86; mem. Ga. Senate, Atlanta, 1975-83; mayor City of Macon, Macon, 1988-92; pvt. practice Macon, 1985—. Judge mcpl. ct. (part time), Macon. 2d lt. U.S. Army; col. USAR. Decorated Bronze Star with two oak leaf clusters, Legion of Merit with oak leaf cluster. Named to U.S. Army Officer Candidate Sch. Hall of Fame. Mem. Ga. Assn. Criminal Def. Lawyers, Macon C. of C. (former bd. dirs.), Macon Bar Assn. Address: 3824 Overlook Ave Macon GA 31204-1325 Office: 201 2nd St Ste 580 Macon GA 31201-8282 also: PO Box 4852 Macon GA 31208-4852 E-mail: wlrmcnlaw@aol.com.

ROBINSON, WARREN LOWE, utilities executive; b. Logan, Utah, Apr. 11, 1950; s. Floyd Comish and Grace (Lowe) R.; m. Ann Decker, May 21, 1977 (div. Dec. 1981); 1 child, Stephanie; m. Joan Cunningham, June 17, 1983; children: Jennifer, John. BBA, Brigham Young U., 1974; MBA, Boise State U., 1976; cert., Stanford U., 1985, Harvard U., 1991. Fin. analyst Intermountain Gas Co., Boise, 1976-77, dir. budgets and fin. planning, 1977-79, mgr. planning services, 1979-80, asst. to pres., 1980-81; v.p., treas., chief fin. officer Great Falls (Mont.) Gas Co., 1981-87, sr. v.p., chief fin. officer, 1987-88. Pres., co-founder, bd. dirs. Mont. Overthrust Energy Found., Great Falls, 1983-87; v.p., treas., co-founder Great Falls Capital Corp., 1984-87; mgr. corp. devel. MDU Resources Group, Inc., 1988-89, treas., asst. sec., 1988-92, v.p., treas., CFO, 1992—. Commr. Garden City, Idaho, 1981. Served with N.G., 1968-75. Mem. Nat. Assn. Corp. Treas., Nat. Investor Rels. Inst., Leadership Bismarck Alumni Assn. (pres., co-founder), Fin. Execs. Inst. Lodges: Rotary (pres. Great Falls chpt. 1985-86, bd. dirs. 1985-87). Republican. Mem. Lds Ch. Office: MDU Resources Group Inc 400 N 4th St Bismarck ND 58501-4092 Home: 1533 Galleon Pl Bismarck ND 58504-8984

ROBINSON, WENDY Y. school system administrator; Under grad., DePauw U., Ind. U.-Purdue U., Ball State U. Tchr. Ward Elem., 1973—86; asst. prin. Meml. Pk. Mid. Sch., 1986—87, Weisser Pk. Elem., 1987—89; prin. Price Elem., 1989—91; area admin., asst. supt. Wayne HS, 1991—95; dep. supt. Fort Wayne Comm. Schs., 1995—2003, supt., 2003—. Office: Fort Wayne Comm Sch 1200 S Clinton St Fort Wayne IN 46802

ROBINSON, WILKES COLEMAN, retired federal judge; b. Anniston, Ala., Sept. 30, 1925; s. Walter Wade and Catherine Elizabeth (Coleman) R.; m. Julia Von Poellnitz Rowan, June 24, 1955; children: Randolph C., Peyton H., Thomas Wilkes Coleman. BA, U. Ala., 1948; JD, U. Va., 1951. Bar: Ala. 1951, Va. 1962, Mo. 1966, Kans. 1983. Assoc. Bibb & Hemphill, Anniston, 1951-54; city recorder City of Anniston, 1953-55; judge Juvenile and Domestic Rels. Ct. of Calhoun County, Ala., 1954-56; atty. legal dept. GM&O R.R., Mobile, Ala., 1956-58; commerce counsel, asst. gen. atty. Seaboard Air Line R.R., Richmond, Va., 1958-66; chief commerce counsel Monsanto Co., St. Louis, 1966-70; gen. counsel, v.p. Marion Labs., Inc., Kansas City, Mo., 1970-79; pres. Gulf and Gt. Plains Legal Found., Kansas City, Mo., 1980-85, also bd. dirs.; atty. Howard, Needles, Tammen & Bergendoff, Kansas City, 1985-86, also bd. dirs.; v.p. S.R. Fin. Group, Inc., Overland Park, Kans., 1986-87; judge U.S. Ct. Fed. Claims, Washington, 1987-97, sr. judge, 1997—. Bd. govs. Kansas City Philharm. Orch., 1975-77. Served with USNR, 1943-44. Mem. Indian Bayou Golf Club, Scottish Rite, Phi Beta Kappa (past treas. Kansas City, Mo. chpt.), Phi Eta Sigma, Phi Alpha Theta, Kappa Alpha. Episcopalian. Home: 12 Weekewachee Cir Destin FL 32541-4426 E-mail: wilkescrob@cox.net.

ROBINSON, WILLIAM ANDREW, health service executive, physician; b. Phila., Pa., Jan. 31, 1943; s. Colonial Washington and Lillian Dorothy Robinson; m. Jacqueline Ellen Garcia, Mar. 28, 1980; 1 child, David Alan; 1 child by previous marriage, William Andrew Jr. BA, Hampton U., 1964; MD, Meharry Med. Coll., 1971; MPH, Johns Hopkins U., 1973. Diplomate Nat. Bd. Med. Examiners; lic. physician, Md. Rotating intern George W. Hubbard Hosp., Nashville, 1971-72, emergency room physician, 1972; med. officer gastrointestinal drug sect., bur. drugs FDA USPHS, HEW, Rockville, Md., 1973-75; dep. dir. office health resources opportunity USPHS, HHS, Rockville, Md., 1975-80, dep. dir. bur. health professions health resources adminstrn., 1980-87, chief med. officer health resources and svcs. adminstn., 1987-89, dep. asst. sec. minority health, dir. office minority health Washington, 1989-91, acting adminstr. health resources and svc. adminstrn. Rockville, Md., 1993-94, chief med. officer health resources and svc. adminstrn., 1991—, dir. Office Pub. Health Affairs, 1996-97, dir. Ctr. for Quality, 1997—. Chmn. sr. execs. performance rev. bd. Office of Asst. Sec. for Health, 1990-91; pub. health svc. rep. 2d Internat. Conf. on Health Promotion, Adelaide, South Australia; health cons. com. on interior and insular affairs U.S. Ho. of Reps., Washington, 1982-83; appointed field faculty dept. family and cmty. health Meharry Med. Coll., 1979; U.S. rep. to WHO Primary Health Care Conf., Alma Ata, Kazakhstan. Mem. nat. editl. bd. Jour. Health Care for the Poor and Underserved, 1991; contbr. articles to profl. jours. Capt. U.S. Army, 1964-67. Recipient Nat. Urban Coalition Cmty. Health Svc. award, 1972, Letter of Appreciation, Chmn. Congl. Black Caucus Health Braintrust, U.S. Ho. of Reps., 1988. Mem. AMA, APHA, Am. Acad. Family Physicians, Blacks in Govt., Fed. Physicians Assn., Nat. Med. Assn., Sr. Execs. Assn., Delta Omega (Alpha chpt.). E-mail: brobinson@hrsa.gov.

ROBINSON, WILLIAM I. sociologist; b. N.Y.C., Mar. 28, 1959; s. Howard Sydney and Jo-Ann Phyllis Robinson; m. Gloconda Lucia Robinson, May 10, 1985 (div. Oct. 9, 2000); children: Amaru Alejandro, Tamara Yoconda; m. Marielle Mayorga, Sept. 27, 2003. BA, Friends World Coll., N.Y.C., 1982; M, U. N.Mex., 1992, PhD, 1994. Editor, reporter Agencia Nueva Nicaragua, Managua, 1982-87; Washington bur. chief Agencia Nueva Nicaragua Internat. News Agy., Washington, 1987-90; news analyst, cons. Latin Am. Data Base, Albuquerque, 1990-94; prof. sociology U. N.Mex., Albuquerque, 1994-96, U. Tenn., Knoxville, 1996-98, N.Mex. State U., Las Cruces, 1998-2001; prof. sociology and global studies U. Calif., Santa Barbara, 2001—. Author: David & Goliath, 1987, A Faustian Bargain, 1992, Promoting Polyarchy, 1996, Transnational Conflicts: Central America, Globalization and Social Change, 2003, A Theory of Global Capitalism, 2004. Mem.: Internat. Studies Assn., Latin Am. Studies Assn., Am. Sociol. Assn., Global Studies Assn., Phi Kappa Phi. Avocation: Latin dance. Office: U Calif Santa Barbara Dept Sociology Santa Barbara CA 93106 Office Phone: 805-893-5607. Business E-Mail: wirobins@soc.ucsb.edu.

ROBINSON, WILLIAM P. academic administrator, consultant, speaker; b. Elmhurst, Ill., Sept. 30, 1949; s. Paul Frederick and Lillian (Horton) R.; m. Bonnie Van Laan, Aug. 10, 1974; children: Brenna Kay, Benjamin Paul, Bailley Kay. Student, Moody Bible Inst., Chgo., 1967-70; AB, U. No. Iowa, 1972; postgrad., Princeton (N.J.) Theol. Sem., 1972-73; MA, Wheaton Coll., 1975; PhD, U. Pitts., 1979. Assoc. minister First Presbyn. Ch., Pitts., 1975-77; instr. U. Pitts., 1977-79; asst. prof. sch. continuing studies Nat. Coll. Edn., Evanston, Ill., 1979-80, dean sch. continuing studies, 1980-84, sr. v.p., 1984-86; pres. Manchester Coll., North Manchester, Ind., 1986-93, Whitworth Coll., Spokane, Wash., 1993—. Bd. dirs. Coun. Indep. Colls., Ind. Colls. Wash., Whitworth Coll.; cons., speaker for U.S. corps. and svc. orgns. Bd. dirs. Wash. Friends of Higher Edn., Spokane Symphony; vol. various orgns., especially prion work and hunger projects. Recipient various acad. awards. Mem. Nat. Assn. Ind. Colls. and Univs., Coun. Ind. Colls., Spokane Country Club, Spokane Club. Presyterian. Avocation: sports. Office: Whitworth Coll Office of Pres 300 W Hawthorne Rd Spokane WA 99218-2515

ROBINSON, ZAN DALE, language educator, writer; b. Abington, Pa., July 15, 1935; s. Paul Roland Robinson and Dorothy Ellen Robinson Nee Philpott; m. Patricia Marion McNaney, Nov. 10, 1961; children: Michael Leo, Zan Dale Jr., Joan Marie, Rand Raymond. BA in Eng., MA in Eng., SUNY, Buffalo, 1974, PhD in Eng., 1990. Prof. Erie C.C., Williamsville, NY, 1979—. Dir. spl. ednl. programs Daemen Coll., Williamsville, NY, 1976—78; adj. lectr. Buffalo State Coll., NY, 1983—2003. Author: (monograph) Revelation: The Adult Learner and the Learning Environment, A Psychoanalytic and Semiotic Interpretation of Herman Melville's Fiction, The Adherance Principle: A Psychoanalytic Interpretation of the Fairy Tale in Relation to Early Childhood Development, (fiction) Ferdie the Fay Meets Flutterby the Butterfly, The Spirit of November: A Psychosemiotic Interpretation of Literature, (textbook) Fundamentals of Writing, Practical Writing Techniques (Ten Editions), Writing Effectively (two Editions), Dynamic Writing Techniques, (anthology) The Workplace, (resource guide) Robinson's Resource Guide for English Majors, Robinson's resource Guide for Writing Resumes and Cover Letters. Chmn. Greater Buffalo Cmty. Housing Resources Bd., Buffalo, 1979—80; chmn. bd. Leadership Ho. Inc., Buffalo, 1999—2001, Fletcher-Green Found., Inc., Buffalo, 2001—03; bd. dirs. Nat. Alliance for Mentally Ill, WNY chpt., Buffalo, 1985—2003, Citizen's Coun. on Human Rels., Buffalo, 1979—85. Recipient One of Top Ten Tchrs. in Western NY, The Buffalo Evening News, 1985, Disting. Alumnus Award, Buffalo State Coll., 1989, 2000, Chancellor's Award for Excellence in Tchg., SUNY, 1997, Brotherhood/Sisterhood Award in Edn., NCCJ, 1998, Pathfinders Award for Edn., Buffalo Edn. Alliance, 1998, Medal of Excellence for Edn. and Svc. for Youth, Berkshire Union Free Sch. Dist., 2001. Mem.: Continuing Edn. Assn. N.Y., Niagara Linguistic Soc., United U. Professions, N.Y. State United Tchrs., MLA, NEA, Nat. Coun. Eng. Tchrs., Am. Fedn. Tchrs. Avocations: professional harmonica player, judge for amateur boxing. Home: 1300 N French Rd Amherst NY 14228 Office: Buffalo State Coll 1300 Elmwood Ave Buffalo NY 14222 E-mail: robinsz@buffalostate.edu.

ROBINSON, ZELIG, lawyer; b. Balt., July 7, 1934; s. Morton Matthew and Mary (Ackerman) R.; m. Karen Ann Bergstrom (div. Oct. 1987); children: John, Christopher, Kristin; m. Linda Portner Strangmann, Dec. 23, 1987. BA, Johns Hopkins U., 1954; LLB, Harvard U., 1957. Bar: Md. 1958. Legis. analyst Md. Ho. of Dels., Annapolis, 1958; tech. asst. IRS, Washington, 1958-60; pvt. practice Balt., 1960-62; assoc. gen. counsel commerce com. U.S. Ho. of Reps., Washington, 1962-64; assoc. Weinberg & Green, Balt., 1964-66; spl. legal cons. commerce com. U.S. Ho. of Reps., Washington, 1966-68; pvt. practice Balt., 1966—70; mem. Gordon, Feinblatt, Rothman, Hoffberger & Hollander, LLC, 1972—. Bd. dir. Durapak Mfg. Co., Balt., Vac Pac, Inc., Balt., Universal Die Casting Co., Inc., Saline, Mich.; chmn. Balt. City Minimum Wage Commn., 1974-82, Md. Pub. Broadcasting Commn., 1991-95; mem. Gov's. Commn. to revise Md. Code, Annapolis, 1968-90. Contbr. articles to profl. jour. Bd. dirs., v.p., sec. Gov.'s Mansion Found., Annapolis, Md.; v.p. bd. dirs. Md. Cmty. and Citizens Fund, Chestertown, Md.; sec. bd. dirs. William Donald Schaefer Civic Fund; bd. dirs. Md. Arts Pl., Balt., Balt. Coalition of Homeowners, 1989—; v.p., bd. dirs. Everyman Theatre, 2002-; mem. Found. for Md. Pub. Broadcasting; sec., trustee Balt. City Hist. Soc.; bd. dirs., pres. Celebration 2000, Inc., 1998—; founder, bd. dirs. Balt. Efficiency and Econ. Found., 1999—; chmn., Balt. City Coun. Transition Commn., 2003. With U.S. Army, 1958. Mem. ABA, Md. State Bar Assn. (laws com., internat. law com.). Democrat. Office: Gordon Feinblatt Rothman Hoffberger & Hollander LLC 233 E Redwood St Baltimore MD 21202-3332 Business E-Mail: zrobinson@gfrlaw.com.

ROBIRDS, ESTEL, state legislator; Mem. Mo. State Ho. of Reps. Dist. 143, 1993—. Home: Rte 2 Box 2919 Theodosia MO 65761 Office: Mo Ho of Reps State Capitol Building Jefferson City MO 65101-1556

ROBISON, CAROLYN LOVE, retired librarian; b. Orlinda, Tenn., Aug. 9, 1940; d. Fount Love and Martha Desha (Jones) R. BA, Denison U., 1962; MLS, Emory U., 1965; PhD, Ga. State U., 1982. Tchr. Dag Hammarshjold Jr. H.S., Wallingford, Conn., 1962-64; asst. libr., lectr. Architecture Libr., Ga. Inst. Tech., Atlanta, 1965-67; head circulation Ga. State U., Atlanta, 1967-71, asst. prof., then assoc. prof., asst. libr., 1971-75, prof., assoc. libr., 1975-98, prof. emeritus, 1998. Active Friends of Atlanta-Fulton County Pub. Libr., 1981—98. Recipient Woman of Achievement award YWCA, 1989. Mem. ALA, AAUP, Ga. Libr. Assn., Delta Kappa Gamma, Phi Kappa Phi, Kappa Delta Pi. Republican. Presbyterian. Home: 1057 Capital Club Cir NE Atlanta GA 30319-2662 Personal E-mail: clrobison@mindspring.com.

ROBISON, CLARENCE, JR., surgeon; b. Tecumseh, Okla., Dec. 9, 1924; s. Clarence Sr. and Margaret Irene (Buzzard) Robison; m. Patricia Antoinette Hagee, May 27, 1951; children: Timothy D., Paul D., John D., Rebecca A. AS, Stanford U., 1943; MD, U. Okla., 1948. Intern Good Samaritan Hosp., Portland, Oreg., 1948-49; fellow pathology and oncology U. Okla., 1949-51; pathologist USAF Hosp., Cheyenne, Wyo., 1951-53; resident in surgery Okla. U. Health Scis.-VA Svc., Oklahoma City, 1953-56; mem. faculty surgery dept. Okla. U. Health Scis., Oklahoma City, 1956-57, clin. prof. surgery, 1957—. Mem. bd. advisors Mercy Health Ctr., Oklahoma City, 1974—81, sec. staff, 1974—84, chief surgery, 1992—95. Presdl. elector Dems., 1960; mem. Commn. Mission Indian Nations Presbytery, 1980—91; elder Presbyn. Ch.; bd. dirs. Okla. Found. Quality Assurance, Oklahoma City, Found. Sr. Citizens, 1964—. Capt. USAF, 1951—53. Fellow: ACS, Am. Cancer Soc. (past pres. Okla. divsn., exec. com., bd. dirs., nat. bd. dirs.), Southwestern Surg. Soc.; mem.: SAR, AMA (del. organized med. staff sect. Oklahoma City 1989—, alt. del. AMA Okla. 1991—93, 1996—98), Oklahoma City Surg. Soc. (pres. 1967—69), Okla. Surg. Assn. (sec., treas. 1966—68), Okla. State Med. Assn. (alt. trustee Okla. 1989—92, trustee 1993—96), Oklahoma County Med. Soc. (bd. dirs. 1989—93), Men's Dinner Club, Petroleum Club, Sportsman Club, Knights Templar, Shriners (Royal Order Jesters), Masons (32 degree). Office: 4200 W Memorial Rd Ste 508 Oklahoma City OK 73120-9331 E-mail: nmi@ionet.net.

ROBISON, EMILY BURNS, musician; b. Pittsfield, Mass., Aug. 16, 1972; d. Paul and Barbara Burns; m. Charlie Robison, May 1999; 1 child, Charles. Performer Blue Night Express, 1984—89; banjo player, guitarist, vocalist Dixie Chicks, 1989—. Performer: (albums) LIttle Ol' Cowgirl, 1992, Ghank Heavens for Dale Evans, 1992, Shouldn't a Told You That, 1993, Wide Open Spaces, 1998 (Maximum Vision Clip of Yr., Billboard, 1998, Best New Country Artist Clip of Yr., Billboard, 1998, Best Country Album, Grammy Awards, 1998, Album of Yr., Acad. Country Music, 1998, Best Selling Album, Can. Country Music Awards, 1999, Song of Yr., WB Radio Music Award, 1999, Album of Yr., ACM, 1999), Fly, 1999 (Best Country Album, Grammy Awards, 1999, Best Selling Album, Can. Country Musc Awards, 2000, Internat. Album, British Country Music Award, 2000, Country Album of Yr., Billboard Awards, 2000, Album of Yr., ACM, 2000, Album of Yr., CMA, 2000), Home, 2002 (Favorite Country Album, Am. Music Awards, 2002, Best Recording Package, Grammy Awards, 2002, Best Country Album, Grammy Awards, 2002). Named Most Significant New Country Act, Country Monitor, 1998, Top New Country Artist, Billboard, 1998, Top Vocal Group, Acad. Country Music, 1998, Country Artist of Yr., Rolling Stone, 1999, Top Country Artist, Billboard, 1999, Internat. Rising Star, British Country Music Awards, 1999, Artist of Yr. (Country), WB Radio Music Award, 1999, Favorite New Artist (Country), AMA, 1999, Vocal Group of Yr., CMA, 1999, Country Artist of Yr., Billboard, 1999, 2000, Entertainer of Yr., CMA, 2000, ACM, 2000, Vocal Group of Yr., 2001, Entertainer of Yr., 2001, Favorite Musical Group or Band, People's Choice Award, 2002, Vocal Group of Yr., Country Music Assn., 2002, others; recipient Horizon award, CMA, 1998. Office: Monument Sony Nashville 34 Music Sq East Nashville TN 37203

ROBISON, FREDERICK MASON, retired financial executive; b. Danville, Ill., May 30, 1934; s. Frederick A. and Katherine L. (Mason) R.; m. Nancy Jane Potter, Aug. 18, 1956; children: Frederick B., Christopher M. BS, U. Ill., 1956, JD, 1959. Tax mgr. Arthur Andersen & Co., Chgo., 1959-65; treas. Warnaco, Inc., Bridgeport, Conn., 1965-76; v.p. Emery Air Freight, Wilton, Conn., 1976-86, treas., 1976-79, sec., 1979-82, controller, 1979-86; v.p., controller Burlington Air Express, Irvine, Calif., 1986-88; sr. v.p. fin., chief fin. officer Sebastain Internat., Inc., Woodland Hills, Calif., 1988-96. Vice chmn. Town Council, Monroe, Conn., 1971-73, mem., 1969-73, bd. edn., Monroe, 1973-79, chmn., 1975-79. Mem. Fin. Execs. Inst. (dir. So. Conn. chpt. 1973-83, pres. 1977-78) Republican. Presbyterian. Home: 508 W Bay St Dunn NC 28334-5602

ROBISON, JUDY A. grants officer, research administrator; d. Earl D. and Louise D. Robison. MS, So. Ill. U., 1975; PhD, Tex. Woman's U., 1989; BE, U. of Ctrl. Ark., 1973. Cert. Am. Assn. of Family and Consumer Scis., 1990. County ext. agt. home economics U. of Ark., Coop. Ext. Svc., Fayetteville, 1974—75, U. of Ark. Coop. Ext. Svc., Waldron, 1975—78, state 4-H agt. and dist. program leader Little Rock, 1978—80, 4-H program specialist, 1980—94, grants officer, 1994—. Consulting Nat. 4-H Coun., 1994; v.p. Ark. Assn. of Family and Consumer Sci., 2002—. Recipient Disting. Svc. Citation, Pulaski County Farm Bur., 1982; grantee, USDA Coop. State Rsch., Edn., and Ext. Svc., 1991—96, USDA Rural Devel., 1997—99. Mem.: Nat. Assn. of Ext. 4-H Agents (Disting. Svc. award 1982), Ark. Assn. of Ext. 4-H Agents (Disting. Svc. award 1982), Ark. Assn. of Coop. Ext. Specialists (Performance award 1990), Pulaski County Home Economics Unit, Nat. Coun. of U. Rsch. Adminstrs., Am. Assn. of Family and Consumer Scis. (v.p., bd. dirs. Ark. affiliate), Am. Coun. on Consumer Interests, Epsilon Sigma Phi (sec. 1991—93, dist. dir., alt. dist. dir. 2000—, Cert. of Meritorious Svc. 1994), Gamma Sigma Delta. Office: U of Ark CoopExt Svc 2301 S University PO Box 391 Little Rock AR 72203

ROBISON, KENT RICHARD, lawyer; b. Reno, Nev., May 22, 1947; s. Burle and Helen Jean (Martin-Szymanski) R.; m. Tonya Robison; 2 children. BA, U. Nev.-Reno, 1969; JD, U. San Francisco, 1972. Bar: Nev. 1972, U.S. Dist. Ct. Nev. 1973, U.S. Ct. Claims 1973, U.S. Ct. Appeals (9th cir.) 1976, U.S. Supreme Ct. 1977, U.S. Tax Ct. 1982. Law clk. Carson City Dist. Atty.'s Office, 1971; dep. pub. defender Washoe County, Reno, 1972-75; ptnr. Johnson Belaustegui & Robison, Reno, 1975-79, Johnson, Belaustegui, Robison & Adams, Reno, 1979-81, Robison, Lyle, Belaustegui & Robb, Reno, 1981-88, Robison, Belaustegui, Robb & Sharp, Reno, 1988-99, Robison, Belaustegui, Sharp & Low, Reno, 1999—. Lectr. West Nev. Community Coll., Reno Police Acad., Calif. Legal Secs., U. Nev., Reno Bus. Coll., assns., socs., others; mem. com. on ct. costs and speedy trials Nev. Supreme Ct.; mem. Nev. State Commn. on Sentencing Felony Offenders, Exec. Com. to Establish Appellate Ct., Commn. to Implement Cameras in the Courtroom, Com. on Rules of Civil Procedure, Ad Hoc Com. for Improved Tech. in Nev. Fed. Courtrooms; mem. No. Nev. Legal-Med. Screening Panel, 1981-85; Washoe County Juvenile Master pro tem, 1975-77; ex-officio mem. ethics com., jury instrn. com. Nev. State Bar. Contbr. articles to law jours. Mem. ABA, ATLA, Am. Bd. trial Advocacy (pres. 1991), Nat. Bd. Trial Advocacy (diplomat civil and criminal), Nev. State Bar Assn. (bd. dirs., bd. govs.), Washoe County Bar Assn., Nev. Trial Lawyers Assn. (past pres., bd. govs.), Nat. Assn. Criminal Def. Lawyers, Am. Bd. Criminal Lawyers, Am. Inns of Ct. (charter, master), Am. Coll. Barristers, Roscoe Pound Found. Republican. Office: Robison Belaustegui Sharp & Low 71 Washington St Reno NV 89503 Office Phone: 775-329-3151. E-mail: krobison@rbslattys.com.

ROBISON, LINDA M. epidemiologist, medical researcher; b. Salt Lake City, Aug. 7, 1948; d. James John and Dorothy Leola Thomas; m. Marvin Henry Robison, June 10, 1971; 1 child, Jonas. BS, U. Utah, 1972, MSPH in Epidemiology, 1984. Health data analyst U. Utah, 1976—79, rsch. assoc., 1980—88; rsch. coord. Wash. State, 1989—. Contbr. articles to profl. jours. Recipient Pharmacy Practice Rsch. award, Am. Soc. of Health Sys. Pharmacists Rsch. & Edn. Found., 1995, Drug Therapy Rsch. award, 1995. Home: 606 Hathaway St Moscow ID 83843 Office: Wash State University Coll of Pharmacy PO Box 646510 Pullman WA 99164 Office Phone: 509-355-1865. Business E-Mail: lrobison@wsu.edu.

ROBISON, OLIN CLYDE, political science educator, former college president; b. Anacoco, La., May 12, 1936; s. Audrey Clyde and Ruby (Cantrell) R.; div.; children: Gordon Reece, Blake Elliott, Mark Edward. BA, Baylor U., 1958, LLD, 1979; D.Phil., Oxford (Eng.) U., 1963; LHD (hon.), Ehrenburger-Johannes Gutenberb U., Mainz, Fed. Republic Germany, 1977, Monterey Inst. Internat. Studies, 1982, Hofstra U, 1988; LLD (hon.), U. Vt., 1989, Middlebury Coll., 2000. Dean students San Marcos (Tex.) Acad., 1963-64; regional

officer Peace Corps, Washington, 1964-65, dir. univ. affairs, 1965-66; spl. asst. dep. under-sec. for polit. affairs Dept. State, Washington, 1966-68; asso. provost for social scis. Wesleyan U., Middletown, Conn., 1968-70; provost, dean faculty, sr. lectr. govt. and legal studies Bowdoin Coll., Brunswick, Maine, 1970-75; prof. polit. sci. Middlebury (Vt.) Coll., 1975-95, pres., 1975-90, pres. emeritus, 1990—, prof. emeritus, 1995—; pres. Salzburg Seminar, 1991—. Chmn. Am. Collegiate Consortium, 1987-94; cons. State Dept., 1968-72, 77-88; bd. dirs. Investment Co. Am., Am. Mut. Fund, Bank of Vt., 1989-92, The Noel Group, N.Y.C, 1989-91, AMCAP, ACMAP Mut. Fund; cons. Paine Webber Mitchell Hutchins Inc., Am. Coun. Life Ins., 1968-81, Washington Forum, Met. Life Ins. Co. Bd. dirs. Atlantic Info. Center for Tchrs., London, 1970-77, Am. Com. on U.S.-Soviet Rels., Washington; chmn. Vt. com. Rhodes Scholarship Trust, 1976-77; bd. dirs. Am. Coun. Young Polit. Leaders, 1968-78, 81-90, Inst. East-West Security Studies, N.Y.C., Nat. Spinal Cord Injury Assn., Washington, Atlantic Coun. U.S., 1973-78, 81-91, U.S. Commn. for United World Coll. Schs.; mem. U.S. Adv. Commn. on Public Diplomacy, 1978-83, chmn., 1978-81, visiting comm. Harvard Div. Sch., Cambridge, Mass., 1980-86, adv. comm. Harvard U., Ctr for Middle Ea. Studies, Cambridge, 1992-96; adviser U.S. del. Conf. on Security and Coop. in Europe, Belgrade, 1977-78; U.S. del. Conf. on Security and Coop. in Madrid, 1980, in Vienna, 1986-87; bd. dirs. Nat. Endowment for Democracy, 1984-92; bd. dirs., chmn. Chatham House Found., 1985-93. Named Ehrenburger Johannes Gutenberg Universität, Mainz, Fed. Republic Germany, 1977; Rockefeller Found./Aspen Inst. fellow, 1978-79; Presdl. fellow Aspen Inst. Humanistic Studies, 1979-80, Harry Luce fellow Aspen Inst., 1982-83. Mem. Internat. Inst. Strategic Studies (London), Soc. Values in Higher Edn., Council Fgn. Rels., Royal Inst. Internat. Affairs (bd. dirs. 2000—). Clubs: Federal City (Washington); Century (N.Y.C.); United Oxford and Cambridge (London). Baptist. Office: Salzburg Seminar The Marble Works PO Box 886 Middlebury VT 05753-0886

ROBISON, PAULA JUDITH, flutist; b. Nashville, June 8, 1941; d. David Victor and Naomi Florence R.; m. Scott Nickrenz; Dec. 29, 1971; 1 child, Elizabeth Hadley Amadea Nickrenz. Student, U. So. Calif., 1958-60; BS, Juilliard Sch. Music, 1963. Founding artist, player Chamber Music Soc., N.Y.C., 1970-90, N.Y. ChôroBand, 1994; co-dir. chamber music Spoleto Festival, Charleston, S.C., 1978-88; Filene artist-in-residence Skidmore Coll., Saratoga Springs, N.Y., 1988-89; mem. faculty New Eng. Conservatory Music, 1991—2001; co-dir. Gardner Chamber Orch., Boston, 1995—. Faculty Juilliard Sch., N.Y.C., 1978-82; annual concert series, Met. Mus. Art, N.Y., 1990—, With Art series, P.S. 1 Art Gallery, N.Y., 2000, Mass. Mus. Contemporary Art, 2001; dir.Vivaldi in the Courtyard, Gardner Mus., Boston, 2002—. Soloist with various major orchs., including N.Y. Philharm., London Symphony Orch.; player, presenter Concerti di Mezzogiorno, Spoleto (Italy) Festival, 1970-2003; commd. flute concertos by Leon Kirchner, Toru Takemitsu, Oliver Knussen, Robert Beaser, Kenneth Frazelle; premiered works by Pierre Boulez, Elliott Carter, William Schuman, Thea Musgrave, Carla Bley, John Tavener; premiered Rio Days Rio Nights, Music Theatre Group prodn. in N.Y.C., 1998; participant Marlboro Music Festival, 1999—; author: The Paula Robison Flute Warmups Book, 1989, The Andersen Collection, 1994, Paula Robison Masterclass: Paul Hindemith, 1995, The Sidney Lanier Collection, 1997, Frank Martin: Ballade, 2002, To a Wild Rose, 2003; co-author: Places of the Spirit, 2003; recs. on CBS Masterworks, Music Masters, Vanguard Classics, New World Records, Omega, Arabesque, Sony Classical, King Recs., Mode Recs., Artemis Recs.; featured in PBS documentary and book: Juilliard. Recipient First prize Geneva Internat. Competition, 1966, Adelaide Ristori prize, 1987, Lifetime Achievement award Nat. Flute Assn., 2004; named Musician of Month, Musical Am., 1979, House Musician for Isamu Noguchi Garden Mus., N.Y.C., 1988; Martha Baird Rockefeller grantee, 1966; Nat. Endowment for Arts grantee, 1978, 86; Fromm Found. grantee, 1980; Housewright Eminent scholar Fla. State U., 1990-91. Recipient Disting. Svc. award, Music Tchrs. Nat. Assn., 1989, Laurence Lesser Presdl. award, 1999, Lifetime Achievement award, Usdan Ctr. for Creative and Perfomring Arts, 2000, Hon. Citizen for Life award, City of Charleston, S.C., 2002, Lifetime Achievement award, Nat. Flute Assn., 2004. Mem. Sigma Alpha Iota (hon.). Office: care Matthew Sprizzo 477 Durant Ave Staten Island NY 10308-3006

ROBISON, SUSAN MILLER, psychologist, speaker, consultant; b. Chgo., Nov. 15, 1945; d. William Louis and Constance Mary (Maloney) Miller; m. Philip Dean Robison, Dec. 27, 1969; 1 child, Christine Gray. BS, Loyola U., Chgo., 1967; MS, Ohio U., 1969, PhD, 1971. Lic. psychologist, Md. Asst. prof. psychology Ohio U., Lancaster, 1970-72; prof. psychology Coll. Notre Dame, Balt., 1972—; pvt. practice Ellicott City, Md., 1982—. Leadership cons. Nat. Coun. Cath. Women, Washington, 1987—99; co-owner BossWoman (leadership seminars and coaching). Author: Sharing Our Gifts, 1987, 2d edit., 1992, Discovering Our Gifts, 1989, 2d edit., 1993, Thinking and Writing in College, 1991. Mem. APA, Assn. for the Advancement Behavior Therapy, Am. Assn. Sex Educators, Counselors and Therapists, Nat. Spkrs. Assn. Avocations: writing, skiing, dance, jogging, quilting. Home: 3725 Font Hill Dr Ellicott City MD 21042-4932

ROBISON, VICTOR JAMES, JR., retired military officer; b. Youngstown, Ohio, Apr. 29, 1920; s. Victor James Robison and Babe Albert. BS, Case Western Res. U., 1942, MA, 1948; Qualified Comms. Officer, US Naval Acad. Grad. Sch., 1943; student, Sorbonne U., Paris, 1949-50, Columbia U., 1950-51. Commd. ensign USN, 1943, advanced through grades to comdr., comms. officer USS Taylor Pacific, 1943-45, tng. officer US Naval Res. Tng. Ctr. Balt., 1952-55, asst. ops. officer USS Worcester Mediterranean and Pacific, 1955-56; US Naval attaché US Embassy, Warsaw, 1957-58; officer in charge Jt. Comm. Ctr. Navy Liaison Group, USN, Ft. Ritchie, Md., 1958-61; US Naval attaché U.S. Embassy, Brussels, 1962-66; asst. curator for Navy Dept., Office Chief of Naval Ops. USN, Washington, 1966-69, ret., 1969; English tchr. Corcoran Coll. Art, Washington, 1969—70; pvt. practice appraiser Navy artifacts and memorabilia Washington and Annapolis, Md., 1970-84. Decorated Order of Leopold II, 1966, Navy Unit Commendation, 13 Battle Stars, USN, others. Mem. VFW, Am. Legion, Fleet Res. Assn., Smithsonian Instn., Beta Theta Pi. Avocations: stamp collecting/philately, jogging, poetry, learning. Home: 423 7th St SE Washington DC 20003-2756

ROBITAILLE, LUC, professional hockey player; b. Montreal, P.Q., Can., Feb. 17, 1966; With Hull Olympiques Major Jr. Hockey League, 1983—84, L.A. Kings, 1984—94, Pitts. Penguins, 1994—95, N.Y. Rangers, 1995—97, L.A. Kings, 1997—2001, Detroit Red Wings, 2001—. Mem. Stanley Cup Championship Team, 2002. Named NHL Rookie of Yr., 1986—87; named to NHL All-Star Team, 1987, 1988, 1990—91, 1992—93; recipient Guy LaFleur Trophy, 1985—86, Can. Hockey Player of Yr. award, 1985—86, Calder Meml. Trophy. Achievements include Scored winning goal for national team of Canada at 1994 World Hockey Championship. Office: Detroit Red Wings Joe Louis Arena 600 Civic Center Detroit MI 48226

ROBLE, CAROLE MARCIA, accountant; b. Bklyn., Aug. 22, 1938; d. Carl and Edith (Brown) Dusowitz; m. Richard F. Roble, Nov. 30, 1969. MBA with distinction, N.Y. Inst. Tech., 1984. CPA, Calif., N.Y. Compt. various orgns. various orgns., 1956-66; staff acct. ZTBG CPA'S, L.A., 1966-67; sr. acct. J.H. Cohn & Co., Newark, 1967-71; prin. Carole M. Roble, CPA, South Hempstead, N.Y., 1971-90; ptnr. Roble & Libman, CPAs, Baldwin, N.Y., 1990-93; prin. Carole M. Roble, CPA, Baldwin, N.Y., 1993—. Speaker, moderator Found. for Acctg. Edn., N.Y., 1971—; lectr. acctg. various schs. including New Sch., Queens Coll., Empire State Coll., Touro Coll., N.Y. Inst. Tech., N.Y.C., Parsons Sch., 1971—. Guest various N.Y. radio and TV stas., 2 noted various newspapers. Treas. Builders Devel. Corp. of L.I., Westbury, N.Y., 1985; dir. Women Econ. Devels. of L.I., 1985-87. Recipient Sisterhood citation Nat. Orgn. Women, 1984, 85, cert. of Appreciation Women Life Underwriters, 1988, Women in Sales, 1982, 83, 84; named top Tax Practitioner Money Mag., 1987, one of Top 100 Most Influential People, Acctg. Today, 1999. Mem. AICPA (mem. small firm advocacy com. 1996—), Am. Acct. Assn. (auditing sect.), Am. Soc. Women Accts. (pres. N.Y. chpt. 1980-81), Am. Woman's Soc. CPAs, Nat. Conf. CPA Practitioners (trustee L.I. chpt. 1981-82, sec. 1982-83, treas. 1983-84, v.p. 1984-85, 1st v.p. 1985-86, pres. 1986-87, nat. nominating com. 1983-84, 88-89, nat. continuing profl. edn. chmn. 1988-90, nat. treas. 1991-94, nat. v.p. 1994-96, exec. v.p. 1996-98, first woman nat. pres. 1998-99), Calif. Soc. CPAs, N.Y. State Soc. CPAs (bd. dirs. Nassau chpt. 1981-86, 91-93, bd. dirs. profl. devel., 1982-86, sec., mem. fin. acctg. standards com. 1990-95), Kiwanis (program chmn. County Seat chpt. 1989-90, sec. 1990-91, pres. 1991-92), Baldwin C. of C. (treas. 1990-93). Avocations: golf, gourmet cuisine, water-skiing, music. Home: 626 Willis St Hempstead NY 11550-8000

ROBLEDO RINCON, EDUARDO, former federal official; b. Tuxtla Gutiérrez, Chiapas, Mexico, Apr. 29, 1947; m. Alejandra Aburto de Robledo; children: Gabino, José Eduardo, Zoé. BA in Polit. Sci. and Pub. Adminstrn., U. Nat. Autónoma Mexico. Pres. adv. coun. League Agrarian Cmtys., Chiapas, Mexico; gen. sub-dir. Nat. Peasant Tng. Ctr. Nat. Peasant Confedn.; asst. sec. for polit. tng. Partido Revolucionario Institucional; acad. sub-dir., prof. Polit. Tng. Inst.; asst. sec. Ordn. Partido Revolucionario Institucional, pres.; tech. sec. tech. adv. coun. Nat. Peasant Confedn.; spl. del., gen. asst. sec. nat. exec. com. Partido Revolucionario Institucional; gen. govt. sec. State Chiapas; fed. congressman, coord. Chiapanecan del. 53rd Legis. Congress of the Union; senator of the republic 55th-56th Leg. Congress of the Union; coord. Spl. Autonomous Commn. for Peace in Chiapas; constnl. gov. State of Chiapas, 1994—95; Mexican amb. to Argentina, 1996—99; sec. Agrarian Reform, 1999—2000; now official Partido Revolutionario Institucional. Office: Partido Rev Inst Insurgentes Norte No 59 Edif 2 Col Buenavista 06359 Mexico

ROBLES, DARLINE P. school system administrator; AA in History, East L.A. Coll., 1968; B in History, Calif. State U., L.A., 1972; MEd, Claremont Grad. Sch., 1976; D in Edn. Policy and Adminstrn., U. So. Calif. Cert. tchr., adminstr. Tchr. Montebello Intermediate Sch., Calif., 1973—79; dir. bilingual program Montebellow Unified Sch. Dist., Calif., 1979—81; prin. Washington Elem., Montebello, Calif., 1981—85, Montebello Intermediate, Montebello, Calif., 1985—88; asst. supt. Montebello Unified Sch. Dist., Montebello, Calif., 1988—91, acting supt., 1991—92, supt., 1992—95, Salt Lake City Sch. Dist., 1995—2002; county supt. schs. L.A. County Office of Edn., 2002—. Office: LA County Office of Edn 9300 Imperial Hwy Rm EC109 Downey CA 90242-2890

ROBLES, ELIODORO GONZALES, consulting company executive, educator; b. Paniqui, Tarlac, The Philippines, July 3, 1923; s. Mariano Abraham and Lucia (Gonzales) R.; m. Rosario Palaganas Lavitoria, Oct. 30, 1964; children: Michael, Elmer, Eliodoro Jr., Marilou, Jonathan, Jay. BS in Polit. Sci., Far Eastern U., 1953; MA in Internat. Rels., Cornell U., 1954; MA in Polit. Economy, Harvard U., 1955, PhD in Polit. Economy, 1959. Cert. tchr., Calif.; cert. C.C. instr., Calif. C.C.; cert. C.C. supr., Calif. C.C. Instr. Far Eastern U., Manila, 1952-53; tech. cons., staff asst. Embassy of the Rep. of Indonesia in the Philippines, 1950-53; spl. asst. on fgn. econ. policies Program Implementation Office of the Pres. of the Philippines, 1962-64; prof. econs. and polit. sci., dean Grad. Sch. Far Eastern U., Manila, 1959-64; econ. officer, dep. dir. for econ., cultural, social affairs S.E. Asia Treaty Orgn. (SEATO), Bangkok, 1964-74; project dir. San Francisco Unified Sch. Dist., 1975-79; sr. assoc. Devel. Assocs., Inc., Walnut Creek, Calif., 1979—; evaluation specialist including polit. economist USAID, various locations, Calif., 1984-85, ednl. adminstrn. specialist Manila and Islamabad, 1987, tng. specialist, Asia Narcotics Edn. Program, 1988-89, polit. economist, 1992—; project dir. tng. and tech. assistance for Native Am. tribes, 1990—2002. Presenter in field. Author: Economic Analysis, 1966, The Philippines in the Nineteenth Century, 1969. Lt. col. Philippine Army, 1941-46; 1st lt. inf. U.S. Army, 1946-49. Fulbright Assn. scholar, 1954; Telluride fellow Cornell U., 1954, Fletcher fellow Harvard U., 1954-55, Newberry fellow Newberry Libr., 1957-58. Mem. Fulbright Assn., Filipino Am. Tchrs. Assn., Far Eastern U. Alumni Assn. (bd. dirs., adviser 1991—), Harvard Club San Francisco. Democrat. Methodist. Avocations: general gardening, orchid growing, stamp and coin collecting. Home: 1335 Greenway Dr Richmond CA 94803-1204 Personal E-mail: eligrobles@yahoo.com.

ROBLES, JOSUE, JR., insurance company executive; b. Rio Piedras, Puerto Rico, Jan. 24, 1946; B in Acctg., Kent State U, 1972; M in Bus. Adminstrn., Ind. State U. CFO, sr. v.p., treas. USAA, San Antonio, 1994—. Mem. Def. Base Closure and Realignment Commn., 1995. Joined U.S. Army, 1966, ret., maj. gen. U.S. Army, 1994. Office: USAA 9800 Fredericksburg Rd San Antonio TX 78288-0002

ROBLES-CERECERES, OSCAR FERNANDO, language educator, researcher, writer; arrived in U.S., 1991; s. Oscar Robles and Piedad Cereceres. BA in Spanish, Universidad Autonoma De Chihuahua, Mex., 1979—91; MA in Spanish, N. Mex. State U., Las Cruces NM, 1991—93; PhD in Spanish, U. Ariz., Tucson, 1993—2002. Libr. Escuela Secundaria Bilingue Isaac Newton, Chihuahua, Mexico, 1985—86; full time tchr. Instituto Tecnologico Y De Estudios Superiores De Monterrey, Chihuahua, Mexico, 1986—90; grad. asst. tchr. N. Mex State U., Las Cruces, N.Mex., 1991—93; evaluator of spanish proficiency U. Ariz., Tucson, 1997—98, grad. assoc. tchg., 1993—98; visitant asst. prof. Angelo State U., San Angelo, Tex., 2001—04; lectr. Calif. State U., Fresno, Calif., 1998—2001. Vis. asst. prof. Dickinson Coll., Carlisle, Pa., 2001—03. Author: (poems) Sangre De Circe, (short stories) Historias De Familia; editor: (literary review) AZAR. Recipient Ignacio R. M. Galbis, Revista "El Cid" / The Citadel, 1998—99, Letras de Oro (finalist), U. Miami, 1994; grantee Doctoral Dissertation, U. Ariz., 1997—98. Mem.: Am. Assn. Teachers Spanish And Portuguese, Sociedad Nacional Hispanica Sigma Delta Pi, Modern Language Assn.

ROBLES-ROMAN, CAROL A. municipal official; b. Bronx, N.Y., 1962; m. Nelson Roman; 1 child, Adriana Roman. BA, Fordham U.; JD, NYU. Bar: N.Y. 1990. Sr. v.p., gen. counsel P.R. Indsl. Devel. Co.; asst. atty. gen. civil rights bur. N.Y. State Dept. of Law; chief staff, counsel to dep. chief adminstrv. judge Hon. Barry Cozier N.Y. State Unified Ct. Sys., spl. insp. gen. bias matters, dir. pub. affairs, spl. counsel to chief adminstrv. judge Hon. Jonathan Lippman; dep. mayor legal affairs, counsel to Mayor Mike Bloomberg City of New York. Counsel to com. promote pub. trust and confidence Unified Ct. Sys. Bd. dirs. N.Y. State Jud. Com. Women and Cts. Named one of N.Y.'s 50 Outstanding Latinas, El Diario/La Prensa. Mem.: NYU Black, Latino, and Asian Pacific Alumni Assn. (pres. 1999—2000). Office: City Hall New York NY 10007

ROBLING, CLAIRE A. state legislator; b. Oct. 22, 1956; m. Tony Robling; 2 children. Student, Coll. St. Catherine. Mem. dist. 35 Minn. Senate, St. Paul, 1996—. Office: 100 Constitution Ave Saint Paul MN 55155-1232 Home: 1169 Butterfly Ln Jordan MN 55352-9476

ROBOCK, ALAN, meteorology educator; b. Boston, Sept. 7, 1949; s. Stefan Hyman Robock and Shirley Ruth (Bernstein) Fox; m. Sherri Lynne Carpini West, May 12, 1990; children: Brian, Daniel. BA, U. Wis., 1970; SM, MIT, 1974, PhD, 1977. Vol. Peace Corps, The Philippines, 1970-72; rsch. scientist Lawrence Livermore (Calif.) Lab., 1973; asst. prof. dept. meteorology U. Md., College Park, 1977-82, assoc. prof., 1982-96, prof., 1996-97; prof. dept. environ. scis. Rutgers U., New Brunswick, NJ, 1998—2003, prof. II, 2003—. Dir. Ctr. Environ. Prediction Rutgers U., 2001-; snow forecaster Montgomery County (Md.) Pub. Schs., 1980-81; state climatologist State of Md., 1991-97; vis. rsch. scientist Princeton U., NOAA/Geophys. Fluid Dynamics Lab., 1994-95. Editor Jour. Climate and Applied Meteorology, 1985-87, Jour. Geophys. Research-Atmospheres, 2000—; assoc. editor Revs. Geophysics, 1994-2000, Jour. Geophys. Rsch.-Atmospheres, 1998-2000; contbr. articles to profl. publs., chpts. to books. Fellow Am. Meteorol. Soc.; mem. AAAS (Congressional sci. fellow 1986-87), Am. Geophys. Union. Avocations: tennis, Bob Dylan music, travel, politics. Office: Rutgers U Dept Environ Scis 14 College Farm Rd New Brunswick NJ 08901-8551 E-mail: robock@envsci.rutgers.edu.

ROBOL, RICHARD THOMAS, lawyer; b. Norfolk, Va., Feb. 8, 1952; s. Harry James and Lucy Henley (Johnson) R. BA, U. Va., 1974; JD, Harvard U., 1978. Bar: Va. 1979, Ohio 1996, U.S. Dist. Ct. (ea. dist.) Va. 1979, U.S. Ct. Appeals (4th cir.) 1979, U.S. Dist. Ct. (we. dist.) Va. 1981, U.S. Supreme Ct. 1982, D.C. 1991, U.S. Ct. Appeals (4th, 6th and 9th cirs.) 1995. Law clk. to presiding justice U.S. Dist. Ct. (ea. dist.) Va., 1978-79; ptnr. Seawell, Dalton, Hughes & Timms, Norfolk, 1979-87, Hunton and Williams, Norfolk, 1987-92; exec. v.p., gen. counsel Columbus Am. Discovery Group, Inc., 1992—. Adj. prof. U. Dayton Law Sch.; asst. prof. mil. sci. Capital U.; pro bono counsel Nat. Commn. for Prevention Child Abuse, Norfolk, 1983, Tidewater Profl. Assn. on Child Abuse, 1983, Parents United Va., 1981-82, Sexual Abuse Help Line, 1983-86; mem. Boyd-Graves Conf. on Civil Procedure in Va., 1981-87. Contbr. articles to law revs.; contbg. editor: International Law for General Practitioners, 1981. Bd. dirs. Va. Opera Assn. Guild, Norfolk, 1983-87, Tidewater br. NCCJ, 1991-92; deacon Ctrl. Bapt. Ch., Norfolk, 1980-83. Maj. USAR, 1992—. Fulbright scholar, 1974. Mem. Va. State Bar Assn. (bd. dirs. internat. law sect. 1984-87, chmn. 1982-83), Va. Young Lawyers Assn. (cir. rep. 1984-88), Va. Assn. Def. Attys., Maritime Law Assn., Norfolk-Portsmouth Bar assn. (chmn. speakers bur. 1987-88), Assn. Def. Trial Attys. (chmn. Va. 1987), Def. Rsch. Inst., 1982-88. Avocations: camping, rowing, scuba diving. Home: 60 Kenyon Brook Dr Worthington OH 43085-3629 Office: Robol and Winkler 555 City Park Ave Columbus OH 43215 Office Phone: 314-559-3839. Business E-Mail: rrobol@columbuscounsel.com.

ROBOLD, ALICE ILENE, retired mathematician, educator; b. Delaware County, Ind., Feb. 7, 1928; d. Earl G. and Margaret Rebecca (Summers) Hensley; m. Virgil G. Robold, Aug. 21, 1955; 1 son, Edward Lynn. BS, Ball State U., 1955, MA, 1960, EdD, 1965. Substitute elem. tchr. Am. Elem. Sch., Augsburg, Germany, 1955-56; instr. Ball State U., Muncie, Ind., 1960-61, tchg. fellow, 1961-64, asst. prof. math. scis., 1964-69, assoc. prof., 1969-76, prof., 1976 98; ret., 1998. Mem. Nat. Coun. Tchrs. Math., Ind. Coun. Tchrs. Math. Mem. Ch. of God.

ROBRENO, EDUARDO C. federal judge; b. 1945; BA, Westfield State Coll., 1967; MA, U. Mass., 1969; JD, Rutgers U., 1978. With antitrust divsn. U.S. Dept Justice, Phila., 1978-81; ptnr. Meltzer & Schiffrin, Phila., 1981-86, Fox, Rothschild, O'Brien & Frankel, Phila., 1987-92; judge U.S. Dist. Ct. for Ea. Dist. Pa., Phila., 1992—. Mem. Jud. Conf. Com. on Bankruptcy Rules. Fellow Am. Law Inst. Office: US Courthouse Rm 3810 Philadelphia PA 19106

ROBSON, DONALD, physics educator; b. Leeds, Eng., Mar. 19, 1937; came to U.S., 1963; s. Albert and Rose Hannah (Parbutt) R.; m. Joy Olivia Burkitt Findlay, Aug. 1960 (div. May 1971); children: Donald Peter, David Ian, Karen Joy; m. Martha Breitenlohner, Aug. 26, 1971 (div. Sept. 1999); m. Kimberly G. Kitchen, Dec. 18, 1999; 1 child, Nadirah Berge. BSc, U. Melbourne, Australia, 1959, MSc, 1961, PhD, 1963. Rsch. assoc. Fla. State U., Tallahassee, 1963-64, asst. prof. physics, 1964-65, assoc. prof., 1965-67, prof., 1967—, chmn. dept. physics, 1985-91, Disting. prof., 1990—2003, emeritus prof., 2003—. Editor: (with J.D. Fox) Isobaric Spin in Nuclear Physics, 1966, Nuclear Analogue States, 1976; assoc. editor Nuclear Physics A., 1972-96; contbr. more than 100 articles to profl. jours. Chmn. bd. trustees Southeastern Univ. Rsch. Assn., 1996-98. Fulbright scholar, 1963-64; A.P. Sloan fellow, 1966-67; Alexander Von Humboldt sr. scientist, 1976-77. Fellow Am. Phys. Soc. (co-recipient Tom W. Bonner prize 1972). Avocations: chess, golf, running. Office: Fla State U Dept Physics Tallahassee FL 32306 Business E-Mail: robson@csit.fsu.edu.

ROBSON, GEORGE T., SR., computer company executive; b. 1947; BS Wharton Sch. of Bus., U. Pa., 1969; MS, SUNY, 1969. Various mgmt. positions IBM, 1969-82; mgmt. Burroughs Corp., 1982-86; v.p., corp. contr. Unisys Corp., Blue Bell, Pa., 1986—89, sr. v.p. CFO, 1990—95; sr vpres, CFO H & R Block Corp, 1996—97; exec vpres, CFO Dendrite Int, 1997—2001. Office: Dendrite Internat Inc 1200 Mt Kemble Ave Morristown NJ 07960

ROBSON, GLENN R. engineering and design company executive; BS in Econs., U. Pa.; MBA, Harvard U. Various positions to mng. dir. investment banking divsn. Morgan Stanley, 1990—2002; sr. v.p., CFO Aecom Tech., LA, 2002—. Office: Aecom Tech 555 S Flower St Los Angeles CA 90071

ROBSON, JUDITH BIROS, state legislator; b. Cleve., Nov. 21, 1939; d. George John and Mary Grace (Millen) Biros; m. Arthur Robson, Sept. 2, 1961; children: Marybeth, Marc, Matthew. BSN, St. John Coll., Cleve., 1961; MS, U. Wis., 1976. RN. Staff nurse Beloit (Wis.) Hosp., 1967-73; nurse practitioner Dr. Ken Gold, Beloit, 1976-78; instr. Blackhawk Tech. Coll., Jonesville, Wis., 1978-87; mem. Wis. Assembly, 1987-98; mem Wis. Senate from 15th dist., Madison, 1998—. Mem. bd. Bedcore, Beloit, 1990, YWCA, Beloit, 1992; sec. Majority Party Caucus, 1990—. Recipient Clean 16 award Environ. Decade. Avocations: biking, skiing, gardening, photography. Office: State Legislature State Capital PO Box 7882 Madison WI 53707-7882

ROBSON, MARTIN CECIL, surgery educator, plastic surgeon; b. Lancaster, Ohio, Mar. 8, 1939; children: Karen Iredell, Douglas Spears, Martin Cecil Robson III. Student, Northwestern U., 1957—59; BA, Johns Hopkins U., 1961, MD, 1964. Diplomate Am. Bd. Surgery, Am. Bd. Plastic Surgery . Intern U. Chgo. Hosps. and Clinics, 1964—65; resident in surgery Balt. City Hosp., 1965—67, Brooke Gen. Hosp., Ft. Sam Houston, Tex., 1967—69; resident in plastic surgery Yale-New Haven Hosp., 1971—73; instr. dept. surgery Yale U. Sch. Medicine, New Haven, 1973—74, asst. prof. plastic surgery, 1973—74, assoc. prof., 1974; assoc. prof., chief plastic surgery U. Chgo., 1974—77, prof. and chief plastic surgery, 1977—83; dir. U. Chgo. Burn Ctr., 1976—83; prof., chmn. divsn. plastic and reconstructive surgery Wayne State U., Detroit, 1983—88; dir. Detroit Med. Ctr. Burn Ctr., 1983—88; Truman Blocker Disting. prof., chief divsn. plastic surgery U. Tex. Med. Br., 1988—93; dir. surg. svcs. Shriners' Burn Inst., Galveston, Tex., 1988—93; prof. surgery U. South Fla., Tampa, 1993—2001, prof. surgery emeritus, 2001—, chair divsn. surgery rsch., 1993—97; chmn. surg. svc. Bay Pines (Fla.) VA Med. Ctr., 1993—97. Chmn., pres. Am. Bd. Plastic Surgery, 1996—97. Mem. editl. bd.: Jour. Trauma. Maj. M.C. U.S. Army, 1967—71, col. M.C. USAR, 1991—97. Recipient Lifetime Achievement award, Assn. Advanced Wound Care, 2003. Fellow: ACS, Royal Coll. Surgeons of Eng. (hon.), Royal Australasian Coll. Surgeons (hon.); mem.: Am. Bd. Med. Specialties, Am. Assn. Plastic Surgery, Wound Healing Soc. (pres. 1995—96, Lifetime Sci. Achievement award 1998), Am. Surg. Assn., Am. Burn Assn. (pres. 1985—86, Disting. Svc. award), Plastic Surgery Rsch. Coun. (chmn. 1983—84), Alpha Omega Alpha, Phi Delta Theta, Nu Sigma Nu. E-mail: mcrobson@earthlink.net.

ROBSON, ROY RAYMOND, historian, educator; b. Erie, Pa., June 19, 1963; s. Joe Brooks and Anita Evanoff Robson; m. Kim Elizabeth Pawlak, July 19, 1987. BA, Allegheny Coll., Meadville, Pa., 1985; MA, U. Pitts., 1987; PhD, Boston Coll., 1992. Asst. prof. history Fayetteville (NC) State U., 1994—97; assoc. prof. history U. Sci., Phila., 1997—. Adj. asst. prof. Boston Coll., Newton, Mass., 1992—94. Author: Solovki: The Story of Russia Told Through Its Most Remarkable Islands, 2004, Old Believers in Modern Russia, 1995; contbr. Seeking God, 1993, The Human Tradition in Modern Russia, 2000, Life Lines: Perspectives on Russian and European Culture, Society, and Politics, 2001; author: (exhibition catalog) Old Believers in Erie, Pennsylvania: Exhibition Catalog, 1998. Parish coun. Our Lady Joy of All Who Sorrow Ch., Phila., 2003—. Recipient Sci. and Religion Course prize, John Templeton Found., 1999; fellow, USA Fulbright Com., 1990, Russian Rsch. Ctr. fellow, Harvard U., 1992—95, Postdoc. fellow, Am. Coun. Learned Socs./Social Scis. Rsch. Coun., 1993—95, Nat. Endowment for the Humanities, 1997; grantee, Internat. Rsch. and Exch. Bd., 1997, Pa. Humanities Coun., 1998. Mem.: Am. Hist. Assn., Am. Assn. Advancement Slavic Studies. Avocation: rowing. Office: University Sci Phila 600 S 43d Philadelphia PA 19104 E-mail: r.robson@usip.edu.

ROBY, CHERYL J. deputy assistant secretary; b. Fall River, Mass. BS in math. cum laude, Bridgewater State Coll. Various positions Naval Tech. Intelligence Ctr., Suitland, Md., 1975-88, Def. Intelligence Agy., 1988-90; with Office of asst. sec. of def., 1991-92; asst. dep. dir. Intelligence Program Evaluation, 1992-93; dir. programs and evaluations, 1993-96; acting prin. dir.

for intelligence Office of Dep. Asst. Sec. of Def., 1996-97, acting dep. asst. sec. of def., 1997-98, dep. asst. sec. of def., 1998—. Office: Dep Asst Sec of Def Programs & Evaluation 6000 Defense Pentagon Washington DC 20301-6000

ROBY, DANIEL ARTHUR, lawyer; b. Anderson, Ind., Aug. 16, 1941; s. Virgil A. and Frances E. R. A.B. with honors, Ind. U., 1963, J.D., 1966. Bar: Ind. 1966, U.S. Dist. Ct. (no. dist.) Ind. 1967, U.S. Dist. Ct. (so. dist.) Ind. 1966, U.S. Ct. Appeals (7th cir.) 1968. Practice law, Ft. Wayne, Ind.; faculty lectr. Ind. U.; mem. Ind. Jud. Nominating Com., 1997-99; mem. Allen County Jud. Nominating Commn., 1983-89. Past pres. Allen County (Ind.) Heart Assn., Northeastern Ind. Heart Assn.; chmn. bd. Ind. affiliate Am. Heart Assn.; past pres. bd. mgrs. Faith Bapt. Ch. Mem. Ind. State Bar Assn., Allen County Bar Assn. (bd. dirs. 1983), Assn. Trial Lawyers Am., Ind. Trial Lawyers Assn. (bd. dirs. 1980—, pres. 1993, named Lawyer of Yr. 1986, Lifetime Achievement award 2004), Am. Arbitration Assn. (bd. arbitrators). Contbr. articles to legal jours. Office: 200 E Main St Ste 520 Fort Wayne IN 46802-1998 Office Phone: 260-423-3366. Personal E-mail: droby@robyhood.com.

ROBY, JASPER, bishop; Sr. bishop, exec. head Apostolic Overcoming Holy Ch. of God, Inc., Birmingham, Ala. Office: Apostolic Overcoming Church of God PO Box 2364 Birmingham AL 35201-2364

ROBY, JOE LINDELL, investment banker; b. Metropolis, Ill., May 22, 1939; s. Gerald C. and Inez (DeLaine) R.; m. Elizabeth Shute, June 17, 1967 (dec. Oct. 1980); m. Hilppa Pirila, June 15, 1984 BA cum laude, Vanderbilt U., 1961; MBA with distinction, Harvard U., 1967. Asst. v.p. Kidder, Peabody & Co., N.Y.C., 1967-72; v.p. Donaldson, Lufkin & Jenrette, N.Y.C., 1972-75, sr. v.p., 1976-83, mng. dir. investment banking, 1984-89, chair. banking grp., 1989-95, COO, 1995-99, pres., 1996-99; CEO, pres. Donaldson, Lufkin & Jenrette (merged with Credit Suisse First Boston in 2000), N.Y.C., 1999-2000; chmn. Credit Suisse First Boston, N.Y.C., 2000—01, chmn. emeritus and sr. advisor, 2002. Bd. dirs. Sybron, Inc., Muskland Group, Inc. Served to lt. USN, 1961-65 Mem. Down Town Assn., Bond Club of N.Y. Clubs: Down Town Assn. (N.Y.C.).

ROBY, MARY LORRAINE, special education educator; b. Balt., Nov. 17, 1952; d. Robert Edelen and Lorraine Teresa Roby. BA in Edn., Loyola Coll., Balt., 1974, MEd, 1977; postgrad., NYU, 2003—. Spl. edn. educator St. Francis Sch. for Spl. Edn., Balt., 1975—77, Balt. County Pub. Schs., Balt., 1977—. Adj. prof. spl. edn. Loyola Coll., Balt., 2000—; dir., choreographer Balt. Area Schs., Essex C.C., Balt. area cmty. theaters, 1977—; ednl. rsch. cons. Johns Hopkins U., Balt., 2001—03; mem. tchg. staff Carver Ctr. for Arts and Tech. magnet sch., Balt., 1993—97. Recipient Excellence in Edn. award, Balt. (Md.) C. of C. Avocations: teaching dance, choreography, musical theater. Office: Loyola Coll 4501 N Charles St Baltimore MD 21210-2699

ROBY, PAMELA ANN, sociologist, educator; b. Milw., Nov. 17, 1942; d. Clark Dearborn and Marianna (Gillman) Roby; m. James Peter Mulherin, July 15, 1977 (div. 1987). BA, U. Denver, 1963; MA, Syracuse U., 1966; PhD, NYU, 1971. Instr. ednl. sociology NYU, N.Y.C., 1966; asst. prof. George Washington U., Washington, 1970-71; asst. prof. sociology and social welfare Brandeis U., Waltham, Mass., 1971-73; assoc. prof. U. Calif., Santa Cruz, 1973-77, prof. sociology and women's studies, 1977—, chair cmty. studies bd., 1974-76, 79, dir. sociology doctoral program, 1988-91, chair sociology dept., 1998-2001. Mem. social sci. rsch. rev. com. NIMH, Washington, 1976—80; vice chair Nat. Commn. Working Women, Washington, 1977—80; cons. James Irvine Found., San Francisco, 1986; mem. sociology program rev. com. Northeastern U., Boston, 1990; mem. anthropology, linguistics and sociology panel NSF, Washington, 1993; assessor Social Scis. and Humanities Rsch. Coun. Can., Toronto, 1993. Co-author: The Future of Inequality, 1970; editor: Child Care: Who Cares? Foreign and Domestic Infant and Early Childhood Development Policies, 1973—75, The Poverty Establishment, 1974; author: Women in the Workplace, 1981; adv. editor: Social Quar., 1990—93, Gender and Society, 1986—89. Vis. scholar, Indian Coun. Social Sci. Rsch., 1979, U. Wash., Seattle, 1991—92; Andrew W. Mellon Sr. scholar, Wellesley Coll., 1978—79. Mem.: Alpha Kappa Delta, Re-Evaluation Counseling (coll. and univ. faculty reference person 1980—), Eastern Sociol. Assn. (exec. coun. mem.-at-large 1973—74), Pacific Sociol. Assn. (v.p. 1996—97), Internat. Sociol. Assn. (rsch. coun. mem.-at-large 1978—82), Am. Sociol. Assn. (chair sect. sex and gender 1974—78, exec. coun. mem.-at-large 1975—78), Sociologists Women in Soc., Soc. Study Social Problems (pres. 1996—97, 1978—80), Phi Beta Kappa. Avocations: camping, hiking, painting, swimming, pen and ink drawing. Office: U Calif Dept Sociology C8 Santa Cruz CA 95064

ROBY, TOM, mathematician, educator; b. Chgo., Aug. 30, 1963; s. Thomas W. and Anne Roby; m. Marjorie Nugent, Jan. 27, 1998; 1 child, Vielle A. BA, Swarthmore Coll., 1985; PhD, MIT, 1991. Rschr. U. Tokyo, 1991—93; vis. asst. prof. Reed Coll., Portland, Oreg., 1993—95; rsch. assoc. U. Wis., Madison, 1995—97; asst. and assoc. prof. Calif. State U., Hayward, 1997—. Author, math cons. Harcourt Sch. Pubs., Orlando, Fla., 1999—; PI and co-dir. Alameda County Collaborative for Learning and Instrn. in Math., Hayward, 2000—. Mathlets editor: Jour. Online Math. and Its Applications, 2000—02; contbr. articles to profl. jours. Grantee Math. Profl. Devel. Inst., U. Calif. Office of the Pres., 2000—; Post-doctoral rsch. fellow, Japan Soc. for the Promotion Sci., 1991—93. Avocations: ethnic dance, racquetball, ancient japanese poetry, linguistics, music. Office: Cal State Hayward Dept Math 25800 Carlos Bee Blvd Hayward CA 94542 E-mail: metis@seki.mcs.csuhayward.edu.

ROBY, WARREN B. humanities educator; b. Wichita, Kans. s. Floyd E. Roby and Betty J. Shanklin; m. Eiko Takamatsu, Jan. 16, 1982; children: Eugene, Edwin, Ethan, Eileen. BA, Wichita State U., 1976; MA, U. Kans., 1986, PhD, 1991. Assoc. prof. modern langs. Wash. State U., Pullman, 1991—2000; prof. modern langs., chmn. John Brown U., Siloam Springs, Ark., 2000—. Vis. prof. Dokkyo U., Soka, Japan, 1998—99. Avocation: genealogy. Office: John Brown U 2000 W University St Siloam Springs AR 72761

ROCCA, CHRISTINA B. federal agency administrator; married; 2 children. BA in History, King's Coll., London, 1980. Intelligence officer CIA, 1982—97; fgn. affairs advisor Senate Sam Brownback; asst. sec. of state South Asian affairs U.S. Dept. of State, Washington, 2001—. Office: US Dept of State South Asian Affairs 2201 C St NW Washington DC 20520-6243

ROCCA, SUE, state legislator; b. May 12, 1949; AS, Ctrl. Mich. Coll. Commr. Macomb County, Mich.; rep. Mich. Dist. 30, 1995-2000. Vice chmn. health policy com. Mich. Ho. Reps., joint com. on adminstrv. rules & regulatory affairs. Office: Office Bd Commrs Macomb County Court Bldg 2nd Fl 40 Gratiot Ct Mount Clemens MI 48043-5719 Address: Mich State Capitol PO Box 30014 Lansing MI 48909-7514

ROCCO, JAMIE ALEXANDER, choreographer, theater director, actor; b. Astoria, NY, Sept. 8, 1956; s. Alexander F. and Jacqueline Rocco; life ptnr. Albert Evans. Author: (musical) Streakin'!; dir.: (musical) Smokey Joe's Cafe (CT. Critics Circle Award, 2002), Guys and Dolls (CT. Critics Circle Award, 2000), (musical - stage and television) Born Of A Dream. Recipient Mary Jane Teall Award, Wichita Theatre Awards, 1999, Outstanding Young Men In Am., Outstanding Young Men In Am. Com., 1997. Mem.: ASCAP, Actors Equity Assoc., Soc. of Stage Directors and Choreographers. Achievements include creating musical staging for Madison Square Garden's prodn. of The Wizard of Oz starring Roseanne, Eartha Kitt and Mickey Rooney.

ROCCO, NIKKI, film company executive; m. Joseph Rocco. Sales dept. Universal Pictures, 1967, asst. to gen. sales mgr., 1981—84, v.p., distbn., 1981—84, 1984—90, sr. v.p., distbn. and mktg., 1990—95, exec. v.p., distbn., 1995—96, pres., distbn., 1996—. Office: Universal Pictures 100 Universal City Plaza Universal City CA 91608*

ROCEK, JAN, chemist, educator; b. Prague, Czech Republic, Mar. 24, 1924; came to U.S., 1960, naturalized, 1966; s. Hugo and Frida (Loebl) Robitschek; m. Eva Trojan, June 26, 1947; children: Martin, Thomas. MS, Tech. U., Prague, 1949, PhD, 1953. Scientist Czechoslovak Acad. Sci., Prague, 1953-57, sr. scientist, 1957-60; vis. scientist U. Coll., London, 1958; research fellow Harvard U., 1960-62; asso. prof., then prof. Cath. U. Am., 1962-66; prof. chemistry U. Ill., Chgo., 1966-95, acting head dept., 1980-81, head dept., 1981-93, vice chancellor rsch., dean grad. coll., 1993-95, acting dean Grad. Coll., 1969-70, dean Grad. Coll., 1970-79, asso. mem. Ctr. for Advanced Studies, 1968-69; ret., 1995. Vis. scholar Stanford U., 1979-80, Cambridge U., 1980 Contbr. articles to profl. jours. Mem. Am. Chem. Soc., AAAS, Czechoslovak Soc. Arts and Scis. in Am., AAUP, Sigma Xi (pres. chpt. 1976-77, 85-86), Phi Kappa Phi. Home: 2636 Laurel Ln Wilmette IL 60091-2202 Business E-Mail: rocek@uic.edu.

ROCH, LEWIS MARSHALL, II, ophthalmic surgeon, medical entrepreneur; b. Mineola, Tex., Aug. 13, 1934; s. Lewis Marshall and Gladys Irene (Hoover) R.; m. Lois Afton Price; children: Lewis Marshall Roch III, Katrina Ann Seitz. BA, U. Tex., Austin, 1955; MD, U. Tex. Southwestern, 1959. Diplomate Am. Bd. Ophthalmology. Intern USPHS Hosp., Boston, 1959-60, resident in ophthalmology New Orleans, 1960-63, dep. chief ophthalmology, 1963-64, chief opthalmology Seattle, Wash., 1964-67; attending ophthalmic surgeon Ball Meml. Hosp., Muncie, Ind., 1967—, chmn. dept. surgery, chmn. clin. staff, 1975, chmn. exec. com., 1980-93; founder, CEO, med. dir. The Eye Ctr. Group, Muncie, 1985—, 1985—, The Surgi Ctr. Group, Muncie, 1985—. Ho. of dels. Ind. State Med. Assn., 1975-87; exec. com. Ind. Acad. Ophthalmology, 1978-82; bd. dirs. Cardinal Health Ptnrs.; clin. asst. prof. Ind. U. Sch. Medicine, 1978—. Chmn. Muncie-Delaware Devel., 2000-2003; active Ball State U. Bus. Forecasting Roundtable, 2000—; exec. v.p. Muncie-Delaware Econ. Devel., 2000-2002; trustee Minnetrista Cultural Ctr., 2002—; bd. dirs. United Way Delaware County, 2003—. Fellow ACS, Am. Acad. Ophthalmology; mem. AMA, Ind. State Med. Assn., Muncie Acad. Medicine (pres. 1981-82), Am. Soc. Cataract and Refractive Surgeons, Am. Coll. Physicians Execs., Muncie-Delaware C. of C. (bd. dirs. 1999-2003). Republican. Achievements include first to work in outpatient ambulatory surgery; innovation in intraocular lens implantation in cataract surgery; integration of physician's practices with hospital health care delivery systems. Home: 2006 E Robinwood Dr Muncie IN 47304-2857 Office: The Eye Ctr Group LLC 200 N Tillotson Ave Muncie IN 47304-3988 Office Phone: 765-289-7073. E-mail: lmroch@comcast.net.

ROCHA, CATHERINE TOMASA, municipal official; BA, U. Mo., 1977, MA, 1979. Cert. mcpl. clk. U. Mo., 1991. Student svc. coord., academic advisor U. Mo., Kansas City, 1979-84; dir. records records dept. Jackson County Courthouse, Kansas City, 1984-87; city clk. Office of the City Clk. City of Kansas City, 1988—. Mem. human rels. adv. commn., 1982-84; mem. bd. zoning commn., 1978-79. Author: (oral history) Black Baseball-The Kansas City Monarch Experience, 1978; editor: newsletter CCFOA, 1991-95. Bd. dirs. Trinity Luth. Hosp. Found., 1996, Women's Found. Gtr. Kansas City; chmn. Westside Fountain Com., 1995-97; former trustee, chmn. auction benefit Westport Alien Ctr.; bd. dirs. Trinity Hosp., 1998-99. Harvard U. fellow, 1990; named 25 Most Influential Hispanic Leaders in Kansas City Dos Mundos newspaper, 1994. Mem. Internat. Inst. Mcpl. Clks. (chmn. big cities com. 1991-94, Harvard grant allocation com. 1994-95, profl. status com. 1995-96), Mexican-Am. Women's Nat. Assn., Friends of Art Coun. (mem. exec. bd.), Southwest Blvd. Merchants Assn. (bd. dirs.), Westside Bus. Assn. (pres. 1996-97). Home: 4545 Wornall Rd Kansas City MO 64111-3270 Office: City of Kansas City Mo Office of the City Clk City Hall 25th Fl 414 E 12th St Kansas City MO 64106-2702

ROCHA, GUY LOUIS, archivist, historian; b. Long Beach, Calif., Sept. 23, 1951; s. Ernest Louis and Charlotte (Sobus) R. BA in Social Studies and Edn., Syracuse U., 1973; MA in Am. Studies, San Diego State U., 1975; postgrad., U. Nev., 1975—. Cert. archivist Am. Acad. Cert. Archivists. Tchr. Washoe County Sch. Dist., Reno, Nev., 1975-76; history instr. Western Nev. C.C., Carson City, 1976; curator manuscripts Nev. Hist. Soc., Reno, 1976-81, interim asst. dir., 1980, interim dir., 1980-81; state adminstr. archives and records Nev. State Libr. and Archives, Carson City, 1981—. Hist. cons. Janus Assocs., Tempe, Ariz., 1980, Rainshadow Assocs., Carson City, 1983—. Co-author: The Ignoble Conspiracy: Radicalism on Trial in Nevada, 1986, The Earp's Last Frontier: Wyatt and Virgil Earp in Nevada 1902-1905, 1988; contbr. to books and govt. study; host weekly radio talk show Sta. KPTL, Carson City, 1988-2000, KUNR/NPR, Reno, 2001-; hist. cons. to documentary Las Vegas, A&E Network, 1996, documentary Truckee and Carson Rivers, PBS Network, 1997, documentary Hoover Dam, PBS Network, 1999, documentary Lake Tahoe, PBS, Network, 2001; dir. documentary Comstock Miners' Unions, Nev. AFL-CIO, 2003. Mem. Washoe Heritage Coun., Reno, 1983-85; editl. bd. Nev. Hist. Soc., Reno, 1983—; mem. Washoe County Dem. Ctrl. Com., Reno, 1984-87; ex-officio mem. Nev. Commn. Bicentennial U.S. Constn., 1986-91. Mem. Conf. Intermountain Archivists (coun. mem. 1979-87, v.p. 1984-85, pres. 1985-86), No. Nev. Pub. Adminstrs. Group (pres. 1986-87), S.W. Labor Studies Assn., State Hist. Records Adv. Bd. (dep. coord. 1984-86, coord. 1986—), Westerners Internat. Nev. Corral (dep. sheriff 1980-81, sheriff 1984-85, mem. state coords. steering com. 1985-87, vice chmn. 1986-87), Soc. Am. Archivists, Western History Assn., Nat. Assn. Govt. Archives and Records Adminstrs., Orgn. Am. Historians. Home: 1824 Pyrenees St Carson City NV 89703-2331 Office: Nev State Libr & Archives 100 N Stewart St Carson City NV 89701-4285

ROCHA, V. MANUEL, former diplomat, international trade consultant; Grad. cum laude, Yale U., 1973; MPA, Harvard U., 1976; M. Internat. Relations, Georgetown U., 1978. Desk officer Dept. State, Honduras, 1981-83, polit. officer U.S. Embassy Santo Domingo, Dominican Republic, 1983, watch officer Ops. Ctr., consul for polit. and econ. affairs, politico-mil. officer U.S. Embassy Tegucigalpa, Honduras, 1987, dep. polit. counselor Mexico City, dep. chief of mission Santo Domingo, 1991-94; dir. Inter-Am. Affairs Nat. Security Coun., Washington; dep. prin. officer U.S. Interests Section Dept. State, Havana, Cuba, dep. chief of mission Buenos Aires, 1997, charge d'affaires, 1997—2000, U.S. amb. to Bolivia, 2000—02; sr. counselor internat. trade and govt. affairs Steel Hector & Davis LLP, Miami, Fla., 2002—. Office: Steel Hector & Davis LLP Ste 4000 200 S Biscayne Blvd Miami FL 33131-2398*

ROCHBERG, GEORGE, composer, educator; b. Paterson, N.J., July 5, 1918; s. Morris and Anna (Hoffman) R.; m. Gene Rosenfeld, Aug. 18, 1941; children: Paul Bernard (dec.), Frances Ruth. BA, Montclair State Tchrs. Coll., 1939, LHD, 1962; BMus, Curtis Inst. Music, 1948; MA, U. Pa., 1949, MusD (hon.), 1988, Phila. Mus. Acad., 1964, Curtis Inst. Music, 1988. Faculty Curtis Inst. Music, 1948-54; Fulbright fellow Am. Acad., Rome, 1950-51; editor, dir. publs. Theo. Presser Co., Bryn Mawr, Pa., 1951-60; chmn. Music dept. U. Pa., 1960-68; ret., 1983; Annenberg prof. humanities U. Pa., 1979. Commd. to compose ballet music for Anna Sokolov, Lincoln Center Fund, 1965; recordings include numerous others; (recipient Gershwin Meml. award 1952, Soc. for Publ. Am. Music award 1956, Koussevitzky commn. 1957, Naumberg Rec. award 1961); Composer: Symphony No. 1, 1948-49, Night Music, 1949, String Quartet No. 1, 1952, Serenata d Estate, 1955, Symphony No. 2, 1956, La Bocca della Verita, 1958, String Quartet No. 2, 1959-61, Blake Songs, 1961, Time-Span (II), 1962, Trio for Violin, Cello and Piano, 1963, Zodiac, 1964, Black Sounds, 1965, Contra Mortem et Tempus, 1965, Music for the Magic Theater, 1965, Symphony No. 3, 1969, Tableaux for chamber ensemble, 1968, String Quartet No. 3, 1972, Violin Concerto premiered by Isaac Stern, 1975, Piano Quintet (Nat. Endowment for Arts commn.), 1975, Symphony No. 4, 1976; monodrama Phaedra, 1976, String Quartet No. 4, 1979 (1st place Kennedy Center Friedheim award), The Confidence Man, an Opera, 1981, Piano Trio No. 2 (for Beaux Arts Trio), 1983, Symphony No. 5, Chgo. Symphony, 1986, Symphony No. 6, Pitts. Symphony, 1987, Muse of Fire for flute and guitar, 1989, Piano Trio No. 3 (for Beaux Arts Trio), 1991, Sonata for Violin and Piano, 1988, Sonata-aria for Cello and Piano, 1992, Concerto for Clarinet and Orchestra, 1994-95, Chromaticism: Symmetry in Atonal and Tonal Music, 1996, Circles of Fire for 2 Pianos, 1997; (chamber concerto for guitar and ensemble) Eden: Out of Time and Out of Space, 1997, Sonata Seria for piano, 1998, Three Elegiac Pieces for Piano, 1999. Served to 2d lt., inf. AUS, 1942-45, ETO. Decorated Purple Heart with cluster; gold medal in music Brandeis Creative Arts award, 1985; Nat. Inst. Arts and Letters grant, 1962; Fromm Found. commn., 1965; Guggenheim fellow, 1957, 1966-67; Nat. Endowment for Arts grant, 1972-73 Mem. Am. Acad. Arts and Scis., Am. Musicological Soc., ASCAP (Life-Achievement award 1999). *I have always clung fast to these fundamentals: that music was given man so he could express the best he was capable of; that the best he was capable of had to do with his deepest feelings; that his deepest feelings are rooted in what I believe to be a moral order in the universe which underlies all real existence.*

ROCHDI, MYRIAM, pharmacist, researcher; b. Eaubonne, Paris, France, Apr. 2, 1964; d. Ahmed and Francoise (Loiseleux) R. PharmD, MS, Sch. of Pharmacy, Paris, 1987. Rsch. fellow Nat. Inst. Health and Med. Rsch., Paris, 1989-94; dir. biopharmaceutics SkyePharma AG, San Diego, 1995—2002; team leader Globomax LLC, Hanover, Md., 2002—. Mem. Am. Assn. Pharm. Sci. Office: Globomax LLC 7250 Parkway Dr Hanover MD 21076 E-mail: myrochdi@yahoo.com.

ROCHE, EAMONN KEVIN, architect; b. Dublin, June 14, 1922; came to U.S., 1948, naturalized, 1964; s. Eamon and Alice (Harding) R.; m. Jane Tuohy, June 10, 1963; children: Eamon, Paud, Denis, Anne, Alice. B.Arch., Nat. U. Ireland, 1945; D.Sc. (hon.), Nat. U. Ireland, 1977; postgrad., Ill. Inst. Tech., 1948; D.F.A. (hon.), Wesleyan U., 1981, Yale U., 1995. With Eero Saarinen and Assocs., Bloomfield Hills, Mich., 1950—61; ptnr. Kevin Roche John Dinkeloo and Assocs., Hamden, 1966—. Prin. works include Ford Found. Hdqs., 1967, Oakland (Calif.) Mus, 1968, Met. Mus. Art, N.Y.C., Creative Arts Ctr., Wesleyan U., Middletown, Conn., 1971, Fine Arts Ctr., U. Mass., 1971, Union Carbide Corp. World Hdqs., Conn., Gen. Foods Corp. Hdqs., Rye, N.Y., 1977, 1978, Conoco Inc. Hdqs., Houston, 1979, Central Pk. Zoo, N.Y.C., 1980, DeWitt Wallace Mus. Fine Arts, Williamsburg, Va., 1980, Bouygues World Hdqs., Paris, 1983, J.P. Morgan and Co. Hdqs., N.Y.C., 1983, UNICEF Hdqs., N.Y.C., 1984, Leo Burnett Co. Hdqs., Chgo., 1985, Corning (N.Y.) Inc. Hdqs., 1986, Merck & Co. Hdqs., N.J., 1987, Dai Ichi Hdqs./Norinchukin Bank Hdqrs., Tokyo, 1989, Nations Bank Hdqs., Atlanta, 1989, Pontiac Marina Pvt. Ltd., Singapore, 1990, Metropolitano, Madrid, 1990, Borland Internat. Headquarters, Scotts Valley, Calif., 1990, Tanjong & Binariang/Ampang Tower, Kuala Lumpur, Malaysia, 1993, Mus. Jewish Heritage Holocaust Meml., N.Y.C., 1993, Tata Cummins Pvt. Ltd., Jamshedpur, India, 1994, Vis. Ctr., Columbus, Ind., 1994, Cummins Engine Co. APEX Mfg. Facility, 1994, Lucent Techs. Hdqs., Murray Hill, N.J., 1996, Wuxi Newage Cummins, Wuxi, China, 1996, Total Sys. Svcs. Corp. Headquarters, Columbus, Ga., 1997, student housing and student union NYU, N.Y.C., 2003, ctrl. athletic facility MIT, Cambridge, 2000, Lucent Tech. R & D Facilities, various locations including The Netherlands and Germany, 2001, Shiodome Block B Devel., Tokyo, 2003, Santander Ctrl. Hispano, Madrid, 2001—, Securities & Exch. Commn. Hdqrs., Washington, 2001—, Bouygues SA Holding Co. Hdqrs., Paris, 2002—, Nat. Conf. Ctr., Dublin, 2002—, Oakland Mus. Calif. Expansion, 2002—. Mem. Fine Arts Commn., Washington; trustee Am. Acad. in Rome, 1968-71, Woodrow Wilson Center for Scholars in Smithsonian Instn. Recipient Creative Arts award Brandeis U., 1967; A.S. Bard award City Club N.Y., 1968, 77, 79; award Gov. of Calif., 1968; N.Y. State award Citizens Union N.Y., 1968; total design award Am. Soc. Interior Design; Pritzker Archtl. prize, 1982; Albert S. Bard award, 1990. Fellow AIA (medal of honor N.Y. chpt. 1968, Gold Medal award 1993, 25-yr. award 1995), AAAS; mem. NAD (academician), AAAL (pres. 1994-97), Am. Acad. Arts and Letters (Brunner award 1965, Gold medal 1990), Académie d'Architecture (Grand Gold medal 1977), Mcpl. Art Soc. N.Y. (Brendan Gill prize 1989), Acad. di San Luca. Office: Kevin Roche John Dinkeloo & Assoc PO Box 6127 20 Davis St Hamden CT 06517-3501 Office Phone: 203-777-7251. E-mail: info@krjda.com.

ROCHE, GAIL CONNOR, editor; b. Phila., Aug. 14, 1953; d. Donald Russell Connor; m. Richard Roche, Nov. 21, 1981; children: Alex James, Clare Evelyn. AB cum laude, Franklin & Marshall Coll., Lancaster, Pa., 1975; MA with distinction, Rider Coll., 1988. Cert. tchr., Pa. Tchr. Pennsbury Schs., Fallsington, Pa., 1975-76, Cen. Bucks Sch., Doylestown, Pa., 1977-79; reporter Trenton Times, N.J., 1979-82; editor Dow Jones & Co., Princeton, N.J., 1982-95; mem. adv. bd. Dow Jones Women's Network, Princeton, 1990-95; tech. editor Bloomberg News, Princeton, 1995-2000; sr. editor Bloomberg Markets, 2000—. Contbr. articles to mags. Mem. Phi Beta Kappa. Home: 23 Jericho Run Washington Crossing PA 18977-1027 Office Phone: 609-750-5097. E-mail: groche@bloomberg.net., groche@bloomberg.net.

ROCHE, GERARD RAYMOND, management consultant; b. Scranton, Pa., July 27, 1931; s. Joseph Arthur and Amelia Jane (Garcia) R.; m. Marie Terotta, Apr. 27, 1957; children: Mary Margaret, Anne Elizabeth, Paul Joseph. BS in Acctg., U. Scranton, 1953; MBA, NYU, 1958. Mgmt. trainee AT&T, Phila., 1955-56; account exec. ABC-TV, N.Y.C., 1956-58; sales and mktg. positions Kordite Corp. subs. Mobil Oil Co., Macedon, N.Y., 1959-63; assoc. Heidrick & Struggles, Inc., N.Y.C., 1964-68, ptnr., 1968—, mgr. N.Y., 1968-73, mgr. East, 1973-77, pres., chief exec. officer, chmn., 1981-2000, sr. chmn., 2000—. Former trustee Cath. U. Am., U. Scranton; mentor Nat. Mentoring Partnership; bd. dirs. Covenant House, N.Y.C. Served to lt. USN, 1953-55. Mem.: Cmty. Anti-Drug Coalitions of am. (bd. dirs.), Knights of Malta, Loblolly Pines Country Club, Blind Brook Club, Sleepy Hollow Country Club, Sky Club, Univ. Club, Yale Club, Alpha Sigma Nu (past treas.). Roman Catholic. Office: Heidrick & Struggles Inc 245 Park Ave Fl 43 New York NY 10167-0152

ROCHE, JAMES G. civilian military employee; B.S., Illinois Inst. of Tech., Chicago, 1960; M.S., U.S. Naval Postgrad. Sch., Monterey, Calif., 1966; Ph.D., Harvard Grad. Sch. of Bus. Admin., Cambridge, Mass., 1972, Illinois Inst. of Tech., 2002; PhD. (hon.), St. Thomas Aquinas College, 2003. Capt. U.S. Navy, 1960-83; Office Sect. Defense, 1975-79; sr. profl. staff mem. Senate Select Com. Intelligence, 1979-81; princ. dep. dir. policy planning staff U.S. Dept. State, 1981-83; Democratic staff dir. U.S. Senate Com. on Armed Svcs., 1983—84; v.p., dir. analysis ctr. Northrop Grumman, 1984-89, v.p., special asst. to chmn., pres., CEO, 1989-91, v.p., adv. devel. planning, 1991—92, chief advanced develop., planning, pub. affairs, 1992—96; corp. v.p., pres. Northrop Grumman's Elec. Sensors, Systems Sector, 1996—2001; secy. air force U.S. Dept. Def., Washington, 2001—. Mem. The Council on Foreign Relations, Internat. Institute of Strategic Studies, Fleet Reserve Assoc. Office: 101 Army Pentagon Rm 3E700 Washington DC 20310-0101

ROCHE, JOHN EDWARD, educator, human resources consultant; b. St. Albans, N.Y., Nov. 11, 1946; s. John F. and Carolyn C. (Miller) R.; m. Valerie Vastola; children: Christopher B., Danielle, Ryan J., Jennifer M. BA, Marist Coll., 1968, MBA, 1975; MS in Edn., SUNY, New Paltz, 1974; EdD, Nova Southeastern U., 1998. Tchr. Kingston (N.Y.) City Schs., 1968-76; employment supr. ACLI Internat. Inc., N.Y.C., 1976-78; dir. pers. Balfour MacLaine Internat., N.Y.C., 1978-80; mgr. employee rels. Harcourt Brace Jovanovich, N.Y.C., 1980-82; nat. dir. pers. Hayt, Hayt & Landau, Great Neck, N.Y., 1982-86; pres. Pers. Mgmt. Svcs., Great Neck, N.Y., 1983-86, Martin-Roche Assocs., Inc., Levittown, N.Y., 1986-94, Human Resources Dept. Inc., Syosset, NY, 1994—2002, L.I. Bus. Network, Inc., 1994-2000, Martin-Roche Internat. Ltd., Plainview, NY, 1992—94; prof. instrnl. tech. N.Y. Inst. Tech., Old Westbury, 1989-2000, chair Sch. Edn. Manhattan Campus, 1997-2000, acting dir. Ctr. Labor & Indls. Rels., 2000; dean Sch. Continuing Studies L.I. U., Bklyn., 2000—. Exec. dir. Jr. Achievement, Kingston, 1972-76, coach Syosset Baseball Assn., CYO Basketball Assn.; mem. Syosset Youth Athletic Commn.; human resource com. mem. Adults and Children with Learning and Devel. Disabilities, 1990-2000; mem. L.I. U. Coun. Deans, Middle States Com. Mem. ASTD, WorldatWork (cert. compensation profl.), Soc. for Human Resource Mgmt. (cert. sr. profl. in human resources), KC (grand knight 1967-68). Republican. Roman Catholic. Avocations: astronomy, photography, painting. Home: 17 Meadow Ln Syosset NY 11791-4126 Office: L I Univ Sch Continuing Studies Brooklyn NY 11201 Office Phone: 718-488-1362. Personal E-mail: jeroche@juno.com. Business E-Mail: jroche@liu.edu.

ROCHE, JOHN JEFFERSON, lawyer; b. N.Y.C., Apr. 12, 1934; s. William and Florence E. (Garvey) R.; m. Judith J. Stackpole, Sept. 4, 1980; 1 child from previous marriage, Forrest B. AB, Brown U., 1957; LL.B., Boston U., 1964. Bar: Mass. 1964, U.S. Tax Ct. 1976. Asst. atty gen. Dept. Atty. Gen., Boston, 1964-67; ptnr. Hale and Dorr, Boston, 1967-90; pvt. practice Cambridge, Mass., 1991-2001; ptnr. Taylor, Ganson & Perrin LLP, Boston, 2001—03. Trustee The Hotchkiss Sch., 1986-91, Archaeol. Inst. Am., 1998—; bd. dirs. Indian Soc. Served with U.S. Army, 1959-62. Fellow Am. Coll. Trusts and Estates, Internat. Acad. Estate and Trust Law; mem. ABA, Mass. Bar Assn., Boston Bar Assn., Masons, Wig and Penn Club (London), Winchester Country Club. Republican. Congregationalist.

ROCHE, JOYCE M. marketing executive; Sales exec. Avon Inc., 1976-91, sr. v.p. mktg., 1991-93, v.p. global mktg., 1993-94; exec. v.p. global mktg. Carson Prods. Co., Savannah, Ga., 1995-96, pres., COO, dir., 1996—98; pres., CEO Girls, Inc. Office: Girls Inc 120 Wall St New York NY 10005-3902

ROCHE, MARK A. consumer products company executive, lawyer; b. 1954; m. Barbara Roche. BA, U. Va.; JD, Cornell U. Bar: N.Y. 1980. From assoc. to counsel Chadbourne & Park LLP, N.Y.C., 1981-88; group gen. counsel Fortune Brands Inc., Deerfield, Ill., 1988-91, Lincolnshire, Ill., 1991-96, v.p., assoc. gen. counsel, 1996-98, v.p., gen. counsel, 1998-99, sr. v.p., gen. counsel, 1999—. Office: Fortune Brands Inc 300 Tower Pkwy Lincolnshire IL 60069-3640

ROCHE DE COPPENS, PETER GEORGE, sociologist, educator; b. Vevey, Switzerland, May 24, 1938; s. George Sebastian and Alice Emmanuela (De Coppens) Roche de C.; m. Marian Karpacz, May 27, 1977 (dec. 1991); m. Marie Teresa Crivelli, Sept. 16, 2002. BS, Columbia U., 1965; MA, Fordham U., 1966, PhD, 1973; MSW, U. Montreal, 1978. Prof. sociology, anthropology East Stroudsburg (Pa.) U., 1970—. Instr. sociology Fordham U., N.Y.C., 1968-69, tchg. fellow, 1965-68; cons. UN, N.Y.C., 1997; v.p. Internat. Inst. Integral Human Studies, Montreal, 1977-97; cons. UN; adv. prof. faculty edn. McGill U., Montreal, 1998—. Author: The Development of the New Man, 1989, 98, The Art of Joyful Living, 1991, The Sociological Adventure, 1991, 96, Divine Light and Fire, 1992, Divine Light and Love, 1994, The Initiatory Path for the Year 2000, 1994, The Levels of Human Counclousness, 1996, Love Vitamins, 1998, Prayer, the royal Path of the Spiritual Tradition, 2003, La Priére la Voie royale de la Tradition Chretienne, 2003, Medicina e Spiritualita, 2003, La Preghiera, Strumento di Guarigione, 2004, Medicine and Spirtuality, 2004, What are Life and Death, 2004, LaScintilla Divina: Il piu grande Mistero e Tesoro, 2004; contbr. articles to mags.; host tv program Soul Sculpture. Office Phone: 570-422-3276. E-mail: proche@esu.edu.

ROCHEFORT, REGINA MARIE, ecologist, botanist; b. Boston, Mass., May 1, 1953; d. John Spencer and Kathleen Alice Rochefort; m. Stephen Thomas Gibbons, Aug. 11, 1984; children: Shane Clinton Gibbons, Taylor Christian Gibbons. BS, Northeastern U., Boston, 1975; MFS, Yale U., New Haven, 1978; PhD, U. Wash., Seattle, 1995. Fire ecologist South Fla. Rsch. Ctr. Everglades Nat. Pk., Ochopee, Fla., botanist Homestead, 1982—84, Mt. Rainier Nat. Pk., Ashford, Wash., 1984—98; sci. advisor North Cascades Nat. Pk. Svc. Complex, Sedro-Woolley, 1998—. Mem.: Soc. of Conservation Biology, Soc. of Ecol. Restoration. Office: N Cascades Nat Pk 810 State Rt 20 Sedro-Woolley WA 98284 E-mail: regina_rochefort@nps.gov.

ROCHELLE, LUGENIA, academic administrator; b. Maple Hill, N.C., July 14, 1943; d. John Edward and Ruby Lee (Holmes) R. BA, St. Augustine's Coll., 1965; MS, N.C. A & T State U., 1969; D of Pedagogy, Barbar-Scotia Coll., 1993. Cert. tchr., N.C. Tchr. French, English Butler High Sch., Barnwell, S.C., 1965-67; instr. English N.C. A & T State U., Greensboro, 1970-77, St. Augustine's Coll., Raleigh, N.C., 1977-86, dir. freshman studies program, 1986-91, dean lower coll., 1991-95, asst. to v.p. acad. affairs, 1991-92; dir. gen. studies, asst. prof. English Voorhees Coll., Denmark, S.C., 1996-98, spl. asst. to pres. external affairs, 1999—2002, dir. Hons. Coll., 1999—, dean, Coll. of General Studies, 2002—. Dir. Mellon program St. Augustine's Coll., Raleigh, 1980-83; adv. bd. cooperating Raleigh Colls., 1986—, Off to Coll., Montgomery, Ala., 1993—; mem. profl. practices commn. N.C. Dept. Pub. Instrn., 1994-96; coord. Title III, 1999-00, coord. Bd. Trustees Rels., 1999-02; dir. Ctr. Excellence in Humanities, Vorhees Coll., April 2000-02; Hostess for Radio Talk Show, Views and News from Voorhees Coll., Sept. 2001-03. Author: English Manual of Writing, 1980, (with others) Off to College, 1997, 98, reprinted, 1999, 2000, 01; editor: Can't Nobody Do You Like Jesus, 1998. Judge oratorical contests, Optimist Club, Raleigh, 1985-93; chair pro tem Raleigh Bicentennial Hist. Com., Raleigh, 1991-92; initiated, effected chartering of Phi Eta Sigma St. Augustine's Coll., 1995; bd. dirs. Garner Rd. YMCA, Raleigh, 1994-1996; coord. Honda Campus All-Star Challenge, 1996—; lay min., sec. vestry St. Philip's Episcopal Ch., 1997—; instnl. rep. S.C. Women in Higher Edn., Voorhees Coll., 1998—. Nat. teaching fellow N.C. A & T State U., Greensboro, 1968-70. NCTE Fellow Nat. Coun. Tchrs. English; mem. ASCD (assoc.), Am. Assn. U. Women (pres. Denmark Br.), Cardinal Club. Avocations: reading, collecting antique birds, travel. E-mail: rochelle@voorhees.edu.

ROCHELLE, ROBERT THOMAS, lawyer, former state legislator; b. Nashville, Nov. 25, 1945; s. James Marcell and Katherine (Purnell) R.; m. Janice Johnson, Aug. 18, 1973; 1 son, Aaron Marcellus. BS, Cumberland Coll. Bar: Tenn. Sole practice law, Lebanon, Tenn.; county atty. Wilson County, Tenn., 1974—87; mem. Tenn. Senate, 1982—2002, Rochelle, McCulloch, Aulds P.L.L.C., 2003—. Democratic del. Nat. Conv. from Wilson County, 1974; coord. 4th Congl. Dist. for Carter for Pres., 1976, 80; state vice chmn. Mondale for Pres., 1984; bd. dirs. YMCA, 1971-76; chmn. Children's Hosp. Fund Drive, 1977-78; legacies chmn. Cancer Crusade, 1977-83; bd. dirs. Wilson County Promotions, Inc. Served with U.S. Army, 1969-71. Decorated Army Commendation medal with oak leaf cluster, Bronze Star, Vietnam Svc. medal; recipient Svc. to Youth award YMCA, 1974; named Outstanding Young Man of Yr., Lebanon Jr. C. of C., 1978. Mem. ABA, Wilson County Bar Assn., Tenn. Bar Assn., U. Tenn. Alumni Assn. (pres. 1974), Lebanon/Wilson County C. of C., West Wilson C. of C. Methodist. Office: 109 Castle heights Ave N Lebanon TN 37087

ROCHELLE, VICTOR CLEANTHUS, lawyer; b. Nov. 4, 1918; s. Floyd Emerson and Goldie Opal (Dunbar) Rochelle; m. Marjorie Armitage, Dec. 20, 1946 (div. 1956); children: Vickie Adrianne, Margo Renee; m. Patricia Ann Leary, Mar. 20, 1964; children: Elizabeth Ann, Linda Raquel. BA, U. Tex., 1940; LLB, Columbia U., 1947. Bar: Tex. 48, U.S. Dist. Ct. Ill. 53. Assoc. Tom Hartley, Atty., Pharr, Tex., 1947—49, Kelly, Looney, McLean & Littleton, Edinburg, Tex., 1949—52; personal injury supr. County Mut. Ins. Co., Chgo., 1952—57, claims mgr., 1957—61, Bloomington, Ill., 1961—69; cons., dir. litigation Country Mut., Country Casualty, Mid-Am., 1969—84; ins. law cons., 1984—. Lectr. in field.; arbitrator Mut. Casualty, 1965—70. Lt. comdr. USN, 1941—45. Mem.: ABA, Am. Judicature Soc., Def. Rsch. Inst., Property Loss Bur., Internat. Assn. Ins. Counsel, McLean County Bar Assn., Ill. Bar Assn., Tex. Bar Assn. Reform. Address: 27 Lateer Dr Normal IL 61761-3925

ROCHESTER, MICHAEL GRANT, geophysics educator; b. Toronto, Ont., Can., 1932; s. Reginald Rochester and Ruth Rochester Konrad; m. Elizabeth Manser, 1958; children— Susan, Fiona, John. BA with honors, U. Toronto, 1954, MA, 1956; PhD, U. Utah, 1959. Aerodynamicist A. V. Roe Can. Ltd., Malton, Ont., 1954-55; lectr. geophysics U. Toronto, 1959-60, asst. prof., 1960-61, U. Waterloo, Ont., 1961-65, assoc. prof., 1965-67, Meml. U. Nfld., St. John's, Can., 1967-70, prof., 1970-98, univ. research prof., 1986—, prof. emeritus, 1998—. Officer Nat. Spiritual Assembly of Baha'is of Can., 1963—92. Grantee, NRC, Natural Scis. and Engring. Rsch. Coun. Can, 1961—2002. Fellow Royal Soc. Can.; mem. Internat. Union Geodesy and Geophysics (Can. nat. com. 1971-75, 84-88), AAAS, Am. Geophys. Union, Can. Assn. Physicists, Can. Geophys. Union (Tuzo Wilson medal, 1986), Internat. Astron. Union (commn. rotation of the Earth 1973—), Royal Astron. Soc. London, Sigma Xi Avocations: hiking, swimming, history. Office: Meml Univ Nfld Dept Earth Scis Saint John's NF Canada A1B 3X5 E-mail: mrochest@mun.ca.

ROCHETTE, LOUIS, retired shipowner and shipbuilder; b. Quebec City, Que., Can., Feb. 19, 1923; s. Evariste and Blanche (Gaudry) R.; m. Nicole Barbeau, Oct. 12, 1968; children: Louise (dec.), Anne, Guy. M. Commerce, Laval U., Que., 1948. Chartered acct., Que. Chief auditor Sales Tax Govt. Que., Quebec City, 1952—55; treas. Davie Ltd., Lauzon, 1955—65; chmn., CEO Davie Ltd., Lauzon, 1976—81; exec. v.p. Marine Industries, Ltd., Montreal, 1965—76; pres., CEO Soconav Inc., Quebec, 1976—86; pres. Gesconav Inc., 1986—. Past chmn. Lloyd's Com. for Can. Author: Le Reve Separatiste, 1969. Bd. dirs. Gov. Coun. for Can. Unity; gov. Laval U. Found, Quebec Opera Found. Pilot RCAF, 1943-45, ETO. Fellow Inst. Chartered Accts. Can., Can. Inst. Mgmt. Accts. Home and Office: 17 Ocelots Road Saint-Anne-Des-Lacs QC Canada JOR 1B0 *Whatever success I have met with throughout my career was mainly achieved through perseverance in the face of what often looked like insurmountable obstacles.*

ROCHINSKI, STEPHEN JAMES, musician, educator; b. Washington, Jan. 20, 1954; s. Stanley James Rochinski, Jr. and Lorraine Agnes Rochinski, Carol Rochinski (Stepmother); m. Laurie Fox, May 24, 1986; children: Anna F., Alex F. Diploma, Berklee Coll. Music, 1980. Freelance guitarist, Washington, 1972—77; freelance guitarist, arranger Boston, 1977—80; guitarist, arranger, music dir. Anthony Tillman Show with The East Coast Brass, 1980—84; prof. Berklee Coll. Music, 1984—. Writer Hal Leonard Corp., Milw., 1995—; jazz clinician numerous nat. and internat. locations, 1996—. Musician: (recording) Until Further Notice, 1993, A Bird In The Hand, 1999, Otherwise, 2001; author: (book) The Jazz Style of Tal Farlow, 1994, The Motivic Basis for Jazz Guitar Improvisation, 1998, composer numerous jazz compositions and arrangements; Jardis Records, Spiesen-Elversberg, Germany, 1999—; contbg. editor (and author): Berklee Press and Advance Music, 1991—; performances with Tal Farlow, Tim Hagans, Jimmy Raney, Attica Zoller, Pete and Conte Candoci, Chuck Redd and Brad Goode. Jazz artist-in-residence Nat. and Internat. locations. Grantee, NEA, 1992, Berklee Coll. Music, 1989, 1994, 1998, 2001. Mem.: Broadcast Music Inc. (writer, pub. affiliate 1991—2003), Rec. Acad. (voting mem. 2001—03). Roman Catholic. Avocations: reading, political affairs, history. Home: 2 Wellington Terr Brookline MA 02445 Office: Berklee Coll Music 1140 Boylston St Faculty Box #273 Boston MA 02215 Office Phone: 617-747-8335. E-mail: srochinski@berklee.edu.

ROCHLIN, PAUL R. lawyer; b. Balt., Dec. 14, 1934; s. Jack and Sara (Levin) Rochlin; m. Lois David, Oct. 25, 1962 (div. 1969); children: Greg, Jennifer; m. Joyce Tretick, July 12, 1973; children: Keith Sopher, Maura Sopher. JD, U. Balt., 1958. Bar: Md. 59, U.S. Dist. Ct. Md. 59. Assoc. Milton Talkin, Balt., 1959—61, Rochlin & Settleman, Balt., 1961—63, ptnr., 1963—78; pres., sr. ptnr. Rochlin Settleman & Dobres, P.A., Balt., 1978—2001. Bd. dirs. Balt. Jewish Coun., 1979. Mem.: Balt. City Bar Assn., Md. Trial Lawyers Assn. (bd. dirs. 1988—92), Md. State Bar Assn., Suburban Club (pres. 2003—). Jewish.

ROCHOWICZ, JOHN ANTHONY, JR., mathematician, mathematics and physics educator; b. Reading, Pa., Mar. 20, 1950; s. John Anthony and Sara Jane (Binckley) R. BS in Math., Albright Coll., 1972; MS in Math., Lehigh U., 1974; secondary edn. cert. math., Albright Coll., 1975; EdD in Ednl. Tech., Lehigh U., 1993. Cert. secondary teaching, Pa. Math. tchr. Bethlehem Cath. H.S., Pa., 1980—81; instr. math. Pa. State U.-Berks, Reading, 1982—84, Kutztown U., Pa., 1983—84, Lehigh County C.C., Schnecksville, Pa., 1994, Alvernia Coll., Reading, 1984, Reading Area C.C., 1984—86; prof. math. Alvernia Coll., 1985—. Recipient Alumni Educator award Albright Coll., Reading, 1987. Mem. AAUP, Math. Assn. Am., Assn. for the Advancement Computing in Edn., Assn. for Ednl. Communications and Tech., Nat. Coun. Tchrs. Math.; contbr. articles to scientific jours. Democrat. Roman Catholic. Avocations: collecting music, computers, calculators, billiards, swimming. Home: 825 Brighton Ave Reading PA 19606-1316 Office: Alvernia College 400 Saint Bernardine St Reading PA 19607-1799

ROCK, ALLAN MICHAEL, ambassador, former Canadian government official; b. Ottawa, Ont., Can., Aug. 30, 1947; s. James Thomas and Anne (Torley) R.; m. Deborah Kathleen, June 24, 1983; children: Jason, Lauren, Andrew, Stephen. BA, U. Ottawa, 1968, LLB, 1971. Certified specialist in civil litigation. Sr. ptnr. Fasken Campbell & Godfrey, Toronto; min. of justice, atty. gen. Govt. of Can., 1993-97, min. of health, 1997—2002, min. of industry, 2002—03; permanent Can. rep. UN, New York, 2004—. Treas. Law Soc. Upper Can., 1992-93; bencher Law Soc., 1983, 87, 91; former chmn. discipline and legal edn. coms.; past chmn. litigation dept. Fasken Campbell Godfrey. Fellow Am. Coll. Trial Lawyers. Office: UN One Dag Hamarskjold Plz 885 Second Ave 14th Fl New York NY 10017

ROCK, ARTHUR, venture capitalist; b. Rochester, N.Y., Aug. 19, 1926; s. Hyman A. and Reva (Cohen) Rock; m. Toni Rembe, July 19, 1975. BS, Syracuse U., 1948; MBA, Harvard U., 1951. Gen. ptnr. Davis & Rock, San Francisco, 1961-68, Arthur Rock & Assocs., San Francisco, 1969-80. Mem. exec. com. Teledyne, Inc., L.A., 1961-94; dir. emeritus, founder, past chmn., chmn. exec. com., lead dir. Intel Corp., Santa Clara, Calif.; bd. dirs. Echelon Corp., San Jose, Calif.; bd. govs. Nasdaq Stock Market, Inc. Trustee Calif. Inst. Tech.; pres. Basic Fund; bd. dirs. San Francisco Opera Assn., 1970-92, San Francisco Mus. Modern Art; mem. vis. com. Harvard U. Bus. Sch., 1982-88. Recipient Medal of Achievement Am. Electronics Assn., 1987, Am. Acad. Achievement, 1989, Lifetime Achievement in Entrepreneurship and Innovation award U. Calif., 1999; named to Jr. Achievement Hall of Fame, 1990, Calif. Bus. Hall of Fame, 1990, Bay Area Bus. Coun. Hall of Fame, 1995, Arents Pioneer medal Syracuse U., 1997, Outstanding Dir., Corp. Am., 1999, SDForum Visionary award, 2001, Bus. Leader of Yr. award Harvard Bus. Sch. Assn. No. Calif., 2002. Office: 1 Maritime Plz Ste 1220 San Francisco CA 94111-3502

ROCK, CHRIS, actor, comedian; b. Andrews, SC, Feb. 7, 1966; m. Malaak Compton, 1996; 1 child, Lola. Appeared on TV in series Saturday Night Live, 1990-93, In Living Color, 1993, The Chris Rock Show, 1997-2000; appeared in films Beverly Hills Cop II, 1987, I'm Gonna Git You Sucka, 1988, Comedy's Dirtiest Dozen, 1988, New Jack City, 1991, Boomerang, 1992, CB4, 1993, Happily Ever AFter: Fairy Tales for Every Child (voice), 1995, The Immortals, 1995, Panther, 1995, Sgt. Bilko, 1996, Beverly Hills Ninja, 1997, Bring the Pain, 1998, Doctor Dolittle (voice), 1998, Lethal Weapon 4, 1998, Dogma, 1999, Spin Doctor, 1999, Jackie's Back, 1999, Nurse Betty, 2000, Down to Earth, 2001, Artificial Intelligence: AI (voice), 2001, Pootie Tang, 2001, Osmosis Jones (voice), 2001, Jay and Silent Bob Strike Back, 2001, Bad Company, 2002, Head of State, 2003; appeared on TV specials, First Person with Maria Shriver, 1990, Saturday Night Live: All the Best for Mother's Day, 1992, 93, Met Life Presents the Apollo Theatre Hall of Fame, 1994, HBO Comedy Half-Hour, 1994, Politically Incorrect, 1994, Saturday Night Live: The Best of Chris Farley, 1998, Saturday Night Live: Bad Boys, 1998, Saturday Night Live: 25th Anniversary, 1999, Best of Chris Rock (prodr., writer), 1999, Chris Rock: Bigger & Blacker (prodr., writer), 1999 (American Comedy award for Funniest Male Performer in a TV Special, 2000), Whatever Happened to Michael Ray? (voice), 2000, The Black Ambition Tour, 2003-2004; film producer (with Nelson George) CB4, 1993; exec. t.v. prodr.: Chris Rock: Bring the Pain, 1997 (Emmy for Outstanding Variety, Music or Comedy Special), The Chris Rock Show, 1997-2000 (Emmy for Outstanding Writing for a Variety or Music Program, 1998), The Hughleys, 1998; albums: Born suspect, 1991, Roll with the New, 1997 (Grammy award for Best Spoken Comedy Album, 1997), Bigger & Blacker, 1999 (Grammy award for Best Spoken Comedy Album, 1999); Author Rock This!, 1998. Recipient Star, Hollywood Walk of Fame, 2003.

ROCK, DOUGLAS LAWRENCE, manufacturing executive; b. Glen Cove, N.Y., Jan. 25, 1947; s. Herb and Beatrice (Vyse) R.; m. Cindy Pegoraro, May 11, 1967 (div. Apr. 1973); 1 child, Jason; m. Mary Sue Bell, Mar. 23, 1991 (div. Jan. 1996). BS in Psychology and Chemistry, Pa. State U., 1968; postgrad., U. Chgo., 1971-73. Rsch. chemist FMC Corp., Princeton, N.J., 1968-69; mfg. system project leader A.O. Smith Corp., Erie, Pa., 1969-71; dir. materials and info. systems Joy Mfg., Michigan City, Ind., 1971-74; dir. info. systems Smith Tool div. Smith Internat. Inc., Irvine, Calif., 1974-75, dir. materials, 1975-77, v.p. mfg., 1977-80, sr. v.p. ops., 1980-82, pres., 1985-87, Drilco div. Smith Internat. Inc., Houston, 1982-85; pres., chief exec. officer Smith Internat. Inc., Houston, 1987—, chmn. bd., 1991—. Bd. dirs. Viad Corp. Named Golden Knight, Nat. Mgmt. Assn., 1983. Mem. Internat. Assn. Drilling Contractors, Am. Petroleum Inst., Petroleum Equipment Suppliers Assn. (bd. dirs. Houston chpt. 1987—, 1st v.p. 1996), Nat. Offshore Industries Assn. (fin. com. 1988, audit com. 1989), Greenspoint Club . Avocations: golf, racquetball, reading. Office: Smith Internat PO Box 60068 16740 Hardy Rd Houston TX 77205

ROCK, JOHN AUBREY, gynecologist and obstetrician, educator; b. Corpus Christi, Tex., Oct. 21, 1946; s. William A. and Burta (Wheeler) R.; children: John Aubrey Jr., Deborah Ellen, Daniel Authur; m. Martha Miller. BS in Zoology, La. State U., Baton Rouge, 1968; MD, La. State U., New Orleans, 1972. From asst. prof. to prof. pediats. Sch. Medicine Johns Hopkins U., Balt., 1978-80, prof. pediatrics Sch. Medicine, 1988-92, dir. reproductive endocrinology Sch. Medicine, 1979-91, dep. dir. Sch. Medicine, 1985-88; chmn. Union Meml. Hosp., Balt., 1991-92; James Robert McCord prof., chmn. dept. ob-gyn. Emory U. Sch. Medicine, Atlanta, 1992—2002; chancellor, prof. obstetrics and gynecology and pediatrics La. State U. Health Scis. Ctr., 2002—. Cons. Dept. Army, Washington, 1982 93, NASA, Houston, 1988—; chmn. ad hoc com. on in vitro fertilization State of Md., 1985. Author: Reparative and Constructive Surgery of the Female Generative Tract, 1983, Endometriosis, 1988, TeLinde's Operative Gynecology, 1991, 9th edit., 2003, Reproductive Endocrinology, Surgery and Technology, 1995; mem. editl. bd. Fertility and Sterility jour., 1986-94, Gynecology Surgery, 1989—. Fellow ACOG; mem. Am. Gynecol. and Obstet. Soc., Soc. Gynecol. Surgeons (pres. 1998-99), Am. Soc. for Reproductive Medicine (pres. 1996-97), Soc. Gynecologic Investigation, Soc. Reproductive Surgeons (pres. 1986), World Endometriosis Soc. (pres. 2000-02), Rotary, Phi Kappa Phi, Alpha Omega Alpha. Methodist. Office: La State U Health Scis Ctr 433 Bolivar St New Orleans LA 70112 Office Phone: 504-568-4800.

ROCK, MARY ANN, artist, educator; b. St. Louis, Mar. 2, 1931; d. Clobert Bernard and Mary Henrietta (Jones) Broussard; m. William Ralph Rock, Mar. 18, 1960 (div. Sept. 1967); 1 child, John Henry C. BS, Bennett Coll., 1952; postgrad., Chgo. Art Inst., 1953-54, So. Ill. U., Carbondale, 1955. Instr. arts and crafts Presidio Hill Sch., San Francisco, 1966-71; dir. gallery Cannery House Gallery, Friday Harbor, Wash., 1974-76; co-founder Island Artisans, Friday Harbor, 1980-85; gallery asst. Waterworks Gallery, Friday Harbor, 1986-95; with European study tour, 1996; patron sponsored painting sabbatical, 2001—03; prin., owner Dream Keeper Art Card Co., 2002—. Guest instr. Spring St. Sch., Friday Harbor, 2001, Friday Harbor, 02; presenter art workshops Friday Harbor Elem. Sch., 1976, 87, Portland CC, 1989, 90. Author, illustrator: DreamKeeper, 1995; brochures, exhibitions include 13th Saloon Internat. del Alpha, Lyon, France, Waterworks Gallery, Friday Harbor, 1986—, 7th Wahtcomb county Mus., Bellingham, 1988, Portland CC, 1990, Chetwynn Stapleton Gallery, Portland, 1989—98. Curator African art exhibit NAACP, San Francisco, 1961. Vt. Studio Ctr. fellow, Johnson, 1999. Democrat. Avocations: collecting ethnic artifacts, skiing, rock climbing, travel, reading.

ROCKART, JOHN FRALICK, information systems researcher; b. N.Y.C., June 20, 1931; s. John Rachac and Janet (Ross) R.; m. Elise Jean Feldmann, Sept. 16, 1961; children: Elise B. Liesl, Scott F. AB, Princeton U., 1953; MBA, Harvard U., 1958; PhD, MIT, 1968. Sales rep. IBM, 1958-61, dist. med. rep., 1961-62, fellow in Africa, 1962-64; instr. MIT, Cambridge, Mass., 1966-67; asst. prof. IBM, Cambridge, Mass., 1967-70, assoc. prof., 1970-74, sr. lectr., 1974—; dir. MIT, Cambridge, 1976—. Bd. dirs. Keane, Inc., Boston, Selective Ins. Group, Branchburg, NJ. Co-author: Computers & Learning Process, 1974, Rise of Managerial Computing, 1986, Executive Support Systems, 1988 (Computer Press Assn. 1989); contbr. articles to profl. jours. Trustee New Eng. Med. Ctr., Boston. Lt. USN, 1953-56. Mem. Assn. for Computing Machinery, Soc. for Info. Mgmt. (bd. dirs. mem. at large 1989-94, acad. v.p. 2003—), Weston (Mass.) Golf Club, Lake Sunapee Country Club (New London, N.H.). Republican. Unitarian Universalist. Home: 150 Cherry Brook Rd Weston MA 02493-1308 Office: CISR MIT Sloan Sch Mgmt 3 Cambridge Ctr NE20-336 Cambridge MA 02142

ROCKAS, ANASTASIA T. lawyer; b. Rochester, N.Y., 1963; BA, Smith-Coll., 1985; JD with hons., U. Conn., 1990. Bar: Conn. 1990, N.Y. 1993. Atty. Skadden, Arps, Slate, Meagher & Flom LLP, N.Y., 1992, ptnr. Office: Skadden Arps Slate Meagher & Flom LLP Four Times Sq New York NY 10036

ROCKBURNE, DOROTHEA GRACE, artist; b. Montreal, Que., Can., naturalized; Student, Black Mountain Coll.; PhD, Coll. of Creative Studies, Detroit, 2002. Milton and Sally Avery Disting. prof. Bard Coll., 1986. Trustee Ind. Curators Inc., N.Y., Art in Gen.; artist in residence Am. Acad. in Rome, 1991; vis. artist Skowhegan Sch. Painting and Sculpture, 1984; Rockefeller Found. resident Bellagio (Italy) Conf. and Study Ctr., 1997. One-woman shows at Sonnabend Gallery, Paris, 1971, New Gallery, Cleve., 1972, Bykert Gallery, NYC, 1970, 72-73, Galleria Toselli, Milan, Italy, 1972-74, Galleria D'Arte, Bari, Italy, 1972, Lisson Gallery, London, 1973, Daniel Weinberg Gallery, San Francisco, 1973, Galerie Charles Kriwin, Brussels, 1975, Galleria Schema, Florence, Italy, 1973, 75, 92, John Weber Gallery, NYC, 1976, 78, Galleria la Polena, Geona, Italy, 1977, Tex. Gallery, Houston, 1979-81, Xavier Fourcade Gallery, NYC, 1981-83, 85-86, David Bellman, Toronto, 1980-81, Margo Leavin, Calif., 1982, Arts Club Chgo., 1987, André Emmerich Gallery, NYC, 1988-89, 91-92, 94-95, Rose Art Mus., 1989, P. Fong & Spratt Galleries, San Jose, Calif., 1991, Sony Music Hdqs., NYC, 1993, Frederick Spratt Gallery, San Jose, 1994, Guild Hall Mus., Easthampton, N.Y., 1995, Portland Mus. Art, Maine, 1996, Ingrid Raab Gall., Berlin, 1997, Art in Gen., NY, 2000, Greenberg, Van Doren, NYC, 2000, Dieu Donné Papermill, NYC, 2003, Jan Abrams Fine Art, NY, 2003; group exhbns. at Whitney Mus. Am. Art, 1970, 73, 77, 79, 82, Mus. Modern Art, NYC, 71, 73, 84, 86, 91, 93-94, Buenos Aires, 1971, Kolner Kunst Market, Cologne, Germany, 1971, Stedelijk Mus., Holland, 1971, Spoleto (Italy) Festival, 1972, Palazzo Taverna, Rome, 1973, Nat. Gallery Victoria, Melbourne, Australia, 1973, Art Gallery NSW, Sydney, 1973, Auckland (New Zealand) City Art Gallery, 1973, Inst. Contemporary Art, London, 1974, Mus. d'Arte de la Ville, Paris, 1975, Galerie Aronowitsch, Stockholm, 1975, Stadtiches Mus., Manchengladbach, Germany, 1975, Galleria D'Arte Moderna, Bologna, Italy, 1975, Art Gallery Ont., Toronto, Can., 1975, Mus. Fine Art, Houston, 1975, Contemporary Arts Ctr., Cin., 1973, 75, 81, Mus. Contemporary Art, Chgo., 1971, 77, 86, Corcoran Gallery of Art, Washington, 1975, 87, Städtisches Mus., Leverkusen, Germany, 1975, Cannaviella Studio d'Arte Rome, 1976, Phila. Coll. Art, 1976, 83, New Mus., NYC, 1977, 80, 84, 83, Renaissance Soc. of U. Chgo., 1976, Lowe Art Mus., U. Miami, Fla., 1976, Inst. Contemporary Art, Boston, 1976, Seibu Mus. Art, Tokyo, 1976, NY State Mus., Albany, 1977, Drawing Ctr., 1977, Kansas City (Mo.) Art Inst., 1977, Smithsonian Inst., Washington, 1977, Kassel, Fed. Republic Germany, 1972, 77, Ackland Art Ctr., Chapel Hill, NC, 1979, 84, Milw. Art Ctr., 1978, 81, Biblioteca Nacional, Madrid, 1980, Gulbenkian Mus., Lisbon, Portugal, 1980, Bklyn. Mus., 1981, 89, Guggenheim Mus., 1982, 88-89, Albright Knox Art Gallery, Buffalo, 1979-80, 88-89, Kuustforeningen Mus., Copenhagen, 1980, Venice Biennale, 1980, Cranbrook (Mich.) Acad. Art, 1981, Mus. Fine Arts, Boston, 1983, Contemporary Arts Mus., Houston, 1983, Norman Mackenzie Art Gallery, U. Regina, Sask., Can., 1983, Galleriet, Sweden, 1983-84, Seattle Art Mus., 1979-84, Nat. Mus. Art., Osaka, Japan, 1984, Fogg Art Mus., Cambridge, Mass., 1984, Am. Acad. and Inst. Arts and Letters, NYC, 1984, 87, LA County Mus. Art, 1984, 86, Wadsworth Atheneum, Hartford, Conn., 1981, 84, Evehart Mus., Pa., 1984, Grey Art Gallery, NYU, 1977, 84, 87, Avery Ctr. Arts, Bard Coll., N.Y., 1985, 87-88, Stamford (Conn.) Mus., 1985, Aldrich Mus., Conn., 1979, 82, 95, Bronx Mus. Arts, N.Y.C., 1985, High Mus., Atlanta, 1975, 81, Phila. Mus. Art, 1986, Nat. Gallery Art, Washington, 1984, 94, 97, Mus. Art, Ft. Lauderdale, Fla., 1986, Nat. Mus. Women in Art, Washington, 1987, Xavier Fourcade

Gallery, 1983, 86-87, LA County Mus. Modern Art, 1986-87, The Hague, The Netherlands, 1986, Carnegie-Mellon Art Gallery, Pitts., 1979, 87, Balt. Mus. Art, 1975-76, 88, Ctr. for Fine Arts, Miami, 1989, Milw. Art Mus., 1989, Cin. Art Mus., 1989, New Orleans Mus., 1989, Denver Art Mus., 1989, Parrish Art Mus., South Hampton, NY, 1990-91, 99, Margo Leavin Gallery, LA, 1991, Guild Hall Mus., East Hampton, NY, 1991, Am. Acad., Rome, 1991, Mus. Contemporary Art, LA, 1991, 99, Hunter Coll., NY, 1991, CentroCultural/Arte Contemporanea, Mexico City, 1991, Hilton, San Jose, Calif., 1992, Hillwood Art Mus., L.I., NY, 1992, Am. Acad. and Inst. Arts and Letters, 1992, Neuberger Mus., 1992, 2000, Kohn-Abrams Gallerie, LA, 1993, Gallery at Bristol Myers Squibb, NJ, 1993-94, Friends of Art and Preservation in Embassies, NYC, 1993, Andre Emmerich Gallery, NYC, 1993, Fred Spratt Gallery, San Jose, Calif., 1994, Raab Galarie, Berlin, 1994, NY Studio Sch., NYC, 1995, 2002, Rose Art Mus., Brandeis U., 1996, Addison Gallery Am. Art Philips Acad., Andover, Mass., 1997, Fine Arts Mus. San Francisco, 1997, Wexner Ctr., Columbus, 1997, Dieu Donne Papermill, Inc., NYC, 1998, Pub. Sch. 1, Long Island City, NYC, 1999, Gemini G.E.L., 1998, Am. Acad. Arts and Letters, 1999, 2001, Parsons Sch. Design, NYC, 1999, David Dorsky Gallery, NY, 2000, Greenberg, Van Doren Fine Art, NYC, 2000, 02, NAD, NYC, 2002, Armory Show, NYC, 2002, Nat. Gallery of Art, 2001, Krannert Art Mus., 2002, Selby Gallery, Fla., 2002, Geffen Contemporary, LA, 2002, Marcus Ritter, NYC, 2002, Bowdoin Coll. Mus. Art, 2002, Reina Sophia Mus., Madrid, 2003, Cleve. Mus. Art, 2003, New Britain (Conn.) Mus. Am. Art, 2003, Mus. New Zealand, 2003, Guggenheim Mus., NYC, 2004, MOCA at Calif. Plz., LA, 2004, others; print exhbns. at Nat. Gallery, Washington, 1994, 97, 2001, Kate Ganz, Ltd., NYC, 2000, David Adamson Gallery, Washington, 2000, Fine Arts Mus. San Francisco, 1997, Bklyn. Mus., 1989, Mt. Holyoke Coll. Art Mus., 1987, Harcus Gallery, Boston, 1985, Xavier Fourcade Gallery, NYC, 1982, Mus. Modern Art, NYC, 1981, 91, Yale U. Art Gallery, New Haven, 1981, New Gallery Contemporary Art, Cleve., 1978, Art Gallery Ont., Toronto, 1978, Stadtiches Mus., Monchengladbach, Germany, 1971; represented in permanent collections Milw. Art Ctr., Mus. Modern Art NYC, Fogg Mus., Cambridge, Mass., Phila. Mus. Art, High Mus. Art, Atlanta, Houston Mus. Fine Arts, Corcoran Gallery, Washington, Mpls. Art Inst., Mpls. Art Mus., Met. Mus. Art, NYC, Guggenheim Mus., NYC, Ludwig Mus., Aachen, Fed. Republic Germany, Holladay, Washington, Saatchi, London, Bard, Albright-Knox Art Gallery, Buffalo, Whitney Mus. Am. Art, NYC, U. Mich., Ann Arbor, Ohio State U., Columbus, Gilman Paper Co., NY, Auckland (New Zealand) City Art Mus., Portland (Oreg.) Art Mus., Aaken Art Mus., Oberlin, Ohio, Highhold Internat., South Africa, U. Ohio Art Gallery, Columbus, HHK Charitable Found., Milw., Art Gallery Ont., Nat. Mus. Women in Art, Washington, Chase Manhattan Bank, NYC; installations: Hilton Hotel, San Jose, Calif., Sony Music Hdqrs., Aldridge Mus., Conn., Edward T. Gignoux Courthouse, Portland, Maine. Recipient Witowsky prize, Art Inst., Chgo., 1976, Creative Arts award, Brandeis U., 1985, Bard Coll., 1986, Alliance for Young Artists and Writers Inc. award, 1997, Jimmy Ernst Lifetime Achievement award in art, Am. Acad. Arts and Letters, 1999, Pike award, Nat. Acad. of Art and Design, 2002, Adolph and Clara Obrig prize, Nat. Acad. Design, 2002, Pollock Krasner award, 2002, Omi Internat. Francis J. Greenberger award, 2003; fellow, Guggenheim fellow, 1972; grantee, Nat. Endowment Arts, 1974, Am. Acad. Rome, 1991. Mem.: AAAL. E-mail: drockburne@earthlink.net.

ROCKEFELLER, DAVID, banker; b. N.Y.C., June 12, 1915; s. John Davison Jr. and Abby Greene (Aldrich) R.; m. Margaret McGrath, Sept. 7, 1940 (dec. Mar. 1996); children: David, Abby A., Neva, Margaret D., Richard G., Eileen M. BS, Harvard Coll., 1936; student, London Sch. Econs.; PhD, U. Chgo., 1940; LLD (hon.), Columbia U., 1954, Bowdoin Coll., 1958, Jewish Theol. Sem., 1958, Williams Coll., 1966, Wagner Coll., 1967, Harvard U., 1969, Pace Coll., 1970, St. John's U., 1971, Middlebury, 1974, U. Liberia, 1979, Rockefeller U., 1980, Am. U., 1987, U. Miami, 1988; DEng (hon.), Colo. Sch. Mines, 1974, U. Notre Dame, 1987. Sec. to Mayor Fiorello H. La Guardia, 1940-41; asst. regional dir. Office Def., Health and Welfare Services, 1941-42; asst. mgr. for. dept. Chase Nat. Bank, N.Y.C., 1946-47, asst. cashier, 1947-48, 2d v.p., 1948-49, v.p., 1949-51, sr. v.p., 1951-55; exec. v.p. Chase Manhattan Bank (Chase Nat. Bank merged with Bank of Manhattan), 1955-57; vice chmn. bd. Chase Manhattan Bank, 1957-61, pres., chmn. exec. com., 1961-69, chmn., 1969-81, CEO, 1969-80. Chmn. Chase Internat. Adv. Com., 1981-99, Rockefeller Group, Inc., 1981-95, N.Y. Clearing House, 1971-78, Ctr. for Inter-Am. Rels., 1966-70, Overseas Devel. Coun., U.S.-USSR Trade and Econ. Coun. Inc.; chmn. Internat. Exec. Svc. Corps., 1964-68; chmn. Rockfeller Ctr. Properties Trust, Inc., 1996—. Author: Unused Resources and Economic Waste, 1940, Creative Management in Banking, 1964. Active Urban Devel. Corp., N.Y. State Bus. Adv. Coun., 1968-72, U.S. Adv. Com. on Reform on Internat. Monetary System, 1973-77, U.S. exec. com. Dartmouth Conf. Bd. Inst. Internat. Econs., Am. Friends of LSE, U.S. Hon. Fellows LSE, Bus. Com. for Arts; founding mem. Commn. on White House Fellows, hon. mem., 1964-65; exec. com., chmn. Downtown Lower Manhattan Assn., 1958-75; trustee Rockefeller U., 1940-95, Carnegie Endowment Internat. Peace, Hist. Hudson Valley, 1981—; chmn. Rockefeller Bros. Fund, 1981-87, vice-chmn., 1968-80; hon. trustee Rockefeller Family Fund; life trustee U. Chgo.; trustee, chmn. bd., exec. com. Mus. Modern Art, 1962-72, 87-93; bd. overseers Harvard Coll., 1954-60, 62-68; co-founder Trilateral Commn., 1973-91, N.Am. chmn. 1981-92, hon. chmn., 1992; hon. chmn. Internat. House, 1940—, dir., 1940-63; pres. Morningside Heights, Inc., 1947-57, chmn., 1957-65; chmn. Am. Soc., 1981-92, hon. chmn., 1992—, N.Y.C. Partnership, 1979-88. Capt. AUS, 1942-45, NATOUSA, ETO. Decorated Legion of Honor France, Order of Arts and Letters; Order of the Liberator San Martin, Argentina, Order of Valor, Rep. of Cameroun, Order of Boyaca, Colombia, Order of Christopher Columbus, Domincan Republica, Nat. Order of Merit, Ecuador, Knight Comdr.'s Cross of the Order of Merit, Germany, Order of the Republic, Guinea, Gwengha Medal of the Rep. of Korea, Order of the Aztec Eagle, Mexico, Order of the Throne, Morocco, Hilal-i'Quaid-e-Azam, Pakistan, Order of Vasco Nunez de Balboa, Panama, Order of Manuel Amador Guerrero, Panama, Nat. Order of Merit/Grand Cross, Paraguay, Order of Merit, Italy, Order of Southern Cross, Brazil, Order of the White Elephant and Order of Crown, Thailand, Order of the Cedars, Lebanon, Order of the Sun, Peru, Nicholas Copernicus award, Porland, Order of Prince Henry the Navigator, Portugal, Nat. Order of the Lion, Rep. of Senegal, Order of Francisco de Miranda, Venezuela, Order of the Humane African Redemption, Liberia, Order of the Crown, Belgium, Nat. Order of Ivory Coast, Grand Cordon Order of Sacred Treasure, Japan, Order Bernardo O'Higgins, Chile, others; recipient Merit award N.Y. chpt. AIA, 1965, Gold medal Nat. Inst. Social Scis., 1967, AIA medal of Honor for City Planning N.Y.C., 1968, Charles Evans Hughes award NCCJ, 1974, World Brotherhood award Jewish Theol. Sem, 1953, C. Walter Nichols award NYU, 1970, Regional Planning Assn. award, 1971; Hadrian award, World Monuments Fund, 1994, U.S. Presdl. Medal of Freedom, 1998. Mem. Council Fgn. Relations (dir. 1949-51, v.p. 1951-70, chmn. 1970-85), Japan Soc. (hon. chmn.), Internat. House (hon. chmn.), Bilderberg Conf., Harvard Club, Univ. Club, Century Club, The Links, The Knickerbocker. Avocation: sailing. Address: 30 Rockefeller Plz Rm 5600 New York NY 10112-0002

ROCKEFELLER, EDWIN SHAFFER, lawyer; b. Sept. 10, 1927; s. Edwin and Nancy Rhea (McCullough) R.; m. Marilie Gould Wallace, Dec. 22, 1952; children: Ben Wallace, Edwin Palmer. AB, Yale U., 1948, LLB, 1951; M in Internat. Pub. Policy, Johns Hopkins U., 1989. Bar: Conn. 1951, D.C. 1956, U.S. Supreme Ct. 1957. Atty. FTC, 1956—61, asst. to gen. counsel, 1958—59, exec. asst. to chmn., 1960—61; pvt. practice Washington, 1961; chmn. adv. bd. bna.antitrust rept., 1961—. Mem. USIA Inspection Team, Pakistan, 1971; adj. prof. Georgetown U. Law Ctr., Washington, 1987. Author: Antitrust Questions & Answers, 1974, Desk Book of FTC Practice & Procedure, 3d edit., 1979, Antitrust Counseling for the 1980s, 1983. Mem.: ABA (chmn. sect. antitrust law 1976—77, ho. of dels. 1979—82), Met. Club, Chevy Chase Club. Office: Ste 1114 2801 New Mexico Ave NW Washington DC 20007-3940

ROCKEFELLER, JOHN DAVISON, IV, (JAY ROCKEFELLER), senator, former governor; b. N.Y.C., NY, June 18, 1937; s. John Davison III and Blanchette Ferry (Hooker) R.; m. Sharon Percy, Apr. 1, 1967; children: John, Valerie, Charles, Justin. BA, Harvard U., 1961; student, Japanese lang. Internat. Christian U., Tokyo, 1957-60; postgrad. in Chinese, Yale U. Inst. Far Eastern Langs., 1961-62. Apptd. mem. nat. adv. council Peace Corps, 1961, spl. asst. to dir. corps, 1962, ops. officer in charge work in Philippines, until 1963; desk officer for Indonesian affairs Bur. Far Eastern Affairs, U.S. State Dept., 1963; later asst. to asst. sec. state for Far Eastern affairs; cons. Pres.'s Commn. on Juvenile Delinquency and Youth Crime, 1964; field worker Action for Appalachian Youth program, from 1964; mem. W.Va. Ho. of Dels., 1966-68; sec. of state W.Va., 1968-72; pres. W.Va. Wesleyan Coll., Buckhannon, 1973-75; gov. State of W.Va., 1977—85; U.S. senator from W.Va., 1985—; mem. vets. affairs com., fin. com., commerce, sci. and transp. com.; chmn. sen. steel caucus, Bipartisan Com. on Comprehensive Health Care. Chmn. Nat. Commn. on Children, natural resources and environ. com. Nat. Govs. Assn., 1981-84, Dem. Tech. and Comms. Com., Sen. Steel Caucus, Bipartisan Com. on Comprehensive Health Care; mem. Vets. Affairs Com., Fin. Com., Commerce, Sci. and Transp. Com. Contbr. articles to mags. including N.Y. Times Sunday mag. Trustee U. Chgo., 1967—; chmn. White House Conf. Balanced Nat. Growth and Econ. Devel., 1978, Pres.'s Commn. on Coal, 1978-80, White House Adv. Com. on Coal., 1980; active Commerce, Sci., and Transp. Com., Fin. Com.; ranking mem. Vet. Affairs Com. Democrat. Presbyterian. Office: US Senate 531 Hart Senate Bldg Washington DC 20510-0001

ROCKEFELLER, RICHARD GILDER, medical association administrator; b. N.Y.C., Jan. 20, 1949; MD, Harvard U., 1979, EdM. Diplomate Am. Bd. Family Practice. Intern Highland Hosp.-U. Rochester, 1979—80, resident family practice, 1980—82; founder, pres. Health Commons Inst., Portland, Maine, 1992—; clin. instr. family medicine Maine Med. Ctr.-Mercy Hosp. Family Practice Residency Program. Chmn. adv. bd. Doctors Without Borders. Bd. dirs. Rockefeller U.; bd. trustees Rockefeller Family Fund, Rockefeller Bros. Fund; bd. dirs. Maine Summer Dramatic Inst. Office: Health Commons Inst PO Box 9715 135 Marginal Way #375 Portland ME 04104-5015

ROCKEFELLER, SHARON PERCY, broadcast executive; b. Oakland, Calif., Dec. 10, 1944; d. Charles H. and Jeanne (Dickerson) Percy; m. John D. Rockefeller IV; children: John, Valerie, Charles, Justin. BA cum laude, Stanford U.; LLD (hon.), U. Charleston, 1977, Beloit Coll., 1978; LHD (hon.), West Liberty State Coll., 1980, Hamilton Coll., 1982, Wheeling Coll., 1984. Founder, chmn. Mountain Artisans, 1968—78; chmn. Corp. Pub. Broadcasting, Washington, 1981—84; bd. dirs. Stas. WETA-TV-FM, Washington, 1987—89, pres., 1989—. Past bd. dirs. Sta. WETA-TV-FM, Washington, pres., 1989—; bd. dirs. Pub. Broadcasting Svc., W.Va. Edn. Broadcasting Authority. Mem.-at-large Dem. Nat. Conv., del., 1976, 1980, 1984; bd. dirs. Rockefeller Bros. Fund. Office: Sta WETA-FM 2775 S Quincy St Arlington VA 22206-2236

ROCKEFELLER, WINTHROP P. lieutenant governor; b. Sept. 17, 1948; s. Winthrop Rockefeller Sr.; m. Lisenne Rockefeller; children: Andrea, Katherine, Winthrop Jr., William, Colin, John, Louis. Student, Oxford U.; grad. Ranch Mgmt. Program, Texas Christian U., 1974. Lt. gov. State of Ark., 1996—. Chmn. Pres. Coun. on Rural Am., 1991-93, Juvenile Justice Adv. Group; bd. dirs. Ark. Crime Commn., Tex. Christian U.; mem. Ark. State Police Commn., 1981-95; pres. Ark. Cattlemen's Assn., 1976-78. Vice-chmn. Winthrop Rockefeller Found., Ark. Cancer Rsch. Ctr., Ark. Arts Found.; founder, chmn. Internat. Billfish Conservation, U.S. Marshal's Assn.; trustee Winthrop Rockefeller Charitable Trust. Mem. Ducks Unlimited (trustee emeritus). Republican. Office: Office of Lt Gov State Capitol Bldg Rm270 Little Rock AR 72201-1088

ROCKENSIES, JOHN WILLIAM, mechanical engineer; b. N.Y.C., May 30, 1932; s. John William and Wilma (Mercz) R.; m. Marion Pauline Peachman, Sept. 16, 1956; children: Kenneth John, Karen Martha Rockensies Steinbeck. B of Mech. Engring., CCNY, 1954, M of Mech. Engring., 1960; postgrad., Bklyn. Polytechnic Inst., 1955, Columbia U., 1956. Registered profl. engr., N.Y. Jet engine performance and compressor devel. Curtiss Wright Corp., Woodridge, NJ, 1954-56; product devel. engr. Sperry Gyroscope Corp., Lake Success, NY, 1956-60; sr. exptl. test engr. Pratt & Whitney Corp., East Hartford, Conn., 1960-62; project engr. Stratos Corp., Bayshore, NY, 1962; prin. propulsion engr. Republic Aviation Corp., Farmingdale, 1963-64; power plant design engr., group and project leader, project engr., engr. specialist and mgr. Grumman Aerospace Corp., Bethpage, 1964-95; retired, 1995; contract staff engr. Northrop-Grumman Corp., Bethpage, N.Y., 1996-98. Mem. SAE E-32 Engine Condition Monitoring com., 1983; lt. comdr. Smithtown Bay Power Squadron, instr. navigation. Author tech. papers in field; co-author chpt. in book. Deacon, trustee, elder First Presbyn Ch. of Smithtown; docent Cradle of Aviation Mus., Garden City, N.Y., 2002-. Recipient Apollo Achievement award NASA, Washington, 1970. Assoc. fellow AIAA (mem. air breathing propulsion tech. com. 1996—, coun. mem. LI sect. 2002—, Chmn.'s award 2003); mem. NSPE, ASME, U.S. Power Squadrons (sr. navigator). Avocations: sailing, boating, jogging, camping, travel, model aircraft. Home: 65 Parnell Dr Smithtown NY 11787-2428 Personal E-mail: jrock8@optonline.net.

RÖCKENWAGNER, HANS, chef, restauranteur; m. Patti Röckenwagner; children: Gina, Roxanne, Hansi. Former mem. staff Zum Adier, Switzerland, Le Perroquet Restaurant, Chgo.; chef, co-owner Röckenwagner, L.A., 1984—. Author: Röckenwagner Cookbook, 1997. Named one of Rising Chefs of Am., James Beard Ho., 1992, 300 Reasons Not to Pack Up and Leave L.A., L.A. mag., 1994. Office: Röckenwagner Edgemar Complex 2435 Main St Santa Monica CA 90405

ROCKETT, JOHN ALEXANDER, fire safety consultant; b. Phila. s. Francis Haynes and Katharine Lee (Stewart) Rockett; m. Abby Burgess, June 8, 1956; children: Angus, Katharine. BS, MIT, 1944; MS, Brown U., 1951; PhD, Harvard U., 1958. Rsch. asst. MIT, Cambridge, Mass., 1951—56; project engr. Pratt & Whitney Aircraft, East Hartford, Conn., 1956—65; dir. basic rsch. Factory Mutual Rsch. Assn., Norwood, Mass., 1966—68; sect. chief U.S. Nat. Bur. Stats., Gaithersburg, Md., 1968—86; cons. Fire Modeling & Analysis, Peterborough, NH, 1986—. With USN, 1944—46. Mem.: Internat. Assn. Fire Safety Soc. (awards com. chmn. 1986—2000), Soc. Fire Protection Engrs. (Harry Bigelstone award). Avocation: skiing.

ROCKETT, THOMAS J. retired management consultant; b. Medford, Mass., June 4, 1934; s. John Francis Rockett and Agnes Mary Connor; m. Sarah Ellen Hough, Oct. 24, 1964; children: Matthew Thomas, Andrew Frank, Daniel Patrick. BS, Tufts U., 1956; MS, Boston Coll., 1958; PhD, Ohio State U., 1963. Rsch. scientist USAF, Dayton, Ohio, 1961—64, Monsanto, St. Louis, 1964—68; asst. lab. dir. Baxter/Am., Evanston, Ill., 1968—71; prof. materials. engring. U. R.I., 1971—85, vice provost rsch. and grad. studies, 1995—2000; dept. chair/prof. U. R.I.19, 1985—95; cons./writer Self-Employed, East Greenwich, RI, 2000—03; ret., 2003. Cons. product devel., innovation, rsch. mgmt. Contbr. articles. Gov. R.I. Bd. for Higher Edn., Providence, 2002—; trustee Kent County VNA Directors, Warwick, 1990—95, Directors East Greenwich Libr., 2000—. Several rsch. grants, 1972—95. Mem.: Am. Mineralogic Soc., Am. Ceramic Soc., Am. Soc. Metals (pres. 1975—2000). Republican. Roman Cath. Achievements include patents for biomaterials; discovery of role of water in deterioration in polymers; cause of phase separation in glass and polymers. Avocations: cross country skiing, golf, reading. Home: 216 Maplewood Dr East Greenwich RI 02818

ROCKEY, EUGENE A., JR., vocational school educator, scriptwriter; b. Louisville, Ky., Sept. 17, 1963; s. Eugene A. Rockey Sr. and Hazel Rockey; 1 child, Krystal. Student, Ky. Coll. Tech., 1986, Ind. U., Lexington, 1996—2004, U. Ky., 1996—2004; A in Elec. Engring. Cert. elec. tech. Internat. Soc. Cert. Electronics Technicians, 1989, consumer elec. journeyman Internat. Soc. Cert. Electronics Technicians, 1990, computer elec. journeyman Internat. Soc. Cert. Electronics Technicians, 1991, lic. TV and radio tech. Ind., 1993. Educator Jefferson State Vocat., Louisville, 1990, Radio Elec. Tech. Sch., Louisville, 1990—93, Ivy Tech. State Coll., Sellersburg, Ind., 1993—2003; advisor, test proctor Skills USA, Sellersburg, 2003; screenplay writer. Author: (plays) Only Time..., 2003. Mem. Am. Ctr. for Law and Justice, Washington, 2003, 700 Club, 2003. With1983 USAF, 1982. Republican. Avocations: soccer, fishing, guitar. Home: PO Box 22091 Louisville KY 40252

ROCKLAND, LAWRENCE HOWARD, psychiatrist, educator; b. N.Y.C., Apr. 13, 1932; s. Milton and Bess Sherry Rockland; m. Charlotte Francis Roberts, June 29, 1957; children: Nancy, Thomas, Peter. BS, Union Coll., 1952; MD, Albany Med. Ctr., 1956. Diplomate Am. Bd. Psychiatry and Neurology. Rsch. psychiatrist NIMH, Bethesda, Md., 1959—61; pvt. practice Scarsdale, Larchmont, NY, 1961—; instr. psychiatry Georgetown Med. Coll., Washington, 1961—63; asst. prof. psychiatry Albert Einstein Coll. Medicine, N.Y.C., 1967—76; assoc. prof. clin. psychiatry Cornell U. Med. Coll., N.Y.C., 1982—99; assoc. prof. psychiatry emeritus Weill/Cornell Med. Coll., N.Y.C., 1999—; assoc. prof. clin. psychiatry U. Mass. Med. Coll., Worcester, 1999—2002. Cons. Montgomery County Child Clinic, Rockville, Md., 1962—66, US Peace Corps, Washington, 1963—66, Carson Adult Family Clinic, Westfield, Mass., 1999—2002. Contbr. articles to profl. jours., chapters to books; author: Supportive Therapy, 1989, Supportive Therapy for Borderlines, 1992, La Terapia di Sostegno, 1994. Surgeon USPHS, 1959—2003. Fellow: Am. Psychoanalytic Assn. (exec. coun. 1976—79, 1985—2001), Am. Psychiat. Assn. (disting.); mem.: Group for Advancement Psychiatry, Sigma Xi, Phi Beta Kappa, Alpha Omega Alpha. Avocations: music, hiking, physical exercise, reading. Home and Office: 7 East Drive Larchmont NY 10538 Office Phone: 914-834-7601.

ROCKLEN, KATHY HELLENBRAND, lawyer; b. NYC, June 30, 1951; BA, Barnard Coll., 1973; JD magna cum laude, New England Sch. Law, 1977. Bar: NY 1978, US Dist. Ct. (so. and ea. dists.) NY 1982, US Dist. Ct. (no. dist.) Calif. 1985. Interpretive counsel NY Stock Exchange, NYC; 1st v.p. E.F. Hutton & Co. Inc., NYC; v.p., gen. counsel, sec. S.G Warburg (USA) Inc., NYC; mem. Proskauer Rose LLP, NYC. Adj. prof. Fordham Sch. Law. Mem. bd. dirs., NY lawyers Pub. Interest; mem. exec. com. lawyers divsn. Am. Friends Hebrew U.; mem. lawyers' divsn. exec. com. ADL; mem. adv. com. NY Women's Bar Found. Mem. NY State Bar Assn., NY Women's Bar Assn., Assn. Bar City NY (v.p., chmn. exec. com., chmn. drugs law com., chmn. fed. legis. com., chmn. libr. com., securities law com., sec. 2d century com., sex law com., young lawyers' com., corp. law com.). Office: Proskauer Rose LLP 1585 Broadway New York NY 10036 Office Phone: 212-969-3755. E-mail: krocklen@proskauer.com.

ROCKMAN, ILENE FRANCES, librarian, educator, editor; b. Yonkers, NY, Nov. 9, 1950; d. Leon and Margaret (Klein) Rockman; m. Fred Gertler, Mar. 9, 1996. BA, UCLA, 1972; MSLS, U. So. Calif., 1974; MA, Calif. Poly. State U., 1978; PhD, U. Calif., Santa Barbara, 1985. Libr. Wash. State U., Pullman, Wash., 1974—75, Calif. Poly. State U., San Luis Obispo, 1975—98, Calif. State U., Hayward, 1998—2001, office of the chancellor, 2001—. Adj. prof. Cuesta Coll., San Luis Obispo, 1982—85; abstracter Women Studies Abstracts, Rush, NY, 1976—91. Contbr. articles to profl. jours.; editor: Reference Svcs. Rev., 1986—; co-author: BLISS-Basic Library Information Sources and Svcs., 1991—95; mem. editl. bd.: Jour. Acad. Librarianship, 2003, Libr. Hi Tech., 1997—, Am. Libr., 1997—99; editor: Integrating Information Literacy into the Higher Education Curriculum: Practical Models for Transformation, 2004. Del. Dem. Nat. Conv., 1984; bd. dirs. Friends of Hayward Pub. Libr., 2001—. Recipient scholarship, Calif. PTA, L.A., 1973, Literati award, MCB Univ. Press, 2001. Mem.: ALA, Total Libr. Exch. (pres. 1979—80), Am. Ednl. Rsch. Assn., Calif. Assn. Rsch. Librs. (mem. exec. bd. 1998—99), Assn. Coll. and Rsch. Librs. (mem. exec. com. edn. and behavioral sci. sect. 1988—90, mem. exec. com. univ. libr. sect. 1999—2002, Disting. Libr. of Yr. Ednl. and Behavioral Sect. 2003), Calif. Libr. Assn. (mem. coun. 1983—86), Spl. Libr. Assn., Am. Assn. Higher Edn., Calif. Reading Assn. (Exemplary Svc. award 1992), Libr. Assocs. Calif. Poly. State U. (exec. sec. 1981—83). Business E-Mail: irockman@calstate.edu.

ROCKOFF, HUGH TOUFF, economist, educator; b. Dayton, Ohio, Feb. 8, 1945; s. Joseph Rockoff and Mildred Touff; m. Hope Corman; children: Jessica, Steven. BA, Earlham Coll., 1967; PhD, U. of Chgo., 1971. Prof. of economics Rutgers U., New Brunswick, NJ, 1971—. Author: The Free Banking Era, 1975, Drastic Measures: A History of Wage and Price Controls, 1984, History of the American Economy, 2002. Mem.: Econ. History Assn. (v.p. 2002—03). Office: Rutgers University 75 Hamilton Street New Brunswick NJ 08901 Office Phone: 732-932-7857.

ROCKOFF, MARK ALAN, pediatric anesthesiologist; b. Jersey City, Apr. 13, 1948; s. Aaron and Rose Rockoff; m. Elizabeth Sceery, Aug. 6, 1978; children: Benjamin, Jillian, Michael. BS, MIT, 1969; MD, Johns Hopkins U., 1973. Diplomate Am. Bd. Pediatrics, Am. Bd. Critical Care, Am. Bd. Anesthesiology. Pediatric intern and resident Mass. Gen. Hosp., Boston, 1973-75, anesthesia resident, 1975-77, assoc. dir. pediatric ICU, 1979-81; neuroanesthesia fellow U. Calif., San Diego, 1978-79; assoc. dir. ICU Children's Hosp., Boston, 1981-89, assoc. anesthesiologist-in-chief, 1988—; med. dir. operating rm., 1992-99; prof. anaesthesia Harvard Med. Sch., Boston, 1999—. Editor jours. Survey of Anesthesiology, 1984-94, Jour. Neurosurg. Anesthesiology, 1994-98. Fellow: Soc. Critical Care Medicine, Am. Acad. Pediats., Am. Soc. Anesthesiologists; mem.: Soc. Pediat. Anesthesia (pres. 1996—98), Am. Bd. Anesthesiology (dir. 2000—). Office: Children's Hosp 300 Longwood Ave Boston MA 02115-5737

ROCKOFF, S. DAVID, radiologist, physician, educator; b. Utica, N.Y., July 21, 1931; s. Samuel and Sarah (Rattinger) R.; m. Jacqueline Garsh; children—Lisa E., Todd E., Kevin D. AB, Syracuse U., 1951; MD, Albany Med. Coll., 1955; M.Sc. in Medicine, U. Pa., 1961. Diplomate: Am. Bd. Radiology. Intern U.S. Naval Hosp., Bethesda, Md., 1955-56; resident and fellow in radiology, USPHS trainee dept. radiology p. of U. Pa., Phila., 1958-61; staff radiologist NIH, Bethesda, Md., 1961-65; asst. prof. radiology Yale U. Sch. Medicine, New Haven, 1965-68, assoc. prof., 1968; asst. attending radiologist Yale-New Haven Med. Center, 1965-68; assoc. prof. radiology Washington U. Sch. Medicine, St. Louis, 1968-71; asst. radiologist Barnes and Allied Hosps., St. Louis, 1969-71; cons. radiologist VA Hosp., St. Louis, 1969-71, Homer G. Phillips Hosp., St. Louis, 1968-71; prof. radiology George Washington U. Sch. Medicine, Washington, 1971—, chmn. dept. radiology, 1971-77, head pulmonary radiology, 1978—, interim chmn. dept. radiology, 1989-90, prof. emeritus radiology, 1993—. Cons. NIH, 1972—; vis. prof. Hadassah U., Beersheba U., Rambam Hosp., Israel, 1977; cons. in radiology VA Hosp., Washington, 1972-77, U.S. Naval Med. Center, Bethesda, 1973-77; mem. diagnostic radiology adv. com. NIH, 1973-76; mem. Cancer Research Manpower Rev. Com., NIH, 1978 Editor-in-chief: Investigative Radiology, 1965-76; editor-in-chief emeritus, 1976—; editor Jour. Thoracic Imaging, 1985; reviewer Jour. Computed Tomography, 1997—; contbr. numerous articles to med. jours. Served with USN, 1955-58; Served with USPHS, 1961-63. Recipient numerous USPHS grants. Fellow Am. Coll. Radiology (pres.-elect D.C. chpt. 1976), Am. Coll. Chest Physicians; mem. Am. Fedn. Clin. Research, D.C. Med. Soc. (mem. med.-legal com. 1975-78), AMA, Radiol. Soc. N.Am. (mem. roster of disting. sci. advisors Rsch. and Edn. Found. 1999), Assn. Univ. Radiologists, Soc. Thoracic Radiology (pres. 1983-84, exec. dir. 1984-87). Home: PO Box 675650 Rancho Santa Fe CA 92067-5650

ROCKOWITZ, NOAH EZRA, lawyer; b. N.Y.C., Apr. 11, 1949; s. Murray and Anna Rae (Cohen) Rockowitz; m. Julie Rachel Levitan, Dec. 24, 1978; children: Shira Aviva, Leora Civia, Dahlia Yaffa. BA, Queens Coll., 1969; JD, Fordham U., 1973. Bar: N.Y. 1974, U.S. Dist. Ct. (so. and ea. dists.) N.Y. 1974, U.S. Ct. Appeals (2d cir.) 1974. Tchr., chmn. social studies dept. Intermediate Sch. 74, Queens, NY, 1969-73; atty. Cahill Gordon & Reindel, N.Y.C., 1973-78; corp. sec., asst. gen. counsel Belco Petroleum Corp., N.Y.C., 1978—85; v.p., gen. counsel Hudson Gen. Corp., Great Neck, NY, 1985-98, sr. v.p., 1998—2001; sr. v.p., gen. counsel GlobeGround N.Am. LLC, Great Neck, 2001—03. Trustee, mem. exec. com., chmn. bd. edn. Solomon Schechter Sch., Westchester, NY; mem. Westchester adv. com. Bd. Jewish Edn. Greater N.Y.; trustee Beth El Synagogue New Rochelle. Mem.: ABA,

Assn. Corp. Counsel, Assn. Bar City of N.Y., N.Y. State Bar Assn., Am. Soc. Corp. Secs., Phi Beta Kappa. Office: GlobeGround NAm LLC 111 Great Neck Rd PO Box 355 Great Neck NY 11022-0355

ROCKSWOLD, GAYLAN LEE, neurosurgeon; b. Valley City, N.D., Dec. 11, 1940; s. E. Palmer and Myrna Christine R.; m. Mary Helen Garnass, June 27, 1964; children: Sarah Beth, Payl Gaylan, Nathan Kristopher. BA, St. Olaf Coll., 1962; MD, U. Minn., 1966, PhD, 1976. Diplomate Am. Bd. Neurol. Surgery. Intern Hennepin County Gen. Hosp., Mpls., 1966-67; gen. surgery resident USPHS Hosp., Balt., 1967-68; med. assoc. sect. neurosurgery Nat. Cancer Inst., Balt., 1969; med. fellow dept. surgery U. Minn., Mpls., 1969; med. assoc. Nat. Cancer Inst., Balt., 1969; from instr. to prof. U. Minn., Mpls., 1974-92, prof., 1992—; chief neurosurgery divsn. Hennepin County Med. Ctr., Mpls., 1977—. Pres. Neurosurgical Assocs., Ltd., Mpls., 1997—; adv. bd. Mpls. Neurosci. Inst.,1992—, v.p. 1998—; presenter in field. Author: (with others) 11 chpts. in books; contbr. over 45 articles in profl. jours. Adv. THINK First Head and Spinal Cord Injury Prevention Program, Mpls., 1990-91; mentor Mentor Connection Program for High Sch. Students, Mpls., 1995-96. Recipient Recognition award Minn. Head Injury Assn., Mpls., 1993; Smith-Kline-French Foreign fellow Malawi, East Africa, 1965. Mem. ACS (Minn. chpt. com. on trauma), AMA (Minn. state chpt.), Am. Assn. Surgery of Trauma, Neurosurg. Soc. Am., Am. Assn. Neurological Surgeons, Congress Neurological Surgeons, Minn. Neurosurg. Soc. (sec., treas., v.p., pres. 1989-95), Hennepin County Med. Soc., Hitchcock Surg. Soc., The Wilderness Soc., Phi Beta Kappa, Alpha Omega Phi. Lutheran. Avocations: sailing, backpacking, reading history and biographies, canoeing, fishing. Office: Hennepin County Med Ctr 701 Park Ave Minneapolis MN 55415-1623 E-mail: rocks001@maroon.tc.umn.edu.

ROCKWELL, BRUCE MCKEE, retired banker and foundation executive; b. Denver, Dec. 18, 1922; s. Robert B. and Florence (McKee) R.; m. Virginia Packard, Apr. 22, 1950; children— David, Jane, Sarah. BA, Yale U., 1945. Exec. sec. to mayor City of Denver, 1947-51; pub. rels. and advt. account exec. William Kostka & Assocs., 1952-53; with Colo. Nat. Bank, Denver, 1953-85, pres., 1970-75, chmn., CEO, 1975-85, also dir.; pres. Colo. Trust, Denver, 1985-91; sr. cons. BBC, Inc., Denver, 1991. Chmn., bd. dirs. The Denver Partnership, Inc., Kaiser Permanente, 1980-92; bd. dirs. Am. Pub. Welfare Assn., 1989-91; chmn. Denver Urban Renewal Authority, 1958-68; nat. coun. Salk Inst., 1978-84; trustee C.C. Denver, Com. Econ. Devel., 1979-85, Denver Symphony Orch., 1974-77, Denver Art Mus., 1965-72, 82-86, Denver Health Authority, 1995—; trustee Colo. Hist. Soc., 1980—, chmn., 1986-87; mem. Colo. Moffat Tunnel Commn., 1997-98. Ensign USNR, 1945-46. Named Colo. Bus. Man of Yr., Colo. Bus. mag., 1976, Rotary Club, 1984. Mem. Assn. Res. City Bankers (dir. 1975-85), Denver C. of C., Univ. Club, Tennis Club. Home: 2800 S University Blvd #18 Denver CO 80210

ROCKWELL, DON ARTHUR, retired psychiatrist; b. Wheatland, Wyo, Apr. 24, 1938; s. Orson Arthur and Kathleen Emily Rockwell; m. Frances Pepitone-Arreola, Dec. 23, 1965; children: Grant, Chad. BA, Wash. U., 1959; MD, U. Okla., 1963; MA in Sociology, U. Calif., Berkeley, 1967. Diplomate Am. Bd. Psychiatry and Neurology. Intern in surgery San Francisco Gen. Hosp., 1963-64; resident in psychiatry Langley-Porter Neuropsychiatric Inst. U. Calif. Med. Ctr., San Francisco, 1964-67; instr. dept. psychiatry U. Calif. Sch. Medicine, Davis, 1969-70, asst. prof., 1970-74, assoc. prof., 1974-80, acting. assoc., dean curricular affiars, 1979-80, acting assoc. dean student affairs, 1980, assoc. dean student affairs, 1980-82, prof., 1980-84; career tchr. NIMH, 1970-72; assoc. psychiatrist Sacramento Med. Ctr.; med. dir. U. Calif. Med. Ctr., Davis, 1982-84; prof., vice chmn. dept. psychiatry and biobehavioral sci. UCLA, 1984-96; dir. UCLA Neuropsychiat. Hosp., 1984-95; chief profl. staff Neuropsychiat. Inst., UCLA, 1984-85, also dir. outpatient svc. Chmn. U. Calif. Hosp. Dir. Council, 1988-89; cons. Nat. Commn. on Marijuana, Washington, 1971-73; mem. Santa Barbara County Civil Grand Jury, 2001-02. Co-author: Psychiatric Disorders, 1982; contbr. chpts. to books; articles to profl. jour. Mem. bd. visitors U. Okla. Sch. Medicine; chmn. hosp. dirs. coun. U. Calif. Hosp.; mem. governing coun. AHA Psychiat. Hosp.; mem. County of Santa Barbara Civil Grand Jury, 2001—02; bd. dir. Bereavement Outreach, Sacramento, 1974—84, Suicide Prevention, Yolo County, 1969—84. Fellow APA (disting. life), Am. Coll. Psychiatrists, Am. Coll. Mental Health Adminstr.; mem. AMA (gov. coun. psych. hosp.), Am. Sociologic Assn., Calif. Med. Assn. (med. staff survey com.), Cen. Calif. Psychiat. Assn. (sec.-pres. 1977-78), U. Okla. Alumni Assn. (trustee 1981-86), Alpha Omega Alpha. Home: 1816 E Las Tunas Rd Santa Barbara CA 93103-1744 Personal E-mail: rockwell@west.net.

ROCKWELL, ELIZABETH DENNIS, retirement specialist, financial planner; b. Houston, Tex., 1921; d. Robert Richard and Nezzell Alderton (Christie) Dennis. Student, Rice U., 1939—40, U. Houston, 1938—39, student, 1940—42, D (hon.), 1999. Purchasing agt. Standard Oil Co., Houston, 1942—66; v.p. mktg. Heights Savs. Assn., Houston, 1967—82; exec. dir. investments CIBC Oppenheimer Corp., Houston, 1982—2001; exec. prof. U. Houston Coll. Bus., 1992—. Contbr.: articles on retirement planning, tax planning and tax options, monthly article 50 Plus sect. for Houston Chronicle newspaper. V.p. Desk and Derrick Club Am., 1960—61; bd. dirs. ARC, 1985—91, Houston Heights Assn., 1973—77; sr. v.p. Oppenheimer, 1986—; mem. found. bd. Coll. Bus. U., Houston, 1990, mem. million dollar roundtable, 1991—, mem. ct. of the table, 1991—, Top of Table, 1996—; mem. U. Houston Sys. Planned Giving Coun., U. Houston Found., 2000—; mem. coll. bus. adv. bd. U. Houston Coll. Bus., 1992—, mem. alumni bd., 1987—95; apptd. trustee U. Houston Sys. Found., Inc.l, 1992; bd. govs. Houston Forum; active Tex. Leader's Round Table, 1994; pres. U. Houston Coll. Bus. Adminstrn. Found., 1986—2000; mem. Houston C.C. Adv. Bd. for Ednl. TV. Named Disting. Alumnae, Coll. Bus. Alum. Assn., U. Houston, 1992, YWCA Outstanding Woman of Yr., 1978; recipient Disting. Alumna, U. Houston Alumni Orgn., 1996, award, Freedoms Found., 2004, Jesse H. Jones award for philanthropy, ARC, 2004, Roger Eichhorn Leadership Svc. award, U. Houston Coll. Engring., 2004. Mem.: Houston Heights Assn. (charter, dir. 1973—77), U.S. Savs. and Loan League (com. on deposit acquisitions and adminstrn.), Soc. Savs. Instns., Fin. Mgrs., Inst. Fin. Edn., Savs. Inst. Mktg. Soc. Am. (Key Person award 1974), Am. Savs. and Loan League (chpt. pres. 1971—72, pres. 1972—73, state dir. 1973—76, Leaders award 1972), Greater Houston Women's Found. (charter), U. Houston Alumni Orgn. (life), U. Houston Bus. Women's Assn. (pres. 1985), Rice U. Bus. and Profl. Women, Harris County Heritage Soc., Friends of Bayou Bend, Forum Club, River Oaks Bus. Women's Exch. Club.

ROCKWELL, ELIZABETH GOODE, dance company director, consultant, educator; b. Portland, Oreg., Sept. 10, 1920; d. Henry Walton and Elizabeth (Harmon) Goode; m. William Hearne Rockwell, Feb. 3, 1948; children: Enid, Karen, William. BA, Mills Coll., 1941; MA, NYU, 1946. Instr. dance Monticello Jr. Coll., Alton, Ill., 1941-42; dir. masters program in dance Smith Coll., Northampton, Mass., 1946-48; 1st dir. dance dept. High Sch. of Performing Arts, N.Y.C., 1948-51, 53-54; dir. Elizabeth Rockwell Sch. Dance, Bedford, N.Y., 1956-86, Rondo Dance Theater Internat. Dance Touring Co., Bedford, 1971-93; tchr. continuing dance classes CCAE, 1994—; with Martha Graham, 1944-46; with Hanya Holm, 1946-48; with José Limon, 1949-52. Mem. adv. ednl. com. Calif. Ctr. for Arts, Escondido, Calif., 1993-95, dir. dance classes, 1994—; tchr. master class, choreographer Waitukubuli Dance Theater, Dominica, 1999; dir. prime dance performance Artists Coming of Age, U. San Diego, 1999. Choreographer (suite of dances) Jazz Suite, 1966, (50-minute dances) Catch the Wind, 1969, Genesis, 1972, (narrative modern ballet) The Executioner, 1974, Decathalon, 1982; dir. (subscription series) Dance-Art-Poetry-Jazz, 1978-79, (dance/music 1600-1900) Stages in Ages, 1981, (Am. dance revivals) Masterpieces of American Dance, 1982-84, Dances of the Decades, 1985-90, (revival & new choreography) Dances of Our Times, 1991; dir. dance workshops for Calif. Ctr. Arts, 1994, 95, 96; creator, founder performing group of older dancers Golden Connections Dance Ensemble of Women, CCAE, (touring San Diego area), 1996—. Bd. dirs. Coun. for Arts in Westchester, White Plains, N.Y., 1978-79, affiliate, 1978— Recipient Medal for Performance, Israeli Army, 1966, Award for Excellence in Arts Edn. Alumnae of High Sch. of Performing Arts, 1990, Tommy Dance award of distinction San Diego Area Dance Alliance, 1999; various grants N.Y. State Coun. on Arts, 1971-93, Coun. Arts in Westchester, 1973-92, dance touring program grant Nat. Endowment for Arts, 1975-79. Mem. Am. Dance Guild, Westchester Dance Coun. (program dir. 1965-69), Assn. Am. Dance Cos., San Diego Area Dance Alliance (bd. dirs. 1995—). Avocations: writing, swimming, touring, reading. Home: 335 Saxony Rd #232 Encinitas CA 92024-2723

ROCKWELL, THEODORE, nuclear engineer; b. Chgo., June 26, 1922; s. Theodore G. and Paisley (Shane) R.; m. Mary Juanita Compton, Jan. 25, 1947; children: Robert C. (dec.), W. Teed, Lawrence E., Juanita C. BS in Engring, Princeton U., 1943, Chem.E. (MS), 1945; grad. courses, Oak Ridge, 1944-49; D.Sc. (hon.), Tri-State U., 1960. Registered profl. engr., D.C. 1964-1990. Process improvement engr. Manhattan Project, Oak Ridge, 1944-45; head shield engring. group Oak Ridge Nat. Lab., 1945-49; nuclear engr., naval reactors br. AEC, also nuclear propulsion divs. Navy Bur. Ships, 1949-55, tech. dir., 1955-64; founding officer, dir. MPR Assos., Inc., Washington, 1964—; research asso. Johns Hopkins U. Center Fgn. Policy Research, 1965-66. Chmn. Atomic Indsl. Forum Reactor Safety Task Force, 1966-72; mem. adv. group artificial heart program NIH, 1966; cons. to Joint Congl. Com. on Atomic Energy, 1967; founding officer, dir. Radiation, Sci. & Health, Inc., 1996—. Author: The Rickover Effect: How One Man Made a Difference, 1992, Creating the New World, 2003; co-author: Shippingport Pressurized Water Reactor, 1958, Arms Control Agreements/Designs Verification, 1968; co-founder Princeton Engr.; editor: Reactor Shield Design Manual, 1956; contbg. editor: New Realities, 1988—92; contbr. sci. articles to profl. publs., non-tech. articles to nat. mags. Mem. adv. council dept. chem. engring. Princeton U., 1966-72. Recipient Disting. Civilian Svc. medal USN, 1960, Disting. Svc. medal AEC, 1960, Lifetime Contbn. award Am. Nuclear Soc. (1st, now known as Rockwell award), 1986. Fellow Am. Nuclear Soc., Am. Soc. Psychical Rsch. (life); mem. AAAS (rep. of Parapsychol. Assn. to AAAS 1975-87), N.Y. Acad. Scis., Soc. for Sci. Exploration, U.S. Psychotronic Assn. (dir. 1988-91), Nat. Inst. for Discovery Sci. (sci. adv. bd. 1995—), Nat. Acad. Engring. (Sigma Xi disting. lectr. 2003—), Authors Guild, Writers Ctr., Washington Ind. Writers, Cosmos Club (Washington), Nat. Press Club. Presbyterian (elder). Achievements include several patents; patent applications for neutron-absorbing cermets and plastics, also others. Address: 3403 Woolsey Dr Chevy Chase MD 20815-3924 E-mail: tedrock@starpower.net.

ROCKWELL, WINTHROP ADAMS, lawyer; b. Pittsfield, Mass., May 7, 1948; s. Landon Gale Rockwell and Ruth (Adams) Lonsdale; m. Barbara Washburn Wood, June 20, 1970; children: Samuel Adams, Madeleine McCord. AB, Dartmouth Coll., 1970; JD, NYU, 1975. Bar: Minn. 1975, U.S. Dist. Ct. Minn. 1975. Asst. newsman fgn. desk N.Y. Times, N.Y.C., 1970-71; asst. to pres. Dartmouth Coll., Hanover, N.H., 1971-72; assoc. Faegre & Benson, Mpls., 1975-79; assoc. chief counsel Pres.'s Commn. on Accident at Three Mile Island, Washington, 1979; assoc. Faegre & Benson, Mpls., 1979-82, ptnr., 1983—. Chmn. diversity com. Faegre & Benson, 1990—95, head gen. litig. group, 1995—2004, mem. mgmt. com., 2004—. Bd. dirs., v.p. Children's Theatre, Mpls., 1982-83; bd. dirs. Actors Theatre St. Paul, 1975-79, Trinity Films, Mpls., 1978-82, Minn. Ctr. for Book Arts, 1996-2003; adv. bd. U. Minn. Joint Degree Program in Law, Health and the Life Scis. Brit.-Am. Project fellow, 1987. Mem. ABA, Minn. Bar Assn., Hennepin County Bar Assn., Am. Agrl. Law Assn., Adirondack 46ers, Adirondack Mountain Club. Avocations: writing, tennis, mountain climbing, gardening. Home: 1901 Knox Ave S Minneapolis MN 55403-2840 Office: Faegre & Benson 2200 Wells Fargo Ctr 90 S 7th St Ste 2200 Minneapolis MN 55402-3901 E-mail: wrockwell@faegre.com.

ROCKWOOD, FREDERICK WHITNEY, insurance company executive; b. Salt Lake City, Dec. 18, 1947; s. Lewis Frederick and Muriel (Whitney) R.; m. Alyce Jolene Edmunds, Aug. 26, 1970; children: Justin, Melissa, Jennifer, Katherine, Elizabeth, David. Student, U. Utah, 1966-67, Columbia U., N.Y.C., 1970; AB in Anthropology, Stanford U., 1972; JD, Harvard U., 1975. Bar: Mass. Corp. strategy cons. Boston Cons., 1975-77; corp. strategy cons. Bain & Co., Boston, 1977; dir. corp. strategy Hillenbrand Industries, Inc., Batesville, Ind., 1977-78, sr. v.p., 1978-85; pres. The Forethought Group, Batesville, 1985—. Mem. adj. faculty U. Mich. Grad. Sch. Bus., 1980; pres., bd. dirs. Rockwood Furniture, Inc., Salt Lake City, 1985—; chmn. curriculum adv. coun. Ind. State Bd. Edn., 1987-92. Rep. Ch. of Jesus Christ of Latter-day Saints, Hong Kong, 1967-69; unit scouting coord. Dan Beard coun. Boy Scouts Am., Cin., 1982-91; bishop Ch. of Jesus Christ, Batesville, 1986-90. Mem. ABA, Fellow Life Mgmt. Inst. (chartered life underwriter 1990, chartered fin. cons. 1992), Am. Mgmt. Assn., Phi Beta Kappa. Republican. Avocations: philately; genealogy. Office: The Forethought Group Forethought Ctr Batesville IN 47006

ROCKWOOD, IRVING E., JR., publisher; b. Norwood, Mass., Dec. 13, 1944; s. Irving E. and Cassie A. (Richardson) R.; m. Nancy E. Wilcox, June 14, 1969; children: Catherine Anne, Margaret Elaine. BA in Polit. Sci., No. Ill. U., 1967, MA in Polit. Sci., 1969. Sales rep. Coll. Divsn. Houghton Mifflin Co., Geneva, Ill., 1970-72, maths. editor Coll. Divsn. Boston, 1972-74; editor, math. and econs. Coll. Divsn. D.C. Heath, Lexington, Mass., 1974-76; gen. editor U. Wis. Press, Madison, 1976-79; exec. editor Longman, Inc., N.Y.C., 1979-85; pres. Irving Rockwood & Assocs., Inc., Chappaqua, N.Y., 1985-89; pub. Dushkin Pub. Group, Guilford, Conn., 1989-95; editor and pub. Choice, Middletown, Conn., 1995—. Mem. rsch. libr. delegation Citizen Amb. Program People to People, S. Africa, 1997; chair grants subcom. Horace Greeley Edn. Fund, Chappaqua, N.Y., 1989-95. Mem. Am. Polit. Sci. Assn., Soc. for Scholarly Pub., Am. Soc. Assn. Execs., ALA, Assn. Coll. and Rsch. Librs. Mem. Ch. of Christ. Avocations: reading, hiking, do-it-yourself projects, choral singing. Office: Choice 100 Riverview Ctr Middletown CT 06457-3401 E-mail: irockwood@ala-choice.org.

ROCKWOOD, MARCIA, magazine editor; Exec. editor Reader's Digest, Pleasantville, N.Y. Office: Reader's Digest Reader's Digest Rd Pleasantville NY 10570-7000

ROCQUE, VINCENT JOSEPH, lawyer; b. Franklin, N.H., Nov. 27, 1945; s. Francis Albert and Mary Helen (O'Grady) R.; m. Emily Adams Arnold, May 31, 1969; children: Amanda Adams, Peter O'Connor, Caroline Quinn. BA magna cum laude, Georgetown U., 1967; JD, Columbia U., N.Y.C., 1970. Bar: D.C. 1971, U.S. Supreme Ct., 1973. Assoc. Hogan & Hartson, Washington, 1970-73; counsel, spl. asst. to Commr. Barbara Franklin, U. S. Consumer Product Safety Commn., Washington, 1973-77; asst. dir. bur. trade regulation U.S. Dept. Commerce, Washington, 1977-80; ptnr. Sullivan & Worcester, Washington, 1980-90; pvt. practice law Washington, 1990—. V.p., co-pres. Janney Pub. Elem. Sch. PTA, Washington, 1982-84; vol. coord. homeless shelters Cath. Charities, Washington and Silver Spring, Md., 1984-90. Staff sgt. USAR, 1969-75. Mem. ABA (adminstrv. law and regulatory practice sect. and internat. law and practice sect.), D.C. Bar (internat. law sect. and adminstrv. law and agy. sect.), Fed. Bar Assn. (adminstrv. law and internat. law sects.), Mid-Atlantic Literary Edification Soc., Nat. Capital YMCA, Phi Beta Kappa. Catholic. Avocations: reading, travel, American Civil War history. Office: Ste 1000 1155 Connecticut Ave NW Washington DC 20036-4306

RODA, JOSEPH FRANCIS, lawyer; b. Lancaster, Pa., June 22, 1949; s. Frank Edward and Mary Virginia (Reeder) R.; m. Dianne M. Nast, Aug. 23, 1980; children: Michael, Daniel, Joseph, Joshua, Anastasia. AB, Harvard Coll., 1971; JD, U. Pa., 1974. Bar: Pa. 1974, U.S. Dist. Ct. (ea. dist.) Pa. 1975, U.S. Dist. Ct. (mid. dist.) Pa. 1981, U.S. Ct. Appeals (3d cir.) 1981, U.S. Supreme Ct. 1982. Law clk. to judge U.S. Dist. Ct. (ea. dist.) Pa., Phila., 1974-75; assoc. Kohn, Savette, Marion & Graf, P.C., Phila., 1975-80; pvt. practice Lancaster, 1980—. Mem. ABA, ATLA, Am. Coll. Trial Lawyers, Pa. Trial Lawyers Assn., Internat. Acad. Trial Lawyers, Pa. Bar Assn. (ho. dels), Lancaster Country Club, Hamilton Club (Lancaster). Home: 1059 Sylvan Rd Lancaster PA 17601-1923 Office: 801 Estelle Dr Lancaster PA 17601-2130 Office Phone: 717-892-3000. E-mail: jroda@rodanast.com.

RODALE, ARDATH HARTER, publishing executive; 5 children. B in art edn., Kutztown U., LLD (hon.), 1995. Chmn. Prevention Mag., Rodale Press, Inc., 1990— ; owner, CEO Rodale Press Inc., Emmaus, Pa., 1990—2002. Chmn. emeritus on the bd. Rodale Inst. Author: Climbing Toward the Light, 1989, Gifts of the Spirit, 1997, Reflections: Finding, Love, Hope and Joy in Everyday Life, 2002. Office: Rodale Press Inc 33 E Minor St Emmaus PA 18098-0099*

RODAMAKER, MARTI TOMSON, bank executive; m. Bill Rodamaker; children: Mackenzie, Meeghan. BA in Econs., U. No. Iowa; MBA in Fin., U. St. Thomas. Credit analyst Marquette Bank, Mpls., 1984—87; field examiner Norwest Bank, 1987—93; from mem. staff to pres. First Citizens Nat. Bank, Mason City, Iowa, 1993—2000, pres., 2000—. Mem. adv. coun. Fed. Res. Iowa. Chmn. Hosp. Found.; treas. campaign YMCA; bd. regents Luther Coll., 2003—. Named One of 25 Women to Watch, U.S. Banker Mag., 2003. Mem.: Iowa Ind. Bankers Assn. (pres. 2001), Mason City C. of C. (bd. dir.). Office: First Citizens National Bank 2601 Fourth St SW Mason City IA 50401-1708

RODAS, DANIEL, academic administrator, management educator; b. Rochester, NY, Dec. 8, 1963; s. Howard M. and Sally V. Rodas. BA cum laude, Williams Coll., Williamstown, Mass., 1985; EdM, Harvard U., 1988; MBA, Stanford U., 1993, PhD, 1998. Asst. to dirs. Harvard Sch. Pub. health, Boston, 1988—99; dep. dir. grad. programs Harvard Sch. Pub. Health, Boston, 1989; asst. to vice provost Stanford U., 1993—97; spl. asst. to exec. v.p. Duke U., Durham, NC, 1997—99, asst. v.p., 1999—2003; provost Southampton coll. LI U., Southampton, NY, 2003 — . Asst. prof. of the practice Duke U., Durham, NC, 1998—2002, assoc. prof. of the practice, 2002—03; vis. asst. prof. NC State, 1999—2003. Author: Resource Allocation in Pvt. Rsch. Universities, 2001. Recipient Rising Star award, Nat. Assn. Coll. and U. Bus. Officers, 1999; grantee Henry J. Kaiser fellowship, Stanford U., 1991—93. Avocations: reading, travel, physical fitness. Office: Office of the Provost Southampton Coll/LIU 239 Monatuk Highway Southampton NY 11968-4198

RODBELL, CLYDE ARMAND, retired distribution executive; b. Atlanta, Aug. 16, 1927; s. Joseph Hirsch and Fannie (Turetzky) R.; m. Cecile Rosenson, Mar. 27, 1949 (div.); children: Marsha, Jeffrey, Keith, Kim; m. Robin Graham McKenzie Rodbell, Dec. 15, 1974; 1 child, Lindsey. BBA, Emory U., 1949. Chmn. Apex Supply Co. Inc., Atlanta, 1949—2002. Co-chmn. George Bush Presdl. Fund Raising, Ga., 1988-89; mem. State of Ga. Electoral Coll., 1989, exec. commr. Am. Bicentenial Pres. Inaugural Bus. Adv., 1989, Pres' Commn. on White House Fellowships, 1989-92. With U.S. Army, 1945. Mem. Wholesale Assn. Ga., Southern Wholesalers Assn., Am. Supply Assn., Standard Club, Rotary Club. Republican. Jewish. Avocations: reading, gardening, antiquing, politics, fund raising. E-mail: rrodbell@aol.com.

RODDICK, ANDY, professional tennis player; b. Omaha, Aug. 30, 1982; s. Jerry and Blanche Roddick. Turned pro, 2000—; winner jr. Grand Slam titles Australian Open and U.S. Open, 2000; quarter-finalist Roland Garros, 2000; singles titles, Atlanta, Houston, Washington U.S. Clay Court Championships, 2001, singles titles, Memphis, Houston, 2002; runner up U.S. Open, 2002; quarterfinalist Indian Wells TMS, 2003; semifinalist Paris TMS, Basel, Tennis Masters Cup, Wimbledon, Australian Open, Washington, 2003; finalist Houston, Memphis, 2003; winner Raiffeisen Internat. Grand Prix, 2003, Stella Artois Championships, 2003, RCA Championships, 2003, Montreal Masters, 2003, Cin. Masters, 2003; winner Grand Slam title U.S. Open, 2003. Mem. U.S. Olympic Tennis Team, Athens, 2004. Host: Saturday Night Live, 2003. Founder The Andy Roddick Found. Recipient Espy Award for Best Male Tennis Player, 2004. Achievements include finishing the year as the youngest player at 18 years, 3 months in the top 200 and as the No. 1 junior in the world, 2000. Avocations: movies, music, skydiving.*

RODDICK, DAVID BRUCE, construction company executive; b. Oakland, Calif., Oct. 31, 1948; s. Bruce Ergo and Hortensia Cabo (Castedo) R.; m. Sharon Ann Belan, May 25, 1975; children: Heather Marie, Christina DeeAnn. BSCE, U. Calif., Davis, 1971. Engr. Bechtel Corp., San Francisco, 1971-77, contract specialist, 1977-78; subcontract adminstr. Boecon Corp., Richland, Wash., 1978-79; constrn. mgr. BE&C Engrs., Inc., Vancouver, Wash., 1979-81; contracts mgr. Boecon Corp., Tukwila, Wash., 1981-83; sr. constrn. mgr. BE&C Engrs., Inc., Wichita, Kans., 1983-84; project mgr., v.p. ops. Carl Holvick Co., Sunnyvale, Calif., 1984-88, also corp. sec. bd. dirs.; v.p., gen. mgr. Brookman Co. div. B.T. Mancini Co., Inc., Milpitas, Calif., 1988-92; v.p., sec., CFO B.T. Mancini Co., Inc., 1992-98, sr. v.p. ops., CFO, corp. sec., 1998-2000, exec. v.p., CFO, corp. sec., 2000—. Mem. devel. com. San Jose (Calif.) Mus. Assn., 1993—95; mem., dir. Constrn. Fin. Mgmt. Assn., 1995—, pres. Silicon Valley chpt., 1999—2000, 2001—02, 2004—; pres. Reed Sch. PTA, San Jose, 1985—88, San Jose Coun. PTAs, 1988—89; trustee, deacon Heart of Valley Bapt. Ch.; bd. dirs. Vinehill Homeowners Assn., 1975—77. Lt. col. C.E. USAR, 1969—99. Decorated Army Achievement medal, 1988, Commendation medal, 1991, 96, 98, meritorious svc. medal, 1998, 99; recipient Calif. State PTA Hon. Svc. award, 1988, Bronze de Fluery medal Army Engr. Assn., 1998. Mem. Am. Soc. Civil Engrs., Res. Officers Assn. (life), Am. Arbitration Assn. (mem. panel arbitrators), Am. Subcontractors Assn., Engr. Regimental Assn. (life), Calif. Aggie Alumni Assn., Ill. State Geneal. Soc., Floor Covering Installation Contractors Assn., Oreg. Calif. Trails Assn., Santa Maria Valley Geneal. Archtl. Engring. Inst. (founding mem.), Soc., Army Engr. Assn. (de Fleury medal 1998), U. Calif.-Davis Century Club, Sigma Nu. Republican. Office: B T Mancini Co Inc 876 S Milpitas Blvd Milpitas CA 95035-6311

RODE, GLENN G. music educator, secondary school educator; b. Chgo., Nov. 10, 1954; s. Emil Cornelius and Dolores Elizabeth Rode. MA, Northeatsern Ill. U., 1986. Band dir. Lake Zurich H.S., Ill., 1979—83; dist. orch. dir. Cons. H.S. Dist. 230, Orland Park, 1983—89; elem. music instr. Chgo. Pub. Schools, 1992—94; band dir. Mather H.S., 1994—2000; dir. bands Payton Coll. Prep H.S., 2000—. Trombonist/condr. various, Chgo., 1976; adj. faculty Morraine Valley C.C., Palos Hills, 1999. Author: Bands of Chicago. Mem.: Internatioanl Trombone Assc., Nat. Assn. Jazz Educators, Nat. Band Assc. Independent. Home: 4926 N Mozart Chicago IL 60625 Office: Payton College Prep High School 1034 N Wells Chicago IL 60610 Personal E-mail: glennrode@hotmail.com. E-mail: glennrode@hotmail.com.

RODE, LEIF, retired real estate personal computer consultant; b. Copenhagen, Aug. 24, 1926; arrived in US, 1948, naturalized, 1960; s. Stig and Kirsten (Bay) Rode; m. Elsa B. Ringressy, Feb. 14, 1992. BS magna cum laude, Columbia U., 1959. Cert. auditor; ChFC, CLU. Mgr. East Asiatic Co., N.Y.C., 1952-54; various auditing positions N.Y. Life Ins. Co., N.Y.C., 1954-70, asst. gen. auditor, 1970-71, gen. auditor, 1971-82, sr. v.p., gen. auditor, 1982-87, cons., 1987-89; real estate agt. Weichert Realtors, Holmdel, N.J., 1989-90, Fraybern Realtors, Holmdel, N.J., 1990-92, Colts Neck (N.J.) Realty, 1992-98; ret, 1998. Mem. Bd. Edn., Colts Neck, 1975—76, v.p., 1976—78; bd. dirs. Sports Found., Inc., Colts Neck, 1973—75, pres., 1975—77; trustee Bayshore Cmty. Hosp., Holmdel, 1986—87. With Royal Danish Navy, 1946—47. Recipient Award of Honor, NY State Soc CPAs, 1960; scholar Merle M Hoover, 1960. Mem.: N.J. Assn. Realtors (mcpl. liaison to Colts Neck Twp 1989—94, new products and technology com. 1990—92, state legis comt 1990—93, vice chair 1992, chmn 1993, bd dirs 1993, real estate personal computer consult 1995—98), Monmouth County Bd Realtors (mem constn and by-laws comt 1989—92, co-chair 1991—92, strategic planning comt 1992—93), Am Soc CLU and Chartered Fin Consults, Inst Internal Auditors. Lutheran. Home and Office: 18 Sandhurst Rd Lakewood NJ 08701 Personal E-mail: llrode@aol.com.

RODEKOHR, DIANE E. state official; A in Bus. Mgmt., Nat. Bus. Inst., 1958. Asst. exec. dir. Associated Gen. Contractors of Wyo., 1963-78; field rep. to Sen. Alan Simpson Wyo., 1978-84; state dir. to Sen. Alan Simpson, 1984-96; state dir. to Sen. Michael Enzi, 1997—. Mem. PEO, Cheyenne C. of C., Rotary (sec. 1995-99). Office: Office Sen Michael Enzi 2120 Capitol Ave Ste 2007 Cheyenne WY 82001-3631

RODELLO, DEBBIE A. state representative; b. Espanola, N.Mex., Nov. 28, 1961; m. Thomas Rodella; children: Thomas Rodella Jr., Kara Rodella. AA, No. N.Mex. C.C., 1982, AA, 1983; student, Coll. Santa Fe. Sec. Materials Sci. Technician, San Juan Pueblo, N.Mex., 1998—. Democrat. Roman Catholic. Home: PO Box 1074 San Juan Pueblo NM 87566 Office: New Mexico State Capitol Rm 201A Santa Fe NM 87501

RODEMEYER, MICHAEL LEONARD, JR., lawyer; b. Balt., May 25, 1950; s. Michael Leonard and Claire Isabel (Gunther) R.; m. Dorrit Carolyn Green, June 7, 1975; children: Justin, Christoffer. AB, Princeton U., 1972; JD, Harvard U., 1975. Bar: Md. 1977, D.C. 1980, U.S. Ct. Appeals (10th cir.) 1980. Atty. Fed. Trade Commn., Washington, 1976-81, atty. advisor, 1981-84; counsel Subcom. on Natural Resources, Agr. Rsch. & Environ., Washington, 1984-88; staff dir., counsel U.S. Ho. of Reps., Washington, 1988-90, house com. on sci., chief dem. counsel, 1990-98; asst. dir. for environment White House Office of Sci. and Tech. Policy, Washington, 1998-99, dem. legis. dir., 1999-2000; exec. dir. Pew Initiative on Food and Biotech., Washington, 2000—. Democrat. Avocations: computing, bicycling. Home: 6000 Harvard Ave Glen Echo MD 20812-1114 Office: Pew Initiative on Food and Biotech 1331 H St NW Ste 900 Washington DC 20005 E-mail: mrodemeyer@pewagbiotech.org.

RODEN, DAN MARK, clinical pharmacologist, cardiologist, medical educator; b. Montreal, Can., Apr. 15, 1950; came to U.S., 1978; s. Rudolph George and Eva (Vonchovsky) R.; m. Rosemary Wetherill, Dec. 29, 1972; children: Mark McKenzie, Paul Joseph, Rosemary Claire. BSc, McGill U., 1970, MD, 1974. Diplomate Am. Bd. Internal Medicine, Am. Bd. Cardiovascular Disease, Am. Bd. Clinical Cardiac Electrophysiology, Am. Bd. Clinical Pharmacology; Lic. physician, Quebec, Canada and Tenn.; Cert. Med. Coun. of Canada, Nat. Bd. Med. Examiners. Intern Royal Victoria Hosp., Montreal, Can., 1974-75, resident, 1975-76, 77-78; pvt. practice Montreal, Can., 1976-77; rsch. fellow clin. pharmacology Vanderbilt U., Nashville, 1978-81, fellow cardiol., 1980-81, asst. prof., 1981-85, assoc. prof., 1985-89, prof. Med. and Pharmacology, 1989—, also dir. divsn. clin. pharmacology, 1992—. Del. 4th U.S.-USSR Symposium on Sudden Death, Birmingham, Ala., 1985; mem. Nat. VA Merit Review Cardiovasc. Disease com., 1986-88, chmn. 1988-89; ad hoc reviewer, Pharmacology Study and Cardiovasc. and Pulmonary Study sects., NIH, mem. Cardiovasc. and Pulmonary Study sect., 1991-94, chmn. 1994-96; adv. panel cardiovasc. and renal drugs, U.S. Phamacopeial Conv., 1990-95; mem. external adv. com., Pharmacological Scis. Tng. Grant, Columbia U., 1992—; mem. Clin. Cardiac Electrophysiology Test Writing com., Am. Bd. Internal Medicine, 1992—; mem. adv. com., Vanderbilt Clin Rsch. Ctr., 1989-91, chmn. 91-92, faculty appointments and promotions, Vanderbilt U. Dept. Med., 1992-95; mem. instl. review bd., Vanderbilt U. Dept. Health Scis., 1991-93, chmn. 1993-94. Author 27 book chpts., over 150 abstracts and 130 articles to profl. jours.; mem. editl. bd. Jour. Cardiovasc. Electrophys., 1990—; mem. adv. bd. The Med. Letter (newsletter), 1991—. Fellow Am. Coll. Physicians, Am. Coll. Cardiology (annual scientific session program com. 1992-93), Royal Coll. Physicians of Can.; mem. Am. Fedn. Clin. Rsch., Am. Soc. Clin. Pharmacology Therapeutics (bd. dirs. 1994—, chmn. cardiovasc. and pulmonary sect., 1995—), North Am. Soc. Pacing and Electrophysiol., Cardiac Electrophysiol. Soc., Biophysical Soc., Am. Soc. Pharmacol. and Experimental Therapeutics, So. Soc. Clin. Investigation, Am. Soc. Clin. Investigation, Am. Heart Assn. (clinician-sci.t award, 1981-86, long-range planning com. 1995—, basic sci. coun. exec. com. 1995—) Office: Vanderbilt U 532B Medical Rsch Bldg 1 Nashville TN 37232-0001

RODEN, JON-PAUL, retired educator, labor union organizer, educational consultant; b. Vernon, Conn., July 15, 1943; s. Paul James and Evelyn Mary Roden. BS, SUNY, Oswego, 1965; MS, Ctrl. Conn. State U., 1970. Cert. pioneer in professionalism Nat. Bd. Profl. Tchg. Stds., registered lobbyist Conn. Gen. Assembly, notary public Conn. Tchr. elem. sch. Vernon Pub. Schs., 1965—68, tchr. anatomy and physiology, 1969—79, tchr. computer sci., 1980—82, dist. chmn. computer sci., 1982—2000, presenter staff devel., 1986—; union organizer Conn. Edn. Assn., Hartford, 2000—02, state treas., 2002—; ret., 2002. Tech. advisor Capitol Region Edn. Coun., 1981-85; presenter Inst. for Tchrs. and Learning, Conn. Dept. Edn., 1990-91, N.E. Holmes Group, Boston, 1994; mem. adv. com. Affiliate Newsletter Svc., 1992-2000; provider mgr. Conn. Dept. Edn., 1994-98; mem. Legis. Task Force on ednl. tech., 1995-97; mem. Legis. Task Force on tchrs. retirement health ins. sys., 2000-2001; mem. Conn. stakeholders com. Nat. Bd. Profl. Tchg. Stds, 1995-2000, cons. 1995; mem. educator preparation program rev. com. Conn. State Bd. Edn., 1996-99; mem. nat. parent-tchr. adv. coun. Am. Online; presenter Nat. Sch. Bd. Assn. Tech. Conf., 1995, 96, 97, 98; keynote spkr. Minn. High Success Consortium, 1997; mem. bd. examiners Nat. Coun. Accreditation Tchr. Edn.; mem. tech. adv. commn. Nat. Coun. State Edn. Affiliates, 1999-2001; presenter NEA, Chgo., 2000; mem. task force on Conn. low performing schs. Assoc. editor: Logo Activities, 1985; writer, editor numerous teaching guides. Pres. U. Conn. Friends of Soccer, 1987—89; corporator Newington (Conn.) Children's Hosp., 1978—98; celebrant Celebration of Excellence Conn. State Dept. Edn., 1991, 1995, 1999; mem. Vernon Rep. Town Com., 1978—98, Vernon Recreation Commn., 1978—84, chmn., 1982—84; mem. Vernon Traffic Authority, 1988—94, vice chair, 1996—; spl. dep. sheriff Tolland County, Conn., 1977—82; bd. gov. Conn. Children's Hosp., 1995—; mem. adv. bd. Vernon Law Enforcement Block Grant, 1997—2000; bd. dir. Hockanum Valley Cmty. Coun., 2003—, exec. com., 2004—. Recipient Ofcl. Citation of Recognition Conn. Gen. Assembly, 1991, 95, 96, Celebration of Excellence Emeritus award Conn. State Dept. Edn., 1999; nominated Disney Tchr. awards, 2000. Mem.: NEA (design com. 1995, conv. del. 1995, presenter 1995, tchr./cons. Washington 1995—, conv. del. 1996, panelist N.E. regional leaders conf. Phila. 1997, panelist N.E. regional leaders conf. Rochester 1999, presenter 2000), ASCD, Conn. Computer Educators, Conn. Edn. Assn. (editl. bd. 1991—), Nat. Coun. State Edn. Affiliates (tech. com. 1999), Shriners, Elks (exalted ruler 1969—70, dist. dep. grand exalted ruler 1973—74, named Elk of the Yr. 2003), Masons, Phi Delta Kappa (exec. bd. 1991—, chpt. pres. 1994—96, selection com. 1995, internat. doctoral dissertation com.). Roman Catholic. Avocations: racquetball, bicycling, skiing. Home: 105 Maple Ave Vernon Rockville CT 06066-5450

RODENBAUGH, MARCIA LOUISE, retired elementary school educator; b. Pitts., Nov. 11, 1942; d. E. Thomas and Lucy Indiana (Fry) Wimer; m. John Anthony Lee, Mar. 21, 1964 (div. Nov. 1971); m. Richard Alan Rodenbaugh, Aug. 3, 1975 (div. Dec. 1989); stepchildren: Ken, Tiffany, Tricia. BA in Edn., Westminster Coll., New Wilmington, Pa., 1964, MEd in Remedial Reading, 1966. Tchr. North Hills Sch. Dist., Pitts., 1964-69, Ctrl. Bucks Schs., Doylestown, Pa., 1969—2001. Fellow Pa. Writing Project, West Chester U., 1990; presenter in field. Author children's books: Marci Books (set of 6), 1983-99. Pres. Maple Leaf Day Care Ctr. Bd., Warminster, Pa., 1971; pres. Wesley Coll. Parents Assn., Dover, Del., 1985-86; vol. Meals on Wheels, Phila. inner-city schs.; bd. dirs. Friends of the Libr., Doylestown br. Bucks County Libr., 2002—, sec. 2003—; local judge History Day, Ursinus Coll.; home tutor. Mem. NEA, Pa. Edn. Assn., Ctrl. Bucks Edn. Assn. Republican. Presbyterian. Avocations: skiing, sailing, writing, piano, church choir. Home: 7-16 Aspen Way Doylestown PA 18901-2756 Office: Ctrl Bucks Sch Dist 315 Weldon Dr Doylestown PA 18901-3525

RODENBERG, JOY D. sports association executive; Student, Wellesley Coll.; grad., Northwestern U. Mem. Jr. Tennis Coun. U.S. Tennis Assn., 1977-87, mem. nominating com., 1985-87, mem. sanctions and schedules com., 1981-87, mem. jr. ranking com., 1977-80, v.p., 1996—, in charge of Cmty. Tennis Devel. Divsn., in charge of Administrn. and Svc. Divsn., chmn. Player Devel. Com., 1988-91, bd. dirs., 1991-97, vol., 1998—. Pres. Missouri Valley Tennis Assn., 1980-84; past umpire U.S. Open. Named to Missouri Valley Hall of Fame, 1994, Nebr. Tennis Hall of Fame, 1989.

RODENBERGER, CHARLES ALVARD, aerospace engineer, consultant; b. Muskogee, Okla., Sept. 11, 1926; s. Darcy Owen and Kathryn Martha (Percival) R.; m. Molcie Lou Halsell, Sept. 3, 1949; children: Kathryn Sue Wilcox, Charles Mark. Student, U. Ark., 1944-45; BS in Gen. Engring., Okla. State U., 1948; MSM.E., So. Meth. U., 1959; PhD in Aero. Engring., U. Tex.-Austin, 1968. Registered profl. engr., Tex. Petroleum engr. Amoco Oil Co., Levelland, Tex., 1948-51; chief engr. McGregor Bros., Odessa, Tex., 1953; petroleum engr. Gen. Crude Oil Co., Hamlin, Tex., 1954; sr. design engr. Gen. Dynamics, Ft. Worth, 1954-60; aerospace engr. NASA, Houston, summer 1962; prof. aerospace engring. Tex. A&M U., College Station, 1960-82, prof. emeritus, 1982—; chmn. bd. Meiller Research, Inc., College Station, 1967-82; pres. JETS, Inc., N.Y.C., 1977-79; cons. Southwest Research Inst., Gen. Motors Corp., Gen. Dynamics. Patentee hypervelocity gun and orthotic device; newspaper columnist: Livestock Weekly, 1986—; mag. columnist, Santa Gertrudis, Tex., 2002. Served with USAAF, 1945; served with USAF, 1951-53. NSF fellow, 1964-65; recipient Disting. Teaching award Tex. A&M U., 1962 Fellow AIAA (assoc.); mem. ASME, NSPE (v.p. 1980-81), Tex. Soc. Profl. Engrs., Am. Soc. for Engring. Edn., Sigma Xi, Kiwanis Club (pres. Cross Plains chpt. 2002-03). Methodist. Home: 8377 FM 2228 Baird TX 79504-4813 Office Phone: 254-725-6816. E-mail: crodenberg@aol.com., car926@aol.com.

RODENBURG, CLIFTON GLENN, lawyer; b. Jamestown, ND, Apr. 5, 1949; s. Clarence and Dorothy Irene (Peterman) R.; m. Donna Michele Stockman, Mar. 1, 1980. BS, N.D. State U., 1971; JD, U. N.D., 1974; M.L.I.R., Mich. State U., 1976. Bar: N.D. 1974, U.S. Dist. Ct. N.D. 1974, U.S. Ct. Appeals (8th cir.) 1974, Minn. 1980, U.S. Supreme Ct. 1980, S.D. 1983, Nebr. 1984, U.S. Dist. Ct. Minn. 1984, U.S. Dist. Ct. Nebr. 1984, Wis. 1985, U.S. Dist. Ct. Wis. 1985, Mont. 1986, U.S. Dist. Ct. Mont. 1986, bd. cert. Creditors' Rights Law, Am. Bd. Cert. Ptnr. Johnson, Rodenburg & Lauinger, Fargo, N.D., 1976—; pres., gen. counsel Rodenburg Group, Inc., Fargo, 1980—. Contbg. editor: The Developing Labor Law, 1976-80; drafter N.D. garnishment statutes, 1982. Mem. Acad. Comml. and Bankruptcy Law Specialists.

RODEO, SCOTT A. surgeon, sports medicine specialist; b. San Jose, Calif., May 6, 1963; MD, Cornell U., 1989. Diplomate American Board of Orthopaedic Surgery. Intern N.Y. Hosp., 1989—90; resident Hosp. Spl. Surg.-Cornell Med. Ctr., N.Y., 1990—94, fellow, 1994—96, assoc. attending orthop. surgeon (sports medicine and shoulder svc.), 1996—; asst. scientist rsch. divsn. (lab soft tissue) Hosp. Spl. Surgery, N.Y., 1996—; assoc. attending orthop. surgeon orthop. surgery N.Y.-Presbyn. Hosp., NY, 1996—; asst. prof. surgery Weill Med. Coll. Cornell U. Med. Ctr., NY, 1996—. Assoc. team physician N.Y. Giants Football Team; provider med. assistance U.S.A. Swimming Team, 1998—; head team physician U.S.A. Swimming Nat. Team World Swimming Championships, Barcelona, 2003; mem. med. staff U.S. Olympic Com. Games XXVIIIth Olympiad, Athens, 2004; head team physician World Championship, Moscow. Mem.: Am. Orthop. Soc. Sports Medicine (3M Basic Rsch. award 1996, Excellence in Rsch. award 2004), Am. Shoulder and Elbow Surgeons (Nominee Charles Neer award 1996), Orthop. Rsch. Soc. (Finalist New Investigator's Recognition award 1995, 1997), Am. Orthop. Assn., U.S.A. Swimming Network Taskforce Injury Prevention (chmn.), U.S.A. Sports Com. (chmn.), Asphalt Green Swim Club (med. cons.). Office: Hosp Spl Surgery 535 E 70th St New York NY 10021 Address: Belaire Bldg 525 E 71st St 1st Fl New York NY 10021

RODER, HANS MARTIN, retired physicist, consultant; b. Schenectady, N.Y., June 30, 1930; s. Johann Nikolaus and Elsa Margarethe (von Kujawa) R.; m. Mary Margaret Ball, Aug. 4, 1951; children: Jenny Brooks, Nicholas, Renate Pearson. BA in Chemistry, U. Colo., 1955, postgrad. in chemistry and physics, 1955-60. Physicist divsn. cryogenics Nat. Inst. Stds. and Tech. (formerly Nat. Bur. Stds.), Boulder, Colo., 1955-66, leader data compilation group, 1966-73, physicist divsn. thermophysics, 1973-87. V.p., sec. Doggie Biscuits, Inc., Breckenridge, Colo., 1989—. Contbr. to books: Technology and Uses of Liquid Hydrogen, 1964, Transport Properties of Fluids, 1990; editor: The Nat. Ski Patrol Ski Mountaineering Man., 1980; contbr. over 75 articles to profl. jours. Patrol leader Nat. Ski Patrol, Loveland Basin, Colo., 1962-87, ski mountaineering advisor, Denver, 1978-85. 1st lt. AUS, 1952-54. Recipient Gold Medal award U.S. Dept. Commerce, 1966, Tech. and Utilization award NASA, 1967, 68, 70, 71; R.B. Scott Meml. award Cryogenic Engring. Conf., 1969. Avocations: skiing, hiking, mountain climbing. Home: PO Box 684 340 W Buffalo Dillon CO 80435

RODERICK, JORDAN M. communications executive; BA, MBA, Dartmouth U. V.p. sales and mktg. United TeleSpectrum, 1985—88; from mem. staff to pres. Internat. Divsn. AT&T Wireless Svcs. Inc., Redmond, Wash., 1988—2000, pres. Internat. Divsn., 2000—. Office: AT&T Wireless Services Inc 7277 164th Ave NE Bldg 1 Redmond WA 98052

RODGER, GINETTE, professional association executive, nurse; b. Amos, Que., Can., Mar. 18, 1943; d. Joseph and Blanche (Gagnon) Lemire; m. William James Rodger; children: Robert, Philippe, Sabrina. Diploma in nursing, U. Ottawa, 1964, BS in nursing, 1966; M.Nursing Adminstrn., U. Montreal, 1971; D.Sci. h.c., U. N.B., 1985. Gen. duty nurse Ottawa Gen. Hosp., Ont., 1964-65; asst. dir. nursing St. Vincent Hosp., Ottawa, summer 1965; gen. duty nurse Queen Mary Hosp. and Jewish Gen. Hosp., Montreal, Que., summer 1966, Hotel-Dieu Hosp., Amos, summer 1967, Queen Mary Hosp., summer 1968; adminstrv. asst. Hosp. Notre-Dame, Montreal, 1968-72, gen. duty nurse, 1972-73, nurse researcher, 1973, asst. dir. nursing, 1973, in-charge nursing research, 1973-74, dir. nursing, 1974-81; exec. dir. Can. Nurses Assn., Ottawa, 1981—, pres., 2000—02. Mem. Can. Council Hosp. Accreditation, 1972-86, chmn., 1981-82; nat. dep. dir. St. John Ambulance for Health Care Program, 1981-86; mem. nat. com. tng. Order of St. John, 1981-86; mem. service adv. com. Victorian Order of Nurses for Can., 1981—; mem. nat. health com. Can. Red Cross Soc., 1981—; mem. Que. council Order of St. John, 1975-81, v.p., 1976-79; pres. Assn. St. John, 1976-79; chmn. nursing edn. com. Que. Ministry Edn., 1978-80; mem. Fedn. Que. Health and Social Affairs Adminstrs., 1975-81; mem. com. essential services Que. Ministry Labor, 1978-80; mem. group dirs. nursing Montreal Univ. Hosps., 1980-81. Decorated Serving Sister Can. Order St. John Ambulance, 1979; recipient Vigor prize Que. Fedn. Health Services Adminstr., 1981; officer St. John Ambulance, 1981; Ryerson fellowship award Ryerson Poly. Inst., 1984—. Mem. Can. Coll. Health Service Execs., Can. Hosp. Assn., Ordre des infirmieres et infirmiers du Quebec, Coll. Nurses Ont., Registered Nurses Assn. Ont., Am. Soc. Hosp. Nursing Service Adminstrn., Can. Nurses Found. (sec.-treas. 1981—), Med. Research Council Can., Can. Nurses Protective Soc. (chief exec. officer, treas.). Office: Can Nurses Assn 50 The Driveway Ottawa ON Canada K2P 1E2

RODGERS, BILLY RUSSELL, chemical engineer, research scientist; b. Fitzgerald, Ga., Sept. 5, 1936; s. Jimmie R. and Ruby Doris (Morris) R.; divorced; children: Cheryl, Donna, Angie, Rusty. AA, U. Fla., 1956, BSChemE with high honors, 1966, MS in Engring., 1967; PhD, U. Tenn., 1980. Project leader Shell Devel. Co., 1968-72; group leader Keene Corp. Fluid Handling, Cookeville, Tenn., 1972-74, Oak Ridge (Tenn.) Nat. Lab., 1974-92; sr. engr. Walk Haydel & Assocs., New Orleans, 1992-94; pres. Rodgers USA Enterprises, Orange Park, Fla., 1992—2002, Intelligent Cons., Orange Park, 1993—2002; qualifying agt./mgr. Rodgers Constrn. Co., 1996—2002; ret., 2002—. Author 3 books in field; contbr. articles to profl. publs. Fellow AIChE (bd. dirs. 1993-97, chmn. fuels and petrochem. divsn. 1992-95, chmn. program com. fuels and petrochem. divsn. 1990-92). Republican. Achievements include 1 patent in field.

RODGERS, DENISE V. medical educator; Chief staff Cmty. Health Network, San Francisco, 1997; assoc. dean for cmty. health Robert Wood Johnson Med. Sch., New Brunswick, NJ, 1997—. Office: Robert Wood Johnson Univ Med Group Clinical Acad Bldg 125 Paterson St Ste 1400 New Brunswick NJ 08901-1977

RODGERS, FRANK, librarian; b. Darlington, Eng., July 28, 1927; came to U.S., 1956; s. Charles Bede and Frances (Page) R.; m. Sarah Louise Edelson, Dec. 18, 1971; children: Hilda Marie, Norah Frances. BA with honors, King's Coll., U. Durham, 1947; diploma librarianship, London U., 1952. Libr. Poplar Tech. Coll., London, 1951-53, St. Martin's Sch. Art, 1953-56; sr. libr. adult svcs. divsn. Akron (Ohio) Pub. Libr., 1956-59; asst. reference libr. U. Ill., 1959-64; chief reference libr., then asst. dir. pub. svcs. Pa. State U. Librs., 1965-69; dir. Portland (Oreg.) State U. Libr., 1969-79; dir. librs. U. Miami, Fla., 1979-97. Mem. Oreg. adv. coun. librs., 1973-74; bd. dirs. Pacific N.W. Bibliog. Ctr., 1973-77; tech. adv. com. librs. Columbia Regional Assn. Govts., 1976-79; vis. fellow U. Southampton Eng., 1975-76; pres. Oreg. Libr. Assn., 1974-75; mem. nominating com. Southeastern Libr. Network, 1984-85; bd. dirs. S.E. Fla. Libr. Info. Network, 1984-97, pres. 1991-92; mem. exec. coun. Assn. Caribbean U. Rsch. and Instl. Librs., 1985-88; chmn. local organizing com. for 1981 and 1987 confs. in Miami; mem. Fla. Libr. Network Coun., 1985-91; NEH challenge grant rev. panel, 1987, Howard U. ann. inspection team, 1989, Reaffirmation com., Tex. Christian U., 1993. Author, editor various libr. publs., guides. Sr. fellow Grad. Sch. Libr. and Info. Sci. UCLA, 1983; grantee Coun. Libr. Resources, 1975-76. Fellow Libr. Assn. U.K.; mem. ALA, Assn. Rsch. Librs. (office mgmt. studies adv. com. 1981-83, stats. and measurements com. 1993-96), Assn. Specialized and Coop. Libr. Agys. (membership promotion com. 1994-96, chair 1990 program com.), Assn. Southeastern Rsch. Librs. (chmn. membership com. 1982-97). Address: 7a Avenida Norte #25 Antigua Guatemala E-mail: frodgers@conexion.com.gt.

RODGERS, FREDERIC BARKER, judge; b. Albany, N.Y., Sept. 29, 1940; s. Prentice Johnson and Jane (Weed) R.; m. Valerie McNaughton, Oct. 8, 1988; 1 child: Gabriel Moore. AB, Amherst Coll., 1963; JD, Union U., 1966. Bar: N.Y. 1966, U.S. Ct. Mil. Appeals 1968, Colo. 1972, U.S. Supreme Ct. 1974, U.S. Ct. Appeals (10th cir.) 1981, U.S. Ct. Appeals (fed. cir.) 2001. Chief dep. dist. atty., Denver, 1972-73; commr. Denver Juvenile Ct., 1973-79; mem. Mulligan Reeves Teasley & Joyce, P.C., Denver, 1979-80; pres. Frederic B. Rodgers, P.C., Breckenridge, Colo., 1980-89; ptnr. McNaughton & Rodgers, Central City, Colo., 1989-91; county ct. judge Gilpin County Combined Cts., Colo., 1987—. Presiding mcpl. judge cities of Breckenridge, Blue River, Black Hawk, Central City, Edgewater, Empire, Idaho Springs, Silver Plume and Westminster, Colo., 1978-96; chmn. com. on mcpl. ct. rules of procedure Colo. Supreme Ct., 1984-96; mem. gen faculty Nat. Jud. Coll. U. Nev., Reno, 1990—, elected to faculty coun., 1993-99, chair 1999, bd. trustees 2004-. Author: (with Dilweg, Fretz, Murphy and Wicker) Modern Judicial Ethics, 1992; contbr. articles to profl. jours. Mem. Colo. Commn. on Children, 1982-85, Colo. Youth Devel. Coun., 1989-98, Colo. Family Peace Task Force, 1994-96. Served with JAGC, U.S. Army, 1967-72; to maj. USAR, 1972-88. Decorated Bronze Star with oak leaf cluster, Air medal. Recipient Outstanding County Judge award Colo. 17th Judicial Dist. Victim Adv. Coalition, 1991; Spl. Community Svc. award Colo. Am. Legion, 1979, Lifetime Achievement award Denver Law Club, 2003. Fellow Am. Bar Found., Colo. Bar. Found. (life); mem. ABA (jud. div. exec. coun. 1989-2000, vice-chair 1996-97, chair-elect 1997, chair 1998-99, mem. Ho. of Dels. 1993—, jud. divsn. del. to ABA nominating com. 2000-01, bd. govs. Dist. 11 2001—), Colo. Bar Assn. (bd. govs. 1986-88, 90-92, 93-99, 2002—, sr. v.p. 2004—), Continental Divide Bar Assn., Denver Bar Assn. (trustee 1979-82), First Jud. Dist. Bar Assn. (trustee 2000-02), Nat. Conf. Spl. Ct. Judges (chmn. 1989-90), Colo. County Judges Assn. (pres. 1995-96), Colo. Mcpl. Judges Assn. (pres. 1986-87), Colo. Trial Judges Coun. (v.p. 1994-95, sec. 1996-97), Denver Law Club (pres. 1981-82), Colo. Women's Bar Assn., Am. Judicature Soc. (bd. dirs. 2003—), Nat. Coun. Juvenile and Family Ct. Judges, Federalist Soc. for Law and Pub. Policy Studies, Judge Advs. Assn., Univ. Club (Denver), Arlberg Club (Winter Park), Marines Meml. Club (San Francisco), Rotary (charter pres. Peak to Peak 2000-2001, Paul Harris fellow 1996). Episcopalian. Office: Gilpin County Combined Trial Cts 2960 Dory Hill Rd Golden CO 80403-8827 Office Phone: 303-582-5522 x16. Business E-Mail: frederic.rodgers@judicial.state.co.us. E-mail: rodgers@abanet.org.

RODGERS, JAMES BEALL, surgeon; b. Martinsburg, W.Va., 1923; s. Decatur Hedges and Anne Leitch (Lancaster) R.; m. Anne English Colcord, Jan. 2, 1950; children: David, Alan, Alice. BA, U. Va., 1945, MD, 1948. Diplomate Am. Bd. Surgery. Intern Colum-Presbyn. Med. Ctr., N.Y.C., 1948-50, resident in surgery, 1952-57; assoc. clin. prof. surgery Columbia P&S, 1956-92; sr. attending surgeon emeritus St. Lukes, Roosevelt Hosp. Ctr., N.Y.C., 1957-92, ret., 1992. Fellow ACS; mem. Century Assn.

RODGERS, JAMES FOSTER, association executive, economist; b. Columbus, Ga., Jan. 15, 1951; s. Laban Jackson and Martha (Jackson) R.; m. Cynthia Lynne Bathurst, Aug. 20, 1975. BA, U. Ala., Tuscaloosa, 1973; PhD, U. Iowa, 1980. Fed. intern Office Rsch. and Stats., Social Security Adminstrn., Washington, 1976-77; rsch. assoc. Ctr. Health Policy Rsch., AMA, Chgo., 1979-80, rsch. dir., 1980-82, asst. to dep. exec. v.p. AMA, 1982-85; dir. AMA Ctr. Health Policy Rsch., Chgo., 1985-96, v.p. health policy, 1996—2003; sr. rsch. exec. Blue Cross Blue Shield Assn., Chgo., 2003—. Contbr. articles on health econs. to profl. jours. Pharm. Mfrs. Assn. grantee, 1978; NSF grantee, 1978; Hohenberg fellow, 1969-70 Mem. Am. Econ. Assn., Am. Statis. Assn. Home: 2233 N Orchard St Chicago IL 60614-3713 Office: Blue Cross Blue Shield Assn 225 N Michigan Ave Chicago IL 60601

RODGERS, JANET AHALT, nursing educator, dean; b. Hershey, Pa. d. Harold A. and Margaret L. (Bittle) Ahalt; m. Terry C. Rodgers. BSN, Wagner Coll., 1957; MA in Psychiat.-Mental Health Nursing, NYU, 1964, PhD Nursing, 1971; cert., N.Y. Med. Coll., 1973. RN, N.Y. Staff N.Y. State Psychiat. Inst., N.Y.C., 1957-59, head nurse, 1959-61; asst. DON Psychiat. Treatment Ctr., N.Y.C., 1961-62; group therapist Creedmoor State Hosp., Queens, N.Y., 1963; instr. Wagner Coll., S.I., N.Y., 1964-66, asst. prof., 1966-68, lectr. psychiat. nursing, 1969-70; asst. prof. psychiat. nursing Lehman Coll. CUNY, 1971-74, coord. psychiat. nursing Lehman Coll., 1971-76, assoc. prof., dep. chmn., 1974-77; prof., chairperson dept. nursing Old Dominion U., Norfolk, Va., 1977-79; cons., 1979-81; prof., chair dept. nursing Lycoming Coll., Williamsport, Pa., 1981-87; dean., prof. Philip Y. Hahn Sch. Nursing U. San Diego, 1987—2003. Vis. assoc. prof. Sch. Nursing U. Pa., 1981; presenter in field. Contbr. articles to profl. jours. Mem. adv. bd. Lee Hawkins Endowment Fund, Norfolk, Va., 1978-83, N.Y.C. Com. for Children, 1973-77, Bronx Health Manpower Consortium Bd., 1975-76, Ea. Va. Health Edn. Consortium, 1977-79; mem. health adv. bd. Divine Providence Hosp.-Cmty. Mental Health Ctr., 1985-87; bd. dirs. Regional Home Health Svcs., Williamsport, Pa., 1982-87, Divine Providence Hosp., Williamsport, 1986-87, San Diego Hospice, 1989-92, Am. Lung Assn. San Diego and Imperial Counties, 1994-96, Am. Heart Assn., 1996-2000, Assn. Calif. Nurse Leaders, 1996-98; bd. trustees Scripps Health, San Diego, 1998-2004, The Whittier Inst. for Diabetes, 2001; exec. ptnr. Cmty. Health Improvement Ptnrs., San Diego County. Recipient Diane F. Cooper Lifetime Achievement Award, 2002. Fellow Am. Orthopsychiat. Assn., Am. Acad. Nursing; mem. ANA, Am. Assn. Colls. Nursing (bd. dirs. 1987-94, pres.-elect 1990-92, pres. 1992-94, Wagner Coll. Alumni Assn. Achievement award 1977), Wagner Coll. Nat. Alumni Assn. (bd. dirs. 1999—), NYU Alumni Assn. (v.p. 1970-72, Mary Barr Alumni award Sch. Nursing 1993), Pi Lambda Theta, Kappa Delta Pi, Phi Kappa Phi, Sigma Theta Tau (Beta Upsilon and Zeta Mu chpts.). Office: U San Diego Hahn Sch Nurs & Health Svcs 5998 Alcala Park San Diego CA 92110-2492 E-mail: rodgers@acosd.edu.*

RODGERS, JOHN HUNTER, lawyer; b. Lubbock, Tex., Jan. 18, 1944; s. James O'Donnell Rodgers and Dorothy (Ulin) Carpenter; m. Anne C. Smith, Nov. 29, 1969; children; Anne Elizabeth, Catherine Hunter. BA, Tex. A&M, 1966; JD, U. Tex., 1969. Bar: Tex. 1969, U.S. Supreme Ct. 1973. Atty. The Southland Corp., Dallas, 1973-79, gen. counsel, 1979-91, sec., 1987-95, sr. v.p., chief adminstrv. officer, 1991-93, exec. v.p., chief adminstrv. officer, 1993-95; pres. Clairemead Corp., Dallas, 1996-2000; sr. v.p., gen. counsel, sec. Am. Pad & Paper Co., Dallas, 1998-2000, pres., 2000—04; prin. J. Hunter & Assocs., Dallas, 2003—. Mem. visual arts com. Tex. A&M U., 1985-94, bd. dirs. student fund enrichment bd., 1986-94; mem. exec. com. Jr. Achievement Dallas, 1988-93; mem. Dallas Citizens Coun., 1992-95; bd. dirs. Boys and Girls Clubs of Greater Dallas, 1998—, vice chmn., 2003—; nat. chair Tulane U. Parents Coun., 1997-98; trustee Goals for Dallas, 1991-92; nat. bd. dirs. Boys and Girls Clubs Am., 1993-98; mem. mktg. com. Dallas Mus. Art, 1994-97. Capt. JAGC, U.S. Army, 1969-73, Vietnam. Mem. ABA, Tex. Bar Assn. (coun. mem. corp. counsel sect. 1988), Dallas Bar Assn., Southwestern Legal Found. (adv. bd. Internat. and Comparative Law Ctr., rsch. fellow 1986-94), Nat. Assn. Convenience Stores (bd. dirs. 1993-95). Roman Catholic. Office: 4655 Insurance Ln Ste 100 Dallas TX 75205 Office Phone: 214-219-7771.

RODGERS, JOHN JOSEPH, III, educational administration consultant, educator; b. Jamaica, N.Y., Oct. 13, 1941; s. John Joseph Rodgers, Edith (McInerney) Rodgers; m. Iris Rodgers; children: Janet, John Joseph IV, Yvette. BS, Fordham U., 1962; Profl. diploma, St. Johns U., 1970, EdD, 1979; postgrad., CUNY, Flushing. Asst. prin. N.Y.C. Bd. Edn., 1972-82; prin. Howard T. Herber Sch., Malverne, N.Y., 1982-85, Norman Thomas H.S., N.Y.C., 1988-96, Matawan Regional H.S., Aberdeen, N.J., 1996-97; cons. on edn1. adminstrn. Valley Stream, NY, 1999—; prof. math. Farleigh Dickinson U., Madison, N.J., 1999-2001; prof. ednl. adminstrn. Coll. New Rochelle, N.Y., 2000-01; dean acad. affairs Five Towns Coll., Dix Hills, NY, 2001—02; acad. dean Bus. Informatics Ctr., The Coll. for Bus., Valley Stream, NY, 2002—. Mem. ASCD, Am. Assn. Sch. Adminstrs., Math. Assn. Am., Nat. Assn. Secondary Sch. Prins. Home: 350-34 N Corona Ave Valley Stream NY 11580-3403 E-mail: jrodgers@thecollegeforbusiness.com., pelicula419@hotmail.com.

RODGERS, JOHNATHAN, broadcast executive; b. San Antonio, Jan. 18, 1946; s. Marion Alford and Barbara (Merriwether) Rodgers; m. Royal Graves Kennedy, Sept. 27, 1976; children: David, Jamie. BA, U. Calif., Berkeley, 1967; MA, Stanford U., 1972; PhD (hon.), Columbia Coll., Chgo., 1991. Writer-reporter Sports Illustrated, N.Y.C., 1966—68; assoc. editor Newsweek, N.Y.C., 1968—72; prodr. WNBC-TV, N.Y.C., 1972—73; reporter WKYC-TV (NBC), Cleve., 1973—74; sta. mgr., news dir. KCBS-TV, L.A., 1978—83; exec. prodr. CBS News, N.Y.C., 1983—86; v.p., gen. mgr. WBBM-TV (CBS), Chgo., 1986—90; former pres. CBS TV Stas., Chgo.; pres. Discovery Networks, US, Bethesda, Md., 1996—2003; pres., CEO TV One, LLC, Lanham, Md., 2003—. Advisor Make-A-Wish Found., Chgo.; bd. dirs. Jr. Achievement, Chgo., Sickle Cell Anemia Found., Chgo., 1986—90, Harold Washington Found., Chgo., 1988—90. With U.S. Army, 1969—71, Korea. Mem.: Nat. Assn. Black Journalists. Home: 3120 Newark St NW Washington DC 20008-3343 Office: TV One, LLC Ste 400 5900 Princess Garden Pkwy Lanham MD 20706*

RODGERS, KIRK PROCTER, international environmental consultant; b. Balt., Oct. 15, 1932; s. Samuel Procter and Florence Eugenia (Besley) R.; m. Karen Frances Johnson, Jan. 3, 1959; children: Brian Kirk, Kimberly Paige. BA in Geography, Yale U., 1954, MS in Natural Resource Conservation, 1956. Timber surveyor U.S. Forest Svc., Colo., Calif., 1953-54; land use planner Balt. (Md.) County Planning Commn., 1955; natural resources specialist, dept. econ. affairs Orgn. of Am. States, Washington, 1960-63, chief natural resources unit, dept. econ. affairs, 1963-69, dir. dept. regional devel. and environment, 1970-96, dir. unit of sustainable devel. and environ., 1996—98, ret. cons., 1998—. Mem. strategic policy coun. Yale U. Sch. Forestry and Environ. Studies, 1992-97; permanent sec. Interamerican Travel Congress, Washington, 1986-94; pres. Besley and Rodgers Inc., Woolford, Md., 1988—; mem. U.S. Sci. Com. on Problems of the Environment, Washington, 1990-93; advisor UN Environment Program, 1986; mem. internat. bd. advisors UN Internat. Environ. Tech. Ctr., Osaka, Japan, 1995-98; bd. advisors Jour. Environ. and Devel., 1992-98; bd. govs. World Water Coun., 1997-98; cons. to Orgn. Am. States & NAFTA Commn. Environ. Coop., 1998—. Author: Physical Resource Investigations for Economic Development, 1969, Integrated Regional Development Planning-Guidelines and Case Studies from OAS Experience, 1984, Conservation in the Big Picture-Development Approaches for the Next Decade, 1992, Ecological and Economic Evaluation of Protected Areas, 1995, The Interamerican Water Resources Network: A Tool for Capacity Building, 1996; contbr. The Careless Technology-Ecological Consequences of Internat. Development, 1970, Managing the Environment in Developing Countries, 1992, Governance in the Western Hemisphere, 1982. Mem. nat. bd. dirs. Fla. Mus. Sci. and Tech., 1994-98; pres. Interam. Water Resources Found., 1997—2001. Lt. (j.g.) USNR, 1956-58. Recipient Grad. fellowship Conservation Found., Yale U., 1955-56, Population Workshop fellowship Ford Found., Washington, 1956; recipient Disting. Alumnus award Yale U. Sch. Forestry and Environ. Studies, 2004. Mem. Am. Soc. for Internat. Devel., Forest Landowners Assn. (chair govtl. affairs 1993-95, pres. 1997-99, exec. com. 1999-), Am. Forest Paper Assn. (mem. pvt. forests bd. dirs.), Am. Water Resources Assn. (hon. mem. 1996), Md. Forests Assn. (bd. dirs. 2000—, pres. 2002-04), Assn. Yale Alumni, (del. 2001-04), Forest Landowners Tax Coun. (bd. dirs. 2003—). Avocations: white water canoeing, hunting, fishing, skiing. Home: 3508 Stoneybrae Dr Falls Church VA 22044-1229 Office: 3508 Stoneybrae Dr Falls Church VA 22044-1229

RODGERS, LAWRENCE RODNEY, internist, educator; b. Clovis, N.Mex., Mar. 9, 1920; s. Samuel Frank and Lillian (O'Connor) R.; m. Ivy Lorna Piper, Aug. 6, 1943; children: Lawrence Rodney (dec.), Ivy Elizabeth, George Piper. BS, West Tex. State U., 1940; MD, U. Tex., 1943. Diplomate Am. Bd. Internal Medicine. Intern Phila. Gen. Hosp., 1943-44, resident in medicine, 1946-49; assoc. internist Tumor Inst., U. Tex. M.D. Anderson Hosp., Houston, 1949—; chmn. dept. medicine Hermann Hosp., Houston, 1966-71; assoc. prof. clin. medicine Baylor U., 1949—; prof. clin. medicine U. Tex., 1972—. Editor: Harris County Physician, 1976-80. Bd. dirs. Tex. Med. Found.; trustee Houston Mus. Med. Sci., 1981. Served to maj. M.C. AUS, 1944-46. Decorated Bronze Star with two oak leaf clusters; recipient Ashbel Smith Disting. Alumnus award U. Tex. Med. Br.-Galveston, 1993, Mastership award Am. Coll. Physicians, 1996. Fellow ACP (gov. for Tex. 1979-83, Laureate Internist Tex. award 1994); mem. AMA (del. 1975-94), Tex. Med. Assn. (elected emeritus), Harris County Med. Soc. (exec. bd. 1978-82, v.p. 1984), Am. Heart Assn., Houston Soc. Internal Medicine (pres. 1974), Houston Acad. Medicine (pres. 1981), Houston Philos. Soc. (pres. 1993-94), Doctor's Club Houston (bd. govs. 1984-88, pres. 1986).

RODGERS, LOUIS DEAN, retired surgeon; b. Centerville, Iowa, Nov. 24, 1930; s. John James and Anna Alice (Spraguer) R.; m. Gretchen Lynn Hendershot, Feb. 19, 1954; children: Cynthia Ann, Elizabeth Dee. MD, U. Iowa, 1960. Diplomate Am. Bd. Surgery. Intern Broadlawns Hosp., Des Moines, 1960-61; resident Meth. Hosp., Des Moines, 1961-65; pvt. practice, Des Moines, 1965-95. Chmn. dept. surgery Iowa Meth. Ctr., Des Moines, 1980-84, chief gen. surgery, 1982-95; clin. assoc. prof. surgery U. Iowa, Iowa City, 1983-95, ret., 1995 . Mem. steering com. gov.'s campaign Iowa Rep. Com., 1982; bd. dirs. Iowa Meth. Med. Found., Des Moines, 1983, Des Moines Synthony, 1984-90, Des Moines Children's Home, 1987-93. Staff sgt. U.S. Army, 1951-54. Recipient Disting. Alumni award Centerville Schs. Found., 1993; named Surg. Tchr. of Yr., Iowa Meth. Med. Ctr., 1978, 84. Fellow ACS (liaison to cancer com. 1973); mem. Western Surg. Assn. (Iowa trauma com. 1983), Iowa Acad. Surgery (pres. 1982-83), Throckmorton Surg. Soc. (pres. 1986), Des Moines Golf and Country. Republican. Home: 13138 Cedar Crest Ln Des Moines IA 50325

RODGERS, MARY COLUMBRO, literature educator, writer, academic administrator; b. Aurora, Ohio, Apr. 17, 1925; d. Nicola and Nancy (DeNicola) Columbro; m. Daniel Richard Rodgers, July 24, 1965; children: Robert, Patricia, Kristine. *Dr.Columbro's parents, Nicola and Nazarena DeNicola Columbro, came from Benevento, Italy to the U.S. in 1919. A tobacco farmer in Italy, Nicola had previously married Assunta Ievolella and immigrated with her in 1905 to Cleveland, Ohio. His wife, Assunta, died during childbirth and Nicola placed his five young children temporarily in Catholic orphanages and returned to Benevento to marry Nazarena DeNicola, a designer dressmaker. Together Nicola and Nazarena raised their combined family of ten children. Educating their children for Catholic professional life was the dream they both shared, encouraging them to achieve a total of nineteen academic degrees.* AB, Notre Dame Coll., 1957; MA, Western Res. U., 1962; PhD, Ohio State U., 1964; postgrad., U. Rome, 1964-65; EdD, Calif. Nat. Open U., 1975, DLitt, 1978. Tchr. English Cleve. elem. schs., 1945-52, Cleve. secondary schs., 1952-62; supr. English student tchrs. Ohio State U., 1962-64; asst. prof. English U. Md., 1965-66; assoc. prof. Trinity Coll., 1967-68; prof. English D.C. Tchrs. Coll. U. D.C., 1968—2000; pres. Md. Nat. U., 1972—; chancellor Open U. Am., 1965—; dean Am. Open U. Acad.; ret., 2000; ind. rschr., writer, 2000—. *From 1945 to 1965, Mary Columbro Rodgers designed, tested and published the multicomponent, open learning methodology which encouraged textbook publishers to provide comprehensive, experience-based literacy texts in K-12 English rather than traditional, classroom-limited, fragmented ones. Since 1965, she has directed the Open University of America which she founded with the Columbro-Rodgers families in Hyattsville, Maryland. This research archetype for college degrees promotes open learning from associate to doctoral levels via distance teaching methods such as telecourses, WWW courses, directed study, correspondence with e-mail, skills tests, learning in paracollegiate agencies, on-the-job training, transfer credits, computer assessment of work experience, and others. "My life as a Catholic scholar has focused on the literate and humane. Both as a student and as a scholar I have made my work a disciplined commitment to English literature, English language, and English pedagogy. My life's goal has been the effective, everyday transmission of humane values defined in my Catholic heritage to younger generations through my teaching, research and writing. My epitaph should read: She saw with the writer's eye and worked with the scholar's tools before she spoke with the teacher's tongue."* Author: A Short Course in English Composition, 1976, Chapbook of Children's Literature, 1977, Comprehensive Catalogue: The Open University of America System, 1978-80, Open University of America System Source Book, V, VII, VII, 1978, Essays and Poems on Life and Literature, 1979, Modes and Models: Four Lessons for Young Writers, 1981, Open University Structures and Adult Learning, 1982, Papers in Applied English Linguistics, 1982, Twelve Lectures on the American Open University, 1982, English Pedagogy in the American Open University, 1983, Design for Personalized English Graduate Degrees in the Urban University, 1984, Open University English Teaching, 1945-85: Conceptual History and Rationale, 1985, Claims and Counterclaims Regarding Instruction Given in Personalized Degree Residency Programs Completed by Graduates of California National Open University, 1986, The American Open University, 1965 to 1985: History and Sourcebook, 1986, New Design II: English Pedagogy in the American Open University, 1987, The American Open University, 1965 to 1985: A Research Report, 1987, The American Open University and Other Open Universities: A Comparative Study Report, 1988, Poet and Pedagogue in Moscow and Leningrad: A Travel Report, 1989, Foundations of English Scholarship in the American Open University, 1989, Twelve Lectures in Literary Analysis, 1990, Ten Lectures in Literary Production, 1990, Analyzing Fact and Fiction, 1991, Analyzing Poetry and Drama, 1991, Some Successful Literary Research Papers: An Inventory of Titles and Theses, 1991, Catalogue for the Mary Columbro Rodgers Literary Trust, 1992, A Chapbook of Poetry and Drama Analysis, 1992, Convent Poems, 1943-1961, 1992, Catholic Marriage Poems 1962, 1979, 1993, Catholic Widow with Children Poems 1979-1993, 1994, First Access List to the Mary Columbro Rodgers Trust by Year, 1994, Nicola Columbro: A Brief Biography, 3d edit., 1994, Biographical Sourcebook I: Mary Columbro Rodgers 1969-1995, 1995, Catholic Teacher Poems, 1945-1995, 1995, Fables and Farm Stories for Fiction Analysis, 1995, Second Access List to the Mary Columbro Rodgers Literary Trust by Alphabet, 1995, Third Access List to the Mary Columbro Rodgers Literary Trust by Subject, 1996, Fourth Access List to the Mary Columbro Rodgers Literary Trust for K-PhD Open Learning-Open University Methods with Data Batches Delineated, 2002, Journals: Reflections and Resolves 1992-2002, 14 vols., 2002, Fifth and Final Access List to the Mary Columbro Rodgers LIterary Trust with Annotations, 2004; contbr. articles to profl. jours. Fulbright scholar U. Rome, 1964-65. Fellow Cath. Scholars; mem. U.S. Distance Learning Assn., Poetry Soc. Am., Nat. Coun. Tchrs. English, Am. Ednl. Rsch. Assn., Am. Acad. Poets, Pi Lambda Theta. Home and Office: Coll Heights Estates 3916 Commander Dr Hyattsville MD 20782-1027 Office Phone: 301-779-0220. E-mail: openuniv@aol.com.

RODGERS, STEPHEN JOHN, lawyer, physician, consultant; b. Phila., July 10, 1943; s. Harry Edward Rodgers and Antoinette Julia Muckenfuss; m. Roberta Elaine Rhine, Sept. 21, 1974; children: Abigail Elizabeth, Rebecca Elizabeth. MD, Hahnemann U., 1969; JD, Widener U., 1989. Bar: Pa. 1990, N.J. 1990; med. lic., Pa., Del., N.J. Pvt. practice in family practice and emergency medicine Del. Pain Clinic, Wilmington, 1975-89, asst. dir., 1989-92; pvt. practice as medicolegal cons. Wilmington, 1992—. Mem. Med. Assistance and Health Svcs. Adv. Bd., N.J., 1996-98; chair Task Force on Ind. Med. Exam., Dept. Labor and Industry, Commonwealth of Pa., 1996-98. Comdr. USN, 1968-75; capt. USNR, 1975—; surgeon gen. N.J. Naval Militia Joint Command. Fellow Am. Acad. Family Physicians, Am. Acad. Disability Evaluating Physicians, Am. Acad. Emergency Medicine, Am. Coll. Legal Medicine; mem. Aerospace Med. Assn., Pa. Bar Assn. (health care com. 1991—), Del. Acad. Medicine, N.J. Acad. Family Physicians (ho. of dels. 1989, 90, 91), Vietnam Vets. of Am. Republican. Roman Catholic. Avocations: equestrian, pro bono veterans and disability advocate. Home: PO Box 54 Alloway NJ 08001-0054 Office: Ste 14 1701 Augustine Wilmington DE 19803 Office Phone: 302-421-9111.

RODGERS, STEVEN EDWARD, tax practitioner, educator; b. Pierre, S.D., Feb. 8, 1947; s. Thomas Edward and Dorothy Zoe (Barker) R.; m. Donna Lynn Joyner, June 10, 1984; 1 child, Michelle Ann. Student, State U. S.D., 1964-65, U. Calif., Berkeley, 1968-72; cert., Coll. for Fin. Planning, 1986-87; fellow, Nat. Tax Practice Inst., 1988-89. CFP, Enrolled Agent. Collection mgr. Cenval Leasing-Ctrl. Bank, Long Beach, Calif., 1972-77; tax preparer Rodgers Tax Svc., Las Vegas, 1977-78; CEO Rainbow Tax Svc. Inc., Las Vegas, 1978—. Pres. Rainbow Tax Svc., Inc., Las Vegas, 1978-90. Author: Marketing To Build Your Tax Practice, 1994. Active Amnesty Internat., Mensa; chmn. Best in the West Edn. Found., Las Vegas, 1994—. Nat. Assn. Enrolled Agents Edn. Found., 1995-96. With U.S. Army, 1965-68, Vietnam. Mem. Nat. Assn. Enrolled Agts. (nat. sec. 1989-90, nat. treas. 1991-92, nat. edn. chair 1994-95, named Tax Educator of the Yr., 1995), Nat. Assn. Enrolled Agents Edn. Found. (chair 1995-96), Nev. Soc. Enrolled Agts. (charter pres. 1985-86, fellow edn. found.), So. Nev. Assn. Tax Cons. (pres. 1981-82), Nat. Soc. Pub. Accts., Vietnam Vets. Am. Home: 1101 Cahill Ave Las Vegas NV 89128-3335 Office: Rainbow Tax Svc Inc 6129 Clarice Ave Las Vegas NV 89107-1401

RODGERS, SUZANNE HOOKER, ergonomics consultant, physiologist; b. Rochester, N.Y., Dec. 26, 1939; d. John Ashmead and Priscilla May (Bodman) Rodgers. AB, Vassar Coll., 1961; PhD, U. Rochester Med. Ctr., 1967. Postdoctoral fellow USPHS Middlesex Hosp., London, 1966-68; ergonomist Eastman Kodak Co., Rochester, N.Y., 1968-82; cons. Rochester, N.Y., 1982—. Author: Working With Backache, 1985; tech. editor, prin. author Ergonomic Design for People at Work, 1983, 86, co-editor, contbr. Kodak's Ergonomic Design for People at Work 2d edit., 2003. Bd. dirs., chmn. com., v.p. Rochester Philharm. Orch. Inc., Rochester, 1969-75; bd. dirs. Opera Theatre Rochester, 1969-75; bd. dirs., chmn. com., pres. Monroe County Bd. Health, Rochester, 1979-88. Mem. Human Factors and Ergonomics Soc., (pres. Western N.Y. chpt. 1971-72), Am. Coll. Sports Medicine. Avocations: photography, sailing, gardening, reading, enjoying silent films. Home and Office: 169 Huntington Hls Rochester NY 14622-1121 Office Phone: 585-544-3587. Personal E-mail: shrodgers@aol.com.

RODGMAN, ALAN, chemist, consultant; b. Aberdare, Wales, Feb. 7, 1924; came to U.S. from Canada, 1954, naturalized, 1961; s. Arch and Margaret (Llewellyn) R.; m. Doris Curley, June 7, 1947; children: Eric, Paul, Mark. BA in Chemistry, U. Toronto, 1949, MA in Organic Chemistry, 1951, PhD in Organic Chemistry, 1953. Rsch. asst. med. rsch. dept. U. Toronto, 1947-51, rsch. assoc., 1951-54; tchr., courses in organic chemistry, phys. chemistry, math. Chem. Inst. Can., 1951-54; sr. rsch. chemist R.J. Reynolds Tobacco Co., Winston-Salem, N.C., 1954-65, head smoke rsch. sect., 1965-75, mgr. analytical rsch., 1975-76, dir. rsch., 1976-80, dir. fundamental rsch. and devel., 1980-87; cons. in field, 1987—. Mem. editl. bd. Tobacco Sci., 1963-67 (Vol. 31 Tobacco Sci. dedicated in his name 1987), Beitrage zur Tabakforschung Internat., 1978-87. Mem. Tobacco Working Group, Nat. Cancer Inst., 1976-77, Tech. Study Group on Cigarette and Little Cigar Fire Safety, 1984-87, Sci. Commn. Cooperation Ctr. for Sci. Rsch. Relative to Tobacco, 1982-84. With Royal Can. Navy, 1942-45. Mem. Coun. for Tobacco Rsch. (industry tech. com. 1956-62, Tobacco Sci. Rsch. Conf. Inaugural Lifetime Achievement award 2003), Chem. Inst. Can., Can. Chem. Soc., Am. Chem. Soc., N.Y. Acad. Scis. Episcopalian. Home: 2828 Birchwood Dr Winston Salem NC 27103-3410

RODIBAUGH, ROBERT KURTZ, retired judge; b. Elkhart County, Ind., July 2, 1916; s. Ralph Leedy and Rose (Kurtz) R.; m. Doris Ann Siekemeyer, Jan. 1, 1942 (dec.); children: David L., Bob K.; m. Eunice Margaret Cline, Nov. 25, 1972. BSc, U. Notre Dame, 1940, JD, 1941. Bar: Ind. 1941, U.S. Dist. Ct. (no. dist.) Ind. 1946, U.S. Ct. Appeals (7th cir.) 1972, U.S. Supreme Ct. 1965. Dep. pros. atty. Ind. 60th Jud. Cir., St. Joseph County, 1948-50, 53-57; judge U.S. Bankruptcy Ct., No. Dist. Ind., South Bend, 1960-99, ret., 1999. Lectr. in law U. Notre Dame, 1973; atty. St. Joseph County Bd. Zoning Appeals, 1958-60. V.p. No. Ind. coun. Boy Scouts Am., 1967-77; bd. dirs. St. Joseph County chpt. ARC, 1970-77. Capt. U.S. Army, 1941-46, PTO. Recipient Silver Beaver award Boy Scouts Am., 1969. Mem. ABA, Seventh Fed. Cir. Bar Assn., Ind. Bar Assn., St. Joseph County Bar Assn. (gov. 1953-56), Comml. Law League, Nat. Conf. Bankruptcy Judges (dir. 1977-79), Exch. Club, Masons, DeMolay Club (Legion of Honor), Shriners, Rotary (South Bend, Ind. chpt.). Office: US Bankruptcy Ct PO Box 7003 401 S Michigan St South Bend IN 46601-2365 Home: 360 Winterset Dr Englewood OH 45322-1630

RODIN, HOWARD ALAN, periodontist; b. Bronx, N.Y., Oct. 21, 1942; s. David and Edna (Fialkow) R.; m. Gail Sandra Stein, July 8, 1967; children: Dennis, Stephanie. BS, Fairleigh Dickinson U., 1964, MS in Physiology, 1966; DDS, Howard U., 1970; cert. in periodontics, Columbia U., 1973. Intern Sydenham Hosp., N.Y.C., 1970-71; staff dept. virology Mt. Sinai Hosp., 1964-66; postdoctoral fellow Fairleigh Dickinson U., Teaneck, NJ, 1971; pvt. practice Babylon, 1973-82, Smithtown, 1978—; staff dept. spl. surgery St. John's Hosp., 1979-81, 85-91. Cons. NYU Med. Ctr./Goldwater Meml. Hosp., 1995-97; planning com. Greater L.I. Dental Meeting, 1973-97, gen. chmn., 1985; asst. clin. prof. periodontics Columbia U., 1986-88; pres. L.I. Acad. Periodontists, 1986-90; mass disaster forensic identification team TWA Flight 800; mem. forensic identification team World Trade Ctr., 2001. Contbr. articles to profl. jours. Fellow Am. Coll. Dentists (chmn. N.Y. sect. 2002), Am. Soc. Forensic Odontology, Internat. Coll. Dentists, Pierre Fauchand Acad., Acad. Dentistry Internat., N.Y. Acad. Dentistry, Suffolk Acad. Medicine (pres. 1992-93, trustee 1990-95), Am. Acad. Osseointegration, Am. Acad. Forensic Scis.; mem. ADA (del., alt. del. 1989-2001), Internat. Assn. Dental Rsch. (periodontal rsch. com. 1984—, implantology rsch. com. 1995—, Hatton award competition 1968), Am. Assn. Oral Biologists, Am. Acad. Periodontology, Suffolk County Dental Soc. (bd. dels. 1981—, pres. 1991), N.Y. State Soc. Periodontists (bd. dirs.), Northeastern Soc. Periodontists, N.Y. Acad. Scis., Suffolk Soc. Forensic Dentistry (exec. com. 1995—), Columbia U. Periodontal Alumni Assn. (trustee 1996—), Sigma Xi, Alpha Omega (pres. 1985-87), Omicron Kappa Upsilon. Office Phone: 631-360-0090.

RODIN, JUDITH SEITZ, former academic administrator; b. Phila., Sept. 9, 1944; d. Morris and Sally R. (Winson) Seitz. m. Paul Verkuil. AB, U. Pa., 1966; PhD, U. Columbia, 1970. Asst. prof. psychology NYU, 1970—72; assoc. prof. Yale U., 1975—79, prof., dir. grad. studies, 1982—89, Philip R. Allen prof. psychology, medicine and psychiatry, 1984—94, chmn. dept. psychology, 1989—91, dean Grad. Sch., 1991—92, provost, 1992—94; pres. U. Pa., Phila., 1994—2004, prof. psychology, medicine and psychiatry, 1994—2004. Chmn. John D. and Catherine T. MacArthur Found. Rsch. Network on Determinants and Consequences of Health-Promoting and Health-Damaging Behavior, 1983-93; vice chair coun. press. U. Rsch. Assn., 1994-95, chair, 1995-96; mem. Ind. Panel to Review Safety Procedures at The White House, 1994-95; chair adv. com. Robert Wood Johnson Found., 1994—; mem. Pres. Clinton's Com. Advisors Sci. and Tech., 1994—; mem. Coun. Competitiveness, 1997—; mem. nominating com. N.Y. Stock Exch., 1998—; bd. dirs. Aetna, Electronic Data Sys., AMR. Author: (with S. Schachter) Obese Humans and Rats, 1978, Exploding the Weight Myths, 1982, Body Traps, 1992; chief editor Appetite Jour., 1979-92; contbr. articles to profl. jours. Mem. Pa. Task Force on Higher Edn. Funding, 1994; bd. dirs. Catalyst, N.Y.C., 1994—; trustee Brookings Inst., 1995—; pres. steering com. Am. Reads, 1997—. Fellow Woodrow Wilson Found., 1966-67, John Simon Guggenheim Found., 1986-87; grantee NSF, 1973-82, NIH, 1981—. Recipient Phila. Award, 2004. Fellow AAAS, APA (bd. sci. affairs 1979-82, pres. divsn. 38 health psychology 1982-83, Outstanding Contbn. award 1980, Disting. Sci. award 1977), Am. Acad. Arts and Scis., Soc. Behavioral Medicicine; mem. AAUW (mem. exec. com. 1996—), Am. Philosophical Soc., Inst. Medicine of NAS, Acad. Behavioral Medicine Rsch., Ea. Psychol. Assn. (exec. bd. 1980-82), Phi Beta Kappa, Sigma Xi (pres. Yale chpt. 1986-87).

RODIN, RITA A. lawyer; b. N.Y., 1968; BS, Boston (Mass.) Coll., 1990; JD, St. John's U., 1990. Bar: N.J. 1994, N.Y. 1994. Law clk. Hon. Thomas C. Platt U.S. Dist. Ct. (ea. dist.) N.Y., 1993—94; atty. Skadden, Arps, Slate, Meagher & Flom LLP, N.Y., 1994—2001, ptnr., 2001—. Office: Skadden Arps Slate Meagher & Flom LLP Four Times Sq New York NY 10036

RODITE, ROBERT R.R. engineering scientist; b. Easton, Pa., Oct. 17, 1942; s. Victor James and Alice Cecilia (Zatovich) R.; m. Patricia Ann Sule, Apr. 8, 1967; children: Colleen P., Robert J. BSEE, Lafayette Coll., 1964; MSEE, Caif. Inst. Tech., 1965. Rsch. engr., mgr. mfg. rsch. lab. IBM, Endicott, N.Y., 1965-70, mfg. engring. mgr. electronic packaging mfg., 1970-72, devel. engring. mgr. electronic packaging engring., 1972-77, program dir. corp. engring., programming & tech. staff Armonk, N.Y., 1977-79, product engring. mgr., sr. engr. multichip module devel. East Fishkill, N.Y., 1979-81, system mgr., sr. tech. staff mem. fin. industry devel. Charlotte, N.C., 1981-92, sr. tech. staff mem. corp. tech. strategy devel. staff Armonk, 1992-93; pres. Rodite Assocs., Inc., Charlotte, 1993—; lectr. math. and bus. Belmont Abbey Coll., 2001—04. Workgroup mem. Am. Nat. Standards Inst. Com. X9B Stds. Com., 1991-97; chmn. IBM Image Processing and Visualization Interdivisional Tech. Liaison Com., 1992-93. Contbr. articles to profl. jours.; patentee in field. Asst. scoutmaster Boy Scouts Am., Charlotte, 1991, 92; mid. sch. basketball asst. coach, Charlotte, 1991-92, 93-94; com. mem. Town County Consolidation Com., Endicott, 1970s; mem. Cath. sch. bd. Diocese of Charlotte, 1988-90; pres. Homeowners Assn., Charlotte, 2001-03. Tau Beta Pi fellow Calif. Inst. Tech., 1964. Mem. IEEE (sr.), Assn. for Info. and Image Mgmt. Internat. (designated Master Info. Tech. 1997, cert. document Image Architech, Laureate of Info. Technologies 1998), Phi Beta Kappa, Tau Beta Pi, Eta Kappa Nu. Avocations: personal computers, travel. Home: 9664 Chaumont Ln Charlotte NC 28277-2140 Personal E-mail: rodite@email.com.

RODKEY, FRANCES THERESA, elementary school educator; b. Germantown, Pa., Sept. 3, 1952; d. Joseph Milton and Elizabeth Jane Parsons; m. Glenn Leroy Rodkey, May 1, 1976; children: Jennifer, Rachel. Student, Immaculata Coll., 1970—72; BS in Elem. Edn., Bloomsburg U., 1975. Cert. emergency edn. Pa., 1986. Substitute tchr. Coatesville Sch. Dist., Pa., 1984—89, tchr. 6th grade, 1989—, head dept. social studies, 2000. Mem.: NEA, Pa. State Edn. Assn. Republican. Roman Catholic. Avocations: reading, camping, hiking. Home: 1111 Oak St Coatesville PA 19320 Office: Coatesville Sch Dist 1515 E Lincoln Hwy Coatesville PA 19320

RODKIN, GARY M. beverage company executive; B.A., Rutgers Univ.; M.B.A., Harvard Business School. Pres., served other mktg. and gen. mgmt. positions Gen. Mills (Yoplait-Colombo yogurt unit); pres. Tropicana N.Am., 1995—98, pres., CEO, 1998—99, PepsiCola N.Am., 1999—2002; Pres. PepsiCo, Beverages and Foods, 2002—03, CEO, 2002—, chmn., 2003—. Office: Pepsi-Cola Inc Purchase NY 10577

RODKIN, LOREE, jewelry artist; Studied film making, art history, design, N.Y.C. Hollywood actors mgr., interior designer; jewelry maker Loree Rodkin Gothic Jewelry, Beverly Hills, Calif. Designer of In Memory Ring to honor friend, lover, or family mem. proceeds donated to Elton John AIDS Found. Office: Loree Rodkin Gothic Jewelry 453 Rodeo Dr Beverly Hills CA 90209 Fax: 310-276-8104. E-mail: lrodkin@instanet.com.

RODMAN, ALPINE C. arts and crafts company executive, photographer; b. Roswell, N.Mex., June 23, 1952; s. Robert Elsworth and Verna Mae (Means) R.; m. Sue Arlene Lawson, Dec. 13, 1970; 1 child, Connie Lynn. Student, Colo. State U., 1970—71, U. No. Colo. Ptnr. Pinel Silver Shop, Loveland, Colo., 1965-68, salesman, 1968-71; real estate salesman Loveland, 1971-73; mgr. Traveling Traders, Phoenix, 1974-75; co-owner Deer Track Traders, Loveland, 1975-85; pres. Deer Track Traders, Ltd., Loveland, 1985—. Author: The Vanishing Indian: Fact or Fiction?, 1985. Mem. Civil Air Patrol, 1965-72, 87-92, dep. comdr. for cadets, 1988-90; cadet comdr. Ft. Collins, Colo., 1968,

70, Colo. rep. to youth tng. program, 1969, U.S. youth rep. to Japan, 1970. Mem. Bur. Wholesale Sales Reps., We. and English Salesmen's Assn. (bd. dirs. 1990), Internat. Platform Assn., Indian Arts and Crafts Assn. (bd. dirs. 1988-94, exec. com. 1989-92, v.p. 1990, pres. 1991, market chmn. 1992), Crazy Horse Grass Roots Club. Office: Deer Track Traders Ltd PO Box 448 Loveland CO 80539-0448 *Personal philosophy: I believe that most good and bad in the world comes out of respect or lack of respect for one's self, fellow man, environment and creator.*

RODMAN, JOHN SLATER, lawyer; b. Boston, June 21, 1953; s. Sumner and Helen (Morris) R.; m. Pamela Taglienti, May 30, 1976; children: Calvin, Lydia. BA, U. Pa., 1975; JD, Boston U., 1978. Bar: Mass. 1978, U.S. Dist. Ct. Mass. 1978, U.S. Ct. Appeals (1st cir.) 1979, U.S. Supreme Ct. 1982, U.S. Dist. Ct. (no. dist.) Ill. 1998. With Gargill, Sassoon & Rudolph, Boston, 1979-89; head of bankruptcy dept. Parker, Coulter, Daley & White, Boston, 1989-94; pvt. practice Boston, 1994—; of counsel Mauser & DiPiano, LLP, Boston, 1999—. Chmn. Newton (Mass.) Hist. Commn.; mem. Chestnut Hill Hist. Dist. Commn., Newton. Mem. Mass. Bar Assn., Boston Bar Assn., Comml. Law League Am., Am. Bankruptcy Inst. Office: 98 N Wash St Ste 305 Boston MA 02114-1913 Office Phone: 617-227-8887. E-mail: jrodman@mauserlaw.com.

RODMAN, LEIBA, mathematician; b. Riga, Latvia, June 9, 1949; came to U.S., 1985; s. Zalman and Haya Rodman; m. Ella Levitan, Feb. 2, 1983; children: Daniel, Ruth, Benjamin, Naomi. Diploma in maths., Latvian State U., 1971; MA in Statis., Tel Aviv (Israel) U., 1976, PhD in Maths., 1978. Instr. Tel Aviv U., 1976-78, sr. lectr., 1981-83, assoc. prof., 1983-85; postdoctoral fellow U. Calgary, Can., 1978-80; from assoc. to full prof. Ariz. State U., Tempe, 1985-87; prof. math. Coll. William and Mary, Williamsburg, Va., 1987—. Author: Introduction to Operator Polynomials, 1989, (with others) Matrix Polynomials, 1982, Matrices and Indefinite Scalar Products, 1983, Invariant Subspaces of Matrices with Applications, 1986, Interpolation of Rational Matrix Functions, 1990, Algebraic Riccati Equations, 1995; co-editor: Contributions to Operator Theory and Its Applications, 1988. Mem. Am. Math. Soc., Internat. Linear-Algebra Soc., Soc. Indsl. and Applied Math. Office: Coll of William & Mary Dept Math PO Box 8795 Williamsburg VA 23187-8795 Business E-Mail: lxrodm@math.wm.edu.

RODMAN, LEONARD C. civil and communication engineering executive; BS in Civil Engring., Iowa State U., 1971; MS in Environ. Engring., U. Mo., 1978. Civil engr. Black & Veatch, Kansas City, Mo., 1971—, group mng. ptnr., head N.Am. divsn. infrastructure bus., CEO, pres., 1998—, chmn. bd. dirs., 2000—. Mem. Iowa State Engring. Coll. Indsl. Adv. Consul. Bd. trustees, cmty./legis. affairs com. U. Mo., Kansas City. Mem.: WEF, NSPE, MSPE, AWWA, ASCE. Office: Black & Veatch 8400 Ward Parkway Kansas City MO 64114 Fax: (913) 458-3511.

RODMAN, LEROY ELI, lawyer; b. NYC, Feb. 22, 1914; s. Morris and Sadie (Specter) R.; m. Toby Chertcoff, Mar. 14, 1943; children: John Stephen, Lawrence Bernard. AB, CCNY, 1933; JD (James Kent scholar), Columbia, 1936. Bar: NY 1937. Pvt. practice, NYC, 1937—43, 1946—; law sec. to US dist. judge Bklyn., 1936; law asst. Am. Law Inst., NYC, 1937; chief food enforcement unit NY Regional Office, OPA, 1942—43; mem. firm Lawrence R. Condon, NYC, 1937—42; ptnr. Joseph & Rodman, NYC, 1946—53; sr. ptnr. Rodman, Maurer & Dansker, NYC, 1964—73, Carro, Spanbock, Londin, Rodman & Fass, NYC, 1973—78, Rodman & Rodman, NYC, 1978—89, Teitelbaum, Hiller, Rodman, Paden & Hibsher, P.C., NYC, 1990—96; of counsel Morrison, Cohen, Singer & Weinstein LLP, NYC, 1996—2003. Edtl. bd.: Columbia Law Rev., 1934-36; Contbr. articles to legal jours. V.p. Ctrl. Synagogue, pres. brotherhood, 1958—60, hon. trustee; bd. dirs. Manhattan coun. Boy Scouts Am., v.p., 1961—68, pres., 1972—75, exec. bd. Greater NY coun. Capt. JAGD U.S. Army, 1943—46. Recipient Certs. Svc., Silver Beaver award Boy Scouts Am., 1962, Eagle Scout. Fellow: Am. Coll. Trust Estate Counsel; mem.: ABA, Judge Adv. Assn., Assn. Bar City NY, NY County Lawyers Assn., Metropolis Country Club (White Plains, NY) (sec. 1976—77, 1980—82, v.p. 1977—78, bd. govs. 1976—82), Univ. Club (NYC), Phi Beta Kappa. Home and Office: 535 E 86th St New York NY 10028-7533

RODMAN, PETER WARREN, government official; b. Boston, Nov. 24, 1943; s. Sumner and Helen Rhoda (Morris) R.; m. F. Veronique Boulad, Apr. 13, 1980; children: Theodora, Nicholas. BA summa cum laude, Harvard U., 1964, JD, 1969; BA, MA, Oxford (Eng.) U., 1966. Staff mem. NSC, Washington, 1969-77; fellow in diplomatic studies Ctr. for Strategic and Internat. Studies, Washington, 1977-83; dir. rsch. Kissinger Assocs., Washington, 1982-83; mem. policy planning council Dept. of State, Washington, 1983-84, dir. policy planning staff, 1984-86; dep. asst. to pres. for nat. security affairs (fgn. policy) NSC, Washington, 1986-87, NSC counselor, spl. asst. to pres. for nat. security affairs, 1987-90; fellow Johns Hopkins Fgn. Policy Inst., Washington, 1990-93; dir. Middle East and Eurasian studies Ctr. for Strategic and Internat. Studies, Washington, 1994-95; dir. nat. security programs Nixon Ctr., Washington, 1995-2001; asst. sec. def. for internat. security affairs Dept. of Def., Washington, 2001—. Author: More Precious Than Peace: The Cold War and the Struggle for the Third World, 1994; sr. editor Nat. Rev., 1991-99; contbr. articles to profl. jours. V.p. World Affairs Coun., Washington, 1996-2001; trustee Freedom House, 1997-2001. Mem. Coun. on Fgn. Rels., Internat. Inst. for Strategic Studies, Atlantic Coun. U.S., Cosmos Club. Office: 2400 Defense Pentagon Rm 4E838 Washington DC 20301-2400 Office Phone: 703-695-4351. E-mail: peter.rodman@osd.mil.

RODMAN, RAYMOND G. insurance company executive; b. Topeka, Kans., Aug. 2, 1946; s. John T. and Wilma D. (Cox-Betts) R.; m. Sherri L. Shughart, Aug. 31, 1968; children: Eric, Erin, Tara, Charisse. BS in Math., Emporia State U., 1970; MBA, Ill. State U., 1980. CLU, ChFC, CPCU, cert. data processing profl. Programmer State Farm Ins., Bloomington, Ill., 1970-72, analyst, 1973-75, team leader, 1975-77, project leader, 1977-80, supt., 1980-86, mgr., 1986-90, IS mgr., 1990—. Chmn. economy subcom., steering com. 2020 Planning Com., Normal, Ill., 1995-96; mem. McLean County Bd., 1990—. Mem. CPCU Soc., CLU Soc. Republican. Baptist. Home: 719 N School St Normal IL 61761-1620 Office: State Farm Insurance 3 State Farm Plz # K2 Bloomington IL 61791-0002

RODMAN, SUE A. wholesale company executive, artist, writer; b. Ft. Collins, Colo., Oct. 1, 1951; d. Marvin F. Lawson and Barbara I. (Miller) Lawson Shue; m. Alpine C. Rodman, Dec. 13, 1970; 1 child, Connie, Lynn. Student, Woodbury Bus./Arts Coll., Calif., 1969, Colo. State U., 1970-73. Silversmith Pinel Silver Shop, Loveland, Colo., 1970-71; asst. mgr. Traveling Traders, Phoenix, 1974-75; co-owner, co-mgr. Deer Track Traders, Loveland, 1975-85; v.p. Deer Track Traders, Ltd., Loveland, 1985—. Author: The Book of Contemporary Indian Arts and Crafts, 1985, also numerous children's articles and short stories. Mem. U.S. Senatorial Club, 1982-87, Rep. Presdl. Task Force, 1984-90; mem. Civil Air Patrol, 1969-73, 87-90, pers. officer, 1988-90. Mem. Internat. Platform Assn., Indian Arts and Crafts Assn., Western and English Sales Assn., Crazy Horse Grass Roots Club. Mem. Am. Baptist Ch. Avocations: museums, piano, recreation research, fashion design. Office: Deer Track Traders Ltd PO Box 448 Loveland CO 80539-0448

RODMAN, SUMNER, insurance company executive; b. Malden, Mass., Aug. 5, 1915; s. Nathan Markel and Sara Ruth (Slater) Rodman; m. Helen Rhoda Morris, July 2, 1942; children: Peter Warren, John Slater. AB cum laude, Harvard U., 1935. CLU. Ins. broker, employee benefits specialist Aetna Life Ins. and Annuity Co., Boston, 1935-98; with Rodman Ins. Agy., Inc., Needham, Mass.; life ins. adviser, 1953—. Pres. Boston Life Ins. and Trust Coun., 1958—59. Bd. dirs. Boston Estate Planning Coun., 1960—85, pres., 1958; mem. Anti-Defamation League B'nai Brith, World Affairs Coun. Boston; chmn. class com. Harvard, 1935; bd. dirs. Jewish Family and Children's Svc., Boston, 1953—85; mem. Am. Jewish Com.; hon. trustee Temple Israel, Boston; bd. dirs. Youth Tennis Found. New Eng., 1963—85, Simons-Gutman Found., 1965—, Alzheimers Assn. Ea. Mass., 1990—97; hon. trustee Combined Jewish Philanthropies of Greater Boston, 1967—. Served to capt. AUS, ETO. Fellow CLU Inst., 1952, 1961. Mem.: New Eng. Tennis Assn. (bd. dirs. 1966—68, Hall of Fame 1992), Am. Soc. CLUs (pres. 1972—73), Boston Life Underwriters Assn. (pres. 1965—66), Am. Coll. (trustee 1971—74), Million Dollar Round Table (life), Wightman Tennis Ctr. Club (Weston, Mass.), Harvard Varsity Club (Boston), Harvard Club (Boston), Newton Club (Mass.), Squash and Tennis Club, Masons, Golden Key Soc. Jewish. Home: 94 Vine St Chestnut Hill MA 02467-3050 Office: Rodman Ins Agy Inc 145 Rosemary St Needham MA 02494-3238 E-mail: srodman@rodmanins.com.

RODNE, KJELL JOHN, healthcare administrator; b. July 6, 1948; came to U.S., 1959; s. Johannes and Margit (Gautun) R.; m. Kathleen Anne Gordon, Sept. 21, 1966; children: Jay Robert, Lee Eric. BS, U. Minn., Duluth, 1971; MSW, 1985; cert., Univ. Assn. Human Resources, 1995; PMA sci. of success diploma, personal computer tng. program diploma,, 1996. Asst. youth dir. YMCA, Duluth, 1967-68; counselor Northwood, Duluth, 1968-71; team leader, 1971-76; social worker, 1976-77; program dir., 1977-85; pers. dir. City of Duluth, 1985-86, adminstrv. asst., 1986-92; mgmt. cons., 1992-93; adminstr. Northwood West, 1993-95; dir. quality assurance, 1995-96; CEO Duluth Bethel Soc., 1996-97; dir. program ops. Youth Continum, New Haven, 1997-2000; dir. St. Croix Boys Camp, 2000—. Bd. dirs. Minn. Coun. Residential Teatment Ctrs., St. Paul, 1977-85, 93-96. Mem. Duluth City Coun., 1978-85, pres., 1981; bd. dirs. United Devel. Achievement Ctr., Duluth, 1981-85, United Way of Duluth, 1981-89, Duluth Econ. Devel. Authority, 1989-92, Arrowhead Growth Alliance, 1990-92, Northspan, 1991-92. Mem. Lake Superior Assn. Labor Mgmt. (bd. dirs. 1989-92), Internat. City Mgrs. Assn. (pub. policy com. 1991-95), Nat. Assn. Homes for Children. Democrat. Home: 1511 N 64th St Superior WI 54880-5958 Personal E-mail: ingolf@aol.com. E-mail: kjr@wilder.com.

RODNEY, JOEL MORRIS, dean, campus executive officer; b. Bklyn., Nov. 9, 1937; s. Samuel Seymour and Jane (Loorya) R.; m. Judith DeStefano, July 22, 1994; children from previous marriage: Jonathan, Adam, Benjamin. BA cum laude, Brandeis U., 1959; PhD, Cornell U., 1965; attended, Inst. Ednl. Mgmt. Harvard U., 1976. From instr. to assoc. prof. Wash. State U., Pullman, 1963-70; chmn. div. social scis., assoc. prof. history Elmira (N.Y.) Coll., 1970-72, coordinator flood relief and community planning, 1973; dean arts and sci., prof. history Widener Coll., Chester, Pa., 1973-76, acting chief acad. officer, dean, 1976-77, chief acad. officer, dean, 1977-81, dir. univ. grad. programs, 1979-81; v.p. acad. affairs Salisbury (Md.) State Coll., 1981-86; provost Rockford (Ill.) Coll., 1986-90; CEO, dean U. Wis. -Washington County, West Bend, 1990—. Editor Albion, 1967-78; contbr. articles to profl. jours. Vice chmn. Md. Gov.'s Com. on Employment of Handicapped, 1985-86, chmn. and mem. Lower Shore divsn., 1983-86; chmn. adv. bd., mem. Crozer-Chester Med. Health Ctr., Chester, 1974-77; project evaluator NEH, 1986, RSA, 1993; mem., sec. Delaware County Mental Health/Mental Retardation Bd., 1975-81; adv. bd. Rehab. Inst. of Chgo., 1988-94; mem. coun. Ct. of Gov.'s Regents Coll., London, 1986-90, Rock Valley Coll. Indsl. Coun., Rockford, 1989-90; bd. dirs. Moraine Symphony Orch., 1990-93, Welcome Home, Inc., 1990—, pres., 1992—; citizens adv. bd. West Bend Bank One, 1991, Washington County Vol. Ctr., 1991-92; bd. dirs. The Threshold, 1992—, vice chair, 1990-2000, chair, 2000; apptd. to State Wis. Coun. Phys. Disabilities, 1994, vice chmn., 1995, chmn., 1996-2000; exec. com. Moraine area Tech. Prep. Coun., 1994—; mem. Wis. Gov.'s Com. on Persons with Disabilities, 1994-97, vice chmn., 1996; mem. adv. bd. S.E. Wis. Area Health Edn. Coun., 1995-96, West Bend Art Mus., 1996-2001, chair, 1999-2001; mem. West Bend C. of C. Ambs., 1995—; mem. Washington County Growth Mgmt. Task Force, 1996—, chair, 1999—; del. Washington County Reps., 1997—; bd. dirs. Kettle Moraine YMCA, 1999—. Recipient Disting. Service award Widener Meml. Sch., 1978, Award of merit Md. Gov.'s Com. on Employment of Handicapped, 1984; named to Legion of Honor, Chapel of Four Chaplains, 1978; honoree West Phila. Vets. and Handicapped Employment Com., 1977. Mem. Am. Assn. Acad. Deans, Conf. on Brit. Studies, Am. Assn. Univ. Adminstrs., Nat. Spinal Cord Injury Assn. (bd. dirs. Ill. chpt. 1988-90), Rotary, Phi Alpha Theta. Republican. Office: U Wis Washington County 400 S University Dr West Bend WI 53095-3619

RODNEY, ROXANNE AUDREY, cardiologist, consultant; BA summa cum laude, Hunter Coll., 1981; MD, Cornell U., 1985. Diplomate Am. Bd. Internal Medicine, Am. Bd. Cardiovasc. Diseases, Am. Bd. Nuc. Cardiology. Resident in internal medicine Montefiore Hosp., Bronx, N.Y., 1985-88; fellow in cardiology N.Y. Med. Coll., Valhalla, 1988-90; fellow in nuc. cardiology Columbia U., N.Y.C., 1990-91; attending physician Columbia-Presbyn. Med. Ctr., N.Y.C., 1991-99; sr. assoc. cons. Mayo Clinic, Jacksonville, Fla., 1999—. Contbr. articles to profl. jours. Mem. Am. Heart Assn. (chair women cardiology com. 1997—, bd. dirs. 1999—), Assn. Black Cardiologists (bd. dirs. 1995-99, chair cardiovasc. diseases women com. 1995—). Office: Mayo Clinic Divsn Cardiology 4500 San Pablo Rd S Jacksonville FL 32224-3899

RODNING, CHARLES BERNARD, surgeon; b. Pipestone, Minn., Aug. 4, 1943; s. Selmer Bernard and Ida Amanda (Selness) R.; m. Mary Elizabeth Lipke, June 15, 1968; children: Christopher Bernard, Soren Piers, Kai Johannes. BS, Gustavus Adolphus Coll., St. Peter, Minn., 1965; MD, U. Rochester, 1970; PhD, U. Minn., 1979. Diplomate Am. Bd. Med. Examiners, Am. Bd. Surgery. Intern, asst. resident dept. surgery U. Rochester Sch. Medicine and Dentistry, 1970-72; assoc. resident to chief resident, med. fellow dept. surgery U. Minn. Health Scis. Ctr., Mpls., 1972-79; prof. dept cell biology and neurosci. U. South Ala., Mobile, 1981—, prof. dept. surgery, 1981—, vice chmn. dept. surgery, 1981—, dir. gen. surgery, 1996—. Field liaison physician Commn. on Cancer-ACS, Chgo., 1984—; mem. med. adv. bd. Ala. Organ & Tissue Ctr., Birmingham, 1988—. Author: Elan Vital, 1988, Wode and Ston, 1988, Sorrowful Wheel, 1989, Ponderings, 1990, The Sea Rises in the West, 1991, Stepping Stones, 1991, Snowbound Below the Firn Line, 1991, Love Knot, 1994, Papering Dreams, 1994, Carry Onward, 1996, Swaying Grass, 1998, Tradition of Excellence: Pictorial History of Surgical Education at the Mobile General Hospital and University of South Alabama College of Medicine and Medical Center, 1999; reviewer: Jour. Histochem. Cytochem., 1988—; contbr. (articles) Clin. Anatomy, —, Surg. Endoscopy, Pharos, Jours. Thoracic Cardiovasc. Surgery, So. Med. Jour., others. Bd. dirs. Mobile Mental Health Ctr., Mental Health Found. of S. Ala., Mobile Med. Mu. Comdr. USN, 1974-81. Recipient Physicians Recognition award AMA, 1980, 85, 88, 91, 95, 99, 02, Bacaner Rsch. award Minn. Med. Found., 1979, Humanism in Medicine award Arnold P. Gold Found., Healthcare Found. N.J., 2002, Howard L. Holley award Med. Assn. State Ala., 2002. Fellow ACS, Internat. Coll. Surgeons (vice regent Ala. chpt. 1989—); mem. Iota Delta Gamma, Alpha Omega Alpha, Phi Kappa Phi. Office: U South Ala Coll Med Allied Health Professions Mobile AL 36617-2293 Office Phone: 251-471-7034. Business E-Mail: crodning@usouthal.edu.

RODNUNSKY, SIDNEY, lawyer, educator; b. Edmonton, Alta., Can., Feb. 3, 1946; s. B. and I. Rodnunsky; m. Teresita Asuncion; children: Naomi, Shawna, Rachel, Tevie, Claire, Donna, Sidney Jr. BEd, U. Alberta, 1966, LLB, 1973; MEd, U. Calgary, 1969, grad. diploma, 1990; BS, U. of State of N.Y., 1988; MBA, Greenwich U., 1990. Served as regional counsel to Her Majesty the Queen in Right of the Dominion of Can.; former gov. Grande Prairie Regional Coll.; now prin. legal counsel Can. Nat. exec., Alta. coord. for gifted children, ombudsman, SIG coord. Mensa Can.; past pres. Grande Prairie and Dist. Bar Assn., Alta Tchrs. Assn., Aspenview. Author: Breathalyzer Casebook; editor: The Children Speak. Decorated knight Grand Cross Sovereign and Royal Order of Piast, knight Grand Cross Order of St. John the Baptist; knight Hospitaller Order St. John of Jerusalem; Prince of Kiev, Prince of Trabzon, Prince and Duke of Rodari, Duke of Chernigov, Count of Riga, Count of St. John of Alexandria; named to Honorable Order of Ky. Colonels; named adm. State of Tex.; recipient Presdl. Legion of Merit. Mem. Law Soc. Alta., Law Soc. Sask., Can. Bar Assn., Inst. Can. Mgmt., Phi Delta Kappa. Address: General Delivery Kugaaruk NU Canada X0B 1K0 Office Phone: 867-769-6211. E-mail: wonderfulschool@hotmail.com.

RODOLFF, DALE WARD, engineer, sales executive, consultant; b. Casa Grande, Ariz., Aug. 5, 1938; s. Norval Ward and Mary Louise (Grasty) Rodolff; m. Kathleen Pennington, Sept. 3, 1960 (div. July 1983); children: David Ward (dec.), Julia Ann. BS in Mining Engring., U. Ariz.; PMD, U. Cape Town; postgrad., Denver Sem. Registered profl. engr., Republic of South Africa. Supt. smelting and fabricating Inspiration Consol. Copper Co., Claypool, Ariz., 1960-72; smelter and refinery supt. Palabora Mining Co, Phalaborwa, Republic of South Africa, 1972-74; asst. mgr. Empress Nickel Mining Co., Gatooma, Zimbabwe, 1974-77; smelter supt. Magma Copper Co., San Manuel, Ariz., 1977-81; v.p., gen. mgr. Sentinel Mgmt. Corp., Tucson, 1981-82; dir., mgr. metallurgy Outokumpu Engring. Inc., Denver, 1982-86, mgr. N.Am., 1986-96, also bd. dirs.; supt. flash smelting and flash converting Kennecott Utah Copper, 1996-97. Cons., pres. D.W. Rodolff Cons. Corp., 1986—; pres. Bus. Performance Svcs., Inc., 1986-90; dir. Grace Ministries, 1995-99; chmn. Mountain Area Crisis Pregnancy Ctr., 2001—. Contbr. articles to tech. jours.; inventor scrap rod feed system, 1970. Pres. Y Men's Club, Miami, Ariz., 1969. Kennecott scholar U. Ariz., 1959. Mem. AIME (metall. soc., soc. mining engrs., chmn. smelter div. 1970, 71, pyro metall. com. 1973-77), Mining and Metall. Soc. Am. Avocations: flying, skiing, christian endeavors. Home and Office: 6527 S Jungfrau Way Evergreen CO 80439-5308

RODOWSKY, LAWRENCE FRANCIS, retired state judge; b. Balt., Nov. 10, 1930; s. Lawrence Anthony and Frances (Gardner) R.; m. Colby Fossett, Aug. 7, 1954; children: Laura Rodowsky Ramos, Alice Rodowsky-Seegers, Emily Rodowsky Savopoulos, Sarah Jones Rodowsky, Gregory, Katherine Rodowsky O'Connor. AB, Loyola Coll., Balt., 1952; LLB, U. Md., 1956. Bar: Md. 1956. Ct. crier, law clk. U.S. Dist. Ct. Md., 1954-56; asst. atty. gen. State of Md., 1960-61; assoc., ptnr. firm Frank, Bernstein, Conaway & Goldman, Balt., 1956-79; judge Ct. Appeals Md., Annapolis, 1980-2000, mem. rules com., 1969-80; sr. status judge Ct. of Spl. Appeals Md., Annapolis, 2001—. Lectr., asst. instr. U. Md. Law Sch., 1958-68, 87-91; reporter jud. dept. Md. Constl. Conv. Commn., 1966-67. Chmn. Gov. Md. Commn. Racing Reform, 1979. Fellow Am. Coll. Trial Lawyers; mem. Md. Bar Assn., Balt. Bar Assn. Roman Catholic. Home: 6614 Walnutwood Cir Baltimore MD 21212-1213 Office: 620 CM Mitchell Jr Courthse 100 N Calvert St Baltimore MD 21202 E-mail: Lawrence.Rodowsky@courts.state.md.us.

RODRIGUE, GEORGE P. newspaper editor; Exec. editor, v.p. news The Press Enterprise, Riverside, Calif., 1998—. Office: The Press Enterprise 3512 14th St Riverside CA 92501-3878

RODRIGUES, AZAEL MAGALHAES, JR., musician; s. Azael Magalhaes Rodrigues and Maria Olga Soares Cunha. Student, U. Sao Paulo, 1975—79. Drummer, composer Pau Brasil, Divina Increnca, Preme, Sao Paulo, 1978—82, Pau Brasil, Preme, Prisma, 1982—87; drummer, composer,. arranger, prodr. Band Z/Gremio Recreativo, 1988—94; mgr., musical prodr. Bourbon St. Music Club, 1995—96; prodr., musician Free lancer/Corda Toda, 1997—2000; mgr., musician Haveli Inc./Free Lancer, Miami. Lectr., tchr. U. Miami, 2002—03. Author: The Rhythm Within: a Brazilian passport to the groove, (music critic) Folha De Sao Paulo; musician (arranger): (c.d.) 23 (Engenho de Dentro, Princesa) (# 1 Hit Parade, 1993); prodr.(composer+arranger): (c.d.) Universal 18 _ Questing for Virtual Transportation. Achievements include One of the three best drummers of the year .Readers pool, Jornal da Tarde. Avocations: tennis, jogging, swimming, travel.

RODRIGUES, RAYMOND JOSEPH, academic administrator; b. Somerville, N.J., May 2, 1938; s. Joseph Batiste and Vera (Fedechena) R.; m. Dawn Droskinis; 1 child, Brad. AB, Rutgers U., 1960, MEd, 1965; PhD, U. N.Mex., 1974. Cert. secondary tchr. From asst. prof. to assoc. prof. English and Edn. U. Utah, Salt Lake City, 1974-78, head dept. secondary education, 1978-79; head dept. Curriculum and Instruction N.Mex. State U., Las Cruces, 1982-86; dir., tchr. edn. U. Colo., Colorado Springs, 1979-82; assoc. acad. v.p. Colo. State U., Ft. Collins, 1986-92; v.p. acad. affairs North Adams (Mass.) State Coll., 1992—. Author: Teaching Writing with a Word Processor, 1986, A Guide Book for Teaching Literature, 1978 Served to 1st lt. U.S. Army, 1960-62. Mem. Nat. Coun. Tchrs. English (exec. bd. conf. English edn. 1984-88, editorial bd. 1987-90). Office: N Adams State Coll Office Vp Academy # Affairs North Adams MA 01247

RODRIGUEZ, ALEXANDER EMMANUEL, professional baseball player; b. NYC, July 27, 1975; s. Victor Rodriguez and Lourdes Navarro; m. Cynthia Scurtis, Nov. 2, 2002. Grad. Westminster Christian Sch., Miami. Baseball player Seattle Mariners, 1995—2001, Tex. Rangers, 2001—03, NY Yankees, 2004—. Co-author: (children's book) Hit a Grand Slam, 1998. Founder Grand Slam for Kids, 1996, Alex Rodriguez Found., 1998. Named Am. League Batting Champion, 1996, Am. League MVP, 2003; named to MLB All-star game, 1996—98, 2000—04; recipient Gold Glove award, 2002, 2003. Achievements include being the third player in major league history with 40 home runs and 40 stolen bases in one season; leading the Am. League in home runs, 2001-03; leading the Am. League in runs scored, 2001, 2003; leading the Am. League in RBI's, 2002. Office: c/o NY Yankees E 161st st and River Ave Bronx NY 10452*

RODRIGUEZ, ANNABELLE, state attorney general; m. Francisco de Jesus-Schuck; 2 children. BA, JD, U. P.R. From asst. solicitor gen. to solicitor gen. P.R. Dept. Justice; ptnr. Martino, Odell & Calabria, Hato Rey, PR, 1993—96; judge U.S. Dist Ct (P.R. dist.), 1996; atty. gen. Commonwealth of P.R., 2001—. Democrat. Office: Atty Gen PO Box 9020192 San Juan PR 00902-0192*

RODRIGUEZ, ANTONIO JOSE, lawyer; b. New Orleans, Dec. 7, 1944; s. Anthony Joseph and Josephine Olga (Cox) R.; m. Virginia Anne Soignet, Aug. 23, 1969; children: Henry Jacob, Stephen Anthony. BS, U.S. Naval Acad., 1966; JD cum laude, Loyola U. of the South, New Orleans, 1973. Bar: La. 1973, U.S. Dist. Ct. (ea. dist.) La. 1973, U.S. Ct. Appeals (5th cir.) 1973, U.S. Dist. Ct. (mid. dist.) La. 1975, U.S. Dist. Ct. (we. dist.) La. 1977, U.S. Ct. Appeals (11th cir.) 1981, U.S. Supreme Ct. 1987, U.S. Dist. Ct. (so. dist.) Miss. 1991, U.S. Ct. Appeals (4th cir.) 1991, U.S. Ct. Appeals (1st cir.) 1997, U.S. Ct. Internat. Trade, 1991. Assoc. Phelps, Dunbar, Marks, Claverie & Sims, New Orleans, 1973-77; ptnr. Phelps Dunbar, New Orleans, 1977-92, Fowler Rodriguez Kingsmill Flint, Gray & Chalos, LLP, New Orleans, 1992—. Prof. law Tulane U., New Orleans, 1981—; mem. nat. rules of the road adv. coun. U.S. Dept. Transp., Washington, 1987-90, chmn. nat. navigation safety adv. coun., 1990-94, mem., 2000—; spkr. on admiralty and environ. Co-author: Admiralty-Limitation of Liability, 1981—, Admiralty-Law of Collision, 1990—; author: (chpt.) Benedict on Admiralty, 1995—; assoc. editor Loyola Law Rev., 1971-73; contbr. articles to profl. maritime and environ. jours. Bd. dirs. Greater New Orleans Coun. Navy League, 1988—, Propeller Club of New Orleans, 1997—. Lt. USN, 1966-70; capt. USNR, 1970-95. Decorated Navy Commendation medal; recipient Disting. Pub. Svc. award U.S. Dept. Transp., 1993. Fellow La. Bar Found.; mem. ABA, La. State Bar Assn., La. State Law Inst., Maritime Law Assn. U.S. (proctor 1975—), New Orleans Bar Assn., Southeastern Admiralty Law Inst., Assn. Average Adjusters U.S., Assn. Average Adjusters U.K., Naval Res. Assn. (chpt. pres. 1982-84), U.S. Naval Acad. Alumni Assn. (chpt. pres. 1981-83), Bienville Club, Phi Alpha Delta, Alpha Sigma Nu. Republican. Roman Catholic. Home: 4029 Mouton St Metairie LA 70002-1303 Office: Fowler Rodriguez Kingsmill Flint Gray & Chalos LLP Texaco Ctr 400 Poydras St 30th fl New Orleans LA 70130-1000 Office Phone: 504-523-2600. E-mail: ajr@frc-law.com.

RODRIGUEZ, ARTURO SALVADOR, labor union official; b. San Antonio, June 23, 1949; s. Arthur Salvador and Felice (Quintero) R.; m. Linda Fabela Chavez, Mar. 30, 1974; children: Olivia, Julie, Arthur. BA in Sociology, St. Mary's U., 1971; MSW, U. Mich., 1973. Various positions United Farm Workers of Am., Keene, Calif., 1973-90, v.p., 1981-93, organizer, 1990-92; pres. United Farm Workers Am. AFL-CIO, Keene, 1993—. Chief instr. UFW Sch., Keene, 1978-79; coord. Edward Kennedy Presdl. Dr., San Antonio, 1980. Office: United Farm Workers Am AFL CIO PO Box 62 La Paz 29700 Woodford Tehachapi Rd Keene CA 93531

RODRIGUEZ, CIRO DAVIS, congressman; b. Dec. 9, 1946; m. Carolina Pena; 1 child. BA, St. Mary's U., 1973; MSW, Our Lady of the Lake U., 1978. Mem. Harlandale Ind. Sch. Dist. Bd., 1975-87; faculty assoc., Worden Sch. Social Work Our Lady of the Lake U., 1987-96; mem. Tex. Ho. of Reps.,

1987-97, 105th-108th Congress from 28th Tex. dist., 1997—. Mem. Mil. Readiness subcom. House Nat. Security Com., Health subcom. House Vets. Affairs Com.; 2d vice chair and health care task force chair Congrl. Hispanic Caucus. Democrat. Roman Catholic. Office: 1507 Longworth HOB Washington DC 20515-4328 also: 1313 SE Military Dr Ste 115 San Antonio TX 78214-2850 Fax: (202) 225-1641.

RODRIGUEZ, DARLENE, newscaster; married. BA in Broadcast Journalism, U. Miami. Reporter Bronxnet Cable TV, Bronx, NY, 1993—94; gen. assignment reporter WCBS NewsRadio 88, N.Y.C., 1994—98; reporter NewsChannel 4, N.Y.C., 1998—, co-anchor Today in New York, 2003—. Recipient Silurian award, 1998, Latina Excellence award, Hispanic mag., 2000. Office: NBC 30 Rockefeller Plz New York NY 10112

RODRIGUEZ, DONNA JEANNE ANGLIN, dietician, writer; b. Albuquerque, July 21, 1953; d. Randolph Sterling and Audrey Miriam (Kubach) Anglin; m. Ralph A. Rodriguez, Feb. 19, 1977. BS, N.Mex. State U., 1975; MS, U. N.Mex., 1996. Cert. nutrition support dietitian; registered dietitian. Clin. dietitian U. N.Mex. Hosp., Albuquerque, 1977-91, nutrition support coord., 1991-95, rsch. coord., 1995-96, vis. prof./lectr., 1996-97; profl. healthcare writer Lovelace Healthcare Innovations, Albuquerque, 1997-98; clin. dietitian West Albuquerque Dialysis Ctr., 1999—. Assoc. editor: (jour.) Support Line, 1996—; contbr. articles to profl. jours., chpts. to books. Mem. Am. Soc. Parenteral and Enteral Nutrition, N.Mex. Soc. Parenteral and Enteral Nutrition, Am. Dietetic Assn., N.Mex. Dietetic Assn., Am. Burn Assn. (chmn. nutrition spl. interest group 1994-96). Avocations: camping, needlecrafts.

RODRIGUEZ, ENSOR, physician, scientist, writer; b. San Juan, P.R., Jan. 11, 1937; s. Ensor A. Rodriguez and Josefina Lopez; m. Aida Lucia Herrera, Sept. 3, 1957; children: Jose E., Mariela, Marisol, David E. MD, U. Salamanca, Spain, 1961; MPH, Harvard U., 1968; PhD, Johns Hopkins U., 1976. Diplomate Am. Bd. Preventive Medicine. Commd. med. officer USAF, 1964, advanced through grades to col., 1976; deputy dir. Aerospace Med. Rsch. Lab., Dayton, Ohio, 1978-80; intern USAF Hosp., Patrick AFB, Fla., 1961—62, resident, 1968—70, med. dir., 1980-82; staff surgeon USAF Sys. Command, Washington, 1982-84; corp. med. dir. Atlantic Richfield Co., L.A., 1984-92; intern Dist. Hosp., Arecibo, P.R.; residency Sch. Pub. Health Harvard U.; resident Sch. Aerospace Medicine USAF; cons. PACT, L.A., 1993—. Fellow Ctr. Performance Humana. Office: PACT 121 S Hope St Apt 2 Los Angeles CA 90012-5002 E-mail: rodensor@sbcglobal.net.

RODRIGUEZ, FERDINAND, chemical engineer, educator; b. Cleve., July 8, 1928; s. José and Concha (Luís) R.; m. Ethel V. Koster, July 28, 1951; children: Holly Edith, Lida Concha. BS, Case Western Res. U., 1950, MS, 1954; PhD, Cornell U., 1958. Devel. engr. Ferro Corp., Bedford, Ohio, 1950-54; asst. prof. chem. engring. Cornell U., 1958-61, asso. prof., 1961-71, prof., 1971—. On sabbatic leave at Union Carbide Corp., 1964-65, Imperial Chem. Industries, Ltd., 1971, Eastman Kodak Co., 1978-79; cons. to industry. Author: Principles of Polymer Systems, 5th edit., 2003; contbr. articles; songwriter:. Served with U.S. Army, 1954-56. Recipient Excellence in Teaching award Cornell Soc. Engrs., 1966, Edn. Achievement award Hispanic Engr. Mag., 1991. Fellow Am. Inst. Chem. Engrs.; mem. Am. Chem. Soc., Soc. Hispanic Profl. Engrs., Soc. Plastics Engrs. Lutheran. Office: Cornell U 267 Olin Hall Ithaca NY 14853 E-mail: FR13@cornell.edu.

RODRIGUEZ, FREDDY, actor; b. Chgo., Jan. 17, 1975; m. Elsie Rodriguez. Actor: (TV series) Oh Grow Up, 1999, Six Feet Under, 2001; (films) The Fence, 1994, A Walk in the Clouds, 1995, Dead Presidents, 1995, The Pest, 1997, Can't Hardly Wait, 1998, Shock Television, 1998, Joseph's Gift, 1998, Payback, 1999, Beyond City Limits, 2001, Pledge of Allegiance, 2002, Chasing Papi, 2003, Dallas 362, 2003. Office: c/o Innovative Artist Talent Agy 7th Fl 235 Park Ave South New York NY 10003*

RODRIGUEZ, GENO (EUGENE RODRIGUEZ), artist, arts administrator; b. N.Y.C., June 2, 1940; s. Eugenio and Juana (Lopez) R.; m. Janice Rooney, Oct., 1966; 1 dau., Samantha Marisol. Student, Internat. Peoples Coll., Elsinor, Denmark, 1961-62; nat. diploma in art, Hammersmith Coll. Art, London, 1966. Founder, pres., exec. dir. Alternative Center for Internat. Arts Alternative Museum, N.Y.C., 1975—; instr. photography Sch. Visual Arts, N.Y.C., 1978-82, Rutgers U., 1977-79; founder, dir. Alternative Mus., 1982. Mem. Artists Cert. Appeals Bd., N.Y.C., 1979, spl. artist task force N.Y. State Council on Arts, 1981; panelist, cons. NEA, Dept. Cultural Affairs N.Y.C.; curator Internet exhbns.; lectr. in field. Exhibited in one-man shows Il Diaframa Gallery, Milan, Italy, 1979, Mus. Contemporary Arts, Caracas, Venezuela, 1979, Real Art Ways Gallery, Hartford, Conn., 1980, Cayman Gallery, N.Y.C., 1980, CEPA Gallery, Buffalo, 1987, Sheldon Meml. Art Gallery U. Nebr., Lincoln, 1989; group shows include Autoren Gallery, Munich, 1980, Miss. Mus. Art, Jackson, 1981, Palacio de Minerias, Mexico City, 1981, J.A.M. Gallery, N.Y.C., 1981, Chrysler Mus., Norfolk, Va., 1981, Am. Indian Gallery, 1982, Roger Litz Gallery, N.Y., 1982, Tweed Gallery, N.J., 1983, Baumgartner Gallery, Washington, 1983, Municipality of Genoa, Italy, 1984, Phila. Arts Alliance, 1985, Jayne H. Baum Gallery, N.Y.C., 1985-86, Gerald Melberg Gallery, Charlotte, N.C., 1985, Eupherat Gallerty, Calif., 1986, N.Y. State Mus., Albany, 1986, Hillwood Art Gallery, N.Y., 1986, Stux Gallery, Boston, 1986, San Diego Mus. Art, 1987, Alternative Mus., N.Y.C., 1987, Graham Modern, N.Y.C., 1987, Internat. Ctr. Photography, N.Y.C., 1987, Haggerty Mus. Art Marquette U., Milw., 1988, Herter Art Gallery U. Mass., 1989, Nat. Mus. Am. Art Smithsonian Instn., 1989; represented in permanent collections Internat. Ctr. Photography, N.Y.C., Mus. City of N.Y., Met. Mus. Art, N.Y.C., Everson Mus. Art, Syracuse, N.Y., Am. Mus. Natural History, N.Y.C., Mus. Contemporary Art, Caracas, Venezula; author: The Islands: Worlds of the Puerto Ricans, 1974, Mira, Mira, Mira Puerto Rican New Yorkers, 1975. Active Clinton/Gore Presdl. Transition Team for Arts and Humanites, 1992. Served with USN, 1959-63. Recipient Phelps-Stokes Fund award, 1977; Ludwig Vogelstien Found. award, 1981; Nat. Endowment for Arts fellow, 1979 Mem. Am. Assn. Mus. (exec. mem. curators com. 1985). Office: Apt 9A 32 W 82nd St New York NY 10024-5622

RODRIGUEZ, ILEANA P. academic administrator, director; d. Justo P. and Arminda Rodriguez; m. Raul F. Marrero, Aug. 5, 1995; 1 child, Sofia I. Marrero. PhD in social and personality psychology, Mich. State U., 1990—99. Grad. asst. Mich. State U., East Lansing, Mich., 1990—94; vis. faculty mem. U. of PR, Mayaguez, PR, 1994—95; dept. chair faculty mem. Triton Coll., River Grove, Ill., 2000—, chairperson, behavioral sci. dept., 2003—. Pres. Latino Network at Triton Coll., River Grove, Ill., 2001—; chair Academic Support Com., Academic Senate, Triton Coll., River Grove, Ill., 2001—03; mem. Ill. Articulation Initiative, Psychology Panel, Springfield, Ill., 2001—. Contbr. articles. Recipient Leadership through Svc. Recognition, by the Pres. of Triton Coll., 2002, Phi Kappa Phi Nat. Honor Soc., Phi Kappa Phi Nat. Honor Soc., 1989. Master: Am. Evaluation Assn.; mem.: Am. Assn. Higher Edn., Midwestern Psychol. Assn. (assoc.), Am. Psychol. Soc. (assoc.). Office: Triton Coll 2000 Fifth Ave River Grove IL 60171 E-mail: irodri10@triton.edu.

RODRIGUEZ, IVAN TORRES, professional baseball player; b. Vega Baja, P.R., Nov. 30, 1971; Catcher Tex. Rangers, 1991—2002, Florida Marlins, 2003, Detroit Tigers, 2004—. Mem. Am. League All-Star Team, 1992-2001, 2004, Am. League Silver Slugger Team The Sporting News, 1994-99, American League MVP, 1999, NLCS MVP, 2003, mem. of World Series Championship Team, 2003. Recipient Gold Glove award, 1992-2001. Office: c/o Detroit Tigers 2100 Woodward Ave Detroit MI 48201*

RODRIGUEZ, JAI, television personality; b. Brentwood, N.Y., June 22, 1977; Actor: (films) The New Guy, 2002; (Broadway plays) Rent, Spinning into Butter, (off broadway plays) Zanna, Don't!, 2003; co-author: (books) Queer Eye for the Straight Guy: The Fab 5's Guide to Looking Better, Cooking Better, Dressing Better, Behaving Better, and Living Better, 2004; culture specialist (TV series) Queer Eye for the Straight Guy, 2003—. Office: Endeavor Talent Agy 9701 Wilshire Blvd Fl 10 Beverly Hills CA 90212*

RODRIGUEZ, JUAN ALFONSO, technology corporation executive; b. Santiago, Cuba, Feb. 10, 1941; came to U.S., 1953; s. Alfonso and Marie Madeleine (Hourcadette) R. BEE, CCNY, 1962; MEE, NYU, 1963. Engr. IBM, Poughkeepsie, N.Y. and Boulder, Colo., 1963-68, engring. mgr., 1968-69; dir. tech. Storage Tech. Corp., Louisville, Colo., 1969-74, v.p. engring., 1974-77, v.p., gen. mgr. disk, 1977-79, v.p., gen. mgr. optical disk Longmont, Colo., 1979-85; pres., CEO Exabyte Corp., Boulder, 1985-87, CEO, 1987-90, chmn., 1987-92; pres. Sweetwater Corp., 1992-93, chmn., 1992-95, also bd. dirs.; prof. elec. and computer engring. and engring. mgmt. U. Colo., 1992—, co-exec. dir. Ctr. for Entrepreneurship, 1994-2000; chmn. Datasonix, 1992-96, Vixel, 1995-99; chmn., CEO Ecrix Corp., 1996—2001; chief technologist, bd. dirs. Exabyte Corp., 2001—03, interim CEO, pres., 2003, chmn., 2003—. Mem. devel. coun. Coll. Engring. U. Colo., 1990-92; Decisionism Corp.; mem. engring. adv. bd. CCNY, bd. dirs. Colo. Advanced Tech. Enterprise, 1994-98; Robert J. Appel Disting. lectr. law and tech. Law Sch. U. Denver, 1990. Patentee in field. Bd. dirs. Boulder YMCA, 1982-87, U. Colo. Artist Series, 1988-92; mem. bd. govs. Boulder County United Way, 1989-93, chairperson campaign, 1992; commr. Colo. Advance Tech. Inst., 1988-92. Recipient Ind. Quality award Rocky Mountain sect. Am. Soc. Quality Control, 1990, Gen. Palmer award for Outstanding Engr. in Industry The Am. Cons. Engrs. Coun. of Colo., 1995; named Boulder Spirit Entrepreneur of Yr., 1989, Entrepreneur of the Decade Boulder C. of C., 1994, Hispanic Engr. of Yr., Entrepreneur Hispanic Engr. Nat. Achievement Awards Coun., 1995, Career Achievement Award Engring. Sch. Alumni CCNY, 2002, Townsend Harris medal Alumni Assn. CCNY, 2003; finalist Entrepreneur of Yr., Arthur Young & Inc Mag., 1989. Fellow IEEE; mem. Computer Soc. of IEEE (mem. steering com. on mass storage 1981-93), Soc. Photo-Optical Instrumentation Engrs., Boulder C. of C. (chmn. entrepreneurs support program 1989), Greater Denver C. of C. (bd. dirs. 1990-91); mem. Beta Gamma Sigma (medallion of Entrepreneurship 2003). Office: Exabyte Corp 2108 55th St Boulder CO 80301

RODRIGUEZ, JULIO, information technology executive; b. N.Y.C., Feb. 6, 1935; s. Julio Rodriguez and Dora Torres; m. Olga Zatsepina, Jan. 8, 1996; children: Richard, Ronald, Anne Marie, Matthew. BS in Edn., SUNY, Cortland, 1957; MA in English, Queens Coll., 1963; cert. in adminstrn., Hofstra U., 1966; MA in Psychology, NYU, 1971. English and comm. arts tchr. Brentwood and East Islip Schs., Suffolk County, N.Y., 1957-65; instr. edn. and psychology Adelphi Suffolk Coll., Oakdale, N.Y., 1965-67; rsch. asst. N.Y. City U. Ctr. for Urban Edn., N.Y.C., 1965-67; dep. dean tchr. edn. Adelphi Suffolk Coll., Oakdale, 1967-69; spl. cons. to pres. N.Y.C. Bd. Edn., N.Y.C., 1969-71; exec. v.p. Monserrat Assoc., N.Y.C., 1971-73; sr. mgr. quality control RCA Corp., Cherry Hill, N.J., 1973-76; exec. dir. Iprus Inst., N.Y.C., 1982-88; pres. Culturelink Corp., N.Y.C., 1988-98; v.p. tng. Global Privacy Solutions, Washington, 1998—. Dir. Mercy Coll. Culture Link Ctr., Dobbs Ferry, N.Y., 1993-95.; U.S. rep. non-govt. orgn. UN Consulate, N.Y.C., 1977-80; spkr., panelist in field; adj. prof. Lehman Coll. CUNY, 1997—. Editor, pub. art/history book: Portraits of the Puerto Rican Experience, 1984; tech. cons. film: The Sun and the Moon, 1988; editor jour. Hispanics and HIV, 1986. Pres. Citizens for Lyndon Johnson, Suffolk County, 1964; mem. com. N.Y.C. Mayoral Transition, 1986. Recipient Civic award Inst. Puerto Rican Culture, 1985. Mem. APA, Am. Anthropol. Assn. Avocations: singing, fishing, travel. Home: 34 Hillside Ave Apt 4C New York NY 10040-4805 E-mail: culturelink@worhdnet.att.net.

RODRIGUEZ, LOUIS JOSEPH, academic administrator, economist, educator; b. Newark, Mar. 13, 1933; m. Ramona Dougherty, May 31, 1969; children: Susan, Michael, Scott. BA, Rutgers U., 1955; MA, La. State U., 1957, PhD, 1963. Dean, Coll. Bus. Adminstrn., Alcee Fortier Disting. prof. Nichols State U., Thibodaux, La., 1958-71; dean Coll. Bus. U. Tex.-San Antonio, 1971-72, v.p. acad. affairs, dean faculty, 1972-73; dean Sch. Profl. Studies U. Houston-Clear Lake City, 1973-75, vice-chancellor, provost, 1975-80; pres. Midwestern State U., Wichita Falls, Tex., 1981—2000; ret., 2000; Hardin Found. prof. Midwestern State U., Wichita Falls, Tex., 1994—. Vice chmn. Coun. Tex. Pub. Univ. Pres. and Chancellors, 1992-93; mem. formula and health professions edn. adv. coms. Tex. Higher Edn. Coordinating Bd. Author 4 books; contbr. over 50 articles to profl. jours. Chmn. bd. Tex. Council on Econ. Edn., Houston, 1981-83; bd. dirs. Joint Council on Econ. Edn., N.Y.C., 1981-83, Goodwill Industries Am., Washington, 1976-82, Robert Priddy Found., 1993-96, Wichita Falls Met. Y.M.C.A., 1999-2000, 4A Economic Devel. Bd., 2000-2003, Wichita Falls Area Cmty. Found., 1999-2001; pres. Wichita Falls Bd. Commerce and Industry, 1988-89, Clear Lake City Devel. Found., Houston, 1976-77, Goals for Wichita Falls, Inc., 1983; mem. internat. adv. com. Tex. Higher Edn. Coordinating Bd.; pres. United Way Greater Wichita Falls, 1998-99. Recipient Tchr. Edn. Supportive Pres. award Am. Assn. Colls. Tchr. Edn., 1991, Disting. Citizen award N.W. coun. Boy Scouts Am., 1998; named Wichitan of the Yr., 1987; Ford Found. grantee, 1964; Fulbright fellow, 1976 Mem. Am. Assn. State Colls. and Univs. (bd. dirs.), So. Assn. Colls. and Schs. (Commn. on Colls.), Assn. Tex. Colls. and Univs. (pres. 1988-89), Rotary (pres. Downtown Wichita Falls club 1990-91). Mem. Ch. of Christ. Home: 2403 N Elmwood Cir Wichita Falls TX 76308-3813

RODRIGUEZ, NANCY, state legislator; b. San Luis, Colo., Mar. 18, 1953; BBA, MBA. Mem. N.Mex. Senate, Dist. 24, Santa Fe, 1996—; mem. edn. com.; mem. fin. com. Democrat. Office: 1838 Camino La Canada Santa Fe NM 87501

RODRIGUEZ, NESTOR JOAQUIN, insurance broker; b. Tulua-Valle, Colombia, Jan. 23, 1959; came to U.S., 1982; s. Pedro Pablo and Edna Lucia R.; m. Ligia Carolina Urroz, Apr. 16, 1988; children: Veronica Alexandra, Mauricio Javier. Degree in Computer Engring., U. INCCA of Colombia, Bogota, 1981; B of Profl. Studies, Barry U., 1989. CLU, ChFC, CFP. V.p. Uniflor, Ltda., Bogota, Colombia, 1979-81; pres. Universal Growers, Inc., Miami, Fla., 1982-84; gen. mgr. The Life Ins. Co. of VA, Miami, Fla., 1985-92, Interamerican Ins. Brokers, Miami, Fla., 1992-96; pres. VMR Ins. Group, Weston, Fla., 1996—. Ins. cons. Best-Dorsey Ins., Inc., Coral Gables, Fla., 1996—; spkr. in field; exec. dir. rsch. book Economic Impact Colombia Community, 1992. Author: (insurance guide) Manual del Inversionista, 1990. Founder The Kiwanis Club of Colombia, 1989; dir. Colombian-Am. C. of C., Miami, 1990-92. Recipient Nat. Quality/Sales/Health awards, Fort Lauderdale, 1987-91, Pres.'s awards The Life Ins. Co. of Va., 1990-92; named to Million Dollar Round Table, 1987. Mem. CLU Soc., ChFC Soc., Nat. Assn. Life Underwriters. Republican. Roman Catholic. Avocations: youth coach soccer, golf, little league coach, biking. Office: VMR Ins Group 2222 Ponce De Leon Blvd Ste 400 Coral Gables FL 33134-5039 Home: 1892 Hidden Trail Ln Weston FL 33327-1456

RODRIGUEZ, RAQUEL, lawyer; b. Miami Beach, Fla., 1961; JD, U. Miami, 1985. Assoc. Greenberg Traurig, P.A., Miami, Fla., 1985—97, shareholder, 1993—97, dir. global affiliations, coord internat. practice group, 1999—2002, with lit. dept. Washington, 2002; exec. dir. Multilaw Multinational Assn. Ind. Law Firms, London, 1997—99; gen. counsel to gov. Office Gov. State of Fla., Tallahassee, 2002—. Adj. prof. U. Miami. Office: Office Gov The Capital Tallahassee FL 32399

RODRIGUEZ, RICK, newspaper executive editor; b. Salinas, Calif., Apr. 5, 1954; Grad., Stanford U., 1976, Guadalajara, Mex. Newspaper intern Salinas Californian; reporter Fresno (Calif.) Bee, Sacramento (Calif.) Bee, asst. mng. editor, mng. editor, 1993—98, exec. editor & sr. v.p., 1998—. Mem. Pulitzer Prize juries 1994, 95. Mem. Am. Soc. Newspaper Editors (bd. dir. 1999-2002, sec. 2002—), Calif. Chicano News Media Assn. (co-founder Sacramento chpt., past bd. dirs.). Office: Sacramento Bee PO Box 15779 Sacramento CA 95852

RODRIGUEZ, RITA MARIA, economist; b. La Havana, Cuba, Sept. 6, 1944; came to U.S., 1960; Tomas and Adela (Mederos) R.; m. E. Eugene Carter, Jan. 7, 1972; 1 child, Adela-Marie R. Carter. BBA, U. PR, 1964; MBA, NYU, 1968, PhD, 1969. Bus. adminstrn. asst. prof., then assoc. prof. Harvard Bus. Sch., Cambridge, Mass., 1969-74, 74-78; fin. prof. U. Ill., Chgo., 1978-82; dir. Export-Import Bank of U.S., Washington, 1982-99. Cons. Polaroid Corp. and Indsl. Devel. Bank in Ecuador (Corporacion Financiera Nacional), 1978-82, U.S. IRS, 1982; bd. dirs. Acad. Fdnl. Devel., Washington, 1989-93; bd. advisors Pew Econ. Freedom Fellows, Washington, 1991-94, World Bank, MIGA, Washington, 2000; bd. dirs. Affiliated Mgrs. Group, Boston, 2000-, Pvt. Export Funding Corp., N.Y., 2001—; sr. fellow Woodstock Theol. Ctr., Georgetown U., Washington, 2002—, ENSCO, Dallas, 2003—. Author: (with E. Eugene Carter) International Financial Management, 1976, 2d edit., 1979, 3rd edit., 1984, (with Heinz Riehl) Foreign Exchange Markets: A Guide to Foreign Currency Operations, 1977, Foreign Exchange Management in U.S. Multinationals, 1980 (with Heinz Riehl) Foreign Exchange and Money Markets, 1983, Japanese, Spanish, Portuguese translations, The Export-Import Bank at Fifty, 1987; co-editor (with G.C. Hufbauer) Ex-Im Bank: Overview, Challenges, and Policy Options in the Ex-Im Bank in the 21st Century, 2001; editor (with Gary Hufbauer) The Ex-Im Bank in the 21st Century; contbr. numerous fin. articles to profl. publs. Bd. dirs. Am. Friends of Turkey, 2001. Recipient Outstanding Achievement award Nat. Coun. of Hispanic Women, 1986; Outstanding Hispanic Achievement award Hispanic Corp. Achievers, 1988; Nat. Leadership award Government The Nat. Network of Hispanic Women, 1989. Mem.: Coun. Fgn. Rels. Roman Catholic. Avocations: gardening, music. Office: 3075 Ordway St NW Washington DC 20008-3255

RODRIGUEZ, ROBERTO ASHLEY, language educator; b. Los Angeles, Calif., June 25, 1956; m. Maria Antonieta Espinoza, Jan. 13, 1959; children: Grace Rios, Marcus John Rios. AA in psychology, Palo Alto Coll., 1991; BA in Spanish, U. Tex., 1996, MA in Hispanic culture, 1999. Course adminstr., developer AT&T, San Antonio, 1992—98; spanish lectr. UTSA, San Antonio, 1998—; spanish instr. St. Philip's Coll., San Antonio, 1999—2002, NW Vista Coll., San Antonio, 2001—. Spanish cons., translator Ind., San Antonio, 1999—; specialist U. Tex., WebCt Specialist, San Antonio, 2001—; student orgn. adv. Theta Chi Omega (The Girls of Theta), San Antonio, 2002—. Fellow: Sigma Delta Phi (life); mem.: Assn. of Tex. Colleges & Universities (assoc.). Achievements include development of web pages for pedagagical use (multimedia). Home: 603 Northtrail Dr San Antonio TX 78216-3714 Office: U Tex San Antonio 6900 N Loop 1604 W San Antonio TX 78249-0644 Office Phone: 210-458-5219. Personal E-mail: ashley40@sbcglobal.net. E-mail: rarodriguez@utsa.edu.

RODRIGUEZ, ROCIO, artist; b. Caibarién, Las Villas, Cuba, 1952; BFA, MFA, U. Ga. One-woman shows include Carl Solway Gallery, Cin., 1982, 1985, Young Harris Coll., Ga., 1986, The Arts Exch., Atlanta, 1989, McIntosh Gallery, 1989, Sandler Hudson Gallery, 1991, 1993, 1995, Studio Exhbn., 1992, Brenau Coll., Gainesville,Ga., 1995, Nexus Contemporary Art Ctr., Atlanta, 1996, Fay Gold Gallery, 1998, Hemphill Fine Arts, Washington, 1999, exhibited in group shows at Birmingham (Ala.) Art Mus., 1989, High Mus. Art, Atlanta, 1990, Nexus Contemporary Arts Ctr., 1991, Galerie Simonne Stern, New Orleans, 1992, Montgomery (Ala.) Mus. Fine Arts, 1994, Michael Solway Gallery, Cin., 1996, Spelman Mus., Atlanta, 1997, New Orleans Mus., 1998, numerous others, Represented in permanent collections; contbr. articles to profl. jours. Recipient So. Regioanl Vis. Artists award, Am. Acad. Rome, 1997; fellow, Ford Found., 1978, Oscar B. Cintas fellow, 1980, Mayor's fellowship in arts, 1990, regional fellow, So. Arts Fedn./NEA, 1990. Office: Fay Gold Gallery 764 Miami Cir Ne Ste 210 Atlanta GA 30324-3026

RODRIGUEZ, SERGIO RAUL, music educator, conductor; b. San Pedro Sula, Cortes, Honduras, Aug. 29, 1961; s. Maria Alicia Mejia and Juan Pablo Rodriguez; m. Silvia Maria Montoya, Dec. 19, 1995; children: Yasmin Elizabeth, Arianna Rocio. MusB, Victoriano Lopez Music Sch., San Pedro Sula, Honduras, 1980, U. Ky., 1993; MusM, Southeastern La. U., 1999. Cert. tchr. Ga. Profl. Standards Com., 1998. Carl Orff music tchr. Exptl. Sch. for Children, Tegucigalpa, Honduras, 1981—95; condr. violin and viola tchr. Nat. Sch. of Music, Tegucigalpa, Honduras, 1994—95, Conservatory of Music Fco. Zelaya, Tegucigalpa, Honduras, 1994—95; music theory, violin and viola tchr. Honduras Nat. U., Tegucigalpa, Honduras, 1994—95; violin and viola tchr. String Acad. of Southeastern La. U., Hammond, 1995—96; orch. dir., violin and viola tchr. Acadiana Conservatory of Music, Lafayette, La., 1996—97; orch. tchr. Dougherty County Sch. Sys., Albany, Ga., 1997—; orch. condr. Dougherty County Youth Symphony Orch., Albany, Ga., 1997—. Violinist Vermont Symphony Orch., Ga., 1986—89, Dartmouth Symphony Orch., Hanover, NH, 1987—89, Harvard-Radcliffe Symphony Orch., Cambridge, Mass., 1988—88, Lexington Philharm., Ky., 1989—93, Baton Rouge Symphony Orch., 1995—97, Albany Symphony Orch., Ga., 1997—, Macon Symphony Orch., Ga., 1998—, Valdosta Symphony Orch., Ga., 1998—. Musician (composer): (string orchestra) A Silvia. Recipient 2d pl. award, Music in the Parks, 2003; scholarship, Longy Sch. of Music, 1987, 1987-1989, Academic Excellence scholarship, U. Ky., 1989, Fellowship Condr., S.C.'s Conducting Inst., 1998. Mem.: Nat. Assn. Music Edn., Music Educators Nat. Conf., Nat. Assn. Music Educators. Achievements include first to Founder and Conductor of The Dougherty County Youth Symphony Orchestra; Founder of the National Youth Orchestra, Honduras. Home: 1026 Forest Glen Dr Albany GA 31707 Office: Dougherty County Youth Symphony Orchestra 1615 Newton Rd Albany GA 31701 Office Phone: 229-431-3352., 229-431-1261. Personal E-mail: sergio.rodriguez@mchsi.com.

RODRIGUEZ, SONIA, dancer; b. Toronto, Ont., Can. Student, Princess Grace Acad., Monaco, 1984—88, Royal Conservatory of Music & Dance, Madrid, 1980—86. Mem. Nat. Ballet Can., Toronto, Canada, 1990—2000, prin. dancer, 2000—. Dancer (ballets) Giselle, The Sleeping Beauty, Coppélia, The Nutcracker, The Merry Widow, Onegin, The Taming of the Shrew, Jewels, Lead pas de deux Désir, Apollo, dancer Cruel World, Terra Firma, The Four Seasons, Madame Butterfly, Romeo & Juliet, La gille mal gardeé, Swan Lake; (films) The Planets, The Four Seasons, (TV films) Gotta Skate 1, Gotta Skate 2. Office: Walter Carsen Ctr Nat Ballet Can 470 Queens Quay West Toronto ON Canada M5V 3K4

RODRIGUEZ, VINCENT ANGEL, lawyer, director; b. Cayey, P.R., 1921; s. Vicente and Maria (Antongiorgi) R. BS, Harvard U., 1941; LLB, Yale U., 1944. Bar: N.Y. 1947. Assoc. Sullivan & Cromwell, N.Y.C., 1944-56, ptnr., 1956—. Mem. Council Fgn. Relations, ABA, Assn. Bar City N.Y., Am. Soc. Internat. Law Clubs: River (N.Y.C.). Home: 4521 Fisher Island Dr Miami FL 33109-0156 Office: Sullivan & Cromwell 125 Broad St Fl 28 New York NY 10004-2489

RODRIGUEZ, WILLIAM JULIO, physician; b. Ponce, P.R., June 18, 1941; BS, MD, Georgetown U., Washington, 1967; PhD, Georgetown U., 1975. Intern Univ. Hosp., San Juan, PR, 1967—68, intern and resident, 1967-72, resident in pediat., 1970—72; fellow Children's Hosp., Washington, 1972-75; attending in infectious disease Children's Hosp. Nat. Med. Ctr., Washington, 1975—; pediat. sci. dir. Office of Counterterrorism and Pediatric Drug Devel. Ctr. for Drug Evaluation and Rsch./FDA, 2000—; med. officer USN, 1968—70. Assoc. chief infectious disease and microbiology rsch. Children's Hosp. Med. Ctr., 1979—80, chmn. infectious disease dept., microbiology rsch., 1983—2000; cons. staff Hosp. for Sick Children, Washington, 1985—2000, Shady Grove Adventist Hosp., Rockville, Md., 1988—2001, Holy Cross Hosp., Silver Spring, Md., 1988—2001, Columbia Hosp. for Women, 1990—2000; prof. emeritus pediat. George Washington Med. Sch., 2000—. Contbr. articles to profl. jours. MARC fellow, XIII, 1973-76. Fellow Infectious Disease Soc.; mem. AAAS, APS, Am. Acad. Pediat., Soc. for Pediat. Rsch., Am. Fedn. Clin. Rsch., Am. Soc. Microbiology, Assn. Puerto Ricans in Sci. and Engring. Office: FDA 7520 Standish Pl HFD 950 Ste 220 Rockville MD 20855 Business E-mail: rodriguezw@cder.fda.gov.

RODRIGUEZ, XAVIER, lawyer; BA, Harvard U., 1983; MPA, JD, U. Tex., 1987. Cert.: Tex. Bd. Legal Specialization (labor and employment law). Ptnr. Fulbright & Jaworski; justice Supreme Ct. State of Tex., 2001—02; atty. pvt. practice, San Antonio, 2002—. Served Judge Advs. Gen's. Corps.; lectr. continuing legal edn. courses. Contbr. chapters to books. Past pres. Respite Care San Antonio; San Antonio C. of C.; vice chmn. State Bd. Educator Certification; mem. bd. dirs. San Antonio Area Found.; mem. adv. bd. to dean St. Mary's U. Sch. Law, U. Tex. at San Antonio Coll. Social and Behavioral Scis. Officer USAR, 1983. Named 40 under 40 Rising Stars, San Antonio Bus.

Jour. Fellow: Tex. Bar Found.; mem.: ABA, State Bar of Tex. (immediate past chmn. labor and employment law sect., standing com. on legal assts.). Office: 300 Convent Ste 2200 San Antonio TX 78205

RODRIGUEZ-CAMILLONI, HUMBERTO LEONARDO, architect, historian, educator; b. Lima, Peru, May 30, 1945; came to U.S., 1963; s. Alfonso and Elda (Camilloni) R.; m. Mary Ann Alexanderson, July 1, 1972; children: Elizabeth Marie, William Howard. BA magna cum laude, Yale U., 1967, MArch, 1971, MPhil, 1973, PhD, 1981. Rsch. asst. Sch. Architecture Yale U., 1964-70, teaching fellow dept. history art, 1971-72, 74-75; chmn. research dept. Centro de Investigacion y Restauracion de Bienes Monumentales Instituto Nacional de Cultura, Lima, 1973; restoration architect OAS, Washington, 1976—; prof. Sch. Architecture Tulane U., New Orleans, 1975-82; prof., dir. Henry H. Wiss Ctr. Theory and History of Art and Architecture, Coll. Architecture and Urban Studies Va. Poly. Inst. and State U., Blacksburg, 1983—, dir. Ctr. for Preservation and Rehab. Tech., Coll. Architecture, 1986—. Vis. prof. U. Ill., Chgo., 1982-83; reviewer, cons. Choice, 1975—; mem. interim bd. dirs. Ctr. Planning Handbook Latin-Am. Art, 1978-87; cons., adviser Internat. Exhbn. and Symposium Latin-Am. Baroque Art and Architecture, 1980; mem. adv. bd. Mountain Lake Symposium on Art and Architecture Criticism, 1985—, Internat. Symposium Luis Barragan, 1990; coord., advisor exhbn. Tradition and Innovation: Painting, Architecture and Music in Brazil, Mex. and Venezuela between 1950-80, 1991, Internat. Art History Colloquium, 1993, 48th Internat. Congress of Americanists, 1994, Congress Internat. Union Architects, 1996, 49th Internat. Congress Americanists, 1997, 2nd European Assn. for Archtl. Edn./Archtl. Rsch. Ctrs. Consortium Conf., 2000; coord., adv. exhbn. Frank Lloyd Wright: An Architect in America, 1995, The Jesuits, Conf. II: Cultures, Scis. and the Arts, 1540-1773, 2002, 1st Internat. Congress on Constrn. History, 2003. Author: (with Walter D. Harris) The Growth of Latin American Cities, 1971; (with Charles Seymour, Jr.) Italian Primitives, The Case History of a Collection and its Conservation, 1972, Religious Architecture in Lima of the Seventeenth and Eighteenth Centuries: The Monastic Complex of San Francisco el Grande, 1984; contbg. editor Handbook of Latin American Studies, 1987—, The Retablo Facade as Transparency: A Study of the Frontispiece of San Francisco, Lima, 1991, Tradición e Innovación en la Arquitectura del Virreinato del Perú, Constantino de Vasconcelos y la Invención de la Arquitectura de Quincha en Lima Durante el Siglo XVII, 1994, (with Graziano Gasparini) Arquitectura Iberoamericana, 1997, Manuel de Amat y Junyent y la Navona de Lima: un ejemplo de diseño urbano barroco del siglo XVIII en el virreinato del Perú, 1999, (with Mehdi Setareh) Monticello's Dome: Development of an Integrated Resource for the Study of Thomas Jefferson's Architecture, 2000, Quincha Architecture: The Development of an Antiseismic Structural System in Seventeenth Century Lima, 2003; contbg. editor: The Dictionary of Art, 1991-96, Encyclopedia of Twentieth Century Architecture, 1999. Named Ellen Battell Eldridge fellow, 1970-72, Robert C. Bates Jr. fellow Jonathan Edwards Coll., Yale U., 1970-71, Social Sci. Rsch. Coun. fellow, 1972-74, Yale Concilium Internat. Studies fellow, 1972-73, Giles Whiting fellow, 1974-75, NEH fellow Columbia U., 1983, Hobart and William Smith Colls. fellow, 1987, U. Ill. fellow, 1990, Edilia De Montequin fellow, 1991, NEH fellow U. N.Mex., 1992. Mem.: KC, Preservation Resource Ctr. (past bd. dirs.), Inter-Am. Inst. Advanced Studies in Cultural History (bd. dirs. 1998—), Blacksburg Regional Art Assn., Assn. for Preservation Tech., Save Our Cemeteries (past bd.dirs.), Nat. Trust Hist. Preservation, New River Valley Preservation League (bd. dirs. 1987—), Assn. Preservation Va. Antiquities, Coll. Art Assn. Am., S.E. section Soc. Archtl. Historians, Soc. Archtl. Historians (bd. dirs. 1977—80, past pres., past sec. South Gulf chpt.), Internat.Archive of Women in Architecture (treas. 1999—2002), Assn. Latin Am. Art, Latin Am. Studies Assn., S.E. Coll. Art Conf., Phi Beta Delta, Tau Sigma Delta. Roman Catholic. Office: Va Poly Inst and State U Coll Architecture & Urban Studies Blacksburg VA 24061-0205 E-mail: hcami@vt.edu. *As an educator across the years, I have come to realize that the true art of teaching consists of reaching both the human mind and the human heart.*

RODRIGUEZ-DIAZ, JUAN E. lawyer; b. Ponce, P.R., Dec. 27, 1941; s. Juan and Auristela (Diaz-Alvarado) Rodriguez de Jesus; m. Sonia de Hostos-Anca, Aug. 10, 1966; children: Juan Eugenio, Jorge Eduardo, Ingrid Marie Rodriguez. BA, Yale U., 1963; LLB, Harvard U., 1966; LLM in Taxation, NYU, 1969. Bar: N.Y. 1968, P.R. 1970. Assoc. Baker & McKenzie, N.Y.C., 1966-68, McConnell, Valdes, San Juan, P.R.; undersec. Dept. Treasury P.R., 1971-73; mem. Sweeting, Pons, Gonzalez & Rodriguez, 1973-81; pvt. practice San Juan, 1981-94, Totti & Rodriguez-Diaz, 1994—. Bd. dirs. Ochoa Indsl. Sales Corp., Ensco Caribe, Inc., Industrias Vassallo, Inc., Triangle Cargo Services, Inc. Bd. govs. Aqueduct and Sewer Authority P.R., 1979-84; mem. adv. com. collective bargaining negotiation of P.R. elec. Power Authority to Gov. P.R., 1977-78; bd. govs. P.R. coun. Boy Scouts Am., mem. transition com., 1984-85; mem. adminstrv. coun. Ballajá, 1993-2000. Mem. N.Y. State Bar Assn., P.R. Bar Assn., AFDA Club, Berwind Country Club, Palmas de Mar Country Club. Office: Suite 1200 416 Ave Ponce De Leon Hato Rey San Juan PR 00918-3418 Office Phone: 787-753-7910. E-mail: JERD@TRDLAW.com.

RODRIGUEZ-FIGUEROA, R. VILMARIE, pharmaceutical executive; b. Aibonito, P.R., Nov. 27, 1961; d. Hector Jose Rodriguez and Aurea Esther Figueroa; m. Efrain Flores-Colon, Aug. 12, 1983; children: Veronica A., André S. BS in Life Scis. magna cum laude, U. P.R., Cayey, 1983; MS in Chemistry magna cum laude, San Diego State U., 1990. Rsch. assoc., grad. teaching asst. San Diego State U., 1984-89; safety and health specialist Rohr, Inc., Chula Vista, Calif., 1989-92; environ. health & safety specialist Beckman Instruments, Carlsbad, Calif., 1992-94; sr. indsl. hygienist San Diego Gas & Elec., 1994-96; assoc. dir. environ. health and safety Ligarn Pharms., San Diego, 1996—. Instr. Southwestern Coll., Chula Vista, 1989—; mem. hearing bd. Air Pollution Control Dist., San Diego, 2000—; cons. Internat. Health & Safety, Chula Vista, 1996—. Cubmaster Boys Scouts Am., Chula Vista, 1999—; tchr. Bonita (Calif.) Valley Christian Ctr., 1992-98; dist. mem., rep. New Progressive Party, Cayey, 1981-83. Mem. Am. Indsl. Hygiene Assn. (spl. interest 1999—), Am. Indsl. Hygiene Assn. (pres. San Diego local sect. 1995-96), Biosafety Network San Diego (dir. 1999—), Indsl. environ. Assn., Binat. Air Quality Alliance. Avocations: mountain biking, baking, choral singing. Office: Ligand Pharms 10275 Sci Ctr Dr San Diego CA 91910-1117

RODRIGUEZ-RODRIGUEZ, PEDRO PABLO, retired veterinarian; b. Yauco, PR, Jan. 15, 1929; s. Domingo and Crescencia Rodriguez; m. Pilar de los Angeles Sampablo-Rodriguez, Jan. 27, 1932; children: Pedro Pablo Rodriguez, David Domingo Rodriguez; 1 child, Maria Jose Gonzalez. BA, U. PR, Mayaguez, 1953—57; BS, U. PR; DVM, U. Pensylvannia, Phila., 1958—62. Cert. Veterinarian Sch. Vet. Medicine, Madrid, 1981. Vet. officer USDA, 1962—88; vet. corps US Army, PR, 1947—90; retired. Pres. Va. NonProfit Honey Bee Rsch. Corp., Virginia Beach, 1997. Cpl. U.S. Army, 1949—53, US and Germany. Recipient Good Conduct Medal, 1951. Mem.: DAV (life; newsletter editor 1991—92). Achievements include research in Use of food grade mineral oil to treat honey bee parasites. Home and Office: Va NonProfit Honey Bee Rsch Corp 2133 Wolfsnare Rd Virginia Beach VA 23454 Personal E-mail: dronebeer@netscape.net.

RODRIGUEZ-SAINS, RENE S. physician, surgeon, educator; b. Santiago, Cuba, July 25, 1952; came to U.S., 1960, naturalized, 1968; s. Emilio Rene Rodriguez and Caridad Sains; m. Juanita Laszlo, Aug. 31, 1974; children: Daniel Rene, Diana. BA cum laude, CUNY, 1973; MD, NYU, 1977. Diplomate Nat. Bd. Med. Examiners, Am. Bd. Ophthalmology. Dermatology rsch. fellow NYU Med. Ctr., N.Y.C., 1973-77, intern dept. medicine, 1977-78; resident in ophthalmology Manhattan Eye, Ear and Throat Hosp., 1978-81, chief resident in ophthalmology, 1980-81, asst. attending surgeon, 1981-85, assoc. attending surgeon Ophthalmic Plastic & Reconstructive Surgery, Ocular Tumor & Orbital Clinic, 1985-89, surgeon dir. Ophthalmic Plastic & Reconstructive Surgery Clinic, 1989-93, surgeon dir., chief Ocular Tumor & Orbital Clinic, 1989-93; attending surgeon, chief Manhattan Eye, Ear And Throat Hosp., N.Y.C., 1993—, attending surgeon ophthalmic plastic and reconstructive surgery clinic, 1993—, dir. internat. fellowship program, 1991—. Heed Ophthalmic Found. fellow Manhattan Eye, Ear and Throat Hosp.-N.Y. Hosp., Cornell U. Med. Ctr., 1981-82, resident instr. dept. ophthalmology, 1983-85; adj. asst. prof. dermatology NYU, 1981-88; clin. asst. prof. ophthalmology, Mt. Sinai Med. Ctr.; attending surgeon Dept. Ophthalmology, Plastic and Reconstructive Surgery divsn., Bronx VA Hosp., 1985-88; clin. asst. prof. Dept. Ophthalmology, NYU Med. Ctr., 1988—. Mem. med. adv. bd. Skin Cancer Found., 1980—; mem. NYU Malignant Melanoma Clin. Coop. Group, 1981—; bd. dirs. Orbital Disease Found., 1994—; mem. Barraquer Inst. Barcelona, Spain, N.Y. Soc for Clin. Ophthalmology. Contbg. editor Jour. Dermatologic Surgery ad Oncology, 1980-90; co-author: Malignant Melanoma, 1979; contbr. articles to med. jours. Fellow Am. Coll. Surgeons, Am. Acad. Facial Plastic and Reconstructive Surgery, Am. Soc. Ophthalmic Plastic and Reconstructive Surgery, N.Y. Acad. Medicine; mem. AMA, N.Y. State Ophthalmol. Soc., Am. Assn. Ophthalmology, Assn. Rsch. in Vision and Ophthalmology, Manhattan Ophthalmologic Soc., N.Y. County Med. Soc., Med. Soc. State N.Y., Am. Acad. Ophthalmology. Office: 799 Park Ave New York NY 10021 Office Phone: 212-535-0315. Personal E-mail: r52surg@aol.com.

RODRIGUEZ-WALLING, MATILDE BARCELO, special education educator; b. Santiago, Cuba, Aug. 15, 1950; d. Humberto Jacinto and Matilde Amelia (Cuervo) Barcelo; m. Luis Alfredo Rodriguez-Walling, June 29, 1973; 1 child, Alfredo Luis. BA, U. Miami, Fla., 1972; MS in Diagnostic Tchg., Fla. Internat. U., 1981; EdS, Barry U., 1988. Cert. ednl. specialist computer edn., Fla. Tchr., chair fgn. lang. dept. Notre Dame Acad., Miami, Fla., 1972-80; tchr., coord. English as 2d lang. adult edn. program Dade County Pub. Schs., Miami, elem. sch. tchr., tchr. middle sch. spl. edn. Homestead, Fla., elem. spl. edn. tchr. Miami, 1986—, behavior mgmt. specialist, exceptional edn. dept. chair; tchr. on spl. assignment Fla. Dept. of Edn., 1994—. Mem. spkrs. bur. Nat. Clearinghouse for Professions in Spl. Edn.; sch. adv. chairperson Blueprint 2000; presenter and spkr. at state and nat. profl. confs.; coord. Fla. Spkrs. Bur.; mem. Fla. Edn. Stds. Commn. Commr. Fla. Edn. Stds. Commn.; mem. State Adv. Com.; mem. Commrs. Blue Ribbon Panel Edn. Governance; co-chair Nat Commn. Improve Spl. Edn. Teaching & Learning. Recipient Gran Orden Martiana, Cuban Lyceum, Miami, 1976. Mem. Coun. Exceptional Children (sec. 1989, v.p. 1990, pres. 1991-92, multicultural chair 1992-93, Mainstreaming Tchr. of Yr. 1983, region finalist Dade County Tchr. of Yr. 1991, Fla. Tchr. of Yr.), Fla. Fedn. Coun. for Exceptional Children (pres. 1997-98, past pres. 1998-99), Coun. Children with Behavior Disorders, Nat. Bd. for Profl. Tchg. Stds. (exceptional needs com.), Internat. Coun. for Exceptional Children (Tchr. of Yr. 1994), Delta Kappa Gamma (Epsilon chpt.). Roman Catholic. Avocations: travel, guitar. Office: Miami-Dade County Pub Schs 1500 Biscayne Blvd Ste 409G Miami FL 33132-1400 Home: 9421 SW 119thCt Miami FL 33186-2007

RODSTEIN, RICHARD M. apparel executive; b. 1955; m. Leslie Rodstein. BA in Econs., UCLA, 1976, MBA, 1978. Exec. Ernst & Young, 1978-83; v.p. fin. K2, Inc. (formerly Anthony Industries, Inc.), L.A., 1983-85, sr. v.p. fin., 1985-88, exec. v.p., 1988-90, pres., COO, 1990—, CEO, 1995—, also bd. dirs. Office: K2 Inc 4900 S Eastern Ave Los Angeles CA 90040 Fax: 323-724-2800.

RODWELL, JOHN DENNIS, biochemist; b. Boston, Oct. 9, 1946; s. William Joseph and Lillian Catherine (Cunningham) R.; m. Ellen M. McCaffrey, Dec. 18, 1971; children: Elizabeth Ann, Sarah Catherine. BA in Chemistry, U. Mass., 1968; MS in Organic Chemistry, Lowell Technol. Inst., 1971; PhD in Biochemistry, UCLA, 1976. Postdoctoral fellow Sch. Medicine U. Pa., Phila., 1976—80; rsch. asst., prof. U. Pa. Sch. Medicine, 1980—81; with Cytogen Corp., Princeton, NJ, 1981—99, v.p. discovery rsch., 1987—88, v.p. R & D, 1989—96, sr. v.p., chief sci. officer, 1996—99; CEO, bd. dirs. eMetagen LLC, Madison, Wis., 2004—. Adj. asst. prof., then adj. assoc. prof. Sch. Medicine, U. Pa., 1981—; series editor Marcel Dekker, Inc., N.Y.C., 1988—98; bd. dirs., treas. Biotech. Consortium, 1994—98; bd. dirs., pres. AxCell Bioscis. Corp., Newtown, Pa., 1996—2002; pres. Rodwell Consulting, New Hope, Pa., 2003—. Patentee, antibody conjugates for compound delivery, antibody metal ion complexes; editor: Antibody Mediated Delivery Systems, 1988; co-editor: Covalently Modified Antigens and Antibodies in Diagnosis and Therapy, 1989. Recipient Nat. Rsch. Svc. award NIH, 1978-80, Thomas Alva Edison Patent award, 1993. Mem. AAAS, Am. Assn. Immunologists, Am. Chem. Soc. (assoc. editor 1989-93), N.Y. Acad. Scis., Soc. Nuc. Medicine. Democrat. Avocations: gardening, photography. Home: 1340 Eagle Rd New Hope PA 18938-9222 Office: Rodwell Consulting 1340 Eagle Rd New Hope PA 18938-9222

RODZIANKO, PAUL, energy and environmental company executive; b. Washington, Oct. 22, 1945; s. Paul and Aimee Rodzianko; m. Chauncie McKeever, May 1987; children: Marina, Alexander. BA, Princeton U., 1967; MA, Inst. Critical Langs., 1967. With GE Co., 1967-76; pres. U.S. Geothermal Corp., N.Y.C., 1976-77, Geothermal Energy Corp., N.Y.C., 1977-83, Geothermal Food Processors, Inc., Fernley, Nev., 1979-82; exec. v.p. Grace Geothermal Corp., 1981-83, bd. dirs., 1981-83; pres. Bay Capital Corp., Oyster Bay, N.Y., 1983-85, Data Port Co., 1985-86; v.p. spl. projects Kvaerner Energy Devel., Inc., Dover, N.J., 1992-95; pres., CEO Tuxedo Venture Mgmt. Group Inc., N.Y.C., 1995—. Bd. dirs. Access (Eurasia), U.S.-Russia Bus. Coun., chmn. Electricity and Gas subcommittee, 2001—; sec. U.S.-Kazakhstan Bus. Assn., 2001—; chmn. bd. dirs., CEO Mt. Hope Hydro, Inc., 1986-92, Halecon, Inc., 1986-92, Kvaerner Venture Inc., 1992-95; v.p. Little Horn Energy Who., 1993; sr. v.p. devel. Access Industries, 2000—; dir. Bogatyr Coal Co., Ekibastuz, Rep. of Kazakstan, 1996—; bd. dirs. Energibolaget i Sverige, Stockholm; chmn. audit com. Comirbank, Ekibastuz, Kazakhstan, 1998-99. Vice chmn. Russian Orthodox Theol. Fund, 1978—; chmn. Am.-Russian Cultural Coop. Found., 2003—; chmn., CEO Mt. Hope Waterpower Project, 1989-92; sr. v.p. bus. devel. and strategic planning Access Industries, 1996—; bd. dirs. Access (Eurasia); mem. Town Coun., Tuxedo, N.Y., 1993-97, vice chmn. Small Bus. Commn., Ekibastuz, Kazakhstan, 1998-99. Fellow Royal Geog. Soc., Explorers Club, New Eng. Soc.; mem. Geothermal Resources Coun. (bd. dirs., chmn. audit com. 1980-82), Nat. Inst. Social Scis., Rockaway Area C. of C. (bd. dirs. 1988-92), U.S.-Kazakhstan Bus. Assn., Camp Fire Club, Tuxedo Club, Rotary (hon., Paul Harris fellow 1988-92), Lions (mem.-at-large). Office: Access Industries Inc 730 5th Ave New York NY 10019-4105

ROE, BENSON BERTHEAU, surgeon, educator; b. L.A., July 7, 1918; s. Hall and Helene Louise (Bertheau) R.; m. Jane Faulkner St. John, Jan. 20, 1945; children: David B., Virginia St. John. AB, U. Calif., Berkeley, 1939; MD cum laude, Harvard U., 1943. Diplomate Am. Bd. Surgery, Am. Bd. Thoracic Surgery (dir. 1971-83, chmn. bd. 1981-83, chmn. exam. com. 1978, chmn. long-range planning com. 1980, chmn. program com. 1977). Intern Mass. Gen. Hosp., Boston, 1943-44, resident, 1946-50; nat. rsch. fellow dept. physiology Med. Sch., Harvard U., Boston, Mass., 1947, instr. surgery, 1950; Moseley Traveling fellow Harvard. U. at U. Edinburgh, Scotland, 1951; asst. clin. prof. surgery U. Calif., San Francisco, 1951-58, chief cardiothoracic surgery, 1958-76, prof. surgery, 1966-89, emeritus prof., 1989—; pvt. practice medicine specializing in cardiothoracic surgery San Francisco, 1952-85. Sr. scientist Cardiovascular Rsch. Inst., 1956-89; cons. thoracic surgery VA Hosp., San Francisco Gen. Hosp., Letterman Army Hosp., St. Lukes Hosp., Blue Shield of Calif., Baxter Labs., Ethicon, Inc.; bd. dirs. Control Laser Corp.; vis. prof. U. Utah, U. Ky., U. Gdansk, Poland, Nat. Heart Hosp., London, U. Ibadan, Nigeria, Sanger Clinic, Charlotte, Rush-Presbyn. Hosp., Chgo., Penrose Hosp., Colorado Springs. Author: Maverick Among the Moguls, 2002; mem. editl. bd. Annals of Thoracic Surgery, 1969-82, Pharos, E-Medicine; editor 2 med. texts; author 21 textbook chpts.; contbr. more than 175 articles to profl. jours. Bd. dirs. United Bay Area Crusade, 1958-70, mem. exec. com., 1964-65; bd. dirs. chmn. exec. com. San Francisco chpt. Am. Cancer Soc., 1955-57; bd. dirs. San Francisco Heart Assn., 1964-72, pres., 1964-65, chmn. rsch. com., 1966-71; mem. various coms. Am. Heart Assn., 1967-70; pres. Miranda Lux Found., 1982-94; trustee Avery-Fuller-Welch Found.; bd. dirs. Internat. Bioethics Inst., Point Reyes Bird Obs. Served with M.C., USNR, 1944-46. Inductee Rowing Hall of Fame, 1979, U. Calif. Athletic Hall of Fame, 1995. Fellow Am. Coll. Cardiology, ACS (chmn. adv. coun. thoracic surgery, program chmn. thoracic surgery, cardiovascular com.), Polish Surg. Assn. (hon.); mem. Am. Assn. Thoracic Surgery (chmn. membership com. 1974-75), AMA (residency rev. com. for thoracic surgery), Am. Surg. Assn., Pacific Coast Surg. Assn., Calif. Acad. Medicine (pres. 1974), Calif. Med. Assn., Soc. Univ. Surgeons, Soc. Thoracic Surgeons (pres. 1972, chmn. standards and ethics com.), Soc. Vascular Surgery (v.p.). Clubs: Cruising of Am, Pacific Union, St. Francis Yacht, Calif. Tennis. Office: U Calif Div Cardiothoracic Surgery U Calif M593 San Francisco CA 94143-0118 E-mail: ghotieg@earthlink.net.

ROE, BYRON PAUL, physics educator; b. St. Louis, Apr. 4, 1934; s. Sam S. and Gertrude Harriet (Claris) R.; m. Alice Susan Krauss, Aug. 27, 1961; children: Kenneth David, Diana Carol. BA, Washington U., St. Louis, 1954; PhD, Cornell U., 1959. Instr. physics U. Mich., Ann Arbor, 1959-61, asst. prof., 1961-64, assoc. prof., 1964-69, prof., 1969—. Guest physicist SSC Lab., 1991. Author: Probability and Statistics in Experimental Physics, 1992, 2d edit., 2001, Particle Physics at the New Millennium, 1996 (Libr. Sci. Book Club selection). CERN vis. scientist Geneva, 1967, 89; Brit. Sci. Rsch. Coun. fellow, Oxford, 1979; recipient inventor's prize CDC Worldtech, Edina, Minn., 1982, 83. Fellow Am. Phys. Soc. Home: 3610 Charter Pl Ann Arbor MI 48105-2825 Office: U Mich Physics Dept 500 E University Ave Ann Arbor MI 48109-1120 E-mail: byronroe@umich.edu.

ROE, CHARLES BARNETT, lawyer; b. Tacoma, June 25, 1932; s. Charles Brown and Gladys Luvena (Harding) Roe; m. Marilyn Marie Quam, July 31, 1954; children: Sharon Lynn Roe De Groot, Jeannine Carole Roe Dellwo. AB, U. Puget Sound, 1953; postgrad. Boalt Hall, U. Calif. Law Sch., Berkeley, 1957—58; JD, U. Wash., 1960. Bar: Wash. 1960, U.S. Dist. Ct. (ea. and we. dists.) Wash. 1960, U.S. Ct. Appeals (9th cir. 1963, U.S. Supreme Ct. 1963, U.S. Ct. Appeals (D.C. cir.) 1964. Asst. atty. gen. depts. natural resources, conservation, water resources and pollution control commn. State of Wash., Olympia, 1960—70, asst. dir. dept. water resources, 1967—69, sr. asst. atty. gen., 1970—90; of counsel Perkins Coie, Olympia, 1991—. Chief counsel Dept. Ecology, 1970—85, Nuclear Waste Bd., 1983—90; counsel natural resources com. Wash. Ho. of Reps., Olympia, 1970; supr. sea grant trainees U. Wash. Law Sch., 1970—72; adj. prof. Gonzaga U. Sch. Law, Spokane, 1973—76, U. Puget Sound Law Sch., 1985—90; contr. Nat. Water Commn., Washington, 1970—71; legis. aide Gov. Daniel J. Evans, 1969—77. Spl. asst. atty gen. State of Mont, Helena, 1983; rep. Western States Water Coun., Salt Lake City, 1970—90; sec. Olympia Audubon Soc., 1962—63; chmn. bd. mgrs. United Chs., 1967—68. 1st lt. USAF, 1954—57. Mem.: SAR, ABA (chmn. water resources com. natural resources sect. 1981—83), Wash. Cts. Hist. Soc. (bd. dirs. 1998—), Wash. State Bar Assn. (chmn. environ. law sect. 1971—72), Rotary, Am. Legion, Masons, Phi Delta Phi, Kappa Sigma. United Ch. Of Christ. Home: 2400 Wedgewood Dr SE Olympia WA 98501-3841 Office: 111 Market St NE Olympia WA 98501-6965 Business E-Mail: croe@perkinscoie.com.

ROE, GERALD BRUCE, director, writer; b. Cushing, Wis., June 16, 1940; s. Fred Walter and Maybell Meranda (Swenson) R.; m. Laurel A. Nagel, Sept. 12, 1964 (dec. Feb. 1990); children: Stephen, David. BA, U. Minn., 1964, postgrad., 1969-71; MA, Coll. St. Thomas, 1967. Tchr. St. Anthony Padua H.S., Mpls., 1965-68, Ctrl. H.S., St. Paul, 1968-69; asst. to dir. bur. recommendations U. Minn., Mpls., 1973; assoc. dir. ednl. placement U. Iowa, Iowa City, 1974—. Co-author: (with Rebecca Anthony) Over 40 and Looking for Work, 1991, The Curriculum Vitae Handbook, 1994, 3d edit., 2003, 101 Grade A Resumés for Teachers, 1994, 3d edit., 2003; contbr. articles to profl. jours. Bd. dirs. Iowa City Cmty. Theatre, 1994-98. Mem. Phi Delta Kappa (chpt. 0005, v.p. 1990-94, pres. 1994-97). Avocation: theater. Office: Univ Iowa Ednl Placement 302 Lindquist Ctr N Iowa City IA 52242-1529 E-mail: gerald-roe@uiowa.edu.

ROE, JOHN H. manufacturing executive; b. 1939; BA, Williams Coll., 1962; MBA, Harvard U., 1964. With Bemis Co. Inc., Mpls., 1964—, plant supt., 1964-67, sales rep., 1967-68, sales mgr., 1968-70, plant mgr., 1970-73, gen. mgr. film div., 1973-76, exec. v.p. ops., 1976-87, pres., chief oper. officer, from 1987, chief exec. officer, 1990—, also bd. dirs., chmn. Office: Bemis Co Inc 222 S 9th St Ste 2300 Minneapolis MN 55402-4099

ROE, MARK J. law educator; b. N.Y.C., Aug. 8, 1951; m. Helen Hsu, Aug. 12, 1974; children: Andrea Hsu, Jessica Hsu. BA, Columbia U., 1972; JD, Harvard U., 1975. Bar: N.Y. 1976. Atty. Fed. Res. Bank, N.Y.C., 1975-77; assoc. Cahill Gordon & Reindel, N.Y.C., 1977-80; prof. Rutgers U. Law Sch., Newark, 1980-86, U. Pa. Law Sch., 1986-88, Columbia U. Law Sch., N.Y.C., 1988-2001, Harvard Law Sch., Cambridge, Mass., 2001—. Author: (book) Strong Managers, Weak Owners: The Political Roots of American Corporate Finance, 1994, Corporate Reorganization and Bankruptcy, 2000, Political Determinants of Corporate Governance, 2003. Business E-Mail: mroe@law.harvard.edu.

ROE, RICHARD C. industry consultant, former home furnishings manufacturing executive; b. Des Moines, Jan. 4, 1930; s. Lloyd E. and Mary E. (Nuzum) R.; m. Sally McGlothlen, Dec. 27, 1952; children: Stephen James, Julie Ann. BS in Gen. Engring, Iowa State U., 1952. Registered profl. engr., Iowa, Ind., Ill. Indsl. engr. Maytag Co., Newton, Iowa, 1952-56; gen. mgr. mfg. Schnadig Corp., Chgo., 1956-66; v.p. mfg. Sealy Inc., Chgo., 1966-76, group v.p., 1976-86, pres., 1987-89; cons. to industry, 1989—. Bd. dirs. Schnadig Corp., Chgo., Restonic Mattress Corp., Chgo. Patentee in field. Former chmn. adv. com. dept. mgmt., mem. adv. coun. Coll. Bus., Iowa State U. Recipient profl. achievement citation in engring. Iowa State U., 1989. Mem. NSPE, Inst. Indsl. Engrs., Internat. Sleep Products Assn. (former chmn., pres., Exceptional Svc. award 1989), Elks. Home: 8355 E Via De La Luna Scottsdale AZ 85258-3223 Office: 4475 E Rustic Knolls Ln Flagstaff AZ 86004

ROE, RICHARD STEVEN, writer, illustrator; b. Bklyn., July 4, 1959; s. Stanley A. and Cynthia V. Roe. BA, SUNY, N.Y., 1982. Cert. Personal Trainer Am. Coun. on Exercise, 1996. Artist, animal keeper Jersey Wildlife Preservation Trust, England, 1978—79; artist Wildlife Conservation Soc., Bronx Zoo, N.Y.C., 1983—93, LA County Mus. of Natural History, LA, 1996—97, LA Zoo, 1996—99. Book, The Dechromization of Sam McGruder, 1996, When Winter Comes, 1989, How Speedy is a Cheetah?, 1987, Dinosaur Days, 1985, Animal Babies, 1985, Animal ABC, 1984. Recipient Citation for Typographic Excellence, Type Directors Club, 1985. Avocations: weight training, reading, travel. Home: 609 Carolina Holly Way Fletcher NC 28732 Personal E-mail: rickroe@mchsi.com.

ROE, ROGER ROLLAND, JR., lawyer; b. Mpls., Dec. 31, 1947; s. Roger Rolland Roe Jr.; m. Paula Speltz, 1974; children: Elena, Madeline. BA, Grinnell Coll., 1970; JD, U. Minn., 1973. Bar: Minn. 1973, U.S. Dist. Ct. Minn. 1974, U.S. Ct. Appeals (8th cir.) 1977, U.S. Supreme Ct. 1978, Wis. 1988, U.S. Dist. Ct. Nebr. 1995, U.S. Dist. Ct. (ea. and we. dists.) Wis. Law clk. to Hon. Judge Amdahl Hennepin County Dist. Ct., Mpls., 1973-74; from assoc. to ptnr. Rider, Bennett, Egan & Arundel, Mpls., 1974-91; mng. ptnr. Yaeger, Jungbauer, Barczak, Roe & Vucinovich, PLC, Mpls., 1992-2000; ptnr. Best & Flanagan LLP, Mpls., 2000—. Mem. nat. panel arbitrators Am. Arbitration Assn.; judge trial practice class and moot ct. competitions law sch. U. Minn.; guest lectr. Minn. Continuing Legal Edn. courses. Fellow Internat. Soc. Barristers; mem. ATLA (guest lectr.), Am. Bd. Trial Advs. (diplomat, Minn. chpt. pres. 1996-97), Million Dollar Round Table. Avocations: golf, downhill skiing. Office: Best & Flanagan LLP 225 S 6th St # 4000 Minneapolis MN 55402 Office Phone: 612-349-5683.

ROE, THOMAS COOMBE, former utility company executive; b. Dover, Del., Sept. 22, 1914; s. John Moore and Elizabeth Lindale (Cooper) R.; m. Emma Lillian Scotton, Oct. 16, 1937 (dec.); children: Thomas C., Margaret Ruth (dec.); m. Carolyn Scotton, May 4, 2002. BS in Elec. Engring. U. Del., 1935; DHL (hon.), Wesley Coll., 1987. With Eastern Shore Public Service, 1936-43; with Delmarva Power & Light Co., 1943—; pres. subs. Delmara Power & Light Co., 1971-76, chmn. bd., 1976-79, dir., 1971-80, ret., 1980. Hon. trustee Peninsula Regional Med. Ctr., Salisbury, Md.; hon. trustee, former chmn. Wesley Coll., Dover, Del.; former trustee Wesley Theol. Sem., Washington. Served with AUS, 1941-45. Mem.: Rotary (past pres.). Republican. Methodist.

ROE, THOMAS LEROY WILLIS, pediatrician; b. Bend, Oreg., Sept. 1, 1936; MD, U. Oregon Health Scis. U., Portland, 1961. Diplomate Am. Bd. Pediatrics. Intern U. Calif., San Francisco, 1961-62, resident, 1962-64; physician Sacred Heart Med. Ctr., Eugene, Oreg.; pvt. practice Peace Health Med. Group, Eugene, 1969—; clin prof. pediatrics U. Oreg., Portland, 1985—. Fellow Am. Acad. Pediatricians; mem. AMA, North Pacific Pediatrics Soc. Office: Peace Health Med Clinic 1162 Willamette St Eugene OR 97401-3568 Office Phone: 541-687-6061. Business E-Mail: troe@peacehealth.org.

ROE, W. BARTON, engineering executive; b. N.Y.C., Aug. 29, 1955; s. Kenneth Andrew R.; m. Lynne Roe, 1983; 4 children. BS in Mech. Engring., U. Pa., 1978; MSEE, Stevens Inst. Tech., 1987. Engr. analyst Sargent & Lundy Engrs., Chgo., 1978-80; engr. Stone & Webster Engring. Co., N.Y.C., 1980-85; supr. mech. thermal group Am. Rocket Co., Camarillo, Calif., 1987; project engr. Burns & Roe Group Inc., Oradell, N.J., 1988-92, v.p. bus. devel., 1992-96, v.p. infrastructure, 1996—2002, v.p. fed. svcs., 2002—, also bd. dirs. Bd. dirs. Polar Molecular Corp., 1991-92. Mem. ASME (sect. dir. 1998-2001), IEEE, NSPE, Greenwich Country Club, Psi Upsilon of Phila. (trustee 2000—). Avocations: golf, skiing. Office: Burns and Roe Group Inc 800 Kinderkamack Rd Oradell NJ 07649 E-mail: broe@roe.com.

ROEBUCK, DEBORAH MAE BRITT, management consultant, educator; b. San Antonio, Tex., Apr. 11, 1952; d. Aubrey Clarence and Marian Lavita Britt; m. Robert Leroy Roebuck; 1 child, Hillary Grace. BSE, N.E. Mo. State U., Kirksville, 1972—74, MA, 1974—75; PhD, Ga. State U., Atlanta, 1986—90. Cert. tchr. Mo., Iowa, 1974. Assoc. prof., mgmt. Kennesaw State U., Ga., 1992—2001, chair, leadership and profl. devel., 2001—. Author: (textbook) Improving Business Communication Skills; contbr. articles to profl. jours. Mem.: Orgnl. Behavior Tchg. Soc., Acad. Mgmt. Baptist. Avocations: travel, reading. Office: Kennesaw State Univ 1000 Chastain Rd Kennesaw GA 30144

ROEBUCK, JAMES RANDOLPH, JR., state legislator; b. Phila., Feb. 12, 1945; m. Cheryl Arrington. BA cum laude, Va. Union U., 1966; MA, U. Va., 1969, PhD, 1977. Lectr. Drexel U., 1970-77, asst. prof., 1977-84; legis. asst. Office of Mayor, Phila., 1984-85; mem. Pa. Ho. of Reps., Harrisburg, 1985—. Chmn. Pa. Legis. Black Caucus, 1998-2000; Democratic chmn. Ho. Edn. Com., 2003; mem. Pa. History and Mus. Commn., 1990-95; bd. dirs. Pa. Higher Ednl. Assistance Agy., 1995-. Author: The Shaping of William Howard Tafts View of East Asia 1900-1908; co-editor: Biographical Dictionary of Internationalists, 1983. Recipient Young Leadership award Hamilton Watch Co., 1966, Outstanding Svc. award Va. Union U. Alumni Assn., 1973, Legion of Honor award Chapel Four Chaplains, 1980. Mem. Nat. Black Caucus State Legislators, Alpha Phi Alpha. Address: 4800 Baltimore Ave Philadelphia PA 19143-3419 Office Phone: 717-783-1000. E-mail: jroebuck@pahouse.net.

ROEDDER, WILLIAM CHAPMAN, JR., lawyer; b. St. Louis, June 21, 1946; s. William Chapman and Dorothy (Reifeiss) R.; m. Gwendolyn Arnold, Sept. 13, 1968; children: William Chapman, Darcley Shane. BS, U. Ala., 1968, JD cum laude, Cumberland U., 1972. Bar: Ala. Law clk. to chief justice Ala. Supreme Ct., Montgomery, 1972; ptnr. McDowell Knight Roedder & Sledge, L.L.C., Mobile, Ala., 1997—. Comments editor Cumberland-Samford Law Rev.; contbr. articles to legal publs. Mem.: ABA (vice chair com. trial tactics, torts and ins. practice 1995—96), Def. Rsch. Inst., Ala. Def. Lawyers Assn., Fedn. Def. and Corp. Counsel (chmn. products liability sect. 1990—93, bd. dirs. 1993—2000, regional v.p. 1994—96, exec. com. 1997—, sec.-treas. 1999—2000, pres.-elect 2000—01, pres. 2001—02, chmn. bd. dirs. 2002—03), Mobile County Bar Assn. (sec., chmn. ethics com. 1988—90, grievance com. 1994—96), Ala. State Bar Assn., Order of Barristers, Curia Honoris, Phi Alpha Delta (pres. 1971—72). Home: 211 Levert Ave Mobile AL 36607-3219 Office: McDowell Knight Roedder & Sledge LLC PO Box 350 Mobile AL 36601-0350 E-mail: broedder@mcdowellknight.com.

ROEDER, RICHARD KENNETH, business owner, lawyer; b. Phila., Oct. 11, 1948; s. Walter August and Gloria (Miller) R.; 1 child, William Frederick; m. Allison Nunn Roeder, June 12, 1999. AB, Amherst Coll., 1970; JD, U. Calif., Berkeley, 1973, Cambridge U., 1973-74. Assoc. Paul, Hastings, Janofky & Walker, L.A., 1974-81, ptnr., 1981-90; founding ptnr. Aurora Capital Group, L.A., 1990—. Office: Aurora Capital Group Ste 2100 10877 Wilshire Blvd Los Angeles CA 90024-4341 Office Phone: 310-551-0101.

ROEDER, ROBERT GAYLE, biochemist, molecular biologist, educator; b. Boonville, Ind., June 3, 1942; s. Frederick John and Helene (Bredenkamp) Roeder; m. Suzanne Himsel, July 11, 1964 (div. 1981); children: Kimberly, Michael; m. Cun Jing Hong, June 2, 1990; 1 child, Maxine. BA summa cum laude (Gilbert scholar), Wabash Coll., 1964, DSc (hon.), 1990; MS, U. Ill., 1965; PhD (USPHS fellow), U. Wash., 1969. Am. Cancer Soc. fellow dept. embryology Carnegie Instn. Washington, Balt., 1969-71; asst. prof. biol. chemistry Washington U., St. Louis, 1971-75, assoc. prof., 1975-76, prof., 1976-82, prof. genetics, 1978-82, James S. McDonnell prof. biochem. genetics, 1979-82; prof. lab. biochemistry and molecular biology Rockefeller U., N.Y.C., 1982—, Arnold O. and Mabel S. Beckmann prof. molecular biology and biochemistry, 1985—. Cons. USPHS, 1975-79, Am. Cancer Soc., 1983-86. Recipient Dreyfus Tchr.-Scholar award Dreyfus Found., 1976, molecular biology award NAS-U.S. Steel Found., 1986, outstanding investigator award Nat. Cancer Inst., 1986-2002, Dickson prize in medicine, 2001, Albert Lasker Basic Med. Rsch. award 2003; co-recipient Lewis S. Rosenstiel award for disting. work in basic med. scis. Brandeis U., 1995, Passano award Passano Found., Inc., 1995, Alfred P. Sloan prize GM Cancer Rsch. Found., 1999, Louisa Gross Horowitz award Columbia U., 1999, Gairdner Found. Internat. award, 2000, ASBMB-Merck Award, 2002; grantee NIH, 1972-, NSF, 1975-79, Am. Cancer Soc., 1979-85. Fellow AAAS, Am. Acad. Arts and Scis., Am. Acad. Microbiology, N.Y. Acad. Scis.; mem. NAS, Am. Chem. Soc. (Eli Lilly award 1977), Am. Soc. Biol. Chemists, Am. Soc. Microbiologists, Harvey Soc. (pres. 1994), Phi Beta Kappa. Office: Rockefeller U 1230 York Ave New York NY 10021-6399 Office Phone: 212-327-7600. Business E-Mail: roeder@rockefeller.edu.

ROEDERER, JUAN GUALTERIO, physics educator; b. Trieste, Italy, Sept. 2, 1929; came to U.S., 1967, naturalized, 1972; s. Ludwig Alexander and Anna Rafaela (Lohr) R.; m. Beatriz Susana Cougnet, Dec. 20, 1952; children: Ernesto, Irene, Silvia, Mario. PhD, U. Buenos Aires, 1952. Research scientist Max Planck Inst., Gottingen, W.Ger., 1952-55; group leader Argentine Atomic Energy Commn., Buenos Aires, 1953-59; prof. physics U. Buenos Aires, 1959-66, U. Denver, 1967-77, U. Alaska, Fairbanks, 1977-93, prof. emeritus, 1993—, dir. Geophys. Inst., 1977-86, dean Coll. Environ. Scis., 1978-82. Vis. staff Los Alamos Nat. Lab., 1969-81; chmn. U.S. Arctic Research Com., 1987-91; sr. adviser Internat. Ctr. Theoretical Physics, Trieste, Italy, 1998—2002. Author: Dynamics of Geomagnetically Trapped Radiation, 1970, Physics and Psychophysics of Music, 1973, 3d edit., 1995, Mecanica Elemental, 2002; contbr. articles to profl. jours. Nat. Acad. Sci. NASA sr. research fellow, 1964-66 Fellow AAAS, Am. Geophys. Union (Edward A. Flinn III award, 2000); mem. Assn. Argentina de Geodestas y Geofisicos (hon.), Nat. Acad. Sci. Argentina (corr.), Nat. Acad. Sci. Austria (corr.), Third World Acad. Scis. (assoc.), Internat. Assn. Geomagnetism and Aeronomy (hon.), Sci. Com. on Solar-Terrestrial Physics (hon.). Lutheran. Achievements include research on plasma and energetic particles in earth's and Jupiter's magnetosphere, policy issues for Arctic, perception of music, information theory. Home: 105 Concordia Dr Fairbanks AK 99709-3029 Office: U Alaska Geophys Inst Fairbanks AK 99775-7320 E-mail: jgr@gi.alaska.edu.

ROEDER VAUGHAN, MIMI, small business owner; b. Balt., Nov. 21, 1948; m. Arky Vaughan; children: Gina Pizza, Kelly Vaughan, Ryan Vaughan. BA, U. Tenn., 1970; postgrad., U. Hawaii, 1972. Founder, CEO Roeder Travel, 1973—, Kailua Property, 1973—, Md. Sch. Travel, 1976—, Roland Park Travel, 1984—92, Falls Road Travel, 1990—. Mem. bd. Augusta Bank, 1990—91. Dir., sec. Civic Works, 1998—2000; pres., founder Baskets and Books, 1995—2000; co-founder Kingston Orphanage Group, 2000. Named One of Md.'s Top 100 Women, Daily Record, 1995, 1999, 2001; recipient Sabre Star award, Am. Airlines, 1999, 2000, Gold Spike award, Amtrak, 1998. Mem.: GBC Leadership (bd. dirs. 2000, class rep. 1995 1995—2000), Network 2000 (co-chair mentoring 1999—2000, membership com. 1998—2000). Office: 9805 York Rd Cockeysville Hunt Valley MD 21030

ROEDIGER, PAUL MARGERUM, hospital administrator; b. Princeton, N.J., June 30, 1932; s. Paul Otto and Helen Mae (Margerum) R.; m. Janice Ann Balint, Aug. 18, 1956; children: Pamela, Matthew, Joan. AB, Princeton U., 1954; MD, Jefferson Med. Coll., 1958. Dir. med. edn. Abington (Pa.) Meml. Hosp., 1965—, chief divsn. gen. internal medicine, 1972-2000. Vestry mem. St. Ann's Episcopal Ch., Abington, 1965—. Fellow ACP, Coll. Physicians of Phila. Home: 1250 Greenwood Ave Jenkintown PA 19046 Office: 1200 York Rd Dixon Bldg Abington PA 19001-3800 Office Phone: 215-481-2603. Business E-Mail: amhgme@amh.org.

ROEG, NICOLAS JACK, film director; b. London, Aug. 15, 1928; s. Jack Nicolas and Mabel Getrude (Silk) R.; m. Susan Rennie Stephen, May 12, 1957; children: Joscelin Nicolas, Nicolas Jack, Lucien John, Sholto Jules; m. Theresa Russell, 1985; children: Maximilian Nicolas Sextus, Statten Jack. Student Brit. schs.; LittD honoris causa, Hull (Eng.) U., 1995; DFA (hon.), CUNY, 2004. Cinematographer films The Caretaker, 1963, Masque of Red Death, 1964, Fahrenheit 451, 1966, A Funny Thing Happened on the Way to the Forum, 1966, Far from the Madding Crowd, 1967, Petulia, 1968; co-dir. film Performance, 1970; dir. films Walkabout, 1970, Don't Look Now, 1973, Glastonbury Fayre, 1973, The Man Who Fell to Earth, 1976, Bad Timing, 1980, Eureka, 1982, Insignificance, 1985, Castaway, 1986, 89, Track 29, 1987, Aria, 1987, The Witches, 1988-89, Cold Heaven, 1990, Heart of Darkness, 1994, Two Deaths, 1994, Hotel Paradise, 1995, Full Body Massage, 1995, Samson & Delilah, 1996; dir. TV films: Sweet Bird of Youth, 1989, Heart of Darkness, 1994; exec. prodr. Without You I'm Nothing, 1989, Young Indy, 1991, The Sound of Claudia Schiffer, 1999-; co-prodr. Rock Concert, 2002; writer (screenplays) Night Train, 2000, Ivanhoe, 2000, History Play, 2004. Decorated comdr. Brit. Empire. Fellow Brit. Film Inst.; mem. Dirs. Guild Am., Dir. Guild Gt. Britain, Acad. Motion Picture Arts and Scis., Assn. Cinematograph, TV and Allied Technicians.

ROEHL, JERRALD J. lawyer; b. Austin, Tex., Dec. 6, 1945; s. Joseph E. and Jeanne Foster (Scott) R.; m. Nancy J. Meyers, Jan. 15, 1977; children: Daniel J., Katherine C., J. Ryan, J. Taylor. BA, U. N.Mex., 1968; JD, Washington and Lee U., 1971. Bar: N.Mex. 1972, U.S. Ct. Appeals (10th cir.) 1972, U.S. Supreme Ct. 1977. Practice of law, Albuquerque, 1972—; pres. Roehl Law Firm P.C. and predecessors, Albuquerque, 1976—. Lectr. to profl. groups; real estate developer, Albuquerque. Bd. advs. ABA Jour. 1981-83; bd. editors Washington and Lee Law Rev., 1970-71. Bd. dirs. Rehab. Ctr. of Albuquerque, 1974-78; mem. assocs. Presbyn. Hosp. Ctr., Albuquerque, 1974-82; incorporator, then treas. exec. com. Ctr. City Coun., 1991-98, law coun. Washington & Lee U. Law Sch., 2002—. Recipient award of recognition State Bar N.Mex., 1975-77. Mem. ABA (award of achievement Young Lawyers divsn. 1975, coun. econs. of law practice sect. 1978-80, exec. coun. Young Lawyers divsn. 1979-81, fellow divsn. 1984—, coun. tort and ins. practice sect. 1981-83), N.Mex. Bar Assn. (pres. young lawyers sect. 1975-76), Albuquerque Bar Assn. (bd. dirs. 1976-79), N.Mex. Def. Lawyers Assn. (pres. 1983-84), Albuquerque Country Club, Albuquerque Petroleum Club, Sigma Alpha Epsilon, Sigma Delta Chi, Phi Delta Phi. Roman Catholic. Home: 4411 Constitution Ave NE Albuquerque NM 87110-5721 Office: Roehl Law Firm PC 300 Central Ave SW Albuquerque NM 87102-3298 Office Phone: 505-242-6900. E-mail: jjr@roehl.com.

ROEHLING, CARL DAVID, architect; b. Detroit, June 25, 1951; m. Barbara K. Jeffries; children: Carl Robert, Kristin Virginia. BS in Architecture, U. Mich., 1973, MArch, 1975. Registered arch., Mich.; cert. Nat. Coun. Archtl. Registration Bd. Architect Minoru Yamasaki and Assocs., Inc., Troy, Mich., 1976-77; TMP Assocs., 1977-81; architect Harley Ellington Pierce Yee Assocs., Inc., Southfield, Mich., 1981-83, Giffels/Hoyem Basso Assocs., Troy, 1983-87, Smith, Hinchman & Grylls Assocs., Inc., Detroit, 1987—. With Chrysler World Hdqs., 1994. Prin. works include CBS/Fox Video Hdqrs., Livonia, Mich. (Honor award Mich. Masonry Inst., 1985), First Ctr. Office Bldg., Southfield, Mich. (Honor award FAIA Mich., 1988), Ind. U. Chemistry Bldg., Bloomington (Honor award AIA Detroit, 1990, AIA Mich., 1990), U. Mich. Aerospace Lab. Bldg., Ann Arbor, 1993, Los Alamos (N.Mex.) Materials Sci. Lab., 1993, others. Mem. AIA (Mich. chpg. pres. bd. dirs. 1989, mem. nat. com. on environ. 1991, Detroit chpt. pres. 1994, Young Arch. of Yr., AIA Detroit, 1986, AIA Mich., 1991, regional dir. 1996—, nat. bd. dirs.), Am. Archtl. Found. (bd. dirs. 1997—), Mich. Archtl. Found. (chmn. pres. scholarship program 1990). Office: Smith Group Inc 500 Griswold St Ste 200 Detroit MI 48226-3808

ROEHMHOLDT, JOHN MICHAEL, urologist, educator; b. Buffalo, Jan. 3, 1960; s. Robert Louis and Mary Elizabeth Roehmholdt; m. Sheliah Joan Jung, Aug. 25, 1990; children: Peter, Max, Julie. BA in Biology summa cum laude, Canisius Coll., Buffalo, 1981; MD cum laude, Albany Med. Coll., 1985. Diplomate Am. Bd. Urology; lic. capt. USCG. Pvt. practice; resident surgery U. Wis. Hosp. and Clinics, Madison, 1985-87, resident in urology, 1987-90; pvt. practice, Amherst, N.Y., 1990—. Clin. instr. urology SUNY, Buffalo, 1996—; mem. staff DeGraff Meml. Hosp., North Tonawanda, N.Y., pres. med. staff, 1995, dir., 1996-97; mem. trustee coun. Kaleida Health Sys., Buffalo, 1998—. Bd. dirs. West Seneca Devel. Ctr. chpt. N.Y. State ARC, 1994—; chmn. stewardship and devel. com. parish coun. Sts. Peter and Paul Ch., Williamsville, N.Y., 1999—, pres. parish coun., 2001-02. Recipient physician's recognition award AMA, 2000. Fellow ACS; mem. AMA (Physicians Recognition award 2000), Am. Urol. Assn., Buffalo Urol. Soc. (pres.-elect 2001-02, pres. 2002-2003), Olcott Yacht Club (N.Y.) (sr. mem., fleet surgeon 1998—), Alpha Omega Alpha. Office: Northtown Urology Assocs PC 3800 Sheridan Dr Amherst NY 14226

ROEHRIG, C(HARLES) BURNS, internist, health policy consultant; b. Brookline, Mass., Jan. 21, 1923; s. Gilbert Haven and Helen (Burns) R.; m. Patricia Joan Orme, July 22, 1952 (dec. 2002); children: Joan Russell Roehrig Vater, Jennifer Orme Roehrig Munn, Charles Burns, Jr. Student, Amherst Coll., 1941-43, Vanderbilt U., 1943-44; MD, U. Md., 1949; cert. in internal medicine, U. Pa., Phila., 1953. Diplomate Am. Bd. Internal Medicine. Intern Boston City Hosp., 1949-50; resident in internal medicine and diabetes Joslin Clinic, New Eng. Deaconess Hosp., Boston, 1952-54; practice medicine specializing in internal medicine and diabetes Boston, 1954-91; chief of staff, pres. med. adminstrv. bd. New Eng. Deaconess Hosp., Boston, 1972-75; dir., mem. exec. com. Blue Shield of Mass., Inc., Boston, 1977-88; exec. com. Met. Boston Hosp. Coun., 1982-86; physician adv. coun. Mass. Hosp. Assn., Burlington, 1982-86. Editor: Today's Internist, Washington, 1987-99; contbr. articles to profl. jours. Bd. dirs. Camping Svcs. Bd., Greater Boston YMCA, 1966—; mem. physician adv. group Health Care Financing Adminstrn., Washington, 1983-88; mem. adv. panel on physician payment and med. tech. Office of Tech. Assessment, U.S. Congress, Washington, 1984-85; chmn. Federated Coun. for Internal Medicine, Washington, 1985-86; trustee New Eng. Deaconess Hosp. Capt. (flight surgeon) USAF, 1949-52. Fellow ACP; mem. AMA (chmn. coun. on long range planning and devel., Chgo.), New Eng. Diabetes Assn. (pres. 1963-64), Mass. Soc. Internal Medicine (pres. 1971-72), Am. Soc. Internal Medicine (pres. 1984-85), Country Club of Hilton Head, Wellesley (Mass.) Country Club. Republican. Episcopalian. Office: 5 Summer Breeze Ct Hilton Head Island SC 29926-2536 Office Phone: 843-681-7713. Personal E-mail: burnsroehrigmd@aol.com.

ROEHRIG, JOHN T. immunologist, educator; BS in Microbiology, U. Ill., 1973; PhD in Microbiology, U. Mo.-Columbia, 1977. Rsch. microbiologist divsn. vector-borne infectious diseases Ctr. Disease Control and Prevention, Fort Collins, Colo., 1981-84, supervisory rsch. microbiologist, 1984—, chief immunochemistry br./sect., 1985-98; chief arbovirus diseases br. Colo. State U., Fort Collins, 1981—, biosafety com. mem., 1981—, affiliate faculty mem. dept. microbiology, 1981—. Presenter in field. Ad hoc reviewer Am. Jour. of Tropical Medicine and Hygiene, Archives of Virology, Infectio and Immunity, Jour. of Gen. Virology, Jour. of Infectious Diseases, Jour. of Med. Virology, Jour. of Virology, Virology and Virus Rsch.; contbr. chpts. to books and numerous articles to profl. jours. Grantee U.S. Army, 1987-90, NATO, 1987-90, WHO, 1989-91. Mem. AAAS, Am. Soc. for Virology, Am. Soc. for Microbiology, Am. Com. for Arthropod-Bone Viruses, Protein Soc., Am. Peptide Soc., Am. Soc. for Tropical Medicine and Hygiene, U. Ill. Alumni Assn., U. Mo. Alumni Assn., Sigma Xi. Office: Divsn Vector Borne Infectious Diseases Ctrs Disease Control PO Box 2087 Fort Collins CO 80522-2087

ROELANDTS, WILLEM P. data processing executive; came to U.S., 1982; BEE, Rijks Hogere Technische Sch., Belgium. Various position including sr. v.p. Hewlett-Packard, 1966—96; CEO, pres. Xilinx, San Jose, 1996—. Spkr. in field. Mem.: Fabless Semiconductor Assn. (pres.), Tech. Network (bd. dirs.), Semiconductor Industry Assn. (bd. dirs.). Office: Xilinx Inc 2100 Logic Dr San Jose CA 95124-3400

ROELL, STEPHEN A. manufacturing executive; CFO Johnson Controls, Inc., Milw. Office: Johnson Controls Inc PO Box 591 Milwaukee WI 53201-0591

ROELLER, HERBERT ALFRED, biology and medical scientist, educator; b. Magdeburg, Germany, Aug. 2, 1927; came to U.S., 1962; s. Alfred H. and Elfriede (Wartner) R.; m. Manuela R. Buresch, Dec. 20, 1957. Abiturium, Christian Thomasius Schule, Halle/Saale, 1946; PhD, Georg August U., Goettingen, 1962; MD, U. Muenster, 1955. Project assoc. zoology U. Wis., Madison, 1962-65, asst. prof. pharmacology, 1965-66, rsch. assoc. zoology, 1966-67, assoc. prof. zoology, 1967-68; prof. biology Tex. A&M U., 1968-83, prof. biochemistry and biophysics, 1974-83, dir. Inst. Devel. Biology, 1973-83, Disting. prof., 1977—, Alumni prof., 1980-85. V.p. rsch. Zoecon Corp., Palo Alto, Calif., 1968-72, sci. adv., 1972-85, chief scientist, Zoecon Rsch. Inst., Palo Alto, 1985-88; sci. advisor Syntex Rsch., Palo Alto, 1966-68, European Cmty., 1988—, Affymax Rsch. Inst., Palo Alto, 1989-96; corp. advisor Symyx Techs., Sunnyvale, Calif., 1996—; mem. adv. panel regulatory biology, divsn. biol. and med. scis. NSF, 1969-72; mem. Internat. Centre Insect Physiology and Ecology, Nairobi, Kenya, 1970—, dir. rsch., 1970-75. Mem. editl. bd. Jour. Chem. Ecology, 1974—; Contbr. articles to profl. jours. Recipient Disting. Achievement award for research Tex. A&M U., 1976. Fellow Tex. Acad. Sci.; mem. German Acad. Naturforscher Leopoldina, AAAS, Am. Soc. Zoologists, Entomol. Soc. Am., Am. Soc. Devel. Biology, Sigma Xi.

ROELLIG, LEONARD OSCAR, physics educator; b. Detroit, May 17, 1927; s. Oscar Otto and Laura K. (Rutz) R.; m. B. Pauline Cowdin, June 20, 1952; children: Thomas Leonard, Mark Douglas, Paul David. AB, U. Mich., 1950, MS, 1956, PhD, 1959. From asst. prof. to prof. physics Wayne State U., Detroit, 1958-78, dean, 1971-72, asso. provost, 1972-76; pres. Central Solar Energy Research Corp., Detroit, 1977; prof. physics CCNY, 1978-96, prof. emeritus, 1996—; vice chancellor acad. affairs CUNY, 1978-83. Vis. prof. Univ. Coll., London, 1968-69, Tata Inst. Fundamental Rsch., Bombay, India, 1973, Paul Scherrer Inst., Villigen, Switzerland, 1991-92; chmn. bd. advisers Midwest Regional Solar Energy Planning Venture, 1977. Co-author: Positron Annihilation, 1967; contbr. articles to profl. jours. Bd. dirs. Luth. Publicity Bur., 1981-91, v.p., 1984-85, pres., 1985-89; v.p. Grosse Pointe (Mich.) Human Rels. Coun., 1969-70. With USN, 1945-46, U.S. Army, 1950-52. Recipient Wayne State U. Fund Research Recognition award, 1963, Probus Club award for acad. achievement, 1968, Probus Club award for acad. leadership, 1977 Mem. Am. Phys. Soc. Home: 4520 Sioux Dr Boulder CO 80303-3733 Office: U Colo Dept Physics Boulder CO 80302 E-mail: loroellig@aol.com.

ROELLIG, MARK D. telecommunications industry executive, lawyer; BS in Applied Maths. with highest distinction, U. Mich., 1976; JD, George Washington U., 1979; MBA, U. Washington, 1988. Assoc. Perry & Smity, Seattle, Reed, McClure, Moceri & Thonn, Seattle; litigation and regulator atty. law dept. U S West, Seattle, 1983-92, v.p. law and litigation sect. Denver, 1992-95, v.p. law and human resources, asst. sec. corp. sect., 1995, exec. v.p. pub. policy and regulatory law, 1996-97, exec. v.p. pub. policy, human resources, law, gen. counsel, 1997—. Mem. Beta Gamma Sigma. Office: US West Inc 1801 California St Ste 4750 Denver CO 80202-2658

ROELOFS, LYLE DEAN, physicist, researcher; b. Grand Rapids, Mich., Dec. 19, 1953; s. Harlan Ray and Cynthia Clara (Van Dyke) R.; m. Lauren Beth Mulder, June 14, 1975; children: Christopher Dean, Brian Alexander. BS, Calvin Coll., 1975; MS, U. Md., 1978, PhD, 1980. Instr. Calvin Coll., Grand Rapids, 1977; rsch. asst., instr. U. Md., College Park, 1977-80; rsch. assoc. Brown U., Providence, 1980-82; asst. prof. physics Haverford (Pa.) Coll., 1982-87, assoc. prof. physics, 1987-93, prof. physics, 1993—. Author: Electricity and Magnetism Simulations, 1995, Handbook of Surface Science, Vol. 1, 1996; contbr. articles to profl. jours. Democrat. Office: Haverford Coll Dept Physics 370 Lancaster Ave Haverford PA 19041-1336

ROELOFS, WENDELL LEE, biochemistry educator, consultant; b. Orange City, Iowa, July 26, 1938; s. Edward and Edith (Beyers) Roelofs; m. Donna R. Gray, Dec. 23, 1989; children: Brenda Jo, Caryn Jean, Jeffrey Lee, Kevin Jon. BA, Central Coll., Pella, Iowa, 1960; PhD, Ind. U., 1964; DSc (hon.) (hon.), Central Coll., Pella, Iowa, 1985, Ind. U., 1986, Hobart and William Smith Colls., 1988, U. of Lund, Sweden, 1989, Free U. Brussels, 1989. Asst. prof. Cornell U., Geneva, NY, 1965—69, assoc. prof., 1969—76, prof., 1976—, Liberty Hyde Bailey prof. insect biochemistry, 1978—, chmn. dept., 1991—. Contbr. articles to sci. jours. Recipient Alexander von Humboldt award in Agr., 1977, Outstanding Alumni award, Central Coll., 1978, Wolf prize for agr., 1982, Disting. Alumnus award, Ind. U., 1983, Nat. Medal of Sci., 1983, Disting. Svc. award, USDA, 1986, Silver medal, Internat. Soc. Chem. Ecology, 1990; fellow postdoctoral fellow, MIT, 1965. Fellow: AAAS, Entomol. Soc. Am. (J. Everett Bussart Meml. award 1973, Founder's Meml. award 1980, Disting. Achievement award Ea. br. 1983); mem.: NAS, Am. Acad. Arts and Sci., Am. Chem. Soc. (Sterling B. Hendricks awar 1994, Spencer award 2001), Sigma Xi. Republican. Presbyterian. Achievements include patents for in field. Home: 4 Crescence Dr Geneva NY 14456-1302 Office: Cornell Univ Dept Entomology Barton Lab Geneva NY 14456

ROEMER, ELIZABETH, astronomer, educator; b. Calif., Sept. 4, 1929; d. Richard Quirin and Elsie Roemer. BA with honors, U. Calif., Berkeley, 1950, PhD (Lick Obs. fellow), 1955. Tchr. adult class Oakland pub. schs., 1950-52; lab technician U. Calif. at Mt. Hamilton, 1954-55; grad. research astronomer U. Calif. at Berkeley, 1955-56; research asso. Yerkes Obs. U. Chgo., 1956; astronomer U.S. Naval Obs., Flagstaff, Ariz., 1957-66; asso. prof. dept. astronomy, also in lunar and planetary lab. U. Ariz., Tucson, 1966-69, prof., 1969-97; prof. emerita, 1997—; astronomer Steward Obs., 1980-97, astronomer emerita, 1997—. Chmn. working group on orbits and ephemerides of comets commn. 20 Internat. Astron. Union, 1964-79, 85-88, v.p. comm. 20, 1979-82, pres., 1982-85, v.p. commn. 6, 1973-76, 85-88, pres., 1976-79, 88-91; mem. adv. panels Office Naval Research, Nat. Acad. Scis.-NRC, NASA; researcher and author numerous publs. on astrometry and astrophysics of comets and minor planets including 79 recoveries of returning periodic comets, visual and spectroscopic binary stars, computation of orbits of comets and minor planets. Recipient Dorothea Klumpke Roberts prize U. Calif. at Berkeley, 1950, Mademoiselle Merit award, 1959; asteroid (1657) named Roemera, 1965; Benjamin Apthorp Gould prize Nat. Acad. Scis., 1971; NASA Spl. award, 1986. Fellow AAAS (council 1966-69, 72-73), Royal Astron. Soc. (London); mem. Am. Astron. Soc. (program vis. profs. astronomy 1960-75, council 1967-70, chmn. div. dynamical astronomy 1974), Astron. Soc. Pacific (publs. com. 1962-73, Comet medal com. 1968-74, Donohoe lectr. 1962), Internat. Astron. Union, Am. Geophys. Union, Brit. Astron. Assn., Phi Beta Kappa, Sigma Xi. Office: U Ariz PO Box 210092 Lunar & Planetary Lab Tucson AZ 85721-0092

ROEMER, HENRY CONRAD, JR., lawyer; Sr. v.p. RJ Reynolds Industries, Inc., Winston-Salem, NC, gen. counsel, sec. Office: R J Reynolds Industries Inc RJR World Headquarters Reynolds Blvd Winston Salem NC 27102

ROEMER, JAMES PAUL, data processing executive, writer; b. Cin., June 6, 1947; s. Charles William and Lillian (Vollman) R.; m. Patricia Pipenger; children: Kimberly, Michelle. Student, U. Cin., 1965-68; A.M.P., U. Va., 1978. Systems analyst Union Central Life Ins. Co., Cin., 1965-70; program and systems mgr. Computer Systems, Inc., Florence, Ky., 1970-72; mgr. data processing Mead Products, Dayton, Ohio, 1972-77; dir. ops. Mead Data Central, Dayton, 1977-78, v.p. ops., 1978-80, acting pres., 1980-81, v.p. product devel., 1981-82, sr. v.p. legal, govt., acctg., sr. v.p. with responsibility for lexis, 1982-89; pres. Michie Group, Charlottesville, Va., 1989-91; pres., COO Bell and Howell Publs. Systems Co., 1991-93; pres., CEO Univ. Microfilms Internat., Ann Arbor, 1994-95; chmn., pres., CEO Bell & Howell, Skokie, Ill., 1995—. Active Harvard, 1989. Mem. Info. Industry Assn., Assn. for Info. and Image Mgmt. Republican. Roman Catholic. Home: 6271 Canterbury Dr Hudson OH 44236-3558 Office: Bell & Howell 3400 W Pratt Ave Lincolnwood IL 60712-ND

ROEMER, KENNETH MORRISON, English language educator; b. East Rockaway, NY, June 6, 1945; s. Arthur Kenneth and Mildred (Allison) R.; m. Claire Marie O'Keefe, June 15, 1968; children: Yvonne Marie, Michael Kenneth. BA in English, Harvard U., 1967; MA in Am. Civilization, U. Pa., 1968, PhD in Am. Civilization, 1971. From asst. to full prof. U. Tex., Arlington, 1971—. Vis. prof. Shimane U., Matsue, Japan, 1982-83, Internat. Christian U., Mitaka, Tokyo, 1988. Author: (scholarly) The Obsolete Necessity, 1976 (nominated for Pulitzer), Utopian Audiences, 2003, Michibata De Deata Nippow (A Sidewalker's Japan), 2002; (textbook) Build Your Own Utopia, 1981; author, editor: (scholarly) America as Utopia, 1981, Approaches to Teaching Momaday's Rainy Mountain, 1988, Native American Writers of the United States, 1997 (Writer of Yr., Wordcraft Cir. 1998); asst. editor: Am. Quar., 1970; mng. editor: Am. Lit. Realism, 1971-88; mem. editl. bd.: Am. Lit., 1993-96. Choir dir. U. Cath. Community, Arlington, 1977-87; bd. dirs. Creative Arts Theatre and Sch., Arlington, 1989-96. Japan Soc. for Promotion of Sci. fellow, 1988; grantee Exxon Edn. Found., 1977-78, ACLS, 1986, NEH, 1992, 94, 96, 98. Mem. MLA (chmn. Native Am. discussion group 1981, publ. com. 1989-91, chmn. Am. Indian lit. divsn. 1995), Soc. for Utopian Studies (pres. 2002—). Office Phone: 817-272-2729. Business E-Mail: roemer@uta.edu.

ROEMER, TIMOTHY J. think-tank executive, former congressman; b. South Bend, Ind., Oct. 30, 1956; m. Sarah Lee Johnston, 1989. BA in pol. sci, U. Calif., San Diego, 1979; MA, PhD in internat. rels., U. Notre Dame, 1986. Staff asst. to congressman John Brademas U.S. Congress, def., trade and fgn. policy advisor to senator Dennis DeConcini; mem. U.S. Congress from 3rd Ind. dist., 1991—2003, mem. economic and ednl. opportunity com., mem. sci. com., mem. edn. and the workforce com., mem. permanent select committee on intelligence; ptnr. Johnston & Assocs., Washington, 2003; pres. Ctr. for Nat. Policy, Washington, 2003—. Adj. prof. Am. U. Mem.: Nat. Commn. Terrorists Attacks U.S. Democrat. Office: Ctr for Nat Policy One Massachusetts Ave NW Ste 333 Washington DC 20001*

ROEN, PHILIP RUBEN, urologist, surgeon, medical educator; b. N.Y.C., Aug. 5, 1914; s. Nathaniel and Ida (Brickman) R.; m. Florence Sonia Gluck, Dec. 23, 1944; children: Janet Leslie. BA, Columbia Coll., 1934, MD, 1938. Diplomate Am. Bd. Urology. Fellow Cleve. Clinic; resident in urology N.Y. Hosp.; dir. urology St. Clare's Hosp., N.Y.C., 1959—; attending urologist Roosevelt Hosp., N.Y.C., 1980—; prof. clin. urology N.Y. Med. Coll., Valhalla, 1980—; ret. Author: Atlas of Genitourinary Surgery, 1951, Atlas of Urologic Surgery, 1967, Male Sexual Health, 1974; contbr. articles to profl. jours. Chmn. profl. rels. Blue Shield, N.Y.C., 1978-80. Mem. ACS, Am. Urol. Assn., N.Y. Urol. Assn., Princeton Club N.Y.C. Office: 220 Madison Ave New York NY 10016-3422

ROEN, SHELDON R. publisher, psychologist; b. N.Y.C. s. Morris Rosenthal and Gussie (Weininger) R.; m. Selma Lois Pollets, 1954; children: Randa M., Marjorie A., Harris L. BS, City U. N.Y., 1950, MA, 1951; PhD, Columbia U., 1955; postgrad., New Sch. Social Research, 1951-53, Harvard Sch. Pub. Health, 1961-62. Diplomate: Am. Bd. Examiners in Profl. Psychology. Tchr. pub. schs., N.Y.C., 1950-53; chief Clin. Psychology Svc., Ft. Sill, Okla., 1955-58; instr. Cameron Coll., Okla. A. and M. U., 1956-58; asst. prof. U. N.H., 1958-60; asst. chief psychol. services Mass. Mental Health Center, Boston, 1960-63; instr. Harvard, 1961-63; rsch. assoc. Med. Sch., 1960-63; dir. rsch. S. Shore Mental Health Center, Quincy, Mass., 1962-66; assoc. prof. dept. psychology Tchrs. Coll., Columbia, N.Y.C., 1966-72; dir. Psychol. Consultation Center, 1966-72; chmn. bd., pres., psychologist Human Scis. Press, N.Y.C., 1972—90. Lectr. L.I. U., summer 1958, Tufts U., 1961-62; mem. N.H. Gov.'s Com. on Spl. Edn., also Study Com. on Mental Health Reorgn., 1961-62; cons. VISTA program OEO, 1966-67; mem. juvenile problems research rev. com. NIMH, 1968-69; mem. research rev. com. Title III Elementary and Secondary Edn. Act project application Ohio Dept. Edn., 1969-72; mem. mental health coordinating com. local sch. dist. 5, N.Y.C., 1969-72; mem., research dir. work incentive program for welfare recipients Wharton Sch. Pa., U.S. Dept. Labor, 1969-72; mem. mental health and community control com. N.Y. Psychologists for Social Action, 1969-72 Authors, editor books.; Editor: Mass. Psychol. Assn. Newsletter, 1963-65, Community Mental Health Jour; contbr. articles to profl. jours. and chpts. to books. Chmn. bd. trustees Bristol Acres Sch., Taunton, Mass., 1965-67. Fellow Am. Psychol. Assn. (mem. com. pre-coll. behavioral scis. 1968-71, founder div. 27 community psychology div. 1969, chmn. subcom. pre-high sch. behavioral sci. 1969-72), Am. Pub. Health Assn., Am. Orthopsychiat. Assn. (com. on research edn. 1965-67), Am. Sociol. Assn.; mem. New Eng. Psychol. Assn. (steering com. 1965-68), N.H. Psychol. Assn. (legis. chmn. 1961-62) Office: 3205 Beacon St Pompano Beach FL 33062-1207

ROENICK, JEREMY, professional hockey player; b. Boston, Jan. 17, 1970; Center Chgo. Blackhawks, 1988—96, Phoenix Coyotes, 1996—2001, Phila. Flyers, 2001—. Played NHL All-Star Games, 1991—94. Named NHL Rookie of Yr., The Sporting News, 1989—90. Office: PA Flyers 1st Union Ctr Complex 3601 S Broad St Philadelphia PA 19148

ROENIGK, MARTIN ALLEN, insurance company executive; b. Cleve., Sept. 19, 1942; s. Henry Herman and Irene Lena (Rini) R.; m. Elise Feutz, July 5, 1965. B.A., Antioch Coll., 1965; M.B.A., U. Chgo., 1967. C.P.A., Conn. Staff auditor Arthur Andersen & Co., Cleve., 1968; with Travelers Inc. Co., Hartford, Conn., 1970-80, v.p., 1980— . Editor, publisher MBS News Bull., 1976— . Pres., Greater Middletown Preservation Trust, Conn., 1981, trustee, 1978—; mem. Republican Town Com., 1981— . Served with U.S. Army, 1968-70. Mem. Am. Inst. C.P.A.s. Club: Musical Box Soc. (trustee). Home: 26 Barton Hl E Hampton CT 06247 Office: Compudyne Corporation 7249 National Dr Hanover MD 21076

ROENS, STEVEN THOMAS, music educator, dean; b. Phila., Mar. 1, 1949; s. Burt Beaudry and Jacqueline Roens; m. Cheryl Anne Clarke, Aug. 18, 1994; stepchildren: David Hart, Sarah Hart, Edward Alexander Hart, Isaac Hart. BA, Swarthmore Coll., Pa., 1971; MFA, Brandeis U., Mass., 1977; DMA, Columbia U., N.Y.C., 1986. Vis. asst. prof. music Wellesley Coll., Mass., 1986—90; assoc. prof. music U. of UT, Salt Lake City, 1990—, assoc. dean, 1998—. Composer: (musical compositions) Time and Again (Commn. from Stony Brook Contemporary Chamber Players), (musical composition) Delicate Arch, In the Night Fields, 1977, Invocation, (piano solo) starry skies, 1978, quartet for clarinet, violin, cello and piano. Mem. League of Composers Internat. Soc. for Contemporary Music, N.Y.C., 1983—86. Fellow, MacDowell Colony, 1987. Mem.: Soc. of Composers. Democrat. Avocations: astronomy, photography, hiking. Office: U of UT Sch of Music 1375 E Presidents Cir Salt Lake City UT 84112 Personal E-mail: steve.roens@music.utah.edu.

ROER, ROBERT DAVID, physiologist, educator; b. NYC, Oct. 15, 1952; s. Edwin Marvin and Dorothy Barbara (Blaymore) R.; m. Marjorie Elizabeth Smith, May 29, 1976; 1 child, Sara Elizabeth. BS, Brown U., 1974; PhD, Duke U., 1979. Asst. prof. U. N.C., Wilmington, 1979-85, assoc. prof., 1985-90, prof., 1990—, dean Grad. Sch., 2002—. Contbr. articles to various jours. and publs. Grantee NSF, NASA, N.C. Biotech. Ctr., N.C. Sea Grant. Mem. AAUP, Am. Physiol. Soc., Soc. Integrative & Comparative Biology, Crustacean Soc., Sigma Xi, Phi Kappa Phi. Office: Univ North Carolina 601 S College Rd Wilmington NC 28403-5955 Office Phone: 910-962-4117. Business E-Mail: roer@uncw.edu.

ROES, NICHOLAS A. communications executive; b. Jersey City, Dec. 26, 1952; s. Nicholas R. and Mimi (Maresca) R.; m. Nancy Bennett. BS in Edn., U. Bridgeport, 1974, MA in Bus. and Pub. Mgmt., 1983; PhD in Addictions Treatment, Westbrook U., 1997. Credentialed substance abuse counselor NY, credentialed alcohol and substance abuse counselor, credentialed justice counselor, registered addiction specialist. Chmn. bd. Tchr. Update, Inc., Saddle River, N.J., 1976—; pres., cons., author Nicholas A. Roes & Assocs., Saddle River, 1979—; mng. ptnr. Barryville (N.Y.) Investors, 1985—; exec. dir. New Hope Manor, residential substance abuse treatment ctr. for women, Barryville, N.Y., 1992—. Dir. NAR Prodns., 1987, Idea Group, Inc., 1986—; instr. Marist Coll., Poughkeepsie, N.Y., 1989—. Author: Helping Children Watch TV, 1978, rev., 1992, America's Lowest Cost College, 1977, 10th edit., 1997, Gambling for Fun, 1988, Pick Your Own, 1989, Solutions for The Treatment Resistant Addicted Client, 2002; editor (newsletter) Tchr. U pdate, 1977; columnist The Investment Column, 1980—, Addiction Profl. Mag., 2003—. Exec. dir. New Hope Manor, Barryville, 1992—; chair alcohol and substance abuse subcom. Sullivan County Cmty. Svcs. Bd. Recipient Cert. of Recognition, N.Y. State Office Alcohol and Substance Abuse Svcs., 2002. Mem. Internat. Assn. Fin. Planners, Direct Mail Club of N.Y., EDPRESS, C. of C., Mensa, Internat. Platform Assn. Avocation: music. Office: Nicholas A Roes & Assocs PO Box 205 Saddle River NJ 07458-0205 Personal E-mail: nickaroes@aol.com.

ROESCH, CLARENCE HENRY, banker; b. Egg Harbor City, N.J., Aug. 22, 1925; s. Joseph Aloysius and Bertha (Heumann) R.; m. Helen Regina Owens, Sept. 25, 1954; children: Kathleen Marie, Helena Patricia, Maryanne Cornelia. BBA, Rutgers U., 1949, postgrad., 1961; certificate, Am. Inst. Banking, 1961; grad., Trust Sch., Bucknell U., 1971. Cert. internal auditor, data processing auditor. Bookkeeper, teller, head teller, asst. sec., trust officer, auditor Egg Harbor Bank & Trust Co., 1949-61; bank examiner Phila. Fed. Res. Bank, 1962-65; chief auditor Am. Bank & Trust Co. of Pa. (name changed to Meridian Bancorp Inc. 1985), Reading, 1966-88, v.p. audit dept., 1968-88, ret. officer, 1988; parish sec. St. Benedict Ch., Plowville, 1989-99; sr. staff auditor Nat. Penn Bank, Boyertown, 1990-97. Census enumerator, 2000; mem. faculty Berks County chpt. Am. Inst. Banking, 1966-68; instr. bank auditing Bank Adminstrn. Inst., U. Richmond, 1968; pres., past mems. chpt. Am. Banking Inst., Atlantic County, N.J., 1958-59. Budget com. Berks County chpt. United Way, 1967-73; bd. dirs. Berks Reading Coun. Camp Fire, 1966-93, chmn. fin. com., 1973, 75, treas., 1974-84; instr. 55 Alive Program AARP, 1989-93. Recipient John Johnston award as outstanding banker N.J., 1955; award U.S. Savs. Bond Com., 1961; Luther Halsey Gulick award for vol. services Camp Fire, 1975; John C. Collier award for outstanding bus. and fin. services, 1981, Blue Ribbon award for vol. services Camp Fire, 1984, award for corp. vol. of yr. Meridian Bancorp Inc., 1984, 85, Outstanding Svc. in Fin. Mgmt. award Camp Fire, 1988. Mem. Inst. Internal Auditors (dir. ctrl. Pa. chpt.), Berks County Bankers Assn., Travelers Protective Assn., Berks Reading C. of C., Bank Administration Inst. (past pres., dir. Penn-Jersey chpt.), Spring Lawn Optimist Club (bd. dirs. 1992, Key Mem. award 1992, chmn. fin. and budget com. 1992-94), St. BEnedict Ch. Prime Timers Srs. Home: 6-E Doral Dr Reading PA 19607-3379

ROESCH, ROBERT EUGENE, dentist; b. July 10, 1951; s. Wilber H. and Vivian (Reese) R.; m. Susan M. Tuttle, Aug. 25, 1973. BA, Midland Luth. Coll., 1973; DDS, U. Nebr., 1976. Pvt. practice, Fremont, Nebr., 1979—; mem. bd. Three Rivers Pub. Health Dept., 2002—. Dental cons. Dodge County Am. Cancer Soc., Fremont, 1984—98. Campaign chmn. Fremont United Way, 1987, v.p., 1988; mem. orgn. com. Main St. Fremont, 1995—, chmn. orgn. com., 1998—2000, 2nd v.p., 1998, 1st v.p., 1999; pres. Sinai Luth. Ch. Coun., Fremont, 1983—84, bd. dirs., 1987—90; mem. endowment com. Sinai Luth. Ch., 1990—94; bd. dirs. Main St. Fremont, 1997—. Master: Acad. Gen. Dentistry (v.p. region 10 1990—91, dir. 1991—93, trustee 1993—94, budget and fin. com. 1994—99, 1997, 1998, 1999, spkr. to house 1999—); fellow: Pierre Fauchard Acad., Am. Coll. Dentistry, Internat. Acad. Dentistry, Internat. Coll. Dentistry; mem.: ADA (del. 2002, alt. del. 2000, 2001, 2003), Acad. Gen. Dentistry, Fremont Indsl. Found., Fremont C. of C. (diplomate 1985—94, vice-chmn. memberships and membership svcs. 1989—90, bd. dirs. 1991—94, vice-chmn. pub. affairs 1992—94), Fremont Wellness Coun. (bd. dirs. 1996—98), Omaha Dist. Dental Soc. (bd. dirs.), Am. Equilibration Soc., Am. Assn. Functional Orthodontists, Am. Orthodontic Soc., Nebr. Dental Assn. (v.p. 2000—02, pres.-elect 2001, pres. 2002), Nebr. Acad. Gen. Dentistry (pub. info. officer 1983—85, sec., treas. 1985—88, pres.-elect 1988—89, pres. 1990—92, exec. dir. 1992—94, cont. edn. chmn. 1994—, legis. chmn. 1997—), Acad. Operative Dentistry, Midland Coll. Alumni (bd. dirs. 1981—87, pres. 1983—84), Dodge County Hist. Soc., Salmon Soc., Fremont Tennis Assn., Fremont Cmty. Players, R.V. Tucker Nebr. Study Club, Tri Valley Dental Study Club (sec.-treas. 1983, v.p. 1984, pres. 1985, v.p. 1989), Midland Luth. Coll. Boosters Club (bd. dirs. 1988—94), Main St. Ambs. (co-chmn. 1997—98, chmn. 1998—2000, pres. 2000), Optimists (bd. dirs. 1981—83, 1984—88, pres. 1987, bd. dirs. Fremont club 1991—93), Am. Legion. Avocations: tennis, travel. Home: 2137 Nye Dr Fremont NE 68025-2210 Office: 553 N Broad St Fremont NE 68025-4930 E-mail: broesch@agd.org.

ROESCH, ROBERTA, writer; d. William A. and Elvira L. Fleming; m. Philip K. Roesch, Aug. 21, 1943 (dec. 2000); children: Jeffrey, Bonnie, Meredith. AA, Centenary Coll., NJ, 1939, D (hon.) in Humane Letter, 1978. Columnist King Features Syndicate, NY, 1961—71; editor Pageant Mag., Conn., 1971—73; freelance writer, 1973—; tchr. Rockland CC, NY, 1975—93, Bergen CC, NJ, 1975—93, Long Ridge Writers Group, NY, 1995—. Author: (book) The Encyclopedia of Depression, 2d edit., 2001, How to be Organized in Spite of Yourself, Time Management for Busy People, The Working Woman's Guide to Managing Time, Smart Talk, You Can Make It Without a College Degree, Women in Action, Money, Jobs, and Futures, There's a Right Job for Every Woman, Anyone's Son, others; contbr. articles to profl. jours. Trustee Westwood Pub. Libr., Westwood, NJ, 1990—; com. mem. Hillsdale United Methodist Ch., Hillsdale, NJ, 1990—. Recipient Journalism award, NJ Libr. Assn., Book and Column awards, NJ Press Women. Mem.: Author's League, Am. Soc. Journalists and Authors. Home: 131 Prospect Ave Westwood NJ 07675

ROESCHEN, MARLENE Y. retired elementary school educator; b. Racine, Wis., Jan. 14, 1948; d. Harold Wilbert and May Leeanna Hertzberger; m. Marc Steven Slomski, Dec. 2, 1966 (dec. May 1974); 1 child, Kim Yvonne Mikulance; m. Terrence Walter Roeschen, Jan. 24, 1981; adopted children: Steven, Andrew, Vaughn, Justin. BA in Elem. Edn., Carthage Coll., 1981; M, Nat. Louis U., 1991. Elem. tchr. Racine Unified Sch., Wis., Paradise Valley Sch., Phoenix. Author: (book of poetry) Remnants of Reflection and Reality, 2002; contbr. Mem.: Internat. Soc. Poets (Poet of Merit 2001, 2002, Best Poet & Poems 2003). Pentecoastal. Avocations: gardening, poetry. Home: N6045 Johnson Rd Burlington WI 53105

ROESER, THOMAS FRANCIS, columnist, commentator; b. Evanston, Ill., July 23, 1928; s. Harold Nicholas Roeser and Frances Catherine Cleary; m. Lillian Kathleen Prescott, Oct. 10, 1959; children: Thomas F. Jr., Mary Catherine, Michael J., Jeanne Marie. BA in English, St. John's U., 1950. Asst. to rep. Albert Quie and rep. Walter Judd U.S. Capitol, Washington, 1958-60; asst. to gov. of Minn. St. Paul, 1960-63; v.p. The Quaker Oats Co., Chgo., 1964-91; asst. sec. of commerce U.S. Commerce Dept., Washington, 1969—; dir. pub. affairs U.S. Peace Corps, Washington, 1970; pres. Thomas F. Roeser & Assocs., Chgo., 1991—. Op-ed columnist Chicago Tribune, 1995-97, Chicago Sun Times, 1997—; dist. prof. pub. policy Roosevelt U., Chgo., 2000; radio talk show host WLS-AM. Author: Father Mac, The Life and Times of Ignatius McDermott, Co-Founder of Chicago's Famed Haymarket Center, 2002. Chmn. Cath. Citizens Ill., Chgo., 1996—, City Club Chgo., 1996—. Kennedy fellow Harvard U., Cambridge, 1977, Woodrow Wilson Internat. fellow, Princeton, N.J., 1979-80, Sr. fellow Heartland Inst., Chgo. Mem. Better Govt. Assn. (bd. dirs. 1980—), Chgo. Athletic Assn., Skyline Club. Republican. Roman Catholic. Office: Thomas F Roeser & Assocs 333 N Michigan Ave Ste 932 Chicago IL 60601-3907

ROESLER, JOHN BRUCE, lawyer; b. Portland, Oreg., Oct. 9, 1943; s. Bruce Emil and Charlotte Amanda (Naess) R.; m. Kathryne Elise Nilsen, Aug. 14, 1965; children: Paul, Mark, Nico. BA, U. Kans., 1966, JD, 1971. Bar: Mo. 1971, N.Mex. 1979, Colo. 1998, U.S. Dist. Ct. (we. dist.) Mo. 1971, U.S. Dist. Ct. N.Mex. 1979, U.S. Dist. Ct. Colo. 1998. U.S. Ct. Appeals (10th cir.) 1979, U.S. Ct. Appeals (5th cir.) 1988, U.S. Ct. Appeals (4th cir.) 1992, U.S. Supreme Ct. 1987. Assoc. The Gage Firm, Kansas City, Mo., 1971-74; civil rights advocate State of N.Mex. Human Rights, Santa Fe, 1977-78; law clk. Hon. Edwin L. Felter N.Mex. Supreme Ct., Santa Fe, 1978-79; asst. dist. atty. Taos (N.Mex.) Dist. Atty.'s Office, 1979-80; asst. spl. pros. Santa Fe Dist. Atty.'s Office, 1980-82; pvt. practice Santa Fe, 1982-97; of counsel Roth, Van Amberg, Gross, Rogers & Ortiz, 1991-94; spl. asst. atty. gen. Colo. Atty. Gen's Office, 1997-99; assoc. Jones & Keller, Denver, 1999-2000; pvt. prac. Denver, 2000—. Instr. John Marshall Law Sch., Chgo., summer, 1974; spkr. edn. law and civil rights issues U. Miami Law Sch., 2000, Nat. Com. for Prevention of Child Abuse, Chgo., 1989, Little Rock, 90, Lorman Educators Svcs., 2004. Author: (books) How To Find the Best Lawyers; In Harm's Way: Is Your Child Safe in School, Beyond Special Education and the IDEA; mem. law rev. U. Kans. Sch. Law, 1970-71; contbr. articles to profl. jours. and Am. Jour. treatise. Mem. Colo. Bar Assn., Denver Bar Assn., Colo. Trial Lawyers Assn. Democrat. Roman Catholic. Avocations: skiing, hiking, gardening. Home: 2571 S Sherman St Denver CO 80210-5725 Office: 303 E 17th Ave Ste 200 Denver CO 80203 Office Phone: 303-832-1282. E-mail: jroesler@lawyer.com.

ROESLER, ROBERT HARRY, media consultant; b. Hammond, La., Oct. 5, 1927; s. Albert N. and Hilda (Schwartz) R.; m. Cloe Alferez, May 7, 1955; children: Kim, Bob, Toby. Student, Tulane U. Mem. sports staff Times Picayune, New Orleans, 1949-94, sports editor, 1964-80; exec. sports editor Times Picayune and States-Item, 1980-94; sports coord. New Orleans Met. Conv. and Visitors Bur., 1994—; CEO Roesler Media Cons. Chmn. faculty coun., Student Publs. Bd., U. New Orleans, 1998-2001. Author: Fair Grounds: Big Shots and Long Shots, 1998. Vice-chmn. Navy Recruiting Dist.; mem. assistance coun., New Orleans, 1992-96. With USN, WWII, Korean conflict. Mem. Profl. Football Writers Assn. Am. (pres. 1976-77, PFWA McCAnn Meml. award NFL Hall of Fame, 1997), Nat. Turf Writers Assn., Football Writers Am., Am. Legion, Navy League U.S., New Orleans Press Club (pres. 1959-60, sports writing awards). Home: 6958 Colbert St New Orleans LA 70124-2334 Office: 2020 St Charles Ave New Orleans LA 70130 Office Phone: 504-288-0403. Personal E-mail: roesler@cox.net.

ROESLER, THOMAS ALLEN, psychiatrist, researcher; b. Seattle, June 23, 1945; s. William Pascoe Roesler and V. Betty Simonsen; m. Carole A. Jenny, Mar. 16, 1974; children: Laura Alice, Amelia Martha Burke. BA, Whitman Coll., 1967; MD, U. Wash., 1972; MA (hon.), Brown U. Diplomate Am. Bd. Psychiatry and Neurology. Intern psychiatry and medicine Phila. Gen. Hosp., 1972—73; resident in psychiatry Hosp. U. Pa., 1972—74; fellow child psychiatry Phila. Child Guidance Clinic, 1974—76; pvt. practice Seattle, 1976—90; clin. faculty U. Wash. Sch. Medicine, Seattle, 1976—90; chmn., dept. psychiatry Providence Med. Ctr., Seattle, 1988—90; consulting psychiatrist C. Henry Kempe Nat. Ctr. Prevention and Treatment of Child Abuse and Neglect, Denver, 1990—92; asst. prof. child psychiatry U. Colo. Sch. Medicine, Denver, 1990—96; staff psychiatrist Nat. Jewish Ctr. Immunology and Respiratory Medicine, Denver, 1992—96, Hasbro Children's Hosp., RI Hosp., and Emma Pemberton Bradley Hosp., Providence, 1996—; dir., Hasbro partial hosp. program Hasbro Children's Hosp., Providence, 1998—; assoc. prof. psychiatry and human behavior Brown Med. Sch., Providence, 2000—. Author: (jour. articles) Jour. AMA, Jour. Am. Acad. Child and Adolescent Psychiatry, Pediat., Child Abuse and Neglect, Families Sys. and Health. Recipient Intern of the Yr., Phila. Gen. Hosp., 1973. Mem.: Helfer Soc., Am. Acad. Child and Adolescent Psychiatry, Am. Psychiat. Assn. Office: RI Hosp 593 Eddy St Providence RI 02903 Office Phone: 401-444-8638. Office Fax: 401-444-2085. E-mail: troesler@lifespan.org.

ROESNER, LARRY AUGUST, civil engineer; b. Denver, Mar. 14, 1941; s. Walter George and Sarah Jane (Merrick) R.; m. Kathleen Ann Fahrenbruch, Dec. 13, 1964; children: David John, Kevin Walter, Nathan August, Melissa Jane. BS, Valparaiso (Ind.) U., 1963; MS, Colo. State U., 1965; PhD, U. Wash., Seattle, 1969. Registered profl. engr., Calif., Colo. From assoc. engr. to prin. engr. Water Resources Engrs., Inc., Walnut Creek, Calif., 1968-77; from assoc. to v.p. Camp Dresser & McKee Inc., Annandale, Va., 1977-85, sr. v.p., dir. water resources Maitland, Fla., 1985-92, chief tech. officer, 1992-98; dean Camp Dresser & McKee Corp. U., 1998-99; Harold H. Short prof. urban water infrastructure systems Colo. State U., Ft. Collins, 1999—, interim head dept. civil engring., 2000. Guest lectr., cons. urban hydrology and surface water quality; NRC exec. com. Wastewater Mgmt. in Urban Coastal Areas, 1992; chair Engring. Found. Conf. Stormwater Mgmt.-Sustainable Urban Water Resources in the 21st Century, 1997, NRC study panel Oil in the Sea, 2001; urban wet weather adv. Water Environ. Rsch. Found.; U.S. del. to joint IHR/IWA com. on urban drainage, 2002. Contbr. articles to profl. jours. Recipient Water Resource Planning and Mgmt. Divsn. Svc. to the Profession award 1999. Fellow ASCE (chmn. 1995 water resources planning and mgmt. divsn. splty. conf., nat. Walter L. Huber civil engring. rsch. prize 1975); mem. NAE, Am. Acad. Environ. Engrs. (diplomate), Am. Water Resources Assn., Water Environ. Fedn. (chmn. urban quality runoff task force 1998), Tau Beta Pi (eminent engr.). Republican. Lutheran. Achievements include development of mathematical models for U.S. government agencies including QUAL-II stream quality model for the EPA; an urban stormwater management model, the dynamic hydraulics model SWMMEXTRAN for storm drainage and sewer systems. Home: 5926 Huntington Hills Dr Fort Collins CO 80525-7118 Office: Colo State U Dept Civil Engring Fort Collins CO 80523-1372 Business E-Mail: larry.roesner@engr.colostate.edu. *An environmental engineer is a caretaker in God's garden, the earth. The challenge for the environmental engineer is to maintain a balance between the needs of people and those of nature so that we may both use and enjoy the garden. It is the responsibility of the environmental engineer to leave the garden a little nicer than he found it.*

ROESNER, PETER LOWELL, manufacturing executive; b. Winchester, Ind., July 3, 1937; s. Lowell LeClair and Martha Christine (Overmyer) R.; children: Peter Lowell II, David Brandon, John Franklin. Student, Durham (Eng.) U., 1957-58; BA, DePauw U., 1959; JD, U. Mich., 1962; MBA, Harvard U., 1964. Bar: Ind. 1962, N.J. 1992. Asst. to pres. Overmyer Corp., Muncie, Ind., 1964-65, corp. sec., 1965-69, pres., 1969-84, also dir.; pres. Clinitemp Inc., Indpls., 1985-88; pres., owner Middletown (N.J.) Interiors Inc., 1993—. Dir. Mchts. Nat. Bank, 1974-84 Trustee Purdue U., 1978. Mem. Ind. Mfrs. Assn. (dir. 1970-82, pres. 1975, chmn. Phoenix Award com. 1974), Glass Packaging Inst. (trustee 1981-84), ABA Episcopalian.

ROESSEL, FAITH, Indian arts and crafts administrator; Bachelor's, Ft. Lewis Coll.; JD, U. N.Mex. Bar: N.Mex., D.C. Legis. asst. to U.S. Senator Jeff Bingaman, Washington; sr. staff atty. Native Am. Rights Fund, Washington; dir. Navajo Nation, Washington Office; dep. asst. sec. Indian Affairs, Washington; staff coord. for White House Domestic Policy Coun.'s Working Group on Am. Indians ans Alaska Natives Dept. of Interior, Washington, spl. asst. to Interior Sec. Bruce Babbitt; chmn. Indian Arts and Crafts Bd., Washington. Bd. dirs. Am. Indians for Opportunity, Child Welfare League Am.; mem. adv. bd. Ariz. U. Law Sch. Mem. ABA, Fed. Bar Assn., Indian Bar Assn. Office: Indian Arts and Crafts Bd 1849 C St NW R4004 Washington DC 20240-0001

ROESSLER, CAROL ANN, state legislator; b. Madison, Wis., Jan. 16, 1948; d. John J. and Lucile E. (Kraner) Murphy; m. Paul Roessler. BS, U. Wis., Oshkosh, 1972. Dir. nutrition program for older adults County of Winnebago, Wis., 1973-82; mem. Wis. Assembly, Madison, 1983-87, Wis. Senate from 18th dist., Madison, 1987—. Instr. pre-retirement planning Fox Valley Tech. Inst., 1978-81. Home: 1506 Jackson St Oshkosh WI 54901-2942 Office: PO Box 7882 Madison WI 53707-7882 E-mail: Sen.Roessler@legis.state.wi.us.

ROESSLER, ERNEST CHRISTIAN, bank executive; b. Pitts., Apr. 7, 1941; s. Ernest George and Edna Melzena (Poor) R.; m. Constance Verne Benner, Jan 20, 1968; children: E. Christian Jr., Todd S., Victoria E. BA, Dartmouth U., 1962; MBA, Amostuck, 1963. Sr. v.p. Mellon Bank, Pitts., 1963-87; supr., chief fin. officer Lane Fin., Northbrook, Ill., 1987-88; pres., CFO Central Carolina Bank, Durham, N.C., 1988—. Pres. Life and Sci. Mus., Durham, 1992—; dir. C. of C., Durham, 1992—. Capt. Air Guard, 1963-72. Mem. Fin. Execs. Inst. (v.p. 1989, pres.), Rotary Internat. (dir.), Duquesne Club, Hope Valley Club. Republican. Presbyterian. Avocations: golf, skiing. Office: CCB Fin Corp 111 S Corcoran St Durham NC 27701-3235 Home: 173 Ascot Park Common Dr Memphis TN 38120-2380

ROESSNER, BARBARA, journalist; b. Elizabeth, N.J., Sept. 16, 1953; d. Gilbert George and Dorothy Anne (Hector) R.; m. Craig William Baggott, Jan. 20, 1982; children: Craig, Taylor, Liam, Katherine, Elizabeth. BA, Wesleyan U., 1975. Reporter, editor Meriden (Conn.) Record-Jour., 1975-78; reporter The Hartford (Conn.) Courant, 1978-81, chief polit. writer, 1981-86, columnist, 1986-90, dep. mng. editor, 1990—. Column distributed worldwide by L.A. Times-Washington Post News Svc. Recipient Best Mag. Column award Soc. Profl. Journalists, 1993, Best Mag. Feature award, 1993. Office: Hartford Courant Co 285 Broad St Hartford CT 06115-3785

ROETHE, JAMES NORTON, lawyer; b. Milw., Jan. 27, 1942; s. Arthur Frantz and Bess Irma (Norton) R.; m. Nita May Dorris, July 15, 1967; children: Melissa Dorris, Sarah Rebecca. BBA, U. Wis., Madison, 1964, JD, 1967. Bar: Wis. 1967, Calif. 1968, U.S. Dist. Ct. (we. dist.) Wis. 1967, U.S. Dist. Ct. (no. dist.) Calif. 1972, U.S. Ct. Claims 1975, U.S. Ct. Appeals (9th cir.) 1980, U.S. Dist. Ct. (ea. dist.) Calif. 1982, U.S. Dist. Ct. (ctrl. dist.) Calif. 1986), U.S. Ct. Appeals (4th cir.) 1988, U.S. Ct. Appeals (2d cir.) 1989. Assoc. Pillsbury, Madison & Sutro, San Francisco, 1971-77, ptnr., 1978-92; sr. v.p., dir. litigation Bank of Am., San Francisco, 1992-96, exec. v.p., gen. counsel, 1996-98, dep. gen. counsel, 1998-99; ptnr. Pillsbury Winthrop LLP, 2000—. Staff atty. Commn. on CIA Activities within U.S., Washington, 1975. Editor: Africa, 1967; editor-in-chief Wis. Law Rev., 1966-67. Bd. dirs. Orinda (Calif.) Assn., 1984-85, pres., 1986; mem. City of Orinda Planning Commn., 1988-94, chmn., 1990, 93; bd. dirs. Calif. Shakespeare Festival, 1993—, pres., 2001-04; bd. visitors U. Wis. Law Sch., 1994-99. Served to lt. USNR, 1967-71. Fellow Am. Bar Found.; mem. ABA, Wis. Bar Assn., Calif. Bar Assn., Bar Assn. San Francisco, Wis. Law Alumni Assn. (bd. dirs. 2000—), Orinda Country Club (pres. 2003-04), Order of Coif, Phi Kappa Phi. E-mail: jimroethe@aol.com., jn@pillsburywinthrop.com.

ROETHEL, DAVID ALBERT HILL, consultant; b. Milw., Feb. 17, 1926; s. Albert John and Elsie Margaret (Hill) R.; children: Elizabeth Jane, Susan Margaret. BS, Marquette U., 1950, MS, 1952; cert., Oak Ridge Sch. Reactor Tech., 1953. Chem. engr. naval reactors br. AEC, Washington, 1952-57; mgr. profl. relations, asst. to exec. sec. Am. Chem. Soc., Washington, 1957-72; exec. dir. Nat. Registry in Clin. Chemistry, Washington, 1967-72, Am. Assn. Clin. Chemists, Washington, 1968-70, Am. Acad. Orthotists and Prosthetists, Am. Bd. Cert. in Orthotics and Prosthetics, 1973-76, Am. Orthotic and Prosthetic Assn., 1973-76, Am. Orthotic and Prosthetists Assn. Found., 1975—76; exec. dir., fellow Am. Inst. Chemists, Washington, 1977-90, bd. dirs., exec. com., 1981-90, exec. dir. Nat. Certification Commn. in Chemistry and Chem. Engring., 1977-90, exec. dir., trustee Am. Inst. Chemists Found., 1982-90, sec., 1990; pres. Peachtree Promotions, 1991—; dir. Chemical Heritage Found., 1992-98; v.p., treas. Cons. Consortium, 1994-98, pres., 1998-2000, bd. dirs., 1992—2003. Sec., vice chmn., then chmn. Intersoc. Com. on Health Lab. Svcs., 1966-72; v.p. Pensions for Profls., Inc., Washington, 1970-72; vice chmn., then chmn. Engrs. and Scientists Joint Commn. on Pensions, 1978-80, vice chmn., 1985-87, chmn., 1988-90, 94-95, sec., 1996-97; mem. Commn. Profls. in Sci. and Tech., 1978-96, sec.-treas., 1979-82, bd. dirs., 1989-96, v.p., 1990-91, exec. com., 1990-93, 95; sec. gen. 7th Internat. Congress in Orthotics and Prosthetics, 1975-76, 2d World Congress in Prosthetics and Orthotics, 1975-77; exec. dir. Am. Orthotic and Prosthetic Assn. Found., 1975-76; chmn. U.S. arrangements Can.-Am. Chem. Congress, 1982-84; bd. dirs. China-U.S. Sci. Exchanges, 1985-89. Editor: Almanac, 1973-76, Chemist, 1977-90. Mem. Md. Gov.'s Com. on Sci. Devel., 1969; bd. dirs. Episcopal Ctr. for Children, 1991-97, sec., 1992-93, pres., 1993-95; mem. Episcopal Sr. Ministries Coun., 2002—. Served with U.S. Army Air Corps, 1944-46, CBI. Recipient Outstanding Svc. award Intersoc. Com. on Health Lab. Svcs., 1972, Appreciation awards Nat. Reg. in Clin. Chemistry, 1972, Engrs. and Sci. Com. on Pensions, 1996, Stewart R. Macdonald award., Consultans Consortium, 2001. Mem.: Washington Soc. Assn. Execs. (bd. dirs. 1986—87, chair bylaws com. 1989—90, govt. affairs coun. 1999—, Md. com., Profl. Achievement award 1986), Washington Acad. Sci. (DCIC rep. 2000—), Chem. Soc. Washington (bd. dirs. 2000—03, treas. 2004), D.C. Inst. Chemists (sec. 1992—94, bd. dirs. 1992—, pres.-elect 1995—97, pres. 1998—99, Honor Scroll award 1999), Am. Inst. Chemists, Coun. Engring. and Sci. Soc. Execs. (bd. dirs. 1983—86), Am. Chem. Soc. (dir. fed. credit union 1967—70, pres. 1968—70), Sports Car Club Am. (local officer 1960—74, bd. dirs. 1964—67, vice chmn., sec. 1967, 1975—76, bd. dirs. 1975—77, historian 1989—), Alpha Chi Sigma Washington Prof. Chpt. (pres. 1963—65, 1995—98, sec. 1998—2003, v.p. 2004—05, bd. dirs. 1986—, newsletter editor 1998—2003), Pi Mu Epislon, Sigma Gamma Chi, Alpha Chi Sigma (pres. 1963—64, nat. dist. counselor 1964—68, nat. profl. rep. Washington chpt. 1986—). E-mail: Droethel@juno.com.

ROETHENMUND, OTTO EMIL, financial and banking executive; b. Thun, Switzerland, Sept. 1, 1928; came to U.S., 1951, naturalized, 1957; s. Franz and Berta (Dallenbach) R.; m. Ermina Grassi, May 7, 1955; children— Robert, Denise. MA, U. Neuchatel, 1948. Mgmt. trainee Kantonalbank, Bern, 1948-51; exec. trainee J. Henry Schroeder Banking and Trust Corp., N.Y.C., 1951-56; with Deak-Perera Group, N.Y.C., 1956—, vice chmn., group partner, 1962—; v.p., then sr. v.p. Deak & Co. (holding co.), 1962-74, exec. v.p., 1974-80, pres., chief exec. officer, 1980-86; pres., dir. Inter-Nation Capital Mgmt. Corp., 1986—. Lectr. internat. monetary and investment seminars. Served to lt. Swiss Army, 1948-51. Decorated knight Mil. Order Sts. Salvador and Brigitta (Sweden). Mem. Explorers Club, Met. Club (N.Y.C.), Westchester Country Club. Home: 2 Shore Rd Rye NY 10580-1031 Office: Inter-Nation Capital Mgmt Corp 230 Park Ave Rm 2600 New York NY 10169-0699 E-mail: oeratincm@aol.com.

ROETT, RIORDAN, political science educator, consultant; b. N.Y.C., Sept. 10, 1938; s. Riordan Jr. and Marion (Underwood) R. BA, Columbia U., 1959, MIA, 1962, PhD, 1968. Postdoctoral fellow Ctr. for Internat. Studies, MIT, Cambridge, Mass., 1966-67; asst. prof., assoc. prof. polit. sci. Vanderbilt U., Nashville, 1967-73; prof. polit. sci. Sch. Advanced Internat. Studies, Johns Hopkins U., Washington, 1973—. Sr. polit. analyst internat. capital markets Chase Manhattan Bank, N.Y.C., 1983-95; sr. advisor World Econ. Forum, Geneva; bd. dirs. Global Ptnrs. Income Fund, Emerging Markets Income Fund I & II, Salomon Bros. Worldwide Income Fund, Emerging Markets Floating Rate Fund, Salomon Bros. 2008 Worldwide Dollar Govt. Term Trut. Editor, co-author: Latin America, Western Europe, and the U.S.: Reevaluating the Atlantic Triangle, 1985, Mexico and the U.S.: Managing the Relationship, 1988, Paraguay: The Legacy of Personalist Politics, 1990, Mexico's External Relations in the 1990's, 1991, Political and Economic Liberalization in Mexico, 1993, The Challenge of Institutional Reform in Mexico, 1995, The Mexican Peso Crisis: International Perspectives, 1996, Brazil Under Cardoso, 1997, Mexico's Private Sector: Recent History, Future Challenges, 1998, Mercosur: Regional Integration, World Markets, 1999, Brazil: Politics in a Patrimonial Society, 5th edit. 1999, Exchange Rate Politics in Latin America, 2000, Latin America in a Changing Global Environment, 2003, Post-Stabilization Politics in Latin America, 2003. Fulbright fellow, 1962. Mem. Latin Am. Studies Assn. (v.p. 1977, pres. 1978), Coun. on Fgn. Rels., Cosmos Club, Univ. Club. Democrat. Roman Catholic. Home: 2301 Connecticut Ave NW Apt 1B Washington DC 20008-1730 Office: Johns Hopkins U SAIS 1740 Massachusetts Ave NW Washington DC 20036-1903 E-mail: rroett@jhu.edu.

ROFF, ALAN LEE, lawyer, consultant; b. Winfield, Kans., July 2, 1936; s. Roy Darlis and Mildred Marie (Goodaile) R.; m. Sonyia Ruth Anderson, Feb. 8, 1954; 1 child, Cynthia Lee Roff Edwards; m. Molly Gek Neo Tan, July 21, 1980. BA with honors and distinction, U. Kans., 1964, JD with distinction, 1966. Bar: Okla. 1967. Staff atty. Phillips Petroleum Co., Bartlesville, Okla., 1966-75, sr. atty., 1976-85, sr. counsel, 1986-94; cons. in Asia, 1995—. Mem. editl. bd. Kans. Law Rev., 1965-66. Precinct com. man Rep. Party, Lawrence, Kans., 1963-64; assoc. justice Kans. U. Chancery Club; mem. Kans. U. Young Reps. Elizabeth Reeder scholar U. Kans., 1965-66, Eldon Wallingford award, 1964-66. Mem. ABA, Okla. Bar Assn., Washington County Bar Assn., Phoenix Club (Bartlesville) (bd. dirs. 1985-86, gen. counsel 1986-91), Order of the Coif, Masons, Hon. Order Ky. Cols., Phi Alpha Delta, Pi Sigma Alpha. Mem. First Christian Ch. Avocation: travel. Home and Office: 2247 Mountain Dr Bartlesville OK 74003-6954

ROFF, J(OHN) HUGH, JR., energy company executive; b. Wewoka, Okla., Oct. 27, 1931; s. Hugh and Louise Roff; m. Ann Green, Dec. 23, 1956; children— John, Charles, Andrew, Elizabeth, Jennifer AB, U. Okla., 1954, LL.B., 1955. Bar: Okla., Mo., N.Y. Law clk. to presiding justice U.S. Ct. Appeals (10th cir.), 1958; atty. Southwestern Bell Telephone Co., St. Louis, 1959-63, AT&T, N.Y.C., 1964-68; v.p., gen. atty. Long Lines, N.Y.C., 1969-73, gen. atty., 1973-74; chmn., pres., chief exec. officer United Energy Resources, Houston, 1974-86; chmn. PetroUnited Terminals Inc., Houston, 1986-98, Roff Resources LLC, Houston, 1998—. Past chmn. Cen. Houston Inc.; mem. adv. bd. Ctr. for Strategic and Internat. Studies, Washington; mem. coun. overseers Jones Sch. Bus. Adminstrn., Rice U.; trustee Baylor Coll. Medicine; past chmn. adv. bd. The Salvation Army, Houston. 1st lt. U.S. Army, 1955-58. Mem. Order of Coif, Phi Beta Kappa, Beta Theta Pi. Clubs: Houston Country, Coronado, Houstonian. Office: 333 Clay St Ste 4300 Houston TX 77002 4103 E-mail: hughroff@roffresources.com.

ROFF, WILLIAM ROBERT, history educator, writer; b. Glasgow, Scotland, May 2, 1929; arrived in U.S., 1969; s. Robert Henry William and Isabella (Anderson) R.; m. Susanne Rabbitt, Aug. 2, 1978; children: Sarah, Emily. BA, U. New Zealand, 1957, MA, 1959; PhD, Australian Nat. U., 1965. Lectr. history Monash U., Australia, 1963-66; lectr., sr. lectr. U. Malaya, Malaysia, 1966-69; assoc. prof. Columbia U., N.Y.C., 1969-73, prof., 1973-90, prof. emeritus, 1990—. Vis. prof. Yale U., 1971, L'Ecole des Hautes Etudes en Scis. Sociales, Paris, 1985; vis. fellow Australian Nat. U., 1974; hon. fellow Edinburgh U., Scotland, 1992—. Author: The Origins of Malay Nationalism, 1967, Bibliography of Malay and Arabic Periodicals, 1972, (with others) The Emergence of Modern Southeast Asia, 2004; author, editor: Kelantan: Religion, Society and Politics, 1973; editor: Islam and the Political Economy of Meaning, 1987. Guggenheim Found. fellow 1973; Rockefeller Found. fellow, 1982. Mem. Royal Asiatic Soc. (life), Assn. for Asian Studies, Asian Studies Assn. Australia, Brit. Soc. for Mid. East Studies, Mid. East Studies Assn. Avocation: parenting. Home: 29 Shore St Cellardyke Fife KY10 3BT Scotland E-mail: williamroff@compuserve.com

ROFFÉ, SARINA, public relations executive; b. Bklyn., Feb. 16, 1955; d. Abe J. and Reneé (Salem) Missry; m. David Roffé, June 4, 1974; children: Simon, Honey, Abraham. BA in Journalism, U. Md., 1992. Reporter Gazette Newspaper, Gaithersburg, Md., 1991—93; news editor Richner Publs., Lawrence, NY, 1993—94; mng. editor Queens Tribune, 1994; interpreter of deaf Montgomery County Pub. Schs., Rockville, Md.; writer, editor freelance Bklyn.; dir. pub. affairs NYC Dept. Juvenile Justice, 1996—2002; founder, exec. dir. NY Speech Ctr., Inc., 1995—; nat. dir. comms. Jewish Nat. Fund, 2002—. Contbg. author: Choices in Deafness-A Parent's Guide, 1987, Cued Speech Resource Guide for Parents, 1993, Jewish Cooking in America, 1994; contbr. articles to profl. jours. Pres. Montgomery County Assn. Hearing Impaired Children, Silver Spring, 1981—83; fundraising v.p., treas. B'nai B'rith Women, Gaithersburg, 1975—93; dir. Magen David Sephradic Congregation Bd., Rockville, 1989—93. Named Best in the Bus., Am. Correctional Assn., 1999; recipient 1st Pl. award, Am. Sephardic Fedn., 1991. Mem.: Am. Sephardi Fedn. (bd. dirs. 2002—), Nat. Cued Speech Assn. (v.p. 1999—2002, pres. 2002—), Sephardic Voters League (v.p. 1999—), Hadassah, Jewish Women Internat., Acad. Women Achievers of the YWCA, Deadline Club. Democrat. Jewish. Avocations: Mid East cooking, Jewish genealogy. E-mail: sarinaroffe@aol.com.

ROG, JOSEPH W. engineering company executive; Chmn., pres., CEO Corrpro Cos., inc., Medina, Ohio. Office: Corrpro Cos Inc 1090 Enterprise Dr Medina OH 44256-1328

ROGAL, ANDREW L. insurance company executive; b. Pitts., Dec. 13, 1948; s. Alvin and Ann (Lawrence) R.; m. Vicki Loveness, Dec. 30, 1971; children: Erin, Lisa, Samuel. BS in Journalism, Northwestern U., Chgo., 1970; JD, U. Pitts., 1975. Law clk. Hon. Hubert I. Teitelbaum, Fed. Dist. Ct. of We. Dist. Pa., Pitts., 1975-77; jr. ptnr. Titus, Marcus & Shapira, Pitts., 1977-80; pres., chief exec. officer Hilb, Rogal and Hamilton Co. of Pitts., Inc., 1987-91, Hilb, Rogal and Hamilton Internat. Ltd., 1991—; exec. v.p. Hilb, Rogal & Hamilton Co., Glen Allen, Va., 1990—. Mem. bd. trustees Children's Hosp., Pitts., mem. investment com.; bd. dirs. Pitts. Ballet Theatre, Jewish Community Ctr., Pitts., United Jewish Fedn., Pitts., Jewish Healthcare Found., Pitts., mem. investment com., mem. distbn. com.; mem. budget and allocations com. United Jewish Fedn. of Pitts. Avocation: skiing. Office: Hilb Rogal & Hamilton Co 4951 Lake Brook Dr Ste 400 Glen Allen VA 23060-9273

ROGALSKI, EDWARD J. university administrator; b. Manville, N.J., Feb. 16, 1942; s. Joseph Stanley and Wladyslawa (Kraszewski) R.; m. Barbara Ann Bogk, June 01, 1968; children: Edward, James, Daniel, David, Christopher. BA, Parsons Coll., 1965; MA, U. Iowa, 1968, PhD, 1985; LittD (hon.), Loras Coll., 1990. Dean of men, asst. dean of students Parsons Coll., Fairfield, Iowa, 1965-67; dean of students St. Ambrose Coll., Davenport, Iowa, 1968-74, v.p. adminstrn., 1974-80, sr. v.p., 1980-86, exec. v.p., 1986-87; pres. St. Ambrose U., Davenport, 1987—. Bd. dirs., past chmn. Genesis Med. Ctr.; bd. dirs. Genesis Health Sys., Genesis Health Svcs. Found., Firstar Bank Davenport N.A.; cons. ednl. divsn. Marriott Corp., 1988—. Past vice chairperson Civil Rights Commn., Davenport, 1975; bd. dirs. Handicapped Devel. Ctr., Davenport, 1987, Jr. Achievement, 1988, Big Brothers-Big Sisters, 1988, Iowa Coll. Found., 1992—. Grantee Kettering Found., 1968. Mem. Iowa Assn. Ind. Colls. and Univs. (exec. com. and past chmn., treas. 1992—), Nat. Assn. Ind. Colls. and Univs. (bd. dirs., past exec. sec.), Am. Assn. Higher Edn., Davenport One (bd. dirs. 1992, exec. com., past chair-elect), Rotary, Phi Delta Kappa. Roman Catholic. Home: 806 W Rusholme St Davenport IA 52804-1928 Office: St Ambrose U 518 W Locust St Davenport IA 52803-2898 E-mail: erogalsi@sau.edu.

ROGALSKI, LOIS ANN, speech and language pathologist; b. Bklyn. d. Louis J. and Filomena Evelyn (Maro) Giordano; m. Stephen James Rogalski, Jun e 27, 1970; children: Keri Anne, Stefan Louis, Christopher James, Rebecca Blair, Gregory Alexander. BA, Bklyn. Coll., 1968; MA, U. Mass., 1969; PhD., NYU, 1975. Lic. speech and lang. pathologist, N.Y. Speech, lang. and voice pathologist Rehab. Ctr. of So. Fairfield County, Stamford, Conn., 1969, Sch. Health Program-P.A. 481, Stamford, 1969-72, pvt. practice speech, lang. and voice pathology Scarsdale, N.Y., 1972—. Cons. Bd. Coop. Ednl. Svcs., 1976-79, Handicapped Program for Preschoolers for Alcott Montessori Sch., Ardsley, N.Y., 1978—; rsch. methodologist Burke Rehab. Ctr., 1977. Mem. profl. adv. bd. Found. for Children with Learning Disabilities, 1978—; bd. dirs. United Way of Scarsdale-Edgemont, 1988-89; instr. religious instr. CCD Immaculate Heart of Mary Ch., Scarsdale, 1991—; bd. dirs. Scarsdale Teen Ctr., Inc., 1998—. Fellow Rehab. Svcs. Adminstrn., 1968-69; N.Y. Med. Coll., 1972-75. Mem. N.Y. Speech & Hearing Assn., Westchester Speech & Hearing Assn., Am. Speech, Hearing & Lang. Assn. (cert. clin. competence), Coun. for Exceptional Children, Assn. on Mental Deficiency, Am. Acad. Pvt. Practice in Speech Pathology & Audiology (bd. dirs., treas. 1983-87, pres. 1987-89), Internat. Assn. Logopedics & Phoniatrics, Sigma Alpha Eta. Office: PO Box 331H Scarsdale NY 10583-8831

ROGAN, ELEANOR GROENIGER, cancer researcher, educator; b. Nov. 25, 1942; d. Louis Martin and Esther (Levinson) G.; m. William John Robert Rogan, June 12, 1965 (div. 1970); 1 child, Elizabeth Rebecca. AB, Mt. Holyoke Coll., 1963; PhD, Johns Hopkins U., 1968. Lectr. Goucher Coll., Towson, Md., 1968-69; rsch. assoc. U. Tenn., Knoxville, 1969-73, U. Nebr. Med. Ctr., Omaha, 1973-76, asst. prof., 1976-80; assoc. prof. Eppley Inst., dept. pharm. scis. U. Nebr., Omaha, 1980-90, prof. dept. pharm. scis. and dept. biochem. & molecular biol, 1990—. Contbr. articles to profl. jours. Predoctoral fellow USPHS, Johns Hopkins U., 1965-68. Mem. AAAS, Am. Assn. Cancer Rsch., Soc. Toxicology. Democrat. Roman Catholic. Home: 8210 Bowie Dr Omaha NE 68114-1526 Office: U Nebr Med Ctr Eppley Inst 986805 Nebr Med Ctr Omaha NE 68198-6805 Office Phone: 402-559-4095. Business E-Mail: egrogan@unmc.edu.

ROGAN, JAMES E. federal agency administrator, former congressman; m. Christine Apffel. BA in Polit. Sci., U. Calif., Berkeley, 1979; JD, UCLA, 1983. Past atty. Lillick McHose and Charles (now Pillsbury, Madison and Sutro), L.A.; past dep. dist. atty. L.A. County; judge Glendale (Calif.) Mcpl. Ct., 1990—93, presiding judge, 1993—94; past mem. Calif. Assembly, 1994—96, assembly majority leader, 1996; mem. U.S. Congress from 27th Calif. dist., 1996—2001; mem. house jud. com., mem. commerce com., asst. minority whip; ptnr. Venable, Baetjer, Howard & Civiletti, Washington, 2001; under sec. of commerce for intellectual property, 2001—; dir. US Patent & Trademark Office, 2001—. Adj. prof. trial advocacy Sch. Law Southwestern U.; adj. prof. criminal law Coll. Law Glendale U.; past adj. prof. criminal law Glendale C.C.; mem. Selective Svc. Sys. U.S. Govt., 1981—. Republican. Office: US Patent & Trademark Office Crystal Plaza 3 Rm 2C02 Washington DC 20231 Fax: 202-225-5828.

ROGAN, RICHARD A. lawyer; b. L.A., Sept. 6, 1950; AB with honors, Hamilton Coll., 1972; JD, U. Calif., 1975. Bar: Calif. 1975. Ptnr. Broad, Schulz, Larson & Wineberg, 1978-94, chmn., 1991-93; ptnr. Jeffer, Mangels, Butler & Marmaro, San Francisco, 1994—, mng. ptnr., San Francisco office, 2002—. Editorial assoc. Hastings Law Jour., 1974-75. Trustee Bentley Sch., 1989-92. Mem. ABA (mem. corp., banking, and bus. sect.), Bar Assn. of San Francisco (mem. comml. law and bankruptcy sect.), Calif. Receivers Forum (bd. dirs. Bay Area chpt.), Delta Sigma Rho. Office: Jeffer Mangels Butler Marmaro-JMBM 2 Embarcadero Ctr 5th Fl San Francisco CA 94111-3823

ROGAN, STEPHEN JOSEPH, software implementation consultant; b. N.Y.C., Dec. 7, 1955; s. Robert F. and Agnes (O'Connor) R.; m. Laurie E. Leblanc, May 27, 1984; children: Daniel, Julianne. BS, Fairfield (Conn.) U., 1977; MBA, Pace U., 1982. CPA, Conn.; cert. prodn. and inventory mgmt.; JAVA cert. Acctg. coord. Greenwich (Conn.) Assocs., 1978-83; br. contr. Nat. Guardian, Norwalk, Conn., 1984-85; contr. L'Amy Inc., Shelton, Conn., 1986-88, v.p. fin. and adminstrn., 1989-93; v.p. ops. Silhouette Optical, Northvale, N.J., 1994-95; cons. Price Waterhouse Coopers (formerly Coopers-Lybrand), Westport, Conn., 1996—. Coach Jr. Boys Basketball, Norwalk; asst. coach Jr. Boys Soccer and Baseball, Norwalk; usher, greeter St. Philip's Ch., Norwalk. Mem. Ednl. Soc. Resource Mgmt., Conn. Soc. CPAs (mem. tech. com.), Mensa, Intertel. Republican. Roman Catholic. Avocations: power boating, downhill skiing, travel, personal computers. Home: 27 Algonquin Rd Norwalk CT 06851-1809 Office: Price Waterhouse Coopers 300 Atlantic St Stamford CT 06901-3522

ROGATZ, PETER, retired physician; b. N.Y.C., Aug. 5, 1926; s. Julian and Sally (Levy) Rogatz; m. Marjorie Plaut, June 10, 1949; children: Peggy Joy, William Peter. BA, Columbia Coll., 1945; MD, Cornell U., 1949; M.P.H., Columbia U., 1956. Intern Lenox Hill Hosp., N.Y.C., 1949-50, resident, 1950-51, VA Hosp., Bronx, N.Y., 1951-52, N.Y. Hosp., N.Y.C., 1952-53; dep. dir. Montefiore Hosp., N.Y.C., 1960-63; dir. L.I. Jewish Med. Center, 1964-68, Univ. Hosp., SUNY, Stony Brook, 1968-71; sr. v.p. Blue Cross/Blue Shield of Greater N.Y., 1971-76; prin., founding ptnr. RMR Health and Hosp. Mgmt. Cons., Inc., Roslyn Heights, N.Y., 1976-84; v.p. med. affairs Vis. Nurse Service, N.Y., 1984-91; med. dir. Staff Builders, Inc., 1992-98. Prof. cmty. medicine SUNY, Stony Brook, 1968—94; mem. N.Y.C. Mayor's Commn. on Delivery of Health Svcs., 1967; v.p. Health and Welfare Coun. of Nassau County, 1968—72; bd. dirs. Cmty. Coun. Greater N.Y., 1974—77; mem. Task Force on N.Y.C. Crisis, 1976—81; chmn. bd. dirs. Cmty. Health Program affiliated with L.I. Jewish Med. Ctr., 1989—94; chmn. bd. dirs. Managed Health Inc., 1990—94. Author: Organized Home Medical Care in New York City, 1956; co-author (with Eli Ginzberg): Planning for Better Hospital Care, 1961; contbr. articles to profl. jours. Bd. dirs. Choice in Dying, 1994—2000, Compassion in Dying of N.Y., 1998—. Recipient Dean Conley award, Am. Coll. Hosp. Adminstrs., 1975; fellow, Commonwealth Fund, 1955. Fellow: ACP, Am. Coll. Preventive Medicine, N.Y. Acad. Medicine, APHA; mem.: N.Y. County Med. Soc., N.Y. State Med. Soc., N.Y. Pub. Health Assn., Am. Hosp. Assn., AMA. Home and Office: 76 Oakdale Ln Roslyn Heights NY 11577-1535 Personal E-mail: rogatz2@aol.com.

ROGEL, EDWARD P. corporate human resources executive; BA in Psychology, Ctrl. Wash. U., 1969. Employee rels. supr. Pulp and Wood Products Weyerhaeuser Co., Everett, Wash., 1969—, area pers. supr. for No. Wash. Region, regional pers. mgr. for S.W. Oreg., pers. mgr. ops., corp. pers., 1970—78, exec. devel. and succession planning mgr. for corp. pers., 1978—86, dir. human resources for Forest Products Co., 1986—88, v.p. human resources Fores Products Co. Timberlands, 1988—94, v.p. human resources and total quality, 1994—2000, v.p. human resources ops., 2000—03, sr. v.p. human resources, 2003—. Mem. MacMillan Bloedel Transition Team for Timberlands and Wood Products, Willamette and Trus Joist Integration Teams, Culture Change Project Weyerhaeuser Co. Co-chmn. facilities fundraiser campaign for Pierce County Jr. Achievement New Experience; bd. chmn. Pierce County Jr. Achievement; mem. conf. bd. Performance Improvement Coun. Recipient Leadership award, Jr. Achievement, 1998. Mem.: Human Resource Planning Soc. (treas., exec. com., past co-chair corp. sponsors), Performance Mfrs. Alliance. Office: Weyerhaeuser Co 33553 Weyerhaeuser Way S Federal Way WA 98063-9777

ROGEL, STEVEN R. forest products company executive; BS in Chem. Engring., U. Wash., 1965. With St. Regis Paper Co., 1965—70; asst. mgr. St. Anne-Nackawic Pulp and Paper, Nackawic, Canada, 1970—72; tech. dir. Willamette Industries, Inc., Albany, Oreg., 1972—95, pres., CEO, 1995—97, Weyerhaeuser Co., Tacoma, 1997—, chmn., 1999—. Bd. dirs. Kroger Co. Trustee Pacific U.; bd. dirs. Pacific Harbors coun. Boy Scouts Am. Mem.: Am. Forest and Paper Assn. (bd. dirs.). Office: 33663 Weyerhaeuser Way S Federal Way WA 98003-9620*

ROGENESS, MARY SPEER, state legislator; b. Kansas City, Kans., May 18, 1941; d. Frederic A. and Jeannette (Hybskmann) Speer; m. Dean Rogeness, Aug. 31, 1964; children: Emily, James, Paul. BA, Carleton Coll., 1963. Computer analyst Dept. Def., Ft. Meade, Md., 1963-66; freelance writer, editor Longmeadow, Mass., 1982-91; mem. Mass. Ho. of Reps, Boston, 1991—. Editor: Reflections of Longmeadow, 1983. Mem. Longmeadow Rep. Town Com., 1983—; bd. dirs. Goodwill Industries Hartford-Springfield, 1996—; mem. Longmeadow Sch. Com., 1982-88. Mem. Am. Legis. Exch. Coun., World Affairs Coun. of Western Mass. Office: Mass House of Reps State House Rm 124 Boston MA 02133

ROGER, JERRY LEE, academic administrator; b. Chase, Kans., Mar. 11, 1945; s. LeRoy J. and Lottie E. (Maphet) R.; m. Tucky Saint Roger, 1995. BS, U. Tulsa, 1966, MA, 1969, EdD, 1975. Cert. tchr., supt., Okla. Math. tchr. Kansas City (Mo.) Pub. Schs., 1966-67, Shawnee Mission (Kans.) Pub. Schs., 1967-71; rsch. asst. Tulsa Pub. Schs., 1972-73, rsch. coord., 1973-81, adminstrv. asst., 1981-90, rsch. dir., 1990-95, dir. planning and assessment, 1995-2000; chmn. U. Phoenix Sch. Gen. Studies, Tulsa, 2000; dir. acad. affairs U. Phoenix, Tulsa, 2001—. Adj. instr. Tulsa Jr. Coll., 1975-88; adj. asst. prof. U. Tulsa, 1980-85; sr. faculty U. Phoenix, Tulsa campus, 1998-2000. Contbr. book revs. to Tulsa Sunday World, 1990-92. Paul Harris fellow; Rotary benefactor. Mem. NEA, Am. Ednl. Res. Assn., Nat. Book Critics Cir., Nature Conservancy, Nat. Conf. for Cmty. and Justice, Phi Delta Kappa. Home: 3504 N Narcissus Ave Broken Arrow OK 74012 Office: U Phoenix 10810 E 45th St Tulsa OK 74146-3818 E-mail: Jerry.Roger@phoenix.edu.

ROGERS, AILENE KANE, retired secondary school educator; b. Jamaica, N.Y., Jan. 17, 1938; d. Daniel H. and Helen (Shirkey) Kane; m. Edward Lee Rogers, Nov. 18, 1961 (dec. Mar. 1998); children: Ruth, John, Helen, Daniel (dec.). BA, Middlebury Coll., 1959; MS in Biology, Am. U., 1963; MS in Environ. Biology, George Mason U., 1998. Asst. dir. program Student Conservation Assn., Charlestown, N.H., 1959-60, dir., 1960; tchg. asst. Am. U., Washington, 1961-62; naturalist Nat. Park Svc., 1966-68; tchr. sci. Hauppauge (N.Y.) Middle Sch., 1972-73, Oak Grove Coburn Sch., Vassalboro, Maine, 1974-75, head sci. dept., 1976-79; tchr. sci. lower sch. Nat. Cathedral Sch., Washington, 1979-82, tchr. sci. upper sch., 1982-2000, head sci. dept., 1989-93, 94-95; ret., 2000; educator Marine Program Cornell Coop. Ext. Suffolk County, 2003—. Counselor Sci. Camp, The Potomac Sch., McLean, Va., 1982—88, dir., 1986—88, co-dir., 1991; cons. Nat. Geographic Soc. Edn. Programs, 1982—92, Greenhouse Crisis Found., 1991; tchr., cons. Nat. Assn. Biology Tchrs., 1993; lectr. Young Assn. Program Smithsonian Inst., Jan., Feb., 1988, 89. Founder Setauket Environ. Ctr., 1970, bd. govs., 1970-72; bd. dirs. Student Conservation Program, 1970-79; cons. Sch. Wide Environ. Edn. Program, N.Y.C., 1978, Population Reference Bur., 1995; chmn. Pittston (Maine) Conservation Commn., 1975-78; co-pres. McLean High Sch. Student-Parent-Tchr. Assn., 1982-84; mem. State Team D.C., Mid-Atlantic Consortium Math. and Sci. Edn.-Dwight D. Eisenhower Nat. Program Math. and Sci. Edn., 1989-94; facilitator Com. for Math. and Sci., Washington, 1993-95; marine sci. tchr. Oceans Program Phillips Acad., Andover, Mass., 1996. Chopinsky fellow for Ukrainian Ednl. Exch., 1994; NSF grantee, 1962. Mem. Nat. Parks and Conservation Assn., Student Conservation Assn., Nature Conservancy (dir. Maine chpt. 1976-78). Home: 91 Little Neck Rd Centerport NY 11721-1615 Office Phone: 631-854-5533 22. Business E-Mail: ar295@cornell.edu. E-mail: akrogers@optonline.net.

ROGERS, ALAN VICTOR, former career officer; b. Hannibal, Mo., Nov. 13, 1942; s. Julian Alan and Gladys Cuneo R.; m. Linda Rae Peterson, May 8, 1966; children: Kimberly Rae, Krista Anne, Peter Alan. BS in Mil. Sci., USAF Acad., 1964; MBA with distinction, Harvard Bus. Sch., 1972; grad. with distinction, Air War Coll., 1980. Commd. 2d lt. USAF, 1964, advanced through grades to maj. gen., 1989, ret., 1993; combat fighter pilot 355th Tactical Fighter Wing, Takhli, Thailand, 1966-67; jet pilot instr. Flying Tng. Wing, Williams AFB, Ariz., 1967-69; student Harvard Bus. Sch., Cambridge, Mass., 1970-72; pers. officer Cols. Group USAF Pentagon, Washington, 1972-75; student Air War Coll., Maxwell AFB, Ariz., 1980; wing comdr. 5th Bomb Wing, Minot AFB, N.D., 1982-84, 96th Bomb Wing (1st B-1 Wing), Dyess AFB, Tex., 1984-86; dir. ops. SAC, Offutt AFB, Nebr., 1986-89; asst. chief of staff ops. Supreme HQ Allied Powers Europe NATO, Mons, Belgium, 1989-91; dir. J-7 Joint Staff, Pentagon, Washington, 1991-93; assoc. Burdeshaw Assocs., Ltd., Bethesda, Md., 1993-94; prin. Gemini Consulting, Morristown, N.J., 1994-97; sr. v.p., gen. mgr. Fed. Defense Group, Am. Mgmt. Sys., Inc., Fairfax, Va., 1997—2002; sr. v.p. CACI Inc., 2003—. Mem. Active Angel Investors, Vienna, 2003—; mem. adv. bd. Infodata, Inc., 2003—; bd. dirs. RGS & Assocs., Inc. Mem., mil. adviser C. of C., Minot, N.D., 1982-84, Abilene, Tex. 1984-86; trustee The Falcon Found., Colorado Springs, 2003—. Decorated Defense Disting. Svc. Medal, Legion of Merit, D.F.C. with two oak leaf clusters, Purple Heart, Def. Superior Svc. medal, Disting. Svc. medal, Def. Disting. Svc. medal; recipient Am. U. Leadership award, 2000. Mem.: Nat. Assn. Corp. Dirs., Nat. Def. Industry Assn. (bd. dirs.), Potomac Officers Club, Daedalians (chpt. pres. 1986), Nat. Eagle Scout Assn., Red River Valley Fighter Pilots Assn., Sabre Soc., USAF Acad. Assn. Grads. (bd. dirs. 1999—), Air Force Assn. Republican. Lutheran. Avocations: skiing, travel, antiques. Home: 4600 32nd Rd N Arlington VA 22207-4406 Office Phone: 703-679-3566. E-mail: alanvrogers@aol.com.

ROGERS, ALICE LOUISE, retired bank executive, writer, researcher; b. McLoud, Okla., Feb. 18, 1929; d. John Edmond and Katy McNora (Williams) Stanka; m. Jesse Ray Rogers, Apr. 18, 1948; children: Jimmy Allen Rogers, Bonnie Kay Calhoun. Student, Am. Inst. Banking, 1967-69. Clk. typist loan dept. Security Pacific Nat. Bank, L.A., 1960-64; office mgr., adminstrv. asst. to v.p. loan adminstn. divsn. City Nat. Bank, Beverly Hills, 1964-75, credit mgr. Pershing Square branch, 1975-77. Author, editor: Dance Bands and Big Bands Reference Book and Price Guide, 1986, Dance Bands, Big Bands and Swing Reference Book and Price Guide, 1993; contbr. articles to DISCoveries mag., Internat. Assn. of Jazz Record Collectors Jour., Joslin's Jazz Jour., Dancing USA mag., Am.'s Registry of Outstanding Profls. Mem.: Big Band Acad. Am. Republican. Avocations: phonograph record collection, researching jazz and dance information, postcard collection. Home: 700 Clark St Apt 108 Deming NM 88030-4589

ROGERS, ARTHUR HAMILTON, III, lawyer; b. Florence, S.C., Apr. 19, 1945; s. Arthur Hamilton Jr. and Suzanne (Wilson) R.; m. Karen Lyn Hess, June 22, 1968; children: Sarah Elizabeth, Thomas Hess. BA, Rice U., 1967; JD, Harvard U., 1970. Bar: Tex. 1970. Assoc. Fulbright & Jaworski LLP, Houston, 1970-74; participating assoc. Fulbright & Jaworski L.L.P., Houston, 1974-77; ptnr. Fulbright & Jaworski, L.L.P., Houston, 1977—; gen. counsel Lifemark Corp., Houston, 1981-82. Sec. Mosher, Inc., Houston, 1984-97. Bd. dirs. Alley Theatre, Houston, 1990—, v.p. fin., 2001—, mem. exec. com., 2001—; bd. dirs. Autry House, 1994-97; mem. exec. com. Rice U. Fund Coun., Houston, 1993-99, vice chmn., 1996-97, chmn., 1997-98. Mem. ABA, State Bar Tex., Assn. of Rice Alumni (treas. 1995-97), Petroleum Club of Houston, The Forest Club. Episcopalian. Home: 5309 Bordley Dr Houston TX 77056-2323 Office: Fulbright & Jaworski LLP 1301 Mckinney St Fl 51 Houston TX 77010-3031 E-mail: arogers@fulbright.com.

ROGERS, BARBARA JEAN (B.J. ROGERS), writer, editor; b. Chgo, Apr. 23, 1949; d. Louis Herman and Bernice (Millunchick) Block; m. Malcolm Leland Rogers Jr., Feb. 17, 1979; children: Anna Elizabeth, Sara Randall. BA cum laude, U. Ill., 1971; MLAS, Vanderbilt U., 1999. Freelance proofreader, copy editor, author Thomas Nelson Pubs., Nashville, 1979-94; v.p. Rogers Graphics, Nashville, 1980-82; proofreader, editor Typecraft Co., Nashville, 1982-88; editor creative svcs. Vanderbilt U., 1993—. Assoc. critic STAGES, 1991—; gen. mgr. Am. Negro Playwright Theatre, Nashville, 1992-94; artistic staff asst. Tenn. Repertory Theatre, Nashville, 1990-93; cast mem., bus. mgr. So. Stage Prodns. and Tenn. Repertory Theatre, 1982, prodn. mgr., 1983, gen. mgr., 1985-86; studio booker, Soundshop, Inc., Nashville, 1977-1979; nat. traffic mgr. Sammy & Co., 1975; post-prodn. coord. Studio Seven, Inc., Chgo., 1973-75; mem. libr. staff Chgo. Hist. Soc., 1968-71. Producer, dir. Nashville Arts Hark Awards, Greater Nashville Arts Found., 1991, Hungry Ear Prodn., 1989, Dark Horse Theatre; dir. Welcome to 1998. Founding mem. Tenn. Repertory Theatre Artistic Co., 1987; co-founder, artistic dir. Nashville Early Music Ensemble; founding pres. Nashville Opera Chorus, 1989, soprano, 1989-97; house mgr., costume designer Dark Horse Theatre/Nashville Shakespeare Festival, 1990-92; costume designer Belmont U. Opera Workshop, Nashville, 1991-97, Actors' Playhouse, Nashville, 1993; box office mgr. Kingston Mines Theatre, Gill Community Arts Ctr., Unity Theatre, Chgo., 1969-75; sec. Bellevue (Tenn.) Civic Coun., 1980-81; edn. ctr. dir. Heartlands Acad. Trust, 1986-90. Mem. AFTRA (bd. dir. Nashville chpt. 1984-92), Actors' Equity Assn. Office: Vanderbilt U Creative Svcs 850 Baker Bldg 110 21st Ave S Nashville TN 37203-2416

ROGERS, BARBARA JEAN, writer, costume designer; b. Mattoon, Ill., June 3, 1947; d. Charley Clarence Chaplin and Charline Poffinbarger; m. Thomas Rogers, Jr., Oct. 4, 1986 (div.). BA, Ea. Ill. U., Charleston, 1974—78. Caregiver to elderly Helen Wright, Sullivan, Ill., 1982—86; costume designer Broadway Bazaar Costumes, Mattoon, Ill., 1988—98; author Meriwether & Red Wheel/Weiser/Conari Press, Yarnell, Ariz., 1994—. Author: (book) Costuming Made Easy, 1998, Instant Period Costumes, 2001, Mystic Glyphs, 2003, Feng Shui In A Day, 2005, (songs) Pray For Today, 2005, Simply Happy Every Day, 2005, 27 Words, 2005. Mem.: Authors Guild. Achievements include being an inspirational spkr. for twenty years; sponsoring a new writer semi-annually to attend the Maui Writers Conf.; speaking at the Nat. Costumers Nat. Assn. Conv. in 2001. Avocations: astrology, hiking, reading, Native American and Eastern mysticism, Tarot. Home: 16932 Juniper Way P.O. Box 1073 Yarnell AZ 85362

ROGERS, BENJAMIN TALBOT, former consulting engineer, solar energy consultant; b. Cleve., Oct. 4, 1920; s. Benjamin Talbot and Marie Aline (Miller) R.; m. Dale Hays, Sept. 11, 1961 (dec. Nov. 1975); children: Leslie, Phyllis. BS in Mech. Engring., U. Wis., 1944. Registered profl. engr., N.Mex., Colo., Ariz., Tex. Mech. engr. Black & Veatch, Kansas City, Mo., 1946-49; staff mem. U. Calif., Los Alamos, N.Mex., 1949-76; cons. engring. Los Alamos, N.Mex., 1949-76, Embudo, N.Mex, 1976-80, 81-2000; ret., 2000. Vis. prof. Ariz. State U., 1980-81, 84; v.p. Barkmann & Rogers Cons. Engrs., Santa Fe, N.Mex., 1964-70. One-man shows include Millicent Rogers Mus., Taos, N.Mex., 1994, Roller Mill Mus., Cleveland, N.Mex., 1995, Ariz. State U. Coll. Architecture, Tempe, 1996, First State Bank Taos, 1997 (Artist of Month 1997), Johnson Gallery, Madrid, N.Mex., 1998-99; contbr. articles to tech. and profl. jours.; 6 patents in field of optics, high speed photography and explosive tech. Commr. Rinconada Cmty. Acequia, Embudo, 1961-70; v.p. adv. bd. Embudo Presbyn. Hosp., 1972; pres. Embudo Valley Health Found., 1974. 1st lt. C.E., 1942-46. Recipient Solar Design award HUD, Dept. of Energy, Solar Energy Rsch. Inst., 1978, Peter van Dresser award N.Mex. Solar Energy Assn., 1983, Maharishi award Maharishi Found., 1984; grantee Graham Found. for Advanced Studies in Fine Arts, 1992, 95. Fellow ASHRAE; mem. ASME (life), NSPE (life), Am. Soc. Materials (life), Nat. Assn. Scholars, Celtic Confederation (founding sec. 2000-2003). Republican. Home: PO Box 2 Embudo NM 87531

ROGERS, BERNARD WILLIAM, military officer; b. Fairview, Kans., July 16, 1921; s. William Henry and Lora (Haynes) R.; m. Ann Ellen Jones, Dec. 28, 1944; children: Michael W., Diane E., Susan A. Student, Kans. State Coll., 1939-40; BS, U.S. Mil. Acad., 1943; BA (Rhodes scholar), Oxford (Eng.) U., 1950, MA, 1954, DCL (hon.), 1983; grad., Command and Gen. Staff Coll., 1954-55, Army War Coll., 1959-60; LLD, Akron U., 1978, Boston U., 1981. Commd. lt. U.S. Army, 1943, advanced through grades to gen., 1974; aide to supt. U.S. Mil. Acad., 1945-46, comdt. cadets, 1967-69; aide to high commr. Austria Gen. Mark W. Clark, 1946-47; bn. comdr. Republic of Korea, 1952; exec. to comdr.-in-chief Far East Command, 1953-54; mil. asst. to Chief Staff U.S. Army, 1956-59; exec. to chmn. (Joint Chiefs of Staff), 1962-66; asst. div. comdr. (1st Inf. Div.), Vietnam, 1966-67; comdg. gen. (5th Inf. Div.), Ft. Carson, Colo., 1969-70; chief legis. liaison Dept. Army, 1971-72, dep. chief of staff for personnel, 1972-74; comdg. gen. U.S. Army Forces Command, 1974-76; chief of staff U.S. Army, 1976-79; supreme allied comdr. Europe; comdr. in chief (U.S. European Command), 1979-87; ret. U.S. Army, 1987. Former bd. dirs. Atlantic Coun. U.S., George C. Marshall Found., Gen. Dynamics Co., Kemper Nat. Ins. Co., Thomas Industries; former sr. cons. The Coca-Cola Co.; chmn. USO World Bd. of Govs., 1988-94. Decorated DSC, Def. DSM with oak leaf cluster, DSM of Army, Navy and Air Force, Silver Star, Legion of Merit with 3 oak leaf clusters, D.F.C. with 2 oak leaf clusters, Bronze Star medal with V device; hon. fellow Univ. Coll., Oxford U.; recipient Disting. Svc. Citation U. Kans., 1984, Disting. Grad. award U.S. Mil. Acad., 1995, Assn. U.S. Army George C. Marshall medal, 1999. Mem.: VFW, Mil. Order of World Wars, Ret. Officers Assn., Assn. Am. Rhodes Scholars, Assn. U.S. Army (bd. dirs.), Soc. 1st Inf. Divsn., Am. Soc. French Legion of Honor, Alibi, Alfalfa, Army and Navy Club, The Pilgrims, Army-Navy Country Club, Phi Delta Theta. Office Phone: 703-448-0188. Personal E-mail: rogers1467@aol.com.

ROGERS, BRENDA GAYLE, educational administrator, educator, consultant; b. Atlanta, July 27, 1949; d. Claude Thomas and Louise (Williams) Todd; m. Emanuel Julius Jones Jr., Dec. 17, 1978; children: Lavelle, Brandon, Albre Jede, Briana Adanne. BA, Spelman Coll., 1970; MA, Atlanta U., 1971, EdS, 1972; PhD, Ohio State U., 1975; postgrad., Howard U., 1980, Emory U., 1986. Program devel. specialist HEW, Atlanta, 1972; rsch. assoc. Ohio State U., Columbus, 1973-75; asst. prof. spl. edn. Atlanta U., 1975-78, program adminstr., 1978—, CIT project dir., 1977-91, exec. dir. Impact project, 1992—. Tech. cons. Dept. Edn., Washington, 1978-93, 96, 97-98, cons. Head Start, 1990-91; cons. Princeton Testing Svcs., 1996—; due process regional hearing officer Ga. State Dept. Edn., Atlanta, 1978-84, adv. bd., 1980-84; regional cons. Access project, 1995—; mem. parent adv. coun. APS, 1988—; cons. program devel. Ga. Respite Care, Inc., 1988-89; mem. exec. bd., pres. PTA Stone Mountain elem. Sch., 1989-92; mem. test verification panel Edn. Testing Svcs., Princeton, N.J., 1995-96; cons. So. Assn. Colls. & Univs., 1998. Mem. Ga. Assessment Project com. Atlanta Pub. Schs. Adv. Coun., 1986—; bd. dirs. Mountain Pines Civic Assn., 1988—; mem. Grady Meml. Hosp. Cmty. Action Network, Atlanta, 1982-83; exec. bd. PTA Shadow Rock Elem. Sch., 1992-94. Recipient disting. svc. award Atlanta Bur. Pub. Safety, 1982, Mountain Sch. PTA, 1995, award Atlanta Pub. Sch. Sys., 1980, 82, 83, 89-90, Disting. Svc. award CAU, 1998; fellow Ohio State U., 1972-74, Howard U., 1980. Mem. NAFE, Assn. for Retarded Citizens, Coun. for Exceptional Children, So. Assn. Colls. and Univs. (cons. com. 1998—), Nat. Assn. Learning Disabilites, Phi Delta Kappa, Phi Lambda Theta. Democrat. Roman Catholic. Avocation: gourmet cooking. Office: Clark Atlanta U James P Brawley Atlanta GA 30314-3913 E-mail: dr.brenda.rogers@mediaone.net.

ROGERS, BRIAN DEANE, librarian; b. New London, Conn., June 26, 1937; s. Albert Nash and Janette (Loofboro) R.; m. Carol Mallett, May 18, 1962; children: Alison, Paul, Amy. BA, Alfred U., 1959; MLS, Rutgers U., 1967. Asst. registrar Salem (W. Va.) Coll., 1964-66; libr. staff Wesleyan U., Middletown, Conn., 1967-75; librarian Conn. Coll., New London, 1975-93, spl. collections libr., 1993-99. Mem. State Adv. Council on Libraries, Hartford, 1976, chair 1977; mem. library bd. Mystic Seaport Maritime Mus., Mystic, Conn., 1987-2001. Contbr. The Battery Park City Broadsheet (N.Y.C.), 1998—. Mem. accreditation teams New England Assn. Sch. & Colls., 1985-90. Served with U.S. Army, 1961-64. Mem. Eugene O'Neill Soc. (bd. dirs. 2001—). Clubs: Columbiad (Meriden, Conn.); Acorn (Hartford, Conn.). Home: 114 Library St Mystic CT 06355-2420 E-mail: bdrog@conncoll.edu.

ROGERS, BRYAN LEIGH, artist, art educator; b. Amarillo, Tex., Jan. 7, 1941; s. Bryan Austin and Virginia Leigh (Bull) R.; m. Cynthia Louise Rice; 1 child, Kyle Austin Rogers. BE, Yale U., 1963; MS, U. Calif., Berkeley, 1966, MA, 1969, PhD, 1971. Design engr. Monsanto Co., Texas City, Tex., 1962; research engr. Rocketdyne, Canoga Park, Calif., 1963-64; research scientist Lawrence Livermore (Calif.) Lab., 1966; lectr. U. Calif., Berkeley, 1972-73; fellow Akademie der Bildenden Künste, Munich, 1974-75; prof. art San Francisco State U., 1975-88; head, prof. sch. art Carnegie Mellon U., Pitts., 1988-99, dir. Studio for Creative Inquiry, 1989-99; dean, prof. Sch. of Art and Design U. Mich., Ann Arbor, 2000—. Fellow Ctr. Advanced Visual Studies MIT, Cambridge, Mass, 1981. Editor Leonardo Jour., San Francisco, 1982-85. One-man shows include: Laguna Beach (Calif.) Mus. Art, 1974, DeSaisset Art Gallery U. Santa Clara, Calif., 1974, San Francisco Mus. Modern Art, 1974, Baxter Art Gallery Calif. Inst. Tech., Pasadena, 1979, Contemporary Crafts gallery, Portland, Oreg., 1987; group exhbns. include: Berkeley (Calif.) Art Ctr., 1969, Hansen-Fuller Gallery, San Francisco, 1970, San Francisco Arts Commn. Gallery, 1984, Clocktower Gallery, N.Y.C., 1984, Otis-Parsons Gallery, L.A., 1985, P.P.O.W. Gallery, N.Y.C., 1985, 18th Internat. Bienal, São Paulo, Brazil, 1985, MIT, Cambridge, 1990, Objects Gallery, Chgo., 1992, ARTEC 93 Internat Biennale, Nagoya, Japan, 1993, Chgo. Cultural Ctr., 1993, Am. Iron and Steel Expo., Pitts., 1993, Pitts. Ctr. for Arts, 1994, Allegheny Coll. Gallery, Meadville, Pa., 1997, Aichi Art Ctr., Nagoya, Japan, 1997. Fellow NEA, Washington, 1981, 82, Deutscher Akademischer Austauschdienst, Fed. Republic of Germany, 1974, NSF, Washington, 1965-69; recipient SECA award San Francisco Mus. Modern Art, 1974. Office: Sch Art & Design Univ Michigan Ann Arbor MI 48109 Office Phone: 734-763-4093. E-mail: blrogers@umich.edu.

ROGERS, C. B. lawyer; b. Birmingham, Ala., July 10, 1930; s. Claude B. Rogers and Doris (Hinkley) Rogers Lockerman; m. Patricia Maxwell DeVoe, Dec. 22, 1962; children: Bruce Lockerman, Evelyn Best, Brian DeVoe. AB, Emory U., 1951, LL.B., 1953. Bar: Ga. 1953. Adj. prof. litigation Emory U., 1968-70; assoc., then partner firm Powell, Goldstein, Frazer & Murphy, 1954-76; partner firm Rogers & Hardin, Atlanta, 1976—. Fellow Am. Coll. Trial Lawyers; mem. Am. Law Inst., Capital City Club (Atlanta). Democrat. Episcopalian. Home: 1829 W Wesley Rd NW Atlanta GA 30327-2019 Office: Rogers & Hardin International Tower 229 Peachtree St NE Ste 2700 Atlanta GA 30303-1638 E-mail: cbr@rh-law.com.

ROGERS, CARLETON CARSON, JR., trade show and convention executive; b. Chgo., Nov. 5, 1935; s. Carleton Carson and Eleanor (Lowell) R.; m. Loretta Zirkel; children: Kirsten Anne, Mark, Brett. BS in Bus. Adminstrn., Am. U., 1957; postgrad., Northwestern U., 1957, Chgo.-Kent Coll. Law, 1957—58. Mgmt. trainee Ill. Bell Telephone Co., Chgo., 1959-61; sales mgr. Programs Internat., Chgo., 1961-64, pres., 1964-71; show mgr. Indsl. & Sci. Conf. Mgmt., Chgo., 1975-78; pres. Expo Mgmt., Inc., Chgo., 1978-82, Trade Expositions and Assoc. Mgmt. Ltd., Chgo., 1982-92, Expn. Mmgt., Inc., Elgin, 1992-99, National Show Mgmt., Inc., Elgin, 1999—. Adj. prof. Roosevelt U., Chgo. Pres. Kane County (Ill.) Young Republican Club, 1962-64; trustee Gail Borden Pub. Libr., Elgin; bd. dirs. Area C Coun. on Aging for Ill., Upper Kane County chpt. Am. Heart Assn., Chgo. Conv. and Tourism Bur.; mem. adminstrv. bd., pres. bd. trustees First United Meth. Ch., Elgin.; sec.-treas. found. pres. Ctr. for Exhbn. Industry Rsch. Mem. Internat. Assn. Exhibit Mgmt. (chmn. bd., recipient Disting. Svc. award), Masons, Shriners, Omicron Delta Kappa, Alpha Tau Omega. Home: 11n937 Almora Ter Elgin IL 60123-4805 Office: Nat Show Mgmt Inc PO Box 7084 Elgin IL 60121-7084 E-mail: expomgmt@juno.com.

ROGERS, CHARLES EDWIN, physical chemistry educator; b. Rochester, N.Y., Dec. 29, 1929; s. Charles Harold and Maybelle (Johnson) R.; m. Barbara June Depuy, June 12, 1954; children: Gregory Newton, Linda Frances, Diana Suzanne. BS in Chemistry, Syracuse U., 1954; PhD in Phys. Chemistry, SUNY at Syracuse U., 1957. Rsch. assoc. dept. chemistry Princeton U., 1957-59, Goodyear fellow, 1957-59; mem. tech. staff Bell Telephone Labs., Murray Hill, N.J., 1959-65; assoc. prof. macromolecular sci. Case Western Res. U., Cleve., 1965-74, prof., 1974-98, prof. emeritus, 1998—. Sr. vis. fellow Imperial Coll., U. London, 1971; assoc. dir. Ctr. for Adhesives Sealants Coatings, Case Western Res. U., 1984-88, dir., 1988-91; co-dir. Edison Polymer Innovation Corp., Ctr. for Adhesives, Sealants and Coatings, 1991-97; cons. to polymer and chem. industries; devel. overseas ednl. instns. Editor: Permselective Membranes, 1971, Structure and Properties of Block Copolymers, 1977; contbr. numerous articles to profl. jours.; patentee in field. Mem.: Adhesion Soc., N.Am. Membrane Soc., Am. Phys. Soc., Am. Chem. Soc. Home: 8400 Rockspring Dr Chagrin Falls OH 44023-4645 Office: Case Western Reserve U Dept Macromolecular Sc Cleveland OH 44106-7202 Office Phone: 216-368-6376. E-mail: charles.rogers@case.edu.

ROGERS, CHARLES RAY, minister, religious organization administrator; b. Grapevine, Tex., Nov. 26, 1935; s. Arlin Avery and Bessie Leone (Deaton) R.; m. Oma Fay Hines, Aug. 21, 1954; children: Sheree Gay Rogers, Charles Denne Ray, Robin Celeste Rogers Eddins. MS in Christian Edn., Faith Bible Coll., 1980, DD in Humanities (hon.), 1981; B of Theology, M of Theology, Ctrl. Am. Theol. Sem., Escuintla, Guatemala, 2000; D of Ministry in Humanities (hon.), Sem. of Theol. Missions, Escuintla, Guatemala, 1992. Pastor various Bapt. chs., Athens, Dallas, Ft. Worth, 1960-64, various interdenominational chs., Houston, Longview, 1965-69; pres. Evangelism in Action, Ft. Worth, 1969—. Bd. dirs. World Ministry Fellowship, Plano, Tex., dir. world missions, 1970—; leader Over 100 Mission, humanitarian trips Evangelism in Action, Ft. Worth, 1976—. Author: Joy, 1979, Handbook for Victorious Living, 1980, How to Develop Christian Love, 1981; vocalist (rec.) Charlie, 1981. Republican. Avocations: golf, tennis, swimming, running, computers. Home: 6417 Rogers Dr Fort Worth TX 76180-4817 Office: Evangelism in Action PO Box 820724 Fort Worth TX 76182-0724 Office Phone: 817-498-3589. E-mail: chasrog@swbell.net.

ROGERS, CHERYL LYNN, music and dance educator; b. Tyler, Tex., Sept. 14, 1949; d. Lewis Barton and Edna Elaine (Hunt) Whisenant; m. Carl Michael Rogers, May 23, 1971; children: Jennifer Leigh, Christopher Lewis. AA, Tyler Jr. Coll., 1969; B. Music Edn., North Tex. State U., 1971; MA, Stephen F. Austin State U., 1972; EdD, Texas A&M U., Commerce, 1997. Math. instr. Kilgore (Tex.) Ind. Sch. Dist., 1972-73, jr. high choral dir., 1973-75; instr. music Tyler Jr. Coll., 1975-88, dir. fine and performing arts, 1988—. Dir. Concert Chorus, Chamber Singers, Harmony and Understanding, Tyler, 1980—; adjudicator All-Region, All-Area Vocal Auditions, Tyler, 1975—. Mem. Tyler Friends of the Gifted, 1990—; social com. mem. Hollytree Country Club, Tyler, 1989-90; v.p. edn. Women's Symphony League, Tyler, 2001—; mem. adminstrv. bd. Marvin United Meth. Ch., Tyler, 1984—; yearbook commn. chmn. Kilgore Music Club, 1974-75. Grad. Teaching fellow Stephen F. Austin State U., 1971-72. Mem. Am. Choral Dirs. Assn., Tex. Music Educators Conf., Tex. Assn. Music Schs. (past pres.), Tex. Jr. Coll. Tchr. Assn., Nat. Assn. Tchrs. Singing, Tex. Choral Dirs. Assn., Young Audiences N.E. Tex. (pres.), Mortar Bd., Alpha Chi, Pi Kappa Lambda, Phi Theta Kappa, Kappa Delta Pi Edn. Honor Soc. Republican. Avocations: needlepoint, reading. Office: Tyler Jr Coll PO Box 9020 Tyler TX 75711-9020 E-mail: crog@tjc.edu.

ROGERS, CINDY L. music educator; b. Washington, Jan. 5, 1959; d. Robert C. and Joyce A. Reef; m. Terry L. Rogers, July 31, 1999; m. David Tuzson, Sept. 4, 1982 (div.); children: Andrew D. Tuzson, Daniel R. Tuzson, Matthew G. Tuzson. MusB in Piano Performance, Capital U., Columbus, Ohio, 1979; MusM in Piano Performance, Wichita State U., Wichita, Kans., 1981. Piano tchr. Rogers Piano Studio, Scottsbluff, Nebr., 2003—. Music dir. Christ the King Cath. Parish, Gering, Nebr., 1995—2003. Mem.: Nat. Guild of Piano Tchrs., Music Tchrs. Nat. Assn. Home: 240405 County Rd G Scottsbluff NE 69361 Office: Rogers Piano Studio 240405 County Rd G Scottsbluff NE 69361 Personal E-mail: clrogers99@hotmail.com. Business E-Mail: clrogers99@hotmail.com.

ROGERS, DAVID, playwright, novelist, actor; b. N.Y.C. s. George and Deborah (Samuels) Rosenberg; m. June Lois Walker, Oct. 14, 1962; children: Dulcy Dru, Amanda Brooke. Student, Am. Theatre Wing Sch., 1948, 49. Author (N.Y.C. prodns.): Ziegfeld Follies, 1957, Vintage '60, 1960, New Faces of 1962, Fun City, 1967, Charlie and Algernon, 1980 (Tony award nomination); author: (London prodns.) Jubilee Girl, 1956, Young at Heart, 1961, Flowers for Algernon, 1979, Killing Jessica, 1986; author: The Hero, 1966, opera, 1966 (winner Prix d'Italia Concorso Internat. Per Opera Radiofoniche e Televisive); author: (TV) The Carol Burnett Show, 1970; author: Oh Eden, 1974, The Bedroom Set, 1976, Somewhere There's Music, 1977, The Great American Alimony Escape, 1979, The In-Laws, 1979; actor(Broadway prodns.): Doubles, 1985,: George Abbott's Broadway, 1987, A Funny Thing Happened on the Way to the Forum, 1997, (Off Broadway): Down the Garden Paths, 2000,: internat. tour Grand Hotel, 1991, (regional theatre appearances): Players Theatre, 1992,: Birmingham Theatre, 1993, Jupiter Theatre, 1993, Great Lakes Theatre Festival, 1994, Phoenix Theatre, 1995, Denver Ctr. Theatre Co., 1996, Repertory Theatre of St. Louis, 1998, Cin. Playhouse in the Park, 1998, Westport Playhouse, 1998, San Jose Repertory Theatre, 1999 (Dean Goodman Choice award), Va. Stage Co., 2000, Fla. Studio Theatre, 2002, Two Rivers Theatre Co., 2002, Merrimack Repertory Theatre, 2003—04, (TV guest appearances): Law and Order, 2000, Law and Order: Criminal Intent, 2001, Law and Order: Special Victims Unit, 2003; writer, performer: (one-man show) Naked on Broadway, 2004. With U.S. Army, 1951—52, Korea. Mem.: AFTRA, SAG, Actors Equity, Broadcast Music Inc., Writers Guild Am. East, Dramatists Guild, Theatre Artists Workshop Westport (bd. dirs. 1985).

ROGERS, DAVID, apparel executive; With Pickwick Internat., Mpls.; pres. Wilson's The Leather Experts, Inc., Brooklyn Park, Minn., 1979—. Office: Wilsons The Leather Experts Inc 7401 Boone Ave N Brooklyn Park MN 55428-1080

ROGERS, DAVID ANTHONY, electrical engineer, educator, researcher; b. San Francisco, Dec. 21, 1939; s. Justin Anthony and Alice Jane (Vessey) R.; m. Darlene Olive Hicks, Feb. 20, 1965; 1 child, Stephen Arthur. BSEE cum laude, U. Wash., 1961, PhD in Elec. Engring., 1971; MSEE, Ill. Inst. Tech., 1964; MDiv cum laude, Trinity Evang. Div. Sch., Deerfield, Ill., 1966. Registered profl. engr., Wash. Assoc. engr. Ford Aero., Newport Beach, Calif., 1961; tech. asst. IIT Rsch. Inst., Chgo., 1963, grad. fellow, 1963-64; predoctoral lectr. U. Wash., Seattle, 1964-65, 66-71, acting asst. prof., 1971-72; asst. prof. State U. of Campinas, Brazil, 1972-77, assoc. prof., 1977-80; assoc. prof. elec. engring. N.D. State U., Fargo, 1980-86, prof.,

1986—2000, prof. elec. and computer engring., 2000—. External MS thesis examiner Poly. Sch. U. Sao Paulo, Brazil, 1974; external PhD thesis examiner Inst. Tech., Banaras Hindu U., India, 1989, 91, 95; rschr. microwaves, fiber optics, electromagnetics, profl. and rsch. ethics, tech. and soc., engring. edn.; faculty seminar (interdisciplinary, multi-cultural and internat. studies 1991-94) N.D. State U.-Bush Found.; presenter N.D. State U.-Bush Found. Industry-Ethics Inst., 1995-96. Co-author: Fiber Optics, 1984; mem. editl. rev. bd. IEEE Transactions Microwave Theory and Techniques, 1987-97; contbr. articles to profl. publs. including IEEE Transactions on Antennas and Propagation, Transactions on Edn., Transactions on Microwave Theory and Techniques, Jour. Quantum Electronics, Electronics Letters, Radio Sci., Engring. Edn., Computers in Edn. Jour. Mem. rev. panel NSF, Quantum Electronics Waves and Beams program, 1989; mem. tech. paper rev. com. Internat. Symposium on Recent Advances in Microwave Tech., China, 1989, 97, Reno, 1991, India, 1993, Ukraine, 1995, Spain, 1999; reviewer procs. ASEE/IEEE Frontiers in Edn. Conf., Phoenix, 1998, San Juan, P.R., 1999, Kansas City, 2000, others; judge N.D. Sci. Olympiad, 1987-95, S.E. N.D. Regional Sci. and Engring. Fair, 1993, 95-96; reviewer SBMO/IEEE MTT-S Internat. Microwave and Optoelectronics Conf., Natal, Brazil, 1997, Belem, Brazil, 2001; vol. examiner FCC Amateur Radio Exams thru Am. Radio Relay League. 2d lt. Signal Corps, U.S. Army, 1961-62. Grantee summer fellow, NSF, 1965, TELEBRAS (Brazil), 1973—80, NSF, 2001—04. Mem. IEEE, IEEE Antennas and Propagation Soc., Am. Soc. Engring. Edn. (internat. and other divsn., grantee summer 1984), N.D. Acad. Sci., Am. Geophys. Union, Applied Computational Electromagnetics Soc., Am. Sci. Affiliation, Am. Radio Relay League (life), Order of Engr., IEEE Edn. Soc., Microwave Theory and Techniques Soc., Sigma Xi, Tau Beta Pi, Eta Kappa Nu. Evangelical. Office: ND State U Elec Computer Engring Dept Fargo ND 58105

ROGERS, DAVID FREEMAN, aerospace engineering educator; b. Theresa, NY, Sept. 3, 1937; s. Lewis Freeman and Gladys Marion Zoller; m. Nancy Ann Nuttall, Sept. 5, 1959; children: Stephen David, Karen Nanci, Ransom Robert. B in Aero. Engring., Rensselaer Poly. Inst., 1959, MS in Aero. Engring., 1960, PhD, 1967. From asst. prof. to prof. U.S. Naval Acad., Annapolis, Md., 1964—2003, dir. aeronautics, 1999—2003, prof. emeritus, 2004—. Fujitsu Rsch. prof. Royal Melbourne Inst. Tech.; hon. rsch. scholar U. Coll. London, 1977-78. Author: Mathematical Elements for Computer Graphics, 1976, 2d edit. 1990; Procedural Elements for Computer Graphics, 1985, 2d edit., 1997, Laminar Flow Analysis, 1992, Flying Adventures, Vols. 1-2, 1999, An Introduction to NURBS, with Historical Perspective, 2001; editor Meml. edit. for P. Bezier, CAD Jour., 2001; mem. editl. bd. Visual Computer, CAD, the Computer Aided Design Jour.; contbg. editor World Beechcraft Soc. Mag., 1995—; contbr. articles to profl. jours. David F. Rogers Chair in Aerospace Engineering named in his honor, 2000. Avocations: flying, photography, sailing. Office: US Naval Acad Aerospace Engring Dept Annapolis MD 21402

ROGERS, DAVID HUGHES, finance executive; b. Chgo., May 21, 1947; s. Joseph Gordon and Viola Winifred (Hughes) R.; m. Bonnie Hope Sinai, 1997; children: Kirsten Morgan, Loren Avery, Daniel Jay. BA, U. Mich., 1968; PhD, Columbia U., 1975. Economist Fed. Res. Bank of Cleve., 1974-75; asst. treas. B.F. Goodrich Co., Akron, Ohio, 1975-82; exec. v.p., chief fin. officer First Tex. Savs. Assn., Dallas, 1982-83; sr. exec. v.p., chief operating officer PriMerit Bank, Las Vegas, 1984-87, pres., dir., 1987-91, vice chmn., 1991-92; COO, The Baird Cos., Las Vegas, 1992-99; v.p., chief fin. officer Norall Labs., Las Vegas, 1999—2001; v.p., relationship mgr. Wells Fargo Bank, Las Vegas, Nev., 2001—04; v.p. Am. Income Life Ins. Co, Las Vegas, 2004—. Adj. prof. econs. C.C. of So. Nev., 1998—. Author: Consumer Banking in New York, 1975; also articles. Bd. dirs. Boulder Dam Area coun. Boy Scouts Am., 1986—; bd. dirs. Nev. Sch. Arts, 1988-98; chmn. Las Vegas Bus. Bank, 1995-99. Office: Am Income Life Ins Co 1771 E Flamingo Rd Las Vegas NV 89119 E-mail: DHRogers14@aol.com.

ROGERS, DAVID J. marketing professional, researcher; s. Virginia Merlene Henry. MBA, U. San Francisco, 2004. Rsch. asst. Human Interaction Lab., San Francisco, 2000—04; sr. rsch. assoc. Culture and Emotion Rsch. Lab., San Francisco, 1999—2004. Rschr. Family Bus. Ctr., San Francisco, 2002—04. Recipient Outstanding Academic Excellence, SFSU Honor's Convocation, 2000, Regional Rsch. award, Western Psychol. Assn., 2002; scholar Rsch. award Stipend, SFSU Coll. of Behavior and Social Scis., 2002; Dean's Rsch. Fellowship, U. San Francisco, 2002—04. Avocations: travel, reading. Personal E-mail: drogers@usfca.edu.

ROGERS, DESIREE GLAPION, utilities executive; b. New Orleans, June 16, 1959; d. Roy and Joyce Glapion; 1 child, Victoria. B in Polit. Sci., Wellesley Coll., 1981; MBA, Harvard U., 1985. Customer svc. mktg. mgr. AT&T, N.J., 1985-87; dir. devel. Levy Orgn., Chgo., 1987-89; founder, pres. Mus. Ops. Consulting Assocs., Chgo., 1989-91; dir. Ill. State Lottery, Chgo., 1991-97; chief mktg. officer Peoples Energy, Chgo., 1997—. Bd. dirs. Mus. Sci. and Industry, WTTW/Ch. 11, Ravinia; trustee Lincoln Park Zoo. Mem. The Econ. Club, Execs. Club. Office: Peoples Energy 130 E Randolph Dr Fl 18 Chicago IL 60601-6207

ROGERS, DONALD ROBERT, retired pathologist; b. Tacoma, Apr. 7, 1932; s. John Robert and Thelma Ethel (Neely) Rogers; m. Georgia Lee Miller, June 9, 1956; children: Steven, Julie. BS, U. Puget Sound, 1954; MD, U. Wash., 1958. Diplomate Am. Bd. Pathology. Intern Mpls. Gen. Hosp., 1958-59; resident U. Wash., Seattle, 1963-66; pathologist Alaska Regional Hosp., Anchorage, 1967-94; ret., 1994. Med. examiner State of Alaska, 1967—94; cons. forensic pathology. Contbr. articles to profl. jours. Nat. del. dir. Am. Cancer Soc., Alaska, 1983—84, bd. dirs., 1967—94. Lt. comdr. USN, 1959—62. Fellow: Coll. Am. Pathologists; mem.: ACS (mem. Anchorage unit 1967—94), Nat. Assn. Med. Examiners, Anchorage Med. Soc. (pres. 1972), Ala. State Med. Assn. (pres. 1989—91), Rotary. Republican. Home and Office: 921 Old Klatt Rd Anchorage AK 99515-3254 Office Phone: 907-349-9104.

ROGERS, EARL LESLIE, artist, educator; b. Oakland, Calif., July 8, 1918; s. Robert Ray and Addie Myrtle (Dice) R.; m. Eileen Estelle MacKenzie, Apr. 9, 1945; children: Leslie Eileen, Brian Donald (dec.). Student, L.A. Valley Coll., 1949-52, Northridge State U., 1958-59, UCLA Extension, 1967, Sergei Bongart Sch. Art, 1967-68; AA, Pierce Coll., 1958; MA equivalency, Merced Coll., 1996. Cert. tchr., Calif. Various positions City of L.A., Van Nuys, Calif., 1948-55, Reseda, Calif., 1955-68; pvt. practice Canoga Park, Calif., 1948-68; art tchr. Mariposa (Calif.) County High Sch., 1969-70; art instr. Merced (Calif.) County Coll., 1970—. Instr. Earl Rogers Studio Workshop, Mariposa, Calif., 1969—; art dir. Yosemite Nat. Park, Calif., 1973; instr. art Asilomar Conf. Grounds, Pacific Grove, Calif., 1980; juror various art orgns., 1971-95; demonstrator Clovis (Calif.) Art Guild, 1971, 89, Sierra Artists, Mariposa, 1972, 81, 82, 84, 91, 2000, Merced Art League, 1976, Yosemite Western Artists, Oakhurst, Calif., 1973, Madera (Calif.) Art Assn., 1978, Chowchilla (Calif.) Art Guild, 1983, 86, 87, 89, 91, Soc. Western Artists, 1981, 89, 93, 97. One-man shows include L.A. City Hall, 1968, Merced Coll., 1969, 1995, Mariposa Title Co. Bldg., 1969, Coffee's Gallery, 1970, Bear Valley Hist. Bon-Ton, Calif., 1999, others, exhibited in group shows at West Valley Artists Assn., 1966—68, L.A. City Hall, 1967, Yosemite Nat. Park, 1973, Soc. Western Artists, 1977—78, Cannon Bldg. Rotunda, Washington, 1982, Mother Lode Gallery, Columbia, Calif., 1977—78, Arbor Gallery, Merced, 1988, 1998, 2001, Gold Country Gallery, 1990—91, Merced Coll., 1969—92, 1996, Mariposa County Arts Coun., 1999, at others, Represented in permanent collections John C. Freemont Hosp., Mariposa, Mariposa County Arts Coun., Mariposa Mus. and History Ctr., Capital Hill Br. Pub. Libr., Seattle. Asst. scout master Boy Scouts of Am., Canoga Park, Calif., 1956-58; art instr. L.A. Recreation Corps, L.A. Parks and Recreation Dept., 1967. Mem. Soc. Western Artists (Neva Rall Meml. award 1978), Mariposa Mus. and Hist. Ctr. (life), Pastel Soc. West Coast. Avocation: piano and books. Home and Office: 5323 State Hwy 49 N Mariposa CA 95338-9503

ROGERS, EARLINE S. state legislator; b. Gary, Ind., Dec. 20, 1934; d. Earl and Robbie (Hicks) Smith; m. Louis C. Rogers, Dec. 24, 1956; children: Keith, Dana. d. Earl and Robbie (Hicks) Smith; m. Louis C. Rogers, Dec.24, 1956; children: Keith, Dana. BS, Ind. U., 1957, MS, 1971. Mem. Ind. State Ho. Reps, 1982-90, Ind. State Senate from 14th dist., 1990—, asst. minority whip, 1995—96. Mem. appointment and claims com. (ranking minority mem.), edn. com., health and provider svcs. com., rules and legis. procedure com. Mem. NAACP, Nat. Coun. Negro Women, League Women Voters, Urban League, Black Prfl. Women, Am. Fedn. Tchrs., Ind. State Tchrs. Assn. Democrat. Avocations: reading, sewing. Office: Ind State Senate Dist 3 200 W Washington St Indianapolis IN 46204-2728 also: 3636 W 15th Ave Gary IN 46404

ROGERS, EDWARD SAMUEL, communications company executive; b. Toronto, May 27, 1933; s. Edward Samuel and Velma Melissa (Taylor) R.; m. Loretta Anne Robinson, Sept. 25, 1963; children: Lisa Anne, Edward Samuel, Melinda Mary, Martha Loretta. BA, Trinity Coll., U. Toronto, 1956; LLB, Osgoode Hall Law Sch., 1961; DSc (hon.), Clarkson U., 1989; LLD (hon.), U. Victoria, 1990; LLD, York U., 1994; LittD, U. of New Brunswick, 2001; LLD, U. of Toronto, 2002, D of sacred letters, 1997. Bar: Ont., 1962. Founder, prin. Rogers Telecomm. Ltd., Toronto, 1960—; pres., CEO Rogers Comm. Inc., Toronto, 1978—, Rogers Cablesystems, Toronto, 1990—96; vice chmn. Rogers Media Inc., Toronto, 1994, Rogers Cable Inc., Toronto, 1997—; chmn. Rogers Wireless Comms. Inc., 1991. Bd. dirs. The Toronto Dominion Bank, Toronto Blue Jays Baseball Club. Bd. dirs. Jr. Achievement Can. Mem. Royal Can. Yacht Club, Albany Club, Granite Club, York Club, Muskoka Golf & Country Club, Rideau Club Ottawa, Lyford Cay Club (gov.), Balboa Bay Club, Sigma Chi (Beta Omega chpt.). Progressive Conservative. Mem. Anglican Ch. Office: Rogers Comm Inc 333 Bloor St E Toronto ON Canada M4W 1G9

ROGERS, ELIZABETH (BETTY) CARLISLE, education educator, consultant; d. Charles Bunyan and Maggie Era (Little) Carlisle; children: Kellie Elizabeth, Sean Lewis. BS, U. Miss., 1972, MS, 1974; PhD, U. Ga., 1997. Chair divsn. sci. and math. Truett-McConnell Coll., Cleveland, Ga., 1974—84; chair dept. math. Lakeview Acad., Gainesville, Ga., 1984—89; prof. math. and edn. Piedmont Coll., Demorest, Ga., 1989—. Pres. BCR Inc., Gainesville, Ga., 1990—; ptnr. The Ednl. Solutions Task Force, Washington, 2000—. Author: (profl. book) A Study of Curriculum and Pedagogy, 1997; editor (contbg. author) Cooperative Learning In Undergraduate Mathematics, 2001; author: (textbook) Mathematics for Agriculture, 2000. Chair, ceremonies and events Spl. Olympics of Ga., 2001—04, Grantee Faculty Devel. in Ga., State of Ga., 1992—95; scholar Carrier Scholarship, Carrier Found.; Tchg. Fellow, U. of Miss., 1971—73. Mem.: Women in Math., Math. Assn. of Am., Alpha Delta Pi (Dorothy Shaw Leadership award), Alpha Lambda Delta (pres.), Kappa Delta Phi (pres.), Phi Kappa Phi. Achievements include research in advantages of coop. learning for undergraduate math. students; history of math. in Ctrl. and South Am. Home: 4733 Highland Rd Gainesville GA 30506 Office: Piedmont Coll Ctrl Ave Demorest GA 30535 Office Phone: 706-778-8500 1235. Personal E-mail: b.rogers@prodigy.net. E-mail: brogers@piedmont.edu.

ROGERS, ELYSE MACFADYEN, communications and foundation executive; b. Kearny, N.J., Sept. 28, 1932; d. Frank H. and Silvia (Simms) MacFadyen; m. Edward W. Rogers, July 18, 1952; children: Pamela, Cynthia, Jenifer RN, Mountainside, 1953; BS, Ind. U., 1957; MA, Purdue U., 1973. Pres. Sci. Syntax Services, Midland, Mich., 1976-81; exec. v.p. OAK Assoc. KK, Tokyo, 1981-84; pres. MAC Internat. Ltd., Tokyo, 1984-87, MAC Internat. Ltd.-USA, Midland, 1987—; asst. v.p. Herbert H. and Grace A. Dow Found., 1990—. Vice chmn. Asian Pacific Council Am. C. of C., Japan, 1985-87; bd. govs. Am. C. of C., Japan, 1985-87. Author: Staying Healthy in Japan, 1983, Cross Cultural Dialogues, 1985, Home Nursing Care, 1978; columnist: Japan Times, Yomiuri Shimbun, and Tokyo Weekender, 1980—; contbr. articles to profl. jours. Bd. dirs. Midland Symphony Orch., 1995-2002, chair, 1998-2000; bd. dirs. MidMich. Health, 1995—, MidMich. Med. Ctr., 1998—, Little Forks Conservancy, 2003—; bd. dirs. MicMich. Vis. Nurse Assn., 1990-96, chair, 1995-96; bd. fellows Saginaw Valley State U., 1997—; bd. govs. Northwood U., 2000—; chair exec. women's bd. Northwood U., 2002—. Recipient Disting. Woman award Mitten Bay Girl Scouts U.S., 1997, Athena award Athena Found., 1998. Mem. Am. Med. Writers Assn. (fellow), Fgn. Exec. Women (founder, pres. 1981-84), Am. Soc. Journalists and Authors, Detroit Women Writers, Mich. Non Profit Assn. (bd. dirs. 1999—), Fgn. Corrs. Club of Japan, Midland Country Club, Rotary, Zonta. Republican. Episcopalian.

ROGERS, ERNEST MABRY, lawyer; b. Demopolis, Ala., Sept. 22, 1947; s. James B. and Ernestine B. (Brewer) R.; m. Jeanne Edwards, Dec. 15, 1979; children: Gilbert B., Katherine B., Mary C. BA, Yale U., 1969; JD, Harvard U., 1974. Bar: Ala. 1974, U.S. Dist. Ct. (no. dist.) Ala. 1975, U.S. Ct. Appeals (5th cir.) 1976, U.S. Ct. Appeals (11th cir.) 1981, U.S. Supreme Ct. 1981, U.S. Ct. Claims 1983, U.S. Ct. Appeals (6th cir.) 1987. Law clk. to judge U.S. Dist. Ct. (no. dist.) Ala., 1974-75; ptnr. Bradley Arant Rose & White LLP, Birmingham, Ala., 1981—. Contbr. articles to profl. jours. Mem. Jefferson County (Ala.) Bd. of Code Appeals, 2001—. Fellow: Am. Coll. Constrn. Lawyers; mem.: Am. Arbitration Assn. (bd. dirs. 2001—), Kiwanis. Episcopalian. Office: One Federal Plaza 1817 5th Ave N Birmingham AL 35203-2104 Office Phone: 205-521-8225. Business E-Mail: emr@bradleyarant.com.

ROGERS, EUGENE JACK, medical educator; b. Vienna, June 13, 1921; came to U.S., 1937; s. Louis and Malvina (Haller) R.; m. Joyce M. Lighter, Feb. 9, 1952; children: Jay A., Robert J. BS, CCNY; M.B., Chgo. Med. Sch., 1946, MD, 1947. Diplomate Am. Bd. Phys. Medicine and Rehab. Intern Our Lady of Mercy Med. Ctr. and Cabrini Meml. Hosps., N.Y.C., 1946-48; resident Madigan Hosp., Tacoma, 1951, Mayo Clinic, Rochester, Minn., 1951, N.Y. Med. Coll. Met. Med. Ctr., 1953-55; USPHS fellow, 1955-56; ship's surgeon U.S. Lines, Grace Lines, N.Y.C., 1948-49; indsl. physician Abraham & Strauss Stores, Bklyn., 1949-51; practice medicine specializing in phys. medicine and rehab. Bklyn., 1956-73; dir. rehab. service, attending physician N.Y. City Hosp. Dept., 1955-73; prof. and chmn. dept. rehab. medicine Chgo. Med. Sch., North Chicago, Ill., 1973—. Cons. N.Y.C. Mayor's Adv. Com. for Aged, 1957; asst. prof. SUNY Downstate Med. Sch., Bklyn., 1958-73; med. dir. Schwab Rehab. Hosp., Chgo., 1973-75; acting chief rehab. service VA Center, North Chicgo, 1975-77; chmn. Ill. Phys. Therapy Exam. Com., 1977-78; examiner Am. Bd. Phys. Medicine and Rehab., 1983; sec., dir. Microtherapeutics, Inc., 1972 Editor: Total Cancer Care, 1975; contbr. articles to med. jours.; contbg. editor Ill. Med. Jour., 1983-89 Served to capt. U.S. Army, 1951-53. Recipient Bronze medal Am. Congress Rehab. Medicine, 1974 Fellow: ACP, Am. Acad. Phys. Medicine and Rehab. (Cert. Appreciation 1993); mem.: Chgo. Med. Sch. Alumni Assn. (asst. treas. 1983—93, treas. 1983—, sec. 1995—97, 1st v.p. 1999, pres. 2001—03, exec. com., Disting. Alumnus award 1980, Presdl. plaque Greater N.Y. chpt.), Chgo. Med. Sch. Faculty Assembly (spkr. 1978—80), Ill. Soc. Phys. Medicine and Rehab (pres. 1983—84), Ill. Med. Soc. (chmn. workmen's compensation com. 1980—83), Odd Fellows (pres. 1961—62), Phi Lambda Kappa (trustee 1980), Alpha Omega Alpha. Home: 1110 N Lake Shore Dr Chicago IL 60611-1054 Office: Rosalind Franklin U Medicine Scis Chgo Med Sch 3333 Green Bay Rd North Chicago IL 60064-3037 Personal E-mail: eugenerogers@worldnet.att.net. *To render good medical care: Prevent disease, evaluate the patient, treat the condition, educate patient and family, restore function, support group referral, on-line medical knowledge maintenance, never neglect or lie to or for patients, never divulging patient med. info. without consent.*

ROGERS, FRED BAKER, medical educator; b. Trenton, N.J., Aug. 25, 1926; s. Lawrence H. and Eliza C. (Thropp) R. AA, Princeton U., 1947; MD, Temple U., 1948; MS in Medicine, U. Pa., 1954; MPH, Columbia U., 1957; spl. student, Johns Hopkins U., 1962. Diplomate: Am. Bd. Preventive Medicine. Intern Temple U. Hosp., Phila., 1948-49, chief resident physician, 1953-54; USPHS fellow Temple U. Sch. Medicine, 1954-55, asst. prof. preventive medicine, 1956-58, assoc. prof., 1958-60, prof., 1960-90, prof. emeritus, 1991—, chmn. dept., 1970-77. Lectr. epidemiology Columbia U. Sch. Pub. Health, 1957-68, Sch. Nursing, U. Pa., 1964-67; cons. USN Hosp., Phila., 1964-73 Author: A Syllabus of Medical History, 1958, Help-Bringers: Versatile Physicians of N.J, 1960, Epidemiology and Communicable Disease Control, 1963, Studies in Epidemiology, 1965, (with A.R. Sayre) The Healing Art, 1966, (with M.E. Cashel) Your Body is Wonderfully Made, 1974; mem. editorial bd. Am. Jour. Pub. Health, 1967-73; contbr. articles to profl. jours. With M.C. USNR, 1950-53, Korea, capt. (ret.) USNR. Recipient Chapel of Four Chaplains award, 1982. Fellow ACP; mem. AMA (past chmn. sect. preventive medicine), Am. Pub. Health Assn., Royal Soc. Medicine of London (hon.), Sigma Xi, Alpha Omega Alpha, Phi Rho Sigma. Clubs: Campus (Princeton); Franklin Inn (Phila.); Charaka (N.Y.C.); Osler (London). Home: 333 W State St Apt 6K Trenton NJ 08618-5722 Office: Temple U Sch Med Philadelphia PA 19140

ROGERS, GAIL ELIZABETH, library director; b. Charlotte, N.C., May 6, 1947; d. James Yates and Marian Elizabeth (Church) Rogers. BA, Salem Coll., 1969; MLS, U. N.C., 1971. Cert. libr., Ga. Br. libr. Atlanta Pub. Libr., 1970-77; br. coord. Dekalb Libr. System, Decatur, Ga., 1977-82; asst. dir. West Ga. Regional Libr., Carrollton, 1982-83, Cobb County Pub. Libr., Marietta, Ga., 1983-90, dir., 1991—. Mem. Leadership Cobb, Cobb County, 1985-86. Mem. ALA, Ga. Libr. Assn. (2d v.p. 1987-89), Southeastern Libr. Assn. (v.p.-pres. elect. 1990-92, pres. 1992-94), Urban Librs. Coun., Kiwanis Club Marietta (bd. dirs. 1991-92, sec. 1992-93, sec.-treas. 1993-94, pres. 1995-96). Office: Cobb County Public Lib 266 Roswell St SE Marietta GA 30060-2005

ROGERS, GARDNER SPENCER, railroad company executive; b. Bryn Mawr, Pa., Sept. 16, 1926; s. Gardner Spencer and Frances (Lloyd) R.; m. Margaret Elizabeth Windsor, July 18, 1954; children: Ann Rogers Wilbanks, Barbara Rogers Coombs. Student, Episc. Acad., 1940-44, MIT, 1944-45; BS, U. Colo., 1951. Registered ret. profl. engr., Calif. With We. Pacific R.R. Co., San Francisco, 1947-70, engr. costs, valuation and stats., 1964-69, asst. to gen. mgr. planning and control, 1969, asst. gen. mgr., 1970; gen. mgr. Civil & Mech. Maintenance Pty. Ltd., Perth, Australia, 1970-77; mgr. We. Australian ops. Fluor Australia Pty. Ltd., 1971-73, gen. mgr. ry. divsn., 1973-77; gen. mgr. Pilbara Industries, 1971-73; dir. budgets and control Consol. Rail Corp., 1978-79, sr. dir. budgets, planning and control, 1980, dir. corp. planning, 1981-87; cons., 1987—2001. Adv. com. on R.R. property ICC, 1966-70; mem. spl. adv. team R.R. Ofcls. to U.S. Govt., 1962. Mng. trustee Daniel B. Gardner Trust, Chgo.; alt. trustee Cathedral Sq. Found., Perth; vestryman Ch. of Eng., 1971-77, mem. synod and provincial synod, 1973-77, mem. diocesan coun., 1974-77, bd. dirs. sch.'s trust, 1975-77; vestryman, chmn. fin. com., sr. warden St. Mary's-by-the-Sea Episc. Ch., Pacific Grove, Calif., 1989-91; vestryman, chmn. stewardship com., jr. warden St. Mark's Epis. Ch., Medford, Oreg., 1996-98. Mem. Instn. Engrs. Australia, Am. C. of C. in Australia (bd. dirs., v.p., chmn. We. Australian exec. com. 1976-77), Swanleigh (chmn. exec. com. 1974-77, coun.), Am. Mgmt. Assn., Am. Ry. Engr. Assn. (sec. com. 11 1983-87), Epis. Diocese of El Camino Real (bd. dirs. 1991-93, lay Eucharistic Min. 1991-94), Diocese of Oreg. (lay Eucaristic Min. 1995—, lic. lay reader 1996—), Ry. and Locomotive Hist. Soc., Soc. of Cin., Mil. Order Loyal Legion (vice comdr.), Colo. Alumni Assn. No. Calif. (pres. 1951-52), Rogue Valley Manor (pres. residents coun. 1999-2000), Berkeley Tennis Club, Pacific Ry. Club, Commonwealth Club, Australian-Am. Club, Alpha Tau Omega (high coun. 1964-68, 82-90). Home: 2410 Rogue Valley Manor Dr Medford OR 97504-4512 Personal E-mail: grogersRVM@charter.net.

ROGERS, GARTH WINFIELD, lawyer; b. Fort Collins, Colo., Nov. 4, 1938; s. Harlan Winfield and Helen Marie (Orr) R.; m. Joanne Kathleen Rapp, June 16, 1962; children: Todd Winfield, Christopher Jay, Gregory Lynn, Clay Charles. BS, U. Colo., 1958, LLB, 1962. Bar: Colo. 1962; U.S. Dist. Ct. Colo. 1962. Law clk. to presiding justice U.S. Dist. Ct., Denver, 1962-63; assoc. Allen, Stover & Mitchell, Ft. Collins, 1963-68; ptnr. Allen, Rogers & Vahrenwald, Ft. Collins, 1968-97; ret., 1997. Articles editor Rocky Mountain Law Rev., 1961-62. Past bd. dirs. Salvation Army, Ft. Collins, Ft. Collins C. of C., United Way of Ft. Collins, Trinity Luth. Ch., Ft. Collins, others; bd. dirs. Poudre Sch. Dist. Bd. Edn. Mem. ABA, Colo. Bar Assn., Larimer County Bar Assn. Avocations: nicaragua projects, participative sports, amateur writing, reading. Office: 215 W Oak St Ste 777 Fort Collins CO 80521-2734

ROGERS, GARY L. former diversified technology and services company executive; BA in Mktg., Fla. State U., 1966. Mem. fin. mgmt. program GE, 1966; mgr., fin. planning & analysis of lamp components op. GE Lighting, Cleveland, 1977—80, gen. mgr., lamp glass & components dept., 1980—81, gen. mgr., gen. purposes control dept., 1981—82; v.p. GE Co., Fairfield, Conn., 1982—86; v.p., gen. mgr., lamp products div. GE Lighting, 1982—86; pres., CEO GE Elec. Distbn. and Control, Plainville, Conn., 1986-90, GE Appliances, Louisville, 1990-92, GE Plastics, Pittsfield, Mass., 1992—2001; sr. v.p. GE Co., 1992—2001, vice chmn., 2001—03. Mem. bd. dirs. Rohm and Haas Co., 2004—.

ROGERS, HAROLD DALLAS (HAL ROGERS), congressman; b. Barrier, KY, Dec. 31, 1937; BA, U. Ky., 1962, LLB, 1964. Bar: Ky. 1964. Pvt. practice, Somerset, Ky., 1967-69; Commonwealth atty. Pulaski and Rockcastle counties, Ky., 1969-80; mem. 97th-108th Congresses from 5th Dist. Ky., 1981—, mem. appropriations com., subcom. homeland security, transp., commerce, justice and state. With KY and NC Nat. Guard, 1957—64. Republican. Office: US Ho of Reps 2406 Rayburn Hob Washington DC 20515-1705

ROGERS, HARVEY DELANO, lawyer; b. Krosniewice, Poland, Jan. 2, 1946; s. Bernard and Rose (Zaltztrager) R.; m. Maria Cimitiere, Dec. 22, 1978; children: Daniel, Randall, Rachel, Amanda. BA, CCNY, 1968, MA, 1970; JD, U. Miami, 1974. Bar: Fla. 1975, U.S. Dist. Ct. (no. and so. dists.) Fla. 1975, U.S. Ct. Appeals (5th cir.) 1975, U.S. Ct. Appeals (11 cir.) 1981, Supreme Ct. Fla. 1975, U.S. Supreme Ct.1980. Sole practice, Miami, Fla., 1974—. Arbitrator Am. Arbitration, Miami, 1975—. Fellow Fla. Criminal Defense Attys.; mem. ABA, Lawyers Title, Fla. Trial Lawyers Assn., Phi Alpha Delta. Avocations: history, sports, fishing. Home: 6401 SW 123rd Ter Miami FL 33156-5560

ROGERS, HON PAULLETTO, researcher, writer; b. Washington, Mich., Aug. 22, 1961; s. Paulleto Rogers I and Dorothy L.R. Rogers; children: Alexis R. Roycia July, Ambre L. Majasticaa, Ericka J. Student, Wayne County C.C.; cert. computer ops., Mother Waddles Sch. Cert. paralegal; notary pub. Pres. C.C.O.A, L.A., 1983; gen. operator CBOU, 1983—; regent agent Security MGN, 1984; collector Nat. Credit Corp., L.A., 1985; craftman Vinyl Indsl. Products, Chgo., 1986; field insp. Mortgage Svcs. Assoc., Inc., 1995; sales cons. Swepo, 1996; legal tech. Probone Legal Svcs., 1997; directorate Prousa Internat. Projects 2001, 1998. Substaining member Rep. Platform Commn., 1986; substaining sponsor Ronald Reagan Presdl. Found., Libr., and Ctr. Pub. Affairs, Ventura County, Calif., 1988; sponsor Statue of Liberty Ellis Island Centennial Commn., 1985, Ronald Reagan Congressional-Vicotry Fund, 1987; advisorate Senate Adv. Coun., 1997; co-founder Justice Inst.; vol. Mother Waddles-Petr. Mission Support; del. at large Del. Adv. Coun.; legal adv. Alexis, Ambre, Dorthy-Lewis, Paul, Paulleto, Rogers, Sutton, Profl. Corp., 2001. Creator, founder The Collectionals Survey. At-large-del. Rep. Presdl. Task Force, 1992—, lobbyist, 1994—; activist U.S. Def. Com., 1985; lobbyist Prousa Legal Corpsusa, 1999; del. Wayne County Clk. Office; Mich. state advisor Rep. Senatorial Com.; mem. Jaycees, 1981, GOPAC, congl. VIP, 1984; GOP Victory Fund sponsor NRCC, 1984; supporter KIDSFIRST YESMI, 2000; assoc. mem. Ch. Tae Adv., 2000—. Decorated Rogers Coat of Arms, Medieval Knight, Chevron, 2000; recipient Cert. Recognition, NRCC, 1990, Cert. Appreciation, Presdl. Commn. A.A., 1990, Presdl. award Rep. Presdl. Legion of Merit, 1994. Mem. Oahspe (assoc.), World Peace Tonite/Freedom Inst. (assoc.), 2nd Ch. of Tae. Avocations: copyrights, activism, lobbying, community reinvesting. Home: PO Box 27473 Detroit MI 48227-0473

ROGERS, HOWARD H. retired chemist; b. N.Y.C., Dec. 26, 1926; s. Julian Herbert and Minnie (Jaffa) R.; m. Barbara Kniaz, Mar. 27, 1954 (div. 1978); children: Lynne, Mark David, Susan; m. Maureen Dohn, Dec. 28, 1978. BS in Chemistry, U. Ill., 1949; PhD in Inorganic Chemistry, MIT, 1953. Research group leader Allis-Chalmers Mfg. Co., West Allis, Wis., 1952-61; sr. tech. specialist Rocketdyne div., Rockwell, Canoga Park, Calif., 1961-70; chief research scientist Martek Instruments, Newport Beach, Calif., 1970-73; scientist Boeing Satellite Systems, Torrance, Calif., 1973—2002; ret., 2002. Developer nickel-hydrogen battery; patentee; contbr. sci. papers to profl. publs. in field. With USN, 1944—46. Recipient Lawrence A. Hyland Patent

award Hughes Aircraft Co., 1987. Mem. Electrochem. Soc. (chmn. So. Calif./Nev. sect. 1976-78), Am. Chem. Soc., Sigma Xi. Home: 18361 Van Ness Ave Torrance CA 90504-5309 Personal E-mail: howard.rogers@alum.mit.edu. *In my 75 plus years of living experience I have found that these two items are vital: focus on what you intend to do, not what you have already done; complete honesty to yourself and to others in interpreting and reporting results is mandatory.*

ROGERS, JACK DAVID, plant pathologist, educator; b. Point Pleasant, W.Va., Sept. 3, 1937; s. Jack and Thelma Grace R.; m. Belle C. Spencer, June 7, 1958. BS in Biology, Davis and Elkins Coll., 1960; MF, Duke U., 1960; PhD, U. Wis., 1963. From asst. prof. to prof. Wash. State U., Pullman, 1963-72, chmn. dept. plant pathology, 1986-99. Contbr. articles to profl. jours. Recipient William H. Weston Teaching Excellence award Mycological Soc. Am., 1992. Mem. Mycological Soc. of Am. (pres., 1977-78), Am. Phytopathol. Soc., Botanical Soc. Am., British Mycological Soc.

ROGERS, JAMES BEELAND, JR., investment company executive; b. Balt., Oct. 19, 1942; s. James Beeland and Ernestine Barbara (Brewer) Rogers. BA cum laude, Yale U., 1964; BA with honors, MA in Politics, Philosophy, Econs., Balliol Coll., Oxford (Eng.) U., 1966. Investment analyst Bache & Co., NYC, 1968-69, R. Gilder & Co., NYC, 1969-70; asst. to chmn. Neuberger & Berman, NYC, 1970-71; with Arnhold and S. Belichroeder, Inc., 1971-73; exec. v.p. Soros Fund Mgmt., NYC, 1973-80; chmn. bd. dirs. Rogers Holdings, 1980—. Adj. prof. Columbia U. Sch. Bus., 1983—85, prof. fin., 1986—90, vis. prof., 1994—96. Host (TV series) The Profit Motive with Jim Rogers, 1989—90, Guinness Record Motorcycle Trip Around World, 1990—92, co-host, commentator various TV shows, 1992—; author: Investment Biker: On the Road with Jim Rogers, 1994, Guiness Record Drive Around the World on Millennium Adventure, 1999—2001, Adventure Capitalist, 2003; columnist:. Home: 352 Riverside Dr New York NY 10025-2731 Office Phone: 212-316-0393. E-mail: jim@jimrogers.com.

ROGERS, JAMES DEVITT, judge; b. Mpls., May 5, 1929; s. Harold Neil and Dorothy (Devitt) R.; m. Leanna Morrison, Oct. 19, 1968. AB, Dartmouth Coll., 1951; JD, U. Minn., 1954. Bar: Minn. 1954, U.S. Supreme Ct. 1983. Assoc. Johnson & Sands, Mpls., 1956-60; sole practice Mpls., 1960-62; judge Mpls. Municipal and Dist. Ct., 1959-91. Mem. faculty Nat. Judicial Coll. Bd. dirs. Mpls. chpt. Am. Red Cross, chmn. service to mil. families and vets. com.; bd. dirs. Minn. Safety Coun., St. Paul, 1988-91; founding dir., sec. Forest Landowners Tax Coun. Served sgt. U.S. Army, 1954-56. Mem. ABA (chmn. nat. conf. spl. ct. judge, spl. com. housing and urban devel. law, traffic ct. program com., chmn. criminal justice sect., jud. adminstrn. div.), Nat. Jud. Coll. (bd. dirs.), Nat. Christmas Tree Grower's Assn. (pres. 1976-78), Mpls. Athletic Club. Congregationalist. Office: 14110 Prince Pl Minnetonka MN 55345-3027

ROGERS, JAMES EDWARD, paper company executive; b. Richmond, Va., Aug. 13, 1945; s. Olin Adair and Marjorie (Aiken) R.; children: James Edward Jr., Catherine, Margaret. BS in Physics, Va. Mil. Inst., 1967; MS in Nuclear Engring., U. Va., 1969; postgrad., Harvard U., 1987. Licensing engr. Va. Electric and Power Co., Richmond, 1969-71; sales engr., sales mgr., v.p. sales and mktg. James River Paper Co., Richmond, 1971-77, 79-82, sr. v.p., gen. mgr., 1977-82; v.p. corp. devel., 1982-87; sr. v.p., group exec., specialty paper bus. James River Corp., Richmond, 1987-92; pres., CEO Specialty Coatings Intl., Richmond, 1992-93; pres. SCI Investors Inc., Richmond, 1993—. Chmn., bd. dirs. Custom Papers Group Inc., Richmond; bd. dirs. Owens and Minor, Inc., Richmond, Wellman, Inc., Shrewsbury, N.J., Caraustar Industries, Inc., Austell, Ga., Marine Devel. Corp., Richmond, Mohawk Paper Mills., Inc., Cohoes, N.Y., Wilson Paper Co., Richmond, Robert Bryan Ltd., Port Royal, Va. 5d. dirs. Richmond Cerebral Palsy Ctr., Richmond Childrens Mus., Maymont Found., Richmond, 1987; mem. men's adv. coun. Va. Home, Richmond, Commonwealth Girl Scouts. Mem. Soc. Internat. Bus. Fellows, Pub. Affairs Group, Storm Trysail Club, Commonwealth Club, Fishing Bay Yacht Club (past commodore), N.Y. Yacht Club. Clubs: Commonwealth (Richmond); Fishing Bay Yacht (Deltaville, Va.) (commodore 1980); N.Y. Yacht (N.Y.C.). Republican. Office: SCI Investors Inc 101 Shockoe Slip Ste O Richmond VA 23219-4144

ROGERS, JAMES EDWIN, geology and hydrology consultant; b. Waco, Tex., Feb. 24, 1929; s. Charles Watson and Jimmie (Harp) R.; m. Margaret Anna Louise Bruchmann, Oct. 10, 1957; 1 child, James Frederick. Student, Rice U., 1947-49, Baylor U., 1953; BS, U. Tex., 1955, MA, 1961. Geologist U.S. Geol. Survey, St. Paul, 1956-59, Alexandria, La., 1959-63, supervisory hydrologist, 1963-85; ind. cons. Alexandria, 1985—. Cons. geol. survey for map State of La., Baton Rouge, 1982-85, mapping com., 1997—, mem. adv. bd. La. geol. survey, 1998—. Author: Water Resources of Kisatchie Well-Field Area Near Alexandria, Louisiana, 1981, Preconstruction and Simulated Postconstruction Ground-Water Levels at Urban Centers in the Red River Navigation Project Area, Louisiana, 1983, Red River Waterway Project - Summary of Ground-Water Studies by the U.S. Geological Survey, 1962-85, 1988; co-author: Water Resources of Vernon Parish, Louisiana, 1965, Water Resources of Ouachita Parish, Louisana, 1972, Water Resources of the Little River Basin, Louisana, 1973. Scoutmaster Boy Scouts Am., Alexandria, 1971, 72. Sgt. U.S. Army, 1950-52, Japan. Fellow Geol. Soc. Am.; mem. Gem Mineral and Lapidary Soc. Ctrl. La. (pres. 1972, 86-87, 94-96), Baton Rouge Geol. Soc., Phi Beta Kappa. Presbyterian. Avocations: coin collecting/numismatics, minerals, genealogy, travel, history. Home and Office: 4008 Innis Dr Alexandria LA 71303-4738

ROGERS, JAMES EUGENE, electric and gas utility executive; b. Birmingham, Ala., Sept. 20, 1947; s. James E. and Margaret (Whatley) R.; m. Robyn McGill (div.); children: Chrissi, Kara, Ben; m. Mary Anne Boldrick, Oct. 28, 1977. BBA, U. Ky., 1970, JD, 1974. Asst. atty. gen. Commonwealth Ky., Louisville; asst. chief trial atty. Fed. Energy Regulation Commn., Washington, dep. gen. counsel litigation and enforcement; law clk. to presiding justice Supreme Ct Ky., Louisville; ptnr. Akin, Gump, Strauss, Hauer & Feld, Dallas, Akin Gump Strauss Hauer & Feld, Houston, 1985-86; formerly pres. Transwestern Pipeline, Houston; pres., CEO, chmn. Cinergy Corp. (formerly PSI Resources, Inc.), Cin., 1994—. Bd. dirs. CINergy Corp., Fifth Third Bank, Edison Electric Inst., Duke Realty Investments, Inc. Trustee Nat. Symphony Orch.; bd. dirs. Cin. Mus. Assn., The Nature Conservancy-Ind. chpt., U. Ky. Bus. Partnership Found. Mem. Ky. Bar Assn., D.C. Bar Assn., Meridian Hills Country Club, Crooked Stick Golf Club, Queen City Club, Met. Club. Baptist. Avocations: tennis, biking, skiing, golf. Office: Cinergy Corp 139 E Fourth St Cincinnati OH 45202-0960

ROGERS, JAMES FREDERICK, banker, management consultant; b. Centerville, Iowa, June 27, 1935; s. John W. and Mildred Holly (Morris) R.; m. Janet L. Marsden, July 27, 1957; children: Jennifer Burke, John William. AB, U. Mo., 1957; postgrad., Rutgers U. Grad. Sch. Banking, 1970-72. With Am. Security and Trust Co., Washington, 1959-85, exec. v.p., 1980-83. Bd. dirs., pres. Am. Security Corp., 1983-85; cons. B.E.I.-Golembe Assocs., 1985-93; chmn. Nat. Bank of No. Va., 1988-89. Commr. Arlington County Planning Commn., 1979-80; asst. treas. Kennedy Ctr. Performing Arts; pres., trustee Leonard Wood Found.; trustee Friends of Nat. Zoo, Greater Washington Rsch. Ctr., Washington Dulles Task Force, Arena Stage, Sch. Commerce U. Va. Officer AUS, 1958-59. Mem. D.C. Bankers Assn. (pres. 1984-85), Davenport Soc., U. Mo., Met. Club (Washington), Chevy Chase Club. Presbyterian. Home: 4201 38th Rd N Arlington VA 22207-4554

ROGERS, JAMES GORDON, JR., art educator; b. Dec. 16, 1944; AB in English, U. Mo., 1967, MA in Art History and Archaeology, 1983, PhD, 1989. Asst. prof. art history William Woods Coll., Fulton, Mo., 1989-90; prof. art history Savannah (Ga.) Coll. Art & Design, 1990-92, Florida So. Coll., Lakeland, Fla., 1992—. Adj. prof. Sch. Arch. and Comty. Design, U. South Fla., 1995-2002; cons. The Design Ctr., 1977—, chair, Dept. of Art and Art History, dir. Melvin Art Gallery, Art & Art History Study Abroad Program, 1999-; lectr. in field. Contbr. articles to profl. jours. Mem. peer rev. com. Fla. Arts Coun.; past bd. dirs. Mid-Mo. chpt. Am. Heart Assn., Sta KBIA Pub. Radio, Columbia, Mo., Columbia Art League, also co-chmn. finance com.; active Nat. Holocaust Meml. Mus. Mem. AAUP, Am. Soc. Hispanic Art Hist. Studies, Soc. Archtl. Historians, Coll. Art Assn. Office: Fla So Coll Lake Hollingsworth Dr Lakeland FL 33803 Office Phone: 863-680-4223. E-mail: jrogers@flsouthern.edu.

ROGERS, JAMES W. trucking executive; BA, Rutgers U. Former sr. v.p., mem. corp. exec. coun. GE Electric Co.; pres., CEO GE Indsl. Control Systems, 1995—98; bd. dirs. SIRVA, Inc., Westmont, Ill., 1999—, chmn. bd. dirs., 1999—, pres., CEO, 2001—02. Prin. Clayton, Dubilier & Rice, Inc.; ltd. ptnr. CD&R Assocs V Ltd. Partnership, CD&R Assocs. VI Ltd. Partnership; stockholder, dir. CD&R Investment Assocs. II, Inc., CD&R Investment Assocs. VI, Inc.; chmn. Brake Bros plc. Office: SIRVA Inc 700 Oakmont Ln Westmont IL 60559*

ROGERS, JEFFERY PAUL, music educator; b. Bloomington, Ill., Jan. 18, 1959; s. Paul Marshall and Ruthannis Hastings Rogers; m. Karen Ann Collegde, Dec. 19, 1981; children: Keith, Renee, Katie. BA, West Va. U., 1981; MS, Western Md. Coll., 1992. Music tchr. K-12 Roane Co. Public Sch., Spencer, W.Va., 1981—82; band dir. FS Key HS, Carroll Co. Public Sch., Westminster, Md., 1982—88; band dir. Westminster HS, 1988—92; asst. prin. North Carroll HS, 1992—99, fine arts supr., 1999—. Recipient Asst. Prin. of Yr., Nat. Assn. Secondary Sch. Prin., Md., 1998. Mem.: Assn. Supervision & Curriculum Devel., Nat. Assn. Music Educators. Office: Carroll Co Public Schs 125 N Ct St Westminster MD 21157-5192

ROGERS, JIMMY DON, county official, writer; b. Tulsa, Okla., Jan. 22; s. J.B. and Marjeita Jean Rogers; m. Dorothy Gail Rogers, Apr. 4, 1992; children: Angi, Jody; children: Rebecca Shackelford, Lonnie Shackelford, Rhonda Shackelford. BA, Ctrl.State Univ., Edmond, Okla., 1980. Cert. tchg. Okla., 1980. Tchr., coach Broken Arrow Pub. Sch., Broken Arrow, Okla., 1980—89; owner, contr. Rogers Constrn., Collinsville, Okla., 1989—92; mgr. Midway Redi Mix, Collinsville, Okla., 1992—95; owner, operator Double R Cafe, Jenks, Okla., 1995—96; bldg. insp. City of Glenpool, Okla., 1996—98; dir. pub. svc. City of Collinsville, Okla., 1998—. Mem. Okla. Mcpl. League, Okla. City, 1999—, Nat. Edn. Assn., 1980—89; judge Okla. Tchrs. English Anthology, Okla. City, 1980—84. Author poetry, (brochure) Oklahoma Western Heritage Inc., 2003. Mem. Collinsville C. of C., Okla., 2004—. Airman 1st class USAR, 1971—77, Okla. Mem.: Okla. Code Enforcement Assn., Internat. Code Coun., Okla. Western Heritage Inc. (v.p. 2004—, Silver Spur 2003). Republican. Assembly Of God. Achievements include first to mem. of support team for Ride 4 Am. program. This group rode horseback from Okla. City to N.Y.C. in 2002 arriving for spl. ceremony at Ground Zero Sept. 5., 2002; the poem from Liberty's View was recited at the ceremony as well as all stops along the way. Avocations: poetry, music, hunting, cowboy. Home: 223 S 10th St Collinsville OK 74021 Office: City of Collinsville 106 N 12th St Collinsville OK 74021 Office Phone: 918-371-1010.

ROGERS, JOE, former lieutenant governor; b. Omaha, Nebraska, July 8, 1964; m. Juanita (Kay); children: Trent, Jordan, Haley. Degree in bus., Colo. State U., 1986; JD, Ariz. State U., 1989. Past law clk. to Hon. Robert Broomfield U.S. Dist. Ct.; assoc. Davis, Graham, and Stubbs, Colo., 1989-93; staff counsel to Senator Hank Brown U.S. Congress, Washington, 1993-95; lt. gov. State of Colo., 1998—2002; pvt. practice lawyer, 2002—. Past atty. Lend A Lawyer Program, Colo. Mem. Denver Bar Assn. (bd. dir. credit union 1990-93), Colo. Bar Assn., Sam Carey Bar Assn. Republican. Office: Joe Rogers PO Box 17287 Denver CO 80217

ROGERS, JOHN HEADLEY, literature and language professor; b. Richmond, Ky., Mar. 8, 1947; s. Glenn Clive and Agnes Amerine R. BA, Ctr. Coll., 1969; MA, Ind. U., 1973, PhD, 1977. Tchr. Pendelton County H.S., Falmouth, Ky., 1969-71; lectr. Ind.-Purdue U., Indpls., 1977-80, Morehead (Ky.) State U., 1980-81; prof. English Vincennes (Ind.) U., 1982—. Contbg. author: British Romantic Poets, 1990, British Romantic Writers, 1991, Continuum Encyclopedia of English Literature; 18th Century Literary Biographers, Encyclopedia of the Essay, 1997; editor: British Short Fiction, 1918-1945, 1996. Pres. Old Town Players Cmty. Theatre, Vincennes, 1993-96, v.p., 1991-93. Mem. AAUP, Nat. Coun. Tchrs. English, Modern Lang. Assn., Popular Culture Assn., Phi Delta Kappa (found. rep., pres. 2000-03, 2004—). Democrat. Methodist. Avocations: theater, travel, reading, music. Home: 1507 E Saint Clair St Vincennes IN 47591-4817 Office: Vincennes U 1002 N 1st St Vincennes IN 47591-1500

ROGERS, JOHN JAMES WILLIAM, geology educator; b. Chgo., June 27, 1930; s. Edward James and Josephine (Dickey) R.; m. Barbara Bongard, Nov. 30, 1956; children: Peter, Timothy. BS, Calif. Inst. Tech., 1952, PhD, 1955; MS, U. Minn., 1952. Lic. geologist, N.C. From instr. to prof. Rice U., Houston, 1954-75, master Brown Coll., 1966-71, chmn. geol. dept., 1971-74; W.R. Kenan Jr. prof. geology U. N.C., Chapel Hill, 1975-97, W.R. Kenan Jr. prof. geology emeritus, 1997—. Author: A History of the Earth, 1993, History and Environment of North Carolina's Piedmont, 1999; co-author: Fundamentals of Geology, 1966, Precambrian Geology of India, 1987; co-editor: Holocene Geology of Galveston Bay, 1969, Precambrian of South India, 1983, Basalts, 1984, African Rifting, 1989, People and the Earth, 1998; regional editor Jour. African Earth Scis., 1982-93; contbr. articles to profl. jours. Fellow Geol. Soc. Am., Geol. Soc. India, Geol. Soc. Africa (hon.); Am. Assn. Petroleum Geologists. Home: 114 Woodbridge Ln Chapel Hill NC 27514 Office: U NC Dept Geology CB 3315 Chapel Hill NC 27599-0001

ROGERS, JOHN MARSHALL, judge, law educator; b. Rochester, N.Y., June 26, 1948; s. Harry Lovejoy III and Virginia Kathryn (Meyers) R.; m. Ying Juan Xiong, 1990. BA, Stanford U., 1970; JD, U. Mich., 1974. Bar: D.C. 1975, Ky. 1980, U.S. Ct. Appeals, U.S. Supreme Ct. Commd. USAR, 1970; appellate atty. civil div. U.S. Dept. Justice, Washington, 1974-78; asst. prof. U. Ky., Lexington, 1978-81, assoc. prof., 1981-86, prof., 1986—2002, prof. emeritus, 2002—; cir. judge U.S. Ct. Appeals for Sixth Cir., 2002—. Vis. prof. Civil Divsn. U.S. Dept. Justice, Washington, 1983-85; Fulbright lectr. Fgn. Affairs Coll., Beijing, 1987-88, Zhongshan U., Guangzhou, People's Republic of China, 1994-95; spl. counsel impeachment com. Ky. Ho. of Reps., 1991. Contbr. articles to profl. jours. Mem. Coun. on Fgn. Rels., Am. Law Inst., Order of Coif, Phi Beta Kappa. Office: 532 Potter Stewart US Courthouse 100 E 5th St Cincinnati OH 45202-3988

ROGERS, JOHN S. retired union official; b. Scranton, Pa., Nov. 19, 1930; Student, U. Wis., 1959-61, U. Mich., 1963; student spl. studies, Am. U., 1965-66, Harvard U. Bus. Sch., 1967. Internat. rep. United Brotherhood of Carpenters and Joiners of Am., Washington, 1958-65, asst. to gen. pres., 1966-74, dir. edn., 1971-82, mem. gen. exec. bd., 1974-78, gen. sec., 1978-91, ret., 1992. Sec.-treas. Suffolk County (N.Y.) Dist. Coun. Carpenters, 1957-58; v.p. N.Y. State Bldg. and Constrn. Trades Council, 1974-78, N.Y. State Fedn. Labor, 1974-78; pres. N.Y. State Coun. Carpenters, 1974-78; vice chmn. N.Y. State Commn. Jobs and Energy; mem. Suffolk County Pub. Employment Rels.s Bd.; vis. lectr. George Meany Ctr. Labor Studies. Author numerous trade union leadership mans. and instructional materials, 1966-79. Bd. dirs. L.I. action com. Assn. Help for Retarded Children, 1956-60; labor co-chmn United Cerebral Palsy, N.Y.C., 1977-78; v.p. Leukemia Soc. Mem. Harvard Trade Union Alumnae Assn. Home: 2713 Cranbrook Dr Boynton Beach FL 33436-5717

ROGERS, JON MARTIN, financial consultant, finance company executive; b. Piedmont, S.C., June 4, 1942; s. James Robert and Eunice (Ashley) Rogers; m. E. Jeanette Owen, June 16, 1962; children: E. Elaine, Jonette Marie, Melissa Anne. BS, Clemson U., 1964, MS, 1966; PhD in Fin. Mgmt., LaSalle U., 1994. CLU; chartered fin. cons. Sales rep. Met. Life, Greenville, SC, 1969-71, dist. sales mgr. Atlanta, 1972-74, regional sales mgr. Milw., 1975-81; ptnr. J&J Enterprises, Piemont, SC, 1975—; regional sales mgr. Liberty Corp., Greenville, 1982-88; chmn. bd. dirs., CEO Rogers Fin. Group LLC, Greenville, 1989-2000, CEO, 2000—. Registered securities rep. Royal Alliance Assocs., Inc., N.Y.C., 1986—; adj. prof. Webster U. Pres. Rep. Precinct, Piedmont, 1988; deacon, chmn. Washington Ch., Pelzer, SC, 1985—87, 1993—94; bd. dirs. Child Evangelism Fellowship, 1988—89. Capt. U.S. Army, 1967—69, Vietnam. Decorated Bronze Star. Mem.: Million Dollar Round Table, Nat. Assn. Securities Dealers, Internat. Assn. Fin. Planners, Nat. Assn. Life Underwriters (v.p. 1972—73, awards), Rotary (bd. dirs., pres. 1996—97), Gideons Internat. Club (S.C. pres. 1985—87). Baptist. Avocations: photography, golf, walking. Home: 21 Fairway Dr Piedmont SC 29673-9167 Office: Rogers Fin Group Inc 7 Boyce Ave Greenville SC 29601 Office Phone: 864-250-1376. E-mail: jrogers6@msn.com.

ROGERS, JUDITH W. federal judge; b. 1939; AB cum laude, Radcliffe Coll., 1961; LLB, Harvard U., 1964; LLM, U. Va., 1988; LLD (hon.), D.C. Sch. Law, 1992. Bar: D.C. 1965. Law clk. Juvenile Ct. D.C., 1964-65; asst. U.S. atty. D.C., 1965-68; trial atty. San Francisco Neighborhood Legal Assistance Found., 1968-69; atty. assoc. atty. gen.'s office U.S. Dept. Justice, 1969-71, atty. criminal divsn., 1969-71; gen. counsel Congl. Commn. on Organization of D.C. Govt., 1971-72; coordinator legis. program Office of Dep. Mayor D.C., 1972-74, spl. asst. to mayor for legis., 1974-79, corp. counsel, 1979-83; assoc. judge D.C. Ct. Appeals, 1983-88, chief judge, 1988-94; cir. judge U.S. Ct. Appeals-D.C. Cir., 1994—. Mem. D.C. Law Revision Commn., 1979-83; mem. grievance com. U.S. Dist. Ct. D.C., 1982-83; mem. exec. com. Conf. Chief Justices, 1993-94. Bd. dirs. Wider Opportunities for Women, 1972-74; mem. vis. com. Harvard U. Sch. Law, 1984-90; trustee Radcliffe Coll., 1982-88. Recipient citation for work on D.C. Self-Govt. Act, 1973, Disting. Pub. Svc. award D.C. Govt., 1983, award Nat. Bar Assn., 1989; named Woman Lawyer of Yr., Women's Bar Assn. D.C., 1990. Fellow ABA; mem. D.C. Bar, Nat. Assn. Women Judges, Conf. Chief Justices (bd. dirs. 1988-94), Am. Law Inst., Phi Beta Kappa. Office: US Ct Appeals Fed Cir 717 Madison Pl NW Washington DC 20001-2866

ROGERS, JULIE, foundation administrator; B, Duke U.; M in tchg., George Wash. U. Staff dir. Coun. DC Com. Human Svcs.; pres. Eugene and Agnes Meyer Found.; joined Meyer Found., 1986—. Founding chair Wash. Regional Assn. Grantmakers, 1992—95; founder Wash. AIDS Partnership, Cmty. Devel. Support Collaborative; dir. Greater Wash. Bd. Trade; bd. mem. Forum Regionals Assn. Grantmakers. Bd. mem. Venture Philanthropy Ptnr., DC Coll. Access Program; adv. com. DC Local Initiatives Support Corp.; bd. Leadership Wash., treas., 1990—91, vice chmn., 1990—91; bd. Found. Ctr., 1991—2000; mem. Federal City Coun., Coun. Found., 2002—. Named one of 100 Most Powerful Women in Wash., Washingtonian mag., 2001; recipient Founder award for leadership and cmty. svc., Leadership Wash., 1997. Mem.: Wash. Women's Forum. Office: Meyer Found 1400 16th St NW Ste 360 Washington DC 20036 Office Phone: 202-483-8294. Office Fax: 202-328-6850.

ROGERS, JUSTIN TOWNER, JR., retired utility company executive; b. Sandusky, Ohio, Aug. 4, 1929; s. Justin Towner and Barbara Eloise (Larkin) R. AB cum laude, Princeton U., 1951; JD, U. Mich., 1954. Bar: Ohio 1954. Assoc. Wright, Harlor, Purpus, Morris & Arnold, Columbus, 1956-58; with Ohio Edison Co., Akron, 1958-93, v.p., then exec. v.p., 1970-79, pres., 1980-91, chmn. bd., 1991-93; ret., 1993. Past mem. coal adv. bd. Internat. Energy Agy. Past pres., trustee Akron Cmty. Trusts, Akron Child Guidance Ctr.; past chmn. Akron Assoc. Health Agys., U. Akron Assocs., Ohio Electric Utility Inst.; past chmn., trustee, mem. exec. com. trustees Akron Gen. Health Sys.; trustee Sisler McFawn Found., Cmty. Health Ventures, Inc., VNS-Hospice Found.; former trustee Stan Hywet Hall & Gardens; past dir. Edison Elec. Inst., Elec. Power Rsch. Inst., Assn. of Edison Illuminating Co.'s. Mem. Portage Country Club, Mayflower Club, Rockwell Springs Trout Club (Castalia, Ohio), Princeton Club (N.Y.C.), Phi Delta Phi, Beta Gamma Sigma. E-mail: jnjrog@neo.rr.com.

ROGERS, KAREN BECKSTEAD, gifted studies educator, researcher, consultant; b. L.A., Nov. 28, 1943; d. Maurice Webster and Helen Dorothy (Nalty) Beckstead; m. William Geoffrey Rogers, Sept. 11, 1965; children: Jeanne Elizabeth Rogers Armstrong, Jennifer Lynn Rogers Hasbrouck, William Carey. BA in Humanities, U. Calif., Berkeley, 1965; MA in Spl. Edn., San Diego State U., 1969; MA in Ednl. Psychology, U. Minn., 1983, PhD in Curriculum and Instrn. Sys., 1991. Cert. elem. tchr., Calif. Pace project coord. West Jr. Paul Schs., 1975-77; Omnibus project dir. Jr. League of Mpls., 1978-83; instr. U. Minn., Mpls., 1985—95; gifted studies instr. U. St. Thomas, Mpls., 1984-87, asst. prof. gifted studies, 1987-93, assoc. prof. gifted studies, 1993-98, prof., 1999—. Cons., Burnsville, Minn., 1978—. Author: Ability Grouping and Gifted Learners, 1991 (Early Scholar award, 1991), Talent Development in Context, 1998, Re-Forming Gifted Education, 2002; contbg. editor Roeper Rev., 1994—, contbg. reviewer Jour. Secondary Gifted Edn., 1994—, Jour. for the Edn. of the Gifted, 1994—, Gifted Edn. Internat., 1998—, Gifted Child Quarterly, 1997—; contbr. 90 articles to profl. jours., 12 chpts. to books. Docent Mpls. Inst. Arts, 1975—. Recipient Lifetime Achievement award Minn. Coun. for Gifted and Talented, 1989. Mem. Coun. for Exceptional Children (pres. The Assn. for the Gifted 1994-96), Nat. Assn. for Gifted Children, Am. Ednl. Rsch. Assn. Democrat. Avocations: art collecting, art history, music appreciation, writing, reading. Home: 14004 Whiterock Rd Burnsville MN 55337-4717 Office: U St Thomas MOH 217 1000 LaSalle Ave Minneapolis MN 55403-2025 Office Phone: 651-962-4386. E-mail: kbrogers@stthomas.edu.

ROGERS, KATE ELLEN, interior design educator; b. Nashville, Dec. 13, 1920; d. Raymond Lewis and Louise (Gruver) R.; diploma Ward-Belmont Jr. Coll., 1940; BA in Fine Arts, George Peabody Coll., 1946, MA in Fine Arts, 1947; EdD in Fine Arts and Fine Arts Edn., Columbia U., 1956. Instr., Tex. Tech. Coll., Lubbock, 1947-53; co-owner, v.p. Design Today, Inc., Lubbock, 1951-54; student asst. Am. House, N.Y.C., 1953-54; asst. prof. housing and interior design U. Mo., Columbia, 1954-56, assoc. prof., 1956-66, prof., 1966-85, emeritus, 1985—, chmn. dept. housing and interior design, 1973-85; mem. accreditation com. Found. for Interior Design Edn. Rsch., 1975-76, chmn. stds. com., 1976-82, chmn. rsch., 1982-85. Mem. 1st Bapt. Ch., Columbia, Mo.; bd. dirs. Meals on Wheels, 1989-91. Nat. Endowment for Arts rsch. grantee, 1981-82. Fellow Interior Design Educators Coun. (pres. 1971-73, chmn. bd. 1974-76, chmn. rsch. com. 1977-78); mem. Am. Soc. Interior Designers, (hon., medal of honor 1975), Am. Home Econs. Assn., Columbia Art League (adv. bd. 1988-93), Pi Lambda Theta, Kappa Delta Pi, Phi Kappa Phi (hon.), Gamma Sigma Delta, Delta Delta Delta (Phi Eta chpt.), Phi Upsilon Omicron, Omicron Nu (hon.). Democrat. Author: The Modern House, USA, 1962; editor Jour. Interior Design Edn. and Research, 1975-78.

ROGERS, KATHERINE DIANE, political consultant, commissioner; b. Concord, N.H., Mar. 7, 1955; d. Albert A. and Alta (Whittier) R. BA, Clark U., Worcester, Mass., 1977. Mem. N.H. Ho. of Reps., Concord, 1992-98; county commr. County of Merrimack, 1998—. Bd. dirs. N.H. Bus. Fin. Authority. Mem. City Coun., Concord, 1991—. Democrat. Lutheran. Home: 4 Jay Dr Concord NH 03301-7831

ROGERS, LEE FRANK, radiologist; b. Colchester, Vt., Sept. 24, 1934; s. Watson Frank and Marguerite Mortimer (Cole) R.; m. Donna Mae Brinker, June 20, 1956; children: Michelle, Cynthia, Christopher, Matthew. BS, Northwestern U., 1956, MD, 1959. Commd. 2d lt. U.S. Army, 1959, advanced through grades to maj., 1967; rotating intern Walter Reed Gen. Hosp., 1959-60; resident radiology Fitzsimons Gen. Hosp., 1960-63; ret., 1967; radiologist Bapt. Meml. Hosp., San Antonio, 1967-68, U. Tex. Med. Sch., San Antonio, 1968-71, dir. residency tng., radiologist Houston, 1972-74; prof., chmn. dept. radiology Northwestern U. Med. Sch., Chgo., 1974-95; editor-in-chief Am. Jour. Roentgenology, Winston-Salem, NC, 1995—2003; prof. radiology U. Ariz. Health Scis. Ctr., 2003—. Fellow Am. Coll. Radiology (past pres.), Am. Roentgen Ray Soc. (past pres.); mem. Assn. Univ. Radiologists (past pres.), Radiol. Soc. N.Am., Am. Bd. Radiology (past pres.), Alpha Omega Alpha. Episcopalian. Home: 8235 N Fairway View Dr Tucson AZ 85742 Office Phone: 520-626-6794. *The source of most problems is previous solutions.*

ROGERS, LINDA LEE, artist; b. Bisbee, Ariz., Aug. 6, 1954; d. Raymond Boyd and Mary Lois Mortenson; m. Richard Alan Rogers, Apr. 23, 1977. BA in Art, Western N.Mex. U., 1997. PADI diver basic/rescue. Keypunch operator WNMU, Silver City, N.Mex., 1973-76, UV Industries, Fierro, N.Mex., 1976-78; data analyst Gray & Gray, Inc., Silver City, N.Mex., 1978-82, 82-90; EMT-I Gila Regional Med. Ctr., Silver City, N.Mex., 1988-92; artist Desert Reef Ind., Pinos Altos, N.Mex. Photographer: Studies in Black and White, 1997, Perspectives V, 1997. Recipient 1st pl. Grant County Art Guild, 1998, Jubilation Gallery, 1998-99, Peterson's Photographic Mag., 1998, 75th Ann. Gila Wilderness Show, 1999, Stellei Gallery, Las Cruces, 1999, Potter's Guild Las Cruces, 2000, Desertreef.com, 2000—. Mem.: Grant County Humane Soc. (bd. dirs. 2000—). Avocations: scuba diving, photography, pottery, environmental issues, animal rights/rescue. Office: Desert Reef Industries PO Box 53078 Pinos Altos NM 88053-3078 E-mail: linda@desertreef.com.

ROGERS, LORENE LANE, university president emeritus; b. Prosper, Tex., Apr. 3, 1914; d. Mort M. and Jessie L. (Luster) Lane; m. Burl Gordon Rogers, Aug. 23, 1935 (dec. June 14, 1941). BA, N. Tex. State Coll., 1934; MA (Parke, Davis fellow), U. Tex., 1946, PhD, 1948; DSc (hon.), Oakland U., 1972; LLD, Austin Coll., 1977. Prof. chemistry Sam Houston State Coll., Huntsville, Tex., 1947-49; research scientist Clayton Found. Biochem. Inst. U. Tex., Austin, 1950-64, asst. dir., 1957-64, prof. nutrition, 1962-80, assoc. dean Grad. Sch., 1964-71, v.p. univ., 1971-74, pres., 1974-79, mem. exec. com. African grad. fellowship program, 1966-71; research cons. Clayton Found. for Research, Houston, 1979-81. Vis. scientist, lectr., cons. NSF, 1959-62; cons. S.W. Research Inst., San Antonio, 1959-62, mem. Grad. Record Exams Bd., 1972-76, chmn., 1974-75; adv. com. ITT Internat. Fellowship, 1973-83; dir. Texaco, Inc., Gulf States Utilities, Republic Bank, Austin. Bd. dirs. Tex. Opera Theatre, Austin Lyric Opera; chmn. bd. trustees Texaco Philanthropic Found.; chmn. council of presidents Nat. Assn. State Univs. and Land-Grant Colls., 1976-77, mem. exec. com., 1976-79; mem. com. on identification of profl. women Am. Council on Edn., 1975-79, mem. com. on govt. relations, 1978-79; mem. target 2000 project com. Tex. A&M U. System; mem. ednl. adv. bd. John E. Gray Inst., Lamar U., Beaumont, Tex. Eli Lilly fellow, 1949-50; Recipient U. Tex. Students Assn. Teaching Excellence award, 1963; Disting. Alumnus award N. Tex. State U., 1972; Outstanding Woman of Austin award, 1950, 60, 71, 80; Disting. Alumnus award U. Tex., 1976; Honor Scroll award Tex. Inst. Chemists, 1980 Fellow Am. Inst. Chemists; mem. AAAS, Am. Chem. Soc. (sec. 1954-56), Am. Inst. Nutrition, Am. Soc. Human Genetics, Nat. Soc. Arts and Letters, Assn. Grad. Schs. (internat. edn. com. 1967-71), Sigma Xi, Phi Kappa Phi, Iota Sigma Pi, Omicron Delta Kappa. Achievements include research in hydantoin synthesis, intermediatry metabolism, biochem. nutritional aspects of alcoholism, mental retardation, congenital malformations. Home: 4 Nob Hill Cir Austin TX 78746-3650

ROGERS, MAL DAVID, JR., chemical engineer; b. July 26, 1922; BSChemE, U. Okla., 1948, M of Chem. Engring., 1949; cert. in nuc. engring., Pa. State U. and Argonne Nat. Lab., 1957. Chem. engr. Pure Oil, Wyo., 1949-51, Shell Chem., Deer Park, Tex., 1951-56; sr. chem., nuclear engr. Gen. Dynamics, Ft. Worth, 1956-59; sr. chem. engr., tech. staff Tex. Instruments, Dallas, 1959-90. Lt. USAF, 1942-45. Decorated DFC, Purple Heart; recipient Air medals with 2 oak leaf clusters USAF. Mem. N.Y. Acad. Scis. Home: 1240 Derby Dr Richardson TX 75080-5834

ROGERS, MALCOLM AUSTIN, museum director, art historian; b. Scarborough, Yorkshire, Eng., Oct. 3, 1948; s. James Eric and Frances Anne (Elsey) R. BA in English Language & Literature, Oxford U.; MA, Magdalen Coll., U. Oxford, Eng., 1976; DPhil, Christ Ch., Oxford U., 1976. Asst. keeper Nat. Portrait Gallery, London, 1974-83, dep. dir., 1983—85, dep. keeper, 1985—94; Ann and Graham Gund dir. Mus. Fine Arts, Boston, 1994—. Noted authority on 16th, 17th & early 18th century portraits. Author: Blue Guide: Museums and Galleries of London, 1983; contbr. articles to profl. publs. Mem. Harvard overseers' com. Visit the Art Mus.; trustee Found. for the Arts, Nagoya, Japan, Wednesday Evening Club of 1777, Club of Odd Volumes. Commander of the British Empire, 2004. Fellow Soc. Antiquaries. Avocations: wine and food, travel, opera. Home: 540 Chestnut Hill Ave Brookline MA 02445-4155 Office: Mus Fine Arts 465 Huntington Ave Boston MA 02115-5597 E-mail: mrogers@mfa.org.*

ROGERS, MARGARET ELLEN JONSSON, civic worker; b. Dallas, Aug. 7, 1938; d. John Erik and Margaret Elizabeth (Fonde) Jonsson; m. Robert D. Rogers; children: Emily, Erik, Laura. Student, Skidmore Coll., 1956—57, So. Meth. U., 1957—60. Civic worker, Dallas. Dir. Sta. KRLD radio, Dallas, 1970-74; dir. 1st Nat. Bank, Dallas, 1976-85, vice-chmn. dirs. trust com.; trustee Meth. Hosps., 1972-82, mem. exec. com., 1977-82, corp. bd. mem., 1990-94, mem. fin. com., 1990-93; bd. dirs. Lamplighter Sch., 1967—; past mem. vis. com. dept. psychology MIT; mem. vis. com. Stanford U. Librs., 1984-90; bd. dirs. Callier Ctr. Communication Disorders, 1967-90, Winston Sch., 1973-85; bd. dirs., mem. exec. com. Episc. Sch., 1976-83; chmn. Crystal Charity Ball; co-chmn. nat. major gifts com. Stanford Centennial Campaign; bd. dirs. Children's Med. Ctr., Hope Cottage Childrens' Bur., Baylor Dental Sch., Dallas Health and Sci. Mus., Dallas YWCA, Day Nursery Assn.; mem. devel. bd. U. Tex., Dallas, 1988-90; bd. govs. The Dallas Found., 1988-95, chmn. investment com. 1991-92; trustee So. Meth. U., mem. investment com., 1988—, chmn. investment com., 1992-99; mem. vis. com. Dedman Coll., 1989-90; life trustee Dallas Mus. Art, mem. investment com.; mem. collectors com. Nat. Gallery Art; bd. dirs. Dallas Arboretum, 1991-92; trustee, mem. fin. com. Monterey Bay Aquarium, 1995—, chair devel. com., 1995-2000, mem. fin. com., 2000—. Mem. internat. coun. Mus. Modern Art; pres. MJR Fund, Jonsson Found. Margaret Jonsson Charlton Hosp. of Dallas named in her honor, 1973. Mem.: The Lamplighter Sch. (life).

ROGERS, MARK CHARLES, anesthesiologist, pediatrician, entrepreneur, educator; b. N.Y.C., Oct. 25, 1942; s. Gerald and Inez (Kaufman) R.; m. Elizabeth Ann London, Dec. 30, 1972; children: Bradley, Meredith. BA, Columbia U., 1964; MD, SUNY, Syracuse, 1969; MBA, U. Pa., 1991; PhD (hon.), U. Ljubljana Slovenia, 1995. Diplomate Am. Bd. Anesthesiology (examiner 1982-96), Am. Bd. Pediatrics. Intern Mass. Gen. Hosp., Boston, 1969-70, resident, 1973-75, Boston Children's Hosp., 1970-71; fellow Duke U. Med. Ctr., Durham, N.C., 1971-73; asst. prof. dept. anesthesiology and critical care medicine Johns Hopkins U., Balt., 1977-79, assoc. prof., 1979-80, prof., chmn. dept., 1980-93, assoc. dean Sch. Medicine, 1990-93, dir. pediatric ICU, 1977-93; CEO Duke Hosp. and Health Network, 1993-96; sr. v.p. Perkin Elmer, Wilton, Conn., 1996-98; pres. Paramount Capital, N.Y.C., 1998—2000; chmn. Genta Pharms., 2001—02, Cardiome Pharma, 2002—, Adherex Pharma, 2002—04, Aptamera, 2004—, Bradmer Ventures, LLC, 2004—. Pres. Critical Care Found., Balt., 1981-96; cons. WHO, Bangkok, 1982-83. Editor in chief: Yearbook of Critical Care, 1983-96, Textbook of Pediatric Intensive Care, 1987, 91, 96, Principles and Practices of Anesthesiology, 1990; editor: Perioperative Management, 1989, dep. editor in chief Critical Care Medicine Jour., 1990-96. Maj. U.S. Army, 1975-77. Recipient Club of Mainz award, Mainz, Fed. Republic of Germany, 1981, award Assn. Univ. Anesthetists, 1980; Fulbright scholar, Ljubljana, Yugoslavia, 1990. Mem. Inst. Medicine. Home: 7772 Fisher Island Dr Fisher Island FL 33109 E-mail: mrogers@bradmer.com.

ROGERS, MICHAEL ALAN, writer; b. Santa Monica, Calif., Nov. 29, 1950; s. Don Easterday and Mary Othilda (Gilbertson) R.; m. Donna Rini, Oct. 9, 2000. BA in Creative Writing, Stanford U., 1972. Assoc. editor Rolling Stone Mag., San Francisco, 1972-76; editor-at-large Outside mag., San Francisco, 1976-78; vis. lectr. fiction U. Calif., Davis, 1980; sr. writer Newsweek mag., San Francisco, 1983—; mng. editor Newsweek InterActive, San Francisco, 1993-97; exec. prodr. broadband divsn. The Wash. Post Co., 1995-96; v.p. Washingtonpost.Newsweek Interactive, 1996—. Editor, gen. mgr. Newsweek.MSNBC.com, N.Y.C., 1998—. Author: Mindfogger, 1973, Biohazard, 1977, Do Not Worry About The Bear, 1979, Silicon Valley, 1982, Forbidden Sequence, 1988; contbr. articles to mags., newspapers. Recipient Disting. Sci. Writing award AAAS, 1976, Best Feature Articles award Computer Press Assn., 1987. Mem. Author Guild, Sierra Club. Achievements include patents for for multimedia storytelling technology. Avocations: travel, hiking. Address: 535 Dean St # 704 Brooklyn NY 11217 E-mail: MR@michaerogers.com.

ROGERS, MICHAEL BRUCE, orthodontist; b. Augusta, Ga., Aug. 25, 1945; s. Bruce Latimer and Dorothy (Baird) R.; m. Elizabeth Bennett, Dec. 21, 1968; children: Bruce, Kay, Alison, Lisa. Student, Emory U., 1963-65, DDS, 1969; cert. in orthodontics, Med. Coll. Ga., 1973. Diplomate Am. Bd. Orthodontists. Pvt. practice orthodontia, Augusta, 1973—. Part-time asst. clin. prof. Sch. Dentistry, Med. Coll. Ga., Augusta, 1973—. Capt. Dental Corps U.S. Army, 1971-73. Army Commendation Medal. Fellow: Ga. Acad. Dental Practice, The Internat. Acad. Dentists, Pierre Fauchard Acad., Ga. Dental Assn. (hon.; spkr. of ho. 1999—2004, v.p. 2004—), Internat. Acad. Dental Studies, Am. Coll. Dentists; mem.: Ea. Dist. Dental Soc. (pres. 1982—83), Med. Coll. Ga. Orthodontic Alumni Assn. (pres. 1981—83), Ga. Assn. Orthodontists (v.p. 1983—84, pres. 1984—85, exemplary svc. award), So. Assn. Orthodontists (spokesperson, sec.-treas. 1993—95, dir. 1995, pres. 2000, Disting. Svc. award 2001—), Am. Assn. Orthodontists (Ga. del., chmn. mem., ethics and jud. conderns, spkr. of house 1995—97, trustee 2002—), ADA (del.), Omicron Kappa Upsilon, Psi Omega (pres. 1967—68). Roman Catholic. Home: 3214 Candace Dr Augusta GA 30909-3259 Office: 3545 Wheeler Rd Augusta GA 30909-6517

ROGERS, MIKE, congressman; b. June 2, 1963; BA, Adrian Coll. Spl. agt. FBI; small bus. owner; mem. Mich. Senate from 26th dist., 1995-2000; vice chmn. judiciary com. Mich. Senate, mem. fin. svc., human resources, labor and vet affairs coms., mem. reappropriations com., mem. tech. and energy commn., mem. banking and fin. com.; mem. U.S. Congress from Mich. 8th dist., Washington, 2001—; mem. fin. svcs. and transp. coms.; mem. Com. on Energy and Commerce. Republican. Office: Dist Office 1327 E Michigan Ave Lansing MI 48912

ROGERS, MIKE, congressman; b. Hammond, Ind., July 16, 1958; m. Beth Rogers; 3 children. BA, Jacksonville State U., 1981, MPA, 1985; JD, U. Birmingham, 1991. Mem. Ala. Ho. Reps., 1994—2002; congressman 3rd Dist. Ala. U.S. Ho. Reps., 2003—. Mem. Calhoun County Commn., 1987—91; active State Rep. Exec. Com., 1990—. Republican. Baptist. Office: 514 Cannon HOB Washington DC 20515-0103

ROGERS, MILLARD FOSTER, JR., art museum director emeritus; b. Texarkana, Tex., Aug. 27, 1932; s. Millard Foster and Jessie Bell (Hubbell) Rogers; m. Nina Olds, Aug. 3, 1963; 1 child, Seth Olds. BA with honors, Mich. State U., 1954; MA, U. Mich., 1958; studied with, John Pope-Hennessy; LHD, Xavier U., 1987. Gosline fellow Victoria and Albert Mus., London, Eng., 1959; curator Am. art Toledo Mus. Art, 1959-67; coord. Ford Found. intern program; dir. Elvehjem Art Ctr., prof. art history U. Wis., Madison, 1967-74; dir. Cin. Art Mus., 1974-94, dir. emeritus, 1994—. Vis. scholar Principia Coll., Elsah, Ill., 1982, Elsah, 84; pres. Mariemont Preservation Found., Ohio, 1982—91, Ohio, 1995—2001; adj. prof. U. cin., 1987—91. Author: Randolph Rogers, American Sculptor in Rome, 1971, Spanish Paintings in the Cincinnati Art Museum, 1978, Favorite Paintings from the Cincinnati Art Museum, 1980, Sketches and Bozzetti by American Sculptors, 1800-1950, 1988, Rich in Good Works: Mary M. Emery of Cincinnati, 2000, John Nolen and Mariemont: Building a New Town in Ohio, 2001. With AUS, 1954—56. Named Outstanding Citizen of Mariemont, 1991. Mem.: Am. Assn. Mus., Assn. Art Mus. Dirs. (hon.), Phi Beta Kappa. Office: 3610 Pleasant St Cincinnati OH 45227 E-mail: nandmrogers@earthlink.net.

ROGERS, NANCY HARDIN, dean, law educator; b. Lansing, Mich., Sept. 18, 1948; d. Clifford Morris and Martha (Wood) Hardin; m. Douglas Langston Rogers, Jan. 30, 1970; children: Lynne, Jill, Kim. BA with highest distinction, U. Kans., 1969; JD, Yale U., 1972. Bar: D.C. 1975, Ohio 1972, U.S. Ct. Appeals (6th cir.) 1973, U.S. Dist. Ct. (no. dist.) Ohio 1974, U.S. Dist. Ct. (so. dist.) Ohio 1975. Law clk. U.S. Dist. Judge Thomas D. Lambros, Cleve., 1972-74; staff atty. Cleve. Legal Aid Soc., 1974-75; vis. asst. prof. Coll. of Law Ohio State U., Columbus, 1975-76, asst. prof., 1976-78, 83-89, assoc. prof., 1989-92, prof., assoc. dean acad. affairs, 1992-97, prof., 1992—, Joseph S. Platt, Porter, Wright, Morris & Arthur prof. law, 1995—2001, vice provost acad. adminstrn., 1999—2001, dean, Michael E. Moritz chair in alternative dispute resolution Michael E. Moritz Coll. Law, 2001—. Adj. prof. Ohio State Coll., 1981-83; vis. prof. law Harvard Law Sch., 2000. Author (with Frank E.A. Sander, Sarah R. Cole, Stephen B. Goldberg): (Book) Dispute Resolution: Negotiation, Mediation and Other Processes), 2003; author: (book with Craig A. McEwen and Sarah R. Cole) Mediation: Law, Policy, Practice, 2nd edit., 1994; mem. (adv. bd.) World Arbitration and Mediation Report, 1991—, Alternatives, 1992—, co-chair (edit. bd. with Frank E.A. Sander) Dispute Resolution mag., 1994—2002; contbr. chapters to books, articles to profl. jours. Bd. dirs. Assn. for Developmentally Disabled, Columbus, 1980-85; Legal Svcs. Corp. 1995-2003. Named Outstanding Prof., Ohio State U. Coll. Law Alumni Assn., 1996; recipient Book prize, Ctr. Pub. Resources for A Student's Guide to Mediation and the Law, 1987, Ctr. Pub. Resources for Mediation: Law, Policy, Practice, 1989, Peacemaker of Yr. award, Comty. Mediation Svcs. Ctrl. Ohio, 1990, Disting. Svc. Recognition, Soc. Profls. in Dispute Resolution, 1990, Whitney North Seymour sr. medal, Am. Arbitration Assn., 1990, Svc. Recognition award, Legal Aid Soc. Columbus, 1996, Ritter award, Ohio State Bar Found for outstanding contbns. to adminstrn. of justice, 1998; grantee Exxon Edn. Found., 1986, William and Flora Hewlett Found., 1990, Ohio State U. Interdisciplinary Seed, 1990, Ohio State U. Symposium, 1992, William and Flora Hewlett Found., 1992—96, Nat. Sci. Found., 1993—95, State Justice Instn., 1994, Fund for Improvement Post-Secondary Edn., U. Mo., 1996—97, William and Flora Hewlett Found., 1997—2003. Mem. ABA (chair, standing com. dispute resolution 1988-91, D'Alemberte-Raven award sect. on dispute resolution 2002), Phi Beta Kappa. Office: Ohio State U Coll Law 55 W 12th Ave Columbus OH 43210-1306 Business E-Mail: rogers.23@osu.edu.

ROGERS, NATHANIEL SIMS, retired banker; b. New Albany, Miss., Nov. 17, 1919; s. Arthur L. and Elizabeth (Bouton) R.; m. Helen Elizabeth Ricks, July 3, 1942; children— Alice, John, Lewis. AB, Millsaps Coll., 1941; MBA, Harvard U., 1947. With Deposit Guaranty Bank and Trust Co., Jackson, Miss., 1947-69, 1st v.p., 1957-58, pres., dir., 1958-69, 1st City Nat. Bank Houston, 1969-81, chmn., 1982-84; pres. 1st City Bancorp. of Tex., Houston, 1970-83, chmn., 1983-85, also bd. dirs.; ret. Chmn. Jackson United Givers Fund, 1957, pres., 1959, bd. dirs., 1958-61; pres. Andrew Jackson area coun. Boy Scouts Am., 1962; trustee Miss. Found. Ind. Colls., 1959-69; past pres., trustee Millsaps Coll.; trustee Methodist Hosp., Houston; chmn. ofcl. bd. Meth. ch. Lt. (s.g.) USNR, 1942-46. Named Outstanding Young Man of Year Jackson Jr. C. of C., 1955. Mem. Am. Bankers Assn. (pres. 1969-70), Miss. Bankers Assn. (pres. jr. banker sect. 1952-53, pres. 1964-65), Robert Morris Assocs. (pres. S.E. chpt. 1954-55, nat. dir. 1959-62), Assn. Res. City Bankers (bd. dirs. 1980-83), Jackson C. of C. (pres. 1962), Houston C. of C. (chmn. 1979-80), Young Pres.'s Orgn., Millsaps Coll. Alumni Assn. (pres. 1955-56), Newcomen Soc., Phi Beta Kappa, Omicron Delta Kappa, Kappa Alpha. Methodist.

ROGERS, OSCAR ALLAN, JR., college president; b. Natchez, Miss., Sept. 10, 1928; s. Oscar Allan and Maria Pinkie (Jackson) R.; m. Ethel Lee Lewis, Dec. 20, 1950; children— Christopher, Christian, Christoff. A.B., Tougaloo Coll., 1950; S.T.B., Harvard U., 1953, M.A.T., 1954; Ed.D., U. Ark., 1960; postgrad. U. Wash., 1968-69; LHD (hon.), Oklahoma City U., 1992,. Ordained to ministry Congl. Ch., 1953, Baptist Ch., 1955, Methodist Ch., 1962. Asst. pastor St. Mark Congl. Ch., Roxbury, Mass., 1951-54; dean-registrar Natchez Jr. Coll., Miss., 1954-56; pres. Ark. Bapt. Coll., Little Rock, 1956-59; dean students prof. social sci. and edn. Jackson State U., Miss., 1960-68, dean Grad. Sch., 1969-84; pres. Claflin Coll., 1984-94, pres. emeritus, 1994—; postdoctoral fellow U. Wash., Seattle, 1968-69; pastor Asbury-Kingsley Charge, Bolton and Edwards (Miss.) United Meth. Ch., 1962-84, Morton (Miss) Cir. United Meth. Chs., 1994-96. Served with USN, 1946-47. Recipient Order of the Palmetto Gov. Campbell (S.C.), 1994, Rabbi Martin Katzenstein award Harvard Div. Sch., 2003. Mem. Conf. Deans of Black Grad. Schs. (pres. 1975-76, treas. 1979-84), AAUP, NAACP, Phi Delta Kappa, Kappa Delta Pi, Alpha Phi Alpha. Democrat. Author: My Mother Cooked My Way Through Harvard with These Creole Recipes, 1973; Mississippi: The View from Tougaloo, 1979, 2d edit., 2002. Home and Office: 5932 Holbrook Dr Jackson MS 39206-2062

ROGERS, PATRICIA LOUISE, education educator, consultant; b. St. Paul, 1956; life ptnr. W. S. Larson. BS, U. Minn., Twin Cities, 1979, MA, 1982, PhD, 1997. Lic. tchr. art and theatre Minn., 1979. Tchr. St. Paul Schs., 1979—82; cancer rschr. U. Minn. Sch. Pub. Health, Mpls., 1984—95; prof. Bemidji (Minn.) State U., 1996—. Cons. and trainer for online tchg. Minn. State Colls. and Univs., Twin Cities, cons., 1998—; spkr. in field. Editor: (book) Designing Instruction for Technology-Enhanced Learning, Ency. of Distance Learning, Teaching, Technologies and Applications; contbr. articles to profl. jours. Vice chair Minn. Online Coun., 2003—04, chair, 2004—. Grantee, Minn. State Colls. and Univs. under a FIPSE Grant, 2001—02; scholar, Fulbright, Coun. for Internat. Exch. Scholars, 2000—01; Dissertation fellow, Getty Ctr. for Arts in Edn., 1996. Mem.: Nat. Art Edn. Assn., Assn. for Ednl. Comm. and Tech., Rotary Internat. (assoc.). Dfl. Office: Bemidji State Univ Rm 343 Ed/Art 1500 Birchmont Dr NE Bemidji MN 56601 Office Phone: 218-755-3781. E-mail: progers@bemidjistate.edu.

ROGERS, PAUL A'COURT, management consulting executive; b. Detroit, Oct. 12, 1939; s. Noel and Jessie (Adams) Rogers; 1 child, Ashley. BSBA, U. Md., 1982. Field engr. Gen. Dynamics, Pomona, Calif., 1962—65, project mgr., 1968—72; field engr. Hughes Aircraft Co., L.A., 1965—68; sys. engr. Sci. Mgmt. Assocs., Riverdale, Md., 1972—73, program mgr., 1975—82, corp. planner, 1982—; pres. R & M Assocs., 1989—; pres., CEO Parinc Corp. Project mgr. Sys. Cons., Washington, 1973—75; bd. dirs. Applied Sys. Planning, Mut. Human Concerns. Served with USNR, 1959—62. Mem.: Am. Soc. Naval Engrs., Project Mgmt. Inst., Am. Mktg. Assn., Am. Mgmt. Assn., Naval Inst. Democrat. Presbyterian. Home: 7524 Republic Ct Alexandria VA 22306 E-mail: paul_acourt@msn.com.

ROGERS, PETER PHILLIPS, environmental engineering educator, city planner; b. Liverpool, England, Apr. 30, 1937; arrived in U.S., 1960, naturalized, 1970; s. Edward Joseph and Ellen (Duggan) R.; m. Suzanne Ogden, Oct. 24, 1998; children: Christopher, Justin. B in Engring., Liverpool U., 1958; MS, Northwestern U., 1961; PhD, Harvard U., 1966. Asst. engr. Sir Alfred McAlpine & Sons Ltd., Cheshire, Eng., 1958-60; mem. faculty Harvard U., 1966—, Gordon McKay prof. environ. engring., 1974—, prof. city planning, 1974—. Mem. Center Population Studies, Harvard U. Sch. Pub. Health, 1974—; cons. World Bank, UN, U.S. Agy. for Internat. Devel., Govt. India, Govt. Pakistan, Govt. Bangladesh, Govt. Nepal, Govt. Italy, Govt. Costa Rica, Commonwealth P.R. Co-author: Urbanization and Change, 1970, Land Use and The Pipe: Planning for Sewerage, 1975, Resource Inventory and Baseline Study Methods for Developing Countries, 1983, Systems Analysis for River Basin Management, 1985, Evaluacion de Projectos de Desarrollo, 1990, America's Waters, 1993, Water in the Arab World, 1994, Measuring Environmental Quality in Asia, 1997, Science with a Human Face, 1997. Mem. World Commn. for Water in 21st Century. Gordon McKay tchg. fellow 1961; Radley rsch. student, 1962-64; doctoral dissertation fellow Resources for Future 1964-65; recipient Clemens Herschel prize Harvard U., 1964; Guggenheim fellow, 1973, 20th Century Found. fellowship, 1989, Maass-White fellow U.S. Army C.E., 2003. Mem. ASCE, Third World Acad. Scis. (corr.), Indian Inst. Agrl. Engring. (life), Cosmos Club (Washington), Cambridge Tennis Club, Sigma Xi. Home: 20 Berkeley St Cambridge MA 02138 Office: Harvard U 116 Pierce Hall Cambridge MA 02138 Office Phone: 617-495-2025. Business E-Mail: rogers@deas.harvard.edu.

ROGERS, RAYMOND JESSE, retired federal railroad associate administrator; b. Eugene, Oreg., Mar. 1, 1941; s. Raymond Everett and Virginia Elaine (Simpkins) R.; m. Joan Katherine Peterson, June 6, 1964 (div. Aug. 1974); 1 child, Virginia Arlene; m. Kim Lien Nguyen, Dec. 26, 1974; children: Kim Lan, Vincent Minh. Student, Santa Rosa (Calif.) Jr. Coll., 1960-61, U.S. Army Non-commd. Officer Acad., Anchorage, Alaska, 1963, U. Md., 1967-74, Fed. Exec. Inst., Charlottesville, Va., 1981. Lic. real estate agt., Va. Sr. asst. mgr. Household Fin. Corp., Md., 1964-67; contract specialist Dept. Navy, Washington, 1967-71; contract svcs. officer AID, Saigon, Vietnam, 1971-76; contracting officer Dept. Transp., Fed. R.R. Adminstrn., Washington, 1976-80, dir. fin. svcs., 1980-84, assoc. adminstr. for adminstrn., 1984—2002, CFO, CIO, 1994—2002, ret., 2002. Leader local group Boy Scouts Am., Vienna, Va., 1987-92, Izaac Walton League of Am., Am. Legion, Am. Assn. of Retired Persons. Sgt. U.S. Army, 1961-64. Decorated Vietnam Civilian Svc. medal. Mem. U.S. Sr. Exec. Svc., Fed. Exec. Inst. Alumni Assn. Avocations: fishing, hiking, camping, waterskiing. Home: 102 Yeonas Dr SW Vienna VA 22180-6557 E-mail: Rayvin78@aol.com.

ROGERS, RICHARD DEAN, federal judge; b. Oberlin, Kans., Dec. 29, 1921; s. William Clark and Evelyn May (Christian) R.; m. Helen Elizabeth Stewart, June 6, 1947; children— Letitia Ann, Cappi Christian, Richard Kurt. BS, Kans. State U., 1943; JD, Kans. U., 1947. Bar: Kans. 1947. Ptnr. firm Springer and Rogers (Attys.), Manhattan, Kans., 1947-58; instr. bus. law Kans. State U., 1948-52; partner firm Rogers, Stites & Hill, Manhattan, 1959-75; gen. counsel Kans. Farm Bur. & Service Cos., Manhattan, 1960-75; judge U.S. Dist. Ct., Topeka, Kans., 1975—. City commr., Manhattan, 1950-52, 60-64, mayor, 1952, 64, county atty., Riley County, Kans., 1954-58, state rep., 1964-68, state senator, 1968-75; pres. Kans. Senate, 1975. Served with USAAF, 1943-45. Decorated Air medal, Dfc. Mem. Kans., Am. bar assns., Beta Theta Pi. Clubs: Masons. Republican. Presbyterian. Office: US Dist Ct 444 SE Quincy St Topeka KS 66683

ROGERS, RICHARD F. construction company executive, architect, engineer; b. Chgo., July 25, 1942; s. Frank S. and Emily H. (Novak) R.; m. Christina L. Rogers, June 30, 1963; children: Mitchell, Cynthia. B in Architectural Engineering, U. Ill., Chgo., 1964. Registered architect, Ill., Wis., Mich., profl. engr., Ill. Architect Einstein Assocs. Inc., Skokie, Ill., 1963-69; v.p. Land Am. Corp., Chgo., 1969-70; project architect M.A. Lombard Constrn. Co., Alsip, Ill., 1970-73; sr. project mgr. W.E. O'Neil Constrn. Co., Chgo., 1973-78; pres. A.C.E. Assocs. Inc., Mt. Prospect, Ill., 1978—. Mem.: AIA. Office: 1306 S Wolf Rd Wheeling IL 60090-6444

ROGERS, RICHARD HILTON, hotel consultant, broker; b. Florence, S.C., May 26, 1935; s. Leslie Lawton and Bessie (Holloway) R.; m. Evelyn Pasciuto; children: Richard Shannon, Leslie Anne. Student, U. N.C., 1953-55; BA in Bus. Adminstrn. cum laude, Bryant U., 1962; postgrad., Memphis State U., 1964; DHL (hon.), Schiller Internat. U. Innkeeper Helmsley Spear, N.Y.C., 1961-62; v.p. Holiday Inns of Am., Memphis, 1962-73; exec. v.p. First Hospitality Corp., Hackensack, N.J., 1974-77; v.p., chief oper. officer Cindy's Inc., Atlanta, 1978-82; v.p. 1982 World's Fair, Knoxville, Tenn.; pres., chief exec. officer Hospitality Internat., Atlanta, 1982-92; dir. franchise devel. Baymont Inns, Milw., 1992, 2000. Developer, operator The Warehouse Rest., Oxford, Miss., 1973-75, Beauregard's Rest., Hattiesburg, Miss., 1975-78, Walter Mitty's Rest., Auburn, Ala., 1980-83. Contbr. to profl. jours. Mem. adv. bd. U. South Fla. With USN, 1954-58, Korea. Mem. Am. Hotel/Motel Assn. (mktg. com. 1986-92, adv. coun. 1987-92, industry adv. bd., chmn.), Economy Lodging Coun. Avocations: sailing, photography. Home and Office: 8525 Hope Vine Roswell GA 30076 Personal E-mail: innkpr@charter.net.

ROGERS, RICHARD HUNTER, lawyer, business executive; b. Flushing, N.Y., Sept. 11, 1939; s. Royden Harrison and Frances Wilma (Hunter) R.; children: Gregory P., Lynne A., Reade H. BS in Bus. Adminstrn, Miami U., 1961; JD, Duke, 1964. Bar: Ill. 1964, Ohio 1973. Atty. Continental Ill. Nat. Bank, Chgo., 1964-65; sr. atty. Brunswick Corp., Chgo., 1965-70; corporate counsel The A. Epstein Cos., Inc. (real estate developers), Chgo., 1970-73; v.p., gen. counsel, sec. Price Bros Co., Dayton, Ohio, 1973-82; v.p., divsn. mgr. Water Systems Tech. div. Price Bros. Co., Dayton, Ohio, 1982-85; pres. Internat. divsn. Price Bros. Co., Dayton, Ohio, 1986—88; pvt. practice law Dayton, 1988—; pres. Richard H. Rogers & Assocs. LPA. Pres. adv. coun. Miami U. Bus. Sch.; bd. dirs. Red and White Club, Miami U.; mem. Washington Twp. Task Force on Future Govt.; trustee Woodhaven, Inc.; mem.

Washington Twp. Zoning Commn., 1990—, chmn., 1999—. Mem. ABA (forum com. on constrn.), Ill. Bar Assn., Ohio Bar Assn., Dayton Bar Assn. (chmn. corp. law dept. com. 1983-84, exec. com. 1986-87, editor Bar Briefs 1990-91), Miami U. Alumni Assn. (pres.), Miami U. Pres.'s Club. Office: 7333 Paragon Rd Ste 200 Dayton OH 45459-4157 Address: PO Box 751144 Dayton OH 45475-1144 Office Phone: 937-438-0555. Personal E-mail: rhrlawoffice@aol.com.

ROGERS, RICHARD MEAD, food service executive; b. Montclair, N.J., Oct. 7, 1942; s. Bernard George and Doris Hayward Rogers; m. Joan Ruperti Gerdau, Oct. 26, 1968; children: Gregory Theophilus, Alec Nicoll Mead. BA in Econ., Hobart Coll., 1963; postgrad., U. Pa., 1964. CFA. Securities analyst Union Svc. Corp., N.Y.C., 1964, 65-67; v.p. White, Weld & Co., Inc., N.Y.C., 1967-74; portfolio mgr. GE Pension Trust, Stamford, Conn., 1974-76; pres. The Otto Gerdau Co., N.Y.C., 1976-89, Rogers Internat. Ltd., Portland, Maine, 1990—. Fundraiser Portland Symphony Orch., 1996—; vestry St. John's Episcopal Ch., Stamford, 1972-76; grand argentier Commanderie De Bordeaux, N.Y.C., 1989—, grand chambellan, 2000—. With USAR, 1964-65. Mem. Choral Art Soc., Camphill Found. (treas. 1996—2001), Prouts Neck Country Club, Prouts Neck Yacht Club, The Cumberland Club. Republican. Avocations: sailing, singing, golf, tennis, chess. Home: Chiara 21 Atlantic Dr Scarborough ME 04074 Office: Rogers International LLC 10 Dana St #301 Portland ME 04101-4087

ROGERS, RICHARD MICHAEL, judge; b. Lorain, Ohio, Dec. 8, 1944; s. Paul M. and Lillie (Morris) R.; m. Sophia Lydia Wagner, Dec. 23, 1967; children: L. Danielle, David K., Marisa D., Matthew D. BA, Ohio No. U., 1966, JD, 1972. Bar: Ohio 1972, U.S. Dist. Ct. (no. dist.) Ohio 1973. Assoc. Martin, Hall & Rogers, Marion, Ohio, 1972-76; ptnr. Rogers & Rogers, Marion, 1976-81; asst. law dir., police prosecutor City of Marion, 1973-74; pub. defender, 1975; asst. county prosecutor Marion County, 1976-81; village solicitor La Rue, Ohio, 1976-81; judge Marion Mcpl. Ct., 1982-88, Common Pleas Ct., 1989—2004, 3d Dist. Ct. Appeals, 2004—; mem. traffic rules rev. commn. Ohio Supreme Ct., 1989—. Judge dist. competition Nat. Bicentennial Competition on Constitution and Bill of Rights, 1988, judge state competition, 1988—, judge nat. competition, 1989, 93, 95; instr. faculty Ohio Jud. Coll. Mem. Marion Active 20/40 Svc. Club, 1973-84, treas., 1976-80, bd. dirs., 1976-84, pres., 1980-81; chmn. bd. dirs., pres., co-founder Marion Area Driver Re-edn. Project, 1974-81; pres. Big Bros./Big Sisters Marion County, 1986-87, bd. dirs., 1984-88; mem. sch. bd. St. Mary's Elem. Sch., 1985-88, v.p., 1986, bd. dirs. Marion Cath. High Sch. Endowment Fund, 1986—, v.p., 1991—; mem. Marion Cath. Jr./Sr. High Sch. Bd., 1988-94, pres., 1990-91; mem. fellow in criminal justice steering com. Marion campus Ohio State U., 1996—; mem. paralegal adv. com. Marion Tech. Coll., 1994-96; trustee Ohio State Bar Found., 1997-99. With U.S. Army, 1968-69. Mem. Ohio State Bar Assn. (modern cts. com. 1982-85, jud. adminstrn. and legal reform com. 1982-93, legis. subcom. of jud. adminstrn. and legal reform com. 1989-93, coun. dels. 1991-93, bd. govs. 1996-99, chmn. govt. affairs com. 1998-99, vice-chair criminal justice com. 2001-02, chmn. jury instrn. com. 2002--), Marion County Bar Assn. (pres. 1985-86), Ohio Jud. Conf. (gen. adminstrn. 1984-85, vice chair family matters video com. 1991—, chmn. subcom. legal matters video, civil law and procedure com. 1991-95, editl. bd. Ohio Jury Instrn. 1995—), Ohio Bar Coll., Marion County Law Libr. Assn. (trustee 1982—, pres. 1991-93), Ohio Common Pleas Judges Assn., Delta Theta Phi, Sigma Pi. Republican. Methodist. Avocations: golf, scuba diving. Home: 310 Edgefield Blvd Marion OH 43302-5802 Office: 3d Dist Ct Appeals 204 N Main St Lima OH 45801 Office Phone: 419-223-1861. *Notable cases include: Hines vs. Thermal-Gard of Ohio, Inc., 1988, applicability of home solicitation sales acts, Augenstein vs. Augenstein, deeds sufficient to convey, reserve life estate, Scioto Conservancy Dist., Establishment of Conservancy Dist.*

ROGERS, RICHARD RAYMOND, cosmetics company executive; b. Houston, Apr. 15, 1943; s. J. Ben and Mary Kay (Ash) R.; student North Tex. State U.; children: Terri, Rick, Ryan. Co-founder Mary Kay Cosmetics, Inc., Dallas, 1963, gen. mgr., 1963-65, v.p., 1965-68, pres., 1968-87, chmn. bd., 1987—, also dir. With USMCR. Named Man of Yr., North Tex. Mktg. Assn., 1968. Republican. Baptist. Office: Mary Kay Cosmetics Inc 16251 Dallas Pkwy Addison TX 75001-6801

ROGERS, RITA DORIS LUCK, family nurse practitioner; b. Lincoln County, Kans., Feb. 6, 1948; d. Ernest F. and Rea N. (Nelson) Luck; m. Eugene W. Rogers, Mar. 15, 1969; children: R. Michelle, Sara J (dec.), Brandon G. Diploma, Wesley Sch. Nursing, 1969; BSN cum laude, Ft. Hays State U., 1992, MSN, 1996. RN, ARNP, Kans., Mo., Nebr.; cert. family nurse practitioner ANCC, AANP. Float, relief charge nurse Wesley Med. Ctr., Wichita, 1969-71; charge nurse Mitchell County Hosp., Beloit, Kans., 1971-72; dir. PHN III Jewell County Health Dept., Mankato, Kans., 1973-74; office nurse Dr. A.T. Llana, Superior, Nebr., 1975-76; head nurse, evening supr. Jewell County Hosp., 1977-97; family nurse practitioner Dr. Judith Butler, Superior, 1997-99; interim dir. nursing Sterling (Kans.) Presbyn. Manor, 1998-99, Kansas City Presbyn. Manor, 1999; nurse cons. Presbyn. Manors Mid-Am., Wichita, Kans., 1999—2003; interim nurse practitioner Statcare Minor Emergency Ctr., Salina, Kans., 2000; edn. spec. Hospice Care of Kans., Wichita, 2004; clin. edn. spec. Presbyn. Manors Mid-Am, Wichita, Kans., 2003—. Allied health adj. faculty Cloud C.C., Concordia, Kans., 1988—' Perkins grant coord. North Ctrl. Kans. Area Vo-Tech., Beloit, 1988; county chair Am. Cancer Soc., Mankato, 1972-74; sec. Jewell County Mental Health Assn., 1973-75; parliamentarian Dist. XII Kans. State Nurses Assn., Topeka, 1975-79; infection control com. Brodstone Meml. Hosp., Superior, Nebr., med. staff mem., 1997-98; mem. nursing standards com. and products specifications com. Presyn. Manors of Mid-Am., 1998—, ind. contractor, Nation's Care Unit, 2003-; cert. leader for Arthritis Found. Aquatics Program, 2004-. Columnist Rap with Rita, 1973-74. County and club leader 4-H, Jewell County, 1977-91, Mitchell County, 2000—; tchr. Sunday sch. Luth. Ch., Mankato, 1979-82. Scholar Kans. Health Found., 1993, Midwest Organ Bank, 1994, Ft. Hays State U., 1994, Dane G. Hansen Found., 1994, Kans. Nurses' Found. Wesley Alumni, 1995. Mem. Am. Acad. Nurse Practitioners, Great Plains Nurse Practitioner Soc., Nebr. Nurse Practitioners, Ft. Hays Grad. Nurses Assn., Ft. Hays Alumni Assn., Sigma Theta Tau. Avocations: gardening, crocheting, computing, family. Home: Rte 2 Box 252 309 N Columbus St Jewell KS 66949-9582 Office: PO Box 20440 6525 E Mainsgate Wichita KS 67208-1440 Fax: 785-428-7929. E-mail: brrogers@nckcn.com.

ROGERS, ROBERT BURNETT, naval officer; b. Plainfield, N.J., May 25, 1931; s. Jack Willoughby and Margaret (Snyder) R.; m. Jeanne Weaver, Mr. 15, 1956 (dec. Sept. 1978); children: Robert Burnett (dec.), Steven Michael, John Weaver, Kathryn Patricia; m. Marolyn Maybelline Templeton, May 25, 1981. BS, U.S. Naval Acad., 1954; MS, George Washington U., 1968. Commd. ensign U.S. Navy, 1954, advanced through grades to rear adm., 1981; comdg. officer U.S.S. Austin, Norfolk, Va., 1977-78; asst. chief of staff Naval Surface Force Atlantic, Atlantic Fleet, Norfolk, 1978-80, dep. comdr. Norfolk, 1982-83; comdr. Destroyer Squadron Eight, Mayport, Fla., 1980-81; dep. chief of staff Supreme Allied Command Atlantic, Norfolk, 1981-82; comdr. Amphibious Group Two, Norfolk, 1983-86; dir. logistics Atlantic Fleet, Norfolk, 1986, ret., 1986. City Commr. Fernandina Beach, 1994, mayor, 1996-97, city commr., 1999-2002. Decorated Legion of Merit with 4 gold stars; recipient William S. Sims award Navy League U.S. Mem. U.S. Naval Inst., Marine Corps. Assn. Roman Catholic. Home: 2056 Oak Marsh Dr Fernandina Beach FL 32034-2407 E-mail: marbob@fdn.com.

ROGERS, ROBERT ERNEST, medical educator; b. West Palm Beach, Fla., Nov. 16, 1928; s. Jessie H. and Willie L. (Bahr) Rogers; m. Barbara Ann Hill, May 16, 1950; children: Robert E., Jr., Stephanie Ann Thompson, Cheri Lee Heck. BS, John B. Stetson U., 1949; MD, U. Miami, 1957. Diplomate Am. Bd. Ob-gyn. Commd. 1st lt. M.C., U.S. Army, 1952, advanced through grades to col., 1971; intern Brooke Gen. Hosp., San Antonio, 1957-58, chief resident ob-gyn, 1960-61; resident in ob-gyn Jackson Meml. Hosp., Miami, Fla., 1958-60; fellow gynecology M.D. Anderson Hosp., Houston, 1965-66; asst. chief ob-gyn Tripler Army Med. Ctr., Honolulu, 1966-69; chmn. ob-gyn Walter Reed Med. Ctr., Washington, 1969-70, Madigan Army Med. Ctr., Tacoma, 1970-74; ret. U.S. Army, 1974; prof. Ind. U. Sch. Medicine, Indpls., 1974—, also chief gynecol. div., 1974—; chief ob-gyn svd. Wishard Meml. Hosp., Indpls., 1983-87. Contbr. articles to profl. jours.; editl. bd. Jour. Am. Coll. Surgeons, 2003—. Mem.: ACOG (chmn. gynecol. practice com., commr. practice), AMA, Internat. Soc. Advancement Humanistic Studies Medicine (pres. 1997—98), Soc. Gynecol. Oncologists, Soc. Gynecol. Surgeons (pres. 1983—84). Office: Ind U Sch Medicine 550 University Blvd Indianapolis IN 46202-5149 Office Phone: 317-849-4026. Personal E-mail: Bobberogers@hotmail.com. Business E-Mail: reroger@iupui.edu.

ROGERS, ROBERT REED, manufacturing executive; b. Oak Park, Ill., Feb. 22, 1929; s. Glen Charles and Lucile (Reed) R.; m. Barbara June Fain, Feb. 22, 1951 (div.); children: Robin, Janeen, Kevin; m. Celeste Sim, Sept. 29, 1993. BS in Chemistry, Berea Coll., 1951; MBA, Ill. Inst. Tech., 1958, postgrad., 1959-62. Asst. mgr. metallurgy rsch. dept. Armour Rsch. Found., Ill. Inst. Tech., Chgo., 1955-56, faculty econs. dept., 1956—62; cons. McKinsey & Co., Inc., 1962-64; mgr. devel. planning, profl. group Litton Industries, Inc., 1964-67; pres. N.Am. subs. Muirhead & Co., Ltd., 1967-68; group v.p. Am. Electric Inc. subs., City Investing Co., 1968-70; pres. Cleartight Corp., 1971-73, Newport Internat. Metals Corp., 1973-76, Kensington Assocs., Inc., Newport Beach, Calif., 1976-83; pres., chmn. bd. Proteus Group, Inc., Newport Beach, 1981-83; pres., chmn. bd. dirs. Comparator Sys. Corp., Newport Beach, 1983-96; chmn. bd. UltraCard, Inc., Newport Beach, 1997-98, Vantage Assocs. Inc., Newport Beach, 1998—. Officer USN, 1951-55. Decorated Knight of Grace Sovereign Order St. John; Machinery and Allied Products Inst. fellow, 1956-62; Berea Coll. grantee. Mem. Navy League, Mensa, Intertel. Democrat. Mem. Ch. Of Religious Science. Office: MagnaCarda Inc 5001 Birch St Newport Beach CA 92660-2116 Home: 206 Harbor Woods Pl Newport Beach CA 92660-7824 Business E-Mail: rrr@magnacardainc.com. E-mail: rogersrr@compuserve.com.

ROGERS, RONALD, public relations executive; Pres., CEO Rodgers & Assocs., L.A. Office: 1875 Century Park E Ste 300 Los Angeles CA 90067-2504

ROGERS, ROSE MARIE, state legislator; b. Wolfeboro, N.H., Sept. 27, 1927; m. Roland N. Rogers (dec.); 2 children. BS, U. N.H., 1949; MSW, U. Conn., 1959. Mem. Ward 1 N.H. Ho. of Reps. (dist. 15), Concord, 1993-94; mem. wildlife and marine resources com. N.H. Ho. of Reps., Concord, 1996—. Active Granite State Sr. Games. Mem. NASW, Am. Assn. Ret. Persons, Acad. Cert. Social Workers. Roman Catholic. Home: 29 Eagle Dr Rochester NH 03868-7038

ROGERS, ROSEMARY, author; b. Panadura, Ceylon, Dec. 7, 1932; came to U.S., 1962; naturalized citizen. d. Cyril Allan and Barbara (Jansze); m. Summa Navaratnam (div.); children: Rosanne, Sharon; m. Leroy Rogers (div.); children: Michael, Adam; m. Christopher Kadison (div.). BA, U. Ceylon. Writer features and pub. affairs info. Associated Newspapers Ceylon, Colombo, 1959-62; sec. billeting office Travis AFB, Calif., 1964-69; sec. Solano County (Calif.) Parks Dept., Fairfield, 1969-74. Part-time reporter Fairfield Daily Republic Author: (novels) Sweet Savage Love, 1974, The Wildest Heart, 1974, Dark Fires, 1975, Wicked Loving Lies, 1976, The Crowd Pleasers, 1978, The Insiders, 1979, Lost Love, Last Love, 1980, Love Play, 1981, Surrender to Love, 1982, The Wanton, 1985, Bound by Desire, 1988, The Tea Planter's Bride, 1995, A Dangerous Man, 1996, Dark Fires: Book 2, 1996, Boomer Babes: A Woman's Guide to the New Middle Ages, 1998, All I Desire, 1998. Mem. Authors Guild of Authors League Am., Writers Guild Am.

ROGERS, ROY STEELE, III, dermatologist, educator, dean; b. Hillsboro, Ohio, Mar. 3, 1940; s. Roy S. Jr. and Anna Mary (Murray) R.; m. Susan Camille Hudson, Aug. 22, 1964; children: Roy Steele IV, Katherine Hudson. BA, Denison U., 1962; MD, Ohio State U., 1966; MS, U. Minn., 1974. Cert. dermatologist, dermatopathologist and immunodermatologist. Intern Strong Meml. Hosp., Rochester, NY, 1966—67; resident Duke U. Med. Ctr., Durham, NC, 1969—71, Mayo Clinic, Rochester, Minn., 1972—73, cons., 1973—, prof. dermatology, 1983—, dean Sch. Health Related Scis., 1991—99. Adv. coun. Rochester Community Coll., 1991-2000. Contbr. over 250 sci. articles to publs. Capt. USAF, 1967-69. Recipient Alumni Achievement award Ohio State U. Coll. Medicine, 1991, Alumni citation Denison U., 1993, Faculty Svc. award Mayo Med. Sch., 1993, Gold medal 2d Med. Sch., Charles U., Prague, 2002; named Disting. Educator, Mayo Clinic, 2004. Mem. Am. Acad. Dermatology (bd. dirs. 1987-91, v.p.-elect 1998, v.p. 1999, Gold Triangle award 2004), Am. Soc. Dermatologic Allergy and Immunology (sec.-treas. 1988-2000), Am. Dermatologic Assn. (v.p. 2002-03), Soc. Investigative Dermatology, Assn. Schs. Allied Health Professions, Dermatology Found. Avocations: travel, family, reading, walking. Office: Mayo Clinic 200 1st St SW Rochester MN 55905-0002 Home: 1924 Greenfield Lane SW # 204 Rochester MN 55902-1083

ROGERS, RUTHERFORD DAVID, librarian; b. Jesup, Iowa, June 22, 1915; s. David Earl and Carrie Zoe (Beckel) R.; m. E. Margaret Stoddard, June 4, 1937; 1 child, Jane Shelley; m. Bernette W. Barton, Feb. 28, 2002. BA, U. No. Iowa, 1936, Litt.D., 1977; MA, Columbia, 1937, BS (Lydia Roberts fellow), 1938; D.Library Adminstrn. (hon.), U. Dayton, 1971. Asst. N.Y. Pub. Library, 1937-38; reference librarian Columbia Coll. Library, Columbia U., 1938- 41, acting librarian, 1941-42, librarian, 1942-45; research analyst Smith, Barney & Co., N.Y.C., 1946-48; dir. Grosvenor Library, Buffalo, 1948-52, Rochester Pub. Library, 1952-54; chief pers. office N.Y. Pub. Libr., 1954-55; chief reference dept., 1955-57; chief asst. librarian of Congress, Washington, 1957-62, dep. librarian of, 1962-64; dir. univ. libraries Stanford U., 1964-69; univ. librarian Yale U., 1969-85, univ. librarian emeritus, 1985—. Founder, chmn. bd. dirs. Rsch. Librs. Group, Inc.; mem. Exam. Com. for Pub. Librarians' Certs., N.Y. State, 1951-54; mem. U.S. Adv. Coun. Coll. Libr. Resources; bd. govs. Yale U. Press; bd. dirs., v.p. H.W. Wilson Found., 1969-98; chmn. program mgmt. com. Internat. Fedn. Libr. Assns. Author: Columbia Coll. Library Handbook, 1941, (with David C. Weber) University Library Administration, 1971; also articles in profl. jours. Served from pvt. to 1st sgt. Air Transp. Command USAAF, 1942-43; from 2d lt. to capt., planning officer, chief, spl. Planning Div., Office Asst. Chief Staff, Plans, Air Transport Command 1943-46. Decorated officier de L'Ordre de la Couronne Belge; recipient U. No. Iowa Alumni Achievement award, 1958, Disting. Alumni award Columbia U. Sch. Libr. Svc., 1992, medal Internat. Fedn. of Libr. Assns., 1977. Fellow Am. Acad. Arts and Scis.; mem. A.L.A. (chmn. com. Intellectual Freedom 1950-51), (1950-60), (2d v.p. 1965-66), (mem. exec. bd. 1961-66), (trustee endowment fund), Assn. Research Libraries (dir., pres. 1967-68), N.Y. Library Assn., AAUP, Bibliog. Soc. Am., Assn. Coll. and Reference Libraries, Blue Key, Kappa Delta Pi, Sigma Tau Delta, Theta Alpha Phi. Clubs: Grolier; N.Y. Library (N.Y.C.), Columbia U. (N.Y.C.), Yale (N.Y.C.); Cosmos (Washington), Kenwood Country (Washington); Roxburghe (San Francisco); Book of Calif. Home (Winter): 1081 Lakemont Ct Winter Park FL 32792-5025 Home (Summer): 525 The High Rd Waynesville NC 28786

ROGERS, SAMUEL SHEPARD See SHEPARD, SAM

ROGERS, SHARON J. education consultant; b. Grantsburg, Wis., Sept. 24, 1941; d. Clifford M and Dorothy L (Beckman) Dickau; m. Evan D Rogers, June 15, 1962 (div. Dec. 1980); m. Joseph Y. Ruth, Dec. 22, 2003. BA summa cum laude, Bethel Coll., St. Paul, 1963; MA in Libr. Sci., U. Minn., 1967; PhD in Sociology, Wash. State U., Pullman, 1976. Lectr., instr. Alfred (N.Y.) U., 1972-76; assoc. prof. U. Toledo, 1977-80; assoc. dean Bowling Green (Ohio) State U. Librs., 1980-84; univ. libr. George Washington U., Washington, 1984-92, asst. v.p. acad. affairs, 1989-92, assoc. v.p. acad. affairs, 1992-97, co-dir. Univ. Teaching Ctr., 1990-97; cons. in higher edn. and librs., 1997—. Mem Online Computer Library Ctr Users Coun, 1985—92; pres. Online Computer Library Ctr Users Coun., 1989—90, rsch. advt. com., 1990—92; trustee Online Computer Library Ctr., 1992—2002; exec dir Assn Libr. and Info. Sci. Edn., 1997—2000. Contbr. articles to profl jours. Bd dirs CapAccess, 1993—97, treas, 1993—95; bd dirs ACLU, Toledo, 1978—84. Fellow Jackson, Univ Minn, 1964—65; grantee NSF, Wash State Univ, 1969—72. Mem.: ALA (exec coun 1987—91, pub comt 1989—93, chair 1990—93), Universal Serials and Book Exchange (bd dirs, treas 1987), Washington Research Library Consortium (bd dirs 1987—90), Am Sociological Asn, Asn Col and Research Libraries (pres 1984—85). Home: 2922 24th St N Arlington VA 22207 E-mail: sroger7@attglobal.net.

ROGERS, SHERRY ANNE, physician; b. Syracuse, N.Y., Apr. 15, 1943; d. Rodney Wellington and Jayne Hammond; m. Robert Hamilton Rogers, June 30, 1970. BA, Syracuse U., 1969; MD, SUNY, 1969-70. Diplomate Am. Bd. Family Practice, 1973, Am. Bd. Environ. Medicine, 1985. Intern Health Scis. Ctr. Syracuse, 1969-70; pvt. practice pediat., Auburn, N.Y., 1970-71; emergency physician Cmty. Gen. Hosp., Syracuse, N.Y., 1971-72; pvt. practice family medicine, Syracuse, 1972-85; pvt. practice environ. medicine, 1978—. Lectr. in field. Author: (book) Tired or Toxic?, 1990, Wellness Against All Odds, 1994, Chemical Sensitivity, 1995, You Are What You Ate, The E.I. Syndrome, 1997, Depression Cured At Last, 1997, No More Heartburn, 2000, The Cure is in the Kitchen, The Scientific Basis of Environmental Medicine Techniques, 2000, Total Wellness, 2000, 2001, Pain Free in 6 Weeks, 2001, Detoxify or Die, 2003; editor (ed environm med sect): Internal Medical World Report, 1992—93; contbr. articles to profl. jours., book Alternative and Complementary Veterinary Medicine, 1998, chapters to books. Fellow: Am. Coll. Nutrition, Am. Coll. Asthma, Allergy and Immunology. Office: NE Ctr Environ Med 2800 W Genesee St Syracuse NY 13219-1451

ROGERS, STEFFEN H. retired academic administrator; m. Athena Rogers. B in Biology, Ga. So. Coll., 1964; PhD in Biology, Vanderbilt U., 1968. Postdoctoral rschr. Johns Hopkins U. Sch. Pub. Health, Balt., 1968—70; asst. prof. biology, acting dean Coll. Arts and Scis. Tulsa (Okla.) U., 1970—91; prof. zoology, dean Coll. Arts and Scis. U. R.I., 1991—96; prof. biology, acting pres., v.p. acad. affairs, provost Clemson (S.C.) U., 1996—2001; pres. Bucknell U., Lewisburg, Pa., 2001—04. Past dir. Okla. Ctr. of Excellence in Molecular Medicine, Tulsa, Mervin Bovaird Ctr. for Studies in Molecular Biology and Biotech., Tulsa; presenter in field.

ROGERS, STEPHEN G. biotechnologist; b. Peoria, Ill. 1 child, Kirsten. AB in Biology/Chemistry, Wabash Coll., 1969, MA in Biology, 1970; PhD in Biology, Johns Hopkins U., 1976. Dir. biotech. projects for Europe Monsanto Cereals Tech. Ctr., Cambridge, Eng.; now dir. Crop Genomics Cereron Genomics subs. Monsanto Co., Boston. Recipient Nat. Medal Tech, 1998. Achievements include development of member of scientific team to first develop foreign genes into plants leading to virus resistance and insect protection traints for crops; integrating modern crop breeding with newer methods for crop i. Avocations: magic, international cooking, travel. Office: Cereron Genomics 45 Sidney St Cambridge MA 02139-4133

ROGERS, STEPHEN HITCHCOCK, former ambassador; b. Flushing, N.Y., June 21, 1930; s. Francis Walker and Julia (Wheeler) R.; m. Kent Brain, June 23, 1956; children: Kryston R. Fischer, F. Halsey, Julia L., John H. BA, Princeton U., 1952; MA, Columbia U., 1956; MPA, Harvard U., 1962. Fgn. svc. officer Dept. of State, 1956-93; econ. counselor Am. Embassy, London, 1970-72; counselor U.S. Mission to OECD, Paris, 1972-75; office dir. Bur. Inter.-Am. Affairs Dept. of State, Washington, 1975-78; econ. counselor Am. Embassy, Mexico City, 1978-82; prof. Nat. Def. U., Washington, 1982-85; econ. counselor Am. Embassy, Pretoria, South Africa, 1986-90, amb. Mbabane, Swaziland, 1990-93. Bd. dirs. Cen. Atlantic Conf., United Ch. of Christ, 2000-03. Lt. (jg) USN, 1952-55. Recipient Outstanding Civilian Svc. award Dept. of Army, 1985. Mem. Am. Fgn. Svc. Assn., Diplomatic and Consular Officers Ret., Nassau Club (Princeton, N.J.). Mem. United Ch. of Christ. Home: 3803 Ivydale Dr Annandale VA 22003-2006

ROGERS, STEVEN RAY, physicist; b. Tachikawa, Honshu, Japan, Dec. 6, 1952; arrived in U.S., 1953; s. Culis Doyle Martin and Mary Lu (Bowles) Rogers; m. Robina Rae Behel, Dec. 27, 1975; children: Miranda Rae, Kellina Gail. BA in Math./Physics magna cum laude, U. No. Colo., 1975; MS in Physics, Kans. State U., 1977. Rschr., instr. Kans. State U., Manhattan, 1975-79; tech. staff ElectroMagnetic Applications, Lakewood, Colo., 1979-82; lead engr. MITRE Corp., Colorado Springs, Colo., 1982—. Cons., advisor sys. survivability and hardening N.Am. Aerospace Def. Command, Air Force Space Command, Colorado Springs, 1982—; adj. prof. Webster U., Colorado Springs, 1994. Contbr. articles to profl. jours. Mentor gifted students Colorado Springs Sch. # 20, 1992—93; host family cadet USAF Acad., Colorado Springs, 1994—98. Recipient Program Recognition award, MITRE Corp., 1988, 1996. Mem.: IEEE (sr.; chmn. Pikes Peak sect. 1993—94), Lambda Sigma Tau, Sigma Pi Sigma. Achievements include co-holder of patent for global situation awareness information distribution system; co-founder of programs that sustain the survivability of NORAD and Air Force Space Command systems; evaluation and integration of NORAD systems. Home: 5510 Broadmoor Bluffs Dr Colorado Springs CO 80906-7971 Office: MITRE Corp 1155 Academy Park Loop Colorado Springs CO 80910-3716

ROGERS, T. GARY, food products company executive; b. 1943; BSME, U. Calif., 1963; MBA, Harvard U., 1968. Assoc. McKinsey & Co., San Francisco; founder, pres. Vintage Ho. Restaurants, Calif. and Tex.; chmn. bd., CEO Dreyer's Grand Ice Cream, Inc., Oakland, Calif., 1977—. Dir. Levi Strauss & Co., Stanislaus Food Products, Gardonjim Farms, The Friends of Calif. Crew. Mem. Bay Area Coun. Mem. Internat. Dairy Foods Assn. (bd. dirs.). Office: Dreyers Grand Ice Cream Inc 5929 College Ave Oakland CA 94618

ROGERS, TERI ELLEN, mathematician, educator; b. Chgo., Nov. 18, 1946; d. Frank and Elaine Augusta (Mullan) Naccarato; m. David Joseph Rogers, Nov. 26, 1971; 1 child, Jeremy. BA, Northwestern U., 1968; MS, Western Ill. U., 1971. Prof. math. Coll. DuPage, Glen Ellyn, Ill., 1986—. Mem.: DAR (chpt. regent 2003—), Am. Math. Assn. Two-Yr. Colls., Math. Assn. Am. Baptist. Avocations: genealogy, square dancing. Office: Coll DuPage Natural Sci Divsn 425 22d St Glen Ellyn IL 60137-6599

ROGERS, THEODORE COURTNEY, investment company executive; b. Lorain, Ohio, Aug. 25, 1934; s. William Theodore and Leona Ruth (Gerhart) Rogers; m. Elizabeth B. Barlow, June 28, 1984; children from previous marriage: Pamela Anne Rogers Harmon, Theodore Courtney Jr. BS in Social Sci., Miami U., Oxford, Ohio, 1956, LHD (hon.), 2001; postgrad., Johns Hopkins U., 1957; MBA summa cum laude, Marquette U., 1968; MALA, St. John's Coll., Annapolis, Md., 2004. With Armco Inc., 1958-80; pres. Olympic Fastening Sys., 1970-74; with Bathey Mfg. Co. subs., 1970, group v.p. indsl. products, 1971-74; exec. v.p. Nat. Supply Co. subs., Houston, 1974-76, pres., 1976-80, v.p. parent co., 1976-79, group v.p. parent co., 1979-80; pres., COO NL Industries, Inc., N.Y.C., 1980-82, pres., CEO, 1982-83, chmn., pres., CEO, 1983-87; chmn. Am. Indsl. Ptnrs., N.Y.C., 1987—. Chmn. Bucyrus Internat., Stanadyne Automotive Corp., Consoltex Inc., Gt. Lakes Carbon Corp.; bd. trustees St. John's Coll. Nat. coun. Theatre Comm. Group; bd. dirs. Lincoln Ctr. Peforming Arts, City Ctr. Music and Drama, Nat. Ocean Industries Assn.; chmn. bd. dirs. Theatre for New Audience; former chmn. Ctr. Cmty. Interests; emeritus chmn. N.Y.C. Ballet; bd. dirs., trustee Ballet Rev. Qur. Lt. USN, 1956—58. Mem.: Poets and Writers (bd. dirs.), Bus. Roundtable, N.Y. Soc. Libr. (trustee), Grolier Club, Univ. Club (Milw.), Met. Club (Washington), Sky Club, Ramada Club, Century Assn. (N.Y.), Achilles Track Club (founder, bd. dirs.), Links Club, Econs. Club (N.Y.), Union Club (Cleve.), Kappa Phi Kappa, Sigma Chi (Significant Sig), Beta Gamma Sigma (bd. dirs.). Office: Am Indsl Ptnr 551 5th Ave Ste 3800 New York NY 10176-0001 Office Phone: 212-983-1399.

ROGERS, THEODORE OTTO, JR., lawyer; b. West Chester, Pa., Nov. 17, 1953; s. Theodore Otto and Gladys (Bond) R.; m. Hope Tyler Scott, Nov. 7, 1981; children: Helen Elliot, Theodore Scott, Robert Montgomery Bond. AB magna cum laude, Harvard U., 1976, JD cum laude, 1979. Bar: N.Y. 1980, U.S Ct. Appeals (2nd cir.) 1984, U.S. Dist. Ct. (so. and ea. dists.) N.Y. 1980, D.C. 1981, U.S. Ct. Claims, 1982, U.S. Supreme Ct. 1983, U.S. Ct. Appeals (6th and 10th cirs.) 1983, U.S. Ct. Appeals (1st cir.) 1984, U.S. Ct. Appeals (fed. cir.) 1986. From assoc. to ptnr. Sullivan & Cromwell, N.Y.C., 1979—. Co-author: (books) Employment Litigation in New York, 1996, Employment

Law DeskBook for Human Resources Professionals, 2001. Mem. U.S. Presdl. Transition Team, 1980. Fellow Coll. Labor and Employment Lawyers; mem. N.Y. State Bar Assn. (co-chair individual rights and responsibilities com. labor and employment law sect.), Assn. of Bar of City of N.Y. (labor and employment law). Republican. Home: 535 E 86th St New York NY 10028-7533 Office: Sullivan & Cromwell 125 Broad St Fl 28 New York NY 10004-2489 E-mail: rogerst@sullcrom.com.

ROGERS, THOMAS FRANCIS, foundation administrator; b. Providence, Aug. 11, 1923; s. Thomas Francis and H. Ann (Flaharty) R.; m. Estelle E. Hunt, July 6, 1946; children: Clare Hibschman, Judith Reynolds, Hope Grove. BS cum laude, Providence Coll., 1945; MA, Boston U., 1949. Rsch. assoc. Radio Rsch. Lab. Harvard U., Cambridge, Mass., 1944-45; TV engr. Bell and Howell Co., Chgo., 1945-46; electronics scientist AF Cambridge Rsch. Ctr., Cambridge, Mass., 1946-54; assoc. group leader MIT Lincoln Lab., Cambridge, 1951-53; lab. head AF Cambridge Rsch. Ctr., Bedford, Mass., 1954-59; div. head and steering com. mem. MIT Lincoln Lab., Bedford, 1959-64; asst. dir. def. rsch. and engring. Office of Sec. Def., Washington, 1964-65, dep. dir. def. rsch. and engring., 1965-67; dir. rsch. and tech. Office of Sec. HUD, Washington, 1967-69; v.p. The Mitre Corp., Washington, Bedford, 1969-72; chmn. The Sophron Found., McLean, Va., 1980—; dir. U.S. Congress Office of Tech. Assessment Study on Civilian Space Stas. and U.S. Future in Space, Washington, 1982-84; from pres. to chief scientist The Space Transp. Assn., Arlington, Va., 1992—. Founding chmn. bd. dirs. External Tanks Corp., Boulder, Colo.; bd. dirs. Internat. Radio Satellite Corp., Washington, Space Destinations Svcs., Inc., 1994—; chmn. bd. dirs. Luna Corp., Great Falls, Va., 1991—; dir. Share Space Found., 2000; chmn. POLARIS Command-Comm. Co., USN, 1960-64; mem. Satellite Comm. Panel, Pres.'s Sci. Adv. Com., 1961-63; mem. Dept. Def. NASA Satellite Comm. Com., 1961-64; U.S.A. del. UN Conf. on Applications of Sci. and Tech. by Lesser Developed Nations, Geneva, 1963; mem. Fed. Aeronautics and Astronautics Coordinating Bd., 1965-67, Fed. Coun. on Sci. and Tech., 1967-69; mem. Space Program Adv. Coun., NASA, 1971-73, chmn. applications com., 1972-73; mem. NAS com. on regional emergency med. comm. systems, 1976-78; mem. space applications bd. com. on NASA space comms. 1986-87; mem. com. on antenna, satellite broadcasting and emergency preparedness for Voice of Am., 1986-88; mem. adv. com. study space transp. U.S. Congrl. Office Tech. Assessment, 1994-95. Contbr. articles to jours., chpts. to books. Trustee X-Prize Found., 1995—. Recipient Outstanding Performance award CSC, 1957, cert. commendation Sec. Navy, 1961, Meritorious Civilian Svc. award and medal, Sec. Def., Constrn.'s Man of Yr. award Engring. News Record, 1969, Space Pioneer award Nat. Space Soc., 1988, Best Vision of the Future award Space Frontier Found., 1997, NASA Disting. Pub. Svc. award, 1999, Pioneer award Visionary Lifetime Achievement award Space Tourism Soc. Fellow IEEE (mem. aerospace policy com., chmn. 1991-95, Profl. Achievement award 1995); mem. Internat. Acad. Astronautics, Cosmos Club (Washington). Home and Office: 5400 Vantage Point Rd # 210 Columbia MD 21044 Office Phone: 410-992-1210.

ROGERS, THOMAS SYDNEY, communications executive; b. New Rochelle, N.Y., Aug. 19, 1954; s. Sydney Michael Rogers Jr. and Alice Steinhardt, m. Sylvia Texon, Oct. 9, 1983; children: Robert, Jessica, Jason. BA, Wesleyan U., 1975; JD, Columbia U., 1979. Bar: N.Y. 1980, U.S. Dist. Ct. (so. and ea. dists.) N.Y. 1980, U.S. Ct. Appeals (D.C. cir.) 1981. Legis. aide to Congressman Richard Ottinger U.S. Ho. Reps., Washington, 1975-76, sr. counsel subcom. telecommunications, 1981-86; assoc. Lord, Day & Lord, N.Y.C., 1979-81; v.p. policy planning and bus. devel. Nat. Broadcasting Co., Inc., N.Y.C., 1987-88; pres. NBC Cable, 1988-89, NBC Cable & Bus. Devel., 1989-99; exec. v.p. NBC, N.Y.C., 1992-99; vice chmn. NBC Internet, N.Y.C., 1999; chmn., CEO Primedia, Inc., N.Y.C., 1999—2003; chmn. TRget Media, N.Y.C., 2003—. Pres., CEO internat. coun. Nat. Acad. TV Arts and Scis., 1994-97, chmn., 1998-99; lectr. in field. Named one of Outstanding Young Men in Am., 1985. Mem. N.Y. State Bar Assn., Internat. Radio and TV Soc. Office: TRget Media 150 E 52d St New York NY 10022

ROGERS, THOMASINA VENESE, federal commissioner; Student, Northwestern U.; JD, Columbia U. Chmn. Adminstrv. Conf. U.S., Washington, 1994-95; presdl. pers. staff The White House, Washington; dep. legal counsel, then legal counsel EEOC, Washington; mem. Occupl. Safety and Health Rev. Commn., Washington, 1998—, chmn., 1999—2002. Bd. dirs. Children's Nat. Med. Ctr. Mem. Am. Arbitration Assn. (bd. dirs.) Office: Occupl Safety and Health Review Commn One Lafayette Ctr 1120 20th St NW Washington DC 20036-3457*

ROGERS, WARD JUNIOR, retired industrial designer; b. Savanna, Ill., May 8, 1924; s. Charles Clarence Rogers and Lucille Mae Woods; m. Marilyn Ruth Edwards, May 30, 1945; children: Douglas, Renee, Toni, Ward J. Grad., Mpls. Sch. Fine Arts, 1947. Chef Old Elm Club, Highland Park, Ill., 1947—49; engr. Clinton Engine, Manquota, Iowa, 1950—51; engr., indsl. designer GE, Morrison, Ill., 1951—71; art dir. Color Arts Inc., Racine, Wis., 1971—74; owner Dairy Bar, Mt. Carroll, 1976—86; custodian US Post Office, Mt. Carroll, 1973—91. Freelance designer Savanna Fabricators, Sterling (Ill.) Ambulance; drafting tchr. local coll.; mem. round table U. Iowa. Author: (column) Remember When, 1980. Pres. Art Guild, Morrison, Ill.; chmn. Mt. Carroll Hist. Soc., 1998—; precinct com. Dem. Party, Morrison, Ill. S/sgt. USMC, 1941—45, PTO, 2d lt. reserves U.S. Army, 1949. Mem.: VFW (life), Indsl. Design Inst., Am. Legion. Avocations: antiques, records, collecting cars, painting. Home: 207 E Rapp St Mount Carroll IL 61053

ROGERS, WAYNE L. political organization administrator; m. Valerie; children: Courtney, Kellyn. MBA, U.S. Naval Acad.; postgrad., Georgetown U. Pres. Synergics, Inc., Annapolis, Md.; chair Md. Dem. Party, Annapolis. Mem. nat. fin. bd., Leadership 2000 com. Dem. Nat. Com. Office: 188 Main St Ste 1 Annapolis MD 21401

ROGERS, WILLIAM, psychologist, behavior specialist, writer, lecturer, journalist; BA in Broadcast Journalism, L.A. Inst. Arts, 1970; BA in Psychology, We. Ill. U., Macomb, 1989; MS in Counseling Psychology, Our Lady of the Lake U., San Antonio, 1991; PhD in Psychology, Columbia Pacific U., San Rafael, Calif., 1993; postgrad., Rollo May Ctr. Social Rsch. Saybrook Inst., San Francisco, 1994. Lic. psychotherapist, ednl. psychologist. Fgn. and domestic correspondent ABC News, NBC News, UPI Internat., KTRH Radio News, WOAI Radio News, 1970-85. Exec. dir. Behavior Rsch. Inst. San Antonio. Author: The Technology of Behavior, 1993, The Behavior Management Handbook, 1994, Creating Positive Behavior, 1995, Recovered Memory and Other Assaults Upon the Mysteries of Consciousness, 1995, Behavior and Consequences, 1997, Kids in Chaos, 1997, Humpty Dumpty was Pushed, 1999; feature stories include Cmty. Responsibility, Behavior and Consequences, 1974, Missing Children, 1984; contbr. articles to profl. jours., TV and radio shows. Recipient George Foster Peabody Nomination Tex. Med. Assn., Wendall mays Pub. Svc. award Tex. Bar Assn., Gov.'s award AP, Tex. Assn. Broadcasters, Radio-T.V. News Dirs. Assn., Tex. Legislature Commendation, League of United Lat. Am. Citizens award Tex. State Network News, Coastal Bend Planning Commn. Spl. Svc. award, Headliner's News award, AP honors (5), UPI awards (13); citation ABA, U.S. Senate, Spl. Citation City of Corpus Christi, Tex., Spl. Resoultion of Commendation Tex.Ho. Reps., Exceptional Recognition Entered Into Perpetuity State of Tex. Archives; recognized as founder of Behavior Mgmt. Philosophy and Methodology (Existential-Realism); commd. Adm. of Tex. Navy. Achievements include patents for electr4omagnetic brain animation; electronic brain animation generator, transcranial magnetic stimulation. Office: Behavior Rsch Inst 4835 Medical Dr # 29882 San Antonio TX 78230

ROGERS, WILLIAM CECIL, political science educator, consultant; b. Manhattan, Kans., 1919; s. Charles Elkins and Sadie (Burns) R.; m. Mary Jane Anderson, Aug. 31, 1941; children: Shelley, Faith, Mary Sarah. BA, U. Chgo., 1940, MA, 1941, PhD, 1943. Asst. to dir. Pub. Adminstrn. Clearing House, Chgo., 1943-47; lectr. internat. relations U. Chgo., 1945-47; asst. prof. U. Va., 1947-48; asso. prof. polit. sci. Western Res. U., 1948-49; dir. World Affairs Center, U. Minn., Mpls., 1949-84; cons. Minn. Internat. Ctr., 1984—. Dir. Program Info. on World Affairs, Mpls. Star and Tribune, 1951-73. Author: Community Education in World Affairs, 1956, A Guide to Understanding World Affairs, 1966, Global Dimensions in U.S. Education: The Community, 1972; co-author The Winter City Book, 1980. Pres. Minn. Jazz Sponsors, 1966-67; chmn. Mpls. Com. on Urban Environ., 1976-80. Mem. Nat. Univ. Extension Assn. (past sec.-treas.), Winter Cities Assn. (co-founder 1982). Home: 219 Chandler Dr Apt 219 St Anthony MN 55421 Office: 711 E River Rd Minneapolis MN 55455-0369

ROGERS, WILLIAM DILL, lawyer; b. Wilmington, Del., May 12, 1927; m. Suzanne Rochford, Sept. 7, 1926; children: William Rogers, Daniel. BA, Princeton U., 1948; LL.B., Yale U., 1951. Bar: D.C. 1952, U.S. Supreme Ct. 1954. Ptnr. Arnold & Porter, Washington, intermittently 1953—; dep. U.S. coordinator Alliance for Progress, AID, 1962-65; pres. N.Y. Ctr. Inter.-Am. Relations, 1965-72; asst. sec. of state inter-Am. relations Dept. State, 1974-76, undersec. of state for econ. affairs, 1976-77; mem. law faculty Cambridge U., Eng., 1982-83. Sr. counselor Bipartisan Commn. on Central Am., 1983-84; vice chmn. Kissinger Assocs. Inc. Author: The Twilight Struggle: The Alliance for Progress and U.S.-Latin-American Relations, 1967. Co-chmn. U.S.-Mexico Binat. Commn.; bd. dirs. Coun. Fgn. Rels., 1981-90. Mem. Am. Soc. Internat. Law (pres. 1971-73), ABA. Office: Arnold & Porter 555 12th St NW Washington DC 20004-1206 Office Phone: 202-942-5915.

ROGERS, WILLIAM FENNA, JR., supermarket executive, management consultant; b. Higgsinville, Mo., Dec. 25, 1912; s. William Fenna and Emily S. (Moose) R.; m. Thelma Ann Hooper, June 15, 1940 (dec. Mar. 1982); m. Ethel Allene Burgess, Aug. 6, 1983; stepchildren: Dorothy H. Nance, Linda H. Connors. BA, Ark. Coll., 1933; postgrad. U. Ark., 1933, Tulane U., 1935, U. Fla., 1938-39. Vocat. adv. Nat. Youth Adminstrn., Little Rock, 1936-38; chief field ops. U.S. Employment Svc., Little Rock, 1938-43, chief supr. tng., Washington, 1946-47; asst. dir. Civilian Pers. Divsn., U.S. Dept. Navy, Washington, 1947-55; mem. productivity team Nat. Mgmt. Coun., Paris, 1952; lectr. U.S. Internat. Fair, Amsterdam, 1963; v.p. indsl. rels. Giant Food, Inc., Washington, 1955-75; mgmt. cons., Falls Church, Va., 1975—; trustee Teamster Warehouse Fund, 1956—, Carpet Layers Funds, 1968—; lectr. Am. U., 1949-69; pres. Chateau Devel. Corp., Fairfax, Va., 1978-83. Mem. selection bd. U.S. Postal Svc., 1969-77; elder New York Ave. Presbyn. Ch., Washington, 1918 72, cons. Lincoln commn., 1984—, chmn., 1989—; elder Falls Church Presbyn. Ch., 1980-83, sunday sch. supt., 1984-88; mem. Falls Church Village Preservation and Improvement Soc., 1967—; chmn. bur. edn. and employment Greater Washington Bd. Trade, 1974-76. Served to lt. comdr. USNR, 1943-64. Mem. ASTD (life), Am. Legion Res. Officers Assn., Naval Res. Assn., Alpha Psi Omega, Kappa Gamma, Pi Kappa Delta, Iota Lambda Sigma. Club: Internat. Town and Country (dir. 1959-61) (Fairfax, Va.). Avocations: golf, fishing. Home: 9229 Arlington Blvd Apt 258 Fairfax VA 22031-2508

ROGERS, WILLIAM WARREN, historian, educator, publishing executive, writer; b. Sandy Ridge, Ala., Aug. 18, 1929; s. Harry Ernest Rogers and Mittie Pate Loftin; m. Miriam Arnold Rogers, June 6, 1951; children: Warren, Arnold, Kate, Amy. BS, MS, Auburn U., Ala., 1951; PhD, U. N.C., Chapel Hill, 1959. With U.S. Army Counter Intelligence Corps, Stuttgart, Germany, 1954—56; instr. U. Md., Stuttgart, Germany, 1955—56; dir. Moody AFB program Fla. State U., Valdosta, Ga., 1958—59, prof. history Tallahassee, 1959—96; vis. prof. Fla. A&M, 1990, Auburn U., Ala., 1993, 1996; dir. Sentry Press, Inc., Tallahassee, 1996—. Bd. editors Fla. Historical Quarterly, 1970—2000; bd, dir Southern Studies, Nachitaches, La.; spkr. on politics and history to groups and orgns. Author: Ante-Bellum Thomas County, 1825-1861, 1963, Thomas County During the Civil War, 1964, The One-Gallused Rebellion, 1970 (Am. Assn. State and Local History award of Merit, 1972), Thomas County 1865-1900, 1973, Transition to the Twentieth Century Thomas County, Ga., 1900-1920, 2002; co-author: Montgomery as the Confederate Capital: A View of a New Nation, 1964, Labor Revolt In Ala.: The Great Strike of 1894, 1965, Stephen S. Renfroe Ala.'s Outlaw Sheriff, 1972, Favored Land: A History of Tallahassee and Leon County, 1972 (Tallahassee/Leon County Historic Preservation Bd. award, 1972), August Reckoning Jack Turner and Racism in Post Civil War Ala., 1973, Convict's, Coal and the Banner Mine Tragedy, 1987, Ala.: The History of a Deep South State, 1994 (James F. Sulzby award, 1995), Fla.'s Clerks of the Circuit Ct. Their History and Experiences, 1996, Fla. Sheriffs: A History 1821-1945, 2001 (James J. Horgan award, 2002), The Croom Faily and Goodwood Plantation, 2001 (Nat. Assn. State and Local History Commendation of Merit, 2002), Ala.'s Response to the Penitentiary Movement, 1829-1865, 2003; editor: Am. Siberia by J.C. Powell, 1976; co-editor: Fla.'s Heritage of Diversity Essays in Honor of Samuel Proctor, 1997; contbr. scholarly articles to profl. jours. Finalist Prof. of Yr., Am. Hist. Assn.; named Outstanding Alumnus, Auburn U.; recipient Coyle Moore award Outstanding Tchg., Fla. State U. Faculty and Student Com., 1972, Lifetime Commitment commendation, Am. Assn. for State and Local History, 1994, Outstanding Tchr. award, Phi Alpha Theta (Fla. State chpt.), 1996; fellow, NEH, 1980; grantee, Am. Philosophical Soc., 1970. Democrat. Avocations: reading, walking, tennis, birdwatching, antique books. Office: Sentry Press Inc 424 E Call St Tallahassee FL 32301 Office Phone: 850-234-7423.

ROGERSON, CRAIG ALLAN, manufacturing executive; b. Detroit, July 4, 1956; s. William Durie and Eunice Clara (Richert) R.; m. Carina Joy Ballato, Sept. 11, 1982; children: Scott Allan, Kristen Joy, Colin William. BS in Chem. Engring., Mich. State U., 1979. Tech. rep. Water Mgmt. Chemicals div. Hercules Inc., Charlotte and Wilmington, N.C., 1979-82, sales rep. Fibers div. Atlanta, 1982-85, market devel. supr., 1985-87, product mgr., 1987-88, nat. sales mgr., 1989-90, dir. ops. Oxford, Ga., 1991-92, bus. dir. Wilmington, Del., 1992-94, sales dir. paper tech. divsn., 1995-96, v.p., gen. mgr. fibers divsn., 1996—. Nat. Merit scholar, 1974. Mem. TAPPI, INDA Assn. Nonwovens Industry, Mich. State U. Alumni Assn. Republican. Lutheran. Avocations: racquetball, golf, travel. Home: PO Box 702 Gwynedd Valley PA 19437-0702 Office: Hercules Inc Hercules Plz Wilmington DE 19801-6101

ROGGE, JAMES ALAN, education educator; b. Akron, Ohio, Mar. 18, 1952; s. Arthur Denver and Violet Rogge; m. Ruth Moss, Dec. 22, 1974. BA, U. South Fla., 1974; MEd, U. Miami, 1976; EdS, Nova U., 1994. Cert. tchr., Fla. Asst. city planner City of Ormond Beach, Fla., 1977-78; tchr. 5th grade Beacon Hill Pvt. Sch., Hollywood, Fla., 1978-79; tchr. social studies/gifted Broward County Schs., Ft. Lauderdale, Fla., 1979-82, 91-92, Dade County Schs., Miami, Fla., 1982-91; instr. reading Broward C.C., Ft. Lauderdale, 1992—, Miami C.C., 1994-97, Nova U., Ft. Lauderdale, 1997—2001. Scholarship com. U. South Fla., Ft. Lauderdale, 1989-91, com. collegewide equal opportunity, 1994-95, multicultural, 2000-01, student success, 2001—, internat. com. co-chmn.; test writer exit exam State of Fla. Grantee, Broward C.C., 1993—94, 2001. Mem. Internat. Reading Assn., Broward County ESOL Coun., Chronicle of Higher Edn. Avocations: travel, speedwalking, skiing, writing, chess. Office: Broward CC North Campus 1000 Coconut Creek Blvd Coconut Creek FL 33066 E-mail: roggej@yahoo.com.

ROGILLIO, KATHY JUNE, musician, piano rebuilder, educator; b. Baton Rouge, La., Nov. 4, 1950; d. David Hunter and Thelma Ruth (Tucker) R. MusB, La. State U., 1972, MusM, 1974. Organist Plains Presbyn. Ch., Zachary, La., 1963-73; teacher's aid Gifted/Talented East Baton Rouge Parish, Baton Rouge, La., 1974-75; staff accompanist La. State U., Baton Rouge, 1975-76; music enrichment tchr. Episcopal H.S., Baton Rouge, 1976-77; organist, choirmaster Grace Episcopal Ch., St. Francisville, La., 1977-82; piano-technician So. U., Baton Rouge, La., 1977-84; apprentice in piano rebuilding and concert tuning, 1978-81; music tchr., organist, choirmaster St. Patrick's Episcopal Day Sch. and Ch., Zachary, La., 1985-86; vis. organist, dir. Numerous Chs., La. and Miss., 1982—; piano rebuilder pvt. practice, Zachary, La., 1986—. Ind. contract work Santi Falcone, Falcone Piano Co., Haverhill, Mass., 1987-88, part time organist/choirmaster St. Patrick's Episcopal Ch., Zachary, La., 1999-2000; pvt. piano tchr. La. Sch. for Visually Impaired, 2000—; recitalist, vis. organist. Arranger: Piano-Trio Arrangement Brahms Intermezzo Opus 118, #2, 1986 (2d pl. Composer's Guild Farmington, Utah, 1986). Treas. Beulah Plains Cemetery Assn., Zachary, La., 1987; mem. Landowners for Equitable Flood Control, Zachary, La., 1994—; Dem. candidate for U.S. Ho. of Reps. from 6th Dist. La., 2000. Mem. Am. Guild Organists, Baton Rouge Musicians' Assn. (exec bd. 1990-92, v.p. 1992-94. pres. 1994-96), La. Endowment for the Humanities, La. Pub. Broadcasting, Pi Kappa Lambda (profl. mus. hons. frat.). Democrat. Episcopalian. Avocations: needlework, cooking, animals. Home and Office: Artist Pianos 18153 Barnett Rd Zachary LA 70791-8114 E-mail: k.rogillio@worldnet.att.net.

ROGIN, GILBERT LESLIE, editor, author; b. N.Y.C., Nov. 14, 1929; s. Robert I. and Lillian Carol (Ruderman) R. Student, State U. Iowa, 1947-49; AB, Columbia, 1951. Editor-at-large Miller Pub., L.A., 1955—. Author: The Fencing Master, 1965, What Happens Next?, 1971, Preparations for the Ascent, 1980. Served with AUS, 1952-54. Recipient award for creative work in lit. Am. Acad. Inst. Arts and Letters 1972 Home: 21 W 10th St New York NY 10011

ROGLIERI, JOHN LOUIS, health facility administrator; b. Plainfield, N.J., June 24, 1939; s. Vito and Grace Mary (DeCristofaro) R.; m. Geraldine Ann Piller, June 15, 1963; children: Maria Roglieri Friedman, Anna Roglieri Healy, John. BSChemE, AB in Applied Scis., Lehigh U., 1960; MD, Harvard U., 1966; MS in Bus., Columbia U., 1978. Diplomate Nat. Bd. Med. Examiners. Intern Bellevue Hosp., Columbia Svc., 1966-67; resident Presbyn. Hosp., N.Y.C., 1969-71, dir. divsn. ambulatory medicine, 1973-75, v.p. ambulatory svcs., 1975-82, dir. employee health svc., 1988-92; fellow Harvard Med. Sch., Boston, 1971-73; asst. dir. lab. computer sci. Mass. Gen. Hosp., 1972-73, dir. ambulatory screening clinic, 1972-73; med. dir. N.Y. Health Plan, Inc., N.Y.C., 1988-92; corp. med. dir. Sanus Corp. Health Sys., Ft. Lee, N.J., 1992-95, NYL Care Health Plans Inc., N.Y.C., 1996-99; physician Web Link, Inc., Englewood, N.J., 2000-2001; med. dir. N.Y. Life Ins. Co., 2001—. Cons. Nat. Ctr. Health Svc. Rsch. and Devel., 1973-75; dir. clin. scholar program Columbia U., 1975-77, asst. prof. clin. medicine Coll. Physicians and Surgeons, 1973—; health edn. cons. Basic Internat. Investments, 1975-76; v.p., bd. dirs. AMARCO Internat., N.Y.C., 1975-85; mem. adv. bd. Western and Upper Manhattan Regional Perinatal Network, Coll. Physicians and Surgeons, N.Y.C., 1975-80; appeared in various TV and radio programs. Author: Odds on Your Life, 1980; mem. editl. bd. Managed Care, 1992—, Jour. Applied Rsch. in Health Adminstrn., 1979-81, Hosp. Physician, 1997—; book rev. cons. Acad. Press, Inc., N.Y.C.; contbr. articles to profl. publs. Capt. USPHS, 1967-69. Mem. APHA, Am. Fedn. Clin. Rsch., Am. Soc. Internal Medicine, N.Y. State Soc. Internal Medicine, Soc. for Rsch. and Edn. in Primary Care Internal Medicine, Nat. Assn. Managed Care Physicians. Roman Catholic. Avocations: surfcasting, woodworking. Office: Columbia Presbyn Med Ctr 161 Fort Washington Ave New York NY 10032-3713

ROGOFF, JEROME HOWARD, psychiatrist, psychoanalyst, forensic expert; b. Detroit, Dec. 21, 1938; s. Abraham Solomon and Sarah Riva (Epstein) R.; (div. 1983); m. Erika Kathleen Keller, Sept. 25, 1983. BA cum laude, Harvard Coll., 1960; MD, Case Western Reserve U., 1965. Diplomate Am. Bd. Psychiatry and Neurology. Physician Peace Corps USPHS, Kathmandu, Nepal, 1966-68; clin. fellow psychiatry Harvard Med. Sch., Boston, 1975-79; staff psychiatrist Westwood (Mass.) Lodge Hosp., 1972-74, assoc. clin. prof. psychiatry Tufts Med. Sch., Boston, 1977-86; assoc. chief, psychiatry and dir., inpatient Psychiatry, day hosp. Faulkner Hosp., Boston, 1975-94; pvt. practice psychiatry, psychoanalysis and forensic psychiatry, 1994—. Cons. psychiatrist Mass. Parole Bd. Probate Ct. Plymouth County, Mass., LEAA, Washington, 1971-78; med. psychiat. dir. ct. diversion program Boston TASC-A, 1974-75; treas., bd. dirs. Guild for Continuing Edn., Boston, 1981-95; founding dir. Law and Psychiatry Resource Ctr., Boston, 1983—; adj. prof. Simmons Sch. Social Work, Boston, 1981-85; lectr. in psychiatry Harvard Med. Sch., Boston, 1986-94, 2001-. Chmn. psychiatry team Combined Jewish Philanthropies, Boston, 1978-83, assoc. chmn. med. team, 1984-87, mem. social planning and allocations com., 1991-98, mem. cmty. svcs. com., 1998—, chmn. chronic mental illness com., 1999-2000, mem. disabilities com., 2000—; bd. dirs. Jewish Vocat. Svc., Boston, 1987-91. Fellow Am. Psychiat. Assn. (Disting., pub. affairs rep. 1988-92, 93-94, budget com. 1996-2002, assembly rep. 2000—, chmn. privacy and confidentiality com. 2003—); mem. AMA, Mass. Psychiat. Soc. (councillor 1988-94, chair pub. affairs com. 1988-92, 93-94, chair nominating com. 1990, 2000, pres.-elect 1998-99, pres. 1999-2000), Am. Acad. Psychiatry and Law, Am. Assn. Pvt. Practice Psychiatrists. Democrat. Avocations: cabinetry, carpentry, cooking, classical music, languages. Home and Office: 659 Chestnut St Waban MA 02468-2035 Office Phone: 617-964-1805. *Two guiding principles, both from my father: "When in doubt, do the right thing." Sounds trite and naive, but turns out in the event to be profound; one almost always knows deep down what the right thing is. "When you are born, you cry, and everyone around you laughs. So live your life that when you come to leave it, you laugh, and everyone around you cries." On my profession of psychiatry and psychoanalysis: psychotherapy adds insight to injury.*

ROGOFF, KENNETH SAUL, economics professor; b. Rochester, N.Y., Mar. 22, 1953; s. Stanley Miron and June Beatrice (Goldman) R.; m. Evelyn Jane Brody, Aug. 18, 1979 (div. 1989); m. Natasha Lance, June 25, 1995; children: Gabriel, Juliana. BA/MA in Econs., Yale U., 1975; PhD in Econs., MIT, 1980. Economist Internat. Monetary Fund, Washington, 1983; economist, sect. chief Internat. Fin. divsn., Bd. Govs. of the Fed. Res. Sys., Washington, 1979-84; assoc. prof. econs. U. Wis., Madison, 1985-89; prof. econs. U. Calif., Berkeley, 1989-92; prof. econs. and internat. affairs Princeton U., 1992—, Charles and Marie Robertson prof. of internat. affairs, 1995-98; prof. econs. Harvard U., 1999—, Thomas D. Cabot prof. pub. policy, 2004—, dir. Ctr. Internat. Devel., 2003—04; econ. counselor, dir. rsch. IMF, 2001—03. Vis. scholar San Francisco Fed. Res., 1990-92, World Bank, Washington, 1989, IMF, Washington, 1988-94. Author books and contbr. articles to profl. jours. Alfred P. Sloan Rsch. fellow, 1986-87, Hoover Instn. Nat. fellow, 1986-87, NSF fellow, 1985—, John Simon Guggenheim fellow, 1998. Fellow World Econ. Forum, Econometric Soc., Am. Acad. Arts and Scis., World Econ. Forum; mem. Am. Econ. Assn.(mem. trilateral commn.), Coun. on Fgn. Rels., Internat. Grandmaster Chess. Office: Harvard U Econs Dept Littauer Ctr Cambridge MA 02138-3001 Office Phone: 617-495-4022. Business E-Mail: krogoff@harvard.edu.

ROGOFF, PAULA DRIMMER, English and foreign language educator; b. N.Y.C. d. George and Florence (Levine) Drimmer; m. Arnold Stevan Rogoff; children: Jeffrey Scott, Eric Todd, Brian Craig. BA cum laude, Hunter Coll., 1961; MEd summa cum laude, William Paterson Coll., 1979. Cert. elem. tchr., ESL tchr., supr., N.J. Tchr. handicapped Herricks Bd. Edn., Williston Park, N.J.; tchr. reading compensatory edn. Oakland (N.J.) Bd. Edn.; tchr., coord. gifted-talented program N. Haldeon (N.J.) Bd. Edn.; ESL adult tchr., h. s. students Passaic County Tech. Inst., Wayne, N.J. Presenter Children's Libr. programs. Named Tchr. of Yr., Passaic County Tech. Inst., 1999-2000. Mem. ASCD, NEA, TESOL, Internat. Platform Assn., N.J. Edn. Assn., Phi Beta Kappa, Phi Lambda Theta, Kappa Delta Pi. Home: 11 Furman Dr Wayne NJ 07470-5304 Office: Passaic County Tech Inst 45 Reinhardt Rd Wayne NJ 07470

ROGOSKI, PATRICIA DIANA, financial executive; b. Chgo., Dec. 29, 1939; d. Raymond Michael and Bernice Rose (Konkol) R. BS in Acctg. and Econs., Marquette U., 1961, postgrad., 1965-66, NYU, 1966-68, St. John's U., N.Y.C., 1975-76; cert. mgmt. acct., 1979. Sr. fin. analyst Blackhawk Mfg. Co., Milw., 1961-66; mgr., sr. analyst Shell Oil Co., N.Y.C., 1966-71; mgr. data processing Bradford Nat./Penn Bradford, Pitts., 1971-75; asst. mgr. fin. controls ITT, N.Y.C., 1975-79; v.p., comptr. ITT Consumer Fin. Corp., Mpls., 1979-80; sr. v.p. fin. ITT Fin. Corp., St. Louis, 1980-84; v.p., exec. asst., group exec. ITT Coins, Secaucus, N.J., 1984-85; pres. Patron S., Ltd., Wilmington, Del., 1986—; CFO, sr. v.p. Guardsmark, Inc., Memphis, 1989-94; sr. v.p. Peoplemark, Inc., Memphis, 1989-94. Bd. dirs. St. Louis Repertory Theater, 1983-84. Named to Acad. Women Achievers, YWCA, N.Y.C., 1980. Mem. Fin. Execs. Inst., Inst. Mgmt. Acctg., Econ. Club, Memphis Symphony Chorus. Avocation: duplicate bridge. Office: Patron S Ltd 2711 Centerville Rd Ste 400 Wilmington DE 19808-

ROGOVIN, JOHN A. lawyer; b. Washington, July 10, 1961; s. Mitchell and Sheila Ann (Ender) R. AB, Columbia U., 1983; JD, U. Va., 1987. Bar: N.Y. 1989, D.C. 1990. Law clk. hon. Laurence Silberman U.S. Ct. Appeals (D.C. Cir.), Washington, 1987-88; assoc. Kramer, Levin et al, N.Y.C., 1988-89,

O'Melveny & Myers, Washington, 1990-92, spl. counsel, 1996-97, ptnr., 1997-2001; dep. transition counsel Presdl. Transition, Little Rock, 1992-93; asst. to atty. gen. U.S. Dept. Justice, Washington, 1993, dep. asst. atty. gen. Civil Divsn., 1993-96; dep. gen. counsel FCC, Washington, 2001—02, gen. counsel, 2003—. Mem. ABA, D.C. Bar Assn. Office: Fed Comm Commn Gen Counsel Washington DC 20554 Business E-Mail: John.Rogovin@fcc.gov.

ROGOVIN, LAWRENCE H. lawyer; b. NYC, June 10, 1932; s. Abraham and Laura R.; m. Saundra Schwartz, Aug. 11, 1957; children: Jayne Lina, Wendy Renee, Evan Lewis. BS in Econ., U. Pa., 1953; LLB cum laude, NYU, 1956. Bar: NY 1956, Fla. 1971. Dep. asst. atty. gen. State of N.Y., 1956-57, asst. atty. gen., 1960-61; assoc. Squadron, Gartenberg, Ellenoff & Plesent and predecessors, N.Y.C., 1962-67, ptnr., 1967-72; pvt. practice Miami, Fla., 1972—74, 1983—98, 2002—; ptnr. Squadron, Ellenoff, Plesent & Lehrer, N.Y.C., 1974-75, Cohen, Angel & Rogovin, North Miami, Fla., 1978-82, Cohen, Rogovin, Reed & Ivans, Miami, 1982-83; v.p., gen. counsel Rare, Inc., Miami, 1998—2002. 1st lt. JAGC, USAFR, 1957-60. Recipient NYU Founders Day award, 1956. Mem.: FBA, ABA, Fla. Bar Assn. Office: Ste 265 South 4000 Hollywood Blvd Hollywood FL 33022 Office Phone: 954-367-0006. Office Fax: 954-272-0225. E-mail: lrogovin@bellsouth.net.

ROGOVIN, MILTON, documentary photographer, retired optometrist; b. N.Y.C., Dec. 30, 1909; s. Jacob and Dora (Shainhouse) R.; m. Anne Setters, Apr. 7, 1942; children: Ellen, Mark, Paula. BS in Optics and Optometry, Columbia U., 1931; MA in Am. Studies, SUNY, Buffalo, 1972; DFA (hon.), U. Buffalo, 1994, Buffalo State Coll., 1994, D'Youville Coll., 1994. Optometrist, Buffalo, 1931-75; freelance documentary photographer, 1958—. Author: Milton Rogovin: The Forgotten Ones, 1985, Portraits in Steel, 1993, Windows That Open Inward, 1999, The Bonds Between Us, 2001, Triptychs, Buffalo's Lower West Side Revisited, 2002, Milton Regovin-The Forgotten Ones, 2003. Served with U.S. Army, 1942-45. Recipient W. Eugene Smith Meml. Fund award, 1983, Gov.'s award N.Y. State Coun. on Arts, 2000; Libr. of Congress acting as repository for Milton Rogovin's negatives and photographs, 1999—. Home: 90 Chatham Ave Buffalo NY 14216-3109 Office Phone: 716-876-4872.

ROGOWICZ, EDWARD JOSEPH, industrial arts, technology educator; b. Glen Lyon, Pa., Apr. 25, 1934; s. Walter Edward Rogowicz and Celia Dutch; m. Jeannine Marie Mentzer, Aug. 22, 1964. BS in Edn., Millersville (Pa.) U., 1961, MS in Edn., 1965. Tchr. Cumberland Valley Sch. Dist., Mechanicsburg, Pa., 1961—65, West Shore Sch. Dist., Lewisberry, Pa., 1965—97, ret., 1997; substitute tchr., 1998—. Vol. Sr. Citizen's People Mover, Hershey, Pa., 1998—; chmn. com. Pa. Sports Hall Fame, Harrisburg, 1995—; program enhancement specialist Neighborhood Ctr. United Meth. Ch., Harrisburg, Pa., 1964—; various positions assistance bd. Dauphin County, Harrisburg, 1985—. With U.S. Army, 1955—57. Mem.: Pa. State Edn. Assn. (legis. com. 1997, v.p. vocational practical arts 1977—97, Recognition award 1997), Tech. Edn. Assn. Pa. (Outstanding Svc. award 1997, 2002), Hershey (Pa.) Optimist Club (pres. 1990—2000, chmn. jr. golf qualifier 1990—2000, chmn. respect for law program 1990—2003). Republican. Roman Catholic. Avocations: films, photography, hunting, fishing, reading. Home: 37 Bromley Ct Hershey PA 17033

ROGOWSKI, WALTER S. corporate executive, lawyer; b. 1929; married. LL.B., U. Wis., 1953; B.A., St. Ambrose Coll., 1959. Atty. Iowa Power & Light Co., 1962-66; with Marmon Group Inc. (Mich.), 1966—, sr. v.p. sec., gen. counsel Marmon Group Inc., Chgo., 1966-83, sr. v.p., gen. counsel, 1983— . Served with U.S. Army, 1956-57. Office: Marmon Group Inc 39 S La Salle St Chicago IL 60603-1603

ROGOWSKY, ROBERT ARTHUR, trade commission operations director, educator; b. Vancouver, B.C., Can., Mar. 12, 1951; s. Michael Randall and Ruth Ann (Wellman) R.; m. Linda Sue George, June 17, 1972; children: Vanessa, Heather, Tara, Nichole, Alexis. BA in Econs., Boston U., 1973; MA in Econs., U. Va., 1975, PhD in Econs., 1982. Asst. prof. dept. econs. George Mason U., Fairfax, Va., 1977-78; rsch. economist Bur. Econs. FTC, Washington, 1979-83; econ. advisor to commrs. Consumer Product Safety Commn., Washington, 1983-84, acting exec. dir., asst. to dir., 1984; pres. Econ. Edn. for Clergy, Inc., Bethesda, Md., 1985-86; exec. asst. to chmn. Internat. Trade Commn., Washington, 1986-87; dep. dir. Bur. Consumer Protection FTC, Washington, 1987-89; dir. office of industries U.S. Internat. Trade Commn., Washington, 1989-92, dir. ops., 1992—; adj. prof. George Mason U. Instr. U. Va., 1976-77; econ. rschr. Am. Enterprise Inst., 1976; econ. rsch. analyst Econ. Policy Office, U.S. Dept. Justice, 1974-75; presenter in field. Contbr. articles to profl. jours. Mem. Am. Mgmt. Assn., Am. Econs. Assn., Assn. Christian Economists. Lutheran. Home: 9542 Locust Hill Dr Great Falls VA 22066 Office: US International Trade Comm Operations 500 E St NW Washington DC 20436-0003

ROGULA, JAMES LEROY, consumer products company executive; b. Rock Island, Ill., Nov. 8, 1933; s. Andrew and Nellie Pearl (Cook) R.; m. Adelaide F. Dittbrenner, May 29, 1960; children: James Lyle, Adelaide Ann, John Andrew. BA, Knox Coll., 1955; MBA, NYU, 1964. Group product mgr. Am. Chicle Co., Long Island City, N.Y., 1958-66; v.p. new product devel. Carter Wallace, Inc., N.Y.C., 1966-72; v.p. new products J.B. Williams Co., N.Y.C., 1972-74; sr. v.p. E.J. Brach & Sons, Chgo., 1974-77; v.p., gen. mgr. A.E. Staley Mfg. Co., Oak Brook, Ill., 1977-80; exec. v.p. Booth Fisheries Corp., Chgo., 1980-82; v.p., gen. mgr. Arm & Hammer div. Church & Dwight, Inc., Princeton, NJ, 1982-90; pres. Am. Candy Co., Richmond, Va., 1990-94; group exec. v.p. N.Am. bus. groups Scotts Co., Marysville, Ohio, 1994—2001; pres., personal care domestic Church & Dwight Co. Inc., Princeton, 2001—. With U.S. Army, 1956-58. Mem. Sunset Ridge Country Club. Home: 370 Old Farm Rd Northfield IL 60693 Office: 469 N Harrison St Princeton NJ 08540-3510

ROHATYN, FELIX GEORGE, ambassador; b. Vienna, May 29, 1928; came to U.S., 1942, naturalized, 1950; s. Alexander and Edith (Knoll) R.; m. Jeannette Streit, June 9, 1956; children: Pierre, Nicolas, Michael; m. Elizabeth Fly, May 31, 1979. BS, Middlebury (Vt.) Coll., 1948; LLD (hon.), Adelphi U., Bard Coll., Hofstra U., 1981, L.I. U., 1981, Middlebury Coll., 1982, Fordham U., 1983; LLB (hon.), NYU, 1979, Brandeis U., 1987. With Lazard Freres & Co., LLC, N.Y.C., 1948—, mng. dir., 1960—97; amb. to France Paris, 1997—2001; pres. Rohatyn Assocs., N.Y.C., 2002—. Bd. dirs. Suez, Lagardere Group, LVMH, Inc.; mem. bd. govs. N.Y. Stock Exch., 1968—72. Served with AUS, 1951—53, Korea.

ROHDE, BRUCE C. food company executive, lawyer; b. Sidney, Nebr., Dec. 17, 1948; BS, BA, Creighton U., 1971, JD cum laude, 1973. Bar: Nebr. 1974, U.S. Dist. Ct. Nebr. 1974, U.S. Tax Ct. 1975, U.S. Ct. Appeals (8th cir.) 1976, U.S. Ct. Appeals (5th cir.) 1979, U.S. Supreme Ct. 1980, U.S. Claims Ct. 1981, U.S. Ct. Appeals (D.C. cir.) 1982. Lawyer, pres. McGrath, North, Mullin & Kratz, Omaha, 1984—96; gen. counsel ConAgra Inc., Omaha, 1984—96, vice chmn., pres., 1996—97, CEO, 1997—, chmn., 1998—. Bd. dirs. Valmont Industries Inc. Vice chmn. bd. dirs. Creighton U.; chmn. bd. dirs. Strategic Air and Space Mus. Mem.: ATLA, ABA (corp., banking and bus. law sect., taxation sect., antitrust law sect., litigation sect.), Omaha Bar Assn., Nebr. Soc. CPA, Nebr. State Bar Assn., Nebr. Assn. Trial Lawyers, Beta Alpha Psi, Beta Gamma Sigma. Address: ConAgra Inc 1 ConAgra Dr Ste 302 Omaha NE 68102*

ROHDE, JAMES VINCENT, software systems company executive; b. O'Neill, Nebr., Jan. 25, 1939; s. Ambrose Vincent and Loretta Cecilia R.; children: Maria, Sonja, Daniele, Olga. B of Comml. Sci., Seattle U., 1962. Chmn. bd. dirs., pres. Applied Telephone Tech., Oakland, Calif., 1974; v.p. sales and mktg. Automation Electronics Corp., Oakland, 1975-82; founder, pres., CEO, chmn. Am. Telecorp, Inc., Redwood City, Calif., 1982-99; founder, vice-chmn., bd. dirs. Ceon Corp., Redwood City, 1999—. Chmn. exec. com., chmn. emeritus Pres.'s Coun. Heritage Coll., Toppenish, Wash., 1985—; chmn. bd. dirs. Calif. chpt. Coun. of Growing Cos., 1990-93. Bd. dirs. Ind. Colls. No. Calif., 1991-93. Named U.S. Dept. Commerce Export Exec. Yr. No. Calif., 1993. Mem. Am. Electronics Assn. (bd. dirs. 1992-94, vice-chmn. No. Calif. coun. 1992-93, chmn. 1993-94). Republican. Roman Catholic. Office: Ceon Corp 720 Bay Rd Redwood City CA 94063-2469 E-mail: jrohde@ceon.com.

ROHLF, F. JAMES, biometrician, educator; b. Blythe, Calif., Oct. 24, 1936; BS, San Diego State Coll., 1958; PhD in Entomology, U. Kans., 1962. Asst. prof. biology U. Calif., Santa Barbara, 1962-65; assoc. prof. statis. biology U. Kans., 1965-69; assoc. prof. biology SUNY, Stony Brook, 1969-72, prof., 1972—, chmn. dept. ecology and evolution, 1975-80, 90-91. Statis. cons. N.Y. Pub. Svc. Commn., 1975-78, IBM, 1977-81, U.S. EPA, 1978-80; vis. scientist IBM, Yorktown Heights, N.Y., 1976-77, 80-81; vis. prof. U. Rome, 1997, 99. Fellow: Am. Acad. Arts and Scis.; mem.: Internat. Fedn. Classification Socs. (pres. 1975—78), Classification Soc. (pres. 1975—78, editl. bd. 1984—, bd. dirs. 1994—2002), Soc. Systematic Biologists, Biometric Soc. Achievements include research and development of statistical methods and software for geometric morphometrics and applications of multivariate analysis to systematics and population biology. Office: SUNY at Stony Brook Dept Ecology And Evolution Stony Brook NY 11794-5245 Office Phone: 631-632-8580. E-mail: rohlf@life.bio.sunysb.edu.

ROHLFING, FREDERICK WILLIAM, lawyer, political consultant, retired judge; b. Honolulu, Nov. 2, 1928; s. Romayne Raymond and Kathryn (Coe) R.; m. Joan Halford, July 15, 1952 (div. Sept. 1982); children: Frederick W., Karl A., Brad (dec.); m. Patricia Ann Santos, Aug. 23, 1983. BA, Yale U., 1950; JD, George Washington U., 1955. Bar: Hawaii 1955, Am. Samoa 1978. Assoc. Moore, Torkildson & Rice, Honolulu, 1955-60; ptnr. Rohlfing, Nakamura & Low, Honolulu, 1963-68, Hughes, Steiner & Rohlfing, Honolulu, 1968-71, Rohlfing, Smith & Coates, Honolulu, 1981-84; pvt. practice Honolulu, 1960-63, 71-81, Maui County, Hawaii, 1988—; dep. corp. counsel County of Maui, Wailuku, Hawaii, 1984-87, corp. counsel, 1987-88; land and legal counsel Maui Open Space Trust, 1992-97, also bd. dirs. Polit. cons., 1996, 98, 2002; magistrate judge U.S. Dist. Ct. Hawaii, 1991-96. Active Hawaii Ho. Reps., 1959-65, 80-84, Hawaii State Senate, 1966-75; US alt. rep. So. Pacific Commn., Noumea, New Caledonia, 1975-77, 1982-84; Maui adv. coun. State Reapportionment Commn., 2001; hon. chmn. Maui coms. George W. Bush for Pres., 2000. Capt. USN, 1951-54, USNR, 1955-87, ret. Mem. Hawaii Bar Assn., Maui Country Club, Naval Intelligence Profls. Avocations: ocean swimming, golf, skiing. Home and Office: 2807 Kekaulike Ave Kula HI 96790

ROHLOFF, CLAIRE MARIE, interior designer, educator; b. Dover, NJ, Mar. 17, 1945; d. Harold Alfred and Margaret Clara (Grether) Rohloff. Diploma, Bryn Mawr Hosp., 1966; BFA magna cum laude, Kean Coll. N.J., 1980; MS in Interior Design, Pratt Inst., 1984; grad., Meridian Shiatsu Inst., 1997. RN N.J., cert. internat. cert. bodywork and massage profl., practitioner Asian bodywork; master gardener. Asst. head nurse neuropsychiat. inst. Morristown (N.J.) Meml. Hosp., 1966-70; clinic nurse Morris County Aftercare Clinic Drug Abusers, Morristown, 1970-72; charge nurse psychiat. unit Overlook Hosp., Summit, N.J., 1975-81, interior design tech. and facilities devel., 1981-83; propr. Innovative Interiors; asst. prof. Kean Coll., 1979-80, prof., 1980-90, Trenton State Coll., 1990-92; co-owner Light lines Holistic Health Ctr., Clinton, N.J., 1992-97; owner, tchg. classes in Shiatsu, Yoga, aromatherapy and Fengh Shui East West Inst. Inc., 1997—2003. Cons. Sweets electronic divsn., McGraw Hill. Mem.: Nat. Assn. Inventors Club, Alpha Sigma Lambda. Presbyterian. Home: 383 Bloomsbury Rd Bloomsbury NJ 08804-3208

ROHM, ROBERT HERMANN, sculptor, educator; b. Cin., Feb. 6, 1934; s. Hermann George and Anna Katherine (Sager) R.; m. Patricia Jean Cutlip, Dec. 6, 1959 (div. 1978); children: Hans Tobin, Kyle Curtis. B in Indsl. Design, Pratt Inst., 1956; MFA in Sculpture, Cranbrook Acad. Art, 1960. Instr. Columbus (Ohio) Coll. Art and Design, 1956-59, Pratt Inst., Bklyn., 1960-65; prof. art U. R.I., Kingston, 1965-95, pres. emeritus, 1996—. One-man shows: O.K. Harris Gallery, N.Y.C., 1970, 72, 73, 75, 77, 80, 83, 84, 86, 89, 92, 94, 97, 99, 2002, Parker St. 470 Gallery, Boston, 1970, 72, Univ. Rochester, N.Y., 1971, N.S. Coll. Art, Halifax, 1970, Worcester Art Mus. (Mass.), 1978, Univ. R.I., 1981, 88, 94, Nielsen Gallery, Boston, 1985, 86, 92, 93, 2001, Wheaton Coll., Norton, Mass., 2002, La Jolla Mus. Contemporary Art, Calif., 1985, Lenore Gray Gallery, Providence, 1990, 93, 95, Wheeler Gallery, Providence, 1996, R.I. Coll., Providence, 1998, Salve Regina U., Newport, R.I., 2003; group shows include Boston Mus., 1974, Whitney Mus., N.Y.C., 1962, 64, 69, 70, 73, 83, Va. Mus., Richmond, 1970, Fogg Mus., Cambridge, Mass., 1971, Seattle Art Mus., 1969, Vancouver Art Mus., B.C., Can., 1970, N.J. State Mus., Trenton, 1969, R.I. State Coun. on Arts, 1973, 82, Vassar Coll., 1971, Inst. Contemporary Art, Boston, 1975, Miss. Mus. Art, Jackson, 1979-80, Grey Art Gallery, NYU, 1980, Montclair (N.J.) Art Mus., 1978, Aldrich Mus. Contemporary Art, Ridgefield, Conn.,1981, 82, SUNY-Plattsburgh, 1981, Zone Gallery, Springfield, Mass., 1982, Cumberland Gallery, Nashville, 1986, 93, Allan Frumkin Gallery, N.Y.C., 1985, Beitzel Fine Arts Inc., N.Y.C., Addison Gallery Am. Art, Andover, Mass., 1989, Nielsen Gallery, Boston, 1990-91, 99, 2004, Soma Gallery, San Diego, 1993, Palo Alto (Calif.) Cultural Ctr., Centre Coll., Danville, Ky., Harn Mus., U. Fla., Gainesville, 2004, Brevard Mus. Art & Sci., Melbourne, Fla., 2004; represented in permanent collections Columbus Gallery Fine Art, Finch Coll., N.Y.C., Pa. State U., Kunsthalle, Zurich, Va. Mus. Fine Arts, Mus. Modern Art, N.Y.C., U. N.Mex., Albuquerque, Albright-Knox Gallery, Buffalo, Whitney Mus. Am. Art, N.Y.C., Met. Mus. Art, N.Y.C., Rose Art Mus., Brandeis U., Waltham Mass., Mus. Fine Art, Boston, Mus. of Contemporary Art, Chgo., Newport (R.I.) Art Mus., Tucson Mus. of Art, Ariz., Flint Inst. Arts, Mich., Butler Inst. Am. Art, Youngstown, Ohio, Munson-Williams Proctor Arts Inst. Mus. Art, Utica, N.Y., Harn Mus., U. Fla., Gainesville. Grantee Guggenheim Found., 1964, R.I. State Council on Arts, 1973, 82, 93, NEA, 1974, 86; recipient Cassandra Found. award, 1967, award Boston 200 Bicentennial Commn., 1975. Achievements include subject of numerous articles in jours. and catalogues. Home: PO Box 1679 Charlestown RI 02813-0909 E-mail: robertrohm@netsense.net.

ROHN, REUBEN DAVID, pediatric educator and administrator; b. Israel, Apr. 12, 1945; came to U.S., 1954; s. Aryeh and Rachel (Brenner) R.; m. Judith Semel, Sept. 6, 1971; 1 child, Karen. BA cum laude, Bklyn. Coll., 1967; MD, N.Y. Med. Coll., 1971. Diplomate Am. Bd. Pediat., Am. Bd. Pediatric Endocrinology, Am. Bd. Pediatrics-Adolescent Medicine. Intern in pediat. Montefiore Hosp., Bronx, N.Y., 1971-72, resident in pediat., 1972-74; fellow in adolescent medicine U. Md. Hosp., Balt., 1974-76; preceptor in pediat. Johns Hopkins U. Sch. Health Svcs., Balt., 1975-76; asst. prof. dept. pediat. Ea. Va. Med. Sch., Norfolk, 1976-82; coord. pediat. clerkship Ea. Va. Med. Sch., Children's Hosp. of King's Daus., Norfolk, 1977-90; prof. dept. pediat. Ea. Va. Med. Sch., Norfolk, 1989—; adj. prof. chemistry Old Dominion U., Norfolk, 1984—; dir. adolescent medicine/endocrinology Children's Hosp. of King's Daus., Norfolk, 1976—. Mem. curriculum com. Ea. Va. Med. Sch., 1977-79, clerkship coords. com. 1977-90, genetics com., 1978-80, evaluation com. 1979-91, chmn. selectives com., 1981-82, ad hoc com. on consultation, 1982-83, student progress com., 1983-85, student health com., 1985-87, LCME com. on curriculum, 1990-92; mem. child abuse com. Children's Hosp. of King's Daus., 1976-80, chmn. adolescent adv. com., 1976-80, patient care com. 1980-94, nutrition com. 1980-94, utilization rev. com., 1980-82, med. records com., 1987-89, gen. med./surg. task force com., 1987-88, chmn. dept. promotions com., 1990—; bd. dirs. Pediat. Faculty Assocs., 1994-98, mgmt. com. Children's Specialty Group, 1998-2000; spkr. in field. Reviewer Jour. Adolescent Health Care, 1986—, mem. editl. bd., 1989-92; contbr. articles to profl. jours. Mem. Norfolk Sch. Health Coun., 1977—, mem. ad hoc com. infant screening program for hypothroidism Commonwealth of Va., 1977-79, cons., 1979—; mem. cmty. adv. bd. Norfolk Adolescent Pregnancy Prevention Svc. Project, 1981-83; bd. dirs. Elizabeth River chpt. Am. Diabetes Assn., 1982-85, South Hampton Roads chpt. 1985-93; mem. adv. com. Norfolk-Virginia Beach Jr. League, 1987-88; judge ann. Health Edn. Fair, Norfolk Pub. schs., 1980-94; pres. VA/Carolines chpt. Soc. Adolescent Medicine, 1998-2000. Recipient grant Bressler Rsch. Fund, 1975-76, Biomed. Rsch. Devel. grant Ea. Va. Med. Sch., 1978, 78-79, 79-80. 81-82, 83-84, Children's Health Found. grant, 1988-89. Fellow: Am. Acad. Pediat. (youth and adolescence com. Va. chpt. 1978—2000); mem.: Lawson Wilkins Pediat. Endocrine Soc., Soc. Adolescent Medicine (abstract reviewer 1984—91), Sigma Xi. Avocations: photography, folk dancing. Home: 4653 Larkwood Dr Virginia Beach VA 23464-5815 Office: Childrens Hosp Kings Daus 601 Childrens Ln Norfolk VA 23507-1910 E-mail: rrohn@chkd.com.

ROHN, WILLIAM R. biotechnology company executive; Sr. v.p. comml. and corp. devel. IDEC Pharms., Inc., San Diego, 1993—96, sr. v.p. comml. ops., 1996—98, pres., COO, 1998—. Office: IDEC Pharmaceuticals Corp 3030 Callan Rd San Diego CA 92121

ROHNER, BONNIE-JEAN, small business owner, computer consultant; b. Waltham, Mass., Aug. 2, 1946; d. Gerrit John and Marjorie Lorraine (Hollis) R.; children: David Harrison Sackett, Amanda Marjorie Sackett. BFA in Fashion, Pratt Inst., Bklyn., 1967; BA in Biology, Adelphi U., Garden City, N.Y., 1983; MS, CIS, U. New Haven, Conn., 1993. Freelance fashion designer, Garden City, 1971-76; owner, mgr. The Printing Workshop, Massapequa, N.Y., 1976-78; personnel mgr. Doron Ltd., Norwich, Conn., 1978-79; computer related trainer Gen. Dynamics, Groton, Conn., 1979-89; acad. computing coord. Three Rivers Com./Tech. Coll., Norwich, 1989-94; owner, mgr. bytestream, Norwichtown, Conn., 1993—. Computer cons. U. New Haven, Groton, 1990-92; tech. advisor Countywide Network Com., 1989-90; sec. Connbug, Rocky Hill, Conn., 1992-93; tech. cons. on Internet Am. Online, 1996—. Mem. NAFE, AAUW, AAUP, ACM, Women's Network of S.E. Conn. Avocations: creative writing, internet.

ROHNER, RALPH JOHN, lawyer, educator, university dean; b. East Orange, N.J., Aug. 10, 1938; AB, Cath. U. Am., 1960, JD, 1963. Bar: Md. 1964. Teaching fellow Stanford (Calif.) U., 1963-64; atty. pub. health div. HEW, 1964-65; prof. law Cath. U. Am. Sch. Law, Washington, 1965—, acting dean, 1968-69, assoc. dean, 1969-71, dean, 1987-95; staff counsel consumer affairs subcom. U.S. Senate Banking Com., 1975-76; cons. Fed. Res. Bd., 1976-83, chmn. consumer adv. council, 1981; cons. FDIC, 1978-80; spl. counsel Consumer Bankers Assn., 1984—. Cons. U.S. Regulatory Coun., 1979-80. Co-author: Consumer Law: Cases and Materials, 1979, 2d edit., 1991; co-author, editor The Law of Truth in Lending, 1984, republished, 2000. Bd. dirs. Migrant Legal Action Program, Inc., Washington, Automobile Owners Action Coun., Washington, Credit Rsch. Ctr., Georgetown U., Am. Fin. Svcs. Assn. Edn. Found. Conf. on Consumer Fin. Law. Mem. ABA, Am. Law Inst., Coll. of Consumer Fin. Svcs. Lawyers. Home: 10909 Forestgate Pl Glenn Dale MD 20769-2047 Office: Cath U Sch Law 620 Michigan Ave NE Washington DC 20064-0001 E-mail: rohner@law.edu. *We learn from those we teach, we are inspired to write by those who read, and we should serve as examples to those who aspire.*

ROHR, DAVIS CHARLES, aerospace consultant, business executive, retired air force officer; b. Burlington, Wis., Oct. 29, 1929; s. Charles Davis Rohr and Dorothy Elizabeth (Hahn) Rohr Larson; m. Gayle Lynn White, Aug. 22, 1959; children— Ellen Louise, Jean Elizabeth Student, Northwestern U., 1947-48; B.Sc., U.S. Mil. Acad., 1952; MA, U. Wash., 1960. Commd. 2d lt. USAF, 1952, advanced through grades to maj. gen, 1980, fighter pilot, 1954-58; asst. prof. history USAF Acad., Colo., 1960-64; fighter pilot, squadron ops. officer Idaho and, Fed. Republic Germany, 1965-69; fighter squadron comdr., 1969-70; country dir. S.Am. Office of Sec. of Def., Washington, 1970-73; exec. officer, dep. dir. maintenance Hdqrs. Tactical Air Command, 1973-75; tactical fighter wing comdr., 1976-79; chief Office of Mil. Coop., Cairo, 1979—81; dir. plans and policy U.S. European Command, Stuttgart, Fed. Republic Germany, 1981-84; dep. comdr. in chief U.S. Cen. Command, MacDill AFB, Fla., 1984-87, ret.; aerospace cons., 1988—. Adj. prof. history Paradise Valley C.C., 1991-94; real estate broker, 1991—. Decorated Def. D.S.M., 2 Def. Superior Service medals, Legion of Merit with cluster, D.F.C., Meritorious Service medal, Air medal with 14 clusters, Air Force Commendation medal, Purple Heart

ROHR, DONALD GERARD, history professor; b. Toledo, Oct. 10, 1920; s. Lewis Walter and Marie (Pilliod) R.; m. Joan Willis Michener, Sept. 14, 1948; children: Karen, Kristin. BA, U. Toronto, Ont., Can., 1943, MA, 1949; PhD, Harvard U., 1958. Instr., then asst. prof. Williams Coll., 1953—59; mem. faculty Brown U., 1959—, prof. history, 1963—86, prof. history emeritus, 1986—, chmn. dept., 1960—65, 1966—69, 1972—74, sec. faculty, 1969—72, assoc. dean faculty and acad. affairs, 1976—81; adminstrv. dir. Howard Fedn., 1989—92. Author: The Origins of Social Liberalism in Germany, 1963, (with Robert Ergang) Europe Since Waterloo, 1967; editor: Travel Diaries of John Carter Brown, 1822-1824. Served with AUS, 1943-46, ETO. Mem. Am. Hist. Assn., Conf. Group Ctrl. European History, Providence Com. Fgn. Rels. (sec. 1968-81, chmn. 1981-92), Thomas Becket Fedn. (v.p. 1983-84, pres. 1984-86), English Speaking Union (pres. Providence br. 1986-88), U. Club, Faculty Club (Providence, pres. 1981-83). Roman Catholic. Home: 71 Grotto Ave Providence RI 02906-5609 Office Phone: 401-863-2131.

ROHR, DWIGHT MASON, news director, radio marketing consultant; b. Covington, Va., July 18, 1952; s. Edward Mason and Betty (Eppling) R.; m. Betty Erwin, Aug. 1, 1977; children: Christopher Mason, Joseph Michael. AAS in Bus. Mgmt., Dabney S. Lancaster C.C., Clifton Forge, Va., 1997. Cert. radio operator; cert. radio mktg. cons. Audio engr. WJBR, Wilmington, Del., 1971-72; announcer WASA/WHDG, Havre de Grace, Md., 1972-73; news dir. mktg. WKEY Inc., Covington, 1974—. Active Stonewall Jackson Area coun. Boy Scouts Am., 1990-99; dir. cmty. rels. ARC, Covington, 1975-98; mem. adv. bd. Salvation Army, Covington, 1995-2001—, Alleghany County chpt. March of Dimes, 2001—, Alleghany Heart Unit, Potts Valley Singers; city coucilman, Covington, 1997-98; mountaineer Amateur Radio Emergency Svc. Recipient Scouter of Yr. awrd VFW Post 1033, 1994, Dist. award of merit Boy Scouts Am., 1995, Silver Beaver, 1998; named to Outstanding Young Men of Am., 1980. Mem. Soc. Profl. Journalists, Radio TV News Dirs. Assn., Masons, Scottish Rite, Eastern Star, Va. Mountain Amateur Radio Club, Covington Ruritan Club. Avocations: amateur radio, broadcasting, coin collecting/numismatics. Home: 347 E Gray St Covington VA 24426-2109 Office Phone: 540-962-1133. Personal E-mail: wkeywiqo@aol.com., wiqo@aol.com., w4spj@aol.com.

ROHR, JAMES EDWARD, diversified financial services company executive; b. Cleve., Oct. 18, 1948; s. Charles E. and Loretta (Kramer) R.; m. Sharon Lynn Chambers, Dec. 29, 1970; children— Julie, James, Kristen. BA, Notre Dame U., 1970; MBA, Ohio State U., 1972. From comml. banking officer to pres. Pitts. Nat. Bank, 1974-89, chmn., CEO, 1989-93, pres., CEO, 1993—; vice-chmn. PNC Bank Corp., 1989-92, pres., 1992—, COO, 1998—; CEO, pres. PNC Fin. Svcs. Group, Inc., Pitts., 2000—, chmn., 2001—. Bd. dirs. Allegheny Techs. Corp., Equitable Resources, Inc., Rand Corp., Black Rock, Inc., PFPC Worldwide, Inc. Bd. dirs. Greater Pitts. coun. Boy Scouts Am., Carnegie-Mellon U.; chair Cultural Trust. Mem. Am. Bankers Assn., Internat. Monetary Conf., Fin. Svcs. Roundtable, Allegheny Conf., Orgn., Pa. Bus. Roundtable. Roman Catholic. Office: PNC Financial Services Group Inc 249 5th Ave Pittsburgh PA 15222-2709

ROHRA, SRIKRISHIN ASSARDAS, cardiologist; b. Mumbai, India, Apr. 15, 1958; arrived in U.S., 1984; s. Assardas Awatmal and Meera (Assardas) Rohra; m. Sheila Srikrishin, Jan. 6, 2002; children: Shalini Srikrishin, Priya Srikrishin. MD, Bombay U., 1981. Cardiologist Bay Area Cardiology Med. Group, Concord, Calif., 1992—. Fellow: Am. Coll. Cardiology; mem.: Am. Heart Assn., AMA. Home: 11 Majestic Oak Ct San Ramon CA 94583 Office: Bay Area Cardiology Med Group 2222 East St Ste 260 Concord CA 94520-2074

ROHRABACHER, DANA, congressman; b. Coronado, Calif., June 21, 1947; s. Donald and Doris Rohrabacher; m. Rhonda Carmont, Aug. 1997. Student, L.A. Harbor Coll., 1965-67; BA in History, Long Beach State Coll., 1969; MA in Am. Studies, U. So. Calif., 1976. Reporter City News Svc./Radio West, L.A.; editorial writer Orange County Register, 1979-80; asst. press. sec. Reagan for Pres. Campaign, 1976, 80; speechwriter, spl. asst. to Pres. Reagan White House, Washington, 1981-88; congressman from 46th dist. U.S. Ho. Reps., Washington, 1989—. U.S. del. Young Polit. Leaders Conf., USSR;

disting. lectr. Internat. Terrorism Conf., Paris, 1985; mem. Internat. Rels. com.; chmn. sci. subcom. on space and aeroractics. Recipient Disting. Alumnus award L.A. Harbor Coll., 1987. Republican. Avocations: surfing, white water rafting. Office: US Ho Reps 2338 Rayburn HOB Washington DC 20515-0546

ROHRABACHER, JANET HAMMOND, geneologist, archivist; b. Williamston, Mich., Apr. 24, 1913; d. Herbert Moore and Anna Eugenia (Lane) Hammond; m. Albert Hazen Rohrabacher (dec.); children: Ardenne Anna Brigham, Jeffrey. Tchg. cert., We. Mich. U., Kalamazoo, 1936; degree in Practical Nursing, McPherson Nursing Sch., Howell, Mich., 1965; student, Mich. State U., East Lansing, 1940. Cert. Geneologist, LPN. Nurse Mich. State Sanatorium, Howell, 1939-41, Ingham County Chest Hosp., Lansing, 1940, Ea. Mich. Sanatorium, Ypsilanty, 1941, McPherson Hosp., Howell, 1942-66; archivist Howell Carnegie Libr., Howell, 1977-2001. Writer Bicentennial History of Howell. Chmn. Livingston County Civil War Obs. Com., 1963; active Bicentennial Com. Howell, 1973-77, Mich. State Sesquicentennial Com., 1985-89; sec. Howell Archives Bd., 1977—. Recipient award, Mich. Geneal. Coun., 1997. Mem. DAR (award 1976), Livingston County Historical Soc. (charter, founder), Livingston County Genealogical Soc. (founder, 1982), Ancient and Honorable Artillery Soc. Mass, Descendents of Early Quakers, Palatines Am., Detroit Soc. Geneol. Rsch., DLKG. Methodist. Avocations: antique collecting, square dancing, genealogical lecturing. Home: 407 W Highland Rd Apt A1 Howell MI 48843

ROHRBACH, HEIDI A. lawyer; b. Buffalo, Jan. 25, 1953; d. William R. and A.T. R.; m. Leonard Lance, Aug. 9, 1996; 1 child, Peter R. Frank. BA, Northwestern U., 1974; JD, Vanderbilt U., 1977 Bar: NY, 1978. V.p., asst. gen. counsel J.P. Morgan Chase & Co., NYC, 1985—2004. Office: J P Morgan Chase & Co 270 Park Ave Fl 40 New York NY 10017-2014 Office Phone: 212-270 5854.

ROHRBAUGH, LISA ANNE, librarian; b. Girard, Ohio, Sept. 17, 1956; d. John Michael and Josephine Antoinette (Oliva) Sultan; m. Paul Hugh Rohrbaugh Jr., July 28, 1979. BA, Youngstown State U., 1978; MLS, Kent State U., 1979. Libr. readers assistance dept. Youngstown (Ohio) Pub. Libr., 1979-86; libr., researcher Ajax Magnethermic Corp., Warren, Ohio, 1986-90; asst. reference libr. Youngstown State U., 1990-93; dir. East Palestine (Ohio) Meml. Pub. Libr., 1993—. Translator articles dealing with electronics and induction heating/melting tech. from Spanish, German and French into English; mem. Ohio Regional Libr. Sys. Reviewer for Libr. Jour. Recipient Quest '91 Creative Scholarship award Youngstown State U., 1991. Recipient People Who Made a Difference award, Vindicator Pub. Co., 2003. Mem. Ohio Libr. Coun., Rotary (pres. E. Palestine (Ohio) 1999-2000, 2003-04). Avocations: reading, cooking, baseball. Office: East Palestine Meml Pub Libr 309 N Market St East Palestine OH 44413-2153 Office Phone: 330-426-3778.

ROHRBAUGH, NOVA R, retired music educator; b. Brodbecks, Pa., Jan. 28, 1915; d. Adam Kaltreider and Florence Viola Grote; m. Norman S Rohrbaugh, Oct. 13, 1934; children: Machree M Baumgardner, Marlet R, Laura J Summers. BM, U. Ext. Conservatory, Chicago, IL, 1961. Music tchr. Conewago Twp., Hanover, Pa., 1956—59; elem. tchr. Southwestern Sch. Dist., Hanover, Pa., 1959—69; music tchr. Conewago Valley Sch. Dist., Hanover, Pa., 1970—74, Spring Grove Sch. Dist., Spring Grove, Pa., 1970—78. Pvt. music tchr., Pa., 1941—2000; church organist. Composer: (choral anthem) I Want to Live for the Master, The Lord is My Light, author several books of poetry including Words from the Heart: Heartstrings More Heartstrings, (childrens book) Chester the Nosy Pig, Daisy the Little Gosling, Benny the Little Goat, Mousey's Ride, Peppy and His Friends and Sonny the Bunny, Curious Molly. Vol. Hanover Hall Nursing Home, Homewood Retirement Ctr, Hanover, Pa., 1982—2001. Recipient Editors Choice Award, Nat. Libr. of Poetry, 1994, 1995. Mem.: AARP (sec. 1986—2000, outstanding svc. to cmty. 1992). Democrat-Npl. United Church Of Christ. Avocations: sewing, quilting, writing poetry and childrens stories. Home: 120 Amy Ln New Oxford PA 17350

ROHREN, BRENDA MARIE ANDERSON, therapist, educator; b. Kansas City, Mo., Apr. 18, 1959; d. Wilbur Dean and Katheryn Elizabeth (Albright) Anderson; m. Lathan Edward Rohren, May 10, 1985; 1 child, Amanda Jessica. BS in Psychology, Colo. State U., 1983; MA in Psychology, Cath. U. Am., 1986. Lic. mental health practitioner, cert. alcohol/drug abuse counselor. Mental health therapist, sr. case mgr. Rappahannock Area Community Svcs. Bd., Fredericksburg, Va., 1986-88, mental health therapist, case mgmt. supr., 1988; rsch. assoc. Inst. Medicine, NAS, Washington, 1988-89; supr. adult psychiat. program Lincoln (Nebr.) Gen. Hosp., 1989, program supr. mental health svcs., 1989-91; adj. instr. S.E. Community Coll., Lincoln, 1990—; assessment & referral specialist Rivendell Psychiat. Ctr., Seward, Nebr., 1993-95; therapist Lincoln Day Treatment Ctr., Lincoln, Nebr., 1993-95. Adj. instr. Coll. of St. Mary, 1994—2001; therapist Rape/Spouse Abuse Crisis Ctr., Lincoln, 1996—2002; substance abuse counselor Independence Ctr., Lincoln, 2002—; computer cons. Syscon Corp., Washington, 1983—84. Author: (report) Bottom Line Benefits: Building Economic Success Through Stronger Families; editor: (newsletter) Alliance for Mentally Ill, Lincoln, 1993-2002. Active Nat. Alliance for the Mentally Ill-Lincoln, Nebr. Domestic Violence/Sexual Assault Coalition. Mem. APA (assoc.), ACA, Nat. Assn. Alcohol and Drug Abuse Counselors, Nebr. Psychol. Assn. (assoc.), Nebr. Counseling Assn Democrat. Roman Catholic. Avocations: interior decorating, reading, landscaping, camping. Home: 3821 S 33rd St Lincoln NE 68506-3806 Office: Independence Ctr 1650 Lake St Lincoln NE 68502 Office Phone: 402-481-5390. Personal E-mail: brenda@neb.rr.com.

ROHRER, HEINRICH, physicist; b. Buchs, Switzerland, June 6, 1933; Diploma in physics, Swiss Inst. Tech., Zurich, 1955, PhD in Physics, 1960; D. Sci. (hon.), Rutgers U., 1987, Marseille (France) U., 1988, Madrid U., 1988, Tsukuba (Japan) U., 1994, Frankfurt (Germany) U., 1996, Tohoku (Japan) U., 2000. Rsch. asst. Swiss Inst. Tech., Zurich, 1960-61; postdoctoral Rutgers U., New Brunswick, N.J., 1961-63; with IBM Rsch. Lab., Zurich, 1963-97; rschr. CSIC, Madrid, 1997-2000, RIKEN, Waco, Japan, 1998, Tohoku U., Sendai, Japan, 1998—. Vis. scholar U. Calif., Santa Barbara, 1974-75. Co-recipient King Faisal Internat. prize for sci., 1984, Hewlett Packard Europhysics prize, 1984, Nobel prize for Physics, 1986, Cresson medal Franklin Inst., Phila., 1987; IBM fellow, 1986; named to Nat. Inventors Hall of Fame, 1994. Fellow Royal Microscopical Soc. (hon.); mem. NAS (fgn. assoc.), Swiss Acad. Tech. Scis., Swiss Phys. Soc. (hon.), Swiss Assn. Engring. and Architecture (hon.), Zurich Phys. Soc. (hon.). Office: Rebbergstr 9d CH 8832 Wollerau Switzerland E-mail: h.rohrer@gmx.net.

ROHRER, JANE CAROLYN, retired gifted education specialist, academic administrator, poet, consultant; b. Faribault, Minn., July 17, 1940; d. Christian A. and Lydia G. (Hilleboe) R.; children: Paula Eisenrich, Lisa Eisenrich, Peter Eisenrich. BS in English, U. Minn., 1962, MA in English, 1964; MA in Edn., Boise (Idaho) State U., 1976; PhD in Spl. Edn./Gifted, Kent State U., 1992; student, Seabury We. Theol. Sem. Tchr. Engligh Lompoc (Calif.) High Sch., 1962-63; gifted and talented facilitator Boise Sch. Dist., 1976-84, spl. edn. cons. tchr., 1984-89, spl. edn. adminstrv. intern, 1989-90; faculty Kent (Ohio) State U., 1991-92; dir. Tchr. Edn. Program Sierra Nev. Coll., Incline Village, Nev., 1993-1996, dean acad. programs, 1995-1996, dean faculty, 1997-99, v.p. acad. affairs, 1999—2002, acting pres., 2001, ret., 2002. Mem. Nev. Statewide Task Force on Tchr. Edn., Nev. State English Framework Commn.; numerous publs. and conf. presentations. Choir dir., La., Japan, Idaho, Ohio, Nev., 1966-98. Whittenberger fellow Boise State U., 1975-76. Mem. Ch. Women United (state pres. 1980), Coun. Exceptional Children (state bd. dirs. 1987-88), Nat. Assn. Gifted Children, S.W. Regional Spl. Edn. Adv. Bd., Idaho Talented and Gifted Assn. (state pres. 1988-89), Nev. Assn. Colls. of Tchr. Edn. (sec.-treas.), Mortar Bd., Phi Beta Kappa, Eta Sigma Upsilon, Pi Lambda Theta, Phi Delta Kappa. Avocations: reading, music, swimming, hiking, writing.

ROHRER, RICHARD JEFFREY, surgeon, educator; b. Columbus, Mar. 14, 1950; s. James William and Nancy Lenore (Acheson) R.; m. Jill Ellen Stein, Nov. 29, 1981; children: Benjamin, Noah. BS, Yale U., 1973; MD, Columbia U., 1977. Surgeon New Eng. Deaconess and Harvard Med. Sch., Boston, 1984—87; surgeon, chief transplantation New Eng. Med. Ctr., Boston, 1988—; vice chmn. dept. surgery Tufts-New Eng. Med. Ctr., Boston, 2004—; prof. surgery Tufts U. Sch. Medicine, Boston, 2004—. Trustee New Eng. Organ Bank, Boston, 1988—, chmn. bd. dirs., 1999—; councillor United Network for Organ Sharing, 1996—, sec., 2000—. Fellow ACS; mem. Am. Soc. Transplant Surgeons, Transplantation Soc., Physicians for Social Responsibility, Assn. for Acad. Surgery, Assn. for Surg. Edn., Soc. Critical Care Medicine. Office: New England Med Ctr Box 40 750 Washington St Boston MA 02111-1526 Office Phone: 617-636-5592.

ROHRER, SUSAN EARLEY, film producer, writer, director; b. Richmond, Va., Mar. 24; d. Charles Marion Jr. and Gloria Jean (Ripley) Earley; m. Mark Brooks Rohrer. BA in Art cum laude, James Madison U. Prodr., dir., co-story writer (tv shows) Never Say Goodbye, 1988 (Emmy award, Humanitas Prize finalist), Terrible Things My Mother Told Me, 1988 (Emmy nomination, Gold award Nat. Ednl. Film Festival); prodr., dir. (TV movies) For Jenny With Love (TV Movie award), Mother's Day, 1989 (3 Image award nominations), prodr., dir., writer (TV show) The Emancipation of Lizzie Stern, 1991 (Angel award, Bronze award Nat. Ednl. Film Festival, Emmy nomination, Monitor award finalist, TV Movie award), If I Die Before I Wake, 1993 (Emmy nomination, Humanitas Prize finalist, Cine Golden Eagle, TV Movie award); dir. (TV show) Sweet Valley High, 1996; dir. TV pilot Dojo Kids, 1996; prodr., dir., co-writer About Sarah, TV movie, 1998 (award of excellence Film Adv. Bd., Best of Festival award Breckenridge Film Festival, The Christopher award, Angel award, N.Y. Festivals finalist); writer (TV movies) Another Pretty Face, 2002, Book of Days, 2003. Recipient Resolution of Recognition Virginia Beach City Coun., 1988. Mem. ATAS, SAG, Writers Guild Am., Dirs. Guild Am. Office: Josh Schechter IPG 9200 Sunset Blvd Ste 520 Los Angeles CA 90069

ROHRMAN, DOUGLASS FREDERICK, lawyer; b. Chgo., Aug. 10, 1941; s. Frederick Alvin and Velma Elizabeth (Birdwell) R.; m. Susan Vitullo; children: Kathryn Anne, Elizabeth Clelia, Alessandra Claire. AB, Duke U., 1963; JD, Northwestern U., 1966. Bar: Ill. 1966. Legal coord. Nat. Communicable Disease Ctr., Atlanta, 1966-68; assoc. Keck, Mahin & Cate, Chgo., 1968-73, ptnr., 1973-97, Lord, Bissell and Brook, Chgo., 1997—. Exec. v.p., dir. Kerogen Oil Co., 1967—;mem. bd. visitors Nicholas Sch. of Environment Duke U., 1991—, chmn., 1993-2001. Co-author: Commercial Liability Risk Management and Insurance, 2 vols., 1978, 86, Lenders Guide to Environmental Law: Risk and Liability, 1993; mem. editl. bd., columnist Ecol. Soc. Am., 2001—; contbr. articles on law to profl. jours. Vice chmn., commr. Ill. Food and Drug Commn., 1970-72. Lt. USPHS, 1966-68. Fellow: Am. Numismatic Soc. (life; chmn. adv. com. 2001—03, trustee); mem.: ABA, William Preston Few Assn. (mem. pres. coun.), Duke U. Alumni Assn., James B. Duke Soc., Selden Soc., Am. Soc. Law and Medicine, Environ. Law Inst., 7th Cir. Bar Assn., Chgo. Bar Assn. (chmn. com. food and drug law 1972—73), Am. Numismatic Assn. (life), Wigmore Club (fellow), Mich. Shores Club, Legal Club. Democrat. Epsicopalian. Home: 520 Brier St Kenilworth IL 60043-1064 Office: Lord Bissell & Brook 115 S La Salle St Ste 3200 Chicago IL 60603-3902 Office Phone: 312-443-0531.

ROHSENOW, WARREN MAX, retired mechanical engineer, educator; b. Chgo., Feb. 12, 1921; s. Fred and Selma (Gorss) R.; m. Katharine Towneley Smith, Sept. 20, 1946; children— John, Brian, Damaris, Sandra, Anne. BS, Northwestern U., 1941; M.Eng., Yale, 1943, D.Eng., 1944. Teaching asst., instr. mech. engring. Yale, 1941-44; mem. faculty Mass. Inst. Tech., 1946-85, prof. mech. engring., 1955-85, dir. heat transfer lab., 1954-85, prof. emeritus, 1985. Bd. dirs. Dynatech Corp., Thermal Process System. Author: (with Choi) Heat Mass and Momentum Transfer, 1961; Editor: Developments in Heat Transfer, 1964, (with Hartnett) Handbook of Heat Transfer, 1973, 3d edit., 1998. Served as lt. (j.g.) USNR, 1944-46; mech. engr. gas turbine div. Engring. Expt. Sta. Annapolis, Md. Recipient Pi Tau Sigma gold medal ASME, 1951; award for advancement sci. Yale Engring. Assn., 1952; merit award Northwestern Alumni, 1955; named hon. alumnus MIT, 2004. Fellow Am. Acad. Arts and Scis., Nat. Acad. Engring., ASME (hon. mem., Heat Transfer Meml. award 1967, Max Jakob Meml. award 1970, ASME medal 2001, Classic Paper award 2003); mem. Sigma Xi, Tau Beta Pi, Pi Tau Sigma. Home: 32 Carroll St Falmouth ME 04105-1908

ROIF, HENRY IRVING, aeronautical engineer, electronic engineer, air transportation executive; b. Lima, Peru, Dec. 15, 1955; came to U.S., 1991; s. Israel Meyer and Raquel (Rotstain) R. BSEE, Nat. U. Engring., Lima, 1984; MS in Aero. Engring., Israel Inst. Tech., Haifa, 1989; comml. pilot, Escuela de Aviacion Civil Peru, Lima, 1981. Flight test engr. Quiet Tech. Venture, Miami, Fla., 1996—; pres., owner Aeroiflight Corp., 2003—. Mem. IEEE (sr.), AIAA, Aerospace and Electronics Systems Soc., IEEE Comm. Soc., Inventors Soc. South Fla. Jewish. Achievements include patents for in fields of medicine and information technology. Avocations: hang gliding, skydiving, outdoors, music, accomplished faith healer, achievements include 17 patents including aircraft landing taxing system, special project for the recovery of the ozone layer, patent pending on automobile automatic steering and cruise guidance control, airport surface movement detection system, electromagnetic fields for protection of airplanes from lightning, automatic parking for airplanes. Office: Aeroiflight Corp 1551 NE 167th St Apt 711 North Miami Beach FL 33162-2964 Fax: 305-947-6082. Office Phone: 305-949-0548. E-mail: hroif@ieee.org.

ROITMAN, JUDITH, mathematician, educator; b. N.Y.C., Nov. 12, 1945; d. Leo and Ethel (Gottesman) R.; m. Stanley Lombardo, Sept. 26, 1978; 1 child, Ben Lombardo. BA in English, Sarah Lawrence Coll., 1966; MA in Math., U. Calif., Berkeley, 1971, PhD in Math., 1974. Asst. prof. math. Wellesley (Mass.) Coll., 1974-77; from asst. prof. to prof. math. U. Kans., Lawrence, 1977—. Author: Introduction to Modern Set Theory, 1990; contbr. articles to profl. jours. Grantee NSF, 1975-87, 92-95. Mem. Assn. Symbolic Logic, Am. Math. Soc., Assn. Women in Math. (pres. 1979-81, Louise Hay award 1996), Kans. Assn. Tchrs. Math., Nat. Assn. Tchrs. Math. Avocation: poetry. E-mail: roitman@math.ukans.edu.

ROITSCH, PAUL ALBERT, pilot; b. Hermosa Beach, Calif., Oct. 15, 1926; s. George Arthur and Margaret (Pattillo) R.; m. Phyllis T.A. McCoy, Aug. 26, 1955; children— Sharon Elise, Alison Carol, Paul Eric. BA, U. So. Calif., 1952; postgrad. U.S. Navy Test Pilot Sch., 1965. Copilot, navigator Pan Am. Airways, San Francisco, 1952-53, pilot, 1955-64, asst. chief pilot tech., Jamaica, N.Y., 1965-69, chief pilot tech., 1969-73, line pilot, 1973-86, pres. Paul Roitsch Assocs., Internat. Aviation Cons., Greenwich, Conn., 1986—, pilot Civil Air Transport, 1954-55; bd. dirs. Pan Am Hist. Found., 1993—, v.p., 1994—, exec. v.p., 1995—. With USN, 1944-49, 53-54. Mem. AIAA, Soc. Automotive Engrs. (airplane handling qualities and flight deck design com., recipient cert. of appreciation 1981), Internat. Soc. Air Safety Investigators. Home: 39 John St Greenwich CT 06831-2608 Office: PO Box 786 Greenwich CT 06836-0786

ROIZEN, MICHAEL F. dean, medical educator, internist; b. N.Y., Jan. 7, 1946; m. Nancy J. Roizen; children: Jeffery, Jennifer. AB in Chemistry with honors, Williams Coll., Williamstown, Mass., 1967; MD, U. Calif., San Francisco, 1971. Intern Beth Israel Hosp., Boston, 1972, resident in medicine, 1973; rsch. assoc. in pharmacology NIH, Bethesda, Md., 1973-75; resident in anesthesia U. Calif., San Francisco, 1977, asst. prof., 1977-81, assoc. prof., 1981-85; prof. internal medicine U. Chgo., 1985—, prof. and chair dept. anesthesia and critical care, 1985—. Panel mem. FDA. Author: Essence of Anesthesia Practice, 1997, RealAge: Are You As Young as You Can Be?, 1999; reviewer numerous anesthesia and med. jours. Mem. Am. Bd. Anesthesiology (assoc.), Am. Bd. Internal Medicine (assoc.), Am. Soc. Anesthesiologists, Soc. of Cardiovascular Anesthesiologists (pres. 1995-97), U.S. Squash Racquets Assn., Alpha Omega Alpha, Phi Beta Kappa. Avocation: squash. Home: MC 4028 5841 S Maryland Ave Chicago IL 60637-1463 Office: U Chgo Sch Medicine Anesthesia Cricital Care 5841 S Maryland Ave Chicago IL 60637-1463 E-mail: mrzz@airway2.bsd.uchicago.edu.

ROIZEN, NANCY J. physician, educator; b. Hartford, Conn. m. Michael F. Roizen; children: Jeffrey, Jennifer. BS, Tufts U., 1968, MD, 1972. Diplomate Am. Bd. Pediats. Staff physician Oakland (Calif.) Children's Hosp., 1976-84; asst. prof. clin. pediats. Johns Hopkins Hosp., Balt., 1984-85; assoc. prof. pediat. and psychiatry U. Chgo., 1985—. Fellow Am. Acad. Pediats.; mem. Soc. for Devel. Pediats. (pres. 1996-98). Office: U Chgo Hosps MC 900 5841 S Maryland Ave Chicago IL 60637-1463

ROIZMAN, BERNARD, virologist, educator; b. Chisinau, Rumania, Apr. 17, 1929; arrived in U.S., 1947, naturalized, 1954; s. Abram and Liudmilla (Seinberg) Roizman; m. Betty Cohen, Aug. 26, 1950; children: Arthur, Niels. BA, Temple U., 1952, MS, 1954; ScD in Microbiology, Johns Hopkins, 1956; DHL (hon.), Gov.'s State U., 1984; MD (hon.), U. Ferrara (Italy), 1991; DSc (hon.), U. Paris, 1997, U. Valladolid, Spain, 2001. From instr. microbiology to assst. prof. Johns Hopkins Med. Sch., 1956—65; mem. faculty div. biol. scis. U. Chgo., 1965—, prof. microbiology, 1969-84, prof. biophysics, 1970—, chmn. com. virology, 1969-85, 88-01, Joseph Regenstein prof., 1981-83, Joseph Regenstein Disting. Svc. prof., 1984—, chmn. dept. molecular genetics and cell biology, 1985-88. Co-founder Aviron, Inc., 1992; convener herpes virus workshop, Cold Spring Harbor, NY, 72; lectr. Am. Found. for Microbiology, 1974—75; mem. spl. virus cancer program devel. rsch. working group Nat. Cancer Inst., 1967—71, cons. inst., 1967—73; mem. steering com. human cell biology program NSF, 1971—74, cons. found., 1972—74; mem. adv. com. cell biology and virology Am. Cancer Soc., 1970—74; chmn. herpes virus study group Internat. Commn. Taxonomy of Viruses, 1971—73; mem. Internat. Microbiol. Genetics Commn. Internat. Assn. Microbiol. Scis., 1974—81; mem. sci. adv. coun. N.Y. Cancer Inst., 1971—88; mem. adv. bd. Leukemia Rsch. Found., 1972—77; mem. herpes-virus working team WHO/FDA, 1978—81; mem. bd. sci. cons. Sloan Kettering Inst., N.Y.C., 1975—81; mem. study sect. exptl. virology NIH, 1976—80; mem. task force on virology Nat. Inst. Allergy and Infectious Disease, 1976—77; mem. external adv. com. Emory U. Cancer Ctr., 1973—81, Northwestern U. Cancer Ctr., 1979—89; cons. Inst. Merieux, Lyon, France, 1979—91; mem. com. to establish vaccine priorities Nat. Inst. Medicine, 1983—85; chmn. sci. adv. bd. Tampa Bay Rsch. Inst., 1983—, chmn. bd. trustees, 1991—. Editor: (book) Herpes Viruses, Vol. 1, 1982, Herpes Viruses, Vol. 2, 1983, Herpes Viruses, Vols. 3 and 4, 1985, The Human Herpesviruses, 1993, Infectious Diseases in an Age of Change, 1995; adv. editor: Progress in Surface Membrane Science, 1972, editor-in-chief: Jour. Infectious Agts. and Disease, 1992—96, mem. editl. bd.: Jour. Hygiene, 1985—91, Infectious Diseases, 1965—69, Jour. Virology, 1970—, Jour. Intervirology, 1972—85, Archives of Virology, 1975—81, Virology, 1976—78, 1983—, Microbiologica, 1978—, Cell, 1979—80, Gene Therapy, 1994; contbr. scientific papers, chapters to books. Trustee Goodwin Inst. Cancer Rsch., 1977—. Named hon. prof., Shandong Acad. Med. Scis., China, 1985; recipient Lederle Med. Faculty award, 1960—61, Cancer Devel. award, USPHS, 1963—65, Pasteur award, Ill. Soc. Microbiology, 1972, Esther Langer award for Achievement in Cancer Rsch., 1974, Outstanding Alumnus in Pub. Health award, Johns Hopkins U., 1984, ICN Internat. prize in Virology, 1988, J. Allyn Taylor Internat. prize in Medicine, 1997, Bristol-Myers Squibb award for Disting. Infectious Disease Rsch., 1998; fellow Travelling, Internat. Agy. Rsch. Against Cancer, Karolinska Inst., Stockholm, 1970; grantee Facutly Rsch. Assoc., Am. Cancer Soc., 1966—71, USPHS/NIH, 1958—, Am. Cancer Soc., 1962—90, NSF, 1962—79; scholar Am. Cancer Soc., Pasteur Inst. Paris, 1961—62. Fellow: Japanese Soc. for Promotion of Sci., Am. Acad. Arts and Scis.; mem.: NAS, Johns Hopkins U. Soc. Scholars, Chinese Acad. Engring. (fgn.), Hungarian Acad. Scis. (fgn.), Brit. Soc. Gen. Microbiology, Am. Soc. Molecular Biology and Biochemistry, Am. Soc. Virology, Am. Soc. Microbiology, Am. Assn. Immunologists, Am. Acad. Microbiology, Inst. Medicine, Quadrangle Club (Chgo.). Home: 5555 S Everett Ave Chicago IL 60637-1968 Office: U Chgo MB Kovler Viral Oncology Labs 910 E 58th St Chicago IL 60637-1432 Office Phone: 773-702-1898. Business E-Mail: barnard.roizman@bsd.uchicago.edu.

ROJANY, LISA ADRIENNE, publishing company executive, writer; b. L.A., Feb. 14, 1964; d. Aviezer Rojany and Mary Marks; m. Kristian Buccieri. B of Comms. magna cum laude, UCLA; cert. in translation, Sorbonne U., Paris; M English and Am. Lit., Brown U. Newspaper journalist UCLA Daily Bruin, Together Newsmag., L.A., 1985-86; English tutor Paris, 1986-87; writer, reviewer TV Guide, L.A., 1987-88; sr. editor Intervisual Books, Santa Monica, Calif., 1991-93; editl. dir. Price Stern Sloan divsn. Penguin Putnam Pub., L.A., 1993-97, Gateway Learning Corp., 1997; west coast publ. dir. Golden Books Family Entertainment, L.A., 1998-2000; editl. dir. bus. devel. MyPotential.com, 2000-01; editor/writer, pres. Editl. Svcs. of L.A., 2001—; v.p., pub. Americhip Books, 2002—. Proofreader MIT U. Press, Cambridge, Mass., 1990, Fidelity, Inc., Boston, 1990, Heinle & Heinle Pubs., Inc., Boston, 1990; correlator, proofreader Houghton Mifflin Co., Boston, 1990; spkr. in field; v.p. and pub. Americhip Books, 2002—. Author: (childrens books) The Hands-on Book of Big Machines, 1992, Exploring the Human Body, 1992 (10 Best New Parenting Books, Child Mag., 1993), King Arthur's Camelot, 1993 (Book of the Month Club selection, 1993), The Story of Hanukkah, 1993, Where's That Pig?, 1993, Santa's New Suit, 1993, Jake and Jenny on the Town, 1993, 1996, Andrews & McMeel Mini Pop-Up Quote Books, 1993, Alice in Wonderland, 1994, Token of Love and Spring Gardens, 1994, Mickey Mouse: Where's the Picnic, 1994, Winnie the Pooh: The Suprise Party, 1994, Make Your Own Valentines, 1994, Make Your Own Valentines, 3d edit., 1996 (Pub.'s Weekly Bestseller list, 1994, 1995), Melvin Martian, Dumbo's Circus Train, 1995, Cinderella's Coach, 1995, The Magic Feather, 1995 (Parents Choice Silver Honor award, 1995), Pandora's Box (CD ROM), 1995, Over in the Meadow (CD ROM), 1995, Tell Me About When I Was a Baby, 1996, Gold Diggers: The Novelization, 1996, Hanukkah Candles, 1995, Dragonheart: The Jr. Novelization, 1996, Giant Animal Fold-Outs: Big Trucks & Bigger Diggers, 1996, Giant Giants & Magic Mermaids, 1996, Hippo & Pals, 1996 (Am. Booksellers Pick of the List, 1995), Kangaroo & Company, 1996 (Am. Booksellers Pick of the List, 1995), Dena Dinosaur, Morty Monster, Wanda Witch, 1996, Code Blue: In the Emergency Room, 1996, Code Blue: Making the Grade, 1996, Leave It to Beaver: The Novelization, 1997, Love You Because...Love, Barbie, 1999, Make Your Own Valentine Cards, 2000; co-author: (books) Fund Your Future, 2001 (NY Times Bus. Hardcover Bestseller list #10, 2002, NY Times hardover bus. bestseller, 2001); ghostwriter: childrens books Dinotopia Pop-Up Book, 1993, Sliding Surprise Books, 1993—97, The Facts of Life, 1994, All Mixed Up, 1994, Little Merlin's Book of Magic Pets, 1994, Claverie Fairytale Theater, 1994. Vol. kids activity days Dutton's Books, Brentwood, Calif., 1996; spkr. UCLA Extension, 1993-98; mem. comms. bd., fin. com. UCLA, 2002-. Recipient one of 10 Best New Parenting Books award Child Mag., 1993. Mem. PEN Ctr. U.S.A. West (editor-in-chief 1992-95), Soc. Children's Book Writers and Illustrators (manuscript reviewer 1995—), Internat. Women's Writing Guild, Author's Guild, Brown Alumni Assn. (interviewer 1995-98), UCLA Alumni Assn. (bd. dirs., comms., fin. com. 2002-2004), Phi Beta Kappa. Avocations: parenting twins, reading, moderating writing groups, rollerblading, walking. E-mail: creativeideaz@comcast.net.

ROJAS, CARLOS, Spanish literature educator; b. Barcelona, Aug. 12, 1928; s. Carlos and Luisa (Vila) R.; m. Eunice Anne Mitcham, Mar. 19, 1966; children: Carlos, Eunice Anne. MA, U. Barcelona, 1951; PhD, U. Cen., Madrid, 1955; PhD (hon.), U. Simón Bólivar, Barranquilla, Colombia, 1985. Teaching asst. U. Barcelona, 1951-52; fgn. asst. U. Glasgow, Scotland, 1952-54; asst. prof. Rollins Coll., Winter Park, Fla., 1957-60, Emory U., Atlanta, 1960-63, assoc. prof., 1963-68, prof., 1968-80, Charles Howard Candler prof. Spanish lit., 1980-96, Charles Howard Candler prof. emeritus, 1996. Author: Auto de fe, 1968 (Premio Nacional de Literatura 1968), Azana, 1973 (Planeta award 1973), El Igenioso Hidalgo y Poeta F.G. asciende a los infiernos, 1980 (Nadal award 1980), El Sueno de Sarajevo, 1982, El Jardin de las Hespèrides, 1988, El Jardin de Atocha, 1990, Yo, Goya, 1990, Proceso A Godoy, 1992, Salvador Dali, or the Art of Spitting on Your Mother's Portrait, 1993, Alfonso de Borbón Habla Con El Demonio, 1995, !Muera La Inteligencia! !Viva La Muerte! Salamanca, 1995, The Garden of Janus, 1996, Crónica

de la Guerra Civil Española, 1996; co-author, contbg. editor Spanish Civil War documents, Momentos estelares de la guerra de España, 1996, La Vida y la Época de Carlos IV, 1997, Los Borbones Destronados, 1997, El bastardo del Rey, 1999, The Garden of the Hesperides, 1999, Puneta La Espaneta, 2000, Despiada Memoria: Memorias, 2002, Diez Crisis del Franquismo, 2003. Recipient Premio Espejo de España award, Madrid, 1984, Encomienda al Mérito Civil, King of Spain, 1986, Univ. Scholar/Tchr. award Emory U., 1987, Arts and Scis. award of Distinction, Emory U., 2001; honoree of yr. Philol. Assn. of Carolinas, 1987, Llave de Barcelona, 2003. Mem. MLA, Am. Assn. Tchrs. Spanish and Portuguese, Assn. Doctores y Licenciados Españoles en los Estados Unidos (bd. dirs.), South Atlantic MLA (hon.). Avocation: painting. Home: 1378 Harvard Rd NE Atlanta GA 30306-2413 E-mail: crojas@emory.edu.

ROJAS, EDDY M. engineering educator; b. San Jose, Costa Rica, Feb. 26, 1969; came to U.S., 1993; s. Jorge L. Rojas and Hannia Molina; m. Denise Murillo, Aug. 10, 1991. MSCE, U. Colo., 1995, MA in Econs., PhD in Civil Engring., U. Colo., 1997. Registered civil engr., Costa Rica. Rschr. Earthquake Engring. Lab. U. Costa Rica, San Jose, 1991, instr., 1991-93; asst. prof. U. Buffalo, 1997—2001, U. Wash., 2001—04, assoc. prof., 2004—. Contbr. papers to profl. jours. Recipient Making Virtual Teams Work award, Constrn. Industry Inst., 2000, Tech. Transfer for Mex. Electrical Contracting Firms award, Electrical Contracting Found., 2000, Automating N.Y. State Dept. Transp. Data Collection, 1998, Millennium Generation award, Electrical Contracting Found., 2001. Mem. ASCE (mem. constrn. rsch. coun. 1997—, computing in constrn. com. 1997—). Roman Catholic. Office: U Washington 116 Architecture Box 351610 Seattle WA 98195-1610 E-mail: er@u.washington.edu.

ROJAS, VICTOR HUGO MACEDO, retired vocational education educator; b. Mollendo, Peru, Jan. 11, 1923; came to U.S., 1944; s. Mariano A. and Maria Santos (Macedo) R.; m. Mary Emily Bush, Apr. 28, 1945 (dec. 1984). AA, Miami-Dade C.C., 1982; BS in Vocat. Edn., Fla. Internat. U., 1986. Cert. tchr., Fla. Engine tech. Nat. Sch., 1943; automotive mechanic various Ford dealerships, Miami, Fla., 1945-60; automotive technician East Tenn. Motors, Knoxville, 1960-63; car and truck salesman Ford Mktg. Inst., 1963; automotive technician Tally-Embry Ford, Inc., Miami, 1964-66, shop foreman, then mgr., 1966-75, master technician, automotive instr., 1973-75; instr. automotive tech. Dade County Pub. Schs., Miami, 1975-91; bus. exec. Internat. Correspondence, 1976; ret., 1991. Adviser, sponsor Vocat.-Indsl. Clubs Am., Miami, 1988-91. Contbr. articles to newspapers. With Armada Peruana, 1940-44, USN, 1945. Recipient Cert. of Achievement Motor Age mag., 1961, 62, St. Mary's Cathedral, Miami, 1988, Automotive Svc. Excellence award Nat. Inst. Automotive Svc., 1975. Mem. Am. Legion (historian 1989), Elks. Democrat. Roman Catholic. Avocations: music, ballroom dancing, reading, writing, photography. Home: 2365 Ainsworth Ave Spring Hill FL 34609-4402

ROJEK, KENNETH JOHN, health facility administrator, hospital; b. Chgo., Aug. 6, 1953; m. Carol Rojek; 2 children. BS with honors, U. Ill., 1975; MBA with honors, Roosevelt U., 1980. Diplomate Am. Coll. Healthcare Execs. Lab. mgr., tech. dir. Rush-Presbyn.-St. Lukes Med. Ctr., Chgo., 1977-80; adminstr. Wyler Children's Hosp., dept. pediatrics U. Chgo., 1980-86; v.p. Parkside Human Svcs., 1986-89, Luth. Gen. Med. Group, S.C., Chgo., 1989-92; sr. v.p. Luth. Gen. Hosp., Park Ridge, Ill., 1992-94, CEO, 1994-2000, Advocate North Side Health Network, 2000—. Adj. faculty U. Minn., St. Francis Coll., Joliet, Ill. Active numerous cmty. and civic orgns., cmty. devel. couns. Fellow Am. Coll. Med. Practice Execs. Med. Group Mgmt. Assn. Office: Ill Masonic Med Ctr 836 W Wellington Chicago IL 60657 E-mail: kenaojek@advocatehealth.com.

ROJO, RUTH M. nutritionist, alternative medicine consultant; b. San Antonio, Tex., Oct. 23, 1938; d. Fernando Sosa and Margie Macias Rojo; 1 child, Amina Ruth. Dr. Naturopathy, Clayton Coll. Natural Health, Birmingham, Ala., 1996, U.S. Sch. Naturopathy, Atlanta, 1999; PhD in Nutrition, Am. Holistic Coll. Nutrition, Birmingham, 1996; Dr. Naturopathic Medicine, Colo. U. Naturopathic Medicine, Denver, 1999. Board Certified Naturopath Am. Naturopathic Med. Certification and Accreditation Bd. Pres. / founder Tex. State Naturopathic Med. Assn., San Antonio, 1998—; Tex. rep. Am. Naturopathic Med. Assn., Las Vegas, Nev., 1998—, bd. dirs., 2000—; founder Tex. Complimentary and Alternative Medicine Assn., 2003; cons. in complimentary and alternative medicine. Lectr. Sun Harvest, San Antonio, 1998—2002, U. Tex., San Antonio, 1998—2002. Author: Priority 1--A Guide to Natural Health. Legis. chair N.E. Bexar County Rep. Women's Club, San Antonio, 2001—02. Recipient Hall of Fame award, Tex. State Naturopathic Assn., 2000. Avocations: painting, walking, reading, sports. Office: Ruth M Rojo ND PhD 8026 Vantage Dr Suite 101 San Antonio TX 78230

ROJO DE SANTOS, ANITA, shop owner, writer; b. Bacamopa Mocorito, Sinaloa, Mexico, Feb. 5, 1941; arrived in US, 1985; d. Rafael Rojo and Mercedes Beltran; m. Raul Santos, June 3, 1972; children: Raul Santos Rojo, Adrian Santos Rojo, Paul Santos Rojo. Owner Rojo Bros. Market, Guamuchil, Sinaloa, Mexico, 1955—84, Santa Anita Pharmacy, Guamuchil, Sinaloa, Mexico, 1960—84, Sombrereria Panama (hat store), Los Mochis, Sinaloa, Mexico, 1972—84; prin. Santa Anita Flowers, L.A., Calif., 1992—. Mem. Commerce Adv. Com., Guamuchil/Los Mochis, Mexico, 1956—84. Author: (book) Amor del Bueno y Mas, 1991, The Grandest Love in the World, 2003. Finalist Hispanic Family of the Yr., Hispanic Am. Family of the Yr. Found., 1990; named hon. vol., Leukemia Soc. of Am., 1988. Avocations: reading, painting. Office: PO Box 2021 LaPuente CA 91746 Office Phone: 626-806-7285. Personal E-mail: anitarojob@yahoo.com.

ROKER, AL, broadcast journalist; m. Deborah Roberts. Grad., SUNY, Oswego. Weathercaster, graphic artist WTVH-TV, Syracuse, N.Y., 1974-76; weathercaster WTTG-TV, Washington, 1976-78, WKYC-TV, Cleve., 1978-83, WNBC-TV, N.Y.C., 1983—; weatherman NBC News Today Show, N.Y.C., 1995—; founder Al Roker Productions, 1994—. Named Best Weatherman, N.Y. mag., 1985. Mem. Am. Meteorol. Soc. (recipient Seal of Approval). Office: NBC News 30 Rockefeller Plz Rm 1420 New York NY 10112-0002

ROKHVARGER, ANATOLY EFIM, materials science and ceramic technology scientist; b. Moscow, July 24, 1937; came to U.S., 1991; s. Efim Laser and Avgustina Naum (Leschiner) R.; m. Zina Gregory Mikhelson, Feb. 17, 1965; 1 child, Avgustina. MS, Mendeleev Chem.-Tech. U., Moscow, 1959, PhD, 1967; cert., Moscow U., 1965; DS, Tech. U., Leningrad, USSR, 1986. Engr. Electronic Industry Design Inst., Moscow, 1959-63; rschr. Bldg. Materials Inst., Moscow, 1964-68; project leader, head dept. Ceramic Industry Analytical Ctr., Moscow, 1969-91; rsch. prof. Poly. U., Bklyn., 1992—; v.p. R&D Nucon Sys., Inc., N.Y.C., N.Y., 1996-2000. Vis. scientist Rutgers U. Ctr. Ceramic Rsch., Piscataway, N.J., 1998-99. Author 5 books, 1 textbook in field; contbr. over 175 articles to profl. jours. Named Among 100 Greatest Innovators of 20th Century Am. Ceramic Soc., Businessman of Yr., The Nat. Rep. Congl. Com. Bus. Adv. Coun., 2003. Achievements include development of nine advanced technological systems and six ceramic products; invention of cost-effective nanotechnology of gas impenetrable and thick-walled ceramics; ultimate safe and durable ceramic containers for nuclear and hazardous waste, including techniques for their mass production and seamless covering using microwave; five U.S. patents in field; invention of industrial nanofabrication of inexpensive high temperature superconductor continuous wire; other shaped and superconducting ceramic products (leads) with superconductive nono-aarchitecture for electrical/electronic needs using Y-BA-CU-O powder, silicone polymer additive/silver power dope. Office: Polytechnic U 6 Metrotech Ctr Brooklyn NY 11201-3840 Office Phone: 718-260-3751. E-mail: aerokhv@aol.com.

ROKITA, TODD, secretary of state; BA in Political Sci., Wabash Coll.; JD, Ind. Univ. Sch. of Law. Atty.; gen. counsel sec. state State of Ind., 1997, dep. sec. of state, sec. state, 2002—. Mem.: Indiana Coun. for Economic Edn. (Director's Circle), St. Thomas More Parish, Indiana State Bar Association's Aviation Law Com. (past chair). Republican. Office: 201 State House Indianapolis IN 46204

ROKKE, ERVIN JEROME, college president; b. Warren, Minn., Dec. 12, 1939; s. Edwin K. and Joan (Ivery) R.; m. Pamela Mae Patterson, June 6, 1962; children: Lisa Mae, Eric Scott. Student, St. Olaf Coll., 1957-58; BS, USAF Acad., 1962; MPA, Harvard U., 1964, PhD in Polit. Sci., 1970. Commd. 2d lt. USAF, 1962, advanced through grades to lt. gen., 1994; intelligence officer Pacific Air Forces, Hawaii, Japan, 1965-68; assoc. prof. dept. polit. sci. USAF Acad., Colorado Springs, Colo., 1968-73, permanent prof., 1976-80, dean of faculty, 1982-86; plans officer NATO Hdqrs., Brussels, 1973-76; air attache Am. Embassy, London, 1980-82, def. attache Moscow, 1987-89; sr. staff Nat. Security Agy., Ft. Meade, Md., 1989-91; dir. intelligence Hdqrs. European Command, Stuttgart, Fed. Republic Germany, 1991-93; assigned to Hdqs. USAF, Washington, 1993-94; pres. Nat. Def. U., Ft. Lesley J. McNair, DC, 1994-97, Moravian Coll. and Moravian Theol. Sem., 1997—. Cons. Dept. State, 1969. Editor: American Defense Policy, 1973. Decorated Def. Disting. Svc. medal, Disting. Svc. medal, Def. Superior Svc. medal, Legion of Merit. Mem. Coun. on Fgn. Rels., Falcon Found. Lutheran. Avocations: reading, skiing, squash. Home: 79 W Church St Bethlehem PA 18018-5821 Office: Moravian Coll 1200 Main St Bethlehem PA 18018-6614 E-mail: chaos01@aol.com.

ROLAND, ALEX FREDERICK, history professor; b. Providence, Apr. 7, 1944; s. George Hayes and Alice Ruth (Thurber) R.; m. Elizabeth Ann Sullivan, June 31, 1979; children: Quentin H. Hopkins, Michael K., Christopher S., Daniel H. BS, U.S. Naval Acad., Annapolis, Md., 1966; MA, U. Hawaii, 1970; PhD, Duke U., 1974. Historian NASA, Washington, 1973-81; assoc. prof. Duke U., Durham, N.C., 1981-87, prof. history dept., 1987—, chair dept. history, 1996-99. Johnson prof. mil. history U.S. Mil. History Inst., Carlisle, Pa., 1988—89; Dr. Leo Shifrin prof. mil.-naval history U.S. Naval Acad., 2001—02; resident fellow Dibner Inst., Cambridge, Mass., 1994—95. Author: Underwater Warfare in the Age of Sail, 1978, Model Research, 1985, The Military-Industrial Complex, 2001; co-author: Men in Arms, 5th edit., 1991, Strategic Computing, 2002; editor: A Spacefaring People, 1985; co-editor: Atmospheric Flight, 2000. Capt. USMC, 1966-70. Mem. Soc. History Tech. (pres. 1995-96), Soc. Mil. History (v.p. 2001-03). Office: Duke U Dept History Durham NC 27708 E-mail: alex.roland@duke.edu.

ROLAND, ANNE, registrar Supreme Court of Canada; b. France, 1947; m. Alphonse Morisette, Dec. 3, 1975; 1 child, Julien. BA Philosophy, Caen, France, 1965; diploma, Inst. Supérieur d'interprétation et de traduction, 1969; lic. in law, Paris, 1969; LLB, U. Ottawa, 1979. Bar: Quebec 1980. Legal trans., revisor, Can., 1971-75; chief trans. svcs. customs and excise Sec. of State, Can., 1975-76; spl. asst. to chief justice Can., 1976-81; chief law editor Supreme Ct. Can., 1981-88, dep. registrar, 1988-90, registrar, 1990. Mem. Can. Bar Assn., Assn. Can. Ct. Adminstrs., Assn. Francophone Jurists, Can. Inst. Adminstrn. Justice, Assn. Reporters Jud. Decisions. Office: Supreme Ct Can Office Reg 301 Wellington St Ottawa ON Canada K1A 0J1 Office Phone: 613-996-9277. E-mail: rolanda@scc-csc.gc.ca.

ROLAND, BILLY RAY, electronics company executive; b. Grandview, Tex., June 12, 1926; s. Marvin Wesley and Minnie Mae (Martin) R.; m. Ruth Ranell Sheets, Mar. 9, 1950 (div. 1982); children: Carl Ray and Darla Kay (twins); m. Linda Sue Leslie, Feb. 21, 1986 (div. Nov. 1991); m. Martha Kay Redford, May 17, 1993. BS, Tex. Christian U., 1954. CPA, Tex. Ticket and baggage agt. Southwestern Greyhound Co., Ft. Worth, 1943-44, 46-51; supr. acctg. dept. Tandy Leather Co., 1954-60; controller, asst. sec., treas. Tandy Corp., 1960-75; v.p., 1978-85; ret.; controller, asst. sec., treas. Tandy Crafts, Inc., 1975-78. V.p., treas. David L. Tandy Found., 1966-2003, dir. emeritus, 2004—; mng. trustee James L. and Eunice West Charitable Trust, 1980-91; treas. Benjamin F. Johnston Found., 1984—. Served with U.S. Army, 1944-46. Mem. AICPA, Tex. Soc. CPAs, Colonial Country Club, Petroleum Club. Republican. Methodist. Home: 8937 Random Rd Fort Worth TX 76179-2739

ROLAND, CATHERINE DIXON, entrepreneur; b. Andalusia, Ala., Mar. 9, 1939; d. Charles and Thelma (Chapman) Dixon; m. Henry F. Roland, Dec. 16, 1966 (div. Nov., 1976); 1 child, Charles H.; stepchild, Vickie Roland Little. Student, Huntingdon Coll., 1954-56; BS, Auburn U., 1956-59; MA in History, U. Ala., Tuscaloosa, 1965-66. Sec. Dixon Lumber Co., Inc., Andalusia, 1969-74, v.p., 1974-78; land and timber owner, mgr. Catherine D. Roland & Co., Andalusia, 1978—. Owner Sta. WCTA, andalusia, 1947-75, bd. dirs., 1972-75; owner, bd. dirs. D & G Property Ltd., Perth, Australia, 1967—, Covington County Bank, 1979—, So. Nat. Corp., 1985—. Chmn. Thelma Dixon Found., Andalusia, 1981—; mem. Rep. Senatorial Inner Cir., Washington, 1980—, 2d Congl. Com., Montgomery, Ala., 1980—, Andalusia Pub. Libr. Friends, Inc., 1981—; mem. adv. coun. Mises Inst. Auburn (Ala.) U., Auburn and Washington, 1983-85, Coll. Bus. Auburn U., 1987—; mem. Com. of 100, Huntington Coll., 1978, trustee, 1978—, vice chmn. bd. trustees 1985-93; bd. dirs. Women Health, Birmingham, Ala., 1978-82, Health Svcs. Found., 1982—, Andalusia Hosp., 1980-82. Named countess Huntingdon Coll., Montgomery, 1978, named to Hall of Honor, 1980; recipient commendation for Outstanding Svc. and Leadership, 1980, Loyalty award, 1988. Mem. DAR, Nat. Soc. Colonial Dames XVII Century, Ams. of Royal Descent, Dames of Magna Charter, Forest Landowners Assn., Ala. Landowners Assns., Ala. Wildlife Fedn., Andalusia Area C. of C., Auburn Alumni Assn., Huntingdon Coll. Alumni Assn. (chmn. Andalusia area chpt. 1983—), Am. Legion, Study Club. Methodist. Avocations: coin collecting/numismatics, reading, horses, tennis.

ROLAND, CHARLES GORDON, physician, medical historian, educator; b. Winnipeg, Man., Can., Jan. 25, 1933; s. John Sanford and Leona (McLaughlin) R.; m. Marjorie Ethel Kyles, 1953 (div. 1973); children: John Kenneth, Christopher Franklin, David Charles, Kathleen Siobhan; m. Connie Rankin, 1979. Student, U. Toronto, Ont., Can., 1952—54; MD, BSc, U. Man., 1958, DSc (hon.), 1997. Intern St. Boniface Hosp., 1958-59; pvt. practice medicine specializing in family medicine Tillsonburg, 1959-60, Grimsby, 1960-64; sr. editor Jour. Am. Med. Assn., Chgo., 1964-69; head sect. publs. Mayo Clinic, 1969-70, chmn. dept. biomed. communications, 1970-77; prof. history medicine, prof. biomed. comm., coord. family practice track, chmn. adminstrv. com. dept. family medicine Mayo Med. Sch., 1971-77; mem. admissions, edn. and curriculum coordinators coms., hon. mem. med. staff West Lincoln Meml. Hosp., Grimsby; mem. grants com. Hannah Inst. History of Medicine, Toronto, 1974-77, 87-91, mem. publs. com., 1991-95; Jason A. Hannah prof. history of medicine McMaster U., Hamilton, Canada, 1977-99, Hannah prof. emeritus, 1999—, assoc. mem. dept. history, 1978-96, chmn. archives com. Faculty of Health Scis., 1983-98; chmn. spl. grants com. Hannah Inst. for History of Medicine, 1981-85; Sid W. Richardson vis. prof. Inst. Med. Humanities U. Tex. Med. Br., Galveston, 1984. Mem. devel. adv. com. Assoc. Med. Svcs., 1999—; inaugural Osler-McGovern lectr. Green Coll., Oxford U., Eng., 2001. Author: (with L.S. King) Scientific Writing, 1968, (with J.P. McGovern) William Osler, The Continuing Education, 1969, Good Scientific Writing, 1971, William Osler's The Master Word in Medicine: A Study in Rhetoric, 1972, (with L.S. Baker) You and Leukemia: A Day at a Time, 1976, (with P. Potter) An Annotated Bibliography of Canadian Medical Periodicals, 1826-1975, 1979, Clarence Meredith Hincks 1885-1964: Mental Health Crusader, 1990, Courage Under Siege: Starvation, Disease and Death in the Warsaw Ghetto, 1992, Harold Nathan Segall: Pioneer Canadian Cardiologist, 1995, Long Night's Journey Into Day: Prisoners of War in the Far East, 1941-45, 2001; editor: (E.P. Scarlett) In Sickness and In Health, 1972; co-editor: An Annotated Checklist of Osleriana, 1976, vol. 2, 2000, Sir William Osler 1849-1919: A Selection for Medical Students, 1982, Health Disease and Medicine: Essays in Canadian History, 1984, Sir William Osler 1849-1919: petite anthologie à l'intention des étudiants in médecine, 1987, Bibliography of Secondary Sources in Canadian Medical History, 1985, 2d edition, 2000, (with J. Bernier) The Collected Essays of Sir William Osler (3 vols.), 1985; editor, author introduction: Medical Topography of Upper Canada, 1985; (with Richard Golden) Sir William Osler: An Annotated Bibiography with Illustrations, 1987; co-editor: The Persisting Osler, 1984, The Persisting Osler II, 1994, The Persisting Osler III, 2001; editor-in-chief Can. Bulletin of Med. History, 1987-90; mem. editl. adv. bd. Can. Family Physician, 1964-72, Chest, 1966-95, Med. Comm., 1971-75, Postgrad. Med. Jour., London, 1967-72, Mayo Clinic Procs., 1969-77, Bioscis. Comm., 1975-80, Ont. Med. Rev., 1979-84, HSTC Jour., 1980-87, Can. Bull. Med. History, 1983-90, Med. History (London), 1982-87, Jour. History of Medicine and Allied Scis., 1991-94, 96—. Mem. bd. curators Osler Libr., McGill U., Montreal, 1981—. Recipient Jason A. Hannah medal Royal Soc. Can., 1994. Fellow AAAS (coun. 1969-74), Am. Med. Writers Assn. (pres. 1969-70); mem. Can. Med. Assn., Am. Assn. History Medicine (sec.-treas. 1976-80, publs. com. 1979-85), Acad. Medicine Toronto (Grogan lecture com. 1978-83), Am. Mil. Inst., Internat. Inst. Prisoners of War, Soc. Internat. d'Histoire de la Medicine (internat. del. for Can. 1983-86), Can. Soc. for History of Medicine (v.p. 1982-87, pres. 1993-95), Soc. Med. History Chgo. (sec.-treas. 1966-69), Can. Ctr. for Studies in Hist. Horticulture (exec. com. 1982-89), Coun. Biology Editors, Med. Hist. Club Toronto (pres. 1977-78), Ont. Hist. Soc., Can. Hist. Assn., Bibliog. Soc. Can., Am. Osler Soc. (sec.-treas. 1975-85, v.p. 1985-86, pres. 1986-87, historian, 1999-), Japan Osler Soc. (hon.), Royal Soc. Medicine (London), Royal Can. Mil. Inst., Champlain Soc. (Toronto), History of Second World War (Can. com.), Soc. Army Hist. Rsch., Univ. Club (Rochester); Osler Club (London), Alpine Club Can., Lit. Club (Chgo.), Sigma Xi. Office: McMaster U 3N10-HSC Med Ctr 1200 Main St W Hamilton ON Canada L8N 3Z5 E-mail: rolandc@mcmaster.ca.

ROLAND, DAVID LEONARD, retired broadcast production educator; b. Port Jefferson, NY, Oct. 2, 1948; s. Leonard Ernest and Dorothy (Stewart) R.; m. Susan Mary Becht, July 10, 1971 (dec. Nov. 1979); m. Theresa Regina Ryan, Dec. 27, 1980. BS, Empire State Coll., 1976; MA, L.I. U., 1981. Tchr. photography Bd. Coop. Ednl. Svcs., Patchogue, NY, 1975—85, tchr. TV prodns., graphic arts module leader, 1985—2003; ret., 2003. Video arts prof. Five Towns Coll., Dix Hills, N.Y. Dir. CBS TV Worth Teaching Video (cert. merit), Camp Pa-gua-tuck Video (Outstanding Svc. award); audio engr. Children of the Cradle. Named Disting. Occupational Tchr. of Yr. State of N.Y., 1988. 020. Vocat. Indsl. Clubs Am. (advisor 1976—, chair), Internat. TV Assn., L.I. Media Arts Com., Assn. of BTC Educators. Home: 523 Washington Ave Riverhead NY 11901-2742

ROLAND, DONALD EDWARD, advertising executive; b. Dalhart, Tex., Nov. 14, 1942; s. Vernon O. Roland and Doris M. (Cox) Roland Hutson; m. Kathleen Marie Bennett, Feb. 1, 1964; children: Aileen, Donald E., Jenny. BS, Calif. State U., L.A., 1964; MA, U. Calif., Riverside, 1967; cert. exec. mgmt., UCLA. Dir. computer graphics Times Mirror Press, L.A., 1966-78, plant mgr., 1978-81, v.p. prodn., 1981-83; group v.p. ops. Treasure Chest Advt., Glendora, Calif., 1983-84, sr. v.p. ops., 1984-93, exec. v.p., 1993-94, pres., CEO, 1995-2000; pres., CEO, chmn. Vertis Inc., Balt., 2000—. Republican. Home: 4 Norwood Rd Annapolis MD 21401-1227 Office: Vertis Inc PO Box 17102 Baltimore MD 21297-1102 E-mail: droland@vertisinc.com.

ROLAND, JOHN, newscaster; b. Pitts., Nov. 25, 1941; s. John Roland and Marion (Costlow) Gingher. BA in English., U. Calif., Long Beach, 1963. Rschr. NBC News, L.A., 1966-69; reporter KTTV, L.A., 1969; anchorman Fox News, N.Y.C., 1970—. Recipient Emmy award, 1978, 83, Pub. Svc. award Am. Fed. Govt. Employees Assn., 1974, Cert. of Appreciation, Goldwater Hosp., N.Y., 1975, N.Y. City Patrolman's Benevolent Assn. Journalism award, 1982, Good Samaritan award Bronx C. of C., 1983, Excelsior award N.Y.C. Coun., 1983, Man of the Yr. award N.Y.'s Finest Found., 1989; named Crimefighter of the Week, N.Y. Daily News, 1983. Mem. N.Y.C. Police Dept. Detective Endowment Assn. (hon.), Sigma Alpha Epsilon. Avocations: boating, tennis, golf. Office: WNYW TV Fox Broadcasting Co 205 E 67th St New York NY 10021-6050

ROLAND, MELISSA MONTGOMERY, accountant; b. Houston, Mar. 6, 1961; d. John Edgar and Mariann (Guggino) Montgomery; m. Larry Dean Roland, Sept. 20, 1984. BBA, Tex. A&M U., 1983. CPA, Tex., cert. fraud examiner, Tex. Audit sr. Arthur Andersen & Co., Houston, 1983-87; cons. mgr.-performance improvement group Ernst & Young, San Antonio, 1988-91; COO Roy Smith Shoes, Inc. d/b/a Accenté, Houston, 1991-96; v.p., COO Third Coast Mgmt., Inc., Jacksonville, Fla., 1996—2004, pres., 2004—. Bd. dirs., treas. Grandparents Outreach, San Antonio, 1989—. Mem. AICPA, Tex. Accts. and Lawyers for the Arts (adv. bd.), Tex. Soc. CPAs, Young Reps., Jr. League Jacksonville, S.W. Found. Forum. Episcopalian. Avocations: running, scuba diving, weightlifting, bicycling. Office: 515 Rutile Dr Ponte Vedra Beach FL 32082-2319 Office Phone: 904-543-9966.

ROLAND, RAYMOND WILLIAM, lawyer, mediator; b. Ocala, Fla., Jan. 3, 1947; s. Raymond W. and Hazel (Dunn) R.; m. Jane Allen, Dec. 28, 1968; children: John Allen, Jason William. BA, Fla. State U., 1969, JD, 1972. Bar: Fla. 1972, U.S. Dist. Ct. (no. dist.) Fla. 1973, U.S. Dist. Ct. (mid. dist.) Fla. 1985, U.S. Ct. Appeals (5th cir.) 1974, U.S. Ct. Appeals (11th cir.) 1983, U.S. Supreme Ct. 1985; cert. cir. ct. mediator. Assoc. Keen, O'Kelley & Spitz, Tallahassee, 1972-74, ptnr., 1974-77; ptnr., v.p. McConnaughhay, Roland, Maida & Cherr, P.A., Tallahassee, 1978-97; owner Roland Mediation Svcs., Tallahassee, 1997—2002; cir. mediator U.S. Ct. Appeals 11th Cir., 2002—. Diplomate mem. Fla. Acad. of Profl. Mediators, Inc.; adj. prof. Bapt. Coll. Fla. Bd. dirs. So. Scholarship Found., Tallahassee, 1985-89, 98-99, v.p. 1989; bd. visitors Bapt. Coll. Fla. Mem. Internat. Assn. Def. Coun., Def. Rsch. Inst., Kiwanis (life, lt. gov. 1984-85), Capital City Kiwanis Club (Kiwanian of Yr. 1978, pres. 1979), Fla. Kiwanis Found. (life fellow). Baptist. Avocations: reading, hiking, camping, golf. Home: 800 Freedom Ln Roswell GA 30075 E-mail: BRoland487@aol.com.

ROLDAN, ULISES, sales and marketing executive; b. P.R. BA, U. Interamericana, Rio Piedras, P.R., 1990. Mktg. mgr. Direct Mktg. and Media Group, San Juan, PR, 1991—95; sales and mktg. mgr. Grupo Editl. Norma USA, San Juan, 1995—. Acting sgt. U.S. Army, 1981—85. Office: Grupo Editorial Norma USA Po Box 195040 San Juan PR 00919-5040

ROLEN, SCOTT BRUCE, professional baseball player; b. Jasper, Ind., Apr. 4, 1975; m. Niki Warner, Feb. 2, 2002. 3d base Phila. Phillies, 1993—2002, St. Louis Cardinals, 2002—. Named Nat. League Rookie Player of Yr., The Sporting News, 1997, Baseball Writers Assn. of Am., 1997; named to Nat. League All-Star Team, 2002—04; recipient Nat. League Gold Glove Award, 1997—2003. Office: c/o St Louis Cardinals 250 Stadium Plaza Saint Louis MO 63102*

ROLETT, ELLIS LAWRENCE, medical educator, cardiologist; b. N.Y.C., July 10, 1930; s. Daniel Meyer and Mary Elaine (Warshaw) R.; m. Virginia Ann Vladimir, Mar. 25, 1956; children: Roderic Lawrence, Barry Vladimir, Daniel Alfred. BS, Yale U., 1952; MD cum laude, Harvard U., 1955. Diplomate: Am. Bd. Internal Medicine, Am. Bd. Cardiovas. Disease. Intern, resident in medicine Mass. Gen. Hosp., Boston, 1955-56, 59-61; asst. resident N.Y. Hosp.-Cornell U. Med. Ctr., N.Y.C., 1956-57; Am. Heart Assn. research fellow Peter Bent Brigham Hosp., Boston, 1961-63; mem. faculty U. N.C., Chapel Hill, 1963-74, then prof., 1971-74; prof. UCLA, 1974-77; chief cardiology VA Wadsworth Hosp., L.A., 1974-77, Dartmouth-Hitchcock Med. Ctr., Hanover, NH, 1977—87; prof. Dartmouth Med. Sch., Hanover, 1977-97, prof. medicine active emeritus, 1997—. Vis. scientist August Krogh Inst., Copenhagen, 1984; mem. merit rev. bd. Cardiovasc. studies VA, 1976-79, chmn., 1978-79; mem. regional rsch. rev. com. New Eng. Am. Heart Assn., 1978-83; mem. sci. bd. Stanley J. Sarnoff Endowment for Cardiovasc. Sci., 1992-97, chmn., 1994-95, bd. dirs., 1997-2000; mem. lit. sect. rev. com. Nat. Libr. Medicine, 1995-99, chmn., 1998-99; dir. Vt.-Karelia (Russia) Med. Project, St. Petersburg Univ. Global Fund. Bd. dirs. N.H. affiliate Am. Heart Assn., 1978-85; pres. N.H. affiliate Am. Heart Assn., 1983-85. Served to capt. M.C. USAF, 1957-59. Recipient Lederle Med. Faculty award, 1965-68, USPHS Career Devel. award, 1967-72; grantee USPHS/NIH, 1964-76, VA Merit Rev. Rsch. Program, 1975-77, Mathers Found., 1984-86, 93-96, Am. Heart Assn., 1989-91. Mem. AAAS, Am. Coll. Cardiology, Am. Fedn. Clin. Rsch., Am. Heart Assn., Am. Physiol. Soc., Internat. Soc. Heart Rsch., Phi Beta Kappa, Alpha Omega Alpha Home: 4 Balch Hill Ln Hanover NH 03755-1622 Office: Dartmouth Med Sch Hanover NH 03755 Office Phone: 603-650-1060. E-mail: ellis.rolett@dartmouth.edu.

ROLEY, V. VANCE, finance educator, academic administrator; b. Nov. 26, 1951; BA in econ. and statistics with honors, U. Calif., Berkeley, 1973; MA in econ., Harvard U., 1976, PhD in econ., 1977. Tchg. fellow Harvard U., 1975—76; sr. staff economist Coun. Econ. Adv., 1979—80; fin. economist Fed. Reserve Bank, Kansas City, 1977—79, asst. v.p., economist, 1981—83; assoc. prof. fin. U. Wash. Bus. Sch., 1983—86, dir. Ctr. Study Banking and Fin. Markets, 1983—86, prof. fin., 1986—, affiliate program prof. fin. and bus. econ., 1986—87, Rainier Nat. Bank prof. banking and fin., 1987—88, Security Pacific Bank Wash. prof. banking and fin., 1988—92, dir. Pacific Rim Fin. Ctr., 1995—96, Seafirst Faculty Scholar banking and fin., 1992—95, Hughes M. Blake prof. bus. adminstrn., 1995—, assoc. dean acad. and faculty affairs, 2000—, interim dean, 2004—. Vis. asst. prof. econ. U. Wash. Bus. Sch., 1979; vis. scholar Fed. Reserve Bank, Kansas City, 1983—90, Kansas City, 1994—; rsch. affiliate Nat. Bureau Econ. Rsch., 1980—92; assoc. Ctr. Pacific Monetary and Econ. Studies, Fed. Reserve Bank, San Francisco, 1990—; editl. adv. bd. Jour. Econ. and Bus., 1989—. Assoc. editor Jour. Internat. Fin. Markets, Instn. and Money, 1989—, Jour. Fin. and Quantitative Analysis, 1996—; author: Structural Model of the U.S. Government Securities Market, 1979; contbr. articles and papers in field. Recipient Merton Miller prize, Jour. Bus., 1998. Office: Dept Fin and Bus Econ UW Bus Sch Univ Wash Box 353200 Seattle WA 98195-3200 Office Phone: 206-685-3622. Office Fax: 206-616-6856. Business E-Mail: vroley@u.washington.edu.

ROLFE, ROBERT MARTIN, lawyer; b. Richmond, Va., May 16, 1951; s. Norman and Bertha (Cohen) R.; m. Catherine Dennis Stone, July 14, 1973; children: P. Alexander, Asher B., Joel A., Zachary A. BA, U. Va., 1973, JD, 1976. Bar: Va. 1976, N.Y. 1985, U.S. Dist. Ct. (ea. and we. dists.) Va. 1976, U.S. Ct. Appeals (4th cir.) 1976, U.S. Ct. Appeals (2d cir.) 1979, U.S. Dist. Ct. (ea. dist.) Mich. 1985, U.S. Ct. Appeals (D.C. cir.) 1985, U.S. Dist. Ct. (so. and ea. dists.) N.Y. 1985, U.S. Ct. Appeals (7th cir.) 1995, U.S. Ct. Fed. Claims, 1997, U.S. Supreme Ct. 1979. Assoc. Hunton & Williams, Richmond, 1976-83, ptnr., 1983—, gen. counsel, co-head litigation, intellectual property and antitrust team, exec. com., 1998—2004. Contbr. articles to profl. jours. Trustee Jewish Family Supporting Found.; bd. dirs. Jewish Family Svcs., Richmond, pres., 1993-95; bd. mgrs., 2d v.p. Congregation Beth Ahabah, 1995-97, 1st v.p., 1997-99. Fellow Am. Bar Found.; mem. ADA (litig. sect.), Va. Bar Assn., Va. State Bar, Richmond Bar Assn., Order of Coif (Alumni award for acad. excellence U. Va. 1976). Home: 18 Greenway Ln Richmond VA 23226-1630 Office: Hunton & Williams Riverfront Plz East Tower PO Box 1535 Richmond VA 23218-1535 also: 200 Park Ave New York NY 10166-0005 Office Phone: 804-788-8466.

ROLFE, RONALD STUART, lawyer; b. N.Y.C., Sept. 5, 1945; s. Nat and Florence I. (Roth) R.; m. Yvonne S. Quinn, Sept. 1, 1979 (div. Apr. 2002); m. Sara Darehshori; children; Andrew, Dare. AB, Harvard U., 1966; JD, Columbia U., 1969. Bar: N.Y. 1969, U.S. Ct. Appeals (2d cir.) 1970, U.S. Dist. Ct. (so. and ea. dists.) N.Y. 1971, U.S. Supreme Ct. 1973, U.S. Dist. Ct. (no. dist.) Calif. 1982, U.S. Ct. Appeals (6th and 5th cirs.) 1982, U.S. Ct. Appeals (9th cir.) 1983, U.S. Dist. Ct. (ea. dist.) Ky. 1984, U.S. Ct. Appeals (7th and 10th cirs.) 1989, U.S. Ct. Appeals (fed. cir.) 1991, U.S. Ct. Appeals (3d cir.) 1992, U.S. Ct. Appeals (4th cir.) 1991. Law clk. to judge U.S. Dist. Ct. (so. dist.) N.Y., 1969-70; assoc. Cravath, Swaine & Moore, 1970-77, ptnr., 1977—. Trustee Allen-Stevenson Sch., 1980—91, pres., 1992—; trustee Lawrenceville Sch., 1987—, v.p., 2001—. Trustee DeLaSalle Acad., 2002—. Fellow: Am. Bar Found.; mem.: ABA, Am. Law Inst., Fed. Bar Coun. (trustee 1989—94), Assn. Bar City NY, NY State Bar Assn., Turf and Field Club (N.Y.C.), Stanwich Club (Greenwich, Conn.), Univ. Club, Union Club. Office: Cravath Swaine & Moore LLP Worldwide Plz 825 8th Ave 40th Fl New York NY 10019-7475 Office Phone: 212-474-1714. Business E-Mail: rrolfe@cravath.com.

ROLFSON, HELEN C. theology studies educator, translator; b. Duluth, Minn., Oct. 4, 1938; d. Neil Edward Rolfson and Isla Elizabeth Hanson. BA, Coll. of St. Teresa, Winona, Minn., 1962; MA, Notre Dame U., Ind., 1967; Dr.ès.Sc.Rel., Université de Strasbourg, France, 1972; postgrad., U. Montreal, 1977. Professed mem. Sisters of St. Francis, Roman Cath. Ch., 1956. Tchr. St. Mary's Elem. Sch., Winona, 1959—60, Pacelli H.S., Austin, Minn., 1962—67; assoc. prof. theology Coll. of St. Teresa, Winona, 1967—81, St. John's U., Collegeville, Minn., 1981—. Bd. dirs. Hill Monastic Microfilm Libr., Collegeville; mem. dialogue team Roman Cath./Pentecostal Dialogues, Vatican City, 1985—97; collaborator translator 1st 3 vols. Repertoire des Institutions Chretiennes, Strasbourg, 1969—71. Translator (bd. editors): (book) Jan van Ruusbroec: Opera Omnia, vols. 1-12, 1981—; translator: Brieven of Gerlac Peters; mem. editl. bd. (series) The Living Flame, 1999—. Mem. ecumenical commn. Diocese of St. Cloud, Minn., 1998—; translator Internat. Com. of English in the Liturgy, Washington, 2002—. Grantee Dillon grantee, St. John's U., 1993—94, 1995—96; European Area Studies grantee, Fulbright Assn., 1988, Transl. grantee, NEH, 1977. Mem.: Cath. Theol. Soc. Am. Roman Catholic. Avocations: reading, viola. Office: Saint John's Univ Sch of Theology PO Box 7288 Collegeville MN 56321 Office Phone: 320-363-2105. E-mail: hrolfson@csbsju.edu.

ROLIN, CHRISTOPHER ERNEST, lawyer; b. Feb. 15, 1940; s. Carl A. and Kate (Northcote) R.; m. Debbie Best, Apr. 1994; children: Whitney, Brett. BA, U. Calif., Berkeley, 1961; JD, U. So. Calif., 1965. Bar: Calif. 1966. Assoc. Meserve, Mumper & Hughes, L.A., 1966—71, ptnr., 1972, Haight, Dickson, Brown & Bonesteel, Santa Monica, Calif., 1974—88, Rodi Pollock, L.A., 1990—96, Newkirk, Newkirk & Rolin, 1996—2000; sole practice Law Office of Christopher Rolin, 2001—. Expert witness on std. of care for attys. Bd. dirs. Legion Lex, 1991—, sec., 1995, v.p., 1996, pres., 1997—98; bd. dirs. Wellness Cmty., 2001. Mem.: Cowboy Lawyers, Lawyers Profl. Liability Assn. (chmn. 2001—03), Am. Arbitration Assn., L.A. County Bar Assn. (bd. dirs., vice chmn. law mgmt.sect. 1994, chmn. 1995—96), Am. Bd. Trial Advs. (bd. dirs. 1994), So. Calif. Def. Counsel (bd. dirs. 1981—85), Optimists (pres. 1989). Home: 3672 Twin Lake Rdg Westlake Village CA 91361-3927 Office: Ste 1200 21031 Ventura Blvd Woodland Hills CA 91364-2229 E-mail: CRolin@ChrisRolin.com., crolin@chrisrolin.com.

ROLINGSON, MARTHA, research archeologist; b. Wichita, Kans., Nov. 6, 1935; BA, U. Denver, 1957; MA, U. Ky., 1963; PhD, U. Mich., 1967. Dir. U. Ky. Mus. Anthropology, Lexington, 1965-68; archeologist Ark. Archeol. Survey, 1968—; dir. rsch. Toltec Mounds Archaeol. State Park, Scott, Ark., 1976—. Mem. Soc. Am. Archaeology, Southeastern Archaeol. Conf. Office: Toltec Mounds Archaeol State Park 490 Toltec Mounds Rd Scott AR 72142

ROLL, DAVID LEE, lawyer; b. Pontiac, Mich., May 1, 1940; s. Everett Edgar and Garnette (Houts) R.; m. Nancy E. Spindle, Aug. 17, 1963; children: Richard, Molly. BA cum laude, Amherst Coll., 1962; JD, U. Mich., 1964. Bar: Mich. 1965, U.S. Dist. Ct. (ea. dist.) Mich. 1965, U.S. Ct. Appeals (6th cir.) 1969, D.C. 1974, U.S. Dist. Ct. D.C. 1975, U.S. Supreme Ct. 1975, U.S. Ct. Appeals (4th cir.) 1976, U.S. Ct. Appeals (D.C. cir.) 1983, U.S. Ct. Appeals (3rd and 11th cirs.) 1985, U.S. Ct. Appeals (9th cir.) 1992, U.S. Ct. Appeals (fed. cir.) 1993. Assoc. Hill, Lewis, Detroit, 1965-70, ptnr., 1970-72; asst. dir. gen. litigation Bur. of Competition Fed. Trade Commn., Washington, 1972-75; ptnr. Steptoe & Johnson, Washington, 1975—, chmn., 1993—98. V.p. bus. devel., bd. dirs. eLawForum, 2000—. Mem. ABA (chair Robinson Patman Act com., antitrust sect. 1984-86, Clayton Act com., antitrust sect. 1986-88, Energy Litigation com., litigation sect. 1992-93, mem. task force on indsl. competitiveness 1987, coun., antitrust sect. 1988-91, author, editor antitrust sect.), Lex Mundi (bd. dirs., chair competition com.). Office: 1330 Connecticut Ave NW Washington DC 20036-1704 E-mail: droll@steptoe.com.

ROLL, IRWIN CLIFFORD (WIN ROLL), advertising, marketing and publishing executive; b. N.Y.C., Aug. 21, 1925; s. Arnold and Bertha (Vogel) R.; m. Marilyn Witlin, Apr. 10, 1949; children: Richard J., Douglas W. BBA magna cum laude, CCNY, 1948; postgrad., Columbia U., 1952. Asst. advt. mgr. Standard Motor Products, Inc., Long Island City, N.Y., 1948-50; advt. and sales promotion exec. RCA, Harrison, N.J., 1950-54; account exec. Fuller & Smith & Ross, Inc., N.Y.C., 1954-59, group v.p., 1959-66; pres., dir. Henderson & Roll, Inc., advt. and pub. relations agy., 1966-77; pres., dir., chief exec. officer Henderson, Roll & Friedlich, Inc., 1977-79; chmn. bd., treas., chief exec. officer, dir. Listfax Corp., nat. computerized info. services co., 1966-79; pres., CEO Win Roll and Co., Inc., N.Y.C., 1979-89, 99—, chmn. bd. Roll-Bender Research, 1980-82, Devonshire Communications, Ltd., 1980-83; sr. v.p. Tradewell Industries, Inc., 1983-87. Exec. v.p. Internat. Mktg. Sys. Inc., 1988-90; pres. Concord Cons. Group, 1990—; corp. devel. dir. Ind. Media Svcs., Inc., 1990-92; pres. Maco Pub. Co., 1992- 94; pres., treas., bd. dirs. Megaworld, Inc., 1994-99. Mem. mktg. com. Nat. Multiple Sclerosis Soc., 1958-98; bd. dirs. Westchester County chpt. Multiple Sclerosis Soc., 1983-89; pres. Rosedale Residential Assn., 1983-85, bd. dirs., 1980-2000. With U.S. Army, 1943-46, ETO. Mem. Ad-Net Nat. Advt. Orgn. (bd. dirs. 1983-90, pres. 1986-88), Beta Gamma Sigma (bd. dirs., v.p. N.Y. Alumni chpt. 1986-89, pres. 1989-91). Home: 2558 Downeyville Ave Henderson NV 89052 Fax: 702-614-5117. E-mail: winroll@webtv.net.

ROLL, JOHN MCCARTHY, judge; s. Paul Herbert and Esther Marie (McCarthy) Roll; m. Maureen O'Connor; 3 children. BA, U. Ariz., 1969, JD, 1972; LLM, U. Va., 1990. Bar: Ariz. 1972, U.S. Dist. Ct. Ariz. 1974, U.S. Ct. Appeals (9th cir.) 1980, U.S. Supreme Ct. 1977. Asst. pros. atty. City of Tucson, 1973; dep. county atty. Pima County (Ariz.), 1973-80; asst. U.S. Atty. U.S. Attys. Office, Tucson, 1980-87; judge Ariz. Ct. Appeals, 1987-91, U.S. Dist. Ct. Ariz., 1991—. Mem. criminal justice mental health standards project ABA, 1980—83, mem. com. model jury instrns. 9th circ., 1994—2001, chair com. model jury instrns. 9th circ., 1998—2001; mem. panel workshop criminal law CEELI Program, Moscow, 1997; mem. U.S. Jud. Conf. Adv. Com. Criminal Rules, 1997—2003. Contbr. Merit Selection: the Arizona Experience, Ariz. State Law Jour., 1991, The Rules Have Changed: Amendments ot the Rules of Civil procedure, Defense Law Jour., 1994, Ninth Cir. Judges' Benchbook on Pretrial Proceedings, 1998, 2000, 2002. Recipient Disting. Faculty award Nat. Coll. Dist. Attys., U. Houston, 1979, Outstanding Alumnus award U. Ariz. Coll. Law, 1992. Mem. Fed. Judges Assn., KC (adv. coun. 1991). Republican. Office: US Dist Ct 405 W Congress Tucson AZ 85701

ROLLAND, CLARA, pianist, educator; b. Budapest, Hungary, Apr. 20, 1916; arrived in U.S., 1939; d. Alexander and Katalin (Stein) Szekely; m. Paul Rolland, Dec. 24, 1940 (dec. Nov. 9, 1978); children: Peter Thomas, John Paul. M, Royal Franz Liszt Acad. Music, 1939; grad., Cleve. Inst. Music, 1941; diploma (hon.), Franz Liszt Acad. Music, 1990. Founder, instr. prep. dept. piano, theory and ear tng. Simpson Coll., Indianola, Iowa, 1941—45; pvt. studio Urbana, Ill., 1946—73; founder fun with music class Fine Arts Ctr., Clinton, Ill., 1966—70; co-dir. Music Divsn. Nat. Acad. Arts, 1973—79. Lectr. in field; judge Three Rivers Piano Competition, St. Louis, 1978. Performer, WILL-FM, 1950. Mem.: Music Tchr. Nat. Assn. (Baldwin Jr. Achievement award 1972, 1973, 1974, 1975, 1977, Mason & Hamlin Tchr. Achievement award 1974, H.S. Auditions winner 1974), Am. String Tchr. Assn. (life), Mu Phi Epsilon (pres. Mu Alpha chpt. 1961).

ROLLAND, DONALD F. printing company executive; Former CEO Big Flower Press, Glendora, Calif.; pres., CEO Treasure Chest Advt., Balt., 1993—. Office: Treasure Chest Advt PO Box 17102 Baltimore MD 21297-1102

ROLLAND, LUCIEN GILBERT, paper company executive, director; b. St. Jerome, Que., Can., Dec. 21, 1916; s. Olivier and Aline (Dorion) R.; m. Marie de Lorimier, May 30, 1942; children: Nicolas, Natalie, Stanislas, Dominique, Christine, Etienne, David. Student, Coll. Jean de Brebeuf, Montreal, U. Montreal, BA, BASc., C.E., also D.C.Sc. (hon.), 1960. Registered profl. engr. With Rolland Paper Co. Ltd. (name changed to Rolland inc. 1979), 1942—, v.p., gen. mgr., 1952, pres., gen. mgr., 1952-78, pres., CEO, 1978—, chmn., pres., CEO, 1984, chmn., CEO, 1985, chmn., 1991. Cons. in field, 1995; chmn. bd. Tarascon, Inc. Bd. govs. Notre-Dame Hosp., Montreal Children's Hosp., Montreal Gen. Hosp., Hôpital Marie Enfant. Decorated Knight Comdr. Order St. Gregory, officer Order of Can. Mem. Can. Pulp and Paper Assn. (hon.), Corp. Profl. Engrs., Montreal Bd. Trade, Province of Que., C of C, Montreal C. of C., Engring. Inst. Can. Home: Apt B-60 1321 Sherbrooke St W Montreal QC Canada H3G 1J4 Office: Tarascon Inc 1200 McGill College #1100 Montreal QC Canada H3B 4G7

ROLLANS, JAMES O. service company executive; b. Glendale, Calif., July 7, 1942; s. Henry Leo and Geraldine Ada (Berg) R.; children: Jodie Helene, Thomas James, Daniel Joseph. BS, Calif. State U., Northridge, 1967. Vice pres., dir. Chase Manhattan Bank, 1976-78; v.p. corp. communications Dart Industries, Los Angeles, 1978-80; v.p. bus. analysis and investor relations Dart & Kraft, Chgo., 1980-82; sr. v.p., CFO Fluor Corp., Irvine, Calif., 1982-99, also bd. dirs., 1998—; pres., group exec. Bus. Svcs., Aliso Viego, Calif., 1999. Bd. dirs. Cupertino Elec.; mem. Flowserve Corp. Bd. dirs. Irvine Med. Ctr. Episcopalian. Avocations: boating; skiing; fishing; hunting. Office: Fluor Corp One Enterprise Dr Aliso Viejo CA 92656

ROLLE, ANDREW, historian, writer; b. Providence, Apr. 12, 1922; m. Frances Squires, Dec. 1945 (div.); children: John Warren, Alexander Frederick, Julia Elisabeth.; m. Myra Moss, Nov. 1983. BA, Occidental Coll., 1943; MA, UCLA, 1949, PhD, 1953; grad., So. Calif. Psychoanalytic Inst., 1976. Am. vice consul, Genoa, Italy, 1945-48; editorial assoc. Pacific Hist. Rev., 1952-53; from asst. prof. to Cleland prof. history Occidental Coll., 1953-88; rsch. scholar Huntington Libr., San Marino, Calif., 1988—. Author: Riviera Path, 1946, An American in California, 1956, reprinted, 1982, The Road to Virginia City, 1960, reprinted, 1989, Lincoln: A Contemporary Portrait, 1961, (with Allan Nevins, Irving Stone) California: A History, 1963, rev. edits., 1963, 69, 78, 87, 98, 2002, Occidental College: The First Seventy-Five Years, 1963, The Lost Cause: Confederate Exiles in Mexico, 1965, 1992, The Golden State, 1967, rev. edit., 1978, 1989, 2000, California, A Student Guide, 1965, Los Angeles, A Student Guide, 1965; Editor: A Century of Dishonor (Helen Hunt Jackson), 1964, Life in California (Alfred Robinson), 1971, Voyage to California (Jour. of Lucy Herrick), 1998; The Immigrant Upraised, 1968, The American Italians: Their History and Culture, 1972, Gli Emigrati Vittoriosi, 1973, reprinted, 2003; (with George Knoles others) Essays and Assays, 1973, (with others) Studies in Italian American Social History, 1975, (with others) Los Angeles: The Biography of a City, 1976, 2d edit., 1991; (with Allan Weinstein and others) Crisis in America, 1977, The Italian Americans: Troubled Roots, 1980, 2d edit. 1985, Los Angeles: From Pueblo to Tomorrow's City, 1981, 2nd edit., 1995, Occidental College: A Centennial History, 1986, John Charles Frémont: Character as Destiny, 1991, Henry Mayo Newhall and His Times, 1992, Westward the Immigrants, 1999. Served to 1st lt. M.I. AUS, 1943-45, 51-52. Decorated Cavaliere Ordine Merito Italy; recipient silver medal Italian Ministry Fgn. Affairs; Commonwealth award for non-fiction; Huntington Library-Rockefeller Found. fellow; resident scholar Rockefeller Found. Center, Bellagio, Italy Fellow Calif. Hist. Soc.; mem. Phi Beta Kappa. Office: Huntington Libr Rsch Div San Marino CA 91108 Office Phone: 626-405-2100 2321.

ROLLE, MARTHA COLLINS (MARTHA TRAUDT COLLINS), lawyer; b. Colorado Springs, Colo., July 23, 1952; d. Verne O.M. and Helen Louise Traudt; m. Alexander F. Rolle; children: Joseph T. Collins, Alexander S. Rolle. BS in Math., U. Nebr., 1974; JD, U. Colo., 1977. Bar: Colo. 1977, N.Y. 1997. Assoc. Holme Roberts & Owen LLC, Denver, 1977-82, ptnr., 1983—, mng. ptnr. London, 2002—. Contbg. author: Rocky Mountain Mineral Law Foundation's Law of Federal Oil and Gas Leases, 1988; author: Hedging Transactions for Oil and Gas Producers: Rocky Mountain Mineral Law Foundation Special Institute, 1995; contbr. articles to profl. jours. Mem. ABA, Colo. Bar Assn., N.Y. Bar Assn., Order of Coif, Phi Beta Kappa. Office: Five Chancery Ln Clifford's Inn London EC4A 1BU England E-mail: marty.rolle@hro.com.

ROLLE, MYRA MOSS See MOSS, MYRA

ROLLER, DUANE WILLIAMSON, archaeologist, educator; b. Lafayette, Ind., Oct. 7, 1946; s. Duane Henry Dubose and Marjorie Fair (Williamson) R.; m. Letitia Jean Kaminski, Feb. 18, 1984. BA, U. Okla., 1966; MA, 1968; PhD, Harvard U., 1971. Asst. prof. Franklin and Marshall Coll., Lancaster, Pa., 1971-74, Wilfrid Laurier U., Waterloo, Ont., 1974-84, assoc. prof. classics, 1982-86; asst. prof. Ohio State U., 1986-89, assoc. prof., 1989-93, prof., 1993-98, prof. Greek and Latin, 1998—. Exec. mem. Can. Archaeol. Inst., Athens, 1982-87; dir. Tanagra Survey Project, Greece, 1985-1990, Southern Messapia Survey, Italy, 1989-1997; vis. prof. classics U. Calcutta, 1995; vis. prof. history U. Wroclaw, 2000. Author: Tanagran Studies, 1989, The Building Program of Herod the Great, 1998, The World of Juba II and Kleopatra Selene, 2003, Messapia, 2003; contbr. editor Internat. Rwy. Traveller; contbr. articles on classical archaeology and classical studies to profl. jours. Charles Eliot Norton fellow Harvard U., 1970; Fulbright scholar, 1995, 2000; recipient rsch. awards Social Scis. and Humanities Rsch. Coun. Can., 1980, 84, Nat. Geographic Soc., 1990, NEH, 1993, 2000. Mem. Archaeol. Inst. Am. Democrat. Avocation: railway passenger travel. Office: Ohio State U Lima OH 45804

ROLLER, MATTHEW BENEDICT, classics educator; b. Denver, July 27, 1966; s. Kent G. and Jean Cason Roller; m. Rhonda R. Van Roekel. BA, Stanford U., 1988; PhD, U. Calif., Berkeley, 1994. Asst. prof. Johns Hopkins U., Balt., 1994—2000, assoc. prof., 2000—04, prof., 2004—. Author: (monograph) Constructing Autocracy: Aristocrats and Emperors in Julio-Claudian Rome; contbr. articles to profl. jours. Fellow dissertation fellow, Mellon Found., 1993—94; fellow in the humanities, 1988—90, 1992—93, jr. fellow, Am. Coun. Learned Societies, 2000—01, Solmsen fellow, Inst. for Rsch. in the Humanities, U. Wis., 2000—01. Mem.: Archaeol. Inst. Am., Am. Philol. Assn. Democrat. Office: Dept Classics Johns Hopkins U 3400 N Charles St Baltimore MD 21218 Office Phone: 410-516-7556.

ROLLER, ROBERT H. dean, finance educator; b. Columbus, Ohio, May 13, 1957; s. Robert F and Emmalou Nunamaker Roller; m. Wanda C Hammack, May 12, 1979; children: Laura Elizabeth, Rachel Marie. BS, Oral Roberts U., Tulsa, 1979; MBA, Oral Roberts U., 1986; PhD, Okla. State U., 1995. Bus. mgr. Cone-Lewis Printing Co., Tulsa, 1979—80; youth pastor Carbondale Assembly of God, Tulsa, 1979—81; assoc. paster First Assembly of God, Warren, Ohio, 1981—85; asst. prof. of bus. Oral Roberts U., Tulsa, 1986—92; asst. prof. of mgmt. Kennesaw State U., Ga., 1992—96; chair, divsn. of bus. & mgmt. Roberts Wesleyan Coll., Rochester, NY, 1996—98, dean, sch. of bus. LeTourneau U., Longview, Tex., 1998—. Commr. Internat. Assembly for Collegiate Bus. Edn., Overland Park, Kans., 1999—. Editl. bd. (acad. jours.) Jour. of Ministry Mktg. and Mgmt., Jourj. of Biblical Integration in Bus.; author: (accreditation manual) IACBE Accreditation Manual; contbr. articles to profl. jours. Mem. class of 2000 Leadership Longview, Tex., 1999—2000; nat. adv. bd. mem. Assembly of God Bible Quiz, Springfield, Mo., 1981—90; league coord. N.E. Tex. Jr. Bible Quiz League, Longview, 2002—04; elder First Assembly of God, Longview, 1998—2004; state coord. Ga. Dist. Bible Quiz, Ga., 1995—96. Named Outstanding Young Man of Am., 1996; fellow Disting. Grad. fellow, Robert Glenn Rapp Found., 1988. Mem.: Internat. Assembly for Collegiate Bus. Edn. (chair bd. of commrs. 2001—02, 2004—05), Okla. Small Bus. Inst. Dirs. Assn. (2nd v.p. 1991—92), Christian Bus. Faculty Assn., Acad. of Mgmt. Assemblies Of God. Avocations: travel, swimming. Office: LeTourneau University School of Business Longview TX 75607-7001 Personal E-mail: rhroller@cox-internet.com. E-mail: bobroller@letu.edu.

ROLLERI, DENISE MARIE, radiation therapist, business owner; b. Phila., Mar. 16, 1950; d. Albert J. and Marie (Fenerty) R. diploma, diploma, Bryn Mawr Sch. Radiol. Tech., Pa., 1976. Chief technologist dept. radiation therapy Bryn Mawr Hosp., 1970-75; sr. staff therapist Thomas Jefferson U. Hosp., Phila., 1976-85; supr. radiation oncology dept. St. Peter's Med. Ctr., New Brunswick, N.J., 1985-87; pres., CEO, R.T. Temps Inc., Wayne, Pa., 1987—, R.T. Career Edn., Wayne, Pa., 1995—. Pres. Radnor (Pa.) Young Reps., 1976-77, Mem. Am. Hosp. Assn., Soc. Radiation Oncology Adminstrs., Am. Soc. Radiol. Tech. Avocations: boating, walking, pet therapy. Office: RT Temps Inc PO Box 404 Wayne PA 19087-0404

ROLLETTE, HAROLD HENRY, insurance company executive; b. Cazenovia, Wis., May 6, 1939; s. Henry Harold and Eva Gertrude (Jessop) R.; m. Joanne Krueger, Oct. 24, 1959 (div. 1964); m. Mary Jean Hirschinger, Aug. 31, 1968 (dec. July 1995); children: Christopher, Renee; m. Nancy Jo Larsen, June 5, 1997. BA, Madison Bus. Coll., Wis., 1962. Underwriter Gen. Casualty Cos., Madison, 1962-66, mktg. rep., 1966-73, sales mgr. Ill. Freeport, 1973-75, br. mgr. Springfield, Ill., 1975-79, asst. mktg. mgr. Madison, 1979-81, br. mgr., resident sr. v.p. Sun Prairie, Wis., 1981—. Bd. dirs. Sun Prairie Indsl. Devel. Corp., 1989—. Mem. Sun Prairie C. of C. (bd. dirs. 1984-86), Leions. Republican. Lutheran. Avocations: woodworking, golf, hunting, fishing. Office: Gen Casualty Cos One General Dr Sun Prairie WI 53596

ROLLICK, MARY BETH, mathematician, educator; d. Paul and RoseMary Breindel; m. Kevin L. Rollick, June 12, 1976; children: Kathleen, Anne. BS, Ind. U. of Pa., 1975; MS, Kent State U., Ohio, 2001. Math. tchr. Holy Family Sch., Stow, Ohio, 1996—97; adj. prof. math. Kent State U., Kent, Ohio, 1997—. Math. acad. trainer Ohio Dept. Edn., Canton, 2002—. Mem.: Nat. Coun. of Tchrs. of Math., Math. Assn. Am. Office: Kent State Univ Mathematics Dept Kent OH 44242

ROLLIN, BERNARD ELLIOT, philosophy educator, consultant; b. NYC, Feb. 18, 1943; s. Phillip and Yetta Ethel (Bookchin) R.; m. Linda Mae Schieber, Aug. 30, 1964; 1 child, Michael David Hume. BA, CCNY, 1964; PhD, Columbia U., 1972. Preceptor Columbia U., NYC, 1968-69; asst. prof. philosophy Colo. State U., Ft. Collins, 1969-73, assoc. prof., 1973-78, prof., 1978—, prof. physiology and biophysics, 1980—, dir. bioethical planning, 1981—, prof. animal sci., Univ. disting. prof., 2000—. Cons. Can., Australian, South African, The Netherlands, and US govt., various univs. and agy. including U. Calif., Berkeley, Wash. State U., U. Fla., USDA, NIH, 1980—, United Airlines, Denver, 1985—, Nat. Livestock Ethics Coun., 1997—, Pfizer, 1998, McDonalds, 1998; lectr. on animal ethics, 1978—. Author: Natural and Conventional Meaning, 1976, Animal Rights and Human Morality, 1981, 2d edit., 1992 (Outstanding Acad. Book award Choice Mag. Am. Assn. U. Libr., 1982, Gustavus Meyers Ctr. award for study of human rights 1993), The Unheeded Cry, 1989, 2nd edit., 1998, The Experimental Animal in Biomedical Research, 1990, vol. 2, 1995, The Frankenstein Syndrome: Ethical and Social Issues in the Genetic Engineering of Animals, 1995, Farm Animal Welfare, 1995, Veterinary Ethics, 1998, Complementary and Alternative Veterinary Medicine Considered, 2003, The Well-Being of Farm Animals: Challenges and Solutions, 2004; mem. editl. bd. Jour. AVMA, Between the Species, Agrl. Ethics, Acta Semiotica et Linguistica, Studies in Animal Welfare Sci., Vet. Forum, numerous others; series editor: Issues in Animal Bioethics; contbr. articles to profl. jour. Recipient Harris T. Guard award Colo. State U., 1981, honors prof., 1983; Waco F. Childers award Am. Humane Assn., 1982, svc. award Colo. Vet. Med. Assn., 1983, Disting. Faculty award Colo. State U. Coll. Vet. Med., 1993, Gustavus Myers Human Rights award 1994, Brownlee award Animal Welfare Found. Can., 1994; named Eddy prof., 2001. Jewish. Avocations: weightlifting, horseback riding, motorcycles. Office: Colo State U Dept Philosophy Fort Collins CO 80523-0001 Office Phone: 970-491-6315. E-mail: bernard.rollin@colostate.edu.

ROLLIN, BETTY, writer, television journalist, lecturer; b. N.Y.C., Jan. 3, 1936; d. Leon and Ida R.; m. Harold M. Edwards, Jan. 21, 1979. BA, Sarah Lawrence Coll., 1957. Assoc. features editor Vogue mag., 1964; sr. editor Look mag., 1965-71; network corr. NBC News, N.Y.C., 1971-80, contbg. corr., 1985—2003; network corr. ABC News Nightline, 1982-84. Contbr. corr. Religion and Ethics Newsweekly PBS; lectr. in field. Profl. actress: on stage and TV, 1958—64; author: I Thee Wed, 1962, Mothers Are Funnier Than Children, 1964, The Non-Drinkers' Drink Book, 1966, First, You Cry, 1976, reissue, 2000, Am I Getting Paid for This?, 1982, Last Wish, 1985, reissue, 1998; columnist: Hers, N.Y. Times; contbr. articles to popular mags. Bd. mem. Death With Dignity Nat. Ctr., 1997—. Office: Care NS Bienstock Inc 1740 Broadway New York NY 10019-4315

ROLLINO, JOHN, academic administrator, writer, physicist, educator; b. N.Y.C., Oct. 11, 1944; s. John Anthony and Edith Ann (Patti) Rollino; m. Florence Alice Fink, Jan. 10, 1970; children: John, Daniel. BS, St. Francis Coll., N.Y.C., 1962—66; PhD, MIT, Cambridge, Mass., 1966—69. Prof., chemistry and physics St. Francis Coll., N.Y.C., 1969—83; computer specialist Walden Sch., N.Y.C., 1983—84; prof., chemistry and physics Upsala Coll., East Orange, NJ, 1984—95; dir., undergrad. physics Rutgers U., Newark, 1995—. Author: (lab manual) Notes for Physics Lab, 1997. Coach Little League, Glendale, NY, 1972—84; crew Clearwater, Poughkeepsie, NY, 1989—. Mem.: Am. Assn. Physics Tchrs., Am. Chem. Soc., Am. Phys. Soc. Avocations: sailing, reading, carpentry, chess, cooking. Home: 45 Wells Ct Bloomfield NJ 07003 Office: Rutgers Univ Physics-Smithhau Newark NJ 07102 Office Phone: 973-353-1573. Business E-Mail: jrollino@andromeda.rutgers.edu.

ROLLINS, ALBERT WILLIAMSON, civil engineer, consultant; b. Dallas, July 31, 1930; s. Andrew Peach and Mary (Williamson) R.; m. Martha Ann James, Dec. 28, 1954; children: Elizabeth Ann, Mark Martin. BS in Civil Engring., Tex. A&M U., 1951, MS in Civil Engring., 1956. Registered profl. engr., Tex., La., Okla. Engring. asst. Tex. Hwy. Dept., Dallas, 1953-55; dir. pub. works City of Arlington, Tex., 1956-63, city mgr., 1963-67; ptnr. Schrickel, Rollins & Assocs., Land Planners-Engrs., Arlington, 1967—. Contbr. articles to profl. jours. Mem. Gov.'s Energy Adv. Coun.; chmn. Tex. Mass Transp. Commn.; bd. dirs. Tex. Turnpike Authority. Served as 1st lt. AUS, 1951-53. Mem. ASCE (Award of Honor Tex. sect. 2002), NSPE, Internat. City Mgmt. Assn., Am. Water Works Assn., Water Pollution Control Fedn., Sigma Xi, Phi Eta Sigma, Tau Beta Pi, Phi Kappa Phi, Chi Epsilon. Home: 3004 Yellowstone Dr Arlington TX 76013-1166 Office: Suite 200 1161 Corporate Dr W Ste 200 Arlington TX 76006-6819

ROLLINS, ALDEN MILTON, documents librarian; b. Billerica, Mass., July 31, 1946; s. Alden Milton and Agnes Morgan (Simpson) R. BA, Am. U., 1968; MLS, U. R.I., 1973. Cert. geneal. record specialist, Bd. for Certification of Genealogists., Vt., N.H. Documents libr. U. Alaska Libr., Anchorage, 1973—. Author: The Fall of Rome: A Reference Guide, 1983, Rome in the Fourth Century A.D., 1991, Vermont Warnings Out, 1995, Vermont Religious Certificates, 2003. With U.S. Army, 1969-71. Mem. Nat. Geneal. Soc., Geneal. Soc. Vt., N.H. Geneal. Soc., New Eng. Hist. Geneal. Soc., N.H. Hist. Soc., Vt. Hist. Soc. (life), Piscataqua Pioneers (life), Am. Congl. Assn. (life). Avocation: genealogy. Home: 221 E 7th Ave Apt 114 Anchorage AK 99501-3639 Office: U Alaska Libr Govt Documents 3211 Providence Dr Anchorage AK 99508-4614

ROLLINS, ALFRED BROOKS, JR., historian, educator; b. Presque Isle, Maine, May 28, 1921; s. Alfred Brooks and Clarissa (Jack) R.; m. Ernestine Emma McMullin, Nov. 6, 1942 (dec. Aug. 28, 1972); children: John Douglas, Nancy Jane, James Scott; m. Faith Kenyon, June 16, 1973 (dec. Mar. 8, 1979); m. Helen Anrod Jones, Feb. 28, 1981. BA, Wesleyan U., Middletown, Conn., 1942, MA, 1946; PhD, Harvard U., 1953. From instr. to prof. history State U. N.Y. at New Paltz, 1948-63; prof., chmn. dept. history State U. N.Y. at Binghamton, 1964-67; dean U. Vt., Burlington, 1967-70, v.p. acad. affairs, 1970-76; pres. Old Dominion U., Norfolk, Va., 1976-85, prof. history, 1976-91, pres. emeritus, prof. emeritus, 1991—. Cons. oral history project John F. Kennedy Library, 1965 Author: Roosevelt and Howe, 1962; Editor narrative: Franklin D. Roosevelt and the Age of Action, 1960, Woodrow Wilson and the New America, 1965; Contbr. articles to profl. jours. Served to 1st lt. USAAF, 1943-46. Decorated D.F.C., Air medal with four clusters. Mem. Am. Hist. Assn., Orgn. Am. Historians, Phi Beta Kappa, Chi Psi.

ROLLINS, ANDREW MARTIN, biomedical engineer, educator; s. Orson Boyd and Barbara Nuttall Rollins; m. Lynn Marie Ameen, Aug. 30, 1996; children: Dominica Ameen, Alexander Ameen, Maxwell Ameen. PhD, Case Western Res. U., 2000. Asst. prof. medicine Case Western Res. U., Cleve., 2000—02, asst. prof. biomedical engring., 2000—.

ROLLINS, ARLEN JEFFERY, osteopathic physician; b. Cleve., June 30, 1946; s. Lee Roy and Celia (Madorsky) R.; m. Deborah Joyce Gross, Dec. 18, 1971 (div.); children: Aaron Jason, Howard Philip, Lee Craig; m. Miriam Rollins, Dec. 29, 2003. AB, Miami (Ohio) U., 1968; DO, Chgo. Coll. Osteo. Medicine, 1973; MS in Occupl. Medicine Environ. Health, U. Cin., 1984. Diplomate Am. Bd. Preventive Medicine. Intern Phoenix Gen. Hosp., 1973-74; resident in environ. health/occupl. medicine Cin. Gen. Hosp.-U. Cin., 1977-77; plant physician Ford Motor Co., Cin., 1974-77, Walton Hills, Stamping Plant Divsn., Cleve., 1987—. Assoc. med. dir. East Side Occupl. Health Ctr., Cleve., 1977-79; med. dir. Ferro Corp., Cleve., 1979—, S.K. Wellman Corp., Cleve., 1979-87, Morgan Matroc, 1979—; pres. Occupl. Health Mgmt. Cons.; cons. occupl. health Ohio Bell Tel. Co., Cleve., 1981-87; cons. Occupl. Health Ctr., Univ. Hosps. of Cleve.; dir. occupl. health program Bedford Med. Ctr. Univ. Hosps. Cleve., 1990-99; corp. med. cons. Cleve.-Cliffs Inc., 1998—. Fellow Am. Acad. Occupl. Medicine, Am. Occupl. Med. Assn., Am. Coll. Preventive Medicine; mem. Ohio State Med. Assn., Cleve. Acad. Medicine (pub. health and immunization com., med.-legal com.), Western Res. Med. Dirs. Assn., Am. Osteo. Assn., Am. Osteo. Acad. Pub. Health and Preventive Medicine (past bd. dirs.). Office Phone: 216-292-6263. Personal E-mail: arlenrollins@att.net.

ROLLINS, DIANN E. nurse, occupational health nurse; b. Newark, Dec. 13, 1943; d. Lewis Paul and Letitia Lavinia Rollins. RN, Meth. Hosp. Sch. Nursing, Phila., 1964; postgrad., Howard U., 1966, Milton Coll., 1969—72, West Chester State Coll., 1972—79; cert. bldg. maintenance, John F. Kennedy Vocat. Tech., 1992; BSN, Thomas Jefferson U., 2000. RN, Pa., N.J. Nurse Meth. Hosp., Phila., 1964—66, 1967—69, Mercy Hosp., Janesville, Wis., 1969—72, Chester County Hosp., West Chester, Pa., 1972—74, Cheyney U., Pa., 1974—75, Embreeulle State Hosp., coatesville, 1976—78; agy. nurse Norristown, Phila., 1978—86, Medox, Olsten, Kimberly, Phila., 1985-86; RN supr. New Ralston House, Phila., 1986-87, 88-89; agy. nurse Kimberly, Quality Care, Olsten, Medox, others, Phila., 1987-89; info. and referral specialist Nat. Mental Health Consumer Self Help Clearing House, Phila., 1992-93; intern ACT NOW Southeastern Mental Health Program, Phila., 1993-94; nursery sch. tchr. Bambino Gesu Child Devel. Ctr., Phila., 1994-99; primary instr. nursing assts. ARC, 2000—01, Clin. Pathways Educators Ins., 2001—02; supplemental staff nurse Breslin Learning Ctr., 2002—, LPN instr., 2003—; staff nurse Bayada Nurses, 2002—; postal nurse (occupl. health nurse) U.S. Post Office, 2003—. Vol. instr. program Franklin Inst., Phila., 1973-74; vol. multimedia first aide instr. ARC, Wilmington, Del., 1975-83; vol. plan II nurse blood mobiles ARC, S.E. Pa., 1982-85. Mem. Alumnae Meth. Hosp. Sch. Nursing, Four Chaplains Legion of Honor. Avocations: reading, writing, walking.

ROLLINS, EDWARD TYLER, JR., newspaper executive; b. Durham, N.C., May 23, 1922; s. Edward Tyler and Bessie (Steed) R.; m. Frances Louise Page, Oct. 5, 1963; children: Edward Tyler III, William Lawson. AB, U. N.C., 1947. V.p., asst. sec. Durham (N.C.) Herald Co., 1949-69, v.p., sec.-treas., 1969-81, pres., pub., 1982-88, chmn., bd. dirs., 1985—. Pres. Durham Radio Corp. Stas. WDNC-AM, WDCG-FM, 1982-88. Bd. dirs. Chowan Coll. Graphic Arts Found., 1986-95; bd. dirs. Sch. of Journalism Found. of N.C., 1982-88; mem. Friends of Duke Art Mus., mem. adv. bd. N.C. Nat. Bank, 1979-89; mem. Gov.'s Bus. Coun. on Arts and Humanities, 1989-90; mem. Duke Pres.'s Art Mus. com., 1994-2001; trustee Meredith Coll., Raleigh, N.C., 1966-69, Durham Pub. Libr., 1961-81; former bd. dirs. Durham Salvation Army; pres. Durham YMCA, 1952; former bd. dirs. Family Svc. Assn.; supporter N.C. Symphony. With U.S. Army, 1943-46. Mem. Newspaper Assn. Am., N.C. Press Assn., So. Newspaper Publs. Assn., The English Speaking Union, Durham C. of C. (bd. dirs. 1969), Kiwanis, Hope Valley Country Club, Univ. Club, Carolina Club. Presbyterian. Office: Durham Herald Co Inc 2828 Pickett Rd Durham NC 27705-5613

ROLLINS, JAMES CALVIN, professional baseball player; b. Oakland, Calif., Nov. 27, 1978; Grad., Encinal HS, 1996. Profl. baseball player Phila. Phillies, 2000—. Co-recipient NL Cool Papa Bell award, Negro League Hall of Fame; named 5th Best Rookie in Major Leagues, Baseball Am., 3d Best in Nat. League; named to Topps Major League Rookie All-Star team, MLB mgrs. . Avocation: recreational activities. Office: Philadelphia Phillies Veterans Stadium 3501 South Broad Street Philadelphia PA 19148

ROLLINS, KEVIN B. computer company executive; m. Debra Rollins; children: Marisa, Stephanie, Lauren, Alex. BS, Brigham Young U., MBA, 1984. Ptnr. Bain & Co., 1984—96; cons. Dell Computer Corp., 1993—96, sr. v.p., corp. strategy, 1996—97, pres. Dell Americas, 1997—2001, vice-chmn., 1997—2001, pres., COO, 2001—04, pres., CEO, 2004—. Mem. Am. Enterprise Inst.; pres. leadership council Brigham Young U., Marriot Sch. Nat. Advisory Council, founder, Rollins Ctr. E-commerce. High tech chmn. Juvenile Diabetes Rsch. Found.; trustee Arts Center Stage; bd. dir. Austin Symphony, KLRU. Office: Dell Computer Corp Hdqs One Dell Way Round Rock TX 78682*

ROLLINS, SONNY (THEODORE ROLLINS), composer, musician; b. N.Y.C., Sept. 7, 1930; s. Walter and Valborg (Solomon) R.; m. Dawn Finney, 1956 (div.); m. Lucille Pearson, Sept. 7, 1959. Ed. high sch., N.Y.C.; ArtsD, Bard Coll., 1992, Long Island U., 1998, Wesleyan U., 1998, Duke U., 1999; D of Music, New Eng. Conservatory of Music, 2002; MusD (hon.), Berklee Coll. Music, 2003. Ann.concert tours in Europe and Asia; more than 100 original compositions recorded including Freedom Suite, Oleo, Airegin, Sonnymoon for Two, Way Out West; composer, musician: (film) Alfie, 1966 (Grammy nomination 1966), (album) This is What I Do, 2001 (Grammy award 2001). Recipient Lifetime Achievement award, Nat. Acad. Recording Arts and Scis., 2004, numerous others; Guggenheim fellow, 1972. Home: RR 9 # G Germantown NY 12526

ROLLINS, TIMOTHY CHRISTOPHER, editor, policy analyst; b. San Diego, May 15, 1959; s. Dean Trueman Rollins and Edith Joan Lampton; m. Gaylene Terry, Aug. 15, 1980 (div. Aug. 6, 1984); m. Helen Elizabeth Cameron, May 8, 1993 (div. Jan. 24, 2003); m. Elyn Marie Jankowski, June 19, 2004; children: Michael Terry, Timothy James, Stephanie Marie. Student, Utah State U., 1979—81, U. Utah, 1982—84. Sr. assoc. editor USA Jour., Jefferson City, Mo., 1998—99; editor and pub. The Am. Partisan, Milw., 1998—; policy analyst Ctr. for the Nat. Security Interest, Arlington, Va., 2001—. Polit. campaigning Com. to Reelect the Pres., Salt Lake City, 1972; vol. Mem. LDS Ch., Milw., 1971—. LCpl. USMC, 1976—79, specialist Army Nat. Guard, 1987—91. Mem.: LDS Ch., Marine Corps. Assn. (assoc.), Assn. of the U.S. Army (assoc.). Republican. Mem. Lds Ch. Avocations: ballroom dancing, baseball, computers, web sites. Office: The American Partisan PO Box 370451 Milwaukee WI 53237-1551 E-mail: rollins@american-partisan.com.

ROLLINSON, FREDERICK (RICK), III, manufacturing executive; BA in Bus. Mgmt., N.C. State U.; MBA, Campbell U. Various positions Nortel Networks, 1984—2001; sr. v.p. Solectron Corp., Milpitas, Calif., 2001—, pres. Ams. Region, 2001—. Mem. adv. coun. Vance Granville C. C.; mem. coun. N.C. Citizens for Bus. and Industry; bd. dirs. Granville County United Way. Office: Solectron Corp 777 Gibraltar Dr Milpitas CA 95035

ROLLMAN, STEVEN ALLAN, communications educator; b. NYC, Aug. 3, 1947; s. Leo and Margot (Seelenberger) R.; m. Nancy Sue Toberen, June 15, 1973; 1 child, Benjamin Allan. BA, C.W. Post Coll., 1970; MA, Ohio U., 1972; PhD, Pa. State U., 1977. Instr. Pa. State U., University Park, 1976; asst. prof. James Madison U., Harrisonburg, Va., 1977-83, assoc. prof., 1983-95, coord. interpersonal communication, 1986-90, prof., 1995—. Cons. various sch. dists., Va., 1978—, Swissair, Zurich, 1971-72; book reviewer Choice, 1982—. Contbr. articles to profl. jours.; founding editor Va. Jour. Comm., 1980-81. Mem. Nat. Comm. Assn., So. States Comm. Assn., Va. Speech Comm. Assn., Internat. Listening Assn. Avocations: computers, music, film, automobiles, tennis. Home: 608 Wyndham Woods Cir Harrisonburg VA 22801-1668 Office: James Madison U Sch Speech Cmn Harrisonburg VA 22807-2106 Office Phone: 540-568-6455. Business E-Mail: rollmasa@jmu.edu.

ROLLS, STEVEN GEORGE, communications executive; Joined BF Goodrich Co., Richfield, Ohio, 1981; asst. treas.; CFO Canadian and aerospace bus.; v.p., controller; exec. v.p. global customer mgmt. and employee care Convergys Corp. (subs. Cin. Bell Inc.), 1998—. Office: Convergys Corp PO Box 1638 Cincinnati OH 45201-1638

ROLOFF, MARVIN L. publishing executive; m. Shirley Sekas, June 27, 1959; children: Reed, Ross, Robyn. BA, Wartburg Coll., 1955; postgrad., U. Iowa, 1956; BD, Wartburg Theol. Sem., 1960, DD (hon.), 1997; ThM, Princeton Theol. Sem., 1961. Ordained to ministry Luth. Ch., 1961. Pastor youth and edn. Grace Luth. Ch., Green Bay, Wis., 1961-65; editor Augsburg Pub. Ho., Mpls., 1965-70, sr. editor children's curriculum divsn. parish edn., 1970-71, curriculum editl. dir. divsn. parish edn., 1971-74, dir. media resources divsn. life and mission in congregation, 1974-76, dir. edn. resources bd. of publ., 1976-87; dir. ednl. resources pub. Pub. Ho. of Evangelical Luth. Ch. Am., 1988-91; v.p. mktg. Augsburg Fortress, Pubs., 1991-93, v.p. customer resources and relationships, 1993-95, acting pres., CEO, 1995-96, pres., CEO, 1996—. Vis. prof. Christian edn. Luther Northwestern Theol. Sem., 1981, 83, 89, instr. Christian Edn. Inst., summers 1976-90; cons., chairperson youth/adult and children's coms. Curriculum Selection Conf. of Armed Forces, 1971-91; mem. resource planning groups Evangelical Luth. Ch. Am.; mem. publ. com. Augsburg Fortress, Pubs. Mem. Assn. Profs. and Rschrs. in Religious Edn., Protestant Ch.-Owned Pubs. Assn. (mem. edn. com., chair armed forces com. 1993—, mem. exec. com., bd. dirs. 1993—), Nat. Coun. Chs. (Augsburg Fortress, Pubs. rep. to ministries in Christian edn. com., mem. unit com. 1988—, mem. budget and fin. com. 1992—, mem. Bible translation and utilization com. 1994—). Protestant Ch.-Owned Pubs. Assn. (pres. 1998—). Office: Augsburg Fortress Pubs 100 S 5th St Ste 700 Minneapolis MN 55402-1219 Fax: 612-330-3583.

ROLPH, MATTHEW G. J. literature and language professor, consultant; s. Gary and Jean Rolph; m. Marlene Lalonde, Apr. 11, 1999. BA in English Lit., Plymouth State Coll., 2000; MEd. in English Edn., Plymouth State U., 2003. Lectr. English Plymouth State U., NH, 2001—. Tech. liaison Plymouth Writing Project (N.H. chpt. Nat. Writing Project), 2002—; asst. dir. Plymouth State Ann. Medieval Forum, NH, 2003—. Mem. editl. bd., mng. editor: anthology High School Voices: NH Student Writing. Mem.: Soc. for Tech. Comm., MLA, Internat. Soc. for Tech. in EDn., Nat. Coun. Tchrs. of English, The Smithsonian Instn., Acad. of Am. Poets, Phi Delta Kappa. Independent. Avocations: civics, creative writing, design and illustration, travel/teaching abroad, educational technology research. Home: 12 Lookout Rd Warren NH 03279 Office: Plymouth State Univ 17 High St Plymouth NH 03264 Business E-Mail: m_rolph@mail.plymouth.edu.

ROLSTON, HOLMES, III, theologian, educator, philosopher; b. Staunton, Va., Nov. 19, 1932; s. Holmes and Mary Winifred (Long) R.; m. Jane Irving Wilson, June 1, 1956; children: Shonny Hunter, Giles Campbell. BS, Davidson Coll., 1953; BD, Union Theol. Sem., Richmond, Va., 1956; MA in Philosophy of Sci., U. Pitts., 1968; PhD in Theology, U. Edinburgh, Scotland, 1958. Ordained ministry Presbyn. Ch. (USA), 1956. Asst. prof. philosophy Colo. State U., Ft. Collins, 1968-71, assoc. prof., 1971-76, prof., 1976—. Vis. scholar Ctr. Study World Religions, Harvard U., 1974-75; official observer UNCED, Rio de Janiero, 1992. Author: Religious Inquiry: Participation and Detachment, 1985, Philosophy Gone Wild, 1986, Science and Religion: A Critical Survey, 1987, Environmental Ethics, 1988, Conserving Natural Value, 1994, Genes, Genesis and God, 1999; assoc. editor Environ. Ethics, 1979—; mem. editorial bd. Oxford Series in Environ. Philosophy and Pub. Policy, Zygon: Jour. of Religion and Sci.; contbr. chpts. to books, articles to profl. jours. Recipient Oliver P. Penock Disting. Svc. award Colo. State U., 1983, Coll. award Excellence, 1991, Univ. Disting. Prof., 1992; Disting. Russell fellow Grad. Theol. Union, 1991, Disting. Lectr., Chinese Acad. of Social Scis., 1991, Disting. Lectr., Nobel Conf. XXVII, Gifford Lectr., U. Edinburgh, 1997; featured in Fifty Key Thinkers on the Environment, 2001, Templeton Prize in Religion, 2003. Mem. AAAS, Am. Acad. Religion, Soc. Bibl. Lit. (pres. Rocky Mountain-Gt. Plains region), Am. Philos. Assn., Internat. Soc. Environ. Ethics (pres. 1989-94), Phi Beta Kappa. Avocation: bryology. Home: 1712 Concord Dr Fort Collins CO 80526-1602 Office: Colo State U Dept Philosophy Fort Collins CO 80523-0001 Office Phone: 970-491-6315. Business E-Mail: rolston@lamar.colostate.edu.

ROM, MARTIN (MELVYN ROM), investor; b. Detroit, Mar. 2, 1946; s. Jack and Thelma (Meyer) R.; m. Barbara Miller, July 12, 1970. BA magna cum laude, U. Mich., 1967. Founder MultiVest, Inc., Southfield, Mich., 1969, pres., 1969-73, chmn. bd., chief exec. officer, 1973-75; pres. Real Estate Securities and Syndication Inst., Nat. Assn. Realtors, Washington, 1975-76, dir., bd. govs., 1972-77; pres. Martin Rom Co., Inc., 1976—. Vice chmn. Sports Illus. Ct. Clubs, Inc., 1977-79; bd. dirs. Mocatta Corp., 1979-80; founder, dir. Real Age, Inc., 1994—; mem. joint com. Nat. Assn. Securities Dealers-Nat. Assn. Realtors, 1975-76; mem. adv. com. on market instruments Commodity Futures Trading Commn., 1975-76; mem. N.A.S.D., Com. on Gold Regulations, 1974-75. Author: Nothing Can Replace the U.S. Dollar . . . and It Almost Has, 1975; Adv. bd.: Housing and Devel. Reporter, Washington. Trustee U. Chgo. Found. Mem. Phi Beta Kappa. Home and Office: 60 Quarton Ln Bloomfield Hills MI 48304-3456 Office Phone: 248-258-0388.

ROMA, AIDA CLARA, artist; b. Phila., July 17, 1924; d. Carlo and Giustina S. R.; widowed; 7 children. Student, Camden County Coll., 1990-99. Dental Dr. Martin Apother, Runnemede, N.J., 1956-66; owner Rogers Auto Sales, Runnemede, N.J., 1966-90; tchr. St. Joseph's Sch., Camden, N.J., 1955-56. Author of poems, Jealousy, 1999, My 2 Best Friends, 2001, "Pal" My Pal, 2004. Art tutor, Haddenfield, N.J.; v.p. Girl Scouts Am., Runnemede, 1964; sec. Boy Scouts Am., 1960; mem. St. Teresa's Choir, 1993—. Atlantic City Choirs. Recipient Internat. Poet award, Artistic Artistry award, England, 2004. Mem. Sons of Italy. Republican. Achievements include invention of Rack on the Back auto addition. Avocation: singing. Home: PO Box 2076 Laurel Springs NJ 08021

ROMAINE, HENRY SIMMONS, investment consultant; b. N.Y.C., May 30, 1933; s. Theodore Cole and Cornelia (Simmons) R.; m. Susan Donaldson; children: Henry, Hilary, Kathryn. BA, Harvard U., 1954. Asst. security analyst Mutual Life Ins. Co., N.Y.C., 1958-60, investment analyst, 1960-61, investment specialist, 1961-64, asst. dir. investments, 1964, dir. investments, 1964-66, asst. v.p. for securities investment, 1966-68, 2d v.p. for securities investment, 1969-71, v.p. for securities investment, 1971-72, sr. v.p., 1972-78, sr. v.p., chief investment officer, 1976-78, exec. v.p., 1978-81, pres., 1981-86; vice chmn., chief investment officer Am. Gen. Corp., Houston, 1986-93. Dir. MONY Life Ins. Co. of Can.; chmn. bd. MONY Real Estate Investors, 1978-86; mem. adv. bd. Chem. Bank, 1974-93. Served with USN, 1954-57. Mem.: Harvard Club. Home: 7 Conquest Ave Sullivans Island SC 29482-9779

ROMAN, ANDREW MICHAEL, lawyer, educator; b. Pitts., Aug. 19, 1951; s. James Andrew and Lois Roman; m. Heather Lynne Harms; children: Rebecca Lynne, Carolyn Elizabeth. BA, Bucknell U., 1973; JD, Duquesne U., 1976. Bar: Pa. 1976. Law clk. U.S. Dist. Ct. (we. dist.) Pa., Pitts., 1976-77; assoc. Eckert Seamans Cherin & Mellott, Pitts., 1977-84, ptnr., 1985-91; dir. Cohen & Grigsby, P.C., Pitts., 1991—, v.p. tech., 1998—2003, exec. v.p., 2003—. Adj. prof. law Duquesne U. Sch. Law, Pitts., 1993—; arbitrator Fed. Ct. Arbitration Panel, Pitts., 1991—; faculty mem. seminar on bad faith litig. in Pa. Nat. Bus. Inst., 1995, 99, 2000-03. Editor-in-chief Duquesne Law Rev., 1976, A New Look at the Broad Form Nuclear Exclusion, Risk Management, 1995. Bd. dirs. Codes Rev. Bd., Mt. Lebanon, Pa., 1991-2003, The Extended Court House, Inc., 1997—; mem. vestry St. Paul's Episcopal Ch., Mt. Lebanon, 1995-98. Recipient Am. Jurisprudence awards Lawyers Coop. Pub. Co., 1974; T. Robert Brennan scholar Duquesne U. Sch. Law, 1974, Duquesne U. Sch. Law scholar, 1975. Mem. ABA, Am. Arbitration Assn. (mem. panel 1991—), Pa. Bar Assn., Allegheny County Bar Assn., Duquesne U. Law Alumni Assn. (treas. 1985-86, bd. dirs. 1988-90, pres. 1992-93). Office: Cohen & Grigsby PC 11 Stanwix St Ste 15 Pittsburgh PA 15222-1312

ROMAN, NANCY GRACE, astronomer, consultant; b. Nashville, May 16, 1925; d. Irwin and Georgia Frances (Smith) R. BA (Joshua Lippincott Meml. fellow), Swarthmore Coll., 1946; PhD, U. Chgo., 1949; D.Sc., Russell Sage Coll., 1966, Hood Coll., 1969, Bates Coll., 1971, Swarthmore Coll., 1976. Asst. Sproul Obs., Swarthmore Coll., 1943-46; asst. Yerkes Obs., U. Chgo., at Williams Bay, Wis., 1946-48, research asso., 1949-52, instr. stellar astronomy, 1952-55, asst. prof., 1955; research asso. Warner and Swasey Obs., Case Inst. Tech., Cleve., summer 1949; physicist radio astronomy br. U.S. Naval Research Lab., Washington, 1955-56, astronomer, head microwave spectroscopy sect., 1956-58, astronomer cons., 1958-59; head observational astronomy program Office Space Flight Devel., NASA, Washington, 1959-60, chief astronomy and solar physics, geophysics and astronomy programs, 1960-64, chief astronomy and relativity programs, 1964-79, program scientist for space telescope, 1979-80; astronomy cons., 1980-89; prin. scientist Astronomical Data Ctr. (NASA), 1981—. With McDonnell Douglas Space Systems, 1988-94. Contbr. articles to sci. periodicals. Trustee Russell Sage Coll., 1973-78; bd. mgrs. Swarthmore Coll., 1979-83. Recipient Fed. Woman's award, 1962; citation for pub. service Colo. Woman's Coll., 1966; 90th Anniversary award Women's Ednl. and Indsl. Union, 1967; NASA Exceptional Sci. Achievement award, 1969; NASA Outstanding Leadership medal, 1978 Fellow AAAS, Am. Astronautical Soc. (William Randolf Lovelace II award 1980); mem. AAUW, Am. Astron. Soc., Internat. Astron. Union (editor symposia 1956-58), Astron. Soc. Pacific. Acheivements include rsch. on stellar clusters, high velocity stars, radio astronomy; 1st noted correlation of metallic lines in stars with their space velocity; asteroid named Roman, 1989. *This guiding principle sounds old fashioned but I have found it useful: "Forget that you are a woman but never forget that you are a lady".*

ROMAN, STANFORD AUGUSTUS, JR., medical educator, dean; b. N.Y.C. s. Stanford Augustas and Ivy L. (White) D.; m. Norma Dabney Roman; children: Mawiyah Lythcott, Jane E. Roman-Brown. AB, Dartmouth Coll., 1964, MA (hon.), 1992; MD, Columbia U., 1968; MPH, U. Mich., 1975. Diplomate Nat. Bd. of Med. Examiners. Intern Columbia U.-Harlem Hosp. Ctr., N.Y.C., 1966—69, resident in medicine, 1969—71, chief resident in medicine, 1971—73; 1972assoc. dir. ambulatory care Columbia U. Harlem Hosp., 1972—73; instr. medicine Columbia U., N.Y.C., 1972—73; asst. physician Presbyn. Hosp., 1972—73; clin. dir. Healthco, Inc., Soul City, NC, 1973—74; dir. ambulatory care, asst. prof. medicine/sociomed. scis. Boston City Hosp., Boston, 1974—78; asst. prof. medicine U. N.C., Chapel Hill, 1973—74; asst. dean Boston U. Sch. Medicine, 1974—78; med. dir. D.C. Gen. Hosp., Washington, 1978—81; from assoc. dean acad. affairs to dep. dean Dartmouth Med. Sch., Hanover, NH, 1981—87, assoc. prof., 1981—87, dep. dean, 1986—87; dean, v.p., prof. medicine Morehouse Sch. Med., Atlanta, 1987—89; sr. v.p., med. and profl. affairs Health and Hosps. Corp., N.Y.C., 1989—90; dean med. sch., prof. cmty. health and social medicine Sophie Davis Sch. Biomed. Edn., 1990—; interim pres. CCNY, 1999—2001. Dir. Boston Comprehensive Sickle Cell Ctr., 1975—78; bd. dirs. Winifred Masterson Burke Rehab. Hosp., White Plains, NY, 1993—94; mem. Dartmouth Hitchcock Med. Ctr. Bd. of Medicine, NY, 1993—2002; mem. bd. trustees Dartmouth Coll., Hanover, NH, 1992—2002. Contbr. to book chpts. and profl. jours. and editls. Fellow N.Y. Acad. Medicine; mem. AMA, APHA, Nat. Med. Assn., N.Y. State Coun. Grad. Med. Edn., N.Y. State Dept. Edn. Bd. Medicine. Democrat. Episcopalian. Avocations: photography, travel, music.

ROMAN, TWYLA I. state legislator; m. John Roman; children: Lisa, Sheryl. Student, U. Akron, 1977-78. Trustee Springfield Twp., 1981-94; mem. Ohio State Ho. Reps., Columbus, 1994—. Mem. Summit County Emergency Mgmt. Planning and Exec. Commn. Mem. MADD, S.E. Bd. of Trade, Ohio Twp. Assn., Summit County Twp. Assn., Brimfield Meml. House Assn.

ROMANCE, MARY C. library director; b. Rabat, Morocco, June 20, 1957; d. Francis Joseph and Ann (Pickert) Romance. BA in Orgnl. Comms. and Mgmt., U. Mich., Ann Arbor, 1979; MLS, Rutgers U., New Brunswick, N.J., 1992. Libr. coord. Bernardsville (N.J.) Pub. Libr., 1991-93; libr. dir. Rockaway

(N.J.) Borough Pub. Libr., 1993-94, Lincoln Park (N.J.) Pub. Libr., 1994-97, Roxbury Twp. Pub. Libr., Succasunna, N.J., 1997—. Mem. planning coun. M.A.I.N. Inc. Mem. Roxbury Area C. of C. (bd. dirs., v.p. 2004), Roxbury Area C. of C. (bd. dirs.). Office: Roxbury Public Library 103 Main St Succasunna NJ 07876-1417

ROMANI, JOHN HENRY, health administration educator; b. Milan, Mar. 6, 1925; s. Henry Arthur and Hazel (Pettengill) R.; m. Barbara A. Anderson; children: David John, Paul Nichols, Theresa A. Anderson. BA, MA, U. N.H., 1949; PhD, U. Mich., 1955. Instr. U. N.H., 1950-51; instr. U. Mich., Ann Arbor, 1954-55, assoc. prof., asst. to assoc. dean Sch. Pub. Health, 1961-69, assoc. v.p., 1971-75, chmn. health planning and adminstrn., 1975-80, prof., 1971-93, prof. emeritus pub. health adminstrn., 1993—, adj. prof. program on the environment, 2004—; interim chair Pub. Health Policy and Adminstrn., 1991-92. Asst. prof. We. Mich. U., 1956-57; assoc. dir. Cleve. Met. Svcs. Commn., 1957-59; assoc. prof. U. Pitts., 1959-61; vice chancellor, prof. U. Wis.-Milw., 1969-71; rsch. fellow Brookings Instn., 1955-56; mem. task force Nat. Commn. on Orgn. Cmty. Health Svcs., 1963-66; dir. staff Sec.'s Com. on Orgn. Health Activities, HEW, 1965-66; dir. Govtl. Affairs Inst., 1969-75, chmn., 1970-72; trustee Pub. Adminstrn. Svc., 1969-75, chmn., 1973-75; mem. Delta Dental Plan Mich., 1972-78, bd. dirs. 1972-78, chmn. consumers' adv. coun., 1975-77; bd. dirs. Ctr. for Population Activities, 1975-81, chmn., 1975-81; lifetime vis. prof. Capital U. Economics and Bus., Beijing, 1996—; vis. rschr. Human Scis. Rsch. Coun., Pretoria, South Africa, 1999—. Author: The Philippine Presidency, 1956; editor: Changing Dimensions in Public Administration, 1962; contbr. articles to profl. jours. Mem. Citizens League, Cleve., 1957-59; mem. Ann Arbor Citizens Coun., 1965-69; bd. dirs. Southeastern Mich. Family Planning Project, 1975-77; trustee Congregational Summer Assembly, 1982-85; commr. Accrediting Commn. on Edn. for Health Svcs. Adminstrn., 1989-95. Served with AUS, 1943-46, ETO. Fellow Am. Pub. Health Assn. (chmn. program devel. bd. 1975-77, exec. bd. 1975-80, governing coun. 1975—, pres. 1979, chmn. publs. bd. 1984-88), Royal Soc. Health (hon.), Am. Polit. Sci. Assn. (life); mem. ASPA (past mem. coun.), Population Assn. Am., Phi Kappa Phi, Pi Sigma Alpha, Pi Gamma Mu, Delta Omega. Home and Office: 2125 Nature Cove Apt 108 Ann Arbor MI 48104

ROMANI, PAUL NICHOLAS, government official; b. LI, NY, May 14, 1943; m. Patricia Elsie Riley, July 26, 1968; children: Michele P., Christopher P. BBA, George Washington U., 1967, MBA, 1968, DPA with distinction, 1975. Lic. real estate broker, Va.; cert. EEO counselor; CFP, CNA; cert. net. engr. Assoc. professorial lectr. George Washington U., 1970-72; sci. adminstr. NSF, Washington, 1972-82; sci. and tech. fellow The White House, Washington, 1982-83, dir. fin. and adminstrn. automated systems div., 1983-85, dir. adminstrv. ops., 1985-91; dir. Fed. Fin. Instns. Exams. Coun., Washington, 1991-98; CEO R3 Cons. Svcs. Inc., 1999—; cons. The White House, Washington, 2001—. Dir. adminstrn., comptr. Pres.' Edn. Summit with Govs., Charlottesville, Va., 1989; cons. to Pres. Nixon's Adv. Coun. on Mgmt. Improvement, 1970. Author: Principal Investigator Guide to Research Proposal Development, 1998; editl. adv. panel Bur. Bus. Practice, 1997—; contbr. articles to profl. jours. Bd. dirs. scholarship fund City of Alexandria, Va., 1992—. Humble Oil fellow, 1968, McGraw-Edison fellow George Washington U., 1971-73; recipient Meritorious Svc. award Exec. Office of the Pres., 1984, Disting. Svc. award Exec. Office of the Pres., 1989, Disting. Svc. award Fed. Fin. Instns. Exam. Coun., 1992, Spl. Achievement award, 1995. Mem.: Soc. Am. Value Engrs., Soc. Gen. Systems Rsch., Supreme Ct. Soc., Am. Soc. Pub. Adminstrn., Tex. State Soc., Alpha Kappa Psi. Roman Catholic. Office: R3 Cons Svcs Inc Mills Bldg 1700 Pennsylvania Ave NW Washington DC 20006-4704 Office Phone: 202-393-7600. E-mail: r-cubed@erols.com.

ROMANO, JOHN FRANCIS, dermatologist; b. S.I., N.Y., July 4, 1948; MD, Cornell U., 1973. Diplomate Am. Bd. Dermatology. Intern Einstein Hosps., N.Y.C., 1973—74; resident in medicine St. Vincent's Hosp., N.Y.C., 1974—76; resident in dermatology N.Y. Hosp., N.Y.C., 1976—78; pvt. practice dermatology N.Y.C., 1979—; attending physician St. Vincent's Hosp., N.Y.C., 1979—; clin. asst. prof. dermatology N.Y. Hosp.-Cornell U., 1979—. Mem.: N.Y. State Dermatologic Soc., Am. Soc. for Laser Medicine and Surgery, Am. Soc. for Dermatologic Surgery, Am. Acad. Dermatology. Avocation: sailing. Office: 36 7th Ave New York NY 10011-6609 Office Phone: 212-242-5815. Business E-Mail: info@romanodermatology.com.

ROMANO, JOSEPH ANTHONY, healthcare education and marketing consultant; b. Bklyn., Sept. 5, 1946; s. Anthony Wilbur and Anne R.; m. Linda Rose Giacalone, Sept. 23, 1972; children: Nicholas Joseph, Christine Dianne. Student, Villanova U., 1964-66; BS Pharm. Sci., Columbia U., 1970, D Pharmacy, 1972. Clin. resident Lenox Hill Hosp., N.Y.C., 1970-72; asst. dean, asst. prof. Columbia U., N.Y.C., 1972-76, SUNY, Buffalo, 1976-78; assoc. dean, assoc. prof. U. Wash., Seattle, 1978-83; assoc. dir. medicine Pfizer Labs., N.Y.C., 1983-85, product mgr., 1985, asst. to pres., 1985-87; sr. v.p., group dir. Hill & Knowlton, Inc., N.Y.C., 1987-88; exec. dir. external affairs Novartis, N.Y.C., 1988-89; pres., COO Visual Med. Mktg., N.Y.C., 1989-92; vice chair Nelson Communications, Inc. Worldwide (divsn. Publicis), N.Y.C., 1992-2001; chmn., CEO SCIENS Worldwide Healthcare Comms., 1996-2001; co-chmn. Nelson Profl. Sales, 1998-2000. Mem. U.S. Nat. Adv. Com. Health Profls., Washington, 1980-86. Co-author: Clinical Pharmacology, 1980, Pharmacy State Board Reviews, 1976, 78, 85, The Vitamin Book, 1985, 99; contbr. articles to profl. jours. Fellow Royal Soc. Health London; mem. Am. Pharm. Assn., Am. Soc. Healthcare Pharmacists, Am. Assoc. Study Headaches, U.S. Golf Assn., Rho Chi. Avocations: photography, stamp collecting/philately, golf, music, cooking. Personal E-mail: josepharomano@earthlink.net.

ROMANO, JOSEPH SCOTT, music educator; b. N.Y.C., Aug. 4, 1971; s. Lydia and Philip Romano. BS in Music Edn. cum laude, Hofstra U., 1993, MA in Humanities with distinction, 1999. Cert. music edn. k-12 N.Y., 1999. Asst. band dir. Divsn. Ave. H.S., Levittown, NY, 1989—95; band dir. Wisdom Ln. Mid. Sch., 1993—95; dir. of bands Gen. Douglas MacArthur H.S., 1995—. Band festival chmn. Nassau Music Educators Assn., 1997—2000. Contbr. articles to profl. jours. Finalist Educator of Yr. award, 21st Century Jour., 1997; nominee Am. Tchr. award, Disney Co., 1999, 2001; recipient Outstanding Tchr., Elks Found., 2001; grantee Rsch., Levittown Tchr.'s Ctr., 1999; Leonard B. Myers endowed scholarship, Hofstra U., 1991. Mem.: World of Wind Ensembles/Symphonic Bands Online, Nat. Band Assn., N.Y. State Schools Music Assn., Music Educators Nat. Conf., Nassau Music Educators Assn. (band festival chmn. 1997—2000), English Folk Song and Dance Soc., Phi Kappa Lambda (hon.), Tri-M Nat. Honor Soc. (life). Home: 1-46 Atlantic Avenue Farmingdale NY 11735 Office: General Douglas MacArthur HS 3369 Old Jerusalem Rd Levittown NY 11756 Office Phone: 516-520-8450 844. Personal E-mail: jrromman@optonline.net.

ROMANO, MICHAEL, chef, restaurant owner; Degree, N.Y.C. Tech. Coll., 1975. Evening line cook Serendipity, N.Y.C., 1971; stage Hotel Bristol, Paris, 1975; chef Hotel Pierre, N.Y.C., 1975, Regine's, Paris and N.Y.C., 1976; commis poissonier, saucier Eugenie les Bains, France; personal chef Switzerland; stage Chapon Fin, Bordeaux, France; chef de cuisine Chez Max, Zurich, Switzerland, La Caravelle, N.Y.C., 1984—88, Union Sq. Cafe, N.Y.C., 1988—, co-owner, 1993—. Author (with Danny Meyer): The Union Square Cafe Cookbook, 1994. Named one of Top Ten Chefs in U.S.A., Food and Wine Mag. Office: Union Sq Cafe 21 E 16th St New York NY 10003

ROMANO, MICHAEL, publishing executive, consultant; b. IndianTown Gap, Pa., Nov. 23, 1952; s. Frank and Patricia Romano; m. Elaine A. Ambrose, July 22, 2000; children: Daniel Martin, Emily Brooke Nielson, Adam Jeffery Nielson. BS in Environ. Health, Colo. State U., 1979. Cert. EMT Colo.; LPN, Wash., Colo. Environ. specialist Hewlett Packard Co., Boise, Idaho, 1979—99; pub. Mill Pk. Pub., McCall, Idaho, 2003—. Fin. cons. E & M Group, McCall, 1999—2003. Mem. capital campaign U. Idaho, Moscow, 2000—03. With U.S. Army, 1971—75. Recipient Best New Children's Book, 2003, Statewide Literacy award. Mem.: Small Publishers Assn. Am. (assoc.). Independent. Home and Office: PO Box 1932 1510 McCall Ave McCall ID 83638 Office Phone: 208-634-1358. E-mail: millparkpublish@aol.com.

ROMANO, NICHOLAS CHARLES, information scientist, educator; b. Poughkeepsie, N.Y., Apr. 8, 1963; s. Nicholas C. and Joan Romano; m. Rosalina Marie Jacobs, Dec. 26, 1998; children: Gabriela Nicola children: Isabella Mercedes. BS in Biology, U. Ariz., 1986, BS in MIS, 1988, MS in MIS, 1994, PhD in MIS, 1998. Sys. programmer Internat. Bus. Machines Corp., Tucson, 1988—91; rsch. assoc. Ctr. for Mgmt. of Info., U. Ariz., Tucson, 1992—98, rsch. scientist, 1998—99; vis. scholar Ctr. for the Mgmt. of Info., U. Ariz., Tucson, 2000—02; asst. prof. MIS dept. MIS Coll. Bus. Adminstrn. U. Tulsa, 1999—2001; asst. prof. dept. mgmt. sci. and info. sys. Coll. Bus. Adminstrn. Okla. State U., Tulsa, 2001—. Software engring. cons. Ventana Corp., Tucson, 1996, Tucson, 1998—99, GroupSystems.Com, Tucson, 2000; reviewer chair Am.'s Conf. on Info. Systems, Dallas, 2002—03; mem. steering com. ISOneWorld Acad. Affairs, 2002—; tech. facilitation cons. U. Ariz. MIS and Arthur Andersen Cons., Tucson, 1998; facilitator nat. bd. advisors Eller Sch. Mgmt., Tucson, 1994; tech. facilitator Inst. for the Future, Tucson, 1993; adj. lectr. dept. MIS U. Ariz., Tucson, 1998—99; tech. and process facilitator Am. Soc. Quality, Tucson, 2002; program co-chair Isoneworld Conf., 2003—04; reviewer chair Am.'s Conf. on Info. Systems, Tampa, Fla., 2003, N.Y.C., 04. Guest editor (journal) Bus. Process Mgmt. Jour., Internat. Jour. Electronic Commerce, Logistics and Info. Mgmt., mem. editl. rev. bd., 2002—. V.p. bd. dirs. Waterford Crossing Home Owners Assn., Broken Arrow, Okla., 2002; United Way charitable contbns. rep. IBM, Tucson, 1990; host computer capers program for jr. H.S. students U. Ariz., Tucson; vol. Cmty. Action Project, Tulsa County Head Start, Foster Head Start, Tulsa, 2000; mem. AJS- Web Academic Conf. Mgmgt. Sys. Steering Com., KC, Broken Arrow, Okla., 2002, Tucson, 1998—2002; lector Thomas More, Cath. Newman Ctr. U. Ariz., Tucson, 1998—99. Recipient U.S. Achievement Acad. award, U.S. Achievement Acad., 1986—87, Nat. Collegiate Bus. award, Nat. Collegiate Bus. Assn., 1987; grantee Free Form Semantic Comment Analysis and Visualization for Usability Studies, U. Tulsa Office of Rsch., 2000, Project Collaboration, Ctr. Aviation Systems/Support Infrastructure, 2002—03, Telecom. Virtual Lab. Devel., Dept. of Edn., 2002—03; scholar Grad. Registration Scholarship, Dept. MIS, U. of Ariz., 1995—96. Mem.: Assn. Info. Sys. (assoc.), Phi Kappa Phi, Beta Gamma Sigma, Golden Key. Conservative. Avocations: numistatics, travel, bottle collecting.

ROMANO, RAY, actor, comedian; b. Forest Hills, N.Y., Dec. 21, 1957; m. Anna Scarpula; 4 children. Stand up comedian; sitcom actor. Actor: (TV series) Everybody Loves Raymond, 1996— (Best Actor, Quality Comedy, Viewers for Quality TV, 1998, TV Critics Assn. award for outstanding ind. achievement in comedy, 1999, nominee Emmy award outstanding lead actor in comedy series, 1999, nominee Golden Globe award best performance by actor in comedy, People's Choice award favorite male TV performer, 2002, nominee Screen Actors Guild award outstanding performance by a male actor in comedy series, 2002, TV Guide award Favorite Actor in a Comedy, Funniest Male Lead in a TV Series at 14th Ann. Am. Comedy Awards); (films) Welcome to Mooseport, 2004, (voice) Ice Age, 2002; TV guest appearances in Dr. Katz Professional Therapist, 1995, The King of Queens, 1998, Hollywood Squares, 1998—, Becker, 1998, Who Wants to Be a Millionaire, 1999; author: Everything and a Kite, 1999; performer: (CD) Ray Ramono: Live at Carnegie Hall, 1999.

ROMANO, SHEILA JUNE, telecommunications industry executive, artist, writer; b. Elko, Nev., June 11, 1951; d. John Lewis and June Florene (Lani) C. BA, U. Nev., 1974. Various svc. positions Citizens Comm. (formerly Alltel-Nevada Inc.), Elko, 1974-78, svc. rep., 1978-84, bus. office supr., 1984-87, bus. supr. Nev. office, 1987-94, bus. supr., state pub. rels. coord., 1994-97, results coord., project mgmt. support person Elk Grove, Calif., 1997, supr. customer ops. escalations and exec. complaints, 1998-2000, specialist state gov. affairs, 2001—02; sr. regulatory analyst Frontier Comm., Elk Grove, 2002—. Active Citizens Amb. program People to People Internat., 1995—98; writer, artist, 1974—. Contbg. author: Fence Post to Fiber, 1998. Officer, organizer Freedom Com., Elko, 1984; mem., treas. Elk Grove Cmty. Action Team, 1997-98. Mem. NOW, AAUW (editor newsletter Elko 1980-82, v.p. programs 1991-93, sec. 1995-96), Soroptimists Internat. (treas. 1992-93, sec. 1993-94, v.p. 1995-96, pres. 1996-97). Office: Frontier PO Box 340 Elk Grove CA 95759-0340

ROMANOFF, MARJORIE REINWALD, retired education educator; b. Chgo., Sept. 29, 1923; d. David Edward and Gertrude (Rosenfield) Reinwald; m. Milford M. Romanoff, Nov. 6, 1945; children: Bennett Sanford, Lawrence Michael, Janet Beth (dec.). Student, Northwestern U., 1941-42, 43-45, Chgo. Coll. Jewish Studies, 1942-43; BEd, U. Toledo, 1947, MEd, 1968, EdD, 1976. Tchr. Old Orchard Elem. Sch., Toledo, 1946-47, McKinley Sch., Toledo, 1964-65; substitute tchr. Toledo, 1964-68; instr. Mary Manse Coll., Toledo, 1968-73; instr. children's lit. Sylvania (Ohio) Bd. Edn., 1977; supr. student tchrs. U. Toledo, 1968—73, 1985—2001, instr. advanced comms., 1977, rschr., 1973-74; instr. Am. Lang. Inst., 1978—2002. Part-time asst. prof. elem. edn. Bowling Green (Ohio) State U., 1978—88; chair rsch. com. Am. Lang. Inst., U. Toledo, 1985—94, asst. prof. elem. edn. in lang. arts, 1985—87, part time asst. prof. elem. edn., ESL specialist, 1978—2002; presenter numerous workshops and demonstrations in children's lit. and analysis of tchr. behavior, 1976—99. Author: Language and Study Skills: For Learners of English, Prentice Hall Regents, 1991. Trustee Children's Svcs. Bd., 1974-76; pres. bd. Cummings Treatment Ctr. for Adolescents, 1978-80; mem. Crosby Gardens Adv. Bd., 1976-82, Cmty. Planning Coun., 1980-84, Citizens Rev. Bd. of Juv. Ct., 1979—; allocations com. Mental Health and Retardation Bd., 1980-81; active Bd. Jewish Edn., 1976—, pres., 1982-84; active Jewish Family Svc., 1978-85, v.p., 1980-85; allocations com. Jewish Welfare Fedn., 1980, 89-91; bd. dirs. Family Life Edn. Coun., 1984-90, sec., 1988-90; budget and allocations com. Jewish Fedn., 1989-93; bd. dirs. Friends Toledo-Lucas County Librs., 1991—, bd. pres., 1991-93; program chair U. Toledo Women's Commn., 1991-93; bd. dirs. Ohio Friends of Pub. Librs., 1992-94; presenter ann. conf. N.W. Ohio Libr. Assn., 1993, Bowling Green State U., 1997; condr. workshop Internat. Conf./Teaching Langs., U. Cin., 1996. Named One of Ten Women of Yr., St. Vincent's Hosp., Guild, 1984, Outstanding Instructional Staff Woman, U. Toledo, 1990, Excellence award Citizen's Rev. Bd., 2003. Mem. Tchrs. English to Speakers Other Langs. (presenter 1986, presenter Internat. TESOL Atlanta 1993), Toledo Libr. Legacy Found., Orgn. Rehab. and Tng. (named Outstanding Woman in Cmty. Svc. 1987), Hadassah (chpt. pres. regional bd. 1961-64), Northwestern U. Alumni Assn., Phi Kappa Phi, Phi Delta Kappa, Kappa Delta Pi (pres./faculty adv. 1971-75, Point of Excellence award 1992), Pi Lambda Theta (chpt. pres. 1978-80, nat. com. 1979-84). Home: 4343 W Bancroft Apt 4B Toledo OH 43615 E-mail: MRR1923@aol.com.

ROMANOFF, MILFORD MARTIN, retired building contractor; b. Cleve., Aug. 21, 1921; s. Barney Sanford and Edythe Stolpher (Bort) R.; m. Marjorie Reinwald, Nov. 6, 1945; children: Bennett S., Lawrence M., Janet Beth (dec.). Student, U. Mich. Coll. Arch., 1939-42; BBA, U. Toledo, 1943. Pres. Glass City Constrn. Co., Toledo, 1951-55, Milford Romanoff, Inc., Toledo, 1956—2003. Co-founder Neighborhood Improvement Found. Toledo, 1960; active Lucas County Econ. Devel. Com., 1979—, Childrens Svcs. Bd. Lucas County, 1981—97, Arthritis Bd. Dirs., Crosby Gardens Bd. Advisors, 1983—96, Toledo Met. Area Govt. Exec. Com., 1996—; citizens adv. bd. Recreation Commn. Toledo, 1973—86; campus adv. com. Med. Coll. Ohio, 1980—; trustee Cummings Treatment Ctr. for Adolescents, 1981—; pres. Toledo Lodge, 1958—59, Cherry Hill Nursing Home, 1964—85; bd. dirs. Anti-Defamation League, 1955—60, Ohio Hillel Orgns., Lucas County Dept. Human Svcs., Arthritis Assn., 1995—, Comprehensive Addiction Svc. Sys., 1998, Kidney Found. Northwestern Ohio, 1986—, sec., 1989; chmn. Comprehensive Addiction Svc. Sys., 1999, Toledo Amateur Baseball and Softball Com., 1979—81; cons. U.S. Care Corp., 1985—; bd. govs. Toledo Housing for Elderly, 1982—84, sec., 1989, pres. bd. govs., 1990—, pres., 1991—; bd. adv. Ret. Sr. Vol. Program, 1987—89, chmn., 1988—90, 1993—, sec. adv. bd., 1990—, bd. dirs., 2000—; vice chmn. adv. bd. Salvation Army, 1986—87, chmn. adv. bd., 1988—90, ct. apptd. spl. advocate adv., bd. treas., 1988—; chmn. Mental Health Adv. Bd., 1983—84, sec., 1989; bd. dirs. Toledo Urban Forestry Commn., 1991—, pres., 1993, 1995, Lucas County Dept. Human Svcs. Bd.; adv. coun. Renaissance Sr. Apts., 1997, chmn. adv. coun., 1999; adv. bd. Lucas Co. Correctional Facility, 1999—; chmn. Compass Bd., 2002—; bd. dirs. Area Office on Aging of Northwest Ohio, 2001, Lucas County Mental Health, 2001; chair Compass Corp. for Recovery Svcs., 2002—; mem. Lucas County Mental Health Bd., 2002, Juvenile Correction Bd., 2003—; bd. dirs. Mental Health Lucas Co.; mem. Juvenile Correction Bd. Lucas County, 2003—; active Dem. Precinct Com., 1975—78; trustee Temple Brotherhood, 1956—58, bd. dirs., 1981—; pres. Ohio B'nai Brith, 1959—60. Mem.: Friends Libr. Bd., Mental Health Bd. of Lucas County, U. Mich. Alumni Assn., Toledo Zool. Soc., Juvenile Justice (adv. bd.), U. Toledo Alumni Assn., Toledo Mus. Art (assoc.), Nat. Coun. on Alcoholism & Drug Dependence, Econ. Opportunity Planning Assn. Greater Toledo (adv. bd.), Hadassah (assoc. Toledo chpt.), Masons (Outstanding Cmty. Svc. award of Lucas County 2001), Zeta Beta Tau. Home: Stratford in the Hills 4343 W Bancroft St Apt 4B Toledo OH 43615-3956

ROMANOFF, RICHARD ARTHUR, music educator, musician; b. Lynn, Mass., USA, May 23, 1979; s. William Kane and Theresa Germaine Romanoff. MusB, The Boston Conservatory, Boston, MA, 1997—2001. Tchg. certification Mass., 2001. Dir. bands Somerville Pub. Schools, Somerville, 2001—; pvt. music tchr. Billerica Pub. Schools, Billerica, 2002—. Creative writing tchr. Boston Symphony Orchestra's Edn. Outreach Program Days in the Arts, 2002; band mgr. Mass. Music Educator's Assn. Northeastern Dist. Festival, Lowell, 2003—04; musican Harvard Summer Pops Band, Cambridge, 1999—2003; musician Boston Bar Assn. Orch., 2003. Composer: (musical for children) Why the Sea is Salt; prodr.: (high school musical prodn.) Cabaret; composer: (musical) World's Fair, (music) Three Pieces for Clarinet, Theme and Variations for Orchestra. Musician First Church, Bedford, 2003. Recipient Student Leadership Award, Boston Conservatory, 2001. Mem.: Somerville Teachers's Assn., Mass. Music Educator's Assn., Mass. Teachers' Assn., MENC: The Nat. Assn. for Music Edn., St. Anthony's Philharm. Democrat. Roman Catholic. Avocations: golf, tennis, baseball. Office: Somerville High School 81 Highland Avenue Somerville MA 02143 E-mail: rromanoff@somerville.mec.edu.

ROMANO-MAGNER, PATRICIA R. English studies educator, researcher; b. N.Y.C., Mar. 22, 1928; d. Al and Nicole (Siriani) Romano; m. Ralpha M. Magner, Dec. 24, 1954. AA, BA, L.A. City Coll.; MA, Calif. State U., L.A.; D (hon.), Stanford U., Cambridge (Eng.) U., Queens Coll. Master tchr. Burbank (Calif.) Unified Sch. Dist., L.A. City Schs., Stanford (Calif.) U. Sch. for the Gifted; prof. Calif. State U., L.A., curriculum lab. asst. LA. Mem. AAUW, AAUP (award 2000), Am. Legion Aux., Sierra Club, Natural Resources Def. Coun., The Friends of the William J. Clinton Presdl. Libr. (founding mem.), Scholarship Soc. of Calif. State U. L.A. Republican. Avocation: horseback riding. Home: 5975 N Odell Ave Chicago IL 60631-2358

ROMANOSKY, LUANN, elementary school educator; d. Thomas Forese and Minnie Ann Bianchini Forese; m. David Charles Romanosky, May 20, 1978; children: David C. Jr., Maria. BS in Elem. Edn., West Chester State Coll., 1976; MS in Elem. Edn., West Chester U., 1983. Cert. middle sch. math. Pa. Dept. Edn., elem. instrnl. II Pa. Dept. Edn. Remedial math. tchr. Chester County Intermediate Unit, Downingtown, Pa., 1976—, chairperson math. program, 1996—. Workshop presenter Chester County Intermediate Unit, Downingtown, 1976—. Mem.: Math. Assn. Am., Nat. Coun. Tchrs. Math., ASCD. Avocations: reading, exercise. Office: Chester County Intermediate Unit 455 Boot Rd Downingtown PA 19335

ROMANOV, VOLODYMYR ALEXEEVICH, computer science educator, researcher; b. Kamynino, Kursk, Russia, Jan. 23, 1960; s. Alexey Filippovich and Olga Sergeevna Romanov; m. Svitlana Egorivna Chystova, Oct. 16, 1981; children: Olga Volodymyrivna, Volodymyr Volodymyrovych. MD, Nat. U., Kharkov, Ukraine, 1983, PhD, 1987. Cert. computer scis. and nuc. physics. Rschr. Nuc. Phys. Lab., Kharkiv, Ukraine, 1983-88; prof. State Tech. Univ. Agr., Kharkiv, 1988-96; head Info. Tech. Ctr., Kharkiv, 1996-2000. Vice-head Coun. Young Rschrs., Kharkiv, 1984-91; editor Regional TV, Kharkiv, 1985-87; prof. State Tech Univ. Agr., Kharkiv, 1996-2000, prof. Newton Coll., Montreal, 2000—. Author: (with S. Troubnikov) Nuclear Forces, 1992, (with I. Furman) Programmed Microcontrollers, 2000; contbr. articles to profl. jours. Mem. Can. Info. Processing Soc. Russian Orthodox. Avocations: russian literature, history, music. Home: Apt 81 4645 Bourret Montreal QC Canada H3W 1K9 Office: 2900 Decarie # 3575 Cote-St Luc Montreal QC Canada H3X 2T8 E-mail: volodymyr_romanov@yahoo.com.

ROMANOWITZ, BYRON FOSTER, architect, engineer; b. Covington, Ky., Nov. 14, 1929; s. Harry Alex and Mildred (Foster) R.; m. Mildred Elaine Gize, June 15, 1957; children: Laura Ann, Mark Walter, Cynthia Ellen. BS in Civil Enginrg, U. Ky., 1951; M.F.A. in Architecture, Princeton, 1953. Instr. sch. architecture Princeton U., 1954; architect Brock & Johnson, Lexington, 1958-59, Johnson & Romanowitz, Architects, Lexington and Louisville, 1960-2000; ret., 2000. Pres. Ky. Bd. examiners and Registration of Archs., 1975-91; instr. U. Ky. Sch. Architecture, 1996, 2000. Prin. works include U. Ky. campus bldgs., 1959-96, Ea. Ky. U. campus bldgs., 1959-77, Centre Coll., Danville, Ky., campus bldgs., 1967-89, Georgetown (Ky.) Coll. campus bldgs., 1964-84, Asbury Coll., Wilmore, Ky., 1972-78, Asbury Theol. Sem., 1978-93, Berea Coll. bldgs., 1978-91, Transylvania U. bldgs., 1974-98, U. Louisville, 1990-98, 11 downtown Lexington office bldgs.; leader Men of Note Orch., 1986—, Jazzberry Jam Combo, 1993—. Mem. Lexington Urban Renewal Commn., 1963-69; chmn. adv. bd. Salvation Army, 1971-72; trustee Midway (Ky.) Coll., 1986-95. With USNR, 1955-58; lt. comdr. Res. Recipient award of merit nat. archtl. competition AIA/Ednl. Facilities Lab., 1966 Fellow AIA (1st honor awards Ky. archtl. competition 1959, 61, 68, 70, 73, 78, 80, 81, pres. East Ky. chpt. 1965); mem. Ky. Soc. Architects (pres. 1966), Masons, Rotary, Lexington Club, Navy League, Tau Beta Pi, Phi Mu Alpha, Phi Sigma Kappa. Home: 2057 Lakeside Dr Lexington KY 40502-3016

ROMANOWSKI, THOMAS ANDREW, physics educator; b. Warsaw, Apr. 17, 1925; came to U.S., 1946, naturalized, 1949; s. Bohdan and Alina (Sumowski) R.; m. Carmen des Rochers, Nov. 15, 1952; children: Alina, Dominique. BS, Mass. Inst. Tech., 1952; MS, Case Inst. Tech., 1956, PhD, 1957. Rsch. assoc. physics Carnegie Inst. Tech., 1956-60; asst. physicist high energy physics Argonne Nat. Lab., Ill., 1960-63, assoc. physicist, 1963-72, physicist, 1972-78; prof. physics Ohio State U., Columbus, 1964-92, prof. emeritus, 1992-98; sr. scientist Argonne Nat. Lab., 1992; physicist U.S. Dept. Energy, Washington, 1992-98; cons. in pvt. practice, 1998—. Contbr. articles to profl. jours. and, papers to sci. meetings, seminars and workshops. With high energy program U.S. Dept. Energy, 1993-98. Served with C.E. AUS, 1946-47. Fellow Am. Phys. Soc., AAAS; mem. Lambda Chi Alpha. Achievements include research in nuclear and high energy physics. Home: 319 Tano Rd Santa Fe NM 87506-8823 Personal E-mail: romanowski@santafe-newmexico.com.

ROMANS, DONALD BISHOP, corporate executive; b. Louisville, Apr. 22, 1931; s. Albert D. and Moneta (Bishop) R.; m. Marilyn Yvonne Neff, June 13, 1953 (dec. Aug. 2000); children: Rebecca Ann, Jennifer. BS, U. Louisville, 1953; MBA, Harvard U., 1958. Mgr. internal auditing and data processing, mem. contr. staff Container Corp. Am., Chgo., 1958-62; successively asst. to pres., asst. treas., treas., v.p. fin., sr. v.p. fin., exec. v.p. Trans Union Corp., Chgo., 1962-81; exec. v.p., chief fin. officer Sunbeam Corp., Chgo., 1981-82, Bally Mfg. Corp., Chgo., 1982-87; fin. cons. Chgo., 1987; pres. Romans and Co., Chgo., 1987-93. Bd. dirs. Burnham Investment Trust, N.Y.C.; trustee PhoenixFunds, Hartford, Conn.; life trustee St. Mary of Nazareth Hosp. Capt. USMCR, 1953-56. Republican. Avocations: tennis, boating. Home: 39 S Sheridan Rd Lake Forest IL 60045-3269 E-mail: dbromans@yahoo.com.

ROMANS, JOHN NIEBRUGGE, lawyer; b. Bklyn., May 23, 1942; s. John McDowell and Helen Pond (Niebrugge) R.; m. Caroline Ward; children: John A., Andrew C. BA, Williams Coll., 1964; LLB, Columbia U., 1967. Bar: N.Y. 1967, U.S. Dist. Ct. (so. and ea. dists.) N.Y. 1971, U.S. Ct. Appeals (2d cir.) 1971, U.S. Ct. Appeals (3rd cir.) 1976, U.S. Ct. Appeals (4th and 7th cirs.) 1987, U.S. Ct. Appeals (9th cir.) 1992, U.S. Ct. Appeals (11th cir.) 1996, U.S. Supreme Ct. 1971. Ptnr. Curtis, Mallet-Prevost, Colt & Mosle, N.Y.C.,

1980—90, Katten Muchin & Zavis, N.Y.C., 1990—98, Rosen Weinhaus, LLP, N.Y.C., 1998—. Lectr. on air law topics at various seminars. Contbr. articles to profl. jours. Trustee Summit (N.J.) Unitarian-Universalist Ch., 1978, Mamaroneck Pub. Libr. Dist., 1990-99; mem. budget com. Village of Mamaroneck, 2001—, chmn, 2002; dir. The Univ. Glee Club NYC, 1993—. Lt. USNR, 1968-71. Mem. Assn. Bar City N.Y. (aero. com. 1983-85, 2004-, chmn. 1986-89, 92-94, 2000, products liability com. 1989-91), Larchmont (N.Y.) Yacht Club. Avocation: sailing. Office: Rosen Weinhaus LLP 40 Wall St 32d Fl New York NY 10005-1304

ROMANSKY, MONROE JAMES, physician, educator; b. Hartford, Conn., Mar. 16, 1911; s. Benjamin and Henrietta (Levine) R.; m. Evelyn Muriel Lackman, Jan. 10, 1943; children: Stephen, Gerald, Michael, Richard. AB, U. Maine, 1933; MD, U. Rochester, 1937. Diplomate: Am. Bd. Internal Medicine. Intern Strong Meml. Hosp.-U. Rochester, N.Y., 1937-38, asst. resident, 1938-39, James Gleason Research fellow studies on relationship of kidneys to hypertension, 1939-40, chief resident, 1940-41, instr. in medicine, 1941-42; investigator Office Sci. Research and Devel., Surgeon Gen. U.S., 1941-42; chief biochemistry and antibiotic research Walter Reed Army Hosp., 1942-46; asso. prof. Sch. Medicine, George Washington U., Washington, 1946—, prof. medicine, 1957—; dir. George Washington U. med. div. D.C. Gen. Hosp., 1950-69; dir. infectious diseases research lab. and infectious diseases div. D.C. Gen. Hosp., 1950-69. Cons. internal medicine antibiotics Walter Reed Army Hosp., Washington, 1946—; Cons. internal medicine antibiotics VA Hosp., Washington, 1952—, NIH, Bethesda, Md., 1953—, Surgeon Gen. USAF, 1966—; mem. Asian influenza adv. com. D.C., 1956-61; mem. ad hoc adv. com. Bur. Medicine FDA, 1966-67; examiner Am. Bd. Internal Medicine, 1965, 67, 69 Editorial bd.: Antimicrobial Agts. and Chemotherapy, 1961-72; Contbr. to profl. jours. Trustees council U. Rochester, 1965— . Served with M.C., AUS, 1942-46. Decorated Legion of Merit; recipient Founders award Tau Epsilon Phi, Disting. Career award U. Maine. Fellow ACP (adv. bd. to gov. D.C. 1969—); mem. Am. Soc. Internal Medicine, Am. Fedn. Clin. Research, Soc. Exptl. Biology and Medicine, Am. Soc. Microbiology, Infectious Diseases Soc. (founding council 1963-66), Soc. Med. Cons. to Armed Forces, Sigma Xi, Alpha Omega Alpha. Clubs: Woodmont Country. Achievements include pioneer work in prolonging action of penicillin, requiring only single daily injection, Romansky Formula, 1944; nutritional studies in obesity as related to weight reduction. Home: 5600 Wisconsin Ave Chevy Chase MD 20815-4405

ROMANZI, KENNETH, toy manufacturing executive; Grad., Babson Coll. With Frito-Lay, Inc.; v.p.-mktg./strategic planning Cadbury Schweppes, 1992—93; pres. and gen. mgr., Fleishmann's divsn. Nabisco, 1993—96, sr. v.p.-sales and customer svc., 1996—2000; pres. and CEO Balducci's Direct, 2000—01, Ultimate Juice Co., 2002—03; pres.-US Toys Hasbro, Inc., 2003—. Office: Hasbro Inc 1027 Newport Ave Pawtucket RI 02862*

ROMARY, THOMAS GERALD, mathematician, educator, writer; b. Ft. Wayne, Ind., July 8, 1943; m. Becky M. Spycyalski, Aug. 16, 1969; children: Tammy M., Tyler T. BS in Math. and Edn., Purdue U., 1966; MS in Math and Edn., St. Francis Coll., 1969; MS in Secondary Adminstrn., Ind. U., 1985. Lic. tchr. Ind., Mich. Tchr. math. various schs., Ind., 1965—78; prof. math. Ind. Inst. Tech., Ft. Wayne, 1978—. Author: (8 book series) Toms Tips, 1996—. Mem.: Nat. Coun. Tchrs. Math. Office: IIT 1600 E Washington Fort Wayne IN 46803 Office Phone: 260-422-5561 x 2286. Business E-Mail: romary@indtech.edu.

ROMAS, NICHOLAS ACHILLES, urologist, educator; b. Endicott, N.Y., Jan. 17, 1936; s. Peter Angelo and Stavroula Romas; m. Serene Karikas, June 19, 1968; children: Stavra Nicole, Eva Maria, Pamela Stephanie. AB, Colgate U., 1958; MD, Columbia U., 1962. Bd. cert. urologist, 1974. Asst. prof. clin. urology Columbia U. Coll. Physicians and Surgeons, N.Y.C., 1970-78, assoc. prof. clin. urology, 1978-89, prof. clin. urology, 1989—; dir. urology St. Luke's-Roosevelt Hosp. Ctr., N.Y.C., 1984—. Editor: Prostate Acid Phosphatase Measurement, 1982; contbr. articles to profl. jours. Maj. USAF, 1968-70. Mem. Am. Urol. Assn. (rsch. com. 1990—, fin. com. 1991—, pub. com. 1998—, pres NY sect. 2003), N.Y. Acad. Medicine (adv. com. 1986—, sec. urology sect. 1987-88, chmn. 1988-89). Greek Orthodox. Achievements include research in the role of prostate acid phosphates in different stages of prostate cancer. Office: St Lukes-Roosevelt Hosp Ctr 1000 10th Ave New York NY 10019-1147 E-mail: nromas@slrhc.org.

ROMASCO, ROBERT G. insurance company executive; BA, Brandeis U., 1969; MBA, Harvard U., 1978. Various mgmt. positions Epsilon Data Mgmt.; prin. Corp. Decisions, Inc.; head corp. mktg. Am. Century Investments; pres., CEO JC Penny Direct Mktg. Svcs.; exec. v.p., chief mktg. officer Cigna Corp., Phila., 2002—. Office: Cigna Corp 1 Liberty Pl Philadelphia PA 19192-1552

ROMBERG, OSVALDO, artist; b. Buenos Aires, 1938; Student, Colegio Nat. Buenos Aires, 1950-55, U. Buenos Aires, 1956-62. One-man shows include Galerie Montagne, Paris, 1992, Galerie Shuppenhauer, Cologne, Germany, 1993, Galerie Heike Curtze, Vienna, 1993, 1996, 1999, Fundacion San Telmo, Buenos Aires, 1993, Sprengel Mus., Hanover, Germany, 1993, Mus. Moderner Kunst, Vienna, 1993, 1996, Gimel Gallery, Jerusalem, 1994, Ingrid Dacic Gallery, Tubingen, Germany, 1994, Galerie Hohenthal und Bergen, Cologne, 1995, Artists Space, N.Y., 1995, Mus. Ludwig, Cologne, 1996, Voxx Galerie, Chemnitz, 1996, Tel Aviv U. Gallery, 1996, 1996, Pa. Acad. Fine Arts, Phila., 1996, Mus. Modern Art, Odessa, Ludwig Mus., Budapest, 1996, Fundacion Xavier Corbero, Barcelona, 1996, Kunstmus. Bonn, Germany, 1997, Kunsthistoriches Mus., Vienna, 1999, Galerie Hohenthal und Bergen, Munich, 1997, Galerie Ingrid Dacid, Tubingen, Germany, 1997, U. Arts, Phila., Domgrabungs Mus., Salzberg and N.Y., 2000, numerous others. Office: 7946 Montgomery Ave Elkins Park PA 19027-2644

ROMBERGER, JOHN ALBERT, scientist, historian; b. Klingerstown, Pa., Dec. 25, 1925; s. Ralph T. and Carrie (Bahner) Romberger; m. Margery Janet Davis, June 17, 1951; children: Ann I., Daniel D. Student, Hershey Jr. Coll., 1947—49; BA, Swarthmore Coll., 1951; MS, Pa. State U., 1954; PhD, U. Mich., 1957; postdoctoral, Calif. Inst. Th., 1957—60. Plant physiologist Forest Physiology Lab., U.S. Forest Svc., USDA, Beltsville, Md., 1961—82; vis. scientist Swedish U. Agrl. Scis., Alnarp, 1983, Inst. Agrl. Scis., Zamosc, Poland, 1985, Agrl. U., Warsaw, 1988. Editor: Internat. Rev. Forestry Rsch., 1963—70, Beltsville Symposia in Agrl. Rsch., 1976—78; contbr. articles to profl. jours.; author: Meristems, Growth and Development in Woody Plants, 1963, 1978; co-author (with Z. Hejnowicz and J.F. Hill): Plant Structure: Function and Development, 1993; co-author: Plant Structure: Function and Development, reprint edit., 2004. With U.S. Army, 1945—46. Recipient Poland U.S. Interacad. Exchange Program fellowship, U. Silesia, Katowice, 1981, 1983. Fellow: AAAS; mem.: Botanical Soc. Am., Hist. Soc. Pa., Pa. German Soc., Soc. for History Tech., Sigma Xi. Home: 320 Tennessee Ave Elizabethville PA 17023-9640 E-mail: jaromber@epix.net.

ROMEO, ANTHONY C. air transportation services executive; b. 1953; married. With Overseas Nat. Airways, Detroit, 1971-76, Fleming Internat., Miami, Fla., 1976-82; pres., dir. Miami Aircraft Support, Inc., 1981—. Prin. Charter Am., Inc., Miami, 1986—, Support Equipment Leasing, Inc., Miami, 1988—. Office: Ste 1220 9100 S Dadeland Blvd Miami FL 33156-7816

ROMEO, JOANNE JOSEFA MARINO, mathematics educator; b. Youngstown, Ohio, Nov. 21, 1943; d. Joseph James and Ann Marie (Bonamase) Marino; m. John Homer Romeo, Aug. 14, 1965; children: Christopher, Chrisanne, Jonathan. BS, Ohio State U., 1965; postgrad., Youngstown State U., 1969-70; MS, Purdue U., 1974; postgrad. in computer sci., U. Tenn., Knoxville, 1982-91. Substitute tchr., Columbus, Ohio, 1964-65; tchr. geometry, math. and French Hamilton Sch. Dist., Columbus, Ohio, 1965-66; tchr. gifted children Bluegrass Elem. Sch., Knoxville, Tenn., 1976-77; tchr. math. and sci. Webb Sch., Knoxville, 1977-85, also developer computer sci. program, 1977-85; headmistress Greenbrier Acad., Sevierville, Tenn., 1985-86; instr. math. Pellissippi State Tech. Community Coll., Knoxville, Tenn., 1986—; dir. religious edn. Sacred Heart Parish, Knoxville, Tenn., 1987—2001; tchr. advanced math. Knox County Sch., Knoxville, Tenn., 2000—. Delegate to go to Russia and Lithuania Ministries of Edn., NCEA. Vol dir. religious edn. Sacred Heart Parish, Knoxville, 1979-87, lay pastoral minister, 1988—. Mem. Nat. Council Tchrs. Math., Nat. Cath. Edn. Assn., Nat. Council Parish and Religious Coordinators and Dirs., Nat. Sci. Tchrs. Assn., Nat. Assn. Exec. Females, Ohio State U. Alumni Assn., Tenn. Assn. Dirs. Religious Edn., Purdue U. Alumni Assn., Alpha Gamma Delta. Republican. Home: 1708 Capistrano Dr Knoxville TN 37922-6302

ROMEO, PETER JOHN, lawyer; b. Darby, Pa., Aug. 1, 1942; s. Joseph Paul and Rose Marie (Beckett) R.; m. Nancy Virginia Schmidt, July 15, 1972; children: Christopher, Jeffrey, Michael. BSBA, Georgetown U., 1964; JD, George Washington U., 1967, LLM, 1969. Bar; Va. 1968, U.S. Dist. Ct. D.C. 1969, U.S. Supreme Ct. 1972; CPA, D.C. Acct. Schumaker & Yates, Washington, 1964-69; atty. U.S. Securities and Exch. Com., Washington, 1969-72, spl. counsel, 1972-79, chief counsel divsn. corp. fin., 1980-84; ptnr. Hogan & Hartson LLP, Washington, 1984—. Author: The Registration Process, 1985 (updated biannually); co-author: Comprehensive Section 16 Outline, 1984 (updated annually), Section 16 Reporting Guide, 1989, Section 16 Forms and Filing Handbook, 1991 (updated biannually), Section 16 Treatise and Reporting Guide, 1994; contbr. articles to profl. jours. Mem. ABA (mem. fed. regulation securities com.), D.C. Bar, Va. State Bar. Roman Catholic. Office: Hogan & Hartson LLP 555 13th St NW Washington DC 20004-1161 Office Phone: 202-637-5805. Business E-Mail: pjromeo@hhlaw.com.

ROMER, DANIEL, university official, psychologist, educator; b. Caracas, Venezuela, Apr. 19, 1947; arrived in U.S., 1948; s. Adolf and Eleanor (Rittermann) R.; m. Lauren B. Alloy, Jan. 4, 1985; 1 child, Adrienne. AB, Dartmouth Coll., 1969; PhD, U. Ill., Chgo., 1974. Rsch. fellow Dept Mental Health, Chgo., 1976-79; vis. asst. prof. Northwestern U., Evanston, Ill., 1979-81; adj. assoc. prof. U. Ill., 1981-89; assoc. rsch. dir. Leo Burnett Co., Chgo., 1982-89; sr. rschr. Annenberg Sch. for Comm., U. Pa., Phila., 1990—2000, sr. fellow Ctr. for Cmty. Partnerships, 1996—, rsch. dir. Inst. for Adolescent Risk Comm., 2001—. Mem. nat. expert panel on adolescent STD prevention Ctr. for Disease Control and Prevention, Atlanta, 2000-01; mem. rev. panels NIH, Washington, 1994-97, 98—. Mem. editl. bd. Jour. Exptl. Social Psychology, 1988-91, Youth and Society, 2001—; contbr. over 60 articles to psychol. and pub. health jours., chpts. to books. Grantee NIMH, 1992—, Ford Found., 1994. Mem. APA, APHA. Office: Annenberg Pub Policy Ctr 3620 Walnut St Philadelphia PA 19104 E-mail: dromer@asc.upenn.edu.

ROMER, ROBERT HORTON, physicist, researcher; b. Chgo., Apr. 15, 1931; s. Alfred Sherwood and Ruth (Hibbard) R.; m. Diana Haynes, June 12, 1953 (dec. Feb. 1992); children: Evan James, David Hibbard, Theodore Haynes; m. Betty Steele, June 25, 1994. BA, Amherst Coll., 1952; PhD in Physics, Princeton U., 1955. Faculty Amherst (Mass.) Coll., 1955—, prof. physics, 1966—2001, prof. emeritus, 2001—. Research asso. Duke, 1958-59; guest physicist Brookhaven Nat. Lab., 1963—; vis. prof. physics Voorhees Coll., 1969-70 Author: Energy—An Introduction to Physics, 1976, Energy Facts and Figures, 1984. NSF fellow Princeton, 1952-55, U. Grenoble, France, 1964-65 Fellow AAAS, Am. Phys. Soc.; mem. Am. Assn. Physics Tchrs. (asso. editor jour. 1968, book rev. editor 1982-88, editor 1988-2001), Phi Beta Kappa, Sigma Xi. Achievements include research in low temperature physics, solar energy, electromagnetic theory. Home: 104 Spring St Amherst MA 01002-2332 E-mail: rhromer@amherst.edu.

ROMER, ROY R. Superintendent Los Angeles Unified School District, former governor; b. Garden City, Kans., Oct. 31, 1928; s. Irving Rudolph and Margaret Elizabeth (Snyder) R.; m. Beatrice Miller, June 10, 1952; children: Paul, Mark, Mary, Christopher, Timothy, Thomas, Elizabeth BS in Agrl. Econs., Colo. State U., 1950; LL.B., U. Colo., 1952; postgrad., Yale U. Bar: Colo. 1952. Engaged in farming in Colo., 1942-52; ind. practice law, 1955-66; mem. Colo. Ho. of Reps., 1958-62, Colo. Senate, 1962-66; owner, operator Arapahoe Aviation Co., Colo. Flying Acad., Geneva Basin Ski Area; engaged in home site devel.; owner chain farm implement and indsl. equipment stores; commr. agr. State of Colo., 1975, chief staff, exec. asst. to gov., 1975-77, 83-84, state treas., 1977-86, gov., 1987-98; chmn. Dem. Nat. Com., 1997—2000; superintendent Los Angeles Unified Sch. Dist., 2000—. Chmn. Gov. Colo. Blue Ribbon Panel, Gov. Colo. Small Bus. Council; mem. agrl. adv. com. Colo. Bd. Agr. Bd. editors Colo. U. Law Rev., 1960-62. Past trustee Iliff Sch. Theology, Denver; mem., past chmn. Nat. Edn. Goals Panel; co-chmn. Nat. Coun. on Standards and Testing; mem. adv. bd. Ad Coun.; former chair Dem. Nat. Com., now chair Dem. Nat. Conv. Com. With USAF, 1952-53. Mem. Dem. Gov.'s Assn. (chmn.), Nat. Gov.'s Assn. (former chmn.), Colo. Bar Assn., Order of the Coif. Democrat. Presbyterian. Office: LA Unified Sch District 333 S Beaudry Ave Los Angeles CA 90017*

ROMERIL, BARRY D. office equipment company executive; CFO Xerox Corp., Stamford, Conn. Office: Xerox Corp PO Box 1600 800 Long Ridge Rd Stamford CT 06904

ROMERO, ANTHONY D. legal association administrator; b. N.Y.C. Grad., Princeton U., Stanford U. With Rockefeller found.; program officer for civil rights and racial justice Ford Founds. Human Rights and Internat. Cooperation Program; exec. dir. ACLU, N.Y.C., 2001—. Dinkelspiel scholar, Stanford U., Cane scholar, Princeton U., Nat. Hispanic scholar, Stanford U., Princeton U. Mem.: Coun. on Fgn. Rels., N.Y. State Bar Assn. Office: ACLU 18th Fl 125 Broad St New York NY 10004

ROMERO, EDWARD L. diplomat, environmental engineering executive; b. Albuquerque, Jan. 2, 1934; m. Cayetana Garcia; 4 children. Student, L.A. State Coll., 1955-59, Citrus Coll. Founder, chmn., CEO, Advanced Scis., Inc. (merged with Commodore Applied Techs.), Albuquerque, 1976-98; amb. to Spain, Am. Embassy, Madrid, 1998—. Former mem. U.S. Trade Rep.'s Svcs. Policy Adv. Com., leader numerous U.S. dels. to Mex.; former mem. fed. adv. com. for trade negotiations; former mem. U.S. del. to Helsinki Accords. Active numerous civic and charitable orgns.; former mem. President's Hispanic Adv. Com.; bd. dirs. Congl. Hispanic Caucus Inst. With U.S. Army, Korea. Recipient numerous awards from various orgns., including Nat. Kidney Found., N.Y. Anti-Defamation League, Nat. Hispanic Scholarship Found., Multiple Sclerosis Soc.; named Nat. Hispanic Businessman of Yr., Hispanic C. of C., 1989. Mem. Albuquerque Hispanic C. of C. (founder). Office: Am Embassy Madrid Spain PS6 61 Box 43 APO AE 09642

ROMERO, JESSE CHARLES, political consultant; b. Corpus Christi, Tex., Nov. 4, 1960; s. Juan Leos and Amelia Ramirez Romero; m. Anna Alicia Arteaga, June 2, 1991; children: Emiliano Sandino, Antonio Cesar, Victor Aetius Emmanuel. BA, S.W. Tex. State U., 1987. Field organizer S.W. Voter Registration Edn. Project, San Antonio, 1987—90; exec. dir. Mexican Am. Legis. Caucus, Austin, Tex., 1991—93; spl. asst. State Senator Rodney Ellis, Austin, Tex., 1994—95; policy analyst Mexican Am. Legal Def. Ednl. Fund, San Antonio, 1995—97; spl. projects dir. Congressman Ciro Rodriguez, San Antonio, 1997—2000; S.W. dir. Ctr. Policy Alternatives, Washington, 2000—03; ptnr. Haley, Romero & Winick, Austin, 2004—. Dir. Adelante Con Clinton, Austin, Tex., 1992; dir. latino vote Dem. Congl. Campaign Com., Washington, 2002. Recipient Aguila Activism award, Mexican Am. Dems., 1992, Chmn.'s Advocacy award, Tex. Assn. Mexican Am. C. of C., 1997. Mem.: YMCA, San Antonio Hispanic C. of C. (legis. adv. bd. 1995—). Roman Catholic. Avocations: basketball, football, softball, weightlifting. Office: Haley Romero & Winick Ste 200 815 Brazos St Austin TX 78701 Personal E-mail: romero.jesse@sbcglobal.net.

ROMERO, JORGE ANTONIO, neurologist, educator; b. Bayamon, P.R., Apr. 15, 1948; s. Calixto Antonio Romero-Barcelo and Antonia (de Juan) R.; m. Helen Mella, June 20, 1970 (div. 1983); children: Sofia, Jorge, Alfredo, Isabel; m. Cheryl Raps, Aug. 1994; 1 child, Jessica. SB, MIT, 1968; MD, Harvard U., 1972. Diplomate Am. Bd. Psychiatry and Neurology. Intern U. Chgo. Hosp. and Clinics, 1972-73; resident Mass. Gen. Hosp., Boston, 1975-78; rsch. fellow in pharmacology NIMH, Bethesda, Md., 1973-75; asst. prof. neurology Harvard Med. Sch., Boston, 1979-92; mem. staff VA Med. Ctr., Brockton, Mass., 1979-92; assoc. physician Brigham and Women's Hosp., Boston, 1980-92; chmn. dept. neurology Ochsner Clin. Baton Rouge, 1993-97; assoc. clin. prof. neurology La. State U. Sch. Medicine, 1996-97; attending physician Baylor U. Med. Ctr., Dallas, 2002—. Cons. Mass. Mental Health Ctr., Boston, 1987-92. With USPHS, 1973-75. Recipient Career Devel. award VA, 1979. Mem. Am. Acad. Neurology. Office: 3600 Gaston Ave Dallas TX 75246 Office Phone: 214-827-5525. E-mail: rneurology@sbcglobal.net.

ROMERO, JOSEFINO TABERNILLA, nurse anesthetist; b. Tayabas, Quezon, The Philippines; came to U.S., 1963; s. Melanio Merca and Teodorica (Tabernilla) R. Diploma, Quezon Meml. Hosp., 1961; cert. nurse anesthetist, Mt. Carmel Hosp., Detroit, 1968; D in Art, U. Found., Malta, 1986. RN, Mich. Psychiat. nurse Nat. Mental Hosp., Manila, 1961-63; operating room nurse St. Vincent Hosp., Worcester, Mass., 1963-64, Michael Reese Hosp., Chgo., 1964-65, Sarnia (Canada) Gen. Hosp., 1965-66; operating room nurse, nurse anesthetist Quezon Meml. Hosp., 1971-72; nurse anesthetist Mt. Carmel Hosp., 1973-74, Brent Hosp., Detroit, 1974-86, Straith Hosp., Southfield, Mich., 1986—. Exhibited paintings in numerous one-man shows including Beijing Internat. Conv. Ctr., 1991, Pontiac Art Ctr., 1989, Troy Libr. and Gallery, 1989, Scarab Club Detroit, 1989, Lawrence St. Gallery, Pontiac, Mich., 1989, Acad. Art Gallery, Paris, 1988, Gallert in the Grove, Canada, 1987, Southfield Civic Ctr., 1986, Electric Fantasy Gallery, 1986, Philippine Orgn. and Filipino Artists, Chgo., 1978, others; exhibited in several group shows including Detroit Press Club, 1989, Mich. Design Ctr., 1988, Philippine Cultural Ctr., Ayala Mus., Casa de Communidad de Tayabas, 1997, Seattle Asian Art Mus., 1997, Gov.'s Mansion-The Philippine, 1998, Galleria Romero, The Philippines, 1998. Named one of Outstanding Men. Mich., City of Detroit, 1976, Outstanding Alumnus quezon Meml. Hosp. Sch. Nursing, 1994; recipient Albert Einstein award Internat. Acad. Found., 1991, Merit award Mich. Ann. Art Festival, 1975, Cert. of Appreciation Gov. of Mich., 1986, Quezon medal honor (The Philippines), 1997. Mem. Am. Assn. Nurse Anesthetists, Mich. Assn. Nurse Anesthetists, Filipino Nurse Assn., Beijing Watercolor Soc., Scarab Club Detroit (bd. dirs. 1988—), Knights of Rizal, Internat. Assn. Educators for World Peace. Roman Catholic. Avocations: photography, travel, tennis. Home: 2230 S Shore Ct Rochester Hills MI 48307

ROMERO, RICHARD M. state legislator, educator; b. Oakland, July 21, 1944; divorced. BS in Edn., U. Albuquerque, 1967; MA in Edn. Adminstrn., N.Mex. State U., 1971. Ednl. adminstr.; mem. N. Mex. Senate, Dist. 12, Santa Fe, 1992—; mem. rules com.; vice chair ways and means com.; pres. N. Mex. Senate, Dist. 12, Santa Fe, 2002—. Mem. Metro bd. YMCA. With USAF, 1968-69. Democrat. Office: 907 Silver Ave SW Albuquerque NM 87102-3002

ROMERO-BARCELO, CARLOS ANTONIO, former congressman, former governor of Puerto Rico, former mayor of San Juan; b. Sept. 4, 1932; s. Antonio S. Romero and Josefina Barceló; m. Kathleen Donnelly, Jan. 2, 1966; children: Juan Carlos, Melinda Kathleen; children by previous marriage: Carlos, Andrés. BA, Yale U., 1953; LLB, U. P.R., 1956; LLD (hon.), U. Bridgeport, 1977. Bar: P.R. 1956. Mem. Herrero-Frank & Romero-Barceló, 1956-58; ptnr. Rivera-Zayas, Rivera-Cestero & Rúa, San Juan, 1958-63, Segurola, Romero & Toledo, San Juan, 1963-68; pres. Citizens for State 51, San Juan, 1965-67; mayor San Juan, PR, 1969-77; gov. P.R., 1977-85; pres. New Progressive Party, San Juan, 1974-85, 89-91; P.R.'s at-large rep. U.S. Ho. Reps., Washington, 1992-2000; mem. edn. and workforce and resources com. 106th Congress, also ranking mem. pub. lands and nat. parks subcom. New Progressive. Office: Centro de Seguros Bldg 701 Ponce de Leon Ave # 412 San Juan PR 00907 E-mail: rbarcelo@prtc.net.

ROMERO-RAINEY, REBECA, bank executive; d. Martin and Cheryl Romero; m. John Rainey. Degree, Wellesley Coll. Pres., CEO Centinal Bank Taos, N.Mex., 1999—, bd. dir., 1999—. Bd. admissions Wellesley Coll. V.p. Taos Chpt. Habitat for Humanity; sec., treas. Bridges Project Edn. Taos; mem. Leadership N.Mex.; treas. N.Mex. Cmty. Found.; bd. dir. Taos (N.Mex.) Feeds Taos; treas. bd. dirs. Rocky Mountain Youth Corps. Named One of 25 Women to Watch, U.S. Banker Mag., 2003. Mem.: Ind. Cmty. Bankers Assn. N.Mex. (bd. dir. 2003—).

ROMESBURG, KERRY D. university president, former state education administrator; b. Akron, Ohio, Mar. 12, 1945; s. Bert Lewis and Edna (Bartlett) R.; m. Judy Kaye Land, July 2, 1965; children: Rod A., Donald A. BA, Ariz. State U., 1967, MA, 1968, PhD, 1972. Tchr. math. East H.S., Phoenix, 1969-70; asst. dir. instl. rsch. Ariz. State U., Tempe, 1972-73; planning analyst Ariz. Bd. Regents, Phoenix, 1973-74; exec. dir. Ariz. Commn. Post Secondary Edn., Phoenix, 1974-75, Alaska Commn. Postsecondary Edn., Juneau, 1975; pres. Utah Valley St. Coll., Orem, Utah, 1996—. Mem. Western Interstate Commn. on Higher Edn., Boulder, Colo., 1977—, chmn., 1981-82; mem. Western Tech. Manpower Coun., 1982—; mem. Nat. Adv. Coun. for United Student Aid Funds, N.Y.C., 1978—. Recipient Outstanding Alumnus award Ariz. State U., 1982; NDEA fellow, 1972. Mem. State Higher Edn. Exec. Officers, Nat. Adv. Coun. State Postsecondary Planning Commns., Am. Assn. Higher Edn., NEA.

ROMEY, WILLIAM DOWDEN, geologist, educator; b. Richmond, Ind., Oct. 26, 1930; s. William Minter and Grace Warring (Dowden) R.; m. Lucretia Alice Leonard, July 16, 1955; children: Catherine Louise Keener, Gretchen Elizabeth Tanzer, William Leonard. AB with highest honors, Ind. U., 1952; student, U. Paris, 1950—51, student, 1952—53; PhD, U. Calif., Berkeley, 1962. Asst. prof. geology and sci. edn. Syracuse (NY) U., 1962-66, assoc. prof., 1966-69; exec. dir. earth sci. ednl. program Am. Geol. Inst., 1969-72; prof., chmn. dept. geology St. Lawrence U., Canton, NY, 1971-76, prof., 1976—93, prof., chmn. dept. geography, 1983-93, prof. emeritus, 1993—. Ednl. cons., 1962—; NAS visitor USSR Acad. Sci., 1967; vis. geoscientist Am. Geol. Inst., 1964-66, 71; earth sci. cons. Compton's Ency., 1970-71; adj. prof. Union Grad. Sch., 1974-2000; bd. rsch. advisors and readers Walden U., 1981-2000; prof. Grad. Sch. Am., 1993-99; travel writer and cruise ship lectr., 1990-; bd. dirs. Ctr. for Internat. Environ. Law, Project on Ethnic Rels.; pres. Peachem Cmty. Housing. Author: (with others) Investigating the Earth, 1967, (with J. Kramer, E. Muller, J. Lewis) Investigations in Geology, 1967, Inquiry Techniques for Teaching Science, 1968, Risk-Trust-Love, 1972, Consciousness and Creativity, 1975, Confluent Education in Science, 1976, Plus Ça Change..., 1996, Illustrated Guide to the Geology of commonly visited sites on the Antarctic Peninsula, South Georgia, and the Falkland Islands, 2004; co-editor: Geochemical Prospecting for Petroleum, 1959; assoc. editor: Jour. Coll. Sci. Tchg., 1972-74, Geol. Soc. Am. Bull., 1979-84, Jour. Geol. Edn., 1980—2003; editor-in-chief: Ash Lad Press, 1975—; contbr. articles to profl. jours. Bd. dirs. Onondaga Nature Ctrs., Inc., 1966—69. Served to lt. j.g. USNR, 1953—57, lt. comdr. res., 1957—66. Woodrow Wilson Found. fellow, 1959-60, 61-62; NSF sci. faculty fellow U. Oslo, 1967-68. Fellow AAAS, Geol. Soc. Am., Explorers Club; mem. Nat. Assn. Geology Tchrs. (v.p. 1971-72), N.Y. Acad. Scis., Nat. Assn. Geology Tchrs. (pres. 1972-73), Assn. Am. Geographers, Am. Geophys. Union, Geol. Soc. Norway, Can. Assn. Geographers, Assn. for Can. Studies in U.S., Phi Beta Kappa, Sigma Xi, Phi Delta Kappa. Home and Office: PO Box 294 East Orleans MA 02643-0294 Office Phone: 508-255-2301.

ROMEYN, PRESCOTT C. venture capitalist; BA, Dartmouth Coll.; MBA, Amos Tuck Sch. Bus. Adminstrn. With merchant banking group Shearson Lehman Hutton, Inc.; various positions including mng. dir. AEA Investors, Inc., 1988—99; mng. dir. Perry Ptnrs., 2000—01; prin. Kohlberg & Co., 2001—. Office: Kohlberg & Co 111 Radio Cir Mount Kisco NY 10549 Office Phone: 914-241-7430. Office Fax: 914-241-7476.

ROMIG, ALTON DALE, JR., materials scientist, educator; b. Bethlehem, Pa., Oct. 6, 1953; s. Alton Dale and Christine (Groh) R.; m. Julie H. Romig. BS, Lehigh U., 1975, MS, 1977, PhD, 1979. Metallurgist, tech. staff Sandia Nat. Labs., Albuquerque, 1979-87, supr. phys. metallurgy, 1987-90, mgr. metallurgy, 1990-92, dir. materials and process scis., 1992-95; dir. Microelectronics and Photonics, 1995-98, Microsys. Sci., Tech. and Components, 1998-99; v.p. Sci. Tech. and Components, 1999—2000, Sci. Tech. & Partner-

ships, Albuquerque, 2000—, chief tech. officer, 2001—. Part time full prof. N.Mex. Inst. Mining and Tech., Socorro, 1981—; Acta/Scripta Metallurgica Lectr., 1993. Author: Principles of Analytical Electron Mecroscopy, 1986, Scanning Electron Microscopy, X-ray Microanalysis and Analytical Electron Microscopy, 1991, Scanning Electron Microscopy and Microanalysis, 1992; editor numerous procs. in phys. metallurgy and electron microscopy; contbr. over 160 articles to sci. jours. Fellow Am. Soc. Metals Internat. (trustee 1992-95, v.p. 1996-97, pres. 1997-98, Outstanding Rsch. award 1992); mem. TMS, Electron Microscopy Soc. Am. (Burton Outstanding Young Sci. medal 1988), Microbeam Analysis Soc. (pres. 1990, Heinrich award for Outstanding Young Sci. 1991), Materials Rsch. Soc., Sigma Xi, Tau Beta Pi. Home: 304 Big Horn Ridge Pl NE Albuquerque NM 87122-1446 Office: Sandia Nat Labs M/S 0513 Divsn 1000 Albuquerque NM 87185 E-mail: adromi@sandia.gov.

ROMIG, EDGAR DUTCHER, clergyman; b. N.Y.C., July 6, 1921; s. Edgar Franklin and Ella Woodruff (Dutcher) R. BA, Princeton U., 1942; MDiv, Episcopal Theol. Sch., Mass., l95l; DD (hon.), Va. Theol. Sem., 1969. Ordained deacon Episcopal Ch., l95l, priest, l952. Asst. minister Trinity Ch., Boston, 1951-53; rector Grace Ch., North Attleboro, Mass., 1953-58, St. Stephen's Ch., Lynn, Mass., 1958-64, Ch. of Epiphany, Washington, 1964-92. Dep. Episcopal Gen. Conv., 1973, 76, 79, 82, 85, 88, 91. Author: Trinity Church in the City of Boston, l953; contbr. articles to various jours. Ambulance driver Am. Field Svc., l942-43, NATOUSA; with AUS, l943-45, ETO. Decorated Bronze Star, Purple Heart. Mem. Century Club (N.Y.C.), Princeton Club (N.Y.C.), Met. Club. Democrat. Home: 4000 Cathedral Ave NW Apt 217B Washington DC 20016-5265

ROMIG, JAMES, composer, educator; b. Long Beach, Calif., Aug. 5, 1971; s. James Lyle and Angela Carroll Romig. MusB, U. of Iowa, 1993, MA, 1996; PhD, Rutgers U., 2000. Vis. lectr. Rutgers U., New Brunswick, NJ, 1998—2000; vis. asst. prof. Bucknell U., Lewisburg, Pa., 2001—02; asst. prof. Western Ill. U., Macomb, Ill., 2002—. Music dir., prin. condr. The Soc. Chromatic Art, N.Y.C., 1997—. Nominee 2003 Awards in Music, AAAL, 2003; recipient Std. award, ASCAP, 1998—2002, Pierre Boulez Workshop award, Carnegie Hall, 1999; fellow, Rutgers U., 1998—99; Meet the Composer grant, 2003. Mem.: ASCAP (Std. award 1999, 2000, 2001, finalist Rudolf Nissim award 2002, Std. award 2002, 1998), Soc. for Music Theory, Composers Guild of NJ., Coll. Music Soc., Am. Music Ctr., Pi Kappa Lambda. Office: Western Illinois University Department of Music Macomb IL 61455 E-mail: jromig@jamesromig.com.

ROMIG, THOMAS J. military officer; b. Manhattan, Kans., Dec. 27, 1948; Grad., Nat. War Coll., Armed Forces Staff Coll.; BS, Kans. State U., 1970; JD with honors, Santa Clara U., 1980. Commd. U.S. Army, 1971, advanced through grades to maj. gen., mil. intelligence officer, Ft. Huachuca, Ariz.; trial counsel, sr. trial counsel, chief of legal assistance and chief criminal law 2d Armored Divsn., Ft. Hood, Tex., 1980—83; instr. internat. and operational law Judge Advocate Gen.'s Sch., Charlottesville, Va., 1984—87, plans officer, pers., plans and tng. office, 1988—90; staff judge advocate 32d Army Air Def. Command, Darmstadt, Germany, 1990—93, chief pers./asst. chief pers., plans and tng. office, 1993—95; staff judge advocate V Corps, Heidelberg, Germany and Taszar, Hungary, 1996—98; asst. judge advocate gen. for mil. law and ops. Office of the Judge Advocate Gen., Rosslyn, Va., 1998, judge advocate gen. Washington. Decorated Legion of Merit, Meritorious Svc. medal with 4 oak leaf clusters, Army Commendation medal, Army Achievement medal, Nat. Def. Svc. medal with 1 bronze service star, Armed Forces Svc. medal, NATO medal. Office: Office of the Judge Advocate General US Army Pentagon Washington DC 20310-1500

ROMIJN-STAMOS, REBECCA, actress, model; b. Berkeley, Calif., Nov. 6, 1972; m. John Stamos, Sept. 19, 1998; children: Jaap Romihn Stamos, Elizabeth Kuizenga Stamos. Attended, U. Calif., Santa Cruz. Model Sports Illustrated, Christian Dior, Victoria's Secret, Biotherm, Clarins, Dillards, Escada, Furla, Got Milk?, J.Crew, La Senza, Liz Claiborne, Matrix Essentials, Maybelline, Pantene Pro V, Tommy Hilfiger, various others. Actor: (films) Dirty Work, 1998, X-Men, 2000, Rollerball, 2002, Femme Fatale, 2002, X2, 2003, The Punisher, 2004, Godsend, 2004; (TV films) Hefner: Unauthorized, 1999; (TV series) Just Shoot Me, 1999—2000. Mailing: c/o Bragman/Nyman/Cafarelli 9171 Wilshire Blvd Ste 300 Beverly Hills CA 90210

ROMINE, JEFFREY LEE, chemist; b. Chicago, Ill., Oct. 13, 1959; s. Edward Lee and Loretta Jean Romine; m. Karen Lynn Lewis, June 12, 1982; children: Jacqueline Marie, Amanda Jean, Joshua Lee, Elizabeth Lynn, Benjamin John, Joseph Ronald. PhD, Ohio State U., 1982—87. Group leader medicinal chemistry Bristol-Myers Squibb, Wallingford, Conn., 1989—. Achievements include patents for Potassium Channel Modulators (3); Platelet Aggregation Inhibitors (2). Office: Bristol-Myers Squibb 5 Research Pkwy Wallingford CT 06492 E-mail: rominej@bms.com.

ROMITA, MAURO CHARLES, plastic surgeon; b. N.Y.C., Jan. 16, 1947; MD, U. Miami, 1973. Diplomate Am. Bd. Surgery, Am. Bd. Plastic Surgery. Resident, fellow NYU Med. Ctr., 1974—81; pvt. practice plastic surgery N.Y.C., 1999—. Attending physician St. Vincent Hosp. Med. Ctr., N.Y.C.; asst. clin. prof. surgery N.Y. Med. Coll. Mem. Boys Town of Italy; bd. govs. Sound Shore Med. Ctr. Mem.: Am. Soc. Plastic Surgeons. Office: 853 5th Ave New York NY 10021-5802*

ROMJUE, JOHN LAWSON, historian, writer; b. Washington, D.C., Oct. 4, 1936; s. Lawson Rodney Romjue, Joanne Romjue; m. Ingeborg Gertrud Schaefer, Mar. 25, 1961; children: Martin John, Kristin Elisabeth. BA in History and Polit. Sci., U. Mo., 1962, MA in Modern European History and German Lit., 1963. Staff historian USN Facilities Enging. Command, Port Hueneme, Calif., 1966—69; command historian US Army Combat Devel. Experimentation, Fort Ord, Calif., 1969—74; staff historian, dep. staff historian field programs Mil. Hist. Office US Army Tng. and Doctrine Command, Fort Monroe, Va., 1974—85, chief hist. studies and publs. Mil. Hist. Office, 1985—98. Author: American Army Doctrine for the Post-Cold War, 1996, The Army of Excellence, 1993, Out of the Riven Century, 2001. Specialist 5 U.S. Army, 1957—61. Grantee Fulbright Commn., 1963—64. Mem.: Va. Writers Club (1st v.p. 1995—96, bd. govs. 1997—2001). Republican. Lutheran. Home: 105 Lochmere Ct Yorktown VA 23693

ROMNEY, CARL F. seismologist; b. Salt Lake City, June 5, 1924; m. Barbara Doughty; children: Carolyn Ann, Kim. BS in Meteorology, Calif. Inst. Tech., 1945; PhD, U. Calif., Berkeley, 1956. Seismologist U.S. Dept. Air Force, 1955-58; asst. tech. dir. Air Force Tech. Applications Center, 1958-73; dep. dir. Nuclear Monitoring Research Office, Def. Advanced Research Projects Agy., 1973-75, dir., 1975-79; dep. dir. Def. Advanced Research Projects Agy., 1979-83; dir. Ctr. Seismic Studies, 1983-91; v.p. Sci. Applications Internat. Corp., 1987—2001. Tech. adviser U.S. reps. in negotiations Test Ban Treaty; mem. U.S. del. Geneva Conf. Experts, 1958, Conf. on Discontinuance Nuclear Weapons Tests, 1959, 60; negotiations on threshold Test Ban Treaty, Moscow, 1974; mem. U.S. del. Peaceful Nuclear Explosions Treaty, Moscow, 1974-75 Contbr. articles to tech. jours. Recipient Exceptional Civilian Service awards Air Force, 1959, Exceptional Civilian Service awards Dept. Def., 1964, 79; Pres.'s award for Distinguished Fed. Civilian Service, for outstanding contbns. to devel. of control system for underground nuclear tests, 1967; Presdl. Rank of Meritorious Exec., 1980; inducted in Hall of Honor, Air Intelligence Agy., 1996. Achievements include research on earthquake mechanism, seismic noise; generation, propagation, detection seismic waves from underground explosions. Home: 4105 Sulgrave Dr Alexandria VA 22309-2629 E-mail: cromney@earthlink.net.

ROMNEY, RICHARD BRUCE, lawyer; b. Kingston, Jamaica, Dec. 29, 1942; came to U.S., 1945, naturalized, 1956; s. Frank Oswald and Mary Ellen (Burton) R.; m. Beverly Cochran, Sept. 11, 1965 (dec. 1984); children: Richard Bruce, Jr., Stephanie Cochran; m. Lynthia H. Walker, Aug. 14, 1988; children: Alisa Dawn, Kristen Elizabeth. BA, U. Pa., 1964; JD, U. Va., 1972. Bar: N.Y. 1973, U.S. Ct. Appeals (2d cir.) 1975. Assoc. Dewey, Ballantine, Bushby, Palmer & Wood, N.Y.C., 1972—80, ptnr., 1981—. Mem. editl. bd. U. Va. Law Rev., 1970-72. Lt. USN, 1964—68. Mem. ABA, N.Y. State Bar Assn., Assn. Bar City N.Y., Order of Coif. Home: 35 Deerfield Rd Chappaqua NY 10514-1604 Office: Dewey Ballantine LLP 1301 Ave Americas New York NY 10019-6022 Office Phone: 212-259-6480. Personal E-mail: rromney@aol.com. Business E-Mail: rromney@dbllp.com.

ROMNEY, SEYMOUR LEONARD, physician, educator; b. N.Y.C., June 8, 1917; s. Benjamin and Anne (Senter) Romney; m. Shirley Gordon, Nov. 4, 1945; children: Benjamin, Tim, Anne. AB, Johns Hopkins, 1938; MD, N.Y. U., 1942. Intern Beth Israel Hosp., Boston, 1942-43; resident Boston Lying-in Hosp., Free Hosp. for Women, Boston, 1946-51; fellow, instr. Harvard Med. Sch., 1947-51, asst. prof. obstetrics and gynecology, 1951-57; prof., chmn. dept. gynecology and obstetrics Albert Einstein Coll. Medicine, N.Y.C., 1957-72, prof., 1972-89, prof. emeritus, 1989—, dir. research gynecol. oncology, 1972—. Dir. obstetrics and gynecology Bronx Mcpl. Hosp. Ctr., N.Y.C., 1957-72; cons. WHO, Geneva, 1969-70. Founding chair Soc. of Physicians for Reproductive Choice and Health; bd. dirs. NARAL, N.Y.; mem. Nat. Abortion and Reproductive Rights Action League, N.Y. Abortion and Reproductive Rights Action League. Served to lt. M.C. USNR, 1943-45. Mem. ACOG, AAAS, Am. Assn. Med. Colls. (life), Am. Gynecol. and Obstet. Soc., Soc. Gynecologic Investigation, Am. Assn. Cancer Rsch., Population Assn. Am., N.Y. Obstet. Soc., N.Y. Acad. Medicine, N.Y. Acad. Sci. Home: Glenbrooke Dr White Plains NY 10605-5008 Office: Einstein Coll Morris Park Ave Bronx NY 10461-2534

ROMNEY, W. MITT, governor; b. Detroit, Mar. 12, 1947; s. George W. and Lenore (Lafount) R.; m. Ann D., Mar. 21, 1969; children: Taggart, Matthew, Joshua, Benjamin, Craig. BA, Brigham Young U., 1971; JD, MBA, Harvard U., 1975. Cons. Boston Consuting Group, 1975-77, Bain & Co., Boston, 1977-78, v.p., 1978-84, chmn., CEO, 1991—2001; mng. ptnr., CEO Bain Capital, Inc., Boston, 1984—2001; pres., CEO Salt Lake Organizing Com. (Winter Olympics), Utah, 1999—2002; gov. State of Mass., 2003—. Bd. dirs. Marriott Corp., Bethesda, Md., Staples Inc., Framingham, Mass., Babbages Inc., Dallas, Tex., Damon Corp., Needham, Mass. Pres. Boston Stake LDS Ch., 1986-1994; adv. bd. Brigham Young U. Sch. Bus., Provo, Utah, 1990—; vis. com. Harvard Bus. Sch., Cambridge, Mass; mem. nat. exec. bd. Boy Scouts Am.; trustee Belmont (Mass.) Hill Sch., 1989—. Baker scholar Harvard Bus. Sch., Cambridge, Mass., 1975. Mem. Belmont Hill Club. Office: Gov Office State House Rm 360 Boston MA 02133 also: Bain Capital 111 Huntington Ave Ste 3500 Boston MA 02199-7615

ROMOFF, JEFFREY ALAN, health care executive; b. N.Y.C., Nov. 30, 1945; s. Richard Warren and Evelyn (Alter) Romoff; m. Vivian Irene Goodman, Aug. 25, 1966 (dec. June 1983); children: Jennifer Ann, Rebecca Lynn; m. Stefania Ferrarese, Dec. 2002. BS magna cum laude in Social Scis., CCNY, 1967; M.Phil. in Polit. Scis., Yale U., 1971. Teaching fellow Yale U., 1969-70, teaching assoc., 1970-71; exec. dir. Central Naugatuck Valley Mental Health Council, Waterbury, Conn., 1971-73; regional programing dir. Western Psychiat. Inst. and Clinic (U. Pitts.), 1973-74, assoc. dir. div. edn. and research, 1974-75; assoc. dir. Western Psychiat. Inst. and Clinic, 1975—86; adj. asst. prof. pub. health U. Pitts., 1981—, instr. psychiatry, 1982—, assoc. v.p. health scis., 1984-86, vice chancellor health scis., 1986-92, sr. vice chancellor for Health Adminstrn., 1992—96; exec. v.p. U. Pitts. Med. Ctr., 1986-92, pres., 1992—. N.Y.C. Regents scholar CCNY, 1963-67 Mem. Am. Hosp. Assn. (governing coun. sect. for mental health and psychiat. scvs. 1986-89), Am. Psychiat. Assn. (chmn. joint com. with Am. Hosp. Assn. 1983-84), Hosp. Assn. Pa., Coun. Psychiat. Svc. Providers (exec. com. 1981-84) Jewish. Home: 3208 Fox Run Rd Allison Park PA 15101-1506 Office: U Pitts Med Ctr Forbes Tower 200 Lothrop St Ste 11045 Pittsburgh PA 15213-2546*

ROMPALA, RICHARD M. chemical company executive; B in Liberal Arts and Chem. Engring., Columbia U.; MBA, Harvard U. Bus. mgr. Olin Corp.; sr. v.p. ops. Mueller Brass Co.; joined PPG Industries, 1985, v.p. corp. devel., group v.p. chems., group v.p. coatings and resins; pres. Valspar Corp., Mpls., 1994, CEO, 1995—, chmn., 1998. Office: The Valspar Corp 1101 Third St S Minneapolis MN 55415

RON, AMOS, computer scientist, educator, mathematician; m. Michal Ron; children: Daphna, Tal, Eyal D. PhD, Tel Aviv U., 1987. Prof. computer sci. and math. U. Wis., Madison, 1988—. Editor in chief Jour. Approximation Theory, Columbus, Ohio, 2000—; coord. Wavelet IDR Ctr., Madison, 1998—. Office: U Wis 1210 West Dayton Madison WI 53706 Office Phone: 608-262-6621. E-mail: amos@cs.wisc.edu.

RONALD, PETER, utilities executive; b. Duluth, Minn., Aug. 26, 1926; s. George W. and Florence (Jones) R.; m. Mary Locke Boyd, Nov. 25, 1950; children: Peter Webb, Pauline Morton, Samuel Herschel. BA, U. Va., 1950. With Louisville Gas & Electric Co., 1950-88, treas., 1962—, v.p., 1969-82, sr. v.p., 1982-88, dir., 1979-89. Bd. dirs., mem. exec. com. Bus. Devel. Corp. Ky., 1967-75, pres., 1971-72; bd. dirs. Louisville Community Chest, 1967-72, v.p., 1969-72; bd. dirs., v.p. Louisville Rehab. Ctr., 1964-82, pres., 1970-71; bd. overseers Louisville Country Day Sch., 1967-70; trustee Children's Hosp. Found., 1978-81, sec.-treas., 1978-81; bd. govs. Captiva (Fla.) Civic Assn., 1990-94, v.p., 1992; commr. Captiva, Fla. Erosion Prevention Dist., 1996-98. With USNR, 1945-46. Mem. Louisville Country Club, Captiva Yacht Club, Zeta Psi. Home: 4710 Indian Hills Green Louisville KY 40207-1366 also: PO Box 877 Captiva FL 33924

RONALTER, CHELSEA MARIA, artist, graphic designer; b. Manchester, N.H., Jan. 30, 1974; d. Donald E. and Lynn Elise Ronalter. AA in Comml. Design and Illustration, Manchester Cmty. Tech. Coll., 1997; AA in Interior Design summa cum laude, Hesser Coll., Manchester, 2001; postgrad., Notre Dame Coll., Manchester, 2001—. Graphic designer Notre Dame Coll., Manchester, NH, 1998—2002; instl. advancement So. NH U., Manchester, 2002—. Event planner Notre Dame Coll., Manchester, NH, 1999—2000. Mem.: Phi Theta Kappa. Roman Catholic. Avocations: art, literature, history. Office: So NH Univ 2500 N River Rd Manchester NH 03106 Home: 31 English Village Rd Apt 305 Manchester NH 03102-2498

RONAN, WILLIAM JOHN, management consultant; b. Buffalo, Nov. 8, 1912; s. William and Charlotte (Ramp) R.; m. Elena Vinadé, May 29, 1939; children: Monica, Diana Quasha. AB, Syracuse U., 1934; PhD, NYU, 1940, LLD, 1969; certificate, Geneva Sch. Internat. Studies, 1933. Mus. asst. Buffalo Mus. Sci., 1928-30; with Niagara-Hudson Power Co., 1931; transfer dept. N.Y.C.R.R., 1932; Penfield fellow internat. law, diplomacy and belles lettres, 1935; Univ. fellow, 1936; editor Fed. Bank Service, Prentice-Hall, Inc., 1937; instr. govt. N.Y. U., 1938, exec. sec. grad. div. for tng. in pub. services, 1938, asst. dir., 1940, asst. prof. govt., dir. grad. div. for tng. pub. service, 1940, assoc. prof. govt., 1946-47, prof., 1947, dean, grad. sch. pub. adminstrn. and social service, 1953-58; Cons. N.Y.C. Civil Service Commn., 1938; prin. rev. officer, negotiations officer U.S. Civil Service Commn., 1942; prin. div. asst. U.S. Dept. State, 1943; cons. Dept. State, 1948, Dept. Def., 1954; dir. studies N.Y. State Coordination Commn., 1951-58; project mgr. N.Y. U.-U. Ankara project, 1954-59; cons. ICA, 1955, N.Y. State Welfare Conf.; adminstrv. co-dir. Albany Grad. Program in Pub. Adminstrn.; 1st dep. city adminstr. N.Y.C., 1956-57; exec. dir. N.Y. State Temporary Commn. Constl. Conv., 1956-58; sec. to Gov. N.Y., 1959-66; chmn. interdept. com. traffic safety, commr. Port Authority N.Y. and N.J., 1967-90, vice chmn., 1972-74, chmn., 1974-77; with UTDC Corp., West Palm Beach, Fla. Trustee Crosslands Savs. Bank; chmn. bd. L.I. R.R., 1966-74; chmn. Tri-State Transp. Com., N.Y., N.J., Conn., 1961-67; chmn. interstate com. New Haven R.R., 1960-63; chmn. N.Y. Com. on L.I. R.R., 1964-65; mem. N.Y. State Commn. Interstate Coop., 1961, N.Y. State Com. Fgn. Ofcl. Visitors, 1961, N.Y. State Coordination Commn., 1960; mem. N.Y. Civil Svc. Commn., Temporary State Commn. on Constl. Conv., 1966-67; chmn. N.Y. State Met. Commuter Transp. Authority, 1965-68, Met. Transp. Authority, 1968-74, Tri-Borough Bridge and Tunnel Authority, 1968-74, N.Y.C. Transit Authority, 1968-74, Manhattan and Bronx Surface Transit Operating Authority, 1968-74; chmn. bd., pres. 3d Century Corp., 1974-94; mem. Commn. Critical Choices for Am., 1973—, acting chmn., 1975—; mem. urban transp. adv. com. U.S. Dept. Transp.; sr. adviser Rockefeller family, 1974-80; pres. Nelson Rockefeller Collection, Inc., 1977 80; trustee Power Authority of State of N.Y., 1974-77; cons. to trustees Penn Ctrl. Transp. Co.; vice chmn. bd. CCX, Inc.; sec.-treas. Sarabam Corp. N.V.; chmn., dir. UTDC (U.S.A.) Inc., 1987-88; chmn. UTDC Corp., 1989-94, Transit Svcs. Corp., 1989-94; cons. Herzog Transit Svcs., 1995-99, Dime Savs. Bank, Metal Powder Products Inc., Flomet Inc., 1997—. Teckna Seal, LLC, 2002--; Internat. Mining and Metals Inc., Quadrant Mgmt. Inc., 1990—, Ohio Highspeed Rail Authority, 1991-93; chmn. N.Y. and N.J. Inland Rail Rate Com.; dir. Nat. Mgmt. Coun., 1951. Author: Money Power of States in International Law, 1940, The Board of Regents and the Commissioner, 1948, Our War Economy, 1943, (with others), articles in profl. jours.; adviser: Jour. Inst. Socio-Econ. Studies. Mem. U.S. FOA, Am. Public Health Assn.; staff relations officer N.Y.C. Bd. Edn.; Mem. Nat. Conf. Social Work, Nat. Conf. on Met. Areas, Citizens Com. on Corrections, Council on Social Work Edn.; bd. dirs. World Trade Club; adv. bd. World Trade Inst.; mem. 42d St. Redevel. Corp., chmn., 1980-94; mem. Assn. for a Better N.Y.; bd. advisers Inst. for Socioecon. Studies, 1977—; dir. Nat. Health Council, 1980-86; dep. dir. policy Nelson Rockefeller campaign for Republican presdl. nomination, 1964; mem. N.Y. State Gov.'s Com. on Shoreham Nuclear Plant, 1983-85, Nassau County Indsl. Devel. Authority, 1982-90, U.S. Dept. Transp. Com. on Washington and Capital Dist. Airports, 1985-86; bd. dirs. Ctr. Study Presidency, 1986-90, Alcoholism Council of N.Y., 1986—; trustee N.Y. Coll. Osteopathic Medicine, 1986-91; v.p. Am. Cancer Soc., Palm Beach. Served as lt. USNR, 1943-46. Mem. ASPA, NEA, Am. Polit. Sci. Assn., Am. Acad. Pub. Adminstrn., Civil Svc. Assembly of U.S. and Can., Internat. Assn. Met. Rsch. and Devel., Nat. Mcpl. League, Mcpl. Pers. Soc., Citizens Union of N.Y., Nat. Civil Svc. League, Am. Acad. Polit. and Social Sci., L.I. Assn. Commerce and Industry (dir.), Internat. Inst. Adminstrv. Scis., Am. Fgn. Law Assn., Internat. Union Pub. Transport (mgmt. com., v.p.), Am. Pub. Transit Assn. (chmn. 1974-76), Nat. Def. Transp. Assn. (v.p. for Mass transit), English Speaking Union (bd. dirs. Palm Beach), Met. Opera Club, Maidstone Club, Devon Yacht Club, Knickerbocker Club, Hemisphere Club, Harvard Club, Creek Club, Wings Club, Traffic Club, Univ. Club, Am. Club Riviera, Beach Club (Palm Beach), Everglades Club. Home: 525 S Flagler Dr West Palm Beach FL 33401-5922 also: Villa La Pointe Du Cap Ave de La Corniche 06230 Saint Jean Cap Ferrat France E-mail: wjramp@aol.com.

RONAY, MATTHEW, sculptor; b. Louisville, 1976; Grad., Md. Inst. Coll. Art, 1998; MFA, Yale U., 2000. One-man shows include Gallery Luhmann, Nils Staerk, Copenhagen, 2002, Galerie Grimm/Rosenfeld, Munich, 2003, Vedanta Gallery, Chgo., 2003, exhibited in group shows at Richard Telles Gallery, L.A., 1999, Andrew Kreps Gallery, N.Y.C., 2000, Exit Art, 2001, Marc Foxx, L.A., 2001, 2002, Dorsky Gallery, L.I., N.Y., 2002, Wattis Inst. for Contemporary Arts, San Francisco, 2002, Logan Gallery, 2002, Gallery Luhmann, Nils Staerk, Copenhagen, 2002, Inst. Contemporary Art, Boston, 2002, Gallery 2 Andrea Rosen, N.Y.C., 2002. Named Invited Exhibitor, 2004 Biennial Exhbn., Whitney Mus. Am. Art, N.Y., 2004; recipient award for set design, N.Y. Internat. Fringe Festival, 2001.*

RONAYNE, MICHAEL RICHARD, JR., academic dean; b. Boston, Apr. 29, 1937; s. Michael Richard and Margaret (Fahey) R.; m. Joanne Maria, Aug. 7, 1971; 1 child, Michelle Eileen. BS, Boston Coll., 1958; PhD, U. Notre Dame, 1962. Instr. chemistry Providence Coll., 1962-63, asst. prof. chemistry, 1963-64; rsch. chemist Panametrics, Inc., Waltham, Mass., 1964-66; asst. prof. chemistry Suffolk U., Boston, 1966-67, assoc. prof., 1967-70, prof., chmn. dept. chemistry, 1970-72, dean Coll. Arts and Sci., 1972—. Reaccreditation vis. team mem. New Eng. Assn. Schs. and Colls., Winchester, Mass., 1974-80, Mass. Dept. Edn., Boston, 1975; mem. acad. adv. com. Mass. Bd. Higher Edn., Boston, 1977. Contbr. articles to sci. jours., profl. publs. Mem. Winchester Sch. Com., 1983-92, chmn., 1984-85, 86-87; mem. Winchester Town Meeting, 1983-98, mem. town capital planning com., 1983-84, town coun. on youth, 1987-88, 89-90; mem. exec. com., bd. dirs. Mass. Bay Marine Studies Consortium, 1985-87; project dir. U.S. Dept. of Edn. Title III Grants. Shell Oil Corp. fellow, 1958-59, AEC fellow 1959-62; recipient Contbns. in Sci. and Edn. citation New Eng. Sch. Art and Design, Boston, 1991; named to Matignon High Sch. Alumni Achievement Hall of Fame, 1997. Mem. AAAS, Am. Chem. Soc., Am. Conf. Acad. Deans, Coun. for Liberal Learning, Am. Assn. for Higher Edn., Sigma Xi, Phi Alpha Theta, Phi Gamma Mu, Sigma Tau Delta, Omicron Delta Epsilon, Sigma Zeta, Pi Sigma Alpha. Office: Suffolk U Beacon Hill Boston MA 02114 E-mail: mronayne@suffolk.edu.

RONCAL, ROGELIO, psychiatrist; b. Bataan, Philippines, 1939; MD magna cum laude, Manila Ctrl. U., 1962. Diplomate Am. Bd. Psychiatry and Neurology, Am. Bd. Forensic Medicine, Am. Acad. Integrative Medicine. Intern French Hosp., N.Y.C., 1963; resident in psychiatry Middletown PC-N.Y. Psychiat. Inst., N.Y.C., 1965-67; physician Horton Meml. Hosp., Middletown, N.Y.; founding dir. Middletown Alcohol Treatment Ctr. (now R. Ward Addictions, Treatment Ctr.), 1974—; pvt. practice., 1974-89; clin. dir. Middletown Psychiat. Ctr., N.Y.; attending psychiatrist Mid Hudson Psychiat. Ctr., New Hampton, N.Y., 1984-95; med. dir. chemical dependency program Pius XII Youth and Family Svcs., 1995—. Instr. clin. psychiat. Columbia U.; psychiatrist N.Am. Province Order Carmelites, 1975-95; med. cons. N.Y. State Divsn. Alcoholism and Alcohol Abuse, 1981-84; pychiat. cons. McQuade Found. for Children, 1974-81; attending psychiatrist N.Y. State Dept. Corrections, 1992-95. Maj. M.C., USAR, 1983. Recipient Life Achievement award Alcoholism and Drug Abuse Coun. Orange County, N.Y., 2001, medal of honor MCU Coll. Medicine, 2000; donor M. Roncal achievement award for acad. excellence given to delinquent youth in group homes served by Pius XII Youth and Family Svcs., 1990-95; named to First Alumni Hall of Fame, Manila Ctrl. U., 2001. Fellow: APA (disting. life), Am. Assn. Integrative Medicine (life; cert.), Am. Psychiat. Assn. (life); mem.: Acad. Internat. Med. Study, Manila Ctrl U. Med. Alumni Assn. (pres. N.E. chpt. 1998, pres. found. in Am. 1999, pres. 2000—), West Hudson Psychiat. Soc. (sec. 1979, pres. 1981), N.Y. State Med. Soc. (task force on smoking cessation 1997—), Am. Soc. Addiction Medicine, Am. Acad. Psyciat. Adminstrn., Am. Coll. Forensic Examiners, Orange County Med. Soc., Am. Coll. Physician Execs., Am. Med. Dirs. Assn., Med. Staff Orgn. Middletown Psychiat. Ctr., Med. Staff Orgn. Mid-Hudson Forensic Psychiat. Ctr. (pres. 1995), Philippino Psychiatrists in Am. (life). Office: Youth and Family Svcs 224 Main St Goshen NY 10924-2157 Fax: 914-294-1402.

RONCHI, DONALD M. psychologist, educator; BS, Marist Coll.; MS, Cornell U., Ithaca, N.Y.; PhD, U. Chgo. Pvt. practice orgnl. psychology; v.p. productivity, Raytheon Supplier Diversity Raytheon Co., Lexington, Mass., 1998—2001, raytheon Six Sigma, supply chain and chief learning officer, 2001—. Vis. scholar Columbia U., N.Y.C., La Universidad de Carabobo, Valencia, Venezuela. Office: Raytheon Co 141 Spring St Lexington MA 02421

RONDE, JOHN HERMAN, author, translator; b. Lonneker, Overyssel, The Netherlands, July 12, 1929; s. Johannes Maria Ronde and Lamberdina Hulsschreuder. BA in Econs., Columbia U., 1973, MA in Social Studies, 1974, MPhil in Geography, 1983. Substitute tchr. NYC HS, 1985-86, 92-93; asst. geographer US Census Bur., NYC, 1988-91. Author: Migration, Social Infrastructure and Urban Devel. in Selected German Cities, and Housing Policy and Supply in the Fed. German Republic (1970-85), 1996, Urban Devel. and Migration in Kiel with Reference to City Ctr. and Fringe Area Devel. Initiatives, 1971-84, Philosophical Interpretations of Modern Science, The Developing New World View of Man and His Activities for The Fulfillment of His Needs, An Introd. To and A Discussion of A Model of The Location of Man and His Activities, or: Geography as a Theory of Man. Mem.: AAAS, Am. Chem. Soc. (nat. affil.), NY Acad. Sci. Democrat. Avocations: bibliophile in history, philosophy of science, music, Bandonion player. Home: 75 East 3rd St C-3 New York NY 10003-9015

RONDEAU, ANN E. career officer; b. San Antonio, Tex. Diploma in History, Eisenhower Coll., 1973; Grad., Officer Candidate Sch., 1974. Commd. 2d lt. USN, 1974, advanced through grades to rear adm.; various assignments to exec. officer Fast Sealift Squad. One, New Orleans, 1987-89; asst. for polit.-mil. analysis Chief of Naval Operation (CNO), 1989-90; various to mil.

asst. to Prin. Deputy Under Sec. of Def. for Policy, 1995-96; assigned to Navy's Quadrenniel Def. Rev. Support Office, 1997—; dep. chief of staff Shore Base Mgmt. N46/U.S. Pacific Fleet. Decorated Def. Superior Svc. medal, Legion of Merit, Def. meritorious Svc. medal (2 times), Navy Meritorious Svc. medal (2 times), Navy Commendation medal (3 times); recipient Groben award for Leadership Eisenhower Coll.

RONDEAU, CLEMENT ROBERT, petroleum geologist; b. Ironwood, Mich., July 6, 1928; BS, Tulane U., 1955. Geol. supr. Texaco, Inc., New Orleans, 1955-63; area mgr. Pubco Petroleum Corp., New Orleans, 1963-69; cons. petroleum geologist Harahan, La., 1969—; owner Natural Gas Exploration Co., Harahan, 1977—. Mem. AAAS, Am. Assn. Petroleum Geologists, Soc. Exploration Geophysicists, New Orleans Geol. Soc., N.Y. Acad. Sci., The Explorers Club, Internat. Platform Assn., Phi Beta Kappa, Sigma Gamma Epsilon. Democrat. Roman Catholic. Home and Office: 612 S Beach Blvd Bay Saint Louis MS 39520-4203 E-mail: gasfinder@aol.com.

RONDEAU, DORIS JEAN, entrepreneur, consultant; b. Winston-Salem, N.C., Nov. 25, 1941; d. John Delbert and Eldora Virginia (Klutz) Robinson; m. Robert Breen Corrente, Sept. 4, 1965 (div. 1970); m. Wilfrid Dolor Rondeau, June 3, 1972. Student Syracuse U., 1959-62, Fullerton Jr. Coll., 1974-75; BA in Philosophy, Calif. State U.-Fullerton, 1976, postgrad., 1976-80. Ordained to ministry The Spirit of Divine Love, 1974. Trust real estate clk. Security First Nat. Bank, Riverside, Calif., 1965-68; entertainer Talent, Inc., Hollywood, Calif., 1969-72; co-founder, dir. Spirit of Divine Love, Huntington Beach, Calif., 1974—; pub., co-founder Passing Through, Inc., Huntington Beach, 1983—; instr. Learning Activity, Anaheim, Calif., 1984—; chmn. bd., prin. D.J. Rondeau, Entrepreneur, Inc., Huntington Beach, 1984—; co-founder, dir. Spiritual Positive Attitude, Inc., Moon In Pisces, Inc., Vibrations By Rondeau, Inc., Divine Consciousness, Expressed, Inc., Huntington Beach, Doris Wilfrid Rondeau, Inc., Huntington Beach, Calif. Author, editor: A Short Introduction To The Spirit of Divine Love, 1984; writer, producer, dir. performer spiritual vignettes for NBS Radio Network, KWVE-FM, 1982-84; author: Spiritual Meditations to Uplift the Soul, 1988. Served with USAF, 1963-65. Recipient Pop Vocalist First Place award USAF Talent Show, 1964, Sigma chpt. Epsilon Delta Chi, 1985, others. Mem. Hamel Bus. Grads., Smithsonian Assocs., Am. Mgmt. Assn., Nat. Assn. Female Execs. Fax: (714) 841-3286. Avocations: long-distance running, body fitness, arts and crafts, snorkeling, musical composition.

RONDEPIERRE, EDMOND FRANCOIS, insurance executive, lawyer; b. N.Y.C., Jan. 15, 1930; s. Jules Gilbert and Margaret Murray (Moore) R.; m. M. Anne Lerch, July 5, 1952; children: Aimee S., Stephen C., Peter E., Anne W. BS, U.S. Mcht. Marine Acad., 1952; JD, Temple U., 1959. Bar: D.C. 1959, Conn. 1988, U.S. Supreme Ct. 1992. Third mate Nat. Bulk Carriers, 1952-53; field rep. Ins. Co. N.Am., Phila., 1955-59, br. mgr., 1959-61, asst. sec. underwriting, 1965-67, asst. gen. counsel, 1967-70, sr. v.p., gen. counsel, 1970-76; v.p., dep. chief legal affairs INA Corp., Phila., 1976-77; v.p., gen. counsel Gen. Reins. Corp., Stamford, Conn., 1977-79, sr. v.p., corp. sec., gen. counsel, 1979-94, sr. v.p., 1994-95; pres., dir. ARIAS-US, 1994—99, dir. emeritus, 1999—. Bd. dirs. Arias-US. Lt. USN, 1953-55. Mem. ABA, Conn. Bar Assn., D.C. Bar Assn., Inter-Am. Bar Assn., Soc. CPCU, Internat. Assn. Def. Counsel (past bd. dirs.), AIDA Reins. and Ins. Arbitration Soc. (dir., pres.), Stamford Yacht Club, Wee Burn Country Club. Roman Catholic.

RONDINARO, PETER DOMINICK, social sciences educator, psychologist; b. Teaneck, N.J., Dec. 24, 1948; s. Peter and Claire Rondinaro; m. Ellen Rondinaro, Nov. 10, 1990; children: Melisa, Alison, Jake. BA, Duquesne U., Pitts., 1971, MS, 1974; PhD, Temple U., Phila., 2003. Lic. psychologist Commonwealth of Pa. sch. psychologist Commonwealth of Pa. Sch. psychologist Wallingford-Swarthmore Sch. Dist., Wallingford, Pa., 1976—77, Salem Sch. Dist., NJ, 1977—78; dir. student devel. Spring Garden Coll., Phila., 1978—92; faculty Jefferson U., Cabrini Coll., Immaculata Coll., Phila., 1992—98; asst. prof. Immaculata (Pa.) U., 1998—. Psychologist Guarding Group, Phila., 1996—98; cmty. advocacy bd. N.W. Ctr. of Mental Health, 1985—92; treas. and bd. mem. Coll. Consortium on Drugs and Alcohol, 1985—92. Lt. USAF, 1971—72. Mem.: APA, Pa. Psychol. Assn. Achievements include research in cooperative learning and test anxiety. Avocations: golf, skiing, reading, yoga. Office: Immaculata Univ Box 670 Immaculata PA 19345 Office Phone: 610-647-4400 3293. E-mail: prondinaro@immaculata.edu.

RONDINELLI, DENNIS A(UGUST), business administration educator, researcher; b. Trenton, N.J., Mar. 30, 1943; s. August P. and Vincentia Rondinelli; m. Soonyoung Chang, Dec. 19, 1976; children: Linda, Lisa. BA, Rutgers U., 1965; PhD, Cornell U., 1969. Asst. prof. urban affairs U. Wis., Milw., 1971-73; assoc. prof. grad. sch. of mgmt. Vanderbilt U., Nashville, 1973-76; assoc. prof. planning Maxwell Sch. of Citizenship and Pub. Affairs Syracuse U., N.Y., 1976-79, prof. social scis., 1979-86; prin. scientist and sr. policy analyst Office for Internat. Programs, Research Triangle Inst., Research Triangle Park, N.C., 1986-90; Glaxo Disting. Internat. Prof. Mgmt. Kenan-Flagler Bus. Sch. Cons. World Bank, U.S. Dept. State, UN Devel. Program, Govts. of Colombia, South Korea, Can., Indonesia, Philippines, China, India, mem. com. of experts on pub. adminstrn., United Nations Econ. and Social Coun., 2002—. Author: Decentralization and Development: Policy Implementation in Developing Countries, 1983, Applied Methods of Regional Analysis: The Spatial Dimensions of Development Policy, 1985, Development Administration and U.S. Foreign Aid Policy, 1987, Urban Services in Developing Countries: Public and Private Roles in Urban Development, 1988, Planning Education Reforms in Developing Countries, 1990, Development Projects as Policy Experiments, 1993, Privatization and Economic Reform in Central Europe, 1994, Expanding Sino-American Business and Trade: China's Economic Transition, 1994, Great Policies: Strategic Innovations in Asia and the Pacific, 1995, Policies and Institutions for Managing Privatization, 1996, Market Reform in Vietnam, 1999, Reinventing Government for the 21st Century, 2003, Beyond Reconstruction in Afghanistan, 2004; mem. editl. adv. bd. Leadership Rev., Jour. Internat. Bus. Edn., Jour. Internat. Devel. Planning; contbr. articles to Jours. Mem. expert com. pub. admin. unecon. and social coun. UN, 2002—. Capt. U.S. Army, 1965—72. Decorated Julio Lieras Order of Merit (Colombia), 1988; recipient Rural Devel. medal Republic of Vietnam, 1971, Ethnic Minorities Devel. medal, 1971, W. Bloomberg award for excellence in futures studies, 1997, Weatherspoon Disting. Rsch. award, 1997; East-West Ctr. sr. fellow, 1975-76, Pacific Basin Rsch. Ctr./Soka U. of Am./Harvard U. rsch. fellow, 1991-92. Avocations: gardening, writing nonfiction. Office: Kenan-Flagler Bus Sch U NC CB #3490 Chapel Hill NC 27599-3490 E-mail: dennis_rondinelli@unc.edu.

RONEN-ZLOTNIK, ELA S. cardiologist, writer; d. Shmuel Zlotnik and Raisa Heifetz; m. Moshe Ronen, Nov. 11, 1973; 1 child, Dinah Shafir-Brown. MD, First Moscow U., 1961. Physician Hosp.#75, Moscow, 1962—68; staff physician Cupat Holim, Jerusalem, 1970—76. Author: Let My People Go. Tchr. Saddelbeck Coll., Mission Viejo, Calif., 2002—03. Fellow, UCLA, 1980—82. Fellow: Nahamaat (corr.). Achievements include research in history.

RONEY, ALICE LORRAINE MANN, poet; b. Hartford, Mich., Dec. 6, 1926; d. Paul Douglass and Margaret Alice (Widener) Mann; m. Robert Kenneth Roney, Oct. 6, 1951; children: Stephen Paul, Karen Margaret. AA, Santa Monica Coll., 1946; BA, UCLA, 1950. Tech. writer Hughes Aircraft Co., Culver City, Calif., 1949—52; chmn. Ebell Jr. Blind Recording, LA, 1959—63; librarian St. Augustine-by-the-Sea Episcopal Day Sch, Santa Monica, Calif., 1961—68. Author: Those Treasured Moments, 1972, The Seeds of Love, 1975, Psalms for My Lord, 1975; co-author: Singing for Joy, 1989, numerous poems. Sch. bd. Episcopalian Ch., 1964—67, asst. directress altar guild, 1967—69, directress altar guild, 1969—71; treas. Diocese of LA Churchwomen, 1970—73. Recipient Ebell Jr. Svc. award, 1959, 2d pl. for poetry creative writing divsn. marina dist., Calif. Fedn. Women's Clubs Fine Arts Festival, 1979, 3d pl. for inspirational poetry, 1979, 2d and 3d pl., 1981, 1st and 2d pl., 1982, 1st pl., 1985, 2d pl., 1986, 3d pl. for light verse, 1980, 1st pl. for children's stories, 1983, 1985. Fellow: World Lit. Acad.; mem.: PEO (pres. chpt. QB 1969—71, 1976—78, 1986—88), Nat. Fedn. State Poetry Socs., Ky. State Poetry Soc., World Poetry Soc. (life), Calif. State Poetry Soc., Internat. Poetry Soc., Santa Monica Bay Woman's Club (1st v.p. 1980—82, pres. 1982—84, 2d v.p. 1984—86, pres. 1986—). Episcopalian. Home and Office: 1105 Georgina Ave Santa Monica CA 90402-2027

RONEY, GLEN E. finance company executive; Chmn., pres., CEO Tex. Regional Bancshares, Inc., McAllen, Tex., 1978—. Office: Texas Regional Bancshares Inc 3900 N 10th Fl Mcallen TX 78501

RONEY, JOHN M. lawyer; b. Wash., D.C., Sept. 21, 1939; m. Barbara Kennedy; children: Christopher, Carley, Kristina. BA, Providence Coll.; JD, Cath. U. Am. Atty. Roney & Labinger, Providence; senator R.I. State Senate, 1994—. Dep. majority leader, vice chair fin., health, edn. welfare R.I. State Senate. Mem. Lawyers for the Arts; bd. dirs. R.I. Legal Svcs.; mem. Leadership R.I., R.I. Coun. on Alcoholism. Mem.: R.I. Bar Assn. (exec. com.). Democrat. Office: Roney and Labinger 344 Wickenden St Providence RI 02903

RONEY, PAUL H(ITCH), federal judge; b. Olney, Ill., Sept. 5, 1921; m. Sarah E. Eustis; children: Susan M., Paul Hitch Jr., Timothy Eustis. Student, St. Petersburg Jr. Coll., 1938—40; BS in Econs., U. Pa., 1942; LLB, Harvard U., 1948; LLD, Stetson U., 1977; LLM, U. Va., 1984. Bar: N.Y. 1949, Fla. 1950. Assoc. Root, Ballantine, Harlan, Bushby & Palmer, N.Y.C., 1948—50; ptnr. Mann, Harrison, Roney, Mann & Masterson (and predecessors), St. Petersburg, Fla., 1950—57; pvt. practice, 1957—63; ptnr. Roney & Beach, St. Petersburg, 1963—69, Roney, Ulmer, Woodworth & Jacobs, St. Petersburg, 1969—70; judge U.S. Ct. Appeals (5th cir.), St. Petersburg, 1970—81, U.S. Ct. Appeals (11th cir.), St. Petersburg, 1981—86, chief judge, 1986—89, sr. cir. judge, 1989—. Adv. com. on adminstrv. law judges U.S. CSC, 1976—77; pres. judge U.S. Fgn. Intelligence Surveillance Ct. of Rev., 1994—2001; lectr. Stetson U. Coll. of Law. With U.S. Army, 1942—46. Fellow: Am. Bar Found.; mem.: ABA (chmn. legal adv. com. Fair Trial-Free Press 1973—76, task force on cts. and public 1973—76, jud. adminstrn. divsn., chmn. appellate judges conf. 1978—79, Gavel Awards com. 1980—83), Jud. Conf. U.S. (subcom. on jud. improvements 1978—84, exec. com. 1986—89, com. to review circuit coun. conduct and disability orders 1991—93), Nat. Jud. Coll. (faculty 1974—75), St. Peterburg Bar Assn. (pres. 1964—65), Fla. Bar Assn., Am. Law Inst., Am. Judicature Soc. (bd. dirs. 1972—76). Office: US Ct Appeals Bank of Am One Progress Plz 200 Central Ave Saint Petersburg FL 33701-3326

RONEY, ROBERT KENNETH, retired aerospace company executive; b. Newton, Iowa, Aug. 5, 1922; s. Louie Earl and Hazel Iona (Cure) R.; m. Alice Lorraine Mann, Oct. 6, 1951; children: Stephen P., Karen Margaret Dahl. BSEE, U. Mo., 1944; MSEE, Calif. Inst. Tech., 1947, PhD, 1950. Engr. rsch. Jet Propulsion Lab. Calif. Inst. Tech., Pasadena, 1948-50, Hughes Aircraft Co., Culver City, Calif., 1950-54, mgr. sys. analysis, 1955-59, dir. tech. R&D, 1960, assoc. mgr. space sys. divsn., 1961-68, mgr. space sys. divsn., 1968-70, v.p. asst. group exec., 1970-85, sr. v.p. corp. tech., 1986-88, ret., 1988. Mem. adv. bd. Dept. Transp. Comml. Space Transp., 1984-87, Engrng. Sch. U. Kans., 1988-91. Lt. (j.g.) USNR, 1944-46, PTO. Recipient Honor award for Disting. Svc. in Engrng. U. Mo.-Columbia, 1979. Fellow IEEE; mem. NAE, Caltech Assocs. Home: 1105 Georgina Ave Santa Monica CA 90402-2027

RONG, YIMING, manufacturing engineering educator; b. Harbin, China, Sept. 3, 1958; arrived in U.S., 1985; s. Yanmo Rong and Kunyi Shen; m. Jiaoshi Dong, June 12, 1984; 1 child, Zhixin (Blake). BS in Mech. Engrng., Harbin U. Sci. & Tech., 1981; MS in Mfg. Engrng., Tsinghua U., Beijing, 1984; MS in Indsl. Engrng., U. Wis., 1987; PhD in Mech. Engrng., U. Ky., 1989. Instr. Tsinghua U., 1984-85; postdoctoral rsch. assoc. U. Ky., Lexington, 1990; asst. prof. mfg. systems So. Ill. U., Carbondale, 1990-96, assoc. prof. mfg. sys., 1996-98; assoc. prof. mfg. engr. Worcester (Mass.) Poly. Inst., 1998—2003, Higgins prof., 2002—. Faculty rsch. assoc. Wright-Patterson AFB, Dayton, Ohio, 1995; vis. assoc. prof. U. Ill., Urbana, 1996; adj. prof. Dalian U. Tech., China, 2000—, Harbin U. Sci. & Tech., 1996—, Huazhong U. Sci. & Tech., Wuhan, China, 1998—; adj. assoc. prof. Tsinghua U., Beijing, 1994—96. Author: (book) Computer-Aided Fixture Design, 1999; editor, organizer Procs. Symposium Mfg. Engrng./Computer-Aided Tooling, 1995, Procs. Symposium Mfg. Engrng./Concurrent Design of Product & Mfg. Processes, 1998, Symposium Mfg. Engrng./Decision Making in Design and Mfg., 1999. Pres. Chinese Friendship Assn., Lexington, 1988—89; faculty advisor Chinese Students and Scholars Assn., 2002—, Chinese Students Assn., 2002—. Recipient Rsch. Initiation award, NSF, 1993—96; grantee Rsch., USAF Office Sci. Rsch., 1995—96, NSF, 1997—2000, 2001, 2001—, Dept. Energy, 2001—, Pratt & Whitney Rsch. Ctr., 1996—97, Caterpillar, 1998—2001, Ford, 1999—2001, Delphi Automotive Sys., 1999—, GE Aircraft Engrs., 2002—. Mem.: ASME, Am. Soc. Metals Heat Treating Soc., Chinese Mech. Engrng. Soc., Am. Soc. Engrng. Edn., Soc. Mfg. Engrs. Achievements include development of of first comprehensive computer-automated modular and dedicated fixture design techniques and systems; of tolerance analysis method for manufacturing and assembly processes with multiple setups; of an automated setup and fixture planning technique and system; of fixture design analysis and verification technique; exploration of flexible fixturing with phase-change materials; modeling of machining chip formation/breaking and heat treatment processes; modeling and simulation of induction hardening processes. Office: Worcester Poly Inst Mech Engring Dept 100 Institute Rd Worcester MA 01609-2280 E-mail: rong@wpi.edu.

RONGEN, RENEE WALL, entrepreneur, consultant, writer; BBA, St. John's U., St. Joseph, Minn., 1983. Nat. accounts mgr. Avis Rent-A-Car, Newport Beach, Calif., 1984—88; mktg. specialist Carlson Companies, Mpls., 1986—89; mktg. product mgr. Lucas Aerospace, Jamestown, ND, 1989—93; pres. Corp. Comm., Erskine, Minn., 1993—98; prin. Ingenuity Concepts Group, Erskine, 1998—. Mem. Minn. Speaker.com, Mpls., 2002—03. Author: (non-fiction inspirational/gift book) Grandy's Quilt.A Gift For All Seasons; prodr.: (audio series) Candid Conversations with an Adoption Attorney, Candid Conversations with an Adoptive Mother; composer: (video/audio series) Life is Short.Live Your Dash; contbr. articles to profl. jours. Bd. trustee Minn. Hosp. Assn., St. Paul, 2002—04; v.p. Riverview Healthcare Orgn., Crookston, Minn., 1996—2004; chairperson Riverview Hospice, Crookston, 1999—2001, NW Minn. Women's Fund, 1997—2000; vol. pub. rels. coord. Am. Cancer Soc., Crookston, 2002—04. Recipient Female Entrepreneur of Yr., Women's Bus. Ctr., 1995. Mem.: Nat. Spkrs. Assn. Avocations: travel, golf, skiing, horseback riding, reading. Office: Ingenuity Concepts Group 39829 Sunset Shores Rd SE Erskine MN 56535 E-mail: renee@reneerongen.com.

RONGEN, THOMAS, professional soccer coach; b. Netherlands, Oct. 31, 1956; arrived in US, 1979; m. Gail Megaloudis, Apr. 13, 1996. AA in Lang., Snellius Lyceum, Netherlands; MA in Phys. Edn. and Recreation, Central Inst. for Training of Sportsleaders, Netherlands. "A" coaching lic. U.S. Soccer Fedn., Dutch coaching lic.; cert. in sports massage Netherlands Sports Fedn. Midfielder/defender LA Aztecs, 1979, Wash. Diplomats, 1980, Strikers, Ft. Lauderdal, 1980-84, 86, Chgo., 1984-86; asst. coach Nova Southeastern U., 1986-92, head coach, 1992-96; coach New England Revolution, 1996-98; head coach DC United, 1999—2001, US Nat. Men's Under-20 Team, 2001—. Dir. coaching and player devel. Plantation (Fla.) Eagles Soccer Club; coach Am. Soccer League All-Star team, 1991. Named MLS Coach of the Yr., 1996, Am. Soccer League Coach of the Yr., 1991. Office: c/o D C United 13832 Redskin Dr Herndon VA 20171-3208

RONK, JAY H. music educator, department chairman; b. Twin Falls, Idaho, Feb. 27, 1954; s. Howard Weaver and Nelda Ruth Ronk; m. V. Suzan Johnson, Dec. 26, 1954; children: Jayson Miles, Rebecca Jean. MusB Edn., Idaho State, Pocatello, 1976. Cert. secondary tchr. Idaho, 1984. Dir. of bands Hillcrest H.S., Midvale, Utah, 1978—; music coord. Sch. Dist. #25, Pocatello, Idaho, 1994—. Bd. dir. Highland Edn. Found.; adj. percussion instr. Idaho State, Pocatello, 1986—87; pres. Gem State Music Conf., 1996—98; dept. chmn. Highland H.S. Fine Arts Dept., 1996—. Musician Idaho State Civic Symphony; deacon Pocatello Bapt. Ch., 2001—04. Recipient Nat. Citizenship Edn. Tchr. Recognition award, VFW, 2003, State of Idaho Tchr. of Yr., VFW and Ladies Aux. of the US, 2003—04, The Thing, Idaho Music Educators Assn., 2002—04, Tchr. of Yr., Am. Legion, 2004. Mem.: NEA, Idaho Edn. Assn., Pocatello Edn. Assn. Office: Highland HS 1800 Bench Rd Pocatello ID 83201 Office Phone: 208-237-1300. Office Fax: 208-237-1350.

RONNING, CHARLOTTE JEAN, foreign language educator; b. Billings, Mont., Dec. 19, 1953; d. Charles and Ruth Alice (Johnson) R. BA, Mont. State U., Billings, 1978, BS, 1980; MA, U. Colo., 1995. Nat. cert. counselor. Sales/office mgr. Clint Faubions, Denver, 1980-81; office mgr. Virginia Horn Travel, Denver, 1981-82; sales, instr. R.B. Bonar & Assocs., Denver, 1982-86; fgn. lang. educator Cherry Creek Schs., Denver, 1987—. Student Fgn. Study League, Europe, 1970; Dale Carnegie course instr., N.Y.C., 1982-87; sponsor Cherry Creek in Costa Rica, 1988. Mem. Fgn. Lang. Proficiency Com., Denver, 1993—; v.p. Bromley Commons, Denver, 1994—, U. Madrid, 1997. Mem. ACA, Colo. Counseling Assn., Chi Sigma Iota, Alpha Lambda Delta, Alpha Mu Gamma, Kappa Alpha Theta. Republican. Presbyterian. Avocations: piano, golf, skiing. Home: 350 Detroit St Apt 207 Denver CO 80206-4361

RONSTADT, LINDA MARIE, singer; b. Tucson, July 15, 1946; d. Gilbert and Ruthmary (Copeman) R. Rec. artist numerous albums including Evergreen 1967, Evergreen Vol. 2, 1967, Linda Ronstadt, The Stone Poneys and Friends, Vol. 3, 1968, Hand Sown, Home Grown, 1969, Silk Purse, 1970, Linda Ronstadt, 1972, Don't Cry Now, 1973, Heart Like a Wheel, 1974, Different Drum, 1974, Prisoner In Disguise, 1975, Hasten Down the Wind, 1976, Greatest Hits, 1976, Simple Dreams, Blue Bayou, 1977, Living in the U.S.A., 1978, Mad Love, Greatest Hits Vol. II, 1980, Get Closer, 1982, What's New, 1983, Lush Life, 1984, For Sentimental Reasons, 1986, Trio (with Dolly Parton, Emmylou Harris), 1986, 'Round Midnight, 1987, Canciones de Mi Padre, 1987, Cry Like a Rainstorm-Howl Like the Wind, 1989, Mas Canciones, 1991, Frenesi, 1992, Winter Light, 1993, Feels Like Home, 1995, Dedicated to the One I Love, 1996, We Ran, 1998, Trio 2, 1999 (with Emmylou Harris & Dolly Parton), Western Wall: The Tucson Sessions (with Emmylou Harris); starred in Broadway prodn. of Pirates of Penzance, 1981, also in film, 1983, off Broadway as Mimi in La Boheme, 1984. Recipient Am. Music awards, 1978, 79, Grammy awards, 1975, 76, 87 (with Emmylou Harris and Dolly Parton), 1988, 89 (with Aaron Neville), 1990 (with Aaron Neville, 1992 (2), 1996, Acad. Country Music award, 1987, 88. Office: Electra Records 75 Rockefeller Plz New York NY 10019-6908

ROOB, RICHARD, manufacturing executive; b. 1932; Degree, Hamilton Coll., 1953; JD, Columbia U., 1956. With Benjamin Moore & Co., Montvale, N.J., 1977—, vice chmn. bd., 1982-84, CEO, chmn. bd. dirs., 1984—. Office: Benjamin Moore & Co 51 Chestnut Ridge Rd Montvale NJ 07645-1862

ROOBOL, NORMAN RICHARD, industrial coatings consultant, educator; b. Grand Rapids, Mich., Aug. 19, 1934; s. Pleune and Henrietta (Sietsema) Roobol; m. Joan Lois Ezinga, Aug. 15, 1957; children: Kerri Linda, Michael Eric, Victoria May, Sara Elizabeth Angelique. BS, Calvin Coll., 1958; PhD in Organic Chemistry, Mich. State U., 1962. Rsch. chemist Shell Oil Co., Emeryville, Calif., 1962-65; asst. prof. chemistry GMI Engring. Inst., Flint, Mich., 1965-68, assoc. prof., asst. head dept. math., sci., 1968-72, prof., 1972-89; pres. NR Painting Cons. Co., Peachtree City, Ga., 1989—. Rhodes prof., Russelsheim, Germany, 1980—81; tchr. short courses paint; cons. coatings application processes; spkr. indsl. painting methods; painting advisor, instr. Outboard Marine Corp., 1986—2001, Bombardier Can., 1988—, Compaq-Asia, Singapore, 1991—, Harley-Davidson, 1992—, Metagal Comercie e Industri, San Paulo, Brazil, 1996—, Decometal S.A., Panama City, Panama, 1997—2001, J. R. McDermott Corp., Jebel Ali, 2000—; adj. prof. Kent (Ohio) State U., 1986—94, Okla. State U., 1994—98, U. Wis., 1992—2001. Author: (book) Painting Problems Solved, 1987, Industrial Paint and Powder Coating Principles and Practices, 3d edit., 2003; monthly columnist, tech. editor: Indsl. Paint and Powder Jour.; contbr. articles to profl. jours. Treas. Fayette (Ga.) Cmty. Hosp., bd. dirs. With Signal Corps U.S. Army, 1954—56. Fellow Johnson, 1957—58, NSF, 1960—62, Dow, 1961—62. Fellow: Am. Inst. Chemists; mem.: AAUP, Assn. Finishings Proc. (v.p. profl. devel. coun.), Soc. Mfg. Engrs. (bd. dirs.), Am. Sci. Affiliation, Pi Tau Sigma (chpt. sr. adviser 1979—86), Alpha Tau Omega, Sigma Xi. Achievements include patents in field. Home and Office: Powder Coating & Painting Cons 507 Haddington Ln Peachtree City GA 30269-3340 Personal E-mail: drroobol@flash.net.

ROOD, DAVID S. linguistics educator; b. Albany, NY, Sept. 14, 1940; s. J. Henry and Pearl B. (Stanley) R.; m. Juliette A. Victor; 1 child, Jennifer. AB, Cornell U., 1963; MA, U. Calif., Berkeley, 1965; PhD, U. Calif., 1969. Instr. U. Colo., Boulder, 1967-69, asst. prof., 1969-77, assoc. prof., 1977-82, prof., 1982—; vis. prof. U. Köln, Germany, 1998-99. Author: Wichita Grammar, 1975, Siouan Languages Archive, 1982; (with others) Beginning Lakhota, 1976; editor Internat. Jour. of Am. Linguistics, 1981-2002; contbr. numerous articles to profl. jours. NSF grantee, 1972-96, NEH grantee, 1972-96, Volkswagen Stiftung grantee, 2000-04. Mem.: Tchrs. English to Speakers Other Langs., Soc. for Study Indigenous Langs. Am. (pres. 2004), Linguistic Soc. Am. Office: U Colo Dept Linguistics 295 UCB Boulder CO 80309-0295 Office Phone: 303-492-2747. Business E-Mail: rood@colorado.edu.

ROOF, ROBERT L. broadcast executive, sales executive; b. Circleville, Ohio, Apr. 15, 1946; s. Roger D. and Doris (Kraft) R.; m. Linda Anderson, Nov. 28, 1969; children: Jennifer, Leslie. BA, Franklin U. Sales, disc jockey Sta. WPKO Radio, Waverly, Ohio, 1969-72, Sta. WSCR Radio, Scranton, Pa., 1972-75; sales Sta. WSPD Radio, Toledo, Ohio, 1975-78, Sta. WTVN Radio, Columbus, Ohio, 1978-81, local sales mgr., 1981-83, gen. sales mgr., 1984-87; v.p., gen. mgr. Sta. WDVE Radio, Pitts., 1987-93, pres., gen. mgr., 1993—. Bd. dirs. Southwest PA Jr. Achievement, Pitts., 1994—. Recipient Bronze Leadership award Jr. Achievement, Pitts., 1994. Mem. Columbus Sales Club (pres. 1982), Pitts. Sales Club (pres. 1989), Pitts. Radio Orgn. (pres. 1994). Methodist. Avocations: golf, hunting, Am. history. Office: Sta WDVE-FM 200 Fleet St Pittsburgh PA 15220-2908

ROOF, SALLY JEAN-MARIE, library and information scientist, educator; b. Cleve., Dec. 29, 1947; d. James William and Marie Monreal Roof; m. Christian John Hoffmann III, Sept. 22, 1973; children: Christian Graham Hoffmann, Joscelyn Nicole Hoffmann, Gavin Leigh Hoffmann. BA in English Lit., Dunbarton Coll. of Holy Cross, Washington, D. C., 1969; MS in Libr. and Info. Sci., Cath. U. of Am., 1972; degree in Profl. Mgmt. (hon.), Miami U., 1976; MA in Elem. Edn., No. Ariz. U., 2001. Cert. tchr. in libr. media ctr. adminstrn. Nat. Bd. of Cert. Tchrs., 2004. Asst. libr. U.S .Postal Svc. Libr., Washington, 1971—72; head of acquisitions George Wash. U. Libr., Washington, 1972—74; libr. adminstr. and mgr. Calgon Corp. Libr. Merck Inc., Pitts., 1974—77; libr. info. specialist U. of Phoenix, 1979—81; reference libr. Grand Canyon U., Phoenix, 1990—91; reference libr. West Campus Libr. Ariz. State U., Phoenix, 1994—95; libr. info. specialist Madison Meadows Sch., Phoenix, 1998—. Libr. cons. U. of Phoenix, 1981—82; presenter Ariz. Libr. Assn., Scottsdale, 2003; mem., presenter People to People Amb. Program Children's Lit. Del., Spokane, Wash., 2004; participant rep., 04; cons. in field. Editor: Serial Titles in the Washington, D. C. University Consortium Libraries, No School Left Behind at Your Library. Librarians Meet Arizona Legislators, 2004; author: (pamphlet) Madison Meadows Library Media Center; designer (school website) Madison Meadows Sch. website. Chmn. grade level patroness Nat. Charity League, Phoenix, 1994—99; pres. Phoenix (Ariz.) Mus. of History, 1991—94. Mem.: ALA (assoc.), Ariz. Libr. Assn. (assoc.), Phi Kappa Phi, Beta Phi Mu, Jr. League of Phoenix. Democrat-Npl. Roman Catholic. Avocations: yoga, fast walking, reading, bicycling. Office: Madison Meadows School 225 W Ocotillo Rd Phoenix AZ 85013 Office Phone: 602-664-7640. Personal E-mail: sroofhoff@cox.net. E-mail: sroof@msd38.org.

ROOK, JUDITH RAWIE, television producer, writer; d. Wilmer Ernest and Margaret Jane (Towle) Rawie; m. Dr. John Holland, 1964 (div. 1978); children: Daryn Simons, Dawn Reinard; m. Tim Rook, 1993. BA, Loyola-Marymount Univ., 1964; postgrad., U. Calif., San Diego, 1978. Syndicated columnist Environ. Forum, 1971-74; dir. IABC, San Francisco, 1982; dir. programming Westinghouse Cable, 1983-85; dir. devel. Embassy/Nelson

Home Entertainment, 1985-87; ptnr. Real Magic, 1987-89; prodr., writer, ptnr. BrantHol Prodns., 1990-93; co-sponsorship Beetle Juice, The Last Emperor, 1987—89; founder, pres. R2 Group, 1990—. Assoc. dir.: (off-broadway play) Arms and the Man, 1967; The Man Who Came to Dinner, 1981; exec. prodr.: Neighborhood Without Bars (Emmy award, 1985, 1986, 1987); prodr., writer: PBS series Focus, 1980; Achieving, 1982 (Emmy award, ACE nominee, PBS nominee); NBC pilot Christmas Comes to Silverton, 1990—93; CNN pilot Clever Encounters, 1991; prodr.: One Creative Moment, Close up: The 60s, 1995—97; assoc. prodr.: Fox Latin Am. Billboard Music Awards, 1998—2000; (TV pilot) Fempresario, 2004; playwright: Theatre 40 Writer's Workshop Anniversary for Three, 2003. Mem. adv. bd. U. Calif. Irvine Screenwriting/Film Prodn., 1996-2000; mem. adv. bd. Univ. Art Mus., 1996-97, co-pres. contemporary coun., 1996-97; mem. exec. bd. Long Beach Mus. Art, 1995-96; bd. dirs. Counseling 4 Kids, 1998—, bd. sec., 2001—; editor, bd. League Women Voters, Santa Monica. Mem. Am. Film Inst., Women in Film (dir. seminars on women in film), IFP West. Democrat. Episcopalian. E-mail: tirook@earthlink.net.

ROOKE, ALLEN DRISCOLL, JR., civil engineer, consultant; b. San Antonio, Oct. 5, 1924; s. Allen Driscoll and Jean Edna (Lackner) R.; m. Betty Ruth Whitson, Oct. 17, 1949; children: Victoria Lynn Lewis, Cornelia Ruth. BSCE, Tex. A&M U., 1957; MSCE, Miss. State U., 1980. Registered profl. engr., Miss. Enlisted U.S. Army, 1942, advanced through grades to brig. gen., ret., 1984; rsch. civil engr. U.S. Army Corps Engrs., Vicksburg, Miss., 1958-83; ptnr. F.B. Rooke & Sons, Woodsboro, Tex., 1964—; sr. engr. Sci & Tech. Corp., Vicksburg, Miss., 1984-95. Bd. dirs. First Nat. Bank, Woodsboro, 1985—. Author/co-author numerous tech. publs. Mem. Res. Officers Assn. U.S. (dept. pres. 1980-82, svc. award 1980, 84), Assn. of U.S. Army, Ret. Officer's Assn. (chpt. v.p. 1985-86), Soc. Am. Mil. Engrs. (post v.p. 1979). Clubs: Army and Navy Vicksburg (pres. 1980, 82). Episcopalian. Avocation: chess.

ROOKE, DAVID LEE, retired chemical company executive; b. San Antonio, Tex., May 2, 1923; s. Henry Levi, Jr. and Annie (Davidson) R.; m. Esthermae Litherland, June 2, 1945; children— Eugene, Mark, Paul, Bruce. BS in Chem. Engring, Rice Inst., Houston, 1944; postgrad., U. Houston. With Dow Chem., Midland, Mich., 1946-88, v.p. ops., 1977-78; pres. Dow U.S.A., 1978-82; v.p. Dow Chem. Corp., 1978-82, exec. v.p., 1982-83, sr. v.p., 1983-86, sr. cons., 1986-88, ret., 1988, also bd. dirs. Bd. dirs. Dow Corning Corp., James Avery Craftsman, Inc. Nat. exec. bd. Boy Scouts Am., 1979-86; bd. dirs. Meth. Mission Home, San Antonio. Served with USNR, 1944-46. Mem. AICE, United Meth. Reporter Found. (Dallas). Methodist.

ROOKS, CHARLES S. foundation administrator; b. Whiteville, N.C., June 29, 1937; BA in English, Wake Forest Coll., 1959; Rockefeller Brothers fellow, Harvard U., 1959-60; MA in Polit. Sci., Duke U., 1964, PhD in Polit. Sci., 1968. Rsch. assoc. Voter Edn. Project, Atlanta, 1969-70, dir. tech. assistance programs, 1970-71, dep. dir., 1971-72; exec. dir. Southeastern Coun. of Founds., Atlanta, 1972-78; dir. mem. svcs. Coun. on Founds., Washington, 1979-80, v.p., 1981-82, acting CEO, 1981-82; exec. dir. Meyer Meml. Trust, Portland, Oreg., 1982—. Instr. polit. sci. Duke U., Durham, N.C., 1963, 65-67; asst. prof. of govt. Lake Forest Coll., Ill., 1967-69; asst. prof. polit. sci. Clark Coll., Atlanta, 1969-71; bd. dirs. Pacific Northwest Grantmakers Forum, Forum of Regional Assns. of Grantmakers; mem. adv. bd. Neighborhood Partnership Fund (Oreg. Cmty. Found.); mem., adv. bd. Giving in Oreg. Coun.; co-chair Northwest Giving Project. Contbr. articles to profl. jours. Home: 2706 SW English Ct Portland OR 97201-1622 Office: Meyer Memorial Trust 425 NW 10th Ave Ste 400 Portland OR 97209-3128

ROOKS, GEORGE MALCOLM, writer, educator, company executive; b. Anderson, S.C., Mar. 5, 1951; s. George and Miriam (Bailey) R.; divorced, 1983; children: George, Brendan; m. Hila Zizov, Feb. 1, 1983; children; Kanon, Maayan. BA in English, U. Ga., 1973; MA in English, U. Calif., Davis, 1975. Mem. faculty U. Calif., Davis., 1976—; owner, CEO Teletext Corp., 1989—. Author: The Book of Losers, 1980, 2d edit., 1988, The Nonstop Discussion Workbook!, 1980, Can't Stop Talking, 1981, 2d edit., 1988, Share Your Paragraph, 1988, 2d edit., 1995, Paragraph Power, 1988, Beat the TOEFL: A Video-Workbook-Computer Series, 1990, Let's Start Talking, 1990, Power TOEFL Deluxe CD Rom and Workbook, 1998, Power 2000 Grammar Review CD rom, 2001, TOEIC Test Master CD Rom, 2001, Power TOEFL Listening CD Rom with Listening Scripts, 2001, The Ttext Word Frequency CD Rom Dictionary for the TOEIC Test, 2003; (with others) Conversar Sin Parar, 1981, Conversations San Fin, 1982, Was Sagen Sie Dazu?, 1983, Japanese Listening and Grammar Exercises for TOEFL, 1996; editor: Vocabulary Enrichment for ESL Students (15 disks), 1994, Grammar Enrichment for ESL Students (9 disks), 1994; contbr. articles to profl. jours. Mem. Calif. Tchrs. ESL, Zionist Orgn. Am. Avocations: tennis, travel. Address: 10 Sara Emanu Tet Vav 77724 Ashdod Israel Office: 710 Valencia Ave Davis CA 95616-0153

ROOMANN, HUGO, architect; b. Tallinn, Estonia, Mar. 25, 1923; came to U.S., 1951, naturalized, 1957; s. Eduard August and Annette (Kask) R.; m. Raja R. Suursoho, Sept. 15, 1945; children— Katrin-Kaja, Linda-Anu. BS, Inst. Tech. Carolo Wilhelmina, Braunschweig, W. Ger., 1950; M.F.A. in Arch. (scholar 1956-57), Princeton U., 1957. Archtl. engr. Austin Co., Roselle, N.J., 1951-54; archtl. designer Epple & Seaman, Newark, 1954-55, 57-61; propr. Hugo Roomann, Cranford and Elizabeth, N.J., 1961-66; ptnr. A.M. Kinney Assocs. (Architects and Engrs.), Cin., N.Y.C. and Chgo., 1966-89. Dir. architecture, v.p. corp. ops. A.M. Kinney, Inc., Cin., 1967, 77, 89; dir. Walter Kidde Constructors, Inc., 1973, A.M. Kinney, Inc., A.M. Kinney Assocs. Inc., Chgo.; pres. Design Art Corp., 1986. Prin. works include Grad. Rsch. Ctr. for Biol. Scis., Ohio State U., 1970, Lloyd Libr., Cin., 1968, offices, labs. and mfg. facilities, Miles Labs., West Haven, Conn., 1969, Am. Mus. Atomic Energy, Oak Ridge, 1975, Renton K. Brodie Sci. Ctr., U. Cin., 1970, EPA Nat. Labs., Cin., 1975, NALCO Tech. Ctr., Naperville, Ill., 1979, Brown & Williamson Corp. Hdqrs., Louisville, 1983, U. Cin. Kettering Lab., 1989; pub.: Urban Growth and the Development of an Urban Sewer System, City of Cincinnati 1800-1915, 2001. Pres. Citizens League, Elizabeth, N.J., 1966, Estonian Heritage Assn. Cin., 1991-94; bd. dirs., pres. Inter-Ethnic Coun. of Greater Cin., 1992-95. Recipient Top Ten Plant award Factory mag., 1967, Top Ten Plant award Modern Mfg. mag., 1970 Mem. AIA (Ohio chpt. award for Renton K. Brodie Sci. Ctr. 1971, for NALCO Ctr. 1980), Cin. Preservation Assn., Princeton Club. Lutheran. Office: 2856 Observatory Ave Cincinnati OH 45208-2340

ROONEY, ANDREW AITKEN, writer, columnist; b. Albany, N.Y., Jan. 14, 1919; s. Walter S. and Ellinor (Reynolds) R.; m. Marguerite Howard, Mar. 21, 1942; children: Ellen, Martha, Emily, Brian. Student, Colgate U., 1942. Writer-producer CBS-TV News, 1959—; newspaper columnist Tribune Co. Syndicate, 1979—. Author: (with O.C. Hutton) Air Gunner, 1944, The Story of Stars and Stripes, 1946, Conquerors' Peace, 1947, The Fortunes of War, 1962, A Few Minutes with Andy Rooney, 1981, And More By Andy Rooney, 1982, Pieces of My Mind, 1984, Word for Word, 1986, Not That You Asked, 1989, Sweet and Sour, 1992, My War, 1995, Sincerely, Andy Rooney, 1999, Common Nonsense, 2002; TV programs include An Essay on War, Mr. Rooney Goes to Washington, Mr. Rooney Goes to Dinner; regular commentator-essayist: 60 Minutes, 1978—. Served with AUS, 1941-45. Decorated Air Medal, Bronze Star; recipient awards for best written TV documentary Writers Guild Am., 1966, 68, 71, 75, 76, Emmy awards, 1968, 78, 81, 82 Office: CBS News 524 W 57th St New York NY 10019-2924

ROONEY, BRENDA LOUISE, epidemiologist, researcher; b. Estherville, Iowa, Jan. 18, 1962; d. Henry Otto and Evelyn Ellen Schauberger; m. Daniel Michael Rooney, July 13, 1985; children: Nicholas Alan, Claire Marie. BS Magna Cum Laude, U. Minn., 1984, MPH, 1987, PhD, 1992. Clin. epidemiologist Gundersen Luth. Health Sys., La Crosse, Wis., 1991—. Rsch. coord. Am. Lung Assn., N.Y.C., 1987—90; cons. Minn. Dept. Health, Mpls., 1990—90. Chair La Crosse Area Health Initiative, La Crosse, Wis., 1997—98; com. chair English Luth. Ch., La Crosse, Wis., 1998—2003; mem. State Task Force for Childhood Lead Poisoning Prevention, Madison, Wis., 1994—95. Recipient YWCA Tribute Outstanding Women, YWCA Coulee Region, 2000, Am. Assn. Health Plans; fellow Predoctoral fellow, Nat. Cancer Inst., 1988-1991. Mem.: APHA, Wis. Pub. Health Assn., Soc. Behavioral Medicine. Dfl. Lutheran. Office: Gundersen Luth Health System 1900 South Ave La Crosse WI 54601 Office Phone: 608-775-2152. E-mail: blrooney@gundluth.org.

ROONEY, DANIEL M. professional football team executive; b. 1932; s. Arthur Joseph and Kathleen (McNulty) Rooney. Former salesman advt., editor Pitts. Steelers Program; now pres. Pitts. Steelers; mem. exec. coms. NFL. Office: Three Rivers Stadium 3400 S Water St Pittsburgh PA 15203-2349

ROONEY, GEORGE WILLARD, lawyer; b. Appleton, Wis., Nov. 16, 1915; s. Francis John and Margaret Ellen (O'Connell) R.; m. Doris I. Maxon, Sept. 20, 1941; children: Catherine Ann, Thomas Dudley, George Willard. BS, U. Wis., 1938; JD, Ohio State U., 1948. Bar: Ohio 1949, U.S. Supreme Ct. 1956, U.S. Ct. Appeals 1956. Assoc. Wise, Roetzel, Maxon, Kelly & Andress, Akron, Ohio, 1949-54; ptnr. Roetzel & Andress, and predecessor, Akron, 1954—; dir. Duracote Corp. Nat. bd. govs. ARC, 1972-78; trustee, mem. exec. bd. Summit County chpt. ARC, 1968, 1975—; v.p. Akron coun. Boy Scouts Am., 1975—; pres. Akron Automobile Assn., 1980-83, trustee, 1983—; chmn. bd. Akron Gen. Med. Ctr., 1981-86, trustee, mem. exec. com., 1986—; trustee Mobile Meals Found., Bluecoats, Inc. Maj. USAAF, 1942-46. Decorated D.F.C. with 2 oak leaf clusters, Air medal with 3 oak leaf clusters; recipient Disting. Community Svc. award Akron Labor Coun.; Disting. Svc. award Summit County chpt. ARC, 1978. Mem. ABA, Ohio Bar Assn. Akron Bar Assn. Am. Judicature Soc., Rotary (past pres.), Portage Country Club (past pres.), Cascade Club (past chmn., bd. govs.), KC. Republican. Roman Catholic. Avocations: golf, travel, gardening. Home: 2863 Walnut Ridge Rd Akron OH 44333-2262 Office: Roetzel & Andress 222 S Main St Akron OH 44308-1533

ROONEY, JOE DON, country musician; b. Baxter Springs, Kans., Sept. 13, 1975; s. Windell and Jo Rooney. Student, A&M Jr. Coll. (Northwestern Okla. A&M). Performer Printers Alley, Nashville, Chely Wright Band; guitarist Rascal Flatts, 2000—. Musician: (albums) East to West, 1993, Rascal Flatts, 2000, Melt, 2002; performer: (songs) "Walk the Llama Llama", Emperor's New Grove (Original Soundtrack), 2000. Recipient Vocal Group Yr., Country Music Assn., 2002, Song Yr. for "I'm Movin On", Acad. Country Music Awards, 2002, Top Vocal Group, 2003. Office: Lyric St Records 19th Ave Nashville TN 37203 Office Phone: 615-963-4848.*

ROONEY, JOHN EDWARD, communications company executive; b. Evergreen Park, Ill., Apr. 24, 1942; s. John Edward and Margaret Wilma (Stolte) R.; m. Germaine Rose Dettloff, June 26, 1965; children: Kathleen, John, Colleen. BS, John Carroll U., 1964; MBA, Loyola U., 1969. Credit analyst Fed. Res. Bank, Chgo., 1964-69, adminstrv. asst., 1969-70; asst. treas. Pullman Inc., 1970-73, asst. contr., 1973-78; v.p. fin. Pullman Standard, 1978-79; sr. v.p. fin. Trailmobile, Chgo., 1979-81; treas. Firestone Tire & Rubber Co., Akron, Ohio, 1981-87, v.p. retail fin. services, 1987-88, sr. v.p. MasterCare Svc. Ctrs., 1988-90; v.p., treas. Ameritech, Chgo., 1990-92; pres. Ameritech Cellular Svcs., Chgo., 1992—. Instr. fin. Ill. Benedictine Coll., 1975-80 Mem. Ohio Mfrs. Assn. (trustee 1983-87), Ohio Pub. Expenditure Coun. (trustee 1986-87), Glen Oak Country Club (Glen Ellyn, Ill.), Boulders Club (Carefree, Ariz.), The Tavern Club (Chgo.). Home: 2S 311 Davis Ct Wheaton IL 60187 Office: Ameritech # 3H 70 2000 W Ameritech Center Dr Hoffman Estates IL 60196-1025

ROONEY, JOHN PHILIP, law educator; b. Evanston, Ill., May 1, 1932; s. John McCaffery and Bernadette Marie (O'Brien) R.; m. Jean Marie Kliss, Feb. 16, 1974 (div. Oct. 1988); 1 child, Caitlin Mairin. BA, U. Ill, 1953; JD, Harvard U., 1958. Bar: Ill. 1958, Calif. 1961, Mich. 1975, U.S. Tax Ct. 1973. Assoc. lawyer Chapman & Cutler, Chgo., 1958-60, Wilson, Morton, San Mateo, Calif., 1961-63; pvt. practice San Francisco, 1963-74; prof. law Cooley Law Sch., Lansing, Mich., 1975—. Author: Selected Cases (Property), 1985; contbr. articles to profl. jours. Pres. San Francisco coun. Dem. Clubs, 1970. 1st lt. U.S. Army, 1953-55. Recipient Beattie Teaching award Cooley Law Sch. Grads., 1979, 90, 92. Fellow Mich. Bar Found.; mem. ABA (real estate fed. tax problems com., title ins. com.), Ingham County Bar Assn., Univ. Club. Democrat. Unitarian Universalist. Office: Cooley Law Sch 300 S Capitol Ave Lansing MI 48933-1586 E-mail: rooneyj@cooley.edu.

ROONEY, KEVIN DAVITT, lawyer; b. Springfield, Mass., June 23, 1944; s. Davitt Michael and Elizabeth Isabel (Wlodyka) R.; m. Annette Eloise Benevento, Nov. 11, 1972; children: Kathryn Denise, Mary Elizabeth. BA, St. Marys Coll., 1966; JD, George Washington U., 1975. Bar: Va. 1975, D.C. 1977. Computer systems analyst VA, Washington, 1967-68, 70-73; chief legal programs and budget Dept. Justice, Washington, 1973-77, exec. asst. to assoc. atty. gen., 1977, asst. atty. gen. for adminstrn., 1977-84; prin. Rooney & Assocs, Washington, 1984-87, 90-94, Rooney & Barry, Washington, 1987-89; assoc. dir. Exec. Office for Immigration Rev. Dept. Justice, Falls Church, Va., 1995-97, asst. dir. Fed. Bur. Prisons Washington, 1997-99, dir. Exec. Office for Immigration Rev. Falls Church, Va., 1999-2001, acting commr. Immigration and Naturalization Svc., 2001—. Bd. dirs., v.p. Joint Action in Cmty. Svcs., Inc., Washington, 1988-94. With U.S. Army, 1968-70. Mem. ASPA, Fed. Bar Assn., Va. Bar Assn., D.C. Bar Assn. Office: Dept Justice Immigration Naturalization 425 Eye St NW Washington DC 20536

ROONEY, MARIA DEWING, photographer; b. N.Y.C., July 25; d. Madeleine L'Engle Franklin; m. John Bryan Rooney, Jan. 21, 1984; children: Bryson, Alexander. BFA, Phila. Coll. Art. Tchr. photography Bishop Bright Grammar Sch., Leamington Spa, Eng., Mid-Warwickshire Sch. of Further Edn., Leamington Spa, 1976-80; photographer, owner The Studios, Shipston-on-Stour, Eng., 1977-80; photographer Gary Studios & Comini Studios, Dallas, 1980-83; pvt. practice Mystic, Conn., 1990—. Exhibitions include Warwick (Eng.) Gallery, Derby (Eng.) Coll. Art Gallery, Bath (Eng.) Pl. Cmty. Ctr., Midland Group Galley, Nottingham, Eng., Wimbledon Sch. Art, London, Warwich U. Arts Ctr., Birmingham, Eng., Essex Art Assn., 1998, R. J. Julia, Madison, Conn., 1998, State Capitol Hartford, Conn., 1999, Emporium Gallery, 2003, Brick Gallery, Essex, Conn., 2003; contbr. photographs Anytime Prayers, 1994, Mothers and Daughters, 1997, Mothers and Sons, 1999, photographs published in Co-Optic Publs., London, 1976—80; prodr.: series greeting cards with personal photography; exhibitions include Brick Gallery, Essex, Conn., 2004, Emporium Gallery, 2004, one-woman shows include, 2004. Mem. Child and Family Svcs. Mem.: AAUW, Mystic Art Assn., Essex Art Assn. (photography award 1997, 2002, 2003). Avocations: sailing, writing. Home and Office: 77 High St Mystic CT 06355 E-mail: vlad0121@aol.com.

ROONEY, MATTHEW A. lawyer; b. Jersey City, May 19, 1949; s. Charles John and Eileen (Dunphy) R.; m. Jean M. Alletag, June 20, 1973 (div. Dec. 1979); 1 child, Jessica Margaret; m. Diane S. Kaplan, July 6, 1981; children: Kathryn Olivia, S. Benjamin. AB magna cum laude, Georgetown U., 1971; JD with honors, U. Chgo., 1974. Bar: Ill. 1975, U.S. Dist. Ct. (no. dist.) Ill. 1975, U.S. Ct. Appeals (7th cir.). 1990. Law clk. to cir. judge U.S. Ct. Appeals (7th cir.), Chgo., 1974-75; assoc. Mayer, Brown, Rowe & Maw, Chgo., 1975-80, ptnr., 1981—. Assoc. editor U. Chgo. Law Rev., 1973. Fellow Am. Coll. Trial Lawyers; mem. ABA, 7th Cir. Bar Assn., Order of Coif, Phi Beta Kappa. Democrat. Roman Catholic. Avocations: jogging, golf. Home: 2718 Sheridan Rd Evanston IL 60201-1754 Office: Mayer Brown Rowe & Maw LLP 190 S La Salle St Ste 3100 Chicago IL 60603-3441 E-mail: mrooney@mayerbrownrowe.com.

ROONEY, MICKEY (JOE YULE JR.), actor; b. Bklyn., Sept. 23, 1920; s. Joe and Nell (Carter) Yule; m. Ava Gardner, Jan. 10, 1942 (div. May 1943); m. Betty Jane Rase, Sept. 30, 1944 (div. 1949); children: Mickey Jr., Timothy; m. Martha Vickers, June 3, 1949 (div.); m. Elaine Mahnken (div. 1958); m. Barbara Thomason, Dec. 1958; children: Kerry, Kyle, Kelly Ann, Kimmy Sue; m. Margie Lang, Sept. 1966 (div. 1967); m. Carolyn Hockett, (div.); 1 adopted child, Jimmy, 1 child, Jonell; m. Jan Chamberlin, July 28, 1978; stepchildren: Chris Aber, Mark Aber. Ed. in, Dayton Heights and Vine Street grammar sch., Pacific Mil. Acad., under tutors. First appeared in vaudeville with parents; then appeared with Sid Gould, numerous TV programs; appeared in motion pictures Judge Hardy's Children, Hold That Kiss, Lord Jeff, Love Finds Andy Hardy, Boys Town, Stablemates, Out West With the Hardys, Huckleberry Finn, Andy Hardy Gets Spring Fever, Babes in Arms, Young Tom Edison, Judge Hardy and Son, Andy Hardy Meets Debutante, Strike Up the Band, Andy Hardy's Private Secretary, Men of Boystown, Life Begins for Andy Hardy, Babes on Broadway, A Yank at Eton, The Human Comedy, Andy Hardy's Blonde Trouble, Girl Crazy, Thousands Cheer, National Velvet, Ziegfeld Follies, The Strip, Sound Off, Off Limits, All Ashore, Light Case of Larceny, Drive A Crooked Road, Bridges at Toko-Ri, The Bold and Brave, Eddie, Private Lives of Adam and Eve, Comedian, The Grabbers, St. Joseph Plays the Horses, Breakfast at Tiffany's, Somebody's Waiting, Requiem For A Heavyweight, Richard, Pulp, It's a Mad, Mad, Mad, Mad World, Everything's Ducky, The Secret Invasion, The Extraordinary Seaman, The Comic, The Cockeyed Cowboys of Calico County, Skidoo, B.J. Presents, That's Entertainment, The Domino Principle, Pete's Dragon, The Magic of Lassie, Black Stallion, Arabian Adventure, Erik the Viking, My Heroes Have Always Been Cowboys, 1991, (voice) Little Nimo: Adventures in Slumberland, 1992, Long Road Home, 1996, Kings of the Court, 1997, Animals, 1997, Babe: Pig in the City, 1998, Internet Love, 1998, The First of May, 1999, (voice) Lady and the Tramp II: Scamps Adventure, 2001, Topa Topa Bluffs, 2002; starred in TV prodns. Pinocchio, 1957, Leave 'Em Laughing, 1981, Bill, 1981 (Emmy, Golden Globe), Senior Trip!, 1981, Bill on His Own, 1983, Little Spies (Acad. Hon. award 1982), It Came upon the Midnight Clear, 1984, Bluegrass, 1988, Legend of Wolf Mountain, 1992, That's Entertainment! III, 1994, Revente of the Red Baron, 1994, Radio Star-die AFN-Story, 1994, The Legend of O.B. Taggart, 1995; appeared on stage in Sugar Babies, 1979, The Will Rogers Follies, 1993; appeared in TV series A Year at the Top, The Mickey Rooney Show; author: I.E. An Autobiography, 1965, Life Is Too Short, 1991, Search for Sonny Skies, 1994, Brother's Destiny (T.V.), 1995, Michael Kael in Katango, 1997, Boys Will be Boys, 1997, Sinbad: The Battle of the Dark Knights, 1998, The First of May, 1998, The Face on the Barroom Floor, 1998, Babe: Pig in the City, 1998; fgn. films: Midsummer Nights Dream, 1937, Words and Music, 1946, Rachels, 1973, To Hong Kong with Love, 1975, Oddessy of the Pacific, 1979. With AUS, WWII. Recipient Spl. Acad. Award, 1940, Tony award for best mus. actor, 1980; named One of Top 10 Money-Making Stars, Herald-Fame Poll, 1938-43 Office: PO Box 3186 Thousand Oaks CA 91359-0186

ROONEY, PAUL GEORGE, mathematics professor; b. N.Y.C., July 14, 1925; s. Geoffrey Daniel and Doris Elizabeth (Babcock) R.; m. Mary Elizabeth Carlisle, June 20, 1950; children: Francis Timothy, Elizabeth Anne, Kathleen Doris, John Edward, James Carlisle. B.Sc., U. Alta., 1949; PhD, Calif. Inst. Tech., 1952. Asst. prof. math. U. Alta., 1952-55; asst. prof. U. Toronto, 1955-60, assoc. prof., 1960-62, prof., 1962-91, prof. emeritus, 1991—. Dir. Commonwealth Petroleum Co., Calgary, 1946-59 Editor in chief Can. Jour. Math. 1971-75; contbr. articles to profl. jours. Bd. dirs. Francis F. Reeve Found., 1954-85. Served with Can. Army, 1943-45. Fellow Royal Soc. Can.; Mem. Can. Math. Soc. (councillor 1960-64, 66-70, 76-78, v.p. 1979-81, pres. 1981-83), Am. Math. Soc., Math. Assn. Am. Office: U Toronto Dept Math 100 St George St Toronto ON Canada M5S 3G1 E-mail: rooney@math.toronto.edu.

ROONEY, PHILLIP BERNARD, service company executive; b. Chgo., July 8, 1944; BA magna cum laude, St. Bernard Coll., 1966. With Waste Mgmt., 1969-97, Service Master Co., Downers Grove, Ill., 1997—2003; chmn. Claddaugh Investments LLC, 2004—. Trustee Notre Dame U.; chmn. sister Cities Internat.; bd. dirs. El Valor. Recipient Semper Fidelis award Marine Corps Scholarship Found., El Valor's Corp. Visionary award, Man of Yr. award Ill. Viet Nam Vets. Mem.: Econ. Club Chgo. (past chmn.). Roman Catholic. Office: 1301 W 35th St Chicago IL 60609 E-mail: prooney78@aol.com.

ROOP, JAMES JOHN, public relations executive; b. Parkersburg, W.Va., Oct. 29, 1949; s. J. Vaun and Mary Louise (McGinnis) R.; m. Margaret Mary Kuneck (div. 1982); m. Susan Lynn Hoell (div. 1989); m. Daisy P. Billue, 1990 (div. 1999). BS in Journalism, W. Va. U., 1971. Various account mgmt. postions Ketchum Pub. Rels., Pitts., 1972-77, v.p., 1977-79, Burson-Marsteller, Chgo., 1979-81; sr. v.p. Hesselbart & Mitten/Watt, Cleve., 1981-84, exec. v.p., 1984-86, pres., 1986-87, Watt, Roop & Co. (formerly Hesselbart & Mitten/Watt), Cleve., 1987-96; chmn., pres., CEO Roop & Co., Cleve., 1996—. Contbr. articles to profl. jours. Mem. Leadership Clevel.; former bd. dirs. Ctr. for Families and Children, Boys Hope, Girls Hope, Kidney Found., Police Athletic League, Econs. Am. Fellow Pub. Rels. Soc. Am. (chmn. investor rels. sect. 1984-85, chmn. honors and awards com. 1995); mem. Nat. Investor Rels. Inst. (pres. Cleve./Akron/Pitts. chpt., sr. investor rels. roundtable), Cleve. Skating Club, Mayfield Country Club, Hermit Club. Republican. Home: 2697 Scarborough Rd Cleveland Heights OH 44106-3241 Office: Roop & Co 650 Huntington Bldg 925 Euclid Ave Cleveland OH 44115-1408

ROOP, JOSEPH MCLEOD, economist; b. Montgomery, Ala., Sept. 29, 1941; s. Joseph Ezra and Mae Elizabeth (McLeod) R.; m. Betty Jane Reed, Sept. 4, 1965; 1 dau., Elizabeth Rachael. BS, Ctrl. Mo. State U., Warrensburg, 1963; PhD, Wash. State U., Pullman, 1973. Economist Econ. Rsch. Svc., USDA, Washington, 1975-79; sr. economist Evans Econs., Inc., Washington, 1979-81; staff scientist Battelle Pacific N.W. Nat. Lab., Richland, Wash., 1981—. Adj. prof. dept. econs. Wash. State U., 1999—; with Internat. Energy Agy., Paris, 1990-91. Contbr. articles to profl. jours. With U.S. Army, 1966—68. Dept. Agr. Coop. State Rsch. Svc. rsch. grantee, 1971-73. Mem. Am. Econ. Assn., Econometric Soc., Internat. Assn. Energy Econs., Am. Statis. Assn. Home: 715 S Taft St Kennewick WA 99336-9587 Office: PO Box 999 MSIN K6-05 Richland WA 99352-0999 Office Phone: 509-372-4245. Personal E-mail: jmroop@verizon.net. Business E-Mail: joe.roop@pnl.gov.

ROOP, MITCHELL A. information scientist; b. Ocala, Fla., Feb. 12, 1955; s. James Q. and Bobbie P. Roop; m. Elizabeth S. Roop, Feb. 14, 1992. BA, U. Fla., 1989; M.Liberal Arts, U. South Fla., 1992. Programmer/tech. writer Rare Comms. Inc., Oldsman, Fla., 1990—94; writer Kronus Inc., Tampa, 1994—97; tech. dir. Sites on Demand, Inc., Tampa, 1997—98, chief tech. officer, COO, 1998—99; CEO MTG Internat., Inc., Tampa, 1999—2002; pres. Mitch Roop, Inc., Tampa, 2002—. Mem. Leadership Tampa, 2002—03; exec. com., bd. dirs. Faces of Courage Found., Inc., Tampa, 2002—; mem. pres.'s coun. U. Fla., Tampa, 2001—. With U.S. Army, 1973—85. Republican. Methodist. Avocations: weight training, martial arts. Office: Mitch Roop Inc 12601 Wood Ibis Way Tampa FL 33624-5717

ROORDA, JOHN FRANCIS, JR., business consultant; b. Evanston, Ill., Jan. 16, 1923; s. John Francis and Sadie M. (Daley) R.; m. Elizabeth Mulcahy, July 2, 1949; children: Elizabeth Roorda Barker, John F., Ann Roorda Hollis. BSChemE, Purdue U., 1943, PhD, 1949. With Shell Oil Co., 1949-83; gen. mgr. combined oil products/chem. econs. dept., 1973-74; v.p. planning and econs., 1974-77; v.p. Shell Devel. Co., Houston, 1977-78; v.p. corp. planning Shell Oil Co., 1978-83; pres. John Roorda, 1983—. Coordinator Exec. Service Corps, Houston, 1985— Served to lt. (j.g.) USNR, 1943-46. Recipient Disting. Engring. Alumnus award Purdue U., 1976, Outstanding Chem. Engr. award Purdue U., 1993. Mem. Sigma Xi. Roman Catholic. E-mail: graycell@houston.rr.com.

ROORDA, PETER, lawyer; b. Harlingen, Friesland, Netherlands, Oct. 25, 1952; came to U.S., 1988; s. Dirk Sidonius and Louise J.M. (Timmermans) R.; m. Geertje Boontje, June 25, 1986; children: Sietske L., Haye F., Tjallingh O.P. Gynmasium-B, Latin Sch., 1972; JD cum laude, U. Groningen, 1978; M of Laws, U. Pa., 1979. Bar: Amsterdam 1980, N.Y. 1990. Assoc. Stibbe, Blaisse & De Jong, Amsterdam, Netherlands, 1980-87; ptnr. Stibbe & Simont, Amsterdam, Netherlands, 1987-88, resident ptnr. N.Y.C., 1988—. Pres. Dutch United Nations Student Assn., Groningen, 1973-74; mem. steering com. Netherlands Lawyers Com. Human Rights, Leiden, 1977-78; mem. adv. bd. Student Publ. Found., Nijmegen, Netherlands, 1977-84; bd. dirs. The Hycliff Assn., Stamford, Conn., 1990—, Netherlands C. of C. in U.S., N.Y.C., 1991, The Netherlands Am. Amity Trust, Washington, 1991—. Greenfield fellow

Human Rights, U. Pa., 1978; recipient German/Dutch Translation award Germany Embassy in The Netherlands, 1972. Mem. ABA (co-chmn. internat. comml. arbitration com. sect. internat. law and practice 1992—), Am. Fgn. Law Assn. (v.p. 1990—), N.Y. State Bar Assn., City Bar N.Y., Netherland Club N.Y. Avocations: gardening, tennis, travel, reading. Office: Stibbe & Simont 335 Madison Ave Rm 1502 New York NY 10017-4605

ROOS, CASPER, actor; b. N.Y.C., Mar. 21, 1925; s. Jacob and Sabina (Uhlenbusch) R.; m. Shirley Anne Nicholson, June 27, 1953; 1 child, Pieter Nicholson. Student, N.Y. Coll. Music. Treas. Actors Equity Found., N.Y.C., 1982-88; co-chmn. research subcom. Nat. Theater Com., N.Y.C., 1983—; chair supv. com. Actors Fed. Credit Union, 1990-2001, 2003—. Prin. actor Shenandoah, N.Y.C., 1975-78, Brigadoon, N.Y.C., 1979-80, My One and Only, N.Y.C., 1982-85, Into the Light, 1986, Man of La Mancha, Zurich, 1988, (Broadway prodn.) Shenandoah Revival, 1989; numerous regional theater prodns. Served with U.S. Mcht. Marines, 1943-46. Mem. Actors Equity (treas. 1982-88, councilor 1964-79, 88-93). Home: PO Box 11 Gilbertsville NY 13776-0011 Office Phone: 800-484-1081 x4081. *Don Quixote wanted to 'add a little grace to the world.' I, too, would like to add a 'little' to this world, whether it be grace or laughter or tears to an audience or service to my colleagues. If, like Don Quixote, I look a little foolish, so be it. I prefer a life of striving for the ultimate to the easier smug acceptance of the status quo.*

ROOS, CHARLES EDWIN, physicist; b. Chgo., Apr. 23, 1927; s. Charles Frederick and Mary Barkuloo Roos; m. Anne Friedrich, Aug. 30, 1952; children: Margit Josephine, Alice Marie, Carlton Friedrich, Charles David. BA in Zoology, U. Tex., Austin, 1948; PhD in Physics, Johns Hopkins U., 1953. Faculty assoc. in physics Johns Hopkins U., Balt., 1953-54; asst. prof. physics U. Calif., Riverside, 1954-59; rsch. fellow Calif. Inst. Tech., Pasadena, 1955-67; assoc. prof. physics Vanderbilt U., Nashville, 1959-65, prof. physics, 1965-89, prof. emeritus, 1989—; chmn. Nat. Recovery Tech., Nashville, 1982—. Regular visitor, Be. Labs., Holmdale, N.J., 1973-76, scientific assoc. CERN, Geneva, Switzerland, 1969-80, founder, dir. Am. Magnetics, Oak Ridge, Tenn., 1966-85, mng. ptnr. Seofon Assocs., Baytown, Tex., 1960—; prin. investigator, NSF, 1955-89, U.S. Dept. Energy, 1970—. Contbr. over 140 articles to profl. jours.; U.S. and fgn. patentee in field. Mem. Condominium bdl, 817 5th Ave. Condominium, N.Y.C., 1975—, pres. bd., 1999—. With USN, 1945-46. Recipient Tibbets award, SBA, 1996, Nat. Conservation medal, DAR, 1992; guest Nobel awards, Royal Acad. Physics, Stockholm, 1989; sr. NATO fellow, NSF, Max Planck Inst., 1968. Fellow Am. Physics Soc.; mem. Cosmos Club. Avocations: cross country skiing, scuba diving. Office: 566 Mainstream Dr Ste 300 Nashville TN 37228-1234 E-mail: ceroos@comcast.net.

ROOS, DANIEL, engineering educator; b. Bklyn., Apr. 12, 1939; s. Sigmund and Anita (Sperling) R.; m. Eva Bonis, June 1, 1969; children— Richard Joseph, Linda Suzanne. BS in Civil Engring, M.I.T., 1961, MS, 1963, PhD, 1966. Mem. faculty MIT, Cambridge, 1963—, assoc. prof. civil engring., 1970-76, prof., 1976—, head transp. systems div., 1977-78, dir. Ctr. for Transp. Studies, 1978-85, dir. Ctr. Tech., Policy and Indsl. Devel., 1985-97, Japan Steel Industry prof., 1985—, mem. Commn. on Indsl. Productivity, 1987-89, assoc. dean engring. systems, 1997—, spl. asst. provost and chancellor, 1996—, co-dir. Ford Indsl. Ptnrships, dir. engring. sys. divsn., 1998—. Founder, dir. Multisystems Inc., Cambridge, 1965—85; chmn. com. to assess advanced vehicle and hwy techs. NRC, 1990—91, mem. com. on fuel economy, 1991—92; dir. Internat. Motor Vehicle Program, 1980—99; co-dir. Lean Aircraft Initiative, 1992—97; mem. coun. indsl. relationships MIT, 1996—97. Author: ICES System Design, 1964; The Future of the Automobile, 1984, Auto Futures, 1990; co-author: Made in America, 1989, The Machine That Changed the World, 1990; contbr. articles to profl. jours. Mem. U.S. Task Force on Transp., 1969. Recipient Shingo Prize for Excellence in Mfg. Rsch., 1994. Mem. ASCE (Frank M. Masters Transp. Engring. award 1989), Assn. Computing Machinery, Ops. Research Soc. (treas. transp. sci. sect. 1970-71), Transp. Research Bd. (chmn. para-transit com. 1974-80, group coun. 1980-84), Coun. Univ. Transp. Ctrs. (pres. 1983). Achievements include developing Dial-A-Ride transp. concept, 1965; dir. Internat. Motor Vehicle. Home: 28 Baskin Rd Lexington MA 02421-6929 Office: MIT Engring Sys Divsn 77 Massachusetts Ave Cambridge MA 02139-4307 Office Phone: 617-253-1661. E-mail: roos@mit.edu.

ROOS, JANE MAYO, art history educator; b. N.Y.C., Feb. 14, 1943; d. Maurice Arthur and Katherine Haverkamp Mayo; m. Michael Roos, Apr. 17, 1971 (div. Dec. 1993); 1 child, Katherine; m. William Howard Griesar, June 12, 1999. BA, Coll. New Rochelle, 1964; MA, Hunter Coll., 1974; PhD, Columbia U., 1981. Editor Holt, Rinehart and Winston, N.Y.C., 1966-71; prof. art history Hunter Coll. and Grad. Ctr. CUNY, N.Y.C., 1985—. Vis. lectr. Christie's Grad. Program Connoisseurship, N.Y.C., 1999—. Author: Early Impressionism and the French State 1866-1874, 1996; co-author: Rodin's Monument to Victor Hugo, 1998, The Landscapes of France, 1995; contbr. articles to profl. jours. Curator A Painter's Poet: Stéphane Mallarmé, 1999. Columbia U. grantee, 1975, 76, 81, Samuel H. Kress Found. grantee, 1977, 78, 79, Rsch. and Travel grantee Am. Coun. Learned Socs., 1987,, CUNY Rsch. and Travel grantee, 1991, 94, 98, 99, 2000, Florence Gould Found. grantee, 1999; Postdoctoral fellow J. Paul Getty Truste, 1987-88. Mem. Coll. Art Assn. Am., Assn. Historians Nineteenth-Century Art. Home: 40 Clinton Ave Dobbs Ferry NY 10522 Office: Hunter Coll and Grad Ctr 695 Park Ave New York NY 10021

ROOS, SYBIL FRIEDENTHAL, retired elementary school educator; b. L.A., Jan. 29, 1924; d. Charles G. and Besse (Weixel) Friedenthal; m. Henry Kahn Roos, May 8, 1949 (dec. Dec. 1989); children: Catherine Alane Cook, Elizabeth Anne Garlinger, Virginia Ann Bertrand. BA in Music, Centenary Coll., 1948; MEd, Northwestern State U., 1973. Cert. elem. edn. tchr., spl. edn. tchr. Tchr. Caddo Parish Schs., Shreveport, 1968-75, Spring Branch Ind. Schs., Houston, 1975-85; vol. Houston Grand Opera/Guild, 1979—, Houston Mus. of Fine Arts/Guild, 1990—, Houston Symphony Soc./Guild, 1997—. Author tchrs. guides. Pres. Nat. Coun. Jewish Women, Shreveport, 1958; bd. dirs. Mus. Fine Arts; area coord. Spl. Olympics, Shreveport, 1974-75; bd. dirs. U. Houston Moore Sch. Music. With USN, 1944-46. Mem. AAUW (pres. Spring Valley Houston chpt. 1985-87), Houston Grand Opera Guild (pres. 1989-91), Houston Symphony League, Houston Ballet Guild, Mus. of Fine Arts Guild (bd. dirs.), U. Houston Sch. of Music (bd. dirs.) Am. Needlepoint Guild, Delta Kappa Gamma (bd. dirs., treas. 1987-89), Phi Mu. Republican. Avocations: music, tennis, needlepoint, volunteering. Home: 10220 Memorial Dr Apt 78 Houston TX 77024-3227 E-mail: s.roos@worldnet.att.net.

ROOSA, JAN BERTOROTTA, clinical psychologist; b. Champaign, Ill., Apr. 19, 1927; s. Walter Laidlaw and Giannina (Bertorotta) R.; m. Joan Herr. BS, U. Ill., 1950; MA, U. Denver, 1951, PhD, 1957. Coord., clin. psychologist Child Rsch. Coun., Kansas City, Mo., 1954-57, dir. neighborhood rsch. project, 1957; supr., psychologist State Hosp., Fulton, Mo., 1957-59; chief of psychotherapy VA Hosp., Kansas City, 1959-63; clin. psychologist in pvt. practice, Kansas City area, 1963—. Dir., co-founder Learning Resource Ctr., Kansas City, 1969-79; dir. Gestalt, Social Competence Inst., Kansas City, 1969-89; active Conflict Resolution of Met. Kansas City; dir. Competence and Cooperation Group, 1992—. Author: Situation-Options-Consequences-Simulation: A Technique for Teaching Social Skills, 1973, Psychological and Social Competence Model and Skills, 1975, 88, 92; creator SOCCSS and SOCCSS: A Decision Making Process, 1973, 96, The Competence and Cooperation Based Program, 1995. Served with USN, 1945-47, 51-52. Mem. APA, Greater Kansas City Psychol. Assn., Mo. Psychol. Assn., Kans. Assn. Profl. Psychologists, Mental Health Profls., Nat. Register Health Providers in Psychology. Office: 9229 Ward Pkwy Ste 365 Kansas City MO 64114-3334

ROOSEVELT, JAMES, JR., health plan executive, lawyer; b. L.A., Nov. 9, 1945; s. James and Romelle (Schneider) R.; m. Ann M. Conlon, June 15, 1968; children: Kathy, Tracy, Maura. AB, Harvard U., 1968, JD, 1971. Bar. Mass. 1971, D.C. 1973, U.S. Ct. Appeals (D.C. cir.) 1973, U.S. Ct. Appeals (1st cir.) 1976, U.S. Supreme Ct. 1975. Assoc. Winthrop, Stimson, Putnam & Roberts, N.Y.C., 1971, Herrick & Smith, Boston, 1975-80, ptnr., 1981-86, Nutter, McClennen & Fish, Boston, 1986-88, Choate, Hall & Stewart, Boston, 1988-98; assoc. commr. for retirement policy Social Security Adminstrn., Washington, 1998-99; sr. v.p., gen. counsel Tufts Health Plan, Waltham, Mass., 1999—. Mem. Dem. Nat. Com., Washington, 1980—, Dem. State Com., Boston, 1980—; trustee Emmanuel Coll., Boston, 1982-92, 95—; trustee Care Group, Inc., Boston, 1996-00, Mt. Auburn Hosp., Cambridge, Mass., 1984-2000, chmn., 1988-92, chmn. bd. overseers, 2000—. Lt. JAGC, USN, 1972-75. Mem. ABA, Boston Bar Assn., Mass. Bar Assn., Am. Health Lawyers Assn. (pres. 2002-03), Mass. Hosp. Assn. (trustee 1987-99, chmn. 1996-97), Harvard Club. Roman Catholic. Avocation: public policy. Office: Tufts Health Plan 333 Wyman St Waltham MA 02451-1282 E-mail: james_roosevelt@tufts-health.com.

ROOSEVELT, PHIL, periodical editor; BA, Tufts U., 1979; MBA, Columbia U., 1985. Editor Am. Banker, Inc., N.Y.C., 1999—. Office: Time Inc 1271 Ave of the Americas New York NY 10020

ROOSEVELT, THEODORE, IV, investment banker; b. Jacksonville, Fla., Nov. 27, 1942; s. Theodore III and Anne Mason (Babcock) Roosevelt; m. Constance Lane Rogers, Aug. 1, 1970; 1 child, Theodore V. AB, Harvard U., 1965, MBA, 1972. Assoc. Lehman Bros., N.Y.C., 1972-76; corp. v.p. Lehman Bros. Kuhn Loeb, N.Y.C., 1976-82; sr. v.p. Lehman Comml. Paper Inc., N.Y.C., 1982-85; mng. dir. Lehman Brothers (formerly Shearson Lehman Bros., Inc.), N.Y.C., 1985—. Chmn., bd. dirs. Lehman Bros. Fin. Products, Inc.; dir. Inst. Environ. and Natural Resources U. Wyo. Mem. N.Y. State Pk. Recreation and Hist. Preservation Commn. City of N.Y.; commr. Hudson River Pk. Conservancy; mem., governing coun. Cultural Inst. Retirement Sys.; trustee Pew Ctr. Global Change, Am. Mus. Natural History, World Resources Inst. Mem.: Fgn. Policy Assn. (gov.), Coun. Fgn. Rels., Trout Unlimited, Wilderness Soc. (vice chmn.), Clove Valley Rod and Gun Club, Econ. Club N.Y., Harvard Club (N.Y.C.), Explorers Club, Heights Casino Club (Bklyn.), Edgartown Yacht Club, Links (N.Y.C.). Republican. Home: 1 Pierrepont St Brooklyn NY 11201-3302 Office: Lehman Bros 745 7th Ave 20th Fl New York NY 10019 Office Phone: 212-526-8363.

ROOT, ALAN CHARLES, diversified manufacturing company executive; b. Essex, Eng., Apr. 11, 1925; arrived in U.S., 1951, naturalized, 1959; s. Charles Stanley and Lillian (Collins) Root. BA, Oxford U., 1943; MA, Cambridge U., 1951; MBA, Stanford U., 1953. Rsch. analyst Dow Chem. Co., Midland, Mich., 1954—55; mgr. mktg. rsch. GE Co., 1955—61; v.p. bus. planning Mosler Safe Co., Hamilton, Ohio, 1961—70; v.p. corp. planning Am. Standard Inc., N.Y.C., 1970—76, sr. v.p. ops. svcs., 1976—86, sr. v.p., 1986—88, sr. advisor, 1989. Trustee 1995 Trust Fund; sr. advisor Unit Ice, 1995—; bd. dirs. Am.-Standard Energy Inc., Amstan Trucking Inc., 1976-86. Trustee, treas. N.J. Chamber Music Soc., 1988—95; mem. Sheriff's Jury, N.Y. Cty., 1971—79; bd. dirs., chmn. Brit. Schs. and Univs. Found., 1970—2002, hon. dir., 2002—. Capt. Brit. Army, 1944—48. Admission to Order of St. John of Jerusalem sanctioned by Her Majesty Queen Elizabeth II, 1986, comdr., 1994. Mem. AIChE (assoc. producer TV series Midland sect. 1955), Pilgrims U.S., Newcomen Soc. N.Am., Univ. Club (N.Y.C.). Home: 4934 Mount Pleasant Ln Las Vegas NV 89113-0114 Fax: 702-227-8885. *Good luck meant that my industrial career drew on the education I enjoyed as a young man. Professional advancement came by building on prior experience at each step and through long-term, managerial continuity.*

ROOT, ALLEN WILLIAM, pediatrician, educator; b. Phila., Sept. 24, 1933; s. Morris Jacob and Priscilla R.; m. Janet Greenberg, June 15, 1958; children: Jonathan, Jennifer, Michael. AB, Dartmouth Coll., 1955, postgrad. Med. Sch., 1954-56; MD, Harvard U., 1958. Diplomate Am. Bd. Pediatrics (mem. bd. 1985—), Am. Bd. Pediatric Endocrinology (mem. bd. 1985-90, chmn. 1990). Intern Strong Meml. Hosp., Rochester, N.Y., 1958-60; resident in pediatrics Hosp. U. Pa., Phila., 1960-62; fellow in pediatric endocrinology Children's Hosp. of Phila., 1962-65; assoc. physician in pediatrics U. Pa. Sch. Medicine, 1964-66, asst. prof. pediatrics, 1966-69; assoc. prof. pediatrics Temple U. Sch. Medicine, Phila., 1969-73, prof., 1973; asst. physician in endocrinology Children's Hosp. Phila., 1965-69; chmn. divsn. pediatrics Albert Einstein Med. Center., Phila., 1969-73; prof. pediatrics U. South Fla. Coll. Medicine, Tampa, 1973—, prof. biochemistry, 1987—, assoc. chmn. dept. pediatrics, 1974-99, dir. sect. pediatric endocrinology, 1973-96. Dir. univ. tchg. svcs. All Children's Hosp., St. Petersburg, 1973-89; mem. Fla. Infant Screening Adv. Coun., 1979—, chmn., 1994—; mem. Hillsborough County Thyroid Adv. Com., 1980; mem. med. adv. com. Nat. Pituitary Agy., 1974-78, mem. growth hormone subcom., 1972-79, 81-85; chmn. Fla. Legis. Infant Screening Task Force, 2002. Author: Human Pituitary Growth Hormone, 1972; editor Endocrinology and Metabolism Current Opinion in Pediats., 1993—; co-editor: (with C. La Cauza) Problems in Pediatric Endocrinology, 1980; mem. editl. bd. Jour. Pediats., 1973-81, Jour. Adolescent Health Care, 1979-95, Jour. Pediat. Endocrinology and Metabolism, 1985—, Jour. Clin. Endocrinology and Metabolism, 1993-96, 2001—, Growth, Genetics and Hormones, 1993—, Pediat. in Rev., 1995-2001; assoc. editor Adolescent and Pediat. Gynecology, 1992-95. USPHS grantee; Birth Defects Found. grantee. Mem. AAAS, Am. Pediatric Soc., Soc. Pediatric Rsch., Lawson Wilkins Pediatric Endocrine Soc. (treas. 1979-88, pres. 1988-89), Endocrine Soc., Am. Acad. Pediatrics, Am. Fedn. Clin. Rsch., Soc. Exptl. Biology and Medicine, Soc. Nuclear Medicine, N.Y. Acad. Sci., Phila. Coll. Physicians, Phila. Endocrine Soc. (bd. dirs. 1971-72, treas. 1973), Dartmouth Coll. Alumni Coun., Dartmouth Club. Office: 801 6th St S Saint Petersburg FL 33701-4816 Business E-Mail: roota@allkids.org.

ROOT, EDWARD LAKIN, education educator, academic administrator; b. Cumberland, Md., Dec. 5, 1940; s. Lakin and Edna Grace (Adams) Root. BS, Frostburg (Md.) State Coll., 1962, MEd, 1966; EdD, U. Md., 1970. Cert. tchr. Md. Tchr. Allegany County Bd. of Edn., Cumberland, 1962-66; grad. fellow U. Md., College Park, 1966-67, fellow, 1967-69; with Frostburg (Md.) State U., 1969-99, prof., head edn. dept., 1980-87, dean, 1987-95, prof., head MEd adminstrn., 1995-99. Mem. Profl. Stds. Bd. Md., Balt., 1980—87, Balt., 1995—99, Cert. Rev. Bd. Md., Balt., 1987—90, Md. Task Force Adminstrn., Balt., 1985—88, Md. Task Force: Prisoners Time and Response, task force tchr. assessment, 1995—97, Md. Task Force Tchr. Quality, 2002—03, Md. Task Force Disadvantaged but Capable Students, 2000—02; chmn. Md. Tchr. Quality Task Group, 2002—03. Mem. Allegany County (Md.) Planning and Zoning Bd. Appeals, 1995—96; gubernatorial appointee Md. State Bd. Edn., 1999—, pres., 2003—. Mem.: ASCD, Nat. Soc. Study Edn., Nat. Assn. Secondary Sch. Prins., Mensa, Masons, Elks, Shriners, Phi Delta Kappa. Democrat. Methodist. Avocations: photography, travel. Home: 100 Pennsylvania Ave Cumberland MD 21502-4236 Office: Frostburg State U College Ave Frostburg MD 21532-1724

ROOT, GERALD EDWARD, legal administrator; b. Gridley, Calif., May 5, 1948; s. Loris Leo Root and Mary Helen (Wheeler) Murrell; m. Tricia Ann Caywood, Feb. 13, 1982 (dec.); children: Jason Alexander, Melinda Ann. AA in Bus., Yuba C.C., Marysville, Calif., 1968; BA in Psychology, Calif. State U., Sonoma, 1974; MA in Social Sci., Calif. State U., Chico, 1977; postgrad., U. San Francisco, 1994—99. Gen. mgr. Do-It Leisure Therapeutic Recreation, Chico, Calif., 1977-79; CETA projects coord. City of Chico, 1980-81; exec. dir. Voluntary Action Ctr., Inc., South Lake Tahoe, 1981-83; devel. dir. Work Tng. Ctr., Inc., Chico, 1983—91; exec. dir. North Valley Rehab. Found., 1986-92; spl. projects adminstrn. officer Superior Ct. of Calif., County of Sacramento, 1992—. Project mgr. Juvenile Detention Alternatives Initiative, 1992-98, Feather River Industries Vocat. Tng., 1991, Creative Learning Ctr. Constrn., 1988-89, Correctional Options-Drug Ct., 1994, Violence Prevention Resource Ctr., 1995-96, Communities That Care-Juvenile Delinquency Prevention Initiative, 1995, Securing the Health and Safety of Urban Children Initiative, 1995-97, Joint Cabinets Youth Work Group/Child Welfare League Am., 1996-97, Task Force on Fairness-The Juvenile Justice Initiative, 1994-97, SacraMentor, Inc., Calif. Wellness Found., 1994-95, Violent Injury Prevention Coalition/Calif. Dept. Health and Human Svcs., 1995-2000, Domestic Violence Coord. Coun., Sacramento County, 1995-98, Family Violence Summit, 1997, Ptnrs. in Protection Conf. 1997 Child Abuse Prevention Coun., The Drug Store, Calif. N.G. drug demand reduction program, 1996-97, disporportionate minority confinement rsch. com. Criminal Justice Cabinet, 1997-99, Court Cmty.-Focused Strategic Plan, 1998-2001, Sunrise Recreation and Park Dist. 10 Yr. Master Plan, 1999-2000, virtual courthouse tour-distance learning, 2001-2002, lang. aides program, 2002-, self-represented litigants action plan initiative, 2000-2003, jud. and ct. staff tng. videos, 2003-2004, early Calif. Ct. history, 2003-, ct. forms stds., 2003-2004, ct. interpreters recruitment, 2004-; steering com. Multicultural Family Violence Prevention Conf., 1996-2001; legis. coord., 2003-2004; presenter in field. Bd. dirs. Cmty. Action Agy., Butte County, Calif., 1990-92, ARC, Butte County, 1989-90, Sunrise Recreation and Park Dist., 1996-2001; adv. bd. Butte C.C. Dist., 1987-92, Cmty. Svcs. Planning Coun., 1994-96; blue ribbon task force for strategic plan Calif. Found. for Parks and Recreation, 2000. Grantee Annie E. Casey Found., USDA, U.S. Dept. Justice, Robert Wood Johnson Found., Calif. Office Criminal Justice Planning, U.S. Dept. Labor, Office Juvenile Justice and Delinquency Prevention, Sacramento Criminal Justice Cabinet, Calif. Wellness Found., Calif. Endowment, Adminstrv. Office of the Cts., 1998-2003; recipient Ralph N. Kleps award Calif. Jud. Coun., 2000. Office: Superior Ct Calif County of Sacramento 720 9th St Sacramento CA 95814-1302 E-mail: rootg@saccourt.com.

ROOT, JAMES BENJAMIN, landscape architect; b. Detroit, Jan. 26, 1934; s. William Jehial and Helen Elizabeth (English) R. BBA, Memphis State U., 1960; B Landscape Architecture, U. Ga., 1966. Registered landscape architect; lic. real estate agt., Va. Asst. prof. W.Va. U., Morgantown, 1973-75, 93; pvt. practice Charlottesville, Va., 1976-85, 91—; site planner LBA, PH&R, Charles P. Johnson & Assocs., Fairfax, Va., 1986-90. Pvt. practice as golf course architect, Charlottesville, 1976—; instr. Parkersburg C.C., 1975, Piedmont Va. C.C., 1981. Author: Fundamentals of Landscaping and Site Planning, 1985; contbr. articles to profl. jours., also poetry. Mem. Planning Commn., Marietta, Ohio, 1972. Mem. Nat. Golf Found., Elks, Va. Writers Club. Avocations: piano, drums. Office: PO Box 7017 Charlottesville VA 22906-7017 E-mail: jamesbroot@aol.com.

ROOT, M. BELINDA, chemist; b. Port Arthur, Tex., May 2, 1957; d. Robert A. and Charlene (Whitehead) Lee; m. Miles J. Root, Nov. 8, 1980; children: Jason Matthew, Ashley Erin. BS in Biology, Lamar U., 1979; MBA, U. Houston, 1994. Asst. chemist Merichem Co., Houston, 1979-81, project chemist, 1982-84, instrument chemist, 1984-85, quality assurance coord., 1986-89, product lab. supr., 1989-91; quality control supr. mfg. Welchem Inc. subs. Amoco, 1991—; mgr. Quality Control Petrolite Corp., 1993; mgr. quality control/quality assurance Akzo-Nobel Chems., Pasadena, Tex., 1994—. Mgr. Quality and Environ. Svcs. (Akzo Nobel Catalysts), 1999—. Editor (newsletter) Merichemer, 1989-91. Mem. MADD, 1989—, PTA, 1988—. Recipient Gulf Shore Regional award Cat Fanciers Assn., 1981, Disting. Merit award, 1990. Mem. Am. Soc. Quality Control (cert. quality auditor, quality engr.), Am. Chem. Soc., United Silver Fancier (sec. 1980-82), Lamar U. Alumni Assn., Houston Area Lab Mgrs. Group (chair 2000-01), Beta Beta Beta (sec. 1978-79), Beta Gamma Sigma. Avocations: camping, gardening. Office: Akzo-Nobel Chem Inc 13000 Baypark Rd Pasadena TX 77507-1104

ROOT, NINA J. librarian, writer; b. 1934; d. Jacob J. and Fannie (Slivinsky) R. BA, Hunter Coll.; MSLS, Pratt Inst.; postgrad., USDA Grad. Sch., 1964-65, CUNY, 1970-75. Reference and serials libr. Albert Einstein Coll. Medicine Libr., Bronx, N.Y., 1958-59; asst. chief libr. Am. Cancer Soc., N.Y.C., 1959-62; chief libr. Am. Inst. Aeros. and Astronautics, N.Y.C., 1962-64; head ref. and libr. svcs. sci. and tech. divsn. Libr. Congress, Washington, 1964-66; mgmt. cons. Nelson Assocs., Inc., N.Y.C., 1966-70; dir. libr. svcs. Am. Mus. Natural History, N.Y.C., 1970-97; freelance mgmt. cons. and libr. planning, 1970-99. Trustee Barnard Found., 1984-91; mem. libr. adv. coun. N.Y. State Bd. Regents, 1984-89, trustee Metro, 1987-92; bd. dirs. Hampden/Booth Libr. Players, 1990-97, Sutton Area Cmty., 1997-2001; trustee Mercantile Libr. N.Y., 1993-95; dir. emerita Libr. AMNH, 1998—. Recipient Meritorious Svc. award Libr. of Congress, 1965, Founders medal SHNH, 1997. Mem. ALA (preservation com. 1977-79, chmn. libr./binders com. 1978-80, chmn. preservation sect. 1980-81, mem. coun. 1983-86), Spl. Librs. Assn. (sec. documentation group N.Y. chpt. 1972-73, 2d v.p. N.Y. 1975-76, treas. sci. and tech. group N.Y. 1975-76, mus. arts and humanities divsn. program planning chairperson-conf. 1977), Archons of Colophon (convener 1978-79), Soc. for Hist. of Natural History (N.Am. rep. 1977-85), N.Y. Acad. Scis. (mem. publs. com. 1975-80, 89-91, archives com. 1976-78, search. com. 1976), Explorers Club. Home: 400 E 59th St New York NY 10022-2342

ROOT, STANLEY WILLIAM, JR., lawyer, retired; b. Honolulu, Mar. 2, 1923; s. Stanley William and Henrietta E. (Brown) R.; m. Joan Louise Schimpf, Sept. 3, 1949; children: Henry, Louise. AB, Princeton U., 1947; LLB, U. Pa., 1950. Bar: Pa. 1950, U.S. Ct. Mil. Appeals 1951, U.S. Supreme Ct. 1971. Ptnr. Foley, Schimpf & Steeley, Phila., 1952-69, Ballard, Spahr, Andrews & Ingersoll, Phila., 1970-91, of counsel, 1992-97; ret., 1998. Lectr. Pa. Bar Assn., 1970-80; bd. dirs. Boardman-Hamilton Co., sec. 1980-98. Exec. v.p. Chestnut Hill Cmty. Assn., Phila., 1978; with Whitpain Farm Assn., Blue Bell, Pa., 1987, 90, pres., 1992-94; with St. Paul's Ch. Vestry, Phila., 1969-75; bd. dirs. Lansdale (Pa.) Med. Group, 1972-95, E.B. Spaeth Found. Wills Hosp., Phila., 1975-88, Chevalier Jackson Clinic, Phila., 1965-88; trustee Civil War Libr. and Mus., 1985-93, v.p., 1989, sec., 1992-93, mem. adv. bd., 1993-95; trustee Soc. Protestant Episc. Ch., Pa. Diocese, 1955-95. Lt. col. U.S. Army, 1942-45, ETO, 1950-52, Korea. Decorated Bronze Star; recipient Pa. Commendation medal State of Pa., 1962. Mem.: Mil. Order Fgn. Wars (comdr. Pa. Commandery 1970), Mil. Order Loyal Legion, Union League, Mil. Order World Wars (comdr. Phila. chpt. 1960—61), Brit. Officers Club, Royal Poinciana Golf Club, Sunnybrook Golf Club. Republican. Episcopalian. Avocations: golf, tennis, fishing. Home: 16 Hounds Run Ln Blue Bell PA 19422-2456 Office: Ballard Spahr Andrews & Ingersoll 51st Fl 1735 Market St Fl 51 Philadelphia PA 19103-7599 Office Phone: 215-864-8306. E-mail: stanislaw16@aol.com.

ROOT, WILLIAM LUCAS, electrical engineering educator; b. Des Moines, Oct. 6, 1919; s. Frank Stephenson and Helen (Lucas) R.; m. Harriett Jean Johnson, Dec. 10, 1918; children: William Lucas Jr., Wendy Elizabeth Root Cate. BEE, Iowa State U., 1940; MEE, MIT, 1943, PhD in Math., 1952. Staff mem. MIT Lincoln Lab., Lexington, Mass., 1952-61, group leader, 1959-61; lectr. Harvard U., Cambridge, Mass., 1958-59; visitor U. Wis., Madison, 1963-64; vis. prof. Mich. State U., East Lansing, 1966, 68, U. Calif., Berkeley, 1966-67; prof. aerospace engring. U. Mich., Ann Arbor, 1961-87, prof. emeritus, 1988—. Visitor U. Cambridge (Eng.), 1970; mem. U.S. Army Sci. Bd., 1979-82. Co-author: Random Signals and Noise, 1958 (Russian and Japanese transls.); assoc. editor: (IEEE) Information Theory Transactions, 1977-79; Soc. Indsl. and Applied Math. Jour. Applied Mathematics, 1962-72; contbr. 65 articles to profl. jours., book chpts. and conf. procs. Served to lt. USMCR, 1943—45. NSF Sr. postdoctoral fellow, 1970, vis. fellow Cambridge Clare Hall, 1970; recipient Claude E. Shannon award IEEE Info. Theory Soc., 1986, Career Achievement award ComCon Conf. Bd., 1987. Life fellow IEEE (vice chmn. adminstrv. com. info. theory group 1965-66); mem. Am. Math. Soc. Home: PO Box 3785 Ann Arbor MI 48106-3785 Office: Univ Mich Dept Aerospace Engring Ann Arbor MI 48109

ROOT, WILLIAM PITT, poet, educator; b. Austin, Minn., Dec. 28, 1941; s. William Pitt and Bonita Joy (Hilbert) R.; m. Judith Carol Bechtold, 1965 (div. 1970); 1 dau., Jennifer Lorca; m. Pamela Uschuk, 1987. BA, U. Wash., 1964; MFA, U. N.C. at Greensboro, 1967; postgrad., Stanford, 1968-69. Asst. prof. Mich. State U., 1967-68; tchr. writing Mid-peninsula Free U., 1969; writer-in-residence Amherst Coll., U. Southwestern La., 1976, U. Mont., 1978, 80, 83-84; with poet-in-schs. program state art councils Oreg., Miss., Idaho, Ariz., Vt., Mont., Wyo., Wash., Tex., 1971—; Distinguished writer-in-residence Wichita State U., 1976; vis. writer in residence U. Mont., 1978, 80, 83-86, Hunter Coll., N.Y.C., 1986—; vis. writer NYU, 1986. Vis. writer Westside Young Men's Hebrew Assn., N.Y.C., 1988; disting. writer-in-residence Pacific Luth. U., 1990. Author: The Storm and Other Poems, 1969, Striking the Dark Air for Music, 1973, The Port of Galveston, 1974, Coot and Other Characters, 1977, 7 Mendocino Songs, 1977, A Journey South, 1977, Fireclock, 1981, Reasons for Going It on Foot, 1981, In the World's Common Grasses, 1981, The Unbroken Diamond: Nightletter to the Mujahideen, 1983, Invisible Guests, 1984, Faultdancing, 1986, Trace Elements from a Recurring Kingdom, 1994; collaborated (with filmmaker Ray Rice) on poetry films Song of the

Woman and the Butterflyman (Orpheus award 1st Internat. Poetry Film Festival 1975), 7 For a Magician, 1976, Faces, 1981. Rockefeller Found. grantee, 1969-70; Guggenheim Found. grantee, 1970-71; Nat. Endowment for Arts grantee, 1973-74; U.S./U.K. Bicentennial Exchange Artist, 1978-79, Wallace Stegner creative writing fellow Stanford U., 1968 69; recipient 1st prize univ. poetry contest Acad. Am. Poets, 1966, Atlantic Young Poet award, 1967, Stanley Kunitz Poetry award, 1981, Guy Owen Poetry Prize, 1982, Pushcart Prize (Poetry), 1977, 1980, 1985; named Poet Laureate of Tucson, 1997-2002. Address: CUNY Hunter Coll Dept Eng 695 Park Ave New York NY 10021-5024 *With Rilke I believe the measure of one's life consists in a growing capacity to engage ever more fully in that dance between what we call will and what we call fate until the result is a contagion of vitality powerful enough to dissipate the spell of habits and to recreate in oneself that first spirit which is intuitive, sympathetic, and clear. Poems simply record the complex effort.*

ROOT-BERNSTEIN, ROBERT SCOTT, biologist, educator; b. Washington, Aug. 7, 1953; s. Morton Ira and Maurine (Berkstresser) Bernstein; m. Michèle Marie Root-Bernstein, Sept. 2, 1978; children: Meredith Marie, Brian Robert. AB, Princeton U., 1975, PhD, 1980. Postdoctoral fellow Salk Inst. for Biol. Studies, La Jolla, Calif., 1981-82, rsch. assoc., 1983-84; from asst. to assoc. prof. Mich. State U., East Lansing, 1987-96, prof., 1996—. Cons. Parke-Davis Pharm. Rsch. Divsn., Ann Arbor, 1990-96, Chiron Corp., 1992-96; mem. adv. bd. Soc. for Advancement Gifted Edn., Chgo., 1987-92; Sigma Xi nat. lectr., 1994-96. Author: Discovering, 1989, Rethinking AIDS, 1993, Honey, Mud, Maggots and Other Medical Marvels, 1997, Sparks of Genius, 1999; columnist The Scis. mag., 1989-92, The Leonardo mag., 2004—; contbr. numerous articles to profl. jours. MacArthur Found. fellow, 1981-86; recipient D.J. Ingle Meml. Writing prize, 1988. Mem. Phi Beta Kappa (hon.), Sigma Xi. Avocations: drawing, painting, photography, cello. Office: Mich State U Dept Physiology Biomed & Phys Scis Bldg East Lansing MI 48824 Office Phone: 517-355-6475 ext. 1101. Business E-Mail: rootbern@msu.edu.

ROPER, DONNA C. archaeologist; Rsch. assoc. prof. dept. Sociology & anthrop. Kans. State U., Manhattan. Mem.: Kans. State Hist. Soc., Nebr. Assn. Profl. Archeologists (pres.). Home: 1924 Bluehills Rd Manhattan KS 66502-4503 Office: Kans State U Dept Sociology Anthrop & Social Work 204 Waters Hill Manhattan KS 66506

ROPER, HARRY JOSEPH, lawyer; b. Bridgeport, Conn., Apr. 15, 1940; BEE, Rensselaer Poly. Inst., 1962; LLB, NYU, 1966. Assoc. Neuman, Williams, Anderson & Olson, 1966-70, ptnr., 1970-90, Roper & Quigg, 1990—2004, Jenner & Block, 2004—. Home: 611 W Fullerton Pky Chicago IL 60614-2613 Office: Jenner & Block 1 IBM Plz 330 N Wabash Ave Chicago IL 60611 Office Phone: 312-923-8303. Business E-Mail: hjroper@jenner.com.

ROPER, HARTWELL H. tobacco company executive; CFO, v.p. Universal Leaf Tobacco Corp., 1992—. Office: Universal Leaf Tobacco Co Hamilton St at Broad PO Box 25099 Richmond VA 23260-5099

ROPER, JOHN HERBERT, historian, educator; b. Greenville, S.C., Aug. 9, 1948; s. Edmund Ravenel and Dorothy (Watson) Roper; m. Margarita Adele Bowers, May 20, 1972; children: John Herbert Jr., James Kyle. AB in History, U. S.C., 1970; AM in History, U. N.C., 1973, PhD in History, 1977; ME in Econs., N.C. State U., 1981. Vis. lectr. U. N.C., Chapel Hill, 1977—77; vis. asst. prof. Fla. Internat. U., Miami, 1978—79; assoc. prof. St. Andrews Coll., Laurinburg, NC, 1979—88; prof. Emory (Va.) & Henry Coll., 1988—96, Richardson prof., 1996—. Author: U. B. Phillips, 1984, C. Vann Woodward, 1987, Paul Green Playwright, 2003. Scoutmaster Boy Scouts Am., Emory, 1990—; vestry, mem. study com. Episc. Ch., Roanoke, Va., 1988—. With N.G. U.S. Army, 1971—77. Mem.: Hist. Soc., So. Hist. Assn., Kiwanis, St. George Tucker Soc. Democrat. Avocations: hiking, camping, swimming. Office: Emory and Henry Coll Dept History Box 947 Emory VA 24327 Office Fax: 276-944-6223. Business E-Mail: jhroper@ehc.edu.

ROPER, JOHN LONSDALE, III, shipyard executive; b. Norfolk, Va., Jan. 19, 1927; s. John Lonsdale II and Sarah (Dryfoos) R.; m. Jane Preston Harman, Sept. 29, 1951; children: Susan Roper, John Lonsdale IV, Sarah Preston Roper Massey, Jane Harman Roper Van Sciver, Katherine Hayward Roper Stout. BSME, U. Va., Charlottesville, 1949; BS in Naval Architecture and Marine Engring., MIT, 1951. CEO, pres. Norfolk Shipbuilding & Drydock Corp., 1985-91, pres., CEO, 1992-98, also bd. dirs.; mgr. Branbleton, LLC, Norfolk, 1998—. Dir. John L. Roper Corp., Cruise Internat., Inc., The Flagship Group Ltd.; pres., dir. Lonsdale Bldg. Corp. Marepcon Corp.-Internat. With USCG, 1945-46. Mem. Shipbuilders Coun. Am. (bd. dirs.). Episcopalian.

ROPER, JOHN MARLIN, SR., federal magistrate judge; b. Greenville, Ala., Dec. 11, 1942; s. Marlin Ross and Ruby Lois (Martin) R.; m. Virginia Gene Kerth, Apr. 2, 1966; 1 son, John Marlin. BS, Auburn U., 1964; JD, Tulane U., 1968. Bar: Ala. 1968, Miss. 1974. Counselor, program dir. Juvenille Delinquency Instn., New Orleans, 1966-69; sr., law clk. to judge U.S. Dist. Ct. (so. dist.) Miss., 1969-75, magistrate judge, 1975—. Mem. Fed. Magistrate Judges Assn. (dir. 5th cir. 1976-82, nat. officer 1982-86, nat. pres. 1986-87, security com. jud. conf. 1987-89, budget com. jud. conf. 1989-97). Methodist. Home: 2012 15th Street #870 Gulfport MS 39501

ROPER, LOUIS H. historian, educator; b. Bloomington, Ind., Nov. 10, 1958; s. Donald M. and Carol A. Roper. BA, Northeastern U., Boston, 1980; JD, SUNY at Buffalo, 1983; PhD, U. of Rochester, NY, 1992. Prof. dept. of history SUNY at New Paltz, NY, 1994—. Chair of history SUNY-New Paltz, NY, 2002—. Author: (history monograph) Conceiving Carolina: Proprietors, Planters, and Plots, 1662-1729. Fellow Alexander O. Vieter fellow, Beinecke Libr., Yale U., 2003—04; grantee Internat. Seminar on the History of the Atlantic World, Charles Warren Ctr. for the Study of Am. History, Harvard U., 1996. Mem.: Omohundro Inst. of Early Am. History and Culture (assoc.), Am. Hist. Assn. (assoc.). Avocations: supporting liverpool football club, cricket. Office: Dept History SUNY New Paltz 75 S Manheim Blvd Ste 6 New Paltz NY 12561-2440 Office Phone: 845-257-3545. Office Fax: 845-257-2735. Business E-Mail: roperl@newpaltz.edu.

ROPER, WILLIAM ALFORD, JR., diversified technology services company executive; b. Birmingham, Ala., Mar. 14, 1946; BA in Math., U. Miss., 1968; grad. in banking, So. Meth. U., 1974; grad. fin. mgmt. program, Stanford U., 1986. Owner, gen. mgr. real estate devel. and wholesale distbn. cos.; loan officer, br. mgr. Deposit Guaranty Nt. Bank, until 1981; various positions, including corp. v.p., treas. Bell & Howell Co., 1981-87; exec. v.p., CFO, Intelogic Trace, Inc., 1987-90; sr. v.p., CFO, Sci. Applications Internat. Corp., San Diego, 1990-2000, corp. exec. v.p., 2000—. Mem. adv. bd. Allendale Mut. Ins. Co., Johnston, R.I.; mng. dir. Carlisle Enterprises, LLC, La Jolla, Calif.; bd. dirs. Cush Automotive Group, San Diego, Network Solutions, Inc., Herndon, Va., Holiday Bowl, San Diego. Chmn. bd. ACCION San Diego; bd. dirs. Alvarado Hosp. Med. Ctr., San Diego; vice chmn. bd. San Diego Conv. Ctr. Corp. Mem. CEO Roundtable, Greater San Diego C. of C. (bd. dirs., exec. com., chmn. fin. com.). Office: Sci Applications International 10260 Campus Point Dr San Diego CA 92121

ROPER, WILLIAM LEE, dean, physician; b. Birmingham, Ala., July 6, 1948; s. Richard Barnard and Jean (Fyfe) R.; m. Maryann Roper, Jan. 14, 1978 AA, Fla. Coll., 1968; BS, U. Ala, 1970, MD, 1974, M.P.H., 1981. Diplomate Am. Bd. Pediatrics, Am. Bd. Preventive Medicine. Intern, resident in pediatrics U. Colo. Med. Ctr., Denver, 1974-77; health officer Jefferson County Dept. Health, Birmingham, 1977-82, 83; White House fellow Washington, 1982-83; spl. asst. to Pres. for health policy, 1983-86; adminstr., Health Care Finance Adminstrn. HHS, Washington, 1986-89; dep. asst. to pres. for domestic policy The White House, Washington, 1989-90; adminstr. Agy. for Toxic Substances and Disease Registry and dir. Ctrs. for Disease Control and Prevention, Atlanta, 1990-93; sr. v.p. Prudential Health Care, Roseland, NJ, 1994-97; pres. Prudential Ctr. for Health Care Rsch., Atlanta, 1993-95; dean, sch. pub. health, prof. medicine and health policy U. NC, Chapel Hill, 1997—2004, dean sch. medicine, vice chancellor med. affairs, CEO U. NC Health Care, 2004—. Mem. Inst. Medicine, Phi Beta Kappa, Alpha Omega Alpha Republican. Home: 10424 Stone Chapel Hill NC 27517-8549 Office: U NC 170 Rosenau Hall Campus Box 7400 Chapel Hill NC 27599-7400*

ROPP, PAUL STANLEY, historian; b. Bloomington, Ill., Mar. 25, 1944; s. Peter and Anna Ropp; m. Marjorie Louise Liechty, Aug. 1, 1965; children: Andrew Gordon, Benjamin Edwin, Amy Su-lin. BA, Bluffton (Ohio) Coll., 1966; MA, U. Mich., 1968, PhD, 1973. Asst. prof. history State Coll. of Ark., Conway, 1973—74; vis. asst. prof. McGill U., Montreal, Canada, 1974—75; from asst. to assoc. prof. history Memphis State U., 1975—84; prof. history Clark U., Worcester, Mass., 1985—. Author: (monograph) Dissent in Early Modern China, 1981, Banished Immortal: Searching for Shuangqing, China's Peasant Woman Poet, 2001; editor: (anthology) Heritage of China, 1990. Mem.: Nat. Com. on U.S.-China Rels., Am. Hist. Assn. (ann. program com. co-chair 2001—02), Assn. Asian Studies (life; nat. program com. 1992—94). Democrat. Unitarian-Universalist. Avocations: music, travel, politics, literature. Home: 40 Chamberlain Pky Worcester MA 01602 Office: Clark U 950 Main St Worcester MA 01610 E-mail: propp@clarku.edu.

ROPSKI, GARY MELCHIOR, lawyer; b. Erie, Pa., Apr. 19, 1952; s. Joseph Albert and Irene Stefania (Mszanowski) R.; m. Barbara Mary Schleck, May 15, 1982. BS in Physics, Carnegie-Mellon U., 1972; JD cum laude, Northwestern U. Sch. Law, 1976. Bar: Ill. 1976, U.S. Patent and Trademark Office 1976, U.S. Dist. Ct. (no. dist.) Ill. 1976, U.S. Ct. Appeals (7th cir.) 1977, U.S. Dist. Ct. (ea. dist.) Wis. 1977, U.S. Ct. Appeals (3d cir.) 1981, Pa. 1982, U.S. Ct. Claims 1982, U.S. Ct. Appeals (fed. cir.) 1982, U.S. Supreme Ct. 1982, U.S. Dist. Ct. (ea. dist.) Mich. 1984, U.S. Dist. Ct. (no. dist.) Calif. 1986. Assoc. Brinks Hofer Gilson & Lione, Chgo., 1976-81, shareholder, 1981—. Adj. prof. patents and copyrights Northwestern U. Sch. Law, Chgo., 1982-97. Contbr. numerous articles to profl. jours. Mem. ABA, Internat. Bar Assn., Internat. Trademark Assn., Am. Intellectual Property Law Assn., Ill. Bar Assn., Intellectual Property Law Assn. Chgo., Chgo. Bar Assn., Univ. Club, Chgo. Yacht Club. Roman Catholic. Office: Brinks Hofer Gilson & Lione Ste 3600 455 N Cityfront Plaza Dr Chicago IL 60611-5599 E-mail: gropski@brinkshofer.com.

ROQUE, FRANCIS XAVIER, auxiliary bishop; b. Providence, Oct. 9, 1928; s. Warren Edward Roque and Mary Loretta Gallagher BA, Saint John's Sem., 1950. ordained priest Roman Catholic, 1953. Parish priest Diocese of Providence, 1953-61; army chaplain U.S. Army, 1961-83; bishop Archdiocese for Mil. Svcs. USA, Washington, 1983—. Served to col. U.S. Army, 1961-83, Vietnam Decorated Bronze Star Roman Catholic. Office: Archdiocese for Mil Svcs USA PO Box 4469 Washington DC 20017-0469 E-mail: froque@milarch.org.

ROREM, NED, composer, author; b. Richmond, Ind., Oct. 23, 1923; s. Clarence Rufus and Gladys (Miller) R. Student, Northwestern U., 1940-42, Curtis Inst., Phila., 1943; BA, Juilliard Sch. Music, 1946, MA, 1948; D.F.A. (hon.), Northwestern U., 1977, Curtis Inst., 1982. Slee prof., composer-in-residence Buffalo U., 1959-61; prof. composition U. Utah, 1965-67, Curtis Inst., 1980—, Yale U., New Haven, 1998—, Manhattan Sch. of Music, 1995—. Guest composer New Music New Haven Series Sch. Music Yale U., 1998, vis. prof., 1998-99; composer-in-residence Lakes Chamber Music Festival, 1999. Composer: symphonies No. 1, premiere Vienna, Austria, 1951, No. 2, premiere La Jolla, Calif., 1956, No. 3, premiere with Leonard Bernstein and N.Y. Philharmonic, 1959, Three Piano Sonatas, 1949, 50, 54, Lento for Strings, 1950, Design for Orch., 1954, Pilgrims for Strings, 1958, Eagles for Orch., 1958, Lions, 1964, Ideas for Easy Orch, 1961, Piano Concerto No. 2, 1951, 3d Piano Concerto, 1970, Eleven Studies, 1959, Water Music, 1966, Sun; for voice and orch., commd. by N.Y. Philharmonic, 1966, Air Music for Orch, 1974 (Pulitzer prize 1976), Assembly and Fall, 1975, Sunday Morning for Orch., 1977, Remembering Tommy, 1981; numerous chorus works, latest being Letters from Paris, 1965; for chorus and orch., commd. by Koussevitzky Found. in Library of Congress, Little Prayers, 1972, Whitman Cantata, 1982, An American Oratorio, 1983, Homer, 1986, Seven Motets, 1986, Te Deum, 1986, What is Pink?, 1987, The Death of Moses, 1987, Goodbye My Fancy, 1988; operas A Childhood Miracle, 1952, Three Sisters Who Are Not Sisters, 1969, Fables, 1970, Bertha, 1968, Miss Julie, 1964 (Ford Found. grantee), Hearing, 1976, Cycles: War Scenes, 1969, Six Songs for High Voice and Orchestra, 1954, Six Irish Poems, 1951, Poems of Love and the Rain, 1964, Ariel for Voice, clarinet and piano, 1971, Last Poems of Wallace Stevens for voice, cello and piano, 1971, Serenade for voice, violin, viola and piano, Women's Voices, 1975, The Nantucket Songs, 1979, Three Calamus Poems, 1982, The Schuyler Songs, 1987, Day Music and Night Music for Violin, 1972-73, Etudes for Piano, 1975, Book of Hours for flute and harp, A Quaker Reader for Organ, 1976, The Santa Fe Songs, 1980, Remembering Tommy, 1980, Views From the Oldest House for organ, 1981, Winter Pages, 1981, Picnic on the Marne, 1982, Dances for Cello, 1983, Violin Concerto, 1984, Organ Concerto, 1985, String Symphony, 1985, Septet: Scenes from Childhood, 1985, Trio: End of Summer, 1985, Quintet: Bright Music, 1988, Diversions for Brass Quintet, 1989, Trio (Spring Music), 1990, Three Organbooks; The Auden Poems, Trio for Violin, Cello, Piano, 1990, Swords and Plowshares (for 4 solo voices and orch.), 1991, Third Quartet, 1991, Fourth Concerto for Piano (left hand) and Orch., 1991, Present Laughter for mixed chorus, piano and brass, 1993, Fourth Quartet, 1994, Songs of Sadness for quartet of baritone, guitar, clarinet and cello, 1994, More Than a Day for countertenor and orch., 1995, Six Variations for Two Pianos, 1995. Evidence of Things Not Seen, 1997; Autumn Music for Violin and Piano, 1997, Six Organ Pieces, 1998, Double Concerto for Violin, Cello and Orchestra, 1998, An Oboe Book, 1999, Another Sleep,, Cello Concerto, 2001 Aftermath, 2002, Pas de Trois (oboe, violin, piano), 2002, Fifth String Quartet, 2002, Flute Concerto, 2002, Mallet Concerto, 2003; commns. for U.S. Bicentennial include compositions for, Cin. Symphony, N.C. Symphony, Nat. Endowment of the Arts, Am. Harp Soc.; Author: The Paris Diary of Ned Rorem, 1966, Music from Inside Out, 1967, The New York Diary, 1967, Music and People, 1968, Critical Affairs, 1970, Pure Contraption, 1973, The Later Diaries, 1974, An Absolute Gift, 1978, Setting the Tone, 1983, Paul's Blues, 1985, The Nantucket Diary, 1987, Settling the Score, 1988, Knowing When To Stop, 1994, Other Entertainment, 1996, Dear Paul, Dear Ned, 1997 (letters between Paul Bowles and Ned Rorem), Lies: A Diary (1986-1999), 2000 A Ned Rorem Reader, 2002; also articles newspapers, mags., Recs. for, Columbia, Decca, Odyssey, Desto, Phillips, Premier, C.R.I., Westminster, Orion, New World Records. Recipient Music Libraries Assn. award for song Lordly Hudson 1948, Gershwin Meml. award 1949, Lili Boulanger award 1950, Nat. Inst. Arts and Letters award 1968, Pulitzer prize in music 1976, Grammy award for Best Orchestral Rec., 1989; Fulbright fellow Paris, 1951-52; Guggenheim fellow, 1957-58, 77-78 Mem.: AAAL (pres. 2000—), ASCAP, PEN, Am. Acad. Arts & Letters (pres. 2000—03), Soc. Friends. Mem. Soc. Of Friends. Address: PO Box 764 Nantucket MA 02554-0764

RORER, JOHN WHITELEY, publisher, consultant; b. Phila., Aug. 4, 1930; s. Ronald Erle and Hazel (Whiteley) R.; m. Beverly Case, June 6, 1953. BS, U. Pa., 1952; MBA, Drexel U., 1956. Credit analyst Phila. Nat. Bank, 1954-56; with Curtis Pub. Co., Phila., 1956-68; dir. purchasing Chilton Pub. Co., Phila., 1968-70; founding pres. Focus Bus. Weekly, Bus. News, Inc., Phila., 1968—, pres., pub., 1974—; owner Pubs. Systems Assocs., Upper Darby, Pa., 1979—. Mem. Phila. World Affairs Council, 1979—. Served to capt. U.S. Army, 1952-54. Mem. Nat. Assn. Bus. Publs. (co-founder, bd. dirs. 1978-81), Nat. Assn. Indsl. Advt., Mktg. and Communications Execs. Assn., Union League Club, Engrs. Club (Phila.), Downtown Club. Republican. Episcopalian. Avocation: economics research. Office: 1015 Chestnut St Philadelphia PA 19107-4305

RORICK, WILLIAM CALVIN, librarian, educator, portrait artist; b. Elyria, Ohio, June 23, 1941; s. Harold R. and Edythe E. (Harris) R.; m. Anne L. Sherbondy, Aug. 21, 1971. BA in Econs. and Bus. Adminstrn., Ohio Wesleyan U., 1963; MusB in Music History and Lit., U. Utah, 1968; MusM in Music History and Lit., Northwestern U., 1970; MLS, Pratt Inst., 1974; MA in Musicology, NYU, 1982; trainee in portraiture, various art schs., workshops. Curator orchestral-choral libr., reference asst., office mgr. Manhattan Sch. Music Libr., NYC, 1970-74; music reference libr. CUNY Queens Coll. Music Libr., Flushing, 1974-96, instr., 1974-79, asst. prof., 1979-96, asst. prof. emeritus, 1996—, mem. senate nominating com., del.-at-large arts divsn., 1984-86. Contbr. articles and revs. to profl. jour. Bd. deacons South Britain (Conn.) Congl. Ch., 1998—2001, historian, 2002. Grantee Rsch. Found CUNY, 1981-84; recipient regional and nat. art awards including Best in Show Conn. Classic Arts Assn. Mem. Am. Musicological Soc., Am. Printing History Assn., Assn. for Recorded Sound Collections, Internat. Assn. Music Libr., Libr. Assn. CUNY (chmn. grants com. 1978-80, mem. publ. com. 1979-81, editor Directory 1980-81, del. 1983-85), Music Libr. Assn. (program chmn. Greater NY chpt. 1977-79, sec.-treas. 1979-81, chpt. chmn. 1983-85, mem. nat. subcom. on basic music collection 1977-79, chmn. nat. membership com. 1979-82, mem. Music Pub. Assn. joint com. 1986-88), Am. Soc. Portrait Artists, Sonneck Soc., Conn. Classic Arts, Inc. (publicity chmn. 1996-99), Soc. Creative Artists of Newtown (corr. sec. 1999-2002), Portrait Soc. of Am., Inc., Portrait Soc. Atlanta, Conn. Soc. Portrait Artists, N.Y. Soc. Portrait Artists (mem. leadership team 2001-02), Portrait Clubs Am. (cert. leader-instr. 2003—), Acad. Artists Assn., Kent Art Assn. (elected artist, bd. dirs. 2003—), Beta Phi Mu. Home: 63 Beacon Hill Dr Southbury CT 06488-1914

RORIE, CONRAD JONATHAN, scientist, naval officer; b. Henning, Tenn., Oct. 28, 1930; s. Elvy and Lena (Jenkins) R.; m. Patricia Paris Cunliffe, Feb. 7, 1952; children: Michael Stephen, Catherine Jean, Patrick Jonathan. BS, Union U., Jackson, Tenn., 1952; MSEE, U.S. Naval Postgrad. Sch., 1961; PhD in Elect. Engring., Vanderbilt U., 1970. Enlisted USN, 1952, advanced through grades to adm., 1971; comdg. officer various ships, 1957-72; comdr. U.S. Naval Surface Weapons Ctr., Dahlgren, Va., 1974-77; dep. comdr. for surface combatants and weapons systems engr. Naval Sea Systems Command, Washington, 1977-81; comdr. Naval Surface Forces Middle Pacific & Naval Base Pearl Harbr, Hawaii, 1981-84. Planning dir. Johns Hopkins U., Applied Physics Lab., 1984—; mem. numerous naval bd. for officer career devel., chmn. Weapons Systems Mgr./Ordnance Adv. Bd. to Naval Postgrad. Sch. President Hawaii Navy Relief Soc. and Red Cross, 1980; chmn. Combined Fed. Campaign Charity Dr., 1981; bd. dirs. Govs. for Navy Charity Retail Store, 1981; commissioning chmn. USS Antietam, 1987, USS Arleigh Burke, 1991; mem. panel Navy/Civilian U. Lab., 1988; mem. curricula rev. com. Naval Postgrad. Sch., 1977-81; bd. dirs. Historic USS Constellation, 1996; mem. warfare sys. adv. panel for 21st century aircraft carriers. Decorated Legion of Merit (4), Meritorious Svc. medal with gold star; recipient Ann. Disting. Alumnus award Union U., 1975, Am. Spirit of Honor medal, APL Disting. Svc. award Johns Hopkins U., 1998; named Tenn. Number One State Future Farmer, 1948; C.J. Rorie annual award for Excellence established in his honor, 1987, Navy Surface Warfare Ctr. established in his honor. Mem. Naval Inst., Am. Soc. Naval Engrs., Nat. Security Indsl. Assn., AIAA, Am. Astronaut. Soc., U.S. Navy League, Armed Forces Communications and Electronics Assn., Mil. Order of Carabao, Masons, Bapt. Club, Sigma Xi, Eta Kappa Nu, Alpha Tau Omega. Home: 12412 Hooper Ct Fulton MD 20759-9645 Office: Johns Hopkins U Applied Physics Lab Johns Hopkins Rd Laurel MD 20707 Personal E-mail: conradrorie@aol.com.

RORIE, NANCY CATHERINE, retired elementary and secondary school educator; b. Union County, NC, May 31, 1940; d. Carl Evander and Mary Mildred (Pressley) Rorie. BA, Woman's Coll. U. N.C., 1962; MEd, U. N.C., 1967; EdD, Duke U., 1977. Cert. curriculum and instrnl. specialist, social studies tchr. for middle and secondary levels, English tchr., N.C. Social studies and English tchr. Guilford County Schs., Greensboro, NC, 1962—67; social studies instr. Lees-McRae Coll., Banner Elk, NC, 1967—76; social studies and English tchr. Monroe (NC) City Schs., 1977—93, Union County Schs., Monroe, 1993—2002; ret., 2002. Mem.: Monroe Aquatics And Fitness Ctr., Kappa Delta Pi, Phi Alpha Theta. Democrat. Southern Missionary Baptist. Home: 2401 Old Pageland Monroe Rd Monroe NC 28112-8163

RORIG, KURT JOACHIM, chemist, research director; b. Bremerhaven, Germany, Dec. 1, 1920; came to U.S., 1924, naturalized, 1929; s. Robert Herman and Martha (Grundke) R.; m. Helen Yonan, Mar. 20, 1949; children: James, Elizabeth, Miriam. BS, U. Chgo., 1942; MA, Carleton Coll., 1944; PhD, U. Wis., 1947. Lectr. Loyola U., Chgo., 1950-62; chemist to dir. Chem. Research G.D. Searle & Co., Chgo., 1947-87; pres. Chemo-Delphic Cons. Ltd., Chgo., 1987—. Adj. prof. chemistry U. Ill., Chgo., 1989—. Patentee in field. Mem. Sch. Bd., Wilmette, Ill., 1969-71. Mem. Am. Chem. Soc. (dir. Chgo. sect.), Am. Soc. Pharm. and Exptl. Therapeutics, N.Y. Acad. Scis., AAAS, Chgo. Chemists Club (past pres.) Presbyterian. Home and Office: 337 Hager Ln Glenview IL 60025-3329 Office Phone: 847-724-2808.

RORISON, MARGARET LIPPITT, reading consultant; b. Wilmington, N.C., Feb. 6, 1925; d. Harmon Chadbourn and Margaret Devereux (Lippitt) Rorison. AB, Hollins Coll., 1946; MA, Columbia U., 1956; Diplôme de langue, L'Alliance Française, Paris, 1966; postgrad., U. S.C., 1967-70, 81—. Market and editl. rschr. Time, Inc., N.Y.C., 1949—55; tchr. classroom and corrective reading N.Y.C. Pub. Schs., 1956—65; TV instr. ETV-WNDT, Channel 13, N.Y.C., 1962—63; grad. asst., TV instr. U. S.C., Columbia, 1967—70; instrnl. specialist in reading S.C. Office Instrnl. TV and Radio S.C. Dept. Edn., Columbia, 1971—81; reading cons. S.C. Office Instrnl. Tech., Columbia, 1982—. Author instrnl. TV series: Getting the Word (So. Ednl. Communications Assn. award 1972, Ohio State award 1973, S.C. Scholastic Broadcasters award 1973), Getting the Message, 1981. Episcopalian. Home: 460 S 23rd St Wilmington NC 28403-0200

RORKE-ADAMS, LUCY BALIAN, pathologist, educator; b. St. Paul, June 22, 1929; d. Aram Haji and Karzouhy (Ousdigian) Balian; m. Robert Radcliffe Rorke, June 4, 1960 (div.); m. Boyce M. Adams, Apr. 16, 2004. AB, U. Minn., 1951, MA, 1952, BS, 1955, MD, 1957. Diplomate Am. Bd. Pathology. Intern Phila. Gen. Hosp., 1957-58, resident anat. pathology and neuropathology, 1958-62, asst. neuropathologist, 1963-67, chief pediat. pathologist, 1967-68, chief neuropathologist, 1968-69, chmn. dept. anat. pathology and chief neuropathologist, 1969-73, chmn. dept. pathology, 1973-77, pres. med. staff, 1973-75; pvt. practice Phila., 1962—; neuropathologist Children's Hosp., Phila., 1965—, pres. med. staff, 1986-88, acting pathologist-in-chief, 1995-2000. Cons. neuropathologist Wyeth Rsch. Labs., Radnor, Pa., 1961—87, Wistar Inst. Anatomy and Biology, Phila., 1967—93; assoc. prof. pathology U. Pa. Sch. Medicine, Phila., 1970—73, prof., 1973—, clin. prof. neurology, 1979—, clin. prof. pediat., 1997—; forensic neuropathologist Office Med. Examiner, Phila., 1977—2004. Author: Myelinization of the Brain in the Newborn, 1969, Pathology of Perinatal Brain Injury, 1982; mem. editl. bd. Jours. Neuropathology Exptl. Neurology, 1980—85, 1993—, Pediat. Neurosurgery, 1984—2002, Child's Nervous Sys., 1984—88, Brain Pathology, 1990—95; contbr. articles to profl. jours. NIH fellow, 1961—62, NIH grantee, 1963—68. Fellow: Coll. Am. Pathologists; mem.: AMA, Phila. Coll. Physicians (trustee 2002, treas. 2004), Burlington County Med. Soc., Am. Neurol. Soc., Am. Soc. Neuroradiology (hon.), Am. Assn. Neuropathologists (exec. coun. 1976—85, v.p. 1979—80, pres. 1981—82, Meritorious Svc. award 1999), Phila. Neurol. Soc. (v.p. 1971—72, editor transactions 1973, pres. 1975—76). Home: 633 E Main St - 6A Moorestown NJ 08057-3027 Office: Childrens Hosp Phila 324 S 34th St Philadelphia PA 19104-4399 Business E-Mail: Rorke@email.chop.edu.

RORRIE, COLIN C., JR., emergency physician; PhD, U. Iowa. Cert. assn. exec. Exec. dir. CEO Am. Coll. Emergency Physicians, Irving, Tex., 1982—. Fellow: Am. Soc. Assn. Execs. (chmn. 2001—02); mem.: Nat. Emergency Medicine Polit. Action Com., Emergency Medicine Found., Medic Alert Found. (chair 1995—98), Am. Assn. Med. Soc. Execs. (pres. 1993—94). Office: Am Coll Emergency Physicians 1125 Executive Cir Irving TX 75038-2522

RORSCHACH, RICHARD GORDON, lawyer; b. Tulsa, Aug. 9, 1928; s. Harold Emil and Margaret (Hermes) R.; m. Martha Kay King, Dec. 23, 1979; children by previous marriage: Richard Helm, Reagan Cartwright, Andrew Maxwell. BS, MIT, 1950; MS, U. Okla., 1952; JD, U. Houston, 1961. Bar: Tex. 1961; lic. prof. engr., Tex. Cons. civil engr. Freese & Nichols, Ft. Worth, 1955; cons. engr. Freese, Nichols & Turner, Houston, 1955-56; petroleum engr. Marathon Oil Co., Bay City, Tex., 1956-57, Houston, 1957-61, atty.,

1961-64; ptnr. Broady, Kells & Rorschsch, Houston, 1964-68, Ragan, Russell & Rorschach, Houston, 1968-80, Kilgore, Tex., 1980—. Mem. exec. com. Colonial Royalties Co., Tulsa, 1970-77; officer Little River Oil & Gas Co., 1980-88; mng. ptnr. Pentagon Oil Co., 1988—; pres. Nat. Assn. Royalty Owners-Tex., 1993-96, bd. trustees, 2004—; chmn. Nat. Assn. Royalty Owners, Inc., 1996-99, bd. dirs., 1999-2000, ad. dirs., 2004—; mem. exec. com. Nat. Assn. Royalty Owners, Inc.; owner, breeder, exhibitor Arabian Horses Shadowbrook Farm, Kilgore, Tex., 1980—. Author: How to Protect Your Royalty Interests: Texas Perspectives, Vols. 1 & 2, 2002. Served to 1st lt. C.E., AUS, 1952-54, Korea. Mem. ASME, ASCE, Tex. Bar Assn., Rotary Club (pres. Kilgore chpt. 1984-85), Sigma Xi, Sigma Alpha Epsilon. Republican. Presbyterian. Home: RR 4 Box 210 Kilgore TX 75662-9023 Office: 1100 Stone Rd PO Box 1934 Kilgore TX 75663-1934

RORTY, RICHARD MCKAY, philosophy educator; b. N.Y.C., Oct. 4, 1931; s. James Hancock and Winifred (Raushenbush) R.; m. Amelie Sarah Oksenberg, June 15, 1954 (div. 1972); 1 son, Jay; m. Mary R. Varney, Nov. 4, 1972; children: Patricia, Kevin. BA, U. Chgo., 1949, MA, 1952; PhD, Yale U., 1956; DHL, Northwestern U., 1992, Fla. Internat. Univ., 1994. Instr. philosophy Yale U., 1955-57; instr. Wellesley Coll., 1958-60, asst. prof., 1960-61; mem. faculty Princeton U., 1961-82, prof. philosophy, 1970-81, Stuart prof. philosophy, 1981-82; Univ. prof. humanities U. Va., 1982—. Author: Philosophy and the Mirror of Nature, 1979, Consequences of Pragmatism, 1982, Contingency, Irony and Solidarity, 1989, Objectivity, Relativism and Truth, 1991, Essays on Heidegger and Others, 1991. Served with AUS, 1957-58. Guggenheim fellow, 1973-74; MacArthur fellow, 1981-86. Mem. Am. Philos. Assn. (pres. Eastern div. 1979), Am. Acad. Arts and Scis. Home: 402 Peacock Dr Charlottesville VA 22903-9725 Office: 412 Cabell Hall Charlottesville VA 22903

ROSA, DOMENICO, mathematics professor; b. L'Aquila, Abruzzi, Italy, Apr. 19, 1947; came to U.S., 1957; s. Emidio Pio and Assunta (Rosa) R.; m. Julia Margaret Pellettier, July 24, 1976; children: Robert Francis, Katherine Elizabeth. BA, Tufts U., 1970; MS, McMaster U., 1971, PhD, 1974. Actuarial asst. The Hartford (Conn.) Ins. Group, 1975-79, sr. actuarial, 1979-83; asst. prof. to prof. Teikyo Post U., Waterbury, Conn., 1983-95, prof., 1995—. Contbr. papers to profl. jours. Mem. Am. Math. Soc., Math. Assn. Am. Democrat. Roman Catholic. Avocations: history, politics. Office: Teikyo Post Univ 800 Country Club Rd Waterbury CT 06708-3240

ROSA, EUGENE ANTHONY, sociologist, environmental scientist, educator; b. Canandaigua, NY, Sept. 20, 1941; s. Louis Gastaldo and Flora Louise (Brevette) R.; m. Jody Ross, Sept. 7, 1985 (div. 1993). BS, Rochester Inst. Tech., 1967; MA, Syracuse U., 1975, PhD, 1976. Research assoc., instr. Stanford U., 1976-78; from asst. to prof. Wash. State U., Pullman, 1978—, prof., 1993—. Cons. Brookhaven Nat. Lab., Upton, N.Y., 1978—, Nuclear Regulatory Commn., Washington, 1978—; vis. prof. London Sch. Econs., 1988, U. Klagenfurt, 1996, 99; chmn. dept., 1996-2001, Edward R. Meyer Disting. prof. natural resources and environ. policy Wash. State U., Pullman, 1996—. Co-author: Risk, Uncertainity and Rational Actioneditor: Public Reactions to Nuclear Power, 1984, Pub. Reactions to Nuclear Waste, 1993; bd. dirs. several profl. jours.; contbr. articles to profl. jours. Mem. nuc. waste adv. coun. Wash. State, 1987—92; mem. NAS Nat. Bd. on Radioactive Waste Mgmt., 2002—. Fellow: AAAS; mem.: Soc. Risk Analysis, Soc. for Human Ecology, Internat. Soc. Assn., Sociol. Rsch. Assn., Am. Sociol. Assn. (Disting. Contbn. award), Sigma Xi. Avocations: conceptual art constrns., skiing, collecting native masks, gardening, collection fine art. Home: 510 East C St Moscow ID 83843 Office: Wash State U Dept Sociology Pullman WA 99164-4020 Office Phone: 509-335-4163. Business E-Mail: rosa@wsu.edu.

ROSA, FREDRIC DAVID, construction company executive; b. Monroe, Wis., Oct. 31, 1946; s. Fredric Carl Rosa and Irene (Sommers) Rosa Figi; m. Melanie A. Downs, May 31, 1986; children: Mark, Katherine. BBA in Mktg., U. Wis., 1968. Dir. mktg. Swiss Colony Stores, Inc., Monroe, 1968-80; pres. Videotape Indsl. Prodns., Inc., Madison, Wis., 1980-82; agt. VR Bus. Brokers, Colorado Springs, Colo., 1982-83; sales rep. NCR Corp., Denver, 1983-85; prin. F. D. Rosa & Assocs., Denver, Aspen and Eagle, Colo., 1985-89; pres. Peak Benefit Cons., Colorado Springs, 1989-95; registered prin. Nexus Fin. Programs, Inc., Colorado Springs, Colo., 1990-92, Nutmeg Securities Ltd., Colorado Springs, 1992-94; sales staff Am. Airlines, Colorado Springs, Colo., 1993-95. Cons. Kolb-Lena Cheese Co., Lena, Ill., 1983-85; instr. The Am. Coll., Bryn Mawr, Pa., 1990-91, A.D. Banker & Co., Overland Park, Kans., 1995-97; owner Fred Rosa Constrn., Colorado Springs, 1990-94, Lakewood, Colo., 1995—. Contbr. articles to trade publs. and newspapers. Mem. Am. Soc. CLU and Chartered Fin. Cons., Mensa, Internat. Legion of Intelligence, Delta Sigma Pi (life). Methodist. Avocations: big game hunting, skiing, camping, travel. Home and Office: Fred Rosa Constrn 2150 Centre Ave Lakewood CO 80526-8118 E-mail: roosa1660@iwon.com.

ROSA, HELEN, dean; Dean U. Central del Caribe Sch. Medicine, Bayamon, PR, 2002—. Office: Univ Central del Caribe Sch Medicine Office Admissions Call Box 60-327 Bayamon PR 00960-6032

ROSA, LINDA, advocate; b. Rhineland, Wis., Feb. 5, 1949; d. Homer Dale and Marcella Ion Streckert Rosa; m. Larry W. Sarner, Aug. 17, 1993; 1 child, Emily. BA in Anthropology, BSN, U. Wis., 1975. RN Wis. Co-founder, pres. South Am. Explorers Club, 1975—90; vol. supr. Hosp. Amazonico, Pucallpa, Peru, 1978; Colo. coord., nat. bd. mem. Nat. Coun. Against Health Fraud, Newton, Mass., 1998—; co-founder, adminstrv. dir. Advocates for Children in Therapy, Loveland, Colo., 2003—; co-founder Citizens for Sci. in Medicine, 2003—. Editor: South American Explorer mag.; co-author: Attachment Therapy on Trial: The Torture and Death of Candace Newmaker. Recipient James Randi Skeptic of the Yr. award, 1995, Sci. and Profl. Integrity trophy, Assn. for Advancement of Behavioral Therapy, 2002. Avocations: belly dancing, gardening, reading. Office: Advocates for Children in Therapy 711 W 9th St Loveland CO 80537 E-mail: rosa@ezlink.com.

ROSA, PETER MANUEL, academic administrator, researcher, education educator; b. NYC, Nov. 22, 1946; s. Pedro and Raquel (Ramirez) R.; m. Pamela Ann Greene, Aug. 10, 1968; children: Kimberly Ann, Peter Martin. BA, Cen. Conn. State U., 1968, MS, 1974; PhD, U. Conn., 1981. Tchr. Bristol (Conn.) Cen. High Sch., 1968-72; admission officer Ctrl. Conn. State U., New Britain, 1972—83; researcher, lobbyist Conn. Dept. Higher Edn., Hartford, 1983—87; higher edn. lobbyist Conn. State Univ. Sys., Hartford, 1987—96, acad. adminstr. New Britain, 1996—98, exec. officer for student affairs, 2003—, chief student affairs officer; v.p. student affairs Ctrl. Conn. State U., New Britain, 1998—2002, v.p. emeritus, 2002—, assoc. prof. higher edn., 2002—. Dean, faculty Nat. Assn. Coll. Admission Counselors Hampton (Va.) Inst., 1988—92. Mem. Latino and Puerto Rican Affairs Commn., 1995—97; bd. dirs. Conn. Assn. of Edn., 1995—99; vice chair New Britain Bd. Edn., 1997—98; alderman New Britain Common Coun., 1989—91, 1993, asst. majority leader, 1989—91, 1993; pres. New Britain Bd. Edn., 1998—99. Fellow Nat. Hispanic Leadership, NJ Dept. Higher Edn., 1985. Mem.: Nat. Assn. Coll. Admission Counselors, New Britain Bd. Edn., Conn. Assn. Latinos/Latinas in Higher Edn. (pres. 1983, 2003—). Democrat. Roman Catholic. Avocations: politics, baseball, reading, music. Home: 521 Shuttle Meadow Ave New Britain CT 06052-1826 Office: Conn State U Sys 39 Woodland St Hartford CT 06105 Office Phone: 860-493-0075. Business E-Mail: rosa@ccsu.edu.

ROSA, RAYMOND ULRIC, retired banker; b. New Britain, Conn., Jan. 30, 1927; s. Kenneth E. and Regina (Chenette) R.; m. Irene M. Asselin, Feb. 5, 1949; children: R. James, David M., Cathryn P., Michael F., Nancy A., Kenneth E. AS, Hillyer Coll., 1949. CPA, Conn. Pvt. practice pub. accounting, Manchester, Conn., 1949-52; auditor Auditors of Pub. Accounts, State of Conn., Hartford, 1952-65; dir. Fed.-State Relations Dept. Finance and Control, Conn., 1965-69; dep. commr. Finance and Control, Conn., 1969-71; sr. v.p., auditor Soc. Savings, Hartford, 1971-90, ret., 1990. Mem. Windsor Locks (Conn.) Bd. Fin., 1973—81; pres. Savs. Bank Forum, 1981—82; trustee, sec.-treas. Mease Manor, Inc., Dunedin, Fla., 1995—2001, vice chmn., 2001—03, chmn., 2003—. Treas. Mental Health Assn. Conn., 1974-77, v.p., 1977-80, pres., 1980-83; bd. dirs. Nat. Assn. Mental Health, 1977-85, v.p. region 1, 1982-83; bd. dirs. Combined Health Appeal of Greater Hartford, 1982-90. Served with USNR, 1944-46. Mem. AICPA, Conn. Soc. CPAs, Conn. Soc. Govtl. Accts., KC, Dunedin Country Club (bd. dirs. 1997-2000, v.p. 1998-99, pres. 1999-00), Suffield Country Club (bd. govs. 1984-91). Home: 2060 Golf View Dr Dunedin FL 34698-2330

ROSADO, RODOLFO JOSE, psychologist, educator; b. N.Y.C., Jan. 9, 1959; s. Rodolfo Jose and Maria (Gonzalez) R.; m. Ruth Laura Morrison, June 11, 1982; children: Emily Hope, Adam Philip. BS in Psychology, Fordham U., Bronx, N.Y., 1979, MA in Clin. Psychology, 1986, PhD in Clin. Psychology, 1992. Diplomate in clin. psychology and child psychology Am. Bd. Psychol. Specialties; lic. psychologist, N.Y., Conn. Psychology tng. fellow N.Y. Med. Coll., Valhalla, 1979-81; clin. psychology intern Hall-Brooke Hosp., Westport, Conn., 1982-83; therapist Child Guidance Ctr., Bridgeport, Conn., 1983-85, office coord., 1985-90, program dir., 1990-93; asst. prof. Fairfield (Conn.) U., 1993-97, program dir. coll. access, 1995-96; pvt. practice specializing in psychol. evaluations Norwalk, Conn., 1993—. Initial Rev. Group profl. reviewer USPHS, Rockville, Md., 1990-95; regional adv. com. Dept. Children & Families, Bridgeport, 1995—; oversight collaborative Bridgeport Futures, 1994-95; faculty co-sponsor SALSA Hispanic Students Assn., Fairfield U., 1995-97; bd. dirs., clin. cons. R.E.A.C.H. Program, Riverside, Conn.; bd. dirs. Side by Side Charter Sch., Norwalk, Conn., 2002--. Author, moderator TV show Conversation in Edn., 1994; co-author proposal Empowerment Zone Grant, 1994; author proposal Comprehensive Child & Adolescent Svc., 1993. Mem. Youth Svc. Bur., City of Bridgeport, 1991-93; family preservation initiative Conn. Dept. Children & Families, Bridgeport, 1995-2000; coach Little League Baseball, 2000-02; asst. coach Biddy Basketball Youth Program, Norwalk, 2001-02; vice chmn. bd. dirs. Side by Side Charter Sch., Norwalk, Conn., 2002—. Recipient N.Y. Regents scholarship, 1975-79, scholarship Fordham U., Bronx, 1975-79, Appreciation award for collaborative support State of Conn. Dept. Children & Families, 1995, Outstanding Contbns. to Latino Cmty. Recognition award Puerto Rican/Latino employees of Human Resources Adminstrn. and Affiliated Agys., Dept. Homeless Svcs. and Adminstrn. for Children's Svcs., 1999. Mem. APA, Am. Coll. Forensic Examiners, Hispanic Assn. Mental Health and Allied Professions (exec. com., treas. 1988-92), Conn. Coalition for Children of Alcoholics (steering com. 1986-87), Sigma Xi. Avocations: racquetball, hiking. Office: 71 East Ave Ste U Norwalk CT 06851

ROSADO, ROSSANA, publishing executive, editor-in-chief; b. Bronx, N.Y. married; 2 children. BA in Journalism, Pace U. Reporter El Diario/La Prensa, N.Y.C., editor-in-chief, 1995—, gen. mgr., pub., 1999—; prodr. pub. affairs programming Sta. WPIX-TV, N.Y.C., 1988, pub. svc. dir. Prodr.: (TV series) Best Talk in Town; contbr. articles to mags. V.p. pub. affairs Health and Hosps. Corp., N.Y.C., 1992. Recipient STAR award, N.Y. Women's Agenda, Emmy award, Broadcaster's award, N.Y. State, Folio award. Office: El Diario La Prensa 345 Hudson St 13th Fl New York NY 10014

ROSALDO, RENATO IGNACIO, JR., cultural anthropology educator; b. Champaign, Ill., Apr. 15, 1941; s. Renato Ignacio and Mary Elizabeth (Potter) R.; m. Michelle Sharon Zimbalist, June 12, 1966 (dec. Oct. 1981); children: Samuel Mario, Manuel Zimbalist; m. Mary Louise Pratt, Nov. 26, 1983; 1 child, Olivia Emilia Rosaldo-Pratt. AB, Harvard U., 1963, PhD, 1971. Asst. prof. cultural anthropology Stanford (Calif.) U., 1970-76, assoc. prof., 1976-85, prof., 1985—, Mellon prof. interdisciplinary studies, 1987-90, dir. Ctr. for Chicano Rsch., 1985-90, chair anthropology, 1994-96, Lucie Stern prof. social scis., 1993—. Author: Ilongot Headhunting 1883-1974, 1980, Culture and Truth, 1989. Recipient Harry Benda prize Assn. for Asian Studies, 1983; Guggenheim fellow, 1993. Fellow Am. Acad. Arts and Scis. Avocations: poetry, swimming, drawing, dance. Office: Stanford U Dept Cultural and Social Anthropology Palo Alto CA 94305-2145 Home: 120 W 15th St Apt 7H New York NY 10011-6792

ROSALES, SUZANNE MARIE, hospital coordinator; b. Merced, Calif., July 23, 1946; d. Walter Marshall and Ellen Marie (Earl) Potter; children: Anita Carol, Michelle Suzanne. AA, City Coll., San Francisco, 1966. Diplomate Am. Coll. Utilization Review Physicians. Utilization review coord. San Francisco Gen. Hosp., 1967-74; mgr. utilization review/discharge planning UCLA Hosp. and Clinics, 1974-79; nurse III Hawaii State Hosp., Kaneohe, 1979-80; review coord. Pacific Profl. Std. Review Orgn., Honolulu, 1980-81; coord. admission and utilization reviewq The Rehab. Hosp. of the Pacific, Honolulu, 1981-85; coord. Pacific Med. Referral Project, Honolulu, 1985-87; dir. profl. svcs. The Queen's Healthcare Plan, Honolulu, 1987-88; utilization mgmt. coord. Vista Psychiat. Physician Assocs., San Diego, 1989; admission coord. utilization review San Francisco Gen. Hosp., 1989-91, quality improvement coordinator, 1991—. Cons. Am. Med. Records Assn. Contbr. articles to profl. jours. Mem. Nat. Assn. Utilization Review Profls. Home: 138 Alta Vista Way Daly City CA 94014-1402 Office: San Francisco Gen Hosp 1001 Potrero Ave San Francisco CA 94110-3594

ROSALSKY, BARBARA ELLEN, artist, home health aide; b. N.Y.C., Nov. 16, 1948; d. Ellis M. Rosalsky and Claire (Schwartz) Rosalsky Shapiro; m. Dennis Robinson. BA, SUNY, Plattsburgh, 1970. Sales girl Cambridge (Mass.) Artist mag., 1970-71; artist Pillar of Fire mag., Zarephath, N.J., 1977; home health aide CMR, Bound Brook, N.J., 1978—; designer New Brunswick (N.J.) Tomorrow, 1980-87; art therapist Middlesex Hosp., New Brunswick, 1981-83. One-woman shows include The Bird and Me, 1980, Highland Pk. (N.J.) Libr., 2003, The City, 2003, exhibited in group shows at Other Artists Other Art, 1983. Mem. Cultural Arts Commn., Piscataway, N.J., 1993—. SUNY Plattsburgh scholar, 1970. Mem. Women's Caucus Art, Marriott Swim Club. Democrat. Avocations: piano, swimming, dance, hiking, print making. Home: 114 Woodland Rd Piscataway NJ 08854-4222

ROSAND, DAVID, art history educator; b. Bklyn., Sept. 6, 1938; s. Johan Herbert and Frieda (Grotenstein) R.; m. Ellen Fineman, June 18, 1961; children: Jonathan, Eric. AB, Columbia Coll., 1959; MA, Columbia U., 1962, PhD, 1965. Instr. art history Columbia U., NYC, 1964-67, asst. prof., 1967-69, assoc. prof., 1969-73, prof., 1973-95, chmn. Soc. of Fellows in the Humanities, 1979-83, Meyer Schapiro prof. art history, 1995—. Co-author (with Michelangelo Muraro): Titian and the Venetian Woodcut, 1976, Titian, 1978; author: Painting in Cinquecento Venice: Titian, Veronese Tintoretto, 1982, rev. edit., 1997; author: (with others) Places of Delight: The Pastoral Landscape, 1988; author: The Meaning of the Mark: Leonardo and Titian, 1988, Painting in Sixteenth-Century Venice, rev. edit., 1997, Robert Motherwell on Paper, 1997, Myths of Venice: The Figuration of a State, 2001, Drawing Acts: Studies in Graphic Expression and Representation, 2002, The Invention of Painting in America, 2004; editor: Titian: His World and His Legacy, 1982; editor: (with Robert W. Hanning) Castiglione: The Ideal and the Real in Renaissance Culture, 1983; editor: Interpretazioni Veneziane, 1984. Mem. bd. advisors CASVA Nat. Gallery Art., 1990-94. Fulbright Commn. fellow, 1962-63; NEH fellow, 1971-72, 85-86, 91-92; John S. Guggenheim Meml. Found. fellow, 1974-75. Mem. Coll. Art Assn. Am., Renaissance Soc. Am. (mem. exec. bd. 1981—), Save Venice, Inc. (bd. dirs.), Ateneo Veneto (fgn.), Am. Acad. Arts and Scis. Home: 560 Riverside Dr New York NY 10027-3212 Office: Columbia U Dept Art History & Archaeology 826 Schermerhorn Hall Mail Code 5517 New York NY 10027 Office Phone: 212-854-4502. Business E-Mail: dr17@columbia.edu.

ROSARIO-OLMEDO, CARMEN GLORIA, principal; b. Mayaguez, P.R., Jan. 4, 1940; d. Rafael and Emilia (Derieux) Rosario; m. William Galindo, Apr. 19, 1968 (div. 1974); m. Ruben Eduardo Olmedo, Dec. 25, 1976. BA, CCNY, 1963; MA, NYU, 1982; profl. diploma, L.I. U., 1987. Cert. elem. prin., asst. prin., sch. dist. adminstr., sch. adminstr. and supr., permanent tchg. cert., N.Y.C. Tchr. N.Y.C. Bd. Edn., 1963-89, asst. prin., 1989-95, prin. I.A., 1995-97, prin., 1997—2001. Curriculum designer Cmty. Sch. Dist. 17, Bklyn., 1965-66, tchr. trainer, 1967-70; exch. tchr. trainer, San Juan, P.R., 1970-71; founder, artistic dir. Children in the Arts, Bklyn., 1979-86; coord. sch. vol. program Pub. Sch. 316, Bklyn., 1988-95. Contbr.: The Mexican Family, 1979, The Chilean Family Structure, 1982. Mem. Puerto Rican Educator's Assn., N.Y.C., 1979—, Atlas, N.Y.C., 1972-93. Recipient Women's Hist. Month award Borough Pres. Office, 1986, NYC Coun. Proclamation award, 2002, Bklyn. Borough Pres. Citation, 2002, NY State Senate 20th Dist. award, 2002, Y State Exec. Chamber Cert. of Merit, 2002, Cmty. Dist. 17 Disting. Service award, 2001; Fulbright scholar, 1972, 82, NDEA grantee U.S. Office Edn. Inst. for Tchg. Disadvantaged Children, 1965-66, exch. program grantee N.Y.C. Bd. Edn., 1970-71. Mem. ASCD, Counsel of Supervisors and Adminstrs., Nat. Assn. P.R. Women, Hispanic Orgn. Latino Actors, Fulbright Assn. (life). Avocations: acting, anthropology, artist, travel, writer, archaeology. Home: 176 Prospect Park W Brooklyn NY 11215-5285 Office: Pub Sch 316 750 Classon Ave Brooklyn NY 11238-4685 E-mail: colmedo@nycboe.nycenet.edu.

ROSASCHI, JIM, librarian; b. Alma, Mich., Apr. 4, 1949; s. Mary Henry and True Rosaschi; m. Gaylene Reynolds, Aug. 22, 1975; children: Nicole, Daniel, MIchelle, Emma. MLS, Brigham Young U., 1979. Cert. K-12 tchrg. Calif., 1982. Dir. Nampa (Idaho) Pub. Libr., 1979—82; mgr. Petaluma br. libr. Sonoma County Libr., Sana Rosa, Calif., 1982—95, mgr. ext. svcs. Santa Rosa, 1985—89, mgr. tech. svcs., 1989—. Pres. Customers of Dynix, Inc., Salt Lake City, 2003—; libr. tech. presentations, Melbourne, Australia, 2003, Edinburgh, Scotland, 04. Adult sunday sch. tchr. Ch. of Jesus Christ of Latter-Day Saints, Santa Rosa, 1998—2002. With US Army, 1969—72. Mem.: Calif. Libr. Assn., ALA, Mormon History Assn. Home: 925 Hyland Dr Santa Rosa CA 95407 Office: Sonoma County Libr 3rd and E St Santa Rosa CA 95404 Office Phone: 707-545-0831.

ROSATI, ALLISON, newscaster; b. Dover, Del., 1963; married; 4 children. Grad. Speech and Comms. cum laude, Gustavus Adolphus Coll., 1985. Gen. assignment reporter Sta. KTTC-TV, Rochester, Minn., 1985, prodr., co-anchor of 6 pm and 10 pm newscasts, 1986—87; gen. assignment reporter Sta. WGRZ-TV, Buffalo, 1987, anchor 6 pm and 10 pm newscasts; anchor, reporter NBC 5, Chgo., 1990—97, co-anchor 10 pm newscast, 1997—, co-anchor weekday 6 pm newscast. Active Big Brothers/Big Sisters; bd. dirs., organizer Bowl for Kids and Celebrity Golf Outing; active Greater Chgo. Food Depository, March of Dimes, Salvation Army, Ronald McDonald House. Recipient 1st Decade award for Most Accomplished Alumna of the Decade, Gustavus Adolphus Coll., Nat. Emmy award, Excellence in Comms. award, Justinian Soc. Chgo., David award for Achievement in Broadcasting, Joint Civic Com. Italian Ams., Dante award, 2001. Office: NBC 454 N Columbus Dr Chicago IL 60611

ROSATO, ANTHONY DOMINICK, mechanical engineer, educator; b. Bklyn., Aug. 28, 1953; s. Michael Joseph and Betty (Rispoli) R. BME, Pratt Inst., 1975; MS in Theoretical and Applied Mechanics, Northwestern U., 1979; MS in Applied Maths., Carnegie Mellon U., 1981, PhD in Mech. Engring., 1985. Devel. engr. Green Fan Co., Beacon, NY, 1975—77; rsch. asst. dept. civil engring. Northwestern U., Evanston, Ill., 1977—79; tchg. asst. mech. engring. and maths. Carnegie Mellon U., Pitts., 1979—82, rsch. asst., 1981—84, rsch. assoc. dept. mech. engring., 1985—86; adj. faculty dept. exact scis. Carlow Coll., Pitts., 1986; asst. prof. mech. engring. N.J. Inst. Tech., Newark, 1987—93, assoc. prof. mech. engring., 1993—2002, prof. mech. engring., 2002—, dir. Particle Tech. Ctr., 1995—99, dir. Granular Sci. Lab., 2000—, coord. undergrad. rsch. in mech. engring., 2000—02. Faculty Gov.'s Sch. in Scis., Drew U., Madison, N.J., 1988; vis. faculty fellow, physicist dept. earth scis. Lawrence Livermore (Calif.) Nat. Lab., 1989, 90; Joliot professorship Ecole Superieure de Physique et de Chimie Industrielles, Laboratoire H.M.P., Paris, 1994; mem. nat. materials adv. bd. NRC, 1995; vis. scientist The Lovelace Insts., Albuquerque, 1995-96; vis. assoc. prof. mech. engring. Worcester Poly. Inst., 1995; assoc. chmn. mech. engring. grad. studies, N.J. Inst. Tech., 2001-2003. Assoc. editor Mechanics Rsch. Comms.; mem. editl. bd. Internat. Jour. Nonlinear Sci. and Numerical Simulation. Chair sci. com. IUTAM Symposium, Cape May, N.J., 1999. Vis. scholar mech. engring, Stanford U., 2003. Fellow ASME; mem. Am. Soc. Engring. Edn. (program chair elect grad. studes divsn. 1995), Am. Acad. Mechanics, N.J. Inst. Tech. Ctr. for Applied Maths., Sigma Xi, Tau Beta Pi, Pi Tau Sigma. Roman Catholic. Office: NJ Inst Tech Mech Engring Dept University Heights Newark NJ 07102 Office Phone: 973-596-5829. E-mail: rosato@adm.njit.edu.

ROSATO, MELISSA ANNE, educator; b. Morristown, NJ, Feb. 26, 1979; d. Arcangelo C. and Ethel Marie Rosato. BS, Coll. of St. Elizabeth, Morristown, NJ, 1994—98; MS, NYU, GSAS, 1999—2001. Tchg. asst. NYU, 1999—2002, lab. asst., 2002; ade Huntington Learning Ctr., NJ, 2003. Mem.: NY Acad. of Sci. Democrat. Roman Catholic. Avocations: reading, running, watercolor. Home: 692 Bliss Dr New Milford NJ 07646

ROSBERG, MERILEE ANN, education educator; b. Oak Park, Ill., June 1, 1942; d. Andrew Clark and Martha (Kester) Adamson; m. William H. Rosberg, Aug. 17, 1963; children: Peter E., Trent W. AB, Augustana Coll., 1963; MA, U. Iowa, 1971, PhD, 1985. Tchr. Cedar Rapids (Iowa) Pub. Schs., 1963-65, Internat. Sch. Kuwait, 1965-67, N. Winnishiek Cmty. Schs., Decorah, Iowa, 1967-69, St. Mark's Luth. Ch. Presch., Cedar Rapids, 1969-71; staff tng. specialist Linn County Day Care Svcs., Cedar Rapids, 1971-76; dir. early childhood program Jane Boyd Comty. House, Cedar Rapids, 1976-86; prof., divsn. chair Mt. Mercy Coll., Cedar Rapids, 1986—. Vis. prof. U. Sts. Cyril & Methodius, Veliko Turnovo, Bulgaria, 1992, Czech Tech. U., Prague, Czech Rep., 1990. Fulbright scholar U. Brunei Darusalam, 1994-95. Mem. Nat. Assn. Early Childhood Edn., Nat. Coun. Tchrs. English, Internat. Reading Assn. (Reading Adminstr. of Yr., Cedar Rapids 2002, Iowa 2002), Orgn. Mondiale Pour L'Education Prescolaire (U.S. nat. com.). Avocations: reading, travel. Home: 1900 Bever Ave SE Cedar Rapids IA 52403-2715 Office: Mt Mercy Coll 1330 Elmhurst Dr NE Cedar Rapids IA 52402-4763 Business E-Mail: merilee@mtmercy.edu.

ROSCH, ELLIOTT CARL, internist; b. N.Y.C., July 29, 1952; s. Maurice Charles and Bea (Horowitz) R. BA, Brown U., 1974; MD, U. Pa., 1978. Diplomate Am. Bd. Internal Medicine. Pvt. practice, Yonkers, N.Y., 1981—; med. dir. Riverside Med. Group. V.p., chmn. homeless svcs. Jewish Coun. Yonkers, 1992—. Office: Riverside Med Group 1010 N Broadway Yonkers NY 10701-1303

ROSCH, JOHN THOMAS, lawyer; b. Council Bluffs, Iowa, Oct. 4, 1939; s. H.P. and Phebe Florence (Jamison) R.; m. Carolyn Lee, Aug. 18, 1961; children: Thomas Lee, Laura Lee. BA, Harvard U., 1961, LLB, 1965. Bar: Calif. 1966, U.S. Dist. Ct. (no. dist.) Calif. 1966, U.S. Dist. Ct. (ea. dist.) Calif. 1967, U.S. Ct. Appeals (9th cir.) 1966. Assoc. McCutchen, Doyle, Brown & Enersen, San Francisco, 1965-72, ptnr., 1972-73, 75-93, Latham & Watkins, San Francisco, 1994—, office mng. ptnr., 1994—99. Bd. dirs. Bur. Consumer Protection, FTC, Washington, 1973-75, bd. dirs. The Eisenhower Inst. Contbr. articles to profl. jours. Fellow Am. Bar Found., Am. Coll. Trial Lawyers; mem. ABA (past chmn. antitrust sect.), State Bar Calif., San Francisco Bar Assn., Calif. State and Antitrust and Trade Regulation Sect. (past sect. chair, Calif. Antitrust Lawyer of Yr. 2003). Republican. Episcopalian. Office: Latham & Watkins 505 Montgomery St Fl 19th San Francisco CA 94111-2552 Business E-Mail: tom.rosch@lw.com.

ROSCH, PAUL JOHN, internist, educator; b. Yonkers, N.Y., June 30, 1927; s. Samuel Joseph and Mary (Gang) R.; m. Lorraine Marie Hunt, June 27, 1951; children: David Carl, Jonathan Hunt, Jane Ellen, Michael Edward, Richard Joseph, Donna Marie; m. Marguerite Delamater, Sept. 12, 1972. AB, Brown U., NYU, 1948, MA, 1950; MD, Albany Med. Coll., 1954. Diplomate Am. Bd. Internal Medicine. Fellow Inst. Exptl. Medicine and Surgery, U. Montreal, Que., Can., 1951-52; intern, asst. resident in medicine Johns Hopkins Hosp., 1954-56; resident in medicine, then chief dept. metabolism Walter Reed Med. Ctr., 1956-58; physician-in-charge nuclear medicine St. John's Riverside Hosp., Yonkers, 1959-67, dir. endocrine clinic, sr. attending physician, 1959-96, vice chief of staff, 1977; chief endocrine clinic St. Joseph's Hosp., 1959, sr. cons. in medicine, 1980—; pres. Am. Inst. Stress, Yonkers, 1978—, sr. cons. in medicine, 1980—; clin. prof. medicine and psychiatry N.Y. Med. Coll., 1980—. Asst. clin. prof. medicine Mt. Sinai Hosp. Sch. Medicine, 1963-67; former adj. prof. medicine in psychiatry U. Md. Sch. Medicine. From asst. to assoc. editor Health Comm. and Informatics;

editor-in-chief Stress Medicine, 1990—; mem. editorial bd. AMA Archives Internal Medicine, Folia Clinica Internat, Jour. Human Stress, Internat. Jour. Psychosomatics, Am. Jour. Health Promotion, Cardiovascular Revs. & Reports, Internat. Jour. Stress Mgmt., Comprehensive Therapy, Jour. Human Behavior; contbg. editor Creative Living; contbr. articles to profl. jours. Bd. govs. Jewish Community Ctr.; bd. dirs. Family Svc. Soc., Mensana Clinic, 1980—; chmn. bd. Internat. Found. Biosocial Devel. and Human Health, 1980—; mem. adv. bd. Image Inst., 1980—. Capt. AUS, 1956-58. Fellow ACP, Internat. Stress Mgmt. Assn. (hon. v.p. 1991—), Am. Coll. Cardiology, Internat. Acad. Medicine, Am. Coll. Angiology, N.Y. Diabetes Assn.; mem. Westchester Diabetes Assn. (pres. 1968), Internat. Law Enforcement Stress Assn. (adv. bd. 1980—), Yonkers Acad. Medicine (bd. govs., pres. 1971), N.Y. Cardiology Soc., Acad. Psychosomatic Medicine, Soc. Behavioral Medicine, N.Y. Acad. Scis., Endocrine Soc., Am. Diabetes Assn., Westchester Soc. Internat. Medicine (past pres.), Stress Mgmt. Assn. (hon. v.p.), N.Y. State Soc. Internal Medicine (pres. 1974), Soc. Nuclear Medicine (bd. dirs.), Am. Fedn. Clin. Rsch., Am. Soc. Internal Medicine, Am. Geriatrics Soc., Elmwood Country Club, Atlantis Golf Club, Breakers Golf Club, St. Andrews Golf Club, La Coquille Club (Palm Beach, Fla.). Home: 10 Old Jackson Ave Hastings On Hudson NY 10706-3203 also: 221 N Country Club Dr Lake Worth FL 33462-1113 Office Phone: 914-963-1200. Personal E-mail: shur124@earthlink.net.

ROSCHER, NINA MATHENY, chemistry professor; b. Uniontown, Pa., Dec. 8, 1938; d. Charles Kenneth and Wilma Pauline (Solomon) Matheny; m. David Roscher, Dec. 27, 1964. BS in Chemistry, U. Del., 1960; PhD in Chemistry, Purdue U., 1964. Phys. chemist Nat. Bur. of Standards, 1958-61; rsch. and teaching asst. Purdue U., West Lafayette, Ind., 1960-64, fellow in chemistry, instr. chemistry, 1964-65; instr. U. Tex., Austin, 1965-67; sr. staff chemist Coca-Cola Export Corp., 1967-68; asst. prof. Douglass Coll., Rutgers U., The State U., 1968-74, asst. dean, 1971-74; dir. acad. adminstrn. Am. U., Washington, 1974-76, assoc. prof. chemistry, 1974-79, prof., 1979—, assoc. dean grad. affairs Coll. Arts and Scis., 1976-79, vice-provost acad. svcs., 1979-82, vice provost for acad. affairs, 1982-85, dean faculty affairs, 1981-85, chair chemistry dept., 1991—. Program dir. sci. edn., NSF, 1986-98; lectr. in field. Contbr. articles to profl. jours. Recipient Disting. Alumna award Purdue Univ. Sch. Sci., 1996, Am. Chem. Soc. award for encouraging women into careers in the chem. scis. Camille and Henry Dreyfus Found., 1996, Presdl. Award for Excellence in Sci., Math. and Engring. Mentoring, 1998; Standard Oil fellow, 1961-62, David Ross fellow, 1963-64, Rutgers U. Rsch. Fund, Biomed. Support grantee. Fellow AAAS, Am. Inst. Chemists (profl. opportunities for women com., pres. dist. inst. chemists 1978-79, sec. 1976-77, fin. com. 1983-87, exec. com., bd. dirs. 1986), Assn. Women in Sci., Am. Chem. Soc. (treas. Monmouth County sect. 1970-72, chair 1974, pres. Washington sect. 1995, profl. programs planning and coord. com. 1976-78, admissions com. 1981-89, 91-96, GM scholar 1956-60, Virgil F. Payne award, others); mem. N.Y. Acad. Scis., AAUA, Soc. Applied Spectroscopy, Sci. Manpower Commn. Profls. in Sci. Home: 10400 Hunter Ridge Dr Oakton VA 22124-1616 Office: Am Univ Dept Chemistry Washington DC 20016-8014 E-mail: NRosche@American.edu.

ROSCIGNO, JOHN ANTHONY, music educator, conductor; b. Bronx, NY, Sept. 26, 1964; s. John and Carolyn Roscigno; m. Amy Christine Amy Andrew, Aug. 13, 1994; children: Andrew John, Isabella Christina. MusB, U. of Ariz., 1982—87; MusM, U. of Ill., 1987—89; D of musical arts, U. of Ariz., 1994—98. Dir. of orchestral studies U. of Ctrl. Ark., Conway, Ark., 1996—2002; music dir., condr. Conway Symphony Orch., Conway, Ark., 1996—2002; asst. prof. of music Auburn U., Auburn, Ala., 1989—92; dir. of orchestral activities U. of Ariz., 1994—96; dir. of orch. studies Calif. State U., Northridge, 2002—; music dir., condr. CSUN Youth Orchestras, Los Angeles, 2002—. Guest condr. Opera Constata, Constata, Romania, 2003, Santa Barbara Dance Theater, Calif., 2003, Plainview Symphony, Plainview, Tex., 2002, So. Ariz. Symphony, 1996. Officer ex-officio Conway Symphony Orch., Conway, Ark., 1996—2002; bd. mem. Tucson Arts Dist. Partnership, 1995. Recipient Semi-finalist, Tokyo Internat. Conducting Competition, 1996; Conducting scholarhips, Aspen Music Festival, 1986, fellowship, U. of Miami, 1993, U. of Ariz., 1994, Grad. Assistantship, U. of Ill., 1987—89, Fine Arts scholarhips, U. of Ariz., 1982—87. Mem.: Am. Symphony Orch. League (assoc.), Am. String Teachers Assn. (assoc.). Home: 7954 Loma Verde Ave Canoga Park CA 91304 Office: California State University Northridge 18111 Nordhoff St Northridge CA 91330-8314 E-mail: jr4915@yahoo.com.

ROSCOE, STANLEY NELSON, psychologist, aeronautical engineer; b. Eureka, Calif., Nov. 4, 1920; s. Stanley Boughton and Martha Emma (Beer) R.; m. Margaret Hazel Brookins, Dec. 21, 1948 (dec.); children: Lee Marin Roscoe Bragg, Jack; m. Elizabeth Frances Lage, Mar. 12, 1977 (dec.); 1 child, Catherine Marie; m. Gayle Buchanan Karshner, Mar. 15, 1990. AB in Speech and English, Humboldt State U., 1943; postgrad., U. Calif., Berkeley, 1942, 46; MA in Psychology, U. Ill., 1947, PhD in Psychology, 1950. Cert. psychologist, Calif. Research asst. U. Ill., Urbana-Champaign, 1946-50, research assoc., 1950-51, asst. prof., 1951-52; assoc. dir. Inst. Aviation, head aviation rsch. lab., Savoy, 1969—75, prof. aviation, psychology, aero. and astronautical engring., 1969—79, prof. emeritus, 1979—; prof. psychology N.Mex. State U., Las Cruces, 1979-86, prof. emeritus, 1986—; with Hughes Aircraft Co., Culver City, Calif., 1952-69, 75-77, dept. mgr., 1962-69, sr. scientist, 1975-77; tech. adviser, cons. in field. Pres. Illiana Aviation Scis. Ltd., Las Cruces, N.Mex., 1976—; v.p. Aero Innovation, Inc., Montreal. Author: Aviation Psychology, 1980, Flightdeck Performance: The Human Factor, 1990, Heydays in Mattole, 1996, Predicting Human Performance, 1997, Keeping the Picture: The Measurement of Flow Control, 1999; editor: Aviation Research Monographs, 1971-72, Heydays in Humboldt, 1991, From Humboldt to Kodiak, 1992; assoc. cons. editor: Human Factors Jour., 1982—, Internat. Jour. Aviation Psychology, 1991—; contbr. more than 200 articles to profl. jours.; patentee, inventor in field. 1st lt. AC, U.S. Army, 1943-46. Fellow APA (divsn. of applied and engring. psychology, Franklin V. Taylor award 1976), Human Factors and Ergonomics Soc. (pres. 1960-61, Jerome H. Ely award 1968, 73, 89, 91, Alexander C. Williams award 1973, Paul M. Fitts award 1974, Pres.'s award 1990), Royal Aero Soc. (Eng.); mem. IEEE, AIAA, Inst. Navigation, Assn. Aviation Psychologists (ann. career award 1978), Aerospace Human Factors Assn. (Paul T. Hansen award 1994), Sigma Xi, Phi Kappa Phi, Phi Sigma, Chi Sigma Epsilon. Home: 2750 Sunnygrove Ave Mckinleyville CA 95519-7912 Office: PO Box 4498 Las Cruces NM 88003-4498

ROSCOPF, CHARLES BUFORD, lawyer; b. Marvell, Ark., Apr. 21, 1928; s. Emmett Lee and Sally Virginia (King) R.; m. Mary Anne Maddox, Aug. 22, 1954; children— Charles David; Ann Karen. Student, Hendrix Coll., 1948-50; JD, U. Ark., 1954. Bar: Ark. bar 1954, U.S. Dist. Cts 1955, 64, U.S. Supreme Ct. bar 1965. Pvt. practice, Helena, Ark., 1954—; assoc. firm Burke, Moore & Burke, 1954-58; ptnr. firm Burke & Roscopf, 1958-64; sr. ptnr. Roscopf and Roscopf, P.A., 1964—. Mem. Ark. Ho. of Reps., 1953-58; del. Ark. Constl. Conv., 1968; mem. Ark. Probate Drafting Com.; mem. Ark. State Bd. Law Examiners, 1973-79; spl. justice Ark. Supreme Ct. Served with USN, 1946-48; served with USAFR, 1962-68. Fellow Am. Bar Found., Ark. Bar Found. (pres. 1995-96); mem. ABA, Ark. Bar Assn. (pres. 1990-91), Am. Law Inst., Rotary (Paul Harris fellow), Masons, Shriners, Kappa Sigma. Methodist. Home: 117 Avalon Pl Helena AR 72342-1715 Office: Helena Nat Bank Bldg PO Box 610 Helena AR 72342-0610 Office Phone: 870-338-3438.

ROSE, AARON, artist; One-man shows include include Paul Kasmin Gallery, 1997, 1999, exhibited in group shows at John Froats Gallery, Cold Springs, N.Y., 1995, Whitney Mus. Am. Art, N.Y., 1997, Susquehanna Art Mus., Pa., 1999, Represented in permanent collections Mus. Fine Arts, Boston, Whitney Mus. Am. Art, N.Y., Met. Mus. Art, Mus. Modern Art, San Francisco. Office: c/o Paul Kasmin Gallery 293 10th Ave New York NY 10001-7003

ROSE, ALBERT SCHOENBURG, lawyer, educator; b. Nov. 9, 1945; s. Albert Schoenberg Sr. and Karleen (Klein) Rose; m. Nancy K. Rose; children: Claudia, Micah Daniel. BSBA, U. Ala., 1967; JD, Washington U., St. Louis, 1970; LLM in Taxation, George Washington U., 1974. Bar: Mo. 1970, U.S. Dist. Ct. (ea. dist.) Mo. 1970, U.S. Tax Ct. 1970, U.S. Ct. Mil. Appeals 1970, U.S. Supreme Ct. 1970. Ptnr. Lewis Rice & Fingersh, St. Louis, 2001—. Adj. prof. law Washington U., 1979-98, Fontbonne Coll., 1993-96. Co-author: Missouri Taxation Law and Practice, 1986, supplement, 1989. Capt. U.S. Army, 1970-74, Korea. Mem.: Civic Entrepreneurs Orgn. (Bd. dirs., sec.), Tax Lawyers Club, Mid.Am. Tax Conf. (chmn.). Office: Lewis Rice & Fingersh 500 North Broadway Ste 2000 Saint Louis MO 63102 E-mail: arose@lewisrice.com.

ROSE, ANITA CARROLL, retired educator; b. New Bedford, Mass., Oct. 14, 1922; d. Louis Arthur and Aline (Chicoine) Carroll; m. Anthony E. Rose, Sept. 24, 1955 (dec.); children: Anthony David, Stephen Arthur. BA, U. Mass., Dartmouth, 1971; MAT, R.I. Coll., 1975. Exec. sec. Berkshire-Hathaway, Inc., New Bedford, 1941—55, New Bedford Cancer Soc., 1956-59; tchr. French and English New Bedford Pub. Schs., 1971-88; ret., 1988. Clk. Friends of Coastline Elderly Svcs., Inc., 1991-93; bd. dirs. Our Lady's Haven, 1995—. Pres. New Bedford Jr. Women's Club, 1950-51, Fairhaven Mothers' Club, 1967-69, book chmn., 1989-91, sunshine chmn., 1991-93, nominating com. chmn., 1993—; v.p. Cath. Women's Club, 1957-59, del. Coun. of Women's Orgns., 1989-91; active Fairhaven Town Mtg., Mass., 1965—; trustee Millicent Libr., Fairhaven, 1980—; rec. sec. Fairhaven Improvement Assn., 1982-99; sec. Fairhaven Rep. Town Com., 1980—; bd. dirs. St. Anne Credit Union, New Bedford, 1988—, asst. treas., investment com. 1991-93, pres., chmn. bd., 1993—; adv. coun. Coastline Elderly Svc. Inc., 1988-92; del. Mass. Rep. Conv., 1974, 82, 86, 90, 94, 98; mem Old Dartmouth Hist. Assn., Friends of the Zeiterion Theatre, Friends New Bedford Festival Theatre. Testimonial dinner in her honor for years of cmty. svc. Fairhaven Improvement Assn., 1997. Mem. AAUW (pres. Coll. Club New Bedford 1983-85, 1st v.p. 1989-91, del. nat. conv. 1981, 83, 85, 93, chmn. nominating com. Mass. divsn. 1988-90, chmn. art study group 1992—, honored Mass. chpt. 1986), Tri-County Music Assn. (pres. 1992-95, bd. dirs. 1988—), R.I. Coll. Alumni Assn., U. Mass.-Dartmouth Alumni Assn., Libr. Assocs. U. Mass.-Dartmouth, Ret. Officers Assn., Am. Ex-Prisoners of War, St. Joseph's Couples Club (pres. 1987-88, 2001-02), Fairhaven Colonial Club (2d v.p. 1988-89), MONETA Assocs. Investment Club (chmn. 1998-99), Republican Club Southeastern Mass., Greater New Bedford Garden Club, Friends of Buttonwood Park Zoo. Avocations: travel, music, theater. Home: 49 Laurel St Fairhaven MA 02719-2817 E-mail: fairhavenacr@msn.com.

ROSE, BEATRICE SCHROEDER (MRS. WILLIAM H. ROSE), harpist, educator; b. Ridgewood, N.J., Nov. 15, 1922; d. Henry William and Ida (LeHovey) Schroeder; m. William Harrison Rose, Apr. 10, 1954; 1 child, Daniel. Student, Inst. Musical Art, 1940—41, Mannes Coll. Music, 1942—44; studies with, Lucile Lawrence and Carlos Salzedo. Concert and radio debut N.Y. World's Fair, N.Y.C., 1939; soloist Damrosch Music Appreciation Hour broadcast, 1940, Duke of Windsor's Save the Children Fund, Nassau, The Bahamas, 1941; assoc. harpist Radio City Music Hall Orch., N.Y.C., 1944-50; various radio and solo performances N.Y. area, 1944-51; concert artist Italy, U.S. and Can., 1952; prin. harpist Houston Symphony, 1953-84; prof. harp Moores Sch. Music, U. Houston, 1953—98. Soloist Contemporary Music Soc., 1959, 60, Houston Chamber Orch., 1969; dir. Christmas Festival of Harps, Houston Harp Ensemble, PBS, 1978, Harps of Gold, 1983; staff harpist Heritage Club, 1987 95, High Tea Ritz Carlton, 1996 97, St. Regis, 1998 2003. Author: Troubadour Harp: A Guide for Teachers and Students, 1976, rev. edits., 1982, 92, The Harp in the Orchestra: A Reference Book for Harpists, Teachers, Composers and Conductors, 2003; co-author; Outline of Six-Year Harp Course for Elementary, Junior and Senior High School, 1966; composer works include Enchanted Harp, rev. edit., 1995; recs. for Houston Symphony, Stokowski, Everest, Capitol, Comissiona, Vanguard Records. Recipient 1st prize Federated Music Clubs Contest, 1936; N.Y. Hour of Music award, 1945. Mem. Am. Harp Soc., Tex. Music Educators Assn. (adjudicator All-State competitions), Nat. Fedn. Music Clubs (harp adviser 1991—), Phi Beta. Home: 1315 Friarcreek Ln Houston TX 77055-6714 Office: U Houston Sch Music Houston TX 77004

ROSE, CAROL ANN, retired air transportation executive; b. Toledo; d. Donald Lucien and Dorothy Josephine (Maus) Edmunds; m. Saul Rose, Feb. 3, 1971 (div. 1976). BA, Kent State U., 1963. Entertainer, restaurant supr. S.S. Aquarama Cruiseship, Cleve., 1961-63; airline reservation agt. United Airlines, Cleve., 1963-68, internat. passenger svc. rep. Miami, Fla., 1969-70, V.I.P. customer svc. receptionist-expediter Phila., 1971-79, account exec., 1980-84, spl. events mgr. Chgo., 1984-87, red carpet club coord., 1987-88, corp. meeting planner, 1988-90, comml. aircraft weight and balance planner Seattle, 1991-96, comms. coord., 1996-98, mktg. and promotion coord., 1998-99, coord. workers compensation-comm./return to work Chgo., 1999—2001; ret., 2001; vol. editor Spiceline cmty. newsletter. Speaker Am. Mktg. Assn., Chgo., 1989. Author: Red Carpet Club Procedure Manual-O'Hare, 1987, Corporate Meeting Planners Manual, 1989, United Airlines Foundation Community Connection Report; Editor: Sky Lines Seattle Station Newsletter, 1992, United Airlines Workers' Compensation Newsletter, 1999. Vol. Relay for Life, Am. Cancer Soc., Angel Flight East, 2004—. Recipient Oustanding Svc. award Airline Passengers Assn., Phila., 1981, Outstanding Contbn. award Muscular Dystrophy Assn.-Jerry Lewis Telethon, Las Vegas, 1985, 86, 89, Leadership award United Way Campaign, Chgo., 1988. Mem. Meeting Planners Assn., Mgmt. Club (v.p. 1983, pres. 1984), Women United (exec. bd. 1982-83), Delta Zeta. Avocations: reading, aerobic walking, writing prose for spl. events, social dancing. Home: 468 Woodruff Trl Mullica Hill NJ 08062-2026

ROSE, CHARLES, television journalist; B in History, JD, Duke U.; postgrad., NYU. Interviewer Sta. WPIX-TV, N.Y.C., 1972; mng. editor Bill Moyers Internat. Report, 1974—; exec. producer Bill Moyers Jour., 1975—; corr. U.S.A.: People in Politics, PBS, 1976; polit. corr. NBC News, 1976-77; co-host A.M. Chgo., 1978; host The Charlie Rose Show Sta. KXAS-TV, Dallas, Ft. Worth, 1979-81, Sta. WRC-TV, Washington, 1981-83; former host, interviewer CBS News Nightwatch, Washington, 1984—; exec. prodr., exec. editor and host The Charlies Rose Show, 1991—; corr. Sixty Minutes II, 1999—. Producer: (TV program) A Conversation with Jimmy Carter (Peabody award). Recipient News and Documentary Emmy award for Conversation with Roger Payne, 1992, Cable ACE award, 1992. Office: 499 Park Ave New York NY 10022-1240

ROSE, CHARLES ALEXANDER, lawyer; b. Louisville, June 14, 1932; s. Hector Edward and Mary (Shepard) R.; m. Moncie Watson; children: Marc, Craig, Lorna, Gordon, Alex, Sara. BA, U. Louisville, 1954, JD, 1960. Bar: Ky. 1960, U.S. Ct. Appeals (6th cir.) 1970, Ind. 1978, U.S. Supreme Ct. 1978. Pvt. practice, Louisville, 1960-63; assoc. Jones, Ewen & McKenzie, Louisville, 1963-65; ptnr. Curtis & Rose, Louisville, 1965-81, Weber & Rose, Louisville, 1981—. Organist Scottish Rite Temple, Louisville. Lt. USAF, 1954-56. Mem. ABA, Ky. Bar Assn., Ind. Bar Assn., Louisville Bar Assn., Am. Soc. Hosp. Attys., Am. Bd. Trial Advocates, Brandeis Soc., Fedn. Ins. Counsel, River Road Country Club, Pendennis Club (Louisville), Jefferson Club. Republican. Episcopalian. Office: 400 W Market St Ste 2700 Louisville KY 40202-3358

ROSE, DANIEL, real estate company executive, consultant; b. N.Y.C., Oct. 31, 1929; s. Samuel B. and Belle (Bernstein) R.; m. Joanna Semel, Sept. 16, 1956; children: David Semel, Joseph Benedict, Emily, Gideon Gregory. Student, Yale U., 1947-50; cert. of proficiency in Russian lang., U.S. Air Force Program, 1951; BA, Syracuse U., 1952; postgrad., U. Paris. With Dwelling Mgrs., Inc., N.Y.C., 1954—, pres., 1960—, vice-chmn., sec.-treas. Baltic-Am. Enterprise Fund, 1994—; dir. Dreyfus Tax Exempt Bond Fund Inc., 1976-82, Dreyfus Money Market Fund, Inc., 1980-82; pres., CEO Rose Assocs., Inc., N.Y.C., 1980-99, chmn., 1999—, 22 Dreyfus Funds, 1992—. Assoc. fellow Pierson Coll. Yale U., 1974—; bd. govs., hon. life mem. Technion-Israel Inst. Tech.; bd. dirs., grants com. Realty Found. N.Y.; vice-chmn. Lionel Trilling seminars Columbia U., 1977—; bd. dirs. Ventures in Edn.; trustee, mem. exec. and compensation and benefits coms. U.S. Trust Co. of N.Y., 1982-92; trustee, vice-chmn. mixed use devel. coun. Urban Land Inst., 1986-93; exec. com. Urban Land Found., 1989—, gov., 1993—; designated Cert. Property Mgr. Inst. for Real Estate Mgmt. Expert adv. to sec. HUD, 1972; expert/cons. to commr. edn. HEW, 1974; cons. HUD panel on urban devel., 1984-86; dir. N.Y. Coun. Humanities, 1980-86, N.Y. Conv. Ctr. Devel. Corp., 1980-90, Get Ahead Found., 1989-98, Fifth Ave. Assn., 1989-98; mem. Governor's Task Force on Housing, 1975, Task Force on Taxation, Mcpl. Assistance Corp., 1976-77, Planning Commn. Theatre Adv. Group, coun. of fellows, vis. com. to grad. faculty, bd. overseers Ctr. for Study of N.Y.C. affairs New Sch. for Social Rsch., overseers com. to visit Ctr. Internat. Affairs Harvard U., 1992-98, Mcpl. Broadcasting System, 1977-78, MIT Ctr. for Real Estate Devel.; donor Daniel Rose chair urban econs., trustee NYU N.Y. Inst. for Humanistic Studies, Mus. of City of N.Y., 1984-90; chmn. bd. trustees, Horace Mann-Barnard Sch., 1971-74, trustee, 1962-89, hon. trustee, 1989—; v.p., assoc. treas., bd. dirs. Police Athletic League of N.Y., vice chmn. Cen. Harlem Facility; founder and pres. Harlem Ednl. Activities Fund Inc., YM & YWHA of the Bronx, 1963-67; v.p. N.Y. Landmarks Conservancy, bd. dirs. 1977-90; bd. dirs. Jewish Cmty. Ctrs. Assn., 1970—, pres. 1974-78, hon. pres. 1978—; v.p. World Confedn. of Jewish Cmty. Ctrs., 1977-83; former trustee and exec. com. mem. Fedn. of Jewish Philanthropies of N.Y., chmn. standing functional com. on cmty. ctrs., 1969-73; ptnr. N.Y.C. Partnership, 1990—; treas., bd. dirs. Citizens Housing and Planning Coun. of N.Y., 1972—; chmn. Dem. platform adv. com., 1984 Nat. Conv.; bd. advisors Dem. Leadership Coun., 1992—, Progressive Policy Inst.; trustee Dem. Nat. Com., 1988; chmn. Del. Svcs. Host Com., N.Y.C.; bd. trustees MBA of N.Y. Scholarship Found., Inc., 1996—. Served with USAF, 1951-54. Mem. Internat. Inst. Strategic Studies (dir. Am. com. for IISS 1987—), Coun. on Fgn. Rels., Fgn. Policy Assn. (bd. dirs. 1971—, chmn. fgn. policy assocs. 1972-75), East-West Inst. (bd. dirs. 1982—, treas. 1988—, co-chmn. fin. com. 1990—, chmn. exec. com. 2000—), Am. Soc. Real Estate Counselors (mem. publs.-rsch. com.), Real Estate Bd. of N.Y. Inc. (chmn. housing com. 1975—, mem. bd. govs. 1977-80, 90—, mem. REBNY Found.), Assn. of Yale Alumni (del.-at-large 1978-81, class of 1951 del. 1986-89), Century Assn. (N.Y.C.), Coffee House, Yale, Union League Club, Cosmos (Washington), Quaker Ridge Country Club, Noyac Country Club, Econ. Club N.Y. Office: Rose Associates Inc 200 Madison Ave Fl 5 New York NY 10016-3912 E-mail: drose@rosenyc.com.

ROSE, DAVID ALLAN, portfolio manager; b. N.Y.C., Feb. 15, 1937; s. Edward William and Marion (Nadelstein) Rose; m. Frances Helaine Dushman, Aug. 16, 1959; children: Evan Denali, Mitchell Franklin. BS in Acctg., Queens Coll., 1958; MBA, Syracuse U., 1968; LLD (hon.), U. Alaska, 1999. Fin. mgr. U.S. Army, Fort Richardson, Alaska, 1961-75, comptroller, 1975; exec. dir. Alaska Mcpl. Bond Bank Authority, Anchorage, 1975-82, Alaska Indsl. Devel. Authority, Anchorage, 1980; co owner Downtown Investment Co., Anchorage, 1980—, Downtown Delicatessen, Inc., Anchorage, 1976—; CEO, Alaska Permanent Fund Corp., Juneau, 1982-92; chmn., CEO, Alaska Permanent Capital Mgmt. Co., Inc., Anchorage, 1992—. Fin. advisor Fin. Green Lake Dam, Sitka, Alaska, 1977, Fin. Dutch Harbor Port, Unalaska, Alaska, 1979—80, Fin. Kenai-Anchorage Pipeline, 1979—80, Fin. Pulp Mill Pollution control, Ketchikan, Alaska, 1979—80. Pres. Alaska Mcpl. League, 1975; chair organizing com. Unity Pk. Found., 2002; chair endowment fund Anchorage Concert Assn., 2002—; mem. City Coun., mem. Borough Assembly City of Anchorage, 1971—75, mem. Mcpl. Assembly, 1975—77, chmn., 1975—77; vice chmn. endowment fund Alaska Pacific U., 1994—2002, chmn., 2002—. Named Pub. Adminstr. of the Yr., ASPA Alaska chpt., 1986; named to Alaska Bus. Hall of Fame, 2003; recipient Golden Man award, Boys Club Alaska, Anchorage, 1974, Meritorious Civilian Svc., U.S. Army, 1975, Pub. Svc. award, City and Borough Juneau, 1986, Lions Internat. award, award for Fundraising, Am. Diabetes Assn., Disting. Svc. medal, State of Alaska, 1999, Shining Light award, Alaska, 2003, Alaskan of the Yr. Denali award, 1997. Mem.: Rotary (awards). Republican. Jewish. Avocations: boating, gardening. Office: Alaska Permanent Capital 900 W 5th Ave Ste 601 Anchorage AK 99501-2044 E-mail: apcm@alaska.net.

ROSE, DEBORAH, epidemiologist; b. NYC, Mar. 14, 1950; d. Frederick Phineas and Sandra (Priest) R.; m. Jan A.J. Stolwijk, Sept. 16, 1990; 1 child, Sarah Leia. BA, Yale U., 1972; SM, Harvard U., 1975; MPH, Yale U., 1977, PhD, 1989. Epidemiologist Nat. Inst. Occupl. Safety and Health, Rockville, Md., 1978-79; assoc. in rsch. II dept. epidemiology and pub. health Yale U., New Haven, Conn., 1986-88, lectr. Sch. Nursing, 1986-88; epidemiologist Nat. Ctr. Health Stats., Hyattsville, Md., 1989—. Cons. to the Min. of Health, Hungary, 1999—. Vice chair bd. dir. Dwight Hall at Yale, New Haven, 1982—, v.p., 2002—; trustee Carnegie Instn. Washington, 2001—, sec., 2004—. Recipient Elm-Ivy award Yale U., 1987, Alumni award Assn. Yale Alumni, 1997, Mary E. Ives award New Haven Free Pub. Libr., 1999. Mem.: APHA, Soc. Epidemiol. Rsch., Sigma Xi. Avocations: computer consulting, bonsai. Home: 4414 Harbour Town Dr Beltsville MD 20705-1081 Office: Nat Ctr Health Stats 3311 Toledo Rd Hyattsville MD 20782 Business E-Mail: debrose@erols.com.

ROSE, DENNIS NORMAN, manufacturing executive; b. Medicine Hat, Alberta, Can., Jan. 5, 1948; came to U.S., 1987, naturalized, 1995; s. Norman Cecil Joseph and Anna (Jorgensen) R.; children: Darren Craig, David Christopher. BS, U. Calgary, Alberta, Can., 1971; MBA, York U., Toronto, Ontario, Can., 1977. Registered profl. engr., Ky., Ind., Fla., Ont., Can. Mgr. mfg. and engring. Canadian GE, Barrie, Canada, 1971—79; v.p. Algonquin Industries, Huntsville, Canada, 1979—85; gen. mgr. Mallory Controls, Woodstock, Canada, 1985—87, v.p. ops. Indpls., 1987—89; mfg. cons., owner, pres. Turnaround, Holmes Beach, Fla., 1988—; exec. v.p. Sargent & Greenleaf, Inc., Nicholsville, Ky., 1989—93; owner, pres. Island CondoCare, Inc., Holmes Beach, Fla., 1992—; v.p., gen. mgr. New Eng. Machinery, Inc., Bradenton, Fla., 1993—99; owner, pres. Quality Screening and Window Repair, Inc., Sarasota, Fla., 1994—95; v.p. Profit Counselors, Inc., Sarasota, Fla., 1996—2000; pres., CEO WCCO Belting, Inc., Wahpeton, ND, 2000—01; pres. Klockner Bartelt, Inc., Sarasota, Fla., 2001—03. Mem. Nat. Soc. Profl. Engrs., Aircraft Owners & Pilots Assn., Am. Soc. for Quality Control. Avocations: piano, skiing, flying, scuba diving. Home: Unit 4B 3701 E Bay Dr Unit 4B Holmes Beach FL 34217-2047

ROSE, DONALD MCGREGOR, retired lawyer; b. Cin., Feb. 6, 1933; s. John Kreimer and Helen (Morris) R.; m. Constance Ruth Lanner, Nov. 29, 1958; children: Barbara Rose Burgess, Ann Rose Weston. AB in Econs., U. Cin., 1955; JD, Harvard U., 1958. Bar: Ohio 1958, U.S. Supreme Ct. 1962. Asst. legal officer USNR, Subic Bay, The Philippines, 1959-62, with Office of JAG The Pentagon, Va., 1962-63; assoc. Frost & Jacobs, LLP, Cin., 1963-70, ptnr., 1970-93, sr. ptnr., 1993-97, ret. ptnr., 1997. Co-chmn. 6th Cir. Appellate Practice Inst., Cin., 1983, 90, mem. 6th Cir. adv. com., 1990-98, chmn. subcom. on rules, 1990-94, chmn., 1994-96. Trustee Friends of Cin. Pks., Inc., 1980-89, 93-98, pres. 1980-86; trustee Am. Music Scholarship Assn., Cin., 1985-88; pres. Social Health Assn. Greater Cin. Area Inc., 1969-72; co-chmn. Harvard Law Sch. Fund for So. Ohio, Cin., 1985-87; pres. Meth. Union, Cin., 1983-85; chmn. trustees Hyde Pk. Cmty. United Meth. Ch., Cin., 1974-76, chmn. coun. on ministries, 1979-81, chmn. adminstrv. bd., 1982-84, chmn. mem. canvass, 1985, chmn. staff parish rels. com., 1988-90, chmn. commn. missions, 1993-95; trustee Meth. Theol. Sch. Ohio, vice chmn. devel. com., 1990-94, sec. 1992-94, chmn. devel. com., 1994-98, vice chmn., 1998, chmn., 1999—2004; loaned exec. United Way, Cin., 1999. Lt. USNR, 1959-63. Mem. Cin. Citizens Police Assn., On Air Reader, Cin. Assn. for Blind, Univ. Club (Cin.), Cin. Country Club, Boothbay Harbor Yacht Club. Republican. Avocations: sailing, golf. Home: 8 Walsh Ln Cincinnati OH 45208-3435 also: 11 Blackstone Rd Boothbay Harbor ME 04538-1943 E-mail: dmrose@fbtlaw.com.

ROSE, DWIGHT DEAN, music educator; b. Omaha, Nebr., Apr. 6, 1970; s. Marvin Alan Rose (Deceased) and Betty Jane Rose. BA, Midland Luth. Coll., Fremont, NE, 1993; MA Music Ed., Univ. Nebr., Omaha, NE, 2002. Music educator Laurel-Concord Schools, Laurel, Nebr., 1993—97; Lyons-Decatur Schools, Lyons, 1997—2003. Recipient Snider Young Band Dir., Nebr. State Bandmasters Assn., 1998. Mem.: Music Educators Nat. Conf., Nebr. Music Educators Assn., Nebr. State Bandmasters Assn. Office: Lyons-Decatur Public Schools PO Box 526 Lyons NE 68038

ROSE, EDITH SPRUNG, retired lawyer; b. N.Y.C., Jan. 7, 1924; d. David L. and Anna (Storch) Sprung; m. David J. Rose, Feb. 15, 1948; children: Elizabeth Rose Stanton, Lawrence, Michael. BA, Barnard Coll., 1944; LLB, Columbia U., 1946. Bar: N.Y. 1947, N.J. 1973. Adminstr. Practising Law Inst.,

N.Y.C., 1947-48; ptnr. Smith, Lambert, Hicks & Miller, Princeton, N.J., 1974-88; counsel to Drinker, Biddle & Reath, Princeton, 1988-91; ret., 1991. Mem. ABA, N.Y. Bar Assn., N.J. Bar Assn., Princeton Bar Assn., Womens Law Caucus of Mercer County, Princeton Club (N.Y.C.). Home: 201 Lambert Dr Princeton NJ 08540-2308

ROSE, ELIHU, real estate executive; b. N.Y.C., Mar. 30, 1933; s. Samuel B. and Belle (Bernstein) R.; m. Susan Wechsler, Feb. 6, 1965; children: Amy, Isabel, Abigail. BS, Yale U., 1954; MA, NYU, 1969, PhD, 1978. Vice chmn. Rose Assocs., N.Y.C., 1956—. Contbr. articles to profl. mil. jours. Former chmn. bd. dirs. Internat. Ctr. Photography; bd. dirs. Sta. WNET (PBS), Lincoln Ctr. Theater, 1992—, Nat. Mus. Am. History, Smithsonian Instn. Fellow Am. Acad. Arts and Scis.; mem. Internat. Inst. Strategic Studies, Coun. Fgn. Rels., Century Assn., Union League Club, Yale Club of N.Y., Army and Navy Club (Washington). Office: Rose Assocs 200 Madison Ave New York NY 10016-3903

ROSE, ELIHU ISAAC, lawyer; b. Bklyn., Nov. 27, 1941; s. Aaron Henry and Frances (Klinger) R.; m. Gail Roberta Cohen, Aug. 22, 1964; children: Melissa Kaye, Heidi Jill. AB, Columbia U., 1963, MBA, 1965; JD, St. John's U., Bklyn., 1968. Bar: N.Y.; CPA, N.Y. Sr. tax acct. Price Waterhouse & Co., N.Y.C., 1967-71; dir. taxes Exec. Monetary Mgmt., Inc., N.Y.C., 1971-79; pres. Elihu I. Rose, P.C., Lake Success, N.Y., 1979—; of counsel Sahn Ward & Baker, PLLC, Garden City, NY, 2003—. Mem. ABA, AICPA, N.Y. State Bar Assn., N.Y. State Soc. CPAs, Bar Assn. Nassau County, Estate Planning Coun. L.I. Office: 1983 Marcus Ave Ste 129 New Hyde Park NY 11042-1016 E-mail: roselaw@sprintmail.com.

ROSE, GEORGE ANDREW, software developer, information systems specialist; b. Mt. Clemens, Mich., Dec. 17, 1950; s. George Hubert and Geraldine Marie (Benoit) R. BA, BSW in Psychology and Biology, Ea. Mich. U., 1975; MBA in Internat. Fin., George Washington U., 1987. Inpatient substance abuse therapist St. Joseph's Hosp., Mt. Clemens, 1974—77; dep. twp. clk. Twp. of Clinton, Mich., 1977—79; social worker Bur. Rehab, Washington, 1979—84; sr. social worker Comprehensive Alcohol and Drug Abuse Ctr., Washington, 1984—88; contract mgmt. UMWA Health and Retirement Funds, Washington, 1988—91; dir. software devel., info. svcs. United Seniors Health Coop., Washington, 1993—98; pres., CEO Portsmouth Group, Inc., Washington, 1997—. Home: 2929 Connecticut Ave NW Ste 306 Washington DC 20008-1435 Office: The Portsmouth Group Inc Ste 605 1522 K St Washington DC 20005 Business E-Mail: georgerose@portsmouthgroup.net.

ROSE, HUGH, management consultant; b. Evanston, Ill., Sept. 10, 1926; s. Howard Gray and Catherine (Wilcox) R.; m. Mary Moore Austin, Oct. 25, 1952; children: Susan, Nancy, Gregory, Matthew, Mary. BS in Physics, U. Mich., 1951, MS in Geology, 1952; MBA with highest distinction, Pepperdine U., 1982. Mgr. Caterpillar, Inc., Peoria, Ill., 1952-66; v.p., mktg. mgr. Cummins Engine Co., Columbus, Ind., 1966-69; pres., CEO Cummins Northeastern, Inc., Boston, 1969-77; pres. Power Systems Assocs., L.A., 1980-83, C.D. High Tech., Inc., Austin, Tex., 1984-87; mgmt. cons. Rose and Assocs., Tucson, 1984, 87—. Polit. cartoonist. Contbr. articles to profl. jours. Bd. dirs. Raymond Alf Mus., Claremont, Calif., 1975—, Comstock Found., Tucson, 1988, Environ. Edn. Exch., 1991, Heart Ctr. U. Ariz., Tucson, 1992. With USAAF, WWII. Fellow AAAS; mem. Acacia, Soc. Vertebrate Paleontology, Beacon Soc. Boston (pres. 1979-80), Algonquin Club Boston (v.p., bd. dirs. 1974-80), Duxbury Yacht Club, Longwood Cricket Club, Skyline Country Club, Phi Beta Kappa, Delta Mu Delta, Sigma Gamma Epsilon, Sigma Pi Sigma, Beta Beta Beta, Sigma Xi, Beta Gamma Sigma. Republican. Presbyterian. Office: Rose & Assocs 5320 N Camino Sumo Tucson AZ 85718-5132

ROSE, HUGH, retired economics educator; b. London, July 20, 1920; came to U.S., 1960, naturalized, 1977; s, William and Ann (Ogus) R. Student, Oxford (England) U., England, 1939-40, 45-47, Nuffield Coll., 1950-52. Lectr. in econs. Rhodes U., South Africa, 1947-50, lectr., 1952-53; lectr. in econs. Exeter U., England, 1954-60; assoc. prof. econs. U. Rochester, N.Y., 1961-63, prof., 1965-70; assoc. prof. econs. U. Toronto, Can., 1963-65; hon. rsch. assoc. Harvard U., Cambridge, Mass., 1969-70; prof. econs. Johns Hopkins U., Balt., 1970-91. Author: Macroeconomic Dynamics, 1991; contbr. articles to profl. jours. With British Army, 1940-45. Home: 112 Cross Keys Rd Apt D Baltimore MD 21210-1536 Office: Johns Hopkins U Dept Econs 3400 N Charles St Dept Econs Baltimore MD 21218-2680 Personal E-mail: hrose@charm.net.

ROSE, ISRAEL HAROLD, mathematics professor; b. New Britain, Conn., May 17, 1917; s. Abraham and Dora (Dubrow) R.; m. Pearl Nitzberg, Jan. 24, 1942 (div. Feb. 1956); 1 son, Steven Philip; m. Susan Ann Lazarus, Mar. 26, 1961; children: Dora, Eric. Student, CCNY, 1934-36; AB, Bklyn. Coll., 1938, A.M., 1941; PhD, Harvard, 1951. Tutor, instr. Bklyn. Coll., 1938-41; instr. Pa. State Coll., 1942-46; asst. prof. U. Mass., 1948-54, assoc. prof., 1954-60; faculty Hunter Coll., 1960-68, prof. math., 1965-68, chmn. dept., 1966-68; prof. math. Lehman Coll., CUNY, 1968-82, prof. emeritus, 1983—, chmn. dept., 1968-72, 80-82, resident prof., 1983—. Vis. asst. prof. Mt. Holyoke Coll., 1951-52, vis. assoc. prof., 1954-55, 58-59; sci. cons. AID, India, summer 1965 Author: A Modern Introduction to College Mathematics, 1959, Algebra: An Introduction to Finite Mathematics, 1963, Vectors and Analytic Geometry, 1968, Elementary Functions: A Precalculus Primer, 1973, (with Esther R. Phillips) Elementary Functions, 1978. NRC predoctoral fellow Harvard, 1946-48; fellow Fund Advancement Edn., 1952-53 Mem. Am. Math. Soc., Math. Assn. Am. (chmn. Met. N.Y. sect. 1973-75), Nat. Council Tchrs. Math., Assn. Tchrs. Math. New Eng. (pres. Conn. Valley sect. 1956-57), Sigma Xi (pres. Hunter Coll. chpt. 1966-67) Home: 18 Floral Dr Hastings On Hudson NY 10706-1202 Office: Lehman Coll Bedford Park Blvd W Bronx NY 10468

ROSE, JALEN, professional basketball player; b. Detroit, Jan. 30, 1973; s. Jeanne R. Student, U. Mich. Guard Denver Nuggets, 1994-96, Ind. Pacers, 1996—2002, Chicago Bulls, 2002—. Named Honorable Mention All-Am., AP, 1991; set Michigan freshman scoring record, 1991; selected as All-Am., Parade Magazine, Third-Team All-Am., USA Today; set Nuggets' rookie record for assists, 1994-95 season; named to All-Rookie Second Team, NBA, 1995 Office: Chicago Bulls United Ctr 1901 W Madison St Chicago IL 60612

ROSE, JAMES TURNER, aerospace consultant; b. Louisburg, N.C., Sept. 21, 1935; s. Frank Rogers and Mary Burt (Turner) R.; m. Daniele Raymond, Sept. 15, 1984. BS with high honors, N.C. State U., 1957. Aero. rsch. engr. NASA, Langley Field, Va., 1957-59; project engr. NASA (Mercury and Gemini), Langley Field, Va. and Houston, 1959-64; program sys. mgr. McDonnell Douglas Astronautics Co (MDAC), St. Louis, 1964-69; mgr. shuttle ops. and implementation (MDAC) McDonnell Douglas Astronautics Co., St. Louis, 1969-72, mgr. shuttle support (MDAC), 1972-74, mgr. space processing programs, 1976-83; dir. electrophoresis ops. in space McDonnell Douglas Astronautics Co (MDAC), St. Louis, 1983-86; dir. space shuttle engring. NASA, Washington, 1974-76, asst. adminstr. comml. programs, 1987-91; aerospace cons., 1992—. Chmn. Fla. Space Bus. Roundtable, 1995-98. Recipient Lindberg award for mgmt. leadership AIAA, 1983, Presdl. Meritorious Rank award, 1989, NASA Exceptional Svc. medal, 1990, Laurels award Aviation Week, 1990, Aerospace Contribution to Soc. award AIAA, 1993. Mem. Phi Kappa Phi. Episcopalian.

ROSE, JEFFREY RAYMOND, economist, educator, negotiator; s. Albert and Thelma R.; m. Sandra Black; 1 child, Adam. BA with honors, U. Toronto, 1968, M.Indsl. Relations, 1983; postgrad., London Sch. Econs., 1968-69. Planner planning dept. City of Toronto, 1976-80; pres. local 79 Can. Union Pub. Employees, Toronto, 1980-83, nat. pres. Ottawa, Ont., 1983-91; dep. min. intergovtl. affairs Govt. of Ont., Toronto, 1991-95; sr. fellow Harrowston program in conflict mgmt.-negotiation U. Toronto, 1995—. Gen. v.p. Can. Labour Congress, 1983—91. Exec. mem. Ont. New Dem. Party, 1982-91; bd. dirs. Inst. for Rsch. on Pub. Policy, 1988-91; mem. fed. coun. New Dem. Party, 1988-91; co-chmn. Ont.-Que. Commn. for Cooperation, 1991-95. Home: 55 Sunnydene Crescent Toronto ON Canada M4N 3J5

ROSE, JIM, broadcast executive; Student, U. of Tex. at Arlington, 1967—68, Draughon's Bus. Coll., Dallas, 1962—63, Elkin's Inst., 1964—65. Program dir., music dir. and dj KHFI FM, Austin, Tex., 1965—66; disc jockey WFAA AM (820 kc) and WFAA (570 kc), Dallas, 1966—68; news announcer KLIF AM, Dallas, 1972; disc jockey KFJZ AM-FM, Ft. Worth, 1973—75; news announcer KBOX AM and KTLC FM, Dallas, 1971—72; program dir., music dir. and disc jockey KBER FM-AM, San Antonio, 1972—73; disc jockey KULF AM, Houston, 1978—81; music dir. and disc jocket KXOL AM, Ft. Worth, 1975—77; disc jockey KIKK FM-AM, Houston, 1977—78, KILT FM, Houston, 1981—82; program dir., music dir. and dj KBUC-FM/AM, San Antonio, 1968—71; disc jockey KILT FM, Houston, 1993—97; program dir. Contract Broadcasting, Houston, 1997—. R-Consevative. United Methodist.

ROSE, JOANNA SEMEL, cultural activist; b. Orange, NJ, Nov. 22, 1930; d. Philip Ephraim and Lillian (Mindlin) Semel; m. Daniel Rose, Sept. 16, 1956; children: David S., Joseph B., Emily, Gideon G. Cert., Shakespeare Inst., U.K., 1951; BA summa cum laude, Bryn Mawr Coll., 1952; postgrad., St. Hilda's Coll., Oxford U., 1953. Mem. exec. com. Am. Friends of St. Hilda's Coll., former chmn.; former pres. bd. dirs., current bd. dirs. Paper Bag Players, NYC; former bd. dir., current mem. adv. coun. Poets and Writers, Inc., NYC; former chmn. adv. bd. Partisan Rev., NYC; former bd. dir., current mem. adv. coun. Nat. Dance Inst., NYC. Bd. dir. Bay St. Theatre, Sag Harbor, Am. Friends Jewish Mus. Greece; assoc. fellow Berkeley Coll. Yale U.; mem. NY Inst. for the Humanities. Former bd. dirs. Eldridge St. Project, N.Y.C. Mem. Cosmopolitan Club, Bryn Mawr Club of NY, LVIS East Hampton. Home: 895 Park Ave New York NY 10021-0327 also: 1 Lily Pond Ln East Hampton NY 11937

ROSE, JOANNE W. rating service executive; BA in Polit. Sci. and History magna cum laude, U. Rochester; JD, Columbia U. Assoc. White & Case, N.Y.C.; sr. mng. dir., gen. counsel Standard & Poor's Rating Svcs. divsn. McGraw Hill, N.Y.C., 1989—99, chair rating policy bd.; exec. mng. dir., structured fin. ratings Standard & Poor's, N.Y.C., 1999—. Office: Standard & Poors 55 Water St New York NY 10041-0003

ROSE, JOEL ALAN, legal consultant; b. Bklyn., Dec. 26, 1936; s. Edward Isadore and Adele R. Rose; m. Isadora Fenig, Apr. 12, 1964; children: Susan, Terri Angstriech. BS in Econs., NYU, 1958; MBA, Wharton Grad. Sch., U. Pa., 1960. Asst. purchasing agt. Maidenform Inc., N.Y.C., 1960-62; personnel dir. E.J. Korvette Inc., N.Y.C., 1962-66; mgmt. cons. Daniel J. Cantor & Co. Inc., Phila., 1966—, sr. v.p., 1987—; mgmt. cons. to legal profession. Coord. Ann. Conf. on Law Firm Mgmt. and Econs. Author: Managing the Law Office; mem. adv. bd. Law Office Economics and Management, 1987; contbg. columnist N.Y. Law Jour., 1984—, Nat. Law Jour. Extra, 1996—, Phila. Legal Intelligencer, 1995—, L.A. Daily Times, 1999—, Legal Times of Washington, 1998—, N.J. Law Jour., 2000-, The Barrister, 1995-; contbr. articles to profl. jours.; bd. editors Acctg. for Law Firms, Law Firm Partnership and Benefits Report, 2001—; editl. adv. bd. Corp. Counsel's Guide to Law Dept. Mgmt. With U.S. Army, 1960, Res., 1960-66. Fellow Coll. of Law Practice Mgmt.; mem. ABA (chmn. acquisition and mergers com., practice mgmt. sect., large law firm interest group), Inst. Mgmt. Cons., Am. Arbitration Assn. (nat. panel), Adminstrv. Mgmt. Soc. (past chpt. pres.), Am. Mgmt. Assn., Assn. Legal Adminstrs. Office: Joel A Rose & Assoc Inc PO Box 162 Cherry Hill NJ 08003-0162

ROSE, JOHN CHARLES, internist, educator; b. N.Y.C., Dec. 13, 1924; s. Hugh Stanley and Marie-Louise (Delury) R.; m. Dorothy Anne Donnelly, June 26, 1948; children— Nancy, Ellen, John Charles, Richard, Christopher. BS, Fordham U., 1946; MD magna cum laude, Georgetown U., 1950, D.Sc. (hon.), 1973; D.C.L. (hon.), Mt. St. Mary's Coll., 1973. Diplomate: Am. Bd. Internal Medicine, Am. Bd. Family Practice. Intern Walter Reed Army Hosp., 1950-51; resident, research fellow Georgetown U., VA hosps., Washington, 1950-54; established investigator Am. Heart Assn., 1954-57; instr., asst. prof. medicine Georgetown U., 1954-57, coord. med. edn., 1957-58, assoc. prof. physiology and biophysics, 1958-60, prof., 1960-91, chmn. dept. physiology and biophysics, 1958-63, dean Sch. Medicine, 1963-73, 78-79, prof. medicine, 1973-91, prof. emeritus, 1991—, vice chancellor Med. Ctr., 1984-87. Assoc. editor Am. Family Physician, 1955-62, chief med. editor, 1962-88; assoc. editor Acad. Medicine, 1992-95; contbr. articles to sci. publs. Trustee Charles E. Culpeper Found., 1986-96. Served to 2d lt. USAAF, 1943-45. Decorated Air medal. Master ACP; mem. Am. Physiol. Soc., Soc. Exptl. Biology and Medicine (nat. councillor 1962-63), Am. Heart Assn. (fellow sect. circulation). Clubs: Cosmos (Washington). Home: 5710 Surrey St Chevy Chase MD 20815-5520 E-mail: jrosemd@earthlink.net.

ROSE, JOHN THOMAS, finance educator, department chairman; b. Ft. Worth, Aug. 20, 1943; s. Paul Pittman and Francis Nan (White) R.; m. Sandra Kaye Rolen, Sept. 5, 1969; children: Melanie Ann, Leah Nan, Lynnelle Renee. BA with honors, Tex. A&M U., 1965; MA, Washington U., St. Louis, 1968, PhD, 1976. Economist Bd. Govs. of FRS, Washington, 1972-82, sr. economist, 1982-84; prof. fin., Harriette L. & Walter G. Lacy, Jr. chair banking Baylor U., Waco, Tex., 1984—, acting chmn. dept. fin. ins. and real estate, 1996-97, chmn. dept., 1997—. Contbr. articles to profl. jours. Bd. visitors Abilene (Tex.) Christian U., 1989-92. Capt. U.S. Army, 1969-71. Decorated Bronze Star; recipient Disting. Bus. Prof. award, Alpha Kappa Psi Favorite Prof. award Hankamer Sch. Bus. Baylor U., 2004; Econ. Devel. Adminstrn. U.S. Dept. Commerce fellow, 1968-69; Ernst & Young Found. Rsch. grantee, 1991. Mem. Am. Fin. Assn., So. Fin. Assn., Southwestern Fin. Assn., Fin. Mgmt. Assn., Omicron Delta Epsilon, Beta Gamma Sigma. Mem. Ch. of Christ. Office: Baylor U Hankamer Sch of Bus Dept Fin Ins and Real Estate One Bear Pl # 98004 Waco TX 76798-8004 Office Phone: 254-710-4140. Business E-Mail: jt_rose@baylor.edu.

ROSE, JONATHAN CHAPMAN, lawyer; b. Cleve., June 8, 1941; s. Horace Chapman and Katherine Virginia (Cast) R.; m. Susan Anne Porter, Jan. 26, 1980; 1 son, Benjamin Chapman. AB, Yale U., 1963; LL.B. cum laude, Harvard U., 1967. Bar: Mass. 1968, D.C. 1972, U.S. Supreme Ct. 1976, Circuit Ct. Appeals 1977, Ohio 1978. Law clk. Justice R. Ammi Cutter, Mass. Supreme Jud. Ct., 1967-68; spl. asst. to U.S. pres., 1971-73; gen. counsel Coun. on Internat. Econ. Policy, 1973-74, The White House; assoc. dept. atty. gen. U.S. Dept. Justice, 1974-75; dept. asst. atty. gen. U.S. Dept. Justice (Antitrust Div.), 1975-77, asst. atty. gen. Office of Legal Policy, 1981-84; ptnr. firm Jones Day, Washington, 1977-81, 84—. Prin. Ctr. for Excellence in Govt.; pres. Yale Daily News Found.; bd. govs. Yale Alumni Assn., 1996-99. 1st lt. U.S. Army, 1969-71. Mem. ABA, D.C. Bar Assn., Mass. Bar Assn., Ohio Bar Assn., Fed. Bar Assn., Am. Law Inst. Clubs: Met, Chevy Chase, Union, Yale, Harvard. Republican. Episcopalian. Office: Jones Day 51 Louisiana Ave NW Washington DC 20001-2113 Business E-Mail: jcrose@jonesday.com.

ROSE, JORDAN PAYMAN, lawyer; b. N.Y.C., Sept. 12, 1944; s. M. Alvin and Rose (Markowitz) R.; m. Beverly Bondy, Oct. 15, 1972. B.A., Alfred U., 1966; J.D. cum laude, Bklyn. Law Sch., 1969; LL.M. in Taxation, Georgetown U., 1979. Bar: N.Y. 1969, D.C. 1971, Calif. 1972, U.S. Tax Ct. 1980. Assoc. Berlack, Israels & Liberman, N.Y.C., 1969-71; counsel select com. U.S. Ho. of Reps., 1972-75; assoc. Herzstein & Maier, San Francisco, 1976-78; ptnr. Tuckman, Sussman, Rose & Kalish, San Francisco, 1979-85, Bronson, Bronson & McKinnon, San Francisco, 1985—; adj. faculty Golden Gate Grad. Sch. Taxation, 1980—; lectr. in field. Mem. Bar Assn. of San Francisco (mem. corp., taxation coms. 1980), State Bar Calif. (mem. bus. law, taxation sects.). Clubs: Bankers, Merchants Exchange (San Francisco); Oakland Hills Tennis. Articles editor Bklyn. Law Rev., 1967-69; contbr. articles to profl. jours. Office: 555 California St Bronson Bronson & McKinnon Suite 3400 Bank of America Ctr San Francisco CA 94104

ROSE, JOSEPH HUGH, clergyman; b. Jewett, Ohio, Nov. 21, 1934; s. Joseph Harper and Lottie Louella (VanAllen) R.; m. Nila Jayne Habig, Feb. 14, 1958; children: J. Hugh II, Stephanie Jayne, David William, Dawnella Jayne. ThB, Apostolic Bible Inst., St. Paul, 1955, DD, 1990. Ordained United Pentecostal Ch. Assoc. min. Calvary Tabernacle, Indpls., 1956-73; Ind. youth sec. United Pentecostal Ch., 1958-60, Ind. youth pres., 1960-72, bd. edn., 1974—, presbyter Ohio dist., 1975-97, hon. life presbyter Ohio, 1997; pastor Harrison Hills Ch., Jewett, Ohio, 1973—. Editor, Ind. Dist. News, 1959-70; narrator radio svc. Harvestime, 1961—. Republican. Mem. United Pentecostal Ch. Avocation: travel. Office: United Pentecostal Ch 8855 Dunn Rd Hazelwood MO 63042-2212 E-mail: jhrhhupc@eohio.net., jhrose@upci.org.

ROSE, KENNETH L. business executive; b. May 14, 1936; BS, Stanford U.; PhD, Carnegie Mellong U. CEO Henkels & McCoy, Blue Bell, Pa., 1987—. Office: Henkels & McCoy 985 Jolly Rd Blue Bell PA 19422-1958

ROSE, KENNETH L. food products executive; BS, U. San Diego. Contr. Teledyne Micronetics divsn. Teledyne Components, 1982—85, v.p. fin. and adminstrn. Teledyne CME divsn., 1985—90, v.p. fin. and adminstrn., 1990—93; corp. contr. Tyson Foods Inc., Springdale, Ark., 1993—, chief acctg. officer, 1995—, sr. v.p. indirect purchasing, aviation and travel, 1995—. Office: Tyson Foods Inc 2210 W Oaklawn Dr Springdale AR 72762-6999

ROSE, KIM MATTHEW, lawyer, educator; b. Gallipolis, Ohio, Mar. 21, 1956; s. Dave and Lois Ann R.; m. Pamela Carol Sims, Aug. 11, 1990. Student, USMA, 1974—76; BBA, Ohio U., 1977; JD, Capital U. Law, 1981; MBA, Ashland Coll., 1988. Bar: Ohio 1981, U.S. Dist. Ct. (so. dist.) Ohio 1981, U.S. Ct. Appeals (6th cir.) 1987, U.S. Supreme Ct. 1988. Asst. prosecutor Knox County Prosecutor, Mt. Vernon, Ohio, 1982-90; with Critchfield, Critchfield & Johnston, Mt. Vernon, 1982—. Adj. prof. Mt. Vernon Nazarene Coll., 1982-2002. Active Met. Housing Authority, Knox County, 1990-2002; adv. bd. Salvation Army, Mt. Vernon, 1991—; bd. dirs. Knox Cmty. Hosp., Mt. Vernon, Ohio, 2000. Maj. USAR, 1974-95. Mem. Ohio State Bar Assn., Knox County Bar Assn. (past pres.), Mt. Vernon Nazarene Coll. Found. (rec. sec. bd. 1995—), Mt. Vernon-Knox County C. of C., Masons. Avocations: flying, skiing, fishing, golf, biking. Home: 1413 Greenbrier Dr Mount Vernon OH 43050-9101 Office: Critchfield Critchfield & Johnston 10 S Gay St Mount Vernon OH 43050-3546 Office Phone: 740-397-4040. E-mail: rose@core.com., kimr@ccj.com.

ROSE, L. STEVEN See JASHEL, LARRY

ROSE, MARIAN HENRIETTA, physics researcher; b. Brussels; (parents Am. citizens); m. Simon Rose, Oct. 20, 1948 (dec. Jan. 1981); children: Ann, James, David, Simon. BA, Barnard Coll., 1942; MA, Columbia U., 1944; PhD, Harvard U., 1947. Teaching fellow Harvard U., Cambridge, Mass., 1945-46; adj. asst. prof. Courant Inst., N.Y.C., 1947-48, rsch. assoc., 1951-65, sr. rsch. scientist, 1965-75; vis. fellow Yale U., New Haven, Conn., 1981-93. Bd. dirs. Minna-James-Heineman Stiftung, Essen, Fed. Republic of Germany. Contbr. articles to profl. jours. Bd. dirs. Jay Heritage Ctr., Rye, N.Y.; mem. Wetlands Control Commn., Bedford, N.Y., 1992-99, Conservation Bd., Bedford, 1989-93; pres. Croton Watershed Clean Water Coalition, 1997—. Mem.: Sierra Club (conservation chair Atlantic chpt. 1992—95, del. at large to Westchester County Environ. Mgmt. Coun. 1994—, chair N.E. regional conservation com. 1995—98, conservation chair Atlantic chpt. 1998—2000, steering com. Atlantic chpt. 2000—02, del. at large N.E. regional conservation com., del. at large Atlantic chpt., exec. com. Atlantic chpt.), Sigma Xi, Phi Beta Kappa. Avocations: skiing, hiking. E-mail: marianr451@aol.com.

ROSE, MARK ALLEN, humanities educator; b. New York, Aug. 4, 1939; s. Sydney Aaron and Rose (Shapiro) R.; m. Ann (Bermingham); 1 son, Edward Gordon. AB(hon.), Princeton, 1961; LittB, Merton Coll., Oxford, Eng., 1963; PhD, Harvard Univ., 1967. Instr. to assoc. prof. in English Yale U., 1967-74; prof. English U. Ill., 1974-77; prof. U. Calif., Santa Barbara, 1977—, chmn. dept. English, 1987-89; dir. U. Calif., Humanities Rsch. Inst., Santa Barbara, 1989-94, chmn. dept. English, 1997—2001, assoc. vice chancellor, 2002—. Author: Heroic Love, 1968; (fiction) Golding's Tale, 1972; Shakespearean Design, 1972; Spenser's Art, 1975; Alien Encounters, 1981; Authors and Owners, 1993; editor: Twentieth Century Views of Science Fiction, 1976; Twentieth Century Interpretations of Antony and Cleopatra, 1977, (with Slusser and Guffey); Bridges to Science Fiction, 1980; Shakespeare's Early Tragedies, 1994; (CD-ROM) Norton Shakespeare Workshops. Woodrow Wilson Fellow, 1961; Henry Fellow, 1961-62; Dexter Fellow, 1966; Morse Fellow, 1970-71; NEH Fellow, 1979-80, 90-91. Mem. MLA, Renaissance Soc. Am., Shakespeare Soc. Am., Phi Beta Kappa. Office: U Calif English Dept Santa Barbara CA 93106 Business E-Mail: mrose@english.ucsb.edu.

ROSE, MARY MABEL, elementary school educator; b. Monticello, Iowa, Dec. 16, 1940; d. Ralph Richard and Flora Birdena (Hawkins) Ganfield; m. Paul Roger Rose, Dec. 30, 1961 (dec. Oct. 1979); children: Lynn Marie, Carol Ann. BA, Upper Iowa U., 1962; postgrad., U. No. Iowa, 1990—93. Cert. profl. tchr., Iowa. Elem. tchr. North Fayette County Cmty. Schs., West Union, Iowa, 1962-67, Marion (Iowa) Ind. Schs., 1963—64; instr. adult edn. West Central Sch. Dist., Iowa, 1967; substitute tchr. Bremer County Schs., Waverly, Iowa, 1974-84; tchr. Waverly-Shell Rock Schs., Iowa, 1984—, early childhood adv. bd., 1990—91. Mem. edn. com. Waverly Trinity Meth. Ch., 1979-84, trustee, 1984-86, mem. fin. com., 1989-92, staff parish relationship com., 1999-2001; vol. Waverly Hosp. Aux., 1984-86. Mem. ASCD, Nat. Assn. for Edn. Young Children, Shell Rock Music Assn. (bd. dirs. 1995-98). Home: 107 S Ridge Dr Waverly IA 50677-3908

ROSE, MATTHEW K. rail transportation executive; Chmn., pres., CEO Burlington No. Santa Fe Corp., 2002—. Office: Burlington No Santa Fe Corp PO Box 961052 Fort Worth TX 76161-0052

ROSE, MERRILL, public relations counselor; b. Beaufort, N.C., Apr. 20, 1955; d. Robert Lloyd Rose and Betty Lou (Merrill) Ellis. Student, U. N.C., 1977. Reporter, editor Consumer News, Washington, 1978-79; v.p. Fraser/Assocs., Washington, 1979-82; sr. assoc. Porter/Novelli, Washington, 1982-85, v.p., 1985-87, sr. v.p., food practice leader N.Y.C., 1989-91, exec. v.p., 1990—, gen. mgr. Chgo., 1991-96; dir. Europe Porter Novelli Internat., Brussels, 1996-98; exec. v.p. Porter Novelli, N.Y.C., 1998-2000; ind. cons., 2000—. Bd. dirs. CARE, 1991-98; bd. visitors U. N.C. Sch. Journalism, Chapel Hill, 1992—; bd. dirs. Friends of Prentice affiliate Northwestern Meml. Hosp., 1993-2000; mem. accrediting com. Accrediting Coun. for Edn. in Journalism and Comm., 1994-2000. Mem. Am. Inst. of Wine and Food, Pub. Rels. Soc. Am. Office: 43 5th Ave Apt 1N New York NY 10003-4368

ROSE, MICHAEL DEAN, lawyer, educator; b. Johnstown, Pa., Oct. 22, 1937; BA, Ohio Wesleyan U., 1959; JD, Case Western Res. U., 1963; LLM, Columbia U., 1967. Bar: Ohio 1963. Assoc. firm Porter, Stanley, Treffinger & Platt, Columbus, Ohio, 1963-66; asst. prof. law Ohio State U., Columbus, 1967-69, assoc. prof., 1969-72, prof., 1972-99, Lawrence D. Stanley prof. law, 1987-99, prof. emeritus, 1999—. Staff asst. to chief counsel IRS, Washington, 1970-71. Author: (with Leo J. Raskind) Advanced Federal Income Taxation: Corporate Transactions, 1978, (with Joseph S. Platt) A Federal Taxation Primer, 1973, Hornbook on Federal Income Taxation, 3d edit., 1988; editor Selected Federal Taxation Statutes and Regulations, 1973-99, Ohio Will Manual, 1986-2002. Mem.: Am. Law Inst. Home: 1327 Friar Ln Columbus OH 43221-1527 Office: Ohio State U 55 W 12th Ave Columbus OH 43210-1338 Business E-Mail: rose.4@osu.edu.

ROSE, MICHAEL ELVIN, oil and gas exploration company executive; b. Beaumont, Tex., Mar. 8, 1947; s. Harold Elvin and Onita (Buckelew) R.; m. Patricia Jan Howell, Aug. 21, 1971; children: Jaime Erin, Dana Lyn. BBA, Lamar U., 1970. CPA, Tex. Various positions Atlantic Richfield Co., Dallas, Midland, Tex., L.A., 1971-77; chief acct. Anadarko Prodn. Co., Houston, 1978-79, asst. contr., 1979-80, contr., 1980-81, v.p., contr., 1981-85, Anadarko

Petroleum Corp., Houston, 1985-86, exec. v.p. fin., chief fin. officer, 1986—2003. Mem. Fin. Execs. Inst., AICPA, Tex. Soc. CPAs. Avocations: golf, hunting, sailing. Home: 43 Silver Iris Way Spring TX 77382-2714

ROSE, MICHAEL LEONARD, film, television and video producer; b. St. Paul, Aug. 9, 1952; s. Robert L. and Beverly Bain (McKee) R.; m. Carol L. King, 1991. BA, UCLA, 1978, MFA, 1990. Media dir. Com. to Bridge the Gap, L.A., 1980-82; producer KPFK Pacifica, L.A., 1982-83, GM, Detroit, 1983-92, Network USA, Inc., Rockville, Md., 1993-96; producer 30-part documentary series Automobiles, 1995—; prodr., writer, dir. Michael Rose Prodns., Santa Monica, Calif., 1996—. Prodr. (film) Character, 1984 (Cine award 1984, 96), (videotape) A New Me, 1985 (U.S. Industry award 1985), Safety Belts for Dummies and People, 1986 (ITVA award, U.S. Industry award, Nat. Com. Films for Safety award), (TV series) Wheels of Survival, History Channel, Dream Machines, Ultimate Autos, History Channel, Great Cars, Wealth TV and PBS, Pvt. Jets, (video) ZZ Top; prodr. (for Travel Channel), Private Jets Revealed, Hot Rod TV; prodr., writer (videotape) I Need the Earth and the Earth Needs Me, 1990 (Cine Golden Eagle award, Nat. Edn. Film and Video award 1991), (film) A Tale of Two Cities, 1990 (Expo of Short Film and Video Award, Outstanding Student Documentaty Bklyn. Arts Coun. 1991); dir. pub. svc. announcement Eye Exam, 1988 (ITVA award 1988); prodr. The Game of Your Life, 1989 (Am. Film and Video award, ITVA award), Precious Cargo, (TV series) Wheels of Survival, Dream Machines, Ultimate Autos. Active, prodr. Mahaffey for Coun. campaign, Detroit, 1989; prodr. radio comml. Friends of the Nuclear Freeze, L.A., 1982. Recipient E.P. Ingersoll award Soc. Automotive Historians, 1998, Nat. Ednl. Media Network award, 1998; scriptwriting grantee Calif. Coun. for Humanities, 1999. Mem.: Dirs. Guild Am., Internat. Documentary Assn. (bd. dirs.). Office Phone: 310-821-0800. E-mail: michaelrose@mrpi.tv.

ROSE, MICHAEL ROBERTSON, evolutionary biology educator, consultant; b. Iserlohn, Germany; s. James Barry and Charlotte Julia Rose; children: Darius, Caitlin, Liam, Muireann. BS, Queen's U., Kingston, Ont., Can., 1975, MS, 1976; PhD, U. Sussex, Eng., 1979. NATO sci. fellow U. Wis., Madison, 1979-81; asst. prof. Dalhousie U., Halifax, N.S., Can., 1981-85, assoc. prof., 1985-87; assoc. prof. evolutionary biology U. Calif., Irvine, 1987-90, prof., 1990—; dir. U. Calif. Intercampus Rsch. Program on Exptl. Evolution, 2004—. Author: Evolutionary Biology of Aging, 1991, Adaptation, 1996, Darwin's Spectre, 1998, Methuselah Flies, 2004. Recipient President's prize Am. Soc. Naturalists, 1992, Busse award World Congress Gerontology, Adelaide, Australia, 1997. Mem. Soc. for Study Evolution. Avocation: music. Office Phone: 949-824-8121. E-mail: mrrose@uci.edu.

ROSE, NOEL RICHARD, immunologist, microbiologist, educator; b. Stamford, Conn., Dec. 3, 1927; s. Samuel Allison and Helen (Richard) R.; m. Deborah S. Harber, June 14, 1951; children: Alison, David, Bethany, Jonathan. BS, Yale U., 1948; MA, U. Pa., 1949, PhD, 1951; MD, SUNY, Buffalo, 1964; MD (hon.), U. Cagliari, Italy, 1990; ScD (hon.), U. Sassari, Italy, 1992; Order of the First Class (hon.), Ctrl. U. Venezuela, 1997. From instr. to prof. microbiology SUNY Sch. Medicine, Buffalo, 1951 73, dir. Center for Immunology, 1970-73, dir. Erie County Labs., 1964-70; dir. WHO Collaborating Center for Autoimmune Disorders, 1968—; prof. immunology and microbiology, chmn. dept. immunology and microbiology Wayne State U. Sch. Medicine, 1973— 82; prof., chmn. dept. immunology and infectious diseases Johns Hopkins U. Sch. Hygiene and Pub. Health, Balt., 1982-93, prof. medicine and environ. health scis., 1982—, prof. molecular microbiology and immunology, 1993—; prof. pathology Johns Hopkins U. Sch. Medicine, 1994—; dir. Johns Hopkins Autoimmune Disease Rsch. Ctr., 1998. Cons. in field. Editor: (with others) International Convocation on Immunology, 1969, Methods in Immunodiagnosis, 1973, 3d rev. edit., 1986, The Autoimmune Diseases, 1986, 2d edit., 1992, 3d edit., 1998, Microbiology, Basic Principles and Clinical Applications, 1983 Principles of Immunology, 1973, 2d rev. edit., 1979, Specific Receptors of Antibodies, Antigens and Cells, 1973, Manual of Clinical Laboratory Immunology, 1976, 6th edit., 2002, Genetic Control of Autoimmune Disease, 1978, Recent Advances in Clinical Immunology, 1983, Clinical Immunotoxicology, 1992, Manual of Human Immunology, 1997; editor in chief Clin. Immunology and Immunopathology, 1988-98; contbr. articles to profl. jours. Recipient award Sigma Xi, 1952, award Alpha Omega Alpha, 1976, Lamp award, 1975, Faculty Recognition award Wayne State U. Bd. Govs., 1979, Pres.'s award for excellence in teaching, 1979, Disting. Service award Wayne State U. Sch. Medicine, 1982, U. Pisa medal, 1986, U. Venezuela medal, 1998; named to Acad. Scholars Wayne State U., 1981; Josiah Macy fellow, 1979 Fellow AAAS, APHA, Am. Acad. Allergy and Immunology, Am. Acad. Microbiology, Assn. Med. Lab Immunologists; mem. Acad. Clin. Lab. Physicians and Scientists, Am. Assn. Immunologists, Am. Soc. Investigative Pathology, Am. Soc. Clin. Pathologists, Am. Soc. Microbiology (hon.; Abbott Lab. Clin. and Diagnostic Immunology award 1993, Profl. Achievement award 2003), Brit. Soc. Immunology, Coll. Am. Pathologists, Societè Française d'Immunologie, Can. Soc. Immunology, Soc. Exptl. Biology and Medicine Coun., Clin. Immunology Soc. (sec., treas., pres. 1993), Austrian Immunology Soc. (hon. mem.), Sigma Xi (pres. Johns Hopkins U. chpt. 1988), Alpha Omega Alpha, Delta Omega. Office: Johns Hopkins U 615 N Wolfe St Baltimore MD 21205-2103

ROSE, PATRICIA, artist, educator; 1 child, Nicholas Flores. BA, U. Calif., Berkeley, 1968; MA, Roosevelt U., 2002. Cert. elem., secondary tchr. Ill. Tchr. Cook and Lake Counties, ., Ill., 1991—95; dir. Ravenswood Gallery and Studios, Chgo., 1995—96; founder, dir. Art Odyssey, Wilmette, Ill., 1997—; tchr. Muslim Cmty. Ctr. Full Time Sch., Morton Grove, Ill., 1999—2000; instr. gifted edn. and arts Sch. of Art Inst., Chgo., 2001. One-woman shows include Union League Club, Chgo., 1999, exhibited in group shows at Montserrat Gallery, N.Y.C., 2000, Ann. Chgo. Art Open, 2000, Art Odyssey, Willmette, 2002, 2003, one-man shows include, 2004. Mem.: Ill. Assn. Gifted Children, Nat. Assn. Gifted Children. Avocations: theater, social science.

ROSE, PAUL LAWRENCE, history educator; b. Glasgow, Scotland, Feb. 26, 1944; m. Susan Ellen Kaplow, June 3, 1969; children: Alexander, Olivia, Zoe, Ariel. BA, MA, Oxford U., Eng., 1968; D in History, U. Paris, 1973. Vis. lectr. UCLA, 1968-69; research assoc. Toronto U., 1969-70; instr. St. John's U., N.Y., 1970-71; APS research fellow Cambridge (Eng.) U., 1974-75; from lectr. to sr. lectr. to reader/research prof. James Cook U., Australia, 1974-84; prof. history Newcastle U., Australia, 1984-85, Haifa (Israel) U., 1985-92, Reuben Hecht prof. Zionist history, 1987-92; Roberts prof. York U., Can., 1990-92; Mitrani prof. Jewish studies/European history Pa. State U., 1992—. Author: The Italian Renaissance of Mathematics, 1975, Bodin and the Great God of Nature, 1980, German Question/Jewish Question, 1990, Wagner-Race and Revolution, 1992, Heisenberg and the Nazi Atomic Bomb Project, 1998, Antisemitisms, 2004. Recipient various research awards; Am. Philos. Soc. grantee, Am. Coun. Learned Socs. grantee, Australian Rsch. Commn. grantee. Fellow Royal Hist. Soc.; mem. Am. Hist. Assn., Inst. for Advanced Study. Avocations: music, chess, billiards. Office: Pa State U Dept History Weaver Bldg 106 University Park PA 16802 E-mail: plr2@psu.edu.

ROSE, PETER EDWARD, former professional baseball player and manager; b. Cin., Apr. 14, 1941; s. Harry Rose; m. Karolyn Ann Englehardt (div.); children: Fawn, Peter; m. Carol Woliung, Apr. 1984; children: Cara, Tyler. Player Cin. Reds, 1963-78, player mgr., 1984-87, mgr., 1987-89; player Phila. Phillies, 1979-83, Montreal Expos, 1984; host weekly radio show Pete Rose on Baseball Sta. WCKY, Cin., 1992; now host syndicated show Talk Sports with Pete Rose Sta. WGTO-AM, Orlando, Fla. Author: (with Bob Hertzel) Charlie Hustle, 1975, Winning Baseball, 1976, (with Peter Golenback) Pete Rose on Hitting, 1985, (with Roger Kahn) Pete Rose: My Story, 1989, Pete Rose: My Prison Without Bars, 2004; TV appearances include Babe Ruth, 1991, Arli$$, 1996, Savage Skies, 1996, Veronica's Closet, 1997, Wrestlemania XIV, 1998, Wrestlemania XV, 1999, Wrestlemania XVI, 2000. Named Nat. League Rookie of Yr., 1963, Most Valuable Player, 1973, Most Valuable Player World Series, 1975, Nat. League Player of Yr. The Sporting News, 1968, Ball Player of Decade, 1979; named to Nat. League All-Star Team, 1965, 67-71, 73-79, 80-81, member of MLB All-Century Team, 1999. Achievements include being second player in baseball history to exceed 4000 hits, all time leader in hits. Office: 1368 Coventry Cir Melbourne FL 32904-8708

ROSE, PETER GRAHAM, gynecologic oncologist; b. Beverly, Mass., Mar. 11, 1955; MD, Boston U., 1955. Cert. in ob-gyn., specialty in gynecol. oncology. Resident in surgery Vanderbilt U., Nashville, 1981-83; resident in ob-gyn. Ohio State U., Columbus, 1983-86; fellow in gynecologic oncology Roswell Park, Buffalo, 1986-88; with Cleve. Clinic. Prof. Case Western Res. U. Mem. ACOG, Am. Soc. Clin. Oncology, Soc. Gynecological Oncology. Office: Cleve Clinic A-81 9500 Euclid Ave Cleveland OH 44129

ROSE, PETER ISAAC, sociologist, writer; b. Rochester, N.Y., Sept. 5, 1933; s. Aaron E. and Lillian (Feld) R.; m. Hedwig Hella Cohen, Mar. 25, 1956; children: Elisabeth Anne, Daniel Eric. AB, Syracuse U., 1954; MA, Cornell U., 1957, PhD, 1959. Mem. faculty Smith Coll., Northampton, Mass., 1960—2003, sr. fellow Kahn Inst., 2000—, Sophia Smith prof. emeritus, 2003—; mem. grad. faculty U. Mass., 1961—. Fulbright prof. U. Leicester, Eng., 1964-65, Kyoto (Japan) Am. Studies Inst., Flinders U., Australia, 1970, U. Vienna, 2004; vis. prof. Wesleyan U., Middletown, Conn., 1966-67, U. Colo., 1968, Yale U., 1970, Clark U., 1970-71, Doshisha U., Kyoto, Japan, fall 1999; vis. scholar Harvard U., 1983, 84-85, vis. prof., spring 1984; vis. scholar Chinese Acad. Social Sci., Beijing, 1986; resident scholar Rockefeller Study Ctr., Bellagio, Italy, summer 1987; vis. fellow St. Catherine's Coll., Oxford, spring, 1995,Stanford U., 1996, Liguria Study Ctr., Bogliasco, Italy, spring 1998, fall 2001. Author: They and We, 1964, 5th edit., 1997, The Subject is Race, 1968, Strangers in Their Midst, 1977, Mainstream and Margins, 1983, Tempest-Tost, 1997, Guest Appearances and Other Travels in Time and Space, 2003; co-author: Sociology, 1977, 2d edit., 1982, Understanding Society, 1978, 3d edit., 1986; editor: The Study of Society, 1967, 4th edit., 1977, The Ghetto and Beyond, 1969, Americans From Africa, 1970, Nation of Nations, 1972, reissued, 1981, Seeing Ourselves, 1972, rev. edit., 1975, Socialization and the Life Cycle, 1979, Working With Refugees, 1986, Interminority Relations in the U.S., 1993, Professorial Passions, 1998, The Dispossessed, 2004; co-editor: Through Different Eyes, 1973. Mem. Am. Sociol. Assn. (mem. coun. 1974-77), Mass. Sociol. Assn. (pres. 1967-68), Soc. Study of Social Problems (v.p. 1968-69), Ea. Sociol. Soc. (v.p. 1970-71, pres. 1991-92). Home: 66 Paradise Rd Northampton MA 01060-2907 Office Phone: 413-585-3515. Business E-Mail: prose@smith.edu.

ROSE, PETER J. delivery service executive; V.p. air divsn. The Harper Group, San Francisco, 1969-81; exec. v.p. Expeditors Internat. Wash. Inc., Seattle, 1981-88, pres., CEO, 1988—, chmn., 1996—. Office: Expeditors Internat Wash Inc 1015 3rd Ave Seattle WA 98104

ROSE, RICHARD LOOMIS, lawyer; b. Long Branch, N.J., Oct. 21, 1936; s. Charles Frederick Perrott and Jane Mary (Crotta) R.; m. Marian Frances Irons, Apr. 1, 1960; children: Linda, Cynthia, Bonnie. BA, Cornell U., 1958; JD, Washington and Lee U., 1963. Bar: N.Y. 1963, Conn. 1966, U.S. Dist. Ct. (so. dist.) N.Y. 1964, U.S. Dist. Ct. Conn. 1966, U.S. Ct. Appeals (2d cir.) 1965, U.S. Supreme Ct. 1970. Assoc. Cummings & Lockwood, Stamford, Conn., 1965-71, ptnr., 1971-91, Kleban & Samor, P.C., Southport, 1991-93; of counsel Whitman Breed Abbott & Morgan, Greenwich, Conn., 1993-95; prin. Roberts, Rose & Bates, P.C., Stamford, Conn., 1995—. Bd. dirs. and sec. Index Corp.; mem. adv. com. Conn. Banking Commr. on Conn. Securities Laws, 1982—; dir. Conn. World Trade Assn. Editor: Washington and Lee Law Rev. Chmn. Fgn. Trade Zone Com. to Mayor of City of Bridgeport, Conn., 1988-90; mem. fgn. trade awareness com. S.W. Area Industry and Commerce Assn., Task Force, 1987-88; bd. dirs. German Sch. of Conn., Inc., 1992—. 1st lt. U.S. Army, 1958-60, Korea. Mem. ABA, Conn. Bar Assn. (exec. com. corp. sect.), Internat. Bar Assn., New Canaan Country Club, Gridiron Club New Canaan, Phi Delta Phi, Omicron Delta Kappa, Phi Delta Theta. Republican. Office: Roberts Rose & Bates PC PO Box 3610 17 Hoyt St Stamford CT 06905

ROSE, ROBERT DIDIER, neurophysiologist; b. Washington, Oct. 10, 1954; s. Richard Contee and Mary Estill (Martin) R. AB, Transylvania U., 1976; MS, Emory U., 1981; PhD, SUNY, Stony Brook, 1986. Tchg. asst. Emory U., 1977-81, SUNY, Stony Brook, 1981-82, NIMH predoctoral rsch. fellow, 1982-84, rsch. asst., 1984-86; rsch. assoc. prof. dept. pharmacology U. Pitts. Med. Sch., 1987-88; clin. neurophysiologist dept. neurosurgery U. Pitts. Med. Ctr., 1992; clin. fellow Ctr. Clin. Neurophysiology U. Pitts. Sch. Medicine, 1992-97; asst. prof. dept. biol. sci. Duquesne U., Pitts., 1988-90; asst. prof. dept. biology Slippery Rock U., Pa., 1991-92; vis. prof. dept. anatomy and histology U. Pitts. Dental Sch., 1998—; COO Neurex, Inc., 1999—. Pres., CEO Neuro-Resource, 1998—; cons. Computational Diagnostics, Inc., Pitts., 1992—; cons. dept. otolaryngology Children's Hosp. of Pitts., 1994—, NuVasive, Inc., 2000—; adj. faculty C.C. Allegheny County, Pitts., 1988—; trainee activities com. Ctr. for Neurosci., U. Pitts., 1988—; naturalist-cons. Queens Coll. Ctr. for Environ. Edn., 1982-84; grant reviewer US-Israel Bination Sci. Found., Tel Aviv, 1990—; mem. panel NSF, Washington, 1990, 92; exec. dir. Childrens Rights Inst., 1999—; bd. dir. Child & Family Advocates; clin. dir. EMG Group, 2000—; bd. dir., PT Works, 2003-; Neurophysiology Program Dir. Integrative Med. Ctr., Atlantic City, 2003-; lectr., reviewer in field. Contbr. articles, chpts., abstracts to profl. publs. Fellow Marine Biol. Lab., Woods Hole, Mass., 1978, Luft-Brückendank fellow Inst. Tierphysiologie und Angewandte Zoologie, Arbeitsgruppe Neurobiologie, Freie U. Berlin, 1979, Deutscher Akademischer Austauschdienst fellow, 1979, NIMH/NRSA fellow SUNY-Stony Brook, 1982-84; grantee Emory U., 1978-81, Freie U., 1979, Hunkele Devel. Fund, 1988, State of Pa., 1989, NSF, 1989-91, Copeland Found., 1992-94, Children's Hosp. of Pitts., 1994, 94-95. Mem. AAAS, Am. Soc. Neurophysiol. Monitoring, Soc. Neurosci. Avocations: white water kayaking, fishing, skiing, rugby. Office: 440 Broadway Pitcairn PA 15140-1447

ROSE, ROBERT EDGAR, state supreme court justice; b. Orange, N.J., Oct. 7, 1939; BA, Juniata Coll., Huntingdon, Pa., 1961; LL.B., NYU, 1964. Bar: Nev. 1965. Dist. atty. Washoe County, 1971-75; lt. gov. State of Nev., 1975-79; judge Nev. Dist. Ct., 8th Jud. Dist., Las Vegas, 1986-88; justice Nev. Supreme Ct., Carson City, 1989—, chief justice, 1993-94, 1999—2000. Office: Nev Supreme Ct Capitol Complex 201 S Carson St Carson City NV 89701-4702

ROSE, ROBERT GORDON, lawyer; b. Newark, June 25, 1943; s. Harry and Ann Shirley (Gordon) R.; m. Ellen Nadley Berkowitz, July 2, 1966; children: Lisa Pauline, Michael Allan. BA, SUNY, Buffalo, 1965; MA, Columbia U., 1969; JD, Seton Hall U., 1974. Bar: N.J. 1974, U.S. Dist. Ct. N.J. 1974, U.S. Ct. Appeals (3rd cir.) 1974, U.S. Ct. Appeals (2nd cir.) 1975. Law clk. to Hon. John J. Gibbons U.S. Ct. Appeals (3rd cir.), Newark, 1974-75; assoc. Pitney, Hardin, Kipp & Szuch, Morristown, N.J., 1975-80, ptnr., 1980—. Mem. com. on unauthorized practice of law N.J. Supreme Ct., 1989-2001, apptd. com. chair, 2000-2001; apptd. lawyers adv. com. U.S. Dist. Ct., Dist. N.J., 2002—; trustee Legal Svcs. N.J., 2001—. Contbr. articles to profl. jours. Recipient Disting. Grad. award Seton Hall U. Law Sch., 2000. Mem. ABA, N.J. Bar Assn., Morris County Bar Assn. (trustee 1989-90). Avocations: travel, stamp collecting/philately. Office: Pitney Hardin Kipp & Szuch Park Ave at Morris County PO Box 1945 Morristown NJ 07962-1945 Office Phone: 973-966-8070. Business E-Mail: rrose@pitneyhardin.com.

ROSE, ROBERT LAWRENCE, financial services company executive; b. N.Y.C., Mar. 10, 1945; s. Martin and Helen (Diamond) R.; m. Andrea Joan Hoffman, Dec. 27, 1964 (div. June 1972); 1 child, Dawn; m. Julia Frances Knipl, Jan. 2, 1974 (div. Mar. 1991; children— Justin, Adam, Andrew. BS, Mich. State U., 1966; JD, U. Mich., 1969; LLM in Taxation, NYU, 1978. Bar: N.Y., Conn., Calif. Assoc. Kindel & Anderson, 1969-72; owner, mgr. Carol's Restaurant, N.Y.C., 1972-74; assoc. gen. counsel Equitable Life Ins. Co., N.Y.C., 1974-77; tax counsel Conn. Gen. Life Ins. Co., Bloomfield, 1977-80, assoc. gen. counsel, 1980-82; chief counsel employee benefits and fin. services CIGNA Corp., Bloomfield, 1982-84, sr. v.p., chief counsel investment group, 1984-89, v.p. corp. acctg. and planning Phila., 1989-95, v.p. strategic growth and devel., 1995-98, v.p. corp. mktg., 1998—. Author: Group Insurance Tax, 1980, Annual Meeting-Annuity Taxation, 1983, Tax Shelters, 1984; editor U. Mich. Law Rev., 1968-69, Duke U. Law Jour., 1978 Mem. Leadership Greater Hartford, 1984, Am. Leadership Forum, 1986. Mem. Am. Council Life Ins. (fin. regulatory policy subcom.), U. Conn. Sch. of Law Ins. Inst. (chmn.), Assn. Life Ins. Counsel, Calif. Bar Assn., Conn. Bar Assn., N.Y. Bar Assn. Avocations: skiing, tennis, travel. Office: CIGNA Corp Two Liberty Pl TL45F 1601 Chestnut St Philadelphia PA 19192-0004

ROSE, ROBERT MICHAEL, materials science and engineering educator; b. N.Y.C., Apr. 15, 1937; s. Lawrence Lapidus and Lillian (Rosen) R.; m. Martha Gibbs, Oct. 15, 1961; children: Cynthia J., James L., Joshua S. BS, MIT, 1958, DSc, 1961. Registered profl. engr., Mass. Asst. prof. materials sci. and engring MIT, Cambridge, 1961-66, assoc. prof., 1966-72, prof., 1972—2003, prof. emeritus, 2003—, dir. MIT Concourse program, 1988—; prof. health scis. and tech. Harvard Med. Sch.- MIT, 1978-90; dir. Cryoelectro Assocs., Wenham, Mass., 1978-90. Author: Structure and Properties of Materials, 1964, Practical Biomechanics for the Orthopedic Surgeon, 1979, 92, The Chicken From Minsk, 1995. Recipient Kappa Delta prize Am. Acad. Orthop. Surgeons, 1973. Mem. Am. Soc. Metals (vice chmn. 1971-72, Bradley Stoughton prize, chmn. 1972-73), Metal Soc. AIME, Boston Yacht Club. Jewish. Home: 18 Morgan St Wenham MA 01984-1114 Office: Room 4-132 MIT 77 Massachusetts Ave Cambridge MA 02139-4301 Business E-Mail: rose@mit.edu. *I would share my thoughts with you if I were satisfied with what I am. But I submit to you that anyone who is truly satisfied with his personal success doesn't understand the nature of his own achievement.*

ROSE, ROBERT NEAL, investment banker; b. Chgo., Feb. 27, 1951; s. James Allan Rose and Hazel (Gordon) Kaufman; m. Anna Yvette Trujillo, Aug. 23, 1981; children: David James, Michelle Elizabeth, Daniel Jonathan. BS, Georgetown U., 1973; MPA, Harvard U., 1995. Trader Salomon Bros., N.Y.C., 1974-75; regional coord. Latin Am. Merrill Lynch Govt. Securities, N.Y.C., 1975-76; dir. fed. govt. affairs Pub. Svc. of N.Mex., Albuquerque, 1977-78; exec. dir. Gov. Jerry Apodaca, Washington, 1979-80; expert cons. U.S. Dept. Commerce, Washington, 1980-81; asst. treas. Am. Express Internat. Bank, N.Y.C., 1981-82; sr. v.p. Refco, Inc., N.Y.C., 1982-84; v.p., mgr. Thomson McKinnon Securities, N.Y.C., 1984-88; sr. v.p. Lehman Bros., N.Y.C., 1988-92; mng. dir. Credit Agricole Futures Inc., N.Y.C., 1992-95; sr. mng. dir. Bear Stearns, N.Y.C., 1995—. Cons. BDM Corp., McLean, Va., 1981-88; Presdl. appointee J. William Fulbright Fgn. Scholarship Bd., 1993-97; bd. adv. Shenandoah U. Sch. Bus., 2001—. Exec. com. Conn. Yankee Coun. Boy Scouts Am., 2000—, v.p. exec. com., 2003—; mem. arrangements com. Dem. Nat. Conv., San Francisco, 1984, mem. site selection com., 1989—90, alt. del., 2004, mem.rules com. L.A., 2000; chmn. nat. fin. coun. Dem. Nat. Com., 1998—99; fin. chmn. Conn. Dem. State Ctrl. Com., 1993, 2003—; trustee Conservative Synagogue of Westport, 2000—02. Wexner Heritage Found. fellow, 1992-94; recipient Disting. Citizen award Conn. Yankee Coun. Boy Scouts Am., 2004. Jewish. Avocations: skiing, tennis. Home: 326 Bayberry Ln Westport CT 06880-1315 Office: 383 Madison Ave New York NY 10179 Office Phone: 212-272-2822. E-mail: robrose@att.net.

ROSE, ROBERT WILLIAM, JR., (ROBIN ROSE), forest regeneration scientist, educator; b. Bryn Mawr, Pa., July 9, 1945; s. Robert William Rose and Anne (Foulke) Corson; m. Marion Bray, Sept. 4, 1977; children: Robert Wistar, Andrew Blair; m. Li-Wen Lee, Apr. 1, 1995. BA in History, U. Conn., 1968; MS in Forestry, U. Vt., 1975; PhD in Forestry, N.C. State U., 1980. Forest regeneration scientist Westvaco Corp., Summerville, S.C., 1979-86; prof., dir. Nursery Tech. Coop. Oreg. State U., Corvallis, 1986—, dir. Vegetation Mgmt. Rsch. Coop., 1993—, pres.-elect faculty senate, 1999. Co-author: Propagation of Pacific Northwest Native Plants, 1998. Served with USAF, 1968-72, Vietnam. Decorated Bronze Star. Mem. Internat. Soc. Tropical Foresters (country v.p. 1999—). Episcopalian. Avocation: nature photography. Home: 2500 NW Princess St Ste 204 Corvallis OR 97330 Office: Oreg State U Forest Sci Dept Jefferson St Corvallis OR 97331

ROSE, ROSLYN, artist; b. Irvington, N.J., May 28, 1929; d. Mark and Anne Sarah (Green) R.; m. Franklin Blou, Nov. 26, 1950; 1 child, Mark Gordon Blue (dec.). Student, Rutgers U., 1949-51, Pratt Ctr. for Contemporary, Printmaking, N.Y.C., 1969; BS, Skidmore Coll., 1976. Artist. One-woman shows include Midday Gallery, Caldwell, N.J., 1972, Caldwell Coll., 1972, Kean Coll., Union, N.J., 1973, Art Corner Gallery, Millburn, N.J., 1974, Brandeis U., Mass., 1974, Newark Mus., 1974, George Frederick Gallery, Rochester, N.Y., 1981, Robbins Gallery, Washington, 1981, Arnot Art Mus., Elmira, N.Y., 1982, Douglas Coll. Rutgers U., New Brunswick, 1987, Nathans Gallery, West Paterson, N.J., 1984, 86, 89, 97, 99, The Pen and Brush, N.Y.C., 1998, New Century Artists Gallery, N.Y.C., 2003; exhibited in group shows at Seattle Art Mus., Portland (Oreg.) Mus., NYU U., Montclair Art Mus., N.J., Women in the Arts, Florence and Naples, Italy, Art Ctr. Athens, Greece, Middlesex County Mus., Piscataway, N.J., New Century Artists, N.Y.C., Noyes Mus., Oceanville, N.J., Grounds for Sculpture, Hamilton, N.J., Mountain Art Show, Bernardsville, NJ, 2002 (Best in Show award), Manhattan Arts Internat., N.Y.C. (Artist Showcase award) 2004, J.W. Starks Galleries, Tex A&M U., 2004, others; represented in permanent collections including N.J. State Mus., Trenton, Citibank of N.Y., Moscow, N.J. State Libr., Trenton, Roddenbery Meml. Libr., Cairo, Ga., Rosenberg Libr., Galveston, Tex., Newark Mus., Newark Pub. Libr., AT&T, BASF Wyandotte Corp., First Fed. Bank, Rochester, Gulf & Western Industries, Irving Trust Co., N.Y., McAllen Internat. Mus., Tex., Nabisco Brands Corp., East Hanover, N.J., Readers Digest Collection, Voorhees-Zimmerli Mus., Rutgers U., New Brunswick, N.J., The Noyes Mus. (study collection), Oceanville, N.J., others; featured artist New Century Artists Gallery, N.Y.C., 1998-2001, 2003, 2004, Internat. Soc. Exptl. Artists, 1999-2000, Period Gallery, Omaha (Dirs. award 2001), Cambridge Art Assn., 2002, Studio Seto, Boston, 2004; creator UNCIF cards, 1979-80. Recipient graphic award Westchester (N.Y.) Art Soc., 1973, Best-in-Show award Livingston (N.J.) Art Assn., 1971, Best-in-Show award N.J. Ctr. for Visual Arts, Summit, 1969, Mixed Media Merit award Salmagundi Club, N.Y.C., 1995, Exptl. Art award Western Colo. Art Ctr., 2000, Period Gallery Alternative Photography award, 2000, 2001; numerous others. Mem.: Nat. Collage Soc. Inc., Internat. Soc. Exptl. Artists, Nat. Assn. Women Artists (v.p. 1997—2001, exec. bd. 2001—03, Innovative Painting award 1990, Hazel Witte Mem. Computer Art award 2003), Pen and Brush Club N.Y.C. (Mixed Media award 1996, 1997, 1998, Photography award 2000, 2001, Best-in-Show award Mountain Art Show 2002). Office: Roslyn Rose Studios 321 Newark St Hoboken NJ 07030-2434 Office Phone: 201-217-9760. Business E-Mail: bluerose@roslynrose.com.

ROSE, SARAH ELIZABETH, genealogist, counselor, web site designer; d. H. S. Agsanian and B. M. Phillips; children: Julie, Tory, Mary, Alesandra, Vinnie, Sasha, Zachary. Grad. with honors, U.S. Army Signal Sch., 1975; grad. with distinction, Non-Commd. Officer's Leadership Acad. U.S. Army, 1977; BA in Social Sci., San Jose State U., 1980; MA in History with honors, Hawking Inst., 2004. Registered profl. genealogist Oreg. Prof. genealogist Heardry. Author: Many Branches, One Tree, 1997, World Wide Roots, 2001, Poetry: A Tribute to Life, 2003, numerous poems. With U.S. Army, 1974—77. Decorated Good Conduct medal, Nat. Def. Svc. medal, weapons medal M-16 U.S. Army; recipient Cold War Recognition Cert., U.S. Dept. Def. Mem.: Nat. Fedn. Poetry Socs., Oreg. Poetry Soc., Internat. Soc. Daus. Utah Pioneers, Pioneers of Kans., Ill. Prairie Pioneers, Am. First Families, Nat. Soc. DAR, The Winthrop Soc. (assoc.), Nat. Soc. Daus. of the Am. Colonists, Nat. Soc. Colonial Dames XVII Century, Pioneer Families Nebr., Women in Mil. Svc. for Am. (charter mem.), Am. Legion. Avocation: collecting Egyptian, African, Native American objects. Address: PO Box 945 Sutherlin OR 97479 Personal E-mail: genealogical2002@yahoo.com.

ROSE, SCOTT A. lawyer; b. Flint, Mich., Feb. 10, 1953; BS with distinction, Ariz. State U., 1975, JD cum laude, 1979. Bar: Ariz. 1979. Chmn. bd. The Cavanagh Law Firm, Phoenix, Ariz. Articles editor Ariz. State Law Jour.,

1978-79. Ariz. Govt. Affairs chmn. Internat. Coun. Shopping Ctrs. Mem. ABA, State Bar Ariz., Maricopa County Bar Assn., Downtown Phoenix Rotary Club 100 (bd. dirs.). Office: The Cavanagh Law Firm 1850 N Central Ave Ste 2400 Phoenix AZ 85004

ROSE, SELWYN H. chemical company executive; b. N.Y.C., May 1, 1933; s. Rubin and Ruth Rosenthal; m. Helen Diana De Mov, July 25, 1957; children: Michelle, Wendy, Suzanne. BS, CCNY, 1954; MS, Ohio State U., 1958, PhD, 1961; MBA with honors, U. Chgo., 1979; CFP, Coll. Fin. Planning, 1994. Sr. rsch. chemist Pennwalk Corp., King of Prussia, Pa., 1961-65; dept. mgr. Horizons Inc., Beachwood, Ohio, 1965-72, dir. rsch., 1972-74; mgr. long range rsch. De Soto Inc., Des Plaines, Ill., 1974-79; dir. rsch., cen. rsch. lab. Borg-Warner Chems., Des Plaines, 1979-85; v.p. tech. Parker Chem. Co., Madison Heights, Mich., 1985-88; gen. mgr. rsch. and devel. Himont Inc., Wilmington, Del., 1988-91, v.p. product devel., 1991-93; pres. SHR Fin. Advisors, Wilmington, 1993—. Contbr. articles to profl. jours.; patentee in field. 1st lt. U.S. Army, 1954-56. Recipient IR 100 award Indsl. Rsch. mag., 1971, award Roon Found., 1979. Mem. Am. Chem. soc., Nat. Assn. Personal Fin. Advisors, Fin. Planners Assn. Achievements include development of polyphosphazene polymers. Home: 1503 Evergreen Ln Wilmington DE 19810-4431

ROSE, STUART, retail executive; Chmn., CEO REX Stores Corp., Dayton, Ohio, 1981—. Office: REX Stores Corp 2875 Needmore Rd Dayton OH 45414-4301

ROSE, SUSAN PORTER, consultant; b. Cin., Sept. 20, 1941; d. Elmer Johnson and Dorothy (Wurst) Porter; m. Jonathan Chapman Rose, Jan. 26, 1980; 1 child, Benjamin Chapman. BA, Earlham Coll., 1963; MS, Ind. State U., 1970; HDL (hon.), Rose-Hulman Inst. Tech., 2002. Staff asst. Congressman Richard L. Roudebush, Washington, 1963-64; asst. dean George Sch., Bucks County, Pa., 1964-66; asst. dir. admissions Mt. Holyoke Coll., South Hadley, Mass., 1966-71; asst. dir. correspondence First Lady (Mrs. Nixon) The White House, 1971-72, dir. of scheduling to First Lady Pat Nixon, 1972-74, to First Lady Betty Ford, 1974-77; spl. asst. to asst. atty. gen. Office Improvements in Adminstrn. Justice, Washington, 1977-79; spl. asst. to dep. asst. atty. gen. Justice Mgmt. divsn. U.S. Dept. Justice, Washington, 1978-81; chief of staff to Barbara Bush V.P. of U.S., Washington, 1981-89; dep. asst. to Pres. of U.S., chief of staff to First Lady Barbara Bush, The White House, 1989-93; commr. U.S. Commn. Fine Arts, 1993-98. Bd. dirs. Barbara Bush Found. for Family Lit.; trustee Bush Presdl. Libr.; mem. alumni coun. Earlhem Coll., 1977—78, pres. alumni assn., 1978—81. Recipient Disting. Alumni award, Earlham Coll., 1992, Ind. State U., 1991. Mem.: Ind. Acad. Home: 5955 Ranleigh Manor Dr Mc Lean VA 22101-2428

ROSE, THOMAS ALBERT, artist, art educator; b. Washington, Oct. 15, 1942; s. Francis John and Ann Elizabeth (Voelkel) R.; m. Mary Melinda Moyer, Aug. 21, 1965; children: Sarah, Jessica. Student, U. Wis., 1960-62; BFA, U. Ill., 1965; MA, U. Calif., Berkeley, 1967; postgrad., Lund (Sweden) U., 1967-68. Instr. U. Calif., Berkeley, 1968-69, N.Mex. State U., Las Cruces, 1969-72; faculty mem. U. Minn., Mpls., 1972—, prof. art, 1983—, Fesler-Lampert chair in humanities, 2001—. Author: Winter Book, 1995, Where Do We Start?, 2003; one-man shows include Clock Tower, N.Y.C., 1977, Truman Gallery, N.Y.C., 1977-78, Rosa Esman Gallery, N.Y.C., 1979, 81, 82, Marianne Deson Gallery, Chgo., 1984-86, Robert Thomson Gallery, Mpls., 1986, 91, 92, 95, Deson Saunders Gallery, Chgo., 1989, Mpls. Inst. Art, 1992, Weisman Art Mus., Mpls., 1994, Tweed Mus., Duluth, Minn., 1995, Steinbaum/Krauss Gallery, N.Y.C., 1996, 99, Brevard Mus. Art, Melbourne, Fla., 1997, Gensler Arch., Washington, 1999, Flanders Gallery, Mpls., 2000, Bernice Steinbaum Gallery, Miami, Fla., 2001, Intermedia Arts, Mpls. Bernice Steinbaum Gallery, 2003; exhibited in group shows at Walker Art Ctr., Mpls., 1974, 76, 77, Whitney Mus. Downtown, N.Y.C., P.S. #1, N.Y.C., 1978, Wave Hill, Bronx, N.Y., 1981, Hirshhorne Mus., Washington, 1981, Am. Ctr. in Paris, 1982, Harvard U. Sch. Architecture, 1983, Cultural Ctr., Chgo., 1983, Hal Bromm Gallery, N.Y.C., Sheldon Mus., Lincoln, Nebr., 1989, Tampa (Fla.) Mus., 1988, MCAD, Mpls., 1996, Minn. Mus. Art, 1996, Socrates Sculpture Park, N.Y.C., Fla. Internat. U., Miami, 1997, Gensler Arch., Washington, 2004; represented in permanent collections Whitney Mus., N.Y.C., N.Y., Getty Inst. L.A. Calif., Walker Art Ctr., Joslyn Mus., Omaha, Park St. Lofts, Springfield, Mass., U. Minn., Mpls., Am. Lung Assn. Target Ctr., Mpls., St. Lukes Episcopal Ch., Mpls.; set designer: Fool for Love, Cricket Theater, Mpls., 1985, Circus, Theater de Jeune Lune, 1986; project dir. Works of Art in Pub. Places for Humphrey Inst. Pub. Affairs, Mpls., 1988; prin. works include Minn. Zoo, Marine Edn. Ctr., Sacred Heart U., Fairfield, Conn., Berniece Steinbaum Gallery, Miami, 1999, Steinbaum residence, 2002, Bennett Meml., Mpls., 2002. Named Rockefeller resident, Bellagio, Italy, 1993; recipient McKnight Artist fellow, 1995, travel fellow, Dayton-Hudson/Jerome, 1990, 1995, Jerome Found. Arts, 1993—94, Mellon Found., 1993, Fesler-Lampert Chair in Humanities, 2002; fellow, Nat. Endowment for Arts, 1977, 1981, Bush Found., 1979, Minn. State Arts Bd., 1979, 1984, McKnight Found., 1981, McKnight Found. Rsch., 1993—96, McKnight Photography, 2002; grantee, Arts Bd. Opportunities, 1993. Home: 91 Nicollet St Minneapolis MN 55401-1513 Office: Univ Minn 208 Studio Arts 23D S Avenue Minneapolis MN 55425 E-mail: rosex001@umn.edu.

ROSE, TODD ALAN, lawyer; b. Merced, Calif., Oct. 26, 1962; s. William Arthur and Mary (Brooks) R.; m. Teresa Gail Suiter, June 1, 1991; children: Miranda Brooke, Savannah Leigh, Emily Jane, Thomas Pierce. BS, Murray State U., 1988; JD, Vanderbilt U. Law Sch., 1991. Bar: Tenn. 1991, U.S. Dist. Ct. (we. dist.) Tenn. 1992. Asst. dist. atty. State of Tenn., Paris, 1994-97; mem. Burch, Porter & Johnson, P.L.L.C., Paris, 1991-94, 97—. Office: Burch Porter & Johnson PLLC 107 W Blythe St Paris TN 38242-4150

ROSE, WILLIAM KENNETH, astronomer, educator; b. Ossining, N.Y., Aug. 10, 1935; s. Kenneth W. and Shirley Hazel (Near) Rose; m. Sheila Luba Tuchman, Apr. 3, 1961; children: Kenneth W., Edward W., Cindy E. AB, Columbia U., 1957, PhD in Physics, 1963. Mem. rsch. staff Princeton (N.J.) U., 1963-67; asst. prof., assoc. prof. MIT, Cambridge, 1967-71; assoc. prof. astronomy U. Md., College Park, 1971-76, prof., 1976—. Author: Astrophysics, 1973, Stars, Galaxies and Cosmology, 1989, Advanced Stellar Astrophysics, 1998; contbr. articles to profl. jours. Office Phone: 301-405-1521. Business E-Mail: wrose@astro.umd.edu.

ROSE-ACKERMAN, SUSAN, law and political economy educator; b. Mineola, N.Y., Apr. 23, 1942; d. R. William and Rosalie Rose; m. Bruce A. Ackerman, May 29, 1967; children: Sybil, John. BA, Wellesley Coll., 1964; PhD, Yale U., 1970. Asst. prof. U. Pa., Phila, 1970-74; lectr. Yale U., New Haven, Conn., 1974-75, asst. prof., 1975-78, assoc. prof., 1978-82; prof. law and polit. economy Columbia U., N.Y.C., 1982-87; Ely prof. of law and polit. econ. Yale U., New Haven, 1987-92, co-dir. Ctr. Law, Econ. and Pub. Policy, 1988—, Luce prof. jurisprudence law and polit. sci., 1992—. Vis. rsch. fellow World Bank, 1995-96. Author: (with Ackerman, Sawyer and Henderson) Uncertain Search for Environmental Quality, 1974 (Henderson prize 1982); Corruption: A Study in Political Economy, 1978, (with E. James) The Nonprofit Enterprise in Market Economies, 1986; editor: The Economics of Nonprofit Institutions, 1986, (with J. Coffee and L. Lowenstein) Knights, Raiders, and Targets: The Impact of the Hostile Takeover, 1988, Rethinking the Progressive Agenda: The Reform of the American Regulatory State, 1992, Controlling Environmental Policy: The Limits of Public Law in Germany and the United States, 1995, Corruption and Government: Causes, Consequences and Reform, 1999 (Levine Prize 2000), (with Janós Kornai) Building a Trustworthy State in Post-Socialist Transition, 2004, (with Kornai and B. Rothstein) Creating Social Trust in Post-Socialist Transition, 2004; contbr. articles to profl. jours.; bd. editors: Jour. Law, Econs. and Orgn., 1984—, Internat. Rev. Law and Econs., 1986—, Jour. Policy Analysis and Mgmt., 1989—, Polit. Sci. Quar., 1988—. Guggenheim fellow 1991-92, Fulbright fellow, Free U. Berlin, 1991-92; fellow Ctr. for Advanced Study in the Behavioral Scis., Stanford, Calif., 2002, Collegium Budapest, 2002. Mem. Am. Law and Econs. Assn. (bd. dirs. 1993-96, 2002-), Am. Econ. Assn. (mem. exec. com. 1990-93), Am. Polit. Sci. Assn., Assn. Am. Law Schs., Assn. Pub. Policy and Mgmt. (policy coun. 1984-88, treas. 1998-2000). Democrat. Office: Yale U Law Sch PO Box 208215 New Haven CT 06520-8215

ROSEANNE, (ROSEANNE BARR), actress, comedienne, television producer, writer; b. Salt Lake City, Nov. 3, 1952; d. Jerry and Helen Barr; m. Bill Pentland, 1974 (div. 1989); children: Jessica, Jennifer, Brandi, Buck, Jake; m. Tom Arnold, 1990 (div. 1994); m. Ben Thomas, 1994. Former window dresser, cocktail waitress; prin. Full Moon & High Tide Prodns., Inc. As comic, worked in bars, church coffeehouse, Denver; produced showcase for women performers Take Back the Mike, U. Boulder (Colo.); performer The Comedy Store, L.A.; showcased on TV special Funny, 1986, also The Tonight Show; featured in HBO-TV spl. On Location: The Roseanne Barr Show, 1987 (Am. comedy award Funniest Female Performer in TV spl., 1987, Ace award Funniest Female in Comedy, 1987, Ace award Best Comedy Spl. 1987); writer, dir., star of TV series Roseanne ABC, 1988-97 (U.S. Mag. 2nd Ann. Readers Poll Best Actress in Comedy Series, 1989, Golden Globe nomination Outstanding Lead Actress in Comedy Series 1988, Emmy award Outstanding Lead Actress in Comedy Series, 1993), The Real Roseanne Show, 2003; actress: (motion pictures) She-Devil, 1989, Look Who's Talking Too (voice), 1990, Freddy's Dead, 1991, Even Cowgirls Get the Blues, 1994, Blue in the Face, 1995, Unzipped, 1995, Meet Wally Sparks, 1997, Home on the Range (voice), 2004; TV movies: Backfield in Motion, The Woman Who Loved Elvis, 1993; appeared in TV spl. Sinatra: 80 Years My Way, 1995; exec. prodr. Saturday Night Spl., Fox-TV; author: Roseanne: My Life as a Woman, 1989, My Lives, 1994; (host) Roseanne Show, 1998-2000, I am Your Child, 1997 (TV), Get Bruce, 1999. Active various child advocate orgns. Recipient Peabody award, People's Choice award (4), Golden Globe award (2), Am. Comedy award, Humanitas award, Nickelodeon Kids Choice award, 1990, Eleanor Roosevelt award for Outstanding Am. Women, Emmy award, 1993.

ROSEBERG, CARL ANDERSSON, sculptor, educator; b. Vinton, Iowa, Sept. 26, 1916; s. Swan Bernard and Selma (Olson) R.; m. Virginia M. Gorman, Aug. 23, 1942. B.F.A., U. Iowa, 1939, postgrad., 1939-41, M.F.A., 1947; postgrad., Cranbrook Acad. Art, summers 1947-48, U. Hawaii, 1950-51, U. Va., summer 1964, Mysore (India) U., summer 1965, Tyler Sch. Art, Temple U., summer 1967. Faculty Coll. William and Mary, Williamsburg, Va., 1947—, prof. fine arts, 1966-82, prof. emeritus, 1982—, William and Mary Heritage fellow, 1968-82. Founding bd. mem. 20th Century Gallery, Williamsburg.; active judge various art groups Exhibited one man shows at Radford Coll., 1962, Roanoke Fine Art Gallery, 1962-63, Norfolk Mus., 1963, Asheville (N.C.) Gallery Art, 1963, Longwood Coll., 1966, Phi Beta Kappa Hall, William and Mary Coll., 1970; 35 yr. retrospective William and Mary Coll., 1982; retrospective Twentieth Century Gallery, 1983; exhibited in numerous group shows; represented in permanent collections at U. Iowa, Springfield (Mo.) Mus., Va. Mus. Fine Arts, Colonial Williamsburg, Chrysler Mus. Norfolk, Rockingham County Citizens Com., Longwood Coll., Farmville, Va., Thalhimer Bros., Inc., Swem Libr., Coll. William and Mary, Patriot's Colony '98, others; designer, creator bronze meml. plaque honoring Donald W. Davis for, Millington Hall, Coll. William and Mary, 1970, bronze plaque honoring William G. Guy, Rogers Hall, 1975; I.L. Jones, Jr., Bruton Parish Ch., 1985. designer: James City County Bicentennial Medallion, 1976; designer, creator Carter O. Lowance Bronze Medallion Marshall-Wythe Sch. Law Coll. William and Mary, 1989, Bronze Medallion honoring 300th Ann. Coll. William and Mary, 1991, Bronze Medallion honoring L. I'Anson Marshall-Wythe Sch. Law, 1991. Served to comdr. USNR, 1941-45, 50-52; ret. Res. Recipient Thomas Jefferson award, 1971, numerous art awards, Cheek award William & Mary, 1993. Fellow Internat. Inst. Arts and Letters; mem. Am. Audubon Artists, Fulbright Assn., Res. Officers Assn. Am., Va. Watercolor Soc., Navy League U.S., Williamsburg German Club, Mid. Plantation Club, Masons, Lambda Chi Alpha. Presbyterian. Home: PO Box 1468 Williamsburg VA 23187-1468

ROSEBERRY, EDWIN SOUTHALL, retired state agency administrator; b. Roanoke, Va., July 4, 1925; s. Edwin Alexander and Gladys Edmonia (Southall) R.; m. Mary Louise Sprengel, Sept. 2, 1949 (dec. 1978); children: Edwin Jr., David, Kevin; m. Alice Proffit Boger, Dec. 27, 1980; 1 stepdaughter, Elizabeth Leigh Boger. BS in Commerce, U. Va., 1949. Registered sanitarian, Hawaii, Va. Store mgr. Allied Arts, Charlottesville, Va., 1949-51; retail credit sales mgr. B.F. Goodrich Co., Charlottesville, 1951-53; environ. health specialist Dept. of Health, Charlottesville, 1953-84, Dept. of Labor, Honolulu, 1987-2000; ret., 1999. Self-employed photographer, Charlottesville, 1949-85, Honolulu, 1985—. Contbr. photographs: The Inward Eye, 1986. Election ofcl. State of Hawaii, Honolulu, 1988—. With USN, 1944-46. Recipient numerous nat. awards Eastman Kodak Co., nat. newspapers, and photography mags., 1951-69. Mem. VFW (life), Am. Indsl. Hygiene Assn., Austrian Hawaiian Club (v.p., bd. dirs. 1985), Antique Auto Assn. (pres. Piedmont region 1964), Hawaii Photo Soc. (v.p. 1989), Elks (tiler and inner guard 1985), Am. Legion (dept. historian, VFW jr. vice commdr.), Mason (32 degree), Shriners (sojourners, heroes of '76, eastern star), Pi Delta Epsilon. Episcopalian. Avocations: photography, stamp collecting/philately, antique automobiles, figure skating. Home: Carriage Hill Apts #302 820 Beverly Dr Charlottesville VA 22911

ROSEBORO, BRIAN CARLTON, federal agency administrator; m. Valeri Roseboro; 2 children. BS in Econs., U. Rochester; MBA, Columbia U., 1983. Chief dealer fng.-exch. desk N.Y. Fed. Res. Bank; v.p. fng.-exch. options 1st Nat. Bank Chgo.; risk mgmt. advisor fgn.-exch. trading Swiss Bank Co., N.Y.C.; dep. dir. mkt. risk mgmt. Am. Internat. Group; asst. sec. fin. mkts. U.S. Dept. Treasury, Washington, 2001—04, acting under-sec., domestic fin., 2003—04, under-sec., domestic fin., 2004—. Office: US Dept Treasury 1500 Pennsylvania Ave Rm 2334 Washington DC 20220*

ROSEBUSH, JAMES SCOTT, marketing professional, international management and public affairs consultant, former government official; b. Flint, Mich., June 1, 1949; s. Kenneth F. and Jacqueline (Porter) R.; m. Nancy Paull, May 18, 1974; children: Claire Haisley, Lauren Culver. BA, The Principia, Elsah, Ill., 1971; MA, Boston U., 1973. Cons., Boston, 1972-76; v.p. Nat. Chamber Found., Washington, 1976-79; assoc. dir. corp. contbn. Std. Oil Co., Cleve., 1979-81; dir. Office Bus. Liaison, U.S. Dept. Commerce, Washington, 1981, spl. asst. to pres. for pvt. sector initiatives, Washington, 1981-82; dept. asst. to Pres., chief staff for First Lady The White House, Washington, 1982-86; pres. James Rosebush & Co., 1986—; CEO Growth Strategy, Inc., OurfamilyManager.com. Lectr. Georgetown U., Washington, 1977-79, George Washington U., Washington, 1977-79; presdl. appointee Nat. Mus. Svcs. Bd. Author: First Lady, Public Wife, 1987; contbr. articles to profl. jours. Mem. rev. com. United Way, Cleve., 1979; mem. cmty. rels. com. Cleve. Orch., 1979; bd. dirs. Phillips Collection Mus., SDC, Inc.; art adv. panel Fed. Res. Bd.; mem. adv. bd. Boston U. Recipient Internat. award Rotary Internat., 1970 Republican. Avocations: tennis, skiing, reading, travel. Office: 1250 24th St NW Ste 350 Washington DC 20037-1124 Office Phone: 202-835-1695. E-mail: jsrosebush@aol.com.

ROSEFF, SCOTT, reproductive endocrinologist; MD, UAG Sch. of Medicine, 1982. Diplomate Reproductive Endocrinology/Infertility Am. Bd. of Obstetrics and Gynecology, 1994, Diplomate Obstetrics and Gynecology Am. Bd. of Obstetrics and Gynecology, 1992. Dir. West Essex Ctr. for Advanced Reproductive Endocrinology (W.E. C.A.R.E.), West Orange, NJ, 1983—. Author: (multiple scientific publications) Various - See C.V. (Mellon Found. Award for Academic Excellence in Sci., 1987). Fellow: Am. Coll. Obstetricians and Gynecologists. Achievements include invention of The Roseff Double-Lumen Insemination Catheter; research in Use of Pycnogenol for treating male infertility; Various scientific endeavors. Office: WE CARE 741 Northfield Ave - Ste 100 West Orange NJ 07052 Office Phone: 973-736-1200. Personal E-mail: doc@reproendo.com. E-mail: doc@reproendo.com.

ROSEFSKY, JONATHAN BENENSOHN, pediatrician; b. Johnson City, N.Y., June 28, 1939; s. I. J. and Elsie S. Rosefsky; m. Sue Perel, 1964; children: Katherine, Douglas, Matthew. AB, Cornell U., 1960; B in Med. Sci., Dartmouth U., 1962; MD, Harvard U., 1964. Diplomate Am. Bd. Pediat., lic. Pa., Va. Intern in surgery Vanderbilt Univ. Hosp., Nashville, 1964-65; resident in pediatrics Children's Hosp. Med. Ctr., Boston, 1965-67; pediatrician USAF Med. Corps, Langley AFB, Va., 1967-69; dir. neonatal ICU United Health Svcs. Hosp., Johnson City, N.Y., 1969-74; pvt. practice Binghamton, N.Y., 1969-86; pres. Notation Systems, Inc., Binghamton, 1981-89; asst. dir. clin. devel. McNeil Consumer Products Co., Ft. Washington, Pa., 1986-89; dir. med. svcs., sr. dir. med. affairs Wyeth-Ayerst Labs., St. David's, Pa., 1989—99; pres. Fluidmotive, Inc., Haverford, Pa., 2000—, Simulatrix, Inc., Haverford, Pa., 2004—. Cons. pediat. N.Y. State Dept. Social Svcs., Albany, 1976—86; FDA adv. com. Gen. Hosp. and Personal Use Devices, Rockville, Md., 1986; industry rep. FDA Adv. Com. on Immunology Devices, Rockville, 1987—93; asst. prof. Pediat. Jefferson Med. Sch., Phila., 1987—. Contbr. articles to profl. jours. Chmn. Citizen's Adv. Com. to Mayor of Binghamton, NY, 1971; active chmn.'s coun. Phila. Mus. Art. Capt. USAF, 1967—69. Recipient Physician's Recognition award, AMA, 2004. Fellow: Am. Coll. Nutrition, Am. Acad. Pediat.; mem.: Harvard Club NYC, Green Valley Country Club. Achievements include invention of back wedge, mole marker, ribbon drive, DecTRR electronic camouflage. Avocations: skiing, swimming, photography, foreign languages, travel. Home: 251 Montgomery Ave Haverford PA 19041-1862 Office Phone: 877-790-7972. E-mail: fluidmotive.inc@att.net.

ROSEGARTEN, RORY, personal manager, television producer, theater producer; b. N.Y.C., Feb. 12, 1962; s. Robert Joel and Rita Honey (Mandel) Rosegarten; m. Wendy Jill Korn, May 4, 1991; children: Danielle Sydney, Ryan Harris. Student, Ariz. State U., 1980-81. Pres. Conversation Co., Ltd., Great Neck, NY, 1983—. Prodr.: (Broadway plays) Late Nite Comic, 1987; (plays) Comfortable Shoes, 2002; (films) Grilled, 2004; exec. prodr.: (albums) Robert Klein: Let's Not Make Love, 1990, Brian Regan: Live, 1997, Ray Romano: Live at Carnegie Hall, 2002, (TV spl.) A Pair of Jokers: Brian Regan and Denis Regan, 1991, Something's Wrong with Regan Boy, 1992, Robert Klein: It All Started Here, 1996, Sketch Pad, 2001, Sketch Pad 2, 2003, (TV series) Everybody Loves Raymond, 1996—, New Joke City, 2000—01, The John Henson Project, 2004, (TV spl., DVD) Clint Holmes: A Night to Remember, 2001; exec. prodr.: (films) Welcome to Mooseport, 2004, Eulogy, 2004. Assoc. trustee North Shore L.I. Jewish Health Sys. Found.; assoc. bd. dir. Parker Jewish Geriat. Inst., New Hyde Park, NY, 1995—98; bd. gov. Comic Relief, 1999—2002. Mem.: NATAS, Friars Club. Avocations: autograph and memorabilia collecting, hockey, water-skiing. Office: The Conversation Company Ltd 1044 Northern Blvd Ste 304 Roslyn NY 11576

ROSE-HEIM, WILLIAM BENTLEY, minister, mediator, business owner, entrepreneur; b. Syracuse, N.Y., Aug. 29, 1955; s. William Bentley and Marilynn Ann Rose; m. Irma Diana Ruiz, Jan. 4, 1975 (div. Oct. 1985); children: Daniel Joseph, Christina Marie, Elizabeth Ann; m. Donna Rae Heim, May 16, 1986; children, Zachariah Shalom, Nathaniel Mir. AA, Riverside (Calif.) City Coll., 1979; BA, Rockhurst Coll., 1980; MDiv, St. Paul Sch. Theology, Kansas City, Mo., 1986; grad., Ark. Leadership Acad., 1997. Ordained to ministry Christian Ch., 1987. Pastoral assoc. Curé of Ars Cath. Ch., Leawood, 1979-83, St. Francis Xavier Cath. Ch., Kansas City, 1983-85; pastoral asst. St. Luke Presbyn. Ch., Kansas City, 1985-87; co-pastor 1st Christian Ch., Odessa, Mo., 1987-93; sr. pastor, 1993-96; mental health therapist West Cen. Mo. Mental Health Ctr., Warrensburg, 1990-95; assoc. regional minister Christian Ch., Ark., 1996-2000; co-pastor N.W. Area Christian Ch. Mid-Am., 2000—; mem. adj. faculty St. Paul. Sch. Theology, 2000—; owner, CEO, Rose-Heim Agy., 2003—, Engage For Success, 2003—. Instr. in theology Rockhurst High Sch., Kansas City, 1980-84; vol. chaplain intern VA Med. Ctr., 1986-89, asst. chief chaplain, 1988; moderator Christian Ch. Mid Am., 1994-96; founder, mediator Helping Hand Dispute Resolution Svcs., 1991-96. Contbr. Cameron Citizen Observer. Co-founder Odessa Alanon Family Group, 1987-90, Odessa R/7 Friends for Youth, 1987—; sec. bd. dirs. Odessa Habitat for Humanity, 1989-90; co-founder Odessa Outreach-West Cen. Mo. Mental Health Ctr., 1990; co-founder, acting exec. dir. Odessa Cmty. Svc. Ctr., 1991; coach Ark. Leadership Acad., 1999—; 2d v.p. Ark. Interfaith Conf.; v.p. Ark. Friends for Better Schs., 1999; mem., bd. dirs. Our House Homeless Shelter, 1997-99; mem. Disciples of Christ Hist. Soc.; pastor, counselor Gen. Conf. Disciples Men, 1998-99; co-founder, sec. Interfaith Disaster Recovery Team, 1998-2000; mem. Renewing Rural Mo., 2000-2002; chaplain Cameron Fire Dept., 2001. Recipient Ark. Traveler award Ark. Leadership Acad., 2000. Avocations: rock-climbing, music composition, writing, woodcraft, Hap Ki Do (brown belt). Home: 705 E 3rd St Cameron MO 64429-1951 Office: Christian Ch MidAm PO Box 353 811 S Walnut Cameron MO 64429 E-mail: brh@nwareacc.org. *Lead us to places You call home by Your good Spirit O my God.*

ROSEL, CAROL ANN, artist; b. Dodge City, Kans., June 12, 1944; d. John Elbert and Mary Claire (Wetmore) Frazier; m. Herbert Carey Zortman, Aug. 21, 1960 (div. Jan. 1989); children: Elaine Marie, Anita Louise, Stanley Dale; m. George D. Rosel, Sept. 22, 1990 (dec. June 1995). Student, Ctrl. Coll., McPherson, Kans., 1961; BFA cum laude, Ft. Hays State U., 1994. Cert. machine embroidery instr. Dress designer Ms. Cosmo Ltd., Wichita, Kans., 1975-76; designer artistic embroidery garments, 1977-80, 99; owner Carol Ann's Gallery, Liberal, Kans.; part time music tchr. W. Mid. Sch., 1999—. Part-time art tchr. U.S. D 443, Dodge City, part-time music tchr.; singer A Touch of Class; developer The Tour (the Life of Christ). One-woman show Ft. Hays Libr., 1993. Mem. Baker Art Ctr., Liberal, 1989—, Hays (Kans.) Arts Coun., 1993, Carnegie Ctr. of Arts, Dodge City, Kans.; solo pianist ch. weddings and comty. functions; mem. Glory Rd. Singers, 1999; mem. cast Wild West Show, 2001—, Touch of Class Ladies Group; vol. Make A Wish Found.; tchr. Sunday sch. Recipient All Am. Scholar Collegiate award, 1994, Grand Champion award State Fair, 1989, 90, 95, 97, 98, Purple Champion award, 1990, others; named Woman of World, 1995-96, Internat. Women of World, 1996-97, Internat. Woman of Yr., 1995-96. Mem.: So. Gospel Music Assn., Baker Art Ctr., Mid. Am. Arts and Crafts Assn., Christian Womens Club, Lions Club, Christian Life Drama Club, Art Club, Pinnacle Honor Soc. Republican. Avocations: piano, singing, dramatics, painting. Home and Office: 2901 Westview Dodge City KS 67801

ROSELLA, JOHN DANIEL, clinical psychologist, educator; b. Phila., Sept. 12, 1938; s. Orazio and Angela Theresa (Cardone) Rosella; m. Rose Mary Theresa Malloy, Nov. 14, 1964; children: Anne-Marie, John Daniel Jr. BS in Psychology, Villanova U., 1961; MEd Temple U., 1966, postgrad. Temple U., 1969—72, PhD Walden U., 1981. Diplomate Am. Bd. Forensic Examiners, Am. Bd. Psychol. Spltys., Profl. Acad. Custody Evaluators, cert. hypnotherapist, lic. psychologist, Pa.; cert. in edn. St. Joseph's U., 1963. Tchr., counselor Father Judge H.S., Phila., 1962—67; counselor Bristol Twp. Sch. Dist., Bucks County, Pa., 1967—69; prof., dept. social & behavioral scis. Bucks County C.C., 1994, subject area coord., 1995, 1968—, founder coll. reading and study skills program, 1968—70, founding chmn. dept. basic studies, 1970—76; dir. psychol. svcs. Fairless Hills (Pa.) Med. Ctr., 1978—89, dir. clin. svcs., 1989—96; asst. clin. prof. Widener U., 1990—. Cons. Office of Vocat. Rehab., 1977—; psychol. cons. Eugenia Hosp.19890, 1980—, Bur. Disability Determination, 1982—, Human Growth Ctr., Inc., 1982—, Crestview North Nursing Home and Rehab. Ctr., 1990—; cons. staff psychologist Attleboro Nursing Home and Rehab. Ctr., 1993—2001, Pickering Manor Nursing Home, 1997—2001; clin. assoc. prof., Dept. Mental Health Scis. Hahnemann U., 1982—94; cons. Bucks County (Pa.) Family Ct., 1985—; grad. clin. supr. Coll. of N.J., 1985—86; grad. counseling intern supr. Rider Coll., 1988—95; participant 1st Internat. Colloquium on Family Health, Sri Lanka, 1983, Australia, 88; ednl. profl. travel Italy and Switzerland, 1991; lectr. in field. Author: Reading and Study Skills: A Counseling Approach, 1970, Effects of the Basic Studies Program on the Academic Achievement of High Risk Students, 1973—74, The Professor and the Law, 1975, Research in Hypnosis for Students, 1976, Marriage and Family Therapy: Its Evolution from Revolution, 1980, others; author: (audiotapes) Developing Successful Study Skills, Guided Imagery Exercises; author: articles. Active Right to Read Task Force, 1972—73; project dir. Fairless Hills Psychiat. Hosp. bldg. program, 1982—83; pres. bd. trustees Friends of the Libr. Found., Bucks County C.C., 1984—; co-founder Newtown Twp. Dem. Party, 1978, 1st vice chmn., 1979—80, Dem. committeeman, 1989—92; mem. 8th Congressional Dist. Adv. Coun. on Health Care, 1981—83; bd. dirs. Valley Day Sch., 1978—81; Bucks County Cmty. Ctrs., 1980—85. Recipient Man of Yr. award, Assn. to

Advance Ethical Hypnosis, 1976, Disting. Tchg. recognition, Phi Theta Kappa, 1981, 1983, Faculty Svc. award, 1989, Profl. AChievement award, Bucks County C.C. Alumni Assn., 1991. Fellow: Pa. Psychol. Assn., Internat. Coun. for Sex Edn. and Parenthood of Am. U.; mem.: APA, Profl. Acad. Custody Evaluators, Pa. Assn. Marriage and Family Therapy, Am. Assn. Marriage and Family Therapy, Am. Coll. Forensic Examiners, Sons of Italy, KC, Am. Legion. Office: Offices at Oxford Crossing Ste 202 333 S Oxford Valley Rd Fairless Hills PA 19030-2626

ROSELLE, DAVID PAUL, university president, mathematics educator; b. Vandergrift, Pa., May 30, 1939; s. William John and Esther Suzanne (Clever) R.; m. Louise Helen Dowling, June 19, 1967; children— Arthur Charles, Cynthia Dowling BS, West Chester State Coll., 1961; PhD, Duke U., 1965; LLD, West Chester U., 1994; hon. degree, Westchester U., Soka U., Japan. Asst. prof. math. U. Md., College Park, 1965-68; assoc. prof. math. La. State U., Baton Rouge, 1968-73, prof., 1973-74, Va. Poly. Inst. and State U., Blacksburg, 1974-87, dean grad. sch., 1979-81, dean research and grad. studies, 1981-83, provost, 1983-87, chmn. Commn. on Rsch., 1981-83, chmn. Commn. on Grad. Studies, 1983-87; prof. U. Ky., 1987-90, pres., 1987-90; prof. math., pres. U. Del., 1990—. Pres. COMAP, Inc., Lexington, Mass., 1986-95; bd. dirs. Wilmington Trust Corp., VTLS, Inc. Editor: Proc. of the First Louisiana Conf. on Combinatorics, Graph Theory and Computing, 1970, Proc. of the Second Louisiana Conf. on Combinatorics, Graph Theory and Computing, 1971; mem. editorial bd. The Bicentennial Tribute to American Mathematics, 1977; contbr. numerous research articles to profl. jours. Mem. Del. Roundtable, 1990—, Bus.and Pub. Edn. Coun., 1990—; trustee Winterthur Mus., 1991—; bd. dirs. Del. Acad. Medicine, 1991—, Med. Ctr. Del., 1991—, mem. USAID adv. com. vol. fgn. aid, 2000—. Named Outstanding Alumnus West Chester State Coll., 1979; Westinghouse Coop. scholar, 1957; NSF grantee, 1965-75; Teaching Excellence Cert., 1978; Digital Equipment grant, 1984; Nat. Coun. Tchrs. Math. Cert. of Appreciation, 1984; founding fellow of Inst. for Combinatorics and Its Applications, 1990; numerous invited addresses at univs. and profl. soc. meetings. Mem. Am. Math. Soc., Math. Assn. Am. (sec., fin. com., exec. com., com. on publs. 1975-84; com. on spl. funds 1985—; chmn. com. on accreditation 1985; numerous other coms.). Home: 47 Kent Way Newark DE 19711-5201 Office: U Del Rm 104 Hullihen Hall Newark DE 19716-0099 E-mail: roselle@udel.edu.

ROSELLE, WILLIAM CHARLES, librarian; b. Vandergrift, Pa., June 30, 1936; s. William John and Suzanne Esther (Clever) R.; m. Marsha Louise Lucas, Aug. 2, 1959; 1 child, Paul Lucas. BA, Thiel Coll., 1958; MLS, U. Pitts., 1963. Lic. profl. guide State of Mont., 1978. Mem. faculty Milton Hershey (Pa.) Sch., 1960-62; trainee Pa. State Library, 1962-63; asst. catalog librarian Pa. State U., 1963-65; engring., math. librarian U. Iowa, 1965-66, library adminstrv. asst., 1966-69, asst. dir. libraries, 1969-71; prof., dir. library U. Wis.-Milw., 1971-89; dir. univ. library system U. Pitts., 1989-90; pvt. cons. Thiensville, Wis., 1991—. Chmn. Morris Fromkin Meml. Lectr. Com., 1972-89; chmn. planning task force on computing U. Wis. System, 1973-74, mem. library planning study com., 1978-79, co-chmn. library automation task force, 1983-85; chmn. computing mgmt. rev. team U. Wis.-Stout, 1976; chmn. Council for U. Wis. Libraries, 1981-82; library cons. Grambling (La.) State U., Viterbo Coll., LaCrosse, Wis., N.C. A&T U., Greensboro, Mt. Mary Coll., Milw., U. Ill. at Chgo., Milw. Sch. Engring., Bklyn. Coll., U. South Ala., Concordia Coll., Milw., Metrics Rsch. Corp., Cardinal Stritch Coll., Milw., N.Y. Inst. Tech., Indiana U. of Pa., Med. Coll. Wis., Wis. Luth. Coll., Milw.; participant Library Adminstrs. Devel. Program, U. Md., 1973, micrographics seminar Nat. Microfilm Assn., 1973, Mgmt. Skills Inst., Assn. Rsch. Libraries, Kansas City, Mo., 1977, Meadowbrook Symposium Midwest Library Network, 1976; mem. sect. geography and map libraries Internat. Fedn. Library Assns. and Instns., 1978-83; mem. bldg. com. Ctr. for Rsch. Libraries, 1980-82. Editorial cons. The Quest for Social Justice, 1983, Current Geographical Publications, 1978-89; contbr. articles to profl. jours. Pres. Thiensville (Wis.) Village Bd., 1987; bd. dirs. Charles Allis Art Mus., 1979-84. Served with AUS, 1958-60. Named Disting. Alumnus, Thiel Coll., 1985 Hon. fellow Am. Geog. Soc.; mem. Spl. Libraries Assn. (spl. citation 1979), ALA (life), Iowa Library Assn. (chmn. audit com. 1968-70, chmn. intellectual freedom com. 1969-70), Wis. Library Assn., Midwest Acad. Librarians Conf. (chmn. 1969-71), AAUP (treas. U. Iowa chpt. 1969-70), Coun. Wis. Libraries (chmn. 1973-74), Soc. Tympanuchus Cupido Pinnatus, Internat. CBX Owners Assn., Milw. Civil War Round Table, Ozaukee Corvette Club, Beta Beta Beta, Beta Phi Mu, Phi Alpha Theta, Phi Kappa Phi, Phi Delta Kappa. Lutheran. Home: 324 Sunny Ln Thiensville WI 53092-1334

ROSELLO, JACQUELINE DELAPP, occupational therapist; d. Joseph K. and Elizabeth C. DeLapp; m. Donald E. Rosello, Aug. 7, 1976; children: Anthony F., Daniel A. AA, Lehigh C.C., Schweinksville, Pa., 1980. Occupl. therapist Reading Rehab. Hosp., Pa., 1980—95, The Highlands at Wyomissing, Pa., 1990—. Instr. in occupl. therapy Pa. State U., Reading, 1995—96. Adv. bd. Wilson Sch. Dist., West Lawn, Pa., 1995—; adv. bd. in occupl. therapy Alvernia Coll., Reading, 2000—. Mem.: Am. Occupl. Therapy Assn. Roman Catholic. Home: 2407 LaSalle Dr West Lawn PA 19609 Office: The Highlands at Wyomissing 2000 Cambridge Ave Wyomissing PA 19610

ROSEMAN, CHARLES SANFORD, lawyer; b. Jersey City, Feb. 26, 1945; s. Leon and Edith (Neidorf) R.; children: Rochelle Lynn, Loren Scott. BA, Calif. State U., 1968; JD, U. San Diego, 1971. Bar: Calif. 1972, U.S. Dist. Ct. (so. dist.) Calif. 1972, U.S. Dist. Ct. (cen. dist.) Calif. 1975, U.S. Supreme Ct. 1980, U.S. Claim Ct. 1990. Assoc. Greer, Popko, Nickoloff & Miller, San Diego, 1972-73; ptnr. Roseman & Roseman, San Diego, 1973-78, Roseman & Small, San Diego, 1978-82, Frank, Roseman, Freedus & Mann, San Diego, 1982-86, Roseman and Mann, 1986-92; pvt. practice San Diego, 1992—; judge pro tem San Diego County Superior Ct., 1975—; also arbitrator, mediator, 1977—; founding ptnr. i2i Resolutions, 2001. Bd. dirs. Glenn Aire Cmty. Devel. Assn., San Diego, 1972-73, Big Bros. San Diego County, 1973-81,; bd. dirs. San Diego County Anti-Defamation League, 1985—; chmn. exec. com. 1984-85, assoc. nat. commr., 1995—; bd. dirs. San Diego County Legal Aid Soc., 1988-89, Tifereth Israel Synagogue, pres. 1982-84, Homeys Youth Found., 2002--. Mem. ABA, ATLA, Fed. Bar. Assn., Consumer Attys. of Calif. (Recognition of Experience award 1985), Calif. Bar Assn., Am. Arbitration Assn. (arbitrator, panel 1985—), San Diego Bar Assn., Consumer Attys. of San Diego (bd. dirs. 1982-84), U. San Diego Sch. Law Alumni Assn. (bd. dirs. 1972-73), B'nai B'rith (pres. 1978). Democrat. Office: Law Offices Charles S Roseman & Assocs 170 Laurel St San Diego CA 92101-1419 Office Phone: 619-544-1500. E-mail: csroseman@rosemanlaw.com.

ROSEMAN, JACK, computer services company executive; b. Lynn, Mass., June 13, 1931; s. Abraham and Bessie (Guz) R.; m. Judith Ann Rosenthal, Feb. 21, 1960; children: Laura, Alan, Shari. BA, Boston U., 1954; MS, U. Mass., 1955. Instr. U. Mass., 1958-60; dir. info. processing CEIR, Inc., Washington, 1960-66; v.p. KMS Tech. Ctr., Washington, 1966-70; pres., bd. dirs. On-Line Systems, Inc., Pitts., 1970-79; pres., chmn. United Computing Internat. subs. of SPRINT, 1979-80; pres., bd. dirs., later chmn. Actronics, 1981-85; pvt. investor, ptnr. J.R. Assocs., Pitts., 1988-92; chmn. of bd. dirs. Omega Systems, 1994-96; CEO/dir. Roseman Inst., 2001—. Disting. adj. prof. Donald H. Jones Ctr. Entrepreneurship, 1992—2000, assoc. dir., 1992—2001; John Thorne prof. entrepreneurship Carnegie Mellon U., 2000—01; dir. emeritus Pitts. High Tech. Coun.; chmn. Cerebellum, Inc., 1997—2000; dir. Roseman Inst., 2002—; bd. dirs. Collaborate, Inc., Ventire, Inc.; advisor Netspoke, Inc., Donald H. Jones Ctr. for Entrepreneurship, Carnegie Mellon U., Akustica, Inc.; bd. dirs. Venture, Inc.; columnist Pitts. Post Gayette, 2001—. Co-author: Outrageous Optimism: Wisdom for the Entrepreneural Journey. Adv. Kobold Found. Recipient Judges' award, Ernst & Young, and Merrill Lynch Inc. mags., 1991. Office Phone: 412-562-1560.

ROSEMAN, MARTIN RICHARD, publisher, consultant, lecturer; b. East Orange, N.J., Aug. 4, 1958; s. Jack Melvin and Esther Shirley (Beshunsky) Roseman; m. Carolina Villacorta, Dec. 8, 2001; children from previous marriage: Fabricio, Shirley. BA, Hampshire Coll., 1980; MS, Rutgers U., 1987. Rschr., editor Consumer Fedn. Am., Washington, 1977; pres. Matrix Audio Video, West Hatfield, Mass., 1980-86; founder, pres. MAC Consulting, Miami Beach, Fla., 1980—; dir. mktg. Profl. Audio Cons., Millburn, N.J., 1986-96; v.p. Les Enfants, South Orange, 1990-97. Chief cons. Sony Latin Am., 2001; lectr. CEDIA Expo, 1999. Profl. musician, 1974—. Lobbyist Pub. Citizen, Washington, 1977; sponsor Save the Children, Westport, Conn., 1991-97; ptnr. NJPIRG, Trenton, N.J.; Frontline sponsor Greenpeace, Washington. Mem. Profl. Audio Video Retailers Assn., Custom Electronics Design and Installation Assn., Home Theater Specialists Assn., Nat. Trust for Hist. Preservation. Democrat. Jewish. Avocations: musical performance and composition, computer science, antiquities. Home and Office: 4335 N Meridian Ave Miami Beach FL 33140-2940 E-mail: info@macmrkt.com.

ROSEMAN, SAUL, biochemist, educator; b. Bklyn., Mar. 9, 1921; s. Emil and Rose (Markowitz) R.; m. Martha Ozrowitz, Sept. 9, 1941; children: Mark Alan, Dorinda Ann, Cynthia Bernice. BS, CCNY, 1941; MS, U. Wis., 1944, PhD, 1947; MD (hon.), U. Lund, Sweden, 1984. From instr. to asst. prof. U. Chgo., 1948-53; from asst. prof. to prof. biol. chemistry, also Rackham Arthritis Research Unit, U. Mich., 1953-65; Ralph S. O'Connor prof. biology Johns Hopkins U., Balt., 1965—, chmn. dept., 1969-73; dir. McCollum-Pratt Inst., 1969-73, chmn. dept. biology, dir., 1988-90. Cons. NIH, NSF, Am. Cancer Soc., Hosp. for Sick Children, Toronto; sci. counselor Nat. Cancer Inst.; Lynch lectr. U. Notre Dame, 1989; Van Niel lectr. Stanford U., 1992. Author articles on metabolism of complex molecules containing carbohydrates and on solute transport.; former mem. editorial bd.: Biochemistry, Jour. Biol. Chemistry. Served with AUS, 1944-46. Recipient Sesquicentennial award U. Mich., 1967, T. Duckett Jones Meml. award Helen Hay Whitney Found., 1973, Rosenstiehl award Brandeis U., 1974, Internat. award Gairdner Found. award, 1981, Townsend Harris award CUNY, 1987, Spl. award 11th Internat. Symposium on Glycoconjugates, 1991, Karl Meyer award Soc. Glycobiology, 1993. Fellow Am. Acad. Microbiology; mem. Am. Soc. Biol. Chemists, Am. Soc. Cell Biology, Am. Acad. Arts and Scis., Nat. Acad. Scis., Am. Chem. Soc., Am. Soc. Microbiologists, Biochem. Soc. Japan (hon.). Office: Johns Hopkins U 34th Charles St Baltimore MD 21218

ROSEMAN, STEVEN A. insurance company executive; BA in Econs., Brandeis U.; JD, U. Pa. Assoc., ptnr. Ervin Cohen & Jessup, Beverly Hills, Calif.; v.p. bus. affairs Worldwide Pay TV Paramount Pictures Corp.; sr. v.p., gen. counsel, sec. Am. Health Properties Inc., Englewood, Colo., 1997—2000; counsel LeBoeus Lamb Green & MacRae LLP, Denver, 2001—02; exec. v.p. Sun Healthcare Group, Albuquerque, 2002—, gen. counsel, 2002—, sec., 2002—. Office: Sun Healthcare Group 101 Sun Ave NE Albuquerque NM 87109*

ROSEMARIN, CAREY STEPHEN, lawyer; b. Englewood, N.J., Aug. 19, 1950; s. Jack L. and Muriel Ruth (Gordon) R.; m. Joan Maxine Lafer, June 17, 1973; children: Benjamin Joseph, Meryl Ruth. BS, U. Mich., 1972; MS, Pa. State U., 1974; JD, U. Tenn., 1978. Bar: Tenn. 1978, Ill. 1982, U.S. Dist. Ct. (ea. dist.) Tenn. 1978, U.S. Dist. Ct. (no. dist.) Ill. 1982. Rsch. assoc. Union Carbide Corp., Oak Ridge Nat. Lab., 1974-80; asst. regional counsel U.S. EPA, Chgo., 1980-86; ptnr. Katten, Muchin, & Zavis, Chgo., 1986-90, Jenner & Block, Chgo., 1990-99; prin. Law Offices of Carey S. Rosemarin, P.C., Northbrook, Ill., 1999—. Participant Israel Environ. Bike Ride to benefit Arava Inst. Environ. Studies, 2004; v.p. facilities Congregation Beth Judea, Long Grove, Ill. Mem. ABA, Tenn. Bar Assn., Chgo. Bar Assn. (chmn. environ. law com. 1985-86), Environ. Law Inst. (assoc.). Jewish. Avocations: licensed glider pilot, bicycling. Office: Law Offices of Carey S Rosemarin PC 500 Skokie Blvd Ste 510 Northbrook IL 60062-2893 Fax: 312-896-5786. Office Phone: 847-897-8000. Business E-Mail: csr@rosemarinlaw.com.

ROSEMBERG, EUGENIA, physician, educator, medical research administrator; b. Buenos Aires, Apr. 25, 1918; came to U.S., 1948, naturalized, 1956; d. Pedro and Fanny (Hestrin) R. BS, Liceo Nacional de Senoritas, Buenos Aires, 1936; MD, U. Buenos Aires, 1944. Intern Hosp. Pirovano, Buenos Aires, 1940-41; resident Hosp. Nacional de Clinicas, U. Hosp., U. Buenos Aires, 1941-44, assoc. in pediatrics, 1943-48; instr. in anatomy Hosp. Nacional de Clinicas, U. Hosp., U. Buenos Aires (Med. Sch.), 1940-46, instr. pediatrics, 1946-48; practice medicine specializing in pediatrics, 1946-48; research in endocrinology, 1948-51, Worcester, Mass., 1955—; Mead Johnson fellow dept. endocrinology Johns Hopkins Med. Sch., Balt., 1948-49; vis. scientist Med. Sch., U. Montevideo, Uruguay, 1950; research fellow NIH, Bethesda, Md., 1951-53, Nat. Inst. Arthritis and Metabolic Diseases, 1951-53, Med. Research Inst. and Hosp., Oklahoma City, 1953; mem. staff Worcester Found. Exptl. Biology, Shrewsbury, Mass., 1953-62; research dir. Med. Research Inst. of Worcester, Inc., 1962—; cons. Center for Population Research, Nat. Inst. Child Health and Human Devel., NIH, 1969-70, chief contraceptive devel. br., 1970-71; prof. pediatrics U. Md. Hosp., Balt., 1970-73; prof. medicine U. Mass. Med. Sch., Worcester, 1972—; mem. staff Worcester City Hosp., 1955-85, sec. human experimentation com., 1965-83, chmn., 1984-85, dir. clin. research, 1972-85. Sec. subcom. on gonadotropins Nat. Hormone and Pituitary Program, Nat. Inst. Arthritis, Diabetes, Digestive and Kidney Diseases, 1965-69, chmn., 1969-85, mem. med. adv. bd., 1969-72, 73-85, sec. subcom. on standards endocrinology study sect., 1968 Author: Gonadotropins, 1968, (with C.A. Paulsen) The Human Testis, 1970, Gonadotropin Therapy in Female Infertility, 1973, (with C. Gual) Hypothalamic Hypophysiotropic Hormones—Physiological and Clinical Studies, 1973; Mem. editorial bd.: Giner, 1970—, Procs. 1st Ann. Meeting Am. Soc. Andrology, supplement, Vol. 8, 1976, Andrologia, 1978—, Jour. Andrology, 1979-82, Internat. Jour. Andrology, 1978—; assoc. editor: Reproduccion, 1970—, Andrologia jour, 1974-77; Contbr. articles and book chpts. on research in endocrinology to med. texts and jours.; Translator: from Spanish Diagnosis and Treatment of Endocrine Disorders in Childhood and Adolescence (L. Wilkins). Patentee in field, U.S., Can., Europe. Fellow AAAS; mem. Am. Med. Women's Assn., Endocrine Soc. U.S. (mem. com. pub. affairs 1971, v.p. 1975-76), Soc. for Research in Biology of Reproduction, Soc. for Study of Reproduction, Am. Fertility Soc., Peru Fertility Soc. (fgn. corr.), N.Y. Acad. Scis., New Eng. Cardiovascular Soc., Am., Mass. heart assns., Argentine Endocrine Soc., Argentine Pediatric Soc., Sociedad Argentine Para El Estudio de la Esterilidad., Pan Am. Med. Women's Alliance, Am. Soc. Andrology (program chmn. 1975-76, exec. council 1976-78, chmn. publ. com. 1975-80, Disting. Andrologist award 1982), Internat. Com. for Study Andrology (exec. council 1976-79)

ROSEN, ADRIENNE, artist, educator; b. St. Louis, Dec. 18, 1940; d. Charles and Rena Gallop; m. Alex Paul Tucker, June 21, 1961 (dec. June 1965); m. Martin M. Rosen, Dec. 1967. BFA, Washington U., St. Louis, 1972. Illustrator, designer Internat. Shoe Co., St. Louis, 1961; owner, illustrator, graphic designer A.R. Art Studio, St. Louis, 1961—; painter portraits of people and pets St. Louis, 1995—. Art tchr. St. Louis Artist Guild; art tchr. Coll. for Kids program Meramec C.C.; pvt. instr. Designer, illustrator (dolls) Bethany Farms Inc., 1990—. Vol. artist Leukemia Soc. Am., St. Louis, 1999, Animal Aid, St. Louis, 1975, Am. Med. Ctr., St. Louis, Cystic Fibrosis Found.; vol. St. Louis Showstoppers for Breast Cancer Rsch. Named Artist of Month, Ballwin, Mo., 2004; recipient 2d pl. award, Jewish Cmty. Ctrs. Assn., St. Louis, 1997, University City Art Assn., St. Louis, 1999, award of mention, South County Art Assn., St. Louis, 1998, Recognition award, Art Happening, 2001—02, 1st pl. award profl. watercolor, Jewish Cmty. Ctrs. Assn., 2002, 2003. Mem.: Greater St. Louis Art Assn. (publicity dir. 1994—99, sec. 1995—98, v.p. 1998—2000, pres. 2000—02, exhibits chair 2002—03, publicity chair 2004—), St. Louis Watercolor Soc. (signature mem.), St. Louis Artist Guild (bd. dirs. 1993—94), Art World Art Assn. Avocations: running races, dance, photography, marathon running. Office: AR Art Studio 1717 Seven Pines Dr Saint Louis MO 63146-3713

ROSEN, ALLEN DAVID, plastic surgeon; b. Bklyn., Mar. 5, 1957; MD, SUNY-Buffalo, 1983. Diplomate Am. Bd. Plastic Surgery with subspecialty in hand surgery. Intern Columbia-Presbyn. Med. Ctr., N.Y.C., 1983—84, resident in surgery, 1984—86, resident in plastic surgery, 1986—88, fellow in hand surgery, 1987; pvt. practice plastic surgery, 1987—; founding ptnr., med. dir. The Plastic Surgery Group, Montclair, NJ, 1995—. Attending plastic surgeon Passaic Gen. Hosp., NJ, Mountainside Hosp., NJ, St. Barnsbes; clin. asst. prof. U. Medicine and Dentistry N.J.; spokesperson Am. Soc. Plastic and Reconstructive Surgery, 1990—. Fellow: ACS; mem.: N.J. Soc. Plastic and Reconstructive Surgery, Am. Cancer Soc. (past pres.). Office: 37 N Fullerton Ave Montclair NJ 07042*

ROSEN, ARTHUR MARVIN, advertising executive; b. N.Y.C., Dec. 28, 1930; s. Joseph and Cornelia (Grob) R.; m. Maureen Elizabeth Reilly; children: Ellen Jessica, Deborah Lynn, Daniel Joshua. BA, CUNY, 1952; MA, Yale U., 1953; postgrad., Columbia U., 1955-57, Dartmouth Coll. Analyst research Dancer-Fitzgerald-Sample, N.Y.C., 1955-56; supr. research Benton and Bowles, N.Y.C., 1956-61; account exec. Young and Rubicam, N.Y.C., 1961-66; v.p. account supr. Grey Advt., N.Y.C., 1966-69; pres. Met. Diagnostic, N.Y.C., 1969-73; v.p. group mgmt. Grey Advt., N.Y.C., 1973-81; exec. v.p. Sudler and Hennessey, N.Y.C., 1981-94; mktg. cons. Himmel Nutrition, Inc., 1994-95, Martin Himmel, Inc., 1994-95. Spkr. in field. Contbr. articles to profl. jours. Pres. Temple Beth Or, Washington Twp., N.J., 1973-74; chmn. Soc. Families, Colgate U., 1983-84; chmn. curriculum com., mem. exec. coun., study leader ILEAD, Dartmouth Coll.; study leader Adventures in Learning, Colby-Sawyer Coll. Cpl. U.S. Army, 1953-55. Republican. Jewish. E-mail: ponderosen@tds.net.

ROSEN, ARYE, microwave, optoelectronics and medicine researcher; b. June 26, 1937; BSEE cum laude, Howard U., 1963; MScE, Johns Hopkins U., 1965; MSc in Physiology, Thomas Jefferson U., 1975; PhD in Elec. Engring., Drexel U., 1993. Registered profl. engr., B.C., Can. Disting. mem. tech. staff Sarnoff Corp. subs. SRI, Princeton, NJ, 1967—2003; assoc. in medicine Jefferson Med. Coll., Phila., 1977—; rsch. prof. Sch. of Biomed. Engring. Sci. and Health Sys. Drexel U., Phila., adj. prof. elec. and computer engring., 1981—2003, acad. prof. of biomed. engring. and elec. engring., 2003—. Mem. com. on sci. and the arts The Franklin Inst., 2003—; mem. tech. staff Sarnoff Corp. subs. SRI, Princeton, NJ, 1967—2003. Co-editor: High-Power Optically Activated Solid-State Switches, 1993, New Frontiers in Medical Device Technology, 1995; contbr. more than 150 articles to profl. jours. Mem. adv. com. John Scott award Phila. Bd. Dirs. City Trusts, 2004—. Recipient Microwave prize 16th European Microwave Conf., 1986, Disting. Alumni award Drexel U. Coll. Engring., Elec. and Computer Engring. Dept., 1997, IEEE MTT-S Microwave Application award, 2000, IEEE Third Millenium medal, 2000, IEEE Reg. I award, 1989. Mem.: IEEE (mem. MMT-S tech. com. for light-wave tech. 1979—, mem. MTT-S tech. program com., chmn. MTT-S tech. com. on biol. effects and med. applications, mem. editl. bd., assoc. editor IEEE Jour. Light-Wave Tech., editl. bd. Transactions on Microwave Theory and Techniques, editl. bd. Microwave and Optical Tech. Letters, mem. tech. com. IEEE Internat. Conf. Microwaves in Medicine 1991, ednl. activities bd., mem.-at-large health care engring. policy com., Disting. Microwave lectr. 1997—2001), Nat. Acad. Engring. Achievements include 55 patents in the fields of engineering and medicine, including Percutaneous Transluminal Microwave Catheter Angioplasty, Method and Apparatus for High Frequency Catheter Ablation, Catheter with Distally Located Integrated Circuit Radiation Generator, Electrical Phase Shifter Controlled by Light, Direct DC to RF Conversion by Impulse Excitation, Light Controlled Antennas, High Power Optical Switch, Radiation Protection Circuit for Protection Against Gamma Ray and Neutron Radiation. Office: Drexel Univ Sch Biomed Engring Sci and Health Sys 3141 Chestnut St Philadelphia PA 19104-2875 Office Phone: 215-895-1913.

ROSEN, BERNARD CARL, sociologist, social psychologist, educator; b. Phila., July 1, 1922; s. Morris and Sophie Slaviter Rosen; m. Shirley Rosenbluth, Sept. 10, 1950; 1 child, Michele Beth. BA, Temple U., 1948; MA, Columbia U., 1950; PhD, Cornell U., 1952. Instr. Yale U., New Haven, Conn., 1952-53; asst. prof. U. Conn., Storrs, 1953-61; prof. U. Nebr., Lincoln, 1961-66, Cornell U., Ithaca, N.Y., 1966-93, prof. emeritus, 1993—. Vis. prof. U. São Paulo, Brazil, 1960-61, Escola Sociologia-Politica, São Paulo, 1963-64, Harvard U., 1966, London Sch. Econs., 1973-74, U. Padua, Italy, 1983-84; cons. Upjohn Inst. for Employment Rsch., 1965, NSF, 1966-89, USAID, 1990, Hunter Coll. Edn. in Depressed Areas Project, 1963, U. Chgo. Study of Adolescence Project, 1963; organizer Conf. on Socialization of Competence, Social Sci. Rsch. Coun., Puerto Rico, 1965, Conf. on Ednl. Aspirations of Can. Youth, Carleton U., Ottawa, 1970, Symposium on Family Structure and Personality, Soc. Rsch. in Child Deve., 1963, Conf. of Personality Deve. Among H.S. Youth, Social Sci. Rsch. Coun., 1963, Nat. Com. for Vis. Scientists, 1978. Author: The Industrial Connection, 1982, Women, Work and Achievement, 1989, Winners and Losers of the Information Revolution, 1998, Masks and Mirrors: Generation X and the Chameleon Personaltiy, 2001, Adolescence and Religion, 1965; co-author: (with A.M. Rattazzi, A. C. Tajoliand D. Capozza) Aspettative Di Istruzione E Occupazione Nei Giovani, 1988; contbr. articles to profl. jours., chpts. to books; co-editor: Achievement in American Society, 1969;ssoc. editor Sociometry, 1966-79; mem. editl. bd. Luso-Brazilian Rev., 1966-71; reviewer jours. in field. With U.S. Army, 1943-46, WW II. Decorated 2 combat stars; ssch. grantee NSF, 1968-73, NIMH, 1956-57, 58-62, Harvard U. 1957, U. Calif., Berkeley, 1964. Avocations: art collecting, travel, visiting museums. Home: 895 Highland Rd Ithaca NY 14850-1475 Office: Dept Sociology Uris Hall Cornell U Ithaca NY 14853

ROSEN, CAROL, editor; b. Chgo., Aug. 21, 1948; d. James Joseph and Colette Ann Cole; m. Phillip Rosen, Aug. 20, 1972; children: Elias, Anna. BA with honors, Cornell U., 1970; MA in History with honors, U. Va., 1971; JD, George Mason U., 2000. Editor U.S. Dept. Labor, Washington, 1972-74, Ctr. for Urban Policy Rsch., New Brunswick, N.J., 1974-76, Cambridge Univ. Press, N.Y.C., 1976-79, Am. Enterprise Inst., Washington, 1979-81, Brookings Instn., Washington, 1981-84, World Bank, Washington, 1984-89, mng. editor, 1989-92, chief editl. and prodn., 1992-97; dir. publs. World Resources Inst., Washington, 1997-99, dir. comms. svs., 1999—, editor-in-chief World Resources, 1999—. Mem. Washington Book Pubs. (officer 1999—). Office: Word Resources Inst 10 G St NE Washington DC 20002-4213

ROSEN, CAROL MENDES, artist; b. N.Y.C., Jan. 15, 1933; d. Bram de Sola and Mildred (Bertuch) Mendes; m. Elliot A. Rosen, June 30, 1957. BA, Hunter Coll., 1954; MA, CUNY, 1962. Tchr. art West Orange (N.J.) Pub. Schs., 1959-85. Co-curator exhibit Printmaking Coun. N.J., Somerville, 1981; exhibit curator 14 Sculptors Gallery, N.Y.C., 1988; collection: Nat. Collection of Fine Arts, Smithsonian Instn., Newark Mus., N.J. State Mus., Bristol-Myers Squibb, AT&T, Noyes Mus., N.Y. Pub. Libr., Zimmerli Art Mus., Mus. of Modern Art, Whitney Mus., Libr. Collection Bklyn. Mus., Victoria & Albert Mus., Nat. Art Gallery, London, Mus. of Tolerance, L.A., Hunterdon Mus. Art, Nat. Mus. Women in Arts, Tel Aviv U. and The Jewish Nat. & U. Libr., Jerusalem, Houghton Libr., Harvard U., Yale U., Clark Art Inst., Skidmore, Williams Coll. Mus. Art, Oberlin Coll., William Paterson U., Stanford U., Smith Coll., Wellesley Coll. Contbr. articles to arts mags. Recipient Hudson River Mus. award, Yonkers, 1983; fellow, N.J. State Coun. Arts, 1980, 1983. Jewish. Avocations: gardening, reading. Home: 10 Beavers Rd Califon NJ 07830-3433 E-mail: earosen@earthlink.net.

ROSEN, CHARLES, II, lawyer; b. New Orleans, Jan. 29, 1925; s. Louis Leucht and Nita (Silverstein) R.; m. Mary Alice Waldauer (div. 1976); children: Charles III, Virginia, Jane, James Louis; m. Sandra Reed (div. 1995); m. Emily Hart, 1995. BA, Tulane U., 1948, LLB, 1951. Bar: La. 1951. Assoc. Rosen, Kammer, Wolff, Hopkins & Burke, New Orleans, 1951-55, Jones, Walker, Waechter, Poitevent, Carrere & Denegre, New Orleans, 1955-58, ptnr., 1958-90; spl. counsel Locke, Purnell, Rain, Harrell (now Locke Liddell & Sapp), New Orleans, 1990-97; of counsel Sullivan Stolier & Resor, New Orleans, 1997—. Past chmn. and mem. exec. com. Golf & Sports Attractions, Inc., ret. mem. fore kids Found. Past trustee Touro Synagogue; hon. trustee Touro Infirmary; chmn. lawyers div. Jewish Fedn. Greater New Orleans, 1969; past chmn. lawyers div. United Fund. 1st lt. U.S. Army, 1944-46, PTO. Mem. ABA, La. Bar Assn., New Orleans Bar Assn., Am. Coll. Real Estate Attys., Anglo Am. Real Property Inst., So. Golf Assn. (past bd. dirs.), New Orleans Golf Assn. (past pres., past bd. dirs.), Tulane Green Wave Club (past bd. dirs.), Lakewood Country Club (past pres., bd. dirs.). Republican. Avocation: golf. Home: 410 Northline Metairie LA 70005-4452 Office: Sullivan Stolier & Resor 909 Poydras St Ste 2600 New Orleans LA 70112-4022 E-mail: attorney@ssrlawfirm.com.

ROSEN, CLIFFORD JAMES, internist; b. Utica, N.Y., Feb. 18, 1950; s. Harry N. and Harriett P. (Rubin) R.; m. Donna Peckham, June 17, 1973; (div. Dec. 1983); 1 child, Aaron; m. Rebecca Harless, Aug. 7, 1986; 1 child, Isaac. BS, U. Maine, 1971; MD, SUNY, Syracuse, 1975. Diplomate Nat. Bd. Med. Examiners, Am. Bd. Internal Medicine. Chief resident in medicine U. Mass./Berkshire Med. Ctr., Pittsfield, 1978-79, instr. medicine, 1978-79; fellow in endocrinology Dartmouth Hitchcock Med. Ctr., Hanover, N.H., 1982-84; cooperating prof. nutrition U. Maine, Orono, 1986-88, rsch. asst. prof., 1988-91, rsch. assoc. prof., 1991-94; clin. assoc. prof. Tufts U. Sch. Medicine, Boston, 1991-94, Boston U. Sch. Medicine, 1993—; rsch. prof. U. Maine, 1995—, prof. nutrition, 1999—. Adv. bd. Inst. Cellular Rsch., Bangor, 1991-93; exec. dir. Maine Ctr. for Osteoporosis Rsch.; chief medicine St. Joseph Hosp., Bangor, 1989-99. Editor-in-chief Jour. Clin. Densitometry, 1998—; editor Osteoporosis in Clin. Medicine, 1995—; contbr. chpts. to books, articles to profl. jours. Founder Physicians for Nat. Health Plan, Maine, 1991; com. person Am. Health Reform Com., Washington, 1993. Recipient Katherine Musgrave award Maine Nutrition Coun., Augusta, 1994, Excellence in Aging Rsch. award Glenn Found., 1996. Mem. Am. Fedn. Clin. Rsch., Soc. of Insulin Growth Factor Rschrs., Endocrine Soc., Am. Soc. Bone Mineral Rsch. (bd. dirs. adult bone and mineral working group 1993—, pub. affairs com. 1994-, pres., 2002-03), Soc. Clin. Densitometry (founding mem.). Democrat. Jewish. Avocations: running, gardening. Home: 16 Mckinley St Bangor ME 04401-3830 Office: St Joseph Hosp Maine Ctr Osteoporosis Rsch Bangor ME 04402 E-mail: rofe@aol.com.

ROSEN, DAVID MICHAEL, public relations administrator, public affairs consultant; b. Cambridge, Mass., Mar. 26, 1945; s. Maynard S. and Irma (Leavitt) R.; m. Nina J. Glick, Apr. 8, 1967; children: Michelle, Elisabeth. BA, Boston U., 1967, MS, 1977. Reporter The Day, New London, Conn., 1968-69, Boston Herald, 1969-73; polit. writer UPI, Boston, 1973-76, State House bur. chief, 1976-77; polit. commentator WGBH-TV, Boston, 1975-77; pub. affairs cons. Boston, 1977-79; pub. info. dir. U.S. Commodity Futures Trading Commn., Washington, 1979-80; dir. pub. rels. Harvard U., Cambridge, Mass., 1980-84, assoc. v.p., 1984-85, U. Chgo., 1986-88; v.p. Nicolazzo Assocs., Boston, 1988; chief of staff Office of Lt. Gov., Boston, 1988-89; v.p. Brandeis U., Waltham, Mass., 1989-93; cons. David Rosen Assocs., Boston, 1993; dir. pub. rels. Yeshiva U., N.Y.C., 1993-99; assoc. v.p. pub. affairs Emerson Coll., Boston, 2000—. Cons. U.S. GAO, Washington, 1977-79, Mass. Ins. Divsn., Boston, 1977-78, Harvard U., 1977-80, Radcliffe Coll., 1993, New Eng. Bd. Higher Edn., 1993, Clark U., 1993, Pilgrim Health Care, 1993; substitute tchr. Boston Pub. Schs., 1967-68. Author: Protest Songs in America, 1977. Avocations: piano, running. Home: 157 Bishops Forest Dr Waltham MA 02452-8800 Office: Emerson Coll Pub Affairs 120 Boylston St Boston MA 02116-4624 Office Phone: 617-824-8540. Business E-Mail: david_rosen@emerson.edu. E-mail: david_rosen@comcast.net.

ROSEN, ELLEN FREDA, psychologist, educator; b. Chgo., Jan. 28, 1941; d. Samuel Aaron and Clara Laura (Pauker) R. BA, Carleton Coll., 1962; MA, U. Ill., 1965, PhD, 1968. Instr. psychology U. Ill., Urbana, 1966-67; prof. Coll. William and Mary, Williamsburg, Va., 1967-99; dean grad. studies and dir. Ctr. for Urban Mental Health Rsch. Chgo. State U., 1999—. Cons. Ctr. for Teaching Excellence Hampton (Va.) U., 1988-94; sr. rsch. scientist Behavioral Rsch. Ctr., Hampton U., 1997-99. Author: Ednl. Computer Software, (with E. Rae Harcum) The Gatekeepers of Psychology, 1993; contbr. articles to profl. jours. Mem. Am. Psychol. Soc. Office: Office Grad Studies LIB 338 Chgo State Univ Chicago IL 60628 E-mail: EF-Rosen@csu.edu.

ROSEN, EVAN MARK, executive communication advisor, journalist; b. N.Y.C. s. Gerald Robert and Lois Ann Rosen; m. Katherine Hirzel. BA, U. Mich., 1983. Reporter Our Town, N.Y.C., 1977—78; copy clk., reporter The N.Y. Post, 1979—80; intern ABC News, N.Y.C., 1980; news dir. WCBN-FM, Ann Arbor, Mich., 1980—81; desk asst. WABC-TV, 1981—82; writer, prodn. asst. WXYZ-TV, Detroit, 1982—83; reporter KODE-TV, Joplin, Mo., 1983—85; reporter, anchor WTOL-TV, Toledo, 1985—93, KICU-TV, San Jose, Calif., 1993—94; chief strategist, mng. ptnr. Impact Video Comm. Inc., San Francisco, 1994—2003, p.CEO, 2004—. Lectr. Stanford U. Ctr. for Profl. Devel., Palo Alto, Calif.; on-air contbr. CNN, Atlanta, 1985—90, CBS News Newspath, N.Y.C., 1985—93; consulting mem. Personal Conferencing Work Group, Santa Clara, Calif., 1993—95. Author: Personal Videoconferencing; columnist Telemedicine Today mag.; contbr. articles to profl. jours., mags.; contbg. editor: Network World Mag., Information Week Mag. Intern Office of U.S. Rep. Ed Koch, Washington, 1977; press aide Ed Koch for Mayor of N.Y. campaign, 1977, Office of The Mayor of N.Y., 1978. Nominee Emmy award, NATAS, 1991; recipient 2d pl. award best spot news coverage-large market, Ohio AP, 1988, Crystal award of excellence, Women In Comm., 1990. Office: Impact Video Comm Inc 1750 Montgomery St San Francisco CA 94111 E-mail: erosen@impactvid.com.

ROSEN, FRED, travel company executive; b. Windsor, Ont., Can., May 19, 1926; arrived in U.S., 1946; s. Harry and Dora Rosen; m. Gertrude Rush, May 13, 1952; 1 child, Robert Martin. Cert. Elec. Tech., Washington U., St. Louis, 1964; AA in Tourism, Forest Park C.C., St. Louis, 1993; Cert. Microcomputers, Meramec C.C., St. Louis, 2000. X-ray maint. staff Keleket X-Ray, Covington, Ky., 1953—54; whse. mgr. Western Shoe Jobbers, St. Louis, 1954—64, prodn. supr., 1977—92; owner Vanity Shoes, Kirkwood, Mo., 1964—77; travel cons. Hausler Travel, St. Louis, 1995—97; owner Accessible Travel, St. Louis, 1997—. Contbg. editor: the Independence, 1997—98; author: (guidebook) How to Travel - A Guidebook for Persons with a Disability, 1997, How to Travel in Canada - A Guidebook for a Visitor with a Disability, 2000. Pres. Kirkwood Noonday Optimist Club, 1971—72; commr. Kirkwood Disabled Commn., 1984—91, Kirkwood Housing Authority, 1977—83, Kirkwood Human Rights, 1974—77; bd. dirs. Mo. Assn. Retarded Citizens, Jefferson City, 1962—65, St. Louis Assn. Retarded Citizens, 1962—89, mem. recreation com., 1962—89. Sgt. 1st class U.S. Army, 1946—53, ETO. Mem.: Masons (worshipful master 1990—91, Achievement award 1991). Jewish. Avocations: dance, cruising. Home: 144 Oakside Ln Saint Louis MO 63122-1211

ROSEN, FRED SAUL, pediatrics educator; b. Newark, May 26, 1930; s. Philip and Amelia (Feld) Rosen. AB, Lafayette Coll., 1951; MD, Western Res. U., 1955; MA (hon.), Harvard U., 1970; DSc (hon.), Lafayette Coll., 1978. From asst. to assoc. prof. pediat. Harvard Med. Sch., Boston, 1966—72, James L. Gamble prof. pediat., 1972—; chief. divsn. immunology Children's Hosp., Boston, 1968—85, program dir. Gen. Clin. Rsch. Ctr., 1977—91; pres. Ctr. for Blood Rsch., Boston, 1987—. Chmn. sci. com. on immunodeficiencies WHO, Boston, 1988—. Author: Dictionary of Immunology, 1989. Pres. Am. Friends of Jenner Appeal, Boston, 1985—. Sr. asst. surgeon USPHS, 1957—59. Recipient E. Mead Johnson award for pediatric rsch., Am. Acad. Pediat., 1970, Gen. Clin. Rsch. Ctrs. Program 4th Ann. award, NIH, 1992; fellow John Simon Guggenheim Meml., 1974. Mem.: Inst. Medicine NAS, Assn. Am. Physicians, Am. Pediatric Soc., Am. Soc. Clin. Investigation, Am. Assn. Immunology, Somerset Club, Harvard Club, St. Botolph Club. Office: The Ctr for Blood Rsch Dept Pediats 800 Huntington Ave Boston MA 02115-6399*

ROSEN, GEORGE, economist, educator; b. St. Petersburg, Russia, Feb. 7, 1920; s. Leon and Rebecca (Rosenoer) R.; m. Sylvia Vatuk; 1 son, Mark. BA, Bklyn. Coll., 1940; MA, Princeton U., 1942, PhD, 1949. Prof. econs. Bard Coll., Annandale-on-Hudson, N.Y., 1946-50; economist Dept. State, Washington, 1951-54, Council Econ. Indsl. Research, Washington, 1954-55, MIT, CENIS, Cambridge, 1955-59, UN, N.Y.C., 1959-60, Ford Found., N.Y.C., Nepal and India, 1960-62, Rand Corp., Santa Monica, Calif., 1962-67; chief economist Asian Devel. Bank, Manila, Philippines, 1967-71; prof. econs. U. Ill.-Chgo., 1972-85, prof. econs. emeritus, 1985—, head dept., 1972-77; fellow Woodrow Wilson Internat. Ctr., Washington, 1989-90. Adj. prof. Johns Hopkins U.-Nanjing U. Ctr. Chinese-Am. Studies, 1986-87; cons. USAID, Egypt, 1994; book rev. editor Econ. Devel. and Cultural Change, 1988-2001; treas. Am. Com. for Asian Econ. Studies, 1990-98; Golden Jubilee spkr. Dept. Commerce Osmania U., Hyderabad, India, 1999; disting. spkr. Ctr. for Advanced Study of Internat. Devel., Mich. State U., East Lansing, 1999. Author: Industrial Change in India, 1958, Some Aspects of Industrial Finance in India, 1962, Democracy and Economic Change in India, 1966, 67, Peasant Society in a Changing Economy, 1975, Decision-Making Chicago-Style, 1980, Western Economists and Eastern Societies, 1985, Industrial Change in India 1970-2000, 1988, Contrasting Styles of Industrial Reform: China and India in the 1980s, 1992, Economic Development in Asia, 1996; contbr. The India Handbook, 1997. Ford Found. fellow NYU, 1971-72; grantee U. Ill., 1977-78, Social Sci. Research Council and Am. Inst. Indian Studies, 1980-81, Am. Inst. Indian Studies, 1983-84, 87-88, Rockefeller Found. Bellagio Study Ctr., 1984. Office: U Ill Dept Econs M/C 144 601 S Morgan St Chicago IL 60607-7121 Home: 5830 S Stony Island Ave 11A Chicago IL 60637

ROSEN, GERALD ELLIS, federal judge; b. Chandler, Ariz., Oct. 26, 1951; s. Stanley Rosen and Marjorie (Sherman) Cahn; m. Laurie DeMond; 1 child, Jacob DeMond. BA, Kalamazoo Coll., 1973; JD, George Washington U., 1979. Researchist Swedish Inst., Stockholm, 1973; legis. asst. U.S. Senator Robert P. Griffin, Washington, 1974-79; law clk. Seyfarth, Shaw, Fairweather & Gerardson, Wash., 1979; from assoc. to sr. ptnr. Miller, Canfield, Paddock and Stone, Detroit, 1979-90; judge U.S. Dist Ct. (ea. dist.) Mich., Detroit, 1990—. Mem. Jud. Evaluation Com., Detroit, co-chmn. 1983-88; adj. prof. law Wayne State U., 1992—, U. Detroit Law Sch., 1994-98; mem. U.S. Jud. Conf. Com. on Criminal Law; lectr. CLE confs., 1996-2002, others. Co-author: Federal Civil Trials and Evidence, 1999, Michigan Civil Trials and Evidence, 2001; contbr. articles to profl. jours. Rep. candidate for U.S. Congress, Mich., 1982; chmn. 17th Congl. Dist. Rep. Com., 1983-85; mem. Mich. Criminal Justice Commn., 1985-87; mem. Birmingham Athletic Club; bd. visitors George Washington U. Law Sch., 2000—; bd. dirs. Focus Hope, 2000—. Fellow Kalamazoo Coll. (sr. 1972); recipient Career Achievement award Rolex/Intercollegiate Tennis Assn. Mem. Fed. Judges Assn. (bd. dirs.). Jewish. Office: US Courthouse 231 W Lafayette Blvd Rm 802 Detroit MI 48226-2707

ROSEN, GERALD HARRIS, physicist, consultant, educator; b. Mount Vernon, NY, Aug. 10, 1933; s. David A. and Shirley (Schapiro) R.; m. Sarah Louise Sweet, June 8, 1963; children: Lawrence A., Karlyn Rosen Aires. BSE, Princeton (NJ) U., 1955, MA, 1956, PhD, 1958. Rsch. assoc. dept. aero. engring. Princeton U., 1958-59, NSF predoctoral fellow, 1956, Inst. Theoretical Physics, Utrecht, Netherlands, 1957-58, NSF postdoctoral fellow Stockholm, 1959-60; tech. cons. weapon sys. evaluation divsn. The Pentagon, 1960; prin. scientist Martin-Marietta Aerospace divsn., Balt., 1960-63; cons. to a tech. v.p. Southwest Rsch. Inst., 1963-66; prof. physics Drexel U., Phila., 1966-73, M.R. Wehr prof. physics, 1973-98, prof. emeritus, 1998—. Cons. fin., indsl. and govt. agys., 1966—. Author: Formulations of Classical and Quantum Dynamical Theory, 1969, A New Science of Stock Market Investing, 1990; assoc. editor Bull. Math. Biology, 1982—; contbr. over 300 articles to profl. jours.; patentee in field. Sponsor San Antonio Chamber Music Soc., 1963-66; mem. Franklin Inst., 1967—; mem. publ. bd. Soc. Math. Biol., 1983— . Guggenheim Jet Propulsion scholar, Princeton U., 1955, Whiton Engring.-Physics scholar, 1955. Fellow Am. Phys. Soc., AAAS; mem. Am. Math. Soc. Home and Office: 415 Charles Ln Wynnewood PA 19096-1604 E-mail: gerosen@yahoo.com. *The meaning of life has transcended human understanding up to the present time, but there are reasons to believe that future discoveries in science will illuminate the significance of life in nature. We must break completely free of non-rational dogma and illusion, and attempt to solve this mystery with factual clues revealed by scientific progress.*

ROSEN, GERALD ROBERT, editor; b. N.Y.C., Nov. 17, 1930; s. Sol and Essie (Shapiro) R.; m. Lois Lehrman, May 9, 1958; 1 son, Evan Mark. BS, Ind. U., 1951, MA, 1953. Intelligence analyst Dept. Def., N.Y.C., 1955-58; assoc. editor Challenge: The Mag. of Econ. Affairs, N.Y.C., 1959-61, mng. editor, 1961-64, 65-66; sr. editor Dun's Rev., N.Y.C., 1964-65, nat. affairs editor, 1967—; exec. editor Dun's Rev. (now Bus. Month), 1978-90; editor IMF survey Washington, 1990-93; mng. dir. Global Insights Svcs., Washington, 1993—. Fin. corr. Westinghouse Broadcasting Co. Served with CIC U.S. Army, 1953-55. Mem. Soc. Am. Bus. and Econ. Writers, N.Y. Fin. Writers Assn., White House Corrs. Assn. Clubs: Nat. Press. Home: 3210 Grace St NW Washington DC 20007-3628 Office Phone: 202-342-1377. E-mail: gerry308@aol.com.

ROSEN, HAROLD A. retired aeronautical engineer; b. New Orleans, Mar. 20, 1926; 2 children. B in Engring., Tulane U., 1947, DSc (hon.), 1975; MS in Electrical Engring., Calif. Inst. Tech., 1948, PhD in Electrical Engring., 1951. With Raytheon Mfg. Comp., 1948; v.p. engring., mgr. Comm. Systems divsn. Space & Comm. Group, Hughes Aircraft Co., 1956—75; v.p. Comm. Systems divsn. Space & Comm. Group, Hughes Aircraft Co., Boeing Satellite Systems, know as Hughes Electronics Corp., 1975—93; cons. Boeing Satellite Systems, 1998—. Astronautical engr. Nat. Space Coun., 1964. Contbr. papers to the field. Named So. Calif. Inventor of Yr., Patent Law Assn. of LA, 1973; named to Nat. Inventors Hall of Fame, 2003; recipient Aerospace Comm. award, AIAA, 1968, Spacecraft Design of Yr. award, 1973, L.M. Ericsson Internat. prize, Sweden, 1976, Lloyd V. Berkner award, Am. Astronaut Soc., 1976, Alexander Graham Bell medal, IEEE, 1983, Nat. medal Tech., Pres. of U.S., 1985, C&C Found. prize, Tokyo, 1985, Arthur C. Clarke award, Sri Lanka, 1990, Draper prize, 1995, Astronautics Engr. award, Nat. Space Club, Golden Plate award, Am. Acad. of Achievements "Gathering of the Great". Tex., Communications award, Am. Inst. of Aeronautics and Astronautics, Emmy, NATAS. Fellow: IEEE (Mervin J. Kelly award 1972), AIAA (Comm. award 1968); mem.: NAE (Charles Stark Draper prize 1995). Achievements include conception of spin stabilized synchronous communication satellite; development of advanced communication and satellite systems; founder of the modern communications satellite industry; patents in field. Avocations: skiing, scuba diving, windsurfing, running. Office: Hughes Space & Communications 2260 E Emperial Way El Segundo CA 90245*

ROSEN, JACQUELINE I. flutist, music educator; b. Los Angeles, Sept. 28, 1952; d. Samuel Morris and Blanche (Seigel) R.; m. James Andrew Meckel, July 14, 1979; children: Sean Aaron, Eric Rosen. Student, Music Acad. of the West, Santa Barbara, Calif., 1973-74; BS in Music, UCLA, 1974; studies with Julius Baker, James Galway, Jean-Pierre Rampal, 1974-80. Freelance musician, Los Angeles, San Francisco and Monterey, Calif., 1974—; mem. Laurel Wind Quintet, 1977-80, Allegra Trio, 1980—, Farrell/Rosen Duo, Carmel, Calif., 1978-87, Terrence Farrell Consort, Carmel, 1980—. Instr. flute pvt. studio, Monterey, 1976—, Monterey Peninsula Coll., 1981-85; instr. Hidden Valley music seminars, Cazadero Music Camp; prin. flutist Hidden Valley Opera, Carmel Valley, Calif., 1976—; condr. master classes numerous Calif. colls., 1982—.; music specialist Salinas City Sch. Dist. Premiere performance (flute-guitar duo) Sonatine for Flute and Guitar, 1981; rec. artist (with Terrence Farrell) Alla Romanza, Merry Christmas; appearances with San Francisco Spring Opera, 1979, Cabrillo Music Festival, 1978-84, Carmel Bach Festival, 1996, 98, 99, Camerata Singers; flutist Michael Culver Trio; editor CTB/Macmillan-McGraw-Hill; radio broadcasts, 1977—. Recipient Southwestern Music Conf. award, 1972; Leonard Bernstein fellow, Tanglewood, 1977. Mem.: Calif. Music Educators Assn., Music Educators Nat. Conf. Avocations: playing jazz, gourmet cooking. Home: 15 Paseo Primero Salinas CA 93908-9110 E-mail: jjmeckel@pacbell.net.

ROSEN, JEFFREY ADAM, federal agency administrator, lawyer; b. Boston, Apr. 2, 1958; m. Kathleen Nichols, May 29, 1982. BA summa cum laude, Northwestern U., 1979; JD magna cum laude, Harvard U., 1982. Bar: D.C. 1982, U.S. Ct. Appeals (fed. cir.) 1983, U.D. Dist. Ct. D.C. 1983, U.S. Supreme Ct. 1986, U.S. Ct. Appeals (11th cir.) 1988, U.S. Ct. Appeals (6th cir.) 1990, U.S. Ct. Appeals (3rd cir.) 1996, U.S. Dist. Ct. (ea. dist.) Mich., U.S. Dist. Ct. (no. dist.) Ill., U.S. Ct. Appeals (4th cir.). Assoc. Kirkland & Ellis, Washington, 1982-88, ptnr., 1988—2003; gen. counsel U.S. Dept. Transp., Washington, 2004—. Adj. prof. Georgetown U. Law Ctr., 1996—2003; mem. Arlington County Hist. Affairs and Landmark Rev. Bd., 1991—93. Mem.: Va. Hist. Soc., U.S. Supreme Ct. Hist. Soc., Am. Law Inst. Office: US Dept Transp 400 Seventh St SW Rm 10428 Washington DC 20590

ROSEN, JON HOWARD, lawyer; b. Bklyn., May 20, 1943; s. Eli and Vera Horowitz Rosen; children: Jason Marc, Hope Terry. BA, Hobart Coll., 1965; JD, St. John's U., 1968; postgrad. in bus., CCNY, 1969—71. Bar: N.Y. 1969, Calif. 1975, Wash. 1977. Atty. FAA, N.Y.C., 1968-71; regional atty., contract adminstr. Air Line Pilots Assn., N.Y.C., Chgo., L.A., San Francisco, 1971-77; pvt. practice Seattle, 1977-80; ptnr. Frank and Rosen, Seattle, 1981-98, Frank Rosen Freed Roberts LLP, Seattle, 1999—2002, The Rosen Law Firm, 2002—. Instr. labor studies Shoreline C.C., 1978-90. Trustee Temple DeHirsch Sinai, 1991-98, v.p., 1998-2000, pres.-elect 2000-01, pres., 2001-03; chair Ward Springs Pk. Steering Com.; mem. African-Am./Jewish Coalition for Justice, Interfaith Alliance. Fellow: Am. Bar Found., Coll. Labor and Employment Lawyers; mem.: ABA (union co-chmn. com. on employee rights and responsibilities 1992—96, union co-chmn. regional programs subcom. 1998—2000, union co-chmn. nat. programs. subcom. 2000—02, union co-chmn. ADR in labor and employment law com. 2002—, co-regional EEOC liaison), Wash. State Trial Lawyers Assn. (past chair employment law com.), Nat. Employment Lawyers Assn. (state steering com. 1990—95, founding state chair), King County Bar Assn. (past chmn. aviation and space law sect., past chmn. Pacific Coast Labor and Employment Law Conf., past chmn. labor law sect.). Office: Rosen Law Firm 705 2nd Ave Ste 1200 Seattle WA 98104-1729 Office Phone: 206-652-1464. E-mail: jhr@jonrosenlaw.com.

ROSEN, JUDAH BEN, computer scientist; b. Phila., May 5, 1922; s. Benjamin and Susan (Hurwich) R.; children— Susan Beth, Lynn Ruth. BSEE, Johns Hopkins U., 1943; PhD in Applied Math., Columbia U., 1952. Rsch. assoc. Princeton (N.J.) U., 1952-54; head applied math. dept. Shell Devel. Co., 1954-62; vis. prof. computer sci. dept. Stanford (Calif.) U., 1962-64; prof. dept. computer sci. and math. rsch. ctr. U. Wis., Madison, 1964-71; prof., head dept. computer sci. U. Minn., Mpls., 1971-92, fellow Supercomputer Inst., 1985—; sr. fellow Supercomputer Ctr., San Diego, 1993—; adj. rsch. prof. dept. computer sci. and engrin. U. Calif. San Diego, La Jolla, 1992—, bioinformatics grad. program faculty, 2001—. Fulbright prof. Technion, Israel, 1968-69, Davis vis. prof. 1980; invited lectr. Chinese Acad. Sci., Peking, 1980, Guilin, 1996, Samos, Greece, 2000; lectr., cons. Argonne (Ill.) Nat. Lab.; mem. Nat. Computer Sci. Bd. Author: Topics in Parallel Computing, 1992; editor: Nonlinear Programming, 1970, Supercomputers and Large-Scale Optimization, 1988; assoc. editor Global Optimization, 1990—, Annals of Ops. Rsch., 1984—; contbr. articles to profl. jours. and procs. Grantee NSF, 1995—, ARPA/NIST, 1994-97. Mem. Assn. Computing Machinery, Soc. Indsl. and Applied Math., Math. Programming Soc., European Acad. Scis. Achievements include research in supercomputers and parallel algorithms for optimization, computation of molecular structure and drug design by energy minimization and homology models, algorithms for structured approximation in signal processing. Office: U Calif San Diego Dept Computer Sci Engring 9500 Gilman Dr La Jolla CA 92093-0114 E-mail: jbrosen@cs.ucsd.edu.

ROSEN, LAWRENCE, anthropologist, educator; b. Cin., Dec. 9, 1941; s. George and Hannah (Persky) Rosen. BA, Brandeis U., 1963; MA, U. Chgo., 1965, PhD, 1968, JD, 1974. Bar: N.C. 1975, U.S. Supreme Ct. 1979. Asst. prof. anthropology U. Ill., Urbana, 1968-70; mem. Inst. Advanced Study, Princeton, NJ, 1970-71; assoc. prof. Duke U., Durham, NC, 1974-77; prof. Princeton (N.J.) U., 1977—, William Nelson Cromwell Prof., 2002. Adj. prof. Columbia U. Law Sch., 1979—; vis. prof. Northwestern U. Law Sch., Chgo., 1985—87, U. Pa. Law Sch., Phila., 1985—86, Georgetown Law Ctr., 1994; Lewis H. Morgan lectr. U. Rochester, 1985; mem. commons Wolfson Coll. Oxford U., Corpus Christi Coll. Cambridge U., 1998—99. Editor: The American Indian and the Law, 1974, Other Intentions, 1995, The Culture of Islam, 2002; co-author: Meaning and Order in Morrocan Society, 1978; author: Bargaining for Reality, 1984, The Anthropology of Justice, 1989, The Justice of Islam, 2000. Legal asst. Native Am. Rights Fund, Boulder, Colo., 1973. Recipient John and Catherine MacArthur Found. award, 1981; vis. scholar, Phi Beta Kappa, 1997; Woodrow Wilson fellow, 1964, Guggenheim fellow, 1981, Fulbright fellow, 1991. Fellow: Am. Anthrop. Assn. E-mail: lrosen@princeton.edu.

ROSEN, LOUIS, physicist; b. N.Y.C., June 10, 1918; s. Jacob and Rose (Lipionski) R.; m. Mary Terry, Sept. 4, 1941; 1 son, Terry Leon. BA, U. Ala., 1939, MS, 1941; PhD, Pa. State U., 1944; DSc (hon.), U. N.Mex., 1979, U. Colo., 1987. Instr. physics U. Ala., 1940-41, Pa. State U., 1943-44; mem. staff Los Alamos Sci. Lab., 1944-90, group leader nuclear plate lab., 1949-65, alt. div. leader exptl. physics div., 1962-65, dir. meson physics facility, 1965-85, div. leader medium energy physics div., 1965-86, sr. lab. fellow, 1985-90, sr. fellow emeritus, 1990—; Sesquicentennial hon. prof. U. Ala., 1981. Mem. panel on future of nuclear sci., chmn. subpanel on accelerators NRC of NAS, 1976, mem. panel on instnl. arrangements for orbiting space telescope, 1976; mem. U.S.A.-USSR Coordinating Com. on Fundamental Properties of Matter, 1971-90. Author papers in nuclear sci. and applications of particle accelerators.; bd. editors: Applications of Nuclear Physics; co-editor Climate Change and Energy Policy, 1992. Mem. Los Alamos Town Planning Bd., 1962-64; mem. Gov.'s Com. on Tech. Excellence in N.Mex.; mem. N.Mex. Cancer Control Bd., 1976-80, v.p., 1979-81; co-chmn. Los Alamos Vols. for Stevenson, 1956; Dem. candidate for county commr., 1962; bd. dirs. Los Alamos Med. Ctr., 1977-83, chmn., 1983; bd. govs. Tel Aviv U., 1986; bd. dirs. Sombillo Nursing and Rehab. Facility, 2004. Recipient E.O. Lawrence award AEC, 1963, Golden Plate award Am. Acad. Achievement, 1964, N.Mex. Disting. Pub. Svc. award, 1978; named Citizen of Yr., N.Mex. Realtors Assn., 1973; Guggenheim fellow, 1959-60; alumni fellow Pa. State U., 1978; Louis Rosen prize established in his honor by bd. dirs. Meson Facility Users Group, 1984; Louis Rosen Auditorium dedicated, 1995; recipient Los Alamos Nat. Lab. medal, 2002. Fellow AAAS (coun. 1989), Am. Phys. Soc. (coun. 1975-78, chmn. panel on pub. affairs 1980, div. nuclear physics 1985, mem. subcom. on internat. sci. affairs 1988). Home: 1170 41st St Los Alamos NM 87544-1913 Office: Los Alamos Sci Lab PO Box 1663 Los Alamos NM 87544-0600 *I have come to believe that only after one has learned to manage and set worthy goals for himself should he attempt to do so for others.*

ROSEN, MARCY B. music educator; b. Phoenix, Dec. 31, 1956; d. Gerald J and Anne R Rosen. MusB, Curtis Inst. of Music, 1972—77. Prof. of cello U. of Del., Newark, 1989—98; blodgett artist in residence Harvard U., Cambridge, Mass., 1992—2002; vis. assoc. prof. of cello Eastman Sch. of Music, Rochester, NY, 1996—97; prof. of cello NC Sch. the Arts, Winston-Salem, 1998—2004, Mannes Coll. of Music, N.Y.C, 1999—; vis. prof. of cello New Eng. Conservatory, Boston, 2000—01; prof. of cello Queens Coll. Aaron Copland Sch. Music, 2003—. Co-artistic dir. Ea. Shore Chamber Music Festival, Easton, Md., 1986—. Musician (cellist): Mendelssohn String Quartet, 1979—. Bd. mem. Violoncello Soc., N.Y.C, 1990. Recipient Prize Winner, Young Concert Artists, 1981, Young Artist of the Yr., Musical Am., 1981, Prize Winner, Young Concert Artists, 1986, Mischa Schneider Meml. award, Walter W. Naumburg Found., 1986.

ROSEN, MARVIN ABRAHAM, music educator; b. Englewood, N.J., May 9, 1953; s. Sidney J. and Clarice M. (Solomon) R.; m. Beata Regina Rzeszodko, Oct. 24, 1986. BA in Music Edn., Trenton State Coll., 1975; MusM in Musicology, Manhattan Sch. Music, 1977; EdM in Music Edn., Columbia U., 1983, EdD in Coll. Tchg., 1985. Piano instr. New Sch. for Music Study, Princeton, N.J., 1979-82; pvt. piano instr. Princeton, 1983—. Pianist Radio Boston WGBH/WNYC/WBAI/NY/WFLN PH, 1993-95; pianist-recital Moniuszko Soc., Warsaw, Poland, 1997; piano soloist for recordings Fred the Cat, Vision of Starry Night; lecture-recital Karlowicz Music Sch., Katowice, Poland, 1997, The Phillips Collection, Washington, 1998; author composer information in booklets; lectr. in field. Host weekly radio program Classical Discoveries WPRB 103.3 FM, Princeton, 1997. Mem. Kappa Delta Pi (Columbia U. chpt.), Princeton Music Club (pres. 1997—). Avocations: classic cd collecting, expert on classical recordings, baseball fan, 50's and 60's pop music. Office: Princeton Univ Store 36 University Pl Princeton NJ 08540-5116

ROSEN, MARVIN SHELBY, lawyer; b. Detroit, Aug. 8, 1947; s. Joseph P. and Rachel K. (Kaplan) R.; m. Sandra Mira Levy, Nov. 22, 1970; children: Joseph H., Bradley J. BA, Columbia U., 1970, JD, MBA, 1973; B in Hebrew Lit., Jewish Theol. Sem., N.Y.C., 1970. Bar: Mich. 1974, Fla. 1984. Assoc. Honigman Miller Schwartz and Cohn, Detroit, 1974-78, ptnr., 1978-84, mng. ptnr., 1984-97; shareholder Ruden, McClosky, Smith, Schuster & Russell, P.A., West Palm Beach, 1997—. Contbr. articles to profl. jours. Mem. bd. overseers List Coll., N.Y.C.; v.p. Pres. Country Club, 1995-99, Jewish Fedn. Palm Beach County, 1992-99; pres. Jewish Cmty. Day Sch., 1987-88;

founding chmn. Commn. for Jewish Edn., 1990-93; pres. Temple Emanu-El, Palm Beach, 2000-2004. Named one of Best Lawyers in Am., 1989—. Mem. Mich. State Bar (chmn. com. on mortgages, land contracts and related security devices real property sect. 1982-84), Detroit Bar Assn. (chmn. real property sect. 1982-83). Office: Ruden McClosky Smith Schuster & Russell PA 222 Lakeview Ave Ste 800 West Palm Beach FL 33401-6148 Fax: 561-514-3401. E-mail: marvin.rosen@ruden.com.

ROSEN, MATTHEW STEPHEN, botanist, consultant; b. NYC, Oct. 7, 1943; s. Norman and Lucille (Cass) R.; m. Deborah Louise Mackay, June 16, 1974 (div. Feb. 1983); children: Gabriel Mackay, Rebecca Mackay; m. Kay Eloise Williams, July 11, 1987. MFSc, Yale U., 1972; BS, Cornell U., 1967. Instr. ornamental horticulture SUNY-Farmingdale, 1968-69; landscape designer Manhattan Gardener, N.Y.C., 1969-70; instr. ornamental horticulture McHenry County Coll., Crystal Lake, Ill., 1972-74; coord. agrl. studies, asst. prof. biology, chemistry Mercer County Community Coll., West Windsor, N.J., 1974-79; adminstr. Des Moines Botanical Ctr., 1979-96, horticulture divsn. mgr., 1996—. Cons. dir. West Mich. Hort. Soc., 1993; nat. judge Communities in Bloom, 2001, 03-04, Winter Lights, 2002-04, Am. in Bloom, 2002; cons. in field. Contbr. articles to profl. jours. Com. chmn. United Way Cen. Iowa, 1982, divsn. chmn. 1983-86, 88-89, 91, 2000, group chmn. 1987, chmn. arts adv. com. 1985-86, pres. 1986, bd. dirs. Arts and Recreation Coun., 1985-86, com. chmn., 1992; career vocat. com. Des Moines Indsl. Sch. Dist., 1986, co-chmn., 1987, ptnrs. for progress com., 1988-90, sci. monitoring program, 1991-92; chmn. Two Rivers Festival, 1987-88; active Des Moines Sister City Program, Kofu, Japan, 1984, delegation, 1989, Naucalpan, Mexico, 1986, 87, Shijiazhuang, China, 1986, 90, 92, 95, 97; vice-chmn. Greater Des Moines Sister City Commn., 2004; edn. com. Am. Assn. Botanical Gardens & Arboretum, membership com., conservation com., bd. dirs., 1997—. Mem. Am. Assn. Botanical Gardens and Arboreta (edn. com.), Greater Des Moines C. of C. (team leader 1984—, chmn. new mem. sales, chmn. 8 O'clock new, Pres. Cabinet award 1983-85, bd. dirs., exec. com. 1995—, Achievement award C. of C. Fedn. 1986, exec. com. 1995-97), East Des Moines C. of C. (bd. dirs. 1992—, v.p., sec. 1993—, pres.-elect 1994, pres. 1995-96, sister cities commn. 1994, china chair 1995—, treas. 1995—, vice chair 2003,04), Greater Des Moines Conv. and Visitors Bur. (chmn. new mem. sales com. 1988-89), Iowa Advt. Rev. Coun., Affiliate Pres.'s Coun. of Chambers (chair 1995, 97), bd. dirs. DM Gen. Hosp., 1994-97, Bd. Coun. Internat. Trade, Latinos Unidos (bd. dirs. 1996-97), Rotary, Phi Kappa Phi, Pi Alpha Xi. Democrat. Jewish. Avocations: photography, reading, model trains, collecting old books, writing. Home: 1042 22nd St West Des Moines IA 50265-2219 Office: Park and Recreation Dept 3226 University Ave Des Moines IA 50317 Office Phone: 515-323-8901. Business E-Mail: msrosen@dmgov.org.

ROSEN, MEYER ROBERT, chemical engineer; b. Bklyn., Mar. 9, 1943; s. Philip and Jeanne (Rosenzweig) R.; children: Carrie, David; m. Selma Schwartz Mirman. BS, Poly. Inst. Bklyn., 1964, MS, 1966. Diplomate, Am. Bd. Forensic Engring. and Tech., cert. forensic examiner, profl. chemist, profl. chem. engr.; fire and explosion investigator Nat. Cert. Bd., Nat. Assn. Fire Investigators. Rsch. engr. Union Carbide Corp., Tonawanda, N.Y., 1966-73, project scientist, 1973-79, devel. scientist Tarrytown and Boundbrook, N.J., 1979-92; dir. chemistry and fire investigation Inter-City Testing and Cons. Corp., Mineola, NY, 1993—; pres. Interactive Cons. Inc., 1993—. Cons. Brookfield Engring. Labs., Stoughton, Mass., 1979-81; cons. to chem. industry; course dir. Ctr. for Profl. Advancement, East Brunswick, N.J., 1994; adj. prof. chemistry Westchester C.C., 1970-84; exec. advisor Am. Bd. Forensic Engring. and Tech.; spkr. in field; forensic litigation expert in field, Vaaler Awards Judge Chemical Processing Mag., 2003. Co-author: Rheology Modifier Handbook: Practical Use & Application, 2000; contbr. articles to profl. jours. Fellow Am. Coll. Forensic Examiners, Royal Soc. Chemistry London (chartered chemist), Am. Inst. Chemists (dir., exec. bd. dirs.), Am. Coll. Forensic Examiners; mem. ASTM (mem. various subcoms.), Am. Inst. of Chem. Engrs., Am. Chem. Soc. (divsn. colloid and surface chemistry, mem. noise com., organizer, session leader nat. mtgs., 2002—), Am. Indsl. Hygiene Assn. (cons. spl. interest group), Am. Soc. Safety Engrs. (v.p.), Assn. Cons. Chemists and Chem. Engrs., Am. Assn. Colorists and Textile Chemists, Am. Med. Writers Assn., Nat. Assn. Sci. Writers, Soc. de Chimie Industrielle (Am. sect.), Nat. Fire Protection Assn., Soc. Indsl. Chemistry (Am. sect.), Am. Assn. Acupuncture and Oriental Medicine, Acupuncture Soc. Pa., Nat. Dental Acupuncture Soc. (exec. bd.), Nat. Alliance of Acupuncture and Oriental Medicine (bd. cert. in pain mgmt.), Nat. Hearing Conservation Assn. Achievements include 21 patents for process for fire fighting foams, antifoams; flocculation of phosphatic slimes, high molecular weight water soluble polymers and flocculating method, process for producing polymer water-in-oil emulsion, process for agglomerating ore concentrate utilizing clay and dispersions of polymer binders or dry powder binders, removal of residual ethylene oxide from poly(ethylene oxide); development of treatment of previously incurable ear disorder, seminar leader in Reflex-Correspondence Training. Publications include Polyox R Water Soluble Resin Worldwide Technical Literature; Rheology of Non-Newtonian Fluids; Energy Medicine; Auriculotherapy; Korean Hand Therapy. Office: Interactive Cons Inc PO Box 66 East Norwich NY 11732-0066 Fax: 516-922-3830. Office Phone: 516-922-2167. Business E-Mail: meyer.rosen@chemicalconsult.com.

ROSEN, MICHAEL HOWARD, real estate executive; b. N.Y.C., May 22, 1943; s. Irving Edward and Lilyan Ruth (Ruttenberg) R.; children: Daniel Matthew, Lenise Gayle. AB, Tufts U., 1965. Lic. real estate broker, N.Y., Md. Exec. v.p., dir. Rosen Orgn., Inc., N.Y.C., 1971-75; v.p. apt. ops. Monumental Properties, Inc. & Monumental Properties Trust, Balt., 1975-79; exec. v.p. Town and Country Mgmt. Corp., Balt., 1979-93; exec. v.p., chief oper. officer Town & Country Trust, Balt., 1993—. Commr. Wellwood Little League Baseball and Pikesville Basketball, 1981-82, Blue Devil Umpire Assn., 1982—, Mason Dixon Umpire Assn., 1989-99, pres., 1998-99; commr. Chesapeake Basin Collegiate Umpire Assn., 1996—, pres., 2000—; commr. W.Va. Inercollegiate Athletic Conf., 1997—, Mason Dixon Colligiate Umpire Assn., 1990—, pres., 2000; divsn. chmn. maj. firms divsn. United Way of Ctrl. Md., 1983-86; chmn. ctrl. mid. team, 1987—; bd. dirs. Cystic Fibrosis Found., 1983-88, Essex C.C. Found., 1990-94, Waxter Ctr. Sr. Citizens Found., 1989-94, Nat. Multi Housing Coun., 1994—, Md. Multi Housing Assn., 1997—; chmn. Life Line Ministries, Md., 1988-92; bd. dirs. Bapt. Family & children's Svcs., 1999—. Mem. Nat. Apt. Assn., Greater Balt. Bd. Realtors. Office: Town & Country Trust 100 S Charles St Ste 1700 Baltimore MD 21201-2777

ROSEN, MICHEL, retired prosthodontist; b. Mulhouse, France, Jan. 25, 1936; came to U.S., 1970; s. Jean-James and Suzanne (Mulstein) R.; m. Naomi Schultz, May 20, 1965; 1 child, Robert. DDS, U. Louis Pasteur, Stasbourg, France, 1962; MSc in Dentistry, Boston U., 1973, DSc in Biology, 1974. Lic. dentist, Mass. Hosp. prin. French Air Force, Dakar, Senegal, 1963—64; pvt. practice Belfort and Antibes, France, 1964—70, various, Mass., 1974—91, 1991—92; ret., 1992; consul gen. Senegal, West Africa, Boston, 1994—2004. Asst. clin. prof., asst. dir. overseas affairs Boston U., 1971-74; asst. clin. prof. Tufts U., Boston, 1980-81; instr. Harvard U., Boston, 1990-91; internat. cons. West Africa. Contbr. articles to profl. jours. Lt. French Air Force, 1985-94; maj. Mass. Mil. Res. Recipient Gold medal City of Nice, France, 1981, Bronze Eagle award City of Nice, France, 1982, Officier de l'ordre du merite award Rep. of Senegal, 1998, Comdr. de l'ordre du Lion Senegal, 2000. Mem. Assn. Mil. Surgeons of U.S., Rabboni Lodge AF and AM, Nat. Sojourners, Assn. of First Corps. of Cadets, Ancient and Hon. Artillery Co. Avocations: diplomacy, travel, reading. Home and Office: 630 Bridgeway Ln Naples FL 34108-2777 Fax: 239-596-5925. E-mail: naomi.michel@comcast.net.

ROSEN, MOISHE, religious organization founder; b. Kansas City, Mo., Apr. 12, 1932; s. Ben and Rose (Baker) R.; m. Ceil Starr, Aug. 18, 1950; children: Lyn Rosen Bond, Ruth. Diploma, Northeastern Bible Coll., 1957; DD, Western Conservative Bapt. Sem., 1986. Ordained to ministry Bapt. Ch., 1957. Missionary Am. Bd. Missions to the Jews, N.Y.C., 1956, minister in charge Beth Sar Shalom Los Angeles, 1957-67, dir. recruiting and tng. N.Y.C., 1967-70; leader Jews for Jesus Movement, San Francisco, 1970-73, exec. dir., 1973-96, founder, 1973—. Speaker in field. Author: Saying of Chairman Moishe, 1972, Jews for Jesus, 1974, Share the New Life with a Jew, 1976, Christ in the Passover, 1977, Y'shua, The Jewish Way to Say Jesus, 1982, Overture to Armageddon, 1991, The Universe is Broken: Who on Earth Can Fix It?, 1991, Demystifying Personal Evangelism, 1992, Witnessing to Jews, 1998. Trustee Western Conservative Bapt. Sem., Portland, Oreg., 1979-85, 86-91, Bibl. Internat. Coun. on Bibl. Inerrancy, Oakland, Calif., 1979-89; bd. dirs. Christian Advs. Serving Evangelism, 1987-91. Named Hero of the Faith, Conservative Bapt. Assn. Am., 1997. Office: Jews for Jesus 90 Miraloma Dr San Francisco CA 94127-1641 Office Phone: 415-661-2263. E-mail: MityMo@aol.com.

ROSEN, MYOR, harpist, educator; b. N.Y.C., May 28, 1917; s. Caesar and Rose (Seidenberg) R.; m. Esther Rosen, May 25, 1941; children: Linda, David. Diploma, Juilliard Sch. Music, 1940. Faculty Juilliard Sch. Music, 1947-69. Prin. harpist, Mexico Symphony Orch., 1941-42, Indpls. Symphony Orch., 1941-42, Mpls. Symphony Orch., 1943-44, staff harpist, CBS, Columbia Records and free lanced, 1945-60, prin. harpist, N.Y. Philharm., 1960-87; Composer incidental music for; NBC series Arts and the Gods, 1946, CBS Camera Three, 1947, Solomon, The King, 1948. Served with U.S. Army, 1945. Mem. Am. Fedn. Musicians, Bohemians. Personal E-mail: roymnesor@juno.com. *Having been the fortunate recipient of a 7-year scholarship through the New York Philharmonic Symphony Society and the Juilliard School of Music when I began my career as a harpist, I can think of no greater honor than my privilege in having been accepted as principal harpist with the same organization which trained me. I now bend my efforts to train future harpists to excel in like manner. In my opinion, the most important function of a teacher is to teach his students how to teach themselves; self-development.*

ROSEN, NATHANIEL KENT, cellist; b. Altadena, Calif., June 9, 1948; s. David Leon and Frances Jean (Kaufman) R.; m. Jennifer Langham, Aug. 27, 1976 (div. 1986); m. Margo Shohl, May 21, 1989 (div. 2001); children: Samuel Gregory, Stella Rosalie. Student, Pasadena (Calif.) City Coll., 1965-67; Mus.B., U. So. Calif., 1971. Teaching asst. U. So. Calif., 1968-75, mem. faculty 7th ann. Gregor Piatigorsky Seminar Sch. Music, 1984; asst. prof. Calif. State U. at Northridge, 1970-76; mem. faculty Manhattan Sch. Music, N.Y.C., 1981—, U. Ill., Urbana, 1988-94; artist-in-residence So. Meth. U., Dallas, 2002—. Prin. cellist, Los Angeles Chamber Orch., 1970-76, Pitts. Symphony, 1977-79, concert cellist worldwide; recordings include Orientale: Romantic Music for the Cello. Recipient 1st prize Naumburg Competition, 1977, 1st prize Moscow Tchaikovsky Competition, 1978; Ford Found. grantee, 1970-71; Rockefeller Found. grantee, 1973-74 Mem. Violoncello Soc. N.Y., Century Assn. N.Y. Office: John Gingrich Mgmt Inc PO Box 1515 New York NY 10023-9462 also: North Star Recordings 95 Hathaway St Providence RI 02907-3760

ROSEN, PAUL PETER, pathologist; b. Bklyn., Aug. 16, 1938; s. George and Beate (Caspari) R.; m. Mary Sue, Aug. 7, 1994; children: Susan Deborah, Jonathan Daniel. BS, Swarthmore Coll., 1960; MD, Columbia U., 1964. Asst. attending pathologist Meml. Hosp., N.Y.C., 1970-73; asst. prof. pathology Cornell U. Med. Sch., N.Y.C., 1972-78; assoc. attending pathologist Meml. Hosp., N.Y.C., 1973-78, attending pathologist, 1978-98; assoc. prof. pathology Cornell U. Med. Sch., N.Y.C., 1978-84, prof. pathology, 1984—; assoc. mem. Sloan Kettering Inst., N.Y.C., 1980-84; mem. tenure title Meml. Sloan-Kettering Cancer Ctr., N.Y.C., 1984-98; sr. cons. pathologist Dickstein Cancer Treatment Ctr., White Plains, N.Y., 1998-99; attending pathologist, chief of breast pathology N.Y. Presbyn. Hosp., N.Y.C., 1999—. Adj. prof. pathology N.Y. Med. Coll., Valhalla, N.Y., 1996-99. Author: Rosen's Breast Pathology, 1996, 2d edit., 2001, Breast Pathology: Diagnosis by Needle Core Biopsy, 1999; co-author: Tumors of the Mammary Gland, 1993; co-editor Pathology Annual, 1977-95, Revs. Pathology, 1996-98; contbr. over 290 articles to profl. jours. Mem. Internat. Acad. Pathology, Am. Soc. Clin. Pathologists, Soc. Surg. Pathologists, N.Y. Acad. Medicine, Am. Soc. Clin. Oncologists.

ROSEN, PETER, health facility administrator, emergency physician, educator; b. Bklyn., Aug. 3, 1935; s. Isadore Theodore and Jessie Olga (Solomon) R.; m. Ann Helen Rosen, May 16, 1959; children: Henry, Monte, Curt, Ted. BA, U. Chgo., 1955; MD, Washington U., St. Louis, 1960. Diplomate Am. Bd. Surgery, Nat. Bd. Med. Examiners, Am. Bd. Emergency Medicine; cert. Advanced Cardiac Life Support Instr., Advanced Trauma Life Support Provider. Intern U. Chgo. Hosps. & Clinics, 1960-61; resident Highland County Hosp., Oakland, Calif., 1961-65; assoc. prof. divsn. emergency medicine U. Chgo. Hosps. & Clinics, 1971-73, prof. divsn. emergency medicine, 1973-77; dir. divsn. emergency medicine Denver City Health & Hosps., 1977-86, 87-89; asst. dir. dept. emergency medicine U. Calif., San Diego Med. Ctr., 1989—, dir. edn. dept. emergency medicine, 1989—, dir. emergency medicine residency program, 1991-2000, dir. emeritus, 2000—. Attending physician Hot Springs Meml. Hosp., Thermopolis, Wyo., Worland (Wyo.) County Hosp., Basin-Graybull Hosp., Basin, Wyo., 1968-71, U. Chgo. Hosps. & Clinics, 1971-77; dir. emergency medicine residency program, divsn. emergency medicine U. Chgo. Hosps. & Clinics, 1971-77; emergency medicine med. advisor State of Colo., 1977-85; dir. emergency medicine residency program Denver Gen. Hosp., St. Anthony Hosp. Systems, St. Joseph Hosp., 1977-88; clin. prof. divsn. emergency medicine Oreg. Health Scis. U., Portland, 1978-89; prof. sect. emergency medicine, dept. surgery U. Colo. Health Scis. Ctr., 1984-89; dep. mgr. med. affairs Denver Dept. Health & Hosps., 1986-87; med. dir. life flight air med. svc. U. Calif., San Diego Med. Ctr., 1989-91; mem. hosp. staff U. Calif., San Diego Med. Ctr., Tri-City Med. Ctr., Oceanside, Calif., 1989—; base hosp. physician, adj. prof. medicine & surgery U. Calif., San Diego Med. Ctr., 1989—; chair med. ethics com., mem. ethics consult team U. Calif., San Diego Med. Ctr., 1990—, mem. recruitment and admissions com., 1992—; lectr. in field; cons. in field. Author: (with others) Case Reports in Emergency Medicine: 1974-76, 1977, Encyclopedia Brittannica, 1978, 85, Principles and Practice of Emergency Medicine, 1978, 86, Protocols for Prehospital Emergency Care, 1980, 84, Cardiopulmonary Resuscitation, 1982, An Atlas of Emergency Medicine Procedures, 1984, Critical Decisions in Trauma, 1984, Emergency Pediatrics, 1984, 86, 90, Controversies in Trauma Management, 1985, Standardized Nursing Care Plans for Emergency Department, 1986, Emergency Medicine: Concepts and Clinical Practice, 1988, 92, The Clinical Practice of Emergency Medicine, 1991, Essentials of Emergency Medicine, 1991, Current Practice of Emergency Medicine, 1991, Care of the Surgical Patient, 1991, Diagnostic Radiology in Emergency Medicine, 1992, Pediatric Emergency Care Systems: Planning and Management, 1992, The Airway: Emergency Management, 1992; contbg. editor, editor abstracts sect. Jour. Am. Coll. Emergency Physicians, Annals of Emergency Medicine, 1976-83; mem. editorial bd. Topics in Emergency Medicine, 1979-82, ER Reports, 1981-83; consulting editor Emergindex Microindex, 1980—; editor in chief Jour. Emergency Medicine, 1983—; contbr. articles to profl. jours. Capt. USMC, 1965-68, lt. col. Res. inactive. Recipient AMA award, 1970, Am. Hosp. Assn. award, 1973. Fellow Am. Coll. Surgeons, Am. Burn Assn., Am. Coll. Emergency Physicians (chmn. edn. com. 1977-79, bd. dirs. Colo. chpt. 1977-80, pres. Colo. chpt. 1981-82, N.C. chpt. award 1976, Outstanding Contbns. and Leadership in Emergency Medicine award 1977, Silver Tongue Debater award 1980, John. D. Mills Outstanding Contbn. to Emergency Medicine award 1984); mem. Am. Trauma Soc. (founding), Soc. Acad. Emergency Medicine (Leadership award 1990), Alpha Omega Alpha Honor Med. Soc. (grad.), Coun. Emergency Medicine Dirs. Office: U Calif 200 W Arbor Dr San Diego CA 92103-1911

ROSEN, RAYMOND, health facility executive; b. Louisville, Feb. 5, 1950; s. Sam and Olga Rosen; m. Deborah Joy Rubinow, June 25, 1972; children: Lisa, Jessica. BS, Pa. State U., 1972; MA, George Washington U., 1974. Adminstrv. resident York (Pa.) Hosp., 1973-74, asst. to pres., 1974-75, asst. adminstr.-adminstrn., 1975-77, asst. adminstr.-med. affairs, 1977-79, adminstr.-med. affairs, 1979-87, v.p. opers., 1987—. Pres. Young Adminstrs. Group Ctrl. Pa., 1980-82, Rabbit Transit, Inc., 1992—, vice chmn., 1989-92, chmn., 1992—; bd. dirs. Fedn. South Ctrl. Pa. Emergency Health Svcs., 1978-92, mem. adv. com., 1992-93, York County Emergency Health Svcs. Coun., 1978-92, Jewish Cmty. Ctr., 1986-91; divsn. chmn. United Way York County, 1988, York County Transp. Auth., 1995—. Fellow: Am. Coll. Healthcare Execs. (regent south ctrl. Pa. 1991—95); mem.: Hosp. Assn. Pa. (planning com. 1992—), Am. Hosp. Assn. Office: York Hosp 1001 S George St York PA 17403-3676

ROSEN, RICHARD LEWIS, lawyer, real estate developer; b. NYC, Mar. 6, 1943; s. Morris and Lorraine (Levy) R.; m. Doris Ellen Bloom, Aug. 28, 1983. BA, Cornell U., 1965; JD, N.Y. Law Sch., 1968; cert., NYU Real Estate Inst., 1980. Bar: N.Y. 1968, U.S. Dist. Ct. (so. and ea. dists.) N.Y. 1972; lic. real estate broker. Pvt. practice, N.Y.C., 1971-73; ptnr. Rosen, Wise, Felzen & Salomon, N.Y.C., 1973-79, Rosen & Felzen, N.Y.C., 1979-84, Rosen, Rudd, Kera, Graubard & Hollender, N.Y.C., 1985-88, Bell, Kalnick, Klee and Green, N.Y.C., 1989-90; shareholder Rosen, Einbinder & Dunn, P.C., N.Y.C., 1990—. Contbg. author: Franchising 101, The Complete Guide to Evaluating, Buying and Growing Your Franchise Business; author: Renewal of Your Franchise: Some Solutions, Franchise Times. Named Ea. States Lightweight Weightlifting Champion, 1968; N.Y. State Regents scholar. Mem. ABA (mem. Forum Com. on Franchising), Am. Assn. Franchises and Dealers (former chmn. legal steering com., chmn. fair franchising stds. com., chmn. alternate dispute resolution com., bd. dirs.), Franchise Lawyers Assn., Am. Franchise Assn., N.Y. State Bar Assn. (founding mem. franchise law com., chmn. mission statement com. of franchise law com.), Nat. Franchise Mediation Program (mem. steering com.), Assn. Bar City N.Y. (panel mem. com. on franchising, panel mem. com. on corp. law), Red Key Hon. Soc., Cornell U., Sphinx Head Hon. Soc., Cornell U., Spiked Shoe Soc., Cornell U., Ea. Intercollegiate Athletic Assn. (named Lightweight Football All Ea. Selection 1963, 64). Avocations: guitar, reading, coaching youth soccer and track, masters track competition. Home: 1 Old Jericho Tpke Jericho NY 11753-1205 Office: Rosen Einbinder & Dunn PC 641 Lexington Ave New York NY 10022-4503 Office Phone: 212-888-7717. Business E-Mail: rlr@redlawfirm.com

ROSEN, RICHARD S. lawyer; b. Charleston, S.C., Aug. 15, 1949; BA, Tulane U., 1971; JD, U. S.C., 1975. Bar: S.C. 1975, U.S. Dist. Ct. S.C. 1975, U.S. Ct. Appeals (4th cir.) 1993, U.S. Supreme Ct. 1993. Mem.: ABA, Am. Bd. Trial Advs., Assn. Trial Lawyers Am., S.C. Trial Lawyers Assn., S.C. Bar (bd. govs. 1991—94, Ho. of Dels. 1984, chmn. 1996, nominating com. 1986—89, continuing legal edn. com. 1995, law practice mgmt. com. 1995, sec. 1999, treas. 2000, pres.-elect 2001, pres. 2002), Charleston County Bar Assn. (exec. com. 1982—83), Soc. Wig and Robe, Charleston Lawyer's Club (pres. 1982). Office: Rosen Rosen & Hagood LLC PO Box 893 134 Meeting St Ste 200 Charleston SC 29402

ROSEN, ROBERT ARNOLD, management company executive, real estate investor; b. N.Y.C., June 19, 1936; s. Louis and Helen (Weiss) R.; m. Florence Cohen, Oct. 23, 1960; children: David S., Kenneth A., Mark A., Emily B. BBA, CUNY, 1957, MBA, 1960; postgrad. (Ford Found. scholar), NYU, 1961; grad., Indsl. Coll. Armed Forces, Air War Coll., 1960, U.S. Air Force U.; various courses, Naval Edn. and Tng. Command. Sales promotion mgr. Leipzig & Lippe, Inc., 1956-58; advt. and sales promotion mgr. Zenith Radio, 1957-62; chmn., pres., founder Am. Bus. Resources Corp., 1963-64; v.p., dir. Royal Bus. Funds Corp., 1964-68; chmn., CEO Rosen Assocs. Mgmt. Corp., Jericho, N.Y., 1983—. V.p. corp. finance div., dir. Brand Grumet & Siegel, Inc., 1969-70; pres. Brand Grumet & Siegel Equities, Inc., 1970; former pres., chief operating officer Bell TV, Inc., N.Y.C.; pres., former chmn. bd. Holmes Protection, Inc.; former chmn. bd., pres. Union Small Bus. Investment Co., 1968-77, Skyway-Laguardia Corp.; dir. past chmn. bd. Okuraya Davos Internat., Inc.; chmn. bd., pres., chief exec. officer, treas. Suburban Broadcasting Corp., 1970-80; chmn., pres. Affiliated Comms. Corp.; vice chmn., pres. Comm. Svcs. Corp.; pres. Wescom Corp.; pres. Androse Corp., 1983—; cons. Asian Devel. Bank, Albert Einstein Coll. Medicine, Nat. Housing Bank of Brazil, 1972-76; mem. U.S. Senatorial Bus. Adv. Bd.; lectr. Baruch Coll. Grad. Sch. Bus., CUNY, 1960-63; adj. prof. Fairleigh Dickinson U. Grad. Sch. Bus., 1968-75; retired pres., retired dean Internat. Inst. Real Estate Studies Ltd.; dir. Ctr. for Real Estate Studies, Adelphi U.; adj. prof. mgmt. NYU; mem. faculty New Sch. for Social Research; guest lectr., mem. bd. advs. Fordham U.; prin. owner, developer shopping ctrs., comml. real estate throughout, U.S.; chmn. UN Trade and Tech. Adv. Mission to Israel, 1972, Econ. Devel. Com./UJA Fedn.; active Nat. Builder Mktg. Bd.; owner, inestor N.Y. Stock Exch. Chmn. Borough Pres.'s of Manhattan Com. on Narcotics Addiction Control, 1970—75; N.Y. mem. adv. coun. USAF Acad.; mem. editl. policy com. Internat. Property Investment Jour. of Hofstra U. Law Sch.; mem. Navy Recruiting Dist., N.Y. Assistance Coun.; chmn. Navy Task Force to Study Navy Budgeting, Acquisition and Procurement; mem. Pres.'s Pvt. Sector Survey on Cost Control (Grace Commn.), N.Y. State Gov.'s Bus. Adv. Coun.; trustee Zachary and Elizabeth M. Fisher Found., Fisher House Found., Inc., North Shore L.I.J. Health Sys.; chmn. econ. devel. com., former bd. dirs. United Jewish Appeal/Fedn.; former mem. corp. adv. bd. Queens Coll.; mem. adv. bd. Roundabout Theatre; bd. dirs. The Film Forum, 1979—86, N.Y.C. Housing Partnership, Housing Partnership Devel. Corp.; bd. dirs., trustee Intrepid, Sea Air Space Mus.; bd. dirs. Fed. Law Enforcement Found. With USAFR and USNR, 1959—90, ret. as capt. USNR, 1990, rear adm. upper half N.Y. Naval Militia, comdr. Divsn. Mil. and Naval Affairs, naval aide to the Gov. Mem. Soc. Internat. Devel., Internat. Inst. Valuers (SCV designation), NRA, Nat. Def. Exec. Res., Chief Execs. Orgn., Nat. lPres.'s Orgn., Young Pres.'s Orgn. (past chmn. Met. chpt.), Real Estate Bd. N.Y., Assn. for Better N.Y., Internat. Coun. Shopping Ctrs., Property Cons. Soc., Nat. Assn. Rev. Appraisers (cert. rev. appraiser), Air Force Assn., Res. Officers Assn., Nat. Guard Assn. (life), Naval Res. Assn. (life), U.S. Naval Inst., Navy League U.S., Naval War Coll. Found. (assoc.), Am. Legion, Naval Militia Assn. (chmn.), Jewish War Vets. U.S., Wine Inst. Group Stony Brook State U. N.Y., Militia Assn. N.Y., U.S. Navy Pub. Affairs Assn., Alpha Delta Sigma, Phi Sigma Delta, Sigma Alpha. Home: 60 Apple Lake Ln PO Box 8 Rhinebeck NY 12572 Office: Rosen Associates Mgmnt Corp 33 South Service Rd Jericho NY 11753-1006 Office Phone: 516-333-2000. E-mail: rar@rosenmgmt.com.

ROSEN, ROBERT THOMAS, analytical and food chemist; b. Concord, N.H., Nov. 5, 1941; s. Maurice J. and Miriam M. (Miller) R.; m. Sharon Lynne Beres, Apr. 23, 1972. BA (cum laude), Nasson Coll.; PhD, Rutgers U. Sr. rsch. scientist Chem. Rsch. and Devel. Ctr., FMC Corp., Princeton, N.J., 1966-84; program dir. analytical support facilities, 1984—; assoc. dir. Ctr. for Advanced Food Technology, Rutgers U., New Brunswick, N.J., 1993—; rsch. prof. food sci. Rutgers U., New Brunswick, 2000—. Contbr. articles and book reviews to profl. jours. Recipient award for best oustanding rsch., Cook Coll./Rutgers U., 2001. Fellow Am. Inst. Chemists, Am. Chem. Soc. (agrl. and food chemistry divsn.); mem. Inst. Food Technologists, Phi Lambda Upsilon (hon.). Achievements include research in gas and liquid chromatography of organic compounds in fruits and vegetables, determination of phytochemicals in food, natural products and the environment by liquid chromatography and mass spectrometry. Home: 347 Harrier Dr Monroe Township NJ 08831-5566 Office: Rutgers U Cook Coll Ctr for Advanced Food Tech New Brunswick NJ 08901 E-mail: Rosen@aesop.rutgers.edu.

ROSEN, ROBERTA, philosophy educator; b. Madawaska, Maine, Aug. 9, 1935; d. Bernard and Dolores (Bourgoin) Dionee; m. Frank Rosen, June 8, 1963; children: Ruth, Rachael, David, Sarah. BA, Gov. State U., University Park, Ill., 1975, MA, 1976; PhD, Walden U., 1977; postdoctoral, K.A.M.I.I. Temple. Free-lance writer, Chgo.; dir. religious edn. ASFU, Chgo.; minister All Souls 1st Universalist Soc., Chgo., 1975—95; prof. philosophy Prairie State Coll., Chicago Heights, Ill., 1976—89. Leader seminars on prevention of child abuse, 1976-1999. Author: (novel) Call Her Dolores, (children's) Johnny Linny's Nightmare; contbr. articles to religious jours. Bd. trustees Gov. State U., Unitarian-Universalist Women's Fedn. Recipient Humanitarian award, Humane Soc. award; named Best Tchr. Mem. Unitarian-Universalist Women's Assn. (life). Address: 2444 Madison Rd Apt 1004 Cincinnati OH 45208-1269

ROSEN, SANFORD JAY, lawyer; b. N.Y.C., Dec. 19, 1937; s. Alexander Charles and Viola S. (Grad) R.; m. Catherine Picard, June 22, 1958; children: Caren E. Andrews, R. Durelle Schacter, Ian D., Melissa S. AB, Cornell U., 1959; LLB, Yale U., 1962. Bar: Conn. 1962, Calif. 1974, U.S. Supreme Ct. 1966. Law clk. to Hon. Simon E. Sobeloff U.S. Ct. Appeals, Balt., 1962-63; prof. sch. law U. Md., Balt., 1963-71; assoc. dir. Coun. on Legal Edn.

Opportunity, Atlanta, 1969-70; vis. prof. law U. Tex., Austin, 1970-71; asst. legal dir. Nat. ACLU, N.Y.C., 1971-73; legal dir. Mex.-Am. Legal Def. Fund, San Francisco, 1973-75; ptnr. Rosen, Remcho & Henderson, San Francisco, 1976-80, Rosen & Remcho, San Francisco, 1980-82; prin. Law Offices of Sanford Jay Rosen, San Francisco, 1982-86; sr. ptnr. Rosen & Phillips, San Francisco, 1986-89; prin. Rosen & Assocs., San Francisco, 1990; sr. ptnr. Rosen, Bien & Asaro, San Francisco, 1991—. Mem. Balt. Cmty. Rels. Commn., 1966-69; mem. com. Patuxent Instn., Md., 1967-69; ad hoc adminstrv. law judge Calif. Agrl. Labor Rels. Bd., San Francisco, 1975-80; interim monitor U.S. Dist. Ct. for no. dist. Calif., San Francisco, 1989, early neutral evaluator, 1987—, mediator, 1993—; judge pro tem San Francisco Superior Ct., 1991—; perm. atty. del. Jud. Conf. U.S. Ct. Appeal for 4th Cir.; atty. del. Jud. Conf. U.S. Ct. Appeals 9th cir., 1996-98. Contbr. articles to profl. jours. Mem. Com. on Adminstrn. of Criminal Justice, Balt., 1968; mem. adv. com. HEW, Washington, 1974-75. Mem. ABA, Assn. Trial Lawyers Am. (chair civil rights sect. 1993-94), Calif. Bar Assn., Bar Assn. San Francisco. Avocations: reading, travel, movies. Office: Rosen Bien & Asaro 155 Montgomery St Fl 8 San Francisco CA 94104-4113 Business E-Mail: srosen@rbalaw.com.

ROSEN, SAUL WOOLF, research scientist, health facility administrator; b. Boston, July 29, 1928; s. David Tsvi and Ida (Hannah) Sadwin; m. Mary Jean Westfall, June 14, 1959 (div. 1986); children: Craig, Laura, David; m. Deborah Susan Kieffer, Nov. 3, 1989. BA cum laude, Harvard U., 1947, MD, 1956; PhD, Northwestern U., 1955. Intern U. Calif. Med. Ctr., San Francisco, 1956-57, resident, 1957-58, sr. res., 1960-61; clin. assoc. Nat. Inst. Arthritis and Metabolic Diseases, Bethesda, Md., 1958-60, sr. investigator NIH, 1961-84; dep. dir. Clin. Ctr. NIH, Bethesda, Md., 1984-90, acting dir. clin. ctr., 1990-94. Vis. scientist Nat. Inst. Med. Rsch., London, 1975-76. Contbr. articles to profl. jours. U.S. Rubber Co. fellow, Northwestern U., 1950. Fellow ACP; mem. Assn. Am. Physicians, Endocrine Soc. Avocations: opera, lexicography, weightlifting. Home: 11801 Rockville Pike Apt 1204 Rockville MD 20852-2728 E-mail: saulrosen@earthlink.net.

ROSEN, SCOTT ALAN, corporate financial executive, financial analyst; b. Randolf Township, N.J., Jan. 17, 1968; s. George Edward Rosen and Lila Tondow; m. Deborah Victoria Rokhsar, Oct. 26, 2003. BS in Econs., Tex. A&M U., 1989. Equity analyst Hoare Govett Asia, Hong Kong, 1989—91; chief rep. Hoare Govett Asia - South Korea, Seoul, 1991—91, Hoare Govett Asia - India, Bombay, 1992—92; dir. rsch. Marlin Ptnrs., Hong Kong, 1993—95; pres., founder Bondtech Internat., Hong Kong, 1995—96; mng. dir. I/B/E/S Internat., Hong Kong, 1996—97; sr. v.p. I/B/E/S Internat. London, 1997—98; dir. rsch. I/B/E/S Internat., N.Y.C., 1999—2000; sr. v.p. Thomson Fin., N.Y.C., 2000—. Exec. v.p. Internet Soc. N.Y., N.Y.C., 1999—2001. Fellow, Jordan Inst., 1988. Achievements include development of Trapeze Research Distribution Network. Avocations: travel, photography, scuba diving, Kendo, Iaido. Office: Thomson Financial 195 Broadway New York NY 10007

ROSEN, STANLEY HOWARD, humanities educator; b. Warren, Ohio, July 29, 1929; s. Nathan A. and Celia (Narotsky) R.; m. Francoise Harlepp, Sept. 5, 1955; children: Nicholas David, Paul Mark, Valerie. BA, U. Chgo., 1949, PhD, 1955; postgrad., Am. Sch. Classical Studies, Athens, Greece, 1955-56; D honoris causa, New U. Lisbon, 1997. Mem. faculty Pa. State U., 1956-94, prof. philosophy, 1966-94; Fulbright research prof. U. Paris, 1960-61; research fellow Humanities Research Inst., U. Wis., 1963-64; Inst. Arts and Humanities research sr. fellow Pa. State U., 1972—, Evan Pugh prof. philosophy, 1985-94; Bowne prof. philosophy Boston U., 1994—, univ. prof., 2000—. Vis. prof. U. Calif., San Diego, 1978, U. Nice, 1981, Scuola Superiore Pisa, 1989; vis. lectr. U. Barcelona, Spain, 1992; Priestly lectr. U. Toronto, 1997; Cardinal Mercier lectr. Louvain U., 1998; Gilson lectr. Institut Catholique, Paris, 2003. Author: Plato's Symposium, 1968, Nihilism, 1969, G.W.F. Hegel, 1974, The Limits of Analysis, 1980, Plato's Sophist: The Drama of Original and Image, 1983, Hermeneutics as Politics, 1987, The Quarrel Between Philosophy and Poetry, 1988, The Ancients and the Moderns, 1989, The Question of Being, 1993, Plato's Statesman: The Web of Politics, 1995, The Mask of Enlightenment, 1995, Metaphysics in Ordinary Language, 1999; editor: The Examined Life: A Treasury of Western Philosophy, 2000, The Elusiveness of the Ordinary, 2002. Research grantee Am. Philos. Soc., 1961; Research grantee Earhart Found., 1971, 73, 81, 2000. Mem. Metaphys. Soc. Am (pres. 1990-91). Home: 117 Brook St Wellesley MA 02482-6632 Office: 745 Commonwealth Ave Boston MA 02215-1401 E-mail: srosen@bu.edu.

ROSEN, STEVEN O. lawyer; b. NYC, Jan. 11, 1949; s. Albert I. and Yvette (Sterenbuch) R.; m. Martha M., July 10, 1983; 1 child, Melissa L. BS Aerospace Engring., SUNY, 1970; MS System and Control Engring., Case Western Reserve, 1975; JD, Lewis & Clark Coll., 1977. Bar: Ill. 1977, Oreg. 1978. Assoc. Lord, Bissell & Brook, Chgo., 1977-79, Miller, Nash, Wiener, Hager & Carlsen, Portland, Oreg., 1979-84, ptnr., 1984-97; pvt. practice Rosen Law Firm, Portland and Salem, Oreg., 1997—. Disting. adj. prof. Lewis & Clark Law Sch., 1986. Mem. ABA (dir. divsns. sect. of litigation 1996-97, chmn. aviation litigation com. 1990-93), Am. Bd. Trial Advocates, Oreg. State Bar Assn. (exec. com. aviation sect. 1984-2001, chmn. 1994-95). Avocations: skiing, bicycling. Address: The Rosen Law Firm 620 SW Main St Ste 702 Portland OR 97205-3030 Office Phone: 503-525-2525. E-mail: rosen@rosenlawfirm.com.

ROSEN, STEVEN TERRY, oncologist, hematologist; b. Bklyn., Feb. 18, 1952; married, 1976; 4 children. MB, Northwestern U., 1972, MD, 1976. Genevieve Teuton prof., med. sch. Northwestern U., 1989—, dir. cancer ctr., 1989—. Dir. clin. programs Northwestern Meml. Hosp., 1989—. Editor-in-chief Jour. Northwestern U. Cancer Center, 1989—, Contemporary Oncology, 1990-95, Cancer Treatment and Rsch., 1995—, In Touch, 1998—. Mem. AAAS, ACP, AMA, Am. Soc. Hematology, Am. Soc. Clin. Oncology, Ctrl. Soc. Clin. Rsch. Achievements include research in hematologic malignancies, lung cancer, breast cancer, biologic and hormonal therapies. Office: Northwestern U Olson Pavilion Rm 8250 303 E Chicago Ave Chicago IL 60611-3093 Office Phone: 312-908-5250. E-mail: s.rosen@northwestern.edu.

ROSEN, THEODORE HOWARD, psychologist, consultant; b. Balt., Aug. 25, 1947; s. Jerome and Mary (Schwartz) R.; m. Linda Peller, Oct. 21, 1973; children: Sara Michelle, Julia Diane. BA, George Washington U., 1969, PhD, 1984; MA, Temple U., 1971. Diplomate Am. Bd. Forensic Examiners. Cons. Human Resources Rsch. Orgn., Alexandria, Va., 1972—76; psychologist U.S. Postal Svc., Washington, 1977—78; pers. psychologist U.S. Office of Personnel Mgmt., Washington, 1978—84; cons. CACI Internat., Arlington, Va., 1984—85; psychologist Bethesda, Md., 1984—; cons. Price Waterhouse, Washington, 1993—95; adj. prof. U. Md., 1983—97, George Washington U., 1983—97; asst. prof. mgmt. sci. George Washington U. Sch. Bus., 1997—; dir. orgnl. behavior and devel. program, 2002—. Presenter profl. orgns. in field. Assoc. editor, reviewer, contbr. articles to profl. jours. Trustee Green Acres Sch., Rockville, Md., 1989-95; pres. Sonoma Citizens Assocs., Bethesda, Md., 1991-93. Mem.: APA, Acad. Mgmt., Soc. Indsl./Organizational Psychology, N.E. Ednl. Rsch. Assn., Met. Baseball Umpires Assn. Avocations: photography, golf, instrumental music, sports officiating. Office Phone: 202-994-1562.

ROSEN, THOMAS J. food and agricultural products executive; 3 children. CEO Rosen's Diversified, Fairmont, Minn., 1986—. Bd. dirs. Morningside Coll., Danish Immigrants Coun. Minn. Mem. Minn. Agro-Growth Coun. Office: Rosen's Diversified 1120 Lake Ave Fairmont MN 56031-1939

ROSEN, WENDY WORKMAN, arts management and publishing executive; b. Miami, Sept. 17, 1954; d. Robert L. and Mildred E. (Duck) Workman; m. Steven David Rosen, June 22, 1972, children: Rebecca, Jeffrey. AS, Santa Fe Coll., 1974; BS, U. Fla., 1976. Cert. exhbn. mgr. Advt. exec. Balt. News Am., 1978-80, Balt. Mag, 1980-82; pres. The Rosen Group, Inc., Balt., 1982—. Cons. Times Pub. Group, Balt., 1982; gen. ptnr. Mill Ctr. Artists Studios, Balt.; pres. Am. Craft Showroom; founder The Buyers Markets of American Crafts, founder Craft Bus. Inst. Author: Crafting as a Business, Cash For Your Crafts; pub.: Niche mag., Am. Style mag., Market Insider. Bd. mem. Craft Emergency Relief Fund. Mem. Natl. Assn. Exposition Mgrs., Glass Art Soc. Democrat. Jewish. Avocation: gardening. Office: The Rosen Agy 3000 Chestnut Ave Ste 300 Baltimore MD 21211-2769

ROSEN, WILLIAM WARREN, lawyer; b. New Orleans, July 22, 1936; s. Warren Leucht and Erma (Stich) R.; m. Eddy Kahn, Nov. 26, 1965; children: Elizabeth K., Victoria A. BA, Tulane U., 1958, JD, 1964. Bar: La. 1964, U.S. Dist. Ct. (ea. dist.) La. 1965, U.S. Ct. Appeals (5th cir.) 1965, U.S. Supreme Ct. 1984, U.S. Dist. Ct. (mid. dist.) La. 1985, Colo. 1989. Assoc. Dodge & Friend, New Orleans, 1965-68, Law Office of J.R. Martzell, New Orleans, 1968-70; pvt. practice New Orleans, 1970-79, 89-90; ptnr. Lucas & Rosen (and predecessor firm), New Orleans, 1979-87, Herman, Herman, Katz & Cotlar, New Orleans, 1987-88, Rosen and Samuel, New Orleans, 1990-95; of counsel Rittenberg & Samuel, New Orleans, 1996-99; founder & dir. Litigation Consultation Svcs., New Orleans, 1996—; ptnr. Rosen & Lundeen, L.L.P., New Orleans, 1999—2002; pvt. practice New Orleans, 2002—. Adj. prof. trial advocacy Law Sch. Tulane U., 1988—, mem. adv. com. paralegal studies program, 1977-86, instr. bus. orgns., 1978, instr. legal interviewing, 1980-81; mem. adv. com. Paralegal Inst. U. New Orleans, 1990—, instr. legal interviewing and investigations, 1986-87; lectr. legal and paralegal fields; lectr. real and demonstrative evidence Nat. Edn. Network, 1993; lectr. new judges seminar La. Jud. Coll., 2000, 01, 02, 03. Author: (with others) Trial Techniques publ. La. Trial Lawyers Assn., 1981; columnist Briefly Speaking publ. New Orleans Bar Assn., 1993-2000. Mem. budget and planning com. Jewish Welfare Fedn., 1970-73; mem. adv. coun. on drug edn. La. Dept. Edn., 1973; mem. profl. adv. com. Jewish Endowment Found., 1982—; mem. exec. com. U.S. Olympic Com., La., 1982-84; bd. dirs. Planned Parenthood La., 1994-2001, Hillel Found. New Orleans, 2003—; pres. Dad's Club, Isidore Newman Sch., 1984-85, Uptown Flood Assn., 1982-85; bd. dirs. Jewish Children's Home Svc., 1973-76, Met. Crime Commn. New Orleans, 1976-82; spl. agt. Office Spl. Investigations USAF, 1958-61. Fellow, Inst. of Politics. Loyola U. Mem. ABA, ATLA (keyperson com. 1986-89, vice chmn. paralegal com. 1986-89, mem. family law adv. com. 1989-90, sec. family law sect. 1990-91, lectr. legal edn. 1979, 81, 83, 86, 88); mem. La. Bar Assn. (vice chmn. pub. rels. com. 1970-73, 88-89, past chmn. state youth drug abuse edn. program, vol. lawyers for arts 1986-96, chmn. sr. counsel com. 1995-96), Am. Arbitration Assn., Nat. Fedn. Paralegal Assn. (adv. coun. 1989-1998), Assn. Atty. Mediators (pres. La. chpt. 1995), Nat. Choice in Dying (legal adv. com. 1992-96), Nat. Edn. Network (lectr. legal edn. 1993), New Orleans Bar Assn. (CLE com. 1990-91, chmn. 1991-92, mem. alternative dispute resolution com. 1996-2000, panel moderator 1997), Inn of Ct. (master 1992—), Rotary Club New Orleans (bd. dirs. 1996-98, 2003—, chmn. legal com. 1996—). Avocation: photography. Office: 210 Baronne St 18th Flr New Orleans LA 70112-4132 Office Phone: 504-523-3300. E-mail: lcsno@aol.com.

ROSENAU, JAMES NATHAN, political scientist, author; b. Phila., Nov. 25, 1924; s. Walter Nathan and Fanny Fox (Baum) R.; m. Norah McCarthy, Aug. 5, 1955 (dec. July 1974); 1 child, Heidi Margaret; m. Pauline Vaillancourt, June 14, 1987 (div. 1993); m. Hongying Wang, Dec. 11, 1993; 1 child: Fan Elizabeth. AB, Bard Coll., 1948; AM, Johns Hopkins U., 1949; PhD, Princeton U., 1957. From instr. to prof. Rutgers U., New Brunswick, N.J., 1949-70; prof. Ohio State U., Columbus, 1970-73; prof. polit. sci. U. So. Calif., L.A., 1973-92; prof. internat. affairs George Washington U., 1992—. Research asst. Inst. Advanced Study, Princeton, N.J., 1953-54; research assoc. Princeton U., N.J., 1960-70; dir. Sch. Internat. Relations U. So. Calif., L.A., 1976-79; dir. Inst. for Transnat. Studies, U. Southern Calif., L.A., 1973-92. Author: Public Opinion and Foreign Policy, 1961, National Leadership and Foreign Policy, 1963, The Dramas of Politics, 1973, Citizenship between Elections, 1974, The Scientific Study of Foreign Policy, 1980, Turbulence in World Politics, 1990, The United Nations in a Turbulent World, 1992, Along the Domestic-Foreign Frontier, 1997, Distant Proximities, 2003; (play) Kwangju: An Escalatory Spree, 1991; co-author: American Leadership in World Affairs, 1984, Global Voices, 1993, Thinking Theory Thoroughly, 1995, 2nd edit., 2000, International Political Economy, 1995, Understanding Globalization, 1998; co-editor: Journeys through World Politics, 1989, Global Changes and Theoretical Challenges, 1989, Governance without Government, 1992, Strange Power, 2000, Information Technologies and Global Politics, 2002. Trustee Bard Coll., Annandale-on-Hudson, 1968-70, Odyssey Theater Ensemble, L.A., 1987-88. With U.S. Army, 1942-46. Ford Found. fellow, 1958-59, Guggenheim fellow, 1987-88; Rsch. grantee NSF, 1970, 73, 78-79, 83, 88, 92, 96, NEH grantee, 1976. Fellow World Acad. Art and Sci.; mem. Internat. Studies Assn. (pres. 1984-85), Am. Polit. Sci. Assn. (exec. council 1975-77) Democrat. Office: 2130 H St NW Washington DC 20052-2521 E-mail: jnr@gwu.edu.

ROSENAU, KIMBERLY MARIE, parochial school educator; d. John Ferdinand and Joan Katherine Rosenau. BS in English Edn., Maranatha Bapt. Bible Coll., Watertown, Wis., 2000. Elem. tchr. Calvary Bapt. Sch., Menomonee Falls, Wis., 2000—. Piano tchr., 1999—. Mem.: Milw. Area Piano Assn. Avocations: reading, writing, piano, church ministries.

ROSENAU, PETE, public relations executive; Owner, powersports franchises, import/export parts and accessories retail and wholesale operation; owner 6 new car franchises Honda, Hyundai, Mazda, Volkswagon, Toyota, Subaru, Mich.; chmn. Franco Pub. Rels. Group, 2002—. Bd. trustees YWCA Western Wayne County. Recipient Quality Dealer award, Time Mag., All-Star Dealer award (twice nominated), Sports Illustrated. Mem.: Henry Ford Cmty. Coll. (mem. found. bd.), BBB (serves exec. com.), Detroit Auto Dealers Assn. (past pres., exec. com., bd. dirs., co-chmn. 1997 and 1998 N.Am. Internat. Auto Shows, mem. bd. dirs. adv. ethics stds.). Office: Franco Pub Rels Group 400 Renaissance Ctr Ste 1050 Detroit MI 48243

ROSENBACH, LEOPOLD, engineer, consultant; b. Walbrzych, Poland, Jan. 10, 1947; came to the U.S., 1969; s. Samuel and Halina (Kormicz) R.; m. Pola Knott, Dec. 23, 1969; 1 child, Coleene Rosenbach. MSEE, Polytechnic, Wroclaw, Poland, 1968. Cert. mfg. engr. Mfg. mgr. Leviton Mfg. Co., Bklyn., 1973-77; mfg. engr. Eagle Electric, Long Island City, N.Y., 1977-78; electric mfg. engr. Standard Motor Products, Long Island City, 1979-83, product devel. mgr., 1984-87, design mgr., 1988-90, engring. mgr., 1991-93, dir. materials, 1994-96, dir. ops., 1996—. Contbr. numerous articles to sci. jours. Mem. IEEE, Am. Soc. Metals, Am. Purchasing Soc., Internat. Soc. for Hybrid Microelectronics (met. chpt. treas. 1988-89, sec. 89-90, pres. 90-91), Soc. Mfg. Engrs. Avocations: music, astronomy. Office: Standard Motor Electronics 170 Sunport Ln Orlando FL 32809-7892 also: 7709 Windbreak Rd Orlando FL 32819-5163 E-mail: leor@smpe.net.

ROSENBAUM, ALLAN, public administration educator, academic administrator, international governance advisor; b. N.Y.C., Oct. 5, 1940; s. Frances Lawrence; m. Judith M. Rosenbaum, June 16, 1963; children: Michelle, Amy. BA, U. Miami, 1962; MS in Edn., So. Ill. U., Carbondale, 1964; MA, U. Calif., Berkeley, 1967; PhD, U. Chgo., 1976. Adminstrv. asst. to lt. gov. State of Ill., Chgo., Springfield, 1968-69; dir. Woodlawn manpower planning survey Ctr. Urban Studies, U. Chgo., 1970-71; asst. prof. polit. sci. U. Wis., Madison, 1971-74, U. Conn., Storrs, 1974-77; sr. assoc., study dir. Nat. Inst. Edn., HEW, Washington, 1977-80; chief cons. appropriations subcom. on edn.-human resources Md. Gen. Assembly, Annapolis, 1981, dir. jobs initiative task force, 1982-83; assoc. prof., dir. Md. Inst. Policy Analysis and Rsch. U. Md. Grad. Sch., Balt., 1981-89, dir. Thomas M. Bradley Ctr. Employment and Tng. Edn.-Rsch., 1985-88; prof. pub. adminstrn., dean Sch. Pub. Affairs and Svcs., Fla. Internat. U., Miami, 1988-94, dir. Inst. for Pub. Mgmt., 1995—, coord. PhD program, 2000—01. Advisor, cons. UN Devel. Program, govts. Argentina, Costa Rica, Paraguay, Peru, Poland, Ukraine, Sierra Leone, U.S. AID, OAS, UN Dept. Econ. and Social Affairs, others; organizer, speaker State Treas.'s Conf. on Capital Debt Affordability in Md., 1987; mem. policy coun. Fla. Inst. Govt., 1988-89; chmn. 1991 ann. conf. program Policy Studies Orgn., 1990-91; co-prin. Consortium for Legis. Devel. in Latin Am., 1990-95; numerous presentations in field; co-chmn. UN Expert Group on Improving Govt. Leadership, chmn. selection com. UN Pub. Svc. Awards. Co-author: Poliscide, 1976, repub., 1989, Local Governence, 1997, Responding to Citizens Needs, 2001, State Modernization and Decentralization - Implications for Education and Training in Public Administration, 2003; editor-in-chief Policy Studies Rev., 1993-97; contbr. articles to profl. jours., chpts. to books and proc. Pres. Reston (Va.) Community Assn., 1987-88; chmn. sci. adv. com. Greater Miami Coalition for Drug Free Community, 1989-96, bd. dirs., 1990-97; mem. govt. rels. com. United Way Dade County, Miami, 1989-94. Fellow Ford Found., 1966-67, Nat. Inst. Mental Health, Pub. Policy fellow U Chgo.., 1967-70, U. Conn., 1975, Inst. for Ednl. Leadership, 1976-77; numerous govt. and found. grants. Mem. Nat. Assn. Schs. Pub. Affairs and Adminstrn. (exec. coun.), Am. Soc. for Pub. Adminstrn., Assn. for Pub. Policy Analysis and Mgmt., Am. Polit. Sci. Assn., Greater Miami C. of C. (task force on homelessness in South Fla. 1989-92, pub. affairs and state affairs coms. 1989-96), Internat. Inst. Adminstrv. Scis. (founding mem. working group on environ. mgmt. 1990-93, exec. coun. 2001-), Internat. Assn. Schs. and Insts. Adminstrn. (task force on women in pub. mgmt. 1990-93, v.p., bd. mgmt., chair ann. conf. 1995, 2000, pres. 2001-), Cosmos Club. Democrat. Jewish. Home: 5000 Riviera Dr Miami FL 33146-1741 Office: Fla Internat U Sch Pub Policy and Mgmt Univ Park Campus Miami FL 33199 E-mail: rosenbau@fiu.edu.

ROSENBAUM, ARTHUR L. ophthalmologist; b. St. Louis, Aug. 20, 1940; s. Harry David and Evelyn Levy Rosenbaum; m. Sandra Dine Rosenbaum, May 28, 1985; 1 child, Steven. BA, U. Mich., 1962; MD, Washington U., St. Louis, 1966. Diplomate Am. Bd. Ophthalmology, lic. physician Calif. Intern Mt. Zion Hosp., San Francisco, 1966—67; resident Jules Stein Eye Inst.-UCLA, 1969—73; chief divsn. pediat. ophthalmology UCLA-Jules Stein Eye Inst., 1985—, vice chmn. dept. ophthalmology, 1990—. Editor: (book) Clinical Strabismus Management, 1999. Maj. USPHS, 1967—69. Mem.: Am. Assn. Pediat. Ophthalmology and Stoabismus (pres. 1987—88), Am. Acad. Ophthalmology (Sr. Honor award 1995). Office: Jules Stein Eye Inst UCLA 200 Stein Plz Los Angeles CA 90024 Office Phone: 310-825-2872. E-mail: rosenbaum@jsei.ucla.edu.

ROSENBAUM, BELLE SARA, appraiser, interior designer, museum director, educator; b. N.Y.C., Apr. 1, 1922; d. Harry and Hinda (Sits) Heimowitz; m. Jacob H. Rosenbaum, Mar. 12, 1939; children: Linda Zelinger, Simmi Brodie, Martin, Arlene Levene. Cert., N.Y. Sch. Interior Design, 1945; MA in Judaic Art, PhD, U. B.C., 1997. Sr. mem. Am. Soc. Appraisers, Washington, 1979—; tchr. Judaica Yeshiva U., 1984—; dir. Mus. Contemporary Judaica; pres. Jarvis Designs, Inc., Union City, N.J., 1955-75, Design Assocs., BLS, Monsey, N.Y., 1970-78; v.p. Lord & Lady Inc., Union City, 1955-70, Cardio-Bionic Scanning, Inc., Spring Valley, N.Y., 1975-78; v.p., treas. Rapitech Sys., inc., 1985; exec. bd. State of Israel Bonds Orgn., 1992—. Author short stories, 1947-48, Chronicle of Jewish Traditions, 1992, Upon Thy Doorposts, 1996; contbr. articles on interior design to profl. jours. Chmn. bd. artifacts Rockland Holocaust Ctr., 1991—; trustee Rockland Ctr. Holocaust Studies, 1994; pres. Ednl. Ctr. Jewish Values Jerusalem Gt. Synagogue, Israel, 1998—; co-chair Nat. Jewish Art Week, 2000; curator arts Holocaust Mus. Rockland County, 2000; Bd. dirs. Midgal Ohr Schs., 1971—, Shaare Zedek Hosp., Jerusalem, 1998—, Jewish Fedn. Rockland County, 1999—, Riverdale (N.Y.) Jewish Mus., 1999—, Am. Guild Judaic Art, 1999—, Judaica Mus. Riverdale, 2001—.

ROSENBAUM, DAVID MARK, engineering executive, consultant, educator; b. Boston, Feb. 11, 1935; s. Frederick and Elizabeth (Gelman) R.; m. Karen Jeanne Smith, Dec. 27, 1964; children: Benjamin Micah, Shoshana Elizabeth. BSc, Brown U., 1956; MS, Renessaler Poly. Inst., 1958; PhD, Brandeis U., 1964. Asst. rsch. prof. Boston U., 1964-65; assoc. prof. Poly. U., Bklyn., 1969-70; pres. Network Analysis Corp., Glen Cove, NY, 1970-72; asst. dir. Office of Nat. Narcotics Intelligence, Washington, 1973-74; cons. to comptr. gen. GAO, Washington, 1975-78; dir. Office of Radiation Programs EPA, Washington, 1978-81; pres. Tech. Analysis Corp., McLean, Va., 1981—. Cons. Dir. of Licensing, AEC, Washington, 1972-73. Author: Super Hilbert Space and the Quantum Time Operator, 1969, Liquefield Energy Gases Safety, 1978, A Statistical Procedure for Testing Pacemakers, 1978, Health Effects of Low-Level Radiation, 1981, A Statistical Procedure for Cluster Recognition with Application to Atlanta Leukemia Data, 1983. Mem. IEEE (sr.), Am. Phys. Soc. Office: Tech Analysts Corp # 202 6723 Whittier Ave Mc Lean VA 22101-4533 Personal E-mail: dmrose@radix.net.

ROSENBAUM, DIANE M. state representative; b. Berkeley, Calif., Nov. 26, 1949; m. Jas Adams. State rep., dist. 42 Oreg. House Rep., Salem, 1999—; pres. Oreg. State Indsl. Union Coun., 1994—; legis. rep. Comm. Workers Am., 1989—. Chair Oreg. Commn. for Women, 1993—. Mem.: ACLU. Democrat. Office: 900 Court St NE H-377 Salem OR 97301 Address: Dist Office 1423 SE Hawthorne Blvd Portland OR 97214

ROSENBAUM, GREG ALAN, merchant banker, consultant; b. Toledo, Aug. 7, 1952; s. Marvin and Ida Edith (Millman) R.; m. Martha Jane Radlo, Sept. 3, 1978; children: Eli Samuel, Eve Hannah, Elliott Jacob. AB, Harvard U., 1974, M in Pub. Policy, JD, Harvard U., 1978. Bar: Ohio 1978, Ill. 1980. Summer assoc. Jones, Day, Reavis & Pogue, Cleve., 1977; tchg. fellow in govt. and social scis. Harvard U., Cambridge, Mass., 1976-78; cons. Boston Consulting Group, Boston and Chgo., 1978-82; v.p. Dyson-Kissner-Moran Corp., N.Y.C., 1982-87; mng. dir. Carlyle Group, Washington, 1987-88; pres. Palisades Assocs., Inc., Bethesda, Md., 1988—. Debating coach Harvard U., 1976-79; dir. Varlen Corp., Naperville, Ill., 1985-99, Richey Electronics, Inc., Garden Grove, Calif., 1993-99, McLaren/Hart Inc., Rancho Cordova, Calif., 1995-2000, Expressions Furniture, Inc., Anaheim, Calif., 1992-97, AMCO Corp., Chgo., 1993-97, The Whaler on Kaanapali Beach, 1999—, PlayCore Holdings, Inc., 2000—. Co-author: The Crime of Poverty, 1973, Beyond Politics, 1974, World Without Plenty, 1975. Dir. Lifeline, A Mental Retardation Partnership, Washington, 1993-98; baseball coach Potomac (Md.) Boys' Club, 1992-96; co-chair Harvard Debate Centennial, 1991—; mem. Harvard Law Sch. 20th Reunion gift com., 1997-98, 25th Reunion gift com., 1998-99. Winner Ames Moot Ct. competition Harvard Law Sch., 1976. Mem. ABA, Am. Forensic Assn. (nat. intercollegiate debate champion 1974, coach nat. intercollegiate debate champion 1979), Am. Acad. Polit. and Social Scis., Ctr. for Study of Presidency, Toledo Bar Assn., Chgo. Bar Assn., Phi Beta Kappa. Democrat. Jewish. Avocations: major league baseball, golf, computers, sports memorabilia. Office: Palisades Assocs Inc 9140 Vendome Dr Bethesda MD 20817-4021

ROSENBAUM, JACOB I. lawyer; b. Cleve., Oct. 4, 1927; s. Lionel C. and Dora (Heldman) R.; m. Marjorie Jean Arnold, Apr. 20, 1952; children: Laura Rosenbaum, Alexander, Judith Bartell. JD, U. N.Mex., 1951. Bar: N.Mex. 1951, Ohio 1952. Pres. Ohio Savs. Assn., Cleve., 1955-60, sr. v.p., 1960-92, also dir.; ptnr. Burke, Haber & Berick, 1955-79, Arter & Hadden, 1979-94, of counsel, 1994—2003, Tucker Ellis & West, 2003—. Pres. Kiwanis Found. of Cleve., 1994—; active Judson Retirement Cmty., Cleveland Heights, Ohio, 1990—, trustee, 1994—2003, pres., 1992; trustee Cleve. Zool. Soc., 1983—, Cleve. Nat. Air Show, 1981—, pres., 1987—90, 1994—, pres. Found., 1995—; trustee Golden Age Ctrs. of Cleve., 1996—; pres. Temple Emanu El, University Heights, Ohio, 1965—67, 1995—. Mem.: Cleve. Execs. Assn. (pres. 1989, chmn. 1990, pres. 2003, chmn. 2004), Greater Cleve. Bar Assn. (pres. 2003, chmn. 2004), Ohio Bar Assn. (chmn. aviation law com. 1981—84), Lawyer-Pilots Bar Assn. (pres. 1981—82, editor jour. 1982—97), Kiwanis Club of Cleve. (pres. 1970—71, 1999—). Democrat. Jewish. Home: 28050 N Woodland Rd Cleveland OH 44124-4521 Office: Tucker Ellis & West 1150 Huntington Bldg 925 Euclid Ave Cleveland OH 44115-1475 Office Phone: 216-696-2480. Business E-Mail: jrosenbaum@tuckerellis.com.

ROSENBAUM, JAMES MICHAEL, judge; b. Ft. Snelling, Minn., Oct. 12, 1944; s. Sam H. and Ilene D. (Bernstein) Rosenbaum; m. Marilyn Brown, July 30, 1972. BA, U. Minn., 1966. Bar: (Minn) 1969, (Ill.) 1970, (U.S. Supreme Ct.) 1979. VISTA staff atty. Leadership Coun. for Met. Open Cmtys., Chgo., 1969-72; assoc. Katz, Taube, Lange & Frommelt, Mpls., 1972-77; ptnr. Rosenbaum & Rosenbaum, Mpls., 1977-79, Gainsley, Squier & Korsh, Mpls., 1979-81; U.S. dist. atty. U.S. Dept. Justice, Mpls., 1981-85; judge U.S. Dist. Ct. Minn., 1985—, chief judge, 2001—. 8th cir. rep. Jud. Conf. U.S., 1997—, mem. exec. com., 1999—2001. Author: (booklet) Guide to Practice Civil Rights Housing, 1972; co-author: U.S. Courts Design Guide, 1991—96;

contbr. U.S. Courts Design Guide. Campaign chmn. People for Boschwitz, Minn., 1978; bd. vis. U. Minn. Law Sch. (pres. 1996-97). Mem.: FBA (bd. dirs.). Republican. Jewish. Office: US Courthouse 300 S 4th St Minneapolis MN 55415-1320

ROSENBAUM, JOAN HANNAH, museum director; b. Hartford, Conn. d. Charles Leon and Lillian (Sharasheff) Grossman; m. Peter S. Rosenbaum, July 1962 (div. 1970). AA, Hartford Coll. for Women, 1962; BA, Boston U., 1964; student, Hunter Coll. Grad Sch., 1970-73; cert., Columbia U. Bus. Sch. Inst. Non Profit Mgmt., 1978; DHL (hon.), Jewish Theol. Sem., 1993. Curatorial asst. Mus. Modern Art, N.Y.C., 1966-72; dir. mus. program N.Y. Council on Arts, N.Y.C., 1972-79; cons. Michal Washburn & Assocs., N.Y.C., 1979-80; dir. Jewish Mus., N.Y.C., 1980—. Mem. adv. bd. Pub. Ctr., N.Y.C.; bd. dirs. Creative Time. Bd. dirs. Artists Space, 1980-93; mem. coun. Am. Jewish Mus., 1981—; mem. policy panel Nat. Endowment Arts, 1982-83. Created knight (Denmark); recipient Disting. Alumni award Boston U. Coll. Libera Arts, 1994, Woman of Distinction award Hadassah, 1997, diploma Chevalier of Order of Arts and Letters (France), 1999; European travel grantee Internat. Coun. Mus., 1972. Mem. Am. Assn. Mus. (cons. 1979—), Assn. Art Mus. Dirs. (com. chair), N.Y. State Assn. Mus. (mem. coun. 1981-90), Art Table. Office: Jewish Mus 1109 5th Ave New York NY 10128-0118

ROSENBAUM, MARK DALE, lawyer; b. Cin., May 9, 1948; s. David A. and Evelyn (Finkelman) R. BA, U. Mich., 1970; JD, Harvard U., 1974. Bar: Calif., U.S. Dist. Ct. (cen. dist.) Calif., 1975, U.S. Ct. Appeals (9th cir.),1975, U.S. Ct. Mil. Appeals, 1977, U.S. Supreme Ct., 1980. Legal dir. ACLU, L.A., 1974—. Adj. prof. U. Mich., UCLA. Democrat. Home: 885 W Kensington Rd Los Angeles CA 90026-4365 Office: 1616 Beverly Blvd Los Angeles CA 90026-5711 E-mail: mrosenbaum@aclu-sc.org.

ROSENBAUM, MICHAEL A. investor relations consultant; b. Chgo., May 13, 1953; s. Robert and Muriel (Caplan) R.; m. Jill Ann Rubenstein, Oct. 12, 1975; children: Susan Brooke, Stephanie Ilyse. BS in Communications, U. Ill., 1974; MBA, Roosevelt U., 1979. Reporter Peoria (Ill.) Jour. Star, 1974, Compass Newspaper, Hammond, Ind., 1974-75; corr. UPI, Chgo., 1975-78; mng. editor Purchasing World Mag., Barrington, Ill., 1978-79; chief Midwest bur. The Jour. of Commerce, Chgo., 1979-83; sr. assoc. The Fin. Rels. Bd., Inc., Chgo., 1983-85, ptnr., 1985-88, sr. ptnr., 1988-90, dep. mng. ptnr., chief oper. officer, 1990—, pres., 1997; ptnr., dir. BSMG Worldwide, 1999—. Author: Selling Your Story to Wall Street: The Art and Science of Investor Relations, 1994; contbr. articles to profl. jours. Chmn. capital campaign Congregation Beth Judea, Long Grove, Ill., 1984-87, v.p. programming & membership, 1993-94; mem. capital campaign com. Infant Welfare Soc., Chgo., 1990-92, dir., 1993-97, v.p., 1994-97. Recipient Ann. Report Excellence award Fin. World Mag., 1988-95, Nat. Assn. of Investment Clubs, 1986, 88-95, Assn. of Publicly Traded Cos., 1988-95, Publicity Club of Chgo., 1989, 96, Equities Mag., 2000. Mem. Nat. Investor Rels. Inst., Nat. Assn. Corp. Dirs., Young Pres.'s Orgn. Jewish. Office: Financial Relations Bd John Hancock Ctr 875 N Michigan Ave Ste 2250 Chicago IL 60611-1805

ROSENBAUM, RICHARD MERRILL, lawyer; b. Oswego, N.Y., Apr. 8, 1931; s. Jack M. and Shirley (Gover) R.; m. Judith Kanthor, June 1, 1958; children: Amy, Jill, Matthew, Julie. BA, Hobart Coll., 1952; JD, Cornell U., 1955. Bar: N.Y. 1956. Ptnr. Rosenbaum, Agnello, Agnello & Levine, Rochester, N.Y., 1955-70; justice Supreme Ct. N.Y. State, 1970-73; ptnr. Nixon, Hargrave, Devans & Doyle, Rochester, 1977-84, 88-98; counsel to chmn. of bd., dir. govt. rels. and pub. affairs. Integated Resources, Inc., 1984-88, also bd. dirs. Dir. Integrated Resources, Inc.; past mem. econ. adv. bd. U.S. Dept. Commerce; bd. dirs., sec. Jonathan Inst.; mem. mediation arbitration panel JAMS/Endispute, 1997, Am. Arbitration Assn., 1998, Empire Mediation, 1998; jud hearing officer, 1997; chmn. N.Y. State Unemployment Ins. Bd., 1998—. Contbr. writings in fields of politics and public affairs, legal opinions to publs., 1984-88. Trustee Hobart Coll., 1971-89; nat. committeeman N.Y. State Rep. Nat. Com., 1977—, rules rev. com., subcom. chmn. conv. procedures, 1977—; del.-at-large Rep. Nat. Conv., 1980, 84, 88, congl. dist. del., 1968, chmn. N.Y. State del., 1976; chmn. Monroe County Rep. Com., 1968-70, N.Y. Rep. State Com., 1973-77, Northeastern Rep. State Chairmen's Assn., 1973-76, Nat. Rep. State Chairmen's Assn., 1975-77; justice of peace Town of Penfield (N.Y.), 1962-66; mem. and asst. majority leader Monroe County Legislature, 1966-68; former mem. coun. SUNY, Brockport; dep. counsel U.S. Senate Majority, 1988; apptd. by Pres. Ronald Reagan, U.S. Holocaust Meml. Coun., reapptd. by Pres. George Bush; apptd. by U.S. Senate to Bd. of Fed. Jud. Ctr. Found., 1989—; bd. dirs. Cardozo Sch. Law Yeshiva U.; bd. dirs. Rochester Mus. & Sci. Ctr., 1978—, gen. chmn. devel. fund drive, 1977—; trustee Rochester Area Colls., 1979—; mem. coun. of governing bds. of Ind. Colls. of State of N.Y., 1979—; apptd. mem. N.Y. Mental Hygiene Council, 1973-77, Nat. Citizens Adv. Com. on Environ. Quality, 1977; past bd. dirs. Jewish Home for Aged, Rochester, bd. dirs. Rochester Philharmonic Orchestra; exec. com. Cornell Law Sch; Rep. candidate for nomination for N.Y. state gov., 1994. Recipient Congl. Medal Honor Ellis Island, 1992, Hobart Coll. Alumni citation. Mem. ABA, N.Y. State Bar Assn. Clubs: Royal Order of Jesters, Masons, Shriners. Jewish. Home: 19 Denonville Rdg Rochester NY 14625-1611 Office: NYS Unemployment Ins Appeal Bd 36 W Main St Ste 789 Rochester NY 14614-1704

ROSENBAUM, STANLEY NED, theology educator; b. Dec. 8, 1939; s. Stanley Menz and Wilma R.; m. Mary Helene Pottker, Sept. 2, 1963; children: Sarah Catherine, William David, Ephraim Samuel. BA, Tulane U., 1961; postgrad., U. Chgo., 1961-64; MA, Brandeis U., 1967, PhD, 1974. Assoc. prof. Dickinson Coll., Carlisle, Pa., 1970-90, counselor Hillel, 1971—, prof. Carlisle, 1990—98; adj. prof. U. of Ky., 1999—. Author: Amos of Israel: A New Interpretation, 1990, Understanding Biblical Israel, A Re-examination of the Origins of Monotheism; contbr. articles to religious publs. Bd. mem. Dovetail Inst. for Interfaith Family Resources. Woodrow Wilson fellow, 1961. Mem. Nat. Assn. Profs. Hebrew, Am. Acad. Religion. Home: 815 Simon Greenwell Rd Boston KY 40107-8524 *Biblical scholarship is a form of worship undertaken by those who cannot sing.*

ROSENBERG, ALAN DAVID, accountant; b. Mt. Vernon, N.Y., Apr. 11, 1946; s. Benjamin Bernard and Miriam (Nierenberg) R.; m. Wendy Patricia Cutler, May 25, 1975; children: Kerri L., Joshua Z., Brian S. BS in Acctg., NYU, 1967; MBA in Taxation, Baruch Coll., 1970. CPA, N.Y. Sr. acct. Ernst & Ernst, N.Y.C., 1967-70; dir. acctg., CFO various firms, N.Y.C., 1970-75; pres. Alan D. Rosenberg, CPA, P.C., N.Y.C., New Rochelle, N.Y., 1975—. Mem. AICPA (mem. tax practice mgmt. com. 1992—), N.Y. State Soc. CPAs, Inst. Mgmt. Accts., Nat. Conf. CPA Practitioners, Alliance of Practicing CPAs, Estate Planning Coun. Westchester County, Tax Soc. NYU. Jewish. Avocations: sports, reading, family activities. Office: 2 W 45th St Ste 1208 New York NY 10036-4212

ROSENBERG, ALAN GENE, newspaper editor; b. Chgo., Sept. 14, 1957; s. Earl David and Lorraine Faith (Blum) R.; m. Avis Beth Gunther-Rosenberg, Apr. 8, 1984; children: Ethan Elijah, Rebecca Greer, Jacob Sigmund. BS in Journalism, Northwestern U., 1978. From state staff reporter to asst. features editor Providence Jour., 1978—. Mem. Am. Assn. Sunday and Feature Editors. Office: Providence Jour 75 Fountain St Providence RI 02902-0050 Office Phone: 401-277-7253. E-mail: alan_rosenberg@projo.com.

ROSENBERG, ALAN STEWART, lawyer; b. N.Y.C., Mar. 29, 1930; s. Louis and Sadye (Knobler) R.; m. Ilse Rosenberg/Klein, Aug. 15, 1963; children: Gary, Robert. BA, Stanford U., 1949; LLB, Columbia U., 1952; LLM, NYU, 1960. Bar: N.Y. 1955. Assoc. Wolf Haldenstein Adler & Freeman, N.Y.C., 1955-56; ptnr., chmn. tax dept. Proskauer Rose Goetz & Mendelsohn, N.Y.C., 1957—92. Contbr. articles to profl. jours. Mem. exec. com., bd. visitors Stanford (Calif.) U. Law Sch., 1982-85, Jewish studies program, 1986—; chmn. bd. N.Y. Alliance for the Pub. Sch., 1988-91; mem. adv. com. on pub. issues Advt. Coun., 1991-94; bd. dirs., sec. Univ.-Urban Schs. Nat. Task Force Inc., 1981-96; mem. bd. visitors Columbia U. Law Sch., 1991-96; trustee Ctr. Ednl. Innovation Pub. Edn. Assn., 2000—; mem. bd advisors Spl. Music Sch Am., 1999—; bd. dirs., treas. Justice Resource Ctr., 1994-97; bd. dirs., mem. exec. com. The Abraham Fund; chmn. bd. dirs. Richalan Found., 1996-2003. Lt. (j.g.) USN, 1952-55. Avocations: amateur opera singer, tennis. Home: 115 Central Park W New York NY 10023-4153 E-mail: aandi98@aol.com.

ROSENBERG, ALEX JACOB, art dealer, curator, fine arts appraiser, educator; b. N.Y.C., May 25, 1919; s. Israel and Lena (Zar) R. Student, Albright Coll., 1935-37, Sch. Phila. Mus. Art, 1937-40; BS, Phila. U., 1948; DHL (hon.), Hofstra U., 1989; DSc in Art, Inst. Superior Art, Havana, Cuba, 2003. completed Personal Property courses, levels I, II, III and IV, Am. Soc. of Appraisers, Uniform Standards of Profl. Appraisal Practice, 1994, 2000. Pres. Anserphone, 1959-66; sec., dir. Gen. Cablevision Tex., 1968-72; v.p., dir. Communicable, Inc., Fla., 1967-71, Gen. Cablevision Palatka, Fla., 1967-71, Beacon Cable Corp., 1966-71; pres., dir. Modern Cable Corp., 1966-71, B.F.C.-C.A.T.V. Corp., 1966-71; v.p., dir. Starfax Corp. Real Estate, 1968-70; gen. ptnr. Lakewood Plaza Assocs., N.J., 1973-92, Rostin Assocs., Austin, Tex., 1970-83; pres. Transworld Art Inc., Alex Rosenberg Gallery and Alba Edits., N.Y.C., 1968-89, Rostin Mgmt. Corp., 1986-89, The Abbot Group, 1987-89, Ardmore Affiliates Ltd., Alex Rosenberg Fine Art, 1985—, Neikrug-Rosenberg Assocs., 1989-97. Lectr. Parsons Sch. Design, N.Y.C., 1979—88; instr. appraising modern art NYU, 1992—95, adj. asst. prof. appraising, 1995—; vis. prof. fine art Inst. Superior Art, Havana, Cuba, 1993—; organizer Henry Moore exhbn. Mus. Budapest, Bratislava and Prague, Hungary, 1993; co-curator Leonoid Sokov, Albright Coll., Reading, Pa., 2002; guest lectr. CUNY, N.Y.C., 2000—03; organizer Henry Moore Exhbn., Havana, 1998. Curator An American Portrait, 1976—78, Mus. Fine Art, Havana, 1992—93, co-curator Romare Bearden as Printmaker, 1992—97, Henry Moore Mother and Child Exhbn., 1987—88, assoc. editor exhbn. catalogue. Trustee Alice Baber Art Fund, 1991-93, Phila. Coll. Textiles and Sci., 1992-95, mem. internat. bd. dirs. Tel Aviv Mus. Art, 1999—, bd. dirs., 2000—; bd. dirs. Artists' Rights Today, 1974-80; mus. adv. bd. Hofstra Mus., Hempstead, N.Y., 1987-92; mem. collection and exhbn. com. Parrish Art Mus., Southhampton, N.Y., 1989-95; mem. adv. com. Pollock-Krasner House and Study Ctr., 2000—; trustee Guttman Inst., 1979-92; mem. exec. bd. Nat. Emergency Civil Liberties Com., 1970-98, treas., 1981-98; trustee Nat. Emergency Civil Liberties Found., 1964-98, chmn., 1992-98; nat. bd. dirs. and bd. dirs. local coun. SANE, 1974-83, bd. dirs. Ctr. for Constitutional Rights, 1998—, v.p. 2003—; trustee, treas. New Lincoln Sch., 1968-71; trustee Givat Haviva Ednl. Found., N.Y.C., 1969—, chmn. exec. com., 1992-99, v.p., 1998—, trustee Stephen Wise Free synagogue, 1967-70, 73-76, 99-2000, Mus. Borough Bklyn., 1986-89; del. 28th World Zionist Congress, Jerusalem, 1972; mem. Cmty. Planning Bd. # 7, 1965-67, 70-72; mem. Lower West Side Anti-Poverty Bd., 1965-66, Lincoln Ctr. Cmty. Coun., 1968-74, Com. for Ind. Civilian Police Rev. Bd., 1967; mem. steering com. Com. Pub. Edn. and Religious Liberty; chmn. Am. Israel Civil Liberties Coalition, 1988-89; Dem. dist. leader, 1964-74, state committeeman, 1970-73, mem. county exec. com., 1964-74; del. Dem. Nat. Convs., 1968, 72; bd. dirs. Raoul Wallenberg Commn. of U.S., 1986-90, chmn., 1990-92; mem. print and drawing coun. Israel Mus., 1980-85; assoc. dir. Snug Harbor Cultural Ctr., S.I., 1982-88; mem. AAA del. to Pres. Coun. of Appraisal Orgns., 1995-96; bd. mem. Ludwig Found. of Cuba, 1995—, Am. Friends Ludwig Found. Cuba, 2000—; mem. Assn. Governing Bds. of Univs. and Colls., 1994-96, Nat. Registry of Forensic Examiners, 1994-96; hon. fellow Tel. Aviv Mus. Art, 2002. Recipient Spl. prize Grenschen Triennial, Switzerland, 1976, Cuban Order of Culture, 1995, Cert. of Commendation, Am. Soc. Appraisers, 1993, Cert. for Disting. Svc., Appraisers Assn. of Am., 1993, Graham J. Littlewood III award for profl. excellence Phila. Coll. of Textiles and Sci., 1996, Alex and Carole Rosenberg Collection, Savannah Coll. of Art and Design, 1999, Alex Rosenberg Gallery Hofstra U., 1996—; hon. fellow Tel Aviv Mus. Art, 2002; named to Bronze Cir., Pres.'s Coun., Albright Coll., 2002, Diploma for Service, Nat. Mus. of Fine Art, Havana, Cuba, 2003. Mem. Am. Soc. Appraisers (sr., bd. examiners 1987-95, personal property com. 1987-89), Appraisers Assn. Am. (cert. mem., bd. dirs. 1990-96, v.p. 1992-94, 1st v.p. 1994, pres. 1994-96), Fine Art Pubs. Assn. (v.p., bd. dirs. 1981-83, pres. 1983-86, treas. 1986-89), Nat. Arts Club (Lifetime Achievement Gold medal 2004). Home and Office: 3 E 69th St New York NY 10021-4943 Fax: 212-628-4769.

ROSENBERG, ALISON P. public policy official; b. Miami, Fla., Sept. 5, 1945; d. Mortimer I. and Gail (Sklar) Podell; m. Jeffrey Alan Rosenberg, May 4, 1969; 1 child, Robert Aaron. BS in Econs., Smith Coll., 1967. Mng. officer Citibank, N.Y.C., 1967-69; legis. aide Senator Charles Percy, Washington, 1969-80; profl. staff mem. Senate Fgn. Rels. Com., Washington, 1981-85; assoc. asst. adminstr. Agy. for Internat. Devel., Washington, 1985-87; dir. African affairs Nat. Security Coun., Washington, 1987-88; dep. asst. sec. for Africa State Dept., Washington, 1988-92; asst. admnstr. for Africa Agy. for Internat. Devel., Washington, 1992-93; lead partnerships specialist (Africa) The World Bank, Washington, 1993—. E-mail: arosenberg@worldbank.org.

ROSENBERG, BRIAN C, academic administrator; BA in English, Cornell U.; MA in English, PhD in English, Columbia U. Tchg. asst. Columbia U., NYC, 1979—80; English instr. Queens Coll., NY, 1980—82; asst. prof. The Cooper Union, NYC, 1982—83; asst. prof. to assoc. prof. to prof. to chmn., dept. of English Allegheny Coll., Meadville, Pa., 1983—98; chief acad. officer to dean of faculty and prof. English Lawrence U., Appleton, Wis., 1998—2003; pres. Macalester Coll., 2003—. Pres. fellowship Columbia U., 1977—78, 1980—81; bd. trustees The Dickens Soc., 2000—. Author: (book) Mary Lee Settle's Beulah Quintet: The Price of Freedom, 1991, Little Dorrit's Shadow's: Character and Contradiction in Dickens, 1996. Mem.: Phi Beta Kappa. Office: Office of the Pres, Macalester Coll 208 Weyerhaeuser Hall 62 Macalester St Saint Paul MN 55105 Office Phone: 651-696-6207.

ROSENBERG, CAROLE, art dealer, real estate broker, foundation executive; b. Bklyn., Nov. 16, 1936; d. Hugo and Mildred (Wilinsky) Clemente; m. Melvyn S. Sponder; m. Jerome A. Halsband; children: Michael S. Halsband, Kenneth L. Halsband; m. Alex J. Rosenberg, May 15, 1977. Student, Hunter Coll., 1954-56; BA, Bklyn. Coll., 1958; postgrad., NYU, 1961-62, 64-65. Tchr. N.Y.C. Sch. System, 1958-59, 61-63, Fla. Sch. System, Miami Beach, 1959-61; gallery owner and dir. Original Graphics/Carole Halsband Gallery, N.Y.C., 1971-76; assoc. editor Transworld Art Inc., N.Y.C., 1974-78; exec. dir., curator Alex Rosenberg Gallery/Transworld Art Inc., N.Y.C., 1978-87; exec. dir., v.p. Ardmore Affiliates Ltd., N.Y.C., 1987—; real estate salesperson N.Y.C., 1986-91; real estate broker Carole Rosenberg Properties Internat. Ltd., 1992—. Treas. 3/69 Owners Corp., N.Y.C.1984-87, pres., 1987-91, v.p., 1991-93; chmn. bd. dirs. Friends of the Hofstra U. Arboretum, Hempstead, N.Y., 1991-94. Editor: (art catalogs) Henry Moore, Howard Kanovitz, Mark Tobey, Lila Katzen, 1975; assoc. editor (portfolio) An American Portrait, 1976. Mem. adv. bd. Women Beyond Borders, 1995—, Ludwig Found. Cuba, 1995—; mem. cmty. bd. Water Mill Ctr., 1999—; internat. bd. mem. Tel Aviv Mus. Art, 1999—; bd. dirs. Am. Friends of the Tel Aviv Mus., 2000—; mem. coun. Friends of Upper East Side Hist. Dist., N.Y.C., 1983—96; pres. Am. Friends of the Ludwig Found. of Cuba, 2000—, Lotos Club Found., 2000—. Recipient Lotos medal of merit, 1995, Mgmt. Achievement Award for Innovation, N.Y. Habitat Mag., N.Y.C., 1989. Mem.: Real Estate Bd. N.Y.C., Art Table, N.Y. Hort. Soc. (Longhouse Res. garden com. 1995—, art com. 2001—), Hort. Alliance of the Hamptons, Nat. Arts Club, Mus. Modern Art, Parrish Art Mus. (patron garden com.), Met. Mus. Art, Guggenheim Mus., Women's City Club Am. Hort. Soc., City Gardens Club, Lotos Club (art com. 1989—, chmn. art com. 1992—98, dir. 1993—99). Democrat. Jewish. Avocation: gardening. Business E-Mail: arfineart@aol.com. E-mail: crosenberg@aflfc.org.

ROSENBERG, CHARLES ERNEST, historian, educator; b. N.Y.C., Nov. 11, 1936; s. Bernard and Marion (Roberts) R.; m. Carroll Ann Smith, June 22, 1961 (div. 1977); 1 child, Leah; m. Drew Gilpin Faust, June 7, 1980; 1 child, Jessica. BA, U. Wis., 1956; MA, Columbia U., 1957, PhD, 1961; DHL, U. Wis., 1997. Fellow Johns Hopkins U., Balt., 1960-61; asst. prof. U. Wis., 1961-63; assoc. prof. U. Pa., Phila., 1965-68, prof. history, 1968—, chmn. dept., 1974-75, 79-83; prof. history of sci. Harvard U., 2001—, chmn. dept. history of sci., 2003—. Bd. dirs. Mental Health Assn. Southeastern Pa., 1973-76, Library Co. of Phila., 1980—, Ctr. Advanced Study Behavioral Scis., 1999—. Author: The Cholera Years: The United States in 1832, 1849 and 1866, 1962, The Trial of the Assassin Guiteau: Psychiatry and Law in the Gilded Age, 1968, No Other Gods: On Science and Social Thought in America, 1976, The Care of Strangers: The Rise of America's Hospital System, 1987, Explaining Epidemics and Other Studies in the History of Medicine, 1992; editor Isis, 1986-89. Nat. Inst. Health Research grantee, 1964-70; Guggenheim Found. fellow, 1965-66, 89-90; Nat. Endowment Humanities fellow, 1972-73; Rockefeller Found. humanities fellow, 1975-76; fellow Inst. Advanced Study, 1979-80, Ctr. Advanced Study in Behavioral Scis., 1982-83. Fellow Am. Acad. Arts and Scis., Am. Philos. Soc.; mem. Inst. Medicine of NAS, Am. Assn. History of Medicine (William H. Welch medal 1969, coun. 1974-76, pres. 1992-94), History of Sci. Soc. (George Sarton medal 1995, coun. 1972-75), Soc. Social History of Medicine (pres. 1981), Orgn. Am. Historians (exec. bd. 1985-88). Home: 76 Brattle Cambridge MA 02138 Office: Harvard U Dept History of Sci Cambridge MA 02138 Office Phone: 617-495-9953. Business E-Mail: rosenb3@fas.harvard.edu.

ROSENBERG, CHARLES MICHAEL, art historian, educator; b. Chgo., Aug. 3, 1945; s. Sandor and Laura (Fried) R.; m. Carol Ann Weiss, June 25, 1967; children: Jessica Rachel, Jasper Matthew. BA, Swarthmore Coll., 1967; MA, U. Mich., 1969, PhD, 1974. Asst. prof. SUNY, Brockport, 1973-80; assoc. prof. U. Notre Dame, Ind., 1980-96, prof., 1996—. Author: 15th Century North Italian Painting and Drawing: Bibliography, 1986, Art and Politics in Late Medieval and Early Renaissance Italy, 1990, Este Monuments and Urban Development in Renaissance Ferrara, 1997; contbr. articles to Art Bull., Renaissance Quar., others. Kress Found. fellow Kunsthistorisches Inst., Florence, Italy, 1971-73, Am. Coun. Learned Socs. fellow, 1977-78, NEH fellow, Brown U., 1979-80, Villa i Tatti, Florence, 1985-86, Rome prize Am. Acad. Rome, 2000-01. Mem. Coll. Art Assn., Renaissance Soc. Am., Centro di Studi Europa Della Corti, Italian Art Soc. Office: Notre Dame U Dept Art Art History & Design Notre Dame IN 46556 E-mail: rosenberg.1@nd.edu.

ROSENBERG, CLAUDE NEWMAN, JR., investment adviser; b. San Francisco, Apr. 10, 1928; s. Claude Newman and Elza (Wolff) R.; m. Louise Jankelson, Dec. 19, 1968; children: Linda Kay, Douglas Claude. BA, Stanford U., 1950, MBA, 1952. Research analyst J. Barth & Co., San Francisco, 1955-62, partner charge research, 1962-70; investment adviser, pres. Rosenberg Capital Mgmt., San Francisco, 1970-96. Lectr. and mem. adv. coun. Grad. Sch. Bus., Stanford; mem. adv. bd. Entrepreneur's Found., Hauser Ctr., Kennedy Sch. Govt., Harvard U.; founding chmn. The Philanthropic Rsch. Inst. (Guide/Star), 1997; founder, chmn. The Newtithing Group, 1997. Author: Stock Market Primer, 1962, rev., 1970, 76, 81, 87, The Common Sense Way to Stock Market Profit, 1968, rev., 1978, Psycho-Cybernetics and the Stock Market, 1970, Investing with the Best, 1986, rev., 1993, Wealthy and Wise, 1994. Bd. dirs. Jewish Welfare Fedn., Presbyn. Children's Cancer Rsch. Ctr., Internat. Hospitality Center, Jewish Cmty. Ctr.; trustee San Francisco Ballet Assn., Univ. High Sch., San Francisco; chmn. adv. coun. Stanford U. Sch. Bus.; chmn., founder Newtithing Group, 1997. Served with USNR, 1951-53. Recipient Arbuckle award Stanford U. Grad. Sch. Bus., 1984, Daniel I. Forrestal Leadership award Assn. of Investment and Mgmt. Rsch. 1992, Lilywhite award Employee Benefit Rsch. Inst., 1994, Bus. Statesman award Harvard Bus. Sch. Assn. of No. Calif., 1995, Lifetime Achievement award San Francisco C. of C., 1997, Fishes and Loaves Philanthropist award Cath. Charities, 1998, Gala Spike award Stanford U., 2004, Lifetime of Giving award Omega Boys Club, 2002, Cert. of Spl. Congl. Recognition for outstanding and invaluable svc. to the cmty. U.S. Ho. of Reps., 2002. Mem. Fin. Analysts San Francisco, Alumni Assn. Stanford U. Grad. Sch. Bus. (pres.) Republican. Jewish religion. Clubs: Family (San Francisco), Concordia-Argonaut (San Francisco), Calif. Tennis (San Francisco), Family (San Francisco). Home: 2465 Pacific Ave San Francisco CA 94115-1237 Office: Steuart Tower Ste 2105 One Market St San Francisco CA 94105

ROSENBERG, DAN YALE, retired plant pathologist; b. Stockton, Calif., Jan. 8, 1922; s. Meyer and Bertha (Naliboff) R.; m. Marilyn Kohn, Dec. 5, 1954; 1 son, Morton Karl. AA, Stockton Jr. Coll., 1942; AB, Coll. of the Pacific, 1949; MS, U. Calif., Davis, 1952. Jr. plant pathologist State of Calif. Dept. Agr., Riverside, 1952-55, asst. plant pathologist Sacramento, 1955-59, assoc. plant pathologist, 1959-60, pathologist IV Riverside, 1960-63, program supr., 1963-71, chief exclusion and detectin, divsn. plant industry, 1971-76, chief nursery and seed svcs. divsn. plant industry, 1976-82, spl. asst. divsn. plant industry, 1982-87; pres. Health Inc., 1972-73. Agrl. cons., 1988—; mem. Citrus Rsch. Adm. Com., U. Calif., Riverside, 1992—; mem. Gov.'s Interagy. Task Force on Biotech., 1986—; agrl. cons. Calif. Avocado Commn., 1994—. Contbr. articles to profl. jours. Served with AUS, 1942-46, ETO. Mem. Am. Phytopath. Soc. (fgn. and regulatory com. 1975—, chmn. 1978, grape diseases and pests 1977-98), Calif. State Employees Assn. (pres. 1967-69), Sacto. Met. C. of C. (internat. trade com. 1993-97), N.Am. Plant Protection Orgn. (industry adv. group), Plant Patents Fruit Trees and Ornamental Trees. Home and Office: 2328 Swarthmore Dr Sacramento CA 95825-6867 Office Phone: 916-929-4620.

ROSENBERG, DAVID, lawyer; b. May 6, 1946; s. Marvin and Helene (Feller) Rosenberg; m. Bernice Leber, June 25, 1989. BA, U. Chgo., 1968; JD, NYU, 1971. Bar: NY 72, U.S. Dist. Ct. (so. and ea. dists.) NY 75, U.S. Supreme Ct. 80, U.S. Ct. Appeals (2d cir.) 81. Atty. N.Y.C. Housing and Devel. Adminstrn., 1971—72; law clk. NY Supreme Ct., 1972—80; assoc., then ptnr. Feldesman & D'Atri, N.Y.C., 1980—81; assoc. Summit Rovins & Feldesman, N.Y.C., 1981—82, ptnr., 1983—89, Marcus Rosenberg & Diamond LLP, N.Y.C., 1989—. Mem. com. character and fitness 1st Jud. Dept., N.Y.C., 1984—; asst. counsel NY Com. Jud. Nomination, 1982—89; mem. adv. coun. N.Y.C. Civil Ct., 1982—98, chmn., 1986—98. Mem.: ABA (real property litigation, corp. sects. 1971—), N.Y.C. Bar Assn. (mem. civil ct. com. 1981—84, mem. judiciary com. 1985—88, chmn. common state cts. superior jurisdiction 1989—93), NY Bar Assn. (real property law sect. exec. com. 1979—88, chmn. landlord and tenant com. 1977—88, vice chmn. class action com. 1985—, 1985—, exec. com. comml. and fed. litigation sect. 1998—). Home: 20 W 86th St New York NY 10024-3604 Office: Marcus Rosenberg & Diamond LLP 488 Madison Ave New York NY 10022-5702

ROSENBERG, DAVID ALAN, military historian, educator; b. N.Y.C., Aug. 30, 1948; s. Sidney and Fay (Breitman) R.; m. Deborah Lee Haines, July 1, 1973; 1 child, Rebecca Haines. BA in History, Am. U., 1970; MA in History, U. Chgo., 1971, PhD in History, 1983. Asst. historian, cons. Lulejian & Assocs., Inc., Falls Church, VA., 1974-75; instr. history U. Wis., Milw., 1976-78; pvt. practice cons., rschr. Chgo., Washington, 1978-82; asst. prof. history U. Houston, University Park, 1982-83; sr. fellow Strategic Concepts Devel. Ctr., Nat. Def. U., Washington, 1983-85; prof. strategy and ops. U.S. Naval War Coll., Newport, R.I., 1985-90; assoc. prof. history Temple U., Phila., 1990-2000, professorial lectr., 2001—; Adm. Harry W. Hill prof. maritime strategy Nat. War Coll., Washington, 1996—2003; sr. strategic rschr. U.S. Naval War Coll., 1998—, asst. to vice chief naval ops., 1996—; dir. Task Force History for chief naval ops. Operation Iraqi Freedom, Global War on Terror, 2003. Mem. U.S. exec. com. four Nation Nuclear History Program, project dir. Berlin Crisis, 1989-95; cons. Office of Sec. Def., 1991-93, Office of Chief of Naval Ops., 1991—, Office of Sec. of Navy, 1992—; mem., chair Sec. Navy's Adv. Subcom. of Naval History, 1995—. Co-quthor: Operational Intelligence in the Age of Global Conflict, OPTINTEL in the U.S. Navy, 1939-1999, 2004; co-editor: (15 vol. book set) U.S. Plans for War, 1945-1950, 1990; contbr. articles to Jour. Am. History (2 awards nat. hist. assns. 1980), 22 others, also 16 book chpts. With USNR, 1982—. Recipient Meritorious Pub. Svc. award Dept. of Navy, 1995, Superior Civilian Svc. medal, 2000; Advanced rsch. scholar U.S. Naval War Coll., 1974-79; Ford Found grantee, 1985-86, MacArthur rsch. grantee 1987-88; MacArthur fellow 1988-93. Mem. Orgn. Am. Historians (Binkley-Stephenson article prize), Soc. for Historians of Am. Fgn. Rels. (Bernath article prize), Soc. for Mil. History, U.S. Naval Inst., Internat. Inst. for Strategic Studies. Jewish.

ROSENBERG, EDWIN HAROLD, systems analyst; b. Balt., June 17, 1949; s. Mervin and Helen Rosenberg. BS, Towson U., 1976, BS, 1984. Rsch. psychologist Gerontology Rsch. Ctr., The Nat. Inst. on Aging, NIH, Balt., 1983—92; programmer analyst Johns Hopkins Health Sys., 1993—. Contbr. articles to profl. jours. Mem.: IEEE (assoc.). Avocations: writing, computers,

robotics, crossword puzzles. Home: 6607-3B Woods Pky Baltimore MD 21222 Office: Johns Hopkins Health System 5300 Alpha Commons Suite 100 Baltimore MD 21224 Personal E-mail: erosenb@comcast.net.

ROSENBERG, ELI IRA, physicist, educator; b. Bklyn., Feb. 19, 1943; s. Milton and Beatrice Rosenberg; m. Wendy Jean Harrod, July 23, 1990; m. Eileen Ewig, Aug. 29, 1965 (div. Dec. 1, 1987); children: Elliot Michael, Evan Robert. BS, CCNY, 1964; MS, U. Ill., 1966, PhD, 1971. Enrico Fermi postdoctoral fellow U. Chgo., 1971—72, instr., 1972—74, asst. prof., 1974—79; assoc. physicist Ames (Iowa) Lab., U.S. Dept. Energy, 1979—81, program dir., 1988—93, physicist, 1981, sr. physicist, 1987—93; asst. prof. Iowa State U., Ames, 1979—81, assoc. prof., 1981—87, prof., 1987—, chmn. dept. physics and astronomy, 2002—. Contbr. more than 300 articles to profl. jours. Grantee, U.S. Dept. of Energy, 1979—. Mem.: Am. Phys. Soc. (life), Sigma Xi, Phi Beta Kappa.

ROSENBERG, ELLEN Y. religious association administrator; married; 2 children. Student, Goucher Coll.; BS in Edn., Mills Coll.; postgrad., Columbia U. Assoc. dean for acad. affairs Marymount Manhattan Coll., N.Y.C.; exec. dir. Women of Reform Judaism/Fed. Temple Sisterhoods, 1992—. Bd. dirs. Mazon, World Union for Progressive Judaism, Jewish Braille Inst. Am., Union Am. Hebrew Congregations. Jewish. Office: WRJ 633 3rd Ave New York NY 10017-6706

ROSENBERG, FRANK BLAUSTEIN, petroleum company executive; b. Balt., Sept. 24, 1958; s. Henry A. Jr. and Eleanor (Kantor) R.; m. Ann Lockwood, Feb. 1, 1986. BS in Chem. Engring., Bucknell U., 1980; MBA, Emory U., 1982. Mktg. and project mgr. Gen. Electric Credit Corp., Chgo., 1982-86; feedstock trader Crown Cen. Petroleum Corp., Houston, 1986—; exec. v.p. Rosemore, Balt., 2003—. Mem. jr. bd. Chgo. Symphony Orch., 1983-86. Mem. Am. Inst. Chem. Engrs. Clubs: Union League of Chgo., Royal Automobile. Avocations: theater, golf. Office: Rosemore Inc Ste 2300 1 N Charles St Baltimore MD 21201*

ROSENBERG, GARY ARON, real estate development executive, lawyer; b. Green Bay, Wis., June 18, 1940; s. Ben J. and Joyce Sarah (Nemzin) R.; m. Gloria Davis, Nov. 1967 (div. 1975); children: Myra, Meredith; m. Bridgit A. Maile, Apr. 9, 1983. BS, Northwestern U., 1962, MBA, 1963; JD, U. Wis., 1966. Bar: Wis. 1966, Ill. 1967. Chmn., dir. The Rosenberg Found., 1960—; atty. U.S. SEC, Washington, 1966-67; pvt. practice Chgo., 1967-74; founder, chmn. bd., CEO UDC Homes, Inc. (formerly UDC-Universal Devel., L.P.), Chgo., 1968-1995; chmn., CEO, dir. Canterbury Devel. Corp., Chgo., 1986—; dir. Olympic Cascade Fin. Corp., Chgo., 1996-98, Nat. Securities, Chgo., 1996—; chair, pres., CEO, dir. OneStop Shop, Inc., Chgo., 1998—; dir. hometouch Ctrs., Inc., Chgo. Mem. adv. bd. Kellogg Grad. Sch. Mgmt. Northwestern U., Evanston, Ill., 1985—, founder, chmn. adv. bd. Kellogg Real Estate Rsch. Ctr., 1986—, adj. prof., 1982—; founder Shadow Hill Entertainment Corp., Beverly Hills, Calif., 1990. Recipient Arts Edn. Svc. award Ill. Alliance for Arts Edn., Chgo., 1988, Kellogg Schaffner Disting. Alumni award Kellogg Grad. Sch. Mgmt., 1993. Mem. Nat. Assn. Home Builders (coun. 1989-90), John Evans Club. Avocations: skiing, hiking, climbing, tennis, golf, reading. Office: hometouch Ctrs Inc Ste 3660 676 N Michigan Ave Chicago IL 60611-2866 E-mail: bamgar@interaccess.com.

ROSENBERG, HAROLD NMI, preventive medicine physician, consultant; b. N.Y.C., Nov. 23, 1921; s. Jacob and Rose Rosenberg; m. Sharon Rosenberg, June 6, 1962; children: Marla Holben, Victor. BA, Drake U.; DO, Phila. Coll. Of Osteo. Medicine, 1951; MS, Columbia Coll. Physicians and Surgeons, 1999. Physician Health Awareness/lifesustainer, N.Y.C., 1999—; cons./advisor LIFESUSTAINER, N.Y.C., 1999—. Pres. Internat. Acad. Of Preventive Medicine, Houston. Author (sr. editor): Book Of Vitamin Therapy/web Site:lifesustainer. With U.S. Army, 1944—46, ETO. Decorated Purple Heart, Bronze Star medal. Mem.: Internat. Acad. Preventive Medicine (pres. 1970—75), Mil. Order Of The Purple Heart (life; sr. vice comdr./N.Y. Dept. 2002—04). Independent-Republican. Hebrew. Avocations: swimming, hiking, painting landscape, portrates. Home: Po Box 678 New York NY 10023 Office: Lifesustainer 37 West 72nd St New York NY 10023 E-mail: hr89@columbia.edu.

ROSENBERG, HENRY A., JR., petroleum executive; b. Pitts., Nov. 7, 1929; s. Henry A. and Ruth (Blaustein) R.; children: Henry A. III, Edward Lee, Frank Blaustein; m. Dorothy Lucibello, June 30, 1984. BA in Econs., Hobart Coll., 1952. With Crown Cen. Petroleum Corp., Balt., 1952—, pres., 1966-75, chmn. exec. com., 1966—, chmn. bd., 1975—, also chief exec. officer. Dir. Am. Trading & Prodn. Corp., USF&G Corp., Signet Banking Corp. Bd. dirs. Johns Hopkins Hosp., Goucher Coll., McDonogh Sch., Nat. Flag Day Found., YMCA Greater Balt., United Way Ctrl. Med., Crohn's and Colitis Found. Md., Nat. Aquarium Balt.; mem. nat. exec. bd., mem. N.E. regional bd., v.p. program group nat. coun., past pres., exec. bd., adv. coun. Balt. Area coun. Boy Scouts Am.; past chmn., mem. adv. bd. William Donald Schaefer Ctr. for Pub. Policy; past chmn. bd. dirs. Balt. Area Conv. and Visitors Assn.; trustee Hobart and William Smith Colls. and Loyola Coll. Med. Mem. Nat. Petroleum Refiners Assn. (chmn., bd. dirs., exec. com.), Nat. Petroleum Coun., 25 Yr. Club Petroleum Industry, Nat. Assn. Mfrs. (bd. dirs.). Office: Crown Cen Petroleum Corp 1 N Charles St PO Box 1168 Baltimore MD 21203-1168

ROSENBERG, HERB, sculptor, educator; b. N.Y.C., Feb. 4, 1942; s. David and Eve Rosenberg; m. Jean Gustavson, Nov. 14, 1976 (div. Nov. 1998); 1 child, Andrew. BA, SUNY, Binghamton, 1964; MFA, Pratt Inst., 1967. Registered art therapist. Dir. art therapy studies N.J. City U., Jersey City, 1971—. Exhibited in solo shows at World's Fair, Brisbane, Australia, 1988, UNESCO, Paris, 1992, Grand Palais, Paris, 1994, BRAS. Bd. dirs. Hurley Found., N.Y.C., 1994—, Ctr. Bros d'Or Cultural Ctr., N.S., Can., 1996—, C.A.S.E. Mus., Jersey City, 1995—. Grantee Jersey City State Coll., 1979, 81, 84, 88; recipient Juror's award Hong Kong Mus. Art, 1992; named Sculptor of Yr., Hudson County Cultural Ctr., 1984. Mem.: Kans. Sculpture Soc., Australian Sculpture Soc., Am. Art Therapy Assn., Internat. Sculpture Soc., Art Therapy Assn. (chair 1984—86), Internat. Expressive Arts Assn., Am. Expressive Arts Assn. E-mail: pneuonce@aol.com.

ROSENBERG, HOWELL K. lawyer; b. Phila., June 30, 1950; s. Martin and Thelma Rosenberg; m. Sondra Kramer, Dec. 25, 1971; children: Sydney, Carrie, Jake. BA in Polit. Sci., Pa. State U., 1971; JD cum laude, Villanova U., 1974. Bar: Pa. 1974, U.S. Dist. Ct. (ea. dist.) Pa. 1976, U.S. Ct. Appeals (4th cir.) 1993, U.S. Ct. Appeals (3d cir.) 1994, U.S. Surpeme Ct. 1997. Asst. dist. atty. Phila. Dist. Attys. Office, 1974—80, asst. dist. atty. chief spl. investigations, 1980—82; assoc. Shein & Brookman, 1982—84; founding ptnr. Brookman, Rosenberg, Brown & Sandler, 1984—. Clin. prof. law Widener Law Sch., Del., 1985—91. Assoc. editor: Villanova U. Law Rev., 1973—74. Bd. dirs. Libr. Co. of Phila. Named Pa. Super Lawyer, 2004. Mem.: ATLA, Phila. Trial Lawyers Assn. (bd. dirs. 2001—), Order of Coif. Office: Brookman Rosenberg Brown & Sandler 305 15th St 17th Fl Philadelphia PA 19102 Office Phone: 215-569-4000. E-mail: hrosenberg@brbs.com.

ROSENBERG, IRWIN HAROLD, physician, educator; b. Madison, Wis., Jan. 6, 1935; s. Abraham Joseph and Celia (Mazursky) R.; m. Civia Muffs, May 24, 1964; 1 child, Ilana. BS, U. Wis., 1956; MD, Harvard U., 1959. Diplomate Am. Bd. Internal Medicine. Intern Mass. Gen. Hosp., Boston, 1959-60, resident, 1960-61; instr. medicine Harvard Med. Sch., Boston, 1965-66, assoc. in medicine, 1966-68, asst. prof., 1968-70; assoc. prof. medicine U. Chgo., 1970-75, prof., 1975-86, Sarah and Harold Lincoln Thomson prof. medicine, 1983-86; prof., dir. USDA Human Nutrition Rsch. Ctr. on Aging Tufts U., Boston, 1986—, Jean Mayer prof., 1993. Mem. food and nutrition bd. Nat. Acad. of Scis., 1971-83, chmn., 1981-83; W.O. Atwater lectr. USDA, 1993. Co-chair local br. Med. Com. on Human Rights, Boston, 1967; mem. adv. bd. Hebrew Coll., Boston, 1987, 91; chmn. bd. dirs. Hillel Found., U. Chgo. With USPHS, 1961-64. Recipient Josiah Macy Faculty award Macy Found., 1974, Goldsmith award Am. Coll. Nutrition, 1984. Fellow AAAS; mem. Am. Soc. for Clin. Nutrition (pres. 1983-84, Herman award 1989), Internat. Life Sci. Inst. (editor nutrition revs. 1989—), Inst. of Medicine, Nat. Acad. Scis. Jewish. Avocations: sports, music, judaica. Office: Tufts U USDA Human Nutrition Rsch Ctr 711 Washington St Boston MA 02111-1525

ROSENBERG, JEROME DAVID, physicist; s. Hyman D. and Hilda (Cantor) R.; m. Shirley Sirota, 1947; children: Jonathan, Hindy. BS in Physics, CCNY, 1948; postgrad., Nat. Bur. Standards Grad. Sch., 1949-52, George Washington U., 1952, U. Md., 1951-53, Cath. U. Am., 1953-54. Engr. officer USCG Acad., 1942, APA-34, 1943-45; dir. microphonics Nat. Bur. Stds.; project mgr., mgr. test nuclear reactor Harry Diamond Labs., Washington, 1952-62; ops. mgr. tech. utilization NASA, Washington, 1962-64, program and project mgr. Nat. Geodetic Satellite Program, Satellites Pageos, GEOS 1 and 2, 1964—72, dep. dir. comm. divsn., 1972-74, dir. tech. applications divsn., 1974-77, dir. office energy programs divsn. bus. mgmt., 1977-78; spl. assignment to solar applications & conservation, barriers and incentive br. Dept. Energy, 1978-79; leader solar energy group Mitre Corp., McLean, Va., 1979-80; prin. cons. energy and environ. divsn. Booz, Allen & Hamilton, Washington, 1980-82; sr. staff officer Bd. Telecomm. and Computer Applications, NRC-NAS, Washington, 1982-85. Exec. dir. NASA Alumni League, Washington, 1986—; mem. Outlook for Space Study Group, NASA planning group to develop U.S. space programs, 1975. Lt. (j.g.) USCG, 1943—44. Recipient NASA Exceptional Svc. medal, 1973. Mem. Fed. Exec. Inst., Sigma Pi Sigma. Office: NASA Alumni League 750 1st St NE Washington DC 20002-4241 Office Phone: 202-336-6136. Personal E-mail: jerry@ssrinc.com.

ROSENBERG, JEROME LAIB, chemist, educator; b. Harrisburg, Pa., June 20, 1921; s. Robert and Mary (Katzman) R.; m. Shoshana Gabriel, Sept. 15, 1946; children— Jonathan, Judith. AB, Dickinson Coll., 1941; MA, Columbia U., 1944, PhD, 1948. Rsch. chemist S.A.M. Labs., 1944-46; Instr. chemistry Columbia U., 1946-48; rsch. assoc. (asst. prof.) inst. Radiobiology and Biophysics, U. Chgo., 1950-53; mem. faculty U. Pitts., 1953-91, chmn. dept. biophysics and microbiology, 1969-71, prof. biol. scis., 1976-91, dean faculty arts and scis., 1970-86, vice provost, 1978-89, chmn. biol. scis., 1989-90, interim chmn. communication, 1991, assoc. dean faculty arts and scis., 1991-92, rsch. integrity officer, 1992—, prof. emeritus biol. scis., 1991—, dir. Jewish studies program, 1991-99. Author: Photosynthesis, 1965; editor, reviser: Outline Theory and Problems of College Chemistry (Schaum), 1949, 58, 66, 80, 90, 97; contbr. articles to profl. jours. NSF sr. fellow Technion Israel Inst. Tech., 1962-63, AEC fellow U. Chgo., 1948-50; recipient Pitts. award Am. Chem. Soc., 1987. Mem. AAUP (nat. coun. 1968-69, pres. Pa. div. 1968-69). Home: 1029 S Negley Ave Pittsburgh PA 15217-1045 Office Phone: 412-624-3007. E-mail: jrosenb@pitt.edu.

ROSENBERG, JILL, realtor, civic leader; b. Shreveport, La., Feb. 17, 1940; d. Morris H. and Sallye (Abramson) Schuster; m. Lewis Rosenberg, Dec. 23, 1962; children: Craig, Paige. BA in Philosophy, Tulane U., 1961, MSW, 1965; grad., Realtor Inst., 1994. Cert. residential specialist Residential Sales Coun. Social worker La. Dept. Pub. Welfare, 1961-62, 63-64; genetics counselor Sinai Hosp., Balt., 1967-69; ptnr. Parties Extraordinaire, cons., 1973-77; realtor assoc. Robert Weil Assocs., Long Beach, Calif., 1982—. Pres. we. region Pres. we. region, 1972—73; v.p. Jewish Cmty. Fedn. Long Beach and West Orange County, 1983—86, bd. dirs., 1982—86; pres. Long Beach Cancer League, 1987—88, exec. bd. dirs., 1984—96; pres. Long Beach Jewish Cmty. Sr. Housing Corp., 1989—91; v.p. fundraising S.E. unit Long Beach Harbor chpt. Am. Cancer Soc., 1989—90; trustee St. Mary Med. Ctr. Found., 1991—2003; pres. nat. conf. NCCJ, 1994—96, bd. dirs., 1989—, Leadership Long Beach, 1992—2000, pres., 1994—95; hon. bd. govs., 2000—; mem. dean's adv. bd. Sch. Bus. Adminstrn. Calif. State U., Long Beach, 2000—04; assoc. coun. Long Beach Edn. Foun., 2003—; bd. dirs. Long Beach Symphony Assn., 1984—85, Westerly Sch. Assoc., 1991—2000, Phoenix Long Beach Mus. Art, 1992—98, Am. Diabetes Assn., Long Beach., Calif., 1997—99, Stramski Children's Devel. Ctr., Long Beach Meml. Med. Ctr., 1998—, Pub. Corp. for Arts, 2002—, Long Beach Day Nursery, 2000—02; leadership devel. chair Pub. Corp. for Arts, 2003—. Recipient Young Leadership award Jewish Cmty. Fedn. Long Beach and West Orange County, 1981, Jerusalem award State of Israel, 1989, Hannah G. Solomon award Nat. Coun. Jewish Women, 1992, Alumnus of Yr. award Leadership Long Beach, 1995, Humanitarian award The Nat. Conf., 1997, Disting. Leadership award Calif. Assn. Leadership Programs, 2000; named Rick Racker Woman of Yr., 1999; scholar La. Dept. Pub. Welfare, 1962, NIMH, 1964. Mem. Rotary Club of Long Beach (bd. dirs. 2000-01). Office: Robert Weil Assocs 5220 E Los Altos Plz Long Beach CA 90815-4251

ROSENBERG, JOEL BARRY, government economist; b. Bronx, NY, Aug. 14, 1942; s. Benjamin and Miriam Dorothy (Yellin) Rosenberg; m. Judith Lynne Jackler, Aug. 26, 1965; children: Jeffrey Alan, Marc David. BA, Queens Coll., 1964, MA, 1966; PhD, Brown U., 1972. Accredited valuation appraiser 2002. Cons. Commonwealth Svcs., Washington, 1970—71; asst. prof. econs. SUNY, Geneseo, 1971—75, Case Western Res. U., Cleve., 1975—76; mgr., industry economist IRS, Washington, 1976—. NDEA fellow Brown U., 1966—69. Contbr. articles to profl. jours. Mem.: Am. Statis. Assn., Nat. Assn. Bus. Economists, Am. Econ. Assn. Home: 16 Flameleaf Ct Gaithersburg MD 20878-5216 Office: IRS 500 N Capitol St NW Washington DC 20221-0003

ROSENBERG, JOHN DAVID, English educator, literary critic; b. N.Y.C., Apr. 17, 1929; s. David and Dorothy Lilian (Shatz) R.; m. Barbara E. Hatch, 1952 (div. 1969); m. Maurine Ann Hellner, June 11, 1972; 1 child, Matthew John. BA, Columbia U., 1950, MA, 1951, PhD, 1960; BA, Clare Coll., Cambridge U., 1953, MA, 1958. Editor-in-chief Columbia Rev., 1949-50; lectr. English Columbia U., N.Y.C., 1953-54, asst. prof., 1962-65, assoc. prof., 1966-67, prof. English, 1967—, William Peterfield Trent prof., 1994—; instr. CCNY, 1954-62; chmn. Columbia Coll. humanities program, 1970-73, dir. grad. studies in English, 1986-89. Vis. prof. English Harvard U., 1968, U. B.C., 1970, Princeton U., 1978; vis. fellow Clare Hall Cambridge U., England, 1969; guest lectr. U.S. Mil. Acad., Cambridge U., Lancaster U. Author: The Darkening Glass: A Portrait of Ruskin's Genius, 1961, The Fall of Camelot: A Study of Tennyson's Idylls of the King, 1973, Carlyle and the Burden of History, 1985; editor: The Genius of John Ruskin, 1963, 2nd edit., 98, Mayhew, 1968, Swinburne: Selected Poetry and Prose, 1968, The Poems of Alfred, Lord Tennyson, 1975; contbr. essays and reviews on English lit. to N.Y. Times Book Rev., N.Y. Rev. Books, Harper's mag., Hudson Rev. and profl. jours. Recipient Clarke F. Ansley award Columbia U., 1960, Disting. Svc. award Columbian Coll. Core Curriculum, 1997; Coun. for Rsch. in Humanities grant-in-aid, 1965; Euretta J. Kellett fellow Cambridge U., 1951-53, Edward Coe fellow, 1956-57, Samuel S. Fels fellow, 1959-60, Am. Coun. Learned Soc. fellow, 1965-66, 70, Lawrence H. Chamberlain fellow, 1965-66, Guggenheim fellow, 1968-69, NEH fellow, 1982-83. Mem. MLA (chmn. exec. com. Victorian divsn. 1970, exec. com. 1979-83), Tennyson Soc., Ruskin Assn., Camp Rising Sun Alumni Assn., Columbia Coll. Alumni Assn. (dir. 1980-82, Alexander Hamilton medal 1994), Phi Beta Kappa. Office: Columbia U Dept English 1150 Amsterdam Ave New York NY 10027-7051

ROSENBERG, KENNETH DAVID, epidemiologist; b. Brooklyn, NY, June 10, 1945; s. Charles Harvey and Florence Rosenberg; m. Gail Lehrman, Sept. 30, 1994; 1 child, Alexander P. BA, Dartmouth Coll., 1967; MD, Tufts U. Sch. Medicine, 1973; MPH, Columbia U. Sch. Pub. Health, 1989. Lic. Medicine NY, 1977, Certified Am. Bd. Preventive Medicine, 1997. Maternal and child health epidemiologist Oreg. Dept. Health Services, Portland, Oreg., 1997—; dir. of epidemiology and rsch. NYC Dept. Health, Bur. Maternity Services and Family Planning, 1993—96; resident in pub. health and preventive medicine NYC Dept. Health, 1977—80; policy analyst Health Policy Adv. Ctr., NYC, 1976—77; resident in pediat. Lincoln Hosp., Bronx, NY, 1973—75. Founder Health U., Boston, 1967—68; project dir. No. New Eng. Student Health Project, Boston, 1968—69; founder/editor Catalyst (periodical), Boston, 1967—70. Mem.: APHA. Avocations: tennis, golf. Office: Oregon Health Divsn 800 NE Oregon St Ste 850 Portland OR 97232 Office Phone: 503-731-4507. E-mail: ken.d.rosenberg@state.or.us.

ROSENBERG, LEON JOSEPH, marketing educator; b. Atlanta, Oct. 9, 1918; s. Harry Manville and Gertrude Dora (Hassenbusch) R.; m. Phylis Jane Israel, Feb. 6, 1943 (dec. Mar. 1976); children: Joanne Rosenberg Larson, Paul Harvey; m. Louise Nachman Mayer, Oct. 15, 1977. BS in Indsl. Mgmt, Ga. Inst. Tech., 1939; MS, Columbia U., 1940; PhD, NYU, 1967. Mem. staff Nat. Retail Mchts. Assn., N.Y.C., 1947-49; sr. rsch. analyst Federated Dept. Stores, Inc., Cin., 1949-52; rsch. dir. Sanger Harris Dept. Store, Dallas, 1952-56, gen. supt., 1956-67; assoc. prof. Coll. Bus. Adminstrn., U. Ark., Fayetteville, 1967-74; prof. mktg. and transp. Sam M. Walton Coll. Bus. Adminstrn., U. Ark., 1975-89; dept. head mktg. and transp. U. Ark., 1986-88, prof. emeritus, 1989—; mktg. cons., sales assoc. Lindsey & Assocs. Inc., Fayetteville, 1990—. Disting. vis. prof. Calif. State U., San Bernardino, 1990. Contbr. articles to profl. jours. Pres. Jewish Family Svc., Dallas, 1960-62, Temple Shalom, Fayetteville, 1992-96; mem. exec. com. Dallas Jewish Fedn., 1963-67; bd. dirs. New Orleans Jewish Children's Regional Svc., 1962-73, 75-2003, Jewish Fedn. Ark., 1992-96; pres. N.W. Ark. unit B'nai B'rith, 1992-2001; bd. dirs. Washington County (Ark.) chpt. Am. Cancer Soc., 1979-86, pres., 1982-83. Capt. USAAF, 1940-46. Mem. Am. Mktg. Assn., So. Mktg. Assn., Nat. Bd. Realtors, Ark. Bd. Realtors, Econs. and Bus. History Soc. (trustee 1986-89), Alpha Phi Omega (Svc. award 1971), Beta Gamma Sigma, Delta Nu Alpha. Home: 1923 E Joyce Blvd # 168 Fayetteville AR 72703 Office: Lindsey & Assocs Inc 3900 Front St Fayetteville AR 72703

ROSENBERG, MANUEL, retail company executive; b. Boston, Apr. 26, 1930; s. Israel and Lillian (Wirin) R.; m. Audray Merle Gold, Aug. 28, 1955; children: Peter Neal, Beth Susan. AB, Harvard U., 1951, MBA, 1953. V.P. Filene's, Boston, 1967-73; pres., chief exec. officer Gimbel's, Phila., 1973-75, chmn. bd., chief exec. officer, 1975-77; exec. v.p. Garfinckel, Brooks Bros., Miller & Rhoads, Inc., Washington, 1977-79, pres., 1979-82, also dir.; chmn. bd., chief exec. officer Morse Shoe, Inc., Canton, Mass., 1982-92. Overseer Beth Israel Hosp., Boston; trustee Mass. Eye and Ear Infirmary, Boston; bd. govs. Am. Jewish Com.; mem. corp. Judge Baker Children's Ctr. Lt. USN, 1953-56. Mem. Univ. Club, Harvard Club. Home: 370 Beacon St Boston MA 02116-1002

ROSENBERG, MARILYN ROSENTHAL, artist, visual poet; b. Phila., Oct. 11, 1934; m. Robert Rosenberg, June 12, 1955; 2 children. B in Profl. Studies in Studio Arts, SUNY, Empire State Coll., 1978; MA in Liberal Studies, NYU, 1993. Represented in permanent collections Avant Writing Collection, The Ohio State U. Librs., Whtiney Mus. Am. Art, Frances Mulhull Ancilles Libr., N.Y.C., numerous one-woman shows including most recently, one-woman shows include Marymount Coll., Tarrytown, N.Y., 1993, McHenry County Coll., Crystal Lake, Ill., 1997, John Jay Coll., N.Y.C., 1999, Westchester CC, Valhalla, N.Y., 2002, numerous group shows including most recently, exhibited in group shows at Fla. Atlantic U., Boca Raton, Fla., 2000, U. Ctrl. Ark., Conway, 2000, Ocean Grove Libr., Victoria, Australia, 2000, City Gallery, Szekesfehervar, Hungary, 2000, The Temple Judea, Elkins Park, Pa., 2001, Art Acad. Cin., 2002, Ohio State U. Librs., Columbus, 2002, Cuesta Coll. Art Gallery, San Luis Obispo, Calif., 2002, Pensacola (Fla.) Mus. Art, 2002, U. Indpls. (Ind.) Gallery, 2002, The Ctr. for Book Arts, N.Y.C., N.Y., 2003, Lowenstein Gallery, Miami, Fla., 2003, Starr Gallery, Newton Ctr., Mass., 2003, The Buddy Holly Ctr., Lubbock, Tex., 2003, Peck Arts Ctr. Gallery, Ctrl. Wyo. Coll., Riverton, 2003, Purdue U. Galleries, Lafayette, Ind., 2003, Wexford (Ireland) Arts Centre, Ellipse Art Ctr., Arlington, Va., 2003, Durango Art Ctr., Colo., 2004. Home: 67 Lakeview Ave W Cortlandt Manor NY 10567-6415

ROSENBERG, MARK B. political science educator, university official; b. Athens, Ohio, Aug. 15, 1949; married; 2 children. BA, Miami U., Oxford, Ohio, 1971; PhD in Polit. Sci., U. Pitts., 1976. Prof. polit. sci. Fla. Internat. U., Miami, 1976—, chmn. Caribbean L.Am. studies coun., 1977-79, founding dir. L.Am. and Caribbean Ctr., 1979—, founding/acting dean Coll. Urban and Pub. Affairs, 1994-97, vice provost for internat. studies, 1996-98, provost, acting pres., 1998—, acting pres., 1999-2000, provost, exec. v.p. acad. affairs, 2000—. Mem. exec. com. OLAM; mem. articulation coordination com. Fla. Bd. Edn.; mem. Coun. of Fgn. Relations, Pacific Coun. on Internat. Realtions. Author, editor, co-editor 6 books; former bd. editors Fla. Trend, Latin Trade; contbr. articles to profl. jours. Presdl. appointee U.S. Customs Dist. Export Coun.; mem. exec. com. OLAM, the Jewish Leadership Inst./Jewish Fedn. Miami; mem. statewide articulation coordination com. Fla. Bd. Edn. Mem. Greater Miami C. of C. (vice chair exec. com. for internat. econ. devel. 1992-94), Coun. Fgn. Rels., Pacific Coun. in Internat. Rels. Office: Fla Internat U University Park Pc 526 Miami FL 33199-0001

ROSENBERG, MARK L. health agency administrator; b. Newark, July 30, 1945; m. Jill Alison Dimond; children: Julie, Ben. BA in Biology magna cum laude, Harvard Coll., 1967, MD cum laude, M of Pub. Policy, Harvard Coll., 1972. Diplomate Am. Bd. Internal Medicine, Am. Bd. Psychiatry and Neurology. Intern Mass. Gen. Hosp., Boston, 1972—73, resident in medicine, 1973—74; resident in preventive medicine Ctrs. for Disease Control, Atlanta, 1975—76; resident in psychiatry Beth Israel Hosp., Boston, 1980—83; clin. prof. dept. cmty. medicine and family practice Morehouse Sch. Medicine, Atlanta, 1984—93; clin. prof. psychiatry Emory U. Sch. Medicine, Atlanta, 1994—99; exec. dir. Task Force for Child Survival and Devel., 1999—; dir. sci. devel., dir. programs Ctr. for Child Well-being, 1999—. Dir. Nat. Ctr. for Injury Prevention and Control, Atlanta, 1994—99, acting assoc. dir. for pub. health practice, 1992—93; dir. divsn. injury control Ctr. for Environ. Health and Injury Control, 1989—92; spl. asst. for behavioral sci., office of dep. dir. CDC, Atlanta, 1989, advisor to dep. dir., 88, asst. dir. for sci. divsn. injury epidemiology and control, 1986—88, liaison officer office program planning and evaluation, 1979—80; assoc. dir. office extramural health programs Harvard Sch. Pub. Health, Boston, 1979—80; clin. fellow in psychiatry Harvard Med. Sch., Boston, 1980—83; vis. prof. dept. cmty. health Emory U. Sch. Medicine, Atlanta, 1984—91, clin. asst. prof. psychiatry, 1985—87, clin. assoc. prof., 1988—93; adj. prof. Emory U. Sch. Pub. Health, Atlanta, 1991—; clin. prof. dept. cmty. health and preventive medicine Morehouse Sch. Medicine, Atlanta, 1993—; staff physician Women's Med. Clinic, Atlanta, 1974—76, Harvard St. Neighborhood Health Ctr., Boston, 1976—77, Winchester (Mass.) Hosp., 1978—83; emergency rm. physician Burbank Hosp., Fitchburg, Mass., 1976—77, Harrington Hosp., Southbridge, Mass., 1976—77; vis. physician dept. psychiatry Grady Meml. Hosp., Atlanta, 1985—; lectr. and cons. in field. Author: Patients: The Experience of Illness, 1980, Violence in America: A Public Health Approach, 1990; mem. editl. bd. Violence and Victims, 1985—88, Violence, Aggression and Terrorism, 1986—; contbr. articles to profl. jours. Active Calif. Wellness Found., 1993—; bd. dirs. southeastern divsn., sci. adv. coun. Am. Suicide Found., 1990—. Recipient Coulter Lecture award, Am. ongress Rehab. Medicine, 1991, William S. one award, Am. Trauma Soc., 1991, Outstanding Achievement award, 1994, World Health Day award, Am. Assn. for World Health, 1993, Disting. Svc. award, Ga. Assn. Family and Marital Therapists, 1994, Disting. Achievement award, Disability Wellness Assn., 1998, Outstanding Svc. medal, USPHS, 2000, Meritorious Svc. medal, 2000, Disting. Svc. medal, 2000; fellow, Mass. Gen. Hosp., 1977—78, Mead-Johnson, 1982; scholar, John Harvard, 1964. Mem.: Alpha Omega Alpha, Inst. of Medicine of NAS, Phi Beta Kappa. Avocation: photography. Home: 972 Oakdale Rd NE Atlanta GA 30307-1272 Office: 750 Commerce Dr Ste 400 Decatur GA 30030

ROSENBERG, MARK LOUIS, lawyer; b. Lexington, Ky., Sept. 21, 1947; s. Edward George and Shirley Lee (Berkin) R.; m. Betty Adler, May 16, 1982; stepchildren: Aaron, Sarah Claxton; children: Eli, Daniel. BA, U. Mich., 1969; JD, harvard U., 1973; LLM in Taxation, Georgetown U., 1985. Bar: D.C. 1973, Md. 1991, U.S. Dist. Ct. D.C. 1973, U.S. Ct. Appeals (D.C. cir.) 1973. Asst. to v.p. George Washington U., 1973-75; counsel U.S. Ho. of Reps., Washington, 1975-77; sr. atty. FTC, Washington, 1977-85; ptnr. Gordon, Feinblatt et al, Washington, 1989-91; prin. Law Offices of Mark L. Rosenberg, 1991—; of counsel The Jacobovitz Law Firm, 1994-97. Mem. Fed. Bar Assn. (dep. sect. coord., Disting. Svc. award 1982, 83, 87). Democrat. Jewish. Home: 6101 Shady Oak Ln Bethesda MD 20817-6027 Office: Law Offices of Mark L Rosenberg 6917 Arlington Rd Ste 301 Bethesda MD 20814-5211

ROSENBERG, MICHAEL, lawyer; b. N.Y.C., Oct. 13, 1937; s. Walter and Eva (Bernstein) Rosenberg; m. Jacqueline Raymonde Combe, Apr. 29, 1966; children: Andrew James, Suzanne Jennifer. AB in Econs. with honors, Ind. U., 1959; LLB, Columbia U., 1962. Bar: NY 1963, US Ct Appeals (2d cir) 1975, US Dist Ct (ea dist so div) Mich 1989. From. dep. asst. atty. gen. to asst. atty. gen. N.Y. State Dept. Law, N.Y.C., 1963-66; assoc. Hellerstein, Rosier & Rembar, N.Y.C., 1966-73; assoc. gen. counsel Gen. Instrument Corp., N.Y.C., 1973-78; from assoc. gen. counsel to dep. gen. counsel U.S. Filter Corp., N.Y.C., 1978-82; v.p., gen. counsel, sec. Alfa-Laval Inc., Ft. Lee, N.J., 1982-88; counsel Becker Ross Stone De Stefano & Klein, N.Y.C., 1988-89; ptnr. Rosenberg & Rich, White Plains, N.Y., 1989-95, Quinn, Marantis & Rosenberg, LLP, White Plains, N.Y., 1995-97, Marantis, Rosenberg & van Nes, LLP, White Plains, 1997-2001; atty. Law Offices of Michael Rosenberg, White Plains, 2001—. Mem Zoning Bd Appeals Town of North Castle, NY, 1995—. Mem.: ABA, Westchester County Bar Assn., NY State Bar Assn. Office: Law Offices of Michael Rosenberg 120 Bloomingdale Rd White Plains NY 10605

ROSENBERG, MICHAEL JOSEPH, financial executive; b. Passaic, NJ, Apr. 19, 1928; s. Emanuel and Sylvia Sarah (Schwartz) R.; m. Judith Ann Melnick, Dec. 6, 1964 (div. 1983); children: Ann Kirsten, Emily Jeanne; m. Kathleen Ann Jennings, Mar. 3, 1990. BS, Upsala Coll., 1951; MBA, NYU, 1955, postgrad., 1955-59. Asst. v.p. Meinhard & Co., N.Y.C., 1953-58, A.J. Armstrong Co., N.Y.C., 1958-59, Sterling Nat. Bank, N.Y.C., 1959-61; exec. v.p. Rosenthal & Rosenthal, Inc., N.Y.C., 1961-96; chmn. Taurus Global, LLC, 2000—. Bd. dirs.chmn. 2004 D.V.L., Inc., N.Y.C.; dir. Am. com. Shenkar U.; mem. deptl. disciplinary com. Supreme Ct. NY Appellate Divsn. Contbr. numerous articles on comml. fin. to newspapers and mags. Bd. dirs., treas. Town Hall Found., NYC, 1982 ; treas. Citizens for Clean Air, NYC, 1984, NY Rd. Runners Found., 2002—; trustee NYU, 1997—. Capt. U.S. Army, 1951-53, Korea; col. NY Guard, 1997—2003. Decorated Silver Star, Bronze Star; recipient Meritorious Svc. award NYU, 1983; Albert Gallatin fellow, 1981. Mem. Albert Gallatin Assocs. (chmn. 1984-87), NYU Bus. Forum (pres. 1981-82), NYU Grad. Sch. Bus. Adminstrn. Alumni Assn. (pres. 1978-79), NYU Ptnrs. (co-chmn. 1987-89, chmn. 1990-93), NYU Club (pres. 1975-77, 82-85), NYU Alumni Assn. (pres. 2004— Avocations: skiing, tennis, running, sailing. Office: 53 Columbus Ave Ste 2 New York NY 10023-6917 Office Phone: 212-581-6546.

ROSENBERG, NORMAN JACK, agricultural meteorologist, educator; b. Bklyn., Feb. 22, 1930; s. Jacob and Rae (Dombrowitz) R.; m. Sarah Zacher, Dec. 30, 1950; children: Daniel Jonathon, Alyssa Yael. BS, Mich. State U., 1951; MS, Okla. State U., 1958; PhD, Rutgers U., 1961. Soil scientist Israel Soil Conservation Service, Haifa, 1953-55, Israel Water Authority, Haifa, 1955-57; asst. prof. agrl. meteorology U. Nebr., Lincoln, 1961-64, assoc. prof., 1964-67, prof. agrl. meteorology, 1967—, prof. agrl. engring., 1975—, prof. agronomy, 1976—, George Holmes prof. agrl. meteorology, 1981-87, prof. emeritus, 1987—, leader sect. agrl. meteorology, 1975-79, acting asst. vice chancellor for research, 1983-85; sr. fellow, dir. climate resources program Resources for the Future, Washington, 1987-92; chief scientist integrated earth studies energy sci. divsn. Battelle Pacific N.W. Nat. Lab., Washington, 1992—2003, lab. fellow emeritus, 2003—; scientist Joint Global Change Rsch. Inst., Pacific N.W. Nat. Lab. and U. Md., 2001—; affiliate mem. Washington Adv. Group, 2003—. Cons. Dept. State AID, NOAA Oak Ridge Assoc. Univs., 1986—87; cons. Elec. Power Rsch. Inst., 1989—92, Sandia Nat. Labs., 1990; mem. numerous ad hoc coms. and mem. standing com. on atmsopheric sci. NAS/NRC, 1975—78, mem. bd. atmospheric sci. and climate, 1982—85; mem. U.S. com. Internat. Geosphere-Biosphere Program, 1984—86; mem. panel on policy implications of climate change, 1990—91; mem. bd. coun. Agrl. Sci. and Tech.; vis. prof. agrl. meteorology Israel Inst. Tech., Haifa, 1968; trustee Nat. Inst. Global Environ. Change, 1992, vice-chmn., 1992—95, chmn., 1996—2000; adj. prof. dept. geography U. Md., College Park, adj. prof. Sch. Natural Resources Sci., 2003; bd. dirs. Ctr. for Rsch. on the Changing Earth Sys., Columbia, Md., 2002. Author: Microclimate: The Biological Environment, 1974, 2d edit., 1983, Chinese transl., 1983, Malay transl., 1987; editor: North American Droughts, 1978, Drought in the Great Plains: Research on Impacts and Strategies, 1980, Greenhouse Warming: Abatement and Adaptation, 1989, Toward an Integrated Impact Assessment of Climate Change: The MINK Study, 1993, Carbon Sequestration in Soils: New Science, Monitoring and Beyond, 1999; editor: (with V.C. Cole and K. Paustian) Mitigation of Greenhouse Gas Emissions by the Agricultural Sector, Spl. issue of Climate Change, 1998; editor: (with R.C. Izaurralde) Storing Carbon in Agricultural Soils: A multipurpose environmental strategy, Spl. issue of Climatic Change, 2001; tech. editor: Agronomy Jour., 1974—79, cons. editor: Agrl. and Forest Meteorology, Climatic Change; contbr. articles to profl. jours. Mem. Intergovernmental Panel on Climate Change, 1993—. Recipient Centennial medal Nat. Weather Svc., 1970; sr. fellow in sci., NATO, 1968, rsch. fellow U. Nebr., 1968, Lady Davis fellow Hebrew U., Jerusalem, 1977, nat. resources fellow Resources for Future, 1986; grantee State of Nebr., 1970-73, NSF, 1971-87, 96, U.S. Dept. Commerce, 1972-74, 80-82, 83-85, 88-89, NASA, 1972-73, 85-86, U.S. Dept. Interior, 1974-75, 77-79, 88—, USDA, 1979-82, 88-89, U. Nebr. Found., 1982, Nat. Ctr. Atmospheric Rsch., 1984-85, U.S. Dept. Energy, 1989-92, G. Gunnar Vetleson Found., 1987-92, UN Environ. Program, 1989, EPA, 1988-89, 98, NASA, 1995-97, 98, NOAA, 1996. Fellow AAAS (com. climate 1984-89, com. global change 1992-96, adv. panel Earth Explorer ency. 1992-95), Am. Soc. Agronomy, Am. Meteorol. Soc. (Outstanding Achievement in Bioclimatology award 1978, councillor 1981-84), Am. Water Resources Assn. (Boggess award, 2004); mem. Am. Assn. State Climatologists (Nebr. rep. 1979-81), Arid Zone Soc. India, Sigma Xi, Alpha Zeta, Gamma Sigma Rho. Clubs: Cosmos (Washington). Jewish. Office: Joint Global Change Rsch Inst 8400 Baltimore Ave College Park MD 20740-2496 Office Phone: 301-314-6753. E-mail: nj.rosenberg@pnl.gov.

ROSENBERG, PAMELA, performing company executive, conductor; b. Los Angeles, Calif., 1945; m. Wolf Rosenberg (dec. 1996); 2 children. Diploma, London Opera Ctr.; B, U. Calif. at Berkely, 1966; M in Russian hist., Ohio State U. Various positions Frankfurt Opera, 1974—87; dir. of ops. Deutscher Schauspielhaus, Hamburg, Germany, 1987—88; mgr., artistic affairs Netherlands Opera, 1988—90; co-gen. dir. Stuggart Opera, 1990—2000; gen. dir. San Francisco Opera, 2001—. Office: San Francisco Opera 301 VanNess Ave San Francisco CA 94102*

ROSENBERG, PAUL I. lawyer; b. Newark, Feb. 26, 1937; BS in Econs., U. Pa. Wharton Sch., 1959; MBA, NYU, 1964, JD, 1970, LLM, 1975. Bar: N.J. 1970, U.S. Dist. Ct. N.J. 1970, N.Y. 1982, U.S. Dist. Ct. (3rd dist.) N.Y. 1982, U.S. Tax Ct. 1983, U.S. Supreme Ct. Ptnr. Fox and Fox LLP, Livingston, 1974—. Mem. Essex Co. Probate Early Settlement panel. Fellow Am. Coll. Trust and Estate Counsel (nat. employee benefits in estate-planning, estate and gift tax com.); mem. ABA, Essex County Bar Assn., NJ State Bar Assn. Home: One Belgrade Terr West Orange NJ 07052 Office: Fox and Fox LLP 70 S Orange Ave Livingston NJ 07039-4994 Office Phone: 973-597-0777.

ROSENBERG, PIERRE MAX, museum director; b. Paris, Apr. 13, 1936; s. Charles and Gertrude (Nassauer) R.; m. Béatrice de Rothschild, July 29, 1981. Baccalauréat, Lycée Charlemagne, Paris; Licence, Law Faculty, Paris; Diplome, Louvre Sch., Paris. Chief curator dept. paintings Musée du Louvre, Paris, 1982-94, pres., dir., 1994—2001. Author: Chardin, 1963, 99, Peyron, 1983, (catalogue) La peinture francaise du XVIIe siècle dans les coll. américaines, 1981, (catalogue) Watteau, 1984, 96, Fragonard, 1987, Frères Le Nain, 1993, Poussin, 1994, G. de la Tour, 1997, D. Vivant Denon, 1999, David, 2002. Mem. Soc. Histoire Art Francais (pres. 1982-84), Com. Francais Histoire Art (pres. 1984-96), Acad. Francaise. Home: 35 rue de Vaugirard 75006 Paris France E-mail: pierre.rosenberg@wanadoo.fr.

ROSENBERG, RALPH, former state senator, lawyer, consultant, educator, foundation administrator; b. Chgo., Oct. 7, 1949; s. Nathan Benjamin and Rhea (Matlow) R.; m. Teresa Marie Sturm, July 11, 1989; children: Jacob Louis, Joel Patrick. BS in Commerce and Bus. Adminstrn., U. Ill., 1972; JD, Drake Law Sch., 1974. Bar: Iowa 1974. Sole practice Rosenberg Law Firm, Ames, Iowa, 1974—; mem. Iowa Ho. of Reps., Des Moines, 1981-90, Iowa Senate, Des Moines, 1990-94. Adj. faculty Des. Moines Area C.C., 1980—, Drake Law Sch., 1992, Upper Iowa U., 1993, Iowa State U., 1994—; dir. Environ. Planning Rsch. Group, Ames, 1976-77; exec. dir. Story County Legal Aid Soc., Nevada, Iowa, 1977-78; asst. Story County atty. County Attys. Office, Nevada, 1979-81; exec. dir., mng. atty. Youth Law Ctr., Des Moines, 1989-92; chair adv. bd. Inst. Pub. Leadership, 1994—; exec. dir. Coalition for Family and Childrens Svcs., 1995-2002; co-chair Iowans United for a Healthy Future; exec. dir. Heartland Sr. Svcs., 2003-04; exec. dir. Iowal Civil Rights Commn., 2004—. Author, editor: Public Interest Law, 1992; author: Family Theory, Law, Policy and Practice, 1994; editor: Descriptive Analysis of Iowa Environmental Agencies, 1977. Past chair Midwest Leadership Inst. of Coun. of State Govt.; bd. dirs. Emergency Residence Project Jewish Cmty. Rels. Commn., Iowa Protection and Advocacy, regional adv. bd. Legal Svcs. Corp. Iowa, Child and Family Policy Ctr.; past bd. dirs. Co-op. Child Care Svcs., Cmty. Action Rsch. Group, Rural Iowa. Recipient Outstanding Contbn. to Well-being of Children award Youth and Shelter Svcs., 1992, Excellence in Svc. award Legal Svcs. Group, 1993, Iowa LWV Cornerstone award, 1994, Iowa Farmers' Union Friend of the Farmer award, 1994, Iowa Consumer Action Network Citizen Svc. award, 1994; named LEgislator of Yr., Sierra Club, 1988, Isaak Walton League, 1993, Common Ground award Inst. of Public Leadership, 1997; named Legis. Conservationist of Yr., Wildlife Soc., 1988, Elected Ofcl. of Yr., Iowa Corrections Assn., 1984. Mem.: Nat. Conf. State Legislators (criminal justice com. 1986—94), Iowa State Bar Assn. Home: 811 Ridgewood Ave Ames IA 50010-5823 E-mail: hn3957@earthlink.net.

ROSENBERG, RAYMOND DAVID, special education educator, consultant; b. Jersey City, Apr. 25, 1951; s. Fabulous Sam and Arlene (White) R.; m. JoAnn Gabriella Simchera, June 10, 1984; 1 child, Anna Teresa. BA, Boston U., 1974; MEd, William Paterson Coll., 1978, MEd in Sch. Adminstrn., 1994, Cert. tchr., N.J. Tchr. reading Passaic County Tech. Vocat. High Sch., Wayne, NJ, 1980-82; specialist learning disabilities North Jersey Devel. Ctr., Totowa, 1983-84; ednl. specialist Div. Devel. Disabilities, Totowa, NJ, 1984-85, tchr. profoundly retarded students, 1987-89, tchr. medically frail, 1990-91; tchr. mildly retarded, emotionally disturbed students North Jersey Devel. Ctr., Totowa, NJ, 1992-93; learning disabilities tchr. Office of Edn., NJ, 1993-96; cons. youth consultation svcs. George Washington Sch. Annex, Hackensack, NJ, 1993-96; learning cons. child study team North Bergen (N.J.) H.S., 1996-98; GED tchr. Bergen C.C. Computer Learning Ctr., Paramus, 1998—. Learning disabilities tchr., cons., 1997-2000; pres. Ednl. Assessment Svcs., Inc., 2002—; mem. child study team and behavioral intervention team West N.Y. Early Childhood Sch., 2002-. With ABA discrete trial learning with PDD autistic students, 2003—; staff Office of the Child Study Team, Garfield, NJ. Recipient Eagle Scout award Boy Scouts Am., Ridgefield, N.J., 1968, 7 tchg. certs., 1978-89. Mem. Nat. Eagle Scout Assn., Pi Lambda Theta (Beta Chi chpt.). Episcopal. Lodge: Order of Arrow. Office: 541 Palisade Ave Garfield NJ 07026 Office Phone: 973-340-5044. E-mail: rayjoanna@nj.rr.com.

ROSENBERG, RICHARD F. physician, radiologist; b. N.Y.C., June 13, 1942; s. Henry J. and Sylvia (Harris) R.; m. Judith Wolf, May 5, 1985; 1 child, Glen. BA, Colgate U., 1964; MD, N.Y. Med. Coll., 1968. Diplomate Am. Bd. Radiology. Intern Met. Hosp., N.Y.C., 1968-69; resident Montefiore Hosp. and Med. Ctr., Bronx, N.Y., 1969-70, 72-74, chief resident, 1974; radiologist Lipsay & Rosenberg, Great Neck, N.Y., 1974-78, dir. gastrointestinal radiology North Shore U. Hosp., Manhasset, N.Y., 1978-82; radiologist, owner Great Neck Radiologists, 1982—. Mem. adv. bd. Bank of Great Neck, 1990-94. Contbr. articles to profl. jours. Lt. comdr. USN, 1970-72. Fellow Am. Coll. Gastroenterology; mem. Am. Coll. Radiology, Alpha Omega Alpha. Republican. Office: Great Neck Radiologists 935 Northern Blvd Great Neck NY 11021-5309 Office Phone: 516-829-4414.

ROSENBERG, RICHARD MORRIS, banker; b. Fall River, Mass., Apr. 21, 1930; s. Charles and Betty (Peck) R.; m. Barbara K. Cohen, Oct. 21, 1956; children: Michael, Peter. BS, Suffolk U., 1952; MBA, Golden Gate U., 1962; LLB, Golden Gate Coll., 1966. Publicity asst. Crocker-Anglo Bank, San Francisco, 1959-62; banking services officer Wells Fargo Bank, N.A., San Francisco, 1962-65, asst. v.p., 1965-68, v.p. mktg. dept., 1968, v.p., dir. mktg., 1969, sr. v.p. mktg. and advt. div., 1970-75, exec. v.p., from 1975, vice chmn., 1980-83, Crocker Nat. Corp., 1983-85; pres., chief operating officer Seafirst Corp., 1986-87, also dir.; pres., chief operating officer, also bd. dirs. Seattle First Nat. Bank, 1985-87; vice chmn. bd. BankAm. Corp., San Francisco, 1987-90, chmn., CEO, 1990-96. Bd. dirs. ABX Air, Inc., Pacific Life, Exigen Group, Health Care Property Investors, Inc.; past chmn. Mastercard Internat.; past. pres. Fed. Res. Adv. Coun. Bd. dirs. San Francisco Symphony, United Way, Buck Inst. for Age Rsch., Am. Ctr. for Wine, Food and the Arts; trustee Calif. Inst. Tech. Jewish. Office: Bank of Am CA5-705-11-01 555 California St San Francisco CA 94104- E-mail: richard.rosenberg@bankofamerica.com.

ROSENBERG, ROBERT ALLEN, psychologist, educator, optometrist; b. Phila., July 31, 1935; s. Theodore Samuel and Dorothy (Bailes) R.; m. Geraldine Bella Tishler, Sept. 3, 1961; children: Lawrence David, Ronald Joseph. BA, Temple U., 1957, MA, 1964; BS, Pa. Coll. Optometry, 1960, OD, 1961. Lic. optometrist, psychologist, Pa. Instr. Pa. Coll. Optometry, Phila., 1962-65, asst. prof., 1965-67; asst. prof. psychology Community Coll. Phila., 1967-76, assoc. prof., 1976—. Pvt. practice optometry, Roslyn, Pa., 1965-95; assoc. in practice optometry, Huntingdon Valley, Pa., 1995-98. Contbr. articles to profl. jours. Named Humanitarian Chapel of Four Chaplains Bapt. Temple, 1980. Fellow Am. Acad. Optometry; mem. Am. Optometric Assn., Pa. Optometric Assn., Bucks-Montgomery Optometric Assn., Alumni Assn. Pa. Coll. Optometry (v.p. 1992-98, sec. 1991—). Avocations: singing, acting, photography, writing, public speaking. Home: 970 Corn Crib Dr Huntingdon Valley PA 19006-3304 Office: Community Coll Phila 1700 Spring Garden St Philadelphia PA 19130-3991

ROSENBERG, ROBERT BRINKMANN, technology organization executive; b. Chgo., Mar. 19, 1937; s. Sidney and Gertrude (Brinkmann) Rosenberg; m. Patricia Margaret Kane, Aug. 1, 1959 (dec. Feb. 1988); children: John Richard, Debra Ann; m. Maryann Bartoli Manrot, June 25, 1989. BSChemE with distinction, Ill. Inst. Tech., 1958, MS in Gas Tech, 1961, PhD in Gas Tech, 1964. Registered profl. engr., Ill. Adj. asst. prof. Ill. Inst. Tech., 1965-69; mem. staff Inst. Gas Tech., Chgo., 1962-77, v.p. engring. rsch., 1973-77; v.p. R & D Gas Rsch. Inst., Chgo., 1977-78, exec. v.p., sr. v.p., 1978-84, v.p., 1984-96; pres. RBR @ Vision, Burr Ridge, Ill., 1996—; bd. dirs. IEA Internat. Ctr. Gas Tech. Info. Tech. program dir. World Energy Congress, 1996—98. Pres. Triangle Frat. Edn. Found., 1974—96, bd. dirs., 1996—2001, dir. emeritus; bd. dirs. Hinsdale Arts Coun., 1977—85, dir. emeritus, 1985—95; mem. adv. coun. U. Tex. Coll. Natural Scis. Found., 1990—95; mem. giving com. Norton Arboretum, 2004—; mem. Hinsdale (Ill.) Home Rule Ad Hoc Com., 1975—77; mem. vis. com. dept. chemistry U. Tex.; bd. advisors Chgo. (Ill.) 502, 2004—; pres. Lake Ridge Club Homeowners Assn., 2001—. Recipient Gas Industry Rsch. award, 1985, Energy Exec. of the Yr. award, 1987, Profl. Achievement award, Ill. Inst. Tech. Alumni Assn., 1991. Mem.: AIChE, Triangle (Svc. Key and Outstanding Alumnus award 1987), Air Pollution Control Assn. (past sect. com. residential pollution sources), Gas Appliance Engrs. Soc. (past trustee), Internat. Gas Union, Atlantic Gas Rsch. Exch., Combustion Inst. (past treas. bd. dirs. ctrl. states sect.), Inst. Gas Engrs., Am. Gas Assn. (oper. sect. award of merit 1989). Achievements include patents for 13 patents in field. Home: 28 Lake Ridge Club Dr Burr Ridge IL 60527-7937 Office: RBR @ Vision 28 Lake Ridge Club Dr Burr Ridge IL 60527-7937 Office Phone: 630-654-3213. Personal E-mail: RBR3@comcast.net.

ROSENBERG, ROBERT CHARLES, housing corporation executive; b. Bronx, N.Y., Oct. 21, 1934; s. Bernard L. and Flora (Popiel) R.; m. Diane Stricof, Jan. 29, 1962 (dec.); children: Andrew, Scott; m. Frances Kaufman, Sept. 11, 1976; stepchildren: Michael Kaufman, Benjamin Kaufman. BS, NYU, 1955, JD (hon.), 1995; LLB, Columbia U., 1958. Bar: N.Y. 1959. Adminstrv. asst. N.Y. State Dept. Law, N.Y.C., 1957-58; assoc. firm Barron Rice & Rochmore, N.Y.C., 1959-62, Carro Spanbock & Londin, N.Y.C., 1962-68; 1st dep. commr. for devel. dept. N.Y.C. Housing and Devel. Adminstrn., 1968-73; 1st sr. v.p., dir. Starrett Corp., N.Y.C., 1973-97; gen. mgr. Starrett City; pres., chmn. bd. Grenadier Realty Corp., 1976-97; pres. Rosenberg Housing Group, 1997—. Lectr. Practicing Law Inst., Real Estate Bd. N.Y.C., Harvard U. Kennedy Sch. of Govt., Beijing Inst. of Design, U. Nancy (France), Columbia U., NYU, others; fed. receiver Chester (Pa.) Housing Authority, 1994—; adj. prof. dept. urban affairs Hunter Coll., N.Y.C., 1998—. Author N.Y. acts for residential constrn., rent. Candidate for N.Y. State Assembly, 1958, 65; sec. N.Y. State Assn. Young Rep. Clubs, 1959-61; bd. dirs., chmn. emeritus Bklyn. Philharm.; bd. dirs. Bklyn. Acad. Music, 1978-99; v.p. Citizens Housing and Planning Coun.; dir. Nat. Housing Conf. Served with USAF, 1958. Mem. ABA, N.Y. State Bar Assn., N.Y. County Lawyers Assn., Nat. Assn. Housing and Renewal Ofcls., Urban Land Inst., N.Y.C. Assn. Builders and Owners (v.p.). Home: 201 E 79th St New York NY 10021-0830 Office: 419 Park Ave S New York NY 10016-8410 E-mail: rcr61@aol.com.

ROSENBERG, ROGER NEWMAN, neurologist, educator, department chair; b. Milw., Mar. 3, 1939; s. Sol J. and Cora D. (Newman) R.; m. Adrienne Turick, June 24, 1962; children— Jennifer, Lara Student, Tufts U., 1957-60; BS, Northwestern U., 1961, MD with distinction, 1964. Diplomate Am. Bd. Psychiatry and Neurology. Intern Harvard Med. Service, Beth Israel Hosp., Boston, 1964-65; resident in neurology Neurol. Inst., Columbia U., N.Y.C., 1965-67, instr. neurology, 1967-68; research assoc. Lab. of Biochem. Genetics, NIH, Bethesda, Md., 1968-70; clin. instr. Howard U. Med. Sch., Washington, 1969-70; asst. prof. neuroscis. Sch. Medicine, U. Calif.-San Diego, 1970-71; assoc. prof. neuroscis. and pediatrics, attending neurologist Univ. Hosp., U. Calif.-La Jolla, 1971-74; prof., chmn. dept. neurology U. Tex. Southwestern Med. Ctr., Dallas, 1973-91, prof. physiology, 1976—, Zale Disting. chair, prof. neurology, 1990—, dir. Alzheimer's Disease Rsch. Ctr., 1989—. Attending neurologist Parkland Meml. Hosp. and Children's Med. Ctr., Dallas, 1974—, Zale Lipshy Univ. Hosp., 1990 ; mem. staff Presbyn. Hosp., Dallas, 1974—, St. Paul's Hosp., Dallas, 1974—; cons. staff VA Hosp., Dallas, 1974—; mem. nat. med. adv. bd. Nat. Ataxia Found., Mpls., 1971—, Myasthenia Gravis Found., 1973; chmn. med. adv. bd., dir. med. sci. research Internat. Joseph Diseases Found., Livermore, Calif., 1977—; lectr. Japanese Soc. Neurology, 1987, 94, Chinese Neurol. Soc., 1987, Spanish Neurol. Soc., 1992; chmn. bd. sci. councilors NINDS/NIH, 1984-86; pres. (hon.), Intl. French Soc. of Neurology Charcot Centenary Symposium, 1993. Editor Jour. Neurogenetics; mem. editl. bd. Neurology, 1977-82, 91-97, Trends in Neurosci., 1980-86, Current Opinion in Neurology & Neurosurgery, 1990—, Jour. of AMA, 1997—; chief editor Archives of Neurology, 1997—; contbr. articles to med. jours. Bd. dirs. Winston Sch., Dallas, 1974-80 1st Woody Guthrie scholar, 1971; USPHS grantee; recipient Disting. Alumnus award Neurol. Inst., N.Y., 1994. Fellow AAAS; mem. Am. Acad. Neurology (chmn. sci. program com. nat. meetings 1979-84, elected councillor exec. bd. 1984-89, pres. 1991-93), Am. Neurochem. Soc., Tissue Culture Soc., Soc. Neurosci., Am. Fedn. Clin. Rsch., Soc. Pediat. Rsch., Internat. Child Neurology Assn., Am. Neurol. Assn. (1st v.p. 1987), Ctrl. Soc. Neurol. Rsch., Can. Congress Neurol. Scis. (hon.), Spanish Neurol. Soc. (hon. 1994), Sigma Xi, Alpha Omega Alpha (Merit award Northwestern U. Alumni Assn. 1986). Home: 4425 Wildwood Rd Dallas TX 75209-2801 Office: U Tex Southwestern Med Ctr Dallas TX 75235 E-mail: RogerRosenberg@utsouthwestern.edu.

ROSENBERG, RUDY, chemical company executive; b. Feb. 26, 1930; came to U.S., 1949, naturalized, 1954; s. Hilaire and Frieda Rosenberg; m. Rose H. Wauters, Nov. 7, 1953; 1 child, Rudy. Student in classical studies, Atheneum Leon Lepage, Brussels, 1946. Buyer Lever Bros., Brussels, 1946-49; head biochem. divsn. Mann Rsch. Labs., N.Y.C., 1954-61, Gallard-Schlesinger, Carle Place, N.Y., 1961-75; pres. Accurate Chem. & Sci. Corp., Westbury, N.Y., 1975—. Prin., v.p., Leeches U.S.A. Ltd. Served with U.S. Army, 1951-53. Mem. Reticuloendothelial Soc. Internat. Clubs: Antique Automobile, Rolls Royce, Puppetry Guild Greater N.Y. Democrat.

ROSENBERG, SAMUEL NATHAN, French and Italian language educator; b. N.Y.C., Jan. 19, 1936; s. Israel and Etta (Friedland) R. AB, Columbia U., 1957; PhD, Johns Hopkins U., 1965. Instr. Columbia U., N.Y.C., 1960-61; lectr. Ind. U., Bloomington, Ind., 1962-65, asst. prof., 1965-69, assoc. prof., 1969-81, prof. dept. French and Italian, 1981-99, prof. emeritus, 2000—, chmn. dept., 1977-84. Author: Modern French CE, 1970, (with others) Harper's Grammar of French, 1983, (with W. Apel) French Secular Compositions of the 14th Century, 3 vols., 1970-72, (with H. Tischler) Chanter m'estuet: Songs of the Trouveres, 1981; translator: (with S. Danon) Ami and Amile, 1981, revised edit., 1996, Lyrics and Melodies of Gace Brulé, 1985, (with H. Tischler) The Monophonic Songs in the Roman de Fauvel, 1991, Lancelor-Grail Cycle, vol. 2, 1993, Chansons des trouvères, 1995, Songs of the Troubadours and Trouvères, 1997, (with others) Early French Tristan Poems, 2 vols., 1998. Pres. Mid-Am. Festival of the Arts, Inc., Bloomington, Ind., 1984-85. Woodrow Wilson Found. fellow, 1959-60; Fulbright fellow, 1960-61; Lilly Faculty fellow, 1986-87. Mem MLA, Am. Assn. Tchrs. French; mem. Medieval Acad. Am., Internat. Courtly Lit. Soc., Am. Literary Translators Assn. (bd. dirs. 2002—), Romance Philology Adv. Bd., Phi Beta Kappa Home: PO Box 1164 Bloomington IN 47402-1164 Business E-Mail: srosenbe@indiana.edu.

ROSENBERG, SARAH ZACHER, retired cultural organization administrator; b. Kelem, Lithuania, Jan. 10, 1931; came to U.S., 1938; d. David Meir Zacher and Rachel Korbman; m. Norman J. Rosenberg, Dec. 30, 1950; children: Daniel, Alyssa. BA in History, U. Nebr., 1970, MA in Am. History, 1973. Rsch. historian U. Mid-Am., Lincoln, Nebr., 1974-78, program developer dept. humanities, 1978-79, asst. dir. div. acad. planning, 1980-81, dir. program devel., 1981-82; exec. dir. Nebr. Humanities Coun., Lincoln, 1982-87, Nebr. Found. for Humanities, Lincoln, 1984-87, Am. Inst. for Conservation Hist. and Artistic Works, Washington, 1987-97, exec. dir. found., 1991-97; program officer, spl. cons. mus. div. NEH, Washington, 1987, external reviewer, 1981, 89; pvt. practice Potomac, Md., 1997—2004; ret., 2004. Lay participant long-range planning conf. Nebr. Bar Assn., Hastings, 1986. Co-editor: The Great Plains Experience: Readings in the History of a Region, 1978; contbr. articles to profl. jours. Action mem. Hadassah, Lincoln, 1961—87, Tifereth Israel Synagogue, Lincoln, 1961—87, Beth El Congregation, Besthesda, Md., 1988—2001, Kol Shalom Congregation, 2001—; bd. dirs. Sta. KUCV, affiliate Nat. Pub. Radio, Lincoln, 1986—87, Lincoln Cmty. Playhouse, Lincoln, 1986—87. NEH grantee, 1981, 86, merit awards, 1983, 87; Humanities Resource Ctr. grantee, Peter Kiewit Found., 1984. Mem. Am. Hist. Assn., Western Hist. Assn., Alpha Theta. Democrat. Home: 8102 Appalachian Ter Potomac MD 20854-4050 Personal E-mail: srosenb435@aol.com.

ROSENBERG, SAUL ALLEN, oncologist, educator; b. Cleve., Aug. 2, 1927; BS, Western Res. U., 1948, MD, 1953. Diplomate Am. Bd. Internal Medicine, Am. Bd. Oncology. Intern Univ. Hosp., Cleve., 1953—54; resident in internal medicine Peter Bent Brigham Hosp., Boston, 1954—61; research asst. toxicology AEC Med. Research Project, Western Res. U., 1948—53; asst. prof. medicine and radiology Stanford (Calif.) U., 1961—65, assoc. prof., 1965—79, chief divsn. oncology, 1965—93, prof., 1970—95; prof. emeritus, 1995—; Am. Cancer Soc. prof. Stanford (Calif.) U., 1983—89, assoc. dean, 1989—92. Chmn. bd. No. Calif. Cancer Program, 1974—80. Contbr. articles to profl. jours. Served to lt. M.C. USNR, 1954—56. Master: ACP; fellow: Am. Coll. Radiology (hon.); mem.: Western Assn. Physicians, Western Soc. Clin. Rsch., Radiation Rsch. Soc., Calif. Acad. Medicine, Assn. Am. Physicians, Am. Soc. Clin. Oncology (pres. 1982—83), Inst. Medicine NAS, Am. Assn. Cancer Rsch., Am. Soc. Therapeutic Radiotherapy Oncology (hon.). Office: Stanford U Sch Medicine Div Oncology 269 Campus Dr Stanford CA 94305

ROSENBERG, SEYMOUR, psychologist, educator; b. Newark, Sept. 7, 1926; s. Morris and Celia (Weiss) R.; children: Harold Stanley, Michael Seth. BS, The Citadel, 1948; MA, Ind. U., 1951, PhD, 1952. Rsch. psychologist USAF, San Antonio, 1952-58, U. Kans., Lawrence, 1958-59, Bell Tel. Labs., Murray Hill, NJ, 1959-65; vis. prof. psychology Columbia U., NYC, 1965-66; prof. psychology Rutgers U., New Brunswick, NJ, 1966—2000, chmn. dept. psychology, 1981-83, 94-95, prof. emeritus psychology, 2001—. Adj. prof. Rutgers U. Med. Sch., 1974—2000; vis. scholar U. Leuven, Belgium, 1983, Belgium, 92, Univ. de Provence, France, 1990; panel mem. NSF, 1970—72. Cons. editor Jours. Personality Social Psychology, 1968-69; assoc. editor,

1970-73; contbr. articles to profl. jours. Served with USN, 1945-46. Grantee, NSF, 1965—90, NIMH, 1966—68; Rsch. scientist grantee, 1968—73, Social Sci. Rsch. Coun. fellow, 1973—74. Fellow APA; mem. Soc. Exptl. Social Psychology, Psychometric Soc., Classification Soc., NY Acad. Sci., Ea. Psychol. Assn. Home: 689 Canal Rd Somerset NJ 08873-7327 Office: Rutgers U Dept Psychology ED Livingston Campus New Brunswick NJ 08903 Office Phone: 732-445-2440. Business E-Mail: srpsych@rci.rutgers.edu.

ROSENBERG, SHELI Z. investment company executive; Degree, Tufts U., Northwestern U. Atty. Cotton, Watt, Jones & King, 1966—70; mng. ptnr. Schiff Hardin & Waite, 1976—80; from gen. coun. to vice-chmn. Equity Group Investments, LLC, Chgo., 1980—2000, vice-chmn., 2000—. Bd. dirs. CVS Corp., Capital Trust, Cendant Corp., Manufactured Home Communities, Inc., Equity Residential Properties Trust, Equity Office Properties Trust, Ventas, Inc.; adv. bd. J.L. Kellogg Grad. Sch. Bus. N.W. Univ. Trustee Rush Presbyn. St. Luke's Med. Ctr., exec. com.; co-founder, pres. Ctr. for Exec. Women, J.L. Kellogg Grad. Sch. Bus., 2001—. Office: Equity Group Investments LLC 737 North Michigan Ave Ste 1405 Chicago IL 60611 E-mail: szr312@aol.com.

ROSENBERG, SHIRLEY SIROTA, publications executive; b. Bklyn. d. Charles and Donia (Rudoy) Sirota; m. Jerome D. Rosenberg; children: Jonathan, Hindy. BA, Bklyn. Coll. Freelance writer, 1968—; contract writer-editor Dept. HEW, Washington, 1968-72; writer, editor Smithsonian Instn., Washington, 1972-77; sr. instr. George Washington U., 1979—99; pres. SSR, Inc., Washington, 1977—. Washington corr. Parent's mag.; cons. NSF, Nat. Task Force on Minorities, Women and the Handicapped in Sci. and Engring., Joseph P. Kennedy Inst., bd. dirs. Office of Commn., U.S. Holocaust Meml. Coun., Humanities mag., NEH, George Washington U. Pubs. Specialist Program, ARC Blood Svcs. Author: The First Oil Rush, 1967, How Children Grow, 1971, Code of Ethics and Professional Standards for Print Media Professionals, 1981, 92, A National Conversation on American Pluralism and Identity, 1995, Living is a Lifelong Process, 1995, Staying Connected: A Guide for Parents on Raising a Teenage Daughter, 2000; editor-author: First Special Report on Alcohol and Alcohol Abuse, Forging Partnerships for Africa's Future, Facility Study, Bureau of Engraving and Printing, The Quest for Theraputic Institution, The Search for the Theraputic Institutiuon, Gender-Based Violence: Emerging Issues in Programs Serving Displaced Persons; contbr. articles to trade and profl. jours.; editor, coord. top level nat. and internat. position papers. Recipient numerous awards. Office Phone: 202-543-1800. E-mail: ssr@ssriac.com.

ROSENBERG, STEVEN AARON, surgeon, medical researcher; b. N.Y.C., Aug. 2, 1940; s. Abraham and Harriet (Wendroff) Rosenberg; m. Alice Ruth O'Connell, Sept. 15, 1968; children: Beth, Rachel, Naomi. BA, Johns Hopkins U., 1960, MD, 1963; PhD, Harvard U., 1968. Resident in surgery Peter Bent Brigham Hosp., Boston, 1963—64, 1968—69, 1972—74; resident fellow in immunology Harvard U. Med. Sch., Boston, 1969—70; clin. assoc. immunology br. Nat. Cancer Inst., Bethesda, Md., 1970—72, chief surgery, 1974—, assoc. editor Jour., 1974—. Mem. U.S.-USSR Coop. Immunotherapy Program, 1974—, U.S.-Japan Coop. Immunotherapy Program, 1975—; clin. assoc. prof. surgery George Washington U. Med. Ctr., 1976—; prof. surgery Uniformed Svcs. U. Health Scis. Contbr. articles to profl. jours.; author: The Transformed Cell: Unlocking the Mysteries of Cancer, 1992. Served with USPHS, 1970-72 Co-recipient Armand Hammer Cancer prize, 1985; named 1990 Scientist of Yr., R&D mag.; recipient Meritorious Svc. medal, Pub. Health Svc., 1981. Mem.: Am. Assn. Cancer Rsch., Am. Assn. Immunologists, Transplantation Soc., Halsted Soc., Surg. Biology Club II, Soc. Surg. Oncology, Am. Surg. Assn., Soc. Univ. Surgeons, Alpha Omega Alpha, Phi Beta Kappa. Office: Nat Cancer Inst Clinical Sci 31 Center Dr Bldg 10 Rm 2042 Bethesda MD 20892-0001

ROSENBERG, THEODORE ROY, financial executive; b. Nyack, N.Y., Aug. 6, 1933; s. Rebecca Sheer R.; m. Eleanor Schmalsteig, Feb. 19, 1956 (div); children: Bradley Scott, Martha Ann; m. Mary Frances McVay, Sept. 21, 1991. BS, U. Conn., 1955; MBA, U. Pa., 1964. Commd. 2nd lt. U.S. Army, 1955, advanced through grades to col., 1976, retired, 1982; portfolio mgr. The Burney Co., Falls Church, Va., 1979—, v.p. mktg., 1982-94, v.p., 1994-95, pres., 1995—2003, CEO, 2003—. Bd. dirs. Army Transp. Mus., U. Conn. Found., 1995-2001; supr. bd. dirs. Bay Creek Cmty. Dist. Decorated Legion of Merit, Bronze Star; recipient Vietnam Medal of Honor, Govt. of Vietnam, 1966; inducted into Alumni Hall of Fame, U. Conn. Sch. Bus. Adminstrn., 1994. Mem. U. Pa. Mid-Atlantic Regional Adv. Bd., Wharton Club of Washington (Man of Yr. 1995). Avocations: scuba diving, snorkeling, golf. Office: The Burney Co 121 Rowell Ct Falls Church VA 22046-3174 Office Phone: 703-531-0400. E-mail: ted@burneycompany.com.

ROSENBERG, TINA, international relations educator, writer; b. 1958; BS, Northwestern U., 1981, MS, 1982. Fgn. policy editl. writer The New York Times, freelance writer New York Times mag., 1983-96, fgn. policy editl. writer, 1996—, mem. editl. bd.; adj. prof. internat. rels. Columbia U., N.Y.C. Vis. fellow Nat. Security Archive; former sr. fellow World Policy Inst., New Sch. U. Author: Children of Cain: Violence and the Violent in Latin America, The Haunted Land:; Facing Europe's Ghosts After Communism (Pulitzer and Nat. Book award, 1996); contbr. articles to publs. Recipient MacArthur Fellowship "genius" award. Office: NY Times Editl Bd 229 W 43rd St New York NY 10036

ROSENBERG, VICTOR I. plastic surgeon, educator; b. N.Y.C., Nov. 15, 1936; s. Leonard C. and Sarah G. (Berger) R.; m. Deborah Iskoe, Jan. 2, 1966; children: Spencer, Ria. AB, NYU, 1957; MD, Chgo. Med. Sch., 1961. Diplomate Am. Bd. Plastic Surgery. Intern Beth Israel Hosp., N.Y.C., 1961-62, resident, 1962-63, 64-66, Beekman Downtown Hosp., 1963-64, Bronx Mcpl. Hosp., 1966-67, Mt. Sinai Hosp., N.Y.C., 1967-68; pvt. practice in plastic surgery N.Y.C., 1968—. Assoc. attending surgeon Beth Isreal Hosp., 1968—; assoc. attending surgeon Beekman Downtown Hosp., 1968—, chief plastic surgery, 1976-80; attending surgeon N.Y. Infirmary-Beekman Downtown Hosp., 1980-98, dir. cosmetic surgery, 1984-97; asst. attending surgeon Mt. Sinai Hosp., N.Y.C., 1968—; asst. clin. prof. Mt. Sinai Sch. Medicine CUNY. Comdr. USN, 1968-70. Fellow ACS, Internat. Coll. Surgeons; mem. Am., N.Y. Regional socs. plastic and reconstructive surgeons, Am. Soc. Aesthetic Plastic Surgery, AMA, Am. Cleft Palate Assn., N.Y. Acad. Medicine, N.Y. State, N.Y. County Med. Socs., Pan Am. Med. Assn. (diplomate sect. plastic surgery), Friars Club. Office: 4 Sutton Pl New York NY 10022-3056

ROSENBERGER, BRYAN DAVID, lawyer; b. Johnstown, Pa., Oct. 8, 1950; s. Clarence Haines and Ida Rae (Neiderheiser) Rosenberger; m. Barbara Leah Byer, July 14, 1977; children: Laura Michelle, Lisa Renee. BS, Juniata Coll., 1971; JD, Coll. of William and Mary, 1974. Bar: Pa 1974. Assoc. Eckert Seamans Cherin & Mellott, Pitts., 1974-82, ptnr., 1983—, chmn. corp. and bus. dept., 1992-98, mem. exec. com., 1994-98, also bd. dirs., chmn. bus. div., 2001—04. Active new leadership bd Pitts. Symphony Soc, 1990—98. Mem.: Allegheny County Bar Assn. Home: 1358 Oakledge Ct Upper Saint Clair PA 15241-3540 Office: Eckert Seamans Cherin & Mellott 600 Grant St Ste 4400 Pittsburgh PA 15219-2702 Office Phone: 412-566-6123. Business E-Mail: bdr@escm.com.

ROSENBERGER, CAROL, concert pianist; b. Detroit, Nov. 1, 1935; d. Maurice Seiberling and Whilamet (Gibson) R. B.F.A., Carnegie-Mellon U., 1955; postgrad., Acad. Performing Arts, Vienna, 1956-59. In charge of artists and repertoire Delos Internat. Mem. artist faculty U. So. Calif., Calif. State U., Northridge, Immaculate Heart Coll.; vis. artist numerous colls. and univs. Internat. concert career, 1964—; New York debut, 1970; appeared several times at Carnegie Hall; soloist Am. Symphony, Nat. Symphony, Royal Philharmonic, San Diego Symphony, Detroit Symphony, Houston Symphony, St. Louis Symphony, Indpls. Symphony, Los Angeles Chamber Orch.; performed world premiere of Buenaventura; piano concerts with Philippine Philharmonic, 1977, Am. Symphony, 1977; recital series in Am., European, Asian music capitals; recordings include Hindemith's Four Temperaments with London Royal Philharm., Water Music of the Impressionists (one of 25 Best Classical CDs of All Time, Stereo Rev., Recording of Yr., Gramophone mag., All-time Gt. Recording, Billboard mag.), works of Beethoven, Schubert, Szymanowski, Night Moods, 1989, Perchance To Dream, Lullabys for Children and Adults, 1989, Reveries: Music of Chopin, Such Stuff as Dreams, Singing on the Water, Mozart Adagios, (with N.Y. Chamber Symphony) Fantasy Variations on a Theme of Youth (Howard Hanson), 1991 (Grammy nomination), Haydn D Major Concerto, Nights in the Gardens of Spain, Beethoven Concerto No. 4, (with Seattle Symphony) Burleske, Piano Concerto of Howard Hanson, (with L.A. Chamber Orch.) Shostakovich 1st Piano Concerto, others; prodr., co-prodr. Music for Young People Series, others; author script for narration of The Firebird (Stravinsky) (Notable Recording award ALA);contbr. articles to music publs. Recipient Steinway Centennial medal, 1954, Critics Choice award Gramaphone mag., 1980, 10/10 award CD Rev. Mem. Nat. Acad. Rec. Arts and Scis. Achievements include being chosen to represent Am. women musicians by Nat. Commn. on Observance Internat. Womens Year, 1976. Office: Delos Internat Inc 1645 Vine St Ste 340 Los Angeles CA 90028-8842

ROSENBERGER, CAROLYN ANN, art educator; b. Beaver Dam, Wis., Nov. 27, 1945; d. Gust Albert and Ethel May (Linck) Pomering; m. Randy Byron Rosenberger, Aug. 3, 1968; 1 child, Shiloh Rae. BS, U. Wis., 1967, postgrad., 1969-94. Founder, advisor Ann. HS Art Show, Iola, Wis., 1967—2002, HS Art Club, 1972—2002; art tchr., supr. Summer Sch. Art Program, Amherst, Wis., 1969—71; supr. to student who won Waupaca (Wis.) Fine Arts Festival, 1969—2002, Milw. Jour. Art Calendar Contest, 1971, 76, 82, 83, 85, Statewide HS Art Day, Oshkosh, Wis., 1979, Oshkosh, 93, Oshkosh, 94, Oshkosh, 97, Oshkosh, 99, Bi-State X-mas Card Design contest, Waupaca, 1985, Waupaca, 1990—93; art tchr. adult night sch. Fox Valley Tech., Iola, 1970—80; in charge HS gifted/talented exhibits, 1990—2002; accepted exhibitor Ctrl. Wis. Art Tchrs. Exhibit, Stevens Point, 1984; judge Wis. Regional Art Assn. Exhibit, Wausau, 1993—2002; founder, chmn. Art on Track Profl. Art/Craft Fair, Iola, 1991—2002. One-woman shows include Judd Gallery, Paoli, 2001, Ctrl. Wis. Cultural Ctr., Wisconsin Rapids, 2002, Ctr. Gallery, Whitewater, Wis., 2002, Judd Gallery, Paoli, Wis., 2001; exhibited in group shows at Wis. Edn. Assn., Madison, 1989 (Purchase award and award of merit, 1990, Purchase award, 1992-94, 96, 98, 2000, 02), Shawano Arts and Crafts Fair, 1990 (2d place prize), Wisconsin Rapids Arts and Crafts Fair, 1990 (1st place award), New London Mid-Winter Art Exhibit, 1991, (prize), 2003 (prize), Winnebagoland Art and Crafts Fair, Oshkosh, 1991, 99, 2002 (prize), 10 State Art Fair, 1992 (Excellence award), Milw. War Meml. Mus., 1992 (Merit award), Art Works Gallery, Green Bay, 1993, Wausau Ctr. for Visual Arts, 1992-94, 98-99, 2001-03, Neville Mus., Green Bay, 1993-95, 97, 99, Bonifas Art Ctr., Escanaba, Mich., Nat. Exhibit Mequon, Wis., 1993-94, Waupaca Fine Arts Festival Exhibit, 1994-2003 (prize and purchase award 1994, Top Purchase award 1998-2002, prize 2003), Marshfield's New Visions Gallery, 1994-95, 97, 2001-02, Nicolet Coll., Rhinelander, 1994, Wausau Ctr. Visual Arts, 1993, 98, 2000-03, Wausau 8-State Mid-Winter Exhibit, 1995, 98, 2000-03, Waupaca Pub. Libr., 1996, 98-99, 03, Alexander House Gallery and Mus., Port Edwards, 1996, Hardy Gallery, 1996, Lawton Gallery, Green Bay, 1999, Art at the Arboretum, Appleton, Wis., 1999-2001, 03, Seippel Ctr., Beaver Dam, Wis., 2000, Prairie Art Ctr., Oshkosh, 2002, Appleton Art Ctr.'s Inaugural Exhibit, 2002, Secura Ins. Co.'s Fine Art Exhbn., Appleton, 2002, 03, Wis. Edn. Assn., Madison, 2002-03. Founding mem. Iola Jaycees, 1976, local dir.; organizer Art in the Pk. Iola Centennial, 1992; leader, camp councilor United Meth. Youth, Iola, 1967—68. Named Jaycette of Yr. Iola Jaycettes, 1979, Tchr. of Yr. Iola-Scandinavia Tchrs. Assn., 1979; recipient Best of Show Trophy winner Scandinavian Fine Arts Show, 1977, 78, 79, 81, 82, 83, Award of Merit, Eagle River Artarama, 1991, 97, Best of Show award Wis. Rapids, 1995, Best of Painting award Marshfield Art Fair, 1996. Mem. Wis. Art Edn. Assn., Nat. Art Edn. Assn., Wis. Women in the Arts, Midwest Watercolor Soc., Wis. Painters and Sculptors Inc., Ctr. for the Visual Arts in Wausau, Hardy Gallery, Northeastern Wis. Arts Coun., Appleton Art Ctr. Methodist. Avocations: painting, camping, photography, pool. Home: PO Box 203 Iola WI 54945-0203 E-mail: carolynrosenberg@hotmail.com.

ROSENBERGER, MARGARET ADALINE, retired elementary school educator, writer; b. Micanopy, Fla., Oct. 30; d. Eugene David and Lillian Adeline (Bauknight) Rosenberger. Student, Stetson U., 1946—48; BA in Edn., U. Fla., 1949, MEd, 1952. Drama sec. Nat. Youth Adminstrn., Gainesville, Fla., 1939—40; civil svc. clk. U.S. Army Camp Blanding, Fla., 1940—46; tchr. J.J. Finley, Gainesville, 1949—52; prin., tchr. Micanopy Jr. H.S., 1952—55; gen. supr. Alachua County Schs., Gainesville, 1955—57, elem. supr., 1958—59; tchr. U.S. Army Dependents' Sch., Heidelberg, Germany, 1957—58; prin. Littlewood Elem. Sch., Gainesville, 1959—73, Prairie View Elem. Sch., Gainesville, 1973—82, ret., 1982; owner Rose Hill Publs. Mem. sch. adv. com. Prairie View Elem. Sch., 1975—82. Co-author: Reflections of Light, 1995; author: My God of Love, Mercy, Miracles and Angels, 1996, Secrets and Songs of Payne's Prairie, 1998, A Teacher's Odyssey, 2001, My Pets and I, 1999, Poems for Children, 2001, My Angels and I, 2001, Spiritual Interpretations of God's Truths, 2002, The Birth and Growth of the Village, 2003, Secrets & Songs at Payne's Prairie, 2004—, The Other Sides Where Love Knows No Color, 2004; author, composer: St. Augustine Song; contbr. articles to The Gainesville Sun, to WLUS Radio Talk Show, 1992-95, poems to mags. & papers. Pres. Govs. Children's Commn., Gainesville, 1956—57; dir. The Village Chorus, Gainesville, 1987—; mem. Gainesville Schs. PTA, 1959—82, PTA Micanopy, 1952—55; Dem. candidate Fla. House Rep., 1974; pianist/organist The Village Vespers on Sunday Evenings, 1990—; bd. dir. Foster Grandparents, Gainesville, 1974—76; chmn. bd. dir. No. Fla. Retirement Village, Inc., Gainesville, Fla., 1982—86, bd. rep. to residents, 1986—, v.p. bd. dir., 1981—82. Mem.: Internat. Soc. Poets, Am. Soc. Composers, Authors & Pub., Micanopy Hist. Soc., Altrusa Internat. Club Gainesville (chmn. internat. com., chmn. newsletter, spkr. for programs), Order of Eastern Star, Delta Kappa Gamma (internat. soc. 1959—). Democrat. Baptist. Avocations: stamp collecting/philately, coin collecting/numismatics, book collecting, post card collecting, creative writing. Home: 410 SW Wacahoota Rd Micanopy FL 32667 Mailing: 8015 NW 28th Pl B 110 Gainesville FL 32606

ROSENBERRY, WILLIAM KENNETH, lawyer, educator; b. St. Louis, Aug. 14, 1946; s. William Hugh and Shirley Anne (Love) Rosenberry; m. Linda Lou Lang, Aug. 24, 1968 (div. Jan. 1985); children: Ashlie Anne, Allison Renee; m. Donna L. Pruitt; stepchildren: Corey David Pruitt, Lindsey Lee Pruitt. BBA, U. Tex., Arlington, 1967; JD, Baylor U., 1970. Bar: Tex. 1970, Colo. 1991, U.S. Dist. Ct. (no. dist.) Tex. 1971, cert.: Coll. State Bar Tex. (specialist in comml. real estate law) 03, Tex. (residential real estate law). Assoc. Hinds & Chambers, Arlington, 1970-71; ptnr. Duke, Rosenberry, Duke & Jelinek, Arlington, 1971-76; pvt. practice, Arlington, 1976—. Mem. faculty U. Tex., 1991—; bd. dirs. Equitable Bank, NA, Arlington, Equitable Bankshares, Dallas; gen. mgr. Triple R. Propertries; escrow officer Am. Title Co., 1984—; assoc. bd. dirs. First Savs. Bank, Arlington. Pres. Pantego Christian Acad. Boosters, Arlington, 1990—92; mem. Arlington City Zoning Bd., 1989—92; bd. dirs. Baylor Bear Found. of Baylor U., Childrens Charities Ft. Worth, v.p., 1999—; bd. dirs. Ft. Worth Charities, Inc. Named, Outstanding Young Men in Am., 1980; recipient Outstanding Part-Time Faculty Tchg. award, U. Tex. Dept. Real Estate and Fin., 1992. Mem.: Arlington Bar Assn. (bd. dirs. 1987), Arlington Rep. Club, Arlington Sportsmans Club. Mem. Pantego Bible Ch. Avocation: Avocations: fishing, hunting, jogging. Office: 3010 W Park Row Dr Arlington TX 76013-2048 Office Phone: 817-461-6601.

ROSENBLAD, HELEN VIOLA, social services coordinator; b. Hutchinson, Kans., Dec. 14, 1923; d. Raymond Grant Streeter and Edith May Hunter; m. Ralph Alexander Rosenblad, June 8, 1946; children: Signe Elizabeth, Eric Lee, Kirstin Patricia, Lars Jon. BA in Sociology, Baker U., 1945. Dir. girls work Kingdom House, St. Louis, 1945—46; youth worker Morgan Meml. Youth and Children's Ctr., Boston, 1946—50; pricer Goodwill Industries, Springfield, Mass., 1950—52; EMT Downs (Kans.) Ambulance Svc., 1985—87; coord. Mother-To-Mother Ministry, Hutchinson, Kans., 1987—91. Transp. cons. S.W. Kans. Area Agy. on Aging, Dodge City, 1970—79. Author: The Flitting of Rose Leaves, 1983, 1997. Leader Girl Scouts, Boston, Springfield, Lowell, Andover, Mass., 1946—60; clothing and foods leader 4H, Winfield, Bushton, Stafford, Kans., 1960—75; bd. mem. Area Agys. on Aging, Kans., 1970—87; founder, mem. Downs Sr. Citizens, Inc, 1983—87; dir. Fed. Commodity Distbn., Osborne County, Kans., 1984—87; founder, mem. Downs Hist. Soc., 1983—87; founder, bd. mem. Interfaith Housing Svcs., Hutchinson, 1990—2003; adv. bd. Youthbuild, Inc., Hutchinson, 1993—96; mem. Hutchinson Cmty. Improvement Commn., 1995—2001, Hutchinson Housing Commn., 1995—; founder, bd. mem. Stepping-Stones for Youth, Inc., Hutchinson, 1997—; delivery person Meals on Wheels, Hutchinson, 1997—; mem. Hutchinson Housing Authority Bd., 1998—. Named Vol. of the Cmty., Hutchinson News, 2002; grantee to establish Sr. Ctr., S.W. Kans. Area Agy. on Aging, Minneola, Kans., 1976, N.W. Kans. Area Agy. on Aging, Downs, 1984. Mem.: Mayor's Task Force for Cmty. Diversity (Hutchinson Ams. with Disabilities Act bd. 2004—), United Meth. Women, United Meth. Ch. (missions com. 1960—). Avocation: geneaology. Home: 814 E 30th 301 Hutchinson KS 67502

ROSENBLATT, ALBERT MARTIN, state appeals court judge; b. N.Y.C., Jan. 17, 1936; s. Isaac and Fannie (Dachs) R.; m. Julia Carlson, Aug. 23, 1970; 1 child, Elizabeth. BA, U. Pa., 1957; LLB (JD), Harvard U., 1960. Bar: N.Y. 1961. Dist. atty. Dutchess County, N.Y., 1969-75, county judge, 1976-81; justice N.Y. State Supreme Ct., 1982-89, chief adminstrv. judge, 1987—89, justice, appellate divsn., 1989-98; judge N.Y. State Ct. Appeals, Poughkeepsie, NY, 1999—. Instr. judge N.Y. State, 1987-89; vis. prof. Vassar Coll., 1993; moderator N.Y. State Fair Trial Free Press Conf., 2000-04; creator Dutchess County 1st consumer protection bur., 1973; instr. newly elected state supreme ct. judges and county judges; asst. dist. attys., 1974, 75; instr. law tng. N.Y. State Police Acad., 1997; lectr. Nat. Dist. Attys. Assn., 1968-74; mem. vis. faculty trial advocacy workshop Harvard Law Sch., 1998, 99. Mem. bd. editors N.Y. State Bar Jour., 1992-99; contbr. articles on law to profl. jours. and popular mags. Bd. dirs. United Way Cmty. Chest, 1970; bd. dirs. Bardavon 1869 Opera House, Dutchess County Hist. Soc.; mem. adv. bd. Jewish Cmty. Ctr., 1987—; pres. Hist. Soc. Cts. of State of N.Y., 2002—; mem. State-Fed. Jud. Coun., 2003—. With USAR, 1960-66. Mem. N.Y. State Bar Assn. (named Outstanding Prosecutor 1974, Outstanding Jud. Svcs. award 1994), N.Y. State Dist. Attys. Assn. (pres. 1974, Frank S. Hogan award 1987, Jud. Svcs. award 1994), Profl. Ski Instrs. Am. (cert. 1984—), Baker St. Irregulars Club (former assoc. editor Baker St. Jour.). Republican. Jewish. Home: 300 Freedom Rd Pleasant Valley NY 12569-5431 Office: 10 Market St Poughkeepsie NY 12601-3228 Office Phone: 845-486-6444.

ROSENBLATT, ALICE F. health products executive; With New England, William M. Mercer, Inc., Mutual of NY; chief actuary, sr. v.p. Blue Cross HMO, 1987—89; sr. v.p., chief acutary Blue Cross/Blue Shield Mass., 1989—93; prin. health and welfare group Coopers & Lybrand, Boston; chief actuary, exec. v.p. integration planning and implementation Wellpoint Health Networks, Inc., 1996—. Commr. Medicare Payment Adv. Commn. Fellow: Soc. Actuaries (bd. dirs.); mem.: Am. Acad. Actuaries (bd. dirs.). Office: Wellpoint Health Networks Inc 1 Wellpoint Way Thousand Oaks CA 91362

ROSENBLATT, ARTHUR ISAAC, architect, former museum director; b. N.Y.C., Aug. 31, 1931; s. Harry and Helen (Satz) R.; m. Ruth Anne Turteltaub, Aug. 5, 1956; children: Paul Mark, Judith Alice. Diploma in architecture, Cooper Union, 1952; BArch, Carnegie-Mellon U., 1956. Registered architect, N.Y. Designer Katzman Assocs., N.Y.C., 1956-57, Isadore & Zachary Rosenfield, N.Y.C., 1957-60, Skidmore, Owings & Merrill-Harrison, Abramovitz, Pomerance and Breines, N.Y.C., 1960-61; chief designer Irwing S. Chanin, Architect, N.Y.C., 1961-65; first dep. commr. N.Y.C. Dept. Parks, Recreation and Cultural Affairs, 1966-68; v.p., vice dir. Met. Mus. Art, N.Y.C., 1968-86; dir. capital projects N.Y. Pub. Libr., N.Y.C., 1982-86; dir. U.S. Holocaust Meml. Mus., Washington, 1986-88; v.p. Grand Cen. Partnership, N.Y.C.; assoc. dir. Bryant Park Restoration Corp., N.Y.C., 1989-95; v.p. 34th St. Partnership, N.Y.C., 1991-95; prin. RKK&G Mus. & cultural Facilities Cons., Inc., N.Y.C., 1995—. Faculty Sarah Lawrence Coll., Bronxville, N.Y., 1967-69; dir. capital projects N.Y. Pub. Libr., N.Y.C., 1982-86; cons. arch. Butler Mus. Am. Art, 1980, Whitney Mus. Am. Art, N.Y.C., 1981, Chrysler Mus. Art, Norfolk, Va., 1982, Internat. Ctr. Photography, N.Y.C., 1985-86, Mus. and Archive Acad. Hebrew Lang., Jerusalem, Newport Harbor Art Mus., 1990-91, J.B. Speed Art Mus., Louisville, 1992, Museo de Arte de Ponce, Ponce, P.R., 1995, P.R. Tourism Co., Commonwealth of P.R., 1995, Museo de Arte de P.R., 1996-2000, Songwriters Hall of Fame Mus., 1997, Am. Craft Mus., 1999, Ctr. Jewish History, 1999, Auschwitz Jewish Cultural Ctr., Poland, 1999, City Mus. of Washington, Hist. Soc. Washington, 2000, Saginaw Art Mus., 2001, Latvian Contemporary Art Ctr., Riga, Latvia, 2001, Hechal Shlomo Ctr. for Jewish Heritage, Jerusalem, Israel; prof. CCNY Sch. Arch., 2002-. Author: Temple of Dendur, 1978, John Wiley & Sons Building Type Basics for Museums, 2000; co-author: Movie Song Catalog, 1993; contbg. author: Building Security, 2004; contbr. articles to mags. and jours. Vice chmn. cmty. planning bd. # 8, N.Y.C., 1964-66; trustee The Cooper Union, 1983-86; commr. N.Y.C. Coun. Environment; pres. Met. Hist. Structures Assn.; presl. appointee Nat. Mus. Svc. Bd. of the Inst. of Mus. and Librs. Svcs., Washington, 1995. With U.S. Army, 1953-55. Nat. Endowment for the Arts grantee, 1981. Fellow AIA (pres. N.Y. chpt. 1982-83, spl. citation 1978, Thomas Jefferson award for pub. architecture 1998), Nat. Acad. Design N.Y. (academician), Nat. Inst. for Archtl. Edn. (bd. dirs. 1978); mem. Mcpl. Art Soc., Archtl. League N.Y. (pres. 1970-72), Met. Hist. Structures Assn. (pres.), Century Assn., Players Club, Salmagundi Club of N.Y. Home: 1158 5th Ave New York NY 10029-6917 Office: 48 W 25th St New York NY 10010-2708 Office Phone: 212-807-0342. E-mail: rkkg@att.net.

ROSENBLATT, JASON PHILIP, English language educator; b. Balt., July 3, 1941; s. Morris D. and Esther (Friedlander) R.; m. Zipporah Marton, June 2, 1964; children: Noah David, Raphael Mark. BA, Yeshiva U., 1963; MA, Brown U., 1966, PhD, 1969. Asst. prof. English U. Pa., Phila., 1968-74, Georgetown U., Washington, 1974-76, assoc. prof., 1976-83, prof. English, 1983—. Vis. lectr. English lit. Swarthmore (Pa.) Coll., 1972-73; cen. exec. com. Folger Inst./Folger Shakespeare Libr., Washington, 1976-88. Author: Torah and Law in "Paradise Lost", 1994; co-editor: Not in Heaven: Coherence and Complexity in Biblical Narrative, 1991; mem. editl. bd. Milton Studies, 1992—; contbr. articles to scholarly publs. Recipient Virginia Graham Healey award, 1998-99; Guggenheim Found. fellow, 1977-78, NEH fellow, 1990-91, Folger Shakespeare Libr./NEH fellow, 1999-2000. Mem. MLA (del. assembly 1989-91, exec. com. div. religion and lit. 1982-86, exec. com. 17th century Eng. lit. 2002—), Milton Soc. Am. (exec. com. 1977-80, James Holly Hanford award 1989, v.p. 1998, pres. 1999), Milton Seminar, Phi Beta Kappa. Democrat. Jewish. Avocations: talmud study, music, swimming. Office: Dept English Georgetown Univ Box 571131 Washington DC 20057-1131 Office Phone: 202-687-7577. E-mail: rosenblj@georgetown.edu.

ROSENBLATT, JOAN RAUP, mathematical statistician; b. N.Y.C., Apr. 15, 1926; d. Robert Bruce and Clara (Eliot) Raup; m. David Rosenblatt, June 10, 1950. AB, Barnard Coll., 1946; PhD, U. N.C., 1956. Intern Nat. Inst. Pub. Affairs, Washington, 1946-47; statis. analyst U.S. Bur. of Budget, 1947-48; rsch. asst. U. N.C., 1953-54; mathematician Nat. Inst. Standards and Tech. (formerly Nat. Bur. Standards), Washington, 1955—, asst. chief statis. engring., 1963-68, chief statis. engring. lab., 1969-78, dep. dir. Ctr. for Applied Math., 1978-88; dep. dir. Computing and Applied Math. Lab., Gaithersburg, 1988-93, dir., 1993-95, guest rschr. Statis. Engring. Divsn., 1996—. Mem. com. on indsl. rels. Dept. Stats. Ohio State U., 1981-90; mem. adv. com. in math. and stats. USDA Grad. Sch., 1971—; mem. Com. Applied and Theoretical Stats., Nat. Rsch. Coun., 1985-88. Mem. editorial bd. Communications in Stats., 1971-79, Jour. Soc. for Indsl. and Applied Math., 1965-75, Nat. Inst. Stds. and Tech. Jour. Rsch., 1991-93; contbr. articles to profl. jours. Chmn. Com. on Women in Sci., Joint Bd. on Sci. Edn., 1963-64. Rice fellow, 1946, Gen. Edn. Bd. fellow, 1948-50; recipient Fed. Woman's award, 1971, Gold medal Dept. Commerce, 1976, Presdl. Meritorious Exec. Rank award, 1982. Fellow AAAS (chmn. stats. sect. 1982, sec. 1987-91), Inst. Math. Stats. (coun. 1975-77), Am. Statis. Assn. (v.p. 1981-83, dir. 1979-80, Founders award 1991), Washington Acad. Scis. (achievement award math. 1965); mem. AAUW, Royal Statis. Soc. London, Philos. Soc. Washington, Internat. Statis. Inst., Caucus Women Stats. (pres. 1976), Assn. Women Math., Exec. Women

Govt., Phi Beta Kappa, Sigma Xi (treas. Nat. Bur. Standards chpt. 1982-84). Home: 2939 Van Ness St NW Apt 702 Washington DC 20008-4628 Office: Nat Inst Stds and Tech 100 Bureau Dr Stop 8980 Gaithersburg MD 20899-8980 E-mail: jrr@nist.gov.

ROSENBLATT, KARIN ANN, cancer epidemiologist; b. Chgo., Apr. 22, 1954; d. Murray and Adylin Rosenblatt. BA, U. Calif., Santa Cruz, 1975; MPH, U. Mich., 1977; PhD, Johns Hopkins U., 1988. Postdoctoral fellow U. Wash., Seattle, 1987-89; staff scientist Fred Hutchinson Cancer Rsch. Ctr., Seattle, 1989-91; asst. prof. U. Ill., Champaign, 1991-97, assoc. prof., 1997—. Vis. scientist Fred Hutchinson Cancer Rsch. Ctr., 1999-2000; vis. scholar U. Wash., 1999-2000. Fellow Am. Coll. Epidemiology; mem. APHA (governing councilor epidemiology sect. 1988-2000), Internat. Epidemiologic Assn., Internat. Genetic Epidemiology Soc., Soc. for Epidemiologic Rsch. Office: Dept Cmty Health 120 Huff Hall MC 588 1206 S 4th St Champaign IL 61820-6920

ROSENBLATT, LOUISE MICHEL, emerita educator; b. Atlantic City, N.J., Aug. 23, 1904; d. Samuel and Jennie (Berman) R.; m. Sidney Ratner, June 1932; 1 child, Jonathan. BA with honors, Barnard Coll., 1925; cert. d'etudes francaises, U. Grenoble, France, 1926; D in Comparative Lit., U. Paris, 1931; postgrad., Columbia U., 1932-34; LHD (hon.), U. Ariz., 1991. Instr. English Barnard Coll., 1927-38; asst. prof. English Bklyn. Coll., 1938-48; assoc. chief Western European sect., chief ctrl. reports sec Bur. Overseas Intelligence, Office War Info., 1943-45; prof. English edn. NYU, N.Y.C., 1948-72, prof. emerita, 1972—. Vis. prof. Rutgers U., 1972-75; mem. faculty insts. in English Northwestern U., Mich. State U., U. Pa., U. Ala., U. Alta. (Can.), Auburn U., U. Mass., 1978-96; vis. prof. U. Miami (Fla.), 1996-2001; participant Conf. Methods in Philosophy and the Scis., sec., 1941-42; cons. in field. Author: L'idée de l'Art pour l'Art, 1931, reprinted, 1976, Literature as Exploration, 1938 (cited as Book of Century by Mus. Edn. 1999), 5th rev. edit., 1995, Arabic transl., 1999, Spanish transl., 2002, Swedish transl., 2002; (with William S. Gray) Reading in an Age of Mass Communication, 1949, Research Development in the Teaching of English, 1963, The Reader, The Text, The Poem: The Transactional Theory of the Literary Work, 1978, rev. paperback edit., 1994; (with Robert Parker) Developing Literacy, 1983; (with Charles Cooper) Researching Response to Literature, 1984; (with Patricia Demers) The Creating Word, 1985, Writing and Reading: The Transactional Theory, 1988; (with Jana Mason) Reading and Writing Connections, 1989; contbr. chpts. to Transactions With Literature, 1990, Handbook of Research on the English Language Arts, 1990, Theoretical Models of the Reading Process, 4th edit., 1994; contbr. articles to profl. jours. Recipient NYU Great Tchr. award, 1972, Nat. Coun. Tchr. English Disting. Svc. award, 1973, Russell award for disting. rsch., 1980, Leland Jacobs award Lit., 1981, Disting. Alumna award Barnard Coll., 1990, Disting. Rsch. award Nat. Conf. Rsch. English, 1990, Lifetime Achievement award John Dewey Soc., 2001, Lifetime Achievement award Nat. Reading Conf., 2002; named to N.J. Lit. Hall of Fame, 1988, Internat. Reading Assn. Hall of Fame, 1992, Outstanding Educator in Lang. Arts, 1999; Franco-Am. Exch. fellow, 1925-26, Guggenheim fellow, 1942-43. Mem. MLA, Am. Soc. Aesthetics, Nat. Coun. Tchrs. English (James C. Squire award 2002), Nat. Conf. Rsch. English, Am. Comparative Lit., Soc. Advancement of Am. Philosophy, Internat. Comparative Lit. Assn., Phi Beta Kappa. Home: 5310 Little Falls Rd Arlington VA 22207

ROSENBLATT, MICHAEL, internist, researcher, academic administrator, educator; b. Lund, Sweden, Nov. 27, 1947; s. Arthur Rosenblatt and Jean (Strosberg) Bialer; m. Patricia Ellen Regenbogen, Aug. 23, 1969; children: Anna Miriam, Adam Richard. AB summa cum laude, Columbia U., 1969; MD magna cum laude, Harvard U., 1973. Diplomate Am. Bd. Internal Medicine. Intern then resident Mass. Gen. Hosp., Boston, 1973-75, clin. rsch. fellow in endocrinology and metabolism, 1975-77, chief endocrine unit, 1981-84; instr. in medicine Harvard U., Boston, 1976-78, asst. prof. medicine, 1978-82, assoc. prof. medicine, 1982-85; v.p. for biol. rsch. Merck Sharp & Dohme Rsch. Labs., 1984-87, v.p. for biol. rsch. and molecular biology, 1987-89, sr. v.p. rsch., 1989-92; dir. divsn. health sci. and tech. Harvard-MIT, 1992-98; Ebert prof. molecular medicine Harvard Med. Sch., Boston, 1992-98; chief divsn. bone and mineral metabolism Beth Israel Hosp., Boston, 1992—2000, 2002—; dean Tufts U. Sch. Medicine, 2003—. Faculty dean acad. programs Beth Israel Deaconess Med. Ctr., Harvard Med., 1996—2000, George R. Minot prof. med., 1996—; exec. dir. Carl J. Shapiro Inst. Edn. and Rsch. at Harvard Med. Sch. and Beth Israel Deaconess Med. Ctr., 1996—2000, pres., 1999—2001. Editor: Atrial Natriuretic Factor Endocrinology and Metabolism Clinics of N.Am., 1987; contbr. numerous sci. articles on parathyroid hormone and calcium metabolism to leading sci. jours. Recipient Vincent du Vigneaud award Gordon Confs., Kingston, R.I., 1986, Fuller Albright award Am. Soc. for Bone and Mineral Rsch., 1986, citation Japan Endocrine Soc., Tokyo, Taiwanese Osteoporosis Soc., Tainan. Fellow AAAS; mem. The Endocrine Soc., Am. Soc. for Biochemistry and Molecular Biology, Am. Soc. for Clin. Investigation, Am. Soc. Bone and Mineral Rsch. (pres. 1997-98), Assn. Am. Physicians, Inter-Urban Clin. Club (pres. 1997-98). Office: Tufts U Sch Medicine 136 Harrison Ave Boston MA 02111-1800

ROSENBLATT, MURRAY, mathematics professor; b. N.Y.C., Sept. 7, 1926; s. Hyman and Esther R.; m. Adylin Lipson, 1949; children: Karin, Daniel BS, CCNY, 1946; MS, Cornell U., 1947, PhD in Math., 1949. Asst. prof. statistics U. Chgo., 1950-55; assoc. prof. math. Ind. U., 1956-59; prof. probability and statistics Brown U., 1959-64; prof. math. U. Calif., San Diego, 1964—. Vis. fellow U. Stockholm, 1953; vis. asst. prof. Columbia U., 1955; guest scientist Brookhaven Nat. Lab., 1959; vis. fellow U. Coll., London, 1965-66, Imperial Coll. and Univ. Coll., London, 1972-73, Australian Nat. U., 1976, 79; overseas fellow Churchill Coll., Cambridge U., Eng., 1979; Wald lectr., 1970; vis. scholar Stanford U., 1982 Author: Statistical Analysis of Stationary Time Series, 1957, Random Processes, 1962, (2d edit), 1974, Markov Processes, Structure and Asymptotic Behavior, 1971, Studies in Probability Theory, 1978, Stationary Sequences and Random Fields, 1985, Stochastic Curve Estimation, 1991, Gaussian and Non-Gaussian Linear Time Series and Random Fields, 2000; mem. editl. bd. Jour. Theoretical Probability. Recipient Bronze medal U. Helsinki, 1978; Guggenheim fellow, 1965-66, 71-72 Fellow Inst. Math Statistics, AAAS; mem. Internat. Statis. Inst., Nat. Acad. Scis. Office: U Calif Dept Math La Jolla CA 92093 also: PO Box 2066 La Jolla CA 92038-2066 E-mail: mrosenblatt@ucsd.edu.

ROSENBLATT, PAUL GERHARDT, judge; b. 1928; AB, U. Ariz., 1958, JD, 1963. Asst. atty. gen. State of Ariz., 1963-66; adminstrv. asst. to U.S. Rep., 1967-72; soel practice, 1971-73; judge Yavapai County Superior Ct., Prescott, Ariz., 1973-84, U.S. Dist. Ct. Ariz., Phoenix, 1984—. Office: US Dist Ct Sandra Day O'Connor Ct Ste 621 401 W Washington St SPC 56 Phoenix AZ 85003-2156

ROSENBLATT, PETER RONALD, lawyer, former ambassador; b. N.Y.C., Sept. 4, 1933; s. William and Therese Amalia (Steinhardt) Rosenblatt; m. Naomi Henriette Harris; children: Therese Sarah Sonenshine, Daniel Harris, David Steinhardt. BA, Yale U., 1954, LLB, 1957. Bar: N.Y. 1959, D.C. 1969. Tchg. asst. history Yale U., New Haven, 1954-55; asst. dist. atty. N.Y. County, 1959-62; assoc. Stroock & Stroock & Lavan, N.Y.C., 1962-66; dep. asst. gen. counsel AID, Washington, 1966; mem. White House staff, Washington, 1966-68; jud. officer, chmn. bd. contract appeals U.S. Post Office Dept., Washington, 1968-69; v.p., dir. EDP Technology, Inc., Washington, 1969-71; chmn. bd. Internat. Devel. Svcs., Washington, 1969-71; spl. cons. to Senator Edmund S. Muskie, 1970-72; practice law Washington, 1972-77, 81-91; founding ptnr. Heller & Rosenblatt, Washington, 1991—. Personal rep. of Pres. with rank amb. to conduct negotiations on future polit. status of Trust Ter. of Pacific Islands, Washington, 1977-81; mem. Mid. East study group Dem. Adv. Coun. Elected Ofcls., 1974-76; bd. dirs. MediSense, Inc., 1983-96. Sec., chmn. exec. com. Coalition for a Dem. Majority, 1973-77, pres., 1983-93; bd. dirs. Com. on Present Danger, 1976-77, 82-93, 2004—; mem. U.S. Nat. Com. Pacific Econ. Cooperation, 1986, sec., 1987-2003; bd. govs. Haifa (Israel) U., 1990-94, 98—; sec.-treas. Fund for Democracy and Devel., 1991-94, pres., 1994—; mem. adv. coun. Nixon Ctr., 1994—; mem. task force on fgn. policy Dem. Policy Commn., 1986; bd. govs. Am. Jewish Com., 1998—, pres. D.C. chpt. 2003-, bd. dirs. UN Watch, 2000—, chmn., bd. govs. Koppelman Inst. on Am. Jewish-Israeli Rels., 1999-2002; bd. advisors Jewish Inst. for Nat. Security Affairs, 2000—; mem. The Alliance for Am. Leadership, 2001—. Postgrad. fellow, Tel-Aviv U., 1971. Mem. ABA, N.Y., D.C. Bar, Coun. Fgn. Rels. Jewish. Office: Heller & Rosenblatt 1101 15th St NW Ste 205 Washington DC 20005-5002 Office Phone: 202-466-4700. E-mail: ffdd@erols.com.

ROSENBLATT, ROGER, writer; b. N.Y.C., Sept. 13, 1940; m. Virginia Rosenblatt; children: Carl, Amy, John. PhD in English and Am. Lit., Harvard U.; hon. doctorate, U. Md., Claremont Grad. Sch., U. Utah, Pace U., Brigham Young U. Briggs-Copeland prof. creative writing Harvard U., 1968-73; dir. edn. NEH, 1973-75; lit. editor The New Republic, 1975-78; columnist Washington Post, mem. editorial bd., 1976-79; essayist, sr. writer Time, 1980-88; essayist MacNeil/Lehrer News Hour, PBS, 1983—; columnist, editor-at-large Life mag., 1989-92; editor-at-large Time, Inc., 1999—2001. Parsons Family Univ. prof. writing Southampton Coll., L.I. U. Author: Black Fiction, 1974, Children of War, 1983 (Robert F. Kennedy Book prize), Witness: The World Since Hiroshima, 1985, Life Itself: Abortion in the American Mind, 1992 (Melcher award), The Man in the Water, 1994, Coming Apart, 1997, Consuming Desires, 1999, Rules for Aging, 2000, Where We Stand, 2002, Anything Can Happen, 2003, (plays) Free Speech in America, 1991, And, 1992, Bibliomania, 1993. Fulbright scholar, Dublin, Ireland, 1965; recipient numerous honors including two George Polk awards, George Foster Peabody award, Emmy award.

ROSENBLATT, ROGER ALAN, physician, educator; b. Denver, Aug. 8, 1945; s. Alfred Dreyfus and Judith Ann (Ginsburg) R.; m. Fernne Schnitzer, Sept. 23, 1942; children: Eli Samuel, Benjamin. BA magna cum laude, Harvard U., 1967, MD cum laude, M in Pub. Health, 1971. Diplomate Am. Bd. Family Practice, Nat. Bd. Med. Examiners. Intern internal medicine U. Wash., Seattle, 1971-72, resident in family medicine, 1974; regional med. cons. region X Pub. Health Service, Seattle, 1974-76, dir. Nat. Health Services Corps., 1976-77; asst. prof. dept. family medicine U. Wash., Seattle, 1977-81, assoc. prof. dept. family medicine, 1981-85, prof., vice chmn. dept. family medicine, 1985—. Cons. U.S. Agy. for Internat. Devel., 1978, Western Interstate Commn. Higher Edn., 1981-82; vis. prof. medicine U. Auckland, New Zealand, 1983-84, Royal Australia Coll. Gen. Practitioners, Victoria, 1984, U. Calgary, 1988, U. Mo., 1988; vis. prof., Fogarty Ctr. Sr. Internat. fellow dept. ob-gyn. NIH, Coll. Medicine, U. Wales, Cardiff, 1992-93. Author: Rural Health Care, 1982; contbr. numerous articles on healthcare to profl. jours. Mem. Beyond War, Physicians for Social Responsiblity. Served with USPHS, 1974-77. Recipient Hanes Rsch. award North Am. Primary Care Rsch. Group, 1996. Mem. Am. Acad. Family Physicians (Hanes Rsch. award 1996), Am. Pub. Health Assn., Soc. Tchrs. Family Medicine (Hanes Rsch. award 1996), Nat. Rural Health Assn., Nat. Council Internat. Health, Nat. Acad. Sci. (elected inst. medicine 1987), Am. Rural Health Assn. (Research award 1985), Phi Beta Kappa. Office: U Wash Dept Family Medicine PO Box 354696 Seattle WA 98195-4696

ROSENBLATT, STEPHEN PAUL, marketing and sales promotion company executive; b. N.Y.C., Feb. 13, 1935; s. Jack Aaron and Ruth (Kloth) R.; m. Dorothy Freedman, Apr. 7, 1962; children: Gregg, Amy, Robert. BEd, NYU, 1957. Tchr. art N.Y.C. Schs., 1957-58; art dir. Morse Internat., N.Y.C., 1958-65; v.p. L.C. Gumbinner Advt., N.Y.C., 1966-71; group mktg. dir. Norcliff Thayer, Tarrytown, N.Y., 1971-75; pres. BMS Mktg. Services, Inc., N.Y.C., 1975-89, The Promotion Group Inc. subs. Doctus PLC, N.Y.C., 1989-91, SPQR Inc., Yorktown Heights, N.Y., 1991-93, ret., 1993. Home: 1451 White Hill Rd Yorktown Heights NY 10598-3543

ROSENBLEETH, RICHARD M. lawyer; b. Phila., Mar. 20, 1932; s. Morris B. and Henrietta (Friedman) R.; m. Judith A. Alesker, June 20, 1954; children— Dori, Lyn BS in Econs., U. Pa., 1954, JD, 1957. Bar: Pa. 1958, U.S. Supreme Ct. 1961. Asst. dist. atty. City of Phila., 1957-62; assoc. Richman, Price & Jamieson, 1962-65; ptnr. Blank, Rome, Comisky & McCauley, Phila., 1965-97; gen. coun. MBIA Muni Svcs. Co., 1998-2001, Arbitation and Mediation Svcs., Phila., 2001—. Mem. Civil Justice Reform Act Adv. Group, U.S. Dist. Ct. (ea. dist.) Pa., 1991—; co-chair Mayor Rendell's Transition Task Force on the Law Dept., 1991; judge pro tem Phila. Ct. Common Pleas, 1992—. Pres. Merion Park Civic Assn., Pa., 1967; mem. Citizens Crime Commn., Phila., 1979-87; commr. Youth Svcs. Coordinating Commn., Phila., 1979-85; Pa. state mem. chair U.S. Supreme Ct. Hist. Soc., 1994-95; pres., Corp. Alliance for Drug Edn., 1998-2000, chmn. Pa. Conv. Ctr. Authority, 1996-2000. Fellow Am. Coll. Trial Lawyers (chmn. Pa. state com. 1993-94), Internat. Acad. Trial Lawyers, Am. Bar Found.; mem. ABA, Pa. Bar Assn., Phila. Bar Assn., Phila. Bar Found. (pres. 1994). Avocations: golf, art collecting. Office: One Logan Sq 8th Fl Philadelphia PA 19103-6998 E-mail: rosenbleeth@blankrome.com.

ROSENBLOOM, BERT, marketing educator, consultant, writer; b. Phila., Feb. 2, 1944; s. Max and Dora (Cohen) R.; m. Pearl Friedman, Aug. 18, 1968; children: Jack Alan, Robyn. BS, Temple U., 1966, MBA, 1968, Ph.D, 1974. Instr. mktg. Rider Coll., Trenton, N.J., 1968-72, asst. prof., 1972-74; asst. prof. mktg. Baruch Coll. CUNY, 1974-76; assoc. prof. Drexel U., Phila., 1976-80, prof., 1980-85, G. Behrens Ulrich prof. mktg., 1985-98, assoc. dean grad. programs, 1994-97, Rauth chair electronic commerce mgmt., 1999—. Vis. scholar Higher Sch. Commerce Paris, 1993; cons. editor mktg. Random House, N.Y.C., 1977—; exec. dir. Safe Guard Sci. E-Commerce Mgmt. Ctr., 1999-2000, sr. rsch. fellow, 2000—; cons. in field; bd. dirs. Reality Landscaping Corp., McKee Real Estate Devel. Corp., RESHARE Corp.—; vis. disting. prof. Hannon U., Japan, 2000; vis. disting. scholar U. St. Gallen, 2000; Disting. vis. fellow Sogang U., Korea, 2001. Author: Marketing Channels, 1978, 3d edit., 2003, Market Functions and the Wholesaler Distribution, 1987, Marketing Channels: A Management View, 5th edit., 1997, 6th edit., 1999, 7th edit., 2003, Retail Marketing, 1981, Direct Selling Channels, 1993, Wholesale Mktg. Channels, 1994; editor Jour. Mktg. Channels, 1989—, Jour. Consumer Mktg., Jour. Global Mktg., Jour. Acad. Mktg. Sci.; contbr. articles to profl. jours. Mem. E-Commerce Commn., Mayor Phila., 1999—. Named Disting. Erskine fellow U. Canterbury, New Zealand, 1986; recipient Outstanding Educator award Chapel of Four Chaplains, 1984, Nomura Fund Collaborative rsch. award U. Rykus, Japan, 1998; rsch. award Distbn. Rsch. and Edn. Found., 1986, rsch. award Direct Selling Found., 1986, 91, 96, Literati Club award for excellence, 2002; Nat. Assn. Wholesaler Distbrs. grantee, 1991; honored as disting. prof. Retail Mktg. Inst. of Australia, 1985. Fellow Acad. Mktg. Sci. (bd. govs. 1978-89); mem. Internat. Mgmt. Devel. Assn. (pres. 1992-94), Am. Mktg. Assn. (v.p. Phila. chpt. 1978-79), Beta Gamma Sigma. Office: Drexel U Sch Bus 32d and Market Sts Philadelphia PA 19104 Office Phone: 215-895-6992. E-mail: rosenblb@drexel.edu.

ROSENBLOOM, DANIEL, investment banker, lawyer; b. New York City, Feb. 11, 1930; s. Sol and Florence (Vogel) R. BA, U. Va., 1951, JD, 1954; LLM, NYU, 1960. Bar: Va. 1954, N.Y. 1956. Atty. Paskus, Gordon, and Hyman, N.Y.C., 1956—61; v.p., sec., gen. counsel Phila. and Reading Corp., N.Y.C., 1962—67; ptnr. First Manhattan Co., N.Y.C., 1968—2002, sr. mng. dir., 2002—. Trustee Nat. Found. for Facial Reconstruction, N.Y. Univ. Med. Ctr., Univ. Va. Law Sch. Found. 1st lt. AUS, 1954—56. Mem. Sunningdale Country Club, Farmington Country Club, Harmonie Club, Atlantic Golf Club, River Club, Phi Alpha Delta, Phi Epsilon Pi. Office: First Manhattan Co 437 Madison Ave New York NY 10022-7001

ROSENBLOOM, DAVID HARRY, political science and law educator; b. N.Y.C., Aug. 27, 1943; s. Jerome and Rita R. BA, Marietta Coll., 1964, LLD (hon.), 1994; MA, U. Chgo., 1966, PhD in Polit. Sci., 1969. Asst. prof. U. Kans., Lawrence, 1969-71; fellow Am. Soc. Pub. Adminstrn. U.S. Civil Svc. Commn., Washington, 1970-71; vis. sr. lectr. Tel Aviv (Israel) U., 1971-73; asst. prof. U. Vt., Burlington, 1973-75, assoc. prof., 1975-78; vis. assoc. prof. Syracuse (N.Y.) U., 1978-79, prof., 1979—88, disting. prof., 1988-90, Am. U., Washington, 1990—. Bd. trustees Marietta Coll., 2003—. Author: (Books) Federal Service and Constitution, 1971, Public Administration, 2004, 6th edit., Public Administration and Law, 1997, Building a Legislative-Centered Public Administration, 2000, Administrative Law for Public Managers, 2003. Mem. Clinton-Gore Transition Team, U.S. Office Pers. Mgmt., Washington, 1992. Recipient Charles Levine Meml. award for excellence and Disting. Rsch. award Am. Soc. for Pub. Adminstrn. and Nat. Assn. Schs. of Pub. Affairs and Administration, Washington, 1992, 93, Thomas Dye award for outstanding svc. Policy Studies Orgn., 1996, Dwight Waldo award for outstanding contbns. to lit. and leadership of Pub. Adminstrn., Am. Soc. Pub. Adminstrn., Washington, 1999, Louis Brownlow Book award Nat. Acad. Pub. Adminstrn., 2001. Fellow Nat. Acad. Pub. Adminstrn. Recipient John Gaus award for exemplary scholarship in joint tradition polit. sci. and pub. adminstrn. Am. Polit. Sci. Assn., 2001. Office: American U 4400 Massachusetts Ave NW Washington DC 20016-8001 Office Phone: 202-885-2361. Business E-Mail: rbloom@american.edu.

ROSENBLOOM, H. DAVID, lawyer; b. N.Y.C., May 26, 1941; s. Milton M. and Rose (Gold) Rosenbloom; m. Carla L. Peterson, June 23, 1968; children: Sarah Alix, Julia Micol. AB, Princeton U., 1962; postgrad. (Fulbright scholar), U. Florence, Italy, 1962-63; JD, Harvard U., 1966. Bar: N.Y. 1967, DC 1968. Spl. asst. to Arthur J. Goldberg U.S. amb. UN, 1966-67; law clk. to Abe Fortas U.S. Supreme Ct., 1967-68; assoc. Caplin & Drysdale, Washington, 1968-72, ptnr., 1972-77, 81—. Spl. asst. to dep. asst. sec. for tax policy Dept. Treasury, Washington, 1977, internat. tax counsel, 1978—81; lectr. Harvard U. Law Sch., 1984—87, 1990—93, 1995—96, 1999, Pub. Fin. Tng. Inst., Taipei, 1985—86, 1989, Stanford U. Law Sch., 1988, Inst. Tecnologico Autonomo d' Mex., 1993, 95, 97, Columbia U. Law Sch., 1997, U. Pa. Law Sch., 1998, U. Commerciale Luigi Bocconi, Milan, 2001, So. African Tax Inst., U. Pretoria, 2002, NYU Law Sch., N.Y.C., 2000—, dir. internat. tax program, 2002—; faculty law U. Sydney, 2001, 03. Home: 2948 Garfield Ter NW Washington DC 20008-3507 Office: 1 Thomas Cir NW Washington DC 20005-5802 Office Phone: 202-862-5037.

ROSENBLOOM, JOSHUA LEVI, economist, educator; b. Boston, Aug. 13, 1958; s. Richard S. and Ruth M. Rosenbloom; m. Mary Lyle McCorison, Sept. 2, 1984 (dec. Apr. 30, 2001); children: Nathan M., Benjamin K., Timothy E.; m. Leslie Anne Bennett, July 20, 2003. BA, Oberlin Coll., 1981; PhD, Stanford U., 1988. Asst. prof. U. Kans., Lawrence, 1988—94, assoc. prof., 1994—99, prof., 1999—2003. Rsch. assoc. Nat. Bur. Econ. Rsch., Cambridge, Mass., 1997. Office: U Kans Econ Dept 1300 Sunnyside Ave Lawrence KS 66045

ROSENBLOOM, LEWIS STANLEY, lawyer; b. Fort Riley, Kans., Feb. 28, 1953; s. Donald and Sally Ann (Warsawsky) R.; children: Micah, Shaina. BA, Lake Forest Coll., 1974; JD with high honors, DePaul U., 1977. Bar: Ill. 1977, U.S. Dist. Ct. (no. dist.) Ill, 1977, U.S. Ct. Appeals (7th cir.) 1979, U.S. Supreme Ct. 1983, U.S. Ct. Appeals (9th cir.) 1987, U.S. Ct. Appeals (3rd cir.) 1993. Sr. acct. Gale, Takahasi & Channon, Chgo., 1973-74; law clk. to Hon. Robert L. Eisen U.S. Dist. Ct. (no. dist.) Ill., Chgo., 1976; assoc. Nachman, Munitz & Sweig, Ltd., Chgo., 1976-82, prin., 1982-87; ptnr., co-chmn. involvency, bankruptcy & bus. reorgn. dept. Winston & Strawn, Chgo., 1987-93; ptnr., sr. corp. reorgn. counsel McDermott, Will & Emery, Chgo., 1994—; chmn. distressed transactions. Mem. bd. advisors to bankruptcy, comml. law advisor Bus. Laws, Inc., 1988—; lectr. in field. Contbr. articles to profl. jours. Mem. adv. com. and fin. subcom. Ill. Bd. Higher Edn., Springfield; mem. state edn. and legal aid subcom. Ill. Coun. on Children and Youth Welfare, Chgo. Coll. scholar Lake Forest Coll., 1973-74. Fellow Am. Coll. Bankruptcy; mem. ABA (bus. bankruptcy com. 1982—, chmn. new and pending bankruptcy legis. com. 1982-85, chmn. transp. reorganizations com. 1985-88), Chgo. Bar Assn. (bankruptcy reorganization com., co-chmn. subcom. on retention and fees 1987-88). Office: McDermott Will & Emery 227 W Monroe St Ste 3100 Chicago IL 60606-5096 Office Phone: 312-984-6943. Business E-Mail: lrosenbloom@mwe.com.

ROSENBLOOM, NORMA FRISCH, lawyer; b. N.Y.C., Dec. 2, 1925; d. Jacob Frisch and Anna (Fox) Frisch Schwartz; m. Philip Rosenbloom, Oct. 31, 1946; children: David, James, Eric. BA, New Sch. Social Rsch., 1951; JD, Rutgers U., Newark, 1979. Bar: N.J. 1979, N.Y. 1980. Mem. faculty, head dept. music Ranney Sch., Tinton Falls, N.J., 1962-74; chief law clk. Monmouth County (N.J.) Prosecutor's Office, 1979-80; assoc. Karasic & Karasic, P.C., Oakhurst, N.J., 1980-82; ptnr. Abrams, Gatta, Rosen & Rosenbloom, Ocean Twp., N.J., 1982-90, Abrams, Gatta, Rosen, Rosenbloom & Sevrin, P.C., 1990-92; of counsel Abrams, Gatta, Falvo & Sevrin, P.A., 1992-99, Abrams Gatta Falvo LLP; legal adv. Epiphany House Inc., Asbury Park, N.J., 1999—. Asst. county counsel Monmouth County, 1987-88; mem. N.J. Supreme Ct. Family Part Practice Com., 1997-98. Sec., mem. exec. bd. Temple Beth Miriam, Elberon, N.J., 1969-74; mcpl. leader Monmouth Beach (N.J.) Dem. Com., 1973—; del. Dem. Nat. Conv., 1976; freeholder rep. to Monmouth County Cmty. Action Program, poverty program, 1975-76; bd. dirs. Cen. Jersey Regional Health Planning Bd., 1973-75; trustee search com. Brookdale C.c., Lincroft, N.J., 1984-85; trustee Planned Parenthood Monmouth County, 1981-88. Recipient award for cmty. involvement Asbury Park-Neptune Youth Coun., 1970. Fellow Am. Acad. Matrimonial Lawyers; mem. ABA, N.J. Women Lawyers Assn. (pres. 1994-95), N.J. State Bar Assn. (mem. legis. com., trustee women in the profession sect.), Women Lawyers Monmouth County. Democrat. Jewish. Avocation: classical pianist. Home: Channel Club Towers Monmouth Beach NJ 07750 Office: Epiphany House 300 4th Ave Asbury Park NJ 07712-6006

ROSENBLOOM, RICHARD SELIG, business administration educator; b. Springfield, Mass., Jan. 16, 1933; s. Irving J. and Lillian (Saks) R.; m. Ruth Miriam Friedlander, Oct. 14, 1956; children: Joshua, Daniel, Rachel. A.B. in Chemistry, Harvard U., 1954, M.B.A., 1956, D.B.A., 1960. Faculty, Harvard Bus. Sch., Boston, 1960—, dir. doctoral program, 1970-74, assoc. dean research and course devel., 1976-80, prof., 1967—; vis. prof. Hebrew U. of Jerusalem, Israel, 1974-75; founder Jerusalem Inst. Mgmt., Tel Aviv, 1974-88; bd. dirs. Lex. Svc. PLC, London, Arrow Electronics Inc., Exec. Info. Systems, Inc. Author: (with others): Technology and Information Transfer, Cases in Operations Management: A Systems Approach. Editor: Research on Technological Innovation, Management and Policy. Pres., Friends of Harvard/Radcliffe Hillel, Cambridge, Mass., 1985—; bd. dirs. Combined Jewish Philanthropies Greater Boston, 1988—. Mem. AAAS, Soc. for History of Technology. Jewish. Office: Grad Sch Bus Adminstrn Harvard U Cambridge MA 02138

ROSENBLUM, BARRY NORTON, physician; b. St. Louis, Jan. 30, 1956; m. Lisa Margaret Oakley, Nov. 29, 2003. MD, U. Mo., Kansas City, 1980. Resident St. Louis U. Sch. Medicine, 1980—85, fellow in facial plastic and reconstructive surgery, 1985—86; asst. clin. prof. Columbia U. Coll. Physicians, N.Y.C., 1985—88; asst. prof. St. Louis U. Sch. Medicine, 1988—91; attending physician Mo. Bapt. Med. Ctr., St. Louis, 1996—2002, pvt. attending physician, 2002—. Contbr. chapters to books, articles to profl. jours. Fellow: ACS. Republican. Avocations: automobile racing, motorcycling, antique gun collecting. Office: Suburban Surgical Associates Inc Ste 600D 3023 N Ballas Saint Louis MO 63105 Personal E-mail: bnrosenblum@msn.com. E-mail: bnr@ssainc.net.

ROSENBLUM, ELLEN F. judge; b. 1951; m. Richard Meeker. BS, U. Oreg., 1971, JD, 1975. Bar: Oreg. 1975. Cir. ct. judge Multnomah County Ct., Portland, Oreg. Trustee Nat. Jud. Coll. Mem.: ABA (bd. govs., sec. 2002—). Office: Multnomah County Courthouse Rm 512 1021 SW 4th Ave Portland OR 97204

ROSENBLUM, ESTELLE H. retired dean, nursing educator; b. Davenport, Iowa, Feb. 8, 1933; d. Dan and Cecil (Spiewak) Masters; m. Sidney Rosenblum, Aug. 30, 1953 (dec. 1988); children: Jay Douglas, Gail Rae, Paul Mitchell; m. Jack Grevey, Mar. 31, 1996; stepdaughter: Eileen Grevey Hillson. Student, U. Iowa, 1950—53; BSN, Wayne State U., Detroit, 1956; MA in Audiology, U. N.Mex., 1971, PhD, 1979; MSN, U. Tex., El Paso, 1981. Head nurse Northville (Mich.) State Hosp., 1956; head nurse, supr. Sister Kenny Polio/Rehab. Hosp., 1957-60; pub. health nurse Englewood County Health Dept., 1961-62; nursing supr. Bernalillo County Indian Hosp., Albuquerque, 1962-63, asst. dir. nursing, 1963-64; clin. tchr. U. N.Mex. Coll. Nursing,

Albuquerque, 1964-65, inst. to prof., 1972-86, dean and prof. nursing, 1986-93, dean and prof. emerita, 1993—; sch. nurse West Mesa H.S., Albuquerque, 1967-69. Internat. nursing cons.; dir. ANA Approved CE program, Profl. Seminar Cons., 1979-89; spkr. Hong Kong Nurse Educators Soc., 1985; founder convenio U. N.Mex. and U. Mex., 1990, first nurse midwifery grad. program, U. N.Mex., 1989, first nurse practitioner program at grad. level, 1987. Author: Fundamentals of Hearing for Health Professionals, 1981; contbr. articles to profl. jours., chpts. to books. Bd. dirs. U. N.Mex. Found., 1996—, bd. sec. 2000-04; docent City of Albuquerque, 1996—; chair recognition com. Jewish Cmty. Ctr., 1998—. USPHS grantee, 1989; recipient Centennial Disting. Alumni award, U. N.Mex., 1989, Helene Fuld award to Coll. Nursing, U. N.Mex., 1987, Sigma Delta Tau Nat. Disting. Alumni award, 1988, State N.Mex. Gov.'s Disting. Svc. award, 1993, Estelle H. Rosenblum Thesis award U. N.Mex. Coll. Nursing, 1995, Nurse of the Yr. Awards "Legend of Nursing" award March of Dimes, 2002, Myrtle Aydelotte award U. Iowa Coll. Nursing, 2004; Rosenblum-Weiss Ctr. for Nursing Excellence in women and children's health care established at U. N.Mex., 2000. Fellow Am. Acad. Nursing; mem. Am. Assn. Colls. of Nursing (emeritus, exec. devel. series 1988-92), Am. Colls. Nursing (bd. dirs. 1990-92), N.Mex. Nurses Assn. (pres. 1975), N.Mex. Health Resources (bd. dirs. 1986-88), The Rotary Club of Albuquerque (Harvest ball fundraiser 1994—), Sigma Theta Tau (founder, pres. Gamma Sigma chpt. 1974-76, Mentor award), Phi Kappa Phi. Office Phone: 713-500-4586. E-mail: Saroj.M.Bahl@uth.tmc.edu.

ROSENBLUM, FRANK MICHAEL, civil engineer, consultant, surveyor; b. Calif., Nov. 12, 1961; s. Jerald and Lois Rosenblum; m. Roberta Rosenblum; 1 child, Jane. BCE, Calif. Poly. State, San Luis Obispo, 1983. Profl. civil engr., Calif., 1987, profl.land surveyor, Calif., 1990. Prin. engr. and pres. Underwood & Rosenblum, Inc., San Jose, Calif., 1993—. Facility planning cons. Calif. Pub. Schs., Calif.; vol. profl. svcs. Calif. State Parks and U.S. Nat. Parks, Calif., 1999—2004. Mem.: ASCE (assoc.), Calif. Assn. of Sch. Bus. Officials (assoc.), Calif. Land Surveyor's Assn. (assoc.), Am. Pub. Works Assn. (assoc.), Coalition for Adequate Sch. Housing (assoc.). Achievements include development of 9-step sch. traffic safety planning sys; digital mapping and planning system. Office: Underwood & Rosenblum Inc Ste A114 1630 Oakland Road San Jose CA 95131 Office Phone: 408-453-1222. Home Fax: 408-453-1207.

ROSENBLUM, JEFFREY IRA, consulting economist; b. N.Y.C., Mar. 12, 1956; s. Charles and Sylvia Lilian (Silverstein) R.; m. Monica Rosales, Sept. 15, 2000. BS, SUNY, Brockport, 1983; PhD, U. Tex., 1992. Analyst Pub. Utility Commn. of Tex., Austin, 1986-91, asst. mgr., 1991-94; mgr. KPMG Peat Marwick LLP, N.Y.C., 1994-96, sr. mgr. Dallas, 1996-99, KMPG LLP (formerly KPMG Peat Marwick), Short Hills, N.J., 1999-2001, Arthur Andersen LLP, Roseland, NJ, 2001—02; pres. Monrosen, Inc., 2002—. Mem. Am. Econ. Assn., Law and Econs. Assn. Home and Office: 108 Old Farm rd Milford PA 18337-9497 Office Phone: 570-296-3388. E-mail: jeff@monrosen.com., jeffr3@mercurylink.net.

ROSENBLUM, JOHN WILLIAM, finance educator; b. Houston, Jan. 1, 1944; s. H. William and Susan (Ullmann) R.; m. Carolyn Edith Jones, Sept. 12, 1964; children: J. Christopher, Kathryn, Nicholas. AB, Brown U., 1965; MBA, Harvard U., 1967, DBA, 1972. Instr. Harvard U. Bus. Sch., Boston, 1969-72, asst. prof., 1972-75, assoc. prof., 1975-79; prof. Darden Grad. Sch. Bus. Adminstrn., U. Va., Charlottesville, 1979-80, assoc. dean, 1980-82, dean, 1982-93, Tayloe Murphy prof., 1993—; dean Jepson Sch. Leadership Studies, U. Richmond, Va., 1996-2000. Bd. dirs. Chesapeake Corp., The Providence Jour. Co., Grantham, Mayo, Van Otterloo, Thomas Rutherford, Inc. Co-author: Strategy and Organization, 1973, (2d edit.), 1977, Cases in Political Economy-Japan, 1980. Bd. dirs. Landmark Vols., Tredeger Nat. Civil War Ctr., Jamestown-Yorktown Found., Inc., Atlantic Challenge, Charlottesville Symphony Orch., Farnsworth Art Mus. Mem. Phi Beta Kappa, Omicron Delta Kappa. Home: 854 Crozet Ave Crozet VA 22932-9803

ROSENBLUM, MARTIN JEROME, ophthalmologist; b. N.Y.C., Apr. 7, 1948; s. Philip and Rita (Steppel) R.; m. Zina Zarin, May 31, 1975; children: Steven David, Richard James. BS, Bklyn. Coll., 1968; MD, U. Ariz., 1973; postgrad., Columbia U., 1977. Diplomate Am. Bd. Ophthalmology, Nat. Bd. Med. Examiners. Intern Cornell U., N.Y.C., 1973-74; resident N.Y. Med. Coll., 1975-78, instr., 1978-79; practice medicine specializing in eye surgery St. Petersburg, Fla., 1979—. Chief ophthalmology Edward White Hosp.; asst. clin. prof. ophthalmology, U. So. Fla.; attending surgeon St. Anthony's Bayfront Med. Ctr., Palms of Pasadena, St Petersburg Gen. Hosp., Am. Soc. for Cataract and Refractive Surgery, Ctr. Spl. Surgery; med. dir. Suncoast Eye Clinic, Pa. Fellow ACS, Am. Acad. Ophthalmology; mem. AMA, Am. Soc. Ophthalmic Plastic and Reconstructive Surgery, Fla. Med. Assn., Fla. Soc. Ophthalmology, Pinellas County Med. Soc., Bayou Country Club. Republican. Jewish. Avocations: tennis, golf, travel, skiing. Home: 9035 Baywood Park Dr Largo FL 33777-4630 Office: 2200 16th St N Saint Petersburg FL 33704-3106 Office Phone: 727-822-4729. Personal E-mail: mjreye@aol.com.

ROSENBLUM, MARVIN, mathematics educator; b. Bklyn., June 30, 1926; s. Isidore and Celia (Mendelsohn) Rosenblum; m. Frances E. Parker, May 30, 1959; children: Isidore, Mendel, Jessie, Rebecca, Sarah. BS, U. Calif.-Berkeley, 1949, MA, 1951, PhD, 1955. Instr. math. U. Calif.-Berkeley, 1954-55; asst. prof. U. Va., Charlottesville, 1955-59, assoc. prof., 1960-65, prof., 1965-2000, Commonwealth prof., prof. emeritus. Mem. Inst. Advanced Study, 1959-60 Served with USNR, 1944—46. Jewish. Office: U Va Dept Math Kerchof Hall Charlottesville VA 22903

ROSENBLUM, MINDY FLEISCHER, pediatrician; b. Bronxville, N.Y., June 5, 1951; d. Herman and Muriel (Gold) Fleischer; m. Jay S. Rosenblum, June 22, 1971; children: Meira, Tamar, Rafi, Rachel. BA, Yeshiva U., 1972; MD, Albert Einstein Coll., 1976. Diplomate Am. Bd. Pediat., Am. Bd. Pediatric Endocrinology. Intern in pediat. Bronx Mcpl. Hosp. Ctr., 1976-77, residency in pediat., 1977-79; fellow in pediatric endocrinology Children's Hosp. of Phila., 1981; asst. prof. U. Pa., Phila., 1981—95; attending physician Bryn Mawr (Pa.) Hosp., 1981—, Lankenau Hosp., Wynnewood, Pa., 1983—; clin. assoc. Children's Hosp. of Phila., 1995—. Fellow Am. Acad. Pediat.; mem. Phila. Pediat. Soc. (bd. dirs. 1988-92), Am. Diabetes Assn., Lawson Wilkins Pediatric Endocrine Soc. Office Phone: 610-642-9200. E-mail: jmr101@comcast.net.

ROSENBLUM, RICHARD MARK, utilities executive; b. N.Y.C., Apr. 28, 1950; s. Victor Sigmund and Julia R.; m. Michele E. Cartier, Aug. 30, 1979; children: Gialisa, Jeremy Scott. BS, MS, Rensselaer Poly. Inst., 1973. Startup engr. Combustion Engring., Inc., Windsor, Conn., 1973-76; engr. So. Calif. Edison Co., Rosemead, 1976-82; project mgr. San Onofre Nuclear Generating Sta., 1982-83, tech. mgr., 1983-84, nuclear safety mgr., 1984-86, mgr. quality assurance, 1986-89, mgr. nuclear regulatory affairs, 1989-93, v.p. engring. and tech. svcs., 1993-95, v.p. distbn., 1996-98, sr. v.p. T&D, 1998—. N.Y. State Regents scholar, 1968-73. Office: 2244 Walnut Grove Ave Rosemead CA 91770-3714 Personal E-mail: rosenblum1@cox.net. Business E-Mail: richard.rosenblum@sce.com.

ROSENBLUM, ROBERT, art historian, educator; b. N.Y.C., July 24, 1927; s. Abraham H. and Lily M. (Lipkin) R.; m. Jane Kaplowitz, June 23, 1977; children: Sophie Lila, Theodore Abraham. BA, Queens Coll., 1948; MA, Yale U., 1950; PhD, NYU, 1956; MA (hon.), Oxford U., 1972; ArtsD (hon.), Queens Coll., 1992. Mem. faculty U. Mich., Ann Arbor, 1955-56, Princeton (N.J.) U., 1956-66, Yale U., New Haven, 1966-67; mem. faculty NYU, N.Y.C., 1967—, prof. fine arts, 1967—. Part-time curator Guggenheim Mus., N.Y.C., 1996—. Author: Cubism and Twentieth Century Art, 1960, Transformations in Late Eighteenth Century Art, 1967, Ingres, 1967, Frank Stella, 1971, Modern Painting and the Northern Romantic Tradition, 1975, The International Style of 1800, 1976, Andy Warhol: Portraits of the 70s, 1979, 19th Century Art, 1984, The Dog in Art From Rococo to Post-Modernism, 1988, The Romantic Child From Runge to Sendak, 1989, Paintings in the Musee d'Orsay, 1989, The Jeff Koons Handbook, 1992, Andy Warhol Portraits, 1993, Mel Ramos: Pop Images, 1994, The Paintings of August Strindberg, The Structure of Chaos, 1995, On Modern American Art, 1999, 1900: Art at the Crossroads, 2000, Introducing Gilbert & George, 2004. Served with U.S. Army, 1945-46. Recipient Frank Jewett Mather award for art criticism, 1981 Fellow: Am. Acad. Arts and Scis.; mem.: Coll. Art Assn.Am., Legion of Honor, L'Ordre Arts et Lettres (commandeur, chevalier). Office: NYU Dept Fine Arts Washington Sq New York NY 10003-6688 Office Phone: 212-998-8185.

ROSENBLUM, WILLIAM F., JR., lawyer; b. N.Y.C., May 11, 1935; AB cum laude, Princeton U., 1957; JD, Columbia U., 1960. Bar: N.Y. 1961, U.S. Dist. Ct. (so. dist.) N.Y. 1965. Gen. atty. Stanley Warner Corp., 1964-66; assoc. Leon, Weill & Mahony, 1967-70, Finley, Kumble, Wagner & Heine, 1970-74; pvt. practice, 1975; v.p. legal affairs Rep. Nat. Bank N.Y., 1976-82; sr. v.p., dep. gen. counsel, corp. sec. Rep. N.Y. Corp., 1987—2001; sr. v.p., dep. gen. counsel HSBC USA Inc., 2000—01; mng. dir., gen. counsel NuVerse Advisors LLC, N.Y.C., 2001—. Mem.: ABA (mem. bus. law sect., mem. futures and derivatives regulation com.), Assn. of Bar of City of N.Y. (fgn. and comparative law com. 2000—, investment mgmt. regulation com.), N.Y. State Bar Assn. (mem. sect. bus. law, futures and derivatives regulation 1990—). Office: Nuverse Advisors LLC 645 Fifth Ave New York NY 10022

ROSENBLUTH, MORTON, periodontist, educator; b. N.Y.C., Sept. 28, 1924; s. Jacob and Eva (Bigeleissen) R.; m. Sylvia Fradin, July 2, 1946; children: Cheryl Bonnie, Hal Glen. BA, NYU, 1943, grad. program in periodontia, oral medicine, 1946, DDS, 1946. Diplomate Am. Bd. Periodontology. Intern Bellevue Hosp., N.Y.C., 1946-47, resident, 1947; individual practice dentistry N.Y.C., 1947-59; individual practice periodontia North Miami Beach, Fla., 1960—; individual practice periodontia, TMJ, implantology Bay Harbor Islands, Fla., 1995—. Periodontist Mt. Sinai Hosp., N.Y., Polyclinic Hosp. and Med. Sch. N.Y., Mt. Sinai Hosp., Miami Beach, Fla., Parkway Gen. Hosp.; chief dental dept. North Miami Gen. Hosp.; chmn. periodontia sect. Dade County Rsch. Ctr.; clin. assoc. prof. divsn. oral and maxillofacial surgery U. Miami Sch. Medicine; assoc. clin. prof. Southeastern U. Health Scis.; assoc. prof. Nova Southeastern U. Coll. Dental Medicine; lectr. throughout U.S.A., Israel, Mexico, Rome, Teheran, Bangkok, Hong Kong, Tokyo, Honolulu, Jamaica, Paris, London, Sicily, Budapest, Berlin, Luxembourg, South Africa and others; vis. lectr. U. Tenn. Dental Coll., NYU Dental Coll.; cons. VA Hosp., Miami. Contbr. articles to profl. jours. Mem. adv. bd. U. Fla. Coll. Dentistry; mem. profl. adv. bd. North Dade Children's Ctr., Hope Sch. Mentally Retarded Children; mem. sci. adv. com. United Health Found.; chmn. Dental divsn. United Fund of Dade County, Combined Jewish Appeal; nat. chmn. Hebrew U. Sch. Dental Medicine; bd. dirs. Health Planning Coun. South Fla.; pres. Condominium Assn.; bd. dirs. and bd. overseers Am. Friends of Hebrew U.; mem. med. adv. bd. Dade-Broward Lupus Found.; trustee Jewish Congregation, 1961-64. With AUS, 1943-44, as capt. USAF, 1951-52. Recipient Maimonides award State of Israel, 1979. Fellow Am. Coll. Dentists, Internat. Coll. Dentists; mem. ADA, Am. Acad. Periodontology, Am. Assn. Hosp. Dental Chiefs, Am. Acad. Dental Medicine, Am. Soc. Advancement Gen. Anesthesia in Dentistry, Am. Soc. Periodontists, Fla. Soc. Periodontists, Northeastern Soc. Periodontists, Fla. Dental Soc. (chmn. coun. on legislation), Miami Dental Soc., Miami Beach Dental Soc., East Coast Dental Soc. (sec.-treas. 1968, pres. 1971-72), North Dade Dental Soc. (pres. 1963-64), Fedn. Dentaire Internat., Fla. Acad. Dental Practice Adminstrn., Alpha Omega (pres. 1978-78, internat. regent 1973-75, internat. editor 1975-77, internat. pres.-elect 1977-78, internat. pres. 1979, chmn. bd. Alpha Omega Found. 1985-90), Am. Dental Interfrat. Coun. (pres. 1981-82), Nocoma Club (pres. 1958-60), NYU Century Club (local chmn.), Jockey Club (bd. govs.), KP, Masons, Kiwanis (bd. dirs. 1965), Chaine Des Rotisseurs (Miami Beach charge de missions). Home: 20281 E Country Club Dr Apt # 1001 Aventura FL 33180 Office: 1048 Kane Concourse Bay Harbor Islands FL 33154-2000 Office Phone: 305-867-0005.

ROSENBURGH, STEPHEN ARUTHUR, corporate financial executive; b. Peterborough, Ont., Can., July 15, 1951; came to U.S., 1993; s. Donald Joseph and Evelyn Mabel (Poole) R.; children: Lara Aislynn, Meghan Lynne, Jana Michelle. BA in Polit. Sci., Laurentian U., 1973; grad diploma in pub. adminstrn., Carelton U., 1974, MA in Adminstrn. and Mktg., 1975; cert. mgmt., Harvard U., 1997. Exec. officer Govt. Ont., Mgmt. Bd. Cabinet, Toronto, Can., 1975-77; sr. v.p. York-Hannover, Toronto, 1977-83; pres. Morewood Industries, Ltd., Ottawa, Ont., 1983-89; sr. v.p. Bramalea, Ltd., Toronto, 1990-91; pres. Carelton County Mgmt., Ottawa, 1989-96, Jordan Homes, Charlotte, N.C., 1993-95; chmn., CEO Enterprise Devel. Internat., Fairfax, Va., 1996—; dir. Consol. Stone Industries, 1998—; pres. U.S. Land Investments, Charlotte, N.C., 1998—. Baptist. Home: 15839 Strickland Ct Charlotte NC 28277-1477

ROSENDAL, HANS ERIK, meteorologist; b. Lyngby, Denmark, July 19, 1931; s. Kaj and Anna Katrine (Hansen) R.; m. Angela Karlos, Dec. 20, 1958; children: Erik P., Dana G., Paul A. BS, U. Wis., 1960; MS, U. Mich., 1965. Meteorologist U.S. Weather Bur., Washington, 1960-65; state climatologist Nat. Weather Svc., Madison, Wis., 1965-73, meteorologist Milw., Wis., 1973-74, Phoenix, 1974-76, Honolulu, 1976—. Editor Mariners Weather Log, 1962-64. Recipient Gold medal U.S. Dept. Commerce, Honolulu, 1992. Fellow Am. Meteorol. Soc. (spl. award 1992). Lutheran. Home: 1242 Mokapu Blvd Kailua HI 96734-1847 Office: Nat Weather Svc U Hawaii at Manoa Honolulu HI 96734 E-mail: hans.rosendal@noaa.gov, rosendalhe@aol.com.

ROSENDALE, GEORGE WILLIAM, aircraft company executive; b. Keenan, Okla., Nov. 4, 1933; s. John Webster and Laura Lee (Schawo) Rosendale; m. Penney Sue Tillotson, Dec. 27, 1964; children: James Christopher, Kathleen Marie, John Charles. Student ., Okla. Bapt. U., 1957—58; student, U. Wichita, 1958—63; BA in English, Wichita State U., 1969, MS in Adminstrn., 1971. Diplomate Pers. Accreditation Inst., 1977. Engring. draftsman Skyline Corp., Wichita, Kans., 1952, Boeing Aircraft Co., Wichita, Kans., 1953, O.A. Sutton Corp., Wichita, Kans., 1956, engring. checker, 1856—56; various positions Cessna Aircraft Co., Wichita, Kans., 1958—98, pers. rep., 1967—69, tng. supr., 1969—73, mgr. employee tng. and devel., 1973—84, mgr. pers. projects, 1984—85, mgr. mgmt. resource devel., 1985—87, adminstr. internat. assembly programs, 1987—88, mgr. material fin. and adminstrn., 1988—98; mgr. material TAD Tech., Wichita, Kans., 1999—2000. Vocat. instr. Wichita Pub. Schs., 1963; pers. adviser Wichita Police Res., 1969—73; treas. Haysville Police Res., 1975—91; chmn. bd. dirs. Corp. Employment Resources, Inc., 1987—88. Area comdr. United Fund, Wichita, 1971; sec. Haysville Jr. Football League, Haysville, Kans., 1973—75; study com. chmn. Wichita Cmty. Planning Coun., 1972—73; mem. Haysville Planning Commn., 1976—86, chmn., 1977—79, 1980—84; exec. com. Kans. State Employment and Tng. Coun., 1979—82. Served with U.S. Army, 1953—56. Recipient Campaign award, United Fund of Wichita, 1969—71, Outstanding Svc. Plaque award, Am. Cancer Soc., 1978—79, 1981—82, SER Individual Support award, 1979, others. Mem.: Optimist (chmn. cmty. svc. 1985—88, v.p. Haysville club 1986—87, pres. 1987—88, lt. gov. Kans. dist. 1988—89, dir. 1989—92), Psi Chi. Home: 424 W Hollywood St Wichita KS 67217-5934

ROSENDHAL, JEFFREY DAVID, federal science agency administrator, astronomer; b. Bklyn., June 21, 1941; s. Louis and Beulah (Goldsmith) R.; m. Sharon E. Katzman, Dec. 27, 1964 (div. Jan. 25, 1989); children: Martin Andrew, Rachel Lynn; m. Ellen R. Anderson, Feb. 14, 1992. BA, Williams Coll., 1962; MS, U. Ill., 1963; PhD, Yale U., 1968. Vis. asst. prof. astronomy U. Wash., Seattle, 1968-69; asst. prof. U. Wis., Madison, 1969-71, U. Ariz., Tucson, 1971-74; with NASA, Washington, 1974—, mgr. advanced programs and tech., astrophysics divsn., 1978-80, asst. assoc. adminstr. advanced planning Office Space Sci., 1980-81, asst. assoc. adminstr. sci. Office Space Sci., Applications, 1981-87, spl. asst. to assoc. adminstr. for space sci. and applications, 1987-89, 92-93, spl. asst. for policy Office Exploration, 1989-90, asst. dir. exploration (internat.) Office Aeronautics, Exploration and Tech., 1990-91, asst. dir. strategic planning Astrophysics Divsn. Office of Space Sci., 1993-96, asst. assoc. adminstr./edn. and outreach Office Space Sci., 1996-2001, edn. and pub. outreach dir. Office of Space Sci., 2001—04, asst. assoc. adminstr. for edn. programs Office of Edn., 2004—. Vis. prof. internat. rels. George Washington U., 1988-89; mem. staff energy subcom. House Sci. Space and Tech. Com., 1992. Mem. editl. bd.: Jour. Brit. Interplanetary Soc., 1988—; contbr. articles to profl. jours. Recipient Team Achievement award European Space Agy., 1983, 85, 86, Presdl. award of Meritorious Exec. in Sr. Exec. Svc., 1987, 2001; NSF grantee, 1971, 72-73; NASA fellow Yale U., 1966-68; hon. Woodrow Wilson fellow, 1962. Fellow: AIAA (assoc.); mem.: Sr. Execs. Assn., Internat. Astron. Union, Internat. Acad. Astronautics, Royal Astron. Soc., Am. Astron. Soc. (divsn. planetary scis.), Astron. Soc. Pacific, Cosmos Club, Phi Beta Kappa. Achievements include discovery of the variability of the microturbulence in early-type high luminosity stars; direction of the selection of flight experiments for every major NASA scientific mission 1980-1988; development of strategic and implementation plans for incorporating education and the public understanding of science into space science research programs and missions; establishment of a national support network for space science education; creation of the largest single program in astronomy and space science education ever undertaken, an effort that is now reaching tens of millions of people every year. Home: 11446 Links Dr Reston VA 20190-4813 Office: NASA Hdqrs Office of Edn Code N Washington DC 20546 E-mail: jeffrosendhal@comcast.net., Jeffrey.D.Rosendhal@nasa.gov.

ROSENDIN, RAYMOND JOSEPH, electrical contracting company executive; b. San Jose, Calif., Feb. 14, 1929; s. Moses Louis and Bertha C. (Pinedo) R.; m. Jeanette Marie Bucher, June 30, 1951 (dec. Feb. 1967); children: Mark R., Patricia A., Debra M., Cynthia C., David R.; m. Nancy Ann Burke, July 6, 1984; children: Raymond M., Callie R., Blake W. Student engring., San Jose State U., 1947-48; BSE.E., Heald's Engring. Coll., San Francisco, 1950. V.p., CEO Rosendin Electric, Inc., San Jose, Calif., 1953-59, exec. v.p., CEO, 1969-75, pres., CEO, 1975-94, chmn., CEO, 1995-2000, chmn., 2000—, former dir. Former dir. Community Bank, San Jose Bd. fellows U. Santa Clara, Calif., 1966-93, pres. bd., 1969-72, bd. regents, 1972-82; bd. dirs. United Way, Santa Clara, 1970-74; O'Connor's Hosp., San Jose, 1979-85, Community Hosp., Los Gatos, Calif., 1968-74. Recipient Man of Yr. award Santa Clara Valley Youth Village, 1963, Optimist of Yr. award Optimist Club, San Jose, 1970 Mem. C. of C. Greater San Jose (past dir.), Nat. Elec. Contractors Assn. (past pres., gov., dir.) Clubs: St. Claire (San Jose). Republican. Roman Catholic. Avocation: boating. Office: Rosendin Electric Inc 880 Mabury Rd San Jose CA 95133-1021

ROSENFELD, ALBERT HYMAN, science and medical writer; b. Phila., May 31, 1920; s. Samuel and Annie (Zeiffert) R.; m. Lillian Elizabeth Snow, Aug. 24, 1948; children: Robert, Shana. BA in History and Social Scis., N.Mex. State U., 1950, DLett (hon.), 1971. Freelance mag. writer, corr., Santa Fe, 1950-56; sci. editor Life mag., N.Y.C., 1956-69; mng. editor Family Health mag., N.Y.C., 1969-71; writer, prodr. Time-Life Video, N.Y.C., 1971-72; sci. editor, columnist Saturday Rev., N.Y.C., 1973-79; cons. on future programs March of Dimes Birth Defects Found., White Plains, NY, 1973—; adj. asst. prof. U. Tex. Med. Br., Galveston, 1973-98. Bd. dirs. RegeneRx, Biopharms., Inc., Bethesda, Md., Totts Gap (Pa.) Med. Rsch. Labs.; mem. sci. bd. Alliance for Aging Rsch., Washington, 1995—. Author: The Quintessence of Irving Langmuir, 1962, The Second Genesis, 1969, Prolongevity II, 1985; co-author: Responsible Parenthood, 1980; contbr. articles to profl. publs. Sgt. U.S. Army, 1942-45, ETO. Recipient award for leadership in med. journalism Lasker Found., 1967, Nat. Mag. award Columbia U., 1975, James P. Grady medal Am. Chem. Soc., 1981. Mem. World Future Soc., Nat. Assn. Sci. Writers, Authors Guild, Coun. for Advancement of Sci. Writing (bd. dirs., past pres.), Smithsonian Assocs., Hastings Ctr. Democrat. Jewish. Avocations: music, sketching, tennis, baseball, hiking. E-mail: alrosenf@westnet.com.

ROSENFELD, ARTHUR F. federal agency administrator; b. Allentown, Pa. m. Carla Toledo. BA, Muhlenberg Coll., 1970; MBA, Lehigh U., 1974; JD, Villanova U., 1979. Bar: D.C. 1979, U.S. Supreme Ct., U.S. Ct. Appeals (4th, 5th and D.C. cirs.). Labor atty. U.S. C. of C., Washington, 1979—84; atty. Hansell & Post, 1984—86; numerous positions including counsel for regulations divsn. employee benefits, spl. ast. to silicitor of labor, assoc. deputy sec. labor U.S. Dept. Labor, 1986—97; sr. labor advisor to chmn. James M. Jeffords Senate Com. Health, Edn., Labor and Pensions, 1997—2001; gen. counsel Nat. Labor Rels. Bd., 2001—. Office: NLRB 1099 14th St NW Washington DC 20570-0001

ROSENFELD, ARTHUR H. physics educator, research director; b. Birmingham, Ala., June 22, 1926; BS in Physics, Va. Poly. Inst., 1944; PhD in Physics, U. Chgo., 1954; DSc (hon.), U. Durham, Eng., 1983. Rsch. assoc. Inst. Nuclear Studies U. Chgo., 1954-55; rsch. assoc. Lawrence Berkeley Lab. U. Calif., Berkeley, 1955-57; asst. prof. to assoc. prof. U. Calif., 1957-63; prof. physics U. Calif., Berkeley, 1963-94, dir. particle data group Lawrence Berkeley Lab., 1964-75, acting chmn. dept. computer sci., 1967-68, leader rsch. group A Lawrence Berkeley Lab., 1971-73, leader energy-efficient bldgs. rsch program Lawrence Berkeley Lab., 1975-83, vice chmn. energy and resources grad. program, 1986-94, dir. Ctr. Bldg. Sci. Lawrence Berkeley Lab., 1986-94, founder, acting dir. Calif. Inst. for Energy Efficiency, 1988-90, prof. emeritus, 1994—; sr. advisor to asst. sec. energy efficiency U.S. Dept. Energy, Washington, 1994-99; commr. Calif. Energy Commn., Sacramento, Calif., 2000—. Vis. prof. Coll. de France, Paris, 1978; co-founder Am. Coun. Energy-Efficient Econ., 1979, chmn., 1981-83, pres., 1984-90, bd. dirs., 1990-94; mem. steering com. advanced customer tech. test maximum energy efficiency Pacific Gas & Electric Co., 1989-98; mem. tech. adv. panel joint com. on energy regulation and environ. State of Calif., 1990-91; mem. Nat. Sci. and Tech. Coun., 1994—, civilian indsl. tech. com, 1994—, co-chmn. subcom. constrn. and bldgs., 1994—. Author: (with E. Fermi and others) Nuclear Physics, 1949, Experimental Meson Spectroscopy, 1968, 3d edit., 1972, Supplying Energy Through Greater Efficiency: The Potential for Conservation in California's Residential Sector, 1983, A New Prosperity: The SERI Solar/Conservation Study, 1991, Scenarios of U.S. Carbon Reductions, Interlaboratory Working Group, 1997; contbr. articles, seminars to profl. jours., confs.; assoc. editor Jour. Computational Physics, 1964-73, Energy and Bldgs., 1979—, Energy, the Internat. Jour., 1985-91; editl. cons. Ency. of Applied Physics, 1988—. Mem. governing bd. Am. Inst. Physics, 1974-77; co-founder Am. Coun. for an Energy Efficient Economy, 1979; chmn. 1981-83, pres. 1984—, mem. adv. com. Calif. Legis. Joint Com. on Energy Regulation and Environ., 1990-91. Recipient Sadi Carnot award US Dept. of Energy, 1993, Star Energy Efficiency for outstanding contbn. in promoting energy efficiency Alliance to Save Energy, 1995. Fellow Am. Physical Soc. (sec., treas. divsn. particles and fields 1967-71, Leo Szilard award for physics in the pub. interest 1986); mem. NAS (panel on policy implications of greenhouse warm 1990—), Fedn. Am. Sci. (coun. 1964-72, 77-81, 83-87, 94-98, 2004—), Am. Inst. Physics (mem. governing bd. 1974-77). Achievements include co-developement of Ultra-Violet Water Works to purify water in villages and slums, 1996; studied under Enrico Fermi at U. Chgo. Office: Calif Energy Commn 1516 9th St Sacramento CA 95814 Office Phone: 916-654-4930. Business E-Mail: AHRosenfeld@LBL.gov.

ROSENFELD, ARTHUR HERBERT, lawyer, publisher; b. Bklyn., May 24, 1930; s. Abraham and Sadie (Albert) R.; m. Lois E. Glantz, Apr. 15, 1956; children: Felicia Ann, Carolyn Jane, Sara Ellen. Student, St. Andrew's U., 1950-51; AB, Union Coll., Schenectady, 1952; JD, Harvard U., 1955; postgrad., CCNY, 1962-63. Bar: N.Y. 1955. Pres. Warren, Gorham & Lamont, Inc., N.Y.C., 1970-81, Internat. Thomson Profl. Pub., N.Y.C., 1981-84; chmn. bd. Rosenfeld, Emanuel Inc., Larchmont, N.Y., 1984-88; pres. Prentice Hall Tax & Profl. Ref., N.Y.C., 1988-89, Maxwell Macmillan Profl. and Bus. Reference Div., Englewood Cliffs, N.J., 1989-92; chmn. Arthur H. Rosenfeld Assocs., 1991—; Civic Rsch. Inst., Inc., 1992—. Mem. ABA, N.Y. State Bar Assn., Am. Assn. Pubs. (exec. coun. 1991), Harvard Club. Democrat. Office: 2067 Broadway Ste 50 New York NY 10023 E-mail: ahrcri@aol.com.

ROSENFELD, AZRIEL, computer science educator, consultant; b. N.Y.C., Feb. 19, 1931; s. Abraham Hirsh and Ida B. (Chadaby) R.; m. Eve Hertzberg, Mar. 1, 1959; children— Elie, David, Tova BA, Yeshiva U., 1950, M.H.L., 1953, MS, 1954, D.H.L., 1955; MA, Columbia U., 1951, Ph.D, 1957; D.Tech. (hon.), Linkoping U., Sweden, 1980; D of Tech. (hon.), Oulu U., Finland, 1994; LHD (hon.), Yeshiva U., 2000. Ordained rabbi, 1952. Physicist Fairchild Controls Corp., N.Y.C., 1954-56; engr. Ford Instrument Co., Long Island City, N.Y., 1956-59; mgr. research electronics div. Budd Co., Long Island City and McLean, Va., 1959-64; prof., dir. Ctr. for Automation Rsch. U. Md., College

Park, 1964-2001, Disting. univ. prof., 1995-2001, prof. emeritus, 2001—. Vis. asst. prof. Yeshiva U., N.Y.C., 1957-63; pres. ImTech, Inc., Silver Spring, Md., 1975-92 Author, editor numerous books; editor numerous jours. Recipient Info. Sci. award Assn. for Intelligent Machinery, 1998. Fellow IEEE (Emanuel R. Piore award 1985), IEEE Computer Soc. (Harry Goode Meml. award 1995), IEEE Sys., Man and Cybernetics Soc. (Norbert Wiener award 1995), Washington Acad. Scis. (Sci. Achievement award 1988), Am. Assn. for Artificial Intelligence (founding), Assn. Computing Machinery (founding); mem. Math. Assn. Am., Machine Vision Assn. (bd. dirs. 1984-88, Pres.'s award 1987), Internat. Assn. Pattern Recognition (pres. 1980-82, K.S. Fu award 1988, founding fellow 1994), Assn. Orthodox Jewish Scientists (pres. 1963-65), Nat. Acad. Engring. of Mex. (corr.). Home: 6701 Park Hgts Ave Apt 3G Baltimore MD 21215-2442 Office: U Md Ctr Automation Rsch Computer Vision Lab College Park MD 20742-3275 E-mail: ar@cfar.umd.edu.

ROSENFELD, HARRY MORRIS, editor; b. Berlin, 1929; s. Sam and Esther Rosenfeld; m. Anne Hahn, Feb. 28, 1953; children: Susan, Amy, Stefanie. BA, Syracuse U., 1952; postgrad., NYU, 1954, Columbia U., 1955-59. With N.Y. Herald Tribune, 1954-66, fgn. editor, 1962-66; mng. editor Herald Tribune News Svc., 1959-62; with Washington Post, 1966-78, fgn. editor, 1969; asst. mng. editor Met. News, 1970-74, Nat. News, 1974-76, Outlook/Book World, 1976-78; editor Times Union and Knickerbocker News, Albany, N.Y., 1978-88, L.A. Herald Examiner, 1985, The Times Union and Sunday Times Union, 1978-96; editor-at-large, columnist The Times Union, Albany, N.Y., 1996—. Dir. daily Watergate coverage for Washington Post (newspaper award Pulitzer Gold medal for pub. svc.); vice-chmn. N.Y. Fair Trial Free Press Conf., 1985-98, vice chmn. emeritus, 1998—; co-chmn. N.Y. State Reporters Com. for Freedom of Press; mem. adv. com. Harvard Journalism Fellowship for Advanced Studies in Pub. Health; Pulitzer juror, 1987-88, 96, 97; chmn. Elder Network of the Capital Region. Commr. N.Y. State Regents Commn. on Libr. Svcs. Recipient Black United Front award, 1973, First Amendment award Anti-Defamation League-B'nai B'rith, L.A., Outstanding Alumni award, Syracuse U. Coll. of Arts and Scis., 1993, Media Responsibility award N.Y. State Martin Luther King Jr. Inst. for Non-Violence, 1993. Mem. Am. Soc. Newspaper Editors, N.Y. State AP Assn. (pres. 1983, 3d pl. column award 1983, 85, 1st pl. column award 1987), N.Y. State Soc. Newspaper Editors, Internat. Press Inst., UPI Fgn. News Com. (rep. for N.E.), Soc. Profl. Journalists (adv. bd. Albany chpt.), and 3 commns. on Cameras in the Cts. (adv. comm.). Office: Times Union PO Box 15000 Albany NY 12212-5000 Office Phone: 518-454-5450. Business E-Mail: hrosenfeld@timesunion.com.

ROSENFELD, JOEL CHARLES, surgeon; b. Phila., Nov. 5, 1948; MD, Jefferson Med. Coll., 1974. Diplomate Am. Bd. Surgery. Intern Pa. Hosp., Phila., 1974-75, resident, 1975-79, fellow in vascular surgery, 1981-82; surgeon St. Luke's Hosp., Bethlehem, Pa., 1987—, gen. surgery residency program dir., 1995—, dir. med. edn., 2002—. Mem. AMA, ACS, Internat. Soc. Cardiovasc. Surgery, Soc. Vascular Surgery, Soc. for Clin. Vascular Surgery, Assn. Program Dirs. Surgery, Assn. for Acad. Surgery. Office: Progressive Physicians 301 W Broad St Bethlehem PA 18015 Office Phone: 610-252-8281. Business E-Mail: rosenfj@slhn.org.

ROSENFELD, MARK KENNETH, real estate developer; b. Jackson, Mich., Mar. 17, 1946; s. Nathan and Marjorie N. (Leopold) R.; children: Edward Robert, Zachary, Alix Caitlin. BA, Amherst Coll., 1968; S.M., MIT, 1970. With Jacobson's, Jackson, 1972—, v.p., real estate group mgr., 1976-78, exec. v.p., 1978-82, pres, 1982-93, chmn., CEO, 1993-96; chmn. Wilherst Developers Inc., 1997—. Bd. dirs. Ramco-Gershenson Property Trust, Kurt Gaum Inc. With U.S. Army, 1969-70. Jewish. Office Phone: 813-250-1717. E-mail: mark.rosenfeld@wilherst.net.

ROSENFELD, MARTIN JEROME, healthcare executive, educator; b. Flint, Mich., Oct. 3, 1944; s. Israel Edward and Lillian Edith (Natchez) R.; m. Marcy Tucker Colman; 1 child, Joshua; stepchildren: Jessica Colman, Zachary Colman. BA, Mich. State U., 1968, MHA, 1978; MBA with high honors, Ind. No. U., 1979. Adminstr. Care Corp., Grand Rapids, Mich., 1969—70, Chandler Convalescent Ctr., Detroit, 1970—71, Grand Cmty. Hosp., Detroit, 1971—73; exec. v.p., CEO Msgr. Clement Kern Hosp. Spl. Surgery, Warren, Mich., 1973—84; pres. M.J. Rosenfeld Assocs., 1984—85; COO Dickinson, Wright, Moon, Van Dusen & Freeman, 1985—88; acting COO New Ctr. Hosp., Detroit, 1995—96; prin. Rosenfeld Partners LLP, Farmington Hills, Mich., 1988—2003; instr. U. Phoenix, 2001—; practice mgr. Tri-County Med. Clinic, Sterling Heights, Mich., 2003—. Instr. Marygrove Coll., 1975-80; assoc. prof. Mercy Coll., Detroit, 1978-80; mem. faculty Inst. on Continuing Legal Edn., Ann Arbor, Mich., Inst. Law Firm Mgmt., Ann Arbor; instr. Legal Tech '87, Chgo. Author papers in field. Mem. editl. bd. The Human-Size Hosp.; mem. panel of experts The Health Care News. V.p. Detroit chpt. Jewish Nat. Fund, 1978—; pres. Cranbrook Village Homeowners Assn., 1977; chmn. Community Hosps. of Southeastern Mich., 1981-84; mem. tech. work group Comprehensive Health Planning Coun. of Southeastern Mich., 1981-84; mem. fin. mgmt. com., mem. hosp. affairs bd. Greater Detroit Area Hosp. Coun., 1981-84; bd. dirs., com. chmn. Detroit Symphony Orch., 1984-90; bd. dirs., mem. fund raising com. Detroit Met. Orch., 1984-87. Mem. ABA, Assn. Legal Adminstrs., Am. Assn. Health Care Cons., Royal Soc. Health, Am. Podiatry Assn. (com. hosps. 1981-84), Warren C. of C. (com. chmn. 1975), Nat. Assn. Legal Search Cons., Nat. Assn. Pers. Svcs., Mich. Assn. Pers. Svcs., Sanford Rose Assocs. Dirs. Assn. (pres. 1993-95, treas. 1995-97). E-mail: tcmcmjr@aol.com.

ROSENFELD, MICHAEL G. medical educator; Prof. dept. medicine U. Calif. Med. Sch., La Jolla, 1996—. Mem.: NAS. Office: U Calif San Diego Sch Medicine Howard Hughes Med Inst 9500 Gilman Dr Room 345 La Jolla CA 92093-0648

ROSENFELD, RONALD A. federal agency administrator; Grad., Law Sch. Sec. of commerce State of Okla.; dep. asst. sec. for single family housing Dept. HUD, 1989, gen. dep. asst. sec. housing, FHA commr., pres. Govt. Nat. Mortgage Assn., 2001—. Office: Dept HUD Govt Nat Mortgage Assn 451 7th St SW Washington DC 20410-9000

ROSENFELD, SARENA MARGARET, artist; b. Elmira, N.Y., Oct. 17, 1940; d. Thomas Edward and Rosalie Ereny (Fedor) Rooney; m. Robert Steven Bach, June 1958 (div. 1963); children: Robert Steven, Daniel Thomas; m. Samson Rosenfeld III, June 5, 1976. Student, Otis/Parson Art Inst., L.A., 1994-98, Idyllwild Sch. Music and Arts, 1994-98. One-woman shows include Robert Dana Gallery, San Francisco, Gordon Gallery, Santa Monica, Calif., Hespe Gallery, San Francisco, Art Expressions, San Diego, L.A., La Jolla, Calif., Aspen, Colo., New Orleans, Honolulu, La Sierra U., Riverside, Calif., U. Enklinik, Bochum, Germany, Ruhr U., Germany, Universitatsklinikum Benjamin Franklin, Berlin, 2002, Gallery 444, San Francisco; artist (group shows) Ergane Gallery, N.Y.C., Orlando Gallery, Sherman Oaks, Calif., Bradford Gallery Blue Sq., Newport Beach, Calif., 2001, L.A., Soho, N.Y.C., Santa Barbara, Calif., Tanglewood, Mass., Johannesburg, South Africa, Coda Gallery, Palm Desert, Calif., Johnson Art Collection, Melrose Ave., L.A. Mem., vol., animal handler Wildlife Waysta., Angeles Nat. Forest, Calif.; vol. animal keeper L.A. Zoo. Recipient Best of Show award Glendale Regional Arts Coun., 1984-85, 1st pl. awards Santa Monica Art Festival, 1982, 83, 84, 85, 86, Sweepstakes award and 1st pl., 1986, Purchase prize awards L.A. West C. of C., 1986-87, Tapestry in Talent Invitational San Jose Arts Coun., 1986, 1st pl. awards Studio City and Century City Arts Couns., 1976-84, 1st award Pacific Palisades Art Affair XII, 1997, Sherman Oaks Fall Arts Festival, 1997. Mem. Nat. Mus. of Women in the Arts. Republican. Home: 6570 Kelvin Ave Canoga Park CA 91306-4021

ROSENFELD, STEVEN B. lawyer; b. N.Y.C., Apr. 12, 1943; s. Eugene David and Laura (Sipin) R.; m. Naomi Eve Winkler, Aug. 21, 1965; children: Kathryn Anne, Elizabeth Jane. BA, Columbia Coll., 1964; LLB, Columbia U., 1967. Bar: N.Y. 1967, D.C. 1984, U.S. Dist. Ct. (so. dist.) N.Y. 1969, U.S. Dist. Ct. (ea. dist.) N.Y. 1970, U.S. Ct. Appeals (2d cir.) 1971, U.S. Ct. Appeals (3d cir.) 1974, U.S. Ct. Appeals (Fed. cir.) 1978, D.C. 1979, U.S. Supreme Ct. 1979, U.S. Ct. Appeals (5th cir.) 1982, U.S. Ct. Appeals (6th and D.C. cirs.) 1984, U.S. Ct. Appeals (4th and 9th cirs.) 1987, U.S. Ct. Appeals (1st cir.) 1989, U.S. Ct. Appeals (10th cir.) 1991. Law clk. to Hon. Charles M. Metzner U.S. Dist. Ct. (so. dist.) N.Y., 1967-68; assoc. Rosenman & Colin, N.Y.C., 1968-71; dep. gen. counsel N.Y. State Commn. on Attica, N.Y.C., Batavia, N.Y., 1971-72; assoc. Paul, Weiss, Rifkind, Wharton & Garrison, N.Y.C., 1972-75, ptnr., 1976—. Lectr. Columbia U. Sch. Law, 1995—2002; chmn. Conflicts of Interest Bd. N.Y.C., 2002—. Contbr. articles to profl. jours. Bd. dirs. N.Y. Assn. New Ams., N.Y.C., 1973-95; trustee Dalton Sch., N.Y.C., 1988-94; trustee Putney Sch. Putney, Vt., 1995-2001, N.Y. Theatre Workshop, 1996—. Mem. N.Y. State Bar Assn. (ho. of dels. 1996-98), Assn. Bar City N.Y. (exec. com. 1992-96, v.p. 1998-99, past mem. various coms.), Legal Aid Soc. (pres. 1989-91, bd. dirs., exec. com. 1978-95). Democrat. Jewish. Avocations: opera and chamber music, theatre, tennis. E-mail: srosenfeld.paulweiss.com. Office: Paul Weiss Rifkind Et Al 1285 Ave of Americas New York NY 10019-6028

ROSENFELD, STEVEN IRA, artistic director, music publisher; b. Bklyn., May 24, 1949; s. Harry Allen and Rosina (DeStefano) R. BA, Southampton Coll., 1971; postgrad., St. Francis Coll., Bklyn., 1975—. Pres. World Wide Mgmt., Yorktown, 1970—; v.p. mktg. JVC, Inc., Maspath, N.Y., 1972-74; v.p., gen. mgr. Audio Mktg. Cons., Yorktown, N.Y., 1976-88; mng. dir. Westchester Shakespeare Festival, N.Y.C., 1987-90; v.p. Barnett Labs., Houston, 1992-93; CEO Apple Pie Products, 1996—; pres., CEO The F.C. Sturtevant Co., 1998—. Founding ptnr. Smoking Caterpillar Music Publ., 2004—, Have Another Hit Music Publ., 2004—; bd. dirs. Neworld Order Recording Co., New Canaan Capitol, Waterline Filter Corp. Editor (newspaper) The Windmill, 1968 69. Mem. Internat. Platform Assn., Audio Engring. Soc. (cert.), Soc. Audio Cons. (cert.), Nat. Trust, Nat. Acad. Rec. Arts and Scis. Jewish. Office Phone: 212-573-6000. Personal E-mail: sirmagic6@aol.com.

ROSENFELD, STEVEN IRA, ophthalmologist; b. N.Y.C., Nov. 18, 1954; s. Frederick and Pearl (Stern) R.; m. Lisa Allyson Klar, June 24, 1978; children: Michael, Julie. BA, Johns Hopkins U., 1976; MD, Yale U., 1980. Diplomate Am. Bd. Ophthalmology, Nat. Bd. Med. Examiners. Intern Yale-New Haven Hosp., 1980-81; resident Barnes Hosp., St. Louis, 1981-84; fellow Bascom Palmer Eye Inst., Miami, Fla., 1984-85; ptnr. in pvt. practice Delray Eye Assocs., Delray Beach, Fla., 1985—. Clin. instr. Bascom Palmer Eye Inst., 1985-90, asst. clin. prof., 1990-96, assoc. clin. prof., 1996—; assoc. examiner Am. Bd. Ophthalmology, Phila., 1993—. Author: The Eye in Systemic Disease, 1990, Lens and Cataract, 1996; contbr. articles to profl. jours. Recipient Harry Rosenbaum Rsch. award Washington U. Sch. Medicine, 1984; named one of Best Doctors in Am., 1996; Heed Ophthalmic Found. fellow, 1984. Fellow ACS, Am. Acad. Ophthalmology (chmn. B.C.S.C. section Lens and Cataract Surgery 2002—), Soc. Heed Fellows; mem. Castroviejo Corneal Soc., Eye Bank Assn. Am., Fla. Med. Assn., Fla. Soc. Ophthalmology, Assn. for Rsch. in Vision and Ophthalmology, Ocular Microbiology and Immunology Group, Phi Beta Kappa, Alpha Omega Alpha. Avocations: tennis, golf, fly fishing, lacrosse. Office: Delray Eye Assocs 16201 South Military Trail Delray Beach FL 33484-6503 Office Phone: 561-498-8100.

ROSENFELD, WALTER DAVID, JR., architect, writer; b. N.Y.C., May 30, 1930; s. Walter David and Florence (Romann) R.; m. Marilyn Smith, Oct. 15, 1954; children: John W., Sarah E., Susannah, Elizabeth A. AB, U. Pa., 1952; postgrad., Ind. U., 1953-54, Yale U., 1954-55, 57-60. Registered architect, Mass., N.H.; cert. Nat. Coun. Archtl. Registration Bds.; cert. constrn. specifier. Draftsman, specifier Perry Dean Stewart, Boston, 1960-67; architect, specifier, v.p., prin. The Architects Collaborative, Cambridge, Mass., 1967-86, also dir., 1980-84; cons. architect Walter Rosenfeld CSI, Newton, Mass., 1986—. Author: The Practical Specifier, 1985; contbg. editor Progressive Architecture mag., 1980-94; contbr. articles to profl. jours. Pres. Friends of Newton Free Libr., Mass., 1970-72; chmn. Newton Ward 1 Dem. Com., 1974-80; vice chmn. designer sel. com. City of Newton, 1976-86; bd. dirs. Mass. Audubon Soc., 1987-99, Mass. Audubon Coun., 01—. Mem. AIA, Constrn. Spcifications Inst. (bd. dirs. Boston chpt. 1980-86, pres. Boston chpt. 1987-88), Boston Soc. Architects. Office: Walter Rosenfeld CSI PO Box 568 Edgartown MA 02539-0568

ROSENFIELD, ALLAN, physician; b. Cambridge, Mass., Apr. 28, 1933; s. Harold Hermann and Beatrice (Garber) Rosenfield; m. Clare Stein, July 31, 1966; children: Paul Allan, Jill Emilie. BA cum laude, Harvard U., 1955; MD, Columbia U., 1959. Diplomate Am. B. Ob-Gyn. Intern, surgical resident Beth Israel Hosp., Boston, 1959—61; resident in ob-gyn Boston Hosp. for Women (now Brigham and Woman's Hosp.), Boston, 1963—66; rep., med. advisor The Population Council and Ministry Pub. Health, Bangkok, 1967—73; asst. dir. tech. assistance div. The Population Council, N.Y.C., 1973—75; prof. ob-gyn Columbia U., N.Y.C., 1975—88, prof. pub. health, 1975—86, DeLamar Prof. pub. health, 1986—, dir. ctr. for population and family health, 1975—88, acting chmn. dept. ob-gyn., 1984—86; dean and delamer sch. pub. health Columbia U. (now known as Joseph Mailman Sch. Pub. Health), N.Y.C., 1986—. Contbr. articles to profl. jours. Capt. USAF, 1961—63. Fellow: ACOG; mem.: APHA, Inst. Medicine of NAS (several coms. and bds.). Jewish. Avocations: tennis, skiing, music. Home: 4 Crosshill Rd Hartsdale NY 10530-3014 Office: Columbia U Joseph Mailman Sch Pub Hlth 600 W 168th St New York NY 10032-3722

ROSENFIELD, GENE, construction executive; CEO, mng. ptnr. Western Pacific Housing, El Segundo, Calif., 1989—. Office: Western Pacific Housing 300 Continental Blvd Ste 390 El Segundo CA 90245

ROSENFIELD, JAMES HAROLD, communications executive; b. Boston, July 18, 1929; s. Harold and Beatrice (Garber) R.; m. Nancy Lee Stenbuck, Oct. 19, 1952; 2 children. BA, Dartmouth Coll., 1952; D of Comml. Sci. (hon.), St. John's U., 1981. TV network sales exec. NBC, N.Y.C., 1954-57; advt. mgr. Polaroid Corp., Boston, 1956-59; v.p. mktg. Airequipt, Inc., New Rochelle, N.Y., 1959-65; TV account exec. CBS, Inc., N.Y.C., 1965-67, dir. daytime sales, 1967-70, v.p. Ea. sales, 1970-75, v.p. network sales adminstrn., 1975-77, v.p., nat. sales mgr., 1977, pres. TV Network Div., 1977-81; exec. v.p. CBS/Broadcast Group, N.Y.C., 1981-83, sr. exec. v.p., 1983-85; chmn., CEO John Blair Communications, Inc., N.Y.C., 1987-93; pres. JHR Assocs., Consulting, N.Y.C., 1993; mng. dir. Veronis, Suhler & Assocs., N.Y.C., 1994-98; pres. JHR & Assocs., 1998—. Bd. dirs. Salon Interactive, Inc., Global Vision-New Media, Columbia U. Sch. Pub. Health. Mem. nat. bd. dirs. Jr. Achievement, Inc.; past alumni trustee Roxbury (Mass.) Latin Sch.; bd. dirs., former chmn. Adv. Coun. With Signal Corps, AUS, 1950-53. Fellow Internat. Acad. TV Arts (life); mem. Internat. Radio TV Soc. (past pres.).

ROSENFIELD, M(ANUEL) C(HARLES), retired history educator, retired coastguard officer; b. Boston, Aug. 23, 1931; s. James Charles and Lillian Francis (Obelsky); m. Dora Rose Empson, Dec. 2, 1961; 1 child, Sarah Elizabeth. BA, Boston U., 1951, MA, 1957; PhD, U. London, 1961. Prof. history S.E. Mass. U. (name changed to the U. Mass.), Dartmouth, 1965-96. Contbr. articles to profl. jours. Rsch. fellow Inst. Hist. Rsch., London, 1961, Mus. of London, 1960; tchg. fellow Boston U., 1957. Fellow Royal Hist. Soc. U.K. (assoc.); mem. Hist. Assn. U.K., Am. Hist. Assn., London and Middlesex Archl. Soc., Bostonian Soc., Boston Athaeneaum. Home: PO Box 395 8 Marion Rd Mattapoisett MA 02739-0395 E-mail: rosenfield1@comcast.net.

ROSENFIELD, RUTH, advertising executive; b. Santa Monica, Calif., Nov. 24, 1962; m. Thomas Andrew Rosenfield, 1989; childen: Charlotte Elyse, Oliver Cole. Student, UCLA, 1980-82; BFA with honors, Art Ctr. Coll. Design, 1985. Art dir. Oglivy & Mather, N.Y.C., 1985-86, Chiat/Day, N.Y.C., 1986-88, Venice, Calif., 1988-91; v.p., assoc. creative dir. Hill Holliday, L.A., 1991-93; freelance art dir. San Francisco and L.A., 1993-95; v.p., creative dir. Publicus & Hal Riney (formerly Hal Riney & Ptnrs.), San Francisco, 1995—. Recipient Comm. Arts award, Cannes awards, Obie awards, Belding awards, Andy awards. Office: Publicus & Hal Riney 2001 The Embarcadero San Francisco CA 94133-5200

ROSENGARTEN, FRANK, retired language educator, retired literature educator, writer; b. N.Y.C., June 13, 1927; s. Herbert and Clae Rosengarten; m. Lucille Vera Lindner, Mar. 4, 1979; m. Lillian Lebrecht Rosengarten, Apr. 27, 1959 (div. 1977); children: Philip, Daniel, Lydia. BA in English, Adelphi Coll., 1950; MA in English, Columbia U., 1951, PhD in Italian, 1962; MA in French, CUNY, 1998, PhD in French, 2000. Instr. Queens Coll., Flushing, NY, 1957—59, assoc. prof. Italian and Comparative Lit., 1967—92; instr. Adelphi U, Garden City, NY, 1957—59; instr. Italian grad. sch. CUNY, N.Y.C., 1959—62, prof. Italian and Comparative Lit., 1967—92; instr. Italian Columbia U., N.Y.C., 1959—62; asst. prof. Case Western Res. U, Cleve., 1962—67, assoc. prof., 1962—67. Founder Rsch. Group on Socialism and Democracy, N.Y.C., 1983. Author: Vasco Pratolini:The Devel. of a Social Novelist, 1965, The Italian Antifascist Press, 1968, Silvio Trentin: Dall'interventismo alla Resistenza, 1980, The Writings of the Young Marcel Proust, 2001; editor: (publication) Rsch. Group on Socialism and Democracy, 1984—2001; co-editor: New Studies in the Politics and Culture of US Communism, 1993; editor: Antonio Gramsci- Letter from Prison, 1994; contbr. articles, essays in English and Italian. Seaman second class USN, 1945—46, Norfolk Va. Fellow NEH, 1967; grantee APS, 1965. Mem.: Adv. bd./The Brecht Forum, Columbia U Seminar on Modern Italian Hist., Modern Lang. Assoc. Achievements include research in co-founder of the Group on Socialism and Democracy. Home: 160 E 84th St, Apt 7D New York NY 10028-2016

ROSENGREN, PAUL GREGORY, lawyer; b. Oakland, Calif., Apr. 3, 1952; s. Jack Whitehead and Patricia Jean (Dorking) R.; m. Nikki Christine Ballard, Aug. 21, 1976. AB, Princeton U., 1974; MBA, JD, U. Calif., Berkeley, 1977. Bar: Calif. 1978, D.C. 1978, U.S. Ct. Appeals (5th cir.) 1979. Assoc. Covington & Burling, Washington, 1978; law clk. to justice U.S. Ct. Appeals (5th cir.), New Orleans and Baton Rouge, La., 1978-79; assoc. Gibson, Dunn & Crutcher, Washington, 1979-85; assoc. gen. counsel Fannie Mae, Washington, 1985-88, v.p., dep. gen. counsel, 1988-2000; gen. counsel, corp. sec. ARMILLAIRE Techs., Inc., Bethesda, 2000—. Note and comment editor U. Calif. Law Rev., 1975-77. Mem. Huntington Met. Area Task Force, Fairfax County, Va., 1984-85; bd. dirs., pres. Heritage Hill Townhouses Assn., Alexandria, Va., 1980-82. Mem. ABA, D.C. Bar Assn., Calif. Bar Assn., Washington Met. Area Corp. Counsel Assn., Am. Corp. Counsel Assn. Avocations: theater, travel, tennis, reading. Office: 10411 Motor City Dr 4th Fl Bethesda MD 20817

ROSENHAUS, STEVEN L. composer, conductor, music educator; b. Bklyn., July 23, 1952; s. Lawrence and Anne S. Rosenhaus; m. Ruth H. Kluger, Aug. 7, 1977. BA in Secondary Edn., Music, Queens Coll., Flushing, 1975; MA in Music Composition, Queens Coll., 1980; PhD in Music Composition and Theory, NYU, 1995. Freelance composer, arranger, condr., author, N.Y.C., 1977—; asst. chief editor Warner Bros. Music Pub., N.Y.C., 1977—80; editor-in-chief Bourne Co. Music Pubs., N.Y.C., 1982—83; adj. instr. NYU, N.Y.C., 1992—96, adj. asst. prof. dept. music, 1997—. Judge Mensa Scholarships of Greater N.Y., N.Y.C., 1991—2002, Morton Gould Young Composers Competition/ASCAP, N.Y.C., 1998, New Music for Young Ensembles, N.M.Y.E., N.Y.C., 1999; condr. N.Y. premier Sussex Celebration, Carnegie Hall, 1998; adj. instr. Nassau C.C., SUNY, Garden City, NY, 1999—; premier Violin Concerto Dresden Days of Contemporary Music, Germany, 2002. Composer: (for band) Symphony for Band, 2003, (musical) FreeTheMusic-.Com, 2002, (film score) Ashes, 2001, Strange Loops (String Quartet No. 1), 1998, (for orch.) Sussex Celebration, 1998, (for violin and orch.) Violin Concerto, 1994, (musical) Critic, 1988, (for viola and cello) Kol Nidre Prelude, 1986, (for piano) The Kiss, 1984, Matilda Variations, 2001, Waltz Rhapsody, 2003, over 100 original works and arrangements, works pub. (Hal Leonard, Warner Bros., E.F. Kalmus, Music-Print Prodns., and recorded on Capstone, Music for a G Day, MPP labels. Recipient ASCAP awards, 1987—2003; grantee Margaret Jory Grant, Am. Music Ctr., 1998, Composition grantee, Am. Composers Forum/Mellon Found., 1998; Meet the Composer grantee, 1997—98, 2002. Mem.: Nat. Acad. of Recording Arts and Scis., ASCAP, Music Theory Soc. of N.Y. State, Am. Music Ctr., Music Theory Soc., Coll. Music Soc., L.I. Composers Alliance, Am. String Tchrs. Assn. (chpt. treas. 1984—91), League of Composers/I.S.C.M. (bd. dirs. 1995—), Pi Kappa Lambda. Avocations: reading, travel, art. Office: Music-Print Prodns PO Box 750458 Forest Hills NY 11375-0458

ROSENHEIM, DONALD EDWIN, electrical engineer; b. N.Y.C., Mar. 23, 1926; s. Seymour Lawrence and Leah Rebecca (Rosenberg) R.; m. Judith Comfort Hyman, June 22, 1958; children— Micah Robert, Jay Aaron. BSEE magna cum laude, Poly. Inst. Bklyn., 1949; MS, Columbia U., 1957. Devel. engr. Servo Corp. Am., 1949-51; mem. rsch. staff IBM ., 1951—, asst. dir. rsch. divsn., 1972-73. Dir. San Jose (Calif.) Rsch. Lab., 1973-83, dir. tech. coordination, 1983-84; asst. dir. Almaden Rsch. Ctr., San Jose, 1984-92 Fellow IEEE; mem. Sigma Xi, Tau Beta Pi, Eta Kappa Nu. Home: 128 Smith Creek Dr Los Gatos CA 95030-2139 Personal E-mail: jdrosenheim@msn.com.

ROSENHEIM, EDWARD WEIL, English educator; b. Chgo., May 15, 1918; s. Edward Weil and Fannie (Kohn) R.; m. Margaret Morton Keeney, June 20, 1947; children: Daniel Edward, James Morton, Andrew Keeney. BA, U. Chgo., 1939, MA, 1946, PhD, 1953. Publicity writer Pub. Relations Service, Chgo., 1939-40; instr. Gary (Ind.) Coll., 1946; faculty U. Chgo., 1947—, prof. English, 1962—, David B. and Clara E. Stern prof., 1980-88, prof. emeritus, 1988—, assoc. chmn. dept. English, 1967-75, dir. broadcasting for univ., 1954-57; dir. Nat. Humanities Inst., 1977-80. Disting. vis. prof. Pa. State U., 1961; Disting. lectr. Nat. Coun. Tchrs. English, 1967; mem. Ill. Humanities Coun., 1982—, pres., 1985-87. Author: What Happens in Literature, 1960, Swift and the Satirist's Art, 1963; editor: Selected Prose and Poetry of Jonathan Swift, 1958, Jour. Gen. Edn., 1954-56; co-editor: Modern Philology, 1968-88. Served to capt. inf. AUS, 1941-46. Recipient Alumni Svc. medal U. Chgo., 1990; Willet Faculty fellow, 1962, Guggenheim Meml. fellow, 1967. Mem. Am. Soc. 18th Century Studies, Johnson Soc. (pres. Central region 1971) Clubs: Quadrangle, Wayfarers, Caxton. Home: One Thomas More Way Apt 3 San Francisco CA 94132 Office: 1050 E 59th St Chicago IL 60637-1559 Office Phone: 773-702-8495.

ROSENHEIM, MARGARET KEENEY, social welfare policy educator; b. Grand Rapids, Mich., Sept. 5, 1926; d. Morton and Nancy (Billings) Keeney; m. Edward W. Rosenheim, June 20, 1947; children: Daniel, James, Andrew. Student, Wellesley Coll., 1943-45; JD, U. Chgo., 1949. Bar: Ill. 1949. Mem. faculty Sch. Social Service Adminstrn., U. Chgo., 1950—, assoc. prof., 1961-66, prof., 1966—, Helen Ross prof. social welfare policy, 1975-96, dean, 1978-83; lectr. in law U. Chgo., 1980-97. Vis. prof. U. Wash., 1965, Duke U., 1984; Helen Ross prof. emerita U. Chgo., 1996—; acad. visitor London Sch. Econs., 1973; cons. Pres.'s Commn. Law Enforcement and Adminstrn. Justice, 1966-67, Nat. Adv. Commn. Criminal Justice Stds. and Goals, 1972; mem. Juvenile Justice Stds. Commn., 1973-78; trustee Carnegie Corp. N.Y., 1979-87; trustee Children's Home and Aid Soc. of Ill., 1981—, chair, 1996-98; chair CHASI Sys. Inc., 1998-2001; dir. Nat. Inst. Dispute Resolution, 1981-89, Nuveen Bond Funds, 1982-97; mem. Chgo. Network, 1983—. Editor: Justice for the Child, 1962; contbr. 2d edit., 1977; editor: Pursuing Justice for the Child, 1976; editor: (with F.E. Zimring, D.S. Tanenhaus, B. Dohrn) A Century of Juvenile Justice, 2002; editor: (with Mark Testa) Early Parenthood and Coming of Age in the 1990s, 1992; contbr. articles to profl. jours. Office: 969 E 60th St Chicago IL 60637-2677 Home: Apt 303 1 Thomas More Way San Francisco CA 94130-2942 E-mail: mrosenhe@midway.uchicago.edu.

ROSENHOUSE, MICHAEL ALLAN, lawyer, editorial consultant; b. Chgo., Nov. 8, 1946; s. Seymour Samuel and Jeanne Mozette (Rosenthal) R. BA, Yale U., 1968; JD, U. Chgo., 1974. Bar: Ill. 1974, N.Y. 1982. Atty. in pvt. practice, Rochester, N.Y. Mng. editor: Am. Jurisprudence, 2d edit., 1991—93, Am. Law Reports (Fed.), 1991—93; editor: (newsletter) Bank Employment Law Report, 1998—99; author: Recent Court. of Appeals Decisions Reflect Strict Interpretation of Procedure Requirements, 2003, Employment Law (Syracuse Law Rev.), 1998; columnist: The Daily Record, 2001—03. Mem.: ABA, N.Y. State Bar Assn., Monroe County Bar Assn. (co-chair Disability Labor and Employment Law Commn. 1998—99), U. Chgo. Club of Rochester

(bd. dirs. 1999—2001), Yale Alumni Assn. (schs. com. 1997—), U. Chgo. Law Sch. Alumni Assn. (bd. dirs. 1977—80). Avocations: squash, tennis, golf. Office: 16 W Main St Rochester NY 14614 Office Phone: 585-232-8500. E-mail: mike@rosenhouse.com.

ROSENKER, MARK VICTOR, federal agency administrator; b. Balt., Dec. 8, 1946; s. Stanley and Irene (Moss) R.; m. Heather Beldon. BA in Communications, U. Md., 1969, postgrad., 1970-71; grad., USAF Air Command and Staff Coll., 1986, USAF Air War Coll., 1990. Asst. to events producer, relief engr. ABC-TV News, Washington, 1968-69; dep. dir. radio and TV Com. Reelect Pres., Washington, 1972; staff asst. to sec. U.S. Dept. Interior, Washington, 1972-73; account exec. Daniel Edelman Pub. Relations, Inc., Washington, 1973-75; dir. comm. Motorized Bicycle Assn., Washington, 1975; dep. press sec. Pres. Ford Com., Washington, 1976; v.p. Electronic Industries Alliance, Washington, 1977—99; asst. exec. dir. for external affairs United Network for Organ Sharing, 1999—2001; dept. asst. to the Pres. The White House, Washington, 2001—02; vice chmn. Nat. Transp. Safety Bd., Washington, 2003—. Bd. of vis. Cmty. Coll. USAF, Maxwell, Ala., 1981-86; apptd. commr. Am. Battle Monument Commn., 1990-94. Active Campaign to Elect Reagan/Bush, Washington, 1980, 84, Campaign to Elect Bush/Quayle, 1988, 92—; sr. advisor Dole/Kemp Campaign, 1995-96, Bush/Cheney Campaign, 2000-01. 1st lt. USAF, 1969-72, maj. gen. USAFR, 1972—. Recipient Chuck Docekal Meml. award, 1987, Am. Battle Monuments Commn. Meritious Svc. award, 1994; decorated D.S.M. USAF, 2002. Mem. Am. Soc. Assn. Execs., Greater Washington Soc. Assn. Execs., Res. Officers Assn. Club, Capitol Hill Club, Army Navy Club. Avocations: sailing, tennis, skiing, golf. Home: 1626 Great Falls St Mc Lean VA 22101-5079 Office: Nat Transp Saftey Bd L'Enfant Plaza NW Washington DC 20006-2202

ROSENKILDE, CARL EDWARD, retired physicist; b. Yakima, Wash., Mar. 16, 1937; s. Elmer Edward and Doris Edith R.; m. Bernadine Doris Blumenstine, June 22, 1963 (div. Apr. 1991); children: Karen Louise, Paul Eric; m. Wendy Maureen Ellison, May 24, 1992. BS in Physics, Wash. State Coll., 1959; MS in Physics, U. Chgo., 1960, PhD in Physics, 1966. Fellow Argonne (Ill.) Nat. Lab., 1966-68; asst. prof. math. NYU, 1968-70; asst. prof. physics Kans. State U., Manhattan, 1970-76, assoc. prof., 1976-79; physicist Lawrence Livermore (Calif.) Nat. Lab., 1979-93, lab. assoc., 1994-95, participating guest, 1995-97; chief scientist C.R. Sci., 1993-98. Cons. Lawrence Livermore Nat. Lab., 1974-79; astronomy instr. Los Positas Coll., 1997; part-time instr. physics Bellarmine Coll. Prep., 1999-2000; full-time instr., 2000-04. Contbr. articles to profl. jours. Woodrow Wilson fellow, 1959-60. Mem. NSTA, Am. Phys. Soc., Am. Assn. Physics Tchrs., Calif. Math. Coun. C.C., Am. Astron. Soc., Soc. for Indsl. and Applied Math., Am. Geophys. Union, Accoustical Soc. Am., Math. Assn. Am., Tubists Universal Brotherhood Assn., Phi Beta Kappa, Phi Kappa Phi, Phi Eta Sigma, Sigma Xi. Republican. Presbyterian. Achievements include research in nonlinear wave propagation in complex media, theoretical physics, fluid dynamics. Personal E-mail: carlrosenkilde@comcast.net.

ROSENKRANTZ, BARBARA GUTMANN, historian of science and medicine; b. N.Y.C., Jan. 11, 1923; d. James and Jeanette (Mack) G.; m. David P. Bennett, Sept. 5, 1942 (div.); 1 child, Louise; m. Paul Rosenkrantz, Apr. 19, 1950 (dec. 1986); children: Judith, Deborah; m. J. Nathaniel Marshall, 1988. AB, Radcliffe Coll., 1944; PhD, Clark U., 1970. Rsch. assoc. Harvard U., Cambridge, Mass., 1970-71, lectr., 1971-73, assoc. prof. history of sci., 1973-75, prof., 1975-93, prof. emeritus, 1993—, chmn. history of sci. dept., 1984-89, master Currier House, 1974-79, faculty adminstr. Author: Public Health and the State, 1972, (with William A. Koelsch) American Habitat, 1973; editor for history Am. Jour. Pub. Health, 1985-89. NIH research grantee, 1970-72; Rockefeller Found. fellow, 1979-80; Ctr. for Advanced Study in Behavioral Scis. fellow Stanford U., 1984, Inst. Medicine fellow; Sherman Fairchild Disting. Scholar, Calif. Inst. Tech., 1989. Fellow Am. Acad. Arts and Scis., Mass. Hist. Soc.; mem. Am. Hist. Assn., History of Sci. Soc., Am. Assn. for History of Medicine. Jewish. Office: Harvard U Dept History Sci Ctr 371 Cambridge MA 02138 Fax: 617-495-3344.

ROSENKRANTZ, DANIEL J. computer science educator; b. Bklyn., Mar. 5, 1943; s. Harry and Ruth (Sirota) R.; m. Carole Jaffee, Aug. 2, 1969; children: Holly, Sherry, Jody, Andrew. BS, Columbia U., 1963, MS, 1964, PhD, 1967. With Bell Telephone Labs., Murray Hill, N.J., 1966-67; info. scientist GE Co. R & D Ctr., Schenectady, N.Y., 1967-77; prof. dept. computer sci. U. Albany-SUNY, 1977—, dept. chair, 1993-99; prin. computer scientist Phoenix Data Systems, Albany, 1983-85. Author: (with P.M. Lewis II and R.E. Stearns) Compiler Design Theory, 1976. Fellow ACM (editor-in-chief jour. 1986-91, area editor for formal langs. and models of computation 1981-86, mem. spl. interest group on mgmt. of data, mem. numerous conf. coms., Sigmod Contbns. award 2001); mem. IEEE Computer Soc., ACM Spl. Interest Group on Automata and Computability Theory (sec. 1977-79). Home: 1261 Cranbrook Ct Niskayuna NY 12309-1203 Office: U at Albany SUNY Dept Computer Sci Albany NY 12222-0001 Office Phone: 518-442-4274. E-mail: djr@cs.albany.edu.

ROSENKRANTZ, LINDA, writer; b. NYC, May 26, 1934; d. Samuel H. and Frances (Sillman) R.; m. Christopher Finch, Feb. 2, 1973; 1 child, Chloe. BA, U. Mich., 1955. Founding editor Auction Mag., N.Y.C., 1967-72; columnist Copley News Svc., San Diego, 1986--. Author: Talk, 1968; co-author: Gone Hollywood, 1979, SoHo, 1981, Beyond Jennifer and Jason, 1988, Beyond Charles and Diana, 1992, Beyond Shannon and Sean, 1992, Beyond Sarah and Sam, 1992, The Last Word on First Names, 1995, Sotheby's Guide to Collecting Animation Art, 1998, My Life as a List: 207 Things About My (Bronx) Childhood, 1999, Beyond Jennifer and Jason, Madison and Montana, 1999, Baby Names Now, 2001, Cool Names, 2003, Telegram! Modern History as Told Through More Than 400 Witty, Poignant, and Revealing Telegrams, 2003. E-mail: lindro@earthlink.net.

ROSENKRANTZ, STEVEN JAY, lawyer; b. N.Y.C., Feb. 4, 1965; s. Michael and Rhona Sue (Dasheff) R. BA, Rutgers Coll., 1987; JD, Rutgers U. Sch. Law, 1991. Bar: Pa. 1994, DC 1996. Rsch. assoc. Fedn. Am. Scientists, Washington, 1993-94; rsch. asst. U.S. Dept. Justice, Washington, 1994-95; fgn. affairs specialist U.S. Arms Control & Disarmament Agy., Washington, 1995-99; spl. asst. office of undersec. state arms control U.S. Dept. State, Washington, 1998-2001, fgn. affairs officer Bur. Arms Ctrl., 2001—. Mem.: Mid. East Inst., Phi Beta Kappa. Avocations: history, classical music, fencing, reading, chess. Home: 1401 Blair Mill Rd Apt 1811 Silver Spring MD 20910-4875 Office: US Dept State Bur Arms Control Office Strat & Theater Def Washington DC 20520 E-mail: rosenkrantzsj@t.state.gov.

ROSENKRANZ, GEORGE, chemical company executive; b. Budapest, Hungary, Aug. 20, 1916; naturalized Mexican citizen, 1949; s. Bertalan and Stella (Weiner) R.; m. Edith Stein, Sept. 20, 1945; children: Robert Peter, Gerald Michael, Richard Thomas. Chem. engr. degree, D of Tech. Scis., ETH, Zurich, Switzerland, 1939, postgrad., 1940-41; D (hon.), U. las Ams. Dir. rsch. Labs. Vieta-Plasencia, Havana, Cuba, 1941-45; from tech. dir. to exec. v.p. Syntex SA (now Sytnex Corp.), Mexico City, 1945-56, pres., chmn. bd., 1956-76, chmn. bd., 1976-81, founding chmn. bd., 1981—, CEO, 1976-80, ret., 1981. Bd. govs. U. Tel Aviv, Israel, bd. govs. emeritus, Israel; mem. coun. Rockefeller U., N.Y.C. Author: The Romex System, A Dynamic Approach to Bidding, Win with Romex, Key to Accurate Bidding, Bid Your Way to the Top, Modern Ideas in Bidding, Bridge: The Bidders Game, Everything You Always Wanted to Know About Trump Leads, Tips for Tops; contbr. articles to profl. jours.; patentee in field. Bd. govs. U. Tel Aviv, Weizmann Inst. Sci., Rehovoth, Israel; mem. coun. Rockefeller U. Decorated Order Vasco Nunez de Balboa Panama; named to, Am. Contract Bridge League Hall of Fame, 2000. Fellow Internat. Coll. Dentists; mem. AAAS, Am. Chem. Soc., Royal Chem. Soc. Gt. Britain, Nat. Acad. Medicine in Mex. (hon.), Chem. Soc. Switzerland, N.Y. Acad. Scis. Home: Parque Via Reforma 1730 Delegación Miguel Hidalgo 11000 Mexico City DF Mexico

ROSENKRANZ, HERBERT S. public health educator; b. Vienna, Sept. 27, 1933; came to U.S., 1948; s. Samuel and Lea Rose (Marilles) R.; m. Deanna Eloise Green, Jan. 27, 1959; children: Pnina Gail, Eli Joshua, Margalit E., Dara V., Jeremy Amiel, Sara C., Naomi, Tsilila. BS, CCNY, 1954; PhD, Cornell U., 1959. Postdoctoral fellow Sloan-Kettering Inst. for Cancer Rsch., 1959-60, U. Pa., Phila., 1960-61; asst. prof. microbiology Columbia U., N.Y.C., 1961-65, assoc. prof., 1965-69, prof., 1969-76; prof., chmn. dept. microbiology N.Y. Med. Coll., Valhalla, 1976-81; prof. Case Western Res. U., Cleve., 1981-90, dir. Ctr. Environ. Health, 1981-84, chmn. dept. environ. health sci., 1985-90; prof., chmn. dept. environ. and occupl. health U. Pitts., 1990—2001, interim dean Grad. Sch. Pub. Health, 1998—2002; rsch. prof. biomed. scis. Fla. Atlantic U., Boca Raton, Fla., 2001—. Recipient award Lalor Found., 1963, Nat. Cancer Inst. Rsch. Career Devel. award, 1965-75. Fellow AAAS, Am. Assn. Cancer Rsch., Am. Soc. Biol. Chemists, Environ. Mutagen Soc., Soc. Toxicology. Jewish. Office: Florida Atlantic Univ Biomed Sci Dept PO Box 3091 777 Glades Rd Boca Raton FL 33431 E-mail: rosenkra@fau.edu.

ROSENKRANZ, LINDA, English educator; b. Bryan, Tex., Jan. 25, 1943; d. Fred Louis and Laura Imogene (Gandy) Rosenkranz; children: Richard Mark Geppert, Nathan Jay Geppert, Gary Patrick Geppert. BA in English, Sam Houston State U., Huntsville, Tex., 1964; MA, U. St. Thomas, Houston, 1991. Coach girls' tennis and basketball Dickinson (Tex.) Ind. Sch. Dist., 1964-66; athletic dir. girls' sports Dickinson H.S., 1964-66; tchr. asst. Sam Houston State U., Huntsville, 1962-63; camp asst. dir. UN/UNESCO, Paris; resident tchr. Brit. prep sch.; faculty English Houston C.C. Sys., 1988—; instr. English S.W. Coll., Houston C.C., 1988—. Contbr. articles and poetry to profl. jours. Dir. Galveston County Head Start, Dickinson, 1966; dir. civic affairs Pleasant Run Farm Civic Assn., Cin., 1973-76; mem. Ashford Hills Civic Assn., Houston, 1993—. Recipient Outstanding Tchr. of the Yr. award Dickinson Ind. Sch. Dist., 1965, Outstanding Young Educator award Texas City Ind. Sch. Dist., 1966, Faculty Assn. Outstanding Tchr. award Houston C.C. Sys., 1998, numerous writing awards; Jesse Jones scholar, 1961. Mem. MLA, Two Yr. C.C. Assn. Avocations: gardening, writing, socio-political issues, literature, current events. Office: SW College/Houston CC Sys 10141 Cash Rd Stafford TX 77477 E-mail: rosenkranz_l@hccs.cc.tx.us.

ROSENKRANZ, ROBERT BERNARD, military officer; b. Paterson, N.J., Sept. 26, 1939; s. Irving Morton and Lucille (Kane) R.; m. Barbara Jean Larson, May 17, 1970; children: Stephen Robert, Deborah Anne, Diana Rebecca, Susan Leslie. BS, U.S. Mil. Acad., 1961; MA, U. Pa., 1969. Commd. 2d. lt. U.S. Army, 1961, advanced through grades to maj. gen., 1992, officer, 1962-65, bn. exec. officer, 1973-74, battery comdr., 1966-67, bn. and brigade comdr., 1977-79, 83-85; assoc. prof. U.S. Mil. Acad., West Point, NY, 1969-72; dir. soviet studies U.S. Army War Coll., Carlisle, Pa., 1981-83; sr. mil. asst. under sec. of def. Pentagon, Washington, 1986-88; dep. dir. Army Ops., Readiness and Mobilization U.S. Army Pentagon, Washington, 1988-89, dir. force programs, 1989-92; comdr. U.S. Army Optec, Washington, 1992-95; sr. v.p. range and logistics svcs. Dyncorp, Reston, Va., 1995-2001; v.p. force mgmt. and logistics MPRI, Alexandria, Va., 2001—04; sr. v.p., gen. mgr. BeamHit, Columbia, Md., 2004—. Decorated Bronze Star, Air medal; recipient Superior Svc. medal U.S. Dept. Def., 1988, D.S.M., 1992, 95. Mem.: Nat. Def. Indsl. Assn., Internat. Test and Evaluation Assn., Assn. of the U.S. Army, Internat. Inst. Strategic Studies. Republican. Jewish. Avocations: jogging, reading, woodworking, golf, racquetball. Home: 3222 Wynford Dr Fairfax VA 22031-2828 Office Phone: 410-309-1500. E-mail: Bob.Rosenkranz@MPRI.L-3com.com., rrosen007@aol.com.

ROSENKRANZ, STANLEY WILLIAM, lawyer; b. N.Y.C., Aug. 20, 1933; s. Jacob and Adele R.; m. Judith Ossinsky, Aug. 14, 1960; children: Jack Michael, Andrew Lawrence. BS in Acctg, U. Fla., 1955, JD with honors, 1960; LLM (Kenneson fellow), NYU, 1961. Bar: Fla. 1960, Ga. 1970, cert.: (tax lawyer). Mem. firm Macfarlane, Ferguson, Allison & Kelly, Tampa, Fla., 1961-68, 71-79; with King & Spalding, Atlanta, 1969-71, Holland & Knight, Tampa, 1979-86, Shear, Newman, Rosenkranz, Burton & Lamb, Tampa, 1986-2000, Ruden McClosky Smith Schuster & Russell, Tampa, 2000—03, Akerman Sentor, 2003, Akerman Senterfitt, Tampa, 2003—. Adj. prof. Grad. Sch. Law, U. Fla., 1975-79, Grad. Coll. Bus. Adminstrn., U. Tampa, 1989, 97-99, Stetson U. Coll. Law. Pres. Congregation Schaarai Zedek, Tampa, 1981-83; bd. dirs. Union Am. Hebrew Congregations, 1990—, v.p. S.E. region, 1988-90, pres., 1992-96. With U.S. Army, 1955-57. Named Young Man of Year Tampa Jaycees, Fla., 1967 Mem. ABA, Am. Coll. Tax Counsel, Am. Law Inst., Fla. Bar Assn., Ga. Bar Assn., Greater Tampa C. of C. (bd. govs., chmn. anti-drug task force). Home: 1125 Shipwatch Cir Tampa FL 33602-5785 Office: Akerman Senterfitt 1000 Ashley Dr Tampa FL 33602-5311 E-mail: srosenkranz@akerman.com.

ROSENMAN, KENNETH D. medical educator; b. N.Y.C., Feb. 25, 1951; AB, Cornell U., 1972; MD, NY Med. Coll., 1975. Bd. cert. internal medicine; bd. cert. occupational and preventive medicine. Asst. prof. U. Mass., Amherst, 1979-81; dir. occupational and environ. health N.J. Dept. Health, Trenton, 1981-86; pvt. practice Plainsboro, N.J., 1986-88; assoc. prof. Mich. State U., East Lansing, 1988-93, prof., 1993—. Office: Mich State U 117 W Fee Hall East Lansing MI 48824-1316 Office Phone: 517-353-1846.

ROSENN, HAROLD, lawyer; b. Plains, Pa., Nov. 4, 1917; s. Joseph and Jennie (Wohl) R.; m. Sallyanne Frank, Sept. 19, 1948; 1 child, Frank Scott. BA, U. Mich., 1939, JD, 1941; LLD, Coll. Misericordia, 1991. Bar: Pa. 1942, U.S. Supreme Ct. 1957. Ptnr. Rosenn & Rosenn, Wilkes Barre, Pa., 1948-54, Rosenn, Jenkins & Greenwald, Wilkes Barre, 1954-87, of counsel, 1988—. Mem. Pa. State Bd. Law Examiners, 1983-93, Pa. Gov.'s Justice Commn., 1968-73, Pa. Crime Commn., 1968-73, Fed. Jud. Nominating Com., Pa., 1977-79, Appellate Ct. Nominating Com., Pa., 1979-81; asst. dist. atty. Luzerne County, Pa., 1952-54. Chmn. United Jewish Appeal Campaign of Wyo. Valley, 1956, 1984, 2003, ARC, Wilkes-Barre, 1959, chair, 1963—65, life bd. dirs., 1991—; pres. Pa. Coun. on Crime and Delinquency, Harrisburg, 1969—71; chmn. United Way Campaign of Wyo. Valley, 1975, chmn. of bd., 1978—80; pres. Temple Israel of Wilkes Barre, 1972—74, chmn. bd., 1974—84, life bd. dir.; bd. dir. Coll. Misericordia, Dallas, Pa., 1976—86, emeritus, 1986—; bd. dir. Hoyt Libr., Kingston, Pa., 1971—78, Nat. Coun. on Crime and Delinquency, N.Y.C., 1969—71, Jewish Cmty. Ctr., Wilkes-Barre, 1964—66, Keystone State Games, Jewish Fedn. Bd. of Greater Wilkes-Barre, St. Vincent de Paul Soup Kitchen, 1987—2000; comdr. Post 395 Am. Legion, Kingston, 1948. Capt. USAAF, 1942—45, ETO. Decorated medal with 6 bronze stars, European combatant cross French Govt.; named Golden Key Vol. of Yr., United Way of Pa., 1989; recipient Erasmus medal, Dutch Govt., Disting. Svc. award in Trusteeship, Assn. Governing Bds., Univs. and Colls., 1990, Disting. Cmty. Svc. award, Greater Wilkes-Barre Soc. Fellows Anti-Defamation League, 1991, Clara Barton honor award, Wyo. Valley chpt. ARC, 1992, Lifetime Achievement award, United Way of Wyo. Valley, 1992, Outstanding Vol. Fundraiser award, Greater Pocono chpt. Nat. Soc. of Fundraising Execs., 1995, honoree, Wyo. Valley Interfaith Coun., 1986, Ethics Inst. N.E. Pa., 2001, 10 Gallon Blood Donor award, ARC, inductee, Jr. Achievement Hall of Fame for N.E. Pa., 1997, President's award, Luzerne County Bar, 2003. Mem. ABA, Pa. Bar Assn., Am. Judicature Soc., The Pa. Soc., B'nai B'rith (pres. Wilkes Barre 1952-53, Cmty. Svc. award 1976), U. Mich. Club N.E. Pa. (pres. 1946-76), Westmoreland Club (Wilkes-Barre), Huntsville Golf Club (Lehman, Pa.). Republican. Jewish. E-mail: hrosenn@rjglaw.com.

ROSENN, MAX, federal judge; b. Plains, Pa., Feb. 4, 1910; s. Joseph and Jennie (Wohl) Rosenn; m. Tillie R. Hershkowitz, Mar. 18, 1934; children: Keith S., Daniel Wohl. BA, Cornell U., 1929; LLB, U. Pa., 1932. Bar: Pa. 1932, U.S. Supreme Ct. 1955, Cts. of Philippines 1946. Gen. practice, Wilkes-Barre, Pa., 1932—70; spl. counsel Pa. Dept. Justice, 1939; asst. dist. atty. Luzerne County, 1942—44; solicitor various mcpl. boroughs, ptnr. Rosenn, Jenkins & Greenwald, Wilkes-Barre, 1954—70; sec. pub. welfare Pa., 1966—67; judge U.S. Ct. Appeals (3rd cir.), 1970—81, sr. judge, 1981—. Criminal procedure rules com. Supreme Ct. Pa., 1958—85; mem. Pa. Commn. to Revise Pub. Employee Laws, 1968—69; Pa. chmn. com. children and youth White House Conf., 1968—70. Contbr. articles to profl. jours. Active Pa. Bd. Pub. Welfare, 1963—66; chmn. study commn. Pa. Gov.'s Coun. for Human Svcs., 1966—67; exec. bd. Commonwealth of Pa., 1966—67; chmn. Commn. Met. Govt., 1957—58, Pa. Human Rels. Commn., 1969—70, Legis.-exec. Task Force Structure for Human Svcs., 1970, Flood Recovery Task Force, 1972; pres. Property Owners Assn. Luzerne County, 1955—57; alt. del. Rep. Nat. Conv., 1964; pres. Wyoming Valley Jewish Com., 1941—42; life trustee Wilkes-Barre Jewish Cmty. Ctr. 1st lt. U.S. Army, 1944—46. Named a U.S. Courthouse in his honor, 1996, libr., U.S. Courthouse at Scranton in his honor, 2002. Fellow: Internat. Acad. Trial Lawyers, Am. Coll. Trial Lawyers; mem.: ABA, Am. Judicature Soc., Am. Soc. Law and Medicine (past assoc. editor), Am. Law Inst., Luzerne County Bar Assn., Pa. Bar Assn., Westmoreland Club, Masons (33rd degree), B'nai B'rith (life; pres. dist. grand lodge 1947—48, bd. govs., chmn. bd. dirs. Anti-Defamation League Pa., W.Va. and Del. 1955—58, nat. commr. 1964—), Alpha Epsilon Pi. Jewish. Office: US Ct Appeals Max Rosenn US Cthse Rm 235 197 S Main St Wilkes Barre PA 18701-1500

ROSENNE, MEIR, lawyer, government agency administrator; b. Iasi, Romania, Feb. 19, 1931; arrived in Israel, 1944; s. Jacob and Mina Rosenhaupt; m. Vera Ayai, June 9, 1959; children: Mihal, Dafna. MA in Polit. Sci., Inst. Polit. Sci., Paris, 1953; LLB, Sorbonne, U. Paris, 1955, PhD in Internat. Law with honors, 1957; grad., Inst. Internat. Studies, Paris, 1953. In govt. service, Israel, 1953—; consul Israel Consulate, N.Y.C., 1967-69; sr. lectr. in polit. sci. U. Haifa, Israel, 1969-71; coordinator Atomic Energy Commn. Israel, 1969-71; chief legal adviser Fgn. Office Israel, Jerusalem, 1971-79; Israeli amb. to France, Paris, 1979-83; Israeli amb. to U.S. Washington, 1983-87; pres. State of Israel Bonds, N.Y., 1989-93; ptnr. Balter, Guth, Aloni & Co., Jerusalem, 1994—. Chmn. overseas com. Jerusalem Bank; bd. dirs. Israel Discount Bank Holding, Ltd. Contbr. articles to newspapers. Chmn. internat. bd. govs. Share-Zedek Hosp., Jerusalem, 1989—94. Sgt. Israeli Air Force, 1948—50. Named comdr., Nat. Order French Legion of Honor; recipient Harold Weil medal, NYU Sch. Law, Elie Wiesel award. Mem.: French Assn. Internat. Law, Am. Soc. Internat. Law, Israeli Bar Assn., Soc. Internat. Law, Internat. Law Soc. France, Internat. Club Washington. Avocations: volleyball, swimming. Office: Balter Guth & Aloni 23 Hillel St Jerusalem Israel E-mail: mrosenne@bgalaw.co.il.

ROSENOF, THEODORE DIMON, historian, educator; b. Newark, Sept. 15, 1943; s. Irving and Josephine Stella (Schmitt) R.; m. Patricia Mary Reilly, Aug. 31, 1985; children: Charles Reilly, Liza. BA, Rutgers U., 1965; MA, PhD, U. Wis., 1970. Vis. instr., vis. asst. prof. history Tex. Tech. U., Lubbock, 1975-77; vis. asst. prof. history Pan Am. U., Edinburg, Tex., 1977-78; rsch. assoc. U. Wis., Madison, 1978-79; asst. prof., assoc. prof. history Mercy Coll., Dobbs Ferry N.Y., 1979-89, prof. history, 1989—. Author: Dogma, Depression, and the New Deal: The Debate of Political Leaders over Economic Recovery, 1975, Patterns of Political Economy in America: The Failure to Develop a Democratic Left Synthesis, 1933-1950, 1983, Economics in the Long Run: New Deal Theorists and Their Legacies, 1933-1993, 1997, Realignment: The Theory that Changed the Way We Think about American Politics, 2003. Mem. Am. Hist. Assn., Orgn. Am. Historians. Democrat. Home: 75 Academy Ave Cornwall On Hudson NY 12520 E-mail: trosenof@hvc.rr.com.

ROSENOW, EDWARD CARL, III, medical educator; b. Columbus, Ohio, Nov. 2, 1934; s. Oscar Ferdinand and Mildred Irene (Eichelberger) R.; m. Constance Donna Grahame, Sept. 7, 1957; children: Sheryl Lynn, Scott Edward. BS, Ohio State U., 1955, MD, 1959; MS in Medicine, U. Minn., 1969. Diplomate Am. Bd. Internal Medicine, Am. Bd. Pulmonary Diseases. Intern Riverside Meth. Hosp., Columbus, Ohio, 1959-60; resident in internal medicine Mayo Grad. Sch. Medicine, Rochester, Minn., 1960-65, clin. fellow in thoracic diseases, 1965-66; cons. in internal medicine (pulmonary diseases) Mayo Clinic, Rochester, 1966; instr. in medicine Mayo Grad. Sch. Medicine, Rochester, 1969-73; asst. prof. medicine Mayo Med. Sch., Rochester, 1973-77, assoc. prof. medicine, 1977-80, prof. medicine, 1980; chmn. divsn. pulmonary and critical care medicine, 1987-94; assoc. dir. internal medicine residency program Mayo Clinic, Rochester, 1977-79, program dir. internal medicine residency program, 1979-84, sec. Mayo staff, 1979; pres. Mayo staff, 1986; Arthur M. and Gladys D. Gray prof. medicine Mayo Clinic, Rochester, 1987-96, prof. emeritus, 1996—. Cons. NASA, Houston. Capt. M.C., U.S. Army, 1962-64. Recipient Alumni Achievement award Coll. Medicine Ohio State U., 1989, Disting. Mayo Clinician award, 1994, Henry S. Plummer Disting. Internist award, 1994, Karis award Mayo Clinic, 1996, Disting. Alumnus award Mayo Found., 1998; Edward W. and Betty Knight Scripps Professorship named in his honor Mayo Med. Sch., 1994, Edward C. Rosenow, III, Outstanding Subsplty. fellow award established in his honor. Fellow ACP (gov. Minn. chpt. 1987-91, Ralph S. Claypoole Sr. award for Lifetime Dedication to Patient Care 1995, Minn. chpt. Laureate award 1994, Disting. Lectr. award 1996), Am. Coll. Chest Physicians (master fellow, editl. bd. CHEST 1973-78, editor spl. case reports 1975-90, com. on postgrad. med. edn. 1978-84, sci. program com. 1982, com. on undergrad. med. edn. 1981-82, co-chmn. sci. program com. Internat. Coll. Chest Physicians meeting, Sydney, Australia, 1985, regent 1984-88, pres. elect 1988-89, pres. 1989-90, pres. Chest Found. 1998—, Endowed Hon. Lectr. in name 2004); mem. AMA, So. Minn. Med. Assn., Minn. Thoracic Soc., Am. Thoracic Soc., Sigma Xi. Office: Mayo Clinic Div Pulmonary Diseases 200 1st St SW Rochester MN 55905-0002

ROSENOW, JOHN EDWARD, foundation executive; b. Lincoln, Nebr., Sept. 15, 1949; s. Lester Edward and Lucille Louise (Koehler) R.; m. Nancy Kay Hadley; children: Matthew, Stacy. BS in Agrl. Engring., U. Nebr., 1971. Dir. of tourism Nebr. Dept. Econ. Devel., Lincoln, 1971-79, interim dept. dir., 1985; founder Nat. Arbor Day Found., 1972, exec. dir. million-mem., 1979-94, pres., 1994—. Co-author: (book) Tourism: the good, the bad, and the ugly, 1979. Democrat. Mem. United Ch. of Christ. Office: Nat Arbor Day Found 211 N 12th St Lincoln NE 68508-1422

ROSENSAFT, LESTER JAY, management consultant, lawyer, consultant; b. Leominster, Mass., Jan. 11, 1958; s. Melvin and Beatrice (Golombek) Rosensaft; m. Elizabeth Amanda Lahti, July 29, 1992; 1 child, Mia Elisabeth. BS in Econs., Wharton Sch., U. Pa., 1978; JD, MBA, Case Western Res. U., 1981; LLM in Corp. Law, NYU, 1983. Bar: Ohio 1981, U.S. Dist. Ct. (no. dist.) Ohio 1982, U.S. Dist. Ct. (all dists.) N.Y. 1982, Mass. 1992. With Cons. to Mgmt., Inc., Cleve., N.Y.C., Boston, Hong Kong, 1977—, v.p., 1977—80, pres., 1980—83, chmn., 1983—85; pvt. practice specializing in corp. and comml. law Ohio, 1981—. Mem. Hall, Rosensaft & Yen, Cleve., Singapore, 1981—90; reorganization law fed. cts., Ohio, 1982—, NY, 1982—; pres., CEO Eljay Devel. Corp., 1985—86; chmn., CEO Logistix Ltd., 1987—90; ptnr. Sanctuary Assocs., Boston, 1988—89; pres., CEO Union Meat Co., East Hartford, Conn., 1989—90, also bd. dirs.; pres. Golub Enterprises II, Inc., 1989—90, also bd. dirs.; COO CCC Fin. Orgn., Cleve., 1992—95, also bd. dirs.; pres., CEO ASA Comm., Inc., N.Y.C., 1995—, also bd. dirs.; pres., CEO ASA Adminstrn., Inc., Chgo, Greensboro, 1999—, also bd. dirs.; mem. fin. and strategic planning com. ASA Acquisition Corp., also bd. dirs.; mem. ASA Mgmt. and Exec. Com., 1995—, ASA Investment Com., 1996—98; v.p. corp. devel. Paramount Sys. Design Group, Inc., N.Y.C., also vice chmn. bd. dirs.; v.p., CFO Chipurnoi Inc., Long Island City, NY, also bd. dirs.; v.p., CFO Kinnerton Industries, N.Y.C., London, 1983—85; vice chmn., gen. counsel GIOIA Couture, Inc., Akron, Ohio, 1984—86, also bd. dirs. Co-author: (book) Industrial Development Survey for City of Leominster, 1978; contbr. articles to profl. jours. Active Combined Jewish Philanthropies; participant 40th Anniversary II Pres.s Mission, 1987; edn1. cons., advisor indsl. devel. and strategic urbanism; cons. federally funded biomedical rsch. projects; chmn. Region V Outreach Mission, 1988; vice chmn. Regional Campaign Leadership Mission, 1991; mem. Russian Resettlement Com., 1988—91, Maj. Gifts Gala Com., 1989; mem. exec. adv. coun. Keene State Coll., 1984—88; assoc. alumni trustee U. Pa., 1991—95, active secondary com. ctrl. Mass., bd. govs., 1992—95; mem. pres.'s soc. Beth Israel Deaconess Hosp., Boston, 2003—. Recipient Grand award, APEX, 1999, Best of Show award, ESMA, 1999, numerous ACE awards, Silver and Gold Quill awards, 1996—99. Mem.: ABA, Coll. Firm Prins., Coun. Cons. Orgns., Inst. Mgmt. Cons. (cert.), Soc. Profl. Mgmt. Cons., Internat. Soc. Strategic Planning Cons., N.Y.C. Reorganization Roundtable, Bankruptcy Lawyers Bar Assn., Assn. Bar City of N.Y.,

Ohio State Bar Assn., Greater Cleve. Bar Assn., Turnaround Mgmt. Assn., Assn. Corp. Growth, N. Ctrl. Mass. C. of C. (indsl. devel. com. 1984—86), Boca Pointe Golf and Racquet Club, Phi Alpha Delta (vice justice). Home: 640 Hammond St 102 Chestnut Hill MA 02467-2310 E-mail: ljrosensaft@aol.com.

ROSENSAFT, MENACHEM ZWI, lawyer, writer, foundation administrator, advocate; b. Bergen-Belsen, Germany, May 1, 1948; arrived in U.S., 1958, naturalized, 1962; s. Josef and Hadassah (Bimko) Rosensaft; m. Jean Bloch, Jan. 13, 1974; 1 child, Joana Deborah. BA, MA, Johns Hopkins U., 1971; MA, Columbia U., 1975, JD, 1979. Bar: N.Y. 1980. Adj. lectr. dept. Jewish studies CCNY, 1972-74, professorial fellow, 1974-75; rsch. fellow Am. Law Inst., 1977-78; law clk. to judge U.S. Dist. Ct. (so. dist.) N.Y., N.Y.C., 1979-81; assoc. Proskauer, Rose, Goetz & Mendelsohn, N.Y.C., 1981-82, Kaye, Scholer, Fierman, Hays & Handler, N.Y.C., 1982-89; v.p., sr. assoc. counsel Chase Manhattan Bank, N.Y.C., 1989-93; spl. counsel Hahn & Hessen, N.Y.C., 1994-95; sr. internat. counsel Ronald S. Lauder Found., N.Y.C., 1995-97; exec. v.p. Jewish Renaissance Found., Inc., N.Y.C., 1996-2000; ptnr. Ross & Hardies, N.Y.C., 2000—03, McGuire Woods LLP, N.Y.C., 2003; spl. counsel Van Der Moolen Specialists USA, LLC, N.Y.C., 2004—. Author: (book) Moshe Sharett Statesman of Israel, 1966, Not Backward to Belligerency, 1969, (poetry) Fragments, Past and Future, 1968; editor: Bergen Belsen Youth Mag., 1965, (book) Life Reborn, Jewish Displaced Persons 1945-1951, 2001; book rev. editor: Columbia Jour. Transnational Law, 1978—79; co-editor (with Yehuda Bauer): (book) Antisemitism: Threat to Western Civilization, 1988; contbg. editor: Reform Judaism, 1993—2002; contbr. articles to publs.; dir., editor-in-chief: Holocaust Survivors' Memoirs Project of World Jewish Congress, 2000—. Chmn. Internat. Network Children Jewish Holocaust Survivors, 1981—84, founding chmn., 1984—; nat. pres. Labor Zionist Alliance, 1988—91; chmn. commn. human rights World Jewish Congress, 1986—91, chmn. exec. com. Am. sect., 1986—90; mem. Gen. Coun. World Zionist Orgn., 1987—92; mem. U.S. Holocaust Meml. Coun., 1994—2004, chmn. content com., 1994—2000, chmn. collections and acquisitions com., 1996—2000, chmn. task force on procs. for com. on conscience, 1996, mem. exec. com., 1996—2003, chmn. governance com., 2001—02; bd. dirs., exec. com. Nat. Com. for Labor Israel, 1988—91, 1995—2001; mem. Am. Zionist Tribunal, 1988—90, chmn., 1990; sec. Am. Zionist Fedn., 1990—93; bd. dirs. Am. Jewish Joint Distbn. Com., 1988—91, Mercaz, 1991—97; mem. exec. com. Nat. Jewish Cmty. Rels. Adv. Coun., 1994—97; organizer, leader demonstration in Germany against Pres. Reagan's visit to Bitburg Cemetery and Bergen-Belsen concentration camp, 1985; del. meeting on recognition of Israel between five Am. Jews and leaders of Palestine Liberation Orgn., 1988; mem. N.Y.C. Holocaust Meml. Commn., 1982—96, chmn. collections com., 1987—89; mem. N.Y. County Dem. Com., 1981—85; mem. nat. adv. bd. United Synagogue Conservative Judaism, 1995—2002, also chmn. United Synagogue del. to Nat. Jewish Cmty. Rels. Adv. Coun., 1994—97; pres. Park Ave. Synagogue, 2003—, sec., 1988—2003, trustee, 1994—; chmn. Sherr Inst. Adult Jewish Studies, 1993—2002. Recipient Parker Sch. recognition of achievement with honors in internat. and fgn. law, 1979, Abraham Joshua Heschel Peace award, 1989, 400th Anniversary medal, City of Warsaw, 1999, commendation Jewish Heritage Week, Comptr. N.Y.C., 1999, Elie Wiesel Holocaust Remembrance award, Israel Bonds, 2003; Harlan Fisk Stone scholar, 1977—79. Mem.: ABA, Phi Beta Kappa. Home: 179 E 70th St New York NY 10021-5109 Office: Van Der Moolen Specialists USA LLC 29th Fl 45 Broadway New York NY 10006 Personal E-mail: mrosensaft@vdm-usa.com.

ROSENSHINE, ALLEN GILBERT, advertising agency executive; b. N.Y.C., Mar. 14, 1939; s. Aaron and Anna (Zuckerman) R.; m. Suzan Weston-Webb, Aug. 31, 1979; children: Andrew, Jonathan. AB, Columbia Coll., 1960. Copywriter J.B. Rundle (advt.), N.Y.C., 1962-65; copywriter Batten, Barton, Durstine & Osborn, N.Y.C., 1965, copy supr., 1967, v.p., 1968, asso. creative dir., 1970, sr. v.p., creative dir., 1975-77, exec. v.p., 1977-80, pres., 1980-82, chief exec. officer, 1981-86, chmn., 1983-86, also dir., mem. exec. com.; pres., chief exec. officer BBDO Internat., N.Y.C., 1984-86, also bd. dirs.; pres., chief exec. officer Omnicom Group, N.Y.C., 1986-88; chmn., chief exec. officer BBDO Worldwide, N.Y.C., 1989—2004, chmn., 2004—. Lectr. gen. studies Bklyn. Coll., 1961-65 Office: BBDO Worldwide Inc 1285 Avenue Of The Americas New York NY 10019-6028

ROSENSTEEL, GEORGE THOMAS, physics educator, nuclear physicist; b. Balt., Sept. 30, 1947; s. Walter St. George and Marie Emily (White) R.; m. Tsetsa Dankova. BSc, U. Toronto, Ont., Can., 1973, PhD, 1975. Can. fellow NRC, 1976-78; prof. physics Tulane U., New Orleans, 1978—, chmn. dept., 1985-91. Vis. fellow Brit. Sci. and Engring. Coun., U. Sussex, Eng., 1986; vis. prof. Nat. Inst. Nuclear Theory, U. Washington, 1992, Inst. Theoretical Physics U. Gent, Belgium, 1999. Contbr. numerous articles to profl. jours. Delivered grad. sch. commencement address Tulane U., 1987; recipient 7 grants NSF, 1979—. Mem. Am. Phys. Soc., Am. Math. Soc., Sigma Xi (young scientist award 1987). Office: Tulane U Dept of Physics New Orleans LA 70118 Office Phone: 504-862-3174. Business E-Mail: george.rosensteel@tulane.edu.

ROSENSTEIN, BERYL JOEL, physician; b. Boston, Jan. 5, 1937; s. Benjamin and Doris (Goldhagen) Rosenstein; m. Carolyn S. Rosenstein, Aug. 31, 1958; children: Susan Eileen, Jonathan David. BA, Boston U., 1957; MD, Tufts U., 1961; M Adminstrv. Sci., Johns Hopkins U., 1987. Diplomate Am. Bd. Pediatrics. Intern in pediatrics Johns Hopkins Hosp., Balt., 1961-62, resident in pediatrics, 1962-64, dir. cystic fibrosis clinic, 1972—2002, v.p. med. affairs, 1994—; prof. pediatrics Johns Hopkins Sch. Med., Balt., 1989—; med. dir. Mt. Washington Pediatric Hosp., Balt., 1988-93. Mem. adv. coun. Cystic Fibrosis Found., Bethesda, Md., 1980—88, trustee, 1986—2003. Author: Pediatric Pearls: Handbook of Pediatrics, 1989, Primary Care of the Newborn, 1992, Cystic Fibrosis, 2000; contbr. articles to profl. jours., chapters to books. Lt. comdr. USPHS, 1964—66. Fellow: Am. Acad. Pediat.; mem.: Am. Pediatric Soc., Alpha Omega Alpha. Avocations: tennis, bicycling, antique cars, travel, art. Office: Johns Hopkins Hosp 327 Park Bldg Baltimore MD 21287-2533

ROSENSTEIN, BRAD, cultural organization administrator, playwright; b. Miami, Fla., July 6, 1964; s. Ira Nathaniel and Patricia Evans Rosenstein; m. Lee Anne Deifer, Oct. 28, 1995; 2 children. BA, U. Pa., 1986. Dance critic and features writer Phila. City Paper, 1986—94; assoc. artistic dir. InterAct Theatre Co., Phila., 1988—90; theatre critic San Francisco Bay Guardian, 1997—2002; dir. programs & edn. San Francisco Performing Arts Libr. & Mus., 2001—. Author (curator): (exhbn. and catalogue) Hirschfeld: A Centennial Celebration; co-curator with William Eddelman (exhibitions) Madame Butterfly: From Puccini to Miss Saigon; author (dir.): (play) Lebensraum (Best Dir., Play Works New Play Competition, 1991); author: Mistletoe; dir.: (play) The Elephant Man, Spell #7, Seduced; co-author (with Michael Morgan): (play) Visions of Langston Hughes; dir.(prodr.): (plays) Tongues & Savage/Love; prodr.: (radio documentary) Voices at the End of the Rainbow, Cayo Hueso - Island of Bones; author (prodr., dir.): (radio play) A Personal Appearance by the Virgin Mary and Other Urgent Messages; co-author, dir. with Alexis Lezin (plays) Tales from Bohemia, co-author, dir. with Dawn-Elin Fraser The Amazing Theatre Trunk Show; author (dir., prodr.): (plays) Players (Pa. Coun. on the Arts Playwriting fellow, 1993); dir.(prodr.): (plays) What Happened: The September 11th Testimony Project; author: (plays) The Vermeer Room (Nat. Play award, 2000), Mandala (Finalist, San Francisco Playwright's Ctr. Internat. Playwriting Competition, 1994); author: (co-dir.) (music-theatre) A Feather on the Breath; author: (co-director) (dance-theatre) Fallen Shadows; author: (dir.) (performance piece) Climbing the Walls. Mem.: Theatre Comm. Group, Theatre Bay Area, Dramatists Guild. Office: Barbara Hogenson Agy Inc 165 W End Ave Ste 19C New York NY 10023

ROSENSTEIN, ELYSE S. secondary school educator; b. Bklyn., Jan. 23, 1951; d. Matthew and Beverly Irene (Gobstein) Piries; 1 child, Michael Howard. BS, Adelphi U., Garden City, NY, 1987, MS, 1994. Cert. tchr. physics and gen sci. NY. Tchr. sci. NYC bd. dirs., 1988—96, Brentwood UFSO, Brentwood, NY, 1996—97; adj. instr. Bklyn. Coll. CUNY, Bklyn., 1997—2000; sci. tchr. Hempstead H.S., Hempstead, NY, 1997—, Malverne H.S., Malverne, NY, 2000—. Mem.: NY Acad. Scis., LI Physics Tchrs. Assn. Avocations: reading, cooking, knitting. Home: 190 Henry St Bellmore NY 11710

ROSENSTEIN, JAMES ALFRED, lawyer, mediator, negotiation facilitator; b. Phila., Jan. 4, 1939; s. Louis Charles and Natalie Selma (Stern) R.; m. Linda Merle Lederman, Sept. 7, 1969; 1 child, Judith Esther AB, Harvard U., 1961, JD, 1968. Bar: Pa. 1968. Assoc. Wolf, Block, Schorr and Solis-Cohen, Phila., 1968-76, ptnr., 1976-97; prin. Rosenstein Assocs., Phila., 1997—. Mem. adv. com. task force on condominiums Joint State Govt Commn., Pa. Gen. Assembly, 1977-79; mem. condominium-coop. steering com. Phila. City Planning Commn., 1980-81 Contbr. articles to profl. jours. Trustee Jewish Fedn. of Greater Phila., 1977—, mem. exec. com., 1989-97, 98-2002, chmn. com. on local svcs., 1986-89, sec., 1987-88, v.p., 1988-94, chmn. com. on allocations and planning, 1989-92; v.p jewish Cmty. Rels. Coun., 1982-85, 89-90, 96-2000, pres., 2000-2002; trustee United Way of Greater Phila., 1979-84, bd. dirs., 1982-85, 91-97; pres. Hillel Greater Phila., 1981-83; vice chmn. Synagogue-Fedn. Coun. Greater Phila., 1995-97, chmn., 1997-99. Lt. USN, 1961-64. Mem. ABA (chmn. devel. and financing of condominium projects 1993-97), Pa. Bar Assn. (chmn. common interest ownership com. 1980-93, chmn. real property divsn. 1993-95, chmn. real property, probate and trust law sect. 1995-96), Phila. Bar Assn. (co-chmn. legis. rels. com. 1996-97, co-chmn. ADR com. 2003—), Am. Coll. Real Estate Lawyers, Coll. Cmty. Assn. Lawyers, Soc. Profls. in Dispute Resolution (co-chmn. comml. sect. 1998-2000), Coun. Jewish Fedns. (bd. dirs. 1986-98, chmn. com. on svcs. to aging 1991-94, chair nat. funding coun. 1996-98, exec. com. 1997-98), United Jewish Cmtys. Fedn. N.Am. (chmn. N.E. region 1998-2001). Office: Rosenstein Assocs 1650 Arch St 22nd Fl Philadelphia PA 19103-2097 E-mail: jrosenstein@earthlink.net.

ROSENSTEIN, MARY ELISABETH MALLORY, retired social worker; b. Los Gatos, Calif., Feb. 25, 1916; d. Merton Shannon and Mabel Beatrice (Penny) Mallory; m. Albert Rosenstein, Sept. 20, 1947; children: Nathan Stewart, Thomas Mallory. AB, U. Calif., Berkeley, 1937; MA in Social Work, U. Chgo., 1950. Lic. clin. social worker, marriage, family and child counselor, Calif. Caseworker Calif. Relief Adminstrn., San Francisco, 1938-40, San Francisco Children's Agy., 1940-42; caseworker foster home placement Oakland (Calif.) Family Svc., 1942-44; psychiat. social worker ARC Hosp. Svc., Oakland and Long Beach, Calif., 1946-51, Calif. Dept. Mental Health, L.A., Long Beach, Santa Ana, Calif., 1950-51; dist. supr. Calif. Dept. Mental Health, L.A., 1951-53; caseworker, acting dir. Family Svc. Assn. Rio Hondo Area, Whittier, Calif., 1954-81; pvt. practice, 1981-91; ret., 1991. Chmn. mental health study LWV, Whittier, 1974-76; workshop leader Montebello (Calif.) Child Study Workshop; chmn. liaison com. San Gabriel Valley Regional County Mental Health, Pasadena, Calif., 1976-81; cons. dist. teen mothers Montebello Unified Sch. Dist. Mem. Whittier Area Coordinating Coun., 1960—; pres. Birney Elem. Sch. PTA, Pico Rivera, Calif., 1957; cellist Rio Hondo Symphony Assn. Orch., Whittier, 1970-97; v.p., membership chmn. UN Assn., Whittier, 1968-97, bd. dirs., 1981, 2004. Recipient commendation Calif. Legislature, 1981, U.S. Ho. of Reps., 1981, County of L.A., 1981, spl. citation UN Assn. U.S.A., 1996. Fellow Soc. for Clin. Social Workers; mem. NASW (diplomate in clin. social work), Acad. Cert. Social Workers, AAUW (Las Distinguitas award 1979), LWV. Democrat. Unitarian Universalist. Avocations: music, gardening, swimming, river rafting, live theater. Address: 7260 Canyon Crest Rd Whittier CA 90602-1929

ROSENSTEIN, NEIL, surgeon, genealogical researcher; b. Cape Town, South Africa, Oct. 31, 1944; came to U.S., 1969; s. Emanuel Boruchovich and Annie (Marine) R.; m. Mavis Joyce Naumann, Jan. 14, 1968; children: Joel, Ari, Moshe Baruch, Rafael Samuel, Jonathan Simcha. MD, U. Cape Town Med. Sch., 1967. Intern Tel Hashomer Hosp., Tel Aviv, 1968-69; surg. resident Mt. Sinai Hosp., Cleve., 1970—73, N.Y.C., 1973—75; mem. surg. staff Trinitas, Elizabeth, NJ, 1975—, The Union Hosp., NJ, 2001—. Author: These Are the Generations, 1969, The Unbroken Chain, 1976, 90, The Margolis Family, 1984, The Gaon of Vilna and his Cousinhood, 1997, The Lurie Legacy: The House of Davidic Royal Descent, 2004; co-author: From King David to Baron David—A Rothschild Saga, 1989, Avnei Zikaron, 1999; editor: Latter Day Leaders, Sages and Scholars, 1982, The Feast and the Fast, 1984. Founder, pres. Jewish Geneal. Soc., N.Y.C., 1977-79; bd. dirs. YMHA, Union, N.J., 1990-2001; mem. adv. bd. Auschwitz Jewish Center Found., N.Y.C., 1999—; founder, dir. Computer Ctr. for Jewish Genealogy; rep. to genealogy com. Ctr. for Jewish History bd. dirs. Yeshiva U., NY, 2001—. Mem. Med. Soc. N.J., Union County Med. Soc. N.J., AmeriGroup NJ, Inc. (med. adv. com.). Republican. Jewish. Home: 185 Shelley Ave Elizabeth NJ 07208-1061 E-mail: Neil@Tali.com.

ROSENSTEIN, PETER D. educational association administrator, consultant; b. N.Y.C., Jan. 23, 1947; s. Heinz and Dorrit Rosenstein. BA, CCNY, 1969; MPA, Baruch U., 1978. Coord. local govt. Mayor's Office, N.Y.C., 1974-77; exec. dir. implementation unit White House Conf. on Handicapped Individuals, Washington, 1978-80; exec. dir. Am. Acad. Physician Assts., Alexandria, Va., 1981-84, Accts. for Pub. Interest, Washington, 1985-89, Nat. Assn. for Gifted Children, Washington, 1989—2003. Trustee U. D.C., Washington, 2000—. Issues coord. Williams for Mayor, Washington, 1998. Mem. Profl. Conv. Mgmt. Assn. (bd. dirs. Capital chpt. 1995-2000), Arts in Action (pres. 1995—), Masons. Democrat. Jewish. Avocations: travel, theater. Office: 1545 18th St Washington DC 20036

ROSENSTEIN, ROBERT BRYCE, lawyer, financial advisor; b. Santa Monica, Calif., Feb. 26, 1954; s. Franklin Lee and Queen Esther (Shall) Rosenstein; m. Sandra L. Michaels; stepchildren: Alana Michaels, Meredith Michaels; children from previous marriage: Shaun Franklin, Jessica Laney, Madeline Frances. BA, Calif. State U., Northridge, 1976; JD, Southwestern U., 1979. Bar: Calif. 1979, U.S. Dist. Ct. (cen. and no. dists.) Calif. 1980, U.S. Tax Ct. 1981; registered environ. assessor. Service rep. Social Security Adminstrn., Los Angeles, 1974-77; tax cons. Am. Tax Assocs., Los Angeles, 1970-78, ptnr., 1978; prin., pres. Robert B. Rosenstein, PC, Los Angeles, 1979-84; ptnr. Rosenstein and Werlin, Los Angeles, 1984-87; pres. Robert Bryce Rosenstein Ltd., Temelula, 1987-99; chief fin. officer BSE Mgmt. Inc., Los Angeles, 1987-90, corp. counsel, 1987-92, sr. v.p. corp. devel., acquisitions, 1990-92; pres. Robert Bryce Rosenstein, a Profl. Law Corp., 1999—, Rosenstein Hitzeman AAPLC, 2004—. Bd. dirs. BSE Mgmt. Inc, Sirius Computer Corp., Spartan Computer, Unicomp, Inc., Diagnostic Engring. Inc.; pres. Will Find Inc., 1986-87; judge pro tem Three Lakes Jud. Dist., 1997—. Judge pro tem Riverside County, Calif., 1996—. Recipient Am. Jurisprudence award Bancroft Whitney; Order of Cheviler. Mem. ABA (taxation and environ. coms., vice chmn. gen. bus. sect. 1995), Assn. Trial Lawyers Am., L.A. Bar Assn. Lodges: Masons, Ionic, Composite. Democrat. Jewish. Avocations: sports, reading, golf. Office: 41877 Enterprise Cir N Ste 200 Temecula CA 92590-5628 Office Phone: 951-296-3888. Business E-Mail: robert@rbradlc.com.

ROSENSTOCK, LINDA, federal agency administrator, medical educator; b. N.Y.C., Dec. 20, 1950; AB in Psychology, Brandeis U., 1971; student, U. B.C., Vancouver, Can., 1971-72; MD, MPH, Johns Hopkins U., 1977. Diplomate Am. Bd. Internal Medicine, Am. Bd. Preventive Medicine; lic. physician and surgeon, Wash. Med. resident then chief resident U. Wash., Seattle, 1977-80, resident in preventive medicine, instr. medicine, 1980-82, asst. prof., 1982-83, 83-87, lectr. environ. health, 1982-83, adj. asst. prof., 1983-86, mem. grad. sch. faculty, 1985—, assoc. prof., 1987-93, prof. medicine and environ. health, 1993—, also dir. programs, 1994—; dir. Nat. Inst. Occupational Safety and Health, Washington, 1997—. Dir. Harborview Med. Ctr., Seattle, 1981-87, acting sect. head, 1992-94; dir. Nat. Inst. Occupational Safety and Health, Washington, 1994—. Assoc. editor Internat. Jour. Occupational Medicine and Toxicology, 1991—; mem. editorial bd. Am. Jour. Indsl. Medicine, 1985-94, Jour. Gen. Internal Medicine, 1987-90, Environ. Rsch., 1987—, Western Jour. Medicine, 1990—; contbr. numerous articles to profl. jours. Mem. exec. bd. Physicians for Human Rights, 1990—; mem. occupl. health adv. bd. United Auto Workers GM, 1990-94, chair, 1993-94; mem. task force on pneumoconioses Am. Coll. Radiology, 1991-94; mem. external adv. panel Agrl. Health and Safety Ctr., 1992-93; mem. adv. com. Ctrs. for Disease Control, 1992-94; mem. com. to survey health effects of mustard gas and lewisite Inst. Medicine, 1992, mem. bd. health promotion and disease prevention, 1993-94; mem. bd. sci. counselors HHS, 1993-94, mem. exec. com. nat. toxicology program, 1994 ; mem. med. adv. bd. Teamsters Internat., 1993-94. Recipient Upjohn Achievement award Harborview Med. Ctr., 1978, Jean Spencer Felton MD award Western Occupational Med. Assn., 1988, Environ. and Occupational Medicine award Nat. Inst. Environ. Health Scis., 1991-94; Robert Wood Johnson scholar, 1980-82, Henry J. Kaiser scholar, 1984-89. Fellow ACP (health promotion subcom. 1989-90, clin. practice subcom. 1990-91), Collegium Ramazzini; mem. APHA (chair membership com. 1983-85, chairperson occupational helath and safety sect. 1985-86, gov. coun. 1986-88), Am. Coll. Occupational Medicine (mem. jud. com. 1989-94), Am. Thoracic Soc. (com. health care policy and clin. practice 1990-93), Internat. Commn. Occupational Health (sci. com. epidemiology in occupational health 1989—), Soc. Gen. Internal Medicine (program planning com. 1987, Glaser award com. 1993-94), Western Assn. Physicians, Pacific Interurban Clin. Club. Office: Nat Inst Occpl Safety and Health 200 Independence Ave SW Rm 715H Washington DC 20201-0004

ROSENSWEIG, DANIEL L. Internet company executive; BA, Hobart Coll., NY. Assoc. pub. PC Mag., 1992—94, v.p., pub., 1994—96; pres. Ziff-Davis Internet Pub. Group, 1996-97; pres., CEO ZDNet, Inc., N.Y.C., 1997—2000; pres. CNET Networks, 2000—02; COO Yahoo!, Inc., Calif., 2002—. Office: Yahoo! Inc 701 First Ave Sunnyvale CA 94089

ROSENSWEIG, RONALD ELLIS, scientist consultant; b. Hamilton, Ohio, Nov. 8, 1932; s. Herman and Deana (Meisel) R.; m. Ruth Evelyn Cohen, Sept. 5, 1954; children— Scott Elliot, Beth Ellen, Perry Ethan. Chem. Engr., U. Cin., 1955; S.M., MIT, 1956, Sc.D., 1959. Asst. prof. dept. chem. engring. MIT, Cambridge, 1959-62; prin. scientist Avco Corp., Wilmington, Mass., 1962-69; pres., tech. dir., co-founder Ferrofluidics Corp., Burlington, Mass., 1969-73, also dir., 1969-85; rsch. assoc. Exxon Corp., Annandale, N.J., 1973-78, sr. rsch. assoc., 1978-85, sci. advisor, 1985-95; internat. rsch. chair Blaise Pascal, Paris, 1996-98. Vis. prof. U. Minn., Mpls., 1980, U. Chgo., 1990, Weizmann Inst. Sci., Israel, 1997. Author: Ferrohydrodynamics, 1985; contbr. articles to profl. jours.; patentee in field Fellow NSF, MIT, 1955-56; recipient IR-100 awards Indsl. Rsch. Pubs., 1968, 69, 71; named Young Engr. of Yr., Avco Corp., 1966, Disting. Engring. Alumnus U. Cin., 1986. Mem. Nat. Acad. Engring., Am. Inst. Chem. Engrs. (Alpha Chi Sigma award for rsch. 1985), Am. Phys. Soc., Magnetic Fluids Conf., Internat. Steering Com. (chmn. 1977-92). Jewish. Home: 34 Gloucester Rd Summit NJ 07901-3023 E-mail: resosen@comcast.net.

ROSENTHAL, ALAN, lawyer; b. Newark, N.J., Apr. 19, 1948; s. Robert Rosenthal; children: Keith Michael Rosenthal, Greg Jason Rosenthal. BA, Syracuse U., 1970, JD, 1974. Bar: N.Y. 1975, U.S. Dist. Ct. (no. and we. dists.) N.Y. 1975. Lawyer Ctr. Cmty. Alternatives, Inc., N.Y. Mem. N.Y. State Bar Assn., Nat. Lawyers Guild, Onondaga County Bar Assn., Nat. Legal Aid and Defender Assn., Bd. of Dir. N.Y. State Assn. of Criminal Defense Lawyers, mem. N.Y. State Defense Assn., Nat. Assn. of Sentencing Advocates. Home: 340 Kensington Pl Syracuse NY 13210-3310 Office: 115 E Jefferson St Ste 300 Syracuse NY 13202-2480 Office Phone: 315-422-5638 227.

ROSENTHAL, ALAN SAYRE, government official; b. N.Y.C., Sept. 30, 1926; s. Morris S. and Elizabeth (Ralph) R.; m. Helen Miller, Sept. 8, 1951; children: Edward S., Susan L., Richard M., James M. AB, U. Pa., 1948; LL.B., Yale U., 1951. Bar: N.Y. 1952. Asst. in instrn. Yale U. Law Sch., 1950-51; law clk. to U.S. Circuit Judge Henry W. Edgerton, Washington, 1951-52; atty. appellate sect., civil div. Justice Dept., 1952-72, asst. chief, 1958-72; admnstrv. judge atomic safety and licensing appeal panel AEC (now Nuclear Regulatory Commn.), Washington, 1972-91, chmn., 1972-88; adminstrv. judge pers. appeals bd. GAO, Washington, 1991-96, chmn., 1992-94; adminstrv. judge atomic safety and licensing bd. panel Nuclear Regulatory Commn., Washington, 1999—. Mem. ethics panel Montgomery County Bd. Edn., 1987-93; lectr. law U. Pa., 1981-83, Am. U., 1991-92. Pres. Kensington Elem. Sch. PTA, 1966-67; pres. North Chevy Chase Swimming Pool Assn., 1974-76; chmn. trustees Cedar Ln. Unitarian Universalist Ch., 1970-71; bd. dirs. Montgomery chpt. ACLU, 1967-69. Served with USAAF, 1944-46. Recipient John Marshall award Justice Dept., 1969, Disting. Svc. award Nuclear Regulatory Commn., 1988. Mem. Order of Coif, Phi Beta Kappa, Pi Gamma Mu, Delta Sigma Rho Home: 3203 Kent St Kensington MD 20895-3210 Personal E-mail: rsnthl@comcast.net.

ROSENTHAL, ALBERT JAY, advertising agency executive; b. Chgo., Sept. 30, 1928; s. Harry and Jennie (Comm) R.; m. Rhoda R. Rosenstein, June 18, 1950; children: Jayne, Michael, James, Nancy. BA, U. Ill., 1950. Reporter Transradio Press., Chgo., 1950-51; columnist Lerner Newspapers, Chgo., 1951-53; creative dir. Elliot, Jaynes & Baruch, Chgo., 1953-61; chmn. Albert Jay Rosenthal & Co., Chgo. and N.Y.C., 1961-85; chmn. Midwest div. HBM/Creamer-Albert Jay Rosenthal, Chgo., 1985-88, Della Femina, McNamee WCRS, Inc., Chgo., 1988-93; chmn. DFM/Tatham, Chgo., 1993; founder, pres. Franchising & Licensing World Ctr., Chgo., 1994-98; v.p. mktg., chief mktg. officer Terry Farms Inc., Wayzata, Minn., 1998—. Weekly columnist Franchising and You, Chgo. Sun-Times. Bd. dirs. Ill. Arts Alliance Found., Ill. Arts Alliance, Court Theatre U. Chgo.; mem. sustaining fund com. Ravinia Festival Assn.; mem. mktg. com. World Bus. Coun., Washington; vice chmn. Chgo. Internat. Film Festival; v.p. Gastro-Intestinal Rsch. Found. U. Chgo. Named one of Chgo. Ten Outstanding Young Men, Chgo. Jr. Assn. of Commerce, 1962, Advt. Man of Yr., Alpha Delta Sigma, 1978, Communicator of Yr., Jewish United Fund, 1988 Jewish. Home: 1110 N Lake Shore Dr Apt 32N Chicago IL 60611-1022

ROSENTHAL, ALBERT LESTER, dermatologist, educator; b. New Bedford, Mass., July 25, 1926; s. Myer and Ruth Naomi (Gourse) R.; m. Carol Ash, July 30, 1969; children: Robert, Jill, Bruce. BA magna cum laude, Tufts U., 1946, MD, 1951. Diplomate Am. Bd. Dermatology. Intern R.I. Hosp., Providence, 1951-52, asst. resident surgery, 1952-53; asst. resident dermatology Mass. Gen. Hosp., Boston, 1955-56; asst. in dermatology NYU, 1958-60; practice medicine specializing in dermatology Trenton, N.J., 1958—; attending dermatologist Mercer Hosp., 1958—, chief dermatologist, 1958-93; chief dermatology Helene Euld Hosp., 1973-85; assoc. in dermatology U. Pa., Phila., 1969-73; assoc. prof. dermatology Hahnemann Med. Coll., Phila., 1973-87, clin. prof. dermatology, 1987—; mem. staff Grad. Hosp. Pa., 1969-73, Hamilton Hosp., chief dermatologist, 1972-76. Contbr. numerous articles on dermatology to med. jours. Trustee Friend of the N.J. State Mus., 1972—, chmn. bd. trustees, 1980-82, v.p. fine arts, 1978-80; gov. appointee adv. coun. N.J. State Mus., 1994-2000; adv. bd. Princeton Sr. Resource Ctr., 1997—, Am. Art Newark Mus., 1998-2002; mem. Mercer County Cultural and Heritage Commn., 1982-2000, chmn., 1984-2000; mem. Mercer County Open Space Preservation Commn., 1992-2000; founding mem. Leader's Soc. Dermatology Found., 1988; gov. appointee Bd. Trustees N.J. State Mus., 2000—. Served to capt., M.C., USAF, 1953-55. Mem. Am. Acad. Dermatology, Pa. Acad. Dermatology, Noah Worcester Dermatology Soc., Phila. Dermatology Soc. (pres. 1984-85), N.J. Dermatology Soc., N.J. Med. Soc., Mercer Med. Soc., AMA. Jewish. Office: 74 Franklin Corner Rd Lawrenceville NJ 08648-2102 E-mail: carosentha@aol.com.

ROSENTHAL, AMNON, pediatric cardiologist; b. Gedera, Israel, July 14, 1934; came to U.S., 1949, naturalized, 1959; s. Joseph and Rivka Rosenthal; m. Prudence Lloyd, July 22, 1962; children: Jonathan, Eben, Nathaniel. MD, Albany Med. Coll., 1959. Intern Buffalo Children's Hosp., 1959-60; resident in pediatrics Children's Hosp. Med. Center, Boston, 1960-62, resident in pediatric cardiology, 1965-68; asso. prof. pediatrics Children's Hosp. Med. Center and Harvard U. Med. Sch., Boston, 1975-77; prof. pediatrics C.S. Mott Children's Hosp., U. Mich., Ann Arbor, 1977—, assoc. dir. dept. pediatrics, 1989-92, dir. pediatric cardiology, 1977-97. Served to capt. M.C. USAF, 1962-65. Recipient Founders award, Am. Acad. Pediat., 2003, Disting. Svc. award, U. Mich., 2003; Amnon Rosenthal endowed professorship, 1994. Mem. Am. Acad. Pediatrics, Soc. for Pediatric Rsch., Am. Pediatric Soc., Am.

Heart Assn., Am. Coll. Cardiology, Am. Bd. Pediatrics, Am. Bd. Pediatric Cardiology (chmn. 1987-88). Office: CS Mott Children's Hosp Ann Arbor MI 48109-0204 Office Phone: 734-936-6703. E-mail: amnonr@umich.edu.

ROSENTHAL, ARNON, science association director; PhD, Hebrew U., Jerusalem. Staff scientist Genentech, Inc.; pres., chief tech. officer Rinat Neurosci. Corp., Palo Alto, Calif., 2001—. Mem. NIH Adv. Com. on Parkinson's Disease and Neuronal Repair. Contbr. articles to profl. jours. Achievements include patents for neuronal factors and receptors. Office: Rinat Neurosci Corp 3155 Porter Dr Palo Alto CA 94304

ROSENTHAL, ARTHUR JESSE, publishing executive; b. N.Y.C., Sept. 26, 1919; s. Arthur J. and Grace (Ellinger) R.; m. Margaret Ann Roth, Dec. 12, 1975; children: James, Kathryn, Paul. BA, Yale U., 1941; postgrad., Harvard U. Bus. Sch., 1942. Spl. asst. to U.S. ambassador to Israel, Jerusalem, 1948; pres., editor in chief Basic Books, Inc., N.Y.C., 1949-72; dir. Harvard U. Press, Cambridge, 1972-90; pub. Hill and Wang, N.Y.C., 1990—. Founding trustee Bank St. Coll. Edn., 1952-68 Editorial bd.: Pub. Interest, Harvard Bus. Rev, Family Process, Yale U. Press. Trustee Austen Riggs Center, Stockbridge, Mass. Served to capt., M.I. U.S. Army, 1942-46. Mem.: Century Assn. (N.Y.C.); St. Botolph (Boston).

ROSENTHAL, CHARLES A., JR., prosecutor; Dist. atty. Harris County, Houston. Office: Ste 600 1201 Franklin St Houston TX 77002-1923

ROSENTHAL, CHARLES MICHAEL, financial executive; b. Bklyn., Nov. 21, 1935; s. David B. and Edna (Lefcort) R.; m. Eva F. Sonnenberg, July 7, 1963; children: Andrea (dec.), Nicole. BA, Colgate U., 1957. Rsch. asst. Fed. Res. Bank N.Y., N.Y.C., 1960-62; v.p. L.M. Rosenthal & Co., Inc., 1962-74; ptnr. 1st Manhattan Co., N.Y.C., 1974—. Dir. Veritas Asset Mgmt. Ltd. Trustee Brown U., Providence, 1992—. Capt. USAF, 1957-60. Mem. East Hampton Tennis Club. Jewish. Home: 784 Park Ave New York NY 10021-3553 Office: 1st Manhattan Co 437 Madison Ave New York NY 10022-7001 Office Phone: 212-756-3200. Business E-Mail: crosenthal@firstmanhattan.com.

ROSENTHAL, DANIEL, investment company executive; BS, U. Chgo., 1975, MBA, 1977. With Deloitte & Touche LLP, 1977-95, provider acctg. and cons. svcs. to fin. instn. clients, 1981-95, ptnr., 1985-95; sr. v.p., CFO Instinet Corp., N.Y.C., 1995—, bd. dirs., sr. mgmt. com., chmn. credit com. Bd. dirs., mem. fin. com. League of Hard of Hearing. Mem. AICPA, N.Y. CPA Soc., N.J. CPA Soc., Ill. CPA Soc.

ROSENTHAL, DONNA MYRA, social worker; b. Rochester, NY, Feb. 23, 1944; d. Harry Lionel and Leila Estelle (Eber) Rosenthal; m. Thomas Robert Kolar, Aug. 5, 1979. BA, George Washington U., 1965; MS, Columbia U., 1967. Cert. social worker. Cmty. organizer Health & Welfare Coun. Nassau County, Uniondale, NY, 1967-68; field rep. NY State Office Aging, NYC, 1968-73; asst. dir. United Neighborhood Houses, NYC, 1973-84; exec. dir. Nat. Down Syndrome Soc., NYC, 1984-94; exec. vice chmn. CLAL-The Nat. Jewish Ctr. for Learning and Leadership, NYC, 1994—. Pres. Exec. Women in Human Svcs., NYC, 1985—89. Pres. Congregation Beth Elohim, Bklyn., 1991-94; pres. Columbia U. Social Work Alumni, NYC, 1989-91; 3rd vice-chmn. adv. coun. Columbia U. Sch. Social Work, 1991-2000, co-chair centennial com., 1995-98, chmn. adv. coun. 2000—; treas. Alumni Fedn. Columbia U., 1995-97, sec., 1997-99, v.p., 1999-2001, pres. 2001-03. Recipient Alumni medal Columbia U., 1991; NIMH fellow Columbia U., 1966-67; Regents scholar, 1961. Avocation: music. Office: CLAL 440 Park Ave S New York NY 10016-8012 Office Phone: 212-779-3300.

ROSENTHAL, DOUGLAS EURICO, lawyer, author; b. N.Y.C., Feb. 12, 1940; s. Jacob and Edna Louise (Muir) R.; m. Erica Switzen Kremen, Nov. 12, 1967; children: Benjamin Muir, Rachel Elizabeth. BA summa cum laude, Yale U., 1961, LLB, 1966, PhD in Polit. Sci. 1970; postgrad., Oxford (Eng.) U., 1962; MA, Columbia U., 1963. Bar: N.Y. 1968, U.S. Supreme Ct. 1976, D.C. 1980. Project dir. Russell Sage Found., N.Y.C., 1968-70; assoc. Fried, Frank, Harris, Shriver & Jacobson, N.Y.C., 1970-74; asst. chief fgn. commerce sect., antitrust divsn. Dept. Justice, Washington, 1974-77, chief, 1977-80; ptnr. Sutherland, Asbill & Brennan, Washington, 1980-88, Coudert Bros., 1989-94, Sonnenschein, Nath & Rosenthal, Washington, 1994—; reporter Am. Law Inst.-Am. Bar Assn. Model Lawyer Peer Rev. Sys., 1980. Adj. prof. Tokyo U. Law Sch., 1992; spkr. USIA, Australia, France, Eng., Can., Germany, Japan; escrow agt. Boesky settlement funds paid to U.S. Govt.; expert in internat. litig. and U.S. Fgn. rels. law; mem. plaintiffs' com. lawsuit against Govt Libya for victims of bombing of Pan Am flight 103. Author: (with D. Baker and others) Antitrust Guide for International Operations, 1977; author: Lawyer and Client: Who's in Charge?, 1972, 2d rev. edit., (with Knighton) National Law and International Commerce: The Problem of Extraterritoriality, 1982, Competition Policy in Hufbauer, Europe, 1992: An American Perspective, 1990; co-editor (with Carl Green) Competition Regulation in the Pacific Rim, 1996; author (with others) Global Competition Policy, 1997; mem. bd. advisors Antitrust and Trade Regulation Reporter, Am. Antitrust Inst., George Washington Jour. Internat. Law and Econ.; mem. editl. bd. CCH Merger Notification and Clearance in Can.; contbr. articles to profl. publs. Mem. Sedona Conf. Working Group on econs. and antittrust Inst. for Consumer Antittrust Studies, Loyola U., Chgo.; committeeman Nassau County (N.Y.) Dem. Party, 1963—65; lifetime mem. corp. Culinary Inst. Am.; mem. Brookings Roundtable on Trade and Investment; mem. trade and competition com. Internat. C. of C. Recipient Edward S. Corwin Nat. award Am. Polit. Sci. Assn., 1971; Henry fellow Balliol Coll., Oxford U., 1962, Nobel Internat. and Woodrow Wilson fellow Columbia U., 1963. Mem. ABA (antitrust sect.), Coun. on Fgn. Rels., Am. Law Inst. (life, adv. com. law governing lawyers), Confrerie des Chevaliers du Tastevin, Mory's Assn., Phi Beta Kappa. Jewish. Office: 1301 K St NW Ste 600 Washington DC 20005-3317 Office Phone: 202-408-6352. E-mail: drosenthal@sonnenschein.com.

ROSENTHAL, EDWARD CHARLES, management science educator; m. Bryony R.V. Kay; 2 children. BS in Math., SUNY, Albany, 1980; MS in Indsl. Engrng. and Mgmt. Sci., Northwestern U., 1981, PhD in Indsl. Engrng. and Mgmt. Sci., 1985. Asst. prof. Temple U., Phila., 1985—91, assoc. prof., 1991—. Contbr. articles to profl. jours. Mem.: Inst. for Ops. Rsch. and the Mgmt. Scis. Office: Fox Sch Bus and Mgmt Temple Univ Philadelphia PA 19122

ROSENTHAL, EDWARD LEONARD, secondary school educator; b. Chgo., June 15, 1948; s. Irving H. and Nina (Kritchevsky) R.; m. Hilary Rosenberg, June 29, 1969; children: Rachel, Rebecca. BS in Sci. and Letters, U. Ill., 1969; MEd in Earth Sci., Northern Ill. U., 1972. Tchr. St. Joseph Sch., Dyer, Ind., 1969-70; tchr., golf coach Joliet (Ill.) Cath. High Sch., 1970-77; tchr., girls golf coach Naperville (Ill.) N. High Sch., 1977—. Chmn. United Multi Family Homeowners, Bolingbrook, Ill., 1974-75; v.p. Ill. Jr. Miss Program, Bolingbrook, 1985-87; trustee Village of Bolingbrook, 1975-81, mayor, 1981-85; bd. dirs. West Suburban Temple Har Zion, 1988-92. Named one of Outstanding Young Men Am., 1975, 82, Ill. Girls' Golf Coach Yr., 1988-89; elected to Ill. Golf Coaches Hall Fame, 1995; recipient Disting. Svc. award, 1974. Mem. NEA, (bd. dirs. 1999—), Ill. Edn. Assn. (bd. dirs., 1992—, exec. com. 1994-98, 2001—, chmn. legis. com. 1987-90), Ill. Earth Sci. Assn., Nat. Sci. Tchrs. Assn., Ill. Girls' Golf Coaches Assn. (pres. 1985-88), Naperville Unit Edn. Assn. (1st v.p. 1990-95), Cmty. Assn. Inst. Ill. (bd. dirs. 1980-83), Ill. Jr. Golf Assn. (bd. dirs.2001-). Jewish. Avocation: golf. Home: 508 Clover Ln Bolingbrook IL 60440-1416 Office: Naperville N High Sch 899 N Mill St Naperville IL 60563-2909 E-mail: edrosenthal@hotmail.com.

ROSENTHAL, FAIGI, librarian; b. Montreal, Que., Can., Sept. 6, 1936; d. Hyman and Anne (Podbere) R.; m. Irwin Rosenthal, Sept. 17, 1964; children: Stephen, Barbara. BA, McGill U., Montreal, 1957, MLS, 1958. Asst. head libr. N.Y. Post, N.Y.C., 1978-86; head libr. N.Y. Daily News, N.Y.C., 1986—. Office: NY Daily News 450 W 33rd St New York NY 10001-2603 Office Phone: 212-210-6395. Business E-Mail: frosenthal@edit.nydailynews.com.

ROSENTHAL, GERT, economist; b. Amsterdam, The Netherlands, Sept. 11, 1935; arrived in Guatemala, 1937; s. Ludwig and Florence (Koengisberger) R.; m. Margit Uhlmann, Oct. 18, 1959; children: Caroline, Deborah, Jacqueline, Susan. BA, U. Calif., Berkeley, 1957, MA, 1958. Economist Nat. Planning Office, Guatemala, 1960-65; sr. ofcl. Ministry of Fin., Guatemala, 1966-67; sr. economist Secretariat of Cen. Am. Common Market, Guatemala, 1967-68; min. of planning Nat. Planning Office, Guatemala, 1969-70, 73-74; fellow Adlai Stevenson Inst. for Internat. Affairs, Chgo., 1971; coord. UN Tech. Assistance Project UN Conf. of Trade and Devel., Geneva, 1972; dir. Mex. office Econ. Commn. for Latin Am., Mexico City, 1975-85, dep. exec. sec. Santiago, Chile, 1986—87, exec. sec., 1988—97; rep. of Guatemala to the United Nations, 1999—. Author: Direct Foreign Investment in Central America, 1973; contbr. articles to profl. jours. Home: Residencial Santo Domingo Ste 5 Calle de los Duelos Antigua Guatemala Office: Permanent Mission of Guatemala to UN 57 Park Ave New York NY 10016-3006 Office Phone: 212-679-4760. E-mail: grosenthal@un.int., grosenthal@guate.net.

ROSENTHAL, HELEN NAGELBERG, county official, advocate; b. N.Y.C., June 6, 1926; d. Alfred and Esther (Teichholz) Nagelberg; m. Albert S. Rosenthal, Apr. 10, 1949 (dec.); children: Lisa Rosenthal Michaels, Apryl Meredith Rosenthal Stuppler. BS, CUNY, 1948; MA, NYU, 1950; postgrad., Adelphia U., L.I. U., Lehman Coll., 1975. Cert. early childhood and gifted edn. tchr., N.Y., N.J., elem. and secondary tchr., Fla. Tchr. gifted students N.Y. Bd Edn., Bklyn., 1949-77, 79-87, Baldwin (N.Y.) Pub. Schs., 1977-79; rep. community affairs County of Dade, Fla., 1988-92; ret., 1992; condo dir. Pembroke Pines, 1999—. Author: Criteria for Selection and Curriculum for the Gifted, 1977, Science Experiments for Young Children, 1982, Music in the Air...and in Our Minds. Dir. Condominium, 1989-91. Recipient Departmental award, 1948. Mem. Concerned Citizens for Educating Gifted and Talented (officer N.Y.C. chpt.), Assn. Gifted and Talented Edn. (N.Y. chpt.), Am. Inst. Cancer Rsch., Bklyn. Coll. Alumni Assn. (pres. Broward-Dade chpt. 1995-96, v.p. membership 1996—).

ROSENTHAL, HERBERT MARSHALL, lawyer; BA, UCLA; JD, Hasting Coll. Law, U. Calif., San Francisco. Bar: Calif. 1962. Formerly exec. dir. State Bar Calif., San Francisco; pvt. practice Millbrae, Calif.; pres. Found. State Bar Calif., San Francisco. Office: PO Box 507 Millbrae CA 94030-0507

ROSENTHAL, HOWARD LEWIS, political science educator; b. Wilkinsburg, Pa., Mar. 4, 1939; s. Arnold Sidney R. and Elinor (Kaufman) (Rosenthal) Lewis; m. Annie Regine Lunel, June 30, 1960 (div. Nov., 1967); children: Illia Rebecca, Jean Laurent; m. Margherita Guastoni Spampinato, Feb. 6, 1968; 1 son, Gil Guastoni. BS, MIT, 1960, PhD, 1964. Asst. prof. polit. sci. U. Calif.-Irvine, 1965-66; asst. prof. and assoc. prof. polit. sci. Carnegie-Mellon U., Pitts., 1966-71, prof., 1971-93; Roger Williams Straus prof. social scis. Princeton U, N.J., 1993—. Vis. prof. Hebrew U., Jerusalem, 1968-69, U. Calif., San Diego, 1976-77, MIT, Cambridge, 1989-90, U. Paris I, 1990; Walras-Pareto lectr. U. Lausanne, Switzerland, 1996; vis. grad. lectr. Fondation Nat. des Scis. Politiques, Paris, 1972-73; disting. vis. prof. Brown U., 2003—. Author: Prediction Analysis of Cross Classifications, 1977, Analysis of Ordinal Data, 1977, Partisan Politics, Divided Government and the Economy, 1995, Flexible Integration: Towards a More Effective and Democratic Europe, 1995, The Realignment of National Politics and Income Redistribution, 1997, Congress: A Political-Economic History of Roll Call Voting, 1997; mem. editl. bd. Pub. Choice, Economics of Governance. Fellow NSF, 1969-92, 98-2003, Ford Found., 1972-73, Social Sci. Rsch. Coun., 1964-65, nat. fellow Hoover Instn., Stanford U., 1979-80; Sherman Fairchild disting. scholar Calif. Inst. Tech., 1982-83; fellow Internat. Ctr. for Econ. Rsch., Turin, Italy, 1991-93, Ctr. for Advanced Study in Behavioral Scis., 1991-92, 98-99, ECARE U. Libre de Brussels, 1995, Russell Sage Found., 2002-03. Fellow Am. Acad. Arts and Scis.; mem. Pub. Choice Soc. (Duncan Black award 1979), Am. Polit. Sci. Assn. (CQ Press award 1985), Am. Econ. Assn. Office: Princeton Univ Politics Dept Princeton NJ 08544-0001

ROSENTHAL, IRA MAURICE, pediatrician, educator; b. N.Y.C., June 11, 1920; s. Abraham Leon and Jean (Kalotkin) R.; m. Ethel Ginsburg, Oct. 17, 1943 (dec.); children: Anne, Judith; m. Irene Farkis-Conn, Apr. 21, 2001. Student, CCNY, 1936-38; AB, Ind. U., 1940, MD, 1943. Intern Lincoln Hosp., N.Y.C., 1943-44; resident in pathology Albert Einstein Hosp., Phila., 1947-48; resident in pediatrics Fordham Hosp., N.Y.C., 1948-49; practice medicine specializing in pediatrics Bklyn., 1950-52; instr. U. Ill. Coll. Medicine, Chgo., 1953, asst. prof., 1953-55, assoc. prof., 1955-63, prof. pediatrics, 1963-90, prof. emeritus, 1990—, head dept., 1973-82; clin. prof. pediatrics Stritch Sch. Medicine Loyola U., Chgo., 1990-91, lectr., 1991-93; clin. assoc. in pediatrics U. Chgo., 1990-91, clin. prof. pediatrics, 1991—. Mem. med. service adv. com. Nat. Found. March of Dimes, 1975-80 Served to capt. U.S. Army, 1944-46. Mem. Am. Pediatric Soc., Soc. Pediatric Research, Acad. Pediatrics, Lawson Wilkins Pediatric Endocrine Soc., Endocrine Soc. Home: 5490 S South Shore Dr Chicago IL 60615-5984

ROSENTHAL, IRENE L. education educator, consultant; b. N.Y.C., Aug. 11, 1949; d. George Joseph and Marie Jennie Licata; m. Lewis Elliott Rosenthal, Oct. 16, 1971; children: Michael George, Sarah Helen, Daniel James. Ph.D., U. Albany, 1997. Cert. K-12 reading tchr. NY, pub. librn. NY. Tchr. reading South Colonie Sch. Dist., Albany, NY, 1997—2001; asst. prof. Coll. St. Rose, Albany, NY, 2001—. Cons. NY State Edn. Dept., Albany, 1997, NY State Libr., Albany, 1999—. Pres. Albany City Area Reading Coun.; v.p. Two-Together, Albany, 2003. Mem.: Internat. Reading Assn. (assoc.). Democrat. Jewish. Achievements include research in study of 6th grade readers. Office: Coll St Rose 432 Western Ave Albany NY 12203 Office Phone: 518-454-2879. Business E-Mail: rosenthi@mail.strose.edu.

ROSENTHAL, IRVING, journalism educator; b. N.Y.C., July 31, 1912; s. Max and Rose Rosenthal; m. Ruth M. Rosenthal, May 22, 1943; children: David, Robert, Risa. BSS, CCNY, 1933, MS, 1934. Reporter N.Y. Times, N.Y.C., 1933; fellow to full prof. dept. English CCNY, 1933-77, chmn. comms. and mass media, 1946-77, asst. to pres., 1933-43; coord. broadcasting courses Sta. WCBS-TV, N.Y.C., 1969-90, emeritus prof., 1977—. Adj. prof. C.W. Post Coll., Brookville, N.Y., 1967-70; editl. cons. Dance mag., 1983-87, Med. Soc. State of N.Y. Editl. adv. bd. Hadassah mag., 1978-96; co-author: Modern Journalism, 1962, A Contemporary Reader, 1961, Art of Writing Made Simple, 1958, Business English Made Simple, 1955. Mem. Silurians, awards chmn. 1989-91. 1st lt. U.S. Army, 1943-45. Mem. Alpha Phi Gamma, Phi Delta Sigma, Phi Delta Kappa. Home and Office: 62 Hampshire Rd Great Neck NY 11023-1537

ROSENTHAL, J. THOMAS, hospital administrator, medical educator; b. Richmond, 1949; BA, Johns Hopkins U.; MD, Duke U., 1974. Intern Johns Hopkins U., Balt., 1970; resident U. Va. Hosp., Charlottesville, Va., 1976, Lahey Clinic Found., Boston, 1980; exec. vice chmn. dept. surgery UCLA Sch. Medicine, 1991, prof. surgery/urology, 1993—, assoc. vice chancellor; dir., vice provost UCLA Med. Group, 1996; chief med. officer UCLA Health Sys.; vice provost UCLA Med. Group Affairs. Office: UCLA Urology/David Geffen Sch Medicine Box 951731 14-214R CHS Los Angeles CA 90095-1731

ROSENTHAL, JACOB (JACK ROSENTHAL), foundation executive; b. Tel-Aviv, June 30, 1935; came to U.S., 1938, naturalized, 1943; s. Manfred and Rachel (Kaplan) R.; m. Holly Russell, Dec. 21, 1985; children by previous marriage: John, Ann; stepchildren: Christopher Russell, Andrew Russell. AB, Harvard U., 1956. Reporter, editor Portland Oregonian, Reporter, 1950-61; asst. dir., dir. public info. U.S. Dept. Justice, Washington, 1961-66; exec. asst. to Undersec. of State, 1966-67; Kennedy fellow Harvard Inst. Politics, 1967-68; nat. urban corr. Life Mag., N.Y.C., 1968-69; urban corr. N.Y. Times, Washington, 1969-73, asst. Sun. editor, mag. editor N.Y.C., 1973-77, dep. editor editl. page, 1977-86, editor editl. page, 1986-93; editor-in-chief N.Y. Times Mag., N.Y.C., 1993-99; pres. N.Y. Times Co. Found., N.Y.C., 2000—. Editor: Kerner Commn. Report on Urban Riots, 1968. Mem. Harvard Crimson Grad. Bd. Recipient Best Editorial award Internat. Labor Press Assn., 1961, Loeb award, 1973, Pulitzer prize for editorials, 1982 Office: NY Times Co 229 W 43d St New York NY 10036-3959 E-mail: rosebud@nytimes.com.

ROSENTHAL, JAMES D. retired federal official, former U.S. ambassador; b. San Francisco, Jan. 15, 1932; BA, Stanford U., 1954; student, Fgn. Svc. Inst., 1960—61, Nat. War Coll., 1974—75. With U.S. Fgn. Svc., 1956—90, adminstrv. officer, 1958—60; polit. officer Saigon, Vietnam, 1961—65; mem. faculty U.S. Mil. Acad., 1965—67; internat. rels. officer Vietnam affairs Dept. State, 1967—70, dir. Vietnam, Laos and Cambodia affairs, 1975—77, dep. dir. mgmt. ops., 1986—90; mem. U.S. del. to Vietnam Peace Talks Paris, 1970—72; dep. chief of mission Bangui, 1972—74, Kuala Lumpur, Malaysia, 1977—79, Manila, Philippines, 1979—83; amb. to Guinea Conakry, 1983—86; exec. dir. Commonwealth Club of Calif., 1990—96.

ROSENTHAL, JANE, film company executive; b. Providence, 1957; d. Martin and Ina; m. Craig Hatkoff; children: Juliana, Isabella. Student, Brown U.; BA, NYU, 1977. Rsch. staff CBS Sports, NY; editor program practices CBS Entertainment, 1977, program exec. miniseries, 1978, assoc. dir. motion pictures for TV, 1979; v.p. feature prodn. Universal Studios, 1984—85; v.p. in charge of motion pictures and TV Walt Disney, 1985—87; v.p. in charge of movies and miniseries Warner Bros. TV, 1987—88; co-founder Tribeca Films, N.Y.C., 1988—, Tribeca Film Festival, N.Y.C., 2002. Prodr.: (films) Thunderheart, 1992, Night and the City, 1992, A Bronx Tale, 1993, Faithful, 1996, Marvin's Room, 1996, Wag the Dog, 1997, Analyze This, 1999, Entropy, 1999, Flawless, 1999, The Adventures of Rocky & Bullwinkle, 2000, Meet the Parents, 2000, Prison Song, 2001, Showtime, 2002, About a Boy, 2002, Analyze That, 2002; (TV series) Tribeca, 1993; exec. prodr.: (films) Nine, 1996, The Repair Shop, 1998; (TV films) Witness to the Mob, 1998, Holiday Heart, 2000, Porn 'n Chicken, 2002. Office: Tribeca Prodns 6th Fl 375 Greenwich St New York NY 10013

ROSENTHAL, JOEL, manufacturing executive; b. Ft. Worth, Oct. 25, 1946; s. Melvin and Jane (Hertzman) R.; m. Susan Ellman, Nov. 15, 1970; children: Jackie Ilene, Harold Joseph. BBA, No. Tex. State U., 1969. V.p. First Street Corp., Ft. Worth, 1969-72; mgr. Edison Jewelers & Distbrs., Ft. Worth, 1972-73; v.p. Yankton Sioux Industries, Wagner, S.D., 1973-81, pres., 1981-85; cons., Canton, S.D., 1985—; pres. Ctrl. Plains Tractor Parts, Sioux Falls, S.D., 1986—. Cons. econ. devel. State of S.D., Pierre, 1985-86; guest lectr. U. S.D., 2003. Chmn. S.D. Rep. Com., 1995-2003; mem. Electoral Coll., 1996, 2000; pres. City Coun., Wagner, 1978-83; trustee Carnegie Libr., Wagner, 1978-83; active Rep. Nat. Com., Washington, 1985-2003, S.D. Jud. Qualifications Commn., 1983-86, Pvt. Industry Coun., Pierre, 1985-86, SD Coun. of Econ. Advs., 2003. Named S.D. Vol. of Yr. Office of Gov., 1983. Republican. Jewish. Home: 6001 S Tomar Rd Sioux Falls SD 57013 Office: PO Box 1818 Sioux Falls SD 57101-1818 Office Phone: 605-334-0021.

ROSENTHAL, JOEL HOWARD, think-tank executive; b. Brookline, Mass., Apr. 28, 1960; s. Edward and Helen R.; m. Patricia Barney, Dec. 7, 1986; children: Sarah, David. BA, Harvard U., 1982; PhD, Yale U., 1988. Pres. Carnegie Coun. on Ethics and Internat. Affairs, N.Y.C., 1995—; adj. prof. N.Y.U., N.Y.C., 1996—. Co-dir. Carnegie Coun./Nat. War Coll. working group on Ethics and the Future of Internat. Conflict; coordinator Carnegie Coun.'s projects on Justice and the World Economy and Ethics and U.S. Fgn. Policy. Author: Righteous Realists, 1991; editor: Ethics and Internat. Affairs, 1990—, Ethics and Internat. Affairs: A Reader (2d edit.), 1999; contbr. articles to profl. jours. Co-dir. NEH 1994 Summer Faculty Inst. on Teaching Ethics and Internat. Affairs, U. Va.; charter author and 1st chmn. Internat. Ethics sect., Internat. Studies Assn. Office: Carnegie Coun 170 E 64th St New York NY 10021-7478

ROSENTHAL, KENNETH W. lawyer; b. Frankfurt, Fed. Republic Germany, Nov. 2, 1929; came to U.S., 1944; s. Ludwig and Florence (Koenigsberger) R.; m. Joan Finkelstein, Apr. 10, 1960; children: Jeffrey, David. BA, Syracuse U., 1951; LLB, U. Calif., San Francisco, 1958. Bar: Calif. 1959, U.S. Dist. Ct. (no. dist.) Calif. 1959, U.S. Ct. Appeals (9th cir.) 1959, U.S. Supreme Ct. 1972. Assoc. Jay A. Darwin, San Francisco, 1959-61; ptnr. Darwin, Rosenthal & Leff, San Francisco, 1961-69; pres. Rosenthal & Leff Inc., San Francisco, 1969-89; of counsel Molligan, Cox & Moyer, San Francisco, 1989-98, Cox & Moyer, San Francisco, 1998—. Del. 9th Cir. Jud. Conf., 1986-89. Contbr. numerous articles to profl. jours. Mem. Nat. Bd. Trial Advocacy (cert.), Am. Bd. Trial Advs. (cert.), Calif. Bar. Assn. (legal specialization sect., civic trial advocacy com., mediator, arbitrator 1993—), San Francisco Bar Assn., San Francisco Trial Lawyers Assn. (bd. dirs. 1976-84, pres. 1984). Democrat. Jewish. Avocations: photography, walking. Office: Cox & Moyer 703 Market St San Francisco CA 94103-2102

ROSENTHAL, LARRY, cosmetic dentist; b. NYC, 1948; married; 1 child. DDS, U. Pa. Sch. Dental Medicine, 1974. Dir. aesthetic continuum Baylor Coll. Dentistry, Dallas, Advanced Program, NYU, U. Ky. Coll. Dentistry; dir. Aesthetic Advantage Inc., Rosenthal Group Aesthetic Dentistry, NY. Named one of Top Cosmetic Dentists in NY, NY Mag., 2004. Mem.: Am. Acad. Cosmetic Dentistry (assoc. editor, AACD Jour.). Office: Rosenthal Group Aesthetic Dentistry 30 E 76th St Ste 5B New York NY 10021 Office Phone: 212-794-9600. Office Fax: 212-794-3644.

ROSENTHAL, LEE H. federal judge; b. Nov. 30, 1952; m. Gary L. Rosenthal; children: Rebecca, Hannah, Jessica, Rachel. BA in Philosophy with honors, U. Chgo., 1974, JD with honors, 1977. Bar: Tex. 1979. Law clk. to Hon. John R. Brown U.S. Ct. Appeals (5th cir.), 1977-78; assoc. Baker & Botts, 1978-86, ptnr., 1986-92; judge U.S. Dist. Ct. (so. dist.) Tex., 1992—. Vis. com. Law Sch. U. Chgo., 1983-86, 94-97, 99-2001; mem. Fed. Jud. Conf. Adv. Com. for Fed. Rules of Civil Procedure, 1996-2003, chair 2003-; chair 1999 Fifth Cir. Jud. Conf.; mem. Am. Law Inst., cons. group on transactional rules of civil procedure and aggregate litigation project. Mem. bd. editors Manual for Complex Litigation, 1999—. Pres. Epilepsy Assn. Houston/Gulf Coast, 1989-91; trustee Briarwood Sch. Endowment Found., 1991-92; bd. dirs. Epilepsy Found. Am., 1993-98, DePelchin Children's Ctr., 2000-; bd. trustees Kinkaid Sch. Fellow Tex. Bar Found.; Mem. ABA, Texas Bar Assn., Houston Bar Assn. Office: US Dist Ct US Courthouse Rm 11535 515 Rusk St Houston TX 77002-2600

ROSENTHAL, LUCY GABRIELLE, writer, educator, editor; b. NYC; d. Henry Moses and Rachel (Tchernowitz) R. AB, U. Mich., 1954; MS in Journalism, Columbia U., 1955; MFA, Yale Sch. Drama, 1961; postgrad. Writers Workshop, U. Iowa, 1965—68. Asst. editor Radiology mag., Detroit, 1955—57; free-lance editl. cons. various pub. houses, lit. agts. NYC, 1957—73; mem. admissions staff Writers Workshop U. Iowa, Iowa City, 1965—68; editor Book-of-the-Month Club, NYC, 1973—74, mem. editl. bd. judges, 1974—79, sr. editl. advisor, 1979—87. Mem. biography jury Pulitzer Prize, 1980; mem. bd. Am. Book Awards, 1981-82; adj. prof. English, NYU, 1986—; mem. guest faculty in writing Sarah Lawrence Coll., 1988-96, regular faculty writing, 1996—; lectr., adj. asst. prof. writing program Columbia U., 1990-96, Humanities faculty, 92nd St. YM/YWCA, 1987; fiction workshop The Writer's Voice, West Side YMCA, summer 1991; adj. prof. NYU Sch. Continuing Edn., 1988; mem. faculty Sarah Lawrence Ctr. for Continuing Edn., 1989, 90; instr. fiction writing course Art Workshop Internat., Assisi, Italy, summer 1993. Plays produced at Eugene O'Neill Meml. Theater Ctr., 1966, 67; author: The Ticket Out, 1983; editor: Great American Love Stories, 1988, The World Treasury of Love Stories, 1995, The Eloquent Short Story: Varieties of Narration, 2004; contbr. articles and revs. to various mags. and periodicals including Washington Post and Chgo. Tribune Book World, Saturday Rev., Ms. mag., Mich. Quar. Rev., NY Times Book Rev.; contbr. fiction to Global City Rev., 1995. Pulitzer fellow critical writing, 1968. Mem. Authors Guild, Authors League, Nat. Book Critics Circle, Women's Media Group (bd. mem. 1979-81), PEN, Phi Beta Kappa, Phi Kappa Phi. Office: Sarah Lawrence Coll Bronxville NY 10708 E-mail: lrosenth@slc.edu.

ROSENTHAL, LYOVA HASKELL See GRANT, LEE

ROSENTHAL, MICHAEL ROSS, academic administrator, consultant; b. Youngstown, Ohio, Dec. 2, 1939; s. Samuel Herman and Frances Vance (Schlesinger) R.; m. Linda Gabler, Sept. 6, 1963; children: Heidi, Erika, Nicolas Gabler. AB, Case Western Res. U., 1961; MS, U. Ill., 1963, PhD,

1965. Asst. prof. chemistry Bard Coll., Annandale, N.Y., 1965-68, assoc. prof. chemistry, 1968-73, prof. chemistry, 1973-84, assoc. dean acad. affairs, 1980-84; v.p. acad. affairs St. Mary's Coll. of Md., St. Mary's City, 1984-89; provost, dean faculty, prof. chemistry Southwestern U., Georgetown, Tex., 1989-96; dep. sec. Md. Higher Edn. Commn., Annapolis, 1996—99; spl. asst. to provost McDaniel Coll., Westminster, Md., 1999—. Acad. cons., ind. and as rep. of Assn. Am. Colls. Author or co-author of numerous articles in jours. of inorganic chemistry and chem. edn. Chmn. Environ. Mgmt. Coun., Dutchess County, N.Y., 1978-84; founding chmn. Heritage Task Force for Hudson River Valley, 1980-84; pres., bd. dirs. Hudson River Heritage, N.Y., 1978-84; bd. dirs. Hudson River Rsch. Coun., 1976-84; teaching assoc. Danforth Found., 1980. Recipient Outstanding Community Svc. award, Dutchess County (N.Y.) Legislature, 1980. Mem. Am. Chem. Soc., The Royal Society (Chemistry, London), Hudson River Environ. Soc., Sigma Xi, Phi Beta Kappa, Phi Lambda Upsilon Democrat. Office: McDaniel Coll 2 College Hill Westminster MD 21157 Office Phone: 410-857-2268. Business E-Mail: mrosenth@mcdaniel.edu. *Those of us who spend our professional lives as educators are subject to many pressures and influences - financial influences, political influences, intellectual influences. I try to remember that in the usually chaotic world of education the only really important thing is the welfare of the student.*

ROSENTHAL, MILTON FREDERICK, chemical and minerals company executive; b. N.Y.C., Nov. 24, 1913; s. Jacob C. and Louise (Berger) R.; m. Frieda Bojar, Feb. 28, 1943; 1 child, Anne Rosenthal Mitro. BA, CCNY, 1932; LLB, Columbia U., 1935. Bar: N.Y. 1935. Rsch. asst. N.Y. State Law Revision Commn., 1935-37; law sec. Fed. Judge William Bondy, 1937-40; assoc. atty. Leve, Hecht & Hadfield, 1940-42; sec., treas. Hugo Stinnes Corp., 1946 48, exec. v.p., treas., CEO, 1948-49, pres., dir., CEO, 1949-64, Minerals and Chems. Philipp Corp., N.Y.C., 1964-67; pres., dir., COO Engelhard Minerals & Chem. Corp., N.Y.C., 1967-71; chmn., pres., CEO, dir. Engelhard Minerals & Chems. Corp., N.Y.C., 1971-81; dir. Salomon, Inc., N.Y.C., 1981-88, dir. emeritus, 1988-98; chmn. Engelhard Corp., N.J., 1981-86. Ret. dir. US-USSR Trade and Econ. Coun., 1974-82, Nat. Coun. US-China Trade, 1977-82; chmn., dir. Romanian-Am. Econ. Coun., 1974-89; dir. Fgn. Policy Assn., 1971-91. Life trustee Mt. Sinai Med. Ctr.; bd. dirs. United Cerebral Palsy Rsch. and Ednl. Found., Inc.; ret. trustee Am. Fedn. Arts, Manhattanville Coll., Purchase Coll. Found. 1st lt. JAG dept. U.S. Army, 1942-45. Mem. Assn. of Bar of City of N.Y., Chgo. Bar Assn., Columbia Law Sch. Alumni Assn., Judge Adv. Assn., Phi Beta Kappa. Home: 450 Woodlands Rd Harrison NY 10528-1220 also: 1602 Quartz Valley Dr Carefree AZ 85377 Office: 3rd Fl 666 3d Ave New York NY 10017

ROSENTHAL, RICHARD JAY, psychiatrist; b. N.Y.C., Jan. 12, 1939; s. Sam and Yvette Loraine (Kapelov) Rosenthal; m. Strawn Rosenthal, Nov. 10, 1984. BA, Cornell U., 1960; MD, Albert Einstein Coll. of Medicine, 1964. Diplomate Nat. Bd. Med. Examiners, Am. Bd. Psychiatry and Neurology. Resident in psychiatry Mt. Sinai Hosp., N.Y.C., 1968; clin. assoc. L.A. Psychoanalytic Inst., 1980; pvt. practice Los Angeles, 1970—; asst. clin. prof. psychiatry UCLA, 1971—; faculty L.A. Psychoanalytic Inst., 1984—; dir. inpatient gambling treatment program Westwood Hosp., 1990—93; chief of psychiatry CPC Westwood Hosp., L.A., 1992—93; supr. attending Cedars Sinai Med. Ctr., L.A., 1982—; co-dir. UCLA Gambling Studies Program, 2003—. Founder/pres. Calif. Coun. on Problem Gambling, 1986—99; com. on impulse disorders APA Task Force on DSM IV, 1988—93; com. on social and econ. impact of path. gambling Nat. Acad. Sci., 1998—99. Contbr. chapters to books, articles to jours. Beit T'Shuvah Residential Treatment Ctr. L.A., 1992—94; adv. com. Little Hoover Commn. on Gambling in Calif., 1997; trustee Mus. Photog. Arts, San Diego. Lt. comdr. USN, 1968—70. Recipient Rsch. award, Nat. Coun. on Problem Gambling, 1993, Herman Goldman award, 1995, Robert Custer award, 2004. Fellow: Am. Psychiat. Assn. (life); mem.: Internat. Dostoevsky Soc., So. Calif. Psychiat. Soc. (ethics com. 1992—), Inst. for the Study of Gambling and Comml. Gaming (adv. bd. 1993—), Am. Acad. Psychiatrists in Alcoholism and Addictions. Achievements include first controlled study of repetitive self mutilation(demonstrated progression and role of dissociation); author of current diagnostic criteria for pathological gambling; co-investigator on first genetic study of pathological gambling (demonstrating physiological predisposition); research establishing the legitimacy of the disorder; founding of California council on problem gaming, started first inpatient treatment program on the west coast, began UCLA gambling studies program, mentored researchers and clinicans. Avocations: photography, fly fishing. Office: 435 N Roxbury Dr Beverly Hills CA 90210 Office Phone: 310-278-3746.

ROSENTHAL, ROBERT, psychology educator; b. Giessen, Germany, Mar. 2, 1933; came to U.S., 1940, naturalized, 1946; s. Julius and Hermine (Kahn) R.; m. Mary Lu Clayton, Apr. 20, 1951; children: Roberta, David C., Virginia. AB, UCLA, 1953, PhD, 1956, U. Giessen, 2003. Diplomate: clin. psychology Am. Bd. Examiners Profl. Psychology. Clin. psychology trainee Los Angeles Area VA, 1954-57; lectr. U. So. Calif., 1956-57; acting instr. UCLA, 1957; from asst. to assoc. prof., coordinator clin. tng. U. N.D., 1957-62; vis. assoc. prof. Ohio State U., 1960-61; lectr. Boston U., 1965-66; lectr. clin. psychology Harvard U., Cambridge, Mass., 1962-67, prof. social psychology, 1967-95, chmn. dept. psychology, 1992-95, Edgar Pierce prof. psychology, 1995-99, Edgar Pierce prof. emeritus, 1999—; disting. prof. U. Calif., Riverside, 1999—. Author: Experimenter Effects in Behavioral Research, 1966, enlarged edit., 1976; (with Lenore Jacobson) Pygmalion in the Classroom, 1968, expanded edit., 1992, Meta-analytic Procedures for Social Research, 1984, rev. edit., 1991, Judgment Studies, 1987; (with others) New Directions in Psychology 4, 1970, Sensitivity to Nonverbal Communication: The Pons Test, 1979; (with Ralph L. Rosnow) The Volunteer Subject, 1975, Primer of Methods for the Behavioral Sciences, 1975, Essentials of Behavioral Research, 1984, 2d edit., 1991, Understanding Behavioral Science, 1984, Contrast Analysis, 1985, Beginning Behavioral Research, 1993, 4th edit., 2002, People Studying People: Artifact and Ethics in Behavioral Research, 1997, (with Ralph L. Rosnow and Donald B. Rubin) Contrasts and Effect Sizes in Behavioral Research: A Correlational Approach, 2000; (with Brian Mullen) BASIC Meta-analysis, 1985; editor: (with Ralph L. Rosnow) Artifact in Behavioral Research, 1969, Skill in Nonverbal Communication, 1979, Quantitative Assessment of Research Domains, 1980, (with Thomas A. Sebeok) The Clever Hans Phenomenon: Communication With Horses, Whales, Apes and People, 1981; (with Blanck and Buck) Nonverbal Communication in the Clinical Context, 1986; (with Gheorghiu, Netter and Eysenck) Suggestion and Suggestibility: Theory and Research, 1989. Recipient Donald Campbell award Soc. for Personality and Social Psychology, 1988, James McKeen Cattell Sabbatical award, 1995-96; co-recipient Golden Anniversary Monograph award Speech Comm. Assn., 1996; named Watson lectr. U. N.H., Lanzetta Meml. lectr. Dartmouth Coll., Bayer lectr. Yale Sch. Medicine, Foa lectr. Temple U., Disting. Alumni lectr. UCLA; Guggenheim fellow, 1973-74, fellow Ctr. for Advanced Study in Behavioral Scis., 1988-89; sr. Fulbright scholar, 1972; recipient Gold Medal for Life Achievement in Sci. of Psychology Am. Psychol. Found., 2003. Fellow AAAS (co-recipient Sociopsychol. prize 1960, co-recipient Behavioral Sci. Rsch. prize 1993), APA (divsn. evaluation, measurement, and stats., co-recipient Cattell Fund award 1967, co-chmn. Task Force on Statis. Inference, Disting. Sci. award for applications of psychology, 2002, Disting. Sci. Contbns. award, 2002, divsn. evaluation, measurement and stats., others), Am. Psychol. Soc. (charter, James McKeen Cattell award 2001); mem. Soc. Exptl. Social Psychology (Disting. Scientist award 1996), Ea. Psychol. Assn. (Disting. lectr. 1989), Mid-we. Psychol. Assn., Mass. Psychol. Assn. (Disting. Career Contbn. award 1979), Soc. Projective Techniques (past treas.), Phi Beta Kappa, Sigma Xi. Office: U Calif Olmsted Hall Riverside CA 92521-0001 Office Phone: 909-827-4503.

ROSENTHAL, ROBERT JON, newspaper editor, journalist; b. N.Y.C., Aug. 5, 1948; s. Irving and Ruth (Moss) R.; m. Inez Katherina von Sternenfels, Nov. 22, 1985; children: Adam, Benjamin, Ariella. BA, U. Vt., 1970. News asst. N.Y. Times, N.Y.C., 1970-73; reporter Boston Globe, 1974-79, Phila. Inquirer, 1979-82, Africa corr., Nairobi, Kenya, 1982-86, fgn. editor, Phila., 1986-91, city editor, 1991-93, asst. mng. editor, daily, 1993-94, assoc. mng. editor, 1994-96, exec. editor, 1996-98, editor, exec. v.p., 1998—2001; mng. editor, v.p. San Francisco (Calif.) Chronicle, 2002—. Recipient Third World Reporting award Nat. Assn. Black Journalists, 1983, Mag. award Overseas Press Club, 1985, Disting. Fgn. Corr. award Sigma Delta Chi, 1985, Mag. Writing award World Population Inst., 1986. Avocations: ice hockey, gardening, fishing, cooking. Office: 1 Stevens Ct Belvedere Tiburon CA 94920-1549

ROSENTHAL, ROBERT M. automotive sales executive; b. Jan. 6, 1928; BS, Temple U. Pres. Rosenthal Chevrolet Co., Arlington, Va., 1954—; CEO Rosenthal Cos., Arlington, 1978—. Office: Rosenthal Cos 1550 Wilson Blvd Ste 700 Arlington VA 22209-2490

ROSENTHAL, SHIRLEY LORD, cosmetics magazine executive, novelist; b. London, Aug. 28; came to U.S., 1971; d. Francis J. and Mabel Florence (Williamson) Stringer; m. James Hussey; m. Cyril Lord; m. David Anderson; m. A. M. Rosenthal, June 10, 1987; children: Mark, Richard. Student, S.W. Essex Coll., London, 1948—50. Reporter London Daily Mirror; fiction editor Woman's Own, 1950-53; features editor Good Taste mag., 1953-56; features, fiction editor Woman and Beauty, 1956-59; women's editor Star Evening newspaper, 1959-60, London Evening Standard, 1960-63, London Evening News, 1963-68; beauty editor Harper's Bazaar, London, 1963-71, N.Y.C., 1971-73; beauty, health editor Vogue mag., Condé Nast Publs., N.Y.C., 1973-75; v.p. corp. rels. Colgate, Helena Rubinstein, N.Y.C., 1975-80; beauty dir. Vogue mag., 1980—95, contbg. editor, 1995—. Chairwoman media coun. The Am. Acad. Dermatology, 1995—; corp. v.p. content iBeauty.com, 1999—2002. Syndicated Field columnist on beauty, health; author 3 beauty books; also novels: Golden Hill, 1982; One of My Very Best Friends, (Lit. Guild Selection), 1985; Faces, 1989; My Sister's Keeper, 1993, The Crasher, 1998. City commr. Craigavon City, No. Ireland, 1963-68. Address: 131 E 66th St New York NY 10021-6129 E-mail: Shirlord3@aol.com.

ROSENTHAL, SOL, lawyer; b. Balt., Oct. 17, 1934; s. Louis and Hattie (Getz) R.; m. Diane Myra Sackler, June 11, 1961; children: Karen Abby, Pamela Margaret, Robert Joel. AB, Princeton U., 1956; JD, Harvard U., 1959. Bar: Md. 1959, Calif. 1961. Law clk. to chief judge U.S. Ct. Appeals, 4th cir., Balt., 1959-60; assoc. Kaplan, Livingston, Goodwin, Berkowitz & Selvin, Beverly Hills, Calif., 1960-66, ptnr., 1966-74, Buchalter, Nemer, Fields & Younger, L.A., 1974-96; of counsel Blanc, Williams, Johnston & Kronstadt, L.A., 1996-2000, Arnold & Porter, 2000—. Bd. dirs. Playboy Enterprises, Inc., Chgo.; arbitrator Dirs. Guild Am., L.A., 1976—, Writers Guild Am., L.A., 1976—, Am. Film Mktg. Assn., 1989—, SAG, L.A., 1992—; negotiator Writers Guild-Assn. Talent Agts., L.A., 1978—; mem. entertainment and large complex case panels Am. Arbitration Assn., 1997—. Founder Camp Ronald McDonald for Good Times, L.A., 1985; charter founder Mus. Contemporary Art, L.A., 1988. Fellow: Coll. Comml. Arbitrators, Am. Bar Found.; mem.: ABA, Beverly Hills Bar Assn. (pres. 1982—83), Acad. TV Arts and Scis. (bd. govs. 1990—92), L.A. Copyright Soc. (pres. 1973—74), Los Angeles County Bar Assn. (trustee 1981—82), Calif. Bar Assn., Phi Beta Kappa. Office: Arnold & Porter 1900 Ave Of Stars Ste 1700 Los Angeles CA 90067-4408 Office Phone: 310-552-2500.

ROSENTHAL, STEVEN SIEGMUND, lawyer; b. Cleve., May 22, 1949; s. Fred Siegel and Natalie Josephine Rosenthal; m. Ilene Edwina Goldstein, Oct. 1, 1983; children: Alexandra M., Eliana D. AB, Dartmouth Coll., 1971; JD, Harvard U., 1974. Bar: Fla. 1974, D.C. 1975, U.S. Supreme Ct. 1978, Calif. 1983. Law clk. judge Malcolm R. Wilkey U.S. Ct. Appeals (D.C. cir.), 1974-75; assoc. Covington & Burling, Washington, 1975-80, Morrison & Foerster, Washington, 1980-81, ptnr., 1981-97, Cooper, Carvin & Rosenthal, PLLC, Washington, 1998-2001, Holland & Knight LLP, Washington, 2001—02, Kaye Scholer LLP, Washington, 2002—. Lawyer rep. Jud. Conf. D.C. Cir., 1981-83, 2004—; mem. adv. com. on procedures U.S. Ct. Appeals D.C. Cir., 2003—. Pres. Family and Child Svcs. Washington, 1986-88, trustee, 1978—. Mem. ABA, Am. Law Inst., Phi Beta Kappa. Republican. Office: Kaye Scholer LLP 901 Fifteenth St NW Ste 1100 Washington DC 20005-2327

ROSENTHAL, SUSAN BARBARA, retired librarian; b. Elberon Park, N.J., Apr. 7, 1946; d. Joseph and Anna (Warar) Rosenthal. BA, Montclair State Coll., 1967; MEd in Libr. Sci., U. Miami, 1973. Cert. media specialist, tchr., Fla., N.J. Tchr. Manasquan Bd. Edn. (N.J.), 1967-71; tech. svcs. libr. Oakland Park (Fla.) Libr., 1978-92, asst. dir., 1992-93, acting dir., 1993, ret. Author: (mag.) Galumph, 1965-67; contbr. A Micro Handbook for Small Libraries and Media Centers, 1983, 2d edit., 1986, 3d edit., 1991. Mem. Humane Soc., Broward County, Fla., 1981, WPBT-TV PBS sta., 1975-2000, So. Mus. Flight, 1997-2004, Friends of the Oakland Park Libr., 1998—, mem. luncheon com., 1999—, mem. planning com., 1999—; charter mem. Mus. of Discovery and Sci., 1989-96, U.S. Holocaust Meml. Mus., 1994—; donor Miami Book Fair Internat., 1990—, Cats Exclusive, Boca Raton (Fla.) Mus. Art, Survivors of the Shoah Visual History Found., Friends of the Oakland Park Libr., Sierra Club, WPBT-TV PBS Sta., Am. Coming Together. Recipient St. Cloud Tchg. award Société d'Enseignement, St. Cloud, France, 1966, 2 awards Libr. Pub. Rels. Coun., winner, 1983, hon. mention, 1985, cert. appreciation U.S. Holocaust Meml. Mus., 1996, 2000. Mem. ALA, AARP, Fla. Libr. Assn., Fla. Pub. Libr. Assn., Broward County Libr. Assn. (treas. 1981-83, continuing edn. com. 1980), Apple Libr. Users Group, Apple Computer Enjoyment Soc. (chpt. sec. 1984-87, corp. sec. 1985-89), Consumers Union, NFO Rsch., Wilderness Soc., World Wildlife Fund, Environ. Def. Fund, People for Ethical Treatment of Animals, Nat. Resources Def. Coun., Nature Conservancy, Nat. Wildlife Fedn., Mensa, actforchange.org, moveon.org, Procrastinators Club Am., Pi Delta Phi. Office: Bibliothèque Lamienne 1522 NE 34th Ct Oakland Park FL 33334-5305 E-mail: su5ro@hotmail.com.

ROSENTHAL, SUSAN R. pediatrician, educator; MD, Mount Sinai Sch. of Medicine, N.Y.C., 1977. Diplomate Pediatrics Am. Bd. Pediatrics, 1981, Pediatric Gastroenterology Am. Bd. Pediatrics, 1990. Intern in Pediatrics Bronx Mcpl. Hosp., N.Y.C., 1977—78; resident Boston Children's Hosp. Med. Ctr., 1978—80; fellow in Pediatric Gastroenterology and Nutrition Mass. Gen. Hosp., Boston, 1980—82; physician dept. Pediatrics Robert Wood Johnson U. Med. Group, New Brunswick, NJ, 1995—. Clin. assoc. prof. Pediatrics Robert Wood Johnson Univ. Hosp., New Brunswick, 1998—, asst. dean of students, 1998—. Office: Clin Acad Bldg Se 6140 125 Paterson St New Brunswick NJ 08901-1977

ROSENTHAL, WILLIAM J. lawyer; b. Balt., Nov. 4, 1920; s. Justin J. and Ray Marian (Stern) Rosenthal; m. Margaret Irwin Parker, July 4, 1956; children: Adriane Leigh, Jacqueline Rae, John Justin. AB, Johns Hopkins U., 1941; LL.B., U. Balt., 1950. Bar: Md. 1950. Adminstrv. asst. Office Price Adminstrn., Washington, 1941-42; assoc. Earle K. Shawe, Balt., 1951-67; ptnr. Shawe & Rosenthal (formerly Earle K. Shawe), Balt., 1967—. Lectr. U. Balt., 1952—56; mem. regional adv. coun. NLRB; vets. rep. Md. Constrn. Adv. Coun., 1946—49; lectr. NYU Conf. Labor Rels., 1981, Boston U. Labor Law Seminar, 1985; expert witness on labor law, legis. and congl. coms. Co-author: The Developing Labor Law; contbr. articles to profl. jours. Served to lt. USNR, 1942—46, ETO. Mem.: ABA, Balt. Bar Assn., Md. Bar Assn., Johns Hopkins Club, Suburban Club Baltimore County (bd. govs., pres.), Spiked Shoe Soc., Pi Delta Epsilon, Omicron Delta Kappa. Home: 8207 Cranwood Ct Baltimore MD 21208-1823 Office: Shawe & Rosenthal Sun Life Bldg Charles Center Baltimore MD 21201 Office Phone: 410-752-1040. E-mail: rosenthal@shawe.com.

ROSENWALD, E. JOHN, JR., former brokerage house executive, former investment banker; b. 1930; AB, Dartmouth Coll., 1952, MBA, 1953. With Bear Stearns Cos. Inc., N.Y.C., 1953—, gen. ptnr., 1962, mem., Office of the Pres., 1985—88, former vice-chmn., sr. mng. dir. Bd. dirs. Hasbro Inc., Nat. Ctr. on Addiction & Substance Abuse, Columbia U.*

ROSENWASSER, DONNA, management consulting company executive; CFO McKinsey & Co., Inc., N.Y.C. Office: McKinsey & Co Inc 55 E 52nd St Fl 18 New York NY 10055-0183

ROSENZWEIG, AMY, biochemist, educator; BA, Amherst Coll., 1988; PhD., MIT, 1992. NIH fellow Harvard Med. Sch., Dana Farber Cancer Inst.; asst. prof. of biochemistry, molecular Biology, and cell biology Northwestern U., 1997—2002, asst. prof. chem., 1997—2002, assoc. prof., 2002—. Recipient Camile and Henry Dreyfus Tchr - Scholar. award; fellow David and Lucile Packard, MacArthur Found., 2003. Office: Northwestern Univ Dept BMBCB Cook Hall 4162 2220 Campus Dr Evanston IL 60208

ROSENZWEIG, CHARLES LEONARD, lawyer; b. N.Y.C., Apr. 12, 1952; s. William and Frieda (Dechner) R.; m. Rya R. Mehler, June 14, 1975; children: Jessica Sara Neweshel, Erica Danielle. AB cum laude, Princeton U., 1974; JD, NYU, 1977. Bar: N.Y. 1978, U.S. Dist. Ct. (ea. and so. dists.) N.Y. 1978, U.S. Ct. Appeals (7th cir.) 1980, U.S. Ct. Internat. Trade 1981, U.S. Ct. Appeals (2d cir.) 1985. Assoc. Graubard, Moskovitz et al, N.Y.C., 1977-85; ptnr. Rand, Rosenzweig, Smith, Radley, Gordon & Burstein LLP, N.Y.C., 1987—. Mem. panel of neutrals comml. divsn. Supreme Ct. State N.Y. Editor NYU Jour. Internat. Law. and Politics. Chmn. of bd. Jewish Cmty. Ctr., Harrison, 1998-2000. Mem. ABA (internat. law sect.), N.Y. State Bar Assn. (co-chair internat. litig. com. 1995-98, mem. exec. com. comml. and fed. litig. sect.), NYU Alumni Assn. (chmn. jour. internat. law and politics alumni 1985-87), Assn. of Commercial Fin. Attys. Avocations: skiing, bicycling, tennis, scuba diving. Office: Rand Rosenzweig et al 605 3rd Ave New York NY 10158-0180 Home: 9 Hadley Rd Armonk NY 10504-2417 Office Phone: 212-687-7070. Business E-Mail: crosenweig@randrote.com.

ROSENZWEIG, HERBERT STEPHEN, stockbroker; b. Phila., Aug. 5, 1943; s. Morton and Helen (Katzen) R.; m. Myra Pauline Saltzburg, June 7, 1964; children: Helene, Michael, Elisa, Jeffrey. BS in Fin., Temple U., 1965. CFP. Stockbroker Walston & Co., Phila., 1967-73, Reynolds Securities, Phila., 1974, Merrill Lynch, Ontario, Calif., 1974—. Vol. Spl. Olympics, 1980-96; chmn. Pomona Valley Coun. Chs. Hunger Walk, 1995-97, 1999-2003; pres. Upland Youth Accountability Bd., 1995-97; mem. San Antonio Heights Citizens Patrol. Mem. Kiwanis (past pres., lt. gov. Divsn. 15 1992-93, Club Kiwanian of Yr., Divsn. Kiwanian of Yr. 1992). Republican. Jewish. Office: 4141 Inland Empire Blvd Ste 150 Ontario CA 91764-5007

ROSENZWEIG, MARK RICHARD, psychology educator; b. Rochester, N.Y., Sept. 12, 1922; s. Jacob and Pearl (Grossman) R.; m. Janine S.A. Chappat, Aug. 1, 1947; children: Anne Janine, Suzanne Jacqueline, Philip Mark. BA, U. Rochester, 1943, MA, 1944; PhD, Harvard U., 1949; hon. doctorate, U. René Descartes, Sorbonne, 1980, U. Louis Pasteur, Strasbourg, France, 1998. Postdoctoral rsch. fellow Harvard U., 1949-51; asst. prof. U. Calif., Berkeley, 1951-56, assoc. prof., 1956-60, prof. psychology, 1960-91, assoc. rsch. prof., 1958-59, rsch. prof., 1965-66, prof. emeritus, 1991—, prof. grad. studies, 1994—. Vis. prof. biology U. Sorbonne, Paris, 1973-74; mem. U.S. nat. com. for Internat. Union Psychol. Sci., NRC and NAS, 1984-96. Author: Biologie de la Mémoire, 1976, (with A.L. Leiman) Physiological Psychology, 1982, 2nd edit., 1989, (with M.J. Renner) Enriched and Impoverished Environments: Effects on Brain and Behavior, 1987, (with D. Sinha) La Recherche en Psychologie Scientifique, 1988, (with W.H. Holtzman, M. Sabourin and D. Bélanger) History of the International Union of Psychological Science, 2000; editor: (with P. Mussen) Psychology: An Introduction, 1973, 2nd edit., 1977, International Psychological Science: Progress, Problems, and Prospects, 1992, (with A.L. Leiman and S.M. Breedlove) Biological Psychology, 1996, 3d edit., 2002, (with S.M. Breedlove and N.V. Watson) 4th edit., 2004; co-editor: (with E.L. Bennett) Neural Mechanisms of Learning and Memory, 1976, (with L. Porter) Ann. Rev. of Psychology, 1968-94, (with K. Pawlik) International Handbook of Psychology, 2000; contbr. articles to profl. jours. Served with USN, 1944-46. Recipient Disting. Alumnus award U. Rochester; Fulbright rsch. fellow; faculty rsch. fellow Social Sci. Rsch. Coun., 1960-61; rsch. grantee NSF, USPHS, Easter Seal Found., Nat. Inst. Drug Abuse. Fellow AAAS, APA (Disting. Sci. Contbn. award 1982, Disting. Contbn. award for Internat. Advancement of Psychology 1997), Am. Psychol. Soc.; mem. NAS, NAACP (life), Am. Physiol. Soc., Internat. Union Psychol. Sci. (hon. life, mem. exec. com. 1996—, v.p. 1980-84, pres. 1988-92, past pres. 1992-96), Internat. Brain Rsch. Orgn., Soc. Exptl. Psychologists, Soc. for Neurosci., Société Française de Psychologie, Sierra Club (life), Common Cause, Fulbright Assn. (life), Phi Beta Kappa, Sigma Xi. Office: U Calif Dept Psychology 3210 Tolman Hall Berkeley CA 94720-1650

ROSENZWEIG, PEGGY A. state legislator; b. Detroit, Nov. 5, 1936; married; 5 children. BS, U. Wis., Milw., 1978; postgrad., Wayne State U. Wis. state assemblyman Dist. 98, 1982-92, Dist. 14, 1993; mem. Wis. Senate from 5th dist, Madison, 1993—. Former ranking minority mem. Health Com. Former dir. comty. rels. Milw. Regional Med. Ctr.; former pres. Med. Coll. Wis. Mem. LWV. Address: 6236 Upper Pkwy N Wauwatosa WI 53213-2430 Office: Wis State Senate State Capitol PO Box 7882 Madison WI 53707-7882

ROSENZWEIG, RICHARD STUART, publishing company executive; b. Appleton, Wis., Aug. 8, 1935; s. Walter J. and Rose (Bahcall) R. BS, Northwestern U., 1957; Advanced Mgmt. Program, Harvard U., 1975. Credit rep. Dun & Bradstreet, Inc., 1958; with Playboy Enterprises, Inc., 1958—, exec. asst. to pres., 1963-73, sr. v.p., dir., 1973-82, dir. mktg., 1974-82, exec. v.p. publs. group, 1975-77, exec. v.p., head West Coast ops., 1977-80, exec. v.p. corp. affairs, 1980-82, exec. v.p., chmn. emeritus, 1982—; pres. Playboy Jazz Festivals, 1989—. Dir. I. Bahcall Industries, Appleton; exec. v.p. (dir. 1973—) Playboy Enterprises; chmn. Alta Loma Enterment, 2000—. Trustee L.A. Film Expn.; mem. 2d decade coun. Am. Film Inst.; bd. dirs. Mus. Contemporary Art, Chgo., Periodical and Book Assn. Am., Internat. Inst. Kidney Diseases of UCLA, Children of Night, Maple Ctr. Beverly Hills; mem., chmn. bd. UCLA Legis. Network, Town Hall of Calif.; adv. bd. West Hollywood Mktg. Corp., 1985—; bd. dirs. So. Calif. ACLU, 1985—; mem. Los Angeles County Mus.; apptd. to blue ribbon com. project West Coast Gateway. With AUS, 1957; chmn. Modern and Contemporary Art Coun. L.A. County Mus. of Art.; pres. Beverly Hills Cultural Ctr.; exec. com. Henry Mancini Inst.; v.p. Faternity of Friends music Ctr. Recipient Do-ers award, 1988, Beverly Hills medal Beverly Hills City Coun., 1993. Mem. Am. Mktg. Aslsn., L.A. Pub. Affairs Officers Assn., UCLA Chancellor's Assocs., Pres.'s Cir., Beverly Hills C. of C. (bd. dirs., visitors' bur., v.p.), Beverly Hills Fine Art Commn. (chmn.), Beverly Hills Econ. Devel. Coun., Founders Circle of Music Ctr., Pub. Affairs Coun., Craft and Folk Art Mus., Pres.' Coun. and Contemporary ARts Coun. L.A. Mus. Contemporary Art, The Am. Cinematheque (groundbreaker), Variety Club So. Calif. (bd. dirs.). Office: Playboy Enterprises Inc 2706 Media Center Dr Los Angeles CA 90065-1733

ROSENZWEIG, SAUL, psychologist, educator, administrator; b. Boston, Feb. 7, 1907; s. David and Etta (Tuttle) R.; m. Louise Ritterskamp, Mar. 21, 1941; children: Julia, Ann. AB summa cum laude, Harvard U., 1929, MA, 1930, PhD, 1932. Research assoc. Harvard Psychol. Clinic, 1929-34, Worcester (Mass.) State Hosp., 1934-43; affiliate prof. Clark U., Worcester, 1938-43; chief psychologist Western State Psychiat. Ins. and Clinic, Pitts., 1943-48; lectr. psychology U. Pitts., 1943-48; assoc. prof. psychology and med. psychology Washington U., St. Louis, 1949-51, prof., 1951-75, prof. emeritus, 1975—; chief psychologist Child Guidance Clinic, 1949-59. Cons., mem. life scis. study sect. NIH, 1964-68; mng. dir. Found. for Idiodynamics and the Creative Process, 1972—; adj. prof. psychology St. Louis U., 1996—. Author: (with Kate L. Kogan) Psychodiagnosis, Grune and Stratton, 1949, Rosenzweig Picture-Frustration Study, 1948, Aggressive Behavior and the Rosenzweig Picture-Frustration Study, 1978, Freud and Experimental Psychology: The Emergence of Idiodynamics, 1986, Sally Beauchamp's Career, 1987, Freud, Jung, and Hall the King-Maker, 1992, 2d edit., 1994; assoc. editor: Jour. Abnormal and Social Psychology, 1950-56; cons. editor: Psychol. Monographs, 1948-57, Zeitschrift für Diagnostische Psychologie und Persönlichkeitsforschung, 1953-58, Diagnostica, 1959—; adv. editor: Jour. Cons. Psychology, 1959-64, Jour. Abnormal Psychology, 1965-67; mem. editorial bd. Aggressive Behavior, 1974—; contbr. articles to profl. jours. Fellow Am. Psychol. Assn. (rep. internat. group for Coordination Psychiatry and Psychol. Methods 1955-61), Am. Psychopathol. Assn.; mem. Internat. Soc. for Research on Aggression (founding pres. 1972-73, archivist 1981-88), Soc. Prof. Emeriti Washington U. (founding pres. 1978), Sigma Xi, Phi Beta Kappa. Home: 8029 Washington Ave Saint Louis MO 63114-6333 Office: Washington U PO Box 1125 Saint Louis MO 63188-1125 Office Phone: 314-429-0080.

ROSES, ALLEN DAVID, neurologist, educator; b. Paterson, N.J., Feb. 21, 1943; BS in Chemistry summa cum laude, U. Pitts., 1963; MD, U. Pa., 1967. Diplomate Am. Bd. Psychiatry and Neurology. Intern Hosp. of the U. Pa., Phila., 1967—68; resident in neurology N.Y. Neurol. Inst., Columbia U., N.Y.C., 1968—70; chief resident divsn. neurology Duke U. Med. Ctr., 1970—71, assoc. in medicine divsn. neurology, 1970—73, asst. prof. medicine divsn. neurology, 1973—76, assoc. prof. medicine divsn. neurology, 1976—79, asst. prof. biochemistry, 1977—89, prof. neurology dept. medicine, 1979—97, prof. neurobiology, 1989—97, Jefferson-Pilot Corp. prof. neurobiology and neurology, 1990—97, chief divsn. neurology dept. medicine, 1977—97; v.p., worldwide dir. genetics Glaxo Wellcome R&D, Research Triangle Park, NC, 1997—. Fellow Nat. Multiple Sclerosis Soc., Lab. Neurochemistry, Divsn. Neurology, Duke U. Med. Ctr., Lab. Virology, Divsn. Pediat. Neurology, Duke U. Med. Ctr., 1971-73, dir. Duke Neuromuscular Rsch. Clinic, 1974—, dir. neurosciences study program Sch. Medicine, 1975-85, investigator Howard Hughes Med. Inst., 1977-81, dir. Duke Muscular Dystrophy Assn. Clinic, 1979—, Joseph and Kathleen Bryan Alzheimer's Disease Rsch. Ctr., 1985—; cons. neurologist N.C. State Hosp. Sys., Cherry Hosp., Goldsboro, 1973-76, N.C. State Hosp. Sys., Lenox Baker Hosp., Durham, 1974—; chmn. internat. sci. adv. com. Australian Neuromuscular Rsch. Inst., 1989-92; sci. adv. Cyprus Isnt. Neurology and Genetics. Assoc. editor Molecular and Cellular Neuroscis., 1989-94; mem. editl. bd. Amyloidosis Jour., 1993-96, Neurobiology of Disease, 1993—, Fondation Ipsen, Rsch. and Perspectives in Neuroscis., 1994—, Alzheimer's Rsch., 1995—, Contemporary Neurology, 1995—, Alezheimer's Disease Rev., 1995—; contbr. articles to profl. jours. Capt. USAFR, 1967-72. Recipient Rsch. Career Devel. award Nat. Inst. Neurol. and Communicative Disorders and Stroke, 1976, Best in the Triangle-Aerobics Instr. award Spectator Mag., 1986, Leadership in Excellence in Alzheimer's Disease award Nat. Inst. Aging, 1988, Met.-Life Found. prize for outstanding med. rsch., 1994, Potamkin prize for Alzheimer's Disease Rsch., 1994, Internat. Alzheimer's Disease award Parke-Davis, 1996, award for muscular dystrophy rsch. Svc. Merchandise, 1997; Basil O'Connor Starter Rsch. grantee Nat. Found. March of Dimes. Fellow Am. Acad. Neurology; mem. Am. Soc. for Clin. Investigation, Am. Soc. for Clin. Rsch., Am. Neurol. Assn. (trustee 1982-84, 96—), Assn. Univ. Profs. Neurology, Assn. Brit. Neurologists (hon. fgn. mem.), Muscular Dystrophy Assn. (genetics task force and rev. com. 1989—, med. adv. com. 1990—, nat. v.p. 1994—), Alzheimer's Assn. (med. sci. adv. com. 1989—, chair 1996—, Sigma Tau award 1990, Rita Hayward Gala award 1994), Phi Beta Kappa. Office: Glaxo Wellcome 5 Moore Dr Research Triangle Park NC 27709

ROSETT, DANIEL J. film company executive; Degree in bus. and econ., U. Calif., Santa Barbara, 1984. CPA. Mgr. KPMG Peat Marwick; with Walt Disney Co., exec. dir. studio ops.; v.p., corp. controller MGM Studios, 1994—95, sr. v.p. fin. ops., 1995—98, exec. v.p. studio fin. and ops., 1998—2001, exec. v.p. mktg. and distribution, 2001—04; pres. United Artists, 2004—. Office: United Artists Corp 10250 Constellation Blvd Los Angeles CA 90067*

ROSHEL, JOHN ALBERT, JR., orthodontist; b. Terre Haute, Ind., Apr. 7, 1941; s. John Albert and Mary M. (Griglione) R.; m. Kathy Roshel; children: John Albert III, James Livingston, Angela Kay. BS, Ind. State U., 1963; DDS, Ind. U., 1966; MS, U. Mich., 1968. Individual practice dentistry specializing in orthodontics, Terre Haute, 1968—. Mem. ADA, Am. Assn. Orthodontists, Terre Haute C. of C., Terre Haute Country Club, Lions, Elks, K.C., Lambda Chi Alpha, Delta Sigma Delta, Omicron Kappa Upsilon. Roman Catholic. Home: 15 E Wedgeway Dr Terre Haute IN 47802-4983 Office: 4241 S 7th St Terre Haute IN 47802-4367 Personal E-mail: drjrosh@aol.com.

ROSHKO, ANATOL, aeronautical engineer; b. Bellevue, Alta., Can., July 15, 1923; came to the U.S., 1950; married, 1957; 2 children. BSc, U. Alta, 1945; MS, Calif. Inst. Tech., 1947, PhD in Aero. Engring., 1952. Instr. math. U. Alta., 1945—46, lectr. engring., 1949—50; rsch. fellow Calif. Inst. Tech., Pasadena, 1952—55, asst. prof. to prof., 1955—85; acting. dir. Grad Aero. Labs, Pasadena, 1985—87; Theodore Von Karman prof. aeronautics Calif. Inst. Tech., Pasadena, 1985—, prof. emeritus, 1994—. Sci. liaison officer Office Naval Rsch., London, 1961-62; cons. McDonnell Douglas Corp., 1954-90, Rocketdyne Corp. Divsn., Rockwell Internat., 1984-90; founding dir. Wind Engring. Rsch. Inc., 1970; mem. Aero. & Space Engring. Bd., 1988-93. Recipient Timoshenko medal ASME, 1999; named to U. Alta. Alumni Wall of Recognition, 1998. Fellow AAAS, AIAA (Dryden Rsch. lectr. 1976, Fluid Dynamics award 1998), Am. Phys. Soc. (Fluid Dynamics prize 1987), Indian Acad. Scis. (hon.), Can. Aeronautics and Space Inst.; mem. NAS, ASME, NAE. Office: Calif Inst Tech Mail Sta 105-50 1201 E California Blvd Pasadena CA 91125-0001

ROSHOLT, ROBERT A. financial executive; b. Mar. 24, 1950; BA, St. Olaf Coll.; MBA, U. Rochester. Asst. v.p. Profit Planning Group First Chicago NBD Corp., Chgo., 1974-82, mem. Treasury Dept., 1982-87, head Treasury Dept., sr. v.p., 1987; former CFO First Chgo. NBD Corp., Chgo.; exec. v.p. First Nat. Bank of Chgo., AON Corp., Chgo.; exec. v.p. for fin. and investments of Nationwide, 2003—. Office: 1 Nationwide Pl Columbus OH 43215

ROSHON, GEORGE KENNETH, manufacturing executive; b. July 30, 1942; s. George Washington III and Ellen Eleanor (Knopf) R.; m. Ella Maye Barndt, Nov. 21, 1964; 1 child, Kirsten Renee. BSEE, Pa. State U., 1964; MS, Drexel U., 1974, postgrad., 1974-75. Registered profl. engr., Pa. Sr. engr. Am. Electronics Labs., Inc., Colmar, Pa., 1966-69; v.p. engring. Acrodyne Industries, Inc., Montgomeryville, Pa., 1969-74; mgr. electric design W-J divsn. Hayes-Albion Corp., Norristown, Pa., 1974-78; mgr. quality assurance PSMBD GE, Phila., 1978-80, mem. exec. com. electronics test coun., 1980-83, mgr. advanced sys. engring., 1983-84, mgr. comm. engring. Malvern, Pa., 1984-86; v.p. quality assurance Hercules Aerospace Display Sys., Inc., Hatfield, Pa., 1986-88, v.p. engring., 1988-90; mgr. Electronics Group Westcode, Inc., Malvern, 1991-92; v.p. mfg. Epitaxx, Inc., West Trenton, N.J., 1992-99, v.p. ops. JDSUNIPHASE Divsn., 1999—. Patentee in field. Served to lt. USNR, 1964-66. Mem. NSPE, Am. Soc. Quality Control (cert. quality engr., quality auditor), Pa. Soc. Profl. Engrs., Gen. Electric Mgmt. Assn., Elfun Soc., Drexel U. Alumni Assn., Pa. State U. Alumni Assn., Tri-County Arabian Horse Assn. Home: 454 Eagle Ln Lansdale PA 19446-1547 Office: 7 Graphics Dr Trenton NJ 08628-1547

ROSHONG, DEE ANN DANIELS, dean, educator; b. Kansas City, Mo., Nov. 22, 1936; d. Vernon Edmund and Doradell (Kellogg) Daniels; m. Richard Lee Roshong, Aug. 27, 1960 (div.). BMusEd., U. Kans., 1958; MA in Counseling and Guidance, Stanford U., 1960; postgrad., Fresno State U., U. Calif.; EdD, U. San Francisco, 1980. Counselor, psychometrist Fresno City Coll., 1961-65; counselor, instr. psychology Chabot Coll., Hayward, Calif., 1965-75, coord. counseling svcs. Livermore, Calif., 1975-81, asst. dir. student pers. svcs., 1981-89, Las Positas Coll., Livermore, Calif., 1989-91, assoc. dean student svcs., 1991-94, dean student svcs., 1991—2003, life coach, 2000—; counselor Experience Unltd., Pleasant Hill, Calif., 2004—. Writer, coord. I, A Woman Symposium, 1974, Feeling Free to Be You and Me symposium, 1975, All for the Family Symposium, 1976, I Celebrate Myself Symposium, 1978, Person to Person in Love and Work Symposium, 1978, The Healty Person in Mind and Spirit Symposium, 1980, Change Symposium, 1981, Sources of Strength Symposium, 1982, Love and Friendship Symposium, 1983, Self Esteem Symposium, 1984, Trust Symposium, 1985, Prime Time: Making the Most of This Time in Your Life Symposium, 1986, Symposium in Healing, 1987, How to Live in the World and Still Be Happy Symposium, 1988, Student Success is a Team Effort, Sound Mind, Sound Body Symposium, 1989, Creating Life's Best Symposium, 1990, Choices Symposium, 1991, Minding the Body, Mending the Mind Symposium, 1992, Healing through Love and Laughter Symposium, 1993, Healing Ourselves Changing the World Symposium, 1994, Finding Your Path Symposium, 1995, Build the Life You Want Symposium, 1996, Making Peace With Yourself and Your Relationships Symposium, 1997, Everyday Sacred Symposium, 1998, Wisdom of the Heart Symposium, 1999, Inner Wisdom Symposium, 2000, Second Half of Life Symposium, 2001, A Celebration of Life Symposium, 2003, Viewing Mental Health and Mental Illness From a Multi-Cultural Perspective Symposium, 2004, others; mem. cast TV prodns. Eve and Co., Best of Our Times, Cowboy; chmn. Falling Awake Symposium, 2002, Celebration of Life Symposium, 2003, Calif. C.C. Chancellor's Task Force on Counseling, Statewide Regional Counseling Facilitators, 1993-95, Statewide Conf. Emotionally Disturbed Students in Calif. C.C.s, 1982—, Conf. on the Under Represented Student in Calif. C.C.s, 1986, Conf. on High Risk Students, 1989. Author: Counseling Needs of Comunity College Students, 1980. Bd. dirs. Teleios Sinetar Ctr., Ctr. for Cmty. Dispute Resolution, 1998—, Pleasanton Youth Collaborative Bd., 1997-2002, Pleasanton Youth Master Plan Bd., 1998—; choir dir., 1996-99; pres. Tri-Valley Unity Ch. bd., 1998, Tri-Valley Haven bd., 2000—, Calif. State U. at Hayward Inst. of Mental Illness and Wellness Edn. bd., 2000—, Ellis Life Coach Tng., 1999—; title III activity dir. Las Positas Coll., 1995-99, dir. pace program, 1999-2003, dir. quest program, 2000-03. Mem.: Calif C.C. Counselors Assn. (svc. award 1986—87, award for Outstanding and Disting. Svc. 1986—87, Pleasanton Mayor's award 2000—01, 2002), Calif. Assn. C. C. (chmn. commn. on students svcs. 1979—84), Assn. Counseling and Devel., Nat. Assn. Women Deans and Counselors, Western Psychol. Assn., Assn. Humanistic Psychologists. Home and Office: 1856 Harvest Rd Pleasanton CA 94566-5456 E-mail: deeroshong@comcast.net.

ROSIC, GEORGE STEVE, lawyer; b. Kenosha, Wis., Dec. 12, 1951; s. Momcilo and Loni R.; m. Mary J. Marselus, June 7, 1976; children: Nicholas Andrew, Gregory George. BA, Knox Coll., 1974; JD, U. Chgo., 1977. Bar: Ill. 1977. Ptnr. Arvey, Hodes, Costello & Burman, Chgo., 1986-91, Wildman, Harrold, Allen & Dixon, Chgo., 1992-94; assoc. gen. counsel MMI Cos., Inc., Deerfield, Ill., 1995-2000; ptnr. Michael Best & Friedrich and predecessor firm, Chgo., 2000—02. Author: The Illinois Corporation, BNA Corp. Practice Series Portfolio, 1986. Mem. ABA, Chgo. Bar Assn. (chair corp. law com. 1995-96), Phi Beta Kappa. Serbian Orthodox. Office: 1603 Orrington Ave Ste 800 Evanston IL 60201

ROSICA, GABRIEL ADAM, manufacturing executive, electrical engineer; b. N.Y.C., Jan. 9, 1940; s. Gabriel J. and Elma (P.) R.; m. Bettina R. Nardozzi, Sept. 8, 1962; children: Gregory A., Julie Ann, Mark A. BA in Math. and Physics, Columbia U., 1962, BSEE, 1963; MSEE, Rensselaer Poly. Inst., 1966; MBA, Boston U., 1971. Registered profl. engr., Mass. Rsch. engr. United Aircraft Research Labs., East Hartford, Conn., 1963-67; mgr. electronic devel. The Foxboro (Mass.) Co., 1967-75, gen. mgr. U.S. div., 1975-77, v.p., 1977-80; pres., chief operating officer Modular Computer Systems, Inc., Ft. Lauderdale, Fla., 1980-82, pres., chmn., chief exec. officer, 1982-88; pvt. practice bus. cons. Boca Raton, Fla., 1988-91; sr. v.p. Elsag Bailey Corp., Pepper Pike, Ohio, 1991-92; exec. v.p. Bailey Controls Co., Wickliffe, Ohio, 1993-94; COO Bailey Control Co., Wickliffe, Ohio, 1994-96; sr. v.p. Keithley Instruments, Solon, Ohio, 1996-2001, exec. v.p., 2001—. Chmn. engring. adv. coun. U. Fla., Gainesville, 1987-90; chmn. hi tech adv. coun. Coll. Boca Raton, Fla., 1987-90. Mem. Pres.'s Coun. Fla. Atlantic U., Boca Raton, 1987-91; trustee Nova U., Ft. Lauderdale, Fla., 1987-94. Recipient Boston U. Chair, 1971, Outstanding Young Engr. of Year award Mass. Soc. Profl. Engrs., 1974. Mem. IEEE (sr. mem.), Am. Electronics Assn. (bd. dirs. 1987, chmn Fla. bd. dirs. 1987-88), Fla. High Tech. and Industry Coun. Home: 35640 Spicebush Ln Solon OH 44139-5063 Office: Keithley Instruments Inc 28775 Aurora Rd Solon OH 44139-1891 E-mail: gabe.rosica@att.net.

ROSIN, LINDSAY ZWEIG, clinical psychologist; b. San Antonio, Oct. 28, 1954; s. Morris and Ethel (Rosenberg) R.; m. Susana Aceituno, Sept. 3, 1981; children: Lauren, Melanie. BA, U. Tex., 1975; MA, Xavier U., 1979; PhD, Fla. Inst. Tech., 1985. Lic. psychologist, Tex. Psychology assoc. Dayton (Ohio) Mental Health Ctr., 1980-81, Cin. Neurological Assocs., Cin., 1981-82; intern VA Med. Ctr., Houston, 1982-83; coord. outpatient services Houston Child Guidance Ctr., Houston, 1983-84; fellow Med. Ctr. del Oro Hosp., Houston, 1984-85; staff psychologist Mid-City Mental Health Mental Retardation, Houston, 1985-89; clin. asst. prof. psychology Baylor Coll. Medicine, Houston, 1985—2001; pvt. practice Houston, 1986—; psychologist St. Joseph Hosp., Houston, 1987—. Psychologist cons. Mid-City Mental Health Mental Retardation, Houston, 1989-2003, Tex. Children's Hosp., 1993-96. Contbr. articles to profl. jours. Recipient Outstanding Contbn. to Psychology award, Ohio Assn. Psychologists, 1982. Mem. Am. Psychol. Assn., Tex. Psychol. Assn., Houston Psychol. Assn., Internat. Neuropsychological Soc., Gerontological Soc. Am. Home: PO Box 20671 Houston TX 77225-0671 Office: 3730 Kirby Dr Ste 825 Houston TX 77098-3979 E-mail: lrosin0000@aol.com.

ROSIN, R. THOMAS, anthropologist, educator; b. L.A., Calif., Feb. 18, 1938; s. Nat Rosin and Elizabeth Kaufman; m. Gail Lee Wread, Oct. 26, 1997; children: Shawn Michelle, Miranda Sahale. PhD, U. Calif. Berkeley, 1968; BA, Reed Coll., 1960. Asst. prof. Carleton Coll., Northfield, Minn., 1966—70; prof. anthropology Sonoma State U., Rohnert Park, Calif., 1970—2002. Author: (journal article) Anthropology & Education Quarterly (selection for Anniversary Edit., 1984), (2 entries) Ency. Vernacular Architecture in World, (book) Land Reform and Agrarian Change.; contbr. articles to profl. jours. Recipient Meritorious Performance and Profl. Promise Award, Sonoma State U., 1987, Meritorious Performance and Profl. Promise award, 1989; Fulbright Rsch. Fellow, Fulbright Found., 1993—94, Sr. Fellowship for rsch. in India, Am. Inst. for Indian Studies, 1987, 1981—82, Travel Grant, NSF, 1978, Rajasthan Studies Conf. Travel Grant to Jaipur, India, Ford Found., Indian Coun. of Social Sci. Rsch., Indian Coun. for Hist. Rsch., 1987, Jr. Fellowship for doctoral rsch., Am. Inst. for Indian Studies, 1963—65, Nat. Def. Fgn. Lang. Fellowship, U.S. Dept. of Edn., 1962—63, Grad. Scholarship, U. Chgo., 1960—62, Nat. Def. Fgn. Lang. fellowship, U.S. Dept. Edn., 1963—64, 1965—66. Fellow: Am. Anthrop. Assn. (assoc.). Achievements include research in demonstration of methodologies for the case study of indigenous computational skills, water management practices, and conceptions about the recycling of wastes in India. Avocations: wilderness exploration, backpacking, bicycle touring. Home: 976 Miller Ave Berkeley CA 94708-1406 Office: Sonoma State University 1801 E Cotati Ave Rohnert Park CA 94928 E-mail: tom.rosin@sonoma.edu.

ROSINEK, JEFFREY, judge; b. N.Y.C., Sept. 13, 1941; s. Isidore and Etta (Kramer) R.; m. Sandra Gwen Rosen, Aug. 7, 1977; 1 child, Ian David. BA in History, U. Miami, 1963; postgrad. in polit. sci., JD, 1974. Bar: Fla. 1974. Tchr. Coral Gables (Fla.) High Sch., 1963-78; sole practice Miami, 1974-76; assoc. Tendrich and Todd, Miami, 1976-77; ptnr. Todd, Rosinek & Blake, Miami, 1984-86; judge Dade County Ct., Miami, 1986-89, 11th Jud. Cir., Fla., 1990—, assoc. adminstr. appeal divsn., 1999—; judge Miami Dade County Drug Ct., 1999—. Instr. Boston U., 1975; mem. faculty Fla. Coll. Advanced Jud. Studies, 1992—, Nat. Jud. Coll., 2000—; lectr., presenter in field of juvenile justice and substance abuse. Contbr. articles to profl. jours. Chmn. Miami Environ. Rsch. Adv. Com., 1969-73; mem. Miami Beach Tranportation commn., Nat. Bicentennial Competition on the Constitution and Bill of Rights com., Dade County Youth Adv. Bd., 1973-75; bd. dirs. U. Miami Law Sch., treas., 1973-75; bd. dirs. U. Miami Law Sch., treas. alumni, jud. dir.; past pres. Dade County Young Dems.; mem. Congl. Civilian Rev. Bd., 1975-90, chmn., 1976-78; bd. dirs., treas. Fla. Congl. Com., Legal Svcs. Greater Miami; chmn., 1976-78; chmn. Dade County adv. Coun. Close-Up Found.; Fla. chmn. Project Concern Internat.; internat. state chmn. Fla. Walk for Mankind, Project Concern, legal adv. com., Kiwanis, 1982-86; v.p. Beth David Congregation, 1982-86; bd. trustees Haven Ctr.; bd. dirs., treas., organizer South Miami-Kendall pro bono project Legal Svc. of Greater Miami, 1983-86; traffic rev. com. Dade County, 1987-92; bd. dirs. Fla. Law Related Edn., 1988—, Adv. Program, 1988—; mem. Miami-Dade County task force for homeless, 1992-94; active Dade Coalition for the Homeless, 1992—, Dade County Homeless Trust, 1993-2001, 2003-, chmn. criminal justice com.; chmn. Beck Mus. Judaica, 1988—; ednl. dir. Tempel Judea; jud. cir. rep. Dept. corrections "Boot Camp" program, 1994-98; 11th jud. cir. organizer, rep. Homeless Alt. Rehab. Tracking Program, 1994—, rep. Comprehensive Homeless Integration Program (CHIP), 1992-94, chair Fla. 1st Annual Edn. Seminar/Retreat, 1995, Eugent P. Spellman Am. Inn of Ct., 1996—, bd. dirs., 2002—, sec., 2003-2004, South Fla. Super Bowl XXXIII Host Com.; 1st v.p. Coral Gables High Sch. Parent-Tchr.-Students Assn., 1995-96, pres., 1996-98; mem. adv. bd. Coconut Grove Art Festival, 2002—. Recipient award Jewish Theol. Sem., 1978, Outstanding Law Student award Merit award Profl. Law Enforcement Assn., appreciation award Liberty City Christian Assn., Dade County Chief of Police Svc. award, 2001. Mem.: ABA (task force reduction of litig. cost and delay 1995—), Fla. Assn. Drug Ct. Profls. (inaugural chair), Nat. Ct. Reporters Assn. (strategic com. 1993—), Am. Judges Assn. (bd. govs. 1988—92, domestic violence com. 1990—96, chair 32d Ann. Edn. Conf., Miami Beach 1992, sec. 1992—93, 2d v.p. 1993—94, 1st v.p. 1994—95, chair fed.-state rels. com. 1994—96, pres. 1996—97, exec. com. 1997, chair nominations com. 1997, coord. Close-UP Found. project 1997—, chair 38th Ann. Edn. Conf., Orlando 1998, edn. com. 1998—, exec. com. 2000—01, Image of Judiciary com.), Bar and Gavel Soc., Wig and Robe (chancellor 1973—74), Fla. Conf. Cir. Ct. Judges (criminal justice com. 1995—), Cuban Am. Bar Assn., Miami Beach Bar Assn. (bd. dirs.), Fla. Bar Assn. (rules com. family law sect. 1984—87, jud. nominating procedures com.), Coral Gables Bar Assn., South Miami-Kendall Bar Assn. (past pres.), Dade County Bar Assn. (criminal cts. com. 1994—), Greater Miami C. of C. (v.p. permanent housing 1996—98, pres. 1999—2000, Carrefour Housing Corp. for homeless), U. Miami Law Sch. Alumni Assn. (sec.-treas. 1985—87, jud. dir. 1987—), Chabad of Dade (bd. dirs. 1999—), Dade Ptnrs., Miami-Dade Lions Club (charter), Key Internat. (pres. 1980—81, 1994—95, sec. 1995—, counselor Fla. dist., Key of Honor 1979, honoree 1984), Biscayne Bay Kiwanis (pres. 1994—, disting. past pres., Major Emphasis chmn., lt. gov. Fla. Dist., Kiwanian of Yr. 1983—84), Kiwanis Internat. (life). Home: 535 Bird Rd Coral Gables FL 33146-1307 Office: 1351 NW 12th St Miami FL 33125-1644 Office Phone: 305-548-5103. E-mail: jefaroz@aol.com.

ROSINSKI, EDWIN FRANCIS, medical educator; b. Buffalo, June 25, 1928; s. Theodore Joseph and Josephine M. (Wolski) R.; m. Jeanne C. Hueniger, Oct. 27, 1951; children: John T., Mary E., Sarah J. BS, SUNY, Buffalo, 1950; EdM, U. Buffalo, 1957, EdD, 1959. Prof. health scis. Med. Coll. Va., Richmond, 1959-66; dep. asst. sec. HEW, Washington, 1966-68; exec. vice chancellor U. Calif., San Francisco, 1968-72, prof., 1972-94; prof. emeritus medicine & pharmacy, 1994—. Adv. Rockefeller Found., N.Y.C., 1962-67, WHO, Geneva, 1962-78, Imperial Com. Health, Tehran, Iran, 1974-77; cons. Stanford Research Inst., Menlo Park, Calif., 1975-79. Author: The Assistant Medical Officer, 1965; contbr. over 100 articles to profl. jours. Served with USAF, 1950-54. Recipient spl. citation HEW, 1968, Merrell Flair award, 1991; named disting. prof. Australian Vice Chancellors Office, 1974, disting. vis. prof. Tulane U., New Orleans, 1983. Fellow AAAS; mem. Assn. Am. Med. Colls. (Merrel Flair award), Am. Ednl. Research Assn., Soc. Health and Human Values (founding mem.), Calif. Pharmacists Assn. (hon.), Phi Delta Kappa. Roman Catholic. Avocation: physical fitness. Home: 80 Sotelo Ave San Francisco CA 94116-1423

ROSITA, ALMA See DAVIES, ALMA

ROSKAM, JAN, aerospace engineer; b. The Hague, The Netherlands, Feb. 22, 1930; arrived in U.S., 1957; s. Kommer Jan and Agatha (Bosman) Roskam; m. Janice Louise Thomas-Barron, Dec. 21, 1994. MA in Aerospace Engring., Tech. U. Delft, 1954; PhD in Aeros. and Astronautics, U. Wash., 1965. Asst. chief designer Aviolanda Aircraft Co., Netherlands, 1954-57; sr. aerodynamics engr. Cessna Aircraft Co., Wichita, Kans., 1957-59; sr. group engr. Boeing Co., Wichita and Seattle, 1959-67; prof. emeritus aerospace engring. U. Kans., Lawrence, 1967—; pres. Design, Analysis and Rsch. Corp., 1991—. Cons. to govt. and industry. Author: Airplane Flight Dynamics and Automatic Flight Controls, 2 vols., 1979; co-author: Airplane Aerodynamics and Performance, 1981, Airplane Design, Part I-VIII, 1986, Roskam's Airplane War Stories, 2002. Served to 1st lt. Royal Netherlands Air Force, 1954—56. Fellow: AIAA, Soc. Automotive Engrs.; mem.: Exptl. Aircraft Assn., U.S. Chess Fedn., Koninklijk Instituut van Ingenieurs, Royal Aero. Soc., Am. Def. Preparedness Assn., Air Force Assn., Internat. Wildlife Assn., Aircraft Owners and Pilots Assn., Omicron Delta Kappa, Sigma Gamma Tau, Tau Beta Pi, Sigma Xi. Office: U Kans 2004 Lea Hl Lawrence KS 66045-0001 Personal E-mail: roskam@sunflower.com. Business E-Mail: roskam@darcorp.com.

ROSKENS, RONALD WILLIAM, international business consultant; b. Spencer, Iowa, Dec. 11, 1932; s. William E. and Delores A.L. (Beving) R.; m. Lois Grace Lister, Aug. 22, 1954; children: Elizabeth, Barbara, Brenda, William. BA, U. No. Iowa, 1953, MA, 1955, LHD (hon.), 1985; PhD, U. Iowa, 1958; LLD (hon.), Creighton U., 1978, Huston-Tillotson Coll., 1981, Midland Luth. Coll., 1984, Hastings Coll., 1981; LittD (hon.), Nebr. Wesleyan U., 1981; PhD (hon.), Ataturk U., Turkey, 1987; LHD (hon.), U. Akron, 1987; DSc (hon.), Jayewardenepura U., Sri Lanka, 1991; LHD (hon.), Am. Coll. of Greece, Athens, 1994. Lic. min. United Ch. of Christ (Congl. and E&R). Tchr. Minburn (Iowa) High Sch., 1954, Woodward (Iowa) State Hosp., summer 1954; asst. counselor to men State U. Iowa, 1956-59; dean of men, asst. prof. spl. edn. Kent (Ohio) State U., 1959-63, assoc. prof., then prof., 1963-72, asst. to pres., 1963-66, dean for adminstrn., 1968-71, exec. v.p., prof. ednl. adminstrn., 1971-72; chancellor, prof. ednl. adminstrn. U. Nebr., Omaha, 1972-76; pres. U. Nebr. System, 1977-89, pres. emeritus, 1989; hon. prof. East China Normal U., Shanghai, 1985; adminstr. USAID, Washington, 1990-92; pres. Action Internat., Inc., Omaha, 1993-96, Global Connections, Inc., Omaha, 1996—. Interim exec. officer Omaha Pub. Libr., 1996-98; mem. Bus.-Higher Edn. Forum, 1979-89, exec. com., 1984-87; mem. govtl. relations com. Am. Council Edn., 1979-83, bd. dirs., 1981-86, vice chair, 1983-84, chair, 1984-85; chmn. com. on financing higher edn. Nat. Assn. State Univs. and Land Grant Colls., 1978-83, vice chmn. com. on financing higher edn., 1983-84, chmn. com. on fed. student fin. assistance, 1981-87; mem. nat. adv. com. on accreditation and instl. eligibility U.S. Dept. Edn., 1983-86, chmn., bd. dirs., 1986; exec. bd. North Cen. Assn., 1979-84, chmn. exec. bd., 1982-84, pres., 1989-90; active Environ. Ams. Bd., 1991-92, Strategic Command Consultation Commn., 1993-96, Nat. Exec. Res. Corps, Fed. Office Emergency Preparedness, 1968-88; chmn. Omaha/Douglas Pub. Bldg. Commn., 1996—. Co-editor: Paradox, Process and Progress, 1968; contbr. articles profl. jours. Mem. Kent City Planning Commn., 1962-66; bd. dirs. United Ch. of Christ Bd. Homeland Ministries, 1968-74, Met. YMCA, Omaha, 1973-77, Mid-Am. council Boy Scouts Am., 1973-77, Midlands United Community Services, 1972-77, NCCJ, 1974-77, Omaha Rotary Club, 1974-77, 93—, Found. Study Presdl. and Congl. Terms, 1977-89, First Plymouth Congl. Ch., 1989-90, Midland Luth. Coll., 1993—, Coun. Aid to Edn., 1985-89, ConAgra Foods, Inc., 1993—, Russian Farm Cmty. Project, Capitol Fed. Found., Topeka, Kans., 1999—, The Silverstone Group, 2004—; trustee Huston Tillotson Coll., Austin, Tex., 1968-81, chmn., 1976-78, Joslyn Art Mus., 1973-77, Nebr. Meth. Hosp., 1974-77, 1st Ctrl. Congregational Ch., Brownell-Talbott Sch., 1974-77, Harry S. Truman Inst., 1977-89, Willa Cather Pioneer Meml. and Ednl. Found., 1979-87; pres. Kent Area C. of C., 1966; mem. Met. Commn. Coll. Found., 1993-96; min.-in-residence Countryside Cmty. United Ch. Christ, Omaha, 2003—. Decorated comdr.'s cross Order of Merit (Germany); recipient Disting. Svc. award Kent, Ohio, 1967, Brotherhood award NCCJ, 1977, Americanism citation B'nai B'rith, 1978, Legion of Honor, Order of DeMolay, 1980, gold medal Nat. Interfrat. Coun., 1987, Agr. award Triumph Agr. Expn., Omaha, 1989, Disting. Alumni Achievement award U. Iowa, 2004; named Nat. 4-H Alumnus, 1967, Outstanding Alumnus, U. No. Iowa, 1974, Midlander of Yr., Omaha World Herald, 1977, King Ak-Sar-Ben LXXXVI, 1980; named to DeMolay Hall of Fame, 1993; named Hon. Consul Gen. of Japan, 1999. Mem. AAAS, APA, AAUP, Am. Coll. Pers. Assn., Assn. Urban Univs. (pres. 1976-77), Am. Ednl. Rsch. Assn., Coun. on Fgn. Rels., Chief Execs. Orgn., Young Pres. Orgn., Scottish Rite (bd. dirs. Omaha coun. 1999-), Lincoln C. of C. (bd. dirs. 1989-90), Masons (33 deg.), Rotary (bd. dirs. Omaha 1974-77, pres. Kent, Ohio chpt., 1970-71), Phi Delta Kappa, Phi Eta Sigma, Sigma Tau Gamma (pres. grand coun. 1968-70, Disting. Achievement award 1980, Disting. scholar 1981), Omicron Delta Kappa (nat. pres. 1986-90, Found. pres. 1986-96). Home: 10849 N 58th Plz Omaha NE 68152 Office Phone: 402-399-0928.

ROSKEY, CAROL BOYD, social studies educator, dean, director; b. Columbus, Ohio, Mar. 9, 1946; d. Clarence Eugene and Clara Johanna (Schwartz) B.; m. Joseph Meeks, Aug. 17, 1968 (div. 1981) m. William Roskey, Nov. 16, 2003; children: Catherine Rachael, Tiffany Johannah. BS, Ohio State U., Mex., 1968; MS, Ohio State U., 1969, PhD, 1972. Rsch. asst., assoc. Ohio State U., Columbus, 1968-71; internship Columbus Area C. of C.,

Ohio, 1970; lectr. Ohio State U., Columbus, 1970, 72; asst. prof. U. Mass., Amherst, 1972-74, Cornell U., Ithaca, N.Y., 1974-78, assoc. prof., 1978-80; legis. fellow Senate Com. Banking, 1984; supr. economist, head housing section USDA, Washington, 1980-85; assoc. prof. housing and consumer econs. U. Ga., Athens, 1985-90, prof., 1990-97, head housing and consumer econs., 1992-97; dean Coll. Family and Consumer Scis. Iowa State U., Ames, 1997—2003, dir. Family Policy Ctr., 2003—. Rsch. fellow Nat. Inst. for Consumer Rsch., Oslo, Norway, 1992; cons. Yale U., 1976-77, HUD, Cambridge, Mass., 1978, MIT Ctr. for Real Estate Devel. Ford Found. Project on Housing Policy; del. N.E. Ctr. for Rural Devel. Housing Policy Conf. Reviewer Home Econ. Rsch. Jour., 1987—01, ACCI conf., 1987—; contbr. articles to profl. mags. Mem. panel town of Amherst Landlord Tenant Bd.; bd. dirs. Am. Coun. Consumer Interests; mem. adv. coun. HUD Nat. Mfg. Housing, 1978-80, 91-93; chair Housing Mfg. Inst. Consensus Commn. on Fed. Standards. Recipient Leader award AAFCS, 1996, Disting. Alumni award Ohio State U., 1999; named one of Outstanding Young Women of Am., 1979; Columbus Womens Chpt. Nat. Assn. Real Estate Bds. scholar, Gen. Foods fellow, 1971-72, HEW grantee, 1978, travel grantee NSF bldg. rsch. bd., AID grantee, USDA Challenge grant, 1995-98. Mem. Am. Assn. Housing Educators (pres. 1983-84), Nat. Inst. Bldg. Sci. (bd. sec. 1984, 85, 89-92, bd. dirs. 1981-83, 85, 87-93), Internat. Assn. Housing Sci., Com. on Status on Women in Econs., Nat. Assn. Home Builders (Smart House contract 1989, treas. bd. human sci. 2001-03), Epsilon Sigma Phi, Phi Upsilon Omicron, Gamma Sigma Delta, Phi Beta Delta, Kappa Omicron Nu (v.p. of programs 1995-96), Phi Kappa Phi, others. Office: Iowa State U 2354 Palmer Ames IA 50011-0001 Office Phone: 515-294-3028.

ROSKI, EDWARD P., JR., professional sports team executive; s. Edward P. Roski, III; m. Gayle Roski. BS in Fin. and Real Estate, U. So. Calif., 1962. Pres. So. Calif.-based Majestic Realty Co.; owner L.A. Kings, 1995—. Dir. Big Bros. of Greater L.A.; bd. govs. Natural History Mus. of L.A. County; bd. dirs. Comerica Bank, Calif. With USMC, 1962-66. Mem. Explorers Club, Soc. Indsl. Realtors. Avocations: bicycling, mountain climbing. Office: Los Angeles Kings Staples Center 111 S Figueroa St Los Angeles CA 90012-2465

ROSKIN, WILLIAM A. communications executive; BBA, City Coll. of NY, 1963; LLB, St. John's U. Sch. of Law, 1966; LLM, NY U. Grad. Sch. of Law, 1968. Staff, law dept. RCA Global Comm., Inc.; gen. counsel City NY Dept. Pers., City Svc. Commn., N.Y.C., 1971—76; v.p., labor rels. Warner Comm., 1976—86; sr. v.p., human resources Coleco Industries, Inc., 1986—88; v.p. human resources, admin. Viacom, Inc., N.Y.C., 1988—92, sr. v.p., human resources, admin., 1992—. Office: Viacom Inc 1515 Bdwy New York NY 10036

ROSKOSKI, JOHN, religious studies educator, coach; b. Rahway, NJ, May 23, 1960; s. Charles Clement and Elaine Magdelene Roskoski; m. Tracy Ann Abrego, Apr. 23, 1995; children: Nicholas Thaddeus, Samuel John. BA in religious studies, Seton Hall, 1981; MA in theology, New Brunswick (NJ) Theol. Sem., 1986; MA in Jewish-Christian studies, Seton Hall, 1990; MPhil in Theology, Fordham U., 2004. Cert. strength trng. instr. YMCA. Tchr. religion St. Michael's High Sch., Jersey City, 1982—83; instr. logic Middlesex CC, Edison, NJ, 1986; strength coach Bishop Ahr High Sch., Edison, 1984—89; tchr. religion Marist High Sch., Bayone, NJ, 1989—91; adj. prof. theol. St. Peter's Coll., Jersey City, 1992—. Contbr. articles to Armbender Mag. Mem.: Assn. Biblical Rsch., Nat. Honor Soc., Theol. Honor Soc. Roman Catholic. Avocations: chess, walking sticks, coin collecting/numismatics, powerlifting. Home: 23 Morse Ave Edison NJ 08817 E-mail: Samson.Jr@verizon.net.

ROSKOSKI, ROBERT, JR., biochemist, educator, author; b. Elyria, Ohio, Dec. 10, 1939; s. Robert and Mary R.; m. Laura Martinsek, Aug. 17, 1974. BS, Bowling Green State U., 1961; MD, U. Chgo., 1964, PhD, 1968. Asst. prof. U. Iowa, Iowa City, 1972-75, assoc. prof., 1975-79, vis. prof., 1993; prof. dept. biochemistry and molecular biology Health Scis. Ctr., La. State U., New Orleans, 1979—; Fred G. Brazda prof. Med. Ctr., La. State U., New Orleans, 1991—. Cons. biochemistry test com. Nat. Bd. Med. Examiners, 1981-84, 2003—; mem. merit rev. bd. for basic scis. VA; mem. rev. com. biol. scis. U. South Fla., 1992-95; mem. rev. com. biochemistry St. George's U. Sch. Medicine, 1997, Kuwait U. Health Scis. Ctr., 2002; cons. Royal Soc. New Zealand. Served with USAF, 1966-69. NIH postdoctoral fellow U. Chgo., 1964-66; NIH spl. fellow Rockefeller U., 1969-71 Mem. Am. Chem. Soc., Am. Soc. Neurochemistry, Soc. for Neurosci., Am. Soc. Biol. Chemists, Am. Soc. Pharmacology and Exptl. Therapeutics, Internat. Soc. Neurochemistry, Assn. Med. and Grad. Depts. Biochemistry (sec. 1994-96, pres. 1997), Coun. Acad. Scos., Greater New Orleans Soc. for Neurosci. (pres. 1982-83). Achievements include condr. research enzymology. Home: 1206 Aline St New Orleans LA 70115-2421 Office: 1100 Florida Ave New Orleans LA 70119-2714 Office Phone: 504-619-8568. Business E-Mail: biocrr@lsuhsc.edu.

ROSKY, BURTON SEYMOUR, lawyer; b. Chgo., May 28, 1927; s. David T. and Mary W. (Zelkin) R.; m. Leatrice J. Darrow, June 16, 1951; children: David Scott, Bruce Alan. Student, Ill. Inst. Tech., 1944-45; BS, UCLA, 1948; JD, Loyola U., L.A., 1953. Bar: Calif. 1954, U.S. Supreme Ct 1964, U.S. Tax Ct 1964; C.P.A., Calif. Auditor City of L.A., 1948- 51; with Beidner, Temkin & Ziskin (C.P.A.s), L.A., 1951-52; supervising auditor Army Audit Agy., 1952-53; practiced law L.A., Beverly Hills, 1954—; ptnr. Duskin & Rosky, 1972-82, Rosky, Landau & Fox, 1982-93, Rosky, Landau & Stahl, Beverly Hills, 1993-99; pvt. practice Beverly Hills, 1999—. Lectr. on tax and bus. problems; judge pro tem Beverly Hills Mcpl. Ct., L.A. Superior Ct.; mem. L.A. Mayor's Community Adv. Council. Contbr. profl. publs. Charter supporting mem. Los Angeles County Mus. Arts; contbg. mem. Assocs. of Smithsonian Instn.; charter mem. Air and Space Mus; mem. Am. Mus. Natural History, L.A. Zoo; supporting mem. L.A. Mus. Natural History; mem. exec. bd. So. Calif. coun. Nat. Fedn. Temple Brotherhoods, mem. nat. exec. bd.; mem. bd. govs. Loyola Sch. Law, L.A. With USNR, 1945-46. Walter Henry Cook fellow Loyola Law Sch. Bd. Govs. Fellow Jewish Chautauqua Soc. (life mem.); mem. Am. Arbitration Assn. (nat. panel arbitrators), Am. Assn. Attys.-CPAs (charter mem. pres. 1968), Calif. Assn. Attys.-CPAs (charter mem., pres. 1963), Calif. Soc. CPAs, Calif., Beverly Hills, Century City, Los Angeles County bar assns., Am. Judicature Soc., Chancellors Assocs. UCLA, Tau Delta Phi, Phi Alpha Delta.; mem. B'nai B'rith. Jewish (mem. exec. bd., pres. temple, pres. brotherhood). Club: Mason. Office: 8383 Wilshire Blvd Beverly Hills CA 90211-2410 Office Phone: 323-655-9757.

ROSKY, THEODORE SAMUEL, insurance company executive; b. Chgo., Apr. 14, 1937; s. Theodore and Lora Marie (O'Connell) R.; m. Jacqueline Reed, Apr. 19, 1958; 1 child, Laura Marie. BA, State U. Iowa, 1959. Various actuarial positions Conn. Gen. Life Ins. Co., Hartford, 1959-66, assoc. actuary, 1967-70, controller, 1970-73, 2d v.p., actuary, 1973, v.p., 1973-78; exec. v.p. Capital Holding Corp., 1978-84, exec. v.p., CFO, 1984-91, exec. v.p., 1991-92; bd. dirs. Legend Funds, 1993-98, SBM Mut. Funds, 1995-97, SBM Certificate Co., 1996-98; fin. svcs. Dory L.P., 1998-99. Instr. State U. Iowa, 1958-59, U. Hartford, 1964-66, U. Conn., 1967-68. Mem. bd. pensions Evang. Luth. Ch. Am., 1974—82, 1984—87, 1989—95; bd. dirs. Hartford Coll. for Women, 1974—78, Macauley Theater, 1983—85, Louisville Fund for the Arts, 1980—97, Louisville Luth. Home, 1983—97, Louisville Orch., 1982—88, 1989—95, Ky. Opera, 1992—2001, Lincoln Found., 1992—2002, Actors Theatre of Louisville, 1995—, New Performing Arts, 1996—98, Oak and Acorn, 1995—2001, Glassworks Found., 2002—03, Pub. Radio Partnership, 2003—04, YMCA Safe Place, 2003—, Sch. Choice Scholarships, 2004—. Recipient award Soc. Actuaries, 1958 Fellow Soc. Actuaries; mem. Am. Acad. Actuaries, Southeastern Actuaries Club. Republican. Lutheran. Home and Office: 2304 Speed Ave Louisville KY 40205-1642

ROS-LEHTINEN, ILEANA, congresswoman; b. Havana, Cuba, July 15, 1952; d. Enrique Emilio and Amanda (Adato) Ros; m. Dexter Lehtinen; 2 children, 2 stepchildren. AA, Miami (Fla.)-Dade C.C., 1972; BA, Fla. Internat. U., 1975, MS, 1987. Prin. Ea. Acad., from 1978; mem. Fla. Ho. of Reps., Tallahassee, 1983—86, Fla. Senate, 1986—89, U.S. Congress from 18th Fla. dist., 1989—; mem. govt. reform com., internat. rels. com. Recipient Nat. Legis. award LULACH, 1999. Republican. Roman Catholic. Office: US Ho of Reps 2160 Rayburn Ho Office Bldg Washington DC 20515-0918

ROSLOW, SYDNEY, marketing educator; b. N.Y.C., July 29, 1910; s. Joseph and Anna (Lipman) R.; m. Irma Sternberg, Oct. 21, 1932; children: Richard Jay, Susan Jane, Peter Dirk. BS, NYU, 1931, MA, 1932, PhD, 1935. Rsch. asst. in market, indsl and pers. rsch. Psychol. Corp., 1931-41; sch. psychologist, mem. Bd. Edn., Hastings on Hudson, N.Y., 1937-48; pub. opinion rsch. program surveys divsn. U.S. Dept. Agr., 1939-43; founder Pulse, Inc., market and audience rsch. in radio, TV, advt., N.Y.C., 1941-78; assoc. prof. Baruch Coll., CUNY, 1967-75; assoc. prof. dept. mktg. Fla. Internat. U., 1976-83, prof. mktg., assoc. dean Coll. Bus. Adminstrn., 1983-90, prof. emeritus, 1990—, acting assoc. dean, 1996. Rschr. in mktg. Contbr. chpts. to books, more than 100 articles to profl. jours. Fellow APA; mem. Am. Mktg. Assn. (pres. Miami chpt. 1980-82), Market Rsch. Coun. (inducted into Hall of Fame, N.Y. 1992), Radio-TV Rsch. Coun. (past pres.), Radio and TV Execs. Soc., Phi Beta Kappa. Office: Fla Internat U North Miami Campus North Miami FL 33181 Home: 1905 Hawaii Ave NE Saint Petersburg FL 33703-3417

ROSMARIN, LEONARD ALAN, dermatologist; b. Bronx, May 29, 1950; s. Jack and Dorothy (Blumenstein) R.; m. Wendy Nevard, June 13, 1976; children: David, Deborah. BA, SUNY, Stony Brook, 1972; MD, NYU, 1976. Intern Montefiore Hosp., Bronx, 1976-77, resident, 1977-80; dermatologist pvt. practice, Whitestone, N.Y., 1981—; instr. dermatology Montefiore Hosp., Bronx, 1980-90; attending physician, cons. dermatology N.Y. Hosp. Med. Ctr. Queens County, 1980—. Fellow Am. Acad. Dermatology; mem. L.I. Dermatologic Soc., Greater N.Y. Dermatologic Soc., Soc. Tropical Dermatology. Jewish. Avocations: exercise, reading, photography, travel. Office: 18-15 Francis Lewis Blvd Whitestone NY 11357

ROSNER, ANN See SEAMAN, BARBARA

ROSNER, DAVID, history educator; b. NYC, Mar. 13, 1947; s. Alex and Sophie (Gordon) R.; m. Kathlyn Conway, July 28, 1979; children: Zachary, Molly. BA, CCNY, 1968; MSPH, Univ. Mass., 1972; PhD, Harvard, 1978. Lectr. Harvard, Boston, 1978-79; asst. prof. Baruch Coll. CUNY, NYC, 1978—80, disting. prof. history, 1996—; asst. prof. Mt. Sinai Sch. Med., NYC, 1978—; assoc. prof. grad. faculty CUNY, NYC, 1984—; prof. history and pub. health Columbia U., NYC, 1998—, dir. ctr. for history and ethics of pub. health. Rep. med. care Am. Pub. Health Assn., Washington, 1983-88; rep. governing coun. Am. Pub. Health Assn., Washington, 1989-92. Author: A Once Charitable Enterprise, 1981; co-author: Deadly Dust, 1991; co-editor: Dying for Work, 1989, Slaves of the Depression, 1987, Deceit and Denial: The Deadly Politics of Industrial Pollution, 2002. Guggenheim fellow John Simon Guggenheim Found., NY, 1989, NEH fellow, Washington, 1983-84; Interperative Rsch. award NEH, Washington, 1987-88, 92-94. Home: 290 Riverside Dr New York NY 10025-5200 Office: Columbia Univ Ctr for History and Ethics Pub Health 722 W 168th St New York NY 10032

ROSNER, JONATHAN LEVI, lawyer; b. N.Y.C., Sept. 4, 1932; s. Oscar S. and Miriam (Reinhardt) R.; m. Lydia Sokol, Dec. 23, 1956; children: Beth, Marianne, Josh. BA, Wesleyan U., Middletown, Conn., 1954; JD, NYU, 1959. Bar: N.Y. 1959, U.S. Dist. Ct. (so. dist.) N.Y. 1962, U.S. Dist. Ct. (ea. dist.) N.Y. 1964, U.S. Ct. Appeals (2d cir.) 1964, U.S. Supreme Ct. 1964, U.S. Dist. Ct. Md. 1969, U.S. Dist. Ct. P.R. 1972, U.S. Ct. Appeals (D.C. cir.) 1976, U.S. Dist. Ct. (ea. dist.) Mich. 1984, U.S. Ct. Appeals (11th cir.) 1984. Law clk. to judge U.S. Dist. Ct. (so. dist.) N.Y., N.Y.C., 1959-60, asst. U.S. atty., 1960-63; ptnr. Rosner, Rosner & McEvoy, N.Y.C., 1963-79; pvt. practice N.Y.C., 1979-85; ptnr. Rosner & Murray, N.Y.C., 1985—2004. Adj. prof. law NYU, 1970-83, Pace U., White Plains, N.Y., 1984-86; chief counsel N.Y.C. Spl. Commn. on Power Failure, 1977, dep. commr., gen. counsel N.Y. State Commn. on Criminal Justice and Use of Force, 1985-87. Co-author: How to Prepare Witnesses for Trial, 1985, Cross-Examination of Witnesses, 1989, Impeachment of Witnesses, 1990. Bd. dirs. Westchester Jewish Cmty. Svcs., 1970-73; trustee Woodlands Cmty. Temple, 1971-76; mem. adv coun. Wesleyan U. Alumni Assn., 1972-79, mem. schs. com. 1964-78, alumni fund class agt. 1954-2000, 04. Mem. ABA, N.Y. State Bar Assn. (com. on grievances 1974-76), Assn. Bar of City of N.Y. (coms. on profl. discipline 1983-87, grievances 1970-74, entertainment 1964-68, 78-82, 93—, ABA-CLE panelist 1976-78), N.Y. County Lawyers Assn., NYU Law Alumni Assn. (bd. dirs. 1965-69, 84-88, 93—), N.Y. County Dist. Attys. Ann. Trial Advocacy Program (faculty 1978-2002). Home: 10 Westhaven Ln White Plains NY 10605-5458 Office Phone: 914-993-0509. E-mail: jlrosner@msn.com.

ROSNER, JONATHAN LINCOLN, physicist, researcher; b. N.Y.C., July 23, 1941; s. Albert Aaron and Elsie Augustine (Lincoln) R.; m. Joy Elaine Fox, June 13, 1965; children: Hannah, Benjamin. BA, Swarthmore Coll., 1962; MA, Princeton U., 1963, PhD, 1965. Research asst. prof. U. Wash., Seattle, 1965-67; vis. lectr. Tel Aviv U., Ramat Aviv, Israel, 1967-69; asst. prof. physics U. Minn., Mpls., 1969-71, assoc. prof., 1971-75, prof., 1975-82, U. Chgo., 1982—. Contbr. numerous articles to profl. and scholarly jours. Alfred P. Sloan fellow, 1971-73, Guggenheim fellow, 2002. Fellow Am. Phys. Soc. Democrat. Jewish. Avocations: fishing, hiking, skiing, amateur radio. Office: U Chgo Enrico Fermi Inst 5640 S Ellis Ave Chicago IL 60637-1433 E-mail: rosner@hep.uchicago.edu.

ROSNER, M. NORTON, business systems and financial services company executive; b. Camden, N.J., Aug. 17, 1931; s. Adolph and Anne (Cotler) R.; m. M. Patricia Eskin, Oct. 18, 1953; children— Robert, Susan, Jan BS in Econs., U. Pa., 1953; MBA, U. Mich., 1965. From acct. to mgr. overhead standards RCA Corp., Camden, N.J., 1953-62; supr. methods and programs, then internal cons. forward model planning Ford Motor Co., Dearborn, Mich., 1962-66; asst. controller, then v.p. planning Singer Co., N.Y.C., 1966-70; treas., then v.p. fin. Popular Services, Passaic, N.J., 1970-72; dir. fin. planning, then asst. controller, then gen. mgr. GSD, then v.p. RE/GSD Xerox Corp., Rochester, N.Y., 1972-90; retired, 1990. Bd. dirs., treas. Parcel Post Assn., N.Y.C., 1970-71; dir. Harbinger, Stamford, Conn.; chmn. Xerox Realty Corp., Stamford. Vice chmn. Compeer, Inc., Rochester, N.Y., 1981-87, chmn., 1987-89; chmn. DP2, Rochester, 1985-87; bd. dirs., treas. Rochester Blue Cross-Blue Shield, 1987-89; dir. Palm Beach County Mental Health Assn., 1992, treas., 1993, v.p., 1994-95, pres., 1995-96; dir. JARC, 1992, v.p., 1993, pres., 1994-96. Recipient Nat. Vol. Action award Pres. U.S. Mem.: U. Mich.; U. Pa. Home: 17831 Heather Ridge Ln Boca Raton FL 33498-6423

ROSNER, ROBERT, astrophysicist, educator; b. Garmisch-Partenkirchen, Bavaria, Germany, June 26, 1947; came to U.S., 1959; s. Heinz and Faina (Brodsky) R.; m. Marsha Ellen Rich, Sept. 5, 1971; children: Daniela Karin, Nicole Elise. BA, Brandeis U., 1969; PhD, Harvard U., 1976. Asst. prof. Harvard U., Cambridge, Mass., 1978-83, assoc. prof., 1983-86; astrophysicist Smithsonian Astrophys. Observatory, Cambridge, 1986-87; prof. U. Chgo., 1987—, William E. Wrather prof., 1998—; chief scientist, assoc. lab. dir. Argonne Nat. Lab., 2002—. Trustee Adler Planetarium, Chgo., 1989-98, chmn. dept. astronomy and astrophysics, 1991-97. Contbr. more than 180 articles to profl. jours. Woodrow Wilson fellow, 1969. Fellow Am. Phys. Soc.; mem. Am. Acad. Arts & Scis., Am. Astron. Soc., Soc. Indsl. and Applied Math., Am. Geophys. Union. Home: 4950 S Greenwood Ave Chicago IL 60615-2816 Office: U Chicago Astrophysics 5640 S Ellis Ave Chicago IL 60637-1433 Business E-Mail: r-rosner@uchicago.edu.

ROSNER, SETH, lawyer, educator; b. N.Y.C., Jan. 6, 1931; s. Oscar S. and Miriam (Reinhardt) R.; m. Sara Jane Sheldon, Dec. 4, 1970 (div. Mar. 1978); m. Ann E. Del Toro, June 23, 1983; 1 child, Rachel Ferrer. AB, Wesleyan U., Middletown, Conn., 1952; JD, Columbia U., 1955; LLM in Comparative Law, NYU, 1960; postgrad., U. Paris, 1960-61. Bar: N.Y. 1955, U.S. Dist. Ct. (so. and ea. dists.) N.Y. 1956, U.S. Supreme Ct. 1967. Ptnr. Rosner & Rosner, N.Y.C., 1955-80; sr. ptnr. Marchi Jaffe Cohen Crystal Rosner & Katz, N.Y.C., 1981-88; pvt. practice N.Y.C., 1989-97, 2001—; counsel Jacobs Persinger & Parker, N.Y.C., 1997-2001. Adj. prof. NYU Sch. of Law, 1961—89. Trustee, v.p. exec. com. Fedn. Jewish Philanthropies, N.Y.C., 1977-86; trustee Jewish Home and Hosp. for Aged, N.Y.C., 1970-95, pres., 1978-82, chmn., 1982-86; bd. trustees Wesleyan U. Middletown, Conn., 1982-86; bd. govs. Josephson Inst. of Ethics, Marina Del Rey, Calif., 1986-99, 2000—, chmn. bd., 2000-03; bd. dirs. Saratoga Automobile Mus., Saratoga Springs, N.Y., 1999—, N.Y. State Judicial Inst. on Professionalism in the Law, 2001—. Lt. USN, 1956-59. Fellow Am. Bar Found. (life); mem. ABA (chmn. gen. practice sect. 1980-81, ethics and profl. responsibility com. 1983-89, chmn. professionalism com. 1992-95, chmn. com. on scope, chmn. com. on lawyer competence 1995-97, bd. govs. 1997-2000, chmn. coordinating coun. Ctr. Profl. Responsibility 2002—), Assn. Profl. Responsibility Lawyers (bd. dirs. 1990-96, pres.-elect 1993-94, pres. 1994-95), Assn. of Bar of City of N.Y. (ethics com. 1970-73), N.Y. State Bar Assn. (chmn. gen. practice sect. 1982-83), Leica Hist. Soc. (bd. dirs., v.p., 2001—). Avocations: writing, photography, Ferrari automobiles. E-mail: sethrosner1@msn.com.

ROSNOW, RALPH LEON, psychology researcher and educator; b. Balt., Jan. 10, 1936; s. Irvin and Rebecca (Faber) R.; m. Mimi Quin Medinger, Aug. 12, 1963. BS, U. Md., 1957; MA, George Washington U., 1958; PhD, Am. U., 1962. Asst. prof. Boston U., 1963-67; assoc. prof. Temple U., Phila., 1967-70, full prof., 1970-2001; vis. prof. London Sch. Econs., 1973, Harvard U., Cambridge, Mass., 1978, 1988-89; Thaddeus Bolton prof. Temple U., 1982—2001, Thaddeus Bolton prof. emeritus, 2002—, dir. social and orgnl. psychology divsn. psychology, 1988-2000. Cons. editor jours. and encys. in psychology and comm.; cons. on rsch. methods and data analysis, 1976—. Author: Paradigms in Transition, 1981; author: (with Robert Rosenthal) The Volunteer Subject, 1975, Essentials of Behavioral Research, 2d edit., 1991; author: Contrast Analysis, 1985, Beginning Behavioral Research, 4th edit., 2002, 5th edit., 2005, People Studying People, 1997, Contrasts and Effect Sizes in Behavioral Research, 2000, author: (with Gary Fine) Rumor and Gossip, 1976; author: (with Mimi Rosnow) Writing Papers in Psychology, 6th edit., 2003; editor (with Robert Rosenthal): Artifact in Behavioral Research, 1969; editor: (with Marianthi Georgoudi) Contextualism and Understanding in Behavioral Science. Recipient George A. Miller award Soc. Gen. Psychology, 1999. Fellow: APA, AAAS, Am. Psychol. Soc.; mem.: Soc. Exptl. Social Psychology. Home: 177 Biddulph Rd Radnor PA 19087-4506

ROSOFF, WILLIAM A. lawyer, executive; b. Phila., June 21, 1943; s. Herbert and Estelle (Finkel) R.; m. Beverly Rae Rifkin, Feb. 7, 1970; children: Catherine D., Andrew M. BS with honors, Temple U., 1964; LLB magna cum laude, U. Pa., 1967. Bar: Pa. 1968, U.S. Dist. Ct. (ea. dist.) Pa. 1968. Law clk. U.S. Ct. Appeals (3d cir.), 1967-68; instr. U. Pa. Law Sch., Phila., 1968-69; assoc. Wolf, Block, Schorr & Solis-Cohen, Phila., 1969-75, ptnr., 1975-96, chmn. exec. com., 1987-88; also vice chmn. bd. dirs. Advanta Corp., Spring House, Pa., 1996—, pres., 1999—. Trustee RPS Realty Trust, 1990-96, Atlantic Realty Trust, 1996—; guest lectr. confs. and seminars on tax law; mem. tax adv. bd. Commerce Clearing House, 1983-94; mem. legal activities policy bd. Tax Analysts, 1978—; mem. Little, Brown Tax Adv. Bd., 1994-96; chmn. bd. dirs. RMH Telesvcs., Inc., 1997-99. Editor U. Pa. Law Rev., 1965-67; mem. bd. contbg. editors and advisors Jour. Partnership Taxation, 1983-2000; contbr. articles to profl. jours. Bd. dirs., past mem. com. on law and social action Phila. coun. Am. Jewish Congress. Fellow Am. Coll. Tax Counsel; mem. Am. Law Inst. (cons. taxation of partnerships 1976-78, assoc. reporter taxation of partnerships, 1978-82, mem. adv. group on fed. income tax project 1982-2000, cons. taxation of pass-through entities 1995-2000, past bd. dirs.), Order of Coif, Beta Gamma Sigma, Beta Alpha Psi. Office: PO Box 918 Spring House PA 19477-0918

ROSOVSKY, HENRY, economist, educator; b. Danzig, Sept. 1, 1927; came to U.S., 1940, naturalized, 1949; s. Selig S. and Sophie (Rosovsky) R.; m. Nitza Brown, June 17, 1956; children— Leah, Judith, Michael. AB, Coll. William and Mary, 1949, LL.D., 1976; A.M. (John E. Thayer scholar), Harvard U., 1953, PhD, 1959; L.H.D. (hon.), Yeshiva U., 1977, Hebrew Union Coll., 1978, Colgate U., 1979, Brandeis U., 1984; PhD (hon.), Hebrew U. of Jerusalem, 1982; LL.D. (hon.), Queen's U., Ont., 1984, U. Hartford, 1984, CUNY, 1986, U. Mass., 1986, Harvard U., 1998; DHL (hon.), Hebrew Coll., Brookline, Mass., 1987, NYU, 1993; DL, St. Mary's Coll. Md., 1989, Jewish Theol. Sem., 1995. From asst. prof. to prof. econs. and history U. Calif.-, Berkeley, 1958-65; chmn. Center Japanese and Korean Studies, 1962-65; prof. econs. Harvard U., 1965—, Walter S. Barker prof. econs., 1975-84, Geyser univ. prof., 1984-96, Geyser univ. prof. emeritus, 1996—, chmn. dept., 1969-72, dean Faculty Arts and Scis., 1973-84; assoc. dir. East Asia Research Center, 1967-69. Mem. Harvard U. Corp., 1985-97; vis. prof. Hitotsubashi U., Tokyo, 1957, Tokyo U., 1962, Hebrew U., Jerusalem, 1965; hon. dir. Japan Fund.; dir. emeritus Corning, Inc.; hon. prof. Centro U. Francisco, De Vitoria, Madrid, 1996. Author: Capital Formation in Japan, 1868-1940, 1961, Quantitative Japanese Economic History, 1961, (with K. Ohkawa) Japanese Economic Growth, 1973, The University: An Owner's Manual, 1990; editor: Explorations in Entrepreneurial History, 1954-56, Industrialization in Two Systems, 1966, Discord in the Pacific, 1972, (with H. Patrick) Asia's New Giant, 1976, (with P. Higonnet, D. Landes) Favorites of Fortune, 1991, (with S. Kumon) The Political Economy of Japan, Vol. 3: Cultural and Social Dynamics, 1992. Chmn. bd. trustees Am. Jewish Congress, 1975-88. Served to 1st lt. AUS, 1946-47, 50-52. Jr. fellow Soc. Fellows, 1954-57; recipient Schumpeter prize Harvard, 1963, Clark Kerr medal U. Calif., Berkeley, 1992. Fellow Am. Acad. Arts and Scis., Am. Philos. Soc.; mem. Am. Econ. Assn., Econ. History Assn., Assn. Asian Studies, Chevalier, Legion of Honor, Order of Sacred Treasure, Star (Japan). Home: 37 Beechcroft Rd Newton MA 02458-2403 Office: Harvard Univ Loeb House 17 Quincy St Cambridge MA 02138-3805 E-mail: hrosovsky@harvard.edu.

ROSOW, STUART L. lawyer; b. N.Y.C., Mar. 28, 1950; s. Bernard and Lillian (Bonime) R.; m. Amy Berk Kuhn. AB cum laude, Yale U., 1972; JD cum laude, Harvard U., 1975. Law clk. to presiding justice U.S. Ct. Appeals (7th cir.), Chgo., 1975-76; assoc. Paul, Weiss et al, N.Y.C., 1976-79, Kaye, Scholer, Fierman, Hays & Handler, N.Y.C., 1979-84, ptnr., 1984-97, Proskauer Rose LLP, N.Y.C., 1997—. Adj. prof. Columbia Law Sch., N.Y.C., 1998—. Mem. ABA, N.Y. State Bar Assn., Assn. of Bar of City of N.Y. Office: Proskauer Rose LLP 1585 Broadway Fl 27 New York NY 10036-8299 Office Phone: 212-969-3150. Business E-Mail: srosow@proskauer.com.

ROSOWSKI, ROBERT BERNARD, manufacturing executive; b. Detroit, July 23, 1940; s. Bernard and Anna (Maciag) R.; m. Kathleen Patricia Bates, Aug. 26, 1961; children: John, Paul, Mary, Judith. BS, U. Detroit, 1962; MBA, Mich. State U., 1974. CPA Mich. Auditor, staff supr. Coopers and Lybrand, Detroit, 1962-71; fin. analyst Masco Corp., Taylor, Mich., 1971-73, controller, 1973-85, v.p., controller, 1985-96, v.p., controller and treas., 1996—2001, v.p., treas., 2001—. Bd. dirs. Detroit Cath. Ctrl. HS, 1999—, Detroit Cath. Ctrl. Alumni Assn., pres. 1999-2002; chmn. Oakwood Hosp. Found., 1990—; trustee Oakwood Healthcare System, 1997—. Mem. Am. Inst. CPA's, Mich. Assn. CPA's, Fin. Execs. Inst. Avocations: golf, fishing, boating, photography. Office: Masco Corp 21001 Van Born Rd Taylor MI 48180-1300 Office Phone: 313-792-6258. Business E-Mail: robert_rosowski@mascohq.com.

ROSS, A. CATHARINE, biochemist, educator; Bachelor's, U. Calif., Davis; Master's, Cornell U., PhD, 1976. Prof. dept. biochemistry Med. Coll. Pa. State U., University Park, Dorothy Foehr Huck chair in nutrition, 1994—. Recipient Mead-Johnson award, Am. Inst. Nutrition. Mem.: NIH (mem. policy panel), AAAS, NAS (mem. policy panel), Fedn. Am. Socs. Exptl. Biology (mem. policy panel), Am. Soc. Cell Biology, Am. Soc. Nutritional Scis. (Osborne and Mendel award), Phi Kappa Phi, Sigma Xi. Office: Pa State U 126 Henderson South University Park PA 16802

ROSS, ALBERTA BARKLEY, retired chemist; b. Moores Hill, Ind., July 26, 1928; d. Lawrence Houston and Stella Olcott (Wright) Barkley; m. Joseph Hansbro Ross, June 2, 1956; children: Mary Angela, Joseph Hansbro Jr., Robert Barkley, Kathleen Jarrell. BS, Purdue U., 1948, Wash. U., 1951; PhD, U. Md., 1957. Tech. libr. Monsanto Chem. Co., St. Louis, 1948-53; rsch. assoc. U. Mich., Ann Arbor, 1957-58; supr. Radiation Chemistry Data Ctr. U. Notre Dame (Ind.), 1964-95; ret., 1995. Mem. Am. Chem. Soc. (chmn. St. Joseph Valley chpt. 1977-78), Sigma Xi (chpt. pres. 1980-81), Iota Sigma Pi.

ROSS, ALLAN ANDERSON, music educator, university official; b. Amesbury, Mass., Jan. 16, 1939; s. Frank Albert and Ruth Ethel (Anderson) R.; m. Barbara Kay Bedford, Apr. 15, 1962; children: Karen Elizabeth, Judith Carol, Donna Susan, Linda Beth, Jason Andrew. AB, U. Rochester, 1961; MusM, Ind. U., 1962, MusD, 1968. Asst. dir. music U. Rochester, N.Y., 1962-65; instr. music Ind. U., Bloomington, 1967-69, asst. prof. music, 1969-71, assoc. prof., dir. undergrad. studies, 1971-73, prof., 1977-79, asst. to dean, 1973-79; dean Shepherd Sch. Music, Rice U., Houston, 1979-81; prof. music U. Okla., Norman, 1981-99, Regents prof. music, 1999-2001, Regents prof. emeritus, 2001—, dir. music, 1981-92, devel. officer Coll. Fine Arts, 1992-93; condr. U. Okla. Symphony Orch., 1993-2001, interim dir. music, 1997-98. Dir. music Trinity Methodist Ch., Rochester, N.Y., 1963-65, First United Meth. Ch., Bloomington, Ind., 1969-79, 1st Christian Ch., Norman, Okla., 1981-91; bd. dirs. Riemenschneider Bach Inst.; bd. dirs., exec. bd. Okla. Summer Arts Inst. Guest condr. and adjudicator at music festivals throughout, U.S.; Author: Techniques for Beginning Conductors, 1976. Bd. dirs. United Way of Norman, Helpline of Norman, Okla. Arts Inst.; mem. gov.'s commn. for Okla. Symphony Orch. NDEA Title IV fellow, 1965. Mem. Music Educators Nat. Conf., Am. Choral Dirs. Assn., Coll. Music Soc., Nat. Assn. Schs. of Music (grad. commn., evaluator), Okla. Music Educators Assn., Phi Mu Alpha Sinfonia, Pi Kappa Lambda. Home: 1879 Rolling Hills St Norman OK 73072-6707

ROSS, BEATRICE BROOK, artist; b. NYC, Mar. 31, 1927; d. Alexander and Ray (Tennenbaum) Brook; m. Alexander Ross, Dec. 23, 1945; children: Robert Alan, Kenneth Jay, Stefani Lynn. Student, Hunter Coll., 1943, CCNY, 1944, Bklyn. Mus. Art Sch., 1959-60, 64-65; pupil of Ruben Tam, Wang Chi Yuan, Leo Manso; scholar, Sch. Chinese Brush Work, 1973. Owner, operator Jean Rosenthal Bea Ross Gallery, Jericho, 1961-64; represented by Gillary Gallery, Jericho, N.Y., Patrician Gallery, West Palm Beach, Fla., Lawrence Gallery, Delray Beach, Fla. Founder Birchwood Art League, 1958-63; lectr. bd. edn., Ont., Can., 1972; ad hoc com. with Lucy Lippard Women in Art, 1970-74; presenter in field. Exhbns. include Women in Art, Huntington, NY, 1972, C.W. Post Coll., 1972, 73-76, Guild Hall Mus., East Hampton, 1969-72, Lever House, Inc., 1969-72, J. Walter Thompson Loan Show, 1970, Whitehouse Gallery, 1970, Park Ave. Synagogue, 1970, Locust Valley Ann., 1970, Nat. Arts Club, 1970, Loeb Student Ctr., NYU, 1969, Suffolk Mus., Stony Brook, NY, 1969, 71, Lynn U., Boca Raton, 1992, NAD, 1968, Audubon Artists, 1968, 70, Silvermine Guild, 1968, 71, Port Washington (NY) Libr., 1968, 70, 76, Profl. Artists Guild LI, 1968, Bklyn. Coll., 1968, Huntington Twp. Art League, Cold Spring Harbor, NY, 1967, Gillary Gallery, Jericho, NY, 1966, 68, 70, 72, 79, 83, Hecksher Mus., 1960, 63, 70, Ho. of Reps., 1965, Library of Congress, 1965, Merrick (NY) Gallery, 1963, North Shore Cmty. Art Ctr. ann., Roslyn, NY, 1959, 62, Birchwood Art League, Jericho, NY, 1958, 61-62, Hofstra U., 1960, City Ctr., NYC, 1960, Emily Lowe Gallery, 1960, Nassau Democratic County Com. ann., 1958, R.A.A. Gallery, NYC, 1969-70, 77, Roosevelt Field Art Gallery, Garden City, N., 1958, Boca Raton (Fla.) City Hall, 1991, Bryant Library, Roslyn, NY, 1973, Women's Interart Ctr., NYC, 1974, Wantagh (NY) Libr., 1975, LIU, 1976, NY Tech., 1974, C.W. Post Coll. Schwartz Libr., 1976, St. Johns U., 1976, Union Carbide, NYC, 1977, Harley U. Ctr. Gallery, Adelphi U., 1976, 82, Lincoln Ctr., NYC, 1978, 82, Gallery 84, NYC, 1981, Jericho Libr., 1984, Donell Libr., NYC, 1991, Am. Properties Inc., Boca Raton, Fla., 1996; represented in pvt. collections, traveling shows in France, Italy and Japan; mus. curated show No. Trust Bank, Boca Mus., Fla., 1992, Nations Bank, Boca Raton Mus., Fla., 1995; author numerous poems. Recipient 1st prize oil Birchwood Art League, 1958; certificate award outstanding contbn. Mid Island Plaza Art League, Hicksville, N.Y., 1961, 2d prize oil, 1962; 1st prize oil, 1970; Benjamin Altman landscape prize N.A.D., 1968; 2d prize Heckscher Mus., Huntington, N.Y., 1970; Benjamin Altman Landscape prize Nat. award Nat. Acad. Design, N.Y.C., 1969, RAA Gallery, 1967-78, Harbor Gallery, Glen Cove, N.Y., 1983-85, Gillary Gallery Jericho, N.Y., 1984, Judge's Recognition award Boca Raton Mus., 1989, others; named to Nat. Women's Hall of Fame; MacDowell fellow, 1975, 80; selected for Unique and Universal South Fla. Artists Slide and Lctr., 1997. Mem. Profl. Artists Guild L.I. (v.p. admissions 1971-74, exec. v.p. 1975-77, 2d prize for group show 1990), Profl. Artists Guild Fla., Boca Raton Mus. Artist Guild, Easthampton Guild-Women in Arts, N.Y. Artists Equity, Nat. Mus. Women in Arts (charter), Gallery 84 (N.Y. 1979-85). Home: 5253 Bolero Cir Delray Beach FL 33484-1302

ROSS, BERNADETTE MARIE-TERESA, librarian; b. New Orleans, Sept. 23, 1948; d. Arnold and Doris Learson. MLS, U. S.C., 1975. Cert. libr., N.C. Instr. Southern U., New Orleans, 1972-74; libr. S.C. State Atty. Gen. Office, Columbia, 1975; head outreach svcs. Forsyth County Pub. Libr. Systems, Winston-Salem, N.C., 1975-77; head libr. Reid Ross Sr. High Sch., Fayetteville, N.C., 1977-85; reference libr. Fayetteville State U., 1989—; head libr. Terry Sanford Sr. High Sch., Fayetteville, 1985—, co-chair sch. renewal process, 1992—. Coord. student forum on sch. violence, 1992—; presenter Fayetteville State U. Ednl. Forum, 1999; dist. rep. Cumberland County Schs. Media Adv. Com., 1997—; cons. in field; mem. Supt.'s Roundtable, 1998; participant N.C. State Libr. Leadership Youth Svcs. Project, 1999-00; coord. Black Pearls: African Am. Films in Transition, 2000. Author: Educator's Guide to the Internet, 1995, Vocational Assessment and the Internet: A Beginner's Guide, 1997; editor newsletters From the Shelf, 1980-85, The Media Express, 1985-89; sect. editor N.C. Libr., 1976; book reviewer N.C. Materials and Evaluation Ctr., Raleigh, 1979. Sec. Cumberland County Friends of the Libr., Fayetteville, 1984-86, pres., 1986-88; adv. bd. arts coun. Umoja Cultural Arts Festival, Fayetteville, 1989; creater, organizer First Charles Chesnutt Film Festival, 1991. Fayetteville Jr. League grantee, 1989—, Florence Rogers Trust grantee, Innovation in Edn. grantee, 1999. Mem. ALA, N.C. Libr. Assn., N.C. High Sch. Libr. Assn. (s.e. dist. dir. 1981-82), N.C. Edn. Assn., N.C. Ctr. for Advancement of Tchg., Cumberland County Edn. Assn., Nat. Coun. Negro Women (charter mem. Fayetteville chpt.), Phi Alpha Theta, Delta Sigma Theta. Home: 502 Nottingham Dr Fayetteville NC 28311-1334 Office: Terry Sanford Sr High Sch 2301 Fort Bragg Rd Fayetteville NC 28303-7035

ROSS, BERNARD, engineering consultant, educator; BME, Cornell U., 1957; MSc in Aero. Engring., Stanford U., 1959, PhD in Aero. and Aerospace Engring., 1965; Diploma, Ecole Nat. Superieure L'Aero., France, 1960; cert., U. Edinburgh, Scotland, 1961. Registered profl. engr., Calif. Structural test engr. Gen. Dynamics Corp., Montreal, Quebec, Can., 1956; servomechanism and control sys. design engr. Marquardt Corp., Van Nuys, Calif., 1957; stress analyst Douglas Aircraft Co., Santa Monica, Calif., 1959; vibration and dynamics engr. ONERA, Paris, 1960; rsch. asst. Stanford U., 1961-63, rsch. assoc., 1963-65; sr. rsch. engr., program mgr. Stanford Rsch. Inst., Menlo Park, Calif., 1965-70; founder, chmn. emeritus Failure Analysis Assocs., San Francisco, 1967—. Vis. prof. U. Santa Clara, Calif., 1970-79; adv. coun. Stanford U., 1991—, cons. prof., 1992—; pres. internat. adv. bd. structural failure, product liability and tech. ins. confs. U. Vienna, 1986—; mem. univ. coun. Cornell U., 1995; reviewer Nat. Acad. Assocs. Program; speaker and lectr. in field. Contbr. articles to Exptl. Mechanics, AIAA Jour., Israel Jour. Tech., Profl. Safeyt, others. Cons. U.S. Consumer Product Safety Commn., Washington. NATO scholar, 1960. Mem. ASME, NSPE, AIAA, AAAS, Am. Soc. Safety Engrs., Am. Soc. Agrl. Engrs., Calif. Soc. Profl. Engrs., Soc. Automotive Engrs., Soc. Exptl. Mechanics, Internat. Soc. for Law, Technology and Ins. Achievements include research in analysis of structural collapse, mechanics of impact and penetration, accident reconstruction, safety warning design for heavy equipment, mechanical failure of machine parts, transportation system design. Office: Exponent Failure Analysis Assocs PO Box 3015 149 Commonwealth Dr Menlo Park CA 94025-1133 E-mail: bross@exponent.com.

ROSS, BEVERLEY LONG, real estate broker; b. Reno, Sept. 1, 1940; d. John Clemons Long and Roma Lucille Barkman; m. Barry L. Ross, Oct. 2, 1959; children: J. Michael, Pamela Jo Ross Snodgrass. BS, Calif. State, Sacramento, 1970; grad., Realtors Inst. Cert. residential specialist, accredited buyer rep. Tchr. Washoe County Schs., Reno, 1961-64; homebound tchr. Prince Georges County, Oxon Hill, Md., 1972-73; kindergarten tchr. Raleigh Pre-Sch., N.C., 1974-75; owner Boise (Idaho) Pre-Sch., 1975-82; realtor United Realty, Boise, 1977-79; assoc. broker, ptnr. Treasure Valley Realty, Boise, 1979-92; broker, owner Bev Ross Realty, Boise, 1992—. Mem. foothill plans com. City of boise, 1990—92; mem. source water assessment adv. com. Idaho Dept. Environ. Quality, Boise, 1998; elder Southminster Presbyn. Ch., 1991—92, corp. pres., treas., 2001—. Recipient Tribute to Women in Industry, Women's and Children's Alliance, 1999. Mem.: Women's Coun. Realtors (pres. 2000), Ada County Assn. Realtors (chair legis. com. 1991, dir. Ada County Realtors Found. 1999—2001, v.p. 2002, pres.-elect 2003, pres. 2004, Disting. Svc. award 1993), Idaho Assn. realtors (chair legis. com. 1992, state dir. continuing edn. task force 1997—98), Nat. Assn. Realtors, Soroptimist Internat. Boise (pres. 1988—89). Avocations: singing, reading, walking, travel. Office Phone: 208-345-7555. E-mail: bev@bevrossrealty.com.

ROSS, CAROL RUTH, holocaust educator; b. Milw., Wis., Dec. 26, 1946; d. James and Syliva Pasch; m. James Ira Ross; children: Michael E., David A. BS in Edn., U. of Wis.-Madison, 1965—69; MA in English, U. of Wis.-Milwaukee, 1970—72. Lic. tchng.grades 7-12, English and French State of Wis., 1969. English tchr. Cedarburg HS, Wis., 1969—70; tchr. Congregation Shalom Schools, Fox Point, Wis., 1972—78; creator and bus. owner Party Art, Milw., 1981—84; co-dir. Congregation Shalom Schools, 1984—85; lectr. and sr. lectr. in english dept. U. of Wis.-Milw., 1986—; lectr. in English dept. Marquette U., Milw., 1987—88; co-dir. Congregation Shalom Schools, 1998—99. Holocaust educator Coalition for Jewish Learning, Milw., 1997—. Author: (article) Milwaukee Journal Oh for the Love of a Blizzard, (booklet) A Party Art Primer; editor (book) Tracking Your Medicine; author: (article) Teaching the Book of Job to Ninth Graders in Alternatives in Religious Education, Another Word of Advice in American Baby Magazine, Collaborative Writing with Middle School and College Students in Middle Ed. Kids on the block puppeteer Maple Dale-Indian Hill Sch. Dist., Bayside, Wis., 1981—; Mitzvah Day co-chair Congregation Shalom, Fox Point, Wis., 1997—99. Recipient Tchg. Excellence Award, U. of Wis.-Milw. English Dept., 1993, Meritorious Svc. Award, Congregation Shalom, 1999. Mem.: Coalition for Jewish Learning, Nat. Coun. of Teachers of English. Avocations: travel, biking, dancing.

ROSS, CATHERINE JANE, lawyer, social policy analyst; b. N.Y.C., Dec. 27, 1949; d. Alexander I. and Wilma (Saltzman) Ross; m. Jonathan Rieder, Mar. 14, 1981. BA, Yale U., 1971, PhD, 1977, JD, 1987. Postdoctoral fellow/rsch. assoc. Yale Bush Ctr. in Child Devel. and Social Policy, New Haven, 1977—79; asst. prof. Yale Child Study Ctr., New Haven, 1979—85; assoc. Paul, Weiss, Rifkind, Wharton & Garrison, New Haven, 1987—94; asst. prof. law, history and edn. Boston Coll. Law Sch., 1994—96; assoc. prof. George Washington U. Sch. Law, 1996—. Vis. prof. U. Pa. Law Sch., 2001; mem. HHS Expert Working Group Adoption, 02; cons. Adminstrn. for Children Youth and Families, HEW, 1979, Conn. Dept. Children and Youth Svcs., 1978—84, ednl. films and radio programs. Joint editor: Child Abuse: An Agenda for Action, 1980. Del. Conn. Task Force on Juvenile Justice, 1979—80; com. mem. Conn. Task Force on Foster Care, 1979—81. Grantee Edna McConnell Clark Found., 1981—82, Herman and Amelia Ehrmann Found., 1979—82, Ford Found., 1980—82, John and Catherine MacArthur Found., 1981; Mellon fellow, Aspen Inst. Humanistic Studies, 1983—84. Fellow: Am. Bar Found.; mem.: ABA (vice chair working group on unmet legal needs of Am.'s children and th 1993—94, steering com. unmet legal needs of children 1993—94, chair 1994—97, co-chair 1997—98, mem. sect. litigation task force children, chair com. children's rights 1999—), Coalition Justice. Jewish. E-mail: cross@law.gwu.edu.

ROSS, CHARLES, artist; b. Phila., Dec. 17, 1937; s. Fred H. and Gertrude (Hill) R.; m. Elizabeth Ginsberg, 1977. AB in Math, U. Calif., Berkeley, 1960, MA in Sculpture, 1962. Exhibited in one-man shows: Dilexi Gallery, San Francisco, 1961, 65, 66, 68, Dwan Gallery, N.Y.C., 1968, 69, 71, Daytons Gallery 12, Mpls., 1968, John Weber Gallery, N.Y.C., 1972, 77, 79, 81, The Clocktower, N.Y.C., 1974, Utah Mus. Fine Arts, Salt Lake City, 1975, Mus. Contemporary Art, La Jolla, Calif., 1976, Chgo., 1976, Inst. Contemporary Art, Phila., 1977, Susan Caldwell Gallery, N.Y.C., 1977, MIT, 1977, Portland Center for Visual Arts, 1981, Sena Gallery, Santa Fe, 1991, Johnson Gallery U. N.Mex., 1992, Humphrey Gallery, N.Y.C., 1995, Mus. de Arte y Diseno Contemporaneo, San Jose, Costa Rica, 1996; exhibited in group shows: Archtl. League of, New York, 1967, Albright Knox Art Gallery, Buffalo, 1967, Finch Coll., N.Y.C., 1967, Aldrich Mus., Ridgefield, Conn., 1967, Nelson Atkins Mus., Kansas City, 1968, Milw. Art Center, 1968, Whitney Mus., N.Y.C., 1969, Art Inst. Chgo., 1969, Art Gallery of Ont., Toronto, 1969, Galeries-pilotes, Lausanne, Switzerland, 1970, Mus. Fine Arts, Boston, 1971, Indpls. Mus. Art, 1974, Neuberger Mus., SUNY, Purchase, 1975, Stadtisches Mus., Leverkusen, Germany, 1975, Phila. Coll. Art, 1977, Hirshhorn Mus., Washington, 1977, Old Customs House, N.Y.C., 1977, Mus. Natural History, N.Y.C., 1977, Leo Castelli Gallery, N.Y.C., 1978, Yale U. Art Gallery, 1978, Dartmouth Coll. Gallery, 1978, Aspen (Colo.) Center for Visual Arts, 1980, Centre Georges Pompidou, Paris, 1980, Renwick Gallery, Smithsonian Instn., Washington, 1980, Mus. Contemporary Art, Chgo., 1981, MIT, Cambridge, 1981, Bard Coll., 1984, Light Gallery, N.Y.C., 1985, Venice Biennale, 1986, Differentes Natures la Defense, Paris, 1992, Anchorage Mus. History & Art, 1994, Richard Humphrey Gallery, N.Y.C., 1995, Kunsthallen Brandts Klaedefabrik, Odense, Denmark, 1996, SITE Santa Fe, 1996, NIT Intercommunication Ctr., Tokyo, Japan, 1997, Biennale de Lyon, France, 2000; commn. include: prism/solar spectrum skylight sculpture for Fed. Bldg. Lincoln, Nebr., 1976, U. Pa., 1977, Dietrich Found., Phila., 1979, Spectrum Bldg, Denver, 1980, Grand Rapids Art Mus., Mich., 1982, Towson State U., Md., 1983, Cumberland Rapid Transit Sta., Chgo., 1983, Linay Corp., Kansas City, Mo., 1985, Plaza of the Americas, Dallas, 1985, Wells Fargo Bldg., San Diego, 1986, San Francisco Internat. Airport, 1987, Anchorage Internat. Airport, 1987, Naugatuck Higher Edn. Ctr., Conn., 1990, Harvard Bus. Sc. Chapel, 1992, French Ministry of Culture Chateau d'Oiron, 1993, Cook Inst., Grand Rapids, Mich., 1996, Dwan Light Sanctuary, United World Coll., Montezuma, N.Mex., 1996, U.S. Fed. Courthouse, Tampa, 1998, Saitama (Japan) U., 1999, Kauffman Found., Kansas City, 2001, Nat. Mus. of the Am. Indian, Smithsonian Inst., Washington, D.C., 2004, Meiji U., Tokyo, 2004; represented in permanent collections Nelson Atkins Mus., Whitney Mus. Am. Art, Berkeley Art Mus., Indpls. Mus. Art, Butler Inst. Am. Art, Herbert F. Johnson Mus. Art Cornell U., GSA Art and Architecture Program, U. Pa., Dietrich Found., Grand Rapids Art Mus., Gen. Elec. Corp., City Chgo., Towson State U., Becton Dickinson Corp., Security Pacific Bank, Found. Ctr., N.Y.C., Wynne Jackson Inc., Albuquerque Mus., Linclay Corp., Witco Chem. Corp., City of San Diego, Walker Art Ctr., City of San Francisco, State of Alaska, Koll Co., Los Angeles County Mus. Art, Mus.de Arte y Diseno Contemporaneo, San Jose, Kunsthallen Brandts Klaedefabrik, Odense, Des Moines Art Ctr., French Ministry of Culture, Frederick A. Weisman Mus., Mpls., Harvard Bus. Sch., Mus. Fine Arts, Santa Fe, United World Coll., N.Mex., Saitama U., Japan, Kauffman Found., Kansas City, Meiji U., Tokyo; works in progress include: Star Axis, architectonic earthwork/naked eye observatory atop a mesa in N.Mex. Author: Sunlight Convergence Solar Burn (Am. Inst. Graphic Arts award 1976); films Sunlight Dispersion, 1972, Solar Eclipse, 1972. Recipient Art and Architecture Collaborations award Boston Soc. Architects, 1993, Interfaith Forum on Religion, Art and Arch. Design award Harvard Bus. Sch. Chapel, 1993, award for distinction for artistic achievement Nat. Coun. Art Adminstrs., 1997. Office: Joyce Schwartz Ltd 17 W 54th St New York NY 10019-5404 *My work deals with the nature of light, time, and planetary motion.*

ROSS, CHARLES THOMAS, lawyer, publisher; b. Albany, Ga., Dec. 17, 1941; s. Elmer Basil and Ivaleen (Joiner) R.; m. Robin Leeger, Aug. 15, 1963 (div. June 1979); 1 child, Ivy Caroline; m. Diane Pipkin, July 21, 1980; 1 stepchild, Elizabeth Anne Creech. B.B.A., U. Ga., 1964; J.D., Vanderbilt U., 1969. Bar: N.C. 1970, U.S. Dist. Ct. (mid. dist.) N.C. 1971, U.S. Dist. Ct. (we. and ea. dists.) N.C. 1975, U.S. Supreme Ct. 1975, U.S. Ct. Appeals (4th cir.) 1978, U.S. Ct. Appeals (3d cir.) 1979. Research asst. N.C. Ct. Appeals, Raleigh, 1969-70; atty. Craige Brawley Liipfert & Ross, Winston Salem, N.C., 1970—; editor, pub., cons. Sports and the Courts, Inc., Winston Salem, 1980— . Co-author: Sports and Law, 1984. Mem. Sedimentation Control Commn., Raleigh, 1973-76; mem. law related edn. adv. com. Dept. Pub. Instrn., Raleigh, 1976— . Served to lt. U.S. Army, 1964-66. Mem. ABA (ho. of dels. 1977-79, chmn. spl. com. youth edn. for citizenship 1980-82, chmn. commn. on pub. understanding about the law 1982-84), N.C. Bar Assn. (chmn. young lawyers div. 1975-76, young lawyers service award 1973-74), Winston Salem C. of C. Republican. Club: Forsyth Country (Winston Salem); Twin City. Home: 130 Sullivan Way Winston Salem NC 27104-4925 Office: Craige Brawley Liipfert and Ross 210 W 4th St Winston Salem NC 27101-2824

ROSS, CHARLOTTE PACK, social services administrator; b. Oklahoma City, Oct. 21, 1932; d. Joseph and Rose P. (Traibich) Pack; m. Roland S. Ross, May 6, 1951 (div. July 1964); children: Beverly Jo, Sandra Gail; m. Stanley Fisher, Mar. 17, 1991. Student U. Okla., 1949-52, New Sch. Social Rsch., 1953. Cert. tchr. Exec. dir. Suicide Prevention and Crisis Ctr. San Mateo County, Burlingame, Calif., 1966-88; pres., exec. dir. Youth Suicide Nat. Ctr., Washington, 1985-93; exec. dir. Death with Dignity Edn. Ctr., San Mateo, Calif., 1994—; pres. Calif. Senate Adv. Com. Youth Suicide Prevention, 1982-84; speaker Menninger Found., 1983, 84; instr. San Francisco State U., 1981-83; conf. coord. U. Calif., San Francisco, 1971—; cons. univs. and health svcs. throughout world. Contbg. author: Group Counseling for Suicidal Adolescents, 1984, Teaching Children the Facts of Life and Death, 1985; mem. editorial bd. Suicide and Life Threatening Behavior, 1976-89. Mem. regional selection panel Pres.'s Commn. on White House Fellows, 1975-78; mem. CIRCLON Svc. Club, 1979—, Com. on Child Abuse, 1981-85; founding mem. Women for Responsible Govt., co-chmn., 1974-79. Recipient Outstanding Exec. award San Mateo County Coordinating Com., 1971, Koshland award San Francisco Found., 1984. Fellow Wash. Acad. Scis.; mem. Internat. Assn. Suicide Prevention (v.p. 1985—), Am. Assn. Suicidology (sec. 1972-74, svc. award 1990), bd. govs. 1976-78, accreditation com. 1975—, chair region IX, 1975-82), Assn. United Way Agy. Execs. (pres. 1974), Assn. County Contract Agys. (pres. 1982), Peninsula Press Club.

ROSS, CLARK GRANT, economics educator; b. Gloucester, Mass., June 24, 1950; s. Norman C. and Helen (Blecher) R. B.A., U. Pa., 1971; Ph.D., Boston Coll., 1975. Asst. prof. dept. econs. College of William and Mary, 1975-76; research scientist U. Mich., 1976-79; asst. prof. econs. Davidson Coll., N.C., 1979-83, assoc. prof., 1983—, chmn. dept., 1983—; cons. in field. Contbr. articles to profl. jours. Mem. Am. Econs. Assn., So. Econs. Assn. Roman Catholic. Home: RR 2 Box 283cc Davidson NC 28036-9802 Office: Dept Economics Davidson Coll Davidson NC 28036

ROSS, COLEMAN DEVANE, accountant, insurance company executive; b. Greensboro, NC, Mar. 18, 1943; s. Guy Matthews and Nancy McConnell (Coleman) R.; m. Carol Louise Morde, Aug. 26, 1965; children: Coleman, Jonathan, Andrew. BSBA, U. NC, 1965, postgrad., 1994, Grad. Sch. Banking of South, 1982—84, Trinity Coll., 1999—, Am. Coll., 2004—. CPA, CPCU, CLU, ChFC. With Price Waterhouse, 1965—99, ptnr., 1977—99; chmn., mng. ptnr. Nat. Ins. Svcs. Group, 1988-94; exec. v.p., CFO Trenwick Group Ltd., 2000—02, The Phoenix Cos., Inc., 2002—03. Bd. dirs. NCCI Holdings, Inc. Bd. dirs. N.E. Region Boy Scouts Am., 1988—, v.p., 1993-96, 2002—, pres. New England area, 1988-91, bd. dirs. Greater N.Y. Coun., 1994—, exec. bd. Conn. Rivers Coun., 1978—, pres., 1985-88; participant Leadership Greater Hartford, 1977; bd. visitors U. N.C., 2001—; bd. dirs. McLean Found., 2003—. Recipient Silver Beaver award Boy Scouts Am., 1987, Silver Antelope award, 1991. Mem. AICPA (reins. auditing and acctg. task force 1979-85, rels. with actuaries com. 1982-85, ins. cos. com. 1985-88, acctg. stds. exec. com. 2002—), N.C. Assn. CPAs, CFA Inst., Soc. Fin. Svc. Profls., CPCU Soc., Chartered Ins. Inst., Fin. Exec. Internat., Internat. Ins. Soc., Assn. Ins. and Fin. Analysts, N.Y. Soc. Security Analysts (com. on improved corp. reporting), Inst. Mgmt. Accountants, Inst. Internal Auditors, Polytechnic Club, Carolina Club, Williams Club. Home: 6 Wild Flower Ln West Simsbury CT 06092-2434 Personal E-mail: coleman.ross@comcast.net.

ROSS, CONNIE L. music educator; b. Pratt, Kans., Nov. 5, 1952; d. Eugene Haile and Alta Ross. BA, Mid-Am. Nazarene U., 1975; MusM in Edn., Fort Hays State U., 1982. Vocal music tchr. USD 483, 1975—82; elem. vocal music tchr. USD 443, Dodge City, Kans., 1982—2004. Pvt. piano tchr. Ch. pianist & accompanist. Mem.: NEA, Music Edn. Nat. Conf., Delta Kappa Gamma (co-chmn. music com.). Home: 2805 Buffalo Dr Dodge City KS 67801

ROSS, CURTIS BENNETT, lawyer; b. Carbondale, Ill., June 7, 1955; s. Bernard Harris and Marian Frager Ross. BS in Acctg., U. Ill., 1977, JD, 1980. Bar: Ill., 1984. Tax staff Arthur Andersen & Co., Chgo., 1980-82; lawyer Jerome H. Torshen, Ltd., Chgo., 1983, Curtis Bennett Ross, Chgo., 1984—. Attorney We Are Concerned, Chgo., 1995-99. Mem. Chgo. Bar Assn., CBA Matrimonial Com., Decalogue Soc. Office: 19 S La Salle St #13 Chicago IL 60603-1401

ROSS, DALE GARAND, therapist, programming consultant, speaker, writer; b. Detroit, May 31, 1948; s. Stanley Anthony and Kathleen Mary (Moore) Jamros. BS in Psychology, Mich. State U., 1970; MSW, Wayne State U., 1980. Cert. social worker Nat. Acad. Cert. Social Workers; cert. counselor Nat. Cert. Counselors; cert. social worker, Mich. Ptnr. Unicorns, Detroit, 1970-76; pres. Realities, Ltd., Birmingham, Mich., 1976-78; counselor I univ. counseling Wayne State U., Detroit, 1980-82, counselor II ednl. resources/disabilities, 1982-84, counselor II, univ. counseling, 1984-85; therapist Substance Abuse Ctr., Warren, Mich., 1985; pvt. practice Southfield, Mich., 1985—. Founding mem. Wellness Networks, Inc., Detroit, 1983-84; 1t pres., chmn. protem, founding mem. Wellness House Mich., 1985-87; part-time instr., developer grad. courses for Sch. of Social Work, Wayne State U., 1991-96, faculty liaison for student group, 1994-96, AIDS rsch. and edn. program and HIV mental health ednl. series, 1993—; pres. Southeastern Mich. Info. and Referral Alliance, 1992-94; cons. in field; presenter programs. Contbr. articles to profl. jours. Mem. steering com. Venereal Disease Action Coalition, United Cmty. Svcs., 1986-92; mem. steering com. Macomb County AIDS Cmty. Coun., chmn., 1988; mem. Hospice AIDS Task Force, 1986-88, AIDS Spkrs. Bur. and AIDS Phone Network, Mich. State Med. Soc., 1987—; program chmn. Motor City Bus. Forum, 1983-84, chmn. cmty. ctr. com., 1982-83; founding mem. work/worship Wellness Alliance Com., 1998; group leader Nat. Conf. for Cmty. and Justice, 1999. Recipient Am. Legion award 1966, Libr. Key award Hazel Park Pub. Schs., 1966; Mich. Bd. Govs. grantee, 1978-79, 79-80. Mem. NASW, Am. Coll. Personnel Assn. (men's task force), Nat. Orgn. for Changing Men (co-chmn. job-work satisfaction task group 1986), Internat. Platform Assn., Mich. Orgn. for Human Rights, World Future Soc., Mich. Alcohol and Addiction Assn. (bd. dirs. 1993-96), Am. Assn. Counseling Devel., Mich. Rainbow Therapist Assn. (co-founder). Avocations: antiques, ceramics. Home: 2366 Earlmont Rd Berkley MI 48072-1838 Office: 206 Americana Plaza 28475 Greenfield Rd Southfield MI 48076-3034 Office Phone: 248-544-7041. E-mail: realitiesunlimited@comcast.net.

ROSS, DANIEL J.J. publishing executive; b. Albany, N.Y., June 2, 1943; AB, Hamilton Coll., 1966; MA, U. Fla., 1969. Prodn. mgr. U. Fla. Press, 1976-80; mktg. mgr. U. Ala. Press, 1980-85; asst. dir. Duke U. Press, 1985-89; editor-in-chief U. Nebr. Press, Lincoln, 1989-95, dir., 1995—2001; dir. editor-in-chief Univ. Ala. Press, 2001—. Office: 20 Rsch Dr Tuscaloosa AL 35487-0380 E-mail: danross@uapress.ua.edu.

ROSS, DANIEL R. lawyer; b. Stamford, Conn., Oct. 20, 1941; s. Adrian E. and Ruth (Hill) R.; m. Faye Zerwekh, Aug. 15, 1965; children: Kevin S., Eric D., David W. SB, MIT, 1963; LLB, U. Pa., 1966. Atty. adviser to Hon. Theodore Tannenwald, Jr. U.S. Tax Ct., Washington, 1966-68; assoc. Drinker, Biddle & Reath, Phila., 1970-77, ptnr., 1977-98, Commons & Commons, Phila., 1998—. Presenter in field. Pres. bd. trustees First United Meth. Ch. Germantown, 1984-2004; bd dirs Smith Playground and Playhouses, Inc, 2003—. Capt. U.S. Army, 1968-70, Vietnam. Mem. ABA (chair com. on income of estates and trusts 1985-87, com. on govt. subcoms. 1988-91, taxation sect.). Avocations: bicycling, skiing, tennis, computers. Office: The Cambridge Ste 1210 2967 W School House Ln Philadelphia PA 19144-5222 Personal E-mail: danrross@aol.com. Business E-Mail: dross@commonslaw.com.

ROSS, DARIUS ALEXANDER, arbitrager and commodities trader, philanthropist, investment banker; b. Laurel, Miss., July 16, 1965; s. Malachi and Alice Audrey (Rodgers) R.; m. Rose Mary Mitchell, Feb. 17, 1995 (div. Dec. 1996); children: Tomika, Alexander, T'mia; m. Linda Johnson, Sept. 17, 1998 (div. Dec. 1999). Student, Chicago State U., 1983-86, Wright Coll., 1984, Internat. Acad. Design, 1985, Lake Forest Coll., 1986, AMA Inst., 1992, World Trade Inst. of N.Y., 1992, U. Pa. Dirs. Inst., 1996-97, Harvard U. Dirs. Inst., 1997, Northwestern U., Evanston, Ill., 1997—, Kennesaw State U., U. Chgo., NYU, Columbia U., N.Y. Inst. Fin., Oxford-Templeton Inst., MIT; cert. divinity & ministry, cert. futurist studies, Abaak Acad., 1999. Cert. bus. broker, merger and acquisition intermediary cons., corp. valuation cons.; lic. real estate comml. broker and appraiser. Pres. Darius Ross Interest Ltd., 1989—, BG III MDW Holdings, 1989—, BG III Ohio Holding, 1989—, BG III Wis., 1989—, BG III Mich., 1989—. Bd. dirs. Rossfinaco, Darfin Holdings, Cacig Group, Creamie Inc., Tamco Holdings, Darl Holdings, Darmac Interest., Ross & Ross Assocs., Altimia Holdings, Tamco Industries, Cacicg Group, Tadar Investments, Rossco Equities, Macross Trading, Ross To Ross Assoc., Daalta Devels., Nelgui Holdings, Katdad Investments, Soumislau Holdings, The 79th St. Entertainment Group, Albaltal Internat., LLC, Macalicon Multi State Holdings, The Ross 7AM Agrl. Co., Dam 7AM Ross Co. Holdings Group LLC. Bd. dirs. Tilman Cmty. Health Clinic, 1997, N.Y.C. H.S. of Econs. and Fin. Benefit Bd./Bus. Adv. Bd., Chgo. Acad. of Performing Arts Benefit Bd.; active Jobs for Youths, 1991-96, George W. Ross African Am. Studies Award and Found., Target 79th St. Redevel. Group, Kennedy King Coll. Computer Info. Sys. Adv. Bd.; mem. Consolidated Corp. Fund of Lincoln Ctr., N.Y. Trust, Chgo. Symphony Orch. Assn., Rep. Senatorial Trust; bd. dirs. DA 7AM Ross Co. Found., Malalic Inst., NWO-3 Charity Trust, D. Alexander Ross Ptnrs. Internat. LLC, Alexisal Internat. Edn. Charities. Recipient award Chgo. Directory of Apparel Mfrs., 1989; named Young Leader, S.W. Herald, 1989, N.Y. Times Heir Column, 1989, YEO/The Bridge Wealthy 100, 1990, Ace Young Entrepreneur of Yr., 1989, 90, YEO Entrepreneur Data Directory, 1993. Mem. ABA (assoc. mem.), NAFE, U.S. Postal Adv. Bd., Chgo. Postal Adv. Bd., Auburn Pk. Postal Adv. Bd., Hyde Pk. Postal Adv. Bd., Urban Bankers Assn., Turnabout Mgmt. Assn., Internat. Assn. Fin. Engrs., Treasury Mgmt. Assn., Chgo. Coun. Fgn. Rels., Am. Bus. Women's Assn. Nat. Assn. Women in Edn., Bus. Brokers Assn., Future Industry Assn., World Trade Assn., Nat. Cmty. Econ. Devel. Assn., Nat. Assn. Corp. Dirs. (sec. Chgo. chpt. 1997), N.Y. Stock Exch. Luncheon Club, Mid-Day Club (Chgo.), Met. Club (Chgo.), Chgo. Merc. Exch. Club, Midam. Club of Chgo., Profl. Security Internat., World Super Projects Fedn., Execs. Club (Chgo.), Mpls. Athletic Club, Univ. Club of Mich. State U., Assn. for Corp. Growth, Nat. Assn. Corp. Treasurers, Coun. Instl. Investors, Nat. Black MBA Assn., Alliance of Bus. Brokers and Intermediaries, Assn. Midwest Bus. Brokers, East Manhattan C. of C., Midwest Assn. Family Bus. Owners, Am. Soc. Corp. Secs., Comml. Fin. Assn., Young Execs. Club, Forest Akers Golf Club, Ohio State U. Faculty Club, Chgo. Athletic Assn., Chgo. Symphony Orch. Assocs., U. R.I. Club, Wellesley Coll. Club, Nat. Bar Assn. Women Lawyers Divsn., Am. Bar Assn., Hispanic Nat. Bar Assn., U. Wash. Faculty Club, World Future Soc., Hispanic Nat. Bar Assoc., Women's Bar Assn., Women's Bar Assn. of DC, Nat. Assn. Women Lawyers, Nat. Assn. Women Execs., Chgo. Social Sports Club, Brown U. Faculty Club, Columbia Faculty HSF Club, U. Del. Faculty Club, U. Pa. Faculty Club, U. Louisville Faculty Club, U. Club Nashville, Hofstra Faculty Club, Texas A&M Faculty Club, U. Texas Faculty Club, U. Wis. Faculty Club, U. Mo. Faculty Club, Harvard Club, Canebrake Golf Club, Polo Club, Powerboat Racing Club, Jai Alai Club, ATV Racing Club, Chariot Racing Club, U. Del. Faculty Club, U. Pa. Faculty Club. Republican. Roman Catholic. Avocations: tennis, soccer, golf, international travel, shooting. Office Phone: 212-414-7679. E-mail: drspktoyou@yahoo.com.

ROSS, DARRIN, composer; Pres. Bad Boi Studios; composer, sound engr. Jam on Prodns., 1984—. Collaborator: with Renee Harris Dance Party USA,: with Renee Harris 1 House Street. Recipient Philly's St. Buzz Producer of Yr. award, 1997. Office: Puremovement PO Box 42009 Philadelphia PA 19101

ROSS, DAVID A. art museum director; b. Malverne, N.Y., Apr. 26, 1949; s. Joshua and Grayce R.; m. Margaret Gronner; children: Lindsay, Emily. BA, Syracuse U.; postgrad., Grad. Sch. Fine Arts, Syracuse. Curator video art Everson Mus. Art, Syracuse, N.Y., 1971-74; dep. dir. program devel. and TV Long Beach Mus. Art, Calif., 1974-77; chief curator Univ. Art Mus., Berkeley, Calif., 1977-82; dir. Inst. of Contemporary Art, Boston, 1982-91; dir., CEO Whitney Mus. Am. Art, 1991-98; dir. San Francisco Mus. Modern Art, 1998—. Active Fed. Adv. Com. om Internat. Exbns., 1990—. Contbr. articles to profl. jours. Mem. Assn. Art Mus. Dirs. Office: San Francisco Mus Modern Art 151 3rd St San Francisco CA 94103-3107

ROSS, DAVID EDMOND, church official; b. Lewiston, Maine, Oct. 1, 1950; s. Rev. and Mrs. Lorne Arla Collins R.; m. Shirley Evelyn Godin, Aug. 19, 1972. BA in Theology cum laude, Berkshire Coll., 1973; MPA, U. Maine, 1989. Ordained to ministry Advent Christian Ch., 1975. Pastor State Road Advent Christian Ch., Presque Isle, Maine, 1973-91; exec. dir. Advent Christian Ch. Gen. Conf., Charlotte, NC, 1991—2003; sr. pastor Fellowship Advent Christian ch., Bethlehem, NC, 2003—. V.p. Maine State Conf. Advent Christian Chs., 1975-76, pres., 1976-81, 86-91; mem. exec. coun. Advent Christian Ch., 1981-90, long range strategy com., 1986—; seminar leader Am. Festival of Evangelism, Kansas City, 1981; dir. Northern Lights Youth Choir, 1974-90. Exec. dir., CEO Advent Christian Gen. Conf., 1991—2003. Office: Fellowship Advent Christian Church 885 Icard Ridge Rd Taylorsville NC 28681 Office Phone: 828-495-8086. E-mail: bethlehemshepherd@hotmail.com.

ROSS, DEBRA BENITA, jewelry designer, marketing executive; b. Carbondale, Ill., May 1, 1956; d. Bernard Harris and Marian (Frager) R. BS, U. Ill., 1978; MS, U. Wis., 1979. Dir. mktg. Ambion Devel., Inc., Northbrook, Ill., 1983-89, Fitness Horizons, Inc., Northbrook, 1989-91, v.p. mktg., 1991-97; owner Benita Ross Designs, Northbrook, 1992—. Home: 1853 Mission Hills Ln Northbrook IL 60062-5760

ROSS, DELMER GERRARD, historian, educator; b. Los Banos, Calif., Nov. 5, 1942; s. Elmer G. and Orva Beth (Dickinson) R.; m. Karen Ann Gibson, June 17, 1977; children: Michelle, Richard. BA, Pacific Union Coll., 1965; MA, U. Calif., Santa Barbara, 1967, PhD, 1970. Instr. Pacific Union Coll., Angwin, Calif., 1968-69; from asst. to assoc. prof. Oakwood Coll., Huntsville, Ala., 1970-76; from assoc. prof. to prof. history Loma Linda U., Riverside, Calif., 1976-91, chmn. dept. history and polit. sci., 1986-90; prof. history and polit. sci. La Sierra U., Riverside, 1991—. Author: Visionaries and Swindlers, 1975, Rails Across Costa Rica, 1976, Rails in Paradise, 1991, Gold Road to La Paz, 1992, Development of Railroads in Guatemala and El Salvador, 1849-1929, 2001, To End a Crooked Trail, 2002; co-author: Hope...Not Ashamed, 2002, Reminiscences of Walter D. Scott, Desert Entrepreneur of the American West, 2003; mem. editl. bd. Adventist Heritage mag., 1987-90. Bd. dirs. Inst. for Research in Latin Am., Mobile, Ala., 1968-82. Mem. Am. Hist. Assn., Assn. 7th Day Adventist Historians (exec. sec. 1973-74, sec.-treas. 1974-75, pres. 1981-82), Assn. Western Adventist Historians, Nat. Railway Hist. Soc., Colo. Railroad Hist. Found. (life), Railway and Locomotive Hist. Soc. Republican. Office: La Sierra U Dept History Riverside CA 92515 E-mail: dross@lasierra.edu.

ROSS, DENNIS E. automotive executive; b. 1951; Bachelors, Law Degree, U. Mich. Tax legis. counsel, dep. asst. sec. Office Tax Policy U.S. Treasury Dept., 1986—89; tax ptnr. Davis Polk and Wardwell, NY, 1989—95; chief tax officer Ford Motor Co., Dearborn, Mich., 1995—2000, v.p., gen. counsel, 2000—. Office: Ford Motor 10th Fl Rm 1060a The American Rd Whq Dearborn MI 48121

ROSS, DIANA ERNESTINE EARLE, singer, actress, entertainer, fashion designer; b. Detroit, Mar. 26, 1944; d. Fred and Ernestine R.; m. Robert Ellis Silberstein, Jan. 1971 (div. 1976); children: Rhonda, Tracee, Chudney; m. Arne Naess, Oct. 23, 1985 (div. 2000, dec. 2004); children: Ross Arne, Evan Olaf. Pres. Diana Ross Enterprises, Inc., Anaid Film Prodns., Inc., RTC Mgmt. Corp., Chondee Inc., Rosstown, Rossville, music pub. Started in Detroit as mem. the Primettes; lead singer until 1969, Diana Ross and the Supremes; solo artist, 1969—; albums include Diana Ross, 1970, 76, Everything Is Everything, 1971, I'm Still Waiting, 1971, Lady Sings The Blues, 1972, Touch Me In The Morning, 1973, Original Soundtrack of Mahogany, 1975, Baby It's Me, 1977, The Wiz, 1978, Ross, 1978, 83, The Boss, 1979, Diana, 1981, To Love Again, 1981, Why Do Fools Fall In Love?, 1981, Silk Electric, 1982, Endless Love, 1982, Swept Away, 1984, Eaten Alive, 1985, Chain Reaction, 1986, Diana's Duets, 1987, Workin' Overtime, 1989, Red Hot Rhythm and Blues, 1987, Surrender, 1989, Ain't No Mountain High Enough, 1989, The Force Behind the Power, 1991, Stolen Moment: The Lady Sings... Jazz & Blues, 1993, Musical Memories Forever, 1993, The Remixes, 1994, A Very Special Season, 1994, Making Spirits Bright, 1994, Take Me Higher, 1995, Voice of Love, 1996, Gift of Love, 1996, The Greatest, 1998, The Real Thing, 1998, Every Day is a New Day, 1999; films include Lady Sings the Blues, 1972, Mahogany, 1975, The Wiz, 1978; NBC-TV spl., An Evening With Diana Ross, 1977, Diana, 1981, numerous others; TV movie Out of Darkness, 1994; author: Secrets of a Sparrow, 1993. Recipient citation V.P. Humphrey for efforts on behalf Pres. Johnson's Youth Opportunity Program, citation Mrs. Martin Luther King and Rev. Abernathy for contbn. to SCLC cause, awards Billboard, Cash Box and Record World as worlds outstanding singer, Grammy award, 1970, Female Entertainer Yr. NAACP, 1970, Cue award as Entertainer Yr., 1972, Golden Apple award, 1972, Gold medal award Photoplay, 1972, Antoinette Perry award, 1977, nominee as Best Actress Yr. Lady Sings the Blues Motion Picture Acad. Arts and Scis., 1972, Golden Globe award, 1972, BET (Black Entertainment Television) Walk Fame award, 1999, Heroes award, NARAS, NY Chpt., 2000; named to Rock and Roll Hall Fame, 1988. Office: c/o Motown Records 825 8th Ave New York NY 10019*

ROSS, DONALD, transportation executive; m. Nancy Ross; 3 children. From mgmt. trainee to br. mgr. Enterprise Rent-A-Car, St. Louis, 1964—71, corp. v.p., 1980—92, sr. exec. v.p., COO, 1992—2001, pres., 2001—, from mgmt. trainee to br. mgr. Kansas City, Mo., 1972—80; also bd. dirs. Bd. dirs. Centric Group, BJC Health Care, Mo. Bapt. Hosp. Bd. dirs. Mcpl. Theatre Assn., St. Louis; past bd. dirs. DeSmet Jesuit HS, Boys Hope/Girls Hope. Mem.: Boone Valley Golf Club (bd. dirs.). Office: Enterprise Rent a Car 600 Corporate Park Dr Saint Louis MO 63105-4211

ROSS, DONALD, JR., English language educator, university administrator; b. N.Y.C., Oct. 18, 1941; s. Donald and Lea (Meyer) R.; m. Sylvia Berger (div.); 1 child, Jessica; m. 2d, Diane Redfern, Aug. 27, 1971; children—Owen, Gillian BA, Lehigh U., 1963, MA, 1964; PhD, U. Mich., 1967. Asst. prof. English U. Pa., Phila., 1967—70; prof. English U. Minn., Mpls., 1970—, dir. composition program, 1982—86, 2002—03, dir. Univ. Coll., 1984—89. Author: American History and Culture from the Explorers to Cable TV, 2000; co-author: Word Processor and Writing Process, 1984, Revising Mythologies: The Composition of Thoreau's Major Works, 1988; co-editor, contbr.: American Travel Writers, 1776-1865, 1997, American Travel Writers, 1850-1915, 1998; contbr. articles to profl. jours. Grantee Am. Coun. Learned Socs., 1976, 90, NSF, 1974, Fund for Improvement of Postsecondary Edn., 1982-85; recipient Disting. Teaching award U. Minn., 1992. Mem. MLA, Assn. for Computers and Humanities (exec. sec. 1978-88), Internat. Soc. for Travel Writing (exec. sec. 2001—). Office: U Minn Dept English 207 Lind Hall 207 Church St SE Minneapolis MN 55455-0152 E-mail: rossj001@umn.edu.

ROSS, DONALD EDWARD, engineering company executive; b. N.Y.C., May 2, 1930; m. Jeanne Ellen McKessy, Apr. 4, 1954; children: Susan, Christopher, Carolyn. BA, Columbia Coll., 1952; BS in Mech. Engring., Columbia U., 1953; MBA, NYU, 1960. Registered profl. engr., N.Y., 14 other states. Engr. Carrier Corp., N.Y.C., 1955-70; v.p. Dynadata, 1970-71; with Jaros, Baum & Bolles, N.Y.C., 1971-2000, ptnr., 1977-2000; ret., 2000. Mem. adv. coun. sch. engring. Columbia U. Mem. adv. coun. Columbia U. Sch. Engring. and Applied Sci. Lt. (j.g.) USN, 1953-55. Fellow ASHRAE, Am. Cons. Engrs. Coun.; mem. ASME, NSPE, Nat. Acad. Engrs., Nat. Bur. Engring. Registration, N.Y. Assn. Cons. Engrs. (pres. 1984-86), Coun. on Tall Bldgs. and Urban Habitat (vice chmn. N.Am., mem. steering group), Univ. Club (N.Y.C.), Columbia U. Sch. Engring. Alumni Assn. (pres. 1997-99), Nassau Country Club, Tau Beta Pi. E-mail: Rossd@jbb.com.

ROSS, DONALD EDWARD, university administrator; b. Mineola, N.Y., June 29, 1939; s. Alexander Walker and Florence M. (Carville) R.; m. Helen Landgren, July 23, 1966; children: Ellen Ross Sarafian, Kevin McAndrew. BFA, N.Y. Inst. Tech., 1962, LLD (hon.), 1978; MS, Hofstra U., 1970. Dean of students N.Y. Inst. Tech., Old Westbury, 1962-68; pres. Wilmington (Del.) Coll., 1968-77; pres., CEO Lynn U. (formerly Coll. of Boca Raton), Fla., 1971—. Chmn. adv. com. U.S. Army Command and Gen. Staff Coll. Bd. dirs. Fla. Endowment Fund, 1989—; trustee Boca Raton Community Hosp., 1990—; mem. governing bd. Philharmonic Orch. Fla., 1990—; mem. U.S. Mil. Screening Com. Named Industrialist of Yr., Greater Boca Raton C. of C., 1992, Man of the Yr., City of Hope; recipient Boy Scouts Am. Leadership Svc. award, Boca Raton award, 1991, LEAH Bridge Builder of the Year, 1999. Mem. Assn. Univ. Pres., Econ. Coun. of Palm Beach County, Royal Palm Yacht and Country, Loggerhead Club, Adirondack League Club, Old Forge Club, City (Boca Raton). Avocations: snowskiing, tennis, reading, travel, golf. Home: 7411 Floranada Addison Res Delray Beach FL 33484 Office: Lynn Univ 3601 N Military Trail Boca Raton FL 33431-5598

ROSS, DONALD HUGH, fraternal organization executive; b. Delta, Ohio, Aug. 19, 1949; s. Hugh Archbald and Margaret Baker (Harlton) R.; m. Mary Lynn Feuerborn, Dec. 21, 1974; children: Jon, Michael. BS, Miami U., Oxford, Ohio, 1971. Auditor Moose Internat., Mooseheart, Ill., 1971-76, dep. supreme sec., 1976-78, asst. comptroller, 1978-83; supreme sec. Supreme Lodge, Mooseheart, Ill., 1983-99; dir. gen., pres., CEO, 1999—. Sec. Mooseheart Bd. Govs., Moosehaven Bd. Govs., 1983-00. Mem. pub. bd. Moose Action publ., Moose mag.; contbr. articles to newspapers and profl. jours. Mem.: Interact (Delta) (pres. 1966-67), Moose (past gov. 1976, Pilgrim Degree of Merit 1983). Republican. Avocations: golf, travel. Home: 1119 Woodland Ave Batavia IL 60510-3049 Office: Supreme Lodge Moose Internat Mooseheart IL 60539-1180

ROSS, DONALD KEITH, retired insurance company executive; b. Rochester, N.Y., July 1, 1925; s. Alexander L. and Althea G. (Granger) R.; m. Mary F. Fyffe, June 4, 1949; children: Catherine (Mrs. Charles P. Lesher), Susan (Mrs. William Gardner Morris, Jr.), Donald Keith, Deborah Anne Holt. B.E., Yale U., 1946; MBA, Harvard U., 1948. With N.Y. Life Ins. Co., N.Y.C., 1948—, exec. v.p., 1974-79, vice chmn., 1979-80, pres., 1980-81, chmn. bd., CEO, 1981-90, chmn. exec. com., 1990-93; ret., 1996. Office: NY Life Ins Co 51 Madison Ave New York NY 10010-1603

ROSS, DONALD ROE, federal judge; b. Orleans, Nebr., June 8, 1922; s. Roe M. and Leila H. (Reed) Ross; m. Janice S. Cook, Aug. 29, 1943; children: Susan Jane, Sharon Kay, Rebecca Lynn, Joan Christine, Donald Dean. JD, U. Nebr., 1948, LLD (hon.), 1990. Bar: Nebr. 1948. Practice law, Lexington, Nebr., 1948—53; mayor City of Lexington, 1953; assoc. Swarr, May, Royce, Smith, Andersen & Ross, 1956—70; U.S. atty. Dist. Nebr., 1953—56; gen. counsel Rep. party, Nebr., 1956—58; mem. Rep. Exec. Com. for Nebr., 1952—53; com. mem. Rep. Nat. Com., 1958—70, vice-chmn., 1965—70; judge U.S. Ct. Appeals (8th cir.), 1970—87, sr. judge, 1987—. Office: Roman L Hruska Courthouse Ste 4226 111 S 18 Plaza Omaha NE 68102-1322

ROSS, DOUGLAS, lawyer; b. L.A., July 12, 1948; s. Mathew and Brenda Butler (Boynton) R.; m. Lynne Rose Maidman, June 14, 1970. AB cum laude, Tufts U., 1970; JD with honors, George Washington U., 1973. Bar: Ohio 1973, D.C. 1980, U.S. Supreme Ct. 1976. Asst. atty. gen., antitrust sect. Office of Ohio Atty. Gen., Columbus, 1973-74; spl. asst. U.S. atty. Ea. Dist. Va., Alexandria, 1977; trial atty. antitrust divsn. U.S. Dept. Justice, Washington, 1975-82; atty. advisor Office of Legis. Affairs, 1984-86, Office of Legal Policy, 1987-89, Office Policy Devel., 1989-92; Supreme Ct. counsel Nat. Assn. Attys. Gen., 1982-91. Ran advocacy project for states to enhance their effectiveness before Supreme Ct., 1982—91; operated clearinghouse on state constl. law, 1987—91; civil divsn. Appellate Staff U.S. Dept. Justice, Washington, 1992—94, Office of Consumer Litigation, 1994—2000, spl. counsel for agr. antitrust divsn., 2000—. Recipient Meritorious award Dept. Justice, 1979, Spl. Achievement award, 1984, 96, 97. Mem. Supreme Ct. Hist. Soc., D.C. Bar Assn., Supreme Ct. Opinion Network (bd. dirs. 1989-91), Arlington County Sports Commn. (chair aquatics com., chmn. subcom. North tract masterplan oversight com., 2004—). Jewish. Home: 3153 19th St N Arlington VA 22201-5103 Office: US Dept Justice 601 D St NW Washington DC 20530-0001 Office Phone: 202-514-1874.

ROSS, E. EARL, small business owner; b. July 3, 1942; s. Edward Earl and Ruth Randles (Loewen) R.; m. Mary Donna Moore, May 31, 1964; 1 son, Damon Moore. BA in Psychology, Central Mo. State U., 1965; MA in Corrections, Webster U., 1976. Reporter Warrensburg (Mo.) Daily Star-Jour., 1965; social worker St. Louis County Welfare Div., Maplewood, Mo., 1966-68; assoc. dist. scout exec. Boy Scouts Am., St. Louis, 1968; dep. juvenile officer St. Louis County Juvenile Ct., Clayton, Mo., 1969-72; program dir. St. Louis County Detention Ctr., Clayton, Mo., 1972-99, asst. supt., 1978-99; CEO Golf-o-Gram, 1999—. Trainer statewide detention staffs; past pres. Historygram, Inc. Recipient Outstanding Detention Program award Nat. Council Juvenile and Family Ct. Judges, 1982. Mem. St. Louis County Juvenile Justice Assn., Am. Mgmt. Assn. Home: 15333 Appalachian Trl Chesterfield MO 63017-1939

ROSS, EDWARD, cardiologist; b. Fairfield, Ala., Oct. 10, 1937; s. Horace and Carrie Lee (Griggs) R.; m. Catherine I. Webster, Jan. 19, 1974; children: Edward, Ronald, Cheryl, Anthony. BS, Clark Coll., 1959; MD, Ind. U., 1963. Diplomate Am. Bd. Internal Medicine; cert. specialist in clin. hypertension Am. Soc. Hypertension. Intern Marion County Gen. Hosp., Indpls., 1963; resident in internal medicine Ind. U., 1964-66, 68, cardiology rsch. fellow, 1968-70, clin. asst. prof. medicine, 1970; cardiologist Capitol Med. Assn., Indpls., 1970-74; pvt. practice medicine, specializing in cardiology Indpls., 1974—. Staff cardiologist Winona Meml. Hosp., Indpls., chief cardiovascular disease, 2000—, med. dir. cardiovascular svcs., 2000—, med. dir. cardiac cath lab, 2000—, chief interventional cardiology, 2000—; staff Meth. Hosp., Indpls., chmn. cardiovasc. sect., 1989-96; chmn. cardiovasc. sect., dir. cardiovasc. ctr. Meth. Hosp., 1990-92; bd. dirs. Meth. Hosp. Heart-Lung Ctr., 1990—, mem. dir. cardiovasc. svcs., 1991-98. Assoc. editor Angiology, Jour. Vascular Disease; sr. editor Jour. Vascular Medicine, 1983—. Mem. Ctrl. Ind. Health Planning Coun., 1972-73; bd. dirs. Ind. chpt. Am. Heart Assn., 1973-74, multiphasic screening East Side Clinic, Flanner Ho. of Indpls., 1968-71; med. dir. Nat. Ctr. for Health Svc. R&D, HEW, 1970; consumer rep. radiologic device panel health FDA, 1988-92; dir. hypertensive screening State of Ind., 1974; J.B. Johnson Cardiovasc. lectr. Nat. Med. Assn., 1991. Capt. MC, USAF, 1966-68. Woodrow Wilson fellow, 1959; Nat. Found. Health scholar, 1955, Gorgas Found. scholar, 1955. Fellow Royal Soc. Promotion of Health (Eng.), Am. Coll. Angiology (v.p. fgn. affairs, sec. 1993—), Internat. Coll. Angiology, Am. Coll. Cardiology, Assn. Black Cardiologists (mem. bd. dirs. 1990-94); mem. NAACP, AMA, Am. Soc. Contemporary Medicine and Surgery, Nat. Med. Assn. (coun. sci. assembly 1985-89), Ind. Med. Soc., Marion County Med. Soc., Am. Soc. Internal Medicine, Am. Heart Assn., Ind. Soc. Internal Medicine (pres. 1987-89), Ind. State Med. Assn. (chmn. internal medicine sect. 1987-89), Ind. Med. Soc., Aesculapean Med. Soc., Hoosier State Med. Assn. (pres. 1980-84, 90-95), Urban League, Alpha Omega Alpha, Alpha Kappa Mu, Beta Kappa Chi, Omega Psi Phi. Baptist. Office: 3231 N Meridian St Ste 700 Indianapolis IN 46208-4668 E-mail: edrossmd@aol.com., rosscath@aol.com.

ROSS, EDWARD JOSEPH, architect; b. Dec. 13, 1934; s. Miriam Ross; children: Linda Joy, Melissa Carol. Student, Boston Archtl. Ctr., 1952-55, 61-62, USAF Surveying Sch., 1955-56, Boston Soc. Civil Engrs., 1956-57, Carl Bolivar Structural Engr., 1962-63. Registered architect, Mass., Calif., N.Y., Fla., N.H., Vt.; cert. Nat. Coun. Archtl. Registration Bds.; lic. constrn. supr., Mass.; expert witness constrn. law. Draftsman, assoc. William W. Drummey, Architect, Boston, 1952-59; job capt., designer Drummey-Rosane-Anderson, Boston, 1959-64; projects architect Maginnis & Walsh & Kennedy, Boston, 1964-69; v.p. William Nelson Jacobs Assocs., Inc., Boston, 1969-73; staff architect Robert Charles Assocs., Inc. Architects, Boston, 1973-74; office mgr. Charles F. Jacobs Assocs., Inc., Cambridge, Mass., 1974-76; cons. architect Linenthal, Eisenberg & Anderson, Boston, 1976-77; staff architect Eisenberg Haven Assocs., Inc., Boston, 1977-78; chief architect, chief inspector Boston Housing Authority, 1978-83; prin. Edward J. Ross, AIA/FARA, Randolph, Mass., 1983-84; architect, sr. assoc., dir. constrn. adminstrn. Stull and Lee, Inc., Boston, 1984-91; practice architecture Randolph, Stoughton, Mass., 1963—. Mem. FCC Tech Plus. Bd. dirs. Linderhof Property Owners Assn., Knollsbrook Condominium Complex.; mem. Ancient and Hon. Arty. Co. of Mass. Staff sgt. USAF; maj. Mass. Mil. Res. Fellow Soc. Am. Registered Architects; mem. AIA, USO (New Eng. Coun.), Am. Assn. Ret. Persons, Am. Arbitration Assn. (nat. panel 1965—), Mass. State Assn. Architects., Constrn. Specifications Inst., Boston Soc. Architects (housing com. 1982-86), Air Force Assn. (pres. Boston chpt.), Mass. Air N.G. Hist. Assn., Mil. Hist. Soc. Mass., Assn., First Corps Cadets, Ten of Us Club, Oxford 100 Condominium Assn. (pres.), Linderhof Golf Course Site One Assn. (pres. 1980-86), Elks, K.P., Am. Legion, Oxford Colony Club of Century Village (v.p.). Address: 201 Oxford 100 West Palm Beach FL 33417-1412

ROSS, E(DWIN) CLARKE, association executive, educator; b. Balt., Sept. 21, 1948; s. Harry Edwin and Margaret Frances (Turner) R.; m. Elizabeth Christine Shannon, Mar. 26, 1988; 1 child, Andrew Clarke. BA, U. Md., 1970, MA, 1974; D of Pub. Adminstrn., George Washington U., 1981. Vol. VISTA, Washington, 1970-71; legis. asst. Nat. Assn. State Mental Health Program Dirs., Washington, 1971-72; from asst. dir. to dir. Govt. Rels. United Cerebral Palsy Assns., Washington, 1972-84; asst. prof. European region Troy State U., Weisbaden, Germany, 1984-86; asst. exec. dir. for fed. rels. Nat. Assn. State Mental Health Dirs., Washington, 1986-93, dep. exec. dir., 1993-95; exec. dir. Am. Managed Behavioral Healthcare Assn., Washington, 1995-98; dep. exec. dir. pub. policy Nat. Alliance for the Mentally Ill., Arlington, Va., 1998-2000; CEO Children and Adults with Attention Deficit/Hyperactivity Disorder, Landover, Md., 2000—. Adj. grad. faculty, Cen. Mich. U., Washington, 1983-84, 87-93, 99—; adj. assoc. prof. U. Md., College Park, 1992-95. Author: Managed Behavioral Health Care Handbook, 2001; contbr. articles to profl. jours. and chpts. to books; author: Endurance as a Virtue: Army of Northern Virginia Civil War Experiences. Vol. Com. for Legal Svcs., Washington, 1970-71; mem. U.S. Olympic Com. on Winter Sports for Disabled, Colo. Springs, Colo., 1983-84; mem. program com. Dem. Club, Annapolis, Md., 1984. Recipient Maternal and Child Health scholarship to Johns Hopkins U., State of Md., 1975. Mem. SAR, Am. Coll. Mental Health Adminstrn., Am. Soc. Pub. Adminstrn., Am. Polit. Sci. Assn., St. Andrew's Soc., Sovereign Mil. Order of Temple of Jerusalem, Beta Gamma Sigma (life). Presbyterian. Avocations: Scottish country dancing, skiing, Scottish and U.S. history. Home and Office: 1718 Reynolds St Crofton MD 21114-2635 E-mail: clarke_ross@chadd.org.

ROSS, EDWIN WILLIAM, rubber company executive; b. Phila., May 28, 1938; s. Edwin Morrison and Frances Louise (Ort) R.; m. Dorothy Anne Reilly, Sept. 24, 1966; children: E. William Jr., Catherine Ross Conlin, James David. BS, Lehigh U., 1960. Chmn. bd., CEO, Key Chems., Inc., Phila., 1965-87, Ross Enterprises, Inc., Villanova, Pa., 1987—; pres., CEO Pelmor Labs., Inc., Newtown, Pa., 1989—; chmn. Pelseal Techs., LLC, Newtown, Pa., 1998—. Mem. adv. bd. Prime Bank, Ft. Washington, Pa., 1995—98. Deacon Bryn Mawr (Pa.) Presbyn. Ch., 1977-81, elder, 1985-91, trustee, 1997-2003, pres. bd. trustees, 2001-2003; bd. dirs. Main Line Adult Day Care Ctr., 1999. Recipient Alumni award Lehigh U. Alumni Assn., 1985. Mem. SAR, MidAtlantic Employers Assn. (chmn. 1995-96), Metal Finishing Suppliers Assn. (pres. 1986-88, 89-90, Munning award 1992), N.E. Phila. C. of C. (chmn. 1983), Lehigh U. Alumni Assn. (bd. dirs. 1997-2000), Swedish Colonial Soc., Sons of the Revolution Soc., St. Andrew's Soc., Colonial Soc., Exch. Club (pres. Frankford-Phila. 1972), Phila. Country Club (pres. 1986-89). Republican. Avocations: downhill skiing, hunting, travel, golf. Home: 1514 Willowbrook Ln Villanova PA 19085-1912 Office: Pelmor Labs Inc 401 Lafayette St Newtown PA 18940-0309 Office Phone: 215-968-3334.

ROSS, ELLIOTT M. pharmacologist, researcher, educator; b. Stockton, Calif., Jan. 16, 1949; married; 1 child. Instr. sect. biochemistry, molecular & cell biology Cornell U., 1974; postdoctoral fellow dept. pharmacology Sch. Medicine U. Va., 1975-77, asst. prof. depts. biochemistry & pharmacology, 1978-81; assoc. prof. dept. pharmacology U. Tex. Southwestern Grad. Sch. Biomed. Scis., 1981-86, chmn. grad. program pharmacology, 1982-89, mem. grad. programs cell regulation, 1991—, mem. grad. program molecular biophysics, 1991-93, 95—, mem. grad. program biochemistry & molecular biology, 1993—, mem. grad. program pharmacology, 1981-91, mem. grad. program cell & molecular biology, 1981-91; prof. dept. pharmacology U. Tex. Southwestern Med. Ctr., Dallas, 1986—, chmn. med. rsch. Vis. asst. prof. dept. pharmacology U. Va. Sch. Medicine, 1977-78. Recipient Goodman & Gikman Drug Receptor Pharmacology award Am. Soc. Pharmacology & Exptl. Therapeutics, 1996. Office: U Tex Southwestern Med Ctr Dept Pharmacology 5323 Harry Hines Blvd Dallas TX 75390-7208

ROSS, EUNICE LATSHAW, judge; b. Bellevue, Pa., Oct. 13, 1923; d. Richard Kelly and Eunice (Weidner) Latshaw; m. John Anthony Ross, May 29, 1943 (dec. Jan. 1978); 1 child, Geraldine Ross Coleman. BS, U. Pitts., 1945, LLB, 1951. Bar: Pa. 1952. Atty. Pub. Health Law Rsch. Project, Pitts., 1951-52; atty. jud. asst., law clk. Ct. Common Pleas Allegheny County, Pitts., 1952-70, dir. family divsn., 1970-72, judge, 1972-96, Commonwealth Ct. Pa., 1997—2004. Adj. law prof. U. Pitts., 1967-73; mem. Bd. Jud. Inquiry and Rev., Commonwealth of Pa., 1984-89, Gov's Justice Commn., 1972-78; mem. orphan's ct. rules com. Supreme Ct. Pa., 1998—. Author: (with others) Survey of Pa. Public Health Laws, 1952, Justice, 1995, Lötschers of Latterbach, Monnonite Heritage Mag., 2003; co-author: Will Contests, 1992; contbr. articles to law publs. Mem. exec. com. bd. trustees U. Pitts., 1980—86, bd. visitors Law Sch., 1985—, bd. visitors Sch. Health, 1986—98; mem. adv. bd. Animal Friends, Pitts., 1973—98; committeewoman for 14th ward, vice chmn. Pitts. Dem. com., 1972; bd. dirs. The Program, Pitts., 1983—87, Pitts. History and Landmarks Found., West Pa. Hist. Soc., West Pa. Conservancy. Named Girls Scouts Woman of Yr., Pitts. coun. Girl Scouts U.S.A., 1975, Alumni of Yr., U. Pitts. Law Sch., 2001; recipient Disting. Alumna award, U. Pitts., 1973, Medal of Recognition, 1987, Alumni award, U. Pitts. Sch. of Law, 2001, Susan B. Anthony award, Women's Bar Assn. Western Pa., 1993, Probate and Trusts award, 1994, cert. of achievement, Pa. Fedn. Women's Clubs, 1975, 1977. Mem.: ABA, Allegheny County Bar Assn. (vice chmn., exec. com. young lawyers sect. 1958—59), Pa. Trial Judges Conf., Scribes, Order of Coif. Home: 1204 Denniston Ave Pittsburgh PA 15217-1329

ROSS, FRANK HOWARD, III, management consultant; b. Charlotte, NC, Aug. 28, 1946; s. Frank Howard Jr. (dec.) and Alma (Richardson) R. (dec.); m. Beverly Hazel Ross, June 30, 1973 (dec.); children: Martha McCausland, Frank Howard IV. BS in Engring., N.C. State U., 1968. Cons. Fails & Assocs., Inc., Raleigh, N.C., 1968-73; ptnr. Ross-Payne & Assocs., Inc., Barrington, Ill., 1973—. Bd. dirs. Gilldorn Savs., Chgo., 1982-85, Brickman Industries, Inc., Chgo., 1980-90; CFO WRT, Inc., Chgo., 1993-95; pres., chmn. bd. dirs. Emerald Capital Investments, Inc., Barrington, 1993-97; adviser, spkr. on constrn. and fin.; bd. dirs. Sherman Plumbing, 1975-95. Author: More $ Through $ Management, 1975, MIS and You, 1978, Planning and Budgeting, 1979, Profit by Design, 1981, Pricing for Profit, 1983, Wealthbuilding, 1984, Equipment Cost Analysis, 1988, Survivial in a Tight Economy, 1988, Associated Landscape Contractors of America Operating Cost Survey, 1989, 91, Cash Flow, 1989, Dealing with the Competition of the 90's, 1990, Designing Your Accounting System, 1991, Bidding in a Tight Market, 1992, Industry's Wage and Benefit Study, 1992, Financing Your Business, 1993, Pricing, 1994, 2d edit., 1997, How Low Can You Go?, 1995, Valuing Your Business, 1998, Posturing for Growth and Prosperity, 1999. Mem. Presbyn. Ch. Barrington. Mem. Inst. Mgmt. Cons., Barrington Hills Country Club, Haig Point Country Club, Sigma Alpha Epsilon. Home and Office: Ross Payne Assocs Inc 536 Eton Dr Barrington IL 60010-2017 Office Phone: 847-381-8939.

ROSS, FRED MICHAEL, organic chemist; b. N.Y.C., Aug. 26, 1921; s. Albert N. and Shirley (Honig) R.; m. Nee Kilar, May 9, 1954; children: Robin, Bonnie, Richard. BS, Mich. Tech. U., 1943. Sr. gas analyst Pure Oil Co., Chgo., 1943-44; chief chem. engr. Multiplate Glass Corp., Jamaica, N.Y., 1945-51; founder, CEO Diamond Dust Co., Inc., Mineola, N.Y., 1952-80; chmn. bd. dirs. Portfolio Mgmt., Inc., Rochester, N.Y., 1976-80; founder, pres. Gemery Corp., Mineola, 1974-80; dir. Indsl. Diamond Assn. of Am., 1977-78; CEO, chmn. Robonard, Inc., Boca Raton, Fla., 1980—. Contbr. over 10 articles to profl. publs. Campaign co-chmn. for R. Shaw for Ariz. Ho. of Reps, 1994. Petty officer USN, 1944-45. Recipient Bd. of Control Silver medal for Outstanding Alumnus Mich. Tech. U., 1978; inducted Mich. Tech. U. Acad. Scis. and Arts, 1997. Fellow Am. Inst. Chemists (life). Achievements include development of process for manufacture of ovate diamonds for use in petroleum bits and geological core drills, process for reclamation and recovery of industrial diamond bearing waste materials. Office: Robonard Inc 10325 Crosswind Rd Boca Raton FL 33498-4757 Office Phone: 561-483-4748. Business E-Mail: fmr@att.net.

ROSS, GERALD FRED, engineering executive, researcher; b. NYC, Dec. 14, 1930; s. Samuel Henry and Jenny (Saltzman) Rozansky; m. Vivian Ida Turkish, Dec. 24, 1953; children: Jayne T. Ross Kaufman, Steven A., Helene B. Ross Joseph. BEE, CCNY, 1952; MEE, Poly. U., 1955, PhD, 1963. Registered profl. engr., N.Y., Mass., Fla. Rsch. asst. U. Mich., Ann Arbor, 1952-53; sr. engr. W.L. Maxson Corp., N.Y.C., 1954-58; rsch. sect. head Sperry Gyroscope Co., Great Neck, L.I., N.Y., 1958-65; dept. mgr. Sperry Rsch. Ctr., Sudbury, Mass., 1965-81; CEO, chmn. ANRO Engring., Inc., Sarasota, Fla., 1981—; chmn. Ana Lux Corp., 2002—. Pres., v.p., treas. Adams Pool Corp., Lexington, Mass., 1968-81. Capt. USAFR, 1953—. Contbg. author 3 books, 1986, 90, 93; contbr. numerous articles to profl. jours.; patentee in field. Fellow Polytechnic U. Fellow IEEE (life; K.C. Black Nerem Best paper award 1974, Pioneer award 2004), Nat. Acad. Engring. (life); mem. Electromagnetics Acad., Lexington Golf Club, Longboat Key Club, Sigma Xi (sr.), Tau Beta Pi, Eta Kappa Nu. Republican. Jewish. Avocations: golf, tennis. Office: ANRO Engring Inc 1800 2d St Ste 730 Sarasota FL 34236-5971 Office Phone: 941-957-3080. E-mail: drgfr@aol.com.

ROSS, GERALD HARVEY, family practice and environmental medicine physician; s. Henry Warburton and Norine Hazel (Bishop) Ross; m. Heather M. Pollett, Aug. 15, 1970; children: Graham D.P., Andrew W.J. BSc, Dalhousie U., 1969, MD, 1974. Diplomate Internat. Bd. of Environ. Medicine, 1989. Med. dir. Nova Scotia Environ. Medicine Clinic, Halifax, Canada, 1970—74; family medicine practice Pvt. Practice, New Minas, Canada, 1974—87; med. fellowship Environ. Health Ctr. - Dallas, Dallas, 1987—89, med. staff, 1989—99; rschr. Gerald H. Ross, M.D., P.L.L.C., Bountiful, Utah, 1999—2004. Chmn. exec. com. Med. Soc. Nova Scotia, Halifax, 1992—93; mem. adv. com. Environ. Hypersensitives Ont. Dept. Health, Toronto, 1989—94; rsch. fellow Breakspeare Hosp. for Environ. Medicine, Kings Langley, Hertfordhsire, England, 1988—89. Co-author reports to Ont. Ministry of Health; contbr. chapters to books, articles to profl. jours., scientific papers. Many leadership positions Ch. LDS, Dallas, 1988—99. Internat. grlloe in Environ. Medicine, Nova Scotia Dept. of Health, 1987—89, Innovations in Edn., Utah grantee, 2003. Fellow: Royal Soc. of Medicine (U.K.), Am. Acad. Environ. Medicine (pres. 1995—97, chair rsch. com. 1991—94, bd. dirs. 1993—98, Award of appreciation for serving as Pres. 1997); mem.: AMA, Assn. Am. Physicians and Surgeons, Am. Coll. Nutrition, Am. Coll. Occupl. and Environ. Medicine, Can. Soc. Environ. Medicine, Coll. Family Physicians of Can., Am. Bd. Environ. Medicine (bd. govs. 1993—2004), Chem. Sensitivity Found. (bd. dirs., grantee 2003—), Can. Med. Assn., Tex. Med. Assn. Conservative-R. Mem. Lds Ch. Avocations: reading advances in science, reading mystery fiction, movies. Office: Gerald H Ross MD PLLC PO Box 115 Bountiful UT 84011

ROSS, HAROLD ANTHONY, lawyer; b. Kent, Ohio, June 2, 1931; s. Jules and Helen Assumpta (Ferrara) R.; m. Elaine Louise Hunt, July 1, 1961; children: Leslie Ann, Gregory Edward, Jonathan Harold. BA magna cum laude, Case Western Res. U., 1953; JD, Harvard U., 1956. Bar: Ohio 1956. Assoc. Marshman, Hornbeck, Hollington, Steadman & McLaughlin, Cleve., 1961-64; pres. Ross & Kraushaar Co., Cleve., 1964—. Gen. counsel Brotherhood of Locomotive Engrs., Cleve., 1966—; adv. bd. mem. Ctr. for Advanced Study of Law and Dispute Resolution Procedures, George Mason U. Sch. Law, 2000—. Trustee Citizens League Greater Cleve., 1969-75, 76-82, pres., 1981-82; active Charter Rev. Com. North Olmsted, 1970, 75. With AUS, 1956-58. Fellow Coll. Labor and Employment Lawyers; mem. ABA (co-chair rwy. and airline labor law sect. 1976-78), Ohio State Bar Assn., Cleve. Bar Assn., Phi Beta Kappa, Delta Sigma Rho, Omicron Delta Kappa. Roman Catholic. Office: 1548 Standard Bldg 1370 Ontario St Cleveland OH 44113-1701 Business E-Mail: haross@ble.org.

ROSS, HOWARD PHILIP, lawyer; b. May 10, 1939; s. Bernard and Estelle (Maremont) Ross; m. Loretta Teresa Benquil, 1962 (div.); children: Glen Joseph, Cynthia Ann, Ryan Reeve; m. Jennifer Kay Shirley, 1984. BS, U. Ill., 1961; JD, Stetson Coll. Law, 1964. Bar: Fla. 1964, U.S. Ct. Appeals (5th cir.) 1965, U.S. Supreme Ct. 1969, U.S. Ct. Appeals (11th cir.) 1981, cert.: civil trial lawyer, bus. litigator. Assoc. Parker & Battaglia and predecessor firm, St. Petersburg, Fla., 1964-67; ptnr. Battaglia, Ross, Dicus & Wein, P.A., St. Petersburg, 1967—, pres., CEO, 1992-99, chmn. bd. dirs., 2000—. Lectr. Stetson Coll. Law, St. Petersburg, 1971—72, adj. prof., 1987. Author: Florida Corporations, 1979; co-author: Managing Discovery in Commercial and Business Litigation, 1993; contbr. articles to profl. jours. Hon. chair St. Petersburg br. Awards Banquet NAACP, 1995; bd. dirs. St. Petersburg Neighborhood Housing Svcs., Inc., 1997, legal counsel, 1997—, pres., 2000—02; bd. dirs. Cmty. Alliance, 1997—2002; chmn. subcom. Citizen Rev. Com. City of St. Petersburg, 1992—94, co-chair, 1994—97. Recipient Woman's Svc. League Best Groomed award, 1979, Fla. Bar Merit citation, 1974, Cmty. Svc. award, NAACP, 1998, Humanitarian award, YMCA of Tampa Bay, 1999, C.W. Bill Young Pinellas Pinnacle award, 2002. Mem.: ABA, Am. Arbitration Assoc. (panel of comml. neutrals 2003—), St. Petersburg Bar Assn., Fla. Bar Assn. (chmn. civil trial certification com. 1993—94), St. Petersburg Area C. of C. (bd. govs. 1990—95, v.p. pub. affairs 1992—93, exec. com. 1992—95, v.p. membership 1993—94, counsel 1994—95, dean entrepreneurial acad. 1996—2003, treas. 2000—02, bd. govs. 2000—, chair-elect 2002—03, chair 2003—, Mem. of Yr. 1993—94). Republican. Jewish. Office: Battaglia Ross Dicus & Wein PA PO Box 41100 980 Tyrone Blvd N Saint Petersburg FL 33710-6382 Office Phone: 727-381-2300. E-mail: hross@brdwlaw.com.

ROSS, HUGH COURTNEY, electrical engineer; b. Dec. 31, 1923; s. Clare W. and Jeanne F. Ross; m. Sarah A. Gordon (dec.); m. Patricia A. Malloy; children: John C., James G., Robert W. Student, Calif. Inst. Tech., 1942, San Jose State U., 1946-47; BSEE, Stanford U., 1950, postgrad., 1954. Registered profl. elec. engr., Calif. Instr. San Benito (Calif.) High Sch. and Jr. Coll., 1950-51; chief engr. vacuum power switches Jennings Radio Mfg. Corp., San Jose, Calif., 1951-62; chief engr. ITT Jennings, San Jose, Calif., 1962-64; pres. Ross Engring. Corp., Campbell, Calif., 1964—. Contbr. articles to tech. jours.; patentee in field. Fellow IEEE (life) (chmn. Santa Clara Valley subsect. 1960-61); mem. Am. Vacuum Soc., Am. Soc. Metals. Avocations: electronics, electric autos, camping, ranching, solar power. Office: 540 Westchester Dr Campbell CA 95008-5012 Office Phone: 408-377-4621.

ROSS, IAN BEAUDOIN, neurosurgeon, educator; b. Montreal, Que., Can., Feb. 29, 1960; came to the U.S., 2000; s. Ian Cathcart and Jacqueline Joan Ross; m. Catherine Sylvia Pitfield, June 1, 1985; children: Felicia Lillian, William Leopold. BSc, McGill U., Montreal, 1981; MD, Queen's U., Kingston, Can., 1985; MSc, U. Toronto, Can., 1992. Asst. prof. U. Man., Winnipeg, Can., 1993-99, assoc. prof., 1999-2000, U. Miss., Jackson, 2000—. Vis. fellow Fondation Rothschild, Paris, 1998-99. Contbr. articles to profl. jours. Recipient Penfield McNaughton award Montreal Neurol. Inst., 1992; fellow Fund award Health Sci. Ctr., Winnipeg, 1998. Fellow ACS, Royal Coll. Surgeons Can. (Clin. Traineeship award 1999); mem. Am. Assn. Neurol. Surgeons, Can. Neurosurg. Soc. (provincial rep. 1998-99). Avocations: reading, skiing, tennis, opera. Home: 3605 Old Canton Rd Jackson MS 39216 Office: U Miss Med Ctr 2500 N State St Jackson MS 39216-4505

ROSS, IAN MUNRO, electrical engineer; b. Southport, Eng., Aug. 15, 1927; came to U.S., 1952, naturalized, 1960; m. Christina Leinberg Ross, Aug. 24, 1955; children: Timothy Ian, Nancy Lynn, Stina Marguerite. BA, Gonville and Caius Coll., Cambridge U., 1948, MA in Elec. Engring, PhD, Cambridge U., 1952; DSc (hon.), N.J. Inst. Tech., 1983, Poly. U., 1988; D of Engring. (hon.), Stevens Inst. Tech., 1983; DSc (hon.), Polytech. U., 1988. With AT&T Bell Labs. (and affiliates), 1952-92, exec. dir. network planning div., 1971-73, v.p. network planning and customer svcs., 1973-76, exec. v.p. systems engring. and devel., 1976-79, pres., 1979-91; pres. emeritus AT&T Bell Labs., Holmdel, 1991—. Bd. dirs. Thomas & Betts Corp., B.F. Goodrich Co., Nacco Industries; chmn. Nat. Adv. Commn. on Semicondrs. Patentee in field. Recipient NASA Pub. Svc. award, 1969, 75, medal Ind. Rsch. Inst., 1987. Fellow IEEE (Founders' medal 1988, Am. Acad. Arts and Scis.; mem. NAS, NAE. Home: 5 Blackpoint Horseshoe Rumson NJ 07760-1500 Office: Lucent Technologies 101 Crawfords Corner Rd Holmdel NJ 07733-1985

ROSS, JAMES OWEN, education educator, researcher; b. Morganton, NC, Sept. 27, 1948; s. Owen and Vivian Chapman Ross; life ptnr. Charles Anthony Staley; 1 child, Juliana Adele. BFA, U. of NC at Greensboro, Greensboro, North Carolina, 1971; AM, Brown U., 1986, PhD, 2003. Prof. Ringling Sch. of Art and Design, Sarasota, Fla., 1974—75, Ctrl. Piedmont C.C., Charlotte, ND, 1976—80, Appalachian State U., Boone, NC, 1983—84, RISD, Providence, 1985—86, U. of Okla., 1987—88, Wentworth Inst. of Tech., Boston, 1990—91; tchg. fellow Brown U., 1990—92; prof. ND State U., 1991—92, Western Carolina U., 1992, U. of Memphis, 1995—96, East Tenn. State U., 1997—98. Building, Preliminary Design Windsor Locks Rapids Exhbn. Ctr. (Interior Design Educators Coun. Internat. Exhbn., Nashville, Tenn., 1995), building interior, Hynes Residence Libr. (Interior Design Educators Coun. Internat. Exhibit, Denver, Colo., 1996). Dem. nominee in NC state senate, 27th dist. NC Dem. Party, NC, 1996; vestry mem. St. Peter's Episcopal Ch., Charlotte, NC, 1981—82; represented bus. in hist. dist. Friends of Fourth Ward Hist. Dist., Charlotte, NC, 1979—82. Tchg. fellow, Brown U., 1990—91. Mem.: Internat. Interior Design Assn. (Presdl. Commendation 1999), AIA (assoc.), Soc. of Archtl. Historians (life). Democrat-Npl. Soc. Of Friends. Achievements include research in impact of nineteenth-century public health movement upon American architecture: Theories of Disease, Ventilation, and Sunlight, 1840-1944. Avocations: travel, back packing, swimming, gardening, cooking. Home: 132 Malbon's Mills Rd Skowhegan ME 04976 Personal E-mail: james.ross.g86@alumni.brown.edu.

ROSS, JAMES ULRIC, lawyer, accountant, educator; b. Del Rio, Tex., Sept. 14, 1941; s. Stephen Mabrey and Beatrice Jessie (Hyslop) R.; m. Janet S. Calabro, Dec. 28, 1986; children: James Ulric Jr., Ashley Meredith. BA, U. Tex., 1963, JD, 1965. Bar: Tex. 1965, U.S. Tax Ct. 1969; CPA, Tex. Estate tax examiner IRS, Houston, 1965-66; tax acct. Holmes, Raquet, Harris & Shaw, San Antonio, 1966-67; pvt. practice Del Rio and San Antonio, Tex., 1968—. Instr. St. Mary's U., San Antonio, 1973-75; assoc. prof. U. Tex., San Antonio, 1975-99, ret. Contbr. articles on U.S. and Internat. Estate Planning and Taxation to legal and profl. jours. Active Am. Cancer Soc., Am. Heart Assn. Mem. ABA, Tex. Bar Assn., Tex. Soc. CPAs, San Antonion Bar Assn., San Antonio Estate Planners Coun. Home: 3047 Orchard Hl San Antonio TX 78230-3078 Office: 730 The Forum 8000 IH 10 W San Antonio TX 78230 Office Phone: 210-349-7400. E-mail: jamesross@justice.com.

ROSS, JEAN M. think-tank executive; Grad., U. Calif., Santa Cruz; M in City and Regional Planning, U. Calif., Berkeley. Asst. rsch. dir. Svc. Employees Internat. Union, Washington; sr. cons. Assembly Human Svcs.; prin. cons. Assembly Revenue and Taxation Com.; exec. dir. Calif. Budget Project, Sacramento, 1994—. Mem. exec. com. Calif. Governance Consensus Project; bd. mem. Inst. on Taxation and Econ. Policy, Washington; mem. adv. com. Calif. Franchise Tax Bd.; spkr. in field. Contbr. articles to profl. jours. Sr. fellow, UCLA Sch. Pub. Policy and Social Rsch., 2000—01. Office: Calif Budget Project Ste 502 921 11th St Sacramento CA 95814-2820*

ROSS, JEFFREY ALAN, research biologist; b. Thayer, Mo., Oct. 19, 1955; s. Ralph and Naomi June (Jacobs) R.; m. Lisa Lynn Pnazek, Apr. 23, 1977; children: Trillian Elise, Jennifer Ariane, Marissa Kerowyn. BS, U. Dallas, 1977; PhD, U. Tex., Dallas, 1982. Predoctoral fellow Robert A. Welch Found., 1979-82; postdoctoral fellow Cancer Ctr. Rsch. div. U. Tex., Smithville, 1982-85; NRC fellow U.S. EPA, Research Triangle Park, N.C., 1985-86, rsch. biologist, 1986-99, chief cancer biology br., 1999—. Contbr. articles to profl. jours. Bd. dirs. 1st Environments Early Learning Ctr., Research Triangle Park, 1989-90, 94-96. John B. O'Hara Found. fellow, 1973-76. Mem. AAAS, Am. Assn. Cancer Rsch., N.Y. Acad. Scis., Genotoxicity and Environ. Mutagen Soc. (bd. dirs. 1991-94, 97-2000). Achievements include research on the formation, repair, and biological consequences of carcinogen DNA adducts.

ROSS, JEFFREY ALLAN, political scientist, educator; b. NYC, Dec. 24, 1947; s. Joseph and Pearl (Epstein) R.; m. Marjorie Appelson, Aug. 30, 1970; children: Craig, Eric, Brian, Allison. BA in Polit. Sci. summa cum laude, SUNY, Binghamton, 1969; PhD in Polit. Sci., U. Minn., 1982. N.Y. State regents' fellow, tchg. asst. U. Minn., Mpls., 1969-71, rsch. asst., 1971-73, instr., 1973, Kirkland Coll., Clinton, N.Y., 1973-78, Huber Found. faculty rsch. grantee, 1973, 74, 77, Mellon Found. grantee, 1974, rsch. prof., 1975-76; instr. govt. Hamilton Coll., Clinton, 1978-80, asst. prof., 1980-82; vis. prof. polit. sci. Syracuse U., 1984; adj. prof. polit. sci. Queens Coll., CUNY, 1987-88; dir. dept. campus/higher edn. affairs Anti Defamation League, 1984—. V.p., bd. dirs. Rsch. Ctr. for Religion and Human Rights in Closed Socs.; exec. bd. Com. for Pub. Higher Edn., chmn., profl. panel mem. Author: (with Ann Cottrell) The Mobilization of Collective Identity: Comparative Perspectives, 1980, Pamyat: Hatred Under Glasnost, 1989, Schooled in Hate: Anti-Semitism on Campus, 1997, Guide for College and University Presidents and Administrators, Responding to Bigotry and Intergroup Strife on Campus, 2001; contbr. articles to profl. jours.; mem. editl. bd. Tchg. Polit. Sci., 1971-81; editor Hamilton Social Sci. Rev., 1977-79; reviewer manuscripts for profl. jours., book pubs. Precinct rep. Dem. Farm Labor Party, Mpls., 1972-73. Mpls. Found., Frances E. Andrews Fund All-Univ. rsch. fellow, surveyor Soviet Jewish emigrants, Israel, 1972. Mem. Am. Polit. Sci. Assn., N.E. Polit. Sci. Assn. (exec coun.), Internat. Polit. Sci. Assn., Internat. Studies Assn., Mongolia Soc., Can.-Mongolia Soc., Comparative Interdisciplinary Studies Soc. (exec. coun.), N.Y. State Polit. Sci. Assn. (v.p. 1982-83, pres. 1983-84), Sound Cyclists Bicycle Club (v.p. 1989-90, 94, pres. 1991-93, chmn. giving coun. 2002—), Norwalk Ski Club (v.p. 1992-93), River Hills Ski Club (exec. bd., pres. 2002—). Democrat. Home: 20 Soundview Loop South Salem NY 10590-2510 Office: Anti-Defamation League 823 United Nations Plz New York NY 10017-3518 Fax: (212) 490-0187. . E-mail: rossj@adl.org. *A satisfying life must be multidimensional. One's community, family and recreation have a necessary place alongside one's career. A fully realized person becomes also a fully realized professional.*

ROSS, JERRY L. astronaut; b. Crown Point, Ind., Jan. 20, 1948; s. Donald J. and Phyllis E. Ross; m. Karen S. Pearson; 2 children. BS in Mech. Engring., Purdue U., West Lafayette, Ind., 1970; MS in Mech. Engring., Purdue U.; Grad. Test Flight Engr., USAF Test Pilot Sch., 1976; DSc (hon.), Purdue U. Commd. 2d lt. USAF, 1970, retired, 2000; rschr. ramjet engring divsn. Air Force Aeropropulsion Lan, Wright-Patterso AFB, Ohio, 1972—74; lab. exec. officer, chief mgmt. ops. office Wright Patterson AFB Labs., Dayton, Ohio, 1974—75; flight test engr., supr. crew mem. 6510th; Flight Test Engring. USAF, Edwards AFB, Calif., 1976—79; payload officer, flight controller Lyndon Johnson Space Center, Houston, 1979—80; astronaut NASA, Houston, 1980—. Named a Distging. Grad. of the USAF Test Pilot Sch.; recipient 13 NASA medals, Victor A. Prather award, Am. Astron. Soc., 1985, 1990, 1999, Defense Superior Svc. Medal with one Oak Leaf, Air Force Legion of Merit, Defense Meritoriious Svc. Medal with 3 Oak leaf Clusters, Air Force Meritious Svc. Medal with one Oak Leaf, Outstanding Flight Test Eng. Award Class 75B. Mem.: Purdue Alumni Assn. (life), Assn. of Space Explorers (life). Achievements include six space flights; over 1133 hours in space, including 44 hours, 9 minutes on seven space walks. Avocations: genealogy, stained glass, racquetball, woodworking, photography. Office: Astronaut Ctr NASA Johnson Space Ctr Houston TX 77058*

ROSS, JIMMY DOUGLAS, retired military officer; b. Hosston, La., May 23, 1936; s. Horace Eugene and Lucile Marie (Pontious) R.; m. Patricia L. Cox, Dec. 18, 1955; children: Sabra, DiAnna, Tony. BS, Henderson State U., 1958; MA in Bus. Mgmt., Central Mich. U., 1975. Commd. 2d lt. U.S. Army, 1958, advanced through grades to 4 Star Gen., 1994, served comdr. co., bn., brigade levels, comdg. gen. 2d Support Command (Corps) VII Corps, 1980-82; dir. transp., energy and troop support Office Dep. Chief of Staff for Logistics, U.S. Army, Washington, 1982-84; chief staff U.S. Army Materiel Command, Alexandria, Va., 1984-86; comdr. U.S. Army Depot System Command, Chambersburg, Pa., 1986-87; dep. chief of staff for logistics U.S. Army, Washington, 1987-92; commdg. gen. U.S. Army Materiel Command, Alexandria, Va., 1992-94; retired, 1994. Bd. dirs. VSE Engring. Co., Stanley Assoc., Inc., Armed Forces Svcs. Corp., Integrated Data Corp., Am. Ecology Corp.; chmn. Def. Industry Conf. Bd.; pres. bd. dirs. Indsl. Coll. of Armed Forces Assn.; pres., COO Cypress Internat., 2000-03; sr. logistics cons. Cypress Internat., Inc., 2004. Dist. commr. Alpine dist. Boy Scouts Am., 1980-82; sr. v.p., COO Biomed. Svcs., ARC Nat. Hdqrs., 1994-99; chmn. Army Sci. Bd.; pres. Buffalo Soldiers Meml. Fund Found., 2001; bd. dirs. Buffalo Soldiers Found., 2001. Decorated D.S.M. with oak leaf cluster, Legion of Merit, Bronze Star, Air medal. Fellow Assn. U.S. Army (sr.); mem. Am. Def. Preparedness Assn., Nat. Def. Transp. Assn., Armed Forces Benefit Assn. (bd. dirs.). Methodist. Home: 4981 Maple Glen Pl Lake Forest FL 32771

ROSS, JOHN, physical chemist, educator; b. Vienna, Oct. 2, 1926; arrived in U.S., 1940; s. Mark and Anna (Krecmar) Ross; m. Virginia Franklin (div.); children: Elizabeth A., Robert K.; m. Eva Madarasz. BS, Queens Coll., 1948; PhD, MIT, 1951; D (hon.), Weizmann Inst. Sci., Rehovot, Israel, 1984, Queens Coll., SUNY, 1987, U. Bordeaux, France, 1987. Prof. chemistry Brown U., Providence, 1953—66, MIT, Cambridge, 1966—80, chmn. dept., 1966—71, chmn. faculty of Inst., 1975—77; prof. Stanford (Calif.) U., 1980—2001, chmn. dept., 1983—89, prof. emeritus, 2001—. Cons. to industries; mem. emeritus bd. govs. Weizmann Inst., 1971—. Author: Physical Chemistry, 1980, Physical Chemistry, 2d edit., 2000; editor: Molecular Beams, 1966; contbr. articles to profl. jours. 2nd lt. U.S. Army, 1944—46. Recipient medal, Coll. de France, Paris, Presdl. Nat. Medal of Sci., 1999, Austrian Cross of Honor for Sci. and Art, 1st class, 2002. Fellow: AAAS, Am. Phys. Soc.; mem.: NAS, Am. Chem. Soc. (Irving Langmuir Chem. Physics prize 1992, Peter Debye award in phys. chemistry 2001, Theodore William Richards medal 2004), Am. Acad. Arts and Sci. Home: 738 Mayfield Ave Palo Alto CA 94305-1044 Office: Stanford U Dept Chemistry Stanford CA 94305-5080 Office Phone: 650-723-9203. Business E-Mail: john.ross@stanford.edu.

ROSS, JOHN, JR., cardiologist, educator; b. N.Y.C., Dec. 1, 1928; s. John and Janet (Moulder) R.; children: Sydnie, John, Duncan; m. Lola Romanucci, Aug. 26, 1972; children: Adan, Deborah Lee. AB, Dartmouth Coll., 1951; MD, Cornell U., 1955. Intern Johns Hopkins Hosp., 1955—56; resident Columbia-Presbyn. Med. Center, N.Y.C., 1960—61, N.Y. Hosp.-Cornell U. Med. center, 1961—62; chief sect. cardiovascular diagnosis cardiology br. Nat. Heart Inst., Bethesda, Md., 1962—68; prof. medicine U. Calif., San Diego, 1968—2000, also dir. cardiovascular div., 1968—91, rsch. prof. medicine, 2000—; prof. cardiovascular research Am. Heart Assn. San Diego Co. Affiliate, San Diego, 1986—99. Mem. cardiology adv. com. Nat. Heart, Lung and Blood Inst., 1975-78, task force on arteriosclerosis, 1978-80, adv. council, 1980-84; bd. dirs. San Diego Heart Assn.; vis. prof. Brit. Heart Assn., 1990. Author: Mechanisms of Contraction of the Normal and Failing Heart, 1968, 76, Understanding the Heart and Its Diseases, 1976; mem. editorial bd. Circulation, 1967-75, 80-88, editor in chief 1988-93, Circulation Research, 1971-75, Am. Jour. Physiology, 1968-73, Annals of Internal Medicine, 1974-78, Am. Jour. Cardiology, 1974-79, 83-88, JOur. Clin. Investigation, 1992-97, Italian Heart Jour., 1999—, JOur. Cardiac Failure, 2000—, Circulation JOur. Japan, 2000—; cons. editor Circulation, 1993—; contbr. chpts. to books, sci. articles to profl. jours. Served as surgeon USPHS, 1956-63. Decorated grande ufficiale Order of Merit of Republic of Italy; recipient Ing. Enzo Ferrari prize for Enzo Ferrari, Modena, Italy, 1989, James B. Herrick award Coun. Clin. Cardiology

Am. Heart Assn., 1990, Mentorship award Am. Heart Assn., 2004. Fellow Am. Coll. Cardiology (master 1998—, v.p. trustee, pres. 1986-87, Disting. Scientist award 1990), ACP; mem. Am. Soc. Clin. Investigation (councillor), Am. Physiol. Soc., Assn. Am. Physicians, Cardiac Muscle Soc., Assn. Univ. Cardiologists, Assn. West. Physicians (councillor). Home: 8599 Prestwick Dr La Jolla CA 92037-2025 Office: U Calif Dept Med M # 0613B San Diego CA 92093

ROSS, JOSEPH COMER, physician, educator, academic administrator; b. Tompkinsville, Ky., June 16, 1927; s. Joseph M. and Annie (Pinckley) R.; m. Isabelle Nevins, June 15, 1952; children: Laura Ann, Sharon Lynn, Jennifer Jo, Mary Martha, Jefferson Arthur. BS, U. Ky., 1950; MD, Vanderbilt U., 1954. Diplomate Am. Bd. Internal Medicine (bd. govs. 1975-81), with added qualifications in pulmonary disease. Intern Vanderbilt U. Hosp., Nashville, 1954-55; resident Duke U. Hosp., Durham, N.C., 1955-57, rsch. fellow, 1957-58; from instr. medicine to prof. Ind. U. Sch. Medicine, Indpls., 1958-70; prof., chmn. dept. medicine Med. U. of S.C., Charleston, 1970-80; vis. prof. Vanderbilt U. Sch. Medicine, Nashville, 1979-80, prof. medicine, 1981-99, prof. medicine emeritus, 1999—, assoc. vice chancellor for health affairs, 1982-99, assoc. vice chancellor for health affairs emeritus, 1999—. Mem. cardiovascular study sect. NIH, 1966-70, program project com., 1971-75; mem. adv. coun. Nat. Heart, Lung and Blood Inst., 1982-86; mem. ad hoc coms. NAS, 1966, 67; mem. Pres.'s Nat. Adv. Panel on Heart Disease, 1972; mem. merit rev. bd. in respiration VA Rsch. Svc., 1972-76, chmn., 1974-76. Mem. editorial bd. Jour. Lab. and Clin. Medicine, 1964-70, Chest, 1968-73, Jour. Applied Physiology,1968 73, Archives of Internal Medicine, 1976-82, Heart and Lung, 1977-86; contbr. articles to profl. jours. Bd. dirs. Nashville Ronald McDonald Ho., past pres.; bd. dirs. Agape, Leadership Nashville, v.p.; mem. adv. com. Davidson County Cmty. Health Agy.; active Tenn. Lung Assn.; elder Ch. of Christ. With U.S. Army, 1945—47. Fellow: ACP, Am. Coll. Cardiology, Am. Coll. Chest Physicians (gov. S.C. 1970—76, chmn. sci. program com. 1973, vice chmn. bd. govs. 1974—75, exec. coun. 1974—80, chmn. bd. govs. 1975—76, pres.-elect 1976—77, pres. 1977—78, chmn. by-laws com. 2002—04, bd. regents 2002—04); mem.: AMA (sect. on med. schs.), Am. Soc. Internal Medicine, So. Soc. Clin. Rsch., Am. Thoracic Soc. (nat. councillor 1972—76), S.C. Med. Soc., Ctr. Social Clin. Rsch., Assn. Profs. Medicine, Assn. Am. Physicians, Am. Soc. Clin. Investigatrion, Am. Physiol. Soc., Am. Fedn. Clin. Rsch. (chmn. Midwest sect.), S.C. Lung Assn. (v.p. 1974—75), Phi Beta Kappa, Alpha Omega Alpha. Office: Vanderbilt U Med Ctr Oxford House Ste 212 Nashville TN 37232-0001 Office Phone: 615-322-1479. E-mail: joseph.ross@comcast.net., joseph.ross@vanderbiltmcmail.edu.

ROSS, JUNE ROSA PITT, biologist, educator; b. Taree, New South Wales, Australia, May 2, 1931; came to U.S., 1957; d. Bernard and Adeline Phillips; m. Charles Alexander, June 27, 1959. BSc with honors, U. Sydney, New S. Wales, Australia, 1953, PhD, 1959, DSc, 1974. Research assoc. Yale U., New Haven, 1959-60, U. Ill., Urbana, 1960-65, Western Wash. U., Bellingham, 1965-67, assoc. prof., 1967-70, prof. biology, 1970—73, prof. emeritus, 1974—, chair dept. biology, 1989-90. Pres. Western Wash. U. Faculty Senate, Bellingham, 1984-85; conf. host Internat. Bryozoology Assn., 1986. Author (with others): A Textbook of Entomology, 1982, Geology of Coal, 1984; editor (assoc.): Palaios, 1985—89; contbr. 130 articles to profl. jours. Recipient J. Wolfensohn Award of Excellence Sydney U. Grad. Union of N.Am., 1995, P. and R. Olscamp Outstanding Rsch. award Western Wash. U., 1986; NSF grantee. Mem.: Internat. Bryozoology Assn. (pres. 1992—95), The Paleontol. Soc. (councillor 1984—86, treas. 1987—93), Australian Marine Scis. Assn., U.K. Marine Biol. Assn. (life). Avocations: hiking, classical music. Office: Western Wash U Dept Biology Bellingham WA 98225-9160 Office Phone: 360-650-3634. Business E-Mail: ross@biol.wwu.edu.

ROSS, KAREN, information technology executive; Founder, pres. Turn-Key Solutions, 1985—90; founder, prin. owner, CEO Sharp Decisions, N.Y.C., 1990—. Office: Sharp Decisions 55 W 39th St New York NY 10018

ROSS, KATHLEEN ANNE, academic administrator; b. Palo Alto, Calif., July 1, 1941; d. William Andrew and Mary Alberta (Wilburn) Ross. BA, Ft. Wright Coll., 1964; MA, Georgetown U., 1971; PhD, Claremont Grad. U., 1979; LLD (hon.), Alverno Coll. Milw., 1990, Dartmouth Coll., 1991, Seattle U., 1992; LHD (hon.), Whitworth Coll., 1992; LLD (hon.), Pomona Coll., 1993; LHD (hon.), Coll. of New Rochelle, 1998; LLD (hon.), U. Notre Dame, 1999, Gonzaga U., 1999; LHD (hon.), Carroll Coll., 2003, Pacific Luth. U., 2004. Cert. tchr., Wash. Secondary tchr. Holy Names Acad., Spokane, Wash., 1964-70; dir. rsch. and planning Province Holy Names, Wash. State, 1972-73; v.p. acads. Ft. Wright Coll., Spokane, 1973-81; rsch. asst. to dean Claremont Grad. Sch., Calif., 1977-78; assoc. faculty mem. Harvard U., Cambridge, Mass., 1981; pres. Heritage U., Toppenish, Wash., 1981—. Cons. Wash. State Holy Names Schs., 1971-73; coll. accrediting assn. evaluator N.W. Assn. Schs. and Colls., Seattle, 1975—; dir. Holy Names Coll., Oakland, Calif., 1979—; cons. Yakama Indian Nation, Toppenish, 1975—; speaker, cons. in field. Author: (with others) Multicultural Pre-School Curriculum, 1977, A Crucial Agenda: Improving Minority Student Success, 1989; Cultural Factors in Success of American Indian Students in Higher Education, 1978. Chmn. Internat. 5-Yr. Convocation of Sisters of Holy Names, Montreal, 1981, 96; TV Talk show host Spokane Coun. of Chs., 1974-76; mem. Nat. Congl. Adv. Com. on Student Fin. Assistance, 2002—. Named Yakima Herald Rep. Person of Yr., 1987, MacArthur fellow, 1997; recipient E.K. and Lillian F. Bishop Founds. Youth Leader of Yr. award, 1986, Disting. Citizenship Alumna award, Claremont Grad. Sch., 1986, Golden Aztec award, Wash. Human Devel., 1989, Harold W. McGraw Edn. prize, 1989, John Carroll awrd, Georgetown U., 1991, Holy Names medal, Ft. Wright Coll., 1981, Pres.'s medal, Estern Wash. U., 1994, First Ann. Leadership award, Region VIII Coun. Advancement and Support Edn., 1993, Wash. State Medal of Merit, 1995, Lifetime Achievement award, Yakima YWCA, 2001, numerous grants for projects in multicultural higher edn., 1974—. Mem. Nat. Assn. Ind. Colls. and Univs., Soc. Intercultural Edn., Tng. and Rsch., Sisters of Holy Names of Jesus and Mary-SNJM. Roman Catholic. Office: Heritage Coll Office of Pres 3240 Fort Rd Toppenish WA 98948-9562 Office Phone: 509-865-8600.

ROSS, LARRY, education educator, researcher; s. Jonathan and Thelma Ross. BA, Case Western Res. U., Cleve., 1993; MA, PhD, U. of Missouri, 1999. Evaluation coord., adj. rschr., grad. instr. U. of Mo., Columbia, 1993—2000; asst. prof. Anthropology U. of Nebr., Omaha, 2000—. Rsch. assoc. The Cleve. Mus. of Natural History, 2001—03. Author: (book) African American Jazz Musicians in the Diaspora, 2003. Group study exch. amb. Rotary Internat., Cleve. Heights, Ohio, 1988—89. Recipient Award for Piano Performance, Internat. Assn. of Jazz Educators, 1990; The Chancellor's G. T. Ridgel Fellowship, U. of Missouri, 1996—99. Mem.: Am. Anthrop. Assn., Delta Kappa Epsilon Internat. Frat. (life; v.p. 1992—93). Office: U of Nebr at Omaha 347F Arts & Scis Bldg Omaha NE 68182 Personal E-mail: drlarryross@bizland.com. E-mail: larry_ross@unomaha.edu.

ROSS, LEONARD LESTER, anatomist, educator; b. N.Y.C., Sept. 11, 1927; s. Aaron Theodore and Shirley (Smolen) R.; m. Marcella Gamel, June 23, 1951 (dec. Aug. 1995); children: Jane, Jill; m. Frances Robb, Nov. 12, 1998; 1 chld, Jennifer. AB, NYU, 1946, PhD, 1954. Asst. prof. U. Ala. Med. Coll., 1954-57; assoc. prof. Cornell U. Med. Coll., 1957-69, prof., 1969-73; vis. prof. Cambridge U., 1967-68; prof., chmn. dept. anatomy Med. Coll. Pa., Phila., 1973-89, exec. v.p., Annenberg dean, 1989-93, pres. and Annenberg dean, 1993-94, provost and Annenberg dean, 1993-96; provost Allegheny U., Phila., 1996-98. Exec. v.p. Allegheny Health, Edn. and Rsch. Found. Assoc. editor: Anat. Record, 1976. Served with M.C., U.S. Army, 1946-47. Recipient Lindback award for teaching, 1976; NIH sr. research fellow, 1967-68 Mem. Am. Assn. Anatomists (exec. com. 1984-88), Soc. Neurosci., Soc. Cell Biology, N.Y. Soc. Electron Microscopists (pres. 1975-76), Assn. Anatomy Chairmen (pres. 1983-84), AAUP (nat. council 1974-77), Sigma Xi. Office: MCP/HU 2900 W Queen Ln Philadelphia PA 19129-1033 E-mail: rossil63@netscape.net.

ROSS, LORETTA J. human rights association executive; Founder, exec. dir. Ctr. Human Rights Edn., Atlanta. Political commentator Good Morning Am., The Donahue Show, The Charlie Rose Show, CNN, BET. Office: Ctr Human Rights Edn PO Box 311020 Atlanta GA 31131-1020

ROSS, MADELYN ANN, newspaper editor; b. Pitts., June 26, 1949; d. Mario Charles and Rose Marie (Mangieri) R. BA, Indiana U. of Pa., 1971; MA, SUNY-Albany, 1972. Reporter Pitts. Press, 1972-78, asst. city editor, 1978-82, spl. assignment editor, 1982-83, mng. editor, 1983-93, Pitts. Post-Gazette, 1993—. Bd. dirs. PG Pub. Co.; instr. Community Coll. Allegheny County, 1974-81; Pulitzer Prize juror, 1989, 90. Mem. Task Force Leadership Pitts., 1985-92; v.p. Old Newsboys Charity Fund; bd. dirs. Dapper Dan Charity. Mem. Am. Soc. Newspaper Editors, Press Club of Western Pa. (pres.). Democrat. Roman Catholic. Avocations: tennis; piano; organ. Office: Pitts Post-Gazette 34 Blvd Of The Allies Pittsburgh PA 15222-1204

ROSS, MALCOLM, minerals consultant; b. Washington, Aug. 22, 1929; s. Clarence Samuel and Helen Hall (Frederick) R.; m. Daphne Dee Virginia Riska, Sept. 1, 1956; children: Christopher A., Alexander MacC. BS in Zoology, Utah State U., 1951; MS in Chemistry, U. Md., 1959; PhD in Geology, Harvard U., 1962. Rsch. mineralogist U.S. Geol. Survey, Washington, 1954-5, 61-74, Reston, Va., 1974-95, scientist emeritus, 1996—; minerals and health cons., 1999—. Prin. investigator lunar sci. program NASA, 1969-74. Author: Asbestos and Other Fibrous Minerals, 1988; contbr. numerous articles to profl. jours. First Lt. U.S. Army, 1952-54. Recipient Disting. Svc. award, U.S. Dept. Interior, 1986; grantee Fulbright Commn., Cyprus, 2000. Fellow Mineral. Soc. Am., Geol. Soc. Am., AAAS; mem. Am. Geophys. Union, Clay Minerals Soc., Mineral Soc. Am. (bd. dirs. treas. 1976-80, v.p. 1990, pres. 1991, Pub. Svc. award, 1990). Achievements include research in on asbestos and asbestos-related disease. Home: 1608 44th St NW Washington DC 20007-2025 Personal E-mail: mrdrr@earthlink.net.

ROSS, MARILYN J. English and communications educator; BA in Am. Studies, U. Miami, Fla., 1969, MA in Am. Studies, 1971, PhD in Higher Edn. Leadership, 1995. Asst. prof. English Fla. Meml. Coll., 1971-84, assoc. prof. English and mass comm. arts, 1985-94, prof. higher edn., 1995—. Founder mass comm. arts program Fla. Meml. Coll., 1980, coord. modern langs., 1999—. Author: Success Factors of Young African American Males at a Historically Black College, 1998, Success Factors of Young African American Women at a Historically Black College, 2003; prodr. over 100 hrs. African Am., Caribbean and Hispanic programming, WLRN-TV. Recipient Outstanding Svc. award Vets. Club, 1979, Outstanding and Dedicated Svc. in Behalf of FMC award Miami Cable Access Corp., 1987, award Fla. Meml. Coll./Black Archives History and Rsch. Found. of South Fla., Inc., 1999. Mem. AAUW, Assn. Ednl. Leadership, Nat. Coun. Tchrs. of English, Epsilon Tau Lambda, Kappa Delta Pi, Phi Lambda Pi, Delta Theta Mu, Phi Kappa Phi, Phi Alpha Theta. Address: Unit F-602 1121 Crandon Blvd Apt F602 Key Biscayne FL 33149-2781

ROSS, MARION, actress; b. Albert Lea, Minn. children: Jim, Ellen. Grad., San Diego State U. Performed with Globe Theatre, San Diego, LaJolla Summer Theatre; Broadway debut in Edwin Booth; starred in touring prodns. of Never Too Late, Barefoot in the Park, The Glass Menagerie, Long Days Journey Into Night, Love Letter, Steel Magnolias, Over The River and Through The Woods, Barefoot in the Park, film debut in Forever Female, 1953; on woman show A Lovely Light, 1988—; TV series include Life with Father, 1953-55, Paradise Bay, 1965-66, Happy Days, 1974-84, Love Boat, 1985-86 (2 Emmy nominations), Bklyn. Bridge, 1991-93 (Emmy nomination for lead actress in a comedy 1992, 93), Hidden in Silence, 1995, Evening Star, 1996, The Great War, 1996, The Third Twin, 1997, About Search, 1998, The Lake, 1998, Drew Carey Show, 1998, That 70's Show, 1998, Touched By an Angel, 1999 (Emmy nomination 1999), The Ladies and the Champ, 2001, The Gilmore Girls, A Family of Strangers. Office: Dale Olson & Assocs 7420 Mulholland Dr Los Angeles CA 90046-1306 Office Phone: 323-876-9331.

ROSS, MATTHEW, lawyer; b. NYC, Dec. 28, 1953; s. Harvey and Cecile (Shelsky) R.; m. Susan Ruth Goldfarb, Apr. 20, 1986; children: Melissa Danielle, Henry Max, Thomas Frank. BS in Econs., U. Pa., 1975; JD, U. Va., 1978. Bar: N.Y. 1979, U.S. Dist. Ct. (so. dist.) N.Y. 1979. Assoc. Cravath, Swaine & Moore, N.Y.C., 1978-84; prin., assoc. gen. counsel KPMG LLP, N.Y.C., 1984-90; prin., deputy gen. counsel Deloitte & Touche USA LLP, N.Y.C, 1990—. Mem. ABA (corp. law sect.), N.Y. State Bar Assn. (corp. banking and bus. law sect.), Assn. of Bar of City of N.Y. (corp. law com.), Beta Gamma Sigma. Avocations: basketball, golf, tennis, skiing. Home: 5 Barker Ln Scarsdale NY 10583-7507 Office: Deloitte & Touche USA LLP 1633 Broadway New York NY 10019-6708 Office Phone: 212-492-3898. Business E-Mail: mross@deloitte.com.

ROSS, MELANIE FRIDL, journalist, writer; d. James Joseph and Harriet Mary Fridl; m. James Martin Ross, Sept. 21, 1991. BA, Northwestern U., 1989, MSJ, 1990. Cert. editor in the life scis. Bd. Editors in the Life Scis., 2000. Reporter The Tampa (Fla.) Tribune, 1990—92; freelance med. writer/editor various, 1992—; sr. med. writer, editor U. Fla., Gainesville, 1992—; asst. dir. U. Fla. Health Science Ctr. Office of News & Comm., Gainesville, 2003—. Editor: (booklet) University of Florida Stylebook and Resource Manual (Fla. Pub. Rels. Assn., Gainesville Chpt., Image Award, 2001); contbr. articles to newspapers, radio. Mem.: Am. Med. Writers Assn. (pres. Fla. chpt. 2001—02, adminstr. of chapters, exec. com. 2003—), Bd. Editors in the Life Scis., Coun. Sci. Editors, Nat. Assn. Sci. Writers, Jr. League Ocala, Inc. (pres.-elect 1998—99, pres. 1999—2000), Ocala Royal Dames for Cancer Rsch. Roman Catholic. Avocations: piano, photography, genealogy. Office: Univ Fla Health Sci Ctr Box 100253 Gainesville FL 32610-0253 Office Phone: 352-392-2621.

ROSS, MICHAEL AARON, lawyer; b. Newark, N.J., Sept. 15, 1941; s. Alexander Ash and Matilda (Blumenthal) R.; m. Leslie Gordon, June 26, 1976; children: Christopher Gordon, Alan Gordon. BA, Franklin and Marshall Coll., 1963; JD, Columbia U., 1966; MS in Econs., U. London, 1967. Bar: N.Y. 1968. Assoc., then ptnr. Shearman & Sterling, N.Y.C., 1967-93; dep. gen. counsel Citigroup, N.Y.C., 1993—2001; gen. counsel Citigroup Internat., 2002—03; counsel Wilmer Cutler Pickering Hale and Dorr LLP, N.Y.C., 2004—. Mem. ABA, N.Y. State Bar Assn., Am. Law Inst., New York County Lawyers Assn., Assn. Bar City of N.Y., Univ. Club. Office: Wilmer Cutler Pickering Hale and Dorr LLP 399 Park Ave 31st Fl New York NY 10022 Office Phone: 212-230-8858. Business E-Mail: michael.ross@wilmerhale.com.

ROSS, MICHAEL CHARLES, lawyer; BA, U. Va., 1970, JD, 1977. Assoc. Latham & Watkins, 1977-85, ptnr., 1985-93; sr. v.p., gen. counsel, sec. Safeway Inc., Oakland, 1993-2000. Office: Safeway Inc 5918 Stoneridge Mall Rd Pleasanton CA 94588-3229

ROSS, MICHAEL FREDERICK, magistrate, lawyer; b. Coral Gables, Florida, Sept. 20, 1950; s. George Thomas Ross and Frances (Brown) Skaro. BA, Yale U., 1973; JD, U. Conn., 1979; MLS, So. Conn. State U., 1981. Bar: Conn. 1979, Fla. 1979, N.J. 1983, Mass. 1984, U.S. V.I., 1985; U.S. Dist. Ct. Conn. 1979, N.J. 1983, Vt. 1984, U.S. V.I. 1985; U.S. Ct. Claims 1980; U.S. Tax Ct. 1980; U.S. Ct. Customs and Patent Appeals 1980; U.S. Ct. Mil. Appeals 1980; U.S. Ct. Appeals (1st, 2d and D.C. cir.) 1980, U.S. Ct. Appeals (5th, 9th and 11th cir.) 1981, U.S. Ct. Appeals (Fed. cir.) 1982, U.S. Ct. Appeals (3d, 4th, 6th, 7th, 8th and 19th cir.) 1983; Temp. Emergency Ct. Appeals 1985; Mashantucket Pequot Tribal Ct. 1995; U.S. Supreme Ct. 1982. Pvt. practice, New Haven, 1979—82; chief adjudicate Conn. Motor Vehicle Dept., Wethersfield, 1980—82; asst. atty. gen. State of Conn., Hartford, 1982—84; pvt. practice Madison, Conn., 1985—; adminstrv. law judge State of Conn. Motor Vehicle Dept., Wethersfield, 1985—; asst. atty. gen. Dept. of Law, St. Croix, 1984—85; magistrate Superior Ct. of Middlesex, New Haven, and New London Counties, Conn., 1988—. Faculty mem. Conn. Bar Assn. Acad. Profl. Devel. of Continuing Legal Edn. 1987, 91. Chmn. Madison Zoning Bd. Appeals, 1991-95. Mem. ABA, Am. Trial Lawyers Assn. (jud.), U.S. V.I. Bar Assn., Mensa, Conn. Def. Lawyers Assn., Conn. Magistrates Assn., Fence Club, Morys Assn. Club, Madison Men's Club. Democrat. Jewish. Office: 48 Mohawk Traill Guilford CT 06437-1107

ROSS, MICHAEL WALLIS, public health educator; b. Palmerston North, New Zealand, Nov. 17, 1951; arrived in U.S., 1993; s. Wallis Malcolm and Lois Verrell (Stewart) R. BA with honors, Massey U., New Zealand, 1974; BS in Med. Sociology, SUNY, 1976; MA in Social-Clin. Psychology, Victoria U. Wellington, New Zealand, 1975; diploma in Tertiary Edn., U. New Eng., Australia, 1984; PhD, U. Melbourne, Australia, 1980; MPH, U. Adelaide, Australia, 1989; M in Health Pers. Edn., U. NSW, Australia, 1991; diploma in STDs, Prince of Songkla U., Thailand, 1992; diploma in Applied Criminology, U. Cambridge, 2003. Mem. Secular Franciscan Order. Postdoctoral fellow U. Helsinki, Finland, 1979; sr. demonstrator psychiatry Flinders U., Adelaide, 1979-85; dir. STD/HIV Epidemiology and Rsch. South Australian Health Commn., Adelaide, 1985-89; assoc. prof. Sch. Cmty. Medicine U. NSW, Sydney, 1989-93; prof. Sch. Pub. Health, U. Tex., Houston, 1993—. Bd. dirs. Kolbe House, Houston, 1994—; chmn. bd. Saving Lives Through Alternate Options, Houston, 2000-. Author: The Married Homosexual Man: A Psychological Study, 1983, Psychovenereology: Personality and Lifestyle Factors in Sexually Transmitted Diseases in Homosexual Men, 1986, (with L.C. Channon-Little) Discussing Sexuality: A Guide for Health Practitioners, 1991; (with L.A. Lewis) A Select Body: The Gay Dance Party Subculture and the HIV/AIDS Pandemic, 1995; (with L. Nilsson Schönnesson) Coping With HIV Infection: Psychological and Existential Responses in Gay Men, 1999; (with L.C. Channon-Little and B.R.S. Rosser) Sexual Health Concerns: Interviewing and History Taking for Health Practitioners, 1999; editor: Homosexuality and Social Sex Roles, 1983, Homosexuality, Masculinity and Femininity, 1985, The Treatment of Homosexuals with Mental Health Disorders, 1988, Psychopathology and Psychotherapy in Homosexuality, HIV/AIDS and Sexuality, 1995; (with W.A.W. Walters) Transsexualism and Sex Reassignment, 1986; (with L. Bennett and D. Miller) Health Workers and AIDS: Rsch., Intervention and Current Issues in Burnout and Response, 1995; co-sci. editor: Surgeon-General's Call to Action on Sexual Health and Responsible Sexual Behavior, 2001; contbr. articles to profl. jour. Recipient U.S. Surgeon Gen.'s Exemplary Svc. award, 2002, Kinsey award, 2003. Fellow APA, Brit. Psychol. Soc., Royal Soc. Health, Royal Inst. Pub. Health and Hygiene, Royal Soc. Arts, New Zealand Psychol. Soc., Soc. for the Sci. Study of Sexuality (pres. 2000-01). Roman Catholic. Avocations: aerobatic flying, reading. Home: 401 Anita St Apt 34 Houston TX 77006-3434 Office: Sch Pub Health U Tex PO Box 20036 Houston TX 77225-0186 Office Phone: 713-500-9652. Business E-Mail: mross@sph.uth.tmc.edu.

ROSS, MIKE, congressman; b. Texarkana, Ark., Aug. 2, 1961; m. Holly Ross; children: Sydney, Alex. BA in Political Sci., U. Ark., 1987. Owner Holly's Health Mart and Home Med. Epuipment; area mgr. Fox Meyer Drug Co.; mem. Ark. Senate, 1990-2001, chair children and youth com.; mem. 107th - 108th Congress from 4th Ark. dist., Washington, 2001—; mem. agr. com., fin. svcs. com., small bus. com.; chief of staff to Lt Gov. of Ark., 1985—89. Democrat. Methodist. Office: 314 Cannon HOB Washington DC 20515-0404

ROSS, MOLLY OWINGS, jewelry designer, sculptor, small business owner, b. Ft. Worth, Feb. 5, 1954; d. James Robertson and Lucy (Owings) R. BFA, Colo. State U., 1976; postgrad., U. Denver, 1978-79. Graphic designer Amber Sky Illustrators and Sta. KCNC TV-Channel 4, Denver, 1977-79; art dir. Mercy Med. Ctr., Denver, 1979-83, Molly Ross Design, Denver, 1983-84; co-owner Deltex Royalty Co., Inc., Colorado Springs, Colo., 1981—, LMA Royalties, Ltd., Colorado Springs, 1993—; art dir., account mgr. Schwing/Walsh Advt., Mktg. and Pub. Rels., Denver, 1984-87, prodn. mgr., 1987-88; jewelry designer Molly O. Ross, Gold and Silversmith, Denver, 1988—. Coun. mem. feminization of poverty critical needs area coun. Jr. League Denver, 1989—90, chmn. children in crisis/edn. critical needs area, 1990—91, chmn. project devel., 1991—92, co-chmn. Done in a Day Cmty. Project 75th Anniversary Celebration, 1991—93, bd. dirs., 1993—94, co-chmn. project IMPACT, 1994—95, exec. v.p. external affairs, 1995—96, co-chmn. cmty. coalitions com., 1996—98; mem. steering com. Denver Urban Resources Partnership, 1995—2002, steering com. chmn., 1996—99; pres.-elect Jr. League Denver, 1989—99, pres., 1999—2000; mem. steering com. Internat. Conf. on Vol. Adminstrn., 2001—02; bd. dirs. Environ. Def. Regional Adv. Bd., 2003—; pres. Four Mile Hist. Pk. Vol. Bd., 1985—86; bd. dirs. Four Mile Hist. Pk. Assn., 1985—86, Hist. Denver, Inc., 1986—87, Denver Emergency Housing Coalition, 1989—90; co-founder, bd. dirs. Ctr. Ethics and Social Responsibility/PREP, 1994—2001, pres. bd. dirs., 1997—99, treas. bd. dirs., 1999—2000; bd. dirs. Jr. League Denver Found., 1998—2002, Excelsior Youth Ctr. Found., 2001—, Friends of Warren Village, 2000—01, Art Reach, 2001—. Named Vol. of Month (March), Jr. League Denver, 1990, Vol. of Yr., Four Mile Hist. Pk., 1988; recipient Gold Peak Mktg. award-team design Am. Mktg. Assn., 1986, Silver Peak Mktg. award-team design Am. Mktg. Assn., 1986, Gold Pick award-art dir. Pub. Rels. Soc. Am., 1980-81, cert. Appreciation USDA, 1999, 2001. Mem. Natural Resources Def. Coun., Physicians for Social Responsibility, Am. Farmland Trust, Nat. Trust for Hist. Preservation, Environ. Def. Avocations: horseback riding, bicycling, hiking, backpacking, pastel drawing.

ROSS, MONTE, electrical engineer, researcher; b. Chgo., May 26, 1932; s. Jacob Henry and Mildred Amelia (Feller) R.; m. Harriet Jean Katz, Feb. 10, 1957; children— Karyn, Dianne, Ethan BS in Elec. Engring., U. Ill., 1953; MS, Northwestern U., 1962. Devel. engr. Chance Vought, Dallas, 1953-54; sr. electronics engr. Motorola, Chgo., 1955-56, project engr., 1957-59, assoc. dir. rsch., 1960-63; dir. rsch. Hallicrafters Co., Chgo., 1964-65; mgr. laser tech. McDonnell Douglas Astronautics Co., St. Louis, 1966-70, dir. laser comms.; program mgr. Laser Space Comms., 1971-87; pres. Ultradata Sys., Inc. (formerly Laser Data Tech.), St. Louis, 1987—2001, CEO, 2001—. Mem. alumni bd. dept. elec. and computer engring. U. Ill., 1985-90; guest lectr. various univs.; cons. NSF. Author: Laser Receivers, 1966; tech. editor Laser Applications Series, vol. 1, 1971, vol. 2, 1974, vol. 3, 1977, vol. 4, 1980; patentee in field. Chmn. Laser Mus. and Space Signal Obs., 1997—. Recipient St. Louis High Tech. Entrepreneur of Yr. award, 1995; McDonnell Douglas Corp. fellow, 1985. Fellow IEEE; mem. Internat. Laser Comms. Soc. (pres. 1988-89), Sigma Xi. Home: 19 Beaver Dr Saint Louis MO 63141-7901 Office: Ultradata Sys Inc 1240 Dielman Ind Ct Saint Louis MO 63132-2212 Business E-Mail: mross@ultradatasystems.com.

ROSS, MURRAY LOUIS, lawyer, business executive; b. Rochester, N.Y., Apr. 26, 1947; s. Charles Allen and Florence L. (Falk) R.; m. Linda Marie Wabschall, Dec. 26, 1970. AB in History, Lycoming Coll., 1969; JD, U. Toledo, 1972. Bar: Pa. 1976. Asst. to exec. v.p. Falk Machinery Inc., Rochester, 1972-74; asst. v.p. Phila. (Pa.) Stock Exch., 1975-78, dir. securities dept., 1978-79, dir. market surveillance, 1979-82, v.p., corp. sec., 1982—; exec. v.p. Shiffrin Selections, Ltd., 1994—. Corp. sec. Phila. (Pa.) Bd. Trade Inc., 1984—, Phila. (Pa.) Depository Trust Co., 1986—, Stock Clearing Corp. Phila., 1986—. Mem. ABA, Phila. Bar Assn., Securities Assn. of Phila. Avocations: wine, golf, ice hockey. Home: 1126 Woodstock Ln West Chester PA 19382-7244 Office: Phila Stock Exchange Inc 1900 Market St Lbby 4 Philadelphia PA 19103-3584

ROSS, NORMAN ALAN, publisher; b. Bklyn., Nov. 1, 1942; s. Robert E. and Bertha (Cohen) Ross; m. Leslie Ann Sandler, Oct. 10, 1969; children: Caroline Beth, Juliet Michelle. BBA, CCNY, 1964, postgrad., 1967-74. Prodn. mgr. Thomas Pub. Co., 1964-67; sys. analyst Reuben H. Donnelley Corp., 1968-70; project mgr. Holt Rinehart & Winston, 1971-73; pres. Clearwater Pub. Co., Inc., N.Y.C., 1973-88, Video Strategies USA, Inc., N.Y.C., 1981-84, Broadside Ltd. pub. Broadside Mag., 1983-87, Norman Ross Pub. Inc., 1987—2002, Acad. Microforms Inc., 1999—2003; exec. dir. Norman Ross Pub., subs. Proquest, 2003—; pres. Ross Pub., Inc., 2003—. Author: (book) Index to the Decisions of the Indian Claims Commission, 1973, Index to the Expert Testimony Before the Indian Claims Commission, 1973, Guide to Yiddish Children's Books from the Yivo Institute, 1989. Mem.: ALA. Home: 392 Central Park W Apt 20-c New York NY 10025-5878 Office: Ross Pub Inc 330 W 58th St New York NY 10019 Business E-Mail: norman@rosspub.com.

ROSS, PATTI JAYNE, obstetrics and gynecology educator; b. Nov. 17, 1946; d. James j. and Mary N. Ross; m. Allan Robert Katz, May 23, 1976. BS, DePauw U., 1968; MD, Tulane U., 1972. Diplomate Am. Bd. Ob-Gyn. Asst. prof. U. Tex. Med. Sch., Houston, 1976—82, assoc. prof., 1982—98, prof., 1998—2004, dir. adolescent ob-gyn., 1976—, dir. student edn., dir. devel. dept. ob-gyn. Cons. in field; spkr. in field; appeared on Lifetime TV network. Contbr. articles to profl. jours. Mem. Rape Coun.; vol. Children's Miracle Network/Hermann's Children's Hosp.; Olympic torch relay carrier, 1996; founder Women's Med. Rsch. Fund, U. Tex. Med. Sch., Houston; bd. dirs. Am. Diabetes Assn., 1982—, Susan Komen Found. Recipient Patti Jayne Ross Professorship, 2004. Mem.: Profl. Women Execs., Orgn. Women in Sci., Am. Women's Med. Assn., AAAS, Soc. Adolescent Medicine, Assn. Profs. Ob-Gyn., Houston Ob-Gyn. Soc., Harris County Med. Soc., Tex. Med. Assn., River Oak Breakfast Club, Sigma Xi. Roman Catholic. Office: 6431 Fannin St #3278 Houston TX 77030-1501 Office Phone: 713-500-6431.

ROSS, PHILIP ROWLAND, retired library director; b. Indiana, Pa., Apr. 7, 1940; s. David Biddle and Miriam Elizabeth (Hill) R.; m. Elaine Lucille George, July 17, 1965; children: Mary Elizabeth, David Bruce. BA, Pa. State U., 1962; MSLS, U. Md., 1969. Postal fin. officer USAF, Tachikawa AFB Tokyo, 1963-65; chief data control and quality control Hdqrs. Air Force Systems Command, Andrews AFB, Md., 1965-68; asst. libr. acquisitions West Liberty (W.Va.) State Coll., 1969-86; dist. mgr. Wheeling (W.Va.) office First Investors Corp., 1986-89, divs. mgr. State of Ark., 1989-92; dir. Lonoke (Ark.) Prairie County Regional Libr. System, 1992-2000; ret., 2000. Founder, treas.-mgr. West Liberty (W.Va.) State Coll. Fed. Credit Union, 1977-82, chmn. bd., 1984-85; co-founder Lonoke County Mus., bd. dirs.; mem. Ark. On Line Network Adv. Com., Little Rock, 1993-96, Libr. Devel. Dist. State Coun., Little Rock, 1993-2000, vice chmn., 1996. Maj. USAF, 1962-68; maj. Res., 1968-84. Decorated various USAF medals and decorations. Mem.: AARP (chpt. v.p. 2003, pres. 2004), ALA, S.E. Libr. Assn., Ark. Libr. Assn. (com. 1994—95, conv. com. 1996, 1997), Assn. Ark. Pub. Librs. (treas.-sec. 1993, 1994, v.p., pres.-elect 1995, pres. 1996), Lonoke C. of C., Lions (pres. 2003, 2004), Am. Legion. Republican. Methodist. Avocations: reading, gardening, refinishing antique furniture. Home: 691 Wayne Elmore Rd Lonoke AR 72086-9126

ROSS, RANDOLPH ERNEST, investor; b. N.Y.C., Mar. 17, 1955; s. David Harvey and Pearl (Frandsen) R.; m. Joan Frances Healey, Apr. 2, 1982. AB in History, Brown U., 1977; MBA in Fin., Columbia U., 1981. CFA; comml. pilot FAA. Nat. editor Sta. WEAN Radio, Providence, 1977-79; rsch. analyst, asst. v.p. Kidder, Peabody & Co., Inc., N.Y.C., 1981-85; rsch. analyst First Manhattan Co., N.Y.C., 1985-86; portfolio mgr. Brundage, Story and Rose, N.Y.C., 1986-92; sr. portfolio mgr., v.p. Bankers Trust Co., N.Y.C., 1992-93; investment strategist, sr. v.p. Kidder, Peabody & Co. Inc., N.Y.C., 1993-94; pvt. investor Bklyn., 1994-96; mng. dir. Morgan Hill Corp., N.Y.C., 1996—2004; pvt. investor, 2004—. Mem. CFA Inst., N.Y. Soc. Security Analysts. Republican. Avocations: commercial pilot, sailing, trap and skeet shooting, architectural and urban history, fiction. Home: 111 Hicks St Ste 4A Brooklyn NY 11201-1638

ROSS, RHODA, artist; b. Boston, Dec. 24, 1941; Student, Skowhegan Sch. Painting, 1986; BFA, RISD, 1964; MFA, Yale U., 1966. Art tchr. Emma Willard School, 1983-85, Nat. Found. For Advancement in Arts, 1985, Ocean County College, 1990, Chautauqua Sch. of Art, 1991, NYU, 1994-, The Lucy Moses School, 1987-; participant Art in Embassies Program Dept of State. One woman shows: Yale U., Pierson Coll., New Haven, 1967, Convent of the Sacred Heart, N.Y., 1976, Municipal Art Soc., N.Y., 1978, Long Island U., N.Y., 1981, Dietal Gallery, Emma Willard Sch., Troy, N.Y., 1983, Marymount Manhattan Coll., N.Y., 1985, N.Y.C. Landmarks Preservation Com. 25th Silver Anniversary, 1990, Frick Gallery, Maine, 1991; perm. collections include: Wilkie, Farr & Gallagher, N.Y., St. Louis Conservatory of Music, The Julliard School, Museum of The City of N.Y., Gracie Mansion, The White House; numerous other pvt. and pub. collections; artwork appears on New Sch. Social Rsch. catalog cover, Gifts and Decorative Accessories Mag. cover, UNICEF greeting card, The New York Times, The Chronicle, ABC-TV. Treas. R.I. Sch. Design Alumni Exec. Com. Fellow Va. Ctr. for Creative Arts; recipient Grumbacher Gold Medal, 1985. Mem. RISD Alumni Assn. (treas., mem. alumni exec. com.), Phi Tau Gamma. Home: 473 W End Ave New York NY 10024-4934 E-mail: rr18@nyu.edu.

ROSS, RICH, broadcast executive; b. NYC, Oct. 7, 1961; BA in internat. rels. and English, U. Pa., 1983; JD, Fordham U., 1986. Mgr. talent rels. Nickelodeon, 1986—90, v.p. talent rels., 1990—92, v.p. program enterprises, 1992—93; sr. v.p. devel. and prodn. FX Networks, 1993—96; sr. v.p. programming and prodn. Disney Channel, 1996—99, exec. v.p., gen. mgr. programming and prodn., 1999—2002, pres., 2002—04, Disney Channel Worldwide, 2004—. Bd. dirs. Cable in the Classroom. Office: Disney Channel 500 S Buena Vista St Burbank CA 91521*

ROSS, RICHARD FRANCIS, veterinarian, microbiologist, educator, dean; b. Washington, Iowa, Apr. 30, 1935; s. Milton Edward and Olive Marie (Berggren) R.; m. Karen Mae Paulsen, Sept. 1, 1957; children: Scott, Susan D.V.M., Iowa State U., 1959, MS, 1961, PhD, 1965. Rsch. assoc. Iowa State U., Ames, 1959—61, asst. prof., 1962—65, assoc. prof., 1966—72, prof., 1972—, assoc. dir., assoc. dean Coll. Vet. Medicine, 1990—92, interim dean, 1992—93, dean Coll. Vet. Medicine, 1993—2000, interim dean, dean Coll. Agr., dir. Agrl. Expt. Sta., 2000—02, Rocky Mt. Lab., Hamilton, Mont.; oper. mgr. Vet. Lab. Inc., Remsen, Iowa, 1961—62; postdoctoral fellow NIAID, Hamilton, Mont., 1965—66. Sr. U.S. scientist Alexander von Humboldt Found., Bonn, Fed. Republic Germany, 1975-76; chmn. Internat. Rsch. Program on Comparative Mycoplasmology, 1982-86; pres. Iowa State U. Rsch. Found., Ames, 1984-86; Howard Dunne meml. lectr. Am. Assn. Swine Practitioners, 1984; mem. adv. bd. Sec. Agr., 1996—; mem. strategic planning task force USDA, 1997-99, mem. safeguarding task force, 2001-02, mem. implementation team, 2003—; bd. govs. ISU Found., 2004—. Contbr. numerous articles to profl. pubs., 1963— Named Disting. Prof., Iowa State U., 1982, Hon. Master Pork Producer, Iowa Pork Producers Assn., 1985; recipient faculty citation Iowa State U. Alumni Assn., 1984, Beecham award for rsch. excellence, 1985, Howard Dunne Meml. award Am. Assn. Swine Practitioners, 1988, Am. Feed Mfg. award for rsch., 1995, Sec. of Agr. award for personal and profl. accomplishment, 1996, Gamma Sigma Delta Merit award for disting. achievement in agr. 2002. Mem. Am. Coll. Vet. Microbiologists (diplomate, vice chmn. 1974-75, sec.-treas. 1977-83), Am. Soc. Microbiology (chmn. div. 1985-86), Internat. Orgn. Mycoplasmology (chair 1990-92, Bd. Dirs. award 2002), AVMA, AAAS, Osborn Research Club, Conf. Rsch. Workers in Animal Diseases (coun. mem., pres. 1992), Assn. Am. Vet. Med. Colls. (pres. 1997-98). Republican. Lutheran. Avocations: fishing, gardening, walking, reading, history. Home: 4022 Stone Brooke Rd Ames IA 50010-2900 Office: Iowa State U Coll Vet Medicine Ames IA 50011-0001 E-mail: rfross@iastate.edu.

ROSS, RICHARD STARR, retired medical school dean, cardiologist, educator; b. Richmond, Ind., Jan. 18, 1924; s. Louis Francisco and Margaret (Starr) Ross; m. Elizabeth McCracken, July 1, 1950; children: Deborah Starr, Margaret Casad, Richard McCracken. Student, Harvard U., 1942—44, MD cum laude, 1947; ScD (hon.), Ind. U., 1981; LHD (hon.), Johns Hopkins U., 1994. Diplomate Nat. Bd. Med. Examiners, Am. Bd. Internal Medicine (subsplty. bd. cardiovasc. disease). Successively intern, asst. resident, chief resident Osler Med. Service, Johns Hopkins Hosp., 1947—54; research fellow physiology Harvard Med. Sch., 1952—53; instr. medicine Johns Hopkins Med. Sch., 1954—56, asst. prof. medicine, 1956—59, assoc. prof., 1959—65, assoc. prof. radiology, 1960—71, prof. medicine, 1965—, Clayton prof. cardiovascular disease, 1969—75; dir. Wellcome Research Lab., Johns Hopkins; physician Johns Hopkins Hosp.; dir. cardiovascular div. dept. medicine, adult cardiac clinic Johns Hopkins Sch. Medicine and Hosp., dir. myocardial infarction research unit, 1967—75; dean med. faculty, v.p. medicine Johns Hopkins U., 1975—90, dean emeritus, 1990—. Sir Thomas Lewis lectr. Brit. Cardiac Soc., 1969; John Kent Lewis lectr. Stanford U., 1972; bd. dirs. emeritus Johns Hopkins Hosp., Francis Scott Key Med. Ctr.; mem. cardiovasc. study sect. Nat. Heart and Lung Inst., 1965—69, chmn. cardiovasc. study sect., 1966—69, mem. tng. grant com., 1971—73, chmn. heart panel, 1972—73, adv. coun., 1974—78; mem. Inst. Medicine, 1976—; chmn. vis. com. Harvard Med. and Dental Sch., 1979—86; bd. overseers Harvard U., 1980—86. Editor: Modern Concepts Cardiovascular Disease, 1961—65, The Principles and Practice of Medicine, 17th-22nd edits., 1968—88; mem. editl. bd.: Circulation, 1968—74, mem. editl. com.: Jour. Clin. Investigation, 1969—73; contbr. numerous articles to profl. jours. Capt. M.C. U.S. Army, 1949—51. Named hon. fellow, UMDS, Guy's and St. Thomas's Hosps., London, 1996; recipient Flexner award, Assn. Am. Med. Coll., 1994. Master: ACP; fellow: Am. Coll. Cardiology (Convocation medal 1990); mem.: Heart Assn. Md. (pres. 1967—68), Am. Heart Assn. (chmn. sci. sessions program com. 1965—67, chmn. publs. com. 1970—73, pres. 1973—74, dir. 1974—77, Gold Heart award 1976, Connor lectr. 1979, James B. Herrick award 1982), Assn. Univ. Cardiologists (councillor 1972—75), Am. Clin. and Climatol. Assn. (pres. 1978—79, councillor 1979—83, Metzger lecture 1986), Am. Soc. Clin. Investigation (councillor 1967—69), Sociedad Peruana de Cardiologie (corr.), Brit. Cardiac Soc. (corr.), Cardiac Soc. Australia and New Zealand (corr.), Assn. Am. Physicians, Am. Physiol. Soc., Am. Fedn. Clin. Rsch., Boylston Med. Soc., Elkridge Club, Interurban Club (pres. 1978), Peripatetic Club, Alpha Omega Alpha, Sigma Xi. Home: 830 W 40th St # 851 Baltimore MD 21211-2181 Office: Johns Hopkins U 1830 E Monument St Baltimore MD 21287 E-mail: rross@jhmi.edu.

ROSS, ROBERT, medical association administrator; Exec. dir., sr. v.p. Muscular Dystrophy Assn., Tucson, pres. Office: Muscular Dystrophy Assn 3300 E Sunrise Dr Tucson AZ 85718-3299

ROSS, ROBERT DONALD, library director; b. N.Y.C., Mar. 28, 1931; s. William and Cecile (Cross) Rosenfeld. BA, CCNY, 1954; postgrad., NYU, 1960—64, Columbia U., 1968; MLS, Rutgers U., 1966. m. Madeleine Ladner, May 28, 1961; children: Jeffrey Laurence, Jodie Dianne. Ref. libr. Bklyn. Pub. Libr., 1965; reader svcs. libr., asst. prof. Suffolk County (N.Y.) C.C., 1966-69; dir. South Brunswick (N.J.) Pub. Libr., 1969-73, Ridgewood (N.J.) Pub. Libr., 1973-95. Adj. prof. Middlesex County C.C., N.J., 1973-76; docent Nev. Mus. Art, 2004—. Mem. exec. bd. South Brunswick Cmty. Coun., 1970-73, Human Rels. Coord. Coun., Ridgewood, 1988-94; mem. adv. com. Nat. Project Ctr. for Films and Humanities, N.Y.C., 1971-75; treas. Bergen-Passaic Regional Libr. Coop., 1987-88, mem. exec. bd., 1986-89; mem. Ridgewood Bicentennial Commn., 1975-76; treas. Temple Emanu-El, Reno, 1998-2000, bd. dirs., 2002-2003; bd. dirs. For the Love of Jazz, Reno, 1998-2000; docent Nev. Mus. Art, 2004—. Mem. ALA (chmn. discussion group com. fundraising and fin. devel. sect. libr. adminstrn. and mgmt. divsn. 1984-85), N.J. Libr. Assn. (libr. devel. com. 1977-93, chmn. edn. for librarianship com. 1982-83, govt. rels. com. 1982, 100th ann. com. 1988-91), Librs. South Middlesex (chmn. 1970-73), North Bergen Fedn. Librs. (chmn. dirs. coun. 1975), Bergen County Coop. Libr. Sys. (pres., treas. 1982-83, 86-87, exec. bd. computer consortium 1987-89, budget com. 1989-94), Ridgewood C. of C. (bd. dirs. 1983-93, treas. 1988-93), Soc. Valley Hosp., Ridgewood Kiwanis (pres. 1982-83, treas. 1987-88, Disting. Club. Pres. award 1983). Home: 4910 Deer Pass Dr Reno NV 89509-0577 E-mail: RRoss328317@aol.com.

ROSS, ROBERT DWAIN, lawyer; b. Dec. 3, 1932; s. George Raymond and Alma Lillian (Putman) Ross; m. Frances Root Mitchell, June 15, 1963; children: Robert Mitchell, Virginia Frances, Mary Starr. Student, So. State Coll., 1951—53; BSL, JD, U. Ark., 1962. Bar: Ark. 1961, U.S. Dist. Ct. (ea. dist.) Ark. 1962, U.S. Supreme Ct. 1966. Law clk. Ark. Supreme Ct., 1961—62, 1963; assoc. Pope, Shamburger, Buffalo & Ross, Little Rock, 1963—65, ptnr., 1965—94; sr. mem. Pope, Ross, Dendy & Cazort PLC, 1994—2002, Pope, Ross PLC, 2002—. Sec., exec. dir. Ark. Constl. Conv., 1980. Bd. dirs. Elizabeth Mitchell Children's Ctr. (now Ctrs. for Youth and Families, Inc.), 1972—78, 1983—96, treas., 1974, 1983, pres., 1978, 1984—85, v.p., 1983; bd. dirs. Quapaw Quarter Assn., 1977—80, pres., 1979. Served with U.S. Army, 1956—58. Recipient Disting. Svc. award, Mental Health Coun. Ark., 1993. Fellow: Ark. Bar Found. (bd. dirs. 1982—85); mem.: ABA, Pulaski County Bar Assn. (bd. dirs. 1978—79), Ark. Bar Assn. (sec.-treas. 1969—72, ho. of dels. 1976—76, 1978—81, mem. exec. coun. 1973, 1975—78, chmn. 1981—82, chmn. judicial nominations com. 1989—94, mem. jud. nominations health law and web oversite coms.). Democrat. Episcopalian. Office: Ste 210 620 W 3rd St Little Rock AR 72201-2223 Office Phone: 501-375-9947.

ROSS, ROBERT EVAN, bank executive; b. Alliance, Ohio, Sept. 22, 1947; s. James Jacob Ross and Eva Mae (Forsha) Bodo; m. Susan Margaret Burd, June 20, 1970; children: Margaret Mae, James William. BBA, Kent State U., 1970; MBA, U. Chgo., 1977. Advisor to fraternities, dean of men's office Kent (Ohio) State U., 1970-71; trainee, supr. of trainees Northern Trust Co., Chgo., 1971-73, jr. analyst, 1973-74, trust rep., 1974-77, trust officer, 1977-81, v.p., div. head for personal fin. planning, 1981-85; portfolio mgr., investment rep. Morgan Stanley, Chgo., 1985-89; pres. Northern Trust Bank in Winnetka, Ill., 1989-92; exec. v.p. Northern Trust Bank/Lake Forest, Ill., 1992-95, vice chmn., 1995-97, pres., CEO, 1997—2001; pres., CEO Northern Trust Bank-Ohio, 2001—. Bd. dirs. No. Trust Bank, Lake Forest, O'Hare, Ill., DuPage, Ill. Bd. dirs. The Camerata Singers of Lake Forest, Lake Forest Symphony, 1992-2001, Ragdale Found., 1999-2000, Cleve. Zool. Soc., 2003; bd. govs. Ill. St. Andrew Soc., 1998-2001; suburban chair United Way North Region, 1993—; mem. centennial commn. on identity, values and comm. Kent State U., 1998; trustee DePaul U., Chgo., Barat Coll. Edn. Found., Kent State U. Found., 2003. Avocations: sports, reading, stock market, painting. Office: No Trust Bank Lake Forest Deerpath And Bank Ln Lake Forest IL 60045

ROSS, ROBERT JON SANFORD, sociology educator; b. N.Y.C., Feb. 1, 1943; s. Irving Barrett and Marsha (Greenblatt) R.; m. Marion Karyl Levenson, June 13, 1965; children: Gabriel Micah Barrett, Rachel Irene. BA, U. Mich., 1963; postgrad., U. Coll., London, 1963-64; MA, U. Chgo., 1966, PhD, 1975. Exec. dir. New U. Conf., Chgo., 1968-69; rsch. assoc. Inst. for Social Rsch., U. Mich., Ann Arbor, 1969-72; from asst. prof. to prof. sociology Clark U., Worcester, Mass., 1972—, chair dept. sociology, 1975-78, 93-99, dir. internat. studies, chair faculty, 2000—. Vis. prof. U. Mich., Ann Arbor, 1977, MIT, Cambridge, 1981, Harvard U., Cambridge, 1989-92, 94-95; William I. Cole prof. sociology Wheaton Coll., 1999; policy analyst Mass. Senate, Boston, 1983-86; cons. Econ. Devel. Indsl. Corp., Boston, 1988-90. Co-author: Global Capitalism: The New Leviathan, 1990; mem. editorial bd. Socialism and Democracy, 1995-99, Slaves to Fashion, 2004; contbr. articles to profl. jours. Mem. Dem. Town Com., Southboro, Mass., 1982—99; bd. dirs. Southboro Open Land Found., Southboro, 1992—2000, Dynamy, Worcester, 1993—. Woodrow Wilson fellow Woodrow Wilson Found., 1963. Mem. Am. Sociol. Assn. (mem. polit. economy of world sys. sect. 2001—, chmn.-elect DEWS sect. 2004), Phi Beta Kappa. Avocations: skiing, running, bicycling, hiking. Office: Clark Univ Dept Sociology 950 Main St Worcester MA 01610-1477 Office Phone: 508-793-7376. Business E-Mail: rjsross@clarku.edu.

ROSS, ROBERT JOSEPH (BOBBY ROSS), college football coach; b. Richmond, Va., Dec. 23, 1935; s. Leonard Aloysius and Martha Isabelle (MMiller) R.; m. Alice Louise Bucker, June 13, 1959; children: Chris, Mary Catherine, Teresa, Kevin, Robbie. BA, Va. Mil. Inst., 1959. Tchr., head football coach Benedictine High Sch., Richmond, 1959-60; tchr., coach Colonial Heights (Va.) High Sch., 1962-65; asst. football coach Va. Mil. Inst., Lexington, 1965-67, Coll. William and Mary, Williamsburg, Va., 1967-71, Rice U., Houston, 1971-72, U. Md., College Park, 1972-73; head football coach The Citadel, Charleston, S.C., 1973-77; head coach U. Md., College Park, 1982-87; head football coach Ga. Inst. Tech., Atlanta, 1987-91; asst. coach Kansas City (Mo.) Chiefs, 1978-82; head coach San Diego Chargers, 1992-96, Detroit Lions, 1997-2001, U.S. Mil. Acad., West Point, NY, 2003—. 1st lt. U.S. Army, 1960-62. Named Coach of Yr., Washington Touchdown Club, 1982, Kodak Coach of Yr., 1990, Bobby Dodd Coach of Yr., 1990, Bear Bryant Coach of Yr., 1990, Scripps-Howard Coach of Yr., 1990, Nat. Coach of Yr., CBS Sports, 1990, Coach of Yr., Walter Camp Football Found., 1990, NFL Coach of Yr. UPI, 1992, Pro Football Weekly, 1992, Pro Football Writers' Assn., 1992, Football News, 1992, Football Digest, 1992, Maxwell Football Club, 1992, AFC Coach of Yr. Kansas City 101 Banquet. Mem. Am. Football Coaches Assn., Coll. Football Assn. (coaching com. 1988-92). Roman Catholic. Office: US Military Acad Bldg 639 Howard Rd West Point NY 10996-1985

ROSS, ROBINETTE DAVIS, publisher; b. London, May 16, 1952; d. Raymond Lawrence and Pearl A. (Robinette) Davis; m. William Bradford Ross, III, Mar. 16, 1979; children: Nellie Tayloe, William Bradford IV. Student, Am. U., 1977-78. Asst. to editor The Chronicle of Higher Edn., Washington, 1978, advt. mgr., 1978-82, advt. dir., 1983-88, assoc. pub., 1988-94, The Chronicle of Philanthropy, 1988-94; publ. The Chronicle of Higher Edn., Washington, 1994—; pub. The Chronicle of Philanthropy, Washington, 1994—. Mem. Am. News Women's Club, City Tavern Club, Mt. Vernon Club. Episcopalian. Office: The Chronicle of Higher Edn 1255 23rd St NW Ste 700 Washington DC 20037-1146

ROSS, RODERIC HENRY, insurance company executive; b. Jamestown, N.Y., July 14, 1930; s. Edwin A. and Mary (Dornberger) R.; m. Patricia Johnson, Aug. 6, 1955; children: Timothy, Amy, Jane, Christopher. BA, Hobart Coll., 1952, LLD (hon.), 1979. CLU, ChFC. Gen. agt. Phila. Life Ins. Co., 1957-70, sr. v.p. mktg., 1972-73, pres., 1973-83, vice chmn., 1983-84; chmn., CEO Keystone State Life Ins. Co., Phila., 1985-2000; ret., 2001. Bd. dirs. PNC Bank Corp., Pitts., Hunt Corp., Phila., PMA Capital Corp., Phila.; past chmn. Ins. Fedn. Pa.; dir. Intergroup Svcs. Corp., Malvern, Pa. Rector's warden St. David's Ch., Radnor, Pa., 1989-90; hon. trustee Hobart-William Smith Colls., Geneva, N.Y., 1972—, chmn. bd., 1983-88. Sgt. U.S. Army, 1952-54. Mem. Am. Soc. CLUs, Nat. Assn. Nat. Assn. Life Underwriters, Million Dollar Round Table (life), Union League (former dir.), Orpheus Club, St. David's Golf Club (Wayne, Pa.), Penna Soc., Pine Valley Golf Club (Clementon, N.J.). Republican. Episcopalian. Avocations: golf, tennis. Home (Summer): PO Box 332 Bemus Point NY 14712-0332 Home: 770 Pugh Rd Wayne PA 19087 E-mail: rodnpatross@aol.com.

ROSS, SCOTT R. psychologist, educator; s. Richard and Margie Ross; m. Tassa Carruthers-Ross. Student, U. Mich., Flint, 1988—92; PhD, Wayne State U., 1998. NIH predoctoral intern Rehab. Inst. Mich., Detroit, 1995—97; APA intern Ann Arbor (Mich.) VAMC, 1997—98. Achievements include research in Five Factor Model of Personality, Malingering in Neuropsychological Assessment, Personality Disorder and Psychopathy. Office: DePauw U 7 Larabee St Greencastle IN 46135 E-mail: srross@depauw.edu.

ROSS, SHELDON JULES, dentist; b. N.Y.C., June 17, 1924; s. Sam and Regina (Rosner) R.; 1 stepson, Nathan Sudnow; m. Carolyn L. M. Loesch, Apr. 26, 1946; children: Jane, Eric, Ellen, Lisa. DDS, NYU, 1949. Diplomate Am. Bd. Periodontology, Am. Bd. Oral Medicine (examiner 1980-85). Pvt. practice periodontology, N.Y.C., 1949—; prof. periodontics and oral medicine NYU Sch. Dentistry, 1949—; resident oral medicine Montefiore Hosp., N.Y.C., 1956-57, charge periodontics, 1951-70, oral medicine, 1951-81, cons., 1981-95; attending charge oral medicine and periodontics Beth Abraham Hosp., Bronx, N.Y., 1961-81, cons., 1981-87. Cons. in oral medicine Goldwater Meml. Hosp., N.Y.C., 1982—; former cons., lectr. periodontics and oral medicine Cabrini Hosp. and Med. Ctr., N.Y.C.; lectr. in field; honored lectr. Internat. Odontological Congress, Maringa, Brazil, 1972. Editor Jour. Oral Medicine, 1971-88, Annals of Dentistry, 1971-88; contbr. articles to profl. jours., chpts. to textbooks. With AUS, 1942-43. Fellow N.Y. Acad. Dentistry (v.p. 1989-90, pres.-elect 1990-91, pres. 1991-92), Am. Acad. Oral Medicine (pres. 1980); mem. ADA, Am. Acad. Oral Medicine, Am. Acad. Periodontology, N.E. Soc. Periodontists, Am. Heart Assn., Omega Kappa Upsilon. Home and Office: 40 Twisting Ln Wantagh NY 11793-1947 *None admit to having any new ideals except loving redemption of some souls: Man expects rational and normal deliberation instead.*

ROSS, SHERMAN, psychologist, educator; b. N.Y.C., Jan. 1, 1919; s. Max Rosenblatt and Rachel (Khoutman) Ross; m. Jean Goodwin, Aug. 18, 1945; children: Norman Kimball, Claudia Lisbeth Overway, Michael Lachlan. BS, CCNY, 1939; A.M., Columbia U., 1941, PhD, 1943. Asst. psychology, research psychologist Columbia U., 1941-44; asst., then assoc. prof. psychology Bucknell U., 1946-50; research fellow N.Y. Zool. Soc., 1948; guest investigator, sci. asso. Jackson Lab., 1947-77; assoc. prof., then prof. psychology U. Md., 1950-60; spl. cons. Psychopharmacology Svc. Ctr. NIMH, 1956-63, asst. chief, 1956-57; exec. sec. edn. and tng. bd., sci. affairs officer APA, 1960-68; prof. psychology Howard U., 1968-89, emeritus, 1989—; exec. sec., staff assoc., assembly of behavioral and social scis. Nat. Acad. Scis.-NRC, 1968-76; lectr. Himmelfarb Mobile U., 1994—. Cons. VA, Human Ecology Fund, Stanford Rsch. Inst., Office Naval Rsch., U.S. Sci. Exhibit, Am. U., HRB-Singer, Inc.; bd. dirs. Interdisciplinary Comm. Assocs., Washington; adv. coun. mem. Woodrow Wilson Rehab. Ctr. Found.; mem. Md. Bd. Examiners Psychology, 1957—58, 1984—89; chmn. bd. dirs. Inst. for Rsch., State College, Pa.; mem. Montgomery County Health Planning Commn., Md. Statewide Health Coordinating Coun., Met. Washington Area Coun. Health Planning Agys.; mem. adv. coun. Emergency Med. Svcs.; v.p. bd. dirs. Mobile Med. care, Inc., Bethesda, Md. Trustee Coord. Coun. Asbury Meth. Village, Gaithersburg, Md. Fellow: APA, Washington Acad. Scis., Royal Soc. Health, Am. Coll. Neuropsychopharmacology; mem.: D.C. Psychol. Assn. (pres. 1982), Md. Psychol. Assn. (pres. 1973—74), Ergonomics Rsch. Soc., Ecol. Soc., Am. Soc. Zoologists, Aerospace Med. Assn., Bethesda Naval Club, Cosmos Club Washington, Psi Chi (nat. pres. 1964—68), Phi Kappa Phi, Sigma Xi (pres. U. Md. 1957—58, pres. Howard U. 1983—84). Home: 382 Russell Ave Gaithersburg MD 20877-2863 Personal E-mail: Ross382@aol.com.

ROSS, STAN, real estate company executive; b. 1939; Degree, Baruch Coll., 1956, LLD (hon.), 1999. Mng. ptnr. E&Y Kenneth Leventhal Real Estate Group; vice chmn. Real Estate Industry Svcs. Ernst & Young LLP, 1995—99; chmn. Lusk Ctr. U. So. Calif., LA, 1999—. Cons. Ernst & Young; bd. dirs. The Irvine Co., Forest City Enterprises, U. Judaism. Trustee Urban Land Inst., gov.; trustee Baruch Coll. Mem.: AICPA (mem. auditing standards bd.). Office: USC LuckCtr Real Estate 331 Ralph andGoldy Lewis Hall Los Angeles CA 90089-0626*

ROSS, STANFORD G. lawyer, government official; b. St. Louis, Oct. 9, 1931; m. Dorothy Rabin, June 9, 1958; children: John, Ellen. AB with honors, Washington U., 1953; JD magna cum laude, Harvard U., 1956. Bar: D.C. 1969, Calif. 1956, N.Y. 1959. Assoc. Irell & Manella, L.A., 1956-57; tchg. fellow, rsch. asst. Harvard Law Sch., 1957-58; assoc. Dewey, Ballantine, Bushby, Palmer & Wood, N.Y.C., 1958-61; asst. tax legis. counsel U.S. Dept. Treasury, 1961-63; prof. law N.Y. U., 1963-67; White House staff asst. to Pres. Johnson, 1967-68; gen. counsel U.S. Dept. Transp., 1968-69; ptnr. Caplin & Drysdale, Washington, 1969-78; commr. Social Security Adminstrn., Washington, 1978-79; ptnr. Califano, Ross & Heineman, Washington, 1980-82, Arnold & Porter, Washington, 1983—2002. Pub. trustee Social Security Trust Funds, Washington, 1990-95; chmn. Social Security Adv. Bd., 1997-2002. Editor: Harvard Law Rev, 1954-56. Mem. ABA, Fed. Bar Assn., Internat. Fiscal Assn., Nat. Acad. Social Ins. Office: Arnold & Porter 555 12th St NW Washington DC 20004-1206

ROSS, STEVEN CHARLES, business administration educator, consultant; b. Salem, Oreg., Jan. 14, 1947; s. Charles Reed and Edythe Marie (Calvin) R.; m. Meredith Lynn Buholts, June 15, 1969; children: Kelly Lynn, Shannon Marie. BS, Oreg. State U., 1969; MS, U. Utah, 1976, PhD, 1980. Cons. IRS Tng. Staff, Ogden, Utah, 1977-80; asst. prof. Marquette U., Milw., 1980-88; assoc. prof. Mont. State U., Bozeman, 1988-89; assoc. prof. bus. adminstrn. Western Wash. U., Bellingham, 1989—. Chmn. acad. coord. commn., Western Wash. U., 1997-2002, mem. faculty senate 2000-02; govt. and industry cons.; cons. editor microcomputing series West Pub. Co. Author 35 books and several articles in computer systems field. Mem. adv. com. Milwaukee County Mgmt., 1981-85, Port of Bellingham, 1990-2000; chmn. 1998 U.S. Sailing Jr. Championships. Capt. U.S. Army, 1969-75. Rsch. fellow U. Utah, 1977-79, Marquette U., 1981-84, Western Wash. U., 1998, 2002, 04. Mem. Internat.

Assn. Computer Info. Sys., Assn. for Computing Machinery, Bellingham Yacht Club (trustee 1992-93, sec. 1993-94, rear commodore, 1994-95, vice commodore 1995-96, commodore 1996-97). Office: Western Wash U Coll Bus and Econs Bellingham WA 98225

ROSS, SUE, entrepreneur, author, fundraising executive; b. Chgo., Feb. 2, 1948; d. Irving and Rose (Stein) R. BA in Secondary Edn., Western Mich. U., 1971; postgrad., Northwestern U., Chgo. State U., U. Ill. Dir. youth employment Ill. Youth Svcs. Bur., Maywood, 1978-79; exec. dir. Edn. Resource Ctr., Chgo., 1979-82; asst. dir. devel. Art Inst. Chgo., 1982-83, mgr. govt. affair, 1983-84, dir. govt. affairs, 1984-85; v.p. devel. Spertus Inst. of Judaica, Chgo., 1985-90; mgmt. and fundraising counsel Sue Ross Enterprises, Chgo. and San Francisco, 1990—; founder, pres. Kid Angels Internat., San Francisco, 1994—. Lectr. Sch. Art Inst., Chgo., 1982-85, Episcopalian Archdioceses, Chgo., 1984, Nat. Soc. Fund Raising Execs., Chgo., 1984-90; instr. DePaul U. Sch. for New Learning, 1987-88, Columbia Coll., Chgo., 1980-91; dep. dir. devel. Lead Internat., 2000-01. Resident counsel for devel. The Joffrey Ballet, 1990-91; resident counsel for devel. The 1995 Children's World Peace Festival; adv. panelist Chgo. Office Fine Arts, 1981-82; v.p., bd. dirs. Lines Contemporary Ballet, 1995—; mem. adv. bd. Silkworm Peace Inst., 1996—; mem. Marin Coun. Agys., dev. dirs. Roundtable 1998—; co-chair Marin Estate Planning Seminar, 1999—; mem. adv. coun. Greater Chgo. Food Depository, 1984-85; exec. com. Chgo. Coalition Arts in Edn., 1981-82; mem. info. svcs. com. Donors' Forum Chgo., 1986-88; mem. Marin Devel. Dirs. roundtable, 1999-2001; mem. internationally renowned Gospel Choir of Glide Meml., 1991-93, San Francisco City Chorus, 1994; mem. com. Congregation Sherith Israel, 1996, San Francisco Angel Club, 1994, dir. devel. and comm. Osher Marin Jewish Cmty. Ctr., 1998-2001. Mem. Am. Fund Raising Profls. (Golden Gate chpt.)), World Affairs Coun. Democrat. Jewish. Avocations: community service, singing. Home and Office: 18 Arcangel Ct Fairfax CA 94930-1102

ROSS, TERENCE WILLIAM, architect; b. Saginaw, Mich., Sept. 27, 1935; s. Oran Lewis and Drucilla (Chadman) R.; m. Patricia Ann Marshall, Sept. 27, 1974; children by previous marriage: Deborah, David. BArch, U. Mich., 1958. Designer Roger W. Peters Constrn. Co., Fond du Lac, Wis., 1958-62; draftsman Kenneth Clark, Arch., Santa Fe, N.Mex., 1962-63, Holien & Buckley, Archs., Santa Fe, 1963-64; office mgr. Philippe Register, Architect, Santa Fe, 1964-68; prin. Register, Ross & Brunets archts./engrs., Santa Fe, 1968-71, Luna-Ross & Assocs., 1971-77; staff CNWC Archs., Tucson, until 1981, ADP Archs., 1981-89; sr. arch. U. Calif., 1989-95; arch. ADP Flour Daniel Archs./Engrs., 1995-97, Ross Assocs. Architects, 1997-2000, ret., 2000. Author: Track of the Cats. Vice chmn. N.Mex. R.R. Authority, 1969-74, sec., 1970-72; bd. dirs. colo., N.Mex. Soc. Preservation of Narrow Gauge; v.p. El Dorado Western Narrow Gauge Railway Found. Recipient award for hist. preservation N.Mex. Arts Commn., 1971, award for outstanding svcs. to cmty. Santa Fe Press Club, 1972; named col. aide-de-camp State of N.Mex., 1968, hon. mem. staff atty. gen. Mem. AIA (chpt. pres. 1970, dir.), Constrn. Specifications Inst., N.Mex. Soc. Architects (dir. 1972), Ariz. Soc. Archs., N.Mex. R.R. Authorities (chmn. joint exec. com. 1970-74), Sacto. Valley Garden Ry. Soc (pres. 1993, dir. 1994-99), San Gabriel Hist. Soc. (hon.), Alpha Rho Chi, Sashay Rounders Sq. Dance Club (pres. 1974), Diamond Squares Sq. Dance Club, Railroad Club (pres. N.Mex. 1969, 70, dir.). Home and Office: 2813 57th St Sacramento CA 95817-2403 E-mail: ross@msn.com.

ROSS, TERRY D. lawyer; b. Glendale, Calif., Aug. 12, 1943; BA, U. Calif., Santa Barbara, 1965; JD, U. Calif., San Francisco, 1968. Bar: Calif. 1969, U.S. Dist. Ct. (so. dist.) Calif. 1969, U.S. Dist. Ct. (ctrl. dist.) Calif. 1992, U.S. Dist. Ct. (no. dist.) Calif. 1999, U.S. Ct. Appeals (9th cir.) 1977, U.S. Supreme Ct. 1983. Ptnr. Gray, Cary, Ware & Freidenrich, San Diego. Mem. panel arbitrators Am. Arbitration Assn. Note and comment editor Hastings Law Jour., 1967-68. Bd. dirs., mem. exec. bd., 1st v.p. E. San Diego Co. YMCA. Mem. ABA (sect. litig.), State Bar Calif., San Diego County Bar Assn. (mem. arbitration panel, superior ct. com., client rels. com.), S.D. Marlin Club, SDMB Boat and Ski Club, Phi Delta Phi. Office: Gray Cary Ware & Freidenrich 4365 Executive Dr Ste 1100 San Diego CA 92121-4297 E-mail: tross@graycary.com.

ROSS, THERESA MAE, secondary school educator; m. H. Richard Ross; 1 child, Gwendolyn Denise. BS, Eastern Mich. U., 1967, MS, 1970; PhD, U. Mich., 1981. Tchr. Jackson (Mich.) Pub. Schs., 1967—68, Ann Arbor (Mich.) Pub. Schs., 1968—69, 1971—; grad. intern Inkster (Mich.) Child Devel. Ctr., 1968—70. HEW Early Childhood fellow, 1969—70. Mem.: NEA, Internat. Platform Assn., Am. Bus. Women's Assn., Assn. Curriculum and Supervision (curriculum cons.), World Orgn. Early Childhood Edn., Mich. Edn. Assn., Ann Arbor Edn. Assn. (lang. arts rep., multicultural coord., motivational spkr., life coach), Delta Kappa Gamma, Beta Sigma Phi, Phi Delta Kappa. Home: 1835 N Franklin Ct Ann Arbor MI 48103-2444

ROSS, THOMAS BERNARD, communications company executive; b. N.Y.C., Sept. 2, 1929; s. Henry M. and Evelyn (Timothy) R.; m. Gunilla Ekstrand, Nov. 2, 1963; children: Maria, Anne, Kristina. BA, Yale, 1951. Reporter Internat. News Svc., 1955-58; reporter UPI, 1958; mem. staff Chgo. Sun-Times, 1958-77, mem. staff Washington Bur., 1958-68, fgn. corr., 1968-70, Washington bur. chief, 1970-77; asst. sec. def. for pub. affairs, 1977-81; dir. corp. comm. Celanese Corp., 1981-82; sr. v.p. corp. affairs RCA Corp., 1982-86; sr. v.p. NBC News, 1986-90; sr. v.p., dir. media rels. worldwide Hill and Knowlton, N.Y.C., 1990-94; spl. asst. to pres., sr. dir. pub. affairs NSC, White House, Washington, 1994-95; v.p. govt. rels. Loral, N.Y.C., 1995—. Author: (with David Wise) The U-2 Affair, 1962, The Invisible Government, 1964, The Espionage Establishment, 1967. Lt. (j.g.) USNR, 1951-54. Nieman fellow Harvard U., 1964; recipient Marshall Field award, 1961, 71; decorated Def. Disting. Pub. Svc. medal. Mem. Coun. on Fgn. Rels., Century Assn. (N.Y.), Elizabethan Club (New Haven), Gridiron Club (Washington). Office: Loral 600 3d Ave New York NY 10016 Home: 120 E 83rd St Apt 5B New York NY 10028

ROSS, WARREN E. dean; BA, MD, U. Fla. Assoc. V.P. of Hosp. Affairs & Dir. J. Graham Brown Cancer Ctr., U. of Louisville, Ky.; Exec. Assoc. Dean & CEO Shands Clinic, U. of Fla. Coll. of Medicine; CEO U. of Fla. Heath System, ML Strategies, Boston; Dean Drexel U. Coll. of Medicine, 1999—. Mem.: Am. Fedn. for Clin. Rsch., Am. Assoc. for Cancer Rsch., Am. Soc. Clin. Oncology. Office: Drexel U Sch Medicine Deans Office, Mail Stop 400 245 N 15th St Philadelphia PA 19102-1192 E-mail: wr23@drexel.edu.

ROSS, WAYNE ANTHONY, lawyer; b. Milw., Feb. 25, 1943; s. Ray E. and Lillian (Steiner) R.; m. Barbara L. Ross, June 22, 1968; children: Gregory, Brian, Timothy, Amy. BA, Marquette U., 1965, JD, 1968. Bar: Wis. 1968, Alaska 1969. Asst. atty. gen. State Alaska, 1968-69; trustee, standing master Superior Ct. Alaska, 1969-73; assoc. Edward J. Reasor & Assocs., Anchorage, 1973-77; prin. Wayne Anthony Ross & Assocs., Anchorage, 1977-83; ptnr. Ross, Gingras & Frenz, Anchorage and Cordova, 1983-84, Ross & Gingras, Anchorage and Cordova, 1985; pres. Ross, Gingras and Miner, P.C., Anchorage, 1986-93, Ross and Miner, P.C., Anchorage, 1993—. Col. area def. counsel Alaska State Def. Force; pres. Tyone Mountain Syndicate, Inc. Alaska Rep. Nat. Committeeman, 1992-98; Republican candidate for Gov. of Alaska, 1998, 2002. Decorated knight comdr. Order of Polonia Restituta (Poland), knight Equestrian Order of the Holy Sepulchure of Jerusalem (Vatican). Mem.: NRA (bd. dirs. 1980—92, 1994—, benefactor), Anchorage Bar Assn., Alaska Bar Assn. (Stanley award), Alaska Peace Officers Assn., Mil. Vehicle Preservation Assn. (v.p. 1994—96), Alaska Territorial Cavalry (sec. 1991—97, 2001—), 49th Territorial Guard Regiment (pres. 1987—94, 1995—96), Smith and Wesson Collectors Assn., Ohio Gun Collectors Assn. (hon. life), Alaska Gun Collectors Assn. (pres. emeritus). Roman Catholic. Home: PO Box 101522 Anchorage AK 99510-1522 Office: Ross & Miner 327 E Fireweed Ln Ste 201 Anchorage AK 99503-2110 Office Phone: 907-276-5307. E-mail: waralaska@alaska.com.

ROSS, WILBUR LOUIS, JR., investment banker; b. Weehawken, N.J., Nov. 28, 1937; s. Wilbur Louis and Agnes (O'Neill) R.; m. Judith Nodine, May 26, 1961 (div. 1995); children: Jessica, Amanda. AB, Yale U., 1959; MBA with distinction, Harvard U., 1961. Assoc. Wood, Struthers and Winthrop, N.Y.C., 1963-64; pres. Faulkner, Dawkins and Sullivan Securities Corp., N.Y.C., 1964-76; sr. mng. dir. Rothschild, Inc., N.Y.C., 1976-2000; CEO News Comms., Inc., N.Y.C., 1996-98; chmn., chief investment officer Rothschild Recovery Fund, N.Y.C., 1997-2000; chmn., CEO WL Ross & Co. LLC, N.Y.C., 2000—. Bd. dirs. Biocraft Labs Inc., Rutherford, N.J., FurVault Inc., N.Y.C., Investors Ins. Co., Lawrence Harbor, N.J., Revere Copper and Brass Co., Stamford, Syms Corp., Secaucus, N.J., Am. Bankruptcy Inst., Washington, Allis Chalmers Corp., Milw., KTI Inc., RH Cement Co., Seoul, Korea, Tong Yang Life Ins. Co., Seoul, Kansai Sawayaka Bank, Osaka, Fresca Credit Card Co., Osaka; fin. advisor equity holders com. Texaco Co., A.H. Robins Co., Pub. Service N.H.; hon. econ. amb. from Korea to APEC Investment, Mont., 1999; chmn. Asia Recovery Fund L.P., WL Recovery Fund LP, Asia Co. Investment Ptnrs. L.P.; chmn. Clarent Hosp. Corp., Internat. Steel Group, Inc., Cleve., 2002—, Ohizumi Mfg. Co., Japan, 2003-, Burlington Industries, 2003-, Marquis Who's Who LLC, 2003-; dir. Nikko Elec. Co., Japan. Treas. N.Y. State Dem. Com., 1980-83, Am. Fedn. Arts, 1993—, The New Mus., 1993—; vice chmn. Bklyn. Mus., 1981—; chmn. univ. coun. com. on art Yale U., 1983-88; chmn. NAD, N.Y.C., 1985—, Am. Art Forum, Smithsonian Instn., 1987—; trustee, vice chmn. Nat. Mus. Am. Art, Washington, 1986-91, chmn., 1991—; trustee, Mus. Am. Fin. History; trustee Sarah Lawrence Coll., 1986—, chmn. art gallery, 1984—; pres. Parrish Art Mus., 1991-95; chmn. N.Y. Hist. Soc., 1993-94; bd. dirs. Smithsonian Inst. Nat. Bd., 1994—, chmn. bd. 1995; nat. chmn. Smithsonian Bicentennial Celebration, 1996; trustee Gustave Hyde Ctr. Nat. Mus. Am. Indian, 2001—, Nat. Mus. Am. Fin. History; bd. dirs. Turnaround Mgmt. Assn., 2001—; chmn. Absolute Recovery Hedge Fund, Ltd., Hamilton, Bermuda, Taiyo Fund, 2003-, Japan Real Estate Recovery Fund, 2003-. With U.S. Army, 1961-63. Fellow Jonathan Edward Coll. of Yale U., Met. Mus. Art; mem. Fin. Analysts Fedn. (chartered), Century Assn., The Bus. Round Table, Southampton Bath and Tennis Club (chmn. bd. dirs.), Harvard Bus. Sch. Club N.Y. (bd. dirs.). Beach Club, Club Colette, Palm Beach Fla. Avocation: collecting art. Office Phone: 212-826-2111. Business E-Mail: wlross@wlross.com.

ROSS, WILLIAM DEE, JR., economist; b. Jackson, Miss., May 16, 1921; s. William Dee and Betty (Biggs) R.; m. Nell Triplett, July 25, 1944; 1 child, William Dee III. BA, Millsaps Coll., 1942; MA, Duke U., 1947, PhD, 1951. Economist U.S. Mil. Govt. for Germany, Berlin, 1945—46; instr. econs. Duke U., Durham, NC, 1946—49; assoc. prof. La. State U., Baton Rouge, 1949—54, prof. econs., 1954—56, dean Coll. Bus. Adminstrn., 1956—76; pres. Fin. Cons. Svcs., Inc., Baton Rouge, 1976—99, Ross Bus. Svcs., Inc., Baton Rouge, 2000—. Bd. dirs. Piccadilly Cafeterias Inc., others; dir. La. Hwy. Fin. Study, La. Legis. Coun., 1953-54; cons. Joint House-Senate Hwy. Com., La. Legislature, La. Dept. Hwys., 1955-56; lectr. exec. devel. programs Mich. State U., Ga. Inst. Tech., La. State U.; mem. dept. econs., fin. and adminstrn. Hwy. Rsch. Bd., Nat. Acad. Scis., Washington, 1957-64; mem. adv. coun. Tax Inst. Am., 1961-63. Author (with B.U. Ratchford) Berlin Reparations Assignment, 1947, Financing Highway Imporvements in Louisiana, 1955, Business in a Free Society, 1966; contbr. articles to profl. jours. Bd. dirs. area coun. Boy Scouts Am. Served to 1st lt. USAAF, 1943-45. Mem. Am. Assn. Collegiate Schs. Bus., Am. Econ. Assn., So. Econ. Assn. (exec. com 1960-62), Nat. Tax Assn. (exec. com. 1960-63, editl. com. Nat. Tax Jour. 1959-62), Am. Fin. Assn., So. Fin. Assn. (pres. 1962-63), Southwestern Social Sci. Assn., Omicron Delta Kappa, Beta Gamma Sigma. Lodges: Rotary. Methodist.

ROSS, WILLIAM JARBOE, lawyer; b. Oklahoma City, May 9, 1930; s. Walter John and Bertha (Jarboe) R.; m. Mary Lillian Ryan, May 19, 1962; children: Rebecca Anne Roten, Robert Joseph, Molly Kathleen. BBA, U. Okla., 1952, LLB, 1954. Bar: Okla. 1954. Since practiced in, Oklahoma City; asst. mcpl. counselor, 1955-60; mem. firm Rainey, Ross, Rice & Binns, 1960—, prin., 1965-99, of counsel, 2000—; pres., CEO Ethics and Excellence in Journalism Found., Inasmuch Found. Mem. bd. visitors U. Okla. Coll. Law; bd. dirs. Ethics and Excellence in Journalism Found., Inasmuch Found., Harn Homestead. Mem. Okla. Bar Assn., Okla. Heritage Assn. (vice chmn. edn. com.), Newcomen Soc., Okla. City Golf and Country Club, Econ. Club, Rotary, Phi Alpha Delta, Beta Theta Pi, KC. Home: 6923 Avondale Ct Oklahoma City OK 73116-5008

ROSS, WILLIAM WARFIELD, lawyer; b. Washington, Oct. 3, 1926; s. W. Warfield and Vera Elfleda (Payne) R.; m. Jennie Fitch, Jan. 30, 1963; children— James, Mary, Billy; m. Nan Robertson, Sept. 25, 1999. AB, St. John's Coll., Annapolis, Md., 1948; LL.B., Yale U., 1951. Bar: D.C. 1951. Legal asst. Exec. Office Pres. Harry S. Truman, 1952-53, Pres. Dwight D. Eisenhower, 1953; atty. appellate sect. civil div. Dept. Justice, Washington, 1954-57; asst. to solicitor FPC, Washington, 1957-59; ptnr. Wald, Harkrader & Ross, Washington, 1963-87, Pepper, Hamilton & Scheetz, Washington, 1987-91. Adj. prof. Cornell U. Grad. Sch. Bus. and Pub. Adminstrn., 1977-80; chmn. D.C. Council Commn. on Bd. Appeals and Rev. of D.C. Govt., 1972 Chmn. Nat. Capital area ACLU, 1966-68; chmn. audit hearing panel Title I ESEA of 1965, 1976-80. Served with USN, 1945-46 Mem. ABA (chmn. sect. adminstrv. law 1978-79), Bar Assn. D.C. (chmn. adminstrv. law sect. 1968-69, gov. 1969-70), D.C. Bar, Fed. Bar Assn., Fed. Energy Bar Assn. (contbr. articles to jour.). Home: 4978 Sentinel Dr Apt 303 Bethesda MD 20816-3573 E-mail: eifraw@comcast.net.

ROSSAVIK, IVAR KRISTIAN, obstetrician, gynecologist; b. Stavanger, Rogaland, Norway, Nov. 3, 1936; came to U.S., 1982; s. Andreas and Bergit (Berge) R.; divorced; children: Line, Anne Britt, Kirsten, Solveig; m. Claudia Lagos, May 23, 1987; children: Claudia Kristina, Eevar Benjamin. MD, U. Oslo, 1962, PhD, 1982. Pvt. practice, medicine, Stavanger, 1974; asst. chief, acting chmn. U. Tromsoe, Norway, 1974-76; clin. fellow Nat. Hosp. of Norway, Oslo, 1976-81, Norwegian Radium Hosp./U. Oslo, 1981-82; pvt. practice Oslo, 1977-82; rsch. asst. prof. Baylor Coll. Medicine, Houston, 1983-86; assoc. prof. U. Okla., Oklahoma City, 1987-93, prof., 1993—2001; owner, cons. Clinica Guadalupana, 2001—. Dir. Ultrasound Svcs., Dept. Ob/Gyn., U. Okla. Inventor Rossavik Growth Equation, 1980; author: (textbook) Practical Obstetrical Ultrasound: With and Without A Computer, 1991 (Italian translation 1998). Lt. Royal Norwegian Navy, 1964-65. Mem. Okla. Sheriffs' Assn. (hon.). Lutheran. Avocations: ultrasonography technology, computer technology, fetal growth studies. Office: Clinica Guadalupana 801 NW 23d St Oklahoma City OK 73106 E-mail: iros@ionet.net.

ROSSBACHER, LISA ANN, university president, geology educator, writer; b. Fredericksburg, Va., Oct. 10, 1952; d. Richard Irwin and Jean Mary (Dearing) R.; m. Dallas D. Rhodes, Aug. 4, 1978. BS, Dickinson Coll., 1975; MA, SUNY, Binghamton, 1978, Princeton U., 1979, PhD, 1983. Cons. Republic Geothermal, Santa Fe Springs, Calif., 1979-81; asst. prof. geology Whittier (Calif.) Coll., 1982-84, Calif. State Poly. U., Pomona, 1984-86, assoc. prof. geol. sci., 1986-91, assoc. v.p. acad. affairs, 1987-93, prof. geol. sci., 1991-93; v.p. acad. affairs, dean faculty Whittier (Calif.) Coll., 1993-95; dean of coll., prof. geology Dickinson Coll., Carlisle, Pa., 1995-98; pres. So. Poly. State U., Marietta, Ga., 1998—. Vis. rschr. U. Uppsala, Sweden, 1984. Author: Career Opportunities in Geology and the Earth Sciences, 1983, Recent Revolutions in Geology, 1986; (with Rex Buchanan) Geomedia, 1988; columnist Geotimes, 1988—; contbr. articles to profl. jours. Recipient scholarship Ministry Edn. of Finland, Helsinki, 1984; grantee Sigma Xi, 1976, NASA, 1983-94. Fellow AAAS (geol. nominating com. 1984-87, chair-elect geology and geography sect. 1997-98, chair 1998-99, past chair 1999-2000); mem. Geol. Soc. Am. Office: So Poly State U 1100 S Marietta Pkwy SE Marietta GA 30060-2855 Office Phone: 678-915-7230.

ROSSE, CORNELIUS, medical educator; Prof. emeritus biol. structure U. Wash., Seattle. Adj prof. emeritus med. edn. U. Wash., Seattle. Named a Disting. Tchr. of Basic Scis. in U.S., 1989. Mem.: Nat. Acad. Sci. Inst. Medicine, Alpha Omega Alpha. Office: Univ Washington G507 Health Scis Ctr Box 357240 Seattle WA 98195 E-mail: rosse@u.washington.edu.

ROSSEL, CARY, corporate financial executive; Student, Hebrew U. Jerusalem, So. Meth. U. Chief fin. officer Glazer's Wholesale Drug, 1991—. Mem.: Alcoholic Beverage Industry Elec. Data Inerchange Coun. (retail subcom. chair). Office: Glazers Wholesale Drug 14860 Landmark Blvd Dallas TX 75240

ROSSELL, CHRISTINE HAMILTON, political science educator; b. Bklyn., Jan. 22, 1945; d. Robert Hamilton and Ann (Bezold) R.; 1 child, Elise. AB, UCLA, 1967; MA, Calif. State U., Northridge, 1969; PhD, U. So. Calif., 1974. Asst. prof. Pitzer Coll., Claremont, Calif., 1973-74; rsch. assoc. U. Md., College Park, 1974-75; asst. prof. Boston U., 1975-82, assoc. prof., 1982-89, prof., 1989—, chair dept. polit. sci., 1992-95. Vis. asst. prof. Duke U., Durham, N.C., 1977-78, U. Calif., Berkeley, 1981; vis. lectr. Canberra (Australia) Coll., 1985; vis. fellow Pub. Policy Inst. Calif., 1999. Author: (with others) Strategies for Effective Desegregation, 1983, Carrot or Stick for School Desegregation, 1990, Bilingual Education in Massachusetts: The Emperor Has No Clothes, 1996; co-editor: Consequences of School Desegregation, 1983, Sch. Desegreation in the 21st Century, 2002. Mem. Citywide Coord. Coun., Boston, 1976-77. Home: 44 High St Brookline MA 02445-7707 Office: Boston U Dept Polit Sci 232 Bay State Rd Boston MA 02215-1403 E-mail: crossell@bu.edu.

ROSSELLINI, ISABELLA, actress, model; b. Rome, June 18, 1952; d. Roberto Rossellini and Ingrid Bergman; m. Martin Scorsese, Sept. 1979 (div. Nov. 1982); m. Jonathan Wiedemann (div.); 1 child, Elettra Ingrid. Student, Finch Coll., 1972, New Sch. for Social Research, N.Y.C. Became model for Lancôme, 1982. Appeared in films A Matter of Time, 1976, Il Pap'occhio, 1980, The Meadow, 1982, White Nights, 1985, Blue Velvet, 1986, Siesta, 1987, Red Riding Hood, 1987, Tough Guys Don't Dance, 1987, Zelly and Me, 1988, Cousins, 1989, Wild at Heart, 1990, Les Dames Galantes, 1990, Death Becomes Her, 1992, The Pickle, 1992, Fearless, 1993, Wyatt Earp, 1994, Immortal Beloved, 1994, The Innocent, 1995, The Funeral, Crime of the Century, 1996, Big Night, 1996, The Real Blonde, 1998, Empire, 2002, Roger Dodger, 2002, The Tulse Luper Suitcases: The Moab Story, 2003, The Saddest Music in the World, 2003, The Tulse Luper Suitcases, Part 2: Vaux to the Sea, 2004; TV films: The Last Elephant, 1990, Lies of the Twins, 1991, Don Quixote, 2000, Monte Walsh, 2003; TV miniseries: The Odyssey, 1997, Merlin, 1998, The Impostors, 1998, Left Luggage, 1998; TV series: Napoléon, 2002; TV guest appearances Friends, 1996, Chicago Hope, 1997, The Simpsons, 1999, Alias, 2004. Office: William Morris Agy attn Pakseghian Planco 1350 Avenue Of The Americas New York NY 10019-4702*

ROSSELLO, PEDRO, former governor; b. San Juan, P.R., Apr. 5, 1944; m. Maga Nevares, Aug. 9, 1969; children: Juan Oscar, Luis Roberto, Ricardo Antonio. BS, U. Notre Dame, 1966; MD, Yale U., 1970; MPH, U. P.R., 1981; LLD (hon.), U. Notre Dame, 1995, U. Mass., 1995. Intern straight surgery Beth Israel Hosp., Boston, 1970-71, resident gen. surgery, 1971-74; resident cardiac and burns Mass. Gen. Hosp., Boston, 1972; resident trauma San Francisco Gen. Hosp., 1973; sr. resident pediat. surgery Children's Hosp., Boston, 1974-75, chief resident, pediat. surgery-urology, 1975-76; instr. surgery Harvard Med. Sch., 1975-76; pvt. practice San Juan, 1976-92; asst. prof. surgery U. P.R., 1978-82, assoc. prof. surgery, 1982-92; dir. Dept. Health City of San Juan, 1985-87; chief surgery San Jorge Hosp., San Juan, 1989-92, med. dir., 1990; gov. Puerto Rico, 1993-2001. Lead gov. So. Regional Project Infant Mortality, 1993-95; chair So. States Energy Bd., 1995-96; chmn. So. Growth Policies Bd., 1999-2000; chair So. Tech. Coun., 1998-99, So. Internat. Trade Coun., 1998-99; mem. intergovtl. policy adv. com. U.S. Trade Rep., 1994-2001; pres. Coun. State Govts., 1998; mem. adv. coun. Welfare to Work Partnership; mem. Dem. Nat. Com.; bd. dirs. U.S.-Spain Coun.; mem. nat. adv. bd. Initiative and Referendum Inst. Contbr. articles to profl. jours. Mem. P.R. Olympic Com., 1982-84, 87-88; v.p. New Progressive Party, 1988-91, pres., 1991-99; mem. exec. com. Edn. Commn. States, 1995-2000; bd. visitors emeritus Georgetown U. Law Ctr., Washington; del. Dm. Nat. Conv., Chgo., 1996, 2000. Capt. USNG, 1970-76. Recipient Pres.'s award U.S. Hispanic C. of C., 1996, Pres.'s award League of United Latin Am. Citizens, 1998, Rolex Achievement award, 1999. Mem. Nat. Govs. Assn. (host 1996 ann. meeting), So. Govs. Assn. (chair 1997-98), Dem. Govs. Assn. (chair 1998), P.R. Tennis Assn. (pres. 1982-84), Caribbean Tennis Assn. (pres. 1983-84), Alpha Omega Alpha. Avocations: jogging, tennis, ocean kayaking. Home: 2217 Aryness Dr Vienna VA 22181-3047

ROSSEN, JORDAN, lawyer; b. Detroit, June 13, 1934; s. Nathan Paul and Rebecca (Rizy) R.; m. Susan Friebert, Mar. 24, 1963 (div. June 1972); 1 child, Rebecca; m. M. Elizabeth Bunn, Jan. 3, 1981; children— N. Paul, Jordan David. BA, U. Mich., 1956; JD, Harvard U., 1959. Bar: Mich. 1960, N.Y. 1998, U.S. Dist. Ct. (ea. dist.) Mich. 1960, U.S. Ct. Appeals (6th cir.) 1966, U.S. Supreme Ct. 1966, U.S. Ct. Appeals (7th cir.) 1974, U.S. Ct. Appeals (D.C. cir.) 1984, U.S. Ct. Appeals (3rd cir.) 1987, U.S. Dist. Ct. (ea. and so. dists.) N.Y. 1999. Assoc. Sullivan, Elmer, Eames & Moody, Detroit, 1960-62; assoc. Sugar & Schwartz, Detroit, 1962-64; asst. gen. counsel UAW, Detroit, 1964-74, assoc. gen. counsel, 1974-83, gen. counsel, 1983-98; of counsel Meyer, Suozzi, English and Klein, N.Y.C., N.Y., 1998—; prof. labor studies Wayne State U., 2000—. Vice pres. N.P. Rossen Agy., Inc., Detroit, 1960-83; gen. counsel Mich. Health & Social Security Research Inst., Inc., Detroit, 1965-83; dir. UAW Job Devel. & Tng. Corp., Detroit, 1984-90; mem. 6th Cir. Jud. Conf. Editor: Mich. Bar Labor Section Publication, 1961-64. Contbr. articles to profl. jours. Pres. Young Democrats, Mich., 1963-65; chmn. Americans for Democratic Action, Mich., 1966-68; chmn. Voter Registration Dem. Party, Mich., 1967. Recipient Human Rights award, City of Detroit, 1978. Mem.: Coll. Labor and Employment Lawyers, Fed. Bar Assn., N.Y. Bar Assn., Mich. Bar Assn. Jewish. Office: 1350 Broadway Ste 501 New York NY 10018-7705 Office Phone: 212-763-7034.

ROSSEN-KNILL, DEBORAH F. academic administrator, English educator; BA in fiction writing, U. Mich., 1982, MFA in fiction, 1985; PhD in English, U. Minn., 1995. Freelance writer Columbia Presbyn. Med. Ctr., N.Y.C., 1988; tech. and bus. writer Hansome Energy Sys., Inc., Linden, NJ, 1986—90; tchg. asst. U. Mich., Ann Arbor, 1983—85, lectr., 1985—86, Madonna Coll., Livonia, Mich., 1986, Sch. Continuing Edn, Divsn. Degree Studies, Gen. Studies Program, NYU, 1987—88, adj. asst. prof., 1989; instr., program in composition and comm., U. Minn., Mpls., 1990—94, asst. coord. upper divsn. composition course, program in composition and comm., 1993—94; vis. scholar Inst. Rsch. in Cognitive Sci., U. Penn., 1994—95; adj. faculty, dept. English U. Penn., 1994—95; postdoctoral fellow Inst. Rsch. in Cognitive Sci., U. Penn., 1995—96; dir. writing program Phila. Coll. Textiles and Sci., 1996—98; dir. Writing Across the U. Penn., 1998—99, dir. Speaking Across the U., 1999; sr. lectr., dept. English U. Rochester, 2000—, dir. coll. writing program, 2000—, dean freshman, 2001—. Tchr. creative writing Huron Valley Women's Prison, Ypsilante, Mich., 1979; co-coord. Guild House Readings, Ann Arbor, Mich., 1985; judge, Icarus contest in fiction, prose and art work NYU, 1988, evaluator bus. sch. essay exam, 88, student adv. gen. studies program, 88; chair, grad. student org. curriculum com. U. Minn., 1990—91, sec. NCTE Student Affiliation, 1991—92; v.p. Grad. Student Org., 1991—92; mem. composition group U. Minn., 1993—94; sec. linguistics panel MMLA, 1994, chair linguistics sessions on dialogue in fiction, 95; spkr. in field. Author: (short stories) Fox Bait, 1988, The Unreal Child, 1985, Booze an' Bo, 1984, co-author (with other) numerous scholary pubs.; co-author: (with others) numerous articles. Finalist, Mark Twain Sesquicentennial Fiction Contest, 1985; recipient P.E.O. Nat. Scholar award, 1994.

ROSSER, ALVIN RAYMON, artist; b. Port Clinton, Ohio, July 5, 1928; s. Samuel Webster and Reba Della Rosser; m. Barbara Emma Roth, June 10, 1953; children: Rachelle Karen, Jill Allyn. BFA, Ohio U., 1950, MFA, 1953; postgrad., Hans Hofmann Sch. of Art, N.Y.C., 1953—54. Comml. artist Mutual Broadcasting System, N.Y.C., 1954; art tchr. Chagrin Falls H.S., Ohio, 1955; instr. Lehigh U., Bethlehem, Pa., 1956—58; artists' rep. Gerard Agy., N.Y.C., 1958—60; art dir. Topper Toy Co., Elizabeth, NJ, 1961—62; scenic designer Harnick-Adams Prodns., N.Y.C., 1963—66; art tchr. Sparta Bd. of Edn., NJ, 1966—89. Exhibited in group shows at Ward Eggleston Gallery, N.Y.C., 1953, Roko Gallery, 1953, Koltnow Gallery, 1953—57, Cleve. Mus.

Art, 1954, N.Y.C. Ctr., 1954, 1955, 1956, 1957, Jersey City Mus., 1959, Montclair Mus., 1967; artist (one-man shows) Ohio U., 1953, Lehigh U., 1955, Paper Mill Playhouse, N.J., 1960, featured artist N.J. State Fair, 2000, Artery Gallery, Milford, Pa., 2000—02; author: (short stories) A Lesson in Love, I Thought My Father was God, 2002. Trustee, v.p. Sussex County Arts Coun., Newton, NJ, 1970—76. Cpl. U.S. Army, 1950—52. Recipient Emerson Poetry award 1st prize, Ohio U., 1954, Skylands Best in Show award, Sussex County Arts Coun., 1989, Skylands Select Best in Show award, 2001, Patrick-Claus award, 2003. Avocations: fishing, gardening, bee keeping, pool hustling, ventriloquy. Mailing: PO Box 76 Sparta NJ 07871-0076

ROSSER, ANNETTA HAMILTON, composer; b. Jasper, Fla., Aug. 28, 1913; d. Carlos Calvin and Jermai Reuben (Gilbert) Hamilton; m. John Barkley Rosser, Sept. 7, 1935 (dec. Sept. 1989); children: Edwenna Merryday, John Barkley Jr. BM, Fla. State U., 1932. Cert. tchr. Fla. Tchr. music Kirby-Smith Jr. High Sch., Jacksonville, Fla., 1932-35; 1st violinist Santa Monica (Calif.) Symphony, 1949-50; concertmaster Ithaca (N.Y.) Chamber Orch., 1948-56, Cornell Univ. Orch., Ithaca, 1948-56, soloist, 1957; 1st violinist Princeton (N.J.) Symphony, 1959-61; concertmaster Madison (Wis.) Symphony Orch., 1963-66, 1st violinist, 1967-82. Composer of over 100 vocal and instrumental compositions including Meditations on Cross, song cycle for 2 voices, flute and piano, 1976, An Offering of Song, book of 48 songs, 1977, Songs of a Nomad Flute, song cycle for soprano, flute and piano, 1978, Six Songs of the T'ang Dynasty for soprano and violin, 1983, Nocturne for violin and piano, 1989, Trio for flute, violin and piano, 1991, Scherzo for flute ensemble, 1991, (book of 21 songs) Another Offering of Song, 1998. Bd. dirs. Madison Opera Guild, 1972-86, Madison Civic Music Assn., 1983-85; past pres. Madison Symphony Orch. League, Ithaca Federated Music Club, Ithaca Composers Club; bd. dirs. Madison Art Ctr., 1979-83, Madison Woman of Distinction, 1980, Madison Civics Club, 1976-79, pres., 1977-78; pres. Art League Madison Art Ctr., 1980-82, Univ. League Scholarship Benefit Concert of Rosser Compositions, U. Wis., MMadison, 2003. Recipient Sr. Svc. award Rotary Club, 1994; original music manuscripts and programs were added to archives of U. Wis.-Madison Music Libr., 1996. Mem. AAUW, Wis. Acad. Scis., Arts, and Letters, Univ. League, Univ. League Bird Study Group, Madison Club, Wis. Acad. Scis., Arts, and Letters, PEO, Phi Kappa Phi, Pi Kappa Lambda, Sigma Alpha Iota. Republican. Presbyterian. Avocations: Chinese snuff bottles, English brass rubbings, birding. Home: 4209 Manitou Way Madison WI 53711-3703

ROSSER, EDWIN MICHAEL, mortgage company executive; b. Denver, Oct. 11, 1940; s. Edwin Michael and Anne (Ratliff) R.; m. Keren Call, July 17, 1969; children: Kevin, William. BS, Colo. State U., 1964; MA, U. No. Colo., 1974. Cert. mortgage banker. Mktg. officer United Bank Mortgage, Denver, 1968-74; dir. nat. accounts PMI Mortgage Ins. Co., Denver, 1974-85; v.p. Moore Mortgage Co., Denver, 1985-87, Pacific First Mortgage Corp., Englewood, Colo., 1987-89; 1st v.p. 1st Nat. Bank, San Francisco, 1990-93; v.p. nat. accounts United Guaranty Corp., 1993—. Bd. dirs. Rocky Mtn. Women's Inst. Photographer represented in Denver Art Mus., The Buffalo in Winter, (1st place award 1981). Steering com. Blueprint for Colo., Govs. Unified Housing Task Force; mem. Colo. Housing Coun. (chmn. 1986-87); bd. dirs. Colo. State U. Found.; mem. adv. bd. Arapahoe County Open Space and Trails, 1999-; mem. Colo. Land Use Commn., 1999, Colo. State Housing Bd., 2003; bd. dirs. The Conservation Campaign, 2004. Fellow Soc. Mortgage Bankers; mem. Am. Planning Assn., Soc. of Cert. Mortgage Bankers (chmn.), Mortgage Bankers Assn. Am. (cert., bd. govs. 1986-90, state and local achievement award 1986, Ernest P. Schumacher award 1988, disting. svc. award 2003, Burton Wood Legis. Svc. award), Colo. Mortgage Bankers Assn. (bd. dirs. 1979-88, pres. 1986, E.C. Spelman award 1978, Lifetime Achievement award 1998), Colo. Assn. Commerce and Industry, Denver Nat. Soc. Real Estate Fin., Mus. Natural History, Denver C. of C., Rocky Mtn. Mutual Housing Assn. (bd. dirs.), Ctr. of Fin. Real Estate (bd. dirs.), Colo. State U. Alumni Assn. (nat. pres. 1985, bd. dirs. 1979-87, mem. found. bd. 1987-91, 93-2000, Honor Alumnus 1984, ha Sasso award Dept. Athletics 1993), Univ. Club, City Club Denver, Nat. Soc. for Real Estate Fin. (CRF designation 1997), Colo. State U. Henry Alumni (Svc. award 2000), Univ. Club, Alpha Sigma Gamma. Republican. Roman Catholic. Avocations: photography, fly fishing. Home: 12478 E Amherst Cir Aurora CO 80014-3306 Office: United Guaranty Residential Ins Co 6312 S Fiddlers Green Cir Englewood CO 80111-4943

ROSSER, ESSIE, minister, counselor, marketing professional; b. Dawson, Ga., Apr. 15, 1939; d. James Andrews and Essie Louise Kimbrough; children: Evelyn Ellington, Augustus Reid, Anthony Reid, Lassels Reid. Student, Corp. Coll., 1968—69; AA, Onondaga C.C., Syracuse, N.Y., 1972; BA, Oswego State Coll., 1974; JD, Atlanta Law Sch., 1982; ThD, 1998; DD, Abotra Bible Inst. and Sem. Trained nursing technician Syracuse Meml. Hosp., NY, 1957—62; employment counselor, dir. People's Employment Agy., Syracuse, 1962—64, CEO, dir. job readiness/placement clients, writer manual Decatur, Ga.; cons. families/food plan Family Food Svs., Fulton, NY, 1964—68; sales dir., CEO Dependable Janitorial Svs., North Syracuse, NY, 1969—73; rsch. supr. Math., Inc., Dayton, Ohio, 1975—77; adminstrv. asst. psychology dept. Clark Coll., Atlanta, 1977—82; min., counselor drug deliverance/prevention counselor ch. Worldwide Word Ministries., Inc., Atlanta. Achievements include development of faith based deliverance programs; drug prevention curricluums beginning with pre-k child, extending through high school presently being established in faith based organizations engaging their help with the drug problem. Avocations: antiques, music, writing, travel. Home: 180 Gibson St Atlanta GA 30316-1453

ROSSER, JAMES MILTON, academic administrator; b. East St. Louis, Ill., Apr. 16, 1939; s. William M. and Mary E. (Bass) R.; 1 child, Terrence. BA, So. Ill. U., 1962, MA, 1963, PhD, 1969. Diagnostic bacteriologist Holden Hosp., Carbondale, Ill., 1961-63; rsch. bacteriologist Eli Lilly & Co., Indpls., 1963-66; coordinator Black Am. studies, instr. health edn. So. Ill. U., Carbondale, 1968-69, asst. prof. Black Am. studies dir., 1969-70, asst. to chancellor, 1970; assoc. vice chancellor for acad. affairs U. Kans., Lawrence, 1970-74, assoc. prof. edn., pharmacology and toxicology, 1971-74; vice chancellor dept. higher edn. State of N.J., Trenton, 1974-79, acting chancellor, 1977; pres., prof. health care mgmt. Calif. State U., Los Angeles, 1979—. Mem. tech. resource panel Ctr. for R&D in Higher Edn., U. Calif., Berkeley, 1974-76; mem. health maintenance orgn. com. Health Planning Coun., State of N.J., 1975-79; mem. standing com. on R&D bd. trustees Ednl. Testing Service, 1976-77; mem. steering com. and task force on retention of minorities in engring. Assembly of Engring. NRC, 1975-78; mem. Bd. Med. Examiners, State of N.J., 1978-79; vis. faculty Inst. Mgmt. of Lifelong Edn., Grad. Sch. Edn., Harvard U., 1979; mem. Calif. State U. Trustees Spl. Long Range Fin. Planning Com., 1982-87; mem. Am. Coun. on Edn., 1979—, AFL/CIO Labor Higher Edn. Coun., 1983—, Nat. Commn. Higher Edn. Issues, 1981-82; mem. The Calif. Achievement Coun., 1983-89, strategic adv. counc. Coll. and Univs. Systems Exch., 1988-91; bd. dirs. Am. Humanities Coun., So. Calif. Am. Humanics, Inc. Coun., United Calif. Bank, Edison Internat., Fedco, Inc.; task force on equality and fairness Texaco, 1999-2002. Author: An Analysis of Health Care Delivery, 1977. Mem. exec. bd., chmn. varsity scouting program L.A. area coun. Boy Scouts Am., 1980—; bd. dirs. Hispanic Urban Ctr., L.A., 1979—, L.A. Urban League, 1982-95, Cmty. TV of So. Calif., Sta. KCET, 1980-89, 98—, United Way, L.A., 1980-91, Orthopaedic Hosp., 1983-86, L.A. Philharm. Assn., 1986-99, Nat. Health Found., 1990-98; mem. Citizen's Adv. Coun. Congl. Caucus Sci. and Tech., 1983—; mem. performing arts coun./edn. coun. Music Ctr., 1984—; minority bus. task force Pacific Bell, 1985-86; bd. govs. Nat. ARC, 1986-91, Mayor's Blue Ribbon Task Force on Drugs, City of L.A., 1988, L.A. Annenberg Met. Project, 1994-2001; Nat. Adv. Coun. on Aging, 1989-93; trustee Woodrow Wilson Nat. Fellowship Found., 1993—; bd. advisors Historically Black Colls. and Univs. and Minority Insts., Dept. Air Force, 1997-2001; bd. dirs. Ams. for the Arts, 1991—; mem. L.A. Adv. Alliance, Pasadena Tournament of Roses, 2000—; mem. Action Forum on Diversity in the Engring. Workforce, Nat. Acad. Engring., 2000—; mem. Calif. Coun. on Sci. and Tech., 1999—; mem. campaign adv. com. The Audubon Ctr. L.A., 2001—. NSF fellow, 1961; NDEA fellow, 1967-68; recipient award of recognition in Edn. Involvement for Young Achievers, 1981, Pioneer of Black Hist. Achievement award Brotherhood Crusade, 1981, Alumni Achievement award So. Ill. U., 1982, Friend of Youth award Am. Humanics, Inc., 1985, Leadership award Dept. Higher Edn. Ednl. Equal Opportunity Fund Program, 1989, Medal of Excellence Gold State Minority Found., 1990, Take Charge of Learning Success award Inst. for Redesign of Learning. Mem. Calif. C. of C. (bd. dirs. 1993—), Alhambra C. of C. (bd. dirs. 1979—), Los Angeles C. of C. (bd. dirs. 1985-90), Am. Assn. State Colls. and Univs., Kappa Delta Pi, Phi Kappa Phi. Roman Catholic. Office: Calif State U LA Office of Pres 5151 State University Dr Los Angeles CA 90032-4226

ROSSER, JOHN BARKLEY, JR., economics professor; b. Ithaca, N.Y., Apr. 12, 1948; s. John Barkley and Annetta Louise (Hamilton) R.; m. Sue A. Vilhauer, Aug. 31, 1968 (div. 1979); children: Meagan Rebecca, Caitlin Elizabeth; m. Marina R. Vcherashnaya, May 24, 1987; 1 child: Alexandra Ashley. BA, U. Wis., 1969, MA, 1972, PhD, 1976. Project specialist Inst. Environ. Studies, Madison, Wis., 1972-75; planning analyst Dept. Natural Resources, Madison, 1975-76; prof. econs. James Madison U., Harrisonburg, Va., 1977—, Kirby L. Kramer Jr. chair of bus. adminstrn., 1996—. Author: From Catastrophe to Chaos: A General Theory of Economic Discontinuities, 1991, (with M.V. Rosser) Comparative Economics in a Transforming World Economy, 1996; editor Jour. Econ. Behavior and Orgn., 2002-; contbr. articles to profl. jours. Mem. Am. Econs. Assn., So. Econs. Assn., N.Y. Acad. Scis. Home: 236 Franklin St Harrisonburg VA 22801-4019 Office: James Madison Univ MSC0204 Dept Economics Harrisonburg VA 22807-0001 Office Phone: 540-568-3212. Business E-Mail: rosserjb@jmu.edu.

ROSSER, RICHARD FRANKLIN, higher education consultant; b. Arcanum, Ohio, July 16, 1929; s. Harold Arm and Margaret (Whitacre) R.; m. Donna Eyssen., Mar. 21, 1951; children— Eric, Carl, Edward. BA, Ohio Wesleyan U., 1951; MPA, Syracuse U., 1952, PhD, 1961. Joined USAF, 1952, advanced through grades to col., 1968; prof. polit. sci. USAF Acad., Colorado Springs, Colo., 1959-73, head dept., 1967-73, ret., 1973; prof. polit. sci., dean Albion (Mich.) Coll., 1973-77; pres. DePauw U., Greencastle, Ind., 1977-86, chancellor, 1986; pres. Nat. Assn. Ind. Colls. and Univs., Washington, 1986-93; cons. in higher edn. pvt. practice, Racine, Wis., 1993—. Author: An Introduction to Soviet Foreign Policy, 1969; contbr. articles to profl. jours. Mem. univ. senate United Meth. Ch., 1980-84; mem. spl. commn. of Chief of Staff on Honor Code U.S. Mil. Acad., 1989; bd. visitors Air U., 1991-94; bd. trustees Ohio Wesleyan U., 1991—; mem. nat. adv. com. Instnl. Quality and Integrity, 1994—; co-chair Citizens for Librs., Grand Traverse County, 1995-96. Decorated Legion of Merit with oak leaf cluster. Mem. Phi Beta Kappa, Omicron Delta Kappa. Unitarian. Home and Office: 31 Sumac Dr Brunswick ME 04011

ROSSET, BARNET LEE, JR., publishing executive; b. Chgo., May 28, 1922; s. Barnet Lee and Mary (Tansey) R.; m. Joan Mitchell, 1950 (div. 1952); m. Hannelore Eckert, Aug. 1953 (div. 1957); 1 child, Peter; m. Cristine Agnini, Mar. 11, 1965 (div. 1979); children: Tansey, Beckett; m. Elisabeth Krug, 1980 (div. 1991; 1 child, Chantal. Ph.B., U. Chgo., 1947; BA New Sch. Social Research, N.Y.C., 1952. Pub., editor Grove Press, Inc., 1951-86, Evergreen Rev., 1957-73, Blue Moon Books, Inc., N.Y.C., 1987-98, Evergreen Rev. Inc., 1998—, Foxrock, Inc., 1995—. Served to 1st lt. Signal Corps AUS, 1942-46. Recipient Ninth Pub. citation PEN Am. Ctr., 1988, Poor Richard's award Small Press Ctr., 1999, Commandeur De L'Ordre Des Arts et Des Lettres, French Govt., 1999, Nat. Book Critics Cir. Lifetime Achievement award, 2001, Curtis Benjamin award Assn. Am. Pubs., 2001, 1st Ann. Hadaha award Paris Rev., 2003. Mem. PEN, Overseas Press Club. Office: 61 4th Ave New York NY 10003-5204 Office Phone: 212-505-6880. Personal E-mail: evergreen@nyc.rr.com.

ROSSETTI, MANUEL DAVID, engineering educator, consultant; BS in Indsl. Engring., U. Cin., 1985; MS in Indsl. and Sys. Engring., Ohio State U., 1988, PhD in Indsl. and Sys. Engring., 1992. Registered profl. engr., Ark., 2001. Asst. prof. systems engring. U. Va., Charlottesville, 1993—99; asst. prof. indsl. engring. U. Ark., Fayetteville, 1999—2002, assoc. prof. indsl. engring., 2003—. Cons. Wal-Mart, Bentonville, Ark., 2000—. Contbr. articles to profl. jours. Lilly Tchg. fellow, U. Va., 1998, Baum Tchg. Enhancement grantee, U. Ark., 2002. Mem.: Inst. Ops. Rsch. and Mgmt. Sci., Inst. Indsl. Engrs., Am. Soc. Engring. Edn. Achievements include research in Queueing, Inventory, Logistics and Transportation; Object Oriented Simulation; Industrial Engineering Education; Application of Industrial Engineering to Healthcare Systems. Office: Univ Ark Dept Indsl Engring 4207 Bell Engineering Ctr Fayetteville AR 72701 E-mail: rossetti@uark.edu.

ROSSETTOS, NICHOLAS J. research and development company executive; AB in Econ., Princeton U.; MS in Acctg., MBA, Northeastern U. Dir. fin. and adminstrn. EnviroBusiness, Inc.; mgr. fin. Centerwatch (subs. Thomson CP); CFO Atlantic Tech. Ventures, Inc., N.Y.C., 2000—. Office: Atlantic Technology Ventures Inc 787 7th Ave New York NY 10019-6018

ROSSEY, PAUL WILLIAM, school superintendent, university president; b. Richmond, Ind., July 7, 1926; s. Chris C. and Lela (Longman) R.; m. Adelaide Elizabeth Finnegan; 1 dau., Joanne Rossey Sczubelek. BS, N.J. City Univ., 1952, Litt. D., 1971; MA, NYU, 1953, Ed.D. (Kellogg Found. fellow 1955), 1958. Head jr. sch. Peddie Sch., Hightstown, N.J., 1952-53; cons., elem. sch. instr. West Hempstead, N.Y., 1953-55; prin. elem. sch. Dobbs Ferry, N.Y., 1955-58; supt. schs. Litchfield, Conn., 1958-60, Scotch Plains-Fanwood, N.J., 1960-67; dist. supt. schs. Nassau County, N.Y., 1967-69; pres. West Chester (Pa.) State U., 1969-74; supt. schs. Millburn-Short Hills, N.J., 1974-92; ret. Lectr. NYU, 1954-67 Contbr. articles to profl. jours. County dir. Boy Scouts Am.; v.p. YMCA; bd. dirs. Garbe Found., Community Fund; trustee NYU, 1970-74, The Peddie Sch., 1974-92; mem. exec. com. N.J. Coun. Edn., 1977-83. With USNR, 1944-46, USMCR, 1972-86; ret. Named Outstanding Alumnus, N.J. City U., 1962; recipient NYU medallion, 1966, Ernest O. Melby award human relations, 1970 Mem. Am. Assn. Sch. Adminstrs. (chmn. N.J. 1965-67), Am. Council Edn., Aircraft Owners and Pilots Assn., N.J. Assn. Sch. Adminstrs. (exec. com. 1964-67, 81-85), Horace Mann League U.S. (nat. pres. 1977-78), Kappa Delta Pi, Phi Delta Kappa. Clubs: Exchange (dir.), N.J. Schoolmasters. Republican. Presbyterian. Home: 219 Summit Ave Summit NJ 07901-2213

ROSSI, ANTHONY GERALD, lawyer; b. Warren, Ohio, July 20, 1935; s. Anthony Gerald and Lena (Guarnieri) R.; m. Marilyn J. Fuller, June 22, 1957; children: Diana L., Maribeth, Anthony Gerald III. BS, John Carroll U., 1957; JD, Cath. U. Am., 1961. Bar: Ohio 1961. Ptnr. Guarnieri & Secrest, Warren, 1961—; former acting judge Warren Municipal Ct. Mem. Mahoning-Shenango Estate Planning Coun., 1968—, past sec.; past pres. Warren Olympic Club; past bd. govs. Cath. U. Am. Law Sch. Coun.; past trustee Trumbull Art Guild, Warren Civic Music Assn. Capt. Transp. Corps, AUS, 1957-65. Mem. ABA, Ohio Bar Assn., Trumbull County Bar Assn. (exec. com. 1975—, pres. 1976-77), Am. Arbitration Assn., Ohio State Bar Found., Ohio Motorist Assn. (corp. mem., trustee 1980-86, 92-98), Wolf's Club, KC, Elks, Ohio Acad. of Trial Lawyers. Home: 2500 Hidden Lakes Dr NE Warren OH 44484-4159 Office: 151 E Market St Warren OH 44481-1102 Office Phone: 330-393-1584. E-mail: ganslaw@netdotcom.com.

ROSSI, DINO J. state legislator, real estate broker; b. Seattle, Oct. 15, 1959; m. Terry Rossi; children: Juliauna, Jake, Joseph. BA in Bus. Mgmtr., Seattle U., 1982. Mem. Wash. Senate, Dist. 5, Olympia, 1996—; mem. energy, tech., and telecom. com. Wash. Senate; mem. natural resources, parks and recreation com.; mem. ways and means com.; mem. capital budget subcom.; mem. joint com. on pension policy. Vol. Sr. Ctr.; co-founder Operation Homefront; past bd. dirs. Boys and Girls Club, Mountains to Sound Greenway Bd. Mem. Rotary (Issaquah). Republican. Office: 109A Irving Newhouse Ofc Olympia WA 98504-0001

ROSSI, ENNIO C. physician, educator; b. Madison, Wis., Apr. 3, 1931; s. Joseph and Esther (D'Amelio) R.; m. Anna Maria Bianchi, June 22, 1957; children: Roberta, Marco. BA, U. Wis., 1951, MD, 1954. Diplomate Am. Bd. Internal Medicine. Intern Ohio State U. Hosps., 1954-55; resident medicine U. Wis. Hosps., 1958-61, fellow, 1961-63; instr. medicine Marquette U., Milw., 1963-64, asst. prof. medicine, 1964-66; assoc. prof. medicine Northwestern U., Chgo., 1966-72, prof. medicine, 1972-96, prof. emeritus, 1996—, chief hematology, 1967-84, chief transfusion medicine, 1984-96. V.p. med. affairs Life Source Blood Ctr., Glenview, Ill., 1988-93; vis. scientist Mario Negri Inst., Milan, 1977. Co-editor: Haemostasis and the Kidney, 1989; sr. editor: Principles of Transfusion Medicine, 1991, 2d edit., 1996. Capt. U.S. Army, 1956-58. Fulbright scholar, U.S. Dept. State, U. Rome, 1955; Nat. Heart, Lung Blood Inst. Transfusion Medicine Acad. awardee, 1983; WHO travelling fellow, 1985. Fellow ACP; mem. Am. Soc. Hematology, Am. Soc. Pharmacology and Exptl. Therapeutics, Am. Assn. Blood Banks (chmn. acad. transfusion medicine com. 1988-93), Internat. Soc. Blood Transfusion. Home: 812 Oak St Apt 302 Winnetka IL 60093-2560

ROSSI, FAUST F. lawyer, educator; b. 1932; BA, U. Tornoto, 1953; JD, Cornell U., 1960. Bar: N.Y. 1960. Tax trialy atty. Dept. Justice, Washington, 1960-61; sole practice Rochester, N.Y., 1961-66; assoc. prof. Cornell U., Ithaca, N.Y., 1966-69, prof., 1970—, assoc. dean, 1973-75, Samuel S. Leibowitz prof. trial techniques, 1982—. Vis. prof. Emory U., 1990; cons. report of fed. class actions Am. Coll. of Trial Lawyers, 1971-72; cons. com. on proposed fed. rules of evidence N.Y. Trial Lawyers Assn., 1970; cons., instr. annual seminar N.Y. State Trial Judges, 1970-78; cons., instr. Nat. Inst. for Trial Advocacy, 1974-75, 80-84, 88; cons. N.Y. Law Revision Commn. Project for N.Y. Code of Evidence, 1978-80. Author: Study of the Proposed Federal Rules of Evidence, 1979, Report on Rule 23 Class Actions, 1972, The Federal Rules of Evidence, 1970, Expert Witnesses, 1991; co-author: New York Evidence, 1997; contbr. articles to profl. jours. Lt. j.g. USN. Recipient Jacobsen prize for tchg. trail advocacy, 1992. Mem. Order of Coif. Office: Cornell U Law Sch Myron Taylor Hall Ithaca NY 14853 Business E-Mail: ffr1@cornell.edu.

ROSSI, JOSEPH ANTHONY, film and television make-up artist, educator; b. Providence, July 10, 1955; s. Michael Thomas and Jennie (Paolucci) R.; m. Christina Elliott; children: Michael Elliott, Sofia Rose. BS, R.I. Coll., 1977. Tchr. film and TV R.I. Coll., Providence, 1983-86, Salve Regina Coll., Newport, R.I., 1983—; owner, prin. Joe Rossi Makeup, Providence, 1977—, 1001 Faces, Providence, 1979—. Make-up artist to Pres. William Clinton and Hillary Rodham Clinton, V.P. Albert Gore; make-up artist Stuck on You, Little Black Book, Moonlight Mile, Hanging By a Thread, Mona Lisa Smile, Goodbye, Hello, Shallow Hal, Osmosis Jones, Passionada, Prozac Nation, Me, Myself, and Irene, Bye, Bye, America, David Mamet's State and Main, Thirteen Days, Lift, The Human Stain, Pink Floyd, syndicated show Crimestoppers 800, First Person, Saturday Night Live, Rivera Live, Wide World Sports, Nat. Geographic Lost Subs K-19, 2004, 1995 Skating Finals ABC-TV, Unsolved Mysteries, Providence, 2004, NBC-TV, ABC-TV The Century, Peter Jennings The Century, Access Hollywood, Entertainment Tonight, News Stand, CNN, also key makeup artist on feature film prodn. Outside Providence, Universal feature Meet Joe Black, original design for world premier prodn. Philip Glass Opera, The Fall of the House of Usher, and Genet's The Balcony, at the Bolshoi Theatre, Russia; spl. make-up effects for BBC, PBS, CBS, ABC, NBC CNBC, and several nat. clients; contbg. author: Stage Makeup, 9th edit. Bd. dirs. R.I. State Coun. on Arts, 1996-2003. Home and Office: 137 Abbott Run Valley Rd Cumberland RI 02864-3249 Office Phone: 401-334-3436. E-mail: jo@rossimakeup.com.

ROSSI, MARIO ALEXANDER, architect; b. Chgo., Apr. 9, 1931; s. Gastone J. and Irma (Giorgi) R.; m. Jo Ann Therese Kneip, Apr. 12, 1958; children: John Vincent, Lyn Ann, Paul Alexander, Mara Ann. BArch, Ill. Inst. Tech., 1955. Architect Omnimetrics, L.A., 1967-78; pvt. practice Seal Beach, Calif., 1975—. Prin. works include fin. models for Calif. Fed. Bank, L.A., First Nat. City Bank, N.Y.C., Glendale (Calif.) Fed. Bank, Wailea, Alexander and Baldwin, Hawaii. Lt. (j.g.) USN, 1955-58. Achievements include research computerized techniques in architecture and economic feasibility land development. Home and Office: 1721 Catalina Ave Seal Beach CA 90740-5710

ROSSI, MARK ANTONY, political consultant, writer; b. Jersey City, Apr. 3, 1965; s. Reynaldo and Florence Mary Rossi; m. Kimberly Jean Morgan, May 4, 2002. AAS in Polit. Sci., C.C. USAF, Ramstein, West Germany, 1989; BA in Polit. Sci., 1991, cert. in cmty. rels. civil svc., 1997. Polit. cons. Rep. Party, 1991—; dir. cmty. rels. HHS, Jersey City, 1995—99. Author: (non-fiction) The Intruder Bulletins: Dark Side of Technology, 2003, Mother Of All Machines, 2002, Sword Of Our Fathers: Essays on the Hardships of Writing, 2002, (fiction) Tracking The Beast, 2001, Grins of Divinity, 2001, (poetry) Persistence of Metaphor, 2001, (drama) Obscentities, 2000, (screenplays) Hellscape Three, 2002, Serpenthouse, 2003, (plays) Gear Fear, 1995, Cross, 1996, Thief in the Mist, 1997. Spkr. Ariz. Breakfast Club, 2000—02. Sgt. USAF, 1984—90. Named Pub. Employee of Yr., City of Jersey City, 1997; recipient Cold War Recognition cert., Dept. of Def., 1999, Essay of Yr. award, Very Spl. Arts N.J., 1997, N.J. Playwright of Yr. award, Bayonne Writer's Group of N.J., 1997. Mem.: Bioethics & Lit. Soc. (life), Am. Legion (corr.; pub. affairs 1999—2003). Avocations: theater, jazz. Home: 1773 E Gail DR Chandler AZ 85225-8714 Personal E-mail: markantonyrossi@aol.com.

ROSSI, PETER HENRY, sociology educator; b. N.Y.C., Dec. 27, 1921; s. Peter Maxim and Elizabeth (Porcelli) R.; m. Alice Schaerr, Sept. 29, 1951; children: Peter Eric, Kristin Alice, Nina Alexis. BS, CCNY, 1943; PhD, Columbia, 1951. Research asso. Bur. Applied Social Research, Columbia U., 1947- 51; asst. prof. Harvard U., 1951-55; prof. dept. sociology U. Chgo., 1955-67; dir. Nat. Opinion Research Center, 1960-67; prof. dept. social relations Johns Hopkins, 1967-74, chmn. dept., 1967-70; dir. research Center for Met. Planning and Research, 1972-74; prof. sociology, dir. Social and Demographic Research Inst., U. Mass., Amherst, 1974-92, Stuart A. Rice prof. sociology, dir., 1984-92, prof. emeritus, 1992—; faculty assoc. Chapin Hall U. Chgo., 1994—. Author: Why Families Move, 1956, The Politics of Urban Renewal, 1962, The Education of Catholic Americans, 1966, New Media and Education, 1967, Ghetto Revolts, 1970, Cities Under Siege, 1971, Evaluating Social Programs, 1972, Roots of Urban Discontent, 1974, Reforming Public Welfare, 1976, Prison Reform and State Elites, 1977, Evaluation: A Systematic Approach, 1979, Money, Work & Crime, 1980, After the Clean-up, 1980, Social Science and Natural Hazards, 1981, Measuring Social Judgements, 1982, Natural Hazards and Public Choice, 1982, Under the Gun, 1983, Applied Sociology, 1983, Without Shelter, 1989, Down and Out in America, 1989, Of Human Bonding, 1990, Just Punishments, 1997, Feeding the Poor, 1999; editor: Am. Jour. Sociology, 1957-58; assoc. editor: Am. Sociol. Rev, 1957-60, Am. Sociologist, 1964-66; editor Social Sci. Research, 1972-89; contbr. articles to profl. and popular jours. Served with AUS, 1942-45. Recipient Alvah and Gunnar Myrdal award for contbns. to evaluation research, 1981; Commonwealth award for contbns. to sociology, 1985; faculty research grantee Social Sci. Research Council, 1959; Carnegie sr. fellow, 1965 Fellow Am. Acad. Arts and Scis.; mem. Am. Sociol. Assn. (sec. 1968-72, pres.-elect 1979-80, pres. 1980-81), Am. Evaluation Assn.

ROSSI, PIERRE MARIE, management consultant; b. Alessandria, Italy, Dec. 30, 1949; s. Vincent Nello and Daisy Desiree (Montmorency) R.; m. Susan Caroline Ellis, Feb. 20, 1990 (div.); 1 child, David; m. Salima Mahzar; 1 child, Elisse. BSc, Royal Malta U., 1971; MBA, IMEDE, Lausanne, Switzerland, 1974. Cons. Arthur D. Little, Boston, 1975-76; contr. ITT, Brussels; exec. C.G.E.R., Brussels, 1976-79; dir., ptnr. Deville Petersen & Assocs., Brussels, 1979-88; exec. I.M.R., Manchester, Eng., v.p. devel. Milan, Italy, 1988-91; v.p. Alexander Proudfoot Productivity Mgmt. Co., Brussels, 1992-95; mng. ptnr. European Inst. Mgmt., London, 1995—. Bd. dirs. P.M.R. Cons. Ltd., London; cons. SAFT (U.K.), SAFT (France) Alcatel Group, Paris, 1990-92; mng. ptnr. European Inst. Mgmt., London, Brussels and Geneva, 1995—; dir. e-consult ltd., 2000—. Author: Une nuit a Pise, 1976, Basic Elements of Europe Accounting, 1991, Total Vision Management, 1995; contbr. articles to profl. publs. Mem. European Acctg. Inst., Inst. Dirs. (London). Avocations: sailing, historic cars, opera, collecting contemporary art. Home: Villa Mara Bierges Belgium Office: European Inst Mgmt 284 Th Decuyper 1200 Brussels Belgium also: EIM (Suisse) SA 16 Chemin des Aulx 1228 Geneva Switzerland

ROSSI, RONALD ALDO, sports association administrator, Olympic athlete; b. Bronx, N.Y., Dec. 2, 1956; s. Aldo D. and Jeanette (Morretta) R.; m. Susan Veltman, Mar. 26, 1983; children: Scott, Lauren. BEE, Manhattan Coll., 1978. Registered profl. engr., N.Y. Mem. computer ops. staff John Blair and Co., N.Y.C., 1978-83, communications engr., 1984; sports program dir. U.S. Luge Assn., Lake Placid, N.Y., 1984-85, exec. dir., 1985—. Com. mem. U.S. Luge Assn., 1978—, athlete's rep., 1980-83; com. mem. U.S. Olympic Com., Colorado Springs, Colo., 1989-90, 93-96. Mem. U.S. Olympic Luge Team, Sarajevo, Yugoslavia, 1984; mem. Olympic team staff, Calgary, Can., 1988, Albertville, France, 1992, Lillehammer, Norway, 1994, Nagano, Japan, 1998, Salt Lake City, 2002. Avocations: luge, golf, softball, movies, computers. Address: US Luge Association 35 Church St Lake Placid NY 12946-1805

ROSSI, STEVEN B. newspaper publishing company executive; m. Rosemary; four children. BA, Ursinus Coll.; MBA, U. Pa., 1974. Gen. mgr., corp. controller IU Internat. Corp.; v.p., gen. mgr. Amerigas Indsl. Gases, 1988-91; v.p., chief fin. officer Knight Ridder, San Jose, Calif., 1987-88, sr. v.p., 1988-91, exec. v.p., 1991-98, sr. v.p. ops., 1998—. Chmn. bd. dirs. Am. Music Theater Festival; bd. dirs. Univ. Arts. Mem. Pa. Newspapers Publ.'s Assn. (bd. dirs.). Office: Knight Ridder 50 W San Fernando St San Jose CA 95113-2429

ROSSIDES, EUGENE TELEMACHUS, lawyer, writer; b. N.Y.C., Oct. 23, 1927; s. Telemachus and Anna (Maravel) R.; m. Elinor Burcham (div.); 1 child, Gale; m. Aphrodite Macotsin, Dec. 30, 1961; children: Michael, Alexander, Eleni. AB, Columbia U., 1949, JD, 1952. Criminal law investigator Office of Dist. Atty., N.Y.C., 1952; assoc. Rogers & Wells, N.Y.C., 1954-56, 61-66, ptnr., 1966-69, 73-92, sr. counsel, 1993—; asst. atty. gen. State of N.Y., N.Y.C., 1956-58; asst. to undersec. Dept. Treasury, Washington, 1958-61, asst. sec., 1969-73. Bd. dirs. Sterling Nat. Bank, N.Y.C. Author: U.S. Import Trade Regulation, 2d edit., 1986, Foreign Unfair Competition, 3d edit., 1991, United States Import Trade Law, 1992, also articles; chief import editor Internat. Trade Reporter, Bur. Nat. Affairs, 1980—; editor: The Truman Doctrine of Aid to Greece: A Fifty-Year Retrospective, 1998, Doing Business in Greece, 1996, U.S. Rels. with Greece and Cyprus, 1990—. Mem. Grace Commn., Washington, 1981-82; chmn. nationalities div. Reagan Bush Com., Washington, 1980; campaign mgr. N.Y.C. Nixon for Pres. Com., 1968, Keating for Senator Com., N.Y. State, 1964; bd. dirs. Eisenhower World Affairs Inst., Washington, Am. Hellenic Inst. Inc. Capt. USAF, 1952-60. Recipient Medal for Excellence, Columbia U., 1972, Young Lawyer's award Columbia Law Sch. Alumni Assn., 1972, Silver Anniversary award NCAA, 1974, John Jay award Columbia Coll. Alumni Assn., 1994. Mem. ABA, N.Y. State Bar Assn., Fed. Bar Assn. Republican. Greek Orthodox. Avocations: tennis, photography. Home: 3666 Upton St NW Washington DC 20008-3125 Office: Clifford Chance Rogers & Wells LLP 2001 K St NW Washington DC 20006-1037

ROSSIER, WILLIAM, trade association administrator; b. 1942; Degree in econs., U. lausanne, 1970. Head diplomatic secretariat Conf. on Security and Cooperation in Europe, 1972-73, dep. head divsn. gen fgn. econ. questions Swiss Diplomatic Svc., 1973-76, counsellor Swiss Mission to Europeqn Cmty., 1976-80; head divsn. in charge of rels. Fed. Office for External Econ. Affairs, Switzerland, 1981-88; chmn. trade and devel. bd. UN Conf. on Trade and Devel., Geneva, 1988—96, pres., 1995—96; plenipotentiary ambassador of Switzerland UN, Geneva; currently sec. gen. EFTA. Chair UN/ECE Com. for Devel. of Trade, OECD Working Party on East West Trade; head divsn. in charge of relations with Western Europe; chmn. gen. coun. World Trade Assn., chmn. working party on accession of Russia; chmn. EFTA Coun., Econ. Commn. ofr Europe. Mem. European Free Trade Assn., Econ. Commn. for Europe. Office: EFTA 9-11 rue de Varembé CH-1211 Geneva Switzerland

ROSSIN, LAWRENCE G. ambassador; b. N.J., Nov. 1952; m. Debra J. McGowan; 2 children. BA in Economics, Claremont Men's Coll., Calif., 1975; student, NATO Def. Coll., Rome, 1988—89. Former dir. Office of South Cen. European Affairs, Dept. of State; U.S. chief of mission in Kosovo U.S. Embassy, Pristina, 1999—2000; U.S. amb. to Croatia, 2001—. Recipient award for Valour and others, U.S. State Dept., Presdl. Disting. Svc. award, 2001. Office: DOS Amb 5080 Zagreb Pl Washington DC 20521

ROSSING, DAVID ROBERT, internist; b. Detroit, Jan. 8, 1949; s. Robert Grangaard and Dolores (Christenson) R.; m. Ann Marie Tkacz, July 30, 1977; children: Brian, Philip. BA, St. Olaf Coll., 1971; MD, U. Tex. Southwestern, 1975; M of Med. Mgmt., Tulane U., 1999. Diplomate Am. Bd. Internal Medicine, Am. Bd. Pulmonary Disease. Intern Emory U. Affiliated Hosps., Atlanta, 1975-76, resident in internal medicine, 1976-78; fellow in pulmonary diseases U. Tex., 1978-80; pvt. practice specialzing in pulmonary medicine, Sioux Falls, SD, 1980—94. Med. dir. Ctrl. Plains Clinic, 1994—2001; v.p. med. affairs Sioux Valley Hosps. and Health Sys., 2001—03; mem. staff McKennan Hosp., Sioux Valley Hosp.; chief med. officer Sioux Valley Hosps. and Health Sys., 2003—; mem. staff Royal C. Johnson VA Hosp.; clin. prof. U. S.D. Sch. Medicine, Sioux Falls. Fellow Am. Coll. Physicians; mem. AMA, Rotary, Phi Beta Kappa. Lutheran. Office: 1305 W 18th St Sioux Falls SD 57117-5039

ROSSING, THOMAS D. physics educator; b. Madison, S.D., Mar. 27, 1929; s. Torstein H. and Luella E. Rossing; children: Karen, Barbara, Erik, Jane, Mary. BA, Luther Coll., 1950; MS, Iowa State U., 1952, PhD, 1954. Rsch. physicist Univac div. Sperry Rand, 1954-57; prof. physics St. Olaf Coll., 1957-71, chmn. physics dept., 1963-69; prof. physics No. Ill. U., DeKalb, 1971—, disting. rsch. prof., chmn. dept., 1971-73. Rschr. Microwave Lab., Stanford (Calif.) U., 1961-62, Lincoln Lab., MIT, Cambridge, Mass., summer 1963, Clarendon Lab., Oxford (Eng.) U., 1966-67, physics dept. MIT, 1976-77; rsch. assoc. Argonne (Ill.) Nat Lab., 1974-76, scientist-in-residence, 1990—; vis. lectr. U. New Eng., Armidale, Australia, 1980-81; vis. exch. scholar to China, 1988; guest rschr. Royal Inst. Tech., Stockholm, 1983, 84, 85, Inst. Perception Rsch., Eindhoven, The Netherlands, 1984, 85, Physikalisch-Technische Bundesanstalt, Braunschweig, Germany, 1988-89; guest rschr. Ecole Nat. Supérieure des Telecomm., Paris, 1996, Luleå U. Tech., Sweden, 1996, U. Calif., San Diego, 1998, Fraunhofer Inst., Stuttgart, Germany, 1998; vis. prof. U. Edinburgh, Scotland, 2003. Author 15 books in field; contbr. more than 350 articles to profl. publs. Recipient Robert Millikan medal, 2000. Fellow AAAS, Am. Phys. Soc., Acoustical Soc. Am. (Silver medal in mus. acoustics 1992), Acoustical Soc. India (hon.); mem. IEEE, Am. Assn. Physics Tchrs. (pres. 1991, Robert A. Milliken medal 2000), Catgut Acoustical Soc., Sigma Xi (nat. lectr. 1984-87), Sigma Pi Sigma. Achievements include research in musical acoustics, psychoacoustics, speech and singing, vibration analysis, magnetic levitation, environmental noise conrol, surface effects in fusion reactors, spin waves in metals, physics education; 9 U.S. and 11 foreign patents in field. Office: No Ill U Physics Dept Dekalb IL 60115 Office Phone: 815-753-6493.

ROSSINI, JOSEPH, contracting and development corporate executive; b. New Rochelle, N.Y., Nov. 25, 1939; m. Antonia Rossini; children: Katherine, Anthony, Andrew. Student, Fordham U., 1965-66, Iona Coll., 1972. Pres. Rossini Contracting Corp., Mt. Vernon, N.Y., 1963—; prin. Rossini Devel. Co., Monticello, N.Y., 1965—. Bd. dirs. Circuit Realty Corp., New Rochelle, 1970-71. Mem. planning bd. City of New Rochelle, 1986-92, mem. bldg. dept. adv. com., 1985; vol. instr. N.Y. State Dept. Environ. Conservation, Albany, 1968-95; vice chmn. New Rochelle Conservative Party, 1984-2001, chmn., 2001—; county committeeman Westchester County Conservative Party; pres., bd. trustees Beechwoods Cemetery, New Rochelle; dir. New Rochelle Neighborhood Revitalization Corp., 1993-96. With USN, 1959-61. Mem. NRA (benefactor life patron), Gen. Contractors Assn. N.Y., Constrn. Industry Coun. Westchester and Hudson Valley, Bldg. Trades Employers Assn., Soc. Explosives Engrs., Deep Founds. Inst., Young Ams. for Freedom, Am. Lauretana Assn., Mensa, Assoc. Gen. Contractors Am., Caths. in Constrn., Tin Can Sailors, Westchester County Firearm Owners Assn., N.Y. State Rifle and Pistol Assn. Roman Catholic. Office: Rossini Contracting Corp 113 Edison Ave Mount Vernon NY 10550-5005 Office Phone: 914-664-4300. Personal E-mail: rossinidigs@aol.com.

ROSSITER, ALEXANDER, JR., news service executive, editor; b. Elmira, N.Y., Mar. 2, 1936; s. Alexander H. and Eleanor (Howell) R.; m. Sylvia Lee Vanlandingham, June 11, 1960; children: Alexander H. III, Jill Jarrell. BA, Rutgers U., 1958; postgrad., Emory U., 1959. With UPI, 1959-92; newsman Atlanta, 1959-61, Richmond, Va., 1961-63; bur. mgr. Cape Canaveral, Fla., 1963-73; sci. editor Washington, 1973-87; exec. editor, 1987-88; exec. editor, sr. v.p., 1988-91; editor, exec. v.p., 1991-92; asst. v.p., dir. news svc. Duke U., Durham, NC, 1992—2001, dir. com. Pratt Sch. Engrs., 2001—02, assoc. dean pub. affairs, 2003—. Mem. nat. adv. bd. Knight Ctr. for Specialized Journalism, Colleg Pk., Md., 1988-92; mem. adv. bd. Med. Journalism Program, U. N.C., Chapel Hill, 2000—. Recipient Grady-Stack medal Am. Chem. Soc., 1987, other journalism awards. Mem. Nat. Assn. Sci. Writers, Edn. Writers Assn. Office: Duke U 305 Teer Bldg Box 90271 Durham NC 27708
Enthusiasm is the key to success. Take on your education, your family responsibilities and your work with enthusiasm and good things will result.

ROSSITER, BRYANT WILLIAM, chemistry consultant; b. Ogden, Utah, Mar. 10, 1931; s. Bryant B. and Christine (Peterson) R.; m. Betty Jean Anderson, Apr. 16, 1951; children: Bryant, Mark, Diane, Steven, Linda, Karen, Matthew, Gregory. BA, U. Utah, 1954, PhD, 1957. Researcher Eastman-Kodak Co., Rochester, N.Y., 1957-63, head color phys. chem. lab., 1963-70, dir. chemistry div., 1970-84, dir. sci., tech. devel., 1984-86; pres. Viratek Inc., Costa Mesa, Calif., 1986-89; sr. v.p. ICN Pharms., Costa Mesa, 1989-90; ret., 1990; pres., CEO WRECON, Inc., Laguna Hills, Calif., 1991-96, ret., 1996. Sr. editor John Wiley & Sons, N.Y.C., 1970—; chmn. bd. Nucleic Acid Rsch. Inst., Costa Mesa, 1987-88; trustee Eastman Dental Ctr., Rochester, 1973-93 (bd. pres. 1982-85); bd. dirs. Verax & Corp. Editor: (chem. treatises) Physical Methods of Chemistry (11 vols.), 1970-76, Physical Methods, (12 vols.), 1986—, Chemical Experimentation Under Extreme Conditions, 1979. Mem. rsch. adv. com. U.S. Agy. for Internat. Devel., Washington, chmn. rsch. adv. com., 1989-92; mem. panel on biosci. Pres.' Coun. Advisors on Sci. and Tech., 1991; mem. adv com. Cornell Internat. Inst. for Food, Agr. and Devel., 1991; presiding officer Ch. Jesus Christ Latter Day Saints, Ea. U.S. and Can., 1959-86, counselor presidency San Diego temple, 1998-2002. 1st lt. USAFR, 1951-58. Named Hon. Alumni Brigham Young U., Provo, Utah, 1982. Fellow AAAS, Am. Inst. Chemists (lectr., Fellows award 1988, Will Judy award Juanita Coll. 1978); mem. Internat. Union Pure and Applied Chemistry (chmn. U.S. nat. com., orignator, chmn. Chemical Rsch. Applied to World Needs com. 1975-87, chmn. Chemical Rsch. Applied to World Needs II The Internat. Conf. on Chemistry and World Food Supplies, 1982), Am. Chem. Soc. (chmn. internat. activities). Avocations: horseback riding, reading, fishing. Home and Office: 25662 Dillon Rd Laguna Hills CA 92653-5800 E-mail: bwr@ni.net.

ROSSITER, ROBERT E. interior auto parts manufacturing executive; b. Detroit, 1946; BBA, Northwood U. With Lear Siegler Inc., 1971-87, former pres. seating div.; pres., chief oper. officer Lear Seating Corp., Southfield, Mich., 1987-2000, also bd. dirs.; CEO, pres. Lear Corp., Southfield, Mich., 2000—, Chmn., 2003—. Office: Lear Seating Corp 21557 Telegraph Rd Southfield MI 48034*

ROSS-LEE, BARBARA, dean, educator; BS Biology and Chemistry, M Tchr. Spl. Populations, Wayne State U.; grad., Mich. State U., 1973; DSc (hon.), N.Y. Coll. Osteo. Medicine; degree (hon.), Wilmington Coll., 2001. Legis. asst. Senator Bill Bradley; chmn. dept. family medicine, assoc. dean health policy Mich. State U. Coll. Medicine; dean Ohio U. Coll. Osteo. Medicine, 1993—2001; dean, v.p. health scis. and med. affairs N.Y. Coll. Osteo. Medicine, 2001—. Lectr. in field; dir. Osteo. Heritage Health Policy Fellowship Program; exec. dir. Inst. Nat. Health Policy and Rsch., NOMA (the osteo. affiliate NMA); mem. bd. dirs. Assn. Acad. Health Ctrs., Nat. Fund Med. Edn., Nat. Health Svs. Corps' Assn. Clinicians Underserved; trustee Found. Appalachian Ohio; participant confs. Contbr. more than 30 scholarly articles med. and health-care issues. Named to Ohio Women's Hall of Fame, 1998; recipient Magnificent 7 award, Bus. and Profl. Women/USA, 1993, Women's Health award, Blackboard African-Am. Nat. Bestsellers, Disting. Pub. Svc. award, Okla. State U. Coll. Osteo. Medicine, Walter F. Patenge medal pub. svc., Mich. State U. Coll. Osteo. Medicine, 2001. Fellow: Am. Osteo. Bd. Family Physicians; mem.: NIH (adv. com. rsch. on women's health), Future Primary Care (Inst. Medicine's com.), U.S. Dept. Health and Human Svs. (nat. adv. com. rural health), Appalachian Health Policy (Appalachian regional commn.'s adv. coun.), AACOM Bd. Govs. (chair-elect exec. coun.), AOA Bur. Profl. Edn., Trilateral Internat. Med. Workforce Group. Achievements include first to be an osteopathic physician to participate in the prestigious Robert Wood Johnson Health Policy Fellowship. Office: NY Coll of Osteopathic Med Old Westbury No Blvd Rockefeller Bldg Rm 107 Westbury NY 11568-8000 E-mail: brosslee@nyit.edu.*

ROSSLER, WILLIS KENNETH, JR., petroleum company executive; b. Houston, Nov. 17, 1946; m. Jennifer Hill West; children: Nancy Rossler Ewing, Deborah Anne, Ryan Konrad, Eric George; 1 stepson, Jason Hill Yelverton. BS in Indsl. Engring., Tex. Tech. U., 1969; grad., Stanford U. Dist. mgr. Tex.-La. ops. Continental Pipe Line Co., Lake Charles, La., 1974-75, mgr. engring. Houston, 1976-77; asst. mgr. corp. planning and devel. Conoco, Inc., Houston, 1977-78; v.p. project devel. PetroUnited, Inc., Houston, 1978-80, pres., 1981-86, also dir. Pres. Village Pl. Cmty. Assn., Houston, 1978, also partnership com. Antwerp Gas Terminal, V.G.N., 1982-85, v.p., gen. mgr. Pilko and Assoc., Inc., Houston, 1986-90; pres., CEO Houston Fuel Oil Terminal Co., 1990—; bd. dirs. Pilko and Assocs., Naylor Industries, Inc., Clean Channel Assn. (chmn.), Greater Houston Port Bur., Grace Presbyn. Sch. Mem. Am. Inst. Indsl. Engrs., Am. Petroleum Inst., Houston Mgmt. Coun., Intensive Mgmt. Devel. Inst. (adv. dir. 1983-84), Ind. Liquid Terminals Assn. (vice chmn. 1986, chmn.-elect 1987), Am. Mgmt. Assn., Tex. Tech. Acad. Indsl. Engrs. (chmn.), Planning Forum (pres. chpt. 1985), Petroleum Club of Houston, Lakeside Country Club. Office: Houston Fuel Oil Terminal Co 16642 Jacintoport Blvd Houston TX 77015-6541 Office Phone: 281-452-3390. E-mail: willis@hfotco.com.

ROSSMAN, RUTH SCHARFF, artist, educator; b. Bklyn. d. Joseph and Elsie (Frankel) Scharff; m. Phillip Rossman; 1 dau., Joanne. Grad., Cleve. Inst. Art, 1934; BS, Case Western Res. U., 1934; postgrad., Kahn Inst. Art, 1947-50, UCLA, 1960. Art instr. Canton (Ohio) public schs., 1934-39, Canton Art Inst., 1937-45, Rustic Canyon Art Center, Los Angeles, 1978-81. One-woman shows at Heritage Gallery, L.A., 1963, 66, Canton (Ohio) Community Ctr., 1967, Marymount Coll., U. Judaism, 1980, L.A. Fedn. Bldg., 1981, 89, Platt Gallery, 1986, 93, 98, others; exhibited in group shows Mus. Modern Art, N.Y.C., Butler Mus., Washington and Jefferson Coll., Denver Mus., Space Mus., Mt. St. Mary's Coll., L.A., M.H. de Young Mus., San Francisco Mus. Art, Venice Art Walk, ann. 1981-94, 96-2000, Univ. Judaism, 1986, 93, Brand Art Gallery, 1987, Platt Gallery, 1998, others; represented in permanent collections Pa. Acad. Fine Arts, Phila., Brandeis-Bardin Inst., U. Redlands, Calif., Nat. Watercolor Soc., Ahmanson Collection, Rocky Mt. Nat., others; paintings included in book The California Romantics: Harbingers of Watercolor, 1987, Retrospective Art Exhibit U. Judaism Platt Gallery, 1998. Chair selection com. for Platt Gallery, U. Judaism, L.A., 1986—. Recipient purchase-cash awards Los Angeles All-City Art Exhbn. Mem. Nat. Watercolor Soc. (pres. 1974-75, juror 75th Ann. Exhbn. 1995).

ROSSMANN, ANTONIO, lawyer, educator; b. San Francisco, Apr. 25, 1941; s. Herbert Edward and Yolanda (Sonsini) R.; m. Kathryn A. Burns, Oct. 6, 1991; children: Alice Sonsini, Maria McHale. Grad., Harvard Coll., 1963, JD, 1971. Bar: Calif. 1972, D.C. 1979, N.Y. 1980, U.S. Supreme Ct. 1980. Law clk. to Justice Mathew Tobriner Calif. Supreme Ct., 1971-72; assoc. Tuttle & Taylor, L.A., 1972-75; pub. advisor Calif. Energy Commn., 1975-76; sole practice San Francisco, 1976-82, 85—; exec. dir. Nat. Ctr. for Preservation Law, 1979-80; mem. McCutchen, Doyle, Brown & Enersen, San Francisco, 1982—85. Adj. prof. law Hastings Coll. Law, 1981-84; vis. prof. UCLA Sch. Law, 1985-87; Fulbright lectr. U. Tokyo, 1987-88; adj. prof. Stanford Law Sch., 1989-90, U. Calif. Sch. Law, Boalt Hall, 1991—. Editor Harvard Law Rev., 1969-71; contbr. articles to legal jours. Bd. dirs. Planning and Conservation League, 1984—, Calif. Water Protection Coun., 1982-83, San Francisco Marathon, 1982-90; pres. Western State Endurance Run, 1991-96, counselor, 1996—; pres., bd. dirs. Toward Utility Rate Normalization, 1976-79. Served to lt. comdr. USN, 1963-68. Mem. Calif. State Bar (chmn. com. on environment 1978-82), U.S. Rowing Assn., U.S. Soccer Fedn. (state referee) L.A. Athletic Club, Harvard Club (San Francisco, N.Y.C.), Harvard Law Sch. Assn. No. Calif. (pres. 1997-2002). Office: 380 Hayes St San Francisco CA 94102-4421 E-mail: ar@landwater.com.

ROSSMANN, JACK EUGENE, psychology educator; b. Walnut, Iowa, Dec. 4, 1936; s. Wilbert C. Rossmann and Claire L. (Mickel) Walter; m. Marilyn Martin, June 14, 1958; children: Ann, Charles, Sarah. BS, Iowa State U., 1958, MS, 1960; PhD, U. Minn., 1963. Lic. psychologist, Minn. Asst. prof. Macalester Coll., St. Paul, 1964-68, assoc. prof., 1968-73, prof., 1973—, v.p. acad. affairs, 1978-86, chair dept. psychology, 1990-2000. Cons. Pers. Decisions Internat., Mpls., 1989—2000, Bush Found., 1993—; cons.-evaluator North Ctrl. Assn., 1975—. Author: (with others) Open Admissions at CUNY, 1975; contbr. articles to profl. jours. Bd. dirs. Twin City Inst. for Talented Youth, St. Paul, 1978-91; trustee United Theol. Sem., New Brighton, Minn., 1984-96. 2d lt. U.S. Army, 1959. Mem.: AAUP (pres. Minn. conf. 1993—95), APA, Minn. Psychol. Assn. (treas. 2001, pres. 2003), Assn. Instl. Rsch., Am. Psychol. Soc. Home: 99 Cambridge St Saint Paul MN 55105-1947 Office: Macalester Coll 1600 Grand Ave Saint Paul MN 55105-1801 Office Phone: 651-696-6110. Business E-Mail: rossmann@macalester.edu.

ROSSMANN, MICHAEL GEORGE, biochemist, educator; b. Frankfurt, Germany, July 30, 1930; s. Alexander and Nelly (Schwabacher) R.; m. Audrey Pearson, July 24, 1954; children: Martin, Alice, Heather. BSc with honors, Polytechnic, London, 1951, MSc in Physics, 1953; PhD in Chemistry, U. Glasgow, 1956; PhD (hon.), U. Uppsala (Sweden), 1983, U. Strasbourg (France), 1984, Vrije U. Brussel, 1990, U. Glasgow (Scotland), 1993, U. York (England), 1994, U. Quebec (Can.), 1998. Fulbright scholar U. Minn., 1956-58; research scientist MRC Lab. Molecular Biology, Cambridge, Eng., 1958-64; assoc. prof. biol. scis. Purdue U., West Lafayette, Ind., 1964-67, prof., 1967-78, Hanley Disting. prof. biol. scis., 1978—, prof. biochemistry, 1975—. Editor: The Molecular Replacement Method, 1972; contbr. more than 400 articles to profl. jours. Grantee NIH, NSF, HFSP; recipient Fankuchen award Am. Crystallographic Assn., 1986, Horwitz prize Columbia U., 1990, Gregori Arminoff prize Royal Swedish Acad. Sci., 1994, Stein & Moore award Protein Soc., 1994, Ewald prize Internat. Union Crystallography, 1996, Cole award Biophys. Soc., 1998, Elion award Internat. Soc. for Antiviral Rsch., 2000, Ehrlich and Darmstaedter prize Paul Erhlich-Fedn., 2001. Mem. Am. Soc. Biol. Chemists, Am. Chem. Soc., Biophys. Soc. (Cole award 1998), Am. Crystallographic Assn. (Fankuchen award 1986), Brit. Biophys. Soc., Inst. Physics., Chem. Soc. (U.K.), AAAS, NAS, Indian Nat. Sci. Acad., Royal Soc., Nat. Sci. Bd., Lafayette Sailing Club. Democrat. Home: 1208 Wiley Dr West Lafayette IN 47906-2434 Office: Purdue U Dept Biol Scis 915 W State St West Lafayette IN 47907-2054 Office Phone: 765-494-4911. E-mail: mgr@indiana.bio.purdue.edu.

ROSSO, JEAN-PIERRE, electronics executive; b. Aix-les Bains, Savoie, France, July 11, 1940; Diploma in civil engring., Ecole Polytechnique, Lausanne, Switzerland, 1964; MBA, U. Pa., 1967. Mgr. fin. and adminstrn. Honeywell, Paris, 1969—70, dir. African divsn., 1970—71, sales dir., 1971—75; pres., CEO Rossignol Ski, Burlington, Vt., 1975—81; dir. gen. Rossignol SA, Voiron, France, 1980—81; v.p. bus. devel. Honeywell Europe SA, Brussels, 1981—83, pres., 1981—94; v.p., gen. mgr. Honeywell Med. Electronics, N.Y.C., 1983—85; group v.p. Honeywell Info. Systems, Mpls., 1985—87; pres., CEO Case Corp., Racine, Wis., 1994—99, chmn., 1996—99; chmn., CEO CNH Global, 1999—. Mem. adv. com. Trade Policy and Negotiations, 2002—02; bd. overseers Wharton Sch.; bd. dirs. ADC Telecoms., Inc., Medtronic, Inc. Mem.: Bus. Roundtable. Avocations: golf, skiing. Office: Case Corp 700 State St Racine WI 53404-3392

ROSSO DE IRIZARRY, CARMEN (TUTTY ROSSO DE IRIZARRY), finance executive; b. Ponce, P.R., Feb. 9, 1949; d. Jorge Ignacio and Carmen Teresa (Descartes) Rosso Castain; m. Alfredo R. Irizarry Sile, Aug. 29, 1967. BBA, U. P.R., Rio Piedras. Vice pres. Alcay Inc., San Juan, P.R., 1972—, also bd. dirs.; v.p. J.I.C. Corp., M.I.C. Corp. Bd. dirs., now pres. bd. Construcciones Urbanas Inc., Internat. Fin. Corp.; organizer Best of Saks Fifth Avenue 1990-2000. Troop leader Girl Scouts U.S.A., 1977-80; bd. dirs. PTA, San Juan, 1978-81, 86-88; activities coord. Colegio Puertorriqueño Niñas, San Juan, 1987-88; judge Miss P.R. Pageant, San Juan 1987-88, 93, 94, 95, Miss World P.R. Pageant, San Juan, 1987-88, Miss World of P.R., 1990; pres. fundacion dept. Oncologia Pediatrica Hosp. Universitario Dr. Antonio Ortiz, 1990-2003; organizer Best of Saks Fifth Avenue Benefit, 1991, 92, 93, 94, 95, pres. 1992, 94, 96; com. mem. Make a Wish Found. Colleccion Alta Moda, 1994; mem. com. Museo Ponce Gala, 1994; mem. com. Museo Ponce Coala, 1994; luminaria J.C. Penney, 1994; destellos de la Moda, 1994, 95-96; pres. Best of Saks 5th Avenue Benefit, 1990-96; organizer Fundacion Oncologica Escada Spring and Summer, 2003. Named to Ten Best Dressed List, San Juan Star, 1986-87, Hall of Fame of Ten Best Dressed, 1989; recipient luminaria J.C. Penney, 1994. Fellow Assn. Porcelanas; mem. Union Mujeres Americanas, Club de Leones (Garden Hills, P.R., Lady of Yr. award 1978), Club Avico Dama, Caparra Country Club (pres. 1985-86), Club de Presidentas, Altrusas, Bankers Club, Club Civicos Damas (judge hat show 1989, in charge spl. events 1992), Mu Alpha Phi. Republican. Roman Catholic. Avocations: china painting, boating, water-skiing. Office: Internat Fin Corp PO Box 8486 Santurce San Juan PR 00910-0486

ROSSOLIMO, ALEXANDER NICHOLAS, management consultant, business executive, corporate director; b. Paris, June 8, 1939; came to U.S., 1952; naturalized, 1958; s. Nicholas S. and Vera A. (Boudakovitch) R.; m. Meryl Louise Stowbridge, Sept. 10, 1977; children: Gregory, Katherine, Elizabeth. Student, Lycée Français of N.Y., 1955—57; BEE with honors, CUNY, 1962; MA in Applied Math., Harvard U., 1963, PhD in Applied Physics, 1973; MBA, MIT, 1973. Cert. in bus. French. Tchg. fellow Harvard U., 1963-65, rsch. asst., 1966-71; fin. analyst Péchiney, Paris, 1972; brand/advt. mgmt. The Clorox Co., Oakland, Calif., 1973-74; project leader The Boston Consulting Group, 1974-77; dir. planning and fin. analysis United Brands, Boston, 1977-80; sr. dir. Digital Equipment Corp., Maynard, Mass., 1980-92; pres. Strategy Assocs. Internat., Newton, Mass., 1992-94, pres., chief exec. officer, 1994—; co-founder, acting CEO, IntellectExchange.com, Inc., 1999—2001. Vis. fellow Harvard U., Cambridge, Mass., 1991-93; bd. dirs. ACG Internat., Chgo.; founding dir. Forum 128, 1996—; bd. dirs. Ctr. for Security and Social Progress, Inc., chmn., 1998—; dir. Law Enforcement Assistance Found., 1999—; mem. bd. advisors Radia Techs. Corp., 2004—. Contbr. numerous articles to bus. and internat. newspapers. Mem. search com. Ecole Bilingue, French-Am. Internat. Sch. of Boston, 1991-93; fund raiser Milton (Mass.) Acad., 1994-97, Phillips Exeter Acad., 1997—, Phillips Andover Acad., 2000—. Recipient award in elec. engring. Blonder-Tongue Co., N.Y.C., 1961, Belden prize, gold medal in math., 1960; NSF postgrad. fellow, 1962-63; ACG Dealmaker Challenge winner, 1995. Mem. Nat. Assn. Corp. Dirs., Bus. Execs. for Nat. Security, Boston Security Analysts Soc., Royal United Svcs. Inst. for Def. Studies (London), French Am. C. of C., Japan Soc. Boston, World Affairs Coun., Internat. Assn. of Macro-Engring. Socs. (mem. commn. on macro-engring.), Assn. for Corp. Growth Boston (chmn. 1995-96), Harvard Club Boston, Harvard Faculty Club, Toastmasters Internat. (pres.), Tau Beta Pi, Eta Kappa Nu. Avocations: jogging, tennis, foreign languages, international organizations, theater. Office: Strategy Assocs Internat PO Box 207 Waban MA 02468-0002 E-mail: arossolimo@yahoo.com.

ROSSON, GLENN RICHARD, building products and furniture company executive; b. Galveston, Tex., Aug. 17, 1937; s. John Raymond and Elsie Lee R.; m. Edwina Lucille Hart, June 2, 1956; children— Darrell Richard, Alex Mark. BBA, Tex. Tech U., 1959. C.P.A., Tex. Supr., accountant Axelson div. U.S. Industries Inc., Longview, Tex., 1960-67, controller, 1968, group financial v.p., 1969, group chmn., 1969-72, v.p., 1973-74, sr. v.p., 1974, exec. v.p., 1974-80, also dir.; pres. Rosson Investment Co., 1980—; chmn. bd. Yorktowne Inc., 1988—. Chmn. bd. dirs. Quality Product Finishing, Inc., 1998—. Mem. Am. Inst. C.P.A.s, Tex. Soc. C.P.A.s, Nat. Assn. Accts. (past nat. dir., past pres.

E. Tex. chpt.), Assn. for Corp. Growth (past pres.). Clubs: Dallas Athletic, TBARM Raquet. Home: 11367 Drummond Dr Dallas TX 75228-1946 Office: 6060 N Central Expy # 560 Dallas TX 75206-5142 E-mail: rosson@gte.net.

ROSSOTTI, BARBARA JILL MARGULIES, lawyer; b. Englewood, N.J., Feb. 28, 1940; d. Albert and Loretta (Jill) Margulies; m. Charles Ossola Rossotti; children: Allegra Jill, Edward Charles. BA magna cum laude, Mount Holyoke Coll., 1961; LLB, Harvard U., 1964. Bar: D.C. 1966. Assoc. Nutter McClennen & Fish, Boston, 1964-65, Covington & Burling, Washington, 1965-72, Shaw, Pittman, Potts & Trowbridge, Washington, 1972-73; ptnr. Shaw Pittman LLP (formerly Shaw, Pittman, Potts & Trowbridge), Washington, 1973—. Trustee Mt. Holyoke Coll., South Hadley, Mass., 1984-99, vice chmn., 1989-94, chmn., 1994-99; trustee Legal Aid Soc., D.C., 1979-92, pres. 1985-89, mem. pres. coun., 1992—; trustee Choral Arts Soc., Washington, 1989-96, 1997-2003, chair, 1993-95; bd. dirs. Washington Home, 1989-93, bd. govs., 1993-, chair, 2002—. Fellow Am. Bar Found.; mem. ABA, Am. Soc. Internat. Law, Internat. Law Assn., D.C. Bar, D.C. Bar Found. (adv. com.). Office: Shaw Pittman 2300 N St NW Fl 5 Washington DC 20037-1172

ROSSOTTI, CHARLES OSSOLA, former federal agency administrator; b. N.Y.C., Jan. 17, 1941; s. Charles C. and V. Elizabeth (Ossola) R.; m. Barbara Jill Margulies, June 9, 1963; children: Allegra Jill, Edward Charles. AB magna cum laude, Georgetown U., 1962; MBA with high distinction, Harvard U., 1974. Mgmt. cons. Boston Cons. Group, 1964-65; prin. dep. asst. sec. Office of Systems Analysis, Dept. Def., Washington, 1965-70, prin. dep. asst. sec. of Def., 1969-70; pres. Am. Mgmt. Systems, Inc., Arlington, Va., from 1970, chief exec. officer, from 1981, chmn. bd., 1989-97; commr. IRS, Washington, 1997—2002. Bd. dirs. Intersolv, Inc. Bd. dirs. Georgetown U., 1969-77, 92-97; chmn. Woodstock Theol. Ctr., 1990-96. Mem. Coun. Fgn. Rels.

ROSSTON, RICHARD MARK, lawyer; b. San Francisco, June 29, 1951; s. Edward William and Maxine G. (Aaron) R.; children: Ryan, Matthew, Jean. BA, Dartmouth Coll., 1973; JD, U. Calif., Berkeley, 1977. Bar: Calif. 1977, Alaska 1978. Shareholder Guess & Rudd, Anchorage, 1977—98; mem. Bogle & Gates, PLLC, Anchorage, 1998—99; ptnr. Dorsey & Whitney, LLP, Anchorage, 1999—. Mem.: ABA, Alaska Bar Assn., Calif. Bar Assn. Office: Dorsey & Whitney LLP 1031 w 4TH Ave # 600 Anchorage AK 99501-1964 Office Phone: 907-276-4557.

ROSSUM, RALPH ARTHUR, political science educator; b. Alexandria, Minn., Dec. 17, 1946; s. Floyd Arthur and June Marion (Carlson) R.; m. Constance Mary Brazina, Aug. 19, 1972; children: Kristin, Brent, Pierce. BA summa cum laude, Concordia Coll., 1968; MA, U. Chgo., 1971, PhD, 1973. Instr. Grinnell (Iowa) Coll., 1972-73; asst. prof. Memphis State U., 1973-77, assoc. prof., 1977-80, Loyola U., Chgo., 1980-83, assoc. dean grad. sch., 1981-82; dep. dir. bur. justice stats. U.S. Dept. Justice, Washington, 1983-84; Alice Tweed Tuohy prof. govt. Claremont (Calif.) McKenna Coll., 1984-88, v.p. and dean of faculty, 1988-91; pres. Hampden-Sydney (Va.) Coll., 1991-92; Salvatori Vis. prof. Claremont (Calif.) McKenna Coll., 1992-93, Salvatori prof. Am. Constitutionalism, 1994—; Fletcher Jones Prof. of Am. Politics U. Redlands, Redlands, Calif., 1993-94. Mem. adv. bd. Nat. Inst. Corrections, U.S. Dept. Justice, 1988-91; mem. Robert Presley Inst. Corrections Rsch. and Tng., State of Calif., 1988-91; dir. Rose Inst. of State and Local Govt., 2000—; mem. nat. bd. dirs. FIPSE, U.S. Dept. Edn., 2002—. Author: Federalism, the Supreme Court and the Seventeenth Amendment, 2001, others; co-author: The American Founding, 1981, American Constitutional Law, 1983, 1987, 1991, 1995, 1999, 2003—, others; editor (sr.): Benchmark, 1983—86; book rev. editor:, 1986—91; contbr. 60 articles to profl. jours., chapters to books. Trustee Episcopal Theol. Sch., Claremont, 1987-91. Ford Found. fellow, 1968-72. Mem. Am. Polit. Sci. Assn. Episcopalian. Office: Claremont McKenna Coll Dept Govt 850 Columbia Ave Claremont CA 91711-3901 Office Phone: 909-607-3392. Business E-Mail: ralph.rossum@claremontmckenna.edu.

ROST, THOMAS LOWELL, plant biology educator; b. St. Paul, Dec. 28, 1941; m. Ann Marie Ruhland, Aug. 31, 1963; children: Christopher, Timothy, Jacquelyn. BS, St. John's U., Collegeville, Minn., 1963; MA, Mankato State U., 1965; PhD, Iowa State U., 1971. Postdoctoral fellow Brookhaven Nat. Lab., Upton, N.Y., 1970-72; asst. to full prof. dept. botany U. Calif., Davis, 1972-82, faculty asst. to chancellor, 1982-83, prof., chmn. plant biology sect., 1994-96, assoc. dean divsn. biol. sci., 1996—2003, exec. assoc. dean, 2003—. Cons. faculty of agronomy U. Uruguay, 1979, 89; vis. fellow Rsch. Soc. Biol. Sci., Canberra, Australia, 1979-80; vis. prof. U. Wroclaw, Poland, 1987, U. Exeter, Eng., 1993. Co-author: Botany: A Brief Introduction to Plant Biology, 1979, Botany: An Introduction on Plant Biology, 1982, 2d edit., 2004; co-editor: Mechanisms and Control of Cell Division, 1977, Plant Biology, 1998; also numerous articles to profl. jours. Served to capt. U.S. Army, 1965-67. Fellow Japan Soc. Promotion of Sci.; mem. Bot. Soc. Am., Soc. Exptl. Biology, Am. Inst. Biol. Sci. Democrat. Roman Catholic. Avocation: community theatre. Office: U Calif Sect Plant Biology Davis CA 95616-8537

ROST, WILLIAM JOSEPH, chemist; b. Fargo, N.D., Dec. 8, 1926; s. William Melvin and Christine Ruth (Hamerlik) R.; m. Rita Cincoski, Sept. 15, 1951; children— Kathryn, Patricia, Carol. BS, U. Minn., 1948, PhD, 1952. From asst. prof. to prof. pharm. chemistry Sch. Pharmacy U. Kansas City, Mo., 1952-63; prof. pharm. chemistry Sch. Pharmacy U. Mo., Kansas City, 1963—. Co-author: Principles of Medicinal Chemistry, 1974, 3d rev. edit., 1988; contbr. articles profl. jours. Mem. Am. Pharm. Assn., Am. Chem. Soc., Sigma Xi, Kappa Psi, Rho Chi, Phi Lambda Upsilon. Home: 709 W 115th Ter Kansas City MO 64114-5597 Office: U Mo Sch of Pharmacy Kansas City MO 64110

ROSTEN, IRWIN, writer, producer, director; Writer-producer news, pub. affairs Sta. KNXT-CBS, Los Angeles, 1954-60; dir. news, pub. affairs Sta. KTLA, Los Angeles, 1960-63; writer-producer, dir. Wolper Prodns., Inc., Los Angeles, 1963-67; chief documentary dept. MGM Studios, Culver City, Calif., 1967-72; pres. Ronox Prodns., Inc., Los Angeles, 1970-87. Writer-prodr.-dir. Nat. Geog. Soc. spls.: Splendid Stones, Elephant, Great Moments with National Geographic, The Thames, Mysteries of the Mind, Gold!, The Legacy of L.S.B. Leakey, The Volga, The Incredible Machine, Grizzly!, The Eerie World of Jacques-Yves Cousteau, National Parks: Playground or Paradise?, numerous other shows including Unsolved Mysteries, The Wolf Men, Ripley's Believe It or Not, Sports Illustrated, Trial by Wilderness, Hollywood: The Dream Factory, Kifaru: The Black Rhinoceros, Birds Do It, Bees Do It, Indestructible People, Journey Into Life, One Man's Noise: Stories of an Adventuresome Oceanographer, Tiger: Lord of the Wild, Celebrate the Century; video prodr. opening ceremonies 1984 Olympic Games, L.A., Interactive Multimedia: Columbus, Evolution/Revolution. Recipient Emmy award Acad. TV Arts and Scis.; recipient Writers Guild Am. award, Peabody award, Am. Med. Writers Assn. award, Christophers award, Ohio State U. award, Saturday Rev. award, CINE Golden Eagle award Mem. Writers Guild Am., Dirs. Guild Am., Acad. TV Arts and Scis., Internat. Documentary Assn.

ROSTER, MICHAEL, lawyer; b. Chgo., May 7, 1945; AB, Stanford U., 1967, JD, 1973. Bar: Calif. 1973, D.C. 1980. Ptnr. McKenna, Conner & Cuneo, L.A. and Washington, 1973-87, Morrison & Foerster, L.A. and Washington, 1987-93; gen. counsel Stanford (Calif.) U., 1993—2000; exec. v.p., gen. counsel Golden West Fin. Corp., Oakland, Calif., 2000—. Bd. dirs. Silicon Valley Bancshares, vice chmn., 1995—98; chmn. Encirq, 1998—2000, Insert Therapeutics, 2000—04. Contbr. articles to profl. jours. Bd. dirs. Pasadena Heritage, 1986-87. Lt. (j.g.) USN, 1969-71. Mem. ABA (chmn. com. on savs. instns. 1985-89, fin. svcs. com. 1981—, banking com. 1989—), Calif. Bar Assn. (chmn. banking com. 1978-79), Am. Corp. Counsel Assn. (chmn. 2000-01), Calif. Bankers Assn. (chmn. 2001—), Stanford U. Alumni Assn. (chmn. 1992), L.A. Athletic Club. Home: 1321 Fairlawn Way Pasadena CA 91105-1002 Office: Golden West Fin Corp 1901 Harrison Oakland CA 94612

ROSTKER, BERNARD, federal official; m. Louise Cowen; children: David, Michael. BS in Econs. and Edn., NYU, 1964; M in Econs., Syracuse U., 1967, PhD in Econs., 1970. Economist Manpower Requirements Directorate Office of the Asst. Sec. of Def. for Sys. Analysis, 1968-70; rsch. economist RAND Corp., 1970-72, program dir. manpower per. and tng. program, 1972-77; prin. dep. asst. sec. for manpower and res. affairs USN, 1977-79, dir. Selective Svc., 1979-81, dir. navy mgmt. program Ctr. for Naval Analyses, 1981-83; dir. sys. mgmt. divsn. Sys. Rsch. and Applications Corp., 1983-84; program dir. force devel. and employment program RAND Corp.-The Arroyo Ctr., 1984-90, assoc. dir., 1984-90; dir. Def. Manpower Rsch. Ctr. RAND Nat. Def. Rsch. Ctr., 1990-94; asst. sec. for manpower and res. affairs USN, 1994—98, spl. asst. to dep. sec. def. for Gulf War illnesses, 1996—; under sec. of the Army, 1998—2000; under sec. for pers. and readiness, 2000—. Office: Spcl Asst Gulf War Illnesses Suite 901 Four Skyline Place 5113 Leesburg Pike Falls Church VA 22041*

ROSTOW, CHARLES NICHOLAS, lawyer, educator; b. Geneva, Mar. 3, 1950; s. Eugene Victor and Edna (Greenberg) R.; m. Heyden White, Oct. 31, 1987; children: Theodore Isaac, Celia A.M. BA, Yale U., 1972, PhD, 1979, JD, 1982. Assoc. Shearman & Sterling, N.Y.C., 1982-85; spl. asst. to legal adviser Dept. State, Washington, 1985-87; dep. legal adviser NSC, Washington, 1987, spl. asst. to Pres., legal adviser, 1987-93; assoc. prof. Coll. of Law U. Tulsa, 1993—95, disting. rsch. prof. Coll. of Law, 1995—98; exec. dir. Mass. Office Internat. Trade and Investment, 1995-98; counsel and dep. staff dir. House Select Comm. on Nat. Security & Mil./Comm. Concerns with the PRC, 1998; staff dir. Senate Select Com. on Intelligence, 1999-2000; Charles H. Stockton prof. internat. law U.S. Naval War Coll., Newport, RI, 2001; gen. coun. U.S. Mission UN, N.Y.C., 2001—. Author: Anglo-French Relations 1934-36, 1984; editor: Akten zur deutschen auswaertigen Politik: 1918-1945, vols. XIV-XXI, 1980-83; contbr. articles to prof. jours. Hon. dir. John Goodwin Tower Ctr. for Polit. Studies, So. Meth. U.; nat. adv. bd. Am. Jewish Com. Mem. Assn. Bar City of N.Y., Coun. Fgn. Rels., Phi Beta Kappa, Cosmos Club, Yale Club (N.Y.C.), Elizabethan Club (New Haven). Jewish. Office: US Mission to the UN 799 UN Plaza New York NY 10017 Office Phone: 212-415-4220.

ROSTOW, ELSPETH DAVIES, political science educator; b. N.Y.C. d. Milton Judson and Harriet Elspeth (Vaughan) Davies; m. Walt Whitman Rostow, June 26, 1947 (dec. Feb. 2003); children: Peter Vaughan, Ann Larner. AB, Barnard Coll., 1938; AM, Radcliffe Coll., 1939; MA, Cambridge (Eng.) U., 1949; LHD (hon.), Lebanon Valley Coll.; LLD (hon.), Austin Coll., 1982, Southwestern U., 1988. Mem. faculty various instns. Barnard Coll., N.Y.C. and MIT, Cambridge, 1939-69; mem. faculty U. Tex., Austin, 1969—, dean div. gen. and comparative studies, 1975-77, prof. govt., 1976—, dean Lyndon B. Johnson Sch. Pub. Affairs, 1977-83, Stiles prof. Am. studies, 1985-88, Stiles prof. emerita, 1988—. Mem. Pres.'s Adv. Com. for Trade Negotiations, 1978-82, Pres.'s Commn. for a Nat. Agenda for the Eighties, 1979-81; rsch. assoc. OSS, Washington, 1943-45; Geneva corr. London Economist, 1947-49; lectr. Air War Coll., 1963-81, Army War Coll., 1965, 68, 69, 78, 79, 81, Nat. War Coll., 1962, 68, 74, 75, Indsl. Coll. Armed Forces, 1961-65, Naval War Coll., 1971, Fgn. Svc. Inst., 1974-77, Dept. of State, Europe, 1973; bd. dirs. U.S. Inst. of Peace, vice chmn., 1991, chmn. 1991-92; co-founder The Austin Project, 1991; mem. Gov.'s Task Force on Revenue, Tex., 1991. Author: Europe's Economy After the War, 1948, (with others) American Now, 1968, The Coattailess Landslide, 1974; editor (with Barbara Jordan) The Great Society: A Twenty-Year Critique, 1986; columnist Austin Am. Statesman, 1985-92; contbr. articles to revs., poems to scholarly jours., newspapers, and mags. Trustee Nat. Acad. Pub. Adminstrn., 1989—95, Sarah Lawrence Coll., 1952—59, So. Ctr. for Internat. Studies, 1990—; bd. visitors and govs. St. Johns Coll., 1986—89; bd. dirs. Barnard Coll., 1962—66, Lyndon Baines Johnson Found., 1977—83, Salzburg Seminar, 1981—89, co-chair sr. fellows, 1997—2001; vis. scholar Phi Beta Kappa, 1984—85; bd. adv. to pres. Naval War Coll., Newport, RI, 1995—99; nat. advisor Commn. on Deliberative Polling, 1999—2001. Decorated Order of St. Joan D'Arc; named Fulbright lectr.; recipient Top Hand award, U. Tex. Ex-Students Assn., 1996, Presdl. citation, U. Tex., 1998, Disting. Alumna award, Barnard Coll., 1998; grantee, USIA, 1983—84, 1990. Mem.: Tex. Philos. Soc. (trustee 1989—95, 1997—2001), Headliners Found. (vice-chmn. 1996—2002), Phi Beta Kappa, Omicron Delta Kappa, Mortar Bd. (hon.), Phi Nu Epsilon (hon.). Home: 1 Wildwind Pt Austin TX 78746-2434 Office: U Tex PO Box Y University Station Austin TX 78713

ROSTROPOVICH, MSTISLAV LEOPOLDOVICH, conductor, music director, musician; b. Baku, USSR, Mar. 27, 1927; s. Leopold and Sofia (Fedotova) Rostropovich; m. Galina Pavlovna Vishnevskaya; children: Olga, Elena. Grad., Moscow Conservatory 1948; numerous hon. doctorate degrees. Faculty mem. Moscow Conservatory, 1953, prof., 1960; head cello and double-bass dept., formerly prof. Leningrad Conservatory; music dir., conductor Nat. Symphony Orch., Washington, 1977-94; hon. prof. Cuban Nat. Conservatory, 1960-78. Pres. Evian Internat. Music Festival. Performer (world concert tours): Moscow Philharm. Orch. Decorated Hon. Knight of Brit. Empire, Comdr. French Legion of Honor, Officer's Cross of Merit Fed. Republic Germany; named Musician of Yr., Music Am., 1987; recipient Stalin prize, 1951, 1953, Lenin prize, 1963, Life in Music prize, 1984, Albert Schweitzer Music award, 1985, Grammy award, 1970, 1977, 1980, 1984, Presdl. Medal Freedom, 1987, Ditson Condr.'s award, Columbia U., 1990, Four Freedoms award, Franklin and Eleanor Roosevelt Inst., 1992. Mem.: Acad. Arts of French Inst.-Forty Immortals, Union Soviet Composers, Am. Acad. Arts and Scis., Brit. Royal Acad. Music (hon.). Address: cø CAMI 165 W 57th St New York NY 10019-2201 also: Gazetny per 13 Apt 79 103009 Moscow Russia

ROSWELL, ROBERT H. federal agency administrator; MD, U. Okla., 1975. Diplomate Am. Bd. Internal Medicine. Resident in internal medicine U. Okla. Sch. Medicine; mem. faculty various med. schs.; fellow in endocrinology and metabolism U. Okla. Sch. Medicine; various leadership positions VA facilities, VA Ctrl. Office, Washington; chief of staff VA med. ctrs., Birmingham, Ala., Oklahoma City; dir. Fla. and P.R. VA healthcare network, Bay Pines, Fla., 1995; exec. dir. Fed. Persian Gulf Vets. Coordinating Bd., 1994—99; under sec. health Dept. Vets. Affairs, Washington, 2002—. Served in U.S. Army, 1978—80, col. M.C. USAR. Office: US Dept Vets Affairs Vets Health Adminstrn 810 Vermont Ave NW Washington DC 20420

ROSZKOWSKI, JOSEPH JOHN, lawyer; b. Pawtucket, R.I., Aug. 11, 1938; s. Joseph J. and Anna T. Roszkowski; m. Geraldine J. Szpila, July 2, 1966. BA, Alliance Coll., 1960; JD, Marquette U., 1964. Bar: Wis. 1964, U.S. Dist. Ct. (ea. dist.) Wis. 1964, R.I. 1965. Ptnr. Zimmerman, Roszkowski & Brenner, Woonsocket, R.I., 1965—. Corporator Fogarty Hosp., North Smithfield, RI, 1976—88; counsel Landmark Med. Ctr., 1989—90. Mem. Nat. Ski Patrol, RI, 1974—83; legal counsel R.I. Tuna Tournament, 1975—; bd. dirs. R.I. Legal Svcs., Providence, 1974—87, Legal Aid Soc., Providence, 1985—. Mem. ABA (ho. of dels. 1996-2003, state del. 2000-2001, 2003—, bd. govs. 2001, 2002, commr. Interest on Lawyers' Trust Accounts 1986-90, 2002—), R.I. Bar Found. (pres. 1990-95), R.I. Bar Assn. (pres. 1985-86), Am. Law Inst., Am. Judicature Soc., Fed. Tax Inst. New England (adv. com. 1985-86), R.I. Med. Examiners, U.S. Jaycees (nat. dir. 1968), Am. Acad. Hosp. Attys. Lodges: Rotary (pres. Cumberland, R.I. 1987). Avocations: skiing, sailing, gardening, tennis. Home: 1o Little St Cumberland RI 02864-1101 Office: Zimmerman Roszkowski & Brenner 1625 Diamond Hill Rd Woonsocket RI 02895-1541 E-mail: jroskow@aol.com.

ROSZKOWSKI, STANLEY JULIAN, retired federal judge; b. Boonville, N.Y., Jan. 27, 1923; s. Joseph and Anna (Christkowski) R.; m. Catherine Mary Claeys, June 19, 1948; children: Mark, Gregory, Dan, John. BS, U. Ill., 1949, JD, 1954. Bar: Ill. 1954. Sales mgr. Warren Petroleum Co., Rockford, Ill., 1954; ptnr. Roszkowski, Paddock, McGreevy & Johnson, Rockford, 1955-77; judge U.S. Dist. Ct. (we. dist.), Rockford, Ill., 1977-98; pres. First State Bank, Rockford, 1963-75, chmn. bd., 1977—; mediator-arbitrator JAMS/ENDISPUTE, Chgo., 1998—. Chmn. Fire and Police Commn., Rockford, 1967-74, commr., 1974—; chmn. Paul Simon Com., 1972; active Adlai Stevenson III campaign, 1968-71, Winnebago County Citizens for John F. Kennedy, 1962, Winnebago County Dem. Cen. Com., 1962-64; bd. dirs. Sch. of Hope, 1960—; mem. Ill. Capital Devel. Bd., 1974— . With USAAF, 1943-45. Decorated Air medal with 2 oak leaf clusters.; recipient Pulaski Nat. Heritage award Polish Am. Congress, Chgo., 1982 Mem. ABA, Ill. Bar Assn., Fla. Bar Assn., Winnebago County Bar Assn., Am. Coll. Trial Lawyers, Am. Judicature Soc., Assn. Trial Lawyers Am., Ill. Trial Lawyers Assn., Am. Arbitration Assn. (arbitrator), Fed. Judges Assn. (bd. dirs. 1988—).

ROTAR, TOMAZ, stock exchange executive; COO, exec. v.p. Ljubljana Stock Exch., Slovenia. Office: Ljubljana Stock Exch Slovenska 56 1000 Ljubljana Slovenia

ROTBERG, EUGENE HARVEY, investment banker, lawyer; b. Phila., Jan. 19, 1930; s. Irving Bernard and Blanche Grace (Levick) R.; m. Iris Sybil Comens; children— Diana Golda, Pamela Lynn. BS, Temple U., 1951; LL.B., U. Pa., 1954; PhD (hon.), Salem-Teikyo U., 1992. Chief counsel Office Policy Research Securities and Exchange Commn., Washington, 1963-66; v.p., treas. World Bank, Washington, 1969-87; exec. v.p. Merrill Lynch & Co., N.Y.C., 1987-90. Served with U.S. Army. Decorated King Leopold II medal (Belgium); recipient Disting. Svc. award Securities and Exch. Commn., 1968; named Alumnus of Yr., Temple U. Home: 7211 Brickyard Rd Potomac MD 20854-4808 Office: 1250 24th St NW Ste 350 Washington DC 20037-1124 Office Phone: 202-944-3810. E-mail: genebanker@aol.com.

ROTBERG, IRIS COMENS, social scientist; b. Phila., Dec. 16, 1932; d. Samuel Nathaniel and Golda (Shuman) Comens; m. Eugene H. Rotberg, Aug. 29, 1954; children: Diana Golda, Pamela Lynn. BA, U. Pa., 1954, MA, 1955; PhD, Johns Hopkins U., Balt., 1958. Research psychologist Pres.'s Commn. on Income Maintenance Programs, Washington, 1968-69, Office Planning, Research and Evaluation, Office Econ. Opportunity, Washington, 1970-73; dep. dir. compensatory edn. study Nat. Inst. Edn., Washington, 1974-77, dir. Office Planning and Program Devel., 1978-82; program dir. NSF, Arlington, Va., 1985-87, 89-91, 1993-96; tech. policy fellow Com. on Sci., Space and Tech., U.S. Ho. of Reps., Washington, 1987-89; sr. social scientist RAND, Washington, 1991-93; rsch. prof. edn. policy Grad. Sch. Edn. and Human Devel. George Washington U., Washington, 1996—. NSF fellow, 1956-58. Home: 7211 Brickyard Rd Potomac MD 20854-4808 Office Phone: 202-994-2735. Business E-Mail: irotberg@gwu.edu.

ROTBERG, ROBERT IRWIN, historian, political economist, educator, editor; b. Newark, Apr. 11, 1935; s. Louis and Mildred S. R.; m. Joanna H. Henshaw, June 17, 1961; children: Rebecca T.H., Nicola S.D., Fiona J.Y. AB, Oberlin Coll., 1955; MPA, Princeton U., 1957; DPhil, U. Oxford, 1960. Asst. prof. history, rsch. assoc. Ctr. for Internat. Affairs Harvard U., 1961-68, rsch. assoc. Ctr. for Internat. Affairs, 1968-95; rsch. dir. Twentieth Century Fund, 1968-71; prof. polit. sci. and history MIT, 1968-87; acad. v.p. for Arts, Scis. and Tech. Tufts U., Medford, Mass., 1987-90; pres. Lafayette Coll., Easton, Pa., 1990-93, World Peace Found., Cambridge, 1993—; coord. Inst. for Internat. Devel. Harvard U., 1993-99, dir. program on intrastate conflict Kennedy Sch., 1999—. Adj. prof. Kennedy Sch. Govt., Harvard U., 1993—; mem. coun. NEH, 1993-99; cons. Dept. State, 1968-78, Commrs. of Middlesex County, Mass., 1976-77. Author: A Political History of Tropical Africa, 1965, The Rise of Nationalism in Central Africa, 1965, Protest and Power in Black Africa, 1970, Joseph Thomson and the Exploration of Africa, 1971, Haiti: The Politics of Squalor, 1971, Africa and Its Explorers, 1971, The Black Homelands of South Africa, 1977, Black Heart: Gore-Browne and the Politics of Multiracial Zambia, 1978, Conflict and Compromise in South Africa, 1980, Suffer the Future: Policy Choices in Southern Africa, 1980, Imperialism, Colonialism and Hunger, 1982, Namibia: Economic and Political Prospects, 1983, South Africa and its Neighbors, 1985, The Founder: Cecil Rhodes and the Pursuit of Power, 1988, rev. edit. 2002, Africa in the 1990s and Beyond: Policy Opportunities and Choices, 1988, From Massacres to Genocide: The Media, Public Policy, and Humanitarian Crises, 1996, Vigilance and Vengeance: NGOs Preventing Ethnic Conflict in Divided Societies, 1996, Haiti Renewed: Political and Economic Prospects, 1997, Burma: Prospects for a Democratic Future, 1998, War and Peace in Southern Africa, 1998, Creating Peace in Sri Lanka, 1999, Peacekeeping and Peace Enforcement in Africa, 2000, Truth v. Justice, 2000, Patterns of Social Capital, 2001, Ending Autocracy, Enabling Democracy, 2002, State Failure and State Weakness in a Time of Terror, 2003, When States Fail: Causes and Consequences, 2004; editor Jour. Interdisciplinary History, 1970—. Chmn. Middlesex County Govtl. Rev. Task Force, 1972; v.p. Cambridge Civic Assn., 1969-72; mem. Lexington Town Meeting, 1973-90, 94—, Lexington Sch. Com., 1974-77; mem. Ciskel Commn., 1979-80; trustee World Peace Found., 1980—, Oberlin Coll., 1983—, Coun. Internat. Exch. Scholars, 1991-95. Rhodes scholar U. Oxford, 1960; Guggenheim fellow, 1970-71; Hazen Found. fellow, 1976-77. Fellow Royal Geog. Soc.; mem. Am. Hist. Assn., African Studies Assn., Coun. on Fgn. Rels., Oberlin Coll. Alumni Assn. (pres. 1981-82). Office: World Peace Fund Belfer Ctr 79 John F Kennedy St Cambridge MA 02138-5758 E-mail: robert_rotberg@harvard.edu.

ROTCH, JAMES E. lawyer; b. Auburn, Ala., Mar. 26, 1945; s. Elroy B. and Martha (Ellisor) R.; m. Darlene Edwards, June 26, 1999; children: Jamison B., Susannah R., Amie L. Vaughn. BS, Auburn U., 1967, postgrad., 1967-68; JD, U. Va., 1971. Bar: Ala. 1971, U.S. Dist. Ct. (no. dist.) Ala. 1973. Rsch. asst. Office Instl. Rsch. Auburn (Ala.) U., 1967-68; clk. U.S. Judiciary System, Birmingham, Ala., 1971-72; assoc. Bradley Arant Rose & White LLP, Birmingham, 1971-76; ptnr. Bradley, Arant, Rose & White LLP, Birmingham, 1976—, administrv. ptnr., 1990-93; chmn. bd. dirs. Kaleidoscope Prodns., Inc. Mem. adv. com. Bioelastics Rsch. Ltd., Birmingham, 1992—, Gov.'s Task Force on Biotechnology, Ala., 1993. Author: The Birmingham Pledge. Pres. adv. com. Birmingham Mus. Art, 1989-92; bd. dirs. Operation New Birmingham, 1990-91, 95—, co-chmn. cmty. affairs com., mem. exec. com.; Coalition for Better Edn., Birmingham, 1990—; active Boy Scouts Am.; bd. dirs. Birmingham Com. for Olympic Soccer, 1994-96, Ala. Sports Found., 1994-98, Entrepreneurial Ctr. Inc., 1996—, chmn., 2002; mem. adminstrv. bd. Canterbury United Meth. Ch., 1991-93; chmn. Birmingham Pledge Found., 2000—; chmn. Biringham Area Tech. Leadership Alliance. Capt. USAR, 1972-78. Named Communicator of Yr., Birmingham Bus. Jour., 2001; recipient Outstanding Achievement award, Operation New Birmingham, 1994, Liberty and Justice award, 2000, Key to Unlocking Door to Adversity award, Mercedes-Benz U.S. Internat., 2002. Mem. ALA, Auburn U. Bar Assn., Birmingham Bar Assn., Internat. Bar Assn., Ala. State Bar Assn. (Merit award 1999-2000), Leadership Birmingham, Leadership Ala. (bd. dirs. 1998--),, Auburn Coll. Liberal Arts (adv. coun.), U. Va. Alumni Assn., Newcomen Soc., Birmingham Regional C. of C. (bd. dirs. 2001, vice chmn. for tech. devel. 2002, chmn.-elect 2003), Auburn U. Alumni Assn., Birmingham Venture Club (bd. dirs. 2001), Country Club of Birmingham, Jockey Club, Summit Club (charter), Kiwanis (sec. 1998-99). Methodist. Avocations: horses, bird hunting, cattle farming, golf. Office: Bradley Arant Rose & White LLP One Federal Pl 1819 5th Ave N Birmingham AL 35203

ROTE, NELLE FAIRCHILD HEFTY, management consultant; b. Watsontown, Pa, May 23, 1930; d. Edwin Dunkel and Phebe Hill (Fisher) Fairchild; m. John Austin Hefty, Mar. 20, 1948 (div. June 1970); children: Harry E. Hefty, John B. Hefty, Susan E. Hefty DeBartolo; m. Keith Maynard Rote, Dec. 16, 1983 (dec. Aug. 1985). Student, Bucknell U., 1961, Williamsport Sch. of Commerce, 1968-69, Pa. State U., 1971-72, 83, Susquehanna U., 1986. Typesetter, page designer Colonial Printing House, Inc., Lewisburg, Pa., 1970-76; account exec. Sta. WTGC Radio, Lewisburg, 1976-78; co-owner Colonial Printing Co., Lewisburg, 1978-83; temp. HATS-Temps, Lewisburg, 1986-89; artist, editor Create-A-Book, Inc., Milton, Fla., 1980-92; census crew leader, spl. svc. Dept. Commerce, Washington, 1990; cons. Create-A-Book, Inc., Gulf Breeze, Fla., 1991—99, 2002—. Children's Playmate Mag., 1942; author: McGruff and Me, 1999, My Christmas Wish, 1999, School Fun Book, 1999, My Fishing Adventure, 1999, From Philadelphia to Flanders, 1917, 2004; co-author: Am. Nursing: A Biog. Dictionary, 2000; contbr. articles to profl. jours.; exhibitions include Union County Libr., Lewisburg, 2003. Proofreader Lewisburg Bicentennial Commn., Lewisburg, 1976; charter mem. Women's Art Mus., Washington; charter sponsor Women in Mil. Svc. Meml., Arlington, Va., 1991; founder, donor Nelle Fairchild Rote Book Fund, Union County Libr.; editor, poet Holiday Newspaper Bus. Assn., Lewisburg, 1987. Recipient Humanitarian recognition, Tri-County Fedn. Women's Clubs, Pa., 1965, Grand prize in Cooking, Milton Std., 1966, Most Profl. Photo award, Lewisburg Festival Arts, 1980, Hon. Mention award, Women in Arts,

Harrisburg, Pa., 1981, Photo Contest award, Congressman Allen Ertel, 1981, 2d pl. Photo award, Union County Fair, 1981, 3d pl. Photo award, 1981, Hon. Mention Photo award, Susquehanna Art Soc., 1981, Silver award for Poetry, World of Poetry, 1990. Mem.: DAR (nat. def. reporter Shikelimo chpt. 1989—95, sec. 1992—95, regent 1995—2001, vice chmn. Pa. State Soc. DAR women vets com. 1998—2001, vice-regent 2001—, Prize for safety poster 1942), Soc. Profl. Journalists, Warrior Run Heritage Soc., Orgn. United Environment, Marine Corps League Aux. (life), Western Front Assn., Civic Club Lewisburg (v.p. 1994—97), Am. Legion Aux. (sgt.-at-arms 2003, Unit 182). Achievements include Initiator for renaming bridge in Watsontown, PA. to "Nurse Helen Fairchild Meml. Bridge" (a WWI Reserve Army Nurse relative), 2002. Home: 1015 St Paul St Lewisburg PA 17837-1213

ROTELL, CYNTHIA A. lawyer; BA, Barnard Coll., 1982; JD, Bklyn. Law Sch., 1990. Bar: Calif. 1990. With Latham & Watkins, L.A., 1990—, ptnr., 1997—. Mem.: L.A. County Bar Assn. (exec. com. bus. and corps. law sect.), State of Calif. Bar Assn. Office: Latham and Watkins LLC 633 W Fifth St Ste 4000 Los Angeles CA 90071

ROTENBERG, MANUEL, physics educator; b. Toronto, Ont., Can., Mar. 12, 1930; came to U.S., 1946; s. Peter and Rose (Plonzker) R.; m. Paula Weissbrod, June 23, 1952; children: Joel, Victor. BS, MIT, 1952, PhD, 1956. Staff Los Alamos (N.Mex.) Nat. Lab., 1955-58; instr. physics Princeton (N.J.) U., 1958-59; asst. prof. U. Chgo., 1959-61; prof. applied physics U. Calif., San Diego, 1961-93, dean grad. studies and research, 1975-84, chmn. dept. elec. engring. and computer sci., 1988-93, rsch. prof., 1993—. Author: The 3-j and 6-j Symbols, 1959; founding editor: Methods of Computational Physics, 1963, Jour. of Computational Physics, 1962; editor: Biomathematics and Cell Kinetics, 1981. Fellow Am. Phys. Soc.; mem. AAAS, Sigma Xi. Office: U Calif San Diego La Jolla CA 92093-0407 Office Phone: 858-534-2726. Business E-Mail: rote@ucsd.edu.

ROTENBERG, MARC STEVEN, public interest advocate, lawyer; b. Boston, Apr. 20, 1960; s. Michael and Karen (Sethur) R.; m. Anna Markopoulos; children: Chaz, Chloe. AB, Harvard Coll., 1982; JD, Stanford U., 1987; student, Georgetown U., 1994—. Bar: Mass. 1987, D.C. 1990. Teaching fellow Harvard U., Cambridge, Mass., 1980-82; exec. dir. Pub. Interest Computer Assn., Washington, 1983-84; instr. Stanford (Calif.) U., 1986-87; counsel Senate Jud. Com., Washington, 1987-88; dir. Washington office Computer Profls. for Social Responsibility, 1988-94; dir. Electronic Privacy Info. Ctr., Washington, 1994—. Adj. prof. law Georgetown Law Ctr., 1991—, Washington Coll. Law, 1997—; sec. Privacy Internat.; mem. adv. panels NSF, ABA, AAAS, ALA, Orgn. for Econ. Coop. and Devel., Paris, Austrian Inst. on Law and Policy, Salzburg. Editor: Technology and Privacy: The New Frontier, 1997; bd. editors Electronic Info. Law Reporter, Govt. Info. Quar., Computer Law and Security Report, Ency. Computer Sci.; contbr. articles to profl. jours. Ford Found. fellow internat. law, 1994; recipient 3rd Pl. U.S. Amateur Chess Championship, 1993. Mem. ABA, Assn. Computing Machines. Avocations: chess, basketball, german expressionism, record producing. Office: Electronic Privacy Info Ctr 666 Pennsylvania Ave SE Ste 301 Washington DC 20003-4335

ROTENBERG, SHELDON, violinist; b. Attleboro, Mass., Apr. 11, 1917; s. Joseph and Jennie (Almer) R.; m. Hilde Sussmann, Jan. 25, 1924; children: David, Steffi. AB, Tufts U., 1939, grad. student, 1939-40; violin pupil of, Felix Winternitz, Georges Enesco, Maurice Hewitt. Tchr. violin, 1947—. Music adviser, cons. pub. schs., Brookline, Mass.; archivist, cons. Boston Symphony Orch., 1992-93. Concertized extensively with the Boston String Quartet sponsored by Elizabeth Sprague Coolidge, including concerts and rec. at the Libr. of Congress, 1948-52, occupies endowed Kasdon-Paley chair, 1st violin sect., Boston Symphony Orch., 1948-91, solo performances with Boston Pops Orch., 1939-41; Boston Symphony rep. as soloist, tchr., mem. orch. in State Dept. cultural exch. program with Japan Philharm., Tokyo, 1968-69; mem. faculty Boston U. Tanglewood Inst., 1979—. Served to capt. AUS, 1942-46. Mem. Harvard Mus. Assn., Tufts U. Alumni Assn. Home: 60 Browne St Brookline MA 02446-7050 Office: care Boston Symphony Orch Symphony Hall Boston MA 02115

ROTFELD, ADAM DANIEL, research institute administrator, government official, government agency administrator; b. Przemyslany, Lwow, Poland, Mar. 4, 1938; s. Leon and Berta Rothfeld; m. Barbara Sikorska, Jan. 15, 1970; 1 child, Alicja. Degree in law and diplomacy, Warsaw U., 1960, postgrad., 1962; PhD in Internat. Law, Jagiellonian U., 1969; habilitation, Inst. Internat. Affairs, Warsaw, 1990. Mem. staff Polish Inst. Internat. Affairs, 1961-89, dep. editor-in-chief monthly, 1963-68, sr. rschr., 1969-77, head European Security Dept., 1978-89; fellow Inst. East-West Security Studies, N.Y., 1984-85; project leader European security Stockholm Internat. Peace Rsch. Inst., 1989—2001, dir., leader security project, 1991—; prof. Warsaw U., 2001—; undersecretary of state Ministry of Fgn. Affairs, Warsaw, 2001—. Negotiator Helsinki Final Act of Conf. for Security and Coop. in Europe, Geneva, 1973-75, Belgrade, 1977-78, Madrid, 1980-83, Vienna, 1986-88; personal rep. chmn.-in-office Trans-Dniester Conflict Region of the Republic of Moldova, 1992-93; mem. numerous internat. coms.; editor, pub. SIPRI Yearbook on Armaments, Disarmament and Internat. Security, 1992—; mem. adv. bd. UNESCO Studies on Peace and Conflict, European Fellowship Programme, Ctr. for European Securities Studies; co-chmn. ind. working group Future Security Agenda for Europe, 1994-96, Stockholm Agenda for Arms Control, 1999. Author: European Security System In Statu Nascendi, 1990; co-editor: (with Walther Stützle) Germany and Europe in Transition, 1991, (with Armand Clesse) Sources and Areas of Future Possible Crisis in Europe, 1995, (with Ian Anthony) A Future Arms Control Agenda, 2001; editor: Military Security and Confidence Building Measures, 1991, Human Rights-International Obligations of Poland, 1989, Building Security in Europe: CBMs and CSCE, 1986; contbr. articles to profl. jours. Pres. Polish UN Student Assn., 1962-64; sec. gen. Polish UN Assn., 1975-80. Recipient award Polish Acad. Scis., 1988, Polish Inst. Internat. Affairs, 1990. Mem.: Nat. Security Coun. Poland, Sci. Coun. of the Inst. for Peace Rsch. and Security Studies (Hamburg, Germany), Swedish Royal Acad. of War Studies, Internat. Inst. Strategic Studies. Avocations: films, reading, walking. Office: Ministry Fgn Affairs Al J Ch Szucha 23 PL-00580 Warsaw Poland

ROTH, ALEDA VENDER, business educator; b. Cleve., Oct. 8, 1945; d. Joseph Patrick and Beatrice Vender; m. G. Douglas Roth, Sept. 26, 1970; children: G. Brian, Lauren Carter. BS in Psychology with honors, Ohio State U., 1968; MSPH in Biostats., U. N.C., 1970; PhD in Ops. Mgmt., Ohio State U., 1986. Chief statistician Ark. Children's Colony Ark. State Dept. Human Svcs., 1968-69; rsch. assoc., epidemiologist Epidemiologic Field Sta. Greater Kansas City Mental Health Found., 1970-72, statis. cons. Epidemiologic Field Sta., 1972-74; nat. dir. stats. dept. ANA, 1972-79; grad. teaching and rsch. assoc. faculty mgmt. sci. Ohio State U., 1979-83, grad. teaching and rsch. assoc. acctg. dept., 1983, instr. computer and info. sys. Coll. Engring., 1983-84, instr. faculty mgmt. sci. Coll. Adminstrv. Sci., 1984-85; asst. prof. Boston U. Sch. Mgmt., 1985-89, prin. investigator retail banking futures project, 1986-94; co-investigator mfg.'s future rsch. Boston U., 1985-89, prin. co-investigator rsch. DTT-UNC gloal vision in mfg., 1989—2001, rsch. assoc. ctr. health rsch. and edn., 1989-93; assoc. prof. dept. health adminstrn. Duke U. Med. Ctr., Durham, 1989-91; assoc. prof. bus. Duke U., Durham, N.C., 1989-93; Disting. Mary Farley Ames Lee prof., chair Global Supply Chain Concentration U.N.C, dept. Tech. and Innovation Mgmt., Chapel Hill, 1993—. Prin. rsch. co-investigator Internat. Svc. Study, 1996—; vis. scholar London Business Sch., 2000; Vis. prof. WHU Vallender Germany, 2001; adj. faculty mem. Sch. Pub. Health, U. N.C., Chapel Hill, 1972-74; mem. Coop. Health Stats. Sys. Adv. Com., Nat. Ctr. Health Stats., DHHS, 1974-76; membership svcs. com. Nat. Decision Scis. Inst., 1989-90; adj. rsch. faculty Boston U. Mfg. Roundtable, 1985-90; rsch. adv. com. U. N.C. Ctr. for Mfg. Excellence, 1989-94; exec. com. U. N.C. Cato Ctr. Applied Bus. Rsch., 1994-97, rsch. com. 1997-99. Author (with M. van der Velde): The Future of Retail Banking Delivery Systems, 1988; author: Retail Banking Strategies: Opportunities for the 1990s, 1990, World Class Banking: Benchmarking the Market Leaders, 1992; author: (with C. Giffi and G. Seal) Competing in World Class Manufacturing: America's 21st Century Challenge, 1990; editor: Facts About Nursing, 1972-73 edit., 1974, 1974-75 edit., 1976, 1980-81 edit., 1981; editor: (with J. Jaeger and A. Kaluzny) The Management of Continuous Improvement: Cases in Health Administration, 1993; dep. editor: Manufacturing and Service Operations Management, 1996—, assoc. editor: Decision Sciences, 1993—2002, Jour. Ops. Mgmt., 1993—2001, 2001—, mem. editl. rev. bd.:, 1998—, area editor: Prodn. and Ops. Mgmt. Jour., 1993—, mem. editl. adv. bd.:, 1991—93, assoc. editor: OM Review, 1992—94, Benchmarking for Quality and Tech. Mgmt., 1993—, mem. editl. bd.: Internat. Jour. Prodn. and Ops. Mgmt., 1995—99, Jour. Svc. Rsch., 1998—, ad hoc referee: Mgmt. Sci., Jour. Ops. Mgmt., Decisions on Scis., Prodn. and Ops. Mgmt. Jour., IEEE Trans.; contbr. articles to profl. jours., chpts. to books. Recipient Book award of excellence Soc. for Tech. Comm., 1992, Kenan Inst. Faculty Rsch. award, 1994, Outstanding Paper award Literati Club, London, 1995, Kenan-Flagler Bus. Sch. Disting. Rsch. award 1996, Best Paper award Acad. Mgmt., 1996, 2000, Best Paper award XXII Brazilian Assn. Post Grad. Courses in Adminstrn., 1998, 99; winner Decision Scis. Inst.'s Interdisciplinary Paper award, 1996, Best Theoretical/Empirical Rsch. Paper award 1985, Doctoral Dissertation award 1985; Anna Dice scholar Ohio State U., 1985; grantee Performance Excellence Coun. of the Conf. Bd., 1991—; NIMH fellow, 1969-70, U. N.C. Cato Ctr. fellow, 1995, Kenan Inst. fellow, 1995-96, Dalton L. McMichael Sr. Rsch. fellow, 1998; Disting. O'Herron Faculty scholar, 1996. Mem. Prodn. and Ops. Mgmt. Assn. (sec. 1988-91, bd. dirs. 1988-94, planning com. ann. conf. 1990-91, session chair ann. mtg. 1991, pres.-elect 2000-02, pres. 2002—), Decision Scis. Inst. (bd. dirs. 1996-98), Phi Kappa Phi, Delta Omega. Office: U NC Kenan-Flagler Bus Sch Chapel Hill NC 27599-3490

ROTH, ALVIN ELIOT, economics educator; b. N.Y.C., Dec. 18, 1951; s. Ernest and Lillian (Caesar) R.; m. Emilie Matarasso, May 22, 1977; children: Aaron Leon, Benjamin Nathaniel. BS, Columbia U., 1971; MS, Stanford U., 1973, PhD, 1974. Asst. prof. dept. bus. adminstrn. and dept. econs. U. Ill., Urbana, 1974-77, assoc. prof., 1977-79, prof., 1979-82; A.W. Mellon prof. econs. U. Pitts., 1982-98; G. Gund Prof. Econs. and bus. Adminstrn. Harvard U., Boston, 1998—. Author: Axiomatic Models of Bargaining, 1979, Game-Theoretic Models of Bargaining, 1985, Laboratory Experimentation in Economics, 1987, The Shapley Value, 1988, (with M. Sotomayor) Two-Sided Matching: A Study in Game Theoretic Modeling and Analysis, 1990, (with J. Kagel) Handbook of Experimental Economics, 1995, (with B. Holmstrom and P. Milgron) Game Theory in the Tradition of Bob Wilson, 2002. Recipient Founders' prize Tex. Instruments Found., 1980; Guggenheim fellow, 1983; A.P. Sloan research fellow, 1984; 10 Outstanding Young Ams. award, 1984; Lanchester prize Ops. Rsch. Soc. Am., 1991. Fellow Econometric Soc., Am. Acad. Arts and Scis.; mem. AAAS, Am. Econ. Assn. Jewish. Home: 89 Rawson Rd Brookline MA 02445-4509 Office: Harvard U Harvard Bus Sch Dept Econs Boston MA 02163

ROTH, CAROLYN LOUISE, art educator; b. Buffalo, June 17, 1944; d. Charles Mack and Elizabeth Mary (Hassel) R.; m. Charles Turner Barber, Aug. 4, 1991. Student, Art Student's League N.Y., 1965, Instituto Allende, San Miguel de Allende, Mex., 1966; BFA, Herron Sch. Art, 1967; MFA, Fla. State U., 1969. Asst. prof. art U. Tenn., Chattanooga, 1969-72; lectr. art So. Ill. U., Carbondale, 1973-75; asst. prof. art U. Evansville, Ind., 1975-80; lectr. art U. So. Ind., Evansville, 1984—. Exhbn. coord., gallery dir. Krannert Gallery, U. Evansville, 1977-79; exhbn. coord., conf. advisor Ind. Women in Arts Conf., Ind. Arts Commn., Evansville, 1978; reviewer in field. One-woman shows include Wabash Valley Coll., Mt. Carmel, Ill., 1994, So. Ind. Ctr. for Arts, Seymour, Ind., 1996, Zionsville (Ind.) Muncie Art Ctr., 1997, Oakland City (Ind.) U., 1998; exhibited in group shows Liberty Gallery, Louisville, 1992, Artlink Contemporary Art Gallery, Ft. Wayne, Ind., 1994, S.E. Mo. Coun. on Arts, Cape Girardeau, 1994, Lexington (Ky.) Art League, 1996, Mills Pond Horse Gallery, St. James, N.Y., 1996, SOHO Gallery, Pensacola, Fla., 1996, Indpls. Art Ctr., 1996, Artemesia Gallery, Chgo., 1997, DelMar Coll., Corpus Christi, Tex., 1998, La. State U., Baton Rouge, 1998, Woman Made Gallery, Chgo., 2002; works appeared in various publs.; represented by Creative Art Gallery, St. Louis, the New Harmony Gallery of Contemporary Art, New Harmony, Ind. Malone fellow visitor to Morocco and Tunisia, 1996. Mem. Nat. Mus. Women in Arts, Met. Mus. Art, Evansville Mus. Arts and Sci., New Harmony Gallery of Contemporary Art, Golden Key Honor Soc. (hon.). Democrat. Mem. Unity Ch. Avocation: travel to study art works in museums and galleries in europe and mex. Home: 10801 S Woodside Dr Evansville IN 47712-8422 Office: U So Ind 8600 University Blvd Evansville IN 47712-3534 E-mail: croth@usi.edu.

ROTH, DANIEL BENJAMIN, lawyer, business executive; b. Youngstown, Ohio, Sept. 17, 1929; s. Benjamin F. and Marion (Benjamin) R.; m. Joann M. Roth; children: William M., Jennifer A., Rochelle. BS in Fin., Miami U., Oxford, Ohio, 1951; JD, Case-Western Res. U., 1956. Bar: Ohio 1956, U.S. Supreme Ct. 1960, D.C. 1983. Chmn. Roth, Blair, Roberts, Strasfeld & Lodge, LPA, Youngstown, 1969—; co-founder, vice chmn. Nat. Data Processing Corp., Cin., 1961-69; chmn., pres., CEO Torent, Inc., Youngstown, 1971—, Morrison Metalweld Process Corp., 1979—2003; vice chmn. McDonald Steel Corp., 1980—, Torent Oil & Gas Co., 1979—2002, Vaughn Indsl. Car & Equipment Co., 1988—2002. Bd. dirs. Gasser Chair Co. Profl. singer: appearances including Steve Allen Show, 1952. Bd. dirs. Youngstown Symphony, Stambaugh Auditorium; bd. dirs. Youngstown Playhouse, v.p., 1991-93; pres. Rodef Sholom Temple, Youngstown, 1982-84. 1st lt. USAF, 1951-53, lt. col. Res., ret. Recipient Mgr. of Yr. award Mahoning Valley Mgmt. Assn., 1989, Man of Yr. award Youngstown YWCA, 1995. Mem. ABA, D.C. Bar Assn., Ohio Bar Assn., Mahoning County Bar Assn., Lawyer-Pilots Bar Assn., Soc. Benchers of Case Western Res. U. Law Sch., Youngstown Club, Pelican Marsh Club (Naples, Fla.), Zeta Beta Tau (nat. v.p. 1964-66), Omicron Delta Kappa, Phi Eta Sigma, Tau Epsilon Rho. Jewish. Office: Roth Blair Roberts Strasfeld & Lodge 600 City Centre One Youngstown OH 44503-1514 Office Phone: 330-744-5211.

ROTH, DARYL, theater producer; b. NJ; m. Steven Roth, 1969; children: Amanda, Jordan. Student, NYU. Prodr., owner Daryl Roth Prodns., N.Y.C.; owner Daryl Roth Theater, 1998—, DR2 Theater, 2002—. Co-anchor PBS show N.Y. Theatre Rev.; spkr. in field; guest lectr. Columbia U., NYU, Harvard Club, Women's Art Coalition. Prodr.: (N.Y. and London prodn.) Three Tall Women (Pulitzer prize, 1994), (Broadway prodn.) Twilight. Los Angeles.1992 (Tony nomination), Camping with Henry and Tom (Outer Critics Circle award, Lucille Lortel award), Defying Gravity, (off-Broadway) Snakebit, How I Learned to Drive (Best Play of Season, 1997, Pulitzer prize, 1998), Old Wicked Songs, 1996 (Pulitzer prize finalist for drama, 1996), Wit (Pulitzer prize for Drama, 1999), Bomb-itty of Errors; (plays) Closer Then Ever, 1987—1888, Nick & Nora, 1991, Proof, 2000—03 (Tony Award for Best Play, 2001), The Tale of the Allergist's Wife, 2000—02, Bea Arthur on Broadway, 2002, The Goat, or Who is Sylvia, 2002 (Tony Award for Best Play, 2002), Medea, 2002—03, Salome, 2003, Anna in the Tropics, 2003—04, Caroline, or Change, 2004—. Established (with husband) Roth Ctr. for Jewish Life, Dartmouth U., 1997; bd. dirs. Lincoln Ctr. Theater, Sundance Inst., Albert Einstein Coll. for Med. Rsch. Named award in her honor Daryl Roth Creative Spirit award, honored (with husband) with the Louis Marshall Award, Jewish Theological Seminary. Office: Daryl Roth Prodns 152 W 57th St Fl 21 New York NY 10019

ROTH, DON, music executive; m. Mary Ellen Roth; children: Florence, Daniel. Gen. mgr. Austin (Tex.) Symphony, 1977-80; mng. dir. Hartford (Conn.) Symphony, 1980-83; exec. dir. Syracuse (N.Y.), 1983—; gen. mgr. San Francisco Symphony, 1987-90; exec. dir. Oreg. Symphony, Portland, 1990-98, pres., 1992-98; exec. dir. St. Louis Symphony Orch.; pres., CEO Aspen Music Festival, 2002—. Office: 2 Music School Rd Aspen CO 81611

ROTH, DUANE J. pharmaceutical executive; Grad., Iowa Wesleyan Coll. Chmn., CEO Alliance Pharm. Corp. Chmn. San Diego Regional Econ. Devel. Corp.; mem. bd. dir. Biotechnology Industry Org., CA Healthcare Inst. Chmn. Am. Heart Assn. Heart Walk; co-chair Children's Hosp. Found.'s Ann. Miracles Weekend. Named IFCD Dir. of Yr. for Corp. Citizenship; recipient AT & T Internat. Bus. Leadership award, San Diego Press Club's Headliner of Yr. award, Making a Difference award, San Diego Citizens Against Lawsuit Abuse, Price Waterhouse Svc. to the Biotechnology Cmty. award, James McGraw Disting. Contbn. award for svc. to San Diego biomed. industry. Office: Alliance Pharm Corp 3040 Sci Park Rd San Diego CA 92121

ROTH, EDIE COWAN, rehabilitation services professional; b. Douglasville, Ga., June 8, 1961; d. Walter Louis and Marion Diana (Hampton) Cowan. BS, Ga. State U., 1999. Color printer sales rep. For More-Meisel Corp., Atlanta, 1982—88; caseworker Dekalb Family and Children's Svcs., Decatur, Ga., 1990—96; disability adjudicator Ga. Disability Determination Sect., Stone Mountain, 1996—. Mem.: ASPCA, S.E. Cave Conservancy SCC, Dogwood City Grotto, Nat. Speleolosical Soc., Nat. Humane Soc., Golden Key, Phi Gamma Mu. Office: Disability Determination Sect PO Box 56 Stone Mountain GA 31083 E-mail: mednak2002@yahoo.com., mewnak@hotmail.com.

ROTH, ERIC, screenwriter; 6 children. Student, Columbia U., UCLA. Screenplays include: The Stranger in 7A, 1972, The Nickel Ride, 1975, The Concorde - Airport '79, 1979, Suspect, 1987, Memories of Me, 1988 (with Billy Crystal), Mr. Jones, 1993, Forrest Gump, 1994 (Acad. award Best Adapted Screenplay), the Postman, 1997, The Horse Whisperer, 1998, The Insider (nominated for Acad., Golden Globe 1999); co-writer: (with Michael Mann) Ali, 2001. Office: care CAA 9830 Wilshire Blvd Beverly Hills CA 90212-1804*

ROTH, ERIC M. lawyer; b. Bklyn., Jan. 16, 1954; BA with distinction in all subjects, Cornell U., 1974; JD, NYU, 1977. Bar: N.Y. 1978; U.S. Dist. Ct. (so., ea. dists.) N.Y. 1978, D.C. 1980; U.S. Supreme Ct. 1981; U.S. Ct. Appeals (2nd. cir.) 1984, (4th, 5th cirs.) 1985, (8th cir.) 1989, (11th cir.) 1995, (9th cir.) 1997. Law clk. to Hon. Lee P. Gagliardi U.S. Dist. Ct., 1977-79; atty. Wachtell, Lipton, Rosen & Katz, N.Y.C. Chmn. bd. dirs. MFY Legal Svcs., Inc. Note and comment editor: NYU Law Review, 1976-77. Mem. ABA, N.Y. State Bar Assn., The D.C. Bar, Fed. Bar Coun., NYU Law Alumni Assn. Inc. (former mem. bd. dirs). Office: Wachtell Lipton Rosen & Katz 51 W 52nd St Fl 29 New York NY 10019-6150

ROTH, GARY NEAL, accountant; b. Santa Monica, Calif., Nov. 30, 1961; s. Lewis David and Beverly Sue (Steel) R.; m. Tiffany Anne Lachtman, Aug. 8, 1998; children: Brandon Steel and Collin Benjamin (twins), Parker Immanuel. BS in Bus. Adminstrn., Calif. State U., Northridge, 1983. CPA, Calif.; cert. tax profl. Clk., field rep. Equifax Svcs., Inc., Santa Monica, Calif., 1979-86; acctg. mgr., contr. OneCard Systems Corp., L.A., 1983-88; sr. tax acct., auditor Pannell Kerr Forster, CPAs, L.A., 1989-91; sr. acct., auditor Getz, Krycler & Jakubovits, CPAs, Sherman Oaks, Calif., 1992-96; sr. acct. London & Co LLP, CPAs, L.A., 1996—. Cons. U.S. Resolution Trust Corp., Denver, 1991. Auditor Stop Cancer, L.A., 1992-96; acct. Fair-Taste of L.A., Santa Monica, Calif., 1989-90; venue acct. L.A. Summer Olympics, 1984; tax preparer Vol. Income Tax Assn., L.A., 1983. Mem. AICPA, Calif. Soc. CPAs, Nat. Soc. Tax Profls., Zeta Beta Tau. Avocations: exercise enthusiast, musician, international traveler. Home: 10464 Lorenzo Pl Cheviot Hills CA 90064 Office: London & Co LLP CPAs 11601 Wilshire Blvd #2040 Los Angeles CA 90025

ROTH, GEORGE STANLEY, biochemist, researcher, physiologist; b. Honolulu, Aug. 5, 1946; s. George Frederick and Laura Ann (Zembrzuski) Roth; m. Mary Jane Fletcher, Mar. 11, 1972; children: Susan Marie, George William. BS, Villanova U., 1968; PhD, Temple U., 1971. Fellow Fels Rsch. Inst., Phila., 1971-72; staff fellow Gerontology Rsch. Ctr. NIH, Balt., 1972-76, rsch. chemist, 1976—, chief molecular physiology and genetics sect., 1984-99, sr. guest scientist, 2000—; pres., CEO Gerotech Inc., 2000—; exec. dir. Am. Aging Assn., 2002—03. Vis. prof. Mehary Med. Coll., Nashville, 1983; Alpha Omega Alpha prof. U. P.R. Med. Sch., San Juan, 1986; chmn. Gordon Rsch. Conf. Biology of Aging, Oxnard, Calif., 1985; rsch. cons. George Washington U., 1977—82; Ben Cohen Meml. lectr. U. Mich., 1998; lectr. Med. Sci. Ctr. Student Sci. program, 1980; Sandoz lectr. gerontology, Basel, Switzerland, 84, Basel, 86, Basel, 94. Contbr. articles to profl. jours.; editor: Exptl. Gerontology, Exptl. Aging Rsch., Proc. Soc.Exptl. Biology and Medicine; co-editor: Chem. Rubber Co. Press Series in Aging, 1981—; mem. editl. bd. Ency. of Aging, 1987—. Co-dir. Ea. Harford County Civic Assn., Bel Air, 1981—88; v.p. Cmty. Coalition Harford County, Bel Air, Md., 1988—90, bd. dirs., 1990—92. Recipient Rsch. award, Am. Aging Assn., 1981, prize for gerontol. rsch., Sandoz Ltd., 1989, Third Age award, Internat. Assn. Gerontology, 1989, Spl. award, Balt. Longitudinal Study Aging, 1991, Equal Opportunity award, NIH, 1995, Merit award, 1996; Sigma Chi scholar, Miami U., Oxford, Ohio, 1989. Fellow: Gerontol. Soc. Am. (chair biol. scis. sect. 1975—76, chair rsch. com. 1978—79, chmn. fellowship com. 1986—87); mem.: Soc. Exptl. Biology and Medicine. Republican. Roman Catholic. Avocations: basketball, fishing, hiking, canoeing. Office: Gerontology Rsch Ctr Nat Inst on Aging 5600 Nathan Shock Dr Baltimore MD 21224-6825

ROTH, GEORGIA MIDDLEBROOKS, accounting educator; d. Melvin Todd and Dorothy Baxter Middlebrooks; m. Charles Nelson Roth, Aug. 16, 1958; children: Stuart Todd, Douglas Spicer, Charles Rankine. BSBA cum laude, U. Ark., 1959, MBA, 1962; postgrad., Tenn. State U. Mem. staff Hancock Mazo & Co., Savannah, Ga., 1959—60; tchr. acctg. Centenary Coll., Shreveport, 1962—65, Union U., Jackson, Tenn., 1965—69, Lambuth U., Jackson, 1969—71; assoc. prof. acctg. Jackson State C.C., 1974—. Chmn. faculty coun. Jackson State C.C., 1985—86, commencement spkr., 1989, chmn. bus. dept., 1990—93; advisor Students in Free Enterprise, Jackson, 1998—99; cert. prof. secs. rev. instr., 1979—99; coll. orientation instr., 1989—99; faculty mem. rep. Tenn. State Bd. Regents, 1985—86. Author: (poem) Lives Changed Forever, 2002. Pres. Jackson Newcomers Club, 1966; mem. Jackson Cotillion Club, 1967—69, Jackson Svc. League, 1972—74; debutante ball chair Jackson Symphony League, 1971, 1985. Sam Walton Free Enterprise fellow, 1998—99. Mem.: Tchrs. of Acctg. in 2-Yr. Colls. (conf. presenter), Zeta Tau Alpha, Beta Gamma Sigma. Methodist. Avocations: tennis, bridge, poetry, growing roses, genealogy. Home: 58 Stonehaven Dr Jackson TN 38305 Office: Jackson State CC 2046 N Parkway Jackson TN 38301 Office Phone: 731-424-3520. E-mail: georgiaroth@bellsouth.net.

ROTH, HAROLD, architect; b. St. Louis, June 30, 1934; s. Samuel and Dorothy (Yawitz) R.; m. Dvora Feigon, Dec. 6, 1959; children: Elizabeth, David. AB, Washington U., 1956; MArch, Yale U., 1957. Designer Warner Burns Toan & Lunde, N.Y.C., 1957; sr. designer Eero Saarinen & Assocs., Roche Dinkeloo & Assocs., Hamden, Conn., 1959-65; ptnr. Harold Roth—Edward Saad, Hamden, Conn., 1965-72; sr. ptnr. Roth & Moore Architects, New Haven, 1973—; critic archtl. design Yale U. Sch. Architecture, New Haven, 1964-98. Pres., trustee Perspecta, Yale Archtl. Jour. Trustee Long Wharf Theatre, New Haven, 1972-98, Conn. Trust for Hist. Preservation, 1983-90; pres. bd. trustees Conn. Architecture Found., 1990-93; bd. govs. Bldg. Stone Inst., 1999-2003; bd. regents Am. Arch. Found., 1999-2001; profl. advisor Western European Architecture Found., 2000—. Officer U.S. Army, 1957-59, Korea. Recipient Design award Nat. Coun. Religious Arch., 1970, 96, Design award New Haven Preservation Trust, 1978, 88, Tucker award Bldg. Stone Inst., 1983, 88, Honor award Concrete Reinforcing Steel Inst., 1983, Design award Portland Cement Assn., 1984, Design award Archtl. Record, 1970, 80, Design award AIA/ALA, 1983, Faculty Design award Assn. Collegiate Schs. of Arch., 1988, Healthcare Facilities Design award Boston Soc. Archs., 1992; fellow Pierson Coll., Yale U., 1978—. Fellow: AIA (chmn. nat. com. on design 1990, bd. dirs. 1992—94, sec. Coll. of Fellows 1998—99, vice-chancellor 2000, chancellor 2001, Design award Conn. 1974, 1978, 1983, 1986, 1988, 1990, 1993, 1997, 1998, Design award New Eng. 1968, 1984, 1992, 2001, N.Y. State Design award of merit 2000). Home: 37 Autumn St New Haven CT 06511-2220 Office: Roth and Moore Architects 65 Audubon St New Haven CT 06510-1205 Office Phone: 203-787-1166. E-mail: hroth@rothandmoore.com.

ROTH, HARVEY PAUL, publishing executive; b. N.Y.C., Feb. 20, 1933; s. Lewis Theodore and Harriet (Wallow) R.; m. Tanya Cohen; children by previous marriage: Andrea Warriner, Matthew Jay; stepchildren: Laura Meryl Becker, Matthew Robert Turetzky. AB, Bklyn. Coll., 1954; LL.B., N.Y. U., 1957. Bar: N.Y. bar 1959. Editor West Pub. Co., N.Y.C., 1959-61; pres. BFL Communications, Inc., Plainview, N.Y., 1961-76, Roth Pub., Inc., Great Neck,

N.Y., 1976—; chmn. Alcove Press, London, 1970-75, Nash Pub. Corp., Los Angeles, 1971-75. Served with U.S. Army, 1957-58. Office: Roth Pub Inc 175 Great Neck Rd Great Neck NY 11021-3313 E-mail: hroth@rothpublishinginc.com.

ROTH, JAMES FRANK, manufacturing company executive, chemist; b. Rahway, N.J., Dec. 7, 1925; s. Louis and Eleanor R.; m. Sharon E. Mattes, June 20, 1969; children by previous marriage: Lawrence, Edward, Sandra. BA in Chemistry, U. W.Va., 1947; PhD in Phys. Chemistry, U. Md., 1951. Research chemist Franklin Inst., Phila., 1951-53, mgr. chemistry lab., 1958-60; chief chemist Lehigh Paints & Chems. Co., Allentown, Pa., 1953-55; research chemist GAF Corp., Easton, Pa., 1955-58; with Monsanto Co., St. Louis, 1960-80, dir. catalysis research, 1973-77, dir. process sci. research, 1977-80; corp. chief scientist Air Products and Chems., Inc., Allentown, 1980-91; indsl. cons., 1991—. Contbr. articles to profl. jours.; mem. editl. bd. Jour. Catalysis, 1976-85, Catalysis Revs., 1973-93, Applied Catalysis, 1981-85; editor for Ams., 1985-88, assoc. editor, 1988-95. With USN, 1943-46. Recipient Richard J. Kokes award Johns Hopkins U., 1977, Chem. Pioneer award Am. Inst. Chemists, 1986, Perkin medal Soc. Chem. Industry, 1988. Mem. NAE, Am. Chem. Soc. (St. Louis sect. St. Louis award 1975, E.V. Murphree nat. award 1976, Indsl. Chemistry award 1991), Catalysis Soc. N.Am. (E.J. Houdry award 1991), Catalysis Club of Phila. (award 1981). Inventor process biodegradable detergents, for acetic acid; U.S., fgn. patents in field. Home: 5440 Eagles Point Cir Apt 205 Sarasota FL 34231-9171

ROTH, JANE RICHARDS, federal judge; b. Philadelphia, Pa., June 16, 1935; d. Robert Henry Jr. and Harriett (Kellond) Richards; m. William V. Roth Jr., Oct. 9, 1965; children: William V. III, Katharine K. BA, Smith Coll., 1956; LLB, Harvard U., 1965; LLD (hon.), Widener U., 1986, U. Del., 1994. Bar: Del. 1965, U.S. Dist. Ct. Del. 1966, U.S. Ct. Appeals (3d cir.) 1974. Adminstrv. asst. various fgn. service posts U.S. State Dept., 1956-62; assoc. Richards, Layton & Finger, Wilmington, Del., 1965-73, ptnr., 1973-85; judge U.S. Dist. Ct. Del., Wilmington, 1985-91, U.S. Ct. Appeals (3d cir.), Wilmington, 1991—. Adj. faculty Villanova U. Sch. Law. Hon. chmn. Del. chpt. Arthritis Found., Wilmington; bd. overseers Widener U. Sch. Law; bd. consultors Villanova U. Sch. Law; trustee Hist. Soc. Del. Recipient Nat. Vol. Service citation Athritis Found., 1982. Fellow Am. Bar Found.; mem. ABA, Fed. Judges Assn., Del. State Bar Assn. Republican. Episcopalian. Office: US Court of Appeals 3rd Circuit 844 King St Lock Box 12 Wilmington DE 19801-1790*

ROTH, JEFFREY JOSEPH, plastic surgeon; b. L.A., Dec. 28, 1965; s. Marvin and Carol Ann (Shapiro) R. BA, Brandeis U., 1988; MD, U. Nev., 1992. MD Calif., Nev., Pa., diplomate Nat. Bd. Med. Examiners, Am. Bd. of Surgery. Intern in surgery Med. Coll. of Pa., Phila., 1992-93; resident in surgery Med. Coll. of Pa. and Hahnemann U., Phila., 1993-95, resident in surg. rsch., 1995-97, sr. surg. resident, 1997-98, chief surg. resident, 1998-99; resident in plastic and reconstructive surgery U. Calif., San Francisco, 1999—2001; fellow in microsurgery and hand/microsurgery U. So. Calif., Calif., 2001—02. Contbr. articles to profl. jours., book chpts. Fellow ACS (assoc.); mem. AMA (pres. med. students sect. Nev. 1989-90), AAAS, Nev. State Med. Assn. (pres. med. student sect. 1989-90), Am. Fedn. Clin. Rsch., Mensa. Office: 299 N Pecos Rd Henderson NV 89074

ROTH, JOE, motion picture company executive; b. N.Y.C., June 13, 1948; BA, Boston U. Prodn. assistant various commls. and feature films, San Francisco; also lighting dir. Pitchel Players, San Francisco, then producer L.A.; co-founder Morgan Creek Prodns., L.A., 1987-89; chmn. 20th Century Fox Film Corp., L.A., 1989-92; founder Caravan Pictures, L.A., 1992-94; chmn. Walt Disney Motion Pictures Group, Burbank, 1994-97, Walt Disney Studios, Burbank, 1997-2000; founder Revolution Pictures, 2000—. Bd. dirs. Pixar Studios, 2000—. Prodr. (films) Tunnel Vision, 1976, Our Winning Season, 1978, Americathon, 1979, Ladies and Gentlemen, the Fabulous Stains, 1981, Final Terror, 1983, The Stone Boy, 1984, Moving Violations, 1985, Off Beat, 1986, Where the River Runs Black, 1986, Streets of Gold, 1986, P.K. and the Kid, 1987, Young Guns, 1988, Skin Deep, 1989, Major League, 1989, Nightbreed, 1990, The Three Musketeers, 1993, Angels in the Outfield, 1994, Low Down Dirty Shame, 1994, Houseguest, 1995, The Jerky Boys, 1995, Heavyweights, 1995, Tall Tale, 1995, While You Were Sleeping, 1995, The Forgotten, 2004; exec. prodr. (films) Cracking Up, 1977, Bachelor Party, 1984, Revenge of the Nerds II: Nerds in Paradise, 1987, Dead Ringers, 1988, Renegades, 1989, Enemies: A Love Story, 1989, The Exorcist III, 1990, Pacific Heights, 1990, Angie, 1994, Before and After, 1996, Tears of the Sun, 2003, Daddy Day Care, 2003, Hollywood Homicide, 2003, Mona Lisa Smile, 2003. Office: Revolution Pictures Inc 14024 Tyler St Sylmar CA 91342*

ROTH, J(OHN) REECE, electrical engineer, educator, researcher, inventor; b. Washington, Pa., Sept. 19, 1937; s. John Meyer and Ruth Evangeline (Iams) R.; m. Helen Marie DeCrane, Jan. 14, 1972; children: Nancy Ann, John Alexander. S.B. in Physics, MIT, 1959; PhD, Cornell U., 1963. Engring. aide Aerojet-Gen. Corp., Azusa, Calif., 1957, 58; aerospace engr. N.Am. Aviation, Canoga Park, Calif., 1959; prin. investigator NASA Lewis Rsch. Ctr., Cleve., 1963-78; prof. elec. engring. U. Tenn., Knoxville, 1999—2002; hon. prof. U. Electronic Sci. and Tech. of China, Chengdu, 1992—; prin. investigator Office Naval Rsch., Washington, 1980-89, Air Force Office Sci. Rsch., Washington, 1981—95, 2001—03, Army Rsch. Office, 1988-93, NASA Langley Rsch. Ctr., Hampton, Va., 1995—98, 2001—03, March Instruments, Inc., Concord, Calif., 1996-98, NSF, 2002—03; prof. elec. engring. U. Tenn., Knoxville, 1978—. Cons. TVA, Chattanooga, 1982-84, BDM Corp., 1987-88, Tenn. Eastman, 1989-90, March Instruments, 1995-98; Procter & Gamble, 1996, 2000; Internat. Eco Scis., 1997-98; Environ. Elements Corp., 1997-2000, Tetra Pak Suisse, 1998-2000, Atmospheric Glow Techs., Inc., 1999—; mem. NAS-NRC Com. on Aneutronic Fusion, 1986-87; spkr. at profl. meetings. Author: Industrial Plasma Engineering, Introduction to Fusion Energy; contbr. articles to profl. jours. Sloan scholar, 1955-59; Ford fellow, 1961-62; recipient B. Otto and Katherine Wheeley award for Excellence in Tech. Transfer, 1999. Fellow IEEE, AIAA (assoc.); mem. Am. Phys. Soc., Am. Nuc. Soc. (exec. com. No. Ohio sect. 1975-78), Nuc. and Plasma Scis. Soc., Am. Soc. Engring. Edn., Knoxville Mus. Art, East Tenn. Soc. of Archaeol. Inst. Am., Sigma Xi (pres. U. Tenn. Knoxville chpt. 1985-86). Clubs: U. Tenn. U. Club (Knoxville). Achievements include 11 US patents. Home: 12359 N Fox Den Dr Knoxville TN 37922-3755 Office: U Tenn Dept Elec Computer Engring 409 Ferris Hall Knoxville TN 37996-2100 Office Phone: 865-974-4446. Business E-mail: jrr@utk.edu.

ROTH, JOHN ROGER, geneticist, biology educator; b. Winona, Minn., Mar. 14, 1939; s. Frederick Daniel and Louise Mae (Wirt) R.; m. Uta Goetz (div.); children: Katherine Louise, Frederick Phillip; m. Sherylynne Harris, Jan. 4, 1986. BA, Harvard U., 1961; PhD, John Hopkins U., 1965. From asst. prof. molecular biology to prof. molecular biology U. Calif., Berkeley, 1967-76; prof. biology U. Utah, Salt Lake City, 1976—2002; prof. sect. microbiology U. Calif., Davis, 2002—, chair sect. microbiology, 2003—. Recipient Disting. Prof. award, 1990, Rosenblatt award, 1990. Mem. NAS, Am. Soc. for Microbiology, Genetics Soc. Am. Office: Univ Calif Microbiology 314 Briggs Hall One Shields Ave Davis CA 95616

ROTH, JOSHUA S. obstetrician/gynecologist, educator; b. N.Y.C., 1940; s. Joseph D. and Gertrude (Sattinger) R.; m. Isadora Roth, Dec. 22, 1962; children: Andrew, Eric. AB, Princeton U., 1962; MD, SUNY Downstate, 1967. Diplomate Am. Bd. Ob-Gyn. Intern, resident ob-gyn L.I. Jewish Med. Ctr., N.Y.C., 1967-71, attending physician, 1971—, pres. med. staff, 1986-87; ob-gyn Bayside, N.Y., 1971—. Clin. asst. prof. Albert Einstein Coll. Medicine; chief ob-gyn Lyster Army Hosp., Ft. Rucker, Ala., 1972-73. Maj. USMC, 1971-73. Fellow: ACS, Queens Gynecol. Soc., Am. Coll. Ob-Gyn.; mem.: Queens County Med. Soc., N.Y. State Med. Soc. Office: 223-01 Union Tpke Bayside NY 11364-3644

ROTH, JUDITH SHULMAN, lawyer; b. N.Y.C., Apr. 25, 1952; d. Mark Alan and Margaret Ann (Podell) Shulman; m. William Hartley Roth, May 30, 1976; children: Andrew Henry, Caroline Shulman. AB, Cornell U., 1974; JD, Columbia U., 1977. Bar: N.Y. 1978, U.S. Dist. Ct. (ea. dist.) N.Y. 1978, U.S. Dist. Ct. (so. dist.) N.Y. 1978, U.S. Ct. Appeals (2d cir.) 1993. Assoc. Phillips Nizer Benjamin Krim & Ballon, N.Y.C., 1978-87, ptnr., 1988—. Lectr. CLE Fordham Law Sch., N.Y.C., 1990. Mem. Cosmopolitan Club. Jewish. Avocations: reading, tennis, golf, art, gardening. Office: Phillips Nizer Benjamin Krim & Ballon 666 5th Ave New York NY 10103-0001 Office Phone: 212-977-9700. Home Fax: 212-535-3617. E-mail: jroth@phillipsnizer.com.

ROTH, KENNETH, human rights advocate; b. Elmhurst, Ill., Sept. 23, 1955; s. Walter and Muriel (Teitell) R.; m. Nina Brodsky, May 29, 1983; children: Lisa, Emma. BA magna cum laude, Brown U., 1977; JD, Yale U., 1980. Bar: N.Y. 1981. Law clk. to Judge Edward Weinfeld U.S. Dist. Ct. for So. Dist. N.Y., N.Y.C., 1980-81; assoc. Paul, Weiss, Rifkind, Wharton & Garrison, N.Y.C., 1981-83; from asst. U.S. atty. to chief appellate atty. criminal div. U.S. Atty.'s Office for So. Dist. N.Y., N.Y.C., 1983-87; assoc. counsel Office Ind. Counsel for Iran/Contra, Washington, 1987; dep. dir. Human Rights Watch, N.Y.C., 1987-93, exec. dir., 1993—. Editor, author numerous reports on human rights worldwide; contbr. articles to newspapers and mags. Mem. Assn. Bar City N.Y., Coun. Fgn. Rels. Office: Human Rights Watch 350 5th Ave Fl 34 New York NY 10118-3499

ROTH, LANE, communications educator; b. N.Y.C., Apr. 10; BA with nat. honors in German, NYU; MA, Fla. State U., 1974, PhD in Mass Comm., 1976. Camera operator Sta. WFSU-TV, Tallahassee, 1973-74; broadcast engr., producer-creator, writer, performer Sta. WFSU-FM, Tallahassee, 1974-76; co-host Sta. WNIN-TV, Evansville, Ind., 1976-77; asst. prof. radio-TV-film U. Evansville, 1976-78; asst. prof. comm. Lamar U., Beaumont, Tex., 1978-82, assoc. prof., 1982—. Bd. dirs. Mental Health Assn. of Jefferson County, pres., 1997, 98; writer, performer fund-raising promos, Sta. KVLU-FM, Beaumont, 1995—. Author: Film Semiotics, Metz, and Leone's Trilogy, 1983; contbr. articles to profl. mags., jours.; contbr. to acad. books. Bd. dirs. Mental Health Assoc. of Jefferson Co., 1993—. Recipient Regents Merit award for excellence in tchg., 1980, Mental Health Assn. award for dedicated leadership, 1999. Mem. Internat. Assn. for the Fantastic in the Arts, Popular Culture Assn. Roman Catholic. Avocations: Jungian psychology, analysis of popular film and tv, singer-impressionist-songwriter. Office: Lamar U Dept Communications Beaumont TX 77710

ROTH, LAWRENCE MAX, pathologist, educator; b. McAlester, Okla., June 25, 1936; s. Herman Moe and Blanche (Brown) R.; m. Anna Berit Katarina Sundstrom, Apr. 3, 1965; children— Karen Esther, David Josef BA, Vanderbilt U., 1957; MD, Harvard U., 1960. Diplomate Am. Bd. Pathology. Rotating intern U. Ill. Research and Ednl. Hosps., Chgo., 1960—61; resident in anat. pathology Washington U. Sch. Medicine, St. Louis, 1961—64; resident in clin. pathology U. Calif. Med. Ctr., San Francisco, 1967—68; asst. prof. pathology Tulane U. Sch. Medicine, New Orleans, 1968—71; assoc. prof. pathology Ind. U. Sch. Medicine, Indpls., 1971—75, prof., 1975—2002, prof. emeritus pathology, 2002—, dir. divsn. surg. pathology. Series editor: Contemporary Issues in Surgical Pathology; mem. editl. bd. Am. Jour. Surg. Pathology, Human Pathology, Seminars in Diagnostic Pathology, Internat. Jour. Gynecol. Pathology, Endocrine Pathology; contbr. articles to med. jours. Served to capt. U.S. Army, 1965-67 Mem. Am. Assn. Investigative Pathologists, U.S. and Can. Acad. Pathology, Am. Soc. Clin. Pathologists, Coll. Am. Pathologists, Internat. Soc. Gynecol. Pathologists, Arthur Purdy Stout Soc. Surg. Pathologists, Assn. Dirs. Anatomic and Surg. Pathology. Home: 7898 Ridge Rd Indianapolis IN 46240-2538 Office: 550 University Blvd Indianapolis IN 46202-5149 E-mail: lroth@iupui.edu.

ROTH, LOREN H. psychiatrist; b. May 9, 1939; m. Ellen A. Roth; children: Jonathan, Alexandra, Elizabeth. BA in Philosophy, Cornell U., 1961; MD cum laude, Harvard U., 1966, MPH, 1972; postgrad., Am. U., 1972-73. Diplomate Am. Bd. Psychiatry and Neurology; lic. physician, Conn., Md., Mass., Pa. Med. intern Univ. Hosps., Western Res. U., Cleve., 1966-67; resident psychiatry Yale U., New Haven, 1969-70, Mass. Gen. Hosp., Boston, 1970-72; staff psychiatrist Ctr. for Studies Crime and Delinquency, NIMH, Rockville, Md., 1972-74; co-dir., dir. law and psychiatry program Western Psychiat. Inst. and Clinic/U. Pitts., 1974—, chief adult clin. svcs., 1983-87, 88-89, chief clin. svcs., 1989-95, co-dir., dir. law and psychiatry program, 1974-94; vice-chmn. dept. psychiatry U. Pitts., 1988-97, asst. prof., 1974-78, assoc. prof., 1978-82, prof., 1982—; v.p. for Managed Care U. Pitt. Med. Ctr., 1993-97; assoc. vice chancellor for edn., health scis. U. Pitts. Sch. Medicine, 1995-97; assoc. sr. vice chancellor health scis. U. Pitts., 1997—; sr. v.p., quality care UPMC Health Sys., 2003—, chief med. officer, 1997—2003. Med. staff Presbyn.-Univ. Hosp., Pitts., 1983—; gen. med. officer Fed. Penitentiary, Lewisburg, Pa., 1967-69; William E. Schumacher disting. lectr. Maine Dept. Mental Health and Mental Retardation, Portland, 1982; mem. commn. on mentally disabled ABA, Washington, 1987; cons. law and psychiatry Dept. Welfare, Commonwealth Pa., 1974; cons. reviewer, site visitor crime and delinquency sect. NIMH, 1977; examiner Am. Bd. Psychiatry and Neurology, 1985. Author: (with others) Informed Consent: A Study of Decisionmaking in Psychiatry, 1984; editor: (with others) Psychiatry, Social, Epidemiologic and Legal Psychiatry, Vol. 5, 1986; contbr. articles to profl. jours., chpts. to books; editorial bd. Criminology, 1974-78, Law and Human Behavior, 1980-85, Internat. Jour. Law and Psychiatry, 1980-88, Behavioral Scis. and the Law, 1987-95; assoc. editor Am. Jour. Psychiatry, 1982-90; cons. editor Criminal Justice and Behavior, 1982-85. Lt. comrd. USPHS Res., 1967—. Recipient Steve Allen award United Mental Health, Inc., 1990; grantee NIMH, 1979, 80-81, 89, Founds. Fund for Rsch. in Psychiatry, 1980-82. Fellow Am. Psychiat. Assn. (Isaac Ray award 1988), Am. Coll. Utilization Rev. Physicians, Am. Coll. Psychiatrists; mem. AMA, Am. Acad. Psychiatry and Law (pres. 1983-84), Group for Advancement Psychiatry (com. on psychiatry and law 1979-80, chmn. 1981-84), Am. Soc. Criminology, Am. Soc. Law and Medicine (bd. dirs. 1982-85), Internat. Acad. Law and Mental Health (bd. dirs.), Am. Psychopath. Assn., Phi Beta Kappa, Phi Kappa Phi. Home: 6820 Edgerton Ave Pittsburgh PA 15208-2803 Office: U Pitts Med Ctr Forbes TWR 200 Lothrop St Ste 11016 Pittsburgh PA 15213-2546 Office Phone: 412-647-4860.

ROTH, MARILYN DOROTHY, information scientist; b. Camden, N.J., Feb. 22, 1948; d. Robert Miller and Hattie May (Richards) Graeff; m. Walter Henry Roth, Apr. 28, 1973 (div. Aug. 1993); children: Walter Robert, Kara Suzanne. Libr. asst. Phila. Elec. Co., 1966-74, 82-90; coord. law libr. PECO Energy Co., Phila., 1990-99; regional offices libr. mgr. Duane Morris Heckscher LLP, Phila., 1999—2001; database support rep. Access PA, Health Sci. Libr. Consortium, Phila., 2001—. Mem. Spl. Libr. Assn., Greater Phila. Law Libr. Assn. (bd. dirs. at large 1995-97, chmn. corp. spl. interest sect. 1997-99, membership com.), Am. Assn. Law Librs. Office: Health Sci Libr Consortium 3600 Market St Philadelphia PA 19104

ROTH, MARJORY JOAN JARBOE, special education educator; b. Ranger, Tex., May 24, 1934; d. James Aloysius and Dorothy Knight (Taggart) Jarboe; m. Thomas Mosser Roth, Jr., Dec. 22, 1959; children: Thomas Mosser III, James Jarboe. BA in English, Rice U., 1957; MEd in Ednl. Adminstrn., U. N.C., Greensboro, 1981. Cert. tchr.-specific learning disabilities, middle grades lang. arts and social studies, intermediate grades, adminstr.-prin., N.C. Tchr. 4th grade Houston Ind. Sch. Dist., 1957-60; specific lang. disabilities instr. Forsyth Tech. C.C., Winston-Salem, N.C., 1976-77; specific learning disabilities tchr. Forsyth Country Day Sch., Winston-Salem, 1977-80; tchr. 5th grade Winston-Salem/Forsyth County Schs., 1982-83, specific learning disabilities tchr. Mt. Tabor High Sch., 1983-86; part time instr. English and Learning Disabilities Forsyth Tech. C.C., 1986-90; founding pres., prin. Greenhills Sch., Winston-Salem, 1990—. Co-author, co-editor booklets. Sunday Sch. dir., tchr. Galloway Meml. Episcopal Ch., 1960-70, pres., treas., sec. Churchwomen, 1963-74; treas. Elkin Jr. Woman's Club, 1962; chmn. Elkin Heart Fund Drive, 1968; bd. dirs. Hugh Chatham Hosp. Auxillary, 1968, Friends of the Elkin Pub. Libr., 1968-74, chmn., 1970-72, chmn., exhibits chmn. summer reading program; pres. South Surry Heart Assn., 1969; mem. Churchwomen of St. Paul's Episcopal Ch., Winston-Salem, 1982—, Fiddle and Bow Folk Music Soc., Winston-Salem, 1992—. Recipient June Lyday Orton award for outstanding svc. in the field of dyslexia, 1997; Forsyth fellow NEH, 1985; grantee in field. Fellow Acad. Orton-Gillingham Practitioners and Educators; mem. ASCD, Children with Attention Deficit Disorder (profl. adv. bd. N.C. Triad chpt. 1990-96), Learning Disability Assn. N.C. (sec., bd. dirs. 1981-86), Internat. Dyslexia Assn. (sec., bd. dirs. Carolinas br. 1981-85, founding pres. N.C. br. 1987-91, bd. dirs. 1987-96, nat. nominating com. 1992-94), Internat. Multisensory Structured Lang. Edn. Coun., Inc. (bd.dirs. 2000-03, mem. coun. 1993—). Republican. Avocations: tennis, hiking, folk music. Home: 940 Fox Hall Dr Winston Salem NC 27106-4431 Office: Greenhills Sch 1360 Lyndale Dr Winston Salem NC 27106-9739

ROTH, MICHAEL, lawyer; b. N.Y.C., July 22, 1931; s. Philip Arthur and Mollie (Breitenbach) R.; m. Jeanny Macoir, Nov. 24, 1957; 3 children BA, Yale Coll., 1953; JD, Columbia U., 1956, M. Internat. Affairs, 1964. Bar: N.Y. 1956. Law assoc. Stroock & Stroock & Lavan, N.Y.C., 1956-63; ptnr. Roth, Carlson, Kwit & Spengler, N.Y.C., 1964-74; chmn. N.Y. State Liquor Authority, N.Y.C., 1974-77; ptnr. Shea & Gould, N.Y.C., 1979-89; of counsel Katten, Muchin, Zavis, Rosenman, N.Y.C., 1989—. Mem. U.S. del. to UN Population Commn., 1969; Rep.-Conservative candidate for N.Y. State atty. gen., 1978; mem. Pres.' Task Force on Internat. Pvt. Enterprise, 1983-84, Pres.' Commn. on Mgmt. AID Programs, 1991-92. Mem. Sunningdale Country Club (Scarsdale, N.Y.). Republican.

ROTH, MICHAEL I. lawyer, corporate financial executive; b. Bklyn., Nov. 22, 1945; s. Harry A. and Sally (Kutin) R.; m. Carole A. Snofsky, Aug. 10, 1968; children— Barrie, Marc, Andrew BS, CCNY, 1967; JD, Boston U., 1971; LL.M., NYU, 1973. Bar: N.Y. 1971. CPA: N.Y. 1973, Conn. 1973. With Coopers & Lybrand, N.Y.C., 1969-76; ptnr. Stamford, Conn., 1976-82; exec. v.p. corp. fin., tax and adminstrn. Primerica Corp. (formerly Am. Can Co.), Greenwich, Conn., 1982-87, exec. v.p., 1987, chief fin. officer, 1987-88; exec. v.p., chief fin. officer MONY Fin. Svcs., N.Y.C., 1989-91; pres., COO, MONY-Mut. Ins. Co., N.Y.C., 1991-94, also bd. dirs., chmn. bd. dirs., CEO, 1994—. Bd. dirs. Mut. of N.Y. Bd. dirs. Child Guidance Ctr., Stamford, 1984-85; trustee Temple BethEl, Stamford, 1984-85 Mem. Am. Inst. CPA's, Conn. Soc. CPA's, Stamford Tax Assn. (pres. 1981-82) Office: The Mutual Life Insurance Company of NY (MONY) 1740 Broadway New York NY 10019-4315

ROTH, MICHAEL STEWART, obstetrician-gynecologist; b. Phila., Oct. 27, 1946; s. William Lester and Sara (Freund) R.; m. Bonnie Abrams, Aug. 29, 1971 (div. Feb. 1992); children: Cheryl, Deborah, Howard; m. Adrienne Lee Kahn, Oct. 30, 1993; 1 child, Alexa. BS in Biology, Albright Coll., 1968; MD, Jefferson Med. Coll., 1972. Diplomate Am. Bd. Ob-Gyn. Intern Temple Hosp., Phila., 1972-73, resident in ob-gyn., 1973-76; fellowship in reproductive endocrinology U. Miami/Jackson Meml. Hosp., 1976-78; hosp. staff mem. Pkwy. Regional Med. Ctr., North Miami Beach, Fla.; clin. asst. prof. U. Miami. Fellow: Am. Coll. Ob-Gyn. (mem. vol. rev. quality care divsn. quality care); mem.: Fla. Endocrine Soc., Miami Ob-Gyn. Soc. (pres. 1998—99), Fla. Ob-Gyn. Soc., Am. Soc. Reproductive Medicine. Office: PO Box 630305 Miami FL 33163-0503

ROTH, OLIVER RALPH, radiologist; b. Culberland, Md., Nov. 30, 1921; s. DeCoursey Andrew and Mabel (Lathrum) R.; m. Virginia McBride, June 2, 1943; 1 child, Tiija. BS, Frostburg State U., 1942; MD, U. Md., 1950; DSc (hon.), Frostburg State U., 1980. Diplomate Am. Bd. Radiology. Resident Johns Hopkins Hosp., Balt., 1954-57; cancer rsch. fellow Middlesex Hosp., London, 1957-58; founder dept. radiation oncology Presbyn. Hosp., Charlotte, N.C., 1958-62; attending radiologist King's Daus. Hosp., Ashland, Ky., 1962-80; radiologist Our Lady of Bellefonte Hosp., Ashland, Ky., 1981-86; mem. faculty Sch. of Allied Health Shawnee State U., Portsmouth, Ohio, 1986-90; prof. radiology Sch. Medicine Marshall U., Huntington, W.Va., 1990—2001, Pikeville Coll. Sch. of Osteo. Medicine, 2000—; cons. in radiology VA Med. Ctr., Huntington, 2001—. Mem. adv. com. Ky. Cancer Commn., 1978. Book reviewer Radiology, 1954-55. Bd. dirs. Boyd County chpt. Am. Cancer Soc., 1978. With USN, 1942-45. Commanded to Buckingham Palace, June 17, 1958; recipient Disting. Alumni award Frostburg State U., 1979. Mem. AMA, Am. Coll. Radiology, Radiol. Soc. N. Am., Am. Radium Soc., Royal Faculty Radiology, Brit. Inst. Radiology, Shriners (Cumberland, Md. chpt.). Democrat. Lutheran. Home: 2912 Cogan St Ashland KY 41102-5230 Office Phone: 304-429-6741. Personal E-mail: tiijaranta@aol.com.

ROTH, PAUL BARRY, dean, educator, emergency medicine physician; b. Glen Ridge, N.J., Oct. 7, 1947; s. Jerome M. and Selma (Leitner) R. BS, Fairleigh Dickinson U., 1969, MS, 1972; MD, George Washington U., 1976; postgrad., U. N.Mex., Albuquerque, 1976-79. Resident in family practice U. N.Mex. Sch. Medicine, Albuquerque, 1976—79; owner, pres. EMS of N.Mex., Albuquerque, 1978-82; owner, mem. of bd. Heights Urgent Care Ctr., Albuquerque, 1980-82; dir. divsn. emergency medicine dept. family, cmty. and emergency medicine U. N.Mex. Sch. Medicine, Albuquerque, 1982-91, prof. emerg. med., 1991—, chair dept. emergency medicine, 1991-93, interim chief med. officer, 1992—93, interim dean, 1994—95, dean, 1995—; interim dir. U. N.Mex. Med. Ctr., Albuquerque, 1994—95; med. dir. disaster medicine Nat. Disaster Med. Sys. Chair disaster com. U. N.Mex. Med. Ctr. Contbr. articles to Annals of EM, Current Practice of EM-Disaster Medicine, Jour. of AMA. Recipient Outstanding Individual Svc. award Nat. Disaster Med. Sys., 1986. Fellow Am. Coll. Emergency Physicians (chair sect. on disaster medicine, 1991-92), Am. Acad. Family Practice; mem. AMA, Soc. for Acad. Emergency Medicine, Am. Coll. Physician Execs., Am. Acad. Family Physicians. Office: U NMex Sch Medicine Dean Basic Med Scis Bldg Rm 177 Albuquerque NM 87131-0001*

ROTH, PETER, broadcast executive; b. Larchmont, N.Y. m. Andrea Roth; 2 children. Student, U. Pa.; grad., Tufts U., 1972. From mgr. to dir. children's programs ABC TV Network, 1976, dir. current programs, 1979, v.p. current prime-time series, 1981; past pres. Stephen J. Cannell Prodns.; pres. prodn. Twentieth Network TV, 1992, pres., 1993, 20th Century Fox TV, 1994, Fox Entertainment Group, L.A., 1996—98, Warner Bros. TV, Burbank, Calif., 1999—. Office: Warner Bros Television 300 Television Plz Bldg 140 Burbank CA 91522-0001

ROTH, PHILIP MILTON, writer; b. Newark, Mar. 19, 1933; s. Herman and Bess (Finkel) R.; m. Margaret Martinson, Feb. 22, 1959 (dec. 1968); m. Claire Bloom, Apr. 29, 1990 (div. June 1994). Student, Newark Coll. of Rutgers U., 1950-51; AB, Bucknell U., 1954; MA, U. Chgo., 1955. Tchr. English U. Chgo., 1956-58; faculty Iowa Writers Workshop, 1960-62; writer in residence Princeton U., 1962-64; adj. prof. U. Pa., 1967-77; disting. prof. Hunter Coll. CUNY, 1989-92. Short story writer, novelist; works pub. in Harper's, New Yorker, Epoch, Commentary, others; reprints in Best Am. Short Stories of 1956, 59, 60, O'Henry Prize Stories of 1960; author: Goodbye, Columbus, 1959 (Nat. Book award for Fiction, 1960), Letting Go, 1962, When She Was Good, 1967, Portnoy's Complaint, 1969, Our Gang, 1971, The Breast, 1972, The Great American Novel, 1973, My Life as a Man, 1974, Reading Myself and Others, 1975, The Professor of Desire, 1977, The Ghost Writer, 1979, A Philip Roth Reader, 1980, Zuckerman Unbound, 1981, The Anatomy Lesson, 1983, The Prague Orgy, 1985, Zuckerman Bound, 1985, The Counterlife, 1987 (Nat. Book Critics Circle award for fiction, 1988), The Facts: A Novelist's Autobiography, 1988, Deception, 1990, Patrimony, 1991 (Nat. Book Critics Circle award for biography/autobiography 1992), Operation Shylock: A Confession, 1993 (PEN-Faulkner award for fiction, 1993), The Conversation of the Jews, 1993, Sabbath's Theater, 1995 (Nat. Book award for fiction, 1995), American Pastoral, 1997 (Pulitzer prize for fiction, 1998), I Married A Communist, 1998 (Amb. Book award of English-Speaking Union), The Human Stain, 2000 (PEN-Faulkner award for fiction, 2000, Prix Medicis Etranger, 2000), The Dying Animal, 2001, Shop Talk: A Writer and His Colleagues and Their Work, 2002. Recipient prize for fiction Paris Rev., 1958, Nat. Inst. Arts and Letters award, 1960, Daroff award Jewish Book Coun. Am., 1960, Medal of Honor for Lit., Nat. Arts Club, 1991, Karel Capek prize Czech Republic, 1994; Guggenheim fellow, 1959-60, Rockefeller fellow, 1966.

ROTH, PHILLIP JOSEPH, retired judge; b. Portland, Oreg., Feb. 29, 1920; s. Harry William and Minnie Alice (Segel) R.; m. Ida Lorraine Thomas, Feb. 22, 1957 (div. 1977); children: Phillip Joseph, David Harry; m. Allison Blake Ramsey, Feb. 14, 1978 (div. 1994). BA cum laude, U. Portland, 1943; JD, Lewis and Clark Coll., 1948. Bar: Oreg. 1948, U.S. Dist. Ct. Oreg. 1949, U.S. Ct. Appeals (9th cir.) 1959, U.S. Supreme Ct. 1962. Dep. atty. City of Portland, 1948-50; dep. dist. atty. Multnomah County, Portland, 1950-52; pvt. practice Portland, 1952-64; cir. judge Multnomah County State of Oreg., Portland, 1964-94, presiding cir. judge, 1970-71, 76-78. Adj. prof. Lewis & Clark U. Law Sch., Portland, 1978-80, standing com., 1972-90; exec. com. Nat. Conf. State Trial Judges, 1980-91. Author: Sentencing: A View From the Bench, 1973; co-author: The Judicial Immunity Doctrine Today: Between the Bench and a Hard Place, 1984, The Brief Jour.; The Dangerous Erosion of Judicial Immunity, 1989. Mem. Oreg. Legislature, 1952-54; Rep. nominee for Congress, 1956; chmn. Oreg. Rep. Ctrl. Com., 1962-64; adv. bd. Portland Salvation Army, 1976—; mem. bd. overseers Lewis and Clark Coll., 1972-90. Named Alumnus of Yr. U. Portland, 1963, Lewis & Clark Law Sch., 1973. Fellow Am. Bar Found.; mem. ABA (chmn. jud. immunity com. jud. adminstrn. divsn. 1982-90, mem. commn. on standards jud. adminstrn. divsn. 1973-77, chmn. conf. state trial judges 1990-91, HBH Comm. on State Justice Initiatives 1994-98, chmn. jud. adminstrn. divsn. 1994-95), Oreg. Bar Assn. (bd. govs. 1961-64), Multnomah County Bar Assn. (pres. 1959), Am. Judicature Soc., Oreg. Cir. Judges Assn. (pres. 1988-89), U. Portland Alumni Assn. (pres. 1967), Lewis and Clark Coll. Alumni Assn. (prs. 1974-76, 80-81), Multnomah Law Libr. Assn. (bd. dirs.), City Club, Univ. Club, Masons, Shriners, Rotary, B'nai B'rith, Delta Theta Phi. Jewish. Home: 2495 SW 73rd Ave Portland OR 97225-3274

ROTH, ROBERT A. newspaper executive; b. Upper Darby, Pa., Mar. 19, 1947; s. Robert Raymond and Ruth Lorrayne (Jonas) R. BA magna cum laude, Carleton Coll., 1969; postgrad., U. Chgo., 1969-71. Co-founder Chgo. Reader, 1971, pub., 1971-94, editor, 1975-90; pres. Chgo. Reader, Inc., 1975—, Washington Free Weekly, Inc., 1982—. Dir. Inst. for Alternative Journalism, San Francisco, 1983-89, Raw Vision, Ltd., London, 1991—, Stonington (Maine) Sea Products, Inc., 2002—. Co-founder Intuit: The Ctr. for Intuitive and Outsider Art, Chgo., 1991, pres., 1991-96, bd. dirs., 1991—; trustee Carleton Coll., Northfield, Minn., 1994-98. Recipient Alumni Disting. Achievement award Carleton Coll., 1989, Donald J. Cowling Cup, 2002; named to Esquire Register, Esquire mag., 1984; named among Who's Who in Chgo. Bus., Crain's Chgo. Bus., 1990, 91, 92, 93, 94, 95, 96. Mem. Assn. Alternative Newsweeklies (pres. 1983-87). Avocations: folk and outsider art, architecture. Office: Chgo Reader 11 E Illinois St Chicago IL 60611-5652

ROTH, ROBERT EARL, environmental educator; b. Wauseon, Ohio, Mar. 30, 1937; s. Earl Jonas and Florence Lena (Mahler) R.; m. Carol Sue Yackee, Aug. 8, 1959; children: Robin Earl, Bruce Robert. BS, Ohio State U., 1959, BS in Secondary Sci. Edn., MS in Conservation Edn., Ohio State U., 1960; PhD in Environ. Edn., U. Wis., 1969. Supr. conservation edn. Ethical Culture Schs., N.Y.C., 1961-63; naturalist, sci. tchr. Lakeside Sch., Spring Valley, N.Y., 1963-65; instr. No. Ill. U., Oregon, 1965-67; asst. prof. Ohio State U., Columbus, 1969-73, assoc. prof., 1973-78, prof. environ. edn. and sci. edn., 1978-2001, prof. emeritus, 2001—, chmn. divsn., 1973-84, coord. office internat. affairs, 1985-89, asst. dir., sch. sec. Sch. Natural Resources, 1989-93, acting dir. Sch. Natural Resources, 1993-94, assoc. dir., 1994-2001, state extension specialist Environ. Edn., 1993-2001. Rsch. & devel. assoc. Mosely & Assocs., Columbus, 1986-89; project cons. NARMA project, U.S. Agy. internat. Devel., Santo Domingo, Dominican Rep., 1982-87; cons. Richard Trott & Assocs., 1988-90, Kinzelman & Kline, 1990-2001, Midwest consortium Internat. Activity, 1995; evaluator Montclair State U., N.J. Sch. Conservation, 1999; workshop leader Carribean Conservation Assn., Bridgetown, Barbados, 1981-83; vis. scholar Indonesian Second U. Devel. project, Jakarta, 1988; AID lectr., Thesolonika, Greece, 1992; bd. supr. Franklin Soil & Water Conservation Dist., 2003—. Exec. editor Jour. Environ. Edn., 1974-91 (Pub.'s prize 1970); contbr. articles to profl. jours. Committeeman Boy Scouts Am., 1983-86; adv. coun. McKeever Environ. Learning Ctr., Pa., 1977-83. Named vis. scholar, Uganda Makerere U., 1989, Pacific Cultural Found., Taipei, Taiwan, 1989, 1999, 2001; recipient Pomerene Tchg. Enhancement award, Ohio State U., 1986, 1995, Environ. Edn. award, Ohio Alliance for the Enrivon., 1992, Outstanding Advising award, Coll. Food Agrl. and Environ. Scis., 1996. Mem.: Sch. Nat. Resource Alumni Assn. (inducted hon. 100), Nat. Sci. Tchrs. Assn. (life), N.Am. Assn. Environ. Edn. (life; bd. dirs. 1972—82, pres. 1977—78, Walt Jeske award 1988, Outstanding Contbns. to Rsch. award 2000). Avocations: swimming, canoeing, camping, fishing, travel. Home: 570 Morning St Columbus OH 43085-3775 E-mail: roth.3@osu.edu.

ROTH, ROBERT HOWARD, psychologist; b. Newark, N.J., Jan. 15, 1933; s. Max and Marion (Gurkewitz) R.; m. Estelle Goldstein, June 16, 1957; children: Lisa C., Neil A. BS, Juilliard Sch., N.Y.C., 1953; MA, Columbia U., 1956, EdD, 1960. Lic. psychologist, N.Y., N.J. Instr. Union Coll., Cranford, N.J., 1959-60, Newark State Coll., Union, N.J., 1960-63; asst. prof. Hunter Coll. CUNY, N.Y.C., 1963-65; assoc. prof. Newark State Coll., Union, N.J., 1965-68, chmn. psychology dept., 1967-71; prof. psychology Kean U., Union, 1968—. Cons. Marlboro (N.J.) Psychiat. Hosp., 1982-97; pvt. practice clin. psychology Madison Med. Ctr. Editor: Contemporary Studies in Psychopathology, 1983, Contemporary Studies in Personality, 1986, Explorations in Mental Disorders, 1987, Personality Structures and Functions, 1989, Psychopathologies and Treatments, 1991, Ego, Self, Person, Context, 1992, 2d edit., 1996, Tempest in the Mind, 1994. Fellow Am. Orthopsychiatric Assn.; mem. APA, AAAS, N.Y. Acad. Scis., N.J. Acad. Scis. (chmn. psychology sect. 1971-73). Home: 111 Gallinson Dr New Providence NJ 07974-2723

ROTH, SANFORD IRWIN, pathologist, educator; b. McAlester, Okla., Oct. 14, 1932; s. Herman Moe and Blanche (Brown) R.; m. Kathryn Ann Corliss, Sept. 3, 1961; children: Jeffrey Franklin, Elisabeth Francyne, Gregory James, Suzannah Joan. Student, Vanderbilt U., 1949-52; MD, Harvard U., 1956. Intern Mass. Gen. Hosp., Boston, 1956-57, resident in pathology, 1957-60, pathologist, 1962-75, Armed Forces Inst. Pathology, 1960-62; asst. prof. Med. Sch. Harvard U., 1962-69, assoc. prof. Med. Sch., 1969-75; pathologist, prof., chmn. dept. Coll. Medicine U. Ark., Little Rock, 1975-81; prof. Med. Sch. Northwestern U., Chgo., 1981—2000, asst. dean admissions, 1998-2000, prof. emeritus, 2000—; chief lab. svc. VA Lakeside Med. Ctr., Chgo., 1981-86. Attending pathologist Northwestern U. Hosp., 1981-2002; vis. prof. pathology Harvard Med. Sch., 2001—; cons. in pathology Mass. Gen. Hosp., 2001—. With M.C. U.S. Army, 1960-62. Mem. AMA, AAAS, Coll. Am. Pathology, U.S.-Can. Acad. Pathology, Soc. for Investigative Dermatology, Mass. Med. Soc. Home: 169 Tisquantum Rd Chatham MA 02633-2578 Office: Fruit St Boston MA 02114 Office Phone: 508-945-2995. E-mail: sroth@partners.org.

ROTH, SARAH EVE, occupational safety professional; b. W. Allis, Wis., Mar. 10, 1971; d. Douglas Fred and Rene'e Alice Roth. BS in Edn., U. of Wis., Whitewater, 1994. Sales assoc. K-Mart, Burlington, Wis., 1988—94; safety asst. Velvac, Inc., New Berlin, Wis., 1993; safety intern Johnson Controls, Inc, Milw., 1994; corp. safety adminstr. Schweiger Industries, Inc., Jefferson, Wis., 1994; tech./product specialist Lab Safety Supply, Janesville, Wis., 1994—; tax specialist H & R Block, Janesville, Wis., 1999—2003; comml. print model Janesville, Wis., 1997—. Program com. chairperson Jefferson County Area Safety Network, Jefferson, 1994. Author: (book) Moments in Time, 2000. Mem.: Am. Soc. Safety Engrs. (pub. comm. dir. 1992, social chair 1993). Non-Denominational. Avocations: writing, dance, piano, weightlifting, golf. Home: 1521 Excalibur Dr Janesville WI 53546 Office: Lab Safety Supply 401 South Wright Rd Janesville WI 53546 Personal E-mail: sarahroth310@hotmail.com. Business E-Mail: s.roth@labsafety.com.

ROTH, SOL, rabbi; b. Rzeszow, Poland, Mar. 8, 1927; came to U.S., 1934, naturalized, 1939; s. Joseph and Miriam (Lamm) R.; m. Debra H. Stitskin, Nov. 26, 1957; children: Steven, Michael (dec.), Sharon. BA, Yeshiva U., 1948, D.D. (hon.), 1977; MA, Columbia U., 1953, PhD, 1966; Rabbi, Yeshiva U. Theol. Sem., 1950; D in Divinity (hon.), Yeshiva U., 1977. Ordained rabbi Orthodox Jewish Congregations, 1950; pres. Rabbinical Council Am., 1980-82, N.Y. Bd. Rabbis, 1976-79; chmn. Israel Commn. Rabbinical Council Am., 1976-78; dean Chaplaincy Sch., N.Y. Bd. Rabbis, 1976-79; Samson R. Hirsch prof. dept. philosophy Yeshiva U., N.Y.C. Rabbi Jewish Ctr. Atlantic Beach, N.Y., 1956-86; rabbi Fifth Ave Synagogue, 1986-2003, rabbi emeritus, 2003—; pres. Religious Zionists Am., 1991-94. Author: Science and Religion, 1967, The Jewish Idea of Community, 1977, Halakhah and Politics: The Jewish Idea of a State, 1988 (Samuel Belkin Meml. Lit. award 1989), The Jewish Idea of Culture, 1997; editor: Morasha. Recipient award Synagogue Adv. Council United Jewish Appeal, 1975; named Rabbi Dr. Sol Roth Chair in Talmud and Contemporary Halakha established at Yeshiva U., 1989. Jewish. Home: 201 E 62nd St New York NY 10021-8026 Office: Yeshiva U Dept Philosophy 500 W 185th St Dept New York NY 10033-3299 Personal E-mail: rothsol@aol.com.

ROTH, STANLEY OWEN, federal agency administrator; BA, Brandeis U.; MA, Johns Hopkins U. Legis. asst. Rep. Stephen Solarz, Washington, 1979-82; staff cons. subcom. on Asian and Pacific affairs U.S. House Fgn. Affairs Com., Washington, 1983-85, staff dir. subcom. on Asian and Pacific Affairs, 1985-92, dir. com. liaison, 1993; dep. asst. for East Asia and Pacific Affairs Sec. of Def., Washington, 1993-94; spl. asst. to pres., sr. dir. Asian affairs Nat. Security Coun., Washington, 1994-96; dir. rsch. and studies U.S. Inst. Peace, Washington, 1996; asst. sec. of state for East Asia and Pacific Affairs U.S. Dept. State, Washington, 1997-2000. Office: US Dept State East Asian and Pacific Affairs 2201 C St NW Washington DC 20520-0001

ROTH, STEVEN, realty company executive; Chmn. bd. Vornado Realty Trust, Saddle Brook, N.J., 1989—. Office: Plz II Park 80 W Saddle Brook NJ 07663

ROTH, SUSAN AUSTIN, author, photographer; b. Wheeling, W.Va., Oct. 2, 1950; m. Mark Schneider, June 27, 1986. Student, Mount Holyoke Coll., 1968-70; BS in Horticulture, Cornell U., 1972, MS in Horticulture, 1974; postgrad., SUNY, Stony Brook, 1974-75. Dir. rsch. Valentine Girards Inc., Malvern, N.Y., 1975-77; assoc. editor Gardening Mag., Villanova, Pa., 1977-79; sr. editor Western Pub., N.Y.C., 1979-85; pres. Susan A. Roth & Co., Stony Brook, N.Y., 1984—. Author, photographer: The Weekend Garden Guide, 1991, The Four Season Landscape, 1994, Better Homes and Gardens Complete Guide to Flower Gardening, 1995, Better Homes and Gardens New Complete Guide to Gardening, 1997, Hot Plants for Cool Climates, 2000, Taylor's Guide to Trees, 2001; book packager, photographer Beds and Borders, 1998, Easy-Care Landscapes, 1995, Backyard Landscaper, 1992, Home Landscaper, 1990 Mem.: Dramatists Guild, Am. Soc. Media Photographers, Authors Guild, Am. Soc. Horitculture, Garden Writers Assn. (Photography award 1990, Mag. Writing award 1991, Book Writing award 1992). Avocations: hiking, gardening, travel, theater. Office: 3 Lamont Ln Stony Brook NY 11790-1611 E-mail: susanaroth@optonline.net.

ROTH, TERESA ANN, broadcast executive; b. Little Rock, July 13, 1961; d. Carl Henry and Peggy Joann (Hartsell) Habig; m. Paul Gerhardt Roth, July 15, 1989 (div. May 1990). BA in Comm., U. Ark., 1983. Camera operator Sta. KATV-TV, Little Rock, 1983-85, writer, prodr., 1985-87, Sta. WSB-TV, Atlanta, 1987-89; exec. prodr., mgr. St. WSB-TV, Atlanta, 1989—. Prodr., dir. documentary Jo's Town, 1998, Jo's Town Shown at ValleyFest, 2000, The Hot Springs Documentary Film Festival, 2000, The Memphis Film Festival, 2001, The N.Y. Internat. Film Festival, 2001, The Kan Film Festival, 2001. Vol. Habitat for Humanity, Atlanta, 1996—; co-founder NATAS Student Connection, Atlanta, 1997—. Recipient Addy award Ad Club, Little Rock, 1986. Mem. NATAS (bd. dirs. 1991—, sec. 1993-95, v.p. 1995-99, nat. trustee 1999—), Promotion and Mktg. Execs., Atlanta Press Club. Avocations: movies, painting, writing, travel. Office: WSB-TV 1601 W Peachtree St NE Atlanta GA 30309-2641

ROTH, THEODORE D. pharmaceutical executive; JD, Washburn U.; LLM in Corp. & Comml. Law, U. Mo. Gen. mgr. Holland Industries, Inc.; gen. counsel SAI Corp., 1977—87; from exec. v.p. & CFO to pres. & COO Alliance Pharm. Corp., San Diego, 1987—98, pres. & COO, 1998—. Office: Alliance Pharmaceutical Corp 3040 Science Park Rd San Diego CA 92121

ROTH, THOMAS, marketing executive; Grad., Western Mich. U. With Tarkenton and Co., Atlanta; founder HR Skills divsn. Nat. Edn. Tng. Group, 1988-92; dir. product devel. Wilson Learning Corp., Eden Prairie, Minn., 1981-88, v.p. product mgmt. in global R & D, 1992-94, v.p. product mgmt. and tng. group, 1994-99, v.p. global cons., 1999—. Cons. IBM, AT&T, Ford Motor Co., Pfizer, E.I. DuPont, Gen. Electric, Oracle, Dow Chem., Lucent, Tex. Instruments, Colgate-Palmolive, Honeywell, others; spkr. in field. Co-author: Creating the High Performance Team, 1987. Office: Wilson Learning Corp Warehouse 8000 W 78th St #175 Minneapolis MN 55439-2536

ROTH, TIM, actor; b. London, 1961; With Glasgow Citizen's Theatre, The Oval House, The Royal Ct. Appeared in play Metamorphosis; films include The Hit, 1985, A World Apart, 1988, The Cook, the Thief, His Wife and Her Lover, 1990, Vincent and Theo, 1990, Rosencrantz and Guildenstern Are Dead, 1991, Jumpin' at the Boneyard, 1992, Reservoir Dogs, 1992, Backsliding, 1993, Bodies, Rest and Motion, 1993, Pulp Fiction, 1994, Rob Roy, 1995 (Acad. award nominee for best supporting actor 1996), Little Odessa, 1995, Four Rooms, 1995, No Way Home, 1996, Everyone Says I Love You, 1996, Hoodlum, 1997, Gridlock'd, 1997, Animals, 1997, Deceiver, 1998, The Legend of the Pianist on the Ocean, 1998, Vatel, 1999, Leggenda del pianista sull'oceano, 1998, Film-Fest DVD: Issue 1-Sundance, 1999, The Million Dollar Hotel, 2000; TV movies include Meantime, Made in Britain, Metamorphosis, Knuckle, Yellow Backs, King of the Ghetto, The Common Pursuit, Murder in the Heartland, 1993; dir.: The War Zone, 1998; TV guest appearance Tales From the Crypt, 1989. Office: Ilene Feldman Agy 8730 W Sunset Blvd Ste 490 Los Angeles CA 90069-2248

ROTH, WILLIAM H, insurance company executive; BSc, MBA in fin. and acctg., Indiana U. CPA. With WellPoint Health Networks; sr. v.p. e.bus. ops. WellPoint; sr. v.p. Blue Cross of Calif., 1998—2000; head of regional ops. UNICARE; cons. Deloitte & Touche; sr. v.p., consumer markets Aetna Inc., 2001—. Office: Aetna Inc 151 Farmington Ave Hartford CT 06156

ROTH, WILLIAM STANLEY, hospital foundation executive; b. N.Y.C., Jan. 12, 1929; s. Sam Irving and Louise Caroline (Martin) R.; m. Hazel Adcock, May 6, 1963; children: R. Charles, W. Stanley. AA, Asheville-Biltmore Jr. Coll., 1948; BS, U. N.C., 1950. Dep. regional exec. Nat. coun. Boy Scouts Am., 1953-65; exec. v.p. Am. Humanics Found., 1965-67; dir. devel. Bethany Med. Ctr., Kansas City, Kans., 1967-74; exec. v.p. Geisinger Med. Ctr. Found., Danville, Pa., 1974-78; found. pres. Bapt. Med Ctrs., Birmingham, Ala., 1978—. Sec. Western Med. Systems, Cherokee Cmty. Homes, Cullman Sr. Housing, Dekalb Sr. Housing, Limestone Sr. Housing, Oxford Sr. Housing. Editor: Torch and Trefoil, 1960—61. Mem.-at-large Nat. coun. Boy Scouts Am., 1972-86; chmn. NAHD Ednl. Fund, 1980-82; ruling elder John Knox Kirk, Kansas City, Mo., Grove Presbyn. Ch., Danville, Pa. Recipient Silver award United Meth. Ch., 1970, Mid-West Health Congress, 1971; Seymour award for outstanding hosp. devel. officer, 1983, 60 Yr. Vet. award Boy Scouts Am., 2001. Fellow Assn. for Healthcare Philanthropy (life, nat. pres. 1975-76); mem. Nat. Soc. Fund Raising Execs. (pres. Ala. chpt. 1980-82, nat. dir. 1980-84, mem. ethics bd. 1993-2000, advanced cert fund raising exec., Outstanding Fund Raising Exec., Ala. chpt. 1983), Mid-Am. Hosp. Devel. Assn. (pres. 1973-74), Mid-West Health Congress (devel. chmn. 1972-74), Am. Soc. for Healthcare Mktg. and Pub. Rels., Ala. Soc. for Sleep Disorders, Ala. Heart Inst., Ala. Assn. Healthcare Philanthropy (pres. 1991-93, chmn. bd. 1993-94), Ala. Planned Giving Coun. (bd. dirs. 1991-2000, pres. 1994-95), Alpha Phi Omega (nat. pres. 1958-62, dir. 1950—, Nat. Disting. Scv. award 1962), Delta Upsilon (pres. N.C. Alumni 1963-65), Rotary (pres. club 1976-77), Relay House, Summit Club, Green Valley Club (bd. govs.), Elks, Order of the Arrow (Nat. Disting. Svc. award 1958), Order of Holy Grail, Order of Golden Fleece. Home: 341 Laredo Dr Birmingham AL 35226-2325 Office: 3500 Blue Lake Dr Ste 101 Birmingham AL 35243-1908 Office Phone: 205-979-8285. Personal E-mail: billroth1@aol.com.

ROTHAAR, SUSANNE ELISABETH, music educator, musician; d. Walter Henry and Lore Rothaar; m. John Paul Haggard, Feb. 14, 2000. BA, U. Utah, 1990; MusM, Wichita State U., 1995. Violinist Utah Chamber Orch., Salt Lake City, 1990—93, Wichita (Kans.) Symphony Orch., 1993—98, Oklahoma City Philharm., 1997—98; mem. violin faculty Wichita State U., 1995—96; pvt. violin instr. Las Vegas, Nev., 1998—2000, Phoenix, 2001 . Lectr. violin pedagogy at various univs. and colls., 2001—; mem. summer music faculty Utah State U., 2000—02, U. Oreg., 2001—02. Author: Teaching Violin Technique, 2002. Mem.: Nat. Symphony Orch. Assn., Music Tchrs. Nat. Assn., Am. String Tchrs. Assn. Avocation: tennis. E-mail: derazy@aol.com.

ROTHAUSEN-VANGE, TERESA JEAN, director, educator; b. Battle Creek, Mich., May 3, 1964; d. Carl Frederick and Sandra Jean Rothausen; m. Jens Henry Rothausen-Vange; children: Caleb Rothausen Williams, Jacob Rothausen Williams, Hannah Williams Rothausen, Ethan Brady Vange. BA, St. Olaf Coll., 1986; PhD, U. Minn., 1994. CPA Minn., 1986. Assoc. prof. of mgmt. U. St. Thomas, Mpls., 1994—, dir. MBA Program, 2002—. Office: U St Thomas 1000 LaSalle Avenue; TMH 441 Minneapolis MN 55403-2005

ROTHBART, STEPHEN TOBIAS, cardiologist; b. 1948; MD, U. Medicine and Dentistry N.J.-N.J. Med. Sch., 1977. Diplomate Am. Bd. Internal Medicine, Am. Bd. Clin. Cardiac Electrophysiology, Am. Bd. Cardiovasc. Disease. Intern N.J. Coll. Medicine, Newark, 1977—78, resident, 1978—80; fellow in cardiology Newark Beth Israel Med. Ctr., 1980—83, dir. cardiac electrophysiology. Clin. asst. prof. N.J. Med. Sch. Named one of Top Drs. in N.Y. Metro Area, Castle Connolly, Top Drs. 2003, N.J. Monthly Mag. Office: Newark Beth Israel Med Ctr 201 Lyons Ave Newark NJ 07112-2027

ROTHBAUM, DAVID, obstetrician-gynecologist; b. N.Y.C., 1958; BA, N.Y.U., 1978; MD, Boston U., 1982. Intern North Shore U. Hosp., Manhasset, NY, 1982-83, resident ob-gyn., 1983-86, attending physician; clin. instr. Sch. Medicine NYU; pvt. practice. Med. cons. News 12 L.I. Fellow ACOG; mem. Am. Assn. Gynecol. Laparoscopists, Am. Fertility Soc. Office: 233 E Shore Rd Great Neck NY 11023-2433

ROTHBERG, ABRAHAM, author, educator, editor; b. NYC, Jan. 14, 1922; s. Louis and Lottie (Drimmer) R.; m. Esther Conwell, Sept. 30, 1945; 1 son, Lewis Josiah. AB, Bklyn. Coll., 1942; MA, U. Iowa, 1947; PhD, Columbia U., 1952. Chmn. editorial bd. Stateside (mag.), N.Y.C., 1947-49; instr. English, creative writing Columbia U., N.Y.C., 1948; instr. English, humanities Hofstra Coll., Hempstead, N. Y., 1947-51; prof. English St. John Fisher Coll., 1973-83, chmn. dept. English, 1981-82; disting. writer-in-residence, vis. prof. Wichita State U., 1985. Editor-in-chief Free Europe Press, N.Y.C., 1952—59, East Europe Mag., 1952—59; mng. editor George Braziller, Inc., N.Y.C., 1959, New Leader mag., N.Y.C., 1960—61; cons. editor New Jewish Ency., 1960—62; writer, editl. con.; European corr. Nat. Observer, Washington, Manchester (Eng.) Guardian, 1962—63; sr. editor Bantam Books, Inc., N.Y.C., 1966—67; cons. editor The New Union Prayer Book, N.Y.C., 1975. Author: Abraham, Eyewitness History of World War II, 1962, The Thousand Doors, 1965, The Heirs of Cain, 1966, The Song of David Freed, 1968, The Other Man's Shoes, 1969, The Boy and the Dolphin, 1969, The Sword of the Golem, 1971, Aleksandr Solzhenitsyn: The Major Novels, 1971, The Heirs of Stalin: Dissidence and the Soviet Regime, 1953-1970, 1972, The Stalking Horse, 1972, The Great Waltz, 1978, The Four Corners of the House, 1981, numerous poems; editor: U.S. Stories, 1949, Flashes in the Night, 1958, Anatomy of a Moral, 1959, A Bar-Mitzvah Companion, 1959, Great Adventure Stories of Jack London, 1967; contbr. articles to profl. jours. Served with AUS, 1943-45. Recipient John H. McGinnis Meml. award for short story, 1970, John H. McGinnis Meml. award for essay, 1973—74, Lit. award, Friends of Rochester Libr., 1980; Ford Found. fellow, N.Y.C., 1951—52. Home: 340 Pelham Rd Rochester NY 14610-3355

ROTHBERG, GERALD, editor, publisher, editor-in-chief; b. Bklyn., Oct. 29, 1937; s. Abraham and Pauline Rothberg; m. Glenda Fay Morris, June 18, 1970 (div. 1988); children: Laura, Abigail. BA, Bklyn. Coll., 1960; postgrad., Dickinson Law Sch., 1962. Spl. projects editor Esquire (mag.), 1963-66; owner, editor, pub., founder Circus (mag.), N.Y.C., 1966—; owner, founder, editor Sci. and Living Tomorrow, 1980—, Who's In, 1981; founder, editor Sports Mirror mag., 1983—, MGF mag., 1985—; Country Mirror mag., 1994—. Author: (novels) Composition 36, 1993, The Six-Hour Song, 1994, Redeeming Esau, 1995, The Esau Swindle, 2003, The Golem Code, 2004. Mem. Periodical and Book Assn. Am. (pres.) Office: Circus Mag 6 W 18th St Ste 2C New York NY 10011-4628 Personal E-mail: circusmag@aol.com.

ROTHBERG, GLENDA FAY MORRIS, lawyer; b. Rome, Ga., Aug. 7, 1946; d. Glenn Howell and Fay (Givens) Morris; m. Gerald Rothberg, June 18, 1970 (div. Jan. 1989); children: Laura, Abigail. AB, Randolph-Macon Woman's Coll., 1968; JD, Benjamin Cardozo Law Sch., 1985. Bar: N.Y. 1986, U.S. Dist. Ct. (so. and ea. dists.) N.Y. 1987, U.S. Supreme Ct. 1990. Law guardian juvenile rights divsn. Legal Aid Soc., N.Y.C., 1988-91; pvt. practice N.Y.C., 1992—. Faculty dir. Inst. for not-for-profit Mgmt. Columbia Bus. Sch., N.Y.C., 1994-98. Vol. Manhattan Mediation Ctr., N.Y.C., 1996-99; chair legal com. N.Y.C. Comptr. Task Force on Open Adoption, 1999—. Fellow Am. Bar Found.; mem. ABA, Assn. of Bar of City of N.Y. (com. chair 1996-99, mem. coun. on children 1999—). Office: 386 Park Ave S Ste 904 New York NY 10016-1001 E-mail: gmrlaw@aol.com.

ROTHBERG, JONATHAN M. medical products executive; BSChemE, Carnegie Mellon U.; MS, MPhil, PhD, Yale U. CEO, pres., chmn. 454 Corp., Branford, Conn., 1991—2002, chmn., 2002—. Office: 454 Corp 20 Commercial St Branford CT 06405

ROTHBERG-BLACKMAN, JUNE SIMMONDS, retired nursing educator, psychotherapist, psychoanalyst; b. Phila., Sept. 4, 1923; d. David and Rose (Protzel) Simmonds; m. Jacob Rothberg, Sept. 7, 1952 (dec. Feb. 2001); children: Robert Rothberg, Alan Rothberg; m. Stanley F Blackman, May 27, 2002. Diploma in nursing, Lenox Hill Hosp., 1944; BS, N.Y. U., 1950, MA, 1959, PhD (NIH fellow), 1965; Diploma in Psychotherapy and Psychoanalysis, Adelphi U., Inst. for Advanced Psychol. Studies, 1987. USPHS traineeship N.Y. U., 1957-59; sr. public health nurse Bklyn. Vis. Nurse Assn., 1951-53; prin. investigator in nursing, homestead study project Goldwater Hosp. and N.Y. U., 1959-61; instr. N.Y. U., 1964-65, asst. prof., 1965-68, assoc. prof., 1968-69, project dir. grad. program rehab. nursing, 1964-69, prof., 1969-87, prof. emeritus, 1987—; dean Adelphi U., Garden City, N.Y., 1969-85, v.p. acad. adminstrn., 1985-86; pvt. practice West Hempstead, N.Y., 1993-97. Pres. David Simmonds Co. Inc., Med. Supply Co., 1982-89; dir., chmn. compensation com. Quality Care, Inc.; cons. to various ednl. and svc. instns.; cons. region 2 Bur. Health Resources Devel., HHS.; speaker on radio and TV; bd. dirs., mem. audit com. Ipco Corp. (formerly Sterling Optical Corp.), 1991. Contbr. articles to profl. jours. Mem. pres's coun. N.Y. U. Sch. Edn., 1973-75; treas. Nurses for Polit. Action, 1971-73; trustee Nurses Coalition for Action in Politics, 1974-76; bd. visitors Duke Med. Ctr., 1970-74; mem. governing bd. Nassau-Suffolk Health Systems Agy., 1976-79; leader People-to-People Internat. med. rehab. del. to People's Republic of China, 1981; mem. com. for the study pain disability and chronic illness behavior Inst. Medicine, 1985-86, com. on ethics in rehab. Hastings Ctr., 1985-87; trustee Paget's Disease Found., 1987-89. Recipient Disting. Alumna award NYU, 1974, recognition award Am. Assn. Colls. Nursing, 1976, Achievers award Ctr. for Bus. and Profl. Women, 1980 Fellow Am. Acad. Nursing (governing coun. 1980-82); mem. Nat. League Nursing (exec. com. coun. of baccalaureate and higher degree programs 1969-73), Am. Nurses Assn. (joint liaison com. 1970-72), Commn. Accreditation of Rehab. Facilities, Am. Congress Rehab. Medicine (pres. 1977-78, chmn. continuing edn. com. 1979-86, 34th Ann. John Stanley Coulter Meml. lectr. 1984, Gold Key award 1984, Edward W. Lowman award 1990), Am. Assn. Colls. Nursing (pres. 1974-76), L.I. Women's Network (pres. 1980-81), Kappa Delta Pi, Sigma Theta Tau, Pi Lambda Theta. Achievements include having June S. Rothberg collection in Nursing Archives, Mugar Meml. Library, Boston U. Home and Office: 3941 Redondo Way Boca Raton FL 33487

ROTHBLATT, DONALD NOAH, urban and regional planner, educator; b. NYC, Apr. 28, 1935; s. Harry and Sophie (Chernofsky) R.; m. Ann S. Vogel, June 16, 1957; children: Joel Michael, Steven Saul. BCE, CUNY, 1957; MS in Urban Planning, Columbia U., 1963; Diploma in Comprehensive Planning, Inst. Social Studies, The Hague, 1964; PhD in City and Regional Planning, Harvard U., 1969. Cert. Am. Inst. Cert. Planners; registered prof. engr., NY. Planner NYC Planning Commn., 1960-62, NY Housing and Redevel. Bd., 1963-66; research fellow Ctr. for Environ. Design Studies, Harvard U., Cambridge, Mass., 1965-71; tchg. fellow, instr., then asst. prof. city and regional planning Harvard U., 1967-71; prof. urban and regional planning, chmn. dept. San Jose (Calif.) State U., 1971—. Lady Davis vis. prof. urban and regional planning Hebrew U., Jerusalem and Tel Aviv U., 1978; vis. scholar Indian Inst. Archs., New Dehli, 1979, Shandong Province, China, 1996, U. Lodz, Poland, 2000, Paris Regional Transp. Authority, France, 2002, Greater London Authority, Eng., 2003, Sydney (Australia) Regional Orgn. of Couns., 2004; vis. scholar, rsch. assoc. Inst. Govtl. Studies, U. Calif., Berkeley, 1980—; cons. to pvt. industry and govt. agys. Author: Human Needs and Public Housing, 1964, Thailand's Northeast, 1967, Regional Planning: The Appalachian Experience, 1971, Allocation of Resources for Regional Planning, 1972, The Suburban Environment and Women, 1979, Regional-Local Development Policy Making, 1981, Planning the Metropolis: The Multiple Advocacy Approach, 1982, Comparative Suburban Data, 1983, Suburbia: An International Assessment, 1986, Metropolitan Dispute Resolution in Silicon Valley, 1989, Good Practices for the Congestion Management Program, 1994, Activity-Based Travel Survey and Analysis of Responses to Increased Congestion, 1995, An Experiment in Sub-Regional Planning: California's Congestion Management Policy, 1995, Estimating the Origins and Destinations of Transit Passengers from On/Off Counts, 1995, Changes in Property Values Induced by Light Transit, 1996, Comparitive Study of Statewide Transportation Planning Under ISTEA, 1997, North American Metropolitan Planning Reexamined, 1999, Government Performance Measures Linking Urban Mass Transportation With Land Use and Accessibility Factors, 2000, Best Practices in Developing Regional Transportation Plans, 2001; editor: National policy for Urban and Regional Development, 1974, Regional Advocacy Planning: Expanding Air Transport Facilities for the San Jose Metropolitan Area, 1975, Metropolitan-wide Advocacy Planning: Dispersion of Low and Moderate Cost Housing in the San Jose Metropolitan Area, 1976, Multiple Advocacy Planning: Public Surface Transportation in the San Jose Metropolitan Area, 1977, A Multiple Advocacy Approach to Regional Planning: Open Space and Recreational Facilities for the San Jose Metropolitan Area, 1979, Regional Transpotation Planning for the San Jose Metropolitan Area, 1981, Planning for Open Space and Recreational Facilities in the San Jose Metropolitan Area, 1982, Regional Economic Development Planning for the San Jose Metropolitan Area, 1984, Planning for Surface Transportation in the San Jose Metropolitan Area, 1986, Expansion of Air Transportation Facilities in the San Jose Metropolitan Area, 1987, Provision of Economic Development in the San Jose Met. Area, 1988, Metropolitan Governance: American/Canadian Intergovernmental Perspectives, 1993, Metropolitan Governance Revisited, 1998; contbr. numerous articles to profl. jours.; dir.: Pub. TV series Sta. KTEH, 1976. Mem. adv. coun. Bay Area Met. Transp. Commn., 1995—. Served to 1st lt. C.E., U.S. Army, 1957-59. Rsch. fellow John F. Kennedy Sch. Govt. Harvard U., 1967-69; William F. Milton rsch. fellow, 1970-71; faculty rsch. grantee, NSF, 1972-82, Calif. State U., 1977-78; grantee Nat. Inst. Dispute Resolution, 1987-88, Can. Studies Enrichment Program, 1989-90, Can. Studies Rsch. Program, 1992-93, Univ. Rsch. and Tng. Program grantee Calif. Dept. Transp., 1993-97; recipient Innovative Tchg. award Calif. State U. and Coll., 1975-79; co-recipient Best of West award Western Ednl. Soc. for Tele-communication, 1976; recipient award Internat. Festival of Films on Architecture and Planning, 1983, Meritorious Performance award San Jose State U., 1986, 88, 90, 96-2001. Mem.: AAUP, Architecture and Urban and Regional Planning (chmn. 1973—75), Calif. Edn. Com. Architecture and Landscape, Internat. Fedn. Housing and Planning, Planners for Equal Opportunity, Am. Planning Assn., Assn. Collegiate Schs. of Planning (pres. 1975—76). Office: San Jose State U Dept Urban & Regional Planning San Jose CA 95192-0185 *My basic view is that we should try to develop ourselves fully and help others do the same, so that we will be able to live in harmony with, and contribute to, our world community.*

ROTHCHILD, DONALD SYLVESTER, political science educator; b. N.Y.C., Aug. 11, 1928; s. Sylvester Edward and Alice Levy Rothchild; m. Edith White, Apr. 23, 1954; children: Derek Edward, Maynard White. BA with high honors, Kenyon Coll., 1949; MA, U. Calif., Berkeley, 1954; PhD, Johns Hopkins U., 1958. From instr. to assoc. prof. Colby Coll., Waterville, Maine, 1957-65; prof. U. Calif., Davis, 1965—, faculty rsch. lectr., 1996-97, fellow Washington Ctr., 2000—01, 2003. Vis. Fulbright lectr. Makerere U., Kampala, Uganda, 1962-64; sr. lectr. U. Nairobi, Kenya, 1966-67; vis. Ford prof. U. Zambia, Lusaka, 1970-71; vis. prof. U. Ghana, Legon, 1975-77, 85, U. Calif., Berkeley, 2002; professorial lectr. Johns Hopkins U., Washington, 1993, 95, 2001, 03; internat. adv. bd. mem. Internat. Negotiation, 1995—, 2001, Africa Today 1968-; vis. scholar Brookings Instn., 1992-93, Ctr. for Internat. Security and Cooperation, Stanford U., 1998-99; mem. steering com., Inst. on Global Conflict and Cooperation, 2003—. Author: Racial Bargaining in Independent Kenya, 1973, Managing Ethnic Conflict in Africa, 1997; co-author: Sovereignty as Responsibility, 1996; co-editor: The International Spread of Ethnic Conflict, 1998, Ending Civil Wars: The Implementation of Peace Agreements, 2002, Sustainable Peace: Democracy and Power-Dividing Institutions After Civil Wars; editor Jour. Nationalism and Ethnic Politics, 1994—; contbr. articles to profl. jours. Internat. observer mission Carter Ctr., Ghana, 1992; rapporteur Friedrich Ebert Found., Kampala, Uganda, 1993; Hubert H. Humphrey spkr. Alumni Assn. Conf., Accra, Ghana, 1994. Sgt. U.S. Army, 1950-52. Disting. Am. Specialist grantee USIA, Thika, Kenya, 1993; Peace fellow U.S. Inst. Peace, Washington, 1994-95. Mem. Internat. Polit. Sci. Assn. (pres. rsch. com. 1988-94), Am. Polit. Sci. Assn., African Studies Assn. Democrat. Avocations: opera, theater, ballet. Home: 208 W 8th St Davis CA 95616-3637 Office: Univ Calif Dept Polit Sci 1 Shields Ave Davis CA 95616-5271 Office Phone: 530-752-2636. Business E-Mail: dsrothchild@ucdavis.edu.

ROTHE, DESIDER J. gynecologist-obstetrician; b. Iger, Hungary, Dec. 24, 1936; came to U.S., 1969; s. Istvan Abonyi and Iren (Husi) R.; m. Nalda L. Findell, July 9, 1990; children; Suzanne, Stephan, Christopher. MD, U. Debrecen, Hungary, 1961. Diplomate Am. Bd. Ob-Gyn. Rsch. fellow U. Med. Scis. Debrecen, 1959-61, intern, 1960-61, resident in ob-stet., 1961-65; rschr. CNRS, Paris, 1966-69; rsch. assoc. N.Y. Blood Ctr., N.Y.C., 1969-70; rsch. assoc. human genetics in pediats. Cornell U. Med. Coll., 1970, chief resident in ob-stet., 1970-72, fellow in ob-stet., 1972; asst. ob-stet. N.Y. Hosp.-Cornell U., 1972; asst. attending in ob-gyn. Lenox Hill Hosp., 1974-78, N.Y. Hosp., 1978—. Clin. assoc. prof. ob-gyn. Cornell U. Med. Coll., N.Y. Hosp., 1978—. Contbr. articles to profl. jours. Recipient Young Scientist award Semmelweis Sci. Soc., 1976. Mem. AMA, ACOG, N.Y. Obstet. Soc., Semmelweis Sci. Soc. Avocations: running, skiing, waterskiing. Office: 653 Park Ave New York NY 10021-5954 Home: 1775 York Ave Apt 9B New York NY 10128-6907

ROTHENBERG, ALAN I. lawyer, professional sports association executive; b. Detroit, Apr. 10, 1939; m. Georgina Rothenberg; 3 children. BA, U. Mich., 1960, JD, 1963. Bar: Calif. 1964. Assoc. O'Melveny & Myers, LA, 1963—66; ptnr. Manatt Phelps Rothenberg & Phillips, LA, 1968—90, Latham & Watkins, LA, 1990—; instr. sports law U. So. Calif., 1969, 1976, 1984, Whittier Coll. Law, 1980, 1984; pres., gen. counsel LA Lakers and LA Kings, 1967—79, LA Clippers Basketball Team, 1982—89; pres. U.S. Soccer Fedn., Chgo., 1990—98; chmn., founder Maj. League Soccer, N.Y.C., 1995. Bd. dirs., pres. Constl. Rights Found., 1987—90; soccer commr. 1984 Olympic Games; chmn., pres., CEO 1994 World Cup Organizing Com., 1990—94; founder, chmn. Major League Soccer, 1994—. Mem.: NBA (bd. govs. 1971—79, 1982—89), ABA, N.Am. Soccer League (bd. govs. 1977—80, Major League Soccer mgmt. com. 1994—), LA Bar Assn., LA County Bar Assn., State Bar Calif. (pres. 1989—90), Order of Coif. Office: Latham & Watkins 633 W 5th St Ste 4000 Los Angeles CA 90071-2005

ROTHENBERG, ALBERT, psychiatrist, educator; b. N.Y.C., June 2, 1930; s. Gabriel and Rose (Goldberg) R.; m. Julia C. Johnson, June 28, 1970; children: Michael, Mora, Rina. AB, Harvard U., 1952; MD, Tufts U., 1956. Diplomate: Am. Bd. Psychiatry and Neurology. Intern Pa. Hosp., Phila., 1956-57; resident in psychiatry Yale U., West Haven (Conn.) VA Hosp., 1957-58, Grace-New Haven Hosp., 1958-59, Yale Psychiat. Inst., New Haven, 1959-60, chief resident, 1960-61; practice medicine specializing in psychiatry New Haven, 1960-61, 1963-75; chief neuropsychiatry Rodriguez U.S. Army Hosp., San Juan, P.R., 1961-63; practice medicine specializing in psychiatry Farmington, Conn., 1975-79, Stockbridge, Mass., 1979-94, Chatham, N.Y., 1994—, Great Barrington, Mass., 1994-98; dir. rsch. Austen Riggs Center, Stockbridge, Mass., 1979-94. Asst. dir. Yale Psychiat. Inst., 1963-64, sr. staff mem., 1964-83; mem. staff Yale-New Haven Med. Ctr., West Haven VA Hosp., U. Conn. Health Ctr., Farmington; cons., mem. editorial bd. various jours. in psychiatry and psychology; instr. dept. psychiatry Yale U. Sch. Medicine, 1960-61, 63-64, asst. prof., 1964-68, assoc. prof., 1968-74, clin. prof., 1974-84; prof. psychiatry U. Conn. Sch. Medicine, Farmington, 1975-79, dir. residency tng., 1976-78, dir. clin. svcs., 1975-78; prin. investigator Studies in the Creative Process, 1964—; vis. prof. Pa. State U., 1971, adj. prof., 1971-78; vis. prof. dept. Am. studies Yale U., 1974-76, U. Capetown Med. Sch., South Africa, 1999, Saltpêtrière Hosp., Paris, 1999; lectr. dept. psychiatry Harvard U. Med. Sch., 1982-86, clin. prof., 1986—; researcher in psychotherapy. Author: (with B. Greenberg) Index of Scientific Writings on Creativity: Creative Men and Women, 1974, Index of Scientific Writings on Creativity: General 1566-1974, 1976; (with C.R. Hausman) The Creativity Question, 1976; The Emerging Goddess: The Creative Process in Art, Science and Other Fields, 1979; The Creative Process of Psychotherapy, 1988; Adolescence: Psychopathology, Normality, and Creativity, 1990; Creativity and Madness: New Findings and Old Stereotypes, 1990, Living Color, 2001; contbr. numerous articles on the creative process, schizophrenia, anorexia nervosa, and psychotherapy to profl. and popular jours. Researcher on creativity in the arts, sci. and tech. Served with M.C. U.S. Army, 1961-63. Recipient Tufts Med. Alumni award 1956, Rsch. Scientist Career Devel. award NIMH 1964, 69, Golestan Found. award 1991, 92, Kovler award MESAB, 1999; Guggenheim Meml. fellow 1974-75, Ctr. Adv. Study in Behavioral Studies fellow 1986-87, Netherlands Inst. for Adv. Study in Humanities and Social Scis. fellow, 1992-93. Fellow Am. Psychiat. Assn. (life), Am. Coll. Psychoanalysts; mem. AAAS, Mass. Psychiat. Soc., Am. Soc. Aesthetics, Rappaport-Klein Group, Sigma Xi. Democrat. Home: PO Box 1002 52 Pine Ridge Rd Canaan NY 12029-3101 Business E-Mail: albert_rothenberg@hms.harvard.edu.

ROTHENBERG, ELLIOT CALVIN, lawyer, author; b. Mpls., Nov. 12, 1939; s. Sam S. and Claire Sylvia (Feller) R.; m. Sally Smalying; children: Sarah, Rebecca, Sam. BA summa cum laude, U. Minn., 1961; JD, Harvard U. (Fulbright fellow), 1964. Bar: Minn. 1966, U.S. Dist. Ct. Minn. 1966, D.C. 1968, U.S. Supreme Ct. 1972, N.Y. 1974, U.S. Ct. Appeals (2d cir.) 1974, U.S. Ct. Appeals (8th cir.) 1975. Assoc. project dir. Brookings Inst., Washington, 1966-67; fgn. svc. officer, legal advisor U.S. Dept. State, Washington, 1968-73; Am. Embassy, Saigon; U.S. Mission to the UN; nat. law dir. Anti-Defamation League, N.Y.C., 1973-74; legal dir. Minn. Pub. Interest Rsch. Group, Mpls., 1974-77; pvt. practice law Mpls., 1977—. Adj. prof. William Mitchell Coll. Law, St. Paul, 1983—; faculty mem. several nat. comm. law and First Amendment seminars. Author: (with Zelman Cowen) Sir John Latham and Other Papers, 1965, The Taming of the Press: Cohen v. Cowles Media Co., 1999, The Taming of the Press, 1999; contbr. articles to profl. and scholarly jours. and books, newspapers, popular mags. State bd. dirs. YMCA Youth in Govt. Program, 1981-84; v.p. Twin Cities chpt. Am. Jewish Com., 1980-84; mem. Minn. Ho. of Reps., 1978-82, asst. floor leader (whip), 1981-82; pres., dir. North Star Legal Found., 1983—; legal affairs editor Pub. Rsch. Syndicated, 1986—; briefs and oral arguments published in full Landmark Briefs and Arguments of the Supreme Ct. of the U.S., Vol. 200, 1992; mem. citizens adv. com. Voyageurs Nat. Pk., 1979-81. Recipient Legis. Evaluation Assembly Legis. Excellence award, 1980, Vietnam Civilian Svc. medal U.S. Dept. State, 1970, North Star award U. Minn., 1961; Fulbright fellow, 1964-65. Mem. ABA, Minn. Bar Assn., Harvard Law Sch. Assn., Am. Legion, Mensa, Phi Beta Kappa. Jewish. Office: 3010 Hennepin Ave S Ste 231 Minneapolis MN 55408-2614 E-mail: srothenbe@aol.com.

ROTHENBERG, HARVEY DAVID, educational administrator; b. May 31, 1937; s. Max and Cecelia Rothenberg; m. Audrey Darlynne Roseman, July 5, 1964; children: David Michael, Mark Daniel. BBA, State U. Iowa, 1960; MA, U. No. Colo., 1961; postgrad., Harris Tchrs. Coll., 1962-63; PhD, Colo. State U., 1972. Distributive edn. tchr. Roosevelt H.S., St. Louis, 1961-63, Proviso West H.S., Hillside, Ill., 1963-64, Longmont (Colo.) Sr. H.S., 1964-69, 70-71; supr. rsch. and spl. programs St. Vrain Valley Sch. Dist., Longmont, 1971-72; chmn. bus. divsn. Arapahoe C.C., Littleton, Colo., 1972-75; dir. vocat., career and adult edn. Arapahoe County Sch. Dist. 6, Littleton, 1975-96; part-time instr. Met. State Coll., Denver, 1975-85, Arapahoe C.C., Littleton, 1975-80, Regis U., 1980—. Dir. faculty, curriculum Sch. Profl. Studies, Regis U., 1996-98, instr., facilitator, 1998—; owner HDR Bus. and Ednl. Consulting, 1988—; owner Shreveport Bombers Indoor Football Team of Indoor Profl. Football League, 1999-2001; vis. prof. U. Ala., Tuscaloosa, summer 1972; dir. Chatfield Bank, Littleton, 1974-83, Yaak River Mines Ltd., Amusement Personified Inc.; pres. Kuytia Inc., Littleton, 1975—; co-owner Albuquerque Lasers. Author: Conducting Successful Business Research, 1996. Mem. City of Longmont Long-Range Planning Commn., 1971-72, pres. Homeowners Bd., 1978-80; mem. Denver Union Sta. renovation com., 2002—; mem. Jefferson County Cmty. Devel. Com., 2003—. Recipient Outstanding Young Educator award St. Vrain Valley Sch. Dist., 1967, Outstanding Vocat. Educator, Colo., 1992, Western Region U.S., 1993. Mem. Am. Vocat. Assn., Nat. Assn. Local Sch. Adminstrs., Colo. Vocat. Assn. (mem. exec. com. 1966-68, treas. 1972-73), Littleton C. of C., Colo. Assn. Vocat. Adminstrs., Colo. Educators for and About Bus., Elks, Masons, Delta Sigma Pi, Delta Pi Epsilon. Home: 7461 S Sheridan Ct Littleton CO 80128-7084 Office Phone: 303-979-6800. Personal E-mail: rothenbergs@msn.com.

ROTHENBERG, JEROME, author, visual arts and literary educator; b. N.Y.C., Dec. 11, 1931; s. Morris and Estelle (Lichtenstein) R.; m. Diane Brodatz, Dec. 25, 1952; 1 son, Matthew. BA, CCNY, 1952; MA, U. Mich., 1953; LittD (hon.), SUNY, Oneonta, 1997. With Mannes Coll. Music, N.Y.C., 1961—70. Vis. prof. U. Calif., San Diego, 1971, 77-84, U. Wis.-Milw., 1974-75, San Diego State U., 1976-77, U. Calif., Riverside, 1980, U. Okla., Norman, 1984; vis. Aerol Arnold prof. English U. So. Calif., 1983; vis. writer in residence SUNY, Albany, 1986, prof. English SUNY, Binghamton, 1986-88; prof. visual arts and lit. U. Calif., San Diego, 1989—, chmn. visual arts, 1990-93; head, creative writing, 1994-95. Poet, freelance writer, 1956—; author: numerous books of poetry and prose including Between, 1967, Technicians of the Sacred, 1968, Poems for the Game of Silence, 1971, Shaking the Pumpkin, 1972, America a Prophecy, 1973, Revolution of the Word, 1974, Poland/1931, 1974, A Big Jewish Book, 1978, A Seneca Journal, 1978, Vienna Blood, 1980, Pre-Faces, 1981, Symposium of the Whole, 1983, That Dada Strain, 1983, New Selected Poems, 1986, Khurbn, 1989, Exiled in the Word, 1989, The Lorca Variations I-VIII, 1990, Apres le jeu de silence, 1991, The Lorca Variations (complete), 1993, Gematria, 1994, An Oracle for Delfi, 1995, Poems for The Millennium, vol. 1, 1995, Seedings, 1996, The Book, Spiritual Instrument, 1996, Poems for the Millennium, Vol. 2, 1998, A Paradise of Poets, 1999, A Book of The Book, 2000, The Case for Memory, 2001, Livre de Temoignage, 2002, A Book of Witness, 2003, María Sabina, 2003, Writing Through: Translations and Variations, 2004; editor, pub. Hawk's Well Press., N.Y.C., 1958-65, Some/Thing mag., 1966-69, Alcheringa: Ethnopoetics, 1970-76, New Wilderness Letter, 1976-86. Served with AUS, 1953-55. Recipient award in poetry Longview Found., 1960, Am. Book award, 1982, PEN Ctr. USA West award, 1994, 2002, PEN Oakland Josephine Miles award, 1994, 96, Alfonso el Sabio award for translation San Diego State U., 2004; Wenner-Gren Found. grantee-in-aide for rsch. in Am. Indian poetry, 1968; Guggenheim fellow in creative writing, 1974; NEA poetry grantee, 1976. Mem. PEN Am. Ctr., New Wilderness Found., World Poetry Acad. Office: care New Directions 80 8th Ave New York NY 10011-5126 Office Phone: 760-436-9923. Business E-Mail: jrothenb@ucsd.edu.

ROTHENBERG, KAREN H. dean, law educator; BA, Princeton U., 1973, MPA, 1974; JD, U. Va., 1979. Dean law sch.'s law and health care program U. Md., 2001—, law educator, 2001—. Formerly practiced with Washington D.C. Law firm of Covington and Burling; worked with a variety of health and med. orgns.; pres. Am. Soc. Law, Medicine and Ethics; lectr. on legal issues in health care; dir. law sch.'s law and health care program U. Md.; spl. asst. to dir., 1995—96. Co-editor-in-chief (jours.) Jour. Law, Medicine, and Ethics; co-editor: (book with Elizabeth Thompson) Women and Prenatal Testing: Facing the Challenges of Genetic Technology; contbr. articles on AIDS, women's health, genetics, right to forego treament. Recipient Joseph Healey Health Law Tchr.'s award, Am. Soc. Law, Medicine and Ethics. Mem.: NIH (sect. on prenatal care, recruitment & ret. of women in clin studies, sect. on ethical, legal and social implications of genetics), Nat. Inst. Child & Human Develop. (adv. coun.), ABA (coordinating group on bioethics and the law), Nat. Action Plan Breast Cancer, Ethics in Reproduction (nat. adv. bd.), Inst. Medicine's Com. (sect. legal and ethical issues for inclusion of women in clin. stud.). Office: U Md Law Sch 515 West Lombard St Baltimore MD 21201 Business E-Mail: krothenberg@law.umaryland.edu.

ROTHENBERG, ROBERT PHILIP, public relations counselor; b. N.Y.C., June 5, 1936; s. Robert Edward and Lillian Babette (Lustig) R. BA, Cornell U., 1956; MS, Boston U., 1958. With publicity dept. Columbia Pictures Corp., N.Y.C., 1959-60; asst. to pres., pub. rels. dir. Harry N. Abrams Pub. Co., N.Y.C., 1960-62; press sec. to gubernatorial candidate William R. Anderson Tenn., 1962; with Rowland Co., N.Y.C., 1963-70, v.p., 1965-67, sr. v.p., 1967-70; ptnr., exec. v.p. Robert Marston and Assocs., N.Y.C., 1970-88, sr. exec. v.p., 1978-88, also bd. dirs.; ptnr., pres. Marston and Rothenberg Pub. Affairs, Inc., N.Y.C. and Washington, 1977-88; chmn., pres. Rothenberg Pub. Rels. Comms. Counsel, N.Y.C., 1988—; v.p. Medbook Publs., Inc., 1995—; dir. pub. rels. BigChange Networks, LLC, Washington and N.Y.C., 1998—. Sr. cons. The Lund Group, Inc. Trustee Mus. of Holography, N.Y.C.; bd. dirs. Found. to Save African Endangered Wildlife; assoc. Nat. Park Found.; counselor Am. Bus. Cancer Rsch. Found., Southport, Conn.; bd. dirs. World Rehab. Fund, N.Y.C., 1982-98; fellow Met. Mus. of Art, 1990—; pres., chmn., bd. trustees St. Bartholomew's Preservation Found., 1992-95; mem. Blue Hill Troupe, Ltd.; bd. dirs. Amas Musical Theatre, Inc., 2002—03. With USAFR, 1959-65. Mem. Internat. Soc. Poets, Pride and Alarm Soc., English-Speaking Union, The Players Club. Unitarian Universalist. Home and Office: 400 E 54th St Apt 29B New York NY 10022-5169

ROTHENBERGER, DAVID ALBERT, surgeon; b. Sioux Falls, S.D., 1947; MD, Tufts U., 1973. Cert. colon and rectal surgery. Intern St. Paul-Ramsey Med. Ctr., 1973-74, resident gen. surgery, 1974-78; fellow colon rectal surgery U. Minn., Mpls., 1978-79; mem. staff Fairview Univ. Med. Ctr., Mpls.; cln. prof. surgery U. Minn., Mpls., chief divsn. colon and rectal surgery, divsn. surg. oncology; dir. U. Minn. Cancer Ctr., Mpls.; former pres. Am. Bd. Colon & Rectal Surgery, Taylor, Mich., mem. advisory council. Fellow ACS, Am. Soc. Colon and Rectal Surgeons (exec. coun., past pres. 1997—), Am. Surg. Assn., Soc. for Surgery of the Alimentary Tract, Western Surg. Assn. also: Mayo Mail Code 806 420 Delaware St SE Minneapolis MN 55455-0374

ROTHENBERGER, JACK RENNINGER, clergyman; b. Boyertown, Pa., Oct. 4, 1930; s. Stuart Henry and Beulah (Renninger) R.; m. Jean Delores Schultz, Sept. 8, 1951; children: Susan Marie, Bruce Wayne. BS, Juniata Coll., 1952; MDiv, Hartford Theol. Sem., 1955; STM, Temple U., 1962; D Ministry, Lancaster Theol. Sem., 1977. Ordained to ministry Schwenkfelder Ch., 1955. Pastor Palm and Lansdale (Pa.) Schwenkfelder Ch., 1955-63, 65-66; stated supply, interim pastor Pa. United Ch. of Christ, 1963-69; chaplain, tchr., coach, dir. admissions Perkiomen Sch., Pennsburg, Pa., 1955-56, 62-67, asst. headmaster, headmaster, coach football backfield, basketball, 1967-69; min. Christian edn. Ctrl. Schwenkfelder Ch., Worcester, Pa., 1969-74, sr. min., 1974-95, exec. min. emeritus, 2000—; interim supply pastor Wentz United Ch. of Christ, Worcester, Pa., 1997-99. Pres. World Christian Endeavor, 1994-2002, Internat. Christian Endeavor, Columbus, Ohio, 1983-87; v.p. World Christian Endeavor, 1990-94; mem. cabinet and bd. Pa. Coun. Chs., 1957—, sec., 1993-97; mem. Pa. Conf. Interch. Coop.; mem. Schwenckfeld Mission Bd., 1957—, Schwenckfelder Bd. Pubs., 1957—, Schwenckfelder Libr. Bd., 1957—, Schwenckfeldian in Exile Soc., 1955—; chmn. expansion com. Schwenckfelder Libr., 2d Heritage Ctr., also others. Author: Casper Schwenckfeld and the Ecumenical Ideal, 1962; editor The Schwenkfeldian mag., 1964-87; contbr. articles to profl. jours. First v.p. Schwenckfeld Manor, Lansdale, 1973-97, pres., 1997-2002; v.p. Meadowood Total Care Retirement Community, Worcester, Pa., 1983-98. Mem. No. Pa. Assn. United Ch. of Christ Ministerium, No. Pa. Ministerium, Methacton Area Ministerium, Montgomery County Sunday Sch. Assn. (past pres.), also others. Republican. Home: 127 Bluebird Xing Lansdale PA 19446-5843 E-mail: jackrothenberger@cs.com. *I extend the hand of fellowship to all believers in the Living Christ regardless of their specific expression of that faith. In a world of constant rapid change we can find direction through faith in the Living God revealed by Jesus.*

ROTHER, JOHN CHARLES, association executive, lawyer; b. Springfield, Mo., Apr. 18, 1947; s. Charles C. and Eleanor J. (Morrison) R. BA with honors, Oberlin Coll., 1969; JD with honors, U. Pa., 1975. Bar: Pa. 1975, D.C. 1977. Appellate litigator NLRB, Washington, 1975-77; counsel Senator Jacob Javits U.S. Senate labor & human resources commn., Washington, 1977-81; staff dir., chief counsel spl. commn. on aging U.S. Senate, Washington, 1981-84; dir. legislation and pub. policy Am. Assn. Ret. Persons, Washington, 1984—. Founding mem. Nat. Acad. Social Ins.; mem. study on quality in managed care Inst. Medicine. Bd. dirs. Corp. for Nat. and Cmty. Svc., Nat. Acad. on Aging, Found. for Accountability; mem. Nat. Com. for Quality Assurance. Named One of 150 Who Make A Difference, Nat. Jour., Washington, 1986. Mem. D.C. Bar, Gerontol. Soc. Am. Office: Am Assn Ret Persons 601 E St NW Washington DC 20049-0001

ROTHERHAM, THOMAS G. diversified financial services company executive; BA, U. Iowa. From mem. staff to exec. ptnr. McGladrey & Pullen LLP, Davenport, Iowa, 1971-88, exec. ptnr., 1988—. Mem. AICPA (SEC regulations com., SEC practice section exec. com.), Minn. Soc. CPAs. Office: McGladrey & Pullen LLP 102 W 2nd St Fl 2 Davenport IA 52801-1803

ROTHERMEL, DAN, humanities educator; b. Paterson, N.J., Dec. 27, 1947; s. Daniel Angstadt and Jean (Archer) Rothermel; m. Hannah Kraai, July 1, 1972; children: Molly Melinda, Robyn Leigh, Jaye Will. BA in Elem. Edn., Ariz. State U., 1970, MA in Elem. Edn., 1974, MS in Phys. Edn., 1981; PhD of Reading and Writing Instrn., U. N.H., 1999. Tchr. Tempe Schs., Tempe, Ariz., 1972—81, Somersworth Schs., Somersworth, NH, 1982—86, Kittery Schs., Kittery, Maine, 1986—96; grad. tchg. asst. U. N.H., Durham, 1996—99; asst. prof. Ea. Conn. State U., Willimantic, 1999—2003; assoc. prof. U. New Eng., Biddeford, Maine, 2003—. Author: Starting Points: How to Set Up a Writing Workshop, 1996, Sweet Dreams, Robyn, 1991. Avocations: bicycling, running, golf, crossword puzzles. Office: Univ New England Dept Edn 11 Hills Beach Rd Biddeford ME 04005

ROTHERMEL, DANIEL KROTT, lawyer, holding company executive; b. West Reading, Pa., Mar. 21, 1938; s. Daniel Grim and Ruth Elizabeth (Krott) R.; m. Sarah Finch, July 9, 1960; children: Anne, Daniel F., K. Melissa. BS, Pa. State U., 1960; JD, Am. U., 1966. Bar: D.C. 1967. Acct. Lukens Steel Co., Coatesville, Pa., 1960-61; pvt. practice Reading, Pa., 1966-68; atty. Carpenter Tech. Corp., Reading, 1968-70, resident counsel, 1970-78, asst. sec., 1972-73, sec., 1973-88, v.p., gen. counsel, sec., 1978-88; pres., chief exec. officer Cumru Assocs. Inc., Reading, Pa., 1989—. Bd. dirs. Sovereign Bank, Sovereign Bancorp, Inc., lead dir., chmn. exec. com. Mem. Inst. Cmty. Affairs, Pa. State U., 1974-78; bd. dirs. Berks County chpt. ARC, 1983-86; mem., chmn. adv. bd. Berks campus Pa. State U., 1982—97; ch. lay leader. Lt. USNR, 1961-66. Mem. ABA, D.C. Bar Assn., Am. Soc. Corp. Secs., U.S. C. of C., Pa. C. of C., Reading-Berks C. of C., Rotary. Republican. Lutheran. Home: 20 Glenbrook Dr Reading PA 19607-9645 Office: Cumru Assocs Inc PO Box 6573 Reading PA 19610-0573

ROTHERMEL, JAMES DOUGLAS, retired finance educator; b. Burton, Tex., Aug. 20, 1918; s. Bailleux Ervin and Nathalie (Ponfick) R.; m. Dorothy Ann Hodde, Aug. 24, 1947; children: James Douglas Jr., Donald Henry. AA, Blinn Coll., 1947; BS, SW Tex. State U., 1949, MEd, 1952; postgrad., U. Houston, 1965-67. Instr. bus. edn. Brenham (Tex.) H.S., 1949-52; prin. Schulenburg (Tex.) H.S., 1952-57, Ganado (Tex.) H.S., 1957-64; instr., chmn. bus. adminstrn. divsn. San Jacinto Coll., Pasadena, Tex., 1964-78, part-time instr., 1978-81; ret., 1981. Councilman City of Brenham (Tex.) High Sch., 1949—52, mayor pro tem, 1988—96; mem. Ret. Sr. Vol. Program (RSVP), 1984—2000, mem. Brazos Valley adv. coun., 1990—97, 2000—, chmn., 1994—97, mem. Washington County adv. coun., 1986—2000, chmn., 1995—2000; organizer, chmn. Washington County Vets. Meml. Plz., 2000—. With 14th Constrn. Bn. USN, 1942—45. Mem. Tex. Ret. Tchrs. Assn., Tex. Bus. Edn. Assn., Brenham Louise Giddings Ret. Tchrs. Assn. (legis. chmn. 1984-2003, pres. 1996-98), Am. Assn. Ret. Persons (legis. chmn. 1982-2003, instr. 55/Alive 1985-98, asst. state coord. 55/Alive 1986-88), Am. Legion (comdr. Schulenburg post 143, comdr. 9th dist. 1961-63, vice comdr. 1959-61, comdr. Buddy Wright post 1997-98), Optimists, Rotary. Republican. Lutheran. Avocations: hunting, fishing, travel, gardening, woodworking. Home: 803 Robinhood Rd Brenham TX 77833-2567

ROTHERMEL, JOAN ASHLEY, artist; b. Winchester, Mass., Mar. 10, 1930; d. Mark Braden Ashley and Anne Jorgenson; m. Harold Christian Rothermel, Dec. 30, 1950; children: Lynn Schoenfield, Lawrence. BFA, Miami U., Oxford, Ohio, 1951, MEd in Art, 1970. Art tchr. Middletown (Ohio) Fine Arts Ctr., 1971-77. Sole juror nat. and state watercolor exhbns., including Ohio Watercolor Soc., Cen. Ohio Watercolor Soc., Capital U., Columbus, Beaufort (S.C.) Art Assn., SC, S.C. Watercolor Soc., Toledo Artists Club, 1982—99; instr. watercolor workshops nat. and state exhbns., including Firelands Area Art League, Norwalk, Ohio, Hilton Head Island Workshops, SC, Wyoming Valley Art League, Wilkes-Barre, Pa., Idaho Watercolor Soc., Boise, St. Louis Artists' Guild, Hawaii Watercolor Soc., Honolulu, 1982—, Kanuga Watercolor Workshops, Hendersonville, NC, 2002; juror of awards Am. Watercolor Soc., 2005. One-woman shows include Middletown, Sandusky, Boston Mills Art Festivals, Penninsula, Ohio, exhibited in group shows at Am. Watercolor Soc., Nat. Watercolor Soc., Allied Artists of Am., Nat. Acad. Design, Rocky Mountain Nat. Watermedia Exhbn., Knickerbocker Artists, Nat. Arts Club, Ohio Watercolor Soc., San Diego Watercolor Soc., Ga. Watercolor Soc., represented in corp. collections and galleries, Owens-Ill. Corp., Toledo, Soc. Bank, Sandusky, Oglesby-Barnitz Bank, Middletown, 1st Nat. Bank, Cen. Bank, Cleve., Livingstine Taylor Gallery, Sandusky, works featured in books, Painting the Spirit of Nature, 1984, Exploring Color, 1985, The Creative Artist, 1990, others, also mags. including, Am. Artist, The Artist's Mag. Mem. Am. Watercolor So. (treas. 1986—, Dolphin fellow, Gold medal honor, Bronze medal, 8 other awards 1983-99), Nat. Watercolor Soc., Allied Artists of Am., Midwest Watercolor Soc., Ohio Watercolor Soc., Knickerbocker Artists, Salmagundi Club. Home: 221 46th St Sandusky OH 44870-4894 E-mail: landolls@kellnet.com.

ROTHERT, MARILYN L., dean, nursing educator; b. June 4, 1939; married; 3 children. BSN cum laude, Ohio State U., 1961; MA in Ednl. Psychol., Mich. State U., 1979, PhD in Ednl. Psychol., 1980. RN, Mich. Staff nurse Univ. Hosp., Columbus, Ohio, 1961; instr. sch. nursing Hurley Hosp., Flint, Mich., 1961-66; asst. instr. sch. nursing Mich. State U., East Lansing, 1967-77, grad. asst. dept. community health sci., 1977-80, asst. prof. Coll. Human Medicine, 1980-82, asst. prof., dir. lifelong edn. Coll. Nursing, 1982-84, asst. prof. Coll. Human Medicine, 1982-84, assoc. prof., dir. lifelong edn. Coll. Nursing, 1984-88, assoc. prof. Coll. Human Medicine, 1984-86, prof., dir. lifelong edn. Coll. Nursing, 1988-92, prof., assoc. dean outreach and profl. devel., 1992-96, prof., dean Coll. Nursing, 1996—. Cons. No. Ill. U., Ohio State U., Mich. State Dept. Natural Resources, Can. Nurses Assn., Mich. Judicial Inst., Med. Coll. Va., U. Wash., Kirtland Coll., Anderson Coll. Contbr. articles to profl. jours. Co-chmn. Capitol Health Event, 1987-88; mem. worksite health subcom. Mich. Dept. Pub. Health; mem. State 4-H Health Com. Coop. Extension Svc., 1972-75, 82—; mem. med. adv. com. Mich. Civil Svc. Health Screening Unit, 1984. Mem. ANA (mem. coun. continuing edn., nurse researchers), Mich. Nurses Assn. (chmn. continuing edn. adv. com. 1989), Soc. for Med. Decision Making, The Brunswik Soc., Soc. for Judgment and Decision Making, Soc. for Rsch. in Nursing Edn., Midwest Nursing Rsch. Soc., Am. Pub. Health Assn., Nat. Ctr. for Health Edn., Nat. League for Nursing, Mich. State U. Faculty/Profl. Women's Assn. (bd. dirs. 1989—), Capitol Area Dist. Nurses Assn. (mem. nom. com. 1986, continuing edn. com. 1984), Phi Kappa Phi. Office: Mich State U Coll Nursing A-230 Life Sci Bldg East Lansing MI 48824

ROTHFELD, MICHAEL B. theatrical productions executive, investor; b. N.Y.C., May 19, 1947; m. Ella M. Foshay, May 22, 1970; 2 children. BA, Columbia U., 1969, MS, MBA, cert. internatl fellows program, Columbia U., 1971. With Time, Inc., 1971-76, assoc. editor Fortune, 1971-74; asst. to chmn. bd. dirs., CEO Time Inc., N.Y.C., 1974-76; with Salomon Bros., N.Y.C., 1976-83, v.p., 1979-83, The First Boston Corp., N.Y.C., 1983-84, mng. dir., 1985-89; gen. ptnr. Bessemer Ptnrs. and Bessemer Holdings, 1989-97, ltd. ptnr., 1997-98. Chmn. bd. dirs. Graphic Controls Corp., 1995-98; bd. vis. Columbia Coll., 1998—, vice chmn. 2002-, bd. adv. Knight-Bagheot program in fin. journalism Grad. Sch. Journalism, 1998—; chmn. Redfields, LLC, Eagle Prodns., LLC, N.Y.C. Prodr. off-broadway prodn., 1999, Gore Vidal's The Best Man, 2000 (winner Drama Desk award, Outer Critics Circle award, Tony nomination). Office: Eagle Productions LLC 200 E 69th St New York NY 10021

ROTHFIELD, LAWRENCE I. microbiology educator; b. N.Y.C., Dec. 30, 1927; s. Joseph and Henrietta (Brown) R.; m. Naomi Fox, Sept. 18, 1953; children: Susan Anne, Lawrence, Jane, John. BA, Cornell U., 1947; MD, NYU, 1951. Intern, then resident Bellevue, Presbyn. hosps., N.Y.C., 1951-53, 55-57; successively instr., clin. asst. prof., asst. prof. NYU Sch. Medicine, 1957-64; from asst. prof. to assoc. prof. Albert Einstein Coll. Medicine, N.Y.C., 1964-68; prof. U. Conn. Sch. Medicine, Farmington, 1968—, chmn. dept. microbiology, 1968-80. Mem. molecular biology rev. panel NIH, 1970-75, microbiology and immunology adv. com. Pres.'s Biomed. Rsch. Panel, 1975, molecular biology rev. panel NSF, 1979-83; mem. microbial physiology and genetics rev. panel NIH, 1990-94, chairperson, 1991-93. Author: Structure and Function of Biological Membranes, 1972; mem. editorial bd. Jour. Membrane Biology, 1969-83, Jour. Biol. Chemistry, 1974-80. With M.C. U.S. Army, 1953-55. Mem. Am. Soc. Biol. Chemists, Am. Soc. Microbiology (chmn. microbial physiology div. 1975). Home: 540 Deercliff Rd Avon CT 06001-2859 Office: U Conn Health Center Farmington CT 06032 Office Phone: 860-679-3581. Business E-Mail: lroth@neuron.uchc.edu.

ROTHFIELD, NAOMI FOX, physician; b. Bklyn., Apr. 5, 1929; d. Morris and Violet (Bloomgarden) Fox; m. Lawrence Rothfield, Sept. 18, 1954; children: Susan, Lawrence, John, Jane. BA, Bard Coll., 1950; MD, NYU, 1955. Intern Lenox Hill Hosp., N.Y.C., 1955-56; instr. NYU Sch. Medicine, 1956-62, asst. prof., 1962-68; assoc. prof. U. Conn. Sch. Medicine, Farmington, 1968-72, prof., 1972—, chief divsn. rheumatic diseases, 1972—99. Contbr. chpts. to books, articles to med. jours. Bd. dirs. Conn. Choral Artists, 1999—. Mem. Am. Soc. Clin. Investigation, Am. Rheumatism Assn., Assn. Am. Physics. Jewish. Home: 540 Deercliff Rd Avon CT 06001-2859 Office: U Conn Sch Medicine Divsn Rheumatic Diseases Farmington CT 06030-0001 Office Phone: 860-679-3604. E-mail: rothfield@nso.uchc.edu.

ROTHKOPF, ARTHUR J. college president; b. N.Y.C., May 24, 1935; s. Abraham and Sarah (Mehlman) Rothkopf; m. Barbara Sarnoff, Dec. 25, 1958; children: Jennifer, Katherine. AB, Lafayette Coll., 1955; JD, Harvard U., 1958. Bar: N.Y. 1959, D.C. 1967. Atty. U.S. Dept. Treasury, N.Y.C., 1958—60, SEC, Washington, 1960—63; assoc. tax legis. counsel U.S. Dept. Treasury, Washington, 1963—66; ptnr. Hogan & Hartson, Washington, 1967—91; gen. counsel U.S. Dept. Transp., Washington, 1991—92, dep. sec., 1992—93; pres. Lafayette Coll., Easton, Pa., 1993—. Bd. dirs. Ins. Svcs. Office, Inc., Jersey City, Bristol West Holdings, Lehigh Valley Partnership. Trustee Fed. City Coun., Washington, 1983—91, Lehigh Valley Hosp.; chair bd. dirs. Coun. Higher Edn. Accreditation; bd. dirs., past chmn. Assn. Ind. Colls. and Univs. Pa. Mem.: The Pa. Soc. (1st v.p.), Harvard Club of N.Y.C., Chevy Chase Club, Met. Club of Washington. Jewish. Home: 515 College Ave Easton PA 18042-7623 Office: Lafayette Coll 316 Markle Hall Easton PA 18042 Office Phone: 610-330-5200. Business E-Mail: rothkopa@lafayette.edu.

ROTHLISBERGER, RODNEY JOHN, music educator; b. Bottineau, N.D., May 13, 1940; s. Forrest John and Ellen Rothlisberger; m. Gay Elaine Mohr, Dec. 20, 1975 (div.). BA, St. Olaf Coll., 1962; MA, Eastman Sch. Music, 1967; DMusA, U. Colo., 1978. Anacortes Washington Pub. Schs., 1962-64; organist, choirmaster U.S. Mil. Acad., West Point, NY, 1965-67; instr., prof. Bowdoin Coll., Brunswick, Maine, 1967-70; instr. Melbourne (Australia) HS, 1973-75; prof. Berea (Ky.) Coll., 1976-77; instr. Concordia Coll., Moorhead, Minn., 1979-81, Moorhead Pub. Schs., 1989-95; prof. Minn. State U., Moorhead, 1995—, chmn. music dept., 2002—. Active Civic Opera Bd., 1996—2002; bd. dir. Fargo-Moorhead Symphony, 2004—; bd. dirs. Luth. Brotherhood, Moorhead, 1988—2002, Red River Boy Choir, Moorhead, 1984—2000, Arts Coun. Fargo-Moorhead, 1985—89. With U.S. Army, 1965—67. Recipient Achievement award, Lake Agassiz Arts Coun., 1987. Mem.: Am. Guild Organists (dean Red River Valley chpt. 1985—87, Minn. state chmn. 1995—2002, chmn. nat. com. membership 1994—2000), Music Educators Nat. Conf., Am. Choral Dirs. Assn., Nat. Assn. Tchrs. Singing. Presbyterian. Avocation: reading. Home: 1021 River Dr Moorhead MN 56560-3369 Office: Minn State U Moorhead 1104 7th Ave S Moorhead MN 56563-0002 Office Phone: 218-477-2966. E-mail: rothlisb@mnstate.edu.

ROTHMAN, BERNARD, lawyer; b. N.Y.C., Aug. 11, 1932; s. Harry and Rebecca (Fritz) R.; m. Barbara Joan Schaeffer, Aug. 1953; children: Brian, Adam, Helene. BA cum laude, CCNY, 1953; JD, NYU, 1959. Bar: N.Y. 1959, U.S. Dist. Ct. (ea. and so. dists.) N.Y. 1962, U.S. Ct. Appeals (2d cir.) 1965, U.S. Supreme Ct. 1966, U.S. Tax Ct. 1971. Assoc. Held, Telchin & Held, 1961-62; asst. U.S. atty. Dept. Justice, 1962-66; assoc. Edward Gettinger & Peter Gettinger, 1966-68; ptnr. Schwartz, Rothman & Abrams, P.C., 1968-78, Ferster, Bruckman, Wohl, Most & Rothman, LLP, N.Y.C., 1978-98, Law Offices of Bernard Rothman, N.Y.C., 1999—. Acting judge Village of Larchmont, 1982-88, dep. Village atty., 1974-81, former arbitrator Civil Ct., N.Y.C., family disputes panel Am. Arbitration Assn.; guest lectr. domestic rels. and family law on radio and TV, also numerous legal and mental health orgns. Author: Loving and Leaving-Winning at the Business of Divorce, 1998; co-author: Family Law Syracuse Law Rev. of N.Y. Law, 1992, Leaving Home, Family Law Review, 1987, Put Your Kids First, Am. Bar Assn. Family Adv. Quar., 2000; contbr. articles to profl. jours. Mem. exec. bd., past v.p. Westchester Putnam coun. Boy Scouts Am., 1975—; past mem. nat. coun., 1977-81; mem. adv. com. N.Y. State PEACE, 1994—; pres. Congregation B'nai Israel, 1961-63, B'nai Brith, Larchmont chpt., 1981-83. Recipient Silver Beaver award Boy Scouts Am., Wood Badge award. Fellow Am. Acad. Matrimonial Lawyers (bd. govs. N.Y. chpt. 1986-87, 91-93), Interdisciplinary Forum on Mental Health and Family Law (co-chair 1986-97); mem. ABA (family law sect., contbr. Family Advocate Quar.), N.Y. State Bar Assn. (exec. com. family law sect. 1982—, co-chmn. com. on mediation and arbitration 1982-88, 93—, com. on legis. 1978-88, com. on child custody 1985-88, com. alt. dispute resolution), Assn. of Bar of City of N.Y. (women in the cts. com. 1996-99), N.Y. State Magistrate Assn., Westchester Magistrate Assn., N.Y. Rd. Runners Club, Limousine 6 Track Club. Democrat. Office: 750 3rd Ave Fl 29 New York NY 10017-2703 Office Phone: 212-983-1999. E-mail: divorcelawyer@att.net.

ROTHMAN, CAROL, theater director; BSS, Northwestern U.; MFA, NYU, 1973. Co-founder Second Stage Theatre, N.Y.C., artistic dir. Mem. nat. adv. bd. Sch. Speech Northwestern U. Dir.: (plays), Williamstown Theatre Festival. Nominee Best Dir. Tony award; recipient OBIE award, Rosamund Gilder award. Office: Second State Theatre 307 West 43rd St New York NY 10036

ROTHMAN, DAVID J. history and medical educator; b. N.Y.C., Apr. 30, 1937; s. Murray and Anne (Beier) R.; m. Sheila Miller, June 26, 1960; children: Matthew, Micol. BA, Columbia U., 1958; MA, Harvard U., 1959, PhD, 1964. Asst. prof. history Columbia U., N.Y.C., 1964-67, assoc. prof., 1967-71, prof., 1971—, Bernard Schoenberg prof. social medicine, dir. Ctr. for Study of Society and Medicine. Fulbright-Hayes prof. Hebrew U., Jerusalem, 1968-69, India, 1982; vis. Pinkerton Prof. Sch. Criminal Justice, State U. N.Y., at Albany, 1973-74; Samuel Paley lectr. Hebrew U., Jerusalem, 1977; Mem. Com. for Study of Incarceration, 1971-74; co-dir. Project on Community Alternatives, 1978-82; chmn. adv. bd. on criminal justice Clark Found., 1978-82; mem. bd. advisors The Project on Death in Am., Open Soc. Inst., 1995-2000, trustee; mem. bd. trustees Open Soc. Inst., 1996—, pres. Inst. on Medicine as a Profession, 2003—. Author: Politics and Power, 1966, The Discovery of the Asylum, 1971; co-author: Doing Good, 1978, Conscience and Convenience: The Asylum and its Alternatives in Progressive America, 1980; (with Sheila M. Rothman) The Willowbrook Wars, 1984; Strangers at the Bedside, 1991, Beginings Count: The Technological Imperative in American Health Care, 1997; editor: The World of the Adams Chronicles, 1976, (with Sheila M. Rothman) On Their Own: The Poor in Modern America, 1972, The Sources of American Social Tradition, 1975, (with Stanton Wheeler) Social History and Social Policy, 1981, (with Norval Morris) The Oxford History of the Prison, 1995, (with Steven Marcus and Stephanie Kiceluk) Medicine and Western Civilization, 1995, (with Sheila M. Rothman) The Pursuit of Perfection, 2003. Recipient Albert J. Beveridge prize Am. Hist. Assn., 1971. Mem. Am. Hist. Assn., N.Y. Acad. Medicine, Phi Beta Kappa. Office: Columbia U Coll Physicians and Surgeons Ctr Study Soc and Medicine 630 W 168th St New York NY 10032-3702

ROTHMAN, DEANNA, electroplating company executive; b. Bklyn., Sept. 20, 1938; d. Frank Philip and Elsie (Goldstein) Dukofsky; m. Edward Rothman, Dec. 8, 1956 (div. July 1984); children: Jeffrey Scott, Michele Dawn, Robert Jay; m. Ronald Friedman, Aug. 17, 1986. B.A., Bklyn. Coll., 1968. Exec. Bronzemaster Co., Bklyn., 1969-80, Perma Plating Co. Inc., Bklyn., 1980-84; pres. Duratron Finishing Corp., Bklyn., 1984—. Skillman Metal Corp., Bklyn., 1987—, Deron Holding Corp., Bklyn., 1992—; v.p. Skillman Realty Corp., Bklyn., 1989—. Sec. Tenants Assn., S.I., 1973-77; v.p. Orgn. Rehab. and Tng., Woodmere, N.Y., 1978-80; sponsor Spl. Olympics; mem. East N.Y. Local Devel. Corp. Mem. Masters Electroplating Assn., Am. Metal Finishers, NAFE, NOW, SCORE. Republican. Avocations: painting, collecing art deco, dance, theatre.

ROTHMAN, EDWARD S. information technology executive, consultant; b. London, Eng., July 4, 1963; s. Louis James and Patricia Eve Rothman; m. Kelly Weems, Oct. 31, 1996; 1 child, Hannah Elizabeth. Chief technol. officer Episys, Cambridge, England, 1987—99; chief info. officer Guardsmark, Memphis, 1999—. Dir. Memphis Housecalls Inc., 2003—. Mem.: Inst. Analysts and Programmers, Royal Automobile Club. Jewish. Achievements include patents for various computer algorithmns. Avocations: chess, mathematics. Home: 30 Lombardy Rd Memphis TN 38111 Office: 22 S 2d Street Memphis TN 38101 Personal E-mail: edwardr@msn.com. E-mail: rothmanedwards@guardsmark.com.

ROTHMAN, FRANK GEORGE, biology professor, academic administrator, biochemical genetics researcher, geneticist; b. Budapest, Hungary, Feb. 2, 1930; came to U.S., 1938; s. Stephen and Irene Elizabeth (Manheim) R.; m. Joan Therese Kiernan, Aug.22, 1953; children: Michael, Jean, Stephen, Maria. BA, U. Chgo., 1948, MS, 1951; PhD, Harvard U., 1955. Postdoctoral fellow NSF, U. Wis., MIT, 1956-58, Am. Cancer Soc., MIT, Cambridge, 1958-59; postdoctoral assoc. MIT, Cambridge, 1957-61; asst. prof. Brown U., Providence, 1961-65, assoc. prof., 1965-70, prof., 1970-97, dean of biology, 1984-90, provost, 1990-95, prof. emeritus, 1997—. Sr. advisor, Project Kaleidoscope, 1999—. Contbr. articles to profl. jours. Served with U.S. Army, 1954-56. Spl. fellow USPHS, U. Sussex, Eng., 1967-68; NSF grantee, 1961-84. Fellow AAAS; mem. Genetics Soc. Am. Personal E-mail: frank_rothman@brown.edu.

ROTHMAN, HENRY ISAAC, lawyer; b. Rochester, N.Y., Mar. 29, 1943; s. Maurice M. and Golde (Nusbaum) R.; m. Golda R. Shatz, July 3, 1966; children: Alan, Miriam, Cheryl, Suri. BA, Yeshiva U., 1964; JD, Cornell U., 1967. Bar: N.Y. 1967. Trial atty. SEC, N.Y.C., 1967-69; ptnr. Booth, Lipton & Lipton, N.Y.C., 1969-87, Parker, Chapin, Flattau & Klimpl, N.Y.C., 1987-2000, Jenkens & Gilchrist Parker Chapin LLP, N.Y.C., 2001—. Bd. dirs. Camp Morasha, Lake Como, Pa., 1982—, vice chmn., 1992-2000; bd. dirs. Assn. of Jewish Sponsored Camps, Inc., 1986-2000; bd. dirs. Yeshiva U. High Schs., N.Y.C., 1984-99, vice chmn. bd., 1990-91, chmn. bd., 1992-95; v.p. Manhattan Day Sch., N.Y.C., 1985-96, bd. dirs.; assoc. v.p. Orthodox Union, N.Y.C., 1990-2000, v.p., 2001—; vice chmn. bd. dirs. Azrieli Grad. Sch. Jewish Edn. and Adminstrn., 2000—. Mem. ABA (com. on fed. regulation of securities), N.Y. State Bar Assn., Assn. of Bar of City of N.Y., Yeshiva U. Alumni Assn. (pres. 1986-88, hon. pres. 1988-90). Office: Jenkens & Gilchrist Parker Chapin LLP The Chrysler Bldg 405 Lexington Ave New York NY 10174-0002 Office Phone: 212-704-6000. Business E-Mail: hrothman@jenkens.com.

ROTHMAN, HOWARD JOEL, lawyer; b. N.Y.C., July 10, 1945; BA, CCNY, 1967; JD, Bklyn. Law Sch., 1971; LLM, NYU, 1972. Bar: N.Y. 1972. From assoc. to ptnr. Marshall, Bratter, Greene, Allison & Tucker, N.Y.C., 1972-82; ptnr. Rosenman & Colin LLP, N.Y.C., 1982-97, Kramer, Levin, Naftalis & Frankel LLP, N.Y.C., 1997—. Mem. adv. panel Commr. Fin. of City of N.Y., 1981-83. Author profl. books and articles. Mem. ABA (corp. tax. com. 1977-87, income from real property com. 1980—), Internat. Bar Assn., N.Y. State Bar Assn. (exec. com. tax sect. 1999-2000, corps. com. 1979-87, partnerships com. 1979—, N.Y.C. tax matters com. 1977—, income from real property com. 1987—), Bur. Nat. Affairs (real estate jour. 1984—, tax mgmt. adv. bd 1979—), Alliance for Young Artists and Writers (bd. dirs.), Poetry Soc. Am. (bd. dirs.), N.Y. Found. for Arts (bd. dirs.).

ROTHMAN, JAMES EDWARD, cell biologist, educator; b. Haverhill, Mass., Nov. 3, 1950; BA summa cum laude, Yale U., 1971; PhD in Biochemistry, Harvard U., 1976; D h.c., U. Regensburg, 1995, U. Geneva, 1997. Fellow MIT, Cambridge, 1976-78; asst. prof., dept. biochemistry Stanford (Calif.) U., 1978—81, assoc. prof., 1981—84, prof., 1984—88; E.R. Squibb prof. molecular biology Princeton (N.J.) U., 1988—91; Paul Marks chair Sloan-Kettering Inst., N.Y.C., 1991—, chmn. program in cellular biochemistry and biophysics, 1991—2003, vice chmn., 1994—2003. Editl. bd. Molecular and Cellular Biology, 1982—84; chmn. Gordon Conf. on Molecular Membrane Biology, 1983; bd. editors Science, 1984—89; editl. com. Ann. Review Biochemistry, 1985—90, assoc. editor, 2003; editl. bd. Cell, 1984—94; study sect., Molecular Cytology NIH, 1990—94, coun., Nat. Inst. Digestive and Kidney Diseases, 1997—99; Devel. Therapeutics Review Group Nat. Cancer Inst., 1997—98; bd. sr. editors Jour. Clin. Investigation, 2002—. Recipient Eli Lily award for Fundamental Rsch. in Biol. Chemistry, 1986, Passano Young Scientist award, 1986, Alexander Von Humboldt award, 1989, Heinrich Wieland prize, 1990, Rosenstiel award in Biomedical Sciences, 1994, V.D. Mattia award, 1994, Fritz Lipmann award, 1995, Mayor's award for Excellence in Sci. and Tech., 1995, Gairdner Found. Internat. award Gairdner Found., 1996, King Faisal Internat. prize in Sci., 1996, Harden medal, 1997, Feodor Lynen award, 1997, Jacobaeus prize, 1999, Heineken prize, 2000, Otto-Warburg medal, 2001, Albert Lasker award for Basic Medical Rsch., Lasker Found., 2002, Louisa Gross Horwitz prize of Columbia U., 2002; Fellow Andrew W. Mellon, 1979-1982; scholar Dreyfus Found. Teacher, 1981-86; commd. as a Kentucky Col., by Gov. State of Kentucky, 1997. Fellow: Am. Acad. of Arts and Sciences, NAS (Richard Lounsbery award 1997); mem.: European Molecular Biology Orgn. (foreign assoc. 1995), Inst. Medicine, NAS. Office: Columbia U Russ Berrie Med Sci Pavilion 1150 St Nicholas Ave Rm 520 New York NY 10032

ROTHMAN, MELVIN L. judge; b. Montreal, Que., Can., Apr. 6, 1930; s. Charles and Nellie (Rosen) R.; m. Joan Elizabeth Presant, Aug. 4, 1954; children: Ann Elizabeth, Claire Presant, Margot Sneyd. BA, McGill U., 1951, B.C.L., 1954. Bar: Que. 1954. Practice law, Montreal, 1954-71; mem. Phillips, Vineberg, Goodman, Phillips & Rothman; judge Superior Ct., Dist. of Montreal, 1971-83, Ct. Appeal of Que., 1983—; dep. judge Supreme Ct. N.W. Territories, 1977—. Mem. Jr. Bar of Montreal (pres. 1963-64), Bar of Montreal (council 1964-65), Institut Philippe Pinel (sec., dir. 1965-70). Home: 487 Argyle Ave Westmount QC Canada H3Y 3B3 Office: Que Ct of Appeal Ct House Cormier Bldg 100 Notre Dame E 10 St Antoine St E Montreal QC H2Y YB6 Canada E-mail: melvin.rothman@sympatico.ca.

ROTHMAN, PAUL ALAN, publishing executive; b. Bklyn., June 26, 1940; s. Fred B. and Dorothy (Regosin) R.; m. Mary Ann Dalson, July 28, 1966 (div. 1992); m. Carol Ann Liske, Sept. 17, 1999; children: Deborah, Diana. BA, Swarthmore Coll., 1962; JD, U. Mich., 1965; LLM in Taxation, NYU, 1967. Bar: NY 1965. Assoc. Dewey, Ballentine, Busby, Palmer & Wood, NYC, 1965-67; v.p. Fred B. Rothman & Co., Littleton, Colo., 1967-85, pres., 1985-2000; chmn. bd. Colo. Plasticard, Littleton, 1983-95; owner LoDo Law Books, Denver, 1998—. Editor: Mich. Law Rev., 1963—65. Home: 1801 Wynkoop St Apt 708 Denver CO 80202-1196 Office: LoDo Law Books 1701 Wynkoop St Union Sta # 300 Denver CO 80202 Office Phone: 720-904-5145.

ROTHMAN, STEVEN R. congressman; b. Englewood, N.J., Oct. 14, 1952; divorced; 2 children. BA, Syracuse U., 1974; JD, Washington U., 1977. Pvt. practice law, 1978-93, 96; judge Bergen County's Surrogate's Ct., 1993-96; mem. U.S. Congress from 9th N.J. dist., 1997—; mem. appropriations com. Mayor City of Englewood, 1983-89; Dem. nominee for Bergen County Freeholder, 1989; Dem. candidate for U.S. House 9th dist., N.J., 1996. Democrat. Jewish. Office: US Ho Reps 1607 Longworth Bldg Washington DC 20515-3009

ROTHMAN, THOMAS EDGAR, production executive; b. Balt., Nov. 21, 1954; s. Donald and Elizabeth (Davidson) R.; m. Jessica Randolph Harper, Mar. 11, 1989; children: Elizabeth, Eleanor. BA, Brown U., 1976; JD, Columbia U., 1980. Ptnr. Frankfurt, Garbus, Klein, N.Y.C., 1982-87; exec. v.p. prodn. Columbia Pictures, Burbank, Calif., 1987-89; sr. v.p. prodn. Samuel Goldwyn Co., L.A., 1989-91, pres. worldwide prodn., 1991—; pres. domestic dist. Twentieth Century Fox Film Group, pres. worldwide prodn. Trustee Sundance (Utah) Inst. Office: Twentieth Century Fox PO Box 900 Beverly Hills CA 90213-0900

ROTHMEIER, STEVEN GEORGE, merchant banker, investment manager; b. Mankato, Minn., Oct. 4, 1946; s. Edwin George and Alice Joan (Johnson) R. BBA, U. Notre Dame, 1968; MBA, U. Chgo., 1972. Corp. fin. analyst Northwest Airlines, Inc., St. Paul, 1973, mgr. econ. analysis, 1973-78, dir. econ. planning, 1978, v.p. fin., treas., 1978-82, exec. v.p., treas., dir., 1982-83, exec. v.p. fin. and adminstrn., treas., dir., 1983, pres., chief operating officer, 1984, pres., chief exec. officer, 1985-86, chmn., chief exec. officer, 1986-89, also bd. dirs.; pres. IAI Capital Group, Mpls., 1989-93; chmn., CEO Great No. Capital, St. Paul, 1993—. Bd. dirs. Gencorp, Precision Castparts, Waste Mgmt., Inc., Am. Coun. on Germany, German Marshal Fund. Chmn. St. Agnes Found. Decorated Bronze Star. Mem. Mpls. Club, Chgo. Club. Republican. Roman Catholic. Office: Great Northern Capital 332 Minnesota St Ste W2900 Saint Paul MN 55101-1377 *Success is not an accident; it is a habit. Success is the result of desire, dedication, sacrifice, mental toughness, hard work— and prayer. And you are not successful until you can share your success with others.*

ROTHSCHILD, AMALIE RANDOLPH, filmmaker, producer, director, digital artist, photographer; b. Balt., June 3, 1945; d. Randolph Schamberg and Amalie Getta (Rosenfeld) R. BFA, R.I. Sch. Design, 1967; MFA in Motion Picture Prodn., NYU, 1969. Spl. effects staff in film and photography Joshua Light Show, Fillmore E. Theatre, N.Y.C., 1969-71; artist-photographer represented by Staley-Wise Gallery N.Y.C., 2004. Still photographer TWA Airlines Pub. Rels. Dept., Village Voice newspaper, Rolling Stone mag., Newsweek mag., After Dark, N.Y. Daily News, others, 1968-72; co-founder, ptnr. New Day Films, distbn. coop., 1971—; owner operator Anomaly Films Co., N.Y.C., 1971—; mem., co-founder Assn. Ind. Video and Filmmakers, Inc., N.Y.C., 1974; bd. dirs., 1974-78; instr. in film and TV, NYU Inst. of Film and TV,

1976-78; cons. in field to various organizations including Youthgrant Program of Nat. Endowment for Humanities, Washington, 1973-76. Exhibitions include Soho Triad Fine Arts Gallery, 1997, 2000, 2002, Gomez Gallery, 1998, 2000, VH-1 Mus. First Gallery, 1999, Govinda Gallery, 2001; (film): Woo Who? May Wilson, 1969, It Happens to Us, 1972, Nana, Mom and Me, 1974, Radioimmunoassay of Renin, Radioimmunoassay of Aldosterone, 1973, Conversations with Willard Van Dyke, 1981, Richard Haas: Work in Progress, 1984, Painting the Town: The Illusionistic Murals of Richard Haas, 1990 (Emily award Am. Film and Video Festival 1990); editor: Doing It Yourself, Handbook on Independent Film Distribution, 1977; author: Live at the Fillmore East, 1999; licensed photograph collections include Corbis/Bettmann Archive, 1994—, Star File Photo Agy., 1997—. Mem. Cmty. Planning Bd. 1, Borough of Manhattan, N.Y.C., 1974-86. Recipient spl. achievement award Mademoiselle mag., 1972; Ind. filmmaker grant Am. Film Inst. 1973; film grantee N.Y. State Coun. on the Arts, 1977, 85, 87, Nat. Endowment Arts, 1978, 85, 87, Md. Arts Coun., 1977, Ohio Arts and Humanities Couns., 1985. Mem.: AIVF, Ind. Documentary Assn., NY Women in Film, Univ. Film and Video Assn. Democrat. Address: 135 Hudson St New York NY 10013-2102 also: Via Carrand 22 Florence 50133 Italy E-mail: a.rothschild@agora.it.

ROTHSCHILD, ANTHONY JOSEPH, psychiatrist; b. N.Y.C., Dec. 2, 1953; s. Ernest Leo and Edith Margot (Chan) R.; m. Judith Anne Shindul, May 19, 1985; children: Rachel Emma, Amanda Joan. AB, Princeton U., 1975; MD, U. Pa., 1979. Diplomate Am. Bd. Psychiatry and Neurology. Intern medicine/neurology Mass. Gen. Hosp., Mt. Auburn Hosp., Boston, 1979-80; resident psychiatry McLean Hosp., Belmont, Mass., 1980-83; instr. in psychiatry Harvard Med. Sch., Boston, 1983-85, asst. prof. psychiatry, 1985-92, assoc. prof. psychiatry, 1992-96; psychiatrist-in-charge depression rsch. unit McLean Hosp., Belmont, 1983-88, assoc. dir. depression rsch. facility, 1985—, clin. dir. affective disease program, 1988-95, clin. dir. ambulatory svcs., 1995-96, dir. mood and anxiety disorders rsch., 1995-96; prof., dir. clin. rsch. dept. psychiatry U. Mass. Med. Ctr., Worcester, 1996—, Irving S. and Betty Brudnick endowed chair psychiatry, 1997—. Examiner Am. Bd. Psychiatry and Neurology, 1987—; reviewer Am. Jour. Psychiatry, Washington, 1985—, Psychiatry Rsch., 1985—, others. Mem. editl. bd. Depression and Anxiety, 1997—; contbr. articles to profl. publs. Fellow Am. Psychiat. Assn., Am. Psychopath. Assn.; mem. Internat. Soc. Psychoneuroendocrinology, Am. Coll. Neuropsychopharmacology (edn. and tng. com. 1996-98, program com. 2000—), Am. Coll. Psychiatrists, Am. Soc. Clin. Psychopharmacology, Mass. Psychiat. Soc. (nominating com. 1997-98, councillor 2000—), Collegicum Internat. Neuropsychopharmacologie. Office: U Mass Med Ctr Dept Psychiatry 361 Plantation St Worcester MA 01605-2323

ROTHSCHILD, DONALD PHILLIP, retired lawyer, arbitrator; b. Mar. 31, 1927; s. Leo and Anne (Office) R.; m. Ruth Eckstein, July 7, 1950; children: Nancy Lee, Judy Lynn Hoffman, James Alex. AB, U. Mich., 1950; JD summa cum laude, U. Toledo, 1965; LLM, Harvard U., 1966. Bar: Ohio 1966, D.C. 1970, U.S. Supreme Ct. 1975, R.I. 1989. Tchg. fellow Harvard U. Law Sch., Cambridge, Mass., 1965—66; instr. solicitor's office U.S. Dept. Labor, Washington, 1966—67; prof. law George Washington U. Nat. Law Ctr., Washington, 1966—89, prof. emeritus, 1989; prof. law N.Y. Law Sch., 1989—96; ret., 1996. Vis. prof. U. Mich. Law Sch., Ann Arbor, 1976; dir. Consumer Protection Ctr., 1971—. Inst. Law and Aging, Washington, 1973—89, Ctr. for Cmty. Justice, Washington, 1974—78, Nat. Consumers League, Washington, 1981—87; v.p. Regulatory Alternatives Devel. Corp., Washington, 1982—; cons. Washington Met. Coun. Govt., 1979—82; counsel Tillinghast, Collins & Graham, Providence, 1989—95, chair human resource group. Author: From the Cockpit of the Rubaiyat, 2002; co-author: Consumer Protection Text and Materials, 1973, Collective Bargaining and Labor Arbitration, 1979, Fundamentals of Administrative Practice and Procedure, 1981; contbr. articles to profl. jours. Chmn. bd. dirs. D.C. Citizens Complaint Ctr., Washington, 1980; mayoral appointee Adv. Com. on Consumer Protection, Washington, 1979—80. Recipient Cmty. Svc. award, Television Acad., Washington, 1981. Mem.: ABA, D.C. Bar Assn., Am. Arbitration Assn., Fed. Mediation and Conciliation Svc., Nat. Acad. Arbitrators, Nat. Assn. Coll. and Univ. Attys. (Brown U.), Fed. Trade Commn. Adv. Coun., Phi Kappa Phi. Jewish. Home: 601 Periwinkle Way C8 Sanibel FL 33957

ROTHSCHILD, ERIC, editor, consultant; b. N.Y.C., Jan. 6, 1937; s. Mortimer Maxwell Rothschild; m. Christine Elizabeth MacLean, Sept. 8, 1961; children: Adam, Alan Joseph. BA, Harvard Coll., Cambridge, Mass., 1954—58; MA in Edn., Boston U., 1961—62. Cert. in supervision Dept. Edn., N.Y., 1977. Social studies tchr. Woodlands H.S., Hartsdale, NY, 1962—64; social studies tchr., dept. head Scarsdale H.S., NY, 1964—98. Cons. Coll. Bd., N.Y.C., 1972—, HarpWeek, Norfolk, Va. Pres. Scarsdale Transfer Edn. Plan, NY, 1977—78; chair, bowl com. Scarsdale Found., NY; pres. Scarsdale H.S. Alumni Assn., NY, 1999—2004. Specialist 4 U.S. Army, 1959—61, Korea. Recipient First H.S. Tchr. Elected to Exec. Bd., Orgn. Am. Historians, 1991—94. Home: 32 Donellan Rd Scarsdale NY 10583-2008 Personal E-mail: ericap5@optonline.net.

ROTHSCHILD, JENNIFER ANN, artist, educator; b. Mesa, Ariz., Aug. 16, 1948; d. Joe Dean and Frances Ann (McFarland) Johnston; m. Harry Ronald Rothschild, Feb. 14, 1981. Diploma, El Camino Jr. Coll., 1968; BA in Art Edn., Calif. State U., 1970. Cert. secondary sch. tchr., Calif. Arts and crafts specialist City of Hawthorne (Calif.) Parks and Recreation, 1966-67; portrait artist Disneyland, Anaheim, Calif., 1970-74; secondary sch. art tchr. Orange (Calif.) Unified Schs., 1972-80; freelance custom apparel designer Honolulu, 1982-94; sculptor, artist, 1994—. One woman show at Roy's Honolulu, 2001, Art Centre Gallery, Honolulu, 1997, Studio 1 Gallery, 2004; corp. artist Arts of Paradise Gallery, Honolulu, 1997—; exhibited in show at City of Manhattan Beach, Calif., 1966, Assn. of Hawaii Artists, 1996—, in book Encyclopedia of Living Artists, 10th edit., 1997. Bd. dirs. Hawaii Tennis Patrons, Honolulu, 1996—, Assn. of Hawaii Artists Show chairwoman, 2002. Recipient scholarship Chouinard Sch. Art Inst., 1965-66, 1st Place Stamp Design award Easter Seals, 1995-96, Hokele Artists award Hawaiian Airlines, 1996, Most Unique Art award Assn. of Hawaii Artists Aloha Show, 1997. Fellow Nat. Mus. Women in Arts; mem. AAUW, Honolulu Art Acad., Assn. Hawaii Artists (v.p. 1996-97, pres. 1999-2000), Hawaiian Pacific Tennis Assn. (rules chmn. 1997), mem. Windward Art Guild, 2002, Nat. League of Am. Pen Women, Hon., chapter, Alpha Omicron Pi. Republican. Presbyterian. Avocations: tennis, reading, writing, painting, sculpting. E-mail: onoaloha@attglobal.net.

ROTHSCHILD, LARRY, former professional baseball executive; b. Chgo., Mar. 12, 1954; m. Jane; children: Charlotte, Claire. Grad., Fla. State U. Pitcher Cin. Reds, 1975-81, minor league pitching coach, 1986, bullpen coach, 1990; with Detroit Tigers, 1981; pitching instr. minor league Atlanta Braves; pitching coach Fla. Marlins, 1997; mgr. Tampa Bay Devil Rays, 1997—2001. Finished 3rd Am. Assn., 1981.

ROTHSCHILD, STEVEN JAMES, lawyer; b. Worcester, Mass., Mar. 23, 1944; s. Alfred and Ilse (Blumenfeld) R. BA, U. Vt., 1965; JD, Georgetown U., 1968. Bar: D.C. 1968, Del. 1969, N.Y. 1992. Ptnr. Skadden Arps Slate Meagher & Flom, Wilmington. Mem. Del. Bd. on Profl. Responsibility, 1992-98, vice chmn., 1993, chmn., 1994-98; vice chmn. rules com. Del. Supreme Ct., 1991-94; chmn. Del. Gov.'s Commn. on Major Comml. Litigation Reform, 1993-94; adj. prof. law Georgetown U. Law Ctr., 2000—; lectr. in law U. Pa. Law Sch., 2001—. Bd. dirs. United Way Del., 93-99, v.p., 1981-84, chmn. 1994-95; bd. dirs. Milton and Hattie Kutz Home, 1972—, pres., 1982-84; pres., Del. Art Mus., 1990-92; bd. trustees U. Del., 1998—. Mem. ABA, Bar Assn. D.C., Assn. of Bar of City of N.Y., Del. Bar Assn. Office: Skadden Arps Slate Meagher & Flom One Rodney Sq PO Box 636 Wilmington DE 19899-0636 E-mail: srothsch@skadden.com.

ROTHSCHILD, STEVEN K. physician, medical educator, researcher; b. Chgo., Ill., Mar. 21, 1957; s. Edward Ernst and Emmy Rothschild; m. Lisa Oppenheim; children: Ruth Oppenheim-Rothschild, Joshua Oppenheim-Rothschild. MD, U. Mich. Coll. of Medicine, Ann Arbor, 1980. Diplomate Am. Bd. Family Physicians Lexington, KY, 1984. Assoc. prof. Rush Med. Coll., Chgo., 1984—; assoc. chmn. clin. programs dept. Family Medicine Rush U. Med. Ctr., Chgo., 1988—. Prin. investigator Rush Virtual Integrated Practice Project, Chgo., 2000—; bd. mem. Health and Medicine Policy Rsch. Group, Chgo., 2002—03. Pres. Congregation Makom Shalom, Chgo., 2001—03; sec. bd. dir. Ctrl. City Housing Ventures, Chgo., 1999—2003. Mem.: Am. Acad. of Family Physicians. Office: Rush Univ Med Ctr 1653 W Congress Pky Chicago IL 60612 E-mail: steven_k_rothschild@rush.edu.

ROTHSTEIN, ANNE LOUISE, education educator, college official; b. Bklyn., Feb. 15, 1943; d. William and Rose Mary (Smith) R. BS, Bklyn. Coll., 1963; MA, Tchrs. Coll. Columbia, N.Y.C., 1965, EdD, 1970. Tchr. Erasmus Hall High Sch., Bklyn., 1963-64, Fort Hamilton High Sch., Bklyn., 1964-66; lectr. Hunter Coll. in the Bronx, N.Y., 1965-68; instr., prof. Lehman Coll., Bronx, 1968—, dept. chair, 1980-83, assoc. dean, 1983-93, assoc. provost/dir. for sponsored program devel., 1993-98. Dir. Lehman Ctr. for Sch./Coll. Collaboratives, Bronx, 1988—; grant specialist for sch./coll. programs, 1985—; small sch. developer, 1999—. Editor, pub. (jour.) Motor Skills: Theory into Practice, 1976-87; chair editorial bd. (jour.) Strategies, 1986-92; author: Research and Statistics, 1985, Motor Learning: Basic Stuff, 1987. Grantee in field. Fellow Rsch. Consortium Am. Alliance, Am. Alliance for Health, Physical Edn., Recreation and Dance; mem. Nat. Assn. for Sport and Physical Edn., Nat. Assn. for Girls and Women in Sport, Assn. for Supervision and Curriculum Devel., Am. Ednl. Rsch. Assn. Avocations: computers, grants consulting. Home: PO Box 3007 Newtown CT 06470-3007 Office: Lehman Coll Bedford Park Blvd W Bronx NY 10468 E-mail: anner@lehman.cuny.edu., arothstein@aol.com.

ROTHSTEIN, BARBARA JACOBS, federal judge; b. Bklyn., Feb. 3, 1939; d. Solomon and Pauline Jacobs; m. Ted L. Rothstein, Dec. 28, 1968; 1 child, Daniel. BA, Cornell U., 1960; LL.B., Harvard U., 1966. Bar: Mass. 1966, Wash. 1969, U.S. Ct. Appeals (9th cir.) 1977, U.S. Dist. Ct. (we. dist.) Wash. 1971, U.S. Supreme Ct. 1975. Pvt. practice law, Boston, 1966-68; asst. atty. gen. State of Wash., 1968-77; judge Superior Ct., Seattle, 1977-80, Fed. Dist. Ct. Western Wash., Seattle, 1980—, chief judge, 1987-94, dir. Fed. Jud. Ctr., 2003—. Faculty Law Sch. U. Wash., 1975-77, Hastings Inst. Trial Advocacy, 1977, N.W. Inst. Trial Advocacy, 1979—; mem. state-fed. com. U.S. Jud. Conf., chair subcom. on health reform; dir. Fed. Jud. Ctr. Recipient Matrix Table Women of Yr. award Women in Communication, Judge of the Yr. award Fed. Bar Assn., 1989; King County Wash. Women Lawyers Vanguard Honor, 1995. Mem. ABA (jud. sect.), Am. Judicature Soc., Nat. Assn. Women Judges, Fellows of the Am. Bar, Wash. State Bar Assn., U.S. Jud. Conf. (state-fed. com., health reform subcom.), Phi Beta Kappa, Phi Kappa Phi. Office: Fed Jud Ctr 1 Columbus Cir NE Washington DC 20002-8003 Office Phone: 202-502-4160.

ROTHSTEIN, FRED C. health facility administrator; b. Cleve. m. Jackie Rothstein; 2 children. BA, Miami U., Oxford, Ohio; MD, Chgo. Med. Sch. U. Health Scis., 1976. Bd. cert. pediatrics and pedatric gastroenterology. Pediat. internship Cleve. Metro Gen. Hosp., Ohio, 1976—77, Rainbow Babies & Children's Hosp., Ohio, 1976—77, pediat. residency, 1977—79, pediat. gastroenterology fellowship, 1979—81, chief divsn. pediat. gastroenterology, practicing physician, pediat. gastroenterologist; dir. dept. pediatrics, sr. v.p. med. affairs Mt. Sinai Med. Ctr., Cleve.; sr. v.p. clin. integration U. Hosps. Health System, Cleve., 1996—2002, acting pres., CEO, 2002—03; pres., CEO U. Hosps. Cleve., 2003—. Asst. prof. pediatrics Case Western Reserve U.; bd. trustees Ctr. Health Affairs (CHA), 2004, Geauga Regional Hosp., Chardon, Ohio, 1997; bd. dirs. BioEnterprise. Contbr. more than 60 peer-reviewed abstracts, articles, and book chapters on issues concerning pediatric gastroenterology. Mem.: N.Am. Soc. Pediat. Gastroenterology and Nutrition, Am. Gastroenterological Assn., Am. Acad. Pediatrics, Am. Coll. Gastroenterology. Office: Univ Hosps Cleve 11100 Euclid Ave Cleveland OH 44106 Office Phone: 216-844-6217.

ROTHSTEIN, GERALD ALAN, retired investment company executive; b. Bklyn., Oct. 18, 1941; s. Manuel and Gertrude (Buxbaum) R.; m. Cynthia Bea Pincus, June 11, 1967; children: Michael Neil, Lori Pamela, Meryl Patricia. BBA, City Coll. N.Y., 1962; MBA, U. Pa., 1965. 1st v.p. Shearson Hammill & Co., N.Y.C., 1966-74, Shearson Hayden Stone, N.Y.C., 1974-75; v.p. William D. Witter, Inc., N.Y.C., 1975-76, Oppenheimer & Co., N.Y.C., 1976-79, sr. v.p., 1979-83, mng. dir., 1983—, dir. rsch., 1986-91, dir. internat. rsch., 1991-95, internat. investment banker, 1995—; mng. dir. internat. money mgmt. CIBC World Markets, N.Y.C., 1998—2004; ret. Bd. dirs. Indocean Diamond Tools, Hamilton, Bermuda, India Pvt. Equity Fund, Mauritius, Gamet, Torun, Poland. Trustee Ctr. for Social and Emotional Edn., N.Y.C. Mem. N.Y. Soc. Security Analysts, Inst. CFA's, Internat. Soc. Fin. Analysts. Office: CIBC World Markets 425 Lexington Ave New York NY 10017 E-mail: gerald.rothstein@verizon.net.

ROTHSTEIN, MARK ALAN, health law and bioethics educator; b. Phila., May 23, 1949; s. Sidney David and Selma (Rosenfeld) R.; m. Laura Friesen, June 9, 1974; children: Julia, Lisa. BA, U. Pitts., 1970; JD, Georgetown U., 1973. Bar: Pa. 1973, D.C. 1974. Atty., adviser Occupational Safety & Health Rev. Commn., Washington, 1973-75; assoc. prof. law Ohio No. U., Ada, 1975-79; vis. assoc. prof. law U. Pitts., 1979-80; prof. law W.Va. U., Morgantown, 1980-85, Health Law and Policy Inst. U. Houston, 1985-2000; dir. Inst. Bioethics Health Policy and Law U. Louisville, 2000—. Author: Medical Screening of Workers, 1984, Medical Screening and the Employee Health Cost Crisis, 1989, Occupational Safety and Health Law, 1990, Employment Law, 1991, Employment Law Treatise, 1994, Genetic Secrets, 1997. Office: Inst Bioethics Health Policy and Law U Louisville 501 E Broadway # 310 Louisville KY 40292 Office Phone: 502-852-4980. E-mail: mark.rothstein@louisville.edu.

ROTHSTEIN, SAMUEL, librarian, educator; b. Moscow, Jan. 12, 1921; arrived in Can., 1922, naturalized, 1929; s. Louis Israel and Rose Rothstein; m. Miriam Ruth Teitelbaum, Aug. 26, 1951; children: Linda Rose, Sharon Lee. BA, U. B.C., 1939, MA, 1940, LLD, 2004; grad. student, U. Calif., Berkeley, 1941-42, grad. student, 1946-47, BLS, 1947; postgrad., U. Wash., 1942—43; PhD (Carnegie Corp. fellow 1951-54), U. Ill., 1954; DLitt, York U., 1971. Teaching fellow U. Wash., 1942-43; prin. libr. asst. U. Calif., Berkeley, 1947; mem. staff U. B.C. Libr., Vancouver, 1947-51, 54-62; acting univ. libr. U. B.C., Vancouver, 1961-62, prof. libr. sci., 1961—86, prof. emeritus, 1986—, dir. Sch. Librarianship, 1961-70. Vis. prof. U. Hawaii, 1969, U. Toronto, 1970, 79, Hebrew U., Jerusalem, 1973; mem. Commn. Nat. Plan Libr. Edn., 1963—; mem. assoc. com. sci. info. Nat. Rsch. Coun. Can., 1962-69; councillor B.C. Med. Libr. Svc., 1971; mem. exec. com. Pacific divsn. Can. Jewish Congress, 1962-69, Internat. House Assn. B.C., 1959-60; mem. Can. Adv. Bd. Sci. and Tech. Info.; mem. cabinet Combined Jewish Appeal of Greater Vancouver, 1992-95; pres. Vancouver Pub. Libr. Trust, 1987-88. Author: The Development of Reference Services, 1955, (with others) Training Professional Librarians for Western Canada, 1957, The University-The Library, 1972, Rothstein on Reference..., 1989; also articles.; co-editor: As We Remember It, 1970. Life mem. bd. dirs. Jewish Cmty. Ctr. of Greater Vancouver, pres., 1972-74; bd. dirs. Jewish Fedn. of Greater Vancouver, 1993-2000. Recipient ALISE award Assn. Library Info. Sci. Edn., 1987, Beta Phi Mu award ALA, 1988. Mem. Can. Libr. Assn. (hon. life), Assn. Am. Libr. Schs. (pres. 1968-69), Can. Assn. Libr. Schs. (hon. life, pres. 1982-84), ALA (coun. 1963-69, Beta Phi Mu award 1988), B.C. Libr. Assn. (hon. life, pres. 1959-60, Helen Gordon Stewart award 1970), Pacific N.W. Libr. Assn. (pres. 1963-64, hon. life), Can. Libr. Assn. (hon. life, coun. 1958-60, Outstanding Svc. to Librarianship award 1986), Bibliog. Soc. Can. (coun. 1959-63), Can. Assn. Univ. Tchrs. Home: 1416 W 40th Ave Vancouver BC Canada E-mail: samuelr@interchange.ubc.ca.

ROTHWELL, ELAINE B. artist; b. Mpls., May 8, 1926; d. Frederick Roscoe and Stella Frances (LaVallee) Bartholomew; m. William Stanley Rothwell, May 10, 1946; children: Suzanne, Amy Verrett, Wendy Rothwell-Lopez, Bart. BFA, San Jose State U., 1966; pvt. study, Woodbury Graphic Studio, Los Altos, Calif., 1975-76, Amaranth Intaglio Workshop, Los Altos, 1985. *Rothwell was first known for her series of 14 etchings using chess imagery and chess positions. This series was featured in a cover story in Chess Life Magazine in March 1979. Her 1983 "Spiritus Loci" series of eight etchings forms a cartographical puzzle. Her later series, "Art History Mysteries" 1994, "Mad Meg Amok" 1997, "Inklings" 1999, "Seasons of Romance" 2002 and "Moons" 2002 are online at www.artbyrothwell.com. By means of figure ground ambiguities and enigmatic images, Rothwell's etchings baffle the viewers' eyes with games of visual discovery.* One-woman shows include Triton Mus. Art, Santa Clara, Calif., 1976, Palo Alto Civic Ctr., Calif., 1977, Stanford Art Spaces, Stanford U., Calif., 1985, 1988, 1989, West Valley Art Mus., Surprise, Ariz., 1996, Roseville Arts Ctr., Calif., 2003, exhibited in group shows at Carnegie Art Ctr., North Tonawanda, N.Y., 1995, 1996, N.J. Ctr. Visual Arts Internat., Summit, 1997, 1998, Brand Libr. and Art Ctr., Glendale, Calif., 1996, Internat. Exhbn. Art League Manatee County, Fla., 1996, Nat. Soc. Artists, 1997, Am. Color Print Soc., 1997, Grand Exhbn. Nat. Competition, Akron, Ohio, 1998, Printwork '98, Barrett Ho., Poughkeepsie, N.Y., 1998, 73d Ann. Internat. Print Competition/Print Ctr., Phila., 1999, Manhattan Arts Internat., 1999, Chautauqua Nat. Exhbn. Am. Art, 1999, No. Colo. Ann. Nat. Exhbns., 1999, 2000, Stage Gallery, Merrick, N.Y., 2000, retrospective exhbns., Gallery 9, Los Altos, Calif., 2002, Gallery II, Nevada City, Calif., 2002, Represented in permanent collections Newberry Libr., Chgo., Triton Mus. Art, Santa Clara, West Valley Art Mus., Brand Libr. Art Ctr., Glendale. Mem.: Am. Color Print Soc., Nat. Mus. Women in Arts (charter), Auburn Old Town Gallery, Triton Mus. Art. Home and Office: 3030 Eagles Nest Auburn CA 95603-5918

ROTHWELL, TIMOTHY GORDON, pharmaceutical company executive; b. London, Jan. 8, 1951; came to us., 1966; s. Kenneth Gordon Rothwell and Jean Mary (Stedman) Davey; m. Joanne Claire Fleming; children: Tiffany, Heather. BA, Drew U., 1972; JD, Seton Hall U., 1976; LLM, NYU, 1979, MBA, 1983. With Sandoz Pharms., East Hanover, N.J., 1972—, patent atty., 1974-77, patent and trademark counsel, 1980-82, mng. ops. planning and adminstrn., 1982-84, dir. mktg. ops., 1984-85, exec. dir. field ops., 1985-86, v.p. field ops., 1986-87, pres. profl. bus. ops., 1987-88, corp. v.p., chief oper. officer, 1988-89; sr. v.p. sales and mktg. Squibb, Princeton, N.J., 1989; gen. mgr. Squibb U.S. Pharm. divsn. Bristol-Myers Squibb, 1991; sr. v.p. mktg. and sales Burroughs-Wellcome, 1992; pres., CEO Sandoz Pharm. Corp., 1995; pres. pharm. op. Rhone-Poulenc Rorer Inc., 1996, pres., bd. dirs., 1996-97; exec. v.p. Pharmacia Corp., 2000—, pres. global country ops. Exec. v.p., pres. pharm. ops. Pharmacia Upjohn, N.J., 1998—. Mem. N.J. State Bar Assn., N.Y. State Bar Assn., Am. Soc. for Pharmacy Law, Nat. Health Care Quality Coun., Am. Found. for Pharm. Exec. (bd. dirs.), N.J. Patent Law Assn. (pres. 1986). Republican. Episcopalian. Avocations: stamp collecting/philately, coaching youth soccer, golf, tennis. Office: Pharmacia Corp 100 Rte 206 North Peapack NJ 07977-0800

ROTI, THOMAS DAVID, judge; b. Evanston, Ill., Jan. 20, 1945; s. Sam N. and Theresa S. (Salerno) R.; m. Donna Sumichrast, July 22, 1972; children: Thomas S., Kyle D., Rebecca D., Gregory J. BS, Loyola U., Chgo., 1967, JD cum laude, 1970. Bar: Ill. 1970, U.S. Dist. Ct. (no. dist.) Ill. 1971, U.S. Ct. Appeals (7th cir.) 1971. Sr. law clk. to Judge Frank McGarr, U.S. Dist. Ct. No. Dist. Ill., 1971-72; assoc. Arnstein, Gluck & Lehr, Chgo., 1972-73, Boodell, Sears et al, Chgo., 1973-75; asst. gen. counsel Dominick's Finer Foods, Inc., Northlake, Ill., 1975-77, v.p., gen. counsel, 1977-97; judge Cir. Ct. Cook County, 2000—. Mem. nat. conf. lawyers and econs. com. Good Mktg. Inst., Washington, 1987—97; mem. Nat. Conf. Cmty. and Justice, Chgo.; legis. com. Ill. Retail Mchts. Assn., Chgo., 1987—97; trustee Nat. Conf. Cmty. and Justice, Chgo., 1995—2000. Trustee Joint Civic Com. Italian Ams., Chgo., 1986-95; mem. Chgo. Coun. EDU-CARE Scholarship Program, 1988. Recipient Am. Jurisprudence award, 1970, Alumni Assn. award Loyola U., 1970. Mem. ABA, Ill. Bar Assn., Ill. Judges Assn., Chgo. Bar Assn., N.W. Suburban Bar Assn., Justinian Soc. Lawyers, Cath. Lawyers Guild Chgo., Phi Alpha Delta, Alpha Signa Nu. Roman Catholic. Office: 2121 Euclid Ave Rolling Meadows IL 60008 Office Phone: 847-818-2536. Personal E-mail: tdroti@comcast.net.

ROTMAN, MARVIN, radiation oncologist, radiologist, educator; b. Phila., Sept. 3, 1933; s. Herman Zelman and Edith (Solomon) R.; m. Marsha Vinson; children: David, Robert, Eve, Sydney. BS, Ursinus Coll., 1954; MD, Thomas Jefferson U., 1958. Asst. clin prof. radiology N.Y. Med. Coll., N.Y.C., 1967-68, asst. prof. radiology, 1968-71, assoc. prof. clin. radiology, 1971-75, prof. radiology, 1975-79; prof., chmn. radiation oncology SUNY Health Sci. Ctr. at Bklyn., 1979—2003, Disting. Svc. prof., chair, 2003—; dir. radiation oncology Kings County Med. Ctr., N.Y.C., 1979—, Long Island Coll. Hosp. Cons. Bklyn. VA Hosp., 1979—. Author textbook: (with others) Introduction to Radiotherapy, 1975, Genito-Urinary Malignancy, 1980; editor textbook: (with others) Clinical Applications of Continuous Infusion Chemotherapy and Conmitant Radiation Therapy, 1986, others; contbr. more than 190 articles to profl. jours., textbooks. Bd. dirs. Young Concert Artists, N.Y.C., 1967—; nat. bd. dirs. Sante Fe Opera, 1987-93. Recipient Gold Medal award, Am. Soc. Therapeutic Radiology and Oncology, 2002, award of honor, Radiol. Soc. N.Am., 1991. Fellow Am. Coll. Radiology (counselor N.Y. State chpt. 1980—), Am. Coll. Radiation Oncology; mem. AMA (mem. radiology residency review com., Am. Bd. Radiology examiner on splty. bds.), Am. Radium Soc. (pres. 1994-96), Soc. Acad. Radiotherapy Programs (pres. 1984-86), N.Y. Cancer Soc. (pres. 1983-84), N.Y. Roentgen Soc. (chmn. radiotherapy sect. 1977-78), Med. Soc. Kings County (chmn. radiotherapy 1981—), Am. Soc. Therapeutic Radiology and Oncology (mem. exec. com., Gold medal), Kings Point Civic Assn. (pres. 2004—)Alpha Omega Alpha. Jewish. Avocations: tennis, piano, art. Office: SUNY Health Sci Ctr at Bklyn Dept Radiation Oncology New York NY 11203 Office Phone: 718-270-2181. Business E-Mail: mrotman@downstate.edu.

ROTNER, PHILIP, lawyer; b. Chgo., Feb. 6, 1947; m. Janet Rotner. AB, U. Calif., 1969; JD, Harvard U., 1972. Bar: Ill. 1972, Mass. 1973, Calif. 1975, N.Y. 1996. Litig. assoc. Gaston, Snow, Motley & Holt, Boston, 1973—74, assoc., 1974—80; ptnr. McCutchen, Doyle, Brown & Ereuen, San Francisco, 1981—95; gen. counsel Deloitte & Touche USA LLP, Broadway, NY, 1995—. Vis. faculty Law Sch. Trial Advocacy Program Harvard U., 1990, 93; spkr. in field. Office: Deloitte & Touche USA LLP 1633 Broadway New York NY 10019-6754 Office Phone: 212-492-4012. Business E-Mail: protner@deloitte.com.

ROTT, HANS C. architect, educator; Prof., chair grad. program Sch. Arch. and Design Va. Tech., Blacksburg. Mem.: Va. Assn. Scholars (bd. mem.). Office: Sch Arch and Design Va Tech 0205 201 Cowgill Hall Blacksburg VA 24061*

ROTT, STEPHEN ROSS, biologist, educator; s. Clarence and Kathy Rott(Stepmother); m. Cindy Kuykendall, Apr. 4, 2004; children: Jennifer Stephannie Purvis, Jason Stewart, Bryan Nathanial. BS, Purdue U., 1968; MEd, Ind. U., 1974. Tchr. Cardinal Ritter HS, Indpls., 1968—74, Carmel (Ind.) HS, 1974—. Recipient Clean Air award, Cleaner Air Com. Indpls., 1990. Mem.: NEA (assoc.), Nat. Assn. Biology Tchrs. (assoc.), Ind. State Tchrs. Assn. (assoc.), Ind. Assn. Biology Tchrs. (life), Sierra Club (assoc.). Avocations: hiking, woodworking, gardening. Office: Carmel Clay Schs 520 E Main Carmel IN 46032

ROTTER, PAUL TALBOTT, retired insurance executive; b. Parsons, Kans., Feb. 21, 1918; s. J. and LaNora (Talbott) R.; m. Virginia Sutherlin Barksdale, July 17, 1943; children: Carolyn Sutherlin, Diane Talbott. BS summa cum laude, Harvard U., 1937. Asst. mathematician Prudential Ins. Co. of Am., Newark, 1938-46; with Mut. Benefit Life Ins. Co., Newark, 1946—, successively asst. mathematician, asso. mathematician, mathematician, 1946-59, from v.p. to exec. v.p., 1959-80, ret., 1980. Mem. Madison Bd. Edn., 1958-64, pres., 1959-64; Trustee, mem. budget com. United Campaign of Madison, 1951-55; mem. bd., chmn. advancement com. Robert Treat council Boy Scouts Am., 1959-64. Fellow Soc. Actuaries (bd. govs. 1965-68, gen. chmn. edn. and exam. com. 1963-65, chmn. adv. com. edn. and exam. 1969-72), Phi Beta Kappa Soc.; mem. Brit. Inst. Actuaries (assoc.), Am. Acad. Actuaries (v.p. 1968-70, bd. dirs., chmn. edn. and exam. com. 1965-66, chmn. rev. and evaluation com. 1968-74), Asso. Harvard Alumni (regional dir. 1965-69), Actuaries Club N.Y. (pres. 1967-68), Harvard Alumni Assn. (v.p. 1964-66),

Am. Lawn Bowls Assn. (pres. SW divsn.). Clubs: Harvard N.J. (pres. 1956-57); Harvard (N.Y.C.); Morris County Golf (Convent, N.J.); Joslyn-Lake Hodges Lawn Bowling (pres. 1989-90). Home: 18278 Canfield Pl San Diego CA 92128-1002

ROTTMAN, ELLIS, public information officer; b. Balt., Apr. 5, 1930; s. Abraham Isaac and Sadie (Harris) R.; m. Carol Parker Donovan, May 30, 1965; children— Marcus, Lisa, Jason, Adam. BS, U. Md., 1952. Assoc. editor Army Times Pub. Co., Washington, 1956-59; editor, dir. pub. relations Am. Fedn. Govt. Employees, AFL-CIO, 1959-65; pub. info. officer U.S. Post Office Dept., 1966-69; editor Manpower mag. Dept. Labor, 1969-75; editor, publs. dir. FDA, Rockville, Md., 1975-78; public info. dir. Labor-Mgmt. Services Adminstrn. Dept. Labor, 1978-84; pub. info. officer Office Sec. of Labor, 1984-94. Served with AUS, 1952-54. Recipient Journalism award Internat. Labor Press Assn., AFL-CIO, 1959, 60, 61, 62, 64; award merit Fed. Editors Assn., 1974, 75, 77, 78 Jewish. Home: 901 N Belgrade Rd Silver Spring MD 20902-3247 Office: 2nd St And Constitution Ave NW Washington DC 20210-0001

ROTTSCHAEFER, WILLIAM ANDREW, philosophy educator; b. Tulsa, June 20, 1933; s. Dirk and Clara (Linsmeyer) R.; m. Marie Therese Schickel. BA, St. Louis U., 1956, MA, 1957, Licentiate in Sacred Theol., 1966; MS, U. Ill., 1969; PhD, Boston U., 1973. Asst. prof. philosophy SUNY, Oswego, 1972-73, Plattsburgh, 1973-75, Lewis & Clark Coll., Portland, Oreg., 1975-79, assoc. prof. philosophy, 1979-85, prof. philosophy, 1985—, prof. emeritus, 2003—. Contbr. articles and revs. to profl. jours.; referee for several scholarly periodicals. Mem. Philosophy of Sci. Assn., Am. Philos. Assn., Inst. for Religion in an Age of Sci., Ctr. for Theology and the Natural Scis. (assoc.), Am. Acad. Religion. Office: Lewis and Clark Coll 0615 SW Palatine Hill Rd Portland OR 97219-7879 Office Phone: 503-768-7479. Business E-Mail: rotts@lclark.edu.

ROTUNDA, DONALD THEODORE, public relations consultant; b. Blue Island, Ill., Feb. 14, 1945; s. Nicholas and Frances (Manna) R. BA, Georgetown U., 1967; MA, London Sch. Econs., 1968, PhD, 1972. Analyst NASA, Washington, 1972; lectr. in econs. U. D.C., 1973; legis. asst. Ho. of Reps., Washington, 1974-76, economist budget com., 1977; mgmt. analyst Office Mgmt. and Budget, Washington, 1977-81; cons., 1981-82; mgr. editorial svcs. United Technologies Corp., Hartford, Conn., 1982-87, Pepsico, Inc., Purchase, N.Y., 1987-89, Union Carbide Corp., Danbury, Conn., 1989-90; dir. editorial svcs. Martin Marietta, Bethesda, Md., 1990-92; cons. pub. rels., 1992—. Contbr. numerous articles to Washington Post, New Republic, Saturday Rev. Roman Catholic. Home: 4431 Klingle St NW Washington DC 20016-3578 Office Phone: 202-345-2587.

ROTUNDA, JOSEPH LOUIS, retail and service company executive; b. Washington, Pa., Jan. 26, 1947; s. Joseph and Louise Rotunda; m. Patricia Lou Comer, Aug. 27, 1966; 1 child, Joseph Jason. BA in Econs., Washington & Jefferson U., 1969. From mgr. to v.p. customer svc. & new stores Montgomery Ward, Chgo., 1969-91; from divsnl. v.p. to exec. v.p., COO Thorn Americas, Wichita, 1991-98; COO, exec. v.p. G&K Svcs., Inc., Minnetonka, Minn., 1998-2000; pres., CEO EZCorp, Inc, Austin, Tex., 2000—, also bd. dirs. Bd. dirs. Easyhome Ltd, Toronto. Mem. Mensa. Home: 3208 Aztec Fall Cove Austin TX 78746 Office: EZCorp Inc 1901 Capital Pkwy Austin TX 78746 E-mail: joe_rotunda@ezcorp.com.

ROTUNDA, RONALD DANIEL, law educator, consultant; b. Blue Island, Ill., Feb. 14, 1945; s. Nicholas and Frances (Manna) R.; children: Nora, Mark. AB magna cum laude, Harvard U., 1967, JD magna cum laude, 1970. Bar: N.Y. 1971, U.S. Ct. Appeals (2d cir.) 1971, U.S. Ct. Appeals (D.C. cir.) 1971, U.S. Ct. Appeals (7th cir.) 1990, U.S. Supreme Ct. 1974, Ill. 1975. Law clk. U.S. Ct. Appeals (2d cir.), 1970-71; assoc. Wilmer, Cutler & Pickering, Washington, 1971-73; asst. majority counsel Watergate Com., U.S. Senate, Washington, 1973-74; spl. cons. Office of Ind. Counsel, Washington, 1997-99; asst. prof. U. Ill. Coll. Law, Champaign, 1974-77, assoc. prof., 1977-80, prof., 1980-93, Albert E. Jenner, Jr. prof. of law, 1993—2002; GMU found. prof. law George Mason U., Arlington, Va., 2002—. Vis. prof. law European U. Inst., Florence, Italy, 1981, U. Ala., 1999; mem. profl. responsibility exam. com. Nat. Conf. Bar Examiners, 1980-87; constl. advisor Supreme Nat. Coun. Cambodia, 1993; cons. Supreme Ct. Moldova, 1996; vis. sr. fellow in constnl. studies Cato Inst., 2000. Author: (with Morgan) Problems and Materials of Professional Responsibility, 1976, 8th edit., 2003; (with Nowak and Young) Constitutional Law, 1978, (with Nowak) 2d edit., 1983, 7th edit., 2004, Modern Constitutional Law: Cases and Materials, 1981, 7th edit., 2003, (with Nowak) Treatise on Constitutional Law, 4 vols., 2d edit., 1992, 5 vols., 3d edit., 1999, Legal Ethics, 2002, 2d edit., 2002. Fulbright research scholar, Italy, 1981, Venezuela, 1986. Fellow Am. Bar Found. (life), Ill. Bar Found. (life); mem. Am. Law Inst. Roman Catholic. Office: George Mason Univ Law School 3301 N Fairfax Drive Arlington VA 22201 Office Phone: 703-993-8041. Business E-Mail: rrotunda@GMU.edu.

ROTUNDO, MARGARET R. state legislator; b. Schenectady, N.Y., July 16, 1949; m. Loring Danforth; 2 children. BA, Mount Holyoke Coll., 1971. Devel. coord. Abington (Maine) Friends Sch., 1976-78; asst. dir. Office of Career Counseling Bales Coll., 1978-80, dir., 1980-86, assoc. dir. Ctr. for Svc. Learning, 1995—; mem. Maine Senate from 21st Dist., Augusta, 2001—, mem. edn. and cultural affairs, state/local govt. coms., 2001—. Bd. dirs. Head Start, 1999—, LA Arts, 1996—; co-chair Lewiston Asjurations Partnership, 1994—; chair Lewiston Sch. Com., 1999—. Mem. Androssoggin Valley C. of C. (bd. dirs. 1996—), Maine Sch. Bds. Assn. (past pres.). Home: 446 College St Lewiston ME 04240 Office: State House 3 State House Sta Augusta ME 04333 Office Fax: (207) 287-1585. E-mail: mrotundo@bates.edu.

ROTZIEN, FREDERICK WILLIAM, III, marketing executive; b. Portland, Oreg., Aug. 9, 1944; s. Frederick William Jr. and Vilma E. (Brandon) R.; m. Yvonne Miller, June 12, 1975 (div. Aug. 1979). Student, Clark Coll. Mktg. pres. Rotzien and Assocs., Portland, 1970-85; mktg. exec. Heartland Farms, Portland, 1985-88; mfg./mktg. pres. Blue Ribbon Market, Portland, 1985-90; mfg. pres. Probe Electronics, Portland, 1985-90; mktg. exec. Adventure Mktg., Portland, 1990-94, Am. Elec. Motorcycle, Portland, 1994—; pres. Rote-Sun Co. LLC, 1997—. Author, editor: World Chart of History, 1988; author: Step by Step Tobacco Guide, 1988. Pres. Oreg. chpt. Young Am. Freedom Portland, 1962, Portland Young Reps., 1968, Oreg. Young Reps., Portland, 1969. Mem. Am. Mktg. Assn. Lutheran. Avocations: fishing, politics, reading, gardening. Home: 13005 NE Broadway St Portland OR 97230-2262

ROUB, BRYAN R(OGER), financial executive; b. Berea, Ohio, May 1, 1941; s. Bernard Augustus and Pearl Irene (Koeblitz) R.; m. Judith Elaine Penman, June 19, 1965; children: Paul, Bradley, Michael. Student, Ohio Wesleyan U., 1959-62; BS, Ohio State U., 1966; MBA, U. Pa., 1978. Mem. audit staff Ernst & Ernst, Cleve., 1966-70; asst. contr. Midland-Ross, Cleve., 1970-73, contr., 1973-81, v.p., 1977-81, sr. v.p., 1981-82, exec. v.p. fin., 1982-84; sr. v.p. fin. Harris Corp., Melbourne, Fla., 1984-93, sr. v.p., CFO, 1993—. Bd. dirs. Fairchild Semicondr.; mem. fin. coun. II Machinery and Allied Products Inst., Washington, 1978-84, coun. I, 1984—, vice chmn., 1994-95, chmn., 1996-98; mem. conf. bd. coun. of CFO's, 1993-96. Mem. adv. coun. Coll. Adminstrv. Scis., Ohio State U., 1978-81; mem. citizen's adv. coun. Westlake (Ohio) Schs., 1981-83; trustee Alcoholism Svcs. Cleve., 1982-84; mem. devel. bd. St. John's Hosp., 1983-84; pres. Westridge Homeowners' Assn., 1977; dir., treas. Tortoise Island Homeowners' Assn., 1988-90; bd. dirs. Easter Seal Soc. of Brevard County, 1993-98. Mem. AICPA, Ohio Soc. CPAs, Fin. Execs. Inst. (treas. N.E. Ohio chpt. 1976-78, bd. dirs. 1980-81, 83-84, v.p. 1981-82, pres. 1982-83, bd. dirs. Orlando chpt. 1984—, v.p. 1985-86, pres. 1986-87, nat. bd. dirs. 1987-90, area v.p. 1990-91, chmn. budget and fin. com. 1988-89, chmn. planning com. 1995-97, v.p. at large 1997-99, vice-chmn. 1999-2000, chmn. 2000-01, office of chmn. 1997-2002), Fin. Execs. Rsch. Found. (trustee 1994-97, 1999-2000), Westwood Country Club, Eau Gallie Yacht Club (bd. govs., treas. 1990-92), Suntree Country Club. Office: Harris Corp 1025 W Nasa Blvd Melbourne FL 32919-0002 Address: 10280 S Tropical Trail Merritt Island FL 32952-6919

ROUBIK, SUSANNE EILEEN, architect; b. Milw., Dec. 1, 1959; d. Joseph Rudolph and Gertrude Mae R. BS in Architecture, U. Wis., Milw., 1981, MArch summa cum laude, 1984; postgrad., Inst. of Architecture Studies, Paris, Barcelona, 1984, Taller de Architecture:, Ricardo Bofill. Registered architect, Ill. Archtl. photographer U. Wis., Milw., 1983-84, archtl. slide curator, 1983-84; sr. archtl. designer Skidmore, Owings & Merrill, Chgo., 1984-90; prin. S.E. Roubik & Assocs.-Design Cons., Chgo., 1990—; cons. KMR Group, Inc., Chgo., 1991-93, World Trade Ctr., Chgo., 1995; pres. Internat. Collaborations Group, Inc., Chgo., 1997—; sr. project mgr. McClier, Chgo., 1999-2000, svc. group dir., 2000-01; assoc., project mgr. Skidmore, Owings & Merrill, Chgo., 2001; pres., founder Feng Shui & Design Inst. Chgo., 2003—, Feng Shui & Design Inst. of Ill., 2003—. Design critic Notre Dame U., U. Wis. Mil., U. Ill. Chgo., Ill. Inst. Tech., Chgo., U. Ohio, Miami, Andrews U.; com. chairwoman CCAIA V.I.P./Protocol 1993 AIA/UIA World Congress Architects, 1991-93; founder, bd. dirs., exec. v.p. Newhouse Architecture Found., 1989-93, sec., 1987-88, dir. internships, 1984-93. Com. chairwoman CCAIA V.I.P./Protocol, 1991—93; bd. directors Rehab. Inst. Chgo., Health Resource Ctr. for Women with Disabilities, 1994—98. Recipient award Nat. Inst. Archtl. Edn., 1984, Piux XI H.S. Alumni award, Milw., 1994. Mem.: AIA (program coord. Chgo. chpt. 1987—89, chmn. real estate com. 1989—91, del. young architects forum 1990—92, steering com. young architects forum 1990—92, bd. dirs. 1990—95, program com. 1991—93, Chgo. award 1984, Chgo. chpt.-Chgo. Bar Assn. Young Arch. award 1987, Young Arch. award 1993), Urban Land Inst. (program com. 1999—2003), Crew: Comml. Real Estate Exec. Women, Women in Planning and Devel. (bd. dirs. 2003—, dir. 2003), Third Coast Design Coop. (v.p. bd. dirs. 1981—84), Third Coast Women in Arch. (founder, pres. 1983), Graphic Artists Guild, Am. Mktg. Assn., Internat. Women Assocs. (chair English group 1998—99, ofcl. photographer 1998—, Kent Coll. of Law-Ill. Inst. Tech. 1998—, libr. internat. rels., consular ball exec. com.), Mid Day Club Chgo. (assoc. bd. dirs. co-chair 1995—96, chair 1996—97). Office: Internat Collaborations Grp 421 W Melrose St Ste 15B Chicago IL 60657-5539

ROUDANE, CHARLES, metal and plastic products company executive; b. L.A., July 16, 1927; s. Rudolph and Irene (Warner) R.; m. Orient Fox, Aug. 20, 1948; children: Mark, Matthew. BSME, Tulane U., 1950. Gen. mgr. Master divsn. Koehring Co., Chgo., 1955-67; gen. sales mgr. Wilton Corp., Schiller Park, Ill., 1967-70; dir. mktg. Flexonics divsn. UOP Inc., Bartlett, Ill., 1970-73, v.p., gen. mgr. divsn., 1973-83; pres., CEO, Resistoflex Co. divsn. Crane Co., Marion, NC, 1983—93; chmn., CEO, ASMC Corp., Chgo., 1993—. Bd. dirs. Ctr. Indsl. Mktg. Planning, Inc., PowRhouse Products, Inc. With AUS, 1945-46. Mem. ASME, Am. Mgmt. Assn. (past trustee, chmn. mktg. coun., mem. internat. coun., elected to Inaugural Wall of Fame 1978), Chgo. Pres. Assn., Newcomen Soc. Gt. Britain. Republican. Presbyterian. Office Phone: 828-274-8700.

ROUECHE, JOHN EDWARD, II, education educator, leadership program director; b. Sept. 3, 1938; s. John Edward and Mary (Harris) R.; m. Suanne Davis; 1 stepchild, Robin Sue Maca; children by previous marriage: Michelle Renee, John Edward III. BA, Lenoir Rhyne Coll., Hickory, N.C., 1960, LittD, 2001, LIID, Lenoir Rhyne Coll., 2001; MA, Appalachian Coll., Boone, N.C., 1961; PhD, Fla. State U., 1964. Dean Gaston Coll., Gastonia, N.C., 1964-67; assoc. rsch. educator UCLA, 1967-69; dir. jr. coll. divsn. Nat. Lab. Higher Edn., 1968-71; assoc. prof. edn. Duke U.; prof. edn., dir. c.c. leadership program U. Tex., Austin, 1971—, Sid W. Richardson regents chair, 1987—. Mem. chancellor's coun. U. Tex. Sys., 1990—, U. Tex. Littlefield Soc., 1992—; lectr. Earl Pullias lectr. U. So. Calif., 1992, Coll. Bd. Disting. Lectr. N.Y.C., 1993, Frances Crain Cook Disting. Lectr. U. Tex., 1994; chmn. nat. ednl. adv. bd. Gt. Am. Res. Ins. Co., 1988-94; co-chair Nat. Adv. Bd. for C.C.s, Invest Learning Corp., 1993-96; chair nat. adv. com. Kaplan Ednl. Partnerships, 1995-98; La Platica Disting. lectr. Ariz. State U., 1999; mem. nat. adv. bd. 3-D Internat., 2000—. C.C. editor Jossey-Bass Publs., 1971-82; editor Creative Teaching Series, Media Systems Corp., 1980-85; mem. editl. bd. C.C. Times, C.C. Jour., 1990-94, others; author 35 books, including Profiles of Excellence in America's Schools, 1986, Access with Excellence, 1987, Shared Vision, 1989, Teaching as Leading, 1990, Under-representation: A Question of Diversity, 1991, Between a Rock and a Hard Place, 1993, The Company We Keep, 1995, Strangers in Their Own Land: Part Time Faculty, 1995, Embracing the Tiger: The Effectiveness Debate and the Community College, 1997, High Stakes, High Performance: Making Remedial Education Work, 1999, In Pursuit of Excellence: The Community College of Denver, 2001, Practical Magic: On the Front Lines of Teaching Excellence, 2003; contbr. over 150 articles and monographs. Pres. Doss Sch. PTA, 1974-75; chmn. bd. N.W. Hills United Meth. Ch., 1973-76. Recipient Disting. Svc. award Nat. Coun. Univs. and Colls., 1990, Disting. Rsch. Publ. award, 1990, 93, 95, 97, Outstanding Alumnus award Appalachian State U., 1979, Disting. Grad. award Fla. State U., 1981, Tchg. Excellence award U. Tex., 1982, Outstanding Rschr. award, 1985, Excellence award for outstanding learned article U.S. Edn. Press Assn., 1983, Disting. Rsch. award Nat. Assn. Devel. Edn., 1984-86, Disting. Rsch. Publ. award Nat. Coun. Student Devel., 1987, Disting. Rsch. award Nat. Coun. Staff, Program, and Orgn. Devel., B. Lamar Johnson Nat. Leadership award League for Innovation in the Cmty. Coll., 1988, Disting. Svc. & Leadership award CCP, INC., 1993, Disting. Faculty award U. Tex., 1994, Disting. Rsch. award Interassn. Student Devel. Orgns., 1995, Chancellor's Leadership award State of Ala., 1995, Career Rsch. Excellence award U. Tex., 1998, Disting. Grad. award Lenoir-Rhyne Coll., 2000; named lifetime amb. for N.C., 1978; Kellogg fellow, 1962-64, Disting. Internat. Leadership award Govt. of South Africa, 2000, 01, Disting. Nat. Svc. award Nat. Coun. Instrnl. Adminstrs., 2001, Disting. Leadership award Tex. Assn. Cmty. Colls., 2003. Mem. Am. Assn. Comty. and Jr. Colls. (bd. dirs. 1989-94, Nat. Leadership award 1986, Disting. Rsch. award coun. colls. and univs. 1990, 94, 96, dist. rsch. sr. scholar award 1994, 96, nat. student devel. inter-assn. rsch. award 1995-96), Am. Assn. Higher Edn., Coun. Univs. and Colls. (past pres., bd. dirs.), Phi Beta Kappa, Phi Delta Kappa. Home: 4700 Lookout Mountain Cv Austin TX 78731-3654 Office: U Tex Austin One University Sta D5600 Austin TX 78712-0378 Office Phone: 512-471-7545.

ROUGIER-CHAPMAN, ALWYN SPENCER DOUGLAS, furniture manufacturing company executive; b. Ostende, Belgium, Feb. 19, 1939; came to U.S., 1970; s. Douglas Alwyn and Simone (Stiernet) Rougier-C.; m. Christine Hayes, Mar. 14, 1964; children: Andrew Douglas, Duncan Peter Chartered Acct., City of London Coll., 1963. Chartered acct., Eng. and Wales; C.P.A., Mich. Articled clk. Spain Bros., London, 1958-64; mgr. Deloitte & Co., Brussels, 1964-70; ptnr. Seidman & Seidman, Grand Rapids, Mich., 1970-81; v.p. planning Steelcase Inc., Grand Rapids, Mich., 1981-83, sr. v.p., CFO, 1983—. Dir. Meijer, Inc. Pres. French Soc., Grand Rapids, Mich., 1974-75; treas., vice chmn. Opera Grand Rapids, 1981-86, pres., 1987-89; treas. Grand Rapids Symphony, 1991-96; bd. trustees Blodgett Meml. Hosp., 1989-98; bd. dirs. Fin. Execs. Inst., Western Mich., 1988-94, pres., 1991-92; mem. fin. com. Spectrum Health, 1998—. Fellow Inst. Chartered Accts. Eng. and Wales; mem. Am. Inst. C.P.A.s (computer exec. com. 1977-81), Mich. Assn. C.P.A.s (auditing standards com. 1973-78) Clubs: Cascade Country, Peninsular (Grand Rapids). Roman Catholic. Avocations: golf, tennis, squash, travel, music. Office: 901 44th St SE Grand Rapids MI 49508-7575

ROUHANI, SHAHROKH, civil engineering/environmental consultant, educator; b. Tehran, Iran, Mar. 28, 1956; came to U.S., 1974; s. Aboutorab and Parirokh (Garakani) R.; m. Firouzeh Yekta, Aug. 18, 1983; children: Nina, Shiva. BSCE, BA in Econs., U. Calif., Berkeley, 1978; SM in Engring., Harvard U., 1980, PhD in Environ. Scis., 1983. Registered profl. engr., Ga. Asst. prof. Ga. Inst. Tech., Atlanta, 1983-90, assoc. prof. civil engring., 1990-96; sr. cons. Dames & Moore, Atlanta, 1990-95; pres. New Fields, Inc., Atlanta, 1995—. NSF vis. scientist Ctr. Geostats., Paris Sch. of Mines, 1987-88; expert mem. ASTM, EPA, U.S. Geol. Survey, Dept. Def. Geostats. Standardization Com., 1991-96. Co-author: Ground Water, 1991; contbr. articles to profl. publs., chpts. to books., also numerous reports, papers in field. Mem. ASCE (award 1991, chmn. nat. ground water hydrology 1991, chmn. task com. on geostatis. techniques in geohydrology 1987-89, sec. water resources com. Ga. sect. 1988, spl. session organizer 1989, 90, contact mem. task com. 1988-90, symposium organizer 1991), Am. Geophys. Union (assoc. editor Water Resources Rsch. 1989-94), Internat. Water Resources Assn., Am. Water Resources Assn., N.Am. Coun. on Geostats., Internat. Geostatis. Assn., Phi Beta Kappa, Tau Beta Pi, Chi Epsilon, Sigma Chi. Office: Newfields Inc 1349 W Peachtree St NW Ste 2000 Atlanta GA 30309-2926 Office Phone: 404-347-9050. Business E-Mail: srouhani@newfields.com.

ROUKEMA, MARGARET SCAFATI, congresswoman; b. West Orange, N.J., Sept. 19, 1929; d. Claude Thomas and Margaret (D'Alessio) Scafati; m. Richard W. Roukema, Aug. 23, 1951; children: Margaret, Todd (dec.), Gregory. BA with honors in History and Polit. Sci, Montclair State Coll., 1951, postgrad. in history and guidance, 1951-53; postgrad. program in city and regional planning, Rutgers U., 1975. Tchr. history, govt., public schs., Livingston and Ridgewood, N.J., 1951-55; mem. U.S. Congress from 7th N.J. dist., Washington, 1981—83, U.S. Congress from 5th N.J. dist., Washington, 1983—2003; vice chair fin. svcs. com., chair housing and community opportunity subcom.; mem. banking com., edn. and the workforce com. Vice pres. Ridgewood Bd. Edn., 1970-73; bd. dirs., co-founder Ridgewood Sr. Citizens Housing Corp.; chairwoman Fin. Inst. and Consumer Credit Sub. Com. U.S. Congress; sponcer Family Med. Leave U.S. Congress; lectr. Rutgers Univ. Trustee Spring House, Paramus, N.J.; trustee Leukemia Soc. No. N.J., Family Counseling Service for Ridgewood and Vicinity; mem. Bergen County (N.J.) Republican Com.; NW Bergen County campaign mgr. for gubernatorial candidate Tom Kean, 1977; bd. mem. Children's Aid and Family Svcs., The Red Cross, Ramapo Coll. Mem. Bus. and Profl. Women's Orgn. Clubs: Coll. of Ridgewood, Ridgewood Rep. Republican. *I have served in several roles in my life. Wife, mother, teacher, public servant. All are personally rewarding; each affords the opportunity to help others in need and to enrich the lives of those around you. As a member of Congress, I find the most rewards are in the knowledge that I can truly make a difference and improve the lives of thousands of people. The challenges are frequently insurmountable, but the rewards are incalculable.*

ROUKIS, THOMAS SEAN, surgeon, podiatrist; b. Queens, NY, May 29, 1971; s. Maryann Louise and Peter Thomas Roukis; m. Sherri Lynn Fernholz, May 5, 2001. DPM, Calif. Coll. Podiatric Medicine, 1997. Diplomate Am. Bd. Podiatric Surgery. Podiatric surg. resident Gundersen Luth. Med. Ctr., La Crosse, Wis., 1997—2000; trauma fellow AO Internat./AO N.Am., Mainz, Germany, 2000; reconstructive foot & ankle surgery fellow Weil Foot & Ankle Inst., Des Plaines, 2000—01; European foot & ankle fellow Am. Coll. Foot & Ankle Surgeons, Germany, 2001. Recipient David A. Stone DPM Meml. award, Calif. Coll. Podiatric Medicine, 1993—94, award for Excellence in Rsch., 1997, Herman F. Foster Meml. award, 1994—95, Gold award in Plastic Surgery, Nat. Post-Graduate Rsch. Symposium, 1999, 3rd pl. Abstract Presentation, 2001, Scott Alter, DPM, Meml. Rsch. award, Podiatry Found. Pitts., 1999, 2nd Pl., Am. Podiatric Med. Writers Assn., 1996, 1st Pl., Langer Biomechanics Group 11th Ann. Writing Contest, 1996; Earl G. Kaplan, DPM scholar, Calif. Coll. Podiatric Medicine, 1993—94, John H. Weed, DPM scholar, 1994—95, Bennett G. Zier, MD scholar, 1995—96, Podiatry Ins. Co. Am. scholar, 1995—96, Merton L. Root, DPM scholar, 1996—97. Mem.: Assn. Study and Application of Methods Ilizarov: Lower Extermity, Ill. Podiatric Med. Assn. (mem. continuing med. edn. com. 2001—04), AO Internat., Am. Podiatric Med. Assn. (mem. podiatric physician mentoring network 2000—04, contbg. editor, expert peer reviewer 2001—04), Am. Coll. Foot and Ankle Surgeons (com. mem. 2000—04, editor, expert peer reviewer 2001—04, 1st pl. 1997, 1st pl. instl. poster presentation 2001, 2nd pl. Manuscript award of excellence 2001, 2nd pl. individual poster presentation 2002). Office: Weil Foot and Ankle Inst 1455 E Golf Rd Ste 131 Des Plaines IL 60016 Business E-Mail: troukis@footankledeformity.com.

ROULAC, STEPHEN E. real estate consultant; b. San Francisco, Aug. 15, 1945; s. Phil Williams and Elizabeth (Young) R.; children: Arthur, Fiona. BA, Pomona Coll., 1967; MBA with distinction, Harvard Grad. Sch. Bus. Adminstrn., 1970; JD, U. Calif., Berkeley, 1976; PhD, Stanford U., 1978. CPA, Hawaii. Asst. constrn. supt., foreman, adminstr. Roulac Constrn. Co., Pasadena, Calif., 1963-66; rsch. asst. Econs. Rsch. Assocs., L.A., 1966-67; assoc. economist Urbanomics Rsch. Assocs., Claremont, Calif., 1967; acquisition auditor Litton Industries Inc., Chgo., Beverly Hills, 1967-68; tax cons. Lybrand, Ross Bros. and Montgomery, L.A., 1968; cons. to constrn. group and corp. planning dept. Owens-Corning Fiberglas Corp., Toledo, 1969-70; CEO Questor Assocs., San Francisco, 1972-83; chmn. nat. mgmt. adv. svcs. Kenneth Leventhal & Co., 1983-84; pres. Stephen E. Roulac & Co., 1985-86; mng. ptnr. Roulac Group of Deloitte Haskins & Sells (Deloitte & Touche), 1987-91; CEO The Roulac Group, Larkspur, Calif., 1992—. Strategic fin. econ. and transactions cons. Roulac Capitol Mkt. Strategies, Roulac Capitol Flows; expert witness, preparer econ. analyses for legal matters including civil trial of Irvine Co., Jewell et. al. vs. Bank of Am., Tchrs. vs. Olympia & York, Calif. Legis., Calif. Corps. Dept., Midwest Securities Commrs. Assn., Nat. Assn. Securities Dealers, SEC, Dept. of Labor, HUD; advisor to investment arm of Asian country, Calif. Pub. Employees Retirement System, U.S. Dept. Labor, numerous others; adj. prof. Tex. A&M U., 1986, U. Chgo., 1985, UCLA, 1983-84, Stanford Grad. Sch. Bus., 1970-79, Pacific Coast Banking Sch., 1978, Hastings Coll. Law, 1977-78, U. Calif., Berkeley, 1972-77, Calif. State U., 1970-71, Northeastern U., 1969-70; keynote speaker, instr. continuing edn. sessions, program chmn., corps., orgns. Author: Real Estate Syndications Digest: Principles and Applications, 1972, Case Studies in Property Development, 1973, Syndication Landmarks, 1974, Tax Shelter Sale-Leaseback Financing: The Economic Realities, 1976, Modern Real Estate Investment: An Institutional Approach, 1976, (with Sherman Maisel) Real Estate Investment and Finance, 1976 (1976 Bus. Book of Yr. The Libr. Jour.); editor-in-chief, pub. Calif. Bicyclist, 1988-95, Tex. Bicyclist, 1989-94, Roulac's Strategic Real Estate, 1979-89; columnist Forbes, 1983, 84, 87, 92, 93, Intuition Network, Ctr Real Estate Rsch. Nortwestern U., Nat. Bureau Real Estate Rsch., New Leaders, World 2000, NACORE/ARES Corp. Rsch. Found., Mystery Sch.; mem. editorial adv. bd. Am. Real Estate and Urban Econs. Assn. Jour., 1977-81, Housing Devel. Reporter, 1978-80, Fin. Edn. Jour., 1976-70, Jour. Housing Rsch., 1996—, Jour. Real Estated Edn. and Practice, 1996—, Jour. Real Estate Lit., 1996—, Jour. Property Valuation and Investment, 1992—, Real Estate Workouts and Asset Mgmt., 1992—; assoc. editor Real Estate Rev., 1993—; editor Jour. Real Estate Rsch., 1992—; contbg. editor Real Estate Law Jour., 1973-78, Real Estate Rev., 1973-75; spl. issue editor Calif. Mgmt. Rev., 1976; editor: Real Estate Syndication Digest, 1971-72, Notable Syndications Sourcebook, 1972, Real Estate Securities and Syndication: A Workbook, 1973, Due Diligence in Real Estate Transactions, 1974, Real Estate Venture Analysis, 1974, Real Estate Securities Regulation Sourcebook, 1975, Questor Real Estate Investment Manager Profiles, 1982, Questor Real Estate Securities Yearbook, 1980-85, Retail Giants and Real Estate, 1986, Roulac's Top Real Estate Brokers, 1984-88, (monograph) Ethics in Real Estate; contbr. articles to profl. jours., newspapers; cassettes; frequent appearer on TV shows including MacNeil/Lehrer Newshour, 1986, Cable News Network, 1987, ABC TV, 1987, KCBS Radio, 1986, WABC Radio, Dallas, 1986. Mem. real estate adv. com. to Calif. Commr. Corps., 1973, Calif. Corp. Commr.'s Blue Ribbon Com. on Projections and Track Records, 1973-74; mem. adv. bd. Nat. Bicycle Month, League of Am. Wheelmen, Ctr. for Real Estate Rsch. Kellogg Grad. Sch. Mgmt., Northwestern U. Named Highest Instr. Student Teaching Evaluations, Schs. Bus. Adminstrn., U. Calif., Berkeley, 1975-76; named to Pomona Coll. Athletic Hall of Fame, 1981; W.T. Grant fellow Harvard U., 1969-70,; George F. Baker scholar Harvard Grad. Sch. Bus. Adminstrn., 1970; Stanford U. Grad. Sch. Bus. fellow, 1970-71. Mem. Strategic Mgmt. Soc., Am. Acad. Mgmt., Am. Fin. Assn., Am. Planning Assn, European Real Estate Soc., Internat. Real Estate Soc., Inst. Mgmt. Cons., ISSSEEM, Soc. Sci. Exploration, Am. Real Estate and Urban Econs. Assn., Intuition Network (bd. dirs.), World Future Soc. (exec. com. and adv. bd. World 2000), Am. Econ. Assn., Am. Real Estate Soc. (pres. 1995-96, award for best paper presented in ann. meeting, 1995, 96), Noetic Soc., Nat. Bur. Real Estate Rsch. (founder, bd. dirs.), Harvard Club N.Y., L.A. Adventures Club. Avocations: arts, antiquarian books, reading, bicycle racing (U.S. team 1990), outdoor activities. Office: The Roulac Group 709 5th Ave San Rafael CA 94901-3202

ROULEAU, R. MICHAEL, retail executive; Co-founder, pres. Office Warehouse; exec. v.p. store ops. Lowe's, 1992-95, pres. contractor yard divsn., 1995-96; CEO Michaels Stores, Inc., Irving, Tex., 1996—, pres., 1997—. Office: Michaels Stores Inc 8000 Bent Branch Dr Irving TX 75063

ROULEAU, REYNALD, bishop; b. St.-Jean-de-Dieu, Que., Can., Nov. 30, 1935; Ordained priest, 1963, bishop, 1987. Bishop Churchill-Hudson Bay, 1987—. Home and Office: Diocese Churchill-Hudson Bay PO Box 10 Churchill MB Canada R0B 0E0

ROUMAN, JOHN CHRIST, classics educator; b. Tomahawk, Wis., May 1, 1926; s. Christ and Soteria (Dedes) R. BA in Greek, Carleton Coll., 1950; MA in Greek, Columbia U., 1951; student, Rutgers U., 1951-53, U. Kiel, Germany, 1956-57, U. Minn., Mpls., 1959-60; PhD in Classics, U. Wis., 1965. German tchr. Seton Hall Preparatory Sch., South Orange, N.J., 1954-56; ancient history tchr. Malverne (N.Y.) High Sch., 1957-59; tchg. asst. in ancient history U. Wis., Madison, 1960-61, rsch. asst. in ancient history, 1961-65; rsch. asst. in Greek epigraphy Inst. Advanced Study, Princeton, N.J., 1962-63; asst. prof. classics U. N.H., Durham, 1965-71, assoc. prof., 1971-91, prof., 1991—, prof. classics emeritus, 1999, co-chmn. Spanish and classics depts., mem. adv. bd. Prof. John C. Rouman classical lectr. series, 1997—. Examiner N.H. State Bd. Edn. in Latin and Greek, 1979-80; judge Warren H. Held Jr. Exam-Contests in Latin and Mythology, 1988—; cons. Nat. Classical Greek Examination, 1980; presenter, lectr. in field; adv. bd. Christos and Mary Papoutsy Disting. Endowed Chair in Bus. Ethics, N.H. Coll./So. N.H. Univ., 2000—; exec. bd. Hellenic Soc. PAIDEIA, NH, 2001. Active Colovos Rd. Com., 1981-82. With USN, 1944-46. Fulbright scholar U. Kiel, 1956-57; recipient Disting. Tchg. award U. N.H. Alumni Assn., 1985, Pericles award Am. Hellenic Ednl. Progressive Assn. and Daus. of Penelope, 1993, Profile of Svc. award U. N.H. Aumni Assn., 2000; Prof. John C. Rouman Classical Lecture Series named in his honor. Mem. Am. Classical League (rep. to TCNE at ann. meeting 1978, mem. fin. com. 1981-82, treas. 1982-83), Am. Philol. Assn. (Nat. Excellence in Teaching Classics award, 1991), Archaeol. Inst. Am., Classical Assn. Can., Classical Assn. New Eng. (mem. exec. com. at-large 1981-84, mem. nominating com. 1983-84, 86-87, pres. 1987-88, Barlow-Beach award 1991, mem. ad hoc com. on elections and appointments), Medieval Acad. Am., Modern Greek Studies Assn., Nat. Assn. Advisors for Health Professions, N.H. Classical Assn. (mem. exec. com. 1965—, chair nominating com. 1986—), Strafford County Greco-Roman Found. (pres. 1978—), Vergilian Soc. Am., Carleton Coll. Alumni Assn. (Alumni award for Dist. Achievement 2000), Phi Kappa Theta (faculty advisor, 1982—, chmn. nat. bd., 1993-94, nat. found. 1993—. Man of Achievement award 2000, Chpt. Advisor award 2002). E-mail: Jrouman@comcast.net.

ROUNCE, ROB, controller; Contr. Hartford (Conn.) Courant. Office: Hartford Courant 285 Broad St Hartford CT 06115-2510

ROUNDS, BARBARA LYNN, psychiatrist; b. L.A., Mar. 17, 1934; d. Ralph Arthur and Florene V. (Heyer) Behrend; divorced 1962; children: Steve, Mike, Pamela, Ronald, Thomas. BA, Stanford U., 1964, MD, 1966; postgrad., San Francisco Psychoanalytic, 1973-81. Diplomate Am. Bd. Psychiatry and Neurology; cert. psychoanalyst. Intern New Orleans Pub. Health Svc., 1966-67; resident psychiat. Mendocino State Hosp., 1967-69, U. Calif. Davis, 1969-70; staff psychiatrist U. Calif. Davis Med. Sch., Sacramento, 1970-77, clin. instr., 1970-76; psychiatrist pvt. practice, Sacramento, 1971—; asst. clin. prof. U. Calif. Davis, Sacramento, 1976-84, assoc. clin. prof., 1984-94. Mem. Am. Psychiat. Assn., Am. Psychoanalytic Assn., AMA, Cen. Calif. Psychiat. Soc. (pres.-elect 1990-91, pres. 1991-92). Democrat. Home: 8910 Leatham Ave Fair Oaks CA 95628-6506 Office: 1317 H St Sacramento CA 95814-1928

ROUNDS, MICHAEL, governor; b. Huron, S.D., Oct. 24, 1954; m. Jean Rounds; 4 children. Degree in polit. sci., S.D. State U. Former ptnr. Fischer, Rounds & Assocs., Inc.; state senator Dist. 24, 1991—2001; senate majority leader State of S.D., gov., 2003—. Mem. bd. Oahe YMCA; v.p. Home and Sch. Assn. St. Joseph Sch.; pres. Pierre-Ft. Pierre Exch. Club. Mem.: Pierre Elks Lodge. Republican. Roman Catholic. Office: Off of Gov 500 E Capitol Ave Pierre SD 57501

ROUNER, LEROY STEPHENS, religious studies educator, philosophy educator; b. Wolfeboro, N.H., Aug. 5, 1930; s. Arthur Acy and Elizabeth Ward (Stephens) R.; m. Rita Rainsford, May 21, 1955; children: Stephen Rainsford, Timothy Nichols, Jonathan Kerr, Christina Elizabeth. AB in English, Harvard Coll., 1953, postgrad., 1956; MDiv, Union Theol. Sem., 1958; PhD, Columbia U., 1961; LHD (hon.), Lynchburg Coll., 1985. Asst. prof. United Theol. Coll., Bangalore, India, 1961-66; prof., then prof. emeritus Boston Univ., 1970—, dir. emeritus Inst. Philos. & Religion. Bd. trustees Jaffna Coll. Funds, Boston, 1975—; bd. trustee endowment fund Am. Coll., Madurai, India, 1975. Author: Within Human Experience, 1969, The Long Way Home, 1989, To Be At Home: Christianity Civil Religion and World Community, 1987; gen. editor: Boston Univ. Studies in Philosophy and Religion, 1981-2003. Chmn. dem. com. Carroll County, N.H., 1971-73; trustee Ella Lyman Cabot Trust. Mem. APA, Internat. Soc. Metaphysics, Soc. Asian & Comparative Philos., Phi Beta Kappa. Democrat. Avocations: rowing, hiking. Home: 223 Maple Ridge Rd Center Sandwich NH 03227-3721 Office: Inst Philos & Religion 745 Commonwealth Ave # 523 Boston MA 02215-1401

ROUNICK, JACK A. lawyer, company executive; b. Phila., June 5, 1935; s. Philip and Nettie (Brownstein) R.; m. Noreen A. Garrigan, Sept. 4, 1970; children: Ellen, Eric, Amy, Michelle. BBA, U. Mich., 1956; JD, U. Pa., 1959. Bar: Pa. 1960, U.S. Dist. Ct. (ea. dist.) Pa. 1960; diplomate Am. Coll. Family Trial Lawyers. Spl. asst. atty. gen., 1963-71; ptnr. Israelit & Rounick, 1960-67, Moss & Rounick, 1968-69, Moss, Rounick & Hurowitz, Norristown, Pa., 1969-72, Moss & Rounick, Norristown, 1972-73, Pechner, Dorfman, Wolffe, Rounick and Cabot, Norristown, 1973-87; v.p., gen. counsel Martin Lawrence Ltd. Edits., Inc., 1987-93, dir., 1984—95, Deb Shops, Inc., 1974—; counsel to firm Wolf Block, Schorr & Solis-Cohen LLP, 1997—. Author: Pennsylvania Matrimonial Practice, 6 vols., 1982; editor Pa. Family Lawyer, 1980-87; bd. editors Family Adv. Fin. chmn. Pa. Young Reps., 1964-66, treas., 1966-68, chmn., 1968-70. Recipient Boss of Yr. award Montgomery County Legal Secs. Assn., 1970, Cert of Appreciation Pa. Bar Inst., 1980. Fellow: Am. Acad. Matrimonial Lawyers (pres. Pa. chpt. 1982—84, gov. 1983—85, v.p. 1985—87, chmn. bd. rev. 1997—), Internat. Acad. Matrimonial Lawyers; mem.: FLS, ABA (coun. family law sect. 1982—87, coun. 2000—03), Scope and Correlation Com., Family Adv. (bd. editors), Friends of Hebrew U. (bd. dirs. 1987—93, nat. coun. trustees 1987—93, pres. Phila. chpt. 1988—91, v.p. 1990—91), Montgomery Bar Assn., Pa. Bar Assn. (past chmn. family law sect. 1978—80, Spl. Achievement award 1979—80). Republican. Jewish. Office: Ste 500 1 Main St Norristown PA 19401-4801 E-mail: JRounick@WolfBlock.com.

ROUNTREE, ASA, lawyer; b. Birmingham, Ala., Aug. 9, 1927; s. John Asa and Cherokee Jemison (Van de Graaff) Rountree; m. Elizabeth Rhodes Blue, Aug. 11, 1951 (dec.); m. Helen Hill Updike, Oct. 10, 1998. AB, U. Ala., 1949; LLB, Harvard U., 1954. Bar: Ala. 1954, U.S. Dist. Ct. (no. dist.) Ala. 1954, U.S. Ct. Appeals (5th cir.) 1955, N.Y. 1962, U.S. Dist. Ct. (so. dist.) N.Y. 1963, U.S. Ct. Appeals (2d cir.) 1963, U.S. Supreme Ct. 1972. Assoc. Cabaniss & Johnston, Birmingham, Ala., 1954-60, ptnr., 1960-62; assoc. Debevoise & Plimpton, N.Y.C., 1962-63, ptnr., 1963-91; spl. counsel Maynard, Cooper, & Gale, P.C., Birmingham, 0991—. Bd. dirs. U. Ala. Law Sch. Found. With U.S. Army, 1945—46, lt. U.S. Army, 1951—53. Mem.: ALA (chmn. litig. sect. 1980—81), Am. Coll. Trial Lawyers, Am. Law Inst., Assn. Bar City of N.Y., N.Y. State Bar Assn., Ala. Bar Assn., Am. Bar Found., Mountain Brook Club (Birmingham), River Club (N.Y.C.). Episcopalian. Office: Maynard Cooper Gale PC 2400 AmSouth/Harbert Plz 1901 6th Ave N Birmingham AL 35203-2618

ROUNTREE, NEVA DIXON, public relations executive; b. Jacksonville, Fla., Dec. 13, 1943; d. Jarma E. and Helen (McIlvaine) Dixon; m. Don C. Rountree, Mar. 23, 1941; 1 child, Don C. III. AB in Journalism, U. Ga., 1964, MA, 1979. Press sec. Underwood for U.S. Senate, Atlanta, 1979-80; account exec. Cohn & Wolfe, Atlanta, 1980-81; v.p. Carl Byoir & Assocs., Atlanta, 1981-84; pres. Rountree Group, Inc., Atlanta, 1985—. Co-chmn. Leadership Sandy Springs, Ga., 1985-86, trustee, 1986—; adv. bd. Northside Found., 1994—; comm. com. Atlanta Com. for Olympic Games, 1990-92. Recipient 1 of 3 Best Run Agys. award Atlanta Bus. Chronicle, 1988, 89; named 25 Hot Smaller Pub. Rels. Agys. by Inside Pub. Rels., 1992, named Best Mktg. Driven Pub. Rels. by Atlanta Bus. Chronicle, 1991, 92. Mem. Pub. Rels. Soc. Am. (Counselors Acad., pres. Ga. chpt. 1994—, George Goodwin award 1992), Pub. Rels. Exch. (bd. dirs. 1987—), U. Ga. Journalism Alumni Assn. (v.p., pres. 1986-89).

ROURKE, BRADLEY KEVIN, public affairs executive; b. L.A., July 29, 1965; s. Daniel Lee and Sherill Anne (Siebert) Rourke; m. Andrea Kay Jarrell, Sept. 19, 1992; children: Carson Jarrell-Rourke, Daniel Jarrell-Rourke. BA, U. Calif., Berkeley, 1987. Dir. scheduling Contr. Gray Davis, L.A., 1992-93; dist. dir. Congresswoman Jane Harman, L.A., 1994; dir. pub. affairs Elec. Bicycle Co., Burbank, Calif., 1995-96; state govt. rels. rep. Northrop Grumman Corp., L.A., 1996-97; prin. Jarrell-Rourke Comm., Pasadena, Calif., 1997; dir. project on campaign conduct Inst. Global Ethics, Camden, Maine, 1997-99, v.p. pub. policy and comms., 1999—2002; dir. external initiatives The Harwood Inst., Bethesda, Md., 2002—03; pub. rsch. cons., 2003—. Dep campaign dir Calif Nat Health Care Campaign, Los Angeles, 1993. Episcopalian. Office: 545 Beall Ave Rockville MD 20850 E-mail: bradrourke@earthlink.net.

ROURKE, MICKEY (PHILIP ANDRE ROURKE JR.), actor; b. Schenectady, NY, Sept. 16, 1953; m. Debra Feuer (div.); m. Carre Otis. Appearences include (films) including 1941, 1979, Heaven's Gate, 1980, Fade to Black, 1980, Body Heat, 1981, Diner, 1982 (Nat. Soc. of Film Critics award best supporting actor 1982), Rumblefish, 1983, The Pope of Greenwich Village, 1984, Year of the Dragon, 1985, Eureka, 1985, 9 1/2 Weeks, 1985, Angel Heart, 1987, A Prayer for the Dying, 1987, Barfly, 1987, Homeboy (also screenwriter), 1988, Johnny Handsome, 1989, Wild Orchid, 1990, The Desperate Hours, 1990, Harley Davidson and the Marlboro Man, 1991, White Sands, 1992, F.T.W., 1994, Fall Time, 1995, Exit in Red, 1996, Bullets, 1996, The Rainmaker, 1997, Love in Paris, 1997, Double Team, 1997, Buffalo '66, 1997, Thursday, 1998, Shergar, 1999, Shades, 1999, Out in Fifty, 1999, The Animal Factory, 2000, Get Carter, 2000, The Pledge, 2001, Spun, 2002, Masked and Anonymous, 2003, Once Upon a Time in Mexico, 2003; (TV movies) Act of Love, 1980, City in Fear, 1980, Rape and Marriage: The Rideout Case, 1980, Thicker Than Blood, 1998.*

ROUS, STEPHEN NORMAN, urologist, educator; b. N.Y.C., Nov. 1, 1931; s. David H. and Luba (Margulies) R.; m. Margot Woolfolk, Nov. 12, 1966; children: Benjamin, David. AB, Amherst Coll., 1952; MD, N.Y. Med. Coll., 1956; MS, U. Minn., 1963. Diplomate: Am. Bd. Urology. Intern Phila. Gen. Hosp., 1956-57, resident, 1959-60, Flower-Fifth Ave. and Met. Hosp., N.Y.C., 1957-59, Mayo Clinic, Rochester, Minn., 1960-63; practice medicine specializing in urology San Francisco, 1963-68; assoc. prof. urology N.Y. Med. Coll., N.Y.C., 1968-72, assoc. dean, 1970-72; prof. surgery, chief div. urology Mich. State U., East Lansing, 1972-75; prof., chmn. dept. urology Med. U. S.C., Charleston, 1975-88; urologist-in-chief Med. U. S.C. and County hosps., Charleston, 1975-88; editorial dir. Norton Med. Books div. W.W. Norton and Co., 1988-94, editorial cons., 1994—; clin. prof. surgery Uniformed Svcs. U. of Health Scis., Bethesda, Md., 1992-2001. Adj. prof. urology Med. U. S.C., 1988-99, prof. emeritus, 1999—; adj. prof. surgery Dartmouth Med. Sch., 1988-91, prof. surgery (urology), 1991-2001, prof. surgery emeritus, 2001—; staff urologist Dartmouth-Hitchcock Med. Ctr., 1991-99; cons. urologist Saginaw VA Hosp., 1971-75, Charleston VA Hosp., 1975-88; hon. cons. St. Peter's Hosp., London, 1981-82; sr. vis. fellow Inst. Urology, London, 1981-82; mil. cons. in urology USAF Surgeon Gen., 1982-85; chmn. alumni devel. com. Mayo Clinic, 1979-82; hon. staff The Exeter Hosp., N.H., 1988—; nat. bd. visitors N.Y. Med. Coll., 1988-97; chief urology VA Med. Ctr., White River Junction, Vt., 1991-2001; mem. reparative justice bd. Vt. Dept. Corrections, 2004—. Author: Understanding Urology, 1973, Urology in Primary Care, 1976, Spanish edit., 1978, Russian edit., 1979, Urology: A Core Textbook, 1985, 2d edit., 1996, The Prostate Book, 1988, latest rev. edit., 2001, (with Judge Hiller B. Zobel) Doctors and the Law: Defendants and Expert Witnesses, 1993, (with Dr. Pamela Ellsworth) The Little Black Book of Urology, 2001; editor Urology Ann., 1987-97, Stone Disease: Diagnosis and Management, 1987; mem. editl. bd. Mil. Medicine, 1984-94; contbr. articles to med. jours. Mem. East Lansing (Mich.) Planning Commn., 1974-75; vestryman, jr. warden All Saints Episcopal Ch., East Lansing, 1973-75, lay reader, mem. diocesan com. on continuing edn., 1975-86; vestryman St. Michael's Episc. Ch., 1979-82, Charleston, S.C., chmn. every mem. canvas, 1979-80, chmn. lay readers, 1983-86; mem. fin. com., lay reader Christ Episc. Ch., Exeter, N.H., 1989-91; lector St. Thomas Episc. Ch., Hanover, N.H., 1991—, vestryman, 1992-96, stewardship chmn., 1992-94, jr. warden, 1994-96; mem. selectman's alt. Hampton Falls Planning Bd., 1989-91; alt. mem. Zoning Bd. Adjustment, Hanover, 1997-2000; bd. trustees, Nat. Hypertension Assn., N.Y.C., 2001-; bd. dirs. Med. Sci. Techs. Inc., Newport News, Va., 2001-. Col. USAFR, 1981-85, col. USAR, 1985-2000, col. AUS, ret., 2001—. Recipient "A" designator in urology, U.S. Army Surgeon Gen., 1986. Fellow ACS, Am. Acad. Pediatrics; mem. AMA, Soc. Univ. Urologists, Internat. Soc. Urology, Am. Urol. Assn., Nat. Urologic Forum, Soc. Pediatric Urology, Brit. Assn. Urol. Surgeons, German Urol. Assn. (hon.), Mayo Alumni Assn. (v.p. 1979-81, pres. 1983-85), Army and Navy Club (Washington), Lotos Club (N.Y.C.), Dartmouth Club of N.Y.C., Sigma Xi, Alpha Omega Alpha (hon.). Republican. Home: 6 Partridge Rd PO Box 10 Etna NH 03750-0010 Personal E-mail: stephen.n.rous@dartmouth.edu.

ROUSE, BISHOP C., JR., quality assurance professional; b. Atlanta, Dec. 4, 1948; s. Bishop C. and Lula Alberta (Woodbury) R.; m. Minnie Eva Loney, Sept. 18, 1968; children: Claudia, Bishop III, Kafi, Adam. BS in Chemistry, Allen U., 1971. Cert. ISO lead accessor. Coating chemist Federal Paperboard, Riegelwood, N.C., 1971-72; process engr., sr. quality engr. Fiber Industries, Shelby, N.C., 1973-82; sr. product engr., dept. mgr., tech. engring. mgr. Duracell Inc., Lancaster, S.C., 1982-96, dir. quality Bethel, Conn., 1996—, leader quality assessment 6 countries, 1996—. Mem. bd. examiners Pres.'s Quality Award, 2000—. Vol. Dept. Correction, 1998—. Recipient Pres.'s Quality award Bd. Examiners, 2000. Mem. Am. Soc. Quality, Am. Chem. Soc. Democrat. Methodist. Avocations: golf, weightlifting, martial arts, music.

ROUSE, CHRISTOPHER CHAPMAN, III, composer, educator; b. Balt., Feb. 15, 1949; s. Christopher Chapman Jr. and Margery (Harper) Rouse; m. Ann Jensen, Aug. 28, 1983; children: Jillian, Alexandra, Adrian 1 stepchild, Angela. MusB, Oberlin Conservatory, 1971; MFA, DMA, Cornell U., 1977; DMus (hon.), Oberlin Coll., 1996, SUNY, Geneseo, 2000. Asst. prof. composition U. Mich., Ann Arbor, 1978—81, Eastman Sch. Music, Rochester, NY, 1981—85, assoc. prof. composition, 1985—91, prof. composition, 1991—2002; mem. faculty Juilliard Sch., 1997—. Composer-in-residence Balt. Symphony Orch., 1986—89, Schleswig Holstein Festival, 1989, Helsinki Bienniale, 1997, Tanglewood Music Ctr., 1997, Pacific Music Festival, 1998, Aspen Music Festival, 1999—; writer numerous musical subjects; historian rock music. Composer for numerous renowned soloists and ensembles, including Yo-Yo Ma, Evelyn Glennie, Emanuel Ax, Dawn Upshaw, Cho-Liang Lin, Charles Castleman, James VanDemark, Jan de Gaetani, Leslie Guinn, Sharon Isbin, Carol Wincenc, William Albright, Soc. New Music, Blackearth Percussion Group, commd. composer Atlanta Symphony, Phila. Orch., N.Y. Philharm., L.A. Philharm., Balt. Symphony, Houston Symphony, Minn. Orch., London Symphony, Cleve. Orch., Detroit Symphony, St. Louis Symphony, Boston Pops, Rochester Philharm., Cleve. Quartet, Boston Pops, Boston Musica Viva, Aspen Music Festival, Chamber Music Soc. Lincoln Ctr., N.Y. Internat. Festival of Arts, Chamber Music Am., New Eng. Conservatory Music, Nonesuch Records, orchestral works programmed by Berlin, Helsinki, Stockholm, N.Y.C., Buffalo, L.A., Rochester Philharms., Orch. Nat. de France, Orch. de Paris, Residentie, Concertgebouw, Vienna and Zurich Tonhalle, New Zealand, Philharmonia, also Vienna, BBC, Berlin, Montreal, Chgo., Boston, St. Louis, Detroit, Balt., Nat., Pitts., Houston, Denver, Milw., Cleve., Minn., Phila., Oakland, Cin., Atlanta, N.J., Utah, Indpls., Memphis, San Francisco, Dallas, Göteboro U., Bournemouth symphony orchs, also The Netherlands, Finnish, Frankfurt, Moscow, Austrian, Flemish, BBC and NHK Tokyo Radio Orchs. Recipient awards, Guggenheim Found., League Composers/ISCM, NEA, Rockefeller Found., Am. Music Ctr., Warner Bros. Record Co., Koussevitzky Found., BMI and Pitney Bowes, Friedheim 1st prize, Kennedy Ctr., 1988, Pulitzer prize for music, 1993, Grammy award, 2002. Mem.: Am. Acad. Arts and Letters (Acad. award 1993). Office: Juilliard Sch 60 Lincoln Center Plz New York NY 10023

ROUSE, DORIS JANE, physiologist, research administrator; b. Greensboro, N.C., Oct. 3, 1948; d. Welby Corbett and Nadia Elizabeth (Grainger) R.; m. Blake Shaw Wilson, Jan. 6, 1974; children: Nadia Jacqueline, Blair Elizabeth. BA in Chemistry, Duke U., 1970, PhD in Physiology and Pharmacology, 1980. Tchr. sci. Peace Corps, Tugbake, Liberia, 1970-71; research scientist Burroughs Wellcome Co., Research Triangle Park, N.C., 1971-76; sr. physiologist Rsch. Triangle Inst., Durham, 1976-83, ctr. dir., 1980-2000, also dir. NASA tech. application team, 1980-2000, dir. Tuberculosis Tech. Transfer Program, 1999—, dir. Global Health, 2001—; portfolio project mgr. Global Alliance for Tuberculosis Drug Devel., 2002—. Adminstr. ANSI Tech. Adv. Group for Wheelchairs, N.Y.C., 1982-86; adj. asst. prof. U. N.C. Sch. Medicine, 1983-92; chair Instl. Rev. Bd., Profl. Devel. Award com., chair salary com. Rsch. Triangle Inst.; mem. adv. bd. Assistive Tech. Rsch. Ctr., 1994-96; portfolio project mgr. Global Alliance for TB Drug Devel., 2002—. Mem. adv. bd. Assn. Retarded Citizens, Arlington, Tex., 1981—88, Western Gerontology Soc., San Francisco, 1982—85; bd. dirs. Simon Found., Chgo., 1983—95; mem. spl. rev. com. small bus. applications Nat. Forum on Tech. and Aging; mem. fund steering com. Academy Venture, 2000—. Recipient Group Achievement award NASA, 1979, 2000, President's award, RTI, 2003. Mem.: Am. Soc. Microbiology, Assn. Fed. Tech. Transfer Execs., Licensing Execs. Soc., Rehab. Engring. Soc. N.Am., Rehab. Engring. Soc. N.Am. (chmn. wheelchair com. 1981—86). Home: 2410 Wrightwood Ave Durham NC 27705-5802 Office: Research Triangle Inst PO Box 12194 Durham NC 27709-2194 Office Phone: 919-541-6980.

ROUSE, IRVING, anthropologist, emeritus educator; b. Rochester, NY, Aug. 29, 1913; s. Benjamin Irving and Louise Gillespie (Bohachek) R.; m. Mary Uta Mikami, June 24, 1939; children: Peter, David. BS, Yale U., 1934, PhD, 1938; D in Philosophy and Letters (hon.), Centro de Estudios Avanzados de Puerto Rico y el Caribe, 1990. Asst. anthropology Yale Peabody Mus., 1934-38, asst. curator, 1938-47, assoc. curator, 1947-54, rsch. assoc., 1954-62, curator, 1977-85, emeritus curator, 1985—; instr. anthropology Yale U., 1939-43, asst. prof., 1943-48; assoc. prof. Yale, 1948-54; prof. Yale U., 1954-69, Charles J. MacCurdy prof. anthropology, 1969-84, prof. emeritus, 1984—. Author monographs on archaeology of Fla., Cuba, Haiti, P.R., Venezuela, Antigua. Recipient Medalla Commemorativa del Vuelo Panamericano pro Faro de Colon Govt. Cuba, 1945, A. Cressy Morrison prize in natural sci. NY Acad. Sci., 1951, Viking fund medal Wenner-Gren Found., 1960, Wilbur Cross medal Yale U., 1992; Guggenheim fellow, 1963-64; fellow Phi Beta Kappa, 1996. Mem. Am. Anthrop. Assn. (pres. 1967-68), Ea. States Archeol. Fedn. (pres. 1946-50), Assn. Field Arch. (pres. 1977-78), Soc. Am. Arch. (editor 1946-50, pres. 1952-53), Nat. Acad. Sci., Am. Acad. Arts and Sci., Arch. Soc. of Conn. (hon. mem.), Fla. Arch. Soc. (hon. mem.), Internat. Assn. Caribbean Arch. (hon. mem.), Soc. Antiquaries (London). Office: Yale U Dept Anthropology PO Box 208277 New Haven CT 06520-8277 E-mail: BIRouse@aol.com.

ROUSE, JAMES J. oil industry executive; b. Memphis; BS in indsl. mgmt., Miss. State. Salary analyst dept. human resources Exxon USA, 1962, mktg. dept., 1968, mgr. retail sales S.E. U.S., 1974, supply dept. Houston, 1976, pub. affairs dept., 1976, human resource dept., 1976, mgr. pub. affairs dept., 1994—96; v.p. Washington office pub. affairs dept. ExxonMobil Corp., Washington, 1996—. Bd. dir. Houston Ballet, St. Joseph Hosp. Found., Exec. Svc. Corp., Houston, Miss. State U. Devel. Found. Office: Ste 710 2000 K St NW Washington DC 20006

ROUSE, JEFF, Olympic athlete, swimmer; b. Fredericksburg, VA, Feb. 6, 1970; Olympic swimmer, Barcelona, Spain, 1992. Recipient 100m Backstroke Silver medal Olympics, Barcelona, 1992, 4—100 Medley Relay Gold Medal Olympics, Barcelona, 1992. Achievements include being the World record holder 100m backstroke long course and short course, 1992. Office: care US Swimming Inc One Olympic Plz Colorado Springs CO 80909 also: 4 Brittany Mdws Atherton CA 94027-4101

ROUSE, JOHN WILSON, JR., technology consultant; b. Kansas City, Mo., Dec. 7, 1937; s. John Wilson and Gail Agnes (Palmer) R.; m. Susan Jane Davis, May 3, 1981; 1 son, Jeffrey Scott. A.S., Kansas City Jr. Coll., 1957; BS, Purdue U., 1959; MS, U. Kans., 1965, PhD, 1968. Registered profl. engr., Mo., Tex. Engr. Bendix Corp., Kansas City, Mo., 1959-64; rsch. coord. Ctr. for Rsch., U. Kans., Lawrence, 1964-68; prof. elec. engring., dir. remote sensing ctr. Tex. A&M U., College Station, 1968-78; Logan prof. engr., chmn. elec. engring. U. Mo., Columbia, 1978-81; dean engring. U. Tex., Arlington, 1981-87; pres. So. Rsch. Inst., Birmingham, Ala., 1987-97, The Rouse Group, Hoover, Ala., 1997—. Mgr. microwave program NASA Hdqrs., Washington, 1975-77. Contbr. articles to profl. jours. Recipient Outstanding Tchr. award Tex. A&M U., 1971; Outstanding Prof. award U. Mo., 1980; Engr. of Yr. Tex. Soc. Profl. Engrs., 1983 Mem. IEEE, Nat. Soc. Profl. Engrs., Am. Soc. Engring. Edn., Internat. Bus. Fellows, Internat. Union Radio Sci., Sigma Xi, Eta Kappa Nu., Tau Beta Pi Home: 11 The Oaks Cir Birmingham AL 35244-1455 Office: The Rouse Group LLC 11 The Oaks Cir Birmingham AL 35244-1455

ROUSE, LEO E. dean, dental educator; Grad., Howard U. Coll. Dentistry, 1973; postgrad. studies in comprehensive dentistry, Watson Army Hosp., 1976—78. Assoc. dean clinical affairs Coll. Dentistry, Howard U., chmn. dept. clinical dentistry, interim dean, 2003—04, dean, 2004. Examiner cons. and mem. exam. devel. com. N.E. Regional Bd. Dental Examiners. With U.S. Army, 1972—97, comdr. and COO U.S. Army, 1995—97, US Army Dental Command, ret. col., 1997—. Recipient Alumni Achievement award, Howard U. Coll. Dentistry, 1997. Fellow: Am. Coll. Dentists; mem.: ADA, Am. Assn. Dental Examiners, Am. Dental Edn. Assn., Nat. Dental Assn., Omicron Kappa Upsilon. Office: Howard Univ Coll Dentistry 600 W St NW Washington DC 20059 Office Phone: 202-806-0440. Business E-Mail: lrouse@howard.edu.

ROUSE, MIKEL, composer; b. St. Louis, Jan. 26, 1957; m. Lisa Mae Boudreau, Jan. 1, 2000. BFA, U. Mo., 1978. Composer in residence Meet The Composer, N.Y.C., 2001—. Composer (dir.): (opera) Dennis Cleveland, Failing Kansas; dir.(composer): (film) The End Of Cinematics, Funding; composer (dir.): (music theater) Cameraworld. Recipient, The Found. for Contemporary Performance Arts, 2002; grantee, Mary Flager Charitable Trust, 1997—98; Edward F. Albee fellow, Edward F. Albee, 1996. Mem.: ASCAP (ASCAP Spl. Award 1990-2003).

ROUSE, RICHARD HUNTER, historian, educator; b. Boston, Aug. 14, 1933; s. Hunter and Dorothee (Hüsmert) R.; m. Mary L. Ames, Sept. 7, 1959; children: Thomas, Andrew, Jonathan. BA, State U. Iowa, 1955; MA, U. Chgo., 1957; PhD, Cornell U., 1963. Mem. faculty UCLA, 1963—, prof. history, 1975—. Assoc. dir. Ctr. Medieval and Renaissance Studies, 1966-67, acting dir., 1967-68; dir. Summer Inst. in Paleography, 1978, chair grad. coun., 1989-90; adv. bd. Hill Monastic Microfilm Libr., St. John's U., Collegeville, Minn., Ambrosiana Microfilm Library, Notre Dame (Ind.) U., Corpus of Brit. Medieval Libr. Catalogues, Brit. Acad. Author: Serial Bibliographies for Medieval Studies, 1969, (with M.A. Rouse) Preachers, Florilegia and Sermons: Studies on the Manipulus Florum of Thomas of Ireland, 1979; (with others) Texts and Transmission, 1983; (with C.W. Dutschke) Medieval and Renaissance Manuscripts in the Claremont Libraries, 1986; (with M.A. Rouse) Cartolai, Illuminators and Printers in Fifteenth-Century Italy, 1988; (with L. Bataillon and B. Guyot) La Production du livre universitaire au moyen age, exemplar et pecia, 1988; (with others) Guide to Medieval and Renaissance Manuscripts in the Huntington Library, 1989; (with M. Ferrari) Medieval and Renaissance Manuscripts at the University of California, Los Angeles, 1991; (with M.A. Rouse and R.A.B. Mynors) Registrum de libris doctorum et

auctorum veterum, 1991; (with M.A. Rouse) Authentic Witnesses: Approaches to Medieval Texts and Manuscripts, 1991; (with M.A. Rouse) Manuscripts and Their Makers: Commercial Book Producers in Medieval Paris 1200-1500, 2 vols., 2000, (with M.A. Rouse) Henry of Kirke-Stede, Catalogus de libris autenticis et apocrifis, 2004; co-editor: Viator: Medieval and Renaissance Studies, 1970-; mem. editorial bd. Medieval and renaissance manuscripts in Calif. libraries, Medieval Texts, Toronto; Medieval Texts, Binghamton, Library Quar., 1984-88, Speculum, 1981-85, Revue d'histoire des Textes, 1986-, Cambridge Studies in Paleography and Codicology, 1990-, Catalogue of Medieval and Renaissance Manuscripts in the Beinecke Rare Book and Manuscript Library Yale University, 1984-, Filologia MedioLatina, 1994-, Manuscripta, 2000-. Am. Coun. Learned Socs. fellow, 1972-73, vis. fellow All Souls Coll., Oxford, 1978-79, Guggenheim fellow, 1975-76, Rosenbach fellow in bibliography U. Pa., 1976, NEH fellow, 1981-82, 84-85, 94-96, Inst. for Advanced Studies fellow Jerusalem, 1991; J.R. Lyell reader in bibliogrpahy U. Oxford, 1991-92; vis. fellow Pembroke Coll., U. Oxford, 1992, Cambridge, 2000-01. Fellow Royal Hist. Soc., Medieval Acad. Am.; mem. Medieval Assn. Pacific (councillor 1965-68, pres. 1968-70), Medieval Acad. Am. (councillor 1977-80), Comité international de paléographie (treas. 1985-90), Comité international du vocabulaire des institutions et de la communication intellectuelles au moyen age, 1987—, Societa internazionale per lo studio del medioevo latino, 1988—. Home: 11444 Berwick St Los Angeles CA 90049-3416 Office: Dept History U Calif Los Angeles CA 90024 Office Phone: 310-825-4168. Business E-Mail: rouse@history.ucla.edu.

ROUSE, ROSCOE, JR., librarian, educator; b. Valdosta, Ga., Nov. 26, 1919; s. Roscoe and Minnie Estelle (Corbett) R.; m. Charlie Lou Miller, June 23, 1945; children: Charles Richard, Robin Lou. BA, U. Okla., 1948, MA, 1952; MALS, U. Mich., 1958, PhD, 1962; student (Grolier Soc. scholar), Rutgers U., 1956. Bookkeeper C & S Nat. Bank, Valdosta, Ga., 1937-41; draftsman R.K. Rouse Co. (heating engrs.), Greenville, S.C., 1941-42; student asst. U. Okla. and Rice U., 1947-48; asst. librarian Northeastern State Coll., Tahlequah, Okla., 1948-49, acting librarian, instr. library sci., 1949-51; circulation librarian Baylor U., 1952-53, acting univ. librarian, 1953-54, univ. librarian, prof., 1954-63, chmn. dept. library sci., 1956-63; dir. libraries State U. N.Y. at Stony Brook, L.I., 1963-67; dean libr. svcs., prof. Okla. State U., Stillwater, 1967-87, univ. libr. historian, 1987-92, chmn. dept. libr. edn., 1967-74. Vis. prof. U. Okla. Sch. Library Sci., summer 1962, N. Tex. State U., summer 1965; acad. library cons.; mem. AIA-Am. Library Assn. Library Bldg. Awards Jury, 1976; bd. dirs. Fellowship Christian Libr. and Info. Specialists. Author: A History of the Baylor University Library, 1845-1919, 1962; editor: Okla. Librarian, 1951-52; co-author: Organization Charts of Selected Libraries, 1973; A History of the Okla. State U. Library, 1992; contbr. articles, book revs., chpts. to publs. in field. Bd. dirs. Okla. Dept. Librs., 1989-92, chmn., 1990-92. 1st lt. USAAF, 1942-45. Decorated Air medal with 4 oak leaf clusters; recipient citation Okla. State Senate, 1987, Rotary Outstanding Achievement award, 1996; named in 150 Prominent Individuals in Baylor's History. Mem. ALA (life, mem. coun. 1971-72, 76-80, 83-84, 84-88, chmn. libr. orgn. and mgmt. sect. 1973-75, planning and budget assembly 1978-79, coun. com. on coms. 1979-80, bldgs. and equipment sect. exec. bd. 1979-80, chmn. bldgs. for coll. and univ. librs. com. 1983 85, chmn. nominating com. libr. history roundtable 1993-94), AARP, (sec. local chpt. 1998-2000), Okla. Libr. Assn. (life, pres. 1971-72, ALA coun. rep. 1976-80, 83-84, OLA Disting. Svc. award 1979, Spl. Merit award 1987), S.W. Libr. Assn. (chmn. coll. and univ. div. 1958-60, chmn. scholarship com. 1968-70), Internat. Fedn. Libr. Assns. (standing com. on libr. bldgs. and equipment 1976-88), Assn. Coll. and Rsch. Librs. (chmn. univ. librs. sect. 1969-70, mem. exec. bd. and rep. to ALA Coun., 1971-72), U. Mich. Sch. Libr. Sci. Alumni Soc. (pres. 1979-80, Alumni Recognition award 1988), mem. Alumni Found. Com., 1992-94, Payne County Ret. Educators Assn. (v.p., pres. elect 1991-92, pres. 1992-93), Okla. State U. Emeriti Assn. (pres. 2000-01), Okla. Hist. Soc. (com. on Okla. Higher Edn. mus. 1985—), Stillwater Rotary Club (pres. 1980-81, Rotarian of Yr. 1999, editor Rotary Weekly bulletin, vol. contbr. local daily newspaper), Beta Phi Mu. Baptist (chmn. bd. deacons 1973). Clubs: Archons of Colophon, Stillwater Rotary (dir. 1978-82, pres. 1980-81). *It is sometimes a hidden influence in our lives which drives us toward a set goal. We ourselves may not recognize the real source of that urge to fulfill a dream. Only after many years was I able to look back and discern the factors in my youth that pushed me toward my goal of attaining a good education. They grew out of the influence that the Great Depression had on my early life. Because of that experience the preparation for a career became my first goal in life, yet the ways and means for achieving it were virtually nonexistent. It was to be, however, and I was fortunate to realize that goal. It causes me to think now that perhaps the degree of determination and endurance one possesses is paced more by adverse condition than by times of comfort and ease.*

ROUSE, TERRIE S. museum administrator; b. Youngstown, Ohio; BA in Intercultural Studies, Trinity Coll., Hartford, Conn.; MA in African History, cert. in African studies, Columbia U. Sr. curator Studio Mus., N.Y.C.; dir. Calif. Afro-Am. Mus., L.A., N.Y. Transit Mus., N.Y.C.; exec. dir. Children's Mus. Maine; pres., CEO, African Am. Mus. (formerly Afro-Am. Hist.-Cult. Mus.), Phila. Vis. art coord. L.A. Festival, 1993. Avocation: collecting african american books and dolls. Office: AfricanAm Mus in Phila 701 Arch St Philadelphia PA 19106-1504 Fax: 215-574-3110.

ROUSE, TERRIE SUZITTE, former museum director; b. Youngstown, Ohio, Dec. 2, 1952; d. Eurad R. and Florence Wilcox; 1 child, Malcom Adam Rouse-West. BA, Trinity Coll., 1974; MS in Profl. Studies, Cornell U., 1977; certificate Internat. Affairs, MA, Columbia U., 1979. Mgr., curator Adam Clayton Powell St. Office Bldg., N.Y.C., 1979-81; sr. curator Studio Mus. Harlem, N.Y.C., 1981-86; dir. mus. N.Y. Transit Mus., Bklyn., 1986—91; dir. Calif. Afro-Am. Mus., 1991—93; artistic exec. dir. Atlanta Ballet, 2002—03. Advisor Bellevue Hosp. Art Bd., 1981—. Contbr. articles to profl. jours. Mem. Conf. Mil. Transp. Ofcls. Named Outstanding Young Women Am., 1981-83. Mem. Am. Assn. Museums (assessor 1981—). Avocations: sewing, reading, exploring harlem, doll collecting. E-mail: trouse3008@aol.com.

ROUSEY, JENNIFER ANN, engineer; b. San Angelo, Tex., Apr. 15, 1970; d. Ronny Preston and Cheryl Evonne Childs; m. Terry Mark Rousey, Dec. 21, 2000; children: Shawn, Aaron Curtis, Andrea. Masters of Engring., Wright State U., Dayton, Ohio, 2002—04; MS, Cameron U., 2000—03, BS in Psychology, 1993—98. Rsch. assoc. SA Technologies, Lawton, Okla., 2003—, L-3 Comm., Ft. Sill, Okla., 1999—2003. Mem.: NSPE, Soc. of Women Engineers, Human Factors and Ergonomics Soc. Personal E-mail: justbeingjen@yahoo.com. E-mail: jen@satechnologies.com.

ROUSH, CHARLES DOW, lawyer; b. Phoenix, Nov. 18, 1937; s. Dow Ben and Mary Elizabeth (Spalding) R.; m. Carol Ann Carrigan, Aug. 18, 1962 (div. Aug. 1984); m. Cecilia Helen Roush, Dec. 18, 1984; children: Charles Dow Jr., Aileen Marie. LLB, U. Ariz., 1966. Bar: Ariz. 1966, U.S. Ct. Appeals (9th cir.) 1970, U.S. Ct. Appeals (8th cir.) 1980, U.S. Supreme Ct. 1982. Assoc. Lewis & Roca, Phoenix, 1966-70; ptnr. Steiner & Roush, Phoenix, 1970-71; judge Maricopa County Superior Ct., Phoenix, 1971-76; ptnr. Treon, Warnicke & Roush, Phoenix, 1976-86, Roush, McCracken, Guerrero & Miller, Phoenix, 1987—. Instr. Nat. Coll. of State Judiciary, Reno, Nev., 1975-80. Editor Ariz. Law Rev., 1965-66. Lt. col. USAF, 1957-62; with Ariz. Air N.G., 1964-78. Fellow Am. Coll. Trial Lawyers, Internat. Soc. Barristers; mem. ATLA. Avocations: raising, breeding, training, selling, and showing horses and ponies. Office: Roush McCracken Guerrero & Miller 650 N 3rd Ave Phoenix AZ 85003-1523

ROUSH, GLENN A. state senator; m. Ardith Roush. Ret. Mont. Power Co.; Dem. senator dist. 43 Mont. State Senate, 1998—, mem. bus. and industry com., mem. hwys. and transp. com., mem. natural resources com. Democrat. Home: PO Box 185 Cut Bank MT 59427-0185

ROUSH, JOHN A. academic administrator; b. Wisconsin; B in English summa cum laude, Ohio U.; M, M, D, Miami U. Exec. asst. to pres. U. of Richmond, 1982—90, v.p. planning, 1990—98; exec. asst. to pres. Miami U.; pres. Centre Coll., 1998—. Contbr. articles to profl. jours. Capt. U.S. Army. Office: Centre Coll 600 W Walnut St Danville KY 40422

ROUSH, SUE, newspaper editor; b. Mason City, Iowa., Dec. 26, 1957; BS in Journalism, Northwestern U., 1980. Mng. editor Universal Press Syndicate, Kansas City, Mo., 1995—. Office: Universal Press Syndicate 4520 Main St Ste 700 Kansas City MO 64111-7701

ROUSH, WILLIAM R. chemistry educator; BS in Chemistry, UCLA, 1974; PhD in Chemistry, Harvard U., 1977. Disting. prof. chemistry dept. Ind. U., Bloomington; Warner Lambert Park Davis prof. chemistry, chair chemistry U. Mich., Ann Arbor, 1997—. Recipient Arthur C. Cope Scholar award Am. Chem. Soc., 1994, Alan R. Day award Phila. Organic Chemist's Club, 1992. Office: U Mich Dept Chemistry Ann Arbor MI 48109

ROUSSEAU, EUGENE ELLSWORTH, musician, music educator, consultant; b. Blue Island, Ill., Aug. 23, 1932; s. Joseph E. and Laura M. (Schindler) R.; m. Norma J. Rigel, Aug. 15, 1959; children: Lisa-Marie, Joseph. B of Mus Edn., Chgo. Mus. Coll., 1953; MusM, Northwestern U., 1954; student, Paris Conservatory of Music, 1960-61; PhD, U. Iowa, 1962. Instr. Luther Coll., 1956-59; asst. prof. Cen. Mo. State Coll., 1962-64; prof. music Ind. U., Bloomington, 1964-88, disting. prof. music, 1988—; prof. U. Minn., 2000—. Guest prof. U. Iowa, 1964, Hochschule fur Musik, Vienna, Austria, 1981-82, Ariz. State U., 1984, Prague Conservatory Music, 1985, Showa Coll. Music, 1996, 98, Tokyo Coll. Music, 1997, Paris Conservatory, 1997; tchr. U. Wis.-Ext., 1969—; R&D of saxophone mouthpieces; music arranger; svc. on numerous acad. coms.; tchr. 1st course in saxophone Mozarteum in Salzburg, Austria, 1991—; mem. jury Munich Internat. competitions, 1987, 90, 2001, pres. of juries, 1991-92; first solo saxophonist to perform on Prague Spring Festival, 1993; mem. jury Can. Nat. Music competition, 1994; juror Japan Wind and Percussion Competition, 1997; v.p. jury Adolphe Sax Internat. Competition, Belgium, 1998. Worldwide concert saxophonist; Carnegie Hall debut, 1965; author: Marcel Mule: His Life and the Saxophone, 1982, Saxophone High Tones, 1978, revised 2d edit., 2003, Method for Saxophone (2 vols.), 1975; performer 1st solo saxophone recitals, several European cities, 1st Am. solo saxophone performance in Japan, 1984; 1st to record concert saxophone on compact disc (Delos); radio broadcasts in Berlin, Bremen, London, Montreal, Ostrava, Paris, Prague, Toronto, Vienna; saxophone recs. for Deutsche Gramophon, Golden Crest, Coronet, Delos, Liscio, ALM, McGill and RIAX. Instr., asst. band leader 25th Infantry Div. U.S. Army, 1954-56. Named Hon. Prof. Music, Prague Conservatory, 1993, Braga Inst., Italy, 2001; recipient Edwin Franko Goldman award, Am. Bandmasters Assn., 1995, Disting. Alumni award, U. Iowa, 1996; grantee, Fulbright Found., 1960—61, Rsch. and Exchange Bd., 1985, NEA, 1986. Mem. N.Am. Saxophone Alliance (pres. 1978-80), Comite Internat. de Saxophone (pres. 1982-85), Coll. Music Soc., Clarinet and Saxophone Soc. (U.K.), Music Tchrs. Nat. Assn. (Tchr. of Yr. award for Ind. 1993), Fulbright Assn. (life), World Saxophone Congress (co-founder 1969, pres. organizing com. 2000--). Office: U Minn Sch Music Minneapolis MN 55455 E-mail: rouss007@umn.edu.

ROUSSEAU, IRENE VICTORIA, artist; children: Douglas, Scott. BA, Hunter Coll., N.Y.C.; MFA, Claremont (Calif.) Grad. Sch., 1969; PhD, N.Y. U., 1977. Tenured prof. William Paterson Coll., Wayne, N.J., 1970-74. Invited spkr. Coll. Art Assn./Women Caucus on Art Conf., L.A., 1985, N.J. Ctr. for Visual Arts, Summit, N.J., 1985, Noyes Mus., 1994, Mus. African Art, 1994, Hillwood Art Mus.-C.W. Post/L.I. U., 2000, AIEMA IX Internat. Conf. on Antique and Medieval Mosaic Rsch., Rome, 2001, Sch. Arch., Weston Art Gallery NJIT, Newark, 2004; guest spkr. Internat. AIEMA Conf., Lausanne, Switzerland, 1997, invited guest spkr. Villeme Colloque Intl. de la Mosaique Antique, Univ. de Lausanne, Switzerland, 1997; spkr. Bridges: Math. Connections in Art, Music and Sci. Exhbns. include Betty Parsons Gallery, N.Y.C., Claremonte Colls., State Mus. Sci. and Industry, L.A., Morris Mus. Arts and Scis., Morristown, N.J., The Bronx Mus. of Art, Galleri Sci. Agnes, Copenhagen/Roskilde, Denmark, Sculptors 5, Madison, N.J., Edmund Sci. Co., Barrington, N.J., AT&T World Hdqrs., Basking Ridge, N.J., N.J. Ctr. for Visual Arts, The Brotherhood Synagogue Holocaust Meml. Gramercy Pk. (mosaic), N.Y.C., 1986, 1st Internat. Art Biennale, Malta, 1995, U. Lausanne (Switzerland), 1997, Internat. Biennale Malta, 1997 (awards), Am. Inst. Archs., N.Y., 1998, Southwestern Coll., Kans., 1999, Lausanne, Switzerland, 2001, BRIDGES, Internat. Joint Conf., 2003; artist in residence Program Greece, 2000; guest spkr. and exhibit Internat. Conf. Internat. Soc. Art, Math., Architecture, Frieburg, Germany, 2002, Internat. Conf. Connections in Math., Music, Art, Sci., and Arch., Granada, Spain, 2003, Internat. Soc. Arts, Math., and Arch. and BRIDGES (Math. Connections in Art, Music, and Sci.) Internat. Joint Conf., Granada, Spain; one person exhibits Weston Gallery Sch. Arch., Newark, 2003, N.J. Inst. Tech. Sch. Arch., 2003, Weston Art Gallery Sch. Arch. NJIT, Newark, 2004; author: Mathematical Connections in Art, Music & Science, 2003, Geometric Mosaic Tiling on Hyperbolic Sculptures, Granada, 2003, Mosaic Art as a Metaphor for Concepts of Science and Mathematics, Rome, 2003, International Society Art, Math, Architecture, 2004; contbr. articles and works of art. Recipient seven 1st prize awards for creative work in N.J., ER Squibb and Sons Sculpture award, AIA N.J. Presentation Design award, 1995, Internat. Art Biennale Malta Installatin award, 1997, Traveling Exhibit throughout Europe and Middle East and Africa of Winners of the 1997 Biennale in Malta, 1997-99. Mem. AIA (profl. affiliate N.J., N.Y., chmn. architecture dialogue com. Presentation award 1995), Internat. Sculptors Assn., Am. Abstract Artists (exhbn. chmn. 1978-79, pres. 1979-82), Fine Arts Fedn. (bd. dirs.), Coll. Art Assn., Women's Caucus on Art (conf. spkr.), Phi Delta Kappa. Home: 41 Sunset Dr Summit NJ 07901-2322 Office Phone: 908-273-3160. Personal E-mail: mosiaicartforms@comcast.net.

ROUSSEAU, LILLIAN MCKIM See PULITIZER, LILLY

ROUSSEAU-VERMETTE, MARIETTE, artist; b. Trois-Pistoles, Que., Can., Aug. 29, 1926; d. Joseph-Herve and Corrinne (Belanger) Rousseau; m. Claude Vermette, Nov. 29, 1952; children: Marc, Jerome. Student, Ecole des Beaux Arts du Que., 1944-48, Studio Dorothy Liebes, San Francisco, 1948-49, Oakland Coll. Arts and Crafts, 1948-49; studied different tapestry techniques in Europe, 1952, 58. Head dept. fibre, visual arts Banff (Alta.) Sch. Fine Arts, Canada, 1979—85. Solo exhbns. include: Musée des Beaux-Arts de Montréal, 1961, Galerie Camille Hébert, Montréal, 1964, New-Design Gallery, Vancouver, B.C., 1964, Galerie Godard-Lefort, Montréal, 1969, Musée du Québec, 1972, Marlborough-Godard Gallery, Toronto, 1974, Centre Culturel Canadien, Paris, 1974, Centre Culturel Canadien, Brussels, 1974, Winnipeg (Man.) Art Gallery, 1976, Grace Borgenicht Gallery, N.Y., 1977, Galerie Alice Pauli, Lausanne, Switzerland, 1978, Brown Grotta Gallery, Wilton, Conn., 1993-2001, Galerie Bernard, Montreal, Can., 2004—, numerous others; group shows include: Nat. Gallery of Can., 1959, Biennale Internationale de la Tapisserie, Lausanne, Switzerland, 1962, 65, 67, 71, 77, Triennale de Milan, 1968, Mus. Modern Art, N.Y.C., 1968-69, Art Gallery of Windsor, Ont., 1977, 81, Musée d'Art Contemporain, Montréal, Mus. Modern Art, Kyoto, Japan, 1977, Mus. Modern Art, Tokyo, 1978, Musée d'Art Contemporain de Montréal, 1979, Biennale, Lodz, Poland, 1981, numerous others; theatrical works include: Théâtre Maisonneuve, Place des Arts, Montréal, 1967, Theatre of the Can. Ctr. of Arts, Ottawa, 1965-68, The JFK Ctr. for Performing Arts, Washington, 1970, Group de la Place Royal, 1968, 69, 73; permanent collections include: Nat. Gallery of Can., Art Gallery of Charlottetown, Can. Pavilion, Osaka, Japan, Québec Pavilion, Osaka, Palais de Justice, Montréal, Mus. Modern Art, Kyoto, Met. Mus., N.Y.C., Chgo. Art Mus., numerous others. Decorated officer Order of Can.; Can. Coun. grantee, 1968; recipient Honor certificate la Conférence Canadienne des Arts, 1974. Subject of numerous articles and books. Office: 373 Rue Morin Saint-Adele QC Canada J8B 2P8

ROUSSEY, ROBERT STANLEY, accountant, educator; b. N.Y.C., July 20, 1935; m. Jeanne Archer, May 8, 1965; children: Robert Scott, John Stephen. BS, Fordham U., 1957. CPA, N.Y., Japan. Staff acct. Arthur Andersen & Co., N.Y.C., 1957-63, mgr. N.Y.C. and Tokyo, 1964-69, ptnr. N.Y.C. and Chgo., 1969-92, dir. auditing procedures, 1977-92; prof. acctg. U. So. Calif., L.A., 1992—. Adj. prof. auditing Northwestern U. Kellogg Grad. Sch. Mgmt., 1990, 91; mem. coll. bus. adminstrn. adv. bd. Fordham U., 1999—. Edit. cons. Handbook of Corporate Finance, 1986, Handbook of Financial Markets and Institutions, 1987; mem. editl. bd. Advances in Accounting, 1987—, Jour. Internat. Acctg. Auditing and Taxation, 1991—, Auditing: A Journal of Theory and Practice, 1994-2002; mem. adv. bd. Internat. Jour. Acctg., 1998—; contbr. articles to profl. jours. Treas., bd. dirs. Kenilworth (Ill.) Community House, 1979-81, Troop 13 Boy Scouts Am., Kenilworth, 1978-80, St. Joseph's Ch. Men's Club, Bronxville, N.Y., 1971-73. With U.S. Army, 1958, 61-62. Mem. AICPA (chmn. EDP auditing stds. com. 1978-81, auditing stds. bd. 1986-90, MAS practice stds. and adminstrn. com. 1990-93, internat. spl. strategy com. 1997-98, internat. auditing stds. subcom. 1998-2002, internat. strategy com. 1998—), Am. Acctg. Assn. (v.p. auditing sect. 1987-90, pubs. com. 1993-96), Info. Systems Audit and Control Assn. (stds. bd. 1986-96, v.p., mem. internat. bd. dirs. 1996—, mem. audit com. 2000-01, internat. pres. 2001-03), Info. Tech. Governance Inst. (internat. pres. 2001-03, mem. internat. bd. dirs. 2003-), Ill. State Soc. CPAs, N.Y. State Soc. CPAs, Inst. Internal Auditors (bd. rsch. advisors 1986-99), Internat. Fedn. Accts. (internat. auditing practices com. 1990-2000, chmn. 1995-2000, EDP audit com. 1980-88, mem. cons. adv. group to internat. auditing and assurance standards bd. 2001-), Met. Club (gov. 1977-78), Tokyo-Am. Club (life), Beaver Creek Club, Beta Alpha Psi, Beta Gamma Sigma. Republican. Roman Catholic. Avocations: skiing, sailing, tennis, Karate. Office: U So Calif Dept Acctg Los Angeles CA 90089-0441

ROUSSO, DANIEL ELLIOTT, facial plastic surgeon, educator; b. Atlanta, Sept. 15, 1955; s. Morris D. and Corine Rousso; m. Nancy Popkin; children: Emily Beth, Craig Morris. BA, Emory U., 1977; MD, Med. Coll. Ga., 1981. Diplomate Am. Bd. Otolaryngology, Am. Bd. Facial Plastic and Reconstructive Surgery. Intern U. S.C. Sch. Medicine, Charleston, 1981-82; resident in otolaryngology Emory U., Atlanta, 1982-86; fellow in facial and plastic surgery McCollough Plastic Surgery Clinic, Birmingham, Ala., 1986-87; priv. practice Birmingham. Mem. staff Eye Found. Hosp., Birmingham; clin. asst. prof. otolaryngology, U. Ala., Birmingham. Co-author: Facial Plastic Surgery Clinic, 1994; contbr. articles to profl. jours., chpts. to books. Mem. AMA, Am. Acad. Facial Plastic and Reconstructive Surgery, Am. Bd. Hair Restoration Surgery (bd. dirs.), Am. Acad. Otolaryngology, Head and Neck Surgery, Internat. Soc. Hair Restoration Surgery (pres. 2000). Office: Rousso Facial Plastic Surgery Clinic 2700 Highway 280 Ste 300-W Birmingham AL 35223-2420 E-mail: drousso@aol.com.

ROUSUCK, J. WYNN, theater critic; b. Cleve., Mar. 19, 1951; d. Morton I. and Irene Zelda (Winograd) R. BA summa cum laude, Wellesley Coll., 1972; MS, Columbia U., 1974. Assoc. editor, program guide, Sta. WCLV-FM, Cleve., 1972-73; theater and film reviewer Cleve. Press, 1973; gen. assignment arts reporter Balt. Sun, 1974-84, theater critic, 1984—. Instr. English Goucher Coll., Towson, Md., 1981; master critic O'Neill Critics Inst., Waterford, Conn., 1990—; theater critic Md. Pub. TV., 1986; spkr. in field. Recipient Dog Writers Assn. Am. awards 1977, 79, Md. chpt. 1st Place Arts Reporting award Soc. Profl. Journalists, 1993, Front Page award, Disting. Criticism Washington-Balt. Newspaper Guild, 1997, 99, 2002, Bill Pryor Meml. grand prize for writing, 1999, Bernie Harrison Meml. award for commentary, 2002; NEH journalism fellow U. Mich., 1979-80, fellow O'Neill Critics Inst., 1982. Mem. Balt. Bibliophiles (bd. dirs. 1982-83), Octavo Plus, Walters Art Gallery, Balt. Wellesley Club (pres. 1978-79). Jewish. Avocations: rare books, art, dogs. Office: The Baltimore Sun 501 N Calvert St Baltimore MD 21278-0001

ROUTH, DONALD K(ENT), psychology educator; b. Oklahoma City, Mar. 3, 1937; s. Ross Holland and Fay (Campbell) R.; m. Marion Starbird Wendler, Sept. 10, 1960; children: Rebecca Ann (dec.), Laura Diane. BA, U. Okla., 1962; PhD, U. Pitts., 1967. Diplomate Am. Bd. Profl. Psychology. Asst. prof. psychology and pediatrics U. Iowa, Iowa City, 1967-70, prof., 1977-85; assoc. prof. psychology Bowling Green State U., Ohio, 1970-71; assoc. prof. U. N.C., Chapel Hill, 1971-77; prof. psychology and pediat. U. Miami, Coral Gables, Fla., 1985—2002, prof. emeritus, 2002—. Chmn. behavioral medicine study sect. NIH, 1983-85 Editor Jour. Pediatric Psychology, 1976-82, Jour. Clin. Child Psychology, 1987-91, Jour. of Abnormal Child Psychology, 1992-98, Am. Jour. on Mental Retardation, 1998-2002, Internat. Clin. Psychologist, 2001—04; contbr. numerous articles to profl. jours., books Pres. Eno River Unitarian Universalist Fellowship, 1976-77; vol. faculty Fla. Gulf Coast U., 2002—. Recipient award for disting. contbn. Soc. Pediatric Psychology, 1981, Presdl. award, 1988; Rsch. Psychologist of Yr. award Fla. Psychol. Assn., 1987, Reconocimiento, El Colegio Nacional de Psicologis de Mex., 1999, Disting. Alumni award Okla. Mil. Acad., 2004. Mem. APA (pres. div. child, youth and family svcs., 1984, pres. div. on mental retardation 1987, pres. divsn. clin. psychol. 1998), Internat. Soc. Clin. Psychology (founder, pres. 1998-99), Disting. Profl. Contbns. to Clin. Psychology (sect. on clin. child psychology 1989, div. clin. psychology, 1992, Nicholas Hobbs award div. child youth and family svcs., 1996, Edgar A. Doll award divsn. mental retardation and devel. disabiities 2001). Democrat. Home: 20131 Seagrove St #402 Estero FL 33928 E-mail: drouth@miami.edu.

ROUTT, MILTON LEE (CHIP), orthopedic trauma surgeon, educator; MD, U. Tex. Med. Br., 1983. Diplomate Am. Assn. Surgeons, 1991. Prof. U. of Wash., Seattle, 1995—. Dir. orthop. trauma fellowship Harborview Med. Ctr., Seattle, 1991—. Recipient Howard Rosen Tchg. award, AO/ASIF, 2001; fellow Jack McDaniel Traveling Fellowship, Arbeitsgemeinshaftfur Osteosynthesisfragen/Assn. Study Internal Fiction, 1990. Mem.: Orthop. Trauma Assn. (life). Office: Harborview Med Ctr 325 Ninth Ave Seattle WA 98104-2499

ROUVILLOIS, PHILIPPE, research and development executive; Gen. adminstr. CEA, Paris, France, 1989-95; chmn. CEA Industrie, Paris, France, 1989-99, Institut Pasteur, Paris, France, 1997—; gen. fin. inspector France Ministry Econ., Fin. and Industry, Paris, France, 1999—. Office: Min Econ Fin and Industry 139 rue de Bercy 75572 Paris Cedex 12 France

ROUX, MILDRED ANNA, retired secondary school educator; b. New Castle, Pa., June 1, 1914; d. Louis Henri and Frances Amanda (Gillespie) R. BA, Westminster Coll., 1936, MS in Edn., 1951. Tchr. Farrell (Pa.) Sch. Dist., 1939-55; tchr. Latin, English New Castle (Pa.) Sch. Dist., 1956-76; ret., 1976. Chmn. sr. H.S. fgn. lang. dept. New Castle Sch. Dist., 1968-76, faculty sponsor sch. fgn. lang. newspapers, 1960-76, Jr. Classical League, 1958-76. Mem. Lawrence County Hist. Soc., Am. Classical League, 1958-76. Mem. AAUW (chmn. publicity, chmn. program com. Lawrence County chpt. 1992-96), Am. Assn. Ret. Persons, Nat. Ret. Tchrs. Assn., Pa. Assn. Sch. Retirees (chmn. cmty. participation com. Lawrence County br. 1976-81, telephone com. Lawrence County br. 1990-98), Coll. Club New Castle (chmn. sunshine com. 1989-91, mem. social com. 1991-92), Woman's Club New Castle (chmn. pub. affairs com. 1988-90, internat. affairs com. 1990-92, program com. 1990-92, telephone com. 1992-99). Republican. Roman Catholic. Avocations: church choir, reading, civic interests. Home: # 302 3345 Wilmington Rd New Castle PA 16105-1038

ROVE, KARL CHRISTIAN, government advisor, consultant; b. Denver, Dec. 25, 1950; s. Louis C. (Jr.) and Reba Louise (Wood) Rove; m. Valerie Wainright Rove, July 10, 1976 (div. Jan. 1980); m. Darby Tara Hickson, Jan. 25, 1986; 1 child, Andrew Madison. Student, U. Utah, 1969—71, U. Md., 1972, George Mason U., 1973—75, U. Tex., 1977. Exec. dir. Coll. Rep. Nat. Com., Washington, 1971—73; spl. asst. to chmn. George Bush Nat. Com., Washington, 1973—75, exec. asst. to co-chmn. Richard Obenshain, 1975, also mem. RC exec. com., 1971—75; fin. dir. Va. Rep. Com., Richmond, 1976; dir. Fund for Ltd. Govt., Houston, 1977—79; dep. dir. Gov. William P. Clements Jr. Com., Houston, 1979—80; dir. Tex. Victory Com., Austin, 1980; spl. asst. for adminstrn., dep. exec. asst. Gov. of Tex., 1980—81; pres. Karl Rove & Co., Austin, 1981—99; polit. advisor and chief strategist George W. Bush gubernatorial and presdl. campaigns, 1993—2001; sr. advisor to George W. Bush Washington, 2001—. Pres. U.S. Youth Coun., Washington, 1975—77, chmn., 1973—77, selection panel, 1973—77; regent Tex. Woman's U., Denton, 1981—83, East Tex. State U., 1990—91; treas. Tex. Women's Employment and Edn. Program, Austin, 1981—83; mem. regional selection panel White House Fellows Commn., 1987—90. Mem. spl. com. on governance Tex. Higher Edn. Coord. Bd., 1989—91; bd. dirs. Tex. Bus. Hall of Fame, 1987—88; mem. Bd. for Internat. Broadcasting, 1991—; bd. visitors McDonald Obs., 1993—. Mem.: Barton Creek Country Club (Austin). Office: The White House 1600 Pennsylvania Ave NW Washington DC 20500

ROVELL, MICHAEL JAY, lawyer; b. Chgo., Mar. 30, 1949; s. Bernard and Charlotte (Schaefer) R.; m. Laurie Strauss, Sept. 2, 1979; children: Brandon, Kendall, Ryan. BA with honors, U. Ill., Chgo., 1969; JD with honors, U. Ill., 1972. Bar: Ill. 1972, U.S. Dist. Ct. (no. and so. dists.) Ill. 1972, U.S. Ct. Appeals (7th cir.) 1973, U.S. Ct. Appeals (8th cir.) 1981, U.S. Supreme Ct. 1983, U.S. Ct. Appeals (5th cir.) 1986, U.S. Ct. Appeals (1st cir.) 1990, U.S. Dist. Ct. P.R. 1992, U.S. Ct. Appeals (10th cir.) 1992, U.S. Ct. Appeals (3rd cir.) 1993, U.S. Ct. Appeals (2nd cir.) 1996, U.S. Ct. Appeals (9th cir.), 1997, Belgium 1997. Assoc. Jenner & Block, Chgo., 1972-78, ptnr., 1979-90; prin. Law Offices of Michael J. Rovell, Chgo., 1990—. Dir. Cook County Spl. Bail Project, 1972-74; chief exec. officer, bd. dirs. Sunbelt Communications, Colorado Springs, Colo., 1976-78; of counsel Wampler, Buchanan & Breen, Miami, Troncoso & Becker, San Juan, P.R., Law Offices of Robert Bright, Oklahoma City and affiliate offices London, Paris, Brussels; bd. editors U. Ill. Law Forum, 1971-72. Bd. dirs. Steppenwolf Theatre, Chgo., 1979-81. Mem. ABA (coord. litigation seminar on electronic surveillance), Ill. Bar Assn., Hillcrest Country Club (Long Grove, Ill.). Avocations: golf, tennis, bowling. Home: 1516 Christina Ln Lake Forest IL 60045-3848 Office: 20 N Clark St Ste 2450 Chicago IL 60602-5002

ROVELSTAD, GORDON H. dentist, researcher; b. Elgin, Ill., May 19, 1921; s. Henry Randolph and Margot Helen (Greenhill) R.; m. Barbara Jean Johnson, Apr. 8, 1945; children: Craig Gordon, Martha Kay, Andrew Todd. Student, St. Olaf Coll., 1939-41; DDS, Northwestern U., Chgo., 1944, MSD, 1948, PhD, 1960; DSc (hon.), Georgetown U., 1970. Diplomate Am. Bd. Pediatric Dentistry. Asst. prof. pediatric dentistry Northwestern U., Chgo., 1946-53; head dental dept. Children's Meml. Hosp., Chgo., 1948-53; ensign USNR, 1943, advanced through grades to capt., 1945-46; with USNTC, Camp Peary, Va., 1954-59; dir. rsch. U.S. Naval Dental Sch., Bethesda, Md., 1960-65; officer in charge U.S. Naval Dental Rsch. Inst., Gt. Lakes, Ill., 1965-69; dir. rsch. USN Dental Corp., Washington, 1969-74; ret., 1974; asst. dean, prof. U. Miss. Sch. Dentist, Jackson, 1974-80; exec. dir. Am. Coll. Dentists, Gaithersburg, Md., 1981-94, exec. dir. emeritus, 1994—; pres. William J. Gies Found., Gaithersburg, Md., 1982-98, pres. emeritus, 1998—. Hon. bd. dirs. William J. Gies Found. for Advancement of Dentistry, Am. Dental Edn. Assn., 2003—. Contbr. articles to profl. jours. Fellow Am. Coll. Dentists (pres., v.p.), Internat. Coll. Dentists, N.Y. Acad. Sci., N.Y. Acad. Dentists; mem. ADA, Am. Acad. Pediatric Dentistry (pres., v.p.), Internat. Assn. Dental Rsch. (pres., v.p., sec.), Rotary Internat., Sigma Xi. Avocations: miniatures, music, golf, fishing. Home: 11301 Tooks Way Columbia MD 21044-1049

ROVELSTAD, MATHILDE V(ERNER), library science educator; b. Germany, 1920; came to U.S., 1951. m. Howard Rovelstad, 1970. PhD, U. Tubingen, 1953; MS in L.S, Catholic U. Am., 1960. Prof. libr. sci. Cath. U. Am., 1960-90, prof. emeritus, 1990—. Vis. prof. U. Montreal, 1969 Author: Bibliotheken in den Vereinigten Staaten, 1974; translator Bibliographia, an Inquiry into its Definition and Designations (R. Blum), 1980, Bibliotheken in den Vereinigten Staaten von Amerika und in Kanada, 1988; contbr. articles to profl. jours. Research grantee German Acad. Exch. Svc., 1969, Herzog August Bibliothek Wolfenbüttel, Germany, 1995. Mem. Internat. Fedn. Libr. Assns. and Instns. (standing adv. com. on libr. schs. 1975-81), Assn. for Libr. and Info. Sci. Edn. Home: Apt HR-T35 719 Maiden Choice Ln Catonsville MD 21228-6231 Office: Cath U Am Sch Libr & Info Sci Washington DC 20064-0001

ROVEN, ALFRED NATHAN, surgeon; came to the U.S., 1949. BA in Psychology, Calif. State U., Northridge, 1969; MD, U. So. Calif., 1977. Diplomate Am. Bd. Plastic and Reconstructive Surgery, Am. Bd. Otolaryngology. Resident in otolaryngology U. So. Calif., 1977-82; clin. chief plastic surgery Cedars Sinai Med. Ctr., L.A., 1989-91; resident in plastic and reconstructive surgery U.C.L.A., 1982-84; clin. chief burns Cedars Sinai Med. Ctr., L.A., 1990-92, clin. chief hands, 1990-92. Qualified med. examiner State of Calif., 1985. Contbr. articles to profl. jours. Physician L.A. Free Clinic, 1995—. Avocation: reading. Office: 5757 Wilshire Blvd 6 Los Angeles CA 90036 Office Phone: 323-937-7733.

ROVER, EDWARD FRANK, foundation administrator, lawyer; b. Oct. 4, 1938; s. Frederick James and Wanda (Charkowski) R.; m. Maureen Wyer, June 15, 1968; children: Elizabeth, Emily, William. AB, Fordham U., 1961; JD, Harvard U., 1964. Bar: N.Y. 1964, U.S. Tax Ct. 1968, U.S. Dist. Ct. (so. dist.) N.Y. 1975, U.S. Supreme Ct. 1994. Assoc. White & Case, N.Y.C., 1964-71, ptnr., 1972—2004; pres. Dana Found., N.Y.C., 2004—. Bd. dirs. Cranshaw Corp., N.Y.C., Harvard-Mahoney Neurosci. Inst., Boston, Waterford Sch., Sandy, Utah, Dana-Farber, Boston, Norton Simon Art Mus., L.A., Rumsey-Carter Found., Geneva, Charles A. Dana Found., N.Y.C.; pres. Dana Found.; sec. Solomon R. Guggenheim Found. Mem. ABA, N.Y. Bar Assn., Assn. Bar City N.Y., Century Assn., Scarsdale Golf Club, Harvard Club, Univ. Club. Avocations: sailing, skiing. Home: 1111 Park Ave New York NY 10128-1234 Office: Dana Found 745 Fifth Ave Ste 900 New York NY 10151 Office Phone: 212-223-4040. E-mail: erover@dana.org.

ROVERA, GIOVANNI AURELIO, medical educator, scientist; b. Cocconato, Italy, Sept. 23, 1940; came to U.S., naturalized, 1984. Student, Liceo Classico Valsalice, Torino, Italy, 1955-58; MD summa cum laude, U. Torino, 1964, postgrad., 1965-68. Diplomate Am. Bd. Anatomic Pathology; lic. physician, Italy, Pa. Postdoctoral fellow Fels Rsch. Inst. Temple U. Sch. of Medicine, Phila., 1968-70, resident in anatomic pathology, 1970-72, chief resident in pathology, 1972; asst. prof. pathology Sch. Medicine Temple U., Phila., 1972-75; assoc. prof. Wistar Inst., Phila., 1975-78, prof., 1979—, assoc. dir., 1988-91, dir., 1991—; Wistar Inst. prof. pathology and lab. medicine Sch. Medicine U. Pa., Phila., 1984—; Wistar Inst. prof. pediatrics U. Pa. Sch. of Medicine, Phila., 1987—. Mem. promotion coms. U. Pa. Sch. of Medicine, The Wistar Inst., 1979—; chmn. grad. tng. program The Wistar Inst., 1981-91; mem. sci. adv. com. Leukemia Soc. Am., 1983-88, Am. Cancer Soc., 1986-90; mem. ad. hoc sci. adv. com. Nat. Cancer Inst., 1985—; mem. NCI Devel. Diagnostic Working Group, 1996; mem. Nat. Cancer Soc. Rev. Group, 1997. Editor: (with H. Koprowski) Current Opinion in Immunology: Cancer and Immunology, 1990; assoc. editor Proceedings Soc. Exptl. Biol. Medicine, 1975-78, Jour. Cellular Physiology, 1978—, Leukemia, 1988—, Haematologica Pathology, 1990—; mem. editorial adv. bd. Haematologica, 1989—. Fellow EURATOM, 1965-66, Ministero della Publica Istruzione, 1966-67; scholar Leukemia Soc., 1974-79; recipient Eagles Fly for Leukemia Lifetime Achievement award, 1996. Mem. Coll. of Physicians of Phila. Achievements include development of techniques of monitoring the extent of residual leukemia in B and T lineage malignancies. Home: 933 Wootton Rd Bryn Mawr PA 19010-2227 Office: The Wistar Inst 3601 Spruce St Philadelphia PA 19104-4265

ROVINE, ARTHUR WILLIAM, lawyer; b. Phila., Apr. 29, 1937; s. George Isaac and Rosanna (Lipsitz) R.; m. Phyllis Ellen Hamburger, Apr. 7, 1963; children: Joshua, Deborah. AB, U. Pa., 1958; LLB, Harvard U., 1961; PhD, Columbia U., 1966. Bar: D.C. 1964, N.Y. 1984. Assoc. Curtis, Mallet-Prevost, Colt & Mosle, N.Y.C., 1964—66; asst. prof. Cornell U., Ithaca, NY, 1966—72; editor Digest of U.S. Practice in International Law U.S. Dept. State, Washington, 1972—75, asst. legal adviser, 1975—81, agt. of U.S. Govt. to Iran-U.S. Claims Tribunal The Hague, Netherlands, 1981—83; of counsel Baker & McKenzie, N.Y.C., 1983—85, ptnr., then sr. ptnr., 1985—. Adj. prof. law Georgetown U., Washington, 1977-81; vis. lectr. law Yale U., 1998. Author: The First Fifty Years: The Secretary-General in World Politics, 1920-1970, 1970; editor: Digest of U.S. Practice in International Law, 1973, 74; co-editor: The Case Law of the International Court of Justice, 1968, 1972, 1974, 1976; bd. editors Am. Jour. Internat. Law, 1977-87; also articles on internat. law. Mem. panel on settlement of transnat. bus. disputes, N.Y. panel Ctr. for Pub. Resources; chmn. law subcom. of internat. adv. coun. on profl. edn. Coun. on Internat. Ednl. Exch.; mem. Coun. on Fgn. Rels. Mem. ABA (chmn. internat. law sect. 1985-86, del. to Ho. of Dels. 1988-90), Am. Soc. Internat. Law (cert. of merit 1974, exec. coun. 1975-77, v.p. 1998-99, pres. 2000-02), U.S. Coun. for Internat. Bus. (arbitration com.), Am. Arbitration Assn. (panel of arbitrators), Assn. Bar City N.Y. (coun. on internat. affairs). Home: 215 East 68th St New York NY 10021 Office: Baker & McKenzie 805 3rd Ave New York NY 10022-7513 E-mail: arthur.w.rovine@bakernet.com.

ROVINSKY, JOSEPH JUDAH, obstetrician, gynecologist; b. Phila., Sept. 4, 1927; s. Israel and Sarah (Blackman) R.; m. Judith S. Levin, June 24, 1964; children: Audrey, John, Jill, Michael, Paul, David. BA, U. Pa., 1948, MD, 1952. Diplomate Am. Bd. Ob-Gyn. Intern U. Pa. Hosp., Phila., 1952-53; resident in ob-gyn Mt. Sinai Hosp., N.Y.C., 1953-58; practice medicine specializing in ob-gyn, 1958—; chmn. dept. ob-gyn City Hosp. Center, Elmhurst, N.Y., 1964-74; prof. ob-gyn Mt. Sinai Sch. Medicine, N.Y.C., 1969-74; prof., chmn. dept. ob-gyn Sch. Medicine Health Scis. Center, SUNY, Stony Brook, 1975-79, prof., 1975-89; chmn. dept. ob-gyn L.I. Jewish Med. Center, 1973-92; prof. ob-gyn. Albert Einstein Coll. Medicine, 1989-94; dir. dept. ob/gyn. Sound Shore Med. Ctr. of Westchester, New Rochelle, 1992—. Mem. obstetric adv. com. N.Y.C. Dept. Health, 1964-92. Author: Medical, Surgical and Gynecological Complications of Pregnancy, 1961, 2d edit., 1965; editor: Davis' Gynecology and Obstetrics, 1968-73. Served to capt., M.C. USAF, 1964-66. Mem. ACS, Am. Coll. Obstetricians and Gynecologists, Am. Soc. Reproductive Medicine, Am. Uro-Gynecologic Soc., N.Y. Acad. Medicine, N.Y. Obstetrical Soc., N.Y. Gynecol. Assn., Med. Soc. State N.Y. Jewish. Office: Sound Shore Med Ctr Westchester 16 Guion Pl New Rochelle NY 10801-5500

ROVIRA, LUIS DARIO, state supreme court justice; b. San Juan, P.R., Sept. 8, 1923; s. Peter S. and Mae (Morris) R.; m. Lois Ann Thau, June 25, 1966; children: Douglas, Merilyn. BA, U. Colo., 1948, LL.B., 1950. Bar: Colo. 1950. Justice Colo. Supreme Ct., Denver, 1979-95, chief justice, 1990-95, ret., 1995. Mem. Pres.'s Com. on Mental Retardation, 1970-71; chmn. State Health Facilities Council, 1967-76; arbiter and mediator Jud. Arbiter Group, Denver. Trustee Temple Buell Found. With AUS, 1943-46. Mem. ABA, Colo. Bar Assn., Denver Bar Assn. (pres. 1970-71), Colo. Assn. Retarded Children (pres. 1968-70), Alpha Tau Omega, Phi Alpha Delta. Clubs: Athletic (Denver), Country (Denver). Home: 4810 E 6th Ave Denver CO 80220-5137 Office: Judicial Arbiter Group 1601 Blake St Denver CO 80202

ROVIT, RICHARD LEE, neurological surgeon; b. Boston, Apr. 3, 1924; s. Samuel and Frances (Ehrenberg) R.; m. Barbara Sayre Margolis, Mar. 29, 1953; children: Sandra Amy Golze, Adam John, Hugh Russel. Grad., U. Mich., 1944; MD, Jefferson Med. Coll., 1950; MSc, McGill U., 1961. Diplomate Am. Bd. Neurol. Surgery (dir. vice chmn. 1986-92). Intern in surgery Beth Israel Hosp., Boston, 1950-51; resident, then chief resident Mass. Gen. Hosp., Boston, 1951-58; USPH fellow in neurology The Nat. Hosp., London, 1956; sr. fellow in neurosurgery Lahey Clinic, Boston, 1957; fellow in neurophysiology and EEG Montreal (Can.) Neurol. Inst., 1958-59; prof. clin. neurosurgery NYU, 1967—; chmn. neurosurgery St. Vincent's Hosp. and Med. Ctr., N.Y.C., 1967-92; prof. neurosurgery N.Y. Med. Coll., Valhalla, 1990—. Editor, author: Trigeminal Neuralgia, 1991; contbr. articles to profl. jours. Trustee Sarah Neuman divsn. Jewish Home and Hosps., N.Y.C., 2004-. Lt. USN, 1952-54. Fellow ACS (v.p. 1994-95), Am. Assn. Neurol. Surgeons (v.p. 1980-81); mem. N.Y. Soc. Neurosurgeons (pres. 1974-76, 79-80), Soc. Neurol. Surgeons, Fairview Country Club (Greenwich, Conn.), Harvard Club of N.Y. Avocations: golf, running. Home: 42 Brite Ave Scarsdale NY 10583-2309 Office: Manhattan Neurosurg 153 W 11th St New York NY 10011-8305 Office Phone: 212-604-7767.

ROVNER, ILANA KARA DIAMOND, federal judge; b. Riga, Latvia, 1938; arrived in U.S., 1939; d. Stanley and Ronny (Medalje) Diamond. AB, Bryn Mawr Coll., 1960; postgrad., U. London King's Coll., 1961, Georgetown U., 1961—63; JD, Ill. Inst. Tech., 1966; LittD (hon.), Rosary Coll., 1989, Mundelein Coll., 1989; DHL (hon.), Spertus Coll. of Judaica, 1992. Bar: Ill. 1972, U.S. Dist . (no. dist.) Ill. 1972, U.S. Ct. Appeals (7th cir.) 1977, U.S. Supreme Ct. 1981, Fed. Trial Bar (no. dist.) Ill. 1982. Jud. clk. U.S. Dist. Ct. (no. dist.) Ill., Chgo., 1972—73; asst. U.S. atty. U.S. Atty.'s Office, Chgo., 1973—77, dep. chief of pub. protection, 1975—76, chief pub. protection, 1976—77; dep. gov., legal counsel Gov. James R. Thompson, Chgo., 1977—84; dist. judge U.S. Dist. Ct. (no. dist.) Ill., Chgo., 1984—92; cir. judge U.S. Ct. Appeals (7th cir.), Chgo., 1992—. Mem. Gannon-Proctor Commn. on the Status of Women in Ill., 1982—84; mem. civil justice reform act adv. com. 7th Cir. Ct., Chgo., 1991—95, mem. race and gender fairness com., 1993—; mem. fairness com. U.S. Ct. Appeals (7th cir.), 1996—, mem. gender study task force, 1995—96; mem. jud. conf. U.S. Com. Ct. Adminstrn. Case Mgmt., 2000—. Ctrl. and East European law initiative vol. ABA, 1997—; trustee Bryn Mawr Coll., Pa., 1983—89; mem. bd. overseers Ill. Inst. Tech./Kent Coll. Law, 1983—; trustee Ill. Inst. Tech., 1989—; mem. adv. coun. Rush Ctr. for Sports Medicine, Chgo., 1991—96; bd. dirs. Rehab. Inst. Chgo., 1998—; bd. visitors No. Ill. U. Coll. Law, 1992—94; vis. com. Northwestern U. Sch. Law, 1993—98, U. Chgo. Law Sch., 1993—96, 2000—03; chair Ill. state selection com. Rhodes Scholarship Trust, 1998—2000. Named Today's Chgo. Woman of the Yr., 1985, Woman of Achievement, Chgo. Women's Club, 1986; named one of 15 Chgo. Women of the Century, Chgo. Sun Times, 1999; named to Today's Chgo. Women Hall of Fame, 2002; recipient Spl. Commendation award, U.S. Dept. Justice, 1975, Spl. Achievement award, 1976, Ann. Nat. Law and Social Justice Leadership award, League to Improve the Cmty., 1975, Ann. Guardian Police award, 1977, Profl. Achievement award, Ill. Inst. Tech., 1986, Louis Dembitz Brandeis medal for Disting. Legal Svc., Brandeis U., 1993, 1st Woman award, Valparaiso U. Sch. Law, 1993, ORT Women's Am. Cmty. Svc. award, 1987—88, commendation def. of prisoners com., Chgo. Bar Assn., 1987, Svc. award, Spertus Coll. of Judaica, 1987, Ann. award, Chgo. Found. for Women, 1990, Arabella Babb Mansfield award, Nat. Assn. Women Lawyers, 1998, award, Chgo. Attys. Coun. of Hadassah, 1999, 1st Woman award, Georgetown U. Law Ctr., 2001, Today's Chicago Woman Hall of Fame, 2002, Hebrew Immigrant Aid Soc. Chgo. 85th Anniversary honoree, 1996, Chgo. Hist. Soc. Trailblazers Award, 2003, Lifetime Achievement award, Decalogue Soc. Lawyers, 2004, First Woman award, Chgo. Bar Assn. Alliance for Women and Women's Bar Assn. Ill., 2000, Vanguard award, Chgo. Bar Assn. and Lesbian and Gay Bar Assn. Chgo., 2004. Mem.: Decalogue Soc. of Lawyers (citation of honor 1991, Merit award 1997), Chgo. Coun. Lawyers, Women's Bar Assn. Ill. (ann. award 1989, 1st Myra Bradwell Woman of Achievement award 1994, 1st Woman Award (in conjunction with Chicago Bar Assn. Alliance for Women) 2000), Fed. Judges Assn., Fed. Bar Assn. (mem. selection com. Chgo. chpt. 1977—80, treas. 1978—79, sec. 1979—80, 2d v.p. 1980—81, 1st v.p. 1981—82, pres. 1982—83, 2d v.p. 7th cir. 1983—84, v.p. 7th cir. 1984—85), Kappa Beta Pi, Phi Alpha Delta (hon.). Office: 219 S Dearborn St Ste 2774 Chicago IL 60604-1803

ROVNYAK, JAMES, mathematician, educator; PhD, Yale U., New Haven, Conn., 1963. Asst. prof. Purdue U., Lafayette, Ind., 1963—66; mem. inst. for Advanced Study, Princeton, NJ, 1966—67; assoc. prof. math. U. Va., Charlottesville, 1967—73, prof. math., 1973—. Contbr. articles to profl. jours. Recipient Physics-Astronomy-Mathematics award, Spl. Libraries Assn., 1994. Mem.: London Math. Soc., Math. Assn. of Am., Am. Math. Soc. Avocation: music. Home: 6861 Castleberry Ct Crozet VA 22932 Office: U Va P O Box 400137 Charlottesville VA 22904-4137 Personal E-mail: rovnyak@virginia.edu.

ROWAN, HENRY M. electrical engineer; b. Raphine, Va. m. Betty Rowan. BS in Elec. Engring., MIT. Founder, chmn. Inductotherm Industries, Inc., Rancocas, N.J. Patentee in field. Glassboro (N.J.) State Coll. renamed in his honor, 1992. Mem. NAE. Achievements include research in frequency tripler circuit utilizing the third harmonic component of transformers, stabilized controlled rectifyer circuit having inductive load and induction heating systems for efficiently melting metals. Office: Inductotherm Industries Inc PO Box 157 10 Indel Ave Rancocas NJ 08073-0157

ROWAN, RICHARD LAMAR, business management educator; b. Guntersville, Ala., July 10, 1931; s. Leon Virgle and Mae (Williamson) R.; m. Marilyn Walker, Aug. 3, 1963; children: John Richard, Jennifer Walker. AB, Birmingham-So. Coll., 1953; postgrad., Auburn U., 1956-57; PhD, U. N.C., 1961. Instr. Auburn (Ala.) U., 1956-57, U. N.C., Chapel Hill, 1958-59, 60-61; lectr. U. Pa., Phila., 1961-62, asst. prof., 1962-66, asso. prof. industry, 1966-73, prof. industry, 1973—. Dir. indsl. research unit, 1989-91; co-dir. Ctr. for Human Resources, 1991—; visitor to Faculty Econs. and Politics Cambridge (Eng.) U., 1972; pvt. sector advisor U.S. State Dept. Com. on Internat. Investment and Multinational Enterprises, OECD, 1982-89; chmn. Labor Relations Council, 1985— . Author: (with H.R. Northrup) The Negro and Employment Opportunity, 1965, Readings in Labor Economics and Labor Relations, 5th edit., 1984, The Negro in the Steel Industry, 1969, The Negro in the Textile Industry, 1970, (with others) Studies of Negro Employment, 1970, Educating the Employed Disadvantaged for Upgrading, 1972, Collective Bargaining: Survival in the 1970's, 1972, Opening the Skilled Construction Trades to Blacks, 1972, The Impact of Government Manpower Programs, 1975, International Enforcement of Union Standards in Ocean Transport, 1977, The Impact of OSHA, 1978, Multinational Bargaining Attempts: The Record, the Cases, and the Prospects, 1980; (with H.R. Northrup) Employee Relations and Regulations in the 80s, 1982; (with others) Multinational Union Organizations in the Manufacturing Industries, (with D.C. Campbell) The Multinational Enterprises and the OECD Industrial Relations Guidelines, 1984, Trade Union Clout Erodes, But For How Long?, 1985, Employee Relations Trends and Practices in the Textile Industry, 1986; contbr. articles to profl. jours. Mem. personnel com. Del. Valley Settlement Alliance, 1966-68. Served with Transp. Corps U.S. Army, 1953-56. Recipient Disting. Alumni award, Birmingham-So. Coll., 2000. Mem. Indsl. Rels. Rsch. Assn. (sec. Phila. 1964-65), Acad. Internat. Bus. Democrat. Episcopalian. Home: 113 Blackthorn Rd Wallingford PA 19086-6046 Office: U Pa Wharton Sch 3733 Spruce St Philadelphia PA 19104-6301

ROWAN, WILLIAM HAMILTON, JR., computer science educator; b. Nashville, Tenn., May 8, 1933; s. William Hamilton and Elizabeth (Lowry) R.; m. Sarah Conley, June 9, 1973; children: Elizabeth, Bill. BE, Vanderbilt U., 1955; PhD, N.C. State U., 1965. Registered profl. engr., Tenn. Jr. engr. Boeing Airplane Co., Seattle, 1955-57; instr. of mechanics Vanderbilt U., Nashville, Tenn., 1959-60; electronics engr. Tenn. State Hwy. Dept., Nashville, 1960-61; grad. student civil engring. N.C. State U., Raleigh, N.C., 1961-64; asst. prof. math. Vanderbilt U., Nashville, 1964-67, assoc. prof. and chmn. computer sci. dept., 1967-71, prof. computer sci., 1971-95, prof. computer sci. emeritus, 1996—. Staff couns. AVCO Corp. aerostructures divsn., Nashville, 1965-70; pres., CEO, On-Line Computing, Inc., Nashville; bd. dirs. On-Line Data, Inc., Nashville, 1974-85. Co-editor: (book) Application of Finite Element Methods in Civil Engineering, 1969; co-author: (book) Computer Methods of Structural Analysis, 1970. 1st lt. U.S. Army, 1957-59. Recipient fellowship grant Ford Found., N.C. State U., Raleigh, 1961-64. Mem. IEEE, Am. Soc. for Engring. Edn., Assn. for Computing Machinery, Phi Kappa Phi, Tau Beta Pi. Avocation: golf. Home: 604 Summerwind Cir Nashville TN 37215-6125 Office: Vanderbilt Univ Box 1679 Sta B Nashville TN 37235 E-mail: whrfl@att.net.

ROWARK, MAUREEN, fine arts photographer; b. Edinburgh, Midlothian, Scotland, Feb. 28, 1933; came to U.S., 1960, naturalized, 1970; d. Alexander Pennycook and Margaret (Gorman) Prezdpelski; m. Robert Rowark, May 3, 1952 (div. July 1965). 1 child, Mark Steven. Student, Warmington Bus. Coll., Royal Leamington Spa, Eng., 1950-51, Royal Leamington Spa Art Sch.; diploma, Speedwriting Inst., N.Y.C., 1961; AS in Edn., St. Clair County Community Coll., Port Huron, Mich., 1977, AA, 1978. Supr. proof reading Nevin D. Hirst Advt., Ltd., Leeds, Eng., 1952-55; publicity asst. Alvis Aero Engines, Ltd., Coventry, Eng., 1955-57; adminstrv. asst. Port Huron Motor Inn, 1964-66; adminstrv. asst. pub. rels. dept. Geophysics and Computer Svcs., Inc., New Orleans, 1966-68; sales mgr. Holiday Inn, Port Huron, 1968-70; adminstrv. asst. Howard Corp., Port Huron, 1971-73; sales and systems coord. Am. Wood Products, Ann Arbor, Mich., 1973-74; systems coord. Daniels & Zermack Architects, Ann Arbor, 1974; systems coord., cataloger fine arts dept. St. Clair County Community Coll., Port Huron, 1976-79; freelance fine arts photographer Port Huron, 1978—. Photographer Patterns mag. front cover, 1978, Erie Sq. Gazette, 1979, Bluewater Area Tourism Bur. brochure, 1989, 92, 95, 97, 2000, 2001, Corits Castle, Lexington, 2002, Port Huron, Can. Legion, Wyo., Ont. Br., 1987, 88—, Grace Episcopal Ch. Mariner's Day, Port Huron, 1987, 92-2001, Homes mag., 1989; founder Bluewater Les Chapeaux Rouge chpt. Red Hat Soc., 2001, initiated and produced Calendar Girls 2005. Photographer (one-woman shows) Grace Episcopal Ch., 1995, Port Huron Mus., 1995, St. Clair River Remedial Action Plan, 1995 (Best in Landscape Category), Mich. Waterways Coun. Girl Scouts Exhibit, 1996, exhibited in internat. shows Ann. Ea. Mich. Internat. Juried Exhbn., yearly, 1981—98 (Award of Excellence, 1982, 1983, Best Photography award, 1995, 1996, 1997), exhibited in group shows Ann. Ea. Mich. Internat. Juried Exhbn., 2000, exhibited in internat. shows Our Town Juried Exhbn., 1997, St. Clair County C.C., 1983, 1986 (Award of Excellence, 1986), Gallery Lambton Juried Exhbn., Sarnia, Ont., Can., 1983—92 (Best Photography, 1988), 1994, 1996, 1997, 2000, Bluewater Bridge Juried Exhibit, 1988, Kaskilaaksontie Exhibit, Finland, 1991 (Par Excellence award), Swann Gallery, Detroit, 1996, St. Clair (Mich.) Art Gallery, Genesis Gallery, Lexington, Mich., others, represented in permanent exhibit Royal Can. Legion, Wyo. Br. Centaph, Capac State Bank, 1996, Grace Episcopal Ch., 1995, Thomas Edison Inn, Port Huron Hosp., 1996, Front Cover "Good Health News", 1997, costume modelling Bluewater Art Assn., 2000, 01, contbr. short stories to mags., photographer Bluewater Percussion Brochure, 2001. Cons., buyer interior decor Grace Episcopal Ch., 1994; active Port Huron Mus., 1978; founder Bluewater Les Chapeaux Rouge (chptr. Red Hat Soc.). Recipient hon. mention Gallery Lambton, Sarnia, 1981, 2d pl. memoir writing women's history month St. Clair County C.C., 1999; winner 2d and 3d place awards Times Herald Newspaper, 1988, 1st place juried photography award Port Huron Art Festival, 1997. Mem. St. Clair County C.C. Alumni Assn., Phi Theta Kappa, Lambda Mu. Democrat. Episcopalian. Avocations: costumes and interior design, travel, theater, memoir writing. Home and Office: 3512 Walnut St Port Huron MI 48060 E-mail: ha-penerth-of-tar@prodigy.net.

ROWDEN, MARCUS AUBREY, lawyer, former government official; b. Detroit, Mar. 13, 1928; s. Louis and Gertrude (Lifsitz) Rosenzweig; m. Justine Leslie Bessman, July 21, 1950; children: Gwen, Stephanie. BA in Econs, U. Mich., Ann Arbor, 1950, JD with distinction, 1953. Bar: Mich. 1953, D.C. 1978. Trial atty. Dept. Justice, 1953-58; legal advisor U.S. Mission to European Communities, 1959-62; solicitor, assoc. gen. counsel, gen. counsel AEC, 1965-74; commr., chmn. U.S. NRC, Washington, 1975-77; 2tnr. Fried, Frank, Harris, Shriver and Jacobson, Washington, 1977—. Served with AUS, 1946-47. Decorated officer Order Legion of Honor Republic of France; Recipient Disting. Service award AEC, 1972 Mem. Am., Fed., Mich., D.C. bar assns., Internat. Nuclear Law Assn., Order of Coif. Home: 7937 Deepwell Dr Bethesda MD 20817-1927 Office: Fried Frank Harris Shriver and Jacobson 1001 Pennsylvania Ave NW Washington DC 20004-2505

ROWE, BOBBY LOUISE, art educator; b. Montgomery, Ala., Feb. 15, 1930; d. Herbert and Louise (Barbaree) R. AB, Montevallo U., 1950; MA, Columbia U., 1959; PhD, Fla. State U., 1974. Cert. tchr. K-12 and jr. coll., Fla. Supr. student tchrs. U. Fla. Coll. Edn., Gainesville; assoc. prof. art edn. Mid. Tenn. State U., Murfreesboro; art edn. dir. Cleve. State U.; art curriculum specialist Palm Beach County Sch. Bd., West Palm Beach, Fla. Fiber artist, computer imagist, digital photographer, writer; lectr., presenter in field. Contbr. articles to profl. jours. Mem. Nat. Art Edn. Assn., Am. Edn. Rsch. Assn., Alpha Delta Kappa. Home: 1505 Ft Clarke Blvd Apt 13108 Gainesville FL 32606-9128 E-mail: artrowe711@aol.com.

ROWE, BONNIE GORDON, music company executive; b. Buford, Ga., May 3, 1922; s. Bonnie Gordon and Alma (Poole) R.; m. Mary Wilburta Shidler; 1 child, Sharon Lynn; m. Gloria Lucille Fairfax, Feb. 17, 1962 (div.); 1 child, Susan Rebecca. Student, Ga. Evening Coll., 1939-41, U. Wichita, 1948-49, Ga. State Coll., 1949-52. Traffic mgr. Bonanza Air Lines, Las Vegas, 1946-48, music tchr., 1948-52; owner Rowe Accordion Distbg. Co., Rowe Accordion Ctr., Atlanta, 1952-56, Atlanta Music Pub. Co., 1956—, B. Rowe Music Co., Atlanta, 1957—. Pres.-treas. B. Rowe Enterprises, Inc., 1973—. Bd. dir. Sandtown Found., Atlanta. Lt. col. USAAF, World War II, ETO. Decorated Air medals with three oak leaf clusters. Mem.: Nat. Assn. Music Mchts., Atlanta Fedn. Musicians (life), The Mil. Order of the World Wars (past comdr. Atlanta chpt.), Internat. Platform Assn., Sandtown Civitan Club (pres., lt. gov., past pres. Met. Atlanta Coun.), Air Force Assn., Res. Officers Assn.,

Travelers Protective Assn., 781st Bomb Squadron Assn. (465th bomb group WWII), Atlanta C. of C., Mil. Officers Assn. Am., Southea. Accordion Assn. (past pres.), Dobbins AFB Officers Club, Elks (exalted ruler 1987, 1988, 1989, past pres. past exalted rulers assn., trustee Union City, state organist Ga. Elks Assn.), Am. Legion, Gamma Delta Phi. Home: 5085 Erin Rd SW Atlanta GA 30331-7810 Office: 6102 Mableton Pkwy Mableton GA 30126-4302

ROWE, CARL OSBORN, business consultant; b. Colorado Springs, Colo., Feb. 3, 1944; s. Prentiss Eldon and Jo Ann (Osborn) R.; m. Dale Robin Oren, Apr. 12, 1984; 1 child, Stefanie Osborn. BA in Govt. cum laude, George Mason U., 1972; M Urban Affairs, Va. Poly. Inst. and State U., 1976. Cert. pub. housing mgr.; cert. mgmt. cons. Spl. clk. FBI, Washington, 1968-71; mgmt. analyst ICC, Washington, 1972-75; dir. policy and mgmt. U.S. Bur. Reclamation, Washington, 1975-82; exec. dir. City of Las Vegas Housing Authority, 1990-94; pres. Rowe Bus. Consulting, Las Vegas, 1982-90, 94-97; exec. dir. So. Nev. Housing Corp., 1994-95; assoc. Success Strategies, Las Vegas, 1995-96; dir. orgn. and mgmt. devel. Fair, Anderson and Langerman, CPAs, Las Vegas, 1997—2003; pres. Clarity Advisors to Mgmt., Las Vegas, 2003—. Bd. dirs. Flowtronics, Inc., Phoenix, Sportstech, Inc., Scottsdale, Ariz., MSP Sys., Inc., Scottsdale; interim dir. Las Vegas-Clark County Libr. Dist. Columnist Las Vegas Bus. Press, 1989-90, 94-96. Exec. dir. So. Nev. Housing Corp., So. Nev. Reinvestment and Affordable Housing Com.; founding bd. dirs., CEO Family Cabinet So. Nev., Affordable Housing Inst. So. Nev.; bd. dirs. Opportunity Village, LLV Alumni Found.; exec. bd. Nat. Assn. Housing and Redevel. Ofcls. Pacific S.W. Regional Conf., Oasis So. Nev. Cmty. Svc. Guild, Las Vegas Cmty. Empowerment Commn.; adv. bd. Cmty. Food Bank Clark County, Clark County Sch. Dist. Choices Program, We Care Program. Decorated USAF Commendation medal; named one of Top 50 over 50 in Las Vegas, Prime Mag., Disting. Men in So. Nev. In Bus. Las Vegas Mag.; recipient Cir. of Excellence award Las Vegas C. of C., 2001. Mem.: Turnaround Mgmt. Assn., Leadership Las Vegas, Assn. for Strategic Planning, No. Calif./Nev. Exec. Dirs. Assn., Pub. Housing Authorities Dirs. Assn. (exec. bd.), Inst. Mgmt. Cons., Nat. Assn. Housing and Redevelopment Ofcls. (exec. bd.), Am. Soc. Pub. Adminstrn. (governing coun.), Am. Mgmt. Assn., Las Vegas C. of C. (pres.-elec, bus. coun. bd. dirs., chmn. bus. a.m. com., chmn. bus. edn. series, leadership coun., prospectors bd., chmn. productivity and partnerships with govt. com.), LLV Alumni Found. (pres.), Rotary, Phi Theta Kappa. Avocations: reading, home improvement, music, cooking, physical fitness. Office: Clarity Advisors to Mgmt 3065 S Jones Blvd Ste 100 Las Vegas NV 89146 E-mail: carl@claritycmc.com.

ROWE, CHARLES ALFRED, artist, designer, educator; b. Great Falls, Mont., Feb. 7, 1934; s. Alfred Lewis and Alice Lillian (Ledbetter) R.; m. Eugenia Dean, July 5, 1958; children: Allison Rene, Jon Garner, Dorian Leigh. Student, Mont. State U., 1952—53, So. Meth. U., 1956—57, U. Chgo., 1959—60; BFA, Sch. Art Inst., Chgo., 1960; MFA, Tyler Sch. Art, 1968. Prin. Charles Rowe Advt., Chgo., 1957-60; graphic designer Am. Can Co., Bellwood, Ill., 1960-62, Abrams-Bannister Engraving, Inc., Greenville, SC, 1962-64; prof. art U. Del., Newark, 1964-97, emeritus prof., 1997—. One-man shows include Tyler Sch. Art, Phila., 1968, Mickelson Gallery, Washington, 1970, 1974, C.M. Russell Mus., Great Falls, 1972—73, 1981, 1992, Pleiades Gallery, N.Y.C., 1977, 1981, Vision of La Herradura, Almuñecar, Spain, 1988, USAF exhbn. Soc. Illustrators, N.Y.C., 1989, 1991, one-woman shows include, 2004, one-man shows include West Chester (Pa.) U., 1992, Soc. Illustrators, N.Y.C., 1993, 2004, exhibited in group shows at C.M. Russell Mus., 1974, 1976, 1978, 1980, 1982—83, 1986—91, Am. Painters in Paris, 1976, Monac-Western Art Exhibit, Spokane, Wash., 1977—78, Easton (Md.) Waterfowl Festival, 1981—82, USAF Nat. Collection, 1987, 1989, 1991, Atrium Gallery, N.Y.C., 1995, 1996, One Small Step, NASA, U. Del., Newark, 1999, Our Own Show, Soc. Illustrators, N.Y.C., 1990—96, 1998—2000, 2002—04, over 220 other exhbns., Represented in permanent collections U. Del., Mont. State Collection, Mont. State U., Del. State Collection, Great Falls Pub. Schs., Michael Landon Prodns., Calif., Meredith Corp., Des Moines, Collection Knissel, Austria, Archives Victoria and Albert Mus., London, artists USAF Nat. Collection, Washington, Jacqueline Pierson, Nice, France, artists USAF Nat. Collection, Washington, NASA Space Mus., Hauptman and Greenwood Collections, N.Y.C., Vera Haas, Dallas, Baker, Honolulu; fabric designer Galleon Fabrics, Inc., N.Y.C., Jones of N.Y., Saks Fifth Ave., Kevin Kilner, Jordan Baker, Hollywood, Calif., 1987, Kevin Kostner Collection, 1997, designer graphics Mont. State Arts Coun., Del. state duck stamp, 1981. With inf. U.S. Army, 1954-56. Ctr. for Advanced Study fellow, 1981-82; grantee U. Del., 1964-79, Nat. Endowment for Arts and Humanities, 1972-73, U. Del. Bicentennial, 1976. Mem. AAUP, Soc. of Illustrators (N.Y.C.). Home: Chapel Hill 133 Aronimink Dr Newark DE 19711-3802 Office: U Delaware Dept Art Newark DE 19711 *In my paintings and other artforms I strive for perfection, uniqueness, and a special inner beauty, but more than that, I try to create art that has a universal quality. This universality makes an artform communicate beyond a specific locale, continent or a limited time reference. All great works of art have this special element regardless of when they were created.*

ROWE, DAVID LEE, financial advisor; b. Colorado Springs, Colo., Jan. 30, 1954; s. Prentiss Eldon and Jo Ann (Osborn) R.; m. Elizabeth Webb, June 21, 1986; children: Schuyler Jourdan, Thomas Prentiss. BA, U. Colo., 1976; Master's degree, Johns Hopkins U., 1979; MBA, NYU, 1995. Asst. to undersec. U.S. Dept. Commerce, Washington, 1979—80; analyst Commodities Rsch. Inst., N.Y.C., 1980—81; fin. advisor Merrill Lynch, N.Y.C., 1981—83, Prudential Wachovia Securities, N.Y.C., 1983—, sr. v.p., asst. br. mgr., 1997—. Mem. cmty. ministry coun. St. Bartholomew's Ch., N.Y.C., 1987-96, mem. vestry, 1997—, treas., 2000—; bd. dirs. 133 E. 80th St. Corp., 1999—; adv. bd. Health Advocates Older People, 2003—. Home: 133 E 80th St New York NY 10021-0317 Office: Wachovia Securities 625 Madison Ave New York NY 10022-1801 Office Phone: 212-303-8738. Business E-Mail: david.rowe@wachoviasec.com.

ROWE, DAVID WINFIELD, lawyer; b. Chgo., Nov. 7, 1954; s. Bernard John and Gertrude Katherine (Johnson) R.; m. Martha Lynn Plott, June 12, 1977; children: Daniel, Peter. BA, Davidson Coll., 1976; PhD in Psychology, U. Tenn., 1981; JD, U. Mich., 1987. Bar: Colo. 1987, U.S. Dist. Ct. Colo. 1987, U.S. Ct. Appeals (10th cir.) 1987, Nebr. 1989, U.S. Dist. Ct. Nebr. 1989. Vis. asst. prof. Davidson (N.C.) Coll., 1981-82; mental health worker Peninsula Psychiat. Hosp., Louisville, Tenn., 1982-84; asst. prof. dept. psychology U. Tenn., Knoxville, 1982-84; assoc. Gorsuch, Kirgis, Campbell, Walker & Grover, Denver, 1987-89; NIMH postdoctoral fellow in law and psychology U. Nebr., Lincoln, 1989-91; ptnr. Kinsey, Ridenour, Becker & Kistler, Lincoln, Nebr., 1991—. Mem. interim study group on foster care Health and Human Svcs. com. Nebr. State Legislature, 1990-91; adj. prof. psychology U. Nebr., Lincoln, 1992-94; bd. dirs., past treas. Lincoln Attention Ctr. for Youth; mem. The Mediation Ctr., Detention Ctr. Adv. Bd., 2003-. Author: (with others) Dimensions of Child Advocacy: Advocating for the Child in Protection Proceedings, 1990, Children Under Three in Foster Care, 1991. Exec. com. Lancaster County Rep. Com., 1991-97, chmn., 1993-95; mem. adv. bd. Juvenile Detention Ctr.; bd. dirs. Lincoln-Lancaster Mental Health Found., 1993-, v.p., 1995-96, pres., 1996-97; mem. Ctrl. Com. Nebr. Rep. Com., 1993-97; mem. adv. bd. Juvenile Detention Ctr., 2003-; bd. dirs. The Arc of Lincoln Lancaster County, 2003-; deacon Westminster Prebyn. Ch., 1996-99. Mem. ABA, Nebr. Bar Assn. (alternative dispute resolution com. 1990—2000), Kiwanis (pres. Lincoln 1997-98). Office: Kinsey Ridenour Becker & Kistler 121 S 13th St#601 PO Box 85778 Lincoln NE 68501-5778 Office Phone: 402-438-1313. E-mail: drowe@krbklaw.com.

ROWE, DIANE ELIZABETH, law clerk; b. Grove City, Pa. BS, Ind. U., 1981; M.Pub. Affairs, Ind. U., Gary, 1983; JD, Loyola U. Chgo., 2000. V.p. Ptnrs. in Contracting Corp., Hammond, Ind., 1983-85; energy conservation programs specialist U.S. Dept. Energy, Argonne, Ill., 1985-89, contracting officer Chgo., 1989-97; law clk. U.S. Dist. Ct. (no. dist.) Ill., Chgo., 2000—. Contbr. articles to profl. jours. Recipient Excellence for the Future award Ctr. for Computer-Assisted Legal Instrn., 1996. Mem.: ABA, Am. Soc. Pub. Adminstrn. (exec. coun. 1985—89, pub. rels. com. chair 1985—89), Fed. Bar Assn., Chgo. Bar Assn., Ill. State Bar Assn. Home: 1313 Azalea Dr Munster IN 46321 Office: US District Court 219 S Dearborn St Chicago IL 60604 E-mail: drowel@att.net., diane_rowe@ind.uscourts.gov.

ROWE, ELIZABETH WEBB, community volunteer; b. Canton, Ohio, Dec. 2, 1957; d. Thomas Dudley Webb and Verity Elizabeth (Voight) O'Brien; m. David Lee Rowe, June 21, 1986; children: Schuyler Jourdan, Thomas Prentiss. AB in History, Mt. Holyoke Coll., 1979. Legal asst. Willkie Farr & Gallagher, N.Y.C., 1979-82, legal asst. supr., 1983-88, adminstrv. asst., 1988-89; outreach dir. St. Bartholomew's Ch., 1989-93, dir. comm., 1991-93; paralegal mgr. Patterson, Belknap, Webb & Tyler LLP, N.Y.C., 1993-98; office mgr. Alpha N.Am., N.Y.C., 1998-2001; co-dir. vols. St. Bartholomew's, 2001—. Legal asst. Cmty. Law Offices, N.Y.C., 1980-82; clerical asst. 17th Precinct Police Detective, N.Y.C., 1981-82. Chair homeless shelter St. Bartholomew's Ch., N.Y.C., 1984-85; vol. Breakfast Feeding Program, 1983-92, mem. Cmty. Ministry Coun., 1986-88, 93-96; mem. N.Y. Jr. League, 1979-94; Pres.'s Coun. Mt. Holyoke Coll., 1988-91; rep. Mt. Holyoke Coll. Alumnae Fund, 1986-89, 94—, class officer, 1989-94; bd. dirs. 509 E. 83d St. Corp., E. 67th St. Owners, Inc., Emma J. Adams Meml. Fund, Mid-Manhattan Ctr., Inc., Knickerbocker Greys; sec. Spl. Events Com. Am. Cancer Soc., NY Chpt. Recipient Mary Lyon award Mt. Holyoke Coll., 1994. Home: 133 E 80th St Apt 2C New York NY 10021-0317 Personal E-mail: ewrowenyc@aol.com.

ROWE, ERNEST RAS, education educator, academic administrator; b. Hot Springs, Ark., July 19, 1933; s. Stephen Paul and Emma Leathia (Martin) R.; m. Carla True Dirk, May 27, 1995. BS with distinction, Ariz. State U., 1955, MEd, 1962, EdD, 1965; postgrad., Gonzaga U., 1975, Dublin City U., Ireland, summer 1989. Tchr. Madison Sch. Dist., Phoenix, 1960-61, Garden Grove (Calif.) Unified Sch. Dist., 1964-66; cons. spl. edn. Ariz. Dept. Pub. Instrn., Phoenix, 1966-67; asst. prof. Idaho State U., Pocatello, 1967-70, assoc. prof., 1970-74, prof. edn., 1974-95, interim chmn. dept. edn., summer 1992; adminstrv. intern Cen. Adminstrn., 1982-83, 94-95. Vis. prof. edn. Calif. State U., Long Beach, summer 1965; adv. mem. Idaho Task Force on Higher Edn., 1982-83; gov. apptd. Idaho commr. to Edn. Commn. of the States, 1979-93, rep. to steering com., 1989-93; elected chmn. Idaho State U. Faculty Senate, 1970, 71-72, 86-87. Contbr. articles to profl. jours. Bd. dirs. Bannock Meml. Hosp., 1975-78; mem. Idaho Bd. Medicine pre-litigation panel for malpractice hearings, 1980-95. 1st lt. U.S. Army, 1955-57. Mem.: AAUP, Am. Inst. Parliamentarians (gov. N.W. region 1992—94, univ. parliamentarian), Nat. Soc. Study Edn., Rotary (pres. Pocatello, Idaho club 1981—82, Tempe, Ariz. club 1995—2000, asst. dist. gov. 1998—99, pres. Chandler, Ariz. club 2002—03), Masons, Phi Kappa Phi (pres. 1972—73, 1987—88). Episcopalian. Avocations: physical fitness, music, travel, photography. Home: 678 N Poplar Ct Chandler AZ 85226-6801 E-mail: errcyrano@cox.net. *Initiative and responsibility are cornerstones of a meaningful personal and professional life. Sadly they are missing in much of contemporary society. Apathy, the absence of civility and self-indulgence appear most prominently at the turn of the century and thus far in the 21st century.*

ROWE, G. STEVEN, state attorney general; m. Amanda Rowe; 4 children. BS, U.S. Mil. Acad.; MBA, U. Utah; JD, U. Maine. Mem. Dist. 30 Maine Ho. of Reps., 1993-95, mem. Dist. 35, 1995—2001; litigation counsel UNUM-Provident; atty. gen. State of Maine, 2001—. With U.S. Army, with USAR. Democrat. Office: State House Station 6 Augusta ME 04333

ROWE, HAHN, composer; Composer: (albums) The New Body, performer with Mimi, with Moby, with David Byrne, Foetus, with Syd Straw, with Swans, with True Mori, Michael Brook, with many others; composer: (films) Clean Shaven, The Transformation, Black Kites, Spring Forward.

ROWE, HARRISON EDWARD, electrical engineer; b. Chgo., Jan. 29, 1927; s. Edward and Joan (Golden) R.; m. Alicia Jane Steeves, Feb. 10, 1951; children: Amy Rogers, Elizabeth Joanne, Edward Steeves, Alison Pickard. BS in Elec. Engring, Mass. Inst. Tech., 1948, MS, 1950, Sc.D., 1952; M of Engring. (hon.), Stevens Inst. Tech., 1988. Mem. tech. staff Radio Research Lab., Bell Labs., Holmdel, N.J., 1952-84; Anson Wood Burchard prof. elec. engring. Stevens Inst. Tech., Hoboken, N.J., 1984-93, prof. emeritus, 1993—. Vis. lectr. U. Calif., Berkeley, 1963, Imperial Coll., U. London, 1968; mem. Def. Sci. Bd. Task Force, 1972-74 Author: Signals and Noise in Communication Systems, 1965, Electromagnetic Propagation in Multi-Mode Random Media, 1999; assoc. editor: IEEE Trans. on Communication, 1974-76; contbr. articles to profl. jours.; patentee in field. Served with USN, 1945-46. Co-recipient Microwave prize, 1972, David Sarnoff award, 1977. Fellow IEEE; mem. Monmouth Symphony Soc., Navesink Country Club, Sigma Xi, Tau Beta Pi, Eta Kappa Nu. Clubs: Shrewsbury Sailing and Yacht, Appalachian Mountain. Unitarian Universalist. Home: 9 Buttonwood Ln Rumson NJ 07760-1045 E-mail: harrisonrowe@comcast.net.

ROWE, HERBERT JOSEPH, retired trade association executive; b. Granite City, Ill., Mar. 25, 1924; s. Herbert Bernard and Maude (Klein) R.; m. Ann Muter, Dec. 2, 1950; children: Douglas H., Stephen F., James D., Edith L., Allen. Student, U. Tex., 1942-43, Purdue U., 1943-44; BS in Mgmt.; BS in Mktg., U. Ill., 1948; LittD (hon.), London Inst. for Applied Research, 1975. With Edward Valves, Inc. (subs. Rockwell Mfg. Co.), 1948-50, Muter Co., Chgo., 1952-71, v.p., 1957-64, pres., 1964-71, treas., 1964-67, chmn. bd., 1965-71, also dir., 1957-71; pres., treas., dir. Wescoil Co., 1964-66, Tri-Axial Corp., 1966-67; v.p., treas. Gen. Magnetic Corp., 1965-67, chmn. bd., 1967-70, dir., 1964-70; chmn. bd., dir.; Pemcor, Inc., Westchester, Ill., 1971-75; assoc. adminstr. external affairs NASA, 1975-78; sr. v.p. Electronic Industries Assn., 1978-89; chmn. Famro Corp., 1989-90; pres. Internat. Electronics Fedn., 1989-90. Sec.-treas. Englewood Elec. Supply Wis., Inc., 1972-75, Rahr's Inc., 1972-75; pres. Enclave of Naples, Inc., 1992-94, treas., 1994-96; pres. Rowe Corp., 1994-97; treas. Quality wholesale Foods of S.W. Fla., 1994-96. Pres. Pokagon Trails coun. Boy Scouts Am., 1964-66, pres. Calumet coun., 1966-68, region 7 exec. com., 1966-72, vice chmn., 1971-72, bd. dirs. East Ctrl. region, 1972-75, mem. nat. program com., 1970-78, 90-94, nat. Cub Scout com., 1970-80, chmn., 1990-94, S.E. regional exec. com., 1975-78, So. regional exec. bd., 1993—, bd. dirs. Nat. Capital Area coun., 1978-90, adv. bd., 1990-94, mem. exec. bd. S.W. Fla. coun., 1992—, mem. nat. exec. com. and exec. bd., 1990-95, nat. adv. bd., 1995—; membership chmn. Nat. Eagle Scouts Assn., 1976-80; corp. campaign chmn. Chgo. Met. Crusade Mercy, 1964-68; chmn. Bd. Edn. Caucus, Flossmoor, Ill., 1962; mem. bd. Flossmoor United Party, 1963-68; mem. U. Ill. Found., 1967—; mem. adv. com. U. Ill. Coll. Commerce and Bus. Adminstrn., 1968-78, 97-2002; bd. dirs. Electronic Industries Found., 1974-94; mem. adv. bd. Air and Space Mus., Smithsonian Inst., 1975-78; active Moorings Presbyn. Ch., Naples, Fla. With USMCR, 1942-46, 50-52. Recipient Silver Beaver award Boy Scouts Am., 1966, Silver Antelope award, 1969, Silver Buffalo award, 1994; NASA team award Bicentennial Expo on Sci. and Tech., Exceptional Svc. medal, 1978, Baden-Powell fellow World Scout Found., 1992. Mem. AIAA, AAAS, Electronic Industries Assn. (hon., bd. dirs. 1967-69, bd. govs. 1969-75, exec. com. parts divsn. 1966-75, vice chmn. parts divsn. 1970-74, chmn. 74-75, bd. dirs. consumer electronics divsn. 1972-75, chmn. world trade com. 1968-70, vice chmn. 1970-73, chmn. membership and scope com. 1972-74, Disting. Svc. award 1989), Am. Loudspeaker Mfrs. Assn. (v.p., dir. 1967-68, pres., bd. dirs. 1968-70), Assn. Electronic Mfrs. (bd. dirs. 1970-73), Nat. Space Club, Nat. Space Inst., Am. Acad. Polit. Social Sci., Am. Soc. Assn. Execs. (vice chmn. internat. sect. 1986-87, chmn. 1987-88), U.S. Naval Inst., Field Mus. Natural History, European Soc. of Assn. Execs., Greater Washington Soc. Assn. Execs., Naples Coun. World Affairs (bd. dirs. 2004—), Explorers Club, Chgo. Art Inst., Am. Legion, Chaine des Rôtisseurs, L'Ordre Mondial, Internat. Wine and Food Soc. (pres. Naples br. 2001-), English Speaking Union (pres. Naples chpt. 1996—, nat. dir. 1997—, regional vice chmn. 2000-03, chmn. 2003—), Conservancy, S.W. Fla., Forum Club of S.W. Fla. (bd. dirs. 2000-2003), Naples Press Club (bd. dirs. 1998-2000), Royal Poinciana Golf Club, Naples Yacht Club, Beta Gamma Sigma, Alpha Phi Omega, Sigma Chi (dir. Kappa Kappa corp. 1954-75, sec. 1971-73, pres. 1973-75, Charles J. Kiler award 1975, Grand Consul's citation 1976). Home: 4601 Gulf Shore Blvd N Apt 12 Naples FL 34103-2214 Personal E-mail: hrowe13@comcast.net.

ROWE, JACK FIELD, retired electric utility executive; b. Minn., May 10, 1927; s. William F. and Anna (Stenborg) R.; m. Mary E. Moen, Mar. 26, 1955; 1 child, Lizette Ann. BEE, U. Minn., 1950. Registered profl. engr., Minn., Wis. With Minn. Power and Light Co., Duluth, 1950-89, asst. to pres., 1966-67, v.p., 1967-68, exec. v.p., 1969-74, pres., 1974-84, CEO, 1978-89, chmn., 1969-93, also bd. dirs. Chmn. bd. dirs., CEO FiberCore, Inc., Minn. Paper, Inc., So. States Utilities, Universal Tel., Inc., Topeka Group, Inc., NorLight, Inc.; mem. exec. bd. Nat. Electric Reliability Coun., 1970-73; vice chmn. Mid-Continent Area Reliability Coun., 1970-71, chmn., 1972-73; mem. bus. and econs. adv. bd. U. Minn., Duluth, 1980. Past bd. dirs., v.p. Duluth Jr. C. of C.; mem. exec. bd. Lake Superior coun. Boy Scouts Am., 1967-75, chmn. Explorers, 1968-72; comml. chmn. Duluth United Fund, 1960-61; vice chmn. Duluth United Way, 1975, chmn., 1976, U.S. Savs. Bond chmn., St. Louis County, Minn., 1974-77; chmn. St. Louis County Heritage and Arts Ctr., 1979-81; pres. N.E. Minn. Devel./Assn., 1981-83; mem. Minn. Bus. Partnership, 1979-88; bd. dirs. Minn. Safety Coun., 1979-85, pres., 1983-84, chmn., 1984-85; bd. dirs. Duluth Downtown Devel. Corp., 1979-81, Duluth Growth Co., 1984-85, Greysolon Mall Corp., 1980-86, Duluth Superior Area Cmty. Found., 1984-86, Duluth Clin. Edn. and Rsch. Found., 1985-86, Benedictine Health Sys., 1985-88; mem. adv. bd. exec. program U. Minn., 1979; adv. coun. Inst. Tech., 1979; mem. Minn. High Tech. Coun., 1982-87. With USNR, 1945-46. Recipient Distinguished Svc. award Duluth Jr. C. of C., 1960, Outstanding Leadership award in energy conversion scis. N.Y.C. sect. ASME, 1980, Outstanding Achievement award U. Minn. Alumni Assn., 1986, Bronze CEO of Decade award Fin. World Mag., 1989; named CEO of Yr., Fin. World mag., 1986, 89; Jack F. Rowe Chair of Engring. named in his honor U. Minn., Duluth, 1986. Mem. NAM (dir. 1975-78), IEEE, Electric Info. Coun. (pres. 1978-82), North Cen. Electric Assn., Duluth C. of C. (pres. 1972-73, exec. com., bd. dirs.), Mpls. Club, Engrs. Club (Duluth), Northland Country Club (Duluth), Naples Yacht Club, Kitchi Gammi (Duluth) (dir. 1979-87, pres. 1985-87), Rotary Club (Duluth) (pres. 1974-75), Moorings Country Club, Internat. Mens Club, Royal Poinciana Golf Club, Masons, Shriners, Jesters, Kappa Eta Kappa. Lutheran. Home: 4735 Villa Mare Ln Naples FL 34103-3473

ROWE, JAMES WILLIAM, SR., engineer; b. Richmond, Va., Mar. 10, 1944; s. William Walter and Margaret Lucille (Brauer) R.; m. Janet O'Neal Parker, Mar. 30, 1968; children: James William, Rhett Nelson. BS, Va. Commonwealth U., 1968. Chief operator City of Richmond, 1974-76; supr. Park 500 divsn. Phillip Morris, Richmond, 1976-79; quality control chemist Gen. Metals Tech., Richmond, 1979-81; process engr. Synertech., Richmond, 1981-83, FN Mfg., Inc., Columbia, S.C., Genicom Corp., Waynesboro, Va., 1988-93, The Am. Hist. Found., Richmond, 1993—. Republican. Baptist. Office: The Am Hist Found 1142 W Grace St Richmond VA 23220-3613

ROWE, JOHN WALLIS, health insurance executive, medical executive; b. Jersey City, June 20, 1944; s. Albert Wallis and Elizabeth (Lynch) R.; m. Valerie Ann DelTufo, Aug. 10, 1968; children: Meredith, Abigail, Rebecca. BS with honors, Canisius Coll., 1966; MD with distinction, U. Rochester, 1970. Diplomate Am. Bd. Internal Medicine, Am. Bd. Nephrology. Resident in internal medicine Harvard Med. Sch., Beth Israel Hosp., Boston, 1970-72; clin. assoc. Nat. Inst. Child Health and Human Devel., Balt., 1972-74; rsch. clin. fellow Harvard Med. Sch., Mass. Gen. Hosp., Boston, 1974-75; from instr. to prof. Harvard Med. Sch., Boston, 1976-88; pres. Mt. Sinai Sch. Medicine, N.Y.C., 1988-99, Mt. Sinai Hosp., N.Y.C., 1988-98; prof. geriatrics and medicine Mt. Sinai Sch. Medicine and Mt. Sinai Hosp., N.Y.C., 1988—; CEO Mt. Sinai-NYU Med. Ctr. and Health Sys., N.Y.C., 1998-2000; pres., CEO, Aetna Inc., Hartford, Conn., 2000—, chmn., 2001—. Chmn. bd. trustees U. Conn.; mem. Medicare Payment Adv. Com., 1997—. Editor: Health and Disease in Old Age, 1982, Geriatric Medicine, 1988, Handbook of the Biology of Aging, 1990, Geriatric Neurology, 1991; author: Successful Aging, 1998; contbr. articles to jours. in field. Lt. comdr. USPHS, 1972-74. MacArthur Found. grantee, 1985-98. Mem. NAS Inst. Med., Gerontol. Soc. Am. (pres. 1988), Am. Fedn. for Aging Rsch. (pres. 1988), N.Y. Yacht Club, Century Assn. Roman Catholic. Avocation: sailing. Home: 300 Central Park W New York NY 10024-1513 Office: Aetna 151 Farmington Ave Hartford CT 06156 E-mail: RoweJW@aetna.com.

ROWE, JOHN WILLIAM, utilities executive; b. Dodgeville, Wis., May 18, 1945; married; 1 son. BS, U. Wis., 1967, JD, 1970. Bar: Wis. 1970, Ill. 1970, U.S. Supreme Ct. 1979, Pa. 1982. Assoc. Isham, Lincoln & Beale, Chgo., 1970-77, ptnr., 1978-80; counsel to trustee Chgo. Milw. St. Paul & Pacific R.R., Chgo., 1979-80; v.p. law Consol. Rail Corp., Phila., 1980-82, sr. v.p. law, 1982-84; pres., chief exec. officer Cen. Maine Power Co., Augusta, 1984-89; pres., CEO New Eng. Elec. System, Westboro, Mass., 1989-98, former bd. dirs.; chmn., pres., CEO Unicom Corp. & Commonwealth Edison Co., 1998-2000; pres., co-CEO Exelon Corp., 2000—. Bd. dirs. UnumProvident Corp., Fleet Boston Fin., Wis. Ctrl. Tranp. Co.; of counsel to trustees Chgo., Milw., St. Paul, Pacific Railroad Co. Bd. trustees Art Inst. Chgo., Chgo. Hist. Soc., Field Mus., Wis. Alumni rsch. Found., Am. Enterprise Inst., Ill. chpt. Nature Conservancy; vice-chmn. Edison Electric Inst.; nat. trustee Northwestern U.; past pres. USS Constitution Mus.; past chmn. Mass. Bus. Roundtable. Mem. Econ. Club. Chgo., Comml. Club Chgo. (civic com.), Order of the Coif, Phi Beta Kappa. Home and Office: Unicom Corp Ten S Dearborn St # 37 Chicago IL 60603

ROWE, LARRY LINWELL, lawyer; b. Bluefield, W.Va. m. Julia; 3 children. BA, W.Va. U., 1970, MPA, JD, W.Va. U., 1976. Bar: W.Va. 1976, U.S. Dist. Ct. (so. dist.) W.Va. 1976, U.S. Ct. Appeals (4th cir.) 1978, U.S. Supreme Ct. 1992. Staff counsel W.Va. Housing Devel. Fund, Charleston, W.Va., 1976-77; sr. law clk. for U.S. Cir. Judge K.K. Hall U.S. 4th Cir. Ct. Appeals, Charleston, 1978-79; pvt. practice Charleston, 1980—. Mem. W.Va. Senate 2001-, House of Del., 1997-00; hearing examiner W.Va. Bd. Regents, Charleston, 1985-89, W.Va. Bd. Medicine, Charleston, 1987-88; adj. law prof. U. Charleston, 1980-81. Bd. mem. W.Va. Artists & Craftsmen's Guild, Charleston, 1980-84, Cedar Lakes' Mountain State Arts & Crafts Fair, Ripley, 1981-82; chmn., mem. Legal Aid Soc. of Charleston, 1981-84; pres. W.Va. Dance Theatre, Charleston, 1981-82. Recipient W.Va. Bd. of Regents scholarship W.Va. Univ. Coll. Law, Morgantown, 1974-76, Cato scholarship, 1974-76. Mem.: Phi Beta Kappa, Order of Coif. Democrat. Office: 4200A Malden Dr Charleston WV 25306-6442 Office Phone: 304-925-1333. E-mail: larrylrowe@larrylrowe.com.

ROWE, MARY P. organizational ombudsman, management educator; b. Chgo., Feb. 18, 1936; married; children: Katherine, Susannah, Timothy. BA in History, Swarthmore Coll., 1957; PhD in Econs., Columbia U., 1971; LLD (hon.), Regis Coll., 1975. With World Council of Chs./Office of UN High Commr. for Refugees, Salzburg and Vienna, Austria, 1957-58; research asst. Nat. Bur. Econ. Research, N.Y.C., 1961; economist planning bd. Office of Gov., V.I., 1962-63; free-lance cons. Nigeria, 1963-66, 1967-69; cons., sr. economist with Ctr. for Ednl. Policy Research, Harvard U. Harvard U., Cambridge, Mass., 1970, cons., sr. economist with Abt Assocs., 1970, tech. dir. early edn. project, 1971-72, cons. economist with Abt Assocs., 1971; dir. Carnegie Corp. Grant Radcliffe Inst., Cambridge, 1972; spl. asst. to pres., ombudsperson MIT, Cambridge, 1973—, adj. prof. Sloan Sch. Mgmt., 1985—. Mem. steering com., program on negotiations Harvard U., 1995—. Mem. editorial bd. Negotiation Jour., 1985—, Alternative Dispute Resolution Report, 1987-90; contbr. articles to profl. jours. Trustee Cambridge Friends Sch., 1969-75; mem. bd. advisors Brookline Children's Ctr., 1971-76; mem. Cambridge Friends Meeting and Com. on Clearness, 1971-78, New Eng. Concerns Com., 1973—, Mass. Policy Adv. Com. on Child Abuse/Neglect, 1977-79, Mass. State Youth Council, 1978-83; mem. Mass. State Employment and Tng. Council, 1975-83, chair, 1980-83; mem. nat. adv. Com. Black Women's Ednl. Policy and Research Network Project/Wellesley Coll. Ctr. for Research on Women, 1980-83; bd. dirs. Bay State Skills Comm., 1980-81, Wellesley Women's Research Ctr., 1984-87; sec. bd. dirs. Bay State Skills Corp., 1981-90; mem. panel on employment disputes Ctr. for Pub. Resources, 1986—. Recipient Meritorious Civilian Svc. award Dept. of Navy, 1993. Mem. Soc. Profls. in Dispute Resolution (chair com. on ombudspersons 1982-92, employment disputes), Calif. Caucus Coll. and Univ. Ombudsmen, Univ. and Coll. Ombudsman Assn., Ombudsman Assn. (co-founder, 1982,

pres. 1985-87, program on negotiation steering com. 1995—, Disting. Neutral Ctr. for Pub. Resources 1990—, covenor, presenter confs. 1982, 84, 85, 88, 89, 90-2003). Office: MIT 10-213 77 Massachusetts Ave Cambridge MA 02139

ROWE, MARY SUE, accounting executive; b. Melrose, Kans., Aug. 31, 1940; d. Gene and Carmen (Glidewell) Woffard; m. Edward Rowe, Nov. 27, 1985; children from previous marriage: Denise, Dynell, Dalene, Denette. Student, MTI Bus. Coll., 1968, Calif. State U., Fullerton, 1969, Broome (N.Y.) Community Coll., 1974-76; cert. Sch. Bus. Mgmt., Calif. State U., San Bernardino, 1986. Variou bookkeeping and secretarial, 1968-76; asst. mgr., acct. RM Dean Contracting, Chenango Forks, N.Y., 1976-80; acctg. asst. Hemet (Calif.) Unified Sch. Dist., 1981-86; dir. acctg. Desert Sands Unified Sch. Dist., Indio, Calif., 1986-91; bus. svcs. cons. ednl. div. Vicenti, Lloyd & Stutzman, CPA, La Verne, Calif., 1991-97; prin. Rowe Cons., 1997—; sch. bus. cons., computer trainer Hemet, Calif., 1997—; dir. fiscal svcs. San Rafael City Schs., Calif., 2002—03. Bd. dirs. Family Svcs. Assn., Hemet, 1982-83, PTA Officer, 1993-95. Mem. NAFE, Calif. Assn. Sch. Bus. Ofcls. (acctg. com., R&D com., vice chmn. 1988-90, chmn. 1990-91, state acctg. adv. com. 1990-92), Calif. Assn. Pub. Purchasing Officers, Riverside Assn. Chief Accts. (co-chmn. 1986-88), Coalition for Adequate Sch. Housing. Republican. Home and Office: 4981 Vailwood Dr Hemet CA 92544-7819 *Personal philosophy: Something good can come of any event no matter how bad it first appears.*

ROWE, MELINDA GRACE, public health service officer; b. Decatur, Ala., Aug. 18, 1953; m. Dana Calvin Craig Jr., Jan. 1, 1994. MD, U. Ala., 1978, MPH, 1985, MBA, 1987. Bd. cert. Am. Bd. Pediatrics, Am. Bd. Preventive Medicine. Pediatrics intern U. Ky., Lexington, 1978-79; pediatrics resident Lloyd Nolan Hosp., Fairfield, Ala., 1979-81; physician Columbus (Miss.) Children's Clinic, 1981, pvt. practice, Winfield, Ala., 1982-84; preventive medicine resident U. Ala., Birmingham, 1984-85; asst. state health officer Pub. Health Area III, Pelham, Ala., 1985-95; dir. health Jefferson County Health Dept., Louisville, 1995—2001; dist. health officer Savannah (Ga.) East Health, 2001—03; commr. of health Lexington Fayette County Health Dept., Lexington, Ky., 2003—. Asst. prof. U. Ala., Birmingham, 1988—, U. Louisville, 1995—. Bd. dirs. Cahaba River Soc., Birmingham, 1988—95, U. Ala.-Birmingham Nat. Alumni Soc., 1988—93, Health Ky., Goodwill Industries. Mem.: Ga. Med. Assn., Ky. Health Depts. Assn. (v.p.), Louisville/Jefferson County Primary Care Assn. (bd. dirs.), Jefferson County Med. Soc., Ky. Pediat. Soc., Ky. Pub. Health Assn. (pres.-elect), Ky. Med. Assn. Methodist. Avocations: reading, walking, travel, music. Home: 2006 Fontaine Rd Lexington KY 40502 Office Phone: 859-288-2300. Business E-Mail: melinda.rowe@ky.gov.

ROWE, MICHAEL DUANE, artist; b. Lykens, Pa., Nov. 5, 1947; m. Kathryn Jean Branoff. Student, Art Inst. Pitts., 1971-72. Exhibited in shows at Art Assn. Harrisburg, Pa., 1985, 86, 87, State Mus. Pa., 1986, 87, Doshi Gallery, Harrisburg, 1987, Cheltenham (Pa.) Art Ctr., 1989, 92, Delaplaine Art Ctr., Frederick, Md., 1989 (1st prize 1989), 90, 91, Immaculata (Pa.) Coll., 1990, U. of the Arts, Phil., 1990, Butler Inst. of Am. Art, Youngstown, Ohio, 1990, 92, Phila. Art Alliance, 1990, Altenative Mus., N.Y.C., 1990, 91, 95, Spaces, Cleve., 1991, Alexandria (La.) Art Mus., 1991, Pa. State U., 1992, Allentown (Pa.) Mus. Art, 1992, Muhlenberg Coll., Allentown, 1992 (award 1992), Michael Stone Gallery, Washington, 1992, Ea. N.Mex. U., 1992, Del. Ctr. for Contemporary Arts, Wilmington, 1993, Laguna Gloria Art Mus., Austin, Tex., 1993, Silvermine Art Guild Exhibit, New Cannan, Conn., 1993, Pa. State U., Univ. Park, 1993, East Tenn. U., Johnson City, 1994, Chrysler Mus., Norfolk, Va., 1994, Davidson (N.C.) Coll. Visual Arts Ctr., 1995, Southern Alleghenies Mus. of Art, 1995, Loretto, Pa., 1996, 97, 99, Susquehanna Art Mus., Harrisburg, Pa., 1998. Whitaker Ctr., Harrisburg, 1999, 2000; represented in permanent collection So. Alleghenies Mus., Loretto, Pa. Grantee Art Matters, Inc., 1988; Pa. Coun. of the Arts fellow, 1993. Episcopalian. Avocations: running, travel, reading. Home: 814 Meadow Ln Camp Hill PA 17011-1545

ROWE, NEIL CHARLES, science educator; b. Chgo., July 18, 1953; s. Charles Louis Rowe and Bonnie Natalie Parsons; life ptnr. Suzanne Elizabeth Turner. PhD in Computer Sci., Stanford U., 1983. Professor U.S. Naval Postgraduate School, Monterey, CA, 1983—2002. Author: (book) Artificial Intelligence through Prolog, 1988, (website) www.cs.nps.navy.mil/people/faculty/rowe/index.html, 2002; contbr. articles to profl. jours., chpts. to books. Mem.: IEEE Computer Soc., ACM, Am. Assn. for Artificial Intelligence. Office: US Naval Postgrad Sch Code CS/Rp 833 Dyer Rd Monterey CA 93943 Business E-Mail: ncrowe@nps.navy.mil.

ROWE, PETER A. newspaper columnist; b. Walnut Creek, Calif., Sept. 7, 1955; s. Raymond Alan and Marion (Green) R.; m. Lynn Hanson, Aug. 13, 1977; children: Kyle, Reid, Alec. BA in History, BA in Journalism, U. Calif., Berkeley, 1977; MSJ, Northwestern U., 1981. Reporter Argus, Fremont, Calif., 1977-80, Va.-Pilot, Norfolk, 1981-84, San Diego Union, 1984-87, asst. features editor, 1987-88, features editor, 1988-92; columnist San Diego Union-Tribune, 1992—. Gannett fellow Northwestern U., 1980-81; Fulbright scholar, 2003. Mem.: Nat. Soc. Newspaper Columnists (pres. 2000—02). Roman Catholic. Office: San Diego Union Tribune PO Box 120191 San Diego CA 92112-0191 Office Phone: 619-293-1227. E-mail: peter.rowe@uniontrib.com.

ROWE, PETER GRIMMOND, architecture educator, researcher; b. Wellington, New Zealand, June 28, 1945; arrived in U.S., 1969; s. Leslie Grimmond and Dorothy Olive (Perkins) Rowe; m. Lauretta Vinciarelli, Oct. 18, 1993; 1 child, Anthony. BArch, Melbourne (Australia) U., 1969; MArch in Urban Design, Rice U., 1971; AM (hon.), Harvard U., 1986. Adj. assoc. prof. human ecology U. Tex. Health Sci. Ctr., Houston, 1977—85; assoc. prof. Sch. Arch./Sch. Pub. Health Rice U., 1977—85, dir. Sch. Arch., 1981—85; prin. Environ. Planning and Design, Houston, 1985—87; dir. urban designs programs Grad. Sch. Design Harvard U., 1985—90, Raymond Garbe prof. arch. and urban design Grad. Sch. Design, 1987—, chmn. dept. urban planning and design Grad. Sch. Design, 1988—92, dean faculty design, 1992—2004; hon. prof. Xi'an U. Arch. and Tech., 1999—. Bd. mem. Can. Arch. Ctr., 1995—; mem. U.S. Gen. Svcs. Adminstrn., Pub. Bldgs. Svc. Nat. Register of Peer Profls., 1996—98; hon. cons. Chair Com. on Arch. Melbourne U., 1997—98, 2002; chmn. rev. com., faculty arch. and town planning Technion U., Israel, 1997; chmn. Dean's Cir., Sch. Arch. Rice U., 1998—2001, mem. Dean's Cir., 2001; mem. ctr. artery corridor adv. group task force City of Boston, 1999—; jury pres. Olympic Village Competition, Athens, Greece, 2000; sr. advisor urban planning and design City of Wenzhou, China, 2000—; jury mem. West Kowloon Reclamation Concept Plan Competition, Hong Kong, 2001—02. Author: Principles for Environmental Management, 1978, Design Thinking, 1987, Making a Middle Landscape, 1991, Modernity and Housing, 1993, Civic Realism, 1997, Asia Modern, 1998, Projecting Beruit, 1998; co-author: Modern Urban Housing in China: 1840-2000, 2001, Architectural Encounters with Essence and Form in Modern China; co-editor: Yi-Ti-Laing-Yi Zhi Jian: Redevelopment in Suzhou, China, 1997, Shan Shiu City: Urban Development in Wenzhou, China, 2001, Environments of Opportunity: Redevelopment on the Waterfront of Las Palmas de Gran Canaria, Spain, 2001; pub., mem. editl. bd.: Harvard Design Mag., 1997—. Fellow: Inst. for Urban Design; mem.: Am. Planning Assn., Boston Soc. Archs. (hon.), Urban Land Inst. (assoc.). Office: Harvard U Grad Sch Design 48 Quincy St Cambridge MA 02138-3000*

ROWE, RICHARD HOLMES, lawyer; b. Waltham, Mass., Jan. 2, 1937; s. Robert C. Rowe and Roberta (Holmes) Hayes; m. Sylvia C. Barrow, Aug. 23, 1963; children: Elizabeth C., Dorothy H., Christopher H. AB, Bates Coll., 1957; JD, Harvard U., 1964. Bar: D.C. 1965, N.Y. 1980. Atty., exec. SEC, Washington, 1964-69, 70-79; v.p. Shareholders Mgmt. Co., L.A., 1969-70; ptnr. Proskauer Rose Goetz & Mendelsohn, Washington, 1979—. 1st lt. USMCR, 1957-60. Mem. ABA, FBA, D.C. Bar Assn., Assn. Bar City of N.Y. Democrat. Office: Proskauer Rose LLP 1233 20th St NW Ste 800 Washington DC 20036-2377

ROWE, SANDRA MIMS, editor; b. Charlotte, N.C., May 26, 1948; d. David Lathan and Shirley (Stovall) Mims; m. Gerard Paul Rowe, June 5, 1971; children: Mims Elizabeth, Sarah Stovall. BA, East Carolina U., Greenville, N.C., 1970; postgrad., Harvard U., 1991. Reporter to asst. mng. editor The Ledger-Star, Norfolk, Va., 1971-80, mng. editor, 1980-82, The Virginian-Pilot and The Ledger Star, Norfolk, Va., 1982-84, exec. editor, 1984-86, v.p., exec. editor, 1986-93; editor The Oregonian, Portland, 1993—. Mem. Pulitzer Prize Bd., 1994-2003, chair, 2003. Bd. visitors James Madison U., Harrisonburg, VA., 1991-95; chair journalism adv. bd. Knight Found.; mem. adv. bd. The Poynter Inst., Medill Sch. Journalism, Northwestern U.; chair bd. visitors Knight Fellowships, Stanford U. Recipient George Beveridge Editor of Yr. award Nat. Press Found., 2003; named Woman of Yr. Outstanding Profl. Women of Hampton Rds., 1987; inducted into Va. Journalism Hall of Fame, 2000. Mem. Am. Soc. Newspaper Editors (pres., bd. dirs. 1992-99), Va. Press Assn. (bd. dirs. 1985-93). Episcopalian. Office: The Oregonian 1320 SW Broadway Portland OR 97201-3499

ROWE, SHERYL ANN, librarian; b. Stephenville, Tex., Sept. 29, 1946; d. Horace Milton and Letha Faye (Hensley) Hughes; m. Darrell Vanoy Rowe, Nov. 27, 1969; children: Jason Burt, Shelley Jean. BA in English, Tarleton State U., Stephenville, 1967; MS in Libr. Sci., Tex. Women's U., Denton, 1986. Cert. tchr. secondary edn. Tchr. Lake Worth H.S., Tex., 1967—69, Aledo H.S., Tex., 1967—73, 1978—84, libr., 1984—. Mem. ALA, Tex. Libr. Assn., Region XI Librs. Assn. (treas. 1984—). Office: Aledo HS 1000 Bailey Ranch Rd Aledo TX 76008-4407 E-mail: srowe@aledo.k12.tx.us.

ROWE, THOMAS DUDLEY, JR., law educator; b. Richmond, Va., Feb. 26, 1942; s. Thomas Dudley and Georgia Rosamond (Stripp) R.; m. Susan Fletcher French, Jan. 5, 2001. BA, Yale U., 1964; MPhil, Oxford U., Eng., 1967; JD, Harvard U., 1970. Bar: D.C. 1971, N.C. 1976. Law clk. to assoc. justice Potter Stewart U.S. Supreme Ct., Washington, 1970-71; asst. counsel adminstrv. practice subcom. U.S. Senate, Washington, 1971-73; assoc. Miller, Cassidy, Larroca & Lewin, Washington, 1973-75; assoc. prof. Duke U. Sch. Law, Durham, N.C., 1975-79, prof., 1979-96, Elvin R. Latty prof., 1996—, assoc. dean for rsch., 1981-84, sr. assoc. dean acad. affairs, 1995-96. Vis. prof. Georgetown U. Law Ctr., Washington, 1979—80, U. Mich. Law Sch., Ann Arbor, 1985, U. Va. Law Sch., Charlottesville, 1991, UCLA Law Sch., 2002, 04; atty. Munger, Tolles & Olson, L.A., 1991; adv. com. on rules of civil procedure U.S. Jud. Conf., 1993—99. Co-author: Federal Courts in the 21st Century: Cases and Materials, 1996, 2002, Civil Procedure, 2004; contbr. articles to profl. jours. Fellow U.S. Dept. Justice, Washington, 1980-81; Rhodes scholar, 1964-67; recipient Disting. Teaching award Duke Bar Assn., 1985. Mem. ABA, Am. Law Inst. Democrat. Office: Duke U Sch Law Durham NC 27708-0360 Office Phone: 919-613-7099.

ROWE, TINA L. government official; b. Griffin, Ga., July 22, 1946; 1 child. Student, FBI Nat. Acad., 1981; AA, Aurora (Colo.) C.C., 1991; BA, Colo. Christian U., 1999. From patrol officer to comdr. patrol dist. 2 Denver Police Dept., 1969-94; U.S. marshal for Dist. Colo., U.S. Marshals Svc., Dept. Justice, Denver, 1994—. Trainer, spkr. cons. operational planning, motivation, leadership. Recipient various awards, including Woman of Yr. award Bus. and Profl. Women's Club, 1994; named Outstanding Law Enforcement officer, Am. Legion, 1999. Mem. FBI Nat. Acad. Assocs., Nat. Sheriffs Assn., Colo. Assn. Chiefs Police, Intenat. Assn. Chiefs of Police, Am. Coll. Forensic Examiners, Am. Bd. Law Enforcement Experts. Baptist. Office: US Marshals Svc Dept Justice 1929 Stout St Rm 324C Denver CO 80294-1929

ROWE, WILLIAM DAVIS, financial services company executive; b. Hibbing, Minn., June 5, 1937; s. Richard Lawrence and Alicia (Davis) R.; m. Bobbie Grace Childress, Apr. 20, 1963; children— Lisa, William BA in Psychology, U. Minn, 1959, postgrad. in indsl. relations and bus. adminstrn., 1960; grad. exec. devel. program, Northeastern U., 1975; grad. Advanced Mgmt. Program, Harvard U., 1980. Dir. personnel, adminstrn. EDP Control Data Corp., Mpls., 1964-70; with Comml. Credit Co. subs. Control Data Corp, 1971-84, 85—; sr. v.p. consumer group, 1975-81; sr. v.p. consumer realty services, 1981-83; sr. v.p. consumer banking services, 1983-84; v.p. market devel. Computer Service Co., Control Data Corp., Mpls., 1984; sr. v.p., chief adminstrv. officer Comml. Credit Co., Balt., 1985-87; pres. Enterprise Bank Network Bank Svcs. Co., Atlanta, 1988-91; exec. mng. dir., vice chmn. Foster Ptnrs. Inc., Peat Marwick Alliance Co., 1991—; pres., COO Foster Ptnrs., 2001—. Bd. dirs. Fla. Corp.; co-owner Spirit of West Land Co., Glenwood Springs, Colo., 2001—; lectr. in field Mem. Mayor's Vol. Council of Equal Opportunity, Balt.; trustee St. Paul's Sch. for Girls, Brooklandville, Md., 1981—; bd. dirs. Boy Scouts Am., Take Stock in Children, 1996—. Served to capt. USMC, 1960-63. Mem. Am. Fin. Services Assn. (bd. dirs. and mem. exec. com. 1980-84, consumer banking adv. com. 1983-84), Am. Mgmt. Assn. (pres.'s roundtable 1976) Republican. Avocations: hunting, skiing, cattle ranching.

ROWE, WILLIAM JOHN, retired newspaper publishing executive; b. Detroit, Jan. 11, 1936; s. Howard Tiedeman and Thelma Irene (Fox) R.; m. Ellen McCabe, Nov. 28, 1959; children: Peter William, Susan Victoria. BA in Journalism and Advt., Mich. State U., 1958. With Chgo. Tribune, 1958-79; pres., gen. mgr. area publs. Suburban Trib., 1977-79; pres., gen. mgr. Merrill Printing Co., Chgo., 1977-79; pres., CEO Peninsula Times Tribune, Palo Alto, Calif., 1979-84; exec. v.p., COO Times Mirror Nat. Mktg., N.Y.C., 1984-85, pres., CEO, 1985-86; pres., pub., CEO Adv. and Greenwich Time, Stamford, Conn., 1986-2001. Bd. dirs. Norwalk Cmty. Tech. Coll. 2nd lt. inf. USAR, 1950. Mem. Newspaper Assn. Am. (pres.), New England Newspaper Assn., Indian Harbor Yacht Club, Landmark Club. Office: Advocate So Conn Newspapers Box 9307 75 Tresser Blvd Stamford CT 06901-3300

ROWE, WILLIAM JOSEPH, internist; b. Cin., Oct. 31, 1927; s. Alvin Harold and Ida Claire (Omansky) R.; m. Mary Elaine Kenkel, Apr. 16, 1955. BS, U. Cin., 1950, MD, 1954. Diplomate Am. Bd. Internal Medicine. Asst. clin. prof. medicine Med. Coll. Ohio, Toledo, 1962-93; chmn. dept. medicine St. Vincent's Hosp., Toledo, 1979-83; chief adv. com. cardiac rehab. N.W. Ohio Heart Assn., Toledo, 1981-83. Del. citizen amb. program to China People to People, 1988. Contbr. articles to profl. jours., including Acta Astronautica, Lancet, Circulation. Capt. USAF, 1955-57. Mem. Aerospace Med. Assn., Nat. Space Soc., Brit. Interplanetary Soc. Republican. Avocations: adventurer, tennis, running, writing, travel. Home: 1485 Bremerton Ln Keswick VA 22947 E-mail: rowerun@aol.com.

ROWELL, BARBARA CABALLERO, retired academic administrator; b. New Orleans, Sept. 5, 1922; d. Albert Henry Wischnewske (stepfather) and Antoinette (Angelo) Caballero; m. J.C. Rowell, Dec. 17, 1941; children: Jerrie Carlene, Kerry Gene, Ricky Ray. AA in Bus. Adminstrn., Okaloosa Walton Jr. Coll., Niceville, Fla.; BA in Social Scis., U. West Fla. Exec. sec. Bishop Enterprises, Ft. Walton Beach; office mgr. and real estate property mgr. Fred Cooke Real Estate, Ft. Walton Beach, Fla.; adminstrv. sec. to v.p. Okaloosa Walton Jr. Coll., Niceville. Leader brownie scouts Girl Scouts U.S., cub scouts Boy Scouts Am.; bd. dirs., mem. curriculum com. U. West Fla. Ctr. for Life Long Learning; chair univ svc. com., pres., began Writing Lab; originator, implementor U. West Fla. Tutor Program, Career Fair, started scholarship program, Proctor Program; mem. curriculum com. U. West Fla.Ctr. for Lifelong Learning, presenter S.E. Conf. Insts. of Learning in Retirement, Charleston, S.C.; gov.'s campaign vol.; state legislature campaign vol.; mem. Sr. Ctr. Life Long Learning, U. West Fla. Mem. AAUW, DAV Aux., Order of Ea. Star (past matron). Avocations: education, travel, reading, gardening, dance, volunteering.

ROWELL, EDWARD MORGAN, retired foreign service officer, lecturer; b. Oakland, Calif., Oct. 13, 1931; s. Edward Joseph and Mary Helen (Mohler) Rowell; m. Lenora Mary Wood, Aug. 23, 1957; children: Edward Oliver, Karen Elizabeth Schuler, Christopher Douglas. BA in Internat. Relations, Yale U., 1953; postgrad., Stanford U., 1964-65, Stanford Bus. Sch., 1970-71. Fgn. service insp. U.S. Dept. State, Washington, 1971-74; dep. dir., econ. officer Office Iberian Affairs, Washington, 1974-75; dep. dir. Office West European Affairs, Washington, 1975-76, dir., 1977-78; minister-counselor U.S. Embassy, Lisbon, Portugal, 1978-83; dep. asst. sec. Bur. Consular Affairs, Washington, 1983-85; U.S. amb. to Bolivia La Paz, 1985-88; U.S. amb. to Portugal Lisbon, 1988-90; U.S. amb. to Luxemburg, 1990-94; sr. assoc. Global Bus. Access, Ltd., 1994—. Bd. dirs. Sourcecorp, Dallas, 1995—. Mem. adv. bd. Portuguese-Am. Leadership Coun. U.S.; mem. Cleveland Park Congregational Ch, Washington, 1956—; trustee Cleveland Park Ch., 2000—03; bd. dirs. Luso-Am Develop Found., 1988—90. With U.S. Army, 1953—55. Decorated grand cross Bolivian Condor of the Andes, grand cross Luxembourg Oaken Crown; recipient State Dept. Superior Honor award, 1983, 1991, Presdl. Honor Award, 1988; grantee, Una Chapman Cox Found., 1984; Yale U. scholar, 1949—52, U. Calif. fellow, 1953. Mem.: Diplomatic & Consular Officers Ret. (gov. 2001—), Arena Stage Assocs., Yale Univ. Alumni Assn., Stanford Univ. Alumni Assn., Wash. Inst. Foreign Affairs (membership com. 1999—), Assn. Diplomatic Studies & Training (pres. 1997—2001), Am. Foreign Svc. Assn. (v.p. 1995—97), Am Acad. Diplomacy (bd. dirs. 2002—), Cosmos Club. Avocations: photography, tennis, music. Home: 5414 Newington Rd Bethesda MD 20816-3316

ROWELL, LESTER JOHN, JR., retired insurance company executive; b. Cleve., Apr. 2, 1932; s. Lester John and Francis Laureen (Corbett) R.; m. Patricia Ann Loesch, Jan. 16, 1953 (div. Sept. 1970); children: Deborah, Cynthia, Gregory, Maureen, Diane; m. Carol Ann Jankowski, Sept. 26, 1970. BS, Pa. State U., 1955; grad. Advanced Mgmt. Program, Harvard U. Bus. Sch., 1971. CLU. Second v.p., field mgmt. Mut. Life Ins. Co. N.Y., N.Y.C., 1969-70, v.p. agys., 1970-72, v.p. sales, 1972-78, sr. v.p., 1978-80; exec. v.p. Provident Mut. Life Ins. Co., Phila., 1980-84, pres., 1984-86, pres., chief oper. officer, 1987, pres., chief exec. officer, 1991-93, chmn., pres., chief exec. officer, 1993-96; ret. Bd. dirs. Pa. State U., The PMA Group. Capt. USMC, 1953-62. Recipient Alumni award Pa. State U., 1972, Disting. Alumni award Pa. State U., 1988; Alumni Fellow Pa. State U., 1987. Republican. Personal E-mail: budrowell@aol.com.

ROWELLO, ROBERT JOHN, communications executive; b. Phila., July 7, 1973; s. Robert Joseph Rowello and Lucy Myers; m. Gertrude Bruner, June 25, 1999; children: Grace Elizabeth, Victor Francis. BSEE, Johns Hopkins U., 1995; MBA, MIT, 1999. Prin. Pittiglio, Rabin, Todd, and McGrath, Waltham, Mass., 1998—2003; v.p. customer svc. Comcast Cable Comm., Voorhees, NJ, 2003—. Mem.: Union League Phila. (assoc.). Office: Comcast Cable Comm 401 White Horse Rd Voorhees NJ 08043

ROWE-MAAS, BETTY LU, real estate investor; b. Apr. 2, 1925; d. Horace Dewitt and Lucy Belle (Spiker) Rowe; children: Terry Lee, Clifford Lindsay, Craig Harrison, Joan Louise. Real estate investor, Saratoga, Calif., 1968—. Mem. Nat. Trust Hist. Preservation, Smithsonian Instn., Archeol. Inst. Am., San Jose Symphony, San Jose Cleve. Ballet, San Francisco Symphony, San Francisco Ballet, M. H. de Young Meml. Mus., Santa Barbara Mus. Art, Calif. Palice of the Legion of Honor, Loberro Theatre Found., Arlington Theater Restoration Fund, Bishop Mus. Hawaii, Friends of Kawai Mus., Friends of Princeville Libr., others; bd. dirs. Valley Inst. Theatre Arts; mem. Saratoga Good Govt., 1970-89; mem. Rt 85 Task Froce, 1978—, treas., 1984-89; treas. Traffic Relief for Saratoga. Mem. LWV, NOW (mem. world affairs coun. No. Calif. chpt.), Commonwealth Calif. Club (life), Santa Barbara Rep. Club, Toastmasters (past treas. Santa Barbara Rep. club # 5). Home: 5035 Kapiolani Loop Princeville HI 96722

ROWEN, MARSHALL, radiologist; b. Chgo. s. Harry and Dorothy (Kasnow) R.; m. Helen Lee Friedman, Apr. 5, 1952; children: Eric, Scott, Mark. AB in Chemistry with highest honors, U. Ill., Urbana, 1951; MD with honors, MS in Internal Medicine, U. Ill., Chgo., 1954. Diplomate Am. Bd. Radiology. Intern Long Beach (Calif.) VA Hosp., 1955; resident in radiology Los Angeles VA Hosp., 1955-58; practice medicine specializing in radiology Orange, Calif., 1960—. Chmn. bd. dirs. Moran, Rowen and Dorsey, Inc., Radiologists, 1969—2002; asst. radiologist L.A. Children's Hosp., 1958; assoc. radiologist Valley Presbyn. Hosp., Van Nuys, Calif., 1960; dir. dept. radiology St. Joseph Hosp., Orange, 1961—, v.p. staff, 1972; dir. dept. radiology Children's Hosp. Orange County, 1964—2002, chief staff, 1977—78, v.p., 1978—83, v.p., trustee, 1990—91, 1992—95; asst. clin. prof. radiology U. Calif., Irvine, 1967—70, assoc. clin. prof., 1979—82, clin. prof. radiology and pediat., 1976—99, pres. clin. faculty assn., 1980—81; trustee Choc. Padrinos; sec. Choco Health Svcs., 1987—89, v.p., 1990—93, trustee, 1995—, Found. Med. Care Orange County, 1972—76, Calif. Commn. Adminstrn. Svcs. Hosp., 1975—79, Profl. Practice Systems, 1990—92, Med. Specialty Mgrs., 1990—2004, St. Joseph Med. Corp., 1993—98; v.p. Found. Med. Care Children's Hosp., 1988—89; v.p., sr. v.p. St. Joseph Med. Corp. IPA, 1995—98; sr. v.p. Orange Coast Managed Care Svcs., 1995—98, Paragon Med. Imaging, 1993—2003, Calif. Managed Imaging, 1994—2004, Alliance Premier Hosps., 1995—96; chmn. bd. dirs. Children's Healthcare Calif., 1995—2002, hon. chmn., bd. dirs., 2003—; corp. mem. Blue Shield Calif., 1995—2002; mem. physician's rev. com. Blue Cross Calif., 1996—2004, mem. Blue Shield coun. advisors, 2001—04. Mem. editorial bd. Western Jour. Medicine; contbr. articles to med. jours. Founder Orange County Performing Arts Ctr., mem. Laguna Art Mus., Laguna Festival of Arts, Opera Pacific, S. Coast Reportory, Am. Ballet Theater, World Affairs Council. Served to capt. M.C., U.S. Army, 1958-60. Recipient Rea sr. med. prize U. Ill, 1953; William Cook scholar U. Ill., 1951, Friend of Children award Children's Hosp. Guild, 1995, Charley award Children's Hosp., 1996. Fellow Am. Coll. Radiology; mem. AMA, Am. Heart Assn., Soc. Nuclear Medicine (trustee 1961-62), Orange County Radiol. Soc. (pres. 1968-69), Calif. Radiol. Soc. (pres. 1978-79), Radiol. Soc. So. Calif. (pres. 1976), Pacific Coast Pediatric Radiologists Assn. (pres. 1971), Soc. Pediatric Radiology, Calif. Med. Assn. (chmn. sect. on radiology 1978-79), Orange County Med. Assn. (chmn. UCI liaison com. 1976-78), Cardioradiology Soc. So. Calif., Radiol. Soc. N.Am., Am. Roentgen Ray Soc., Am. Coll. Physician Execs., Soc. Chmn. Radiologists Children Hosp., Center Club, Sports Club (Irvine), Phi Beta Kappa, Phi Eta Sigma, Omega Beta Phi, Alpha Omega Alpha. Office: 1201 W La Veta Ave Orange CA 92868-4213 Office Phone: 714-771-8171. Personal E-mail: romarsh@aol.com.

ROWEN, RUTH HALLE, musicologist, educator; b. N.Y.C., Apr. 5, 1918; d. Louis and Ethel (Fried) Halle; m. Seymour M. Rowen, Oct. 13, 1940; children: Mary Helen Rowen, Louis Halle Rowen. BA, Barnard Coll., 1939; MA, Columbia U., 1941, PhD, 1948. Mgmt. ednl. dept. Carl Fischer, Inc., N.Y.C., 1954-63; assoc. prof. musicology CUNY, 1967-72, prof., 1972—, mem. doctoral faculty in musicology, 1967—. Author: Early Chamber Music, 1948, reprinted, 1974; (with Adele T. Katz) Hearing-Gateway to Music, 1959, (with William Simon) Jolly Come Sing and Play, 1956, Music Through Sources and Documents, 1979, (with Mary Rowen) Instant Piano, 1979, 80, 83, Symphonic and Chamber Music Score and Parts Bank, 1996; contbr. articles to profl. jours. Mem. ASCAP, Am. Musicol. Soc., Music Library Assn., Coll. Music Soc., Nat. Fedn. Music Clubs (nat. musicianship chmn. 1962-74, nat. young artist auditions com. 1964-74, N.Y. state chmn. Young Artist Auditions 1981, dist. coord. 1983, nat. bd. dirs. 1989-2000, rep. UN 1991-2000), N.Y. Fedn. Music Clubs (pres.), Phi Beta Kappa Home: 115 Central Park West At 25D New York NY 10023-4153 *Opportunity grows with each constructive thought.*

ROWEN, SHARON MARIE, journalist, photographer; d. Kenneth Wade Rowen and Dorothy May (Lowe) Rowen. AS, No. Okla. Coll., 1992; B. A. Journalism in Journalism, U. Ctrl. Okla., 2001. Photographer Am. Studios, Ponca City, Okla., 1994—98; sports writer The Vista, Edmond, Okla., 2001; sports editor Blackwell (Okla.) Jour. Tribune, 2002; copy editor Ark. City (Kans.) Traveler, 2003—. Office: Arkansas City Traveler 200 E Fifth Ave Arkansas City KS 67005 Office Phone: 620-442-2400. Personal E-mail: rowen70@hotmail.com. E-mail: newsdesk@arkcity.net.

ROWLAND, ALLEN R. grocery company executive; With Albertson's, Boise, 1971, various positions to sr. v.p. various cities, 1971-96; pres., COO Smith's Food & Drug Ctrs., 1996-97; pres., CEO, dir. Winn-Dixie Stores, Inc., Jacksonville, Fla., 1999—. Office: Winn-Dixie Stores Inc 5050 Edgewood Ct Jacksonville FL 32254-3699

ROWLAND, ARTHUR RAY, librarian; b. Hampton, Ga., Jan. 6, 1930; s. Arthur and Jennie (Goodman) R.; m. Jane Thomas, July 1, 1955; children: Dell Ruth, Anna Jane. AB, Mercer U., Macon, Ga., 1951; M. Librarianship, Emory U., 1952; postgrad., Oxford U., 1989. Circulation asst. Ga. State Coll. Library, 1952, circulation librarian, 1952-53; librarian Armstrong Coll., Savannah, Ga., 1954-56; head circulation dept. Auburn U. Library, 1956-58; librarian, assoc. prof. library sci. Jacksonville U., 1958-61, Augusta Coll., 1961-76, prof., libr., 1976-91, libr. emeritus, 1991—. Lectr. libr. edn. U. Ga., 1962-66; trustee Augusta-Richmond County Pub. Libr., 1980-93, pres. bd. trustees, 1983-85, v.p. bd., 1988-91; trustee Augusta Regional Libr., chmn., 1984-85; trustee East Cen. Ga. Regional Libr., 1987-93, chmn., 1988-91; chmn. Gov.'s Conf. on Ga. Librs. and Info. Svcs., 1977; del. White House Conf. on Librs. and Info. Sci., 1979; cons. on libr. mgmt. to Govt. of Indonesia, 1986. Author: Bibliography of the Writings of Georgia History, 1966, A Guide to the Study of Augusta and Richmond County, Georgia, 1967, (with Helen Callahan) Yesterday's Augusta, 1976, (with James E. Dorsey) A Bibliography of the Writings on Georgia History 1900-1970, rev. edit., 1978, (with Marguerite F. Fogleman) Reese Library Genealogical Resources, 1988, supplement, 1990, Goodman Cousins, 1988, Rowland Cousins, 1990, New Guide to the Study of Augusta, 1990, Index to City Directory of Augusta, Georgia, 1841-1879, 1991, More Goodman Cousins, 1993, My Fair Grandmother, 1994, Distant Cousins, The Huguenots Connecting Rowland, Bulloch, de Bourdeaux, DeVeaux and Roosevelt Families of S.C., N.C. and Ga., 1995, The Bessent Family of Georgia, 1995, Reeves Family of Georgia, 1996, Descendants of Wiley Reeves, 1996, Rowland-Huckaby Connections, 1996, Georgia Almanacs, 1996, Rowland Family of Virginia, North Carolina and Georgia and Beyond, 1998, Atkinson Family in Virginia, 1998, Ancestors of David Jackson, 1998, Ancestors of Rachael Hines Lewis, 1998, Ancestors of Elizabeth Proctor in Virginia and England, 1998, Ancestors of Martha Whitehead, 1998, Wiley Reeves, His Descendants and Ancestors, 1999, John Rowland, Immigrant, 2000, Reeves Family in England, Virginia, North Carolina, Georgia and Beyond, 2000, The Mississippi Branch of the Rowland Family, 2000, Ancestors and Connections of Dunbar Rowland, 2000, Printing in Louisville, 2000, Confederate Printing in Augusta, Ga., 2000, Goodman Family of N.C., Ga. and Beyond Their Cherokee Indian Heritage, 2000, Hillhouse Family of Wash., Ga., 2000, Printing in Wash., Ga., 2000, Jacob Martin Hugenot of Charleston, S.C., 2000, John Gensel of Charleston, S.C., 2000, Bessent Family, 2000, Rowland Faimly in Ga., 2000, Printers of Augusta, Georgia, 1786-1900, 2003, Printing in Milledgeville, Georgia, 2003, Preliminary Checklist of Penfield, Georgia Imprints, 2003, A Preliminary Checklist of Georgia Imprints, 1763-1860, 2003, Civil War Marriages Richmond County, Georgia, 2004, Grocers, Butchers, Baker and Others, 2004, 1890 Census of Augusta and Richmond County Georgia, 2004; editor: Reference Services, 1964, Historical Markers of Richmond County, Georgia, rev. edit., 1971, The Catalog and Cataloging, 1969, The Librarian and Reference Service, 1977, Reminiscences of Augusta Marines, 1985; supervising editor (with Heard Robertson) Jour. Archibald Campbell, 1981; contbr. to profl. jours. V.p. Ga. Libr. Assn. Trustees and Friends, 1989-91. With USN, 1948-49. Recipient Nix-Jones award for disting. service Ga. Library Assn., 1981, Town and Gown award Augusta Coll. Alumni Assn., 1985. Mem. ALA, Am. Assn. State and Local History, Bibliog. Soc. Am., Southeastern Libr. Assn. (hon. life, exec. bd. 1971-72), Ga. Libr. Assn. (hon. life, 2d v.p. 1965-67, 71-73, 1st v.p., pres.-elect 1973-75, pres. 1975-77, chmn. budget com. 1977-79, adv. to pres. 1979-83, 85-92), Ctrl. Savannah River Area Libr. Assn. (past pres., editor union list of serials 1967), Duval County Libr. Assn. (past v.p.), Nat. Geneal. Soc., Ga. Geneal. Soc., N.C. Geneal. Soc., Va. Geneal. Soc., Augusta Geneal. Soc., Richmond County Hist. Soc. (curator 1964-91, pres. 1967-69, founder, editor Richmond County History), Huguenot Soc. S.C., Ga. Hist. Soc. (curator emeritus), Ga. Bapt. Hist. Soc., Nat., Young Men's Libr. Assn. (v.p. 1988-91), Ga. Trusts for Hist. Preservation, Hist. Augusta (trustee emeritus), Soc. Ga. Archivists, Kappa Phi Kappa. Baptist. Address: One Seventh St Ste 1503 Augusta GA 30901 E-mail: RRow999@aol.com.

ROWLAND, DAVID JACK, retired academic administrator; b. Columbus, Ohio, June 17, 1921; s. David Henry and Ethel (Ryan) R.; m. Mary Ellen Stinson, Apr. 8, 1944; children: David Allen, Ryan Stinson, Sue Ellen Rowland Summers. BS, Ohio U., 1949; MA, U. Ala., 1951; LittD (hon.), Athens State Coll., 1967; LLD (hon.), Jacksonville State U., 1969. Pres. Walker Coll., Jasper, Ala., 1956-88, chancellor, 1988-95; interim pres. U. Ala./Walker Coll., 1995-96; ret., 1996. Bd. dirs. First Nat. Bank, Jasper, first Comml. Bancshares, Birmingham, Ala.; chmn. Ala. ACT Bd., Tuscaloosa, 1968—; real estate developer. Wildlife columnist and illustrator. Chmn. Jasper Indsl. Bd., 1987—; commr. Ala. Mining commn., Jasper, 1976—; mem. Ala. Employer Guard Res. commn., Birmingham, 1988—; trustee Walker Coll.; chmn. adv. bd. Jasper Salvation Army; vice chmn. Walker County Human Resource Coun. Col. U.S. Army, 1942-46, ATO. Decorated Legion of Merit; recipient Silver Beaver award Boy Scouts Am., 1972; named to Ala. Sr. Citizen Hall of Fame. Mem. Res. Officers Assn. (pres. Jasper chpt.), Summit Club, Met. Dinner Club, Rotary (pres. Jasper 1967-68, Paul Harris fellow), Masons, Ala. Silver Hair Legislature. Avocations: tree farmer, growing christmas trees, wildfowl carver. Home: 1000 Valley Rd Jasper AL 35501-4925

ROWLAND, ESTHER E(DELMAN), retired dean; b. NYC, Apr. 12, 1926; d. Abraham Simon and Ida Sarah (Shifrin) Edelman; m. Lewis P. Rowland, Aug. 31, 1952; children: Andrew, Steven, Judith. BA, U. Wis., 1946; MA, Columbia U., 1948, MPhil, 1984; cert. in bioethics, Columbia U./Albert Einstein, 1996. Instr. in polit. sci. CCNY, 1947-51, Mt. Holyoke Coll., South Hadley, Mass., 1948-49; dir. health professions adv. bd. U. Pa., Phila., 1971-73; adviser to pre-profl. students Barnard Coll., N.Y.C., 1974-79, dean for pre-profl. students, 1980-93, assoc. dean studies, 1989-95; ret., 1995—. Proofreader Monthly Review, N.Y.C., 1997-2003. Mem. exec. com. Nat. Emergency Civil Liberties Com., N.Y.C., 1975-90; mem. exec. com. Women's Counseling Project, 1981-86. Mem. N.E. Assn. Health Professions Advisers (exec. com. 1973-74), N.E. Assn. Pre Law Advisors (exec. com. 1981-83, 85-86), Neurol. Inst. Aux., N.Y.C. Found. Sr. Citizens (ombudsman 1997-99), Aux. Am. Acad. Neurologists (exec. bd. 1999-2001). Home: 404 Riverside Dr New York NY 10025-1861 E-mail: eerowland@aol.com.

ROWLAND, FRANK SHERWOOD, chemistry professor; b. Delaware, Ohio, June 28, 1927; m. Joan Lundberg, 1952; children: Ingrid Drake, Jeffrey Sherwood. AB, Ohio Wesleyan U., 1948; MS, U. Chgo., 1951, PhD, 1952, DSc (hon.), 1989, Duke U., 1989, Whittier Coll., 1989, Princeton U., 1990, Haverford Coll., 1992, Clark U., 1996, U. East Anglia, 1996; LLD (hon.), Ohio Wesleyan U., 1989, Simon Fraser U., 1991, U. Calgary, 1997; laurea honoris causa, U. Urbino (Italy), 1998; DSc, Carleton Coll., 1998, Gustavus Adolphus Coll., 1997, Occidental Coll., 1998, Kanagawa Univ., Japan, 1999, LaTrobe U., Australia, 2000, U. Waterloo, Can., 2001, Ohio State U., 2002. Instr. chemistry Princeton (N.J.) U., 1952—56; asst. prof. chemistry U. Kans., 1956—58, assoc. prof. chemistry, 1958—63, prof. chemistry, 1963—64, U. Calif., Irvine, 1964—, dept. chmn., 1964—70, Aldrich prof. chemistry, 1985—89, Bren prof. chemistry, 1989—94, Bren rsch. prof., 1994—. Humboldt sr. scientist Fed. Republic Germany, 1981; chmn. Dahlem (Germany) Conf. on Changing Atmosphere, 1987; vis. scientist Japan Soc. for Promotion Sci., 1980; co-dir. western region Nat. Inst. Global Environ. Change, 1989—93; del. Internat. Coun. Sci. Unions, 1993—98; fgn. sec. NAS, 1994—2002, Korean Acad. Sci. Tech.; lectr., cons. in field; mem. ozone commn. Internat. Assn. Meteorology and Atmospheric Physics, 1980—88, hon. life mem., 1996, mem. commn. on atmospheric chemistry and global pollution, 1979—91; mem. acid rain peer rev. panel U.S. Office of Sci. and Tech., Exec. Office of White House, 1982—84; mem. vis. com. Max Planck Inst., Heidelberg and Mainz, Germany, 1982—96; ozone trends panel mem. NASA, 1986—88; chmn. Gordon Conf. Environ. Scis.-Air, 1987; mem. Calif. Coun. Sci. Tech., 1989—95; mem. exec. com. Tyler Prize, 1992—. Contbr. articles to profl. jours. Named to, GTE Acad. All-Am. Hall of Fame, 2000; recipient numerous awards including, John Wiley Jones award, Rochester Inst. Tech., 1975, Disting. Faculty Rsch. award, U. Calif., Irvine, 1976, Profl. Achievement award, U. Chgo., 1977, Billard award, N.Y. Acad. Sci., 1977, Tyler World Prize in Environ. Achievement, 1983, Global 500 Roll of Honor for Environ. Achievement, UN Environment Program, 1988, Dana award for Pioneering Achievements in Health, 1987, Silver medal, Royal Inst. Chemistry U.K., 1989, Wadsworth award, N.Y. State Dept. Health, 1989, medal, U. Calif. Irvine, 1989, Japan prize in Environ. Sci., 1989, Dickson prize, Carnegie-Mellon U., 1991, Albert Einstein prize, World Cultural Coun., 1994, Nobel Prize in chemistry, 1995, Alumni medal, U. Chgo., 1997, Nevada medal, 1997; fellow Guggenheim Found., 1962, 1974. Fellow: AAAS (pres.-elect 1991, pres. 1992, chmn. bd. dirs. 1993), Am. Geophys. Union (Roger Revelle medal 1994), Am. Phys. Soc. (Leo Szilard award for physics in pub. interest 1979); mem.: NAS (co-DATA com. 1977—82, com. atmospheric scis., solar-terrestial com. 1979—83, sci. com. on problems environment 1986—89, bd. environ. studies and toxicology 1986—91, com. on atmospheric chemistry 1987—89, Infinite Voyage film com. 1988—92, Robertson Meml. lectr. 1993, chmn. com. on internat. orgns. and programs 1993—2002, chmn. office of internat. affairs 1994—2002, co-chmn. interacad. panel 1995—2000, mem. exec. com. 2000—02, coun. 1994—2002), Academia Bibliotheca Alexandrinae, Inst. Medicine, Am. Philos. Soc., Am. Meteorol. Soc. (hon.), Korean Acad. Sci. Tech., European Acad. Arts, Scis. and Humanities, Am. Chem. Soc. (chmn. divsn. nuclear sci. and tech. 1973—74, chmn. divsn. phys. chemistry 1974—75, E.F. Smith lectureship 1980, Orange County award 1975, Tolman medal 1976, Zimmerman award 1980, Environ. Sci. and Tech. award 1983, Esselen award 1987, Peter Debye Phys. Chem. award 1993), Am. Acad. Arts and Scis., Sigma Xi, Phi Beta Kappa. Home: 4807 Dorchester Rd Corona Del Mar CA 92625-2718 Office: U Calif Irvine Dept Chemistry 571 Rowland Hall Irvine CA 92697-2025 E-mail: rowland@uci.edu.

ROWLAND, HOWARD RAY, mass communications educator; b. Eddy County, N.Mex., Sept. 9, 1929; s. Lewis Marion and Ursula Lorene (Hunt) R.; m. Meredith June Lee, Apr. 19, 1951; children: Runay Ilene Olson, Rhonda Lee Fisher. B in Journalism, U. Mo., 1950; MS in Journalism, So. Ill. U., 1959; PhD, Mich. State U., 1969. Feature writer Springfield (Mo.) Newspapers, Inc., 1954; newspaper editor Monett (Mo.) Times, 1954-55; edtl. writer So. Ill. U., Carbondale, 1955-59; pub. rels. dir. St. Cloud (Minn.) State U., 1959-86, asst. dean, 1986-87, 88-90; dir. Ctr. for British Studies, Alnwick, Eng., 1987-88, 90-91. Emeritus prof. St. Cloud State U., 1991—; cons. Conf. of Campus Ombudsmen, Berkeley, 1971; recorder Seminar on Fund Raising, Washington, 1985; bibliographer Higher Edn. Bibliography Yearbook, 1987. Author: American Students in Alnwick Castle, 1990, St. Cloud State University—125 Years, 1994, Big War, Small Town, 2003; editor: Effective Community Relations, 1980; sect. editor: Handbook of Institutional Advancement, 1986; author book revs. Chair All-Am. City Com., St. Cloud, 1973-74. With U.S. Army, 1951-53. NDEA doctoral fellow Mich. State U., 1967-69; recipient Appreciation award Mayor of St. Cloud, 1974, Disting Svc. award Coun. for Advancement and Support Edn., 1985. Mem. Soc. of Profl. Journalists (Minn. chpt. pres. 1963-64, dep. dir. 1965-67), Coun. for Advancement and Support of Edn. (dist. 5 chair 1977-79, Leadership award 1979), Phi Delta Kappa (Mich. State U. chpt. pres. 1968-69, St. Cloud State Univ. chpt. pres. 1978-79). Presbyterian. Avocations: writing, fishing, travel, photography, antiques. Home: 29467 Kraemer Lake Rd Saint Joseph MN 56374-9646 Personal E-mail: rjrowland@mymailstation.com. *Striving to achieve is more rewarding than striving to succeed. Achievement brings personal satisfaction more fulfilling than recognition and compensation.*

ROWLAND, JAMES RICHARD, electrical engineering educator; b. Muldrow, Okla., Jan. 24, 1940; s. Richard Cleveland and Imogene Beatrice (Angel) R.; m. Jonell Condren, Aug. 24, 1963 (dec. May 1991); children: Jennifer Lynn, Angela Janel; m. Mary Anderson, Jan. 2, 1995. BSEE, Okla. State U., 1962; MSEE, Purdue U., 1964, PhD in Elec. Engring., 1966. Registered profl. engr., Okla. Instr. Purdue U., West Lafayette, Ind., 1964-65; from asst. to assoc. prof. Ga. Inst. Tech., Atlanta, 1966-71; from assoc. to full prof. Okla. State U., Stillwater, 1971-85; prof., chmn. dept. elec. and computer engring. U. Kans., Lawrence, 1985-89, prof., 1985—. Cons. Lockheed-Ga. Co., Marietta, 1966-71, U.S. Army Missile Command, Huntsville, Ala., 1969-79, Sandia Nat. Labs., Albuquerque, 1979, Puritan-Bennett, Lenexa, Kans., 1992. Author: Linear Control Systems, 1986; mem. editorial adv. bd. Computer and Elec. Engring., 1971-98; co-contbr. 60 articles to profl. jours. Fellow IEEE (edn. soc. pres. 1982-83, Centennial medal 1984, edn. soc. Achievement award 1986, edn. conf. award 1988, Region 5 Oustanding Educator award 1995, Svc. award 2002), Am. Soc. Engring. Edn. (dir. grad. div. 1987-89, Midwest sec. chair 2001-02), Eta Kappa Nu (dir. 1989-91), Kiwanis. Republican. Baptist. Avocations: golf, gardening. Home: 2424 Free State Ct Lawrence KS 66047-2831 Office: U Kans Dept Elec Engring & Computer Sci 2001 Eaton Hall Lawrence KS 66045 E-mail: jrowland@ku.edu.

ROWLAND, JOHN ARTHUR, lawyer; b. Joliet, Ill., Mar. 6, 1943; s. John Fornof and Grace Ada (Baskerville) R.; children: Sean B., Keira L. BA, U. Notre Dame, 1965; JD, U. San Francisco, 1968. Bar: Calif. 1969, U.S. Dist. Ct. (no. dist.) Calif. 1982, U.S. Dist. Ct. (ctrl. dist.) Calif. 1998. Asst. dist. atty. San Francisco Dist. Atty.'s Office, 1971-81; assoc. Ropers, Majeski, Kohn and Bentley, San Francisco, 1982—, ptnr., 1985—. Pres., South of Market Boys, San Francisco, 1981. Served to capt. U.S. Army, 1969-71, Korea. Recipient Commendation San Francisco Bd. Suprs., 1981, Merit award Mayor of San Francisco, 1982. Mem.: Am. Bd. Trial Advocates. Roman Catholic. Office: Ropers Majeski Kohn and Bentley 333 Market St Ste 3150 San Francisco CA 94105 Office Phone: 415-274-6311.

ROWLAND, KYLA FAYE, gospel songwriter; b. LaFollette, Tenn., Aug. 11, 1945; d. William Kyle and Eulalia Faye Martin; m. Bobby Dwayne Mullins, Mar. 1, 1991;; children: Shellie Allyson Kinard, Barry Nelson. Songwriter WORD Music, Nashville, 1976—84, Gt. RM Pub., Morristown, Tenn., 1984—95; spkr. Kyla Rowland Ministries, Morristown, Tenn., 1990—; pres., author, songwriter My Abby Pub., Morristown, Tenn., 1998—; author, songwriter Daywind Records, Nashville, 2001—; radio host, syndicated program Everyday Life, Tenn., 2003—. Coord. Pigeon River Revival, Pigeon Forge, Tenn., 2001—. Author: Between Me And The Storm, Girl Talk; composer: (southern gospel song) There Rose A Lamb (Dove Award and Singing News Song Of Yr., 1993). Republican. Baptist. Avocations: cooking, reading. Office: My Abby Publishing LLC PO Box 11 Morristown TN 37815 Personal E-mail: kyla72@hotmail.com. E-mail: kyla72@hotmail.com.

ROWLAND, LANDON HILL, diversified holding company executive; b. Fuquay Springs, N.C., May 20, 1937; s. Walter Elton and Elizabeth Carr (Williams) R.; m. Sarah Fidler, Dec. 29, 1959; children: Sarah Elizabeth, Matthew Hill, Joshua Carr. BA, Dartmouth Coll., 1959; LL.B., Harvard U., 1962. Bar: Mo. Assoc. Watson, Ess, Marshall & Enggas, Kansas City, Mo., 1962-70, ptnr., 1970-80; v.p. Kansas City So. Industries, Inc., 1980-83, pres., chief oper. officer, 1983-86, pres., chief exec. officer, 1987—, also bd. dirs.; pres., chief exec. officer Kansas City So. Ry. Co., 1990-91, chmn., 1990—. Lectr. antitrust law U. Mo. Kansas City; chmn. DST Systems, 1983—. Co-author West's Mo. Practice Series. Trustee Midwest Rsch. Inst., Kansas City, Mo.; chmn. bd. dirs. Swope Ridge Health Care Ctr.; bd. dirs. Lyric Opera of Kansas City, Am. Royal, Jacob L. & Ella C. Loose Found.; chmn. Met. Performing Arts Fund. Mem. ABA, Mo. Bar Assn., Phi Beta Kappa. Clubs: Kansas City Country, Kansas City, River. Home: Ever Glades Farm 12717 NE Mt Olivet Rd Kansas City MO 64166-1236 Office: Stilwell Financial Inc 920 Main St Kansas City MO 64105-2008

ROWLAND, LEWIS PHILLIP, neurology educator, editor, clinical investigator; b. Bklyn., Aug. 3, 1925; s. Henry Alexander and Cecile (Coles) Rowland; m. Esther Edelman Rowland, Aug. 31, 1952; children: Andrew Simon, Steven Samuel, Joy Rosenthal. BS, Yale U., 1945, MD, 1948; doctorate (hon.), U. Aix-Marseilles, France, 1986, U. Padua, 1996. Diplomate Am. Bd. Psychiatry and Neurology. Intern New Haven Hosp., 1949-50; asst. resident N.Y. Neurol. Inst., 1950-52, fellow, 1953; clin. assoc. NIH, Bethesda, Md., 1953-54; practice rsch. medicine, specializing in neurology N.Y.C., 1954-67, Phila., 1967-73, N.Y.C., 1973—; asst. neurologist Montefiore Hosp., N.Y.C., 1954-57; vis. fellow Nat. Inst. Med. Rsch., London, 1956; from asst. prof. to prof. neurology Columbia Coll. Physicians and Surgeons, 1957-67, prof. dept. neurology, 1973—, chmn. dept. neurology, 1973-98; prof., chmn. dept. neurology U. Pa. Med. Sch., 1967-73; from asst. neurologist to attending neurologist Presbyn. Hosp., 1957-67; co-dir. Neurol. Clin. Rsch. Ctr., 1961-67, dir. neurology svc., 1973-98, attending neurologist, 1973—, pres. med. bd., 1991-94. Cons. Harlem Hosp., 1973—; mem. med. adv. bd. Myasthenia Gravis Found., pres., 1971-73; med. adv. bd. Muscular Dystrophy Assocs., Nat. Multiple Sclerosis Soc., N.Y.C. Multiple Sclerosis Soc., 1977-92, Com. to Combat Huntington's Disease; chmn. med. adv. bd. N.Y.C. Multiple Sclerosis Soc. 1977-92; pres. Parkinson's Disease Found., 1979-; mem. tng. grants com. Nat. Inst. Neurol. Disorders and Stroke, NIH, 1971-73, bd. sci. counselors, 1978-83, chmn., 1981-83, mem. nat. adv. coun., 1986-90, cons. to dir., 2000-01. Mem. editl. bd. Archives of Neurology, 1968-76, Advances in Neurology, 1969—, Italian Jour. Neurol. Sci., 1979—99, Handbook of Clin. Neurology, 1982—, New Eng. Jour. Medicine, 1990-2000, Med. Letter, 1990-97, Jour. Neurol. Sci., 1991—, Jour. Neuromuscular Disorders, 1991-97, Clin. Neurosci., 1995-98; editor-in-chief Neurology, 1977-87, Neurology Today, 2001—; assoc. editor Medlink, 1995—. With USNR, 1942-44; with USPHS, 1953-54. Mem. Am. Neurol. Assn. (pres. 1980, hon. mem. 1989—), Am. Acad. Neurology (pres.-elect 1987-89, pres. 1989-91, hon. mem. 1997—), Phila. Neurol. Soc. (pres. 1972), Assn. Rsch. Nervous Mental Disease (pres. 1969, trustee 1976—, v.p. 1980, chmn. bd. trustees 1992-98), Assn. Univ. Profs. Neurology (sec. 1971-74, pres. 1978), Am. Acad. Neurol. Found. (pres. 1996, chair bd. trustees 1997-99), Ea. Pa. Multiple Sclerosis Soc. (chmn. med. adv. bd. 1969-73, trustee 1999—); hon. mem. Neurol. Socs. France, Poland, Can., Europe, Italy, Gt. Britain, Spain, Japan. Home: 404 Riverside Dr New York NY 10025-1861 Office: Columbia-Presbyn Med Ctr Neurological Inst 710 W 168th St New York NY 10032-2603 Office Phone: 212-305-8551. E-mail: lpr1@columbia.edu.

ROWLAND, PLEASANT, publisher, toy company executive; m. Jerry Frautschi. Grad., Wells Coll., 1962. Elem. tchr. Mass., Calif., Ga. and N.J.; TV news reporter, anchor KGO-TV, San Francisco; v.p. Boston Ednl. Rsch. Co., 1971-78; pub. Children's Mag. Guide, 1981-89; founder, pres. Pleasant Co., 1986—; vice chmn. Mattell, 1998—. Named one of 12 Outstanding Entrepreneurs, Inst. Am. Entrepreneurs, 1990, one of Am.'s Top 50 Women Bus. Owners, Working Women mag., 1993-98; recipient Best and Brightest in Mktg. award Advt. Age, 1993, Mem. Internat. Women's Forum, Com. of 200. Office: Pleasant Co/Am Girl 8400 Fairway Place PO Box 998 Middleton WI 53562-0998

ROWLAND, RALPH THOMAS, retired architect; b. Elizabeth, N.J., Oct. 10, 1920; s. Thomas Aloysius and Anna Frances (McQuaid) R.; m. Bernice Barbara Cannizzo, Sept. 7, 1946; children: Glenn Thomas, Mark Louis, Roy Joseph, Lisa Rowland Majewski. Student, Manhattan Coll., 1937-38, Columbia U., 1945-49. Archtl. field supr., specifier Voorhees Walker Foley & Smith, N.Y.C., 1945-50; specifier, project mgr. Sargent Webster Crenshaw & Folley, Watertown, N.Y., 1951-53; pvt. practice Hamden, Conn., 1958-65; field supr. Fletcher Thompson, Inc., Bridgeport, Conn., 1954-56, project mgr., 1957, 65-73, asso., 1969-73, v.p., 1973-81, dir. archtl. research, 1981-85, adv. coun., 1994-98. Chmn. Conn. Bldg. Code Standards Com., 1978-82; vice chmn. Conn. State Codes and Standards Com., 1982-86; cons. in field. Editorial chmn.: Conn. Architect Mag., 1966-74; project mgr. design, St. Vincents Med. Center, Bridgeport. Mem. Cheshire Planning Commn., 1966-72, chmn., 1967-68; pres. Hamden C. of C., 1964, New Eng. Bldg. Code Assn., 1989; mem. Cen. Naugatuck Valley Regional Planning Agy., 1966-74, chmn., 1969; mem. Cheshire Democratic Town Com., 1960-70, treas., 1963-69; mem. Conn. Archtl. Sch. Task Force, 1987-88. With USN, 1942-45. Fellow AIA; mem. AIA Conn. (past pres.), AARP (pres. Cheshire chpt. 1995-97), Conn. Bldg. Ofcls. Assn., Cheshire C. of C. Roman Catholic. Home: 201 N Rolling Acres Rd Cheshire CT 06410-2119

ROWLAND, RANDALL G. urologist; b. Springfield, Ill., May 14, 1947; BS, Northwestern U., 1969, PhD, 1971, MD, 1972. Diplomate Am. Bd. Urology. Urology faculty Ind. U. Sch. Med., Indpls., 1978-97; prof., James F. Glenn chair of urology U. Ky. Coll. Med., Lexington, 1997—. Office: U Kentucky Divsn Urology MS 283 800 Rose St Lexington KY 40536-0298 E-mail: rrowlan@uky.edu.

ROWLAND, RHONDA STOCKTON, mathematician, educator; b. Farmville, Va., Jan. 22, 1955; d. Ronald William and Frances (Abbott) Stockton; m. Michael Alan Rowland, Aug. 9, 1975. BS in Math., Longwood U., 1976. Profl. tchg. cert. Va. Tchr. Math. Charlotte County Pub. Schs., Charlotte Court House, Va., 1976—90, Prince Edward County Pub. Schs., Farmville, Va., 1990—. Recipient Outstanding Young Educator, Jaycees, 1996. Mem.: Prince Edward Coun. Tchrs. Math. (Outstanding Secondary Math. Tchr. 2001, H.S. Tchr. of Yr. 2004), Va. Coun. Tchrs. Math. (Tchr. of Yr. 2004), Nat. Coun. Tchrs. Math., Phi Kappa Phi, Alpha Delta Kappa (chaplain). Baptist. Avocations: cross stitch, reading, collecting small Christmas trees, rubber stamping, collecting cookbooks. Home: 3832 Farmville Rd Farmville VA 23901 Office: Prince Edward County HS 35 Eagle Dr Farmville VA 23901

ROWLAND, ROBERT ALEXANDER, III, lawyer; b. McAllen, Tex., Apr. 27, 1943; s. Robert Alexander Jr and Marguerite (Gerry) Rowland; m. Victoria Nalle, Apr. 2, 1977; children: Julia Marie, Emily Nalle. BS, Tex. A&M U., 1966; JD, George Washington U., 1972. Bar: Tex. 1972, U.S. Dist. Ct. (so. dist.) Tex. 1973, U.S. Ct. Appeals (5th cir.) 1973, U.S. Supreme Ct. 1976, U.S. Dist. Ct. (no. dist.) Tex. 1979, U.S. Dist. Ct. (we. dist.) Tex. 1982, U.S. Dist. Ct. (ea. dist.) Tex. 1983. Law clk. U.S. Ct. Appeals (5th cir.), Houston, 1973-74; assoc. Vinson & Elkins, Houston, 1975-81; ptnr. Susman, Godfrey & McGowan, Houston, 1982—88; mng. dir. Johnson and Gibbs, Houston, 1988-91; ptnr. Hutcheson & Grundy, LLP, Houston, 1992-94; chmn., CEO Associated Counsel of Am., 1995—; ptnr. Roach & Rowland, Houston, 2003—. Bd. dirs. Vol. Ctr., Houston, 1975—84, pres., 1982—83; founding mem., bd. dirs. Tex. Accts. and Lawyers for Arts, 1979—92, pres., 1989—91; mem. devel. coun. Sch. Liberal Arts Tex. A&M U., 1992—, mem. devel. coun. George Bush Sch. Govt. and Pub. Svc., 2004—; co-chmn. Mayor's Transition Com. for Parks, City of Houston, 1992—94; candidate for State Rep., Tex. Legis. Dist. 134, Rep. Primary, 2002; mem. fin. com. Harris County Rep. Party, 2002—; bd. dirs. United Reps. of Harris County, 2002—; mem. Mission Outreach coun. Christ Ch. Cathedral, 2002—, chmn., 2004—, mem. "C" Club, 2004—; bd. dirs. Contemporary Art Mus. Houston, 1974—80, 1991—94; bd. dirs. Sarah Campbell Blaffer Gallery of Art U. Houston, 1989—94; bd. dirs. Tex. Opera Theater, 1988—89, Houston Pks. Bd., 1993—, chmn., 2003—; bd. dirs. Nat. Recreation and Pk. Assn., 1992—95, Cultural Arts Coun., Houston, 1981—86, Pk. People Inc., 1979—2001, pres., 1991—92, chmn. Endowment Com., 1994—. Capt. U.S. Army, 1966—69, Vietnam. Fellow: Tex. Bar Found., Houston Bar Found.; mem.: Houston Young Lawyers Assn. (bd. dirs. 1975—79, pres. 1978—79), State Bar Tex., Houston Bar Assn. (dir. 1979—88, sec. 1984—85, chmn. law and art com. 1984—85, 2d v.p. 1985—86), Coronado Club, River Oaks Country Club, Phi Delta Phi. Episcopalian. Home: 2010 Chilton Rd Houston TX 77019-1502 Office: Associated Counsel Am Inc Ste 125 4605 Post Oak Pl Houston TX 77027-9744 Office Phone: 713-840-7100. Personal E-mail: wickr@swbell.net. Business E-Mail: rob@robrowland.com.

ROWLANDS, DAVID THOMAS, pathology educator; b. Wilkes-Barre, Pa., Mar. 22, 1930; s. David Thomas and Anna Jule (Morgan) R.; m. Gwendolyn Marie York, Mar. 1, 1958; children: Julie Marie, Carolyn Jane. MD, U. Pa., 1955. Diplomate: Am. Bd. Pathology, Am. Bd. Allergy and Immunology. Intern Pa. Hosp., Phila., 1955-56; resident Cin. Gen. Hosp., 1956-60; asst. prof. U. Colo., 1962-64, Rockefeller U., 1964-66; assoc. prof. Duke U., Durham, N.C., 1966-70; prof. pathology U. Pa., Phila., 1970-82, chmn. dept. pathology, 1973-78, prof. medicine, 1979-82; prof., chmn. dept. pathology U. So. Fla., Tampa, 1982-91, assoc. dean, 1983-84, prof. pediatrics, 1986-91; med. dir. Lifelink Tissue Bank, 1991-93. Mem. editorial bd.: Am. Jour. Pathology, 1971-81, Developmental and Comparative Immunology, 1977-79. Served with USNR, 1960-62. Recipient Lederle Med. Faculty award U. Colo., 1964, Jacob Ehrenzeller award Pa. Hosp., 1976 Mem. Am. Assn. Pathologists, Internat. Acad. Pathology, Am. Soc. Clin. Pathology, Am. Assn. Immunologists, Coll. Am. Pathologist, Arthur Purdy Stout Soc. Presbyterian. Home: 13804 Cypress Village Cir Tampa FL 33618-8406 Office Phone: 813-974-0745.

ROWLANDS, GENA, actress; b. Cambria, Wis., June 19, 1936; d. Edwin Merwin and Mary Allen (Neal) R.; m. John Cassavetes (dec.); children: Nicholas, Alexandra, Zoe. Student, U. Wis., Am. Acad. Dramatic Art, NYC.

Theatrical appearance include The Middle of the Night, 1956; Actress: (films) including The High Cost of Loving, 1958, Lonely Are The Brave, 1962, A Child is Waiting, 1962, Spiral Road, 1962, Faces, 1968, At Any Price, 1970, Minnie and Moscowitz, 1971, Woman Under the Influence, 1973, Two Minute Warning, 1976, Opening Night, 1977, The Brinks Job, 1978, One Summer Night, 1979, Gloria, 1980, Tempest, 1982, Love Streams, 1983, Light of Day, 1987, Another Woman, 1988, Once Around, 1990, Ted and Venus, 1991, Night on Earth, 1992, Silent Cries, 1993, Parallel Lives, 1994, Anything for John, 1995, Something to Talk About, 1995, The Neon Bible, 1995, Enfants de Salaud, 1996, Unhook the Stars, 1996, Hope Floats, 1997, She's so Lovely, 1997, The Mighty, 1997, Paulie, 1998, The Weekend, 1999, Taking Lives, 2004, The Notebook, 2004, (TV movies) A Question of Love, 1978, Strangers, 1979, Thurday's Child, 1983, Early Frost, 1986, The Betty Ford Story, 1987, Montana, Face of a Stranger, 1991 (Emmy award, Leading Actress in a Mini-Series or Special, 1992), Parallel Lives, 1994, Best of Friends for Life, 1996, Ljuset häller mig sållskap, 2000, Color of Love: Jacey's Story, 2000, Wild Iris, 2001, Hysterical Blindness, 2002, (Emmy award best supporting actress in TV movie, 2003), Charms for the Easy Life, 2002, The Incredible Mrs. Ritchie, 2003; numerous other TV appearances. Mem. Actors Equity Assn., Screen Actors Guild, AFTRA, Am. Guild Variety Artists.

ROWLETT, RALPH MORGAN, archaeologist, educator; b. Richmond, Ky., Sept. 11, 1934; s. Robert Kenny and Daisy (Mullikin) R.; m. Elsebet Sander-Jorgensen, Aug. 25, 1963 (div. Jan. 1986); children: Rolf Arvid, Erik Kenneth; m. Elizabeth Helen Dinan, Apr. 21, 1989 (div. Oct. 1995); 1 child, Helen Holly. Student, U. Ky., 1952-53; BA summa cum laude, Marshall U., 1956; postgrad., U. London, 1962-63; PhD, Harvard U., 1968. Instr. anthropology U. Mo., Columbia, 1965-67, asst. prof., 1967-69, assoc. prof., 1969-75, prof., 1975—. Postdoctoral fellow Ghent U., 1969 Co-author: Neolithic Levels on the Titelberg, Luxembourg, 1981, Meeting Anthropology Phase to Phase, 2000; anthropology editor Random House Unabridged Dictionary of English, 1980—; editor: Horizons and Styles, 1993, Horizons and Styles in West Eurasiatic Archaeology; developer thermoluminescence dating of flint, 1972; co-developer electron spin resonance dating of flint, 1981. 1st lt. arty., U.S. Army, 1956-58. Decorated officer Legion de Merit (Luxembourg); named Ky. col., 1976; grantee NSF, 1973-75, 76-79, 82-83, Svc. Archeologique de Neuchatel, 1989, British Coun., 1993, Acad. of Romania, 1996, Internat. Rsch. and Exch. Bd., 1997. Fellow Am. Anthrop. Assn.; mem. AAAS, Archaeol. Inst. Am., Soc. Am. Archaeology, Societe Prehistorique de Luxembourg, Societe Archeologique Champenoise, English Heritage, Palomino Horse Breeders Assn., Sigma Xi. Green Party. Mem. Christian Ch. (Disciples Of Christ). Home: Hollywell Hill 1197 State Road Ww Fulton MO 65251-5106 Office: Univ Mo Dept Anthropology Columbia MO 65211-0001 E-mail: rowlettR@missouri.edu.

ROWLETTE, HENRY ALLEN, JR., social worker, counseling psychologist; b. Phila., July 8, 1947; s. Henry Allen Sr. and Ophelia Alberta (Kilson) R.; m. Geraldine Lee Stevens, Mar. 1972 (div. Mar. 1986); children: Cessandra N., Deaeon D., Christiene A.; m. Carolyn Rowlette; 1 child, Janetta M.; m. Ann Laura Rowe, Mar. 19, 1989. BA, Cheyney State Coll., 1970; MEd, Boston U., 1981; MSW, Temple U., 1988; PhD, Suffield Coll. and Univ., 2003. Cert. sch. social worker, N.J.; lic. clin. social worker; diplomate Am. Psychotherapy Assn., Nat. Bd. Cognitive Behavioral Therapists; ordained minister Bapt. Ch. Cardiac monitor technician Bapt. Med. Ctr., Little Rock, 1982-83; mental health technician The Horsham Clinic, Ambler, Pa., 1984; psychiat. technician The Lower Bucks Hosp., Bristol, Pa., 1984-90; mental health technician The Helene Fuld Med. Ctr., Trenton, N.J., 1988-90, psychiat. social worker, 1988-92; profl. sch. social worker The Willingboro (N.J.) Sch. Dist., 1990—96. Dist. crisis intervention team Willingboro Sch. Dist., 1994-96; therapist The N.J. State Prison, Trenton, 1996-98, The Southwoods State Prison, Bridgeton, N.J.; clinician Kennedy Meml. Health Ctr., Cherry Hill, N.J., 1998—, The Lumberton Schs./Sch. Social Worker, Lumberton, N.J., 1998; behavioral cons. Founds. Behavioral Health, Willow Grove, Pa., 1999; mental health technician The Children's Hosp. Phila., 1999-2000. Clin. social worker Phila. Prison System, 2000; mem. NAACP, Trenton, 1990. With U.S. Army, 1971-79, U.S. Army Candidate Sch., 1975. Mem. NASW, Am. Assn. Christian Counselors, Omega Psi Phi (Delta Upsilon chpt.), Phi Delta Kappa (Trenton chpt.), Am. Psychotherapy Assn., Nat. Bd. Cognitive Behavioral Therapists, Nat. Bd. Addiction Examiners, Nat. Assn. Forensic Counselors. Democrat. Baptist. Avocations: fishing, reading, computer technology/games. Home: 18 Foxchase Dr Burlington NJ 08016-3044 Office Phone: 609-346-0880. Personal E-mail: rowlettejr@msn.com.

ROWLEY, BEVERLEY DAVIES, medical sociologist; b. Antioch, Calif., July 28, 1941; d. George M. and Eloise Davies; m. Richard B. Rowley, Apr. 1, 1966 (div. 1983). BS, Colo. State U., 1963; MA, U. Nev., 1975; PhD, Union Inst., 1983. Social worker Nev. Dept. Pub. Welfare, Reno, 1963-65, Santa Clara County Dept. Welfare, San Jose, Calif., 1965-66; field dir. Sierra Sage coun. Camp Fire Girls, Sparks, Nev., 1966-70; program coord. divsn. health scis. Sch. Medicine U. Nev., 1976-78, program coord., health analyst office rural health, 1978-84, acting dir. office rural health, 1982-84; exec. asst. to pres. Med. Coll. of Hampton Rds., Norfolk, Va., 1984-87; rsch. mgr. Office Med. Edn. Info. AMA, Chgo., 1987-88, dir. dept. data systems, 1988-91; dir. med. edn. Maricopa Med. Ctr., Phoenix, 1991-99; pres. Med. Edn. and Rsch. Assocs., Inc., Phoenix, Chgo., 1999—, Med. Edn. & Rsch. Assocs., Tempe, Ariz., 1999—; vis. prof. Ariz. State U. East, Mesa, 1999-2000, profl. and personal coach, 2004—. Various positions as adj. prof. and lectr. in health scis. U. Nev. Sch. of Medicine, 1972-75; lectr. dept. family and cmty. medicine U. Nev., 1978-84, asst. dir., evaluator Health Careers for Am. Indians Programs, 1978-84; cons. Nev. Statewide Health Survey, 1979-84; interim dir. Health Max, 1985-86; asst. prof. dept. family and cmty. medicine Med. Coll. of Hampton Rds., Norfolk, Va., 1985-87. Editor of five books; contbr. numerous articles to profl. jours. Mem. Am. Sociol. Assn., Nat. Rural Health Assn. (bd. dirs. 1986-88), Assn. Behavioral Sci. and Med. Edn. (pres. 1986), Assn. Am. Med. Colls. (exec. coun. 1993-95), Coun. Acad. Scis. (adminstrv. bd. 1992-97), Assn. Hosp. Med. Edn. (bd. dirs. 1997—), Delta Delta Delta. Achievements include development of three computer systems including AMA-FREIDA; four internet-based educational programs for physicians. Avocations: hiking, skiing, gardening, sewing, ceramics. Office: MERA Inc 8850 S Los Feliz Dr Tempe AZ 85284-3430 E-mail: BRowley@MERAInc.com.

ROWLEY, CHARLES KERSHAW, economics professor; b. June 21, 1939; came to U.S., 1984; s. Frank and Ellen (Beal) R.; m. Betty Silverwood, June 19, 1961 (div. 1971); m. Marjorie Isobel Spillets, July 17, 1972; children: Amanda, Sara. Lectr. U. Nottingham, Eng., 1962-65; lectr., then sr. lectr. U. Kent, Canterbury, Eng., 1970-72; prof. econs. U. Newcastle, Eng., 1972-83, George Mason U., Fairfax, Va., 1984—, Duncan Black prof. econs., 2000—. Gen. dir. John Locke Inst., 1989—, sr. rsch. assoc. Ctr. for Study of Pub. Choice, 1987-92; cons. Office Fair Trading, London, 1980-83; rsch. assoc. Wolfson Coll., Oxford, 1984—; program dir. in econs. and the law James M. Buchanan Ctr., 2000—. Author numerous books in econ. and law; editor: Pub. Choice, 1990—; contbr. articles to profl. jours. Grantee Bank of Eng., 1965, Social Sci. Rsch. Coun., London, 1970-72, Dept. Environ., London, 1974-80, Bradley Found., 1988—, Liberty Fund, 1990, 93, John M. Olin Found., 1986. Mem. Mont Pelerin Soc., Am. Econ. Assn., Royal Econ. Soc., Pub. Choice Soc. European Pub. Choice Soc. (pres. 1980-82). Home: 5188 Dungannon Rd Fairfax VA 22030-5414 Office: George Mason U Dept Econs 4400 University Dr Fairfax VA 22030-4444 Office Phone: 703-934-6934. Business E-Mail: crowley@gmu.edu.

ROWLEY, GEOFFREY HERBERT, management consultant; b. Harrow, Middlesex, Eng., Nov. 10, 1935; came to U.S., 1962; s. Herbert and Muriel Jessie (Nicolls) R. BA, Bristol (Eng.) U., 1958; cert. indsl. adminstrn., Glasgow (Scotland) U., 1962; MBA, Harvard U., 1964. Purchasing officer Pirelli Ltd., London, 1958-61; rsch. assoc. Assn. for Internat. Rsch., Inc., Cambridge, Mass., 1964-68, v.p., 1968—2002, cons. in expatriate compensation, 1964—. Lectr. in field; dir. U. Bristol Found., Inc. Contbr. articles to profl. jours. Served with Royal Navy, 1953-55. Mem. Am. Compensation Assn., Inst. for Human Resources, Brit. Ins. Mgmt., Harvard Club. Home: 11 Berkeley Pl Cambridge MA 02138-3411 E-mail: GH.Rowley@verizon.net., GHRowley@aol.com.

ROWLEY, GLENN HARRY, lawyer; b. Hyannis, Mass., May 16, 1948; s. Harold Frederick and Olive Nellie (Jones) R.; 1 child, Brewster Westgate. BBA, U. Mass., 1970; JD with cum laude, Western New Eng. Coll., 1980. Bar: Mass. 1980, U.S. Dist. Ct. Mass. 1980, U.S. Tax Ct. 1981, cert.: Nat. Elder Law Found./ABA (elder law atty.). Staff mem. Cape Cod Planning and Econ. Devel. Commn., Barnstable, Mass., 1975-76; staff, estate planning tax dept. Coopers and Lybrand, Springfield, Mass., 1980-81; legal assoc. Roberts and Farrell, West Chatham, Mass., 1982-84; ptnr. Roberts, Farrell & Rowley, West Chatham, 1984-97; pvt. practice Chatham, Mass., 1997—. Cons. Local Citizen Scholarship Trusts, Harwich and Chatham, Mass., 1985—. Contbr. (weekly news column) The Enterprise, others; contbr. articles to profl. jours. Founding mem. Brewster (Mass.) Conservation Trust, 1984; elected mem. Brewster Hist. Dist. Com., 1975; adv. bd. The May Inst., The Cape Cod Writers Ctr., Inc. With USN, 1971-74, Iceland. Recipient Am. Jurisprudence awards Lawyers Co-op. Pub. Co., 1978, 79. Mem. Mass. Bar Assn., Ocean Edge Exec. Club, Profl. Writers of Cape Cod, Cape Cod Estate Planning Coun., Nat. Acad. Elder Law Attys., Phi Delta Phi. Avocations: travel, writing. Home: Annaniases Knoll/Sheep Pond Brewster MA 02631 Office: The Marketplace PO Box 1489 26 George Ryder Rd S West Chatham MA 02669 Office Phone: 508-945-1000. E-mail: glennh.rowley@verizon.net.

ROWLEY, JANET DAVISON, physician; b. NYC, Apr. 5, 1925; d. Hurford Henry and Ethel Mary (Ballantyne) Davison; m. Donald A. Rowley, Dec. 18, 1948; children: Donald, David, Robert, Roger. PhB, U. Chgo., 1944, BS, 1946, MD, 1948; DSc (hon.), U. Ariz., 1989, U. Pa., 1989, Knox Coll., 1991, U. So. Calif., 1992, St. Louis U., 1997, St. Xavier U., 1999, Oxford (Eng.) U., 2000, Lund U., Sweden, 2003, Dartmouth U., 2004. Diplomate Am. Bd. Med. Genetics. Rsch. asst. U. Chgo., 1949—50; intern Marine Hosp., USPHS, Chgo., 1950—51; attending physician Infant Welfare and Prenatal Clinics Dept. Pub. Health, Montgomery County, Md., 1953—54; rsch. fellow Levinson Found., Cook County Hosp., Chgo., 1955—61; clin. instr. neurology U. Ill., Chgo., 1957—61; USPHS spl. trainee Radiobiology Lab. The Churchill Hosp., Oxford, England, 1961—62; rsch. assoc. dept. medicine and Argonne Cancer Rsch. Hosp. U. Chgo., 1962—69, assoc. prof. dept. medicine and Argonne Cancer Rsch. Hosp., 1969—77, prof. dept. medicine and Franklin McLean Meml. Rsch. Inst., 1977—84, Blum-Riese Disting. Svc. prof., dept. medicine and dept. molecular genetics and cell biology, 1984—, Blum-Riese Disting. Svc. prof. dept. human genetics, 1997—, interim dep. dean for sci. biol. scis. divsn., 2001—02. Bd. sci. counsellors Nat. Inst. Dental Rsch., NIH, 1972—76, chmn., 1974—76; mem. Nat. Cancer Adv. Bd., Nat. Cancer Inst., 1979—84, Nat. Adv. Coun. for Human Genome Rsch. Inst., 1999—; adv. com. Frederick Cancer Rsch. Facility, 1983—84; bd. sci. counsellors Nat. Human Genome Rsch. Inst., NIH, 1994—99, chmn., 1994—97; adv. bd. Howard Hughes Med. Inst., 1989—94, MD Anderson Cancer Ctr., 1998—; vis. com. dept. applied biol. scis. MIT Corp., 1983—86; bd. sci. cons. Meml. Sloan-Kettering Cancer Ctr., 1988—90; adv. com. Ency. Britannica U. Chgo., 1988—96; W. Jack Stuckey Jr. lectr. Tulane Career Ctr., 1996; Presdl. Symposium Am. Soc. Pediatric Hematology/Oncology, 1995; lectr. in field; mem. coun. adv. Internat. Geneminica Rsch. Inst., 2004—; mem. sci. adv. bd. Meml. Sloan-Kettering Cancer Ctr., 2004. Co-founder, co-editor: Genes, Chromosomes and Cancer, mem. editl. bd.: Oncology Rsch., Cancer Genetics and Cytogenetics, Internat. Jour. Hematology, Genomics, Internat. Jour. Cancer, Leukemia, past. mem. editl. bd.: Blood, Cancer Rsch., Hematol. Oncology, Leukemia Rsch.; contbr. chapters to books, articles to profl. jours. Adv. com. for career awards in biomed. scis. Burroughs Wellcome Fund, 1994—98; selection panel for Clin. Sci. award Doris Duke Charitable Found., 2000—02, 2004; mem. Pres.'s Adv. Coun. on Bioethics, 2001—; mem. med. rsch. material command leukemia program U.S. Army, 2002—; mem. selection com. Rosalind Franklin young investigator award, 2004; nat. adv. com. McDonnell Found. Program for Molecular Medicine in Cancer Rsch., 1988—98; adv. bd. Leukemia Soc. Am., 1979—84; selection com. scholar award in biomed. sci. Lucille P. Markey Charitable Trust, 1984—87; trustee Adler Planetarium, Chgo., 1978—; med. adv. bd. G&P Charitable Found., 1999—. Co-recipient Charles Mott prize, GM Cancer Rsch. Found., 1989; named Chicagoan of Yr., Chgo. mag., 1998; recipient First Kuwait Cancer prize, 1984, Esther Langer award, Ann Langer Cancer Rsch. Found., 1983, A. Cressy Morrison award in natural scis., N.Y. Acad. Scis., 1985, Past State Pres. award, Tex. Fedn. Bus. and Profl. Women's Clubs, 1986, Karnofsky award and lecture, Am. Soc. Clin. Oncology, 1987, Antoine Lacassagne Lique prize, Nat. Francaise Contre le Cancer, 1987, King Faisal Internat. prize in medicine (co-recipient), 1988, Katherine Berkan Judd award, Meml. Sloan-Kettering Cancer Ctr., 1989, Steven C. Beering award, U. Ind. Med. Sch, 1992, Robert de Villiers award, Leukemia Soc. Am., 1993, Kaplan Family prize for cancer rsch. excellence, Oncology Soc. Dayton, 1995, Cotlove award and lecture, Acad. Clin. Lab. Physicians and Scientists, 1995, Nilsson-Ehle lecture, Mendelian Soc. and Royal Physiographic Soc., 1995, The Gairdner Found. award, 1996, medal of honor, Basic Sci. Am. Cancer Soc., 1996, Nat. Medal of Sci., 1998, Lasker award for clin. scis., 1998, Woman Extraordinaire award, Internat. Women's Assocs., 1999, Golden Plate award, Am. Acad. Achievement, 1999, Women Achieving Excellence award, YWCA of Met. Chgo., 2000, Philip Levine award, Am. Soc. Clin. Pathology, 2001, Emile M Chamot award, State Microsurg. Soc. Ill., 2001, Mendel medal, Villanova U., 2003, Benjamin Franklin medal, Am. Philos. Soc., 2003, Dist. Alumni Award, U. Chgo., 2003. Fellow: AAAS (nominating com. 1998); mem.: NAS (chmn. sect. 41 1995—99, mem. com. 2004), Inst. Medicine (coun. 1988—90), Cancer Rsch. (lectr. 2003, G.H.A. Clowes Meml. award 1989, Charlotte Friend award 2003), Am. Soc. Hematology (lectr. Millenium Symposium 1999, Presdl. Symposium 1982, Dameshek prize 1982, Ham-Wasserman award 1995, Henry M. Stratton medal 2003), Genetical Soc., Am. Soc. Human Genetics (pres.-elect 1992, pres. 1993, Allen award and lectr. 1991, Disting. Sci. lectr. 2003), Am. Philos. Soc., Am. Acad. Arts and Scis. (nominating com. 1998), Alpha Omega Alpha, Sigma Xi (William Proctor prize for sci. achievement 1989). Episcopalian. Home: 5310 S University Ave Chicago IL 60615-5106 Office: U Chgo 5841 S Maryland Ave Rm 2115 Chicago IL 60637-1463 Office Phone: 773-702-6117. Business E-Mail: jrowley@medicinebsd.uchicago.edu.

ROWLEY, LARRY LEE, education educator; b. N.Y.C., May 27, 1969; s. Stanley Norman and Lillian Hazel Rowley; m. Stephanie Ann Johnson, Dec. 30, 1995; 1 child, Lawrence Jacob. BA in Commn., Old Dominion U., 1991; MEd in Social Founds., U. Va., 1995, PhD in Higher Edn., 1999. Admissions counselor Old Dominion U., Norfolk, Va., 1992—94; grad. asst. U. Va., Charlottesville, 1994—95; doctoral intern Piedmont Va. C.C., Charlottesville, 1996—97; acad. coord. Kenan Inst. Pvt. Enterprise, Chapel Hill, NC, 1997—98; asst. to exec. assoc. dean Sch. Medicine U. NC, Chapel Hill, 1999—2000, postdoctoral scholar, 2000; rsch. fellow U. Mich., Ann Arbor, 2000—03, asst. prof., 2003—. Proposal reviewer Am. Edn. Rsch. Assn., 2000—. Contbr. articles to profl. publs., chpt. to book. Mem. men's fellowship 2d Bapt. Ch., Ann Arbor, 2002—. Mem.: Assn. for Study of Higher Edn., Am. Acad. Politics and Social Sci., Jefferson Lodge Prince Hall Affiliation (jr. deacon 1995—), Old Dominion U. Alumni Assn. (mem. exec. bd. 2000—), Omicron Delta Kappa, Phi Kappa Phi. Independent. Baptist. Avocations: reading, public speaking, chess, athletics, golf. Home: 7915 Briarbrook Dr Ypsilanti MI 48197 Office: U Mich 610 E University Ann Arbor MI 48109-1259 E-mail: llrowley@umich.edu.

ROWLEY, MAXINE LEWIS, home economics and consumer educator, writer; b. Provo, Utah, Sept. 23, 1938; d. Max Thomas Lewis and Illa Lewis Sanford; m. Arthur William Rowley, Sept. 23, 1960; children: Anne, Jenefer. BA (Ford Found. scholar), Brigham Young U., 1960, PhD in Edn. Adminstrn., 1989; BS, U. Utah, 1974; MA, Utah State U., 1980. Promotion writer Sta. ABC KCPX-TV, 1960; extension home economist USDA, 1961; mgmt. trainee Deseret Book Co., Salt Lake City, 1969; dept. chair Patricia Stevens Career Coll., Salt Lake City, 1970; chair consumer and homemaking dept. Sand Ridge Jr. H.S. Weber Sch. Dist., Roy, Utah, 1975, learning experience designer, 1976-78; consumer and home econs. faculty Utah State U., Logan, 1978-79; spl. appointee to Utah State U. by the Utah State Bd. Edn., 1978-86; intern Gladys Chalkley Brannegan Am. Home Econ. Assn., 1993; chair dept. family life and home econs. Brigham Young U., 1988, 1999—2002. Instrumental writer Utah State U. Found., 1979; faculty Brigham Young U., 1979. Author: NCFR Public Policy Handbook, 1997; (filmstrips, texts and tchrs. guide) CHECS, 1979; (curriculum guide) Operation: Free Enterprise, 1982, Curriculum of Food Sci., Nutrition, vol. I, 1990, vol. II, 1992, vol. III, 1993; co-author: Legacy, vol. I, 1998. Active ward, stake and region positions Ch. of Jesus Christ of Latter-day Saints; leader 4-H Club, coun. mem., adv. bd.; leader Girl Scouts U.S.A., Young Homemakers; active State Text Book Evaluation Com., 1978-86, U. Utah Evaluation Com., 1979; edn. and rsch. com. Am. Cancer Soc., State of Utah, 1993-94; mem. Utah Women's State Legis. Coun., 1998-2003. Named Outstanding Leader Am. Edn., 1976, Nat. Tchr. of Yr., 1977, Outstanding Tchr. in Dept., Brigham Young U., 1984-94, Outstanding Voccat. Edn. Leader, State of Utah, 1996, Nat. Honor Roll in vocat. edn. Nat. Assn. Vocat. Family and Consumer Scis., 1999. Mem.: NEA, Am. Edn. Rsch. Assn. (Nat. chair, HERSIG 2001—03), Utah Assn. Family and Consumer Scis. (disting. svc. award 2003), Worldwide Orgn. Women (internat. bd. dirs. 1999—2003, women's legis. coun. State of Utah 1998—2004), Vocat. Home Econs. Tchrs. (nat. chmn. public rels. and legis. coms. 1978), Home Econs. Edn. Assn., Am. Edn. Rsch. Assn. (nat.chair Home Econs. Related Spl. Interest Group 2000—03, marriage, family & human devel. dept. 2002—), County Welfare Com., Utah Edn. Assn. (award for womens awareness task force project 1976), Utah Nutrition Coun. (chair 1995), Utah Coun. for Improvement Edn., Utah Vocat. Assn., Utah Home Econs. Assn., Am. Vocat. Assn., Am. Assn. Family and Consumer Scis. (nat. v.p., bd. dirs., chair ann. meeting, bd. liaison publs. 1995—97, nat. com. publs. 1999—), Am. Home Econs. Assn. (contbr., author yearbook 1984, Nat. Leadership award 1993), Nat. Assn. Vocat. Home Econs. Tchrs., Spurs, White Key (pres. 1960), Gamma Phi Omicron, Phi Kappa Phi, Kappa Omicron Nu (advisor 1980—, Nat. award of excellence 1999, nat. endowment honoree 1989, nat. leadership endowment 2001). Home: 9801 Lampton Cir South Jordan UT 84095-9211 E-mail: maxine_rowley@byu.edu.

ROWLEY, PETER TEMPLETON, pediatrician, educator; b. Greenville, Pa., Apr. 29, 1929; s. George Hardy and Susan Mossman (Templeton) R.; m. Carol Stone, Mar. 19, 1967; children: Derek Stone, Jason Templeton. AB magna cum laude, Harvard U., 1951; MD, Columbia U., 1955. Diplomate: Am. Bd. Internal Medicine. Intern med. service N.Y. Hosp.-Cornell Med. Center, 1955-56; clin. assoc. Nat. Inst. Neurol. Disease and Blindness, NIH, 1956-58; asst. resident, then resident Harvard Med. Service, Boston City Hosp.; asst. in medicine Harvard U. Med. Sch. and researcher Thorndike Meml. Lab., 1958-60; hon. research asst. dept. eugenics, biometry and genetics Univ. Coll., U. London, 1960-61; postdoctoral fellow dept. microbiology NYU Sch. Medicine, 1961-63; asst. prof. medicine Stanford U., 1963-70; assoc. prof. medicine pediatrics and genetics U. Rochester, 1970-75, prof. medicine, pediatrics, genetics and microbiology, 1975—, prof. oncology, 1991—, chmn. div. genetics, 1990—; physician, pediatrician Strong Meml. Hosp., 1970—. Mem. N.Y. State Exec. and Adv. Coms. on Genetic Disease, 1979—; WHO vis. scholar Inst. Biol. Chemistry, U. Ferrara, Italy, 1970. Editor (with M. Lipkin Jr.): Genetic Responsibility: On Choosing Our Children's Genes, 1974; co-editor: Genetic Testing. With USPHS, 1956-58. Recipient Excellence in Teaching award U. Rochester Class of 1976, 1973; NRC fellow, 1960-63; Buswell research fellow, 1970-71, 71-72 Fellow ACP, Am. Coll. Genetics; mem. Am. Fedn. Clin. Rsch., Am. Soc. Hematology, Am. Soc. Human Genetics (social issues com. 1980-89, program com. 1993-96), N.Y. State Health Rsch. (sci. bd. 1997—). Office: U Rochester Med Sch Div Genetics PO Box 641 601 Elmwood Ave Rochester NY 14642-0001 Business E-Mail: peter_rowley@urmc.rochester.edu.

ROWLEY, ROBERT DEANE, JR., bishop; b. Cumberland, Md., July 6, 1941; s. Robert Deane Sr. and Alice Marquerite (Wilson) W.; m. Nancy Ann Roland, June 27, 1964; children: Karen Gordon Rowley Butler, Robert Deane III. BA, U. Pitts., 1962, LLB, 1965; LLM, George Washington U., 1970; MDiv, Episcopal Sem. of S.W., 1977, DD (hon.), 1989. Ordained deacon Episcopal Ch., 1977; priest, 1978; bishop, 1989. Bar: Pa. 1965, U.S. Supreme Ct. 1970. Dean of students St. Andrew's Priory Sch., Honolulu, 1977-80; canon St. Andrew's Cathedral, Honolulu, 1979-81; rector St. Timothy's Episcopal Ch., Aiea, Hawaii, 1981—89; canon to bishop Diocese of Bethlehem (Pa.); bishop Diocese of Northwestern Pa., Erie, 1989—; pres. 3rd prov., 1993—2002. Capt. USN, 1966-92. Mem. Erie County Bar Assn., Erie Club, Lake Shore Country Club. Episcopalian. Home: 810 Huntington Dr Erie PA 16505-1087 Office: Diocese of Northwestern Pa 145 W 6th St Erie PA 16501-1001 E-mail: rdrowleyjr@aol.com.

ROWLEY, WILLIAM ROBERT, retired surgeon; b. Omaha, June 7, 1943; s. Robert Kuhlmeyer and Dorothy Eleanor (Larson) R.; m. Eileen Ruth Murray, Aug. 11, 1968; children: Bill II, Jeff, Jill. BA in Psychology, U. Minn., 1966, MD, 1970. Diplomate Am. Bd. Surgery. Commd. lt. USN, 1972, advanced through grades to rear admiral, 1994; intern U. Calif., San Diego, 1970-71, gen. surgery resident, 1971-72, Naval Regional Med. Ctr., Phila., 1973-76, peripheral vascular surgery fellow San Diego, 1977-78, staff surgeon Phila., 1977, staff vascular surgeon San Diego, 1978-85, chmn. dept. surgery, 1985-88, dir. surg. svcs., 1987-88; asst. chief of staff for plans and ops. Naval Med. Command S.W. Region, San Diego, 1988-89; dep. comdr. Nat. Naval Med. Ctr., Bethesda, Md., 1989-91; comdg. officer Naval Hospital, Camp Pendleton, Calif., 1991-93; dep. asst. chief for health care ops. Navy Bur. of Medicine and Surgery, Washington, 1993-94, asst. chief for plans, analysis and evaluation, 1994-95; commdr. Naval Med. Ctr., Portsmouth, Va., 1995-98; surgeon U.S. Atlantic Fleet, 1998—2002; sr. med. futurist Inst. for Alternative Futures, 2000—. Program dir. vascular surgery fellowship Naval Hosp., San Diego, 1980-85, gen. surgery residency, 1985-89; assoc. prof. surgery Uniformed Svcs. U. for Health Scis., Bethesda, 1985-2002. Fellow ACS; mem. AMA, Am. Coll. Physician Execs., Am. Coll. Healthcare Execs. Avocations: backpacking, boating.

ROWLING, J.K. (JOANNE KATHLEEN ROWLING), writer; b. Gloucestershire, England, July 31, 1965; d. Peter and Anne Rowling; m. Jorge Arantes, Oct. 16, 1992 (div. 1993); 1 child, Jessica; m. Neil Murray, Dec. 26, 2001; 1 child, David. Attended, Exeter U.; degree (hon.), Napier U., 2000, Dartmouth Coll., 2000, Univ. of Exeter, 2000, Univ. of St. Andrews, 2000. Former rschr. Amnesty International; teacher Scotland, 1990—94. Author: (novels) Harry Potter and the Philosopher's Stone, 1997 (Children's Book of the Year, British Book Awards, 1998, Gold Winner, Smarties Book Prize, 1997, Birmingham Cable Children's Book Award, Young Telegraph Paperback of the Year, Sheffield Children's Book Award, Sorcieres Prix, 1999, Premio Cento per la Letteratura Infantile, 1998), Harry Potter and the Sorcerer's Stone (U.S. title), 1998 (Anne Spencer Lindbergh Prize in Children's Literature, 1998, ABBY Award, American Booksellers Assoc., 1999), Harry Potter and the Chamber of Secrets, 1998 (Gold Winner, Smarties Book Prize, 1998), Harry Potter and the Prisoner of Azkaban, 1999, Harry Potter and the Goblet of Fire, 2000, Quidditch Through the Ages, 2001, Fantastic Beasts & Where to Find Them, 2001, Harry Potter and the Order of the Phoenix, 2003. Named Officer of the Most Excellent Order of the British Empire (O.B.E.) by Charles, Prince of Wales. Office: Christopher Little Literary Agency 10 Eel Brook Studios 125 Moore Park Rd London SW6 4PS England*

ROWLINGSON, JOHN CLYDE, anesthesiologist, physician, educator; b. Syracuse, N.Y., Aug. 3, 1948; s. John Winthrop and Genevieve Estelle (Mahan) R.; m. Rosemary Colette Laney, Oct. 26, 1974 (div. 1992); children: Kristen, Andrew; m. Karen Wheeler, Aug. 4, 2001; stepchild, Isaac. BS, Allegheny Coll., 1970; MD, SUNY, Buffalo, 1974. Intern Millard Fillmore Hosp., Buffalo, 1974-75; resident in anesthesiology U. Va., Charlottesville, 1975-77; fellow in anesthesia pain mgmt. U. Va. Med. Ctr., 1977-78; asst. prof. anesthesiology U. Va. Sch. Medicine, Charlottesville, 1978-82, assoc. prof., 1982-86, prof., 1986—, tenured prof., 1995—. Assoc. dir. Pain Mgmt. Ctr., U. Va. Health Sci. Ctr., 1978-79, dir., 1980-98, dir. acute pain svc., 1987—. Author: Regional Anesthesia, 1984; co-editor: Handbook of Critical Care Pain Management, 1993. Recipient Nils Lofgren award ASTRA, 1999; Nat. Inst. Handicapped Rsch. fellow, 1983-87, Pain fellow 1977-78. Fellow

Am. Coll. Anesthesiology; mem. Am. Soc. Anesthesiologists, Am. Soc. Regional Anesthesia (rsch. grantee 1977, pres. 1996-97), Am. Pain Soc., Internat. Assn. Study of Pain, Am. Acad. Pain Medicine (editl. bd. Anesthesia Analg 1996—, Reg. Anesthesia and Pain Medicine, 1997—). Methodist. Avocations: running, tennis, skiing, biking. Home: 5006 Lake Tree Ln Crozet VA 22932 Office: U Va Hlth Sys Health Sci Ctr Anesthesiology PO Box 800710 Charlottesville VA 22908-0710 Office Phone: 434-924-2283.

ROWNY, MICHAEL J. communications executive; b. Tokyo, Apr. 10, 1950; s. Edward L. Rowny; m. Melissa Blake. Student, U. Pa., Phila., 1968-70; BS, MIT, 1972; JD, Georgetown U., 1977. Profl. staff mem, U.S. Senate Fin. Com., Washington, 1974-78; asst. to ambassador Spl. Trade Rep., Geneva, Switzerland, 1978-79; dep. staff dir. The White House, Washington, 1979-80; v.p., sec. Avenir Group, Inc., Washington, 1981; v.p. strategic planning and ventures Bendix Corp., Southfield, Mich., 1981-83; sr. v.p. fin. MCI Communications, Washington, 1983-86; CEO Hermitage Holding Co., Washington, 1986-89; chmn., pres., CEO Ransohoff Co., Hamilton, Ohio, 1989-92; exec. v.p., CFO ICF Kaiser Internat., Vienna, Va., 1992-94; exec. v.p. MCI Communications Corp., Washington, 1994-99; bd. dirs. Step 9 Software Corp., Fairfax. Bd. dirs. Avenir Group, Inc., Bloomfield Hills, Mich.; chmn. bd. dirs. Embratel, Rio de Janeiro.

ROWSON, RICHARD CAVANAGH, publisher; b. Hollywood, Calif., Apr. 7, 1926; s. Louis Cavanagh and Mable Louise (Montney) R.; m. Elena Louisa Costabile, Nov. 22, 1952; children: Peter Cavanagh, John Cummings. AB, U. Calif., Berkeley, 1946; certificate, Sorbonne, 1949; MIA, Columbia U., 1950. Trainee Fgn. Policy Assn., 1950; dir. World Affairs Council R.I., 1951-52; with Fgn. Policy Assn., 1951-62, dir. finance and devel. n.e. region; with Radio Free Europe, 1962-69, dir. policy and planning, 1964-69; dir. spl. studies Praeger Pubs., Inc., N.Y.C., 1969-77, pres., 1975-77, Pergamon Press, 1977-80, R.R. Bowker, 1980. Dir. Duke U. Press, 1981-90, sr. cons. editor, 1990-91; dir. Am. U. Press, 1989-91, cons. acquisitions, 1992-94, cons. pub., dir., 1994-97; pub. Woodrow Wilson Ctr. Press, 1992-93; v.p. Nat. Exec. Svc. Corps, 1999-2000; dir. Exec. Svc. Corps. of Washington, 2000-03; pub. cons., lectr.; pres. Coun. for Cmty. of Democracies, 2003—; condr. workshops in field. Contbr. articles to profl. jours. Served to lt. (j.g.) USNR, 1944-47. Mem. Am. Assn. Advancement Slavic Studies, N.Y. Acad. Scis., U. Calif. Alumni Assn., Columbia U. Alumni Assn., Pomona Coll. Alumni Assn., Overseas Press Club. Democrat. Home: 4701 Connecticut Ave NW Washington DC 20008-5633 E-mail: rcrowson2@aol.com., rowson@ccd21.org.

ROY, ABHRA, process engineer, researcher; b. Calcutta, India, Sept. 21, 1966; m. Kuhu Banerjee, Aug. 4, 1972. PhD in Mech. Engring., Indian Inst. Tech., Kharagpur, India, 1998. Post doctoral rsch. scientist SUNY, Stony Brook, NY, 1998—2000; rsch. engr. CFD Rsch. Corp., Sunnyvale, Calif., 2000—. Reviewer Jour. Heat Transfer; contbr. articles to profl. jours. Recipient Univ. Gold medal, Jadavpur U., Calcutta, India, 1994. Mem.: Sigma Xi (life). Achievements include help in designing world's largest diameter silicon tube growth system. Home: 745 S Bernardo Ave Apt 52C Sunnyvale CA 94087 Office: 2880 Lakeside DR STE 226 Santa Clara CA 95054-2821 Personal E-mail: abhra_roy@yahoo.com. E-mail: axr@cfdrc.com.

ROY, AMIT H. agricultural executive; Pres.,ceo Internat. Fertilizer Devel. Ctr., Sheffield, Ala. Office: Internat Fertilizer Develop Ct PO Box 2040 Muscle Shoals AL 35662-2040

ROY, ARUNDHATI, writer; b. Bengal, India, 1961; d. Mary Roy. Author (also actor): (films) In Which Annie Gives it Those Ones; author: (screenplays) Electric Moon, (book) The God of Small Things, 1997 (Man Booker prize for fiction, 1997), (essays) The End of Imagination, The Greater Common Good. Office: Random House Inc 201 E 50th St, 22nd Fl New York NY 10022

ROY, ASIM, business educator; b. Calcutta, India, May 5, 1948; arrived in U.S., 1975; s. Samarendra Nath and Chhaya (Mukherjee) R.; m. Suchandra Mukherjee, Feb. 10, 1974; 1 child, Sion Roy. BE, Calcutta U., 1971; MS (scholar), Case Western Res. U., 1977; PhD, U. Tex., 1979. Foreman, supr. Guest, Keen, Williams, Calcutta, 1972—74; mgr. optimization group Execucom Systems Corp., Austin, 1980-82; asst. prof. U. Nebr., Omaha, 1983, Ariz. State U., Tempe, 1983-89, assoc. prof., 1989-99, prof., 1999—. Vis. prof. Stanford (Calif.) U., 1991; cons. Mid-Am. Steel Corp., 1976-77, Fabri-Centre, Inc., Cleve., 1976; pres., CEO Decision Support Software, Inc., 1984-98, Autolearn, Inc., 2003—. Author: (software) IFPS/Optimum and Maxima, Autolearn; contbr. articles to profl. jours. Calcutta U. Merit scholar, 1967, U. Tex. Rsch. scholar, 1978-80; grantee NSF. Mem. IEEE, Inst. Mgmt. Sci. (program chmn. 1990), Ops. Rsch. Soc. Am. (gen. chmn. 1993), Internat. Neural Network Soc. Hindu. Achievements include patents in field. Home: 5771 W Gail Dr Chandler AZ 85226-1232 Office: Ariz State U Sch of Business Tempe AZ 85287

ROY, CHUNILAL, psychiatrist; b. Digboi, India, Jan. 1, 1935; came to Can., 1967, naturalized, 1975; s. Atikay Bandhu and Nirupama (Devi) R.; m. Elizabeth Ainscow, Apr. 15, 1967; children: Nicholas, Phillip, Charles. MB, BS, Calcutta Med. Coll., India, 1959; diploma in psychol. medicine, Kings Coll., Newcastle-upon-Tyne, Eng., 1963. Intern Middlesborough Gen. Hosp., Eng., 1960-61; jr. hosp. officer St. Luke's Hosp., Middlesborough, Eng., 1961-64, sr. registrar, 1964; sr. hosp. med. officer Parkside Hosp., Macclesfield, Eng., 1964-66; sr. registrar Moorehaven Hosp., Ivybridge, Eng., 1966; reader, head dept. psychiatry Maulana Azad Med. Coll., New Delhi, 1966; sr. med. officer Republic of Ireland, County Louth, 1966; sr. psychiatrist Sask. Dept. Psychiat. Services, Can., 1967-68; regional dir. Swift Current, Can., 1968-71; practice medicine specializing in psychiatry Regina, Sask., Can., 1971-72; founding dir., med. dir. Regional Psychiat. Ctr., Abbotsford, B.C., Can., 1972-82. With dept. psychiatry Vancouver Gen. Hosp., 1983—; cons. to prison adminstrs.; hon. lectr. psychology and clin. prof. dept. psychiatry U. B.C., clin. prof. emeritus, 2000; ex-officio mem. Nat. Adv. Com. on Health Care of Prisoners in Can.; cons. (hon.) psychiatrist Vancouver Hosp.; advisor Asian chpt. Psychosomatic Medicine, World Congress of Law and Medicine, New Delhi, 1985; appointed hon. consul for Burkina Faso, 1997; appointed auditor Med. Svcs. Com. B.C., 1997; appointed advisor mental health Govt. West Bengal, India, 1999; pres. organizing com. World Mental Health Assembly, 1999, clinical prof. emeritus, Dept. of Psychiatry, UBC, 2000-. Author: (with D.J. West and F.L. Nichols) Understanding Sexual Attacks, 1978, Hospital or Prison Memories; co-author: Oath of Athens, 1979;; assoc. editor Internat. Jour. Offender Therapy and Comparative Criminology, 1978—; field editor Jour. of Medicine and Law; corr. editor Internat. Jour. Medicine; mem. bd. Internat. Law Medicine, 1979—; mem. editl. rev. bd. Evaluation, 1977—; contbr. articles to profl. jours. Recipient merit awards Dept. Health, Republic of Ireland, 1966, Can. Penitentiary Svc., 1974, Correctional Svcs. Can., 1983, citation by pres. U. B.C., 1983, Letten Saugstad Found., Chevalier de l'ordre de la Legion d'honneur, France, 2003; Awarded Order of Francisco Fajardo Gov. of Caracas, 1998, Legacy award Vancouver Travel and Conv. Ctr., 1998, Chevalier de l'Ordre de la Légion d'honneur award Pres. Chirac, France, 2003. Fellow: Pacific Rim Coll. Psychiatrists (founder), Royal Coll. Psychiatry (Eng.), Royal Coll. Physicians and Surgeons (Can.); mem.: B.C. Psychiat. Assn. (pres. 1995—96), U. Calcutta Med. Assn. of Am. (pres. 2000), World Assembly for Mental Health (pres. 2001), World Assn. Health, Culture and Environ. (sec.-gen. 1995, award 1995), Internat. Conf. on Health, Culture and Contemporaray Soc. (chief advisor Bombay 1989), Internat. Coll. Psychosomatic Medicine (adv. Asian chpt.), Can. Physicians Interested in South Asia (v.p. 1989, pres. 1990), Indian Psychiat. Assn. (life), Australian Acad. Forensic Sci. (corr.), Internat. Found. for Tng. in Penitentiary Medicine and Forensic Psychiatry (founding pres. 1980), Assn. Physicians and Surgeons Who Work in Can. Prisons (founding pres. 1974), Internat. Acad. Legal Medicine and Social Medicine, Can. Psychiat. Assn., Can. Med. Assn., Internat. Coun. Prison Med. Svcs. (founding sec.-gen. 1977), World Psychiat. Assn. (sec., vice chmn. forensic psychiatry 1983), Consul Burkina Faso (hon.), Vancouver Multicultural Soc. (bd. dirs. 1992—93), Order of St. John (knight 1992). Home: 2439 Trinity St Vancouver BC Canada V5K 1C9 Office: 1417-750 W Broadway Vancouver BC Canada V5Z 1J4 Fax: (604) 872-0302.

ROY, DAVID TOD, Chinese literature educator; b. Nanking, China, Apr. 5, 1933; s. Andrew Tod and Margaret (Crutchfield) R.; m. Barbara Jean Chew, Feb. 4, 1967. AB, Harvard U., 1958, AM, 1960, PhD, 1965. Asst. prof. Princeton U., 1963-67; assoc. prof. U. Chgo., 1967-73, prof., 1973—99, prof. emeritus, 1999—, chmn. com. on Far Eastern Studies, 1968-70, chmn. dept Far Eastern Langs. and Civilizations, 1972-75. Author: Kuo Mo-jo: The Early Years, 1971; contbr.: How to Read the Chinese Novel, 1990, Minds and Mentalities in Traditional Chinese Literature, 1999; co-editor: Ancient China: Studies in Early Civilization, 1978; translator: The Plum in the Golden Vase or Chin P'ing Mei, vol. 1, 1993, vol. 2, 2001. Served with U.S. Army, 1954-56. Ford Found. fellow, 1958-60, Jr. fellow Harvard Soc. Fellows, 1960-63, fellow Fulbright-Hays Commn., 1967, Chgo. Humanities Inst. fellow, 1994-95; grantee Am. Coun. Learned Socs., 1976-77, NEH, 1983-86, 95-96. Mem. Am. Oriental Soc., Assn. for Asian Studies. Clubs: Quadrangle (Chgo.). Democrat. Home: 5443 S Cornell Ave Chicago IL 60615-5603 Office: U Chgo 1050 E 59th St Chicago IL 60637-1559 E-mail: davidroy@midway.uchicago.edu.

ROY, DELLA MARTIN, materials science educator, researcher; b. Merrill, Oreg., Nov. 3, 1926; d. Harry L. and Anna (Cacka) Martin; m. Rustum Roy, June 8, 1948; children: Neill R., Ronnen A., Jeremy R. BS, U. Oreg., 1947; MS, Pa. State U., 1949, PhD, 1952. Various rsch. pos. Pa. State U., University Park, 1952—60, sr. rsch. assoc. geochemistry, 1960—62, sr. rsch. assoc. materials sci. engring., 1962—69, assoc. prof. materials sci. engring., 1969—75, prof. materials sci. engring., 1975—. Cons. in field; chmn. status of cement, concrete materials adv. bd., Washington, 1977—80; spl. adv. concrete durability NRC, 1985—. Editor: Instructional Modules in Cement Science, 1985, Jour. Cement & Concrete Rsch., 1971—; contbr. articles to profl. jours. Fellow: AAAS, Am. Concrete Inst. (Can. Ctr. Mineral and Energy Tech. award 1989, Keynote address 1980), Mineral. Soc. Am., Inst. Concrete Tech. (hon.), Am. Ceramic Soc. (trustee 1990—, Jeppson Medal award 1982, Copeland award 1987); mem.: NAS (exec. com., transp. rsch. bd. 1991—), Internat. Acad. Ceramics, Nat. Acad. Engring. (acad. adv. bd. 1989—, membership policy com. 2001—), Coun. Materials Rsch. Soc. (chmn. cement symposia 1980—81, 1986—88, trustee 1988—90). Democrat. Office: Pa State U Hastings Rd 110 Materials Rsch Lab State College PA 16802 Office Phone: 814-865-1196.

ROY, DONALD, artist, poet; b. Lafayette, La., Aug. 2, 1950; s. Albert and Geraldine Roy. Chaplain PTO, 1992-98; with Gumbeaux Mag., 1994—. Motivational spkr., 1995—. Editor: Creative Consultant (Editors Choice award 2000); author bi-mo. Perimeter, 2001; author: (book) Aesthetics Reflection, 2001; author poetry. Co-founder S.W. La. Black Mus., Lake Charles, La., 1999; asst. dir. The Langston Hughes Poetry Contest, Lake Charles, 2000; co-dir. The Zora Neal Hurston Writers Award, Lake Charles, 2000, The Play God's Trombones, Lake Charles, 2001; co-founder Gathering of Artist Spring Festival, Lake Charles, 2001; vol. voter registration Lake Charles, 1997—; activist for civil rights; advocate for human rels. Recipient Recognition in Achievement U.S. and La. State senates, 2000, Poet of the Yr. award Gumbeaux Mag., 1997, Dr. Nancy Shephard Arts Ensemble Writers award, 2000, Outstanding Achievement award Dist. 3, Ward I, Police Juror, Opelousas, La., 2001, Exceptional Leadership award Ladies of Focus, 2001. Avocations: drama, modern dance, theater, youth activities. Home: 932 N Division St Lake Charles LA 70601

ROY, DONALD H. political scientist, educator; b. Hartford, Conn., July 29, 1944; s. Donald H. and Madeline M. (Reynolds) Roy; m. Bernice P. Koffler, Sept. 1, 1968 (div. Aug. 1996); children: Daniel, Marisa. BA, Bard Coll., 1966; MA, Georgetown U., 1968; postgrad., U. St. Andrews, UK, 1970—72; PhD, U. Notre Dame, 1977. 5th grade tchr. Cross (SC) Area Schs., 1968—70; asst. prof. polit. sci. Carroll Coll., Helena, Mont., 1978—82; mgr., dir. rsch. Dallas C. of C., 1983—87; asst. prof. polit. sci. Jefferson C.C., Louisville, 1987—89; assoc. prof. polit. sci. Ferris State U., Big Rapids, Mich., 1989—. Vis. asst. prof. U. Notre Dame, Ind., 1977—78. Author: Public Policy Dialogues, 1994, Reuniting America, 1996, Dialogic Resurgence of the Public Intellectual, 2001. Campaign adv. Andy Everman for Mott C.C. Trustee, Flint, Mich., 2001, 2003; quality of life pollster Big Rapids City Govt., 1993; campaign mgr. Andy Everman for State House Dist. 48, 2004. Richard Weaver fellow, Intercollegiate Studies Inst., 1971, Scaife fellow, U. Notre Dame, 1975—76. Mem.: Mich. Citizens for Water Conservation, Cath. League, Amnesty Internat. Roman Catholic. Avocation: foreign films. Office: Ferris State Univ 820 Campus Dr Big Rapids MI 49307 Home: 901 Colburn Ave Big Rapids MI 49307 Office Phone: 231-591-2764.

ROY, ELMON HAROLD, minister; b. Russell Springs, Ky., Dec. 17, 1924; s. Leslie C. and Olza (Gosser) R.; m. Retha Adkins; children: Joel, Michael. BA in Theology, So. Missionary Coll., 1953; MA, Belin U., 1958, Spalding U., 1970; PhD in Theology, Pacific We. U., 1966; postgrad., Andrews Theol. Seminary, 1974; LLD, Coll. St. Thomas, 1982. Ordained to ministry, 1959. Assoc. pastor, Bucyrus, Ohio, 1955-56, Akron, Ohio, 1956-57; pastor East Liverpool, Ohio, 1957-60, Coudersport, Pa., 1960-64, Huntsville, Ala., 1964-65, Louisville, 1965-71; chaplain Pleasant Grove Hosp., Louisville, 1971—75; pastor Springfield, Ohio, 1975-85, Wooster, Ohio, 1985-88; chaplain Louisville, 1989—. Cons. religious liberty, 1983-88; chaplain Jefferson County Ct. Author: In Remembrance of Redemption, 1996, Courage for Hospital Days 1973, Earth's Coming Events, 1968, Israel's Early Leaders, 1984, Moments of Meditation, 1975, The Word for These Times, 1988, Morning is Coming, 1989, Something to Live By, 1958, Prescription for Personal Peace, 1995, Decisions Determine Destiny, 1994; contbr. numerous articles to mags. Pres. South Oldham Ch. Coun., 1971-72; mem. Ohio conf. bd. edn., 1985-88. With USN, 1943-46. Recipient Outstanding Cmty. Svc. award Pleasant Grove Hosp., Commrs. Commendation award Wayne County, Ohio Senate Commendation award, Gov.'s Outstanding Kentuckian award; decorated six battle stars, knight Sovereign Order of St. John of Jerusalem, Knights of Malta, Hospitallers, comdr. Star of Peace Fedn. des Combattants En Europe, Tenn. Col., Ky. Adm., Croix De Guerre, Cross of Valor, Royal Afghanistan Order of Crown of Amanullah, Order of Polonia Restituta; named hon. citizen of Tenn., hon. sheriff Clark County, Ohio, hon. Ky. Sec. of State, Ky. Amb.; named to Order Ky. Cols. Fellow Philos. Soc. Gt. Britain, Huguenot Soc., Royal Soc. Arts; mem. SAR (chaplain Louisville-Thruston chpt. 1974-75), Am. Acad. Religion, Ky. Hist. Soc., Order Founders and Patriots of Am., East Liverpool Ministerial Assn. (sec., treas. 1960), Coudersport Ministerial Assn. (v.p. 1971-72), Soc. Ky. Pioneers. Address: 2417 W Highway 22 Crestwood KY 40014-9481

ROY, MICHAEL JOSEPH, higher education administrator; b. Kankakee, Ill., Aug. 15, 1945; s. Raymond Joseph and Barbara Elizabeth (Gulczynski) R.; m. Joanne Lee Isley, June 5, 1971; 1 child, Amanda. BS, Mont. State U., 1967; MBA, Ctrl. Mich. U., 1970; EdD, Western Mich. U., 1994. Acct. Mont. State U., Billings, 1967-70; acct., asst. contr. Ctrl. Mich. U., Mt. Pleasant, 1971-75, contr., 1975-78; chief acct. No. Mich. U., Marquette, 1978-81, asst. v.p. fin., contr., 1981-91, interim v.p. fin. and adminstrn., treas., 1991-93, v.p. fin. and adminstrn. and treas., 1993—. Trustee No. Mich. U. Devel. Fund, 1991—; bd. dirs. Mich. Univs. Self-Ins. Corp., Detroit, 1985-97; bd. dirs., treas. No. Initiatives, Marquette, 1992—; allocation com. mem. United Way of Marquette, 1980-91; pres., dir. Marquette Area Cath. Edn. Fund, Marquette, 1988-90; chair fin. coun. St. Louis the King Parish, Marquette, 1985—. Mem. rotary Club of Marquette (treas. 1997—). Roman Catholic. Avocations: woodworking, skiing. Office: Northern Michigan Univ 1401 Presque Isle Ave Marquette MI 49855-5305

ROY, PATRICK, professional hockey player; b. Quebec City, Que., Can., Oct. 5, 1965; Goaltender Montreal Canadiens, 1984—95, Colo. Avalanche, 1995—2003. Mem. Stanley Cup Championshio team, 1986, 93, 96, 2001. Named to NHL All-Rookie Team, 1985—86, NHL All-Star 2d Team, 1987—88, 1990—91, NHL All-Star 1st Team, 1988, 1989, 1989—90, 1991—92, Sporting News All-Star Team, 1988—89, 1989—90, 1991—92; recipient Cpmm Smythe Trophy as Playoff MVP, 1986, William M. Kennings Trophy, 1986—89, 1992—92, Trico Goaltender award, 1988, 1989, 1989—90, Georges Vezina Trophy, 1988—89, 1989—90, 1991—92.

ROY, RALPH LORD, clergyman; b. St. Albans, Vt., Sept. 30, 1928; s. Howard Allen and Olive Lydia (Corliss) R.; m. Margaret Ellen Finlay, Feb. 12, 1960 (dec.); 1 child, Joyce Victoria. BA, Swarthmore Coll., 1950; MA, Columbia U. and Union, Theol. Seminary, 1952. Ordained to ministry United Meth. Ch. as deacon, 1952, as elder, 1961. Asst. minister Met. Community United. Meth. Ch., N.Y.C., 1957-60; minister Grace United Meth. Ch., N.Y.C., 1960-63, Greene Ave./Knickerbocker United Meth. Ch., Bklyn., 1964-68, Cuyler Warren St. Community Ch., Bklyn., 1968-70, United Meth. Ch., Clinton, Conn., 1970-74, Mary Taylor United Meth. Ch., Milford, Conn., 1974-79, First United Meth. Ch., Meriden, Conn., 1979-94, pastor Thomaston, Conn., 1994-99, United Meth. Ch., East Berlin, Conn., 2000—01, First and Summerfield United Meth. Ch., New Haven, 2001—02. Author: Apostles of Discord, 1953, Communism and the Churches, 1960; contbr. articles to profl. jours. Chaplain Meriden (Conn.) Police Dept., 1981-92; radio ministry, 1983-; newspaper columnist, 1999--. Home: 697 S End Rd Unit 37 Plantsville CT 06479-1843 E-mail: ralphlroy@aol.com. *When I consider the magnificence and vastness of the universe, I can be overwhelmed by childlike marvel. That's one key aspect of God's creation. Another is the almost infinite variety, complexity, and beauty of life on our planet, all of it interdependent, making it urgent that we dwell together in harmony, mutual respect and peace.*

ROY, ROBERT RUSSELL, toxicologist; b. Mpls., Sept. 14, 1957; s. Rudolph Russell and Arlene Charlotte (Miller) R.; m. Barbara Jane Richie, Oct. 10, 1987; children: Andrew, Katherine. BA cum laude, Augsburg Coll., 1980; MS, U. Minn., 1986, PhD, 1989. Bd. cert. in toxicology. Toxicologist, project mgr. Pace Labs., Inc., Mpls., 1989-90; toxicologist Minn. Dept. Health, Mpls., 1990-93, Minn. Regional Poison Ctr., St. Paul, 1990-97; team leader, toxicology specialist 3M, St. Paul, 1997—, sr. toxicology specialist, 2000—. Lectr. U. Minn., Mpls., 1986-90, Midwest Ctr. Occupl. Health and Safety, St. Paul, 1990—, instr., 1989; adj. assoc. prof. U. Minn., 1993—; mem. grad. faculty in toxicology and pub. health U. Minn.; adj. asst. prof. emergency medicine Oreg. Health Sci. U., Portland. Mem. Mt. Carmel Luth. Ch. Coun., Mpls., 1983-85. Mem. Soc. Toxicology, Am. Indsl. Hygiene Assn., Delta Omega. Home: 6301 Oxbow Bend Chanhassen MN 55317-9110 Office: Corp Toxicology 3 M Ctr Bldg 220-2E-02 Saint Paul MN 55144-1000 Office Phone: 651-736-3692. E-mail: rroy@mmm.com.

ROY, ROBERT WILLIAM, artist, educator; b. Worcester, Mass., Oct. 7, 1945; s. Vincent Charles and Rita Marie R.; m. Laurie Jean Zephir, Aug. 1, 1981; children: Patrick Zephir, Roy. BFA magna cum laude, U. Mass., 1969; MFA, Yale U., 1971. Instr. Sch. of the Worcester Art Mus., 1972-81; prof., chair painting dept. Montserrat Coll. of Art, Beverly, Mass., 1988—. Adj. instr. Mount Wachusett C.C., Gardner, Mass., 1982-98, mem. adv. bd., 1997—; vis. lectr. U. Lowell, Mass., 1982-83, Worcester State Coll., 1986-87; vis. critic Smith Coll., Northampton, Mass., 1983, vis. artist, U. Southern Maine, 2002, Artist-in-residence, Burren Coll. Art, Ireland, 2004. Exhibited in group shows at Rose Art Mus., Brandeis U., 1977, Williams Coll. Mus. Art, 1977, Danforth Mus. Art, 1981, 1994, 2001, Hudson River Mus., 1984, Worcester Art Mus., 1984, Berkshire Mus., 1984, 1986, Brainerd Art Gallery, State Univ. Coll. at Potsdam, N.Y., 1983, 1986, Siegfried Gallery/Ohio U., 1987, John Szoke Gallery, N.Y.C., 1988, Fitchburg Art Mus., 1988, Laguna Gloria Art Mus., 1989—90, DeCordova Mus., 1991, Cragin Fife Gallery, Brookline, Mass., 1995, U. Ariz., 1996, Butler Inst. Am. Art, 1998, Boston U., 1999, 2001, Fed. Res. Bank, Boston, 1999, Montserrat Coll. Art, 2000, Ben Shahn Galleries, William Paterson U., Wayne, N.J., 2002, The European Biennial of Contemporary Art, Frankfurt, Germany, 2002, The Liverpool (Eng.) Biennial, 2002, U. Galleries, Ill. State U., Normal, Ill., 2003, River Gallery, Ipswich, Mass., 2003, Schitkamp Gallery, Clark U., Worcester, Mass., 2003, Art Gallery, U. N.H., Durham, U. Alberta, Edmonton, Can., 2004; artist (permanent collections) Mus. Modern Art, N.Y.C., Danforth Mus. Art, Trenton State Coll.; Represented in permanent collections U. Alta., Edmonton, Can. Fellow Yale U., Norfolk, Conn., 1968, Mass. Artists Found., Boston, 1977; Ford Found. Faculty grantee, 1976, 78, 80, Cornelia Foss Fellow, 2003. Mem. L.A. Printmaking Soc., Coll. Art Assn. N.Y.C., Boston Printmakers, Southern Graphics Coun. Home: 95 Regan St Gardner MA 01440-4015 Office: Montserrat College of Art 23 Essex St # Beverly MA 01915-4508 Office Phone: 978-922-8222.

ROY, RUSTUM, interdisciplinary educator, materials researcher; b. Ranchi, India, July 3, 1924; came to U.S., 1945, naturalized, 1961; s. Narendra Kumar and Rajkumari (Mukherjee) R.; m. Della M. Martin, June 8, 1948; children: Neill, Ronnen, Jeremy. BSc with honors, Patna (India) U., 1942; MSc, Patna (India) U., India, 1944; PhD, Pa. State U., 1948; DSc (hon.), Tokyo Inst. Tech., 1987, Alfred U, 1993. Research asst. Pa. State U., 1948-49, mem. faculty, 1950—, prof. geochemistry, 1957—, prof. solid state, 1968—, chmn. solid state tech. program, 1960-67, chmn. sci. tech. and soc. program, 1977-84, dir., 1984-89, dir. materials research lab., 1962-85, Evan Pugh prof., 1981—, Evan Pugh prof. solid state emeritus, 1999—; sr. sci. officer Nat. Ceramic Lab., India, 1950; mem. com. mineral sci. tech. Nat. Acad. Scis., 1967-69, com. survey materials sci. tech., 1970-74; exec. com. chem. div. NRC, 1967-70, nat. materials adv. bd., 1970-77, mem. com. radioactive waste mgmt., 1974-80, chmn. panel waste solidification, 1976-80, chmn. com., 1976-81. Mem. com. material sci. and engring. NRC, 1986-89; mem. Pa. Gov.'s Sci. Adv. Com.; chmn. materials adv. panel Gov.'s Sci. Adv. Com., 1965-80; mem. adv. com. on engring. NSF, 1968-72, adv. com. to ethical and human value implications sci. and tech., 1974-76, adv. com. div. materials rsch., 1974-77; Hibbert lectr. U. London, 1979; cons. to industry; mem. adv. com. Coll. Engring., Stanford U., 1984-86; internat. sci. lectr. NRC, 1991-92; vis. prof. materials Ariz. State U., 1999—; vis. prof. medicine U. Ariz., 1999—. Author: Honest Sex, 1968, Crystal Chemistry of Non-metallic Materials, 1974, Experimenting with Truth, 1981, Radioactive Waste Disposal, Vol. 1, the Waste Package, 1983, Lost at the Frontier, 1985; founding editor-in-chief: Materials Rsch. Bull., 1966—, Jour. Materials Edn., 1980-2000, Bull. Sci. Tech. and Soc, 1981-2000, Materials Rsch. Innovations, 1997—; contbr. over 1000 articles to profl. jours., 25 patents in field. Chmn. bd. Dag Hammarskjold Coll., 1973-75; chmn. ad hoc com. sci., tech. and ch. Nat. Council Chs., 1966-68. Sci. policy fellow Brookings Instn., 1982-83; recipient Ellis Island medal of hon., 1996; named to Order of the Rising Sun with Gold Rays status in Japanese Emperor's birthday honors list, 2002. Fellow: AAAS (chmn. chemistry sect. 1985), Mineral. Soc. Am. (award 1957), Am. Phys. Soc., Indian Acad. Scis. (hon.), Am. Ceramic Soc. (Sosman lectr. 1975, Orton lectr. 1984, disting. life, Educator of Yr. 1993); mem.: U.S. Nat. Acad. Engring., Materials Rsch. Soc. (pres. 1976, founder), Am. Soc. Engring. Educators (Centennial medal 1993, Hall of Fame 1993), Am. Chem. Soc. (Petroleum Rsch. Fund award, 1960, Dupont award for Chem. of Materials 1993), Fine Ceramics Assn. Japan (Internat. award), Ceramic Soc.Japan (hon. Centennial award 1991), Mineral Soc. Am., Fedn. Materials Socs. (Nat. Materials Advancement award 1991), Russian Acad. Scis. (elected fgn.), Engring. Acad. Japan (elected fgn.), Indian Nat. Sci. Acad. (elected fgn.), Royal Swedish Acad. Engring. Scis. (elected fgn.). Home: 528 S Pugh St State College PA 16801-5312 Office: 102 Materials Research Lab University Park PA 16802-4800 E-mail: rroy@psu.edu. *My major responsibility to the increasingly unified world culture, as a scientist supported largely by the public, is to integrate into its emerging radically pluralist yet globally unifying Religion, the insights from Science and the impact of Technology on the human condition. As a Christian Radical Pluralist, I am committed to presenting to my fellow humans—especially all non-scientists, from Presidents and CEOs to the person in the street—an accurate picture of the whole truth about my scientific "advances" and those of others—their limited and ambivalent nature and their relatively minor position in the sum total of human concerns.*

ROY, TAPON, statistician, researcher; b. Chapel Hill, NC, Apr. 3, 1958; s. Samarendra Nath and Bani Sen Roy. AB in Chemistry, U. NC, 1980, MS in Pub. Health Biostatistics, 1982. Statistician Ciba-Geigy, Summit, NJ, 1982—84; sr. statistician Boehringer Ingelheim, Ridgefield, Conn., 1984—. Presenter in field. Contbr. over 25 peer-reviewed articles and notes to profl. jours. including Antimicrobial Agents and Chemotherapy, Biometrics, Jour. Chemometrics, Jour. Math. Chem., Jour. Math. Physics, Jour. Med. Chem., Jour. Pharm. Biomedical Analysis, Jour. Pharm. Sci., Jour. Phys. Chem., Jour. Stat. Comp. Simul.; reviewer: numerous statistical and sci. jours. Fellow: Royal Statis. Soc.; mem.: Inst. Math. Stats., Pharm. Rsch. and Mfrs. Assn.,

Am. Statis. Assn., Biometric Soc. Achievements include research in development and implementation of resampling, robust, and error propagation techniques in biology, chemistry, medicine, pharmaceuticals, and physics. Avocations: reading, theater, photography. Office: Boehringer Ingelheim 900 Ridgebury Rd Ridgefield CT 06877 E-mail: troy@rdg.boehringer-ingelheim.com.

ROY, WILLIAM GLENN, sociology educator; b. Rochester, N.Y., Mar. 22, 1946; s. James Rider and Nona Alice (Monks) R.; m. Alice Madeleine Royer, Apr. 3, 1976; children: Margaret Alice, Joseph Edward. BA, Emory U., 1968; PhD, U. Mich., 1977. Prof. UCLA, 1976—. Author: Socializing Capital: The Rise of the Large Industrial Corporation in America, 1997, Making Societies: The Historical Construction of Our World, 2001. Woodrow Wilson fellow, 1968; rsch. grantee NSF, 1987. Mem. Phi Beta Kappa. Avocation: genealogy. Office: UCLA Dept Sociology Los Angeles CA 90095

ROY, WILLIAM ROBERT, physician, lawyer, former congressman; b. Bloomington, Ill., Feb. 23, 1926; s. Elmer Javan and Edna Blanche (Foley) R.; m. Jane Twining Osterhoudt, Sept. 1947; children: Robin Jo, Randall Jay, Richelle Jane, William Robert, Renee Jan, Rise Javan. BS, Ill. Wesleyan U., 1946; MD, Northwestern U., 1949; JD with honors, Washburn U., 1970. Pvt. practice medicine, 1955-70, 79-89; mem. 92d-93d congresses from 2d Dist. Kans., 1971-75; exec. dir. Kans. Med. Edn. Found., 1976-94; newspaper columnist, 1989—. Former dir. Sentry Ins.; Democratic candidate for U.S. Senate, 1974, 78. Mem. Inst. Medicine of Nat. Acad. Scis. Democrat. Methodist. Home: 6137 SW 38th Ter Topeka KS 66610-1307

ROYAL, DARRELL K. university official, former football coach; b. Hollis, Okla., July 6, 1924; s. Burley Ray and Katy Elizabeth (Harmon) R.; m. Edith Marie Thomason, July 26, 1944; children: Marian (Mrs. Abraham Kazen III) (dec.), Mack, David (dec.), BS in Bus, U. Okla., 1950. Former head football coach, then dir. athletics U. Tex., now asst. to univ. pres. Author: Darrell Royal Talks Football, 1963. Recipient Horatio Alger award, 1996, Contbns. to Coll. Football award Nat. Coll. Football Award Assn., 2002; named Coach of Yr., Football Coaches Assn., 1963, 70, Tex. Sports Writers, 1961, 63, 69, 70, Southwesterner of Yr., 1961, 62, 63; named to U. Tex. Longhorn Hall of Fame, 1976, Tex. Sports Hall of Fame, 1976, Jim Thorpe Okla. Hall of Fame, 1977, Nat. Football Hall of Fame, 1983, Coach of Decade for 1960's, ABC; Darrell K. Royal Meml. Football Stadium, U. Tex. named in his honor, 1996; inducted into Southwestern Bell Cotton Bowl Hall of Fame, 1998, Okla. Heritage Soc. Hall of Fame, 2000; football field at Hollis H.S. named in his honor, 2003. Mem.: Delta Upsilon. Presbyterian. Office: U Tex SRH2 101 Austin TX 78712

ROYAL, HENRY DUVAL, nuclear medicine physician; b. Norwich, Conn., May 14, 1948; MD, St. Louis U., 1974. Diplomate Am. Bd. Internal Medicine; Am. Bd. Nuclear Medicine. Intern R.I. Hosp., Providence, 1974, resident in internal medicine, 1975-76; resident in nuclear medicine Harvard Med. Sch., Boston, 1977-79; from assoc. to staff physician Barnes Hosp., St. Louis, 1987—; from assoc. to cons. staff physician Children's Hosp., St. Louis, 1987—; prof. Washington U., St. Louis, 1993—. Co-team leader health effects sect. Internat. Atomic Energy Agy. Internat. Chernobyl Project, 1990; exec. dir. Am. Bd. Nuclear Medicine, 2004—; mem. com. on assessment of CDC radiation studies NRC/NAS, 1993-98; mem. sci. com. 1 and 4 Nat. Coun. on Radiation Protection and Measurements, 1993—; mem. coun. Nat. Coun. on Radiation Protection, 1996—, bd. dirs., 2000—; adv. com. environ. hazards Vets., 1997—; exec. dir. Am. Bd. Nuc. Medicine, 2004—. Contbr. articles to profl. jours. Mem.: Soc. Nuc. Medicine (v.p. 2002, pres. 2003), Alpha Omega Alpha. Office: Acad Faculty Mallinckrodt Inst Radiology 510 S Kingshighway Blvd Saint Louis MO 63110-1016 Office Phone: 314-362-2809. Business E-Mail: royalh@mir.wustl.edu.

ROYAL, WILLIAM HENRY, retired real estate developer, architect; b. Jackson, Tenn., Dec. 16, 1924; s. Joe Henry and Millie Earline (Anderson) R.; m. Odell Peebles, June 16, 1943; children: William H. Jr., Frederick E., Diana, Carolyn M., Wanda H. Diploma, Chicago Tech. Coll., 1959; student, MIT, 1969, '73, U. Neb., 1971-76, U. Minn., 1974-76. Reg. architect, Ill., Mo. Architect, engr. U.S. Army Engr. Dist., Detroit, 1957-61, gen. architect St. Paul, 1959-62, supr. architect Chgo., 1962-70, gen. architect Omaha, Neb., 1970-73; architect, job captain Ellerbe & Co., St Paul, 1962; cons. FREBO, U.S. Postal Svc., St. Paul, 1973-77; constr. mgr. H.Q. U.S. Postal Svc., Washington, 1977-80; pres. William H. Royal & Assoc., Inc., Lake St. Louis, Mo., 1987—2002, Chgo., 1995-97, St. Louis Airport Devel. Corp., 1988-89; v.p. Steelgrade Corp., Clayton, Mo., 1991-93; sec.-treas. Am. Community Telecomms. System, Inc., Ferguson, Mo., 1992-97; pres. Royal King Constrn. Co., St. John, Mo., 1995-97. Author: (tng. manual) Architect Engineer Contracts, 1970; editor: Master Planning, Kinloch Redevelopment, 1987. Steward, United Meth. Ch., Omaha, 1970-73; urban cons. United Meth. Ministries, Omaha, 1970-73, Youth Coord., United Meth. Ch., Omaha, 1971-73; mem. Douglas County Parole Bd., Omaha, 1971-72. Recipient Commendation U.S. Postal Svc., Washington, 1976, Svc. award, 1980, letter of Appreciation, 1982; nominee Rockefeller Pub. Svc. award, U.S. Postal Svc., St. Paul, 1976. Avocations: computer programming, fishing, travel. Home: 1 Berry Ct Lake Saint Louis MO 63367-1921 Office: William H Royal & Assocs 1 Berry Ct Lake Saint Louis MO 63367-1921 Office Phone: 636-561-2735.

ROYBAL-ALLARD, LUCILLE, congresswoman; b. Boyle Heights, Calif., June 12, 1941; d. Edward Roybal; m. Edward T. Allard; 4 children. BA in Speech, Calif. State U., L.A., 1965. Former mem. Calif. State Assembly, 1987—93; mem. U.S. Congress from 34th Calif. dist., 1993—; mem. appropriationscom.; mem. Ho. Com. on Standards of Official Conduct. Democrat. Office: Ho of Reps 2330 Rayburn Bldg Washington DC 20515-0533

ROY-BURMAN, PRADIP, molecular biology and virology educator; b. Comilla, Bengal, India, Nov. 12, 1938; came to U.S., 1963; s. Prafulla Nath and Mrinalini (Barman) Roy-Burman; m. Sumitra Ghosh, Nov. 26, 1963. BSc. with honors, Calcutta (India) U., 1956, MSc., 1958, PhD, 1963. Rsch. assoc. dept. biochemistry Sch. of Medicine U. So. Calif., L.A., 1963-66, Dernham sr. rsch. fellow in oncology Am. Cancer Soc., 1966-71, asst. prof. dept. biochemistry, 1967-72, assoc. prof. dept. pathology and biochemistry, 1972-78, prof. dept. pathology and biochemistry and molecular biology, 1978—, vice chmn. dept. pathology, 1987—2003. Interim chmn. dept. molecular microbiology and immunology, U. So. Calif., L.A., 1995-97; mem. pathology B study sect., NIH, 1990-94, 99-2003, reviewers res., 1994-98, ad hoc mem. sci. tech. rev. bd. for biomed. behavioral rsch. facilities NCRR, NIH, 1997—, prostate cancer rsch. program review panel, Dept. of Def., 2001—; chmn. NIH, NCI Spl. Emphasis Rev. Panels, 1998—; chmn. symposium internat. congress biochem. molecular biology, 1994, co-chmn. symposium internat. cancer congess, 1994, chmn. workshop on pathogenesis of animal retrovirus, session immune interaction, 1996; spkr. in field. Author (with others) books; contbr. articles to profl. jours.; book reviewer; inventor novel transcription regulatory elements for gene transfer vectors, mouse models for human prostate cancer, others; mem. editl. bd. Hematological Oncology, 1987—97, Cancer Biology and Therapy, 2001—. Rsch. grantee Am. Cancer Soc., NIH, Am. Diabetes Assn., Wright Found., Martell Found. Mem. Am. Soc. for Microbiology, Am. Soc. for Biol. Chemists and Molecular Biology, Am. Assn. Cancer Rsch., Am. Soc. Investigative Pathology, Internat. Assn. for Comparative Rsch. on Leukemia and Related Diseases. Democrat. Hindu. Avocations: writing, hiking, golf. Office: Keck Sch Of Medicine Hmr 210B 2011 Zonal Ave Los Angeles CA 90033 Office Phone: 323-442-1184. Business E-Mail: royburma@usc.edu.

ROYCE, BARRIE SAUNDERS HART, physicist, researcher; b. Eng., Jan. 10, 1933; came to U.S., 1957, naturalized, 1978; s. Vincent Pateman Hart and Kathlene (Saunders) R.; m. Dominique J.M. Vallee, May 7, 1964; children: Vincent Rene Hart, Marc Edward Hart. BSc in Physics, King's Coll., U. London, 1954, PhD, 1957. Rsch. assoc. Carnegie Inst. Tech., 1957-60, Princeton U., 1960-61, mem. faculty, 1961—2003, prof. applied physics and materials scis., 1978—2003, prof. emeritus, 2003—, acting dean grad. affairs Sch. Engring. and Applied Sci., 2003—; master of Dean Mathey Coll., 1986-94. Mem. editl. adv. bd. Jour. Photoacoustics, to 1984. Mem. Princeton Borough Zoning Bd. Adjustment, 1980-93, chair, 1993—. Grantee NSF, Air Force Office Sci. and Rsch., Army Rsch. Office. Mem. Am. Phys. Soc., Sigma Xi. Office: Princeton U D416 Duffield Hall Eq Princeton NJ 08544-0001

ROYCE, EDWARD R. (ED ROYCE), congressman; b. Los Angeles, Oct. 12, 1951; m. Marie Porter. BA, Calif. State U., Fullerton. Tax mgr. Southwestern Portland Cement Co.; mem. Calif. Senate, 1983-93, U.S. Congress from 40th Calif. dist. (formerly 39th), 1993—; mem. banking and fin. svcs. com., internat. rels. com. Vice chmn. Public Employment and Retirement Com.; mem. Bus. and Profs. com., Indsl. Rels. com.; legis. author, campaign co-chmn. Proposition 15 Crime Victims/Speedy Trial Initiative; author nation's 1st felony stalking law, bill creating Foster Family Home Ins. Fund, legis. creating foster parent recruitment and tng. program; mem. Banking and Fin. Svcs. Com., Internat. Rels. Com. Named Legis. of Yr. Orange County Rep. Com., 1986, Child Adv. of Yr. Calif. Assn. Svc. for Children, 1987. Mem. Anaheim C. of C. Republican. Office: US Ho Reps 2202 Rayburn Ho Office Bldg Washington DC 20515

ROYCE, PAUL CHADWICK, medical administrator; b. Mpls., July 2, 1928; BA, U. Minn., 1948, MD, 1952; PhD, Case Western Res. U., 1959. Diplomate Am. Bd. of Internal Medicine. Intern U. Chgo. Clinics, 1952-53; fellow NSF Case Western Res. U., Cleve., 1953-54, 56-58, Upjohn fellow, 1958-59; resident internal medicine Bronx Mcpl. Hosp., N.Y., 1959-61; asst. prof. of medicine Albert Einstein Coll. of Med., N.Y.C., 1961-69; sr. staff endocrinologist Guthrie Clinic, Sayre, Pa., 1970-81; assoc. prof. of medicine Hahnemann Med. Sch., Phila., 1973-81; emeritus prof. medicine Med. Coll. Pa./Hahnemann U., 1996—; dean and prof. clin. sci. and physiology Sch. Medicine U. Minn., Duluth, 1981-87; sr. v.p., clin. dir. Monmouth Med. Ctr., Long Branch, N.J., 1987-94; med. dir. The Segal Co. N.Y., 1995-98; prin. Royce Assocs., Atlantic Highlands, N.J., 1995—; tutor Writing Ctr., Monmouth U., NJ, 2001—. Producer, host TV prgram Doctors on Call, 1983-87 (Nat. Friends of Pub. Broadcasting Hill award 1987). Lt. USNR, 1954-56. Mem. Harvey Soc., Am. Physiol. Soc., Fedn. Am. Scientists, Physicians for Social Responsibility, Sigma Xi, Alpha Omega Alpha. Avocations: skiing, bicycling, canoeing. Office: Royce Associates 9 Prospect Rd Atlantic Highlands NJ 07716-1721

ROYCE, RAYMOND WATSON, lawyer, rancher, citrus grower, invester; b. West Palm Beach, Fla., Mar. 5, 1936; s. Wilbur E. and Veda (Watson) R.; m. Catherine L. Setzer, Apr. 21, 1979; children: Raymond, Steven, Nancy, Kathryn, Ryan. BCE, U. Fla., 1958, JD, 1961. Bar: Fla. 1961, U.S. Dist. Ct. (so. dist.) Fla. 1961, U.S. Ct. Appeals (5th cir.) 1961, U.S. Ct. Appeals (11th cir.) 1981. With Scott, Royce, Harris & Bryan P.A., Palm Beach, Fla., 1962-99; pres. Scott, Royce, Harris, Bryan, Barra and Jorgensen, P.A., Palm Beach Gardens, Fla., 1982-99; ptnr. Holland & Knight LLP, West Palm Beach, 1999—. Bd. supvs. No. Palm Beach Improvement Dist., 1995-99. Mem. Fla. Bar (bd. govs. 1974-78), Fla. Blue Key, Phi Delta Phi. Democrat. Presbyterian. Home: 5550 Whirlaway Rd Palm Beach Gardens FL 33418-7735 Office: Holland and Knight LLP 222 Lakeview Ste 1000 West Palm Beach FL 33401-4027 Office Phone: 561-650-8316.

ROYER, KATHLEEN ROSE, pilot; b. Pitts., Nov. 4, 1949; d. Victor Cedric and Lisetta Emma (Smith) Salway; m. Michael Lee Royer, June 6, 1971 (div. Aug. 1975). Student, Newbold Coll., 1968-69; BS, Columbia Union Coll., 1971; MEd, Shippensburg U., 1974; student, Lehigh U., 1974-75. Cert. tchr. Pa. Music. Music tchr. Harrisburg (Pa.) Sch. Dist., 1971-77; flight instr. Penn-Air, Inc., Altoona, Pa., 1977; capt., asst. chief pilot Air Atlantic Airlines, Centre Hall, Pa., 1977-80; capt., chief pilot Lycoming Air Svc., Williamsport, Pa., 1980-81; govs. pilot Commonwealth of Pa., Harrisburg, 1981-87; flight engr. Pan-Am, N.Y.C., 1987-91; pilot, 1st officer B737 United Airlines, Chgo., 1992-96, 1st officer B767 N.Y.C., until 1996, Washington, 1996-99; flight officer B747-400 JFK Internat. Airport, Jamaica, NY, 1999—2001, capt. Airbus 320, 2001—. Frist woman pilot/engr. crew mem. on 747 Pan Am. Airlines, 1989—91, chief pilot, cons. Mem.: UAL-Airline Pilot Assn. (coord. critical incident stress program 1994—96), Flight Engrs. Internat. Assn. (scheduling rep. 1989, scheduling dir. 1990, 1st vice chmn., mem. bd. adjustments 1989, v.p. dir. scheduling 1991—92), Internat. Soc. Women Airline Pilots, Whirley Girls (Washington), 99's (local chair Ctrl. Pa. chpt. 1987—92), Hershey Country Club. Republican. Avocations: owner/flying 1965 Cessna 180, golf, music, reading. Home: 34 Lazy Eight Dr Daytona Beach FL 32128 Office: San Francisco Intl Airport San Francisco CA

ROYER, ROBERT LEWIS, retired utility company executive; b. Louisville, Jan. 2, 1928; s. Carl Brown and Martha Helen (Garrett) R.; m. Carol Jean Pierce, June 24, 1950; children: Jenifer Lea, Todd Pierce, Robert Douglas. BS in Elec. Engring., Rose Hulman Inst. Tech., 1949. Registered profl. engr., Ky. With Louisville Gas and Electric Co., 1949-91, asst. v.p. ops., 1962-63, asst. v.p., asst. gen. supt., 1963-64, v.p., gen. supt., 1964-69, v.p. ops., 1969-78, exec. v.p., 1978, pres., chief exec. officer, 1978-89; chmn., 1989-91; dir. Louisville Gas and Electric Co., 1972-91, chmn. emeritus, 1991—; dir. LG8E Energy Corp., 1990-91. Mem. exec. bd. East Cen. Area Reliability Coun., 1978-89; mem. Ky. Energy Resources Commn., 1975-79; mem. energy task force Gov.'s Econ. Devel. Commn., 1976-79; mem. Ky. Energy Rsch. Bd., 1978-88; v.p. Ind.-Ky. Electric Corp., 1979-89; dir. Ohio Valley Transmission Corp., 1978-90, Ohio Valley Electric Corp., 1979-89, Citizens Fidelity Corp. & Citizens Fidelity Bank and Trust Co., 1976-90. Mem. exec. bd. Old Ky. Home Coun. Boy Scouts Am., v.p. dist. ops., 1970-75, 79-80, 1st v.p., 1981-82, pres., 1982-84, commr., 1975-79, rep. to nat. coun., 1975-84, 95—, mem. regional bd., 1985—, S.E. region area pres., 1988-93, NESA nat. com., 2003—; bd. dirs. East End Boys Club, 1975-78, Louisville Indsl. Found., 1980-86, Ky. Coun. Sci. and Tech., 1987-92; trustee Spirit of Louisville Found., 1978-90, J. Graham, Brown Found., 1980—; bd. mgrs. Rose Hulman Inst. Tech., 1979—; bd. dirs. Ky. Derby Mus., 1991-93, Leadership Louisville Found., 1985-91, Alliant Health Sys., 1989-94; mem. Louisville Devel. Com., 1979-83. Served with U.S. Army, 1953-55. Recipient Silver Beaver award Boy Scouts Am., 1975, Disting. Eagle award, 1989, Silver Antelope award, 1990; elected to the du Pont Manual HS Alumni Hall of Fame, Louisville, KY. Mem. IEEE, Am. Radio and Relay League, Execs. Club Louisville (dir. 1980-83), Louisville Automobile Club (dir. 1974-96, treas. 1977-79, v.p. 1979-81, pres. 1981-83, nat. adv. coun. 1982-86), Louisville Area C. of C. (dir. 1978-80), Hurstbourne Country Club, Pendennis Club, Nat. Eagle Scout Assn. (nat. com. 2003—), Rotary. Methodist. Home and Office: 4014 Norbourne Blvd Louisville KY 40207-3806

ROYER, THOMAS JERRY, financial planner; b. Coshocton, Ohio, June 17, 1943; s. Walter H. Sr. and Francis (Guerke) R.; m. Felipa T. Pagal, Dec. 24, 1965; children: Matthew Vincent, Brian Eugene, Nicholas Alexander. Student, Xavier U., 1979, Coll. for Fin. Planning, Denver, 1986. Cert. fin. planner. Agt. Met. Life Ins. Co., N.Y.C., 1966-68, mgr., 1968-70; gen. agt. Summit Nat. Life Ins. Co., Akron, Ohio, 1970—, Community Nat., Worthington, Ohio, 1989, Life USA, 1990, Am. Life & Casualty, 1997; prin. Royer & Co., Fairfield, Ohio, 1985-88; founder, pres. Group-10 Fin., Fairfield, 1988—; founder, CEO United Group Mktg., Cin., 1993, Altamonte Springs, Fla., 1996. Mem. Inst. Cert. Fin. Planners, Nat. Exchange Club. Republican. Roman Catholic. Avocations: golf, swimming, physical fitness. Office: Group-10 Fin 2790 Mack Rd Fairfield OH 45014-5129 also: United Group Mktg 921 Douglas Ave Ste 208 Altamonte Springs FL 32714-5202

ROYER, TOM A. entomologist, educator; b. Cherokee, Iowa; s. Don and Dorothy Royer; m. Joleen Royer; children: Kelly, Kevin. BS, Iowa State U., Ames, 1973—78; MS, S.D. State U., Brookings, 1980—83; PhD, Tex. A&M U., College Station, 1987—90. Ext. specialist U. Ill. Coop. Ext. Svc., Edwardsville, 1991—92, ext. educator, 1992—97; asst. prof. Okla. State U., Stillwater, 1997—2003, assoc. prof., 2003—. Contbr. chapters to books. Mem.: Soc. Southwestern Entomologists (pres.-elect 2004—), Entomol. Soc. Am. (chair, sect. E 2002—03), Gamma Sigma Delta, Sigma Xi, Phi Kappa Phi. Office: Okla State Univ 127 NRC Stillwater OK 74078 Office Phone: 405-744-5531. E-mail: tom.royer@okstate.edu.

ROYER, WILLIAM A. language educator; b. Indpls., July 13, 1948; s. Donald Criswell Royer and Martha Louise Fesler. AB, Hamilton Coll., Clinton, N.Y., 1970; MA, Ind. U., 1972. Tchg. asst. Ind. U., Bloomington, Ind., 1970—72; tchr. McCallie Sch., Chattanooga, 1972—, fgn. lang., 1981—95, dept. chair, 1984—97. NEH grantee, 1981, 1985, 1987, MLA grantee, 1987. Mem.: Am. Coun. Tchg. of Fgn. Lang., Am. Assn. Tchrs. French, MLA. Home and Office: McCallie Sch 500 Dodds Ave Chattanooga TN 37404 Office Phone: 423-493-5859.

ROYHAB, RONALD, journalist, editor; b. Lorain, Ohio, Oct. 6, 1942; s. Halim Farah and Elizabeth Della (Naiser) R.; m. Roberta Lee Libb, Apr. 20, 1969; children: David Libb, Aaron Nicholas. Reporter Lorain Jour., 1966-69; reporter spl. assignment Scripps Howard Cin. Post, 1971-72; investigative reporter Scripps Howard Cleve. Press, 1972-75; chief bur. Scripps Howard Ohio Bur., Columbus, 1975-78; asst. mng. editor Scripps Howard News Svc., Washington, 1978-81; mng. editor Scripps Howard El Paso (Tex.) Herald Post, 1981-83; asst. mng. editor Scripps Howard Pitts. Press, 1983-92; assoc. editor Pitts. Post Gazette, 1992-93; mng. editor Toledo Blade, 1993-97, exec. editor, 1997—; v.p. Toledo Blade Co., 2004—. Bd. dirs. Toledo Blade Co. With USAR, 1964-70. Decorated knight Order St. Antioch; recipient 7 awards for Excellence Cleve. Newspaper Guild, 1972-75, Spl. Sect. awards Pa. Newspaper Pubs. Assn., 1985, 86, 88; named to DeMolay Legion of Honor, 1997; Am. Polit. Sci. Assn. fellow, 1970-71. Mem. Am. Soc. Newspaper Editors, AP Soc. Ohio (pres. 2000-01), Ohio Newspaper Assn., Toledo Press Club (pres. 2002-03). Eastern Orthodox. Home: 27262 Fort Meigs Rd Perrysburg OH 43551-1230 Office: Toledo Blade 541 N Superior St Toledo OH 43660-0002 Office Phone: 419-724-6161. Personal E-mail: royhab@theblade.com.

ROYLE, CYNTHIA, editor; Student, Brigham Young U.; B Comms., U. Del. Copy editor, reporter, bur. chief, state editor, city editor, city-state editor News Jour., Wilmington, Del.; enterprise editor Jour. News, White Plains, NY, 1995—97, mng. editor Rockland edit., 1997, now sr. mng. editor. Office: Jour News 1 Gannett Dr White Plains NY 10604*

ROYLE, DAVID BRIAN LAYTON, television producer, journalist; came to U.S., 1974; s. John Hardy Layton and Jessie Monica (Pringle) R.; m. Cornelia Boardman Service; children: William Brian Layton, Richard John Boardman. BA cum laude, U. N.C., 1978; MA, U. Minn., 1985. Journalist Northcliffe Newspapers, Stoke-on-Trent, England, 1979-82; news producer Ctrl. Ind. TV, Birmingham, England, 1982-83; producer Inside Story, N.Y.C., 1984-86; pres. New Atlantic Prodns., N.Y.C., 1986-89, David Royle Prodns., N.Y.C., 1989—. Field prodr. Am. Detective in Russia, ABC, L.A., 1992; exec. prodr. Target: Mafia, A&E, CBS, 1993; prodr. TV Nation, NBC, BBC, 1994, Wall St. Jour. TV, 1995; pres. Pub. Media Inc., N.Y.C., 1992-97; dir. The Russian Archive, 1992—; sr. prodr. Nat. Geog. TV, Washington, 1996-98, exec. prodr., 1998—, sr. v.p. prodn., 2000—. Prodr.: (tv shows) Rupert Murdoch: Press Baron Who Would Be King, PBS, 1985 (Emmy nomination), Assignment Africa, PBS, 1986 (Emmy nomination), Senator Sam, PBS, 1988 (Ohio State award, Cine Golden Eagle), Inside Gorbachev's USSR, PBS, 1989 (George Polk award, DuPont-Columbia U. Gold Baton); (TV series) The Eagle and The Bear, ABC/A&E, 1993 (Cine Golden Eagle), Dr. Frank, PBS, 1994 (Cine Golden Eagle, Regional Emmy award), TV Nation, NBC/BBC, 1994 (Prime Time Emmy award), Emerging Powers: Brazil, PBS/NHK Japan, 1996, Trauma: Life and Death in the E.R., TLC, 1996, Nat. Geographic Explorer, TBS, 1999— (5 Emmy awards, Emmy nominations), Inside Base Camp, Nat. Geog. Channel, 2001 (Emmy award, 2001), Taboo, 2002—04, National Geographic's Most Amazing Moments, 2004, Liberia, America Dream?, 2004 (Edward R. Murrow award). Gov. Clifton Coll., Bristol, Eng., 1997—. Morehead scholar, 1974-78, scholar Rotary Internat., 1983; NJ Arts fellow, 1995; named Hon. Citizen, Mpls., 1983; recipient Excellence award U. Minn. Sch. Journalism & Mass Comm., 2000. Mem. NATAS, Soc. Profl. Journalists, Writers Guild of Am. Avocations: running, sailing, photography, reading. Office: Nat Geog TV 1145 17th St NW Washington DC 20036-4701

ROYS, JOHN E. chemist; b. Muskegon, Mich., Jan. 8, 1953; s. Viola Allison and Everett Courtland Roys, Fred Allison (Stepfather); m. Louise Hendrickson, Feb. 16, 1955; 1 child, Andrew. BS Biology minor Chemistry, No. Ill. U., DeKalb IL, 1975. Tech. chemist Avery Dennison Performance Films Div., Schererville, Ind., 1990—; engr. and quality mgr. product devel. Smurfit Laminations, Schaumburg, Ill., 1981—90. Quality supr. Gaurdian Packaging, Batavia, Ill., 1978—81; product devel. engr Laminating and Coating, Schamburg, Ill., 1977—78; quality & tech. svc. Std. Packaging, Elgin, Ill., 1975—77. Author technical papers. Active mem. M.A.V. Firesword a non for profit comty. svc. orgn., Portage, Ind., 1999—2004. Achievements include patents in field.

ROYSTER, PAUL BARNETT, publishing executive; b. Opelika, Ala., June 23, 1953; s. Wimberly Calvin and Betty Jo (Barnett) Royster; m. Sandra Jane Remus, Aug. 8, 1987; children: Elizabeth, James. AB, Princeton U., N.J., 1975; MA, U. Mich., 1976; PhD, Columbia U., N.Y.C., 1984. Asst. editor The Libr. of Am., N.Y.C., 1980—93, prodn. mgr., 1982—93, CFO, 1987—93; project editor Barron's Ednl. Series, Hauppauge, NY, 1994; design and prodn. mgr. Yale U. Press, New Haven, 1994—2002; dir. Univ. of Nebr. Press, Lincoln, 2002—. Prof. English U. Nebr., Lincoln, 2003—. Home: 6710 Park Crest Ct Lincoln NE 68506 Office: Univ of Nebraska Press 233 N 8th St Lincoln NE 68588

ROYSTON, IVOR, scientific director; b. Belford, Eng., Apr. 29, 1945; m. Colette Carson. BS in Human Biology, John Hopkins U., 1967, MD, postgrad., John Hopkins U., 1970. Diplomate Am. Bd. Internal Medicine, Am. Bd. Med. Oncology. Intern in internal medicine Stanford (Calif.) U. Hosp., 1970-71, resident in internal medicine, 1971-72; staff assoc. div. virology Bur. of Biologics (formerly div. Biologic Stds. at NIH), Bethesda, Md., 1972-73, chief viral oncology sect., div. virology, 1973-75; postdoctoral fellow Div. Oncology, Dept. Medicine, Stanford U. Med. Ctr., 1975-77; asst. prof. medicine Div. Hematology/Oncology, U. Calif. Sch. Medicine, San Diego, 1977-82; staff physician San Diego Vets. Adminstrn. Med. Ctr., 1977-78, clin. investigator, 1978-81; dir. Cell Surface Marker Lab. Cancer Ctr., U. Calif., San Diego, 1981-90; chief oncology sect. med. svc. San Diego VA Med. Ctr., 1982-84; assoc. prof. medicine hematology/oncology divsn. U. Calif., 1982-90, dir. clinical immunology program cancer ctr., 1984-90, prof. medicine, 1990-91; pres., sci. dir. San Diego Reg. Cancer Ctr., 1990—. Bd. dirs. UniSyn Techs., Inc., San Diego, 1991—, Somatix Therapy Corp., Alameda, Calif.; adj. prof. medicine U. Calif. San Diego, Sch. Medicine, 1990—; founder, dir., cons. Hybritech, Inc., La Jolla, 1978-86, IDEC Pharms., Inc., LaJolla, 1985-92; immunology com. Cancer and Leukemia Group B., 1980-91; vice chmn. immunology com., 1981-91; cons. mem. biol. response modifiers program decision, network com., Div. of Cancer Treatment, Nat. Cancer Inst., 1982-85; mem. Clin. Cancer Program Project Rev. Com., Nat. Cancer Inst., 1983-88, Long Range Planning com. U. Calif. Cancer Ctr.; mem. adv. com. U. Calif. San Diego Biotechnology Transfer Faculty; co-dir. Internat. Conf. Monoclonal Antibody Immunoconjugates for Cancer, 1986—, Internat. Conf. Gene Therapy of Cancer, 1992—; mem. merit rev. bd. oncology Dept. Vets. Affairs, 1992—. Editorial bd. Jour. of Biol. Response Modifiers, Hybridoma; assoc. editor Jour. of clin. Lab. Analysis, Antibody, Immunoconjugates and Radio Pharmaceuticals, Molecular Biology of Cancer; frequent reviewer Cancer Research, Blood, Jour. of Clin. Oncology; adv. bd. CRC Critical Rev. in Oncology/Hematology. Bd. trustees La Jolla Mus. of Contemporary Art, 1985-86, La Jollar Playhouse, 1986-91, Francis Parker Sch., San Diego, 1989—; bd. dirs. Am. Cancer Soc. With USPHS, 1972-74. Ford Found fellowship, 1969-70; recipient Johns Hopkins Med. Soc. award 1970, Clin. Investigator award VA, 1978-81; named Bus. Leader of Yr., San Diego Venture Group, 1990, Man of Yr., 1991. Fellow ACP; mem. AAAS, Am. Soc. of Microbiology, Am. Fedn. for Clin. Rsch., Am. Assn. for Cancer Rsch., Am. Soc. for Clin. Oncology, Internat. Assn. for Comparative Rsch. on Leukemia, Am. Soc. of Hematology, Transplantation Soc., Am. Assn. of Immunologists, Am. Soc. Clin. Investigation. Achievements include patents for monoclonal antibody compositions specific for single antigens in antigen aggregates;

immunoglobulin secreting human hybridomas from a cultured lymphoblastoid cell line. Address: San Diego Regional Cancer Ctr Ste 200 2099 Science Park Rd San Diego CA 92121 Office: CancerVax Corp 5931 Darwin Ct Carlsbad CA 92008

ROZANTINE, GAYLE STUBBS, clinical psychologist; b. Atlanta, Dec. 1, 1944; d. William L. and Louise (Cash) Stubbs; children: Kathryn Patricia, Webb Black III, Gregory William, Benjamin Stubbs, John Paul; m. Barry Rozantine. BA in Psychology, Agnes Scott Coll., 1965; MA in Tchg., Emory U., 1966; MA in Clin. Psychology, Western Carolina U., 1990; PhD, U. Tenn., 1995. Lic. psychologist, Ga.; diplomate Am. Acad. of Experts in Traumatic Stress; cert. domestic violence counselor. Tchr. Fulton Co. Bd. Edn., Ga., 1967-68; psychology resident Med. Coll. of Ga., Augusta, 1994-95, clin. fellow, 1995-96; rsch. psychologist Pain Evaluation and Intervention Program Dept. of VA Med. Ctr., Augusta, 1995-98; staff psychologist Compass Health Systems, Miami Beach, Fla., 1998, Charter Savannah Bevioral Health System, Ga., 1999-2000; CEO Ctr. Health and Well-Being, 2000—. Mem. critical incident stress debriefing team Med. Coll. Ga.; disaster mental health response team ARC; presenter in field. Mem. Am. Psychol. Assn., Coastal Area Psychologists, Ga. Psychol. Assn., Ga. Breast Cancer Coalition and Fund, Nat. Assn. of Forensic Counselors, Nat. Register Health Svc. Providers in Psychology. Office: The Ctr for Health and Well-Being PC 400 Commercial Ct Savannah GA 31406 Office Phone: 912-352-9500 ext 105. E-mail: grozantine@quietawakening.com.

ROZARIO, DIANE MARIE, publishing executive; b. Landstuhl, Germany, July 19, 1963; arrived in U.S., 1963, d. Michael Milton and Rosemary Ann Oethen; divorced; children: Autumn, Savannah, Bethany, Benedict. BA, Grinnell Coll., 1985. Reverse placement specialist Am. Field Svc., N.Y.C., 1985—87; adminstrv. sec. 1199 Home Core Benefit Fund, N.Y.C., 1989—90; pub. Patter Pub., Burlington, Iowa, 1992—. Adminstrv. asst. J&M Displays, Inc., Yarmouth, Iowa, 2002—. Author: Immunization Resource Guide, 1992, Immunization Resource Guide, 4th edit., 2000. Mem.: Nat. Vaccine Info. Ctr., Soc. Creative Anachronism. Roman Catholic.

ROZEK, THOMAS M. health facility administrator; Pres. Children's Hosp. of Mich.; sr. v.p. Detroit Med. Ctr.; pres. & CEO Miami Children's Hosp., 1999—. Bd. trustees Fla. Hosp., 2001; bd. dirs. Children's Trust of Miami-Dade County, 2003. Office: Miami Children's Hosp 3100 SW 62nd Ave Miami FL 33155

ROZELL, HERBERT, state legislator, construction executive; b. Welling, Okla., Nov. 30, 1931; s. Horace Berry and Myrtle Lee (Knight) R.; m. Carol Margaret Randall; children: Mike, Rene. BS, Northeastern State U., Tahlequah, Okla., 1954, MEd, 1967; postgrad., U. Ark., 1971. Tchr., coach, Haskell, Okla., 1954-57; asst. prin. Tahlequah High Sch., 1960-64, prin., 1965-70; Okla. Senate, Oklahoma City, 1976—. Chmn. com. higher edn., ethics com., 1983, transp. com., 1984, rules com., fin. com., appropiations com., edn. com., budget com.; vice-chmn. common edn.; asst. majority floor leader. Mem. city coun., Tahlequah, 1967-76, Tahlequah Hosp. Bd. Mem. Jaycees (charter pres. Tahlequah chpt.), Tahlequah Alumni Assn. (past pres.). Democrat. Baptist. Home: 1106 W 4th St Tahlequah OK 74464-7317 Office: RR 1 Tahlequah OK 74464-9801

ROZELLE, LEE THEODORE, physical chemist, researcher; b. Rhinelander, Wis., Mar. 9, 1933; s. Theodore and Alice (Omholt) R.; m. Barbara J. Ingli, June 21, 1955; children— David, Steven, Carolyn, Ann, Kenneth BS, U. Wis., 1955, PhD, 1960. Rsch. chemist DuPont Corp., Circleville, Ohio, 1960-63; prin. scientist-tech. coord. Honeywell Corp., Mpls., 1963-67; dir. chemistry div. North Star Rsch. Inst., Mpls., 1967-74; v.p. R&D USCI div. C.R. Bard, Billerica, Mass., 1974-77; dir. engring. tech. div. Mellon Inst., Pitts., 1977-78; dir. rsch. and devel. Permutit Co., Monmouth Junction, N.J., 1978-80; v.p. rsch. and devel. Gelman Scis., Inc., Ann Arbor, Mich., 1980-82; v.p. sci. and tech. Culligan Internat. Co., Northbrook, Ill., 1982-87; assoc. dir. rsch. Olin Chems. Rsch. div. Olin Corp., Cheshire, Conn., 1987-92; cons. in water treatment tech., mktg. and mgmt., 1992—; pres., cons. Water Solutions, Inc., 1995—; exec. v.p. Puraq Water Systems, Inc., 1996—. Cons. in field; mem. Nat. Drinking Water Adv. Council EPA, 1987-90; mem. small bus. inovative rsch. com. U.S. EPA, 1999—. Contbr. chpts. to books, numerous articles to profl. jours. Bd. dirs. Unitarian Ch., Andover, Mass., 1974-77 NIH fellow, 1958-60; recipient Spl. Hominum award Nat. Sanitation Found., 1988. Fellow Am. Inst. Chemists; mem. AAAS, Am. Chem. Soc., Am. Soc. Artificial Internal Organs, Health Industry Mfrs. Assn. (chmn. spl. activities com.), Water Pollution Control Fedn., Water Quality Assn. (chmn. sci. adv. com., Award of Merit 1989), Am. Water Works Assn., Assn. Met. Water Agencies, Filtration Soc., Pacific Water Quality Assn. (bd. dirs. 1987-90, Robert Gans award 1988), Am. Soc. Agrl. Engring., Internat. Water Supply Assn., European Membrane Soc., N.Am. Membrane Soc., Asociacion Interamericano De Ingenieria Sanaitaria y Ambiental, Sigma Xi, Eta Phi Alpha, Phi Lambda Upsilon. Home and Office: 626 23rd St N La Crosse WI 54601-3825 *My professional goal has always been to make significant contributions to the well being of our society through science. Goals have been accomplished from contributions to water purification to health care.*

ROZEN, JEROME GEORGE, JR., research entomologist, museum curator and research administrator; b. Evanston, Ill., Mar. 19, 1928; s. Jerome George and Della (Kretchmar) R.; m. Barbara L. Lindner, Dec. 18, 1948; children: Steven George, Kenneth Charles, James Robert Student, U. Pa., 1946-48; BA, U. Kans., 1950; PhD, U. Calif.-Berkeley, 1955. Entomologist in taxonomy U.S. Dept. Agr., 1956-58; asst. prof. entomology Ohio State U., 1958-60; assoc. curator dept. entomology Am. Mus. Natural History, N.Y.C., 1960-65, curator hymenoptera, 1965—, chmn. dept. entomology, 1960-71, dep. dir. research, 1972-86. Field expdns. in U.S., Europe, Mex., Trinidad, Argentina, Chile, Brazil, Peru, Venezuela, Morocco, Pakistan, Republic of South Africa, Namibia, Israel, Egypt, Kyrgzstan, Turkey; adj. prof. CUNY, 1968—. Contbr. numerous sci. articles on bees (Apoidea) and beetles (Coleoptera). Fellow AAAS; mem. Am. Inst. Biol. Scis., Entomol. Soc. Am. (editor misc. publs. 1959-60), Soc. Study of Evolution, Soc. Systematic Biology, N.Y. Entomol Soc. (pres. 1964-65), Washington Entomol. Soc., Pacific Coast Entomol. Soc., Kans. Entomol. Soc., Orgn. Biol. Field Stas. (pres. 1990), Internat. Soc. Hymenopterists (co-organizer, Bee Course, 1999-). Home: 55 Haring St Closter NJ 07624-1709 Office: Am Mus Natural History Central Park West New York NY 10024-5192 Office Phone: 212-769-5466.

ROZENBERG, LANA, cosmetic dentist; b. 1968; DDS, U. Pacific Sch. Dentistry, 1994. Dir. Dental Day Spa, NY. Named one of NY Top Cosmetic Dentists, NY Mag., 2002, 2004. Avocations: boating, golf, skiing, tennis, financial investments. Office: Dental Day Spa 45 W 54th St Ste 1B New York NY 10019 Office Phone: 212-265-7724. Business E-Mail: office@rozenbergdds.com.

ROZENBLAT, ANATOLY ISAACOVICH, manufacturing engineer, inventor; b. Moscow, Aug. 25, 1938; came to the U.S., 1990; s. Isaac Saimolovich Rozenblat and Natalie Ivanovna Fedorisheva; m. June 27, 1964 (div. 1979) children: Inna, Moshe. BS in Mech. Engring., Inst. Marine Engrs., Odessa, Ukraine, 1967; BS in Computer Sci., East-West U., 1997. Cert. mech. and mfg. engring. Adminstrv. staff Ship Repair and Shipbldg. Plant, Odessa, 1970-80; project engr. Sci. Prodn. Assn., Odessa, 1980-89; pvt. practice scientist and inventor Chgo., 1990—. Mem. Internat. Biog. Ctr., Eng., 1995, adv. bd. Am. Biog. Inst., N.C., 1996; presenter 26th Israel Conf., 1996, 27th Israel Conf., 1998. Author: Regression Analysis of Ship Speed in Waves and The Tropics, 1997, Rozenblat's Innovations For The Twenty-First Century, 1998; contbr. articles to profl. jours.; patentee in field. With Russian Air Force, 1964. Mem. ASME, Soc. Mfg. Engrs., Soc. Naval Architects and Marine Engrs., Nat. Congress Inventors Orgns. Avocations: chess, literature, music, travel, nature. Home: Apt 2606 10 E Ontario St Chicago IL 60611-4770

ROZMAN, GILBERT FRIEDELL, sociologist, educator; b. Mpls., Feb. 18, 1943; s. David and Celia (Friedell) R.; m. Masha Dwosh, Jan. 25, 1945; children: Thea Dwosh, Noah Dwosh. BA, Carleton Coll., Northfield, Minn., 1965; PhD (Woodrow Wilson fellow 1965-66), Princeton U., 1971. Mem. faculty Princeton U., 1970—, prof. sociology, 1979—, Musgrave prof. sociology, 1992—. Mem. com. studies Chinese civilization Am. Council Learned Socs., 1975-80; mem. U.S.-USSR Bi-Nat. Commn. Humanities and Social Scis., 1978-86, IREX Univ. Coun., 1998-2001. Author: Urban Networks in Ch'ing China and Tokugawa Japan, 1973, Urban Networks in Russia, 1750-1800, and Premodern Periodization, 1976, Population and Marketing Settlements in Ch'ing China, 1982, A Mirror for Socialism: Soviet Criticisms of China, 1985, The Chinese Debate About Soviet Socialism 1978-85, 1987, Japan's Response to the Gorbachev Era, 1985-1991: A Rising Superpower Views a Declining One, 1992, Northeast Asia's Stunted Regionalism: Bilateral Distrust in the Shadow of Globalization, 2004; co-author: The Modernization of Japan and Russia, 1975; editor: The Modernization of China, 1981, Soviet Studies of Premodern China: Assessments of Recent Scholarship, 1984, Japan in Transition: From Tokugawa to Meiji, 1986, The East Asian Region: Confucian Heritage and Its Modern Adaptation, 1991, Dismantling Communism: Common Causes and Regional Variations, 1992, Russia and East Asia: The 21st Century Security Environment, 1999, Japan and Russia: The Tortuous Path to Normalization, 1949-1999, 2000. Guggenheim fellow, 1979-80; grantee NSF, NEH, Social Sci. Rsch. Coun., Nat. Coun. for Soviet and E. European Studies, U.S. Inst. Peace, Woodrow Wilson Internat. Ctr. Mem. Assn. Asian Studies, Am. Sociol. Assn., Am. Assn. Advancement Slavic Studies. Home: 20 Springwood Dr Trenton NJ 08648-1048 Office: Princeton U 149 Wallace Hall Princeton NJ 08544-0001 Office Phone: 609-258-5094. E-mail: grozman@princeton.edu.

ROZMAN, JAMES D. church administrator; b. Lynwood, Calif., Sept. 5, 1950; s. Clyde A. and Mae A. Rozman. AA, Coll. San Mateo, 1970; BS, We. Bapt. Coll., Salem, Oreg., 1977; MDiv, Talbot Theol. Sem., La Mirada, Calif., 1981; D of Ministry, Biola U., La Mirada, Calif., 1989; grad., USAF Acad. Instr. Sch., 1984, USAF Squadron Officer Sch., 1988, Air Command and Staff Coll., 1994, USAF Air War Coll., 1996; cert. wing chaplain course, Air U., Maxwell AFB, 2001. Cert. in clin. pastoral edn., 1998. Commd. USAF, 1980, advanced through ranks to lt. col., installation chaplain, 1981-84, installation staff chaplain Sondrestrom Air Base, Greenland, 1984-85, protestant chaplain Travis AFB, Calif., 1985-87, Tactical Air Command site chaplain Griffiss AFB, N.Y., 1987-89, sr. protestant chaplain San Vito dei Normanni, Italy, 1989-91, protestant chaplain Langley AFB, Va., 1991-94, sr. protestant chaplain Tinker AFB, Okla., 1994-97, sr. parish chaplain Travis AFB, 1998—2001, wing chaplain L.A. AFB, Calif., 2001—04; clin. pastoral edn. resident Walter Reed Army Med. Ctr., Washington, 1997-98. Acting sr. chaplain, USAF Chapel Team, Apr. 1995 Oklahoma City Bombing Rescue Effort, Tinker AFB, Okla. Mem. VFW (life), Mil. Chaplains Assn. (life), Air Force Assn. (life), Air Force Sgts. Assn. (life), Mil. Officer Assn. Am. (life), Assn. Clin. Pastoral Edn., Assn. Calif. Sch. Adminstrs., Internat. Assn. Christian Sch. Adminstrs., Internat. Assn. Christian Early Educators, Biola U. Alumni Assn., We. Bapt. Coll. Alumni Assn., Am. Legion. Republican. Baptist. Avocations: walking, travel, swimming, reading. Home: 1656 Betty Ct Santa Clara CA 95051-2910 Office: 1900 Monterey Dr San Bruno CA 94066 Personal E-mail: therozman@juno.com.

ROZNOVSCHI, MIRELA, law librarian, writer; b. Tulcea, Romania, Apr. 10, 1947; d. Iancu and Hrisula Roznovschi; 1 child, Maximilian Adrian Atanasiu. MA in Romance Langs., U. of Bucharest, Bucharest, Romania, 1965—70; M of Info. Sci., Pratt Inst., New York, 1993—96. Cert. Internet Tech. NYU, 1997. Columnist, lit. editor Tomis lit. mag., Constanta, Romania, 1970—74; sr. columnist Magazin, Bucharest, Romania, 1979—89; sr. columnist, bd. dirs. Romania Libera, Bucharest, Romania, 1989—91; faculty, reference libr. internat. and fgn. law NYU Law Libr., New York, NY, 1996—. Cons. Ctrl. European U., Budapest, Hungary, 1999—2002. Author (as Mirela Roznoveanu): Always in the Autumn, 1988, Life on the Run, 1997, Platonia, 1999, Time of the Chosen, 1999; author: numerous poems. Recipient Officer Nat. Order Faithful Svc. of Romania, Pres. of Romania, 2000. Mem.: Assn. Am. Law Schs., Romanian Writers' Guild, Am. Assn. Law Librs. (chair fgn. comparative and internat. law spl. interest sect. 2004—), Am. Soc. Internat. Law, Beta Phi Mu Theta Chpt. Office: NYU Law Libr 40 Washington Square S New York NY 10012

ROZUMNYJ, JAROSLAV, literature educator, researcher; b. Honcharivka, Ukraine, Sept. 6, 1925; s. Hryhory and Anna (Parubocha) R.; m. Oksana Olha Hrycenko, Mar. 10, 1938; children: Larysa, Roman, Istan, Ruslan. BA with honors, Theol. Sem., Culemborg, Netherlands, 1950; MA, U. Ottawa, Ont., Can., 1958, PhD, 1968. Lectr. Laurentian U., Sudbury, Ont., 1960-63; asst. prof. Western Mich. U., Kalamazoo, 1963-64, U. Man., Winnipeg, Can., 1964-71, head dept., 1976-89, prof. lit., 1989—, sr. scholar, 1997. Vis. prof. U. Ottawa, 1972, Ukrainian Cath. U., Rome, 1987; dean Faculty of Philosophy, Ukrainian Free U., Munich, Germany, 1995-96; vis. rsch. scholar Macquarie U., Sydney, 1989; mem. internat. adv. bd. U. Kiev-Mohyla Acad., 1992—, hon. prof., 1996. Editor: New Soil--Old Roots: The Ukrainian Experience in Canada, 1983, I Was Nineteen... KM Academia, 2001, Yesterday, Today, Tomorrow: The Ukrainian Community in Canada, 2004; co-editor: Jubilee Collection of the Ukrainian Academy of Arts and Sciences, 1976; lit. editor: Anthology of Musical Compositions on the Poems of M. Shashkewych, 1992; editor Can. vol. Ency. of Ukrainian Diaspora, 7 vols.; editor-in-chief: Collection of Scholarly Papers, 1996; mem. editl. bd. Suchasnist, 1984-91. Pres. Ukrainian Cultural and Ednl. Ctr., Winnipeg, 1970-73; pres. Can. Friends of Rukh in Ukraine, Winnipeg, 1990-92; Can. rep. U. Kiev-Mohyla-Acad., 1992—; bd. govs. Man. Mus. Man and Nature, Winnipeg, 1976-80; pres. Markian Shashkevych Inst., Winnipeg, 1999—. Recipient Outreach Activities award U. Man., 1986, Order of the Eternal Flame in Silver World Conf. Ukranian Scouts, 1994, Taras Shevchenko medal Ukrainian Can. Congress, 1995, Petro Mohyla Silver medal Nat. U. Kyiv Mohyla Acad., 2003; honored Festschrift, Can. Inst. Ukranian Studies, 2000. Mem. Ukrainian Acad. Arts and Scis. in Can. (pres. 1977-80, v.p. 1995—), Schevchenko Sci. Soc. U.S., Internat. Assn. Ukrainian Studies. Home: 801 Cambridge St Winnipeg MB R3M 3G3 Canada E-mail: rozumnyj@ms.umanitoba.ca.

ROZZELL, SCOTT ELLIS, lawyer; b. Texarkana, Tex., Apr. 12, 1949; s. George M. and Dora Mae (Boyett) Rozzell; m. Michelle Miller Rozzell; children from previous marriage: Stacey Rozzell Murphree, Kimberly Marie. BA, So. Meth. U., 1971; JD, U. Tex., 1975. Bar: Tex. 1975, U.S. Dist. Ct., 1975, U.S. Dist. Ct. (all dists.) 1977, U.S. Ct. Appeals (1st, 3d, 9th cirs.) 1977, U.S. Ct. Appeals (5th and D.C. cirs.) 1976. Assoc. BakerBotts, LLP, Houston, 1975-82, ptnr., 1983-94, sr. ptnr., 1995-2000; exec. v.p., gen. counsel CenterPoint Energy, Inc., Houston, 2001—. Mem. State of Tex. Aircraft Pooling Bd., 1997-2002; devel. bd. U. Tex. Health Sci. Ctr. Houston, 1992-2003; mem. Tex. Commn. for Lawyer Discipline, 2001-03, chair 2002-03; bd. advisors Houston (Tex.) C.C. Sys. Bd. dirs. Manned Space Flight Edn. Found., Inc., 1997—, vice chair 2000-, Tex. Aviation Hall of Fame, 2001—; vice-chmn. Cancer Counseling Inc., Houston, 1991-92; mem. so. regional adv. bd. Inst. Internat. Edn., 2002—; vice chmn. Assn. Electric Cos. Tex. Fellow Tex. Bar Found. (sustaining life), Houston Bar Found. (sustaining life, bd. dirs. 1991-93, chair 1993), Am. Bar Found. (life); mem. ABA, State Bar Tex. (bd. dirs. 1997-2000), Houston Bar Assn. (bd. dirs. 1991-95, pres. 1996-97), Fed. Energy Bar Assn., Houston Young Lawyers Assn. (bd. dirs. 1978-82, pres. 1983-84), Coronado Club, Houstonian. Republican. Presbyterian. Avocation: flying vintage airplanes. Home: 1229 Post Oak Park Houston TX 77027 Office: CenterPoint Energy Inc 1111 Louisiana 46th Floor PO Box 4567 Houston TX 77210-4567 Office Phone: 713-207-1502. Business E-Mail: scott.rozzell@centerpointenergy.com.

ROZZI, CHRISTINE M. mathematician, educator; b. Reading, Pa., Dec. 25, 1967; d. Lorenzo and Lola E. Rozzi. BSE, Millersville (Pa.) U. of Pa., 1990. Tchr. math. and computers Ctrl. Cath. HS, Reading, 1991—98, Girard Coll., Phila., 1998—99; tchr. math Leysin (Switzerland) Am. Sch., 1999—, dean, 2003—. Mem.: Nat. Coun. Tchrs. Math., Math. Assn. Am. Home: 3531 Kutztown Rd Laureldale PA 19605

RUAN, LIAN JIN, library director; arrived in U.S., 1986; d. Yong-dong Jin and Jin-xiu Dai; m. Zhong-jin Ruan, June 24, 1987; children: Gordon J., George J. BA in World History, Peking U., Beijing, 1984; MA in African History, U. Calif., L.A., 1988; MLS, U. Ill., 1990. Rsch. info. specialist Ill. Fire Svc. Inst., Champaign, 1990—99, dir., head libr., 1999—. Newspaper cataloger Ill. State Hist. Libr., Springfield, 1990, manuscript cataloger, 90; libr. cons. Champaign Fire Dept., 1990—. Contbr. articles to profl. jours. Recipient Chancellor's Academic Profl. Excellence award, U. Ill. Mem.: ALA (mem. Illinet network adv. coun. 2003—), Spl. Libr. Assn. (downstate bd. dirs. Ill. chpt. 2002—04, Diversity Leadership Develop. award 2003), Chinese Heritage Assn. (vice prin. chinese sch. 1998—99, prin. chinese sch. 1999—2000, bd. dirs. 2000—03), Internat. Fire Libr. Consortium (adv. com. 1997—2001). Office: Ill Fire Svc Inst Univ Ill 11 Gerty Dr Champaign IL 61820 Office Phone: 217-265-6107. E-mail: lruan@fsi.uiuc.edu.

RUB, TIMOTHY F. museum director; BA in Art History, Middlebury Coll., 1974; MA in Art History, NYU, 1979; MBA, Yale U., 1987; postgrad., Harvard U., 1998. Curatorial intern Met. Mus. Art, 1983; lectr. art and archtl. history Cooper-Hewitt Mus./Parsons Sch. Design, Stevens Inst. Tech., 1979-84; guest curator Bronx Mus. Arts, N.Y., 1985-86; curator Cooper-Hewitt Mus., N.Y.C., 1983-87; assoc. dir. Hood Mus. Dartmouth Coll., Hanover, N.H., 1987-91, dir., COO, 1991-2000; dir. Cin. Art Mus., 2000—. Office: Cin Art Mus 953 Eden Park Dr Cincinnati OH 45202-1596

RUBACK, RICHARD BARRY, psychologist, educator; b. Omaha, Mar. 29, 1950; s. Norman and Mary (Piha) Ruback; m. Jasmin K. Riad, Aug. 27, 2002. BA, Yale U., 1972; JD, U. Tex., 1975; MS, U. Pitts., 1977, PhD, 1979. Bar: Tex. 1975, Ga. 1981, US Supreme Ct. 1995. Asst. prof., assoc. prof. psychology Ga. State U., Atlanta, 1979-88, prof., 1988-96; prof. dept. sociology Pa. State U., Univ. Pk., 1996—, dir. Ctr. for Rsch. on Crime and Justice, 1997—2001. Co-author: Social Psychology of the Criminal Justice System, 1982, After the Crime: Victim Decision Making, 1992; Social and Psychological consequences of violent victimization, 2001; co-editor: Interpersonal Violent Behaviors, 1995; editor Criminal Justice Rev., 1992-1997. Fulbright fellow Coun. Internat. Exch. Scholars, 1985-86, 93-94,Indo-Am. fellow, Indo-US subcommission on Ed. and Culture, 1988; Fulbright-Hays fellow US Dept. Edn., 1991, vis. fellow Nat. Inst. Justice US Dept. Justice, 1986-87, jud. fellow US Supreme Ct., 1995-96; recipient Justice Tom C. Clark award Supreme Ct. Hist. Soc., 1996. Fellow APA; fellow SPSSI; mem. Am. Psychology-Law Soc., Soc. Exptl. Social Psychology. Democrat. Jewish.

RUBARDT, PETER CRAIG, conductor, educator; b. Oakland, Calif., Aug. 7, 1958; s. Kenneth and Betty (Maspero) R.; m. Hedi Salanki; children, Daniel, Vivienna. BA, U. Calif., Berkeley, 1981; M of Music, SUNY, Stony Brook, 1984; student, Hochschule fur Musik, Vienna, 1984-86; D Mus. Arts, Julliard Sch., 1989. Prof., conductor SUNY, Purchase, 1989-90, Rutgers U., New Brunswick, N.J., 1991-96; resident conductor N.J. Symphony, Newark, 1990-93; assoc. conductor Syracuse (N.Y.) Symphony, 1993-97; music dir., condr. Greater Pensacola (Fla.) Symphony Orch., 1997—. Guest conductor various orchs. Condr. rec. Bach Concerti, 1988. Fullbright fellow USIA, 1984-86; Bruno Walter scholar, Julliard Sch., 1986-88. Mem. Am. Symphony Orch. League, Condrs. Guild. Democrat. Home: 8774 Thunderbird Dr Pensacola FL 32514 Office: Pensacola Symphony Orch PO Box 1752 Pensacola FL 32598-1752 Office Phone: 850-435-2533.

RUBASH, HARRY E. orthopedist, surgeon; s. Harry L. and Agnes M. Rubash; m. Kimberly E. Ertman, Aug. 19, 1978; children: Bradley, Steven, Kristen. BS, U. Pitts., 1975, MD, 1979. Diplomate Am. Bd. Orthopedic Surgery. Dir. joint replacement svc. Oakland VA Med. Ctr., Pitts., 1985—87, asst. chief orthopaedic surgery, 1985—87, chief orthopaedic surgery, 1987—95; chief divsn. of adult reconstructive surgery U. Pitts. Sch. of Medicine, Pitts., 1987—97, clin. vice chmn. dept. orthopedic surgery, 1994—97; chief, dept. of orthopaedic surgery Mass. Gen. Hosp., Boston, 1998—. Pres. Pa. Orthopaedic Soc., 1994; treas. Orthopaedic Rsch. Soc., Rosemont, Ill., 1998—2001; bd. dirs. Assn. for Arthritic Hip and Knee Soc., 1991. Editor: The Adult Knee; author: (textbook) Pelvic and Acetabular Fractures. Mem. governing bd. Western Pa. chpt. Arthritis Found., Pitts., 1994—98; state chmn. Pa. Joint Parade, Pitts., 1995—97; co-chmn. Arthritis Found. Joint Walk, Boston, 1998—99; hon. co-chmn. Ladies Hosp. Aid Soc. Ball, Pitts., 1996. Recipient Ranawt award, Knee Soc. /Am. Acad. Orthopaedic Surgeons, 2001, John Charnley award, Hip Soc., 2003. Mem.: Interurban Club, Internat. Hip Soc., Am. Orthopaedic Assn. (mem. program com. 2000). Avocations: golf, fly fishing, hunting, boating. Office: Orthopaedics Mass Gen Hosp 55 Fruit Street White 607 Boston MA 02114 E-mail: hrubash@aol.com.

RUBBERT, PAUL EDWARD, engineering executive; b. Mpls., Feb. 18, 1937; s. Adolf Christian and Esther Ruth Rubbert; m. Mary Parpart, Oct. 6, 1958 (div. 1985); children: Mark, David, Stephen. BS with high distinction, U. Minn., 1958, MS in Aero. Engring., 1960; PhD in Aerodyn., MIT, 1965. Rsch. engr. The Boeing Co., Seattle, 1960-62, 65-72, unit chief aerodyns rsch., comml. airplane group, 1972—, tech. fellow, 1989. Cons. NASA, 1989—, aeronautics adv. com., aerospace rsch. and tech. subcoms.; corp. vis. com. MIT, 1990—; served on various coms. Nat. Rsch. Coun. Panel; aerodyns. cons. GM; speaker in field. Contbr. articles to profl. jours. Recipient Arch T. Colwell Merit award Soc. Automotive Engrs., 1968, Wright Brothers Lectureship in Aeronautics Am. Inst. of Aeronautics and Astronautics, 1994 Fellow AIAA (Outstanding Tech. Mgmt. award Pacific Northwest sect., disting. lectr., assoc. editor jour., past mem. fellow selection com., dir., chmn. various workshops and coms.), Royal Aero. Soc.; mem. NAE. Achievements include three patents in field. Home: PO Box 299 Pollock ID 83547-0299

RUBELI, PAUL E. gaming company executive; b. 1943; married. BS, U. Notre Dame; MBA, Columbia U., 1967. Assoc. A.T. Kearney Inc., Chgo., 1969-73; v.p., gen. mgr. Bunker-Ramo Corp., 1973-76; group v.p. Baker Industries, Parsippany, N.J., 1976-79; exec. v.p. and pres. Ramada Inns Inc., Phoenix, 1979-89; pres., CEO Aztar Corp., Phoenix, 1989—, chmn., 1991—. Served to 1st lt. AUS, 1967-69. Office: Aztar Corp 2390 E Camelback Rd Ste 400 Phoenix AZ 85016-3479

RUBELLO, DAVID JEROME, artist; b. Detroit, Sept. 3, 1935; s. Ludovico and Girolama (Trupiano) R.; m. Mary Anne Keithan, Oct. 14, 1978. BFA, Am. Acad. Art, Rome, 1961; MFA, U. Mich., 1972; cert., Acad. Fine Art, Copenhagen, 1966. Lect. art U. Mich., Ann Arbor, 1973-74; asst. prof. art Pa. State U., University Park, 1974-80; assoc. prof. art Towson (Md.) State U., 1980-81; assoc. prof. U. Mich., Ann Arbor, 1988-90. One man shows include Cade Gallery, Royal Oak, Mich., 1987; exhibited in group shows at Detroit Inst. Art, 1987, GMB Gallery Internat., Bloomfield Hills, Mich., 1991, Kresge Art Inst., 1989, Kalamazoo Art Inst., 1990, 91, Photo Nat. 2, Ella Sharp Mus., Jackson, Mich., BBAA, Birmingham, Mich., Arts Coun., Traverse City, Mich., 1995-96, Patrimonio Invitational Wayne State U., Detroit, 1996, Ann. Celebrate Mich. Artists P.C. Art Ctr., Rochester, 1994, 95, 96, Art Ctr., Mt. Clemens, Mich., 1997, Crative Art Ctr., Pontiac, Mich., 1997; exhibited Null Dimension, Fulda, Germany, 1988, Systematica Constructive Art, Madrid, 1989, B4 Pub. Invitational, London, 1990, Archive 90s, Amsterdam and London, Konkrete Miniatures Invitational, Amsterdam, 1991, Planet Art Gallery, Capetown, South Africa, 1999, Detroit Focus, 2000; contbr. articles to profl. jours. including The Structurist, 1999, 2002. Recipient awards for art work; featured professional artist profile B&W Fine Art Photography Mag., June 2001.

RUBEN, AUDREY H. lawyer, arbitrator, actress; m. Robert J. Ruben; children: Pamela, James B. BA, NYU, 1948; MA, Columbia U., 1953; JD, St. John's U., 1976. Bar: N.Y. 1977, U.S. Dist. Ct. (so. and ea. dists.) N.Y. 1977, U.S. Supreme Ct. 1982. Law intern Westchester Dist. Atty.'s Office, White Plains, NY, 1975, Westchester Legal Svcs., White Plains, 1976-77; assoc. Pierro, Colangelo & Killea, Port Chester, N.Y., 1979-84; legal adminstr. Poloron Products, Harrison, N.Y., 1984-86; pvt. practice Rye, N.Y., 1986-90. Arbitrator N.Y. State Office of Ct. Adminstrn., 1979-90, Am. Arbitration Assn., 1980—, Better Bus. Bur., 1980—, N.Y. Stock Exch., 1991—, Nat. Assn. Securities Dealers, 1991—, Pacific Stock Exch., 1993—; mediator Westchester Med. Ctr. Cluster, Westchester County, N.Y., 1984-90; law guardian Family Ct., Westchester County, 1979-84; guardian ad litem Surrogates Ct., Westches-

ter, 1978-84. Theatre critic (newspaper) L.I. Herald; movie reviewer Saddleback Valley News; freelance children's book reviewer; actress cmty. and summer theatre; actress Readers Repertory Theatre. Commr. Human Rights Commn., Rye, 1984-89, Rye Cable TV Commn., 1989-90; pres. LWV of Rye, 1971-73; bd. dirs. pub. rels. com. Community Media Orgns.; bd. dirs. Rye Youth Coun., 1974-80; mem. Mission Viejo Cultural Arts com.; MME Modjeska chpt. Orange County Performing Arts Ctr. Mem. ABA, AAUW, Am. Arbitration Assn., N.Y. State Bar Assn., N.Y. Women's Bar Assn., Westchester County Bar Assn., Portchester/Rye Bar Assn., Internat. Fedn. Women Lawyers, Am. Judges Assn., Columbia U. Club of So. Calif., Rye Woman's Club. Avocations: theater, swimming, aerobics, skiing, dance. Home and Office: 21285 Amora Mission Viejo CA 92692-4930

RUBEN, IDA GASS, state senator; b. Washington, Jan. 07; d. Sol and Sonia E. (Darman) Gass; m. L. Leonard Ruben, Aug. 29, 1948; children: Garry, Michael, Scott, Stephen. Del. Md. Ho. of Dels., Annapolis, 1974-86; mem. Md. Senate, Annapolis, 1986—, majority whip, 1995-99, pres. pro-tem, 2000—. Chair Montgomery County House Delegation, 1981-86, Montgomery County Senate Delegation, 1987—; mem. house econ. matters com., 1974-85, house ways and means com., 1985-86, legis. policy com., 1991—, vice-chair senate budget and taxation com., 1997-99, joint budget and audit com., 1991—, exec. nominations com., 1991—, joint protocol com., 1991—, chair, senate budget and tax., subcom. on pub. safety, transp., econ. devel. and natural resources, 1995-99, mem. joint com. on spending affordability, 1995—, mem. capital budget subcom., 1995—; mem. Gov.'s Motor Carrier Task Force, 1989—; conv. chair Nat. Order Women Legislators, 1980. Chair Women Legislators Caucus Md., 1982-84; trustee Adventist Health Care Mid-Atlantic, Takoma Park, Md.; bd. dirs. Ctrs. for Handicapped, Silver Spring, Md.; former internat. v.p. B'nai Brith Women. Recipient Cert. Appreciation Ctrs. for Handicapped, 1987, Meritorious Svc. award Safety and Survival, 1989, Cover Those Trucks award AAA Potomac, 1989, Leadership Laurel award Safety First Club Md., 1989, Woman of Valor award B'nai B'rith Women, 1991, Pub. Affairs award Planned Parenthood Md., 1992, ESOL support recognition Montgomery County Pub. Schs., 1992, Appreciation award Fraternal Order Police, 1992, John Dewey award Montgomery County Fedn. Tchrs., 1992, ARC of Md., 1992, Safety Leader award Advocates for Hwy. and Auto Safety, 1993, Disting. Svc. award Gov.'s Commn. Employment of People with Disabilities, 1993, award Faculty Guild U. Md. for support of faculty and univ., 1993, Sincere Appreciation award for commitment to Md.'s youth Md. Underage Drinking Prevention Coalition, 1994, Faithful Svc. to citizens Montgomery County award Montgomery County Assn. of Realtors, 1994; named Most Effective Pub. Ofcl. by residents of Silver Spring, 1990, one of 100 Most Powerful Women in Washington Metro Area by Washingtonian Mag., 1994, 97, Legislator of Yr. award Nat. Commn. Against Drunk Driving, 1995, Legislator of Yr. award Montgomery County Med. Soc., 1995, Carmen S. Turner Achievement in Cmty. Svc. award Montgomery County Dept. Transp., 1995, Safety Leader award Advocates for Hwy. and Auto Safety, 1996, Legislator of Yr. award AAA, Potomac, Md., 1997, Vince and Larry award Md. Com. for Safety Belt Use, 1997, Legislative Leadership award Montgomery County, 1998, Leadership award Olney Theater Ctr., 1998, Legislator of Yr. award Greater Montgomery County C. of C., 1999, Hwy. Safety Herd award Advocates for Hwy. and Auto Safety, 1999, One of Md.'s Top 100 Women, The Daily Record, 1994, 97, 2001, 03, Am. Lung Assn. Appreciation award in protecting youth from tobacco industry, 2000, Olney Theater honoree contbns. Olney Theatre and arts in Md., 2000, Pub. Policy Leadership award Am. Cancer Soc., 2002, M.A.D.D. Award of Exellence, 2002, Disting. Pub. Svc. award Am. Lung Assn. of Md., 2003, Disting. Legislator award Md. Impaired Driver Coalition, 2003, others; named to Washington, Md., Del., Pa. Svc. Sta. Assn. Hall of Fame, 1994, Suburban Md. Transp. Priorities outstanding leadership in transp. pub. policy adminstrn., 2000; Md. Coll. Art and Design honoree, 2000. Mem. Coun. State Govts. (com. on suggested legislation), Hadassah. Democrat. Jewish. Home: 11 Schindler Ct Silver Spring MD 20903-1329 Office: Md State Senate 422 Miller Senate Office Bldg 11 Bladen St Annapolis MD 21401-8012 Office Phone: 301-858-3634. Business E-Mail: ida_ruben@senate.state.md.us.

RUBEN, LAWRENCE, real estate developer, building company executive, lawyer; b. Bklyn., Sept. 28, 1926; s. Irving and Minnie (Sruelif) R.; m. Selma Belfer, Dec. 20, 1952; children: Richard Gordon, Lenore Denise, Rochelle Gail Ruben Kivell. BA, NYU, 1949; LLB, Bklyn. Law Sch., 1951. Bar: N.Y. 1952. Gen. practice law, N.Y.C., 1952-53; pres. Ru-Min Constrn. Co., N.Y.C., 1953-54; exec. v.p. Belco Petroleum Corp., N.Y.C., 1954-64, dir., 1954-85; v.p. Fundamental Bldg. Corp., 1952—; pres. Randall Devel. Co., Aragon Devel. Corp., Lawrence Ruben Co., Inc.; ptnr. Lexington Madison Co., Tower Plaza Assocs., Devonshire Assocs., Boylston Ptnrs., Devonshire Constrn. Co. Inc., Lawrence Assocs., Granite Ptnrs., Inc., Harper-Lawrence; pres. Washington Mgmt. Corp. Mem. adv. bd. NYU Real Estate Inst.; mem. Rockefeller U. Counc.; med. ctr. adv. bd. N.Y. Hosp. Cornell Med. Ctr.; bd. dirs. NY UJA; bd. Govs. Am. Jewish Com. Chmn. N.Y. Builders and Realtors Fellowship Fund; trustee Nat. Jewish Ctr. for Immunology and Respiratory Medicine, Denver; patron Albert Einstein Coll. Medicine; sponsor Grad. Sch. Sci.; bd. dirs. Cardoza Sch. Law at Yeshiva U.; chmn. United Jewish Appeal, Scarsdale, N.Y., 1974-75; mem. pres.'s coun. Meml. Sloan Kettering Cancer Ctr. With AUS, 1945-46. Mem. ABA, Fenway Golf Club, Boca Rio Golf Club, Harmonie Club. Office: 600 Madison Ave New York NY 10022-1615

RUBEN, LEONARD, retired art educator; b. St. Paul, June 3, 1921; s. Theodore and Elizabeth (Hauchman) R.; m. Sue Levey; children: James M., Elizabeth A., Nancy L., Thomas C. Diploma with hon., Pratt Inst., 1948, BFA, 1952; MA, Columbia Tchrs. Coll., 1961; PhD, NYU, 1970. Designer L.W. Frolich, N.Y.C., 1949-52; art dir. Young & Rubicam, N.Y.C., 1952-60; art group head North Advt., N.Y.C., 1960-62; instr. Columbia U. Tchrs. Coll., N.Y.C., 1962-63; assoc. creative dir. Compton Advt., N.Y.C., 1962-64; v.p. assoc. creative dir. J.M. Mathes, N.Y.C., 1964-68; exec. creative dir. Lake Spiro Shurman, Memphis, 1968-69; asst. prof. art Northeast La. U., Monroe, 1969-71, U. Tex., Austin, 1971-74, assoc. prof., 1974-79, prof. art, 1979-82, F.J. Heyne Centennial Prof. in Communication, 1983-87. Design cons. B.B. Martin Pub. Co., Austin, 1978; creative dir. Heart Assn., Austin, 1973. Precinct chmn. Dems., Lake Travis, Tex., 1979; chmn. advt. com. Austin Community Coll., 1980-84. 1st lt. U.S. Army, 1940-46, ETO, PTO. Decorated Bronze Arrowhead, Presdl. Unit emblem; recipient numerous awards including Advt. Appreciation award City of Houston, 1980, Thomas McCartin Tchg. Excellence award, 1983, Founders Day award NYU, 1971; Leo Burnet Creative Excellence Endowment, 1986, Frank Rizzo Meml. Creative grant Tracy-Locke, 1986. Mem. 27th Infantry Div. Assn., 105th (226th) Field Arty Assn., Dallas Soc. Visual Communication. Jewish. Home: 2033 Dolina Dr Virginia Beach VA 23464-8210

RUBEN, ROBERT JOEL, pediatric otorhinolaryngolist, educator; b. N.Y.C., Aug. 2, 1933; s. Julian Carl and Sadie (Weiss) R.; children: Ann, Emily, Karin, Arthur. AB, Princeton U., 1955; MD, Johns Hopkins U., 1959. Intern Johns Hopkins Hosp., Balt., 1959-60, resident, 1960-64, dir. neurophysiology lab., div. otolaryngology, 1958-64; practice specializing in pediatric otorhinolaryngology N.Y.C., 1964—; asst. prof. otorhinolaryngology N.Y. U. Sch. Medicine, 1966-68; mem. staff hosps. Montefiore Med. Ctr., Bronx Med. Hosp. Ctr., N. Cen. Bronx Hosp., Montefiore Med.; mem. staff hosps. Jacobi Hosp., Bronx, NY, Children's Hosp. at Montefiore; prof., chmn. Montefiore Med. Ctr., Bronx Mcpl. Hosp. Ctr., N. Cen. Bronx, Bronx, 1979-99; prof. Montefiore Med. Ctr., Bronze Mcpl. Hosp. Ctr., N. Cen. Bronx, Bronx, N.Y., 1999—; prof. pediatrics Albert Einstein Coll. Medicine, Bronx, 1983—, assoc. prof. otorhinolaryngology N.Y.C., 1968-70, prof., chmn. dept. otolaryngology, 1970-98, prof. dept. otolaryngology, 1970—, chmn. emeritus dept. otolaryngology, 1998—, disting. univ. prof., 1998—; prof. pediatrics Albert Einstein Coll. Medicine and Montefiore Med. Ctr., 1983—. Chmn. Nat. Com. for Rsch. and Neurol. and Communicative Disorders, pres., 1982-84; bd. dirs. Am. Bd. Otolaryngology-Head and Neck Surgery, 1989—; chmn. ENT devices com. FDA, 1993-96. Editor-in-chief: Internat. Jour. Pediatric Otorhinolaryngology, 1979—. Bd. dirs. N.Y. League Hard of Hearing, 1969-75, 76-85, Friends of Princeton U. Libr., chmn. coun., 2001—. Served to surgeon USPHS, 1964-66. Recipient Rsch. award Am. Acad. Ophthalmology and Otolaryngology, 1962, Edmund Prince Fowler award Am. Rhinological-Laryngological-Otological Assn., 1973, Gold medal Best Didactic Film, IX World Congress Otorhinolaryngology, 1977, Pres.'s award Am. Acad. Otolaryngology-Head and Neck Surgery, 1992, Johns Hopkins U. Soc. of Scholars, 1993, George E. Schambaugh Otology prize, 1996. Fellow ACS, N.Y. Acad. Medicine; mem. AMA, Am. Assn. Anatomists, Audiology Study Group N.Y. (pres. 1964-66), Acoustical Soc. Am., Am. Acad. Ophthalmology and Otolaryngology, Soc. Univ. Otolaryngologists, Am. Otol. Soc. (sec.-treas. rsch. fund 1979—, award of merit 2004), Soc. for Ear, Nose and Throat Advances in Children (pres. 1973), Assn. for Rsch. in Otolaryngology (pres. 1985-86), Am. Acad. Pediat. (chmn. otol. bronchoesphology 1983-85), Am. Soc. Pediat. Otolaryngology (historian 1986-95), Am. Soc. Pediat. Otolaryngologists (historian 1986-93, pres.-elect 1993-94, pres. 1994-95), Nat. Inst. Deafness and Other Comm. Disorders (adv. coun. 1989-93), Am. Laryngol. Soc., Grolier Club. Home: 1025 5th Ave Apt 12C S New York NY 10028-0134 Office: Montefiore Med Ctr 111 E 210th St Bronx NY 10467-2401 Office Phone: 718-920-2484.

RUBEN, ROBERT JOSEPH, lawyer; b. N.Y.C., Apr. 9, 1923; m. Audrey H. Zweig, Nov. 20, 1949; children: Pamela Joan, James Bradford. BS, Columbia U., 1943; MA, Harvard U., 1948; LL.B., Fordham U., 1953. Bar: N.Y. 1954. Exec. trainee Chase Nat. Bank, N.Y.C., 1948-49; economist, 1949-53; assoc. Milbank, Tweed, Hope & Hadley, N.Y.C., 1953-55; assoc., then ptnr. Shea & Gould, N.Y.C., 1955-90; sec. Gen. Battery Corp., Reading, Pa., 1963-73, Fiat Metal Mfg. Co., Inc., Plainview, N.Y., 1961-64, Filtors, Inc., East Northport, N.Y., 1961-64, Trans-Industries, Inc., 1969-2001, dir., 2001—; asst. sec. Elgin Nat. Industries, 1975-88. Asst. judge City Ct., Rye, N.Y., 1977-90; arbitrator Nat. Assn. Securities Dealers, 1990—, Pacific Stock Exch., 1992—, Am. Arbitration Assn., 1990—, N.Y. Stock Exch., 1994—. Trustee Rye Hist. Soc.; bd. dirs. Carver Center, Port Chester, N.Y., 1972-90. Served with AUS, 1943-46. Decorated Combat Inf. medal. Mem. ABA, N.Y. State Bar Assn., Assn. Bar of City of N.Y., Harvard Club (N.Y.C.), Harvard-Radcliffe Club So. Calif., Columbia U. Club So. Calif., Beta Gamma Sigma, Zeta Beta Tau. Home: 21285 Amora Mission Viejo CA 92692-4930

RUBENFELD, STANLEY IRWIN, lawyer, director, mediator, arbitrator; b. N.Y.C., Dec. 7, 1930; s. George and Mildred (Rose) R.; children: Lise Susan, Kenneth Michael, Andrew James, Victoria Louise, Alexandria Elizabeth; m. Madeleine Conway, Nov. 5, 2000. BA, Columbia U., 1952, JD, 1956. Bar: N.Y. 1956. Practice law, N.Y.C., 1956—2002, 1965-68; assoc. Shearman & Sterling, 1956-65, ptnr., 1965-68, N.Y.C., 1968-93, of counsel, 1994—2002. Arbitrator and mediator NASD; mediator U.S. Fed. Ct., IRS Panel, CPR Panel; arbitrator NYSE, Internat. C. of C.; bd. dirs. Brit. Gas US Holdings, Inc., BG Energy Fin. Inc., BGLNG Svcs., Inc., South Shore Music, Inc. Editor-in-chief Columbia Law Rev., 1955-56; contbr. articles to profl. jours. Past pres. Port Washington (N.Y.) Cmty. Chest; former bd. dirs. Residents for a More Beautiful Port Washington. Lt. (j.g.) USNR, 1952-54. Stone scholar, 1951-52, 54-55, 55-56; Rockefeller Found. grantee, 1955 Mem. ABA, N.Y. State Bar Assn. (tax sec., past chmn. fgn. activities com., reorgn. corp.), Assn. Bar City N.Y. (past chmn. com. on recruitment lawyers), Nat. Assn. Law Placement (past bd. dirs., exec. com.), Columbia U. Law Sch. Alumni Assn. (bd. visitors, adviser, past bd. dirs.), Columbia Coll. Alumni Assn., Tax Club (past chmn.), Phi Delta Phi, Tau Epsilon Phi (past pres.). Office Phone: 203-227-1162.

RUBENS, SIDNEY MICHEL, physicist, technical advisor; b. Spokane, Wash., Mar. 21, 1910; s. Max Zvoln and Jennie Golda (Rubinovich) R.; m. Julienne Rose Fridner, May 11, 1944; 1 child, Deborah Janet. BS, U. Wash., 1934, PhD, 1939. Instr. U. So. Calif., L.A., 1939—40; rsch. assoc. UCLA, 1940—41; physicist Naval Ordnance Lab., Washington, 1941—46, Engring. Rsch. Assocs., St. Paul, 1946—52; mgr. physics Univac divsn. Sperry Rand, St. Paul, 1958—61, dir. rsch., 1961-66, staff scientist, 1969—71, dir. spl. projects, 1971—75, cons., 1975—81; tech. advisor Vertimag Sys. Corp., 1981—, Advanced Rsch. Corp., Mpls., 1986—. Lectr. U. Pa., 1960-61; mem. adv. subcom. on instrumentation and data processing NASA, 1967-69; mem. panel on computer tech. NAS, 1969. Author: Amplifier and Memory Devices, 1965; contbg. author: Magnetic Recording—The First Hundred Years, 1999. Hon. fellow U. Minn., 1977—. Fellow IEEE (Magnetic Soc. info. storage award 1987, Millennium medal 2000); mem. AAAS, N.Y. Acad. Scis., Am. Phys. Soc., Am. Geophys. Union, Acad. Applied Sci., Minn. Acad. Sci., Am. Optical Soc., Phi Beta Kappa, Sigma Xi, Pi Mu Esilon. Achievements include patents in magnetic material and devices. Home: 1077 Sibley Hwy Apt 506 Saint Paul MN 55118-3616 Office: Advanced Rsch Corp 815 14th Ave SE Minneapolis MN 55414-1515

RUBENSTEIN, ALBERT HAROLD, industrial engineering and management sciences educator; b. Phila., Nov. 11, 1923; s. Leo and Jean (Kaplan) R.; m. Hildette Grossman, Sept. 11, 1949; children: Michael Stephen, Lisa Joan. BS in Indsl. Engring. magna cum laude (Sr. prize econs.), Lehigh U., 1949; MS in Indsl. Engring, Columbia, 1950, PhD in Indsl. Engring. and Mgmt, 1954; DEng (hon.), Lehigh U., 1993. Asst. to pres. Perry Equipment Corp., 1940-43; rsch. assoc. Columbia U., 1950-53; asst. prof. indsl. mgmt. MIT, 1954-59; prof. indsl. engring. and mgmt. scis. Northwestern U., 1959-97; emeritus prof., 1997—; Walter P. Murphy prof. Northwestern U., 1986—, dir. Ctr. for Info. Tech., 1986-97; pres. Internat. Applied Sci. and Tech. Assos., 1977—; vis. prof. U. Calif., Berkeley; pres. Sr. Strategy Group, 1995—. Adj. prof. U. Calif., San Diego, 1997—; cons. to govt. and industry. Dir. Narragansett Capital Corp. Author books and articles in field. Served with inf. AUS, World War II. Decorated Purple Heart, Combat Inf. badge.; Recipient Lincoln Arc Welding Found. prize paper, 1948, Pioneer in Innovation Mgmt. award Ctr. Innovation Mgmt., 1992; Omicron Delta Kappa annual fellow, 1949-50; Fulbright research fellow, 1955 Fellow IEEE (editor trans. 1959—, Engring. Mgr. of Yr. award 1992), Soc. Applied Anthropology; mem. AAAS (chmn. indsl. sci. and tech. sect. 1997—), Inst. Mgmt. Scis. (sr. mem., dir. studies for coll. on R & D 1960—, v.p. rsch. and edn. 1966-68) Home and Office: 1630 Chicago Ave Apt 2010 Evanston IL 60201-6025

RUBENSTEIN, ARTHUR HAROLD, academic administrator, educator, dean, internist; b. Johannesburg, Dec. 28, 1937; arrived in U.S., 1967; s. Montague and Isabel (Nathanson) R.; m. Denise Hack, Aug. 19, 1962; children: Jeffrey Lawrence, Errol Charles. MB BCh, U. Witwatersrand, 1960, DSc (hon.) in Medicine, 2002. Diplomate Am. Bd. Internal Medicine. Intern, then resident Johannesburg Gen. Hosp., 1961, 63-65, 66-67; fellow in endocrinology Postgrad. Med. Sch., London, 1965-66; fellow in medicine U. Chgo., 1967-68, from asst. prof. to assoc. prof., 1968-74, prof., 1974-97, Lowell T. Coggeshall prof. med. sci., 1981-97, assoc. chmn. dept. medicine, 1975-81, chmn., 1981-97; attending physician Mitchell Hosp., U. Chgo., 1968-97; dean, CEO, Gustave L. Levy disting. prof. Mt. Sinai Sch. Medicine, N.Y.C., 1997—2001; exec. v.p., dean U. of Pa. Health Sys., Sch. of Med., Phila., 2001—. Mem. study sect. NIH, 1973-77, Hadassah Med. Adv. Bd., 1986-95, adv. coun. Nat. Inst. Arthritis, Metabolism and Digestive Diseases, 1978-80; chmn. Nat. Diabetes Adv. Bd., 1982, mem., 1981-83. Mem. editl. bd. Diabetes, 1973-77, Endocrinology, 1973-77, Jour. Clin. Investigation, 1976-81, Am. Jour. Medicine, 1978-81, Diabetologia, 1982-86, Diabetes Medicine, 1987-91, Annals of Internal Medicine, 1991-96, Medicine, 1992—; contbr. articles to profl. jours. Mem. Gov.'s Sci. Adv. Coun. State of Ill., 1989-96. Recipient David Rumbough Meml. award Juvenile Diabetes Found., 1978. Master ACP (John Phillips Meml. award 1995); fellow South African Coll. Physicians, Royal Coll. Physicians (London), N.Y. Acad. Medicine; mem. Am. Soc. for Clin. Investigation, Am. Diabetes Assn. (Eli Lilly award 1973, Banting medal 1983, Solomon Berson Meml. lectr. 1985), Brit. Diabetes Assn. (Banting lectr. 1987), Endocrine Soc., Am. Fedn. Clin. Rsch., Ctrl. Soc. Clin. Rsch. (v.p. 1988, pres. 1989), Assn. Am. Physicians (treas. 1984-89, councillor 1989-94, v.p. 1994-95, pres. 1995-96), Am. Bd. Internal Medicine (bd. govs. 1985-93, exec. com. 1990-93, chmn. 1992-93), Residency Rev. Com., Am. Acad. Arts and Scis., Inst. Medicine (coun. 1991-96), Assn. Profs. Medicine (councillor 1991-94, v.p. 1994-95, pres. 1995-96, Robert Williams award 1997), Assn. Am. Med. Colls. (mem. coun. of deans adminstrv. bd. 2002—). Office: U Penn Sch Med 295 John Morgan Bldg, 3620 Hamilton Walk Philadelphia PA 19104

RUBENSTEIN, ATOOSA BEHNEGAR, editor-in-chief; b. Iran, 1973; arrived in U.S., 1978; m. Ari Rubenstein, 1998. BA in Polit. Sci., Barnard COll., 1993. Fashion asst., assoc. fashion editor, fashion edit to sr. fashion editor Cosmopolitan Mag., 1993—95, editor-in-chief, 1998—2003, Seventeen Mag., 2003—. Office: Seventeen Mag 1440 Broadway 13th Fl New York NY 10018

RUBENSTEIN, BERNARD, orchestra conductor; b. Springfield, Mo., Oct. 30, 1937; s. Milton and Evelyn Marion (Friedman) R.; m. Ann Warren Little, Aug. 28, 1961; children: Tanya, Stefan Alexei. B.Mus. with distinction, Eastman Sch. Music, U. Rochester, 1958; M.Mus., Yale U., 1961. Assoc. prof. conducting, dir. orch. orgns. Northwestern U., Evanston, Ill., 1968-80; music dir. San Juan Symphony, Durango, Colo., 1997—2001, Farmington, N.Mex., 1997—2001, Fargo-Moorhead Symphony, 2003—. Asst. condr. R.I. Philharm. Orch., 1961-62; condr. music dir. Santa Fe Symphony Orch., 1962-64; condr. Greenwood Chamber Orch., Cummington, Mass., 1968-79; asst. condr. Stuttgart Opera, 1966-68; condr., music dir. Music for Youth, Milw., 1970-80; assoc. condr. Cin. Symphony Orch., 1980-86; music dir. Tulsa Philharm., 1984-96, condr. laureate, 1996—; music dir. San Juan Symphony, 1997-2001; guest condr. numerous orchs. including Milw. Symphony Orch., St. Paul Chamber Orch., Guadalajara Symphony Orch., Berlin Radio Orch., Frankfurt Radio Orch., Grant Park Orch., Chgo., die reihe, Vienna, Austrian Radio Orch., Eastman Philharm., Halle Symphony Orch., E. Ger., Warsaw Philharm., St. Louis Little Symphony, W. German Radio Orch., Palazzo Pitti Orch. Florence, Italy, Frankfurt Opera, Tonkuenstler Orch., Vienna, S.W. German Radio Orch., Baden-Baden, Jerusalem Symphony, Anchorage, Hamilton, Ont., Hartford Conn., L.A. Chamber Orch., Austin (Tex.) Symphony, Am. Composers Orch. N.Y.C., Nat. Opera of Mongolia, Cuban Nat. Symphony, Havana, Orquesta de Oriente, Santiago de Cuba. Winner internat. conducting competition Serate Musicale Fiorentine, 1965; Fulbright scholar, 1964-66; recipient Charles Ditson award Yale U., 1961, Martha Baird Rockefeller award, 1966-68 Mem. Am. Symphony Orch. League, Condrs. Guild. Office: 1070 Governor Dempsey Dr Santa Fe NM 87501-1078 E-mail: baton@ix.netcom.com.

RUBENSTEIN, DAVID AARON, military officer, healthcare administrator; b. Rockville Centre, N.Y., Nov. 23, 1954; s. Robert R. and Mona Sydney (Feder) R.; m. Patricia Barrier, Mar. 18, 1978; children: Sarah Elizabeth, William Robert. BS in Health Edn., Tex. A & M U., 1977; MHA, Baylor U., 1989; M of Mil. Arts and Sci., Command and Gen. Staff Coll., 1990. Commd. 2d lt. U.S. Army, 1977, advanced through grades to col., 1999, med. platoon leader 3d inf. div., 1977-79, ops. officer 3d med. battalion, 1979-80, pers. officer 307th med. battalion, 1981-82, co. comdr., 1982-83, mil. instr. Acad. of Health Scis. Ft. Sam Houston, Tex., 1984-87, grad. student, 1987-88, adminstrv. resident William Beaumont Army Med. Ctr. Ft. Bliss, Tex., 1988-89, grad. student Command and Gen. Staff Coll. Ft. Leavenworth, Kans., 1989-90; adminstrv. asst. Office of the Army Surgeon Gen. Army Med. Svc. Corps, Washington, 1990-92; chief coordinated care Army Hosp., Ft. Belvoir, Va., 1992-93; hosp. comdr. 18th Mobile Army Surg. Hosp., Ft. Lewis, Wash., 1994-96; grad. student Army War Coll., Carlisle Barracks, Pa., 1996-97; dep. comdr. Eisenhower Army Med. Ctr., Ft. Gordon, Ga., 1997-99; hosp. comdr. 21st Combat Support Hosp., Ft. Hood, Tex., 1999-2001, 1999-2000; cmdr. Landstuhl Regional Med. Ctr., Germany, 2001—03; chief of staff Europe Regional Med. Commd., 2003—04; cmdr. 30th Med. Brigade, 2004. Pres. Health Orgn. Network, El Paso, Tex., 1989, Healthcare Execs. Ctrl. Savannah River Area, 1998-99; participant U.S. Army seminar Baylor U., Ft. Sam Houston, 1989. *Commander Rubenstein is the commander (CEO) of the Army's only forward deployed medical brigade; he is responsible for the health of 46,000 soldiers and for providing a complex healthcare system under combat conditions. He recently received recognition as the uniformed services senior healthcare executive of the year and the Army-Baylor University alumni of the year. David serves as a Governor on the American College of Healthcare Executive's Board of Governors. The college is a 30,000 member professional society dedicated to excellence of healthcare executives. He serves as healthcare administration consultant to the Army Surgeon. In this role, he is responsible for developing excellence in Army healthcare administration.* Author leadership seminar; reviewer books Lehigh U. Press, 1990, Mil. Rev. Jour., Mil. Medicine; contbr. articles to profl. jours. Religious lay leader Office of the Jewish Chapel, Ft. Bragg, 1982-83, Ft. Bliss, 1988-89, Ft. Leavenworth, 1989-90, Bosnia-Herzegovina, 1999-2000; fund drive coord. United Fund, Ft. Leavenworth, 1989; vol. Muscular Dystrophy Assn., Washington, 1990-91. Decorated Legion of Merit; recipient Fed. Healthcare Leadership award, 2003. Fellow: Am. Coll. Healthcare Execs. (regent 2000—02, gov. 2002—, Regent's award 1993); mem.: VFW, Assn. of U.S. Army, Am. Hosp. Assn., Assn. Mil. Surgeons of U.S. Republican. Jewish. Avocations: private flying, running, civil war medical support research, reading. Office Phone: 011-49-6221-17-2233. Business E-Mail: david.rubenstein@us.army.mil.

RUBENSTEIN, EDWARD, physician, educator; b. Cin., Dec. 5, 1924; s. Louis and Nettie Rubenstein; m. Nancy Ellen Millman, June 20, 1954; children: John, William, James. MD, U. Cin., 1947. House staff Cin. Gen. Hosp., 1947—50; fellow May Inst., Cin., 1950; sr. asst. resident Ward Med. Svc., Barnes Hosp., St. Louis, 1953—54; chief of medicine San Mateo County Hosp., Calif., 1960—70; assoc. dean postgrad. med. edn., prof. medicine Stanford (Calif.) U., 1971—, emeritus, active. Faculty Stanford Photon Rsch. Lab.; affiliated faculty Stanford Synchrotron Radiation Lab., 1971—; maj. materials facilities com. NRC, 1984—85, Nat. Steering Com. 6 GeV Electron Storage Ring, 1986—. Author (textbook): Intensive Medical Care; editor: Synchotron Radiation Handbook, 1988, vol. 4, 1991, Synchotron Radiation in the Biosciences, Molecular Medicine; mem. editorial bd.: Sci. Am., Inc., 1991—94; editor (textbook): Sci. Am. Medicine, 1978—94; editor: (series) Molecular Cardiovascular Disease, 1995, Molecular Oncology, 1996, Molecular Neuroscience, 1998. With USAF, 1950—52. Named Disting. Scientist, SvrroMed, Inc., 2003; recipient Kaiser award for outstanding and innovative contbns. to med. edn., 1989, Albion Walter Hewlett award, 1993. Master: ACP (Laureate 2002); fellow: AAAS, Royal Soc. Medicine; mem.: Am. Clin. and Climatol. Assn., Soc. Photo-Optical Engrs., Western Assn. Physicians, Calif. Acad. Medicine, Inst. Medicine, APS, Alpha Omega Alpha. Achievements include research in mechanisms of autoimmunity, dysfunction of the choroid plexus and cerebrospinal fluid circulatory system, synchrotron radiation, and molecular chirality. Office: Stanford Med Ctr Dept Medicine Stanford CA 94305

RUBENSTEIN, HOWARD JOSEPH, public relations executive; b. NYC, Feb. 3, 1932; s. Samuel and Ada (Sall) R.; m. Amy Forman, Dec. 17, 1959; children: Roni, Richard, Steven. AB, U. Pa., 1953; student law, Harvard, 1953; LL.B. (Dean's scholar), St. Johns Sch. Law, 1959, LLD (hon.), 1990. Bar: NY 1960. Pres. Rubenstein Assocs., Inc. pub. rels. cons., N.Y.C., 1954—; asst. counsel judiciary com. U.S. Ho. of Reps., 1960; cons. U.S. Fgn. Claims Commn., 1961-62; cons. joint legis. com. child care needs N.Y., 1965-66; adviser SBA, 1965-66. Mem. Gov.'s Com. on Sale of World Trade Ctr., 1981, Mayor's Com. on Holocaust Commemoration, 1981—, NY State Task Force on Energy Conservation, Dept. Housing, 1981-83, Mayor's Coun. Econ. Bus. Advisors, 1991-93; co-chmn. Holocaust Commn., 1993—; v.p. Jewish Cmty. Rels. Coun., 1988-94, advisor, 1995—; past dir. Brownsville Boys Club; bd. dirs. Provide Addict Care Today, Police Athletic League, NY chpt. March of Dimes; active U.S. Internat. Coun., 1977-81, Commn. on Status of Women, 1982-89, NYC Commn. Operation Welcome Home, 1991—; trustee Ctrl. Park Conservancy; mem. Mayor's Bus. Adv. Coun., 1996—; advisor NY Commn. on Status of Women, 1995—; comm. advisor Gov.'s Com. Jerusalem 3000, 1996—; bd. dirs. Albert Einstein Coll. Medicine, 1997—; bd. govs. Jewish Cmty. Rels. Coun., 1999—; exec. com. Real Estate Bd. NY, 1985—, NYC & Co., 2001—, Partnership for NYC, 2004—. Mem. Assn. Better N.Y. (mem. exec. com. 1972—), Phi Beta Kappa, Beta Sigma Rho. Jewish (dir. congregation). Home: 993 5th Ave New York NY 10028-0105 Office: Rubenstein Assoc Inc 1345 Avenue Of The Americas New York NY 10105-0302 Office Phone: 212-843-8080.

RUBENSTEIN, JACOB SAMUEL, rabbi; b. Rosenheim, Germany, July 17, 1949; came to U.S., 1951; s. David and Eva (Bergman) R.; m. Deborah Powell, Sept. 1, 1969; children: Shira, Daniel, Jonathan, Yoheved. BA, Hebrew U., Jerusalem, 1972; MA, Harvard U., 1976. Ordained rabbi, 1972. Chief justices Ashkenazic and Sephardic Rabbinic Cts., Jerusalem, 1972; rabbi Congregation Beth Sholom, Milford, Mass., 1975-77, Providence, 1977-84, Young Israel of Scarsdale, N.Y., 1984—. Trustee Westchester Jewish Conf., White Plains, 1986-98; vice chmn. rabbinic adv. bd. N.Y. United Jewish Appeal Fedn., 1990-92, exec. officer Westchester Rabbinical Coun., 1986—; vice chmn. Nat. Rabbinic Cabinet of United Jewish Appeal, N.Y.C., 1990-93; pres. Westchester (N.Y.) Bd. Rabbis, 1990-93; nat. chmn. United Jewish Appeal-Rabbinic Cabinet, 1993-95, pres., 1995-96; pres. Rabbinical Coun. of Am., 1997-99, hon. pres. 1999-2000. Contbr. to: Rabbinical Council of America Sermon Manual, 1982, 84, 85, 87-88, 91-92, HaDarom, Torah for Today, 1990, Theological and Halaknic Reflections on the Holocaust; mem. Congl. Acad. Rev. Bd., 1986-89. Mem. Blue Ribbon Panel on Anti-Bias Crime, Westchester County-White Plains, N.Y., 1988; mem. adv. bd. Washington Inst. for Jewish Leadership and Values, 1988—. Recipient City of Peace award Israel Bonds, 1978, Dr. and Mrs. Abraham Stern Svc. award Yeshiva U., 1983, Rabbinical Leadership award Ohr Hameir Theol. Sem., 1985, Rabbinic Svc. award United Jewish Appeal, 1987, Samuel W. and Rose Hurowitz award United Jewish Appeal Fedn., 1993, Ohev Torah award Ariel Am. Friends of Midrasha, 1995, award Nat. United Jewish Appeal, 1993, Orthodox Union Nat. Rabbinical Leadership Centennial medallion, 1999. Mem. Rabbinical Coun. Am. (exec. bd., chmn. legis. and pub. affairs coms. 1985-97), Religious Zionists Am., Inst. for Pub. Affairs (chm rabbinical adv. com 1990-93), Bet Din of Am., The Orthodox Jewish Caucus. Office: Young Israel of Scarsdale 1313 Weaver St PO Box 103H Scarsdale NY 10583-8603 *Physical and social forces govern my life. But in the area of moral freedom, no matter how strong and overwhelming the limitations and mysteries, I can be sovereign, and under the burden of conditioning and conflict motivate my life.*

RUBENSTEIN, JEROME MAX, lawyer; b. St. Louis, Feb. 16, 1927; s. Jacob J. and Anne (Frankel) R.; m. Judith Hope Grand, July 31, 1954; children— Edward J., Emily Rubenstein Muslin, Daniel H. AB, Harvard U., 1950, LLB, 1955. Bar: Mo. 1956, U.S. Dist. Ct. (ea. dist.) Mo. 1956, U.S. Ct. Appeals (8th cir.) 1956. Mem. English lit. faculty U. So. Philippines, Cebu, 1950-51; law clk U.S. Dist. Ct., St. Louis, 1955-56; assoc. Lewis, Rice, Tucker, Allen & Chubb, St. Louis, 1956-64, Grand, Peper & Martin, St. Louis, 1964-65, ptnr., 1965-66; jr. ptnr. Bryan Cave, St. Louis, 1966-67, ptnr., 1968-97, of counsel, 1998—. Dir. Commerce Bank, N.A. Bd. dirs. Independence Ctr., St. Louis, 1985-88, The Arts and Edn. Coun. Greater St. Louis, 1991-99. Served with USN, 1945-46. Bd. dirs. Independence Ctr., St. Louis, 1985. Served with USN, 1945-46 Mem. ABA, Mo. Bar Assn., St. Louis Bar Assn., Mo. Athletic Club, Harvard Club of St. Louis (pres. 1982-83, bd. dirs. 1983-90). Jewish. Avocations: jogging; tennis. Home: 7394 Westmoreland Dr Saint Louis MO 63130-4240 Office: Bryan Cave 1 Metropolitan Sq Ste 3600 Saint Louis MO 63102-2750

RUBENSTEIN, JOSHUA SETH, lawyer; b. Bklyn, Aug. 5, 1954; s. Seth and Elaine (Freedman) Rubenstein; children: Mary-Jane, Kenan, Rebecca, Marlena, Isaac. BA magna cum laude, Columbia U., 1976, JD, 1979. Bar: NY 1980, NJ 1980, US Dist. Ct. (ea. and so. dist.) NY 1980, US Dist. Ct. NJ 1980, US Tax Ct. 1986. Assoc. Fried, Frank, Harris, Shriver & Jacobson, NYC, 1979-82, KMZ Rosenman LLP, NYC, 1982-88, ptnr., 1988—, mem. mgmt. com., 1994—98, chmn., 1998—2002, chmn. trusts and estates dept., 1995—; mng. ptnr. KM2 Rosenman LLP, NYC, 2002—, Charlotte, 2002. Mem. adv. com. surrogate's ct. Office Ct. Adminstrn., 1997—; mem. adv. coun. Law Sch. Trusts, Wills and Estate Planning Columbia U., 1997—; lectr. in field. Author: Answer Guide New York Surrogate's Court, 2004; contbr. articles to legal publ. Dir., sec. Irvington Inst. Med. Rsch., 1991, treas., 1991—92, sec., 1992—93, co-pres., 1993—94, pres., 1994—2000, vice-chmn., 2000—; mem. legis. com., mem. devel. com., mem. bd. governance com., mem. Madeleine Borg com., chmn., mem. exec. com., 1994—; mem. profl. adv. com. Lincoln Ctr., NY Philharm., Mus. Modern Art, Met. Mus. Art, Columbia U., Columbia U. Law Sch., Mus. Art and Design; chmn. estates and trust splty. group, chmn. splty. group task force, mem. exec. com. lawyers divsn. United Jewish Appeal-Fedn., 1989—99; trustee Jewish Bd. Family and Children's Svc., 1991, v.p., 1998—. Named Best Lawyers in NY, NY Mag.; recipient James H. Fogelson award, Lawyer's divsn. United Jewish Appeal Fedn., 1993, Trusts and Estate Lawyers award, 2001. Fellow: NY State Bar Found., Am. Coll. Trusts and Estate Counsel (mem. state laws com.); mem.: ABA, Soc. Trust and Estate Practitioners, Internat. Acad. Estate and Trust Law (academician 1997—), Assn. Bar City of NY, NJ Bar Assn. (real property and probate sect., mem. adv. com. rels. legis. and exec. brs.), NY State Bar Assn. (trust and estate law sect., treas. 1997—98, sec. 1998—99, chair elect 1999—, vice chmn. legis. com. 1988, chmn. 1988—91, co-chmn. ad hoc com. rev. proposals EPTL adv. com. N.Y. State 1991—, mem.-at-large exec. com. 1992—95, liaison to legis. policy com. 1995—, chair 2000—01, Pres.'s Pro Bono Svc. award 1991, Exec. Com. award 1992, 1995, 1996), Practising Law Inst. (mem. estate adv. com., lectr. 1984—, Hadassah estate planning seminar faculty and adv. bd. 1993—), Phi Beta Kappa. Democrat. Jewish. Office: KMZ Rosenman 575 Madison Ave Fl 22D New York NY 10022-2511 Office Phone: 212-940-7150.

RUBENSTEIN, LEONARD, engineering company executive; b. N.Y.C., June 18, 1931; s. William and Sylvia (Jaffe) R.; m. Reva Scharf, Jan. 1951 (div. 1960); m. Geraldine Marilyn Porper, Aug. 14, 1965 (dec. Sept. 2000); children: Alan, Elaine, Philip, Ruth, Jennie. BS in Physics, Poly. Inst. N.Y., 1964. Registered profl. engr. NY, NJ, Del., Ga. Equipment engr. We. Elec., NYC, 1957-66; elec. engr. Gibbs & Hill, NYC, 1966-69; chief engr. Kiegl Lighting, NYC, 1969-72; project mgr. Stone & Webster, NYC, 1972-87; v.p. engring. Laramore Douglas & Popham, NYC, 1988-90; v.p., dir. engring. Gibbs & Hill, NYC, 1990-92; markter NPS, Florham Pk., NJ, 1992-95; pres., prin. Rubenstein Engring. PC, NYC, 1975—. Devel., pipeline project, Costanza-Trieste, Italy. Contbr. articles to profl. publs. Chmn. Walt Whitman Ind. Dems., Bklyn., 1966-68, chmn. West Bklyn. Ind. Dems., 1964-66; bd. dir. NY Gilbert & Sullivan Players, NYC, 1993—, 450 West End Corp, 1984-88; mem. bd. mgr. McBurney YMCA, 1988-97. With US Army, 1951-53. Mem. IEEE (sr., chmn. NY sect. 1995-96, asst. editor Today's Engr. 1997-98, Region I award 1985, 94, 96), NSPE, Soc. Mfg. Engr. (charter mem. Vision Soc., sr. mem. Robotics Internat.), Power Engring. Soc. (chmn. NY/LI chpt. 1984-85). Achievements include development of first large scale waterless power plant; design of first commercial power plant using air stored in salt mines. Avocations: handball, music. Home and Office: 8 W 65th St New York NY 10023 Office Phone: 212-629-6501.

RUBENSTEIN, LEONARD SAMUEL, communications executive, ceramist, painter, photographer; b. Rochester, N.Y., Sept. 22, 1918; s. Jacob S. and Zelda H. (Gordon) R.; m. (dec. 1983); children: Carolinda, Eric, Harley. Student, Case Western Res. U., 1938; BFA cum laude, Alfred U., 1939; postgrad., U. Rochester, 1940-41. Creative dir. Henry Hempstead Advt. Agy., Chgo., 1949-55; v.p., exec. art dir. Clinton E. Frank Advt. Agy., Chgo., 1955-63; v.p., nat. creative dir. Foster & Kleiser divsn. Metromedia, Inc., L.A., 1967-73; ret. Metromedia, Inc., L.A., 1984, v.p. corp. creative cons., 1984-88. Guest lectr. U. Chgo.; instr. Columbia Coll., Chgo., Fashion Inst., L.A.; creator Smithsonian exhibition Images of China: East and West, 1982; lectr. in field. Author: (with Charles Hardison) Outdoor Advertising, 1967; contbr. articles to profl. jours.; one-man show at Calif. Mus. Sci. and Industry, 1970; two-person shows at Palos Verdes Art Ctr., 1987; one-man shows: Palos Verdes Art Ctr., 1998, Distinctive Edge Gallery, San Pedro, Calif., 2003; exhibited in group shows; writer, prodr.: (video) Paul Soldner, Thoughts on Creativity, 1989, High-Tech/Low-Tech: The Sci. and Art of Ceramics, 1994; represented in permenant collections Smithsonian Instn. Renwick Gallery, Am. Ceramic Soc. Ross C. Purdy Ceramic Mus., Internat. Mus. Ceramic Art Alfred U., Laguna Mus. Art, Calif. Past pres. Art Dirs. Club Chgo. Recipient Spl. Citation, Art Dirs. Club Chgo. Mem. Soc. Typog. Arts (past dir.), Am. Ceramic Soc. (bd. dirs. So. Calif. design chpt. 1998), Am. Craft Coun., Inst. Outdoor Advt. (past plans bd.), L.A. County Mus. Art, Mus. Contemporary Art L.A. (charter), Palos Verdes (Calif.) Art Ctr., B'nai B'rith, Zeta Beta Tau. Home and Office: 30616 Ganado Dr Rancho Palos Verdes CA 90275 *Personal philosophy: I have a disdain for the trendy, the superficial and the transient.*

RUBENSTEIN, PAMELA SILVER, manufacturing executive; b. Lansing, Mich., May 12, 1953; d. Neil M. and Leah Rebecca (Coffman) Silver; m. Alec Robert Rubenstein. BA in Linguistics, U. Mich., 1974; MA in teaching English to spkrs. of other langs., Columbia U. Tchrs. Coll., 1976; MA in Linguistics, U. Ill., 1978, doctoral studies in linguistics, 1978-80. Instr. Columbia U. Tchrs. Coll., N.Y.C., 1976, U. Ill., Urbana, 1978, libr. Linguistic Dept., 1978-79; asst. libr. Ill. State Geol. Survey, 1979-80; tchr. Congregation Temple Israel, Springfield, Ill., 1980-81; adminstr., tchr. Springfield Bd. Jewish Edn., 1981-82; instr. Comm. Divsn. Lincoln Land C.C., Springfield, 1981-82; tchr. Cmty. Hebrew Sch., Charleston, SC, 1982-83; instr. The Citadel and Coll. of Charleston, 1983; legal sec. Gibbs & Holmes, Charleston, 1984, May, Oberfell & Lorber, South Bend, Ind., 1984-88; instr. U. Notre Dame, Ind., 1987; tchr. Triton Sch. Corp., Bourbon, Ind., 1988-89; v.p., asst. treas. Allied Splty. Precision, Inc., Mishawaka, Ind., 1989—. Mem. next generation team Nat. Tool and Machining Assn., 2003—. Contbr. articles to profl. jours. Mem. Temple Beth-El Sisterhood, South Bend, 1987—, Hadassah (life mem.). Mem. Michiana Gem and Mineral Soc. (treas. 1995-98, 2004). Office: Allied Splty Precision Inc 815 E Lowell Ave Mishawaka IN 46545-6480 Business E-Mail: pamr@aspi-nc.com.

RUBENSTEIN, STEVEN PAUL, newspaper columnist; b. L.A., Oct. 31, 1951; s. Victor Gerald and Florence (Fox) R.; m. Caroline Moira Grannan, Jan. 1, 1989; children: William Laurence, Anna Katherine. BA, U. Calif., Berkeley, 1977. Reporter L.A. Herald Examiner, 1974-76, San Francisco Chronicle, 1976-81, columnist, 1981—. Office: San Francisco Chronicle 901 Mission St San Francisco CA 94103-2905

RUBENZER, STEVEN JAMES, forensic psychologist; b. West Bend, Wisc., Oct. 27, 1957; s. James Richard Rubenzer and Prisilla Rubenzer-Pontius; m. Traci Nguyen, Dec. 30, 1996 (div. Dec. 30, 2000); children: Zachary, Kaelin. BS, Univ. Wis., Oshkosh, 1980; MS, Univ. Houston, Houston, 1985, PhD, 1990. Pvt. practice, Houston, 1992—. Cons. in field, Houston, 1992—. Contbr. chapters to books, articles to profl. jour.; author: book on personalities of U.S. pres. Mem.: APA. Achievements include invention of fumble creation techniques (football).

RUBERSON, JOHN RUSSELL, entomology educator; b. San Jose, Calif., Nov. 8, 1958; s. James and Joyce Ruberson; m. Mary Lu Hyde, Nov. 7, 1980; children: Joshua, Christina, Matthew, Jonathan. BS, Brigham Young U., 1980—82, MS, 1982—84; PhD, Cornell U., 1984—89. Postdoctoral rsch. assoc. Cornell U., Ithaca, NY, 1989, U. Ark., Fayetteville, 1989—92, USDA-ARS, Tifton, Ga., 1992—94; rsch. scientist U. Ga., Tifton, asst. prof. entomology, 1994—97, assoc. prof. entomology. Editor: (book) Handbook of Pest Management, Predatory Heteroptera: Their Ecology and Use in Biological Control, author 38 refered publ. in jour.; editor: Environ. Entomology; editl. bd. Bio. Control. Scoutmaster, dist. com. chair Boy Scouts Am., Tifton, 1992—2004. Mem.: Ga. Entomol. Soc., Internat. Orgn. Biol. Control (v.p. 2000—02), Entomol. Soc. Am. (subsection Calif. chair 1994—96). R-Conservative. Lds. Avocations: photography, camping/outdoors activity, reading, natural history, world history. Office: Dept Entomology Univ Ga Rainwater Rd Tifton GA 31794 E-mail: ruberson@tifton.uga.edu.

RUBIN, ALAN, physician; b. Phila., 1923; s. Hyman and Miriam (Magil) R.; m. Helen Metz, May 1, 1947; children: Alan, Stephen, Blake. MD, U. Pa., 1947. Diplomate Am. Bd. Ob-Gyn. Intern Hosp. Pa., Phila., 1947-48, resident in ob-gyn., 1949-52; trainee Nat. Cancer Inst., Phila., 1950-51; fellow in pharm. U. Pa., Phila., 1948-49; mem. staff Grad. Hosp., Phila.; clin. prof. ob-gyn. Temple U., Phila. Clin. prof. ob-gyn. U. Pa., Phila. Contbr. more than 150 articles to profl. jours. Fellow ACS, Royal Soc. for the Promotion of Health; mem. Am. Coll. Ob-Gyn., Sigma Xi, Alpha Omega Alpha.

RUBIN, ALAN A. pharmaceutical and biotechnology consultant; b. N.Y.C., July 10, 1926; s. Harry and Gertrude R.; m. Helen M. Feinstein; children: Jeffrey, Ronald, Howard. BS, NYU, 1950, MS, 1953, PhD, 1959. Pharmacologist Schering Corp., Bloomfield, N.J., 1954-64; dir. pharmacology Endo Labs., Garden City, N.Y., 1964-70, v.p. rsch., 1970-74; dir. rsch. DuPont Pharms., Wilmington, Del., 1974-82, dir. sci. info. and tech., 1982-87; dir. licensing tech. DuPont Merck Pharms., Wilmington, Del., 1987-91; cons. ARA Assoc., Rockland, Del., 1991—. Bd. dirs. Redox Pharms., Greenvale, N.Y. Editor: Search for New Drugs, 1972, New Drugs: Discovery and Development, 1978; contbr. articles to profl. jours. With U.S. Army, 1944-46. Mem. AAAS, Am. Soc. Pharmacology and Exptl. Therapeutics, Soc. Exptl. and Biol. Medicine, N.Y. Acad. Sci. Home: 207 Hitching Post Dr Wilmington DE 19803-1914 Office: ARA Assoc PO Box 244 Rockland DE 19732-0244 Personal E-mail: alannar@msn.com.

RUBIN, ALAN J. engineering educator; b. Yonkers, N.Y., Mar. 20, 1934; s. Jerome and Lydia R.; m. Ann Kopyt, June 17, 1962; 1 dau., Sara. BS in Civil Engring, U. Miami (Fla.), 1959; MS in San. Engring, U. N.C., Chapel Hill, 1962, PhD in Environ. Chemistry, 1966. Civil engr. FAA, Ft. Worth, 1959-60; asst. prof. U. Cin., 1965-68; prof. civil engring. Ohio State U., Columbus, 1968-91, prof. emeritus, 1991—; with U.S. Geol. Survey, Columbus, 1991-93. Vis. prof. Technion, Haifa, 1984. Editor 4 books on environ. chemistry; contbr. articles profl. jours. Served with AUS, 1953-55. Mem. Am. Water Works Assn., Water Pollution Control Fedn., Internat. Assn. Water Pollution Research. Achievements include research on giardia cysts, metal ion chemistry, flotation techniques, disinfection, flocculation, coagulation, adsorption, and other physical-chemical treatment processes. Home: 1438 Sherbrooke Pl Columbus OH 43209-3113 Office: Ohio State Univ Dept Civil and Environtl Engring Columbus OH 43210-1058 E-mail: arubin@columbus.rr.com.

RUBIN, ALBERT LOUIS, internist, nephrologist, educator; b. Memphis, May 9, 1927; s. Malcolm M. and Sarah Anne (Bryan) R.; m. Carolyn M. Diehl, Sept. 28, 1953; 1 child, Marc. Student, Williams College, 1944-45, MIT, 1945-46; MD, Cornell U., 1950. Diplomate Am. Bd. Internal Medicine. Intern Bellevue Hosp., N.Y.C., 1950-51, resident internal medicine, 1951-54, fellow nephrology, 1954-55, physician-in-charge, 1953-61; established investigator Am. Heart Assn., N.Y.C., 1958-63; dir. Rogosin Labs., Cornell U. Med. Coll., N.Y.C., 1963—, The Rogosin Kidney Ctr., N.Y.C., 1971—, The Rogosin Inst., N.Y.C., 1983—; prof. biochemistry, surgery, medicine Cornell U. Med. Coll., N.Y.C., 1969—; surgeon The N.Y. Hosp., N.Y.C., 1969—. Com. on sci. and tech. aspects of processing materials in space NRC, NYC; dir. affiliations and patient referrals N.Y. Hosp.-Cornell Med. Ctr., 1977-80; bd. dirs., bd. incorporators neurosci. rsch. program MIT. Author: Physical Diagnosis: A Textbook and Workbook in Methods of Clinical Examination, 1972, Humoral Aspects of Transplantation, 1976, Manual of Clinical Nephrology, 1980; cons. editor Am. Jour. Medicine, Time mag., 1959-94. With USN, 1944-45. Recipient Hoeing award Nat. Kidney Found., 1982. Mem. ACP, AAAS, Am. Soc. for Artificial Internal Organs, Transplantation Soc., Sigma XI. Home: 220 Allison Ct Englewood NJ 07631-4301 Office: The Rogosin Inst 505 E 70th St 2d Fl Rm 230 New York NY 10021-9809

RUBIN, AMY ROCHELLE, speech-language pathologist; b. Bronx, N.Y., May 24, 1972; d. Ronald Gary and Susan E. Langus; m. Adam Theodore Rubin, Aug. 21, 1994; 1 child, Sarah Alexis. BS, Ohio U., 1994; MA, Edinboro U. of Pa., 1996. Cert. clin. competence Am. Speech Lang. Hearing Assn., lic. speech lang. pathology Md., advanced profl. cert. in tchg. Md., 2003. Speech lang. pathologist Anne Arundel County Pub. Schs., Annapolis, Md., 1996—; pvt. practice Arnold, Md., 1999—. Pres. Hillel, 1993—94; collegiate pres. United Jewish Appeal, 1992—93. Mem.: Am. Speech Lang. Hearing Assn., Md. Speech Lang. Hearing Assn. (state edn. advocacy leader 2001—04, Svc. award 2003), Sigma Kappa (parent's club chairperson, jewler 1992—94). Democrat. Jewish. Avocations: crafts, reading, movies. Home: 600 Quaker Ridge Ct Arnold MD 21012 Office: Anne Arundel County Pub Schs 500 Marlboro Rd Glen Burnie MD 21061 Personal E-mail: lucyruby2003@yahoo.com.

RUBIN, ARNOLD E. lawyer; b. Phila., Dec. 8, 1935; s. Harry and Nettie Rubin. BS, Drexel Univ., 1958; JD, Temple Univ., 1961. Bar: Pa. 1962, U.S. Supreme Ct. 1965, Ct. of Common Pleas Del. County, Pa. 1962. Atty. Public Defender, Delaware Co., Pa., 1965-69, first. asst., 1970-74; pvt. practice Delaware Co., Pa., 1974—. Author, lectr., instr. Dist. Justice Sch., 1974, 75, 76, 77; mem. election bd. 2d Precinct Upper Providence, 2002, minority judge elections, 2002—. With U.S. Army, 1961-75. Mem. Masonic Lodge (floor worker 1979-87). Democrat. Jewish. Office: 211 W State St Media PA 19063-3139 Office Phone: 610-565-5300 ext. 10.

RUBIN, ARTHUR HERMAN, retired university official, consultant; b. N.Y.C., Aug. 14, 1927; s. Samuel and Bessie (Moritt) R.; m. Janice Levy, Apr. 9, 1950 (div. 1965); children: Renee Ellen, Linda Joy; m. Audrey M. Schmidt, July 1, 1973. BS, NYU, 1950, MA, 1951. Adminstrv. asst. to asst. dean Sch. Edn. NYU, 1947-54, lab. asst. bus. edn. dept., 1950-54, instr., 1954-56, program dir. grad. students orgn., 1954-63, dir. tours, 1955-58, coord. summer sessions activities, 1959-64, dir. Bur. Pub. Occasions, 1963-74, asst. v.p. pub. occasions, 1974-75, dir. extramural affairs Coll. Dentistry, 1976, assoc. dean adminstrn., 1976-80, adj. asst. prof. behavioral scis. and cmty. health, 1976-80, dir. alumni rels. Sch. of Med., 1980-95, dir. spl. events med. ctr., 1988-95; cons. to Office Alumni Rels. NYU Sch. Medicine, 1995-2000; cons. to Office Spl. Events, NYU Med. Ctr., 1995-2000, ret., 2000. Tchr. Patrick Henry Jr. High Sch., N.Y.C., 1949-58; acting asst. prin. Robert F. Wagner Jr. High Sch., N.Y.C., 1958-63; cons. in field. Trustee Agnew Found., 1967—. Recipient NYU Presdl. citation, 1971, GSO award, 1980, Ernest O. Melby award Sch. Edn. Alumni Assn., 1976, citation Bus. Edn. Assn. Met. N.Y., 1976, Sesquicentennial award NYU Alumni Fedn., 1982, Meritorious Svc. award, 1985, dir. Emeritus citation, 1992. Mem. Ea. Bus. Tchrs. Assn. (chmn. exhibits 1953-74, exec. bd. 1969-71, pres. 1972-73, award 1974), Bus. Edn. Assn. Met. N.Y. (exec. bd. 1962-83), Nat. Bus. Edn. Assn. (exec. bd. 1972-74, conv. mgr. 1974-92, Disting. Svc. award 1992, Cert. of Appreciation 1992), N.Y. Acad. Pub. Edn. (bd. dirs. 1979-98, pres. 1992-94), NYU Edn. Alumni Assn. (v.p. 1961-62, 64-67), NYU Club (bd. govs. 1972-78, 79-89, v.p. 1983-86, chmn. bd. 1986-87), Princeton Club N.Y., Delta Pi Epsilon Rsch. Found. Inc. (bd. dirs. 1990-92), Delta Pi Epsilon (Svc. awards Alpha chpt. 1971, 81). Home: 2605 Houghton Lean Macungie PA 18062-9506

RUBIN, BENJAMIN ARNOLD, microbiologist, immunologist, medical educator, researcher; b. N.Y.C., Sept. 27, 1917; s. Eli and Helen Sarah (Arenoff) R.; m. Mae Koenig, Aug. 31, 1951. BS, CCNY, 1937; MS, Va. Polytech. Inst. & State U., 1938; PhD, Yale U., 1947. Asst. dir. Circle Analytical Lab., N.Y.C., 1938-40; chief lab. and radiology U.S. Army C.E., Nfld., also Cen. Am., 1940-44; asst. chief microbiologist Scherly Rsch. Lab., Lawrenceburg, Ind., 1944; rsch. asst. Yale U., New Haven, 1944-47; chief microbiologist Broockhaven Nat. Lab., L.I., 1947-52, Syntex, Mexico City, 1952-54; prof. pub. health and preventitive medicine Coll. of Medicine Baylor U., Houston, 1954-60; mgr. biol. rsch. Wyeth, Radnar, Pa., 1960-84; rsch. prof. Phila. Coll. Osteo. Medicine, 1984-95; ret. Cons. GE, Valley Forge, Pa., 1972-80, U.S. Congressional com. energy and commerce, 1976-80, biological applications of space. Contbr. over 150 articles to sci. jours. Named to Inventors Hall of Fame, 1992; recipient John Scott award and medal, 1982, Proctor medal Phila. Drug Exchange, 1993; named Inventor of Yr., 1985. Achievements include invention of bifurcated needle in Smallpox eradication program. Home: 50 Belmont Ave Apt 601 Bala Cynwyd PA 19004-2428 Office: Phila Coll Osteo Medicine 4150 City Ave Philadelphia PA 19131-1610

RUBIN, BLAKE DOUGLAS, lawyer; b. Phila., Jan. 11, 1955; s. Alan and Helen (Metz) R.; m. Deborah F. McIlroy, Oct. 30, 1982; children; Bret Andrew, Keith Michael. BA, Haverford Coll., 1976; MBA with distinction, JD cum laude, U. Pa., 1980. Bar: Pa. 1980, D.C. 1988, U.S. Dist. Ct. (ea. dist.) Pa. 1980, U.S. Ct. Appeals (3d cir.) 1980. Assoc. Wolf, Block, Schorr & Solis-Cohen, Phila., 1980-84; atty., Office of Tax Legis. Counsel U.S. Dept. Treasury, Washington, 1984-87; ptnr. Steptoe & Johnson, Washington, 1987—2000, Arnold & Porter, Washington, 2000—. Adj. prof. grad. tax program Villanova (Pa.) U., 1982-84; mem. adv. bd. Nat. Inst. on Real Estate Taxation; frequent speaker in field. Mem. adv. coun. Washington Tax Rev., Tax Mgmt. Real Estate Jour., Jour. Real Estate Taxation; contbr. articles to profl. jours. Mem. ABA (taxation sect.), Order of Coif, Beta Gamma Sigma, Beta Alpha Psi. Republican. Avocations: tennis, swimming, sailing. Home: 5120 Sangamore Rd Bethesda MD 20816-2326 Office: 555 12th St NW # 816 Washington DC 20004-1200 Office Phone: 202-942-5828. Business E-mail: blake_rubin@aporter.com.

RUBIN, CATHY ANN, retired educator; b. Denver, July 17, 1948; d. Harry Phillip and Charlotte Ruth (Brinig) R. BA, Colo. State U., 1970; MA, U. No. Colo., 197l. Cert. tchr., Colo. Tchr. Adams County Dist. 50 Schs., Westminster, Colo., 1971-72; tchr. educationally handicapped Jefferson County Pub. Schs., Golden, Colo., 1972-98. Typist, bookkeeper Kenmark-Shaw's Jewelers, Denver, 1966—. Sec.-treas. Hillel Found., Denver, 1979-81; fundraiser Women's Am. Orgn. for Rehab. through Tng., Denver, 1979—; bookkeeper Religious Coalition for Abortion Rights, Denver, 1982-90; vol. TV PBS sta., Denver, 1978, Muscular Dystrophy Assn., Colo. AIDS Project; vol. usher DCTC, 1999—. Democrat. Jewish. Avocations: music, reading, sailing, knitting, needlepoint. Home: 3500 S Ivanhoe St Denver CO 80237-1123

RUBIN, CHANDA, professional tennis player; b. Lafayette, La., Feb. 18, 1976; d. Edward and Bernadette Rubin. Grad., Episcopal Sch. Acadiana, 1993. Mem. USTA Jr. Devel. Team, 1989, USTA Nat. Team, 1990; prof. tennis player, 1991—. Mem. U.S. Pan Am. Team, 1995, U.S. Fed Cup Team, 1995—97, 1999, 2003—04, U.S. Olympic Team, Atlanta, 1996, U.S. Women's Olympic Tennis Team, Athens, 2004. Founder The Chanda Rubin Found. Recipient 3 U.S. Jr. Titles; winner U.S. nat. title and Rolex Orange Bowl 12s crown, 1988; named Most Improved Female Player, Tennis Mag., 1995, Female Athlete of Yr., U.S. Tennis Assn., 1995, Most Caring Athlete, USA Weekend Mag., 1997; finalist (with Testud) U.S. Open.; winner 7 Career Singles titles and 10 Career Doubles titles, WTA Tour. Office: USTA 70 W Red Oak Ln White Plains NY 10604-3602 also: Advantage International 1751 Pinnacle Dr Ste 1500 Mc Lean VA 22102-3833*

RUBIN, DAVID LEE, humanities educator, publisher; b. Indpls., Sept. 30, 1939; s. Ira Bertram and Jeanne Iva (Gamso) R.; m. Carolyn Dettman, June 12, 1965; 1 child, Timothy Craig. BA, U. Tenn., 1962; cert., U. Paris, 1963; MA, U. Ill., 1964, PhD, 1967. Instr. French U. Ill., Urbana, 1966-67; asst. prof. U. Chgo., 1967-69, U. Va., Charlottesville, 1969-74, assoc. prof., 1974-82, prof. French, 1982-2001, mem. Fulbright selection com., 1996—, mem. com. on comparative lit., 1997-2001, prof. emeritus, assoc. univ. seminar program, 2001—; seminar dir. Folger Inst., 1989. Chair poetry bd. Va. Quar. Rev., 2003—, Great Books discussion leader Jefferson Inst. Lifelong Learning, 2001-; assoc. ctr. advanced studies U. Va., 1979, 80-81, 87, 93, 99-2000; founder Rookwood Press, 1992—; cons. Can. Coun., Etudes littéraires françaises, NEH, numerous univ. presses; lectr., spkr. in field. Author: Higher Hidden Order, 1972, The Knot of Artifice, 1981, A Pact with Silence, 1991; editor: The Selected Poetry and Prose of John T. Napier, 1972, La poésie française du premier 17e siècle, 1986, 2d edit., 2004, Sun King, 1991; co-editor: La Cohérence Intérieure, 1977, Convergences, 1989, The Ladder of High Designs, 1991, The Fulbright Difference, 1993; founding editor Continuum, 1989-93, EMF: Studies in Early Modern France, 1994-2002, EMF Critiques, 1994-2002, Rookwood Texts, 1997—, Rookwood Reprints, 2002—; mem. editl. bd. Purdue Studies in Romance Literatures, 1975-2001, Oeuvres et Critiques, 1976-2001, French Rev., 1986-94; Am. corr. Cahiers Maynard, 1973-2001, Cahiers Tristan L'Hermite, 1989-2001; contbr. articles to profl. jours., chpts. to books. U.S. State Dept. Fulbright fellow, 1963—64, fellow, Woodrow Wilson Found., 1963—64, Guggenheim Found., 1980—81, Hewlett fellow, summer, 1997, The Shape of Change: Studies in Honor of David Lee Rubin, 2002. Mem. MLA, ACLU, Phi Beta Kappa (mem. selection com. U. Va. Book prize 2004—). Avocations: reading, travel, exercise. Home: 520 Rookwood Pl Charlottesville VA 22903-4734

RUBIN, DAVID M. dean, educator; BA in Am. History, Columbia U.; MA in Comm., Stanford U., PhD in Comm., 1972. Mem. faculty and chair dept. journalism NYU; prof. Syracuse U., dean Newhouse Sch. Pub. Comm.,

1990—. Juror Pulitzer Prize, journalism, 1998, 99. Contbr. articles to profl. jours. Mem. adv. bd. Syracuse Opera. Avocations: dogs, music. Office: Syracuse U 215 University Pl Syracuse NY 13244-0001

RUBIN, DONALD BRUCE, statistician, educator, research company executive; b. Washington, Dec. 22, 1943; s. Allan A. and Harriet Rubin; m. Kathryn M. Kazarow; children: Scott Wilk, Paul Stuart. AB magna cum laude, Princeton U., 1965; MS, Harvard U., 1966, PhD, 1970. Rsch. statistician Ednl. Testing Svc., Princeton, N.J., 1971-75, chmn. stats., 1975-79, sr. statis. advisor, 1979-81; pres. Datamatrics Rsch. Inc., Waban, Mass., 1981—; prof. U. Chgo., 1982-84, Harvard U., Cambridge, Mass., 1984—, chmn. stats., 1985-94, 2000—, John L. Loeb Prof. Stats., 2002—. Author: Handling Nonresponse in Sample Surveys by Multiple Imputation, 1980, Multiple Imputation for Nonresponse in Surveys, 1987, classic edit., 2004; author: (with others) Incomplete Data in Sample Surveys (Vol. 2): Theory and Bibliography, 1983; co-author: (with R.J.A. Little) Statistical Analysis With Missing Data, 1987, 2d edit., 2002, (with A. Gelman, J. Carlin. H. Stern) Bayasian Data Analysis, 1995, 2d edit., 2003, (with R. Rosenthal and R. Rosnow) Contrasts and Effect Sites in Behavioral Research: A Correlational Approach, 2000; co-editor: (with P.W. Holland) Test Equating, 1982; contbr. over 300 articles to profl. jours. Recipient Parzen prize for statis. innovation, 1996; Woodrow Wilson Grad. fellow, 1965; NSF Grad. fellow, 1965, 68, John Simon Guggenheim fellow, 1977-78. Fellow AAAS (chmn. stats. 1992), Am. Statis. Assn. (editor jour. 1980-82, dir. 1980-82, statistician of yr. Boston chpt. 1995, Chgo. chpt. 2000, S.S. Wilks medal 1995), Inst. Math. Stats. (coun. mem. 1990-92, 99-2001, Fisher lectr. 2004); mem. NAS (com. on nat. stats. 1989-92, mem. panel on confidentiality data 1989-92, panel on bilingual edn. 1990-92, working group on statis. analysis of com. on basic rsch. in behavioral and social scis. 1985-86, panel statis. in 21st century 1995, other coms.), AAAS, Am. Acad. Arts and Sci., Biometric Soc., Internat. Assn. Survey Statisticians, Internat. Statis. Inst., Psychometric Soc., Royal Statis. Soc. Office: Harvard U Dept Statistics Cambridge MA 02138 Office Phone: 617-495-5498. E-mail: rubin@stat.harvard.edu.

RUBIN, ELIZABETH D. health insurance company official; b. Gloversville, N.Y., Mar. 28, 1970; d. Lewis and Barbara Gayle Vant; m. Dana Fredric Rubin, May 23, 1999. BA, Emory U., 1992; MPA, Columbia U., 1995. Cert. profl. Acad. Healthcare Mgmt. Mktg. coord. Thomas Jefferson U. Hosp., Phila., 1992-93; sr. fin. analyst NYLCare Health Plans, 1995-98; dir. fin. control Empire Blue Cross Blue Shield, N.Y.C., 1998—. Fellow Columbia U. Sch. Internat. and Pub. Affairs, 1994-95. Mem. Healthcare Fin. Mgmt. Assn, Hadassah Women's Orgn. (life). Avocations: fitness walking, tennis. E-mail: elizabeth.rubin@empirehealthcare.com.

RUBIN, E(RWIN) LEONARD, lawyer; b. Chgo., Jan. 11, 1933; s. Samuel and Frances Birdie (Rabin) R.; m. Stephanie Siegel, Mar. 4, 1961 (div. Dec. 1981); children: Matthew, Suzanne; m. Audrey Gay Holzer, May 8, 1983; children: Margot, Bette. Student, U. Ill., Urbana, 1948-51; AB, U. Miami, 1956, JD, 1959. s. N.Y. 1960, Ill. 1962, U.S. Dist. Ct. (no. dist.) Ill. 1962, U.S. Ct. Appeals (7th cir.) 1990, U.S. Ct. Appeals (5th cir.) 1998. Assoc. Hays, St. John A&H, N.Y.C., 1960—62, Devoe, Shadur, Mikva, Chgo., 1962—65; gen. counsel Playboy Enterprises, Inc., Chgo., 1965—78; ptnr. E. Leonard Rubin Law Offices, Chgo., 1978—81, Epton, Mullin & Druth Ltd., Chgo., 1981—86, Brinks, Hofer, Gilson & Lione, Chgo., 1986—96, Gordon & Glickson, LLC, Chgo., 1996—2002, Sachnoff & Weaver, Ltd., Chgo., 2002—. Adj. prof. U. Ill., Northwestern U. Law Sch., Loyola U. Sch. Law, John Marshall Law Sch. Pres. Lawyers for Creative Arts, Chgo., 1983-85; bd. dirs. Wisdom Bridge Theatre, Chgo., 1983-85; mem., bd. dirs. Appletree Theater of Highland Park. Cpl. U.S. Army, 1953-5, ETO. Mem. ABA, Ill. Bar Assn., Chgo. Bar Assn. (bd. mgrs. 1983-85, chmn. various coms., dir. Christmas Spirits Satire Show 1965-99), Union Internat. Des Avocats (pres. intellectual property commn. 1997-2000), Copyright Soc. Am. (trustee, past pres. midwest chpt.). Jewish. Home: 270 Sunset Dr Northfield IL 60093-1047 Office: Sachnoff & Weaver Ltd 30 S Wacker Dr Ste 2900 Chicago IL 60606 Office Phone: 312-207-6464. Business E-Mail: elrubin@sachnoff.com.

RUBIN, GEORGE, real estate executive; Grad., Lafayette Coll. Pres., trustee Preit-Rubin Inc., Phila.; with Rubin Orgn., Inc., 1970—; pres. acquisitions Pa. Real Estate Investment Trust, Phila., 1987—. Bd. dirs. Lafayette Coll., Elwyn Inst., Thorncroft Therapeutic Horseback Riding, Inc.; active various civic orgns. Office: Pa Real Estate Investment Trust 200 S Broad St Ste 300 Philadelphia PA 19102-3803

RUBIN, GERALD MAYER, molecular biologist, biochemistry educator; b. Boston, Mar. 31, 1950; s. Benjamin H. and Edith (Weisberg) R.; m. Lynn S. Mastalir, May 7, 1978; 1 child, Alan F. BS, MIT, 1971; PhD, Cambridge (Eng.) U., 1974, ScD, 2002. Helen Hay Whitney Found. fellow Stanford U. Sch. Medicine, Calif., 1974-76; asst. prof. biol. chemistry Sidney Farber Cancer Inst.-Harvard U. Med. Sch., Boston, 1977-80; staff mem. Carnegie Instn. of Washington, Balt., 1980-83; John D. MacArthur prof. genetics U. Calif., Berkeley, 1983—. Investigator Howard Hughes Med. Inst., 1987—, v.p. biomed. rsch., 2000-01, v.p., dir. planning Janelia Farm Campus, 2001-03, v.p., dir. Janelia Farm Rsch. Campus, 2003—. Recipient Young Scientist award Passano Found., 1983, U.S. Steel Found. award Nat. Acad. Scis., 1985, Eli Lilly award in biochemistry Am. Chem. Soc., 1985, Genetics Soc. Am. medal, 1986. Mem. NAS, Inst. of Medicine, Am. Acad. Arts and Scis. Office: Howard Hughes Med Inst 4000 Jones Bridge Rd Bethesda MD 20815-6789 E-mail: rubing@hhmi.org.

RUBIN, GERROLD ROBERT, advertising executive; b. Evanston, Ill., Mar. 31, 1940; s. Bennie George and Anita (Perich) R.; m. Barbara Ann Nieman, Sept. 5, 1962; children: John, Ann. BS in Radio, TV, Film, Northwestern U., 1962. Account exec. Leo Burnett Advt., Chgo., 1962-67, account supr. Toronto, Ont., 1967-68, Needham, Harper Steers, Chgo., 1968-73, account dir. Los Angeles, 1973-78; mgmt. rep. Needham, Harper & Steers, Chgo., 1978-81, pres., CEO Los Angeles, 1981-86, Rubin, Postaer & Assocs., Santa Monica, Calif., 1986—. Bd. dirs. Country Music Assn., Nashville, 1983— , Presbyterian. Office: Rubin Postaer & Assocs 1333 2nd St Santa Monica CA 90401-1100

RUBIN, HANAN, retired insurance company executive; b. N.Y.C., Mar. 9, 1927; s. Hyman and Esta (Greenberg) R.; m. Mona Klein, June 29, 1958; children: Eric Stuart, Karen Jill Rubin Dauber, Wendy Risa Rubin Axelrod. AB magna cum laude, NYU, 1948, PhD in Math., 1953. Cert. internal auditor, info. sys. auditor. Tchg. asst. math. NYU, 1946-48, instr. math., asst. rsch. scientist Courant Inst. Math. Scis., 1948-51, instr. math., assoc. rsch. scientist, 1951-53, asst. prof. math., rsch. scientist, 1954-58, instr. Bell Telephone Labs., 1954-56; staff mathematician, cons. IBM, 1958-59, cons. analytical svcs. dept., 1959-60, asst. mgr., 1960, mgr., 1960-62; head computer group, sr. supervisory scientist TRG, 1962-64; tech. asst. to pres. Gen. Applied Sci. Labs., 1964-67; corp. staff mem., dir. edn. & tng. Computer Applications Inc., 1967-69; exec. asst. Met. Life Ins. Co., 1972-75, asst. v.p., 1975-77, v.p., 1977-91; ret., 1991. Vis. asst. prof. math. U. Tenn., 1953-54; cons. Union Carbide Nuc. Co., Oak Ridge, Tenn., 1953-66; vis. mathematician Brookhaven Nat. Lab., Upton, N.Y., 1957; co-chair Stony Brook Conf. Advances Computing SUNY, 1966; mem. bi-county task force com. computer applications medicine Nassau Heart Assn., Mineola, N.Y., 1971-72; chair ad hoc EFT com. Life Office Mgmt. Assn., 1978. Contbr. numerous articles to profl. jours. Bd. dirs. South Nassau Cmtys. Hosp., Oceanside, 1980-2002, dir. emeritus, 2002—, treas. bd. dirs., 1985-89, 1st v.p. bd. dirs., 1989-90; bd. dirs. Winthrop South Nassau U. Health Sys., Mineola, Oceanside, 1996-2001. With USN, 1945-46. Rockefeller fellow NYU, 1948. Mem. Phi Beta Kappa, Tau Kappa Alpha, Sigma Xi. Achievements include publication of solution to long-standing problem in mathematical theory of ocean waves; research in aerospace technology, artificial intelligence, atomic energy, controlled nuclear fusion, electronic funds transfer, information theory, management science and telecommunication systems. Avocations: computing, golf, music. Home: 359 Green Ct Oceanside NY 11572-5615

RUBIN, HARRY MEYER, entertainment and software industry executive; b. N.Y.C., Dec. 21, 1952; s. Martin J. and Helene Rubin; m. Cathy Hemery, May 26, 1990; children: Gabriella, James. BA, Stanford U., 1974; MBA, Harvard U., 1976. Investment banker Wertheim & Co., Inc., N.Y.C., 1976-77; fin. mgr. Am. Airlines, Inc., N.Y.C., 1977-79; dir. fin. planning-entertainment, electronics groups RCA Corp., N.Y.C., 1979-81; CFO RCA Videodiscs, RCA Home Video, RCA Cable RCA Entertainment Group, N.Y.C.; v.p. strategic planning RCA Corp., group v.p. fin. and bus. affairs RCA entertainment ops., 1981-86; gen. mgr. Home Video Gen. Electric Co., 1986-87; v.p., gen. mgr. home video div. NBC, Inc., 1988-93; exec. v.p. GT Interactive Software Corp., 1994-98; pres. GT Interactive Internat., 1998-2000; pres. internat. Infogrames, Inc., 2000-01; sr. exec. v.p. and head of worldwide pub. Atari Inc., 2001—. Dir., co-head exec. com. RCA/Columbia Pictures Worldwide Video; founding ptnr. Samuel Adams Beer; founding dir. Arts & Entertainment Network. Mem. Phi Beta Kappa, 22 Club. Avocations: travel, foreign languages. Home: 784 Park Ave New York NY 10021-3553 Office Phone: 212-726-6523.

RUBIN, HARVEY, publishing executive; b. N.Y.C., Mar. 1, 1933; s. Joseph and Esther Rubin; m. Judith Lowe; children: Jonathan, James, Elizabeth. BA, Columbia Coll., 1954, BS, 1955; MS, NYU, 1960. Indsl. engr. Curtiss-Wright Corp., Woodridge, NJ, 1955—58; adminstrv. asst. Bulova R&D, Woodside, NY, 1958—60; v.p. Continental Copper & Steel, N.Y.C., 1960—69; pres., dir. Primary Industries, N.Y.C., 1969—75, Satra Corp., N.Y.C., 1975—79; pub., gen. ptnr. Pindar Press, N.Y.C., 1980—. Pres. Columbia Coll. Alumni Assn., N.Y.C., 1980—82. Recipient Alumni medal, Columbia U., 1982. Mem.: Univ. Club. Avocations: tennis, skiing, bridge. Office: Pindar Press 12 E 49th St New York NY 10017

RUBIN, HERBERT, lawyer; b. Lisbon, Conn., June 4, 1918; s. Simon and Rose (Berko) R.; m. Rose Luttan, July 6, 1941; children: Barbara, Caroline, Donald. AB, CCNY, 1938; JD, NYU, 1942. Bar: N.Y. 1942, U.S. Dist. Ct. (so. and ea. dists.) N.Y. 1951, U.S. Supreme Ct. 1956, U.S. Ct. Appeals (2d, 3d, 4th, 6th, 9th, 10th, 11th and D.C. cirs.). Assoc. Newman & Bisco, 1942; faculty NYU Law Sch., 1946-50, 57-62; prof. creditors' rights Rutgers U. Law Sch., 1949-57; pvt. practice, 1946-56; ptnr. Sereni, Herzfeld & Rubin, and successor Herzfeld & Rubin, N.Y.C., 1956—, sr. ptnr., 1968—. Instr. mil. law U.S. Army, 1944-46; prof. constl. law L.I. U., 1963-68; trustee North Shore L.I. Jewish Hosp. Editor-in-chief NYU Law Rev., 1940-41; bd. editors N.Y. Law Jour., 1971—; contbr. articles to profl. jours. Mem. N.Y. State Banking Bd., 1975-85, N.Y. State Jud. Selection Com., 1975-83, Sen. Moynihan's Jud. Selection Com., 1982-2000, Sen. Schumer's Jud. Selection Com., 1999—, City Charter Revision Commn., 1998-2001; trustee Am. Assn. Jewish Lawyers and Jurists. 1st lt. Signal Corps, AUS, 1942-46. Recipient award NCCJ, 1967, United Jewish Appeal, 1968, 97, Israel Bonds, 1973, NYU Law Assn. award 1987, Judge Weinfeld award, 1992. Fellow Am. Bar Found.; mem. ABA (mem. coun. N.Y. state), N.Y. State Bar Assn., Queens County Bar Assn. (pres. 1970), Assn. Bar City Of N.Y., Fed. Bar Coun., Jewish Lawyers Guild (award 2001). Office: Herzfeld & Rubin 40 Wall St Fl 54 New York NY 10005-2301 Office Phone: 212-471-8500.

RUBIN, IRVIN I. plastics company executive; b. Bklyn., Feb. 27, 1919; children: Jesse, Julie. BS in Chemistry, CCNY, 1938; postgrad., Bklyn. Coll., 1939-40. Pres. Robinson Plastics Corp., Bklyn., 1940-42, 44—; engr. Montrose Chem., Newark, 1942-45; prin. Robinson, Lewis & Rubin, Inc., N.Y.C., 1957-70. Adj. prof. plastics N.Y. Inst. Tech., 1960-63; mem. Plastics Ednl. Commn., Adv. Bd. Vocat. and Extension Edn., Bd. Edn. N.Y.C., 1960-71; cons. Dupont, Am. Optical, Kodex. Author: Injection Molding Theory and Practice, 1973; editor: Handbook of Plastic Materials and Processes, 1990. Named to Plastics Hall of Fame. Fellow Soc. Plastic Engrs. (pres. N.Y. sect.).

RUBIN, JAMES P. international affairs analyst, public affairs administrator; b. N.Y.C., 1960; BA in Polit. Sci., Columbia U., 1982, M in Internat. Affairs, 1984. Rsch. dir. Arms Control Assn., Washington, 1985-89; profl. staff mem. U.S. Senate Com. on Fgn. Rels.; sr. fgn. policy advisor to Sen. Joseph R. Biden, Jr.; sr. advisor, spokesman for U.S. Rep. to UN, Madeleine K. Albright; dir. fgn. policy, spokesman for Clinton/Gore '96 Campaign; asst. sec., chief spokesman Pub. Affairs Bur., Washington, 1997-2000; pub. spkr., commentator, author, London, 2000—. Cons. on nuclear arms control issues Senate Fgn. Rels. Com., 1985-89. Recipient John Jay award for disting. profl. achievement Columbia Coll., Columbia U., 1998, Disting. Svc. award Sec. State, 2000.

RUBIN, JOEL EDWARD, consulting company executive; b. Cleve., Sept. 5, 1928; s. Morris and Pearl (Jacobs) R.; m. Lucille Schutmaat, Dec. 18, 1953; children: Brian G., Jennifer L., Rebecca R. BS, Case Inst. of Tech., 1949; MFA, Yale U., 1951; PhD, Stanford U., 1960. Exec. v.p. Kliegl Bros. Lighting, N.Y.C., 1954-85; prin. cons. Joel E. Rubin & Assocs., N.Y.C., 1985-93; prin. cons. theater planning Artec Cons. Inc., N.Y.C., 1993—. Co-author: Theatrical Lighting Practice 1954; author: Technological Development of Stage Lighting 1960. Member Coll. of Fellows of Am. Theatre, John F. Kennedy Ctr. for the Performing Arts, Washington. Recipient Golden Triaga, Prague Quadrennial, 1987, Zlatou medal, 1991, 1st time award Bus. Com. for the Arts, Forbes Mag., 1987; recipient Founders' award U.S. Inst. for Theatre Tech., 1972, 79, Nat. award, 1990, Lifetime hon. membership award, 1996, Spl. citation, 1996; Dr. Joel E. Rubin Founder's award named in his honor U.S. Inst. Theatre Tchrs., 2000; Internat. Student Rsch. grants established in his honor U.S. Inst. Theatre Tchrs., 2000. Fellow Am. Theatre Assn. (v.p. 1961-63), U.S. Inst. of Theatre Technology (pres. 1963-64); mem. Am. Nat. Theatre Acad. (bd. dirs. 1971-75), Internat. Theatre Inst. of the U.S. (bd. dirs. 1975-79), Nat. Coun. of Arts and Govt. (bd. dirs. 1975-79), Internat. Orgn. Theatre Architects and Scenographers (U.S. chmn., rep. 1968-98, pres. 1971-79, Gold medal award 1996), Illuminating Engring. Soc. Avocations: collecting books, stage design, lincolniana. Home: 24 Edgewood Ave Hastings On Hudson NY 10706-2024 Office: Artec Cons 114 W 26th St New York NY 10001-6812 Office Phone: 212-242-0120. E-mail: booksjoel@aol.com.

RUBIN, KENNETH ALLEN, lawyer; b. Rockville Centre, N.Y., Nov. 24, 1947; s. Albert Alton and Marion (Osterweis) R.; m. Susan Kurman, Sept. 14, 1980; children: Jennifer, Kelly. BS, Cornell U., 1969, MS, 1971, JD, 1973. Bar: D.C. 1974, N.Y. 1974, U.S. Ct. Appeals (D.C. crct.) 1974, U.S. Ct. Appeals (5th crct. 1975, U.S. Ct. Appeals (4th, 9th and 10th crct.) 1976, U.S. Ct. Appeals (3d, 8th and 11th crcts.) 1986, U.S. Supreme Ct. 1992. Trial atty. Dept. Justice, Washington, 1973-74; sr. ptnr. Morgan, Lewis & Bockius LLP, Washington, 1974—. Adj. prof. USDA Grad. Sch., Washington, 1977-85, U. Ala., Huntsville, 1978-91, Antioch U., Washington, 1978; lectr. Cornell U., Ithaca, N.Y., 1979—. Author: What the Business Executive Needs To Know about U.S. Environmental Laws and Liabilities, 1991, (manual) A Tidal Wave of Lawsuits and Regulations Flood the Once-Placid Waters of Drinking Water Utilities, 2000, Oil Spill Reporting Manual, 2002. Mem. adv. com. Cornell Ctr. for Environment. Mem. ABA, Am. Water Works Assn., Swiss Club Washington, Cornell Club Washington. Office: Morgan Lewis & Bockius LLP 1111 Pennsylvania Ave NW Washington DC 20004 E-mail: karwaterlawyer@aol.com.

RUBIN, KENNETH PHILLIP, gastroenterologist; b. Hoboken, N.J., 1950; MD, U. Medicine and Dentistry N.J.-N.J. Med. Sch., 1975. Diplomate Am. Bd. Internal Medicine, Am. Bd. Gastroenterology. Intern Bronx Mcpl. Hosp. Ctr., N.Y.C., 1975—76, resident in internal medicine, 1976—79; fellow in gastroenterology Mt. Sinai Hosp., N.Y.C., 1979—81; pvt. practice Englewood, NJ. Asst. clin. prof. medicine Mt. Sinai Sch. Medicine, N.Y.C., 1991—; affiliated physician Englewood Hosp. and Med. Ctr., NJ. Named one of Top Drs. in N.Y. Metro Area, Castle Connolly, Top Drs. 2003, N.J. Monthly Mag. Office: Englewood Hosp and Med Ctr 420 Grand Ave Englewood NJ 07631-4141

RUBIN, LAWRENCE GILBERT, physicist, laboratory manager; b. Bklyn., Sept. 17, 1925; s. Harry E. and Ruth (Feirberg) R.; m. Florence Ruth Kagan, Feb. 11, 1951; children: Michael G., Richard D., Jeffrey N. Student, Cooper Union, N.Y.C., 1943, 46-47; BS in Physics, U. Chgo., 1949; MA in Physics, Columbia U., 1950. Staff mem., physicist research div. Raytheon Co., Waltham, Mass., 1950-64; group leader Nat. Magnet Lab., MIT, Cambridge, Mass., 1964-78, divsn. head high magnetic field facility, 1978-93; advisor to high magnetic field facility, 1994-95; vis. scientist MIT, 1996—. Mem. NAS adv. panel Nat. Bur. Standards, 1976-82, 85-90; bd. dirs. Lake Shore Cryotronics, Inc., Columbus, Ohio; gen. chmn. 6th Internat. Temperature Symposium, Washington, 1982, 7th Internat. Temperature Symposium, Toronto, Ont., Can., 1992, 8th Internat. Temperature Symposium, Chgo., 2002; chmn. adv. com. Physics Today Buyers' Guide; contbg. editor Physics Today; organizer Am. Physical Soc. Tutorial program. Mem. editl. bd. Rev. Sci. Instruments, 1968-70, 79-81; contbr. articles to physics jours. With U.S. Army, 1943-46, ETO. Fellow IEEE (life, chmn. Keithley award com. 2002—), Am. Phys. Soc. (organizer and 1st chmn. instrument and measurement sci. group 1985); mem. Instrument Soc. Am. (sr.), Am. Vacuum Soc. Jewish. Home: 1504 Centre St Newton Center MA 02459-2447 Office: MIT Bldg NW14 1209 170 Albany St Cambridge MA 02139-4208 Office Phone: 617-253-5517. Business E-Mail: lrubin@mit.edu.

RUBIN, LEONARD SIDNEY, physiologist, educator, researcher; b. New York, Ny, Aug. 27, 1922; s. Hyman Hersh and Toba Rubin; m. Blanche Rubin, Mar. 30, 1950; children: Beth S., Joshua T., Matthew M. BS Chemistry, CUNY, New York, NY, 1943; PhD Neuroscience, NY Univ., New York, NY, 1950. Instr. NY Univ., New York, NY, 1943—44, rsch. assoc., 1950—53; chief psychophysiology br. Med. Labs, Army Chem. Corps., Edgewood, 1953—57; assoc. prof. Univ. Pa, Sch. of Medicine, Philadelphia, 1960—81; rsch. cons. Childrens Hosp. of Phila., Philadelphia, 1960—65; prof. Temple Univ. Med. Coll., Philadelphia, 1970—75; rsch. cons. St. Christopher's Hosp. for Children, 1964—67; cons., behavioral toxicology FDA, 1976—81; prof. Phila. Coll. of Med., Philadelphia, 1982—92; cons., biostatistics Cellcor Corp., Boston, 1988—92; prof., physiology/pharmacology Phila. Coll. of Osteo. Med., Philadelphia, 1981—. Armed forces nrc com. on vision, Washington, 1956—57; armed forces nrc com. on bioacoustics, Washington, 1956—57. Editl. cons. Jour. Studies on Alcohol, Jour. Nervous and Mental Disease, Psychophysiology, Psychopharmacologia, Am. Jour. Psychiatry. US Army, 1944—46. Recipient Social Sci. Rsch. Award, Inst. of Math., Stanford U., 1955, A.E. Bennet Award, Soc. of Biol. Psychiatry, 1961; scholar Fgn. Exch. Scholar, NAS, Yugoslavia, 1974. Fellow: Am. Psychol. Soc., Soc. of Biol. Psychiatry, Am. Psychol. Assn.; mem.: Soc. for Psychophysiological Rsch., Acad. of Psychosomatic Medicine, Sigma Xi. Jewish. Achievements include Author, In Numerous Research Journals, 1952-1996. Avocation: studying philosophy, art, and music. Home: 706 Powder Mill Lane Wynnewood PA 19096-4035

RUBIN, LEWIS J. physician, researcher; b. New York, NY, Aug. 5, 1950; s. Theodore and Erna Rubin; m. Juanita Rose Brooks; children: Lauren, Rose Sheelah, Jai Sheelah. MD, Albert Einstein Coll. of Medicine, 1972—75. Am. Bd. Internal Medicine ABIM/ Wash., DC, 1978. Prof. of medicine U. of Calif. San Diego, 1999—. Fellow: ACP, Am. Coll. Chest Physicians, Am. Heart Assn., Royal Coll. Physicians UK; mem.: Am. Soc. Clin. Investigation. Achievements include basic and clinical research in cardiopulmonary diseases, leading to drug developments and new treatments. Home: 6404 Avenida Wilfredo La Jolla CA 92037 Office: University of California San Diego 9300 Campus Point Drive La Jolla CA 92037 E-mail: ljrubin@ucsd.edu.

RUBIN, MELVIN LYNNE, ophthalmologist, educator; b. San Francisco, May 10, 1932; s. Morris and May (Gelman) R.; m. Lorna Isen, June 21, 1953; children: Gabrielle, Daniel, Michael. AA, U. Calif., Berkeley, 1951, BS, 1953; MD, U. Calif., San Francisco, 1957; MS, State U. Iowa, 1961. Diplomate Am. Bd. Ophthalmology (bd. dirs. 1977-83, chmn. 1984). Intern U. Calif. Hosp., San Francisco, 1957-58; resident in ophthalmology State U. Iowa, 1958-61; attending surgeon Georgetown U., Washington, 1961-63; asst. prof. surgery U. Fla. Med. Sch., Gainesville, 1963-66, assoc. prof. ophthalmology, 1966-67, prof. ophthalmology, 1967—97, prof. emeritus, 1997—, chmn. dept. ophthalmology, 1978-95, eminent scholar, 1989-97, eminent scholar emeritus, 1997. Author: Studies in Physiological Optics, 1965, Fundamentals of Visual Science, 1969, Optics for Clinicians, 1971, 2d edit., 1974, 25th ann. edit., 1995, The Fine Art of Prescribing Glasses, 1978, 3d edit., 2004; editor: Dictionary of Eye Terminology, 1984, 4th edit., 2001, Eye Care Notes, 1989, revised edit., 2001, Taking Care of Your Eyes, 2003; cons. editl. bd. Survey Ophthalmology; contbr. more than 100 articles to profl. jours. Co-founder Citizens for Pub. Schs., Inc., ProArteMusica Gainesville, Inc., 1969, pres., 1971-73; mem. Thomas Ctr. Adv. Bd. for the Arts, 1978-84, nat. sci. adv. bd. Helen Keller Eye Rsch. Found., 1989-96; bd. dirs. Hippodrome State Theater, 1981-87, Friends of Photography Ansel Adams Ctr., 1991-97; trustee U. Fla. Performing Arts Ctr., 1995—2004. With USPHS, 1961-63. Recipient Best Med. Book for 1978 award Am. Med. Writers Assn., 1979, Shaler Richardson award for svc. to medicine Fla. Soc. Ophthalmology, 1995; M.L. Rubin Ann. Lectureship established in his honor by Fla. Soc. of Ophthalmology, 1993. Fellow ACS, Am. Acad. Ophthalmology (sec., dir. 1978-92, pres. 1988, Sr. Honor award 1987. Guest of Honor 1992), Found. Am. Acad. Ophthalmology (bd. trustees, 1988-95, chmn., 1992-94), Joint Commn. on Allied Health Pers. in Ophthalmology (Statesman of Yr. award 1987); mem. Assn. Rsch. in Vision and Ophthalmology (trustee 1973-78, pres. 1979), Retina Soc., Macula Soc., Club Jules Gonin, N.Y. Acad. Sci., Fla. Soc. Ophthalmology, Am. Ophthal. Soc. (coun. 1998-2002), Pan Am. Soc. Ophthalmology, Ophthalmic Photographers Soc., Alachua County Med. Soc., Fla. Med. Assn., AMA (editorial bd. Archives of Ophthalmology 1975-85), Sigma Xi, Alpha Omega Alpha., Phi Kappa Phi. Office: U Fla Med Ctr PO Box 100284 Gainesville FL 32610-0284 Business E-Mail: mrubin@eye.ufl.edu.

RUBIN, MICHAEL HARRY, lawyer, educator; b. Baton Rouge, Jan. 13, 1950; s. Alvin B. and Janice (Ginsberg) R.; m. Ayan J. (Liss), June 11, 1972; children: Bethany, Gillian. BA(hon.), Amherst Coll., 1972; JD, La. State U., 1975. Bar: La., 1975; U.S. Ct. Appeals (5th cir.) 1975; U.S. Dist. Ct. (mid., ea. and we. dists.) La., 1976; U.S. Supreme Ct., 1982. Ptnr. Sanders, Downing, Kean, and Cazedessus, Baton Rouge, 1983-93, McGlinchey and Stafford, Baton Rouge, 1993—. Adj. prof. La. State U. Law Sch., 1976. Author: Louisiana Security Devices, Cases, 2003; contbr. articles to law jour. Mem.: La. State Bar, U.S. Fifth Cir. Bar (past pres.), So. Conf. Bar Pres. Office: McGlinchey & Stafford One American Pl 9th Fl Baton Rouge LA 70825

RUBIN, PATRICIA, internist; b. Apr. 27, 1962; MD, Wright State U., 1988. Cert. internal medicine. Resident in internal medicine U. Cin., 1988-91; fellow in cardiology U. Hosp., Cleve., 1991; rsch. fellow in cardiology U. Wash. Sch. Medicine, Seattle, 1993—; pvt. practice Cardiology One, Kent, Ohio. Recipient Clinician Scientist award Am. Heart Assn., 1995-96. Mem. ACP, AMA, ACC. Office: Cardiology One Box 8086 1330 Mercy Dr NW Ste 200 Canton OH 44708-2624

RUBIN, PATRICIA LEE, art historian; BA summa cum laude, Yale U., 1976; MA with distinction, Courtauld Inst., 1978; PhD, Harvard U., 1986. Mem. I Tatti Adv. Com., 1996—; reader Cambridge U. Press, 1996—, Yale U. Press, 1996—; acting dir. Harvard U. Ctr. for Renaissance Studies, 1997; cons. BBC, 1995—99; external examiner Manchester U.; adv. bd. Medici Archive Project; spkr. in field; conf. presenter. Mem. editl. bd. Art History, 1995—96, 1996—99, Renaissance Studies, 1995—99, exhbn. revs. editor, 1995—96, 1996—99; contbr. articles to profl. jours. Recipient Eric Mitchell prize for Giorgio Vasari Art and History, 1996. Mem.: Ente Raccolta Vinciana, Soc. for Renaissance Studies (coun. mem. 1995—99). Office: Courtauld Inst Art Somerset House Strand London WC2R ORN England

RUBIN, PAUL HAROLD, economist; b. Boston, Aug. 9, 1942; s. Joseph and Freda (Goldhagen) R.; m. Marcia Ann Claybon, June 15, 1964 (dec. Feb. 1973); children: Joseph Saul, Rachel Beth; m. Mariam Hope Moss, July 26, 1985. BA, U. Cin., 1963; PhD in Econs., Purdue U., 1970. Prof. econs. U. Ga., Athens, 1968-82; sr. staff economist Pres. Coun. Economic Advisers, Washington, 1981-82; prof. econs. Baruch Coll. and the Grad. Ctr., N.Y.C., 1982-83; head, consumer protection Bur. Econs., FTC, Washington, 1983-85; chief economist Consumer Product Safety Commn., 1985-87; v.p. Glassman-Oliver Economic Cons., Inc., Washington, 1987-91; prof. econs. Emory U., Atlanta, 1991—, prof. econs. and law, 1999—, Candler Dobbs prof. econs. and law, 2001—. Adj. prof. George Washington U. Law Ctr., Washington, 1985-89. Author: (book) Congressmen, Constituents and Contributors, 1982,

Bus. Firms and the Common Law, 1983, Mng. Bus. Transactions, 1990, Tort Reform by Contract, 1993, Darwinian Politics: The Evolutionary Origin of Freedom, 2002, Privacy and Comml. Use of Personal Info. (foreword by Senator Orin Hatch, with Thomas Lenard), 2001; editor-in-chief: Managerial and Decision Economics; contbr. articles profl.jours. Mem. Am. Econ. Assn., So. Econ. Assn. (v.p. 1994-96), Am. Law and Econs. Assn., Pub. Choice Soc. Fellow. Republican. Office: Emory U Dept Econs Atlanta GA 30322-0001 Office Phone: 404-931-0493. E-mail: prubin@emory.edu.

RUBIN, PHYLLIS GETZ, health association executive; b. N.Y.C., Aug. 6, 1937; d. Joseph and Sylvia (Rosenberg) Getz; m. James Milton Rubin, Oct. 28, 1961; children: Felicia Sue, Andrea Faith. BA, Syracuse U., 1959; MA, Columbia U., 1961, Adelphi U., 1975. Physical edn. tchr. Hicksville (N.Y.) Pub. Schs., 1959-93; bd. dirs., pres. Assoc. Am. Acad. Allergy, Asthma and Immunology. Producer: (video) Aerobic Dancercise for Children, 1987. Bd. dirs. COPAY, Great Neck, N.Y., 1986-91; v.p., sec. Pierpont Condominium Bd., 1986-90. Recipient Founder's Day award PTA, 1986. Mem.: N.Y. State Alliance for Health, Phys. Edn., REcreation and Dance (program spkr. 1984, 85, 93, v.p. Nassau zone 1987—2000, Zone Svc. award 1993). Avocations: tennis, reading, meditation, golf. Office Phone: 516-972-2342.

RUBIN, RICHARD ALLAN, lawyer; b. N.Y.C., June 19, 1942; s. Louis Max and Ruth Ann (Goldman) R.; m. Susan Deborah Levitt, June 18, 1966; children: Karen, Jill. BS, Queens Coll., 1964; JD, Bklyn. Law Sch., 1967; LLM, NYU, 1968. Bar: N.Y. 1967. Assoc. Schwartz and Frank, N.Y.C., 1968—69, Javits and Javits, N.Y.C., 1969—71; ptnr. Wolf Haldenstein Adler Freeman Herz & Frank, N.Y.C., 1972—76, Parker Chapin LLP, N.Y.C., 1977—2000, Jenkens & Gilchrist, Parker Chapin LLP, N.Y.C., 2001—. Lectr. Am. Mgmt. Assn., N.Y. Bar Assn. Mem. ABA. Office: Jenkens & Gilchrist Parker Chapin LLP Chrysler Bldg 405 Lexington Ave New York NY 10174-0002

RUBIN, ROBERT E. former secretary of treasury; b. N.Y.C., Aug. 29, 1938; s. Alexander and Sylvia (Seiderman) R.; m. Judith Leah Oxenberg, Mar. 27, 1963; children: James Samuel, Philip Matthew. AB summa cum laude, Harvard U., 1960; postgrad., London Sch. Econs., 1960-61; LLB, Yale U., 1964; DHL (hon.), Yeshiva U., 1996. Bar: N.Y. 1965. Assoc. Cleary, Gottlieb, Steen & Hamilton, N.Y.C., 1964-66, Goldman Sachs & Co., N.Y.C., 1966-70, ptnr., 1971, mem. mgmt. com., 1980, vice chmn., co-chief oper. officer, 1987-90, co-sr. ptnr., co-chmn., 1990-92; asst. to Pres. for econ. policy, head nat. econ. coun. Exec. Office of Pres., The White House, Washington, 1993-95; sec. U.S. Dept. of the Treasury, Washington, 1995-99; chmn. exec. com. Citigroup, 1999—. Mem. Pres.'s Adv. Com. for Trade Negotiations, Washington, 1980-82, mem. adv. com. on tender offers SEC, Washington, 1983, Gov.'s Commn. on Trade Competitiveness, 1987, regulatory adv. com. N.Y. Stock Exch., 1988-90, adv. com. internat. capital markets Fed. Res. Bank N.Y., 1989-93, Securities and Exch. Commn. Market Oversight and Fin. Svcs. Adv. Com., 1991-93, Gov.'s Adv. Panel on Fin. Svcs., 1988-89; ptnr., bd. dirs. N.Y.C. Partnership Inc., 1991-93; bd. dirs. Ctr. for Nat. Policy, 1982-93, vice chmn., 1984; bd. dirs. N.Y. Futures Exch., N.Y.C., 1979-85, Chgo. Bd. Options Exch. Inc., 1972 76; trustee Mt. Sinai Hosp., 1977, vice chmn., 1986; trustee Sta. WNET-TV, 1985-93; mem., trustee Carnegie Corp. of N.Y., 1990-93; mem. Mayor's Coun. Econ. Advisors, 1990, Gov.'s Coun. on Fiscal and Econ. Priorities, 1990-92. Trustee Am. Ballet Theatre Found., Inc., N.Y.C., 1969-93, trustee Collegiate Sch., 1978-84; mem. bd. overseers' com. to visit econs. dept. Harvard U., 1981-87, com. on univ. resources, 1987-92; mem. fin. com. N.Y. campaign Mondale for Pres., 1983-84; mem. investment adv. coun. N.Y.C. Pension Fund, 1980-89; chmn. Dem. Congl. Dinner, Washington, 1982; Dems. for the 80s, 1985-89, Dems. for the 90s, 1989-90; chmn. N.Y.C. host com. 1992 Dem. Conv., 1989-92; mem. Commn. Nat. Elections. Recipient award Nat. Assn. Christians and Jews, N.Y.C., 1977, Disting. Leadership in Govt. award Columbia Bus. Sch., 1996, Euromoney Mag. award Fin. Min. Yr., 1996, Medal for High Civic Svc. award Citizens' Budget Com., 1997, Fgn. Policy Assn. medal, 1998, "Chmn." award Washington Greater Boys/Girls Clubs, 1998, Intrepid Sea Air Space Mus. award, 1998, Jefferson award Am. Inst. Pub. Svc., 1998, Award of Merit Yale U., 1998, Global Leadership award UN Assn., 1998, Paul Tsongas award, 1998. Mem. Phi Beta Kappa, Harvard Club (N.Y.C.), Century Country Club (Purchase, N.Y.). Democrat. Jewish.*

RUBIN, ROBERT JAY, toxicologist; b. Boston, Mar. 25, 1932; s. Edward and Ruth (Lichter) R.; m. Frances Stone, Sept. 5, 1954 (dec. Nov. 1981); children: Ellen Joyce, Howard Scott, Steven Glen; m. Idalea Kofsky, Aug. 28, 1983; stepchildren: David Wolfe, Jennifer Sirota, Aaron Wolfe. BA, U. Mass., 1953; MS, Boston U., 1955, PhD, 1960. Diplomate Am. Bd. Toxicology. Postdoctoral fellow Yale U. Sch. of Medicine, New Haven, Conn., 1960-64; asst. prof. pharmacology Kans. U. Med. Ctr., Kansas City, 1964; asst. prof. toxicology Johns Hopkins Sch. of Pub. Health, Balt., 1964-67, assoc. prof. toxicology, 1967-73, prof. toxicology, 1973-98, prof. emeritus, 1998—. Cons. in toxicology, 1978—; adv. bd. Johns Hopkins Sch. of Pub. Health, Balt., 1985-86. Contbr. articles to profl. jours. including Toxicology and Applied Pharmacology, Jour. Toxicology and Environ. Health, Environ. Health Perspectives, many others. Pres. Stevenswood Community Assn., Balt., 1970-71; treas. Canton Square Community Assn., Balt., 1993-94. Postdoctoral fellowship NIH, Yale U., 1960-64, Career Devel. award NIH, Johns Hopkins U., 1969-74. Mem. Soc. of Toxicology (pres. Nat. Capital Area chpt. 1994-95, pres. risk assessment specialty sect. 1999-2000), Am. Soc. Pharmacology and Exptl. Therapeutics, Delta Omega (chmn. membership com. 1990-92). Avocation: travel to foreign countries. Office: 2212 Preservation Green Ct Sun City Center FL 33573-4417 E-mail: rrubin@jhsph.edu.

RUBIN, ROBERT JOSEPH, internist, consultant; b. Bklyn., Feb. 7, 1946; s. B. Norman and Suzanne (Fried) R.; m. Fran Auerbach, June 14, 1970; children: Elyse Beth, David Jon. AB, Williams Coll., 1966; MD, Cornell U., 1970. Diplomate Am. Bd. Internal Medicine. Intern New England Med. Ctr. Hosps., Boston, 1970-71, resident, 1971-72, 74-76; epidemic intelligence officer, respiratory disease and spl. pathogens, divsn. viral diseases Ctr. for Disease Control, 1972-74; asst. dean govt. affairs Tufts U., 1979-84, assoc. prof. medicine, 1981-84. Chief renal divsn. Lemuel Shattuck Hosp., Boston, 1979-81; asst. sec. planning and evaluation U.S. HHS, Washington, 1981-84; clin. assoc. prof. Georgetown U., Washington, 1984-95, clin. prof., 1995—; exec. v.p. ICF, Inc., 1984-88; pres. Health and Scis. Internat., 1988-92, Lewin ICF Inc., 1992, Lewin-VHI, Inc., 1992-96, Lewin Group, 1996-99, CEO, 1999-2001. Contbr. articles to profl. jours. With USPHS, 1972-74, asst. surgeon gen., 1981-84. Robert Wood Johnson Health Policy fellow, 1977 Mem. ACP, AMA, Am. Soc. Nephrology, Internat. Soc. Nephrology, Mass. Med. Soc., Kenwood Club, Potomac Club, Williams Club, Phi Beta Kappa. Republican. Jewish.

RUBIN, ROBERT SAMUEL, lawyer; b. Cin., Apr. 25, 1954; s. Carl B. and Gloria W. R.; m. Virginia K. Carson, May 14, 1983; children: John C., Claire W., Elizabeth K. LLB, U. Wales, Aberystwyth, Eng., 1976; JD, U. Cin., 1979. Bar: Ohio 1979, U.S. Dist. Ct. (so. dist.) Ohio 1979. Assoc. Brown, Cummins & Brown, Cin., 1979-82, Porter, Wright, Morris & Arthur, Cin., 1982-88, partner, 1988-92; ptnr. Cohen Todd Kite & Stanford, Cin., 1992—. Mem. arbitration rules com. U.S. Dist. Ct. (so. dist.) Ohio 1984, fed. mediation panel, 1990—; lectr. Nat. Bus. Inst., 1994, 99; mem. oversight adv. bd. Lunken Airport, 2000—, chmn. bd. dirs., 2001—. Author: Fundamentals of Commercial Lending Law. Mem. cmty. initiatives com., cert. com. United Way and Cmty. Chest, 1995—. Mem. Ohio Bar Assn. (banking law com. documentation chmn.), Cin. Bar Assn., U. Cin. Coll. Law Alumni Assn. (trustee 1988-90), Univ. Club. Home: 3693 Kroger Ave Cincinnati OH 45226-1931 Office: Cohen Todd Kite & Stanford 1200 Chiquita Ctr 250 East 5th St Cincinnati OH 45202-3176

RUBIN, ROBERT SAMUEL, investment banker; b. Boston, Sept. 22, 1931; s. Jesse Abraham and Rose (Solomon) R.; m. Martha Lucy Adams, Dec. 15, 1956; children: Rebecca, David, James, Nathaniel. BA, Yale U., 1953; MBA, Harvard Coll., 1955. With Lehman Bros., 1958-70, ptnr., 1967-70; mng. dir., bd. dirs. Lehman Bros. Kuhn Loeb, Inc., N.Y.C., 1970-84; mng. dir. Salomon Smith Barney, Inc., N.Y.C., 1989—2001; sr. v.p. Bank One, 2002—. Trustee Bklyn. Hosp.; chmn. Bklyn. Mus.; bd. dirs. St. Ann's Sch. 2nd lt. AUS, 1955-58. Home: 218 Columbia Hts Brooklyn NY 11201-2105 Office: Bank One 320 Park Ave New York NY 10022

RUBIN, ROBERT TERRY, psychiatrist, researcher, educator; b. Los Angeles, Aug. 26, 1936; s. Joseph Salem and Lorraine Grace (Baum) R.; m. Lynne Esther Mathews, Mar. 10, 1962 (div. Dec. 1980); children: Deborah, Sharon, Rachel; m. Ada Joan Mickas, Jan. 18, 1985. AB, UCLA, 1958; MD, U. Calif., San Francisco, 1961; PhD, U. So. Calif., 1977. Diplomate Am. Bd. Psychiatry and Neurology. Intern Phila. Gen. Hosp., 1961-62; resident in psychiatry Sch. Medicine UCLA, 1962-65, asst. prof. psychiatry, 1965-71, prof. psychiatry, 1972; prof. Pa. State U., Hershey, 1972-93; prof. neuroscis. Coll. Medicine Drexel U., Pitts., 1992—, prof. psychiatry, dir. Ctr. Neurosci. Rsch. Allegheny Campus, 1992—. Cons. Naval Health Rsch. Ctr., San Diego, 1969-70; mem. Brain Rsch. Inst. UCLA, 1969—; assoc. dir. Pitts. Tissue Engring. Initiative, 1994—; trustee Kinsey Inst. Sex Rsch., Ind. U., 1986-90. Contbr. articles to profl. jours. With USNR, 1967-69. Recipient Rsch. Sci. Devel. awards NIMH, 1972-77, Rsch. Scientist award, 1982, 87, 93. Fellow: AAAS, Am. Coll. Psychiatrists, Am. Psychiat. Assn.; mem.: Internat. Soc. Psychoneuroendocrinology (pres. 1984—87). Avocations: swimming, bagpiping. Office: Allegheny Gen Hosp Ctr Neurosci Rsch 320 E North Ave Pittsburgh PA 15212-4756 Office Phone: 412-359-3235. Business E-Mail: rubin@wpahs.org.

RUBIN, ROBERTA GAIL, pathologist; b. Bklyn., Apr. 2, 1934; d. Victor and Pearl Berger Rubin; m. Walter D'Ull; children: Leon Jesse, Victoria Roslyn. MD, SUNY, Bklyn., 1958. Pathologist Chilton Meml. Hosp., Pompton Plains, N.J., 1968-98; dir. lab. Livingston (N.J.) Cmyt. Hosp., 1987-88; assoc. pathologist Bronx Lebanon Hosp. Ctr., 1967-68; staff pathologist Maimonides-Coney Island Med. Ctr., Bklyn., 1964-67; dir. MDS Lab., Wayne, N.J., 1973-89. Clin. instr. pathology SUNY, Bklyn., 1964-67, Albert Einstein Sch. Medicine, Bronx, 1967-68. Sec., treas. bd. Morris Area Cmty. Fedn., Whippany, N.J., 1989—. Fellow: Coll. Am. Pathologists; mem.: N.J. Soc. Pathologists (bd. dirs. 1989—2001), Found. Am. Med. Women's Assn. (treas. 2001—), Nat. Coun. Women's Health (pres. 1999—2001), Am. Women's Hosp. Assn. (chmn. 1993—), Am. Med. Women's Assn. (v.p. fin. 1993, Camille Mermod award 1995). Avocations: doll art collector, cosmology, reading. Home: 10 Woodland Ave Glen Ridge NJ 07028

RUBIN, RONALD, real estate executive; With Richard I. Rubin and Co., Inc., 1953—; chmn., CEO Rubin Orgn., Inc.; CEO, trustee Pa. Real Estate Investment Trust. Bd. dirs. PECO Energy Corp. Chair Ctr. City Dist., Phila. Mem. Greater Phila. C. of C. (past pres.). Office: Pa Real Estate Investment Trust 200 S Broad St Ste 300 Philadelphia PA 19102-3803*

RUBIN, ROSE MOHR, economics professor; b. Montgomery, Ala., Nov. 20, 1939; d. Michael and Bernice (Solomon) Mohr; m. Richard M. Rubin, June 20, 1963; children: Mark, Debra. BS, Wellesley Coll., 1961; MA, Emory U., 1966; PhD, Kans. State U., 1968. Economist OEA, State of Kans., Manhattan, 1969-70; asst. prof. Miss. State U., Starkville, 1970-77; resident in pub. svc. NSF, Fort Worth, 1980-81; asst. prof. econs. U. North Tex., Denton, 1977-84, assoc. prof., 1984-90, prof., 1990-94; chair dept. econs. U. Memphis, 1994-96, prof. econs., 1996—. Faculty fellow Johns Hopkins U., Balt., 1986-87; vis. fellow Brookings Inst., Washington, 1987 Bd. dirs. Vis. Nurses Assn., Ft. Worth, 1987-90, Temple Beth El, Ft. Worth, 1988-91, Plough Towers, Memphis, 1998—. Assoc. Danforth Found., 1981-87; grantee Robert Wood Johnson Found., 1987-88, Andrus Found. grantee Am. Assn. Ret. Persons, 1990-94. Mem.: Mo. Valley Econs. Assn. (bd. dirs. 1998—), Midsouth Acad. Econs. and Fin. (exec. bd. 1983—87, v.p. 1991—92), Assn. for Social Econs. (exec. coun. 1988—90), Southwestern Social Sci. Assn. (treas. 1990—93, v.p. 1998—, pres. 2000—01), Southwestern Econs. Assn. (treas. 1981—89, v.p. 1989—99, pres.-elect 1990—91, pres. 1991—92), Phi Kappa Phi, Omicron Delta Epsilon, Golden Key (hon.), Phi Chi Theta (hon.). Office: U Memphis Fogel Coll Bus and Econs Dept Econs Memphis TN 38152-0001

RUBIN, SAMUEL HAROLD, internist, consultant; b. N.Y.C., July 24, 1916; s. Joseph and Esther (Goldfarb) R.; m. Audrey Arndt, Nov. 20, 1943; children: James E., David A. AB, Brown U., 1938; MD, St. Louis U., 1943; MS, U. Chgo., 1957; DSc (hon.), N.Y. Med. Coll., 1997. Diplomate: Am. Bd. Internal Medicine. Intern Jewish Hosp., St. Louis, 1943-44; resident St. Louis U. Group Hosp., 1944-45, St. Mary's Hosp., Kansas City, Mo., 1945-46; practice medicine Asbury Park, N.J., 1948-61; vol. faculty mem. N.Y. Med. Coll., 1948-61, assoc. prof. dept. medicine, 1962-65, prof., 1965—, dir. Inst. Human Values in Med. Ethics, 1984-86; chief med. service N.Y. Med. Coll.-Met. Hosp. Center, 1966-71, assoc. dean, 1971-72, exec. dean, 1972-74, dean, v.p. acad. affairs, 1975, provost, dean, 1977-83, provost, dean emeritus, 1983—, cons., 1983—. Mem. bd. trustees St. Clares' Hosp., N.Y.C., 1985-2000, N.Y. Med. Coll., 1988-94. Contbr. articles to med. jours. With M.C. AUS, 1946-48. NIH program dir. grantee, 1966-71 Fellow A.C.P.; mem. N.Y. Acad. Sci. Home: 425E Heritage Hills Dr Somers NY 10589-1912

RUBIN, SANDRA MENDELSOHN, artist; b. Santa Monica, Calif., Nov. 7, 1947; d. Murry and Freda (Atliss) Mendelsohn; m. Stephen Edward Rubin, Aug. 6, 1966. BA, UCLA, 1976, MFA, 1979. Instr. Art Ctr. Coll. Design, Pasadena, Calif., 1980, UCLA, 1981. One-woman exhbns. include L.A. Louver Gallery, 1982, 92, 2003, L.A. County Mus. Art, 1985, Fischer Fine Arts, London, 1985, Claude Bernard Gallery, N.Y.C., 1987; group exhbns. include L.A. County Mus. Art, 1977, 82, 83, L.A. Mcpl. Art Gallery, 1977, 83, 93, L.A. Contemporary Exhbns., 1978, L.A. Inst. Contemporary Arts, 1978, Newport Harbor Art Mus., Newport Beach, Calif., 1981, Odyssia Gallery, N.Y.C., 1981, Nagoya (Japan) City Mus., 1982, Long Beach (Calif.) Mus. Art, 1982, Brooke Alexander Gallery, N.Y.C., 1982, Laguna Beach (Calif.) Mus. Art, 1982, Jan Baum Gallery, L.A., 1984, San Francisco Mus. Art, 1986, Claude Bernard Gallery, N.Y.C., 1986, Struve Gallery, Chgo., 1987, Boise (Idaho) Mus., 1988, Judy Youen's Gallery, London, 1988, Tatistscheff Gallery, Inc., Santa Monica, Calif., 1989, Tortue Gallery, Santa Monica, 1990, Contemporary Arts Forum, Santa Barbara, Calif., 1990, San Diego Mus. Art, 1991, Fresno (Calif.) Met. Mus., 1992, Jack Rutberg Fine Arts, L.A., 1993, San Jose Mus. Art, 2003, Pasadena Mus. Calif. Art, 2004. Recipient Young Talent Purchase award L.A. County Mus. Art, 1980; Artist's Fellowship grant NEA, 1981, 91. Avocations: gardening, exercise, reading, singing. E-mail: smr@pacific.net.

RUBIN, SAUL, producer, writer, labor and civil rights organizer; b. N.Y.C., Feb. 8, 1921; m. Gloria Stone, Dec. 8, 1942; children: Jonathan, Susan, Raymond. Grad., Coll. of William and Mary. Exec. v.p. U. Judaism, L.A., 1959; pres. Tantalus Inc., Nat. Comm. Found., 1978-80; media cons. dept. humanities U. So. Calif., L.A.; creator Beyond Sound, deaf prodn. co. Prodr., author more than 1000 TV programs, many documentaries. Capt. USAF, 1941—46, ETO. Decorated Silver Star, Purple Heart, D.F.C., 9 Air Medals, 5 Oak Leaf Clusters and Silver Cluster, Battle Ribbons for European Theatre of War and Anti-Submarine Svc.; recipient over 120 awards, 2 Emmy awards, Ace award for pioneering in prodn. of sign lang. news programs, 2001. Office: 3876 Carpenter Ave Studio City CA 91604-3729 E-mail: srubin1@flash.net.

RUBIN, SETH ISAIAH, psychologist; b. Alexandria, La., Mar. 6, 1945; BA, Northwestern U., 1966, MA, 1968, PhD in Psychology, 1971. Diplomate in psychoanalysis and analytical psychology; cert. profl. qualification in psychology; lic. psychologist, Pa., Calif., Ariz., Mass. Outpatient psychology fellow Hosp. U. Pa., 1978-80; tng. candidate, diploma candidate C.G. Jung Inst., Zurich, 1982-87; instr. dept. psychology Northwestern U., 1969-70; asst. prof. dept. psychology U. Ill. at Chgo. Circle, 1970-72; asst. rsch. prof. dept. psychiatry Med. Coll. Pa., 1974-75; asst. prof. dept. cmty. medicine U. Pa., 1975-76, asst. prof. dept. rsch. medicine, 1976-77, asst. prof. dept. ob-gyn., 1976-83, clin. assoc. dpet. psychiatry, 1987-88, clin. asst. prof./clin. assoc prof. psychology in psychiatry, 1987-92; allied health profl. Phila. Psychiat. Ctr., 1988-92; allied health affiliate, clin. psychologist Calif. Pacific Med. Ctr., 1994—. Adj. prof. Union Grad. Sch., 1989-96, Calif. Sch. Profl. Psychology, Berkeley/Alameda, 1992—; vis. prof. psychology Saybrook Inst., 1994-95; lectr. in field; dir. James Goodrich Whitney Clinic, C.E. Jane Inst. San Franciso, 2004. Contbr. articles to profl. jours. Fellow Am. Coll. Advanced Practice Psychologists, Internat. Coll. Prescribing Psychologists; mem. APA, Internat. Assn. for Analytical Psychology, Am. Soc. Clin. Psychopharmacology, Assn. Grad. Analytical Psychologists of the C.G. Jung Inst., San Francisco Jung Inst. (dir., James Goodrich Whitney Clin.), Soc. for Psychotherapy Rsch., others. Office: 2019 A Webster St San Francisco CA 94115-2329 Office Phone: 415-771-5115. E-mail: sirseth@well.com.

RUBIN, STANLEY CREAMER, producer; b. N.Y.C., Oct. 8, 1917; s. Michael Isaac and Anne (Creamer) R.; m. Elizabeth Margaret von Gerkan (actress Kathleen Hughes), July 25, 1954; children: John, Chris, Angela, Michael. Student, UCLA, 1933-37. Writer Universal Studios, Universal City, Calif., 1940-42, Columbia Pictures, Los Angeles, 1946-47; writer, producer NBC-TV, Burbank, Calif., 1948-49; theatrical film producer various studios, 1949-55, Rastar Prodns., Columbia Pictures, 1988-91; TV producer CBS-TV, Los Angeles, 1956-59, Universal Studios, Universal City, 1960-63, 20th Century-Fox, Los Angeles, 1967-71, MGM Studios, Culver City, Calif., 1972-77; pres. TBA Prodns., Los Angeles, 1978—. Producer theatrical films including The Narrow Margin, 1950, My Pal Gus, 1950, Destination Gobi, 1951, River of No Return, 1952, Promise Her Anything, 1966, The President's Analyst, 1967, Revenge, 1989; co-producer White Hunter, Black Heart, 1990; TV prodns. include G.E. Theatre, 1959-63, Ghost and Mrs. Muir, 1968-69, Bracken's World, 1969-71; writer, producer TV film The Diamond Necklace, 1948 (Emmy award 1949); producer TV films including Babe, 1975 (Hollywood Fgn. Press Golden Globe award, Christopher medal), And Your Name is Jonah, 1978 (Christopher medal 1979), The Story of Satchel Paige, 1980 (Image award 1981); exec. producer TV prodn. Escape from Iran: The Canadian Caper, 1981. Producer spl. programming Dem. Nat. Conv., San Francisco, 1984, Columbia Pictures and Rastar Prodns., 1988-91. 1st lt. USAAF, 1942-46. Mem. Writers Guild Am. (dir. 1941-42), Producers Guild Am. (bd. dirs. 1968-74, pres. 1974-79, v.p. 1987-94, bd. dirs. 1994-2000), Acad. Motion Picture Arts and Scis., Acad. TV Arts and Scis. (bd. govs. 1971, 73), Phi Beta Kappa. Home and Office: 8818 Rising Glen Pl Los Angeles CA 90069-1222 E-mail: tbaprez@aol.com. *I'm still too young to sum up my life, but here's a thought in progress: Stay curious.*

RUBIN, STEPHEN CURTIS, gynecologic oncologist, educator; b. Phila., May 24, 1951; s. Alan and Helen (Metz) R.; m. Anne Loughran, May 30, 1985; children: Michael, Elisabeth. BS, Franklin & Marshall U., 1972; MD, U. Pa., 1976. Diplomate Am. Bd. Ob-gyn. (mem. divsn. gynecol. oncology 1997-2003), Nat. Bd. Med. Examiners. Intern in ob-gyn. Hosp. of Univ. Pa., Phila., 1976-77, residency in ob-gyn., 1977-80, fellow in gynecologic oncology, 1980-82; asst. prof. ob-gyn. Med. Coll. Pa., Phila., 1982-85, dir. surg. gynecology, 1982-85, chief gynecol. oncology, 1984-85; asst. mem. gynecol. staff Meml. Sloan-Kettering Hosp., NYC, 1985-90, assoc. mem., 1990-93; asst. prof. ob-gyn Cornell U. Med. Coll., NYC, 1985-90, assoc. prof., 1990-93; prof. ob-gyn., chief gynecologic oncology U. Pa., Phila., 1993—, Franklin Payne prof., gyn. oncology, 2003—. Editor: Ovarian Cancer, Cervical Cancer, Chemotherapy of Gynecologic Cancer, Uterine Cancer; contbr. over 250 articles to profl. publs. Recipient Career Devel. award Am. Cancer Soc., 1987, Boyer award Meml. Sloan-Kettering; grantee Nat. Cancer Inst., 1991, 96, 98, 99. Mem. ACS, ACOG, Am. Soc. Clin. Oncology, Soc. Gynecol. Oncologists (Pres.'s award 1993), Am. Gynecol. and Obstet. Soc., Soc. Gynecologic Investigation, Soc. Pelvic Surgeons, Gynecol. Cancer Found. (Karin Smith award 1996). Office: U Pa Med Ctr 3400 Spruce St Philadelphia PA 19104-4206 Office Phone: 215-662-3326.

RUBIN, STEPHEN D. food products executive; BBA, JD, U. Wis. Pres. Vita Food Products, Inc., Chgo., 1982—, dir., 1982—, chmn. bd. Office: Vita Food Products Inc 2222 W Lake St Chicago IL 60612*

RUBIN, STEPHEN EDWARD, publishing executive, editor, journalist; b. N.Y.C., Nov. 10, 1941; s. Irving and Evelyn (Halprin) R. BA, NYU, 1965; MS, Boston U., 1966. Editor UPI, N.Y.C., 1966-69; freelance writer N.Y.C., 1969-82; founder, dir. Writers Bloc, N.Y.C., 1976-82; editor Vanity Fair Mag., N.Y.C., 1982-83; exec. editor Bantam Books, N.Y.C., 1984-85, v.p., editorial dir., 1985-88, sr. v.p., editor-in-chief adult fiction and non-fiction, 1987-88, sr. v.p., pub., editor-in-chief adult fiction and non-fiction, 1988-90; pres., pub. Doubleday divsn. Bantam Doubleday Dell Pub. Group, N.Y.C., 1990-95; chmn., CEO Bantam Doubleday Dell Internat. Divsn., London, 1995-98; pres., pub. Doubleday Divsn. Bantam Doubleday Dell Pub. Group (now Doubleday Broadway Group), N.Y.C., 1998—. Author: The New Met in Profile, 1974 Avocations: listening to musical performances, collecting records, tapes and cds, reading, exercising. Office: Random House Inc 1745 Broadway New York NY 10019

RUBIN, SUSAN M. neurologist; b. N.Y.C., Aug. 14, 1956; BS in Speech Pathology, MS in Speech Pathology, Northwestern U.; MD, U. Ill., 1988. Diplomate Am. Bd. Neurology. Intern Luth. Gen. Hosp., Park Ridge, Ill., 1989—90, staff neurologist; resident in neurology Northwestern U. Med. Ctr., Chgo., 1990—93, fellow in neurophysiology, 1993—94; staff neurologist Highland Park (Ill.) Hosp., Holy Family Hosp.; dir., founder Women's Neurology Ctr., Dept. Neurology, Glenbrook Hosp., Glenview, 2001—. Clin. instr. dept. neurology Feinberg Sch. Medicine, Northwestern U., Chgo. Contbr. articles to profl. jours.; peer reviewer Headache jour., 2000. Named one of Chgo.'s Best Drs. in Neurology, Castle Connolly, 1999, 2000; recipient Edward R. Henderson Meml. Student award for geriat. rsch., Murer Healthcare Consultants and Gerontology Ctr. U. Ill.-Chgo., 1988, E.A. Codman award for rsch., 1988. Mem.: Am. Epilepsy Soc., Am. Headache Soc., Am. Acad. Neurology, Alpha Omega Alpha. Office: Glenbrook Hosp 2100 Pfingsten Rd Glenview IL 60025

RUBIN, THEODORE ISAAC, psychiatrist, writer; b. Bklyn., Apr. 11, 1923; s. Nathan and Esther (Marcus) R.; m. Eleanor Katz, June 16, 1946; children: Jeffrey, Trudy, Eugene. BA, Bklyn. Coll., 1946; MD, U. Lausanne, Switzerland, 1951; grad., Am. Inst. Psychoanalysis, 1964. Resident psychiatrist Los Angeles VA Hosp., 1953, Rockland (N.Y.) State Hosp., 1954, Bklyn. State Hosp., 1955, Kings County (N.Y.) Hosp., 1956; chief psychiatrist Women's House of Detention, N.Y.C., 1957; mem. faculty Downstate Med. Sch., N.Y. State U., 1957-59; pvt. practice N.Y.C., 1956—. Tng. and supervising psychoanalyst Am. Inst. for Psychoanalysis of Karen Horney Clinic and Ctr.; mem. faculty Am. Inst. Psychoanalysis, 1962—; pres. emeritus bd. trustees Am. Inst. Psychoanalysis. Author: Jordi, 1960, Lisa and David, 1961, Sweet Daddy, 1963, In The Life, 1964, Platzo and the Mexican Pony Rider, 1965, The Thin Book by a Formerly Fat Psychiatrist, 1966, The 29th Summer, 1966, Cat, 1966, Coming Out, 1967, The Winner's Note Book, 1967, The Angry Book, 1969, Forever Thin, 1970, Emergency Room Diary, 1972, Doctor Rubin Please Make Me Happy, 1974, Shrink, 1974, Compassion and Self-Hate, An Alternative to Despair, 1975, Love Me, Love My Fool, 1976, Reflections in a Goldfish Tank, 1977, Alive and Fat and Thinning in America, 1978, Reconciliations, 1980, Through My Own Eyes, 1982, One to One, Understanding Personal Relationships, 1983, Not to Worry, The American Family Book of Mental Health, 1984, Overcoming Indecisiveness, 1985, Lisa and David, The Story Continues, 1986, Miracle at Bellevue, 1986, Real Love, 1990, Child Potential, 1990, Anti-Semitism: A Disease of the Mind, 1990, Little Ralphie and The Creature, 1998; mem. editl. bd. Am. Jour. Psychoanalysis; also articles, columns.; co-writer (TV movie) Lisa and David, 1998. Served as officer USNR, World War II. Recipient Adolf Meyer award, Assn. Improvement Mental Health, 1963. Fellow Am. Acad. Psychoanalysis; mem. N.Y. County Med. Soc., Am. Psychiat. Assn., Assn. Advancement Psychoanalysis, Authors Guild, Contemporary Authors, Writers Guild East. Office: 113 1/2 E 62nd St New York NY 10021-7301 Office Phone: 212-751-0495.

RUBIN, VERA COOPER, astronomer, researcher; b. Phila., July 23, 1928; d. Philip and Rose (Applebaum) Cooper; m. Robert J. Rubin, June 25, 1948; children: David M., Judith S. Young, Karl C. Allan. BA, Vassar Coll., 1948; MA, Cornell U., 1951; PhD, Georgetown U., 1954, DHL (hon.), 1997; DSc (hon.), Creighton U., 1978, Harvard U., 1988, Yale U., 1990, Williams Coll., 1993, U. Mich., 1996, Ohio State U., 1998, Smith Coll., 2001, Grinnell Coll., 2002. From rsch. assoc. to asst. prof. Georgetown U., Washington, 1955-65; physicist U. Calif., LaJolla, 1963-64; astronomer Carnegie Inst., Washington, 1965—2001, sr. fellow, 2001—. Chancellor's Disting. prof. U. Calif., Berke-

ley, 1981; vis. com. Harvard Coll. Obs., Cambridge, Mass., 1976—82, 1992—2002, Space Telescope Sci. Ins., 1990—92; Beatrice Tinsley vis. prof. U. Tex., 1988; Commonwealth lectr. U. Mass., 1991; Yunker lectr. Oreg. State U., 1991; Bernhard vis. fellow Williams Coll., 1993; Oort vis. prof. U. Leiden, The Netherlands, 1995; lectr. in field, Chile, Russia, China, Armenia, India, Japan, Europe; trustee Assoc. Univs., Inc., 1993—96; mem. Pres. Commn. to Select U.S. Nat. Medal Sci. Awardees, 1995—98, chair, 1997—98; Pres.'s disting. visitor Vassar Coll., 1987; Halley lctr. Oxford Univ., 1997; bd. dir. Sci. Service, 2002—. Assoc. editor: Astrophys. Jour. Letters, 1977—82, mem. editl. bd.: Sci. Mag., 1979—87, mem. sr. editl. bd.:, 2001—. Named to Nat. Sci. Bd., 1996—2002; recipient U.S. medal of Sci., 1993, Gold medal, Royal. Astorn. Soc. London, 1996, Weizmann Women and Sci. award, 1996, Helen Hogg prize, Can. Astron. Soc., 1997, John Scott Award, City Of Phila., 2001, Peter Gruber Internat. prize in cosmology, 2002. Mem.: NAS (space sci. bd. 1974—77, chair sect. on astronomy 1992—95), Am. Acad. Arts and Scis., AAAS, Am. Philos. Soc., Assn. Univ. Rsch. in Astronomy (trustee 1973—76, 1994—96), Pontifical Acad. Scis., Internat. Astron. Union (pres. commn. on galaxies 1982—85, chair U.S. nat. commn. 1999—2001), Am. Astron. Soc. (coun. 1977—80, Russell prize lectr. 1994), Phi Beta Kappa (scholar 1982—83). Democrat. Jewish. *As an observational astronomer, it is my aim to obtain data of highest quality in order to answer questions concerning the universe in which we live. In spite of our enormous ignorance, each day offers exciting opportunities to learn a little more. This is the real joy of doing science.*

RUBIN, WILLIAM, editor; b. N.Y.C., Jan. 10, 1928; s. Herman and Molly (Goodman) R.; m. Claire Levine, Aug. 30, 1953; children: Deborah E., Joan S., Howard I. BA, Bklyn. Coll., 1953. Tech. editor Drug Trade News, N.Y.C., 1952-63; dir. pub. info. Nat. Vitamin Found., N.Y.C., 1958-61; editorial dir. FDC Reports & Drug Rsch. Reports, Washington, 1963-64; proprietor Sci. Reports and Projects, Bethesda, MD., 1964-67; editor Internat. Med. News Group, Rockville, Md., 1967-91; editorial cons., 1992—. Editor Clin. Psychiatry News, Family Practice News, Internal Medicine News, Ob-Gyn. News, Pediatric News, Skin & Allergy News, Internat. Med. News Group. Bd. dirs. Washington chpt. Am. Found. for Suicide Prevention; chmn. Md. Adv. Coun. on Arthritis and Related Diseases; bd. dirs. Reginald Lourie Ctr. for Infants and Young Children; mem. spkrs' bur. Met. Washington chpt. Arthritis Found.; vice chmn. Montgomery County (Md.) Libr. Bd. With USAAF, 1946-47. Mem. Nat. Assn. Sci. Writers (life), Am. Med. Writers Assn., N.Y. Acad. Scis., Nat. Press Club. Avocations: book accumulating, reading history, woodworking.

RUBIN, ZICK, psychology educator, lawyer, writer; b. N.Y.C., Apr. 29, 1944; s. Eli and Adena Rubin; m. Carol Moses, June 21, 1969; children: Elihu James, Noam Moses BA, Yale U., 1965; PhD, U. Mich., 1969; JD, Harvard U., 1988. Bar: Mass., 1988. Asst. to assoc. prof. Harvard U., Cambridge, Mass., 1969—76; Louis and Frances Salvage prof. social psychology Brandeis U., Waltham, Mass., 1976—89, adj. prof. psychology, 1989—96; law clk. chief judge U.S. Ct. Appeals (1st cir.), 1988—89; assoc. Palmer & Dodge, Boston, 1990—93, counsel, 1994—2001; of counsel Hill & Barlow, Boston, 2001—03; prin. Law Office of Zick Rubin, Boston, 2003—. Chmn. com. behavioral scis. Yale U. Coun., New Haven, 1981-86; mem. Adams Papers adminstrv. com. Mass. Hist. Soc., 2001—. Author: Liking and Loving, 1973, Children's Friendships, 1980; co-author: Psychology, 1993; editor: Doing Unto Others, 1974, Relationships and Development, 1986; contbg. editor: Psychology Today, 1980-85; editorial bd.: Harvard Law Rev., 1986-88. Recipient Socio-Psychol. prize AAAS, 1969, Nat. Media award Am. Psychol. Found., 1980; grantee NSF, NIMH, Ford Found., Social Sci. Research Council, Found. Child Devel. Mem. ABA, Boston Bar Assn., Am. Psychology-Law Soc., Authors Guild, Text and Acad. Authors Assn. (mem. coun. 1994-95), Phi Beta Kappa. Clubs: Elihu (New Haven). Jewish. Office Phone: 617-965-9425. E-mail: zrubin@zickrubin.com.

RUBINFELD, JOSEPH, biotechnology company executive; Rsch. scientist Schering-Plough Corp., Colgate Palmolive Co., other pharm. rsch. cos.; v.p., dir. rsch. & devel. Bristol-Myers Co.; sr. dir. Cetus Corp., 1987—90; co-founder, c.p., COO Amgen, 1980—91; chmn., CEO, pres. SuperGen, Inc., Dublin, Calif., 1991—. Office: SuperGen Inc 4140 Dublin Blvd Ste 200 Dublin CA 94568

RUBINFIEN, LEO H. photographer, filmmaker; b. Chgo., Aug. 16, 1953; Student, Reed Coll.; BFA, Calif. Inst. Arts, 1974; MFA, Yale U., 1976. Instr. in photography Swarthmore Coll., 1977, Sch. Visual Arts, N.Y.C., 1978-87; assoc. prof. art Fordham U., 1981-87; represented by Robert Mann Gallery, N.Y.C.; mem. faculty Gallatin Sch., NYU, 2001—. Mem. grad. faculty Sch. of Visual Arts, NYU, 2002—; vis. lectr. Cooper Union, 1982; vis. prof. Nusashino Fine Arts U., Tokyo, 2002. One man shows include Castelli Gallery, N.Y., 1981, Fraenkel Gallery, San Francisco, 1982, 86, Robert Mann Gallery, N.Y.C., 1994, 2001, Met. Mus. Art, N.Y.C., 1992, Seibu Art Forum, Tokyo, 1993, Cleve. Mus. Art, 1994, Seattle Art Mus., 1994, Robert Mann Gallery, N.Y.C.; exhibited in group shows at Internat. Ctr. Photography, N.Y., 1981, Inst. Contemporary Arts, London, 1981, San Francisco Mus. Modern Art, 1981, George Eastman House, Rochester, N.Y., 1981, Corcoran Gallery, Washington, 1981, Mus. Modern Art, N.Y., 1984, Met. Mus. Art, 2001, Tokyo Met. Mus. Photography, 2002; dir., co-author (film) The Money Juggler, 1988, My Bed in the Leaves, 1990; author: (books) A Map of the East, 1992, 10 Takeoffs 5 Landings, 1994, Shomei Tomatsu: Skin of the Nation, 2004, (essays) A Love-Hate Relations, Artforum, 1978, Investigations of a Dog, 1999, Guesses About the Work of Wu Yiming, 1999, The Poetry of Plain Seeing, 2000, Perfect Uncertainty, 2001, The Mask Behind the Face, 2004. Fellow Guggenheim Found., 1982-83, Asian Cult. Coun., 1984, Internat. Ctr. Advanced Studies, 1998—, Japan Found., 2002, Asian Cult. Coun., 2002 Home: 1 Furnace Dock Rd Croton On Hudson NY 10520-1406 Personal E-mail: oscawana@earthlink.net.

RUBIN-KATZ, BARBARA, sculptor, human services administrator; b. Springfield, Mass., May 3, 1931; d. Samuel and Jane (Freeman) Kurn; m. Emanuel Rubin, Mar. 27, 1955 (div. Dec. 1984); children: Raphael, Jonathan, Daniel, Rebecca; m. Robert Nathan Katz, June 15, 1986. BA, U. Ariz., 1952; MSW, Simmons Coll., 1955; MPH, Columbia U., 1977; postgrad. in Sculpture Studies, Phila. Coll. Art, 1981-85. Rschr. Bellevue Hosp., N.Y.C., 1970-75; health svcs. coord. Fedn. Jewish Agencies, N.Y.C., 1977-79, assoc. dir. planning Phila., 1979-84; sculptor Brookline, Mass., 1985—. Prin. works include sculpture at Mass. Gen. Hosp., Villa Campana, Tucson, Worcester Poly. Inst., Regency Park, Brookline, Mass; exhibited in group shows at Copley Soc. Boston shows, 1990—, New Eng. Sculptors Assn. shows, 1987—, The Roxbury Latin Sch., 1991, Jr. League Boston Decorator's Showhouse, Walpole, Mass., 1994, Fanuiel Hall, Boston, 1994, Prestige Gallery, Danvers, Mass., 1995, Michael Allen Gallery, Brookline, Mass., 1996, Curtis Gallery Lenox, Mass., 1996—, Festival Arts, Newton, 1997, Curtis Gallery, Lenox, Mass., 1997, 98, Worcester Poly. Inst., 1997-98, Bradford (Mass.) Coll., 1999; contbr. articles to profl. jours. Mem. Copley Soc. Boston (Copley Artist award 1992), New Eng. Sculptor's Assn. (bd. dirs. 1993), Brookline Coun. for Arts and Humanities. Home: 1731 Beacon St Apt 1403 Brookline MA 02445-5329

RUBINO, VICTOR JOSEPH, academic administrator, lawyer; b. N.Y.C., Dec. 25, 1940; s. Joseph V. and Olympia (Gayda) R.; 1 child, Victor Gayda. BA in Govt., Cornell U., 1962, LLB, 1965. Bar: N.Y. 1965, U.S. Dist. Ct. (so. dist.) N.Y. 1969. Staff atty. Westchester Legal Svcs., White Plains, N.Y., 1968-71; assoc. Squadron Ellenoff Plesent & Lehrer, N.Y.C., 1971; treas., program officer Council on Legal Edn., N.Y.C., 1971-79; assoc. dir. Practising Law Inst., N.Y.C., 1979-83, exec. dir., 1983—. Democratic candidate for N.Y. State Assembly, 1970; chmn. Rye (N.Y.) Human Rights Commn., 1975-76. Served to capt. U.S. Army, 1966-68. Mem. ABA, Assn. Bar City N.Y. Office: Practising Law Inst 810 7th Ave Fl 26 New York NY 10019-5818 Home: 810 7th Ave New York NY 10019-5818

RUBINOVITZ, SAMUEL, diversified manufacturing company executive; b. Boston, Dec. 26, 1929; s. Benjamin Ephraim and Pauline (Kaufman) R.; m. Phyllis Ann Silverstein; children: David Jay, Robert Neal. BS, MIT, 1951, MS, 1952. Sales engr. Clevite Transistor Products, Waltham, Mass., 1954-63; sales mgr. EG&G Inc., Wellesley, Mass., 1963-72, divsn. mgr., 1972-79, v.p., 1979-86, sr. v.p., 1986-89, exec. v.p., 1989-94; ret., 1994. Bd. dirs. Richardson Electronics Ltd., Chgo., Kronos Inc., Chelmsford, Mass., LTX Corp, Westwood, Mass. 1st lt. USAF, 1952-54. Democrat. Jewish. E-mail: Srubinovitz@Kronos.com.

RUBINSON, HOWARD ALAN, physician; b. Bklyn., Aug. 24, 1949; s. Samuel and Hilda (Cohen) R.; m. Carol Berman, May 16, 1976; children: Roger, Abby. AB, Cornell U., 1971; MD, Hahnemann Med. Coll., Phila., 1975. Diplomate Am. Bd. Radiology. Radiology instr. Sch. Medicine U. Miami, Fla., 1979-81, asst. prof. radiology, 1981-84; mem. attending staff North Beach Hosp., Ft. Lauderdale, Fla., 1984-89, North Ridge Med. Ctr., Ft. Lauderdale, Fla., 1989—, Hollywood (Fla.) Med. Ctr., 1998—, Parkway Regional Med. Ctr., 2001—; attending staff Holy Cross Hosp., Ft. Lauderdale, Fla., 2004—. Contbr. articles to profl. jours. Mem. Am. Coll. Radiology, Am. Soc. Emergency Radiology, Soc. Breast Imaging, Radiol. Soc. N.Am., Am. Roentgen Ray Soc., Soc. Thoracic Radiology, South Fla. Radiol. Soc. (pres. 1996-97), Fla. Radiol. Soc., Fla. Med. Assn., Broward County Med. Assn. Office: North Ridge Med Ctr Dept Radiology 5757 N Dixie Hwy Fort Lauderdale FL 33334-4135 E-mail: hrubinson@mindspring.com.

RUBINSTEIN, ALAN JAY, lawyer; BA, U. Miami, 1963; JD, U. Fla., 1965. Bar: Fla. 1965, U.S. Supreme Ct. 1971; cert. marital & family lawyer Fla. Bar. 1985. Ptnr. Goldberg, Rubinstein & Buckley, 1965—88; pvt. practice Ft. Myers, Fla., 1988—. Lectr. in field. Contbr. articles to profl. jours. Fellow Am. Acad. Matrimonial Lawyers (chair-person sub bd. examiners Fla. chpt.); mem. ABA (family & econs. law sects.), Fla. Bar Assn. (bd. examiners, exec. com. 1980-88), Lee County Bar Assn. Office: PO Box 368 Fort Myers FL 33902-0368

RUBINSTEIN, ELLIS MARC, science association director; b. N.Y.C., Dec. 4, 1945; s. Samuel and Estelle (Ellis) R.; m. Joanna Rubinstein. BA in English Lit. magna cum laude, U. Calif., Berkeley, 1967, postgrad., 1967-68, CCNY, 1973-74. Tchr., to chmn. English dept. Henley Sch., N.Y.C., 1968-71; copy editor to mng. editor IEEE Spectrum, N.Y.C., 1973-85; mng. editor Science 85/Science 86, Washington, 1985-86; acting mng. editor Natural History, N.Y.C., 1986; sr. editor Newsweek, N.Y.C., 1987; editor The Scientist, Phila., 1988-89; from news editor to editor Science, Washington, 1989—2002; pres., CEO N.Y. Acad. Scis., N.Y.C., 2002—. Author, editor articles in field, including cover story for Newsweek mag., 1987 (AAAS/Westinghouse award 1988). Recipient various Nat. Mag. awards, 1980, 83, 86. Fellow AAAS; mem. IEEE, Am. Soc. Mag. Editors, Nat. Assn. Sci. Writers. Office: NY Acad of Sciences 2nd E 63rd St New York NY 10021 Office Phone: 212-838-0230 201.

RUBINSTEIN, ERNEST, librarian, educator; b. Queens, N.Y., July 11, 1952; s. Jack and Jeanne Rubinstein; life ptnr. Paul Glassman. BA, Brandeis U., 1974; AMLS, U. Mich., 1977; MTS, Harvard U., 1979; MA, Hebrew Union Coll., 1985; PhD, Northwestern U., Evanston, Ill., 1995. Indexer H.W. Wilson Co., Bronx, NY, 1984—88; editor Am. Theological Libr. Assn., Chgo., 1988—90; reference libr. North Park Coll., Chgo., 1990—94; libr. Interchurch Ctr., N.Y.C., 1994—; book rev. Publs. Weekly, N.Y.C., 1999—. Asst. adj. prof. humanities NYU, N.Y.C., 1995—; adj. faculty New Sch., N.Y.C., 2001—. Author: (non-fiction) Episode of Jewish Romanticism, 1999. Vol. peer counselor Horizons, Chgo., 1992—94, Aids Pastoral Care Network, Chgo., 1992—94. Mem.: Am. Acad. Religion. Jewish. Home: 200 Cabrini Blvd Apt 42 New York NY 10033 Office: Interchurch Ctr 475 Riverside Dr Rm 900 New York NY 10115 Personal E-mail: ehr3@nyu.edu.

RUBINSTEIN, EVA (ANNA), photographer; b. Buenos Aires, 1933; d. Arthur and Aniela (Mlynarska) R.; m. William Sloane Coffin Jr., 1956 (div. 1968); children: Amy, Alexander (dec.), David. Ballet tng., Paris, N.Y.C., Calif., 1938-53; student, Scripps Coll., 1950-51, UCLA, 1952-53; student in photography, Lisette Model, 1969, Jim Hughes, 1971, Ken Heyman, 1970, Diane Arbus, 1971. Lectr. numerous workshops, seminars, confs.; instr. photo seminars Lodz Film Sch., Poland, 1986, 86-87. Dancer, actress: off-Broadway and Broadway, including original prodn. The Diary of Anne Frank, 1955-56; European dance tour, 1955; one-person shows of photographs include Underground Gallery, N.Y.C., 1972, Dayton Art Inst., Ohio, 1973, Arles Festival, France, 1975, Canon Photo Gallery, Amsterdam, 1975, Neikrug Gallery, N.Y.C., 1975, 79, 81, 82, 85, La Photogalerie, Paris, 1975, Friends of Photography, Carmel, Calif., 1975, Galerie 5.6, Ghent, Belgium, 1976, Gallery Trochenpresse, Berlin, 1977, Frumkin Gallery, Chgo., 1977, Galeria Sinisca, Rome, 1979, Hermitage Found. Mus., Norfolk, Va., 1982, Photographers Gallery, London, 1983, Galerie Forum Labo, Arles, France, 1983, Galerie Nicephore, Lyon, France, 1983, Image Gallery, Madrid, 1984, Muzeum Sztuki, Lodz, Poland, 1984, Il Diaframma/Canon Gallery, Milan, 1984, A.R.P.A. Gallery, Bordeaux, 1984, Chateau d'Eau, Toulouse, France, 1985, Galerie Demi-Teinte, Paris, 1985, Associated Artist Photographers galleries in Warsaw, Krakow, Lodz, Katowice and Gdansk, Poland, 1985-86, Foto/Medium/Art Gallery, Wroclaw, Poland, 1986, Visions Gallery, San Francisco, 1986, Canon Galerie, Paris, 1986, Salone Internat. SICOF, Milan, 1987, St. Krzysztof Gallery, Lodz, 1987, L'Image Fixe, Lyon, 1988, Artotheque, Grenoble, 1988, Neikrug Photographica, N.Y.C., 1989, Heuser Art Ctr. Gallery, Bradley U., Peoria, Ill., 1989, 3-os Encontros da Imagem, Braga, Portugal, 1989, Bibliotheque Nat. Galerie Colbert, Paris, 1989, Galerie Picto-Bastille, Paris, 1989-90, Portfolio Gallery, London, 1990, Vaison-La-Romaine, France, 1990, Hist. Mus. of City of Lodz, 1990, Galerie Artem, Quimper, France, 1993, Galerie F.N.A.C. Etoile, Paris, 1994, other F.N.A.C. galleries (France, Belgium, Spain), 1994-97, Galerie Augustus, Berlin, 1995, L'Imagerie, Lannion, France, 1995, Zacheta Gallery, Warsaw, 1996, Salon of Modern Art B.W.A., Bydgoszcz, Poland, 1997, Galleries of Polish Insts., Sofia, Bulgaria, Berlin, Moscow, Bratislava, Slovakia, I. Beszkova Gallery, Plewen, Bulgaria, 1997, Hungarian Mus. Photographic Art, Budapest, 1997, LTF Gallery, Lodz, Poland, 1998, Konfrontacje Fotograficzne, Gorzow Wielopolski, Poland, 1998, Centrum Kultury Zamek, Poznan, Poland, 1998, Mus. Regionalny, Wrzesnia, Poland, 1998, Galeria Korytarz, Jelenia Gora, Poland, 1998, Galeria Foto-Medium-Art, Wroclaw, Poland, 1998, Galeria Pusta, Centrum Kultury, Katowice, Poland, 1998, Teatr Wielki, Lodz, Poland, 2000, Gallery Europa Club, NY, 2003; group shows include, Internat. Salon, Krakow, Poland, 1971, Delgado Mus., New Orleans, 1972, Neikrug Gallery, 1972, 73, 75, Salone Internationale, Milan, Italy, 1973, Photo-OVO, Montreal, Que., Can., 1974, Nat. Portrait Gallery, London, 1976, Hera Gallery, R.I., 1977, Musee National d'Art Moderne Georges Pompidou, Paris, 1977, Centre Culturel de l'ouest Aquitain, Bordeaux, France, 1978, Fotografiska Museet, Stockholm, 1978, Nat. Arts Club, N.Y.C., 1979, Chrysler Mus., Norfolk, 1979, Maine Photog. Gallery, 1981, Floating Found. Photography, N.Y.C., 1970, 71, 72, 73, 79, 82, Ffoto Gallery, Cardiff, Wales, 1983, Musée d'Art Moderne de la Ville de Paris, 1987-88, Boca Raton (Fla.) Mus., 1989, Galerie PICTO Bastille, Paris, 1989, Galerie Arena, Arles, 1989-90, Settimana della Fotografia, Palermo, 1990, Festival de l'Image, Le Mans, France, 1993, Quimper (France), 1995, Galerie Camera Obscura, Paris, 1996, Zacheta Gallery, Warsaw, 2002, Lodz Photographic Soc., 2002, Polish/Am.Photographers, Polish Consulate, NY, 2003, Gutman Libr., Harvard, 2003; represented: in permanent collections Library of Congress, Washington, Met. Mus. Art, N.Y.C., Bibliotheque Nationale, Paris, Musee Reattu, Arles, France, Kalamazoo Inst. Arts, Israel Mus., Jerusalem, Fotografiska Museet, Stockholm, Muzeum Sztuki, Lodz, Poland, Histo Mus. of City of Lodz, others; author: Eva Rubinstein, 1974, Eva Rubinstein, I Grandi Fotografi, 1983, 2 ltd. edit. portfolios with introductions by John Vachon and André Kertész, Lodz: Brief Encounters, 1998, Eva Rubinstein: Fotografie, 1967-1990; contbr. photographs in various books, mags., profl. jours. *Making photographs is my way of exploring the questions that keep me alive by ever leading to further questions.*

RUBINSTEIN, FREDERIC ARMAND, lawyer; b. Antwerp, Belgium, Apr. 20, 1931; came to U.S., 1942; s. Samuel N. and Steffa (Warrenreich) R.; m. Susan August, Dec. 24, 1968; 1 child, Nicolas Eric August Rubinstein. BA, Cornell U., 1953, JD, 1955. Bar: N.Y. 1955. Assoc. Law Offices of I. Robert Feinberg, N.Y.C., 1955-60, Guggenheimer & Untermyer, N.Y.C., 1960-65, ptnr., 1965-85, Kelley Drye & Warren LLP, N.Y.C., 1985—. Vice chmn. zoning & planning com. Local Community Bd. # 6, N.Y.C., 1980-86. Mem. ABA (bus. law sect., emerging growth ventures subcom., chmn. 1988-96). Office: Kelley Drye & Warren LLP 101 Park Ave New York NY 10178-0002

RUBINSTEIN, MARK ISAAC, physician; b. Havana, Cuba, 1957; MD, Jefferson Med. Coll., 1983. Diplomate Am. Bd. Otolaryngology, Am. Bd. Facial Plastic and Reconstructive Surgery. Intern Pa. Hosp., Phila., 1983-84, resident in surgery, 1984-85; resident in otolaryngology, head and neck surgery U. Mich., Ann Arbor, 1985-89; mem. staff Fairfax (Va.) Hosp., 1989—, Fair Oaks (Va.) Hosp., 1989—; mem. courtesy staff Reston (Va.) Hosp., 1989—; clin. asst. prof. Georgetown U. Hosp., Washington; chief otolaryngology Fairfax Hosp., 2000—. Mem. AMA, Am. Acad. Otolaryngology-Head and Neck Surgery, Am. Acad. Facial Plastic and Reconstructive Surgery, Med. Soc. Va., Wash. Met. Ear, Nose and Throat Soc. (pres. 1996-97), Va. Soc. Otolargyngology Head and Neck Surgery, Fairfax County Med. Soc. Office: 8316 Arlington Blvd Ste 300 Fairfax VA 22031-5216

RUBINSTEIN, MOSHE FAJWEL, engineering educator; b. Miechow, Poland, Aug. 13, 1930; came to U.S., 1950, naturalized, 1965; s. Shlomo and Sarah (Rosen) R.; m. Zafrira Gorstein, Feb. 3, 1953; children: Iris, Dorit. BS, UCLA, 1954, MS, 1957, PhD, 1961. Designer Murray Erick Assos. (engrs. and archs.), L.A., 1954-56; structural designer Victor Gruen Assos., L.A., 1956-61; asst. prof. UCLA, 1961-64, assoc. prof. dept. engring., 1964-69, prof., 1969—, chmn. engring. sys. dept., 1970-75, program dir. modern engring. for execs. program, 1965-70. Cons. Pacific Power & Light Co., Portland, Oreg., Northrop Corp., U.S. Army, NASA Rsch. Ctr., Langley, Tex. Instruments Co., Hughes Space System Divsn., U.S. Army Sci. Adv. Com., Kaiser Aluminum and Chem. Corp., IBM Corp., TRW. Author: (with W.C. Hurty) Dynamics of Structures, 1964 (Yugoslavian transl. 1973), Matrix Computer Analysis of Structures, 1966 (Japanese transl. 1974), Structural Systems, Statics Dynamics and Stability, 1970 (Japanese transl. 1979), Patterns of Problem Solving, 1975, (with K. Pfeiffer) Concepts in Problem Solving, 1980, Tools for Thinking and Problem Solving, 1986; IEEE Press Videotapes; Models for People Driven Quality, 1991, Quality through Innovation, 1991, Creativity for Ongoing Total Quality, 1993, Relentless Improvement, 1993, (with I.R. Firstenberg) Patterns of Problem Solving, 2d edit., 1995, (with I.R. Firstenberg) The Minding Organization, 1999 (Portuguese/Japanese transl. 2000, Spanish/Chinese/Russian transls. 2001). Recipient Disting. Tchr. award UCLA Acad. Senate, 1964, Western Electric Fund award Am. Soc. Engring. Edn., 1965, Disting. Tchr. trophy Engring. Student Soc., UCLA, 1966; Sussman prof. for disting. visitor Technion-Israel Inst. Tech., 1967-68; named Outstanding Faculty Mem., UCLA Engring. Alumni award, 1979, Outstanding UCLA Civil Engring. Alumni award, 1990, Outstanding Faculty Mem., State of Calif. Command Coll., 1987, 88, 89, 94, 95; Fulbright-Hays fellow, Yugoslavia and Eng., 1975-76; voted one of UCLA's Top 20 Profs. of the Century. Mem. ASCE, Am. Soc. Engring. Edn., Seismol. Soc. Am., Sigma Xi, Tau Beta Phi. Achievements include research in use of computers in structural systems, analysis and synthesis; problem solving and decision theory; creativity and innovation in the organization. Home: 10488 Charing Cross Rd Los Angeles CA 90024-2646 Office: UCLA Sch Engring & Applied Sci Los Angeles CA 90024 Office Phone: 310-825-7731. Business E-Mail: mrubinst@ucla.edu.

RUBINSTEIN, PHYLLIS M. lawyer; BA in English, Pa. State U., 1966; JD, Temple U., 1977. Bar: Pa. 1977, D.C. 1980, Va. 1982. Jud. clk. to Hon. Israel Packel Phila. Supreme Ct., 1977-78; with Samuel B. Hornstein & Assocs., Doylestown, Pa., 1978-79; adj. instr. Inst. Paralegal Tng., Phila., 1979; counsel Hunton & Williams, Richmond, Va., 1981-95; dir. McCandlish Kaine & Grant, Richmond, 1995—. Speaker in field. Past condominium adv. bd. Commonwealth of Va.; exec. bd. Comml. Real Estate Women, Jewish Family Svcs.; past bd. dirs. B'Nai B'rith Youth Orgn., Beth Sholom Home Ctrl. Va. Mem. ABA (coun., real property, probate and trust law sect. 1993-99, chair diversity com., past chair com. ethics and professionalism, past task force on Applying Fed. Legis. to Congress, past standing com. on membership of real property, probate and trust law sect., past vice-chair com. on significant decisions of real property, probate and trust law sect., former mem. real estate fin. com., liaison to ethics 2000 commn.), Va. Bar Assn., Va. State Bar, Met. Richmond Women's Bar Assn. Home: 1905 Oakway Dr Richmond VA 23233-3513

RUBINSTEIN, RUTH P. medical educator, researcher; arrived in US, 1954; d. Eliezer and Sara (Calderon) Pilas; children: Jonathan, Jay, Sari. BSN, NYU, 1956; MA in Sociology, Rutgers U., 1968, PhD, 1975. RN NY. Instr. psychiat. nursing Belleview Hosp., NYC, 1956—61, Rutgers U., Newark, 1961—66; tchr. sociology Fashion Inst. Tech., NYC, 1985—. Presenter in field. Author: Dress Codes Meaning and Messages in American Culture, 1994, 2d edit., 2000, Society's Child Identity Clothing and Style, 1999. Grantee, NIMH, 1968—71, NEH, 1981, 1988. Mem.: Soc. for the Study of Symbolic Interaction, Soc. for the Study of Social Problems, Am. Sociol. Assn. Office: Fashion Inst Tech 27th St at 7th Ave New York NY 10001 Office Fax: 212-217-7095. Business E-Mail: ruth-rubinstein@fitnyc.edu.

RUBLE, BERNARD ROY, minister, labor relations and human resources consultant, educator; b. Greensburg, Indiana, Apr. 4, 1923; s. Jesse Emery and Marietta (Ward) Ruble; m. Mary Helen Rullman, Dec. 22, 1946; children: Barry Reece, Blane Rodney. BS, Ind. Univ., Bloomington, 1949; postgrad. transactional analysis, Midwest Inst. Human Understanding, 1972—75. Asst. mgr. Morris 5 and 10 Stores, Greensburg, Ind., 1941; store keeper Public Svc. Co., Ind., Greensburg, 1941—43; asst. mgr. personnel Kroger Co., Cin., 1949—51, mgr. personnel Madison, Wis., 1951—56, Ft. Wayne, Ind., 1956—58, Cleve., 1958—73, mgr. labor rels. Erie mktg. area Solon, Ohio, 1973—84; faculty Kroger Edn. Ctr., Cin., 1978—84. Educator Cleve. State U.; trustee Meat Cutters Health and Welfare Fund, 1971—79, Retail Clks. Union Health and Welfare Fund, Akron, 1970—88, No. Ohio Hospice Coun., 1981—84. Active United Appeal Greater Cleve., Cmty. Chest Greater Cleve., Met. Health Planning Corp., Ohio; hosp. vol. Vis. Nurses Assn., Ohio, Home Health Care, Ohio, Hospice We Res., Ohio; adv. com. Family Health Care, Washington, 1977—78; v.p. trustee Urban League Greater Cleve., 1968—75; trustee Cmty. Health Found., Ohio, Greater Cleve. Interchurch Coun., 1993—99; mem. bd. dirs. Nedan Hosp. Coun.; team rep. B.R. Ruble Racing, Burton, Ohio. Served in USAF, 1943—45. Mem.: Chesterland Ministerial Assn., Indsl. Rels. Rsch. Assn. (pres.), Cleve. Pers. Assn., Am. Soc. Pers. Adminstrn. (charter), Soc. Advancement Mgmt. (trustee Madison chpt. 1952—55), Photog. Soc. Am., Sertoma (trustee Madison 1952—56, Ft. Wayne 1957—58, charter), Masons, Alpha Kappa Psi. Home and Office: 8644 Ranch Dr Chesterland OH 44026-3132 Office Phone: 440-729-4691.

RUBLEY, CAROLE A. state legislator; b. Bethel, Conn., Jan. 18, 1939; d. George B. and Evelyn M. (Maloney) Drumm; m. C. Ronald Rubley, Aug. 25, 1962; children: Lauren M. Rubley Simpson, Stephen R., Kristin Rubley Vaughan. BA in Biology, Albertus Magnus Coll., 1960; MS in Environ. Health, West Chester U., 1988. Tchr. biology Danbury (Conn.) High Sch., 1960-62, Waltham (Mass.) High Sch., 1962-63; real estate salesperson Henderson-Dewey, Wayne, Pa., 1976-81; solid waste coord. Chester County Health Dept., West Chester, Pa., 1981-88; environ. cons. Environ. Resources Mgmt., Exton, Pa., 1988-92; mem. Pa. Ho. Reps., Valley Forge, 1992—. Mem. environ. resources, energy, consumer affairs, fin. and children and youth com. House of Reps.; mem. Pa. 21st Century Environ. Commn.; vice-chair environ. com. NCSL, task force on protecting Democracy, chair environ. and natural resources com. Author: (with others) Leading Pennsylvania into 21st Century, 1990. Chmn. Ea. Chester County Regional Planning Commn., 1976-85; vice chmn. planning commn. Tredyffrin Twp., Berwyn, Pa., 1976-86, mem. bd. suprs., 1987-92; bd. dirs. Pa. Resources Coun., exec. v.p., 1988-92. Mem. LWV (pres. Upper Main Line chpt. 1976-78, Involved Voter of Yr. award 1993), Pa. Environ. Coun., Green Valleys Assn., Open Land Conservancy. Republican. Roman Catholic. Avocations: aerobics, tennis, hiking, reading, travel. Home: 621 Vassar Rd Wayne PA 19087-5312

RUBNER, MICHAEL, international relations educator, university administrator; b. Tel Aviv, Aug. 3, 1940; came to U.S., 1956; s. Maurice and Eva Edith (Katz) R.; m. Audrey Ann Pfingst, Feb. 16, 1969; children: Daniel, Jessica.

BA, Rockford (Ill.) Coll., 1962; MA, Marquette U., 1964; PhD, U. Calif., Berkeley, 1975. Instr. James Madison Coll. Mich. State U., East Lansing, 1970-75, asst. prof., 1975-80, assoc. prof., 1980-85, prof., 1985—. Univ. faculty grievance ofcl. Mich. State U., 1989-2004 Co-author: The Palestinian Problem and U.S. Policy, 1986; contbr. articles to profl. jours. Pres. Jacob Schiff B'nai B'rith Lodge 694, Lansing, 1980-93; pres. Congregation Shaarey Zedek, East Lansing, 2002-04. Mem. Acad. Polit. Sci., Internat. Studies Assn. (governing coun. Midwest divsn. 1986-92), U.S. Arms Control Assn., Midwest Consortium for Internat. Security Studies, Phi Beta Kappa (pres. Epsilon of Mich. 1983-84), Alpha Sigma Nu, Phi Beta Delta. Democrat.

RUBNITZ, MYRON ETHAN, pathologist, educator; b. Omaha, Mar. 2, 1924; s. Abraham Srol and Esther Molly (Jonich) R.; m. Susan Belle Block, Feb. 9, 1952; children: Mary Lu Rubnitz Roffe, Peter, Thomas (dec.), Robert. BSc, U. Nebr., 1945; MD, U. Nebr., Omaha, 1947. Diplomate Am. Bd. Pathology. Intern Mt. Sinai Hosp., Cleve., 1947-48; fellow Mt. Sinai Hosp., N.Y.C., 1948-49; resident in pathology Michael Reese Hosp., Chgo., 1949-51; pathologist VA Hosp., Hines, Ill., 1953-56, chief labs., 1956-93, cons., 1993—; assoc. prof. pathology Loyola U. Med. Sch., Maywood, Ill., 1963-70, prof., 1970-99, prof. emeritus, 1999—. Adj. prof. Ill. State U., Normal, 1979-96, 2003—, U. St. Francis, Joliet, Ill., 1989—, Ea. Ill. U. Charleston, 1991—, Western Ill. U., Macomb, 1991—; clin. instr. Augustana Coll., Rock Island, Ill., 1991—. Chmn. candidates com. Village Caucus, Winnteka, Ill., 1969-70; bd. dirs. Chgo. Commons Assn., 1968—, North Shore Sr. Ctr., 1998—; mem. New Trier High Sch. Caucus, Winnetka, 1972-74. With AUS, 1943-46, PTO; 1st lt. M.C., U.S. Army, 1951-53. Fellow Am. Soc. Clin. Pathologists, Coll. Am. Pathologists; mem. Internat. Acad. Pathology, Assn. VA Pathologists (pres. 1982-84), Chgo. Pathology Soc., Lake Shore Country Club (Glencoe, Ill.), Mich. Shores Club (Wilmette, Ill.). Avocations: electronics, tennis, travel. Home: 979 Sheridan Rd Winnetka IL 60093 Office Phone: 847-441-0920. Personal E-mail: northfieldoc@juno.com.

RUBOTTOM, GEORGE MILTON, foundation administrator, chemist; b. London, Mar. 19, 1940; s. Alphonso Milton and Lorna Annie Rubottom. AB, Middlebury Coll., 1962; PhD, MIT, 1967. Lectr. Bucknell U., Lewisburg, Pa., 1968—70; asst. prof. U. PR, Rio Piedras, 1970—75; assoc. and full prof. U. Idaho, Moscow, 1975—84; program dir. in chemistry NSF, Arlington, Va., 1984—. Exec. sec. edn., human resources com. Nat. Sci. Bd., Washington, 1987—2000; mem. dir.'s rev. bd. NSF, Arlington, 1987—2000. Author: (book) Academic Excellence: The Sourcebook, 2001; reviewer: jour. Jour. Org. Chem., Tetrahedron, Tetrahedron Letters. Scuba instr. YMCA, Washington, 1994—. Grantee, NIH, 1973—78, Petroleum Rsch. Fund, 1971—72, 1979—81; Postdoctoral fellow, NIH, 1967—68. Mem.: Am. Chem. Soc., Sigma Xi, Phi Kappa Phi, Phi Beta Kappa. Achievements include research in new methods for the oxidation of C-C double bonds; new methods for the preparation and cleavage of cyclopropanols. Office: NSF 4201 Wilson Blvd Arlington VA 22230 Business E-Mail: grubotto@nsf.gov.

RUBOTTOM, ROY RICHARD, JR., retired diplomat and educator, consultant; b. Brownwood, Tex., Feb. 13, 1912; s. Roy Richard and Jennie Eleanor (Watkins) R.; m. Billy Ruth Young, Dec. 23, 1938; children: Eleanor Ann Rubottom Odden, Frank, John. BS, So. Meth. U., 1932, MA, 1933; postgrad., U. Tex.; LLD, Southwestern Coll., Winfield, Kans., 1968, Ctrl. Meth. Coll., Fayette, Mo., 1985. Asst. dean student life U. Tex., 1937-41; apptd. fgn. svc. officer, 1947; sec. of embassy and consul, 1947-49; officer-in-charge Mex. affairs State Dept., 1950, dep. dir. Middle Am. Affairs, 1951, dir., 1952-53; 1st sec. embassy Madrid, 1953; counselor of embassy, 1954; dir. U.S. Ops. Mission, 1954-56; asst. sec. of state for inter-Am. affairs, 1957-60; U.S. Ambassador to Argentina, 1960-62; advisor Naval War Coll., Newport, R.I., 1962-64; v.p. So. Meth. U., Dallas, 1964-71, prof. polit. sci. emeritus, 1975—; dir. Ctr. of Ibero-Am. Civilization, 1975-77; pres. U. Americas, Puebla, Mex., 1971-73; dir. Office Internat. Affairs, Dallas, 1985-87. Co-author: Spain and the U.S. Since W.W. II, 1984. Active Scouting U.S.A. Served with USNR, 1941-46. Recipient Silver Beaver award Boy Scouts Am., 1975, Inter-Am. award Boy Scouts Am., Silver Buffalo, 1993. Mem. Lambda Chi Alpha, Pi Sigma Alpha. Lodges: Rotary. Methodist. Home: 7831 Park Ln Apt 51B Dallas TX 75225-2039

RUBRIGHT, JAMES ALFRED, paperboard and packaging company executive; b. Phila., Dec. 17, 1946; s. James Alfred and Helen Lucille (Evans) R. (deceased); m. Mary Elizabeth Angelich, Dec. 30, 1987; children: Noah Michael, Benjamin James, Jami Anne, Nathaniel Drew, James McCurdy, William Angelich. BA, Yale U., 1969; JD, U. Va., 1972. Bar: Ga. 1972. Ptnr. King & Spalding, Atlanta, 1972-94; sr. v.p., gen. counsel Sonat Inc., Birmingham, 1994-97; pres. So. Natural Gas Co. subs. Sonat Inc., Birmingham, 1997-98; exec. v.p. Sonat Inc., Birmingham, 1998-99; CEO Rock-Tenn Co., Norcross, Ga., 1999—. Office: Rock-Tenn Co 504 Thrasher St Norcross GA 30071-1914

RUBRUM, ERICA COURTNEY, family therapist, school counselor; b. N.Y.C., Feb. 20, 1965; d. Walter and Rhoda (Metviner) R.; m. Todd Schaffhauser, Sept. 29, 1996, c. Olivia Morgan. BA, U. Mass., 1987; MS in Edn., L.I. U., 1990; MS in Counseling, Queens Coll., 1992. Registered sch. counselor, N.Y. Mgr. Am. Leisure, N.Y.C., 1988-90; family therapist Counseling and Psychotherapy Group, Merrick, N.Y., 1990-94; sch. counselor Herricks Pub. Schs., New Hyde Park, N.Y., 1992-94; pvt. practice family therapy Roslyn, N.Y., 1994—; social worker Big Bros./Big Sisters, Levittown, N.Y., 1995-96; supervising therapist New Image Med., Huntington, N.Y., 1995-96; sch. counselor Carle Place Pub. Schs., 1996-2000, Hollow Hills Pub. Schs., 2000. Vp. One to One: L.I.'s Disability Support and Outreach Group, Islip, N.Y., 1993—; family therapist Family Wellness Ctr., Smithtown, N.Y., 2000—. Mem. ACA, Am. Assn. Marriage and Family Therapists, Am. Psychotherapy Assn., Nassau Counselors Assn. (exemplary practice award 1992, 95). Office: 56 Sherrard St Roslyn Heights NY 11577-1713

RUCCI, ANTHONY JOSEPH, health care products and services executive; b. Youngstown, Ohio, Sept. 19, 1950; BS, Bowling Green State U., 1972, MA, 1976, PhD in Inds l and Organizational Psychology, 1978. Asst. dir., pers. adminstr. Mahoning County Mental Health and Retardation Bd., Youngstown, Ohio, 1972-74; cons., grad. student Bowling Green (Ohio) State U., 1974-78; cons. LWFW Inc., Dallas, 1978-79; pers. planning specialist Baxter Internat. Inc., Deerfield, Ill., 1979-80, mgr. pers. planing, 1980-85; v.p. orgn. and human resource planning Am. Hospital Supply Corp. Am. Hosp. Supply Corp., 1985-86; sr. v.p. human resources Baxter Internat. Inc., Deerfield, Ill., 1986-92. Instr. Bowling Green State U., 1974-78, Davis Jr. Coll., 1975-77, U. Tex. at Dallas, 1979, U. Ill., Chgo. Cir., 1981, Lake Forest Grad. Sch. Mgmt., 1983; invited speaker confs., socs., forums, seminars; mem. White House Fellows Regional Selections Panel, Chgo., 1988, 89. Cons. editor, mem. editorial bd. Jour. Applied Psychology, 1982-86; assoc. editor Human Resource Planning Jour., 1989; editorial reviewer Jossey-Bass Pub. Co., 1991; contbr. articles to profl. jours. Mem. Chancellor's Exec. Adv. Bd., U. Ill. at Chgo.; bd. dirs. Lake Forest Grad. Sch. Mgmt., 1984-87; mem. Human Resource Mgmt. Adv. Bd. U. Mich. Sch. Bus. Adminstrn. Mem. APA, The Bus. Roundtable (bd. dirs., employee rels. com.), Adv. Coun. on Human Resources Mgmt. of the Conf. Bd. (bd. dirs.), Coun. on Orgn. and Mgmt. of the Conf. Bd. (bd. dirs.), Soc. Indsl./Organizational Psychology, Human Resource Planning Soc. (bd. dirs. 1986-90), Human Resource Mgmt. Assn. Chgo. (bd. dirs. 1986-89), Antaean Soc., Sigma Xi, Omicron Delta Kappa. Office: Baxter Internat Inc 1 Baxter Pkwy Deerfield IL 60015-4625

RUCH, CHARLES P. academic administrator; b. Longbranch, N.J., Mar. 25, 1938; s. Claud C. and Marcella (Pierce) R.; m. Sally Joan Brandenburg, June 18, 1960; children: Cheryl, Charles, Christopher, Cathleen. BA, Coll. of Wooster, 1959; MA, Northwestern U., 1960, PhD, 1966. Counselor, tchr. Evanston (Ill.) Twp. High Sch., 1960-66; asst. prof. U. Pitts., 1966-70, assoc. prof., dept. chmn., 1970-74; assoc. dean sch. edn. Va. Commonwealth U., Richmond, 1974-76, dean sch. edn., 1976-85, interim provost, v.p., 1985-86, provost, v.p., 1986-93; pres. Boise (Idaho) State U., 1993—. Cons. various univs., govtl. agys., ednl. founds. Author or co-author over 50 articles, revs., tech. reports. Mem. Am. Psychol. Assn., Am. Ednl. Research Assn., Phi Delta Kappa. Office: Boise State U 1910 University Dr Boise ID 83725-0399 E-mail: cruch@boisestate.edu.

RUCHELMAN, LEONARD ISADORE, urban studies and public administration educator; b. Bklyn., June 28, 1933; s. Jacob and Sarah (Rosenblum) R.; m. Diana G. Hoffberger, Feb.11, 1961; children: Lauren, Charles. BA, Bklyn. Coll., 1954; PhD in Polit. Sci., Columbia U., 1965. Vis. asst. prof. dept. polit. sci. W.Va. U., Morgantown, 1962-64; assoc. prof., chair polit. sci. Alfred (N.Y.) U., 1964-69; assoc. prof., dir. urban studies Lehigh U., Bethlehem, Pa., 1969-75; prof., chmn. dept. urban studies and pub. adminstrn. Old Dominion U., Norfolk, Va., 1975-92, dir. Ctr. for Regional Studies, 1986-90, Eminent Scholar of Pub. Adminstrn., 1992—2002. Mem. editorial com. on socio-polit. influences Coun. on Tall Bldgs. and Urban Habitat, Bethlehem, 1975—. Author: Big City Mayors, 1969, Police Politics, 1974, The World Trade Center, 1977, A Workbook in Program Design for Public Managers, 1985, A Workbook in Redesigning Public Services, 1989. Cities in the Third Wave, 2000. With U.S. Army, 1954-56. Mem. AAUP, Am. Soc. Pub. Adminstrn. (pres. Tidewater chpt. 1977-78), Urban Affairs Assn., Am. Polit. Sci. Assn. E-mail: lruchelm@odu.edu.

RUCINSKI, ROBERT LAWRENCE, musician, educator; b. Jersey City, N.J., Sept. 2, 1977; s. Robert Charles and Doris Barbara Rucinski. BS, MusM, Mass. Inst. Tech., Cambridge, Mass., 1999; MSChemE, Mass. Inst. tech., Cambridge, Mass., 2000. Music dir. Booth Prodn., Worcester, Mass., 2000—, Reagle Players, Waltham, Mass., 2001—; tchr., music dir. Bromfield Sch., Harvard, Mass., 2001—; music dir. Arundel Barn playhouse, Arundel, Maine, 2002; tchr. music dir. Walnut Hill Sch., Natick, Mass., 2003—. Dir. MIT Concert Band, Cambridge, Mass., 2000—; host/coord. John Philip Sousa Nat. Jr. Hon. Band, Harvard, Mass., 2001—; music dir. various theatre orgn., Mass., 1995—.

RUCKDESCHEL, DAVID CLAUDE, music educator; b. Abbington, Pa., Aug. 13, 1974; s. John and Susan Elizabeth Ruckdeschel; m. Michelle Lynn Weber, Aug. 17, 1996; 1 child, Lucas Daniel. B in Music Edn., U. Ky., 1996; M in Music Edn., Murray State U., 2003. Band dir. Crittenden County Schs., Marion, Ky., 1997—2001, Daviess County Middle Sch., Owensboro, Ky., 2001—. Mem.: NEA, Ky. Edn. Assn., Ky. Music Edn. Assn., Nat. Assn. for Music Edn., Music Educators Nat. Conf., Gamma Beta Phi. Home: 1262 Morgantown Rd Whitesville KY 42376 Office: Daviess County Middle Sch 1415 E 4th St Owensboro KY 42303

RUCKELSHAUS, WILLIAM DOYLE, investment company executive; b. Indpls., July 24, 1932; s. John K. and Marion (Doyle) R.; m. Jill Elizabeth Strickland, May 11, 1962; children: Catherine Kiley, Mary Hughes, Jennifer Lea, William Justice, Robin Elizabeth. BA cum laude, Princeton U., 1957; LL.B., Harvard U., 1960. Bar: Ind. 1960. Atty. Ruckelshaus, Bobbitt & O'Connor, Indpls., 1960-68; dep. atty.-gen. Ind., 1960-65; chief counsel office atty.-gen. Ind., 1963-65; minority atty. Ind. Senate, 1965-67; mem. Ind. Ho. of Reps., 1967-69, majority leader, 1967-69; asst. atty.-gen. charge civil div. Dept. Justice, 1969-70; adminstr. EPA, Washington, 1970-73; acting dir. FBI, 1973; dep. atty. gen. U.S., 1973; mem. firm Ruckelshaus, Beveridge, Fairbanks & Diamond, Washington, 1974-76; sr. v.p. law and corp. affairs Weyerhaeuser Co., Tacoma, 1976-83; adminstr. EPA, Washington, 1983-85; pres. William D. Ruckelshaus Assocs., 1985-88; mem. firm Perkins Coie, Seattle, 1985-88; chmn. bd., CEO Browning-Ferris Industries, Inc., Houston, 1988-95, chmn., 1995—99; founder, prin., also bd. dirs. Madrona Investment Group, LLC, 1996—; strategic dir. Madrona Venture Group, Seattle, 1999—; chmn. World Resources Inst., Washington D.C., 1999—. Bd. dirs. Cummins Engine Co., Nordstrom, Inc., Weyerhaeuser Co., Inc., Vykor, Inc. Rep. nominee for U.S. Senate, Ind., 1968; apptd. by Pres. Clinton to serve as U.S. envoy to Pacific Salmon Treaty with Can., 1997-98; apptd. by Pres. Bush as commr. Commn. on Ocean Policy, 2001—; chmn. Salmon Recovery Funding Bd., Wash. Mem. World Resource Inst. (chmn. 1998—), Fed. Bar Assn., Ind. Bar Assn., D.C. Bar Assn., Indpls. Bar Assn. Office: Madrona Investment Group LLC 1000 2nd Ave Ste 3700 Seattle WA 98104-1053 Office Phone: 206-674-3008. E-mail: bill@madrona.com.

RUCKENSTEIN, ELI, chemical engineering educator; b. Botosani, Romania, Aug. 13, 1925; arrived in U.S., 1969; m. Velina Rothstein, May 15, 1948; children: Andrei, Lelia. BSChemE, Poly. Inst., Bucharest, Romania, 1949, PhD, 1967, Tech. U., Bucharest, 1993. Prof. Poly. Inst., Bucharest, 1949—69; vis. prof. U. London, 1969; NSF sr. scientist Clarkson Coll. Tech., Potsdam, NY, 1969—70; prof. U. Del., Newark, 1970—73, SUNY, Buffalo, 1973—81, disting. prof., 1981—. Vis. Humbolt prof. Bayreuth U., Germany, 1986; Gulf vis. prof. Carnegie Mellon U., Pitts., 1988—89; disting. lectr. U. Waterloo, 1985, U. Mo., 1983; Fair Meml. lectr. U. Okla., 1987; Colburn Symposium lectr. U. Del., 1988, Robert L. Pigford meml. lectr., 99; Van Winkle lectr. U. Tex., 1989; Berkeley lectr., 97; Robert A. Welch Found. lectr., 97; Barnett F. Dodge disting. lectr. Yale U., 1998. Contbr. articles to profl. jours. Named Merk Disting. lectr., Rutgers U., 1992; recipient Nat. award, Romanian Dept. Edn., 1958, 1964, Tchg. award, 1961, George Spacu award, Romanian Acad. Sci., 1963, Sr. Humbolt award, Alexander von Humbolt Found., 1985, Creativity award, NSF, 1985, Nat. Medal of Sci., 1998. Mem.: AIChE (Alpha Chi Sigma award 1977, Walker award 1988, Founders award 2002), NAE, Am. Chem. Soc. (Kendall award 1986, Jacob F. Schoellkopf medal 1986, Langmuir Disting. Lectr. award 1994, E.V. Murphree award 1996, Nat. Medal of Sci. 1998). Office: SUNY Dept Chem Engring 303 Furnas Hall Buffalo NY 14260-4200 Business E-Mail: feaeliru@acsu.buffalo.edu.

RUCKER, DONALD W. emergency physician, educator, consultant; b. Montreal, Que., Can. came to U.S., 1960; s. Klaus G. and Daisy Rucker. AB, Harvard U., 1977; MD, U. Pa., 1981; MBA, Stanford U., 1987, MS, 1988. Diplomate Am. Bd. Internal Medicine, Am. Bd. Emergency Medicine. Product mgr. Datamedic, Waltham, Mass., 1988-93; emergency physician Beth Israel Hosp., Boston, 1990—2000; instr. Med. Sch. Harvard U., Boston, 1992—2000; v.p., chief med. officer Siemens Med. Solutions, 2000—. Emergency physician Univ. Pa. Health System, 2000—. Fellow Am. Coll. Emergency Physicians. also: 51 Valley Stream Pkwy Malvern PA 19355-1406

RUCKER, DOUGLAS PENDLETON, JR., lawyer; b. Richmond, Va., Dec. 26, 1945; s. Douglas Pendleton and Margaret (Williams) R.; m. Marian F. Copeland; 1 child, Louise Meredith. BA, Hampden-Sydney Coll., 1968; JD, U. Va., 1972. Bar: Va. 1972, D.C. 1986, U.S. Dist. Ct. (ea. and we. dists.) Va. 1972, U.S. Ct. Appeals (4th cir.) 1982, U.S. Supreme Ct. 1982, U.S. Ct. Claims 1995. Assoc. Sands, Anderson, Marks & Miller, Richmond, Va., 1972-76, mem., 1977—, also bd. dirs. Mem. adv. com. Richmond Renaissance; active St. John's Episcopal Ch., mem. vestry, 1994—98, register, 1996, jr. warden, 1997, sr. warden, 1998, trustee, 1994—; bd. dirs., vice chmn. James River Devel. Corp. With Va. Army N.G., 1968—74. Mem.: ABA, Met. Richmond C. of C., Bar Assn. D.C., Soc. Colonial Wars in the State of Va., Richmond Bar Assn. (real estate sect., bd. dirs. 1994—97), Va. Bar Assn. (constrn. law chmn. 1992, real estate and bus. law sects., exec. com. 1992—97, pres. 1996), Va. Law Found. (bd. dirs. 1998—2004), Am. Bar Found., Twenty-Three Hundred Club, Commonwealth Club. Office: Sands Anderson Marks & Miller PO Box 1998 Richmond VA 23218-1998 Business E-Mail: DRucker@sandsanderson.com.

RUCKER, KENNETH LAMAR, law enforcement officer, educator, military officer; b. Atlanta, July 16, 1961; s. Jack Lamar and Priscilla Anne (Anderson) R.; m. Kerri Lynn Hairston; children: Kenneth Lamar II, Kerbi Lynn. BSBA, Brenau U., 1991; MPA in Pub. Mgmt., Ga. State U., 1993; postgrad., U. Ga., 1993—. Cert. peace officer, supr., Ga., field tng. officer, law enforcement exec.; cert. supply corps, Navy Supply Corps Sch., 1997. Law enforcement officer Met. Atlanta Rapid Transit Authority, 1984-93; sch. resource officer Fulton County Bd. Edn., Atlanta, 1993-95; field facilitator Cmtys. in Schs. of Ga., Inc., Atlanta, 1995-97, field facilitator Cross Roads program, 1995-97; chief of police Fulton County Schs. Police Dept., 1997—. Bd. dirs. Benefactors of Edn., Inc., Atlanta; cons. pub. security Fulton County Bd. Edn., Atlanta, 1993-95; supply corps officer Navy Supply Corps Sch. USNR, Athens, 1997; bd. advisors Fulton County Pub. Safety Tng. Ctr., 2000—; tng. cons. Internat. Assn. of Chiefs of Police, 2000—. Sunday sch. tchr., deacon Simpson St. Ch. of Christ, Atlanta, 1991—; youth motivator Atlanta Pub. Schs., 1988—. Commd. officer Supply Corps, USNR, 1995—. Doctoral fellow U. Ga. Mem. Am. Soc. Pub. Adminstrn., Internat. Assn. Chiefs of Police, Nat. Orgn. Black Law Enforcement Execs., Nat. Forum Black Pub. Adminstrs., Ga. Assn. Chiefs of Police, Benefactors of Edn., Inc. (bd. dirs. 1996-99), Brenau U. Alumni Club (bd. dirs. 1999—), Ga. State U. Alumni Club, U.S. Naval Inst., Naval Res. Assn., Res. Officer's Assn., Navy Supply Corps Assn., Fulton County Pub. Safety Tng. Ctr. (Bd. of advisors 1999—, v. chmn., 2003—); Pi Alpha Alpha, Pi Sigma Alpha, Omicron Delta Kappa (cir. pres. 1992-93). Avocations: computer tech., reading, photography, classical music, fitness. Home: 1835 Jenny Ln Lithia Springs GA 30122-2857 Office: Fulton County Schs Police Fulton County Bd Education 786 Cleveland Ave SW Atlanta GA 30315-7239 E-mail: rucker@fulton.k12.ga.us.

RUCKER, ROBERT D. state supreme court justice; b. Canton, Ga. married; 3 children. BA, Ind. U.; JD, Valparaiso Sch. of Law; LLM, U. Va. Dep. prosecuting atty., Lake County, Ind.; city atty. City of Gary, Ind.; pvt. practice East Chicago; justice Ind. State Supreme Ct., Indpls., 1999—. Former vice chmn. Ind. Commn. for Continuing Legal Edn. Bd. dirs. Legal Svcs. of N.W. Ind. Decorated Vietnam Vet. Office: State House Rm 312 200 W Washington St Indianapolis IN 46204-2798

RUCKMAN, ROGER NORRIS, pediatric cardiologist; b. Washington, Dec. 15, 1944; s. Norris Elliott and Eugenia (Campbell) R.; m. Kathleen Anne Smith; children: Robert, Karen, Stephen, Jonathan. BA in Chemistry, Williams Coll., Williamstown, Mass., 1966; MD, U. Va., 1970. Intern Peter Bent Brigham Hosp., 1970-71; resident Med. Ctr. Hosp. of Vermont, 1973-75; fellow in cardiology Children's Hosp., Boston, 1975-77; asst. prof. pediatrics U. Nebr., Omaha, 1977-79, George Washington U., Washington, 1980-82, assoc. prof. pediatrics, 1982-90, prof. pediatrics, 1990—; pediatric cardiologist Children's Hosp. Nat. Med. Ctr., Washington, 1980—, chmn. cardiology, 1986-89. Contbr. articles to profl. jours. Served to capt. U.S. Army, 1971-73. Recipient Disting. Service award, Am.-Korea Found., 1972; NIH grantee, 1982—. Fellow Am. Acad. Pediatrics, Am. Coll. Cardiology; mem. Am. Heart Assn., Teratology Soc., Soc. Pediatric Research, Columbia Country Club (Chevy Chase, Md.). Republican. Presbyterian. Avocations: tennis, golf. Office: CNMC Dept Cardiology 111 Michigan Ave NW Washington DC 20010-2916 Office Phone: 202-884-2020. Business E-Mail: rruckman@cnmc.org.

RUDA, HOWARD, lawyer, finance company executive; b. N.Y.C., Sept. 7, 1932; s. Menahem and Lucy (Gillenson) R.; m. Leah E. Zeliger, Sept. 22, 1963; 1 child, Amy. BA, CCNY, 1954; JD, Columbia U., 1959. Bar: N.Y. 1959, U.S. Dist. Ct. (so. and ea. dists.) N.Y. 1959. Assoc., then ptnr. Laporte & Meyers, N.Y.C., 1959-63; staff atty., then gen. counsel Meinhard Comml. Corp., N.Y.C., 1963-68; with C.I.T. Group Holdings, Inc., N.Y.C., 1968-87, asst. gen. counsel, 1968—; gen. counsel, v.p., dir. C.I.T. Corp., C.I.T. Leasing Corp., N.Y.C., 1973-84; counsel Hahn & Hessen, N.Y.C., 1987—. Lectr. Practicing Law Inst., Banking Law Inst.; dir. Am. Bankruptcy Inst., 1982-91; arbitrator Am. Arbitration Assn. Editor: Asset Based Financing, Jour. of Bankruptcy Law and Practice. Served with U.S. Army, 1954-56. Fellow Am. Bar Found., Am. Coll. Comml. Fin. Lawyers (regent 1992-95); mem. ABA (chmn. equipment financing com. 1982-85, chmn. ad hoc bulk sales com. 1987-90), Am. Law Inst., Phi Beta Kappa. Jewish. Home: 8 Mirrielees Rd Great Neck NY 11021-2928 Office: Hahn & Hessen 488 Madison Ave New York NY 10022 E-mail: hruda@hahnhessen.com.

RUDACILLE, SHARON VICTORIA, medical technologist; b. Ranson, W.Va., Sept. 11, 1950; d. Albert William and Roberta Mae (Anderson) Rudacille. BS cum laude, Shepherd Coll., 1972. Med. technologist VA Ctr., Martinsburg, W.Va., 1972—. Instr. Sch. Med. Tech., 1972—76, assoc. coord. edn., 1976—77, edn. coord., 1977—78, quality assurance officer clin. chemistry, 1978—80, lab. svc. quality assurance and edn. officer, 1980—84, clin. chemistry sect. leader, 1984—86, staff med. technologist, 1986—94, supervisory med. technologist, 1994—95, sr. med. technologist, 1995—; adj. faculty mem. Shippensburg (Pa.) State Coll., 1977—78, Shepherd Coll., 1977—78. Mem.: Shepherd Coll. Alumni Assn., W.Va. Soc. Med. Technologists, Am. Soc. Clin. Pathologists, Am. Soc. Med. Tech., Sigma Pi Epsilon. Bapt. Home: PO Box 14 Ranson WV 25438-0014

RUDCZYNSKI, ANDREW B. academic administrator, medical researcher; b. Nottingham, England, Sept. 7, 1947; came to U.S., 1951; s. Richard B. and Krystyna Z. R.; m. Andrea Skalny, Oct. 16, 1976 (div. Oct. 1990); children: Christina, Thomas. BSc in Biology/Biochemistry, McGill U., 1969; PhD in Immunology, Syracuse U., 1974; MBA in Adminstrn., So. Ill. U., 1984. Prin. investigator scrub typhus project divsn. Rickettsiology U.S. Army Med. Rsch. Infectious Diseases, Ft. Detrick, Md., 1974-76; rsch. assoc. dept. biology Mich. Cancer Found., Detroit, 1976-77, rsch. scientist dept. immunology, unit chief immunology unit Breast Cancer Prognostic Study, 1977-80; asst. dir. Office Rsch. and Grants U. Md. Ea. Shore, Princess Anne, 1980-83; extramural assoc. Office Extramural Rsch. and Tng., Office of Dir. NIH, 1981-82; asst. dir. Office Rsch. & Sponsored Programs Rutgers U., Piscataway, N.J., 1983-84, dir., 1984-99, asst. v.p. rsch. adminstrn., 1985-93, assoc. v.p. rsch. policy and adminstrn., 1993-99; assoc. v.p. fin., exec. dir. rsch. svcs. U. Pa., Phila., 1999—. Field reader strengthening devel. instns. program U.S. Dept. Edn., 1990; mem. Chancellor's task force instrn. and rsch. infrastructure support N.J. Dept. Higher Edn., 1992. Contbr. articles, abstracts to profl. jours. Capt. U.S. Army Med. Svc. Corps, 1974-76. Recipient traineeship award NSF, 1969-71; predoctoral fellow NIH, 1973-74. Mem. AAAS, Nat. Coun. Univ. Rsch. Adminstrs. (profl. devel. com. 1988-90, region II program com. 1989-90, chmn. region II 1990-92, nat. program com. 1994-95), Coun. Govtl. Rels. (fed. mgmt. devel. com. 1989-90, bd. dirs. 1998-2003, tech. transfer and ethics com. 1998-99, chair rsch. compliance and adminstrn. com. 1999-2003), Beta Gamma Sigma, Sigma Xi. Roman Catholic. Home: 2033 Rodman St Philadelphia PA 19146-1359 Office: Univ Pa Office Rsch Svcs 3451 Walnut St Ste P-221 Philadelphia PA 19104-6205

RUDD, D(ALE) F(REDERICK), chemical engineering educator; b. Mpls., Mar. 2, 1935; m. 1964; 2 children. BS, U. Minn., 1956, PhD in Chem. Engring., 1960. Asst. prof. chem. engring. U. Mich., Ann Arbor, 1960-61; from asst. prof. to prof. U. Wis., Madison, 1961-94, Schlicter emeritus prof. chem. engring., 1994—. Co-author: (book) Strategy of Process Enging., 1968, Process Synthesis, 1973, Strategy of Pollution Control, 1977, Petrochemical Tech. Assessment, 1981, Microkinetics of Heterogeneous Catalysis, 1993. Named J.S. Guggenheim fellow, 1970; recipient Allan P. Colburn award, 1971. Mem. Nat. Acad. Engring., 1978. Achievements include contributions to the knowlege of process engineering.

RUDD, DAVID WILLIAM, management consultant, chemical engineer, consultant; b. Floral Park, N.Y., Dec. 31, 1931; s. Edward Lynn and Joanna (McSorley) Rudd; m. Harriet Fay Sart, Aug. 8, 1953; children: Rebecca, Rachel. BA in Chemistry, Colby Coll., 1953; MS in Phys. Chemistry, Northeastern U., 1962. Rsch. chemist Monsanto Chem. Co., Everett, Mass., 1956-58, Kendall Co., Walpole, Mass., 1958-60, Metal Hydrides, Beverly, Mass., 1960-62; sr. staff engr. Western Electric Co., North Andover, Mass., 1969-78; mem. rsch. staff Engring. Rsch. Ctr., Princeton, NJ, 1978-80; co-founder, dir. David W. Rudd Assocs., mfg. cons., 1985—. Iso-9000 auditor, 1993; co-owner cert. tree farm, Sumner, Maine. Vol. tutor program Mass. Pub. Sch., Lawrence, 1991. With 7th Cav. U.S. Army, 1953—55. Co-recipient Malcolm Baldrige Nat. Quality award, with AT&T's Transmission Divsn., 1992; recipient Engring. Excellence award, Western Electric Co., 1969, C. B. Sawyer Meml. award, 1974, Vol. Tutoring Program award, AT&T, 1991, Lucent Tech. Patent award, 1999. Mem.: We. Electric Engring. Excellence Soc. (pres. 1977—83), Svc. Corp Ret. Execs., Tel. Pioneers Am. (life), Western Foothills Heritage Trust, McLaughlin Found., Sumner Hist. Soc. (bd. dirs. 1996—). Achievements include research in surface chemistry, permeability of metals to hydrogen, rocket propellant synthesis infrared method of Q evaluation synthetic quartz, crystal growth, printed circuit tech., metal

joining; computer-integrated mfg. techniques, statis. quality control, soldering tech., environ. modifications of mfg. processes, ISO 9,000 auditor; patents for for growth of synthetic quartz; research in infra red analysis of quartz; computer control of symthetic quartz crystal growth process. Home: 489 Valley Rd Sumner ME 04292-3402 Office Phone: 207-388-2362. Business E-Mail: davhar@megalink.net.

RUDD, GERALD PATRICK, ophthalmologist; b. Larned, Kans., Oct. 27, 1947; s. Gerald Vern and Olive Irene Rudd; m. Kangsun Yi Stone; children: Michael B. Stone, Sarita Rohonie, Samuel McArthur. BA in Chemistry, Ottawa (Kans.) U., 1969; DO, Kirksville Coll. Osteo. Med., 1976; cert. in leprology, Schieffelin Leprosy Rsch. Ctr., Kirigiri, India, 1976; postgrad., Stanford U., 1981. Diplomate in Osteo. Medicine and Surgery Nat. Bd. Examiners. Intern Riverside Osteo. Hosp., Trenton, Mich., 1976-77; commd. lt. USPHS, 1977, advanced through grades to comdr., 1985; resident in ophthalmology USPHS Hosp., San Francisco, 1980; resident in ophthalmology, then chief resident Walter Reed Army Med. Ctr., Washington, 1981-83, fellow in vitro-retinal disease and surgery, 1983-85; gen. med. officer Winslow (Ariz.) Indian Health Ctr., 1977-79, clin. dir., 1979-80; asst. chief ophthalmology, chief vitreo-retinal surgery Ophthalmology Svc., Gallup (N.Mex.) Indian Med. Ctr., 1985-88; vitreo-reginal surgery and gen. ophthalmology practice Omni Eye Svc., Phoenix, 1988-89, CIGNA Health Plan, Tempe, Ariz., 1989—90, Santa Fe, 1990-91, Eye Clinic, Las Vegas, N.Mex., 1990-91; asst. chief ophthalmology, chief vitreo-retinal surgery Trippler Army Med. Ctr., Honolulu, 1991-94, chief ophthalmology, 1994-96, chief vitreo-retinal surgery ophthalmology svc., 1996-97. Chief EENT clinic, chief ophthalmology svc., chief cons. in ophthalmology to comdg. gen. for S.E. regional med. command Dwight D. Eisenhower Army Med. Ctr., Ft. Gordon, Ga., 1997—2000; instr. dept. surgery F. Edward Hebert Sch. Medicine Uniformed Svcs. U. of Health Scis., Bethesda, Md., 1984—2000; instr. U. Hawaii Sch. Medicine, Honolulu, 1992—97; chief of vitreo-retinal surgery Phoenix Indian Med. Ctr., 2001—. Contbr. articles to profl. jours. Life mem. Rep. Nat. Com. Named Rep. of the Yr., Rep. Nat. Com., 2000; fellow Med. Assistance Programs Internat., Reader's Digest, 1976; scholar Citizens Honors, Ottawa U., 1965—69. Mem.: DAV, Ariz. Ophthal. Soc., Ariz. Osteo. Med. Assn., Walter Reed Alumni Assn., Commemorative Air Force, SAR. Avocation: history. Office: Phoenix Indian Med Ctr Ophthalmology Dept Phoenix AZ 85016

RUDD, NICHOLAS, investor, consultant; b. N.Y.C., Mar. 18, 1943; s. Emmanuel and Lucie Lia Rudd; m. Judith Carol Anderson, 1995; children: Alexis Henry, Kenneth Charles. BA, Columbia U., 1964, MBA, 1967. Mem. staff Ford Motor Co., N.Y.C., 1964-65, Young & Rubicam Inc., N.Y.C., 1968-99, sr. v.p. mgmt. svcs., 1980-90, chief info. officer, 1990-95; chief knowledge officer Wunderman Cato Johnson, N.Y.C., 1996-99; prin. Venture Mgmt. Svcs., Inc., 1999—2003, Anderson Rudd Co., 2003—; mktg. chair Stamford Symphony Orch., 2003—. Dir. emeritus Nat. Choral Coun., chmn., 1993-95, Veritas Therapeutic Cmty. Found.; bd. mem. A Better Chance of Westport. Mem. Beta Gamma Sigma. Office: 20 Sea Spray Rd Westport CT 06880

RUDD, RICKY, race car driver; b. Chesapeake, Sept. 12, 1956; m. Linda Rudd; 1 child, Landon. Profl. race car driver NASCAR, 1975—, team owner, driver, 1993—. Named Winston Cup Rookie of Yr., 1977, winner, Riverside, 1983, Banquet Frozen Foods 300, 1989, Bud at the Glen, 1990, TranSouth 500, 1991, Peek Antifreeze 500, 1992, Miller Genuine Draft 400, 1993, Slick 50 300, 1994, Dura Lube 500, 1995, Winston Cup, 1996, AC Delco 400, 1996, Miller 500, 1997, Brickyard 400, 1997, NAPA Autocare 500, 1998, 9th in NASCAR standings, 1995. Office: c/o NASCAR PO Box 2875 Daytona Beach FL 32120-2875

RUDDER, ERIC, information technology executive; married; 2 children. Grad. with honors, Brown U., 1988. Gen. mgr. Visual Studio Microsoft, Redmond, Wash., v.p. tech. strategy, sr. v.p. Developer and Platform Evangelism. Office: Microsoft One Microsoft Way Redmond WA 98052-6399

RUDDICK, PATSY RUTH, retired librarian; b. Arma, Kans., Dec. 16, 1932; d. Joseph Clarence and Eva (Alumbaugh) R. AA, Parsons Jr. Coll., 1952; BS in Edn., Pitts., Kans. State Coll., 1954; MA, U. Denver, 1963. English tchr. Garden City (Kans.) Jr. High Sch., 1954-62; dir. libr. svcs. Garden City Community Coll., Garden City, 1963-94. Active 1st United Meth. Ch., Garden City, RSVP bd. dirs., 1994-1999, 2003—; sec., Friends of Finney County Libr., 1995—, docent and vol., Finney County Hist. Mus., 1994—, v.p. Emmaus House bd., 1991-92, treas., 1992-94, sec., 1994-96. Mem. ALA, Kans. Libr. Assn., Finney County Libr. Assn. (pres. 1985-87), NEA (Kans. State Reading Cir. 1982-86), Kans. Nat. Edn. Assn., Am. Assn. Ret. Persons (adv. coun. on aging), Delta Kappa Gamma (pres. 1966-68).

RUDDLE, NANCY HARTMAN, microbiology educator, microbiologist, researcher; b. St. Louis, Apr. 3, 1940; d. David Eugene and Josephine (Odell) Hartman; m. Francis Hugh Ruddle, Aug. 1, 1964; children: Kathlyn, Amy. BA, Mt. Holyoke Coll., 1962; PhD, Yale U., 1968. Rsch. assoc. Yale U., New Haven, 1968-71, postdoctoral fellow, 1971-74, rsch. assoc., 1974-75, asst. prof., 1975-80, assoc. prof., 1980-91, prof. epidemiology and immunobiology, 1991—, head divsn. epidemiology of microbial diseases, 1990—. Panel mem. Am. Cancer Soc., 1987-91; study sect. mem. NIH, 1991—. Contbr. articles to profl. jours. Recipient Am. Cancer Soc. Faculty Rsch. award; fellow Am. Cancer Soc. postdoctoral fellow, Damon Runyon postdoctoral fellow; grantee NIH grantee, Am. Cancer Soc. grantee, Multiple Sclerosis Soc. grantee. Office: Yale Univ Sch Medicine 60 College St New Haven CT 06510-3210

RUDDY, FRANCIS (FRANK) HENRY, nuclear physicist; b. Worcester, Mass., Sept. 10, 1941; s. Raymond Francis and Marguerite Bernadette Ruddy; m. Geraldine Claire Vilandre, Aug. 11, 1942; children: Jeremy Kim, Matthew Brian, Jennifer Martha Luster, Marc Raymond. Ph D, Simon Fraser U., Can., 1968; AM, Wash. U., St. Louis, Mo., 1965; A B, Clark U., 1963. Postdoctoral assoc. SUNY, Stony Brook, NY, 1968—72; asst. prof. Wash. State U., Pullman, Wash., 1972—77; sr. scientist Westinghouse Hanford Co., Richland, Wash., 1977—85; cons. scientist Westinghouse Electric Co., Pitts., 1985—. Editor: (book) Reactor Dosimetry: Radiation Metrology and Assessment (George Westinghouse Signature Award, 1989, 1999). Recipient award of Appreciation, ASTM, 1991, 1994, 1997, 2000. Mem.: ASTM (symposium com. chmn. 1994—2000), Am. Nuc. Soc. Achievements include 20 U.S. patents; More than 100 peer-reviewed scientific publications. Office: Westinghouse Electric Company 1332 Beulah Rd Pittsburgh PA 15235-5081 E-mail: ruddyfh@westinghouse.com.

RUDDY, FRANK, lawyer, former ambassador; b. NYC, Sept. 15, 1937; s. Francis Stephen and Teresa (O'Neil) Ruddy; children: Neil, David, Stephen. AB, Holy Cross Coll., 1959; MA, NYU, 1962, LLM, 1967; LLB, Loyola U., New Orleans, 1965; PhD, Cambridge U., Eng., 1969. Bar: D.C., N.Y., Tex., U.S. Supreme Ct. Faculty Cambridge U., 1967-69; asst. gen. counsel USIA, Washington, 1969-72; sr. atty. Office of Telecomm. Policy, White House, Washington, 1972-73; dep. gen. counsel USIA, Washington, 1973-74; counsel Exxon Corp., Houston, 1974-81; asst. adminstr. AID (with rank asst. sec. state) Dept. State, Washington, 1981-84; U.S. ambassador to Equatorial Guinea, 1984-88; gen. counsel U.S. Dept. Energy, Washington, 1988-89; v.p. Sierra Blanca Devel. Corp., Washington, 1989-92; ptnr. Ruddy & Muir, Washington, 1998—. Vis. scholar Johns Hopkins Sch. Advanced Internat. Studies, 1990—94; dep. chmn. UN Referendum for Western Sahara, 1994. Author: International Law in the Enlightenment, 1975; editor: American International Law Cases (series); editor in chief Internat. Lawyer; contbr. articles to legal jours. Bd. dirs. African Devel. Found., Washington, 1983-84, Human Life Internat., 1999—; mem. Coun. of Am. Ambs., Washington, 1988—. Served with USMCR, 1956-61 Mem.: ABA (chmn. treaty compliance sect. 1991—93), Hague Acad. Internat. Law Alumni Assn., Internat. Law Assn., Am. Soc. Internat. Law, Dacor House, Cosmos Club (Washington), Knights of Malta. Republican. Roman Catholic. Office: Ruddy and Muir 1717 K Street NW Ste 600 Washington DC 20036 Home: 203 Croydon Ave Rockville MD 20850-4145 Office Phone: 202-835-0055. Personal E-mail: fruddy@hotmail.com. E-mail: global@globalltd.com.

RUDDY, JAMES VINCENT, JR., tax advocate; b. N.Y.C., June 15, 1941; s. James Vincent Ruddy and Stella Rotas; m. Judy Anne Garland, Mar.21, 1964 (div. Feb. 1998); children: David George, James Vincent, Jason Nicholas; m. Gwyn Goettig, Nov. 2000. BS Elec. Engring., U.S. Missile Warfare Sch., 1964; JD, LaSalle U., 1966; BS in Aeronautical/Astron. Engring., AET in Indsl. Engring., Embry Riddle Aeronautical U., 1968; diploma in securities law, ITT Hartford Group, 1969, diploma in life, health and accident insurance law, diploma in property and casualty insurance law, ITT Hartford Group, 1972; BS, MS, PhD emphasis in human nutrition, Am. Coll. Nutrition, 1995; D of Naturopathy, Clayton Sch. of Medicine, 1996; diploma in real estate, real estate appraisal law, U. Conn., 1972; MS in Computer Sci., Inst. of Computer Sci.; diploma in Fed. Tax Practice, Nat. Tax Practice Inst.; LLM, Washington Law Sch. Lic. real estate broker, ship capt. and master seaman for inland and ocean waters USCG; cert. gen. appraiser, environ. assessor phase I, II, and III, livestock agrl. assessor. Embalmer Rhee Lowe Funeral Home, Miami, 1960-63; instr. Embry-Riddle Aero Inst., Daytona Beach, Fla., 1966-68; rsch. engr. Avco Lycoming, Stratford, Conn., 1968-72; cons., pres. Cons. Assocs., Milford, Conn., 1979-97; tax advocate Sleepy Eye, Minn., 1994—, Goettig Erickson, Sleepy Eye, 1997—; adminstr. Profl. Arbitration Assn., 1999—. Author: Jet and Rocket Propulsion, 1967; six patents in electro-mechanical design. With U.S. Army, 1963-69. Mem.: AIAA, N.Y. Acad. Scis., Nat. Tax Practice Inst. Grad. Fellows Orgn., Nat. Assn. Enrolled Agts., Environ. Assessment Assn., AAIS, Innovation Group. Roman Catholic. Avocations: oceanography, flying, computers, preventative medicine. Office: Goettig Ruddy Ltd 128 Main St W Sleepy Eye MN 56085-1328

RUDDY, JAMES W. lawyer; b. 1949; AB, U. Mich., 1971; JD, Wayne State U., 1973. Bar: Wash. 1974, Mich. 1974. Assoc. gen. counsel Safeco Corp., 1984-89, v.p., gen. counsel, 1989—, now sr. v.p., gen. counsel. Office: Safeco Corp Safeco Plz T 22 Seattle WA 98185-0001

RUDE, BRIAN DAVID, utilities company executive; b. Viroqua, Wis., Aug. 25, 1955; s. Raymond and Conelee (Johnson) R.; m. Karen Thulin; children: Erik, Nels. BA magna cum laude, Luther Coll., 1977; MA, U. Wis., Madison, 1994. Mem. Wis. Assembly, Madison, 1982-84, Wis. Senate, Madison, 1984-2000; pres. Wis. State Sen., 1993-96, 98. With corp. comms. The Trane Co., La Crosse, Wis., 1981-85; dir. external rels. Dairyland Power Coop. Mem. LaCrosse C. of C. (chair), Lions, Sons of Norway, Norwegian-Am. Hist. Assn. (bd. dirs.), WWTC Found., Rotary. Republican. Lutheran. Avocations: reading, gardening, travel, fishing. Home: 307 Babcock St PO Box 367 Coon Valley WI 54623-0367 Office: 3200 East Ave S PO Box 817 La Crosse WI 54602 E-mail: bdr@dairynet.com.

RUDEE, MERVYN LEA, engineering educator, researcher; s. Mervyn C. and Hannah Rudee; m. Elizabeth Eager, 1958; children: Elizabeth Diane, David Benjamin. BS, Stanford U., 1958, MS, 1962, PhD, 1965. Asst. prof. materials sci. Rice U., Houston, 1964-68, assoc. prof., 1968-72, prof. materials sci., 1972-74; prof. U. Calif. San Diego, La Jolla, 1974—, founding provost Warren Coll., 1974-82, founding dean Sch. Engring., 1982-93, coord. grad. program on materials sci., 1994-99, faculty athletic rep., 1999—; interim dean engring. U. Calif., Riverside, 1995-97. Vis. scholar Corpus Christi Coll., Cambridge, Eng., 1971-72; vis. scientist IBM Thomas J. Watson Rsch. Ctr., Yorktown Heights, N.Y., 1987; dir. fellows program Calif. Coun. on Sci. and Tech., 1999-2000. Pres., bd. trustees Mus. Photographic Art, San Diego, 1995-96; trustee The Burnham Inst., 1998—, The Glen Canyon Inst., 1999—. Lt. (j.g.) USN, 1958-61. Guggenheim fellow, 1971-72. Fellow AAAS; mem. Microscopy Soc. Am., Materials Rsch. Soc., Tex. Soc. Electron Microscopy (hon., pres. 1966), Sigma Xi, Tau Beta Pi. Office: U Calif San Diego Dept Elec & Computer Enging La Jolla CA 92093-0407 Office Phone: 858-534-8998. E-mail: rudee@ucsd.edu.

RUDEL, JULIUS, conductor; b. Vienna, Mar. 6, 1921; came to U.S., 1938, naturalized, 1944; s. Jakob and Josephine (Sonnenblum) R.; m. Rita Gillis, June 24, 1942 (dec. May 1984); children: Joan, Madeleine, Anthony Jason. Student, Acad. Music, Vienna; diploma in conducting, Mannes Coll. Music, 1942; diploma hon. doctorates, U. Vt., 1961, U. Mich., 1971; doctorates hon. causa, Pace Coll., Manhattan Coll., 1994, Mannes Coll. Music, 1994, Manhattanville Coll., 1994, Manhattan Sch. Music, 1996. With N.Y. City Opera, 1943-79, debut, 1944, gen. dir., 1957-79, 3rd St. Music Sch. Settlement, 1945-52, mus. dir. Chautauqua Opera Assn., 1958-59, Caramoor Festival, Katonah, N.Y., 1964-76, Cin. May Festival, 1971-72, Kennedy Ctr. Performing Arts, 1971-75; music advisor Wolf Trap Farm Pk., 1971, Phila. Opera, 1978-81; condr. Spoleto (Italy) Festival, 1962-63; music dir. Buffalo Philarm. Orch., 1979-85, debut as condr. Met. Opera, 1978, San Francisco Opera, 1979, Vienna State Opera, 1976, Royal Opera, Covent Garden, 1984, Rome Opera, 1987, Opera de la Bastille, 1992, Teatro Colon, Buenos Aires, 1992, Royal Danish Opera, Copenhagen, 1993, L.A. Opera, 1995; dir. prodn.: Kiss Me Kate, Vienna Volksoper Opera, 1956; prin. ghest condr. Palm Beach Opera, 2003; guest condr. Chgo. Symphony, Phila. Orch., N.Y. Philharm., Boston Symphony, Detroit Symphony, Israel Philharm., Paris Opera, Munich Opera, Hamburg State Opera, Vienna State Opera, other symphonic, operatic orgns. in U.S. and Europe. Decorated Croix du Chevalier in arts and letters France; recipient gold medal Nat. Arts Club, 1958, citation Nat. Assn. Am. Composers and Conductors, 1958, citation Nat. Fedn. Music Clubs, 1959, Ditson award Columbia, 1959, Page One award in music Newspaper Guild, 1959, hon. insignia for arts and sci. Govt. of Austria, 1961, Handel medallion for music City N.Y., 1965, citation Nat. Assn. Negro Musicians, 1965, citation Nat. Opera Assn., 1971, comdr.'s Cross German Order Merit, 1967, hon. lt. Israeli Army, 1969, Julius Rudel award for young condrs., Pan Am./Pan African award for humanism, 1981, Peabody award, 1985, Disting. Achievement award Kurt Weill Found., 2000. Office: c/o Shuman Assocs 120 W 58th St Apt 8D New York NY 10019-2126 Office Phone: 212-315-1300.

RUDELIUS, WILLIAM, marketing educator; b. Rockford, Ill., Sept. 2, 1931; s. Carl William and Clarissa Euclid (Davis) R.; m. Jacqueline Urch Dunham, July 3, 1954; children: Robert, Jeanne, Katherine, Kristi. BS in Mech. Engring., U. Wis., 1953; MBA, U. Pa., 1959, PhD in Econs., 1964. Program engr., missile and space vehicle dept. Gen. Electric Co., Phila., 1956-57, 59-61; sr. research economist North Star Research Inst., Mpls., 1964-66; lectr. U. Minn., Mpls., 1961-64, asst. prof. mktg. Coll. Bus. Adminstrn., 1964, assoc. prof., 1966-72, prof., 1972—. Co-author: (with W. Bruce Erickson) An Introduction to Contemporary Business, 1973, rev. 4th edit., 1985, (with Eric N. Berkowitz, Roger A. Kerin and Steven W. Hartley) Marketing, 1986, rev. 7th edit., 2003, (with Krzysztof Przybytowski, Roger A. Kerin and Steven W. Hartley) Marketing na Przykładach, 1998, (with others) Mapketkht, 1st Russian edit., 2001; contbr. articles to profl. jours. Served USAF, 1954—55. Home: 1425 Alpine Pass Minneapolis MN 55416-3560 Office: U Minn Dept Applied Econs 130 Classroom Office Bldg 1994 Buford Ave Saint Paul MN 55108-6040 Office Phone: 612-624-4788. E-mail: rudelius@umn.edu.

RUDENSTINE, NEIL LEON, former academic administrator, educator; b. Ossining, NY, Jan. 21, 1935; s. Harry and Mae (Esperito) R.; m. Angelica Zander, Aug. 27, 1960; children: Antonia Margaret, Nicholas David, Sonya. BA, Princeton U., 1956; BA (Rhodes Scholar), Oxford U., 1959, MA, 1963; PhD, Harvard U., 1964. Instr. dept. English Harvard U., Cambridge, Mass., 1964-66, asst. prof., 1966-68; assoc. prof. English Princeton (N.J.) U., 1968-73, prof. English, 1973-88, dean of students, 1968-72, dean of Coll., 1972-77, provost, 1977-88, provost emeritus, 1988—; exec. v.p. Andrew W. Mellon Found., N.Y.C., 1988-91; pres. Harvard U., Cambridge, Mass., 1991-2001, prof. English, 1991-2001, pres. emeritus, 2001—. Chair bd. ArtStor, A.W. Mellon Found., 2001—. Author: Sidney's Poetic Development, 1967, Pointing Our Thoughts, 2001; (with George Rousseau) English Poetic Satire, 1972; (with William Bowen) In Pursuit of the PhD, 1992. Trustee Princeton U., N.Y. Pub. Libr., Courtauld Inst. Art, London, Goldman Sachs Found. 1st lt. arty. U.S. Army, 1959—60. Hon. fellow New Coll./Oxford U., Emmanuel Coll./Cambridge U., 1991. Fellow Am. Acad. Arts and Scis.; mem. Am. Philos. Soc., Coun. on Fgn. Rels., Com. for Econ. Devel. Office: AW Mellon Found 140 E 62d St New York NY 10021 Business E-Mail: nlr@mellon.org.

RUDER, DAVID STURTEVANT, lawyer, educator, government official; b. Wausau, Wis., May 25, 1929; s. George Louis and Josephine (Sturtevant) R.; m. Susan M. Small; children: Victoria Chesley, Julia Larson, David Sturtevant II, John Coulter; m stepchildren: Elizabeth Frankel, Rebecca Wilkinson. BA cum laude, Williams Coll., 1951; JD with honors, U. Wis., 1957, LLD, 2002. Bar: Wis. 1957, Ill. 1962. Of counsel Schiff Hardin & Waite, Chgo., 1971-76; assoc. Quarles & Brady, Milw., 1957-61; asst. prof. law Northwestern U., Chgo., 1961-63, assoc. prof., 1963-65, prof., 1965—, William W. Gurley meml. prof. of law, 1994—, assoc. dean Law Sch., 1965-66, dean Law Sch., 1977-85; chmn. Securities and Exch. Commn., Washington, 1987-89; ptnr. Baker & McKenzie, Chgo., 1990-94, sr. counsel, 1994-99. Cons. Am. Law Inst. Fed. Securities Code; planning dir. Corp. Counsel Inst., 1962-66, 76-77, com. mem., 1962-87, 90—; adv. bd. Ray Garrett Jr. Corp. and Securities Law Inst., 1980-87, 90—; vis. lectr. U. de Liege, 1967; vis. prof. law U. Pa., Phila., 1971; faculty Salzburg Seminar, 1976; mem. legal adv. com. bd. dirs. N.Y. Stock Exch., 1978-82; mem. com. profl. responsibility Ill. Supreme Ct., 1978-87; adv. bd. Securities Regulation Inst., 1978—, chmn., 1994-97; bd. govs. Nat. Assn. Securities Dealers, 1990-93, chmn. Legal Adv. Bd., 1993-96, Arbitration Policy Task Force, 1994-97; trustee Fin. Acctg. Found., 1996-2002, Internat. Acctg. Stds. Com. Found., 2000—; mem. Internat. Acctg. Stds. Com. Strategy Working Party, 1997-99; chmn. Securities and Exch. Commn. Hist. Soc., 1999—2004; chmn. Mut. Fund Dirs. Forum, 1999—. Editor-in-chief: Williams Coll. Record, 1950-51, U. Wis. Law Rev., 1957; editor: Proc. Corp. Counsel Inst, 1962-66; contbr. articles to legal periodicals. 1st lt. AUS, 1951-54. Fellow Am. Bar Found.; ABA (sec. bus. law 1970—, coun. 1970-94, com. chmn., mem. various coms.), Chgo. Bar Assn., Wis. Bar Assn., Am. Law Inst., Order of Coif, Comml. Club of Chgo., Lawyers Club Chgo., Gargoyle Soc., Phi Beta Kappa, Phi Delta Phi, Zeta Psi. Home: 325 Orchard Ln Highland Park IL 60035-1939 Office Phone: 312-503-8444.

RUDER, USHA C. pathologist; b. Bangalore, India, May 9, 1943; arrived in U.S., 1969; d. Subramanian and Kamala; m. Chunilal B. Ruder, Dec. 4, 1969; children: Sharmila, Sonali. Pre-med., Sophia Coll.; MD, G.S. Med. Coll. Diplomate Am. Bd. Pathology, 1975, lic. N.Y., 1972. Intern G.S. Med. Coll., Bombay; resident L.I. Jewish Hosp., N.Y.C.; pathologist, dir. Cath. Med. Ctr., N.Y.C., 1975—97, chair, 1997—. Office: St Vincent Cath Med Ctr 152-11 89th Ave New York NY 11432

RUDER, WILLIAM, public relations executive; b. N.Y.C., Oct. 17, 1921; s. Jacob L. and Rose (Rosenberg) R.; m. Betty Cott, May 23, 1980; children: Robin Ann, Abby, Brian, Michal Ellen, Eric. BSS, City Coll., N.Y., 1942. With Samuel Goldwyn Prodns., 1946-48; pres. Ruder & Finn, Inc., N.Y.C., 1948-80, William Ruder Inc., 1981—. Asst. sec. commerce, 1961-62; Tobe lectr. Harvard Grad. Sch. Bus., 1962; mem. grad. adv. bd. City Coll. N.Y., Baruch Sch. Bus., N.Y.C.; cons. State Dept.; bd. dirs. W.P. Carey & Co., Inc.; trustee Continuum Health Ptnrs., Inc. Author: The Businessman's Guide to Washington. Bd. dirs. Bus. Com. for Arts, Jewish Bd. Guardians, Chamber Music Soc. Lincoln Ctr., Fund for Peace, Project Return Found.; exec. com. United Way Am.; trustee, chmn. Manhattanville Coll., Purchase, N.Y., 1974-75; trustee Com. for Econ. Devel., St. Lukes/ Roosevelt Hosp.; bd. overseers Wharton Sch. U. Pa.; mem. pres.'s coun. Meml. Sloan-Kettering Cancer Ctr.; chmn. bd. ACCESS. Capt. USAAF, 1941-45. Mem. UN Assn. U.S.A. (nat. policy panel dir., trustee com. for econ. devel.). Home: PO Box 230 East Hampton NY 11937 Office: Ruder Finn Inc 301 E 57th St New York NY 10022-2900

RUDERMAN, ARMAND PETER, health economics educator, consultant, volunteer; b. Bklyn., Nov. 19, 1923; s. Louis and Lillian (Prigohzy) R.; m. Alice Helen Holton, June 17, 1948 (dec. June 2003); children: Ann, Mary, William, John. SB, Harvard U., 1943, MA, 1946, PhD, 1947; MBA, U. Chgo., 1944. Prof. econs. various U.S. univs., 1946-50; statistician, economist ILO, Pan.-Am. Health Orgn., WHO, 1950-67; chmn. sci. working group on social and econ. aspects of tropical disease research WHO/TDR, 1979-83; prof. health adminstrn. U. Toronto, Ont., Can., 1967-75; founding dean adminstrv. studies Dalhousie U., N.S., Can., 1975-80, prof. health adminstrn., 1981-89, prof. emeritus, 1989—. Vis. prof. Nat. U. Singapore, 1982-83, adj. prof. health adminstrn. U. S.C., 1983—; cons. in field. Contbr. articles to profl. jours. Bd. dirs. Northwood Manor, 1987-89, Northwestern Gen. Hosp., Toronto, 1991-96, Baker Ctr., 2000—; mem. Etobicoke Bd. Health, 1991-95; cmty. adv. com. Toronto Hosp., 1992-95, 97-02; region 3 exec. com. Ont. Hosp. Assn., 1994-96. Mem. Royal Econ. Soc. E-mail: apeterr@idirect.com.

RUDERMAN, WARREN, chemist; b. N.Y.C., Jan. 7, 1920; s. Jack and Mollie (Ettin) R.; m. Carol Carver Schmied, June 15, 1945; children: Barbara, Clifford, William, Genevieve. PhD, Columbia U., 1949. Rsch. scientist, lectr. in chemistry Columbia U., N.Y.C., 1947-54; pres., founder Isomet Corp., Oakland, N.J., 1954-73; founder, chmn., CEO, pres. INRAD Inc., Northvale, NJ, 1973—2000; founder, pres. INCRYS, Demarest, NJ, 2002—. Chmn. bd. trustees Demarest Bapt. Ch. Fellow N.Y. Acad. Scis.; mem. Am. Chem. Soc., Am. Phys. Soc., Optical Soc. Am. Republican. Office: INCRY Inc 45 Duane Ln Demarest NJ 07627 Office Phone: 201-768-0403. E-mail: warrud@optonline.net.

RUDGE, HOWARD J. corporate lawyer; BA, BS, Bucknell U., 1958; JD, George Washington U. Nat. Law Ctr., 1964. Bar: D.C. 1964, Va. 1964. V.p., gen. counsel Conoco, Inc., 1988-90, sr. v.p., gen. counsel, 1990-94, Du Pont De Nemours & Co., Wilmington, Del., 1994—. Office: DuPont De Nemours & Co 1007 Market St Wilmington DE 19801-1227

RUDICH, STEVEN MARK, surgeon; b. Bklyn., N.Y., Dec. 30, 1958; s. Sheldon Seymor and Lois Lee Rudich; m. Donna Marie Cirasole, May 25, 1991; children: Jacquelyn Shea, Alexander David. MD, Mt. Sinai Sch. of Medicine, N.Y.C., 1989; PhD, CUNY, 1987. Diplomate Am. Bd. Surgery. Attending surgeon Univ of Calif., Davis Med. Ctr, Sacramento, 1996—99; dir., organ perfusion svcs. Univ of Mich., Ann Arbor, 1999—2002; dir., liver transplant svcs. Univ of Cin. Coll. of Medicine, 2002—. Cons. Barr Labs., Woodcliff Lake, NJ, 2003—. Fellow: ACS; mem.: Ctrl. Surg. Assoc, Am. Assoc for the Study of Liver Diseases, The Transplantation Soc., Internat. Soc. of Organ Preservation, Assoc for Acad. Surgery, Am. Hepato-Pancreato-Biliary Assn., Internat. Liver Transplantation Soc., The Cin. Surg. Soc., The Frederick Coller Soc., Am. Soc. of Transplant Surgeons (Young Investigator Award 2001), Sigma Xi. Achievements include research in Use of extracorporeal support to improve donor organs. Office: Univ of Cincinnati Coll of Medicine 231 Albert Sabin Way PO Box 670558 Cincinnati OH 45267-0558 Office Phone: 513-558-3892. E-mail: rudichs@uc.edu.

RUDICK, A. JOSEPH, research and development company executive; BA in Chemistry, Williams Coll., 1979; MD, U. Pa., 1983. Ptnr. Assoc. Ophthalmologists PC, NY, 1988—; co-founder Healthdesk Corp., 1993, dir., 1993—98; v.p. Paramount Capital, Inc., 1994—98; founder Optex (subs. Atlantic Tech. Ventures, Inc.), Channel (subs. Atlantic Tech. Ventures, Inc.), Atlantic Tech. Ventures, Inc., bus. cons., 1997—98, pres., 1999—2000, dir., 1999—, 2000—. Office: Atlantic Technology Ventures Inc 787 7th Ave New York NY 10019-6018

RUDIGER, LANCE WADE, secondary school educator; b. Bklyn., Mar. 27, 1948; s. H.F. and Muriel Marie (Staudermann) R.; 1 child, Heidi. BS in Chemistry, SUNY, Albany, 1976; MEd, St. Lawrence U., 1982. Cert. tchr., N.Y. Tchr. chemistry Potsdam H.S., 1982—, chmn. dept. sci., 1992—. Adj. prof. Canton (N.Y.) Coll. Tech., Mater Dei Coll., Ogdensburg, N.Y., Empire Coll., Albany, 1986—; tchr. Inst. Chem. Edn.-Sci. demonstration; bd. dirs., treas. St. Lawrence Valley Tchrs. Learning Ctr., Canton; sci. coord. Upward Bound St. Lawrence U.; program com., bd. dirs. N.Y. Assn. State Computers & Tech. in Edn.; writer for N.Y. State Regents chemistry core curriculum; mem. N.Y. State Part D Performance Regents Test Devel. Com.; mem. SED Regents Benchmark Commn.; item writer NYS Chem. Regents; mem. NYSED-McGraw Hill Chemistry Regents Anchor Com. Co-author: Chemistry Environment, 1990. Bd. dirs. March of Dimes N.Y. State, Syracuse, N.Y. State chemistry regional and state coord. mentor; mem. environ. mgmt. bd. St. Lawrence County, 1997-, edn. com. chair, 1999-, vice chair, 2003-; mem. bd.

examiners Nat. Coun. Accreditation Tchr. Edn., 2001—. Recipient Newmast award NASA, 1987, Dreyfus Master Tchr. award, 1989, Fulbright Symposium award Australia, 2002; grantee NSTA-FDA, 2003, Am. Chem Soc., Woodrow Wilson Found., Binghamtom U. Step Program, St. Lawrence Valley Tchrs. Ctr., 1991-98, Sweetwater Found., Miami U. (Ohio), 1995, Johns Hopkins Space Grant Consortium, Wright Ctr. for Aerospace and Space Engring., Reynolds Metals Excellence in Edn., 1990-94, Cornell U. Sci. Workshop, IRIS; named solar sys. amb. Jet Propulsion Lab., NASA. Mem. Nat. Sci. Tchrs. Assn. (local leader, manuscript review adv. panel The Sci. Tchr., sci. safety com. 2000, webwatchers 2001, Exxon BaP key leader and North Country liaison), Nat. Radio Astronomy Obs. (assoc., mentor astronomy workshop), Am. Astron. Soc. (tchr. resource agent 1996-98, Leadership Workshop award 1998), Sci. Tchrs. Assn. N.Y. State (bd. dirs. 1990—, chmn. sect. 1992—, fin. com. 2000—, grant com. chair, presenter at convs. 1988—, hospitality chair ann. conf. NYSC & TE 1996, 98, 2000, del.-at-large 2004-), North Country Conservation Edn. Assn. (life), USCG Acad. Nat. Parents Assn. (bd. dirs. 1997-98), N.Y. State Tchr. Cert. Exam Adv. Com., Canton Club, Lions (past pres. Waddington, N.Y., Pres.'s award, bd. dirs. Canton, pres. 1997 98, treas. 1998-99, dir. 1999-2003), Potsdam Kiwanis (charter, bd. dirs. 1989-91), Phi Delta Kappa (rsch. dir., v.p. program 1999, v.p. membership, pres. 2001—). Home: 54 Court St Canton NY 13617-1159 Office: Potsdam High School Leroy St Potsdam NY 13676-1798

RUDIN, ANNE, retired mayor, nursing educator; b. Passaic, N.J., Jan. 27, 1924; m. Edward Rudin, June 6, 1948; 4 children BS in Edn., Temple U., 1945, RN, 1946; MPA, U. So. Calif., 1983; LLD (hon.), Golden Gate U., 1990. RN, Calif. Mem. faculty Temple U. Sch. Nursing, Phila., 1946-48; mem. nursing faculty Mt. Zion Hosp., San Francisco, 1948 49; mem. Sacramento City Council, 1971-83; mayor City of Sacramento, 1983-92; ind. pub. policy cons. Pres. LWV, Riverside, 1957, Sacramento, 1961, Calif., 1969-71, Calif. Elected Women's Assn., 1973—; trustee Golden Gate U., 1993-96; mem. adv. bd. U. So. Calif., Army Depot Reuse Commn., 1992-94; bd. dirs. Sacramento Theatre Co., 1992-99, Japan Soc. No. Calif., Sacramento Symphony, 1993-96, Calif. Common Cause, 1993 -96, Sacramento Edn. Found., 1993-2004; v.p. Sacramento Traditional Jazz Soc. Found.; pres. bd. dirs. Natomas Basin Conservancy; foreman Sacramento County Grand Jury, 2000-01. Recipient Women in Govt. award U.S. Jaycee Women, 1984, Woman of Distinction award Sacramento Area Soroptimist Clubs, 1985, Civic Contbn. award LWV Sacramento, 1989, Woman of Courage award Sacramento History Ctr., 1989, Peacemaker of Yr. award Sacramento Mediation Ctr., 1992, Regional Pride award Sacramento Mag., 1993, Humanitarian award Japanese Am. Citizen's League, 1993, Outstanding Pub. Svc. award Am. Soc. Pub. Adminstrn., 1994; named Girl Scouts Am. Role model, 1989, Cmty. Svc. Recognition award, Japanese Am. Citizens League, 1999, Sacramento Traditional Jazz Soc. Hall of Fame, 2000.

RUDIN, SCOTT, film and theatre producer; b. N.Y.C., July 14, 1958; Prodn. asst., asst. to theatre prodrs. Kermit Bloomgarden and Robert Whitehead; casting dir. motion pictures and theatre, prodr. with Edgar Scherick, exec. v.p. prodn. 20th Century Fox, 1984-86, pres. prodn., 1986-87; founder Scott Rudin Prodns., 1990—. Prodr. (films) Mrs. Soffel, 1984, Flatliners, 1990, Pacific Heights, 1990, Regarding Henry, 1991, Little Man Tate, 1991, The Addams Family, 1991, Sister Act, 1992, Jennifer Eight, 1992, Life With Mikey, 1993, The Firm, 1993, Searching for Bobby Fischer, 1993, Sister Act 2, 1993, Addams Family Values, 1993, I.Q., 1994, Nobody's Fool, 1994, Sabrina, 1995, Clueless, 1995, Up Close and Personal, 1996, Ransom, 1996, Marvin's Room, 1996, The First Wives Club, 1996, In and Out, 1997, Twilight, 1998, The Truman Show, 1998, A Civil Action, 1998. Wonder Boys, 1999, Rules of Engagement, 1999, Brokeback Mountain, 1999, Angela's Ashes, 1999, South park: Bigger, Longer and Uncut, 1999 (exec.), Bringing Out the Dead, 1999, Sleepy Hollow, 1999; (TV movies) Revenge of the Stepford Wives, 1980, He Makes Me Feel Like Dancing, 1982 (Outstanding Children's Program Emmy award 1982, Feature Documentary Acad. award 1982); (theatre) Passion, 1994 (Best Musical Tony award 1994), Indiscretions, 1995, Hamlet, 1995, Seven Guitars, 1995, Skylight, 1997, A Funny Thing Happened on the Way to the Forum, 1996, On the Town (with the N.Y. Shakespeare Festival), 1997, The Chairs, 1998, The Judas Kiss, 1998, (London) Closer, 1998, The Blue Room, 1998, Closer, 1999, Amy's View, 1999, Wide Guys, 1999, Copenhagen, 1999 (Tony Award); (off broadway) Stupid Kids, 1998, The Most Fabulous Story Ever Told, 1999, Shaft, 2000. Office: Scott Rudin Prodns c/o Starr & Co 350 Park Ave 9th Fl New York NY 10022

RUDLIN, DAVID ALAN, lawyer; b. Richmond, Va., Nov. 4, 1947; s. Herbert and Dorothy Jean (Durham) R.; m. Judith Bond Faulkner, Oct. 4, 1975; 1 child, Sara Elizabeth. BA with high distinction, U. Va., 1969, JD with honors, 1973. Bar: Va. 1973, U.S. Dist. Ct. (ea. dist.) Va. 1975, U.S. Ct. Appeals (4th cir.) 1975, U.S. Ct. Appeals (10th cir.) 1980, U.S. Ct. Appeals (2d cir.) 1983, U.S. Supreme Ct. 1979. Assoc. gen. counsel U.S. Commn. on Orgn. of Govt. for Conduct Fgn. Policy, Washington, 1973-75; assoc. Hunton & Williams, Richmond, 1975-82, ptnr., 1982—. Adj. faculty civil litigation, appellate practice, libel litigation Duke Univ. Law Sch., Univ. Richmond, T.C. Williams Sch. of Law, Washington and Lee Sch. of Law, William and Mary Sch. of Law, U. Va. Sch. of Law; faculty mem. Boulder and S.E. Regional programs Nat. Inst. Trial Advocacy; faculty mem. Am. Law Inst. ABA. Author: (book chpts.) Toxic Torts: Litigation of Hazardous Substances Cases, 1983, 2d edit., 1992, Federal Litigation Guide, 1989, Corporate Counselor's Guide to Environmental Law, 1989, Sanctions: Rule 11 and Other Powers, 1992, Business and Commercial Litigation in Federal Courts, 1997, Corp. Counsel's Guide to ADR Techniques, 1999, Successful Partnering Between Inside and Outside COunsel, 1999; contbr. articles to profl. jours. and mags., chpts. to books; mem. bd. editl. advisors The Environ. Counselor, Chesterland, Ohio, 1989—, The Toxics Law Reporter, Washington, 1988—. Alumni Metro Leadership Richmond, 1988-89. Mem. ABA (chmn. litig. sect. environ. litig. com. 1985-88, co-chmn. litig. sect. liaison with jud. com. 1988-91, vice-chmn. toxic and hazardous substances and environ. law com. tort and ins. practice sect. 1988-91, co-liaison to standing com. on environ. law from environ. litig. com. litig. sect. 1988-92, dir. div. IV litig. sect. 1991-95, litig. sect. co-chair programs subcom. first amendment and media litig. com. 1993—, mem. litig. sect. task force on specialization 1994—, co-chair litigation sect., 1997, specialization 1994—, mem. litigation sect. task foce on justice sys. 1994—, litigation sect. liaison to ABA jud. adminstrn. divsn. task force on reducion of litigation cost and delay 1995—, co-chair litigation sect. 1997 ann. meeting Washington 1995-97, chair toxic torts and environ. litigation committee sect. of Environment, Energy and Resources 1997-2000; council mem. litigation sect. 1997-2000, co-chair report card on the litigation section, 2000), Am. Arbitration Assn. (Va. mediation panel 1996—), Va. Bar Assn. (chair joint com. on alt. dispute resolution with Va. State Bar 1991-97, exec. com. mem.), Richmond Bar Assn. (chmn. mem. com. 1988-91, mem. judiciary com. 1991-94, mem. continuing legal edn. com. 1994-96), Va. Assn. Def. Attys., CPR Inst. Dispute Resolution (products liability com. 1988, 97—, judge Ann. Awards in Alt. Dispute Resolution 1990—, mem. panels disting. neutrals Va. 1997—), Va. Bar Assn. (mem. exec. com. 2001), Internat. Assn. Def. Counsel. Office: Hunton & Williams LLP Riverfront Pla E Tower 951 E Byrd St Richmond VA 23219-4074 Fax: 804-788-8218. E-mail: arudlin@hunton.com.

RUDLOFF, WILLIAM JOSEPH, lawyer; b. Bonne Terre, Mo., Feb. 19, 1941; s. Leslie W. and Alta M. (Hogenmiller) R.; m. Rita Howton, Aug. 5, 1965; children: Daniel, Andrea, Leslie, Susan. AB, Western Ky. U., 1961; JD, Vanderbilt U., 1965. Bar: Ky. 1965, Tenn. 1965, U.S. Supreme Ct. 1975, U.S. Ct. Appeals (sixth cir.) 1981. U.S. magistrate Western Dist. Ky., 1971-75. NDEA fellow U. Nebr., 1961-62, U. Ky. fellow. Fellow: Ky. Bar Found. (life; charter); mem.: Internat. Acad. Litigators (diplomate), Ky. Acad. Trial Attys., Am. Coll. Legal Medicine, Trial Attys. Am., Def. Rsch. Inst., Am. Counsel Assn., Am. Bd. Trial Advocates. Home: 126 Broadway St Smiths Grove KY 42171-8258 Office: 553 E Main St Bowling Green KY 42101-2256 E-mail: rudloff@aol.com.

RUDMAN, JOAN ELEANOR, artist, educator; b. Owensburg, Ind., Oct. 7, 1927; d. William Hobart and Elizabeth Joaquin (Edington) Combs; m. William Rudman, June 9, 1951; children: Mary Beth, Pamela Ann. BA, Mich. State U., 1949, MA, 1951. Tchr. Arlington Jr. and H.S., Poughkeepsie, NY, Rippowam H.S., Stamford, Conn., North Branch Club, West Dover, Vt.; artist, demonstrator Round Hill Cmty. House, Greenwich; artist-in-residence So. Vt. Arts Ctr., Manchester, Peony Festival at Hildene, Manchester, 2000; jury of selection Hudson Valley Art Assn., 1971—, pres., 2000; selection and awards juror 2d Bergen County Mus. Open Mems. Juried Awards-Allied Artist, NY; dir. Watercolor Workshops, Greenwich; liaison to Metro Mus. Catharine Lorillard Wolfe Art Club; watercolor lectr. and demonstrator tri-state area.; chair Millennium-Larry Rivers Show, Art Soc. of Old Greenwich benefit, 1999—; juried show, 1996—2002; agt. Larry River's Band; guest spkr., guest tchr. 2-day workshop Vt. Watercolor Soc., Chester; watercolor juror Walter Brooks Meml. Watercolor Show, Rowaton, Conn. One-woman shows include Burning Tree Country Club, Greenwich, Town and Country Club, Hartford, Conn., U. Conn., Stamford, Conn. Valley Art Gallery, New Milford, So. Vt. Arts Ctr., Manchester, The Nathaniel Witherall Gallery, Greenwich, Burke Rehab. Ctr., White Plains, N.Y.; exhibited in group shows at Wadsworth Antheneum, 1970, Mus. of Am. Art, New Britain, Conn., So. Vt. Art Ctr., Manchester, 1980-81, Nature Ctr., Westport, Conn., 1979-80, Mus. Fine Arts, Springfield, Mass., 1977, Wadsworth Antheneum, 1970, Mus. Am. Art, New Britain, Conn., Nat. Arts Club Open Show, 1969, 78-79, 81-82, Salmagundi Club, N.Y.C., 1978-80, 82, Am. Watercolor Soc., N.Y.C., 1974, 77, 82, Nat. Acad. Design, 1986, 94, W.C. Founder's Show, Art Soc. Old Greenwich, 1999, Walter Brooks Meml. Watercolor Show, Rowayton, Conn., 2000; represented in permanent collection Kresge Mus., East Lansing, Mich., others; contbr. chpts. to books. Art dir. Round Hill Cmty. Guild; active North Stamford Congl. Ch., asst. assoc. curiator of healing through Art at Christ Ch., Grennwich; founding mem. Nat. Mus. Women in the Arts, Washington. Recipient Nat. Art League awards, 1969, 71, 72, 73, Art Soc. Old Greenwich award, 1989, 94, 99, Windsor Newton award, 1982, YWCA Greenwich Contemporary Women's Art Exhibit award, 1985, Best in Show award Art Soc. Old Greenwich, 1991, 1st Prize Graphics award Art Soc. Old Greenwich, 1994, 2nd Prize award Watercolor, Vol. of Yr. plaque, 1997. Mem. NAD, AAUW (New Canaan chpt.), Am. Watercolor Soc. (bd. dirs., asst. editor newsletter), Acad. Artists, Inc., Hoosier Salon (awards 1975-76), Am. Artists Profl. League (50th Nat. Exhbn. award 1978), Hudson Valley Art Assn. (pres. 2000—, bd. dirs., publ. rels. editor, designer catalog and brochure, awards 1970, 80—, pres.), Conn. Watercolor Soc. (award 1978), Conn. Artists 33, Whiskey Painters Am. (award 1978), Conn. Women Artists, Catharine Lorillard Wolfe Art Club (chmn. 1989-90, co-chair 1994, v.p. 1992-94, awards 1989-90), Pen and Brush (award 1977-78, 97), Nat. League Am. Pen Women (awards 1967, 69, 76-87, treas. 1990—), Nat. Press Club, Columbia U. Alumni Club (hon.), Nat. Soc. DAR (mem. Stamford chpt., historian, good citizens chair), Mich. State Alumni Club, Delta Phi Delta (hon.), Phi Kappa Phi (hon.), Alpha Xi Delta. Republican. Home: 274 Quarry Rd Stamford CT 06903-5004

RUDMAN, PAUL LEWIS, judge; b. Bangor, Maine, Mar. 26, 1935; s. Abraham Moses and Irene (Epstein) R.; m. Inez Lee Kolonel, Oct. 8, 1961; Andrew Isaac, Carole Sue. AB, Yale Coll., 1957; JD, George Washington U. Sch. Law, 1960. Bar: Maine 1960, D.C. 1960; U.S. Dist. Ct. Maine, 1961. Ptnr. Rudman & Winchell, Bangor, 1960-92; justice Maine Supreme Jud. Ct., Bangor, 1992—. Capt. Maine Air NG, 1960-66. Office: Maine Supreme Jud Ct Penobscot County Courthouse 97 Hammond St Bangor ME 04401

RUDMAN, SOLOMON KAL, magazine publisher; b. Phila., Mar. 6, 1930; s. Benjamin and Lena (Holtzman) R.; m. Lucille Steinhauer, June 29, 1958; 1 child, Mitchell. BS in Edn., U. Pa., 1951; MS in Edn., Temple U., 1957; LHD (hon.), Holy Family U., Phila. Chmn. dept. spl. edn. Franklin D. Roosevelt Sch., Bristol Twp., Pa., 1960-68; pub. premier record/ radio trade Fri. Morning Quarterback, Cherry Hill, Pa., 1968—. Bd. dirs. Variety Club, NARAS, Crime Commn., Pa., N.J., Del.; co-host Merv Griffin TV Show, 1981-82; music expert Today Show, 1981-82, Tomorrow Show, 1981-82, Tom Snyder TV Show; host Phila. Franklin Inst. Sci. and Fels Planetarium mobile sci. programs, entertainment shows to Phila.-N.J. Sr. Citizens' homes, children's and vets. hosps.; co-host, talent booker Easter Seals Telethon; creator h.s. jazz piano competition U. the Arts, Phila., e-books for the recording industry Pub.: (mag.) MQB (Modern QB) for Modern Rock Music; prodr. CD's of advance hits N.Am. radio stas.; launched music trade mag. Pro QB, launched Q-Beatl. Bd. dirs. Phila. Broadcast Pioneers; sponsor carillon bells Ave. of Arts, Phila., Franklin Inst. Travelling Sci. Show to Phila. elem. schs., 100th Anniversary Jewish Fedn. Phila.; bd. dirs. Citizens' Crime Commn.; sponsor 1st ann. classical piano H.S. competition, Chestnut Hill Coll.; co-sponsor purchase and distbn. of dictionaries to Phila. Elem. Sch. pupils (in memory of Ennis Cosby), Robotics Competition Phila. h.s., NJ United Cerebral palsy Marathon Dance, Rutgers U.; sponsor Franklin Inst. Time Capsule, Phila., Jewish Fedn. Atrium, Phila.; co-sponsor Succeeding By Reading Program; active Phila. Middle Schs., Jewish Book week, Phila. Ave. of Arts., Newspapers In Edn., others; founder Kal and Lucille Rudman Inst. for Entertainment Studies, Phila., 1974. Recipient Lifetime Achievement award Phila. Music Conf., Lifetime Music Achievement award Delaware Valley Music Poll., Presdl. Citation, Citizens Crime Com., Plaque on Walk of Fame, Ave. of the Arts, Enforcement award Nat. Marines; named to Broadcast Pioneers Hall of Fame Phila.; named Penndelphia Humanitarian of Yr. Mem. Phila. Music Alliance (bd. dirs.), Nat. Arthritis Found. (bd. dirs.), NARAS (bd. dirs.), Masons, Phila. Police Commrs. Club. Office: Friday Morning Quarterback 1930 Marlton Pike E Cherry Hill NJ 08003-2150

RUDMAN, WARREN BRUCE, former senator, lawyer, think tank executive; b. Boston, May 18, 1930; s. Edward G. and Theresa (Levenson) R.; m. Shirley Wahl, July 9, 1952; children: Laura, Alan, Debra. BS, Syracuse (N.Y.) U., 1952; LL.B., Boston Coll., 1960. Bar: N.H. 1960, D.C. Mem. firm Rudman & Gormley, Nashua, N.H., 1960-69; counsel to Gov. Walter Peterson, Concord, N.H., 1970; atty. gen. State of N.H., Concord, 1970-76; mem. firm. Sheehan Phinney Bass & Green, 1976-80; U.S. Senator from N.H., 1981-92; co-founder, co-chmn. Concord Coalition, 1992—; ptnr. Paul, Weiss, Rifkind, Wharton & Garrison, N.Y.C., Washington, 1993—. Deputy chmn. Fed. Reserve Bank of Boston. 1993, mem. bd. dirs. Chubb Corp., 1993—, Raytheon Corp., 1993—, Dreyfus Corp., 1993—. Founder, chmn. bd. trustees Daniel Webster Jr. Coll., 1965—, trustees Boston Coll., Aspen Inst., Valley Forge, Mil Acad.; chmn., founder New Eng. Aero. Inst., v. chmn. Pres. Fgn. Intelligence adv. bd.; sr. adv. com. Inst. of Politics John F. Kennedy Sch. Capt. AUS, 1952-54, Korea. Decorated Bronze Star, Combat Inf. Badge. Mem. Am. Legion. Republican. Office: Paul Weiss Rifkind Wharton & Garrison 1615 L St NW Ste 1300 Washington DC 20036-5694

RUDNER, SARA, dancer; b. Bklyn., Feb. 16, 1944; d. Henry Nathaniel and Jeannette (Smolensky) R.; 1 child, Edward Eli Rudner Marschner. AB in Russian Studies, Barnard Coll., 1964; MFA in Choreography, Bennington Coll., 1999. Dancer Sansardo Dance Co., N.Y.C., 1964-65, Am. Dance Co. at Lincoln Ctr., N.Y.C., 1965, Shakespeare Festival Touring Children's Show, N.Y.C., 1966; featured dancer Twyla Tharp Dance Found., N.Y.C., 1966-85; artistic dir., dancer Sara Rudner Performance Ensemble, N.Y.C., 1977—; guest dancer Joffrey Ballet, N.Y.C., 1973, Pilobolus Dance Theatre, N.Y.C., 1975, Lar Lubovitch Dance Co., N.Y.C., 1975-76; guest lectr., choreographer grad. dance dept. UCLA, 1975. Dir. dance Sarah Lawrence Coll.; tchr. master workshop NYU Theater Program, 1988-90; pres., artistic dir. Heart Dance, Inc. Choreographer: Palm Trees and Flamingoes, 1980, Dancing for an Hour or So, 1981; Minute by Minute, 1982, Eight Solos, 1991, Heartbeats, Inside Out, 1993; (with Jennifer Tipton and Dana Reitz) Necessary Weather, 1994; (with Rona Pondick, Robert Feintuch and Jennifer Tipton) Mine, 1996, Alley Theater-The Greeks part I and II, 1997, Heartbeat/mb with Christopher Janney and Mikhail Barysnikov, 1998. Choreographer Dancing-on-View St. Mark's Ch., N.Y.C., 1999, Santa Fe Opera. Grantee Creative Artists Pub. Svc. Program, N.Y., 1975-76, N.Y. State Coun. on Arts, 1975-78, Nat. Endowment for Arts, 1979-81, 91-92, 94-97; Guggenheim fellow, 1981-82; recipient N.Y. Dance and Performance award, 1984.

RUDNICK, BEN, software professional, retail automotive executive; b. Minerva, N.Y., July 11, 1976; s. Joseph Y. and Patricia Rudnick. BS in Biomed. Engring., Boston U., 1998. Cons. DataSage, Inc., Reading, Mass., 1998-99, project mgr., 1999-2000; CEO, Automotive Anything, Harrisburg, N.C., 2000—; product mgr. Vignette, Inc., Waltham, Mass., 2000—. Fax: 781-487-2800.

RUDNICK, IRENE KRUGMAN, lawyer, former state legislator, educator; b. Columbia, S.C., Dec. 27, 1929; d. Jack and Jean (Getter) Krugman; m. Harold Rudnick, Nov. 7, 1954 (dec.); children: Morris, Helen Gail. AB cum laude, U. S.C., 1949, JD, 1952. Bar: S.C. 1952. Individual practice law, Aiken, SC, 1952—; now ptnr. Rudnick & Rudnick; instr. bus. law U. S.C., Aiken, 1962—; tchr. Warrenville Elem. Sch., 1965-70; supt. edn. Aiken County, 1970-72; mem. S.C. Ho. of Reps., 1972—78, 1980—84, 1986—94. Pres. Adath Yeshurun Synagogue; active Aiken County Dem. Party, S.C. Dem. Party; hon. mem. Aiken Able-Disabled. Recipient Citizen of Yr. award, 1976-77, Bus. and Profl. Women's Career Woman of Yr., 1978, 94, Aiken County Friend of Edn. award, 1985, 93, Outstanding Legis. award Disabled Vets., 1991, Citizen of Yr. award Planned Parenthood, 1994, Sertoma Svc. to Mankind award, 1996. Mem. AAUW, Aiken Able-Disabled (hon.), Aiken Hist. Soc., Hist. Aiken Found., Alpha Delta Kappa, Order Eastern Star, Hadassah Sisterhood, Am. Legion Aux. Office: PO Box 544 135 Pendleton St NW Aiken SC 29801-3859 Office Phone: 803-648-2565.

RUDO, MILTON, retired manufacturing company executive, consultant; b. Balt., Jan. 17, 1919; s. Saul E. and Bertha (Berkowitz) R.; m. Roslind Mandel, Mar. 27, 1943; children: Stephanie Ellen, Neil Dennis. BA, Johns Hopkins U., 1940; AMP, Harvard U., 1964. Various positions Brunswick Corp., Skokie, Ill., 1940-66, corp. v.p., pres. Bowling divsn. Chgo., 1966-74, group v.p. recreation bus., 1974-84, ret., 1984, cons. to the CEO, 1984-87; dir., cons. to the CEO Donlen Leasing Corp., Skokie, 1986-90. Pres. Nat. Bowling Hall of Fame and Mus., 1979. Capt. AUS, 1942-45, ETO. Recipient ann. award N.Y. Mktg. Club, 1960, Industry Svc. award, 1973; named to Bowling Hall of Fame, 1984. Mem. Nat. Bowling Coun. (pres. 1972), Briarwood Country Club, Hamlet Country Club (Delray Beach Fla.). Home (Summer): 1777 Balsam Rd Highland Park IL 60035-4343

RUDOFF, SHELDON, lawyer; b. Bklyn., May 29, 1933; s. Raphael and Goldie (Gorelick) R.; m. Hedda Muller, Nov. 22, 1964; children: Shaindy, Sara, Simone. BA cum laude, Yeshiva Coll., 1954; JSD cum laude, NYU, 1958; ordination, RIETS, 1957. Bar: N.Y. 1958, U.S. Dist. Ct. (so. and ea. dists.) N.Y. 1958, U.S. Supreme Ct. 1978. Ptnr. Shatzkin, Cooper & Rudoff, N.Y.C., 1970-84, Goodkind, Labaton, Rudoff & Sucharow, N.Y.C., 1984—; pres. Union Orthodox Jewish Congregation Am., 1990-94, hon. pres., 1994—; pres. Beth Din Am., 1996—. V.p. Yeshiva Coll. Alumni, N.Y.C., 1962-64; pres. Young Israel West Side, N.Y.C., 1969-72; sec. Orthodox Union, 1972-76, v.p., 1976-78, sr. v.p., 1978-84, chmn. bd., 1984-90, pres. 1990-94, mem. exec. com. World Zionist Orgn.; trustee Fedn. Jewish Philanthropies, 1980-91, United Jewish Appeal. Recipient Pres.'s award Orthodox Union, N.Y.C., 1972, Nat. Leadership award Nat. Conf. Synagogue Youth, N.Y.C., 1974, Kesser Shem Tov award Ortohdox Union, 1995. Mem. ABA, N.Y. State Bar Assn., Assn. Bar City N.Y. (transp. com. 1976—). Office: Goodkind Labaton Rudoff & Sucharow 100 Park Ave New York NY 10017-5516 E-mail: srudoff@glrslaw.com.

RUDOLPH, ABRAHAM MORRIS, pediatrician, educator; b. Johannesburg, Republic of South Africa, Feb. 3, 1924; s. Chone and Sarah (Feinstein) Rudolph; m. Rhona Sax, Nov. 2, 1949; children: Linda, Colin, Jeffrey. MBBCh summa cum laude, U. Witwatersrand, Johannesburg, 1946, MD, 1951; D (hon.), Rene Descartes U., Paris, 1996. Instr. Harvard Med. Sch., 1955—57, assoc. pediat., 1957—60; assoc. cardiologist in charge cardiopulmonary lab. Children's Hosp., Boston, 1955—60; dir. pediatric cardiology Albert Einstein Coll. Medicine, 1960—66, prof. pediat., assoc. prof. physiology, 1962—66; vis. pediatrician Bronx Mcpl. Hosp. Ctr., N.Y.C., 1960—66; prof. pediat. U. Calif., San Francisco, 1966—94, prof. physiology, 1974—88, Neider prof. pediatric cardiology, prof. ob-gyn and reproductive scis., 1974—94, chmn. dept. pediat., 1987—91, prof. pediatr. emeritus, 1994—; practice medicine, specializing in pediatric cardiology San Francisco. Mem. cardiovasc. study sect. NIH, 1961—65; mem. nat. adv. heart coun., 1968—72; established investigator Am. Heart Assn., 1958—62; career scientist Health Rsch. Coun., N.Y.C., 1962—66; Harvey lectr. Oxford (Eng.) U., 1984; inaugural lectr. 1st Nat. Congress Italian Soc. Perinatal Medicine, 1985. Editl. bd. Pediat., 1964—70, Circulation, 1966—74, 1983—88, assoc. editor Circulation Rsch., 1970, Pediatric Rsch., 1970—77; editor: Rudolph's Pediatrics, Rudolph's Fundamentals of Pediatrics; contbr. articles to profl. jours. Recipient Merit award, Nat. Heart, Lung and Blood Inst., 1986, Arvo Yllpo medal, Helsinki (Finland) U., 1987, Jonxis medal, Children's Hosp. Groningen, 1993, Nils Rosen von Rosenstein award, Swedish Pediat. Soc., 1999. Fellow: AAAS, Am. Assn. Adv. Sci., Royal Coll. Physicians (London), Royal Coll. Physicians (Edinburgh); mem.: Am. Heart Assn. (Rsch. Achievement award 1991, Founding Disting. Scientist award 2003), Am. Pediatric Soc. (coun. 1985—92, v.p. 1992—93, pres. 1993—94, Howland award 1999), Soc. for Pediatric Rsch. (coun. 1961—64), Soc. for Clin. Investigation, Am. Phys. Soc., Am. Acad. Pediat. (past chmn. sect. on cardiology, E. Mead Johnson award for rsch. in pediat. 1964, Borden award 1979, Lifetime Med. Edn. award 1992, Joseph St. Geme leadership award Pediat. 1993, Founder award, cardiology sect. 2001), NAS Inst. Medicine. Office: U Calif Cardiovascular Rsch Inst Calif Rm M1331 Box 0544 San Francisco CA 94143-0544 Office Phone: 415-476-9311. Business E-Mail: amrudolph@pedcard.ucsf.edu.

RUDOLPH, ALLEN, secondary school educator, consultant; b. San Jose, Calif., Apr. 28, 1951; BS in polit. sci., Santa Clara U., 1969—73, MA in history, 1977—80, MA ednl. adminstrn., 1981—83; MA in polit. sci., Stanford U., 1995—96, MA in liberal arts, 1997—2002. Tchr. Eldorado HS, Las Vegas, 1975—76, Santa Ynez HS, Calif., 1976—77, Marello Prep. HS, Santa Cruz, Calif., 1977—79, Campbell HS, Calif., 1979—80, Los Gatos HS, Calif., 1980—. Summer sch. prin. Los Gatos HS, 1986—89; coll. bd. cons. Ednl. Testing Svc., Princeton, 1987—; adj. prof. De Anza Cmty. Coll., Cupertino, Calif., 1990—2002. Editor: (newsletter) SCCCSS Hotline; contbr. articles to jour. Planning commissioner-chair and vice-chair Planning Commn., Los Gatos, 1989—95; gen. plan com. chair Gen. Plan Com., Los Gatos, 1989—95; hist. preservation com. mem. Hist. Preservation Com., Los Gatos, 1989—95; trails com. mem. Trails Com., Calif., 1989—95. Recipient Rockefeller Scholar, Rockefeller Found., 1984, Ford Found. Scholar, Ford Found., 1985, Tchr. Yr. for Town of Los Gatos, Los Gatos Weekly, 1992, Cert. Appreciation-Student Poll Worker Coord., Santa Clara County Registrar of Voters, 2000; fellow Madison Found. Fellowship, US Congress, 1994; scholar WICHE Internship, WICHE, 1980; Calif. Instrnl. Improvement Grants, Calif. Dept. Edn., 1984, 1985, 1986. Mem.: NEA (assoc.), Orgn. Am. Historians (assoc.), Amnesty Internat. (assoc.), ACLU (assoc.), Sierra Club (assoc.). D-Liberal. Avocations: reading, music, golf, sports. Home: 258 Jared Ln Los Gatos CA 95030 Office: Los Gatos HS 20 HS Ct Los Gatos CA 95030 Office Phone: 408-354-2730. Personal E-mail: arudolph@lghs.net.

RUDOLPH, ANDREW HENRY, dermatologist, educator; b. Detroit, Jan. 30, 1943; s. John J. and Mary M. Rudolph; children: Kristen Ann, Kevin Andrew. MD cum laude, U. Mich., 1966. Diplomate Am. Bd. Dermatology. Intern Univ. Hosp., U. Mich. Med. Ctr., Ann Arbor, 1966-67, resident dept. dermatology, 1967-70; pvt. practice medicine specializing in dermatology, 1972—. Asst. prof. dermatology Baylor Coll. Medicine, Houston, 1972-75, assoc. prof., 1975-83, clin. prof., 1983—; chief dermatology svc. VA Hosp., Houston, 1977-82; mem. staff Meth. Hosp., Tex. Children's Hosp., St. Luke's Episcopal Hosp. Mem. editl. bd. Jour. Sexually Transmitted Diseases, 1977-85; contbr. to med. publs. Served as surgeon USPHS, 1970-72. Regent's scholar U. Mich., 1966. Fellow Am. Acad. Dermatology; mem. AMA, Am. Dermatol. Assn., So. Med. Assn., Tex. Med. Assn., Harris County Med. Soc., Houston Dermatol. Soc. (past pres.), Tex. Dermatol. Soc., Internat. Soc. Tropical Dermatology, Dermatology Found., Skin Cancre Found., Am. Venereal Disease Assn. (past pres.), Am. Soc. Dermatol. Surgery, Soc. Investigative Dermatology, S. Ctrl. Dermatol. Congress, Mich. Alumni Assn. (life), Alpha Omega Alpha, Phi Kappa Phi, Phi Rho Sigma, Theta Xi. Office: 6560 Fannin St Ste 724 Houston TX 77030-2768

RUDOLPH, CARL J. insurance company executive; Chartered life underwriter; cert. mgmt. acct.; CPA; cert. cash mgr. Dir. fin. planning & control sys. Aid Assn. Lutherans, Appleton, Wis., 1971-86, v.p., controller, 1986-97, v.p.,

controller, treas. corp. fin. svcs., 1997-99, sr. v.p., CFO, 1999—. Mem. Fin. Execs. Inst., Treasury Mgmt. Assn., AICPAs. Office: Aid Assn Lutherans 4321 N Ballard Rd Appleton WI 54919-0001

RUDOLPH, FREDERICK, history educator; b. Balt., June 19, 1920; s. Charles Frederick and Jennie Hill (Swope) R.; m. Dorothy Dannenbaum, June 18, 1949; children: Marta R. MacDonald, Lisa R. Cushman. BA, Williams Coll., 1942, Litt.D., 1985; MA, Yale U., 1949, PhD, 1953; LHD, U. Rochester, 1994, Wilkes U., 1998. Instr. history Williams Coll., 1946-47; asst. instr. Yale, 1949-50; mem. faculty Williams Coll., 1951—, prof., 1961—, Mark Hopkins prof. history, 1964-82, emeritus, 1982—, chmn. Am. civilization program, 1971-80. Williams Coll. marshal, 1978-87; vis. lectr. history and edn. Harvard U., 1960, 61; vis. prof. Sch. Edn., U. Calif.-Berkeley, 1983; mem. commn. plans and objectives Am. Council Edn., 1963-66; mem. study group on postsecondary edn. Nat. Inst. Edn., 1980-83; mem. com. on baccalaureate degrees Assn. Am. Colls., 1981-85; vis. assoc. Ctr. Studies in Higher Edn., U. Calif.-Berkeley, 1983 Author: Mark Hopkins and the Log, 1956, rev. edit. 1996, The American College and University: A History, 1962, rev. edit., 1990 (Japanese translation, 2003), Curriculum: A History of the American Undergraduate Course of Study Since 1636, 1977, rev. edit., 1993; editor: Essays on Education in the Early Republic, 1965, Perspectives: A Williams Anthology, 1983; exec. editor: Change, 1980-84, cons. editor, 1985-92. Founding mem. Berkshire County Hist. Soc., 1962, v.p., 1962-66, pres., 1966-68, bd. dirs., 1974-76; trustee Hancock-Shaker Cmty. Inc., 1974-91, Wyoming Sem., 1976-79, Bennington Mus., 1985-95; bd. dirs. Armand Hammer United World Coll. Am. West, 1993—. Capt. AUS, 1942-46. Guggenheim fellow, 1958-59, 68-69; recipient Frederic W. Ness award Assn. Am. Colls., 1980, Rogerson cup Williams Coll., 1982, Disting. Svc. award Wyo. Seminary, 1986. Mem. AAUP, Nat. Acad. Edn., Mass. Hist. Soc. (fellow), Am. Hist. Assn., Am. Studies Assn., Phi Beta Kappa. Democrat. Home: PO Box 515 Williamstown MA 01267-2800

RUDOLPH, GILBERT LAWRENCE, lawyer; b. L.A., Aug. 23, 1946; s. Martin and Marion R.; Susan Ilene Fellenbaum, Sept. 18, 1983; children: Samara Lisa, Felicia Beth. BA, Ariz. State U., 1967; postgrad., Am. U., Washington, 1967-69; JD, U. Cin., 1973. Bar: D.C. 1973, U.S. Dist. Ct. D.C. 1974, U.S. Ct. Appeals (D.C. cir.) 1974, Ariz. 1975, U.S. Dist. Ct. Ariz. 1975, Calif. 1979. Assoc. Streich, Lang, Weeks & Cardon, P.A., Phoenix, 1975-78; ptnr. Gilbert L. Rudolph, P.C., Phoenix, 1978-87; sr. mem. O'Connor, Cavanagh, Anderson, Killingsworth & Beshears, P.A., Phoenix, 1987-99; shareholder Greenberg Traurig LLP, Phoenix, 1999—. Lectr. on lending issues. Bd. dirs. Temple Chai, 2002—, Make-A-Wish Found. of Am., 1984—89, Aid to Adoption of Spl. Kids, Ariz., 1995—2003. Fellow Am. Coll. Consumer Fin. Svcs. Lawyers; mem. ABA (com. on consumer fin. svcs. bus. law sect. 1981—, com. on comml. fin. svcs. 1989—, mem. com. on uniform comml. code 1992—), Conf. on Consumer Fin. Law (governing com. 1986—). Republican. Jewish. Office: Greenberg Traurig LLP Ste 700 2375 E Camelback Rd Phoenix AZ 85016 Office Phone: 602-445-8206. E-mail: rudolphg@gtlaw.com.

RUDOLPH, JOHN, construction executive; MS, U. Santa Clara. Exec. v.p. Rudolph & Sletten, Inc., Foster City, Calif., president, 1997—, chief exec. officer, 1998—. Office: Rudolph & Sletten Inc 989 E Hillsdale Blvd Foster City CA 94404-2113

RUDOLPH, KATHLEEN ANN, insurance company executive; b. Minnetonka, Minn., Feb. 22, 1962; d. Russell Edward and Joan Lou Schaub; m. Stephen Mark Rudolph, May 26, 1991. BA, DePauw U., 1984. Underwriter The Hartford, Brea, Calif., 1985-88, sales supr. Southington, Conn., 1988-93, underwriting mgr., 1993-96, strategic underwriting dir., 1996-98, dir. outsourcing, 1998-99, v.p. ops. ea. divsn., 1999-2000, underwriting v.p., 2000—. Mem. Delta Delta Delta. Avocations: travel, interior designing, reading, gardening. Office: The Hartford 200 Executive Blvd Southington CT 06489 E-mail: krudolph@thehartford.com.

RUDOLPH, LAVERE CHRISTIAN, library director; b. Jasper, Ind., Dec. 24, 1921; s. Joseph Frank and Rose (Stradtner) R. AB, DePauw U., 1948; B.D., Louisville Presbyn. Sem., 1951; PhD, Yale, 1958; student, U. Zurich, Switzerland, 1960; M.L.S., Ind. U., 1968. Ordained to Ministry Presbyn. Ch., 1950; pastor in Ind. and Conn., 1950-54; mem. faculty Louisville Presbyn. Sem., 1954-69, prof. ch. history, 1960-69; lectr. history U. Louisville, 1965-69; rare books bibliographer Van Pelt Library U. Pa.; head tech. services Lilly Library, Ind. U., 1970-78, curator of books, 1978-86, librarian emeritus, 1987—. Author: Hoosier Zion, 1963 (Thomas Kuch award Ind. U. Writers Conf. 1964), Story of the Church, 1966, Francis Asbury, 1966, Indiana Letters, 1979, Religion in Indiana, 1986, Hoosier Faiths, 1995. Served to capt. USAAF, 1940-46. Mem.: Presbyn. Hist. Soc., Am. Soc. Ch. History, Phi Beta Kappa. Democrat. Home: 2455 Tamarack Trail apt 101 Bloomington IN 47408 Office: Ind U Library Bloomington IN 47405

RUDOLPH, MAYA, actress, comedienne; b. Gainesville, Fla., July 27, 1972; d. Richard and Minnie (Riperton) Rudolph. BA in photography, U. Calif., Santa Cruz, 1994. Former backup singer The Rentals. Actor: (TV series) Saturday Night Live, 2000—, City of Angels, 2000, (guest star) Chicago Hope, 1996—97,: (TV films) The Devil's Child, 1997; (films) Gattaca, 1997, Chuck & Buck, 2000, Duets, 2000, Duplex, 2003, 50 First Dates, 2004. Office: 30 Rockefeller Plaza New York NY 10112

RUDOLPH, SCOTT, pharmaceutical executive; b. 1958; s. Arthur Rudolph. Dir., chmn. of bd., CEO NBTY, Inc., Bohemia, NY, 1986—. Past chmn. of bd. dirs. Dowling Coll., Long Island, NY, 1997—2000; vice chmn. Dowling Coll. Bd., 2004—. Office: NBTY Inc 90 Orville Dr Bohemia NY 11716

RUDOLPH, WALLACE MORTON, law educator; b. Chgo., Sept. 11, 1930; s. Norman Charles and Bertha (Margolin) R.; m. Janet L. Gordon, Feb. 14, 1964 (div. Jan. 1998); children: Alexey, Rebecca, Sarah; m. Mimi Longworth, Mar. 22, 1998; children: Haille, Bryon. BA, U. Chgo., 1950, JD, 1953. Bar: Ill. 1953, U.S. Ct. Mil. Appeals 1954, U.S. Supreme Ct. 1954, Nebr. 1962, Wash. 1978. Rsch. assoc. Ford Found., 1953-54, Ford Found. (Project in Law and Behavior Sci.), 1954-55; instr. U. Chgo. Law Sch., 1959; assoc. Antonow & Fink, Chgo., 1960-61; asst. prof. law U. Nebr., Lincoln, 1961-63, assoc. prof., 1963-64, prof., 1965-76, U. Puget Sound Sch. Law, 1976-94, dean, 1976-80; prof. Seattle U. Sch. Law, 1994—. Vis. prof. law U. Wis., 1980-81, U. Ill., 1984; chair excellence in law Memphis State U. Law Sch., 1991; mem. Commrs. Uniform State Law, 1973-77; judge Ct. Indsl. Rels., Nebr., 1975-77; mem. Wash. Jud. Coun. and COm. II, 1976-80, Pub. Employment Rels. Commn., Wash., 1977-97; dean U. Orlando, 1997-98. Author: Handbook for Correctional Law; contbr. articles to profl. jours.; author: Model Criminal Procedure Code, 1975, Model Sentencing and Corrections Act, 1978, Amicus Curiae Brief, Wash. State Supreme Ct. 1979. Bd. dirs. LIMIT, 1992-94, Nebr. chpt. ACLU, 1965-72; mem. Nebr. Dem. Contact Com., 1973-74, 75-76; chmn. Firt Congl. Dist. Dem. Party, 1975-76; mem. exec. com. Unitarian Ch., Lincoln, 1965-67. With JAGC, U.S. Army, 1954-57. Mem. AAUP, ABA, Soc. Criminology, Am. Law Inst., Am. Arbitration Assn. E-mail: wallace.rudolph@celebration.fl.us.

RUDOLPHSEN, WILLIAM M. retail executive; BS in Acctg., Marquette U.; MBA, DePaul U. With Walgreen Co., Deerfield, Ill., 1977—, dir. 3d party acctg., 1995—98, divisional v.p. acctg., contr., 1998—2004, sr. v.p., CFO, 2004—. Office: Walgreen Co 200 Wilmot Rd Deerfield IL 60015

RUDY, DAVID ROBERT, physician, educator; b. Columbus, Ohio, Oct. 19, 1934; s. Robert Sale and Lois May (Arthur) R.; m. Rose Mary Sims; children by previous marriage: Douglas D., Steven W., Katharine L. Rudy Hoffer, Hunter A. Elam. BSc, Ohio State U., 1956, MD, 1960; MPH, Med. Coll. Wis., 1995. Diplomate Am. Bd. Family Practice, Am. Bd. Preventive Medicine. Intern Northwestern Meml. Hosp., Chgo., 1960-61; resident in internal medicine Ohio State U. Hosp., 1963-64; resident in pediatrics Children's Hosp., Columbus, Ohio, 1964; pvt. family practice Columbus, 1964-75; dir. residency program Riverside Meth. Hosp., Columbus, 1975-85; dir. family practice residency Monsour Med. Ctr., Jeannette, Pa., 1985-88; dir. residency Bon Secours Hosp., Grosse Pointe, Mich., 1988-91; prof., chmn. Finch U. Health Scis., Chgo. Med. Sch., Dept. Family Preventive Medicine, 1991-95, 97—; prof. Pomerene chair family medicine Ohio State U., 1995-97. Editor, contbr. (textbook) Family Medicine for the House Officer; author: Family Medicine Q & A: NMS Series; contbr. articles to profl. jours. Capt. flight surgeon MC. USAF, 1961—63; col. USAFR (ret.). Recipient USAF Commendation medal. Fellow Am. Acad. Family Physicians; mem. AMA, Ill. State Med. Assn. Republican. Office: Chgo Med Sch Finch U Clinic 3333 Green Bay Rd North Chicago IL 60064-3037

RUDY, ELLEN BEAM, nursing educator; b. Moundsville, W.Va., May 5, 1936; d. William Henry and Mary Ellen Beam; m. Theodore Rudy, June 13, 1959; children: Richard, Alan, William. BSN, Ohio State U., 1958; MPA, U. Dayton, 1974; MSN, U. Md., 1977; PhD, Case Western Res. U., 1980. Cmty. health staff nurse Columbus (Ohio) Pub. Health Nursing Svc., 1958-60; supr. in-svc. instr. Henry County Hosp., New Castle, Ind., 1960-66; emergency room staff nurse St. Elizabeth Med. Ctr., Dayton, Ohio, 1970-73; instr. critical care Johns Hopkins Hosp., Balt., 1975-76; assoc. prof., program dir. Kent (Ohio) State U. Adult Program, 1978-84; adminstrv. assoc. U. Hosp. Cleve., 1985-90; assoc. prof., chmn. MSN Case Western Res. U., Cleve., 1985-88, prof., chair acute care nursing, 1988-90, assoc. dean rsch., 1990-91; dean, prof. U. Pitts. Sch. Nursing, 1991—. Author: (with others) Critical Care Nursing, 1992 (Am. Jour. Nursing Book of Yr. 1993); contbr. articles to profl. jours. Grant reviewer NIH Nursing Student Sect., Washington, 1990-93; provider expert testimony Senate Appropriations Com., Washington, 1993, Health Care Forum, Washington, 1993. Edward J. and Louise Mellen Endowed Chair in Acute Care Nursing, 1989-91; fellow Am. Acad. Nursing, 1988; rsch. grantee NIH Nat. Ctr. for Nursing Rsch., 1989-91, 91-94. Mem. ANA, AACN, Am. Heart Assn., Nat. Kidney Found. (co-chair critical care task force 1988-91), Coun. Nurse Researchers. Office: Univ Pitts Sch Nursing 350 Victoria Building Pittsburgh PA 15261-2403 Home: 7815 Lydia Dr Lewis Center OH 43035-8076

RUDY, JOEL S. retired fraternal organization administrator; b. Bklyn., Jan. 20, 1941; s. Sidney T. and Selma Rudy; m. Marlene Yourga, Nov. 24, 1965; children: Lisa Michele, Brian Scott, Julia. BS in Biology, Bethany Coll., 1962; MA in Sociology, Kent State U., 1964; cert. in Ednl. Mgmt., Harvard U., 1985. Instr. sociology, asst. dean students Hunter Coll., CUNY, Bronx, N.Y., 1964-67; assoc. dir. housing, dir. resident student devel. U. Miami, Coral Gables, 1967-71; dean student resident life, asst. v.p. Kent (Ohio) State U., 1971-76; dir. residence life U. Ohio, Athens, 1976-78, assoc. dean students, then dean of students, 1978-95, v.p., dean, 1995-98, v.p. and dean emeritus, 1999—; exec. dir. Phi Kappa Tau Nat. Fraternity, Oxford, Ohio, 1998—2001, exec. v.p., COO, 2001—02; spl. asst. to juvenile and probate judge Union County, Ohio. Sr. fellow Acad. Leadership U. Md., College Park, 1999—. Pres. Athens City Sch. Bd., 1987-91; vice chmn. Athens County Red Cross, 1997-99, Athens County Heart Fund, 1980-81; trustee Phi Kappa Tau Nat. Found., 2002—. Recipient Phil Tripp Outstanding award Ohio Coll. Pers. Assn., Gerald Saddlemire award Ohio Coll. Pers. Assn.; named Hon. Alumnus, Ohio U., 1995. Mem. Ohio Assn. Student Pers. Adminstrn. (pres. 1983-84), Rotary, Golden Key Nat. Honor Soc., Phi Kappa Phi, Phi Delta Kappa, Omicron Delta Kappa. Democrat. Jewish. Avocations: boating, volunteer work. Home: 19 Roxbury Dr Athens OH 45701 E-mail: rudyhome@aol.com.

RUDY, KATHLEEN VERMEULEN, small business owner; b. Grand Rapids, Mich., Dec. 29, 1931; d. John Weston and Geneva (Swiet) Vermeulen; m. Fredrick Albers Yonkman, June 9, 1953 (div. Sept. 1980); children: Sara Yonkman Davis, Margriet Yonkman Finnegan, Nina Tower; m. Raymond Bruce Rudy, Nov. 14, 1981. BA, Hope Coll., Holland, Mich., 1953. Owner Kate's Antiques, 1974-2000. Editor mag. Jr. League of Boston, 1960's, Scarsdale Jr. League, 1960's. Bd. dirs. Jr. League of Boston, 1960s, Greenwich Cmty. for Human Svcs., 1970s-80s, Neighbor to Neighbor, Greenwich, 1980-98; trustee Hope Coll., 1986-96; chmn. Mary Fund com. Ladies Golf Tournament, 1985; mem. Women's Nat. Rep. Club, N.Y.C., 1995—, bd. govs., 1997—; mem. Hope Coll. Pres.'s Task Force, 1997-99; treas. Women's Nat. Rep. Club, 2000-2002, chmn. nominating com. 2000—, 2d v.p., 2002-. Mem. Jr. League of Phoenix, Greenwich Country Club, Dorset Field Club, Kappa Alpha Theta. Republican. Congregationalist. Avocations: tennis, golf, antiques, travel. Home and Office: 37 Lismore Ln Greenwich CT 06831-3741 E-mail: RayRudy@worldnet.att.net.

RUDY, RAYMOND BRUCE, JR., retired food company executive; b. L.A., Apr. 24, 1931; s. Raymond Bruce and Wrena Margaret (Higgins) R.; m. Kathleen Vermeulen; children: Bruce Rudy, Alice M.R. Price, Barbara R. Frith. BS, UCLA, 1953; MBA, Xavier U., Cin., 1960. Brand mgr. Procter & Gamble, Cin., 1956-62; product mgr. Hunt-Wesson Foods, Fullerton, Calif., 1962-63; group v.p. Gen. Foods Corp., White Plains, N.Y., 1963-79; pres. Oroweat Foods Co. subs. Continental Grain Co., N.Y.C., 1979-83; chmn., pres. Arnold Foods Co., Inc., Greenwich, Conn., 1984-86; pres. Affiliates of Best Foods subs. CPC Internat., Englewood Cliffs, N.J., 1987-89; ret., 1989; chmn., CEO, New Hampton, Inc., 1993-94; dep. chmn. Snapple Natural Beverages, Inc., 1992-94; mng. dir. J.W. Childs Assoc., 1995—; chmn. Personal Care Group, Inc., 1996-98. Chmn. Beltone Electronics Corp., 1997-2000, Internat. Diverse Foods, 1998-99, Empire Kosher Poultry, Inc., 1997-2000, Am. Safety Razor, 2000—, Hartz Mountain Corp., 2001-04, The Meow Mix Co., 2002-03; dbd. dirs. Pinnacle Foods Corp., Widmer Bros. Brewing, Inc. With U.S. Army, 1954-56. Mem. Greenwich Country Club, Dorset Field Club, The Links, The Boulders. Congregationalist.

RUDY, RUTH CORMAN, former state legislator; b. Millheim, Pa., Jan. 3, 1938; d. Orvis E. and Mabel Jan (Stover) Corman; m. C. Guy Rudy, Nov. 21, 1956; children: Douglas G., Donita Rudy Koval, Dianna F. Degree in x-ray tech., Carnegie Inst., 1956; student, Pa. State U., 1968-71. Clk. of cts. County of Centre (Pa.), Bellefonte, 1976-82; rep. Pa. Gen. Assembly, Harrisburg, 1982-96. Mem. Dem. Nat. Com., 1980—, chair women's caucus, 1989-91; past pres. Pa. Fedn. Dem. Women, Harrisburg; pres. Nat. Fedn. Dem. Women, 1987-89; mem. exec. com. Dem. Nat. Com., 1987-89; candidate U.S. Congress, 5th Dist., 1995-96; rep. Nat. Dem. Inst. for Internat. Affairs, 1997—; rep. to Yemen, 1997. Mem. Gov. Rendell's Transition Team on Agr., 2003. Named Woman of Yr. Pa. Fedn. dem. Women, 1982, Centre County Living Legend, 2000. Methodist. Achievements include patent for hair spray face shield.

RUDY, WILLIS, historian; b. N.Y.C., Jan. 25, 1920; s. Philip and Rose (Handman) R.; m. Dorothy L. Richardson, Jan. 31, 1948; children: Dee Dee, Willis Philip, Willa. BSS, CCNY, 1939; MA, Columbia U., 1940, PhD, 1948. Instr. CCNY, 1939-49; instr., lectr. Harvard U., 1949-53, 57-58; prof. Mass. State Coll., Worcester, 1953-63; prof. history Fairleigh Dickinson U., Teaneck, N.J., 1963-82, prof. emeritus, 1982—. Mem. editorial bd. Fairleigh Dickinson U. Press, 1966-77. Author: The College of the City of New York, A History, 1847-1947, 1949, 1977; The American Liberal Arts College Curriculum, 1960; Higher Education in Transition, 1958, 68, 76, 97; Schools in an Age of Mass Culture, 1965; The Universities of Europe: A History, 1984; Total War and Twentieth Century Higher Learning, 1991, The Campus and a Nation in Crisis: From the Revolution to Vietnam, 1996, Building America's Schools and Colleges, 2003. Mem. Orgn. Am. Historians, Phi Beta Kappa. Home: 161 W Clinton Ave Tenafly NJ 07670-1916 Office: Fairleigh Dickinson U Dept Of Hist Teaneck NJ 07666 *As a teacher, my greatest reward has been to see people get involved in the sheer joy of learning new things and seeking answers to the big questions that life proposes. As a writer, my enduring satisfaction has come from the opportunity to explore the seemingly chaotic events of human history in the hope of finding a meaningful and instructive pattern.*

RUDY, YORAM, biomedical engineer, biophysicist, educator; b. Tel Aviv, Feb. 12, 1946; arrived in U.S., 1973; s. Nahum and Yaffa (Krinkin) R. BSc, Technion/Israel Inst. Tech., Haifa, 1971, MSc in Physics, 1973; PhD in Biomed. Engring., Case Western Res. U., 1978. Asst. prof. dept. biomed. engring. Case Western Res. U., Cleve., 1981-86, assoc. prof., 1986-89, prof., 1989—, prof. dept. of physiology and biophysics, 1991—, prof. dept. medicine, 1992—. Dir. cardiac bioelectricity rsch. and tng. ctr., vis. prof. Technion/Israel Inst. Tech., 1982-83, U. Parma, Italy, 1986, 87, U. Utah, Salt Lake City, 1990, Tel-Aviv (Israel) U., 1991, Russian Acad. of Scis., St. Petersburg, 1997, U. Berne, Switzerland, 1998; mem. cardiovascular and pulmonary study sect. NIH, 1984-88; Rijlant disting. lectr. Internat. Congress on Electrocardiology, 2000; Ueda Meml. lectr. Japanese Soc. Electrocardiology, 2002. Mem. editl. bd. Jour. Electrocardiology, Jour. Cardiovasc. Electrophysiology, Cardiovasc. Rsch., Cardiac Electrophysiology Rev.; contbr. articles to profl. jours. Grantee NIH, 1985—, Am. Heart Assn., 1990-95, NSF, 1987-94; recipient Gordon K. Moe Prof. award, 1997, NIH-Nat. Heart, Lung and Blood Inst. Merit award, 1998. Fellow IEEE, Am. Physiol. Soc., Am. Inst. Med. and Biol. Engring.; mem. NAE, Am. Heart Assn., Biophys. Soc., Biomed. Engring. Soc. (sr., Disting. Lectr. award 2001). Achievements include development of a novel imaging modality for non-invasive imaging of cardiac electrical events from electrical potentials measured on the body surface (electrocardiographic imaging, ECGI), of theoretical models of cardiac excitation at the cellular, sub-cellular and tissue levels; elucidation of the cellular mechanisms of cardiac arrhythmias and the role of tissue architecture in arrhythmogenesis. Office: Case Western Res U Dept Biomed Engring Cleveland OH 44106-7207

RUDZITIS, ROLAND TALIS, music educator; b. Mpls., Sept. 6, 1960; s. Talivaldis and Irene Rudzitis; m. Leah Marie Canfield, Oct. 14, 1988; children: Justina Marie, Tija Melinda, Talis Grant, Jansons Dallas, Talana Larel, Jezron James, Taaron Lee, Tezra Jael. BS in Instrumental Music, Bethel Coll., 1990. Tchr. music Meadow Creek Christian Sch., Andover, Minn., 1992—. Musician Horizons Cmty. Ch., Ham Lake, Minn. Republican. Evangelilcal. Office: Meadow Creek Christian Sch 3037 Bunker Lk Blvd NW Andover MN 55304

RUE, DOUGLAS MICHAEL, technical application consultant; b. Pensacola, Fla., Apr. 9, 1964; s. Barbara J. Rue; m. Andra O'Neal, 1995; 1 child, Christian Michael Rue. AA in Bus., AA in Computer Sci., Pensacola (Fla.) Jr. Coll., 1984; BS in Computer Sci. cum laude, St. Augustine's Coll., 1988; MS in Telecomms., DePaul U., 1990. Data sys. analyst Internat. Paper, Memphis, 1990-91, project analyst, 1991-94; tech. cons. Sprint, L.A., 1994—, sr. tech. applications cons. Universal City, Calif., 1998—, Jacksonville, Fla., 1999—. Instr. DeVry Inst., Pomona, Calif., 1994. With U.S. Army Res., 1985-91.

RUEB, SHEREE A. social services administrator; b. Lincoln, Nebr., Aug. 23, 1960; d. Larry Hawkins, Annette Hawkins; m. Brent G. Rueb, July 7, 1985. BA, Hastings Coll., 1979—83; MA, Witchita State U., 1989—91. V.p. Mental Health Assn. South Ctrl. Kans., Wichita, 1991—95; state dir. Green Thumb, In.c, Arlington, Va., 1995—97; dir. sr. work experience ARC, Wichita, 1997—. Adv. bd. Reno County Workforce, Hutchinson, Kans., 1998—; bd. dirs. Kans. Workforce Investment, Hays, 1997—; adv. bd. Sedgwick County Workforce Partnership, Wichita, 1998—. Vice chair Older Workers Task Force State of Kans., 1997—. Mem.: Harvey County Archl. Assn. (sec., treas. 1995—, pres. 1996—98). Avocation: historic architecture, historic preservation. Office: ARC Midway KS Chpt 707 N Main Wichita KS 67203

RUEBEL, MARION A. university president; b. Manson, Iowa; B in Biol. Scis., U. No. Iowa, 1958, M in Sch. Adminstrn., 1962; PhD in Ednl. Adminstrn., Iowa State U., 1969. Asst. prof. secondary edn. U. Akron, 1970—73, dept. chmn., assoc. prof., 1973, asst. dean Coll. Edn., dean Univ. Coll., exec. asst. to pres., interim sr. v.p., dir. alumni affairs and govtl. rels., prof. edn.; pres. St. Vincent-St. Mary H.S., 1994—96, U. Akron, 1996—99, trustee prof., 1999—. Bd. dirs. Ohio Aerospace Inst., Northeastern Ohio Univs. Coll. Medicine; mem. Ohio Scis. and Tech. Coun. Contbr. articles to profl. jours. Office: Univ of Akron Stitzleis Alumni Ctr Buchtel Common Akron OH 44325-2602

RUEBHAUSEN, OSCAR MELICK, retired lawyer; b. N.Y.C., Aug. 28, 1912; s. Oscar and Eleonora J. (Melick) R.; m. Zelia Krumbhaar Peet, Oct. 31, 1942. AB summa cum laude, Dartmouth Coll., 1934; LLB cum laude, Yale U., 1937. Bar: N.Y. 1938, U.S. Supreme Ct. 1945. Assoc. Debevoise, Stevenson, Plimpton & Page, N.Y.C., 1937—42, Lend-Lease Adminstrn., Washington, 1942—44; gen. counsel Office Sci. Rsch. and Devel., Washington, 1944—46; ptnr. Debevoise and Plimpton, 1946—64, presiding ptnr., 1972—81, of counsel, 1984—87; counselor to ednl. instn., 1988—99; retired, 1999. Editor: Pension and Retirement Policies in Colleges and Universities, 1990; contbr. articles to profl. jours. Chmn. Commn. on Coll. Retirement, 1984-93; spl. adviser atomic energy to gov. N.Y. State, 1959; vice chmn. N.Y. State adv. com. on atomic energy, 1959-62; chmn. N.Y. State Gov.'s Task Force on protection from radioactive fallout, 1959; mem. Pres.'s Task Force on Sci. Policy, 1969-70, Pres.'s Sci. Adv. Com. Panel on Chems. and Health, 1970-72, Commn. on Critical Choices for Am., 1973-77, adv. com. Carnegie Commn. on Sci., Tech. and Govt., 1988-93; chmn. UN Day, N.Y. State, 1962, chmn. Spl. N.Y. Com. on Ins. Holding Cos., 1967-68; mem. U.S. govt. panel on Privacy and Behavioral Rsch., 1965-66; mem. presdl. panel Chronic Renal Disease, 1966-67; sec., dir. Fund Peaceful Atomic Devel., Inc., 1954-72; dir. Carrie Chapman Catt Meml. Fund, 1948-58; chmn. bd. Bennington Coll., 1957-61, 62-67; trustee Hudson Inst., Inc., 1961-71; trustee Russell Sage Found., chmn. bd., 1965-80; vice-chmn. N.Y.C. Univ. Constrn. Fund, 1966-69; mem. Coun. on Fgn. Rels., Nat. Com. on U.S.-China Rels.; mem. New Sch. Univ. Instl. Policy Com., 1991-2000; bd. dirs. Greenwall Found., 1956-95, chmn., 1982-91, chmn. emeritus, 1991—; bd. dirs. Scripps Clinic and Rsch. Found, 1983-89. Recipient U.S. Presdl. Cert. of Merit, 1948. Mem. ABA, N.Y. State Bar Assn., Yale Law Sch. Assn. (exec. com. and pres. 1960-62, chmn. 1962-64), Assn. of Bar of City of N.Y. (pres. 1980-82, pres. and bd. dirs. fund 1980-82), Order of Coif, Century Club (N.Y.C.), River Club (N.Y.C.), Phi Beta Kappa, Sigma Phi Epsilon. Home: 450 E 52nd St New York NY 10022-6448

RUECKERT, FREDERIC, retired plastic, reconstructive and hand surgeon; b. Boston, Oct. 24, 1921; s. Frederic and Elizabeth (Howe) R.; m. Joan Dodge, May 31, 1947; children: Nancy Lee, Patricia, William Dodge, Carolyn. AB, Hamilton Coll., 1945; MD, Columbia U., 1947. Diplomate Am. Bd. Plastic Surgery, Nat. Bd. Med. Examiners; lic. physician, N.Y., N.H. Intern internal medicine Bellevue Hosp., N.Y.C., 1947-48; resident gen. surgery Am. U. Hosp., Beirut, 1948-50; fellow surg. pathology Columbia-Presbyn. Hosp., N.Y.C., 1950-51; resident gen. surgery Dartmouth-Hitchcock Med. Ctr., Hanover, N.H., 1953-54, staff surgeon, 1956-86; resident plastic surgery, teaching fellow plastic surgery U. Pitts. Med. Ctr., 1954-56; mem. faculty Dartmouth Med. Sch., Hanover, 1956—, prof. plastic surgery, 1974-86, prof. plastic surgery emeritus, 1986—; cons. plastic surgery VA Hosp., White River Junction, Vt., 1956—2001. Contbr. articles to profl. jours., chpts. to books. Mem. Sch. Bd. Edn., Hanover, N.H., 1964-67; trustee Northfield (Mass.) Mt. Hermon Sch., 1969-71, 80-90. With USNR, 1943-45; flight surgeon USAF, 1951-53. Recipient Lamplighter award Northfield Mt. Herman Sch., 1991. Mem. AMA, ACS, Am. Assn. Plastic Surgeons, Am. Assn. Med. Colls., Am. Soc. Plastic Surgeons (bd. dirs. 1980-83, 84-86), Plastic Surgery Ednl. Found. (bd. dirs. 1978-87, pres. 1985-86), Plastic Surgeons Assn. Am. (pres. 1984-85), Internat. Confederation Plastic, Reconstructive and Aesthetic Surgeons, Am. Soc. Aesthetic Plastic Surgeons, New Eng. Surg. Soc., Northeastern Soc. Plastic Surgeons, New Eng. Soc. Plastic and Reconstructive Surgeons (pres. 1969-71), N.H. State Med. Soc., Grafton County Med. Soc. (pres. 1974-75), Univ. Club (N.Y.C.). Republican. Presbyterian. Avocations: swimming, tennis, skiing, photography, wood carving. Home: 18 Berrill Farms Ln Hanover NH 03755-3213 E-mail: frjdr@aol.com.

RUECKERT, ROLAND RUDYARD, retired virologist, educator; b. Rhinelander, Wis., Nov. 24, 1931; s. George Leonard and Monica Amelia (Seiberlich) R.; m. Ruth Helen Ullrich, Sept. 5, 1959; 1 child, Wanda Lynne. BS in Chemistry, U. Wis., 1953, PhD in Oncology, 1960. Fellow Max Planck Inst. for Biochemistry, Munich, 1960-61, Tübingen, Fed. Republic Germany, 1961-62; asst. rsch. virologist virus lab. U. Calif., Berkeley, 1962-65; asst. prof. biophysics lab. U. Wis., Madison, 1965-69, assoc. prof. biophysics lab., 1969-73; prof. Inst. for Molecular Virology, Madison, 1973-85, dist. rsch. prof., 1985-96, prof. emeritus, 1996-97. Mem. viology study sect. NIH, Bethesda, Md., 1981-85; pres. Am. Soc. Virology, 1989-90. With U.S. Army,

1953-55. Recipient William D. Stovall award, U. Wis., 1953, Marie Christine Kohler award U, Oneida County Tree Farmer of the Yr., 2001. Achievements include research in dodecahedral model for picornavirus structure and assembly, molecular biology of picornaviruses (polio 8 common cold), structure 8 biology of small insect viruses, mechanism of neutralization by antibodies and antivirals. Home: 2234 W Lawn Ave Madison WI 53711-1952 Office Phone: 608-262-6949. Business E-Mail: rrruecke@facstaff.wisc.edu.

RUECKERT, WILLIAM HOWE, literature educator, writer; b. Cleve., Nov. 4, 1926; s. Frederic and Elizabeth (Howe) Rueckert; m. Betty Lynn Ehlers, Jan. 30, 1954 (div. Aug. 1980); children: Theron K., Quentin H., Jordan F.B., Morgan P.; m. Barbara Lissner Fields, Aug. 5, 1980. BA, Williams Coll., 1950; MA, PhD, U. Mich., 1956. Instr. English Russell Sage Coll., Troy, NY, 1954—56, Oberlin (Ohio) Coll., 1956—57; from instr. to assoc. prof. U. Ill., Urbana, 1957—65; from assoc. prof. to prof. English U. Rochester, 1965—74; prof., chmn. English dept. SUNY, Geneseo, 1974—88, emeritus prof. English, 1988—. Vis. prof. U. Wash., Seattle, 1971, U. Victoria, BC, Canada, 1976. Author: Kenneth Burke and Drama of Human Relations, 1963, 2d edit., 1982, Glenway Wescott, 1965, Encounters with Kenneth Burke, 1994, Faulkner from Within: Destructive and Generative Being in the Novels of William Faulkner, 2003; editor: Critical Responses to Kenneth Burke, 1969, Letters from Kenneth Burke to William H. Rueckert 1959-1987, 2002; co-editor (with Angelo Bonadonna): On Human Nature - A Gathering While Everything Flows, 2003; editor: Essays Toward a Symbolic of Motives, 2003. Active Nature Conservancy, Thousand Islands Land Trust, Save the River, Clayton, NY; vol. Antique Boat Mus., Clayton, NY. With USN, 1945—46, Japan. Fellow, Nat. Humanities Inst. U. Chgo., 1977—78. Mem.: MLA (life), Assn. for Study of Lit. and Environ., Kenneth Burke Soc. (life, 1st pres. 1990). Democrat. Avocations: collecting and restoring antique St. Lawrence sailing skiffs, poetry. Home: 17 Keswick Way Fairport NY 14450 Home (Summer): PO Box 473 Clayton NY 13624 Personal E-mail: whrueckert@aol.com.

RUEDENBERG, KLAUS, theoretical chemist, educator; b. Bielefeld, Germany, Aug. 25, 1920; came to U.S., 1948, naturalized, 1955; s. Otto and Meta (Wertheimer) R.; m. Veronika Kutter, Apr. 8, 1948 (dec. Jan. 2004); children: Lucia Meta, Ursula Hedwig, Annette Veronika, Emanuel Klaus. Student, Montana Coll., Zugerberg, Switzerland, 1938-39; licence es Scis., U. Fribourg, Switzerland, 1944; postgrad., U. Chgo., 1948-50; PhD, U. Zurich, Switzerland, 1950; PhD (hon.), U. Basel, Switzerland, 1975, U. Bielefeld, Germany, 1991, U. Siegen, 1994. Research assoc. physics U. Chgo., 1950-55; asst. prof. chemistry, physics Iowa State U., Ames, 1955-60, assoc. prof., 1960-62, prof., 1964-78, disting. prof. in sci. and humanities, 1978-91, disting. prof. emeritus, 1991—, sr. chemist Ames Lab., U.S. Dept. Energy, 1964-91, assoc., 1991—. Prof. chemistry Johns Hopkins, Balt., 1962-64; vis. prof. U. Naples, Italy, 1961, Fed. Inst. Tech., Zurich, 1966-67, Wash State U. at Pullman, 1970, U. Calif. at Santa Cruz, 1973, U. Bonn, Germany, 1974, Monash U. and CSIRO, Clayton, Victoria, Australia, 1982, U. Kaiserlautern, Germany, 1987; lectr. univs., rsch. instns. and sci. symposia, 1953—. Contbr. articles to profl. jours.; assoc. editor: Jour. Chem. Physics, 1964-67, Internat. Jour. Quantum Chemistry; Chem. Physics Letters, 1967-81, Lecture Notes in Chemistry, 1976—, Advances in Quantum Chemistry, 1987—; editor-in-chief Theoretica Chimica Acta, 1985-97; hon. editor Theoretical Chemistry Accounts, 1997—. Co-founder Octagon Center for the Arts, Ames, 1966, treas., 1966-71, also bd. dirs. Guggenheim fellow, 1966-67; Fulbright sr. scholar, 1982. Fellow: AAAS, Internat. Acad. Quantum Molecular Scis., Am. Inst. Chemists, Am. Phys. Soc.; mem.: AAUP, Am. Chem. Soc. (Midwest award 1982, Nat. Award in Theoretical Chemistry 2002), Phi Lambda Upsilon, Sigma Xi. Office Phone: 515-294-5253.

RUEDRICH, RANDY, political party official; BS, M in Engring., Tex. A& M in Engring., PhD, Tex. A&M U. Commr. Alaska Oil & Gas Conservation Commn., 2003—; gen. mgr. Doyon Drilling; sr. drilling engr. Arco's Alaska; from fin. chmn. to state chmn. Alaska Rep. Party, 1986—2000, chmn., 2000—. Office: 1515 W 13th Ave Anchorage AK 99501

RUEDY, RALPH H. diplomat, consultant; b. Cedar Rapids, Iowa, Aug. 26, 1943; s. Fred Christian and Marie Louise (Hergert) Ruedy; m. Shirley Eloise Wallace, July 18, 1970; children: Carolyn, Elizabeth, Daniel. BS, Iowa State U., 1965; MA, Duke U., 1972, PhD, 1977. Dep. dir. Fulbright Office U.S. Info. Agy., Washington, 1987—91; dep. Pub. Affairs Officer Am. Emb. Moscow, 1995—97; dir. Office of Pub. Diplomacy for New Ind. States Dept. State, Washington, 1999—2001; ret., 2001. Cons. Am. Emb. Chisinau, Moldova, 2002. Elder Providence Presby. Ch., Fairfax, Va., 1997—2001. Lt. comdr. USN, 1965—69, Vietnam. Recipient Seal of City, Krefeld, Germany City Coun., 1983. Mem.: Am. Fgn. Svc. Assn., Amana Heritage Soc., Hist. Staunton Found. Avocations: gardening, fishing, historic preservation. Home: 4528 Braeburn Dr Fairfax VA 22032

RUEGER, DANIEL SCOTT, horticulture educator; b. Flint, Mich., May 16, 1957; s. William John and Barbara Jane (Ledford) R.; m. Michel Sharon Holzbach, July 22, 1989; children: Danielle Sharon, Christina Anne, Michael Scott. BS in Agr., MS in Agr. Edn., Ohio State U., 1980. Cert. profl. vocational, horticulture teacher, Ohio. Mgr. Idle R's Farms, Plain City, Ohio, 1973-77; research services worker O.M. Scott & Sons Co., Marysville, Ohio, 1977; tng. counselor Cen. Ohio Rural Consortium, Delaware, 1978; supt. parks grounds City of Delaware, 1979; tchr. horticulture Ashland (Ohio) City Schs., 1980—. Co-author: Success Handbook, 1980. Sustaining mem. Rep. Nat. Com., 1980-92; lay leader Emmanuel Meth. Ch., 1988-94; chmn. adminstrv. bd., 1990-91, 2003. Named Citizen of Yr. Citizens Commn. for the Right to Keep and Bear Arms, 1986, 87, 88, Disting. Patriot Concil for Inter-Am. Security. Mem. NEA, Nat. Assn. Agrl. Educators, Inc., Ohio Edn. Assn. (state coun. ednl. polit. action com. 1988-91, profl. devel. com. 1990-98), North Cen. Ohio Edn. Assn. (exec. com. 1986—), Ohio Assn. Agrl. Educators (hort. state chmn. 1988-92, Outstanding Agrl. Edn. Program 1992), Assn. for Career and Tech. Edn., Ohio Assn. for Career and Tech. Edn., Ashland City Tchrs. Assn. (pres. 1988-89), Ohio State U. Alumni Assn., Air Force Assn., Future Farmers Am. Alumni Assn., Orgn. for Secondary Students Enrolled in Agrl. Edn., Ohio Forestry Assn., Bass Angler Sportsmen Soc., Gamma Sigma Delta, Phi Delta Kappa. Avocations: reading, aviation, swimming, fishing, stamp collecting/philately. Office: Ashland High Sch 1440 King Rd Ashland OH 44805-3635 E-mail: darueger@ashland-city.k12.oh.us.

RUEGG, DONALD GEORGE, retired railway company executive; b. LaJunta, Colo., Sept. 11, 1924; s. George Albert and Cecilia Corrine (Decker) R.; m. Ruth Carson, June 27, 1946 (dec. 1963); m. Mary Ann Eichelberger, June 24, 1964. BA, Dartmouth Coll., 1947; MBA, U. Chgo., 1972. Stenographer Atchison, Topeka & Santa Fe Ry. Co., Pueblo, Colo., 1942-51, supr., trainmaster various locations, 1951-68, asst. to v.p. info. systems Topeka, 1968-69; asst. to v.p. ops. Atchison Topeka & Santa Fe Ry. Co., Chgo., 1969-72, gen. mgr. Los Angeles, 1972-73; asst. v.p. ops. Atchison, Topeka & Santa Fe Ry. Co., Chgo., 1973-78, v.p. ops., 1978-83, exec. v.p., 1983-86. Served with USN, 1943-46. Republican. Roman Catholic.

RUEGGEBERG, ERNA M. nursing consultant, nursing administrator, researcher; b. Balt., Md., Aug. 31, 1924; d. Frederick Carl and Selma Augusta (Heimann) Rueggeberg. BSN, U. Colo., 1947; MA in Ednl. Adminstrn., U. Chgo., 1958; DHL (hon.), Carthage Coll., 1985. RN, Ill. Dept. Profl. Regulation. Staff nurse U. Colo. Med. Ctr.-Colo. Gen. Hosp., Denver, 1947—49, Denver Gen. Hosp., 1949, head nurse pediats., 1949—52; acting supr. pediats. U. Colo. Sch. Nursing, 1952—53; instr. pediats. Sch. Nursing U. Colo., Boulder and Denver, 1953—56; instr. pediat. nursing U. Kans. Sch. Nursing, Lawrence and Kansas City, 1955—56, asst. chair, assoc. prof., 1956—60; asst. head, asst. prof. Cen. Mo. State Coll., Warrensburg, Mo., 1960—61, head, asst. prof., 1961—63; dir. chmn., dir. basic nursing edn. Lutheran Gen., Park Ridge, Ill., 1963—88; ret., 1988. Adviser Alumni Assn., Luth. Gen. and Deaconess Hosp. Sch. Nursing, Park Ridge, 1988—; coordinating coun. rep. Health Careers Coun. Ill., mem. adv. bd., bd. and exec. com., 1965—68. Commd. min. Stevens Ministry Program, St. Louis, 1991. Recipient Spiritus Christi award, Concordia Coll., 1981, Sr. award for outstanding health manpower achievement, Health Careers Coun. Ill., 1968. Mem.: ANA, AAUP, North Suburban Assn. for Health Resources (chmn. nursing and allied health edn. allied health edn. com. 1973), Ill. Coun. Hosp. Schs. Profl. Nursing, Nat. League for Nursing, Internat. Coun. Nurses, U. Colo. Sch. Nursing Alumni Assn. (membership dir. 1978—), Assoc. Alumni U. Colo. (membership dir. 1947—), U. Chgo. Alumni Assn. (life; membership dir. 1958—), Pi Lambda Theta (life; Chgo. chpt.). Lutheran. Avocations: gardening, gourmet cooking, attending concerts, lectures, and plays, travel, planned tours. Home: 217 N Main St Mount Prospect IL 60056-2410

RUEGGER, PHILIP T., III, lawyer; b. Plainfield, N.J., Oct. 14, 1949; s. Philip T. Jr. and Gloria Marie (McLaughlin) R.; m. Rebecca Lee Huffman, Aug. 3, 1974; children: Sarah, Britt, Michael. AB, Dartmouth Coll., 1971; JD, U. Va., 1974. Bar: N.Y. 1975. Assoc. Simpson Thacher & Bartlett, N.Y.C., 1974-81, ptnr., 1981—, chmn. exec. com., head corp. dept. Mem. Assn. Bar City N.Y., Phi Beta Kappa. Clubs: Manursing Island (Rye, N.Y.), Apawamis (Rye). Home: 275 Grace Church St Rye NY 10580-4201 Office: Simpson Thacher & Bartlett 425 Lexington Ave Fl 15 New York NY 10017-3954 E-mail: pruegger@stblaw.com.

RUEGSEGGER, DONALD RAY, JR., radiological physicist, educator; b. Detroit, May 29, 1942; s. Donald Ray and Margaret Arlene (Elliot) R.; m. Judith Ann Merrill, Aug. 20, 1965 (div.); children: Steven, Susan, Mark, Ann; m. Patricia Ann Mitchell, Oct. 16, 1999. BS, Wheaton Coll., 1964; MS, Ariz. State U., 1966, PhD (NDEA fellow), 1969. Diplomate Am. Bd. Radiology. Radiol. physicist Miami Valley Hosp., Dayton, Ohio, 1969—, chief med. physics sect., 1983—. Physics cons. X-ray dept. VA Hosp., Dayton, 1970-73; adj. asst. prof. physics Wright State U., Fairborn, Ohio, 1973-74, clin. asst. prof. radiology, 1976-81, clin. assoc. prof. radiology, 1981—, group leader in med. physics, dept. radiol. scis. Med. Sch., 1978-85. Mem. AAAS, Am. Assn. Physicists in Medicine (pres. Ohio River Valley chpt. 1982-83, co-chmn. local summer sch. arrangements com. 1986), Am. Coll. Radiology, Am. Coll. Med. Physics (founding chancellor), Am. Phys. Soc., Ohio Radiol. Soc., Health Physics Soc. Home: 6252 Donnybrook Dr Centerville OH 45459-1837 Office: Radiation Therapy Miami Valley Hosp 1 Wyoming St Dayton OH 45409-2722 Office Phone: 937-208-4058.

RUEHLE, CHARLES JOSEPH, pathologist, military officer; b. May 26, 1943; s. John Donald and Alta (Brown) R.; m. Nellie Backus, Aug. 5, 1972. DVM, Iowa State U., 1967; MD, U. Iowa, 1973; MS, 1973. Diplomate Am. Bd. Preventive Medicine, Am. Bd. Pathology. Commd. 2d lt. USAF, 1964; advanced through grades to col., sr. flight surgeon, 1984; chief flight surgeon, 1987; chief Vet. Svc., Grissom AFB, Ind., 1967-69; resident in aerospace medicine Brook AFB, Tex., 1973-75; resident in pathology Wilford Hall USAF Med. Ctr., Lackland AFB, Tex., 1975-79; with div. aerospace pathology Armed Forces Inst. Pathology, Washington, 1979-88; chief div. aerospace pathology, 1982-85; chmn. dept. forensic scis., 1985-88; sec. Joint COm. Aviation Pathology, 1984-88; exec. asst. to fed. air surgeon FAA, Washington, 1988—93, sr. aviation med. examiner, 1989—, mgr. appeals & special projects branch, 1993—. Adj. asst. prof. prevetive medicine Uniformed Services U. Health Scis. lectr. aerospace pathology; cons. USAF Sugeon Gen., 1987. Fellow Am. Soc. Clin Pathologists, Aerospace Med. Assn.; mem. Am. Acad. Forensic Scis. AMA, USAF Flight Surgeons, Nat. Sojourners, Assn. Mil. Surgeons U.S., Internat. Soc. Air Safety Investigators, Air Force Assn., Alpha Zeta, Gamma Sigma Delta, Omega Tau Sigma (gov. 1967-75), Cosmos Club. Republican. Presbyterian. Home: 1000 Lower Pindell Rd Lothian MD 20711-2704 Office: Fed Air Surgeon FAA 800 Independence Ave SW Washington DC 20591-0001

RUEHLICKE, CORNELIA IRIS, painter; b. Berlin; m. Mark Z. Alpert. MFA, Acad. Fine Arts, Germany, 1979; degree, Pratt Inst., 1980. Spl. projects designer Austen Display Co., Inc., N.Y.C., 1981—85; display designer Colonial Decorative Display Co., Inc., N.Y.C., 1983; assoc. designer Trim Corp. of Am., N.Y.C., 1985; asst. dir. Pindar Gallery, N.Y.C., 1985—88; artist indep., 1979—. One-woman shows include Gasteig Cultural Centre, Germany, 1986, Somerset County Coll., NJ, 1987, The Consulate Gen. of Germany, N.Y.C., 1988, Goethe Inst., German Cultural Centre, Can., 1988, Monmouth Coll. Art Gallery, NJ, 1990, The O'Keefe Centre for the Arts, Can., 1993, exhibited in group shows at The Guggenheim Mus., N.Y.C., 1993, Mus. of Modern Art De La Commanderie d'Unet Bordeaux, France, 1993, The New England Fine Arts Inst., Mass., 1993, San Diego Art Inst., Calif., 1994, Paula Cooper Gallery, N.Y.C., 1995, San Francisco Mus. of Modern Art, Calif., 1996, Whitney Mus. of Am. Art, N.Y.C., 1997, Artsforum Gallery, 1999, Consulate Gen. of Fed. Rep. of Germany, Germany, 2000, Elizabeth Found. for the Arts, N.Y.C., 2001—02, exhibited in group shows, various CD covers; (various video productions); various silkscreen and photo etchings, Represented in permanent collections Sankai Juku-Buto Dance Co., Hampton Arts Commn., Va., Kalani Honua Cultural Ctr., Hawaii, Art Space, Japan, Haag & Haag Gmbh., Germany, Duszinsky Gmbh., exhibited in group shows at Palm Springs Desert Mus., Calif., 1993, Elizabeth Found. for the Arts, NYC, 2001—03, one-woman shows include NJ Ctr. for Visual Arts, Morristown, NJ, 2004. Recipient Mayor's Purchase award, Hampton Arts Commn., 1993, Marc Printmaking award, Peninsula Fine Arts Ctr., 1994. Fellow: Elizabeth Found. for the Arts. Avocations: travel, sports, dance, music.

RUEHLMANN, VIRGINIA JUERGENS, foundation creativity director, writer; b. Cin., Dec. 31, 1924; d. Arthur Henry and Florence Johanna (Doogan) Juergens; m. Eugene Peter Ruehlmann, Aug. 30, 1947; children: Virginia Wiltse, E Peter, Margaret Straus, Andrea Cornett, Gregory, James, Mark, Rick. BS in Edn., U. Cin., 1946, M in Adminstrn., 1948. Swimming instr. Williams YMCA, Cin., 1942-43; recreation leader City of Cin., 1942-43; camp dir. U. Cin. Girls Summer Camp, 1943-45; instr. U. Cin., 1946-47, Wellesley Coll., Wellesley, Mass., 1947-48; homemaker Cin., 1948-84; dir., rschr., editor, writer, creativity dir. Helen Steiner Rice Found., Cin., 1984—. With Revell Pub., Baker Book House, Grand Rapids, Mich., 1984—; consult Gibson Greeting, Cincinnati, Ohio, 1989—. Ed, compiler: devotional and inspirational books, author (of prayers); researcher:; co-author: (activity book) Making Family Memories, 1994, From the Heart Daily Devotional, 1992, Joy for the Heart, 1992, Gifts of Love, 1992, Blossoms of Friendship, 1992, A Book of Thanks, 1993, A Book of Comfort, 1994, Wings of Encouragement, 1995, A Book of Prayer, 1995, A Book of Hope, 1996, A Book of Courage, 1996, Eyes of Tenderness, 1997, An Old Time Christmas, 1997, Celebrating the Golden Years, 1998, Our Family Treasury, 1998, God's Promises from A to Z, 1999, Mother, I Love You, 1999, Gift's of Love, 2d edit., 2000, An Instrument of Your Peace, 2001, Moments of Celebration, 2002, Moments of Comfort, 2002, Moments of Friendship, 2002, Moments of Love, 2002, Awake My Soul and Sing, 2003, The Poems & Prayers of Helen Steiner Rice, 2003. Chair Spec Olympics Greater Cin., 1974; pres Freedom Found Valley Forge, Cincinnati, Ohio, 1974—76; mem Western Hamilton County Econ Coun, Nat Fedn Rep Women, Rep Women's Club Hamilton County; pres Cath Social Serv SW Ohio, 1984—86; trustee Glenmary Missions, 1989—91; mem nat adv bd United Theological Sem; Athenaeum Ohio. Named Woman of the Yr, Cincinnati Enquirer, 1977, Lady Equestrian Order Holy Sepulchre Jerusalem, 1989; named to Ohio Women's Hall of Fame, 1991. Mem.: Guideposts Nat. Adv., Mortar Bd, Donors Forum Ohio, Coun Founds, Argus Club, Queen City Club, Cincinnati Women's Club. Roman Catholic. Avocation: activities with 25 granchildren. Home: 1523 Anderson Ferry Rd Cincinnati OH 45238-3632 Office: Helen Steiner Rice Found 221 E Fourth St Atrium 2 # 2100 Cincinnati OH 45202-4122 E-mail: hsrice@fuse.net.

RUELLAN, ANDREE, artist; b. N.Y.C., Apr. 6, 1905; d. André and Louise (Lambert) R.; m. John W. Taylor, May 28, 1929. Student, Art Students League, 1920-22; art schs., France and Italy. Guest instr. Pa. State Coll., summer 1957 One-man shows include Paris, 1925, Weyhe Galleries, N.Y.C., 1928, 31, Maynard Walker Galleries, 1937, 40, Kraushaar Galleries, 1945, 52, 56, 63, 80-81, Phila. Art Alliance, 1955, S.I. Mus., 1958, nat. exhbns., Carnegie Inst., Whitney Mus., Art Inst. Chgo., Corcoran Gallery, Internat. Expn., San Francisco, Artists for Victory Exhbn., N.Y.C., other cities U.S.; retrospective exhbns., Storm King Art Ctr., Mountainville, N.Y., 1966, Lehigh U., 1965, Woodstock Artists Assn., 1977, Ga. Mus. of Art, 1993, Hyde Collection, Glens Falls, N.Y., 1993, Gibbs Mus of Art, Charleston, S.C., 1993, Prints Gallery at Parkbest, Kingston, N.Y., 1995; drawing retrospective Kaushaar Galleries, 1990, 93, Ga. Mus. Art, Athens, 1993, The Hyde Collection, Glen Falls, N.Y., 1993, Gibbs Mus. Art, Charleston, S.C., 1993, Butler Inst., 1996, Grolier Club, 1996-97; executed murals in Emporia, Va., Lawrenceville, Ga.; represented in permanent collections at Met. Mus. Art, Whitney Mus. Am. Art, N.Y.C., Fogg Mus., Harvard U., Phila. Mus., Storm King Art Ctr., William Rockhill Nelson Mus., Kansas City, Mo., Duncan Phillips Gallery, Washington, Springfield Mus., Norton Gallery, Art Mus., New Britain, Conn., Libr. of Congress, Ency. Brit., IBM Collections, Art Inst., Zanesville, Ohio, U. Ga., S.I. Mus., Butler Inst., Pa. State U., Lehigh U., Columbia (S.C.) Mus. Art, The Whatcom Mus., Washington, Springville (Utah) Mus. Art, S.C. State Mus., Wichita Art Mus., Telfair Mus., Savannah, Ga., drawing retrospective Butler Inst. Am. Art, 1996; also numerous pvt. collections. Recipient 3d prize for painting Charleston Worcester Mus. Biennial, Jan. 1938; 1,000 grant in arts Am. Acad. and Inst. Arts and Letters, 1945; Pennell medal Pa. Acad., 1945; medal of Honor and purchase Pepsi-Cola Paintings of Year, 1948; Dawson Meml. medal Pa. Acad., 1950; Purchase award N.Y. State Fair, 1951; Drawing award Ball State Tchrs. Coll.; Guggenheim fellow, 1950-51; recipient Kuniyoshi award, 1994. Mem. Woodstock Artists Assn. (Sally Jacobs award 1981), Art Students League (life), Nat. Mus. Women in Arts Home: 54 Garrison Rd Bearsville NY 12409-9510

RUESCHEMEYER, MARILYN SCHATTNER, sociology educator; b. NYC, June 3, 1938; d. Julius Schattner and Bela Wax; m. Dietrich Rueschemeyer, June 14, 1962; children: Julia Yael, Simone Margalit. BA in Sociology, Queens Coll., 1959; MA in Sociology, U. Toronto, Can., 1965; PhD in Sociology, Brandeis U., 1978. Asst. prof. RISD, Providence, 1981-87, assoc. prof., 1987-93, prof. sociology, 1994—. Fellow Russian Rsch. Ctr., Harvard U., Cambridge, Mass., 1986—; adj. prof. sociology Brown U., Providence, 1987—; adj. prof. internat. rels. Brown U. Watson Inst., Providence, 1996—; adv. bd. Sociol. Analysis, 1998-2000; sr. assoc., mem. St. Anthony's Coll., Oxford U., 1979, 82, 97; vis. fellow dept. sociology Hebrew U. of Jerusalem, 1990. Author: Profl. Work and Marriage: An East West Comparison, 1981; co-author (with Golomshtok and Kennedy): Soviet Emigré Artists, 1985; editor: Women in the Politics of Post Communist E. Europe, 1994, 1998; co-editor (with D. Rueschemeyer and B. Wittrock): Participation and Democracy East and West, 1998; co-editor: (Comparison) (with Linda Cook and Mitchess Orenstein) "Left Parties and Social Policy in Post Communist Europe", 1999. Founding mem. Women's Polit. Caucus R.I.; active Reform Dems. R.I.; founder Friday Group, Providence, 1971—; bd. mem. RISD-Brown Hillel, 1990-2002. Rsch. grantee Internat. Rsch. and Exchs. Bd., Washington, 1984, 86, 91, 92, 97, Am. Coun. Learned Socs., 1987, 88. Fellow: Swedish Colloquium for Advanced Study in Social Scis.; mem.: Women East and West, German Studies Assn., Am. Sociol. Assn. (chair com. on internat. sociology 1993—96, rep. to Am. Assn. Advancement Slavic Studies), Am. Assn. for Advancement Slavic Studies (bd. dirs. 1996—99, 2001—). Office: Watson Inst for Internat Studies Brown Univ Providence RI 02912-9042 E-mail: marilyn_rueschemeyer@brown.edu.

RUESINK, ALBERT WILLIAM, biologist, plant sciences educator; b. Adrian, Mich., Apr. 16, 1940; s. Lloyd William and Alberta May (Foltz) R.; m. Kathleen Joy Cramer, June 8, 1963; children: Jennifer Li, Adriana Eleanor. BA, U. Mich., 1962; MA, Harvard U., 1965, PhD, 1966. Postdoctoral fellow Swiss Fed. Inst. Tech., Zurich, 1966-67; prof. biology Ind. U., Bloomington, 1967—, spl. asst. to Pres. for Faculty Rels., 1999—. Recipient Amoco Teaching award Ind. U., 1980 Mem. AAUP (pres. chpt. 1978-79, 90-91), Am. Soc. Plant Physiologists, Bot. Soc. Am. Democrat. Mem. United Ch. of Christ. Home: 2605 E 5th St Bloomington IN 47408-4286 Office: Ind U Dept Biology 1001 E 3d St Bloomington IN 47405 Office Phone: 812-855-5555. Business E-Mail: ruesink@indiana.edu.

RUETER, THOMAS JAMES, federal judge; b. 1955; BA, U. Scranton, 1977; JD, Dickinson U., 1980. Bar: Pa. 1980. Law clk. to Hon. Joseph L. McGlynn, Jr., U.S. Dist. Ct. for Ea. Dist. Pa., Phila., 1980-82; assoc. White & Williams, Phila., 1982-85; asst. U.S. atty. for ea. dist. Pa., U.S. Dept. Justice, Phila., 1985-90, chief narcotics sect., 1990-94. Notes editor Dickinson Law Rev., 1979-80; contbr. articles to law jours. Office: 601 Market St Rm 3038 Philadelphia PA 19106-1714

RUETTGERS, MICHAEL CADET, electronics executive; b. Muskogee, Okla., Dec. 11, 1942; s. John J. and Florence J. (Nunn) Ruettgers; m. Maureen Lee Sanders, July 12, 1969; children: Polly K., Christopher M., Abigail G. BS, Idaho State U., 1964; MBA, Harvard U., 1967. Engring. planner LTV Aerospace Co., Detroit, 1964—68; bus. area mgr. Raytheon Co., Lexington, Mass., 1968—81; sr. v.p., gen. mgr. Keane Inc., Boston, 1981—86; COO TFS Inc., Chelmsford, Mass., 1987—88; pres., COO EMC Corp., Hopkinton, Mass., 1988—2000, CEO, 1992—2001, chmn., bd. dirs., 2001—. Bd. dirs. Keane Inc., TFS Inc. Republican. Roman Catholic. Avocations: hunting, fishing. Office: EMC Corp 171 South St Hopkinton MA 01748-2222

RUF, H(AROLD) WILLIAM, JR., retired lawyer, corporation executive; b. Madison, Wis., July 1, 1934; s. Harold W. and Margaret (Dottridge) R.; m. Suzanne Williams, Aug. 25, 1962 (div. Jan. 1978); m. Jocelyn C. Ruf, Nov. 21, 1981; children: David W., Margaret E., Katharine S. BS, U. Wis., 1960, JD, 1962. Bar: Wis. 1962, Ohio 1963. Field atty. N.L.R.B., Cleve., 1962-65; counsel Oglebay Norton Co., Cleve., 1965-74, dir. indsl. rels., 1974-78, v.p., 1978-94; v.p. adminstrn. and legal affairs Oblebay Norton Co., Cleve., 1994-97; ret. Pres. bd. trustees Moreland Ct. Condo. Assn. Mem.: Cleve. Skating Club. Home: 13515 Shaker Blvd Cleveland OH 44120-5602

RUFE, LAURIE J. museum director; b. Pa. m. Mike Rufe. BA in Art History, Va. Commonwealth U. Intern Richmond Fine Arts Mus., Hist. House Mus.; with Mercer Mus., Doylestown, Pa.; oral history project Wyo.; with Douglas County Coun. for the Arts and Humanities, Colorado Springs; dir. Custer County Art Ctr., Mont.; dep. dir. Roswell (N.Mex.) Mus. and Art Ctr., Roswell, 1987—98; dir. Tucson Mus. Art, 1998—2002, 2002—. Office: Tucson Mus Art 140 N Main Ave Tucson AZ 85701*

RUFF, CHERYL ANDERSON, health facility administrator; BS, U. S.C., 1981. Intern U. S.C. Sch. Pharmacy, 1978-81; sr. student extern, relief pharmacist, cons., clin. ptnr. John Nates Pharmacy, Columbia, S.C., 1981-96; office coord., mgr., co-owner, clin. office-base pharmacist John M. Woodward M.D., Columbia, 1983-94; staff pharmacist S.C. Dept. Mental Health/Bryan Psychiat. Hosp., Columbia, 1994; dir. pharmacy D.T.E.C., Inc., Germantown, Tenn., 1994-96, Charter Rivers Behavioral Health Sys., West Columbia, S.C., 1994-96; cons. pharmacist Luth. Svcs., White Rock, S.C., 1996; adminstr., chief drug inspector S.C. Dept. Labor, Licensing and Regulation Bd. Pharmacy, Columbia, 1996—; assoc. prof. Sch. Pharmacy U. S.C. Mem. pharmacy adv. com. Midlands Tech. Coll. Active St. Joseph's Cath. Ch., Crayton Mid. Sch. PTO. Mem. Nat. Assn. Bds. Pharmacy Bd. (multi-state pharmacy jurisprudence examination program, item writer, examiner, com. on constn. and bylaws 1998), S.C. Pharm. Assn., 5th Dist. Pharm. Assn., S.C. Soc. Health Care Pharmacists, Med. Reps. Columbia. Address: PO Box 11927 Columbia SC 29211-1927

RUFF, EDWARD CARR, retired investment company executive; Grad., U. San Francisco, 1962. CPA. Acct., ptnr. mgmt. cons. divsn. Coopers & Lybrand, N.Y.C., 1962-76; CFO, Interstate/Johnson Lane, Charlotte, N.C., 1976-97, COO, 1997-2000. Past chpt. pres., dir. Fin. Execs. Inst.; allied mem. N.Y. Stock Exch. Contbg. author: The Stock Market Handbook. Charter mem. nat. adv. bd. Salvation Army, treas., mem. exec. com., chairperson Charlotte adv. bd., 1984-86; trustee Belmont Abbey Coll. Mem. Nat. Assn. Securities Dealers (prin.), Charlotte Rotary Club, KM, Charlotte Bus. Coun. Office: Interstate/Johnson Lane Corp IJL Fin Ctr PO Box 1012 Charlotte NC 28201-1012

RUFF, L. CANDY, state legislator; m. Gregory W. Ruff. Student, U. Kans. Rep. dist. 40 State of Kans., 1993—. Democrat. Home: 321 Arch St Leavenworth KS 66048-3421 Office: Kans Ho of Reps State Capitol Topeka KS 66612

RUFF, LINDY, professional hockey coach; m. Gaye Ruff; children: Brett, Eryn, Brian and Madeleine (twins). Defenseman Lethbridge Hockey Team, Buffalo Sabres, 1979-89, New York Rangers, 1989-91; player/asst. coach Rochester, 1991-92, San diego Gulls; asst. coach Fla. Panthers; head coach Buffalo Sabres, 1997—. Vol. Children's Hosp., Buffalo, Muscular Dystrophy Assn. Named Buffalo Sabre's Rookie of the Yr., 1980. Avocations: fishing, boating, golf. Office: c/o Buffalo Sabres 1 Seymour H Knox Iii Plz Buffalo NY 14203-3007

RUFF, ROBERT LOUIS, neurologist, physiology researcher; b. Bklyn., Dec. 16, 1950; s. John Joseph and Rhoda (Alpert) R. BS summa cum laude, Cooper Union, 1971; MD summa cum laude, PhD in Physiology, U. Wash., 1976. Diplomate Am. Bd. Neurology and Psychiatry. Asst. neurologist NY Hosp., Cornell Med. Sch., NYC, 1977-80; asst. prof. physiology and medicine U. Wash., Seattle, 1980-84; assoc. prof. neurology Case Western Res. Med. Sch., Cleve., 1984-92, prof. neurology and neuroscis., 1993—, residency dir., neurology dept., 1994—2003, vice chair neurology dept., 1995—2004; chief dept. neurology Cleve. VA Med. Ctr., 1984—2003, chief phys. medicine and rehab. svc., 1998—2000, mgr. rehab. and spinal cord injury and disorder product line, 1999—2003; med. dir. Functional Elec. Stimulation Ctr., Cleve., 2000—; chief Spinal Cord Injury and Dysfunction Svc., Cleveland VA Med. Ctr., 2003—; dir. rehab. rsch. svc. Office R & D Dept. VA Ctrl. Office, Washington, 2004—. Adv. Child Devel. and Mental Retardation Ctr., Seattle, 1980-84, Burien Devel. Disability Ctr., Wash., 1982-84; mem. med. adv. bd. Muscular Dystrophy Assn., Seattle, 1984, NE Ohio chpt. Multiple Sclerosis Soc., 1986—; mem. adv. bd. for Neurology Dept. Vets. Affairs, 1989—, mem. study sect. for rehab. career devel. awards; chmn. med. adv. bd. N.E. Ohio chpt. Myasthenia Gravis Found., 1987—, trustee, 1993—, nat. med. adv. bd., 1988—, grant and fellowship com., 1990—. Assoc. editor: Neurology, 1994—96, mem. editl. bd., 1996—97, assoc. editor: Jour. Rehab. Rsch. and Devel., 2000—, ad hoc reviewer: various profl. and sci. jours., mem. editl. bd.: Jour. Rehab. and Devel., 1999—; contbr. articles to profl. jours., chapters to books. Nat. bd. dir. Myasthenia Gravis Found., 1994—, Doctor's award, 2002. Recipient Tchr. Investigator award NIH; NSF fellow, 1971; NIH grantee, Muscular Dystrophy Assn. grantee, Dept. Vets. Affairs, Rsch. Enhancement Advanced Ctr. awards, 1999—, Dr. award Myasthenia Gravis Found. Am., 2002; NY State Regents med. scholar, 1971. Fellow Am. Heart Assn. (stroke coun.), Am. Acad. Neurology (scientific issues com., legis. action com.); mem. AMA, IEEE, Am. Paraplegia Soc., Am. Soc. Neuro-Rehab., Am. Physics Soc., Neurosci. Soc., Biophys. Soc., Am. Neurol. Assn., NY Acad. Sci., Am. Geriatrics Soc., Am. Physiol. Soc., Sigma Pi Sigma (v.p. 1970-71), Alpha Omega Alpha (v.p. 1975-76). Home: 4026 Princeton Blvd South Euclid OH 44121 Office: VA Med Ctr 10701 East Blvd Ste 127W Cleveland OH 44106-1702 Office Phone: 216-791-3800 5219. Business E-Mail: robertlruff@aol.com.

RUFFALO, MARK, actor; b. Kenosha, Wis., Nov. 22, 1967; m. Sunrise Coigney, 2000; 1 child, Keen. Actor: (films) Rough Trade, 1993, A Song For You, 1993, There Goes My Baby, 1994, Mirror, Mirror 2:Raven Dance, 1994, A Gift From Heaven, 1994, Mirror, Mirror III: The Voyeur, 1995, The Dentist, 1996, The Last Big Thing, 1996, Blood Money, 1996, Safe Men, 1998, 54, 1998, A Fish in the Bathtub, 1999, Ride with the Devil, 1999, You Can Count on Me, 2000, Committed, 2000, Life/Drawing, 2001, The Last Castle, 2001, XX/XY, 2002, Windtalkers, 2002, My Life Without Me, 2003, View From the Top, 2003, In the Cut, 2003, Eternal Sunshine of the Spotless Mind, 2004, 13 Going On 30, 2004; (TV films) On the 2nd Day of Christmas, 1997, Houdini, 1998; (TV series) The Beat, 2000; (films) The Destiny of Marty Fine, 1996; writer: films The Destiny of Marty Fine, 1996; exec. prodr., actor: (films) We Don't Live Here Anymore, 2004. Office: William Morris Agy One William Morris Pl Beverly Hills CA 90212*

RUFFER, DAVID GRAY, museum director, former college president; b. Archbold, Ohio, Aug. 25, 1937; s. Lawrence A. and Florence A. (Newcomer) R.; m. Marilyn Elaine Taylor, Aug. 23, 1958; children: Rochelle Lynne, Robyn Lynne, David Geoffrey. BS, Defiance Coll., 1959; MA, Bowling Green State U., 1960; PhD, U. Okla., 1964. Spl. instr. U. Okla., 1963-64; asst. prof. biology Defiance Coll., 1964-68, asso. prof., 1968-73, faculty dean, 1969-73; provost Elmira (N.Y.) Coll., 1973-78; pres. Albright Coll., Reading, Pa., 1978-91, U. Tampa, Fla., 1991-94; exec. dir. Dayton (Ohio) Soc. Natural History, 1995-99; pres., exec. dir. Children's Mus. of the Valley, Youngstown, Ohio, 2001—. Author: Exploring and Understanding Mammals, 1971; contbr. articles to profl. jours. NSF grantee, 1965, 67; Ohio Biol. Survey grantee, 1968-69 Fellow AAAS; mem. Am. Assn. Museums, Rotary, Sigma Xi. Presbyterian. Home: 167 Mill Creek Rd Youngstown OH 44512-1402 E-mail: mdruffer@aol.com.

RUFFER, JOYCE SELLARS, poet, artist; b. Cairo, Ga. children: Charles Scott Mason, Jeffrey Dewayne Mason. Artist, all mediums. Author: (poetry) Rose Moon. Named Best Poet 1994, Nat. Libr. Poetry, Poet of Yr., Internat. Soc. Poets, 1996; recipient Editor's Choice award Nat. Libr. Poetry, Poetic Achievement award, Am. Poetry Soc. Avocations: spiritual enhancement, birding, nature photography, marine ecology, feline appreciation. Home: 2000 US Highway 199 Crescent City CA 95531-9364 Fax: 707 464-7557. E-mail: Jpolli@cc.northcoast.com.

RUFFIN, JOHN, federal agency administrator, researcher; b. New Orleans, June 29, 1943; s. Wesley and Olivia Ruffin; m. Angela Beverly, Aug. 24, 1968; children: John Wesley, Meeka Dionne, Beverly Alaina. BS, Dillard U., 1965; MS, Atlanta U., 1967; PhD, Kans. State U., 1971; postgrad., Harvard U., 1975-77. Instr. biology So. U., Baton Rouge, 1967-68; asst. prof. biology Atlanta U., 1971-74; assoc. prof. Ala. A&M U., Huntsville, 1974-75; prof. biology, chmn. dept. N.C. Cen. U., Durham, 1978—, dean Coll. Arts and Scis., 1986—90; assoc. dir. research, minority health NIH, 1990—2001; dir. Nat. Ctr. on Minority Health and Health Disparities, NIH, 2001—. Adv. bd. N.C. Bd. Sci. and Tech., 1983—; chmn. MARC study sect. NIH, Bethesda, Md., 1979-81, com. mem. MARC study sect., 1984-87. Contbr. numerous articles to sci. jours. Grantee NIH, 1976; Cabot Research fellow, 1976. Mem. AAAS (nominating com.), Botanical Soc. Am., N.C. Acad. Scis., Assn. Southeastern Biologists, Assn. Environ. and Exptl. Botany. Office: Nat Ctr Minority Health & Health Disparities MSC 5465 6707 Democracy Blvd Ste 800 Bethesda MD 20892-5465*

RUFFIN, PAUL DEAN, English language educator; b. Millport, Ala., May 14, 1941; s. David Clarence and Zealon (Robinson) R.; m. Sharon Marie Krebs, June 21, 1973; children: Genevieve, Matthew. BS, Miss. State U., 1964, MA, 1967; PhD, Univ. So. Miss., 1974. Instr. Eng. Univ. So. Miss., Hattiesburg, 1971-72, Miss. State Univ., Starkville, 1972-74; prof. Eng. Sam Houston State Univ., Huntsville, Tex., 1975—. Dir. Tex. Rev. Press, Huntsville, 1992—. Author: Circling, 1996, Our Women, 1985, The Man Who Would Be God, 1993, Islands, Women and God, 2001, Pompeii Man, 2002, The Book of Boys and Girls, 2003, This the Matter Is: The Selected Poetry and Prose of Robert Holland, 2003; editor: That's What I Like About the South, 1993; editor Tex. Rev., 1976—. With U.S. Army, USNG, 1959-65. Mem. Tex. Inst. Letters, Conf. Coll. Tchrs. Eng., South Ctrl. Modern Lang. Assn. Avocations: writing, gardening, woodworking. Home: 2014 Ave N 1/2 Huntsville TX 77340

RUFFING, ANNE ELIZABETH, artist; b. Bklyn. d. John Paul and Ruth Elizabeth (Price) Frampton; m. George W. Ruffing, Mar. 29, 1967; 1 dau., Elizabeth Anne. BS, Cornell U., 1964; postgrad., Drexel Inst. Tech., 1966. One-woman exhbns. include, IBM, 1966, Hall of Fame, Goshen, N.Y., 1971, group exhbns. include, Internat. Women's Arts Festival, World Trade Center, N.Y.C., 1975-76, Berkshire Mus., Pittsfield, Mass., 1965, 76, Cooperstown (N.Y.) Mus., 1969; represented in permanent collections, Met. Mus. Art, Bklyn. Mus., Library of Congress, Harvard U., Smithsonian Instn., N.Y. Hist. Soc. Johnston Hist. Mus., Atwater Kent Mus., Albany Inst. History and Art, Whitney Mus. Am. Art, Boston Public Library. Recipient 1st place Eric Sloane award, 1974; Internat. Women's Year award Internat. Women's Art Festival, 1976 Address: 1031 Lewis Farm Rd Zebulon NC 27597

RUFFNER, CHARLES LOUIS, lawyer; b. Cin., Nov. 7, 1936; s. Joseph H. and Edith (Solomon) R.; m. Mary Ann Kaufman, Jan. 30, 1966 (div. 1993); children: Robin Sue, David Robert; m. Nanette Diemer, Feb. 26, 1995. BSBA in Acctg., U. Fla., 1958; JD cum laude, U. Miami, 1964. Bar: Fla. 1964, U.S. Dist. Ct. (so. and Mid. dists.) Fla. 1964, U.S. Ct. Appeals (5th cir.) 1964, U. S. Ct. Appeals (11th cir.) 1984, U.S. Claims Ct. 1966, U.S. Tax Ct. 1966, U.S. Supreme Ct. 1969; cert. in taxation. Trial atty. tax divsn. Dept. Justice, Washington, 1964-67; pres. Forrest, Ruffner, Traum & Hagen, P.A., Miami, Fla., 1967-78, Ruffner, Hagen & Rifkin, P.A., Miami, 1978-81; tax ptnr. Myers, Kenin, Levinson, Ruffner, Frank & Richards, Miami, 1982-84; pres. Charles L. Ruffner, P.A., 1984—. Lectr. Fla. Internat. U., Miami. Author: A Practical Approach to Professional Corporations and Associations, 4 edits., 1970, (column) Tax Talk, Miami Law Rev.; editor Miami Law Rev., 1963-64; contbr. numerous articles on taxation to law jours. Named One of Best Lawyers in Am., 1999—. Mem. ABA, Fed. Bar Assn., Fla. Bar (exec. coun. tax sect. 1967-92, 95—, amicus curiae in test case of validity profl. corps.), Dade County Bar Assn., South Fla. Tax Litigation Assn. (chmn. 1986-00), Phi Alpha Delta, Phi Kappa Phi. Office: 8830 SW 67th Ct Miami FL 33156-1700 Office Phone: 305-669-1904. E-mail: cruff7117@aol.com.

RUFFNER, FREDERICK G., JR., book publisher; b. Akron, Ohio, Aug. 6, 1926; s. Frederick G. and Olive Mae (Taylor) R.; m. Mary Ann Evans, Oct. 8, 1954; children: Frederic G. III, Peter Evans. BS, Ohio State U., 1950. Advt. mgr. Jim Robbins Co., Royal Oak, Mich., 1950-52; research mgr. Gen. Detroit Corp., 1953-54; pres. Gale Research Co., Detroit, 1954-87, Omnigraphics, Inc., 1987—. Editor: Ency. of Assns, 1956-68, Code Names Dictionary, 1963, Acronyms and Initialisms Dictionary, 1965, Allusions Dictionary, 1985; pub. Gold Coast Mag., 1992—; patentee in field. Bd. dirs. Friends of Detroit Pub. Libr., pres., 1975-76; mem. exec. bd. Detroit coun. Boy Scouts Am., 1974—, v.p., 1976-82; pres. Coun. for Fla. Librs., 1979—; trustee Bon Secours Hosp., Grosse Pointe, Mich., 1980-81; v.p. Etruscan Found., Florence, Italy, 1980—; pres. Mich. Ctr. for the Book, 1990, Literary Landmarks Assn., Gold Coast Jazz Soc., Ft. Lauderdale, 1992—; bd. dirs., v.p. Ohio State U. Found., Bonnet House, Ft. Lauderdale, 1992. 1st lt. AUS, 1944-46. Decorated Bronze Star, Combat Inf. award; recipient Centennial award Ohio State U., 1970, Benjamin Creativity award Assn. Am. Pubs., 1985, Career medal Ohioana Libr. Assn., 1988, Lifetime Achievement award Am. Libr. Trustees Assn., 1992; named to Entrepreneurs Hall of Fame, Nova U. Mem. Am. Antiquarian Soc., ALA (hon. life), Am. Mgmt. Assn., Am. Assn. Mus., Detroit Hist. Soc., Am. Hist. Print Collectors Soc., Bibliog. Soc. Am., Sierra Club, Pres. Assn., Audubon Soc., Am. Name Soc., Early Am. Industries Assn., Nat. Press Club (Washington), Ephemera Soc., Johnny Appleseed Soc., Navy League, Newcomen Soc., Cen. Bus. Dist. Assn. Detroit (vice-chmn. 1985-87), Jazz Forum (Grosse Pointe Farms, Mich.), Nat. Trust Hist. Preservation, Fairfield Heritage Soc., Archives Am. Art, Pvt. Librs. Assn., Friends Ft. Lauderdale Pub. Libr. (pres. 1974-78), Phileas Soc. (pres. 1985—), Ohio State U. Club (pres. Detroit club 1958, nat. chmn. Ohio State U. campaign, 1985-88), Masons, Shriners, Book Club, Detroit Athletic Club, Econ. Club, Prismatic Club (pres. 1990), Fontenada Soc. (pres. 1990-91), Detroit Club, Country Club Detroit, Ocean Reef Club, Grosse Pointe Yacht Club, Coral Ridge Yacht Club, Lauderdale Yacht Club, Princeton Club, Salmagundi Club, Grolier Club, Century Assn., Marco Polo Club, Faculty Club Ohio State U., Old Club, Commonwealth Club (San Francisco), Gross Pointe Club, Wawetonong Club, Tau Kappa Epsilon. Republican. Presbyterian. Home: 221 Lewiston Rd Grosse Pointe MI 48236-3519 also: 1000 Flamingo Isle Dr Fort Lauderdale FL 33301-2670 also: 901 E Las Olas Blvd Fort Lauderdale FL 33301-2320 Address: Omnigraphics Inc 615 Griswold St Detroit MI 48226-3415

RUFFO, MICHAEL, painter; b. S.I., Mar. 9, 1954; s. Thomas Anthony and Marie (Papa) Ruffo; m. Lorelei Ann Perez, July 5, 1995. BFA, Sch. Visual Arts, N.Y.C., 1991. Exhibited in group shows at Salmagundi Club, 1992—93, 1995—99, Agora Gallery, 1998—99, World Fine Art, 1999, Knickerbocker Gallery, 1999, Hiram Blauvelt Mus., 1999, Nexus Gallery, 1999—2001, NYU, 2000, Green County Coun. Arts, 2002, Gordon Green Gallery, 2002, Mountaintop Gallery, 2003—04, Represented in permanent collections U.S. Dept. State; patentee lockable lid support. Recipient Excellence award, Manhattan Arts Internat. Competition, 1997—98, 1999. Mem.: Nurture Art (reigstry artist), N.Y. Artists Cir. Registry, Orgn. Ind. Artists, N.Y. Artists Equity Assn. Roman Catholic.

RUFFOLO, ROBERT R. research and development company executive; b. Yonkers, N.Y., Apr. 14, 1950; BS in Pharmacology summa cum laude, Ohio State U., 1973, PhD in Pharmacology, 1976. Adj. prof. dept. pharmacology McGill U. Sch. Medicine, Montreal, Canada, 1982—89; chmn. cardiovasc. rsch. com. Lilly Rsch. Labs., 1983—84; adj. prof. divsn. pharmacology Ohio State U. Coll. Pharmacy, Columbus, 1989—; adj. prof. dept. pharmacology Baylor U. Sch. Medicine, Houston, 1990—; bd. visitors U. Wis. Sch. Pharmacy, Madison, 1993—96; spl. rev. cons. NIH, Nat. Inst. on Drug Abuse, 1984; mem. site visit com. U. Chgo., Nat. Heart, Lung and Blood Inst., 1988; mem. subcom. for receptor nomenclature and drug classification: adrenoceptors Internat. Union for Pharmacology, 1990—, mem. com. for receptor nomenclature and drug classification. Named disting. vis. prof., U. Houston, 1994, Malone-Booker lectr. in pharmacology, Howard U., 1995; recipient fellowship, Am. Found. for Pharm. Edn., 1973—76, PRAT fellowship, Nat. Ints. of Gen. Med. Scis., 1977—78, Cert. of Appreciation, FDA, Com. for Advanced Sci. Edn., 1989, Albert Szentgyorgy medal, 1997, Lorenzini Gold medal, Lorenzini Med. Sci. Found., 1999. Mem.: SAG, Am. Soc. for Pharmacology and Exptl. Therapeutics (chmn. symposium of peripheral alpha-adrenergic receptors 1983, mem. program com. 1984—89, chmn., organizer 1990, mem. subcom. on pharmacology in industry 1990—92, mem. nomination com. 1992—93, mem. com. on indsl.-acad. rels. 1993—94, sec.-treas. 1994—97, mem. fin. com. 1994—97, coun. mem. 1994—97, mem. investment subcom. 1995—96, chmn. fin. com. 1995—96, mem. Sollman Award selection com. 1997, coun. mem. 1999—, Travel award 1981, 1984, John Jacob Abel award 1988, John V. Croker lectr. 1998), Brit. Pharmacol. Soc., Fedn. of Am. Socs. Exptl. Biology (mem. publs. com. 1989—), Soc. Critical Care Medicine, Mid-Atlantic Pharmacology Soc., Phi Kappa Phi. Office: Wyeth Rsch Pharm R&D 500 Arcola Rd Collegeville PA 19426

RUFIN, CARLOS, finance educator, consultant; arrived in US, 1982; s. Antonio and Ligia Rufin; m. Sandra Pastrana, Aug. 22, 1962; children: Catalina, Teresa, Mariana. BA in Econs., Princeton U., 1986; MA in Econs., Columbia U., 1987; PhD, Harvard U., 2000; Gen. Course Diploma, London Sch. of Economics, London, England, 1984—85. Cons. Stone & Webster Mgmt. Consultants, N.Y.C., 1987—89; fin. mgr. Imperial Chem. Industries, Barcelona, 1989—93; exec. cons. Levitan & Assocs., Boston, 1994—98, London Econs., Cambridge, 1998—2000; asst. prof. of mgmt. Babson Coll., Babson Park, Mass., 2000—. Ind. cons., 2000—. Author book and articles on polit. economy of privatization and deregulation of the electric power industry. Mem. Cuitadans pel Canvi, Barcelona, 2001—04. Recipient John I. Dixon, Class of '48, Meml. scholarship, Princeton U., 1984—85, Kidder, Peabody & Co. scholarship, 1985—86, grad. fellowship, Grad. Sch. of Arts and Scis., Columbia U., 1986—87, David Rockefeller Ctr. for Latin Am. Studies, Harvard U., 1996—97, Joseph R. Crump fellowship, John F. Kennedy Sch. of Govt., 1998—99. Mem.: Assn. of Pub. Policy Analysis and Mgmt., Acad. of Internat. Bus., Acad. of Mgmt. Office: Babson Coll 231 Forest St Babson Park MA 02457-0310 Home: 144 Wildwood Ave Arlington MA 02476 Office Phone: 781-239-6411.

RUFRANO, GLENN, real estate company executive; Co-chmn. The Peabody Group; ptnr., pres., COO, CFO The O'Connor Group, 1983—2000; CEO New Plan Excel Realty Trust, N.Y.C., 2000—. Bd. dirs. TrizecHahn Corp.; adj. prof. NYU Real Estate Inst. Mem.: Nat. Assn. Real Estate Investment Trusts (bd. govs.), Internat. Coun. Shopping Ctrs., Urban Land Inst. Office: New Plan Excel Realty Trust 1120 Ave of the Americas New York NY 10036*

RUGABER, WALTER FEUCHT, JR., interim university president, newspaper executive; b. Macon, Ga., Nov. 29, 1938; s. Walter Feucht— Edith Almeda (Maynard) R.; m. Sally Sanford, Oct. 6, 1962; children— Leslie, Christopher, Mark BS, Northwestern U., 1960. Corr., editor N.Y. Times, 1965—78; v.p., exec. editor Greensboro Daily News & Record, NC, 1978—82; pres., pub. The Roanoke Times, Va., 1982—2000; pres. Landmark Pub. Group, 1995—99; interim pres. Hollins U., Roanoke, Va., 2001—02. Mem. Pulitzer Prize Bd., 1990-99. Bd. dirs. United Way of Roanoke Valley, Va., 1982—88, Roanoke Sympony Soc., 1985—91, pres., 1986—88; trustee Hollins U., 1993—2002. Mem. Am. Newspaper Pubs. Assn., Am. Soc. Newspaper Editors, So. Newspaper Pubs. Assn. E-mail: wrugaber@swva.net.

RUGE, DANIEL AUGUST, retired neurosurgeon, educator; b. Murdock, Nebr., May 13, 1917; s. August Daniel and Mary Louise R.; m. Greta Piper, June 12, 1942; children: Charlotte, Thomas. BA, N. Central Coll., Naperville, Ill., 1939, Sc.D., 1971; MD, Northwestern U., 1945, PhD, 1961. Intern Wesley Meml. Hosp., Chgo., 1945-46, resident, 1949-50, Passavant Meml. Hosp., Chgo., 1946-49, VA Hosp., Hines, Ill., 1950-52; practice medicine specializing in neurosurgery Chgo., 1952-76; prof. surgery Northwestern U., Chgo., 1973-76; professorial lectr. George Washington U., Washington, 1976-86, ret., 1986; dep. dir. spinal cord injury service VA Central Office, Washington, 1976-80, dir., 1980-81, 85-86, ret., 1986; physician to pres. U.S., White House, 1981-85. Author: Spinal Cord Injuries, 1969, Spinal Disorders: Diagnosis and Treatment, 1977; editor: Jour. Am. Paraplegia Soc., 1976-88. Trustee North Cen. Coll., 1960—, chmn. bd., 1974-77. Lt comdr. USN, 1954-56. Recipient Service award Northwestern U., 1966, Merit award Northwestern U., 1983; Outstanding Alumnus award N. Central Coll., 1978, Meritorious Service award VA, 1986. Fellow A.C.S.; mem. AMA, Am. Assn. Neurol. Surgeons, Central Surg. Assn., James IV Assn. Surgeons. Republican. Presbyterian. Home: 240 S High St Denver CO 80209-2628

RUGEN, KAREN, manufacturing executive, corporate communications specialist; Head corp. comms. Hyatt Hotels Corp., 1978—94; chief comm. officer Boston Chicken Co., Boston, 1994—98; sr. v.p. corp. comms. and pub. affairs Rite Aid Corp., Camp Hill, Pa., 1999—. Office: Rite Aid Corp 30 Hunter Ln Camp Hill PA 17011

RUGGE, HENRY FERDINAND, medical products executive; b. South San Francisco, Oct. 28, 1936; s. Hugo Heinrich and Marie Mathilde (Breiholz) R.; m. Sue Callow, Dec. 29, 1967. BS in Physics, U. Calif., Berkeley, 1958, PhD in Physics, 1963. Sr. physicist Physics Internat. Co., San Leandro, 1963-68; dir. adminstrn. and fin. Arkon Sci. Labs., Berkeley, Calif., 1969-71; v.p. Norse Systems, Inc., Hayward, Calif., 1972-74, Rasor Assocs., Inc., Sunnyvale, Calif., 1974-81, v.p., gen. mgr., 1983-87, exec. v.p. fin., 1988-89, pres., chief exec. officer, 1990—; chmn. UltraVision, Inc., Calgary, Alta., Can., 1993-96, also bd. dirs., 1993—; pres., CEO Mission Med., Inc., Fremont, Calif., 1997-99. Pres. Berlinscan, Inc., Sunnyvale, 1981-82; cons. The Rugge Group, Berkeley, 1987-90; bd. dirs. Rasor Assocs., Inc., Space Power Inc., Analatom, Inc. Patentee in area med. devices. U. Calif. scholar, 1954-58. Mem. Am. Heart Assn., Berkeley Bicycle (treas. 1983-84), Phi Beta Kappa. Avocations: bicycle racing, wine, food. Home: 46 Hiller Dr Oakland CA 94618-2302 Office: Mission Med Inc 5670 Stewart Ave Fremont CA 94538-3174 E-mail: hrugge@missionmed.com.

RUGGIE, JOHN GERARD, political science educator, diplomat; b. Graz, Austria, Oct. 18, 1944; came to U.S., 1967; s. Josef and Margaret (Macic) R.; m. Mary Zacharuk, May 21, 1965; 1 child, Andreas John. BA, McMaster U., 1967; MA, U. Calif., Berkeley, 1968; PhD, U. Calif., 1974; LLD (hon.), McMaster U., 2000. Asst. prof. polit. sci. U. Calif., Berkeley, 1974-78, prof. internat. rels. San Diego, 1987-91, dir. inst. global conflict and cooperation, 1989-91; prof. polit. sci. Columbia U., N.Y.C., 1978-87, prof. polit. sci., internat. affairs, 1991-97, dean Sch. Internat. and Pub. Affairs, 1991-96; Kirkpatrick prof. internat. affairs Harvard U., 2001—. Dir. Ctr. for Bus. and Govt. Harvard U., 2002—; asst. sec. gen. UN, N.Y.C., 1997—2001, spl. advisor sec. gen., 2003—. Author: Winning the Peace, 1996, Constructing the World Polity, 1998; editor: 4 books; contbr. over 60 articles to profl. jours. Named Internat. Studies Assn. Disting. scholar, 1999; recipient Hubert H. Humphrey award outstanding pub. svc., Am. Polit. Sci. Assn., 2000. Fellow Am. Acad. Arts Sci.; mem. UN Assn. (bd. dirs. 1985—), Fgn. Policy Assn. (bd. govs. 1992-95), Coun. Fgn. Rels. Avocations: skiing, scuba, tennis. Office: Kennedy School of Govt Harvard University Cambridge MA 02138 E-mail: john_ruggie@harvard.edu.

RUGGIERO, ALESSANDRO G. physicist, researcher; b. Rome, Apr. 10, 1940; came to the U.S., 1970; s. Ettore Antonio Ruggiero and Irma Zuppa; m. Amalia Lucia Comis, Feb. 7, 1965; children: Sara, Filippo. PhD in Physics, U. Rome, 1964. Physicist CERN, Geneva, 1966-69, Fermilab, Batavia, Ill., 1970-84; sr. physicist Argonne (Ill.) Nat. Lab., 1985-86; divsn. head Brookhaven Nat. Lab., Upton, N.Y., 1987-92, sr. physicist, 1993—. Cons. Dept. Energy, 1985—. Author, editor: Crystalline Beams, 1995, Hadron Colliders, 1996; editor: Stability of Particle Motion, 1992. Fellow Am. Phys. Soc.; mem. N.Y. Acad. Scis. Republican. Roman Catholic. Avocations: history, phylosophy. Home: 33 Inlet View Path W East Moriches NY 11940 Office: Brookhaven Nat Lab PO Box 5000 Upton NY 11973 E-mail: agr@bnl.gov.

RUGGIERO, ANTHONY WILLIAM, chemical company executive; b. Mt. Vernon, N.Y., May 27, 1941; s. Jerome and Mary (Nanti) R.; m. Elaine M. Tornese, Sept. 27, 1964; children: Alicia Marie, Audrey Loren. BS in Econs., Fordham U., 1963; MBA in Fin., Columbia U., 1964; P.M.C. in Acctg., Iona Coll., 1977. V.p. fin. E. R. Squibb & Sons, Princeton, N.J., 1969-83; sr. v.p., chief fin. officer, dir. Squibb Corp., Princeton, N.J., 1983-89; sr. v.p., contr. Bristol-Myers Squibb Co., N.Y.C., 1990; sr. v.p., CFO, Reader's Digest, Pleasantville, N.Y., 1990-95; sr. v.p., CFO Olin Corp., Norwalk, Conn., 1995-99, exec. v.p., CFO, 1999—, also bd. dirs. Bd. dirs. Carlisle Cos., Inc. Recipient Statistics award Am. Statis Assn., 1963 Mem. Fin. Execs. Inst. (CFO adv. coun.). Office: Olin Co PO Box 4500 Norwalk CT 06856-4500

RUGGIERO, GUIDO, historian, educator; s. Guido and Margaret Ruggiero; m. Laura Giannetti. BA, U. of Colo., 1966; MA, UCLA, 1967, PhD, 1972. Prof. of history U. of Miami, Coral Gables, Fla., 1994—97; Josephine Berry Weiss chair in the humanities Pa. State U., U. Pk., Pa., 1997—2003; chair dept. of History U. of Miami, Coral Gables, Fla., 2003—. Prof. of history U. of Conn., Storrs, 1987—94; from instr. to assoc. prof. U. of Cin., 1971—87; editor studies in the history of sexuality Oxford U. Press, N.Y.C., 1985—2002. Author: (history book) Binding Passions: Tales of Magic, Marriage and Power, 1993, The Boundaries of Eros: Sex Crime and Sexuality in Renaissance Venice, 1985, Violence in Early Renaissance Venice, 1980; editor: A Companion to the Worlds of the Renaissance, 2002; co-editor: (encyclopedia) Encyclopedia of European Social History from 1350 to 2000, 6 vols., 2001, (history book) History from Crime; Johns Hopkins, 1994, Microhistory and the Lost Peoples of Europe, 1991, Sex and Gender in Historical Perspective, 1990; co-editor, co-transl.: literature book Five Comedies from the Italian Renaissance, 2003. Recipient NEH fellowship Harvard's Villa I Tatti, NEH, 1990—91, NEH fellowship Inst. for Advanced Studies, Princeton U., 1981—82; fellow, John Simon Guggenheim Found., 1991. Mem.: Ateneo Veneto (fgn., elected). Office: Dept History Ashe 619A U of Miami PO Box 248107 Miami FL 33124

RUGGIERO, MATTHEW JOHN, bassoonist; b. Phila., Sept. 18, 1932; s. Pompeo and Theresa (Ciampa) R.; m. Nancy Cirillo, Apr. 2, 1961; children: Eleanor, Claudia, Lisa. Diploma, Curtis Inst. Music, 1957; AA, Harvard U., 1982, BA cum laude, 1984, MA, 1987; PhD, Boston U., 1993. Second bassoonist Nat. Symphony Orch., Washington, 1957-60; asst. prin. bassoonist Boston Symphony Orch., 1961-89; prin. bassoonist Boston Pops Orch., 1974-89; ret., 1989. Mem. faculty Boston U., 1963—, New Eng. Conservatory Music, 1963— Served with U.S. Army, 1954-57. Boston U. Profs. Program scholar and fellow, 1989.

RUGGIERO, RENATO, former Italian government official; b. Naples, Italy, Apr. 9, 1930; JD, U. Naples, 1953. With Italian Diplomatic Svc., Sao Paulo, Moscow, Washington, counselor Belgrade, 1966, counsellor social affairs Permanent Mission European Cmtys., 1969, pres. Com. European Cmtys., 1970-73, dir.-gen. regional policy, 1973-77, com. spokesperson, 1977; coord. dept. EEC Italian Ministry Fgn. Affairs, 1978, diplomatic counsellor of pres. of coun., 1979, chef cabinet Min. Fgn. Affairs, 1979, permanent rep. European

Cmtys., 1980-84, dir.-gen. econ. affairs, 1984-85, sec.-gen., 1985-87, min. fgn. trade, 1987-91; dir.-gen. World Trade Orgn., Geneva, 1995—99; vice chmn. Schroder Salomon Smith Barney Internat., London, 1999—2001; chmn. Gruppo Campari SPA, Milan, 2001; min. fgn. affairs Govt. of Italy, 2001—02. Decorated knight grand cross Order of Merit, knight comdr. Order St. Michael and St. George (Eng.); grand cordon Order of Sacred Treasure (Japan); knight Grand Croce (Italy); knight grand cross Equestrian Order St. Gregory the Great (Vatican). Mem.: bd. of dir., Fiat S.p.A., 2001-, bd. of dir., Inst. of Internat. Econ., 2002-.

RUGGLES, RUDY LAMONT, JR., international security advisor; b. Evanston, Ill., Nov. 11, 1938; s. Rudy Lamont and Ruth (Cain) R.; m. Cecelia Ann Consorte, July 20, 1974 (div. 1996); m. Sara Joyce Silbernagel, Feb. 3, 1998; children— Rudy, Christopher, Daniel, Andrew. BA, Harvard U., 1960, MBA, 1966. Sr. assoc. physicist IBM Rsch. Labs., Poughkeepsie, NY, 1960-64; corp. planning cons. corp. hdqrs. IBM, Armonk, N.Y., 1966-71; sr. mem. profl. staff Hudson Inst., Croton-on-Hudson, N.Y., 1971-75, pres., 1975-79, also dir.; prin. Cresap, McCormick & Paget, Inc., 1979-82; ptnr. The Phila. Mgmt. Cons. Group, Inc., 1982—; mng. dir. New China Group, Inc., 1982—. Chmn. residential solicitation United Fund, Pound Ridge, N.Y., 1969; mem. parents com. St. Paul's Sch., Concord, N.H.; dir. Danbury Hosp. and Danbury Hosp. Devel. Fund, Conn., 1978—, med. affairs com.; chmn. fin. com. Pound Ridge Community Ch., 1969-70; bd. dirs. Harry Frank Guggenheim Found., 1982—; bd. visitors Sch. Langs. and Linguistics Georgetown U.; trustee New Canaan Country Sch., The Newberry Libr.; mem. Ridgefield (Conn.) Drug and Alcohol Commn.; treas., bd. dirs. Nat. Coun. Alcoholism and Drug Dependence; chmn. bd. dirs. Midwestern Conn. Coun. on Alcoholism. With C.E., U.S. Army, 1962. Fellow Explorers Club; mem. Hudson Inst. (hon.), N. Am. Soc. Corp. Planning (dir. 1966-72), Internat. Inst. Strategic Studies, Internat. Map Collectors Soc., James Caird Soc., Ends of the Earth (hon.), Harvard Club of N.Y.C., Sigma Xi (hon.).

RUGO, STEVEN ALFRED, architect; b. Washington, June 1, 1953; s. Alfred Joseph and Lena (Aubrey) R.; m. Mary Lourie Blackett, Nov. 11, 1978 (div. Jan. 1983); m. Laura Secord de Frise, June 25, 1988; children: Peter William, Aubrey Secord. Student, Ripon Coll., 1971-73, Harvard U., 1973; BArch, Syracuse U., 1976. Assoc. firms Booth/Hansen, Booth Nagle & Hartray, Booth & Nagle, Chgo., 1976-81; pvt. practice architecture Rugo/Raff Ltd., Chgo., 1982—. Assoc. bd. mem. Rush Presbyn., St. Lukes Med. Ctr., Chgo., Art Inst. Chgo. Mem. AIA, Met. Planning Coun., Chgo. Archtl. Club, Southeast Ravenswood Assn., Racquet Club, Saddle and Cycle, Arts Club, Spring Island Club. Episcopalian. Avocations: painting, printmaking. Office: 20 W Hubbard St Chicago IL 60610-4623

RUH, EDWIN, ceramic engineer, consultant, researcher; b. Westfield, N.J., Apr. 22, 1924; s. Harry John and Martha A. (Grasing) R.; m. Elizabeth J. Mundy, June 14, 1952; children: Edwin Jr., Elizabeth Jeanne. BS in Ceramic Engring. with honors, Rutgers U., 1949, MS in Ceramic Engring., 1953, PhD in Ceramics, 1954. Registered profl. engr., Pa. Rsch. engr. Harbison Walker Refractories Co., Pitts., 1954-57, asst dir. rsch., 1957-70; dir. rsch. Harbison Walker Refractories Div. Dresser Ind., Pitts., 1970-73, dir. advanced tech., 1973-74; v.p. rsch. Vesuvius Crucible Co., Pitts., 1974-76; adj. prof. Carnegie Mellon U., Pitts., 1976-84; rsch. prof. Rutgers U., New Brunswick, NJ, 1984—94. Pres. Ruh Internat., Inc., Pitts., 1976-2003. Author: Refractories for the Chemical Process Industries, 1984; editor Metallurgical Transactions, 1979-84; author chpts. to books; contbr. articles to profl. jours. With U.S. Army, 1943-46, ETO. Fellow: Am. Ceramic Soc. (disting. life mem., pres. 1985—86, Founders award Phila. sect. 1989, Bleininger award Pitts. sect. 1990); mem.: AIME, AAAS, Keramos (nat. pres. 1970—72, Greaves-Walker Roll of Honor 1976), Australasian Ceramic Soc., Acad. Ceramics (prof.), Iron and Steel Soc., Minerals, Metals and Materials Soc., Ceramic Assn. N.J. (pres. 1991—92, Ann. award 1988), Nat. Inst. Ceramics Engrs. (P.A.C.E. award 1963, Greaves-Walker award 1999). Republican. Presbyterian. Avocations: antiques, antique autos. Home: 892 Old Hickory Rd Pittsburgh PA 15243-1112 E-mail: edemruh@adelphia.net.

RUHL, MARY B. lawyer; BA, Wilson Coll., 1971; MA, U. Wis., 1973, JD, 1977. Bar: Calif. 1977, Wis. 1977. With Latham & Watkins, L.A., 1977—, ptnr. Mem.: Wis. State Bar Assn., Calif. State Bar Assn. Office: Latham and Watkins LLP 633 W Fifth St Ste 4000 Los Angeles CA 90071

RUHLMAN, HERMAN C(LOYD), JR., manufacturing executive; b. Warren, Pa., Jan. 17, 1949; s. Herman Cloyd and Virginia Lee (Wimer) R.; divorced; children: Brian, Jason, Chad; m. Lorraine; stepchildren: Bethany, Michelle, Randy. BS in Indsl. Tech., Calif. (Pa.) State Coll., 1974. Gen. mgr. Rand Machine Products, Inc., Falconer, N.Y., 1974-80, pres., chmn. bd. dirs., 1980—; pres. Spartan Tool Co., Gerry, N.Y., 1986—. Active Boy Scouts Am. With USAF, 1968-72. Mem. Epsilon Pi Tau. Republican. Home: PO Box 284 15 Annis St Frewsburg NY 14738-9564 Office: PO Box 72 Allen St Extension Falconer NY 14733 Business E-Mail: rand@madbbs.com.

RUHM, THOMAS FRANCIS, retired lawyer, investor; b. Bridgeport, Conn., June 8, 1935; s. Herman David and Martica (Sturges) R.; m. Michele Wood, Oct. 5, 1974; children: Wendy Sturges, Thomas Wood. BA, Yale U., 1957; JD, Havard U., 1962. Bar: N.Y. 1963, U.S. Dist. Ct. (so. and ea. dists.) N.Y. 1964, U.S. Ct. Appeals (2d cir.) 1969. Assoc. Shearman & Sterling, N.Y.C., 1962-70; asst. gen. counsel Bessemer Securities Corp., N.Y.C., 1970-96, v.p., 1981-96; ret., 1996. Chmn. legal aspects venture capital investing Practicing Law Inst., NY and San Francisco, 1979-81; lectr. on venture capital NYU Grad. Sch., 1986-90, Concordia Coll., Bronxville, NY, 1999-2001; expert on fed. securities law, venture capital legal matters, investment tax policy, Fed. Res. monetary policy; witness during 1980s fed. tax hearings; adj. prof. fin. St. John's U., 2000-03. Contbg. author: Technology and Economic Policy, 1986; contbr. articles to profl. jours. Commr. upper div. Eastchester (NY) Youth Soccer League, 1990-91, coach, 1985-91, dir. coaching 1995-96; sr. warden Christ Ch., Bronxville, NY, 1991-94; chmn. fin. com. 1982-1986, Vestry mem., 1981-1986 and 1990-1994, past v.p. and treas. Bronxville Sch. PTA; treas., bd. dir. Friends of Bronxville Pub. Libr., 1997-2000; mem. Quogue (NY) Cultural Com., 1998—; treas. Quogue Hist. Soc., 2003; mem. Blue Hill Troupe, Ltd., 1972—. Lt. (j.g.) USNR, 1957-59, 61-64. Lt. USNR. Mem. Naval Order of U.S., N.Y. Commandery, St. Andrew's Soc., Am. Scottish Found., Univ. Club (mem. coun. 2000—2004), Bronxville Field Club, Quogue Field Club, Quogue Beach Club. Republican.

RUI, HALLGEIR, cancer researcher; b. Rissa, Norway, Dec. 13, 1961; came to U.S., 1989; s. Tarald Martin and Gerd (Neverlien) R. MD, U. Oslo, 1987, PhD in Pathology, 1988. Lic. med. doctor, Norway. Clin. resident in surgery and internal medicine Notodden (Norway) Hosp., 1987-89; postdoctoral fellow Lee Moffitt Cancer Ctr. and Rsch. Inst., Tampa, 1989-91; scientist Nat. Cancer Inst., Frederick, Md., 1991-95; asst. prof. Uniformed Svcs. U. Health Scis. Sch. Medicine, Bethesda, Md., 1995-2001, assoc. prof., 2001—02; assoc. prof. oncology Georgetown U. Lombardi Cancer Ctr., Washington, 2002—. Contbr. over 80 articles to profl. jours. Norwegian Sci. Coun. fellow, 1983-87, Fulbright fellow, 1989, Fogarty fellow, 1989-95. Mem. AAAS, Am. Assn. Cancer Rsch., Internat. Cytokine Soc., Endocrine Soc. Achievements include research in identifying mechanisms of prolactin receptor signal transduction through Jak-Stat and Shc-Ras pathways; identifying Stat5 as a prognostic tumor marker in human breast cancer. E-mail: ruih@georgetown.edu.

RUINA, JACK PHILIP, electrical engineer, educator; b. Rypin, Poland, Aug. 19, 1923; arrived in U.S., 1927, naturalized, 1932; s. Michael and Nechuma (Warshaw) R.; m. Edith Elster, Oct. 26, 1947; children: Ellen, Andrew, Rachel. BEE, CCNY, 1944; MEE, Poly. Inst. Bklyn., 1949, DEE, 1951. Rsch. fellow Microwave Rsch. Inst., Poly. Inst. Bklyn., 1948-50; from instr. to assoc. prof. elec. engring. Brown U., 1950-54; rsch. assoc. prof. coordinated sci. lab. U. Ill., 1954-59, rsch. prof., prof. elec. engring., 1959-63; prof. elec. engring. MIT, 1963—, v.p. for spl. labs., 1966-70. U.S. observer Antarctica, 1964; on leave to U.S. Govt., 1959-63, pres. Inst. Def. Analysis, 1964-66; dep. for rsch. to asst. sec. air force, 1959-60; asst. dir. for def. rsch. and engring. Office Sec. Def., 1960-61; dir. Advanced Rsch. Projects Agy., Dept. Def., 1961-63; mem. panel Presdl. Sci. Adv. Commn., 1963-72, sci. adv. bd. USAF, 1964-67, adv. bd. and panels for Dept. Def., HEW, Dept. Transp., ACDA, Office Tech. Assessment, NSF, NSC, 1963—; mem. gen. adv. com. ACDA, 1969-74; sr. cons. Office Sci. and Tech. Policy, The White House, 1977-80; chmn. com. on environ. decision making NAS, 1974-77; bd. dirs. Mitre Corp. Recipient Fleming award, 1962, Disting. Alumnus award Poly. Inst. Bklyn., 1970, One Hundred and Twenty Fifth Anniversary medal CCNY, 1973. Fellow IEEE, AAAS, Am. Acad. Arts and Scis.; mem. Internat. Sci. Radio Union. Office: MIT Dept Elec Engring 292 Main St Cambridge MA 02142-1014 Home: 130 Mount Auburn St Apt 409 Cambridge MA 02138-5779 E-mail: ruina@mitre.org.

RUIZ, COOKIE, performing company executive; BA in English, Spanish, Wright St. U., Dayton, Ohio. Cert. Fund Raising Executive, 2002. Pres. Jr. League, Austin, Tex.; dir. fund devel. Ballet Austin, 1996-97, gen. mgr., 1997—99, exec. dir., 1999—. Recipient American Red Cross Clara Barton Medal of Honor. Mem.: bd. Austin Convention & Visitors Bureau, Assoc. of Fundraising Professionals, bd. trustees, Dance USA. Office: Ballet Austin 3002 Guadalupe St Austin TX 78705-2818*

RUIZ, HECTOR, information technology executive; b. Negras, Mex. B of Elec. Engring., M of Elec. Engring., U. Tex.; D in Elecs., Rice U., 1973. Various positions Tex. Instruments, Dallas; pres. Motorola's Semiconductor Products Sector, Advanced Micro Devices, Inc., Sunnyvale, Calif., 2000—02, CEO, 2002—. Bd. dirs. Eastman Kodak Co. Apptd. by Pres. Adv. Com. Trade Policy and Negotiations; mem. Govs. Task Force Econ. Growth; apptd. by Gov. G.W. Bush Tex. Higher Edn. Coord. Bd.; mem. adv. coun. Coll. Engring. U. Tex. Named to, Hispanic Engr. Nat. Awards Conf. Hall of Fame, 2000; fellow, Internat. Engring. Consortium, 2002. Mem.: Hispanic Profl. Engrs. (apptd. bd. dirs.). Office: Advanced Micro Devices Inc 1 AMD Pl Sunnyvale CA 94088*

RUIZ, MACEDONIO, entomologist; b. De tamazula, Mexico, Dec. 4, 1961; arrived in US, 1988; s. Macedonio and Enedina (Sanchez) Ruiz; m. Gloria Ruiz, Feb. 24, 1990; children: Favio, Alex, Emilia. BS in Agronomy, U. Guadalajara, 1985. Cert. entomologist Md., Mass.; advanced level integrated pest mgmt. in indsl., institutional and residential specialist U. Purdue, 1998. Tchr., sr. rschr. depts. entomol. and botany U. Guadalajara, Autlan, 1985—88; pest control adv. Entomol. Sys. Inc., Corona, Calif., 1992—93; svc. specialist, entomologist Steritech Group, Inc., Charlotte, NC, 1993—. Cons. Discovery Pl., Charlotte, 2001—. Mem.: Entomol. Soc. Am. Democrat. Roman Catholic. Avocations: coin collecting/numismatics, Tae Kwon Do, soccer. Home: 14926 Bridle Trace Ln Pineville NC 28134 Office: Steritech Group Inc 7600 Little Ave Charlotte NC 28226 Office Phone: 704-541-5660. Office Fax: 704-541-6051. Personal E-mail: macy4111@netzero.net.

RUIZ, MICHELE, newscaster; Anchor, reporter KTLA, Los Angeles, 1991—98; gen. assignment reporter NBC4, Los Angeles, 1998—99, co-anchor, Channel 4 News at 6, 1999—. Recipient LA Press Club Award, 2002, Local Emmy Award, 2003. Mem.: Nat. Assn. of Hispanic Journalists, Radio TV News Dirs. Assn., Investigative Reports and Editors Inc. Office: NBC4 3000 W Alameda Ave Burbank CA 91523

RUIZ, PEDRO, psychiatrist; b. Cuba, Dec. 31, 1936; MD, U. Paris VI, 1964. Intern Jackson Meml. Hosp., Miami, Fla., 1965, resident in psychiatry, 1966-68; prof. psychiatry U. Tex./Houston Health Sci. Ctr., 1969—. Mem.: Am. Psychiat. Assn. (v.p. 2003—), Am. Assn. Social Psychiatry (pres. 2000—02), Am. Coll. Psychiatrists (pres. 2000—01), Am. Bd. Psychiatry and Neurology (pres. 2002—). Office: U Tex-Houston Health Sci Ct Mental Sci Inst 1300 Moursund St Houston TX 77030-3406 Office Phone: 713-500-2799. Business E-Mail: pedro.ruiz@uth.tmc.edu.

RUIZ, RAMON EDUARDO, history professor; b. Sessions Ranch, Calif., Sept. 9, 1921; s. Ramon and Dolores (Urueta) R.; m. Natalia Marrujo, Oct. 14, 1944; children— Olivia, Maura. BA, San Diego State Coll., 1947; MA, Claremont Grad. Sch., 1948; PhD, U. Calif., Berkeley, 1954. Asst. prof. U. Oreg., Eugene, 1955-57, So. Meth. U., Dallas, 1957-58; prof. Smith Coll., Northampton, Mass., 1958-69; prof. Latin Am. history U. Calif. at San Diego, 1969-91, prof. emeritus, 1991—, chmn. dept. history, 1971-76, chmn. divsn. humanities, 1972-74; mem. project grant com. NEH, 1972-73, 75-77, dir. pub. programs divsn., 1979-80; Ralph Chase lectr. San Angelo State U., 2000. Vis. prof. Facultad de Economia, Univ. de Nuevo Leon, Mexico, 1965-66, Coll. de Sonora, Mexico, summer 1983, Pomona Coll., 1983-84, Coll. de Michoacan, Mexico, summer 1986, 87, Univ. Nacional Autonoma de Mexico, fall 1992; scholar-in-residence Colegio de la Frontero Norte, Mexico, 1994-96; MacArthur Found. nominator, 1981-82; mem. project grant com. Ford Found. Author: Cuba: The Making of A Revolution, 1968 (One of Best History Books, Book World Washington Post 1968), Mexico: The Challenge of Poverty and Illiteracy, 1963, An American in Maximillians's Mexico, 1865-1866, 1959; (with James D. Atwater) Out From Under; Benito Juarez and Mexico's Struggle for Independence, 1969; (with John Tebbel) South by Southwest: The Mexican-American and His Heritage, 1969, Interpreting Latin American History, 1970, Labor and the Ambivalent Revolutionaries: Mexico, 1911-23, 1975, The Mexican War: Was it Manifest Destiny?, 1963, The Great Rebellion: Mexico, 1905-1924, 1980 (Hubert C. Herring prize), The People of Sonora and Yanqui Capitalists, 1988, Triumphs and Tragedy: A History of the Mexican People, 1992 (named One of Five Best History Books 1991-92, L.A. Times, Gold Medal award Commonwealth Club San Francisco 1993, History Book Club selection); (with Olivia Teresa Ruiz) Reflexiones Sobre la Identidad de los Pueblos, 1996, On the Rim of Mexico: Encounters of the Rich and Poor, 1998, Memories of a Hyphenated Man, 2003. Served to lt. USAAF, 1943-46. William Harrison Mills traveling fellow in internat. rels., 1950; John Hay Whitney Found. fellow, 1950; Fulbright fellow Mex., 1965-66; fellow Ctr. for Advanced Study in Behavioral Scis., 1984-85, Rockefeller Resident, Bellagio Study Ctr., 2003, Ena H. Thompson lectureship, Pomona Coll., 1995; recipient Am. Philos. Soc. grant in aid, 1959, Nat. medal Humanities Pres. U.S., 1998. Mem. Am. Hist. Assn. (Beveridge prize com. 1974-76), Conf. Latin Am. History, Chicano-Latino Faculty Assn. U. Calif. (pres. 1989-91), Phi Beta Kappa, Sigma Delta Pi. Home: PO Box 1775 Rancho Santa Fe CA 92067-1775 Personal E-mail: reruiz@ucsd.edu.

RUIZ, VANESSA, federal judge; b. San Juan, P.R., Mar. 22, 1950; d. Fernando and Irma (Bosch) Ruiz-Suria; married; m. David E. Birenbaum, Oct. 22, 1983; stepchildren: Tracy, Matthew. BA, Wellesley Coll., 1972; JD, Georgetown U., 1975. Bar: D.C. 1972. Assoc. Fried, Frank, Harris, Shrives & Kampelman, Washington, 1975—83; sr. mgr., counsel Sears World Trade Inc., Washington, 1983—87; founding ptnr. Sloan, Lehner & Ruiz, Washington, 1987—89; ptnr. Pepper, Hamilton & Scheetz, Washington, 1989—91; dep. corporation counsel, legal counsel div. D.C., Washington, 1991—93, prin. dep. corporation counsel, 1993—94, corporation counsel, 1994; assoc. judge D.C. Ct. of Appeals, Washington, 1994—. Spkr. in field. Recipient Judge of the Year award, Hispanic Bar Assoc., 2001. Mem.: ABA, Inter-Am. Bar Assn. Office: DC Ct of Appeals 500 Indiana Ave NW Fl 6 Washington DC 20001-2131*

RUIZ, VICKI LYNN, history professor, department chairman; b. Atlanta, May 21, 1955; d. Robert Paul and Erminia Pablita (Ruiz) Mercer; m. Jerry Joseph Ruiz, Sept. 1, 1979 (div. Jan. 1990); children: Miguel, Daniel; m. Victor Becerra, Aug. 14, 1992. AS in Social Studies, Gulf Coast Community Coll., 1975; BA in Social Sci., Fla. State, 1977; MA in History, Stanford U., 1978, PhD in History, 1982. Asst. prof. U. Tex., El Paso, 1982-85, U. Calif., Davis, 1985-87, assoc. prof., 1987-92; Andrew W. Mellon prof. Claremont (Calif.) Grad. Sch., 1992-95, chmn. history dept., 1993-95; prof. history Ariz. State U., Tempe, 1995—, chair dept. Chicano studies, 1997—. Dir. Inst. of Oral History, U. Tex., El Paso, 1983-85, minority undergrad. rsch. program U. Calif., Davis, 1988-92. Author: Cannery Women, Cannery Lives, 1987, From Out of the Shadows, 1998 (Choice Outstanding Book of 1998); editor: Chicana Politics of Work and Family, 2000; co-editor: Women on U.S.-Mexican Border, 1987, Western Women, 1988, Unequal Sisters, 1990, 3d edit., 1999. Mem. Calif. Coun. for Humanities, 1990-94, vice chmn., 1991-93. Fellow Univ. Calif. Davis Humanities Inst., 1990-91, Am. Coun. of Learned Socs., 1986, Danforth Found., 1977. Mem. Orgn. Am. Historians (chmn. com. on status of minority history 1989-91, nominating com. 1987-88, exec. bd. 1995-98), Immigration History Soc. (exec. bd. 1989-91), Am. Hist. Assn. (nat. coun. 1999—), Am. Studies Assn. (nominating bd. 1992-94, nat. coun. 1996-99), Western History (nominating bd. 1993-95). Democrat. Roman Catholic. Avocations: walking, needlecrafts. Office: Ariz State U History Dept Tempe AZ 85287

RUIZ-VALERA, PHOEBE LUCILE, law librarian; b. Barranquilla, Colombia, Jan. 27, 1950; d. Ramon and Marion (Mehlman) Ruiz-Valera; m. Thomas Patrick Winkler, Mar. 27, 1981. BA cum laude, Westminster Coll., 1971; MLS, Rutgers U., 1974; MA, NYU, 1978. Libr. trainee Passaic (N.J.) Pub. Libr., 1973-74, reference libr., 1974; libr. assoc. cataloger NYU Law Libr., N.Y.C., 1974-79, asst. curator, cataloger, 1979-81; libr. III, cataloger Rutgers U. Libr., New Brunswick, N.J., 1981-82; chief cataloger Assn. Bar City N.Y., 1982-85, head tech. svcs., 1985-99; tech. svcs. libr. Cleary, Gottlieb, Steen and Hamilton, N.Y.C., 1999—. Mem. Am. Assn. Law Librs., Am. Translators Assn. (cert. translator English to Spanish), Law Libr. Assn. Greater N.Y., Reforma, Salalm. Democrat. Presbyterian. Office: 1 Liberty Plz Fl 43 New York NY 10006-1404 E-mail: pruiz-valera@cgsh.com.

RUKEYSER, LOUIS RICHARD, economic commentator; b. N.Y.C., Jan. 30, 1933; s. Merryle Stanley and Berenice Helene (Simon) Rukeyser; m. Alexandra Gill, Mar. 3, 1962; children: Beverley Jane, Susan Athena, Stacy Alexandra. AB, Princeton U., 1954; LittD (hon.), N.H. Coll., 1975; LLD (hon.), Moravian Coll., 1978, Mercy Coll., 1984, Am. U., 1991; DBA (hon.), Southeastern Mass. U., 1979; LHD (hon.), Loyola Coll., 1982, Johns Hopkins U., 1986, Western Md. Coll., 1992; D in Fin. (hon.), Roger Williams U., 1997. Reporter Balt. Sun newspapers, 1954—65; chief polit. corr. Evening Sun, 1957—59; chief London bur. The Sun, 1959—63, chief Asian corr., 1963—65; sr. corr., commentator ABC News, 1965—73, Paris corr., 1965—66, chief London bur., 1966—68, econ. editor, commentator, 1968—73; econ. columnist McNaught Syndicate, 1976—86, Tribune Media Services, 1986—93. Internat. lectr. in field. Host (TV series) Wall St. Week With Louis Rukeyser, 1970—2002; host: (TV series) Louis Rukeyser's Wall St., 2002—; author: How to Make Money in Wall Street, 1974 (Lit. Guild selection, 74, 76), 1976, What's Ahead for the Economy: The Challenge and the Chance, 1983 (Lit. Guild selection, 84), 1985, Louis Rukeyser's Bus. Almanac, 1988, 1991, Louis Rukeyser's Book of Lists, 1997, Right on the Money, 1998; editor-in-chief: newsletters Louis Rukeyser's Wall St., 1992—, Louis Rukeyser's Mutual Funds, 1994—. With U.S. Army, 1954—56. Recipient Overseas Press Club award, 1963, Overseas Press Club citation, 1964, G.M. Loeb award, U. Conn., 1972, Janus award for excellence in fin. news programming, 1975, George Washington Honor medal, Freedoms Found., 1972, 1978, award, N.Y. Fin. Writers Assn., 1980, Free Enterprise Man of the Yr. award, Tex. A&M U. Ctr. for Edn. and Rsch. in Free Enterprise, 1987, Women's Econ. Roundtable award, 1990, 1st Hero of Wall St. award, The Mus. of Am. Fin. History, 1998, Malcolm S. Forbes award for excellence in advancing fin. understanding, Fin. Planning Assn., 2000. Office: 586 Round Hill Rd Greenwich CT 06831-2724

RUKEYSER, M. S., JR., television consultant, writer; b. NYC, Apr. 15, 1931; s. Merryle Stanley and Berenice (Simon) Rukeyser; children: Jill Victoria, Patricia Bern. Student, U. Va., 1948-52. Reporter Albany (N.Y.) Times-Union, 1949, Internat. News Service, N.Y.C., 1951; TV publicist Young & Rubicam, Inc., N.Y.C., 1952-57; with NBC, 1958-80, 81-88, dir. news info., 1962, v.p. press and publicity N.Y.C., 1963-72, v.p. corp. info., 1972-74, v.p. pub. info., 1974-77, exec. v.p. pub. info., 1977-80, 81-84, exec. v.p. corp. communications, 1984-88; v.p. comm. Newsweek Inc., 1980-81; sr. v.p. GTG Entertainment, 1988-90; pres. Rukeyser Communications, N.Y.C., 1990—. Sr. fellow Freedom Forum Media Ctr., 1991-92. Author (with Grant Tinker): Tinker in Television: From General Sarnoff to General Electric, 1994. With U.S. Army, 1953—54. Office: Apt 1213 616 Clearwater Park Rd West Palm Beach FL 33401-6250 E-mail: budruk@aol.com.

RUKEYSER, ROBERT JAMES, manufacturing executive; b. New Rochelle, N.Y., June 26, 1942; s. Merryle Stanley and Berenice Helene (Simon) R.; m. Leah A. Spiro, July 26, 1964; children: David Bern, Peter Lloyd. BA, Cornell U., 1964; MBA with distinction, N.Y.U., 1969. Bond analyst Dun & Bradstreet, N.Y.C., 1964-65, Standard & Poors, N.Y.C., 1965-66; mktg. rep. data processing div. IBM, N.Y.C., 1967-72, regional mktg. staff, 1973-74, mktg. mgr., 1974-76, corp. mgr. internal communications and editl. programs Armonk, N.Y., 1976-79, mgr. communication ops. Franklin Lakes, N.J., 1979-81; pub. affairs dir., asst. to chmn. Fortune Brands, Inc. (formerly Am. Brands, Inc.), N.Y.C., 1981-83, v.p. pub. affairs, asst. to chmn., 1983-85, v.p. office products Old Greenwich, Conn., 1986-87, v.p. ops., 1987-89, sr. v.p. corp. affairs, 1990-99. Bd. dirs. Fortune Brands (formerly Am. Brands Inc.); mgmt. cons. and author, 2000—. Bd. dirs., chair fin. com., mem. exec. com. The Hole in the Wall Gang Camp.; treas., bd. dir., Assn. of Hole in the Wall Camps; bd. dirs., mem. exec. com. Stamford Ctr. for Arts.

RUKEYSER, WILLIAM SIMON, journalist; b. N.Y.C., June 8, 1939; s. Merryle Stanley and Berenice (Simon) R.; m. Elisabeth Mary Garnett, Nov. 21, 1963; children: Lisa Rukeyser Burn, James William. AB, Princeton U., 1961; rsch. student, Cambridge (Eng.) U., 1962—63; LittD (hon.), Maryville Coll., 2002. Copyreader Wall St. Jour., 1961-62, staff reporter, 1963-67; assoc. editor Fortune mag., 1967-71, mem. bd. editors, 1971-72; founding mng. editor Money mag., N.Y.C., 1972-80; mng. editor Fortune mag., 1980-86; dir. internat. bus. devel. Time Inc., 1986-88; editor in chief, exec. v.p. Whittle Communications, Knoxville, Tenn., 1988-91; chmn., CEO, Whittle Books, Knoxville, 1991-94; pres. William Rukeyser, Inc., Knoxville, 1994—; editl. dir. Corporate Board Member mag., 1998—; contbg. editor CNN, 1995-97. Commentator Good Morning America, ABC-TV, 1978-85, CBS Radio Stas. News Svc., 1979-86; mem. nat. adv. coun. Maryville (Tenn.) Coll., 1998—; mem. adv. bd. Ctr. of Inquiry in Liberal Arts Wabash Coll., Crawfordsville, Ind., 2001—. Mem. jud. com. Union County (N.J.) Med. Soc., 1977-80; co-chair capital campaign Nat. Mental Health Assn., 1984-85; mem. liaison com. U. Tenn. Med. Ctr., 1992-99; vice chmn. U. Health Sys. Inc., 1999—; chmn. bd. dirs. Knoxville Jazz Orch., 2001—. Office: 1001 First Tennessee Plz Knoxville TN 37929 Personal E-mail: wsr@finehand.com.

RULAND, MILDRED ARDELIA, retail executive, retail buyer; b. Draketown, Ga., Aug. 11, 1918; m. Harry Morse Ruland, Aug. 19, 1947; children: Hal Morse, Judy Lee Ruland Rigas. BS, West Ga. Coll., 1966. Elem. tchr., New London, Conn., 1947-48, Atlanta, 1948-51, Rome, Ga., 1951-81; mgr. McBrayer Bros. Furniture Co., Rome, 1981—. Rosenwald Found. scholar, 1941-42. Mem. NEA, Nat. Fedn. Ind. Bus. (corr. sec. 1975—), Ga. Edn. Assn. (del. 1964-74), Ga. Home Furnishings Assn., Twickham Garden Club, Rome Pride Assn., Rome C. of C., Alfa Delta Kappa. Republican. Baptist. Avocations: dance, swimming, bowling, hiking, singing.

RULAND, RICHARD EUGENE, English and American literature educator, critic, literary historian; b. Detroit, May 1, 1932; s. Eugene John and Irene (Janette) R.; m. Mary Ann Monaghan; children: Joseph, Michael, Paul, Susan; m. Birgit Noll. BA, Assumption Coll. U. Western Ont., Can., 1953; MA, U. Detroit, 1955; PhD, U. Mich., 1960. Instr., then asst. prof. English and Am. studies Yale U., New Haven, 1960-67, Morse rsch. fellow, 1966-67; prof. English and Am. lit. Washington U., St. Louis, 1967—, chmn. dept. English, 1969-74; chmn. comparative lit. program, 1993-94. Vis. Bruern prof. Am. lit. Leeds (Eng.) U., 1964-65; vis. Fulbright prof. U. Groningen, The Netherlands, 1975, Sch. of English and Am. Studies U. East Anglia, Eng., 1978-79; vis. disting. prof. Am. lit. Coll. of William and Mary, 1980-81. Author: The Rediscovery of American Literature: Premises of Critical Taste, 1900-1940, 1967, America in Modern European Literature: From Image to Metaphor, 1976, (with Malcolm Bradbury) From Puritanism to Postmodernism: A History of American Literature, 1991 (paperback 1992), translation into Czech and Hungarian, 1997; editor: Walden: A Collection of Critical Essays, 1967, The Native Muse: Theories of American Literature, Vol. I, 1972, 76, A Storied Land: Theories of American Literature, Vol. II, 1976; contbr. articles to profl.

jours. Guggenheim Rsch. fellow, 1982-83. Mem. Assn. Depts. English (pres. 1974). Avocation: jazz musician. Office: Washington U Dept English Saint Louis MO 63130 E-mail: rruland@artsi.wustl.edu.

RULE, CHARLES FREDERICK (RICK RULE), lawyer; b. Nashville, Apr. 28, 1955; s. Frederick Charles and Mary Elizabeth (Malone) R.; m. Ellen Friedland, May 13, 1976 BA, Vanderbilt U., 1978; JD, U. Chgo., 1981. Bar: U.S. Ct. Appeals. (D.C. cir.) 1983. Law clk. U.S. Ct. Appeals (fed. cir.), Washington, 1981-82; spl. asst. to asst. atty. gen. Antitrust div. Dept. Justice, Washington, 1982-83, dep. asst. atty. gen. policy planning, 1984-85, acting asst. atty. gen., then dep. asst. atty. gen. regulatory affairs, 1985-86, asst. atty. gen., 1986-89; ptnr. Covington & Burling, Washington, 1989-2001, Fried, Frank, Harris, Shriver & Jacobson, Washington, 2001—. Legal, econ. analyst Lexecon, Inc., Chgo., 1979-80 Mem. Bar of D.C. Ct. Appeals, Phi Beta Kappa, Phi Eta Sigma. Republican. Presbyterian. Office: Fried Frank Harris Shriver & Jacobson 1001 Pennsylvania Ave Nw Washington DC 20004-2505 Office Phone: 202-639-7300. Business E-Mail: ruleri@ffhsj.com.

RULE, JOHN CORWIN, history professor; b. Evanston, Ill., Mar. 2, 1929; s. Corwin V. and Elaine (Simons) R. AB, Stanford U., 1951, MA, 1952, Harvard U., 1955, PhD, 1958. Tutor and fellow Harvard U., Cambridge, Mass., 1956-58; instr. Northeastern U., Boston, 1955-56; from instr. to prof. history Ohio State U., Columbus, 1958—; vis. asst. prof. Western Res. U., Cleve., 1961; vis. prof. Johns Hopkins U., Balt., 1968. Editor and contbg. author: Louis XIV and the Craft of Kingship, 1970; editor: Louis XIV, 1974, Letters from the Hague and Utrecht, 1711-1712, 1979, The Reign of Louis XIV, 1990. Folger Shakespeare Library fellow, 1968, 1970; Huntington Library fellow, 1978; Am. Council Learned Socs. fellow, 1981 Fellow Royal Hist. Soc. (London); mem. Soc. for French Hist. Studies (sec. 1963-70, assoc. editor jour. 1975-86, co-pres. 1989-91), Signet Soc., Crichton Club. Democrat. Home: 118 E Beck St Columbus OH 43206-1110 Office: Dept History Ohio State U 230 W 17th Ave Rm 106 Columbus OH 43210-1367

RULIS, RAYMOND JOSEPH, manufacturing company executive, consultant; b. New Britain, Conn., June 2, 1924; s. James Alexander and Eva (Ragauskas) R.; m. Thelma Pelchat, June 16, 1949 (dec.); children: Elaine, Jeffery, Catherine, Elizabeth, Amy, Daniel, Jean; m. Virginia Kleene, Oct. 9, 1999. BSME, U. Conn., 1949; postgrad., U. Conn., Ohio State U., Northeastern U., 1949-58; student, Fed. Exec. Inst., Charlottesville, Va., 1976. Devel. engr. Hamilton Standard, U.T.C., Windsorlocks, Conn., 1951-55; mgr. fuel controls Lycoming Textron, Stratford, Conn., 1955-59; mgr. controls and accessories GE, Lynn, Mass., 1959-62; successively program mgr. sert spacecraft, chief spacecraft engr., chief launch vehicle engr., chief engring design, program mgr. QCSEE program NASA Lewis Rsch. Ctr., Cleve., 1962-81; v.p. rsch. and. devel. Textron Turbocomponents Group, Walled Lake, Mich., 1981-92; cons., 1992—. Cons. Joint FAA/NASA Civil Aero Rsch. Document Study, 1972, Cruise Missile PRogram, 1977-78, C-17 Aircraft Source Selection Bd., 1978, Tri-Svcs. Propulsion Group, 1976-78; chmn. Conf. on Short Haul Systems, NASA, 1976; mem. exec. coun. Aerospace Industries Tech. Coun., 1988-89. Contbr. articles to profl. jours.; patentee in field. Chmn. Boy Scouts Am. Fund Drives, Cleve., 1976-78; mem. Coun. on World Affairs, Cleve., 1976-81. With U.S. Army, 1943—46. Decorated Combat Infantryman's badge, Bronze Star medal, Purple Heart. Mem. Am. Helicopter Soc. (chmn. tech. session 1970), AIAA (chmn. tech. session 1965), Detroit Engring Soc., KC. Roman Catholic. Avocation: golf. Office: RJR Cons 9 Outpost Ln Hilton Head Island SC 29928-3820

RULISON, JOSEPH RICHARD, investment advisor; b. Syracuse, N.Y., May 14, 1956; s. Laurence M. and Catherine (Fox) R.; m. Karen Richards, Sept. 6, 1980; children: Elizabeth, Mallorie, Morgan, Abigail. BA, St. John Fisher Coll., 1978. Account exec. Prudential-Bache Securities, Rochester, 1982—84; investment exec. Tucker Anthony & R.L. Day, Inc., Rochester, 1984—89; ptnr., exec. v.p. Marsh Capital Mgmt., Rochester, 1989—96; pres., CEO Rulison & Co., Inc., Rochester, 1996—2001; founder, gen. mgr. Muniflow, Rochester, 2001—; sr. v.p. Bank of Am. Adv. Svcs. Trustee, past chmn. bd. trustees, past pres., hon. trustee Geva Theatre; chmn. bd. trustees St. John Fisher Coll.; former treas. Monroe County Rep. Com.; chmn. County Monroe Indsl. Devel. Agy., Monroe County Greater Outdoor Sports Facility-Frontier Field, Monroe County Mid-Sized Arts Com.; past councilman Brighton Town Bd.; past mem. Brighton Planning Bd., Master Plan Com., Archtl. Rev. Bd.; vice-chmn. Empire Zone of Monroe County. Mem. Genesee Valley Club (former gov., house chmn.), Oak Hill Country Club. Roman Catholic. Avocations: politics, theater, art, wine, golf. Office: Fleet Govt Adv Svcs NY-UT-37602C 1 East Ave Rochester NY 14638 E-mail: Joseph_R_Rulison@fleet.com.

RUMAKER, MICHAEL, writer, English educator; b. Phila., Mar. 5, 1932; s. Michael Joseph and Winifred Marvel Rumaker. Honors degree in writing, Black Mountain Coll., 1955; MFA, Columbia U., 1970. Lectr. writing New Sch. for Social Rsch., NYC, 1967-71; tchr. writer, mem. intellectual resources pool Tappan Zee H.S., Orangeburg, NY, 1965-69; instr. writing workshops Rockland Ctr. for Arts, West Nyack, NY, 1975-78; adj. lectr. Rockland C.C., Suffern, NY, 1978-87; writer-in-residence CCNY, CUNY, 1969-71, adj. prof., 1985—. Author: (novels) The Butterfly, 1962, English edit., 1968, A Day and a Night at the Baths, 1979, My First Satyrnalia, 1981, To Kill a Cardinal, 1992, German edit., 1997, Pagan Days, 2000, Russian edit., 2002, (non-fiction) An Immodest Proposal, 2004, (short stories) Gringos and Other Stories, 1967, 2nd edit., 1991, German edit., 1968, English edit. (Exit 3), 1966, (memoir) Robert Duncan in San Francisco, 1996, Black Mountain Days, 2003, (poems) Pizza and other Selected Poems, 2004, (plays) Queers (Schwul), 1970, 2004. Mem. Nat. Writers Union. Literary Agent: Harold Ober Assocs 425 Madison Ave Rm 1001 New York NY 10017-1183 Business E-Mail: mr6213@tco.com.

RUMAN, SAUL I. lawyer; b. Chgo., May 12, 1925; s. James A. and Pauline (Scharfer) R.; m. Beverlee Mahan, June 17; children: Loral Ruman Conrad, Melissa Ruman Stewart, Elizabeth Ruman Plumlee. BS, Ind. U., 1949, JD with distinction, 1952. Bar: Ind. 1952, U.S. Supreme Ct. 1963, U.S. Dist. Ct. Ind. 1952, U.S. Ct. Appeals (7th cir.) 1962. Atty. pvt. practice, Hammond, Ind., 1952—; mng. ptnr. Ruman, Clements & Holub, P.C., 1990. Former lectr. bus. law Ind. U. N.W.; mem. faculty numerous insts. on law; mem. com. on rules of practice and procedure Supreme Ct. Ind., 1983-92, Ind. Jud. Nominating Commn., 1990; mem. Ind. Supreme Ct. character and fitness com., 1975—. Pres. Ind. U. Sch. Law Alumni Assn., 1972-73, bd. visitors, 1973; bd. advisors N.W. Campus Ind. U., 1973-85, class rep., 1983; faculty Nat. Inst. Trial Advocacy, 1984-86; trustee Ind. Legal Svcs. Fund, 1978, 84. With usn, 1942-45. Fellow Internat. Acad. Trial Lawyers (dir. 1980-86); mem. Ill. Trial Lawyers Assn., Ind. Bar Assn. (chmn. trial lawyers sect. 1970-71), Ind. Trial Lawyers Assn. (emeritus dir., pres. 1980-81, lifetime achievement award 1997), Coll. Fellows, Assn. Trial Lawyers Am., Am. Bd. Trial Advocates, Order of Coif. Office: 5261 Hohman Ave Hammond IN 46320-1721 Office Phone: 219-933-7600.

RUMBAUGH, CHARLES EARL, arbitrator, mediator, educator, lawyer, speaker; b. San Bernardino, Calif., Mar. 11, 1943; s. Max Elden and Gertrude Maude (Gulker) R.; m. Christina Carol Pinder, Mar. 2, 1968; children: Eckwood, Cynthia, Aaron, Heather. BS, UCLA, 1966; JD, Calif. Western Sch. Law, 1971; cert. in advanced mgmt., U. So. Calif., 1993. Bar: Calif. 1972, U.S. Dist. Ct. (cen. dist.) Calif. U.S. Ct. Appeals (9th cir.), U.S. Supreme Ct. Engr. Westinghouse Electric Corp., Balt., 1966-68; legal counsel Calif. Dept. of Corps., L.A., 1971-77, Hughes Aircraft Co., L.A., 1977-84, asst. to corp. dir. contracts, 1984-89, asst. to corp. v.p. contracts, 1989-95; corp. dir. contracts/pricing Lear Astronics Corp., 1995-97; pres. Ctr. for Conflict Resolution, 1998-99; pvt. practice in sispute resolution as arbitrator, mediator, pvt. judge. Former EEOC mediator, adminstrv. law judge; mem. arbitration and mediation panels ArbitrationWorks, 1994—2002, Nat. Assn. Security Dealers, Franchise Arbitration & Mediation, Inc., L.A. County Superior Ct., Santa Barbara County Superior Ct.; mem. panel pvt. alt. dispute resolution neutrals U.S. Ct. Fed. Claims; armed svcs. bd. of contract appeals panel of pvt. alt. dispute resolution neutrals, DLA panel of dispute neutrals, also settlement officer U.S. Dist. Ct.; alternative dispute resolution panel World Bank; adj. prof. Calif. State U.; spkr. in field. Mem. editl. bd. Nat. Contract Mgmt. Jour., 1996-00; contbr. articles to profl. jours. Counselor Boy Scouts Am., L.A., 1976—; mem. City of Palos Verdes Estates (Calif.) Citizen's Planning Com., 1986—90; judge pro tem L.A. County Superior Ct., L.A., 1991—2000. Fellow: Nat. Contract Mgmt. Assn. (pres. L.A./South Bay chpt. 1991—92, nat. dir. 1992—93, nat. v.p. southwestern region 1993—95, founder, chmn. alt. dispute resolution com., cert. profl. contracts mgr., nat. bd. advisors, Fellow of Yr. award 1994, Nat. Achievement award 2001); mem.: FBA (pres. Beverly Hills chpt. 1992—93), ABA (founder fed. contracts dispute resolution com. dispute resolution sect, forum on franchising, forum on constrn. industry, pub. contract law sect., internat. law sect., vice chair strategic alliance com.), Inst. Supply Mgmt. (chmn. fed. acquisitions, subcontract mgmt. group), Am. Arbitration Assn. (arbitrator, mediator), Christian Legal Soc., Aerospace Industries Assn. (chmn. procurement techniques com. 1987—88, 1993—94), Soc. Profls. in Dispute Resolution (chmn. internat. sector com. 1996—2000, past bd. dirs. L.A. chpt.), State Bar Calif. (chmn. franchise law com. 2002—03, vice chmn. ADR commn. 2001—, Wiley W. Manual pro bono award 1992), Nat. Def. Indsl. Assn. (vice-chmn. west coast legal subcom. 1994—2000, procurement planning com. 1994—), Calif. Dispute Resolution Coun. (cons. to qualifications com. 1997—99). Avocations: camping, skiing, jogging, equestrian. Office: PO Box 2636 Rolling Hills CA 90274 E-mail: adroffice@rumbaugh.net.

RUMBAUGH, MAX ELDEN, JR., professional society administrator; b. Ada, Okla., Dec. 11, 1937; s. Max E. and Gertrude (Gulker) R.; m. Joan E. Brockway; children: Maria Rumbaugh Gross, Max E. III. BS in Engring., U.S. Mil. Acad., 1960; MS in Engring. Scis., Purdue U., 1965, MBA, 1972. Instr. Purdue U., West Lafayette, Ind., 1964-65; corp. officer Midwest Applied Sci. Corp., West Lafayette, 1965-72; chief engr. advanced tech. Schwitzer div. Wallace-Murray Corp., Indpls., 1972-77, dir. research, 1977-81; mgr. engring. activities div. Soc. Automotive Engrs., Warrendale, Pa., 1981-84, v.p., asst. gen. mgr., 1984-86, exec. v.p., 1986—2002, exec. v.p. emeritus, 2002—; pres. Performance Rev. Inst., 1991—2001. Pres. Soc. Rsch. Adminstrs. Internat., 1973-74; chmn. Ind. sect. Soc. Automotive Engrs., 1978-79; bd. dirs., exec. com. Am. Nat. Standards Inst., N.Y.C., 1986-2002; bd. dirs. Intelligent Transp. Soc. of Am., 1992-2004, mem. exec. com., 1998—. Author mag. column Focus, 1986-2002. Bd. dirs. Jr. Achievement Western Pa., Pitts., 1986-98, YMCA, North Hills, Pitts., 1985-94; sec. Intelligent Transp. Soc. Am. Bd. Dirs., 2000-04. 1st lt. U.S. Army, 1960-63, Mem. ASME, Am. Soc. Assn. Execs., Coun. Engring. and Sci. Soc. Execs. (bd. dirs. 1990-97, sec. 1993-94, v.p. 1994-95, pres. 1995-96), Soc. Automotive Engrs. of China (hon.), Soc. Automotive Engrs. of India (hon.), Russian Internat. Acad. Engring., Intelligent Transp. Soc. Am. (bd. dirs. 1992—, sec. 2000-, chmn. fin. com. 2000-03), Russian Acad. Quality Problems, Rotary (bd. dirs. 1982-84, 93-97, v.p. 1994-95, pres. 1995-96, chmn. youth exch. 2003—). Avocations: skiing, photography. Home: 8731 E San Pablo Dr Scottsdale AZ 85258- Office: Soc of Automotive Engrs Inc 400 Commonwealth Dr Warrendale PA 15086-7511

RUMBLEY, PHILIP LEE, music educator, musician, photographer; b. Alice, Tex., Jan. 8, 1956; s. Jack Edward and Rose Mary Rumbley; m. Karen Gay Stevens, Feb. 14; 1 child, Philip Prescott. BA in visual arts, U. Tex., 1981. Photographer T.B. Butler Publ. Co., Tyler, Tex., 1984—90, U. Tex. Health Ctr., Tyler, Tex., 1990—; adj. faculty music Tyler Jr. Coll., Tex., 2000—. Contract musician, 1989—. Author: (jour article) Am. Jour. Medicine, 1991, several oral presentations. Recipient First Pl. Sports Photography, United Press Internat., 1984, Outstanding Achievement, 1985, Second Pl. News Photography, N.E. Tex. Press Assn., 1986, Third Pl. News Photography, 1987, Katie award News Reporting, Dallas Press Club, 1988, Outstanding Vol. award, Tex. Asthma Camp. Mem.: Tex. Music Educators Assn., BioComm. Assn. (past pres.), Tex. Press Assn., Nat. Press Photographers Assn. Home: 1810 S Sneed Tyler TX 75701 E-mail: phil.rumbley@uthct.edu.

RUMBOUGH, STANLEY MADDOX, JR., industrialist; b. N.Y.C., Apr. 25, 1920; s. Stanley Maddox and Elizabeth (Colgate) R.; m. Nedenia Hutton, Mar. 23, 1946 (div. 1966); children: Stanley H., David P. (dec.), Nedenia Colgate; m. Margaretha Wagstrom, Dec. 21, 1967 (div. 1990); m. Janna Herlow, Mar. 8, 1990. AB, Yale U., 1942; postgrad. in bus. adminstrn., NYU, 1947-51. Vice pres., dir. Willis Air Service, Teterboro, N.J., 1946-47; v.p., dir. White Metal Mfg. Co., Hoboken, N.J., 1945-61, pres., 1960-61; pres., dir. Metal Container Corp., 1950-59, Am. Totalisator, Balt., 1956-58; chmn. bd. Extrusion Devel. Corp., 1959-61; co-founder, chmn. bd. Elec. Engring. Ltd., 1960-69; chmn. bd. Wallace Clark & Co., 1962-69; co-founder, dir. Trinidad Flour Mills, 1961-72, Jamaica Flour Mills, 1963-66; dir. Telemedia Inc., 1980-89. Spl. asst. to sec. Dept. Commerce, 1953; spl. asst. White House charge exec. br. liaison, 1953-55; founder Washington D.C. Tennis Patrons Found. Chmn. U.S. Com. for UN, 1957-58; co-founder Citizens for Eisenhower, 1951; vice chmn. Citizens for Eisenhower-Nixon Com., 1952; trustee Young Pres. Found., 1957-70, pres., 1962-65; bd. dirs. N.Y. World's Fair Corp., 1961-70, Nat. Conf. on Citizenship, 1973—2003, Population Resource Ctr., 1978-92, Planned Parenthood of Palm Beach Area, 1979-95, Planned Parenthood Fedn. Am., 1981-84, Kravis Ctr. Performing Arts; co-chmn., bd. dirs. Palm Beach Civic Assn.; trustee Libr. for Presdl. Papers, 1966-70, Internat. House, 1959—, Fgn. Policy Assn., 1961-70, Am. Health Found., 1972-76; Capt. USMCR, 1942-46. Decorated Air medal (8), D.F.C. (2). Mem. Chief Execs. Orgn., World Pres.'s Orgn. (founding), Young Pres.'s Orgn. (founding), Def. Orientation Conf. Assn., Racquet and Tennis Club, Internat. Lawn Tennis Club, Maidstone Club, Seminole Club, Bath and Tennis Club, Everglades Club, Nat. Golf Links Am. Club, Zeta Psi. Republican. Home: 655 Island Dr Palm Beach FL 33480-4744 Office: 44 Cocoanut Row Ste B103 Palm Beach FL 33480-4069

RUMJAHN, DIANA, academic administrator; Bachelor's degree, San Francisco State U., 2003. Registrar's office specialist San Francisco State U., 1988—93, admissions office adminstrv. asst., 1993—98, adminstrv. coord. cinema, 1998—2000, dept. mgr. cinema, 2000—. Contbr. poetry to anthologies (Editor's Choice award, 1995, 1996). Fellow: Internat. Biog. Assn. (life); mem.: Calif. State Employees Assn., Am. Biog. Inst. (adv. bd. 1994—), Golden Key Nat. Honor Soc. (life). Avocations: travel, golf, gardening, sculpting, writing. Home: PO Box 591536 San Francisco CA 94159

RUML, TREADWELL, English language educator; b. N.Y.C., Mar. 22, 1952; s. Alvin and Zona Ruml; m. Laura Susan Funkhouser, Dec. 30, 1990; children: James Alvin Treadwell, John Jordan Beardsley. AB, Harvard Coll., 1974, JD, 1977; PhD, U. Va., 1989. Assoc. Nutter, McClennan & Fish, Boston, 1977-80; lectr. in English U. Va., Charlottesville, 1989-90; asst. prof. Calif. State U., San Bernardino, 1990-94, assoc. prof., 1994—. Contbr. articles to profl. jours. Sec. faculty senate Calif. State U., San Bernardino, 1998-99. Mem. Am. Soc. for Eighteenth-Century Studies, Western Soc. for Eighteenth-Century Studies (pres. 1998-99, sec.-treas. 1999—) Samuel Johnson Soc. So. Calif. (newsletter editor 1999—). Office: Calif State U Dept English 5500 University Pkwy San Bernardino CA 92407-2318

RUMLER, ROBERT HOKE, agricultural consultant, retired association executive; b. Chambersburg, Pa., Apr. 4, 1915; s. Daniel Webster and Jennie (Sellers) R.; m. Frances Jeannette Montgomery, June 7, 1939 (dec. 1983); children: Craig M., Karen A. Loden; m. Hazel Miller-Karper, Aug. 23, 1986 (dec. 1998). BS, Pa. State U., 1936. Asst. county agt. U. Mo., 1936-37; county agrl. agt. Pa. State U., 1937-45; asst. mgr., editor agrl. promotion divsn. E. I. duPont de Nemours & Co., Inc., Wilmington, Del., 1945-48; asst. exec. sec., COO, Holstein-Friesian Assn. Am., 1948-53, 53-75, exec. sec., CEO, 1975-81, exec. chmn., 1981-82, chmn. emeritus, 1982—. Pres. Holstein-Friesian Svcs., Inc., 1968-81; agribus. cons., 1982—; hon. mem. Holstein-Friesian de Mex. (C.A.); bd. dirs., chmn. Vt. Nat. Bank, Vt. Fin. Svcs., Inc., 1957-88; mem. U.S./USSR Joint Com. Agrl. Cooperation; past chmn. U.S. Agrl. Export Devel. Coun., FAS-USDA; mem. coordinating group Nat. Coop. Dairy Herd Improvement program USDA, 1964-80; mem. agrl. policy adv. com. USTR/USDA Multilateral Trade Negotiations, 1973-87, mem. agrl. tech. adv. com., 1987-95. Contbg. editl. writer Holstein World. Trustee Ea. States Expn., trustee emeritus, 1993—; trustee Assoc. Industries Vt.; past bd. dirs. Internat. Stockmans Ednl. Found.; chmn. adv. bd. Pa. State U., Mont Alto, 1988-98, chmn. 1990-94, emeritus 1998; bd. advisors Pa. State U., Harrisburg, 1990-94. Recipient Disting. award Nat. Dairy Herd Improvement Assn., 1974, Disting. Svc. award Nat. Agrl. Mktg. Orgn., 1977, Cert. of Appreciation, USDA, 1982, Disting. Svc. award Holstein Assn., 1985; named Dist. Alumnus Pa. State U. Coll. Agr., 1978, 2000, Dairy Industry Man of Yr., World Dairy Expo, 1979, Headliner-of-Yr. Livestock Publs. Coun., 1995, Internat. Person of Yr. World Dairy Expo, 1996, 1st Disting. Alumnus AZ Fraternity Penn State, 1996, Disting. Alumnus, Pa. State U. Coll. Agrl., 2000; named to Internat. Livestock Hall of Fame, 1987; Robert H. Rumler scholarhip founded in his name. Fellow Agr. Adventures; mem. Purebred Dairy Cattle Assn. (dir., exec. com.), Nat. Soc. Livestock Record Assns. (past pres., dir., Disting. Svcs. award 1981), Am. Dairy Sci. Assn. (Disting. Svc. award 1977), Agri-Bus. Found. (All-Time Gt. award 1981), Nat. Dairy Shrine (Dairy Hall of Fame 1976), N.E. Master Farmers Assn. (hon. master farmer 1999, Pa. Farm Bur. Disting. Svc. to Agr. award 1999), U.S. Animal Health Assn., Kiwanis, Masons, Elks, Alpha Zeta (hon. roll 1997), Gamma Sigma Delta. Mem. United Ch. of Christ. Home: 937 Wallace Ave Chambersburg PA 17201-3884 E-mail: bobrumler@pa.net.

RUMMEL, ANDREW THOMAS, music educator, musician; b. Peoria, Ill., May 28, 1974; s. Fidelia Anne Rummel. MusB in edn., Ill. State U., 1992—97, MusM in performance, 1997—99. Prin. tuba USAF Heritage Am. Band, Langley AFB, Va., 1999—; adj. prof. of tuba Norfolk State U., 2001—. Sr. airman USAF, 1999—2003, Langley AFB. Decorated Airman of Yr. Air Combat Command Pub. Affairs. Home: #105 1563 N King St Hampton VA 23669 Personal E-mail: iplaytuba@yahoo.com.

RUMMEL, EDGAR FERRAND, retired lawyer; b. New Bern, NC, June 29, 1929; s. Robert French and Reba Jeanette (Burgess) R.; m. Lillian Hildebrandt, Dec. 28, 1954. BA, Ohio State U., 1955; JD, DePaul U., 1965; LLB, U. London, Eng., 1973; LLM, George Washington U., 1978. Bar: U.S. Dist. Ct. D.C. 1967, U.S. Ct. Appeals (D.C. cir.) 1968, U.S. Supreme Ct. 1971, Md. 1980. Atty.-adviser Dept. Army, Washington, 1971-74, 78, counsel U.S. Army Real Estate Agy., Frankfurt, W.Ger., 1975-77, supervisory atty.-adviser, asst. divsn. chief Office of Chief of Engrs., Dept. Army, Washington, 1977-83; sr. atty. adv. Office of Judge Advocate Gen., Dept. Army, Washington, 1983-85, trial atty., 1987; spl. asst. U.S. Atty. Dist. Colo., 1985-87, ret. 1987; chmn. mineral leasing com. Dept. Def., 1981-84; active Oreg. Nat. Trial Adv. Council, 1983-84. With AUS, 1947-51. Mem. Md. State Bar Assn. Democrat. Episcopalian (vestryman 1981-84). Home: 7812 Adelphi Ct Hyattsville MD 20783-1848

RUMMEL, HAROLD EDWIN, real estate development and retail sales executive; b. Youngstown, Ohio, Oct. 4, 1940; s. Harold Edward and Florence Louise (Hill) R.; children: Timothy B., Jonathan S., Briana. BS, U. Fla., 1963. Writer, editor President's coun., Fla., 1958-70; polit. campaign mgr. various state and congressional campaigns, Tallahassee, 1971-79; sr. v.p. Fla. Fed. Saving Bank, St. Petersburg, Fla., 1979-86; pres., CEO Rummel Co. including The Rummel Real Estate Group, Inc., HardwareUSA.net, St. Petersburg, Fla., 1986—, Woodland Bay Group Inc., Mobile, Ala., 1986—. Pres., CEO Rummel Group Inc., Summer Court Inc., Azalea Apts. Inc., Oak Knoll Inc., Bay Vista Inc. Active in civic and polit. orgns. Democrat. Avocations: nature, wildlife photography, travel. Home: 1682 Oceanview Dr Tierra Verde FL 33715-2500 Office: Rummel Cos 1641 1st Ave N Saint Petersburg FL 33713-8935 Home: 1002 Charleston St Mobile AL 36604 E-mail: rumgroup@aol.com.

RUMMEL, ROBERT WILAND, aeronautical engineer, writer; b. Dakota, Ill., Aug. 4, 1915; s. William Howard and Dora (Ely) R.; m. Marjorie B. Cox, Sept. 30, 1939; children: Linda Kay, Sharon Lee, Marjorie Susan, Robert Wiland, Diana Beth. Diploma in Aero. Engring., Curtiss Wright Tech. Inst. Aerosci., 1935. Stress analyst Hughes Aircraft Co., Burbank, Calif., 1935-36, Lockheed Aircraft Corp., Burbank, 1936; draftsman Aero Engring. Corp., Long Beach, Calif., 1936, Nat. Aircraft Co., Alhambra, Calif., 1936-37; chief engr. Rearwin A/C & Engines, Inc., Kansas City, Kans., 1937-42; chief design engr. Commonwealth A/C, Inc., Kansas City, 1942-43; v.p. engring. Trans World Airlines, Inc., Kansas City, Mo., 1943-59, v.p. planning and rsch., 1959-69, v.p. tech. devel., 1969-78; pres. Robert W. Rummel Assocs., Inc., Mesa, Ariz., 1978-87; aerospace cons., 1987—. Commnr. Presdl. Commn. Space Shuttle Challenger Accident, 1986; chmn. nat. rsch. coun. Aero Space Engring. Bd. Fellow Inst. Aero. Scis., Soc. Automotive Engrs.; mem. NAE, Masons (32 deg.), Shriners. Home and Office: 1189 Leisure World Mesa AZ 85206-3067 Office Phone: 480-396-9030. E-mail: RWRummel@aol.com.

RUMOHR, FLOYD, performing company executive, educator; b. Detroit, Mar. 3, 1963; s. Floyd Thomas Rumohr and Grace Lois Meuter. BFA, Wayne State U., 1985; MFA, Temple U., 1988. Assoc. edn. dir., master tchg. artist Theatre New Audience, N.Y.C., 1989—94; artistic dir. Stages Learning, Bklyn., 1984—. Bd. pres. Stages Learning, 1994—2004. Fellow, Temple U., 1986—88; grantee, Robert Sterling Clark Found., Ctr. Arts Edn., NY Cmty. Trust - Worldwide Holdings Fund, Jenesis Group, Independence Cmty. Fellow: Empire State Partnerships Summer Seminar (tchg. fellow 2003—04). Achievements include design of education program that has received four Empire State Partnerships awards from the New York State government. Office: Stages of Learning 138 South Oxford Street #1-B Brooklyn NY 11217 E-mail: floyd@stagesoflearning.org.

RUMP, KENDALL E. air transportation executive; b. Valparaiso, Ind., Sept. 15, 1960; s. Erwin E. and D. Jean Rump. BSBA, Ball State U., 1982. Sales rep. CF Airfreight, Richmond, Va., 1982-83, account mgr. Norfolk, Va., 1984-85, terminal mgr. Saginaw, Mich., 1985-86; v.p., co-owner CCX Express Svcs., Inc., Richmond, 1987-91, exec. v.p. Norfolk, 1991-94, pres., 1993-96; pres., co-owner KRB Couriers, Inc., Norfolk, 1994-96; pres. Express Cargo Svcs., Inc., Norfolk, 1996-98; exec. v.p. Custom Express Cargo, Inc., Norfolk, 1999-2000; v.p. ops. HBI Priority Freight, Inc., Washington, 2000—. Advisor com. Dulles Washington Airport Task Force, 1992-93. Recipient Top 75 Alumni award Ball State U., 1994. Mem. Nat. Air Freight Trucking Alliance, Washington Air Cargo Assn., Balt.-Washington Air Cargo Assn., Hampton Rds. Air Cargo Assn. (1st v.p. 1991, pres. 1992, bd. dirs. 1993, Past Pres. award 1992), Air and Expedited Motor Carrier Assn., Richmond Export-Import Club, Hampton Rds. Traffic Club (fund raiser, program chair joy fund 1992-93, advisor 1993), Richmond Traffic Club, Delta Nu Alpha (sec. 1984). Office: HBI Priority Freight Inc 13894 Redskin Dr Herndon VA 20171 Fax: 757-857-4687.

RUMSCHITZKI, DAVID SHELDON, chemical engineering educator; BS in Chem. Engring. and Math., Cooper Union, 1978; MS in Chem. Engring., U. Calif., Berkeley, 1979, PhD in Chem. Engring., 1984. Process engr. Stauffer Che. Co., Dobbs Ferry, N.Y., summer 1978; rsch. engr. Mobil R&D Corp., Paulsboro, N.J., summer 1984; asst. prof. dept. chem. engring. CCNY, 1983-84, 85-89, assoc. prof., 1990-96, prof., 1997—. Vis. scientist Max Planck Inst. fur Biophys. Chemistry, Gottingen, Germany, 1985, dept. molecular biology Rsch. Inst. Scripps Clinic, La Jolla, Calif., 1988-89, dept. biophysics Rohr U. Bochum, Germany, 1996-97. Alexander von Humboldt fellow, 1996-97; recipient Frederick Urban Meml. scholarship for excellence in chem. engring., 1978, Harry W. Reddick Fund prize and medal for math., 1978, Standard Oil Co. fellowship, 1978, 79, Presdl. Young Investigator award NSF, 1987-93, Best Papter award ASME Bioengring. Divsn., 1995-96, Melville medal ASME, 1996. Mem. Sigma Pi Sigma, Tau Beta Pi, Sigma Xi. Office: Dept Chem City Coll NY 140th St Convent Ave New York NY 10031 E-mail: David@che.ccny.cuny.edu.

RUMSEY, VICTOR HENRY, electrical engineering educator emeritus; b. Devizes, Eng., Nov. 22, 1919; s. Albert Victor and Susan Mary (Norman) R.; m. Doris Herring, Apr. 2, 1942; children: John David, Peter Alan, Catherine Anne. BA, Cambridge U., 1941, DSc in Physics, 1972; DEng, Tohoku U., Japan, 1962. With U.K. Sci. Civil Service, 1941-48; asst. to assoc. prof. Ohio State U., 1948-54; prof. U. Ill., 1954-57, U. Calif., Berkeley, 1957-66, prof. elec. engring. and computer scis. San Diego, 1966-87, prof. emeritus, 1987—, dept. chmn., 1977-81. Author 1 book in field; contbr. articles to profl. jours.; patentee in field. Recipient George Sinclair award Ohio State U., 1982, John Kraus Antenna award IEEE Antennas and Propagation Soc., 2004; Guggen-

heim fellow. Fellow IEEE (Morris Liebman prize, John Kraus award Antennas and Propagation), Union Radio Scientifique Internationale, Internat. Astron. Union; mem. Nat. Acad. Engring. Home: 1171 Bohemian Ln Occidental CA 95465-9115

RUMSFELD, DONALD HENRY, secretary of defense; b. Chgo., July 9, 1932; AB, Princeton U., 1954; hon. degree, De Paul U. Coll. Commerce, Ill. Coll., Lake Forest Coll., Park Coll., Tuskegee Inst., Nat. Coll. Edn., Bryant Coll., Claremont (Calif.) Grad. Sch., Ill. Wesleyan U., RAND Grad. Sch., Hampden-Sydney Coll. Adminstrv. asst. U.S. Ho. of Reps., 1957-59; with A.G. Becker & Co., Chgo., 1960-62; mem. 88th-91st Congresses from 13th Ill. dist., Pres. Richard Nixon's Cabinet, 1969-73; dir. OEO, asst. to pres., 1969-70; counsellor to Pres., dir. econ. stabilization program, 1971-72; U.S. ambassador and permanent rep. to NATO, 1973-74; chief of staff for Pres. Gerald Ford, mem. Cabinet, 1974-75; sec. U.S. Dept. Defense, Washington, 1975—77; pres., chief exec. officer, then chmn. G.D. Searle & Co., Skokie, Ill., 1977-85; spl. envoy of Pres. Ronald Reagan to Mid. East, 1983-84; sr. advisor William Blair & Co., Chgo., 1985-90; chmn., chief exec. officer General Instrument Corp., Chgo., 1990-93; chmn. bd. dirs. Gilead Scis., Inc., Foster City, Calif., 1997—2001; sec. U.S. Dept. Defense, Washington, 2001—. Bd. dirs. Amylin Pharms., Inc., Asea Brown Boveri, Ltd., Tribune Co.; bd. trustees RAND Corp., 1977—; chmn. U.S. Commn. to Assess the Ballistic Missile Threat to the U.S., 1998; commr. U.S. Fed. Trade Deficit Rev. Commn., 1999, U.S. Commn. to Assess Nat. Security Space Mgmt. and Orgn., 2000—. Naval Aviator USN, 1954-57. Recipient Presdl. Medal of Freedom, 1977, George Catlett Marshall award, Woodrow Wilson award, Dwight David Eisenhower medal. Republican. Office: Dept Defense 1000 Defense Pentagon Washington DC 20301-1000

RUMYANTSEV, SERGEY L. research scientist, educator; b. St.Petersburg, Russia, June 26, 1954; arrived in U.S., 1998; s. Lev S. Rumyantsev, Galina S. Rumyantseva; m. Irina D. Shurygina, Apr. 29, 1952; children: Vladimir, Irina, Alexandra Rumyantseva. Master, Inst. Elec. Tech., St. Petersburg, 1977; PhD, State Tech. U., St. Petersburg, Russia, 1987; DSc, Ioffe Inst., St. Petersburg, Russia, 1997. Sr. engr. "Svetlana" Corp., St. Petersburg, Russia, 1980—88; leading scientist Ioffe Inst. of Russian Acad. Scis., St. Petersburg, Russia, 1989—; rsch. prof. Rensselaer Poly. Inst., Troy, NY, 1998—. Vis. rschr. Simon Frazer U., Vancouver, Canada, 1996—98. Editor: (book) "Handbook Series of Semiconductor Parameters, v.1: Elementary Semiconductors and A3B5 Compounds, Si, Ge, C, GaAs,GaP,GaSb, InAs,InP,InSb., 1996, Handbook Series of Semiconductor Parameters, v.2: Ternary and Quarternary A3B5 Compounds, AlGaAs, GaInP, GaInAs, GaInSb, GaAsSb, InAsSb, GaInAsP, GaInAsSb., 1999; author: (book) Properties of Advanced Semiconductor Materials: GaN, AlN, InN, BN, SiC, SiGe, 2000; contbr. articles to profl. jours., chapters to books. Recipient prize for the best paper, Ioffe Inst., 1989, 1995, prize for the best paper of Solid State Electronics Divsn., 1999, 2000. Achievements include research in physics of semiconductors and semiconductor devices; microwave devices; wide band gap semiconductors (SiC, GaN, CdS); noise in microwave and optical devices; power Si, SiC, GaN devices; Si bipolar and Field Effect Transistors; organic semiconductors. Office: Rensselaer Polytech Inst CII 9015 110 8th St Troy NY 12180 Office Phone: 518-276-2908. Business E-Mail: roumis2@rpi.edu.

RUNBECK, LINDA C. state legislator; b. June 11, 1946; m. Richard Runbeck; 1 child. BA, Bethel Coll., 1968. Former mem. Minn. Ho. of Reps., St. Paul; mem. various coms.; U.S. senator from Minn., 1993—. Mem. govt. ops. and reform com., mem. jobs, energy and cmty. devel com., others; advt. exec. Mem. League Women's Voters. Home: 48 E Golden Lake Rd Circle Pines MN 55014-1725 Office: Minn State Senate State Capitol Building Saint Paul MN 55155-0001

RUND, DOUGLAS ANDREW, emergency physician; b. Columbus, Ohio, July 20, 1945; s. Carl Andrew and Caroline Amelia (Row) Rund; m. Sue E. Padavana, 1980; children: Carie, Emily, Ashley. BA, Yale U., 1967; MD, Stanford U., 1971. Lic. physician Ohio, diplomate Nat. Bd. Med. Examiners, Am. Bd. Family Practice, Am. Bd. Emergency Medicine . Intern U. Calif. San Francisco-Moffett Hosp., 1971—72; resident in gen. surgery Stanford U., 1972—74, Robert Wood Johnson Found. clin. scholar in medicine, 1974—76; med. dir. Mid-Peninsula Health Svc., Palo Alto, Calif., 1975—76; clin. instr. dept. medicine and preventive medicine Stanford U. Med. Sch., 1975—76; assoc. prof., dir. divsn. emergency medicine Ohio State Coll. Medicine, 1982—87, dir. emergency medicine residency program, assoc. prof. dept, 1976—87, prof., chmn. dept. preventive medicine, 1988—90, prof., chmn. dept. emergency medicine, 1990—, prof., interim chmn. dept. family medicine, 1994—95, assoc. dean, 2001—; pres. Ohio State Univ. Physicians, 2002—. Attending staff Ohio State U. Hosps., 1976—; med. dir. CSCC, Emergency Med. Svcs. Dept.; pres. Internat. Rsch. Inst. Emergency Medicine; sr. rsch. fellow NATO: Health and Med. Aspects of Disaster Preparedness, 1985—87; vis. epidemiology and injury control U. Edinburgh, Scotland, 1987; working group, emergency and critical care in space NASA, 2001—; bd. dirs. Am. Bd. Emergency Medicine, 1988—97, sr. editor in tng. exam., 1989—, pres., 1995—; pres., chmn. bd. dirs. Physicians of the Ohio State U. (POSU), 2002—; med. dir. Worthington Fire Dept. Author: Triage, 1981, Essentials of Emergency Medicine, 1982, 2d edit., 1986, Emergency Radiology, 1982, Emergency Psychiatry, 1983, Environmental Emergencies, 1985; editor: Emergency Medicine Ann., 1983—84, Emergency Medicine Survey, Annals of Emergency Medicine, Annals of Emergency Medicine Symposium, 1986; editor: (in chief) Ohio State Series on Emergency Medicine, Emergency Medicine Observer, 1986—87; mem. editl. bd.: Physician, Sports Medicine, Emergency Med. Svcs.; co-author: Family Medicine Priciples and Practice, 1978, 2d edit., 1983; contbr. articles to profl. jours. Recipient Douglas A. Rund Disting. Faculty award, Dept. Emergency Medicine, 2003. Fellow: Am. Coll. Emergency Physicians (task force on substance abuse and injury control, Outstanding Contbn. to Edn. award 1992); mem.: IAAA, Internat. Soc. for Emergency Med. Svcs. (med. dir.), Columbus Med. Forum (pres. 1993—), Soc. Acad. Emergency Medicine (chmn. internat. com. 1991—), Assn. Acad. Chairs Emergency Medicine (pres. 1992—93), Nat. Inst. on Alcohol Abuse and Alcoholism, Alpha Omega Alpha. Office: Ohio State U 146 Means Hall 1654 Upham Dr Columbus OH 43210-1240

RUNDELL, ARDEN GRABKE, musician; b. Chico, Calif., Dec. 16, 1961; d. Harold Salisbury and Lois Jean Grabke; m. Robert Glenn Rundell, Aug. 7, 1994; 1 child, Miriam. BA in Psychology, Western Wash. U., 1985, MBA, 1986; PhD in Bus. Adminstrn., Ariz. State U., 1995. Compensation/benefits adminstr. Spacelabs Med., Redmond, Wash., 1986—88; benefits adminstr. Children's Hosp., Seattle, 1989—90; rsch./tchg. asst. Ariz. State U., Tempe, 1990—95; adj. prof. bus. N.W. Coll., Kirklan, Wash., 1996—98; project cons. fin. Bank Am., Seattle, 1997—2000. Violinist Beaverton (Oreg.) Chamber Symphony, 1996—97, Bellevue (Wash.) Philharm., 1997—. Co-author: Handbook of Human Resource, 1995. Violinist Eastside Foursquare Ch., Kirkland, 2000—. With N.G. U.S. Army, 1980—86. Scholar, Western Wash. U., 1985—86. Mem.: Acad. Mgmt. Democrat. Pentacostal. Avocations: applied research, music, computer languages, astronomy, physics. Home: 6521 SE Couger Mt Way Bellevue WA 98006

RUNDELL, ORVIS HERMAN, JR., psychologist, educator; b. Oklahoma City, June 16, 1940; s. Orvis Herman and Virginia Reid (George) R.; m. Jane Shannon Brians, June 25, 1966; children: Leslie Jane, Anne Reid. BS, U. Okla., 1962, MS, 1972, PhD, 1976. Lab. mgr. Okla. Ctr. Alcohol and Drug-Related Studies, Oklahoma City, 1969-76, staff scientist, 1974—. Asst. prof. psychiatry and behavioral scis. U. Okla. Health Sci. Center, 1976—; dir. clin. physiology and sleep disorders ctr. Columbia Presbyterian Hosp., Oklahoma City, 1982-2001; clin. dir. Diagnostic Sleep Ctr. of Dallas, 1989-93; ptnr. Sleep Medicine Assocs., 1994—, Sleep Assocs., 2000—, Sleep Remedies, LLC, 2002—; dir. Columbia Sleep Ptnrs. Program, 1996-2001; clin. dir. The Sleep Clinic, Oklahoma City, 2000—, Sleep Labs PRN, 2001—; cons. in field; instl. rev. bd. U. Okla. Health Sci. Ctr., 1989-2001. Contbr. articles to profl. jours., chpts. in books; asst. editor Alcohol Tech. Reports, 1976-90; cons. editor Psychophysiology, 1974-2001. Bd. dirs. Hist. Preservation, Inc., Oklahoma City, 1978-90. With USAR, 1963-69. Grantee, Nat. Inst. Drug Abuse, Nat. Inst. Alcohol Abuse and Alcoholism. Fellow Am. Acad. of Sleep Medicine; mem. N.Y. Acad. Scis., Psi Chi, Phi Gamma Delta. Home: 431 NW 20th St Oklahoma City OK 73103-1918 Office: 5530 N Francis Oklahoma City OK 73118 Fax: 405-879-2476. Office Phone: 405-767-6970. E-mail: zzzs@cox.net.

RUNDIO, LOUIS MICHAEL, JR., lawyer; b. Chgo., Sept. 13, 1943; s. Louis Michael Sr. and Germaine Matilda (Pasternack) R.; m. Ann Marie Bartlett, July 10, 1971; children: Matthew, Melissa. BS in Physics, Loyola U., Chgo., 1965, JD, 1972. Bar: Ill. 1972, U.S. Dist. Ct. (no. dist.) Ill. 1972, U.S. Ct. Appeals (7th cir.) 1974, U.S. Dist. Ct. (ea. dist.) Mich. 1983. Assoc. McDermott, Will & Emery, Chgo., 1972-77, ptnr., 1978—. Served to 1st lt. U.S. Army, 1965-68, Vietnam. Mem. ABA, Chgo. Bar Assn. Home: 676 Skye Ln Barrington IL 60010-5506 Office: McDermott Will & Emery 227 W Monroe St Ste 3100 Chicago IL 60606-5096

RUNDLE, KATHERINE FERNANDEZ, state's attorney; b. Washington, 1951; BEd, U. Miami, Fla., 1973; MA, U. Cambridge, Eng., 1976. Asst. state's atty. Dade County, Miami, Fla., dep. chief, chief, state's atty. 11th Jud. Cir., 1993—. Office: Dade County 11th Judicial Cir 1350 NW 12th Ave Miami FL 33136-2102

RUNDLETT, ELLSWORTH TURNER, III, lawyer; b. Portland, Maine, Jan. 12, 1946; s. Ellsworth Turner II and Esther (Stevens) R.; m. Lisa Warren, Oct. 25, 1964 (div. June 1967); 1 child, Ellsworth Turner IV; m. Jamie Donnelly, June 7, 1982 (div. 1986); m. Marilyn DeJenzano, Aug. 17, 1994. AB cum laude, Bowdoin Coll., 1968; JD, U. Maine, 1973. Bar: Maine 1973, U.S. Dist. Ct. Maine 1973, U.S. Ct. Appeals (1st cir.) 1973; cert. civil trial specialist, Nat. Bd. Trial Advocacy; diplomate Nat. Coll. Advocacy. Bowdoin Coll. intern U.S. Senate, Washington, 1967; law clk. Superior Ct. Maine, Portland, 1972-73; asst. corp. counsel City of Portland, 1973-76; ptnr. Childs, Rundlett, Fifield, Shumway and Altshuler, Portland, 1980—. Author: Maximizing Damages in Small Personal Injury Cases, 1991; contbr. legal articles to Maine Bus. Digest, 1978-84. Pres. Pine Tree Alcohol Treatment Ctr., Windham, Maine, 1978-80; trustee Portland Players, Inc., South Portland, Maine, 1977-84, pres., 1985-87. Mem. ATLA, Cumberland County Bar (trustee 1983-84, 86-87, v.p. 1988-90, pres. 1990), Maine Bar Assn. (bd. govs. 1991—), Maine Trial Lawyers Assn. (pres. 2000-01), U. Maine Law Alumni (bd. dirs. 1984-87, v.p. 1988, pres. 1989, bd. govs. 1991—), Cumberland Club, Portland Club (gov. 1983-86), Bowdoin Club of Portland (pres. 1978). Office: Childs Rundlett & Fifield 257 Deering Ave Portland ME 04103-4858 Office Phone: 207-773-0275. E-mail: derry@maine.rr.com.

RUNFOLA, ROSS THOMAS, lawyer, educator, writer, journalist, poet; b. Buffalo, Aug. 30, 1943; s. Joseph Paul and Isabelle Louise (Santi) R.; children: Jennifer, Ross Thomas. BA summa cum laude, SUNY, Buffalo, 1965, MA, 1968, PhD, 1973, JD, 1981. Bar: N.Y. 1982. Prof. social scis. Medaille Coll., Buffalo, 1969—; asst. prof. SUNY, Buffalo, 1970-73; sports columnist Buffalo New Times, Buffalo, 1973-74; co-anchor Sta. WUTV, Buffalo, 1974; reporter Buffalo Courier Express, Buffalo, 1975-76; columnist Spree mag., Buffalo, 1979-82; asst. Erie County Pub. Adminstr., Buffalo, 1981; ptnr. Fiorella, Leiter & Runfola, Buffalo, 1982-86; spl. matrimonial counsel Matusick, Spadafora & Verrastro, Buffalo, 1986-87; ptnr. Siegel, Kelleher & Kahn, Buffalo, 1987—2002. Dir. Matrimonial Mediation Ctr. Author: Jock: Sports and Male Identity, 1980; contbr. numerous articles to profl. jours.; chief film scriptwriter: Organized Sports: Are They Good for Young People, 1975. Active Mayor's Energy Task Force City of Buffalo, 1973, commn. Human Rights and Cmty. Relations, 2000, Minority task group for 8th judicial dist., 2000, Attica Prison Task Force, N.Y., 1973, Western N.Y. Consortium on Higher Edn., 1974, Erie County (N.Y.) Task Force on Physical Edn. and Recreation for Meeting the needs of the Handicapped, 1974, Instl. Task Force Pvt. Colls. Western N.Y., 1974, Western N.Y. Higher Edn. Task Force, 1975, Legis. Adv. Com. N.Y. State Assembly, 1976, Children's Hosp. Adolescence Program, 1978, Western N.Y. Heart Assn., 1978, Southern Poverty Law Ctr., 1978—, Erie County Dem. Com., 1978—, Step Family Assn. Western N.Y., 1983—, Frontier Dem. Club, 1983—; mem. adv. com. United Way Buffalo, 1991—; bd. dirs. Monsignor Carr Inst., Just Buffalo Lit. Ctr., 1996. Named One of Ten Best Coll. Profs. Western N.Y. Buffalo News, 1987, Prof. of Yr. Medaille Coll., 1998, Leadership Buffalo for Outstanding Leadership and Cmty. Commitment, 1999; recipient 1st pl. award oral competition Greater Buffalo Poetry Slam, 1998, Social Svcs. award Nat. Conf. for Community and Justice, 1998. Mem. ABA, AAUP, N.Y. State Bar Assn., Erie County Bar Assn. (vice chmn. matrimonial and family law com. 1992—), N.Y. State United Tchrs., N.Y. State Coun. Divorce Mediation, Am. Acad. Family Mediators (designated cons.), Am. Trial Lawyers Assn. Roman Catholic. Avocations: writing, reading, bicycling, cross country skiing. Home: 96 Cleveland Ave Buffalo NY 14222-1610 also: 18 Agassiz Cir Buffalo NY 14214-2601

RUNG, GEORGE W. physician; b. Altoona, Pa., Dec. 18, 1957; s. Wilbur Karl and Emma May (Peterson) R.; m. Catherine Ann Kline, June 9, 1979; children: Katrina, Allison, Jonathan, Christopher. BS, Juniata Coll., 1978; MD, Pa. State U., 1982. Diplomate Am. Bd. Anesthesiology; cert. in pain mgmt. Intern Pa. State U. Hosp., Hershey, 1983, anesthesia resident, 1984-85; asst. prof. Pa. State U., 1986, assoc. prof., 1993—; anesthesia/crit. care fellow U. Western Australia, Perth, 1985-86. Vis. scientist and univ. sabbatical, U. Copenhagen, Denmark, 1995; fellow Project Hope, Guayaqil, Equador, 1992. Author: A Practice of Cardiac Anesthesia, 1991, 95, Anesthesia for Vascular Surgery, 1993; contbr. articles to profl. jours. Vis. scientist, Pa. State U., Denmark, 1995. Mem. Am. Soc. Anesthesiologists, Am. Soc. Regional Anesthesiologists, Internat. Anesthesia Rsch. Soc. Home: 222 E Granada Ave Hershey PA 17033-1343 Office: Anesthesia Assocs Lancaster 133 E Frederick St Lancaster PA 17602-2222 E-mail: georgerung@earthlink.net.

RUNGE, DONALD EDWARD, food wholesale company executive; b. Milw., Mar. 20, 1938; s. Adam and Helen Teresa (Voss) R.; divorced; children: Roland, Richard, Lori. Grad., Spencerian Coll., Milw., 1960. Fin. v.p. Milw. Cheese Co., Waukesha, Wis., 1962-69; dir. Farm House Foods Corp., Milw., 1966-89, pres., 1966-89, CEO, treas., 1984-89, chmn., pres., 1985-89; chmn., CEO Retailing Corp. Am., Milw., 1982-89; CEO, treas. Drug Sys. Inc., Milw., 1984-89; chmn. Drug Sys. Inc. (now Retailing Corp. of Am.), Milw., 1985-89; pres. TDC, 1987-89; chmn., pres. Runge Industries, Gen. Growth, Inc., 1989—. Bd. dirs. Convenient Food Mart, CasaBlanca Industries, Inc., City of Industry, Calif., Palm Beach Opera, 1992—; sec. The Diana Corp., Milw., 1985-86, treas. 1986—, pres. 1987-96; chmn. Economy Dry Goods Co. Inc.; treas. Fairbanks Farms Inc.; adv. Adventist. Office Phone: 561-625-4844. *I believe there is very little in life that cannot be accomplished if a person truly wants to attain the goal.*

RUNGE, JEFFREY WILLIAM, federal agency administrator; m. Ginny Runge; children: Emily, Will. B, U. of South; MD, U. S.C., 1981. Diplomate Am. Bd. Emergency Medicine. Resident Charlotte Meml. Hosp. and Med. Ctr., 1984; faculty emergency medicine residency Carolinas Med. Ctr., Charlotte, NC, 1984; dir. Carolinas Ctr. Injury Prevention and Control; nat. hwy. traffic safety adminstr. U.S. Dept. Transp., Washington, 2001—. Mem.: N.C. Med. Soc. (spkr.), N.C. Coll. Emerency Physicians (past pres.), Am. Coll. Emergency Physicians (trauma care and injury control com., rsch. com.). Office: US Dept Transp Nat Hwy Traffic Safety Adminstr 400 7th St SW Washington DC 20590

RUNGE, KAY KRETSCHMAR, library director; b. Davenport, Iowa, Dec. 9, 1946; d. Alfred Edwin and Ina (Paul) Kretschmar; children: Peter Jr., Katherine. BS in History Edn., Iowa State U., 1969; MLS, U. Iowa, 1970. Pub. svc. libr. Anoka County Libr., Blaine, Minn., 1971-72; cataloger Augustana Coll., Rock Island, Ill., 1972-74; dir. Scott County Libr. Sys., Eldridge, Iowa, 1974-85, Davenport (Iowa) Pub. Libr., 1985—2001, Des Moines Pub. Libr., 2001—. V.p. Quad-Cities Conv. and Visitors Bur., 1992—97, Quad-Cities Grad. Study Ctr., 1992—2001, Downtown Davenport Devel. Corp., 1992—2000, Hall of Honor Bd., Davenport Ctrl. H.S., 1992—95, Brenton Bank Bd., 1995—2001, Wells Fargo Bank Bd., 2001; steering com. Quad-Cities Vision for the Future, 1987—91, Humanities Iowa, 1993—2000, chair, 1998—99; bd. govs. Iowa State U. Found., 1991—; citizens adv. coun. Iowa State U., 1998—2000, Leadership Iowa, 1998—99; adv. bd. U. Iowa Sch. Libr. Sci., 1999—, adj. prof., 2000—01; devel. bd. Iowa State U. Found., 2000—; mem. Greater Des Moines Leadership, 2002—03; mem. dean's adv. bd. Liberal Arts and Sci. Coll. Iowa State U., 2004—; bd. dirs. River Ctr. for Performing Arts, Davenport, 1983—97, Iowa State U. Rsch. Pk., 1998—2000, Quest Ednl. Corp., 1999—2002, Hamilton/Kaplan U., 2002—, Davenport One, Downtown Devel., 2000—01; chmn. bd. dirs. Am. Inst. Commerce, 1989—98. Recipient Svc. Key award Iowa State U. Alumni Assn., 1979, ALA/ALTA Nat. Advocacy Honor Roll award, 2000; named Quad City Panhellenic Woman of Yr., 1998. Mem. ALA (chmn. libr. adminstrs. and mgrs. div., fundraising sect. 1988, bd. dirs., Exhibits Round Table 2003-), Iowa Libr. Assn. (pres. 1983, Mem. of Yr. award 2000), Pub. Libr. Assn. (bd. dirs. 1990-99, pres. 2000-01), Iowa Edn. Media Assn. (Intellectual Freedom award 1984), Alpha Delta Pi (alumni state pres. 1978). Lutheran. Office: Des Moines Pub Libr 100 Locust St Des Moines IA 50309-1791

RUNK, FRED J. insurance company executive; CFO Am. Fin. Group, Inc., Cin. Office: American Financial Group Inc 1 E 4th St Cincinnati OH 45202 Office Fax: (513) 579-2113.

RUNKLE, DONALD L. electronics executive; BSME, MSME, U. Mich.; M in Mgmt. Sci. (Sloan fellow, MIT. Various pos., including chief engr. powertrain and racing, dir. advanced vehicle engring., others GM; v.p., gen. mgr. Delphi Saginaw Steering Systems, 1993—96; gen. mgr. Delphi Energy and Engine Mgmt. Systems, 1996—2000; exec. v.p. Delphi Corp., Troy, Mich., 2000—03, pres., Dynamics and Propulsion sector, 2000—03; vice chmn. Delphi Corp. Enterprise Techs., Troy, Mich., 2003—. Mem.: Soc. Mfg. Engrs., Soc. Automotive Engrs., Shingo Prize Acad. (Wu Mfg. Leadership award 2003), Pi Tau Sigma, Tau Beta Pi. Achievements include patents for rotary engine mounting. Office: World Hdqrs Adelphi Corp 5725 Delphi Dr Troy MI 48098-2815

RUNKLE, MARTIN DAVEY, library director; b. Cin., Oct. 18, 1937; s. Newton and Ilo (Neal) R.; m. Nancy Force, Aug. 7, 1965; children: Seth, Elizabeth. BA, Muskingum Coll., 1959; MA, U. Pitts., 1964, U. Chgo., 1973. Library systems analyst U. Chgo., 1970-75, head cataloging librarian, 1975-79, asst. dir. tech. services, 1979-80, dir. library, 1980—. Sr. lectr. grad. library sch. U. Chgo., 1977-90. Fulbright grantee, 1965. Mem. ALA. E-mail: maru@midway.uchicago.edu.

RUNNALLS, DAVID, think-tank executive; BA, U. Toronto, 1966; MIA, Columbia U., 1968. Sr. advisor Internat. Devel. Rsch. Ctr., UN Devel. Program; dir. Environment and Sustainable Devel. Program Inst. for Rsch. on Pub. Policy; pres., CEO Internat. Inst. for Sustainable Devel., Winnipeg, Canada, 1999—, also bd. dirs. Bd. mem. China Coun. Working Group on Trade and the Environment, Internat. Inst. for Environment and Devel., London, World Environment Ctr., N.Y.C., Pollution Probe; Can. bd. mem. IUCN; bd. mem. World Conservation Union; com. chair World Conservation Congress, Montreal, Canada, 1996. Office: Internat Inst for Sustainable Devel 6th Fl 161 Portage Ave East Winnipeg MB Canada R3B 0Y4*

RUNNALLS, OLIVER JOHN CLYVE (JOHN RUNNALLS), nuclear engineering educator; b. Barrie Island, Ont., Can., June 26, 1924; s. John Lawrence and Ethel May (Arnold) Runnalls; m. Vivian Constance Stowe, Sept. 13, 1947; children: David John, Catherine Ruth. BSc, U. Toronto, 1948, MSc, 1949, PhD, 1951. Registered profl. engr., Ont. R & D scientist Atomic Energy of Can., Ltd., Chalk River, Ont. and Paris, 1951-71; sr. adviser uranium and nuclear energy Energy, Mines and Resources Can., Ottawa, Ont., 1971-79; prof. energy studies U. Toronto, 1979-89, chmn. Ctr. Nuclear Engring., 1983-89; prof. emeritus nuclear engring. and energy studies, 1989—; chmn. bd. Inst. Hydrogen Systems, 1983-89. Pres. O.J.C. Runnalls & Assocs., Ltd. Contbr. Decorated Queen's Silver Jubilee medal; named to Engring. Hall of Distinction, U. Toronto, 2001; recipient B.T.A. Bell Commemorative medal, Can. Mining Jour., 1979. Fellow: Can. Acad. Engring., Royal Soc. Can.; mem.: Can. Nuclear Soc., Can. Nuclear Assn. (bd. dirs., past chmn., Ian F. McRae award 1980). Achievements include patents in field. Home and Office: 65 Court St E Ste 509 Mississauga Ontario Canada L5G4V3

RUNNER, SHARON, state representative; m. George Runner; children: Micah, Rebekah. Student, Antelope Valley (Calif.) Coll. Dir. pub. rels. Desert Christian Schs., 2002—; realtor Red Carpet Real Estate Co.; owner Runner Group; mem. Calif. Assembly, 2002—. Del. Rep. Nat. Conv., 1996, 2000; chair heartwalk Am. Heart Assn.; dir. Antelope Valley Crime Task Force; dir. gift found. Antelope Valley Hosp.; dir. Antelope Valley Vols., CareNet Pregnancy Resource Ctr. Antelope Valley, Friends in Action; dir. adv. coun. Healthy Homes; dir. bd. dirs. United Way. Mem.: Lancaster C. of C. (bd. dirs.). Reform. Baptist. Office: PO Box 942849 Rm 2174 Sacramento CA 95814 Address: 747 W Lancaster Blvd Lancaster CA 93534

RUNNICLES, DONALD, conductor; b. Edinburgh, Scotland, Nov. 16, 1954; Student, Edinburgh U., Cambridge U., London Opera Ctr.; DMus (hon.), U. Edinburgh, 1995. Music dir. San Francisco Opera, 1992—. Office: San Francisco Opera War Meml Opera House 301 Van Ness Ave San Francisco CA 94102-4509

RUNNION, HOWARD J., JR., banker; b. Hot Spring, N.C., May 23, 1930; s. Howard Jackson and Blanche Mae (Elam) R.; m. Betty Ann Bishop, June 30, 1951; children: Debra Joy Sizemore, Jill Marie Glenn. BS, U. N.C., 1952. Various postions Wachovia Bank and Trust Co.-Wachovia Corp., Winston-Salem, N.C., 1952—; ret. vice chmn., former dir. Depository Trust Co., N.Y.C., 1985-95; chmn. bd. PSA Treasury Com, 1984-85. Ret. vice-chmn, CFO Wachovia Corp.; bd. dirs. SI Corp. Chmn. bd. trustees Coll. Found. Raleigh, 1978-95. Mem. Res. City Bankers Assn., Pub. Securities Assn. (dir. 1976-79, 84-85) Clubs: Forsyth Country, Roaring Gap. Lodges: Elk. Republican. Presbyterian. Avocation: golf. Home: 3521 York Rd Winston Salem NC 27104-1346 Office: Wachovia Corp PO Box 3099 Winston Salem NC 27102-3099 Office Phone: 336-732-6552.

RUNQUIST, LISA A. lawyer; b. Mpls., Sept. 22, 1952; d. Ralf E. and Violet R. BA, Hamline U., 1973; JD, U. Minn., 1976. Bar: Minn. 1977, Calif. 1978, U.S. Dist. Ct. (ctrl. dist.) Calif. 1985, U.S. Supreme Ct. 1995. Assoc. Caldwell & Toms, L.A., 1978-82; ptnr. Runquist & Flagg, L.A., 1982-85; pvt. practice Runquist & Assocs., L.A., 1985-99, Runquist & Zybach LLP, L.A., 1999—. Mem. adv. bd. Exempt Orgn. Tax Rev., 1990—, Calif. State U. L.A. Continuing Edn. Acctg. and Tax Program, 1995—. Mem. editl. bd.: ABA Bus. Law Today, 1994—2002. Mem. ABA (bus. law sect.coun. 1995-99, com. on nonprofit corps. 1986—, chair 1991-95, coun. mem. 1995-99, subcom. current devels. in nonprofit corp. law 1989—, chair 1989-91, subcom. rels. orgns. 1989—, chair 1987-91, 95-98, subcom. legal guidebook for dirs. 1986—, ad hoc com. on info. tech., 1997—, chair 1997-98, co-chair, 1998—2002, sect. liaison to ABA tech. coun. 1997-2000, subcom. model nonprofit corp. act, partnerships and unincorp. bus. orgns. com. 1987—, state regulation of securities com. 1988-99, corp. laws com. 1999-, subcom. guidebook for dirs. of closely held corps. chair 2000—, sec. of taxation exempt orgns. com. 1987—, tax), Calif. Bar Assn. (bus. law sect., nonprofit and unincorp. orgns. com. 1985-92, 93-96, 97—, chair 1989-91), Christian Legal Soc., Ctr. Law and Religious Freedom, Christian Mgmt. Assn. (dir. 1983-89). Office: 10821 Huston St North Hollywood CA 91601 E-mail: lisa@runquist.com.

RUNTE, ROSEANN, academic administrator; b. Kingston, N.Y., Jan. 31, 1948; arrived in Can., 1971, naturalized, 1983; d. Robert B. and Anna Loretta (Schorkopf) O'Reilly; m. Hans-Rainer Runte, Aug. 9, 1969. BA summa cum laude, SUNY, New Paltz, 1968; MA, U. Kans., 1969, PhD, 1974; DLitt (hon.), Acadia U., 1989, Meml. U., 1990, U. Vest Timisoara, 1996, U. Arad, 2001; Assoc. (hon.), Moraine Valley C.C., 2003. Lectr. Bethany Coll., W.Va., 1970—71; lectr. adult studies St. Mary's U., Halifax, Canada, 1971—72; from lectr. to assoc. prof. Dalhousie U., Halifax, Canada, 1972—83, asst. dean, 1980—82, chmn. dept. French, 1980—83; pres. U. Sainte-Anne, Pointe-de-l'Eglise, Canada, 1983—88; prin. Glendon Coll., Toronto, Canada, 1988—94; pres. Victoria U., 1994—2001, Old Dominion U., 2001—. Bd. dirs. Banque

Nationale, Va. Advanced Carrier and Shipbldg. Integration Ctr. Author: Brumes Bleues, 1982, Faux-Soleils, 1984, Birmanie Blues, 1993; editor: Studies in 18th Century Culture, vols. VII, VIII, IX, 1977—79, A Canadian in Love, 2000, The Passionate Mind, 2000; lit. rev. editor: French Rev., 1988—94; editor: Lit. Rsch., 1994—97; co-editor: Man and Nature, 1982, Le Development Regional, 1986—87, From Orality to Literature, 1991, Lectures Canadiennes, 1993, Visions of Beauty, 1995, The Foundation for International Training: 25 Years of International Development, 2001; co-translator: Local Development, 1987; mem. editl. bd. Purdue Romance Lang. Series, 2001—. V.p. Can. commn. UNESCO, 1991—92, pres., 1992—96; vice-chair exec. bd. Found. for Internat. Tng., 1994—95, chair bd., 1995—2000; internat. adv. bd. Expo 2000, 1995—2000; v.p. Assn. Internat. des études québecoises, 1999—2001; mem. Internat. Women's Forum, 1998—; chair comm. internat. edn. Am. Coun. on Edn., 2004—; chair accreditation com. visit NCAA, 2004—; commr. Southeastern Accreditation Commn., 2004—; chair Gottschalk Prize Com., 1994; chair publs. com. Hannah Found., 1989—92; vice-chair bd. Gardiner Mus., 1994—2001; mem. Commn. Langs. Instrn., Ontario, Canada, 1999—2001; chair prix du salon Livre Com., 1998; hon. life mem. UNESCO, 2003; bd. dirs. Assn. Med. Svcs., 1989—92; adv. bd. Nat. Libr., 1984—91; bd. dirs. Urban League, United Way. Decorated Order of Can., Ordre du Mérite France, Order Acad. Palmes; recipient Fr. Coppée award, French Acad., 1989, Queen Elizabeth Jubilee medal, 2002, Zonta award, 2004; Regents scholar, SUNY, 1965, Title IV grantee, NDEA, 1968. Fellow: Royal Soc. Can., Soc. Study Values in Edn., World Acad. Arts and Scis.; mem.: Royal Coll. Physicians and Surgeons (exec. com.), Soc. for Study Higher Edn. (bd. dirs. 1988—90), Can. Soc. 18th Century Studies (pres. 1975—76), Atlantic Soc. 18th Century Studies (pres. 1972—76), Can. Fedn. Humanities (pres. 1982—84), Internat. Assn. of Comparative Lit. (treas. 1985—91, sec. 1991—94), Internat. Soc. 18th Century Studies (assoc. treas. 1983—87), World Parliament of Cultures, Club of Rome (exec. com. 1999—), Knights of Malta (grande dame 1991—), Phi Delta Kappa, Delta Kappa Gamma. Home: 5000 Edgewater Dr Norfolk VA 23508 Office: Old Dominion U Norfolk VA 23529 Office Phone: 757-683-3159. E-mail: rrunte@odu.edu.

RUNTSCH, CLARENCE FREDERICK, sculptor; b. Verdigre, Nebr., Mar. 13, 1923; s. Albert and Anna Marie (Czekay) R.; m. Alice Jean McCabe, Aug. 2, 1947 (div. Mar. 1977); 1 child, Teresa Ann Runtsch Duffett. Student, Texas A&M, 1942, Cumming Sch. of Art, Des Moines, 1946-48, Drake U., 1947, Kansas City Art Inst., 1948-50; BFA, U. Kansas City, 1950; student, Kansas City Art Inst., 1950-51; MFA, Univ. Tennessee, 1956. Artist/designer Mus. Natural History, Kansas City, 1951-52; illustrator Civil Svc., U.S. Army, Kansas City, 1952-54; chief designer Am. Mus. Atomic Energy, Oak Ridge, Tenn., 1954-76. Artist/sculptor ltd. edits. and commns., 1951—; principal works include collections at Smithsonian Inst., 1961, U.S. Marine Corps. Mus., 1993, Buffalo Bill Hist. Ctr., 2000, art in corp. and pvt. collections, U.S., Switzerland, Germany. Tech. Sgt. USMC, 1942-46. Recipient 5 Combat Stars USMC, Presdl. Unit Citation. Mem. Am. Soc. Arms Collectors, Smoky Mountain Gun Collectors (charter life mem., pres. 1964), Oak Ridge Art Ctr. (dir. 1956-59), Sertoma (charter pres. 1966—), Southeastern Antique Arms Collectors (charter life mem., dir. 1977—), Free and Accepted Masons (life mem.), Elks. Avocations: collecting and researching antique weapons, collecting indian beadwork. Home: 131 E Vanderbilt Dr Oak Ridge TN 37830-6182

RUNYAN, CHARLES KENT, education educator; b. Cape Girardeau, Mo., Oct. 20, 1950; s. Charles Shelby and Jean Murrill Runyan; m. Linda Sue Stear, Sept. 2, 1972; children: Charles Keith, Jaime Lynn Peterson, Jonathon Scott. BS in Lang. Arts, Marshall U., 1972, MA in Ednl. Adminstrn., 1974; EdD in Ednl. Leadership, W.Va. U., 1988. Tchr., coach Hurricane (W.Va.) H.S., 1972—89; prof. curriculum and instrn. Pittsburg (Kans.) State U., 1989—. Mem. steering com. Kansas City (Kans.) Tchg. Fellows, Kansas City, 1998—; co-dir. Kans. Tchr./Mentor Acad., 2000—; dir. Putnam City Induction Program, Winfield, W.Va., 1986—88; presenter in field; cons. numerous sch. dists. and higher edn. instns.; adj. asst. prof. Marshall U.; mem. nat. task force Nat. Coun. State Classrooms for 21st Century; mem. various coms. Kans. State Dept. Edn. Author: Developmental Induction Programs, 1991, Restructuring the American School, 1997; contbr. articles to profl. jours. Pres. Pittsburg Unified Sch. Dist. Bd. Edn., 1997—98; chmn. bd. dirs. Kans. Tchrs. Credit Union, Pittsburg, 2000—. Named Tchr. of Yr., Putnam C. of C., 1989. Mem.: NEA, Assn. Tchr. Educators, Midwest Ednl. Rsch. Assn., Phi Delta Kappa (pres., chpt. del., Svc. Key 1998, Ednl. Leadership award 1989). Avocations: basketball, golf. Home: 2203 S Homer Pittsburg KS 66762 Office: Pittsburg State U 117 Hughes Hall Pittsburg KS 66762 E-mail: krunyan@pittstate.edu.

RUNYAN, TIMOTHY JACK, historian, educator; b. Gary, Ind, Aug. 9, 1941; s. Jack Elmore and Mavis Lydia (Lewis) R.; m. Laurie Ann Blackmore, July 25, 1964; children: Christopher T., Michael A. BS, Capital U., 1963; MA, U. Md., 1965, PhD, 1972. Instr. U. Md., Coll. Park, 1969, Cleve. State U., 1969-71, asst. prof., 1971-74, assoc. prof., 1974-87, prof. dept. history, 1987-97, asst. dean Coll. Arts and Sci., 1976-79, dir. classical and medieval studies, 1978-86, chmn. dept. art, 1981-82, chmn. dept. modern lang., 1982-86; chmn. dept. history, 1991-94. Vis. prof. Oberlin (Ohio) Coll., 1989; vis. prof., dir. Program in Maritime Hist. and Nautical Arch. East Carolina U., NC, 1994-96, prof., program dir., 1997—; editor Am. Neptune, Jour. of Maritime Hist., Peabody Essex Mus., Salem, Mass., 1990-95. Author: European Naval and Maritime Hist., 300-1500, 1985; editor: Ships, Seafaring and Soc., 1987 (John Lyman Book award 1988), To Die Gallantly: The Battle of the Atlantic, 1994 (selection of Mil. Book Club); contbr. articles to scholarly publ. Mgr. Cleve. Commn. on Higher Edn., 1976-79; pres. Gt. Lakes Sci. Ctr., Cleve., 1987-91, vice chair bd. trustees, 1991-94, trustee, 1987—; gov. appointee to Ohio 1992 Commn., Columbus, 1989-92; chmn. sect. interior Nat. Maritime Heritage Grants Com., 1997—. Recipient Award of Achievement for Mus. N. Ohio Live, 1991; Am. Philos. Soc. grantee, 1973, 76; NOAA Ocean Exploration grantee, 2002-03, 2004. Fellow Royal Hist. Soc. (London); mem. Internat. Commn. Maritime History (exec. coun. 1985—, treas. 1990-95, v.p. 1995—), N.Am. Soc. Oceanic History (pres. 1980-84), Nat. Maritime Alliance Bd. (treas. 1992-97, chair 1997—), Nat. Maritime Hist. Soc. (adv bd. 1989—), Gt. Lakes Hist. Soc. (pres. 1985-95), Medieval Acad. Am. (nominating com. 1985-87, chair 1990-91, endowment campaign com. 1990-95), Midwest Medieval Hist. Conf. (pres. 1981-82), Assn. Gt. Lakes Maritime History (v.p. 1984-87). Episcopalian. Avocations: sports, travel. Home: 101 Wesley Rd Greenville NC 27858-6532 Office: East Carolina Univ Maritime Studies Eller House Greenville NC 27858-4353

RUNYON, KEITH LESLIE, lawyer, newspaper editor; b. Louisville, Oct. 3, 1950; s. Leslie Thomas and Marjorie Fillmore (Fisher) R.; M. Amelia Payne Sweets, Dec. 29, 1979; children; Amelia Brown Payne, Keith Leslie Jr. Student, U. London, 1971; BA cum laude, U. Louisville, 1972, JD, 1982. Staff writer Courier-Jour., Louisville, 1972-77, staff atty., 1984-86; staff atty., assoc. editor Louisville Times and Courier Jour., 1977-86, forum editor, 1986-90; editl. page editor, 1990-92; editor opinion pages, 1992-96; opinion editor, 1996—. Moderator Ky. Author Forum, 1996-2001. Editor: (novels) The Forum and Book Editor, 2001—. Nat. bd. dirs. English-Speaking Union U.S., N.Y., 1976-79, pres. Ky. br., Louisville, 1986-87; pres., dir. U. Louisville Alumni Assn., 1987-93; mem. exec. com. Louisville com. on fgn. rels., 1985-87, Leadership Louisville, 1990-91; clk. Session Calvin Presbyn. Ch., Louisville, 1986-88; mem. St. Francis in the Fields Ch., Harrods Creek, Ky.; bd. dirs. Walden Theatre, Louisville, 1999-2001; alumni council, Brandeis Sch. of Law, 2001—. Recipient William E. Leidt award The Episc. Ch. of U.S., 1975, Roy Howard award (shared) Scripps Howard Journalists Nat. for Pub. Svc., 1976; named Alumnus of Yr., U. Louisville, 1991, disting. alumnus U. Louisville Sch. Law, 1996; Ctr. Fgn. Journalists fellow, 1993, Bingham fellow, 1995-96. Mem. ABA, Ky. Bar Assn., Louisville Bar Assn., Nat. Conf. Edit. Writers (editor The masthead, 1994-96), Soc. Profl. Jours. (Outstanding Editl. Writing award, 1983, 84, 85, Outstanding Criticism award 1997, 98). Home: Nitta Yuma Harrods Creek KY 40027 Office: Courier-Jour and Louisville Times Co 525 W Broadway Louisville KY 40202-2206

RUOCCHIO, PATRICIA JEANNE, writer; b. New Haven, Conn., June 18, 1958; d. William Robert and Margaret Strom Ruocchio. BA cum laude, Harvard U., 1982. Freelance writer, 1982—. Writing instr. Manic-Depressive Depressive Assn., Boston chpt., 2000—01, Arlington (Mass.) Sch. Sys., 2000—02, Belmont (Mass.) Sch. Sys., 2001; guest lectr. Boston U., 2002. Contbr. articles to newspapers, jours. and mags. Recipient Three Editor's Choice Award, N.Am. Open Poetry Contest, 1989. Home: 54B Thayer Rd #2 Belmont MA 02478

RUOF, RICHARD ALAN, minister, poet, writer; b. Lancaster, Pa., Oct. 11, 1932; s. Robert Jacob and Geneva May (Devers) Ruof; m. Anne Margaret Demos; children: Mark Alan Demos Ruof, Anne Tracy Demos Ruof, Richard James Demos Ruof. AB, Franklin and Marshall Coll., 1954; MDiv, Lancaster (Pa.) Theol. Sem., Union Theol. Sem., Richmond, Va., 1960; STM, Luth. Theol. Sem., Gettysburg, Pa., 1974; DMin, McCormick Theol. Sem., 1981. Ordained to ministry United Ch. Christ, 1960. Pastor Harrisville (Va.) Charge of United Ch. Christ, 1959-62, Thurmont (Md.) Charge, 1962-67, First Congl. Ch., Cortland, NY, 1967-77, St. Paul's United Ch. Christ of Hamlin, Fredericksburg, Pa., 1977-82, St. John's United Ch. Christ, Egg Harbor City, NJ, 1982-87, Friedensburg, Pa., 1987-94, pastor emeritus, 1994. Author: (spiritual poems) Songs of the Lesser Servants, 2003, Melting World, 2004, Return of the Martyrs, 2004. Mem. Egg Harbor City Bd. Edn., 1984; registrar-treas. Susquehanna Assn. N.Y. Conf., United Ch. Christ, 1968—74. With USNR, 1954—56.

RUOFF, A. LAVONNE BROWN, English language educator; b. Charleston, Illinois, Apr. 10, 1930; d. Oscar and Laura Alice (Witters) Brown; m. Milford Anthony Prasher, Aug. 19, 1950 (div. 1964); m. Gene W. Ruoff, June 10, 1967; children: Stephen Charles, Sharon Louise(dec.). Student, U. Ill., 1948—50; BS in Edn., Northwestern U., Ill., 1953, MA in English, 1954, PhD in English, 1966. Instr. to asst. prof. Roosevelt U., Chgo., 1961—66; asst. prof. English U. Ill., Chgo., 1966—69, assoc. prof., 1969—81, prof., 1981—94, prof. emeritus, 1994. Interim dir. D'Arcy McNickle Ctr. for Am. Indian History, Newberry Libr., 1999-2000; editor Am. Indian Lives series U. Nebr. Press, Lincoln, 1985—; mem. Am. lit. com. Internat. Exch. of Scholars, Washington, 1987-90, chair, 1989-90; NEH dir. Summer Seminars for Coll. Tchr. on Am. Indian Lit., 1979, 83, 89, 94. Author: American Indian Lit., 1990; Lit. of the Am. Indian, 1990; editor: The Moccasin Maker, 1987, 2d edit., 1998; Wynema, 1997; From the Deep Woods to Civilization and Indian Boyhood, 2001; (with Jerry W. Ward, Jr.) Redefining Am. Lit. History, 1990; (with Donald Smith) Life, Letters and Speeches of George Copway, 1997. Bd. dir. Am. Indian Coun. Fire Chgo., 1980-88. Recipient Lifetime Achievement award Before Columbus Found., 1998, Lit., MLA and Assn. for Study of Am. Indian Lits. award for Outstanding Contbn., 1993; MELUS award for Outstanding Contbn. to Multiethnic Lit., 1986; named Writer of Yr. for Annotation/Bibliography, Wordcraft Circle of Native Writers and Storytellers, 1999; Writer of Yr. for Series Editing Am. Indian Lives; Svc. award Wordcraft Cir. of Native Writers, 2003; NEH fellow, 1992-93, U. Ill. Chgo. Inst. for Humanities fellow, 1990-91; NEH Rsch. Divsn. grantee, 1981. Mem.: MLA (co-chair lit. of people of color com. 2000—01, exec. coun. 2002—, chair discussion group Am. Indian lit., del. assembly organizing com., award for lifetime scholarly achievement 2002), Assn. for Study of Am. Indian Lits., Multi-ethnic Lit. in the U.S., Am. Studies Assn. Business E-Mail: lruoff@uic.edu.

RUOFF, CYNTHIA OSOWIEC, foreign language educator; b. Chgo., Mar. 1, 1943; d. Stephen R. and Estelle (Wozniak) O.; m. Gary Edward Ruoff, June 5, 1965; children: Gary S., Laura A. AB, Loyola U., 1965; MA, Western Mich. U., 1973; PhD in French Lang. and Lit., Mich. State U., 1992. Tchr. Kalamazoo (Mic.) Pub. Schs., 1965-68; asst. prof. Western Mich. U., Kalamazoo, 1980—. Asst. prof. Western Mich. U.; spkr. in field. Contbr. articles to profl. jours. Mem. MLA, N.Am. Soc. Seventeenth-Century French Lit., Am. Assn. Tchrs. French, Am. Soc. Phenomenology and Aesthetics, L'Alliance Française, Soc. Interdisciplinary French Seventeenth-Century Studies, Phi Sigma Iota, Pi Delta Phi. Avocations: piano, skiing. Office: Dept Fgn Langs & Lit Western Mich Univ Kalamazoo MI 49008 *Reach beyond intelligence and reason by experiencing the beauty, harmony, grandeur, and mystery of the cosmos..to achieve a higher understanding and truth.*

RUOHO, ARNOLD EINO, pharmacology educator; b. Thunder Bay, Ont., Can., Nov. 26, 1941; s. Eino Armas and Toini Helen (Kuusisto) R.; m. Marjorie Denise Anderson, Aug. 21, 1965; children— David, Daniel, Jonathon BS in Pharmacy, U. Toronto, Ont., Can., 1964; PhD in Physiol. Chemistry, U. Wis.-Madison, 1970. Helen Hay Whitney postdoctoral fellow U. Calif.-San Diego, 1971-74; asst. prof. pharmacology U Wis.-Madison, 1974-80, assoc. prof., 1980-84, prof., 1984—, acting chair dept. pharmacology Med. Sch., 1994-95, chair, 1995—, S. Jonathan Singer prof. and chair pharmacology, 1997—. Cons. NIH, Bethesda, Md., 1984— Contbr. articles to profl. jours., chpts. to books Den leader local council Boy Scouts Am., Madison, 1975-77, mem. at large, 1979—; hockey coach, 1983— . Grantee March of Dimes, 1975-78, Pharm. Mfrs., 1975-76, NIH, 1975— Mem. AAAS. Lutheran.

RUOSLAHTI, ERKKI, medical research administrator; b. Puumala, Finland; B.Medicine, U. Helsinki, Finland, 1961, MD, 1965, Dr.Medicine, 1967; Dr.Medicine (hon.), U. Lund, Sweden, 1991. Rsch./teaching asst. dept. serology and bacteriology U. Helsinki, 1964-66; head blood group dept. State Serum Inst., Helsinki, 1966-68; NIH rsch. fellow Calif. Inst. Tech., 1968-70; asst. prof., acting assoc. prof. dept. serology U. Helsinki, 1970-75; prof. bacteriology and serology U. Turku, Finland, 1975-76; sr. rsch. scientist dept. immunology City of Hope, Duarte, Calif., 1976; dir. immunobiology divsn. immunology City of Hope Nat. Med. Ctr., Duarte, 1978-79; assoc. sci. dir. La Jolla (Calif.) Cancer Rsch. Found., 1979-80, v.p., COO, 1982-89; sci. dir. La Jolla (Calif.) Cancer Rsch. Found. (now The Burnham Inst), 1980—, pres., CEO and dir. Cancer Ctr., 1989—. Adj. prof. dept. pathology U. Calif., San Diego, 1980—; mem. sci. adv. bd. Helen Keller Eye Rsch. Found., Birmingham, Ala., 1989—; mem. pathobiochemistry study sect. Nat. Cancer Inst., 1981-85; Robert and Estelle Stadtler lectr. U. Tex., Sys. Cancer Ctr., 1984, Burton L. Baker Meml. lectr. U. Mich., Ann Arbor, 1987, Harvey Soc. lectr., 1988, Jeanette Piperno Meml. lectr. Temple U., Phila., 1989, G.H.A. Clowes award and lectr. Am. Assn. Cancer Rsch., 1990, Karl H. Beyer lectr. U. Wis., 1990, Walter Hubert lectr. 33d Ann. Meeting, Brit. Assn. for Cancer Rsch., 1992. Contbr. over 300 articles to profl. jours.; editl. bd. mem. Matrix, 1991—, Internat. Jour. Cancer, 1979—, Ann. Rev. of Cell Biology, 1987-90, Jour. Cell Biology, 1987-89, Jour. Biol. Chemistry, 1985-88, Cancer Rsch., 1979-82; reviewing editor Science, 1989—; editor-in-chief Cell Regulation, 1989-91. Recipient Barbara Robert Meml. medal French Soc. of Connective Tissue, 1988, Outstanding Investigator award Nat. Cancer Inst., 1986-93, Robert J. and Claire Pasarow Found. award, 1991, Lella Gruber Cancer Rsch. award Am. Acad. Dermatology, 1993, Abbott award Internat. Soc. for Oncodevelopmental Biology and Medicine, 1995, Gairdner Found. Internat. award Gairdner Found., 1997. Fellow Am. Acad. Arts and Scis.; mem. Finnish Acad. Scis. Office: The Burnham Inst 10901 N Torrey Pines Rd La Jolla CA 92037-1062

RUOTSALA, JAMES ALFRED, historian, writer; b. Juneau, Alaska, Feb. 17, 1934; s. Bert Alfred and Eva (Karppi) E.; m. Janet Ann Whelan, July 31, 1987; stepchildren: Theresa Cowden, Douglas Whelan, Peggy MacInnis, Michael Whelan, Bruce Whelan, Charlene Rhodes. Student, U. Md., 1960—61, Basic Officers Sch., Maxwell AFB, 1964, Air U., 1985; AA, U. Alaska, Kenai, 1990; BA in Photography, Shaftesbury U., 1997, MA in Journalism, 2001. Asst. divsn. mgr. Macmillan Pub. Co., 1964-80; mgr. Denny's Restaurants, 1980-82; dir. mktg. and sales Air Alaska, 1982-89; state security supr., lt. Knightwatch Security, Juneau, 1990-96; ret., 1996. Archival dir. Alaska Aviation Heritage Mus., 1987-90. Author: Lockheed Vegas in Southeast Alaska, 1980, We Stand Ready, 1986, Eielson, Father of Alaskan Aviation, 1986, Pilots of the Panhandle, The Early Years 1920-1935, 1997, Alaska Wings, 2002, Alaskans Stood Ready, 2002; Alaska's Aviation Heritage Air Alaska newspaper; contbr. articles to profl. jours. Journalist 1st class USN, 1951-56; sgt. U.S. Army, 1958-64; 1st sgt. USAR, 1983-94; ret. USAR, 1994; col. Alaska State Def. Force, 1985-98, ret. Decorated Korean Svc. medal with 2 combat stars, Korean Presdl. unit citation, UN Svc. medal, Nat. Def. Svc. medal, Vietnam Svc. medal, Meritorious Svc. medal with 2 oak leaf clusters, Army Commendation medal with 4 oak leaf clusters; recipient USAF Brewer Aerospace award, Grover Leoning award, Paul E. Garber award, 1984-85, State of Alaska Gov.'s Cert. Appreciation, 1983, Mayor's Pub. Svc. award, Anchorage, 1985, Commendation from Gov. of Alaska, 1993, 94, 18th Session Alaska Legis. Cert. Recognition, 1993, 94, Cert. of Appreciation, Pres. Bill Clinton, 1994. Mem.: Am. Aviation Hist. Soc., Aviation and Space Writers Assn., Pioneers of Alaska (sec. 1988, v.p. 1989, pres. 1990, Igloo 33, treas. 1994—95, pres. 2002—, Igloo 6, Cert. Appreciation 1988, Alaskan of Yr. award 2000), Am. Legion (historian, post 25 comdr. 2002—04), Res. Officers Assn. (pub. affairs officer 1985—), VFW (sr. vice comdr. 1995, post quartermaster 1996—99, sr. vice comdr. 2000, post comdr. 2001—02), U.S. Naval Inst., Ret. Officers Assn., Masons. Lutheran. Home: 2723 John St Juneau AK 99801-2020

RUPEKA, ROBERT W. court administrator; b. Youngstown, Ohio; s. Robert E. and Donna J. Rupeka. BA in Polit. Sci./Mgmt., Case Western Res. U., 1993. Cons. Prodigal Media Co., Youngstown, Ohio, 1993-94; adminstr. Mahoning County Clk. of Cts., Youngstown, 1994-2000; ct. adminstr. Mahoning County Common Pleas Cts., Youngstown, 2000—. Media/polit. cons., Youngstown, 1993-99. Mem., v.p. Mahoning County Alcohol and Drug Addiction Svcs. Bd., Youngstown, 1998-2001. Mem. Ohio Assn. for Ct. Adminstrn., Mahoning/Shenango Case Western Res. U. Alumni Assn. (pres. 1999-2000). Office: Mahoning County Common Pleas Ct 120 Market St Youngstown OH 44503 Office Fax: (330) 740-2088.

RUPEL, DIMITRIJ, diplomat; b. Apr. 7, 1946; Degree in Comparative Lit. and Sociology, U. Ljubljana, Slovenia, 1970; PhD in Sociology, Brandeis U., 1976. Lectr., asst., assoc. prof. U. Ljubljana, 1970-92, prof., 1992—; min. Ministry Fgn. Affairs, Slovenia, 1990-93; mem. Nat. Assembly, Rep. of Slovenia, 1993-95; mayor City of Ljubljana, 1995-97; ambassador to U.S., Mex. Washington, 19972000; min. of fgn. affairs Republic of Slovenia, 2000—. Office: Ministry of Foreign Affairs Presernova 25 1000 Ljubljana Slovenia

RUPERT, DAVID ROY, human resources manager; b. St. Louis, Mo., Dec. 24, 1952; s. Johnnie Rupert and Josephine Whitfield; 1 child, Michael Charles. BS in Social Sci., Culver-Stockton Coll., 1975; MA in Social Science, N.E. Mo. State U., 1977. Rule 31 Mediator: Tenn. Supreme Ct. 1999; cert. Sr. Profl. Human Resources Human Resources Certification Inst., 2003. Mgr. staffing & diversity programs Oak Ridge Nat. Lab., 2000—03, mgr. human resources, 2003—. Human resources generalist Oak Ridge Nat. Lab., 1998—2000, dir., work force diversity, 1991—98, mgr., univ. programs, 1988—91; rep. employee rels. Union Carbide, Oak Ridge, 1979—88; sales rep. We. Auto, Oak Ridge, 1977—79. Contbr. articles to profl. jours. Chmn., supervisory com. Y-12 Fed. Credit Union, Oak Ridge, 2001—. Mem.: Nat. Mgmt. Assn. (past nat. dir. 1993—98), Knoxville Cmty. Mediation Assn. (life), Youth Haven, Inc. (pres. 1982—88), Oak Ridge Rotary (life). Home: PO Box 7085 Oak Ridge TN 37831 Office: Oak Ridge National Laboratory One Bethel Valley Rd Oak Ridge TN 37831 Office Phone: 865-576-2433.

RUPERT, DONALD WILLIAM, lawyer; b. Clearfield, Pa., Oct. 15, 1946; s. Donald Lee and Dorothy Mae (Bonsall) R.; m. Patricia A. Rupert, June 21, 1969. BS in Chemistry, Miami U., Ohio, 1968; JD, Washburn U., Topeka, 1976. Bar: Tex. 1976, Ill. 1978, U.S. Ct. Appeals (Fed. cir.) 1978, U.S. Dist. Ct. (so. dist.) Tex. 1977, U.S. Ct. Appeals (7th cir.) 1981, U.S. Dist. Ct. (no. dist.) Ill. 1979, U.S. Supreme Ct., 1992. Assoc. Arnold, White & Durkee, Houston, 1976-78, Kirkland & Ellis, Chgo., 1978-83, ptnr., 1983-86; ptnr. Neuman, Williams, Anderson & Olson, Chgo., 1986-90; founding ptnr. Roper & Quigg, 1990-93; ptnr. Keck, Mahin & Cate, Chgo., 1993-96; ptnr. Mayer, Brown, Rowe & Maw, LLP, Chgo., 1996—; cons. USAF, Dayton, Ohio, 1974-81. Contbr. articles to profl. jours. Served to capt. USAF, 1968-74. Miami U. Undergrad. Rsch. fellow, 1967, Grad. Rsch. fellow, 1968. Mem. ABA, Am. Intellectual Property Law Assn., Tex. Bar Assn., Phi Kappa Phi. Democrat. Presbyterian. Office: Mayer Brown Rowe & Maw 190 S La Salle St Ste 3100 Chicago IL 60603-3441 Home: 2310 Marcy Ave Evanston IL 60201

RUPERT, DOROTHY, state legislator; b. Meadow Grove, Nebr., Oct. 20, 1926; m. Richard Rupert. BA, Nebr. Wesleyan U., 1948; MA, U. Colo., 1967; postgrad., Harvard U., 1993. Tchr., counselor various high schs., 1948-96; dir. counseling svcs. statewide Colo., 1977-78; developer, dir. Displaced Homemaker Program, 1979-80; mem. Colo. Ho. of Reps., Denver, 1986-94, Colo. Senate, Denver, 1994—, mem. health, environment, welfare and instns. com., mem. jud. com., mem. state local govt. com. Attendee UN Beijing Conf., 1995, Peace & Justice Internat. Conf., Bolivia, 1992, Helsinki, 1995. Mem. Thornton City Coun., 1958-61. Mem. Colo. Counselors Assn. (past pres.), Nat. Human Rights Commn. for Counselors, Nat. Order Women Legislators (bd. dirs.), NOW, Nat. Abortion Rights Action League, AAUW, Amnesty Internat., World Internat. League for Peace and Freedom. Democrat. Office: State Capitol 200 E Colfax Ave Ste 274 Denver CO 80203-1716

RUPERT, ELIZABETH ANASTASIA, retired dean; b. Emlenton, Pa., July 12, 1918; d. John Hamilton and Eva Blanche (Elliott) R. Diploma, Altoona Sch. Commerce, 1936; BS in Edn., Clarion State Coll., 1959; MSLS, Syracuse U., 1962; PhD, U. Pitts., 1970. Sec. Quaker State Oil Refining Corp., 1939-56; tchr., libr. Oil City Area Schs., 1959-61; libr. Venango campus Clarion (Pa.) U., 1961-62, prof. Sch. Libr. Sci., 1962-70, dean Sch. Libr. Sci., Coll. Libr. Sci., 1971-85; prof. emeritus, 1994. Interim pres. Clarion U., spring 1977; acct. William Rupert Mortuary, Inc., 1948-88. *Recognized by calligraphic citation, December 20, 1985, by the Council of Deans of Clarion University of Pennsylvania for having provided the "leadership which was the catalyst for excellence that brought national recognition to Clarion University and the College Library of Science."* Author: Pennsylvania Practicum Program for School Librarians: An Appraisal, 1970; mem. ad hoc edit. com. Pa. Media Guidelines, Pa. Dept. Edn., 1976, author (with others) Encyclopedia of Library and Information Science, 1984. Bd. dirs. Knox Pub. Libr., 1991-97; mem. Abscurf; mem. numerous bds. and couns. Church of God. Recipient Disting. Faculty award Clarion U. Alumni Assn., 1976, Disting. Svc. award, 1986, Disting. Alumni award, 1987, Zonta Internat. Women of Achievement award, 1987. Mem. Beta Phi Mu, Pi Gamma Mu. Republican. Home: PO Box H Knox PA 16232-0608

RUPERT, HOOVER (LYNN HOOVER RUPERT), minister, writer; b. Madison, N.J., Nov. 3, 1917; s. Lynn Hoover and Hazel L. (Linabary) R.; m. Hazel Pearl Senti, June 22, 1941; children— Susan (Mrs. William Newbry), Elizabeth (Mrs. Warren W. Wright). AB, Baker U., 1938; A.M., Boston U., 1940, M.Div. cum laude, 1941; student (summers), Garrett Bibl. Inst. and Northwestern U., 1942, Union Theol. Sem., 1943; D.D., Adrian Coll., 1952, Baker U., 1966; L.H.D., Milliken U., 1974. Ordained to ministry Methodist Ch., 1940; asst. pastor First Meth. Ch., Baldwin, Kans., 1936-38, St. Mark's Meth. Ch., Brookline, Mass., 1938-41; pastor Thayer-St. Paul, Kans., 1941-43, First Ch., Olathe, Kans., 1943-45; dir. youth dept. Gen. Bd. Edn. Meth. Ch., Nashville, 1945-50; pastor 1st Meth. Ch., Jackson, Mich., 1950-59, 1st United Meth. Ch., Ann Arbor, Mich., 1959-72, Kalamazoo, 1972-83; faculty dept. religion Fla. So. Coll., Lakeland, 1983-89; adj. faculty Wesley Theol. Sem., Washington, 1989-93. Dean Mich. Meth. Pastors Sch., 1959-65; mem. Jud. Coun. United Meth. Ch., 1968-88, sec., 1976-88, sec. emeritus, 1988; chaplain Epworth Summer Assembly, Ludington, Mich., 1984-98; Bible lectr. Asbury Meth. Village, 1990-2004. Author: Prayer Poems on the Prayer Perfect, 1943, Christ Above All (editor), 1948, Youth and Evangelism, 1948, Youth and Stewardship, rev. edit., 1960, Your Life Counts (editor), 1950, What Methodists Believe, rev. edit., 1959, John Wesley and People Called Methodists, 1953, I Belong, 1954, And Jesus Said, 1960, Enjoy Your Teen-Ager, 1962, A Sense of What is Vital, 1964, The Church in Renewal, 1965, Divine Demands: God's Commandments, 1966, My People are Your People, 1968, Where is thy Sting?, Christian Perspectives on Death, 1969, What's Good About God?, 1975 God Will See You Through, 1976, An Instrument of Thy Peace, 1982, The High Cost of Being Human, 1986, Why Didn't Noah Swat Both Mosquitoes, 1993, Up to Your Armpits in Alligators, 1996; writer, syndicated weekly mag. column Accent on Living; newspaper feature Talking to Teens; other publs., periodicals, and newspapers. Trustee Bronson Hosp., 1972-88, Adrian Coll., 1952-67, Asbury Meth. Village, 1996-2000; pres., bd. dirs. Youth for Understanding, 1970-83, Ann Arbor United Fund, YMCA-YWCA. Recipient Distinguished Alumnus award Boston U., 1969; Lucinda Bidwell Beebe fellow Boston U., 1941 Mem. World Meth. Council, Nat. Council Chs.,

Mark Twain Soc., Nat. Forensic League, Pi Kappa Delta, Alpha Psi Omega. Lodges: Mason, Rotary (Paul Harris fellow 1983), Chi Rho. Home: 403 Russell Ave Gaithersburg MD 20877-2811

RUPERT, JOHN EDWARD, retired savings and loan executive, business and civic affairs consultant; b. Cleve., Oct. 19, 1927; s. Edward J. and Emma (Levegood) R.; m. Virginia Carlson, Oct. 27, 1951; children: Kristen Foote, Karen Rupert Keating, David. BA, Cornell U., 1949, LL.B., 1951; certificate, Grad. Sch. Savs. & Loan, Ind. U., 1958. With Broadview Savs. & Loan Co., Cleve., 1953-86, v.p., 1964-74, mng. officer, 1965-86, pres., chief exec. officer, 1974-86, chmn., 1979-86. Mem. Cleve. Real Estate Bd., 1955-86; mem. Lakewood (Ohio) Bd. Edn., 1971-77, pres., 1975-77; v.p., trustee Lakewood Hosp., 1966-71; trustee exec. com. of Cleve. Zool. Soc., 1980—, pres., 1987-92, chmn., 1992-97; trustee Cleve. Orch., 1971-98; trustee WVIZ Ednl. TV, 1971-97, life trustee, 1997—; v.p., trustee, exec. com. Greater Cleve. Reads, 1991—; mem. Cornell U. Coun., 1971—, pres., 1977; mem. adv. bd. Cornell Coll. Arts and Scis., 1980—, trustee, Ohio Audubon Soc., 2003-; trustee Med. Ctr. Corp., 1987-96, chair, 1990-96; trustee Internat. Ctr. for Preservation of Wild Animals, 1991—2002; bd. dirs. Shoals Marine Lab. Adv. Coun., 1994—, Ohio Canal Corridor, 2001—. With USAF, 1951-53. Mem. Cleve. Interfaith Housing Corp. (pres. 1971-2003), Inst. Fin. Edn. (pres. 1970), Cleve. Real Property Inventory (pres. 1976-), Ohio Motorists Assn. (corp. bd.), Delta Kappa Epsilon, Phi Delta Phi, Sphinx Head Soc. Clubs: Cleve. Yachting, Cornell (Cleve.) (trustee); Cornell (N.Y.C.). Home and Office: 18129 W Clifton Rd Cleveland OH 44107-1037 E-mail: rup18129@aol.com.

RUPNOR, JENNIFER, journalist; BA in Broadcast Journalism, U. Wis., Eau Claire, 2000. Mem. radio news staff WAXX-WAYY, 1997—2000; reporter, prodr. WEAU-TV, Eau Claire, Wis., 2000, anchor NewsCenter 13 sunrise and noon, 2000—. Avocations: baseball, mysteries. Office: WEAU-TV P oBox 47 Eau Claire WI 54702

RUPP, GEORGE ERIK, not-for-profit administrator; b. Summit, NJ, Sept. 22, 1942; s. Gustav Wilhelm and Erika (Braunoehler) R.; m. Nancy Katherine Farrar, Aug. 22, 1964; children: Katherine Heather, Stephanie Karin. Student, Ludwig Maximilians U., Munich, Germany, 1962-63; AB, Princeton U., 1964; BD, Yale U., 1967; post grad., U. Sri Lanka, Peradeniya, 1969-70; PhD, Harvard U., 1972. Ordained to ministry Presbyn. Ch. USA, 1971, faculty fellow in religion, vice chancellor Johnston Coll., U. Redlands, Redlands, Calif., 1971-74; asst. prof. Harvard Div. Sch., Harvard U., Cambridge, Mass., 1974-76, assoc. prof., 1976-77, prof., dean, 1979-85; prof., dean acad. affairs U. Wis., Green Bay, 1977-79; prof. pres. Rice U., Houston, 1985-93, Columbia U., NYC, 1993—2002; pres. Int. Rescue Comm., NY, 2002—. Bd. dir. Com. for Econ. Devel., Inst. Internat. Edn., InterAction. Author: Christologies and Cultures: Toward a Typology of Religious Worldviews, 1974, Culture Protestantism: German Liberal Theology at the Turn of the Twentieth Century, 1977, Beyond Existentialism and Zen: Religion in a Pluralistic World, 1979, Commitment and Community, 1989; contbr. articles to profl. jour. Danforth Grad. fellow, 1964-71 Mem.: AAAS, Soc. Values in Higher Edn., Coun. Fgn. Rels., Am. Acad. Religion. Office: International Rescue Committee 122 East 42nd Street New York NY 10168

RUPP, RALPH RUSSELL, audiologist, educator, author; b. Saginaw, Mich., Apr. 12, 1929; s. Martin Carl and Veronica Marie (Riethmeier) R. BA, U. Mich., 1951, MA, 1952; PhD, Wayne State U., 1964. Speech and hearing cons. Detroit Pub. Schs., 1955-60; exec. dir. Detroit Hearing and Speech Center, 1960-62; assoc. in audiology Henry Ford Hosp., Detroit, 1962-65; prof. audiology U. Mich., Ann Arbor, 1965-89; coord. audiology Eastern Mich. U., 1985-93, cons. in audiology, 1994—, U. Mich., 1994—. Cons. St. Joseph Mercy Hosp., Ann Arbor, Ann Arbor VA Hosp., Mott Children's Health Ctr., Flint, Mich., Pontiac (Mich.) Gen. Hosp., U. Mich. Health Svcs.; pres. Detroit Hearing Ctr., 1966. Author: (with James Maurer) Hearing and Aging: Tactics for Intervention, 1979, (with Kenneth Stockdell) Speech Protocols in Audiology, 1980; contbr. articles to profl. jours. Served with Med. Service Corps, U.S. Army, 1953-55. Named Disting. Alumnus, Saginaw High Sch., 1981, Outstanding Grad., Wayne State U. Fellow Am. Speech, Lang. and Hearing Assn. (Editor's award); mem. Acad. Rehab. Audiology (past editor Jour.), Mich. Speech and Hearing Assn. (pres. 1954, Disting. Service award, past editor Jour, honor award). Home: 3163 Plymouth Rd Ann Arbor MI 48105-3203

RUPP, SHERON ADELINE, photographer, educator; b. Mansfield, Ohio, Jan. 14, 1943; d. Warren Edmund Rupp and Frances (Hanson) Christian. BA in Sociology and Psychology, Denison U., 1965; MFA in Photography, U. Mass., 1982. Teaching asst. in photography Hampshire Coll., Amherst, Mass., 1981; instr. photography Northfield (Mass.) Mt. Hermon Sch., 1982-83, U. Mass., Amherst, 1984, Holyoke (Mass.) Community Coll., 1986, 87-88; vis. asst. prof. photography Hampshire Coll., 1985, 87; vis. lectr. photography Amherst (Mass.) Coll., 1994. Guest artist, lectr. Boston Mus. Sch., Portland (Maine) Sch. Art, NYU, U. Mass., Deerfield (Mass.) Acad., Hartford Sch. Art/U. Hartford-Conn., Springfield Mus. Fine Arts, Mass., Bard Coll, N.Y., Mass. Coll. Art, Boston, others; guest lectr. Carpenter Ctr., Harvard U., Cambridge, Mass., 2000. One-woman shows include Tisch Sch. Arts NYU, 1987, Portland Sch. Art, 1989, Hart Gallery, Northampton, Mass., 1992, O.K. Harris Gallery, N.Y.C., 1992, Cleve. Mus. Art, 2000; two-person shows include Columbus (Ohio) Mus. Art, 1997—98, Springfield (Mass.) Tech. C.C., 1997; Exhibited in group shows at Mus. Modern Art, N.Y.C., 1991, 1999—, Springfield Mus. Fine Art, 1993, U. Mass., Amherst, 1993, Dirs. Guild, L.A., 1994, Manchester (N.H.) Inst. Arts and Scis., 1995, Weber State U., Utah, 1995, Grand Ctrl. Terminal, N.Y.C., 1995, Photog. Resource Ctr. 3d Biennial, Boston, 1995, DeCordova Mus., Lincoln, 2000—, Smithsonian Arts and Scis., Washington, 2001, Denison U. Art Gallery, Granville, Ohio, 2002, Around the House, A.N. Bush Gallery, Salem, Oreg., 2002, Boston Mus. Fine Arts, 2002—03, Guild Hall, East Hampton, N.Y., 2003, Smith Coll. Mus. Art, Northampton, Mass., 2004, Represented in permanent collections De Cordova Mus., Mus. Modern Art, N.Y.C., Fogg Art Mus. at Harvard U., Hallmark Collection of Photography, Kansas City, Columbus Mus. Art, The J. Paul Getty Mus., L.A., Mus. Fine Arts, Boston, Rose Art Mus. Brandeis U., Mead Art Mus. Amherst Coll., Smith Coll. Mus. Art, Danforth Mus. Art, Springfield Tech. C.C. Found., Carpenter Ctr. for Visual Arts Harvard U., The Smithsonian; photographs (including cover photo) in Double-Take Mag., winter 1998. Bd. dirs. Zone Art Ctr., 1987-94. Recipient Mass. Fellowship award in photography Artist Found., 1984, 87; visual artist fellow Nat. Endowment for the Arts, 1986, 94, Guggenheim fellow, 1990. Avocations: hiking, bicycling, writing. Home and Office: 364 Hatfield St Apt C Northampton MA 01060-1541 E-mail: sheron@crocker.com.

RUPPE, ARTHUR MAXWELL, retired lawyer; b. Boone, N.C., Dec. 15, 1928; s. Arthur Monroe and Floye (Robinson) Ruppe; m. Ruth Marie Ledford; children: Ruth Carol, Sharon Marie, Arthur Maxwell, Jr., Susan Lunette. AA, Gardner Webb Coll., 1947; AB, U. N.C., 1949, JD, 1952. Bar: N.C. 1952, U.S. Dist. Ct. (ea. dist.) N.C. 1955, U.S. Ct. Mil. Appeals 1968, cert.: (mediator). Asst. staff, judge advocate U.S. Army, Ft. Bragg, NC, 1952—55; sole practice Fayetteville, NC, 1955—98; mediator, 1997—2003. Served to 1st lt. U.S. Army, 1952—55. Mem.: ABA, Cumberland County Bar Assn. (pres. 1982—83), 12 Jud. Dist. Bar Assn., N.C. State Bar, N.C. Bar Assn. (patron), K.P. Democrat. Baptist. Avocations: travel, reading. Home: 336 Summertime Rd Fayetteville NC 28303-4658

RUPPEL, HOWARD JAMES, JR., sociologist, sexologist, educator; b. Orange, N.J., July 22, 1941; s. Howard J. and Lillian M. (Wordley) R.; m. Barbara Margaret Wiedemann, June 3, 1967. BA, St. Joseph's Coll., Ind., 1963; MA, No. Ill. U., 1968; postgrad., U. Iowa, 1968-76; EdD, Inst. for Advanced Study Human Sexuality, 1993, PhD, 1994. Diplomate Am. Bd. Sexology; cert. sexologist Am. Coll. Sexologists. Instr. social sci., debate coach St. Francis H.S., Wheaton, Ill., 1963-65; instr. sociology St. Dominic Coll., St. Charles, Ill., 1966-67, Cornell Coll., Mt. Vernon, Iowa, 1969-70, asst. prof., 1970-72, lectr., 1972-73; rsch. dir. Social Sci. Rsch. Assocs., Cedar Rapids, Iowa, 1973-80; founder, co-dir. Ctr. for Sexual Growth and Devel., Mt. Vernon, 1980-95; instr. Sch. Social Work, U. Iowa, 1976-78, adj. asst. prof., 1979-81, adj. assoc. prof., 1981-96, prof., 1997—. Exec. dir. Soc. for Sci. Study of Sexuality, 1988—, Found. for the Sci. Study of Sexuality, 1989-98, Am. Assn. Sex Educators, Counselors and Therapists, 1996—; prof. Inst. Advanced Study Human Sexuality, 1996—; cons. Iowa Dept. Social Svcs., Families Inc., West Branch, A&E Network (Biography); bd. dirs. The Human Outreach and Achievement Inst., Boston, 1988-90, Inst. Advanced Study Human Sexuality, 1995—. Co-editor: Sexuality and the Family Life Span, 1983; assoc. editor Ann. Rev. of Sex Rsch., 1992, 93, 94, 95, 96, 97, 98, 99; contbr. articles on complex orgns., marriage and the family, sexual attitudes and behavior, childhood and preadolescent sexuality, methodology and child care theory to profl. publs. NSF fellow, 1968. Fellow Am. Acad. Clin. Sexologists; mem. Am. Sociol. Assn., Nat. Coun. Family Rels., Iowa Coun. Family Rels. (sec. 1983-84, treas. 1985), Changing Family Conf. (bd. dirs. 1983-87), Soc. Sci. Study of Sex Inc. (bd. dirs. 1983-88, pres. Midcontinent Region 1984-85, treas. 1986-88, chmn. membership com. 1983-85, chmn. exhibits com. 1983-88, ann. meeting chmn. 1986), Am. Assn. Sex Educators, Counselors and Therapists (exec. dir. 1996—, cert. sex educator), Harry Benjamin Internat. Gender Dysphoria Assn., Coun. Assns. for Sexual Sci., Health and Edn. (del.), Inst. for the Advanced Study of Human Sexuality Alumni Assn., Alpha Kappa Delta, Alpha Sigma Lambda (hon.). Democrat. Office: 103 A Ave S Ste 2-b Mount Vernon IA 52314-1400

RUPPERSBERGER, CHARLES ALBERT, III, congressman; b. Balt., Jan. 31, 1946; s. Charles Albert Jr. and Margaret (Wilson) R.; m. Kay Murphy, Dec. 28, 1968; children: Charles Albert, Jill Ann. BA, U. Md., 1967; JD, U. Balt., 1970. Bar: Md. 1972, U.S. Supreme Ct. 1977. Social worker Balt. City Schs., 1967-69; claims adjuster U.S. Fidelity and Guaranty Co., Balt., 1969-70; law clk. to presiding justice Balt. County Cir. Ct., Towson, 1970-72; asst. state's atty. Balt. County State's Atty., Towson, 1972-80; ptnr. Ruppersberger, Winter, Clark & Mister, Timonium, Md., 1980—; mem. U.S. Ho. Reps. from 2nd Md. dist., 2003—. Chief of investigation div. State's Atty.'s Office, Towson, 1972-80; liaison Balt. County Police Dept. and Md. State Police, 1973-80. Coach, v.p. Cockeysville (Md.) Recreation Council, 1978—; campaign mgr. for senator Francis X. Kelly, Annapolis, Md., 1980-85; councilman Balt. County Council, 1985—; legal council Balt. County Athletic League; pres. Topfield condominium Assn., Cockeysville, 1975-78, Greater Timonium Community Council, 1980—, co-chmn. fundraising U. Hosp.; bd. dirs. Timonium (Md.) Meth. Ch., 1984—. Recipient Appreciation award Balt. County Order of Fraternal Police, 1977, Cert. of Appreciation Balt. County Police, 1979; named one of Outstanding Young Marylanders Jaycees, 1979. Mem. Md. Bar Assn. (grievance com.), Balt. County Bar Assn. (chmn. bench-bar com.), Nat. Coll. Dist. Attys. (advisor 1974-80), U. Md. Alumni Assn. (v.p.), U.S. LaCrosse Team. Lodges: Masons. Democrat. Methodist. Office: 1630 Longworth Ho Office Bldg Washington DC 20515-2002

RUPPERT, JOHN LAWRENCE, lawyer; b. Chgo., Oct. 7, 1953; s. Merle Arvin and Loretta Marie (Ford) R.; m. Katharine Marie Tarbox, June 5, 1976. BA, Northwestern U., 1975; JD, U. Denver, 1978; LLM in Taxation, NYU, 1979. Bar: Colo. 1978, U.S. Dist. Ct. Colo. 1978, Ill. 1979, U.S. Tax Ct. 1981. Assoc. Kirkland & Ellis, Denver, 1979-84, ptnr., 1984-88, Ballard, Spahr, Andrews & Ingersoll, Denver, 1988-96; shareholder Brownstein Hyatt Farber & Strickland, P.C., Denver, 1996—. Lectr. U. Denver Coll. Law, fall 1984-92; adj. prof. law grad. tax program, 1993-94; sec. Capital Assocs., Inc., 1989-96; sec. Brothers Gourmet Coffees, Inc., 1995-2000; asst. sec. Renaissance Cosmetics, Inc., 1996-98; sec. Skillset Software, Inc., 2000-01; asst. sec. Rhythms NetConnections Inc., 2000-01. Contbr. articles to profl. jours. Mem. ABA, Colo. Bar Assn. (mem. exec. coun. tax sect. 1985-89), Denver Bar Assn. Office: Brownstein Hyatt Farber & Strickland PC 410 17th St Fl 22D Denver CO 80202-4402 Office Phone: 303-223-1170. Personal E-mail: jruppert53@aol.com. Business E-Mail: jruppert@bhf-law.com.

RUPPERT, RUPERT EARL, lawyer, political consultant; b. Nov. 22, 1943; s. Paul Edward and Sarah Elizabeth (Morgan) R.; children: Jason, Ryan, Bradley, Matthew. BA, Ohio State U., 1968; JD, Capital U., 1976. Bar: Ohio 1976. Asst. to gov. State of Ohio, Columbus, 1971—74, asst. to atty. gen., 1974—77, spl. counsel to atty. gen. and to asst. atty. gen., 1977—93; ptnr. Ruppert, Bronson & Ruppert, Franklin, Ohio, 1977—. Dir., atty. Miami Valley Bank of S.W. Ohio, Franklin, 1979—89. Mem. Franklin City Charter Commn., 1978, Franklin CSC, 1978—79; v.p. Franklin City Schs. Bd. Edn., 1980—95, pres., 1983, 1992, 1994, Franklin City Planning Commn., 1990—92; trustee Franklin Twp., 1995—; pres. Franklin City Planning Commn., 1998—; mem. Warren County Dem. Com., 1978—80, chmn., 1978—80, Warren County Brown for Atty. Gen., 1978; dep. campaign mgr. William J. Brown for Gov., Ohio, 1982; state campaign mgr. U.S. Sen. John Glenn, 1986. With U.S. Army, 1968—70, Vietnam. Decorated Bronze Star; named Citizen of Yr., City of Franklin, 1992, Franklin C. of C., 1993; named to, Ohio Vets. Hall of Fame, 2002; recipient Presdl. award for outstanding civic achievment among Vietnam vets, 1979. Mem.: VFW, Ohio Trial Lawyers, Warren County Bar Assn. (pres. 2002—03), Ohio Bar Assn., Am. Legion. Home: 11 Kentwood Dr Franklin OH 45005-1657 Office: PO Box 369 Franklin OH 45005-0369

RUPPRECHT, NANCY ELLEN, historian, educator; b. Coeur d'Alene, Idaho, Sept. 23, 1948; d. George John and Nancy Berneeda (Baird) R. BA with honors, U. Mo., 1967, MA, 1969; PhD, U. Mich., 1982. Acad. dir. pilot program U. Mich., Ann Arbor, 1971-73, lectr. in women studies, 1973-75; vis. lectr. history U. Mo., St. Louis, 1976-77; vis. instr. of history Wash. U., St. Louis, 1977-79, Grinnell (Iowa) Coll., 1979-81; asst. prof. Oakland U., Rochester, Mich., 1981-83; asst. prof. of history Mid. Tenn. State U., Murfreesboro, 1985-91, assoc. prof., 1991-97, prof. history, 1997—. Dir. women's studies program Middle Tenn. State U., 1988—, publicity dir. women's history month, 1989-92, mem. faculty senate, 1992-95; bd. dir. Remember the Women. Mem. editl. bd. German Studies Rev., 1999—; contbr. articles to profl. jours. Bd. adv. Remember the Women Found. Mem.: NOW, AAUW, AAUP (chpt. v.p. 1988—89, pres. 1989—93), Remember the Women (bd. mem.), Assn. Faculty and Adminstrv. Women (chpt. pres. 1995—), Concerned Faculty and Adminstrv. Women (chpt. v.p. 1993—95, chpt. pres. 1995—96), Women in Higher Edn. in Tenn., German Studies Assn., Mid Tenn. Women's Studies Assn., Holocaust Studies Assn., So. Humanities Assn., So. Hist. Assn. (chair nominating com. European divsn. 1996—97, mem. exec. com. 1996—, mem. program com. 1997—2000, chmn. program com. 2001—02, vice chair European divsn. 2002—03, chair European divsn. 2003—), S.E. Women's Studies Assn., Am. Hist. Assn. Home: 1106 Jones Blvd Murfreesboro TN 37129-2310 Office: Middle Tenn State U 275 Peck Hall Murfreesboro TN 37132-0001

RUPRACHT, WILLIAM GEORGE, chaplain; b. Central Square, N.Y., Apr. 18, 1945; s. William S. and Neva Mae House Rupracht; 1 child, Kimberly Coker. BA, Carson-Newman Coll., 1971; grad., Air Command and Staff Coll.; MDiv, New Orleans Bapt. Theol., 1974; D of Ministry, San Francisco Theol. Sem., 1982. Cert. clin. chaplain Coll. Chaplains, 1978. Pastor 1st Bapt. Ch., White Castle, La., 1971-74; staff chaplain Audie L. Murphy VA Hosp., San Antonio, Tex., 1975-77; instr. USAF Chaplain Sch., Maxwell AFB, Ala., 1978-91; sr. IMA to command chaplain Air Force Materiel Command, Wright-Patterson AFB, Ohio, 1991-94, Air Force Space Command, Peterson AFB, Ohio, 1991-94; chief chaplain svc. VA Med. Ctr., Tuscaloosa, Ala., 1997; IMA to directorate of chaplain svcs. Wilford Hall Med. Ctr., Lackland AFB, Tex., 1997—. Mem. writer's bd. CAP, Maxwell AFB; mem. USAF Chaplain Recruiting Team, USAFR, Denver; pastoral cons. Ala. Coll. Cmty. Health Scis., Tuscaloosa, U. Ala. Sch. Dentistry, Tuscaloosa; lectr. CAP Chaplain Svc. Writer's Study Guide. Author: (book) Pastoral Care to Huntington Patients and Families, 1982; editor: (book) Department of Veteran Affairs Chaplain Service Manual M-2, Part II, 1993. State pk. vol. Mt. San Jacinto, Palm Springs, Calif.; past comdr. Am. Legion, Northport, Ala., 1980; founding bd. dirs. West Ala. AIDS Bd., Tuscaloosa; past pres. West Ala. AIDS Edn. Com., Tuscaloosa; devel. mem. Hospice of West Ala., Tuscaloosa; state chaplain Nat. Huntington's Disease Assn., Birmingham, Ala. Col. USAFR, 1978. Decorated Meritorious Svc. medal; recipient 4 Chaplains Legion of Merit, Am. Legion; named Pub. Citizen of Yr., NASW. Mem.: Mil. Chaplains Assn., Mins. in Med. Edn. (nat. sec., treas., comdr.), Coll. Chaplains, Leadership VA Alumni Assn. (life; founding mem.), Am. Legion (post 208). Southern Baptist. Avocation: travel. Home: 145 Sage Dr Palm Springs CA 92264-6461 Home Fax: 760-322-4602. E-mail: billybama@aol.com.

RURY, JOHN LESLIE, education educator; b. Syracuse, NY, Apr. 6, 1951; s. John and Virginia (Gould) R.; m. Ellen Kennedy, June 18, 1981 (div. Oct. 1992); children: Aaron, Derek; m. Aida Alaka, May 12, 1995. AB, Fordham U., 1973; MS in Edn., CUNY, 1975; PhD, U. Wis., 1982. Instr. history Wayne State U., Detroit, 1980-83; asst. prof. history Antioch Coll., Yellow Springs, Ohio, 1983-84; asst. prof. edn. Ohio State U., Columbus, 1984-87; from assoc. to prof. DePaul U., Chgo., 1987—2003, chmn. dept. edn. policy studies & rsch., 2003; prof. U. Kans., 2003—, chmn. Dept. Tchg. and Leadership, 2003—. Program chmn. Midwest History Edn. Soc., Chgo., 1989-90; core group Policy Rsch. Action Group, Chgo., 1993-99; pub. policy coun. Harris Sch., U. Chgo., 1997; sr. program officer, Spencer Found., Chgo., Ill., 1999-2002, sr. adv., 2002-03. Author: Education and Women's Work, 1991, Education and Social Change, 2002; editor: Seeds of Crisis, 1993 (Cambrnus prize 1993), DePaul University, 1998; editor Am. Edn. Rsch. Jour., 1992-96; mem. editl. bd. History of Education Quarterly, 1985-89. Rsch. grantee Nat. Inst. Edn., Washington, 1979-80, Spencer Found., Chgo., 1985, Radcliffe Coll., Cambridge, Mass., 1987; Spencer fellow Nat. Acad. Edn., Stanford, Calif., 1986-87. Mem. Am. Hist. Assn., Am. Ednl. Rsch. Assn. (v.p. 1997-99), History of Edn. Soc. (v.p. 1996-97, pres. 1997-98), John Dewey Soc. Office: U Kansas 418 JR Pearson Hall 1122 West Campus Rd Lawrence KS 66045

RUSAW, SALLY ELLEN, librarian; b. Potsdam, N.Y., Apr. 24, 1939; d. Ralph Clinton and Marion Ellen (Jenack) R. BS in Edn., Potsdam Coll., 1964; MLS, SUNY, Albany, 1975. Cert. libr. media specialist, pub. libr., permanent tchr. N-6, N.Y. Tchr. grade 7th-9th Diocese of Ogdensburg, N.Y., 1960-74, cons. office edn., 1975-78; assoc. libr. Mater Dei Coll., Ogdensburg, 1974-89, head libr., 1989-99, SUNY, Potsdam, 2000—. Vol. Ogdensburg Correctional Facility, 1982-95, Riverview Correctional Facility, Ogdensburg, 1987—; lector, Eucharistic min. Rite for Christian Initiation of Adults catechist St. Mary's Cathedral; vol. Ogdensburg Cath. Ctrl. Sch., sch. bd., 1995-2000. Named Vol. of Yr. Ogdensburg Correctional Facility, 1985, Outstanding Vol. Riverview Correctional Facility, 1991; Nat. Def. Edn. Act grantee, 1965. Mem. ALA, N.Y. Libr. Assn., North Country 3Rs Coun., North Country Ref. and Rsch. Resources Coun. (trustee 1994-99). Roman Catholic. Avocations: music, reading, berrying, outdoor activities, swimming.

RUSCH, GERALD ALLEN, financial representative; b. Milw., July 8, 1937; s. Herman A. and Martha H. (Gebauer) R.; m. Joan R. Ruehlman, Dec. 29, 1961; children: Susan, Heidi. BA, U. Wis., 1960. Area rep. Wis. Heart Assn., Milw., 1960-61, Tex. Heart Assn., Austin, 1961-63; comms. cons. Wis. Telephone, Milw., 1963-74; sole proprietor Rusch Ins., Eau Claire, Wis., 1974—. Contbr. articles to mags. 1st lt. USAR, 1960-67. Named Agent of Yr. Eau Claire Gen. Agents and Mgrs. Assn., 1980. Mem. Nat. Assn. Fin. Profls., Million Dollar Roundtable, Phi Sigma Epsilon. Avocations: photography, walking, reading, classical music. Office: Northwestern Mut Fin Network 4330 Golf Ter Ste 209 Eau Claire WI 54701-4688 Home (Winter): 14071 Brant Point Cir #621 Fort Myers FL 33919 Home (Summer): 4224 W Robin Meadows Ln Eau Claire WI 54701

RUSCH, THOMAS WILLIAM, manufacturing executive; b. Alliance, Nebr., Oct. 3, 1946; s. Oscar William and Gwen Falerne (Middleswart) R.; m. Gloria Ann Sutton, June 20, 1968 (div. Oct. 1979); children: Alicia Catherine, Colin William; m. Lynn Biebighauser, Jan. 17, 1981. BEE, U. of Minn., 1968, MSEE, 1970, PhD, 1973; MS in Mgmt. of Tech., U. Minn., 1993. Sr. physicist cen. rsch. 3M Co., St. Paul, 1973-77, rsch. specialist cen. rsch., 1977-79; project scientist phys. electronics div. Perkin Elmer Corp., Eden Prairie, Minn., 1979-83, sr. project scientist phys. electronics div., 1983-85, lab mgr. phys. electronics div., 1985-87, product mgr. phys. electronics div., 1987-88, sr. product mgr. phys. electronics div., 1988-93; v.p. product devel. Chorus Corp., St. Paul, 1993-94; pres. Creekside Techs. Corp., Plymouth, Minn., 1994—; v.p. Xoft microTube, Inc., Plymouth, 1998—2001; chief tech. officer Xoft MicroTube, INc., Fremont, Calif., 2001—. Editor: X-rays in Materials Analysis, 1986; co-author: Oscillatory Ion Yields, 1977; patentee in field. Recipient IR100 award for transfer vessel Rsch. and Devel. mag., 1981, IR100 award for energy analyser, 1985. Office: 49000 Milmont Dr Fremont CA 94538

RUSCH, VALERIE WILLIAMS, thoracic surgeon; b. N.Y.C., Oct. 16, 1951; AB in Biochemistry, Vassar Coll., 1971; MD, Columbia U., 1975. Diplomate Nat. Bd. Med. Examiners, Am. Bd. Surgery, Am. Bd. Thoracic Surgery. Intern in gen. surgery U. Wash., Seattle, 1975-76, resident in gen. surgery, 1975-80, resident in cardiothoracic surgery, 1980-82; faculty assoc. dept. of thoracic surgery M.D. Anderson Cancer Ctr., Houston, 1982-83; thoracic surgeon Harborview Med. Ctr., Seattle, 1983-86, assoc. staff mem., 1986-89; thoracic surgeon Group Health Coop. of Puget Sound, Seattle, 1983-84; chief cardiothoracic surgery VA Hosp., Seattle, 1986-87; thoracic surgeon Univ. Hosp., Seattle, 1983-89; mem. courtesy med. staff Pacific Med. Ctr., Seattle, 1987-89; assoc. attending surgeon thoracic svc. Meml. Sloan-Kettering Cancer Ctr., N.Y.C., 1989-94, attending surgeon, 1994—, chief thoracic surgery, 2000—. Asst. prof. div. cardiothoracic surgery U. Wash., 1983-88, assoc. prof., 1988-89; asst. mem. divsn. clin. rsch. Fred Hutchinson Cancer Rsch. Ctr., Seattle, 1985-89; assoc. mem. Meml. Hosp., Meml. Sloan-Kettering Cancer Ctr., N.Y.C., 1989-94, mem., 1994—; assoc. prof. surgery Cornell U. Med. Coll., N.Y.C., 1989-95, prof. surgery Cornell U. Med. Coll., 1995—; mem. cancer clin. investigations rev. com. Nat. Cancer Inst., 1991-98. Mem. editorial bd. Jour. Thoracic and Cardiovascular Surgery, 1992—; guest reviewer The Annals of Thoracic Surgery, Cancer Rsch., Chest, Gastrointestinal Endoscopy Thorax; contbr. articles to profl. publs.; author abstracts in field. Grantee NIH, 1985-89, Deknatel Corp., 1986-87, Bard Electro Med. Systems, 1989, NeoRx Corp., 1989-90, Pfizer Corp., 1995-98. Fellow ACS (Henry Harkins award Wash. state chpt. 1979), Am. Coll. Chest Physicians; mem. Am. Assn. Thoracic Surgery (mem. program com. 1994, 95, 96), Soc. Thoracic Surgeons, Assn. Acad. Surgery, Soc. Surg. Oncology (mem. com. tng. 1993-95, mem. edn. com. 1993-95), Am. Soc. Clin. Oncology, (mem. program com. 1993, 96, bd. dirs. 2002—), Am. Thoracic Soc., N.Y. Cancer Soc., Internat. Assn. for Study of Lung Cancer, North Pacific Surg. Assn., Am. Med. Women's Assn., Seattle Surg. Soc., Henry Harkins' Surg. Soc., M.D. Anderson Assocs., Gen. Thoracic Surg. Club, Alpha Omega Alpha. Office: Meml Sloan-Kettering Cancer Thoracic Surgery Svc 1275 York Ave New York NY 10021-6094 Office Phone: 212-639-8695. Business E-Mail: ruschv@mskcc.org.

RUSCH, WILLIAM GRAHAM, religious organization administrator; b. Buffalo, Dec. 23, 1937; s. William Godfrey and Hope (French) R.; m. Thora Joan Ellefsen, Sept. 2, 1967. BA, SUNY, Buffalo, 1959, MA in Classical Langs., 1960; MDiv, Luth. Theol. Sem., Phila., 1963; PhD, Oxford (Eng.) U., 1965; DD (hon.), Yale U., 1995. Ordained to ministry Evang. Luth. Ch., 1966. Assoc. pastor Evang. Luth. Ch. of the Holy Trinity, N.Y.C., 1966-68; asst. prof., chmn. dept. classical langs. Augsburg Coll., Mpls., 1968-71; assoc. exec. dir. div. Theol. Studies Luth. Coun. in the USA, 1971-78; adj. prof. The Gen. Theol. Sem., N.Y.C., 1978-82, 95; exec. dir., asst. to Bishop Evang. Luth. Ch. in Am., Chgo., 1987-96; dir. Commn. on Faith and Order Nat. Coun. of Chs. of Christ USA, N.Y.C., 1996-2001; exec. dir. Found. for Faith and Order, N.Y.C., 2001—. Adj. prof. Luth. Theol. Sem., Philadelphia., 1998—; vis. lectr. Waterloo Luth. Theol. Sem., 1969; adj. prof. theology Fordham U., N.Y.C., 1984-86; mem. cen. com. World Coun. Chs., 1991-98, mem. standing com. faith and order commn., 1991—; adj. faculty Yale Div. Sch., 1999—; St. John's Disting. prof. Luth. Theol. Sem., Phila., 2002-03; scholar-at-large Graymoor Ecumenical Inst., 2002-03. Author: The Trinitarian Controversy, Ecumenism: A Movement Toward Church Unity; contbr. articles to profl. jours. Samuel Trexler fellow of N.Y. Synod Luth. Ch. in Am., 1964, 65. Mem. Am. Acad. Religion, Am. Soc. Christian Ethics, Am. Soc. Ch. History, Internat. Assn. Coptic Studies. Lutheran. Avocations: book collecting, chess, tennis. Office: Found for Faith and Order 99 Park Ave 298A New York NY 10016 Personal E-mail: ruschgrif@worldnet.att.net.

RUSCHA, EDWARD, artist; b. Omaha, Dec. 16, 1937; m. Danna Knego, 1967; children: Edward Joseph. Studied at, Chouinard Art Inst., Los Angeles, 1956-60. Numerous vis. artist positions including UCLA, 1969-70. Author: Twentysix Gasoline Stations, 1962, Various Small Fires, 1964, Some Los Angeles Apartments, 1965, The Sunset Strip, 1966, Thirtyfour Parking Lots, 1967, Royal Road Test, 1967, Business Cards, 1968, Nine Swimming Pools, 1968, Crackers, 1969, Real Estate Opportunities, 1970, Records, 1971, A Few Palm Trees, 1971, Colored People, 1972, Hard Light, 1978; noted for numerous graphite, gunpowder and pastel drawings, over 200 limited-edit. prints; producer, dir.: films Premium, 1970, Miracle, 1974; works include (paintings) Standard Station, Amarillo, Tex., 1963; Annie, 1963, Smash, 1963, Electric, 1964, (mural) Miami-Dade Pub. Library, Fla., 1985; one-man exhbns. include Minn. Inst. Arts, 1972, Nigel Greenwood Ltd., London, 1970, 73, 80, Leo Castelli Gallery, N.Y.C., (10 shows) 1973—, Albright-Knox Art Gallery, Buffalo, 1976, Stedelijk Mus., Amsterdam, 1976, Ft. Worth Art Mus., 1977, San Francisco Mus. Modern Art, 1982, Whitney Mus. Am. Art, 1982, Vancouver Art Gallery, 1982, Contemporary Arts Mus., Houston, 1983, Los Angeles County Mus. Art, 1983, James Corcoran Gallery, Los Angeles, 1985, also others; exhibited in group shows at 64th Whitney Biennial, 1987, Centre Pompidou, Paris, 1989, Mus. Boymans—van Beuningen, Rotterdam, The Netherlands, 1990, Ghislaine Hussenot, Paris, 1990, Fundacio Caixa, Barcelona, Spain, 1990, Serpentine Gallery, London, 1990, Mus. Contemporary Art, L.A., 1990-91, Robert Miller Gallery, N.Y.C., 1992, Thaddaeus Ropac, Salzburg, Austria, 1992; represented in permanent collections including Mus. Modern Art, Los Angeles County Mus. Art, Whitney Mus., Hirshhorn, Washington, Miami-Dade Pub. Libr., Denver Pub. Libr., Getty Ctr., L.A., also others. Guggenheim fellow; Nat. Endowment Arts grantee. Mem.: Am. Acad. Arts and Letters. Office: 90 Gagosian Gallery 980 Madison Ave New York NY 10021-1848 also: 35 S Venice Blvd Venice CA 90291

RUSCHER, CHARLES B. finance educator, consultant; b. Freeport, N.Y., July 22, 1956; s. Thomas E. and Barbara A. B. Ruscher; m. Dianne S. Witters, Oct. 26, 1957; 1 child, Kristin R. BA in Bus. Adminstrn., Bridgewater Coll., 1978; grad., Campbell U., 1987; MBA, James Madison U., 1989; grad., East Carolina U., 1989; PhD in Fin., U. Ariz., 1999. Plant contr., fin. acct. Am. Brands, Crozet, Va., 1979—83; bus./personal fin. planner Am. Express Fin. Svcs., Charlottesville, Va., 1983—85; comml. loan/trust officer 1st Am. Bank Va., Harrisonburg, 1985—90; fin. instr. James Madison U., Harrisonburg, 1990—92; fin. cons. U. Ariz., Tucson, 1992—95; fin. prof. James Madison U., Harrisonburg, 1995—99, U. Ariz., Tucson, 1999—; fin. cons., interim CFO Ardext Techs., Tucson, 2001. Fin. cons. Cruscher Fin. Cons. Svcs., Tucson, 1990—; dir. Small Bus. Devel. Ctr. Bd., Tucson, 1990—; trainer Intrados Internat. Mgmt. Group, Fed. Fin. Instns. Exam. Coun., 1991. Dir. Bridgewater (Va.) Coll. Estate Planning Bd., 1986—87; panelist Bus. Devel. Fin. Corp. Summit, Tucson, 2000. Fellow: Eller Entrepreneurship Ctr.; mem.: Fin. Mgmt. Assn. Internat. (faculty advisor 1990—), Beta Gamma Sigma (treas. 1992). Avocations: travel, hiking, reading, reading financial journals and books. Home: 5789 N Camino Del Sol Tucson AZ 85718 Office: U Ariz Dept Fin McClelland Hall 315R Tucson AZ 85721 E-mail: ruscher@bpa.arizona.edu.

RUSCIANO, GISSELA LILIANA, purchasing agent; d. Victor Raul and Olga Sarela Pezo; m. John Michael Rusciano, Sept. 23, 1995; 1 child, Joseph Tyler. B, Calif. Poly. U., Pomona, 1991, U. Calif., Riverside, 1997, cert. purchasing mgr., 1999. Cert. arch., AIA, 1987. Architect, designer Clignett and Assocs., Upland, Calif., 1985—87; materials/purcahsing mgr. ELE Corp., Fontana, Calif., 1986—96; materials mgr. Connor Mfg. Svcs., Corona, Calif., 1996—2003; procurement mgr. Irvin Aerospace Inc, Santa Ana, Calif., 2003—. Cons. Black and Decker, Lake Forest, Calif., 2003. Mem.: Nat. Assn. Purchasing Mgrs. (assoc.; treas. 1991—92, cert.). Home: 504 Turtle Crest Dr Irvine CA 92603 Office: Irvin Aerospace Inc 3701 W Warner Ave Santa Ana CA 92704 Personal E-mail: grusciano007@yahoo.com.

RUSCONI, LOUIS JOSEPH, marine engineer; b. San Diego, Calif., Oct. 10, 1926; s. Louis Edward and Laura Ethelyn (Salazar) R.; m. Virginia Caroline Bruce, Jan. 1, 1972. BA in Engring. Tech., Pacific Western U., 1981, MA in Marine Engring. Tech., 1982; PhD in Marine Engring. Mgmt., Clayton U., 1986. Cert. nuclear ship propulsion plant operator, surface and submarine; diplomate naval ship nuclear propulsion system. Enlisted USN, 1944, electrician's mate chief, 1944-65, retired, 1965; marine electrician planner U.S. Naval Shipyard, Vallejo, Calif., 1965-72; marine elec. technician Imperial Iranian Navy, Bandar Abbas, Iran, 1974-79; marine shipyard planner Royal Saudi Navy, Al-Jubail, Saudi Arabia, 1980-86. Cons. in marine engring., 1986—. Author: Shipyards Operations manual, 1980, poetry (Golden Poet award 1989, Silver Poet award 1990). Mem. Rep. Presdl. Task Force, Washington, 1989-90, trustee, 1991. Mem. IEEE, U.S. Naval Inst., Soc. of Naval Architects and Marine Engrs. (assoc. mem.), Fleet Res., Nat. Geographic Soc. Avocations: creative writing, poetry, martial arts. Home: PO Box 100 Darby MT 59829-0100

RUSE, JOAN RIEHLE, genealogist; b. Flint, Mich., Oct. 3, 1931; d. Louis Clemens Riehle and Matilda Kathryn McAfee; m. Ronald Ruse, June 6, 1953; children: James M., Deirdre J. Asst. to editor Coal Mining mag., Pitts., 1949—50; asst. buyer U.S. Steel Corp., Pitts., 1950—60; editor, pub. Die Familie Riehle Geneal. Newsletter, Flossmoor and Olympia Fields, Ill., 1981—86; genealogist Die Familie Riehle, Olympia Fields and Frankfort, Ill., 1980—.

RUSH, AUGUSTUS JOHN, psychiatrist, educator; b. Glen Ridge, N.J., Dec. 15, 1942; s. Augustus John Jr. and Helen Rush; 1 child, Matthew; m. Dee Miller, May 31, 1986; 1 child, Augustus John III. AB in Biochemistry cum laude, Princeton U., 1964; MD, Columbia U., 1968. Intern Northwestern U., Chgo., 1968-69; resident U. Pa., Phila., 1972-75; asst. prof. U. Okla. Health Scis. Ctr., Oklahoma City, 1975-78; assoc. prof. U. Tex. Southwestern Med. Ctr., Dallas, 1978-83, Betty Jo Hay prof., 1983-88, Betty Jo Hay Disting. Chair in Mental Health, 1988—. Dir. Mental Health Clin. Rsch. Ctr., Dallas, 1987—. thor: Beating Depression, 1983; co-author: Cognitive Therapy of Depression, 1979, Cognitive Therapy of Depressed Adolescents, 1994; editor: Short-Term Psychotherapies for Depression, 1982; co-editor: Depression: Basic Mechanisms Diagnosis and Treament, 1986—; assoc. editor Biol. Psychiatry, 1994—. Fellow Am. Psychiat. Assn., Am. Coll. Psychiatrists, Am. Coll. Neuropsychopharmacology; mem. Soc. for Psychotherapy Rsch. (pres. 1984-85), Soc. for Biol. Psychiatry (sec.-treas. 1990-94, v.p. 1994, pres. 1996-97). Office: Ste 225B 6363 Forest Park Rd Dallas TX 75390-9086

RUSH, BOBBY L. congressman; b. Ga., Nov. 23, 1946; m. Carolyn Rush; 5 children. BA in Polit. Sci., Roosevelt U., 1974; MA in Polit. Sci., U. Ill., 1992. Fin. planner Sanmar Fin. Planning Corp.; assoc. dean Daniel Hale Williams U.; ins. agent Prudential Ins. Co.; city alderman Chgo., 1984-93; democratic committeeman Chgo. 2nd ward, 1984, 88, Central Ill., 1990; dep. chmn. Ill. Democratic Party, 1990; mem. U.S. Congresses from 1st Ill. Dist., 1993—. Chmn. Environ. Protection, Energy and Pub. Utilities com., Budget and Govt. Operations com., Capitol Devel. com., Hist. Landmark Preservation Com.; mem. Commerce com. Former mem. Student Non-Violent Coordinating com.; founder Ill. Black Panther Party; past coord. Free Breakfast for Children, Free Med. Clinic. With US Army, 1963-68. Recipient Ill. Enterprise Zone award Dept. Commerce and Community, Operation PUSH Outstanding Young Man award, Henry Booth House Outstanding Community Svc. award, Outstanding Bus. and Profl. Achievement award South End Jaycees, Chgo. Black United Communities Disting. Polit. Leadership award. Democrat. Office: US Ho of Reps 2416 Rayburn House Office Bldg Washington DC 20515-1301

RUSH, DOMENICA MARIE, health facilities administrator; b. Gallup, N.Mex., Apr. 10, 1937; d. Bernardo G. and Guadalupe (Milan) Iorio; m. W. E. Rush, Jan. 5, 1967. Diploma, Regina Sch. Nursing, Albuquerque, 1958. RN N.Mex.; lic. nursing home adminstr.; cert. legal nurse cons., 2004. Charge nurse, house supr. St. Joseph Hosp., Albuquerque, 1958-63; dir. nursing Cibola Hosp., Grants, 1960-64; supr. operating room, dir. med. seminars Carrie Tingley Crippled Children's Hosp., Truth or Consequences, N.Mex., 1964-73; adminstr. Sierra Vista Hosp., Truth or Consequences, 1974-88, pres., 1980-89; clin. nursing mgr. U. N.Mex. Hosp., 1989-90; adminstr. Nor-Lea Hosp., Lovington, N.Mex., 1990-94; with regional ops. divsn. Presbyn. Healthcare Svcs., Albuquerque, 1994—, regional ops., 1994—2004; adminstr. Sierra Vista Hosp., Truth or Consequences, N.Mex., 1995—2003; regional adminstr. Presbyn. Healthcare Svcs., 2003—04; founder Rush Health Consulting Svc., 2004—. Bd. dirs. N.Mex. Blue Cross/Blue Shield, 1977-88, chmn. hosp. relations com., 1983-85, exec. com. 1983—; bd. dirs. Region II Emergency Med. Svcs. Originating bd. SW Mental Health Ctr., Sierra County, N.Mex., 1975; chmn. Sierra County Personnel Bd., 1983—. Recipient Frank Gabriel award N.Mex. Hosp. Health Sys. Assn., 2003, Govenor's award Emergency Med. Svcs., 2003, Govs.award for Outstanding Woman, N. Mex., 2004; Named Lea County Outstanding Woman, N.Mex. Commn. on Status of Women, Woman of Yr. for Lea County, N.Mex.; 1993. Mem. Am. Coll. Health Care Adminstrs., Sierra County C. of C. (bd. dirs. 1972, 75-76, svc. award 1973, Businesswoman of the Yr. 1973-74), N.Mex. Hosp. Assn. (bd. dirs., sec.-treas., pres.-elect, com. chmn., 1977-88, pres. 1980-81, exec. com., 1980-83, 84-85, recipient meritorius svc. award 1988), N.Mex. So. Hosp. Coun. (sec. 1980-81, pres. 1981-82), Am. Hosp. Assn. (N.Mex. del. 1984-88, regional adv. bd. 1984-88). Republican. Roman Catholic. Avocations: raising thoroughbred horses, cooking. Home: 1100 N Riverside Dr Truth Or Consequences NM 87901-9789 Office: 800 E 9th Ave Truth Or Consequences NM 87901-1954

RUSH, GEOFFREY, actor; b. Toowomba, Queensland, Australia, July 6, 1951; married; 2 children. Actor: (plays) Wrong Side of the Moon, 1971, Lock Up Your Daughters, 1972, Assault With a Deadly Weapon, 1972, Twelfth Night, 1972, 1983, 1984, Ruling Class, 1972, You're a Good Man Charlie Brown, 1972, Puss in Boots, 1972, Juno and the Paycock, 1973, Expresso Bongo, 1973, National Health, 1973, The Imaginary Invalid, 1973, Suddenly at Home, 1973, Aladdin, 1973, Hamlet on Ice, 1973, Godspell, 1974, The Rivals, 1974, The Philanthropist, 1974, Present Laughter, 1974, Jack and the Beanstalk, 1975—77, King Lear, 1978, 1988, Point of Departure, 1978, Clowneroonies, 1978, Waiting for Godot, 1979, On Our Selection, 1979, Teeth and Smiles, 1980, Revenger's Tragedy, 1981, No End of Blame, 1982, You Can't Take It With You, 1981, A Midsummer Night's Dream, 1982, 1983, Mother Courage, 1982, Silver Lining, 1982, The Prince of Homburg, 1982, Royal Show, 1983, Blood Wedding, 1983, Netherwood, 1983, 1984, The Marriage of Figaro, 1983, Pal Joey, 1983, The Blind Giant is Dancing, 1983, Sunrise, 1983, Benefactors, 1986, On Parliament Hill, 1987, Shepherd on the Rocks, 1987, The Winter's Tale, 1987, Tristram Shandy-Gent, 1988, Les Enfants du Paradis, 1988, The Importance of Being Earnest, 1988, 1990—91, 1992, Troilus & Cressida, 1989, The Diary of a Madman, 1989, 1990, 1992 (Variety Club award for Stage Actor of Yr., 1989, Sydney Theatre Critics Cir. award for Most Outstanding Performance, 1989, Victorian Green Rm. award for Best Actor, 1990), Marat/Sade, 1990, The Comedy of Errors, 1990, The Government Inspector, 1991, Uncle Vanya, 1992, The Dutch Courtesan, 1993, Oleanna, 1993, Hamlet, 1994, 1995; (films) Hoodwink, 1980, Starstruck, 1981, Twelfth Night, 1985, On Our Selection, 1994, Five Easy Pizzas, 1994, Children of the Revolution, 1995, Shine, 1996 (Oscar award for Best Actor, 1996, BAFTA award Best Actor, 1996), Oscar & Lucinda, 1997, Shakespeare in Love, 1998 (BAFTA award Best Supporting Actor, 1999), Elizabeth, 1998, Mystery Men, 1999, House on Haunted Hill, 1999, Quills, 2000 (NY Film Critics Online award for best actor, 2000), The Taylor of Panama, 2001, Lantana, 2001, Frida, 2002, The Banger Sisters, 2002, Swimming Upstream, 2003, Ned Kelly, 2003, Finding Nemo (voice), 2003, Pirates of the Caribbean: The Curse of the Black Pearl, 2003, Intolerable Cruelty, 2003; (TV series) Consumer Capers, 1979—81, Menotti, 1980—81, The Burning Piano, 1992, Mercury, 1996; dir.: (plays) Clowneroonies, 1978—80, Animal Acts, 1984—86, Teen Ages, 1984—86, Carols-By-Lazerlight, 1984—86, The 1985 Scandals, 1986, Pearls Before Swine, 1986, Pell Mell, 1986, 1987, 1988, The Merry Wives of Windsor, 1987, The Popular Mechanicals, 1987, 1988, 1992, Les Enfants du Paradis, 1989, The Wolf's Banquet, 1989, Popular Mechanicals 2, 1992, Aristophane's Frogs, 1992; co-translator The Government Inspector, 1991, writer (with George Whaley) (TV film) Clowning Around, 1992, (with John Clarke) (play) Aristophane's Frogs, 1992, Call Me Sal, 1996, Children of the Revolution, 1997, Les Misérables, 1998. Office: Creative Artists Agy 9830 Wilshire Blvd Beverly Hills CA 90212-1804

RUSH, HERMAN E. television executive; b. Phila., June 20, 1929; s. Eugene and Bella (Sacks) R.; m. Joan Silberman, Mar. 18, 1951; children: James Harrison, Mandie Susan. BBA, Temple U., 1950. With Ofcl. Films, 1951-57; owner Flamingo Films, 1957-60; with Creative Mgmt. Assos., N.Y.C., 1960-71, pres. TV divsn., 1964-71, exec. v.p. parent co., dir., 1964-71; ind. prodr., 1971-75; prodr. Wolper Orgn., 1975-76; pres. Herman Rush Assos., Inc. (Rush-Flaherty Agy. subs.), 1977-78, Marble Arch TV, Los Angeles, 1979-80, Columbia Pictures TV, Burbank, Calif., 1980-87; chmn., CEO, Coca-Cola Telecom., 1987-88, Rush Assocs., Inc., Burbank, 1988—, Katz/Rush Entertainment, Beverly Hills, Calif., 1990-96, New Tech Entertainment, LLC, Beverly Hills, 1996—; chmn., CEO internet content provider East Cap. Fin. Corp.; chmn. emeritus E Cap. Fin. Corp.; mng. ptnr. Media Consulting Assocs. CEO Infotainment Internat., Inc.; pres., chmn. Royal Animated Art, Inc.; Entertainment Industries Coun.; owner, exec. prodr. The Montel Williams Talk Show, 1991-2004; mem. bd. advisors Smart Video Techs., Inc. Trustee Sugar Ray Robinson Youth Found., 1967-75; pres. Retarded Infant Svcs., N.Y.C., 1957-63; bd. dirs. U.S. Marshall's Svc. Found., Just Say No Found.; conferee White House Conf. for a Drug Free America, 1987, 88. Mem. Acad. TV Arts and Scis., Hollywood Radio and TV Soc., Producers Caucus. Clubs: Friars, Filmex. Office: Rush Entertainment Group 11766 Wilshire Blvd Ste 800 Los Angeles CA 90025 Office Phone: 310-478-5279. E-mail: hermanrush@aol.com.

RUSH, JEFFREY, JR., federal agency administrator; b. Kansas City, Kans. m. Dawn Rush; 2 children. B, Baker U.; JD, George Mason U. Criminal investigator USDA, Hyattsville, Md., 1971—75, with supervisory criminal investigation Kansas City, Mo., 1975—78, asst. regional inspector gen. Chgo., 1978—80, regional inspector gen., 1980—83, dep. asst. inspector gen., 1983—94; acting inspector gen. Peace Corp, 1993; inspector gen. USAID, 1994—99, Dept. Treasury, Washington, 1999—. With U.S. Army, 1968—71. Mem.: ABA, DC Bar Assn., Va. State Bar Assn. Office: Dept of the Treasury Inspector General 1500 Pennsylvania Ave Washington DC 20220

RUSH, JULIA ANN HALLORAN (MRS. RICHARD HENRY RUSH), artist, writer; b. St. Louis, Oct. 25, 1927; d. Edward Roosevelt and Flavia Hadley (Griffin) Halloran; m. Richard Henry Rush, Aug. 15, 1956; 1 child, Sallie Haywood. Student Washington U., St. Louis, 1945-47; B.A., George Washington U., 1949. One-woman shows: Fort Amador Officers Club, Panama Canal Zone, El Panama Hotel, Panama, George Washington U., Statler Hotel, Roosevelt Hotel, Washington, Newspaper Women's Club, Washington, Waukegan Library, Ill., Epworth Heights Hotel, Ludington, Mich.; exhibited in group shows: Panama Art League, Corcoran Gallery; represented in permanent collections: U. Panama; also pvt. collections; model John Robert Powers Agy., 1950; sec.-treas., dir. N.Am. Acceptance Corp., 1956-58; v.p. Rush and Halloran, Inc., 1957-58, ptnr., 1954-57; research asst. to husband's bi-weekly newsletter Art/Antiques Investment Report, 1973—, articles in Wall St. transcript, 1971—. Illustrator: Antiques As An Investment (author Richard H. Rush), 1968; research asst.: Investments You Can Live With and Enjoy (author: Richard H. Rush), 1974, 2d, edit., 1975, 3d edit., 1976; Photographer: Automobiles as an Investment, 1982; Investing in Classic Cars, 1984. Recipient 1st prize (Panama) Newspaper Women's Club, 1953; First Prize Panama Art League, 1953. Mem. DAR, Nat. League Am. Penwomen, Florence Crittenton Circle (rec. sec. 1968-69), Kappa Kappa Gamma. Club: Washington, Royal Palm Yacht (No. Ft. Myers, Fla.), Boca West Golf and Country (Boca Raton, Fla.)

RUSH, NORMAN, author; b. San Francisco, Oct. 24, 1933; s. Roger and Leslie (Chessé) R.; m. Elsa Scheidt; children: Jason, Liza. BA, Swarthmore Coll., 1956. Dealer antiquarian books, 1960-78; instr. English, history Rockland C.C., Suffern, N.Y., 1973-78; co-dir. Peace Corps, Botswana, 1978-83; freelance writer, 1983—. Author: Whites, 1986, Mating, 1991 (Nat. Book award for fiction 1991, Internat. Fiction prize Irish Times and Aer Lingus 1992), Mortals, 2003. Recipient Rosenthal award Nat. Acad. and Inst. Arts and Letters, 1987; fellow Nat. Endowment for Arts, 1986, Guggenheim fellow, 1987, Bellagio residency fellow Rockeller Found., 1990. Mem. PEN Am. Ctr.

RUSH, RICHARD HENRY, financial executive, writer, lecturer; b. N.Y.C., Mar. 6, 1915; s. Henry Frederick and Bessie (Vreeland) R.; m. Julia Ann Halloran, Aug. 15, 1956; 1 dau., Sallie Haywood. *Dr. Rush is the great grandson of Philip Freneau, "The Poet of the American Revolution" who is credited as having saved the country from "monarchy" through his publication of the "National Gazette". He is the great grandnephew of General Phil Kearny, Civil War general and New Jersey's most prominent soldier. The grandnephew of America's first Consul General and Minister to Japan, Townsend Harris, who through his determined negotiating of the American Japanese trade treaty, signed in 1858, opened Japan to trade with the west. Harris, before going to Japan, founded the free College of the City of New York as President of the New York Board of Education.* BA summa cum laude, Dartmouth Coll., 1937, MCS, 1938; MBA with highest distinction, Harvard U., 1941, DCS (Littauer fellow), 1942. Dir. aviation U.S. Bur. Fgn. and Domestic Commerce, 1945-46; chief economist, chmn. planning com. All Am. Aviation (U.S. Air), 1943-45; dir. aircraft divsn. Nat. Security Resources Bd., 1948-51; Washington rep. to J. Paul Getty, 1951-52; ptnr. Rush & Halloran, 1953-58; pres., chmn. bd. N.Am. Acceptance Corp., Atlanta, also Washington, 1956-59; owner Richard H. Rush Enterprises, Greenwich, Conn., also Washington, 1953-73; prof., chmn. dept. finance and investments Sch. Bus. Adminstrn., Am. U., Washington, 1967-70, 77-79. Author: Art as an Investment, 1961, A Strategy of Investing for Higher Return, 1962, The Techniques of Becoming Wealthy, 1963, Antiques as an Investment, 1968, The Wrecking Operation: Phase One, 1972, Investments You Can Live With and Enjoy, 1976, Techniques of Becoming Wealthy, 1977, Automobiles as an Investment, 1982, Selling Collectibles, 1982, Collecting Classic Cars for Profit and Capital Gain, 1984, Collector Cars: Classics for the New Century, 2001; contbr. over 700 articles to newspapers, mags. and profl. jours.; editor series of books on starting businesses for U.S. Dept. Commerce; contbg. editor Wall St. Transcript, 1971-97, Art/Antiques Investment Report, 1972-97. Trustee, exec. com. Finch Coll., 1968-72. Recipient Pres.'s med., CCNY, 1997. Mem. Am. Mktg. Assn. (chmn. nat. com.), Am. Econ. Assn., Am. Statis. Assn., Internat. Platform Assn., AAUP, Harvard Club (N.Y.C.), Royal Palm Yacht Club (Ft. Myers), Phi Beta Kappa, Phi Kappa Phi, Omicron Delta Kappa. Episcopalian.

RUSH, RICHARD R. academic administrator; Pres. Calif. State U. Channel Islands, Camarillo. Office: Calif State U Channel Islands 1 University Dr Camarillo CA 93012 E-mail: richard.rush@csuci.edu.

RUSH, W. MARVIN, trucking executive; CEO Rush Enterprises Inc., San Antonio, 1969—. Office: Rush Enterprises Inc PO Box 34630 San Antonio TX 78265-4630

RUSHEN, ELIZABETH RAE MARSHALL, director; b. Nampa, Idaho, Dec. 2, 1962; d. Monce Raymond Marshall and Nona Lou DeDual, Charles Edward DeDual (Stepfather); m. Anthony Rushen, June 20, 1997; children: Jesse Isaac, Jennifer Elizabeth, Teneah Marie. AAS in Mass Communication/TV Prodn., Portland C.C., 1987; BS in Arts and Letters, Portland State U., 1990. Fin. aid student employee Portland C.C., 1985—87, Portland State U., 1987—90, fin. aid specialist, 1990—95, fin. aid office coord., 1995—97, fin. aid specialist, 1997—99, fin. aid counselor, 1999—2003, student loan coord., 1999—2003; fin. aid coord., Adult Degree Programs Warner Pacific Coll., 2004—. Policy coun. mem. Albina Head Start, Portland, 1995—98. Recipient Grand prize, Courtesy Ford & KPTV, 2000, cert. Merit, Bur. Fire, Rescue and Emer. Svcs., 2001. Mem.: AAUP (assoc.; unit rep. 1999—2003), Western Assn. Student Fin. Aid Adminstrs. (assoc.), Oreg. Assn. Student Fin. Aid Adminstrs. (assoc.), Oreg. Pub. Employees Union (assoc.). Democrat. Eckankar/The Ancient Science Of Light And Sound. Achievements include Coordinated delivery of over $70 million dollars in student loan funds to students in one year; Successfully, using one person CPR, gave man every possible chance of recovery until EMS until could arrive and administer shocks to restore pulse and breathing. He was alert upon transport; Successfully, using Red Cross training, assisted unknown bus passenger in full diabetic seizure, until emergency help arrived; Successfully, using Red Cross training, assisted and created action plan for student predisposed to epileptic grand mal seizures. Avocations: reading, photography, singing, piano, travel. Home: 3906 SE Kelly St Portland OR 97202 Office Phone: 503-317-1091. Personal E-mail: rushenee@comcast.net. E-mail: erushen@warnerpacific.edu.

RUSHER, WILLIAM ALLEN, writer, commentator; b. Chgo., July 19, 1923; s. Evan Singleton and Verna (Self) R. AB, Princeton U., 1943; JD, Harvard U., 1948; DLit (hon.), Nathaniel Hawthorne Coll., 1973. Bar: N.Y. 1949. Assoc. Shearman & Sterling & Wright, N.Y.C., 1948-56; spl. counsel fin. com. N.Y. Senate, 1955; assoc. counsel internal security subcom. U.S. Senate, 1956-57; pub., v.p. Nat. Review mag., N.Y.C., 1957-88, also bd. dirs.; Disting. fellow The Claremont Inst., 1989—. Mem. Adv. Task Force on Civil Disorders, 1972. Author: Special Counsel, 1968, (with Mark Hatfield and Arlie Schardt) Amnesty?, 1973, The Making of the New Majority Party, 1975, How to Win Arguments, 1981, The Rise of the Right, 1984, The Coming Battle for the Media, 1988; editor: The Ambiguous Legacy of the Enlightenment, 1995; columnist Universal Press Syndicate, 1973-82, Newspaper Enterprise Assn., 1982—; played role of Advocate in TV program The Advocates, 1970-74. Chmn., bd. dirs. Media Rsch. Ctr., Washington, 2001—, Nat. Rev. Bd., 1957-88, 90—; bd. advisors Ashbrook Ctr., Ashland, Ohio, past chmn.; past vice chmn. Am. Conservative Union; past trustee Pacific Legal Found., Sacramento. Served as 2d lt. to capt., USAAF, 1943-45, India-Burma Theater. Recipient Disting. Citizen award NYU Sch. Law, 1973. Mem. ABA, Univ. Club (N.Y.C. and San Francisco), Met. Club (Washington). Anglican. Home and Office: 850 Powell St San Francisco CA 94108

RUSHING, PHILIP DALE, retired social worker; b. Carbondale, Ill., Mar. 15, 1932; S. Paul and Beulah Myrl (Benton) R.; m. Linda North, July 5, 1958 (div. July 1964); 1 child, Lisa Anne Rushing Burrow; m. Rosalie Anne Sturm, Aug. 20, 1966. BA, So. Ill. U., 1958; MSW, Washington U., St. Louis, 1960. Bd. cert. diplomate, ACSW; lic. social worker, Ill. Child welfare worker Ill. Dept. Pub. Welfare, Salem, East St. Louis, 1958-60, child welfare supr. East St. Louis, 1960-63; field rep. Nat. Assn. for Retarded Children, Dallas, Denver, 1963-65; dir. social svcs. A.L. Bowen Children's Ctr., Harrisburg, Ill., 1965-68; asst. zone dir. for mentally retarded Ill. Dept. of Mental Health, Harrisburg, 1968-74; regional coord. for devel. disabilities Ill. Dept. of Mental Health & Devel. Disabilities, Marion, 1974-83; social work adminstr. Choate Mental Health & Devel. Ctr., Anna, Ill., 1983-95; ret., 1995. Adj. asst. prof. So. Ill. U. Rehab. Inst., Carbondale, Ill., 1968-78; bd. dirs. Southeastern Ill. Pastoral Counseling Ctrs., chmn. pers. com., 1996-98. Bd. cert. diplomate ACSW; lic. clin. social worker. Bd. deacons First Presbyn. Ch., Harrisburg, 1974-77, bd. trustees, 1978-80, bd. elders, 1980-83, 96-98, 2003—. With USN, 1951-55, Korea. Fellow Am. Assn. on Mental Retardation (life, chmn. social work divsn. Ill. chpt. 1973-74); mem. NASW (chmn. East St. Louis br. 1962). Home: 6542 Hwy 13 W Harrisburg IL 62946-4142 E-mail: prrushing@juno.com.

RUSHING, TONNIE AUSTIN PAGE, musician, educator; b. Hartwell, Ga., Mar. 6, 1940; d. George Wilson and Ruth Smith Page; m. Roger Kendall Vichery, June 18, 1960; children: George Kendall, Carol Page; m. Charles Maynard Rushing, Aug. 18, 1979; stepchildren: Joan E., Brian C., Susanne E. BS in Edn., Athens (Ga.) State Coll., 1973; cert. in Computer Tech., Trident Tech. Coll., 1992, Sylvan Learning Ctr., 1996; cert. in Sign Lang., Trident Tech. Coll., 1997. Musician, Ga., 1958—; prin., owner Opus 11 George Bed & Breakfast, 1988—97; afternoon activities dir. O'Quinn Preschool-Kindergarten, 2001. Dir. music Summer Stock Theater, Morristown, Tenn., 1969; music educator Covenant Sch. Fine Arts Enrichment, 1976—79; music dir. Young Charleston Theatre Co., 1988, 96; mem. founding com. Covenant Fine Arts Enrichment Sch., Decatur, 1976; mem. adv. com. Coun. Arts John C. Calhoun State Coll., Decatur. Singer: North Ala. Charleston Symphony, St. Micheal's Ch., Grace Episc. Ch., Choir Eng. Tour, 1981—2002; musician: French Protestant Ch., 1988—96; author: Huguenots and the Legacy, 1994; dir.: (recording) Huguenot Psalter, 1991; jacket cover, Huguenot Psalter, 1991. Pres. Decatur (Ga.) Civic Chorus; vol. Crisis Ctr. Mental Health Ctr., Decatur, 1971—79; mem. comprehensive planning com. City Hartwell, Ga., 2003; bd. dirs. Preservation Soc., 2004, Hart County Hist. Soc., 2004; music asst. 2d

Presbyn. Ch., Charleston, SC, 1988; sect. leader St. Michaels Ch., Charleston, 1998—2001; elder Hartwell 1st Presbyn. Ch., 2004; bd. dirs. Charleston (S.C.) Symphony Orch. Chorus and Chamber Choir. Mem.: PTA, Am. Guild Organists, Presbyn. Assn. Musicians, Charleston (S.C.) County Med. Auxiliary, Nat. assn. Mental Illness, Hartwell Women's Club, Sigma Alpha Iota. Republican. Home: 175 E Johnson St Hartwell GA 30643

RUSHNELL, SQUIRE DERRICK, author, speaker, television executive; b. Adams Center, N.Y., Oct. 31, 1938; s. Reginald Grant and Erica Mifanwy Redwood Sedgemore (Squire) R.; children: Robin Tracy, Hilary Adair, Squire Grant Sedgemore. Ed., Syracuse U., 1956-60. Disc jockey Stas. WOLF, WHEN and WFBL, Syracuse, N.Y., 1958-61, Sta. WTRL, Bradenton, Fla., 1961-62; exec. prodr. Sta. WBZ AM-TV, Boston, 1962-67; program dir. KYW News-Radio, Phila., 1968; exec. prodr. Kennedy & Co. Sta. WLS-TV, Chgo., 1969-71, program dir., 1971-73; v.p. programs ABC-owned TV stas., N.Y.C., 1973-74; v.p. children's TV ABC Entertainment Network, N.Y.C., 1974-78; v.p. Good Morning Am. and children's programs ABC-TV Network, N.Y.C., 1978-81, v.p. long range planning and children's TV, 1981-87; v.p. late night and children's TV ABC Entertainment, N.Y.C., 1987-89; pres. Rushnell Comm. & Pub., Inc., 1990-96; pres., CEO GoodLife TV Network, Washington, 1996—2001; motivational spkr., 2001—. Author: The Kingdom Chums Greatest Stories, 1986, When God Winks: How the Power of Coincidence Guides Your Life, 2001; co-author: Broadcast Programming, 1981, Broadcast/Cable Programming, 1985, rev. edit., 1989, 1993. Recipient Emmy awards, 1975-88, TV Critics Circle award, 1976, all for outstanding children's TV programming, Am. Children's TV Festival award, 1985, 87. Mem. NATAS, Nat. Acad. Arts and Scis., Internat. Radio and TV Soc., Action for Children's TV (award for outstanding children's TV programming). E-mail: squire@whengodwinks.com.

RUSHTON, ALAN R. physician, medical historian; b. Oak Park, Ill., Mar. 10, 1949; s. Raymond H. and D. Loree (Swan) R.; m. Nancy Spencer, May 5, 1973; children: Andrew, Daniel. AB in Chemistry, Earlham Coll., 1971; PhD in Genetics, U. Chgo., 1975, MD, 1977. Diplomate Am. Bd. Pediatrics, Am. Bd. Med. Genetics. Resident, intern Yale U.-New Haven (Conn.) Hosp., 1977-80; physician Hunterdon Med. Ctr., Flemington, N.J., 1980—; assoc. clin. prof. pediatrics Robert Wood Johnson Med. Sch., New Brunswick, N.J., 1980—. Lectr. genetics Princeton (N.J.) U., 1980 84; adj. prof. Med. U. Ams., Nevis, West Indies. Author: Genetics and Medicine in the United States 1800-1922, 1994. Fellow Am. Acad. Pediatrics, Am. Coll. Med. Genetics, N.Y. Acad. Medicine, Royal Soc. Medicine; mem. Am. Assn. History Medicine, History Sci. Soc. Office: Hunterdon Pediatric Assocs 6 Sand Hill Rd Ste 202 Flemington NJ 08822-4600

RUSHTON, LYNN NOELLE, artist; b. Dallas, Dec. 28, 1967; d. Harold R. and Mary Ann (Wagliardo) Hawkins; m. James Edward Rushton III, June 11, 1994; children: James Edward Burne-Jones, Charles Laurent Cosley-Daubigny. BA in Comm. and Fine Art, Vanderbilt U., 1990; postgrad., Tulane U., 1990-92. Intern (devel.) Kenndy Ctr., Washington, 1990; intern Nat. Mus. Am. Art, Washington, 1990. Guest lectr. Austin Peay State U., Tenn., 1998. Gallery representation includes Estelle Stair Gallery, Rockport, Tex., 1996-97, Pace Collection, 1996-97, Beaux Arts, Dallas, 1996, Visual Effects, Dallas, 1996-99, Wally Workman Gallery, Austin, 1997—, Continental Gallery, 2001; one-woman shows Celebrity Cafe, Dallas, 1996, Sarratt Gallery, Nashville, 1998, Deep Ellum Ctr. for Arts, Dallas, 1999, Plano (Tex.) Art Ctr., 1999, Quadrangle, 2000, Wally Workman Gallery, Austin, 2001; two-person show at Annarella Gallery, Georgetown, 2002; group shows Aardvark Gallery, Garland, Tex., 1996, Dallas Visual Art Ctr., 1996, 98, Richardson Civic Arts Co., Richardson Pub. Libr., 1997, Irving (Tex.) Art Ctr., 1997, Visual Art League, Lewisville, Tex., 1997 (merit award), Associated Creative Artists Awards Show, 1999, Slidell Cultural Ctr., 1999, Assemblage, L.A., 1999, Soc. Outdoor Painters 1997-2000; represented in permanent private collections. Mem. Oil Painters Am., Associated Creative Artists (bd. dirs. 1999—), Tex. Visual Arts Assn., Soc. Outdoor Painters, Jr. League Dallas, Dallas Vanderbilt Alumni (pres. 1997-98), Lakewood Svc. League (bd. dirs. 1997—). Home: 8350 Santa Clara Dr Dallas TX 75218-4342

RUSHTON, WILLIAM JAMES, III, insurance company executive, director; b. Birmingham, Ala., Apr. 23, 1929; s. William James and Elizabeth (Perry) R.; m. LaVona Price, Aug. 19, 1955; children: William James IV, Deakins Ford, Tunstall Perry. BA magna cum laude, Princeton U., 1951; LL.D. (hon.), Birmingham So. Coll., 1981. Asso. actuary Protective Life Ins. Co., Birmingham, Ala., 1954-59, dir., 1956—, agt., 1959-62, v.p., 1962-63, agy. v.p., 1963-67, pres., from 1967, pres., chief exec. officer, 1969-82, chmn., 1982—; pres. Protective Life Corp., Birmingham, 1981-82, CEO, chmn., 1982-92, chmn., 1992-94, chmn. emeritus, 1994—. Dir. Ala. Power Co., The Southern Co., Amsouth Bank N.A., Amsouth Bancorp. Trustee So. Rsch. Inst., Children's Hosp., Birmingham So. Coll., Highland Day Sch.; mem., deacon 1st Presbyn. Ch., Birmingham, chmn. bd. deacons, 1960—; chmn. United Way campaign, 1977, pres., 1986, life mem., 1993; chmn. Leadership Birmingham, United Way, Indsl. Health Coun.; mem. adv. com. Meyer Found., Greater Birmingham Found. (chmn.). Capt. arty., U.S. Army, Korea. Decorated Bronze Star; named to Ala. Acad. of Honors, 1979; recipient Disting. Eagle Scout award Boy Scouts Am., 1980, Brotherhood award NCCJ, 1990. Fellow Soc. Actuaries; mem. Am. Council Life Ins. (dir.), Am. Life Conv. (state v.p. 1975), Am. Life Ins. Assn. (Ala. v.p. 1975), Health Ins. Assn. Am. (dir. from 1982), Million Dollar Round Table, Birmingham C. of C. (dir.) Clubs: Rotary (bd. dirs. 1973-74, treas. 1978-79, pres. 1988-89), Mountain Brook Country, Redstone. Office: Protective Life Corp 2801 Highway 280 S Birmingham AL 35223-2407

RUSIE, RUTH LOUISE, literacy educator; b. Russiaville, Ind., Oct. 13, 1918; d. Volna Ernest and Mamie Audrey (Gallion) Ritz; m. Horace Robert Rusie, June 28, 1941; children: James Frederick, David Robert, John Lindley. BA, DePauw U., 1940; MS, Ind. U., 1972. Elem. sch. tchr. Met. Sch. Dist. Martinsville (Ind.), 1958-72, spl. reading tchr., 1972-80; coord. Martinsville Literacy Coalition, 1982—. Mem. Ind. Right-to-Read Com., 1975-78; mem. adv. bd., participant Reading is Fundamental, Martinsville, 1992-96. Composer music for elementary students The Stupid Thief, 1972. Bd. dirs. Martinsville Edn. Found., 1991—, Cmty. Found. of Morgan County, 2001—, People Respecting Individuality and Diversity in Everyone (P.R.I.D.E.), 1997—, co-pres., 2002—, Cmty. Concerts N.Y.C., 1994—, co-pres., 2003-2004; bd. dirs., treas. Morgan County Pub. Libr., Martinsville, 1984-2001; mem. com. on food Habitat for Humanity, Martinsville, 1997—; mem. Martinsville Arts Coun., 1981—, dir., 1981—; driver cancer patients ARC, Martinsville, 1981-2000, dir., 1986-92; dir. vol. desk Morgan County Meml. Hosp., Martinsville, 1982-94; driver Meals-On-Wheels, Martinsville, 1985—; grand marshall Morgan County Fall Foliage Festival Parade, Martinsville, 1993; adv. bd. United Way Ctrl. Ind., 2003-2004, mem. solutions coun., 2004—; elder Presby. Ch., 2004—; trustee Morgan County Pub. Libr. Found., 2004—; mem. edn. devel. program Morgan County Habitat for Humanity, 2004—; bd. dirs. NBA, 2004—. Named Citizen of Yr., Kiwanis, 1990, Rotary, 1993; recipient Cmty. Spirit award, H.S. Nat. Honor Soc., 1992, Mayor's award for literacy, Mayor and City Ofcls., 1993, Excellence of Cmty. Svc. award, DAR, 1995, Ind. Jefferson award, Am. Inst. Pub. Svc./Indpls. Star, 1996, Svc. to Mankind award, Morgan County Sertoma Club, 2002, S.W. Ind. Dist. Sertoma Internat., 2003. Mem. Martinsville Woman's Club (pres. 1957-59), Martinsville Literary Club, Coterie (pres. 1986-88), Monday Afternoon Art Club, Foxcliff Golf Club (pres. 1981-82), Kappa Kappa Kappa (pres. 1956-57, province officer 1957-59). Presbyterian. Avocations: reading, bell and singing ch. choirs, bridge, opera, theater.

RUSKAUP, CALVIN, therapist, history professor; b. St. Louis, Feb. 5, 1939; s. Henry and Viola (Vogt) R.; m. Chandricka Maharaj, Apr. 1, 1991. BSc, U. Mo., St. Louis, 1967; PhD, Ohio State U., 1979. Diplomate Am. Psychotherapy Assn., Am. Assn. Integrative Medicine. Co-founder Cmty. Broadcasting-Sta. WFAC, Columbus, Ohio, 1975-77; lectr. Ohio State U., 1975-79; designer Trimobile Safety Car, Aspen, Colo., 1980-81; pastoral counselor United Luth. Ch., Knoxville, Tenn., 1982—85, pres. Hilo, Hawaii, 1986—. Spkr. World Parliament Scientists, 2000. Chmn. Commn. to Stop Violence, 1999-2000; editor Patriot Press, 1997-98; Patriot and Libertarian parties U.S. presdl. candidate, 1996. Mem. AAAS Sr. Scientists Engrs. (emeritus), Am. Anthropol. Assn., Acad. Polit. Sci., Orgn. Am. Historians, Assn. Transpersonal Psychology, N.Y. Acad. Scis., Am. Psychoanalytic Assn., Pub. Rels. Soc. Am., Nat. Press Club, Circumnavigators Club.

RUSKIN, JOSEPH RICHARD, actor, director; b. Haverhill, Mass., Apr. 14, 1924; s. Ely and Betty Edith (Chaimson) Schlafman; m. Barbara Greene; 1 child, Alicia. Grad., Carnegie Inst. Tech., 1949. Founder Rochester (N.Y.) Arena Theatre, 1949-52. Actor N.Y. stage plays, 1952-58, Theatre Group, UCLA, Mark Taper Forum, 1959—, (films) Fall of Legs Diamond, 1959, Magnificient Seven, 1960, Escape from Zahrein, 1963, Robin and the Seven Hoods, 1965, Prizzi's Honor, 1985, Longshot, 1987, Indecent Proposal, 1992, Spider-Man, 1994, (voice) Star Trek: Insurrection, 1998, King Cobra, 1999, The Scorpion King, 2002; regular appearances various TV programs, 1952—; TV appearance: Alias, 2002; dir. Houston Alley, 1965-69; freelance dir., 1969—. Served with USNR, 1943-46. Mem. AFTRA, SAG, Actors Equity Assn. (nat. coun.). Home: 1326 Devon Ave Los Angeles CA 90024-5346

RUSKIN, RICHARD A. obstetrician-gynecologist; b. New Rochelle, N.Y., Oct. 1, 1919; MD, Duke U., 1944. Intern Kings County Hosp., Bklyn., 1944; resident in ob.-gyn. N.Y. Polyclinic Hosp., N.Y.C., 1947-49, 51-52, N.Y. Lying-In Hosp., N.Y.C., 1949-51; sr. attending ob.-gyn. N.Y. Hosp., 1952—, St. Lukes-Roosevelt Hosp. Ctr., N.Y.C., 1973—. Clin. prof. ob.-gyn. Cornell U. Med. Sch., 1970—. Fellow Am. Coll. Ob.-Gyn., ACS; mem. AMA, N.Y. Gynecol. Soc. Home: 415 E 52nd St New York NY 10022-6424

RUSKIN, ROBERT STERLING, association executive; b. Washington, Nov. 27, 1945; s. Robert Edward and Thelma (Gipe) R.; m. Rebecca Lynne Wilson, Aug. 11, 1967; 1 child, Brant Edward. BA, Washington Coll., Chestertown, Md., 1967; MA, W.Va. U., 1969, PhD, 1971. Lic. psychologist Va., D.C. Prof. dept. psychology Georgetown U., Washington, 1971-86, chmn. dept. psychology, 1976-85, dir. Ctr. for Personalized Instrn., 1977-80, dir. Teaching Resource Ctr., 1985-86; chief psychol. assessor leadership devel. U. Md., College Park, 1984—; prin. investigator and project dir., consortium univs. rsch fellows program U.S. Army Rsch. Inst., Washington, Alexandria, 1985—; nat. rsch. fellow U.S. Dept. Edn., Washington, 1986-87; affiliate prof. psychology George Mason U., Washington, 1989—; prin. investigator Consortium & Office of Substance Abuse Prevention, Washington, 1990-93; dir. programs and rsch. Consortium of Univs. of Washington Metro. Area, 1987-88, v.p., 1989—. Psychol. cons. DuPont Corp., Seaford, Del., 1986-88; psychol. cons. Consortium of Univs. of D.C., 1984—; cons. in field; rep. of U.S. to UNESCO Planning Meeting, Paris, 1979. Co-author: Behavioral Instruction: An Evaluative Review, 1977; editor manuscript: Consortium Research Fellows Program; editor The Jour. of Personalized Instrn., 1975-81, Revista a Tecnologia Educativa, 1976-83. Battelle Inst. Disting. Acad. Rsch. fellow U.S. Army Rsch. Inst., 1984-86. Fellow APA, Am. Psychol. Soc. (charter); mem. AAAS, D.C. Psychol. Assn., Va. Psychol. Assn., Psi Chi. Methodist. Avocations: golf, fishing. Home: 309 W Alex Ave Alexandria VA 22302 Office: Consortium of Univs of Wash 1 Dupont Cir NW Washington DC 20036-1110

RUSLING, BARBARA N(EUBERT), real estate broker; b. St. Louis, Nov. 27, 1945; d. Ralph L. and Rosemary (Stroot) Neubert; m. Randolph H. Wieser, Apr. 23, 1966 (div. Nov. 1983); children: Keith, Steve, Eric; m. Robert Best Rusling, Aug. 2, 1985. BA, Vanderbilt U., 1966; postgrad., Baylor U., 1975. Lic. real estate broker. Appraisal intern Smith Real Estate, Waco, Tex., 1975; resident real estate broker Sanger Suburban Realty, Waco, 1975-81, sales mgr., 1981-83; pres., gen. mgr. Coldwell Banker Hallmark Realty, Waco, 1983-99; with Coldwell Banker Jim Stewart, Realtors, 1999—; commr. Tex. Gen. Svcs. Commn., 1997—2002; regent Tex. State Tech. Coll., 2002—. Mem. from dist. 57 Tex. State Ho. Reps., 1995-97. Chmn. bd. dirs. YWCA, Waco, 1976-79; dir. Leadership Waco Program, 1986-87; various positions Hist. Waco Found.; bd. dirs. Waco Civic Theatre, treas., 1999-2001; bd. dirs. Family Counseling Ctr., 1991-96, United Way, 1992-98, Family Abuse Ctr., 1993-2002, 2004—, Waco Better Bus. Bur., 1994-99. Mem. Tex. Assn. Realtors (edn. com., strategic planning com. 1983-95, realtor lawyer com. 1985-93), Realtors Nat. Mktg. Inst. (cert.), Waco Bd. Realtors (past bd. dirs., salesman of yr. 1979), Waco C. of C. (bd. dirs. 1990-93), Am. Heart Assn. (McLennan County bd. dirs. 1997—, pres. 1999-2000), Waco Sailing Club, Kappa Delta. Home: 1635 Meandering Way China Spring TX 76633-2905 Office: Coldwell Banker 500 N Valley Mills Dr Waco TX 76710-6007 Office Phone: 254-776-0000. E-mail: brusling@aol.com.

RUSMISEL, STEPHEN R. lawyer; b. N.Y.C., Jan. 27, 1946; s. R. Raymond and Esther Florence (Kutz) R.; m. Beirne Donaldson, Sept. 6, 1980 (div. Jan. 1984); 1 child, Margo Alexander; m. Melissa J. MacLeod, Aug. 24, 1985 (div. Oct. 1996); children: Benjamin William, Eric Scot Kunze, Erin Lea Kunze; m. Teresa R. Paterniti, June 28, 1997; 1 child, Sarah J. Lamendola. AB, Yale U., 1968; JD, U. Va., 1971. Bar: N.Y. 1972, U.S. Ct. Appeals (2d cir.) 1974, U.S. Dist. Ct. (so. dist.) N.Y. 1975. Assoc. Winthrop, Stimson, Putnam & Roberts, N.Y.C., 1971-80, ptnr., 1980-2000, Pillsbury Winthrop LLP, N.Y.C., 2001—. Aux. officer Bedminster Twp. (N.J.) Police, 1976—. Mem. Practicing Law Inst., Am. Arbitration Assn. (arbitrator 1976—), Far Hills Polo Club (Annandale, N.J.), Ausable Club (St. Huberts, N.Y.), Essex Hunt Club (Peapack, N.J.), Phi Delta Phi. Republican. Avocations: polo, flying, carpentry, gardening, poetry. Home: Shadowline Farm Bedminster NJ 07921 Office: Pillsbury Winthrop LLP One Battery Park Plz New York NY 10004-1490 E-mail: srusmisel@pillsburywinthrop.com.

RUSS, JOANNA, author; b. N.Y.C., Feb. 22, 1937; d. Evarett and Bertha (Zinner) R. BA in English with high honors, Cornell, U., 1957; M.F.A. in Playwriting and Dramatic Lit, Yale U., 1960. Lectr. in English Cornell U., 1967-70, asst. prof., 1970-72; asst. prof. English, Harpur Coll., State U. N.Y. at Binghamton, 1972-75, U. Colo., 1975-77; assoc. prof. English, U. Wash., 1977-90, prof., 1984-90. Author: Picnic on Paradise, 1968, And Chaos Died, 1970, The Female Man, 1975, We Who Are About To, 1977, Kittatinny: A Tale of Magic, 1978, The Two of Them, 1978, On Strike Against God, 1980, The Adventures of Alyx, 1983, The Zanzibar Cat, 1983, How To Suppress Women's Writing, 1983, Extra (Ordinary) People, 1984, Magic Mommas, Trembling Sisters, Puritans and Perverts: Feminist Essays, 1985, The Hidden Side of the Moon, 1987, To Write Like a Woman, 1995, (nonfiction) What Are We Fighting For, 1998; also numerous short stories. Mem. Sci. Fiction Writers Am. (Nebula award for best short story 1972, Hugo award for best novella 1983).

RUSSE, CONRAD THOMAS CAMPBELL, accountant; b. Bethesda, Md., July 15, 1954; s. Frederick William Jr. and Constance Oakman (Fagan) R.; m. Deborah Joyce Thompson, June 14, 1980; children: Thomas Campbell, Catherine Alexandra, Caroline Saunders. BS, Duke U., 1977; MBA, Ga. State U., 1982. CPA, Ga., Tenn., N.C. Estimator Advance Builders, Inc., Smyrna, Ga., 1978; contractor B&B Drywalls, Marietta, 1979-81; acct. Evans, Snyder & Co., Atlanta, 1981-82; tax acct. Peat Marwick Mitchell & Co., Charlotte, N.C., 1982-85, Ernst & Whinney & Co., Chattanooga, 1985-86; tax mgr. Costello, Strain & Co, CPAs, Chattanooga, 1986-89; prin. Thomas C. Russe, CPAs, Chattanooga, 1989—. Bd. dirs., treas. Visually Impaired Tng. and Learning Ctr., Chattanooga, 1988-93, Chattanooga Tax Practitioners, 1987-95. Membership chmn. Cherokee Area coun. Boy Scouts Am., Chattanooga, 1987, 88; bd. dirs. Allegro Dance Theater, 1990-92; bd. dirs. Small Bus. Devel. Ctr., 1995—. English Speaking Union scholar, 1972-73. Mem. N.C. Assn. CPAs, Ga. Soc. CPAs (mem. taxation com. 1993—, tax forum com. 1995—), Tenn. Soc. CPAs (taxation com. 1990, 92, tax liaison com. 1992-95, small bus. com. 1999), Chattanooga Estate Planning Coun., Chattanooga Area C. of C. (seminars chmn. small bus. coun. 1987, 88, steering com. small bus. coun. 1986-95), CPA Club (bd. dirs. 1991-92), CPA-Atty. Forum (pres. 1992-94), Chattanooga Civitan Club. Episcopalian. Avocations: reading, antique refinishing, biking. Home: PO Box 4322 Chattanooga TN 37405-0322 Office: PO Box 4322 Chattanooga TN 37405-0322

RUSSEL, WILLIAM BAILEY, engineering educator; b. Corpus Christi, Tex., Nov. 17, 1945; m. 1972; 2 children. BA, MS in Chem. Engring., Rice U., 1969; PhD in Chem. Engring., Stanford U., 1973. NATO fellow applied math. Cambridge U., 1973-74; from asst. prof. to assoc. prof. chem. engring. Princeton U., N.J., 1974-83, prof., 1983—, chmn. dept. chem. engring., 1987-96, dir. Materials Scis. Inst., 1996-98, dean graduate sch., 2002—. Olaf A. Hougen prof. U. Wis., 1984 Mem.: Math. Rsch. Soc., Am. Chem. Soc., Soc. Rheology (pres. 2001—03, Bingham award 1999), NAE, AIChE (William H. Walker award 1992). Office: Princeton U 205 Nassau Hall Princeton NJ 08544 Office Phone: 609-258-3035. E-mail: gradeean@princeton.edu.

RUSSELL, ALAN JAMES, chemical engineering and biotechnology educator; b. Salford, Lancashire, Eng., Aug. 8, 1962; came to U.S., 1987; s. Francis Anthony and Yvonne (Heilbrunn) R.; m. Janice Elaine Quoresimo, Sept. 19, 1987; children: Hannah Justine Serena, Vincent Anthony Alexander, Christian Sebastian, Trevor Alan James, Emily Christine Samantha. BSc with honors, U. Manchester, U.K., 1984; PhD, Imperial Coll., London, 1987. NATO rsch. fellow MIT, Cambridge, 1987-89; chmn., Nickolas DeCecco prof. dept. chem. engring. U. Pitts., 1989-2001, assoc. dir. Ctr. for Biotech., 1991-2001, dir. program in advanced biomaterials, prof. surgery; dir. McGowan Inst. for Regenerative Medicine. Prof. biochemistry and molecular genetics U. Pitts. Med. Ctr.; exec. dir. Pitts. Tissue Engring. Initiative; founder Alerhan Techs., Inc., Agentase, LLC; cons. to chem. and pharm. industries, 1988—. Contbr. articles to profl. jours. Recipient Presdl. Young Investigator award NSF, 1990, Chancellor's Disting. Rsch. award U. Pitts., 1993; NATO fellow, 1988, Am. Inst. Med. and Biol. Engrs. fellow, 1998. Mem. Am. Chem. Soc. (session chmn. 1990-91, awards 1989, 93), Biochemistry Soc., Am. Inst. Chem. Engrs., Tissue Engring. Soc. N.Am. (pres.). Lutheran. Achievements include pioneering use of protein engineering to alter rationally the pH dependence of enzymes; discovery of the phenomenon of enzyme memory in organic solvents, biotechnological destruction of chemical weapons. Office: McGowan Inst 401 Scaife Pittsburgh PA 15261 Home: 530 Salem Heights Dr Gibsonia PA 15044-6136

RUSSELL, ALLAN DAVID, lawyer; b. Cleve., May 6, 1924; s. Allan MacGillivray and Marvel (Codling) R.; m. Lois Anne Robinson, June 12, 1947, m. Patricia A. Ellis, March 8, 2003; children: Lisa Anne, Robinson David, Martha Leslie. BA, Yale U., 1945, LLB, 1951. Bar: N.Y. 1952, Conn. 1956, Mass. 1969, U.S. Supreme Ct. 1977. Atty. Sylvania Electric Products, Inc., N.Y.C., 1951-56, div. counsel Batavia, N.Y., 1956-65, sr. counsel, 1965-71; sec., sr. counsel GTE Sylvania Inc., Stamford, Conn., 1971-76; asst. gen. counsel GTE Svc. Corp., 1976-80, v.p., assoc. gen. counsel, 1980—83; pvt. practice Redding, Conn., 1983—. Sec., dir. mktg. subs. Sylvania Entertainment Products Corp., 1961-67; sec. Wilbur B. Driver Co. Dist. leader Rep. Party, New Canaan, Conn., 1955-56; sec. bd. dirs. Youth Found., Inc., 1981-83, bd. dirs., 1985-2001, pres., 2000-01; mem. planning commn., Redding, Conn., 1987-89; mem. Redding Bd. Ethics, 1990-96, chmn., 1992-96; warden Christ Ch. Parish, Redding, 1987-89; bd. dirs. Mark Twain Libr., 1988-94, 2002—, v.p., 1988-89, pres., 1990-92. With USAAF, 1943—46. Mem. SAR, Assn. of Bar of City of N.Y., Conn. Bar Assn. (exec. com. corp. counsel sect. 1986-90), Am. Soc. Corp. Secs., St. Nicholas Soc., Collie Club Am. Found., Inc. (v.p., dir. 1986 89, pres. 1989-90), Soc. Colonial Wars, Yale Alumni Assn. (sec. local chpt. 1953-56), Yale Club of Danbury (pres. 1990—), Phi Delta Phi. Home: 9 Little River Ln Redding CT 06896-2018

RUSSELL, ALLEN STEVENSON, retired aluminum company executive; b. Bedford, Pa., May 27, 1915; s. Arthur Stainton and Ruth (Stevenson) R.; m. Judith Pauline Sexauer, Apr. 5, 1941. BS, Pa. State U., 1936, MS, 1937, PhD, 1941. With Aluminum Co. Am., 1940-82, assoc. dir. rsch., 1973-74; v.p. Alcoa, Pa., 1974-78; v.p. sci. and tech. Pitts., 1978-81; v.p., chief scientist, 1981-82. Adj. prof. U. Pitts., 1981-86 Contbr. articles to profl. jours.; patentee in field. Named IR-100 Scientist of Yr., 1979; Pa. State U. alumni fellow, 1980; K.J. Bayer medalist, 1981; recipient chem. Pioneer award Am. Inst. Chemists, 1983 Fellow Am. Soc. Metals (Gold medal 1982), AIME (James Douglas gold medal 1987), Am. Inst. Chemists; mem. NAE (coun. 1978-84), Am. Chem. Soc., Sigma Xi. Republican. Presbyterian. Home: 20 Wild Laurel Ln Hilton Head Plantation Hilton Head Island SC 29926 E-mail: alsrus@msn.com.

RUSSELL, ANTONETTE PATRICE, lawyer; b. Belfield, Saint Mary, Jamaica, June 3, 1971; d. Leleith Lemour and Rainford Augustus Kelly(Stepfather). JD, U. Nebr. Lincoln, 1997; BSBA, Nova Southeastern U., 1994; AA in Bus. Adminstrn., Broward C.C., Fort Lauderdale, Florida, 1993. Bar: Supreme Ct. Fla. 1997, Ct. Appeals D.C. 1999. Staff atty. Cath. Charities Legal Svcs., Miami, Fla., 1998—2000; supervising counsel Cath. Charities Legal Svcs.-Broward, Lauderdale Lakes, Fla., 2001—04; ptnr. Cameron & Russell, PA, Hollywood, Fla., 2004—. Mem.: ABA, Broward County Bar Assn., Am. Immigration Lawyers Assn., Nat. Notary Assn. Avocations: reading, travel, sports. Office: Cameron & Russell PA Emily Plz Ste 302 3900 Hollywood Blvd Hollywood FL 33021 Office Phone: 954-986-8630. Personal E-mail: lawyer_aprussell@yahoo.com.

RUSSELL, BRUCE ALAN, SR., social scientist, educator; b. Findlay, Ohio, May 15, 1943; s. Bruce Albert and Arlene A. Russell; children: Catherine Amber, Bruce Arthur. BA in English Lit., U. Rochester, 1965, MA in Edn., 1968; PhD, Columbia Pacific U., 1992. Class 1, Level 2 profl. tchg. cert. Mont. Office of Pub. Instrn., 2001. Instr. U. of Mont., Missoula, Mont., 1975—76; lectr. Sydney U., Australia, 1976—79; dept. chmn./tchr. Busby Sch. of the No. Cheyenne & Lodge Grass H.S., Mont., 1984—91; prof. MSU Billings & Rocky MT Coll., Mont., 1989—90; dean of arts and sciences & vp for academic affairs Columbia Commonwealth U., 2000—01; dir. Mountain States Social Rsch., Missoula, Mont., 1991—. Reviewer Humanity and Soc. (Jour.), Worcester, Mass., 2000—; guest lectr. Fgn. Policy Assn. Gt. Decisions Program, Missoula, Mont., 1996—2002. Author: (social science book) Dimensions of Alienation, (education book) Strategies in Native American Education, (general audience book) Update 2000. Lobbying activities Western Prison Project, MT People's Action, & MT Health Care Consortium, Missoula/Helena, Mont., 2001—03. Sp5 psychometrician U.S. Army, 1967—70, Fort Sam Houston. Mem.: Assn. for Humanist Sociology. Achievements include research in education mostly focused on individualized instruction. Avocation: singing. Home: 313 S 4th W Missoula MT 59801 Office: Mountain State Social Research PO Box 8745 Missoula MT 59807 E-mail: mssrbooks@montana.com.

RUSSELL, C. EDWARD, JR., lawyer; b. Portsmouth, Va., Aug. 19, 1942; BA, Hampden-Sydney Coll., 1964; LLB, Washington & Lee U., 1967. Bar: Va. 1967. Law clk. to Hon. John A. MacKenzie U.S. Dist. Ct. (ea. dist.) Va., 1967-68; atty. Kaufman & Canoles, Norfolk. Mem. ABA (bus. law sect., real property, probate and trust law sect.), Va. State Bar (bus. law sect., real property sect., health law sect.), Va. Bar Assn. (bus. law sect., real estate sect., chmn. young lawyers sect. 1977), Omicron Delta Kappa, Phi Alpha Delta. Office: PO Box 13368 Norfolk VA 23506-0368 E-mail: cerussell@kaufcan.com.

RUSSELL, CANDACE LEIGH, musician, educator; b. Louisville, Aug. 11, 1967; d. James Franklin and Marcella Matilda True; m. Douglas Andrew Russell, Aug. 4, 2000. MusB, U. Louisville, 1989, MusM, 1991, B in Music Edn., 1994; Mus D, U. S.C., 2004. Trumpet instr. U. Louisville, 1989—95, Augusta (Ga.) State U., 2001—. Adj. prof. music U. S.C., Aiken, 2001—; prin. trumpet Lake Murray Symphony Orch., Lexington, SC; trumpet Columbia (S.C.) Cmty. Concert Band. With U.S. Army, 1995—2001. Recipient Lucille Parrish Vets. award, Scholarchis Nat. Orgn. Music Clubs. Mem.: Music Edn. Nat. Conf., Music Tchr. Nat. Assn., Internat. Trumpet Guild. Home: 252 Willow Forks Rd Lexington SC 29073 Personal E-mail: crjazz@sc.rr.com.

RUSSELL, CAROLYN B. state legislator; b. Greenville, N.C., June 19, 1944; d. Oscar Dixon and Naomi (Grey) Barnes; m. Douglas M. Russell; children: Susannah, Douglas, Meredith. B, M in Clin. Psychology, East Carolina U. Psychologist, Fla., S.C.; pers. dir. O'Berry Ctr., Goldsboro, N.C.;

mem. N.C. Ho. of Reps., 1991—. Bd. dirs. Green Lamp Bd.; bd. dirs. Smart Start early childhood devel. program Avocations: baking bread, gourmet cooking, reading, boating. Office: State Legislative Bldg Raleigh NC 27603

RUSSELL, CHARLES HARRY, music educator, restaurant manager; b. Flint, Mich., Oct. 7, 1962; s. Harry Charles and Sandra Kay Russell; m. Pamela Rene Flewelling, Aug. 20, 1983; children: Alena, Angela, Charles. BA, U. Michigan, Flint, Michigan, 1992; MusB in Edn., U. Michigan, Flint, 2002. Sr. asst. restaurant mgr. Taco Bell, Flint, 1987—; trumpet tchr. Herter Music Ctr., Flint, 1997—. Composer: (music) Your Memory Will Live, 1991, If Only, 1990. Recipient Eagle Scout, Boy Scouts of Am., 1980. Mem.: Mich. Band and Orch. Assn., Music Educator Nat. Conf. Home: 4379 Regency Rd Swartz Creek MI 48473 Personal E-mail: cruss9299@aol.com.

RUSSELL, CHARLIE L. writer; b. Monroe, La., Mar. 10, 1932; s. Charlie L. and Katie O. Russell; children: Katheryn K., Joshua E. BS in English, U. San Francisco, 1959; MSW, NYU, 1966; MFA, U. Calif., San Diego, 1986. Author: (play) Five on the Black Hand Side, 1969, (film script) Five on the Black Hand Side, 1972 (Image award, NAACP, 1972), (novels) The Worthy Ones, 2002. With U.S. Army, 1953—55, Korea. Home: 1413 Neilson St Berkeley CA 94702 E-mail: charlierussell@attbi.com.

RUSSELL, CHARLOTTE SANANES, biochemistry educator, researcher; b. N.Y.C., Jan. 4, 1927; d. Joseph and Marguerite (Saltiel) Sananes; m. Joseph Brooke Russell, Dec. 20, 1947; children: James Robert, Joshua Sananes. BA, Bklyn. Coll., 1946; MA, Columbia U., 1947, PhD, 1951. Asst. prof. chemistry CCNY, N.Y.C., 1958-68, assoc. prof., 1968-72, prof., 1972—, prof. emerita, 2001—. Peer reviewer NSF, NIH; ad hoc reviewer sci. jours. including Jour. Bacteriology, Biochemistry. Contbr. articles to profl. jours. Mem. AAAS, AAUP, AAUW (internat. fellowship panel 1986-89), Am. Soc. Biochemistry and Molecular Biology, Am. Chem. Soc., Amnesty Internat., Urgent Action Network, Sigma Xi. Office: CCNY Dept Chemistry 138th St & Convent Ave New York NY 10031 Office Phone: 212-650-6681. E-mail: chrcc@mail.sci.ccny.cuny.edu.

RUSSELL, CLIFFORD SPRINGER, economics and public policy educator; b. Holyoke, Mass., Feb. 11, 1938; s. Kenneth Clifford and Helen Alwilda (Springer) R.; m. Louise Pancoast Bennett, Feb. 3, 1965 (div. June 1985); m. Susan Vanston Reid, Sept. 7, 1985; stepchildren: Timothy Taylor Greene, Elizabeth Claussen Greene (dec.). BA, Dartmouth Coll., 1960; PhD, Harvard U., 1968. Sr. rsch. assoc. Resources for the Future, Washington, 1968-70, fellow, 1970-73, sr. fellow, 1973-85, div. dir., 1981-85; prof. econs. and pub. policy Vanderbilt U., Nashville, 1986—, dir. Vanderbilt Inst. for Pub. Policy Studies, 1986—. Valfrid Paulsson vis. prof. environ. econs. Beijer Inst., Royal Swedish Acad. Scis., Stockholm, 1997. Author: Drought and Water Supply: Implications of the Massachusetts Experience for Municipal Planning, 1970, Residuals Management in Industry: A Case Study of Petroleum Refining, 1973, Steel Production: Processes, Products and Residuals, 1976, Environment Quality Management: An Application to the Lower Delaware Valley, 1976, Freshwater Recreational Fishing: The National Benefits of Water Pollution Control, 1982, Enforcing Pollution Control Laws, 1986, Applying Economics to the Environment, 2001; contbr. articles to profl. jours. Trustee, treas. Environ. Def. Fund, N.Y.C., and Washington, 1973-85; mem. Tenn. Gov.'s Energy Adv. Bd., Nashville, 1989-94; trustee Tenn. Environ. Coun., Nashville, 1989-96; pres. 1992-95. Lt. USN, 1960-63. Mem. Assn. Environ. and Resource Econs. (bd. dirs. 1983-85, chmn. workshop com., pres. 1993-94). Avocations: tennis, fly fishing, sailing, boat building. Home: 1222 Clifftee Dr Brentwood TN 37027-4105 Office: Vanderbilt Inst Pub Policy Studies 1207 18th Ave S Nashville TN 37212-2807 E-mail: cliff.russell@vanderbilt.edu.

RUSSELL, CRISTEL ANTONIA, finance educator; d. Salvador Juan and Louisette Davy; m. Dale Wesley Russell. Diploma, Ecole Superieure des Sciences Commerciales D'Angers, Angers, France, 1994; MBA, So. Ill. U., 1995; PhD, U. of Ariz., 2000. Assoc. prof. San Diego State U., 2000—. Editl. rev. bd. mem. Jour. of Consumer Rsch., Madison, Wis., 2002—. Contbr. articles to profl. jours. Recipient Mktg. Innovation award, Proctor and Gamble Co.; grantee Rsch. grantee, Mktg. Sci. Inst. Mem.: Assn. for Consumer Rsch. Avocations: running, travel, social marketing. Office: San Diego State Univ 5500 Campanile Dr San Diego CA 92182 Office Phone: 619-594-0209. Office Fax: 619-594-3272. E-mail: crussell@mail.sdsu.edu.

RUSSELL, CYNTHIA M. college president; Pres. Clinton Jr. Coll., Rock Hill, S.C., 1994—. Office: Clinton Jr College 1029 Crawford Rd Rock Hill SC 29730-5152

RUSSELL, DAN M., JR., federal judge; b. Magee, Miss., Mar. 15, 1913; s. Dan M. and Beulah (Watkins) R.; m. Dorothy Tudury, Dec. 27, 1942; children— Ronald Truett, Dorothy Dale, Richard Brian. BA, U. Miss., 1935, LL.B., 1937. Bar: Miss. bar 1937. Practice in, Gulfport and Bay St. Louis, Miss.; U.S. judge So. Dist. Miss., 1965—; now sr. judge. Lt. comdr. U.S. Naval Intelligence, 1941-45. Recipient U.S. Supreme Ct. Justice Scalia award, 2000. Founder's Day award Gulfport Rotary Club, 2001. Mem. Miss. Bar Assn., Hancock County Bar Assn., Hancock and Harrison Counties Bar Assn., Bay St. Louis Rotary Club (hon.), Gulfport Rotary Club (hon.), Am. Inns Ct. (hon. Russell-Blass-Walker chpt.), Federalist Soc. (adv. bd. Miss. chpt.), Hancock County C. of C., Tau Kappa Alpha. Clubs: Rotarian (pres. Bay St. Louis, Miss. 1946). Office: 2012 15th St Ste 614 Gulfport MS 39501-2036

RUSSELL, DAVID EMERSON, mechanical engineer, consultant, writer; b. Jacksonville, Fla., Dec. 20, 1922; s. David Herbert and Wilhelmina Russell. BMech Engring., U. Fla., 1948; postgrad., Oxford (Eng.) U. Registered profl. engr., Fla., Ga. Mech. engr. United Fruit Co., N.Y.C., 1948-50; civilian mech. engr. U.S. Army C.E., Jacksonville, 1950-54; mech. engr. Aramco, Saudi Arabia, 1954-55; v.p. Beiswenger Hoch and Assocs., Inc., Jacksonville, Fla., 1955-57; owner, operator David E. Russell and Assocs., Cons. Engrs., Jacksonville, 1957-98; cons. engr., 1998—. Author: The Old Arabia and the New Arabia-An American Engineer in Saudi Arabia 1954 and Again in 1982, 2004; contbr. articles pub. to profl. jours. Chmn. Jacksonville Water Quality Control Bd., 1969-73; bd. dirs. Jacksonville Hist. Soc., 1981-82; mem. Jacksonville Bicentennial Commn., 1973-79. 2d lt. AUS, 1943-46, PTO. Recipient Outstanding Svs. award City of Jacksonville, 1974. Mem. ASME (chmn. N.E. Fla. 1967-68), Nat. Soc. Profl. Engrs., ASHRAE, Fla. Engring. Soc. Univ. Club (Jacksonville), Jacksonville Humane Soc. (life). Episcopalian. Achievements include 5 patents including the ability to detect the arrival of important mail at a remote location. Avocations: world travel, boating, classical music. Home and Office: 4720 Timuquana Rd Jacksonville FL 32210-8231 Office Phone: 904-573-9884.

RUSSELL, DAVID L. federal judge; b. Sapulpa, Okla., July 7, 1942; s. Lynn and Florence E. (Brown) R.; m. Dana J. Wilson, Apr. 16, 1971; 1 child, Sarah Elizabeth BS, Okla. Bapt. U., 1963; JD, Okla. U., 1965. Bar: Okla. 1965. Asst. atty. gen. State of Okla., Oklahoma City, 1968-69, legal adviser to gov., 1969-70; legal adviser Senator Dewey Bartlett, Washington, 1973-75; U.S. atty. for Western dist. Okla. Dept. Justice, 1975-77, 81-82; ptnr. Benefield & Russell, Oklahoma City, 1977-81; judge U.S. Dist. Ct. (we. dist.) Okla., Oklahoma City, 1982—, chief judge, 1994—2002. Lt. comdr. JAGC, USN, 1965-68. Selected Outstanding Fed. Ct. Trial judge Okla. Trial Lawyers Assn., 1988. Mem. Okla. Bar Assn., Fed. Bar Assn. (pres. Oklahoma City chpt. 1981), Order of Coif (alumnus mem.), Jud. Conf. U.S. (mem. exec. com. 2003-). Republican. Methodist. Office: US Dist Ct US Courthouse 200 NW 4th St Oklahoma City OK 73102-3026 Office Phone: 405-609-5100.

RUSSELL, DAVID O. film director, film producer, scriptwriter; b. N.Y.C., N.Y., Aug. 20, 1958; m. Janet Grillo. Grad., Amherst Coll., 1981. Dir.: (films) Hairway to the Stars, 1990, (writer, exec. prodr.) Spanking the Monkey, 1994, (writer) Flirting with Disaster, 1996, Three Kings, 1999; prodr.: The Slaughter Rule, 2002; actor: Adaptation, 2002. Office: Apt 2B 250 W 99th St New York NY 10025-5442*

RUSSELL, DAVID WILLIAMS, lawyer; b. Lockport, NY, Apr. 5, 1945; s. David Lawson and Jean Graves (Williams) R.; m. Frances Yung Chung Chen, May 23, 1970; children: Bayard Chen, Ming Rennick. AB, Dartmouth Coll., 1967, MBA, 1969; JD cum laude, Northwestern U., 1976. Bar: Ill. 1976, Ind. 1983. English tchr. Talledega (Ala.) Coll., 1967; math. tchr. Lyndon Inst., Lyndonville, Vt., 1967-68; asst. to pres. for planning Tougaloo (Miss.) Coll., 1969-71, bus. mgr., 1971-73; law clk. Montgomery, McCracken, Walker & Rhoads, Phila., 1975; with Winston & Strawn, Chgo., 1976-83; ptnr. Klineman, Rose, Wolf & Wallack, Indpls., 1983-87, Johnson, Smith, Pence, Densborn, Wright & Heath, Indpls., 1987-99, Bose McKinney & Evans, Indpls., 1999—2004, Harrison & Moberly, Indpls., 2004—. Cons. Alfred P. Sloan Found., 1972-73; dir. Forum for Internat. Profl. Svcs., 1985—, sec., 1985-88, pres. 1988-89; U.S. Dept. Justice del. to U.S. China Joint Session on Trade, Investment & Econ. Law, Beijing, 1987; leader Ind. Products Trade Fair, Kawachinagano, Japan, 1996; lectr. Ind. law Ind. Gov.'s Trade Mission to Japan, 1986, internat. law Ind. CLE Forum, 1986-96, 2000-03, chmn., 1987, 89, 91, 2001-03; adj. prof. internat. bus. law Ind. U., 1993-95; nat. selection com. Woodrow Wilson Found. Adminstrv. Fellowship Program, 1973-76; vol. Lawyers for Creative Arts, Chgo., 1977-83; dir. World Trade Club of Ind., 1987-93, v.p., 1987-91, pres., 1991-92; dir. Ind. Swiss Found., 1991—; dir. Writer's Ctr., Indpls., 1999—, treas., 2001-; dir. Asian Am. Alliance, 1999—, Friends of Taiwan Assn., Inc., 2001—; dir. Ind. Soviet Trade Consortium, 1991-99, sec., 1991-92; v.p., bd. dirs. Ind. Sister Cities, 1988—; dir. Internat. Ctr. Indpls., 1988-92, v.p. 1988-89; Ind. dist. enrollment dir. Dartmouth Coll., 1990-99; dir. Carmel Sister Cities, 1993—, v.p. 1995-96, pres. 1997-99, chmn., 1999—; v.p., gen. coun. Lawrence Durrell Soc., 1993—; internat. affairs adv. bd. Kelley Sch. Bus., Ind. U., 2001—, Ind. U. Law Sch., 2003—; bd. advisors Ctr. for Internat. Bus. Edn. and Rsch. Krannert Grad. Sch. Mgmt. Purdue U., 1995—; dir., v.p., gen. coun. Global Crossroads Found., Inc., 1995—; mem. bd. arbitrators NASD, 1999—; mem. Ind. Dist. Export Coun., 1999—. Named Hon. fellow, Ctr. for Internat. Legal Studies, 2002—, Internat. Bus. Person of Yr., World Trade Club of Ind., 2002, Sagamore of the Wabash, 2002, Jan. 15, 2002 David Williams Russell Day in his honor, Indpls., Ind. Super Lawyer, 2004; Adminstrv. fellow, Woodrow Wilson Found., 1969—72. Mem. ABA, ACLU, Ill. Bar Assn., Ind. Bar Assn. (vice chmn. internat. law sect. 1988-90, treas. 2002-, chmn. 1990-92, 2002-, co-chmn. written publs. com. 1997-99), Indpls. Bar Assn., Dartmouth Lawyers Assn., Indpls. Assn. Chinese Ams., Chinese Music Soc., Dartmouth Club of Ind. (sec. 1986-87, pres. 1987-88), Internat. Bar Assn., Zeta Psi. Presbyterian. Home: 10926 Lakeview Dr Carmel IN 46033-3937 Office: Harrison & Moberly LLP 2100 First Ind Plz 135 N Pennsylvania St Indianapolis IN 46204-2400 Office Phone: 317-639-4511 ext. 133. Business E-Mail: drussell@h-mlaw.com.

RUSSELL, DONALD GLENN, oil company executive; b. Kansas City, Mo., Nov. 24, 1931; s. Virgil G. and Mae (Agey) R.; m. Norma Jean Robertson, Mar. 21, 1953; children— Karen, Steven BS in Math. and Physics, Sam Houston State U., 1953; MS in Math. and Physics, U. Okla., 1955. Engr. Shell Oil Co., Midland, Houston, New Orleans and N.Y.C., 1956-72, gen. mgr. info. and computer services Houston, 1972-76, spl. assignment SIPC London, 1976, v.p. corp. planning Houston, 1977-78, v.p. internat. exploration and prodn., 1978-80, v.p. prodn., 1977-86; pres. Shell Devel. Co., Houston, 1986—; chmn. & CEO Prime Natural Resources Inc., Houston. Mem. AIME (bd. dirs., v.p. 1973), Soc. Petroleum Engrs. of AIME (bd. dirs. 1970, pres. 1974, John Franklin Carll award 1980, disting. mem. award 1984), Nat. Acad. Engring., Natural Gas Supply Assn. (vice chmn. exec. com.), Am. Petroleum Inst., U. Okla. Assocs. Presbyterian. Avocations: golf, game bird hunting. Office: Duke Energy 5400 Westheimer Rd 5L65 Houston TX 77056-5302

RUSSELL, DOUGLAS CAMPBELL, cardiologist; b. Oxford, Eng., July 26, 1945; came to U.S., 1989; s. David Syme and Marion Hamilton (Campbell) R.; m. Mercedes Dumas, Nov. 16, 1975; 1 child, Georgina Mercedes. BA with 1st class honors, Cambridge U., 1966, MB, BChir, 1969, MD, 1981; PhD, Edinburgh (Scotland) U., 1979. House officer Charing Cross Hosp. Med. Sch., London, 1970-71, sr. house officer, 1971-73, Hammersmith Hosp., London, 1973; registrar cardiology London Chest Hosp., 1973-75; rsch. asst. Med. Rsch. Coun. Edinburgh U., 1975-77, Brit. Heart Found. fellow, 1977-79, lectr. medicine, 1979-83, sr. lectr., sr. rsch. fellow cardiovascular rsch. unit, 1983-89; prof. medicine, chief cardiology U. Va. Sch. Medicine, Salem (Va.) VA Med. Ctr., Roanoke, 1989-97; prof. medicine U. Wis., Madison, 1997—; chief cardiology VA Hosp., Madison, 1997—. Cons. cardiologist Royal Infirmary Edinburgh, 1983-89. Contbr. articles to med. jours. Rsch. grantee British Heart Found., Chest Heart and Stroke Assn., Thyssen Found., Scottish Home & Health, Pharm. Cos., 1976-89; John French Meml. lectr. Arterosclerosis Discussion Grp, Oxford, 1979. Fellow Am. Coll. Cardiology, Royal Coll. Physicians; mem. British Cardiac Soc., British Soc. Cardiovascular Rsch. (treas. 1984-87), Internat. Soc. Heart Rsch., British Med. Assn. Baptist. Avocation: orchid culture.

RUSSELL, EDWARD FRANCIS, humanities educator, social sciences educator; s. Francis S. and Katherine A. Russell; m. Linda Delores Fitzpatrick, Apr. 25, 1999. BA in History, Lewis U., 1966; MA in History, No. Ill. U., 1972; MA in Polit. and Justice Studies, Govs. State U., 2000. H.s. tchr. 6-12 State of Ill., 1966. Tchr./dean/counselor St. Francis Acad., Joliet, Ill., 1966—90; full-time faculty divsn. scis. and humanities Robert Morris Coll., Chgo./Orland Park, Ill., 1991—. Chair adminstrn. com. St. Jude Joliet Pastoral Coun., 1994—2004. Mem.: Am. Polit. Sci. Assn., Am. Hist. Assn. (assoc.), Consumers Union (life), Will County Hist. Soc. (life). Roman Catholic. Avocations: golf, computers, cardiovascular workouts. Office: Robert Morris Coll 43 Orland Square Dr Orland Park IL 60462 Office Phone: 708-226-3825. Personal E-mail: mredrmc@aol.com.

RUSSELL, ELBERT WINSLOW, neuropsychologist; b. Las Vegas, N.Mex., June 4, 1929; s. Josiah Cox and Ruth Winslow Russell; children from previous marriage: Gwendolyn Marie Harvey, Franklin Winslow, Kirsten Nash, Jonathan Nash; m. Sally Lynn Kolitz, Apr. 2, 1989. BA, Earlham Coll., Richmond, Ind., 1951; MA, U. Ill., 1953; MS, Pa. State U., 1958; PhD, U. Kans., 1968. Clin. psychologist Warnersville (Pa.) State Hosp., 1959-61; clin. neuropsychologist VA Med. Ctr., Cin., 1968-71, dir. neuropsychology lab. Miami, Fla., 1971-89, rsch. psychologist, 1989—. Adj. prof. Nova U., Ft. Lauderdale, 1980-87, U. Miami Med. Sch., 1980-94, U. Miami, 1979—. Author: (with C. Neuringer and G. Goldstein) Assessment of Brain Damage, 1970; (with R.I. Starkey) Halstead Russell Neuropsychology Evaluation System (manual and computer program), 1993; contbr. articles to profl. jours. Fellow APA, Am. Psychol. Soc., Nat. Acad. Neuropsychology; mem. Sigma Xi. Democrat. Mem. Soc. Of Friends. Home: 6091 SW 79th St Miami FL 33143-5030 Office: 9350 S Dixie Hwy Ph 3 Miami FL 33156-2944 Office Phone: 305-670-2284.

RUSSELL, EUGENE ROBERT, SR., engineering educator, administrator; b. Cromwell, Conn., Aug. 24, 1932; s. Arland William and Annie Margaret (LeBlanc) R.; m. Mary Lou Conner, June 29, 1957; children: Theresa, Janice, Eugene Jr., Anna, Ruth, Julie, Susan, Paul, Carol, Cecilia. BSCE, U. Mo., Rolla, 1958; MS in Civil Engring., Iowa State U., 1965; PhD, Purdue U., West Lafayette, Ind., 1974. Registered profl. engr., Iowa, Ind. Asst. bridge engr. State of Calif. Pub. Works, Sacramento, 1958-62; asst. area constrn. engr. Iowa Hwy. Commn., Grinnell, 1962-63; rsch. asst. soils Iowa State U., Ames, 1963-65; asst. prof. Ind. Inst. Tech., Ft. Wayne, 1965-69; rsch. assoc. Purdue U., West Lafayette, 1969-74; assoc. prof. Kans. State U., Manhattan, 1974-80, prof. civil engring., 1980—2002, dir. Ctr. for Transp. Rsch. and Tng., 1990—2002, assoc. dir. Mid-Am. Transp. Ctr., 1995-99, Mark and Margaret Hulings prof. civil engring., 1997—2002, prof. emeritus, 2002—. Contbr. more than 80 articles to profl. jours. With USN, 1951-53. Fellow ASCE (life mem., br. pres.), Inst. Transp. Engrs.; mem. Am. R.R. Engring. & Maintentance Assn., Transp. Rsch. Bd. (univ. rep., mem. emeritus com. A3AO5), Transp. Rsch. Forum, Am. Soc. Engring. Edn., Nat. Assn. Railroad Passengers, Roadway Safety Found., Nat. Assn. County Engrs., Am. Pub. Works Assn., Sigma Xi (chpt. honor mem.), Chi Epsilon. Home: 3424 Dickens Ave Manhattan KS 66503-2413 Office: Kansas State Univ Dept Civil Engring 2118 Fiedler Hall Manhattan KS 66506

RUSSELL, FRANCIA, ballet director, educator; b. Los Angeles, Jan. 10, 1938; d. W. Frank and Marion (Whitney) R.; m. Kent Stowell, Nov. 19, 1965; children: Christopher, Darren, Ethan. Studies with, George Balanchine, Vera Volkova, Felia Doubrouska, Antonina Tumkovsky, Benjamin Harkarvy; student, NYU, Columbia U.; degree (hon.), Seattle U., 2003. Dancer, soloist N.Y.C. Ballet, 1956-62, ballet mistress, 1965-70; dancer Ballets USA/Jerome Robbins, N.Y.C., 1962; tchr. ballet Sch. Am. Ballet, N.Y.C., 1963-64; co-dir. Frankfurt (Fed. Republic Germany) Opera Ballet, 1976-77; dir., co-artistic dir. Pacific N.W. Ballet, Seattle, 1977—; dir. Pacific N.W. Ballet Sch., Seattle. Affiliate prof. of dance U. Wash. Dir. staging over 100 George Balanchine ballet prodns. throughout world, including Russia and China, 1964—. Named Woman of Achievement, Matrix Table, Women in Comm., Seattle, 1987, Gov.'s Arts award, 1989, Dance Mag. award, 1996, Brava award Women's U. Club, 2003. Mem. Internat. Women's Forum. Home: 2833 Broadway E Seattle WA 98102-3935 Office: Pacific NW Ballet 301 Mercer St Seattle WA 98109-4600*

RUSSELL, FRANK ELI, retired newspaper publishing executive; b. Kokomo, Ind., Dec. 6, 1920; s. Frank E. and Maude (Wiggins) R.; children: Linda Carole Russell Atkins, Richard Lee, Frank E. III, Rita Jane Russell Eagle, Julie Beth Russell; m. Nancy M. Shover, Oct. 5, 1991. AB, Evansville Coll., 1942; JD, Ind. U., 1951; LLD (hon.), U. Evansville, 1985; HHD (hon.), Franklin Coll., 1989. Bar: Ind. 1951; CPA, Ind. Ptnr. George S. Olive & Co., Indpls., 1947-53; exec. v.p. Spickelmier Industries, Inc., Indpls., 1953-59; bus. mgr. Indpls. Star & News, 1959-77; v.p., gen. mgr. Ctrl. Newspapers, Inc., Indpls., 1977-79, pres., 1979-95, chmn., bd. dirs., 1996-98; ret., 1998; also bd. dirs. Ctrl. Newsprint; pres. Bradley Paper Co., also bd. dirs. Past chmn. adv. bd. Met. Indpls. TV Assn., Inc.; trustee retirement trust Ctrl. Newspapers, Inc.; chmn. retirement com. Hoosier State Press. Bd. dirs. Ariz. Cmty. Found., 1992-96, Eiteljorg Mus., 1994—; trustee, chmn. bd. Nina Mason Pulliam Charitable Trust, 1997—. Recipient Life Salvation award Salvation Army, 1989, Disting. Alumni award Ind. U. Sch. Law, 1989, Life Trustee award U. Evansville, 1991, Ralph D. Casey award, 1997. Mem. ABA, AICPA, Ind. Bar. Assn., Indpls. Bar Assn. (past bd. dirs., past treas.), Ind. Assn. CPAs (past dir.), Tax Execs. Inst. (past pres.), Ind. Assn. Credit Mgmt. (dir., v.p.), Inst. Newspaper Controllers and Fin. Officers (dir., past pres.), Ind. Acad. Ind. Assn. Colls., Midwest Pension Conf. (Ind. chpt.), Newspaper Advt. Bur. (bd. dirs.), Salvation Army (life mem. award), Columbia Club, Meridian Hills Country Club, Masons, Shriners, Order of Coif, Phi Delta Phi, Sigma Alpha Epsilon. Methodist. Office: Nina Mason Pulliam Charitable Trust 135 N Pennsylvania St Ste 1200 Indianapolis IN 46204-1956

RUSSELL, GEORGE ALLEN, composer, theoritician, author, conductor; b. Cin., June 23, 1923; s. Joseph and Bessie (Sledge) R.; 1 son, Jock Millgardh; m. Alice Norbury, Aug. 4, 1981. Grad. h.s.; ed. in pupil composition, Stephan Volpe, 1949. Apptd. mem. faculty New England Conservatory Music, 1969. Also tchr. in Sweden, Norway, Finland, U.K., Italy, Austria, Germany, France and Japan; mem. panel Nat. Endowment of Arts, 1975-76 Composer (with Dizzy Gillespie); 1st composition featuring jazz and Latin influences Cubana-Be, Cubana Bop; presented Carnegie Hall, 1947; performed John F. Kennedy's People to People Music Festival, Washington, 1962, Philharmonic Hall, Lincoln Center, 1963, tours of Europe with Newport Jazz Festival, 1964, jazz orchestras 1970—; performed original compostions with large and small European ensembles for radio, TV and new music socs., in Scandinavia, Italy, Sweden, W.Ger., also other parts Europe, 1964-70; Carnegie Hall performance, 1975; participant 1st White House Jazz Festival, 1978; recs. for RCA Records, Decca, Prestige, Capitol, Atlantic, Columbia, Contemporary, Blue Note, Soul Note, numerous others.; commd. composer maj. jazz work, Brandeis U., 1957, Norwegian TV; other commns. include original music for ballet Othello, 1967, Norwegian Cultural Fund, 1st choral work Listen to the Silence, 1971, Columbia Recs., Living Time for big band featuring Bill Evans, 1975, Swedish Radio for orch., 1977, 81, 83, Mass. Council on the Arts, 1983, Boston Musica Viva, 1987, work for orch. New Eng. Presentors, 1988, work for Relache New Music Ensemble, 1989; sponsor Am. Music Week, 1985, 86; artist-in-residence Glasgow Internat. Festival, 1990, Ezz-thetics with Don Ellis, Dave Baker, et al, N.Y. Big Band, New York, N.Y., Electronic Sonata for Souls Loved By Nature, The Essence of George Russell; tours of U.K., Europe, Japan with George Russell Living Time Orch., 1986—; co-commn. Swedish Concert Inst. and Brit. Coun., 1995; recordings Label Bleu, 1989, 96; seminars: Paris Conservatoire Nat. Superier, Royal Coll. Music, Stockholm, Huddersfield Contemporary Music Festival, Guildhall, others, 1986-96; author: Lydian Chromatic Concept of Tonal Organization, 1953, 59, 98. Recipient Outstanding Composer award Metronome mag., 1958, New Star Composer award Downbeat mag., 1961, Nat. Endowment for the Arts award, 1969, 76, 80, 81, Jazz Masters fellow, 1989; recipient Nat. Music award Am. Music Conf., 1976, numerous awards for recs.; Guggenheim fellow, 1969, 72; Nat. Endowment for Arts grantee, 1979; MacArthur Found. fellow, 1989. Mem. Internat. Soc. Contemporary Music, Norwegian Soc. New Music, Am. Fedn. Musicians, Royal Coll. Music (fgn. mem.). Address: care Concept 1770 Massachusetts Ave Ste 182 Cambridge MA 02140-2808 E-mail: lydconcept@aol.com.

RUSSELL, GEORGE HAW, video production company executive; b. Neosho, Mo., May 22, 1945; s. Kenneth L. and Marjorie (Haw) R.; m. Suzanne Bennett, June 1, 1967; children: Margaret Anne, Marjorie Jane, Karen Lee, George Andrew. BA, La. State U., 1967. Ednl. Video Network, Huntsville, 1990—; ptnr. The Sam Houston Group Ltd. Liability Partnership, Huntsville, 1991—. Producer ednl. videos Nombres et Couleurs, 1988 (Silver Apple award 1988), Napoleon, 1989 (Silver Apple award 1989), Bullfight, 1990, The French Revolution, 1990; exec. producer Spain's Historic Cities, 1992, Munich's Oktoberfest, 1992, The New Nutriton Pyramid, 1992, The Visual Language of Design, 1992, Florence, 1993, Joan of Arc, 1993, New Food Guide Pyramid, 1993, Cleaning and Maintaining Your VCR, 1993, Arts and Crafts of Mexico, 1993, Understanding Geysers and Hot Springs, 1993, Thoreau at Walden Pond, 1993, French Markets, 1993, Great Zimbabwe, 1993. Bd. govs. Tex. Com. on Natural Resources, Dallas, 1979—; bd. dirs. Gibbs-Powell House Mus., Huntsville, 1984—, Natural Area Preservation Assn., Dallas, 1986—; chmn. forest practices Lone Star Sierra Club, Austin, Tex., 1984—; chmn. Fed. Forest Reform, Washington, D.C., 1991—. 1st lt. U.S. Army, 1971-74. Recipient spl. achievement award Sierra Club, San Francisco 1985, chpt. conservation award 1987, environ. heroes for centennial 1991; named Citizen of Month, Huntsville Item 1988. Democrat. Methodist. Avocations: environmental advocacy, historic building restoration, collecting antiques and folk art. Home: 1409 19th St Huntsville TX 77340-5056 Office: Ednl Video Network 1401 19th St Huntsville TX 77340-5057 E-mail: ghr@cyberclone.net.

RUSSELL, HARRIET SHAW, social worker; b. Detroit, Apr. 12, 1952; d. Louis Thomas and Lureleen (Hughes) Shaw; m. Donald Edward Russell, June 27, 1980; children: Lachante Tyree, Krystal Lanae. BS, Mich. State U., 1974; AB, Detroit Bus. Inst., 1976; BA in Pub. Adminstrn., Mercy Coll., Detroit, 1988; MSW, Wayne State U., 1992. Factory staff Gen. Motors Corp., Lansing, Mich., 1973; student supr. tour guides State of Mich., Lansing, Mich., 1974; mgr. Ky. Fried Chicken, Detroit, 1974-75; unemployment claims examiner State of Mich. Dept. Labor, Detroit, 1975-77, asst. payment worker, 1977-84, social svcs. specialist, 1984-90; pres. Victory Enterprises, 1991; social worker Detroit Bd. Edn., 1992—. Ind. contractor Detroit Compact; moderator Mich. Opportunity Skills and Tng. Program, 1985-86. Vol. Mich. Cancer Soc., East Lansing, 1970-72, Big Sisters/Big Bros., Lansing, 1972-73; elected rep. Mich. Coun. Social Svcs. Workers; spkr. Triumphant Bapt. Ch., Detroit, 1976-80; chief union steward Mich. Employees Assn., Lincoln Park, 1982-83; leader Girl Scouts U.S.; area capt. Life Worker Project Program; bd. dirs. Neighborhood Found., 1995-97. Wayne State U. scholar, 1990-91, Deans scholar, 1991-92; recipient Outstanding Work Performace Merit award Mich. Dept. Social Svcs., 1979, Unsung Hero award Neighborhood Found., 1995; elected to Wayne State Sch. Social Work Bd., 1992-98. Mem. NAFE, Am. Soc. Profl. and Exec. Women, Assn. Internat. Platform Spkrs., Mich. Coun. Social Svcs. Workers, Nat. Fedn. Bus. and Profl. Womens Clubs Inc. U.S.A. (elected del. to China), Nat. Assn. Black Social Workers, Wayne State U. Social Work Alumni Assn. (bd. dirs. 1992-98), Delta Sigma Theta. Democrat. Baptist. Office: PO Box 361 Lincoln Park MI 48146-0361

RUSSELL, HELEN DIANE, retired museum curator, educator; b. Kansas City, Mo., Apr. 8, 1936; d. Harry Fay Russell and Georgia Mae (Canfield) Haeberle. AB, Vassar Coll., 1958; PhD, Johns Hopkins U., 1970; postgrad., Inst. for Advanced Study, Princeton, N.J., 1980-81. Mus. curator Nat. Gallery Art, Washington, 1964-90, curator of Old Master Prints, 1990-98. Professorial lectr. The Am. U., Washington, 1966-82, adj. prof. Art History, 1982—. Author: Rare Etchings of G.B. and G.D. Tiepolo, 1972, Jacques Callot, 1975, Claude Lorrain, 1982 (Barr award 1984), EVA/AVE: Woman in Renaissance and Baroque Prints, 1990. Woodrow Wilson Foun. fellow, 1958-59; Univ. fellow, Johns Hopkins U., 1961-63; Kress Found. fellow, 1973; Nat. Endowment for Arts fellow, 1980-81. Mem. Coll. Art Assn., Renaissance Soc. Am., Print Coun. Am., Vassar Club. Avocations: poodles, photography.

RUSSELL, HENRY GEORGE, structural engineer; b. Tewkesbury, Eng., June 12, 1941; came to U.S., 1968. BE, Sheffield U., Eng., 1962, PhD, 1965. Registered structural engr., Ill.; registered profl. engr., Wash., Minn. Rsch. fellow Bldg. Rsch., Eng., 1965-68; structural engr. Constrn. Tech. Labs., Inc. (formerly Portland Cement Assn.), Skokie, Ill., 1968-74, mgr., 1974-79, dir., 1979-88, pres., 1989-91, v.p. 1991-94; v.p. Henry G. Russell, Inc., Glenview, Ill., 1994-95. Contbr. articles to profl. jours. Named one Those Who Made Marks in 1992, Engring. News Record. Fellow Am. Concrete Inst. (Delmar L. Bloem award 1986, Wason medal 1992, Anderson award 1994); mem. Prestressed Concrete Inst. (Martin P. Korn award 1980). Office: 720 Coronet Rd Glenview IL 60025-4457

RUSSELL, HERMAN JEROME, retired real estate developer company executive; b. Atlanta, Dec. 23, 1930; s. Rogers and Maggie (Goodson) R.; m. Otelia Hackney, Aug. 18, 1956; children: Donata C., Jerome, Michael. Student, Tuskegee Inst., 1949-53. CEO H.J. Russell & Co., Atlanta, 1952—2003, chmn. bd., 1952—; chmn. bd., chief exec. officer Concessions Internat. Inc., Los Angeles, 1959—. Bd. dirs. Citizens Trust Co. Bank, Atlanta (chmn.), Ga. Power Co., Wachovia Corp., Ga. Ports Authority. Bd. dirs. Butler St. YMCA, Tuskegee U., Atlanta C. of C.; trustee Morris Brown Coll., Atlanta; nat. adv. bd. Ga. Inst. Tech., Ga. State U. Coll. Bus. Adminstrn. Recipient Meritorious Alumni award Tuskegee Inst. Alumni Assn., 1967, Black Enterprise mag. ann. achievement award, 1978, Top Hat award New Pittsburg Courier, 1980, award for outstanding achievement in breaking new ground on road to democracy in housing Nat. Assn. Real Estate Brokers, 1980, Disting. Humanitarian award Nat. Jewish Ctr. for Immunology and Respiratory Medicine, 1986, Chief Exec. Officer of Yr. award Atlanta Bus. League, 1986, Tree of Life award Jewish Nat. Fund, 1985, Bus. and Youth award Jr. Achievement, 1979, Nat. Alumni award Tuskegee U., 1968, Equal Opportunity Day award Atlanta Urban League, 1972; Drum Major for Justice award in Bus. Ga. State U. Coll. Bus. Adminstrn., 1982; named to Pres.'s Club, Morehouse Sch. Medicine, 1986, Nat. Black Coll. Alumni Hall of Fame, 1986, Bus. Hall of Fame, Ga. State U. Coll. of Bus. Adminstrn., 1985, Entrepreneurs Hall of Fame, Atlanta U. Sch. Bus., 1982, Dow Jones Entrepreneurial Excellence award Dow Jones & Co. Inc. and Wall Street Journal, 1992, Atlanta Bus. Hall of Fame award Junior Achievement, 1992, Horatio Alger award, Horatio Alger Assn. Am., Entrepreneur of Yr. award Nat. Black and Ga. MBA assn., 1991. Mem. Atlanta C. of C. (bd. dirs., past pres. 1981), U.S. C. of C., NAACP (life), Cen. Atlanta Progress, Atlanta Commerce Club, Atlanta Action Forum, Phi Beta Sigma. Mem. Methodist Episcopal Ch. Office: H J Russell & Co 504 Fair St SW Atlanta GA 30313-1299

RUSSELL, HORACE ORLANDO, theology studies educator; b. Clarendon, Jamaica, Nov. 3, 1929; Came to the U.S., 1988; s. Cleveland Augustus and Rowena Nerissa (Gordon) R.; m. Beryl Joyce Redman, Aug. 31, 1957; children: Elisabeth Jennifer, Jonathan Paul Carey, Heather Dawn Marie. BD, Calabar Theological Coll., London, 1954; BA, St. Catherine Coll., Oxford, 1957; PhD, Regent's Park Coll., Oxford, 1972. Ordained Baptist min. Febr. 10, 1958. Prof. church history United Theol. Coll. W.I., U. W.I., Jamaica, 1958-76, pres., 1972-76; sr. pastor East Queen, Kingston Jamaica Bapt. Union, 1976-89; dean of chapel, prof. hist. theology Ea. Bapt. Theol. Sem., Phila., 1989—. Mem. faith and order commn. World Coun. of Ch., Geneva, Switzerland, 1968-90, world assoc. of Christian commn., London, 1969—; v.p. Jamaica Baptist Union, 1980; vice moderator Faith and Order Commr. World Coun. Ch., 1986-90. Author: Five Words of Love, 1982, The Baptist Witness, 1983, Foundations and Anticipations-The Baptist Story in Jamaica 1783-1892, 1993, Jamaica Mission W.I. to West Africa, 1999; founder, editor: Carribean Jour. of Religious Studies, 1966. Mem. nat. commn. on unemployment Govt. of Jamaica, 1969, mem. pub. svc. commn., 1980-88, mem. nat. commn. on drug abuse, 1984-89, chair nat. heritage trust, 1988-89, cultural devel. commn. 1987-88. Recipient Jamaica Prime Minister's medal Jamaican Govt., 1984, Marcus Garvey medal Marcus Garvey Internat., 1984, Jamaica Council of Churches award Churches of Jamaica, 1986. Mem. Am. Soc. of Ch. History, West Indies Group of Univ. Tchrs., Soc. for the Study of Black Religion, Hist. Soc. of Great Britain, Univ. Lodge English Masons (chaplain 1970), Oxford Soc. Baptist. Avocations: photography, creative writing. Home: 1030 E Lancaster Ave Bryn Mawr PA 19010 Office: Ea Baptist Theological Seminary 6 E Lancaster Ave Wynnewood PA 19096-3430 E-mail: horussell@aol.com., horussell@ebts.edu.

RUSSELL, IRWIN EMANUEL, lawyer; b. N.Y.C., Jan. 24, 1926; m. Suzanne Russell, Nov. 15, 1968. BS in Econs., U. Pa., 1947; JD, Harvard U., 1949. Bar: N.Y. 1949, Calif. 1971. Atty. office chief counsel Wage Stabilization Bd., Washington, 1951-53; pvt. practice N.Y.C., 1954-71; founder, chmn., dir. RAI Rsch. Corp., Hauppage, N.Y., 1954-91; exec. v.p., treas., dir. The Wolper Orgn., Inc., L.A., 1971-76; pvt. practice Beverly Hills, Calif., 1977—; bd. dirs. The Walt Disney Co., 1987—2001. With USAAF, 1944-45. Home: 10590 Wilshire Blvd Apt 1402 Los Angeles CA 90024-4563 Office: 9401 Wilshire Blvd Ste 760 Beverly Hills CA 90212-2933 Office Phone: 310-777-3630. Business E-Mail: ierussell@pacbell.net.

RUSSELL, JAMES ALVIN, JR., college administrator; b. Lawrenceville, Va., Dec. 25, 1917; s. Dr. James Alvin and Nellie M. (Pratt) R.; m. Lottye J. Washington, Dec. 25, 1943; children: Charlotte Justyne, James Alvin III. BA, Oberlin Coll., 1940; BS, Bradley U., 1941, MS, 1950, spl. insts.; EdD, U. Md., 1967; spl. insts., Wayne U., U. Mich., U. Ill., NSF. Prof., dir. div. engring., also prof. edn. div. grad. studies Hampton Inst., 1950-71; pres. St. Paul's Coll., Lawrenceville, 1971-81; dir. instructional programs and student services Va. C.C. System, 1981-82; chmn. div. profl. studies W.Va. State Coll., 1982-86, acting pres., 1986-87, exec. asst. to pres., 1987-88; pres. So. W.Va. C.C., 1988-89, ret., 1989. Pres. Peninsula Council Human Relations, 1961-65. United Negro Coll. Fund fellow, 1966-67. Mem. IEEE, Am. Soc. Engring. Edn., Am. Assn. Univ. Adminstrs., Am. Vocat. Assn., Am. Tech. Edn. Assn., Nat. Assn. Indsl. Tech., Am. Assn. for Higher Edn., Nat. Assn. for Equal Opportunity in Edn., Brunswick C. of C., Sigma Pi Phi, Alpha Kappa Mu, Iota Lambda Sigma, Omega Psi Phi. Home: 811 Grandview Dr Dunbar WV 25064-1175

RUSSELL, JAMES FRANKLIN, lawyer; b. Memphis, Mar. 21, 1945; s. Frank Hall and Helen (Brunson) R.; m. Marilyn Land, June 1, 1968 (div. May 1976); children: Mary Helen, Myles Edward; m. Linda Hatcher, July 9, 1977; 1 child, Maggie Abele. BA, Rhodes Coll., 1967; JD, Memphis State U., 1970. Bar: Tenn. 1971, U.S. Dist. Ct. (we. dist.) Tenn. 1971, U.S. Ct. Appeals (6th cir.) 1971, U.S. Dist. Ct. (no. dist.) Miss. 1976, U.S. Ct. Appeals (5th cir.) 1977, U.S. Ct. Appeals (8th cir.) 1987. Assoc. Nelson, Norvell, Wilson, McRae, Ivy & Sevier, Memphis, 1971-75; ptnr. Stanton, Russell & Challen, Memphis, 1975-78, Russell, Price, Weatherford & Warlick, Memphis, 1978-82, Price, Vance & Criss, Memphis, 1982-85, Apperson, Crump, Duzane & Maxwell, Memphis, 1985-97, 1985-97; cir. ct. judge Divsn. II 30th Jud. Dist., 1997—. V.p. mid-south chpt. Am. Red Cross, Memphis, 1992-94; treas. Epilepsy Found. West Tenn., Memphis, 1992-94. Mem. ABA, Nat. Assn. R.R. Trial Counsel, Internat. Assn. Def. Counsel, Tenn. Bar Assn., Tenn. Def. Lawyers Assn., Memphis Bar Assn. (pres. 1992). Episcopalian. Avocations: golf, skiing. Home: 1045 Reid Hooker N Eads TN 38028-6958 Office: Shelby County Courthouse 140 Adams Ave Memphis TN 38103-2000

RUSSELL, JAMES WEBSTER, JR., newspaper editor, columnist; b. Shreveport, La., Nov. 30, 1921; s. James Webster and Aline (Faulk) R.; m. Jean Buck, June 29, 1949; children: Nancy Russell Dearr, Eileen Russell Goure. BA, La. State U., 1942. Fla. mgr. Internat. News Service, 1946-51; bur. chief UPI, Tallahassee, 1951-52; regional editor U.P.I., Atlanta, 1953-57; asst. city editor Miami (Fla.) Herald, 1957-58, bus.-fin. editor, 1958-74, fin.-econ. columnist, 1974—99. Guest lectr. U. Miami, Fla. Internat. U., Miami-Dade Community Coll., La. State U. Contbr. articles to: Fla. Trend, Times of London, N.Y. Times, Gentlemen's Quar. Trustee Fla. So. Coll. Served with USAAF, 1942-45. Recipient Eagle award Invest-in-Am. Nat. Coun., 1976; decorated Air medal with eleven oak leaf clusters; inducted La. State U. Sch. of Mass Comms. Hall of Fame, 1998. Mem. Soc. Am. Bus. Writers, Lambda Chi Alpha, Sigma Delta Chi. Republican. Methodist (chmn. ch. council on ministries 1971-72). Home: 4800 SW 64th Ct Miami FL 33155-6133

RUSSELL, JAMES WILLIAM, neurologist, neuroscientist, electrophysiologist; b. Salisbury, Rhodesia, Jan. 1, 1960; s. William and Olive Russell; m. Jane, Nov. 3, 1990; 3 children. Student, U. Oxford, Eng., 1982-83; MB, ChB, U. Rhodesia, 1984; postgrad., Mayo Clinic, Rochester, Minn., 1991-93; MS, U. Mich., 2001. Diplomate in neurology and electrodiagnostic medicine Am. Bd. Am. Bd. Psychiatry and Neurology; diplomate Am. Bd. Electrodiagnostic Medicine; lic. physician, Iowa, Mich.; fellow Royal Coll. of Physicians, 2003. Intern in medicine and surgery U. Hosps. and Coll. Medicine U. Rhodesia, Salisbury, 1984-85; resident in internal medicine U. Hosps. and Coll. Medicine U. Zimbabwe, 1985-86; resident in internal medicine Pembury and Lewisham Hosps., London, 1986-88, S.E. Thames Regional Neurology Ctr., Brook Hosp., London, 1986-88; resident in neurology U. Iowa Coll. Medicine and Univ. Hosps., Iowa City, 1988-91; rsch. fellow in neurosci. Mayo Postgrad. Med. Sch., Rochester, Minn., 1991-92; clin. peripheral nerve fellow Mayo Clinic, Rochester, 1992-93; clin. assoc. in electrophysiology and neuromuscular disease Nat. Insts. Neurologic Diseases and Stroke/NIH, Bethesda, Md., 1993-95; instr. residents and fellow dept. neurology U. Mich., Ann Arbor, 1995—, assoc. prof., 2003—; assoc. chief neurology Ann Arbor VA Med. Ctr., 1997—. Lectr. med. student neurology rotation U. Iowa Coll. Medicine, 1989—91, lectr., organizer neurology residents' confs., 1988—91, lectr. phys. therapists grad. courses, 1989—91, mem. quality assurance com., 1989—91; organizer, presenter confs. Peripheral Nerve Ctr., electromyography residents and fellows Mayo Clinic, 1991—93, lectr. neurology grand rounds and postgrad. neurosci., 1991—93; lectr. electrophysiology and neuromuscular confs. Nat. Inst. Neurologic Diseases and Stroke, NIH, 1993—95, assoc., 1993—95, instr. electrophysiology and neuromuscular disease fellows and residents, 1994—; spkr. numerous confs. in field; cons. NIH Intramural Program, 1996; grant reviewer NIH FDA Orphan Products Divsn., 1996—; grant reviewer Am. Diabetes Assn., 2002—, Juvenile Diabetes Rsch. Found., 2001—, NIH, 2002—, VA, 2004—; dir. Ann Arbor VAMC Neurology Electrophysiology Lab.; assoc. prof. U. Mich., 2003; grant reviewer Veteran's Adminstrn., 2004—. Contbr. numerous articles to profl. publs., confs.; ad hoc reviewer for neurology (Jour. AMA, diabetes and neurosci. jours.). Grantee NIH, Juvenile Diabetes Rsch. Found., VA. Fellow: Am. Acad. Electro-Diagnostic Medicine, Royal Coll. Physicians (London); mem.: Endocrine Soc., Am. Soc. Cell Biology, Soc. Neurosci., Am. Acad. Electrodiagnostic Medicine, Peripheral Nerve Soc., Am. Autonomic Soc., Juvenile Diabetes Rsch. Found., Am. Diabetes Assn., Am. Acad. Neurology, Royal Coll. Physicians (Edinburgh and Glasgow). Evangelical. Avocations: golf, equestrian activities. Office: U Mich 4410 Kresge III 200 Zina Pitcher Pl Ann Arbor MI 48109-2205 E-mail: jruss@umich.edu.

RUSSELL, JEFFREY BURTON, historian, educator; b. Fresno, Calif., Aug. 1, 1934; s. Lewis Henry and Ieda Velma (Ogborn) R.; m. Diana Emily Mansfield, June 30, 1956; children: Jennifer, Mark, William, Penelope. AB, U. Calif., Berkeley, 1955, A.M., 1957; PhD, Emory U., 1960. Asst. prof. U. N.Mex., Albuquerque, 1960-61; jr. fellow Soc. of Fellows, Harvard U., Cambridge, Mass., 1961-62; mem. faculty U. Calif., Riverside, 1962-75, prof. dept. history, 1969-75, assoc. dean grad. div., 1967-72; dir. Medieval Inst.; Michael P. Grace prof. medieval studies U. Notre Dame, South Bend, Ind., 1975-77; dean grad. studies Calif. State U., Sacramento, 1977-79; prof. history U. Calif., Santa Barbara, 1979—, prof. religious studies, 1994—. Author: Dissent and Reform in the Early Middle Ages, 1965, Medieval Civilization, 1968, A History of Medieval Christianity: Prophecy and Order, 1968, Religious Dissent in the Middle Ages, 1971, Witchcraft in the Middle Ages, 1972, The Devil: Perceptions of Evil from Antiquity to Primitive Christianity, 1977, A History of Witchcraft: Sorcerers, Heretics, and Pagans, 1980, Medieval Heresies: a Bibliography, 1981, Satan: The Early Christian Tradition, 1981, Lucifer: The Devil in the Middle Ages, 1984, Mephistopheles: The Devil in the Modern World, 1986, The Prince of Darkness, 1988, Ruga in Aevis, 1990, Inventing the Flat Earth: Columbus and the Historians, 1991, Dissent and Order in the Middle Ages, 1992, A History of Heaven: The Singing Silence, 1997, Essays in Honor of Jeffrey B. Russell, 1998; contbr. articles in field to profl. jours. Fulbright fellow, 1959-60; Am. Council Learned Socs. grantee, 1965, 70; Social Sci. Research Council grantee, 1968; Guggenheim fellow, 1968-69; Nat. Endowment for Humanities sr. fellow, 1972-73 Fellow Medieval Acad. Am.; mem. Medieval Assn. Pacific, Am. Soc. Ch. Histor Am. Acad. Religion, Astron. Soc. Pacific, Sierra Club. Home: 4798 Calle Camarada Santa Barbara CA 93110-2053 Office: U Calif Dept History Santa Barbara CA 93106 E-mail: russell@history.ucsb.edu.

RUSSELL, JESSE E. communications executive; b. Nashville, Apr. 26, 1948; married; 4 children. BSEE, Tenn. State U., 1972; MSEE, Stanford U., 1973. Mem. tech. staff AT&T Bell Labs., 1972-78, supr. spl. svc. circuit design group, 1978-81, head network performance objectives dept., 1981-82, head integrated loop systems design dept., 1982-84, head cellular base sta. software design dept., 1984-86; dir. cellular telecomm. lab. AT&T, 1986-88, dir. cellular transmission lab., 1988-91, chief tech. officer network wireless systems bus. unit, 1991-92, v.p. advanced wireless tech. lab., 1991-92, chief wireless architect, 1992-95; v.p. advanced comm. lab. AT&T Labs., Florham Park, N.J., 1996—. Mng. dir. AT&T Wireless Comm. Ctr. of Excellence, 1992-95; vice gen. chmn. Internat. Universal Personal Comm. Conf., San Diego, 1994; spkr. Rural Telecomm. Assn., Arizona/Mex. Telecomm. Conf., 1995, Nat. Comm. Forum, 1995, European Commn., Spain, 1995. Contbr. articles to profl. jours.; patentee in field. Named. U.S. Black Engr. of Yr. for Best Contbns. in Digital Cellular and Microcellular Tech., U.S. Black Engr. Mag., 1992; recipient Am.'s New Leadership Class award Esquire Mag., 1985, Outstanding Scientist award Nat. Soc. Black Engrs., 1982, Sci. of Yr. award Nat. Tech. Assns. Inc., 1980. Fellow IEEE (cert. appreciation Balt. sect. 1982, bd. govs. vehicular tech. soc., chmn. tech. program 38th Vehicular Tech. Conf. 1988, 43d Vhicular Tech. Conf. 1993); mem. Nat. Acad. Engring. (electronic engring. sec., computer sci. and engring. sect.), Telecomm. Industry Assn. (chmn. cellular radio and common carrier sect. 1987-92, chmn. mobile and personal comm. divsn., assoc. bd. dirs.), Electromagnetic Energy Assn. (chmn. bd. dirs.), Am. Mgmt. Assn. (info. tech. coun.), Tau Beta Pi, Eta Kappa Nu (Outstanding Svc. award 1983, Outstanding Young Elec. Engr. of Yr. 1980). Home: 2 Thames Ave Piscataway NJ 08854-5229 Office: AT&T Labs 180 Park Ave Florham Park NJ 07932-1004

RUSSELL, JOHN FRANCIS, retired librarian; b. Mt. Carmel, Ind., Apr. 30, 1929; s. David Freeman and Bertha (Major) R.; m. Edith Raymond Hyde, June 27, 1953; 1 child, Anne Marie. BA, DePauw U., 1951; postgrad., Ind. U., 1951-52; MA, Johns Hopkins U., 1954; student, Cath. U. Am., summer 1955; MS, Grad. Sch. Libr. Sci./Drexel, U., 1977. Tchr. English Park Sch. Balt., 1954-75, chmn. dept., 1957-75; tchr. speech, dir. Ira Aldridge Players Morgan State Coll., fall 1965-66; tchr. drama Loyola Coll., 1964, 66. Editor: The Secondary School Theatre, 1972-74. Pres. Tchrs.'s Assn. Ind. Sch. Balt. Area, 1960-62, adv. bd., 1966-67, chmn. com. on English, 1966-68; exec. com. Assn. Ind. Md. Sch., 1967-68; dir., costumer Johns Hopkins U. Playshop, 1963-64; lectr. Lecture Group, Woman's Club Roland Park, others, 1964—; bd. dirs. Balt. area coun. World Federalists U.S.A., 1961-67, vice chmn., 1964-67, nat. exec. coun., 1963-65; bd. dirs. Ctr. Stage, 1964-77; dir. Blvd. Players, pres., 1960-67; dir. Pasadena Little Theatre, v.p., 1979-83, pres., 1983-85, 2d v.p., 1990—; dir. Center Stage Players, New Image Theatre, Theatre Network of Houston, U.S.A. Theatre, Actors Conservatory Tex., v.p., 1990-91, Glenbrook United Meth. Ch. Drama Ministry; bd. dirs. Unicorn Sch. Acting, 1996—, v.p., 1997—; adv. com. Am. H.S. Theatre Festival, 1975; mem. adminstrv. bd. St. Mark's United Meth. Ch., 1957-67, Towson United Meth. Ch., 1967-77, First United Meth. Ch., Houston, 1980-89; adminstrv. coun., vice-chmn. Glenbrook United Meth. Ch., 1997, chmn. pastor-parish rels. com., 1998, lay del., 1999, 2000, lay leader 1999—; sec. Festival Angels, 1982-2001 (Outstanding Svc. award 1991); cmty. vol. svcs. com., ARC, 1985-90; comprehensive volunteerism adv. com., Sheltering Arms, 1986-89. Recipient Nat. Citation of Merit Am. Shakespeare Festival, 1961, Theatre Goddess award U.S.A. Theatre, 1998, Critics Choice award Houston Post, 1984; certs. of appreciation Sheltering Arms, 1986-89, cert. of recognition, 1988. Mem. Am. Assn. Cmty. Theatre, Harris County Heritage Soc., Am. Film Inst., Drama League, Am. Theatre Assn. (v.p. Mid-Atlantic dist. 1967-68, pres. 1968-69, nat. dir. 1970-73, Mid-Atlantic chpt. award for achievement and contbn. to theatre 1973), Secondary Sch. Theatre Assn. (v.p. devel. 1974-75), Tex. Non-Profit Theatre, Nat. (bd. dirs. 1969), Md. Coun. Tchrs. English (pres. 1969-70), Capital Area Media Educators Orgn. (exec. com. 1970-73, screening chmn. 1971-73), ALA, Tex. Libr. Assn. (audiovisual chmn. conv. planning com. 1981), Coun. Info. and Referral Svcs. (newsletter editor 1984-86), Tex. Alliance Info. and Referral Svcs. (conv. speaker 1981, 83, 84, 85), Alliance of Info. and Referral Svcs. (conv. speaker 1985), Houston Pub. Libr. Staff Assn. (pres. 1981-82), Literacy Vols. Am. (sec. Houston 1984-87, adv. bd. 1989-91, 95-96, bd. dirs. 1992-95, chmn. program com. 1991-93), Reading, Edn. and Devel. Coun. (recruitment chmn., exec. com. 1984-86), Cultural Arts Coun. of Houston/Harris County, Park Pl. Civic Club (exemplary svc. award 1991), AARP (bd. dirs. chpt. 1172 1998—, v.p. 1999-2000, 01-02, pres. 2003—), Phi Beta Kappa, Phi Eta Sigma, Beta Phi Mu. Home: 7817 Grove Ridge Dr Houston TX 77061-1405 E-mail: jrussell10@houston.rr.com.

RUSSELL, JOHN JOSEPH, English educator; b. Orange, N.J., Dec. 4, 1949; s. James Francis and Catherine Mary Russell. BA, Seton Hall U., 1973; MA, U. Chgo., 1979, Seton Hall U., 1982; PhD, Fordham U., 1991. Assoc. prof. English Union County Coll., Cranford, NJ, 1987—. Author: (book) Hamlet and Narcissus, 1995. Office: Union County Coll 1033 Springfield Ave Cranford NJ 07016 E-mail: russell@ucc.edu.

RUSSELL, JOHN S. contract research organization executive; b. 1954; BA, U. N.C., 1977; MA, Columbia U., 1978; JD, Harvard U., 1985. Editor trade books dept. Houghton Mifflin Co., N.Y.C., 1978—82; atty. Reasearch Triangle Park, NC, 1986—98; exec. v.p., gen. counsel, sec. Quintiles Transnational, Research Triangle Park, NC, 1998—. Author: Favorite Sons, 1992 (Sir Walter Raleigh award for fiction, 1993). Chmn. Opera Co. N.C. Office: Quintiles Transnational Riverbirch Bldg PO Box 13979 4709 Creekstone Dr Ste 200 Research Triangle Park NC 27709

RUSSELL, JOSEPH ALLEN, instrumentation and controls engineer, consultant; b. Lompoc, Calif. s. Clark Earl and Nanice Mercedis (Poett) Russell; m. Nancy Bolson, July 3, 1971 (div. 1981); children: Elizabeth, Rosalind; m. Reevah Simon, July 18, 1999. Student, Allen Hancoc Coll., Santa Maria, Calif., 1968-70, Calif. Polytechnic Inst., San Luis Obispo, Calif., 1970-71. Registered profl. engr., Calif. Electro optical engr. Electro Optical Industries, Santa Barbara, Calif., 1971-73; designer, field engr. Stearns/Roger, Denver, 1973-74; instrumentation and controls engr. C.F. Braun, Alhambra, Calif., 1974-76; technician, supr. S.C.E., Rosemead, Calif., 1976-84, constrn. supt., 1984-85; project mgr. De La Guerra Power, Santa Barbara, 1985-87; sys. engr. Fairfield Energy, Ft. Fairfield, 1988; project engr. G.W.F. Power Sys., Walnut Creek, Calif., 1989-92; chief telescope engr. Mt. Wilson Obs., Pasadena, Calif., 1992—2003. Tech. expert for profl. engring. test Price & Assocs., Pomona, Calif., 1991. Candidate state sen. Libertarian Party, West L.A., 1985. Achievements include patent for storage ring fusion energy generator. Office: De La Guerra Power Inc PO Box 41955 Los Angeles CA 90041-0955

RUSSELL, JOYCE ANNE ROGERS, librarian; b. Chgo., Nov. 6, 1920; d. Truman Allen and Mary Louise (Hoelzle) Rogers; m. John VanCleve Russell, Dec. 24, 1942; children: Malcolm David, John VanCleve. Student, Adelphi Coll., 1937; BS in Chemistry, U. Ky., 1942; M.L.S., Rosary Coll., 1967; postgrad., Rutgers U., 1970-71. Research chemist Sherwin Williams Paint Co., Chgo., 1942-45; reference librarian Chicago Heights (Ill.) Pub. Library, 1959-61; librarian Victor Chem. Works, Chicago Heights, 1961-62; lit. chemist Velsicol Chem. Corp., Chgo., 1964-67; chemistry librarian U. Fla., Gainesville, 1967-69, interim assoc. prof., 1967-69; librarian Thiokol Chem. Corp., Trenton, N.J., 1969-73; supr. library operations E.R. Squibb Co., Princeton, N.J., 1973-80, sr. research info scientist, 1980-91. Mem. library adv. commn. Mercer Community Coll., 1979—; adv. asso. Rutgers U. Grad. Sch. Library and Info. Scis., 1978— Editor: Bibliofile, 1967-69; contbr. articles to profl. jours. Mem. PTA, 1950-66; den mother Cub Scouts, 1952-59. Mem. Spl. Libraries Assn. (sec., dir., v.p., pres. Princeton-Trenton 1971, 75-80), Am. Chem. Soc. (bus. mgr., sec., dir. Trenton sect. 1969-78), AAUW, Mortar Board, Beta Phi Mu, Sigma Pi Sigma, Chi Delta Phi, Pi Sigma Alpha. Home: 1189 Parkside Ave Trenton NJ 08618-2625

RUSSELL, JUDY C. government agency administrator; children: Christopher, Michael, Catherine. BA cum laude, Dunbarton Coll. of the Holy Cross, Washington; MLIS, Cath. U. Am., Washington. Libr. Office of Tech. Assessment; staff mem. program of policy studies in sci. and tech. George Washington U., Washington; staff mem. COMSAT Labs.; dir. fed. depository libr. program Govt. Printing Office, Washington, dir. office of electronic info. svcs., 1991—96, supt. documents 2003—; dir. govt. svcs. divsn. IDD Ent., 1996—98; dep. dir. Nat. Commn. on Librs. and Info. Scis., 1998—2003. Cons. in field. Recipient Spl. award, Fed. Computer Week's Fed. 100: The Readers' Choice awards, 1993. Office: Govt Printing Office 732 N Capitol St NW Washington DC 20401

RUSSELL, KENNETH CALVIN, metallurgical engineer, educator; b. Greeley, Colo., Feb. 4, 1936; s. Doyle James and Jennie Frances (Smith) R.; m. Charlotte Louise Wolf, Apr. 13, 1963 (div. 1978); children: David Allan, Doyle John. Met.E., Colo. Sch. Mines, 1959; PhD, Carnegie Inst. Tec., 1963. Engr. Westinghouse Rsch. and Devel. Ctr., 1959-61; NSF postdoctoral fellow Physics Inst., U. Oslo, 1963-64; asst. prof. metallurgy M.I.T., Cambridge, 1964-69, assoc. prof., 1969-78, prof. metallurgy, 1978—, prof. nuc. engring., 1979—. Contbr. articles to profl. publs. Served as 2d lt. U.S. Army, 1959-60. DuPont fellow, 1961-62; NSF fellow, 1962-63 Mem.: Metallurgical Soc. Am. Inst. Mining, Metallurgical and Petroleum Engrs., Am. Phys. Soc. Office: MIT Rm 13-5050 Cambridge MA 02139 E-mail: kenruss@mit.edu.

RUSSELL, KERI, actress; b. Fountain Valley, Calif., Mar. 23, 1976; Actress in films: Honey, I Blew Up the Kid, 1992, The Curve, 1998, Mad About Mambo, 1999, We Were Soldiers, 2002; TV series include: MMC, 1989, Mickey Mouse Club, 1991-93, Emerald Cove, 1993, Daddy's Girls, 1994, Malibu Shores, 1996, Roar, 1997, Felicity, 1998-2002; TV films include: MMC in Concert, 1993, The Babysitter's Seduction, 1995, The Lottery, 1996, When Innocence is Lost, 1997, Eight Days a Week, 1997, Cinderelmo, 1999; TV guest appearances include: Boy Meets World, 1993, Married...with Children, 1987, 7th Heaven, 1996. Winner Golden Globe for best performance by an actress in a TV series for Felicity, 1999. Office: The Gersh Agy 232 N Canon Dr Beverly Hills CA 90210-5302

RUSSELL, KURT VON VOGEL, actor; b. Springfield, Mass., Mar. 17, 1951; s. Bing Oliver and Louise Julia (Crone) R.; m. Season Hubley, Mar. 17, 1979 (div.), 1 son, Boston; 1 son (with Goldie Hawn), Wyatt Russell. Student, pub. schs. Profl. baseball player, 1971-73. Actor in numerous films including The Absent Minded Professor, 1961, It Happened at the World's Fair, 1963, Follow Me Boys, 1966, The One and Only Genuine Original Family Band, 1968, The Horse in the Grey Flannel Suit, 1968. The Computer Wore Tennis Shoes, 1970, The Barefoot Executive, 1971, Fools' Parade, 1971, Now You See Him Now You Don't, 1972, Charley and the Angel, 1972, Superdad, 1974, The Strongest Man in the World, 1975, Used Cars, 1980, Escape from New York, 1981, The Thing, 1982, Silkwood, 1983, Swing Shift, 1984, The Mean Season, 1985, The Best of Times, 1986, Big Trouble in Little China, 1986, Overboard, 1987, The Winter People, 1988, Tequila Sunrise, 1988, Winter People, 1989, Tango and Cash, 1989, Backdraft, 1991, Unlawful Entry, 1992,

Captain Ron, 1992, Tombstone, 1993, Stargate, 1994, Executive Decision, 1996, Escape from L.A., 1996 (also writer, producer), Breakdown, 1997, Soldier, 1998, 3000 Miles To Graceland, 2001, Vanilla Sky, 2001, Dark Blue, 2002, Miracle, 2004; TV series include Travels with Jamie McPheeters, 1963-64, The New Land, 1974, The Quest, 1976; TV movies include Search for the Gods, 1975, The Deadly Tower, The Quest (pilot), 1975, Christmas Miracle in Caulfield USA, 1977, Elvis, 1979, Amber Waves, 1988; TV guest appearences include The Fugitive, Daniel Boone, Gilligan's Island, Lost in Space, The FBI, Love American Style, Gunsmoke, Hawaii Five-O. Served with Calif. Air N.G. Recipient numerous auto racing trophies, 10 baseball awards, 5 acting awards, 1 golf championship. Mem. Profl. Baseball Players Assn., Stuntman's Assn. Achievements include being the World championship Class Modified Stock, 1959 Race of Champions, Las Vegas. Office: Creative Artists Agy 9830 Wilshire Blvd Beverly Hills CA 90212-1825

RUSSELL, LIANE BRAUCH, retired geneticist; b. Vienna, Aug. 27, 1923; came to U.S., 1941; d. Arthur and Clara (Starer) Brauch; m. William Lawson Russell (dec.), Sept. 23, 1947; children: David Lawson, Evelyn Ruth. AB, Hunter Coll., 1945; PhD, U. Chgo., 1949; ScD (hon.), Hunter Coll., N.Y.C., 1999. Fellow U. Chgo., 1945-46, teaching asst., 1946-47; rsch. asst. Jackson Lab., Bar Harbor, Maine, 1945, 46; rsch. staff mem. Oak Ridge (Tenn.) Nat. Lab., 1947-75, sect. head., 1975-95, sr. rsch. fellow, 1988—2001; ret., 2002. Sci. advisor U.S. Del. at 1st Atoms for Peace Conf., Geneva, Switzerland, 1955; mem. numerous sci. bds. including Nat. Research Council com. on energy and environment, 1975-77, com. on biol. effects of ionizing radiation, 1977-80, bd. on environ. studies and toxicology, 1981-90, Nat. Council on Radiation Protection and Measurement Task Group, Washington, 1975-77, Genetox Program EPA, Washington, 1979—, Internat. Com. for Protection Against Environ. Mutagens and Carcinogens, Lausanne, Switzerland, 1977-83, Internat. com. on standardized genetic nomenclature for mice, 1977-91, office of tech. assessment, scientific adv. panel, 1985-86; mem. task group Internat. Agy. for Research on Cancer, Hanover, Fed. Republic of Germany, 1979, EPA review panel on mutagenicity guidelines, 1985-86; adj. faculty U. Tenn., 1980-. Assoc. editor Mutation Rsch., 1976-96, Environ. Mutagenesis, 1980-83; editor TCWP Newsletter, 1966—; editor: (book) Genetic Mosaics and Chimeras, 1979; contbr. more than 165 articles to profl. jours. Founder Tenn. Citizens for Wilderness Planning, Oak Ridge, 1966, pres. 1967-70, 86-87; active numerous environ. groups. Corp. fellow Union Carbide, 1983; corp. fellow Martin Marietta, 1985, sr. corp. fellow, 1988; recipient Merit award Mademoiselle, 1955, Roentgen medal City of Remscheid-Lennep, 1973, Disting. Assoc. award U.S. Dept. Energy, 1987; named to Hunter Coll. Hall of Fame, 1979, Sol Feinstone Environ. Achievement award SUNY, 1987, Lifetime Achievement award Tenn. Environ. Coun., 1990, Vocational Svc. award Oak Ridge Rotary, 1992, Marjorie Stoneman Douglas award Nat. Parks Conservation Assn., 1993, Enrico Fermi award U.S. Dept. Energy, 1993, Lifetime Environ. Conservation award Tenn. Dept. Environ. & Conservation, 2000. Fellow AAAS, Environ. Health Inst.; mem. Nat. Acad. Scis., Environ. Mutagen Soc. (pres. 1984-85, EMS award 1993), Genetics Soc. Am., Tenn. Environ. Honor Soc. Avocation: environ. acitivism.

RUSSELL, LOUISE BENNETT, economist, educator; b. Exeter, N.H., May 12, 1942; d. Frederick Dewey and Esther (Smith) B.; m. Robert Hardy Cosgriff, May 3, 1987; 1 child, Benjamin Smith Cosgriff. BA, U. Mich., 1964; PhD, Harvard U., 1971. Economist Social Security Adminstrn., Washington, 1968-71, Nat. Commn. on State Workmen's Compensation Laws, Washington, 1971-72, Dept. Labor, Washington, 1972-73; sr. economist Nat. Planning Assn., Washington, 1973-75; sr. fellow Brookings Instn., Washington, 1975-87; rsch. prof. Inst. for Health, Health Care Policy and Aging Rsch. Rutgers U., New Brunswick, N.J., 1987—, prof. econs., 1987—. Chmn. health care policy divsn. Rutgers U., 1988—. Author: Technology in Hospitals, 1979, The Baby Boom Generation and the Economy, 1982, Is Prevention Better Than Cure, 1986, Evaluating Preventive Care: Report on a Workshop, 1987, Medicare's New Hospital Payment System: Is It Working, 1989, Educated Guesses: Making Policy About Medical Screening Tests, 1994, (with MR Gold, JE Siegel and MC Weinstein) Cost-Effectiveness in Health and Medicine, 1996; also numerous articles. Mem. U.S. Preventive Svcs. Task Force, 1984-88; co-chair Panel on Cost Effectiveness in Health and Medicine DHHS, USPHS, 1993-96. Mem. Inst. Medicine of NAS (com. to study future pub. health 1986-87, bd. on health scis. policy 1989-91, com. on clin. practice guidelines 1990-91, com. on setting priorities for practice guidelines 1994, nat. cancer policy bd. 2001—). Office: Rutgers U Inst for Health Care Policy 30 College Ave New Brunswick NJ 08901-1283

RUSSELL, MARJORIE ROSE, manufacturing executive; b. Welcome, Minn., Sept. 3, 1925; d. Emil Frederick and Ella Magdalene (Sothman) Wohlenhaus; m. Kenneth Kollmann Russell, Sept. 15, 1947 (div. May 1973); children: Jennie Rose, Richard Lowell, Laura Eloise, James Wesley. Student, Northwestern Sch., Mpls., 1944-45, St. Paul Bible Inst., 1946-47. Cook U. Minn., Mpls., 1943-45; maintenance person U. Farm Campus/N.W. Schs., St. Paul, 1945-46; clk. Kresge Corp., Mpls., 1945; cook, waitress, mgr. Union City Mission Bible Camp, Mpls., 1944-47; caterer for v.p. Gt. No. R.R., St. Paul, 1947; custodian Old Soldiers Home, St. Paul, 1946; nurse Sister Elizabeth Kenney Polio Hosp., St. Paul, 1946; seamstress Hirsch, Weis, White Stag, Pendleton, Mayfair, Portland, Oreg., 1960-72; owner, operator, contract mgr., creative designer The Brass Needle, Portland, 1972—. Contractor Forrester's Sanderson Safety, Scotsco, Nero & Assocs., Gara Gear, Portland, 1972—, Columbia Sportswear; tchr. Indo Chinese Cultural Ctr., Portland, 1982; mfr. of protective chaps and vests for the Pacific Northwest hogging industry. Designer, producer Kisn Bridal Fair, 1969; composer: He Liveth in Me, 1968; prodr. Safety Chaps for Loggers. Sec. Model Cities Com., Portland, 1969; com. mem. Neighborhood Black Christmas Parade, Portland, 1970; custume designer Local Miss Jr. Black Beauty Contest, Portland, 1973; nominating com. Nat. Contract Mgmt. Assn., Portland, 1978; mem. nominating com. Multi-Cultural Sr. Adv. Com., 1988-91. Mem. NAFE, Urban League, Urban League Guild (historian 1991-92), Am. Assn. Ret. Persons, Nat. Contract Mgmt. Assn. Democrat. Mem. United Ch. of Christ. Avocations: music, swimming, painting, gardening, arts. Home and Office: The Brass Needle 2809 NE 12th Ave Portland OR 97212-3219

RUSSELL, MARK, comedian; b. Buffalo, Aug. 23, 1932; s. Marcus Joseph and Marie Elizabeth (Perry) Ruslander; m. Alison Kaplan, Dec. 17, 1978; children: Monica, John, Matthew. Student, George Washington U., 1952; LittD, Union Coll., 1987; LHD, Canisius Coll., 1988, Goucher Coll., 1990; LLD (hon.), D'Youville Coll., 2004. Lectr., public speaker. Polit. comedian, featured performer Shoreham Hotel, Washington, 1961-81; prin. Mark Russell Comedy Spls., Pub. Broadcasting Svc., 1975—, Mark Russell's 25th Anniversary Special, 2000 (Silver Telly award 2000); host Mark Russell's England, PBS-TV, 1988, Mark Russell's Irish Fling, 1993, Mark Russell's Great Ala. Trek, 1994, Mark Russell's Tour de France, 1995, Mark Russell's Viva Italia, 1996; co-host NBC's Real People, 1979-84; regular contbr. Good Morning Am., ABC-TV, Inside Politics Weekend, CNN; author: Presenting Mark Russell, 1980; syndicated columnist via Tribune Media Svcs., 1975. Served with USMC, 1953-56. Recipient Mark Twain award Internat. Platform Assn., 1980, 86, 4th Ann. Lucy award Shea's Buffalo, 1992, Nat. Humor Treasure award Nat. Humor Conf., 1995, SOAR St. Elizabeth Ann Seton award Washington, 1995, Washingtonian of the Yr. Washingtonian Mag., 1996, Disting. Washingtonian award Univ. Club, 2001. Mem. AFTRA, Am. Fedn. Musicians. Office: PO Box 9904 Washington DC 20016-8904 Office Phone: 202-362-5045. E-mail: mail@markrussell.net.

RUSSELL, MARLOU, psychologist; b. June 2, 1956; d. William Herman and Carole Eleanor (Musgrove) McBratney; m. Jan Christopher Russell, Sept. 9, 1989. BA, U. Ariz., 1981; MA, Calif. Grad. Inst., 1983, PhD, 1987. Lic. psychologist, marriage, family and child counselor. Asst. to pres. Western Psychol. Svcs., L.A., 1978-81; crisis counselor Cedars-Sinai Med. Ctr., L.A., 1980-84; psychotherapist PMC Treatment Sys., L.A., 1984-85, Beverly Hills Counseling Ctr., 1984-85, Comprehensive Care Corp., L.A., 1985-86; pvt. practice L.A., 1986—. Counselor Brotman Med. Ctr., L.A., 1982-83, Julia Ann Singer Ctr., L.A., 1984; bd. dirs. Los Angeles Commn. Assaults Against Women, 1987-89. Author: Adoption Wisdom: A Guide to the Issues and Feelings of Adoption, 1996; adoptee, reunion expert www.adopting.org, 1999—. Mem. Internat. Assn. Eating Disorders Profls., Women in Health (bd. dirs. 1993-94), Women's Referral Svc., Calif. State Psychol. Assn., Calif. Assn. Marriage & Family Therapists (bd. dirs. 1993-94), Am. Adoption Congress, Westside Bus. Womens Assn. (bd. dirs. 1993-94). Democrat. Office: 1452 26th St Ste 103 Santa Monica CA 90404-3042 Office Phone: 310-829-1438. Personal E-mail: marlourussell@hotmail.com.

RUSSELL, MARY WENDELL VANDER POEL, non-profit organization executive; b. N.Y.C., Feb. 6, 1919; d. William Halsted and Blanche Pauline (Billings) Vander Poel; m. George Montagu Miller, Apr. 5, 1940 (div. 1974); children: Wendell Miller Steavenson, Gretchen Miller Elkus; m. Sinclair Hatch, May 14, 1977 (dec. July 1989); m. William F. Russell, June 24, 1995 (dec. Apr. 1996). Pres. Miller Richard, Inc., Interior Decorators, Oyster Bay, NY, 1972—2000; bd. dirs. Eye Bank Sight Restoration, N.Y.C., pres., 1980-88, hon. chair, 1988—2002; v.p. Manhattan Eye Ear and Throat Hosp., N.Y.C., 1978-90; sec. Cold Spring Harbor Lab., N.Y., 1985-89, 92-97; mem. DNA Learning Ctr. Bd., 1991-97; bd. dirs. DNA Learning Ctr., 1997-2000; sec. Cold Spring Harbor Lab, 1992-97, hon. trustee, 1998—. V.p. North Country Garden Club, Nassau County, N.Y., 1979-81, 1983-85; dir. Planned Parenthood Nassau County, Mineola, N.Y., 1982-84, Hutton House C.W.Post Coll.,Greenvale, N.Y., 1982—; chair Hutton House, 1992-94. Recipient Disting. Trustee award United Hosp. Fund, 1992. Mem. Colony Club (N.Y.C.), Church Club (N.Y.C.), Piping Rock Club (Long Island), Order St. John Jerusalem (N.Y.C.). Republican. Episcopalian. Home: Mill River Rd # 330 Oyster Bay NY 11771-2733 E-mail: ydnewr@aol.com.

RUSSELL, MARYANNE, photographer; Grad., NYU; student, Internat. Ctr. Photography. Staff photographer Time Inc.; owner Maryanne Russell Photography Inc., 1986—. Photographer (works appeared at) Acad. Art Coll., San Francisco, Lobet Gallery, NYC, Grant Gallery, Chelsea Art Gallery, (group exhbns.) Sephora's Flagship store. Mem.: Am. Soc. Media Photographers, NY Women in Comm. (Liz Hoover award 1994). Achievements include photography clients AT&T, Christian Dior, HBO, NY Giants, Paramount Pictures, People mag., Time Warner Inc., Viacom, and many others. Office: Maryanne Russell Photography Inc 230 E 52nd St Ste 1B New York NY 10022 Office Phone: 212-308-8722.

RUSSELL, MICHAEL JAMES, lawyer; Cert. in German, U. Vienna, 1979; BA summa cum laude, Gettysburg Coll., 1980; MA, JD, Vanderbilt U., 1984. Bar: Pa. 1984, DC 1985, U.S. Supreme Ct. 1995. Atty. USDA, Washington, 1984-85; majority counsel subcom. on juvenile justice senate judiciary com. U.S. Senate, Washington, 1985-86, minority gen. counsel subcom. on constn., 1987, legis. dir. to Senator Arlen Specter, 1987-90; senate staff mem. Congrl. Crime Caucus, 1987-90; dep. dir. Nat. Inst. Justice U.S. Dept. Justice, Washington, 1990-93, acting dir., 1993-94; pres. Russell & Assocs., Washington, 1994-96; sr. pub. safety advisor Corp. Nat. Svc., Washington, 1994-96; dep. chief of staff to Senator Ben Nighthorse Campbell, Washington, 1996—2001; dep. asst. sec. for policy and budget (enforcement) U.S. Dept. Treasury, Washington, 2001—03; staff dir. govt. affairs subcom. on fin mgmt., the budget and internat. security U.S. Senate, Washington, 2003—. Office: 446 Hart Senate Office Bldg Washington DC 20510

RUSSELL, NAS'NAGA R. illustrator; b. Dayton, Ohio, Apr. 13, 1941; s. Willard Dudly and Kathryn Louise (Pangborn) R.; m. Harriet Ann Russell, June 1967 (div. 1973); 1 child, Jamie Noelle; m. Barbara Jane Mullins, Sept. 14, 1983. Grad. h.s. Mgr. AAAirlines, Ft. Worth, 1970-74; writer Harper & Rowe, N.Y.C., 1974-75; owner, dir. Art Gallery, Kettering, Ohio, 1979-83. Dir., owner Nas'Naga Enterprises, Inc. Pro., Centerville, Ohio, 1980-83; lectr., spkr. in field. Author, illustrator: Indians' Summer, 1975, Western Writers of America, 1975-1980, Dayton's Society of Painters and Sculptors, 1978-1980, Faces Beneith The Glory, 1979, Darker Side of Glory, 2000; columnist Western Mag., Oslo, Norway, 1976-79; co-author: Poetry Anthology, 2004. Airlines rep. Okla. for Indian Opportunity, Tex., 1970—74; steering com. Newark state mound project Ohio Hist. Soc., 2000. With USN, 1959—63. Recipient Humanitarian Svc. award Oklahomians for Indian Opportunity, Norman, Okla., 1973, United Cerebeal Palsy, Dayton, 1984, Outstanding Artistic Achievement award Green County Ohio, Xenia, 1975. Avocations: archery, painting, research. Home: 3000 B E Main St #359 Columbus OH 43209 Office Phone: 614-270-5938.

RUSSELL, NORMAN J.W. biotechnology company executive; PhD in Physiology, Glasgow U., Scotland. Head biotech. AstraZeneca Pharms., head internat. genomics, head target discovery, head biol. sci. and tech.; pres., CEO, bd. dirs. Lynx Therapeutics, Hayward, Calif., 1999—. Office: Lynx Therapeutics Inc 25861 Industrial Blvd Hayward CA 94545

RUSSELL, PAUL EDGAR, electrical engineering educator; b. Roswell, N.Mex., Oct. 10, 1924; s. Rueben Matthias and Mary (Parsons) R.; m. Lorna Margaret Clayshulte, Aug. 29, 1943; children: Carol Potter, Janice Russell Cook, Gregory. BSEE, N.Mex. State U., 1946, BSME, 1947; MSEE, U. Wis., 1950, PhDEE, 1951. Registered elec. engr., Ariz. From instr. to asst. prof. elec. engring. U. Wis., Madison, 1947-52; sr. engr., design specialist Gen. Dynamics Corp., San Diego, 1952-54; from prof. to chmn. elec. engring. dept. U. Ariz., Tucson, 1954-63; dean engring. Kans. State U., Manhattan, 1963-67; prof. Ariz. State U., Tempe, 1967-90; dir. engring. Ariz. State U. West, Phoenix, 1985-88; dir. Sch. Constrn. and Tech. Ariz. State U., Tempe, 1988-90. Cons. in field, 1954—; programs evaluator, mem. engring. commn. Accreditation Bd. for Engring. and Tech., N.Y.C., 1968-81. Contbr. articles to jours. and chpts. to books. Served as sgt. U.S. Army, 1944-46. Recipient Disting. Service award N.Mex. State U., 1965. Fellow IEEE (life, chmn. Ariz. sect. 1960), Accreditation Bd. Engring. and Tech.; mem. Am. Soc. Engring. Educators. Home: 5902 E Caballo Ln Paradise Valley AZ 85253

RUSSELL, PAUL SNOWDEN, surgeon, educator; b. Chgo., Jan. 22, 1925; s. Paul Snowden and Carroll (Mason) R.; m. Allene Lummis, Sept. 24, 1952; children— Katherine Swift, Paul Snowden, Allene, Laura Rice. Student, Groton (Mass.) Sch., 1939-41; PhB, U. Chgo., 1944, BS, 1945, MD, 1947; MA (hon.), Harvard U., 1962. Diplomate Am. Bd. Surgery, Am. Bd. Thoracic Surgery. From surg. intern, to resident Mass. Gen. Hosp., 1948-56, asst. surgery, 1957-60, chief gen. surg. svcs., 1962-69, chmn. com. on rsch., 1973-76; postdoctoral fellow USPHS, 1954-55; from tchg. fellow to clin. assoc. surgery Harvard Med. Sch., 1956-60, John Homans prof. surgery, 1962-98, John Homans Disting. prof. surgery, 1998—; assoc. prof. surgery Columbia Coll. Phys. and Surg., 1960-62; assoc. attending surgeon Presbyn. Hosp., NYC, 1960-62; assoc. vis. surgeon Francis Delafield Hosp., NYC, 1960-62, 74-94. Mem. com. tissue transplantation NRC-Nat. Acad. Scis., 1963-71, com. trauma, 1963-68; ad hoc com. to study clin. investigation and edn. in USN, 1971-73; allergy and immunology study sect. USPHS, 1963-65, chmn. allergy and immunology study sect. B, 1965-67; mem. transplantation and immunology com. Nat. Inst. Allergy and Infectious Diseases, 1967-69, chmn., 1970; mem. com. on cancer immunotherapy Nat. Cancer Inst., 1974-79. Contbr. papers in field.; Editorial bd.: Archives Surgery, 1963-72, Surgery, 1963-71, Transplantation, 1965-79, Annals of Surgery, 1966—, Transplantation Procs, 1966—, Jour. Immunology, 1977-80. Trustee Pine Manor Coll., Chestnut Hill, Mass., 1963-76, Groton Sch., 1964-79, The Conservation Law Found., 1997—; bd. dirs. Boston Fulbright Com., 1968, pres., 1980—; mem. corp. Jackson Lab.; trustee Worcester Found. for Biomed. Rsch. With USAF, 1951-53. Fellow ACS, Royal Soc. Medicine; mem. AAAS, Am. Acad. Arts and Scis., Am. Assn. Immunologists, NY Acad. Scis., Mass. Med. Soc., New Eng. Surg. Soc., Boston Surg. Soc. (pres. 1994), Soc. Univ. Surgeons, Soc. Exptl. Biology and Medicine, Halsted Soc., Whipple Soc., Internat. Soc. Surgery, Am. Surg. Assn., Transplantation Soc. (pres. 1970), Polish Acad. Sci. (fgn.), Sigma Xi. Home: 32 Lawrence Rd Chestnut Hill MA 02467-1230 Office: Dept Surgery Mass Gen Hosp Boston MA 02114

RUSSELL, PEGGY TAYLOR, soprano, educator; b. Newton, N.C., Apr. 5, 1927; d. William G. and Sue B. (Cordell) Taylor; m. John B. Russell, Feb. 23, 1953; children: John Spotswood, Susan Bryce. MusB in Voice, Salem Coll., 1948; MusM, Columbia U., 1950; postgrad., U. N.C., Greensboro, 1977; student, Am. Inst. Music Studies, Austria, 1972, student, 1978; student of Clifford Bair, Nell Starr (hon.), Salem Coll., Winston-Salem, N.C.; student of Edgar Schofield, Chloe Owen, N.Y.C.; student opera-dramatics, Boris Goldovsky, Southwestern Opera Inst.; student of Ande Andersen, Max Lehner, Graz, Austria. Mem. faculty dept. voice Guilford Coll., Greensboro, NC, 1952—53, Greensboro Coll., 1971—72; pvt. tchr. voice Greensboro, 1963—. Co-founder, v.p. sales, mktg. Russell Textiles, Inc., Greensboro, 1988; vis. instr. in voice U. N.C., Chapel Hill, 1973—77; founding artistic dir., gen. mgr. Young Artists Opera Theatre, Greensboro, 1983, staged and produced 18 operatic prodns., 1983—91; gues lectr. opera workshop U. N.C., Greensboro, 1990—91; lectr. opera Friends of Weymouth, Southern Pines, NC, 1994; lectr. on music history and opera, High Point, NC, Ctr. Creative Leadership, Greensboro, 1979—80, 1st Presbyn. Ch., 1982. Singer: debut in light opera as Gretchen in The Red Mill, 1947; singer: (debuts) Rosalinda in Die Fledermaus, 1949, Lola in Cavalleria Rusticana, 1951, Violetta in La Traviata, 1953, Fiordiligi in Cosi fan Tutte, 1956; singer: Marguerite in Faust, 1967, First Lady in The Magic Flute, 1972, mem. Greensboro Oratorio Soc., 1955—59; singer: (soprano soloist) The Messiah, 1952, 1958, The Creation, 1955, Solomon, 1958, Presbyn. Ch. of the Covenant, 1958—71; singer: guest appearances Sta. WFMY-TV, 1958—62; singer: (soprano soloist) Greensboro Symphony Orch., 1964, 1980, Ea. Music Festival Orch., 1965, Greensboro Civic Orch., 1980; singer: (soloist in numerous recitals). Judge Charlotte Opera Guild Auditions, 1994; mem. Friendship Force of Guilford County, Netherlands, 1985, 1987; bd. dirs. Music Theater Assocs., Greensboro Friends of Music, N.C. Lyric Opera, Piedmont Opera Theatre. Grantee N.C. Arts Coun. and NEA, 1991. Mem.: Piedmont Triad Coun. Internat. Vis. (Appreciation award Nat. Coun. Internat. Visitors 1994), N.C. Symphony Soc., Civic Music Assn. (chmn. 1963—64), Atlanta Opera Guild, Broadway Theater League (chmn. 1961—63), Symphony Guild (dir. 1977—78), Greensboro Music Tchrs. Assn. (pres. 1966—67), Music Educators Nat. Conf., N.C. Fedn. Music Clubs (dir. 1956—58), Nat. Assn. Tchrs. of Singing (state gov. 1976—82, coord. Regional Artist Contest 1982—84), Ctrl. Opera Svc., Nat. Opera Assn. (chmn. regional opera cos. com. 1985—91, judge vocal competition auditions 1991, 1992, 1994, chmn. trustees Cofield Endowment 1991), Weatherspoon Art Mus. Guild, English Speaking Union (bd. dirs. Greensboro chpt., chmn. Shakespeare competition 1995), Guilford County Planning/Devel. Office (Forecast 2015 com.), Greensboro Preservation Soc., Greensboro City Club. Home: 3012 W Cornwallis Dr Greensboro NC 27408-6730

RUSSELL, RALPH TIMOTHY, insurance company executive, mayor; b. Foley, Ala., May 26, 1948; s. Ralph Joseph and Dorothy Eleanor (Peterson) R.; m. Sandra Earle Schultz, May 30, 1970; children: Karen, Kevin, Kenton. BS in Acctg., U. Ala., 1970; MBA, U. South Ala., 1975. Chartered property casualty underwriter. Pres. Baldwin Mutual Ins. Co., Foley, Ala., 1972—; mayor City of Foley, 1996—. Bd. dirs. Baldwin Mutual Ins. Co., 1976—, Riviera Utilities, Foley, 1976—, Gulf Coast Title Ins. Co., Foley, 1978—, Colonial Bank, Foley, 1991—. Pres. South Baldwin United Way, 1981-82; nat. v.p. U. Ala. Alumni Assn., Tuscaloosa, 1978-79; chmn. Foley Pub. Libr., 1975-84, St. Margaret's Ch. Bd., Foley, 1989-90, Baldwin County Econ. Devel. Alliance, South Ala. Regional Planning Commn.; treas. South Baldwin Hosp.; mayor City of Foley, 1996—; bd. dirs. Bus. Coun. Ala. Paul Harris fellow, 1986. Mem. Nat. Assn. Mut. Ins. Cos. (chmn. bd. dirs. 1986-94), Ala. Ins. Planning Com. (bd. dirs.), Ins. Edn. Found. (bd. dirs. 1991-94), Soc. CPCU (pres. 1982), South Baldwin C. of C. (past pres.), Ala. League Municipalities (ecec. com.). Roman Catholic. Home: 117 W Rosetta Ave Foley AL 36535-2223 Office: Baldwin Mutual Ins Co 315 E Laurel Ave Foley AL 36535-2617

RUSSELL, RICHARD DONCASTER, geophysicist, educator, geoscientist; b. Toronto, Ont., Can., Feb. 27, 1929; s. Richard Douglas and Ada Gwennola (Doncaster) R.; m. Virginia Ann Reid Clippingdale, Aug. 11, 1951; children: Linda Jean, Morna Ann, Mary Joyce. BA, U. Toronto, 1951, MA, 1952, PhD, 1954. Asst. prof. physics U. Toronto, 1956-58, prof., 1962-63; assoc. prof. physics U. B.C., Vancouver, Canada, 1958-62, prof. geophysics, 1963-91, prof. emeritus, 1991—, head dept. geophysics, 1968-72, head dept. geophysics and astronomy, 1972-79, bd. govs., 1978-81, assoc. dean sci., 1980-83, assoc. v.p. acad., 1983-86. Sec.-gen. Inter-Union Commn. on Geodynamics, 1976-80; profl. geoscientist. Author (with John Arthur Jacobs and J. Tuzo Wilson): Physics and Geology International Series in the Earth Sciences, first edit., 1959, Physics and Geology McGraw-Hill International Series in the Earth and Planetary Science, 2d edit., 1973; author: (with Richard Doncaster and Ronald McCunn Farquhar) Lead Isotopes in Geology Interscience, 1960. Fellow Royal Soc. Can.; mem. Am. Geophys. Union, Can. Geophys. Union (J. Tuzo Wilson medal 1992). Home: 226-4955 River Rd Delta BC Canada V4K 4V9 Office: U BC Dept Earth & Ocean Scis Vancouver BC Canada V6T 1Z4

RUSSELL, RICHARD M. federal agency administrator; Grad., Yale U. Staff mem. subcom. on oceanography, Gulf of Mexico and Outer Continental Shelf U.S. Ho. of Reps. Com. on Merchant Marine and Fisheres, 1993—94; from profl. staff for the subcom. on energy and environment, staff dir. for subcom. on tech. to dep. chief of staff for sci. com. U.S. Ho. Reps. Com. on Sci., 1995—2001; chief of staff Office Sci. and tech. Policy Exec. Office of the Pres., Washington, assoc. dir. Office Sci. and Tech. Policy, 2001—. Office: Exec Office of the Pres Sci and Tech Policy EEOB 17th & Pennsylvania Ave NW Washington DC 20502

RUSSELL, RICHARD OLNEY, JR., cardiologist, educator; b. Birmingham, Ala., July 9, 1932; s. Richard Olney and Louise (Taylor) R.; m. Phyllis Hutchinson, June 15, 1963; children: Scott Richard, Katherine Hutchinson, Meredith Cooper, Stephen Wilbon. AB cum laude, Vanderbilt U., 1953, MD, 1956. Diplomate Am. Bd. Internal Medicine, 1964, Am. Bd. Cardiovascular Disease, 1967. Intern Peter Bent Brigham Hosp., Boston, 1956-57, resident, 1959-60, 63-64; fellow in cardiology Med. Coll. Ala., Birmingham, 1960-62, instr., 1962-63; instr. medicine U. Ala., Birmingham, 1964-65, asst. prof., 1965-70, assoc. prof., 1970-73, prof., 1973-81, clin. prof., 1981—; pvt. practice medicine specializing in cardiology Birmingham, 1981—. Mem. Jefferson County Bd. Health, 1977-81, chmn., 1979 Author: (with Charles Edward Rackley) Hemodynamic Monitoring in a Coronary Intensive Care Unit, 1974, 2d rev. and enlarged edit., 1981, Coronary Artery Disease: Recognition and Management, 1979, (with others) Radiographic Anatomy of the Coronary Arteries: An Atlas, 1976, Acute Ischemic Syndromes in American College of Cardiology Self Assessment Program, 1993; mem. editorial bd. Circulation, 1976-80, Am. Jour. Cardiology, 1977-82, Heart and Lung, 1978-83, Chest, 1978-83, Ala. Jour. Med. Scis, 1977-80, Jour. Am. Coll. Cardiology, 1987-90; section editor for Case Studies for Cardiosource for Am. Coll. of Cardiology, 2001--; contbr. articles to profl. jours. Distbn. com. Greater Birmingham Found., 1984-90; exec. bd. Birmingham area coun. Boy Scouts Am., 1987—, v.p., 1990-96, coun. commr., 1996-98; vice chmn. Vulcan dist., 1988-89, chmn., 1989-91, bd. dirs. S.E. region, 1990-92, bd. dirs. southern region, 1992—; bd. dirs. Ctrl. Ala. United Way, 1988-92; mem. Newcomen Soc., 1988—; chmn. exec. com. Birmingham Bapt. Med. Ctr., Montclair, 1995, pres.-elect med. staff, 1998-99, pres. 1999-2000; chmn. Nat. Eagle Scout Assn. Scholarship Com. So. Region, 2001-03; asst. coun. cmmr. Greater Ala. Coun., 1998-2000, coun. commr., 2001—; bd, mem, Am. Bd of Cardiovasular Disease, 1991-96. Capt. U.S. Army. Decorated Commendation medal; recipient Dist. Award of Merit, Boy Scouts Am., 1991, Silver Beaver award, 1990, Disting. Eagle Scout, 1999, Silver Antelope award 2001; NIH rsch. fellow, 1966-67. Fellow: ACP, Am. Coll. Cardiology (bd. govs. 1979—81, trustee 1984—85, 1989—94, ann. sci. session program chmn. 1994, disting. fellowship 2001, Ala. chpt. named lectureship in honor); mem.: Med. Assn. State Ala. (spkr. house counselors dels. 1989—94, Laureate award 1999), Birmingham Soc. Internists (pres. 2001—03), Birmingham Cardiovascular Soc. (pres. 1981), Jefferson County Med. Soc. (v.p. 1982, pres. 1984), So. Soc. Clin. Investigation, Am. Fedn. Clin. Rsch., Am. Coll. Chest Physicians (bd. regents 1985—91), Am. Heart Assn. (pres. Ala. affiliate 1975—76, v.p. so. region 1986—87, task force on practice guidelines 1998—2000), Royal Soc. Medicine, NY Acad. Scis., Kiwanis (Brimingham sec. 1984—85, disting. pres. 1994—95), Leadership Birmingham, Omicron Delta Kappa, Alpha Omega Alpha, Phi Beta Kappa. Home: 4408 Kennesaw Dr Birmingham AL 35213-1826 Office: Ala Heart Inst 880 Montclair Rd 1st Fl Birmingham AL 35213

RUSSELL, RICHARD R. industrial executive; CEO Gen. Chem. Group, Hampton, N.H., 1991-99; pres., CEO Gentek, 1999—. Office: Gentek Inc Liberty Ln Hampton NH 03842

RUSSELL, ROBERT HILTON, Romance languages and literature educator; b. Oak Park, Ill., Dec. 26, 1927; s. Melvin Alvord and Gladys (Hilton) R.; m. June Adele Thayer, Oct. 27, 1956. AB, Knox Coll., 1949; A.M., Harvard U., 1950, PhD, 1963; A.M., Dartmouth Coll., 1968. Instr. Romance langs. and lits. Dartmouth Coll., 1957-61, asst. prof., 1961-63, assoc. prof., 1963-67, prof., 1967-91, prof. emeritus, 1991—. Vis. prof. Spanish, U. San Diego, 1989, 90, 91, Knox Coll., 1993; guest lectr. Trinity Coll., Dublin, 1967, U. Salamanca, 1977, U. Leeds, 1978, Oxford U., 1978, U. P.R., 1987. Author: The Christ Figure in Misericordia, 1968; translator: Our Friend Manso, 1987. Corporate mem. United Ch. Bd. Homeland Ministries, 1963-69; N.H. del. Gen. Synod, United Ch. Christ, 1973, 75; corporator Internat. Inst. in Spain. Mem. MLA, Asociación Internacional de Hispanistas, Asociación Internacional de Galdosistas, Phi Beta Kappa. Democrat. Home: 17 Willow Spring Cir Hanover NH 03755-2901 Office: 6072 Dartmouth Hall Hanover NH 03755-3511

RUSSELL, ROBERT JACKSON, music educator, conductor; b. Roanoke, Va., Oct. 3, 1948; s. Herbert Jackson and Gwendolyn Mitchell Russell; m. Linda Lloyd, May 18, 1974; children: Peter Jackson, Benjamin Rajiv. BA, Wake Forest U., N.C., 1971; MusM, U. of NC, 1975; Dr. of Musical Arts, U. of Colo., 1979. Prof. music U. of So. Maine, Portland, 1979—. Music dir. The Choral Art Soc., Portland, Maine, 1979—. Pres. Am. Choral Dirs. Assn., Portland, Maine, 1989—91. Recipient Disting. Choral Dir. award, Am. Choral Dirs. Assn., 1993. Home: 76 Hartley St Portland ME 04103

RUSSELL, ROBERT LEONARD, professional association executive; b. July 18, 1916; s. Charles Arthur and Edna Mabel (Yearwood) R.; m. Jeanne Lucille Tackenberg, May 21, 1942 (dec. Feb. 1990). Student, St. Petersburg C.C., 1971-72; BS, U. Mid. Fla., 1973, MS, 1974. Reporter Peoria (Ill.) Jour., 1939-42, 46-47, Chgo. Daily News, 1947-57; asst. exec. dir. Profl. Golfers Assn., Dunedin, Fla., 1957-65; exec. dir. United Vol. Svcs., San Mateo, Calif., 1965-66; reporter St. Petersburg (Fla.) Evening Ind., 1967-70; exec. v.p. Fla. Health Care Assn. (formerly Fla. Nursing Home Assn.), Orlando, 1970-77, Mortgage Bankers Assn. Fla., Orlando, 1977-90, Mortgage Bankers Assn. Cen. Fla., Orlando, 1978-94, Mortgage Bankers Ednl. Found. Fla., Orlando, 1986-90; CEO B. & B. Trust, Ltd., 1994—. Adminstr. Fla. Health Care Self Insurers Fund, 1972-78; sec.-treas. Mortgage Bankers Fla. Polit. Action Com., 1977-85, treas., 1987-90; pres. Profl. Assn. Svcs., Inc., 1977-81, 90-94, chmn. bd., 1981-90; CEO B. & B. Trust, Ltd., 1994—. Editor: Profl. Golfer mag., 1957-65, Nat. Golfer mag., 1965-66, Communicator, 1977-80, Bull., 1980-81, The Messenger, 1981-90, the newsletter, 1980-94, The Knightly News, 1996—; exec. editor Rx Sports and Travel mag., 1966-67. Elder Park Lake Presbyn. Ch., Orlando, 1979-83, St. Paul's Presbyn. Ch., Orlando, 1983-87, Presbyn. Ch. of Lakes, 1987-93; mem. coord. coun. Presbytery of Cen. Fla., 1989-90; active Holy Family Cath. Ch., Orlando, 1993—; fin. sec. Holy Family Dr. Phillips Coun., KC, 1994—; mem. Holy Family Parish Planning Forum, Orlando, 1996—, mem. liturgy com.; mem. core com. SW FallFest, 1997—. With USAAF, 1942-46. Mem. NRA (life), KC, Am. Soc. Assn. Execs. (cert.), Fla. Soc. Assn. Execs., Cen. Fla. Soc. Assn. Exec., Am. Coll. Health Care Adminstrs. (fellow emeritus), Fla. Sheriffs Assn. (hon.), Mortgage Bankers Assn. Fla. (hon. life), Mortgage Bankers Assn. Cen. Fla. (hon. life), U.S. Basketball Writers Assn. (life, pres. 1956-57), Am. Legion (life). Republican. Home: 7316 Lismore Ct Orlando FL 32835-6150 Office: PO Box 916 Windermere FL 34786-0916

RUSSELL, ROBIE GEORGE, lawyer; b. Moscow, Idaho, July 7, 1948; s. George Robie Russell and Jean Ray (Atkinson) O'Reilly; m. Nancy Kay Olson, May 31, 1975; children: George Robie, Erin Kay. BS in Polit. Sci., Pub. Adminstrn., U. Idaho, 1972, cert. in Pub. Adminstrn., 1974, JD, 1978. Bar: Idaho 1979, U.S. Dist. Ct. Idaho 1979, U.S. Ct. Claims 1980, U.S. Ct. Appeals (9th cir.) 1980, U.S. Tax Ct. 1981, U.S. Ct. Appeals (fed. cir.) 1985, U.S. Supreme Ct. 1985, Wash. 1991. Dep. atty. gen. State of Idaho, Boise, 1979-81, sr. dep. atty. gen., div. chief, 1981-86; regional adminstr. region 10 U.S. EPA, Alaska, Idaho, Oregon, Wash., 1986-90; pres. Environ. Property Mgmt., Inc., Bainbridge Island, Wash., 1991-93; of counsel Ryan Swanson & Cleveland, Seattle, 1993-94; atty. Russell & Assocs., Seattle, 1995—. Counsel Idaho Sec. of State, Boise, 1982-86. Contbg. author: Idaho Media Law Handbook, 1986; editor: Idaho Cities Mag., 1974-75, (newsletter) Local Govt. Legal News, 1981-86; contbr. articles to profl. jours. Pres., treas. Lincoln Day Assn., Boise, 1979-86; vice-chmn. Selective Svc. Bd., Boise, 1983-86; chmn., vice-chmn. Ada County Reps., Boise, 1984-86; chmn. Combined Fed. Campaign, 1988; mem. Puget Sound Fed. Exec. Bd., 1986-90; mem. Am. Ctr. Internat. Leadership, Soviet Union/Poland delegation, 1989; active Boy Scouts Am. Named one of Outstanding Young Men in Am., 1980—. Mem. ABA, Idaho State Bar Assn., Wash. State Bar Assn. (CLE com.), Boise Bar Assn., King County Bar Assn., Nat. Inst. Mcpl. Law Officers, Assn. Idaho City Attys. (sec., treas. 1981-86, founder), Assn. Idaho Cities (advisor 1981—, Boyd Martin award 1985), Phi Alpha Delta, U. Idaho Alumni Assn. (bd. dirs. 1973-74), Sons and Daus. Idaho Pioneers, U. Idaho Vandal Scholarship Fund (Moscow, Idaho) (chpt. pres., bd. dirs. 1975—, nat. v.p. 1987-89, nat. pres. 1989-90, Vandal Booster of Yr. 1985). Republican. Avocations: stamp collecting/philately, fishing, gardening, music, lit. Home: PO Box 10667 Bainbridge Island WA 98110-0667 Office: Russell & Assocs 76 S Main St Seattle WA 98104-2514

RUSSELL, SUE ANN, clinical psychologist; b. Connersville, Ind., Apr. 14, 1949; d. Hugh B. Russell and Martha Jane Meyer. BS, U. Colo., 1971; MDiv, Abilene Christian U., 1981; PhD in Clin. Psychology, U. N.D., 1992. Intern Psychol. Svcs. Ctr. U. N.D., Grand Forks, 1986-92; intern Stone Ctr. Wellesley Coll., Grand Forks, 1991-92; rsch. psychologist women's drinking project U. N.D., Grand Forks, 1986-92; pvt. practice Grand Forks, 1993—. Founding fellow Jean Baker Miller Tng. Inst. of Wellesley Coll., 1996. Contbr. articles to profl. jours. Missionary to Africa Tonga Tribe, Zambia, South Africa, 1972—74. Fellowship Nat. Inst. on Alcohol Abuse and Alcoholism Nat. Inst. of Mental Health, 1991-92, Nat. Rsch. Svc. award 1988-91; pre-doctoral rsch. fellow Stone Ctr. of Wellesley Coll., 1991-92. Mem. Am. Psychol. Assn. (clin. psychology of women), N.D. Psychol. Assn., Assn. of Prevention and Cruelty to Animals. Avocations: American Eskimo dogs, creating wildlife sanctuary and natural prairie habitat on 290 acres. Office: 628 7th Ave S Ste B Grand Forks ND 58201-4854 Office Phone: 701-746-8737.

RUSSELL, TERRENCE JOSEPH, lawyer; b. Jacksonville, Fla., Sept. 26, 1944; AA, St. Leo Coll., 1964; BA, U. Fla., 1966; JD, Fla. State U., 1968. Bar: Fla. 1969. Law clk. to Hon. W.O. Mehrtens U.S. Dist. Ct. (so. dist.) Fla., 1969; atty. Ruden, McClosky, Smith, Schuster & Russell, P.A., Ft. Lauderdale, Fla. Mem. appellate restructure commn. Fla. Supreme Ct., 1985—86, mem. nominating com., 1994—, chmn. nominating com., 1997, 98; mem. Fed. Magistrate's merit selection panel, 1985; vice-chmn. 17th Jud. Cir. Nominating Com., 1982—84, chmn., 1985—86; mem. spl. com. representation of death sentenced inmates Fla. Bar, bd. govs., 1987—91, pres., 2001—02. Bd. govs. Nova U. Law Sch., 1981, chmn., 1993—97; bd. dirs. Broward County Legal Aid Svcs., 1985—86. Mem.: ATLA, ABA (ho. of dels. 2000—04, sects. litig., legal edn.), Fla. Bar Found. (bd. dirs. 1992—98, pres. 2004—), Fla. State U. Law Sch. Alumni Assn. (pres. 1985), Am. Bd. Trial Advs., Am. Bar Found., Acad. Fla. Trial Lawyers (coll. diplomates), Broward County Trial Lawyers Assn., Broward County Bar Assn. (chmn. spl. com. legal malpractice ins. 1978, bar-bench liaison com. 1978, jud. selection and tenure com. 1978—79, exec. com. 1980, 1981, pres. 1984—85), Gold Key, Delta Theta Phi. Office: Ruden McClosky et al PO Box 1900 Fort Lauderdale FL 33302-1900 Office Phone: 954-527-2460.

RUSSELL, TERRY, construction executive; Pres. John Wieland Homes, Atlanta, 1989—. Office: John Wieland Homes 1950 Sullivan Rd Atlanta GA 30337-5706

RUSSELL, THEODORE EMERY, diplomat; b. Madras, India, Nov. 21, 1936; s. Paul Farr and Phyllis Hope (Additon) R.; m. Sara Mather (Stedman) Russell, Sept. 3, 1960; children: Douglas Richmond Russell, Richard Mather Russell. BA, Yale U., 1958; MA, Fletcher Sch. Law & Diplomacy, 1960, MALD, 1961; sr. tng., Nat. War Coll., 1980—81. Fgn. svc. officer Dept. State, Italy, Czechoslovakia, Washington, 1963-80, dep. office dir. (EUR/RPE) Washington, 1981-83; dep. chief mission Copenhagen, 1983-87, Prague, Czechoslovakia, 1988-91; dep. asst. adminstr. for internat. activities EPA, Washington, 1992-93; amb. to Slovak Republic Bratislava, Slovakia, 1993-96; dep. comdt. internat. affairs Army War Coll., Carlisle, Pa., 1996-99; dir. internat. rels. MHz Networks, 2001—03; internat. security affairs cons., 2001—. Adj. fellow CSIS; councillor Atlantic Coun. Mem. Army-Navy Club, Fgn. Svc. Assn., Nat. War Coll. Alumni Assn. Avocations: hiking, fishing, history. Home and Office: 1833 Briar Ridge Ct Mc Lean VA 22101-4233

RUSSELL, THOMAS, retired British government official; b. Melrose, Scotland, May 27, 1920; s. Thomas and Margaret Thomson (Wilkie) R.; m. Andrée Irma Désfossés, Jan. 2, 1951 (dec. May 1989). MA, St. Andrews U., Scotland, 1941; diploma in anthropology, Cambridge (Eng.) U., 1947. Dist. commr. Colonial Adminstrv. Svc., Solomon Islands, 1948-51, 54-56, asst. sec. Western Pacific high commn., 1951-54; adminstrv. officer on secondment to col. Office, London, 1956-57; dep. fin. sec. Western Pacific high commn. Colonial Adminstrv. Svc., Solomon Islands, 1956-65, fin. sec., 1965-70, chief sec., 1970-74; gov. Cayman Islands, 1974-81; Cayman Islands govt. rep. U.K., 1982-2000; ret., 2000. Author: (pub.) I Have The Honour To Be, 2003. Capt. Brit. armed forces, 1940-46, North Africa and Italy, prisoner of war, Germany. Named Comdr. of Order of Brit. Empire, The Queen of England, 1970, Companion of the Order of St. Michael and St. George, The Queen of England, 1980. Fellow Royal Anthropol. Inst. (hon.); mem. Royal Commonwealth Parliamentary Assn. (Cayman Islands br. pres. 1974-81, hon.), Royal Commonwealth Ex-Svcs. League (mem. coun. 1982—, chmn. welfare com. 1993—), Pacific Islands Soc. (mem. coun. 1989-2001, past chmn.), Caledonian Club, Royal Commonwealth Soc. Mem. Ch. of Scotland. Avocations: archaeology, anthropology. Home: Hassendean, Gattonside Melrose TD6 9NA Scotland

RUSSELL, THOMAS ARTHUR, lawyer; b. Corona, Calif., Aug. 2, 1953; s. Larry Arthur Russell and Patricia Helena (Collins) Heath; m. Mary Ellen Leach, June 20, 1992; children: Trevor James, Elizabeth Mary, John Thomas. BS, U. Calif., Berkeley, 1976; JD, U. So. Calif., 1982. Bar: Calif. 1983, U.S. Dist. Ct. (cen. dist.) Calif. 1983, U.S. Ct. Appeals (9th cir.) 1986, U.S. Supreme Ct. 1988. Law clk. Calif. Ct. Appeals, L.A., 1981; assoc. Graham & James, Long Beach, Calif., 1982-88; ptnr. Woolley & Russell, Long Beach, 1988—2002; gen. counsel Port of L.A., 2002—. Spkr., panelist Nat. Marine Bankers Assn., Chgo., 1987—, Conf. on Consumer Fin. Law, 1995—; bd. dirs. Internat. Bus. Assn. So. Calif., 1989-96, pres., 1994-95. Contbg. author Benedict on Admiralty, 1995—, Recreational Boating Law, 1992, Moore's Federal Practice, Admiralty Vol., 1997—; editor Boating Briefs, 1991-96. Bd. dirs. World Trade Ctr. Assn., L.A.-Long Beach, Long Beach Area C. of C.; hon. mem. Am. Vessel Documentation Assn., 1995. Mem. ABA (Bronze Key award 1982, maritime fin. subcom., chmn. 1994-2002, vice chmn. 2002—), Maritime Law Assn. U.S. (proctor 1988—, chmn. recreational boating com. 2002—), Maritime Arbitration Assn. U.S. (pres. 1999—), Calif. Bar Assn., L.A. County Bar Assn., Calif. Yacht Brokers Assn. (Merle Parke award 1996, 2002). Republican. Roman Catholic. Avocations: tennis, skiing. Home: 2339 Port Lerwick Pl Newport Beach CA 92660 Office: 425 S Palos Verdes St San Pedro CA 90731

RUSSELL, THOMAS R. medical association administrator; Intern San Francisco Gen. Hosp., 1966—67; resident, gen. surgery U. Calif, San Francisco, 1971—75, 1967; with Calif. Pacific Med. Ctr., 1975—, chmn, dept. surgery, 1980—; exec. dir. ACS, 2002—; currently with San Francisco Surgical Assocs. Fellow U. Calif., 1979—, bd. governors, 1990—93, regent, 1993—. Office: ACS 633 N Saint Clair St Chicago IL 60611-3234 also: San Francisco Surgical Assocs 2100 Webster St, Ste 520 San Francisco CA 94115

RUSSELL, WILLIAM JOSEPH, educational association administrator; b. Boston, Sept. 23, 1941; s. Stanley Whiteside and Helen Rita R.; m. Frances Marie Chapdelaine, June 25, 1967; 1 son, Scott David. BS, Boston Coll., 1963; M.Ed., Northeastern U., 1966; PhD, U. Calif., Berkeley, 1971. Head math. dept. Oceana, Pacifica, Calif., 1966-71; asst. for fed. and profl. affairs Am. Ednl. Research Assn., Washington, 1971-73, dep. exec. dir., 1973-74, exec. dir., 1974—2002. Adv. bd. Edn. Resource Info. Center Ednl. Testing Center, Princeton, N.J., 1975-87; exec. officer Nat. Council on Measurement in Edn., Internat. Assn. Computing in Edn., 1987-89. Editor: Ednl. Researcher, 1979-90. Mem. Am. Ednl. Research Assn., Phi Delta Kappa. Roman Catholic. Home: 1443 Creekside Ct Vienna VA 22182-1701 Office: AERA 1230 17th St NW Washington DC 20036-3078 E-mail: bill-fran@lycos.com.

RUSSELL, WILLIAM STEVEN, finance executive; b. Evanston, Ill., Aug. 5, 1948; s. John W. and Lillian H. Russell; m. Susan M. Hanson, Aug. 20, 1972. BS, So. Ill. U., 1970. CPA, Ill. Sr. staff auditor Arthur Andersen & Co., Chgo., 1972-76; acctg. mgr., controller, asst. sec. and treas. Lawter Internat., Inc., Northbrook, Ill., 1976-86, treas., sec., 1986-87, v.p. fin., treas. and sec., 1987-96, pvt. investor, 1996—. Served with U.S. Army, 1970-72. Mem. Am. Inst. CPA's, Beta Alpha Psi, Beta Gamma Sigma. Roman Catholic. Home and Office: 51 Park Lane Park Ridge IL 60068-2834

RUSSERT, TIMOTHY JOHN, broadcast journalist, executive; b. Buffalo, May 7, 1950; m. Maureen Orth; 1 child, Luke. BA, John Carroll U., 1972; JD, Cleve. State U., 1976; also 33 hon. degrees. Bar: NY, DC. Spl. counsel US Senate, 1977—82; counselor NY Gov.'s Office, 1983—84; with NBC News, 1984—; moderator, mng. editor Meet the Press, 1991—; anchor The Tim Russert Show CNBC, 1994—; sr. v.p., Washington bureau chief NBC News. Nat. polit. analyst Today program and NBC Nightly News with Tom Brokaw; supr. NBC News Today program live broadcasts from Rome, 1985; overseer prodn. prime time spl. A Day in the Life of Pres. Bush, 1990, A Day in the Life of Pres. Clinton, 1993; has covered 8 U.S./Russian Summits, Geneva, Malta, Washington, Moscow, Vancouver; lectr. at more than 30 univs. Author: Big Russ and Me: Father and Son-Lessons of Life, 2004. Recipient Alumni Spl. Achievement award, Cleve.-Marshall Coll. Law, Pres.'s medal, Trocaire Coll., Dean's award, Cleve.-Marshall Coll. Law, John Peter Zenger award, N.Y. State Bar Assn., 1992, Disting. Grad. award, Nat. Cath. Educator's Assn., 1995, Spl. Achievement Alumni medal, John Carroll U. Fellow: Commn. European Cmtys. Office: NBC News Meet the Press 4001 Nebraska Ave NW Washington DC 20016-2733*

RUSSETT, BRUCE MARTIN, political science educator; b. North Adams, Mass., Jan. 26, 1935; s. Raymond Edgar and Ruth Marian (Martin) R.; m. Cynthia Margaret Eagle, June 18, 1960; children: Margaret Ellen, Mark David, Lucia Elizabeth, Daniel Alden. BA magna cum laude, Williams Coll., 1956; diploma in econs., Cambridge (Eng.) U., 1957; MA, Yale U., 1958, PhD, 1961, Uppsala U., 2002. Instr. MIT, Cambridge, 1961-62; asst. prof., then assoc. prof. Yale U., New Haven, 1961-68, prof., 1968—, Dean Acheson prof. internat. rels. and polit. sci., 1985—, chair dept. polit. sci., 1990-96, dir. UN studies, 1993—. Vis. prof. Columbia U., 1965, U. Mich., 1965-66, U. Libre Brussels, 1969-70, U. N.C., 1979-80, Richardson Inst., London, 1973-74, Netherlands Inst. Advanced Study, 1984, Tel Aviv U., 1989, U. Tokyo, 1996, Harvard U., 2001; prin. cons. pastoral letter on peace Nat. Conf. Cath. Bishops, Washington, 1981-83; co-dir., secretariat ind. working group Future of the UN, 1993-96. Author: World Handbook of Political and Social Indicators, 1964, What Price Vigilance?, 1970 (Kammerer award Amn. Polit. Sci. Assn. 1971), Interest and Ideology (with E. Hanson), 1975, Controlling the Sword, 1990, Grasping the Democratic Peace, 1993, The Once and Future Security Council, 1997, (with John Oneal) Triangulating Peace, 2001, (with Francis Oakley) Governance, Accountability, and the Future of the Catholic Church, 2004, others; editor: Jour. Conflict Resolution, 1972—; contbr. articles to profl. jours. Grantee NSF, 1964, 65, 69, 77, 79, 85, 88, 89, 90, 95, 98, Ford Found., 1993, 94, 97, John and Catherine MacArthur Found., 1988, 91; Fulbright-Hays fellow, Belgium and Israel, 1969, 89; John Simon Guggenheim Found. fellow, 1969, 77; German Marshall Fund fellow, 1977. Fellow Am. Acad. Arts and Scis.; mem. AAUP, Am. Polit. Sci. Assn. (coun. 1984-86), Internat. Studies Assn. (pres. 1983-84), Peace Sci. Soc. Internat. (pres. 1977-79). Avocations: tennis, classical music, hiking. Home: 70 Martin Ter Hamden CT 06517-2333 Office: Yale U Dept Polit Sci PO Box 208301 New Haven CT 06520-8301 E-mail: bruce.russett@yale.edu.

RUSSI, GARY D. academic administrator; BSc, Southwestern Oklahoma State U., 1969; PhD, U. Kansas, 1972. With U.S. Army various mgmt. positions, 1969—92; tchr., rsch. asst. Kansas U., 1969; various positions such as project coord. and v.p., rsch. and strategic planning et al. Drake U., 1973—93; v.p. acad. affairs Oakland U., 1993—95, interim pres., 1995—96, pres., 1996—. Contbr. articles to profl. jours.; author book reviews. Mem. bd. Automation Alley, Oakland County Bus. Roundtable; bd. trustees Citizens Rsch. Coun. of Mich., Crittenton Hosp.; chair, bd. dirs. Rochester Hills Strategic Planning Process; pres. coun. Mid-Continent Athletics Conf.; chair, bd. dir. Mich. Virtual U. Recipient Rho Ci Soc. undergrad. rsch. award, Southwestern Oklahoma State U., 1969, Merck Rsch. award, 1996, Disting. Alumni award, 1998, George Wibby Athletic award, Oakland U., 2002. Office: Oakland U Rochester MI 48309

RUSSIANO, JOHN See MILES, JACK

RUSSIN, JONATHAN, lawyer, consultant; b. Wilkes-Barre, Pa., Oct. 30, 1937; s. Jacob S. and Anne (Wartella) R.; m. Antoinette Stackpole, Oct. 6, 1962; children: Alexander, Andrew, Benjamin, Jacob. BA, Yale U., 1959, LLB, 1963. Bar: D.C. 1963. Guide interpreter Am. Nat. Exhibit, Moscow, 1959; rsch. asst. Law Faculty U. East Africa, Dar es Salaam, Tanganyika, 1961-62; regional legal adviser for Caribbean AID, 1967-69; ptnr. Kirkwood, Kaplan, Russin & Vecchi, Santo Domingo, Dominican Republic, 1969-74, Washington, 1974-78, Kaplan Russin & Vecchi, Madrid, 1978-81, Washington, 1981-92; ptnr., dir. Russian practice group Russin & Vecchi, Moscow, 1992—. Washington rep. for Moscow Patriarchate of Russian Orthodox Ch.; convener adv. coun. Inst. for European, Russian and Eurasian Studies, George Washington U.; mem. adv. bd. Caribbean Am. Directory; trustee St. Nicholas Cathedral, Washington, St. Vladimir's Orthodox Theol. Sem., Crestwood, N.Y., 1985-93; legal adviser Orthodox Ch. in Am. Contbr. articles to profl. jours. Bd. dirs. Nat. Coun. Internat. Visitors, Washington, 1987—93, Fund for Democracy and Devel., Washington, 1993—, MUCIA Global Edn. Group, Inc., 1996—2000, Delphi Internat., Washington, 1988—2000, Dominican Am. Cultural Inst., Santo Domingo, 1988—92. Recipient Order of St. Vladimir, Moscow Patriarchate, Russian Orthodox Ch., 1991. Mem. ABA, Inter-Am. Bar Assn., Yale Club N.Y., Yale Club Washington. Office: 815 Connecticut Ave NW Ste 650 Washington DC 20006-4004 Office Phone: 202-822-6100.

RUSSIN, ROBERT ISAIAH, sculptor, educator; b. N.Y.C., Aug. 26, 1914; s. Uriel and Olga (Winnett) R.; m. Adele Mutchnick, May 21, 1937; children: Joseph Mark, Lincoln David, Uriel Robin. BA, CCNY, 1933, MS, 1935; postgrad., Beaux Arts Inst. Design, 1935—36. Tchr. sculpture Cooper Union Art Inst., N.Y.C., 1944-47; prof. art U. Wyo., Laramie, 1947-86, prof., artist-in-residence, 1976-85, Disting. prof. emeritus, 1985—. One-man shows Tucson Fine Arts Ctr., 1966, Colorado Springs (Colo.) Fine Arts Ctr., 1967, Palm Springs (Calif.) Desert Mus., Chas. G. Bowers Meml. Mus., Judah L. Magnes Meml. Mus., Berkeley, Calif.; retrospective one-man exhbn. Nat. Gallery Modern Art, Santo Domingo, Dominican Republic, 1976, Tubac Ctr. of the Arts, Ariz., 1987, Old Town Gallery-Park City, Ut., Riggins Gallery, Scottsdale, Ariz., 1989, Fine Arts Mus., U. Wyo., 1991; sculpture commns. include 2 8-foot metal figures, Evanston (Ill.) Post Office, 1939, three life-size carved figures, Conshohocken (Pa.) Post Office, 1940, Benjamin Franklin Monument, U. Wyo., 1957, Bust of Lincoln, Lincoln Mus., Washington, (now in Gettysburg Mus.), 1959, Lincoln Monument atop summit Lincoln Hwy., (now U.S. Interstate 80), Wyo., 1959, monumental bas-relief bronze Cheyenne (Wyo.) Fed. Bldg., 1966, two carved wood walls, Denver Fed. Bldg., 1966, monumental fountain, City of Hope Med. Ctr., L.A., 1966-67, statue, Brookhaven (N.Y.) Nat. Lab., 1968, life-size bronze sculpture fountain, City of Hope, 1969, Pomona Coll., 1973, monumental bronze sculpture Prometheus Natrona County (Wyo.) Pub. Libr., 1974, Man and Energy, Casper (Wyo.) C. of C., 1974, 12-foot marble carving Menorah Med. Ctr., Kansas City, Mo., 1975, Einstein and Gershwin medals Magnes Meml. Mus., Berkeley, Nat. Mus. Art, Santo Domingo, 1975, monumental fountain, Galleria d'Arte Moderna, Santo Domingo, 1977, Duarte Monument, Santo Domingo, 1977, 30 foot steel and water fountain monument City Hall, Casper, 1980, marble and bronze monument, Lincoln Centre, Dallas, 1982, acrylic steel and bronze monument, Herschler State Office Bldg., Cheyenne, 1984, marble monument, U. Wyo., Laramie, 1985, portrait head Charles Bluhdorn, chmn. Gulf & Western, 1975, portrait bust Pres. J. Balaguer of Dominican Republic, 1975, portrait head G. Wilson Knight, Shakespearean actor and scholar, 1975, 2 12-foot bronze figures The Greeting and the Gift for Bicentennial Commn., Cheyenne, 1976, monumental marble head of Juan Pablo Duarte liberator Dominican Republic, Santo Domingo, 1976, monumental marble, Pan Am. Family, Dominican Republic, 1977, marble sculpture Trio, U. Wyo., 1985, Isaac B. Singer medal for Magnes Mus., 1983, monumental Holocaust Figure Tucson Jewish Cmty. Ctr., 1989, granite monument Chthonodynamis, Dept. Energy Bldg., Washington, 1992, bust Hon. Milward Simpson, 1993, bust James Forest U. Wyo., 1993, bronze statue Univ. Med. Ctr., Tuscon, Head, Gov. Stanley Hathway, Cheyenne, Wy. 1995; Head, Pres. Franklin D. Roosevelt, Rotunda (pres. hosp. Bethesda, Md.), 4 monumental figures Nat. Jewish Rsch. and Med. Ctr., Denver, 2003; contbr. articles to profl. jours. Recipient awards sec. fine arts U.S. Treasury, 1939, 40, Lincoln medal U.S. Congress, 1959, Alfred G.B. Steel award Pa. Acad. Fine Arts, 1961, medal of Order of Duarte Sanchez y Mella, Dominican Republic, 1977; Inst. fellow Beaux Arts Inst. Design, 1935-36; Ford Found. fellow, 1953. Mem. Nat. Sculpture Conf. (exec. bd.), Sculptors Guild, Nat. Sculpture Soc., AIA, AAUP, Coll. Art Internat. Inst. Arts and Letters, Phi Beta Kappa (hon.). Home: 61 N Fork Rd Centennial WY 82055 also: 1160 W Placita Salubre Green Valley AZ 85614-1334 Office Phone: 520-625-8384. E-mail: stoneman1914@aol.com.

RUSSMAN, IRENE KAREN, artist; b. Chgo., Mar. 10, 1942; d. Andrew Earl and Irene Margaret Kane (Barthley) James; m. James Ora Duffy, Jan. 27, 1963 (div. Oct. 20, 1993); children: Dawn Ann Duffy, James Sean Duffy, Maureen Marie Duffy; m. Stephen George Russman, Aug. 10, 2002. BA, Wash. State U., 1985, MFA, 1989; student summer workshops, Red Deer Coll., 2001, Pitchuk Sch. of Glass, 2001. Exhibitions include Galeria 5, Caracas, Venezuela, 1989, Acad. Arts, Riga, Latvia, 1990, Union Gallery, Pullman, Wash., 1991, Chase Gallery, Spokane, Wash., 1992, Virginia Inn, Seattle, 1993, Wash. State U./U. Ill., 1994, Gallery X "Out of the Box", Art Inst. Chgo., 1995, juried summer workshop, Pilchuck Glass Sch., Seattle, 2001. Represented in permanent collections Johanna Bur. Handicapped, Chgo., Gordon Gilkey Collection, Portland Art Mus., Modern Art Gallery, Leningrad, Russia, Neill Pub. Libr., Vetreria 2001, S.R.L., Murano, Italy, The Nat. Marble Mus., Yreka, Calif., The National Marble Museum. Bd. dirs. Pullman/Moscow Regional Airport; mem. Global Vols. Project, Ostuni, Italy, 1998, Passport Time Forest Svc., 2000. Recipient Civic Appreciation award, City of Pullman Mayor Pete Butkus, 1984. Mem.: Red Hat Soc., Palouse Folklore Soc., Bella Vita Lodge Number 2285. Avocations: folk dancing, flying, travel, gardening. Home: 3014 Lorne St SE Olympia WA 98501 Personal E-mail: irussman@hotmail.com.

RUSSO, ALEXANDER PETER, artist, educator; b. Atlantic City, June 11, 1922; s. Peter Joseph and Lillian Mary (Soma) R.; 1 child, Eugenie. Student, Pratt Inst., 1940-42, Swarthmore Coll., 1946-47; S.S., Bard Coll., 1947; B.F.A. (Breevort-Eickenmeyer fellow), Columbia U., 1952; postgrad., Acad. Fine Arts, Rome, 1952-54, Inst. Advanced Fine Arts, 1977-79. Instr. New Orleans Acad. Art, 1948-49; asst. prof. art U. Buffalo, 1955-58; instr. in graphic design Parsons Sch. Design, 1958-60; chmn. dept. drawing and painting Corcoran Sch. Art, 1961-70, chmn. faculty, acting dean, 1967-70; lectr., thesis adv. George Washington U., 1961-70; prof. Hood Coll., Frederick, Md., 1970-90, prof. emeritus, 1990—, chmn. dept. art, 1970-87. Vis. guest prof. art Instituto Allende, San Miguel de Allende, Mexico, 1993-94; panelist Md. State Coun. Arts, Balt., 1981-82; reviewer art programs Md. State Bd. Edn., 1981—; guest art critic Southampton Press, N.Y., 1989, 91; cons. in field. One-man shows include Corcoran Gallery Art, Washington, 1946, 64, Chiurazzi Gallery,

Rome, 1953, Cavallino Gallery, Venice, Italy, 1954, U. So. Ill., 1955, Frank Rehn Gallery, N.Y.C., periodic exhbns., 1954-74, Phoenix II Gallery, Washington, 1983, Ingber Gallery, N.Y.C., 1983, Washington Gallery Art, 1963, Franz Bader Gallery, Washington, 1967, Internat. Monetary Fund, Washington, 1968, 79, Agra Gallery, Washington, 1971, Benson Gallery, Bridgehampton, L.I., 1976, Phoenix Fine Arts, Frederick, 1981, Benton Gallery, Southampton, N.Y., 1985, 86, 88, 90-91, Arlene Bujese Gallery, East Hampton, N.Y., 1994-95, 97-98, Hood Coll., Frederick, Md., 1991, Western Md. Coll., Westminster, 1991, Bell Gallery, Seattle, 1991-92, Gettysburg (Pa.) Coll., 1989; group exhbns. include Salon de la Marne, Paris, 1945, Met. Mus. Art, N.Y.C., 1948, Bordighera Internat., Italy, 1953-54, Mus. Modern Art, Madrid, 1953, Sala di Esposizione delle Biblioteca Americano, Rome, 1953, Whitney Mus. Am. Art, N.Y.C., 1960, Mus. Modern Art, N.Y.C., 1969, Guild Hall, East Hampton, N.Y., 1976, East Hampton Avant-Garde, A Salute to the Signa Gallery, 1990, NAS, Washington, 1984, Bell Gallery, Seattle, 1990, Illustrator's Club, N.Y.C., 1991, Armory Exhbn., N.Y.C., 1991, Inst. Alleude, San Niguel de Allende, Mex., 1994, Fulbright Assoc. 20th Anniv. Art Exhibition, 1997, Josh Kligerman Gallery, San Miguel de Allende, Mex., 1994; represented in permanent collections Albright-Know Gallery, Buffalo, Columbia U., N.Y.C., Delgado Mus. Art, New Orleans, Corcoran Gallery Art, Fiat Automobile Co., Rome, Nat. Collection Smithsonian Inst., Washington, Fed. Ins. Deposit Corp., Washington, Gettysburg Coll. Pa.; author: Profiles on Women Artists, 1985, The Challenge of Drawing, 1986, (poetry) Vignettes, 1996. Served with USNR, 1942-46. Fellow Guggenheim Found., 1947-48, 49-50,Edward McDowell Found., 1956, Hood Coll. Hodson teaching fellow, 1983; Fulbright grantee for painting and research, Rome, 1952-54, U.S.-Indo Subcommn. on Edn. and Culture grantee, India, 1984. Office: PO Box 1377 Wainscott NY 11975-1377 also: Arlene Bujese Gallery 66 Newtown Ln East Hampton NY 11937-2400 Office Phone: 631-324-4914. *Success is an equivocal matter. "Outward success", no doubt, is meaningful and necessary to most people in terms of fulfilling goals or for some similar reason. "Interior success" is more difficult to achieve, for it means the labor of a developing soul, and, more often than not, the relinquishing of what most would consider to be "material success." Whatever I have achieved in the way of outward or material success, therefore, is but a minute reflection of that which I would wish to achieve on the spiritual level. There is a long way to go.*

RUSSO, ANTHONY JOSEPH, public relations professional; b. N.Y.C., Oct. 23, 1953; s. Lucio and Tina (Iarossi) R. BA cum laude, Alfred U., 1974; MA, Columbia U., 1975; PhD, Claremont Grad. Sch., 1982. Asst. to chmn. Mocatta Metals, N.Y.C., 1982-83; account exec. Gavin Anderson and Co., N.Y.C., 1983-85; sr. account exec. Adams and Reinhart, N.Y.C., 1985; dir. corp. rels. Geto and DeMilly, N.Y.C., 1985-86; v.p. Cameron Assocs., N.Y.C., 1986-88; CEO Euro RSCG Life NRP, N.Y.C., 1988—; chmn. Madison Life Scis. Mem. editl. bd.: Jour. Comml. Biotech., Bio People. Bd. dirs. March of Dimes, Target Autism Genome. Mem. APA, Pub. Rels. Soc. Am., Psi Chi. Democrat. Office: Euro RSCG Life NRP 200 Madison Ave 7th Fl New York NY 10016 also: Euro RSCG Life NRP Berkshire Ho 168-173 High Holborn WCIV 7AA England also: Euro RSCG Life NRP Paris 2 Allee de Longchamp 92281 Suresnes Cedex France also: 100 California St San Francisco CA 94111 also: 10509 Vista Sorrento Pkwy San Diego CA 92121

RUSSO, IRMA HAYDEE ALVAREZ DE, pathologist; b. San Rafael, Mendoza, Argentina, Feb. 28, 1942; came to U.S, 1972; d. Jose Maria and Maria Carmen (Martinez) de Alvarez; m. Jose Russo, Feb. 8, 1969; 1 child, Patricia Alexandra. BA, Escuela Normal MTSM de Balcarce, 1959; MD, U. Nat. of Cuyo, Mendoza, 1970. Diplomate Am. Bd. Pathology. Intern Sch. Medicine Hosps., Argentina, 1969-70; resident in pathology Wayne State U. Sch. Medicine, Detroit, 1976-80. Rsch. asst., instr. Inst. Histology and Embryology Sch. Medicine U. Nat. of Cuyo, 1963-71, assoc. prof. histology Faculty Phys., Chem. and Math. Scis., 1970-72; rsch. assoc. Inst. Molecular and Cellular Evolution U. Miami, Fla., 1972-73; rsch. assoc. exptl. pathology lab. divsn. biol. scis. Mich. Cancer Foun., Detroit, 1973-75, rsch. scientist, 1975-76, vis. rsch. scientist, 1976-82, asst. mem., pathologist, 1982-89, assoc. rsch. mem., 1989-91, co-dir. pathology reference lab., 1982-86, chief exptl. pathology lab., 1989-91; co-dir. Mich. Cancer Found. Lab. Svcs., 1986-91; mem. Fox Chase Cancer Ctr., 1991—; dir. anatomic pathology Am. Oncologic Hosp. Dept. Pathology, 1991-92; dir. Lab. Svcs., 1992-94; chief molecular endocrinology sect. Breast Cancer Rsch. Lab. Fox Chase Cancer Ctr., 1994—; chief resident physician dept. pathology Wayne State U. Sch. Medicine, 1978-80, asst. prof., 1980-82; mem. staff Harper-Grace Hosps., Detroit, 1980-82; adj. prof. Pathology and Cell Biology Jefferson Sch. Medicine/Thomas Jefferson U., 1992—, chairperson Basic Breast Biology Study Sect. U. Calif. Breast Cancer Program, 1997, mem. endocrinology panel peer rev. com. breast cancer rsch. program U.S. Army R & D Command, 1994, 95, 96, 2002, 03, chairperson endocrinology peer rev. com., 1996; ad-hoc mem. biochem. endocrinology study sect. NIH, DHHS, 1994, metabolic pathology study sect., 1996-97; mem. European Commn. Cancer Prevention, 1994—; mem. bd. sci. counselor, sec. health and human svcs. Nat. Toxicology Program Bd., 1994-98; mem. Internat. Life Scis. Inst.-Risk Sci. Inst. Mammary Working Group, 1992—; pres., founder League of Women Against Cancer, Rydal, Pa., 1994—; guest lectr. dept. obstetrics Sch. Medicine U. Nat. of Cuyo, 1965-71; mem. resource devel. subcommittee of the profl. advisory com., Latinas Living Beyond Breast Cancer, 2000—; mem. Breast Cancer Res. Sci. Review Panel, N.J.commr. on cancer rsch., Trenton, N.J., 1997, 2000. Editor-in-chief Jour. Women's Cancer, 1997—; contbr. articles to profl. jours. Rockefeller grantee, 1972-73; Nat. Cancer Inst. grantee, 1978-81, 84-87, 94-99, 2003—, Am. Cancer Soc. grantee 1988-89, 91-94, U.S. Army Med. R&D Command grantee, 1994-99, 2003—; recipient Shannon award Nat. Cancer Inst./NHHSS, 1992-94, Gold medal Inst. U. Dexeus, Barcelona, Spain, 2000. Mem. AAAS, Soc. Española Senología y Patología Mamaria, Nat. Cancer Inst. (breast cancer working group, breast cancer program 1984-88), Nat. Alliance Breast Cancer Orgns. (med. adv. bd. N.Y.C. chpt. 1986—), Ea. Coop. Oncology Group, Coll. Am. Pathologists, Am. Soc. Clin. Pathologists, Am. Assn. Cancer Rsch., Am. Assn. Clin. Chemistry, Internat. Coll. Physicians and Surgeons, Women in Cancer Rsch., The Endocrine Soc., Internat. Assn. Against Cancer, Sigma Xi, Food Quality Protection Act, Sci. Review Bd., Fed. Insecticide Fungi and Rodenticide Act. Adivsory Panel, EPA. Roman Catholic. Office: Fox Chase Cancer Ctr 333 Cottman Ave Philadelphia PA 19111 Office Phone: 215-728-4781. Business E-Mail: I_Russo@fccc.edu. E-mail: Lowac@msn.com.

RUSSO, JOSE, pathologist; b. Mendoza, Argentina, Mar. 24, 1942; came to U.S., 1971; s. Felipe and Teresa (Pagano) R.; m. Irma Haydee, Feb. 8, 1969; 1 child, Patricia Alexandra. BS, Agustin Alvarez Nat. Coll., 1959; MD, U. Nat. Cuyo, 1967. Instr. Inst. Gen. and Exptl. Pathology Med. Sch., Mendoza, 1961-66; asst. prof. Inst. Histology and Embryology, 1967-71; Rockefeller Found. postdoc. fellow Inst. Molecular and Cellular Evolution U. Miami, 1971-73; chief exptl. pathology lab. Mich. Cancer Found., Detroit, 1973-81; assoc. clin. prof. pathology Wayne State U., Detroit, 1979-91, chmn. dept. pathology, 1981-91; chmn. dept. pathology, sr. mem. Fox Chase Cancer Ctr., Phila., 1991-94, sr. mem., dir. Breast Cancer Rsch. Lab., 1994—; sci. dir. League of Women Against Cancer. Mem. Mich. Cancer Found., 1982-91; adj. prof. pathology Jefferson Sch. Medicine, Univ. Penn. Sch. Medicine, Phila. Author: Tumor Diagnosis by Electron Microscopy, vol. 1, 1986, vol. 2, 1988, vol. 3, 1990, Immunocytochemistry in Tumor Diagnosis, 1985; editor-in-chief Jour. of Women's Cancer; contbr. over 380 articles to profl. jours. USPHS grantee, 1978, 80, 84, 88, 90, 93, 94, 95, 98, 2000, 02, grantee Am. Cancer Soc., 1982, Dept. of Def., 1999-2002; NRC Argentina fellow, 1967-71. Mem. Am. Assn. Cancer Rsch., Am. Soc. Cell Biology, Soc. Exptl. Biology and Medicine, Tissue Culture Assn., Am. Soc. Clin. Pathology, Internat. Acad. Pathology, Am. Coll. Pathology, Sigma Xi Roman Catholic. Office Phone: 215-728-4782.

RUSSO, JOSEPH MARIA, public affairs executive; b. Cheverly, Md., Aug. 13, 1950; s. Frank N. Russo and Theresa E. McIntyre; m. Nancy E. Meier, Apr. 4, 1992; children: Emily E., Amy M. Student, Ohio U., 1968-69; BA, Fordham U., 1972; postgrad., New Sch. Social Rsch., 1972-73. Spl. projects writer Prentice-Hall Inc., Englewood Cliffs, N.J., 1972-73; writer, editor Peat Marwick Mitchell & Co., N.Y.C., 1973-76; publs. officer U.S. Trust Co., N.Y.C., 1976-79; acct. supr. Harshe-Rotman & Druck, N.Y.C., 1979-80; v.p. Norstar Bank, Newburgh, N.Y., 1981-83, First Jersey Nat. Corp., Jersey City, 1983-84, The Hertz Corp., Park Ridge, N.J., 1984-2000; v.p. pub. affairs and corp. comm. Niagara Mohawk, Syracuse, N.Y., 2000—. Recipient Joseph Meddill Patterson award NY Daily News, 1971. Mem. Pub. Rels. Soc. Am. (Silver Anvil 1988), Commerce and Industry Assn. N.J. (bd. dirs. 1998-2000), The Wisemen, The Princeton Club N.Y. (assoc.). Republican. Presbyterian. Avocations: golf, fishing, painting. Home: PO Box 922 354 Sarah Wells Trl Goshen NY 10924-5107 Office: Niagara Mohawk 300 Erie Blvd W Syracuse NY 13202-4250 also: 293 Westbrook Hills Dr Syracuse NY 13215

RUSSO, MELISSA, reporter; BA, Tufts U., Boston; MS in Journalism, Columbia U., N.Y.C. Intern Office Media Rels. White House, Washington; assoc. producer, video journalist Time Inc. Mag. Group, 1987—92; polit. reporter N.Y. News 1, N.Y.C., 1992—98, NewsChannel4 NBC, N.Y.C., 1998—. Recipient Gold Typewriter award, N.Y. Press Club, 1997. Mem.: The Inner Circle. Office: NBC 30 Rockefeller Plz New York NY 10112

RUSSO, PATRICIA F. communications executive; BA, Georgetown U.; postgrad. in advanced mgmt., Harvard U., 1989. Sales and mktg. mgmt. exec. IBM, 1973-81; with AT&T (now Lucent Techs. Inc.), 1981—; pres. bus. unit Bus Comm. Sys., 1992-96; exec. v.p. strategy bus. devel. and corp. ops. Lucent Techs., Inc., Murray Hill, NJ, 1997-99, exec. v.p., CEO svc. provider networks Warren, NJ, 1999—2000; pres., CEO Lucent Techs. Inc., Murray Hill, 2002—, chmn., 2003—; pres., COO Eastman Kodak, 2000—02. Bd. dirs. Xerox Corp., Schering-Plough Corp., N.J. Mfrs. Ins. Co., Georgetown U. Office: Lucent Techs 600 Mountain Ave New Providence NJ 07974*

RUSSO, RENE, actress; b. Calif., Feb. 17, 1954; m. Dan Gilroy, Mar. 14, 1992; 1 child, Rose. Fashion model Eileen Ford Agy. Film appearances include Major League, 1989, Mr. Destiny, 1990, One Good Cop, 1991, Freejack, 1992, Lethal Weapon 3, 1992, In the Line of Fire, 1993, Major League 2, 1994, Outbreak, 1995, Get Shorty, 1995, Tin Cup, 1996, Ransom, 1996, Buddy, 1997, Lethal Weapon 4, 1998, The Adventures of Rocky and Bullwinkle, 1999, The Thomas Crown Affair, 1999, Showtime, 2002, Big Trouble, 2002; TV appearances include (series) Sable, 1987, A Salute to Clint Eastwood, 1996. Office: Progressive Artists Agy 400 S Beverly Dr Ste 216 Beverly Hills CA 90212-4404 Address: 8046 Fareholm Dr Los Angeles CA 90046*

RUSSO, RICHARD, writer; Writer, Camden, Maine. Author: Mohawk, The Risk Pool, Nobody's Fool, Straight Man. Home: 3 High St Camden ME 04843

RUSSO, ROY LAWRENCE, retired electronic design automation engineer; b. Kelayres, Pa., Nov. 6, 1935; s. Peter John and Mary (Fudge) R.; m. Elizabeth Jean Tautkus, Dec. 26, 1959; children: Mark, Keith, Aileen, Linda. BSE.E., Pa. State U., 1957, MSE.E., 1959, PhD.E.E., 1964. Asst. prof. elec. engring. Pa. State U., University Park, 1964-65; mgr., staff mem. IBM Research, Yorktown Heights, N.Y., 1965-77, mem. research staff, 1983-85, mgr. design automation lab., 1985-94; sr. engr. Gen. Tech. div. IBM, Hopewell Junction, 1977-81, mgr. strategy, 1981-82; cons. prof. elec. engring Stanford U., 1982-83; retired, 1994. Editor-in-chief IEEE Computer Soc., 1983-85; co-inventor ink jet printer correction system. Treas. St. Patrick's Ch., Yorktown Heights, 1975-77. Recipient Invention Achievement award IBM, 1978, Outstanding Contbn. award IBM, 1968, 89, Outstanding Writing award Pa. State U., 1967 Fellow IEEE (dir. computer disvn. 1989); mem. IEEE Computer Soc. (pres. 1986-87, Svc. award, Centennial medal 1984, Richard E. Merwin award 1992), Eta Kappa Nu.

RUSSO, ROY R. lawyer; b. Utica, N.Y., July 26, 1936; BA, Columbia U., 1956; LLB cum laude, Syracuse U., 1959. Bar: N.Y. 1959, D.C. 1967, U.S. Supreme Ct. 1969. Atty. FCC, 1959—66; ptnr. Cohn and Marks LLP, Washington, 1966—. Mem. Order of Coif, Phi Alpha Delta. Democrat. Home: 6528 Bowie Dr Springfield VA 22150-1309 Office: Cohn and Marks LLP 1920 N St NW Ste 300 Washington DC 20036-1622

RUSSO, THOMAS ANTHONY, lawyer; b. N.Y.C., Nov. 6, 1943; s. Lucio F. and Tina (Iarossi) R.; m. Nancy Felipe, June 18, 1966 (div. 1974); m. Janice Davis, June 10, 1977 (div. 1979); m. Marcy C. Appelbaum, June 16, 1985; children: Morgan Danielle and Alexa Anne (twins), Tyler James. BA, Fordham U., 1965; MBA, JD, Cornell U., 1969. Bar: N.Y., 1970, U.S. Ct. Appeals (2d cir.) 1971, U.S. Dist. Ct. (so. and ea. dists.) N.Y. 1971, U.S. Ct. Appeals (7th cir.) 1982. Staff atty. SEC, Washington, 1969-71; assoc. Cadwalader, Wickersham & Taft, N.Y.C., 1971-75; dir. divsn. trading and markets Commodity Futures Trading Commn., Washington, 1975—77; ptnr., mem. mgmt. com. Cadwalader, Wickersham & Taft, N.Y.C., 1977-92; vice chmn., chief legal officer, mng. dir. Lehman Bros., N.Y.C., 1993—. Vice chmn. bd. trustees, mem. exec. com. Inst. for Fin. Markets; bd. dirs. Rev. Securities and Commodities Regulation, N.Y.C.; trustee, chmn. exec. com., chmn. devel. com. Inst. Internat. Edn.; trustee NYU Downtown Hosp.; mem. adv. com. SEC Hist. Soc.; mem. nat. bd. trustees, exec. com. and nominating com., chmn. pension investments com., vice chmn. fin. and audit com. March of Dimes; mem. monitoring com. The Group of Thirty; mem. U.S. Coun. for Internat. Bus. Author: Regulation of the Commodities Futures and Options Markets; co-author: Regulation of Brokers, Dealers and Securities Markets, Supplement Markets; editorial bd. mem. Internat. Jour. Regulatory Law and Practice; practitioner bd. advisors Stanford Jour. of Law.; mem. editl. bd. Futures and Derivatives Law Report. Mem. ABA (mem. subcom. on exec. coun., fed. regulation of securities, derivative instruments subcom., regulation of futures and derivative instruments), Assn. of Bar of City of N.Y. (chmn. internat. law sub com. of the com. on commodities regulation 1984-85, chmn. com. commodities regulations 1981-82), D.C. Bar Assn., Fgn. Policy Assn., Econ. Club N.Y. Office: Lehman Bros Inc 745 7th Ave 31st Fl New York NY 10019-6801 E-mail: trusso1@lehman.com.

RUSSO, VINCENT BARNEY, music educator; b. Carmel, Calif., Oct. 19, 1944; s. Salvatore Dody and Betty Lou (Posey) R. BA, San Francisco State U., 1967, MA, 1969; lic. de concert, Ecole Normale de Musique, Paris, 1973; PhD, U. Calif., San Diego, 1978. Assoc. in voice U.S. Internat. U., San Diego, 1976-83; assoc. in music Internat. U., London, 1979-80; adj. prof. Tex. Christian U., Ft. Worth, 1986-88, asst. prof. vocal performance pedagogy, 1988-95; faculty Coll of the Redwoods, Mendocino, Calif., 1996—. Apprentice artist Santa Fe Opera Co., 1971; tching. asst., rsch. asst. U. Calif., San Diego, 1974-78; baritone San Diego Opera Co., 1976-82; asst. editor, editor Jour. Rsch. in Singing, Ft. Worth, 1978-95; music coach, dir. Inst. Vocal Studies, Ft. Worth, 1981-88. Baritone soloist French Radio TV, 1971; performer The Merry Widow, PBS, 1977; editor: Jour. Rsch. in Singing and Applied Vocal Pedagog, 1987-95; vocal dir. Gloriana Opera Co., 1995—, Opera Fresca, 1996—; appeared at Mendocino Music Festival, 1996, 97, 98, 99, 2000, 01, 02, 03. Recipient Alexander Saunderson award Met. Opera San Francisco, 1969, Young Artist award Nat. Fedn. Music Clubs, 1969, 77, Harriet H. Wooley and Frank Huntington Beebe award, 1972, 73, William M. Sullivan Music Found. award for European audition, 1974. Mem. Internat. Assn. Rsch. in Singing (gen. sec. 1987-95), Nat. Assn. Tchrs. Singing (Singing Artist award 1971), Coll. Music Soc. Avocations: bicycling, hiking, movies, theater.

RUSSONIELLO, JOSEPH PASCAL, lawyer; b. Jersey City, Oct. 12, 1941; s. Sabin G. and Justine B. (Terraciano) R.; m. Moira F. Ward, Aug. 29, 1969. B in Social Sci., Fairfield U., 1963; JD, NYU, 1966. Bar: N.J. 1967, Calif. 1969. Spl. agt. FBI, Washington, 1966-67; dep. dist. atty. City and County San Francisco (Calif.) Dist. Atty. Offices, 1969-75; assoc. Cooley Godward Castro Huddleson & Tatum, San Francisco, 1975-78; U.S. atty. U.S. Dept. Justice (no. dist.) Calif., San Francisco, 1982-90; ptnr. Cooley Godward L.L.P., San Francisco, 1978-82, 90—. Pres., bd. dirs. San Francisco (Calif.) Law Sch., 1996—; analyst KTVU-Ch. 2, Oakland, Calif., 1994—. Pres. Northgate Cottages, Napa, Calif., 1988—; chmn. Catholics for Truth and Justice, San Francisco, 1991—; v.p. Mid-Pacific region Nat. Italian Am. Fedn., 1996-99. Recipient Man of Yr. award NIAF, 1986, Man of Yr. award St. Thomas More Soc., San Francisco, 2000, Assumpta award Trustees St. Mary's Cathedral, 2000, Papal Pro Ecclesia medal, 2000; named Alumni of Yr.-Pub. Sector, NYU Law Sch., 1991. Fellow Am. Coll. Trial Lawyers; mem. Am. bd. Trial Lawyers (adv.), McFetridge Inn of Ct. (barrister). Republican. Avocations: tennis, golf, reading, playing the saxophone. Office: Cooley Godward LLP 1 Maritime Plz San Francisco CA 94111-3404 E-mail: Russonielloj@cooley.com.

RUSSOTTI, PHILIP ANTHONY, lawyer; b. N.Y.C., Mar. 24, 1948; s. Philip Armond and Yolanda (Morelli) R.; m. Mary Wolfe, Jan. 20, 1973 (div. Mar., 1996); children: Thomas, Matthew, Peter; m. Kathleen Kettles, May 25, 1996. BA, Columbia U., 1970; JD, St. John's U., Queens, N.Y., 1973. Bar: N.Y. 1974, U.S. Dist. Ct. (so. dist.) N.Y. 1974, U.S. Dist. Ct. (ea. dist.) N.Y., 1980, U.S. Ct. Appeals (2nd cir.) 1982, U.S. Ct. Appeals (D.C. cir.) 1989, U.S. Ct. Internat. Trade 1986, U.S. Ct. Fed. Claims, 2000, U.S. Supreme Ct., 1997; bd. cert. civil trial atty. Nat. Bd. Trial Advocacy, 1997, U.S. Ct. Fed. Claims, 2000. Bur. chief, Supreme Ct. trial bur. asst. dist. atty. N.Y. County Dist. Atty.'s Office, N.Y.C., 1973-80; pvt. practice N.Y.C., 1980-84; partner Russotti & Barrison, N.Y.C., 1985-89, Wingate, Russotti & Shapiro, N.Y.C., 1990—. Lectr. in the field. Gen. counsel Italian Am. Repertory Theatre, N.Y., 1985-90; mem. Prospect Park Alliance, Bklyn., 1996—. Recipient Am. Jurisprudence awards Bancroft Whitney & Lawyers Co-op, 1971, 73. Mem. ABA, ATLA, N.Y. State Bar Assn., N.Y. State Trial Lawyers Assn. Roman Catholic. Home: 433 3rd St Brooklyn NY 11215-2949 Office: Wingate Russotti Shapiro 420 Lexington Ave Rm 2750 New York NY 10170-2793 E-mail: prussotti@yahoo.com.

RUST, EDWARD BARRY, JR., insurance company executive, lawyer; b. Chgo., Aug. 3, 1950; s. Edward Barry Sr. and Harriett B. (Fuller) R.; m. Sally Buckler, Feb. 28, 1976; 1 child, Edward Barry III. Student, Lawrence U., 1968-69; BS, Ill. Wesleyan U., 1972; JD, MBA, So. Meth. U., 1975. Bar: Tex. 1975, Ill. 1976. Mgmt. trainee State Farm Ins. Cos., Dallas, 1975-76, atty. Bloomington, 1976, sr. atty., 1976-78, asst. v.p., 1978-81, v.p., 1981-83, exec. v.p., 1983-85, pres., CEO, 1985—87, CEO, chmn., 1987—. Pres. and bd. dirs. State Farm Investment Mgmt. Corp., State Farm Internat. Services, Inc., State Farm Cos. Found.; bd. dirs. exec. and investment coms. State Farm Annuity and Life Ins. Co., State Farm Mut. Automobile Ins. Co., State Farm Life Ins. Co., State Farm Fire and Casualty, State Farm Gen. Trustee Ill. Wesleyan U., 1985—; mem. adv. coun. Grad. Sch. Bus. Stanford U., 1987-94; mem. bus. adv. coun. Coll. Commerce and Bus. Adminstrn. U. Ill. Mem. Am. Enterprise Inst., Bus. Roundtable (chmn. edn. task force), Tex. State Bar Assn., Ill. Bar Assn., Am. Inst. Property and Liability Underwriters (trustee 1986-96), Ins. Inst. Am. (trustee 1986-96), Ins. Inst. for Highway Safety (vice chmn.), Nat. Alliance of Bus. (chmn. 1998—), Ill. Bus. Roundtable (chmn. 1998—). Office: State Farm Ins Cos 1 State Farm Plz E-12 Bloomington IL 61710-0001*

RUST, JOHN HOWSON, JR., lawyer, state legislator; b. May 21, 1947; s. John Howson and Laura Jeanne (Johnson) R.; m. Susan Byrne, Aug. 15, 1970; children: John W., Thomas A., Robert B. BA, U. Va., 1969, JD, 1972. Bar: Va. 1972, U.S. Dist. Ct. (ea. dist.) Va. 1973, U.S. Ct. Appeals (4th cir.) 1975, U.S. Supreme Ct. 1976. Mem. firm Rust & Rust, P.C. Mem. Ho. of Dels., Commonwealth of Va., 1980-82, 97-2001. Office: PO Box 460 10370 Main St Fairfax VA 22030-0460 E-mail: johnhr@erols.com.

RUST, LIBBY KAREN, fundraising and public relations counsel; b. York, Maine, Feb. 8, 1951; d. Myron Davis and Meta Mildred (Libby) R. BA, Wheaton Coll., 1973; MS, Columbia U., 1977. Day care field asst. Childhood Ednl. Enrichment Program, Waterville, Maine, 1974—75; cons. Ctr. for Cmty. Planning and Cons., N.Y.C., 1975—76; intern Morgan Guaranty Trust Co., N.Y.C., 1976; staff asst. subcom. on mental health Task Force on N.Y.C. Fiscal Crisis, 1976—77; auditor AT&T, N.Y.C., 1977; budget examiner Legis. Office of Budget Rev., N.Y.C., 1977—78; exec. dir. Strafford County Human Svcs., Dover, NH, 1978—79; dir. allocations and agy. rels. United Way, Inc., Portland, Maine, 1979—82, planning and allocations divsn. dir., 1982—84; exec. dir. Seacoast United Way, Portsmouth, NH, 1984—87; dir. devel. Am. Cancer Soc., L.A., 1987—88; assoc. dir. St. Vincent Med. Ctr., L.A., 1988—89; dir. ann. giving St. Joseph Hosp. Found., Orange, Calif., 1989—91, asst. dir. devel., 1991—93; dir. devel. Cmty. Health Svcs., Inc., Portland, Maine, 1993—94; exec. dir. York County Tech. Coll. Found., 1994-99; founder The Rust Comm. Group, 1999—. Mem. budget com. Town of York, 1979-80; trustee Kents Hill Sch., 1991-93, York Pub. Libr., 1999-2002, Mercy Hosp. VNA-Homecare, Pine Tree Soc., Maine. Mem. Assn. Fundraising Profls. No. New Eng. (pres. 2003), Jr. League Portland. Republican. Office: PO Box 1227 York Harbor ME 03911-1227

RUST, LOIS, food company executive; Pres. Rose Acre Farms, Seymour, Ind., 1989—. Office: Rose Acre Farms PO Box 1250 Seymour IN 47274-3850

RUST, PATRICIA JOAN, television/film production company executive, writer, producer; b. LA, Sept. 24, 1958; d. William Evans Jr. and Jacquelyn (Knox) R. BA, UCLA, 1978, postgrad., 1978-80, 87-89; student, Am. Film Inst. Writer, producer PBS, L.A., 1978-79, creator, host On Cue; corr. ABC-TV, L.A., 1979-82; pres. Patricia Rust Prodns., L.A., 1982—. Host, writer, creator, producer numerous syndicated spls., 1982-89; writer, producer comedy shows and spls. ABC, NBC, CBS and PBS; spkr. in field. Film and TV writer, story editor: including network comedy spls., TV movies, episodes; author: The King of Skittledeedoo, 1999, 2d edit., 2001 (Parents' Choice award winning literacy book); assoc. editor: Prodrs. Guild Mag., 1990—; contbr. L.A. Times Kids Page. Pres., founder, The Rust Found. for Literacy, 1999—; founder JackietheAngel.com, 1999, PowerforKids.com, 2000. Recipient Golden Mike award Radio and TV News Assn., Hollywood, 1984, Humanitarian Book award for best children's book, 2001; named Best Network Comedy Writer NBC, 1990; winner comedy writing competition Am. Film Inst., 1989. Mem. NATAS, Hollywood Radio and TV Soc., Producers Guild, Writers Guild Am., Am. Film Inst., Daily Bruin Alumni Assn. (pres.). Office: Patricia Rust Prodns # 924 12021 Wilshire Blvd # 924 Los Angeles CA 90025-1206 E-mail: patricia@powerforkids.com.

RUST, ROBERT FRANCIS, retired publishing executive; b. Herrick, S.D., Oct. 26, 1927; s. Charles William and Agatha Susan R.; m. Wilma Lorraine LeBeau, Oct. 18, 1948; children: Randal, Roberta, Ann, Mary. Student, U. Houston, 1950-53. Billing clk. Armour Fertilizer Works, Houston, 1950-53; v.p. Gulf Pub. Co., Houston, 1953-98. With USAF, 1948-49.

RUST, WILLIAM DAVID, JR., retired structural engineer; b. Washington, Oct. 11, 1931; s. William David and Anna Mae (Lyles) R.; m. Eunice Charles Williams, Oct. 24, 1953; children: Diann Yvonne Rust-Tierney, Cheryl Frances, William Douglas. BS in Civil Engring., Howard U., 1954; postgrad., Cath. U. Am., 1956-57; MS in Engring., George Washington U., 1962; postgrad., U. Va., 1973-74. Registered profl. engr., Mass. Naval architect Phila. Naval Shipyard, 1954; structural engr. U.S. Gen. Svcs. Adminstrn., Washington, 1956-92; ret. 1992. Lectr. civil engring. Fed. City Coll. (now U. D.C.), Washington, 1973; mem. com.Interagency Seismic Safety, Washington, 1978-90, ASCE, Found. and Excavation Stds., N.Y.C., 1978-95, AISC, Steel Specification Simplification, Chgo., 1980-81; mem. coms. Fed. Constrn. Coun., Washington, 1978-90. Pack com. chmn. Boy Scouts Am., Washington, 1968; clk. session Northminster Presbyn. Ch., Washington, 1972; commr. genn. assembly Presbyn. Ch. U.S., Ft. Worth, 1973. Lt. C.E., U.S. Army, 1954-56. Fellow ASCE; mem., NSPE, Structural Stability Rsch. Coun. (mem.-at-large), Tau Beta Pi (life). Achievements include administration of development of first nationwide microfilming of design and construction drawings system for the U.S. General Services Adminstration. Home: 7600 Alaska Ave NW Washington DC 20012-1469 Personal E-mail: w.rustjr@worldnet.att.net.

RUSTAY, JENNIFER B. lawyer; b. Kansas City, Mo., Jan. 30, 1973; m. Allen Harrington Rustay, Sept. 29, 2001. BA, Baylor U., 1995, JD, 1997. Bar: Tex. 1997, U.S. Dist. Ct. (no., so., ea. and we. dists.) Tex., Dist. of Colo., U.S. Ct. Appeals (5th cir.). Law clk. Hon. Sam Johnson U.S. Ct. Appeals (5th cir.), Austin, Tex., 1997—98; atty. Bracewell & Patterson, Houston, 1998—2001, Hagans, Bobb & Burdine, 2001—. Office: Hagans Bobb & Burdine 3200 Travis 4th Fl Houston TX 77006 Office Phone: 713-222-2700.

RUSTHOVEN, PETER JAMES, lawyer; b. Indpls., Aug. 12, 1951; s. Richard and Henrietta (Iwema) R.; children from previous marriage: Julia Faith, David James; m. Linda C. Bennett, Dec. 28, 1987; children: Mark Bennett, Matthew Boyd. AB magna cum laude, Harvard U., 1973, JD magna cum laude, 1976. Bar: Ind., 1976. Assoc. Barnes, Hickam, Pantzer & Boyd, Indpls., 1976-81; assoc. counsel to Pres. of U.S., White House, Washington, 1981-85; of counsel Barnes & Thornburg, Indpls., 1985-86, ptnr., 1987—. Counsel Presdl. Commn. on Space Shuttle Challenger Accident, 1986; spl. cons. U.S. Atty. Gen.'s Adv. Bd. on Missing Children, 1988; adj. fellow Hudson Inst., 1989-91, adj. sr. fellow, 1991—; sr. fellow Ind. Policy Rev. Found., 1991—; bd. advisors Indpls. Lawyers Chpt. Federalist Soc., 1993—, mem. nat. practitioners coun., 1995—. Contbr. monthly column The Am. Spectator mag., 1973-79; mem. bd. editors Harvard Law Rev., 1974-76, case editor, 1975-76; contbr. articles to nat. mags. Bd. dirs. Ednl. Choice Charitable Trust, 1994—, Legal Svcs. Orgn. Indpls., 1977-79; precinct committeeman Marion County Rep. Ctrl. Com., Indpls., 1978-81; state media dir. Ind. Reagan for Pres. Com., 1979-80, Ind. Reagan-Bush Com., 1980; speechwriter nat. Reagan for Pres. Campaign, 1980; mem. legal policy adv. bd. Washington Legal Found., 1989—, transition counsel's office Bush-Cheney Presdl. Transition, 2001; candidate for Rep. nomination for U.S. Senate, Ind., 1998. Grantee Inst. Politics, Harvard U., 1972. Mem. Ind. Bar Assn., Indpls. Bar Assn., Phi Beta Kappa. Roman Catholic. Avocations: golf, contract bridge, baseball memorabilia collecting. Office: Barnes & Thornburg 1313 Merchants Bank Bldg 11 S Meridian St Ste 1313 Indianapolis IN 46204-3535 Office Phone: 317-231-7289. Business E-Mail: peter.rusthoven@btlaw.com. E-mail: peter.rusthoven@hotmail.com.

RUSTIN, RUDOLPH BYRD, III, surgeon, educator; b. Charleston, S.C., May 14, 1957; s. Rudolph Byrd and Mary Pringle (Herrin) R.; m. Sandra Lee Talbott, Nov. 28, 1985; children: Jonathan, Jeffrey. BS in Chemistry cum laude, Hampden Sydney Coll., 1979; MD, Med. U. S.C., 1983. Diplomate Am. Bd. Surgery, Am. Bd. Colon and Rectal Surgery. Intern Cleve. Clinic Found., 1983-84, resident, 1984-88, chief resident gen. surgery, 1987-88, fellow, 1988-89; private practice colon rectal surgery Charleston, 1989—; clin. assoc. surgery Med. U. S.C., Charleston, 1989—. Active staff Roper Hosp., Charleston, St. Francis Xavier Hosp.; med. dir. Commun-i-Care, 2002; presenter in field. Fellow ACS, Am. Soc. Colon Rectal Surgeons, Southeastern Surgical Congress; mem. Med. Soc. S.C., S.C. State Med. Assn., S.C. Med. Assn. (del.), So. Med. Assn., Charleston County Med. Soc., Phi Beta Kappa. Office: 125 Doughty St Ste 770 Charleston SC 29403-5764

RUSU, SIR ANDREW PETER (SIR ANDREW RUSU BARON ROCHEFORT), ambassador, lawyer; b. Arad, Romania, Mar. 24, 1949; s. Andrew and Yank Rusu. Eötvoös Jorant, Law Sch., Budapest, Hungary, 1981; BA, Trinity Coll., 1997. Consul gen., amb. Holy See of Antioch, N.Y.C., 1991—; amb. at large Diplomatic Mission of Liberia, N.Y.C., 1997—. Internat. law cons. Rep. senatorial Innter Cir., Washington, 1993, Round Table, 1996. Mem. N.Y. Acad. Scis., Am. Inst. of Sci. and Tech., Knight of Malta (chevaliers). Avocations: reading, tennis, travel, swimming. Office: Diplomatic Mission of Liberia 95-09 43rd Ave Flushing NY 11373 E-mail: andrewrusu@aol.com.

RUSZKIEWICZ, CAROLYN MAE, newspaper editor; b. Tucson, Nov. 10, 1946; d. Robert Frank and Charlotte Ruth (Hadley) Knapton; m. Joseph Charles Ruszkiewicz, July 11, 1969. BA, Calif. State U., Long Beach, 1971, MA, 1973. Reporter Long Beach (Calif.) Press-Telegram, 1968-85, consumer editor, 1985-86, lifestyle editor, 1986-89, regional news editor, 1989-91, city editor, 1991-95, asst. mng. editor, 1995-97, mng. editor, 1997—. Avocations: swimming, walking, reading. Office: Long Beach Press Telegram 604 Pine Ave Long Beach CA 90844-0003

RUTA, THOMAS V. professional sports team executive, accounting executive; married. BS summa cum laude, Fordham U., 1966; MBA with distinction, Pace U.; postgrad. in law, Fordham U. CPA, N.Y., N.J., Minn. Founding ptnr. Behan, Ling & Ruta CPAs, P.C., N.Y.C., now chmn., pres.; ltd. ptnr. Pitts. Penguins; mem. Hockey Holdings & Mgmt. Group. Office: 358 5th Ave 9th Fl New York NY 10001 Office Phone: 212-695-7003. E-mail: truta@blrcpaspc.com.

RUTAN, CHARLES R. musician; b. May 10, 1966; s. Frank and Peggy (Hendry) Rutan; m. Catherine Mayer, May 29, 1999; children: Gwendolyn, Sophia. MusB in Composition summa cum laude, U. Arts, Phila., 1992; postgrad. in music instrn., Chestnut Hill Coll., 1994; postgrad., Piping Ctr., Glasgow, Scotland, 1998. Cert. tchr. Pa. CEO, founder Bagpipes FAO, Phila.; mgr., prin. oboist Chestnut Hill Orch. Performed for Pres. George Bush, Mrs. Tom Ridge, Queen Noor, Regent of Jordan; opened for Rod Stewart Trump Taj Majal, Atlantic City; piper MiGaea Yacht; prin. bagpipe Reading Symphony Orch.; performed USMC, U.S. Army and USN Ceremonies, Guiness Stout and U.S. Airways Promotions, Tom Polis Golf Classic; featured on various TV programs, mags., newspapers, including Phila. Weddings, Modern Bride mags., ABC, NBC, CBS, CNN, Finnish Nat. TV, Irish Am. Newspaper; ceremonial piper retirement ball for Phila. Episcopal Bishop; piper installation ceremonies Phila. Archdiocesan parishes, Presbytery ofcls., organ dedication ceremonies; performer Irish Uilleann (Union) Pipes, World Bagpipes. Composer (symphonic music): 3 symphonies, numerous choral works, works for bagpipes. Mem.: ASCAP (spl. composer award 1994), Friends of Scotland's Classic Malts, Music Educators Nat. Conf., Eastern U.S. Pipeband Assn., Am. Fedn. Musicians, Internat. Double Reed Soc. Office Phone: 800-544-4028. E-mail: bagpipesfao@worldnet.att.net.

RUTAN, ELBERT L. (BURT RUTAN), aircraft designer, aircraft company executive; b. 1943; s. George and Irene R.; m. BS in Aero. Engring., Calif. State Polytech. U., 1965. Flight test project engr. Air Force Flight Test Ctr., Edwards AFB, Calif., 1965-72; dir. Bede Test Ctr., Kans., 1972-74; pres. Rutan Aircraft Factory, Mojave, Calif., 1974—; founder, CEO Scaled Composites Inc., Mojave, Calif., 1982—; v.p. Beech Aircraft, 1985. Designer more than 100 aircraft including VariViggen, Solitaire, Defiant, Raytheon Beechcraft Starship, Proteus, Boomerang and other kits; designer Voyager aircraft, first to fly around-the-world without stopping, refueling; company made history with first private manned mission to space in SpaceShipOne. Recip. Spirit of St. Louis Medal, Am. Soc. Mech. Engrs., 1987, Best Design Award, Exptl. Aircraft Assn.; Air medal, 1970, Stan Szik design contbn. trophy, 1972, EAA Outstanding New Design, 1975-76, 78; Dr. August Raspet Meml. award, 1976, ABC World News Tonight Person of the Week, 1986, Collier trophy for ingenious design and devel., Nat. Aeronautic Assn., 1986, Presdl. Citizens medal, 1986, FAI gold medal for Voyager Constrn., 1987, medal for the City of Paris, 1987, NASA langley Rsch. Ctr. dirs. award, 1987, Soc. of NASA Flight Surgeons, W. Randolph Lovelace award 1987, medal of Outstanding Achievement and disting. leadership, 1987, Soc. of exptl. test pilots, 1987, Aviation Man of the Yr, 1987, Lindbergh Eagle award, 1987, USAF 40th anniversary award, 1987, The City of Genoa, Italy, Christopher Columbus Internat. Communications medal, 1987, British gold medal, 1987, Outstanding Engring. achievement awards, 1988, Franklin medal, 1987, Disting. inventor award 1988, Meritorious Svc. award, 1988, Internat. Aerospace Hall of Fame Honoree, 1988, medal of achievement, 1989, Crystal Eagle award, 1989, Meritorious Civilian Svc. medal, 1989, Leroy Randle Grumman medal, 1989, Structures, Structural Dynamics and Materials award AIAA, 1991. Mem. NAE. Office: Scaled Composites Inc Mojave Airport 1624 Flight Line Mojave CA 93501-1663 Office Phone: 661-824-4541. Office Fax: 661-824-4174.*

RUTAN, RICHARD GLENN (DICK RUTAN), aircraft company executive, aviator; b. Loma Linda, Calif., July 1, 1938; s. George and Irene Rutan; m. Kris Rutan; children: Holly, Jill stepchildren: Shannon, Kelly. BS, Am. Tech. U., 1975; D Sci. and Tech. (hon.), Cen. New Eng. Coll., 1987; HHD (hon.), Lewis U., 1989. Commd. 2d lt. USAF, 1959, advanced through grades to lt. col., 1976, ret., 1978; prodn. mgr., chief test pilot Rutan Aircraft Factory, Mojave, Calif., 1978-81; pres. Voyager Aircraft Inc., Mojave, 1981-94. Mng. dir. Bob Pond Race Team, 1989-91; profl. lectr., 1986—. Rep. nomination to 42d Congrl. Dist. (Calif.), 1992. Decorated Silver Star, DFC with silver oak leaf cluster (5), Purple Heart, Air medals (16); recipient Louis Bleriot medal Fedn. Aeronautique Internationale, 1982, Collier trophy Nat. Aeronautic Assn., 1986, Presdl. Citizen's Medal of Honor, 1986, Godfrey L. Cabot award Aero Club New Eng., 1987, Patriot of Yr. award, 1987, Newsmaker of Yr. award Aviation Writers Am., 1987, Daedalian Disting. Achievement award, 1987, Lindbergh Eagle award San Diego Aerospace Mus., 1987, Iven C. Kincheloe award Soc. Exptl. Test Pilots, 1987, Gold medal Royal Aero Club, Grande Medallion, Medalle de Ville Paris Paris Aero Club, World Record for flying the Voyager in a 1st closed circuit, great circle distance around-the-world, non-stop, non-refueled flight, numerous others. Office: PO Box 359 Mojave CA 93502-0359*

RUTANEN, ROY STEWART, producer, television personality; b. Putnam, Conn., July 1, 1947; s. Phyllis Morse Rutanen; children: Rene, Jade Babey, Jessica Smith, Sarah. BA, U. Mass., 1998. TV reporter, anchor Sta. KENS-TV, San Antonio, 1982-87; TV reporter Sta. KMOL-TV, Tex., 1987-88; anchor, reporter Sta. XTRA-TV, San Diego, 1988-89; writer, prodr., dir. Electronic Scribe, Southbridge, Mass., 1990-2000; talk-show host Sta. WESO-TV, Southbridge, 1998-99, Sta. 13-10 WORC-TV, Worcester, Mass., 1999—. Dir. opers. Artist Devel. Complex, Southbridge, Mass. Author, narrator (documentary) Holy Ground, 1996; (video) Welcome to Strubridge, 1999; author, prodr. (documentary) Reflections of Belchertown, 2000; Writer, prodr. Rehabilitative Resources, Inc., 2000 (Telly award 2001). Active Am. Cancer Soc., Southbridge, 1999. With U.S. Army, 1966-69. Recipient 2d pl. Tex. AP, 1982, Best Feature award Soc. Profl. Journalists, 1984, award of Honor Tex. Safety Assn., 1984, Media award of the Yr., 1986, 2 Golden Mike awards, 1988, 2 Telly awards, 1996. Home and Office: 901 N Woodstock Rd Southbridge MA 01550 Fax: 508-764-3572. E-mail: royr2000@juno.com.

RUTENBERG-ROSENBERG, SHARON LESLIE, retired journalist; b. Chgo., May 23, 1951; d. Arthur and Bernice (Berman) Rutenberg; m. Michael J. Rosenberg, Feb. 3, 1980; children: David Kaifel and Jonathan Reuben (twins), Emily Mara. Student, Harvard U., 1972; BA, Northwestern U., 1973, MSJ., 1975; cert. student pilot. Reporter-photographer Lerner Home Newspapers, Chgo., 1973-74; corr. Medill News Service, Washington, 1975; reporter-newsperson, sci. writer UPI, Chgo., 1975-84; ret., 1984. Interviewer: exclusives White House chief of staff, nation's only mother and son on death row; others. Vol. Chgo.-Read Mental Health Ctr. Recipient Peter Lisagor award for exemplary journalism in features category, 1980, 81; Golden Key Nat. Adv. Bd. of Children's Oncology Service Inc., 1981; Media awards for wire service feature stories, 1983, 84, wire service news stories, 1983, 84, all from Chgo. Hosp. Pub. Relations Soc. Mem. Profl. Assn. Diving Instrs., Nat. Assn. Underwater Instrs., Hon. Order Ky. Cols., Hadassah, Sigma Delta Chi, Sigma Delta Tau Home: 745 Marion Ave Highland Park IL 60035-5123

RUTES, WALTER ALAN, architect; b. N.Y.C., Sept. 21, 1928; s. Jack and Sarah (Ogur) R.; m. Helene Darville, Apr. 2, 1952; children: Daniel J., Linda Lee. B.Arch. (Sands Meml. medal 1950), Cornell U., 1950; fellow city planning, MIT, 1951; postgrad., Harvard U. Grad. Sch. Design, 1978. Cert. Nat. Council Archtl. Registration Bds. Assoc. ptnr. Skidmore, Owings & Merrill, N.Y.C., 1951-72; v.p. John Carl Warnecke & Assocs., N.Y.C., 1972-74; staff v.p. Intercontinental Hotels Corp., N.Y.C., 1974-80; dir. architecture Holiday Inns, Inc., Memphis, 1980-83; dir. design The Sheraton Corp., Boston, 1983-85; chmn 9 Tek Ltd. Devel. Cons., 1985—. Chmn. adv. bd. Hult Fellowships for Constrn. Industry, 1968-75, Architects and Engrs. Com. New Bldg. Code, 1968; mem. zoning adv. com. N.Y.C. Planning Commn., 1970; lectr. in field, 1968—; mem. steering com. UNESCO Council Tall Bldgs. and Urban Habitat, 1980—; vis. prof. Cornell-Essec Grad. Program; vis. prof. Nova U. Author: Hotel Planning and Design, 1985, Hotel Design, Planning and Development, 2001; (software) SHAPE, Megatrends and Marketecture; contbr. articles to profl. jours.; prin. works include Lincoln Center Library for Performing Arts, N.Y.C., 1967, Am. Republic Ins. Co. Nat. Hdqrs., Des Moines, 1967, HUD Apts., Jersey City, 1972, Merrill Lynch Bldg., N.Y.C., 1973, Tour Fiat, Paris, 1974, Aid Assn. for Luths. Nat. Hdqrs., Appleton, Wis., 1976, Semiramis Intercontinental Hotel, Cairo, 1985, Intercontinental, Jeddah, 1983, Embassy Suites Internat., 1985, Universal City Hotel Complex, L.A., 1986, TechWorld Conv. Hotel, Washington, 1986, Sheraton Fairplex Conv. Ctr., L.A., 1992, Orlando Conv. Ctr. Hotel, 1993, Winter Olympiad Media Complex, Norway, 1993, Ephesus Resort Complex, Turkey, 1986, Royal Christiania Hotel, Oslo, Norway, 1991, EuroFrance Leisure Park Complex, Cannes, 1993, Kuna Hills Multi Resort, Guam, 1994. Recipient Platinum Circle award Hotel Design Industry, 1988. Fellow AIA; mem. Ethical Culture Soc. Office: 8501 N 84th Pl Scottsdale AZ 85258-2419 also: 25 Richbell Rd White Plains NY 10605-4110

RUTFORD, ROBERT HOXIE, geologist, educator; b. Duluth, Minn., Jan. 26, 1933; s. Skuli and Ruth (Hoxie) R.; m. Marjorie Ann, June 19, 1954; children: Gregory, Kristian, Barbara. BA, U. Minn., 1954, MA, 1963, PhD, 1969; DSc (hon.), St Petersburg State Tech U., Russia, 1994. Football and track coach Hamline U., 1958-62; rsch. fellow U. Minn., 1963-66; asst. prof. geology U. S.D., 1967-70, assoc. prof., 1970-72, chmn. dept. geology, 1968-72, chmn. dept. physics, 1971-72; dir. Ross Ice Shelf Project U. Nebr., Lincoln, 1972-75; dir. divsn. Polar Programs NSF, Washington, 1975-77; vice chancellor for research and grad. studies, prof. geology U. Nebr., 1977-82, interim chancellor, 1980-81; pres., prof. geoscis. U. Tex., Dallas, 1982-94, Excellence in Edn. Found. prof. of geoscis., 1994—. U.S. del. to Sci. Com. on Antarctic Rsch., 1986-2002, v.p., 1996-98, pres., 1998-2002, mem. exec. com., 2002--; chmn. NRC Polar Rsch. Bd., 1991-95. Mem. editl. bd. Issues in Sci. and Tech., 1991-94. Trustee Baylor Coll. Dentistry, 1989—96. 1st lt. U.S. Army, 1954-56. Recipient Antarctic Svc. medal, 1964, Disting. Svc. award NSF, 1977, Ernie Gunderson award for svc. to amateur athletics S.D. AAU, 1972, Outstanding Achievement award U. Minn., 1993, "M" Club Lifetime Achievement award, 1995. Fellow Geol. Soc. Am.; mem. Antarctican Soc. (pres. 1988-90), Arctic Inst. N.Am., Explorers Club, Am. Polar Soc. (hon.), Philos. Soc. Tex., St. Petersburg Acad. Engring. (Russia), Tex. Acad. Sci., Nebr. Acad. Sci., Cosmos Club, Sigma Xi. Lutheran. Home: 1882 Quail Ln Richardson TX 75080-3456 Office: Univ Tex Dallas Geosciences Program Richardson TX 75083-0688

RUTH, BYRON EDWARD, civil engineering educator; b. Chgo., Mar. 25, 1931; s. Edward Luther and Evelyn Pearl (Wells) R.; m. Margarete Rohweder, Sept. 10, 1960; children: Boyd Owen, Toni Karen. BS, Mont. State U., 1955; MS, Purdue U., 1959; PhD, W.Va. U., 1967. Registered profl. engr., Ind., W.Va., Fla. Field engr. Walter H. Knapp, Drummond Island, Mich., 1959; asst. dir. R & D, Symons Mfg. Co., Des Plaines, Ill., 1960-61; instr. civil engring. W.Va. U., Morgantown, 1961-67, asst. prof., 1967-70; assoc. prof. civil engring. U. Fla., Gainesville, 1970-77, prof., 1977-2000, prof. emeritus, 2000—. Cons. transp., materials and design. Contbr. numerous articles to profl. jours. With U.S. Army, 1956-58. Recipient Ronald D. Kenyon rsch. award, 1996. Mem. ASCE, ASTM (chmn. D04 exec. com. 1993-94), Assn. Asphalt Paving Technologists (hon., pres. 1986), Transp. Rsch. Bd. (chmn. com. A2D05 1994-99, mem. SuperPave com., 1997-2003), Can. Tech. Asphalt Assn. (hon.), Sigma Xi, Tau Beta Pi. Achievements include patents for concrete forming equipment. Office: U Fla Dept Civil and Coastal Engring Gainesville FL 32611-6580

RUTH, DEBORAH ANN, music educator; b. Brookline, Mass., July 25, 1950; d. Neil J. and Mary E. Valerio; m. Gregory J. Ruth, May 1, 1971; children: Melissa, Geoffrey, Jonathan, Stephen, Jennifer. MusB summa cum laude, Columbia Coll., Columbia, SC, 2000. Pianist, music ministry assoc. Fellowship Baptist Ch., Lexington, SC, 1995—; instr. piano Columbia Coll., Columbia, SC, 2001—. Adjudicator keyboard auditions Richland Sch. Dist. II Tri-Dist. Arts, Columbia, SC, 2003—04. Co-dir. summer music camp Fellowship Baptist Ch., Lexington, SC, 2001—04. Mem.: Columbia Music Tchrs. Assn. (mem. exec. bd. 2000—, corr. sec. 2001—03, v.p. programs. 2003—04, adjudicator keyboard auditions 2002—04), SC Music Tchrs. Assn., Music Tchrs. Nat. Assn. Office: Musical Arts Studios Columbia Coll 1301 Columbia College Dr Columbia SC 29203-5949

RUTH, EDWARD KEITH, information systems specialist, management consultant; b. Louisville, June 28, 1960; s. William Edward and Lillian Loretta (Wyatt) R. BS in Bus. Data Processing, BA in Econs., William Carey Coll., 1982; MBA, Oklahoma City U., 1990; EdD in Adult Edn., Okla. State U., 1997. Cert. data processor, computer prof., project mgmt., profl., Inst. Certification Computing Profls., Ill., PMP Project Mgmt. Inst., Pa. Sr. sys. analyst IV Miss. State Tax Commn., Jackson, 1982-96; sr. sys. programmer Cooper Industries, Vicksburg, Miss., 1985-86, Hertz Corp., Oklahoma City, Okla., 1986-90; applications platform mgr. Acxiom Corp., Conway, Ark., 1991-92; sr. product developer Teubner & Assocs., Stillwater, Okla., 1992-93; sr. software developer BMC Software, Austin, Tex., 1996-98; sr. info. tech. specialist IBM, Lexington, Ky., 1998-2000. Contbr. articles to profl. jours. Mem. Project Mgmt. Inst., Nat. Sys. Programmers Assn., Am. Vocat. Ednl. Rsch. Assn., Mgmt. Sci. Inst. Republican. Baptist. Avocations: art, travel, reading, music. Home and Office: 1424 Willus Dr Laurel MS 39440-1467 E-mail: edruthfax@yahoo.com.

RUTH, JAMES PERRY, financial planning executive; b. Washington, Feb. 27, 1946; s. Robert Walker and Virginia Null Ruth; m. Kathleen McHugh, Aug. 10, 1968; children: Heather Lynn, Michael James. BS in Bus. and Public Adminstrn., U. Md., 1970; postgrad., Am. Coll., Bryn Mawr, 1971-83. CLU, CFP, chartered fin. cons. agt., Northwestern Mutual Life Ins. Co., Washington, 1967-74. Gen. agt. Indpls. Life, Rockville, Md., 1974-82; partner Fox, Ruth & Middledorf, Rockville, 1975-82; mgr. Mfrs. Fin. Svcs., Rosslyn, Va., 1982-84; pres. Potomac Fin. Group, 1984—. Contbr. articles to profl. publs.; quoted in N.Y. Times, U.S. News and World Report, USA Today, others. Past pres. Jelleff Boys' Club; past pres. Montgomery County Police Boys' and Girls' Club; chmn. bd. dirs. Asbury Meth. Village Found. Named Outstanding Young Man Am., U.S. Jaycees, 1979. Mem. Nat. Assn. Ins. and Fin. Advisors (pres. Md. chpt. 1995-96), Nat. Assn. Securities Dealers, Suburban Md. Assn. Ins. and Fin. Advisors (past pres., H.L. Meyer Meml. award 1980), Fin. Planning Assn., Suburban Md. Estate Planning Coun. (past pres.), Million Dollar Round Table. Lutheran. Home: 508 Lawson Way Rockville MD 20850 Office: Ste 420 18310 Montgomery Village Ave Gaithersburg MD 20879-3553 Business E-Mail: jruth@pfgroup.org.

RUTH, RODNEY, musician, music consultant, contractor, educator; b. Robesonia, Pa., Sept. 12, 1934; s. Herbert J. and Pearl (Rentz) R.; m. Gloria Mae Kauffman, Nov. 14, 1953; 1 child, Tiffany Tunisia. MusB, Manhattan Sch. Music, 1960; MA, Columbia U., 1964. Freelance musician; music cons., contractor Meadowlands Sports Complex, various theaters and performing arts ctrs., individual conductors and performers, bands, orchs., festivals, N.J., N.Y., Pa., 1957—; tchr. Paterson (N.J.) Bd. Edn., 1961-98. Performed with USAF Band, 1953-57; music contractor for world premiers (musicals) Lucifer, Laugh a Little, Cry a Little, Shoemakers Holiday, Love Games, Las Vegas Laugh-In '75. Scholar Manhattan Sch. Music, N.Y.C., 1958-60. Mem. Nat. Edn. Assn., Music Educators Nat. Conf., Am. Fedn. Musicians. Avocations: travel, gardening, golf. Home and Office: Rod Ruth Music 129 Schuyler Rd Allendale NJ 07401-1836 E-mail: rodruthmusic@aol.com.

RUTH, SHIELA GRANT, music educator; b. Sagamiono, Japan, May 12, 1955; came to U.S., 1957; d. Allan Francis and Eiko (Nagasawa) Grant; m. Terrence Allan Ruth, Sept. 8, 1979. BA, Frostburg State Coll., 1977. Health care asst. Deaton Med. Ctr., Balt., summer 1974, 75, Nursing Staff, Annapolis, Md., 1977; sub. tchr. Anne Arundel County Schs., Md., 1977-78; tchr. piano/organ Jordan Kitts, Glen Burnie, Md., 1978-79; music asst. Lindale Jr. H.S., Ferndale, Md., 1986-90, Harundale Presbyn. Ch., Glen Burnie, 1990—; tchr. piano/organ Severn, Md., 1977—. Mem. Md. State Music Tchrs. Assn., Music Tchrs. Nat. Assn., Anne Arundel Music Tchrs. Assn. (corr. sec. 1997—), Delta Omicron (warden 1975-77), Sigma Delta Pi. Republican. Presbyterian. Avocations: playing piano, touring civil war battlefields, ice skating. Home: 753 Rosewood Rd Severn MD 21144-2069 Office: Harundale Presbyn Ch 1020 Eastway Glen Burnie MD 21060-7303

RUTHCHILD, ROCHELLE GOLDBERG, education educator; b. Jersey City, N.J., Nov. 30, 1940; d. Samuel A. and Ruth (Raichelson) Goldberg; 1 child, Rafael A. BA, Hofstra U., 1962; MA, U. Rochester, 1964, PhD, 1976. Instr. Cardinal Cushing Coll., Brookline, Mass., 1969-72, Goddard-Cambridge Grad. Program, Cambridge, Mass., 1971-74, core faculty, 1974-79, Plainfield, Vt., 1979-81; asst. prof. Vt. Coll. of Norwich U., Montpelier, 1981-82, prof. grad. studies, 1988—2001; dir. Russian Sch. Norwich U., Northfield, Vt., 1988-94; assoc. Davis Ctr. for Russian Studies Harvard U., 1980—; prof. grad. studies Vt. Coll. of Union Inst. and U., Montpelier, 2001—. Author: (book) Women in Russian and the Soviet Union: An Annotated Bibliography, 1994; contbr. articles to profl. jours. Jewish Women's Archive mem. Temple Israel, Boston, 1996—. N.Y. State Regents scholar, 1958-62; grantee Internat. Rsch. and Exchs., Leningrad, Moscow, 1966-67, 78-79, 95, NEH, 1996, Dana Grant, 1997-98, others. Mem. Assn. for Women in Slavic Studies (bd. dirs. 1990—, pres./co-founder, 1988-90). Jewish. Office: Grad Program Regional Offic 137 Coolidge St Brookline MA 02446-5807 Office Phone: 617-738-9524.

RUTHERFORD, ALAN, manufacturing executive; With Crown Cork Co. Belgium N.V., 1974-86, European contr., 1986-89; with Crown Cork & Seal Co., Inc., Phila., 1989-90, contr., 1990-91, sr. v.p. fin. and adminstrn., CFO, 1991-92, exec. v.p., CFO, 1992—, bd. dirs., 1991—. Bd. trustees Thomas Jefferson U. Fellow Chartered Inst. Mgmt. Accts. U.K. Office: Crown Cork and Seal Co Inc One Crown Way Philadelphia PA 19154-4599

RUTHERFORD, JIM, professional sports team executive; b. 1948; 1 child, Andrea. Goal tender Detroit Red Wings, Pitts., Toronto, L.A. profl. hockey teams, 1969-82; dir. hockey ops Compuware Sports Corp., 1982-94; gen. mgr. Windsor (Ont.) Spitfires, 1984-88, head coach, 1986-87; dir. hockey ops. Detroit Ambassadors, 1989-91, coach, dir. hockey ops., 1991-92, Detroit Jr. Red Wings (formerly Ambassadors), 1992-94; COO KTR Hockey Ltd. Partnership, Hartford, Conn., 1984—; pres., gen. mgr., chief operating officer Hartford Whalers (renamed Carolina Hurricanes), 1994—. Mem. Team Can. hockey world championships, Vienna, 1977, Moscow, 79; player rep. 5 seasons Red Wings. Recipient Exec. of Yr. award, Can. Hockey League, 1993, Ont. Hockey League, 1994. Achievements include directing Windsor Spitfires to 1988 Meml. Cup finals; leading Detroit Ambassadors to first-ever playoff in 1992; winning Emms Divsn. championship with Jr. Red Wings in 1994; bringing 1st Am.-based Ont. Hockey League franchise to Detroit, 1989; securing Nat. Hockey League approval of KTR purchase of Hartford Whalers from Conn. Devel. Authority, 1994. Office: Carolina Hurricanes 1400 Edwards Mill Rd Raleigh NC 27607-3624

RUTHERFORD, JOHN SHERMAN, III, (JOHNNY RUTHERFORD), professional race car driver; b. Coffeyville, Kans., Mar. 12, 1938; s. John Sherman and Mary Henrietta (Brooks) R.; m. Betty Rose Hoyer, July 7, 1963; children: John Sherman, Angela Ann. Student, Tex. Christian U., 1956. Profl. race car driver, 1959-94; ret., 1994; driver super-modified race cars, sprint cars, stock cars, midgets, sports cars, Indy cars, Trans-Am cars and formula 5000. Mem. Indy Car Racing Inc.; dir. spl. events Indy Racing League, 1995—; pace car driver for Championship Auto Racing Teams, 1992-95; auto racing cons. Pennzoil Products-Racing Divsn.; lectr. in field. Author: (autobiography) Lone Star J.R., 2000; host: TV show The Racers; race commentator TV show, NBC, ESPN, CBS, ABC; appeared in numerous TV commercials; art work included in traveling exhbn. Art and Athletes; TV and radio pub. services messages for Nat. Safety Council, Calif. Hwy. Patrol, U.S. Marines, Muscular Dystrophy Assn., Cystic Fibrosis Assn., Boy Scouts, Camp Fire, Jewel Charity, Shriner's Hosp., Tex. Soc. to Prevent Blindness, Air N.G. Hon. state chmn. Am. Cancer Soc., Tex., Tarrant County Soc. to Prevent Blindness, Emergency Medicine Found., Ft. Worth Kidney Assn., Ft. Worth Burn Ctr.; Ind. chmn. Am. Heart Assn.; hon. mem. bd. dirs. Tex. chpt. Speedway Children's Charities, 1998—. CARA Charities, 2000--; bd. dirs. Indy HOF and Oldtimers, 2002—. Served with USMC Res., 1955—61. Named Ft. Worth Newsmaker of Yr., 1974, Driver of Yr. Sport Mag., 1976, Driver of Yr. Auto Race Writers and Broadcasters Am., 1974, 80, Olsonite Driver of Yr., 1980, Corvette Challenge's Sportsman of Yr., 1988, Motorsports amb., 1993; recipient Jim Clark award, 1969, Extra Mile award, 1973, Jim Malloy award, 1974, Eddie Sachs award, 1975, Louie Meyer award, 1992; chosen for Internat. Race of Champions, 1974, 76, 77, 78, 79, 84, chosen Fast Masters, 1993; elected to Tex. Sports Hall of Fame, 1981, Indy 500 Hall of Fame, 1987, Boys Clubs Am.'s Celebrity Hall of Fame, 1987, Tex. Auto Racing Hall of Fame, 1988, Nat. Sprint Car Hall of Fame, 1995, Internat. Motorsports Hall of Fame, 1996, Tex. Motorsports Hall of Fame, 2003. Mem. Fedn. Internat.

Automobile, Internat. Motors Sports Assn., Exptl. Aircraft Assn., Warbirds of Am., Confederate Air Force, Internat. Aerobatic Club, League Auto Racing (sec., bd. dirs.), Championship Drivers Assn. (bd. dirs.), Nat. Rifle Assn., Air Force Assn., Air Power Coun., Blue Angels Assn., Ft. Worth Boat Club, Shady Oaks Country Club, Speedway Club, Lions. Achievements include winning 27 championship car races; winner Indianapolis 500, 1974, 76, 80, second place, 1975; set new world's record for stock cars, Daytona Beach, Fla., 1963; set record at Indpls. 500, 1973; at Mich. Internat. Raceway, 1984; U.S. Auto Club Nat. Sprint Car champion, 1965; Nat. Driving champion USAC and CART, 1980; oldest driver (48) to win a 500 mile Indy Car Race, 1986. E-mail: lonestarjr@hotmail.com., bettyr4tx@msn.com. *I am a firm believer in the fact that a person can do anything in this world he or she wants to as long as you have desire. People have to set goals, things to achieve. No one ever remembers who finished second. Luck is where preparation meets opportunity.*

RUTHERFORD, MICHAEL FRANCIS, retired music educator; b. Detroit, Apr. 28, 1926; s. Michael Joseph Rutherford and Frances Catherine Busam; m. Pauline Groves, Oct. 24, 1953. MusB in Violin, Jordan Conservatory Music, Indpls., 1949; MusM in Musicology, Ind. U., 1961. Tchr. music Galveston Pub. Schs., Galveston, Ind., 1949—50, Troy Twp. Consol. Sch., Tell City, Ind., 1953—54, Reitz Meml. H.S., Evansville, Ind., 1956—59, Tennyson Pub. Sch., Tennyson, Ind., 1959—60, Tell City-Troy Twp. Schs., Tell City, 1960—80; ret., 1980. Author: St. Michael on the Hill, 1986, Perry County: Then and Now, 2000. Sp/2 U.S. Army, 1954—56. Mem.: Ind. Hist. Soc. Roman Catholic. Avocations: performing music, historical research, gardening. Home: 10279 State Rd 37 Tell City IN 47586

RUTHERFORD, PAUL HARDING, physicist; b. Shipley, Yorkshire, Eng., Jan. 22, 1938; came to U.S., 1965, naturalized, 1976; s. Joseph William and Annie (Harding) R.; m. Audrey Jones Irvine, Oct. 31, 1959; children— Andrea Christine, Julia Irvine. BA, Cambridge (Eng.) U., 1959, MA, PhD, Cambridge (Eng.) U., 1963. Research asso. Princeton (N.J.) U. Plasma Physics Lab., 1962-63, mem. research staff, 1965-68, research physicist, 1968-71, sr. research physicist, 1971-99, head theoretical div., 1972-80, dep. asso. dir. for research, 1978-80, asso. dir. research, 1980-95. Chair tech. adv. com. Internat. Thermonuclear Exptl. Reactor, 1992-99; research asso. U.K. Atomic Energy Authority Culham (Berkshire, Eng.) Lab., 1963-65; lectr. astrophys. scis. Princeton U. Co-author: (with R.J. Goldston) Introduction to Plasma Physics, 1995; mem. bd. assoc. editors Physics of Fluids, 1973-75; mem. editl. bd. Nuclear Fusion, 1980-99. Recipient E.O. Lawrence award U.S. Dept. Energy, 1983, Disting. Career award Fusion Power Assocs., 1998. Fellow Am. Phys. Soc. Home: 10 Burr Dr Princeton NJ 08540-1950 Office: Plasma Physics Lab PO Box 451 Princeton NJ 08543-0451 E-mail: rutherfo@pppl.gov.

RUTHERFORD, ROBERT BARRY, vascular surgeon; b. Edmonton, Alta., Can., July 29, 1931; s. Robert Lyon and Kathleen Emily (Gunn) R.; m. Beulah Kay Folk, Aug. 20, 1955; children: Robert Scott, Lori Jayne, Holly Anne, Trudy Kaye, Jay Wilson. BA in Biology, Johns Hopkins U., 1952, MD, 1956. Surgeon U. Colo. Health Sci. Ctr., Denver; emeritus prof. surgery U. Colo., Denver, 1996—. Editor: (texts) Management of Trauma, 1968, 4 edits., Vascular Surgery, 1978, 5th edition, 2000, An Atlas of Vascular Surgery, Vol. 1, 1993, Vol. 2, 1998, Decision Making in Vascular Surgery, 2001; editor quar. rev. Seminars in Vascular Surgery. Fellow ACS, Royal Coll. Surgeons Glasgow, Soc. for Vascular Surgery (disting. fellow); mem. Phi Beta Kappa, Alpha Omega Alpha. Republican. Unitarian Universalist. Avocations: skiing, biking, wind surfing, sailing. Office: 345 Small Shore Trl Oakland ME 04963-4317

RUTHERFORD, THOMAS TRUXTUN, II, county commissioner, former state senator; b. Columbus, Ohio, Mar. 3, 1947; s. James William and Elizabeth Whiting (Colby) R.; m. Linda Sue Rogers, Aug. 28, 1965 (div.); 1 child, Jeremy Todd. BBA, U. N.Mex., 1970, JD, 1982. Page, reading clk. N.Mex. State Legislature, 1960-65; mem. N.Mex. Atty. Gen. Environ. Adv. Commn., 1972; radio broadcaster Sta. KOB Radio and TV, 1963-72; mem. N.Mex. Senate, Albuquerque, 1972-96, majority whip, 1978-88. Chmn. rules com. N.Mex. State Senate, chmn. econ. devel. and new tech. interim. com., mem. sci. and new tech. oversight com., majority fl. leader, 1996; pres. Rutherford & Assocs., Albuquerque, 1978—83; pvt. practice, Albuquerque, 1983—; gen. counsel Nat. Fraternal Order of Police, 1996—2001; commr., chair Bernalillo County Commn., 1996—; lobbyist The Rutherford Group, 1996—; bd. dirs. Hispano C. of C., Kirtland Partnership Com., Albuquerque Econ. Devel., Camp Sierra Blanca Youth Detention Ctr., N. Mex. Bus. Weekly Top 100 Power Brokers, 1996—; past chmn. Albuquerque Cable TV Adv. Bd.; mem. S.W. Regional Energy Coun., N.Mex. Gov.'s Commn. on Pub. Broadcasting; bd. dirs., v.p. Rocky Mountain Corp. for Pub. Broadcasting; mem. Am. Coun. Young Polit. Leaders; del. mission to Hungary, Austria, Greece, 1983; mem. Fgn. Trade Adv. Com. Bd. Econ. Devel. and Tourism; trade del. People's Republic of China, 1985; local govt. del. Switzerland, 2001. Mem. Leadership N.Mex. Class of 2004; bd. dirs. Nat. Assn. Counties, N.Mex. Assn. Counties. N.Mex. Broadcasting Assn. scholar, 1970. Home: 1910 Ridgecrest Dr SE Albuquerque NM 87108-4530 also: PO Box 81256 Albuquerque NM 87198

RUTHERFORD, VICKY LYNN, special education educator; b. Florence, S.C., Sept. 12, 1947; BS, Hampton U., 1969, MA, 1971; PhD, Mich. State U., 1991. Cert. tchr. French, spl. edn., reading specialist, Va., tchr. spl. edn., S.C. Social worker day care Hampton (Va.) Dept. Social Svc., 1970-72; reading therapist, asst. dir., dir. Bayberry Reading Clinic, Hampton, 1973-77; tchr. reading, English, counselor York County Schs., Yorktown, Va., 1977-85; staff advisor, asst. to course coord. Mich. State U., East Lansing, 1985-90; tchr. autism Florence (S.C.) Dist. 1 Sch. Sys., 1992-96, tchr. emotionally impaired, 1996—2003, City of Refuge, Gardena, Calif., 2004—. Instrnl. designer: Addiction Severity Index #1, 1987, #2, 1988, Managing a Diverse Workforce, 1990; designer, trainer: Project Teach, 1991; designer, developer: (video) Camp Takona Summer Experience, 1992. Bass guitarist, Sun. sch. sec., youth worker, Sun. sch. supt. Progressive Ch. of Jesus, Florence, 1992-98, Greater Zion Tabernacle Apostolic Ch., Florence, 1998—. Fellow Mich. Dept. Edn., 1987-89. Mem. Internat. Reading Assn. Office: Rogers Mid Sch 365 Monrovia Ave Long Beach CA 90803

RUTHERFORD, WILLIAM B. corporate financial executive; BS in Acctg., U. Tampa. With HCA Inc., 1986—, chief fin. officer ea. group, 1996—. Office: HCA Inc 1 Park Plz Nashville TN 37203

RUTHERFORD, WILLIAM DRAKE, investment executive; b. Marshalltown, Iowa, Jan. 14, 1939; s. William Donald and Lois Esther (Drake) R.; m. Janice W. Rutherford, Feb. 4, 1965 (div. Mar. 1982); children: Wayne Donald, Melissa Drake; m. Karen Anderegg, Jan. 2, 1994. BS, U. Oreg., 1961; LLB, Harvard U., 1964. Bar: Oreg. 1964, U.S. Dist. Ct. Oreg. 1966. Assoc. Maguire, Kester & Cosgrave, Portland, Oreg., 1966-69; house counsel May & Co., Portland, 1969-70, pvt. practice, 1970-71, McMinnville, Oreg., 1971-84; mem. Oreg. Ho. of Reps., Salem, 1977-84; state treas. State of Oreg., Salem, 1984-87; chmn. Oreg. Investment Coun., Salem, 1986-87; exec. v.p., dir. U.S. and Australia ops. ABD Internat. Mgmt. Corp., N.Y.C., 1987-88, pres., chief exec. officer, bd. dirs., 1988-89; pres., bd. dirs. Societé Gen. Touche Remnant, 1990-93; dir. spl. projects Metallgesellschaft Corp., N.Y.C., 1994-95; mng. dir. Macadam Capital Ptnrs., Portland, 1995-96; CEO Fiberboard Asbestos Compensation Trust, Portland, 1997; prin. Rutherford Investment Mgmt. LLC, 1998—. Chmn. bd. dirs. Metro One Telecomms. Author: Who Shot Goldilocks, 2004. Bd. dirs. Portland Opera Assn., 1995-99. Recipient Contbn. to Individual Freedom award ACLU, 1981 Mem. Nat. Assn. State Treas. (exec. v.p. 1985, 86, pres. western region 1985, 86), Nat. Assn. State Auditors, Comptr. and Treas. (exec. com. 1987). Office: 10300 S W Greenburg Rd Ste 115 Portland OR 97223 E-mail: WRutherford@rutherfordinvestment.com.

RUTHERFURD, JOHN, financial information company executive; LLB, Harvard Law Sch., 1966; AB, Princeton U., 1962. V.p., chief of staff Chase Info. Svcs. Group, 1980—85; founder Interactive Data Corp., 1968, pres., 1985—89, 1990—95; exec. v.p. Dun & Bradstreet Fin. Info. Svcs., 1989—90; mng. dir., new bus. develop. Moody's Investors Svc., NYC, 1995-96, chief adminstr. officer, 1996-98, pres., 1998—2000; pres., CEO Moody's Corp., NYC, 2000—, chmn., 2003—. Office: Moodys Corp 99 Church St New York NY 10007*

RUTHMAN, THOMAS ROBERT, manufacturing executive; b. Cin., May 24, 1933; s. Alois H. and Catherine (Gies) R.; m. Audrey J. Schumaker, Mar. 17, 1979; children: Thomas G., Julia C., Theresa K. Grad., LaSalle U., 1970. With Ruthman Pump and Engring. Inc. (formerly Ruthman Machinery Co.), Cin., 1953—, gen. mgr., 1964-70, v.p., 1970-74, pres., 1974—, pres., owner, 1981—. Pres. Gusher Pumps, Inc., Fulflo Spltys. Co., Gusher Pumps of New Castle, Cin., Williamstown (Ky.), Dry Ridge, Calif.; pres., owner, dir. Great Lakes Pump & Supply, Mich.; owner BSM Pump Corp, North Kingston, R.I., Negel Pump Co.; pres., owner Birmingham (Eng.) Pump Supply, Ruthmann Pumpen, GMBH, Germany. Home: Princess del Mar Unit 1202 174 S Collier Blvd Marco Island FL 34145-4333 Office: 1212 Streng St Cincinnati OH 45223-2643

RUTIGER, PAUL, lawyer, educator; b. Chgo., May 17, 1945; s. Daniel and Ellen Hayes Rutiger; m. Lucy Merrin, Apr. 17, 1978; children: Patrick, Jonathan, Pamela. BA, Providence Coll., 1966; JD, U. Miami, 1971; PhD, Yale U., 1975. Bar: Conn. 1979, Mass. 1980. Ptnr. Rutiger, Johnson, & Allen, New Haven, 1973—85, Meriks, Rutiger, & Allen LLC, Hinsdale, Mass., 1986—. Prof. Harvard Law Sch., 1995—. Mem.: ABA, Mass. Lawyers Assn. (pres. 2003—). Avocations: fantasy football, mythology, woodcarving. Office: Meriks Rutiger & Allen LLC 771 New Windsor Rd Hinsdale MA 01235-9365

RUTKOFF, ALAN STUART, lawyer; b. Chgo., May 31, 1952; s. Roy and Harriet (Ruskin) R.; m. Mally Zoberman, Dec. 22, 1974; children: Aaron Samuel, Jordana Michal, Robert Nathaniel. BA with high distinction, U. Mich., 1973; JD magna cum laude, Northwestern U., 1976. Bar: Ill. 1976, U.S. Dist. Ct. (no. dist.) Ill. 1976, U.S. Ct. Appeals (7th cir.) 1977, U.S. Ct. Appeals (3d cir.) 1978, U.S. Supreme Ct. 1981, U.S. Ct. Appeals (5th cir.) 1983, U.S. Ct. Appeals (8th cir.) 1990, U.S. Dist. Ct. (we. dist.) Wis. 1996, U.S. Ct. Appeals (6th cir.) 2003. Assoc. Altheimer & Gray, Chgo., 1976-80; ptnr. Kastel & Rutkoff, Chgo., 1980-83, Holleb & Coff Ltd., Chgo., 1983-84, McDermott Will & Emery LLP, Chgo., 1984—. Pres. N. Suburban Synagogue Beth El, Highland Pk., Ill., 1999-2001. Mem. ABA, Chgo. Bar Assn., Order of Coif. Home: 801 Timberhill Rd Highland Park IL 60035-5148 Office: McDermott Will & Emery 227 W Monroe St Ste 4400 Chicago IL 60606-5096 Office Phone: 312-984-7751. Business E-Mail: arutkoff@mwe.com.

RUTLAND, ROBERT J. transportation executive; Chmn., CFO Allied Holdings, Decatur, Ga., 1994—. Office: Allied Holdings 160 Clairemont Ave Ste 200 Decatur GA 30030-2534

RUTLEDGE, CHARLES OZWIN, pharmacologist, educator; b. Topeka, Oct. 1, 1937; s. Charles Ozwin and Alta (Seaman) R.; m. Jane Ellen Crow, Aug. 13, 1961; children: David Ozwin, Susan Harriett, Elizabeth Jane, Karen Ann. BS in Pharmacy, U. Kans., 1959, MS in Pharmacology, 1961; PhD in Pharmacology, Harvard U., 1966. NATO postdoctoral fellow Gothenburg (Sweden) U., 1966-67; asst. prof. U. Colo. Med. Ctr., Denver, 1967-74, assoc. prof., 1974-75; prof., chmn. dept. pharmacology U. Kans., Lawrence, 1975-87; dean, prof. pharmacology Purdue U., West Lafayette, Ind., 1987—2002, exec. dir. Discovery Park, 2001—, interim vice provost rsch., 2002—04. Contbr. articles on neuropharmacology to profl. jours. Grantee NIH, 1970-87. Mem. AAAS, Am. Soc. Pharmacology and Exptl. Therapeutics (councillor 1982 84, sec.-treas. 1990-93, pres. 1996-97), Am. Assn. Coll. Pharmacy (chmn. biol. scis. sect. 1983-84, chmn. coun. faculties 1986-87, chmn. coun. deans 1993-94, com. implement change pharm. edn. 1989-92, pres. 1996-97), Soc. for Neurosci., Am. Pharm. Assn. Avocations: gardening, skiing. Home: 40 Brynteg Est West Lafayette IN 47906-5643 Office: Purdue U Hovde Hall Rm 313 610 Purdue Mall West Lafayette IN 47907-2040 Office Phone: 765-494-6209. Business E-Mail: chipr@purdue.edu.

RUTLEDGE, JOANNE, artist, consultant; b. Indpls., Dec. 17, 1941; d. Edward John and Dorothy Louise (Bachelor) Underwood; m. Kenneth Clay Smith, Sept. 7, 1963 (div. May 1990); children: Elizabeth, Kenneth Clay, Jr., Andrew; m. Mark Alan Rutledge, July 31, 1993. RN, St. Vincent's Sch. Nursing, Indpls., 1962; BSN, Ind. U., 1979. Staff RN Children's Hosp., Washington, 1962—63, St. Vincent's Hosp., Indpls., 1963—64, Women's Hosp. Spl. Care Nursery, Indpls., 1990—97; nurse cons. Hosp. Care for Indigent Ind. State Program, Indpls., 1995—. Ptnr. Collective Art Gallery, Indpls., 2003—. Exhibitions include Ind. State Fair, Ind. Heritage Arts, Southside Art League Regional Show. Docent Indpls. Mus. Art, 1983—; reading tutor Kiwanis Project, 2002—; active various coms. Children's Mus. Guild, 1975—; v.p. Indpls. Athletic Club Art Bd. Found., 1990—. Recipient Billy Cothran Landscape award, Indpls. Art Ctr., 1985. Mem.: Ind. Plein Art Painters Assn., Stutz Artist's Assn., Ind. Artist's Club (assoc.), Proctor Club (pres. 1994—95). Roman Catholic. Avocations: travel, photography, hiking, canoeing, attending concerts and theater. Home: 1019 W 75th St Indianapolis IN 46260-3408 Office: Ind Hosp Care for the Indigent 402 W Washington St Indianapolis IN 46204

RUTLEDGE, LOUIS C, entomologist; b. Mooreland, Okla., May 30, 1931; s. Henry Rutledge and Tema Croissant; m. Gerda Horr Rutledge (dec.); children: Reuben L, David C. BS, Okla. State U., 1963; MS, U. Md., 1970. Entomologist U.S. Army, 1963—73; civilian employee entomologist Dept. of the Army, San Francisco, 1974—93; ret., 1993. Contbr. scientific papers. Major U.S. Army, 1949—73. Decorated Commendation medal U.S. Army, Meritorious Svc. medal; recipient Rsch. and Develop. Achievement award, Dept. of the Army, 1989. Avocations: reading, science, history, nature study. Home: 11 Circle Way Mill Valley CA 94941

RUTLEDGE, PETER J. federal agency administrator; b. Somerville, NJ, June 19, 1949; BSME, Rutgers U., 1971; M Indsl. Engring., Tex. A&M U., 1974; M Sci. Reliability Engring., U. Md., 1993, PhD in Reliability Engring., 1997. Mech. engr. Delaval Steam Turbine Co., Trenton, NJ, 1972; safety engr. Army Materiel Command Intern Tng. Ctr., Texarkana, Tex., 1972—74, Picatinny Arsenal, Dover, NJ, 1974—75; chief engring. br. safety office Army Materiel Command, Alexandria, Va., 1975—83; tech. advisor Dir. Army Safety, the Pentagon, Washington, 1983—85; dep. dir. occupl. safety and health Safety and Occupl. Health Policy Directorate Office of Sec. of Def., Washington, 1985—88; with NASA, Washington, 1988—, dir. space flight SMA divsn., 1996—97, dir. enterprise safety and mission assurance divsn. Office Safety and Mission Assurance, 1997—. Office: NASA Hdqrs Mail Code Q 300 E St NW Washington DC 20546-0579

RUTLEDGE, ROGER KEITH, lawyer; b. Knoxville, Tenn., Dec. 27, 1946; s. Joseph P. and Jean Mae (Karnes) R.; m. Lily Mee Kin Hee, June 6, 1970; children: Amelia Leilani, Sarah Elizabeth. BA in History with honors, U. N.C., 1968; JD cum laude, Am. U., 1977. Bar: Tenn. 1977, U.S. Dist. Ct. (we. dist.) Tenn. 1978, U.S. Supreme Ct. 1982. Served in U.S. Peace Corps, Nepal, 1968-70; fgn. service officer U.S. Dept. State, Washington and Italy, 1971-76; ptnr. Rutledge & Rutledge, Memphis, 1977—. Pres. Jabez Burns Inc., 1998-99. Editor fiction Carolina Quar., 1967-68; assoc. editor Am. U. Law Rev., 1976-77. Mem. campaign com. Albert Gore Jr. U.S. Senate, Shelby County, 1984, for pres. campaign, 1988, 2000; bd. chmn. United Meth. Neighborhood Ctrs., Inc., 1992. Mem. ABA, Tenn. Bar Assn., Memphis Bar Assn. (editor Bar Forum 1986, asst. editor 1987). Democrat. Methodist. Office: Rutledge & Rutledge 1053 W Rex Rd Memphis TN 38119-3819 *Notable cases include: Fite vs. First Tenn. Prodns. Credit Assn., which involved age discrimination in employment, 1988; Capital Tool & Mfg. vs. Maschinenfabrik Herkules, which involved trade secret law and internat. injunction, 1988.*

RUTLEDGE, VIRGIE MARILYN, elementary school educator; b. Hamilton, Ohio, Jan. 23, 1950; d. Benjamin John and Virgie Jones Hann; m. Dennis Eugene Rutledge, Aug. 1, 1969; children: Brian, Aaron. BS in Edn., Miami U., Oxford, Ohio, 1988; MEd, Miami U., 1994. Elem. tchr. Hamilton City Schs., 1988—. Tchr. mentor Hamilton City Schs., 1999. Ch. elder Christ the King Luth. Ch., West Chester, Ohio, 2000—. Martha Holden Jennings scholar U. Dayton, 1998-99. Mem. Phi Delta Kappa Internat., Delta Kappa Gamma Soc. Internat. Republican. Avocations: reading, hiking, cooking. Office: Martha Holden J Found 710 Halle Bldg 1228 Euclid Ave Cleveland OH 44115-1831

RUTNER, ALAN, wholesale grocery executive; CFO Purity Wholesale Grocers, Boca Raton, Fla. Office: Purity Wholesale Grocers Ste 100 5400 Broken Sand Blvd NW Boca Raton FL 33487 Office Fax: (561) 994-9629.

RUTSALA, VERN A. poet, English language educator, writer; b. Feb. 5, 1934; s. Ray Edwin and Virginia Mae (Brady) R.; m. Joan Merle Colby, Apr. 6, 1957; children: Matthew, David, Kirsten. BA, Reed Coll., 1956; MFA, U. Iowa, 1960. Instr. Lewis and Clark Coll., Portland, 1961-64, asst. prof., 1964-69, assoc. prof., 1969-76, prof., 1976—. Vis. prof. U. Minn., Mpls., 1968-69, Bowling Green (Ohio) State U., 1970; writer-in-residence U. Idaho, Moscow, 1988, Redlands (Calif.) U., 1979; chair English dept. Lewis and Clark, Portland, 1986-89. Author: The Window, 1964, Laments, 1975, The Journey Begins, 1976, Paragraphs, 1978, Walking Home from the Icehouse, 1981, Backtracking, 1985, Ruined Cities, 1987, Selected Poems, 1991, Little-Known Sports, 1994, Greatest Hits: 1964-02, 2002, A Handbook for Writers, 2004, The Moment's Equation, 2004. With U.S. Army, 1956-58. Guggenheim Found. fellow, 1982-83, NEA fellow, 1975, 79, Masters fellow Oreg. Arts Commn., 1990; recipient Carolyn Kizer prize Western Oreg. State Coll., 1988, N.W. Poets prize N.W. Rev., 1975, Hazel Hall award Oreg. Inst. Lit. Arts, 1992, Juniper prize U. Mass. Press, 1993, Duncan Lawrie prize Arvon Found., 1994, Carolyn Kizer prize, 1997, Richard Snyder prize, 2004. Mem. AAUP, AWP, PEN, Poetry Soc. Am. Avocations: drawing, painting, watching the ocean, sports.

RUTSCHKE, ANNAMARIE, artist; b. Santa Barbara, Calif., June 29, 1965; d. Benjamin Wiley Jordan and Jeannette Irene Rutschke; m. Robert Allan Bryant, July 31, 1988 (div. 1996); child: Phillip Dale Dodge Jr. File clk. San Luis Welding Supply, San Luis Obispo, Calif., 1983; customer svc. clk. The Living Picture, Alameda, Calif., 1984, 7-11, Alameda, 1985-86; clk. Def. Subs. Reg. Pacific, Alameda, 1987-88; pers. clk. Def. Depot Tracy, Alameda, 1988-90; adminstrv. clk. Gen. Svcs. Adminstrn., San Francisco, 1990, purchasing agt., 1990-96, adminstrv. technician, 1996-99; legal clk. IRS Dist. Counsel, San Francisco, 1999-2000. Freelance artist. Co-coord. Fed. Recycling Coun., 1992, 93; operator Muscular Dystrophy Assn., Arroyo Grande, Calif., 1980. Republican. Lutheran. Avocations: art, writing, computer programming, web design, cooking. E-mail: mommyofanangel38@aol.com.

RUTSKY, LESTER, retired textiles executive, writer; b. NYC, May 23, 1924; s. Samuel and Bess (Millman) Rutsky; m. Elaine Selesnik, Aug. 30, 1959. Student viola, Stuyvesant House, 1935—37, Christadora House, 1937—38. Co-writer (songs) You're Gonna be Sorry; contbr. articles to profl. jours.; author: numerous poems. Recipient Paul Elliot Meml. award, Poetry Soc. Mich., 1982, 1st pl., Ind. State Poetry Soc., Poetry Clubs Ind. Democrat. Avocations: painting, violin, piano. Home: 2930 W 5th St Brooklyn NY 11224

RUTSTEIN, SEDMARA ZAKARIAN, piano educator, concert pianist; b. Kazan, Russia, Oct. 18, 1937; came to U.S., 1974; d. Suren and Ekaterina (Todorovskaya) Zakarian; m. Alexander Rutstein, Aug. 29, 1958; 1 child, Alla. D in Music, Leningrad State Conservatory, USSR, 1961, diploma (hon.), 1959. Prof. Leningrad State Conservatory, 1961-73; artist-in-residence Grinnell (Iowa) Coll., 1974—76; prof. Oberlin (Ohio) Conservatory, 1976—. Recording artist, classical piano music XVIII through XX centuries, 1972—. Grantee Oberlin Coll., 1984-98. Mem. Am. Music Tchrs. Assn. Avocations: reading, music, travel. Home: 226 N Prospect St Oberlin OH 44074-1035 Office: Oberlin Coll Conservatory of Music Oberlin OH 44074 Office Phone: 440-775-8250. Business E-Mail: sedrut@oberlin.net.

RUTSTEIN, STANLEY HAROLD, apparel retailing company executive; b. Wilkes-Barre, Pa., July 1, 1941; s. Sydney D. and Bessie H. (Cohen) R.; m. Jo Ella Rutstein; children— Wendy Sue, Michael Scott, Lynne Elizabeth. Student, Wilkes Coll., 1959-61; grad., Advanced Mgmt. Program, Harvard U., 1975. Buyer Barbara Lynn Stores, Inc., N.Y.C., 1961-63; buyer, then mdsg. mgr. Casual Corner div. U.S. Shoe Corp., Enfield, Conn., 1963-71, pres., 1971-76; pres., cons., dir. U.S. Shoe Corp., Cin., 1976-79; pres. Commonwealth Trading, Inc., Stoughton, Mass., 1979-85, Chadwick's of Boston Ltd., 1983-85; cons. Commonwealth Trading, Inc., 1985—; pres. Trim Trends, Inc., Boston, 1986-87, chmn., 1987-91; chmn., chief exec. officer, pres. Narragansett Clothing Co., Tiverton, R.I., 1987-90, also bd. dirs.; bd. dirs. Reynolds Bros. Inc., 1989-95; pres., CEO S/J Designs Inc., 1989—2002, DBA, Northeast Knitters, Wagner Realty, Bradenton, Fla., 2002—. Bd. dirs. The Icing, Inc., Sycamore Shops, Inc. Bd. dirs. Ptnrs. for Disabled Youth, 1992. Mem. Young Pres. Orgn. Office: Wagner Realty 3639 Cortez Rd West Bradenton FL 34210 Home: c/o The Water Club 1281 Gulf of Mexico Dr #203N Longboat Key FL 34228 Office Phone: 941-727-2800. E-mail: nextmoveboston@aol.com.

RUTT, JAMES P. design company executive; BSc, MIT. Mem. staff THE SOURCE, 1980-82; co-founder, sr. v.p. tech. Bus. Rsch. Corp., 1982-84; gen. mgr., v.p. tech. First Call Corp., 1984-86; cons. various, 1986-93; COO performance divsn. CDA Investment Techs., Inc., 1993-94; chief tech. officer The Thomson Corp., 1994-99; CEO Network Solutions, Inc., Herndon, Va., 1999—2000; chmn. Analog Design Automation Inc., 2001—. Bd. dirs. Market Switch Corp; adv. bd. Engenia Software and Knowledge Sys., Inc.; spkr. in field. Office: Analog Design Automation Inc 233 Metcalf St Ottawa ON Canada K2P 2C2

RUTTAN, VERNON WESLEY, agricultural economist, educator; b. Alden, Mich., Aug. 16, 1924; s. Ward W. and Marjorie Ann (Chaney) R.; m. Marilyn M. Barone, July 30, 1945; children: Lia Marie, Christopher, Alison Elaine, Lore Megan. BA, Yale U., 1948; MA, U. Chgo., 1950, PhD, 1952; LLD (hon.), Rutgers U., 1978; D Agrl. Sci. ((hon.), U. Kiel, Germany, 1986, Purdue U., 1991. Economist TVA, 1951-54; prof. agrl. econs. Purdue U., 1954-63; staff economist President's Council Econ. Advisers, 1961-63; economist Rockefeller Found., 1963-65; head dept. agrl. econs. U. Minn., St. Paul, 1965-70, Regent's prof., 1986-99, Regent's prof. emeritus, 2000—. Pres. Agrl. Devel. Council, N.Y.C., 1973-77 Author: (with Y. Hayami) Agricultural Development: An International Perspective, 1971, 85, Agricultural Research Policy, 1982, U.S. Development Assistance Policy, 1996, Technology, Growth and Development, 2001, Social Science Knowledge and Economic Development, 2003. Recipient Alexander von Humboldt award, 1985. Fellow AAAS, Am. Acad. Arts and Scis., Am. Agrl. Econs. Assn. (pres. 1971-72, Publ. award 1956, 57, 62, 66, 67, 71, 79, 85, 97); mem. NAS. Home: 1666 Coffman St Apt 112 Saint Paul MN 55108-1326 Office: Dept Applied Econs U Minn Saint Paul MN 55108

RUTTENBERG, CHARLES BYRON, lawyer; b. Reading, Pa., Nov. 16, 1922; s. Abraham David and Mollie Belle (Rabinowitz) Ruttenberg; m. Arden Honore Suk, July 29, 1955; children: Victoria Arden, Valerie Honore, Alexandra Anne. Student, Yale U., 1941—42; BA, U. Va., 1946; LLB, U. Pa., 1949. Bar: DC. With Covington & Burling, Washington; gen. counsel NSF, Washington, Nat. Found. Arts Humanities, Washington, 1949-69; ptnr. Arent, Fox, Kintner, Plotkin & Kahn, Washington, 1969—; fed. mediator US Dist. Ct., 1998—, DC Superior Ct., 2000—. Chmn. legis. bur., mem. exec. com., bd. dirs., gen. counsel Greater Washington Bd. Trade, 1983—92, Nat. Assn. Rec. Merchandisers, Video Software Dealers Assn., 1980—95. Editor, mem. mng. bd.: U. Pa. Law Rev., 1947—49. Gen. counsel Nat. Opera Inst., 1985—95; co-chmn. U. Pa. Law Sch. Alumni Fund, Washington, 1983—91; chmn. lawyers com. DC Commn. Arts, 1972—75; gen. counsel People to People Music Program, Washington, 1970—91; trustee, gen. counsel Wolf Trap Found. Performing Arts, Vienna, Va., 1981—91, Nat. Inst. Music Theatre, Washington, 1969—90; gen. counsel, bd. dirs. Am. Film Inst., 1969—91; trustee U. DC, 1990—94; bd. dirs., pres. Cosmos Club Hist. Preservation Found., 1987—; bd. dirs., v.p., exec. com. Iona Sr. Svcs., 1997—; bd. dirs. Washington Area Lawyers for Arts, 1984—95, Greater Washington Rsch. Ctr.,

1980—95; mem. adv. bd. DC Lottery, 2002—. With USAF, 1942—46, capt. USAFR, 1946—55. Recipient Outstanding Svc. awards, US Govt., 1967, 1968. Mem.: ABA, Arts Internat. (gen. counsel), U. Pa. Law Alumni Assn. (pres. 1967—71, bd. dirs. 1967—78), Washington Athletic Club (bd. govs. 1969—74), Mitchell Law Club, St. Alban's Club, Cosmos Club (bd. mgmt. 2000—03, gen. counsel 2003—), Phi Beta Kappa. Home: 4735 Butterworth Pl NW Washington DC 20016-4459 Office: Arent Fox Kintner Plotkin & Kahn 1050 Connecticut Ave NW Ste 500 Washington DC 20036-5303 Office Phone: 202-857-6082. E-mail: ruttenbc@arentfox.com., cbruttenberg@aol.com.

RUTTENBERG, FRANK Z. lawyer; b. San Antonio, June 4, 1954; BBA, U. Tex., 1976; JD, St. Mary's U., 1979; LLM in Taxation, NYU, 1982. Bar: Tex. 1979. Lawyer Strasburger & Price, L.L.P., San Antonio; ptnr. Bracewell & Patterson, San Antonio, 1999—. Office: Bracewell & Patterson One Alamo Ctr 106 S Saint Marys St Ste 800 San Antonio TX 78205-3603

RUTTENBERG, RUTH A. economist; b. Washington, D.C., Feb. 16, 1948; d. Stanley Harvey and Gertrude Leah Bernstein Ruttenberg; children: Estye Ross, Jack Ross. BA in Econs. with honors, U. Wis., 1969; M in City Planning, U. Pa., 1971, PhD in City Planning, 1981. Prof. Bradford Coll., 1972—73; sr. assoc. Ruttenberg, Kilgallon & Assocs., Inc., Washington, 1973-86; pres. Ruth Ruttenberg & Assocs., Bethesda, Md., 1986—; sr. staff assoc. George Meany Ctr. for Labor Studies, Nat. Labor Coll., 2001—. Sr. lectr. Am. U., Washington, 1973—75; asst. prof. Howard U., Washington, 1975—82; adj. faculty U. Md., College Park, Md., 1974—; mem. Bd. Equalization and Rev., Washington, 1981—82; sr. economist Occupl. Safety and Health Adminstrn., Washington, 1979—80; dir. Nat. Clearinghouse for Worker Safety and Health Tng., Bethesda, 1995—2000; co-chair Instnl. Rev. Bd., Ctr. to Protect Workers Rights, Washington, 1996—; peer rev. mem. U.S. Dept. Energy, Washington, 1996, 97. Author: Occupational Safety and Health in the Chemical Industry, 1981; mem. editl. rev. bd. Indsl. Rels. Rsch. Assn., 2002—. Bd. dirs. Group Health Assn., Washington, 1982-88, 90-94; bd. dirs., Consumer Health Found., Washington, 1994—; bd. dirs. Children's Internat. Summer Villages, Washington, 1994—. Woodrow Wilson fellow, 1969-70; Bicentennial grantee Govt. Sweden, 1978. Democrat. Avocations: reading, kayaking, travel. Office: Ruth Ruttenberg & Assocs Inc 5107 Benton Ave Bethesda MD 20814-2807 Office Phone: 301-571-4226. E-mail: rruttenberg@comcast.net., rruttenberg@georgemeany.org.

RUTTENBERG, SUSANN I. health sciences administrator; b. Chgo., Apr. 7, 1943; d. William and Audrey A. Kray; m. Harold Seymour Ruttenberg, Aug. 11, 1963 (div. Oct. 1977); children: Adam, Michael, Leslie. BS, Northwestern U., 1964; MBA, U. Calif., Irvine, 1993. Writer, prodr. Kragie Newell & Assocs., Des Moines, 1977-80, Nat. Cable Prodns. and Teleshopper, 1980-81; owner, mgr. Rib Joint, Des Moines, 1978-81; gen. mgr. Stuart Anderson's Black Angus, Ariz. and Calif., 1982-87; various adminstr. positions in pediats. U. Calif., Irvine, 1988-93, adminstr. child devel. ctr., 1997-98, adminstr. dermatology, 1996—, adminstr. phys. medicine and rehab., 1999—. V.p. U. Calif. Irvine GSM Healthcare Alumni, 1995—2002; mem. exec. bd. Acad. Bus. Officers Group, 2000—03, chair exec. bd., 2000—01, ADA/M bd. dirs., 2000—04, chair IT com., 2003—04. Editor, contbr.: (cookbook) Child's Play, 1989; editor, writer newsletter UCInsights on Pediatrics, 1995; author: Never Let'em Catch You With Your Bed Rails Down, 2003; contbr. Executive Decisions in Dermatology, 2000—04. Women's chair United Jewish Appeal, Des Moines, 1975; bd. dirs. Child Guidance Ctr., Des Moines, 1976-77, Cmty. Telephone Coun., Des Moines, 1978-81; mem. dir.'s coun. U. Calif. Irvine Chao Family Comprehensive Cancer Ctr., 1998—; vol. rep., sec. bd. dirs. Rancho Mirage, Calif. C. of C., 1984-86. Northwestern U. scholar, 1963-64; U. Calif. Irvine Coll. Medicine Career Devel. award, 1992-93, Healthsci. Adminstr. of Yr. award, U. Calif. Chancellor. Mem.: Assn. Dermatology Adminstrs./Mgrs. (chair newsletter com. 2001, chair comms. com. 2002—03, bd. dirs. 2002—), Assn. Profs. Dermatology, Med. Group Mgmt. Assn. Avocations: cooking, reading, literacy tutoring, dance, travel. Office: U Calif Irvine C340 Med Scis I Irvine CA 92697-0001

RUTTER, ALAN, federal agency administrator; m. Melanie Rutter; children: Sarah, Elizabeth. BA, MPA, U. Tex. Fed. R.R. adminstr. U.S. Dept. Transp., Washington, 2001—; dep. exec. dir. Tex. High-Speed Rail Authority, 1995; dir. transp. policy State of Tex.; served Tex. Govs. Bill Clements and Mark White, 1984—90. Office: US Dept Transp Fed RR Adminstrn 1120 Vermont Ave NW 7th Flr Washington DC 20005

RUTTER, FRANCES TOMPSON, publisher; b. Arlington, Mass., Apr. 12, 1920; d. Harold F. and Mildred F. (Wheeler) Tompson; m. John H. Ottemiller, Mar. 24, 1943; children: Joan Tompson Gillum, John Tompson; m. William D. Rutter, Oct. 26, 1970. AB magna cum laude, Pembroke Coll., Brown U., 1941; postgrad., Mt. Holyoke Coll., 1942-43. Res. book librarian Brown U., 1941-42; annotator ship's papers John Carter Brown Library, Providence, 1943-44; librarian Sci. Service, Washington, 1944-45; ptnr. Shoe String Press, Hamden, Conn., 1952-58; sec., treas. Shoe String Press, Inc., 1958-68, pres., treas., 1968-80, also bd. dirs.; sec.-treas., dir. Tompson-Malone, Inc., book mfrs., 1967-80; pres., treas., dir. Tompson & Rutter, Inc., 1980-89. V.p. class 1941 Pembroke Coll., 1967-73, 76-91, pres., 1973-76, head class agt., 1979-85, bequests and trust chmn., 1979-90, 40th reunion gift com., 1980, co-chair 50th reunion gift com., 1990-91, 55th reunion gift com., 1995-96; spl. projects adv. panel N.H. Commn. on Arts, 1980-84; mem. natural resources com. Grantham, 1980; mem. Grantham Planning Bd., 1981-87, sec., 1981-83, chmn., 1985-87; chmn. Grantham Recycling Com., 1988-89, Grantham Hist. Soc., 1992-96, Habitat for Humanity-Kearsarge/Sunapee chpt., 1989-94; mem. Diocesan Altar Guild Bd., 1990-93, sec., 1991-92; vol. Mary Hitchcock Meml. Hosp. Aux., 1991-2003; mem. vestry St. Paul's Episc. Ch., 1997-2000, jr. warden, 1998-2000; assoc. Holy Cross Monastery, West Park, N.Y. Mem. Friends of Fernald Libr. of Colby-Sawyer Coll., ACLU (life), LWV (editor newsletter 1987-89), Assoc. Alumni Brown U. (bd. dirs. 1981-83), Nicholas Brown Soc., Pembroke Ctr. Assocs. (coun. 1984-86), Soc. for Preservation N.H. Forests, Episcopal Peace Fellowship, Phi Beta Kappa. Episcopalian. Home: 80 Azalea Cir # 19 White River Junction VT 05001 Personal E-mail: franbill@valley.net.

RUTTER, JEREMY BENTHAM, archaeologist, educator; b. Boston, June 23, 1946; s. Peter and Nancy Kendall (Comstock) R.; m. Sarah Robbins Herndon, Jan. 31, 1970; children: Benjamin Ryerson, Nicholas Kendall. BA in Classics with honors, Haverford Coll., 1967; PhD in Classical Archaeology, U. Pa., 1974; MA, Dartmouth Coll., 1993. Vis. asst. prof. dept. classics UCLA, 1975-76, from asst. prof. to prof. dept. classics, 1976—, prof. humanities, 2001—, chmn. dept. classics, 1992-98, 2003—. Participant excavations West Germany, 1966, Italy, 1968-69, Greece, 1972, 73-74, 75, 77, 78, 80-81, 84-86, 88-89, 91—; mem. numerous coms. Am. Sch. Classical Studies, Athens. Author: Lerna III: The Pottery of Lerna IV, 1995; contbr. numerous articles, reviews to profl. jours. With U.S. Army, 1969-71, Vietnam. Woodrow Wilson fellow, 1967-68; NDEA fellow U. Pa., 1968-69, 71-73; Olivia James Traveling fellow Archeol. Inst. Am., 1974-75; NEH rsch. grantee, 1979-81; travel grantee Am. Coun. Learned Socs., 1982; sr. faculty grantee, 1985-86, 91-92, 2001-02. Mem. Am. Schs. Oriental Rsch., Archaeol. Inst. Am. (numerous coms.), Classical Assn. New England, Phi Beta Kappa, Hesperia (edtl. adv. bd). Home: 47 Eagle Rdg Lebanon NH 03766-1900 Office: Dept Classics Dartmouth College Hanover NH 03755-3506 Office Phone: 603-646-2910. E-mail: jeremy.rutter@dartmouth.edu.

RUTTER, MARSHALL ANTHONY, lawyer; b. Pottstown, Pa., Oct. 18, 1931; s. Carroll Lennox and Dorothy (Tagert) R.; m. Winifred Hitz, June 6, 1953 (div. 1970); m. Virginia Ann Hardy, Jan. 30, 1971 (div. 1992); children: Deborah Frances, Gregory Russell, Theodore Thomas; m. Terry Susan Knowles, Dec. 19, 1992. BA, Amherst (Mass.) Coll., 1954; JD, U. Pa., 1959. Bar: Calif 1960. Assoc. O'Melveny & Myers, Los Angeles, 1959-64, Flint & MacKay, Los Angeles, 1964-67, ptnr., 1967-72, Rutter Hobbs & Davidoff, Los Angeles, 1973—. Bd. dirs. Ojai Festivals Ltd., 2001. Gov. The Music Ctr. of L.A. County, 1978-86, 89-92; bd. dirs. Music Ctr. Operating Co., 1992-96; bd. dirs. Chorus Am., Washington, 1987-96, pres., 1993-95; bd. dirs. L.A. Master Chorale Assn., 1964—, pres., 1980-92, chmn. 1992-96, vice chmn., 1996-2001; vestryman All Saints Ch., Beverly Hills, Calif., 1983-86, 88-90. Mem. ABA, Assn. Bus. Trial Lawyers (bd. dirs. 1980-82), L.A. County Bar Assn., Beverly Hills Bar Assn., Century City Bar Assn., English-Speaking Union (various offices L.A. chpt. 1963-91), L.A. Jr. C. of C. (bd. dirs. 1964-67). Democrat. Episcopalian. Avocations: classical and choral music, golf, stamp collecting/philately. Home: 1045 S Orange Grove Blvd Apt 10 Pasadena CA 91105-1795 Office: Rutter Hobbs & Davidoff Ste 1700 1901 Ave of Stars Los Angeles CA 90067-6018 Fax: 310-286-1728. E-mail: mrutter@rutterhobbs.com.

RUTTER, MICHAEL LLEWELLYN, child psychiatry educator; b. Brummanna, Lebanon, Aug. 15, 1933; arrived in Eng., 1936; s. Llewellyn Charles and Winifred Olive (Barber) R.; m. Marjorie Heys, Dec. 27, 1958; children: Sheila Carol, Stephen Michael, Christine Anne. MB, BChir, U. Birmingham, Eng., 1955, MD with honors, 1963; diploma in psychol. medicine, U. London, 1961; degree (hon.), U. Leiden, 1985, Cath. U., 1990, U. Birmingham, 1990, U. Edinburgh, 1990, U. Chgo., 1993, U. Minn., 1993, U. Ghent, 1994; degree, U. Warwick, 1999, U. East Anglia, 2000, U. North London, 2000. Various tchg. positions in pediat., neurology, internal, 1955-58; registrar then sr. registrar Maudsley Hosp., London, 1958-62; mem. sci. staff MRC Social Psychiatry Rsch. Unit, London, 1962-65, sr. lectr. then reader U. London Inst. Psychiatry, 1966-73, prof. child psychiatry, 1973-98, hon. dir. MRC Child Psychiatry unit, 1984-98, Social Genetic and Devel. Psychiatry Rsch. Ctr., 1994; prof. devel. psychopathology Inst. Psychiatry, 1998—. Nuffield med. traveling fellow Albert Einstein Coll. Medicine, N.Y.C., 1961-62; fellow Ctr. for Advanced Study in Behavioral Scis., Stanford, Calif., 1979-80; hon. prof. U. Amsterdam, 2001. Author: Helping Troubled Children, 1975, Maternal Deprivation Reassessed, 2nd edit., 1981, (with H. Giller) Juvenile Delinquency: Trends & Perspectives, 1983, (with M. Rutter) Developing Minds: Challenge and Continuity Accross the Lifespan, 1993, (with H. Giller, A. Hagell) Antisocial Behavior by Young People, 1998, (with T. Moffitt, A. Caspi and P. Silva) Sex Differences in Antisocial Behavior: Conduct Disorder, Delinquency and Violence in the Dunedin Longitudinal Study, 2001; co-editor: Child and Adolescent Psychiatry, 4th edit., 2002, Stress, Risk and Resilience In Children and Adolescents: Processes, Mechanisms and Interventions, 1994, Psychosocial Disorders in Young People: Time Trends & Their Causes, 1995, Antisocial Behavior by Young People, 1998, Autism: A Reappraisal of Concepts and Treatment, 1978, Development Through Life: A Handbook For Clinicians, 1994; editor: Scientific Foundations of Developmental Psychiatry, 1980, Developmental Neuropsychiatry, 1983. Recipient Am. Assn. Mental Deficiency rsch. award, 1975, C. Anderson Aldrich award Am. Acad. Pediat., 1981, Disting. Sci. Contbn. award APA, 1995, Castilla del Pino prize for achievement in psychiatry, Spain, 1995, Lifetime Achievement award IMFAR, 2002, G. STanley Hall award APA, 2003; named Goulstonian lectr. Royal Coll. Physicians, 1973, Salmon lectr. N.Y. Acad. Medicine, 1979, Adolf Meyer ward lectr. APA, 1985; Belding travelling scholar, 1963; Rock Carling fellow, 1979, Royal Soc. fellow, 1987. Fellow Royal Soc. Medicine (London, hon.), Royal Coll. Pediat. and Child Health (hon. founding fellow 1996), Royal Coll. Psychiatrists (London, hon.), Kings Coll. London, Brit. Acad.; mem. AAAS (fgn. hon.), Internat. Soc. Rsch. in Child and Adolescent Psychiatry (pres. 1997-99), U.S. Nat. Acad. Edn. (fgn. assoc.), Brit. Pediat. Assn. (hon.), Assn. Child Psychology and Psychiatry (chmn. 1973-74), Brit. Psychol. Soc. (hon. fellow), Am. Acad. Child Psychiatry (hon. membership), NAS (fgn. assoc. Inst. Medicine, Sarnat Internat. prize in mental health 2001), Soc. Rsch. in Adolescence (John P. Hill award for excellence in theory devel. and rsch. 1992), Soc. Rsch. Child Devel. (pres. 1999-2001), Inst. Child Health (London, hon. fellow 1996), Internat. Acad. Rsch. in Learning Disabilities, Academia Europaea (founding mem.), Acad. Med. Scis. (founder). Home: 190 Court Ln London SE21 7ED England Office: SGDP Rsch Centre P080 Inst Psychiatry DeCrespigny Park London SE5 8AF England Office Phone: 44 2078480882. E-mail: j.wickham@iop.kcl.ac.uk.

RUTTER, NATHANIEL WESTLUND, geologist, educator; b. Omaha, Nov. 22, 1932; s. John Elliot and Karleen (Ludden) R.; m. Mary Marie Munson, Sept. 11, 1961; children: Todd, Christopher. BS, Tufts U., 1955; MS, U. Alaska, 1962; PhD, U. Alta., 1965, DSc honoris causa, 2001. Geologist Venezuelan Atlantic Refining Co., 1955-58; research scientist Geol. Survey Can., Calgary, 1965-74, head urban projects sect. Ottawa, 1974; environ. advisor Nat. Energy Bd., Ottawa, 1974-75; assoc. prof. dept. geology U. Alta., Edmonton, 1975-77, 77-80, prof., chmn. dept., 1980-89, 77-96, prof. dept. atmospheric scis., 1996-97, univ. prof., 1997—, assoc. dean. faculty sci.; pres. Can. nat. com. Internat. Geol. Correlation Program, UNESCO, 1996-97. Pres. Internat. Union Quaternary Rsch. Congress, 1982-87; mem. Internat. Geosphere-Biosphere Program: A Study of Global Change, 1988-94; mem. rsch. com. Can. Global Change Program, 1992-94; chmn. global change com. INUQA, 1991-95; hon. prof. Chinese Acad. Sci., Beijing, 1994—; disting. lectr. Sigma Xi, 1995-97; mem. sci. bd. Internat. Union of Geol. Scis.-UNESCO, 1997—. Contbr. numerous articles to profl. jours.; assoc. editor Arctic, Geosci. Can. Quaternary Rsch.; mem. editl. bd. Quaternary Sci. Revs., Quaternary Rsch., Estonia Jour. Sci., Arctic; editor-in-chief Quaternary Internat. Grantee Natural Scis. and Engring. Rsch. Coun. Can.; grantee Energy, Mines and Resources; named Officer Order of Can., 2001; recipient Queen's Golden Jubilee medal, 2003. Fellow Royal Soc. Can.; mem. Assn. Profl. Engrs., Geologists and Geophysicists of Alta., Internat. Union Quaternary Rsch. (v.p. 1982-87, pres. 1987-91, hon. 1999), Can. Quaternary Assn. (v.p. 1981-82, Johnston medal 1997), Geol. Soc. Am. (mgmt. bd. dirs. quaternary geol. and geomorphology divsn. 1982-84, Disting. Career award 2003), Geol. Assn. of Can. (J. Willis Ambrose medal 1998), Internat. Assn. Quaternary Rsch. (hon.), Explorer's Club, Cosmos Club. Home: Rural Route 3 Stony Plain AB Canada T7Z 1X3 Office: U Alta Dept Earth & Atmospheric Scis Edmonton AB Canada T6G 2E3 E-mail: nat.rutter@ualberta.ca.

RUTTINGER, GEORGE DAVID, lawyer; b. Detroit, Jan. 17, 1948; s. George Jacob and Margaret Mary (Smith) R.; m. Camille Ann Larson, Oct. 4, 1975; children: Jacob Charles, David Hayes, Philip George. AB with high distinction and honors, U. Mich., 1970, JD magna cum laude, 1973. Bar: Calif. 1975, D.C. 1975, U.S. Dist. Ct. D.C. 1975, U.S. Dist. Ct. Md. 1987, U.S. Ct. Appeals (D.C. and 4th cirs.) 1984, U.S. Ct. Appeals (1st cir.) 1988, U.S. Supreme Ct. 1984, U.S. Dist. Ct. (ea. dist.) Mich. 1995, U.S. Ct. Appeals (6th cir.) 1996, U.S. Ct. Appeals (3d cir.) 1999, U.S. Ct.Appeals (9th cir.) 2002. Law clk. to Hon. Malcolm R. Wilkey U.S. Ct. Appeals, Washington, 1973-74; assoc. Latham & Watkins, L.A., 1974, Crowell & Moring LLP (formerly Jones, Day, Reavis & Pogue), Washington, 1975-79, ptnr., 1980—. Author: (with others) Containing Legal Costs: ADR Strategies for Corporations, Law Firms and Government, 1988; contbr. articles to profl. jours. Fellow Am. Bar Found. Office: Crowell & Moringm LLP 1001 Pennsylvania Ave NW Fl 10 Washington DC 20004-2595 E-mail: gruttinger@crowell.com.

RUTZ, RICHARD FREDERICK, physicist, researcher; b. Alton, Ill., Feb. 9, 1919; s. Erwin William and Esther Norma (Brooks) R.; m. Mary Lamsom Lambert, June 10, 1945; children— Frederick R., Carl R., William L. BA, Shurtleff Coll., Alton, Ill., 1941; MS, State U. Iowa, 1947. Staff mem. Sandia Corp., Albuquerque, 1948-51; mem. staff, mgr. IBM T.J. Watson Sr. Rsch. Ctr., Yorktown Heights, N.Y., 1951-87. Contbr. articles to profl. jours.; patentee numerous semicond. devices With U.S. Maritime Svc., 1941-42, USAAF, 1942-46. Fellow IEEE; mem. Am. Phys. Soc. Home: 9 Burgundy Ct Grand Junction CO 81503-1212 E-mail: rfrutz@frontier.net.

RUUD, CLAYTON OLAF, engineering educator; b. Glassgow, Mont., July 31, 1934; s. Asle and Myrtle (Bleken) R.; children: Kelley Astrid, Kirsten Anne; m. Paula Kay Mannino, Feb. 24, 1990. BS in Metallurgy, Wash. State U., 1957; MS in Materials Sci., San Jose State U., 1967; PhD in Materials Sci., U. Denver, 1970. Registered profl. engr., Calif., Colo. Asst. remelt metallurgist Kaiser Aluminum & Chem. Corp., Trentwood, Wash., 1957-58; devel. engr. Boeing Airplane Co., Seattle, 1958-60; mfg. rsch. engr. Lockheed Missiles & Space Corp., Sunnyvale, Calif., 1960-63; rsch. engr. FMC Corp., San Jose, 1963-67; sr. rsch. scientist U. Denver, 1967-79; prof. indsl. engring. Pa. State U., University Park, 1979—. Founder, developer, and co-director of quality and manufacturing management masters degree Pa. State U.; cons. in field; bd. dirs. Denver X-Ray Inst. Inc., Altoona, Pa. Editor series: Advances in X-Ray Analysis, Vol. 12-22, 1970-80, Nondestructive Character of Materials, Vol. 1-6, 1983-1996; editor X-Ray Spectometry, 1975-87; editl. com. Nondestructive Testing and Evaluation, 1991-1995; contbr. chpts. to books. Chmn. Nat. Acad. Sci. Safe Drinking Water Com., Washington, 1976-78. Recipient IR 100 award, 1983, Gov.'s New Product Award, Pa. Soc. Profl. Engrs., 1988. Fellow ASM Internat. (chmn. Resid. Stress Conf. 1989-91); mem. Internat. Ctr. for Diffraction Data, Soc. Mfg. Engrs., Metall. Soc. of AIME. Achievements include patents in x-ray analysis and residual stress measurement; invention of fiber optic based position sensitive scintillation X-ray detector, instrument for simultaneous stress and phase composition measurement; development of an X-ray diffraction instrument for manufacturing process quality control. Office: 310 Leonhard University Park PA 16802 Business E-Mail: cor1@psu.edu.

RUVA, CHRISTINE LORRAINE, psychologist, educator; b. Syracuse, N.Y., June 8, 1963; d. Joseph John and Donna Elizabeth Ruva; m. Kenneth Banas, June 25, 1988. AAS in Food Svc. Adminstrn., Onondaga C., Syracuse, 1983; BA in Psychology, U. Tampa, 1990; MA in Psychology, U. South Fla., 1997, PhD in Psychology, 2001. Cert. correction/probation office Fla., 1991. Kitchen supr. Fairway Restaurant, Syracuse, 1982—86; sous chef Andrews Upstairs, Tallahassee, 1986—87, Phoebe's Garden Cafe, Syracuse, 1987—88, Raymond's Restaurant, Safety Harbor, Fla., 1988—90; correction/probation officer Dept. Corrections, Pinnellas Park, Fla., 1991—93; grad. tchg. asst. U. South Fla., Tampa, 1994—2000, asst. prof., 2001—. Com. mem. Psychology Dept., IRB Com., Tampa, 2001—03; rschr. Alcohol and Substance Use Inst., Tampa, 2000—01. Contbr. articles to profl. jour. Recipient Provost award for outstanding tchg., U. South Fla., 2000, Provost commendation for outstanding tchg., 1999, Eve Levine Grad. Tchg. award, Dept. Psychology, U. South Fla., 1999. Mem.: APA, Am. Psychol. Soc., Am. Psychology-Law Soc. Avocations: mountain and road biking, in-line skating, dog-training, hiking, snorkeling. Office: Univ of South Florida Sarasota/Manatee Coll of Arts and Sci 5700 No Tamiami Trail PMC 101 Sarasota FL 34243

RUVITUSO, DONNA M. editor, publishing executive; b. Bronx, Jan. 1, 1958; d. Edwin and Marie Begley; m. James R. Ruvituso, Apr. 12, 1981; 1 child, James R. Jr. BA in English, Fordham U., 1980. Sr. mng. editor Bantam Books, NY, 1980—89, Simon & Schuster/Pocket Books, NY, 1989—2001; exec. mng. editor HarperCollins Pubs., NY, 2001—. Mem.: Phi Beta Kappa. Avocations: reading, walking.

RUWE, ROBERT P. federal judge; b. 1941; Grad., Xavier U., 1963; JD, No. Ky. U., 1970. Chief counsel IRS Dept. Treasury, 1970-87; judge U.S. Tax Ct., Washington, 1987—. Office: US Tax Ct 400 2nd St NW Washington DC 20217-0002

RUXIN, PAUL THEODORE, lawyer; b. Cleve., Apr. 14, 1943; s. Charles and Olyn Judith (Koller) R.; m. Joanne Camy, May 25, 1965; children: Marc J., Sarah. BA, Amherst Coll., 1965; LLB, U. Va., 1968. Bar: Ill. 1968, U.S. Dist. Ct. (no. dist.) Ill. 1968, U.S. Ct. Appeals D.C. 1972. Assoc. Isham, Lincoln & Beale, Chgo., 1968-73, ptnr., 1974-77; ptnr., chmn. energy utilities sect. Jones Day, Cleve., 1977—. Mem. editl. com. Yale U. edit. Boswell Papers, 2003—. Mem. Hudson Archtl. and Hist. Bd. Rev., 1981-81; mem. Folger Shakespeare Libr. Com., 1999—; exec. bd. Greater Cleve. Boy Scouts Am., 1978-90; bd. dirs. Cleve. chpt. ARC, 1991-97. Mem. ABA, Ohio State Bar Assn. (pub. utilities sect.), Bar Assn. Greater Cleve., Fed. Energy Bar Assn. (com. chmn. 1981), Chgo. Bar Assn., Club at Soc. Ctr., Rowfant Club, Chgo. Club, Caxton Club, Grolier Club, Chgo. Lit. Club. Office: Jones Day 77 W Wacker Dr Fl 35 Chicago IL 60601-1662 also: 901 Lakeside Ave Cleveland OH 44114-1116 Office Phone: 312-782-3939. E-mail: paultruxin@jonesday.com.

RUYBALID, LOUIS ARTHUR, social worker, community development consultant; b. Allison, Colo., Apr. 6, 1925; s. Mike Joseph and Helen Mary (Rodriguez) R.; m. Seraphima Alexander, June 12, 1949; children: Mariana, John. BA, U. Denver, 1946-49, MSW, 1951; PhD, U. Calif., Berkeley, 1970; Professor Ad-Honorem (hon.), Nat. U., Caracas, Venezuela, 1964. Social worker, Ariz., Calif., Colo., 1951-62; advisor community devel. Unitarian Service Com., Caracas, 1962-64, U.S. Agy. for Internat. Devel., Rio de Janeiro, Brazil, 1964-66; area coordinator U.S. Office Econ. Opportunity, San Francisco, 1966-68; prof., dept. head U. So. Colo., Pueblo, 1974-80; licensing analyst State of Calif., Campbell, 1984—; prof. sch. of social work Highlands U., Las Vegas, N.Mex., 1988-89. Cons. UN, Caracas, 1978, Brazilian Govt., Brazilia, 1964-66, Venezuelan Govt., Caracas, 1962-64. Author: (books) Favela, 1970, Glossary for Hominology, 1978, (research instrument) The Conglomerate Hom., 1976. Mem. exec. com. Pueblo (Colo.) Regional Planning Com., 1974-79, Nat. Advisory com. The Program Agy. United Presbyn. Ch., 1978-79. Served with USN, 1944-46. Recipient Pro Mundo Beneficio medal Brazilian Acad. Human Sci., Sao Paulo, 1976; United Def. Fund fellow U. Calif., Berkeley, 1961-62, Cert. World Leadership Internat. Leaders of Achievement, 1988-89. Mem. NASW (cert.), Ethnic Minority Commn., IMAGE (nat. edn. chair), Am. Hominol. Assn. (nat. pres. 1975-79), U. Calif. Alumni Assn., AARP (minority spokesperson), Phi Beta Kappa, Phi Sigma Iota. Democrat. Avocations: tennis, boxing history. Home and Office: Ruybalid Assoc Inc 129 Calle Don Jose Santa Fe NM 87501-2364 *Personal philosophy: As a personal credo, I have adopted the philosophy of the Pueblo Indians of New Mexico which is: Amity, not conquest, stability, not strife, conservation, not waste, restraint, not aggression, I embrace the conviction that human energy should be used to care for the primal needs of people!.*

RUYLE-HULLINGER, ELIZABETH SMITH (BETH RUYLE), consultant, municipal financial advisor; b. Oct. 26, 1946; d. Daniel Lester and Mae (Coley) Smith; m. Craig Harlan Hullinger, Oct. 24, 1985; children: Leigh Ann Ruyle, Clint (dec.), Bret. AA, St. Petersburg Jr. Coll., 1966; BA in English, U. Fla., 1968; MPA, U. Ga., 1975. Rsch. asst. Emory U., Atlanta, 1969—70; health planner Met. Coun. for Health, Atlanta, 1970-72; govtl. rels. coord. Atlanta Regional Commn., 1972-76, govtl. affairs coord., 1976-78; exec. dir. South Suburban Mayors' and Mgrs. Assn., East Hazel Crest, Ill., 1978-2000; pres. Chgo. Southland Econ. Devel. Alliance, 1999-2000; exec. v.p., dir. Ehlers & Assocs., Naperville, Ill., 2000—. Exec. dir. South Towns Agy. Risk Mgmt., 1980-98, South Towns Area Benefits Coop., 1983-89, South Towns Bus. Growth Corp., 1983-90; cons. Planning Devel. Svc., Tinley Park, Ill., 1986—. Contbr. articles to profl. and devel. mags. Mem. World's Fair Adv. Com., Chgo., 1986, Met. Planning Coun., 1990-2000, Cook County Tax Reform adv. coun., South Suburban Arts Coun., 1987, Coun. Urban Econ. Devel., 1986; adv. coun. Urban Innovations, Chgo., Chgo. Assembly Project; mem. Regional Partnership, 1985-2000; bd. dirs. South Suburban Hosp., 1987-96, mem. governing coun., 1999—; bd. dirs. Fin. Cmty. Devel. Corp., 1998-2000; mentor U. Chgo. Sch. Pub. Policy. Mem. Internat. City Mgmt. Assn., Ill. City Mgmt. Assn., Met. City Mgrs. Assn., Ill. Govtl. Fin. Officers Assn., Ill. Tax Increment Assn., Plank Road Trail Assn., Lambda Alpha. Methodist. Home: 17255 66th Ct Tinley Park IL 60477-3501 Office: Ehlers & Assocs 550 Warrenville Rd Ste 220 Lisle IL 60532-5500 Office Phone: 630-271-3332. E-mail: bruyle@ehlers-inc.com.

RUYTER, NANCY LEE CHALFA, dance educator; b. Phila., May 23, 1933; d. Andrew Benedict Chalfa and Lois Elizabeth (Strode) McClary; m. Ralph Markson (div.); m. Hans C. Ruyter, Dec. 7, 1968 (dec. Jan. 1998). BA in History, U. Calif., Riverside, 1964; PhD in History, Claremont Grad. Sch., 1970. Tchr. theater dept. Pomona Coll., 1965-72; instr. dance program U. Calif., Riverside, 1972-76, acting chair dance program, 1974-75; instr. dance dept. UCLA, 1976; instr. phys. edn. dept. Orange Coast Coll., 1976-77; asst. prof. dept. phys. edn. and dance Tufts U., 1977-78; asst. prof. phys. edn. dept. Calif. State U., Northridge, 1978-82; from asst. prof. to full prof. dance dept. U. Calif., Irvine, 1982—, assoc. dean Sch. Fine Arts, 1984-88, 95-96, chair dept. dance, 1989-91. Presenter in field. Appeared with Jasna Planina Folk Ensemble, 1972-77, 78-79, Di Falco and Co., 1955-57; choreographer, dir. numerous coll. dance prodns.; contbr. articles, revs. to profl. publs.; author: Reformers and Visionaries: The Americanization of the Art of Dance, 1979, The Cultivation of Body and Mind in Nineteenth-Century American Delsartism, 1999. Mem. Am. Soc. Theatre Rsch., Bulgarian Studies Assn., Congress on Rsch. in Dance (bd. dirs. 1977-80, pres. 1981-85), Folk Dance Fedn.,

Internat. Fedn. Theatre Rsch., Soc. Dance Rsch., Soc. Ethnomusicology, Soc. Dance History Scholars (steering com. 1980-81), Spanish Dance Soc., Theatre Libr. Assn. Office: U Calif-Irvine Dept Dance Irvine CA 92697-0001 Business E-Mail: nlruyter@uci.edu.

RYALL, JO-ELLYN M. psychiatrist; b. Newark, May 25, 1949; d. Joseph P. and Tekla (Paraszczuk) R. BA in Chemistry with gen. honors, Rutgers U., 1971; MD, Washington U., St. Louis, 1975. Diplomate Am. Bd. Psychiatry and Neurology. Resident in psychiatry Washington U., St. Louis, 1975-78, psychiatrist Student Health, 1978-83, asst. prof. clin. psychiatry, 1983—2003, assoc. prof. clin. psychiatry, 2003—. Inpatient supr. Malcolm Bliss Mental Health Ctr., St. Louis, 1978-80, pvt. practtice medicine specializing in psychiatry, St. Louis, 1980—. Bd. dirs. Women's Self Help Ctr., St. Louis, 1980. Fellow: APA (pres. ea. Mo. dist. br. 1983—85, sect. coun. AMA 1986—99, dep. rep. to assembly 1994—97, rep. 1997—2001, chair bylaws com. 2000—03, dep. rep. area 4 2001—); mem.: AMA (alt. del. Mo. 1988—90, 1993—94, del. 1995—, mem. coun. on constn. bylaws 1998—, vice chair 2002—04, chair 2004—), Manic Depressive Assn. St. Louis (chmn. bd. dirs. 1985—89), Mo. State Med. Assn. (vice spkr. ho. of dels. 1986—89, spkr. 1989—92), St. Louis Met. Med. Soc. (del. to state conv. 1981—86, councilor 1985—87, v.p. 1989, del. to state conv. 1993—), Am. Med. Women's Assn. (pres. St. Louis dist. br. 1981—82, regional gov. VIII 1986—89, pres. St. Louis dist. br. 1992, spkr. ho. of dels. 1993—96), Washington U. Faculty Club. Office: 9216 Clayton Rd Ste 105 Saint Louis MO 63124-1515

RYALL, MARTY, former political organization administrator; Campaign mgr. U.S. Senator Paul Coverell, Ga., 1998; nat. dep. polit. dir. Elizabeth Dole for Pres., 1999; campaign mgr. Tom Gallagher for U.S. Senate, Fla., 2000; exec. dir. Republican Party Del., 2000; with Bush/Cheney Recount Team, Fla., 2000; exec. dir. Republican Party of Ark., state chmn., 2002—03. Republican.

RYAN, ALLAN ANDREW, JR., lawyer, author, lecturer; b. Cambridge, Mass., July 3, 1945; s. Allan Andrew and Anne (Conway) R.; m. Nancy Foote, June 30, 1978; children: Elisabeth, Andrew. AB, Dartmouth Coll., 1966; JD magna cum laude, U. Minn., 1970. Bar: D.C. 1972, Mass. 1985. Law clk. to assoc. justice Byron R. White U.S. Supreme Ct., 1970-71; assoc. Williams, Connolly & Califano, Washington, 1974-77; asst. to Solicitor Gen. U.S., Washington, 1977-80; dir. office of spl. investigations, Dept. Justice, Washington, 1980-83, spl. asst. to atty. gen., 1983; pvt. practice law, 1983-85; with office of gen. counsel, Harvard U., 1985—2001; dir. intellectual property Harvard Bus. Sch., 2001—. Presenting counsel Internat. Commn. Inquiry on Kurt Waldheim, London, 1988; adj. prof. Law Sch., Boston Coll., 1989—, Harvard U., 1997—. Author: Quiet Neighbors: Prosecuting Nazi War Criminals in America, 1984. pres., editor-in-chief: Minn. Law Rev., 1969-70. Mem. exec. com. New Eng. region Anti-Defamation League, 1990—; chair Ctr. on Civil Rights and Pub. Policy, 2003—; bd. dirs. Facing History and Ourselves Nat. Found., 1985—92; mem. adv. bd. Holocaust and human rights rsch. project Boston Coll. Law Sch., 1984—. Capt. USMC, 1971—74. Recipient Internat. Human Rights award Anti-Defamation League, 1986, leadership award Anti-Defamation League, 1997. Mem. ABA, Boston Bar Assn. Office: Harvard Bus Sch Publ 60 Harvard Way Boston MA 02163 Office Phone: 617-783-7849. E-mail: ryan@hbsp.harvard.edu.

RYAN, ARTHUR FREDERICK, insurance company executive; b. Bklyn., Sept. 14, 1942; s. Arthur Vincent and Gertrude (Wingert) R.; m. Patricia Elizabeth Kelly; children: Arthur, Kelly Ann, Kevin, Kathleen. BA in Math., Providence Coll., 1963. Area mgr. Data Corp., Washington, 1965-72; project mgr. Chase Manhattan Corp. and Bank, N.Y.C., 1972-73, 2d v.p., 1973-74, v.p., 1974-75, ops. exec., 1978-82, exec. v.p., from 1982, vice-chmn., then pres., chief operating officer, 1990-94; chmn., CEO Prudential Ins. Co. Am., Newark, N.J., 1994—. Mem. policy and planning com.; bd. dirs., chmn. audit com. Depository Trust Co.; past mem. exec. com., Cedel (European Depository); past chmn. steering com., program mgr. CHIPS Same Day Settlement, N.Y. Clearing House. Past bd. dirs. Urban Acad. N.Y.C. Lt. U.S. Army, 1963-65. Mem. Am. Bankers Assn. (vice chmn. ops. and automation div. and govt. rels. coun., past chmn. internat. ops. com., bd. dirs., Regeneron Pharmaceuticals, NY, 2003-. Office: Prudential Ins Co Am Prudential Plaza 24th Fl 751 Broad St Newark NJ 07102-3714

RYAN, BRENDAN, advertising executive; BA in History, Fordham U.; MBA, Wharton U. V.p. mktg. Citibank; product mgmt. Gen. Foods; head account mgmt. dept., bd. dirs. OMW, N.Y.C.; with Ogilvy & Mather; pres., CEO FCB N.Y.; CEO FCB Worldwide, N.Y.C. Mem. Citizens Crime Commn., N.Y.C.; bd. dirs. Citymeals-On-Wheels, Regis H.S. Office: Foot Cone & Belding FCB 100 W 33RD St #5 New York NY 10001-2921

RYAN, CANDACE IRENE, writer, director, editor; d. Lilburn Terry and Maureen Adell Ryan; children: Elizabeth Maureen Solomon, Virginia Violet Hildenbrand. AA in human rels., Bridgeport U., 1976—79; BA in journalism, Rice U., 1965—68. Human Relations-Death & Life. Abused Woman & Children of CT, 1978. Adv. bd. Barrington Rev. of the Arts, Westport, Conn., 1976—85; councilor Inner Cities Volunteers of CT, Stamford, Conn., 1976—89; asst dir. & advisor CT. Commn. on the Arts, Westport, Conn., 1977—89. Roving editor Family & Moral Issues, Sacremento, Calif., 1993—. Author: Detecting! The Midnight Tattler, over 20 novels, 14 short stories. Sec. World Wildlife Found., San Diego, 1990—93; asst. advisor Women & Children Outreach Org., Sacramento, 1991—2003; asst. editor Wolferts Retreat Ctr. for the Arts, Stamford, Conn., 1980—90. Recipient Journalism Excellence, Fairfield U., 1982, 6 Poetry awards, 1976—2004; Louis Webber grant, Century Acceptance Assoc., 1990—92. Fellow: Mystery Writers Assoc. (corr.; sr. writer 2000); mem.: Beta Corp. Agy. Consortium (v.p. 1981—91), US Travel Industry (rep. China 1984, Israel 1985, France 1986), Quota Club Internat. (sec. 1984—88), Eagles Club of Am. (corr.; mem. 2000, Volunteers above and Beyond the Call of Duty 2001). R-Conservative. Bapt. Achievements include research in Human Relations-Death & Survivors. Avocations: writing, reading, camping, travel. Home: 1419 Eckman Ave Chula Vista CA 91911 Office: Ghost & Greative Writers Co 1419 Eckman Ave Chula Vista CA 91911 Personal E-mail: criamhere@cox.net. E-mail: g&cw@cox.net.

RYAN, CLARENCE AUGUSTINE, JR., biochemistry educator; b. Butte, Mont., Sept. 29, 1931; s. Clarence A. Sr. and Agnes L. (Duckham) R.; m. Patricia Louise Meunier, Feb. 8, 1936; children: Jamie Arlette, Steven Michael (dec.), Janice Marie, Joseph Patrick (dec.). BA in Chemistry, Carroll Coll., 1953; MS in Chemistry, Mont. State U., 1956, PhD in Chemistry, 1959. Postdoctoral fellow in biochemistry Oreg. State U., Corvallis, 1959-61, U.S. Western Regional Lab., Albany, Calif., 1961-63; chemist U.S. Dept. of Agrl., Albany, 1963-64; asst. prof. biochemistry Wash. State U., Pullman, 1964-68, assoc. prof., 1968-72, prof., 1972—, Charlotte Y. Martin disting. prof., 1991—, chmn. dept. agrl. chemistry, 1977-80, fellow Inst. Biol. Chemistry, 1980—. Faculty athletics rep. to PAC-10 & NCAA Wash. State U., 1991-94, 96-97; vis. scientist dept. biochemistry U. Wash., 1981; vis. scientist Harvard U. Med. Sch., 1982, Bert and Natalie Vallee vis. prof., 1997; res. adv. bd. Kemin Industries, Des Moines, 1981—, Plant Genetics, Davis, Calif., 1987-89; rsch. adv. bd. Frito-Lay, Inc., Dallas, 1982, Plant Genetic Engring. Lab., N.Mex. State U., Las Cruces, 1986-89, Noble Found., 1996-2002; mem. NRC rev. bd. Plant Gene Exptl. Ctr., Albany, 1990-93; mgr. biol. stress program USDA Competitive Grants Program, Washington, 1983-84; former mem. adv. panels for H. McKnight Found., Internat. Potato Ctr., Lima, Peru, Internat. Ctr. Genetic Engring. and Biotech., New Delhi, Internat. Ctr. Tropical Agr., Cali, Colombia, Internat. Tropical Agr., Ibandan, Africa; mem. grant rev. panels NSF, USDA, DOE, NIH; co-organizer Internat. Telecom. Symposium on Plant Biotech.; mem. adv. bd. Bert and Natalie Vallee Found., Harvard Med. Sch., 1997-2000. Mem. editl. bd. several biochem. and plant physiology jours.; contbr. articles to profl. publs., chpts. to books; co-editor 2 books. Trustee Carroll Coll., Helena, Mont., 1998-2002; mem. rsch. adv. bd. Danforth Plant Sci. Ctr., St. Louis, 1998—. Grantee USDA, NSF, NIH, Rockefeller Found., McKnight Found.; recipient Merck award for grad. rsch. Mont. State U., 1959, Alumni Achievement award Carroll Coll., 1986, Pres.'s Faculty Excellence award in rsch. Wash. State U., 1986; named to Carroll Coll. Alumni Hall of Fame, 1981, Carroll Coll. Basketball Hall of Fame, 1982; named 1 of 100 centennial disting. alumni Mont. State. U., 1993; Career Devel. grantee NIH, 1964-74, non-resident fellow Noble Found., 1996-2002. Fellow Am. Acad. Microbiology; mem. AAAS, NAS (elected 1986), Am. Chem. Soc. (Kenneth A. Spencer award 1992), Am. Soc. Plant Physiologists (Steven Hales prize 1992), Am. Soc. Exptl. Biology, Biochem. Soc., Am. Peptide Soc., Internat. Soc. Chem. Ecology (Silverstein-Simione award 1997), Internat. Soc. Plant Molecular Biology (bd. dirs.), Phytochem. Soc. N.Am., Nat. U. Continuing Assn. (Creative Programming award 1991), Phi Kappa Phi (Recognition award 1976). Democrat. Avocations: fishing, basketball, golf. Office: Wash State Univ Inst Biol Chemistry Pullman WA 99164-0001 Office Phone: 509-335-3304.

RYAN, CYNTHIA RHOADES, lawyer; b. Wilmington, Del., Feb. 6, 1954; d. Harry Edris and Patricia Irene (Dux) Rhoades; m. John G. Christfield, Aug. 6, 1977 (div. 1984); m. Matthew C. Ryan, Oct. 10, 1993. BA in Polit. Sci., U. Del., 1976; JD, Widener U., 1979. Bar: Del. 1979, U.S. Supreme Ct. 1989. Dep. atty. gen. State of Del., Wilmington, 1979-85; staff counsel permanent subcom. investigations U.S. Senate, Washington, 1985-87; trial atty. criminal div. U.S. Dept. Justice, Washington, 1987-88, sr. atty. DEA, 1988-91, assoc. chief counsel internat. law sect., 1991-96; chief counsel Office of the Chief Counsel, Drug Enforcement Administrn., 1996—. Mem. ABA, Del. Bar Assn., Internat. Assn. of Chiefs of Police, Alpha Sigma Alpha. Avocations: sports, gardening, gourmet cooking, piano, tenor banjo.

RYAN, DANIEL JOHN, university administrator; b. Buffalo, June 5, 1960; s. Michael E. and Joan F. R.; m. Sandra Suffoleto, Aug. 19, 1989. BA in Pol. Sci., Canisius Coll., Buffalo, 1982, MS in Edn., 1992; PhD in Edn., SUNY, Buffalo, 1997. Fin. cons. First Albany Corp., Buffalo, 1982-84; confidential investigator County of Erie, Buffalo, 1984-87; econ. mkt. analyst City of Buffalo, Buffalo, 1987-90; asst. dir. career planning Canisius Coll., Buffalo, 1990-97, asst. dean students svcs., 1997—; dir. career planning and placement SUNY, Buffalo. Lectr. Buffalo and Erie County Pub. Libr., Buffalo, 1990—; dir. career planning and placement SUNY Buffalo. Author: A Job Search Handbook for People with Disabilities. Pres. Univ. Dist. N. Buffalo Civic Assn., Buffalo, 1990-91; v.p. Kiwanis Club of N. Buffalo, 1987-88; vice chmn. City of Buffalo rep. Com., 1989-91, sec. 1993-95; chmn. Delaware Ward Rep. Com., 1985-91. Recipient Edward A. Parish award, Ea. Assn. Colls. and Employers. Mem. Nat. Assn. Student Personnel Admininstrn.(region II Outstanding New Profl.), N. Buffalo Community Devel. Corp., Assn. for Higher Edn. and Disabilities. Republican. Avocations: reading, raquetball. E-mail: dryan@buffalo.edu.

RYAN, DANIEL LEO, bishop; b. Mankato, Minn., Sept. 28, 1930; s. Leonard Bennett and Irene Ruth (Larson) R. BA, Benedictine U., 1952; JCL, Pontificia Università Lateranense, Rome, 1960. Ordained priest Roman Cath. Ch., 1956, consecrated bishop Roman Cath. Ch., 1981. Parish priest Roman Cath. Diocese, Joliet, Ill., 1956—82, chancellor, 1965—78, vicar gen., 1977—79, aux. bishop, 1981—84, bishop Springfield, Ill., 1984—99. Roman Catholic. Office: Diocese of Springfield PO Box 3187 1615 W Washington St Springfield IL 62702-4757 E-mail: dlryan@dio.org.

RYAN, DAVID ALAN, computer specialist; b. Cin., Nov. 13, 1961; s. James Patrick and Virginia Ann (Stewart) R. BS, Wright State U., 1983; MS, Tex. A&M U., 1988. Statistician U.S. Bur. of Census, Washington, 1988-92, computer specialist, 1992—. Vol. math. modeling Soil Conservation Svc., Washington, 1991-96; math. and. probability vol. Washington Opera, 1992—; data entry/programming vol. Opera Am., Washington, 1990-91; hist. rschr. Gasby's Tavern Mus., Alexandria, Va., 1991-94; mem. Bravo! for the Washington Opera, 1991-95. Recipient Vol. Svc. award Soil Conservation Svc., 1992, 93. Mem. Am. Statis. Assn., Capitol PC Users Group, Ballston-Va. Square Civic Assn. (exec. com. 1995—, sec. 1996—, NCAC rep. 1997-98), The Washington Opera Guild, The Washington Opera Camerata, The DC Wagner Soc. Achievements include building a supercomputer at home in 2000. Avocations: classical music, ethnomusicology, history, geography, travel. Office: Bur of Census/CES Ste 208 Washington Plz II Washington DC 20233-6300

RYAN, DAVID J. food products executive; Gen. ptnr. Copley Venture Ptnrs. EcoScience Corp., founding investor, dir., chmn. bd. dirs., 1995—. Office: EcoScience Corp 17 Christopher Way Eatontown NJ 07724-3325 Address: EcoScience Corp 10 Alvin Ct East Brunswick NJ 08816 Fax: 732-676-3031.

RYAN, DAVID THOMAS, lawyer; b. Torrington, Conn., Apr. 18, 1939; s. Edward John and Margaret (Murphy) R.; m. Dale Anderson, Aug. 21, 1965; children: Rachael Anderson, Conor Anne. BS, U. Md., 1961; LLB, Georgetown U., 1965. Bar: Conn. 1966, U.S. Dist. Ct. Conn. 1967, U.S. Ct. Appeals (2d cir.) 1969, U.S. Ct. Appeals (fed. cir.) 1982, U.S. Claims Ct. 1983, U.S. Supreme Ct. 1992. Ptnr. Cooney, Scully & Dowling, Hartford, Conn., 1966-77, Robinson & Cole, Hartford, 1977—. Fellow Am. Coll. Trial Lawyers; mem. Am. Bd. Trial Advs., Conn. Trial Lawyers Assn. (bd. dirs.). Home: 126 Westerly Ter Hartford CT 06105-1117 Office: Robinson & Cole 280 Trumbull St Ste 26 Hartford CT 06103-3509 Office Phone: 203-275-8200. E-mail: dryan@rc.com.

RYAN, DENNIS, information technology executive; Software engr. IBM; product mktg. mgr., engring. mgr. Apple Computer; group mgr. for info. mgmt. products FileMaker (formerly Claris Corp.); v.p. mktg. EO, Inc., 1991—98; pres., CEO Allegis Corp., San Francisco, 1998—. Office: Allegis Corp 1550 Bryant St Ste 220 San Francisco CA 94103

RYAN, DON, state legislator; b. Great Falls, Mont., Dec. 21, 1951; m. Terri Ryan; children: Bill, Annie, Sean. BA, U. Mont., 1976. Eligibility technician Mont. Social and Rehab. Svc., 1985-89; tchr., coach Stevensville, Mont., 1989-94; clk., recorder Cascade County, Mont., 1993-95; daycare owner Lil-Pals and Playmates, 1995—. Mem. Lincoln Sch. PTA, 1999-2000; past pres. Ancient Order Hibernians, 1990—; campaign worker Friends of Pat Williams, 1991-92; trustee Great Falls Pub. Schs., 1995—, mem. transp. subcom., 1998, chair long-range bldg. planning com., 1998—. Mem. Nat. Sch. Bds. Assn. (del. Fed. Rels. Network 1993-95), Mont. Sch. Bds. Assn. Roman Catholic. Office: 2101 Seventh Ave S Great Falls MT 59405 E-mail: donterryan@aol.com.

RYAN, EDWARD W. economics professor; b. Plainfield, NJ, Aug. 23, 1932; s. Edward A. and Helen R. (Shannon) R.; m. Georgian Hurley, Dec. 17, 1966; children: Sarah, Jennifer. BS, U. Pa., 1955; MA, Duke U., 1957; LHD (hon.), Manhattanville Coll., 2003. Lectr. Fordham U., N.Y.C., 1956-57; instr. Iona Coll., New Rochelle, N.Y., 1958-60; Ryan-Bacardi prof. econs. Manhattanville Coll., Purchase, N.Y., 1958—, Doc. of Humane Letters (L.H.D.), 2003. Dir. Econ. Freedom Inst. Author: In the Words of Adam Smith: The First Consumer Advocate, 1990, Liberty, Virtue and Happiness: The Story of Economic Freedom in America, 2000. Mem.: Econ. History Assn., Assn. Pvt. Enterprise Edn., Am. Econ. Assn. Roman Catholic. Home: 25 Jefferson Rd Scarsdale NY 10583-6411 Office: Manhattanville College 2900 Purchase St Purchase NY 10577-2132 E-mail: edwryan1@aol.com.

RYAN, ELLEN BOUCHARD, psychology educator, gerontologist; b. Holyoke, Mass., 1947; arrived in Can., 1982; d. Raoul Rosario and Etiennette Marie Bouchard; m. Patrick J. Ryan, July 12, 1969; children: Lorraine Yvette, Dennis Patrick, Kevin Myles. BA, MA, Brown U., 1968; PhD, U. Mich., 1970. Asst. prof. psychology U. Notre Dame, 1970-76, assoc. prof., 1976-81, prof., 1981-82, chmn. dept., 1978-82; prof. psychiatry McMaster U., Hamilton, Canada, 1982—, dir. Ctr. for Gerontol. Studies, 1985-95, prof. gerontology, 1987—. Editor: Attitudes Toward Language Variation, 1982, Language Communication and The Elderly, 1986, Intergenerational Communication, 1994, Language Attitudes, 1994, Communication, Aging and Health, 1996. Grantee NICHD, 1972-75, NSF, 1976-79, Nat. Inst. Edn., 1979-82, Natural Scis. and Engring. Rsch., 1983-89, Gerontol. Rsch. Coun. of Ont., 1983-85, Ont. Ministry Health, 1986-89, Soc. Sci. and Humanities Rsch. Coun., 1986—. Fellow APA, Gerontol. Soc. Am., Can. Psychol. Assn.; mem. Internat. Assn. of Lang. and Social Psychology, Can. Assn. Gerontology. Roman Catholic. Home: 346 Brookview Ct Ancaster ON Canada L9G 4C2 Office: McMaster U Dept Psychiatry 1200 Main St W Hamilton ON Canada L8N 3Z5 Office Phone: 905-525-9140 ext. 24995. E-mail: ryaneb@mcmaster.ca.

RYAN, FRANK HARRY, plastic surgeon; b. May 21, 1960; BS, U. Mich., 1982; MD, Ohio State U. Coll. Of Medicine, 1986. Surgical residency Cedars-Sinai Med. Ctr., U. Missouri & UCLA Med. Ctr., 1986—94; plastic surgeon priv. practice, Beverly Hills, 1994—. Mem. adv. bd. A. Craig Matthias Found. Founder Bony Pony Ranch Found., Malibu. Avocations: boating, fishing, golf, skiing, tennis. Office: 9675 Brighton Wy Ste 340 Beverly Hills CA 90210 also: Bony Pony Ranch Found 9663 Santa Monica Blvd Ste 785 Beverly Hills CA 90210

RYAN, FRANK J. construction executive; Pres., COO Air Products and Chems., Inc.; bd. dirs. Southdown, Inc., Houston, 1993—, chmn. bd. dirs., 1995—, mem. compensation and benefits com., nominating com. Office: Detection System 130 Perinton Pkwy Fairport NY 14450

RYAN, GEORGE H. former governor, pharmacist; b. Maquoketa, Iowa, Feb. 24, 1934; s. Thomas J. and Jeanette (Bowman) R.; m. Lura Lynn Lowe, June 10, 1956; children: Nancy, Lynda, Julie, Joanne, Jeanette, George. BS in Pharmacy, Ferris State Coll., Big Rapids, Mich. Mem. Ill. Ho. of Reps., 1973-82, minority leader, 1977-80, speaker, 1981-82; lt. gov. State of Ill., 1983-91, sec. of state, 1991-98, gov., 1999—2003. Mem. Kankakee County Bd., 1966-72, chmn., 1971-72; chmn. Ill. Literacy Coun., 1991—. With U.S. Army, Korea. Recipient Humphrey award Am. Pharm. Assn., 1980, Top award Ill. chpt. DARE, 1989, Govt. Leadership award Nat. Commn. Against Drunk Driving and MADD Govt. Leader Against Drunk Driving award, 1994-95, City Club of Chgo. Man of Yr. award, 1995. Mem. Am. Pharm. Assn., Ill. Pharm. Assn., One Hundred Club, Masons (33d degree). Lodges: Elks, Moose, Shriners. Republican. Methodist. Home: 912 S Greenwood Ave Kankakee IL 60901-5211

RYAN, GEORGE WILLIAM, manufacturing executive; b. Sinking Springs, Ohio, Oct. 13, 1939; s. Winson Mark and Mary Edith (Smalley) R.; 1 child: Gina Kristin. Student, Wilmington Coll., 1962. Process engr. B.F. Goodrich Co., Marietta, Ohio, 1962-66; product dev. mgr. Chrysler Corp., Sandusky, Ohio, 1966-70; asst. tech. mgr. Inmont Corp., Toledo, Ohio, 1970-72; tech. mgr. Occidental Petroleum, Burlington, N.J., 1973; owner Ryan Devel. Corp., Peebles, 1973-88; prin. Ironwood Valley Ranch, Ohio, 1986—. Substitute tchr. Adams County Sch. Dist.; cons. Hooker Chem. Corp., Burlington, NJ, 1973; expert Internat. Exec. Svc. Core. Bd. dirs., pres. Missionary Evang. Ch. of Christ; mem. Adams County Workforce Commn; mem. Rep. Presdl. Roundtable, 2001, 04. Mem. Soc. Plastic Engrs., Peebles Ind. Inc. (sec., treas., bd. dirs., 1984-88)., Adams County Mfg. Assn., Presdl. Roundtable. Republican.

RYAN, HAROLD MARTIN, judge; b. Detroit, Feb. 6, 1911; s. Martin and Ida Ryan; m. Lilliana Wargnier, Sept. 4, 1944; children: Kathleen, Nancy, Harold Jr., John, Theresa. Student, Mich. State U., 1930-31; JD, U. Detroit, 1935. Bar: Mich. 1935, U.S. Supreme Ct. 1935. Atty., 1935—; asst. pros. atty. Wayne County, Detroit, 1942-45; state senator Mich. 1st Dist., Lansing, 1948-61; U.S. congressman 14th Congrl. Dist. Mich., Washington, 1961-65; cir. ct. judge Wayne County, Detroit, 1978-85. With USAFR, 1961-66. Democrat. Roman Catholic. Avocations: golf, football, history. Home: 28601 Little Mack Ave Saint Clair Shores MI 48081-3012

RYAN, HENRY BUTTERFIELD, historian, consultant; b. Chgo., July 4, 1931; s. Henry Butterfield and Dorothy Marie (Webster) Ryan; m. Patricia Burns Ryan, Nov. 28, 1957; 1 child, William Warrington. BS, Northwestern U., 1952; MPA, Harvard U., 1972; PhD, U. Cambridge, Eng., 1979. With publs. divsn. U.S. Gypsum Co., Chgo., 1952—56; with Milton Kreines Co., Chgo., 1956—57; asst. editor World Book Ency., Chgo., 1957—59; mng. editor Inland Printer/Am. Lithographer, Chgo., 1959—61; fgn. svc. officer U.S. Info. Agy., Washington, 1961—86, trainee, 1961—63, info. officer U.S. Emb. Brasilia, 1963—65, radio officer U.S. Emb. Rio de Janeiro, 1965—68, press attache U.S. Embassy, 1968—69, nat. security rev. staff Washington, 1969—71, cultural attache U.S. Embassy Oslo, 1972—75, with Bur. European Affairs Washington, 1978—79, dir. editl. svcs. Office Congl. and Pub. Liaison, 1979—81, spokesperson, 1980—81, cultural attache U.S. Emb. Canberra, Australia, 1982—86. Vis. scholar St. Anthony's Coll., Oxford (Eng.) U., 1986; vis. fellow Clare Hall Cambridge (Eng.) U., 1987; consulting sr. historian History Assocs. Inc., Rockville, Md., 1990—95; assoc. Inst. for Study of Diplomacy, Georgetown U., Washington, 1991—; cons. Assn. for Diplomatic Studies and Tng., Arlington, Va., 1992—96; writer History News Svc., 1997—. Author: The Vision of Anglo-America, 1987, The Fall of the Guevara, 1998, (booklet) A Brief History of United States Diplomacy, 1996; contbr. Govt. Exec. mag., 1992—95, articles to newspapers and mags. Tutor, asst. dir., then dir., bd. mem. Saturday Learning Ext. Program, Washington, 1991—2001. Mem.: Orgn. Am. HIstorians, Cambridge Soc. Washington, Kennedy Sch. Govt. Alumni Assn., Harvard Club Washington. Avocation: playwriting.

RYAN, J. BRUCE, healthcare management consulting executive; b. Southbridge, Mass., Mar. 28, 1944; s. Charles J. and Doris (Olney) R.; m. Sarah E. Pattison, Aug. 16, 1993. BSBA in Fin., U. Mass., 1972, MSBA, 1975; MA in Econs., U. Wash., 1976. Regional v.p. Amherst Assocs. Inc., Atlanta, 1976-85; exec. v.p. Jennings Ryan & Kolb, Inc., Atlanta, 1985—; CFO, Cross Country Cons., 2002—. Mem. editl. rev. bd. Healthcare Fin. Mgmt.; contbr. articles to profl. jours. With U.S. Army, 1968-70. Mem. Healthcare Fin. Mgmt. Assn. (Helen M. Yerger/L. Van Seawell best article award 1990), Fin. Mgmt. Assn. Avocation: sailing. Home: 1060 Kentucky Ave NE Atlanta GA 30306-3534 Office: Jennings Ryan & Kolb Inc 17 Executive Park Dr NE Ste 500 Atlanta GA 30329-2225

RYAN, JAMES, insurance company executive; b. Pitts., Jan. 21, 1937; s. Martin Charles and Lucy Elizabeth (Misklow) r.; m. Marlene Sullivan Ryan, Jan. 27, 1973. BA, U. Pitts., U. Louisville. Cert. ins. wholesaler. Chmn. Market Finders Ins. Corp., Louisville, 1972—. Com. chmn. Am. Assn. Mng. Gen. Agts., 1988-89; pres. Ky. Lloyd's Agts. Assn., 1985—; bd. dirs. Nat. Assn. Profl. Surplus Lines Office, Inc., 1983-86; pres. Ky. Surplus Lines Assn., Louisville, 1988-89; mem. adv. coun. Essex Ins. Co., 1991-93, Am. Equity Ins. Co., Scottsdale, Ariz., 1999. Pub. in Best Rev., 1995. Mem. Ky. Thoroughbred Owners & Breeders, Inc., Hon. Order of Blue Goose Internat., Kosair Shrine Temple, Hon. Order of Ky. Col. Named Adv. Coun. Colony Ins. Co., Glen Allen, Va., 1991-93, Hamilton Ins. Co., 1993, Cardinal Ins. Co., 1991-93. Mem. Profl. Ins. Agts., Ind. Ins. Agts. Assn., Am. Assn. Mng. Gen. Agts. (cert., chmn. adv. com. 1991-92, bd. dirs. 1994-96, v.p. zone 2 1995-96, pres.-elect 1996-97, pres. 1997-98), Nat. Assn. Profl. Surplus Lines Offices (chmn. legis. com. 1988-89, Published Best Rev. 1995), Am. Assn. of Gen. Agts. Republican. Roman Catholic. Avocations: breeding and racing thoroughbred horses, golf. Office Phone: 502-423-1800.

RYAN, JAMES DANIEL, history professor; b. Buffalo, Nov. 29, 1938; s. James Daniel Ryan and Antoinette Marie La Teer; m. Jeanne Anne Ryan, Apr. 15, 1963; children: James Daniel III, Julia Regina, Matthew George. BA in Philosophy, St. Bonaventure U., 1960; MS in Edn., Canisius Coll., 1962; PhD in History, NYU, 1972. Prof., dept. chair dept. history CUNY, Bronx C.C., 1970—2002, resident prof., 2002—; dir. spl. projects Bronx C.C., 1985—2002, coord. humanities divsn., 1995—2001. Author: (book) U.N. Under Kurt Waldheim, 2001; contbr. articles to profl. jours. Pres. bd. dirs. Columbus Park Corp., N.Y.C., 1973—. Grantee NEH, 1981, 96, travel grantee Am. Coun. Learned Socs., 1990. Mem. Medieval Acad. Am., Am. Hist. Assn., Soc. for Study of Crusades, Am. Cath. Hist. Assn., Ea. C.C. Social Scis. Assn. (Disting. Svc. award 1992, bd. dirs. 1986-92), Medieval Club. N.Y. (pres. 1994-96). Democrat. Roman Catholic. Avocations: fishing, woodworking, music. Home: 100 W 94th St New York NY 10025 Office: CUNY Bronx C C University Ave and W 181st Bronx NY 10453

RYAN, JAMES E. former state attorney general; b. Chgo., Feb. 21, 1946; m. Marie Ryan; children: John, Jim, Matt, Amy, Patrick, Anne Marie(dec.). BA in Polit. Sci., Ill. Benedictine Coll., 1968; JD, Ill. Inst. Tech., 1971. Bar: Ill. 1971. Asst. state's atty. criminal divsn. DuPage County State's Atty.'s Office, 1971—74, 1st. asst. state's atty., 1974—76; founder Ryan & Darrah; state's atty. DuPage County State's Atty.'s Office, 1984—94; atty. gen. State of Ill., 1994—2002. Disting. fellow Benedictine U., Lisle, Ill., 2003—. Named Lawyer of Yr., DuPage County Bar Assn., 1997; recipient numerous awards from various orgns. including, Nat. Assn. Counties, Alliance Against Intoxicated Motorists. Mem.: Ill. State's Attys. Assn. (past pres., Ezzard Charles award). Republican. Roman Catholic.

RYAN, JAMES LEO, federal judge; b. Detroit, Mich., Nov. 19, 1932; s. Leo Francis and Irene Agnes Ryan; m. Mary Elizabeth Rogers, Oct. 12, 1957; children: Daniel P., James R., Colleen M. Hansen, Kathleen A. LLB, U. Detroit, 1956, LLD (hon.), 1986, BA, 1992; LLD (hon.), Madonna Coll., 1976, Detroit Coll., 1978, Thomas M. Cooley Law Sch., Lansing, Mich., 1986. Atty. Waldron, Brennan & Maher, 1960—62; pvt. practice Redford Twp., Mich., 1962—66; Justice of peace, 1963—66; judge 3d Cir. Ct. of Mich., 1966—75; justice Mich. Supreme Ct., 1975—86; judge U.S. Ct. Appeals (6th cir.), 1985—2000, sr. judge, 2000—. Faculty Nat. Jud. Coll., Reno; adj. faculty, bd. dirs. Ave Maria Sch. Law; adj. prof. Thomas M. Cooley Law Sch., 1979—85, U. Detroit, 1974—. Contbr. articles to profl. jours. Capt. JAGC USNR, 1957—92, ret. mil. judge USNR. Mem.: USNR Lawyers Assn., Detroit Bar Assn., Fed. Bar Assn., State Bar Mich., Fed. Judges Assn., K.M., K.C. Office: US Ct Appeals US Courthouse 231 W Lafayette Blvd Detroit MI 48226-2700

RYAN, JAMES THOMAS, organizational consultant, business owner; b. Auburn, N.Y., Aug. 28, 1947; s. Thomas Francis and Gertrude Helen (Whalen) R.; m. Anne Peduto, June 15, 1974; children: Thomas Michael, Jennifer Lynn, Kathleen Meghan. AA, Auburn C.C., 1967; BA, Ohio State U., 1972; MBA, Gannon U., 1979. Cert. sr. profl. in human resources Human Resource Cert. Inst. Sales rep. Gallery of Homes, Rochester, N.Y., 1974-75, Johnson & Johnson, Erie, Pa., 1975-77; pers. mgr. Singer, Erie, Pa., 1977-80; employee rels. mgr. Frito-Lay, Vancouver, Wash., 1980-85; corp. dir. human resources Welch's, Westfield, N.Y., 1985-94; pres. The North Coast Consulting Group, Erie, 1994—; owner Express Personnel Svcs., 2001—. Mem. adv. coun. Gannon U., Erie, 1990-95; mem. human resources coun. Am. Mgmt. Assn., N.Y.C., 1989-95. Mem. Pres. Club, Republican Party, Washington, 1995, Senatorial Inner Cir., 1992-95. With USAF, 1968-72, Vietnam. Mem. ASTD, Soc. Human Resources Mgmt., Kahkwa Club, Erie Club, Rotary Club. Roman Catholic. Avocations: golf, reading, travel. Home: 5410 Mintwood Ct Erie PA 16506-3935 Office: Express Personnel Svcs 2503 W 15th St Erie PA 16505 E-mail: james.ryan@expresspersonnel.com.

RYAN, JAMES WALTER, physician, medical researcher; b. Amarillo, Tex., June 8, 1935; s. Lee W. and Emma E. (Haddox) R.; children: James P.A., Alexandra L.E., Amy J.S. AB in Polit. Sci., Dartmouth Coll., 1957; MD, Cornell U., 1961; D.Phil., Oxford U. (Eng.), 1967. Diplomate Nat. Bd. Med. Examiners. Intern, Montreal (Que.) Gen. Hosp., McGill U., Can., 1961-62, asst. resident in medicine, 1962-63; USPHS research asso. NIMH, NIH, 1963-65; guest investigator Rockefeller U., N.Y.C., 1967-68, asst. prof. biochemistry, 1968; investigator Howard Hughes Med. Inst., 1968—71; assoc. prof. medicine U. Miami (Fla.) Sch. Medicine, 1968-79, prof. medicine, 1979-95, mem. vasc. biology ctr., 1995-00; prof. anesthesiology, pharmacology and toxicology Med. Coll. Ga., Augusta, 1995-00; sr. cons. ntGen, 2000—. Sr. scientist Papanicolaou Cancer Rsch. Inst., Miami, 1972-77; hon. med. officer to Regius prof. medicine Oxford U., 1965-67; vis. prof. Clin. Rsch. Inst. Montreal, 1974; mem. vis. faculty thoracic disease divsn., dept. internal medicine Mayo Clinic, 1974; vis. prof. Montreal Gen. Hosp./McGill U., 1985. Contbr. numerous articles on biochem. rsch. and pathology to sci. jours.; patentee in field. Rockefeller Found. travel awardee, 1962; William Waldorf Astor traveling fellow, 1966; USPHS spl. fellow, 1967-68; Pfizer travelling fellow, 1972; recipient USPHS Rsch. Career Devel. award NIH, 1968, Louis and Artur Luciano award for research of circulatory diseases McGill U., 1984-85. Mem. AAAS, Am. Physiol. Soc., Am. Chem. Soc., Biochem. Soc., Am. Soc. Biochemist and Molecular Biology, Am. Heart Assn. (mem. coun. cardiopulmonary diseases 1972—, coun. for high blood pressure rsch. 1976—), Microcirculatory Soc., Oxford and Cambridge Club (London), Sigma Xi. Baptist. Home: 3047 Lake Forest Dr Augusta GA 30909-3027 Office: ntGen 3047 Lake Forest Dr Augusta GA 30909 E-mail: james.ryan14@comcast.net.

RYAN, JANE FRANCES, corporate communications executive; b. Bronxville, N.Y., Nov. 1, 1950; d. Bernard M. and Margaret M. (Griffith) R.; m. Kevin Horan, Dec. 26, 1982; 1 child, Kevin. BS in Journalism, Ohio U., 1972; MBA in Mktg., Golden Gate U., 1990. Asst. promotion mgr. Fawcett Publs., Greenwich, Conn., 1972-75; mktg. coordinator Fawcett Mktg. Services div. CBS, Greenwich, Conn., 1975-78; dist. sales mgr. CBS Publs., San Francisco, 1978; prodn. mgr. Cato Inst., San Francisco, 1979-81; account supr. Bus. Media Resources, Mill Valley, Calif., 1981-90, dir. mktg. svcs., 1990-93; dir. publs. RAND Corp., Santa Monica, Calif., 1993—. Office: RAND 1700 Main St Santa Monica CA 90401-3297

RYAN, JEANNE VANYO, music educator; b. Bklyn., July 30, 1930; d. Joseph John and Veronica Zupko; m. Joel Kenneth Ryan, Oct. 21, 1961 (dec.); children: Vanessa, Joel Bradley, Darrell. Student, NYU, 1951, Queens Coll., 1958—61. Pvt. piano tchr., Bklyn., 1948—62, Bowie, Md., 1972—. Musician: (piano debut) Steinway Concert Hall, 1951, WNYC Radio Young Am. Artists Series, 1955—56. Bd. Concert Pianists League. Pres. Whitehall PTA, Bowie, 1975—77; leader Girl Scouts USA, Boys Scouts Am., 1970—80; election judge Rep. Party, Bowie, 1992—2002. Mem.: Bowie Music Tchrs. (pres. 1992—94), Md. State Music Tchrs. (chmn. theory 1995, chmn. spring festival 1995—97, chmn. theory 2002, 2004), Kenilworth Women's Club (pres.). Avocations: bridge, reading, crossword puzzles, music, games.

RYAN, JOAN, food company executive; BS in Acctg., U. Ill. CPA, Ill. With Price Waterhouse Co., Baxter Healthcare Corp., Kewaunee Sci. Corp.; divsn. contr., CFO NutraSweet Co.; v.p. fin., CFO Ameritech Small Bus. Svcs., 1995-98, Alliant Foodservice, Inc., Deerfield, Ill., 1998-2000; CFO, Tellabs, Inc., Lisle, Ill., 2000—03; sr. v.p., CFO SIRVA, Inc., Westmont, Ill., 2003—. Bd. dirs. Fed. Signal Corp. Bd. dirs. Boys and Girls Club Chgo. Office: Tellabs Operations 1415 W Diehl Rd Naperville IL 60563-2359*

RYAN, JOHN DUNCAN, lawyer; b. Portland, Oreg., Dec. 20, 1920; s. Thomas Gough and Virginia Abigail (Hadley) R.; m. Florence A. Ryan, Jan. 30, 1970 (dec. 1987); m. Virginia Kane Wilson, June 15, 1996. BS, Fordham U., 1943; JD, Lewis & Clark Coll., Portland, 1950. Bar: Oreg. 1950. Pvt. practice, Portland, 1950—. Adj. instr. Northwestern Sch. Law Lewis & Clark Coll., 1953-70. Author: (poems) Expressions, 1993, Expressions II, 1995, (book) Expressions, 1988, 1999, Cooking with John Ryan, 2002. Sgt. Air Corps, U.S. Army, 1942-46, ETO. Recipient St. Thomas More award Catholic Lawyers for Social Justice, 1993. Mem. ABA (Oreg. delegate 1985-93, chmn. spl. com. on law & literacy 1991-93), Am. Coll. Trial Lawyers, Am. Trial Lawyers Assn., Oreg. State Bar (bd. govs. 1963-67), Oreg. Trial Lawyers Assn. (Trial Lawyer of Yr. 1993), Multnomah County Bar Assn. (Professionalism award 1997), Washington County Bar Assn. Home and Office: 503 SW Colony Dr Portland OR 97219-7763 Personal E-mail: ryan98@theriver.com.

RYAN, JOHN M. lawyer; b. Glen Ridge, N.J., May 18, 1936; AB, Dartmouth Coll., 1958; LLB, U. Va., 1963. Bar: Va. 1964. Lectr. at law Marshall-Wythe Sch. Law Coll. William and Mary, 1976-86; ptnr. Vandeventer Black LLP, Norfolk, Va.; gen. counsel Va. Internat. Terminals, Inc. Trustee John Marshall Found., Contemporary Art Ctr. Va.; commr. Arts and Humanities Commn., City of Virginia Beach; dir. Contemporary Art Ctr. Va.; bd. dirs. Children's Health Sys., Inc., Greater Norfolk Corp. Fellow: Va. Law Found., Am. Bar Found., Am. Coll. Trial Lawyers; mem.: ABA (labor rels., litigation sect.), So. Conf. Bar Pres., Nat. Conf. Bar Pres., Va. State Bar, Norfolk-Portsmouth Bar Assn., Maritime Law Assn. U.S. (chmn. stevedore and maritime terminals com.), Va. Bar Assn. (pres. 1988), S.E. Admiralty Law Inst., James Kent Am. Inn of Ct. (past pres.), 4th Cir. Jud. Conf. Office: Vandeventer Black LLP 500 World Trade Ctr Norfolk VA 23510-1679 E-mail: jryan@vanblk.com.

RYAN, JOHN MICHAEL, landscape architect; b. Chgo., Sept. 27, 1946; s. Terrance Joseph and Norma (Morris) R.; m. Victoria Jean Wheetley, June 26, 1986; children: Micheline Giannasi-Mennecke, Tony Giannasi, Nick Giannasi, Andrew Morris Jennings, Melissa Contance Victoria, Cameron Michael Montgomery. B in Landscape Architecture, U. Ill., 1969. Registered landscape architect, Ill., cert. Mich., registered Ariz., Ind., Wis., Tenn., cert. CLARB. Assoc. landscape architect Carl Garnder & Assocs., Inc., Chgo., 1969-71; sr. landscape architect Collaborative Rsch. & Planning, Chgo., 1971-73; v.p. Michael L. Ives & Assocs., Inc., Downers Grove, Ill., 1973-84; pres. Ives/Ryan Group, Inc., Naperville, 1984—. Prin. works include renovation of Old Orchard Shopping Ctr., Skokie, Ill., Lake Katherine Nature Preserve, Palos Heights, Ill., Crystal Tree Residential Golf Course Cmty., Orland Park, Ill., Corporetum Office Campus, Lisle, Ill., Maravilla Rainforest Atrium, Vernon Hills, Ill. Trustee Wheaton Evangelical Free Ch., 2000—. Recipient Nat. Landscape award Am. Assn. Nurserymen, 1988, 92, Key award in landscape arch. Home Bldrs. Assn. Greater Chgo., 1981, 84, 90, Best Project Grand award Interiorscape mag., 2001. Mem. Am. Soc. Landscape Archs. (Merit award 1991, 94, 96), Assoc. Landscape Contractors Am. (Environ. Improvement Grand award 1997, 2000, Environ. Improvement honor award 2000), Ill. Landscape Contractors Assn. (Gold award 1991, 96, 2001, Silver award 1986, 90, 93, 2001, Merit award 1988, 91), Chgo. Hort. Soc., Perennial Plant Assn. (Nat. Honor award 1993), Morton Arboretum. Avocations: gardening, travel. *My life is committed to raising my dear children to the best of my ability in a loving christian atmosphere, which I believe to be my true purpose for being here. As a professional landscape architect, if I can enhance or improve the environment for my children and their children, I have made a worthwhile professional contribution to my perceived purpose in life.*

RYAN, JOHN R. career officer; m. Diane L. Ackerman; children: Tricia, Kelly, Julie. Graduate, USN Acad., 1967; MSc in Adminstrn., George Washington U., 1975. Enlisted USN, 1968, advanced through grades to vice adm.; naval aviator Patrol Squadron 8, 1969-72; various assignments Naval Acad., 1972-75; served on USS Nimitz, 1975-77; adminstrv. officer Commander Patrol Wing Five, 1977-80; ops. officer Patrol Squadron Twenty-Six, 1980-81; various assignments Patrol Squadron Eleven, 1981-83, Office of Chief of Naval Ops., 1983-85; military asst. to exec. sec. Immediate Office of Sec. Defense, 1985-86; comdr. Patrol Squadron Thirty-One, Moffett Field, 1986-87; exec. asst. to dep. chief naval ops. Office of Chief of Naval Ops., 1987-88; comdr. Patrol Wing Ten, Moffett Field, 1988-90; various assignments U.S. Pacific Command, 1990-93; commdr., patrol wings US Pacific Fleet/Commdr., Anti-Submarine Warfare Forces, U.S. Pacific Fleet, 1993-95; commdr., maritime surveilance and reconnaissance force, us sicth fleet commdr., fleet air mediterranean/commdr. Maritime Air Forces, 1995-98; supt. USN Acad., 1998—. Decorated D.S.M., Legion of Merit with two gold stars, Meritorious Svc. medal with two gold stars.

RYAN, JOHN WILLIAM, academic administrator; b. Chgo., Aug. 12, 1929; s. Leonard John and Maxine (Mitchell) R.; m. D. Patricia Goodday, June 20, 1949; children: Kathleen Elynne Ryan Acker, Kevin Dennis Mitchell, Kerrick Charles Casey. BA, U. Utah, 1951; MA, Ind. U., 1958, PhD, 1959, LLD (hon.), 1988, U. Notre Dame, 1978, Oakland City Coll., 1981, St. Joseph Coll., 1981, Hanover Coll., 1982, DePauw U., 1983, U. Ma., 1983, Manchester Coll., 1983, U. Evansville, 1985, Wabash Coll., 1986, Ind. U., 1988; DLitt (hon.), U. St. Thomas, 1977; D Pub. Adminstrn., Nat. Inst. Devel. Adminstrn., Thailand, 1991; LLD (hon.), U. Md., 1994. Rsch. analyst Ky. Dept. Revenue, Frankfort, 1954-55; vis. rsch. prof. U. Thammasat, Bangkok, Thailand, 1955-57; asst. dir. Inst. Tng. for Pub. Svc. Ind. U., 1957-58; successively asst. prof., assoc. prof. polit. sci., assoc. dir., Bur. Govt. U. Wis., 1958-62; exec. asst. to pres., sec. of univ. U. Mass., Amherst, 1962-63, chancellor Boston, 1965-68; v.p. acad. affairs Ariz. State U., 1963-65; v.p., chancellor regional campuses Ind. U., Bloomington, 1968-71, pres., 1971-87, pres. emeritus, 1987—, prof. polit. sci., 1968-95, prof. pub. and environ. affairs, 1981-95, prof. emeritus, 1995—; cons. AID, 1991-92; chancellor SUNY, Albany, 1996—2000, chancellor emeritus, 2000—; hon. prof. Moscow State U., 1999. Interim pres. Fla. Atlantic U., 1989, U. Md., Balt., 1994; bd. dirs. Ind. U. Found., chmn. 1972-87; chmn. Nat. Adv. Bd. on Internat. Edn. Programs, 1985-89; chancellor SUNY System, 1996-2000. Contbr. articles to profl. jours. Bd. govs. Pub. Broadcasting Svc., 1973-82; bd. visitors Air U., 1974-81; chmn. Air Force Inst. Tech Subcom., 1976-81; mem. univ. adv. com. Am. Coun. Life Ins.; bd. dirs. Corp. Community Coun., 1976; mem. nat. adv. coun. Pan Am. Games, 1985; mem. adv. bd. Assocs. for Religious and Intellectual Life, 1984—; active United Way Ind. Centennial Commn. Mem. Am. Soc. Pub. Adminstrn. (pres. Ind. chpt. 1969-70, nat. chpt. 1972-73, nat. coun. from 1970, Ind. Soc. Chgo. (non-resident v.p. from 1976, Am. Polit. Sci. Assn., Assn. Asian Studies, Am. Coun. Edn., Assn. Am. Univs. (chmn. 1981-82), Nat. Acad. Public Adminstrn., Ind. Acad., Explorers Club, Adelphia (hon.), Columbia Club (Indpls.), Skyline Club, Cosmos Club (Washington), Athenaeum (London), KC, Equestrian Order of Holy Sepulchre, Elks, Phi Kappa Phi, Phi Alpha Theta, Pi Sigma Alpha, Beta Gamma Sigma, Kappa Sigma (worthy grand master 1985-87). Office: Ind U SPEA 415 1315 E 10th St Bloomington IN 47405-1701 E-mail: chancem123@aol.com., ryan@indiana.edu.

RYAN, JOHN WILLIAM, association executive; b. Manchester, N.H., Sept. 16, 1937; s. William Charles and Mary Ann (Marcoux) R.; m. Carol Jean Battaglia, Sept. 17, 1960; children: James, Kathleen, John, Michael. AB, St. Anselm Coll., 1959; MA, Niagara U., 1960; PhD, St. John's U., 1965. Asst. prof. history Gannon U., Erie, Pa., 1965-66; edn. specialist, div. grad. programs U.S. Office Edn., Washington, 1966-68, regional coordinator, grad. acad. programs, 1968-70; dir. univ. programs Univ. Assocs., Inc., Washington, 1970-72; asst. to pres., sec. Council of Grad. Schs. in U.S., Washington, 1972-80; exec. v.p. Renewables Research Inst., Annandale, Va., 1980-81; exec. dir. Worcester (Mass.) Consortium Higher Edn., 1981-89, N.H. Coll. and Univ. Coun., Manchester, 1989-93; cons.; exec. dir. Mass. Vet. Med. Assn., Marlborough, Mass., 1993-98; cons., 1998—. Contbr. articles to profl. jours. Bd. dirs. No. Va. C.C., 1999—, Loudoun Healthcare, Inc., 2000—, Loudoun County Econ. Devel. Commn., 2000.

RYAN, JOSEPH, lawyer; b. Seattle, Feb. 11, 1942; s. John Joseph and Jane (Wing) R.; m. Mary Katherine Gavin, Aug. 10, 1963; children: Michael Gavin, Kathleen Ann, Jennifer Jo. BA, U. Washington, 1964; JD, Columbia U., 1967. Bar: Calif. 1968, N.Y. 1983, D.C. 1983. Ptnr. O'Melveny & Myers, L.A., 1976—93, mng. ptnr., 1993—94; sr. v.p., gen. counsel Ritz-Carlton Hotel Co., LLC, Atlanta, 1994—; exec. v.p., gen. counsel Marriott Internat., Inc., Washington, 1994—. Tchr., lectr. N.Y. Law Jour. Author: Stating Your Case: How To Interview for a Job as a Lawyer, 1982, Take or Pay Contracts: Alive and Well in California, vol. 192, 1987, Current Investment Banking Activities in the United States, vol. 2, #15 M&A Report, 1988; co-author (with Lorin Fife) The Urban Lawyer, 1987; contbr. articles to law publs. Bd. dirs. Pasadena Playhouse, L.A., 1981-92, Planetary Soc., Pasadena, 1981, Westridge Sch., L.A., 1982-91, Natural History Mus. Los Angeles County, 1988-93. Capt. U.S. Army, 1968-70. Mem. ABA, N.Y. Bar Assn., L.A. County Bar Assn., D.C. Bar Assn., Calif. Bar Assn., Nat. Assn. Bond Lawyers (legis. com.). Republican. Roman Catholic. Avocations: running, biking, camping, hunting and fishing, boating. Home: 10836 Alloway Dr Potomac MD 20854-1503 Office: Marriott Internat Inc 10400 Fernwood Rd Bethesda MD 20817*

RYAN, JOSEPH F. criminal justice professor; b. N.Y.C., Jan. 27, 1949; s. Henry Martin and Anita (Vanderburg) R.; married; children: Robert M., Daniel J., Nora Jean. BA in Criminal Justice, John Jay Coll., MA in Criminal Justice, 1978; PhD in Sociology, Fordham U., 1984. Detective N.Y.C. Police Dept., 1968-91; assoc. prof. Pace U., N.Y.C., 1991—, chmn. dept. pub. adminstrn./criminal justice, 1995—. Cons. Urban Inst., Washington, 1995—; peer rev. Nat. Inst. Justice, Washington, 1990—; lectr. Indian Health Svc., Albuquerque, 1991-96. Co-author 1 book; mem. editl. rev. bd. Am. Jour. Police, 1995—. Vis. fellow Nat. Inst. Justice, Washington, 1991-93. Mem. Am. Soc. Criminology. Avocations: reading, canoeing, hiking, biking, museums.

RYAN, JOSEPH W., JR., lawyer; b. Phila., June 24, 1948; s. Joseph W. Sr. and Marie R. (Hillgrube) R.; m. Mary Pat Law, Sept. 11, 1971; children: Caitlin, Joseph W. III. BA, St. Joseph's U., Phila., 1970; MA, Villanova U., 1971; JD, U. Va., 1978. Bar: Ohio 1978, U.S. Supreme Ct. 1982. Ptnr. Porter, Wright, Morris & Arthur, Columbus, Ohio, 1978—. Lectr. Sch. Dentistry Ohio State U., Columbus, 1982-89, Continuing Legal Edn. Inst., 1984—; mem. trial acad. faculty Internat. Assn. Def. Counsel, Boulder, Colo., 1994. Author: Use of Demonstrative Evidence, 1985; assoc. editor Litigation News, 1986—, editor in chief, 2000-02. Trustee Columbus Zool. Assn., 1980-90; bd. dirs. Columbus Speech and Hearing Ctr., 1988-99, pres., 1995-96. Mem. ABA, Ohio State Bar Assn., Columbus Bar Assn., Internat. Assn. Def. Counsel, Am. Arbitration Assn. (panel of arbitrators). Republican. Roman Catholic. Office: Porter Wright Morris & Arthur 41 S High St Ste 30 Columbus OH 43215-6101 Office Phone: 614-227-2000. E-mail: jryan@porterwright.com.

RYAN, JOYCE ETHEL, artist, author; b. Atlanta, Aug. 29, 1949; m. Jim Cyril Klar, Apr. 5, 1975. BFA, U. Ga., 1972. Instr. Marsh Draughon Coll., Atlanta, 1972-73; retail store mgr. Army & Air Force Exch. Svc., Dallas, 1974; illustrator U.S. Army Logistics Ctr., Ft. Lee, Va., 1975-77; graphics mgr. Ecosystems Internat., Millersville, Md., 1980-82; freelance art studio dir. Seoul, 1983-85; pres. Butterfly Books, Ariz., 1985—. Instr. Cochise Coll., Sierra Vista, 1986. Illustrator, author: Seoul Sketches, 1985, Scenes of Southern Arizona, 1986, Seoul Travel Guide, 1987, Traveling with Your Sketchbook, 1990, The Happy Camper's Gourmet Cookbook, 1992, Calligraphy: Elegant and Easy, 1994, Drawing at Home, 1996, America's Best Cheesecakes, 1998, Fifty Years of Excellence: Texas Watercolor Society, 1999, America's Best RV Cookbook, 2003. Mem.: Art Ctr. Corpus Christi, San Antonio Watercolor Group. Avocations: drawing, painting. Office Phone: 210-494-0077. E-mail: texaswavelady@hotmail.com.

RYAN, KELLY, lawyer; b. N.Y.C., July 18, 1963; d. Robert Gerard and Edith Shaffer Ryan. BA, Tulane U., New Orleans, 1985; JD, Georgetown U., Washington, 1988; LLM, Cambridge U., Eng., 1989. Bar: N.Y. 1990, Wash. 1992. Assoc. gen. counsel Office of Gen. Counsel, INS, Washington, 1992—98, chief refugee and asylum law divsn., 1998—2002; dep. asst. sec. Dept. of State Bur. Population, Refugees and Migration, 2002—. Recipient Commrs. award for meritorious svc., INS, 1998, 2000. Roman Catholic.

RYAN, KENNETH EUGENE, engineer; b. Guilford, N.Y., Apr. 3, 1936; s. Julian Nichols and Irene M. Ryan; m. Nancy Race, Aug. 29, 1959; children: Patrick, Kathleen, Timothy, Maureen. BS, Cornell U., 1958, MS, 1959. Registered profl. engr., N.Y. With various mobile equipment mfrs., 1959-66; rsch. assoc. Cornell U., Ithaca, N.Y., 1966-69; sr. project engr. Raymond Corp., Greene, N.Y., 1969—. Chmn. Zoning Bd. Appeals, Oxford, N.Y., 1973-83; chmn. com. North Guilford (N.Y.) Ch., 1989-91; mem. Oxford Planning Bd., 1970—. Mem. Nat. Soc. Profl. Engrs., Soc. Exptl. Stress Analysis. Avocation: photography. Home: 221 Ryan Rd Oxford NY 13830-9801

RYAN, KEVIN V. lawyer; married; 2 children. BA in History, Dartmouth Coll.; JD, U. San Francisco. Prosecutor Alameda County Dist. Atty.'s Office; judge San Francisco Mcpl. Ct., 1996—98; mem. San Francisco Superior Ct., 1999, presiding judge criminal divsn.; U.S. atty. No. Dist. Calif., 2002—. Bd. dirs. No. Calif. High Intensity Drug Trafficking Area Working Group; mem. Pres. Bush's Corp. Fraud Task Force; apptd. mem. subcom. Controlled Substances and Terrorism and Nat. Security, appointed to Jud. Coun.'s Exec. Legis. Action Network, Chief Justice of Calif. Supreme Ct.; appointed to Criminal Law Planning Com. of Calif. Continuing Jud. Studies Program, Governing Com. of Calif. Ctr. for Jud. Edn. and Rsch.; appointed to Adult Probation Dept.'s Oversight Com., Presiding Judge for Cts.; mem. exec. com. San Francisco Superior Ct.; mem. exec. com. Am. Inn of Cts., U. San Francisco Sch. Law; bd. govs. U. San Francisco Law Soc.; bd. trustees Schs. of Sacred Heart, San Francisco; mem. faculty Intensive Trial Advocacy Program, U. San Francisco Sch. Law; lectr. in field. Recipient Mcpl. Ct. Trial Judge of Yr., San Francisco Trial Lawyers' Assn., 1998. Office: No Dist Calif 450 Golden Gate Ave San Francisco CA 94102

RYAN, KEVIN WILLIAM, virologist, researcher, science educator, clinical research administrator; b. Ft. Dodge, Iowa, Dec. 8, 1952; s. Joseph Michael Ryan and Etoile Evelyn Werth; m. Mary Ellen Lyman, June 1, 1974; children: Matthew Lyman, Mark Joseph. BS, U. Iowa, 1978; PhD, U. Mich., 1984. Staff fellow Nat. Inst. Allergy and Infectious Diseases, NIH, Bethesda, Md., 1984-86; rsch. asst. dept. virology and molecular biology St. Jude Children's Rsch. Hosp., Memphis, 1986-89, asst. mem., 1989-98; asst. prof. pathology U. Tenn. Coll. Medicine, Memphis, 1994-98; sci. rev. adminstr. Nat. Inst. Allergy and Infectious Diseases, NIH, Rockville, Md., 1998-2000; program officer virology vaccine and prevention rsch. prog. divsn. AIDS, Nat. Inst. Allergy and Infectious Diseases, NIH, Bethesda, Md., 2000—; deputy chief Prevention Scis. Br., 2001—02, chief, 2002—, lead program officer grant-supported internat. clin. rsch. in HIV/AIDS prevention, 2001—; mem. working group NIAID, Comprehensive Internat. Program for Rsch. in AIDS (CIPRA), 2001—. Prin. investigator Nat. Inst. Allergy and Infectious Diseases, 1992—98; lead program officer HIV prevention trials network HPTN, 2002—; govt. project officer HIV Network Prevention Trials Internat. Master Contract for AIDS Rsch. NIAID, 2002—04; NIAID Rep. HPTN Prevention Leadership Group, 2002—. Contbr. articles to profl. jours., chpts. to tech. manuals. Fellow postdoctoral Mich. Cancer Rsch. Inst., U. Mich., 1982. Mem.: Am. Soc. for Microbiology. Roman Catholic. Avocations: woodworking, golf. Office: Nat Inst Allergy and Infectious Diseases Divsn AIDS 6700-b Rockledge Dr Bethesda MD 20892-0001

RYAN, L. TIMOTHY, chef, educator, academic administrator; b. Pitts. m. Lynne Ryan; 2 children. BS, U. New Haven; MBA, U. New Haven Sch. Bus. Adminstrn.; graduated, Culinary Inst. Am., 1977; EdD, U. Pa., Pa. Graduate Sch. Edu., Phila. Cert. Master Chef 1985. Asst. chef Ben Gross' Restaurant, Irwin, Pa.; exec. chef La Normande, Pitts.; joined Culinary Institute Am., Hyde Park, NY, 1982, exec. v.p., v.p. edu., dir., culinary edu., dept. head, culinary edu., chef-instructor, pres., 2001—. Developer Am. Bounty Restaurant. Author: The Culinary Olympics Cookbook, 1984, 1988, New Professional Chef, Techniques of Healthy Cooking, An American Bounty; editl. adv. com. mem.: Cheers, Seafood Bus., Take Out Bus. magazines, former chmn. editl. coun.: Nat. Culinary Review; contbr. to videos and television shows. Named to Am. Acad. Chefs, 1990; recipient Gold medals, Pitts. Culinary Arts Salon, 1981, Eastern Regional Olympic Tryouts, 1982, Gourmet Fair, Japan, 1983, Honor Roll Am. Chefs, Food & Wine magazine, 1983, Chef Yr. award, Am. Culinary Fedn., 1998, Presdl. medal, World Assn. Cooks Societies, 1998, Hon. Doctorate Foodservice medallion, N.Am. Assn. Food Equipment Manufacturers, Grand prize of show, Internat. Feinschmecker Parade, Austria. Mem.: Am. Culinary Fedn. (Pitts. chpt. bd. dirs. 1981—82, pub. rels. chair 1982—83, apprenticeship chair, Mid-Hudson chpt. 1982—84, culinary com. 1983—, team capt., U.S. culinary team 1984, master chef com. 1985—, team capt., U.S. Team, Culinary World Cup Competition 1986, team capt., U.S. culinary team 1988, N.E. v.p. 1991—93, nat. pres. 1995—96, chmn. bd. 1996—97, team mgr., U.S. team, Salon Culinaire Mondial 1987, team mgr., U.s. team, Internat. World Culinary Arts Festival, four Gold Medals and World Championship (Hot Food Competition), Internat. Culinary Competition, Germany 1988, two team Gold medals, Salon Culinaire Mondial, Basel, Switzerland 1987, Team grand prize, Culinary World Cup Competition, Luxembourg 1986, Team medal for culinary excellence, Salon Culinary Art, NY 1985, Two gold medals and silver cup, Internat. Culinary Competition, Germany 1984). Achievements include launching the world's first bachelor's degree program in Culinary Arts Management and Baking and Pastry Arts Management; developing a highly successful publishing program; expanding the continuing education programs. Office: Culinary Inst Am 1946 Campus Dr Hyde Park NY 12538-1499*

RYAN, LEO VINCENT, business educator; b. Waukon, Iowa, Apr. 6, 1927; s. John Joseph and Mary Irene (O'Brien) Ryan. BS, Marquette U., 1949; MBA, DePaul U., 1954; PhD, St. Louis U., 1958; postgrad., Catholic U. Am., 1951-52, Bradley U., 1952-54, Northwestern U., 1950; LLD, Seton Hall U., 1988; DHL, Ill. Benedictine U., 1997. Joined Order Clerics of St. Viator, Roman Cath. Ch., 1950. Faculty Marquette U., Milw., 1957-65, dir. continuing edn. summer sessions, coord. evening divsns., 1959-65, prof. indsl. mgmt., 1964; prof., chmn. dept. mgmt. Loyola U., Chgo., 1965-66; dep. dir. Peace Corps, Lagos, Nigeria, 1966-67, dir. Western Nigeria Ibadan, 1967-68; asst. superior gen. and treas. gen. Clerics of St. Viator, Rome, 1968-69, dir. edn. Am. province Arlington Heights, Ill., 1969-74; pres. St. Viator H.S., 1972-74; dean, prof. mgmt. U. Notre Dame Coll. Bus. Adminstrn., Ind., 1975-80; dean DePaul U. Coll. Commerce, 1980-88, prof. mgmt., 1980-99; Wicklander prof. ethics DePaul U., 1993-94; prof. emeritus, 1999. Dir. Peace Corps tng. programs Marquette U., 1962-65; adj. prof. human devel. St. Mary's Coll., Winona, Minn., 1972-74; mem. sch. bd. Archdiocese Chgo., 1972-75, vice-chmn., 1973-75, nat. edn. com. U.S. Cath. Conf., 1971-75, exec. com., 1973-75; nat. adv. bd. Benedictine Sisters of Nauvoo, 1973-83; nat. adv. coun. SBA, 1982-85, vice-chmn. minority bus., 1982-85, exec. com. Chgo. chpt., 1982-84; vis. prof. U. Ife, Ibadan, 1967-68,; chmn. trust audit com. First Bank-Milw., 1980-85, chmn. audit and examination com., 1985-90, adv. coun., 1991-93; bd. dirs. Henricksen & Co., Inc., 1978—; fin. commn. Clerics of St. Viator, 1978-, provincial chpt., 1985-97, 2001-03, devel. adv. bd. 1996-2001, new foundations com. 1996-98, alt. mem., 1997-2001, provincial coun., 2001-03, coord. coun., U.S., Belize, Columbia, 2001-03, comprehensive devel. coun., 2004; Fulbright prof. Adam Mickiewicz U., Poland, 1993-95; vis. prof. Helsinki Sch. Econs., 1992-2002, Polish-Am. Ctr., U. Lodz, 1998, Poznan Acad. Econs., 1991, 1999—; co-chair bus. and profl. com. Archdiocese of Chgo. Sesquetennial Com. Out Reach Divsn. Ctrl. Planning Group, 1993-94; vis. prof. Notre Dame, 2000, Helsinki Sch. Econs., 2000; adv. bd. Sch. of Bus. Univ. Kiev, Ukraine, 2001. Author: Human Action in Business, 1996, Etyka Biznesu, 1997, 4th edit., 2000, From Autarcy to Market: Polish Economics and Politics, 1945-1995, 1998, 2d edit., 1999, Students Focus on Business Ethics, 2000, Praxiology and Pragmatism, 2002, Poland: A Transformational Appraisal, 2003; mem. editl. bd. Internat. Jour. Value Based Mgmt., 1983-2003, Bus. Ethics Quar., 1983-2004, European Bus. Jour., 1990-2002, Mid Atlantic Jour. of Bus., 1990-2002. Mem. Pres.'s Com. on Employment Handicapped, 1959-65, Wis. Gov.'s Com. on Employment Handicapped, 1959-65, Wis. Gov.'s Com. on UN, 1961-64, Burnham Park Planning Commn., 1982-88; bd. dirs. Ctr. Pastoral Liturgy U. Notre Dame, 1976-79; trustee Lake Forest Grad. Sch. Mgmt., 1989-91, St. Mary of Woods Coll., 1978-81, Cath. Theol. Union, U. Chgo., 1992-95, Divine Word Coll., 1997—; regent Seton Hall U., 1981-87, mem. acad. affairs com., 1981-87, chmn., 1983-87; dir. Ctr. for Enterprise Devel., 1992-95; elected fellow St. Edmunds Coll. Cambridge U., 1992—; mem. Cath. Commn. Intellectual and Cultural Affairs, 1992—, Cath. Campaign for Am., 1994-98; bd. dirs. Internat. Bus. Ethics Inst., Am. Grad. Sch. Internat. Mgmt., 1995-97; mem. adv. com. Mgmt. Edn. in Poland, U. Md., College Park, 1995-2000; active Iowa Gov. Heartland Leadership Coun., 2003—. Recipient Freedom award Berlin Commn., 1961, chieftancy title Asoju Atoaja of Oshogbo Oba Adenle I, Yorubaland, Nigeria, 1967, B'nai B'rith Interfaith award, Milw., 1963, Disting. Alumnus award Marquette U., 1974, DePaul U., 1976, Tchr. of Yr. award Beta Alpha Psi, 1980, Centennial Alumni Achievement award Marquette U., 1981, Boland Meml. Disting. Alumni award, St. Louis, 1989, Disting. Alumni and Bicentennial awards Jesuit Bus. Schs., 1989, Pres.' award St. Viator H.S., 1992, Medal of Merit Adam Mickiewicz U., 1995, Excellence in Tchg. award Adam Mickiewicz U., 1997, Ill. Ernst and Young Entrepreneur Supporter award, 1999, Vincentian U. Ethics Scholar award, 2000, Centennial award Dominican U. for lifetime leadership and bus. ethics Dominican U. Sch. Bus., 2002; Brother Leo V. Ryan award named in his honor Cath. Bus. Edn. Assn., 1962; Ryan Scholars in Mgmt. established in his honor DePaul U., 1989, Outstanding Svc. award, 1991-93, Commerce Alumni award of merit, 1997; DePaul Creativity Ctr. named in his honor, 1997, trustee; named hon. life chmn. Nat. Adv. Com., Ryan Creativity Ctr., Creative Cutting Edge award, 1999; Ryan Scholarship named in his honor St. Viator H.S., 1992, Lion award, 1997, trustee, 2000-01, gov., 2001-; named Man of Yr. Jr. C. of C., Milw., 1959, Marquette U. Bus. Adminstrn. Alumni Man of Yr., 1974; named Disting. Vis. Term Prof. Seton Hall U., 2001; Milw. Bd. Realtors traveling fellow, 1964, Nat. Assn. Purchasing Agts. faculty fellow, 1958, German Am. Acad. Exch. Coun. fellow, summer 1983, Presdl. fellow Am. Grad. Sch. Internat. Mgmt., 1989, vis. scholar, 1995, Malone fellow in Islamic studies, 1990, fellow Kosciuszko Found. Adam Mickiewicz U., 1990; scholar-in-residence Mgmt. Sch. Imperial Coll. Sci. and Tech. U. London, 1988; vis. scholar U. Calif., Berkeley, 1989; USIA Acad. Specialists grantee, Poland, 1991-93; fellow St. Edmund's Coll. Cambridge U., 1992; named vis. rsch. fellow Von Hugel Inst., 1992-93; scholar-in-residence Am. Grad. Sch. Internat. Mgmt., 1995; guest scholar Kellogg Inst. Internat. Studies U. Notre Dame, 1997. Mem. Cath. Bus. Edn. Assn. (nat. pres. 1960-62, nat. exec. bd. 1960-64), Assn. Sch. Bus. Ofcls. (nat. com. chmn. 1965-67), Am. Assembly Collegiate Schs. Bus. (com. internat. affairs 1977-84, chmn. 1981-84, bd. dirs. 1981-87, program chmn. 1979-80, exec. com., chmn. projects/svc. mgmt. com. 1984-86), Am. Fgn. Svc. Assn., Am. Assn. Profl. Ethics (bd. dirs. 1996-98), Am. Philat. Soc., Allamakee County Hist. Soc. (charter life), Acad. Internat. Bus., Acad. Mgmt. (social issues div., chmn. membership com. 1990-91), Ancient Order of Hibernians, Nat. Returned Peace Corps Assn., Atomic Vets. Assn., August Derleth Soc., Chgo. Area Return Peace Corps Vols., Econ. Club Chgo., Chgo. Coun. Fgn. Rels., Coun. Fgn. Rels. (diplomat cir. 1998), European Bus. Ethics Network Poland (hon. 1998), Soc. Bus. Ethics (mem. exec. com. 1991—, pres. 1993-94, adv. bd. 1995-97), Assn. Social Econs. (life), Assn. Christian Economists, Iowa Hist. Soc., Iowa Postal History Soc., Iowa Heartland Leadership Coun., Fulbright Assn. (life), Internat. Assn. for Bus. and Soc. (founder), Internat. Soc. for Bus., Econs. and Ethics (charter), Internat. Trade and Fin. Assn. (founder, bd. dirs. 1989-92, 96-98, v.p. membership 1991-92, 96-97), Internat. Learned Soc. Praxiology, (hon. life, internat. adv. bd. praxiology ann.), Polish Inst. Arts and Scis. in Am., Postal History Soc., DePaul Inst. Bus. and Profl. Ethics (founder 1984, adv. bd. 1984-94, Founders award 1999), USS Mt. McKinley Reunion Assn. (life, hon. chaplain AGC-7 1989-96, Disting. Svc. award 1991, 96), Friends of Nigeria, Alpha Sigma Nu, Alpha Kappa Psi (bd. dirs. found. 1985-91, vice-chmn. 1987-91, chmn. scholarship com. 1987-91, chmn. devel. com. 1987, exec. com. 1990-91, Bronze Disting. Svc. award 1949, Silver Disting. Svc. award 1958, Recognition medal, 2001), Beta Alpha Psi, Beta Gamma Sigma (co-chair 75th Anniversary com. Ill., faculty advisor DePaul chpt. 1986-92), Century Travel Club (Silver award), Delta Mu Delta, Pi Gamma Mu, Tau Kappa Epsilon. Office Phone: 847-870-4903. Personal E-mail: LeoRyan@viatorians.com.

RYAN, LEONARD EAMES, judge; b. Albion, N.Y., July 8, 1930; s. Bernard and Harriet Earle (Fitts) R.; m. Ann Allen, June 18, 1973; 1 child, Thomas Eames Allen-Ryan. Grad., Kent Sch., 1948; AB, U. Pa., 1954; JD, NYU, 1962. Bar: D.C. 1963, N.Y. 1963, U.S. Ct. Appeals (D.C. cir.) 1963, U.S. Dist. Ct. (so. and ea. dists.) N.Y. 1965, U.S. Ct. Appeals (2nd cir.) 1966, U.S. Supreme Ct. 1967. Field engr. constrn. U.S. Steel Fairless Works, Morrisville, Pa., 1951-52; reporter Upper Darby (Pa.) News, 1954; newsman AP, Pitts., Phila., Harrisburg, N.Y.C., 1955-62; reporter, spl. writer on law N.Y. Times, 1962-63; info. adviser corp. hdqrs. IBM, N.Y.C., 1963; trial atty. firm Perrell, Nielsen & Stephens, N.Y.C., 1964-66; trial atty. civil rights div. Dept. Justice, Washington, 1966-68; asst. to dir. bus. affairs CBS News, N.Y.C., 1968; program officer Office Govt. and Law, Ford Found., N.Y.C., 1968-74; pvt. practice law, cons. pub. affairs, N.Y.C., 1974-91; v.p., sec. W. P. Carey & Co., Inc., N.Y.C., 1977—82; impartial hearing officer Edn. for All Handicapped Children Act of 1975, 1976-91; per diem adminstrv. law judge N.Y. State Agys., 1976-91; hearing examiner N.Y. State Family Ct., 1980-81; apptd. U.S. adminstv. law judge, 1991; adminstv. law judge Office Hearings and Appeals, San Rafael, Calif., 1991—93, Phila., 1993-94, N.Y.C., 1994—. Arbitrator Small Claims Ct., N.Y.C., 1974-84; bd. dirs. Community Action for Legal Svcs. Inc., N.Y.C., 1971-77, vice-chmn., 1975-77; co-chmn. Citizens Com. to Save Legal Svcs., N.Y.C., 1975-76; bd. dirs. Lower East Side Svc. Ctr., N.Y.C., 1977-89. Author: (with Bernard Ryan Jr.) So You Want to Go Into Journalism, 1963; contbr. articles to profl. jours. Served with USAR, 1950-57. Mem. Am. Judicature Soc., Assn. of Bar of City of N.Y., N.Y. State Bar Assn., St. Elmo Club (Phila.), Heights Casino (Bklyn.). Home: 32 Orange St Brooklyn NY 11201-1634 Office: 111 Livingston St Brooklyn NY 11201-5078

RYAN, LINDA LEE, sculptor, art educator; b. Bartlesville, Okla., Mar. 12, 1952; d. Howard Allen and Mary Ardis Ryan; m. Louie Kistler III, July 6, 1997. BA, Mont. State U., 1974; MA, Ctrl. Wash. U., 1979; MFA, W.Va. U., 1981; postgrad., Internat. Acad. Bilden deKunst, Salzburg, Austria, 1986. Ceramics instr. Ketterer Art Ctr., Bozeman, Mont., 1972; jewelry instr. Coll. of Great Falls, Mont., 1975; tchg. asst. Ctrl. Wash. U., Ellensburg, 1976-79, W.Va. U., Morgantown, 1979-80; art prof. Casper (Wyo.) Coll., 1982—. Trustee, chair exhbns. and collections com. Nicolaysen Art Mus., Casper, 1994-2000; mem. com. task force Western States Arts Fedn., Santa Fe, N.Mex., 1991; co-chair Arts 500 Wyo. Arts Alliance, 1985-88; guest artist Idaho State U., Pocatello, 1987, 90, 10th Ann. Dunconnor Jewelry Workshop, Taos, N.Mex., 1987, U. Mont., Missoula, 1989, Western Wyo. Coll., Rock Springs, 1989, 94, 99, CC Theatre, Casper, 1994, N.W. C.C., Powell, Wyo., 1995, others; panelist, juror in field. One woman shows at St. Katherine's Women's Coll., St. Paul, 1984, Sarah Spurgeon Gallery Ctrl. Wash. U., 1978, Crew Gallery, Seattle, 1979, Alderson-Broddus Coll., Philippi, W.Va., 1980, Creative Arts Ctr., W.Va. U., 1981, Transition Gallery Idaho State U., 1987, Visual Arts Ctr. Gallery Casper Coll., 1989, Davis Gallery Idaho Satte U., 1990, WW Coll. Art Springs, 1991, 94, Goodstein Gallery Casper Coll., 1996; exhibited in group shows at Meadows Gallery, Denton, Tex., 1992, Paris Gibson Sq. Mus. Art, Great Falls, Mont., 1992, Nichlaysen Art Mus., 1992, 93, 99, CC Visual Arts Gallery, 1993, 94, 95, 96, 97, 98, 2000, Wyo. Arts Coun. Traveling Artbox Project, 1994-95, 1999-2000, Sarah Spurgeon Gallery, 1995, Wyo. Arts Coun. Gallery, 1995, U. N.D., 1995, West Wyo. Coll., others; represented in permanent collections at Wyo. State Mus., Casper Coll., Inkfish Gallery, Denver, Scottish Arts Coun., Edinburgh, Crew Gallery; contbr. to books, periodicals and newspapers. Visual arts fellow Wyo. Arts Coun., 1989, 2000; grantee Wyo. Arts Coun., 1995. Mem. Wyo. Alliance for Art Edn., Nicolaysen Art Mus. (trustee 1994-2000), Denver Art Mus., Internat. Sculpture Ctr., Soc. N.Am. Goldsmiths, Delta Phi Delta. Avocations: cross country skiing, weightlifting. Office: Casper Coll 125 College Dr Casper WY 82601-4612 E-mail: lryan@caspercollege.edu.

RYAN, LISA KATHLEEN, education educator, consultant; b. Morgantown, W.Va., July 9, 1958; d. Richard Stoetzer and Ellen Stewart Wagner; m. Gill Diamond, Aug. 31, 1997; m. Niall Patrick Ryan, Oct. 3, 1981 (dec. Oct. 1, 1993); children: Allison Kathleen, Michael Richard Diamond, Sara Elana Diamond. BS in microbiology, Penn State U. Coll. of Sci., 1976—80; MS in med. microbiology, W.Va. U. Med. Sch., 1980—83; PhD in toxicology, U. of Pitts. Grad. Sch. of Pub. Health, 1986—92. Rsch. biologist, immunotoxicology br. U.S. EPA, Rsch. Triangle Pk., NC, 1995—2000; asst. prof., dept. of pathology UMDNJ-New Jersey Med. Sch., Newark, 2000—. Ord regional sci. advisor, epa region 2, U.S. EPA Office of Sci. Policy, Washington, 1998—2000; rsch. fellow in medicine Mass. Gen. Hosp./Harvard Med. Sch., Boston, 1992—95. Contbr. articles to profl. jours. Recipient Re-entry to Rsch. Supplemental award, NIH NIAID, 2000—03, Individual Nat. Rsch. Svc. award, NIH NHLBI, 1994—97; Rsch. Grant Co-Investigator, 2003—, Student Rsch. award, Allegheny-Erie Regional Chpt. of the Soc. of Toxicology, 1991, Devel. of an ELISA for Endotoxin Detection, Hyclone Diagnostics/Travenol Laboratories, 1981—82. Mem.: AAAS, Sigma Xi, Am. Conf. of Govtl. Indsl. Hygenists, Am. Thoracic Soc., Am. Soc. for Microbiology, Soc. for Leukocyte Biology, Am. Assn. of Immunologists, Soc. of Toxicology. Democrat-Npl. Jewish. Achievements include patents for polymyxin agarose-lipopolysaccharide antigen and associated method. Avocations: swimming, ice skating, piano, clarinet, alpine skiing. Office: UMDNJ-New Jersey Medical School 185 South Orange Ave Newark NJ 07101 Personal E-mail: ryanlk@umdnj.edu. E-mail: ryanlk@umdnj.edu.

RYAN, LOUIS FARTHING, lawyer; b. Richmond, Va., Mar. 18, 1947; s. Louis Anthony and Catherine Louise (Farthing) R.; m. Prudence Elwell Hartshorn, Sept. 5, 1970. BSE, Princeton U., 1969; JD, U. Va., 1973. Bar: Va. 1973. Mgmt. cons. Arthur Andersen & Co., Boston, 1969-70; assoc. firm Kaufman and Canoles, Norfolk, Va., 1973-77; sec. Landmark Communications, Inc., Norfolk, 1977—, v.p., gen. counsel, 1985-88, exec. v.p., gen. counsel, 1988—, exec. v.p. fin., 1995-96. Sec. TeleCable Corp., Norfolk, 1984-85, v.p., gen. counsel, 1985-88., exec. v.p., gen. counsel, 1988-95. Bd. dirs. Feldman Chamber Music Soc., 1975-77, Jr. Achievement Tidewater, 1979-81, adv. coun., 1986—; bd. dirs., exec. com. Va. Symphony, 1979-89, pres., 1983-84; vol. United Way, 1975-88, chmn. campaign Norfolk divsn., 1988; mem. Norfolk Harborfest Com., 1979; mem. allocation com. Bus. Consortium for Arts Support, South Hampton Roads, 1987-95; chmn. auction Sta. WHRO-Pub. TV, 1987; bd. dirs., exec. com. Planning Coun., Norfolk, Va., 1988-93; bd. dirs. Leadership Hampton Rds., 1990—, chmn. budget com., 1993, chmn. bd., 1993-95, chmn. nominating com., 1997; mem. exec. adv. coun. Coll. Bus. and Pub. Adminstrn., Old Dominion U., 1990-96; mem. exec. steering com. Hampton Roads Black Achiever Program, 1990-92, mem. Forward Hampton Roads, 1990-91; mem. memberships com. Chrysler Mus., 1991, com. 101 of Future of Hampton Roads, Inc., 1992—; bd. dirs. Norfolk Assembly, 1991-95, Norfolk Festevents, 1994—. Mem. ABA, Va. Bar Assn., Va. State Bar (chmn. bus. law sect. 1980-81), Norfolk-Portsmouth Bar Assn., Am. Newspaper Pubs. Assn. (legal affairs com. 1986—), Hampton Roads C. of C. (bd. dirs. 1989-94, Norfolk divsn. 1990—, treas. 1994), Town Point Club, Norfolk Yacht and Country Club, Country Club Va. Episcopalian. Office: Landmark Communications Inc 150 W Brambleton Ave Norfolk VA 23510-2018

RYAN, MARIANNE ELIZABETH, lawyer; b. Ft. Knox, Ky., Nov. 15, 1964; d. John L. and Frances J. (McIntosh) R. BA, Trinity Coll., 1986; JD, Yale U., 1991; MS in Info., U. Mich., 2003. Bar: Ill. 1991, U.S. Dist. Ct. (no. dist.) Ill. 1991. Assoc. Pattishall, McAuliffe, Newbury, Hilliard & Geraldson, Chgo., 1991-93; internet editor Law Jour. EXTRA! The N.Y. Law Pub. Co., N.Y.C., 1994-95; rsch. scholar Nat. Ctr. for Philanthropy and the Law NYU Sch. Law, 1996-99; tech. coord. Americorps/Project F.I.R.S.T., N.Y.C., 1999-2000; VISTA svc. leader Americorps/Ohio Campus Compact, Yellow Springs, Ohio, 2000—01; resident fellow Lloyd Hall Scholars Program, U. Mich., Ann Arbor, 2002—03, Cmty. Info. fellow Alliance for Cmty. Tech., 2002—. Adj. prof. trademark and copyright law John Marshall Law Sch., Chgo., 1993. Exec. editor Yale Jour. on Regulation. Mem. MLA, Copyright Soc. US, Computer Profls. for Social Responsibility, Internet Soc., Internet Corp. for Assigned Names and Numbers, Am. Acad. Religion, Phi Beta Kappa. Home: 702 S Clarizz Blvd Bloomington IN 47401-5520 E-mail: marianne@aya.yale.edu.

RYAN, MARK ANTHONY, architect, lawyer; b. Council Bluffs, Iowa, Sept. 6, 1964; s. Paul Elmer and Darreline Kay (Wyland) Ryan; m. Shelli Ann Hagerbaumer, Sept. 26, 1992. BA in Architecture with distinction, Iowa State U., 1987; JD summa cum laude, Creighton U., 2003. Registered profl. arch., Wis.; bar: Iowa, 2003, Nebr. 2004. Project arch. U.S. Army CE, Omaha, 1987-90, arch., security engr., 1990-91, environ. project mgr., 1991-96; owner, arch. Ryan Designs, Omaha, 1987—; project mgr. Bovis Constrn. Corp. and Bovis Lend Lease, Omaha, 1997-2000; CEO Ad Hoc Comm. Resources, LLC, Omaha, 1999—, gen. counsel, 2004—. Bd. advisors Fitness Plus, Council Bluffs, Iowa, 1990—92; expert witness, Iowa, Nebr., 1991—; law clk. West Corp., 2002; intern law clk. U.S. Dist. Ct., Nebr., 2003. Chmn. City Devel. Commn., Council Bluffs, Iowa, 1992; trustee San. and Improvement Dist. No. 142, Douglas County, Nebr., 1995—96. Scholar, State of Iowa, 1982; Valentino scholar, 2001, Lane Found. scholar, 2002, Abrahams scholar, 2002. Mem.: ATLA, ABA, AIA (sec. S.W. Iowa sect. 1991, treas. 1992, v.p. 1993, pres. 1994—96), Nebr. State Bar Assn., Iowa Bar Assn., Nat. Trust Hist. Preservation, Golden Key, Phi Delta Phi, Tau Sigma Delta, Phi Kappa Phi. Avocations: architectural restoration, bicycling, freshwater aquatics. Home and Office: Ad Hoc Communication Resources 9030 Raven Oaks Dr Omaha NE 68152-1759 Business E-Mail: mark@adhoccr.com.

RYAN, MARLEIGH GRAYER, language educator; b. N.Y.C., May 1, 1930; d. Harry and Betty (Hurwick) Grayer; m. Edward Ryan, June 4, 1950; 1 child, David Patrick. BA, NYU, 1951; MA, Columbia U., 1956, PhD, 1965; Cert., East Asian Inst., 1956; postgrad., Kyoto U., 1958-59. Research assoc. Columbia U., N.Y.C., 1960-61, lectr. Japanese, 1961-65, asst. prof., 1965-70, assoc. prof., 1970-72; vis. asst. prof. Yale U ., New Haven, 1966-67; assoc. prof. U. Iowa, Iowa City, 1972-75, prof., 1975-81, chmn. dept., 1972-81; prof. Japanese SUNY, New Paltz, 1981-98, dean liberal arts and scis., 1981-90, prof. emeritus, 1999—; assoc. in rsch. Reischauer Inst. for Japanese Studies, Harvard U., Cambridge, Mass., 1999—, chair study group on Asian Am. Lit., 2000—02. Vice chmn. seminar on modern Japan, Columbia U., 1984-85, chmn., 1985-86; co-chmn. N.Y. State Conf. on Asian Studies, 1986, editor, 1993-99, mem. exec. com., 1993-96, sec., 1993-99, co-chmn., 1998. Co-author: (with Herschel Webb) Research in Japanese Sources, 1965; author: Japan's First Modern Novel, 1967, The Development of Realism in the Fiction of Tsubouchi Shoyo, 1975; assoc. editor: Jour. Assn. Tchrs. Japanese, 1962-71, editor, 1971-75. East Asian Inst. fellow Columbia U., 1955; Ford Found. fellow, 1958-60; Japan Found. fellow, 1973, Woodrow Wilson Ctr. Internat. Scholars fellow, 1988-89; recipient Van. Am. Disting. Book award Columbia, 1968 Mem. MLA (sec. com. on teaching Japanese Lang. 1962-68, mem. del. assembly 1979-87, mem. exec. com. div. Asian lit. 1981-86), Assn. Tchrs. Japanese (exec. com. 1969-72, 74-77), Assn. Asian Studies (bd. dirs. 1975-78, N.E. asian coun. 1975-78, coun. of confs., 1993-96), Midwest Conf. Asian Studies (pres. 1980-81) *Studying the most difficult language in the world has taught me patience and tact. One learns what it is to sit completely still at the Japanese No theatre and absorb wondrous sights and sounds in an atmosphere of absolute peace. Discovering the stillness in movement is perhaps the most important lesson we in the West can derive from our Asian experience.*

RYAN, MARY A. diplomat; b. New York, N.Y., Oct. 1, 1940; BA, St. John's Univ., 1963, MA, 1965. With Foreign Service, Dept. of State, 1966—; consular and adminstrv. officer, 1966-69; personnel officer Am. Embassy, Tegucigalpa, Honduras, 1970-71; consular officer Am. Consulate Gen., Monterrey, Mexico, 1971-73; adminstrv. officer Bur. of African Affairs, Dept. of State, Washington, 1973-75, post mgmt. officer, 1975-77; career devel. officer Bur. of Personnel, Dept. of State, 1977-80; adminstrv. counselor Abidjan, Ivory Coast, 1980-81, Khartoum, Sudan, 1981-82; inspector, Office of Insp. Gen. Dept. of State, Washington, 1982-83, exec. dir. Bur. of European and Can. Affairs, 1983-85, exec. asst. to Under Sec. of State for Mgmt., 1985-88; ambassador to Swaziland, 1988-90; dep. asst. sec. Bur. of Consular Affairs, Washington, 1990; dir. Kuwait task force, 1990-91; ops. dir. UN spl. commn. on elimination of Iraqi weapons, 1991; dep. asst. sec. Bur. European & Can. Affairs, Washington, 1991-93; asst. sec. Bur. of Consular Affairs, Washington, 1993—, career amb., 1999. Office: Dept State Bureau of Consular Affairs 2201 C St NW Washington DC 20520-0001

RYAN, SISTER MARY JEAN, health facility executive; LHD, Webster U., 1994, U. Mo., St. Louis, 2003, Lindenwood U., 2003. Pres., CEO SSM Health Care, 1986—. Presenter in field. Co-author: CQI and the Renovation of an American Health Care System: A Culture Under Construction, 1997. Mem. Excellence in Mo. Found.; chair Taking Care/A Health Forum for Women Religious, Madison, Wis.; bd. dirs. Inst. for Healthcare Improvement, United Way of Greater St. Louis; sec. Hawthorn Found. of Mo.; mem., treas., bd. dirs. St. Louis Regional Chamber and Growth Assn.; bd. dirs. SSM Health Care of Okla., SSM Health Care of Wis., SSM Health Care-St. Louis. Named one of 20 Disting. Women/St. Louis Area, 25 Most Influential Women in Bus. in St. Louis; recipient Brotherhood/Sisterhood award, Nat. Conf. Cmty. and Justice, Gov.'s Quality Leadership award, State of Mo., Corp. that Makes a Difference award, Internat. Women's Forum. Office: SSM Health Care Sys Inc 477 N Lindbergh Blvd Saint Louis MO 63141

RYAN, MEG, actress, film producer; b. Fairfield, Conn., Nov. 19, 1961; m. Dennis Quaid, 1991 (div. 2001); 1 child, Jack Henry. Student, NYU. Appearences include (TV) One of the Boys, 1982, As The World Turns, 1982-84, Wild Side, 1985, (films) Rich and Famous, 1981, Amityville 3-D, 1983, Top Gun, 1986, Armed and Dangerous, 1986, Innerspace, 1987, Promised Land, 1987, D.O.A., 1988, The Presidio, 1988, When Harry Met Sally, 1989, Joe Versus the Volcano, 1990, The Doors, 1991, Prelude to a Kiss, 1992, Sleepless in Seattle, 1993, Flesh and Bone, 1993, When a Man Loves a Woman, 1994, Restoration, 1994, I.Q., 1994, French Kiss, 1995, Two for the Road, 1996, Courage Under Fire, 1996, Addicted to Love, 1997, Anastasia (voice), 1997, City of Angels, 1998, Hurlyburly, 1998, You've Got Mail, 1998, Hanging Up, 1999, Proof of Life, 2000, Kate & Leopold, 2001, In the Cut, 2003, Against the Ropes, 2004; owner Prufrock Pictures movie prodn. co.; prodr.: French Kiss/Paris Match, 1995, Two for the Road, 1997, Northern Lights, 1997 (TV, exec. prodr.), Lost Souls, 2000, The Wedding Planner, 2001, Desert Saints, 2002. Recipient Golden Apple award Hollywood Women's Press Club, 1989, Woman of Yr. award Hasty Pudding Theatricals, 1994, ShoWest Conv. Actress of Yr. award, 1999, Am. Comedy Award, 1990, 1994, Women in Film Crystal Award, 1995. Office: care ICM c/o Steve Dontanville 8942 Wilshire Blvd Beverly Hills CA 90211-1934

RYAN, MELBAGENE T. retired food and nutrition service director; b. Arkadelphia, Ark., Jan. 6, 1927; d. Horace Samuel and Eunice Bridges (Moorman) Tull; m. Wayne Stuart Ryan, Dec. 26, 1954. BS in Edn., Henderson U., 1948; M in Edn., Tex. Women's U., 1951. Tchr. Eudora (Ark.) Pub. Schs., 1948-52; dir. food services Tex. Christian U., Ft. Worth, 1952-53, Tex. Women's U., 1953-58; dir. food and nutriton service Irving (Tex.) Ind. Sch. Dist., 1958-85. Project dir. to develop stds. excellence with a self study and evaluation Tex. Sch. Food Svc. Assn., 1985-88; cons. in field. Co-author and project dir.: (with others) Youth Advisory Council Resource Manual, 1978-79, Effective Food Service Management Using Computers, 1982. With child nutrition Tex. Sch. Food Svc. Assn., Washington, 1974-79; with legis. Am. Sch. Food Svc. Assn., Irving, 1980-85; mem. Denton Co. Hist. Commn., 1997—, Denton Co. Courthouse-on-the Square Mus., chmn. 1998—; mem. adv. bd. Lake Forest Good Samaritan Village, 1998—, Tex. Woman's U. Centennial Celebration, 2001, planning com., 1998-99, Denton Good Samaritan Village, 2003; chmn. Bayless Selby House Mus., 2002—. Recipient Food Facilities Design award Instns. Volume Feeding Awards Program, New Orleans, 1977, Trend Setter award, North Tex. Brokers Assn., Dallas, 1978; Melbagene Ryan Scholarship named in her honor by Dallas Profl. Friends, 1985. Mem. Denton Dietetic Assn. (pres. 1977-78), Tex. Dietetic Assn., Am. Dietetic Assn. (chmn. joint com. 1979-82), Tex. Sch. Food Svc. Assn. (pres. 1975-76, nutrition edn. 1975), Am. Sch. Food Svc. Assn. (conf. com. 1977-78, 1982-83), Tex. Women's U. Alumni Assn. Methodist. Home and Office: 1121 Ryan Rd Denton TX 76210-5539

RYAN, MICHAEL D. state supreme court justice; BA, St. John's U., Collegeville, Minn., 1967; JD, Ariz. State U., 1977. Dep. county atty. Maricopa County Atty.'s Office, 1977—85; judge pro tempore Superior Ct. State of Ariz., 1985—86, judge, 1986—96; vice chief judge Ariz. Ct. Appeals, Divsn. 1, 2001—02, judge, 1996—2002; justice Ariz. Supreme Ct., 2002—. Chair com. on keeping the record Ariz. Supreme Ct., 2004—; mem. adv. com. Nat. Ctr. for State Cts., Ctr. for Effective Pub. Policy, also State Justice Inst.'s Nat. Solutions Project, 2003—; vice chair Ariz. Sate Bar Task Force on Persons with Disabilities in the Profession2002; chair Scottsdale Jud. Appts. Adv. Bd., 1999—2002; mem. Ariz. Atty. Gen.'s Capital Case Commn., 2000—02, Maricopa County Resource Site Team for Ctr. for Sex Offender Mgmt., 1996—2000; -=. Infantry platoon comdr. USMC, 1968, Vietnam. Mem.: Maricopa County Bar Assn. (bd. dirs. 1987—91, 1997—2002, chair task force recruitment and retention of women and minorities 1997—2004). Office: Ariz Supreme Ct 1501 W Washington Phoenix AZ 85007-3231

RYAN, MICHAEL LOUIS, controller; b. Corning, Iowa, Feb. 22, 1945; s. Leo Vincent and Elda May (Lawrence) R. AAS in Constrn. Tech., Iowa State U., 1965; BS in Acctg., Drake U., 1972. CPA, Iowa, Wyo. Acct. Ernst & Ernst, Des Moines, 1972-75, Becker, Herrick & Co., Pueblo, Colo., 1975-78; pvt. practice acctg. Gillette, Wyo., 1978-81; acct. Karen M. Moody, CPAs, Sheridan, Wyo., 1981-85; contr. T-C Investments, Inc., Sheridan, 1985—; ptnr. WHG Partnership, Sheridan, 1991—; v.p. Bosley-Ryan Constrn., Inc., Sheridan, 1993—. With spl. forces U.S. Army, 1966-68, Vietnam. Mem. AICPA (tax div.), Wyo. Soc. CPAs, Am. Legion (fin. officer 1977-81), Lodge (sec. Sheridan club 1982-90, pres. 1989), Phi Kappa Phi, Beta Alpha Psi, Beta

Gamma Sigma. Democrat. Roman Catholic. Home: 735 Canby St Sheridan WY 82801-4907 Office: T-C Investments Inc 1566 Terra Ave Sheridan WY 82801-6125 E-mail: mkryan@wavecom.net.

RYAN, NOLAN, former professional baseball player; b. Refugio, Tex., Jan. 31, 1947; s. Lynn Nolan and Martha (Hancock) Ryan; m. Ruth Elsie Holdruff, June 26, 1967; children: Reid, Reese, Wendy. Student, Alvin Jr. Coll., Tex., 1966—69. Pitcher N.Y. Mets, N.Y.C., 1966—71, Calif. Angels, 1972—79, Houston Astros, 1980—88, Texas Rangers, 1989—93; cattle rancher, China Grove, Ray and Gonzalvez Tex.; owner The Bass Inn, Waterfront Steakhouse and Grill, Express Bank (sold to First Community Capital in 2002); owner, Texas league farm club team The Round Rock Express, Round Rock, Tex.; investor, ptnr. The Express Bank of Texas, Round Rock, Tex., 2003—. Commr. Tex. Parks and Wildlife Commn., 1995—2001, vice chmn., 1995—97. Author (with Steve Jacobson): Nolan Ryan: Strike-Out King, 1975; author: (with Bill Libby) Nolan Ryan: The Other Game, 1977; author: (with Joe Torre) Pitching and Hitting, 1977; author: (with Harvey Frommer) Throwing Heat: The Autobiography of Nolan Ryan, 1988; author: (with Tom House) Nolan Ryan's Pitcher's Bible, 1991; author: (with Jerry Jenkins) Miracle Man: Nolan Ryan, The Autobiography, 1992; author: (with others) Kings of Hill, 1992. Founder, bd. dirs. The Nolan Ryan Found.; bd. dirs. The Justin Cowboy Crisis Fund, Texas Water Found., Natural Resources Found., Tex. With AUS, 1967. Named Am. League Pitcher of Yr., Sporting News, 1977; named to All-Star Team, Am. League, 1972, 1973, 1975, 1979, Nat. League, 1981, 1985, Baseball Hall of Fame, 1999. Achievements include holding over 50 Major League records including most seasons pitched (27), most strikeouts (5,714) and most no-hit games (7). Office: Round Rock Express 3400 E Palm Valley Blvd Round Rock TX 78664*

RYAN, PATRICK G. diversified financial services company executive, director; b. Milw., May 15, 1937; m. Shirley Welsh, Apr. 16, 1966; children: Patrick Jr., Robert J., Corbett M. BS, Northwestern U., 1959. Sales agt. Penn Mut., 1959-64, Pat Ryan & Assocs., 1964-71; chmn., pres. Ryan Ins. Group Inc., Chgo., 1971-82; pres., chief exec. officer Combined Internat. Corp. (now Aon Corp.), Northbrook, Ill., 1982—, bd. dirs., 1982—; chmn., pres., CEO Aon Corp., Chgo., 1990—. Bd. dirs. Sears Roebuck and Co., Chgo., Tribune Co., Chgo. Trustee Rush-Presbyterian-St. Luke's Med. Ctr., Chgo., chmn. bd. trustees; trustee Northwestern U., Field Mus. Natural History, Chgo.

RYAN, PATRICK M. lawyer; m. Barbara E. Ryan; children: Michael, Jason, Megan. BA, U. Okla., 1967, JD, 1969. Bar: Okla., U.S. Dist. Ct. (we. and ea. dists.) Okla., U.S. Ct. Appeals (10th cir.), U.S. Ct. Mil. Appeals, U.S. Supreme Ct. Ptnr. Crowe & Dunlevy, Oklahoma City, 1974—81; pres., dir. Ryan, Geister & Whaley, Oklahoma City, 1982—95; U.S. atty. for western dist. Okla. Office of U.S. Atty., Oklahoma City, 1995—99; pvt. practice Ryan & Whaley, 1999—. Editor: Okla. Law Rev. Trustee World Neighbors, 1994—97; active St. John the Bapt. Chat. Ch., Edmond, Okla. With JAGC USAF, 1969—74. Recipient Leadership award, Okla. County Bar Assn., 1989. Fellow: Internat. Acad. Trial Lawyers, Am. Coll. Trial Lawyers (mem. Okla. state com. 1990—95), Okla. Bar Found. (v.p. 1978, 1980); mem.: ABA, Okla. Bar Assn. (gov. bd. govs. 1990—93, mem. young lawyers sect.), Order of Coif. Office: 119 N Robinson Ave Ste 900 Oklahoma City OK 73102-4617

RYAN, PATRICK MICHAEL, lawyer; b. Chgo., May 26, 1944; s. Edward Michael and Kathleen Teresa (Crimmins) R.; m. Holly Ann Daleske, Aug. 31, 1968; children: Rebecca Eileen, Brendan Patrick, Abigail Christine, Lucas Christopher. BA, St. Mary's Coll., Winona, Minn., 1966; JD, Marquette U., 1969. Bar: Wis. 1969. Law clk. Wis. Supreme Ct., Madison, 1969-70; ptnr. Quarles & Brady LLP, Milw., 1970—2001, chmn., mng. ptnr., 2002—. Dir. and officer several pvt. bus. corps. Mem. ABA, Wis. Bar Assn., Milw. Bar Assn., University Club. Avocations: reading, sports. Home: 363 Huntington Dr Cedarburg WI 53012-9507 Office: Quarles & Brady LLP 411 E Wisconsin Ave Ste 2550 Milwaukee WI 53202-4497 Office Phone: 414-277-5000. E-mail: pmr@quarles.com.

RYAN, PAUL, congressman; b. Janesville, Wis., Jan. 29, 1970; son. Paul and Betty R. BS in Econs. and Polit. Sci., Miami (Ohio) U., 1992. Aide to Sen. Bob Kasten (R-Wis.), Washington; legis. dir. U.S. Senate, Washington; economic advisor, speechwriter Empower Am., Jack Kemp, Bill Bennett, Washington; mktg. cons. Ryan Inc., Central, Janesville; mem. U.S. Congress from 1st Wis. dist., 1999—; mem. ways and means com.; mem. joint econ. com. Defeated former Kenosha City Coun. Pres. Lydia Spottswood in 1998 to succeed two-term Rep. Mark Neumann, who ran unsuccessfully for the Senate. Mem. Janesville YMCA, Janesville Bowmen Inc. and Ducks Unlimited. Republican. Roman Catholic. Office: 1217 Longworth Ho Office Bldg Washington DC 20515-4901

RYAN, PRISCILLA E. lawyer; AB, Marquette U., 1969; JD, Loyola U., Chgo., 1982. Bar: Ill. 1982. With IRS, 1986-87; atty.-advisor Office Tax Policy, U.S. Treasury Dept., Washington, 1988-89; ptnr. Sidley & Austin, Chgo. Frequent spkr. on employee benefits. Contbr. articles to profl. jours. Mem. ABA. Office: Sidley & Austin 1 S First National Plz Chicago IL 60603-2000 Fax: 312-853-7036.

RYAN, RAYMOND D. retired steel company executive, insurance and marketing firm executive; b. Big Timber, Mont., Feb. 7, 1922; s. Robert Allen and Elsie (Beery) R.; m. Eunice Dale Burnett, Jan. 17, 1943; children: Raymond Brant, Brenda Ruth, Ronald Dale. BA, U. Mont., 1948, JD (hon.), 1970; LLM, NYU, 1949. Bar: Mont. 1948. Various fin. officer positions U.S. Steel and subsidiaries in U.S. and Venezuela, 1949-75; v.p., treas. U.S. Steel, 1975-83; pres. The Evergreen Group Inc., Stamford, Conn., 1984-94, chmn., 1995-96, Evergreen Benefits Inc., 1996-99, The Money Suite Co., Missoula, Mont., 1999—. With mil. police AUS, 1943-45, ETO. Mem. ABA, Met. Club (N.Y.C.), Phi Sigma Kappa, Phi Delta Phi. Home: PO Box 160601 Big Sky MT 59716-0601 Office Phone: 406-995-3397. Personal E-mail: rayd@moneysuite.com. *Although luck and ambition are the basis of many apparently successful careers, true success comes from hard work, ethical relationships, dedication, and a willingness to accept responsibility.*

RYAN, RICHARD J. emergency medicine physician; b. Tarrytown, N.Y., Apr. 28, 1964; MD, N.Y. Med. Coll., 1990. Diplomate Am. Bd. Emergency Medicine. Intern U. Cin., 1990-91, resident in emergency medicine, 1991-94; v.p. Vanguard Med. Inc., Cin., 1997—; asst. prof. U. Cin., 1994—. Dir. emergency medicine The Jewish Hosps., Cin., 1997—. Office: U Cin Dept Emergency Medicine 231 Albert Sabin Way Cincinnati OH 45267-0769 E-mail: Richard.Ryan@uc.edu.

RYAN, ROBERT COLLINS, lawyer; b. Evanston, Ill., Sept. 15, 1953; s. Donald Thomas and Patricia J. (Collins) R.; m. Joanne Kay Holata, Nov. 5, 1983. BA in Econs., BS in Indsl. Engring. with high honors, U. Ill., 1976; JD, Northwestern U., 1979. Bar: Ill. 1979, Nev. 1999, US Dist. Ct. (no. dist.) Ill. 1980, US Dist. Ct. Nev. 2001, US Ct. Appeals (Fed. cir.) 1982, US Patent Office, 1979, US Supreme Ct. 1984. Assoc. Allegretti, Newitt, Witcoff & McAndrews, Ltd., Chgo., 1979-83, ptnr., 1983-88; founding ptnr. McAndrews, Held & Malloy, Ltd., Chgo., 1988-96, of counsel, 1998—2000; v.p. digital gen. sys., Inc. CNASDAQ DGIT, 2001—03; ptnr. Nath & Assocs. PLLC, Washington and Reno, 2003—. Chief legal and intellectual property officer, exec. v.p. StarGuide Digital Networks, Inc., Reno, 1996-2003; mem. Ian Burns & Assocs., P.C., Reno, 1998-2003; of counsel Pauley, Petersen, Kinne & Fejer, Hoffman Estates, Ill., 1998-2002; lectr. engring. law Northwestern U. Tech. Inst., Evanston, Ill., 1981-85, adj. prof. engring. law, 1985-90; lectr. patent law and appellate practice John Marshall Law Sch., 1991-93, adj. prof. patent law and appellate advocacy, 1993-2000; mem. faculty Nat. Jud. Coll., Reno, Nev., 1998-2000; mem. alumni bd. mech. and indsl. engring. dept. U. Ill., Urbana, 1996—; lectr. U. Nev., Reno, 2003—. Exec. editor Northwestern Jour. Internat. Law & Bus., 1978-79; contbr. articles to profl. jours. Bd. dirs. Washoe Assn. Retarded Citizens, Reno, 1997—, sec., 2001, 1st v.p., 2002-03. James scholar U. Ill., 1976. Mem. ABA, Fed. Cir. Bar Assn., Intellectual Property Law Assn. Chgo., Licensing Execs. Soc., Tau Beta Pi, Phi Eta Sigma, Alpha Pi Mu, Phi Kappa Phi. Home: 95 Rimfire Cir Reno NV 89509-2989 Office: StarGuide Digital Networks Inc 750 W John Carpenter Fwy Ste 700 Irving TX 75039-2508

RYAN, ROBERT JOHN, endocrinology educator and researcher; b. Cin., July 18, 1927; s. Robert M. and Marian J. (Hoffman) R.; m. Elizabeth E. Kennedy, Apr. 18, 1954 (div. Jan. 1980); children: Kathleen, Michel, Robert, Thomas, James, Barbara; m. Gloria A. Patton, May 15, 1981 (div.); m. Diane E. Casper, Sept. 12, 1986. Student, Xavier U., 1945, 47-48; MD, U. Cin., 1952. Resident U. Ill., Chgo., 1953-57, asst. prof., 1959-63, assoc. prof., 1963-67; rsch. fellow Tufts U., Boston, 1957-59; assoc. prof. Mayo Clinic, Rochester, Minn., 1967-71; prof. medicine Mayo Med. Sch., Rochester, 1971-81, Bartells prof., 1983, prof. biochemistry and molecular biology, 1981-90, prof. emeritus, 1990—. Mem. study sect. NIH, 1970-73, chmn., 1972-73; mem. population ctrs. com. NICHD, 1974-78, 81-85, chmn., 1982-85. Contbr. articles to profl. jours. SErved with U.S. Army, 1945-46. NIH grantee, 1960-90; recipient Daniel Drake medal U. Cin., 1990. Mem. AAAS, Endocrine Soc. (coun. 1974-77,, v.p. 1977-78, Robert H. Williams award 1984), Soc. Study Reprodn. (v.p. 1986-87, pres. 1987-88, Carl Hartman award 1991), Am. Soc. Biol. Chemistry, N.Y. Acad. Sci., Am. Sco. Clin. Investigation. Republican. Avocation: stamp collecting/philately.

RYAN, SEAN, information technology executive; BA, Columbia U.; MBA, UCLA. With Chem. Bank, GAP, SegaSoft Networks; v.p. bus. devel. Listen.com, San Francisco, 1999—2000, pres., 2000—, CEO, 2001—. Office: Listen.com 2012 16th St San Francisco CA 94103

RYAN, SHEILA A. nursing educator, former dean; Diploma in nursing, Creighton Meml. St. Joseph's Hosp. Sch. Nursing, 1967; BSN, U. Nebr., 1969; MSN in Psychiat. Nursing, U. Calif., San Francisco, 1971; PhD in Clin. Nursing Rsch., U. Ariz., 1981. Asst. prof. nursing Creighton U., Omaha, 1971—76, dean nursing, 1977—86; dean Sch. Nursing, dir. Med. Ctr. Nursing U. Rochester, NY, 1986—99; prof., Charlotte Peck Lienemann and Alumni Disting. Chair Coll. Nursing U. Nebr. Med. Ctr., Omaha. Fellow: Am. Acad. Nursing; mem.: Inst. for Healthcare Improvement, Nat. League Nursing (treas. 1993, pres. 1996—97), Inst. Medicine (treas.-sec.), Am. Internat. Health Alliance (bd. dirs. 1999—). Office: UNMC Coll Nursing Rm 4030 985330 NE Medical Ctr Omaha NE 68198-5330

RYAN, STEPHEN JOSEPH, JR., ophthalmologist, educator; b. Honolulu, Mar. 20, 1940; s. S.J. and Mildred Elizabeth (Farrer) Ryan; m. Anne Christine Mullady, Sept. 25, 1965; 1 child, Patricia Anne. AB, Providence Coll., 1961; MD, Johns Hopkins U., 1965. Intern Bellevue Hosp., N.Y.C., 1965—66; resident Wilmer Inst. Ophthalmology, Johns Hopkins Hosp., Balt., 1966—69, chief resident, 1969—70; fellow Armed Force Inst. Pathology, Washington, 1970—71; instr. ophthalmology Johns Hopkins U., Balt., 1970—71, asst. prof., 1971—72, assoc. prof., 1972—74; prof. ophthalmology Keck Sch. Medicine, U. So. Calif., L.A., 1974—, chmn. dept. ophthalmology, 1974—95, dean, 1991—2004, sr. v.p. for med. care, 1993—2004, Grace and Emery Beardsley Chair in Ophthalmology, med. dir., Doheny Eye Inst. (formerly Estelle Doheny Eye Found.), 1977—86, pres., Doheny Eye Inst. (formerly Estelle Doheny Eye Found.), chief of staff, Doheny Eye Hosp., 1985—88; acting head ophthalmology div., dept. surgery Children's Hosp., L.A., 1975—77. Mem. adv. panel Calif. Med. Assn., 1975—. Editor (with M.D. Andrews): A Survey of Ophthalmology--Manual for Medical Students, 1970; editor: (with R.E. Smith) Selected Topics on the Eye in Systemic Disease, 1974; editor: (with Dawson and Little) Retinal Diseases, 1985; editor: (with others) Retina, 1989; editor:, 2000; assoc. editor: Ophthalmol. Surgery, 1974—85, mem. editl. bd.: Am. Jour. Ophthalmology, 1981—, Internat. Ophthalmology, 1982—, Retina, 1983—, Graefes Archives, 1984—; contbr. articles to med. jours. Recipient cert. of merit, AMA, 1971, Louis B. Mayer Scholar award, Rsch. to Prevent Blindness, 1973, Rear Adm. William Campbell Chambliss USN award, 1982, Mildred Weisenfeld Award for Lifetime Achievement in Vision Rsch., Fight for Sight, 2000. Mem.: AMA, Jules Gonin Club, Rsch. Study Club, Nat. Eye Care Project, Retina Soc., Macula Soc., Pan-Am. Assn. Microsurgery, L.A. Acad. Medicine, Pacific Coast Oto-Ophthal. Soc., Los Angeles County Med. Assn., Calif. Med. Assn., L.A. Soc. Ophthalmology, Assn. Univ. Profs. of Ophthalmology, Pan-Am. Assn. Ophthalmology, Am. Ophthal. Soc., Am. Acad. Ophthalmology and Otolaryngology (award of Merit 1975), Wilmer Ophthal. Inst. Residents Assn., Soc. Scholars of Johns Hopkins U. (life). Office: 1450 San Pablo St Los Angeles CA 90033

RYAN, THOMAS JOHN, academic cardiologist, physician; b. Manhasset, N.Y., Dec. 19, 1928; s. Mark J. Ryan and Margaret M. Rooney; m. Nancy Therese Cooney, June 12, 1954; children: Kathie Steinberg, Amy, Beth Ryan Walter, Thomas John Jr., Paula, Jennifer Brown. BA, Holy Cross Coll., Worcester, Mass., 1950; MD, Georgetown Med., Washington, DC, 1954. Diplomate Nat. Bd. of Med. Examiners Pa., 1954, cert. Am. Bd. of Internal Medicine Pa., 1962, Subspecialty Bd. Cardiovascular Disease Pa. Chief cardiology St. Elizabeth's Hosp., Boston, 1961—71; instr. in medicine Harvard Med. Sch., Boston, 1961—71; asst. prof. of medicine Tufts Med. Sch., Boston, 1963—68, assoc. prof. medicine, 1968—71; chief cardiology Boston U. Med. Ctr., Boston, 1971—94; prof. medicine Boston U. Sch. of Medicine, Boston, 1971—, sr. cons. in cardiology, chief emeritus, 1994—. Author: (265 articles pub.) In Peer Reviewed Med. Jours., 24 book chpts. in medical texts. Advisor Dept. of Pub. Health, Boston, 1979—96, med. N.Y. State adv. com. N.Y.C., 1991—2003; med. adv. panel Tech. Assessment Group-Blue Cross, Chgo., 2001—03. Capt. Med. Corps. U.S. Army, 1955—57, Ft. Banks, Mass. Recipient Disting. Leadership award, Am. Heart Assn., 1980, Paul Dudley White award, 1982, Alpha Omega Alpha, Nat. Med. Honor Soc., 1985, Lawrence B. Ellis Lectureship, Harvard Med. Sch., 1986, Gold Heart award, Am. Heart Assn., 1991, The Best Doctors in Am., Woodward/White, Inc., 1994, James B. Herrick award, Coun. on Clin. Cardiology, Am. Heart Assn., 1996, The Stokes Lectureship, Irish Cardiac Soc. Royal Coll. of Physicians and Surgeons, Dublin, Ireland, 1996, Chairman's award, Am. Heart Assn., 2001; fellow Fullbright Scholar, Fullbright Com., Washington, DC, 1990—91. Fogarty Sr. Internat. Fellowship, Oxford U., 1990—91. Master: Am. Coll. Cardiology (bd. govs. 1980—83, bd. trustees 1986—93, Disting. Fellowship award 1998), ACP; fellow: European Soc. Cardiology, Soc. Geriatric Cardiology, Irish Cardiac Soc. (hon.); mem.: WHO, NIH (mem. subspecialty bd. cardiovasc. medicine 1986—92, mem. cardiology adv. com. 1990), Am. Heart Assn. (pres. 1984—86), Cardiovasc. Health Initiative Developing Countries (mem. sci. adv. com.), Internat. Health, Inst. Medicine (mem. bd. 1995—98), InterAm. Soc. Cardiology (pres. 1992—95), Assn. Profs. Cardiology, Assn. Univ. Cardiologists, New Eng. Cardiovasc. Soc. (pres. 1973), Roxbury Soc. Med. Improvement, Am. Fedn. Clin. Rsch., Am. Clin. and Climatol. Assn., Mass. Med. Soc. Independent. Roman Catholic. Achievements include early contributor to development of coronary arteriography and the conduct of randomized clinical trials and is internat. recognized as an authority on ischemic heart disease. Avocations: history of western civilization and medicine, classical music, sailing, skiing, golf. Office: Boston Univ Sch of Medicine 88 East Newton St Boston MA 02118

RYAN, THOMAS L. environmentalist; BBA, U. Tex. With Pricewaterhouse-Coopers, 1988—96; from mem. staff to pres., COO Svc. Corp. Internat., Houston, 1996—2000, pres., 2000—, COO, 2000—. Office: Service Corporation Internat 1929 Allen Pkwy Houston TX 77019*

RYAN, THOMAS M. drug store chain executive; b. 1953; Pharmacist CVS Corp., Woonsocket, RI, from 1975, numerous managerial positions v.p. pharmacy ops., sr. v.p. pharmacy, exec. v.p. pharmacy, exec. v.p. stores; pres., CEO CVS Pharmacy, Inc. (then part of Melville Corp.), Woonsocket, RI, from 1993; vice chmn., COO CVS Corp., 1996—98, pres., CEO, 1998—, chmn., 1999—. Bd. dirs. Fleet Fin. Group, Reebok Internat. Ltd., Yum Brands!, Inc. Office: CVS Corp One CVS Dr Woonsocket RI 02895*

RYAN, THOMAS PHILLIP, writer, editor; b. Atlanta, Apr. 23, 1945; s. Christopher Cornelius Ryan and Mildred Ruth Ryan Coker, John Edward Coker (Stepfather). BBA, Ga. State U., 1968, MBA, 1970; PhD, U. Ga., 1977. Dir. statis. cons. Case Western Res. U., Cleve., 1996—2000; vis. prof. U. Mich., Ann Arbor, 2000—01; external staff Nat. Inst. Standards and Tech., Gaithersburg, Md., 2001—. Cons. in field. Author: (book) Statistical Methods for Quality Improvement, 1989, 2000, Modern Regression Methods, 1997; contbr. articles to profl. jours.; editl. rev. bd. Jour. of Quality Tech., 1990—. Fellow: Am. Soc. for Quality, Royal Statis. Soc., Am. Statis. Assn. Avocations: sports, weightlifting. Office Phone: 678-574-9860. Business E-Mail: tpryan@nist.gov. E-mail: tpr42345@aol.com.

RYAN, THOMAS W. treasurer manufacturing company; b. Detroit, Jan. 28, 1947; m. Barbara L. Schembri, Sept. 6, 1968; children: Thomas III, Kristie, Kelly, Stephanie, Michael. BSBA, Wayne State U., 1969. Contr. Leader Internat. Industries, 1973; contr. Kenosha mfg. complex Am. Motors Corp., Wis., 1974-78, contr. mktg., 1978-80, dir. fin. planning, 1981-82, dir. internat. operations, 1982-85; v.p. A.O. Smith Corp., Milw., 1985—, treas., 1987-95; treas., contr., 1990-95; v.p. and CFO Tenneco Automotive Inc., Lake Forest, Ill.; exec. v.p. & CFO Federal-Mogul Corp., Southfield, Mich., 1997-2000, Allied Waste Industries, Inc., Scottsdale, Ariz., 2000—. Trustee Wis. Nat. Multiple Sclerosis Soc., Milw., 1986; mem. Zoning Bd. of Appeals, Whitefish Bay, Wis., 1987; bd. dirs., treas. A.O. Smith Found., 1987. Mem. Fin. Exec. Inst., Nat. Assn. Accts. Office: Allied Waste Industries Inc Chief Fin Officer 15880 N Greenway-Hayden Loop Ste 100 Scottsdale AZ 85260

RYAN, TIMOTHY, congressman; b. Niles, OH, July 16, 1973; BA in Polit. Sci., Bowling Green State U.; JD, Franklin Pierce Law Ctr. Mem. Ohio Senate from 32d dist., Columbus, 2001—02, U.S. Ho. of Reps. from 17th OH dist., 2003—. Trustee Found. Extended. Mem. KC, Sons Italy, Internat. Narcotics Enforcements Offices Assn., Ancient Order Hibernians, Elks. Democrat. Office: 222 Cannon House Off Bldg Washington DC 20515

RYAN, TIMOTHY P. academic administrator; m. Louise Schreiner; children: Katherine, Rebecca. BA in Econs., U. New Orleans, 1971; PHD in Econs., Ohio State U., 1978. Mem. faculty Coll. Bus. U. New Orleans, 1976—, formerly Hibernia prof. econs., former dean Coll. Bus. Adminstrn., interim exec. vice chancellor, COO, 2003, chancellor, 2003—. Recipient Alumni Assn. Excellence in Tchg. award, U. New Orleans, 1982, Homer L. Hitt Disting. Alumnus award, 1987. Office: Office of the Chancellor U New Orleans 2000 Lakeshore Dr New Orleans LA 70148*

RYAN, UNA SCULLY, health sciences professional, medical educator; b. Kuala Lumpur, Malaysia, Dec. 18, 1941; d. Henry and Amy (Yee) Scully; m. Allan Dana Callow, May 26, 1989; children: Tamsin Randlett, Amy Jean Susan Ryan. BSc in Zoology, Chemistry & Microbiology, Bristol (Eng.) U., 1963; PhD in Cell Biology, Cambridge (Eng.) U., 1968. Fellow dept. biology U. Va., Charlottesville, 1964-66; fellow dept. medicine U. Miami, Fla., 1966-67, adj. asst. prof. biology, 1968-71; dir. lab. for ultrastructure studies Howard Hughes Med. Inst., Miami, 1967-71; from instr. to assoc. prof. medicine U. Miami Sch. Medicine, 1967-80, prof. medicine, 1980-89; sr. scientist Papanicolaou Cancer Rsch. Inst., Miami, 1972-77; rsch. prof. surgery Washington U. Sch. Medicine, St. Louis, 1990—; dir. health scis. Monsanto Co., St. Louis, 1990-93; pres., CEO T Cell Scis., Needham, Mass., 1993-98; rsch. prof. medicine Boston U. Sch. Medicine, 1993—; pres., CEO AVANT Immunotherapeutics, Needham, Mass., 1998—. Dir. course W. Alton Jones Cell Sci. Ctr., 1979-81; dir. Hybridoma Facility, U. Miami, 1986-89; chair local organizing com. Internat. Coun. on Thrombosis and Hemostasis, 1984; chair Rev. Com. for Extracellular Matrix Interactions in Lung, 1983; chair various revs. NHLBI; mem. various rev. and adv. coms. Author: J. Tissue Culture Methods, 1987, Pulmonary Endothelium in Health Disease, 1987, Endothelial Cells, 1988, Vascular Endothelium: Receptors and Transduction Mechanisms, 1989; editor: Tissue & Cell, 1981-87; rev. editor: In Vitro, 1986; reviewer profl. jours.; contbr. articles to profl. jours. UK state scholar, 1960, Country Major scholar, 1960; D.S.I.R. rsch. fellow, 1964, 65, Ethel Sargant Rsch. fellow, 1964-65, Sci. Rsch. Coun. fellow, 1966; recipient Louis and Artur Lucian award for rsch. in circulatory diseases, 1984, Merit award Nat. Heart, Lung and Blood Inst., 1986, Lillie award Woods Hole, Marine Bill, Lab., 1989, Order of Brit. Eagle, 2002. Mem. Am. Soc. Cell Biology, Soc. Neurosci., Tissue Culture Assn., Internat. Soc. Heart Rsch., Am. Heart Assn. (coun. on basic rsch., coun. on circulation, cardiopulmonary coun.), Am. Physiol. Soc., Am. Microcirculatory Soc., European Soc. Microcirculation, Am. Thoracic Soc. (dir. course on culture of pulmonary endothelial cells), Internat. Soc. Applied Cardiovascular Biology, N.Y. Acad. Scis., Fla. Soc. Electron Microscopy, Sigma Xi. Office: AVANT Immunotherapeutics 119 4th Ave Needham MA 02494-2725

RYAN, VINCE, lawyer; b. Houston, Aug. 12, 1947; m. Teresa Pamela Rodriguez; 2 children. BA in English, U. Houston, 1969, JD, 1974; MA in History, Rice U., 1979. Bar: Tex. 1974. Assoc. James Patrick Smith, 1974—75, Thomas P. Duncan, Houston, 1975-76, Smith and Conner, Houston, 1976-79, Watrous, Joyce and Ryan, Houston, 1980-81; divsn. chief commrs. ct. divsn. Office of the Harris County Atty., Tex., 1981-83, first asst., 1983-88; of counsel Sinex & Stephenson, Houston, 1988—; regional mng. atty. Clame Linebarger, Houston, 1996-98; of counsel Linebarger Goggan, Houston, 1998—. Dir. legal rsch. svc. U. Houston; adj. faculty U.S. Army Command and Gen. Staff Coll., 1988—. Mem. Dist. C Houston City Coun., 1988—94; alt. City of Houston rep. Houston-Galveston Area Coun., 1989—94; pres. Region 14, Tex. Mcpl. League, 1993—94; bd. dirs. Panama Canal Commn., 1995—99. With U.S. Army, 1969—72, Vietnam, with U.S. Army, 1991, lt. col. USAR. Grad. fellow, 1977—78, Rsch. fellow, 1978—79. Office: Linebarger Goggan et al LLP 1301 Travis Ste 300 Houston TX 77002-6602 Office Phone: 713-844-3463. Business E-Mail: vincer@publicans.com.

RYAN, WILLIAM, executive; B in Psychology, MEd. Ptnr. Neuhaus Ryan Wong, South San Francisco. Office: 601 Gateway Blvd Ste 900 South San Francisco CA 94080-7006

RYAN, WILLIAM FRANCIS, priest; b. Renfrew, Ont., Can., Apr. 4, 1925; s. William Patrick Ryan and Helen Mary Doneg BA, Montreal U., 1951; MA in Labor Rels., St. Louis U., 1953; postgrad., Heythrop Coll., Oxon, Eng.; STL, St. Albert Coll., Louvain, 1958; PhD in Econs., Harvard U., 1964. Ordained priest Roman Catholic Ch., 1957. Asst. prof. econs. Loyola Coll., Montreal, Que., Can., 1963-65; nat. dir. Social Justice Office Can. Conf. Cath. Bishops, Ottawa, Ont., 1964-70, gen. sec., 1984-90; founding dir. Ctr. of Concern, Washington, 1970-78; nat. supr. Jesuit Order, Toronto, Ont., Can., 1978-84; chancellor Sch. Theology Regis Coll., Toronto, 1978-84; vis. sr. rsch. fellow Can. Inst. for Internat. Peace and Security, Ottawa, 1990-91; chair on Cath. social thought St. Paul U., Ottawa, 1991-92; 2001dir. Jesuit Project on Ethics in Politics, Ottawa, 1992. Exec. sec. Inter-religious Peace Colloquium, Washington, 1975-78; bd. dirs. Roncalli Internat. Found., Montreal, 1979-83, North/South Inst., Ottawa, 1979-91; spl. advisor to Internat. Devel. Rsch. Ctr., Ottawa, 1993-2000; coord. Jesuit Ctr. for Social Faith and Justice, 1997—; lectr. in field. Author: The Clergy and Economic Growth in Quebec, 1966, Culture, Spirituality and Economic Development—Opening a Dialogue, 1995, Our Way of Proceeding, in the Lab, The Temple and The Market: Reflections at the Intersection of Science, Religion and Development, 2000; co-author: Religious as Contemplatives in the 80's, 1984, The Lab, The Temple and The Market: Expanding the Conversation, 2001; translator: The Primacy of Charity in Moral Theology, 1961; subject of biography Faith and Freedom—The Life and Times of Bill Ryan sj, by Jamie Swift and Bob Chodos, 2002; contbr. articles to profl. jours. Mem. Am. Econs. Assn. Roman Catholic. Avocations: hiking; skiing. Office: 169 Sunnyside Ave Ottawa ON Canada K1S 0R2

RYBAK, JAMES PATRICK, engineering educator; b. Cleve., Mar. 16, 1941; s. John Anthony and Irene Marcella (Kovar) R.; m. Linda Louise Watkins, Oct. 12, 1968. BSEE, Case Western Res. U., 1963; MS, U. N.Mex., 1965; PhD, Colo. State U., 1970. Registered profl. engr., Colo. Mem. tech. staff Sandia Nat. Labs., Albuquerque, 1963-66; rsch. asst., NDEA fellow Colo. State U., Ft. Collins, 1966-70, postdoctoral fellow, 1970-72; prof. engring. and math. Mesa State Coll., Grand Junction, Colo., 1972—, asst. v.p. acad. affairs, 1986-88, v.p. acad. affairs, 1988-98. Contbr. articles to profl. publs. including

IEEE Transactions, Engring. Edn., Popular Electronics, Elektrosvyaz (Russia), Radio (Russia). Mem. adv. bd. Grand Mesa Youth Svcs., Grand Junction, 1986-88; bd. dirs. Hilltop Rehab. Hosp., Grand Junction, 1989-93, Salvation Army, Grand Junction, 1993—. NEDA fellow, 1968-70, THEMIS fellow, 1970-72. Mem. IEEE, Am. Soc. Engring. Edn. (vice chmn. Rocky Mountain sect. 1974-75, chmn. 1975-76). Avocation: amateur radio. Home: 314 Quail Dr Grand Junction CO 81503-2527 Office: Mesa State Coll 1175 Texas Ave Grand Junction CO 81501-7605

RYBAK, R.T. mayor; m. Megan O'Hara; 2 children. Gen. mgr. WCCO TV & WCCO Radio; v.p. Internet Broadcast Sys.; pub., mgr., bus. ops. Twin Cities Reader; mayor City of Minneapolis, Minn., 2001—. Founder, mem. bd. Save the Water in Mpls.; served Minn. Soc. Architects, Night of the Penguin, Hennepin Ave. Adv. Com., Adv. Fedn. Minn., Eiji Oue Inaugural Com.; coach Little League Baseball, Youth Soccer; vol. reader Minn. Pub. Sch.; co-coord. Bill Bradley for Pres., 2000; co-chair Tony Bouza for Gov., 1994; bd. dir. Residents Opposed to Airport Racket. Democrat. Office: 350 S Fifth St 331 City Hall Minneapolis MN 55415 Office Phone: 612-673-2700. Office Fax: 612-673-2305.

RYBCZYK, JOSEPH ANTHONY, physicist, researcher, writer; b. Phila., Oct. 19, 1935; s. Frank Rybczyk and Isabella Slivak; life ptnr. Dolores Brannan; m. Ruth Diane Menendez, Dec. 30, 1955 (div.); children: Brian Keith, Deborah Gale, Karen Marie. Author: (theoretical physics) Millennium Theory of Relativity. Achievements include research in Theory of Natural Motion; Millennium Theory of Relativity; Time and Energy; The Laws of Acceleration; Time and Energy, Inertia and Gravity; Millennium Relativity Velocity Composition; Relativistic Motion Perspective; Millenium Relativity Acceleration Composition. Personal E-mail: jrybczyk@msn.com.

RYBCZYNSKI, WITOLD MARIAN, architect, educator, writer; b. Edinburgh, Scotland, Mar. 1, 1943; arrived in Can., 1953; s. Witold Kasimir and Anna Jadwiga (Hofman) Rybczynski; m. Shirley Hallam, Nov. 15, 1974. Diploma, Loyola Coll., Montreal, 1960; B.Arch., McGill U., 1966, M.Arch., 1972, DSc (hon.), 2002. Pvt. practice architecture, Montreal, 1970-82; research assoc. McGill U., Montreal, 1972-75, asst. prof. architecture, 1975-80, assoc. prof., 1980-86, prof., 1986-93; Meyerson prof. of Urbanism U. Pa., 1994—. Cons. UN, Manila, 1976, Internat. Devel. Rsch. Ctr., Ottawa, 1977, Banco de Mex., 1979—80. Author: Paper Heroes: A Review of Appropriate Technology, 1980, Taming the Tiger: The Struggle to Control Technology, 1983, Home: A Short History of an Idea, 1986, The Most Beautiful House in the World, 1989, Waiting in the Weekend, 1991, Looking Around: A Journey Through Architecture, 1992, A Place for Art, 1993, City Life, 1995, A Clearing in the Distance, 1999, One Good Turn, 2000, The Look of Architecture, 2001, The Perfect House, 2002; contbg. editor: Saturday Night, 1990—2001; mem. adv. bd. Ency. Americana; founding editor: Wharton Real Estate Rev., 1996—. Mem. adv. coun. Inst. Classical Archs., 2003—; mem. adv. bd. Chgo. Humanities Festival, 2003—; advisor Libr. Am. Landscape History, 2002—, mem. U.S. commn. fine arts, 2004—. Recipient QSPELL Lit. prize for nonfiction, 1988, 1989, Prix Paul-Henri Lapointe, 1988, Progressive Arch. Design award, 1991, Jurzykowski Found. award, 1993, Athaneum Lit. prize, 1997, 2001, Christopher award, 2000, J. Anthony Lukas prize, 2000; Ballard Real Estate scholar, 1994—95. Fellow: AIA (hon.); mem.: US Commn. Fine Art. Office: Grad Sch Fine Arts U Pa Meyerson Hall Philadelphia PA 19104 E-mail: rybczyns@pobox.upenn.edu.

RYBERG, W. GREG, state legislator, food store executive; b. Eau Claire, Wis., Oct. 5, 1946; s. Walter G. and Patricia C. Ryberg; m. Elizabeth Rose Denkewalter, Dec. 28, 1968; children: Amy, Kyle, Shana. BS, Marquette U., 1968. Pres. R & H Maxxon, Inc. (Depot Food Stores), Aiken, S.C.; CEO, REI, Inc.; mem. S.C. Senate, Columbia, 1993—. Mem. corrections and penology com., judiciary com., labor, commerce and industry com., transp. com. Mem. U.S. Army N.G., 1968-74. Named Businessperson of Yr., Greater Aiken C. of C., 1994. Republican. Office: 512 Gressette Bldg Columbia SC 29202 also: PO Box 1077 Aiken SC 29802-1077

RYBERG, WILLIAM A. orchestra executive; BMus, Western Wash. State U., 1980; MMus, Ind. U., 1983. Teller, loan officer, br. mgr., regional mgr. Ranier Nat. Bank; v.p., area mgr. West One Bank, Tacoma; v.p., dist. mgr. Key Bank, Wash., 1993-96; exec. dir. Bellingham (Wash.) Festival of Music, 1996-98; pres. Grand Rapids (Mich.) Symphony, 1998—2004, Oreg. Symphony Orch., Portland, 2004—. Office: 921 SW Wahington Ste 200 Portland OR 97205*

RYBIN, VITALYI OLEGOVICH, research scientist; b. Moscow, Dec. 6, 1957; came to U.S., 1992; s. Oleg Aleksandrovich and Valentina Alekseevna R.; m. Irina Victorovna, Jan. 12, 1979; 1 child: Andrew Vitalevich. MS in Biochemistry, Moscow State U., 1980; PhD in Enzymology, USSR Cardiology Rsch. Ctr., Moscow, 1986. Jr. investigator Cardiology Rsch. Ctr., Moscow, 1983-87, rsch. assoc., 1987-89, sr. investigator, 1989-92; vis. assoc. rsch. scientist Columbia U., N.Y.C., 1992-95, assoc. rsch. scientist, 1995—. Author: (book chpts.) Lung Biology in Health and Disease, vol. 65, 1993, G Proteins, 1996; contbr. articles to profl. jours. Mem. Am. Soc. Pharmacology and Exptl. Therapeutics. Avocation: stamp collecting/philately. Home: 138 Panorama Dr Edgewater NJ 07020 Office: Columbia U 630W 168 St New York NY 10032 E-mail: vrybin4609@aol.com.

RYCHLAK, JOSEPH FRANK, psychology educator, theoretician; b. Cudahy, Wis., Dec. 17, 1928; s. Joseph Walter and Helen Mary (Bieniek) R.; m. Lenora Pearl Smith, June 16, 1956; children: Ronald, Stephanie. BS, U. Wis., 1953; MA, Ohio State U., 1954, PhD, 1957. Diplomate Am. Bd. Examiners in Profl. Psychology. Asst. prof. psychology Fla. State U., Tallahassee, 1957-58, Washington State U., Pullman, 1958-61; assoc. prof., then prof. psychology St. Louis U., 1961-69; prof. psychology Purdue U., West Lafayette, Ind., 1969-83, interim dept. head, 1979-80; prof. Loyola U. Chgo., 1983-99, Maude C. Clarke prof. humanistic psychology, 1983—, prof. emeritus, 1999—. Dir. Human Relations Ctr., Pullman, Wash., 1958-61; research cons. AT&T, 1957-82. Author: The Psychology of Rigorous Humanism, 1977, 2d edit., 1988, Discovering Free Will and Personal Responsibility, 1979, A Philosophy of Science for Personality Theory, 2d edit., 1981, Personality and Life Style of Young Male Managers, 1982, (with N. Cameron) Personality Development and Psychopathology, 2d edit., 1985, Artificial Intelligence and Human Reason: A Teleological Critique, 1991, Logical Learning Theory: A Human Teleology and Its Empirical Support, 1994, In Defense of Human Consciousness, 1997, The Human Image in Postmodern America, 2003; assoc. editor Psychotherapy: Theory, Rsch. and Practice, 1965-76, Jour. Mind and Behavior, 1985-94. With USAF, 1946-49. Named Outstanding Contbr. to Human Understanding, Internat. Assn. Social Psychiatry, 1971. Fellow Am. Psychol. Assn. (div. 24 pres. 1977-78, 86-87), Am. Psychol. Soc.; mem. Soc. Personality Assessment, Phi Beta Kappa. Roman Catholic. Home: 12974 Abraham Run Carmel IN 46033 Office Phone: 317-816-0073. E-mail: rychlak1@juno.com. *From my father I learned to have a sense of purpose, work hard, and assume responsibility. From my mother I learned not to take myself too seriously, and to realize that my achievements are never entirely up to me.*

RYDALCH, ANN, federal agency administrator, former state senator; m. Vernal Rydalch. BS in Business Educ., Idaho State U. Mem. Idaho Senate, 1983—1990, chmn. Fed. Lab. Consortium Tech. Transfer, 2001- . Past mem. Idaho Bicentennial Commn.; former vice chmn. Idaho Republican Com. Office: ID Natl Energy & Envrn Lab PO Box 1625 MS 3810 2525 N Fremont Ave Idaho Falls ID 83415-3810

RYDELL, CATHERINE M. former state legislator; b. Grand Forks, N.D., May 8, 1950; d. Hilary Harold and Catherine F. (Ireland) Wilson; m. Charles D. Rydell, 1971; children: Kimberly, Jennifer, Michael. BS, U. N.D., 1971. Mem. N.D. Ho. of Reps., 1985—, mem. supreme ct. judicial planning, govt., vet. affairs com., past rep. caucus leader; exec. dir. Am. Acad. Neurology, St. Paul. Coord. cmty. svc. Bismarck Jr. Coll.; bus. mgr. surg. svc. St. Alexius Med. Ctr. Bd. dirs. Mission Valley Family, YMCA, N.D. Early Childhood Tng. Ctr., Ronald McDonald Found., CHAND; mem. state adv. bd. Casey Family Program, Juvenile Justice; mem. lay adv. bd. St. Alexius; mem. regional adv. bd. Luth. Social Svcs.; mem. N.D. State Centennial Com., N.D. State Mus. Art. Recipient Outstanding Svc. award Tobacco Free N.D., Legislator of Yr. award Children's Caucus, Guardian of Bus. award Nat. Fedn. Ind. Bus. Mem. Philanthropic and Edn. Orgn. Sisterhood, N.D. Med. Assn. (v.p.), Gamma Phi Beta. Office: Am Acad Neurology 1080 Montreal Ave Saint Paul MN 55116-2386

RYDÉN, BENGT GUNNAR, retired stock exchange executive; b. Stockholm, Oct. 30, 1936; s. Gunnar H. and Ragnhild L. (Soederbaum) Rydén; m. Monica I.H. Tillberg, May 18, 1961. MBA, Stockholm Sch. Econs., 1960, PhD, 1972. Dep. chief economist Fedn. Swedish Industries, Stockholm, 1965-66; editor-in chief Swedish "Veckans Affärer", Stockholm, 1971-73; chief exec. Ctr. Bus. and Policy Studies, Stockholm, 1974-84, Stockholm Stock Exch., 1985-98, exec. chmn., 1998-99; vice chmn. Swedish Acctg. Stds. Coun., 1989—2002; ret., 2002. Chmn. Internat. Fedn. Stock Exchs., 1995—97, Mus. Nat. Antiquities, Sweden, 1998—, Hallvarsson & Halvarsson AB, Sweden, 1999—, Seventh Swedish Nat. Pension Fund, 1999—, Pantor Engring. AB, 2000; bd. dirs. Found. Fin. Rsch., Sweden, Svenskt Rekonstruktionskapital AB, Sweden, 2003—, HEX Integrated Markets, Oy, Finland, 2003—; mem. Com. of Wise Men on the Regulation of European Securities Mkts., 2000—01, Govt. Commn. on Restoration Pub. Trust in Bus., 2002—. Fellow, Indsl. Inst. Econ. and Social Rsch., 1966—70. Fellow: Swedish Acad. Auditing, Royal Swedish Acad. Engring. Scis. E-mail: bengt.ryden@halvarsson.se.

RYDEN, JOHN GRAHAM, publishing executive; b. N.Y.C., Dec. 19, 1939; s. Albert Graham and Margaret Keating (Bastable) R.; m. Barbara Dee Kelly, June 19, 1962; children: Linda, Patricia. AB, Harvard U., 1961. Sales rep. McGraw-Hill Book Co., 1965-68; editor coll. dept. Harper & Row, 1968-71, editor in chief coll. dept., 1971-74; editor in chief, asst. dir. U. Chgo. Press, 1974-78, assoc. dir., 1978-79; dir. Yale U. Press, New Haven, 1979—; chmn. bd. trustees Yale Univ. Press, London, 1981—. Mem. adminstr. bd. The Papers of Benjamin Franklin, 1979—; chmn. adv. bd. Beacon Press, 1983—. Mem. editl. bd. Public Historian, 1980-86, Scholarly Publishing, 1992-95, The Yale Editions of the Private Papers of James Boswell, 1993—; adv. bd. The Yale Review, 1992—. Trustee Orch. New Eng., 1980-2000, pres., 1983-86, chmn., 1995-2000; bd. dirs. Fund for Free Expression, 1990-96; mem. Helsinki Watch Com., 1992-96. With USNR, 1962-65. Berkeley Coll. fellow Yale U. Mem. Assn. Am. Publs. (bd. dirs. 1990-94), Assn. Am. U. Presses (bd. dirs. 1980-83, 87-90, pres. 1988-89), Conn. Acad. Arts and Scis., Internat. Assn. Scholarly Pubs., Grads. Club, New Haven Lawn Club, Hasty Pudding Club (Cambridge, Mass.), Yale Club (N.Y.C.), Century Assn. (N.Y.C.). Office: Yale Univ Press PO Box 209040 New Haven CT 06520-9040 also: Yale U Press 302 Temple St New Haven CT 06511-6601

RYDER, BEVERLY, utilities executive; BA in Econs., Stanford (Calif.) U.; MBA in Fin., U. Chgo. From dir. strategic alliances So. Calif. to corp. sec. Edison Internat., Rosemead, Calif., 1972—96, corp. sec., 1996—, v.p. cmty. involvement, 2000—. Trustee Stanford (Calif.) U.; commr. LA (Calif.) City Employees' Retirement Bd. Bd. dir. United Way, LA. Office: Edison International 2244 Walnut Grove Ave Rosemead CA 91770

RYDER, DONALD J. military career officer; b. Haverstraw, N.Y. m. Lisa Jones; children: Brock, Donald Jr. BS in Edn., N.E. La. U.; MS in Mgmt., Fla. Inst. Tech.; grad., US Army Command and Gen. Staff Coll., US Army War Coll. Commd. officer US Army, 1971, advanced through grades to brig. gen., various positions, platoon leader, 501st mil. police co., 1st armored divsn., comdr., 463d mil. police co. (EG) Fort Leonard Wood, Mo., S-4, 16th mil. police brigade Fort Bragg, NC, S-3 503d Mil. Police Bn. Ft. Bragg, NC, corrections staff officer HQ TRADOC Ft. Monroe, Va., exec. officer, dep. chief of staff for pers. adminstrn., S-3 18th Mil. Police Brigade V (US) Corps Frankfurt, Germany, dep. brigade comdr. 18th Mil. Police Brigade V (US) Corps, comdr. 93d Mil. Police Bn. V (US) Corps, comdr. 418th Base Support Bn., comdr. 14th Mil. Police Brigade, 21st Theater Army Area Mannheim, Germany, provost marshal gen.; sec. of the gen. staff US Army Europe and Seventh Army, Heidelberg, Germany, exec. officer to the comdr. in chief, dep. comdg. gen. 21st Theater Army Area Command Kaiserslautern, Germany; dep. comdg. gen. US Army Chem. and Mil. Police Ctrs. and Ft. McClellan, Ala., 1998-99; comdt. US Army Mil. Police Sch., Ft. Leonard Wood, Mo., 1999—, Fort McClellan, Ala., 1999—, Army Criminal Investigation Divsn., 2002—. Decorated Legion of Merit with two oak leaf clusters, Bronze Star, Meritorious Svc. medal with oak leaf cluster, Army Commendation medal with three oak leaf clusters, S.W. Asia Svc. medal with two campaign stars, Armed Forces Svc. medal, Humanitarian Svc. medal, NATO medal. Office: Military Police Sch Fort Leonard Wood MO 65473-8907*

RYDER, EDWARD FRANCIS, secondary school educator; b. Lynn, Mass., Mar. 25, 1931; s. Edward W. and Theresa (Callahan) R. BSBA, Salem State U., 1954, EdM in Edn., 1973; EdM in Bus. Edn., Boston U., 1956. Cert. tchr., Mass. Bus. tchr. North Quincy (Mass.) H.S., 1968—. Owner, pub. Sunnyside Pub. Co., 1975—. Author: The Art of Playing Bingo and Winning Consistently, 1980, The Art of Entering Sweepstakes and Winning Consistently, 1981, How To Save a Fortune Using Refunds and Coupons, 1983, How to Unlock the Secrets of Winning and Good Luck, 1983, How You Can Achieve Total Success Through Self-Hypnosis, 1984, Where to Buy Everything Wholesale--A Book of Lifetime Savings, 1984, A Guide to Over 1,000 Things You Can Get--For Free!, 1984, The Art of Betting Horses and Winning Consistently, 1985, Blackjack: How to Play and Win Like an Expert, 1985, Hot Dice! How to Leave the Table a Winner, 1986, Winning Secrets of a Poker Master, 1986, Picking Winners at the Harness Races, 1987, Winning Consistently at the Greyhound Races, 1987, Lucky Slots!! How to Beat the Casino Bandits, 1988, Secrets of Winning at Casino Roulette, 1988, Keno: The Art of Playing and Winning, 1989, How to Play and Win at Casino Baccarat, 1989, Secrets of Winning at Video Poker, 1990, Winning Secrets of a Master Sports Bettor--Football, 1991, Winning Secrets of a Master Sports Bettor--Basketball, 1992, Winning Secrets of a Master Sports Bettor--Baseball, 1992; all publs. updated, 1997. Roman Catholic. Home: 28 Sunnyside Rd Lynn MA 01905-1105 Office: Sunnyside Pubs 51 Willow St # 29 Lynn MA 01901-1108 Personal E-mail: hardwoodhoudini@aol.com.

RYDER, GENE ED, retired United States Air Force training administrator; b. Canyon, Tex., Sept. 19, 1932; s. Johnny Allen and Rilda (New) R.; m. Mary Louise Wilson, Feb. 16, 1958; children: Carlyn, Katherine, Anita, Valerie. BA in Govt. cum laude, St. Mary's U., 1965; MEd, Our Lady of the Lake U., 1968; PhD in Adminstrn., The Union Inst., 1979. Instr. USAF, Scott, Keesler & Lackland AFB, 1958-65, tng. specialist, 1965-69, tng. evaluator, 1969-72, curriculum coord., 1972-75, supr. curriculum devel., 1975-78, supr. tng. evaluation, 1978-83, tng. advisor, 1983-92, chief tng. policy Randolph AFB, Tex., 1992-95; ret., 1995. Chmn. affiliated schs. adv. panel C.C. of Air Force, Maxwell AFB, Ala., 1984-88; co-chmn. USAF Tng. and Instrnl. Sys. Career Program, Randolph AFB, 1992-95; apptd. to Tex. State Bd. Profl. Counselors, 1995-2001. Author: Basics of Sunday School Leadership: A Guide for Lay Leaders, 1982. Dir. edn. Calvary Hills Bapt. Ch., San Antonio, 1981-94; coord. state scripture Gideons Internat., Nashville, 1991-94; elected mem. Tex. State Rep. Exec. Com., 1994-2000; del. Rep. Nat. conv., 2000. With USAF, 1953-56. Mem.: Air Force Assn., Am. Legion. Home: 1502 Copperfield Rd San Antonio TX 78251-3324

RYDER, HAL, theater educator, director; b. Evanston, Ill., Aug. 21, 1950; s. Lee Sigmund and Katherine (Philipsborn) Rosenblatt; m. Caroline Margaret Ogden, Nov. 17, 1976 (div. 1991) Student, U. Ariz., 1968-72, U. Miami, summer 1971; cert. in drama, Drama Studio London, 1973; BA in Drama, U. Wash., 1987. Drama specialist Rough Rock (Ariz.) Demonstration Sch., 1971-72; artistic dir. Mercury Theatre, London, 1973-75, Fringe Theatre, Orlando, Fla., 1976-79; dir. Drama Studio London, 1980-82, interim adminstrv. dir., 1985; artistic dir. Alaska Arts Fine Arts Camp, Sitka, 1987, Shakespeare Plus, Seattle, 1983-92; full prof. Cornish Coll. Arts, Seattle, 1982-98; prof., 1998—; producer theatre Cornish Coll. Arts, Seattle, 1987-97, acting-chmn. theatre dept., 1990, 2001, pres. faculty senate, 1999-2001; artistic dir., exec. dir. Open Door Theatre, 1992-98, exec. dir., 1998-00, artistic dir., 2002—03, Snoqualmie Falls Forest Theatre, 1992-94; founder, v.p., CEO Ednl. Arts Resource Svcs., Inc., 1996—; producing artistic dir. Seattle Pub. Theatre, 2001—. Creative cons. Sea World Fla., Orlando, 1979; lit. mgr. Pioneer Square Theatre, Seattle, 1983; space mgr. Seattle Mime Theatre, 1986-87. Author: Carmilla, 1976, (with others) Marvelous Christmas Mystery, 1978; editor: Will Noble Blood Die, 1987, The New Emperor's New Clothes, 1990, Hamlet & Juliet, 1997, Solos Shakespeare Monologue Database, 2000; dir. over 175 stage plays; appeared in over 40 prodns. Artistic dir. Seattle Pub. Theater, 2001. Recipient Faculty Excellence award Seafirst Bank, Seattle, 1988. Mem. SAG, AFTRA, Am. Fedn. Tchrs. (pres. faculty senate Cornish chpt. 1999—), Alpha Kappa Lamda. Democrat. Jewish. Avocations: writing, cooking, gardening, travel, scuba diving. Office: Cornish Coll Arts 710 E Roy St Seattle WA 98102-4604 Home: 2130 124th St SE Everett WA 98208-6624

RYDER, HENRY C(LAY), lawyer; b. Lafayette, Ind., Feb. 18, 1928; s. Raymond Robert and Mina Elizabeth (Arnold) R.; m. Ann Sater Clay, Nov. 29, 1952 (dec.); children: David C., Sarah Paige Hugon, Anne Ryder O'Keefe; m. Velma Iris Dean, Aug. 27, 1976 BS, Purdue U., 1948; LLB, U. Mich., 1951; LLD, Hanover Coll., 1998. Bar: Mich. 1951, Ind. 1952, U.S. Dist. Ct. (so. dist.) Ind. 1953, U.S. Ct. Appeals (7th cir.) 1957, U.S. Supreme Ct. 1981. Assoc. Buschmann, Krieg, DeVault & Alexander, Indpls., 1953-57, ptnr., 1957-60, Roberts & Ryder and successor firms, Indpls., 1960-86, Barnes & Thornburg (merger), Indpls., 1987-95, of counsel, 1996—. Pres. Ind. State Symphony Soc. Inc., 1979-82, bd. dirs., 1972-91, trustee, 1991—; chmn. United Way of Greater Indpls., 1984; vice chmn. Greater Indpls. Progress Com., 1979-86, chmn., 1987-89, mem. exec. com., 1979-2000; trustee Purdue U., 1983-89, Hanover Coll., 1979-2003, chmn., 1988-98; bd. dirs. Hist. Landmark Found. of Ind., 1985-96, chmn., 1992-95; bd. dirs. Purdue Rsch. Found., 1992—; hon. v.p. Ind. Soc. Chgo.; com. bd. IUPUI U. Libr., 1998—, chmn. 2003—04; bd. govs. Heartland Film Festival, 2000—. Lt. U.S. Army, 1951-53. Recipient Jefferson award Indpls. Star, 1983, Whistler award Greater Indpls. Progress Com., 1989; Sagamore of the Wabash, 1984; named Man of Yr., B'nai B'rith Soc., 1984, Ind. Acad., 1992, Lifetime Achievement award Nat. Soc. Fund Raising Execs., 1999. Fellow: Ind. Bar Found., Am. Bar Found.; mem.: ABA, Indpls. Bar Assn., Ind. Bar Assn., Ind. C. of C. (bd. dirs. 1991—94), Purdue U. Alumni Assn. (pres. 1975—77, Alumni Svc. award 1982, Citizenship award 1989), Indpls. Lit. Club, Kiwanis (Downtown Indpls. pres. 1983, Civic award 1981), Columbia Club (bd. dirs. 1987—90, sec. 1988, pres. Columbia Club Found. 1990—95, trustee 1990—, Benjamin Harrison award 1983, Columbian of Yr. award 2002), USAC Benevolent Found. (bd. dirs., pres. 1999—), USAC Properties (sec., bd. dirs.), U.S. Auto Club (bd. dirs., Pres.'s award 1989, Eddie Edenburn award 2000), Lawyers Club of Indpls. (pres. 1966). Republican. Presbyterian. Office: Barnes & Thornburg 11 S Meridian St Indianapolis IN 46204-3535 Office Phone: 317-231-7521.

RYDER, KENNETH WILLIAM, pathologist, educator; b. Mobile, Ala., May 1, 1945; BA, Knox Coll., 1967; PhD, Ind. U., 1972; MD, U. Ill., Chgo., 1975. Asst. prof. Ind. U. Sch. Medicine, Indpls., 1978-83, assoc. prof., 1983-88, prof., assoc. chair, 1986—; chief of svc. Wishard Meml. Hosp., Indpls., 1986-99; med. dir. Vencor Hosp. Lab., Indpls., 1995-2001; exec. dir. bus. devel. lab. svcs., dir. chemistry labs., outreach svcs./point of care testing Clarian Health Ptnrs., Indpls., 2000—; chief pathologist VA Med. Ctr., Indpls., 2000-01. Author: Interferographs, 1987, 2nd Edit., 1991; (with others) Difficult Diagnoses, 1991; contbr. articles to profl. jours. Fellow Coll. Am. Pathologists, 1979, Nat. Acad. Clin. Biochemistry, 1989. Office: Ind U Sch Medicine Meth Hosp Pathology Svc 1701 N Senate Ave Rm AG002A Indianapolis IN 46202-5306 E-mail: kryder@iupui.edu.

RYDER, MARY RUTH, English language educator; b. Bloomington, Ill., Apr. 1, 1950; d. Bernard Leroy and Ruth Marie (Blacker) R. BA, Monmouth Coll., 1972; MA, Ill. State U., 1981; PhD, U. Ill., 1987. Tchr. English and Latin, Monmouth (Ill.) H.S., 1972, Normal (Ill.) Cmty. H.S., 1972-85; asst. prof. English, Ill. State U., Normal, 1985-89; prof. English, S.D. State U., Brookings, 1989—, Disting. prof. English, 2002—, coord. grad. studies in English, 1993—2003. Author: Willa Cather and Classical Myth, 1990 (Mildred Bennett Prize for Disting. Cather Scholarship, Classical and Modern Lit. Quar. Incentive award). Mem. MLA, Willa Cather Pioneer Meml. and Ednl. Found., Phi Kappa Phi, Alpha Xi Delta. Methodist. Office: SD State U Dept English Brookings SD 57007-0001

RYDER, ROBERT P. BS in Acct., U. Scranton. CPA AICPA. Acct. Price Waterhouse, N.Y.C.; with PepsiCo, 1989—2002; sr. v.p. Am. Greetings Corp., Cleve., 2002—, CFO, 2002—. Office: American Greetings Corp 1 American Rd Cleveland OH 44144-2398*

RYDER, WINONA (WINONA LAURA HOROWITZ), actress; b. Winona, Minn., Oct. 29, 1971; d. Michael and Cynthia (Istas) Horowitz. Films include: Lucas, 1986, Square Dance, 1987, Beetlejuice, 1988, Great Balls of Fire, 1989, Heathers, 1989, Edward Scissorhands, 1990, Mermaids, 1990, Welcome Home, Roxy Carmichael, 1990, Night On Earth, 1992, Bram Stoker's Dracula, 1992, Age of Innocence, 1993 (Golden Globe for Best Supporting Actress, 1994, Academy award nominee, Best Supporting Actress, 1993), The House of the Spirits, 1994, Reality Bites, 1994, Little Women, 1994 (Acad. Awd. nom., Best Actress), How to Make An American Quilt, 1995, Looking for Richard, 1995, The Crucible, 1996, Boys, 1996, Alien Resurrection, 1997, Celebrity, 1998, Girl, Interrupted, 1999, Autumn in New York, 1999, Lost Souls, 2000, Mr. Deeds, 2002, S1mOne, 2002, The Day My God Died (narrator), 2003 Hollywood Walk of Fame-2000.

RYDHOLM, RALPH WILLIAMS, advertising agency executive; b. Chgo., June 1, 1937; s. Thor Gabriel and Vivian Constance (Williams) R.; m. Jo Anne Beechler, Oct. 5, 1963; children: Kristin, Erik, Julia. BA, Northwestern U., 1958, postgrad. in bus. adminstrn., 1958-59; postgrad. Advanced Mgmt. Program, Harvard U., 1982. Acct. trainee, copywriter Young & Rubicam Advt., Chgo., 1960-63; copywriter Post-Keyes-Gardner Advt., Chgo., 1963, E. H. Weiss Advt., Chgo., 1963-65; copy group head BBDO Advt., Chgo., 1965-66; with J. Walter Thompson Advt., Chgo., 1966-86, creative dir., v.p., 1969-76, exec. creative dir., 1976-86, sr. v.p., 1972-80, exec. v.p., dir., 1980-86; exec. v.p., chief creative officer, dir. Ted Bates Worldwide, N.Y.C., 1986-87; mng. ptnr., chmn. mgmt. com., chief creative officer, chmn., CEO, EURO RSCG Tatham Advt., Chgo., 1987-98; bd. dirs. Euro RSCG, USA; pres. R2 Cons., 1999—; spl. counsel J. Walter Thompson, 1999-2000. Bd. dirs., ops. com., chmn. creative com., vice chmn., 1996, chmn., 1997-98; Am. Assn. Advt. Agys. guest spkr. Ad Age Workshop, 1969, 77, 86, Adweek Seminar, 1993, CLIO awards, 1995; keynote spkr. Stephen B. Kelly Awards, 1993, CEBA Awards, 1997; chmn. CEBA Awards, 1997. Mem. assoc. bd. Newberry Libr. Assn., Friends com. Northwetern U.; bd. dirs., adv. coun. leadership coun. Chgo. Pub. Edn. Fund; Prin. for a Day Chgo. Pub. Schs., 1998, 1999, 2000, 2001, Chgo. Pub. Schs., 2002; former chmn. bd. dirs. Am. Scandinavian Coun.; dir. Am. Assn. Advt. Agys. Found., 1997—99. Staff sgt. USAF, 1959—65. Recipient Clio awards, Internat. Broadcast award, Lion awards, Cannes Film Festival, Addy awards; named one of Top 100 Creative Ad People Ad Daily, 1972, Advt. Exec. of Yr. Adweek, 1991, Best Man in Advt. McCalls and Adweek, 1992; named to Creative Leader Hall of Fame, Wall St. Jour., 1994. Mem. ASCAP, Am. Advt. Fedn. (Silver medal Lifetime Svc. 1997), Chgo. Advt. Fedn., Chgo. Com. Coun. on Fgn. Rels., Saddle and Cycle Club, Econ. Club Chgo. (bd. dirs. 1996-98), Northwestern Club Chgo., Harvard Club Chgo., Harvard Club Boston, Harvard Club N.Y.C., Execs. Club Chgo., Tavern Club, Carlton Club, Chikaming Country Club (Mich.), Dunes Club (Mich.), Lost Dunes Club (Mich.), Internat. Club, Hon. Order Ky. Cols., Openlands, Friends of the Parks, Friends of Chgo. River, Fernwood, Art Inst. Chgo., Lincoln Park Zoo, Phi Delta Theta. E-mail: rydholm@aol.com.

RYDSTROM, CARLTON LIONEL, chemist, chemicals consultant; b. Indpls., Dec. 4, 1928; s. Carlton Lionel and Sara Ann (McNeese) R.; m. Kathleen O'Leary, Oct. 2, 1954 (dec.); children: Carlton L. III, Michael, Mary (dec.), Leslie, Patricia, Timothy, Molly. BS in Polymer Chemistry, N.D. State U., 1951; MS in Phys. Chemistry, U. Puerto Rico, Rio, Piedras, 1953. Chemist Am. Marietta Co., Kankakee, Ill., 1951—52; chemist, plant mgr. Chinamel Paints, Hato Rey, PR, 1952—53; tech. mgr. Midwest Synthetics (Valspar),

Rockford, Ill., 1953—55; mng. ptnr. Norcote Co., St. Petersburg, Fla., 1955—71; pres. C.M. Industries, Inc., St. Petersburg, 1971—74, Tuftop/Norcote Coatings, Inc., St. Petersburg, 1974—80; owner Rydstrom Lab., Inc., St. Petersburg, 1980—. Bd. dirs. Stacote Finishes, Ltd., W.I.; cons. Sch. Bds. State of Fla., 1981—, paint and adhesive industries. Pres. parish coun. St. Jude Cath. Cathedral Parish, 1977-78, 78-79, 97—; pres. St. Vincent de Paul Pinellas Dist., St. Petersburg, 1988-91; nat. secretariat Cursillo Movement, Roman Cath. Ch., Dallas, 1985-88; dir. Cursillo Movement, Diocese of St. Petersburg, 1995-97; dir. St. Vincent de Paul Food Ctr., St. Petersburg, 1988—; chmn. Waterfront Planning Com., St. Petersburg, 1959; mem. bd. dirs. St. Petersburg Cath. H.S., 1977-80; trustee N.D. State U. Devel. Found., 1998—. Fellow N.Y. Acad. Sci., Am. Inst. Chemists; mem. Nat. Assn. Corrosion Engrs., Soc. Coatings Tech. (chmn./pres. 1958-59, Disting. Svc. award 1975), Fla. Paint and Coating Assn. (treas., dir. 1959-75), St. Vincent dePaul Soc. (Top Hat award 1991), Jr. C. of C. (DSA 1960). Republican. Roman Catholic. Avocations: golf, gardening, travel, public speaking, working with needy. Home and Office: 6300 25th Ave N Saint Petersburg FL 33710-4128 E-mail: budrydstrom@msn.com.

RYERSON, DENNIS, editor; b. Ames, Iowa, Apr. 20, 1948; children: Carey, Kirsten. Student, Iowa State U., U. No. Iowa. Announcer, news dir. Sta. KWBG, Boone, Iowa; reporter, then city editor Cedar Falls Record, 1969—73; news editor Scottsbluff (Nebr.) Star-Herald, 1973—74; editl. page editor Vancouver (Wash.) Columbian, 1974—83; chief editl. writer, then editl. dir. Cleve. Plain Dealer, 1983—88; mng. editor news Denver Post, 1988—89; editor editl. pages Des Moines Register, 1989-94; exec. editor Great Falls (Mont.) Tribune, 1994-95; v.p., editor Des Moines Register, 1995—2001; editl. page editor San Jose Mercury News, 2001—03; v.p., editor The Indianapolis Star, 2003—. Appeared on TV shows including Good Morning America, MacNeil/Lehrer News Hour, CBS Morning News, NPR's All Things Considered. Mem. Nat. Conf. Editl. Writers (past pres.), Am. Soc. Newspaper Editors. Office: VP & Editor The Indianapolis Star 307 N Pennsylvania St Indianapolis IN 46204

RYERSON, LISA M. academic administrator; BA in English cum laude, Wells Coll., Aurora, N.Y., 1981; MS, SUNY. Asst. dir. admissions Wells Coll., Aurora, NY, 1981—84, assoc. dean of students, 1984—87, dean of students, 1991—94, v.p. to exec. v.p., 1994—95, pres., 1995—. Vice chair bd. of mng. dir. Ind. Coll. Funf of N.Y.; chair exec. bd. Pub. Leadership Edn. Network, Washington; bd. mem. Women's Coll. Coalition, Washington. Mem. exec. com. Cayuga County C. of C., Auburn, NY. Office: Wells Coll 170 Main St Aurora NY 13026

RYERSON, PAUL SOMMER, lawyer; b. Newark, Oct. 2, 1946; s. Robert Paul and Audrey Mae (Sommer) R.; m. Susan Jean Duckrow, Aug. 7, 1971 (div. Apr. 1995); children: James Sommer, Jill Carin; m. Kenswynn Black, Jan. 26, 2002. BA, Wesleyan U., 1968; JD, Columbia U., 1971. Bar: N.Y. 1972, D.C. 1972, U.S. Ct. Appeals (D.C. cir.) 1973, U.S. Dist. Ct. D.C. 1973, U.S. Supreme Ct. 1976, U.S. Ct. Appeals (5th cir.) 1979, U.S. Ct. Appeals (4th cir.) 1980. Law clk. to judge Jack B. Weinstein U.S. Dist. Ct. ea. dist. N.Y., 1971-72; assoc. Arnold & Porter, Washington, 1972-79, ptnr., 1980 89, Jones Day, Washington, 1989—. Contbr. articles to profl. publs. Mem. ABA, D.C. Bar Assn. Home: 5809 Nicholson Ln North Bethesda MD 20852-5719 Office: Jones Day 51 Louisiana Ave NW Washington DC 20001-2113 Office Phone: 202-879-3939. E-mail: psryerson@jonesday.com.

RYERSON, WILLIAM NEWTON, non profit organization executive; b. Phila., Mar. 9, 1945; s. W. Newton and Jean (Hamilton) R.; m. Leta C. Finch, Dec. 6, 1975. BA, Amherst Coll., 1967; M.Phil., Yale U., 1971. Dir. student intern program Population Inst., Washington, 1971-73, dir. youth and student div., 1973-79; dir. devel. Planned Parenthood Southeastern Pa., Phila., 1979-81; assoc. dir. Planned Parenthood No. New Eng., Burlington, Vt., 1981-86; pres. Ryerson & Assocs., fundraising counsel, Shelburne, Vt., 1986-2000; exec. v.p. Population Comm. Internat., NYC, 1986-98; pres. Population Media Ctr., Shelburne, Vt., 1998—. Co-author: Population Activist's Handbook, 1974, Communicating Sustainability, 2000, Entertainment-Education and Social Change-History, Research and Practice, 2003. NASA trainee in biology, Yale U., 1967-70. Mem.: Phi Beta Kappa, Sigma Xi (assoc.). Home: PO Box 580 Shelburne VT 05482-0580 Office: PO Box 547 Shelburne VT 05482-0547 Office Phone: 802-985-8156. E-mail: ryerson@populationmedia.org.

RYGIEL, EDWARD K. chemical engineer; BSChemE, U. Toronto. Pres., CEO MDS Capital Corp., Toronto, Canada; exec. v.p. MDS Inc. Chmn. bd. Henosol Inc., Mississauga, Ont., Canada; bd. dirs. NPS Pharm., Inc., MDS Nordion, Can. NeuroSci. Can. Partnership. Office: Henosol Inc 2585 Meadowpine Blvd Mississauga ON L5N 8H9 Canada also: MDS CapitalCorp 100 International Blvd Toronto ON M9W 6J6 Canada E-mail: info@mdscapital.com.

RYKWERT, JOSEPH, architecture and art history educator; b. Warsaw, Apr. 5, 1926; arrived in Eng., 1939; s. Szymon Mieczyslaw and Elizabeth (Melup) R.; m. Anne-Marie Sandersley, Feb. 14, 1972; 1 child from previous marriage, Simon Sebastian; 1 stepchild, Marina Joanna Engel. Student, Archtl. Assn., London, 1944-47; MA, U. Cambridge; PhD, Royal Coll. Art, London, 1970; MA (hon.), U. Pa., 1988; DSc (hon.), U. Edinburgh, 1995; D (hon.), U. Cordoba, 1998, U. Bath, Eng., 2000, U. Rome, 2004. Libr., tutor Royal Coll. Art, 1960-67; prof. art, chmn. dept. U. Essex, Colchester, Eng., 1967-81; Slade prof. fine arts U. Cambridge, 1980, reader in architecture, 1981-87; Paul Philippe Cret prof. architecture, prof. art history U. Pa., Phila., 1988-98, prof. emeritus, also chmn. PhD program in architecture. Andrew Mellon prof. Cooper Union, N.Y.C., 1977; George Lurcy prof. Columbia U., N.Y.C., 1986; commr. Venice (Italy) Biennale, 1974-77; mem. jury Parc de la Villette Competition, Paris, 1982, Wolf Found. Prize, Jerusalem, 1983; trustee Cubitt Trust, London, 1986-98; sr. scholar Getty Ctr. for History Art and Humanities, 1 992, 93; co-editor catalogue, curator Alberti Exhbn., Mantua, Italy, 1994. Author: The Golden House, 1947, The Idea of a Town, 1963, 76, 88, Church Building, 1966, On Adam's House in Paradise, 1972, 82, The First Moderns, 1980, 84, The Necessity of Artifice, 1982, (with Anne-Marie Rykwert) The Brothers Adam, 1985; editl. transl.: On the Art of Building (L.B. Alberti), 1989, 91, The Dancing Column, 1996, The Seduction of Place, 2000; editor Res. jour., Peabody Mus., Cambridge, Mass., 1979—. Mem. steering com. UNESCO Conf. on Urbanism, 1989-91. Decorated Chevalier des Arts et des Lettres, Govt. of France, 1985; recipient Alfred Jurzykowski Found. award, 1990, Accademia di San Luca, 1993. Mem. Polish Acad. of Arts and Scis., Coll. Art Assn., Comite Internat. des Critiques d'Arch. (pres.), Savile Club (London). Office: U Pa Dept Architecture 210 S 34th St 207 Meyerson Hall Philadelphia PA 19104-6311 E-mail: rykwert@pobox.upenn.edu.

RYLAND, V. WALLACE, business developer; b. Alexandria, Va., July 30, 1969; s. Virgil Wallace Ryland and Ann Louise Sedberry. BA in Liberal Arts, U. Tex., 1991. Instr. English Fork Union (Va.) Mil. Acad., 1991-93; receiver/sales NCH Corp., Irving, Tex., 1994-96; account exec. Contractor's Register, Jefferson Valley, N.Y., 1996-98; pub., v.p. Marcoa Pub., Houston, 1998-2000; dir. bus. devel. blue-silicon, San Jose, Calif., 2000—. Pub., mem. Greater Houston Partnership, 1998—. Mem. Tex. Ex-Students Assn. Mem. Masons (grand lodge # 127, Marshal 1991-92), Fork Union Mil. Acad. Alumni Assn., Woodlands C. of C. (pub.), Sugar Creek Country Club, Chi Phi (alumni chmn. 1991). Republican. Avocations: writing, golf, sailing. Home: E 311 Everett Palo Alto CA 94301 Office: blue-silicon 70 Bonaventura Dr San Jose CA 95134 E-mail: vwr3@yahoo.com.

RYLAND, WALTER H. lawyer; b. Richmond, Va., Jan. 23, 1943; s. John William and Evelyn (Quillin) R.; m. Madelaine Aerni, July 10, 1976; children: Mark Vanley, Caroline Aerni. BA, Washington & Lee U., 1965, LLB, 1967. Chief dep. atty. gen. Office of the Atty. Gen. of Va., Richmond, 1978-82; ptnr. Williams, Mullen, Christian & Dobbins, Richmond, 1983—. Counselor, Va. Mus. Fine Arts, Richmond, 1983—; pres. J. Sargeant Reynolds Found., Richmond, 1990; legal adv., Southeastern Legal Found., Atlanta, Ga., 1989—. Co-editor: Racial Preferences in Government Contracting (Nat. Legal Ctr. for the Pub. Interest), 1993. Sec. bd. trustees Washington Internat. U. Va., 1989-91; bd. dirs. Coun. for Am. First Freedom, Richmond, 1988-92; pres. Theatre Va., Richmond, 1987-88; sec. Communication Disorders Found., Richmond, 1986-88; chmn. Cultural Art Ctr. at Glen Allen Found. Mem. ABA, Va. Bar Assn., Richmond Bar Assn. Office: Williams Mullen Clark & Dobbins 2 James Ctr 1021 E Cary St Richmond VA 23219-4000

RYLANDER, HENRY GRADY, JR., mechanical engineering educator; b. Pearsall, Tex., Aug. 23, 1921; married; 4 children. BS, U. Tex., 1943, MS, 1952; PhD in Mech. Engring., Ga. Inst. Tech., 1965. Design engr. Steam Div., Aviation Gas Turbine Div., Westinghouse Elec. Corp., 1943-47; from asst. to assoc. prof. mech. engring. U. Tex., Austin, 1947-68, research scientist, 1950, prof. mech. engring., 1968—, Joe J. King prof. engring., 1980—. Cons. engr. TRACOR, Inc., 1964-69; founding dir. Ctr. for Electromechanics, U. Tex., 1977-85, chmn., mech. engring. dept., 1976-86. Named Disting. Grad. Coll. Engring., U. Tex., Austin, 1989. Fellow ASME (Leonardo da Vinci award 1985); mem. ASME. Office: U Tex Coll Engring C2200 Austin TX 78712 E-mail: hgr@mail.utexas.edu.

RYLANDER, ROBERT ALLAN, financial service executive; b. Bremerton, Wash., Apr. 8, 1947; s. Richard Algot and Marian Ethelyn (Peterson) R.; children: Kate, Erik, Meagan. BA in Fin., U. Wash., 1969; postgrad., U. Alaska, 1972-74. Controller Alaska USA Fed. Credit Union, Anchorage, 1974-77, mgr. ops., 1977-80, asst. gen. mgr., 1980-83, exec. v.p., COO, 1983—; pres., CEO Alaska Option Svcs. Corp., 1983—97. Chmn. Alaska USA Mortgage, Inc., Anchorage, 1992—, Alaska Option Svcs. Corp., Anchorage, 1997—, Alaska USA Trust Co., Anchorage, 1997—. Served to capt. USAF, 1969-74. Avocations: audio electronics, music, home theater. Home: PO Box 220587 Anchorage AK 99522-0587 Office: Alaska USA Fed Credit Union PO Box 196613 Anchorage AK 99519-6613

RYLANT, CYNTHIA, author; b. Hopewell, Va., June 6, 1954; d. John Tune and Leatrel (Rylant) Smith; 1 child, Nathaniel. BA, U. Charleston, 1975; MA, Marshall U., 1976; MLS, Kent State U., 1981. English instr. Marshall U., Huntington, W.Va., 1979-80, U. Akron, Ohio, 1983-84; children's libr. Akron (Ohio) Pub. Libr., 1983. Part-time lectr. Northeast Ohio Univs. Coll. Medicine, Rootstown, Ohio, 1991—. Author: (picture books) When I Was Young in the Mountains, 1982 (Caldecott Honor book, 1983, English Speaking Union Book-Across-the-Sea Amb. of Honor award, 1984, Am. Book award nom., 1983), Miss Maggie, 1983, This Year's Garden, 1984, Waiting to Waltz: A Childhood (verse), 1984 (Nat. Coun. for Social Studies Best Book, 1984), A Blue-Eyed Daisy (in U.K. as Some Year for Ellie), 1985 (Children's Book of Yr., Child Study Assn. Am., 1985), The Relatives Came, 1985 (Horn Book Honor book, 1985, Children's Book of Yr., Child Study Assn. Am., 1985, Caldecott Honor book, 1986), Every Living Thing (stories), 1985, A Fine White Dust, 1986 (Newbery Honor Book, 1987), Night in the Country, 1986, Birthday Presents, 1987, Children of Christmas (in U.K. as Silver Packages and Other Stories), 1987, All I See, 1988, A Kindness, 1989, Mr. Grigg's Work, 1989, Soda Jerk (verse)1990, A Couple of Kooks (stories), 1990, Appalachia: The Voices of Sleeping Birds, 1991 (Boston Globe/Horn Book Honor book for nonfiction, 1991), Best Wishes, 1992, An Angel for Solomon Singer, 1992, Missing May, 1992 (Newbery Medal, 1992), The Dreamer, 1993, I Had Seen Castles, 1993, The Everyday Books, 1993, The Old Lady Who Named Things, 1996, Whales, 1996, Bookshop Dog, 1996, Blue Hill Meadows, 1997, Poppleton, 1997, Poppleton and Friends, 1997, Cat Heaven, 1997, Blue Hill Meadows and the Much-Loved Dog, 1997, Scarecrow, 1998, Bear Day, 1998, Tulip Sees America, 1998, Poppleton Everyday, 1998, Poppleton Forever, 1998, Bird House, 1998, Islander, 1998, Bless Us All, 1998, Cobble Street Cousins in Aunt Lucy's Kitchen, 1998, Bunny Bungalow, 1999, Cookie-Store Cat, 1999, Poppleton in Spring, 1999, Cobble Street Cousins: Some Good News, 1999, Cobble Street Cousins: Special Gifts, 1999, Poppleton in Fall, 1999, Give Me Grace, 1999, Heavenly Village, 1999, Poppleton Through and Through, 2000, Wonderful Happens, 2000, Thimbleberry Stories, 2000, Let's Go Home, 2000, Little Whistle, 2000, In November, 2000, Poppleton Has Fun, 2000, Little Whistle's Dinner Party, 2001, Little Whistle's Medicine, 2001, Ticky-Tacky Doll, 2001, The Great Gracie Chase, 2001, Poppleton in Winter, 2001, Summer Party, 2001, Good Morning Sweetie Pie and Other Poems for Little Children, 2002, Old Town in the Green Groves, 2002, Wedding Flowers, 2002, (Mr. Putter and Tabby series) Walk the Dog, 1994, Bake the Cake, 1994, Pour the Tea, 1994, Pick the Pears, 1995, Fly the Plane, 1997, Row the Boat, 1997, Toot the Horn, 1998, Take the Train, 1998, Paint the Porch, 2000, Feed the Fish, 2001, (The High-Rise Private Eyes series) Case of the Climbing Cat, 2000, Case of the Missing Monkey, 2000, The Case of the Puzzling Possum, 2001, The Case of the Troublesome Turtle, 2001, (Henry and Mudge series) Henry and Mudge, 1987, Henry and Mudge in Puddle Trouble, 1990, Henry and Mudge Take the Big Test, 1991, Henry and Mudge in the Green Time, 1992, Henry and Mudge under the Yellow Moon, 1992, Henry and Mudge in the Sparkle Days, 1993, Henry and Mudge and the Forever Sea, 1993, Henry and Mudge Get the Cold Shivers, 1993, Henry and Mudge and the Happy Cat, 1994, Henry and Mudge and the Bedtime Thumps, 1991, Henry and Mudge and the Long Weekend, 1992, Henry and Mudge and the Wild Wind, 1992, Henry and Mudge and the Careful Cousin, 1994, Henry and Mudge and the Best Day of All, 1995, Henry and Mudge in the Family Trees, 1997, Henry and Mudge and the Sneaky Crackers, 1998, Henry and Mudge and the Starry Night, 1998, Henry and Mudge and Annie's Good Move, 1998, Henry and Mudge and the Snowman Plan, 1999, Henry and Mudge and Annie's Perfect Pet, 1999, Henry and Mudge and the Funny Lunch, 1999, Henry and Mudge and the Tall Tree House, 1999, Henry and Mudge and Mrs. Hopper's House, 1999, Henry and Mudge and the Great Grandpas, 1999, Henry and Mudge and a Very Special Merry Christmas, 1999, Henry and Mudge and the Wild Goose Chase, 1999, Henry and Mudge and the Big Sleepover, 1999, Henry and Mudge and the Tumbling Trip, 1999, Henry's Puppy Mudge Has a Snack, 2001, Henry's Puppy Mudge Takes aBath, 2001. Office: Simon & Schuster Children's 4th Floor 1230 Ave of The Americas New York NY 10020*

RYLES, GERALD FAY, private investor, business executive; b. Walla Walla, Wash., Apr. 3, 1936; s. L. F. and Janie Geraldine (Bassett) R.; m. Ann Jane Birkenmeyer, June 12, 1959; children— Grant, Mark, Kelly. BA, U. Wash., 1958; MBA, Harvard U., 1962. With Gen. Foods Corp., White Plains, NY, 1962—66, Purex Corp., Ltd., Lakewood, Calif., 1966-68; cons. McKinsey & Co., Inc., Los Angeles, 1968-71; with Fibreboard Corp., San Francisco, 1971-79, v.p., 1973-75, group v.p., 1975-79; with Consol. Fibres, Inc., San Francisco, 1979-88, exec. v.p., 1979-81, pres., dir., 1981-86, chief exec. officer, 1986-88; cons. Orinda, Calif., 1988-90; with Interchecks Inc., 1990-92, pres., CEO, 1990-92; bus. exec., pvt. investor, 1992-94; chmn. bd., CEO Microserv, Inc., Kirkland, Wash., 1994—2001, chmn. bd., 2001—03. Bd. dirs. Halifax Corp., Giant Campus, Inc. Mem. adv. com. Ctr. for Tech. and Entrepreneurship, U. Wash. Bus. Sch. Served to capt. U.S. Army, 1958-66. Mem.: Harvard Bus. Sch. Assn., U. Wash. Alumni Assn. Republican. Episcopalian. Home: 127 3rd Ave Apt 301 Kirkland WA 98033-6177 Personal E-mail: g.ryles@verizon.net.

RYMAN, ROBERT TRACY, artist; b. Nashville, May 30, 1930; s. William Tracy and Nora (Boston) R.; m. Lucy Lippard, 1961 (div. 1966); children: Ethan, Ryman; m. Merrill Wagner, Jan. 31, 1969; children: William Tracy, George Corydon. Exhibited one man shows: Paul Bianchini Gallery, 1967, Solomon R. Guggenheim Mus., N.Y.C., 1972, Kunsthalle, Basel, Switzerland, 1975, Palais des Beaus-Arts, Brussels, 1974, Stedelijk Mus., Amsterdam, Netherlands, 1974, Whitechapel Gallery, London, 1977, Centre Pompidou, Paris, 1981, Sidney Janis Gallery, N.Y.C., 1981, Kunsthalle, Dusseldorf, Germay, 1982, Bonnier Gallery, N.Y.C., 1983, Daniel Weinberg Gallery, L.A., 1983, Galerie Maeght LeLong, Paris, 1984, Rhona Hoffman Gallery, Chgo., 1985, Leo Castelli Gallery, N.Y.C., 1986, Galerie Maeght LeLong, N.Y.C., 1986, Pace Gallery, N.Y.C., 1990, DIA Art Found., N.Y.C., 1988-89, Konrad Fischer Gallery, Dusseldorf, Fed. Republic Germany, 1987, Pace Gallery, N.Y., Tate Gallery, London, MMA, N.Y., San Francisco Mus. Modern Art, Walker Arts Ctr., Mpls.; group shows: Biennal Whitney Mus. Am. Art, N.Y.C., 1977, Stedelijk Mus., Amsterdam, 1978, Art of the 70's, Venice Bennale, Italy, 1980, Haus der Kunst, Munich, 1981, Stedelijk Mus., Amsterdam, 1983, Whitney Mus. Am. Art, 1983, Skowhegan Sch. of Painting and Sculpture Medal, 1987, Whitney Biennal Exhbn, 1987; Mus. Modern Art, N.Y.C., 1985, Carnegie International, 1985; represented permanent collections: Mus. Modern Art, N.Y.C., Milw. Art Center, Stedelijk Mus., Amsterdam, Whitney Mus. Am. Art, pvt. collections; apptd. commr. City of N.Y. Art Commn. Mem. AAAL, Am. Acad. Arts and Scis., Mcpl. Art Soc. N.Y. (bd. dirs. 1991—). Home: 17 W 16th St New York NY 10011-6301 Studio: 637 Greenwich St New York NY 10014-3306 *There is never a question of what to paint, but only how to paint. The "how" of painting is the image, the end product.*

RYMAR, JULIAN W. manufacturing executive, director; b. Grand Rapids, Mich., June 29, 1919; m. Margaret Macon Van Brunt, Dec. 11, 1954; children: Margaret Gibson, Gracen Macon, Ann Mackall. Student, Grand Rapids Jr. Coll., 1937—39, U. Mich., 1939—41, Wayne State U., 1948—52, Rockhurst Coll., 1952—53, Naval War Coll., 1954—58. Entered as aviation cadet USN, 1942; comdg. officer Naval Air Res. Squadron, 1957—60, staff air comdr., 1960—64; advanced through grades to capt. USN, 1964; chmn. bd., CEO, dir. Grace Co., Belton, Mo., 1955—90; chmn. bd. dirs. Shock & Vibration Rsch. Inc., 1956—66; chmn. bd., CEO Bedtime Story Fashions. Bd. dirs. Am. Bank & Trust. Mem. Kans. City Hist. Soc.; adv. bd. dirs. St. Joseph Hosp.; trustee Missouri Valley Coll., 1969—74; pres. Ryman Found.; active Sch. Am. Rsch., Inst. Am. Arts, Mus. N.Mex. Found., Spanish Colonial Art Soc.; mem. Episcopal Ch.; bd. dirs. Bros. of Mercy, St. Luke's Hosp. Mem.: Soc. Profl. Journalists, Friends of Art (exec. bd. 1971—74, pres., chmn. bd. govs.), Spanish Colonial Arts Soc., Mus. Indian Arts and Culture, Mus. Internat. Folk Art, Mus. Fine Arts, Mus. N.Mex. Found., Santa Fe Symphony, Soc. Fellows of Nelson Gallery Found. (exec. bd. 1972—77), Mil. Order World Wars, Navy League U.S. (pres. 1959—60, dir. 1960—70), Rockhill Homes Assn. (v.p.), Sch. Am. Rsch., Inst. Am. Indian Art, Quiet Birdman Club, Arts Club of Washington, Press Club, Univ. Mich. Club, Sigma Delta Chi. Episcopalian.

RYMARCSUK, JIM ARTHUR, aerospace industry executive, consultant; b. Chgo., July 2, 1964; s. Louis Arthur and Hazel Annabelle (Oas) R.; m. Jennifer Ann Field, Aug. 26, 1989. BSME, Stanford U., 1986, MS in Astronautical Engring., 1987; MBA in Mgmt., Golden Gate U., 1989; MS in Tech. and Policy, MIT, 1993; grad., Internat. Space U., Toulouse, France, 1992. Rsch. technician Stanford Linear Accelerator Ctr., 1983-84; engring. technician U.S. Army Corps of Engrs., Warsaw, Mo., 1983-85; well test engr. Schlumberger Internat., Aberdeen, Scotland, 1985; rsch. fellow NASA-Lewis Rsch. Ctr., Cleve., 1986; internat. advisor Russian Space Enterprises MIT/Moscow Aviation Inst., Cambridge, MAss., 1992-93; engagement mgr., cons. McKinsey & Co., Washington, 1993-97; dir. mktg. and investment planning Lockheed Martin Corp., Bethesda, Md., 1997—. Advisor, cons. Nat. Ctr. for Therapeutic Riding, Washington, 1994-96; organizer, presenter NASAs Space Grant Program, Cambridge, 1991-92; pro bono cons. MIT Aerospace Engring. Dept., Cambridge, 1996. Contbr. articles to profl. jours. 1st lt. USAF, 1987-90. Fellow Smithsonian Inst., 1996—, NSF, 1990-93, Stanford U., 1987; nat. finalist White House Fellows, 1997. Mem. Stanford Engring. Assn. (bd. dirs. 1984-85), Nat. Geog. Soc., Nat. Trust for Hist. Preservation. Avocations: english riding, sailing, hiking, international travel. Office: Lockheed Martin Corp 6801 Rockledge Dr Bethesda MD 20817-1877

RYMER, ILONA SUTO, artist, retired art educator; b. N.Y.C., Dec. 1, 1921; d. Alexander and Elizabeth (Komaromy) Suto; m. Robert Hamilton Rymer, Mar. 27, 1944 (dec. Dec. 1999); children: Thomas Parker, Shelley Ilona. BA, Long Beach State U., 1953, MA, 1954. Tchr., cons. Long Beach (Calif.) Sch. Dist., 1953-56; tchr. Orange (Calif.) Sch. Dist., 1956-58; tchr., cons. Brea (Calif.)-Olinda Sch. Dist., 1958-80; ind. artist, designer Graphic Ho. Studio, Santa Ynez, Calif., 1980—, Stampa-Barbara, Santa Barbara, Calif., 1990—. Lectr. folk art Brea Sch. Dist., 1975—80. Author: (instrn. book) Folk Art U.S.A., 1975 (Proclamation City of Brea, 1975); art editor, feature writer, illustrator: Arabian Conneciton mag., 1985—86; needlepoint designer Backstictch Store, Solvang, Calif., 1982—83; one-woman shows include Liberty Bell Race Track, Pa., Gallery Los Olivos, Calif., 2004, exhibited in group shows at Liberty Bell Race Track, 1970—, Dennas Mus. Ctr., Northwestern Mich. Coll., 2001, Nat. Exhbn. Am. Watercolor, 2002, Adirondack's Nat. Exhbn. of Am. Watercolors, Old Forge, N.Y., 2002—, commission, Pres. Regan's portrait on his stallion, Reagran Libr., Simi Valley, Calif., Khemosabi and Ruth, 1995. Co-founder, mem. Gallery Los Olivos, pres., 1993—. Recipient 1st pl. Seminar award, Rex Brandt, 1961, Affiliate award, Laguna Art Mus., 1967, Best of Watercolor award, Orange County Fair, 1969, Bicentennial trip to France, Air France, 1975, Proclamation for Tchg., City of Brea, 1980, Theme award, Santa Barbara County Fair, 1991. Mem.: Artist Guild Santa Ynez Valley, Ctrl. Coast Art Assn., Santa Barbara ARt Assn., Calif. Gold Coast Watercolor Soc. (signature). Presbyterian. Studio: PO Box 822 Santa Ynez CA 93460-0822 Personal E-mail: ilonarymer@aol.com.

RYMER, PAMELA ANN, federal judge; b. Knoxville, Tenn., Jan. 6, 1941; AB, Vassar Coll., 1961; LLB, Stanford U., 1964; LLD (hon.), Pepperdine U., 1988. Bar: Calif. 1966, U.S. Ct. Appeals (9th cir.) 1966, U.S. Ct. Appeals (10th cir.), U.S. Supreme Ct. Dir., polit. rsch. and analysis Goldwater for President Com., 1964; v.p. Rus Walton & Assoc., Los Altos, Calif., 1965—66; assoc. Lillick McHose & Charles, L.A., 1966—75, ptnr., 1973—75, Toy and Rymer, L.A., 1975—83; judge U.S. Dist. Ct. (cen. dist.) Calif., L.A., 1983—89, U.S. Ct. Appeals (9th cir.), L.A., 1989—. Faculty The Nat. Jud. Coll., 1986-88; mem. com. summer ednl. programs Fed. Jud. Ctr., 1987-88, mem. com. appellate judge edn., 1996-99; chair exec. com. 9th Cir. Jud. Conf., 1990; mem. com. criminal law Jud. Conf. U.S., 1988-93, Ad Hoc com. gender-based violence, 1991-94, fed.-state jurisdiction com., 1993-96; mem. commn. on structural alternatives Fed. Cts. Appeals, 1997-98. Mem. editorial bd. The Judges' jour., 1989-91; contbr. articles to profl. jours. and newsletters. Mem. Calif. Postsecondary Edn. Commn., 1974-84, chmn., 1980-84; mem. L.A. Olympic Citizens Adv. Commn.; bd. visitors Stanford U. Law Sch., 1986-99, trustee, 1991-2001, chair, 1993-96, exec. com., chmn. bd. trustees com. acad. policy, planning and mgmt. and its ad. hoc. com. athletics., chmn. bd. visitors Sch. Law, 1987—; bd. visitors Pepperdine U. Law Sch., 1987—; mem. Edn. Commn. of States Task Force on State Policy and Ind. Higher Edn., 1987-89, Carnegie Commn. Task Force Sci. and Tech. Jud. and Regulatory Decision-making, 1990-93, Commn. Substance Abuse Coll. and Univ. Campuses, 1992-94, commn. substance abuse high schs. Ctr. Addiction and Substance Abube Columbia U.; bd. dirs. Constnl. Rights Found., 1985-97, Pacific Coun. Internat. Policy, 1995—, Calif. Higher Edn. Policy Ctr., 1992-97; Jud. Conf. U.S. Com. Fed.-State Jurisdiction, 1993, Com. Criminal Law, 1988-93, ad hoc com. gender based violence, 1991-94; chair exec. com. 9th cir. jud. conf., 1990-94. Recipient Outstanding Trial Jurist award L.A. County Bar Assn., 1988; named David T. Lewis Disting. Jurist-in-Residence U. Utah, 1992. Mem. ABA (task force on civil justice reform 1991-93, mem. coord. com. agenda civil justice reform in Am. 1991), State Bar Calif. (antitrust and trade regulation sect., exec. com. 1990-92), L.A. County Bar Assn. (chmn. antitrust sect. 1981-82, mem. editl. bd. The Judges Jour. 1989-91, mem. com. professionalism 1988—, numerous other coms.), Assn. of Bus. Trial Lawyers (bd. govs. 1990-92), Stanford Alumni Assn., Stanford Law Soc. Soc. Calif., Vassar Club So. Calif. (past pres.). Office: US Ct Appeals 9th Cir US Court of Appeals Bldg 125 S Grand Ave Rm 600 Pasadena CA 91105-1621

RYN, CLAES GÖSTA, political science educator, author, research institute administrator; b. Norrköping, Sweden, June 12, 1943; permanent resident of U.S., 1979, naturalized, 2002; s. Gösta Karl and Cecilia Edit (Blom) R.; m. Marianne Carin Tedhagen, Aug. 30, 1969; children: Charlotte, Viveka, Elisabet. Fil.kand. (MA), Uppsala (Sweden) U., 1967, postgrad., 1969—71, Syracuse U., 1968—69; PhD, La. State U., 1974. Asst. prof. politics Cath. U. Am., Washington, 1974-78, assoc. prof. politics, 1978-82, prof. politics, 1982—, asst. dean Sch. Arts and Scis., 1977-79, chmn. dept. politics, 1979-85. Adj. prof. govt. Georgetown U., 2002—; vis. assoc. prof. U. Va., Charlottesville, 1981; co-founder, chmn. Nat. Humanities Inst., Washington, 1984—; referee, evaluator NEH, Dept. Edn., USIA, pubs., jours., others; dir. various confs. and lecture series; mem. Richard M. Weaver fellowship selection com., 1980—; faculty sponsor Earhart Found., 1989—; awards com. Ingersoll Prizes, 1990; mem. Salvatori doctoral fellowship selection com. Intercollegiate Studies Inst., 1990—; lectr. series Peking U., May 2000; appearances on TV and radio. Author: (with Bertil Häggman) Nykonservatismen i USA, 1971, Democracy and the Ethical Life, 1978, 2d rev. edit., 1990, Will, Imagination

and Reason, 1986, 2d rev. edit., 1997, Individualism och gemenskap, 1986, The New Jacobinism, 1991, Unity Through Diversity (in Chinese), 2001, A Common Human Ground, 2003, America the Virtuous, 2003; editor: Humanitas, 1992—; co-editor (with George Panichas), author (with others): Irving Babbitt in Our Time, 1986; editor, author introduction for other volumes; contbr. articles to profl. jours.; mem. editl. bd. Modern Age, 1981—, Marknadsekonomisk Tidskrift, Sweden, 1986-92, This World, 1992—; editl. columnist Svenska Dagbladet, Sweden, 1996—. Mem. vestry St. Francis Episcopal Ch., Potomac, Md., 1986-88. Served with Swedish Army, Royal Life Company I 4 Regt., 1963, Signal Corps, 1967-68. Rsch. fellow various orgns., including Earhart Found., 1980-81, 87-88, Wilbur Found., 1980-81, 90, 93-94; Disting. Fgn. scholar Peking U., 2000; recipient award King of Sweden, 1983, Will Herberg award Disting. Faculty Svc. Intercollegiate Studies Inst., 2003; named Outstanding Grad. Prof., Cath. U. Am., 1992. Mem. Phila. Soc. (trustee 1999, 2d v.p. 2000-01, pres. 2001-02). Episcopalian. Home: 10008 Crestleigh Ln Potomac MD 20854-1820 Office: Cath Univ Am Dept Politics Washington DC 20064-0001

RYNEARSON, W. JOHN, foundation administrator; b. Grosse Point, Mich., Oct. 10, 1948; s. William J. and Anna Lee (Hutto) R.; m. Justine M. Pointer, Aug. 28, 1971; children: Jill, Amy, Julie. Cert. in French, Sorbonne U., Paris, 1967; BA in Mktg./Econs., Jacksonville U., 1970, MAT, 1973. Instr. Duval County Schs., Jacksonville, Fla., 1970-73, Fla. Jr. Coll., Jacksonville, 1973-74; territory mgr. Burroughs Corp., Jacksonville, 1974-76; Mideast, Far East sales administr. Coleman Co., Wichita, Kans., 1976-77, Asia sales mgr., 1977-79, Asia, Europe mktg. mgr., 1979-82; v.p. mktg. O'Brien Co. divsn. Coleman Co., Seattle, 1982-84; pres., gen. mgr. Knight Internat., Seattle, 1984-85; CEO, exec. v.p., found. sec., bd. dirs. Civitan Internat., Birmingham, Ala., 1985—. Com. chmn. Shoreline Community Coll. Internat. Studies, Seattle, 1984-85. Contbr. numerous articles to profl. jours. Sunday sch. tchr., dir. youth program Emmanual Bapt. Ch., Jacksonville, 1975-76; bd. dirs., missions bd. Faith Chapel, Wichita, 1976-82, bd. mgr., 1976-82, Redmond (Wash.) Assembly of God, 1982-85. Mem. Am. Soc. Assn. Execs. (cert. assn. exec. 1991), Am. Mktg. Assn., Civitan. Republican. Avocations: sailing, skiing, car restoration. Office: Civitan Internat PO Box 130744 Birmingham AL 35213-0744 E-mail: rynearson@juno.com.

RYNESKA, JOHN JOSEPH, military career officer; b. Lebanon, Tenn., Sept. 13, 1946; m. Judith Ailene Moore; children: Jennifer, Kristine, Ashley, Kimberly, John. BBA, U.S. Mil. Acad., 1968; MA in Bus. Adminstrn., Webster U., 1979; grad., Command and Gen. Staff Coll., Nat. War Coll., 1979. Commd. 2nd lt. U.S. Army, 1988, advanced through grades to maj. gen., 1997, various positions, G3 exercise officer So. European Task Force, with, 1975-78, tactics instr., field artillery br. rep. West Point, N.Y., 1979-82, bn. S3, divsn. asst. fire support coord. 82d Airborne Divsn. Ft. Bragg, N.C., 1982, bn. comdr. 2d Bn. (Airborne), 319th Field Artillery, 1985-88, asst. dep. dir. ops., J3 Joint Staff, 1988-90, comdr. 7th Inf. Divsn. (Light) Artillery Ft. Ord, Calif., 1990, comdr. Battle Command Tng. Program Ft. Leavenworth, Kans., 1992-94, comdr. XVIII Airborne Corps Artillery Ft. Bragg, N.C., 1994, dep. comdr. JTF 190; asst. chief of staff, C3/J3/G3 Combined Forces Command U.S. Forces Korea/Eighth U.S. Army, 1996; dep. commdg. gen. XVIII Airborne Corps and Ft. Bragg U.S. Army, 1998—. Decorated Def. Disting. Svc. medal, Silver Star, Legion of Merit with oak leaf cluster, Bronze Star with two oak leaf clusters, Def. Meritorious Svc. medal with oak leaf cluster, Meritorious Svc. medal with oak leaf cluster, 23 Air medals. Avocation: golf. Office: Dep Command Gen Xviii Airborne Corps Fort Bragg NC 28310-0001

RYNKIEWICZ, STEPHEN MICHAEL, journalist; b. Sheboygan, Wis., Oct. 20, 1955; s. Walter Paul and Ruth Catherine (Van Hercke) R.; m. Brenda Gail Russell, Sept. 27, 1986. BA, U. Wis., 1976. Various staff assignments Chgo. Sun-Times, 1979-97, real estate editor, 1990-97; Internet prodr. Chgo. Tribune, 1997—. Pres. Ill. Freedom of Info. Coun., 1991-93; mem. profl. faculty Columbia Coll., Chgo., 1998. Pres. Chgo. Headline Club, 1991-92, treas., 2001-02; chmn. Peter Lisagor Awards for Exemplary Journalism, 2002—. Recipient Online Journalism award for pub. svc., 2002. Mem. Soc. Profl. Journalists (regional dir. 1992-95, sec. treas. 1995-96, membership chair 1997-98, diversity chair 1996-97), Nat. Soc. Real Estate Editors (bd. dirs. 1999-2000), Sigma Delta Chi Found. (bd. dirs. 1995-96). Office: Ste 400 435 N Michigan Ave Chicago IL 60611-4001

RYNN, NATHAN, physics educator, consultant; b. N.Y.C., Dec. 2, 1923; s. Meyer and Rose (Wolkerwiczer) Rynkowsky; m. Glenda Brown, June 24, 1989; children by previous marriage: Jonathan, Margaret, David. BSEE, CCNY, 1944; MS, U. Ill., 1947; PhD, Stanford U., 1956. Rsch. engr. RCA Labs., Princeton, N.J., 1947-52; rsch. asst. Stanford U., Palo Alto, Calif., 1952-56, rsch. assoc., 1958; mem. tech. staff Ramo-Woolridge, L.A., 1956-57; supr. Huggins Labs., Menlo Park, Calif., 1957-58; rsch. staff physicist Princeton U., 1958-65; prof. physics U. Calif.-Irvine, 1965-94, prof. physics emeritus, rsch. prof. physics, 1994—. Vis. prof. Ecole Polytechnique Fed. of Lausanne, Switzerland, 1984-90, Ecole Polytechnique, Paris, and other European univs. and labs., 1973-80; indsl. sci. advisor/cons., 1964—; com. mem. Plasma Sci. Com. Nat. Rsch. Coun.; founder and leader plasma physics rsch. facility (the Q-Machine). Contbr. articles and revs. to profl. jours. With USN, 1944-46. Grantee NSF, U.S. Dept. Energy, Air Force Geophys. Lab.; Fulbright sr. fellow, 1978. Fellow Am. Phys. Soc., IEEE, AAAS; Sigma Xi. Office: U Calif Dept Physics & Astronomy Irvine CA 92697-4575 Office Phone: 949-824-5944. E-mail: nrynn@uci.edu.

RYPSTRA, ANN, zoology educator; PhD, Pa. State U., 1982. Prof. zoology Miami U., Oxford, Ohio; also dir. Ecology Rsch. Ctr., Oxford, Ohio. Reviewer NSF. Contbr. articles to sci. jours., including Animal Behaviour, Jour. Arachnology, Oikos. Rsch. grantee NSF. Office: Miami U Dept Zoology Oxford OH 45056

RYSER, HUGUES JEAN-PAUL, pharmacologist, educator, cell biologist; b. Chaux-de-Fonds, Switzerland, June 11, 1926; arrived in U.S., 1958, naturalized, 1972; s. Ernest Jacob and Marthe Alice (Zimmermann) Ryser; m. Carol Leigh Pierson, June 10, 1961; children: Marc Alain, Jeannine, Eve. MD, U. Berne, Switzerland, 1953, Dr. Med., 1955. Instr. pharmacology Harvard U. Med. Sch., Boston, 1960-62, assoc. in pharmacology, 1962-64, asst. prof. pharmacology, 1964-69; assoc. prof. cell biology and pharmacology U. Md. Med. Sch., Balt., 1969-70, prof., 1970-72; prof. pathology and pharmacology Sch. Medicine, Boston U., 1972—2003, prof. biochemistry, 1981—2003; prof. pub. health Sch. Pub. Health, Boston U., 1980—2003, prof. emeritus, 2003—, 2003—. Contbr. articles to profl. jours. Bd. dirs. Am. Cancer Soc., Mass., 1983—97. Recipient Lederle Med. Faculty award, 1964—67, Rsch. Career Devel. award, Nat. Cancer Inst., 1968—69, St. George medal, Am. Cancer Soc., 1996; grantee, Nat. Cancer Inst., 1972—97; NIH Rsch. grantee, 1961—69, 1997—2000, Instnl. Rsch. grantee, Am. Cancer Soc., 1975—2000, Pediat. AIDS Found. grantee, 1997—99. Fellow: AAAS; mem.: Am. Soc. Biochemical Molecular Biology, Am. Soc. Exptl. Pharmacology and Therapeutics, Am. Soc. Cell Biology, Am. Assn. Cancer Rsch. Home: 503 Annursnac Hill Rd Concord MA 01742-5414 Office: Boston U 715 Albany St Boston MA 02118-2526 Office Phone: 617-638-4503. Business E-Mail: hryser@bu.edu. *My purpose as an educator is to engage in the creative process of making important knowledge exciting. As a scientist, I am driven by curiosity and derive pleasure from being at the cutting edge of a field, however narrow it may be.*

RYSKAMP, BRUCE E. publishing executive; b. Grand Rapids, Mich., 1941; AB, Calvin Coll., 1962; MBA, Mich. State U., 1964. With R. H. Donnelly Corp., 1964-82; with Zondervan Pub. House Zondervan Corp., Grand Rapids, 1983—, v.p. book and bible pub. Zondervan Pub. House, 1986-93, pres., CEO, 1993—. Office: Zondervan Pub House 5300 Patterson Ave SE Grand Rapids MI 49512-9512

RYSKAMP, CHARLES ANDREW, museum executive, educator; b. East Grand Rapids, Mich., Oct. 21, 1928; s. Henry Jacob and Flora (DeGraaf) R. AB, Calvin Coll., 1950; MA, Yale U., 1951, PhD, 1956; postgrad., Pembroke Coll., Cambridge U., 1953-54; Litt.D., Trinity Coll., Hartford, 1975; L.H.D., Union Coll., 1977. Nathan Hale fellow Yale U., 1954-55; instr. English Princeton U., 1955-59, asst. prof., 1959-63, assoc. prof., 1963-69; curator English and Am. lit. Univ. Library, 1967-69, prof., 1969—. Procter & Gamble faculty fellow, 1958-59; jr. fellow Council of Humanities, 1960-61, John E. Annan preceptor, 1961-64; dir. Pierpont Morgan Library, N.Y.C., 1969-87, dir. emeritus, fellow (hon.), 1997—; dir. Frick Collection, N.Y.C., 1987-97, dir. emeritus, fellow (hon.), 1997—; dir. vis. Inst. Advanced Study, Princeton, 1997-99; exhbn. of drawings, Pierpont Morgan Libr., 2001; mem. adv. bd. Skowhegan Sch. Painting and Sculpture, Pvt. Papers of James Boswell, Yale U.; vis. com. dept. drawings Pierpont Morgan Libr.; bd. adv. Princeton U. Art Mus. Author: William Cowper of the Inner Temple, Esq, 1959, William Blake, Engraver, 1969; editor: (with F.A. Pottle) Boswell: The Ominous Years, 1963, The Cast-Away, 1963, Wilde and the Nineties, 1966, William Blake: The Pickering Manuscript, 1972, (with J. King) The Letters and Prose Writings of William Cowper, vol. I, 1979, vol. II, 1981, vol. III, 1982, Vol. IV, 1984, Vol. V, 1986, (with R. Wendorf) The Works of William Collins, 1979, (with J. Baird) The Poetical Works of William Cowper, vol. I, 1980, vols. II-III, 1995, (with J. King) William Cowper: Selected Letters, 1989, Report to the Fellows of the Pierpont Morgan Library, vols. 16-21, 1969-89, Charles Ryskamp and Friends, 1999, (with Scott Westrem) The Works of John Chalkhill, 1999, Of Cabbages and Kings, 2004. Trustee, mem. exec. com. Mus. Broadcasting, 1977-87; trustee John Simon Guggenheim Meml. Found., Libr. of Am., Amon Carter Mus., trustee emeritus; past mem. vis. com. dept. paintings conservation Met. Mus. Art; patron William Blake Trust; mem. bd. mgrs. Lewis Walpole Libr., Yale U.; bd. dirs., v.p. Gerard B. Lambert Found.; past v.p. Frederick R. Koch Found.; mem. Venetian Heritage. Decorated Order St. John of Jerusalem, comdr. Order Orange Nassau, The Netherlands, officer Order Leopold II, Belgium, comdr. Order of Falcon, Iceland; recipient Peter Stuyvesant award Dutch Am. West-India Co., 1987, Gold medal Holland Soc., 1991. Mem. Am. Acad. Arts and Scis., Am. Philos. Soc., Museums Coun. N.Y.C. (past v.p.), Keats-Shelley Assn. Am. (past v.p.), Master Drawings Assn. (past pres.), Met. Opera Assn. (bd. advisors), Drawing Soc. (nat. com.), Am. Assocs. Royal Nat. Theatre, Bibliog. Soc. Am., Acad. Am. Poets, Am. Antiquarian Soc., Assn. Art Mus. Dirs. (past pres.), N.Y. Geneal. and Biog. Soc. (spl. corr.), Neuropathy Assn. (nat. adv. coun.), Cowper Soc., Assn. Internationale de Bibliophilie (com. of Honor), Found. French Mus. (adv. bd.), Wordsworth Rydel Mount Trust, Grolier Club, Century Assn., Lotos Club, Knickerbocker Club, Elizabethan Club (New Haven), Roxburghe Club (London).

RYSKAMP, KENNETH LEE, federal judge; b. 1932; m. Karyl Sonja Ryskamp; 1 child, Cara Leigh. AB, Calvin Coll., 1954; JD, U. Miami, 1956. Bar: Fla. 1956, Mich. 1957, U.S. Supreme Ct. 1970. Law clk. to presiding judge Fla. Ct. Appeals 3d Dist., 1957-59; pvt. practice Miami, Fla., 1959-61; ptnr. Goodwin, Ryskamp, Welcher & Carrier, Miami, 1961-84; mng. ptnr. Squire, Sanders & Dempsey, Miami, 1984-86; judge U.S. Dist. Ct. (so. dist.) Fla., Miami, 1986—. Office: US Dist Ct 701 Clematis St Rm 416 West Palm Beach FL 33401-5112

RYU, KYOO-HAI LEE, physiologist; b. Seoul, Republic of Korea, Sept. 5, 1948; came to U.S., 1972; d. Hee Soon and Jung Ock Lee; m. David Tai-Hyung Ryu, May 13, 1978; children: Eugenia, Christina, John. BS, Yonsei U., Seoul, 1971; PhD, U. Minn., 1981. Postdoctoral fellow U. Minn., Mpls., 1980-81, staff scientist, 1981-82; sr. rsch. assoc. Wright State U., Dayton, Ohio, 1985-91; administr. Ohio Ctr. of Cosmetic Surgery, Bellefontaine, Ohio, 1991—. Home: 15 Bexley Ave Springfield OH 45503-1103 Office Phone: 937-390-3277. Personal E-mail: kryu@bizwoh.rr.com.

RYU, WOONG HWAN, electrical engineer; b. Incheon, Republic of Korea, May 24, 1971; s. Jewan Ryu and Sim Kim; m. Jung Seok Park, June 22, 1996; children: Young Jin, Erin Angella. BS, Kwangwoon U., Seoul, 1994; MSc, Korea Advanced Inst. Sci. and Tech., Daejeon, 1997, PhD, 2001. Assoc. engr. Samsung Electronics, Kyungki-Do, Republic of Korea, 1997—2001; vis. assoc. rsch. fellow Gintic Inst. Mfg. Tech., Singapore, 2000—01; analog engr., staff Intel Corp., Folsom, Calif., 2001—. Contbr. articles to profl. jours., scientific papers to profl. confs. Tchr., counselor Open Door Social Welfare Ctr., Seoul, 1990—97. Mem.: IMAPS (assoc.), IEEE (assoc.). Achievements include patents pending for voltage plane with high impedance link; patents for clock distribution module of digital system using RF interconnection (also Korean patent). Office: Intel Corp 1900 Prairie City Rd Folsom CA 95630-9599 Home: 1550 Iron Point Rd Apt 325 Folsom CA 95630-7806 Personal E-mail: whryu00@orgio.net. E-mail: woong.hwan.ryu@intel.com.

RYUN, JAMES RONALD, congressman; b. Wichita, Kans., Apr. 29, 1947; m. Anne Carol Snider; 4 children: Ned, Drew, Catharine, Heather. BA, U. Kansas. Founder, pres. Jim Ryun Sports, Inc.; mem. U.S. Ho. of Reps. from 2nd Kans. dist., 1996—, comm. on armed services, comm. on the budget, comm. on financial services. Participant Olympic Games, 1964, 68, 72. Recipient Silver medal 1500 meter run Olympic Games, 1968; held world record in the mile, 1500 meters, 800 yards. Republican. Office: 2433 Rayburn Ho Office Bldg Washington DC 20515-1602 also: 800 SW Jackson Ste 100 Topeka KS 66612-1205

RZEWNICKI, JANET C. state official; b. May 21, 1953; d. Robert Myers; m. Victor Rzewnicki, June 3, 1972. BS in Acctg. and Fin. with distinction, U. Del. CPA. Sr. acct. KPMG Peat Marwick, Wilmington, Del., 1978-80; corp. acct. internat. sect. Hercules Inc., Wilmington, 1980-81; acctg. instr. U. Del., Newark, 1980-82; pvt. practice acctg. Wilmington, 1981-82; state treas. State of Del., Dover, 1983-97; dir. investments banking Am. Fronteer, N.Y.C., 1998-99. Mem. Del. Econ. Adv. Coun. Leader People to People Del., China, 1985; treas., bd. dirs. March of Dimes, Newark, 1979—; former bd. dirs. United Way of Del., Wilmington, 1980-82; active Gov.'s Coun. on Devel. Fin., 1982-95. Mem. AICPA, Nat. Assn. State Treas. (pres. 1989), Nat. Assn. State Auditors, Contrs. and Treas. (pres. 1998), Del. Soc. CPAs, Pa. Inst. CPAs, Am. Soc. Women Accts. (bd. dirs. 1981), Beta Gamma Sigma. Republican. Office: Am Fronteer 10th Fl 30 Wall St Fl 10 New York NY 10005-2201

RZEZNIK, JOHNNY, singer, musician; b. Buffalo, N.Y., Dec. 5, 1965; Lead singer, guitarist Goo Goo Dolls, 1985—. Guitarist: (albums) First Release, 1987, Goo Goo Dolls, 1987, singer, guitarist: (albums) Jed, 1989, Hold Me Up, 1990, Superstar Car Wash, 1993, Boy Named Goo, 1995, Dizzy Up the Girl, 1998, Gutterflower, 2002, (songs) Iris, City of Angels soundtrack, 1998 (nominated for three Grammy Awards.), I'm Still Here, Treasure Planet soundtrack, 2002; guest appearance (TV series) Charmed, 2000, (albums) Birdland (with the Yardbirds), 2003; singer, composer: (TV series) Good Morning Miami, 2002. Office: Warner Brothers Records 3300 Warner Blvd Burbank CA 91505

SA, JULIE (SHIA RI XIANG), former councilwoman, former mayor, real estate developer; b. Korea, Dec. 15, 1950; came to U.S., 1973, naturalized, 1982; married. Degree in Polit. Sci., Dong-A U., Korea. Owner restaurant chain, China Doll; councilwoman City of Fullerton, Calif., 1992-94, 96-99, mayor, 1994-95; founder Golden Age World, Inc., Republic of Korea. Rep. bd. Orange County Sanitation Dists.; rep. to Tri-City Park Authority, City of Fullerton. Mem. Fullerton C. of C., Orange County Korean C. of C., Orange County Chinese C. of C.

SA, PING, statistician, educator; PhD in Stats., U. S.C., 1990. Asst. prof. stats. U. North Fla., Jacksonville, 1991—96, assoc. prof. stats., 1996—2004, prof. stats., 2004—. Contbr. articles to profl. jours.

SAAB, DEANNE KELTUM, real estate appraiser, real estate broker; b. Allentown, Pa., Jan. 27, 1945; d. James A. and Agnes G. (Hanzlik) S. BA, Cedar Crest Coll., 1966; MS, U. Calif., Santa Barbara, 1973; realtors cert., Pa. State U., 1978. Cert. appraiser Assoc. Appraisal Inst., Pa., 1991; cert. sales profl. Nat. Assn. Home Builders, 1994. Tchr. Ojai (Calif.) Unified Sch. Dist., 1966-74; pvt. practice Allentown, 1978—; owner Heritage Gardens, Allentown, 1981—; pres., treas. DeAnne & Assocs., Inc., Allentown, 1987—. Co-founder, treas. performance group Lehigh Valley Folk Music Soc., 1996. Mem. AAUW (various offices, Best State Newsletter award 1987), Nat. Assn. Realtors, Pa. Assn. Realtors, Allentown Lehigh Valley Assn. Realtors, Cedar Crest Coll. Alumnae Assn. (class rep., various offices), Lehigh Valley Guild Craftsmen (various offices). Avocations: gourd, herbal crafting, painting, folk music performance. Home and Office: 1360 Dorney Ave Allentown PA 18103-9731

SAAD, FATHY ZAKI, medical association administrator, physician; b. Cairo, Dec. 6, 1941; s. Zaki Zolta and Monira Saad; m. Samira Shenoda, Apr. 25, 1970; children: Ihab, Irene. Med. degree in surgery, medicine, Ain Shams U., Cairo, 1967; MPH, U. So. Fla., 1991. Med. dir. Daimler-Chrysler-Corp., Ind. Foundry, 1999—2001, Indsl. Med. Ctr. Lakeland, Fla., 2001—02, Rogers State Prison, Med. Coll. Ga., Reidsville, 2002—; med. practitioner Nigerian Med. Coun., Lagos, Nigeria, 1973—84; chief med. officer Ondo Gen. Hosp., Ondo State, Nigeria, 1977—84; med. fellow in occupl. and environ. medicine U. South Fla., 1998. Cert. med. rev. officer, 2001—. Named People's Dr., His Royal Majesty, The Ele Kole Ikole, Ekiti, Ondo State, Nigeria, 1983; recipient Appreciation of Svc., U. South Fla., 1993. Mem.: APHA, AMA, Am. Soc. Addiction Medicine, Am. Coll. Occupl. and Environ. Medicine. Republican. Avocation: reading. Office: Rogers State Prison Med Coll Ga 200 Rogers Rd Reidsville GA 30453

SAAD, GERMAINE H. finance educator, researcher; b. Bany-Suef, Egypt, Nov. 26, 1944; d. Hozayen and Helpis Saad; m. Ayoub Barsoum Ayoub, Feb. 5, 1972; 1 child, Mariane Ayoub; 1 child, Sameh Ragheb. PhD, Wharton Sch., U. of Pa, Philadelphia, PA, 1980, MA, 1978; MBA, Cairo U., Guiza, Egypt, 1970, B in Comm., 1964. Educator Widener U., Chester, Pa., 1986—, CUNY, New York, NY, 1982—84, Ain-Shams U., Cairo, Egypt, 1980—86, U. of Pa, Philadelphia, Pa., 1978—80, grad. asst., 1975—78; demonstrator and educator Cairo U., Guiza, Egypt, 1964—74. Editl. bd. mem. Bus. Jour., New Haven, 1991—, Jour. of Mgmt. Systems, Arlington, Va., 1989—95; cons. Ctrl. Agy. for Organizations and Administrations, Cairo, 1984—86. Contbr. more than 45 articles to profl. jours. Fund raising participant Am. Soc. for Cancer, Philadelphia, Pa., 1999—2001; vol. Abington Meml. Hosp., Abington, Pa., 1999; bd. mem. St. George Orthodox Ch., Norristown, Pa., 1997—2002. Christian-Orthodox. Avocations: painting, travel, artwork. Home: 1847 Watson Road Abington PA 19001 Office: Widener University One University Place Chester PA 19013 E-mail: germain.h.saad@widener.edu.

SAADA, ADEL SELIM, civil engineer, educator; b. Heliopolis, Egypt, Oct. 24, 1934; came to U.S., 1959, naturalized, 1965; s. Selim N. and Marie (Chahyne) S.; m. Nancy Helen Hernan, June 5, 1960; children: Christiane Mona, Richard Adel. Ingénieur des Arts et Manufactures, École Centrale, Paris, 1958; MS, U. Grenoble, France, 1959; PhD in Civil Engring, Princeton U., 1961. Registered profl. engr., Ohio. Engr. Société Dumez, Paris, 1959; research assoc. dept. civil engring. Princeton (N.J.) U., 1961-62; asst. prof. civil engring. Case Western Reserve U., Cleve., 1962-67, asso. prof., 1967-72, prof., 1973—, chmn. dept. civil engring., 1978-98, Frank H. Neff prof. civil engring., 1987. R.J. Carroll Meml. lectr. Johns Hopkins U., 1990; cons., lectr. soil testing and properties Waterways Expt. Sta. (C.E.), Vicksburg, Miss., 1974-79; cons. to various firms, 1962— . Author: Elasticity Theory and Applications, 1974, 2d edit., 1993; contbr. numerous articles on soil mechanics and foundation engring. to profl. jours. Recipient Telford Prize Instn. of Civil Engrs., U.K., 1995, Disting. Leadership award Cleve. Tech. Socs., 2001. Fellow ASCE (named Outstanding Civil Engr. of Yr. Cleve. sect. 1992); mem. Internat. Soc. Soil Mechanics, ASTM, One Two One Athletic Club. Achievements include invention of pneumatic analog computer and loading frame. Home: 3342 Braemar Rd Shaker Heights OH 44120-3332 Office: Case Western Res U Dept Civil Engring Case Sch Engring Cleveland OH 44106 Office Phone: 216-368-2427. E-mail: axs31@po.cwru.edu.

SAADA, JACQUES, legislator; b. Tunis, Tunisia, Nov. 22, 1947; married; 4 children. BA in Applied Linguistics, U. Que.; grad., McGill U. Pres. Polytrad Ltee, 1977—97; CEO B&B Translation, 1978—93; mem. Canm. Parliament, 1997—; parliamentary sec. to the solicitor gen. Can., 1998—2000; dep. govt. whip, 2001—03; min. responsible for Dem. reform, 2003—; leader Govt. House Commons, 2003—. Chair St. Lawrence Protestant Sch. Bd., 1987—90. Office: House of Commons Ottawa ON Canada K1A 0A6 also: Ste 115B 7400 Taschereau Blvd Brossard PQ Canada J4W 1M9*

SAADEH, CONSTANTINE KHALIL, internist, health facility administrator, educator; b. Beirut, Sept. 6, 1957; came to U.S., 1982; s. Khalil Constantine and Angel Janet (Iskendarian) S.; m. M. Celeste Gaylor; 2 children: Charles, McKenzie. BS in Biology-Chemistry, Am. U. Beirut, 1978, MD, 1982. Diplomate Nat. Bd. Med. Examiners, Am. Bd. Internal Medicine, Am. Bd. Allergy and Immunology, Am. Bd. Internal Medicine, Am. Bd. Rheumatology, Am. Bd. Geriatrics, Am. Acad. Pain Mgmt. Intern U. Miami, Jackson Meml. Hosp., Fla., 1982-83, resident in medicine, 1983-85; fellow in clin. immunology Baylor Coll. of Medicine, Houston, 1985-87; fellow in rheumatology U. Colo. Health Sci. Ctr., Denver, 1987-88, instr. dept. internal medicine, 1988-89; acting chief med. svc. VA Med. Ctr., Amarillo, Tex., 1989, med. svc. staff physician, 1989—; asst. prof. dept. internal medicine Tex. Tech U. Health Scis. Ctr., Amarillo, 1989-91, assoc. prof. internal medicine and pediatrics, dir., 1991—, regional chair internal medicine, dir. residency program, 1992-98, assoc. prof. dept. microbiology and immunology, 1992—, clin. prof. dept. microbiol./immun., internal med., pediats., 1998—; pvt. practice Allergy ARTS, Amarillo, Tex.; pres. Amarillo Ctr. for Clin. Rsch., 2000—. Chief medicine N.W. Tex. Hosp., Amarillo, 1999-2001; lectr. in field. Contbr. articles to profl. jours. Fellow ACP, Am. Acad. Allergy and Immunology, Am. Coll. Rheumatology; mem. AMA, So. Med. Assn. (chmn. rheumatology sect. 1996-97, sec. internal medicine sect. 1997-99, assoc. councilor 1998-99). Home: 3000 S Hughes St Amarillo TX 79109-3515 Office: 1901 Medi Park Ste 2050 Amarillo TX 79106-2109 also: Allergy ARTS Ste 2050 Amarillo TX 79106 Office Phone: 806-353-7000. Business E-Mail: aarts@allergyarts.com.

SAAK, YUNGYEE JENNIFER SU, materials engineer; d. Yingming and Yachin Su; m. Aaron Saak, Aug. 16, 2003. BS, Cornell U., Ithaca, N.Y., 1996; PhD, Northwestern U., Evanston, Ill., 2001. Materials engr. GE Global Rsch., Niskayuna, NY, 2001—. Contbr. articles to profl. jours. Fellow, Northwestern U., 1996—97, GE Faculty for the Future, 2000—01; scholar Thermal Spray Sscholar, Internat. Thermal Spray Soc., 2000—01, John McMullen Dean scholar, Cornell U., 1992—96. Mem.: ASTM, The Materials Soc. (chpt. v.p. 2002—03), Am. Ceramic Soc. Achievements include patents pending for Environmental barrier coatings for ceramic composites. Avocation: pottery/wheel throwing. Office: General Electric Global Research One Research Cir Niskayuna NY 12309 E-mail: saakj@research.ge.com.

SAAL, HOWARD MAX, clinical geneticist, pediatrician, educator; b. N.Y.C., Aug. 20, 1951; s. Josef and Ester (Morgenstern) S.; m. Cara Tina Schweitzer, May 3, 1987; 1 child, Rebecca. BS, U. Mass., Amherst, 1973, MS, 1975; MD, Wayne State U., 1979. Intern pediatrics U. Conn. Med. Ctr., 1979-80; resident pediatrics U. Conn. Health Ctr., 1980-82; fellow med. genetics U. Wash. Sch. Medicine, 1982-84; dir. cytogenetics U. Conn. Health Ctr., Farmington, 1984-87; vice chmn. med. genetics Children's Nat. Med. Ctr., Washington, 1987-93, head clin. genetics Cin., 1993—. Asst. prof. pediats. George Washington U., Washington, 1987-93, assoc. prof. pediats., 1993; assoc. prof. clin. pediats. U. Cin. Sch. Medicine, 1993—, prof. pediats., 2000—. Contbr. articles to profl. jours. Mem. med. adv. com. Nat. Neurofibromatosis Found., N.Y.C., 1987—; mem. health profl. adv. com. March of Dimes, Arlington, Va., 1991-93; bd. dirs. Capital Area March of Dimes, 1993. Tng. grantee NIH, 1979-82. Fellow Am. Acad. Pediats. (chmn. exec. com. for sect. on genetics and birth defects 1999-2003), Am. Coll. Med. Genetics; mem. Am. Soc. Human Genetics, Soc. Craniofacial Genetics (sec.-treas. 1990-96), ACGME (med. genetics residency com). Avocation: photography. Home: 3715 Monets Ln Cincinnati OH 45241-3847 Office: Cin Childrens Hosp Med Ctr 3333 Burnet Ave Cincinnati OH 45229-3026 Office Phone: 513-636-4760.

SAALFELD, FRED ERICH, science educator, researcher; b. Joplin, Mo., Apr. 9, 1935; s. Eric Arthur and Milla (Kessler) S.; m. Elizabeth Renner, Nov. 22, 1958; 1 child, Fred E. Jr. (dec.). BS cum laude, So. East Mo. State U., 1957; MS in Phys. Chemistry, Iowa State U., 1959, PhD in Phys. Chemistry, 1961. Instr. Iowa State U., Ames, 1961—62; chemist Naval Rsch. Lab, Washington, 1962—63, head mass spectrometry sect., 1963—74, head physical chm. br., 1974—76, supt. chem. divsn., 1976—82; chief scientist Office Naval Rsch., London, 1979—80, dir. rsch. Arlington, Va., 1982—87, dir., 1987—93, dep. chief naval rsch., tech. dir., 1993—98, exec. dir., tech. dir., 1998—2002; sr. fellow Potomac Inst. for Policy Studies, 2002—; disting. rsch. prof. Ctr. for Tech. and Nat. Security Policy Nat. Def. U., 2003—04. Author more than 500 publications, reports, presentations on applications of mass spectrometry to fields of combustion, laser, environ. analysis. Recipient Disting. Rank awards U.S. Pres., Washington, 1989, 96, Meritorious Rank award U.S. Pres., Washington, 1986, Robert Conrad award Sec. USN, Washington, 1988, Disting. Civilian Svc. award Sec. of Def./Dept. Def., 1999; named Fed. Exec. of Yr., Fed. Exec. Inst., Washington, 1991, named Fred E. Saalfed award for lifetime achievement in sci., Chief Naval Rsch., 2001; sr. fellow Potomac Inst. Policy Studies, 2002—. Fellow AAAS, mem. Am. Chem. Soc. (councilor 1973-89), Am. Soc. Mass Spectrometry (sec. 1970-74), Combustion Inst., Chem. Soc. Washington (pres. 1972). Achievements include provision for science base for life support systems used in enclosed environments; development of educational programs used by USN for scientist training. Office Phone: 703-887-2197. Personal E-mail: fsaalfeld@cox.net.

SAALI, STEPHEN JOSEPH, banker; b. St. Louis, May 8, 1964; s. Donald Francis and JoAnn (Connaway) S.; m. Linda Ann Nestola, Sept. 16, 1989; 1 child, Alexandra Morgan. BA, Brown U., 1986; MBA, Columbia U., 1988. Mgmt. trainee Republic Nat. Bank, N.Y.C., 1988-90; asst. treas. Republic N.Y. Corp., N.Y.C., 1990-91, asst. v.p., 1991-93, v.p., 1993-94, 1st v.p., 1994-96, sr. v.p., 1996-98, mng. dir., 1998, pres., 1998. Avocations: tennis, travel, personal fitness. Office: Republic New York Corp 452 5th Ave New York NY 10018-2706

SAAM, ROBERT HARRY, human resources specialist, consultant; b. Toledo, Mar. 7, 1947; s. Robert J. and Dorothy H. (Kinney) Saam; m. Pamela Soder, Oct. 30, 1982; children: Robert C., Cara B., Stacia J. BA, U. Toledo, 1970; MS in Ednl. Psychology, U. Wis., 1993. Investigative supr. Ohio Civil Rights Commn., Cleve., 1973-76; councillator U.S. EEO Commn., Cin., 1976-79; mgr. labor rels. Internat. Minerals and Chems., Mundelein, Ill., 1979-85; dir. human resources svcs. Rexnord, Inc., Brookfield, Wis., 1985-87; v.p., owner Thompson Cons. Ltd., Brookfield, 1987-2000; sr. v.p. Lee Hecht Harrison, Brookfield, 2000—. Contbr. articles to profl. jours. Mem.: Am. Assn. Counseling and Devel. Home: 646 N 77th St Milwaukee WI 53213-3512 Office: 17700 W Capitol Dr Brookfield WI 53045-2006 Office Phone: 262-953-2108. E-mail: Rob_Saam@LHH.com.

SAARI, DONALD GENE, mathematician, economist; b. Ironwood, Mich., Mar. 9, 1940; s. Gene August and Martha Mary (Jackson) S.; m. Lillian Joy Kalinen, June 11, 1966; children: Katri, Anneli. BS, Mich. Technol. U., 1962; PhD, Purdue U., 1967, DSc (hon.), 1989, U. Caen, France, 1998, Mich. Tech. U., 1999. Research astronomer Yale U., New Haven, 1967-68; prof. dept. math. Northwestern U., Evanston, Ill., 1968-2000, prof. econs., 1988-2000, Pancoe prof. math., 1995-2000, chmn. dept., 1981-84; prof. U. Nanjing (China), 1995; disting. prof. econ., math U. Calif., Irvine, 2000—, dir. Ctr. for Decision Analysis, dir. Inst. Math. Behavioral Sci., 2003—. Cons. Nat. Bur. Standards, Gaithersburg, Md., 1979-86, Commn. 9, Internat. Astron. Union, 1985-91; nat. com. math. Nat. Rsch. Coun., 1997-2003, chair 2001-03, math./sci. edn. bd., 2001—, Bd. Internat. Sci. Orgns., 2001-03, NRC, 2004—; bd. dirs. Inst. Math. Behavior Scis.; chair trustees Math. Sci. Rsch. Inst., 2004—. Assoc. editor Jour. Econ. Behavior and Orgn., 1988-94, Celestial Mechanics and Dynamical Astronomy. 1989-97, Econ. Theory, 1990—, Social Choice and Welfare, 1997—, Qualitative Theory of Dynamical Sys., 1999—, Positivity, 2000—. Recipient Duncan Black award, Pub. Choice Soc., 1991, Chauvenet prize Math. Assn. Am., 1995, Ford prize Math. Assn. Am., 1985, Allendorfer award Math. Assn. Am., 1999; Guggenheim fellow, 1988-89. Mem. NAS, AAAS, Am. Math. Soc. (chief editor bull. 1999—, mem. coun. 1999—), Am. Astron. Soc., Am. Acad. Arts and Scis., Soc. Indsl. and Applied Math. (editor jour. 1981-88), Econometric Soc. Office: U Calif Dept Econs Dept Math Irvine CA 92697-5100 Business E-Mail: dsaari@uci.edu.

SAAVEDRA, CHARLES JAMES, banker; b. Denver, Nov. 2, 1941; s. Charles James and Evangeline Cecilia (Aragon) S.; m. Ann Helen Taylor, 1967; children: Michael, Kevin, Sarah. BSBA, Regis U., Denver, 1963; postgrad., U. Calif., San Francisco, 1964-66. V.p. Western States Bankcard Assn., San Francisco, 1969-77; dir. info. systems World Airways, Inc., Oakland, Calif., 1977-79; v.p. computer svcs. First Nationwide Bank, San Francisco, 1979-83; sr. v.p. Wells Fargo Bank, San Francisco, 1983-92, Union Bank Calif., San Francisco, 1992—. Instr. Programming & Systems Inst., San Francisco, 1968-69; lectr. Am. Mgmt. Assn., 1984—. Pres. Richt Direction Project Contra Costa County; bd. dirs. No. Calif. Family Ctr. With USNR, 1963-64. Mem. Data Processing Mgrs. Assn. (bd. dirs., chmn. program com. 1981), Am. Nat. Stds. Inst., Am. Bankers Assn., San Francisco Jaycees, Commonwealth Club Calif., Lake Lakewood Assn., Alpha Delta Gamma. Home: 210 Lakewood Rd Walnut Creek CA 94598-4826 Office: Union Bank Calif 350 California St San Francisco CA 94104-1476 Office Phone: 925-980-0911.

SABA, SHOICHI, manufacturing executive, director; b. Tokyo, Feb. 28, 1919; s. Wataru and Sumie (Uemura) S.; m. Fujiko Saito, 1945 (dec.); children: Hiroko, Kazuhisa (dec.), Shunji. Grad., Imperial U., Tokyo, 1941. With Toshiba Corp., Tokyo, 1942-87, mng. dir., 1972-74, exec. v.p., 1974-76, sr. exec. v.p., 1976-80, pres., CEO, 1980-86, chmn., exec. officer, 1986-87, adviser to bd., 1987—; pres. Japanese Indsl. Stds. Com., 1994—2001. Dir. numerous cos.; adviser Japan Fedn. Econ. Orgns., 1994—. Chmn. nat. bd. govs. Nat. Assn. Boy Scouts of Nippon, 1994—; chmn., bd. trustees Internat. Christian U., 1998-2004. Office: Toshiba Corp 1-1 Shibaura 1-chome Minato-ku Tokyo 105-8001 Japan

SABA, WALTER PEDRO, health education communications executive; b. Lima, Peru, Apr. 29, 1955; came to U.S., 1991; s. Elias S. and Gabriela E. (Salomon) S.; m. Flor D. Giusti, Dec. 4, 1980; children: Elias G., Paulina T. Diploma in Film Studies, Conservatoire Libre de Cinema, Paris, 1977; M in Health Sci., Johns Hopkins U., 1993. Video producer Cath. U. of Peru, Lima, 1978-88; inf. coord. Nat. Program on AIDS, Lima, 1988-91; program officer Johns Hopkins U., Balt., 1993-97, sr. program officer, 1997—. Recipient Global Media award The Population Inst., Washington, 1996, Silver Apple award Nat. Ednl. Media Network, Oakland, Calif. 1996. Mem. Am. Pub. Health Assn. Office: Johns Hopkins U 111 Market Pl Ste 310 Baltimore MD 21202-7112 E-mail: wsaba@jhuccp.org.

SABADIE, FRANCISCA ALEJANDRA, lawyer, interpreter, translator; b. New Orleans, July 7, 1947; d. Alfonso and Margaret Gibbons (Burke) S.; m. Robert Thomas Dwyer, Jan. 6, 1973. BA, Newton Coll., 1968; JD, Loyola U., 1975. Bar: N.Y. 1976, U.S. Dist. Ct. (so. and ea. dists.) N.Y. 1976, U.S. Ct. Appeals (2nd cir.) 1977. Clk. Sessions, Fishman, Rosenson, Snelling, Boisfontaine, New Orleans, 1973-75; assoc. Shearman-Sterling, N.Y.C. and Paris, 1975-84; real estate developer London, 1985-87; pvt. practice Scarsdale, N.Y., 1987—. Mem. pub. affairs com. Jr. League Ctrl. Westchester (N.Y.); freedom writer Amnesty Internat.; bd. trustees Nativity Mission Ctr. Mem. Assn. Bar City of N.Y. (mem. entertainment com. 1998—). Roman Catholic. Avocations: music, bicycling, cooking, reading, theater, travel. Office: One Walworth Ave Scarsdale NY 10583-1417 Fax: 914-723-6679.

SABAT, ROBERT HARTMAN, magazine editor; b. Newark, Aug. 28, 1957; s. Charles and Marilyn Ruth (Hartman) S.; m. Jessica Schilling Fine, Oct. 15, 1989; children: Nathaniel, Olivia. BA, Brandeis U., 1980. Mng. editor Penthouse mag., N.Y.C., 1986-91, Connoisseur mag., N.Y.C., 1991-92, Lear's mag., N.Y.C., 1992-94, Interview mag., N.Y.C., 1994-95, Smart Money mag., N.Y.C., 1995-99, exec. editor, 1999—2002; dep. editor US Weekly mag., N.Y.C., 2002—03; mng. editor GQ mag., N.Y.C., 2003—04; personal fin. editor The Wall St. Jour., N.Y.C., 2004—. Office: The Wall St Jour 200 Liberty St New York NY 10281 Personal E-mail: robertsabat@hotmail.com.

SABATINI, DAVID DOMINGO, cell biologist, biochemist; b. Bolivar, Argentina, May 10, 1931; came to U.S., 1961; m. Zulema Lena Sabatini, 1960; children: Bernardo L., David M. MD, U. Litoral, Rosario, Argentina, 1954; PhD in Cell Biology, Rockefeller U., 1966. Instr., lectr., assoc. prof. cell biology Inst. Gen. Anatomy and Embryology, U. Buenos Aires, 1957-60; dir. admissions Sch. Medicine U. Buenos Aires, 1957-60; Rockefeller Found. fellow Sch. Medicine Yale U., 1961; rsch. assoc. cell biol. lab Rockefeller U., N.Y.C., 1961-63, from asst. prof. to assoc. prof. cell biology, 1966-72; prof., chmn. dept. cell biology Sch. Medicine NYU, 1972-74, Frederick L. Ehrman prof., chmn. dept. cell biol. Sch. Med., 1975—, dir. MD-PhD program, 1987-97. Wendell Griffith Meml. lectr. St. Louis U., 1977; Mary Peterman Meml. lectr. Meml.-Sloan Kettering Inst., N.Y., 1977; 25th Robert J. Terry lectr. Wash. U., 1978; 3d ann. Keith R. Porter lectr. cell biology, 1994; vis. prof. Coll. France, Paris, 1986, George Washington U., 1986; 7th Ann. Kenneth F. Naidorff Meml. lectr. Columbia U., 1989; fellow Nat. Acad. Medicine, Argentina, 1956; UNESCO fellow Biophysics Inst., Rio de Janeiro, 1957; Pfizer traveling fellow, 1972; mem. molecular biology study sect. NIH, 1973-77, chmn., 1976-77; mem. bd. basic biology Nat. Rsch. Coun., 1986-89. Editor Jour. Cell Biology, 1971—, Jour. Cellular Biochemistry, 1980-84, Molecular & Cellular Biology, 1980-82, Procs. NAS USA, 1985—, Biol. Cell, 1986—, Current Opinions Cell Biology, 1990—; mem. editl. bd. Procs. NAS, 1993-96. Mem. sci. adv. com. Irma T. Hirshcl Charitable Trust, 1979-85; bd. dirs. Pub. Health Rsch. Inst., 1980-88; bd. sci. dirs. Jane Coffin Childs Meml. Fund, 1980-86, Nat. Inst. Diabetes Digest Kidney Disease, 1982-86; sci. adv. com. Robert Wood Johnson Found. Minority Med. Faculty Devel. Program, 1987—, Human Frontier Sci. Program, 1991—, chair molecular grants, 1994—; mem. sci. rev. com. Pew Internat. Fellows Program, 1990—, med. adv. bd., 1989-93, internat. program, 1994—; mem. sci. adv. com. Inst. d'Embryologie Cellular Mol., Coll. France, 1994—;, Ctr. Adv. Biotech. and Medicine, 1996—; mem. Alfred P. Sloan Jr. award selection com. GM Cancer Rsch. Found., 1996—. Recipient Samuel Roberts Noble Rsch. Recognition award, 1980. Fellow AAAS, Am. Acad. Microbiology, N.Y. Acad. Sci.; mem. NAS (chmn. cell and devel. biology sect. 1994-96), Am. Soc. Cell Biology (pres. 1978-79, coun. mem. 1974-77, E. B. Wilson award 1986), Harvey Soc. (v.p. 1985-86, pres. 1986-87), Argentine Med. Assn. (hon.), French Acad. Sci. (fgn. assoc., Charles Leopold Mayer prize 1988), Am. Soc. Biol. Chemistry, Am. Soc. Microbiology, N.Y. Soc. Electron Microbiology ((pres. 1971), Am. Assn. Anatomy (chair cell biology, neurobiology, exec. coun. 1992—), Inst. Medicine. Office: NYU Sch Medicine 550 1st Ave Rm 659 New York NY 10016-6481

SABATINI, NELSON JOHN, health care executive; b. Rochester, N.Y., Jan. 20, 1940; s. John R. and Ida M. (Ceconi) S.; m. Marilyn Jean Gromala, Jan. 19, 1963; children— John Nelson, Michael Christopher Student, Lewis Coll., Lockport, Ill., 1958-62; BA in Psychology, George Washington U., 1971, postgrad. Claims rep. Social Security Adminstrn., Chgo., 1962-65, various positions Balt., 1965-79, dep. dir. disability programs, 1979-81, exec. asst. to commr., 1981-82, assoc. commr., 1982—, dep. commr., 1983-88; dep. sec. health and mental hygiene State of Md., 1988, sec. health and mental hygiene, 1991—95, 2003; v.p. Univ. Md. Med. Systems, 1995, exec. v.p., 1995—. Named Disting. Marylander of Yr. 1993; recipient Sec.'s cert. HHS, 1975; Commr.'s citation Social Security Adminstrn., 1977, 81; Presdl. Merit Rank award Pres. of U.S., 1984 Roman Catholic. Avocations: sailing, tennis. Office Phone: 410-767-6505.

SABATINI, WILLIAM QUINN, architect; b. Pitts. s. William L. and Lydia M. (Contento) S.; m. Carol Anne Christoffel, Feb. 26, 1972; children: Quinn, Jay, Jillian. BA, Franklin & Marshall Coll., 1971; MArch, U. N.Mex., 1978. Registered arch., N.Mex., Nev.; cert. Nat. Coun. Archtl. Registration Bds. Intern Jess Holmes, Arch., Albuquerque, 1974-78; project mgr. Jack Miller & Assocs., Las Vegas, 1978-81; sr. design arch. HNTB, Kansas City, Mo., 1981-84; prin. Holmes Sabatini Assocs. Arch. (now Dekker Perich Sabatini), Albuquerque, 1984—. Prin. works include Ctrl. Campus Bookstore U. N.Mex. (Merit award N.Mex. Soc. Archs. 1977), Luna County Courthouse, Deming, N.Mex. (Honor award N.Mex. Hist. Preservation Soc. 1978), James R. Dickinson Libr. U. Nev., Las Vegas (Merit award AIA 1981, Honor award Nev. Soc. Arch. 1981), Reno Conv. Ctr. (Merit award Nev. Soc. Archs. 1983), Corp. Hdqs. Nev. Power Co., Las Vegas (Honor award Nev. Soc. Archs. 1983), YMCA, Las Vegas (Honor award Nev. Soc. Archs. 1983), Sanctuary Remodel St. Johns United Meth. Ch., Albuquerque (Best Interiors award N.Mex. Bus. Jour. 1986), The Presidio Office Bldg., Albuquerque (Best Bldgs. award and Best Interiors award N.Mex. Bus. Jour. 1987, Project of Yr. award Assoc. Gen. Contractors N.Mex. 1987), Suarez Residence, Albuquerque (Merit award N.Mex. Soc. Am. 1988), Fire Sta. Number 13 and Fire Marshall's Office, Albuquerque (Merit award Albuquerque Conservation Soc. 1987, Best Bldgs. award N.Mex. Bus. Jour. 1988), Santa Fe Imaging Ctr. (Citation of Excellence, Modern Health Care Mag., AIA com. on healthcare 1989, Best Bldgs. award N.Mex. Bus. Jour. 1989), Health Scis. Bldg. U. N.Mex. (Best Bldgs. award N.Mex. Bus. Jour. 1989), U.S. Port of Entry, Columbus, N.Mex. (Best Bldgs. award N.Mex. Bus. Jour. 1989, Honor award N.Mex. Soc. Archs. 1990, GSA Design award U.S. Gen. Svcs. Adminstrn. 1990), Student Svcs. Bldg., Albuquerque TVI (Best Bldgs. award N.Mex. Bus. Jour. 1989, Merit award Albuquerque Conservation Soc. 1990), Expansion and Renovation Albuquerque Conv. Ctr. (Best Bldgs. award N.Mex. Bus. Jour. 1990), Lovelace Multi-Specialty Clinic Facility, Albuquerque (Merit award N.Mex. Soc. Archs. 1991), Pete's Playground U. N.Mex. Hosp. (Honor award N.Mex. Soc. Archs. 1992, Best Bldgs. Spl. award N.Mex. Bus. Jour. 1993), Nursing Unit Remodel U. N.Mex. Hosp. (Excellence award Am. Soc. Interior Designers 1992), 3.5 Meter Telescope Kirtland AFB, N.Mex. (Honor award AIA 1993). Bd. dirs. Albuquerque Chamber Orch., 1988, Hospice Rio Grande, 1992-94; mem. adv. bd. Balloon Mus., 1989-91; mem. adv. bd. St. Pius High Sch., 1993-96. With USAR, 1971-78. Mem. AIA (bd. dirs. Albuquerque chpt. 1986-87). Roman Catholic. Office: Dekker Perich Sabatini 6801 Jefferson St NE Albuquerque NM 87109-4379

SABATINO, CARMEN, mayor; Former tchr. Modesto City Sch. Dist., Calif.; restaurant owner; mayor City of Modesto, Calif., 1999—. Founder Modesto Basketball Assn.; chair Audit Com. Office: City Hall PO Box 642 Modesto CA 95353-0642 E-mail: csabatino@ci.modesto.ca.us.

SABAU, CARMEN SYBILE, chemist; b. Cluj, Romania, Apr. 24, 1933; naturalized U.S. citizen; d. George and Antoinette Marie (Chiriac) Grigorescu; m. Mircea Nicolae Sabau, July 11, 1956; 1 child, Isabelle Carmen. MS in Inorganic and Analytical Chemistry, U. C.I. Parhon, Bucharest, Romania, 1955; PhD in Radiochemistry, U. Fridericiana, Karlsruhe, Fed. Republic of Germany, 1972. Chemist Inst. Atomic Physics, Bucharest, Romania, 1956—74, Argonne (Ill.) Nat. Lab., 1976-98; ret., 1998; chemist Joint Inst. of Nuclear Rsch., Dubna-Moscow, 1974—75. Author: Ion-exchange Theory and Applications in Analytical Chemistry, 1967; contbr. articles to profl. jours. Mem. World Romanian Coun.; del. NGO/DPJ Conf. on Human Rights. Internat. Atomic Energy Agy. fellow, 1967-68, Humboldt fellow, 1970-72. Mem. Am. Romanian Acad. Arts and Sci., Internat. Soc. Intercomm. of New Ideas, Alexander von Humboldt Assn. Am., Alpha Friends of Antiquity. Home: 689 Banbury Way Bolingbrook IL 60440-1057 Office: Argonne Nat Lab 9700 Cass Ave Bldg 205 Argonne IL 60439-4837 E-mail: Carmen_Sabau@hotmail.com.

SABB, ANNMARIE LOUISE, chemist, researcher; b. New Brunswick, N.J., Sept. 21, 1942; d. Frank John and Marianne Previte; m. Frederick Joseph Sabb, Aug. 1, 1965; children: Frederick William, Jacqueline Marie. BA, Douglass Coll., New Brunswick, N.J., 1964; MS, Rutgers U., 1974; PhD, Princeton U., 1986. Sci. info. chemist FMC Corp., Balt., 1965—68; rsch. chemist Am. Cyanamid, Princeton, NJ, 1969—74; sr. scientist Ayerst Rsch., Princeton, NJ, 1986—88; sr. rsch. scientist Wyeth-Ayerst Rsch., Princeton, NJ, 1989—90, prin. scientist, 1991—2001; prin. rsch. scientist Wyeth Rsch., Princeton, NJ, 2002—. Grad. coll. faculty fellow Princeton U., NJ, 1992—93; conf. chair, co-organizer Strategic Rsch. Inst., N.Y.C., 1997—99; grant reviewer NIH, Washington, 1999—2001; sci. adv. bd. Inst. for the Study of Aging, N.Y.C., 1999—; editl. adv. bd. Bentham Sci. Publishers, Hilversum, Netherlands, 2002—. Editor: (journal issue on alzheimer's disease) Current Topics in Medicinal Chemistry; author: (article:drugs for dementia) Drug Development Research; inventor (drugs for psychiatric disorders) Wo 0242304, (drugs for cognition) Us 6239134, (drugs for dementia in alzheimer's) Us 5468875; author: (journal articles on medicinal chemistry) Bioorganic & Medicinal Chemistry Letters, (review on amyloid protein in alzheimer's) Current Opinion in Investigational New Drugs, (review on cholinergic agents) Current Opinion in Therapeutic Patents, (article on form b of molybdenum cofactor) Journal of Organic Chemistry. Recipient Phoenix award to Princeton Sect., Am. Chem. Soc., 1991, Patent award, Wyeth-Ayerst Rsch., 1997—2001. Mem.: Soc. for Neuroscience, Am. Chem. Soc. (pres. of Princeton sect. 1990—91), Sigma Xi, Iota Sigma Pi, Phi Beta Kappa. Achievements include patents in field of antidementia agents, drugs for neurological illness, antipsychotic agents, others; discovery and synthesis of a novel heterocyclic ring system with activity at the human 5-HTZC receptor (drugs for schizophrenia); preparation of (1,4) diazocino (7,8,1-hi) indole derivatives as antipsychotic and anti obesity agents. Office: Wyeth Rsch Cn 8000 Princeton NJ 08543 8000 E-mail: sabba@wyeth.com.

SABEL, BRADLEY KENT, lawyer; b. Charleston, Ill., Oct. 6, 1948; s. Walter Bernard and Charlotte (Ahlstrom) Sabel; m. Nancy Jean Parker, Apr. 4, 1984. BA, Vanderbilt U., 1970; JD, Cornell U., 1975; MS in Bus. Policy, Columbia U., 1983. Bar: NY 1976. Atty. Fed. Reserve Bank NY, NYC, 1975-80, asst. counsel, 1980, sec., asst. counsel, 1981-85, assoc. counsel, 1985-87, counsel, 1988-93, counsel, v.p., 1993-94; counsel Shearman & Sterling, NYC, 1994-97, ptnr., 1997—. Contbr. articles to profl. jours. Bd. dirs., treas. NY Chamber Orch., NYC, 1985—87. With U.S. Army, 1970—72. Mem.: Assn. Bar City NY (chmn. banking law com.). Home: 2 Midland Gdns Apt 4E Bronxville NY 10708-4727 Office: 599 Lexington Ave Fl C2 New York NY 10022-6030 Office Phone: 212-848-8410. E-mail: bsabel@shearman.com.

SABELHAUS, MELANIE R. government agency administrator; b. Cleve. m. Bob Sabelhaus; 2 children. BS in Journalism, Ohio U. With IBM, 1972—86; founder, CEO Exclusive Interim Properties Ltd., Balt., 1986—97; v.p. global sales Bridgestreet Accommodations, 1997—98; dep. adminstr. SBA, Washington, 2002—. Co-chair Nat. Summit on Women in Philanthropy; bd. dirs. United Way, Alzheimer's Assn. of Ctrl. Md. Recipient Outstanding Vol. Fundraiser of the Yr. award for Md., Assn. of Fundraising Profls., 2002. Office: Small Bus Adminstrn 409 Third St SW Washington DC 20024-3203

SABER, ALAN A. surgeon; arrived in U.S., 1992; s. Abb A. and Sue A. Saber; m. Dalia D. Saber; children: Sara S. children: Jason S., Angie S. MD, Alexandria U., 1984, MChir, 1988. Surg. resident Mt. Sinai Sch. Medicine, N.Y.C., 1993—95, surg. rsch. fellow, 1995—97, surg. resident, 1997—99, chief surg. resident, 1999—2000; clin. fellow minimally invasive surgery Cleve. Clinic Fla., Ft. Lauderdale, 2000—01; asst. prof. surgery Mich. State U., Kalamazoo, 2001—, chief sect. minimally invasive surgery, 2001—. Med. clerkship coord. Mich. State U., 2001—. Author: (book) eMEDICINE; reviewer Jour. Investigative Surgery, 2001—. Fellow: ACS, Am. Soc. Bariatric Surgery (assoc.); mem.: Am. Soc. Gastrointestinal Endoscopic Surgeons. Achievements include research in Computer Tomograpgic Mapping Of Anatomical Landmarks During Laparoscopy. Avocations: fishing, swimming, reading. Office: Michigan State Univ 1000 Oakland Dr Kalamazoo MI 49008 E-mail: saber@kcms.msu.edu.

SABERS, RICHARD WAYNE, state supreme court justice; b. Salem, S.D., Feb. 12, 1938; s. Emil William and Elrena Veronica (Godfrey) S.; m. Colleen D. Kelley, Aug. 28, 1965 (dec. Feb., 1998); children: Steven Richard, Susan Michelle, Michael Kelley; m. Ellie Schmitz, June 9, 2000. BA in English, St. John's U., Collegeville, Minn., 1960; JD, U. S.D., 1966. Bar: S.D. 1966, U.S. Dist. Ct. S.D. 1966, U.S. Ct. Appeals (8th cir.) 1983. From assoc. to ptnr. Moore, Rasmussen, Sabers & Kading, Sioux Falls, S.D., 1966-86; justice Supreme Ct. S.D., Pierre and Sioux Falls, 1986—. Mem. editorial bd. U. S.D. Law Rev., 1965-66. State rep. March of Dimes, Bismarck, N.D., 1963; bd. dirs. St. Joseph Cathedral, Sioux Falls, 1971-86; trustee, bd. dirs. O'Gorman Found., Sioux Falls, 1978-86; active sch. bd. O'Gorman High Sch., Sioux Falls, 1985-86. Lt. U.S. Army, 1960-63. Named Outstanding Young Religious Leader, Jaycees, Sioux Falls, 1971. Mem. ABA, S.D. Bar Assn., Inst. Jud. Adminstrn., St. John's Alumni Assn. (pres. Sioux Falls chpt. 1975-91). Republican. Roman Catholic. Avocations: tennis, skiing, sailing, sports, wood carving. Office: SD Supreme Ct 500 E Capitol Ave Pierre SD 57501-5070 Home: 5218 S Sweetbriar Ct Sioux Falls SD 57108-2855 Office Phone: 605-367-5926.

SABERSKY, ROLF HEINRICH, mechanical engineer; b. Berlin, Oct. 20, 1920; came to U.S., 1938, naturalized, 1944; s. Fritz and Berta (Eisner) S.; m. Bettina Sofie Schuster, June 16, 1946; children— Carol, Sandra. BS, Calif. Inst. Tech., 1942, MS, 1943, PhD, 1949. Devel. engr. Aerojet Gen. Co., 1943-46, regular cons., 1949-70; asst. prof. Calif. Inst. Tech., Pasadena, 1949-55, asso. prof., 1955-61, prof. mech. engring., 1961-88, prof. emeritus, 1988—. Cons. various indsl. orgns. Author: Engineering Thermodynamics, 1957, Fluid Flow, 4th edit., 1999; contbr. articles to profl. jours. Fellow ASME (Heat Transfer Meml. award 1977, 50th anniversary award Heat Transfer Div 1988); mem. Sigma Xi, Tau Beta Pi. Home: 1135 Calle De Los Amigos Santa Barbara CA 93105-5467 Office: Calif Inst Tech Divsn Engring & Applied Sci Pasadena CA 91125-0001 E-mail: sabersky@cox.net.

SABHARWAL, RANJIT SINGH, mathematician; b. Dhudial, India, Dec. 11, 1925; came to U.S., 1958, naturalized, 1981; s. Krishan Ch and Devti (An) S.; m. Pritam Kaur Chadha, Mar. 5, 1948; children— Rajinderpal, Amarjit, Jasbir. BA with honors, Punjab U., 1944, MA, 1948; MA U. Calif, Berkeley, 1962; PhD, Wash. State U., 1966. Lectr. math. Khalsa Coll., Bombay, India, 1951-58; teaching asst. U. Calif., Berkeley, 1958-62; instr. math. Portland (Oreg.) State U., 1962-62, Wash. State U., 1963-66; asst. prof. Kans. State U., 1966-68; assoc. prof. math. Calif. State U., Hayward, 1968-74, prof. math., 1974-92, prof. emeritus math., 1992—. Author papers on non-Desarguesian planes. Mem. Am. Math. Soc., Math. Assn. Am., Sigma Xi. Address: 25179 Old Fairview Ave Hayward CA 94542-1355

SABILI, ERLINDA ASA, internist, psychiatrist, pastoral care minister; b. San Juan, Batangas, The Philippines, Sept. 27, 1959; came to U.S., 1991; d. Marciano Acorda and Rita Lalvces (Asa) S. BS in Med. Tech., U. Santo Tomas, Manila, 1976, MD, 1982. Registered med. technician, The Philippines. Intern U. Santo Tomas Hosp., 1982-83, pre-resident and resident dept. internal medicine, 1987-90; physician Antipolo (Rizal, The Philippines) Rural Health Clinic, 1983; missionary physician Sister of St. Paul, Manila, 1984-87; physician-in-charge Patronato de Sra. de Lourdes Free Clinic, Manila, 1984-95, 90-91; pastoral care vol. St. Elizabeth's Hosp., Elizabeth, N.J., 1991-93; sr. resident in internal medicine and psychiatry Albert Einstein Med. Ctr., Phila., 1993—. Presenter in field. Contbr. articles to med. jours. Vol. physician Archdiocese of Bulacan, The Philippines, 1985-86, San Antonio Feeding Ctr. for Malnourished Children, Manila, 1989-91; vol. Homeless Shelter Dwelling Place, N.Y.C., 1991-93; pastoral care vol. Albert Einstein Healthcare Network, Phila., 1993—; choir leader, pastoral care vol. to Filipino cmty. St. Mary's Cath. Ch., Elizabeth, 1991-93. Recipient young investigator's award Philippine Coll. Cardiology, 1990; Laughlin fellow Faughlin Found., 1997. Mem. AMA, ACP, Am. Psychiat. Assn., Am. Assn. Medicine and Psychiatry, Philippine Med. Assn., U. Santo Tomas Med. Alumni Assn., U. Santo Tomas Med. Mission. Avocations: playing guitar, poetry, singing, cooking, gardening. Home: 3207 Friendship St Philadelphia PA 19149-1516 Office: Albert Einstein Med Ctr 5501 Old York Rd Philadelphia PA 19141-3018

SABIN, JOHN ROGERS, physics educator; b. Springfield, Mass., Apr. 29, 1940; s. Henry Bowman and Elizabeth (Rogers) S.; m. Claudia Ball, 1963 (div. 1978); children: Peter Bowman, Amanda Ball; m. Birgit Horn, Aug. 8, 1987; children: Lene Elizabeth Horn, Niels Kristian Horn. AB, Williams Coll.,

1962; PhD, U. N.H., 1966. Asst. prof. chemistry U. Mo., Columbia, 1968—71; assoc. prof. physics U. Fla., Gainesville, 1971—77, prof., 1977—, dir. info. tech., Coll. Liberal Arts and Scis., 1998—, interim chmn. dept. physics, 2002; adjungeret prof. U. So. Denmark, 1992—. Guest prof. Odense (Denmark) U., 1980-92, Nordita prof., Odense, 1982-83, Fulbright prof., 1986, 91. Editor Advances in Quantum Chemistry; assoc. editor Internat. Jour. Quantum Chemistry; mem. editl. bd. Croatia Chemica Acta, 2000—. Fellow Am. Phys. Soc.; mem. Am. Chem. Soc., Danish Phys. Soc., Danish Chem. Soc. Home: 415 NW 23rd St Gainesville FL 32607-2618 Office: U Florida Dept Physics PO Box 118435 Gainesville FL 32611-8435 Office Phone: 352-392-1597. E-mail: sabin@qtp.ufl.edu.

SABIN, PAUL EDGAR, not-for-profit developer; b. Rochester, N.Y. s. Edgar and Mabelle S.; m. Onalee Rae Barton, 1962 (div. Dec. 1978); m. Linda Emerson, 1979; children: Craig Alan, Laural Ann, Todd Aaron. BA in Psychology, Lycoming Coll., 1962; MDiv, Pacific Sch. Religion, 1966; MSW, Barry U., 1981. Pastor Ontario St. Meth. Ch., Buffalo, 1966-70; exec. sec. Meth. Metro, Buffalo, 1970-74; exec. dir. Man-to-Man Assoc., Columbus, Ohio, 1974-75, Watson Homestead Found., Painted Post, N.Y., 1975-79; dir. social svcs. Meth. Hosp., Jacksonville, Fla., 1981-89; pres., CEO Meth. Children's Home, Jackson, Miss., 1989-94; dir. devel. La. Meth. Children's Home, Ruston, 1994—. Exec. dir. Watson Homestead Found. Elizabeth Hay Bechtel fellow Pacific Sch. Religion, 1965. Mem. NASW (La. bd. dirs. 1997), Academy Cert. Social Workers, People to People Internat., Rotary. Democrat. Avocations: golf, photography. Home: 2702 Huntington St Monroe LA 71201-2520 Office: La Meth Childrens Home 901 S Vienna St Ruston LA 71270-5829

SABIN, WILLIAM ALBERT, writer; b. Paterson, N.J., May 29, 1931; s. David and Esther (Goodman) S.; m. Marie Frances Noonan, May 31, 1958; children— Margaret, John, Katherine, Christopher, James BA in English, Yale U., 1952, MA in English, 1956. Pub. bus. and office edn. McGraw Hill Book Co., N.Y.C., 1973-78, editor in chief bus. books, 1979-86, pub. bus. books, 1987-90. Author: The Gregg Reference Manual, 10th edit., 2004; co-author: College English: Grammar and Style, 1967. Served as cpl. U.S. Army, 1952-54, ETO Home: 540 Fogler Rd Bristol ME 04539-3101

SABINSON, HARVEY BARNETT, theatrical organization administrator; b. N.Y.C., Oct. 24, 1924; s. Samuel and Sarah Sabinson; m. Sarah S. Sabinson, Aug. 15, 1944; children: Eric, Allen. BS, Queens Coll., 1947. Theatrical publicist, NY, 1946—73; dir. spl. projects League Am. Theatres & Prodrs., N.Y.C., 1976-82, exec. dir., 1982-95. Vis. prof. theatre adminstrn. Yale U. Sch. of Drama, New Haven, 1966-70. Author: Darling, You Were Wonderful, 1977. Recipient Lifetime Achievement award United Jewish Appeal Fedn., 1990, Lifetime Achievement Tony award, 1995, Theatre Hall of Fame Founder's award, 1996; named to Townsend Harris Alumni Assn. Hall of Fame. Mem. Actor's Fund of Am. (trustee 1990—), Broadway Assn. (bd. dirs. 1977—2003), Theater Devel. Fund (bd. dirs. 1992-96), Berkshire Theatre Festival (trustee 1995-2001), Mayor's Midtown Citizens Com., Coll. Fellows of Am. Theatre. Avocation: theater.

SABISTON, DAVID COSTON, JR., surgeon, educator; b. Onslow County, N.C., Oct. 4, 1924; s. David Coston and Marie (Jackson) S.; m. Agnes Foy Barden, Sept. 24, 1955; children: Anne Sabiston Leggett, Agnes Sabiston Butler, Sarah Coston. BS, U. N.C., 1944; MD, Johns Hopkins U., 1947; DSc (hon.), U. Madrid. Successively intern, asst. resident, chief resident surgery Johns Hopkins Hosp., Balt., 1947—53; successively asst. prof., assoc. prof., prof. surgery Johns Hopkins U. Med. Sch., Balt., 1955—64; Howard Hughes investigator Johns Hopkins Med. Sch., Balt., 1955—61; Fulbright rsch. scholar U. Oxford, England, 1960; rsch. assoc. Hosp. Sick Children, U. London, 1961; James B. Duke prof. surgery, chmn. dept. Duke Med. Sch., Durham, NC, 1964—94, chmn. dept. thoracic surgery, 1964—94; chief of staff Duke U. Med. Ctr., Durham, 1994—96, dir. internat. programs, 1996—. Chmn. Accreditation Coun. for Grad. Med. Edn., 1985—86. Editor: Textbook of Surgery, Essentials of Surgery, Atlas of General Surgery, Atlas of Cardiothoracic Surgery, A Review of Surgery; co-editor: Gibbon's Surgery of the Chest, Companion Handbook to Textbook of Surgery; chmn. editl. bd.: Annals of Surgery, mem. editl. bd.: Annals Clin. Rsch., ISI Atlas of Sci.: The Classics of Surgery Libr., Surgery, Gynecology and Obsetrics, Jour. Applied Cardiology, Jour. Cardiac Surgery, World Jour. Surgery. Capt. M.C., AUS, 1953—55. Named named Disting. Physician, U.S. Va., 1995; recipient Career Rsch. award, NIH, 1962—64, N.C. award in Sci., 1978, Disting. Achievement award, Am. Heart Assn. Sci. Coun., 1983, Michael E. DeBakey award for Outstanding Achievement, 1984, Significant Sigma Chi award, 1987, Coll. medalist, Am. Coll. Chest Physicians, 1987. Mem.: ACS (chmn. bd. govs. 1974—75, regent 1975—82, chmn. bd. regents 1982—84, pres. 1985—86), James IV Assn. Surgeons (bd. dirs. U.S. chpt.), Soc. Internat. De Chirurgie, Soc. Thoracic Surgeons Gt. Britain and Ireland, Soc. Surg. Chairmen (pres. 1974—76), Johns Hopkins U. Soc. Scholars, Soc. Surgery Alimentary Tract, Soc. Thoracic Surgery, Surg. Biology Club II, Halsted Soc., Soc. Univ. Surgeons (pres. 1968—69), Soc. Vascular Surgery (v.p. 1967—68), Internat. Soc. Cardiovasc. Surgery, Soc. Clin. Surgery, Am. Assn. Thoracic Surgery (pres. 1984—85), So. Surg. Assn., Am. Surg. Assn. (pres. 1977—78, sec. 1969—73, pres. 1973—74), Inst. Medicine of NAS, Am. Bd. Surgery (chmn. 1971—72, diplomate), Philippine Coll. Surgeons (hon.), Surg. Congress Assn. Espanola de Cirujanos (hon.), French Surg. Assn. (hon.), Japanese Coll. Surgeons (hon.), Brazilian Coll. Surgeons (hon.), Colombian Surg. Soc. (hon.), German Surg. Soc. (hon.), Royal Australasian Coll. Surgeons (hon.), Royal Coll. Surgeons Ireland (hon.), Royal Coll. Physicians and Surgeons Can. (hon.), Asociación de Cirugía del Litoral (Argentina) (hon.), Royal Coll. Surgeons Eng. (hon.), Royal Coll. Surgeons Edinburgh (hon.; editl. bd. jour.), Phila. Acad. Surgery (hon.), Ill. Surg. Soc. (hon.), University Club, Cosmos Club (Washington), Alpha Omega Alpha (Disting. Tchr. award 1992), Phi Beta Kappa. Home: 1528 Pinecrest Rd Durham NC 27705-5817 Office: Duke U Med Ctr PO Box 2600 Durham NC 27715-2600

SABLAN, DAVID J. marketing professional, political organization worker; Pres. D.J. Sabian and Co., 1999—; chmn. Rep. Party Guam, 2000—. Vice chmn. Guam State Coun. Vocat. Edn., 1988—90, chmn., 1991—94; mem. Gov.'s Task Force Tourism, 1987—89. Office: Guam Republican Party Chmn PO Box 2846 Hagatna GU 96932*

SABLE, BARBARA KINSEY, retired music educator; b. Astoria, L.I., N.Y., Oct. 6, 1927; d. Albert and Verna (Rowe) Kinsey; m. Arthur J. Sable, Nov. 3, 1973. BA, Coll. Wooster, 1949; MA, Tchrs. Coll. Columbia U., N.Y.C., 1950; DMus, U. Ind., 1966. Office mgr., music dir. Sta. WCAX, Burlington, Vt., 1954; instr. Cottey Coll., 1959-60; asst. prof. N.E. Mo. State U., Kirksville, 1962-64, U. Calif., Santa Barbara, 1964-69; prof. music U. Colo., Boulder, 1969—, prof. emeritus, 1992—. Author: (novels) The Vocal Sound, 1982; contbr. poetry and short stories to lit. jours. Mem.: Colo. Music Tchrs. Assn., AAUP, Nat. Assn. Tchrs. Singing (past state gov., assoc. editor bull.). Democrat. Avocation: poetry. Home: 3430 Ash Ave Boulder CO 80305-3432 Office: U Colo PO Box 301 Boulder CO 80309-0301 Business E-Mail: bks@sable-boulder.com.

SABLE, ROBERT ALLEN, gastroenterologist; b. Bklyn., June 21, 1948; s. Benjamin and Sara (Dickstein) S.; m. Valerie P. Kubie Kopelman, July 1, 1969 (div. Mar. 1982); 1 child, Jesse; m. Ellen Sue Finer, May 29, 1982; children: Scott, Eric. BS, MIT, 1969; MD, Albert Einstein U., 1973. Bd. cert. in internal medicine, gastroenterology and geriatrics Am. Bd. Internal Medicine. Staff physician N.Y. Telephone Co. Mid Manhattan Med. Dept., N.Y.C., 1978-81; physician Riverdale Gastroenterology Cons., Bronx, N.Y., 1981—. Chief gastroenterology St. Barnabas Hosp., Bronx, 1982-2003, pres. med. bd., 1985-90; pres. divsn. coun. Montefiore Med. Ctr., 2001-03. Contbr. articles, reports, revs. to profl. jours. Fellow ACP, Am. Coll. Gastroenterology; mem. AMA, Am. Gastroenterologic Assn., Am. Soc. for Gastrointestinal Endoscopy. Avocations: stamp collecting/philately, coin collecting/numismatics. Office: Riverdale Gastroenterol Con 3765 Riverdale Ave Bronx NY 10463-1845 Office Phone: 718-543-3636. E-mail: ra.sable@verizon.net.

SABLIK, MARTIN JOHN, research physicist; b. Bklyn., Oct. 21, 1939; s. Martin C. and Elsie M. (Fuzia) S.; m. Beverly Ann Shively, Nov. 26,1965; children: Jeanne, Karen, Marjorie, Larry. BA in Physics, Cornell U., 1960; MS in Physics, U. Ky., 1965; PhD, Fordham U., 1972. Jr. engr. The Martin Co., Orlando, Fla., 1962-63; instr. half-time U. Ky., Lexington, 1963-65; rsch. assoc. Fairleigh Dickinson U., Teaneck, N.J., 1965-67, instr. physics, 1967-72, asst. prof., 1972-76, assoc. prof., 1976-80; sr. rsch. scientist Southwest Rsch. Inst., San Antonio, 1980-87, staff scientist, 1987—. Local chmn. Intermag. Conf., San Antonio, 1995; mem. adv. bd. Conf. on Properties and Applications of Magnetic Materials, 1990—, Workshop on advances in Measurement Techniques and Instrumentation for Magnetic Properties Determination, 1994, Magnetic Materials, Measurements and Modeling Symposium, 1996, Magnetic Materials, Measurements and Microstructure Symposium, 1998, Symposium Magnetic Materials for Magnetoelectronic Devices, 2000; mem. exec. bd. Topical Group on Magnetism and Its Applications, 1996-97; mem. program com., assoc. editor Intermag 2000, Toronto. Mem. editl. bd.: Nondestructive Testing and Evaluation, 1989—; contbr. articles to profl. jours.; mem. editl. bd.: IEEE Transactions on Magnetics, 2002—, assoc. editor:, 2003—. Recipient Imagineer award Mind Sci. Found., 1989. Fellow Am. Soc. Nondestructive Testing (chmn. So. Tex. sect. 1983-84, 2001-02); mem. IEEE (sr.), Am. Phys. Soc., Am. Geophys. Union. Roman Catholic. Office: SW Rsch Inst PO Box 28510 San Antonio TX 78228-0510 E-mail: msablik@swri.org.

SABLOFF, JEREMY ARAC, archaeologist; b. N.Y.C., Apr. 16, 1944; s. Louis and Helen (Arac) S.; m. Paula Lynne Weinberg, May 26, 1968; children: Joshua, Saralinda. AB, U. Pa., 1964; MA, PhD, Harvard U., 1969. Asst. prof., asso. prof. Harvard U., Cambridge, Mass., 1969-76; asso. prof. anthropology U. Utah, Salt Lake City, 1976-77; curator anthropology Utah Mus. Natural History, Salt Lake City, 1976-77; prof. anthropology U. N.Mex., Albuquerque, 1978-86, chmn. dept., 1980-83; Univ. prof. anthropology and the history and philosphy of sci. U. Pitts., 1986-94, chmn. dept. anthropology, 1990-92; Charles K. Williams II dir. U. Mus., U. Mus. Term prof. anthropology U. Pa., Phila., 1994—2004, prof. anthropology, curator Mesoamerican archaeology, 1994—2004, Edmund J. and Louise W. Kahn endowed term prof. in the scial scis., curator Mesoamerican archaeology, 2004—. Sr. fellow for Pre-Columbian Studies, Dumbarton Oaks, 1986-92, chmn. 1989-92. Author: (with G.R. Willey) A History of American Archaeology, 1974, 2d edit., 1980, 3d edit., 1993, Excavations at Seibal: Ceramics, 1975, (with C.C. Lamberg-Karlovsky) Ancient Civilizations: The Near East and Mesoamerica, 1979, 2nd edit., 1995, (with D. A. Freidel) Cozumel: Late Maya Settlement Patterns, 1984, The Cities of Ancient Mexico, 1989, rev. edit., 1997, The New Archaeology and the Ancient Maya, 1990, (with G. Tourtellot) The Ancient Maya City of Sayil: The Mapping of a Puuc Region Center, 1991; editor(with C.C. Lamberg-Karlovsky) The Rise and Fall of Civilizations, 1974, (with C.C. Lamberg-Karlovsky) Ancient Civilization and Trade, 1975, (with W.L. Rathje) A Study of Changing Pre-Columbian Commercial Systems, 1975, American Antiquity, 1977-81, (with G.R. Willey) Scientific American Readings in Pre-Columbian Archaeology, 1980, Simulations in Archaeology, 1981, Supplement to the Handbook of Middle American Indians: Archaeology, 1981, Archaeology: Myth and Reality: A Scientific American Reader, 1982, Analyses of Fine Paste Ceramics, 1982, (with D. Meltzer and D. Fowler) American Archaeology: Past and Future, 1986, (with E.W. Andrews V) Late Lowland Maya Civilization: Classic to Postclassic, 1986, (with J.S. Henderson) Lowland Maya Civilization in the Eighth Century A.D., 1993, Tikal: Dynasties, Foreigners, and Affairs of State, 2003. Pres. Kolb Found., 1995-2004; chair Smithsonian Coun., 1999-2001, chair sci. adv. commn., 2001-03. Nat. Geog. Soc. grantee, 1972-74; NSF grantee, 1983-88; NEH grantee, 1990-91 Fellow AAAS (sec. H. chair 1994-95), Am. Anthrop. Assn., Royal Anthrop. Inst., Soc. Antiquaries London; mem. NAS, Am. Philos. Soc., Soc. Am. Archaeology (pres. 1989-91), Am. Acad. Arts and Sci., Internat. Soc., Comparative Study of Civilizations, Sigma Xi. Office: U Pa Mus Archaeology and Anthropology 33d and Spruce Sts Philadelphia PA 19104-6324

SABO, MARTIN OLAV, congressman; b. Crosby, ND, Feb. 28, 1938; s. Bjorn O. and Klara (Haga) S.; m. Sylvia Ann Lee, June 30, 1963; children: Karin, Julie. BA cum laude, Augsburg Coll., Mpls., 1959; postgrad., U. Minn., 1961-62. Mem. Minn. Ho. of Reps. from 57B Dist., 1960-78, minority leader Dem.-Farmer-Labor party, 1969—73, speaker, 1973-78; mem. U.S. Ho. of Reps. from 5th Minn. Dist., 1979—; chmn. Dem. Study Group; dep. majority whip 96th to 103rd Congresses; mem. permanent select com. on intelligence 102d Congress; chmn. Ho. Budget Com. 103d Congress; ranking minority mem. house budget com. 104th-106th Congress, mem. standards of official conduct com., appropriations com., ranking minority mem. subcom. on homeland security. Former mem. Nat. Adv. Commn. on Intergovtl. Rels.; past pres. Nat. Legis. Conf.; bd. regents Augsburg Coll. Mgr., player Dem. Congl. Baseball Team, 1987—. Recipient Disting. Alumni citation Augsburg Coll., Arms Control Leadership award Employees Union, Local 113, SEIU, AFL-CIO; named One of 200 Rising Young Leaders in Am. Time mag., 1974; Man of Yr. Mpls. Jr. C.of C., 1973-74, One of Ten Outstanding Young Men of Yr. Minn. Jr. C. of C., 1974; inducted Scandinavian Am. Hall of Fame, 1994. Mem. Nat. Conf. State Legis. Leaders (past pres.), ranking minortiy mem. on subcommittee on Homeland security 108th Congress. Democrat. Office: 2336 Rayburn Bldg Washington DC 20515-2305

SABO, RICHARD STEVEN, electrical company executive; b. Walkertown, Pa., Jan. 1, 1934; s. Alex S. and Elizabeth (Haluska) S.; m. Gail P. Digon, Feb. 15, 1954; children: Gailyn J., Richard A., Kerry S., Dale A. BS in Edn., California (Pa.) U., 1955; MS in Edn., Edinboro (Pa.) U., 1965. Tchr. Northwestern Sch. Dist., Albion, Pa., 1955-65; prodn. technician The Lincoln Electric Co., Cleve., 1965-66, staff asst. mktg., 1966-70, mgr. pub. rels., 1971-86, asst. to chmn., 1986-96, dir. cop. comms. and investor rels.; also exec. dir. James F. Lincoln Arc Welding Found.; ret., 1999. Editor: The Procedure Handbook of Arc Welding, 1994, 10 other books on arc welding; contbr. numerous articles to profl. jours. Chmn. Area Recreation Bd., Chesterland, Ohio, 1970, West Geauga Boosters, Chesterland, 1973-77; mem. adv. bd. Breckenridge Village, 2003—. Recipient Svc. award Future Farmers Am., 1970—, Svc. award U.S. Skill Olympics, 1980, Lakeland Community Coll. award, 1990, Ohio State U. Hon. Welding Engring. Alumni award, 1990, Calif. U. (Pa.) medallion of Distinction, 1990, Internat. Bus. Exec. of Yr. Internat. Acad. of Bus. Disciplines, 1997. Mem. Am. Welding Soc. (vice chmn. edn. and fin. com., mem. fin. com. 1988-94, speaker, various awards, Plummer lectr. 1992), Am. Soc. for Engring. Edn., Am. Inst. Steel Cons. (mem. edn. com. 1986—), Steel Plate Fabricators Assn. (past chmn. promotions com., mem. bd. dirs. profit sharing coun. 1991-99—), California U. Alumni Assn. (trustee 1983-99—). Lodges: Masons. Republican. Presbyterian. Avocations: golf, hunting, fishing, classical music.

SABOL, CAROLYN A. lawyer, government official; b. Pitts., Nov. 5, 1957; m. Gerald Kirschner, Mar. 15, 1986; 2 children. BA magna cum laude, U. Dayton, 1979; JD with honors, George Washington U., 1982. Bar: Pa. 1982, D.C. 1983, U.S. Supreme Ct. 1991. Dep. gen. counsel Fed. Bur. Prisons, Dept. Justice, Washington, 1982—. Com. chmn. pack 1250 Cub Scouts Am. Mem. Psi Chi. Roman Catholic. Office: Dept Justice Fed Bur Prisons 320 1st St NW Rm 754 Washington DC 20534-0002

SABOLCIK, GENE, manufacturing executive; b. Duquesne, Pa., July 19, 1951; s. Theodore George and Loretta Ann (Repcik) S.; m. Cathy O. Sexton, Dec. 31, 1986; 1 child, Eva Marie. BA in Econs., U. Pitts., 1973, MBA in Fin., 1974. Sr. fin. analyst LTV Steel Co., Pitts., 1974-78; mgr. systems and controls Empire-Detroit Steel Co., Mansfield, Ohio, 1978-81; asst. controller Midland Brake Co., Owosso, Mich., 1981-83; controller Akzo Coatings (Netherlands), Atlanta, 1983-86, Contel Texocom, Atlanta, 1986-87; dir. fin. Contel Material Mgmt. Co., Atlanta, 1987-93; gen. mgr. C.P. Internat., Grand Haven, Mich., 1993—; CFO Engine Power Components, Grand Haven, 1997, Spectra Products, Grand Haven, 1999-2000, Spectra Group, Grand Haven, 2000—. Cons. in field; chmn. bd. dirs. Old Time Tangibles, Atlanta. Mem. Atlanta Zoo Soc., King of Prussia (Pa.) Fire Co. Mem. Contel Profl. Devel. Assn., VFW, MADD, Slovak Club. Republican. Roman Catholic. Avocations: golf, auto racing, bodybuilding. Home: 11840 Lakeshore Dr Grand Haven MI 49417-9649

SABOT, RICHARD HENRY, economics educator, researcher, investor, entrepreneur; b. NYC, Feb. 16, 1944; s. Arnold G. and Victoria (Gomberg) S.; m. Judith A. Plunkett, Sept. 9, 1969; children: Diana, Christopher, Oliver, Julia. BA, U. Pa., 1966, Oxford U., 1968, MA, 1970, DPhil, 1973. Rsch. officer Inst. Econs. and Stats. Oxford (Eng.) U., 1972-74; rsch. economist World Bank, Washington, 1974-84; John J. Gibson prof. econs. Williams Coll., Williamstown, Mass., 1984-99, John J. Gibson prof. econs. emeritus, 1999—. Chmn., co-founder Tripod Inc., 1992-2000 (now Terra Lycos, Inc.); also bd. dirs.; econ. advisor Office of the Exec. V.P., Interam. Devel. Bank, Washington, 1994-98; sr. rsch. fellow Internat. Food Policy Rsch. Inst., Washington, 1987-92; sr. rsch. fellow policy rsch. dept. World Bank, 1992-94; cons. OECD Devel. Ctr., Paris, 1971-74, Internat. Inst. Applied Sys. Analysis, Vienna, Austria, 1982-83, Harvard Inst. Internat. Devel., Cambridge, Mass., 1985-88, World Bank, 1985—; co-founder, chmn. Eziba; ptnr. Peabody-Sabot Ventures; bd. dirs. Old Westbury Venture Fund II, Village Venture Svcs., Old Westbury Global Pvt. Equity Fund., Internat. Exec. Svc. Corps., Bosemer Trust; former chmn. bd. Geek Corps. Author: Economic Development and Urban Migration, 1979, Education Productivity and Inequality, 1990, The East Asian Miracle, 1993, Making Schools Work, 1995; editor: Migration and the Labor Market in Developing Countries, 1982, Unfair Advantage, 1991, Opportunity Foregone: Education in Brazil, 1996, Development Strategy and Management of the Market Economy, 1997, Beyond Tradeoffs, 1998; contbr. numerous articles to scholarly jours. Nat. panel on the econ. of ednl. reform Pew Found., 1991-95; trustee Nat. Child Rsch. Ctr., Washington, 1978-81; nat. bd. Fund for Improvement Post-Secondary Edn., Washington, 1987-91; bd. overseers Coll. Arts and Scis., U. Pa., Colby Coll. Rsch. grantee Ford Found., Mellon Found., Rockefeller Found., MacArthur Found., World Bank; Fulbright fellow, Thouron fellow, Danforth fellow; Hon. fellow Pembroke Coll., Oxford U. Mem. Am. Econ. Assn., Royal Econ. Soc., United Oxford and Cambridge U. Club (London), Williams Club (N.Y.C.), Mt. Greylook Ski Club (bd. dirs. 1984-85). Avocations: hiking, yoga, flyfishing, cross country skiing, swimming. Home: Birch Hollow Oblong Rd Williamstown MA 01267 Office: Eziba 90 Marshall St North Adams MA 01247-2454 E-mail: dick@eziba.com.

SABOUSKY, RICHARD ANTHONY, adult education educator; b. Oil City, Pa., Mar. 15, 1961; s. Robert Michael and Helen Pauline Sabousky. BS, Clarion U. Pa., 1984, MS, 1986; PhD, Kent State U., 1996. Cert. tchr. mentally and physically handicapped Pa. Tchr. Riverview Intermediate Unit, Shippenville, Pa., 1985—92; mem. faculty Clarion U. Pa., 1992—. Cons. Youth Alternatives, Oil City, Pa., 2001—, AC Valley Sch. Dist., St. Petersburg, Pa., 2002—, Mars (Pa.) Home for Youth, 2002—. Author: (chpt.) Transition Planning for Secondary Students with Disabilities, 2001. Recipient Disting. Alumni award, Clarion U. Venango Campus, 2002. Mem.: Coun. Exceptional Children. Home: 17 W Sixth St Oil City PA 16301 Office: Clarion U Pa 840 Wood St Sped Ctr Oil City PA 16301 E-mail: sabousky@clarion.edu.

SABREE, YAHYA AGIN, music educator; s. Oscar and Jerusha Fuller; m. Geneva Haneefah Richardson, Aug. 30, 1944. MS, Troy State U., 1999. Cert. educator Ga. Profl. Std. Commn. Instr. instrumental Bibb County Schs., Macon, Ga., 1998—2000; instr. band, music Dougherty County Sch. Sys., Albany, 2000—. With U.S. Army, 1968—69. Mem.: Music Educators Assn. (assoc.). Avocations: music, hunting, fishing.

SABSAY, DAVID, library consultant; b. Waltham, Mass., Sept. 12, 1931; s. Wiegard Isaac and Ruth (Weinstein) S.; m. Helen Glenna Tolliver, Sept. 24,1 966. AB, Harvard U., 1953; BLS, U. Calif., Berkeley, 1955. Circulation dept. supr. Richmond (Calif.) Pub. Library, 1955-56; city libr. Santa Rosa (Calif.) Pub. Library, 1956-65; dir. Sonoma County Library, Santa Rosa, 1965-92; libr. cons., 1992—. Coordinator North Bay Coop. Library System, Santa Rosa, 1960-64; cons. in field, Sebastopol, Calif., 1968—. Contbr. articles to profl. jours. Commendation, Calif. Assn. Library Trustees and Commrs., 1984. Mem. Calif. Library Assn. (pres. 1971, cert. appreciation 1971, 80), ALA. Clubs: Harvard (San Francisco). Home and Office: 667 Montgomery Rd Sebastopol CA 95472-3020 E-mail: dsabsay@sonic.net.

SABSHIN, MELVIN, psychiatrist, educator, medical association administrator; b. N.Y.C., Oct. 28, 1925; s. Zalman and Sonia Sabshin; m. Edith Goldfarb, June 12, 1955; 1 child, James K. BS, U. Fla., Gainesville, 1944; MD, Tulane U., New Orleans, 1948. Diplomate Am. Bd. Psychiatry and Neurology. Assoc. dir. Michael Reese Hosp. Psychosomatic and Psychiat. Inst., Chgo., 1953-61; prof., head dept. psychiatry U. Ill. Coll. Medicine, Chgo., 1961-74; med. dir. Am. Psychiat. Assn., Washington, 1974-98; ret. Author Depression, 1960, Psychiatric Ideology, 1961; Normality, 1978; Normality and Life Cycle, 1984 With U.S. Army, 1944. Recipient Bowen award Am. Coll. Psychiatrists, 1978, Disting. Psychiatrist award, 1985 Mem. Am. Coll. Psychiatrists (pres. 1974-75). Home: 2801 New Mexico Ave NW Washington DC 20007-3921

SABY, JOHN SANFORD, physicist, consultant; b. Ithaca, N.Y., Mar. 21, 1921; s. Rasmus S. and Maude Emily (Sanford) S.; m. Mary Elizabeth Long, June 9, 1945; children: Arthur D., Thomas S., Joseph A., Jean E. BA, Gettysburg (Pa.) Coll., 1942, Sc.D. (hon.), 1969; MS, Pa. State U., 1944, PhD, 1947. Lab. instr. Gettysburg Coll., 1940-42; instr. Cornell U., 1947-50; with Gen. Electric Co., 1951-82, mgr. semicondr./solid state, 1954-56, mgr. lamp phenomena research Cleve., 1956-82; cons., 1982—; mem. vis. com. biol. and phys. scis. Case Western Res. U., chmn., 1969. Co-author: Principles of Transistor Circuits, 1953; patentee in field. Fellow: IEEE (past com. officer); mem.: Cleve. Assn. Rsch. Dirs. (pres. 1963—64), Am. Phys. Soc., Nat. Assn. Watch and Clock Collectors, Phi Sigma Kappa, Phi Kappa Phi, Sigma Xi, Phi Beta Kappa. Home: Carolina Village # 295 Hendersonville NC 28792-3900

SACCO, DAVID J. neurosurgeon; b. Boston; m. Jodi Sacco. Degree in biochemistry and cell biology, U. Calif., San Diego; MD, Loyola U., Chgo. Lic. physician Tex., Mass. Intern in gen. surgery, resident in neurol. surgery U. Ky.; fellow in pediat. Children's Hosp. Boston/Harvard Med. Sch.; clin. asst. prof. neurol. surgery U. Tex. Southwestern Med. Sch., Dallas; attending neurosurgeon Children's Med. Ctr. Dallas, Med. City Dallas Hosp., Tex. Scottish Rite Hosp. for Children. Presenter in field. Contbr. articles to profl. jours. Mem.: Alpha Omega Alpha. Office: Children's Med Ctr-Neurol Surgery 1935 Motor St Dallas TX 75235

SACCO, JOHN MICHAEL, accountant; b. N.Y.C., Oct. 17, 1952; s. Anthony Carmine and Angelina (Pellegrino) Sacco. BS, St. John's U., 1974. CPA CPA. Staff acct. Price Waterhouse & Co., N.Y.C., 1974-75; semi-sr. acct. Seidman & Seidman, CPAs, White Plains, N.Y., 1976-77; sr. acct. Diamond Internat. Corp., N.Y.C., 1977-79, Burns Internat. Security Svcs., Inc., Briarcliff Manor, N.Y., 1979-81; acctg. mgr. Burns Integrated Sys., Inc., Briarcliff Manor, NY, 1981-83; pvt. practice White Plains, N.Y., 1978—. Mem.: AICPA, N.Y. Soc. CPA (mem. peer rev. com., mem. bus. valuations com., mem. cooperation with bankers and credit grantors, mem. acctg. and auditing com.). Republican. Roman Catholic. Home: 197 Upper Shad Rd Pound Ridge NY 10576-2237 Office Phone: 914-253-8757.

SACERDOTE, PETER M. investment banker; b. Turin, Italy, Oct. 15, 1937; came to U.S., 1940; s. Giorgio S. and Luciana (Levi) S.; m. Bonnie Lee Johnson, June 18, 1967; children: Alisa, Alexander, Laurence. BEE, Cornell U., 1960; MBA, Harvard U., 1964. Assoc. investment banking divsn. Goldman, Sachs & Co., N.Y.C., 1964-69, v.p. investment banking divsn., 1969-73, gen. ptnr., 1973-90, ltd. ptnr., 1990-99, adv. dir., 1999—. Bd. dirs. Hexcel Corp., Qualcomm, Inc., San Diego, Franklin Resource, San Mateo, Calif.; in charge Pvt. Fin. Dept., 1974-80, The Corp. Fin. Dept., 1980-87, Merch Bank, 1987-90; chmn. Committments, Credit and Investment Cons., 1987-90, GS Capital Partnership; adj. prof. Columbia Grad. Sch. Bus., 1984-86; nat. chmn. HBSFD, Milton (Mass.) Acad. Trustee Day Sch., N.Y.C., 1980-85; chmn. Alumni Bd. Harvard Bus. Sch., 1990-92; bd. visitors Fuqua Sch. Duke U., 1990-96; bd. overseers Cornell Med. Coll.; bd. dirs. Nantucket Conservation Found., coun. on fgn. rels. Served to lt. (j.g.) USNR, 1960-62. Mem. Harvard Club N.Y.C., River Club N.Y.C., Downtown Assn., Nantucket Yacht Club, Stanwich Golf Club, Country Club of the Rockies, Sankaty Head Golf Club, Nantucket Golf Club, Eagle Springs Golf Club. Office: Goldman Sachs & Co 85 Broad St Fl 10 New York NY 10004-2434

SACHA, ROBERT FRANK, osteopathic physician; b. East Chicago, Ind., Dec. 29, 1946; s. S. Frank John and Ann Theresa S.; m. Linda T. LePage, 1988; children: Joshua Jude, Josiah Gerard, Anastasia Levon, Jonah Bradley. BS, Purdue U., 1969; DO, Chgo. Coll. Osteo. Medicine, 1975; PharmD, Creighton U., 2004. Diplomate Am. Bd. Pediatrics, Am. Bd. Allergy and Immunology. Pharmacist, asst. mgr. Walgreens Drug Store, East Chicago, Ind., 1969-75; intern David Grant Med. Ctr., San Francisco, 1975-76, resident in pediatrics, 1976-78; fellow in allergy and immunology Wilford Hall Med. Ctr., 1978-80; staff pediatrician, allergist Scott AFB (Ill.), 1980-83; practice medicine specializing in allergy and immunology Cape Girardeau, Mo., 1983—. Assoc. clin. instr. St. Louis U., 1980—; clin. instr. Purdue U., 1971-72, Pepperdine U., 1975-76, U. Tex.-San Antonio, 1978-80, assoc. clin. instr. So. Ill. U. Pres., Parent Tchrs. League; bd. gov. Chgo. Coll. Osteopathic Medicine. Maj. M.C. USAF, 1975-83, comdr. USNR. Named one of Top Pediatricians 2002-2003, Pediatric Allergy, Immunology. Fellow Am. Coll. Allergy, Am. Coll. Chest Physicians, Am. Acad. Pediatrics, Am. Acad. Allergy-Immunology, Am. Assn. Cert. Allergists; mem. ACP, AMA, Am. Acad. Allergy, Assn. Mil. Allergists, Am. Coll. Emergency Physicians, Mil. Surgeons and Physicians. Republican. Lutheran. E-mail: bsacha@charter.net.

SACHAR, DAVID BERNARD, gastroenterologist, educator; b. Urbana, Ill., Mar. 2, 1940; s. Abram Leon and Thelma (Horwitz) Sachar; m. Joanna Maud Belford Silver, Aug. 29, 1961; children: Mark Benson, Kenneth Hulbert Belford(dec.). BA magna cum laude, Harvard Univ., 1959, MD cum laude, 1963. Cert. Am. Bd. Internal Medicine, diplomate Am. Bd. Gastroenterology. Intern Beth Israel Hosp., Boston, 1963-65, resident in internal medicine, 1967-68; asst. chief clin. rsch. Pakistan SEATO Cholera Rsch. Lab., Dhaka, Bangladesh, 1965-67; resident in gastroenterology Mt. Sinai Hosp., NYC, 1968-70; instr. to prof. medicine Mt. Sinai Sch. Medicine, NYC, 1970-92, first Burrill B. Crohn prof. medicine, 1992-99; dir. divsn. gastroenterology Mt. Sinai Hosp., NYC, 1983-99, vice chmn. dept. medicine, 1992-99, dir. emeritus, 1999—. Co-chmn. with work group on inflammatory bowel disease NIH, 1973—75; expert adv. panel gastroenterology and nutrition U.S. Pharmacopeial Conf., 1980—85; co-founder, sec., treas. Burrill B. Crohn Rsch. Found., NYC, 1984—; chmn. rsch. devel. com. Nat. Found. Ileitis and Colitis, 1984—89; K. H. Koster meml. lectr. Danish Soc. Gastroenterology, 1992; mem. Gastroenterology Leadership Coun. Task Force Fellowship Curriculum, 1994, Internat. state art lectr. Falk Symposia, Germany, 1996; twentieth ann. Norman Tanner meml. lectr. St. George's Hosp. Med. Sch., London, 1997; internat. state art lectr., Belgium, 98, Brit. Soc. Gastroenterology, 1998, World Congresses Gastroenterology, Austria, 1998, Turkish Soc. Gastroenterology, 1998, World Congresses Gastroenterology, Italy, 1999, Hungarian Soc. Gastroenterology, 1999, Hellenic Soc. Gastroenterology, 1999; chmn. GI adv. bd. Solvay Pharm., Inc., 2000—02; internat. state art lectr. Falk Symposia, Germany, 2000—02; 25th ann. Nana Svartz meml. lectr., Örebro, Sweden, 2000; co chmn. 40th ann. post grad. course Portuguese Soc. Gastroenterology, 2000; internat. state art lectr., Italy, 01, Portuguese Soc. Gastroenterology, 2003; mem. GI adv. com. FDA, 2004—. Editor: seven books and monograms on gastroenterology; contbr. chapters to books, over 200 articles to profl. journals. Trustee Bangladesh Coun. Asia Soc., NYC, 1972—75, Englewood Cliffs Bd. Edn., 1973—75. Sr. surgeon, comdr. USPHS, 1965—67. Recipient Jacobi Medallion for Disting. Achievement, Mt. Sinai Alumni Assn., 1994, Alexander Richman Commemorative award for Humanism in Medicine, 1996, Norman Tanner medal, St. George's Hosp. Med. Sch., 1997, Gold Headed Cane award, 1997. Master: Am. Coll. Gastroenterology (mem. program dir. com. 1991—, Henry Baker Presdl. Lectr. 1989); fellow: ACP; mem.: Internat. Orgn. Study of Inflammatory Bowel Disease (first Am. elected chmn. 1989—92, chmn. task force clin. phenomics 1992—), Crohn's and Colitis Found. Am. (mem. grant rev. com. and coun. 1990—94, Disting. Svc. Award 1991, N.Y. Gov. Medal 1992), Am. Gastroent. Assn. (first chmn. clin. tchg. project 1984—90, mem. 1990—93, mem. nominating com. 1993—94, chmn. immuno inflammatory disorders sectional nominating com. 1995, mem. 1998—, Disting. Educator Award 1996), Brazilian Soc. Gastroenterology (patron 2003), Alpha Omega Alpha, Phi Beta Kappa. Achievements include co developer of oral rehydration therapy for diarrhea; development of resources and standards for clin. tchg. in gastroenterology; established Joanna and David B. Sachar International Award and Visiting Professorship in Inflammatory Bowel Disease. Office: Mt Sinai Med Ctr One Gustave L Levy Pl New York NY 10029

SACHAR, LOUIS, writer; b. East Meadow, N.Y., Mar. 20, 1954; married, 1985; 1 child. Student, Antioch Coll.; BA, U. Calif., Berkeley, 1976; JD, Hastings Coll. Law, San Francisco, 1980. Part-time atty. Author: (children's books) Sideways Stories From Wayside School, 1978 (1979 Children's Choice Book), Johnny's in the Basement, 1981, Someday Angeline, 1983, Sixth Grade Secrets, 1987, There's A Boy in the Girls' Bathroom, 1987, The Boy Who Lost His Face, 1989, Wayside School is Falling Down, 1989, Dogs Don't Tell Jokes, 1991, Marvin Redpost: Kidnapped at Birth?, 1992, Marvin Redpost: Is He a Girl?, 1993, Marvine Redpost: Why Pick on Me?, 1993, Alone in His Teachers' House, 1994, Wayside School Gets a Little Stranger, 1995, Holes, 1998 (finalist Nat. Book Award), Class President, 1999, Stanley Yelnat's Survival Guide to Camp Green Lake, 2003. Winner 1999 Newberry medal for Holes. Mem. Soc. Children's Book Writers and Illustrators, Authors Guild. Office: c/o Farrar Straus & Giroux 19 Union Sq W New York NY 10003-3304*

SACHAROW, BEVERLY, gerontologist; b. N.Y.C. d. Jules and Mary (Trupine) Levy; m. Stanley Sacharow, June 18, 1961; children: Scott Hunter, Brian Evan. BA, Rutgers U., 1980, M in Gerontology Edn., cert. ednl. gerontology, Rutgers U., 1983. Rschr. U. Pa., Robert W. Johnson Hosp., New Brunswick, N.J., 1976-81; dir. Gerontology Inst. N.J., Milltown, 1983—, Gerontology Inst. N.J., Pa., N.Y., Milltown, 1996—. Tour guide, rsch. leader, del. on tour of geriatric facilities, Moscow, Kiev and St. Petersburg, Russia, 1992; invited reporter White House Conf. on Aging, Washington, 1996; conf. planner in gerontology and social work issues and health; cons. assisted living industry, long term care nursing homes. Editor (newsletter) Update on Aging, 1983; video prodr. over 300 gerontology video catalog, 1998—. Mem. adv. com. Gov. Conf. on Aging, Trenton State Coll., 1981; mem. adv. bd. East Brunswick (N.J.) Office on Aging, 1982; planner Brandeis U. Women Study Group. Mem. Am. Soc. on Aging, Nat. Coun. on Aging (mem. press for nat. conf.), Sigma Phi Omega. Avocations: travel, golf. Office: Gerontology Inst PO Box 345 Milltown NJ 08850-0345 E-mail: geronusa@aol.com.

SACHAROW, STANLEY, chemist, consultant, writer; b. N.Y.C., Oct. 8, 1935; s. Max and Fannie (Rosenberg) S.; m. Beverly Lynn Levy, June 18, 1961; children: Scott Hunter, Brian Evan. AB, Hunter Coll., 1957, MA, 1965. Engr. Standard Packaging Corp., Clifton, N.J., 1960-65; sales engr. Archer Aluminum, Winston-Salem, N.C., 1965-67; tech. svc. mgr. Reynolds Metals Co., Richmond, Va., 1967-84; exec. dir. The Packaging Group Inc., 1984—. Author: Food packaging, 1970; Principles of Packaging Development, 1972; A Packaging Primer, 1979; Packaging Regulations, 1979. Contbr. articles to profl. jours. Recipient Golden Keys award Club Printing N.Y., 1969, Best Tech. Article award Chilton Press, 1974. Mem. Packaging Inst., Am. Chem. Soc., Coblentz Soc., Inst. Dirs. (U.K.), Inst. Packaging (U.K.), Napoleonic Soc. (Clearwater, Fla.), Victorian Soc. (Phila.). Republican. Avocations: antiques, writing, napoleonic battles. Home: 70 Valley Forge Dr East Brunswick NJ 08816-3278 Office: Packaging Group Inc PO Box 345 Milltown NJ 08850-0345

SACHDEO, RAJESH C. neurologist, educator; b. India; MD, Christian Med. Coll., Ludhiana, Panja, India, 1973. Diplomate Am. Bd. of Psychiatry and Neurology, 1982. Intern Christian Med. Coll. Hosp., Ludhiana, India, 1973; rotating resident VA Hines and Loyola Univ. Med. Ctr., Maywood, Ill., 1974—75; fellow in Neurophysiology and Epilepsy St. Lukes Med. Ctr., Chgo., 1979—80; physician divsn. neurosurgery, dept. neurology Robert Wood Johnson Univ. Med. Group, New Brunswick, NJ, 1985—. Clin. prof. Neurology Robert Wood Johnson Univ. Hosp., New Brunswick, NJ, 1987—. Office: Clin Acad Bldg Ste 6100 125 Paterson St New Brunswick NJ 08901-1977

SACHER, BARTON STUART, lawyer; b. Birmingham, Ala., Apr. 9, 1948; s. Martin R. and Inez (Zuckerman) S.; 1 child, Joseph Alan; m. Susan Angela Anton, Sept. 30, 1976. BS, U. Ala., 1970, JD, 1973. Law clk. to judge S. Pointer U.S. Dist. Ct., Birmingham, 1973-74; assoc. Berkowitz, Lefkowitz & Patrick, Birmingham, 1974-77; atty. investigations, trial counsel SEC, Washington, 1977-79, chief of investigations and enforcement Atlanta Region, 1979-85; ptnr. Tew, Jorden, Schulte & Beasley, Miami, 1986-90; pres., dir., ptnr. Sacher, Zelman, Van Sant, Paul, Beiley, Hartman, Rolnick & Waldman PA, Miami, 1990—. V.p., trustee Temple Israel of Greater Miami, Inc.; v.p., dir. Alex Muss H.S., Israel; regional dir. ADL, Nat. Fin. Com., Dem. Party, Dem. Leadership Coun.; mem. S.E. regional coun. Union Am. Hebrew Congregations. Mem. ABA, Fed. Bar Assn., Fla. Bar Assn., D.C. Bar Assn., Ala. State Bar Assn., Greater Miami C. of C. (trustee), Grove Isle Club. Jewish. Office: Sacher Zelman et al 1401 Brickell Ave 7th Fl Miami FL 33131-3506

SACHER, RONALD ALAN, hematologist; b. Johannesburg, Feb. 6, 1946; s. Barney and Doris S.; m. Heather, Feb. 3, 1970; children: Gregory Neill, Samantha Anne. BSc, Witwatersrand U., 1965, MBBCh, 1969. Intern in medicine, surgery Baragwanath Hosp., Johannesburg, 1970; sr. house office pediat. Johannesburg Children's Hosp., 1972; registrar hematology South African Inst. Med. Rsch., Johannesburg, 1974-75; from asst. prof. to prof., head dept. lab. medicine Georgetown U. Sch. Medicine, Washington, 1980-2000; prof., dir. Hoxworth Blood Ctr. U. Cin. Med. Ctr., 2000—. Chmn. med. adv. bd. Chesapeak chpt. ARC, 1992-2000, scientific review com. for blood transfusion scis., 1981-87, med. adv. com. Washington chpt., 1980-2000. Fellow Royal Coll. Physicians and Surgeons of Can.; mem. AAAS, Am. Assn. Blood Banks (chmn. several nat. & internat. meetings 1982, nat. co-chmn. pediat. hemotherapy com. 1982-83, chmn. 1983-87, tech. & scientific workshop com. 1987-94, chmn. 1991-94, chmn. continuing edn. com. 1994), Coll. Am. Pathology, Internat. Soc. Thrombosis and Hemostasis, Am. Soc. for Clin. Pathology, Am. Fedn. Clin. Rsch., Am. Soc. Hematology, Am. Assn. of Blood Banks, Am. Clin. Climate Soc. Office: U Cin Med Ctr Hoxworth Blood Ctr 3130 Highland Ave Cincinnati OH 45267-0055 Office Phone: 513-558-1201. Business E-Mail: ronald.sacher@uc.edu.

SACHER, STEVEN JAY, lawyer; b. Cleve., Jan. 28, 1942; s. Albert N. and Cecil P. (Chessin) S., m. Colleen Marie Gibbons, Nov. 28, 1970; children—Alexander Jerome, Barry Elizabeth, William Paul. BS, U. Wis., 1964; JD, U. Chgo., 1967. Bar: D.C. 1968. Assoc. solicitor Employee Retirement Income Security Act U.S. Dept. Labor, Washington, 1974-77; spl. counsel com. on labor and human resources U.S. Senate, Washington, 1977-79, gen. counsel, 1980-81; ptnr. Pepper, Hamilton & Scheetz, Washington, 1982-88; shareholder Johnson & Gibbs, Washington, 1988-94; ptnr. Kilpatrick Stockton LLP, Washington, 1994—. Adj. prof. law Georgetown U. Law Ctr., 1977; co-chair sr. editors Employee Benefits Law and Annual Supplements, Bur. Nat. Affairs, Washington, 1991-2000. Mem. adv. bd. BNA Pension and Benefits Reporter; mem. editorial bd. Benefits Law Jour., Jour. Pension Planning and Compliance. Founding mem. ERISA Roundtable, Washington. Fellow Coll. Labor and Employment Lawyers, Am. Coll. Employee Benefits Counsel (charter); mem. ABA (mgmt. co-chmn. com. on employee benefits, sect. on labor and employment law 1988-91, chmn. prohibited trans. subcom., com. on employee benefits, sect. on taxation 1986-91), D.C. Bar Assn. Office: Kilpatrick Stockton LLP 607 14th St NW Ste 900 Washington DC 20005 Office Phone: 202-508-5840. Business E-Mail: ssacher@kilpatrickstockton.com.

SACHS, DAVID HOWARD, surgery and immunology educator, medical researcher; b. N.Y.C., Jan. 10, 1942; s. Elliot and Elsie (Hurvitz) S.; m. Kristina Olsson, Mar. 15, 1969; children: Michelle, Jessica, Karin, Teviah. AB, Harvard U., 1963; DES, U. Paris, 1964; MD, Harvard U., Boston, 1968. Intern in surgery Mass. Gen. Hosp., Boston, 1968-69, resident in surgery, 1969-70, dir. transplantation biology rsch. ctr. surgery dept., 1991—; chief immunology br. Nat. Cancer Inst., Bethesda, Md., 1982-90; prof. surgery and immunology Harvard U. Med. Sch., 1991—. Capt. PHS, 1970-91. Avocations: gardening, fishing, windsurfing, skiing. Office: Mass Gen Hosp East Bldg 149-9019 13th St Boston MA 02129

SACHS, GREG ALAN, preventive medicine physician; BA in Biology with honors, U. Chgo., 1977—81; MD, Yale U., 1981—85. Diplomate Am. Bd. Internal Medicine, 1988, cert. in Geriatrics Am. Bd. Internal Medicine, 1990. Resident, internal medicine U. Chgo. Hosps. & Clinics, 1985—87; fellow, geriatric medicine U. Chgo., 1987—90, fellow, clin. med. ethics, 1988—90, asst. prof., medicine, 1990—97, dir., ethics consultation svc., 1992—95, asst. dir., MacLean Ctr. for Clin. Med. Ethics, 1993—99, dir., required ambulatory geriatrics rotation for medicine residents, 1993—97, assoc. prof., medicine, 1997—, found co-dir., The Memory Ctr., 1999—, dir., Hartford Found. Ctr. of Excellence in Geriatrics, 2000—, founding sect. chief, geriatrics, 2000—. Mem. editl. bd. Alzheimer's Disease and Assoc. Disorders, An Internat. Jour., 1995—, Second Opinion, 1999—2002, Jour. of Am. Geriatrics Soc., 2000—, reviewer for various jours. Mem. Cook County State's Atty.'s Task Force on Removal of Life-Sustaining Treatment, 1989—90; mem., cmty. ethics com. Chgo. Coun. for Jewish Elderly, 1990—94; reviewer, grant proposals on end-of-life care Retirement Rsch. Found., 1995—; mem., social sci., humanities, and policy adv. bd. The Brookdale Found., 1998—2000. Mem.: ACP, Nat. Alzheimer's Assn. (mem., ethics adv. panel 1995—, bd. dirs., Chgo. chpt. 1998—2000, chair, ethics adv. panel 2000—), Gerontological Soc. Am., Am. Geriatrics Soc. (mem., ethics com. 1992—, rep., coalition for quality end-of-life care 1996—99, chair, ethics com. 1998—2001, mem., pub. policy adv. group 2001—, New Investigator award 1994), Phi Beta Kappa, Alpha Omega Alpha. Office: Univ Chgo Dept Medicine MC6098 5841 S Maryland Ave Chicago IL 60637-1470*

SACHS, HARLEY LUTHER, writer, educator; s. Jack Samson Sachs and Miriam (Not For Publication); m. Ulla Deborah (Not For Publication), May 15, 1960; children: Anna-Lena Toledo, Belinda Bee Toby, Cynthia Yolanda Bustos. BA, Ind. U., 1953, MAT, 1957; PhD, Ind. Christian U. Instr. So. Ill. U., Alton, 1963—65; assoc. prof. Mich. Technol. U., Houghton, 1965—86; asst. prof. Aalborg U. Ctr., Aalborg, Denmark, 1986—87; prof. emeritus Mich. Technol. U., 1986—. Author: The Mystery Club and the Dead Doctor, The Search for Jesse Bram, Ben Zakkai's Coffin, (short stories) A Troll for Christmas and other Stories, Threads of the Covenant: the Jews of Red Jacket. County commr. Houghton County, 1969—71. With U.S. Army, 1953—55. Recipient First prize for essay, H.G. Roberts Found., 1988, award for excellence, Soc. for Tech. Communication, Chgo. chpt., 1989. Mem.: Willamette Writers, Upper Peninsula Mich. Writers (pres., v.p., Ed Powers Meml. award Humor 1997, Lifetime Achievement award 2002). Avocation: sailing. Home: 113 W Houghton Ave Houghton, MI MI 49931 Office: Idevco 2545 SW Terwilliger Blvd Apt 222 Portland OR 97201 Personal E-mail: hlsachs@mtu.edu. E-mail: hlsachs@mtu.edu.

SACHS, HOWARD F(REDERIC), federal judge; b. Kansas City, Mo., Sept. 13, 1925; s. Alex F. and Rose (Lyon) S.; m. Susanne Wilson, 1960; children: Alex Wilson, Adam Phinney. BA summa cum laude, Williams Coll., 1947; JD, Harvard U., 1950. Bar: Mo. 1950. Law clk. U.S. Dist. Ct., Kansas City, Mo., 1950-51; pvt. practice law Phineas Rosenberg, Kansas City, 1951-56; with Spencer, Fane, Britt & Browne, 1956-79; U.S. dist. judge Western Dist. Mo., Kansas City, 1979—, chief dist. judge, 1990-92, now sr. judge. Contbr. articles to various publs.; contbr. chpt. to Mid-America's Promise, 1982. Mem. Kansas City Commn. Human Rels., 1967-73; chmn. Jewish Community Rels. Bur., 1968-71, Kansas City chpt. Am. Jewish Com., 1963-65; mem. exec. com. Nat. Jewish Community Rels. Adv. Coun., 1968-71; pres. Urban League Kansas City, 1957-58, Kansas City chpt. Am. Jewish Congress, 1974-77; co-chmn. Kansas City chpt. NCCJ, 1958-60; mem. Kansas City Sch. Dist. Desegregation Task Force, 1976-77; pres. Jackson County Young Democrats, 1959-60; treas. Kennedy-Johnson Club, Jackson County, 1960. Served with USNR, 1944-46. Mem. ABA, Mo. Bar, Kansas City Bar Assn., Am. Judicature Soc., Lawyers Assn. Kansas City, Dist. Judges Assn. (8th cir., pres. 1992-94), Phi Beta Kappa. Office: US Dist Ct US Courthouse 400 E 9th St Kansas City MO 64106-2607

SACHS, JEFFREY DAVID, economist, educator; b. Detroit, Nov. 5, 1954; s. Theodore and Joan Sachs; m. Sonia Ehrlich Sachs; children: Lisa, Adam, Hannah. BA summa cum laude, Harvard U., 1976, MA in Econs., 1978, PhD in Econs., 1980; degree (hon.), St. Gallen U., Switzerland, 1990, Lingnan Coll. Hong Kong, 1998, Varba Econs. U., Bulgaria, 2000, Iona Coll. N.Y., 2000. Prof. internat. trade Harvard U., Cambridge, Mass., 1984—2002; prof. sustainable devel. Columbia U., N.Y.C., 2002—, dir. Earth Inst., 2002—. Dir. Harvard Inst. Internat. Devel. Harvard U., 1995—99; chmn. commn. on macroecons. and health WHO, 2000—01; dir. Ctr. for Internat. Devel. Harvard U., 1998—2002; spl. advisor to sec. gen. Kofi Annan UN, N.Y.C., 2002—; cons. in field. Author: Poland's Jump to the Market Economy, 1993; co-author: Macroeconomics in the Global Economy, 1992. Mem.: Inst. Medicine, 2004. Office: The Earth Inst at Columbia Univ 314 Low Libr MC 4327 535 West 116th St New York NY 10027 Office Phone: 212-854-8704.

SACHS, JOHN PETER, carbon company executive; b. Duesseldorf, Germany, 1926; married. BAChemE, Ill. Inst. Tech., 1948, MAChemE, 1950, PhDChemE, 1952. Various mgmt. positions in research and devel., engring. and ops. Union Carbide Corp., 1951-66; v.p. ops. then group v.p. Great Lakes Carbon Corp., N.Y.C., 1966-78; pres., chief exec. officer Gt. Lakes Carbon Corp., N.Y.C., 1978-86; chmn. bd., dir. Gen. Refractories Co., 1978-85; mng. ptnr. J.P. Sachs Assocs., Mgmt. Cons., New Canaan, Conn., 1987—99. Trustee Fairfield U., 1978-92; bd. dirs. Kneissl-Dachstein 1992—, Peridot, 1989-98. Mem. Am. Inst. Chem. Engrs. (pres. 1985) Home and Office: JP Sachs Assocs 67 Dunning Rd New Canaan CT 06840-4009

SACHS, LEO, geneticist, educator; b. Leipzig, Germany, Oct. 14, 1924; s. Elijah and Louise (Lichtblau) S.; m. Pnina Salkind; 4 children. BSc, U. Wales, Bangor, 1948; PhD, Trinity Coll., Cambridge U., 1951; DHC (hon.), Bordeaux U., 1985; MD (hon.), Lund U., 1997. Rsch. scientist John Innes Inst., 1951-52; mem. sci. staff Weizmann Inst. Sci., Rehovot, Israel, 1952—, prof., chmn. genetics dept., 1962—, Otto Meyerhof prof. molecular biology, 1968. Mem. Israeli Acad. Sci. and Humanities, 1975; hon. fellow U. Wales, Bangor, 1999. Contbr. articles to sci. jours. Recipient Israel prize for natural sci., 1972; named Fogarty Internat. scholar NIH, 1972, Harvey Lecture, 1972; recipient Rothschild prize in biol. scis., 1977, Wolf prize in medicine, 1980, Bristol-Myers award for disting. achievement in cancer rsch., 1983, Royal Soc. Wellcome Found. prize, 1986, Sloan prize GM Cancer Rsch. Found., 1989, Warren Alpert prize Harvard Med. Sch., 1997, Emet prize in life scis., 2002. Fellow Royal Soc., 1997; mem. U.S. Nat. Acad. Scis. (fgn. assoc. 1995), Academia Europaea (fgn. 1998), Internat. Cytokine Soc. (hon. life 2001). Office: Weizmann Inst Sci Dept Molecular Genetics Rehovot 76100 Israel Business E-Mail: leo.sachs@weizmann.ac.il.

SACHS, MARGARET V. law educator; b. Washington, Nov. 10, 1951; d. Jeremiah and Thelma S. AB, Harvard U., 1973, JD, 1977. Bar: NY 1978. Law clk. U.S. Ct. Appeals, 2d cir., N.Y.C., 1977-79; assoc. Simpson Thacher & Bartlett, N.Y.C., 1979-81; from asst. to assoc. prof. Sch. Law U. Bridgeport, Conn., 1982-86; assoc. prof. Sch. Law Widener U., Wilmington, Del., 1986-90, U. Ga., Athens, 1990-95, prof. Sch. Law, 1995-97, Robert Cotten Alston prof. Sch. Law, 1997—. Author (with Nagy and Painter): Securities Litigation and Enforcement: Cases and Materials, 2003; mem. editl. bd.: Jour. Legal Edn., 1995—98; contbr. articles to profl. jours. Mem. exec. com. on securities regulation Am. Assn. Law Schs., 2003—. Mem.: Am. Law Inst., Am. Assn. Law Schs. (exec. coun. sect. on bus. assocs. 1993—96), Phi Beta Kappa. Presbyterian. Home: 458 Highland Ave Athens GA 30606-4316 Office: U Ga Sch Law Herty Dr Athens GA 30602 E-mail: mvs@uga.edu.

SACHS, MARILYN STICKLE, author, lecturer, editor; b. NYC, Dec. 18, 1927; d. Samuel and Anna (Smith) Stickle; m. Morris Sachs, Jan. 26, 1947; children: Anne, Paul. BA, Hunter Coll., 1949; MSLS, Columbia U., 1953. Children's libr. Bklyn. Pub. Libr., 1949-60, San Francisco Pub. Libr., 1961-67. Author: Amy Moves In, 1964, Laura's Luck, 1965, Amy and Laura, 1966, Veronica Ganz, 1968, Peter and Veronica, 1969, Marv, 1970, The Bears' House, 1971 (Austrian Children's Book prize 1977, Recognition of Merit award George C. Stone Ctr. for Children's Books 1989), The Truth About Mary Rose, 1973 (Silver Slate Pencil award 1974), A Pocket Full of Seeds, 1973 (Jane Addams Children's Book Honor award 1974), Matt's Mitt, 1975, Dorrie's Book, 1975 (Silver State Pencil award 1977, Garden State Children's Book award 1978), A December Tale, 1976, A Secret Friends, 1978, A Summer's Lease, 1979, Bus Ride, 1980, Class Pictures, 1980, Fleet Footed Florence, 1981, Hello...Wrong Number, 1981, Call Me Ruth, 1982 (Assn. Jewish Librs. award 1983), Beach Towels, 1982, Fourteen, 1983, The Fat Girl, 1984, Thunderbird, 1985, Underdog, 1985 (Christopher 1986), Baby Sister 1986, Almost Fifteen, 1987, Fran Ellen's House, 1987 (award Bay Area Book Reviewers Assn. 1988, Recognition of Merit award George C. Stone Ctr. for Children's Books 1989), Just Like A Friend, 1989, At the Sound of the Beep, 1990, Circles, 1991, What My Sister Remembered, 1992, Thirteen, 1993, Ghosts in the Family, 1995, Another Day, 1997, Suprise Party, 1998, Jo Jo & Winnie, 1999, Jo Jo & Winnie Again, 2000, The Four Ugly Cats in Apartment 3D, 2002; co-editor: (with Ann Durell) Big Book for Peace, 1990 (Calif. Children's Book award 1991, Jane Addams Children's Book prize 1991); reviewer books N.Y. Times, San Francisco Chronicle, 1970—. Mem. PEN, ACLU, Sierra Club, Authors' Guild. Democrat. Jewish. Avocations: reading, walking, baseball. Home: 733 31st Ave San Francisco CA 94121-3523

SACHS, MURRAY B. audiologist, educator; BS in Elec. Engring., MIT, 1962, MS in Elec. Engring. and Auditory Physiology, 1964, PhD in Elec. Engring. and Auditory Physiology, 1966. Teaching asst., dept. elec. engring. MIT, 1962—64, instr., dept. elec. engring., 1964—66; rsch. scientist US Navy Underwater Sound Lab., New London, Conn.; postdoctoral fellow U. Cambridge, 1968—69; asst. prof. biomedical engring. John Hopkins U. Sch. Medicine, Balt., 1970—74, assoc. prof. biomedical engring., 1974—80, prof. biomedical engring., 1980—, prof. neuroscience, 1981—, prof. otolaryngology-head and neck surgery, 1983—, dir. Ctr. Hearing Sci., 1986—91, Massey prof., dir. Whitaker Biomed. Engring. Inst., 1991—. Mem. com. comm. and control Internat. Union Pure and Applied Biophysics, 1975—80; mem. comm. disease panel and basic sci. task force Nat. Inst. Neurol. and Communicative Disorders and Stroke, NIH, 1977—78, chmn. communicative disease rev. com., 1977—79, ad hoc adv. com., 1979—86; ad hoc prog. project adv. com. Kresge Hearing Rsch. Inst., U. Mich., 1982—; sci. program adv. com. Nat. Inst. Neurol. and Communicative Disorders and Stroke, NIH, 1984—86; ad hoc prog. project adv. com. (cochlear implants), dept. otolaryngology-HNS U. Iowa Sch. Medicine, 1984—93; investigator Jacob Javitz Neuroscience, 1985; ad hoc program project adv. com., cochlear implant program MIT, 1986—; bd. scientific counselors Nat. Ctr. for Rsch. Resources, NIH, 1995—. Contbr. articles to profl. pubs.; edit. bd. Hearing Rsch., 1978—. Lt. USNR, 1966—68, US Navy Underwater Sound Lab., New London, Conn. Named Whitaker Disting. Lectr., Biomedical Engring. Soc., 2000; recipient von Bekesy medal, Acoustical Soc. Am., 1998, Merit award, Assn. for Rsch. Otolaryngology, 1999. Fellow: AAAS (chmn. acad. coun. 1994); mem.: NAE, Assn. for Rsch. in Otolaryngology (coun. mem. 1982—), Am. Acad. Otolaryngology-HNS (rsch. com. 1986—), Am. Inst. for Med. and Biol. Engring. (founding fellow 1992, chair-elect, Coll. Fellows 1996—97), NAS (com. on hearing and bioacoustics 1985—88, Inst. Medicine 1990), Eta Kappa Nu, Tau Beta Pi, Sigma Xi. Office: Johns Hopkins U Sch Medicine 720 Rutland Ave Baltimore MD 21205-2109 Office Phone: 410-955-3131. Office Fax: 410-955-0549. Business E-Mail: msachs@bme.jhu.edu.*

SACHS, SAMUEL, II, museum director; b. N.Y.C., Nov. 30, 1935; s. James Henry and Margery Sachs; m. Susan McAllen (div.); children: Katherine, Eleanor; m. Jerre S. Hollander (div.); 1 child, Alexander; m. Elizabeth M. Gordon; 1 child, Hadley Elizabeth. BA cum laude, Harvard U., 1957; MA, NYU Inst. Fine Arts, 1962. With Mpls. Inst. Arts, 1958-60; asst. dir. U. Mich. Mus. of Art, Ann Arbor, 1963-64; chief curator Mpls. Inst. Arts, 1964-73, dir., 1973-85, Detroit Inst. Arts, 1985-97; dir., CEO Frick Collection, N.Y.C., 1997—. Bd. dirs. Internat. Com. on Fine Arts, Art Mus. Image Consortium, IFAR, NINCH, Japan Soc. Decorated knight 1st class Order North Star

(Sweden); Order of Dannebrog (Denmark). Mem. Am. Assn. Museums, Assn. Art Mus. Dirs., Century Assn., Harvard Club. Home: 1112 Park Ave # 16B New York NY 10128-1235 Office: Frick Collection 1 E 70th St New York NY 10021-4907 E-mail: sachs@frick.org.

SACHS, STEPHEN MARK, political scientist, consultant; b. NYC, Aug. 19, 1938; s. Edgar Frank and Hilda Dorethy Sachs; m. Leah M. Ingraham, Feb. 2, 1988. BA with hons., U. Va., 1960; MA, U. Chgo., 1962, PhD, 1968. Asst. prof. We. Ky. U., 1965—66; from lectr. to asst. prof. Ind. U., South Bend, 1965—69; from asst. prof. to prof. emeritus Ind. U.-Purdue U. Indpls., 1969—2002. Adj. prof. Kirkwood C.C., Cedar Rapids, Iowa, 1988, The Econ. U., Prague, Czech Republic, 1993; past co-coord. rsch. action team Orgn. Devel. Inst., 1986—; cons. in field. Editor: Workplace Democracy, 1977—86; sr. editor Workplace Democracy, 1986—90; co-editor: Nonviolent Change, 1986—; co-author (with Richard Goldstein): Applied Poverty Research: Who Benefits?, 1983; co-author: (with Ladislav Rusmich) Lessons From the Failure of the Communist Economic System, 2003; contbr. numerous articles to profl. jours. Mem. Consortium on Peace Rsch., Edn., and Devel., 1992—2002, mem. interim bd., 2001—02, bd. dir., 1992—95, 2000—01. Recipient Book award, Policy Studies Assn., 1997, Outstanding Svc. award, Am. Indian Ctr. Ind., 2000; grantee, Pub. Svcs. Adminstrn., 1980—82, Ind U.-Purdue U. Sch. Liberal Arts, 1994, Ind. U.-Purdue U. SLA, 2001. Mem.: Peace and Justice Studies Assn. (sect. on new polit. sci. chair 1976-77, 1982-83, program coord. 1983—84, treas. 1978—79), Am. Polit. Sci. Assn. (Charles E. Merrium award com. 1976, steering com. 1992—99, sect. on environ. and transformational politics 1992—, program co-chmn. 2001—03), Native Am. Policy, Native Am. Studies Assn. Indigneous Studies Network (steering com. 1994—, program coord. 1999—2000, coord. 1999—, co-editor 2000—, editor Indigenous Policy). Home: 4820 Broadway St Indianapolis IN 46205 Office Phone: 317-924-5968.

SACHSMAN, DAVID BERNARD, communications educator; b. NYC, Aug. 16, 1945; s. Edgar and Susan (Sassower) S.; m. Judith Mittleman, Mar. 15, 1967; children: Jonathan William, Susanne Elizabeth. BA in English, U. Pa., 1967; AM in Comm., Stanford U., 1968, PhD in Comm., 1973. Asst. prof., lectr. Calif. State U., Hayward, 1969-71; asst. prof. Rutgers U., New Brunswick, N.J., 1971-76; spl. corr., copy editor The Home News, New Brunswick, N.J., 1974-77; assoc. prof. Rutgers U., New Brunswick, N.J., 1976-88; sr. Fulbright-Hays scholar U. Nigeria, Nsukka, 1978-79; chairperson dept. journalism Rutgers U., New Brunswick, 1983-88; adj. assoc. prof. U. Medicine and Dentistry of N.J., Piscataway, 1987-89; dean, prof. Calif. State U., Fullerton, 1988-91; west chair of excellence in comm., pub. affairs U. Tenn., Chattanooga, 1991—. News cons., writing coach Sta WRCB-TV, Chattanooga, 1996—98; mem. editl. bd. Mass. Comm. Rev., 1976—; prin. investigator externally funded rsch. New Brunswick, N.J., Fullerton, Calif., 1977—91; cons. in field. Co-editor: Media Casebook, 1972; co-author: Media: An Introductory Analysis of American Mass Communications, 1972, 3d rev. edit., 1982, The Press and the Suburbs: The Daily Newspapers of New Jersey, 1985, Environmental Risk and the Press, 1987, Environmental Reporter's Handbook, 1988, The Civil War and the Press, 2000, Reporter's Environmental Handbook, 2003; editor (assoc.): Advances in Telematics, 1983—86, Mass Comm. Rev., 1984—87; contbr. articles to profl. jours. Trustee The Daily Pennsylvania, Inc., Phila., 1985-88; bd. dirs. Girl Scout Coun. of Orange County, 1989-91, Moccasin Bend Girl Scout Coun., Chattanooga, Tenn., 1992—; bd. dirs., v.p. Girls Inc. of Chattanooga, 1991-94. Recipient award for Rsch. and Journalism, N.J. Chpt. Soc. for Profl. Journalists, 1984, 86, 88, 89; grantee Hazardous Substance Mgmt. Rsch. Ctr., 1985-89, 1985-90, Calif. Dept. Transp., 1990. Mem. Assn. for Edn. in Journalism and Mass Comm., Internat. Comm. Assn., Soc. of Environ. Journalists, Nat. Speech Comm. Assn., Investigative Reporters and Editors, Radio-TV News Dirs. Assn., N.J. Profl. Chpt. Soc. Profl. Journalists (pres. 1981-83, bd. dirs. 1984-88), Alpha Phi Gamma, Kappa Tau Alpha. Avocations: reading, films, tv, walking, music. Home: 1002 Centennial Dr Chattanooga TN 37405-4256 Office: U Tenn at Chattanooga Dept 3003 210 Frist Hall Chattanooga TN 37403 Office Phone: 423-425-4219. Business E-Mail: david-sachsman@utc.edu.

SACHTLER, WOLFGANG MAX HUGO, chemistry professor; b. Delitzsch, Germany, Nov. 8, 1924; came to U.S., 1983; s. Gottfried Hugo and Johanna Elisabeth (Bollmann) S.; m. Anne-Lore Luise Adrian, Dec. 9, 1953; children: Johann Wolfgang Adriaan, Heike Kathleen Julia, Yvonne Rhea Valeska. Diplomchemiker, Tech. U., Braunschweig, Ger., 1949; Dr.rer.nat. (Ph.D), 1952. Research chemist Kon-Shell Lab., Amsterdam, Netherlands, 1952-71, dept. head, 1972—83; extraordinary prof. chemistry U. Leiden, Netherlands, 1963-83; V.N. Ipatieff prof. Northwestern U., Evanston, Ill., 1983-96; chmn. Gordon Research Conf. Catalysis, N.H., 1985. Rideal lectr. Faraday div. Royal Soc. Chemistry, 1981; F. Gault lectr., 1991. Mem. editl. bd. Jour. Catalysis, 1976-88, Applied Catalysis, 1983-87, Catalysis Letters, 1987—, Advances in Catalysis, 1987—, Catalysis Today, 1996—, Catalysis Reviews, 1997—; contbr. numerous articles to sci. jours. Recipient Deutsche Gesellschaft Mineraloel und Kohle Kolleg award, 1991. Fellow AAAS; mem. Royal Netherlands Acad. Scis., Internat. Congress Catalysis (pres. coun. 1992-96), Royal Dutch Chem. Soc. (hon. mem. catalysis divsn.), Am. Chem. Soc. (E.V. Murphee award 1987, Petroleum Chemistry award 1992), Catalysis Soc. N.Am. (Robert L. Burwell award 1985, E. Houdry award 1993). Home: 2141 Ridge Ave Apt 2D Evanston IL 60201-2788 Office: Northwestern U 2137 Sheridan Rd Evanston IL 60208-0001 Office Phone: 847-491-5263. Business E-Mail: wmhs@northwestern.edu.

SACIA, JIM, state representative; Degree in Psychology, Speech, U. Wis., River Falls. Pres., CEO NITE Equip. Inc.; former spl. agent FBI; mem. Ill. Ho. of Reps., 2003—. Mem. Winnebago County Bd. With U.S. Army. Republican. Office: 210 N Stratton Office Bldg Springfield IL 62706 Address: 19 S Chicago Ave Freeport IL 61032

SACK, EDGAR ALBERT, electronics company executive; b. Pitts., Jan. 31, 1930; s. Edgar Albert and Margaret Valentine (Engelmohr) S.; m. Eugenia Ferris, June 7, 1952; children: Elaine Kimberley, Richard Warren. BS, Carnegie-Mellon U., 1951, MS, 1952, PhD, 1954. Dept. mgr. Westinghouse Rsch. Lab., Pitts., 1960-63; engring. mgr. Westinghouse Microelectronics, Balt., 1963-65, ops. mgr., 1965-67, divsn. mgr., 1967-69; div. v.p. Gen. Instrument Corp., Hicksville, NY, 1969-73, group v.p., 1973-77, sr. v.p., 1977-84; pres., CEO Zilog Inc., Campbell, Calif., 1984-98, also chmn. bd. dirs.; pres. Productivity Assocs., Coronado, Calif.; founder, chmn. CDT, Inc., San Jose, Calif., 1998-99. Bd. dirs. Enfo-Web, Inc., Mountainview, Calif., LXi, Inc., Mountainview; vis. com. elec. engring. dept. Carnegie-Mellon U., 1969-74; mem. indsl. adv. coun. SUNY, Stony Brook, 1979-83; mem. adv. com. on solid state electronics Poly. Inst. Tech., 1981-83. Author: Forward Controllership Business Management System, 1989, 2nd edit., 1993; patentee in field. Mem. Action Com. L.I, 1982-84; bd. dirs. Coronado Shores Assn. # 7, 2000-04, landscaping and recreational com., 2000-, chair, 2002-03, treas., 2004; mem. Sharp Coronado Hosp. Aux.; sec. San Diego Imperial Coun. of Vols., 2002; bd. dirs. Coronado Hosp. Found., 2003, chair projects and allocations com., 2004. Recipient 2nd Ann. Hammerschlag Disting. Lectr. award Carnegie Mellon U., 1995. Fellow IEEE, Poly. Inst. Tech.; mem. Semicondr. Industry Assn. (dir. 1982-85), Carnegie Mellon Alumni Assn. (Merit award 1981), Eta Kappa Nu (Outstanding Young Elec. Engr. 1959), Huntington Yacht Club (vice comdr. 1977), Tau Beta Pi (finalist San Francisco Entrepreneur of Yr. award 1991), Phi Kappa Phi. Home and Office: 1780 Avenida Del Mundo Unit 404 Coronado CA 92118-4011 Personal E-mail: esack@pacbell.net.

SACK, GEORGE HENRY, JR., molecular geneticist; b. Balt., Apr. 17, 1943; s. George Henry and Sophia Ann (Philippi) S. BA, Johns Hopkins U., 1965, MD, 1968, PhD, 1974. Diplomate Bd. Med. Genetics, Bd. Med. Examiners. Intern Johns Hopkins Hosp., Balt., 1968-69, asst. resident, 1969-70, fellow genetics, 1975-76; rsch. fellow Johns Hopkins Sch. Medicine, Balt., 1970-73; asst. prof. dept. medicine Johns Hopkins U., Balt., 1976-84, assoc. prof. dept. medicine and biol. chemistry, 1984—; molecular biologist Kennedy Inst., Balt., 1982-93, dir. exec. health program, 1996—. Contbr. articles to profl. jours. Maj. USAR, 1973-75. Andrew W. Mellon scholar Johns Hopkins U., 1976, Kennedy Found. scholar, 1982-85. Fellow Am. Coll. Med. Genetics; mem. AMA, AAAS, Am. Soc. Human Genetics, Phi Beta Kappa. Office: Johns Hopkins Hosp Outpatient Ctr 601 N Caroline St Baltimore MD 21287-0005 Office Phone: 410-955-2374. Business E-Mail: gsack@jhmi.edu.

SACK, JAMES MCDONALD, JR., radio and television producer, marketing executive; b. London, Ky., Oct. 11, 1948; s. James McDonald and Ruth Elmore (Bryant) S.; m. Cheryl S. Gremaux, July 13, 1969 (div. June 1974); 1 child, Graehm McDonald; m. Svetlana Antsulevich, Oct. 14, 1999. BA in History, Ind. U., 1975, MS in Telecomm., 1976. Coord. Latin Am. Ednl. Ctr., Ft. Wayne, Ind., 1979-81, Mayor's Office, Ft. Wayne, Ind., 1981-83; producer WMEE-WQHK Radio, Ft. Wayne, Ind., 1983-85; owner, operator Festival Mgmt. and Devel., Ft. Wayne, Ind., 1984—; owner Lily Co., Ft. Wayne, Ind., 1991—2001; region sales mgr. Plan Mgmt., Ft. Wayne, Ind., 1995-96; v.p. comm., mktg. United Way of Allen County, Ft. Wayne, Ind., 1989-96; owner The Sack Co., 1996—. Pub. affairs prodr. WBYR/WFWA, Ft. Wayne; co-founder, treas. Vurpar Project (aid to Romania), 1999—. Producer radio documentary, 1985 (First Pl. award Ind. Broadcasters Assn., 1985), producer WFWA-PBS Eye on the Arts, 1987-89. Founder, pres. Germanfest of Ft. Wayne, 1981-92; pres. cable TV program adv. coun. City of Ft. Wayne; founder Ft. Wayne-Gera (Germany) Sister City Affilation; commr. Ind. Hoosier Celebration, 1988; dir. Ind. Highland Games, 1992, cons., 1993-99; mktg. dir. Germanfest of Ft. Wayne, 1996-98; pres. cmn. adv. bd. Ft. Wayne Cable Fund, 2000—; bd. dirs. Ft. Wayne Sister Cities Com., 2000—; v.p. Ft. Wayne Sister Cities, 2004—; v.p. Ft. Wayne Sister Cities, Inc., 2004—. Named Ky. Col., 1991. Mem. German Heritage Soc. (founder, bd. dirs. 1986-99), Ind. German Heritage Soc. (founder, bd. dirs. 1986-92, Gov.'s Commendation award 1983), N.Am. Sängerbund (sec. 1985-86), Männerchor Club (Ft. Wayne), Ft. Wayne Sport Club (sec. 1985-86, trustee 1987-89). Lutheran. Avocations: flying, politics, linguistics, travel. Home and Office: 902 West Rudisill Fort Wayne IN 46807 Office Phone: 260-744-1285.

SACK, KEVIN, news correspondent; b. Jacksonville, Fla., Oct. 11, 1959; 1 child. BA in History with honors, Duke U., 1981. Reporter Atlanta Constitution, 1981—89; met. corr. N.Y. Times, 1989, bur. chief Albany, N.Y., bur., 1990—95, bur. chief,, nat. corr. Atlanta bur., 1995—2002; nat. corr. Atlanta bur. L.A. Times, 2002—. Co-recipient Pulitzer prize for nat. reporting, 2001, George Polk award, 2001; recipient Rotary Found. fellowship, U. Witwatersrand, Johannesburg, South Africa, 1983, N.Y. Legis. Corrs. Assn. award for best statehouse coverage, 1992. Mem.: Atlanta Press Club (bd. dirs. 1997—2000). Office: LA Times Atlanta Bur Ste 1105 229 Peachtree St NE Atlanta GA 30303

SACK, ROBERT DAVID, judge, law educator; b. Phila., Oct. 4, 1939; s. Eugene J. and Sylvia I. (Rivlin) Sack; BA, U. Rochester, 1960; LLB, Columbia U., 1963. Bar: N.Y. 1963. Law clk. to judge Fed. Dist. Ct. of N.J., 1963—64; assoc. Patterson, Belknap & Webb, N.Y.C., 1964—70; ptnr. Patterson, Belknap, Webb & Tyler, N.Y.C., 1970—86, Gibson, Dunn & Crutcher, N.Y.C., 1986-98; sr. assoc. spl. counsel U.S. Ho. of Reps. Impeachment Inquiry, 1974; judge U.S. Ct. Appeals (2d cir.), 1998—. Lectr. Practising Law Inst., 1973—97, Columbia U. Law Sch., 2001—04, mem. bd. visitors, 2000—; adv. bd. Media Law Reporter. Author: Libel, Slander, and Related Problems, 1980, 2d edit., 1994, CD-ROM edit., 1995, Sack on Defamation-Libel, Slander, and Related Problems, 3d edit., 1999; co-author: Advertising and Commercial Speech, a First Amendment Guide, 1999; contbr. articles to profl. jours. Chmn. bd. dirs. Nat. Council on Crime and Delinquency, 1982—83; trustee seminars on media and society Columbia U. Sch. Journalism, 1985—92, N.Y.C. Commn. on Pub. Info. and Comm., 1995—98; v.p., bd. dirs. William F. Kerby and Robert S. Potter Fund. Fellow: Am. Bar Found.; mem.: ABA (bd. govs. forum com. on comm. law 1980—88), Assn. Bar City N.Y. (chmn. comm. law com. 1986—89). Office: US Circuit Ct for 2d Circuit 40 Foley Sq New York NY 10007-1502

SACK, SYLVAN HANAN, lawyer; b. Phila., Dec. 26, 1932; s. Isidore F. and Mollye (Bellmore) S.; m. Ellen L. Foreman, Aug. 13, 1972; children: Reuben H., Sara I. MS in Bus. Adminstrn, Pa. State U., 1956; JD, U. Balt., 1964. Bar: Md. 1964, U.S. Tax Ct. 1967, U.S. Supreme Ct. 1970; C.P.A., Md. Pvt. practice, Balt., 1967—; assoc. counsel Safety First Club of Md., 1975-78, spl. counsel, 1979—. Gov. Md. chpt. Retinitis Pigmentosa Found., 1974-75 Contbr. articles to profl. jours. Chmn. Indsl. Toxicology NIOSH Function, 1977, Occupational Disease Forum, 1979, OSHA and Diseases in Workplace Seminar, 1981. Mem. Fed. Bar Assn. (gov. chpt. 1968—, chmn. bd. govs. 1969-70, chmn. environ. law program 1984), ABA (chmn. subcom. sect. taxation 1972-75), Md. Bar Assn., Assn. Trial Lawyers Am.; mem. Md. Trial Lawyers Assn. (lectr. toxic torts 1983 conv.) Home: 27 Brightside Ave Baltimore MD 21208-4802 Office Phone: 410-484-1484.

SACKETT, SUSAN DEANNA, film and television production associate, writer; b. N.Y.C., Dec. 18, 1943; adopted d. Maxwell and Gertrude Selma (Kugel) S. BA in Edn., U. Fla., 1964, MEd, 1965. Tchr. Dade County Schs., Miami, Fla., 1966-68, L.A. City Schs., 1968-69; asst. publicist, comml. coord. NBC-TV, Burbank, Calif., 1970-73; asst. to Gene Roddenberry, creator Star Trek, 1974-91; prodn. assoc. TV series Star Trek: The Next Generation, 1987-91, writer, 1990-91. Lectr. and guest spkr. Star Trek convs. in U.S., Eng., Australia, 1974-. Author, editor: Letters to Star Trek, 1977; co-author: Star Trek Speaks, The Making of Star Trek--The Motion Picture, 1979, You Can Be a Game Show Contestant and Win, 1982, Say Goodnight Gracie, 1986; author: The Hollywood Reporter Book of Box Office Hits, 1990, 2d edit., 1996, Prime Time Hits, 1993, Hollywood Sings, 1995, Inside Trek: My Secret Life with Star Trek Creator Gene Roddenberry, 2002. Mem. ACLU, Writers Guild Am., Nat. Writers Union, Am. Humanist Assn., Humanist Soc. Greater Phoenix (pres. 2000—), Mensa, Sierra Club. Democrat.

SACKHEIM, ROBERT LEWIS, aerospace engineer, educator; b. N.Y.C., N.Y., May 16, 1937; s. A. Frederick and Lillian L. (Emmer) S.; m. Babette Freund, Jan. 12, 1964; children: Karen Holly, Andrew Frederick. BSChemE, U. Va., 1959; MSChemE, Columbia U., 1961; postgrad., UCLA, 1966-72. Project engr. Comsat Corp., El Segundo, Calif., 1969-72; project mgr. TRW, Redondo Beach, Calif., 1964-69, sect. head, 1972-76, dept. mgr., 1976-81, mgr. new bus., 1981-86, lab. mgr., 1986-90, dep. ctr. dir., 1990-93, ctr. dir., 1993-99; asst. dir, chief engr. for space propulsion systems Marshall Space Flight Ctr, NASA, Huntsville, Ala., 1999—. Instr. UCLA engring. ext., 1986, Continuing Engring. Edn., U. Ala., Huntsville, 2001; mem. adv. bds. NASA, Washington, 1989—; mem. peer rev. bd. various univs. and govtl. agys., 1990—; mem. Nat. Rsch. Coun./Aeronautics and Space Engring. Bd., 1994—; guest lectr. various univs. and AIAA short courses. Author: Space Mission Analysis and Design, 1991, Space Propulsion Analysis and Design, 1994, Space Launch and Transportation Systems, 2004; contbr. chpt. to book, more than 200 articles to profl. jours., confs. Mem. adv. bd. L.A. Bd. Edn., 1990-92; fund raiser March of Dimes, L.A., 1970-90, YMCA, San Pedro, Calif., 1974-86. Capt. USAF Reserve, 1960-63. Recipient Group Achievement awards (12) NASA, 1970, 78, 86, 2000, 2001, Sustained Svc. award AIAA, 2000, medal for outstanding tech. leadership NASA, Propulsion Outstanding Contbns. award French Acad. Aero/Astro., 2002, NASA/Dir.'s commendation, 2003, Presdl. Rank award for disting. fed. civil svc., TRW Chmn. awards. Fellow AIAA (chmn. com. 1980-83, chmn. L.A. sect. 1997, chmn. Ala./Miss. sect. 2000, 2001, J.H. Wyld Propulsion award 1992, Shuttle Flag award 1984, Martin Schilling award 2001, Hermann Oberth award 2002, Holgar Toftoy award 2003), Internat. Acad. Astronautics, Nat. Acad. Engring., Sigma Xi. Achievements include 8 patents for spacecraft propulsion systems, controls, devices and components. Office: Office of Dir Marshall Space Flight Ctr Huntsville AL 35812 Office Phone: 256-544-1938.

SACKLER, ARTHUR BRIAN, lawyer; b. Utica, N.Y., June 9, 1950; s. Joseph Leon and Leonore (Guttman) S.; m. Linda J. Cimarusti, May 27, 1979; children: Joshua Michael, Jenna Rachel. B.A., Syracuse U., 1970, J.D., 1973; LL.M., Georgetown U., 1979. Bar: N.Y. 1974, D.C. 1975, U.S. Dist. Ct. D.C. 1979, U.S. Supreme Ct. 1979, U.S. Ct. Appeals (D.C. cir.) 1981. Appeals examiner U.S. Civil Service Commn., Washington, 1973-75, atty. advisor, 1975-76, trial atty., 1976-79; gen. counsel Nat. Newspaper Assn., Washington, 1979-82; dir. pub. policy devel. Time Warner, Washington, 1982-92, v.p. law and pub. policy, 1992—; mng. dir. Mailers Coun., 1990—; mem. Joint Washington Media Com., 1979—, Am. Copyright Council, Washington, 1984-86; faculty communications law Practicing Law Inst., 1980, forum com. on communications law seminar, 1980; instr. Am. Press Inst., 1980-82. Editor and contbr.: Federal Laws Affecting Newspapers, 1981; founder, editor newsletter News Media Update, 1979-82; contbr. articles to profl. jours., newspapers. Pres. Birnam Wood Community Assn., Potomac, Md., 1983-84; sec., treas. Potomac Springs Community Assn., Potomac, Md., 1986-87. Mem. ABA (chmn. postal matters com., adminstrv. law sect.), D.C. Bar Assn., Fed. Communications Bar Assn., Fed. Bar Assn., Mag. Pubs. Am. (govt. rels. coun. N.Y.C. 1982-85, 92—), Am. Advt. Fedn. (govt. relations com. Washington 1984—), Direct Mktg. Assn. (govt. relations com. 1986—), Am. Tort Reform Assn. (bd. dirs. 1987-88, corp. steering com. 1986-88), Assn. Am. Pubs. (postal com. N.Y.C. 1983—). Jewish. Clubs: Nat. Press, Bethesda Country. Office: Time Warner Inc 800 Connecticut Ave NW Ste 800 Washington DC 20006-2718

SACKMAN, DAVE, marketing executive; married; 3 children. BA in Anthropology, U. Calif. Pres., CEO Lieberman Rsch. Worldwide, L.A.; dir. rsch. Columbia Pictures; dir. mktg. Winchell's; dir. mktg. dept. group health svcs. Am. Med. Internat. Active Young Pres. Orgn. Mem. Mktg. Rsch. Assn. (mem. strategic planning com., mem. exec. forum on rsch. quality, mem. exec. com. nat. bd. dirs.). Avocations: basketball, tennis. Office: Liberman Rsch Worldwide 1900 Ave Of Stars Los Angeles CA 90067-4301

SACKMANN, INGE-JULIANA, astrophysicist; b. Schönau, Germany, Feb. 8, 1942; came to U.S., 1971; d. Emil Sackmann and Lilly Stelter; m. Robert Frederick Christy, Aug. 4, 1973; children: Ilia Juliana Lilly Christy, Alexandra Roberta Christy. BA, U. Toronto, Ont., Can., 1963, MA, 1965, PhD, 1968. Postdoctoral fellow U. Göttingen, Germany, 1968-69, Max-Planck-Inst. for Physics and Astrophysics, Munich, 1969-71; rsch. assoc. U. Hamburg Obs., Germany, 1971, Jet Propulsion Labs., Pasadena, 1974-76; rsch. fellow Calif. Inst. Tech., Pasadena, 1971-74, sr. rsch. fellow, 1976-81, faculty assoc., 1981—. Recipient Zonta Club award in math. and physics, 1961-62, Math. and Physics Soc. prize, 1962-63, AAAS award in math. and physics, 1962-63, McLennan prize in math. and physics, 1963-64, Loudon Gold medal in math. and physics, 1963-64, Chant award, 1963-64, Alexander von Humboldt award, 1970-71; co-recipient B'nai B'rith award, 1961-62; 1st alumni scholar U. Toronto, 1959-60, 60-61, Ont. scholar, 1959-60, 1st Alumni scholar, 1962-63, Gamma Phi Beta scholar, 1963-64, Nat. Rsch. Coun. Can. scholar, 1963-64, 64-65, 66-67, 68-69, 69-70; U. Toronto Open fellow, 1965-66. Mem. Internat. Astron. Union, Am. Astron. Soc., Orgn. of Women in Sci. Achievements include scientific findings in carbon creation, preditions of lively future of the sun. Home: 1230 Arden Rd Pasadena CA 91106-4146 Office: U Calif Inst Tech 1201 E California Blvd Pasadena CA 91125-0001 E-mail: ijsekrl@caltech.edu.

SACKNER, MARVIN ARTHUR, physician; b. Phila., Feb. 16, 1932; s. Albert B. and Goldie Mildred (Haber) S.; m. Ruth Karsch, June 24, 1956; children: Sara, Deborah, Jonathan. BS, Temple U., 1953; MD, Jefferson Med. Coll., 1957. Diplomate Am. Bd. Internal Medicine. Intern Phila. Gen. Hosp., 1957-58, med. resident, 1958-61; ACP rsch. fellow U. Pa., Phila., 1961-64; chief pulmonary disease Mt. Sinai Hosp., Miami Beach, Fla., 1964-74, dir. med. svcs., 1974-91, dir. med. svcs. emeritus, 1992—; prof. medicine U. Miami, Fla., 1973—. Gov., chmn. pulmonary disease exam. bd. Am. Bd. Internal Medicine, 1977-80; chief exec. officer Non-Invasive Monitoring Systems, Inc., Miami Beach, Fla., 1986—. Author: Scleroderma, 1966; editor: Diagnostic Techniques in Pulmonary Disease, Parts I and II, 1980; mem. editorial bd. Fla. Med. Assn., 1974, Am. Rev. Respiratory Physiology, 1976-80, Jour. Applied Physiology, 1976-80, Annals Internal Medicine, 1979; patentee in field; contbr. articles to profl. jours. Pres. Art in Pub. Places, Inc., 1975-78; co-dir. Ruth and Marvin Sackner Archive of Concrete and Visual Poetry, 1979—; bd. dirs. Ctr. for Book Art, N.Y.C., 1987-93; mem. libr. com. Mus. Modern Art, N.Y.C., 1990-94. NEA grantee, 1977-78, Nat. Heart, Lung and Blood Inst. grantee, 1966—, others. Fellow ACP, Am. Coll. Chest Physicians; mem. Am. Thoracic Soc. (pres.1980), Am. Physiol. Soc., Grolier Club N.Y.C. Jewish. Office: Nims Inc 1666 79th St CSWY #400 Miami Beach FL 33141-4133

SACKS, CHARLES BERNARD, physician, educator; b. Cleve., May 14, 1939; s. Jerry and Frances (Shifrin) S.; m. Lora Jane Glickman, May 2, 1993; children: Eliza, Aaron. BA, Ohio State U., 1961, MD, 1965. Staff psychiatrist Washington Vets. Hosp., 1971-77; asst. clin. prof. Georgetown U., Washington, 1971—; staff psychiatrist Reston Clinic, Fairfax City, Md., 1976-77, Drug Treatment Adminstrn., Washington, 1971-72, Washington Free Clinic, 1971-73, Arlington & Fairfax City Hosp., 1977-88, Group Health Assocs., Washington, 1984-86; psychiatrist pvt. practice, McLean, Va., 1977—, Greenbelt, Md., 1977—; dir. Chevy Chase Psychiat. Clinic, Washington, 1987-89; Mt. Vernon Mental Health Ctr., 1994—. Maj. U.S. Army, 1969-71. Decorated Bronze medal with Oak Leaf Cluster. Mem. Am. Psychiat. Assn. Avocations: sailing, photography, music, reading, sports. Office: 6201 Greenbelt Rd College Park MD 20740-2354 also: 1313 Vincent Pl Mc Lean VA 22101-3615

SACKS, DAVID G. retired distilling company executive, lawyer; b. N.Y.C., Jan. 6, 1924; s. Irving and Jeannette (Greenhoot) S.; m. Marcella Rosen; children: Jonathan E., Deborah A., Judith A., Joshua M. AB, Columbia U., 1944, LL.B., 1948. Ptnr. Simpson Thacher & Bartlett, N.Y.C., 1961-67, sr. ptnr., 1967-76, counsel, 1981-83; chief adminstrv. officer Lehman Bros., Inc., N.Y.C., 1976-81; exec. v.p. fin. adminstrn. The Seagram Co. Ltd., Montreal, Que., Can., 1983-86, pres., chief operating officer, 1986-89, also bd. dirs.; exec. v.p. fin. adminstrn. Joseph E. Seagram & Sons, N.Y.C., 1983-86, pres., chief operating officer, 1986-89; vice chmn. The Seagram Co. Ltd. and Joseph E. Seagram & Sons, Inc., Montreal and N.Y.C., 1989-91, ret., 1991. Pres. United Jewish Appeal, Fedn. Jewish Philanthropies, N.Y.C., 1989-92. Cpl. USAAF, 1943-46 Office: Office of David G Sacks 800 3d Ave 4th Fl New York NY 10022

SACKS, DAVID HARRIS, historian, humanities educator; b. Bklyn., Dec. 14, 1942; s. Fred and Lillian Pearl (Levy) S.; m. Eleanor Darby Woodward, July 25, 1971. BA magna cum laude, Bklyn. Coll., 1963; AM in History, Harvard U., 1965, PhD in History, 1977. Lectr. history U. Mass., Boston, 1977-79; preceptor in expository writing Harvard U., Cambridge, Mass., 1979-80, lectr. in history and lit., 1980-83, rsch. affiliate Ctr. for European Studies, 1983-86; asst. prof. history and humanities Reed Coll., Portland, Oreg., 1986-89, assoc. prof., 1989-93, prof., 1993—2003, Richard F. Scholz prof. history and humanities, 2003—. Vis. prof. history Yale U., 1998—99; vis. fellow (life mem.) Clare Hall, Cambridge U., 2001—02; mem. bd. advisors Yale Ctr. for Parliamentary History. Author: Trade Society and Politics in Bristol, 1500-1640, 1985, The Widening Gate: Bristol and the Atlantic Economy, 1450-1700, 1991; editor: Thomas More, Utopia, 1999, (with Donald R. Kelley) The Historical Imagination in Early Modern Britain: History, Rhetoric, and Fiction, 1500-1800, 1997; mem. bd. editors Jour. of History of Ideas; contbr. articles to profl. jours. Recipient fellowships Folger Shakespeare Libr., Washington, 1989-90, Woodrow Wilson Internat. Ctr. for Scholars, 1992-93, John Simon Guggenheim Meml. Found., 1992-93, NEH, 2001-02, ACLS, 2001-02, John Carter Brown Libr., 2002-03. Fellow Royal Hist. Soc.; mem. N.Am. Conf. Brit. Studies (chair nominating com. 1993-95, exec. sec. 1995-98), Am. Hist. Assn. (program com. 1993-95, Leo Gershey prize com. 1992-95, mem. coun. 2001-04, rsch. divsn. 2002-04), Renaissance Soc. Am. (Phyllis Goodhart Gordan prize com. 2002-03). Office: Reed Coll 3203 SE Woodstock Blvd Portland OR 97202-8199 Home: 6214 SE 36th Ave Portland OR 97282

SACKS, HERBERT SIMEON, psychiatrist, educator, consultant; b. N.Y.C., Nov. 29, 1926; s. Maxwell Lawrence and Anne (Edelstein) S.; m. Helen Margery Levin, Dec. 26, 1948; children— Eric Livingston, Katharine Bird, Douglas Lowell, Russell Avery AB magna cum laude, Dickinson Coll., 1948; MD, Cornell U., 1952. Diplomate Am. Bd. Psychiatry and Neurology and subspecialty Child and Adolescent Psychiatry. Clin. assoc. Western New Eng. Psychoanalytic Inst., New Haven, 1955-63; intern in pediatrics Yale-New Haven Med. Ctr., 1952-53; jr. asst. resident in psychiatry Yale Psychiat. Inst., 1953-54; sr. asst. resident in psychiatry, USPHS fellow Yale-New Haven Med.

Ctr., psychiat. out patient dept., 1954-55; USPHS fellow in child psychiatry Yale U. Child Study Ctr., 1955-57; clin. dir. Mid-Fairfield Child Guidance Ctr., Norwalk, Conn., 1957-59; cons. Expt. in Internat. Living, Putney, Vt., 1962-69; sr. cons. U.S. Peace Corps, Washington, 1962-69; cons. AID, U.S. Dept. State, Office of Sahel, West Africa, 1974-84, Neurosci. Consultation Group, Grosse Point Farms, Mich., 1984-94; clin. prof. child and adolescent psychiatry Child Study Ctr., Yale U. Sch. Medicine, New Haven. Co-investigator, co-dir. Senegal River pilot health research program, New Haven and West Africa, 1976-78, co-investigator, co-dir. health sector, design team Senegal River integrated devel. project, 1981-83; vis. lectr. Yale Coll., 1969-71; mem. com. reviewers Dept. Commerce Nat. Bur. Standards, Inst. for Computer Scis. and Tech., Washington, 1975-77; mem. exec. com. Nat. Commn. on Confidentiality of Health Records, 1975-80 Author: Hurdles: The Admissions Dilemma in American Higher Education, 1978; contbg. author chpts. in books, articles on confidentiality, juvenile justice, higher edn., issues of youth in transition, other topics; author monographs Mem. Conn. Juvenile Justice Commn., Hartford, 1975-80; bd. advisors Dickinson Coll., Carlisle, Pa., 1980-85. Served to lt. (j.g.) U.S. Navy, 1944-46; PTO Fellow AMA, ACPO, Am. Psychiat. Assn. (trustee 1988-94, v.p. 1994-96, pres. 1997-98), Am. Acad. Child and Adolescent Psychiatry, Am. Orthopsychiat. Assn., Am Coll. Psychiatrists; mem. Conn. Psychiat. Soc. (pres. 1976-77), Conn. Coun. Child and Adolescent Psychiatrists (pres. 1972-73), World Fedn. for Mental Health, Phi Beta Kappa. Avocations: farming, photography, fishing, lawn bowling. Home: 110 Laurel Rd New Haven CT 06515-2426 Office: 260 Riverside Ave Westport CT 06880-4804 also: Yale U Child Study Ctr PO Box 207900 New Haven CT 06520-7900

SACKS, IRA STEPHEN, lawyer; b. N.Y.C., Dec. 6, 1948; s. Marvin Leonard and Mildred (Finkelstein) S.; m. Deborah DiNolfo, children: James, Jennifer, Allison, Gillian. BS, MIT, 1970; JD, Georgetown U., 1974. Bar: N.Y. 1975, U.S. Dist. Ct. (so. and ea. dists.) N.Y. 1975, U.S. Ct. Appeals (2d cir.) 1975, U.S. Ct. Appeals (3d cir.) 1984, U.S. Supreme Ct. 1985, U.S. Ct. Appeals (9th cir.) 1986, U.S. Ct. Appeals (11th cir.) 1987, U.S. Ct. Appeals (D.C. and fed. cirs.) 1993. Assoc. Kaye, Scholer, Fierman, Hays & Handler, N.Y.C., 1974-82, ptnr., 1983-87, Fried, Frank, Harris, Shriver & Jacobson, N.Y.C., 1988—2003, Gursky and Ptnrs., N.Y.C., NY, 2003—. Contbr. articles to profl. jours. NSF fellow, 1970. Mem. ABA, Supreme Ct. Hist. Soc., N.Y. State Bar Assn., Assn. of Bar of City of N.Y. Democrat. Jewish. Avocations: tennis, skiing. Home: 105 Old Colony Rd Hartsdale NY 10530-3610 Office: Gursky and Ptnrs 1350 Broadway New York NY 10018 E-mail: isacks@aol.com.

SACKS, OLIVER WOLF, neurologist, writer; b. London, July 9, 1933; Came to U.S., 1960; s. Samuel and Muriel Elsie (Landau) S. BA, U. Oxford, 1954; MA, BM, BCh, Middlesex Hosp., London, 1958; DHL (hon.), Georgetown U., 1990, Coll. Staten Island, CUNY, 1991; DS (hon.), Tufts U., 1991, N.Y. Med. Coll., 1991. Intern in medicine, surgery and neurology Middlesex Hosp., 1958-60; rotating intern Mt. Zion Hosp., San Francisco, 1961-62; resident in neurology UCLA, 1962-65; I.D. fellow in neuropathology and neurochemistry Albert Einstein Coll. Medicine, N.Y.C., 1965-66, instr. neurology, 1966-75, asst. prof., 1975-78, assoc. prof., 1978-85, clin. prof. neurology, 1985—. Cons., speaker, lectr. in field; hon. lectureships in field. Author: Migraine, 1970, Awakenings, 1973, rev. paperback edit., 1990 (Hawthornden prize 1975), A Leg To Stand On, 1984, The Man Who Mistook His Wife for a Hat, 1985, Seeing Voices: A Journey into the World of the Deaf, 1989, An Anthropologist on Mars, 1995, The Island of the Color Blind, 1996. Recipient Felix Mart-Ibanez book award MD mag., 1987, Oskar Pfister award APA, 1988, Harold D. Vursell Meml. award Am. Acad. and Inst. Arts and Letters, 1989, Odd Fellows book award, 1990, Scriptor award U. So. Calif., 1991, profl. support award Nat. Headache Found., 1991; open scholar in biology Queen's Coll., Oxford U., 1950, Theodoe Williams scholar in anatomy, 1953, med. rsch. scholar, 1954; Guggenheim fellow, 1989. Mem. Am. Acad. Neurology (presdl. citation 1991), Am. Acad. Arts & Letters, N.Y. State Med. Soc., N.Y. Inst for the Humanities, Alpha Omega Alpha. Office: 2 Horatio St Apt 3G New York NY 10014-1638

SACKS, PATRICIA ANN, librarian, consultant; b. Allentown, Pa., Nov. 6, 1939; d. Lloyd Alva and Dorothy Estelle (Stoneback) Stahl; m. Kenneth LeRoy Sacks, June 27, 1959. AB, Cedar Crest Coll., 1959; MS in Libr. Sci., Drexel U., 1965. News reporter Call-Chronicle, Allentown, 1956-59, 61-63; reference libr. Cedar Crest Coll., Allentown, 1964-66, head libr., 1966-73; dir. librs. Muhlenberg and Cedar Crest Colls., Allentown, 1973-94; dir. libr. svcs. Cedar Crest Coll., 1994; sr. fellow Lehigh Valley Assn. Ind. Colls., 1994-97, Ctr. Agile Ptnrs. in Edn., 1997-98; info. svcs. cons., 1998—. Del. On Line Computer Library Ctr. Users Council, Columbus, Ohio, 1977-84; cons. colls./health care orgns., libr. orgns. 1981—. Author: (with Whildin Sara Lou) Preparing for Accreditation: A Handbook for Academic Librarians, 1993; mem. editl. bd. Jour. Acad. Librarianship, 1982-84. Mem. United Way Lehigh Valley Coms., 1993—97; trustee Cedar Crest Coll., 1985—89; bd. dirs. John and Dorothy Morgan Cancer Ctr., 1994—96. Named Outstanding Acad. Woman, Lehigh Valley Assn. for Acad. Women, 1984, Muhlenberg Coll. Outstanding Adminstr., 1987, Alumni Tricorn awrd Muhlenberg Coll., 1989, Alumnae Achievement award Cedar Crest Coll., 1994. Mem. ALA (chmn. copyright com. 1985-87), Assn. Coll. and Rsch. Librs. (chmn. stds. and accreditation com. 1976-78, 81-84), Lehigh Valley Assn. Ind. Colls. (chmn. librs. sect. 1967-81, 88-92), AAUW, LWV, Wildlands Conservancy, Appalachian Mountain Club, Phi Alpha Theta, Phi Kappa Phi, Beta Phi Mu. Democrat. Home: 2997 Fairfield Dr Allentown PA 18103-5413

SACKS, ROBERT D. educational administrator, fund raiser; b. N.Y.C., Oct. 29, 1931; s. Robert and Hortense (Saperstein) S.; divorced; children: David Robert (dec.), Michael Alan. BA, Amherst Coll., 1953; MS, Juilliard Sch., 1956; postgrad., Columbia U., 1951, 52, NYU, 1959-62, U. Paris (Sorbonne), 1962-63. Instr. SUNY, Buffalo, 1963-65; asst. prof. Antioch Coll., Yellow Springs, Ohio, 1965-69; assoc. prof. Temple U., Phila., 1969-73; dean of faculty Phila. Musical Acad., 1973-75; assoc. dir. Transactional Dynamics inst., Glenside, Pa., 1976-82; exec. dir. Keswick Theatre, Glenside, 1982-84, Delaware Valley Coun. of Am. Youth Hostels, Inc., Phila., 1993-99. Commn. on Higher Edn. of the Mid. States Assn. Colls. and Schs. rep. in evaluation of colls. for accreditation/renewal of accreditation, 1974-75. Vol. Hoeffel for Congress, Montgomery County, Pa., 1996, 98, 99—, U.S. Senator Harris Wofford for Re-election, 1995; chmn. Amherst Coll. Vols. for Stevenson, 1952. With U.S. Army, 1957-59. Fulbright scholar, 1962-63; grantee Danforth Found., 1966-67, Ford Found., 1966-67, N.Y. State Regents fellow, 1960-61, Millicent James scholar and Univ. fellow NYU, 1961-62. Mem. Nat. Trust for Hist. Preservation, Preservation Pa. Avocations: gardening, woodworking, water sports.

SACKS, TEMI J. public relations executive; b. Phila. d. Jule and Adeline (Levin) S. BA, Temple U. Pubs. editor Del. Valley Regional Planning Commn., Phila.; comms. assoc. Fedn. Jewish Agys., Phila.; exec. v.p., mng. dir. consumer and healthcare divsns. Lobsenz-Stevens Inc., N.Y.C.; exec. v.p., dir. nat. healthcare practice Shandwick, N.Y.C.; sr. v.p. Noonan-Russo, N.Y.C.; pres. T.J. Sacks & Assocs. Inc., N.Y.C. Mem. Healthcare Businesswomen's Assn., Healtcare Mktg. Assn., Women Execs. in Pub. Rels. Avocations: painting, skiing, americana antiques, jewelry design. Office Phone: 212-787-0787. E-mail: tjsacks@tjsacks.com.

SACKSTEDER, ELIZABETH M. lawyer; AB summa cum laude, Princeton U., 1980; JD, Yale U., 1988. Bar: N.Y. 1989, U.S. Dist. Ct. (so. and ea. dists.) N.Y. 1989, U.S. Ct. Appeals (2d cir.) 1994. Law clk. to Hon. Eugene H. Nickerson, U.S. Dist. Ct. for Ea. Dist. N.Y., N.Y.C., 1988-89; ptnr. Sidley & Austin, N.Y.C., 1995—. Mediator U.S. Dist. Ct. for So. Dist. N.Y. Coordinating articles editor Yale Law Jour., 1988. Mem. Am. Arbitration Assn. (arbitrator, mediator). Office: Sidley & Austin 875 3d Ave New York NY 10022 Fax: 212-906-2021. E-mail: esackste@sidley.com.

SACKSTEDER, FREDERICK HENRY, former foreign service officer; b. N.Y.C., July 12, 1924; s. Frederick H. and Denise (Dorin) S.; m. Evelyn M. Blickensderfer, Oct. 14, 1977; children by previous marriage: Frederick Henry, III, Timothy W. BA, Amherst Coll., 1947; postgrad., Sch. Advanced Internat. Studies, Washington, 1947. Asst. to exec. v.p. Internat. Standard Electric Corp., N.Y.C., 1948-49; joined U.S. Fgn. Service, 1950; Kreis resident officer U.S. High Commn. for Germany, 1950-52; vice consul, consul, sec. Am. embassy, Lyon, France, 1952-55, Madrid, 1959-61, Barcelona, Spain, 1962-65, Tunis, Tunisia, 1967-69; internat. relations officer Dept. State, 1955-59; 65-67; mem. U.S. Mission to UN, 1969-72, Internat. Boundary and Water Com., El Paso, Tex., 1972-75; consul gen. Hermosillo, Sonora, Mexico, 1975-79; bd. examiners Fgn. Service, Dept. State, 1979-81, expert cons. Bur. Personnel, 1981-86. Mem. U.S. del. to UN Gen. Assembly, N.Y.C., 1969-71. Mem. UN Trusteeship Coun., 1970-71, U.S. rep., 1971; pres. El Paso chpt. UN Assn., 1973-75. Lt. (j.g.) USNR, 1943-46. Mem. Fgn. Service Assn., Diplomatic and Consular Officers Ret., Council Fgn. Relations (chmn. Charlottesville com.). Lodges: Rotary (local club pres. 1988-89). Home: The Westchester Apt 344 4000 Cathedral Ave NW Washington DC 20016-5280

SACKSTEDER, THOMAS MICHAEL, corporate executive, entrepreneur, writer; b. Dayton, Ohio, July 27, 1950; s. Harry Pius and Mary Kay (Liebhardt) S.; m. Teresa Ann Nevius, Oct. 12, 1968 (div. Sept. 1980); children: Lori Ann, Kristi Marie, Julie Kay. Student, Sinclair Community Coll., 1968-72, Wright State U., 1972-73, Grand Valley State Coll., 1978-79, Lourdes Coll., 1994-95. Installer Western Electric, Dayton, 1968-69; sales rep. Smith Corona Mcht., Dayton, 1969-70; office mgr. Indsl. Machinery, Dayton, 1970-71; advisor Bell Pub. Rels., Dayton, 1972-73; sales mgr. Washington Nat. Ins., Dayton, 1974-81, Am. Fidelity Assurance Co., 1981-95; gen. ptnr. Innovative Benefits Resource Ltd., 1995—. Gen. ptnr., Annuity Compliance Specilaists, ptnr., Christopher Blake Family Wellness Assn., benefits cons. Ind. State Tchrs. Assn. Ins. Trust, Indpls., 1986-91. Bd. dirs. Mental Health Assn., Dayton, 1971-75, Good Samaritan Mental Health Ctr., 1972-75; campaign mgmt. for polit. candidates and issue oriented policies, 1972—. Mem. Ohio Assn. Sch. Bus. Ofcls. (legis. com. 1993-95), Assn. of Sch. Bus. Ofcls., Natl. Tax Shelter Annuity Assn., Employers Counc. on Flexible Compensation, Natl. Assn. of Life Underwriters, Buckeye Assn. Sch. Adminstrs., Jaycees, Kiwanis. Roman Catholic. Avocations: golf, swimming, writing, research, martial arts. Address: Innovative Benefits Resource Ltd Annuity Compliance Specialists PO Box 70 Holland OH 43528-0070 E-mail: tom.sacksteder@lbracs.com.

SACKTON, FRANK JOSEPH, public affairs educator; b. Chgo., Aug. 11, 1912; m. June Dorothy Raymond, Sept. 21, 1940. Student, Northwestern U., 1936, Yale, 1946, U. Md., 1951-52, BS, 1970, grad., Army Inf. Sch., 1941, Command and Gen. Staff Coll., 1942, Armed Forces Staff Coll., 1949, Nat. War Coll., 1954; MPA, Ariz. State U., 1976, DHL (hon.), 1996. Mem. 131st Inf. Regt., Ill. N.G., 1929-40; commd. 2d lt. U.S. Army, 1934, advanced through grades to lt. gen., 1967; brigade plans and ops. officer (33d Inf. Div.), 1941, PTO, 1943-45; div. signal officer, 1942-43; div. intelligence officer, 1944; div. plans and ops. officer, 1945; sec. to gen. staff for Gen. MacArthur, 1947-48; bn. comdr. 30th Inf. Regt., 1949-50; mem. spl. staff Dept. Army, 1951; plans and ops. officer Joint Task Force 132, PTO, 1952; comdr. Joint Task Force 7, Marshall Islands, 1953; mem. gen. staff Dept. Army, 1954-55; with Office Sec. Def., 1956; comdr. 18th Inf. Regt., 1957-58; chief staff 1st Inf. Div., 1959; chief army Mil. Mission to Turkey, 1960-62; comdr. XIV Army Corps, 1963; dep. dir. plans Joint Chiefs Staff, 1964-66; army general staff mil. ops., 1966-67; comptroller of the army, 1967-70; ret., 1970; spl. asst. for fed./state relations Gov. Ariz., 1971-75; chmn. Ariz. Programming and Coordinating Com. for Fed. Programs, 1971-75; lectr. Am. Grad. Sch. Internat. Mgmt., 1973-77; vis. asst. prof., lectr. public affairs Ariz. State U., Tempe, 1976-78; founding dean Ariz. State U. Coll. Public Programs, 1979-80; prof. public affairs Ariz. State U., 1980—, finance educator, v.p. bus. affairs, 1981-83, dep. dir. intercollegiate athletics, 1984-85, dir. strategic planning, 1987-88. Contbr. articles to public affairs and mil. jours. Mem. Ariz. Steering Com. for Restoration of the State Capitol, 1974-75, Ariz. State Personnel Bd., 1978-83, Ariz. Regulatory Coun., 1981-93. Decorated D.S.M., Silver Star, also Legion of Merit with 4 oak leaf clusters, Bronze Star with 2 oak leaf clusters, Air medal, Army Commendation medal with 1 oak leaf cluster, Combat Inf. badge. Mem. Ariz. Acad. Public Adminstrn., Pi Alpha Alpha (pres. chpt. 1976-82) Clubs: Army-Navy (Washington); Arizona Country (Phoenix). Home: 12000 N 90th St Unit 3072 Scottsdale AZ 85260-8643 Office: Ariz State U Sch Pub Affairs Tempe AZ 85287-0603 Business E-Mail: frank.sackton@asu.edu.

SACRE, ANTONIO, playwright; b. Boston, 1968; BA in English, Boston Coll.; MA in Theater Arts, Northwestern U. Lectr., spkr. in field. Author: (plays) The Barking Mouse, (cassette) Looking for Papito (Parent's Choice Gold award, 1996, Gold award Nat. Assn. Parenting Publ., 1997), Water Torture, The Barking Mouse, and Other Tales of Wonder (Notable Recipient award ALA, 2001); performer: NYC Internat. Fringe Theater Festival, 1997 (Best in Fringe Festival award, 1997, 1999), others. Ethnic and Folk Arts fellow, Ill. Arts Coun., 1998. Home: PO Box 3444 Hollywood CA 90078-3444

SADAN, MARK, photographer, film producer, artist; AA, Am. Acad. Dramatic Arts, N.Y.C., 1963; MFA, NYU, 1969; MEd, U. Mass., Amherst, 1974. Pres., dir. Kiva Film, N.Y., Mass., 1969—75; prodr., dir. short films Sesame St., 1969—72; dir., photo film unit Anti Poverty Program, N.Y.C., 1966—67. Artist (films) Rosebud, Laughing Bear, Ann Arbor Film Festival, 1965—68, prodr., dir. Ecology Probe Planet Earth 74, The New Norway 81, photographer (books) Meditations of the Blessed Beauty, Tablet of Carmel, 1990—93; one-man shows include Nat. Photo Gallery, Riga, Latvia, 1989—90, exhibitions include Am. Mus. Dance, 2000—02. Recipient Medal of Excellence for Photographic Art, Latvian Nat. Photographic Soc., 1990, Cine Golden Eagle, Cine Film Awards, 2003. Mem.: Sunday Photo Group (dir., lectr. 1982—2004), Film Video Workshop (founder, dir. 1969—74). Avocations: dance, photography, swimming, travel, movies. Home: PO Box 207 Ossining NY 10562 Office Phone: 914-762-0219. E-mail: marksadan13@hotmail.com.

SADAO, SHOJI, architect; b. Los Angeles, Jan. 2, 1927; s. Riichi and Otatsu (Kodama) S.; m. Tsuneko Sawada, Apr. 8, 1972. B.Arch., Cornell U., 1954; Fulbright scholar, Waseda U., Tokyo, 1956-57. Designer Geodesics, Inc., Raleigh, N.C., 1954-56; job capt. Edison Price, Inc., N.Y.C., 1959-64; v.p. Fuller & Sadao (P.C.), Long Island City, N.Y., 1965—. Assoc. prof. archtl. design Sch. Architecture and Environ. Design, SUNY, Buffalo, 1976-77. Works include Dymaxion World Map, 1954; co-designer works include, U.S. Pavilion at Montreal Expo 67. Trustee Isamu Noguchi Found., Long Island City, N.Y., 1967—, exec. dir., 1989-2003. With AUS, 1945-49. Mem.: The Century Assn., Japan Soc. Address: Fuller & Sadao 32-37 Vernon Blvd Long Island City NY 11106-4926

SADDLEMYER, ANN (ELEANOR SADDLEMYER), humanities educator, critic, theater historian; b. Prince Albert, Sask., Can., Nov. 28, 1932; d. Orrin Angus and Elsie Sarah (Ellis) S. BA, U. Sask., 1953, DLitt, 1991; MA, Queen's U., 1956, LLD (hon.), 1977; PhD, U. London, 1961; DLitt (hon.), U. Victoria, 1989, McGill U., 1989, Windsor U., 1990, U. Toronto, 1999, Concordia U., 2000. Lectr. Victoria (B.C.) Coll., 1956-57, instr., 1960-62, asst. prof., 1962-65; assoc. prof. U. Victoria, 1965-68, prof. English, 1968-71, Victoria Coll. U. Toronto, 1971-95; prof., dir. Grad. Ctr. for Study of Drama, U. Toronto, 1972-77, 85-86; prof. emerita Dept. English, Comparative Lit. Grad Ctr. for Study of Drama, U. Toronto, 1995—; sr. fellow Massey Coll., 1975-88, master, 1988-95, master emerita, 1995—; Berg prof. NYU, 1975. Adj. prof. U. Victoria. Dir. Theatre Plus, 1972-84; dir. Colin Smythe Pubs.; author: (with Robin Skelton) The World of W.B. Yeats, 1965, In Defence of Lady Gregory, Playwright, 1966, Synge and Modern Comedy, 1968, J.M. Synge Plays Books One and Two, 1968, Lady Gregory Plays, 4 vols., 1970, Letters to Molly: Synge to Maire O'Neill, 1971, Letters from Synge to W.B. Yeats and Lady Gregory, 1971, Collected Letters of John Millington Synge, Vol. 1, 1983, vol. II, 1984, Theatre Business, The Correspondence of the First Abbey Theatre Directors, 1982, (with Colin Smythe) Lady Gregory Fifty Years After, 1987, Early Stages: Theatre in Ontario, 1980-1914, 1990, J.M. Synge: The Playboy of the Western World and Other Plays, 1995; (with Richard Plant) Later Stages: Theatre in Ontario, 1914-1970s, 1997, Becoming George--The Life of Mrs. W.B. Yeats, 2002; co-editor Theatre History in Canada, 1980-86; editorial bds. Modern Drama, 1972-82, English Studies in Can., 1973-83, Themes in Drama, 1974-93, Shaw Rev., 1977—, Research in the Humanities, 1976-90; Irish Univ. Rev., 1970—, Yeats Ann., 1982-86; Studies in Contemporary Irish Lit., 1986—, Irish Studies Rev., 1997; contbr. articles to profl. jours. Recipient Brit. Acad. Rose Mary Crawshay award, 1986, Disting. Svc. award Province of Ont., 1985, U. Toronto Alumni award of excellence, 1991, award yeats Soc. N.Y. 2001; named Disting. Dau. of Pa., 1992, Woman of Distinction in Letters, Toronto, YWCA, 1994; Officer of Order of Can., 1995; Can. Coun. scholar, 1958-59, fellow, 1968, Guggenheim fellow, 1968, 77, sr. rsch. fellow Connaught, 1985. Fellow Royal Soc. Can., Royal Soc. Arts; mem. Internat. Assn. Study Anglo-Irish Lit. (chmn. 1973-76), Assn. Can. Theatre Rsch. (pres. 1976-77), Can. Assn. Irish Studies, Assn. Can. Univ. Tchrs. English. Home: 10876 Madrona Dr Sidney BC Canada V8L 5N9 E-mail: saddlemy@uvic.ca.

SADDLER, DONALD EDWARD, choreographer, dancer; b. Van Nuys, Calif., Jan. 24, 1920; s. Elmer Edward and Mary Elizabeth (Roberts) Saddler. Student, Los Angeles City Coll., 1939; dance pupil of, Carmalita Maracci, Anton Dolin, Anthony Tudor, Madame Anderson Ivantzova. Mem. Ballet Theatre, N.Y.C., 1940-43, 46-47; asst. dir., then artistic dir. Harkness Ballet, N.Y.C., 1964-70. Exec. v.p. Rebekah Harkness Found., 1967—69; mem. exec. bd. Internat. Ballet Corp., 1979; prodr. Delacorte Theatre N.Y. Dance Festival; guest artist Valerie Bettis Co. Dancer Grand Canyon Suite, 1937, High Button Shoes, 1947, Dance Me a Song, 1950, Bless You All, 1950, The Song of Norway, 1951, Winesburg, Ohio, 1958, The Golden Round, 1960, The Castle Period, 1961, Happy Birthday, Mr. Abbot!, 1987, with Ballet Theatre, N.Y.C. Bluebeard, Billy the Kid, Swan Lake, Aurora's Wedding, Les patineus, Lilac Garden, Gala Performance, Romeo and Juliet, Peter and the Wolf, Follies, 2001; dir.: (TV films) Holiday Hotel, 1950; choreographer theatre Blue Mountain Ballads, 1948, Wish You Were Here, 1952, Wonderful Town, 1952, John Murray Anderson's Almanac, 1953, Tobia la Candida Spia, 1954, La patrona di raddio di luna, 1955, Shangri-La, 1956, Buona notte Bettina, 1956, L'adorabile Giulio, 1957, Winesburg, Ohio, 1958, This Property is Condemned, 1958, Un trapezio per Lisistrata, 1958, When in Rome, 1959, Un manderino per Teo, 1959, Dreams of Glory, 1961, Milk and Honey, 1961, Sophie, 1963, Morning Sun, 1963, To Broadway, With Love, 1964, No, No, Nanette, 1971, Much Ado About Nothing, 1972, Fanfare Gala, 1973, Good News, 1973, Tricks, 1973, The Merry Wives of Windsor, 1974, Miss Moffat, 1974, A Midsummer Night's Dream, 1975, A Doll's House, 1975, A Gala Tribute to Joshua Logan, 1975, Rodgers and Hart, 1975, The Robber Bridegroom, 1975, 1976, Koshare, 1976, Vaudeville, 1976, Dear Friends and Gentle Hearts, 1976, Icedancing, 1978, The Grand Tour, 1979, A Long Way to Boston, 1979, Happy New Year, 1980, Hey Look Me Over!, 1981, Pardon, Monsieur Moliere, 1982, On Your Toes, 1983, The Loves of Anatol, 1985, The Golden Land, 1985, Broadway, 1987, The Student Prince, 1987, Teddy and Alice, 1987, My Fair Lady, 1993, tours The Boys from Syracuse, Aida, La Perichole, The Merry Widow, Tropicana, We Take This Town, 1962, Knickerbocker Holiday, 1971, No, No, Nanette, 1971—73, Good News, 1973—74, Hellzapoppin', 1976—77, On Your Toes, 1984, (films) April in Paris, 1952, By the Light of the Silvery Moon, 1953, Young at Heart, 1954, The Main Attraction, 1963, The Happy Hooker, 1973, Radio Days, 1987, (TV films) Holiday Hotel, 1950, (TV series) The Perry Como Show, 1950, Canozionissima, 1959—60, Bell Telephone Hour, 1961—64, (TV films) Much Ado About Nothing, 1973, (TV miniseries) Tony Award Broadcasts, 1973, 1975—78, 1983, Verna: U.S.O. Girl, 1978; dir.(theatre): Berlin to Broadway with Kurt Weill, 1972, George Abbott...A Celebration, 1976, Life with Father, 1982, I Hear Music...of Frank Loesser and Friends, 1984, State Fair Music Hall, 1957, 1959, Carousel Theatre, 1958, Stratford Shakespeare Festival, 1979; prodr.(theatre): The Sol Hurok Birthday Gala, 1973, The 30th Anniversary of City Center Theatre, 1975, (with Martin Feinstein): The Pre-Inaugural Ballet-Opera Gala, 1981,: The Dance Collection Gala, 1972, The 35th Anniversary of the Am. Ballet Theatre, 1975, The Cynthia Gregory Gala. Recipient Dance Mag. award, 1984, Lifetime Achievement award, Theatre Development Fund, 2001. Address: Coleman-Rosenberg 155 E 55th St Apt 5D New York NY 10022-4051

SADDLER, GEORGE FLOYD, government economic adviser; b. Memphis, Sept. 27, 1925; s. Henry Rutherford and Ludorn Myrtle (Woods) S.; m. Pauline Evelyn McKissack, Jan. 3, 1944 (dec. Aug. 1988); children: Paula Frederica, Paulette Yvonne. BS, NYU, 1950; postgrad., Northwestern U., Chgo., 1954, U. Chgo., 1961-62. Supr. acctg. dept. Aldens, Inc., Chgo., 1950-57; sr. acct. City of Chgo., 1957-65; internat. adminstrn. officer U.S. Dept. State, Washington, 1965-68; chief budget sect. UN, N.Y.C., 1968-74; dir. fin. UN Devel. Program, N.Y.C., 1974-78; minister-counselor U.S. Mission to UN, N.Y.C., 1978-81; asst. dir. gen. UNESCO, Paris, 1981-86; sr. econ. adviser U.S. Mission to UN, N.Y.C., 1986-89; sr. advisor, cons. UN Orgns., 1989-96. Pres. Assn. Former Internat. Civil Servants in N.Y., 1994—2002, Riverdale chpt. of the UN Assn. of the U.S., 1995—99; pres., CEO, Fedn. Assns. of Former Internat. Civil Servants, 1999—. Treas. The Hague Appeal for Peace, 2000—; chmn. N.Y. Ralph J. Bunche Centenary Com.

SADE, DONALD STONE, anthropology educator; b. Charleston, W.Va., July 17, 1937; s. Samuel and Charlotte Tracy (Stone) S.; m. Bonita Diane Chepko, Dec. 24, 1971 (div. Feb. 1994); children: Irony Cuervo del Norte, Omen Ondatra; m. Kerry L. Knox, Nov. 24, 1994. Grad., N.Y. State Ranger Sch., 1957; student, Hamilton Coll., 1957-60; AB, U. Calif., Berkeley, 1963, PhD, 1966. Instr. anthropology Northwestern U., Evanston, Ill., 1965-66, asst. prof., 1966-70, assoc. prof., 1970-75, prof., 1975-95, sr. lectr., 1995—97; scientist-in-charge Cayo Santiago, U. P.R., 1970-77; prof. emeritus Northwestern U., 1997—. Founder, pres. North Country Inst. for Natural Philosophy, Inc., Mexico, N.Y., 1980— Sr. author: Basic Demographic Observations on Free-Ranging Rhesus Monkeys, 3 vols., 1985; editor: The North Country Naturalist, Vol. 1, 1987. Recipient Merit cert., Eastman Sch. Music., 2002; grantee, NSF, 1967—. Mem. Animal Behavior Soc., Guild Am. Luthiers, Nature Conservancy, Adirondack Mountain Club, Adirondack Coun., Classical Guitar Soc. Upstate NY. Office: North Country Inst for Natural Philosophy Inc 18 Emery Rd Mexico NY 13114-3331 *...and all I've done for want of wit, to memory now I can't recall. (Irish ballad).*

SADEGH, ALI M. mechanical engineering educator, researcher, consultant; b. Tehran, Iran, Sept. 1, 1950; came to U.S., 1974; s. Saleh S. Mir-Mohamad-Sadegh and Asam Lotfi; m. Guita Miremadi, July 10, 1980; children: Mietra, Cameron, Mona, Jasmin, David. BSME, Arya-Mehr U. Tech., Tehran, 1972; MSME, Mich. State U., 1975, PhD in Mechanics, 1978; postgrad., U. Mich., 1979. Registered profl. engr., Mich.; cert. mfg. engr. Design engr. Nat. Radio engrng. sect., Tehran, 1972-74; rsch. and teaching asst. Mich. State U., East Lansing, 1975-78; asst. prof. Arya-Mehr U. Tech., 1979-81; vis. asst. prof. Mich. State U., 1981-82; asst. prof. CUNY, N.Y.C., 1982-87, assoc. prof., 1987-91, prof., 1991—, chmn. dept. mech. engrng., 1992-96, tchr. courses in solid mechanics, design and CAD/CAM. Cons. Devel. Iranian Heavy Industries, Tehran, 1979-81; tech. cons. AC Rochester Gen. Motors Co., 1986-92; forensic engr., 1990—; cons. and presenter in field. Contbr. over 100 articles to profl. jours.; 7 patents in field. U. Mich. scholar, Ann Arbor, 1978-79; recipient 36 Rsch. awards NSF, AT&T Found., PSC-CUNY, others. Fellow ASME (Best Paper award 1992, Melville medal 1993), Soc. Mfg. Engrs. (chmn. chpt. 320); mem. Am. Acad. Mechanics, Biomed. Engrs. Soc., Sigma Xi. Achievements include patents in field. Home: 787 Oneida Trl Franklin Lakes NJ 07417-2216 Office: CUNY Dept Mech Engring 140th St and Convent Ave New York NY 10031

SADEGHI-NEJAD, ABDOLLAH, pediatrician, educator; b. Meshed, Iran, Apr. 29, 1938; s. Abdolhossein and Azizeh (Jabbari) S.-N.; m. Marion M. Marquardt, Jan. 26, 1974; children; Nathan R., Adrienne R. BA, Beloit Coll., 1960; MS in Pathology, MD, U. Chgo., 1964. Diplomate Am. Bd. Pediatrics. Intern then resident U. Chgo., 1964-67; fellow pediatric endocrinology Tufts-New Eng. Med. Ctr., Boston, 1967-69, U. Calif., San Francisco, 1969-70; from asst. prof. to prof. pediatrics Tufts-New Eng. U., Boston, 1970—; chief pediatric endocrinology and metabolism divsn. New Eng. Med. Ctr., Boston, 1989—. Author and co-author books and articles. Mem. town meeting Town of Brookline, Mass., 1987-2001, mem. adv. com., 1993-99; founder, mem. Friends of Lost Pond. Fellow Am. Acad. Pediatrics; mem. Am.

Pediatric Soc., Am. Diabetes Assn., Endocrine Soc., European Soc. Pediatric Rsch., Lawson Wilkins Pediat. Endocrine Soc., Soc. Pediat. Rsch. Office: Tufts-New Eng Med Ctr 750 Washington St Boston MA 02111-1526

SADER, CAROL HOPE, former state legislator; b. Bklyn., July 19, 1935; d. Nathan and Mollie (Farkas) Shimkin; m. Harold M. Sader, June 9, 1957; children: Neil, Randi Sader Friedlander, Elisa Sader Waldman. BA, Barnard Coll., Columbia U., 1957. Sch. tchr. Bd. Edn., Morris, Conn., 1957-58; legal editor W. H. Anderson Co., Cin., 1974-78; freelance legal editor Shawnee Mission, Kans., 1978-87; mem. Kans. Ho. of Reps., 1987-94. Chair Ho. Pub. Health and Welfare Com., 1991-92; chair Joint Ho. and Senate Com. on Health Care Decisions for the 90's, 1992; vice chair Ho. Econ. Devel. Com., 1991-92; policy chair Ho. Dem. Caucus, 1993-94; appointee Kans. jud. qualifications commn. Kans. Supreme Ct., 1995—; apptd. Kans. Racing and Gaming Commn., 2003-2004, Kans. State Bd. Healing Arts, 2003—. Pres. LWV, Johnson County, 1983—85; mem. State of Kans. LWV Bd., 1986—87; pres. Johnson County Found. Aging, 2002—; mem. Johnson County Charter Commn., 1999; mem. exec. bd. Johnson County C.C. Found., 2000—03; mem. adv. group Kans. Gov.'s B.E.S.T. Team, 2002—; dem. candidate for Kans. Lt. Gov., 1994; mem. Jewish Cmty. Rels. Bd., 1999—; chmn. bd. trustees Johnson County C.C., Overland Park, Kans., 1984—86, trustee, 1981—86; bd. dirs. United Cmty. Svcs. of Johnson County, Shawnee Mission, 1984—92, Jewish Vocat. Svc. Bd., 1983—92, House of Menuha, 1998—99, Appleseed Found. Kans., 1999—2001; bd. dirs., exec. bd. Midwest Ctr. Holocaust Edn., 1999—; chmn. Kans. State Holocaust Commn., 1991—94; pres. MAINstream Coalition, 1995—97, vice chair, 1998—2003; v.p. Kans. Advocates for Better Care, 1998—2001. Recipient Trustee award Assn. of Women in Jr. and C.C., 1985, awards Kans. Pub. Transit Assn., 1990, AARP, 1992, Assn. Kans. Theater, 1992, Nat. Coun. Jewish Women, 1992, Kans. Assn. Osteo. Medicine, 1992, Kans. Chiropractic Assn., 1992, United Com. Svcs. Johnson County, 1992, Disting. Pub. Svcs. award Johnson County, 1993, Hallpac Kans. Pub. Svc. award Hallmark Cards, Inc., 1993, Eddie Jacobsen award B'nai B'rith, 1994, Cmty. Svc. award House of Menuha, 1998, The Pillar award Greater K.C. Women's Political Caucus, 2003, Stand-Up, Speak-Out award Mainstream Coalition, 2003. Mem. Coun. Women Legislators, Phi Delta Kappa. Democrat. Avocations: grandparenting, lakehouse, theater, travel. Home: 8612 Linden Dr Shawnee Mission KS 66207-1807

SADICK, NEIL SCOTT, dermatologist; b. Bronx, NY, June 1, 1951; s. Harry and Shirley (Tompkins) Sadick; m. Amy Rose Kamin, July 22, 1989; 1 child, Sydney Kamin. BA, SUNY, Binghamton, 1973; MD, SUNY, Syracuse, 1977. Diplomate Am. Bd. Internal Medicine, 1980, Am. Bd. Dermatology, 1983, Am. Acad. Cosmetic Surgery, 2000, Am. Bd. Hair Restoration Surgery, 2001. Pvt. practice, NYC, 1983—; mem. adv. bd. Dermatologic Soc. Greater NY, 1994—; clin. prof. dermatology Cornell U, Monroe Coll. Surg. advisor Archives Dermatology. Author: (book) Your Hair, Helping to Keep It, 1994; asst. editor (jour.) Jour. Am. Acad. Dermatology, 1994—; author: (book) Sclerotherapy of Varicose Veins, 1996; asst. editor (jour.) Jour. Aesthetic and Cosmetic Surgery, —. Mem.: Am. Soc. Dermatological Surgery (bd. dirs.), Am. Cancer Soc. (summer fellow 1977), Manhattan Met. Dermatology Soc. (pres. 1995—96), NY Acad. Medicine, Dermatology Found. (vice chmn. 1993—), Am. Soc. Cosmetic Surgery (bd. dirs.), Am. Acad. Dermatology (adv. bd. 1995—), Dermatologic Soc. Greater NY (adv. bd. 1994, pres. 1995—96), Am. Coll. Phlebology. (pres. 2002—04, bd. dir., Jobst award 1990), LI Dermatology Soc. Avocations: tennis, travel, antique pens. Office: 772 Park Ave New York NY 10021-4153 Office Phone: 212-772-7242. Business E-Mail: nssderm@sadickdermatology.com.

SADIK, MARVIN SHERWOOD, art consultant, former museum director; b. Springfield, Mass., June 27, 1932; s. Harry Benjamin and Florence (Askinas) S. AB magna cum laude, Harvard U., 1954, A.M., 1960; D.F.A. (hon.), Bowdoin Coll., Brunswick, Maine, 1978. Curatorial asst. Worcester (Mass.) Art Mus., 1955-57; curator Mus. Art Bowdoin Coll., 1961-64, dir., 1964-67, Mus. Art U. Conn. at Storrs, 1967-69, Nat. Portrait Gallery, Washington, 1969-81. Author: Colonial and Federal Portraits at Bowdoin College, 1966, The Drawings of Hyman Bloom, 1968, The Paintings of Charles Hawthorne, 1968, Edith Halpert and the Downtown Gallery, 1968, The Life Portraits of John Quincy Adams, 1970, Christian Gullager: Portrait Painter to Federal America, 1976, Portraits of George Bellows, 1981; co-author: American Portrait Drawings, 1980. Decorated knight Order Dannebrog Denmark; recipient Detur prize Harvard Coll., 1952, Maine State Art award, 1975, gold medal for exceptional svc. Smithsonian Instn., 1981; Harris fellow, 1957-61; Barr fellow, 1957-61; fellow Belgian Art Seminar, 1956. Fellow Pierpont Morgan Library; mem. Am. Antiquarian Soc., Colonial Soc. Mass. (corr.) Clubs: Century Assn, Grolier. Home: PO Box 6360 Scarborough ME 04070-6360

SADIK, NAFIS, United Nations administrator; b. Jaunpur, India, Aug. 18, 1929; d. Iffat Ara and Mohammad Shoaib; m. Azhar Sadik, 1954; 5 children. Student, Loretto Coll., Calcutta, India, Dow Med. Coll., Karachi, Pakistan, Johns Hopkins U., LHD (hon.), 1989, Brown U., 1993, Duke U., 1995; LLD, Wilfrid Laurier U., 1995; DSc (hon.), U. Mich., 1996, Claremont U., 1996; LHD (hon.), Philippines U., 1997; DSc (hon.), Long Island U., 1997; LHD (hon.), Nepal Tribhuvan U., 1998; DSc, Tulane U., 1999. Intern ob-gyn. City Hosp., Balt., 1952-54; civilian med. officer in charge of women's and children's wards various Pakistani armed forces hosps., 1954-63; resident physiology Queens U., Kingston, Ont., Can., 1958; head health sect. Planning Commn. on Health and Family Planning, Pakistan, 1964; dir. planning and tng. Pakistan Ctr. Family Planning Coun., 1966-68, dep. dir.-gen., 1968-70, dir.-gen., 1970-71; tech. advisor UN Fund for Population Activities, 1971-72, chief programme divsn., 1973-77, asst. exec. dir., 1977-87, exec. dir., 1987—; under-sec.-gen. UN, 1987—. Sec.-gen. Internat. Conf. on Population and Devel., 1994, Soc. for Internat. Devel. (pres. 1994-97). Writings include: Population: National Family Planning Programme in Pakistan, 1968, Population: the UNFPA Experience, 1984, Population Policies and Programmes: Making a Difference: Twenty-five Years of UNFPA Experience, 1994, Lessions learned from Two Decades of Experience, 1991, Making a Difference: Twenty-Five Years of UNFPA Experience, 1994; contbr. articles to profl. jours. Recipient Hugh Moore award; Paul Harris fellow Rotary, 1997. Fellow Royal Coll. Ob-Gyn. Avocations: bridge, reading, theater, travel. Office: UN Population Fund 220 E 42nd St Fl 19 New York NY 10017-5806

SADILEK, VLADIMIR, architect; b. Czechoslovakia, June 27, 1933; came to U.S., 1967, naturalized, 1973; s. Oldrich and Antoine (Zlamal) S.; m. Jana Kadlec, Mar. 25, 1960; 1 child, Vladimir. PhD in City Planning summa cum laude, Tech. U. Prague, 1957. Lic. architect, 28 states. Chief architect State Office for City Planning, Prague, 1958-67; architect, designer Bank Bldg. Corp., St. Louis, 1967-70, assoc. architect San Francisco, 1970-74; owner, CEO Bank Design Cons., San Mateo, Calif., 1974-81, West Coast Devel. Co., San mateo, 1975—; pres., CEO Orbis Devel. Corp., San mateo, 1981—. Served with Inf. of Czechoslovakia, 1958. Recipient awards of excellence Bank Bldg. Corp. and AIA for planning and Design of fin. instns. in Hawaii and Calif., 1971, Ariz., N.Mex. and Tex., 1972, Colo. and Wyo., 1973, Idaho, Oreg., Wash., 1974. Republican. Roman Catholic. Home: 80 Orange Ct Burlingame CA 94010-6516 Office: 1777 Borel Pl San Mateo CA 94402-3509

SADLER, DAVID G(ARY), management executive; b. Iowa City, Mar. 14, 1939; s. Edward Anthony and Elsie June (Sherman) S.; m. Karen Sadler; children: Michael Robert, Katherine Louise. Student, St. Ambrose Coll., 1957-59; BS in Indsl. Adminstrn. and Prodn., Kent State U., 1961. Various mgmt. positions Ford Motor Co., Lorain, Ohio, 1962-67, Sperry-New Holland, Lebanon, Ohio, 1967-71; mgr. mfg. Allis Chalmer, Springfield, Ill., 1971-72; dir. mfg. Purolator, Inc., Fayetteville, N.C., 1972-73; v.p. mfg. farm equipment and ops. truck div. White Motor Co., Eastlake, Ohio and Chgo., 1973-78; corp. v.p. mfg. Massey Ferguson Ltd., Toronto, Ont., Can., 1978-80, Internat. Harvester, Chgo., 1980-81, sr. v.p. ops. staff, 1981-82, v.p. bus. devel., 1982, pres. diversified group, 1982-83, pres. internat. group, 1983-85; pres. AMI, Inc., Chgo., 1985-86; vice chmn., chief exec. officer Savin Corp., Stamford, Conn., 1986, chmn., chief exec. officer, 1986-89, also bd. dirs.; pres. Asset Mgmt. Internat., Westport, Conn., 1989-95; chmn., CEO, Rowe Internat., Grand Rapids, Mich., 1995-2000, also bd. dirs., 2000—01; CEO Merisel, Inc., El Segundo, Calif., also bd. dirs.; chmn., CEO, bd. dirs. Global Motorsport Group, Inc., Morgan Hill, Calif., 2002. CEO, bd. dirs. Global Motorsport Group, Inc., Morgan Hill, Calif., 2002—. Bd. dirs. greater Chgo. Safety Coun., 1981-84; mem. adb. bd. Hellmond Assocs. Opportunity Fund II. Roman Catholic. Home: 751 Bradford Farms Ln NE Grand Rapids MI 49525-3348 E-mail: davidgsadler@aol.com.

SADLER, DENNIS, supervisor; b. Dyersburg, Tenn., July 14, 1960; s. Gene and Dotsy Ramona Sadler; m. Felicia Ann Sadler, Jan. 25, 1985; children: Elizabeth Nicole, Nathan Michael. BS in ch. ministry, Crichton Coll., 1985—88; MS in edn., U. of Memphis, 1999—2003. Profession Teacher's License Tenn. Dept. of Edn., 2000. Owner Sadler Constrn. Co., Halls, Tenn., 1993—98; correctional tchr. supr. TN Dept. Correction, Henning, Tenn., 1998—. Adv. bd. Dyersburg State C.C.; Criminal Justice, Dyersburg, Tenn., 2003—03. County commr. Lauderdale County, Halls, Tenn., 1998—; alderman Town of Halls, Halls, Tenn., 2001—; county chmn. Lauderdale County Rep. Party, Ripley, Tenn., 2000—04; regional coord. Van Hilleary for Gov., Tenn.; ordained deacon So. Bapt., Tenn., lic. preacher; vice-chmn. Lauderdale County C. of C., Ripley, Tenn., 2001—. Sgt. U.S. Air Force, 1978—82, Seymour Johnson Air Force Base. Decorated Marksmanship U.S. Air Force. Mem.: Tenn. State Employee's Assn. (assoc.), Kappa Delta Pi Internat. Honor Soc. in Edn. Conservative-R. Southern Bapt. Office: West Tennessee State Penitentiary PO Box 1150 Henning TN 38041

SADLER, ELLIOTT, race car driver; b. Emporia, Va., Apr. 30, 1975; s. Herman and Bell Sadler. Student, James Madison U. Named winner, Late Model Stock Cars Winston Racing Series, 1994, South Boston Speedway Track, 1995, Core States Advantage 200, 1997, Myrtle Beach, 1997, Gateway Internat. Raceway, 1997, Bristol, 1998, Winston Cup, 2001; recipient Busch Pole award, 1997, 2d pl., Kroger 250, 1998. Avocations: golf, basketball, hunting. Office: c/o Wood Bros Racing 21 Performance Dr Stuart VA 24171

SADLER, GRAHAM HYDRICK, library administrator; b. Sikeston, Mo., Aug. 17, 1931; s. Philip Landis and Montie Pearl (Hydrick) S.; m. Betty A. Grugett, Nov. 22, 1950; children— Graham Hydrick, Lee, Susan, Harrison BS, S.E. Mo. State Coll., 1952; M.L.S., Emory U., 1957. Asst. libr. S.E. Mo. State Coll., Cape Girardeau, 1954-61; adminstrv. libr. Kinderhook Regional Libr., Lebanon, Mo., 1961-66; dir. Fort Lewis Coll. Libr., Durango, Colo., 1966-67; assoc. prof. librarianship Kans. State Tchrs. Coll., Emporia, 1967-69; asst. libr., dir. community svc. Denver Pub. Libr., 1970-77; dir. County of Henrico Pub. Libr., Richmond, Va., 1978-94, ret., 1994. Mem. adv. com. Office of Library Service to Disadvantaged, 1978-91. Mem. ALA (membership com. 1989-92).

SADLO, KENNETH LOUIS, poet, writer; b. St. Louis, Oct. 16, 1969; s. Kenneth Edward Sadlo, Mary Ann Cherrick. Student, St. Louis U., 1988—89, Lincolnland C.C., Springfield, Ill., 1991—92. Author: (CD) The Sound of Poetry, 2001, The Silence Within, 2001, The Best Poems and Poets of 2001, 2002. Liaison Quincy U. "The Falcon", Ill., 1992—93. Scholar John J. McDaniel scholar, 1984—88. Home: 11733 Lindemere Des Peres MO 63131

SADOCK, BENJAMIN JAMES, psychiatrist, educator; b. N.Y.C., Dec. 22, 1933; s. Samuel William and Gertrude S.; m. Virginia Alcott, Oct. 20, 1963; children: James William, Victoria Anne. AB, Union Coll., 1955; MD, N.Y. Med. Coll., 1959. Rotating intern Albany (N.Y.) Hosp., 1959-60; resident Bellevue Psychiat. Hosp., N.Y.C., 1960-63; instr. psychiatry Southwestern Med. Sch., Dallas, 1964-65, N.Y. Med. Coll., N.Y.C., 1965-67, asst. prof., 1967-71, assoc. prof., 1972-74, prof., 1975-80, dir. student health psychiatry, 1980—; prof. psychiatry NYU Sch Medicine, 1981-99, Menas S. prof. psychiatry, 2000—, vice chmn. dept. psychiatry, 1984—, faculty scholar, 2000—. Attending physician Lenox Hill Hosp.; attending psychiatrist Tisch Univ. Hosp. of NYU Med. Ctr., Bellevue Hosp.; cons. psychiatrist Franklin Delano Roosevelt VA Hosp., 1970-78, U.S. Dept. State, 1980-81, P.R. Inst. Psychiatry, 1976-80; examiner Am. Bd. Psychiatry and Neurology, 1970-80; mem. conf. on recert. Am. Bd. Med. Spltys.-Am. Psychiat. Assn., 1974; mem. Commn. on Continuing Edn. in Psychiatry, NIMH-Am. Psychiat. Assn., 1974-75. Co-author: Comprehensive Group Psychotherapy, 1971, 3d edit., 1993, Synopsis of Psychiatry, 1972, 8th edit., 1998, The Sexual Experience, 1976, Study Guide Modern Synopsis of Psychiatry, 1983, 8th edit., 2003, Comprehensive Textbook of Psychiatry, 7th edit., 2000, Pocket Handbook of Clinical Psychiatry, 1991, 3d edit., 2001, Comprehensive Glossary of Psychiatry and Psychology, 1991, Pocket Handbook of Drug Treatment in Psychiatry, 1992, 3d edit., 2000, Pocket Handbook of Psychiatric Emergency Medicine, 1993, Pocket Handbook of Primary Care Psychiatry, 1996; contbr. articles on psychiat. edn., individual and group psychotherapy, diagnosis and treatment of psychiat., sexual disorders to med. jours.; contbr. to Ency. Americana. Fellow Am. Psychiat. Assn. (treas. N.Y. County dist. br. 1973-76, mem. conf. on psychiatry and med. edn. 1967), N.Y. Acad. Medicine, A.C.P.; mem. AMA, Med. Soc. County and State N.Y., Am. Group Psychotherapy Assn., World Psychiat. Assn., Royal Soc. Medicine (London), Psychiat. Soc. N.Y. Med. Coll. (founder, pres. 1975-79), N.Y. Med. Coll. Alumni Assn. (gov. 1965-90), NYU-Bellevue Psychiat. Soc. (pres. 1981—), Alpha Omega Alpha. Office: 4 E 89th St New York NY 10128-0636 also: NYU Med Ctr 550 1st Ave New York NY 10016-6402 E-mail: bjs6@nyu.edu.

SADOCK, KAREN, editor, writer; b. Detroit, Feb. 12, 1943; d. Warren Siebren and Daisy Annie (Taylor) Nauta; m. Geoffrey Johnston Sadock, Sept. 4, 1971; 1 child, Katharine Cordelia Johnston Sadock. AB, U. Mich., 1965; MDiv, Gen. Theol. Sem., N.Y.C., 1975. Assoc. editor Wards Automotive Reports, Detroit, 1966-68; tech. editor Freuhauf Corp., Detroit, 1968-71; author's editor Mt. Sinai Med. Ctr., N.Y.C., 1975-97, spl. projects mgr., Dean's Office, 1997—, asst. dir. sci. integrity, 1999—. Editor med. scholarly articles New Eng. Jour. Medicine, Circulation, others; author articles on Christian spirituality. Mem. Cavalier King Charles Spaniel Clubs U.S.A., Confraternity of Penitents. Republican. Roman Catholic. Avocations: figure skating, quilting. Home: 67 W Shore Ave Dumont NJ 07628-2332 E-mail: Karen.Sadock@saintbruno.org.

SADOFF, ROBERT LESLIE, psychiatrist, educator; b. Mpls., Feb. 8, 1936; s. Max and Rose C. (Karroll) S.; m. Joan A Handleman, June 21, 1959; children: Debra, David, Julie, Sherry. BA, U. Minn., 1956, BS, 1957, MD, 1959; MS, UCLA, 1963. Intern L.A. VA Hosp., 1959—60; resident in psychiatry UCLA, 1960—63; asst. prof. psychiatry Temple U., Phila., 1966—72; clin. prof. U. Pa., Phila., 1972—; pvt. practice Jenkintown, Pa., 1965—. Lectr. law Villanova U., 1972-85. Author: (with Marvin Lewis) Psychic Injuries, 1975, Forensic Psychiatry, 1975, 2d edit., 1988, Legal Issues in the Care of Psychiatric Patients, 1982, Violence and Responsibility, 1988, (with Robert I. Simon) Psychiatric Malpractice, 1992; editor: Psychiatric Clinics of North America, 1984. Bd. dirs. Joseph T. Peters Inst., Phila., 1980-92. Capt. M.C., U.S. Army, 1963-65. Recipient Earl Bond award U. Pa., 1979, VII ann. Nathaniel Winkelman award Phila. Psychiat. Ctr., 1988. Fellow: Am. Coll. Legal Medicine, Am. Psychiat. Assn. (Manfred Guttmacher award 1993); mem.: Internat. Acad. Law and Mental Health (Philippe Pinel award 1995), Internat. Soc. for Philos. Enquiry (mentor 1987—), Am. Acad. Psychiatry and Law (pres. 1971—73), Am. Coll. Psychiatrists, Am. Red Magen David for Israel (nat. pres. 1986—2001). Avocation: collecting antique books in law and medicine. Office: The Pavilion Ste 326 261 Old York Rd Jenkintown PA 19046 Office Phone: 215-887-6144. E-mail: bobsadoff@aol.com.

SADOSKI, MARK CHRISTIAN, education educator; b. Bristol, Conn., June 2, 1945; s. Waldmyr John Sadoski and Ruth Elaine (Gustafson) Kantorski; m. Carol Ann Bove, June 28, 1969; 1 child, Thomas Christian. BS, So. Conn. State U., 1968, MS, 1973; PhD, U. Conn., 1981. Cert. reading, English, social studies tchr. Tchr., reading cons. Milford (Conn.) Pub. Schs., 1968-81; assoc. faculty So. Conn. State U., New Haven, 1978-81; prof. edn. Tex. A&M Univ., College Station, 1981—. Author: Conceptual Foundations of Teaching Reading, 2004, (with Allan Paivio) Imagery and Text: A Dual Coding Theory of Reading and Writing, 2001; mem. editl. bd. Reading Rsch. Quar., 1989—, Jour. Reading Behavior, 1990-95, Reading Psychology, 1990—, Jour. Literacy Rsch., 1995—, Document Design, 1998—, Reading and Writing, 2001—; contbr. over 80 articles to profl. jours. and books. Accident prevention counselor S.W. region FAA, 1989-91. Recipient Disting. Alumnus award So. Conn. State U., 1994. Mem. Internat. Reading Assn. (outstanding dissertation award com. 1983-85, finalist Outstanding Dissertation award 1982), Nat. Reading Conf. (Outstanding Book award com. 1994-99), Am. Ednl. Rsch. Assn. (outstanding book award com. 1994-2000), Soc. for Sci. Study of Reading (chair pubs. com. 1996-97), Phi Kappa Phi. Avocations: reading, cinema. Office: Tex A&M Univ Dept tlac 4232 TAMU College Station TX 77843-4232 E-mail: msadoski@tamu.edu.

SADOVE, STEPHEN IRVING, retail executive; b. Washington, July 25, 1951; s. A. Robert and Harriet (Tenenbaum) S.; m. Karin Sadove; children: Stacy, David, Laurie. BA, Hamilton Coll., 1973; MBA, Harvard U., 1975. Asst. product mgr. desserts divsn. Gen. Foods Corp., White Plains, N.Y., 1975-76, assoc. product mgr., 1976-77, product mgr., 1977-80, group product mgr., 1980-82, category mgr., 1982-84, mktg. mgr., 1984-86; bus. unit mgr. meals divsn. Gen. Foods Corp., White Plains, 1986-88; v.p., gen. mgr. Gen. Foods Corp., White Plains, 1988-89, exec. v.p., gen. mgr. desserts divsn., 1989-91; pres. Clairol, Inc., Stamford, Conn., 1991-96, Bristol-Myers Squibb Beauty Care, Stamford, 1996-97, Bristol-Myers Squibb Beauty Care and Nutritionals, Stamford, 1998—2001; vice-chmn. Saks Inc., N.Y.C., 2002—. Bd. dirs. Saks Inc., Ruby Tuesday Inc. Trustee Hamilton Coll., Hazelden. Avocations: tennis, golf, reading, arts. Office: Saks Inc 12 E 49th St New York NY 10017 Home: 7 Hickory Pine Ct Purchase NY 10577

SADOW, HARVEY S. health care company executive; b. N.Y.C., Oct. 6, 1922; s. Nat. and Frances Donna (Saveth) S.; m. Sylvia June Riber, Dec. 22, 1944 (div. 1966); children: Harvey Jr., Suzanne Gail, Todd Forrest, Gay Summer; m. Jacqueline Lucille Clavel, Jan. 24, 1969 (div. 1993); 1 adopted child, Daniel Jean Marie; m. Mary Morrissey McSwiggan, July 13, 1995. BS, Va. Mil. Inst., Lexington, 1947; MS, U. Kans., 1949; PhD, U. Conn., 1953, DSc (hon.), 2000. Intelligence officer CIA, Washington, 1951-53; assoc. dir. rsch. Lakeside Labs., Inc., Milw., 1953-56; med. rsch. cons. Milw., 1956; dir. clin. rsch. U.S. Vitamin & Pharm. Corp., N.Y.C., 1957-64, v.p. R & D, 1964-68; sr. v.p. scientific affairs USV Pharm./Revlon Corp., N.Y.C., 1969-71; pres., CEO Boehringer Ingelheim, Ltd. (named changed to Boehringer Ingelheim Pharms., Inc. 1984), Ridgefield, Conn., 1971-88, Boehringer Ingelheim Corp., Ridgefield, 1984-88, chmn. bd., 1988-90. Chmn. bd. Roxane Labs., Inc., Columbus, Ohio, 1981-88, Boehringer Ingelheim Animal Health, Inc., St. Joseph, Mo., 1981-88, Henley Co., N.Y.C., 1986-88, U. Conn. Rsch. and Devel. Corp., Storrs, 1984-87; bd. dirs. Anika Therapeutics, Inc., Trega Bioscis., Inc., chmn. 2000-01, Cortex Pharms., Inc., Irvine, Calif., chmn. bd., 1991-99; bd. dirs. Cholestech Corp., Hayward, Calif., chmn. bd. 1992-2000; adv. bd. Salk Inst. Biotechnology-Indsl. Assocs., Inc., La Jolla, 1988-90; chmn. bd. dirs. Acacia Bioscis. Inc., 1996-99, Rosetta Inpharmatics, Inc., 1999-2001. Co-author: Oral Treatment of Diabetes, 1967; contbr. articles to profl. jours. Bd. dirs. Pharm. Mfrs. Assn., 1983-90; chmn. Pharm. Mfrs. Assn. Found., 1988-90; bd. dirs. Conn. Bd. Higher Edn., Hartford, 1977-83, Govs. Tech. Adv. Bd., Hartford, 1984-87; mem. Conn. Commn. on Bus. Opportunity, Def. Diversification and Indsl. Policy, 1991-93; mem. bd. visitors Va. Mil. Inst., Lexington, 1987—, pres. bd., 1991-95; chmn. bd. Conn. Law Enforcement Found., Hartford, 1981-86, 92-97, U. Conn. Found., Storrs, 1984-87; chmn., pres.' coun. Am. Lung Assn., N.Y.C., 1986-87, York Sch., Monterey, Calif., 1988-89; trustee Conn. Coll., Groton, 1991-96, Aldrich Mus. Contemporary Art, Ridgefield, Conn., 1991-98. Decorated Disting. Svc. Cross, Fed. Republic of Germany, 1987; recipient Univ. medal U. Conn., 1987, Citizen of Yr. Conn. Chief of Police Assn., 1988, Recognition award Nat. Hypertension Assn., 1990, Humanitarian award Am. Lung Assn. Conn., 1993, Disting. Svc. award Conn. Innovations, Inc., 1996, Va. Mil. Inst. Found., 1998. Mem. Am. Soc. for Clin. Pharmacology and Therapeutics, Am. Fedn. for Clin. Rsch., Am. Diabetes Assn., Danbury C. of C. (Abraham Ribicoff Community Svc. award City of Danbury 1987, bd. dirs. 1978-81), Union League (N.Y.C.), Landmark Club (Stamford, Conn.), Masons, Sigma Xi, Sigma Pi Sigma, Phi Lambda Upsilon. Avocations: art collecting, photography, music, writing, golf. Home and Office: 1000 Mason St Apt 904 San Francisco CA 94108-1919 Personal E-mail: hssadow@aol.com.

SADOWSKI, CAROL JOHNSON, artist; b. Chgo., Mar. 20, 1929; d. Carl Valdamar Johnson and Elizabeth Hilma (Booth) Johnson Chellberg; m. Edmund Sadowski, July 9, 1949; children: Lynn Carol Mahoney, Christie Sadowski Cortez. AAS, Wright Coll., Ill., 1949. Tchr. art Malverne H.S., NY, 1968-69; artist Valley Stream, NY, 1968-76, Hollywood, Fla., 1976—. Guest spkr. Mus. Art, Ft. Lauderdale, Fla., 1991; Libr. League, Oakland Park, 1985; Boca Raton, Fla. Mus., others; TV appearances on WCGB, Gainesville; WSVN, Miami; Storer and Hollywood Cable; Artist Guild, Boca Raton Mus.; Broward C.C., Hollywood, Fla. One woman shows include Mus. Fla. History, Tallahassee, 1984-85, 87; Hist. Mus. South Fla., Miami, 1986; Thomas Ctr. Arts, Gainesville, Fla., 1985, 87; Elliott Mus., Stuart, Fla., 1987; Hemingway Mus. and Home, Key West, Fla., 1986; I.G.F.A. Fishing Hall of Fame Mus., Dania, Fla., 1999, Alliance Francaise de Miami, 1995; commd. painting St. Agustin Antigua Found., St. Augustine, Fla., 1985, Atlantic Bank, Ft. Lauderdale, Fla., Bonnet House Fla. Trust, Ft. Lauderdale, Hollywood Art & Culture Ctr., Hemingway Mus., San Francisco de Paula, Presdl. Palace, Havana, Tropical Art Gallery, Naples, Fla., 1981-83, Tequesta (Fla.) Art Gallery, 1985-89, Gingerbread Square Gallery, Key West, 1990—, Wally Findlay Galleries, Inc., Palm Beach and N.Y.C., DeBruyne Fine Arts Gallery, Naples, 1998—, Patricia Cloutier Gallery, Tequesta, Fla., 1992-2003. Mem. Ft. Lauderdale Mus. Art; Hollywood Art and Culture Ctr. Recipient Hemingway medal, Ernest Hemingway Mus., Cuba, 1990; appreciation award City of Hollywood; Chgo. Art Inst. scholar; Salmagundi Club N.Y. scholar. Mem. Internat. Platform Assn.; Broward Art Guild; Fla. Hist. Assn.; Ernest Hemingway Soc.; Chopin Found.; Am. Inst. for Polish Culture; Alliance Francaise de Miami; Women in the Arts Nat. Mus. (charter mem.). Avocations: travel, bicycling, swimming, reading. Home: 1480 Sheridan St Apt B 17 Hollywood FL 33020-2295 Personal E-mail: esadowski@msn.com. *I try to do my best at what I love to do; not for money or fame, but for self satisfaction.*

SADOWSKI, CHESTER PHILIP, JR., real estate executive; b. Pensacola, Fla., May 28, 1946; s. Chester P. and Florence Edna (Perry)S.; m. Jerriann Gibson Steller, Oct. 4, 1975; children: Julie K., Charles P., Robert T., David A. BSBA, U. Fla., 1968. CPA, Fla. Sr. auditor Arthur Andersen & Co., Tampa, Fla., 1969-74, U.S. Home Corp., Clearwater, Fla. and Houston, 1974-77, audit mgr., 1977-81, sr. audit mgr., 1981-82, audit dir., 1982-85, controller, 1985-87, sr. v.p., controller, chief acctg. officer, 1987—2003; cons., 2003—. Mem.: AICPA (real estate com. N.Y.C. 1986—89), Inst. Mgmt. Accts., Fla. Inst. CPA's. Office: 6445 Sweet Gum St Katy TX 77493 Office Phone: 713-818-3486.

SADOWSKI, RICHARD J. former publishing executive; b. Mar. 26, 1947; Publ. Press-Telegram, Long Beach, Calif., 1992—97; pres., publ. St. Paul Pioneer Press, 1997—2001. Office: St Paul Pioneer Press 345 Cedar St Saint Paul MN 55101-1057

SADRUDIN, MOE, humanitarian organization executive; b. Hyderabad, India, Mar. 3, 1943; arrived in U.S., 1964; m. Azmath Qureshi, 1964; 3 children. BSME, Osmania U., Hyderabad, 1964; MS in Indsl. Engring., NYU, 1966; IE, MBA, Columbia U., 1970. Cons. project engr. Ford, Bacon & Davis, N.Y.C., 1966; staff indsl. engr. J.C. Penney, N.Y.C., 1966-68; sr. cons. Drake, Sheahan, Stewart & Dougall, N.Y.C., 1968-70, Beech-Nut Inc. subs. Squibb Corp., N.Y.C., 1970-72; founder, pres. Azmath Constrn. Co., Englewood, NJ, 1972-77; crude oil cons., fgn. govt. rep., 1977—88; pres. A-One Petroleum Co., Fullerton, Calif., 1985—95; chmn., CEO, Universal Humanitarian Found., Fullerton, 1989—. Govt. advisor Puerto Rico, 1980-82, Dominica, 1983-84, St. Vincent, 1981-82, Kenya, 1983-84, Belize 1984-85, Costa Rica 1983-86, Paraguay 1984-87. Chmn. Universal Humanitarian Found., 1989—; active in bldg. 50 charitable hosps., 9000 schools, India, 25 hosps., 3000 schools, Bangladesh; active LA World Affairs Coun. Mem.: Internat. Platform Assn. Address: Universal Humanitarian Found 2656 Camino Del Sol Fullerton CA 92833-4806 Office Phone: 714-526-0633. E-mail: UniHumFound@aol.com. *Personal philosophy: I learned from a young age*

that acquisition of knowledge, developing honesty and integrity and service to humanity in the form of charity, love and struggle to help the poor and needy, are the main foundation stones of a successful life. I believe that acquisition of wealth is only a means to an end and not an end in itself. With accumulation of wealth, one has to care for the underprivileged and try to improve their lot.

SADYKOVA, VERA PHILIPPOVNA, librarian, educator; b. Dneprostroy, Zaporozhie, Ukraine, Mar. 4, 1933; arrived in Kazakhstan, 1947; d. Yabtchenko and (Phesik) Philipp; m. Albert Sadykov, May, 13, 1956; children: Aleksey, Gennady. Grad., Kazakh State U., Alma-Ata, 1957, Inst. Culture, Leningrad, Russia, 1966. Cert. libr., philologist. Libr. Sci. and Tech. Libr. Kazakhstan, Almaty, 1960-62, asst. dir., 1964-65, dir., 1965-88, chief libr., 1988-94, mgr. sci.-methodical dept., 1962-64, 94—, instr. advanced courses, 1962—, head sci. rsch. sector, 1998. Instr. advanced courses Kazakh State Inst. Sci. and Tech. Info., Almaty, 1962—, Sci. and Tech. Libr. Ctr. Profl. Devel., Kazakhstan, Kirgizia, Tadzhikistan, Uzbekistan, 2000-. Author brochures; mem. editl. bd. Nautchnie i Technitcheskie Biblioteki, 1990-91, New Jour. Libr. World, 2002-; contbr. articles to profl. jours. Mem. presidium Trade Unions Com. of State Instns. Ofcls., Almaty, 1971-86. Recipient medals and hon. degree Honoured Worker of Kazakh Soviet Socialist Republic, Presidium of Supreme Soviet USSR, 1970, 83, 84, bronze medals Exhbn. Econ. Achievements of USSR, 1969, 74, 81. Avocations: collecting books, gardening. Office: Sci & Tech Libr Kazakhstan S Mukanov 223B 480077 Almaty Kazakhstan E-mail: rntbb@nursat.kz., orb@os.kz.

SAEED, SY ATEZAZ, psychiatrist, physician; b. Karachi, Pakistan, Nov. 15, 1956; came to U.S., 1985; s. Syed M. Laiq and Tanwira Begum; m. Janel Rene Saeed, June 29, 1991; children: Zack Allen, Karen Kelsey, Sophia Marie. MD, Dow Med. Coll., 1982; MS, St. Francis U., 1987. Diplomate Am. Bd. Psychiatry and Neurology, Am. Bd. Med. Psychotherapists; cert. in psychiat. adminstrn. mgmt. Dir. edn. in psychiatry U. Ill. Coll. Medicine, Peoria, 1993-95, chmn. dept. psychiatry, 1995—2004; prof., chmn. dept. psychiatric medicine East Carolina U., Brody Sch. Medicine, Greenville, NC, 2004—. Clin. dir. North Cen. Network of Ill., Peoria, 1998-2004; advisor Regional D&MDA of Am., Peoria, 1993-03. Contbr. articles to profl. jours. Mem. Am. Assn. Psychiat. Adminstrs. (coun. mem., editor Psychiat. Adminstr.), Am. Coll. Psychiatrists, Am. Psychiat. Assn., Cen. Ill. Psychiat. Soc. (pres. 1995-97) Office: East Carolina Univ Brody Sch Medicine Dept Psychiatric Med 600 Moye Blvd Greenville NC 27858 Office Phone: 252-744-2660. E-mail: saeeds@mail.ecu.edu.

SAEGER, REBECCA, advertising executive; B in Psychology and Polit. Sci., Muhlenberg Coll., 1976; MBA, U. Pa., 1980. Various positions including sr. v.p., group dir. for Lever Bros. and Am. Express Ogilvy & Mather, NY, 1980—91; sr. v.p., group mgmt. supr., dir. account mgmt. Foote, Cone & Belding, San Francisco, 1991—97; exec. v.p. advt. and brand mktg. svcs. Visa USA, 1997—2001; exec. v.p. brand mgmt. and mktg. comm. Charles Schwab Corp., San Francisco, 2004—. Mem. exec. mgmt. com. Visa USA. Mem. mktg. com. San Francisco Symphony; mem. adv. bd. World Congress Sports. Mem.: Assn. Nat. Advertisers (bd. dirs.). Office: The Charles Schwab Corp 101 Montgomery St San Francisco CA 94104*

SAEGESSER, MARGUERITE M. artist; b. Bern, Switzerland, May 27, 1922; came to U.S., 1974; d. Wilhelm and Fanny (Kuepfer) Ruefenacht; m. Max Saegesser, May 27, 1952; 1 child, Francisca Marguerite; stepchildren: Anne-Marie Logan, Elisabeth, Barbara, Ursula L'Eplattenier. Solo exhbns. include De Saisset Mus., Santa Clara, Calif., 1995, Smith Andersen Gallery, Palo Alto, Calif., 1981, 85, 89, 91, 92, 95, Galerie Schindler, Bern, 1968, 90, Art Fair, Basel, Switzerland, 1990, many others; group exhbns. include Long Beach, Calif., 1971, Bienne Open Air Sculpture Show, Switzerland, 1958, 62, 66, Soc. Painters & Sculptors, Bern, 1945-46, 52, 56. Grantee Swiss Endowment Arts, 1995. Mem. South Bay Area Women's Caucus for Arts. Democrat. Home: 840 Mesa Ave Palo Alto CA 94306-3709

SAEKS, ALLEN IRVING, lawyer; b. Bemidji, Minn., July 14, 1932; m. Linda J. Levin; 1 child, Adam Charles. BS in Law, U. Minn., 1954, JD, 1956. Bar: Minn. 1956, U.S. Dist. Ct. Minn. 1956, U.S. Ct. Appeals (8th cir.) 1957, U.S. Ct. Appeals (fed. cir.) 1959, U.S. Supreme Ct. 1959, U.S. Ct. Appeals (11th cir.) 1997; cert. civil trial specialist. Asst. U.S. atty. Dept. Justice, St. Paul, 1956-57; assoc. Leonard Street and Deinard, Mpls., 1960-63, ptnr., 1964—. Adj. prof. law U. Minn. Law Sch., 1960-65; chmn. Lawyer Trust Acct. Bd., Interest on Lawyers Trust Accounts, 1984-87; nat. bd. dir. Equal Justice Works. Chmn. Property Tax Com., 1986—87; bd. dirs. Citizens League, Mpls., 1984—87; pres. Jewish Cmty. Rels. Coun of Minn. and the Dakotas, 1994—96. 1st lt. JAGC U.S. Army, 1957—60. Recipient City of Mpls. award, 1996, Lifetime Commitment award Cardozo Soc., 2001. Fellow Am. Bar Found. (life); mem. ABA (commn. on interest on lawyers trust accts. 1990-93), Minn. State Bar Assn. (ethics task force, 2003, Pres. award 2003), Fund for the Legal Aid Soc. (chmn. 1997-98, Law Day Testimonial award 1996), Hennepin County Bar Assn. (pres. 1983-84), Order of Coif, Phi Delta Phi. Office: Leonard Street and Deinard 150 S 5th St Ste 2300 Minneapolis MN 55402-4238 Office Phone: 612-335-1548. Business E-Mail: ais1548@leonard.com.

SAEKS, RICHARD EPHRAIM, engineering executive; b. Chgo., Nov. 30, 1941; s. Morris G. and Elsie E. S. BS, Northwestern U., 1964; MS, Colo. State U., 1965; PhD, Cornell U., 1967. Registered profl. engr., Tex. Elec. engr. Warwick Mfg. Co., Niles, Ill., 1961-63; asst. prof. dept. elec. engring. U. Notre Dame, 1967-71, assoc. prof., 1971-73; assoc. prof. depts. elec. engring., math. Tex. Tech U., Lubbock, 1973-77, prof., 1977-79, Paul Whitfield Horn prof. elec. engring., math. computer sci, 1979-83; prof., chmn. elec. engring. Ariz. State U., 1983-88; dean Armour Coll. Engring. Ill. Inst. Tech., 1988-91, Motorola prof., 1991-92; v.p. engring. Accurate Automation Corp., 1992-2000, chief tech. officer, 2000—. Cons. Research Triangle Inst., 1978-80, Marcel Dekker Inc., 1978-80. Author: Generalized Networks, 1972, Resolution Space Operators and Systems, 1973, Interconnected Dynamical Systems, 1981, System Theory: A Hilbert Space Approach, 1982; contbr. articles to profl. jours.; Editor: Large-Scale Dynamical Systems, 1976, Rational Fault Analysis, 1977, The World of Large Scale Systems, 1982. Recipient Disting. Faculty Research award Tex. Tech U., 1978 Fellow: AIAA, IEEE; mem.: IEEE Systems Men and Cybernetics Soc. (pres. 1998—99). Achievements include patents for in field.

SAENGER, BRUCE WALTER, consulting firm executive; b. Hanover, N.H., July 16, 1943; s. Werner Hugo and Natalie Bertha (Brown) S.; m. Cheryl Jeanne Bouchard, Nov. 6, 1976. BA, Pa. State U., 1969; postgrad., Am. Coll., Bryn Mawr, Pa., 1979, Coll. Fin. Planning, Denver, 1980. CPCU; ChFC; CLU. Agt. Nationwide Ins., Lansdale, Pa., 1969-73, dist. sales mgr. Springfield, Mass., 1973-75, Am. Mut., Braintree, Mass., 1975-77; dir. mktg. Bankers LIfe & Casualty, Chgo., 1977-78; pres., founder Sales Tng. Techniques, Southboro, Mass., 1979-81, The Saenger Orgn., Medway, Mass., 1981—. Mem. faculty Notre Dame U., South Bend, Ind., 1977-78, Northeastern U., Boston, 1984-92; mem. RHU Commn., Washington, 1979-81; dir. Northeastern U. Inst. Inst., Boston, 1985-93; mem. Mass. Ins. Dept. Continuing Edn. Rev. Com., 1985—; program dir. U. Del. Ins. Program, 1989-91; acad. cons. Mass. Soc. Lic. Ins. Advisers, 1995—; cons. in field. Author: Series 6 Study Book, 1983, Series 22 Study Book, 1984, Tax Shelter Market Guide, 1985, Marketing Mutual Funds, 1985, also articles. Bd. dirs. Lansdale Gen. Hosp., 1971-73, New Directions Theater Co., 1988-91; mem. Medway Bus. Couhn., 1989-94, pres., 1990-92. With U.S. Army, 1960-66. Recipient Ednl. Achievement award Profl. Ins. Agts. Assn., 1983; named Outstanding Fin. Exec. of Yr., Fin. Mgmt. Assn., 1993. Fellow Soc. CLUs (ednl. adv., bd. dirs. 1987-91), Soc. CPCUs (ednl. adv.), Life Mgmt. Inst. (Outstanding Lectr. award 1984); mem. Internat. Assn. Fin. Planners (ednl. adv., bd. dirs. 1986-92, pres. 1989-91), Internat. Assn. for Fin. Planning (chmn. bd. dirs. 1990-92), Soc. Cert. Ins. Counselors, Life Underwriters Assn., Inst. CFP (v.p. edn., bd. dirs. 1990-91), Mass. Assn. Health Underwriters (pres. 1992-93, Boston Bus. Ethics award 2001). Republican. Roman Catholic. Avocation: skiing. Home: 68 Orchard St Millis MA 02054-1018 Office: The Saenger Orgn 77 Main St Medway MA 02053-1812

SAENZ, MICHAEL, college president; b. Laredo, Tex., Oct. 25, 1925; s. C.A. and Pola R. Saenz; m. Nancy Elizabeth King; children: Michael King, Cynthia Elizabeth. BS in Acctg. with honors, Tex. Christian U., 1949, MEd, 1952; PhD in Econs., U. Pa., 1961. Dep. collector IRS, Ft. Worth, Dallas, 1949-52; adminstr. United Christian Missionary Soc., Bayamon, P.R., 1954-57, 59-65, exec. sec. Indpls., 1965-71; acad. dean Laredo (Tex.) Jr. Coll., 1971-74; pres. N.W. campus Tarrant County Coll., 1975—. Founder Nat. Comm. Coll. Hispanic Coun., 1985, bd. dirs., 1985—, pres., 1989-91; founder, co-dir. Nat. Hispanic Leadership Inst., 1989—; trustee Tex. Christian U., Brite Div. Sch., 1973-2001. Bd. dirs. Civic Ballet of Laredo, Ft. Worth chpt. NCCJ, Juliette Fowler Homes, Dallas; chmn. Aztec dist., dir. Gulf Coast coun. Boy Scouts Am., 1971-75; gov. Career Devel. Ctr., Arlington, Tex.; chmn. Laredo's Bicentennial Com., 1973-76; trustee, bd. dirs. United Way Ft. Worth, 1979-88; mem., vice moderator gen. bd. Christian Ch. (Disciples of Christ), 1991-93. Mem. Am. Assn. Cmty. Colls. (bd. dirs. 1991-94), Commn. Internat. Edn. Am. Coun. Edn., Tex. Jr. Coll. Tchrs. Assn., Tex. Assn. Jr. Coll. Instructional Adminstrs., Am. Acad. Polit. and Social Scis., Urban Ministries in Higher Edn., Civic Music Assn. Laredo, Rotary. Home: 4427 Tamworth Rd Fort Worth TX 76116-8127 Office: Tarrant County Coll NW Capmus 4801 Marine Pkwy Fort Worth TX 76179

SAENZ, NANCY ELIZABETH KING (MRS. MICHAEL SAENZ), civic worker; b. Greenville, Tex., Jan. 28, 1930; d. Henry M. and Vallie (Wheatley) King; m. Michael Saenz, July 28, 1950; children— Michael King, Cynthia Elizabeth. Saenz Ward. A.B. with honors, Tex. Christian U., B.S. magna cum laude, 1952; postgrad. Hartford Sem. Found., 1952-53, Escuela de Idiomas, 1953, Lexington Theol. Sem., 1953. Missionary, United Christian Missionary Soc., Indpls., serving in P.R., 1954-65; bd. dirs. Adminstrv. Bd. Christian Chs., P.R., 1950-65; chmn. dept. Christian edn. Christian Chs., P.R., 1962-64, sec., 1959-61, state dir., 1963; dept. Christian edn. P.R. Council Chs., 1959-64, sec., 1959-60; sec. and counsellor State Christian Women Fellowship of Christian Chs., P.R., 1955-57, 59-63, dist. chmn. Ind. and Tex., 1968-75, adminstrv. com. Tex., 1971-74; mem. Internat. Christian Women's Fellowship Quadrennial Coms., 1974-82; mem. gen. bd. Christian Ch. in U.S. and Can., 1974-78, 80; pres. Christian Ch. in S.W., 1976-78. Sec., Disciples of Christ Acad. PTA, Bayamon, P.R., 1962-63; mem. state com. Home for Aged, United Ch. Women, P.R., 1963; women's com. Ind. State Symphony Soc., 1967—; women's com. Internat. Christian U. Japan, 1962-64, 65-72, pres. Indpls. chpt. 1967-68; mem. vocational-tech. adv. council Laredo Ind. Sch. Dist., 1971—; vol. coordinator Am. Bible Soc., 1971—; dir. Vol. Center Met. Tarrant County, 1982-93. Bd. dirs. Greater Indpls. Fedn. Chs., 1970-71; bd. dirs. Planned Parenthood Assn. Webb County, 1972-74, pres.-elect, 1974-75; bd. dirs. Civic Ballet Laredo, 1972-75; mem. adv. com. Tarrant County Vol. Center, 1976-81, chmn., 1980; mem. Mercy Hosp. Aux., 1973-75, pres.-elect, 1974-75; interim dir. Ft. Worth Council Chs., 1979, pres., 1981; pres. Ch. Women United, Fort Worth, 1980; bd. dirs. ch. fin. council Christian Ch. (Disciples of Christ) U.S. and Can., 1979-83. Mem. Irvington Union of Clubs (exec. bd. 1966—, 2d v.p. 1968-70), Young Mothers Club Irvington (v.p. 1965, pres. 1967), Marion County Guardian Home Guild (pres. 1968-70), Art Assn. Indpls., Art League, Civic Music Laredo, AAUW, Laredo and Fort Worth Pan Am. Roundtable, Thistle Hill, Docent Guild, Tex., Tex. Christian U., Tex. Christian U. Alumni Assn. (life), Ft. Worth Women's Club, Assn. Vol. Ctrs. (pres. 1990-91), Alpha Chi, Phi Sigma Iota. Clubs: Rotary Anns, Women's College (R.P.); Irvington Women's Laredo Tuesday Music and Lit. (pres. 1973-74), Women's City. Author: Winds of Change, 1968; Step by Step, 1984. Home: 4427 Tamworth Rd Fort Worth TX 76116-8127

SAENZ, VELMA LISA, plant protection and quarantine officer; b. McAllen, Tex., June 10, 1972; d. Osvaldo and Olga Saenz. BS in animal sci., Tex. A&M, 1994. Eligibility specialist Tex. Dept. Human Sci., Rio Grande, 1995—96; plant protection quarantine officer U.S. Dept. Agr., McAllen, Tex., 1996—. Mem.: Tex. A&M Alumni. Avocations: scrapbooks, photography, Web surfing. Home: 8631 N L Homa Rd Mission TX 78574 Office: USDA 320 N Main Rm 119 Mcallen TX 78501

SAFA, AFSHIN AKHAVAN, oncologist, researcher; came to the U.S., 1984; s. Mansour Safa. BS, UCLA, 1991; MD, U. Calif., San Diego, 1995. Diplomate Am. Bd. Radiology. Intern U. Calif., San Diego, resident Los Angeles; radiation oncologist UCLA, 1992—. Radiologicol Soc. N.Am. rsch. grantee Am. Bd. Radiology, 1998. Mem. Radiol. Soc. N.Am., Am. Radium Soc., Am. Soc. Therapeutic Radiology. Avocations: skiing, scuba, tennis. Office: San Monica Cancer Treatment Ctr 2428 Santa Monica Blvd 200 UCLA Medical Plaza Santa Monica CA 90404 E-mail: safa@radonc.ucla.edu.

SAFADI, MOHAMMAD OUSSAMA, engineering educator; arrived in U.S., 1978; BSE, Calif. State U. Northridge, 1982; MSE, UCLA, 1985, grad. civil engring., PhD of Civil Engring., UCLA, 1991. Lectr. UCLA, 1991—95; adj. prof. U. So. Calif., L.A., 1991—. Pres. Applied Math. and Engring. Rsch. Industry of Calif., L.A., 1991—. Home: PO Box 24344 Los Angeles CA 90024

SAFAI, BIJAN, physician, investigator; b. Ardestan, Iran, Mar. 26, 1940; came to U.S., 1968; s. Abdol-Khalegh Safai and Kanom-Sadat Sadjaddi; m. Vera Plaskon, Sept. 16, 1978; 1 child: Matthew. MD, Tehran U., Iran, 1965; DSc, U. Gutenburg, Sweden, 1981. Diplomate Am. Bd. Dermatology, Am. Bd. Internal Medicine. Intern Nassau County Med. Ctr., East Meadow, N.Y., 1968-69; resident N.Y.U. Med. Coll. VA Hosp., N.Y.C., 1969-70; resident in dermatology N.Y.U. Med. Coll., N.Y.C., 1971-73; fellow in immunology Sloan-Kettering Inst. for Cancer & Allied Diseases, N.Y.C., 1973-74; from asst. attending physician to chief dermatology svc. Meml. Hosp., N.Y.C., 1974-93; from assoc. to attending physician in dermatology N.Y. Hosp., N.Y.C., 1980-93; dir. dermatology Westchester County Med. Ctr., Valhalla, N.Y., 1993—; from asst. prof. to prof. in medicine/dermatology Cornell U. Med. Coll., N.Y.C., 1974-93; prof., chmn. dept. dermatology N.Y. Med. Coll., N.Y.C., 1993—, prof. dept. microbiology and immunology, 1994—. Teaching clin. asst. in dermatology NYU Med. Coll, N.Y.C., 1973-74; adj. mem. Rockefeller U., N.Y.C., 1982-84; rsch. assoc. Sloan-Kettering Inst. for Cancer and Allied Diseases, N.Y.C., 1977-79, asst. mem., 1979-83, assoc. mem., 1983-88; assoc. mem. Memorial Sloan-Kettering Cancer Ctr., N.Y.C., 1983-88, mem. 1988-93; mem. grad. sch. med. scis. N.Y. Med. Coll., Valhalla, 1994—; mem. adv. bd. Skin Cancer Found., 1982—; sec. dermatology sect. N.Y. Acad Medicine, 1988-89, chmn. 1989-90; mem. med. adv. bd. Cancer Rsch Instn., 1997—. Mem. editl. bd. Cancer Investigation, 1984-88, AIDS Rsch. and Human Retroviruses, 1986-90, Jour. of Acquired Immune Deficiency Syndromes, 1988—; contbr. numerous articles on immunodermatology to profl. jours. Mem. AIDS adv. task force, NCI/NIH, 1982-85; mem. AIDS Etiology task force, NCI, 1982-85; mem. ad hoc study sect. for AIDS, NIH, 1982-88; mem. spl. dermatology rev. group, GM2 study sect., NIH, 1990-96; mem. spl. rev. team NCI Intramural Rev., Lab. of Tumor cell Biology, 1987, 92, Medicine br., NCI, 1996; mem. study sect. on HIV, NCI, 1996; mem. spl. rev. group FDA Intramural Rev., 1995. Mem. AMA, Internat. Soc. Tropical Dermatology, Am. Fedn. for Clin. Rsch., Am. Acad. Dermatology (mem. AIDS com. 1989-91, task force on cutaneous oncology 1988-9, mem. adv. coun. 1988-91), Am. Dermatol. Soc. for Allery and Immunology, Soc. for Investigative Dermatology, Med. Soc. of State of N.Y., Med. Soc. of County of N.Y., N.Y. State Soc. Dermatology, Dermatol. Soc. of Greater N.Y., N.Y. County Health Svs. Rev. Orgn., N.Y. Acad. Scis., N.Y. Dermatol. Soc. (pres 1990-91, sec., treas. 1989-90), Dermatology Found., Z & E Fisher Med. Found. (pres. 1993—). Home: 340 E 64th St New York NY 10021-7503 Office: NY Med Coll Dept Dermatology Valhalla NY 10595 also: 625 Park Ave New York NY 10021-6545 E-mail: safai@aol.com.

SAFARS, BERTA See FISZER-SZAFARZ, BERTA

SAFDIE, MOSHE, architect; b. Haifa, Israel, July 14, 1938; s. Leon and Rachael Esses; m. Nina Nusynowicz, Sept. 6, 1959 (div. 1981); children: Taal, Oren; m. Michal Ronnen, June 7, 1981; children: Carmelle, Yasmin. BArch, McGill U., 1961; LLD (hon.), 1982; DSc (hon.), Laval U., 1988; DFA (hon.), U. Victoria, 1989. With H.P.D. Van Ginkel, architect, Montreal, Que., Can., 1961-62, then Louis I. Kahn, Phila., 1962-63; assoc. David, Barrott and Boulva, Montreal, 1964; pvt. practice, Montreal, 1964—, 1970—; pvt. practice (prin. office), 1978—; pvt. practice, Toronto, 1985—; Ian Woodner Studio prof. architecture and urban design Harvard U. Grad. Sch. Design, 1984-89. Prin. works include Tomb of Yitzhak Rabin, Jerusalem, Mamilla Hilton Hotel, Jerusalem, Skirball Mus. and Cultural Ctr., L.A., Ford Ctr. for Performing Arts, Vancouver, B.C., Can., Libr. Sq., Vancouver, Ottawa City Hall, Ont., Rosovsky Harvard-Radcliffe Hillel, Cambridge, Mass., Elwyn Rehab. Ctr., Tel Aviv, Neve Ofer Ctr., Tel Aviv, Harvard Bus. Sch. Morgan Hall and '59 Chapel, Cambridge, Esplanade Apts., Cambridge, Musee des Beaux Arts, Montreal, Nat. Gallery Can., Ottawa, Colegio Hebreo Maguen David, Mexico City, Musee de la Civilisation, Que., Cambridge Ctr., Ardmore Habitat Apts., Singapore, Kibbutz Idmit (Israel) Housing, Callahan Residence, Birmingham, Ala., Hebrew Union Coll., Jerusalem, Yad Vashem Transport and Children's Meml., Jerusalem, Hosh Dist. Restoration, Jerusalem, Coldspring New Town, Balt., Block 38 Housing, Jerusalem, Yeshiva Porat Yosef, Jerusalem, Habitat '67, Montreal. Recipient Massey medal in architecture, Lt. Gov. Can. gold medal, urban design concept award HUD, 1980, internat. design award in urban design Am. Soc. Interior Designers, 1980, Prix d'Excellence in architecture Que. Order Architects, 1988, Gov. Gen.'s medal for architecture, 1992, Richard J. Neutra award, 1993, RAIC Gold medal Royal Architectural Inst. of Canada, 1995 Fellow AIA, Royal Inst. Architects Can. (Gold Medal 1995); mem. Order of Can., Order Architects Province Que., Ont. Assn. Architects. Office: 100 Properzi Way Somerville MA 02143-3798 also: Ste 301 165 Avenue Rd Toronto ON Canada M5R 3S4 also: 7 Shlomo Hamelech Jerusalem 94182 Israel

SAFE, KENNETH SHAW, JR., fiduciary firm executive; b. Providence, Oct. 13, 1929; s. Kenneth Shaw and Louise (King) S.; m. Elizabeth Kelley, Dec. 20, 1952; children: Hope, Elizabeth, Kenneth (dec.), Thorn and Edith (triplets). AB, Harvard U., 1951. Intelligence officer CIA, Washington, 1954-56; with trust dept. Old Colony Trust Co., Bank of Boston, 1956-59; registered rep. Tucker, Anthony & R.L. Day, Boston, 1959-68; ptnr. Welch & Forbes, Boston, 1968—2002, mng. ptnr., 1983—2002. Pres. Travelers Aid Soc. Boston, 1980-82, Cmty. Workshops, Inc., Boston, 1968-72; asst. treas. Wellesley (Mass.) Coll., 1970-80; trustee Georgiana Goddard Eaton Meml. Trust, Boston, 1975-2002, G. Howland Shaw Found., Boston, 1977-2002; treas. Woods Hole (Mass.) Oceanographic Inst., 1981-92, Mass. Soc. Cin.; bd. dirs. Beverly Land Co., Providence, 1982—; trustee R.I. Hosp., Providence; trustee Crossroads for Kids, Inc., Boston; bd. dirs. Boston Port and Seaman's Aid Soc. With CIC, U.S. Army, 1952-54. Mem. Boston Security Analysts Soc., Somerset Club, Duxbury Yacht Club, Marshall St. Hist. Soc., Masons, Country Club. Republican. Episcopalian. Avocations: sailing, skiing, hunting, snorkeling. Home: 207 King Caesar Rd Duxbury MA 02332-3912 E-mail: ksafe@welchforbes.com.

SAFE, STEPHEN H. science educator; b. Belleville, Ont., Can., May 14, 1940; BSc, Queen's U., Ont., 1962, MSc, 1963; PhD, Oxford (Eng.) U., 1965; DSc (hon.), U. Guelph, 1996. Rsch. asst. Oxford U., 1966; rsch. assoc. Harvard U., Cambridge, Mass., 1967; assoc. rsch. officer Nat. Rsch. Coun. Can., 1968—73; assoc. prof. U. Guelph, Canada, 1973—77, prof., 1977—81; prof. vet. physiology and pharmacology Tex. A&M U., College Station, 1981—, Chester J. Reed chair in toxicology, 1983, st. scientist. Inst. Occupl. and Environ. Medicine, 1983—, disting. prof., 1984—. Sid Kyle chair in toxicology, 1992. Cons. Environ. Criteria and Assessment Office EPA, Washington, 1983—, cons. sci. adv. bd., 1984—; adj. prof. U. Guelph, Guelph, 1985—; mem. steering com. Can. Ctr. for Toxicology, 1979—; mem. internat. adv. bd. Dioxin Symposia, 1980—; coun. mem. Nat. Adv. Environ. Health Scis., 1984—88; sci. advisor Tex. Air Control Bd., 1990; mem. external adv. bd. Environ. Health Ctr. U. Calif.-Davis, 1992—; mem. EDSTAC working group U.S. EPA, 1997; mem. com. on gender differences in susceptibility to environ. factors Inst. Medicine, 1997; mem. sci. adv. bd. Avax Techs., 1998—; Quest lectr. Queen's U., 1980; disting. lectr. toxicology U. Nebr. Med. Sch., 1986; MillerComm lectr. U. Ill., 1990; Eli Lilly Sci. and Soc. lectr. Ind. State U., 1995; Samuel H. Kuna disting. lectr. Rutgers U., 1996; Charles W. Gowdey disting. lectr. U. Western Ont., 1996; McEwen lectr. Queen's U., 1998. Mem. editl. adv. bd.: Jour. Toxicology Environ. Health, Jour. Biochem. Toxicology, Jour. Women's Cancer, others; co-editor: Environ. Toxin Series; toxicology editor: Chemosphere. Recipient rsch. grants in field, rsch. scholarship, NSERC, 1962, Toxicology scholarship, Burroughs Wellcome, 1989, Queen's Silver Jubilee medal, 1978, Award for Health, Safety or Environ. Chemistry, Royal Soc. Chemistry, 1984. Mem.: Soc. Toxicology (mem. edn. com. 1989—), Chem. Inst. Can., Can. Fedn. of Biol. Socs., Am. Assn. for Cancer Rsch., Am. Soc. for Mass Spectrometry, Am. Coll. Toxicology, Am. Chem. Soc., Chem. Soc., Can. Soc. for Toxicology, Internat. Soc. for Study of Xenobiotics, Sigma Xi (Award for Excellence in Rsch. 1977). Achievements include research in molecular biology of endocrine disruption chemicals; mechanisms of toxicity; breast cancer: mechanisms and therapeutics. Office: Tex A&M U Dept Vet Physiology and Pharmacology 4466 TAMU College Station TX 77843-4466

SAFER, DEBRA LYNN, psychiatrist; d. Daniel Jacob and Elaine Safer. BA, U. Calif., Berkeley, 1987. Cert. psychiatrist Med. Bd. Calif. Resident in psychiatry Stanford (Calif.) U. Sch. Medicine, 1994—98, NIMH rsch. fellow, 1998—2000, asst. clin. prof., 2000—03, asst. prof. psychiatry, 2004—. Mem.: Am. Psychiat. Assn. Democrat. Achievements include research in efficacy of psychotherapeutic treatment for eating disorders. Avocations: films, reading. Office: Stanford U Med Ctr 401 Quarry Rd Stanford CA 94305-5722 Business E-Mail: dlsafer@stanford.edu.

SAFER, JOHN, artist, lecturer, banker, real estate developer; b. Washington, Sept. 6, 1922; s. John M. and Rebecca (Herzmark) S.; m. Joy Scott; children: Janine Whitney, Thomas. AB, George Washington U., 1947; LLB, Harvard U., 1949. Chmn. NationsBank/DC, 1980-92; chmn. exec. com. Fin. Gen. Bankshares, 1977-80; bd. dirs. Nat. Air and Space Mus., The Shakespeare Guild, Materia. Represented in permanent collections at Balt. Mus. Art, Corocoran Gallery Art, Dayton Art Inst., Frederik Meijer Sculpture Gardens, Folger Shakespeare Libr., Nat. Air and Space Mus., Washington Tennis Ctr., High Mus. Art, Atlanta, Milw. Mus. Art, Harvard Law Sch., Harvard Bus. Sch., Hofstra U., Mayo Clinic, Fla., Phila. Mus. Art, San Francisco Mus. Art, Duke U. Med. Ctr., Embry-Riddle Aero. U., Georgetown U., George Washington U., Williams Coll., Scripps Rsch. Inst., Daniel Webster Coll., Am. Hosp., Paris, Embassy of U.S., London, Nassau, Beijing, New Delhi, Fayetteville (NC) Mus. Art, Nat. Jewish Mus., Nat. Peace Inst., Ponce (PR) Mus. of Art, UN, NYC, corps. including Celanese Corp., NY, Crown Equipment Corp., New Bremen, Ohio, First Union Bank of Md., Bank of Am. Ctr., Norfolk, Va., Gen. Mills Corp., Mpls Rosemont Co., Atlanta, West Chase Corp., Houston, numerous others; author: John Safer, Sculptor, Art in Flight,1990, The Sculpture of John Safa, 1982. 1st lt. USAAF, 1942-46. Mem.: Cosmos, Burning Tree, Harvard, Woodmont (Washington), Lyford Cay (Nassau), Linville Ridge (N.C.). Office: PO Box 6720 Mc Lean VA 22106-6720 Office Phone: 703-276-7766.

SAFER, MORLEY, journalist; b. Toronto, Ont., Can., Nov. 8, 1931; came to U.S., 1964; s. Max and Anna (Cohn) Safer; m. Jane Fearer; 1 child, Sarah. Student, U. Western Ont., 1952. With Reuters, London, Eng., 1955; corr., producer Canadian Broadcasting Corp., 1955-60, writer, London corr., 1961-64; corr., producer BBC, 1961; corr. CBS, London bureau, 1964; Vietnam corr. CBS, 1965—70; London bureau chief, 1967—70; corr. & co-editor 60 Minutes news program CBS-TV, 1970—. Writer-corr. news documentary The Second Battle of Britain", 1976; host One for the Road: A Conversation with Charles Kuralt and Morley Safer, 1994; prin. reporter CBS Reports. Author: Flashbacks: On Returning to Vietnam, 1990. Recipient Polk award LI U., 1965, Sigma Delta Chi award, 1965, Paul White award Radio and TV, News Dirs. Assn., 1966, Emmy for Lenell Geter's in Jail, 60 Minutes broadcast, 1984, 3 Overseas Press Club awards, 14 Emmy awards, 3 George Foster Peabody awards, 2 Alfred I. duPont-Columbia U. awards, Robert F. Kennedy Journalism 1st prize for School for the Homeless report, 2002, George Polk Lifetime Achievement award, 2003; named Chévalier dans l'Ordre des Arts et des Lettres, French Government, 1995. Fellow Royal Coll. Bloviation (Edinburgh). Office: c/o 60 Minutes 524 W 57th St New York NY 10019-2902

SAFF, EDWARD BARRY, mathematics professor; b. N.Y.C., Jan. 2, 1944; s. Irving H. and Rose (Koslow) S.; m. Loretta Singer, July 3, 1966; children: Lisa Jill, Tracy Karen, Alison Michelle. BS with highest honors, Ga. Inst. Tech., 1964; PhD, U. Md., 1968. Asst. prof. U. Md., 1968; post-doctoral rschr. Imperial Coll., London, 1968-69; asst. prof. math. U. South Fla., 1969-71, assoc. prof., 1971-76, prof., 1976-86, disting. rsch. prof., 1986—2001, dir. Ctr. for Math. Svcs., 1978-83, dir. Inst. for Constructive Math., 1985—2001, dir. Ctr. for Constructive Approximation, 2001—. Sr. vis. fellow Oxford U., 1978. Author: (with A.D. Snider) Fundamentals of Complex Analysis, 1976, 3d edit., 2003, (with A.W. Goodman) Calculus, Concepts and Calculations, 1981, (with A. Edrei and R.S. Varga) Zeros of Sections of Power Series, (with V. Totik) Logarithmic Potentials with External Fields, 1997; editor (with R.S. Varga) Pade and Rational Approximation: Theory and Applications, 1977, (with R.K. Nagle) Fundamentals of Differential Equations, (with R.K. Nagle) Fundamentals of Differential Equations and Boundary Value Problems, 1993, (with D.S. Lubinsky) Strong Asymptotics for Extremal Polynomials Associated with Weights on R., 1988; editor-in-chief Constructive Approximation Jour., 1983—, Computational Methods and Function Theory Jour., 2001—; editor Jour. Approximation Theory, 1990—, Cambridge Univ. Press, 1995—. Founds. Comp. Math, 1999—. Fulbright fellow, 1968-69, Guggenheim fellow, 1978; NSF grantee, 1970-72, 80—; Hon. prof. Zhejiang Normal U. Mem. Am. Math. Soc., Math. Assn. Am., Sigma Xi. Office: Ctr for Constructive Approximation Vanderbilt Univ Dept of Mathematics Nashville TN 37240

SAFFAR, JEAN-MARC, healthcare consultant; b. Paris, May 1, 1965; s. Max and Michele S.; m. Claudia Moss, Feb. 13, 1994; children: Etty, Charles. MD, Paris Sch. Medicine, 1991, BS in Biostats., 1995; MS in Health Policy, Dauphine Sch. Mgmt., Paris, 1995; PhD in Pub. Health, Amiens Sch. Medicine, France, 1997; MS in Healthcare Mgmt., Harvard U., 1997; MBA, U. Mich., 2000. Internist Paris Hosp., 1991-93; pub. health rschr. Regional Health Obs., Amiens, France, 1994-96; sr. cons. KPMG Peat Marwick, Boston, 1997-98; sr. mgr. A.T. Kearney, Cambridge, Mass., 1998—2002. Cons. in field. Lt. French Army, 1993-94. Mem. French Med. Bd., French Assn. Pub. Health Profls., Harvard Club N.Y., U. Mich. Bus. Sch. Alumni Assn., Harvard Alumni Assn. Avocations: video editing, french movies, backgammon, skiing. Home: 1365 York Ave #12E New York NY 10021 Office: True North Capital 375 Park Ave Ste 2309 New York NY 10152 E-mail: jean-marc.saffar@post.harvard.edu.

SAFFELL, JOHN EDGAR, retired history educator; b. North Georgetown, Ohio, July 22, 1916; s. Byron Edgar and Athalia Isabel (Anderson) S.; m. Helen Weaver, Oct. 8, 1955. AB, Mount Union Coll., 1937; AM, Western Res. U., Cleve., 1938, PhD, 1965; LHD, Mount Union Coll., 1996. Elem. sch. prin. Bd. Edn., Stark County, Ohio, 1939-41; tchr. Harvey Sr. H.S., Painesville, Ohio, 1941-43; rsch. analyst U.S. Army, Tokyo, 1945-47; faculty mem. history Mt. Union Coll., Alliance, Ohio, 1948-82; ret., 1982—. Owner cattle farm, Homeworth, Ohio, 1955-89. Author: Sesquicentennial History of Mount Union College, 1996, Title: Wake the Echoes. With U.S. Army, 1943-45. Mem. Am. Hist. Assn., Orgn. Am. Historians, Ohio Acad. History, Free and Accepted Masons, Alliance Country Club. Republican. Presbyterian. Home: Copeland Oaks 7-314 800 S 15th St Sebring OH 44672

SAFFER, ALFRED, retired chemical company executive; b. N.Y.C., Dec. 3, 1918; s. Louis and Ruth (Mirkis) S.; m. Ruth Lillian Rudow, Jan. 31, 1942 (dec. Dec. 1983); children: Anita Carolyn Horowitz, Martin Kenneth; m. Doris Barbara Graubard, June 18, 1985 (dec. 1999). AB in Chemistry, NYU, 1939, MS in Chemistry, 1941, PhD, 1943. Research chemist Princeton (N.J.) U., 1943-46; sr. research assoc. Firestone Tire and Rubber Co., Akron, Ohio, 1946-48; dir. research Sci. Design Co., Inc., N.Y.C., 1948-57, v.p. mfg.; pres. Catalyst Devel. Corp., Little Ferry, N.J., 1957-69; exec. v.p. Halcon Internat., Inc., N.Y.C., 1963-69; vice chmn. ret. Halcon SD Group, Inc., N.Y.C., 1978-81; exec. v.p. Oxirane Corp, Princeton, 1969-76; pres. Oxirane Internat., Princeton, 1976-78. Bd. dirs. Norwood Venture Co., N.Y.C. Contbr. articles to profl. jours.; patentee in field. Trustee Internat. Ctr. for Disabled, N.Y.C., 1978—; assoc. trustee North Shore U. Hosp., Manhasset, N.Y., 1981—; active instl. rev. bd. Boca Raton (Fla.) Community Hosp., 1992—. Fellow Am. Inst. Chemists (Chem. Pioneer award, 1982); mem. Nat. Acad. Engring., Am. Chem. Soc., Soc. Chem. Industry. Clubs: Glen Oaks (Old Westbury, N.Y.); Delaire Country (Delray Beach, Fla.). Avocation: golf. Home: 16629 Ironwood Dr Delray Beach FL 33445-7050 E-mail: fredsaffer@aol.com.

SAFFER, JUDITH MACK, lawyer; b. N.Y.C., June 10, 1942; d. Gilbert and Rose (Elizer) Mack; m. Brian H. Saffer, June 13, 1965; children: Amy, Ian. BA, NYU, 1965, LLB, 1967. Bar: N.Y. 1968, U.S. Ct. Appeals (2d cir.) 1975. Sr. counsel ASCAP, N.Y.C., 1968-86; asst. gen. counsel Broadcast Music, Inc., N.Y.C., 1986—. Bd. dirs., v.p. Symphony Space; sec. Found. for Creative Am. Mem. ABA (council, I.P. sect.), Am. Intellectual Property Law Assn. (bd. dirs.,v.p.), Copyright Soc. U.S.A. (past pres.). Home: 77 Winchip Rd Summit NJ 07901-4142 E-mail: jsaffer@bmi.com.

SAFFERMAN, ROBERT SAMUEL, microbiologist, researcher; b. Bronx, N.Y., Dec. 19, 1932; s. Irving and Rose (Schuler) S.; m. Jewel S. Reisman, June 7, 1958; children— Karen M., Sharon L., Steven I. BS, Bklyn. Coll., 1955; PhD, Rutgers U., 1960. With USPHS, Cin., 1959-64; with Dept. Interior, Cin., 1964-70, U.S. EPA, Cin., 1970—; chief virology sect. Environ. Monitoring and Support Lab. EPA, Cin., 1974-88, chief virology br. Environ. Monitoring Systems Lab., 1988-94; chief virology and parasitology br. Environ. Monitoring Sys. Lab., Cin., 1994-95; chief biohazard assessment rsch. br. Nat. Exposure Rsch. Lab., 1995—. Mem. Internat. Com. on Taxonomy of Viruses. Recipient Spl. Service award San. Engring. Ctr., USPHS, 1963; Gans medal Soc. Water Treatment and Examination, Eng., 1970; named Fed. Employee of Yr., Cin., 1974 Fellow Am. Acad. Microbiology; mem. Am. Soc. Microbiology, Sigma Xi. Office: 26 Martin Luther King Dr W Cincinnati OH 45268-0001 Home: 263 Branch Creek Ct Dayton OH 45458-3287

SAFFIOTTI, UMBERTO, pathologist; b. Milan, Jan. 22, 1928; came to U.S., 1960, naturalized, 1966; s. Francesco Umberto and Maddalena (Valenzano) S.; m. Paola Amman, June 21, 1958; children: Luisa M., Maria Francesca. MD cum laude, U. Milan, 1951, splty. diploma occupational medicine cum laude, 1957. Intern Inst. Pathol. Anatomy U. Milan, 1951-52, asst. to chmn. occupational medicine, chief lab. pathology, Inst. Occupational Medicine, 1956-60, fellow Inst. Gen. Pathology, 1957-60; rsch. asst. oncology, rsch. assoc. Chgo. Med. Sch., 1952-55, from asst. prof. to prof. oncology, 1960-68; mem. staff Nat. Cancer Inst., NIH, Bethesda, Md., 1968—, assoc. dir. carcinogenesis, 1968-76, chief lab. exptl. pathology, 1974-98, acting head Registry of Exptl. Cancers, 1988-98; scientist emeritus, 1998—; adj. prof., Environ. & Occ. Hlth. The George Washington U., Washington, 2000—. Mem. pathology B study sect., NIH, 1964-68; former mem. various adv. coms. govt. agys.; mem. cancer prevention com. Internat. Union Against Cancer, 1959-66, panel on carcinogenicity, 1963-66; chmn. ad hoc com. evaluation low levels environ. carcinogens HEW, 1969-70. Co-editor books; contbr. articles to profl. jours. Bd. dirs. Rachel Carson Trust, 1976-79. Recipient Career Devel. award NIH, 1965-68, Superior Svc. Honor award HEW, 1971, Pub. Interest Sci. award Environ. Def. Fund, 1977, Spl. Recognition award USPHS, 1980 Fellow NYAS; mem. AAAS, Am. Assn. Cancer Rsch. (pres. Chgo. chpt. 1966-67), Am. Soc. Investigative Pathology, Internat. Commn. Occupational Health, Soc. Occupational and Environ. Health (councillor 1972-76, v.p. 1976-78, pres. 1978-82), Soc. Toxicology, Mineralogical Soc. of Am., Sigma Xi. Democrat. Home: 5114 Wissioming Rd Bethesda MD 20816-2259 Office: NIH Nat Cancer Inst 6116 Executive Blvd Rm 7064 Bethesda MD 20892-8314 Business E-Mail: saffiotti@nih.gov.

SAFFIR, HERBERT SEYMOUR, structural engineer, consultant; b. N.Y.C., Mar. 29, 1917; s. A.L. and Gertrude (Samuels) S.; m. Sarah Young, May 9, 1941; children: Richard Young, Barbara Joan. BS in Civil Engring. cum laude, Ga. Inst. Tech., 1940. Registered profl. engr., Fla., N.Y., Tex., P.R., Miss.; lic. land surveyor, Fla. Civil engr. TVA, Chattanooga, 1940, NACA, Langley Field, Va., 1940-41; structural engr. Ebasco Services, N.Y.C., 1941-43, York & Sawyer & Fred Severud, N.Y.C., 1945; engr. Waddell & Hardesty, Cons. Engrs., N.Y.C., 1945-47; asst. county engr. Dade County, Miami, Fla., 1947-59; cons. engr. Herbert S. Saffir, Coral Gables, Fla., 1959—. Adj. prof. civil engring. Coll. Engring., U. Miami, 1964—; adviser civil engring. Fla. Internat. U., 1975-80; cons. on bldg. codes Govt. Bahamas; cons. on engring. in housing to UN; mem., chmn. Met. Dade County Unsafe Structures Bd., 1977-92; mem. Biltmore Evaluation Panle, 1982-83; mem. Bldg. Code Evaluation Task Force after Hurricane Andrew; mem. Am. Nat. Stds. Inst. Commn. Bldg. Design Loads, Nat. Adv. Group on Glass Design, Dade County Bldg. Code Com. 1993-96; mem. U. Miami/Coral Gables Community Rels. Com., 1993-96; cons. to govt. and industry, condr. seminars, Australia and Ga. Tech.; reviewer for NSF; mem. bd. adjustment City of Coral Gables, 1994-97, mem. budget bd., 1997-2001; presenter seminars in field. Author: Housing Construction in Hurricane Prone Areas, 1971, Nature and Extent of Damage by Hurricane Camille, 1972, Evaluation of Structural Damage Caused by Hurricanes, 1993; contbg. author: Wind Effects on Structures, 1976, Hurricane! Coping with Disaster, 2002; editor: Wind Engr., 1986-92; editor Manual of Wind Damage Investigation; contbr. articles to profl. jours.; designer Saffir/Simpson hurricane scale. With N.Y. Guard, 1942-43, AUS, 1943-44, WWII. Recipient Outstanding Service award Fla. Profl. Engrs., 1954, Pub. Service award Nat. Weather Service, 1975, Disting. Service award Nat. Hurricane Conf., 1987; named Miami Engr. of Year, 1978, 94, Gov.'s Design award, 1986, Gov. Gilchrist award for Profl. Excellence, 1988, Albert H. Friedman Community Svc. award, 1992, Engring. award Nat. Hurricane Conf., 1997; named to Ga. Tech. Engring. Hall of Fame, 1995; Herbert S. Saffir Miami-Dade Permitting and Inspection Ctr. named in his honor, 2002. Fellow Fla. Engring. Soc. (award for outstanding tech. achievement 1973, Cmty. Svc. award 1980, Lifetime Achievement award 2003, disting. engr. award 2003), Coll. Engrs. P.R. (Disting. Engr. award 2002); mem. ASCE (hon., past pres., sec., aerodynamics com. 1983—, mem. mitigation of wind damage com. 1985—, chmn. com. on damage investigation 1989—, mem. com. A7 on design loads for bldgs. 1972—), Soc. Am. Mil. Engrs., Am. Concrete Inst., ASTM (mem. com. performance bldg. constrn.), Internat. Assn. for Bridge and Structural Engring., Colegio de Ingenieros P.R., Am. Meterol. Soc., Am. Arbitration Assn., Wind Engring. Rsch. Coun. (past bd. dirs., Svc. award 1990), Am. Assn. for Wind Engring., Coral Gables C. of C. (bd. dirs., past pres., past chmn.), Tau Beta Pi, Chi Epsilon (hon.). Clubs: Country of Coral Gables. Home: 4818 Alhambra Cir Coral Gables FL 33146-1643 Office: Consulting Engineers 350 Sevilla Ave Ste 108 Coral Gables FL 33134-6617 Office Phone: 305-444-2611.

SAFFIR, LEONARD, public relations executive; b. N.Y.C., Apr. 19, 1930; s. Abraham and Gertrude S.; m. Patricia Roemer (div. 1980); children: Andrew, Michelle; m. Wendy McConaughy (div. 1992); 1 child, Samantha; m. Eleanor Unger, 1997. Student, Syracuse U., 1948-51. Editor, bur. chief Internat. News Service, Dallas, Tokyo, 1953-58; producer Eng., Australia, Asia, 1958-60; ptnr. Haft, Saffir, Siegel Pub. Relations & Advt., N.Y.C., 1960-62; asst. pub. N.Y. Standard, 1962-63; cons. Ferdinand Marcos, 1964; pub. Latin Am. Times, N.Y.C., 1965; exec. v.p. Franchises Internat., N.Y.C., 1965-69; press sec., chief of staff to Senator James Buckley U.S. Senate, Washington, 1970-76; pub., editor The Trib, N.Y.C., 1977-78, The Sun, Bridgehampton, N.Y., 1978-84; exec. v.p. Porter/Novelli, N.Y.C., 1984-90; pres. Jay DeBow & Ptnrs., N.Y.C., Fla., 1989-90, Leonard Saffir & Assocs. Pub. Rels., 2000—; investigative reporter, columnist Lake Worth Herald, 2001—03. CEO Adventures One, 1998-2000, Celebrity Stores.com, 1998-2000. Author: Power Public Relations, 1992, Power Public Relations: How to Master the New PR, 2000. Campaign mgr. Marchi for Mayor, N.Y.C., 1973, Buckley for Senator, N.Y., 1976. Served as sgt. USMC, 1951-53. Recipient Silver Anvil and Big Apple awards Pub. Rels. Soc. Am., Mayor's award City of N.Y., others. Mem. Authors Guild, Overseas Press Club (pres. 1988-89). Home: 6137 Rainbow Circle Lake Worth FL 33463 Office Phone: 561-289-3100. Personal E-mail: lenpr@bellsouth.net.

SAFFMAN, PHILIP G. mathematician, educator; b. Leeds, Eng., Mar. 19, 1931; s. Sam Ralph and Sarah (Rebecca) S.; m. Ruth Arion, Sept. 2, 1954; children: Louise J., Mark E., Emma E. BA, Trinity Coll., Cambridge U., 1953, MA, PhD, Cambridge U., 1956. Asst. lectr. applied math. Cambridge U., 1958-60; reader in applied math. Kings Coll., London U., 1960-64; prof. fluid mechanics Calif. Inst. Tech., Pasadena, 1964-69, prof. applied math., 1969-95, Theodore von Kármán prof. applied math. and aeros., 1995—. Contbr. articles to profl. jours. Trinity Coll. fellow, 1955-59; recipient Otto Laporte award, Am. Physical Soc., 1994, Fluid Dynamics Award, Am. Inst. Aeronautics and Astronautics, 1995. Fellow Am. Acad. Arts and Scis., Royal Soc. London. Office: 217-50 Firestone Calif Inst Tech Pasadena CA 91125

SAFFO, PAUL, communications executive; BA, Harvard Coll.; LLB, Cambridge U.; JD, Stanford U. Bar: N.Y., Calif. Dir. Inst. For The Future, Menlo Park, Calif., 1985—. Author: Dreams in Silicon Valley; contbr. columns to Wired; contbr. essays to profl. jours. including L.A. Times, N.Y. Times, Fortune, Byte, PC Computing, Infoworld. Office: Inst For The Future 2744 Sand Hill Rd Menlo Park CA 94025-7020

SAFFRAN, KALMAN, entrepreneur, venture capitalist; b. Boston, Dec. 28, 1947; s. Max and Marion (Patick) S. BA, Northeastern U., 1971; postgrad., MIT, 1971-72. Lic. real estate broker, Mass. Mgr. sys. MIT, 1972-76; corp. cons. United Brands Co., Boston, 1977-78; CEO Monitrex Corp., Boston, 1977-82; pres. Kalman Saffran Assocs., Inc., Newton, Mass., 1978—2000; bd. advisers Prism Venture Ptnrs. Bd. advisors Blackstone Bank and Trust Co., Boston; mem. network implementation panel U.S. Energy Research and Devel. Adminstrn., Washington, 1975-76; mem. computer com. MIT Lab. for Nuclear Sci., 1975-76. Mem. Data Processing Mgmt. Assn., Assn. Computing Machinery, Soc. for Info. Mgmt., IEEE, Mensa. Republican. Jewish. Home: 1564 Commonwealth Ave W Newton MA 02465-2806 Office: Kalman Saffran Assocs Inc PO Box 66033 Newton MA 02466-0001 Office Phone: 617-527-2000.

SAFFURI, KHALED AHMAD, cultural organization executive; b. Beirut, July 28, 1956; came to U.S., 1981; s. Ahmad Hasan Saffouri and Siham Sihani; m. Jeniffer Ann Hall, Aug. 28, 1994 (div. Aug. 1997). BA in Bus. Adminstrn., USIA, Calif., 1985; MA in Mgmt., U. Redlands, Calif., 1987. Dir. Mid. East affairs Am.-Arab Anti-Discrimination Com., Washington, 1987-90; asst. exec. dir. Nat. Assn. Arab-Americans, Washington, 1990-93, Am. Muslim Coun., Washington, 1994-97; exec. dir. Am. Task Force for Bosnia, Washington, 1992-98, Islamic Inst., Washington, 1998—. Co-author: (book) Islam and Free Market, 1998. Moslem. Office: Islamic Inst Found 1920 L St NW Ste 200 Washington DC 20036-5036

SAFIAN, KEITH FRANKLIN, hospital administrator; b. Bklyn., June 22, 1950; s. Jack I. and Harriet S. (Cohen) S.; m. Ellen Rita Babat, May 18, 1974; children: Elizabeth Anne, Alexander William. BS in EE and Indsl. Engring., SUNY, Buffalo, 1972; MBA, U. Pa., 1974. Asst. dir. Kings County Hosp. Ctr., Bklyn., 1974-76; asst. adminstr. NYU Med. Ctr., N.Y.C., 1977-80, assoc. adminstr., 1981-84, sr. assoc. adminstr., 1984-85; adminstr. St. John's Episcopal Hosp., Far Rockaway, N.Y., 1985-89; pres., CEO Phelps Meml. Hosp. Ctr., Sleepy Hollow, N.Y., 1989—. Bd. dirs. Addabbo Family Health Ctr., Arverne, N.Y., 1987-89, Rockaway Devel. and Revitalization Corp., Far Rockaway, 1988-89; bd. dirs. The ExcelCare Sys., Bronxville, N.Y., 1993-99, chmn. 1995-98; bd. dirs. No. Met. Hosp. Assn., Newburgh, N.Y., 1989—, mem. exec. com., 1993-98, 2000-04, chmn., 1996, 2003, treas., 2001, vice chmn. 2002. Fellow Am. Coll. Healthcare Execs.; mem. Hosp. Adminstrs. Club of N.Y., Health Assn. N.Y. State (trustee 1996-982, 2003—). Home: 16 Brokaw Ln Great Neck NY 11023-1160 Office: Phelps Memorial Hosp 701 N Broadway Tarrytown NY 10591-1096

SAFIAN, LEROY SCHELLER, radiologist; b. N.Y.C., Dec. 15, 1916; s. Harry Markus and Frances (Scheller) S.; m. Renée Morgenstern Bonis, June 15, 1946 (div. Feb. 1952); m. Helen Hoffman, Jan. 25, 1953 (div. Nov. 1962). BS, NYU, 1938; MD, Med. Coll. Va., 1943. Diplomate Am. Bd. Radiology. Instr. radiology N.Y. Med. Coll., N.Y.C., 1962-64; asst. radiologist Coney Island Hosp., Bklyn., 1965-69, assoc. radiologist, 1969-70; asst. radiologist Maimonides Med. Ctr., N.Y.C., 1966-70; attending radiologist Golden Isles Hosp., Hallendale, Fla., 1970-71; instr. radiology Columbia Coll. Physicians & Surgeons, 1972-75, Montefiore Med. Ctr., Bronx, 1975-87; asst. prof. radiology Albert Einstein Coll. Medicine, Bronx, 1975-88; asst. attending radiologist North Cen. Hosp., Bronx, 1975-84, assoc. attending radiologist, 1984-86. Hon. radiologist North Cen. Hosp., Bronx, 1986—. Author articles on radiology and plastic surgery; cons. editor Urban & Schwarzenberg Med. Pubs. Recipient Cert. of Merit, Mallinckrodt Pharms., 1981 Overseas Fellow Royal Soc. Medicine; mem. Am. Coll. Legal Medicine (assoc.), NY Acad. Sci., NY Med. Soc. (grievance com.), Fla. Med. Soc., Univ. Club, various radiol. soc. Home: 301 E 66th St New York NY 10021-6205

SAFIAN, ROBERT, managing editor; b. Mount Vernon, N.Y., Apr. 20, 1964; m. Mary Safian; children: Matthew, Nicholas. BA in History magna cum laude, Brown U., 1987. Summer intern, then reporter, then exec. editor The Am. Lawyer, 1987—94; sr. editor, then articles editor SmartMoney, 1994—97; head personal fin. coverage divsn. Fortune, 1997—98; mng. editor Money Mag., N.Y.C., 1998—2004; exec. editor Time mag., N.Y.C., 2004—. Tchr. legal affairs reporting Columbia U. Sch. Journalism, 1993—96; guest lectr. Harvard Law Sch., 1993. Named one of 40 Under 40, Crain's N.Y. Bus. Office: Time Inc Rockefeller Ctr New York NY 10020-1393

SAFIAN, SHELLEY CAROLE, advertising executive; b. Bklyn., May 29, 1954; d. Jack Israel and Harriet Sara (Cohen) S. BFA, Parsons Sch. Design, 1975. Asst. art dir. Axelrod and Assocs., N.Y.C., 1975-77; art dir. Sta. WDBO-TV-AM/FM, Orlando, Fla., 1978-80; owner, pres. Safian Comm. Svcs., Inc., Winter Park, Fla., 1981—, Bonté Sportswear, Winter Park, Fla., 1993-97. Mem. adv. com. Career Edn., Orange County, Fla., 1981—88, chmn., 1982—83; adj. prof. Internat. Acad. Design and Tech., 2000—; adj. prof. City Coll., Casselberry, Fla., 2000—. Exec. producer/dir. March of Dimes Telethon, Orlando, 1984; bd. dirs. Boy Scouts Am., 1987-91; exec. dir. United Cerebral Palsy Telethon, Orlando, 1982-83; pub. rels. liaison United Cerebral Palsy, Orlando, 1983-84; founder Career Dir. for Deaf, Orlando, 1985; trustee, pub. rels. chair Nat. Multiple Sclerosis Soc., 1991-92, bd. dirs., 1990, 91. Recipient 1st pl. Addy awards Orlando ADvt. Fedn., 1981, 87, 88, 89, 1st pl. Addy award, 2d pl. awards, merit awards, 1982, 84, 85, 87, 88, Nat. Telly award Bronze Statue, 1988, Up and Coming award Price Waterhouse/Orlando Bus. Jour., 1988, Pro-Mark 1st pl. awards Fla. Coun. Shopping Ctrs., 1989, 90, merit award, 1990, Telly award Bronze finalist, 1989, 91; named Tchr. of the Quarter, 2001. Mem. Broadcast Promotion and Mktg. Execs. Assn. (Silver Medalion 1983, nat. finalist 2 Silver Microphone awards 1986, 87), Broadcast Designer's Assn. (bd.d irs. 1980-82), Am. Women in Radio and TV (bd. dirs. 1980-81). Republican. Avocation: horseback riding. Office: Safian Communications Svcs PO Box 1016 Winter Park FL 32790-1016

SAFIRE, WILLIAM, journalist, writer; b. NYC, Dec. 17, 1929; s. Oliver C. and Ida (Panish) S.; m. Helene Belmar Julius, Dec. 16, 1962; children: Mark Lindsey, Annabel Victoria. Student, Syracuse U., 1947—49. Reporter N.Y. Herald Tribune Syndicate, 1949-51; corr. WNBC-WNBT, Europe and Mid. East, 1951; radio-TV prodr. WNBC, N.Y.C., 1954-55; v.p. Tex McCrary, Inc., 1955-60; pres. Safire Pub. Rels., Inc., 1960-68; spl. asst. to Pres. Nixon, Washington, 1969-73; polit. columnist N.Y. Times, Washington, 1973—. Trustee Syracuse U.; chmn. Dana Found. Author: The Relations Explosion, 1963, Plunging into Politics, 1964, Safire's Political Dictionary, 1968, rev. edit., 1972—78, Before the Fall, 1975, Full Disclosure, 1977, Safire's Washington, 1980, On Language, 1980, What's the Good Word?, 1982; author: (with Leonard Safir) Good Advice on Writing, 1982; author: I Stand Corrected, 1984, Take My Word for It, 1986, Freedom, 1987, You Could Look It Up, 1988, Words of Wisdom, 1989; author: (with Leonard Safir) Leadership, 1990; author: Language Maven Strikes Again, 1990, Fumblerules, 1990, Coming to Terms, 1991, The First Dissident, 1992, Lend Me Your Ears, 1992, 1998, 2004, Good Advice on Writing, 1992, Quoth the Maven, 1993, Safire's New Political Dictionary, 1993, In Love with Norma Loquendi, 1994, Sleeper Spy, 1995, Watching My Language, 1997, Spread the Word, 1999, Scandalmonger, 2000, Let a Simile Be Your Umbrella, 2001, No Uncertain Terms, 2003, The Right Word, 2004. Mem. Pulitzer Bd., 1995-2004. With AUS, 1952-54. Recipient Pulitzer prize for Disting. Commentary, 1978. Republican. Office: NY Times 1627 I St NW Washington DC 20006-4007 Business E-Mail: safire@nytimes.com.

SAFIZADEH, M. HOSSEIN, finance educator; BBA, Iran Inst. Banking; MBA, PhD, Okla. State U. Prof. ops. and strategic mgmt. dept. Carroll Sch. Mgmt., Boston Coll., 1997—, interim dean, 2003—. Editl. bd. mem. Prodn. and Ops. Mgmt. Office: Boston Coll Carroll Sch Mgmt Fulton Hall 454A 140 Commonwealth Ave Chestnut Hill MA 02467 Office Phone: 617-552-0476. Business E-Mail: hossein.safizadeh.1@bc.edu.

SAFLEY, JAMES ROBERT, lawyer; b. Cedar Rapids, Iowa, Sept. 19, 1943; s. Robert Starr and Jean (Engelman) S.; m. Dianne Lee McInnis; children: Anne Michele, Jamie Leigh. BA, U. Iowa, 1965; JD, Duke U., 1968. Bar: Minn. 1968, U.S. Ct. Appeals (4th, 5th, 6th, 7th, 8th, 9th and 11th cirs.), U.S. Supreme Ct. Law clk. U.S. Dist. Ct. Minn., Mpls., 1968-69; assoc. Robins, Kaplan, Miller & Ciresi, Mpls., 1969-74, ptnr., 1974—. Bd. visitors Duke Law Sch., 2004—. Mem. adv. coun. Women's Intercollegiate Athletics, U. Minn., 1988-94; mem bd. visitors Duke Law Sch, 2004—. Mem. ABA, Minn. State Bar Assn. (antitrust sect. chmn. 1985-87), Hennepin County Bar Assn., Duke Law Alumni Assn. (bd. dirs 2001-03), Phi Beta Kappa. Office: Robins Kaplan Miller & Ciresi 2800 LaSalle Pla 800 Lasalle Ave Ste 2800 Minneapolis MN 55402-2015 Office Phone: 612-349-8274.

SAFONOV, MICHAEL GEORGE, electrical engineering educator, consultant; b. Pasadena, Calif., Nov. 1, 1948; s. George Michael and Ruth Garnet (Ware) S.; m. Nancy Kelshaw Schorn, Aug. 31, 1968 (div. Oct. 1983); 1 child, Alexander; m. Janet Sunderland, Feb. 25, 1985; 1 child, Peter. BSEE, MSEE, MIT, 1971, EE, 1976, PhDEE, 1977. Electronic engr. Air Force Cambridge Rsch. Lab., Hanscom AFB, Mass., 1968-71; rsch. asst. MIT, Cambridge, 1975-77; prof. elec. engring. U. So. Calif., L.A., 1977—, assoc. chmn. dept., 1989-93, vice chmn. engring. faculty coun., 2001—02, chmn. engring. faculty coun., 2003—04. Vis. scholar Cambridge (Eng.) U., 1983-84, Imperial Coll., London, 1987, Calif. Inst. Tech., Pasadena, 1990-91; cons. Honeywell Systems and Rsch. Ctr., Mpls., 1978-83, Space Systems div. TRW, Redondo Beach, Calif., 1984, Northrop Aircraft, Hawthorne, Calif., 1985-91, also numerous others. Author: Stability and Robustness of Multivariable Feedback Systems (hon. mention Phi Beta Kappa 1981); co-author: (book and software) Robust-Control Toolbox, 1988; assoc. editor IEEE Trans. on Automatic Control, 1985-87, Internat. Jour. Robust and Nonlinear Control, 1989-93, Sys. and Control Letters, 1995—. Awards com. chair Am. Automatic Control Coun., 1993-95. Lt. (j.g.) USNR, 1972-75. Rsch. grantee Air Force Office Sci. Rsch., 1978—, NSF, 1982-84. Fellow IEEE; mem. AIAA (sr.), Common Cause. Republican. Office: U So Calif Dept EE Sys MC 2563 3740 McClintock Ave # 310 Los Angeles CA 90089-2563 Business E-Mail: msafonov@usc.edu. *Consider first only the very simplest problem--but strive for a representation of the simplest problem that generalizes.*

SAFRIT, MARGARET, physical education educator; Chair dept. phys. edn. U. Wis., Madison; chair dept. health and fitness Am. Univ., Washington, prof. emeritus. Presenter in field. Author several books; editor Rsch. Quarterly. Mem. AAHPERD (chair measurement and evaluation coun., Gulick award 1994), Am. Acad. Phys. Edn. Higher Edn. (pres.), Internat. Soc. Measurement and Evaluation (founder, pres.).

SAFT, STUART MARK, lawyer; b. N.Y.C., Feb. 17, 1947; s. Stanley and Dorothy (Ligerman) S.; m. Stephanie C. Optekman, June 6, 1970; children: Bradley S., Gordon D. BA, Hofstra U., 1968; JD, Columbia U., 1971. Bar: N.Y. 1972, Fla. 1975, U.S. Dist. Ct. (so. dist.) N.Y. 1975, U.S. Supreme Ct. 1990. Ptnr. Wolf Haldenstern Adler Freeman & Herz, N.Y.C., 1988—. Chmn. bd. dir. Coun. of N.Y. Coops., N.Y.C., 1981-, Nat. Coop. Bank; chmn. N.Y.C. Workforce Investment Bd.; chmn. bd. dir., CEO Pvt. Industry Coun. N.Y.C., 1994-2000; bd. dir. Am. Women's Econ. Devel. Corp., Nat. Assn. Housing Coops., S.L.E. Lupus Found.; adj. asst. prof. NYU, Real Estate Inst. Author: Commercial Real Estate Forms, 3 vols., 1987, Commercial Real Estate Transactions, 1989, Commercial Real Estate Workouts, 1991, Real Estate

Development: Strategies for a Changing Market, 1990, Commercial Real Estate Leasing, 1992, Real Estate Investor's Survival Guide, 1992, Commercial Real Estate Financing, 1993, Commercial Real Estate Forms, 3d edit., 8 vols., 2001, Commercial Real Estate Transactions, 2d edit., 1995, Commercial Real Estate Workouts, 2d edit., 1996; contbg. editor: The Real Estate Finance Jour., 1989—; contbr. articles to profl. jours. Capt USAR, 1968—76. Mem. ABA, Am. Coll. Real Estate Lawyers, N.Y. Bar Assn., Fla. Bar Assn. Office: Wolf Haldenstein Adler Freeman & Herz 270 Madison Ave New York NY 10016-0601 Office Phone: 212-545-4710. E-mail: saft@whafh.com.

SAFYER, STEVEN MICHAEL, medical administrator, educator; b. New York, NY, Feb. 16, 1949; MD, Albert Einstein Coll. of Med., 1982. Cert. internal medicine . Intern Montefiore Med. Ctr., Bronx, NY, 1978—82, resident, 1983—85, v.p. med. affairs, 1997, sr. v.p., chief med. officer, 1998—; assoc. prof., dept. medicine Albert Einstein Coll. Medicine, 1987—, assoc. prof., dept. epidemiology & population health, 1987—. Office: MMC Centennial Bldg 111 E 210 St 4th Fl Bronx NY 10467*

SAGAFI-NEJAD, TAGI, business educator; b. Bainabaj, Khorasan, Iran, Dec. 19, 1941; arrived in U.S., 1968, m. Nancy Gail Black Sagafi-nejad, Nov. 22, 1967; children: Jahan Crawford Reza, David Joseph Hossein. MA, U. Pa., 1971, PhD, 1979. Lectr. U. Pa., Phila., 1974-76; asst. prof. U. Wash., Seattle, 1976-80, U. Tex., Austin, 1980-84; assoc. prof. Loyola Coll., Balt., 1984-93, prof., 1993—, dept. chair, 1995-96, prof. emeritus, 2002—; Keating-Crawford chair in internat. bus. Stillman Sch. Bus., Seton Hall U., 2002—03; Killam Disting. prof., dir. PhD program in internat. bus. Tex. A&M Internat. U., 2003—. Cons. UN Indsl. Devel. Orgn., 1982—84, UN Ctr. on Transnat. Corp., 1993 , U.S. Congress, 1983—84; lectr., spkr. in field. Author: Technology Transfer Trilogy, 1980, 1981; editl. bd. Transnational Corp., 1993—. Recipient Best Paper award Acad. of Mgmt., 1994, Pacific Asia Mgmt. Inst., U. Hawaii, 1988. Mem. Acad. of Internat. Bus. (chair N.E. chpt. 1988-93), Iranian Scholars Assn. (founding mem., v.p. 1989-90), Middle East Studies Assn., Middle East Inst., Strategic Mgmt. Soc. Democrat. Avocations: gardening, golf, painting, walking. Office Phone: 956-326-2512. E-mail: Tagi.Sagafi@tamiu.edu.

SAGAL, KATEY, actress; b. L.A., Jan. 19, 1954; d. Boris Sagal and Sara Zwilling; m. Jack White, 1993 (div. 2000). Student, Calif. Sch. of the Arts. Former back-up singer for various performers including Bob Dylan, Etta James; (with Bette Midler) former mem. The Harlettes. Actress: (stage prodns.) Martha Rose and the Miners, 1982, My Beautiful Lady, (TV series) Mary, 1986, Imagine That, 2002, (TV movie) The Failing of Raymond, 1971, Mother Goose Rock 'n' Rhyme, 1990, She Says She's Innocent, 1991, Trail of Tears, 1995, Mr. Headmistress, 1998, Chance of a Lifetime, 1998, God's New Plan, 1999, Smart House, 1999, (films) Maid to Order, 1987, The Good Mother, 1988, Following Tildy, 2002; regular (TV series) Married...With Children, 1987-97, (voice) Recess, 1997, (voice) Futurama, 1999, Tucker, 2000, 8 Simple Rules...for Dating My Teenage Daughter, 2002—. Mem. Actors' Equity Assn., Assn. TV and Radio Artists. Office: Progressive Artists Agy Inc 400 S Beverly Dr Ste 216 Beverly Hills CA 90212-4404*

SAGAN, M. J. architectural firm executive; m. Craig L. Haft; children: Nicholas, Claire, Owen. BA arch., Pa. State Univ., Pa., 1982. Lic. NY, NJ, and CT, cert. NCARB. Assoc., staff designer George F. Henschel, Jr., AIA, 1982—83; assoc./project arch. Becker, Becker & Lamont, Inc., New Canaan, Conn., 1983—84; assoc. Shope Reno Wharton Assoc., Greenwich, Conn., 1984—; v.p. Anderson/Schwartz Arch., N.Y.C., 1988—; pc Anderson Arch., N.Y.C., 1996—. Exhibitions include Negotiating Domesticity/ The Greenwich Arts Coun., Greenwich, 2003, Princeton Pub. Libr., 2003. Recipient EDRA/Places Design Award, Abercrombie & Fitch office campus, 2003, Build. Team Project of the Yr.- Grand Award, Abercrombie & Fitch office campus and distbn. ctr., 2003, Good Design is Good Bus. Award, Abercrombie & Fitch, Hollister Co., 2002, Project Award, Hudson River Pk., 2002, Design Award. Arch. Award, AIA/ New York Chpt., 2000, Design Award, Interior Arch. Citation, 1998, Design Award, Interior Arch., 1999, Design Award, Distinction, Environ., AIA/ New York Chpt., ID Mag., 1996, Design Award, Interior Arch. Award, Lake Sebago House, Maine, 1995, Design Award, AIA New York Chpt., ID Mag., 1994, Gold Award, 1994. Several selected publications from 1986-2002 in mag. such as: Arch. Record, House & Garden, The New York Times, Interior Design, Vogue, Diseno Interior 70, House Beautiful, Abitare, and Record Interiors. Office: Anderson Arch PC 555 W 25th St New York NY 10001

SAGARIN, J. DANIEL, lawyer; b. Bridgeport, Conn., Feb. 15, 1941; s. Philip H. Sagarin; m. Mary Demotses; children: Joshua, Mark, Raphael. BA magna cum laude, Lehigh U., 1962; JD, Yale U., 1965. Bar: Conn. 1965, U.S. Dist. Ct. Conn. 1965, Mass. 1966, U.S. Dist. Ct. Mass. 1966, U.S. Ctp Appeals (2d cir.) 1967, U.S. Supreme Ct. 1972, U.S. Claims Ct. Law clk. to Hon. Robert C. Zampano, U.S. Dist. Ct. for Conn., Hartford, 1965-66, asst. U.S. atty., 1967-70, spl. master spl. masters program, 1988—; ptnr. Hurwitz, Sagarin & Slossberg, LLC, Milford, Conn., 1970—. Tutor Yale Law Sch., New Haven, 1965-66, lectr. trial practice, 1976-84. Fellow Am. Coll. Trial Lawyers (state chair 2001-03), Conn. Bar Found.; mem. ABA, ATLA, Conn. Bar Assn. (exec. com. criminal law sect. 1970—, fed. practice com. 1985—), Conn. Trial Lawyers Assn. Home: 72 Vineyard Pl Guilford CT 06437-3237 Office: Hurwitz Sagarin & Slossberg LLC 147 Broad St Milford CT 06460-4742

SAGAWA, SHIRLEY SACHI, lawyer; b. Rochester, NY, Aug. 25, 1961; d. Hidetaka H. and Patricia (Ford) S.; m. Gregory A. Baer; children: Jackson Ford Baer, Matthew Sagawa Baer, Thomas Arthur Baer. AB, Smith Coll., 1983; MSc, London Sch. Econs., 1984; JD, Harvard U., 1987. Bar: Md. 1988. Chief counsel youth policy, labor and human resources com. U.S. Senate, Washington, 1987-91; sr. counsel and dir. family and youth policy Nat. Women's Law Ctr., Washington, 1991-93; spl. asst. to Pres. Clinton for domestic policy, 1993; exec. dir., mng. dir., exec. v.p. Corp. for Nat. and Comty. Svc., Washington, 1993-97; exec. dir. Learning First Alliance, Washington, 1997-98; dep. asst. Pres. Clinton, dep. chief staff First Lady The White House, Washington, 1998-2001; ptnr. sagawa/jospin, 2001—. Co-author: Common Interest, Common Good, Creating Value Through Business and Social Sector Partnership, 1999. Exec. bd. Orgn. for Pan-Asian Am. Women, Washington, 1987-89; mem. Women of Color Leadership Coun., 1991-92; vice-chair, bd. dirs. Nat. Cmty. Svc. Commn., 1991-93; trustee Am. Folklife Ctr., Libr. Congress, 1996-97; commr. Head Start Fellowships Commn., 1996-97; bd. dirs. My Sister's Place, 1996-98, Jumpstart, 1998, Campus Outreach Opportunity League, 1997-98, Nat. Inst. Dispute Resolution, 1997-98, Nat. Womens Law Ctr., 2003—, Nat. AmeriCorps Assn., 2004—, Nat. Assn. Childcare Resource and Referral Agencies, 2004—. Recipient Philip V. McGance award Coun. for Advancement of Citizenship, 1991, cert. of recognition Nat. Coun. Jewish Women, 1989, Alexandrine medal Coll. St. Catherine, St. Paul, 1995, Alec Dickson Servant Leader award Nat. Youth Leadership Coun., 2002; named one of 25 most influential working women Working Mother Mag., 1999; recipient Alec Dickson Servant Leader award, National Youth Leadership Council, 2002; Harry S. Truman scholar, 1981; Smith Coll. Alumnae Assn. fellow, 1983, AAUW fellow, 1986. Mem. Md. Bar Assn. Democrat. Episcopalian. Home: 3000 Greenvale Rd Chevy Chase MD 20815 E-mail: shirleysagawa@comcast.com.

SAGAWA, YONEO, horticulturist, educator; b. Olaa, Hawaii, Oct. 11, 1926; s. Chikatada and Mume (Kuno) S.; m. Masayo Yamamoto, May 24, 1962 (dec. Apr. 1988); children: Penelope Toshiko, Irene Teruko. AB, Washington U., St. Louis, 1950, MS, 1952; PhD, U. Conn., 1956. Postdoctoral rsch. assoc. biology Brookhaven Nat. Lab., Upton, NY, 1955—57, guest in biology, 1958; asst. prof., then assoc. prof. U. Fla., 1957—64; dir. undergrad. sci. ednl. rsch. participation program NSF, 1964; cons. biosatellite project NASA, 1966—67; prof. horticulture U. Hawaii, 1964—; dir. Lyon Arboretum, 1967—91; assoc. dir. Hawaiian Sci. Fair, 1966—67, dir., 1967—68; rsch. assoc. in biology U. Calif., Berkeley, 1970—71; rsch. assoc. Bishop Mus., Honolulu, 1992—, Bot. Rsch. Inst. of Tex., 1993—, Hawaii Tropical Bot. Garden, 1995—; external assessor U. Pertanian, Malaysia, 1994—. Mem. Internat. Orchid Commn. on Classification, Nomenclature and Registration; fellow Inst. voor Toepassing van Atoomengerie in de Landbouw, U. Agr., Wageningen, The Netherlands, 1979-80; mem. sci. adv. bd. Nat. Tropical Bot. Garden, Kauai, Hawaii; councilor Las Cruces Bot. Garden, Costa Rica; cons. FAO, Singapore, 1971, USAID-Agribus. Assistance Program, Vols. in Overseas Coop. Assistance, UN Devel. Program-UN Internat. Short Term Adv. Resources; dir. Hawaii Tropical Bot. Garden; hon. scientist Rural Devel. Adminstrn., Republic of Korea, 1998—; cons. Fiji-N.Z. Bus. Coun., 1996, 97, 98, 99, 2000; cons. IRETA, Western Samoa, 1997, 98, 2003; cons. Nat. Hort. Rsch. Inst., Suwon, Republic of Korea, 1998, 2000. Editor: Hawaii Orchid Jour., 1972-99, Pacific Orchid Soc. Bull., 1966-71; mem. editl. bd. Allertonia, 1976; mem. editl. adv. bd. Jour. Orchid Soc. India, 2002—; contbr. numerous articles to profl. jours. Trustee Friends of Honolulu Bot. Gardens, 1973-99 Recipient Disting. Svc. award South Fla. Orchid Soc., 1968, Grand prize for Poster, 1st Nagoya Internat. Orchid Show, 1990, Cert. of Achievement Garden Club Am., 1995, Digest Doer's Profile, 2000, Gold award Hawaii Orchid Growers Assn., 1996; grantee Am. Orchid Soc., Atomic Energy Commn., NIH, HEW, Inst. Mus. Svcs., Stanley Smith Hort. Trust, Honolulu Orchid Soc. Fellow Am. Orchid Soc. (hon. life, Gold medal for outstanding contbns. and svcs. 1999); mem. AAAS, Internat. Assn. Hort. Sci., Am. Assn. Hort. Sci., Am. Inst. for Biol. Scis., Bot. Soc. Am., Hawn Bot. Soc. (past v.p.), Internat. Assn. Plant Tissue Culture, Internat. Palm Soc., Am. Anthurium Soc. (hon. life), Pacific Orchid Soc. (trustee 1994), Kaimuki Orchid Soc. (hon. life), Honolulu Orchid Soc. (hon., life), Lyon Arboretum Assn. (trustee 1974-91), Garden Club Honolulu (hon., life), Aloha Bonsai Club, Sigma Xi, Gamma Sigma Delta, Phi Kappa Phi (past pres., v.p., councillor U. Hawaii chpt.). Democrat. Office: U Hawaii TPSS St John Rm 102 3190 Maile Way Honolulu HI 96822-2279 Fax: 808-956-3894. Business E-Mail: yoneo@hawaii.edu.

SAGE, ANDREW GREGG CURTIN, II, corporate investor, manager; b. Bryn Mawr, Pa., Mar. 11, 1926; s. Henry W. and Eleanor (Purviance) S.; m. Sara Wakefield, Sept. 29, 1956; children: Andrew Gregg Curtin III, Sally. Mem. staff DeCoppet & Doremus (odd lot stock house), N.Y.C., 1946-47, Sage & Co., N.Y. Stock Exchange Specialists, N.Y.C., 1947-48; assoc. Lehman Bros., N.Y.C., 1948-60, gen. ptnr., 1960-68, mng. ptnr., 1969, pres., 1970-73, vice chmn., 1973-77, mng. dir., 1977-82, Lehman Bros. Kuhn Loeb, Inc., 1977-82, Shearson Lehman Bros., Inc., 1982-87, sr. cons., 1987-90; pres., CEO, dir. Robertson CECO Corp., Boston, 1992-93, chmn. bd. dirs., 1994—, Chgo. Bd. dirs. Tom's Foods, Am. Superconductor Corp.; pres., treas. Sage Land Devel. Co., pres., bd. dirs. Sage Capital Corp. Served with USAAF, 1944-46. Home: PO Box 937 Wilson WY 83014-0937 E-mail: agesage@earthlink.net.

SAGE, ANDREW PATRICK, JR., systems engineer, management educator; b. Charleston, S.C., Aug. 27, 1933; s. Andrew Patrick and Pearl Louise (Britt) S.; m. LaVerne Galhouse, Mar. 3, 1962; children: Theresa Annette, Karen Margaret, Philip Andrew. BS in Elec. Engring, The Citadel, 1955; SM, MIT, 1956; PhD, Purdue U., 1960; DEng (hon.), U. Waterloo, Can., 1987, Dalhousie U., Halifax, Nova Scotia, Can., 1997. Registered profl. engr., Tex. Instr. elec. engring. Purdue U., 1956-60; assoc. prof. U. Ariz., 1960-63; mem. tech. staff Aerospace Corp., Los Angeles, 1963-64; prof. elec. engring. and nuclear engring. scis. U. Fla., 1964-67; prof., dir. Info. and Control Scis. Center, So. Methodist U., Dallas, 1967-74; head elec. engring. dept. So. Meth. U., 1973-74; Quarles prof. engring. sci. and systems U. Va., Charlottesville, 1974-84, chmn. dept. chem. engring., 1974-75, chmn. dept. engring. sci. and systems, 1977-84, assoc. dean, 1974-80; First Am. Bank prof. info. tech. George Mason U., Fairfax, Va., 1984—, assoc. v.p. for acad. affairs, 1984-85, dean Sch. Info. Tech. and Engring., 1985-96, univ. prof., founding dean emeritus, 1996—. Cons. Martin Marietta, Collins Radio, Atlantic Richfield, Tex. Instruments, LTV Aerospace, Battelle Meml. Inst., TRW Sys., NSF, Inst. Def. Analyses, Planning Rsch. Corp., MITRE, Engring. Rsch. Assocs., Software Productivity Consortium; gen. chmn. Internat. Conf. on Sys., Man and Cybernetics, 1974, 87; mem. spl. program panel on sys. sci. NATO, 1981-82; trustee, cons. Ctr. Naval Analysis, 1990-94. Author: Optimum Systems Control, 1968, 2d edit., 1977, Estimation Theory with Applications to Communications and Control, 1971, System Identification, 1971, An Introduction to Probability and Stochastic Processes, 1973, Methodology for Large Scale Systems, 1977, Systems Engineering: Methodology and Applications, 1977, Linear Systems Control, 1978, Economic Systems Analysis, 1983, System Design for Human Interaction, 1987, Information Processing in Systems and Organizations, 1990, Introduction to Computer Systems Analysis, Design, and Applications, 1989, Software Systems Engineering, 1990, Decision Support Systems Engineering, 1991, Systems Engineering, 1992, Systems Management for Information Technology and Software Engineering, 1995, Handbook of Systems Engineering and Management, 1999, Introduction to Systems Engineering, 2000; assoc. editor IEEE Transactions on Systems Sci. and Cybernetics, 1968-72; editor: IEEE Transactions on Systems, Man and Cybernetics, 1972-98; assoc. editor: Automatica, 1968-81; editor, 1981-96; mem. editl. bd. Systems Engring, 1968-72, IEEE Spectrum, 1972-73, Computers and Elec. Engring., 1972, Jour. Interdisciplinary Modeling and Simulation, 1976-80, Internat. Jour. Intelligent Sys., 1986—, Orgn. Sci., 1994—; editor Elsevier North Holland textbook series in sys. sci. and engring., 1970-88, John Wiley textbook series on sys. engring. and mgmt., 1989—; co-editor-in-chief Jour. Large Scale Sys.: Theory and Applications, 1978-88, Info. and Decision Technologies, 1988-94, Info. and Sys. Engring., 1995-96; editor in chief Sys. Engring., 1998—; co-editor in chief Info., Knowledge and Sys. Mgmt., 1999—; contbr. articles to profl. jours. Recipient Norbert Wiener award, 1980, Joseph G. Wohl career award, 1991, Superior Pub. Svc. award Sec. of the Navy, 1994; Case Centennial scholar, 1980, Award Washington Soc. of Engrs., 1996. Master: IEEE Sys./Man and Cybernetics Soc. (pres. 1984—85); fellow: AAAS (chmn. sect. M 1990), IEEE (life M. Barry Carlton award 1970, Centennial medal 1984, Outstanding Contbn. award 1986, Donald G. Fink prize 1994, Simon Ramo medal 2000), Internat. Coun. on Sys. Engring. (Pioneer award 2002); mem.: Nat. Acad. Engring., Inst. for Ops. Rsch. and Mgmt. Sci., Washington Soc. Engrs. (award 1996), Am. Soc. Engring. Edn. (Frederick Emmonds Terman award 1970, Centennial cert. for exceptional contbn. 1993), Internat. Fedn. Automatic Control (Outstanding Svc. award), Inst. Mgmt. Scis., Tau Beta Pi, Eta Kappa Nu (eminent mem. award 2002), Sigma Xi. Home: 8011 Woodland Hills Ln Fairfax VA 22039-2433 Office: George Mason U Sch Info Tech Fairfax VA 22030-4444 Office Phone: 703-993-1506.

SAGE, JACOB I. neurologist, educator; b. Sept. 26, 1946; s. Joseph and Fern (Ginsburg) S.; m. Cynthia Fox; children: Naomi, Rebecca, Abigail. AB, U. Chgo., 1968; MD, U. Pitts., 1972. Intern Yale-New Haven Hosp., 1972-73; resident in neurology U. Pitts., 1976-78; fellow in neurochemistry Cornell Med. Coll., N.Y.C., 1978-80; asst. prof. neurology U. Medicine and Dentistry of N.J., New Brunswick, 1980-86, assoc. prof., 1986-90, prof. neurology, 1990—, dir. movement disorders divsn., 1995—. Mem. sci. adv. bd. Am. Parkinsons Disease Assn., N.Y.C., 1995—. Author: Parkinson's Disease: A Guide for Patients, 1996; editor: Practical Neurology of the Elderly, 1996; contbr. articles to profl. jours. Fellow Am. Neurol. Assn.; mem. Acad. of Neurology. Avocations: skiing, gardening. Office: UMDNJ Robert Wood Johnson Med Sch Dept Neurology New Brunswick NJ 08903 E-mail: sage@umdnj.edu.

SAGE, MARTIN LEE, chemistry professor; b. N.Y.C., Mar. 4, 1935; s. Joseph and Fannie Sage; m. Gloria Arline Welt, June 15, 1958; 1 child, Daniel Simon. AB, Cornell U., 1955; MA, Harvard U., 1958, PhD, 1959. Postdoctoral fellow Brandeis U., Waltham, Mass., 1959-61; asst. prof. U. Oreg., Eugene, 1961-67; assoc. prof. Syracuse (N.Y.) U., 1967-82, prof. chemistry, 1982—, dir. sci., tech. and society program, 1991—. Vis. assoc. prof. Tel Aviv U., 1977-78; visitor Oxford (Eng.) U., 1985-86. Mem. AAAS, AAUP (pres. Syracuse U. chpt. 1988-89), Am. Phys. Soc., Am. Chem. Soc., Nat. Assn. for Sci., Tech., and Soc., Sierra Club, Phi Beta Kappa (Syracuse U. chpt. 2003-). Office: Syracuse U CST 1-014 Syracuse NY 13244

SAGE, WEBSTER LEGENE, JR., ophthalmologist; b. St. Louis, Oct. 22, 1925; s. Webster LeGene and Alice Virginia (Gollehon) S.; m. Claudine New, May 20, 1952 (dec. June 1986); children: Bryan LeGene, Evan Webster; m. Shirley Barr, Jan. 2, 1988. BS, U. Ariz., 1949; MD, Baylor U., 1953. Diplomate Am. Bd. Ophthalmology. Intern Good Samaritan Hosp., Phoenix; resident Loma Linda (Calif.) U.; pvt. practice Phoenix, 1956—. Chmn. dept. ophthalmology Good Samaritan Hosp., Phoenix, 1960-62, St. Joseph's Hosp., Phoenix, 1971-72; cons. Ariz. Bd. Med. Examiners, Phoenix; owner Surg. Eye Ctr. Ariz., Phoenix, 1985—. Chmn. bd. of elders and deacons Camelback Christian Ch., Scottsdale, Ariz. Maj. U.S. Army, 1962-64. Fellow ACS (life), Am. Acad. Ophthalmology, Internat. Coll. Surgeons; mem. Ariz. Ophthalmological Soc. (pres. 1963-64), Phoenix Ophthalmological Soc. (pres. 1967-68), Kiwanis Club, Paradise Valley Country Club, Phoenix Country Club. Avocations: travel, photography. Home: 8210 N Charles Dr Paradise Valley AZ 85253-2405 Office: 5133 N Central Ave Ste 100 Phoenix AZ 85012-1438

SAGE-GAVIN, EVA MARIE, retail executive; b. Boston, Sept. 26, 1958; d. Ross Francis and Theresa Veronica (Bufalo) S.; m. Dennis Gavin. BS in Indsl. Relations, Cornell U., 1980. Affirmative action personnel specialist Xerox Corp., Washington, 1980-81; compensation analyst Xerox Corp, Rochester, N.Y., 1981-82, sales recruiter Boston, 1982, employment mgr., 1983, systems mktg. rep., 1983-85; personnel mgr. Xerox Corp., L.A., 1985—86; human resources mgr. Xerox Corp, Irvine, Calif., 1986; dir. human resources Pepsi Co., 1991, v.p. corp. human resources, Taco Bell; sr. v.p. human resources Disney Consumer Products, 1997—2000, Sun Microsystems, Inc., 2000—03; exec. v.p. human resources Gap Inc., 2003—. Mem. career adv. bd. Emmanuel Coll., Boston, 1983-85. Mem. Am. Soc. Personnel Adminstrn., Women in Mgmt., Xerox Women's Network (edn. com. 1988), Kappa Kappa Gamma. Democrat. Roman Catholic. Avocations: skiing, travel, boating, sailing, aerobics. Office: Gap Inc 2 Folsom St San Francisco CA 94105

SAGER, CLIFFORD J. psychiatrist, educator; b. N.Y.C. s. Max and Lena (Lipman) S.; m. Anne Scheinman; children by previous marriage: Barbara L., Philip T., Rebecca J., Anthony F. BS, Pa. State U., 1937; MD, NYU, 1941; cert. in psychoanalysis, N.Y. Med. Coll., 1949. Diplomate: Am. Bd. Psychiatry and Neurology. Rotating intern Montefiore Hosp., N.Y.C., 1941-42; AUS Capt.,chief neurologist 312th and 42nd Psychiatry Hosp., 1942—46; sr. special resident in psychiatry Bellevue Hosp., N.Y.C., 1946—48; practice medicine specializing in psychiatry N.Y.C. and East Hampton, N.Y., 1946—; dir. therapeutic services, assoc. dean, dir. tng. Postgrad. Ctr. Mental Health, 1948-60; vis. psychiatrist, med. bd. Flower and Fifth Ave Hosp., 1960-71, Met. Hosp., 1960-71; dir. psychiat. tng. and edn. N.Y. Med. Coll., 1960-71; attending psychiatrist Bird S. Coler Hosp., 1960-71; clin. dir. N.Y. Med. Coll., 1960-63, assoc. prof. psychiatry, 1960 65, prof., 1966 71, dir. partial hosp. programs and family treatment and study unit, 1964-71; clin. prof. psychiatry Mt. Sinai Sch. Medicine, 1971-80; assoc. dir. psychiatry Beth Israel Hosp. for Family and Mental Therapy; chief of psychiatry Gov. Hosp., 1970-74; dir. family therapy Mt. Sinai Sch. Medicine, 1974-80; prof. clin. psychiatry N.Y. Hosp.-Cornell Univ. Med. Ctr., 1980—; attending psychiatrist N.Y. Hosp.-Payne Whitney Clinic, 1980—2002; dir. marital and family clinic N.Y. Hosp., 1991—2000; prof. emeritus Cornell U. Coll. Medicine, 2000—. Attending psychiatrist Mt. Sinai Hosp., 1971-80; chief behavioral scis. Gouverneur Hosp.; chief family treatment unit Beth Israel Med. Ctr., 1970-74, assoc. dir. psychiatry family and group therapy, 1971-74; psychiat. dir. Jewish Family Svc., 1974-77; dir. family psychiatry Jewish Bd. Family and Childrens Svcs., 1978-90; dir. Remarried Consultation Svc., 1976-90; dir. Tng. and Sex Therapy Clinic, 1974-90; psychiat. dir. Employee Consultation and Corp. Health Programs, 1980-83; faculty, supr. Contemporary Ctr. Advanced Psychoanalytic Studies; chief neuropsychiatry 42d and 312th Gen. Hosp.; psychiat. cons. Employee Consultation Svc. and Corp. Health Svcs., 1983-1992. Author: Marriage Contracts and Couple Therapy, 1976, Intimate Partners, 1979, Treating the Remarried Family, 1983; 4 other books; mem. editorial bd. Am. Jour. Orthopsychiatry, 1960-69, Internat. Jour. Group Psychotherapy, 1968—, Family Process, 1969-92, Divorce and Remarriage, 1977—, Comprehensive Rev. Jour. Family and Marriage, 1978—; cons. Sexual Medicine, 1974-82; co-editor, founder Jour. Sex and Marital Therapy, 1974—; mem. editorial bd.: Jour. Marriage and Family Counseling, 1977—, Internat. Jour. Family Counseling, 1977—; author or contbr. some 100 sci. articles to jours. Capt. M.C. U.S. Army, 1942—46, with M.C. U.S. Army, 1942—46. Recipient Am. Family Therapy Assn. award for Outstanding Contribution to Family Therapy 1983, Assn. Marriage and Family Therapists award for Outstanding Contributions to the field of Marital and Family Therapy, 1984. Fellow Am. Psychiat. Assn. (life), Am. Orthopsychiat. Assn. (life), Acad. Psychoanalysis (charter), Am. Group Psychotherapy Assn. (pres. 1968-70, dir. 1962-74), Soc. Med. Psychoanalysis (pres. 1960-61, dir. 1958-62, pres.-elect 1997-99), Am. Assn. Marital and Famiy Therapists; mem. AMA (life), Am. Soc. Advancement Psychotherapy (dir. 1954-67), N.Y. Soc. Clin. Psychiatry, Soc. for Sex Therapy and Rsch. (pres. 1976-77, bd. dirs. 1953-58) PAIRS Found. (bd. dirs. 1985—). Home and Office: 35 East 75th St New York NY 10021-2761

SAGER, DONALD JACK, librarian, consultant, former publisher; b. Milw., Mar. 3, 1938; s. Alfred Herman and Sophia (Sagan) Sager; m. Sarah Ann Long, May 23, 1987; children: Geoffrey, Andrew. BS, U. Wis., Milw., 1963; MSLS, U. Wis., 1964. Sr. documentalist AC Electronics divsn. GM, Milw., 1958-63; teaching asst. U. Wis., Madison, 1963-64; dir. Kingston (N.Y.) Pub. Libr., 1964-66, Elyria (Ohio) Pub. Libr., 1966-71, Mobile Pub. Libr., 1971-75, Pub. Libr. Columbus and Franklin County, Ohio, 1975-78; commr. Chgo. Pub. Libr., 1978-81; dir. Elmhurst Pub. Libr., Ill., 1982-83, Milw. Pub. Libr., 1983-91; pub. Highsmith Press, Ft. Atkinson, Wis., 1991-2000; pres., CEO Gossage Sager Assocs. LLC, N.Y.C., 2000—. Secy Online Computer Library Ctr, 1977—78, disting vis scholar, 1982; chmn investment comt PLA Pub Library, 1985—89, chmn mus comt, 1989—91, mem hist comt, 1993—95, chmn PLA nat conf comt, 1986—88; bd dirs Coun Wis Libraries, 1982—91, Urban Libraries Coun, 1985—93, secy, 1991—93; adj faculty Univ Wis, Milwaukee, 1984—91; consult in field. Author: (book) Reference: A Programmed Instruction, 1970, Binders, Books and Budgets, 1971, Participatory Management, 1981, The American Public Library, 1982, Public Library Administrators Planning Guide to Automation, 1983, Managing the Public Library, 1984, Small Libraries, 1992, Small Libraries, 3d rev ed, 2000; co-editor: Urban Library Management Trends, 1989; contbg. editor: Public Libraries, 1990—2000; contbr. articles to profl jours. Pres Milwaukee Civic Alliance, 1990—91; chmn Milwaukee United Way Campaign, 1984; pres Milwaukee Westown Asn, 1987—90; treas. Congl. Ch. Deerfield, Ill., 2002—; bd dirs Goethe House, 1985—91. With AUS, 1956—58. Mem.: ALA (councilor-at-large 1995—2003, policy monitoring comt, awards comt, chmn core values task force), Library Admin Asn Wis (chmn 1987—88), Wis Library Asn Found (chmn 1986—88), Wis Library Asn, Chicago Book Clin, Ill Library Asn, Pub Library Asn (pres 1982—83, bd dirs, vpres, pres-elect), Exchange Club Milwaukee (pres 1988—89). Office Phone: 312-961-5536. Business E-Mail: dsager@gossagesager.com.

SAGER, MADELINE DEAN, lawyer; b. Turlock, Calif., Feb. 9, 1946; d. Paul Kenton and Jean Madeline (Ferguson) Dean; m. Gregory Warren Sager, June, 1970; children: Jeannette Carolyn, Robert Dean. BA, Sacramento State U., 1967; JD, U. Calif., Davis, 1970. Bar: Calif. 1971, U.S. Dist. Ct. (ea. dist.) Calif. 1971, U.S. Dist. Ct. (no. dist.) Calif. 1973. Atty. Blackmon, Isenberg, Moulds & Blicker, Sacramento, 1971-72, Redwood Legal Assistance, Ukiah, Calif., 1972-77, Sager & Sager, Ukiah, Willits, Calif., 1977-87, Leonard J. LaCasse, Ukiah, Calif., 1990—2002, Nelson & Riemenscheider, Ukiah, Calif., 2002—. Dir. Law Libr. Bd., Ukiah, 1985. Sec. PTA, Calpella, Calif., 1989-90; mem. sch. site coun. Redwood Valley (Calif.) Mid. Sch., 1992-93; treas., dir. Ukiah Dolphin Swim, 1994-97; meet dir. Soroptimist Swim Meet, Ukiah, 1996. Mem. Mendocino County Bar Assn. (pres. 1986), Pacific Swimming (ofcl. 1995-98), Music Boosters Ukiah H.S. Democrat. Presbyterian. Avocations: hiking, camping, music, travel. Home: PO Box 72 Redwood Valley CA 95470-0072 Office: Nelson and Riemenscheider 106 N School St Ukiah CA 95482

SAGER, PHILIP TRAVIS, research physician, cardiologist, cardiac electrophysiologist; b. N.Y.C., Jan. 23, 1956; s. Clifford Julius and Ruth (Levy) Sager; m. Linda Sager. BS in Chemistry and Biology, MIT, 1977; MD, Yale U., 1982. Diplomate Am. Bd. Internal Medicine, Am. Bd. Cardiology, Am. Bd. Cardiac Electrophysiology. Resident, fellow in cardiology Yale U., New Haven, 1982—88; asst. prof. medicine Sch. Medicine, U. So. Calif., L.A., 1988-90, asst. dir. electrophysiology, 1988-90, dir. Pacemaker Ctr., 1988-90;

asst. prof. medicine Sch. Medicine, UCLA, 1990-96, assoc. prof. medicine, 1996—2001; dir. cardiac electrophysiology West L.A. VA Med. Ctr., 1990—2001; sr. dir., U.S. lead physician Astrazeneca Inc., Wilmington, Del., 2004—; dir. cardiac rsch. Schering-Plough Rsch. Inst., 2001—; clin. prof. medicine UMDNJ Med. Sch., 2002—. Mem. cardiology adv. com. VA, Washington, 1990-94; cons. electrophysiology ACGME, Chgo., 1995-2001; vis. prof. Kern Med. Ctr., Bakersfield, Calif., 1991, 94, U. Iowa Sch. Medicine, 1994, Northwestern U. Sch. Medicine, 1994, Yale U. Sch. Medicine, 1995, U. Calif., San Francisco, 1996; topic leader, ICH Expert Working Group on the Clin. QT Initative, 2002—; cons. pharm. cos.; clectr. in field. Contbr. chpts. to books, numerous articles to profl. jours.; reviewer sci. jours. and sci. mags. Recipient many rsch. grants, including Am. Heart Assn., 1996. Fellow ACP, Am. Heart Assn., Am. Coll. Cardiology; mem. Am. Fedn. Clin. Rsch., Nat. Assn. Pacing and Electrophysiology (program dirs. com. 1992-2001, govt. com. 1994-2001, co-chair program dirs. com. 1997-2001), Phi Beta Kappa, Alpha Omega Alpha. Avocations: travel, bicycling, scuba diving, reading history, movies. Office: AstraZeneca 1800 Concord Pike PO Box 15437 Wilmington DE 19850-5437 Personal E-mail: philip.sager@astrazeneca.com. Business E-Mail: psager@alum.mit.edu.

SAGER, WILLIAM FREDERICK, retired chemistry educator; b. Glencoe, Ill., Jan. 22, 1918; s. Fred Anson and Alta (Stansbury) S.; m. Marilyn Olga Williams, Dec. 26, 1941; children: Karen Louise Sager Dickinson, Judith Lynn Sager Peyton), Kathryn Gwen Sager Potts. BS in Chemistry, George Washington U., 1939, MA in Organic Chemistry, 1941; PhD in Organic Chemistry, Harvard U., 1948. Research chemist The Texas Co., 1941-45; prof. chemistry George Washington U., 1948-65, U. Ill.-Chgo., 1965-86, prof. emeritus, 1986—, chmn., 1965-80. Cons. to govt. and industry, 1952—. Founder, pres. Sager Innovations, Inc. Patentee (U.S. patents on evergy saving devices.). Recipient Disting. Service award U. Ill. Alumni Assn., 1985; Guggenheim fellow, 1954-55. Mem. Am. Chem. Soc., Sigma Xi, Alpha Chi Sigma. Home: 1552 John Anderson Dr Ormond Beach FL 32176-3567 Office: Dept Chemistry U Ill-Chicago Chicago IL 60680

SAGERHOLM, JAMES ALVIN, retired naval officer; b. Uniontown, Pa., Dec. 23, 1927; s. Frithiof Norris and Margaret Blocher S.; m. Margaret Ann Herrlich, June 7, 1952; children— Lisa Marie, Ann Denise, Jeannine Louise, Mark Christian BS, U.S. Naval Acad., 1952. Commd. ensign U.S. Navy, 1952, advanced through grades to vice admiral, 1983, exec. officer USS Sproston, 1961—63, navigator USS Seadragon, 1965, exec. officer blue crew USS Mariano G. Vallejo, 1966-67, comdg. officer gold crew USS Kamehameha, 1968-71, head gen. purpose warfare forces group Office of Chief Naval Ops., 1971, dep. exec. dir. Chief Naval Ops. Exec. Panel, 1972, exec. sec. Chief Naval Ops. Exec. Bd., 1973, comdr. Naval Intelligence Support Ctr., 1974-75, dep. dir. naval intelligence Chief Naval Ops., 1975-76, comdr. South Atlantic Force, U.S. Atlantic Fleet, 1976-78, dir. Office of Program Appraisal, Office of Sec. Navy, 1978-81, chief naval edn. and tng., 1983-85; exec. dir. Pres. Fgn. Intelligence Adv. Bd. White House, Washington, 1981-82; ret., 1985. Chmn. bd. dirs. Piedmont Environ. Coun., 1987-89; v.p. for nat. affairs Gen. George C. Marshall Home Found., 1990-91. Bd. trustees Balt. Polytech. Inst. Found., 2000-03. Decorated D.S.M., Legion of Merit, Meritorious Service medal; named Disting. Alumnus, Balt. Poly. Inst. Mem. Naval Submarine League, U.S. Naval Inst., K.C. Roman Catholic. Avocations: golf, civil war history. Home: 414 Rockfleet Rd Unit 102 Lutherville Timonium MD 21093-7582

SAGERMAN, ROBERT HOWARD, radiation oncologist; b. N.Y.C., Jan. 23, 1930; s. Irving R. and Ethel Sagerman; m. Malyne Sagerman, Dec. 23, 1954; children: Jason E., Eric S., Evan C., Roger F. BS, NYU, 1951, MD, 1955. Diplomate Am. Bd. Radiology. Intern Meadowbrook Hosp., Mineola, N.Y., 1955-56; resident Charity Hosp., New Orleans, 1956-57; instr. Tulane U., New Orleans, 1956-57; resident Montefiore Hosp., Bronx, N.Y., 1959-61; asst. prof. Stanford (Calif.) U., 1961-64, Columbia U., N.Y.C., 1964-68; prof. SUNY Health Sci. Ctr., Syracuse, 1968—2003, prof. emeritus, 2003—. Cons. radiologist Crouse Irving Meml. Hosp., Syracuse, St. Joseph's Hosp., Syracuse, Community Gen. Hosp., Syracuse, VA Hosp., Syracuse, 1968—. Author, co-editor: Radiotherapy of Intraocular and Orbital Tumors, 1993, 2d edit., 2003, Age Related Molecuar Degeneration, 2001. Capt. USAF, 1957-59. Mem. Radiol. Soc. N.Am. (Erskine lectr. 1992). Office: SUNY Health Sci Ctr 750 E Adams St Syracuse NY 13210-1834 E-mail: sagermar@upstate.edu.

SAGESER, KENDALL WAYNE, mineral exploration executive; b. El Reno, Okla. s. Albert John and Louise Pauline Sageser; m. Jane E. Conrad, Mar. 28, 1959; children: Janice Lucy Runnels, Daniel Scot, David Mark. BS in Mining Engring., S.D. Sch. Mines & Tech., Rapid City, 1962, BS in Geol. Engring., 1963; MS in Geology, Stanford U., Palo Alto, Calif., 1964. Exploration geologist Shell Oil Co., Oklahoma City, 1964-65; geologist, sr. geologist U.S. Steel Corp., Pitts., 1965-72; exploration mgr. Asia Essex Minerals Co., Singapore, 1972-76; exploration mgr. U.S.A. U.S. Steel Corp., Salt Lake City, 1976-81; v.p. Essex Minerals Co., Pitts., 1981-83; v.p., sr. v.p. Santa Fe Pacific Gold Corp., Albuquerque, 1985-96; sr. assoc. Behre Dolbear & Co. Inc., Corrales, N.Mex., 1996—. Mem. Pres. Club, Rep. Party, Corrales, N.Mex., 1997-99, Rep. Senatorial Inner Cir., Corrales, 1997-99; life mem. Rep. Nat. Com., Coralles, 1995-99. Fellow Geol. Soc. Am., Soc. Econ. Geologists; mem. AIME (dir. Ctrl. N.Mex. sect. 1986-90, pres. local sect. 1988-89), Geol. Soc. Nev. Avocations: classical history, astronomy, mountain climbing, white-water canoeing, skiing. Home and Office: Behre Dolbear & Co Inc 490 Manierre Rd Corrales NM 87048-8338 E-mail: ksageser@aol.com.

SAGET, BOB, director, actor, comedian, writer; Grad. film studies, Temple U., 1978. Host 2002 Winter Olympics. Appeared at Carnegie Hall, Las Vegas, Atlantic City, The Comedy Store, The Improv, Calif.; actor (films) Critical Condition, 1986, 1998, Half Baked, 1998; (TV) Full House, 1987-95; actor, exec. prodr. Father and Scout, 1994, Jitters, 1997; dir., exec. prodr. For Hope, 1997; co-host The Morning Program, 1986; host, writer: America's Funniest Home Videos, 1989-97; dir., actor, writer: HBO Comedy Hour: In The Dream State; dir. Dirty Work, 1998, Mind of the Married Man, 2001; dir., actor Becoming Dick, 2000; actor WB series Raising Dad, 2001—. Address: Brillstein/Grey Entertainment 9150 Wilshire Blvd Ste 350 Beverly Hills CA 90212-3453

SAGHIR, ADEL JAMIL, artist, painter, sculptor; b. Beirut, May 27, 1930; came to U.S., 1973; s. Jamil Khalil and Aisha Rachid (Mirii) S.; m. Jindriska Antonin Moucka, Aug. 24, 1968; children: Jamil, Ryan. BA, Am. U., Beirut, 1968, diploma in tchg., 1973; MFA, Pratt Inst., 1975; postgrad., NYU, 1976-79. Asst. prof. Fine Arts Inst., Lebanese U., Beirut, 1963-73; lectr. Am. Beirut U. Coll., 1972-73; adj. prof. Western Conn. State U., Danbury, 1988—; instr. sculpture, mural painting, art history Silvermine Sch. Art, New Canaan, Conn., 1989-98. Artist various murals and tapestries. Recipient 4th prize Alexandria Biennale, Egyptian Govt., 1963, 1st prize silk tapestries Nat. Contest Lebanon, 1965, 1st prize major sculpture monuments, 1966, 1st prize City Ctr. Sculpture Contest, 1969; Fine Arts scholar, Germany, Munic Acad., 1958-60; Fulbright-Hayes fellow NYU, N.Y.C., 1973-79. Mem. Internat. Soc. Advancement of Living Traditions in Art, Washington Pl. Artists Assn. (pres. 1977-80), Lebanese Artists Assn. (v.p. 1964-73). Avocations: gardening, fishing, upland hunting. Home: 20 Newfane Rd New Fairfield CT 06812-4721 Office: Western Conn State U 181 White St Danbury CT 06810-6826 Personal E-mail: ajsaghir@net.net.

SAGINOR, SIDNEY V. management consultant; b. London, May 28, 1909; s. Phillip Saginor Sr. and Polly Miller; m. Ruth K. Saginor, Dec. 13, 1935; children: Mark L., Gail J. Slater. BSME, Case Res. U., 1933. Registered profl. engr.; lic. real estate broker. Estimator, engr. Johns-Manville Corp., Cleve., 1928-35; mech. engr., heat transfer specialist Carbide & Carbon Chems. Corp., 1935-39; prodn. mgr. Davey Compressor Co., 1939-41, gen. mgr., 1941-46; 1st v.p., dir. Robinson Clay Products Co., Akron, Ohio, 1946-53; v.p. tech. svcs. Gladding, McBean & Co., L.A., 1953-57, v.p. corp. tech. planning & overseas assignments, 1958-61, v.p., gen. mgr. tech. ceramics divsn., 1961-64; exec. v.p., dir. Ilco Corp. (formerly Ind. Lock Co.), Fitchburg, Mass., 1964-67, pres., CEO, 1969-73; mgmt. cons., 1967-69, 73—. Fin. advisor Federally Registered Investment Advisor, Washington, 1975—; bd. dirs., CFO San Fernando Valley Mental Health Assn., Van Nuys, Calif., 1983-93, advisor, 1983—. Bd. dirs. Fitchburg C. of C., 1964-73; chmn. indsl. comm. Fitchburg Red Cross, 1966. Lt. U.S. Army Corps Engrs., 1939-43. Recipient Cert. Merit Office Sci. R&D Com., 1945. Mem. ASME (life, award), SAG, Nat. Soc. Profl. Journalists (life), Nat. Soc. Ceramic Engrs., Am. Ceramic Soc. (Emeritus award), Indsl. Rsch. Inst., Inc., Am. Mgmt. Assn., Nat. Clay Pipe Rsch. Corp., Am. Legion, Masons, Rotary, LA Press Club, Jonathan Club, Sigma Delta Chi. Home and Office: 5455 Zelzah Ave Unit 126 Encino CA 91316-2287 Office Phone: 818-705-6346.

SAGMEISTER, EDWARD FRANK, retired military officer, business owner; b. NYC, Dec. 10, 1939; s. Frank and Anna (Unger) S.; m. Anne Marie Ducker, Aug. 18, 1962; children: Cynthia Anne, Laura Marie, Cheryl Suzanne, Eric Edward. BS, U. San Francisco, 1962; MBA, Syracuse U., 1968; postgrad., Air Command and Staff Coll., 1977, Air War Coll., 1981. Commd. 2d lt. USAF, 1963, advanced through grades to lt. col., pers. officer, 1963, aide-de-camp, 1965; dir. pers. sys. Alaskan Air Command, 1968; sys. design and program analysis officer HQ USAF, The Pentagon, 1971; spl. asst. of the sec. Air Force Pers. Coun. USAF, 1975; dir. pers. programs and assignments HQUSAF Europe, 1979; Air Force dep. asst. inspector gen., 1982; ret. USAF, 1984; dir. devel. Am. Cancer Soc., Riverside, Calif., 1984-87; cons. Redlands, Calif., 1987-92; chmn. of bd., pres., CEO Hospitality Pub and Grub, Inc., San Bernardino, Calif., 1992—2002. Instr. Am. Internat. U., L.A., 1987; program dir. Am. Radio Network, L.A., 1987; ptnr., owner Midway Med. Ctr., San Bernardino, 1990-91; mem. Juvenile Justice and Delinquency Prevention Commn. San Bernardino County, 2003—. Foreman pro-tem San Bernardino County Grand Jury, 1990-91; mem. Redlands 2000 Com., 1988; campaign cabinet mem. Arrowhead United Way, San Bernardino, 1986-87, loaned exec., 1985; exec. dir. Crafton Hills Coll. Found., Yucaipa, Calif., 1988; vol. San Bernardino County Dept. Probation, 1985-88; mem. Redlands Cmty., Chorus, 1988-90; vice-chmn., charter mem. Redlands Human Rels. Commn., 1994-97, chmn., 1996-97; mem. Redlands Youth Accountability Bd., San Bernardino County, 1994-97, treas. 1996; mem. supt.'s human rels. adv. com., Redlands Unified Sch. Dist., 1996-97; vol. dir. music therapy program Loma Linda U. Med. Ctr., 2002—; active Inland Master Chorale, 2001-02; commr. Juvenile Justice and Delinquency Prevention Commn. San Bernardino County, 2003—. Mem. Mil. Officers Assn., Nat. Soc. Fundraising Execs., (dir., charter mem. Inland Empire chpt. 1987-88), Empire Singers (v.p. 1987), Air Force Assn. Republican. Roman Catholic. Avocations: travel, music, singing, tennis, reading. Home: 503 Sunnyside Ave Redlands CA 92373-5629

SAGURTON, WILMA, retired secondary school educator, musician, historian; b. Mendham, N.J., Feb. 19, 1916; d. David Minard and Nanna Mae (Mockridge) Lewis; m. James R. Sagurton, Sept. 24, 1937; children: Joan, Frances Seigle, James, David. BA bio., chem., music and geology, Montclair, 1937; dipolma math, Seton Hall, 1950; MA teaching Handicapped, Montclair State, 1971. Asst. bio. tchr. Montclair State U., 1936—37; tchr. sci. Bd. Of Edn., Bloomfield, 1937—62; tchr. elementary Bd. of Edn., Passaic, 1962—65; tchr. Sceep (Inner City), Newark, 1960—; organist, choir dir. Catholic Church, Mendham, 1950—63; tchr. piano private, 1940—; ret., 1980. Founder Mus. of Old Randolph, Randolph, NJ, 1985—. Co-author: Lewises of Combs Hollow, 1985; author: And then there was Lighting, 2002, Fireplace Cooking with Recipes, 2004. Local historian Mendham Township, 1984—; sec. Auxiliary Engine Company, Mendham, NJ, 1965; lectr. Nat. Register of historic sites, 1990—. Recipient Local Historian of the Yr., Heritage Com., 1991, Outstanding Vol. Cmty Svc. award, Mendham Twp., Athletic Letter, Fencing, Montclair State, 1933—37. Mem.: Chester Historical Soc., N.J. Retired Tchrs. Assn., Brookside Engine Co. No. 1 Auxiliary (life), John Ralston Historical Assn., CRAFTS, Garden Club (life; sec. 1989—91), Kappa Delta Pi. Democrat. Episcopalian. Avocations: music, photography, piano, historic preservation. Home: 159 Mountainside Rd Mendham NJ 07945

SAGY, MAYER, critical care physician; b. Isreal, Mar. 8, 1949; m. Yocheved Sagy; children: Liat, Ifat, Noa. MD, Sackler Sch. Medicine, Tel Aviv, Isreal, 1972. Bd. cert. pediatrics, critical care med. Asst. dir. PICU Chaim Sheba Medical Ctr., Tel Aviv, 1984—89; dir. pediat. critical care Morristown Mem. Hosp., NJ, 1989—91; chief pediat. critical care Schneider Children's Hosp., New Hyde Park, NY, 1991—; dir. critical care North Shore Long Island Jewish Health Sys., 2001—. Fellow: Am. Coll. Chest Physician; mem.: Soc. Critical Care Med., N.Y. Soc. Pediat. Critical Care Med. Office: Schneider Childrens Hosp 269-01 76 Ave New Hyde Park NY 11040 Office Fax: 718-470-0159. E-mail: sagym@lij.edu.

SAH, CHIH-TANG, electrical and computer engineering educator; b. Beijing, Nov. 10, 1932; s. Adam Peng-tung and Shu-shen Huang; m. Linda Chang, Nov. 29, 1959; children: Dinah W.Y., Robert L.Y. BS Physics, BSEE, U. Ill., 1953; MSEE, Stanford U., 1954, PhD, 1956; D honoris causa, U. Leuven, Belgium, 1975. Research assoc. Stanford Electronics Lab., Palo Alto, Calif., 1956; sr. mem. tech. staff Shockley Transistor Corp., Palo Alto, 1957-59; head, mgr. physics dept. Fairchild Semiconductor Lab., Palo Alto, 1959-64; prof. physics and elec. engring. U. Ill., Urbana, 1962-88, dir. Ill. Solid State Electronics Lab.; Pittman Eminent Scholar chair, grad. research prof., chief scientist Coll. Engring. U. Fla., Gainesville, 1988—. Cons. Jet Propulsion Lab., Dept. Energy, Pasadena, Calif., 1976-85, Harry Diamond Lab., Washington, 1974-75, IBM Corp., N.Y, numerous other electronics firms 1964-88; advisor Intel Corp., Oreg., Calif., other semicondr. mfrs., 1988—; program dir. 1st generation Si VLSI tech. Fairchild Corp., 1959-64. Author: Fundamentals of Solid-State Electronics, 1991, Transistor Reliability in Fundamentals of Solid-State Electronics—Solution Manual, 1996; co-developer Complementary Metal-Oxide Semiconductor circuit, 1962, other tech. discoveries and inventions; co-discoverer Si P-N junction diode phenomena (Sah-Noyce-Shockley Theory), 1957; co-inventor deep-level transient spectroscipy (Sah, Tasch, Yau), 1966-71, and DVIC diagnosis for deep-submicron transistor design and reliability (Sah, Neugroschel), 1996; contbr. 250 articles to profl. jours. Recipient first high tech. award Asian American Mfg. Assn., 1982; named 1 of 1000 World's Most Cited Scientists, 1965-78. Fellow IEEE (life, IRE Browder J. Thompson prize 1963, J.J. Ebers award 1980, Jack Morton award 1989), AAAS, Am. Physical Soc., Franklin Inst. (life mem., Cert. of Merit award 1975); mem. Nat. Acad. Engring., Academia Sinica (academician). Office: U Fla 216 Larsen Hall Gainesville FL 32611-6200

SAHA, ARUN KUMAR, engineering educator, researcher; b. Gauripur, Assam, India, May 7, 1967; s. Ramani Mohan and Arati Saha; m. Mira Saha, Apr. 26, 1970; 1 child, Arunima. B Mech. Engring., Gauhati U., Assam, India, 1990; M Mech. Tech., Indian Inst. Tech., Kanpur, India, 1994; PhD, Indian Inst. of Tech. Kanpur, India, 1999. Lectr. Jorhat Engring. Coll., Jorhat, India, 1992; asst. exec. engr. Oil & Natural Gas Corp., Sibsagar, India, 1993; post doctoral rsch. assoc. SUNY, Stony Brook, NY, 1999—2000, La. State U., Baton Rouge, 2000—. Contbr. chapters to books, articles to profl. jours. and confs. (Best Paper Award, 2000). Avocations: painting, art, gardening.

SAHA, ASIS KUMAR, cardiologist; b. Calcutta, West Bengal, India, June 14, 1941; came to U.S., 1966; s. Asoke Kumar and Swarna Prabha Saha; m. Barbara Ann Bialy, June 23, 1968; children: Kamala, Tiara, Michael, Stephen. MBBS, Calcutta U., 1963. Diplomate Am. Bd. Internal Medicine and Cardiovascular Diseases. Intern Med. Coll., Calcutta U., 1963; rotating intern Willingdon Hosp., New Delhi, India, 1964-65; rotating resident Safdarjung Hosp., New Delhi, 1965-66; rotating intern St. Peter's Gen. Hosp., Rutgers U., New Brunswick, N.J., 1966-67, med. resident New Burnswick, N.J., 1967-69, chief med. resident, 1969-70; cardiology fellow Mt. Sinai Med. Ctr., Miami Beach, Fla., 1970-72; staff cardiologist Kissimmee (Fla.) Meml. Hosp., 1973—, chmn. dept. medicine, 1973-87, 90—, dir. cardiopulminary dept., 1974-80, trustee, 1978—; practice medicine specializing in cardiology Kissimmee, 1973—. Mem. active staff Fla. Hosp. Kissimmee and Orlando, Orlando Regional Healthcare Sys. at St. Cloud and Orlando, Osceola Regional Hosp., Columbia Pk. Med. Ctr., Orlando, Heart of Fla. Hosp., Haines City, Fla. Fellow Am. Coll. Cardiology, Am. Coll. Chest Physicians, Coun. Clin. Cardiology, Am. Coll. Angiology, Internat. Coll. Angiology; mem. ACP, Am. Soc. Echocardiology, Am. Soc. Geriatric Medicine, Am. Soc. Nuclear Cardiology (founding), Am. Heart Assn. (pres. Ctrl. Fla. chpt. 1980, lic. in nuclear cardiology), Com. of 100, Kissimmee C. of C. Democrat. Hindu. Avocations: gardening, swimming, skiing. Office: 201 Hilda St Kissimmee FL 34741-2320

SAHA, SAMAR KANTI, electronics engineer, educator; arrived in U.S., 1981; s. Phani Bhusan and Mahamaya Saha. PhD, Gauhati U., India, 1981; MS in Engring. Mgmt., Stanford U., Calif., 1992. Asst. prof., elec. engring. So. Ill. U., Carbondale, 1982—84; sr. product engr. Nat. Semiconductor, Santa Clara, Calif., 1984—90; staff engr., R & D LSI Logic Corp., Santa Clara, 1990—92; prin. engr., tech. CAD Nat. Semiconductor, Santa Clara, 1992—95; prin. engr., advanced devel. Tex. Instruments, Santa Cruz, 1995—97; mgr., tech. CAD Philips Semiconductors, San Jose, 1997—2000; mgr., tech. modeling Silicon Storage Tech., Inc., Sunnyvale, 2000—. Contbr. scientific papers to profl. jours. Recipient Outstanding Achievement, Analog Divsn. Nat. Semiconductor, 1988, Tchg. Contbn., EE Dept., U. Nev. Las Vegas, 2002. Mem.: IEEE (mem. compact modeling com. 2001—04), Internat. Soc. Optical Engring. (corr.). Achievements include patents in field; research in scaling considerations for high performance 25 nm metal-oxide-semiconductor field-effect transistors; effects of inversion layer quantization on channel profile engineering for nMOSFETs with 0.1 m channel lengths; development of efficient approach for integrated circuit fabrication technology. Home: 286 Aspenridge Dr Milpitas CA 95035 Office: Silicon Storage Tech Inc 1171 Sonora Ct Sunnyvale CA 94086 Office Phone: 408-720-5478. Personal E-mail: samar@ieee.org. E-mail: ssaha@sst.com.

SAHA, UTTAM KUMAR, environmental scientist, researcher; b. Mirzapur, Pabna, Bangladesh, Sept. 30, 1961; s. Sachindra Nath and Gopi Rani Saha; m. Rupa Rani Saha, Mar. 1, 1962; 1 child, Anupam. PhD, Iwate Univ., Japan, 1996—99. Cert. profl. agrologist Bangladesh Agrl. Inst., 1987. Asst. prof. Bangabandhu Shiekh Mujibur Rahman Agrl. Univ., Salna, Bangladesh, 1993—99; vis. rsch. fellow Japan Soc. Promotion Sci., Tokyo, 1999—2001; postdoctoral rsch. fellow U. Saskatoon, Canada, 2001—03; vis. fellow Natural Sciences and Engring. Rsch. Coun. Can. Office: APCRC 25845 County Rd 20 Harrow ON Canada Office Phone: +1-519-738-2251. Business E-Mail: sahau@agr.gc.ca.

SAHAI, HARDEO, medical statistics educator; b. Bahraich, India, Jan. 10, 1942; m. Lillian Sahai, Dec. 28, 1973; 3 children. BS in Math., Stats. and Physics, Lucknow U., India, 1962; MS in Math., Banaras U., Varanasi, India, 1964; MS in Math. Stats., U. Chgo., 1968; PhD in Stats., U. Ky., 1971. Lectr. math. and stats. Banaras U., Varanasi, India, 1964—65; asst. stats. officer Durgapur Steel Plant, India, 1965; statistician Rsch. and Planning divsn. Blue Cross Assn., Chgo., 1966; statis. programmer Cleft Palate Ctr. U. Ill., 1967; statis. programmer Chgo. Health Rsch. Found., 1968; mgmt. scientist Mgmt. Sys. Devel. Dept. Burroughs Corp., Detroit, 1971—72; from asst. prof. to prof. dept. math. U. P.R., Mayaguez, 1972—82; vis. rsch. prof. Dept. Stats. and Applied Math. U. Ceara, Brazil, 1978—79; sr. rsch. statistician Travenol Labs., Inc., Round Lake, Ill., 1982—83; chief statistician U.S. Army Hqrs., Ft. Sheridan, Ill., 1983—84; sr. math. statistician U.S. Bur. Census Dept. Commerce, Washington, 1984—85; sr. ops. rsch. analyst Def. Logistics Agy. Dept. Def., Chgo., 1985—86; prof. Dept. Biostats. and Epidemiology U. P.R. Med. Scis., San Juan, 1986—. Cons. P.R. Univ Cons., P.R. Driving Safety Evaluation Project, Water Resources Rsch. Inst., Travenol Labs., Campo Rico, P.R., U.S. Bur. Census, Washington, Lawrence Livermore Nat. Lab., Calif., others; vis. prof. U. Granada, Spain, U. Veracruzana, Mex., patrimonial prof. stats., 1997—; vis. prof. U. Nacional de Colombia, U. Nacional de Trujillo, Peru, 1993-94, hon. prof. stats., 1994—; adj. prof. dept. math. U. P.R. Natural Scis. Faculty, 1995—; Patrimonial prof. stafs U. Veracruzana, 1997—. Author: Statistics and Probability: Learning Module, 1984; author: (with Jose Berrios) A Dictionary of Statistical Scientific and Technical Terms: English-Spanish and Spanish-English, 1981, (with Wilfredo Martinez) Statistical Tables and Formulas for the Biological Social and Physical Sciences, 1996, (with Anwer Khurshid) Statistics in Epidemiology: Methods, Techniques and Applications, 1996, (with Satish C. Misra and Michael Graham) Quotations on Probability and Statistics with Illustrations, 2000, (with Anwer Khurshid) A Pocket Dictionary of Statistics, 2000, (with Mohammad I. Ageel) The Analysis of Variance: Fixed, Random and Mixed Models, 2000, (with Wilfredo Martnez) Statistical Glossary: English-Spanish, 2000, (with Lucas López Segovia and Hector W. Colón-Rosa) A Glossary of Medical Epidemiologic and Demographic Statistics: English-Spanish, 2002, (with Mario M. Ojeda) Un Manual de Distribuciones t, x2y F Centrales Y No Centrales, 2000, (with Mario M. Ojeda) A Glossary of Computer and Management Terms: English/Spanish, 2000, (with Mario M. Ojeda) Comparisons of Approximations to the Percentiles of Noncentral t, x2 and F Distributions, 2001, (with A. Khurshid) Pocket Dictionary of Statistics, 2001, Noncentral t, x2y and F Distributions, 1998, Analysis of Variance for Random Models, Vol. 1: Balanced Data and Vol. 2: Unbalanced Data, 2002; mem. editl. bd. Sociedad Colombiana de Matematicas, P.R. Health Scis. Jour.; contbr. editor Current Index to Stats.; reviewer Collegiate Microcomputer, Comm. in Statistics, Indian Jour. Stats., Jour. Royal Statis. Soc. (series D, The Statistician), New Zealand Statistician, Biometrics, Can. Jour. Stats., Technometrics, Problems, Resources and Issues in Math. Undergrad. Studies; contbr. more than 150 articles and papers to profl. and sci. jours., numerous articles to tech. mags. Active Dept. Consumer Affairs Svcs. Commonwealth of P.R., San Juan, Dept. Anti-Addiction Svcs., Commonwealth of P.R., San Juan., Inst. of AIDS, Municipality of San Juan, VA Med. Ctr. of San Juan, Caribbean Primate Rsch. Ctr., Ctr. Addiction Studies Caribbean Ctrl. U. Recipient Dept. Army Cert. Achievement award, 1984, U. Ky. Outstanding Alumnus award, 1993, medal of honor U. Granada, 1994, plaque of honor U. Nacional de Trujillo, 1994; fellow Coun. Sci. and Indsl. Rsch., 1964-65, U. Chgo., 1965-68, Harvard U., 1979, Fulbright Found., 1982; U.P. Bd. Merit scholar, 1957-59, Govt. India Merit scholar, 1959-64; grantee NSF, 1974-77, NIMH, 1987-90, 91—, NIDA, 1991—. Fellow AAAS, Am. Coll. Epidemiology, Inst. Statisticians (charter statistician), Inst. Math. and Its Applications (charter mathematician), N.Y. Acad. Scis., Royal Statis. Soc.; mem. Internat. Statis. Inst., Internat. Assn. Tchg. Stats., Soc. Epidemiol. Rsch., Inst. Math. Stats., Bernouilli Soc. for Math. Stats. and Probability, Internat. Biometric Soc., Am. Soc. for Quality Control, Am. Stats. Assn., Japan Statis. Soc., Can. Statis. Soc., Inter-Am. Statis. Inst., Internat. Assn. Statis. Computing, Sch. Sci. and Math. Assn., Sigma Xi. Avocations: religious studies, philosophy, reading, gardening. Home: Urb Mayaguez Terrace 7083 Calle B Gaudier Texidor Mayaguez PR 00682-6617 E-mail: hsahai@centennialpr.net.

SAHANI, DUSHYANT V. radiologist, educator; b. Nagpur, MS, India, June 2, 1969; arrived in U.S., 1999; s. Vasudeo H. and Sulochana V. Sahani; m. Nita N. Nagpal, Feb. 26, 1995; 1 child, Vyoma. MB BS, P.D.M. Med. Coll., 1992; DMRD, Tata Cancer Hosp., 1995, MD, 1996; D, Nat. Bd., 1996. House officer Pediat. Centenar Hosp., Mumbai, India, 1992; house officer Medicine Masina Gen. Hosp., Mumbai, 1992—93; clin. asst., clin. assoc. P.D. Hinduja Hosp., Mumbai, 1996—98; rsch. fellow, clin. fellow Mass. Gen. Hosp., Boston, 1999—2002; clin. instr. Harvard Med. Sch., Mass. Gen. Hosp., Boston, 2002—. Contbr. articles to profl. jours., chpts. in books. Recipient First Time Presenter award, Soc. Gastrointestinal Radiology, 2002. Fellow: Radiol. Soc. N.Am. (Rsch. Trainee award 2001), Am. Roentgen Ray Soc. (Bronze medal 2002, 2003). Avocations: reading, kayaking. Home: 5 Stone Rd Arlington MA 02474 Office: Mass Gen Hosp 55 Fruit St Boston MA 02114

SAHATJIAN, MANIK, retired nurse, retired psychologist; b. Tabris, Iran, July 24, 1921; came to U.S., 1951; d. Dicran and Shushanig (Der-Galustian) Mnatzaganian; m. George Sahatjian, Jan. 21, 1954; children: Robert, Edwin. Nursing Cert., Am. Mission Hosps.-Boston U., 1954; BA in Psychology, San Jose State U., 1974, MA in Psychology, 1979. RN Calif. Head nurse Am. Mission Hosp., Tabris, 1945-46; charge nurse Banke-Melli Hosp., Tehran, 1946-51; vis. nurse Vis. Nurse Assn., Oakland, Calif., 1956-57; research asst. Stanford U., 1979-81, Palo Alto (Calif.) Med. Research Found., 1981-84; documentation supr. Bethesda Convalescent Ctr., Los Gatos, Calif., 1985-86; sr. outreach worker City of Fremont (Calif.) Human Svcs., 1987-90, case mgr., 1990-97; ret., 1997. Guest rsch. asst. NASA Ames Lab., Mountain View, Calif., summers 1978, 79. Author (with others) psychol. research reports. Mentor elem. sch. children, 1997-2002; pro bono tchg./counseling for srs. who are home bound, Bay Area, Calif., 1999—; pro bono tchr. peer counseling

trainers for srs. Armenian Cmty. Santa Clara, Calif., St. Andrew Ch. Fulbright scholar, 1951; Iran Found. scholar, 1953; Morgan-Segal scholar for peer counseling tng., 1998. Mem. AAUW, Western Psychol. Assn., Am. Assn. Sr. Counseling. Democrat. Mem. St. Andrew Armenian Church. Achievements include fluency in Armenian, Farsi, Turkish, familiarity in Spanish, Russian, French langs. Avocations: painting, classic dance. Home: 339 Starlite Way Fremont CA 94539-7642

SAHATJIAN, RONALD ALEXANDER, science foundation executive; b. Cambridge, Mass., Oct. 1, 1942; s. Vartan and Roxy (Abrahamian) S.; m. Jean Khachadoorian, July 15, 1966; 1 child, Jennifer. BS in Chemistry, Tufts U., 1964; MS in Chemistry, U. Mass., 1968, PhD in Chemistry, 1969. Scientist color photographic rsch. lab. Polaroid Corp., Cambridge, 1971-73, sr. scientist color photograhic rsch. lab., 1973-75, sr. rsch. group leader photographic/optical materials, 1976-79, program mgr. polacolor transparency projects, 1979-81, mgr. applications rsch. lab., 1980-84; dir. R & D Chem. Fabrics Corp., Merrimack, N.H., 1984-87; v.p. corp. tech. Boston Sci. Corp., Watertown, Mass., 1987—. Mem. adv. bd. Franklin Inst., Boston, 1989—. Contbr. articles to Jour. Polymer Sci., Macromolecules, Radiology. Fellow Am. Inst. Chemists; mem. ASTM, Radiol. Soc. N.Am., Watertown C. of C. (bd. dirs. 1991—). Achievements include 58 U.S. and internat. patents. Home: 29 Saddle Club Rd Lexington MA 02420-2121 Office: Boston Sci Corp 1 Boston Scientific Pl Natick MA 01760-1536 E-mail: sahatjian@bsci.com.

SAHID, JOSEPH ROBERT, lawyer; b. Paterson, NJ, Feb. 14, 1944; s. Joseph James and Helen (Vitale) Sahid; m. Serra Yavuz; children: Annunziata, Joseph, Olivia. BS, Rutgers U., 1965; LLB, U. Va., 1968. Bar: NY 1973, US Dist. Ct. NY, US Ct. Appeals (2d and 3d cirs.), US Supreme Ct. Staff mem. Nat. Commn. Causes Prevention Violence, Washington, 1968-69; cons. Pres.'s Commn. Campus Unrest, Washington, 1970; assoc. Cravath, Swaine & Moore, NYC, 1972-77, ptnr., 1977-93, cons., 1994-97; ptnr. Barrack, Rodos & Bacine, NYC, 1995—96; pvt. practice NYC, 1996—. Mediator US Dist. Ct. (so. dist.) NY, NY Civil Ct.; arbitrator NY cts. Author: (book) Rights in Concord, 1969; co-author: Law and Order Reconsidered, 1969; contbr. articles to profl. jours. Lt. USCG, 1968—72. Mem.: ABA, Assn. Bar City NY (profl. discipline com.), NY State Bar Assn. (profl. discipline com. 2001—03, profl. responsibility com., coun. children com.). Address: 845 3rd Ave Fl 20 New York NY 10022-6601 Office Phone: 212-308-5930. E-mail: sahid@nysbar.com.

SAHINALP, SULEYMAN CENK, computer scientist; b. Ankara, Turkey, Jan. 18, 1969; married, Apr. 4, 1968. PhD, U. Md., 1997. Rschr. Bell Labs., Murray Hill, NJ, 1996—97; asst. prof. Warwick U., 1997—99, Case Western Res. U., Cleve., 1999—, Glennan tchg. fellow. Rschr. U. Pa., Phila., 1997—99; PC chmn. Combinatorial Pattern Matching Symposium, 2003; mem. numerous internat. confs. and symposia in computer sci.; Glennan Teaching Fellow. Contbr. articles to profl. jours. Fellow, Fulbright Found.; grantee, NSF, NASA, NIH, Charles B. Wang Found. Mem.: Ctr. for Computational Genomics. Achievements include 2 U.S. patents, 2 pending US patents on data compression and circuit layouts.

SAHOO, SANGRAMA KESARI, physical chemist, researcher; b. Cuttack, Orissa, India, Jan. 5, 1973; s. Purna Chandra and Kumudini Sahoo; m. Sujata Sahoo, Dec. 2, 2001. BS, Utkal U., Bhubaneswar, India, 1992, MS, 1995; PhD in Chemistry, Indian Inst. of Petroleum, Dehradun, India, 2000. Rsch. scholar Ravenshaw Coll., Cuttack, India, 1995—96; CSIR jr. rsch. fellow Indian Inst. of Petroleum, Dehradun, India, 1996—98, CSIR sr. rsch. fellow, 1998—2000; NSF post-doc rsch. assoc. U. Mass., Lowell, 2000—02; rsch. assoc. U. Akron, Ohio, 2002—. Author: (scientific monograph) Understanding the Mechanism of Polymerization of Engring. Polymeric Materials by In-situ NMR Spectroscopy: Poly(Phenols), ACS Symp. Ser. 2002, 834, 258-269., 2002; contbr. articles to sci. jours. Recipient Narayanee Mohanty award, Ravenshaw Coll., India, 1995; GATE fellowship, Govt. of India, 1995, NET fellowship, CSIR, India, 1996, Travel grant to ACS Nat. Meeting, New Orleans, La., CSIR and DST, India, 1999, Am. Chem. Soc., 1999. Mem.: Internat. Soc. of Magnetic Resonance, Am. Chem. Soc., Indian Soc. for Analytical Scientists (life). Achievements include research in NMR Methods for structural characterization of polymers. Office: U Akron 190 E Buchtel Commons Akron OH 44325-3601 E-mail: sahoo@uakron.edu.

SAHOTA, AMRIK, medical researcher, educator, lab administrator; s. Sadhu Milkhy and Rao Kaur; m. Nirmala Thapar; children: Aneil, Jessica. BS in Biochemistry, Bath U., 1974; MS in Medicinal Chemistry, Loughborough U., 1976; PhD in Med. Genetics, Guy's Hosp. Med. Sch., London U., 1980. Diplomate Clin. Molecular Genetics Am. Bd. of Med. Genetics, 1993; Chartered Biologist Inst. of Biology, U.K., 2002. Postdoctoral fellow Aston U., Dept Molecular Scis., Birmingham, England, 1980—83; biochemist Gen. Hosp., Dept Hematology, Birmingham, England, 1983—85; rsch. assoc. Ind. U., Dept. Biology, Bloomington, Ind., 1985—87; lab. dir. Ind. U. Med. Sch., Dept Med. and Molecular Genetics, Indpls., 1988—98; prof. genetics Rutgers U., Dept. Genetics, Piscataway, NJ, 1998—; lab. dir. Robert Wood Johnson U. Hosp., Dept. Pathology, New Brunswick, NJ, 2001—. Cons. Indpls.-Marion County Forensic Sci. Lab., 1991—98; adj. prof. dept. pathology Robert Wood Johnson Med. Sch., U. Medicine and Dentistry, NJ, 2001—. Author: (book chpt.) The Metabolic and Molecular Bases of Inherited Disease; editor: (conf. proceedings) Purine and Pyrimidine Metabolism in Man; author: (sci. rsch. paper) Jour. of Histochemistry and Cytochemistry, Exptl. Nephrology, Kidney Internat., Clin. Transplantation, Neurology, Am. Jour. Physiology, Exptl. Hematology, Proceedings Nat. Acad. Scis., Clin. Biochemistry. Adminstr. India Cmty. Ctr., Indpls., 1996; com. mem. Boy Scouts, Indpls., 1992—95; asst. troop leader with activities and transp. Girl Scouts, Indpls., 1997—99, Hillsborough, NJ, 2000—02; communicator Hillsborough Twp. Bd. of Edn., NJ, 2002. Fellow, Am. Coll. of Med. Genetics, 1996, Inst. of Biology, U.K., 2002. Mem.: Assn. Molecular Pathology, Royal Coll. Pathologists, Soc. for Study of Inborn Errors of Metabolism, Brit. Soc. of Human Genetics, Am. Soc. of Human Genetics, Am. Assn. of Clin. Chemistry, AAAS. Achievements include research in Genetic basis of kidney stone disease. Avocations: travel, reading, health and fitness. Office: Rutgers Univ Dept Genetics Nelson Labs 604 Allison Rd Piscataway NJ 08854-8082

SAHOTA, GURCHARN SINGH, mechanical engineer; b. Talwandi Jattan, Punjab, India, Jan. 4, 1940; arrived in US, 1971, naturalized, 1980; s. Karam Singh and Amar Kaur (Nijjar) S.; m. Gurvindar Kaur Johal, May 4, 1966 (dec. Mar. 1978); 1 child, Saryadvinder Singh; m. Kamaljit Kaur Grewal, Jan. 10, 1979; children: Parmeet Kaur, Sonia K. BS in Mech. Engring., Punjab U., 1961; MS in Mech. Engring., NJ Inst. Tech., 1977. Engr. Heavy Elecs., Bhopal, India, 1962—70; mfg. engr. Engelhard Industries, Union, NJ, 1974—76; sr. plant engr., supr. plant engring. group Am. Cyanamid Co., Stamford, Conn., 1976—93; mgr. plant engring. Cytec Industries Inc., Stamford, 1994—. Home: 34 Duke Dr Stamford CT 06905-1017 Office: Cytec Industries Inc 1937 W Main St Stamford CT 06902-4516 Office Phone: 203-321-2435. Business E-Mail: gurcharn.sahota@cytec.com.

SAHR, MORRIS GALLUP, financial planner; b. Schenectady, Nov. 28, 1928; s. Nathan and Esther (Gallup) S.; m. Sarah Diane Eisenberg, Dec. 23, 1956; children: Evelyn, David, Janet. AB, U. Oreg., 1951, MA, 1953; PhD, Calif. Open U., Oakland, 1978. CFP. Pres. Deposit Mgmt. Svc., Inc., Palmyra, Va., 1978—. Pres. Am. Coll. Funding. Author: Nine Ways to Beat the High Cost of College, 1999, Annuity Owners' Mistakes, 2002; co-author: Your Book of Financial Planning, 1983, Encyclopedia of Financial Planning, 1984, The Financial Planner, 1986, Financial Planning Can Make You Rich, 1987. Chmn. Fairfax County Planning Commn., 1964-68; del. White House Conf. on Aging, 1980, U.S. Congl. Adv. Bd., 1984-87; bd. dirs. Fairfax Indsl. Devel. Authority, 1985-95; adjudicator Am. Arbitration Assn., 1988-99; del to China, People to People Amb. Program, 2000. Recipient award Danforth Found.; named 1 of Top 200 Planners in U.S., Money Mag.; hon. fellow Kennedy Libr., 1985; Paul Harris fellow, 1989. Mem. Internat. Assn. Fin. Planning (founder, 1st pres. Metro Washington chpt.), Inst. Cert. Fin. Planners (nat. govt. affairs com.), Am. Assn. Practicing Fin. Planners (past pres.), Internat. Assn. of Registered Fin. Cons., Rotary (pres. Fairfax 1984-85, Srs. Project Internat. award). Home and Office: DMS Inc 61 Wildwood Dr Palmyra VA 22963-2225 E-mail: dms@ntelos.net.

SAIBLE, STEPHANIE IRENE, magazine editor; b. Mobile, Ala., Sept. 11, 1954; d. Lewis J. Slaff and Phoebe-Jane (Berse) Meiss. Student, Va. Commonwealth U., 1972—75. Editorial asst. Woman's World Magazine, Englewood, NJ, 1980—81, service copywriter, 1981—83, assoc. articles editor, 1983—84, articles editor, 1984—85, sr. editor features dept., 1985—86, sr. editor services dept., 1986, now editor-in-chief, 1994—. Contbr. articles to Woman's World, Modern Bride, New Body, Celebrity Beauty, Trim and Fit, Ladies Home Jour. Named Wonder Woman of the Yr., Bus. Jour., N.J., 1986. Mem.: Women in Comms. Office: Woman's World Mag 270 Sylvan Ave Englewood Cliffs NJ 07632-2521

SAIDA, TOYOYASU, chemical and biochemical engineer; b. Tokyo, Jan. 18, 1935; came to U.S., 1985; s. Tameo and Fukiko Saida; m. Mariko Itano, Jan. 16, 1960; children: Tetsuo, Miyoko Asahi, Takashi Saida. BS, U. Tokyo, 1958. Registered profl. engr., Japan. Ops. engr. Toyo Gas Chems. Corp., Niigata, Japan, 1958-59; rschr. Tokyo Inst. of Tech., 1959-61; rsch. engr. Mitsui-Toatsu Chems. Ltd., Yokohama, Japan, 1961-69, chief rsch. engr., 1969-78; mgr. process rsch. divsn. Toyo Engring. Corp., Mobara, Japan, 1978-84, adv. bd. mem. Chiba, Japan, 1984-85; sr. v.p. BW Biotec, Inc., Chgo., 1985-86; gen. mgr. Hazarmacorp Rsch. Ctr., Tsukuba, Japan, 1987-95; mng. dir. Saida & Assocs., Deerfield, Ill., 1997—. Author: Handbook of Membrane Technology, 1978, Handbook of Bioprocess, 1985, Cellulose, 1986. Recipient Excellent Invention of Yr. Sci. and Tech. Agy., 1965. Mem. Am. Chem. Soc., Soc. of Chem. Engrs. Japan. Achievements include invention of innovative new synthetic method of urea, large scale manufacturing process of single cell protein from n-paraffin, fuel alcohol manufacturing process from lignocellulosics, volume reduction method of radioactive wastes with liquid phase oxidation. Home and Office: 431 Kelburn Rd Apt 315 Deerfield IL 60015-4367 E-mail: tomsaida@aol.com.

SAIDEL, GERALD MAXWELL, biomedical engineering educator; b. New Haven, May 27, 1938; BChemE, Rensselaer Poly Inst., 1960; PhD, Johns Hopkins U., 1965. Asst. prof. Case Western Res., 1967-73, assoc. prof., 1973-81, prof., 1981—, dept. chair., 1987-98. Bd. dirs. MIMS Ctr.; dir. Ctr. for Modeling Integrated Metabolic Sys. Mem.: AIMBE, Biomed. Engring. Soc. (pres. 1986—87). Office: Case Western Res U Dept Biomed Engring Cleveland OH 44106

SAIDI, PARVIN, hematologist, medical educator; b. Teheran, Iran, Mar. 21, 1932; came to U.S., 1946; d. Ahmad and Fatemeh (Ashouri) S.; m. Allahverdi Farmanfarmaian, May 27, 1958; children: Dellara Farmanfarmaian Terry, Kimya Farmanfarmaian Harris. BS, Smith Coll., Northampton, Mass., 1952; MD, Harvard U., 1956. Diplomate Am. Bd. Internal Medicine, subspecialty hematology and med. oncology. Intern medicine UCLA Med. Ctr., 1956-57; resident internal medicine U. Calif., San Francisco, 1957-59; NIH rsch. fellow hematology U. Calif. Hosps. and Children's Med. Ctr., San Francisco, 1959-61, 63-64; asst. prof. medicine U. Medicine & Dentistry N.J.-Rutgers Med. Sch., New Brunswick, 1968-71, assoc. prof., 1971-74; prof. U. Medicine & Dentistry N.J.-Robert Wood Johnson Med. Sch., New Brunswick, 1974—, chief divsn. hematology and oncology, dept. medicine, 1972—, Robert Wood Johnson U. Hosp., New Brunswick, 1981—. Cons. internist, hematologist, oncologist St. Peter's Med. Ctr., New Brunswick, Douglass Coll., Rutgers U., New Brunswick, VA Hosp., Lyons, N.J., Muhlenberg Hosp., Plainfield, N.J., Princeton (N.J.) Med. Ctr.; dir. Melvyn H. Motolinsky Lab. Hematology Rsch., N.J. Regional Comprehensive Hemophilia Care Program; mem. Gov.'s Adv. Coun. on AIDS; chmn. N.J. Regional Comprhensive Hemophilia Care Program Adv. Bd.; chmn. HHS region II Comprehensive Hemophilia Diagnostic and Treatment Ctrs., 1984-85, 89-90, 94-95, 99-2000; chmn. med. adv. bd. Hemophilia Found. N.J.; mem. med. adv. exec. com. N.J. Blood Svcs. Cons. editor Am. Jour. Medicine; contbr. articles to profl. jours. Recipient disting. svc. award for rsch. in leukemia Melvyn H. Motolinsky Rsch. Found., 1977, Humanitarian award Hemophilia Assn. No. N.J., 1978. Fellow ACP (mem. sci. program com. N.J. region), Acad. Medicine N.J.; mem. Am. Soc. Hematology (edn. com.), N.J. Hemophilia Assn. (chmn. med. adv. com., spl. award, Dr. L. Michael Kuhn Meml. award 1996), Coop. Oncology Group N.J. (exec. com., chairperson subcom. on lymphoma), Am. Heart Assn. (coun. on thrombosis), Am. Fedn. Clin. Rsch., Royal Soc. Medicine (affiliate), Am. Soc. Clin. Oncology, World Fedn. Hemophilia, Alpha Omega Alpha, Phi Beta Kappa, Sigma Xi. Office: Robert Wood Johnson Med Sch 1 Robert Wood Johnson Pl New Brunswick NJ 08901-1928

SAIED, JAMES GUY, conductor, consultant; b. Wirt, Okla., June 14, 1915; s. Oscar and Minnie (Adwan) S.; m. Helen Louella Ricker, Feb. 14, 1943; children: James Robert, Delia Ann Pierson. Ba, East Cen. U., Ada., Okla., 1936; postgrad., Vandercook Sch. Music. Cert. pub. sch. tchr. Band dir. Stroud (Okla.) Pub. Schs., 1936, Guthrie (Okla.) Pub. Schs., 1937-40, El Reno (Okla.) Pub. Schs. and Jr. Colls., 1940-42; ret. Music industry exec.; condr. of Univ., profl., mil. and community bands nationwide; cons., condr. John Sousa Concerts, 1981—. Found, condr. Oil Capitol Concert Band, Tulsa, 1959-62; condr. Tulsa Starlight Profl. Band, 1967-70; bd. dirs. Okla. Soc. Crippled Children, 1980—, Jr. Achievement, 1982-84. With U.S. Army, 1942-45, ETO. Decorated Bronze Star; named Disting. Alumnus East Cen. U., 1990; recipient Honor medal DAR, 1988, Order of Merit, John Philip Sousa Found., 1991, Nat. Good Citizen award SAR, 1992, Phi Beta Mu Internat. Outstanding award, 1990, George Washington Honor medal Freedoms Found., 1992, Will Rogers Ann. Spirit award, 1999, Outstanding Contbn. to Music Edn. award Okla. Bandmasters Assn., 1999, Okla. Gov.'s Arts Cmty. award, 2000. Mem. Nat. Assn. Music Merchants (bd. dirs. 1962-65, 71-74), Am. Bandmasters Assn. (hon. award 1988), Nat. Band Assn. (Citation of Excellence 1984, 86), Associated Concert Bands of Am., Rotary (pres. 1976-77, Outstanding Rotarian of Yr. dist. 6110 1981), Masons, Knife & Fork Club (pres. 1977-78), Kappa Kappa Psi (Disting. Svc. to Music award 1989). Democrat. Methodist. Home: 5832 S Florence Ave Tulsa OK 74105-7424 Office: PO Box 4684 Tulsa OK 74159-0684 Personal E-mail: jsaied@cox.net.

SAIF, LINDA J. animal scientist; Bachelor's, Coll. Wooster, 1969; master's, Ohio State U., 1971, doctorate in Microbiology/Immunology, 1976; doctorate (hon.), Ghent U., Belgium, 2003. Prof. OARDC Ohio State U., Wooster, 1979—, disting. univ. prof., 2002—. Contbr. articles to profl. jours. Mem.: NAS. Office: Food Animal Health Rsch Program OARDC 118 Food Animal Health Bldg Wooster OH 44691

SAIFER, MARK GARY PIERCE, pharmaceutical executive; b. Phila., Sept. 16, 1938; s. Albert and Sylvia (Jolles) S.; m. Phyllis Lynne Trommer, Jan. 28, 1961 (dec.); children: Scott David, Alandria Gail; m. Merry R. Sherman, June 26, 1994. AB, U. Pa., 1960; PhD, U. Calif., Berkeley, 1966. Acting asst. prof. zoology U. Calif., Berkeley, 1966, fellow, 1967-68; sr. cancer rsch. scientist Roswell Park Meml. Inst., Buffalo, 1968-70; lab. dir. Diagnostic Data Inc., Palo Alto, Calif., 1970-78; v.p. DDI Pharms., Inc., Mountain View, Calif., 1978-94, Oxis Internat., Inc., 1994-95; v.p., sci. dir. Mountain View Pharms., Inc., Menlo Park, Calif., 1996—, also bd. dirs. Lectr., expert witness in field. Author, patentee in field:, mem. editl. bd.: Current Pharm. Biotechnology Jour. Mem. AAAS (life), Am. Assn. Pharm. Scientists, Parenteral Drug Assn. Home: 1114 Royal Ln San Carlos CA 94070-4277 Office: Mountain View Pharms Inc 3475 Edison Way Ste S Menlo Park CA 94025-1821 E-mail: saifer@mvpharm.com.

SAIKEVYCH, IRENE A. pathologist; b. Perth Amboy, N.J., Oct. 16, 1950; d. Victor C. and Maria (Shomber) S.; divorced; 1 child, Natalie S. White. BA in Chemistry, U. Ill., 1972; MD, Northwestern, 1976. Diplomate Am. Bd. Med. Genetics; cert. pathologist. Resident Northwestern U., Honolulu, 1976-81; fellow in cytogenetics U. Hawaii, Honolulu, 1982-84, dir. cytogenetics rsch. lab., 1985-92, asst. prof. to assoc. prof. Dept. Pathology, 1982-92; med. dir. clin. cytogenetics Dept. Pathology St. Francis Hosp., Honolulu, 1988-92; staff pathologist Presbyn. Hosp., Charlotte, N.C., 1993—, dir. genetic svcs., 1993—. Contbr. numerous articles to profl. jours. Fellow Am. Coll. Med. Genetics (founder); mem. AAAS, AMA, Coll. Am. Pathologists (cytogenetics resource com. 1987—), Am. Soc. Human Genetics, Am. Soc. Hematology. Avocations: classical music, hiking, dance, painting, reading. Office: Presbyn Hosp Path Lab Med 200 Hawthorne Ln Charlotte NC 28204-2515

SAIKI, PATRICIA (MRS. STANLEY MITSUO SAIKI), former federal agency administrator, former congresswoman; b. Hilo, Hawaii, May 28, 1930; d. Kazuo and Shizue (Inoue) Fukuda; m. Stanley Mitsuo Saiki, June 19, 1954; children: Stanley Mitsuo, Sandra Saiki Williams, Margaret C., Stuart K., Laura H. BA, U. Hawaii, 1952. Tchr. U.S. history Punahou Sch., Kaimuki Intermediate Sch., Kalani High Sch., Honolulu, 1952-64; sec. Rep. Party Hawaii, Honolulu, 1964-66, vice chmn., 1966-68, 82-83, chmn., 1983-85; rsch. asst. Hawaii State Senate, 1966-68; mem. Hawaii Ho. of Reps., 1968-74, Hawaii State Senate, 1974-82, 100th-101st Congresses from 1st Hawaii dist., Washington, 1987-91; adminstr. SBA, Washington, 1991-93. Mem. Pres.'s Adv. Coun. on Status of Women, 1969-76; mem. Nat. Commn. Internat. Women's Yr., 1969-70; commr. We. Interstate Commn. on Higher Edn.; fellow Eagleton Inst., Rutgers U., 1970; fellow Inst. of Politics, Kennedy Sch. Govt., Harvard U., 1993; bd. dirs. Bank of Am.-Hawaii, Landmark Systems Corp., Internat. Asset Recovery Corp.; mem. nat. selection com. Innovations in Am. Govt., Ford Found., Harvard U., 1999-2002. Mem. Kapiolano Hosp. Aux.; sec. Hawaii Rep. Com., 1964-66, vice chmn., 1966-68, chmn., 1983-85; del. Hawaii Constl. Conv., 1968; alt. del. Rep. Nat. Conv., 1968, del., 1984, Rep. nominee for lt. gov. Hawaii, 1982, for U.S. Senate, 1990, for. gov. Hawaii, 1994; mem. Fedn. Rep. Women; trustee Hawaii Pacific Coll.; past bd. govs. Boys and Girls Clubs Hawaii; mem. adv. coun. ARC; bd. dirs. Nat. Fund for Improvement of Post-Secondary Edn., 1982-85; past bd. dirs. Straub Med. Rsch. Found., Honolulu, Hawaii's Visitors Bur., Honolulu, Edn. Commn. of States, Honolulu, Hawaii Visitors Bur., 1983-85; trustee U. Hawaii Found., 1984-86, Hawaii Pacific Coll., Honolulu; bd. govs. East West Ctr., 2003—. Republican. Episcopalian. Avocation: golf. Home: 784 Elepaio St Honolulu HI 96816-4710

SAIL, JOHN, computer company executive; Co-founder, exec. v.p. SAS Inst. Inc., Cary, NC, 1976—. Office: SAS Inst Inc 100 SAS Cmpus Dr Cary NC 27513-2414

SAILORS, PAMELA RENE', philosophy educator; d. Rebecca Jane and Wilmer Larry Sailors. BA, Wesleyan Coll., Macon, Ga., 1990; PhD, U. Ga., 1996. Assoc. prof. S.W. Mo. State U., Springfield, 1996—. Contbr. articles to profl. jours. Mem. ethics com. Cox Health Systems, Springfield, Mo., 1998—2003; mem. St. John's Health Sys. Instl. Rev. Bd., Springfield, Mo., 1998—2003. Mem.: Feminist Ethics and Social Theory Soc., Soc. for Women in Philosophy, Am. Soc. for Bioethics and Humanities, Am. Philos. Soc., Phi Eta Sigma (hon.). D-Liberal. Methodist. Avocations: running, hiking, travel. Office: SW Mo State Univ 901 S National Ave Springfield MO 65804

SAIN, CHARLES (HACK SAIN), civil engineer, surveyor; b. New Market, Ala., Jan. 20, 1923; s. Will Oris and Clayta (Speck) Sain; m. Marie Myers, Aug. 8, 1942; children: Charles R., Elizabeth Lester Stockdale, Ann Marie Hays; m. Helen Weil, Mar. 18, 2000. BSCE, U. Fla., 1949. Registered profl. engr., Ala., Ariz., Colo., Conn., Fla., Ga., Ill., Ind., Iowa, Kans., Ky., La., Minn., Miss., N.J., N.Y., N.C., Okla., Pa., S.C., S.D., Tenn., Vt., Va., W.Va., Wis. V.p. engring. Moss-Thornton Co., Inc., Leeds, Ala., 1946-59; gen. mgr. Vecellio & Grogan, Beckley, W.Va., 1960-64; v.p. engring. A.E. Burgess Co., Inc., Birmingham, Ala., 1964-67; pres. Charles H. Sain Assocs., Birmingham, 1968-89, Sain South Engring., Birmingham, 1978-89; CEO, chmn. bd. dirs. Sain Assocs., Inc., Birmingham, 1989—. Bd. visitors civil engring. dept. Coll. Engring. U. Ala., Birmingham; lectr. Auburn U., 1971, 72. Author: (with others) Standard Handbook for Civil Engineers, 1968, 4th edit., 1996; contbr. articles to profl. jours. Bd. dirs. State of Ala. Toll Bridge Authority, 1970-74; city engr. City of Vestavia Hilla, Ala., 1976-88, City of Homewood, Ala., 1976-80; vice chmn., bd. dirs. Ala. Bapt. Retirement Ctrs., Montgomery, 1986-93; mem. Vestavia Hills, Ala. Bd. Zoning Adjustment, 1986-90; vice chmn. Jefferson County Bd. Zoning Adjustment, 1986—; mem. Vestavia Hills Bapt. Ch., 1991—, deacon. Lt. U.S. Army, 1944-46. Named Engr. of Yr. Ala., Engring. Found. Coun. U. Ala.-Birmingham, 1999. Mem. NSPE, ASCE (program chmn. Ala. chpt. 1966, equipment maintenance com. 1958-78, Life Achievement award), Am. Soc. Mil. Engrs., Internat. Platform Assn., Internat. Coun. Shopping Ctrs. (water quality com., environ. site assessment com., lectr., Disting. Svc. award 1996), Birmingham C. of C. (environ. ethicc com., lectr.), Tau Beta Phi, Sigma Tau. Avocations: golf, reading. Office: Sain Assocs Inc 244 W Valley Ave Ste 200 Birmingham AL 35209-3616 E-mail: hsain@sain.com.

SAINER, ARTHUR, writer, theater educator; b. N.Y.C., Sept. 12, 1924; s. Louis and Sadie (Roth) S.; m. Maryjane Treloar, Apr. 18, 1981; children: Douglas M., Stephanie M., Jane M., Ross M. BA, Washington Sq. Coll., N.Y.C., 1946; MA, Columbia U., 1948. Tchr. C.W. Post Coll., Bennington Coll., Vt., 1967-69, Adelphi U., Garden City, N.Y., 1974-75, S.I. Community Coll., 1974-75; faculty Wesleyan U., Middletown, Conn., 1977-80, Hunter Coll., N.Y.C., 1980-81; assoc. prof. theatre Middlebury Coll., Vt., 1981-83; theater faculty New Sch. for Social Rsch., N.Y.C., 1985—, Sarah Lawrence Coll., Bronxville, N.Y., 1990—; play dir. Boat Sun Cavern Middlebury Coll., Vt., 1983; drama critic Village Voice, N.Y.C., 1961—; play dir. Lord Tom Goldsmith at Theatre for New City, N.Y.C., 1979, Witnesses at Open Space, N.Y.C., 1977, Poor Man Rich Man, Theatre for the New City, 1992. Editor: Village Voice, 1962; author: (plays) Jews and Christians in the End Zone, 2000 (Nat. Found. for Jewish Culture award), The Burning Out of 82, 1997, The Celebration Reclaimed, 1993-95, Images of the Coming Dead, 1980, After the Baal-Shem Tov, 1979, Carol in Winter Sunlight, 1977, The Children's Army Is Late, 1974, Cruising Angel, 1984, Sunday Childhood Journeys to Nobody at Home (Berman award), 1984, (criticisms), The New Radical Theatre Notebook, 1975, 97, The Sleepwalker and the Assassin, 1964, Zero Dances, 1998, The Burning Out of 82, 1997; reporter: Nat. Endowment for Arts, Washington, 1979-82. Panelist Vt. Council on the Arts, Montpelier, 1982, 83; panelist N.Y. State Council on the Arts, 1976-78. Ford Found. grantee, 1979, 80; recipient grant Office for Advanced Drama Research, U. Minn., 1967, award for Grab Your Hat John Golden Found., 1946 Address: 59 Railroad Pl #304 Saratoga Springs NY 12866-2161 *From the Burning Out of 82: Francis: But finally, who is going to do my work? No one is going to do it. Lev: Each will do his work. But in the end only God's work amounts to anything. Francis: And does that make you happy? Lev: It makes me useful.*

SAINI, VASANT DURGADAS, computer software company executive; b. Mumbai, Jan. 31, 1952; arrived in U.S., 1974; s. Durgadas D. and Pushpa (Sethi) S.; m. Sonia Juneja, May 20, 1983; children: Isha Seyjal, Kaasha Priyal. B Tech. Electronics, Ind. Inst. Tech., Kharagpur, 1974; MSEE, U. Rochester, 1975, PhD in Elec. Engring., 1979. Asst. prof. elec. engring. U. Rochester (N.Y.), 1980-88; pres., CEO Advanced Computer Innovations, Inc., Pittsford, N.Y., 1988—. Cons. All-Pro Printers, Rochester, 1986, W. Main Ultrasound Group, Rochester, 1986; software developer Dantec Electronics, Denmark, 1987—89, Brother Industries Ltd., Japan, 1992—93, U. Rochester, 1993—96, Brother Industries Ltd., 1995—2001, Manpower Internat., USA, 1993—94, 1995—96, DataEase Internat., USA, 1992—94, Wholly Genes, Inc., 1994—, Automated Legal Sys., Inc., 1996—, The Technology Group, 1996—2000, Nota Bene, 1994—, Expert Ease, Inc., 1997—2000, Info Access, Inc., 1997, Duxbury Sys., 1997—, McDonnell Douglas Helicopter Sys., 1997, U. of Rochester Med. Ctr., 1998—99, Sungard Planning Solutions, 1999—, TenDotZero (U.K.) Ltd., 2000—01, Boss Info. Sys., Switzerland, 2001, ProDoc, Inc., 1998—, Brit. Aerospace, U.K., 1999—, Wire2 Ltd., UK, 2001—, Aportis Techs. Inc., 2001—03, Fonix Corp., 2002—, Internet Access Techs. Inc., 2002, SimDesk, Inc., 2002—, Newslink Ltd., 2002—03. Coauthor: Doppler Echocardiography, 1985, 2d edit., 1992; also articles. Mae Stone Goode Found. grantee, 1979-81. Avocations: indo-jazz music, mathematics of music, squash. Home: 19 Roxbury Ln Pittsford NY 14534-4202 Office Phone: 585-383-1939. E-mail: vsaini@acil.com.

SAINT, EVA MARIE, actress; b. Newark, July 4, 1924; d. John Merle and Eva Marie (Rice) S.; m. Jeffrey Hayden, Oct. 28, 1951; children: Darrell, Laurette. BA, DFA, Bowling Green State U., 1946; student, Actors Studio, after 1950. Appeared in various radio and TV dramatic shows, N.Y.C., 1947—; theater roles include The Trip to Bountiful, 1953 (Outer Circle Critics award, N.Y. Drama Critics award 1953), The Rainmaker, 1953, Winesburg, Ohio, 1970, The Lincoln Mask, 1972, Summer and Smoke, 1973, Desire Under the Elms, 1974, The Fatal Weakness, 1976, Candida, 1977, Mr. Roberts, First Monday in October, 1979, Duet for One, 1982-83, The Country Girl, 1986 (L.A. Dramalogue award 1986), Death of a Salesman, 1994, Love Letters, 1994-2004, On the Divide, 1994-2004; appeared in films On the Waterfront, 1954 (Acad. Award for best supporting actress 1955), That Certain Feeling, 1956, Raintree Country, 1957, A Hatful of Rain, 1957, North by Northwest, 1959, Exodus, 1961, All Fall Down, 1962, 36 Hours, 1963, The Sandpiper, 1964, The Russians are Coming, The Russians are Coming!, 1965, Grand Prix, 1966, The Stalking Moon, 1969, Loving, 1970, Cancel My Reservation, 1972, Nothing in Common, 1986, Mariètte in Ecstacy, 1995, I Dreamed of Africa, 2000, Because of Winn-Dixie, 2003; TV dramas include The Macahans, 1976 (Emmy nom.), The Fatal Weakness, 1976, Taxi!!, 1978 (Emmy nom.), A Christmas to Remember, 1978, When Hell Was in Season, 1980, The Curse of King Tut's Tomb, The Best Little Girl in the World, 1981, Splendor in the Grass, 1981, Love Leads the Way, 1983, Jane Doe, 1983, Fatal Vision, 1984, The Last Days of Patton, 1986, A Year in the Life, 1986, Breaking Home Times, 1987, I'll Be Home for Christmas, 1988, Voyage of Terror: The Achille Lauro Affair, 1990, People Like Us, 1990 (Emmy award 1990), Palomino, 1991, Kiss of the Killer, ABC, 1992, My Antonia, 1994, After Jimmy, 1996, Time to Say Goodbye, 1997, Titanic, 1997; (documentary) Primary Colors: The Story of Corita, 1991; (with Bill Moyers) Children in America's Schools, 1997, Papa's Angels, 2000, Open House, TV-CBS, 2003; (feature films) Because of Winn-Dixie, 2004, Don't Come Knocking, 2004.

ST. AMAND, JANET G. government relations lawyer; b. N.Y.C., Feb. 27, 1953; d. Leonard Marsh and Glenda Weaver St. A.; children: Nikolai, Peter. BA, Arcadia U., 1975; JD, Georgetown U., 1980. Bar: D.C. 1981, N.Y. 1989. Legis. counsel Congressman Jim Coyne, Washington, 1981-83, Congressman Tom Carper, Washington, 1983-85, Sen. John Heinz, Washington, 1985-86, Am. Bankers Assn., Washington, 1986-87; asst. resident counsel J.P. Morgan, N.Y.C., 1987-90; counsel Fin. Svcs. Coun., Washington, 1990-93; fed. dir., counsel Household Internat., Washington, 1993—. Mem. Leadership Coun., Salvation Army, 1994—; trustee Arcadia U. (formerly Beaver Coll.), Glenside, Pa., 1999—, alumni bd. dirs., 1995—; trustee Womenin Housing and Fin. Found.; mem. Tax Coalition, 1999—. Recipient Mary Armstrong Wolf award Arcadia U., 1999. Mem. Women in Housing & Fin. (bd. dirs. 1991-95, mem. of yr. 1993), Univ. Club, Columbia Country Club, Exchequer Club, Tax Coalition. Presbyterian. Avocations: reading, travel, jogging, politics. Home: 5423 33rd St NW Washington DC 20015 Office: Household Internat 1401 I St NW # 520 Washington DC 20005 E-mail: jgst.amand@household.com.

ST. ANTOINE, THEODORE JOSEPH, retired law educator, arbitrator; b. St. Albans, Vt., May 29, 1929; s. Arthur Joseph and Mary Beatrice (Callery) S.; m. Elizabeth Lloyd Frier, Jan. 2, 1960; children: Arthur, Claire, Paul, Sara. AB, Fordham Coll., 1951; JD, U. Mich., 1954; postgrad., U. London, 1957-58. Bar: Mich. 1954, Ohio 1954, DC 1959. Assoc. Squire, Sanders & Dempsey, Cleve., 1954; assoc., ptnr. Woll, Mayer & St. Antoine, Washington, 1958-65; assoc. prof. law U. Mich. Law Sch., Ann Arbor, 1965-69, prof., 1969—, Degan prof., 1981-98, Degan prof. emeritus, 1998—, dean, 1971-78. Pres. Nat. Resource Ctr. for Consumers of Legal Svcs., 1974—78; mem. pub. rev. bd. UAW, 1973—, chmn., 2000—; spl. counselor on workers' compensation Gov. of Mich., 1983—85; chmn. UAW-GM legal svcs. plan, 1983—95; reporter Uniform Law Commrs., 1987—92; mem. Mich. Atty. Discipline Bd., 1999—, vice-chmn., 2000—02, chmn., 2002—; life mem. Clare Hall, Cambridge (Eng.) U. Co-author: (with R. Smith, L. Merrifield and C. Craver) Labor Relations Law: Cases and Materials, 4th edit., 1968, 10th edit., 1999; editor: The Common Law of the Workplace: The Views of Arbitrators, 1998; contbr. articles to profl. jours. 1st lt. JAGC U.S. Army, 1955—57. Fulbright grantee, U. London, 1957—58. Mem. ABA (past sec. labor law sect., coun. 1984-92), Am. Bar Found., State Bar Mich. (chmn. labor rels. law sect. 1979-80), Nat. Acad. Arbitrators (bd. govs. 1985-88, v.p. 1994-96, pres. 1999-2000), Internat. Soc. Labor Law and Social Security (U.S. br. exec. bd. 1983—, vice chmn. 1989-95), Am. Arbitration Assn. (bd. dirs. 2000—), Indsl. Rels. Rsch. Assn., Coll. Labor and Employment Lawyers, Order of Coif (life). Democrat. Roman Catholic. Home: 1421 Roxbury Rd Ann Arbor MI 48104-4047 Office: U Mich Law Sch 625 S State St Ann Arbor MI 48109-1215 Office Phone: 734-764-9348. Business E-Mail: tstanton@umich.edu.

ST. AUBYN, RONALD ANTHONY, pediatrics nurse; b. Vineland, N.J., Nov. 30, 1954; s. Richard Francis and Rita Margaret (DeFeo) St. A. BSN, Northwestern State U., Natchitoches, La., 1980. RN, La. High-risk infant homecare nurse Physicians Prescription Svcs., Shreveport, La., 1982-86; nursing dir., neonatal cons. Quality Care, Inc., Shreveport, 1985-86; poison info. specialist La. Poison Control Ctr., Shreveport, 1987; pediatric clin. supr. La. State U. Med. Ctr., Shreveport, 1988-92, pediatric edn. nurse, 1993—. Mem. ANA, La. State Nursing Assn., Soc. of Pediatric Nurses of La., Krewe Club of Aesclepius, Royalty Club, Beta Beta Beta. Home: 865 Sewanee Pl Shreveport LA 71105-2245

ST. CLAIR, DONALD DAVID, lawyer; b. Hammond, Ind., Dec. 30, 1932; s. Victor Peter and Wanda Small; m. Sergine Anne Oliver, June 6, 1970 (dec. June 1974); m. Beverly Joyce Tipton, Dec. 28, 1987. BS, Ind. U., 1955, MS, 1963, EdD, 1967; JD, U. Toledo, 1992. Bar: Ohio 1992, U.S. Dist. Ct. (no. dist.) Ohio 1993, U.S. Supreme Ct., 1996. Assoc. prof. Western Ky. U. Coll. Edn., Bowling Green, 1967-68, U. Toledo, 1968-77, prof., 1977-92; atty., ptnr. Garand, Bollinger, & St. Clair, Oregon, Ohio, 1992-97; pvt. practice Law Offices Donald D. St. Clair, Toledo, 1997—. Mem. Ohio Coun. Mental Health Ctrs., Columbus, 1978-79; dir. honors programs U. Toledo. Author: (poetry) Daymarks and Beacons, 1983, Impressions from an Afternoon in a Paris Courtroom, 1998; contbr. articles to profl. jours. Organizer Students Toledo Organized for Peace, 1970-71; mem. Lucas County Dem. Party, 1990—. With U.S. Army, 1955-57. Mem. ABA, AAU (nat. bd. dirs. 1973-74), Am. Inns of Ct., Ohio Bar Assn., Toledo Bar Assn., Ohio Acad. Trial Lawyers, Toledo Power Squadron (comdg. officer 1981), Bay View Yacht Club, Ohio Criminal Def. Lawyers Assn., Lucas County Bar Assn., Maumee Valley Criminal Def. Lawyers Assn., Ottawa County Bar Assn., Masons (32 degree), Shriners, Ancient Order Friars, Phi Alpha Delta. Home: 3836 Wheatlands Rd Sylvania OH 43560-3552 Office: PO Box 23185 Toledo OH 43623-0185 Office Phone: 419-841-7000. E-mail: stclairlaw@attglobal.net.

ST. CLAIR, HAL KAY, electrical engineer; b. L.A., Oct. 11, 1925; s. Millard T. and Ruth (McGrew) St. C.; m. Jane Creely, June 24, 1949; children: Gregory, Russell, Elizabeth; m. Bereniece Langham, Mar. 6, 1998. Student, U. So. Calif., 1943-44; BS, U. Calif.-Berkeley, 1946, MS, 1948. Research engr. Marchant Calculators, Emeryville, Calif., 1948-52; project engr. RCA, Camden, N.J., 1953-54; program mgr. IBM, San Jose, Calif., 1954-69, tech. staff Boca Raton, Fla., 1969-72, mgr. input/output devel., 1972-75, mgr. gen. lab. devel., 1975-81, mgr. small comml. systems engring., 1981-83, ergonomics adviser div. hdqrs. staff White Plains, N.Y., 1983-85, devel. edn. mgr., 1986-88, ret., 1988. Instr. U. Calif. Extension Div., 1951-52; tech. adv. U.S. Nat. Com. Internat. Electrotechnical Commn., 1967-69. Mem. Republican Central Com. of Calif., 1962-66. Served to lt. (j.g.) USNR, 1943-46. Mem. IEEE, SAR, Mensa, Phi Beta Kappa, Sigma Xi, Tau Beta Pi, Eta Kappa Nu. Home: 17187 Prado Pl San Diego CA 92128-2163 E-mail: StClair@cal.Berkeley.edu.

ST. CLAIR, JESSE WALTON, JR., retired savings and loan executive; b. Phila., Jan. 15, 1930; s. Jesse Walton and Susan Elizabeth (Leath) St. C.; m. Elizabeth Anne Bartlett, Oct. 6, 1951; children: Jesse Walton III, Susan Elizabeth, Bruce Bartlett, Anne Leath. BA, Coll. of William and Mary, 1951; MBA, U. Pa., 1958; postgrad., Harvard U., 1968. Trainee Fed. Res. Bank, Phila., 1955-57; with Girard Trust Bank, Phila., 1957-78, asst. treas., 1960-64, asst. v.p., 1964-67, v.p., 1967-70, sr. v.p., 1970-75, exec. v.p., 1976-78; pres., chief exec. officer First Nat. Bank of Allentown (Pa.), 1978-82; chmn., chief exec. officer Wilmington Savs. Fund Soc., 1982-90, ret., 1990. Trustee emeritus endowment fund Coll. William and Mary; former mem. exec. bd. Delmarva coun. Boy Scouts Am.; past trustee Wesley Coll. With USN, 1951-55. Mem. Wilmington Country Club, Theta Delta Chi. Republican. Methodist. Home: 4011 Springfield Ln Greenville Wilmington DE 19807

ST. CLAIR, THOMAS MCBRYAR, mining and manufacturing company executive; b. Wilkinsburg, Pa., Sept. 26, 1935; s. Fred C. and Dorothy (Renner) St. C.; m. Sarah K. Stewart, Aug. 1, 1959; children— Janet, Susan, Carol. AB, Allegheny Coll., 1957; MS, MIT, 1958; grad. advanced mgmt. program, Harvard U. With Koppers Co., Inc., Pitts., 1958-88, asst. to gen. mgr. engring. and constrn. div., 1966-69, comptroller, asst. treas., 1969-78, pres. Engineered Metal Products Group, 1978-83, v.p., asst. to chmn., 1983-84, v.p., treas., chief fin. officer, 1984-88; sr. v.p., chief fin. officer Phelps Dodge Corp., Phoenix, 1989-99; retired, 1999. Trustee Allegheny Coll.; bd. dirs. Pitts. Theol. Sem. Mem. Fin. Execs. Inst., Duquesne Club (Pitts.), Allegheny Country Club (Sewickley, Pa.). Presbyterian.

ST. CLAIRE, FRANK ARTHUR, lawyer; b. Charlotte, N.C., June 16, 1949; BS, MIT, 1972; JD, NYU, 1975. Bar: Tex. 1975, U.S. Dist. Ct. (no. dist.) Tex. 1985; bd. cert. in comml. real estate law. Assoc. James H. Wallenstein, Dallas, 1975-78; v.p. Wallenstein & St. Claire, Dallas, 1978-81; pres. Frank A. St. Claire, P.C., Dallas, 1981-84; ptnr. St. Claire & Case, P.C., Dallas, 1984-88, pres., 1988-93; chmn. bd. Sunbelt Empire Title Co., Dallas, 1983-88; pres. St. Claire & Assocs., Dallas, 1993—; chmn. real estate section Godwin & Carlton, P.C., Dallas, 1994-96; ptnr., chmn. real estate sect. Strasburger & Price, L.L.P., Dallas, 1996-2000; CEO EnsureLink, 2001; pres. StClaireNet, 2001—. Author: Texas Condominium Law, 1986; co-author: Texas Real Estate Guide, 2000; contbr. articles to profl. jours. Ofcl. del. Dallas to Baltic Legal Conf., Riga, Latvia, 1990. Mem. Am. Coll. Mortgage Attys. (chmn. pubs. com. 1998—, mem. programs com. 1998—), Tex. Bar Assn. (study of uniform condominium act com., legis. liaison com. 1981-85, vice chmn. 1981-82, chmn. 1982-85, chmn. condominium and coop. housing com. 1985-89, title ins. com., mem. coun. real estate, probate and trust coun. 1991-95, treas. 1996-97, sec., chair-elect 1997-98, chair 1998-99), Dallas Bar Assn., Cmty. Assn. Inst. (bd. dirs. Dallas-Ft. Worth chpt. 1984-85, 87-89, pres.-elect 1989-90), Real Estate Fin. Exec. Assn. (asst. sec. 1996-97), Real Estate Coun., Am. Coll. Real Estate Lawyers (planning com. 1990-98, chmn. practice tech. com. 1993-96, mem. common interest ownership com. 1986-98, alternative dispute resolution com. 1993-95), Tex. Coll. Real Estate Attys. (chmn. projects com. 1991-92, bd. dirs. 1994-98), Internat. Assn. of Attys. and Execs. in Corp. Real Estate (website com. 1997-2001). Episcopalian.

ST. CYR, MARGARET ANN (PEGGY ST. CYR), writer; b. Phila., May 1, 1932; d. Thomas Russell Reiling and Margaret Mary Cannon; m. Raymond Paul St. Cyr, May 14, 1952; children: Mary Louise, Sharon Ann, Margot Elizabeth, Daniel Paul, Mark Dennis. AA, Mesa (Ariz.) C.C., 1977. Sec. to asst. contr. U. Pa. Hosp., Phila., 1965—67; sec. to chmn. dept. pathology Woman's Med. Coll., Phila., 1967—68; exec. sec. to asst. supt. Mesa Pub. Schs., 1969—81; advt. coord. Latter-day Sentinel, Phoenix, 1981—82; profl. writer, 1982—. Spkr. Family History Soc. Ariz. Author: From Conversion to Commitment, 1996, One Fold, One Shepherd, 1999. Sec. MARC Bd., Mesa, 1969—70, Mesa Constn. Week Com., 1972—74, Dist. 29 Reps., Mesa, 1996, 4th vice chmn., 1997, 2d vice chmn., 1998, 1st vice chmn., 1999; precinct committeeman Dist. 18 Reps., 1994—. Served with Women's Army Corps U.S. Army, 1950—51. Named Vol. of Yr., Maricopa County Reps., 1997; recipient, Chapel of 4 Chaplains, Phila., 1967, cert. appreciation, Maricopa County Reps., 1996, Lincoln Day award, 1999. Mem. Lds Ch. Avocations: acting, singing, choir directing. Home: 724 S Kachina Mesa AZ 85204

SAINTE-CROIX, JUDITH LYNN, composer, performing arts educator, consultant; d. Roy Hayden Reher and Jeanne Marie Hadd; life ptnr. Marcelo Mella; m. David Michael Martin (div.); 1 child, Adrian Christopher Martin. Mus M in Composition, Ind. U. Sch. Music, Bloomington, Ind., 1975. Dir. Sonora Ho., Inc., Ny, NY, 1976—; arts edn. cons. Guggenheim Mus., N.Y., 1992—96; arts edn. musical composition cons. Lincoln Ctr. Inst., N.Y., 1993—, Orch. of St Lukes, N.Y., 1995—; arts edn. musical composition cons. Bklyn Philharm., Bklyn., 2001—. Adv. bd. Am. Composers Forum - NYC Chpt., N.Y.C., 1997—2000; concert dir. Mu Phi Epsilon - NYC Chpt., N.Y., 1991—92; pres. NY Women Composers, NY, 1983—85. Author: Everything You Need to Know about Meditation; composer: (orch.) Love Brings Good Fortune (Gaudeamus, 1979, Martha Baird Rockefeller Fund, 1979), Renewal recorded on Capstone Record's Diverse Light (LI Composers Forum Rec. Grant, 2000), Rise Up! The Enemy is Us (Am. Composers Forum Devel. award, 1998), Dear One (Composer and Librettist Studio at New Dramatists, N.Y.C., 1997), From Far Beyond the Blue Sky (Queens Chamber Band Commn., N.Y.C., 1999), Renewal (N.Y. Found. for the Arts Fellow award in Composition, 2002), Kachina Piano Preludes (N.Y. State Coun. on the Arts Commissioning award, 1994), Vision I (Mu Phi Epsilon Commissioning award, 1991), Vision II (Commd. by Heliosphere for Merkin Hall Concert in N.Y.C., 1997), Vision III (Chamber Music Am. Commissioning award, 2001), Anodos: The Goddess Arising (Premiered by the Canton Ohio Symphony), Shake It! Mambo (621 Found. Grant and Commn., 1990), Inspiration Overture (Am. Composers Forum Commn., 1991), Flashtrack (BMI Film Scoring Workshop, 1994), Heart Like a Wild River (Premiere by Orch. of St Lukes at the DIA Art Found., N.Y.C., 1998), Burning in the Center (Premiered by NC Symphony); composer: (with drummer Bob Fish) Gateway to Eternity: The Song of the Angel of Fulfillment (Milenium Commissioning award from the R.I. Philharm., 1999); composer: (lectr. and workshop leader) (nat. tour of woodwind quintet) Vision III (Nat. Endowment for the Arts Spl. Touring award, 2002); composer: (lecturer and workshop leader) (regional tour) (Dept. of Cultural Affairs Touring Grant, 2002); composer: (Operas) Topography of Light (New Dramatist Devel. Grant, 2000), The Vine of the Soul (Jerome Found. Grant, 1999); dir.: (Operas) Reflection on the Ancient Forests of the Temperate Rainforest (Nat. Geog. Cable Networks Conservancy Project, 2002); composer: (Operas) The Rainbow Mother Weaves Hummingbird Dream Bundles (Meet the Composer Commissioning award, 1991); performer; composer: (cd release) Visions of Light and Mystery (Mary Cary Flagler Rec. award, 1999); performer; composer: (Operas) The Vine of the Soul (Concordia Career Advancement award, 2003); performer; composer The Art of Triumph (Atlantic Ctr. for the Arts Fellowship, 2002); performer; composer: (piano music) Kachina Piano Preludes (Wurlitzer Found. Fellowship, 1995), Visions of Light and Mystery (Heathcote Arts and Jerome Found. Grants, 1998); performer. Mem. Greenpeace, N.Y., 2001—03. Recipient Gaudeamus Composition Competition, 1979, Concordia Career Advancement Award, NY Found. for the Arts, 2003; grantee Arts in Edn. Grants, NY State Coun. on the Arts, 1989—2003, Devel. of the Sonora Ensemble, a contemporary music and media ensemble, Nat. Endowment for the Arts, 1983; Artist Fellowship in Compostion, NY Found. for the Arts, 2002, Art Omi Vis. Artist, 2003. Fellow: Creative Assoc., Wurlitzer Found., Atlantic Ctr. for the Arts Assoc. Artist; mem.: LI Composers Forum (Rec. Award 2000), Am. Composers Forum (adv. bd. - nyc chpt. 1997—2000), Am. Music Ctr., Mu Phi Epsilon (program dir. 1991—92). Achievements include creation of an original musical voice that blends contemporary, compositional elements & lyricism with indigenous folk materials of the Americas incorporating theatrical surprises; development of unique workshops that promote the creative process in children and adults. Avocations: bicycling, hiking, mountain climbing, literature, healing arts. Home: 484 West 43rd St Apt 44-Q New York NY 10036 Office: Sonora House Inc 484 West 43rd St Ste 44-Q New York NY 10036 Personal E-mail: sonorahouse@prodigy.net. Business E-Mail: sonorahouse@prodigy.net.

ST. FLEUR, MARIE P. state representative, state legislator; Degree, Univ. Mass. at Amherst; JD, Boston Coll. Law Sch., 1987. State rep. legis., 1999—. Chair Edn., Arts & Humanities Com., 2004. Ho. vice chairperson Counties; com. mem. Edn., Arts and Humanities, Housing and Urban Devel. Democrat. Office: State Ho Rm 473G Boston MA 02133 Office Phone: 617-722-2060.

ST. FLORIAN, FRIEDRICH GARTLER, architect, educator; b. Graz, Austria, Dec. 21, 1932; came to U.S., 1967, naturalized, 1973; s. Friedrich and Anna Maria (Prassl) G.; m. Livia Campanella, Jan. 12, 1967; children: Alisia, Ilaria. Diploma in architecture, U. Graz, 1958; MS in Architecture, Columbia U., 1962. Instr. architecture Columbia U., N.Y.C., 1962-63; asst. prof. R.I. Sch. Design, Providence, 1963-70, assoc. prof., 1974-77; principal architect Friedrich St.Florian Architect, Providence, 1978—; prof. architecture R.I. Sch. Design, 1980—, chmn. div. archtl. studies, 1977-78, dean of architecture, 1978-88, chief critic European Honors Program, 1991-93. Vis. asso. prof. MIT, Cambridge, 1970-71, 74-75 Works exhibited Nat. Inst. Architects, Rome, 1967, 14th Triennale, Milan, 1968, Moderna Museet, Stockholm, 1969, Hayden Galelry, MIT, 1973, Mus. Modern Art, N.Y.C., 1975, Drawing Ctr., N.Y.C., 1979, Walker Art Ctr., Mpls., 1980, Georges Pompidou Ctr., Paris, 1994, Centre de Cultura Contemporania, Barcelona, 1994. Recipient Nat. Endowment for Arts award, 1972-73, 76-77, 79, 26th ann. Progressive Architecture Mag. award, 1979; Ctr. for Advanced Visual Studies fellow MIT, 1970-77, Rome Prize fellow, fellow Am. Acad. in Rome, 1985. Mem. AIA. Design architect for the National World War II Memorial, Washington, D.C. Office: RI Sch Design Arch Dept Providence RI 02903 also: Friedrich St Florian AIA 112 Union St Providence RI 02903*

SAINT-FORT, RAYMOND PAUL, writer; b. Independ., Haiti, Aug. 18, 1932; arrived in U.S., 1967; s. Joseph Saint-Fort and Mathilde Cuvier; m. Ulna Adeclat, Jan. 16, 1971; 1 child, Ketsia. Author: L'volution Du Jeu De Dame En Haiti, 1960, Damkarate, 1989, Checkers Documents Pour L'Histoice, 1967, Checkers the Hearing of a Deaf Man, 1989, (novels) Naked Vangeance, 2004. Mem.: Soc. of Children Book Writers & Illustrators. Achievements include patents for plug-lock, 1978; auto anti-theft, 1994. Avocations: checkers, writing, reading, travel, inventing. Home: 1195 East 46th St Brooklyn NY 11234

ST. GEORGE, JOYCE, conflict and crisis management educator, writer; b. N.Y.C., June 19, 1951; d. Salvatore and Gloria (Munoz) St. G.; m. Francis Patrick Canavan, Dec. 11, 1982; 1 child, Kathleen. B, John Jay Coll., 1974; grad., NYU, 1980. Diplomate Am. Acad. Experts in Traumatic Stress. Spl. anti corruption investigator N.Y. State Atty. Gen.'s Office Criminal Justice, N.Y.C., 1973-79; pres. Pact Tng., New Kingston, N.Y., 1980—; rape crisis counselor, cons. St. Vincent's Hosp. Rape Crisis Program, N.Y.C., 1976-87; expert witness in sexual assault Queens County Dist. Atty.'s Office Spl. Victims Divsn., N.Y.C., 1985-90; instr. New Sch. Social Rsch., N.Y.C., 1984-86; instr., writer Columbia U., N.Y.C., 1988-89; expert witness rape trauma syndrome Queens County Dist. Atty.'s Office, N.Y.C., 1985-90; co-founder, dir. pact tng. and drama based tng. Cons., instr. U.S. Dept. Justice, N.Y.C., 1990-94; dir. Ctr. Theater Techniques in Edn., New Haven, Conn., 1985—. Author: Conflict Management in Hospital Settings, 1988, Perfect Cover, 1994. Recipient Disting. Alumna award John Jay Coll. Criminal Justice, 1994. Office: Pact Tng LLC PO Box 106 New Kingston NY 12459 Fax: 845-586-4277. E-mail: pactrain@catskill.net.

ST. GEORGE, JUDITH ALEXANDER, author; b. Westfield, N.J., Feb. 26, 1931; d. John Heald and Edna (Perkins) Alexander; m. David St. George, June 5, 1954; children: Peter, James, Philip, Sarah Anne. BA, Smith Coll., 1952. Author: Turncoat Winter, Rebel Spring, 1970, The Girl with Spunk, 1975, By George, Bloomers!, 1976, The Chinese Puzzle of Shag Island, 1976, The Shad Are Running, 1977, The Shadow of the Shaman, 1977, The Halo Wind, 1978, The Halloween Pumpkin Smasher, 1978, Mystery at St. Martin's, 1979, The Amazing Voyage of the New Orleans, 1980, Haunted, 1980, Call Me Margo, 1981, The Mysterious Girl in the Garden, 1981, The Brooklyn Bridge: They Said It Couldn't Be Built, 1982 (Am. Book award, N.Y. Acad. of Sci. award), Do You See What I See?, 1982, In The Shadow of the Bear, 1983, What's Happening to My Junior Year?, 1983, Who's Scared? Not Me!, 1984, The Mount Rushmore, 1985 (Christopher award), Panama Canal: Gateway to the World, 1989 (Golden Kite award), The White House, 1990, Mason and Dixon's Line of Fire, 1991, Dear Dr. Bell...Your Friend Helen Keller, 1992, Crazy Horse, 1994, To See With the Heart: The Life of Sitting Bull, 1996, Betsy Ross: Patriot of Philadelphia, 1997 (N.Y. Sons of the Am. Revolution award), Sacagawea, 1997, In the Line of Fire: President's Lives at Stake, 1999, So You Want To Be President?, 2001 (Caldecott medal, 2001), John and Abigail Adams: An American Love Story, 2001, So You Want to be an Inventor?, 2002, You're On Your Way, Teddy Roosevelt, 2004. Adv. coun. on children's lit. Rutgers U., 1977-94; chmn. ednl. com. Bklyn. Bridge Centennial Commn., 1981-83; tchr. creative writing York Correctional Instn., Niantic, Conn. Mem. Soc. Children's Book Writers, Author's Guild. Episcopalian. Avocations: tennis, hiking, travel. Home: 8 Binney Rd Old Lyme CT 06371-1445

ST. GEORGE, SHERYL LEA, air transportation executive, writer; b. New Albany, Ind., Dec. 12, 1957; d. Willard Nevil and Linda Marie Cook; children: Eric Robert, Jess Randall. BA in Applied Math., Weber State U., 1986; MBA, Univ. Phoenix, 2002. Analyst, sr. analyst McDonnell Douglas, Long Beach, Calif., 1986—90; sr. fin. analyst Am. Airlines, Tulsa, Okla., 1990—93, fin. mgr., 1993—. Conservative. Avocations: travel, literature, family, music. Home: 15306 Winding Creek Dr Collinsville OK 74021 Office: American Airlines 3900 N Mingo Rd Tulsa OK 74158 Office Phone: 918-292-2795.

ST. GEORGE, WILLIAM ROSS, lawyer, retired naval officer, consultant; b. Southport, N.C., Nov. 19, 1924; s. William B. and Ila (Ross) St. G.; m. Emma Louise Bridger, June 10, 1950; children— Victoria Butler, William Ross, Susan Bridger. BS, U.S. Naval Acad., 1946; JD, George Washington U., 1953. Bar: D.C. 1953, U.S. Supreme Ct. 1964, Calif. 1980. Commd. ensign U.S. Navy, 1946, advanced through grades to vice adm., 1973; comdg. officer U.S.S. Josephus Daniels, 1969-70; comdr. Cruiser-Destroyer Flotilla 11, also comdr. Cruiser-Destroyer Flotilla 3, 1973; dep. and chief staff to comdr.-in-chief U.S. Pacific Fleet, 1973-76; comdr. Naval Surface Force, U.S. Pacific Fleet, 1976-79, ret., 1979; sole practice San Diego, 1980—. Decorated D.S.M. with oak leaf cluster, Legion of Merit, Bronze Star. Presbyterian. Home: 862 San Antonio Pl San Diego CA 92106-3057 E-mail: williamstgeorge@aol.com.

ST. GERMAIN, FERNAND JOSEPH, retired congressman; b. Blackstone, Mass. s. Andrew Joseph and Pearl (Talaby) St. Germain; m. Rachel O'Neill, Aug. 20, 1953 (dec.); children: Laurene, Lisette. PhB in Social Sci, Providence Coll., 1948, LLD, 1965; LLB, Boston U., 1955; JSD (hon.), Suffolk U., 1976; DCL (hon.), Our Lady of Providence Sem., 1968; DBA (hon.), Bryant Coll., 1981; D in Pub. Svc. (hon.), Roger Williams Coll., 1981; LLB, Brown U., 1985. Bar: R.I. 1956, Fed. 1957, U.S. Supreme Ct. 1983. Mem. R.I. Ho. of Reps., 1952-60, 87th to 100th Congresses from 1st R.I. Dist., 1961-1989, chmn. house com. on banking fin. and urban affairs, 1980-88; ret., 1988. Served with AUS, 1949-52. Recipient Silver Shingle award for disting. public service Boston U. Sch. Law Alumni Assn., 1981, Alumni award disting. pub. service Boston U. Sch. Law, 1982 Mem. ABA, R.I., Bar Assn. Fed. Bar Assn., alumni assns. Our Lady of Providence Sem., Providence Coll., Boston U. Law Sch., Am. Legion. Democrat. Home: 2990 E Palouse River Dr Trlr 409 Moscow ID 83843-8872

ST. GERMAINE-LATTIG, CHARLES EDWIN, political writer; b. Rhinelander, Wis., Feb. 12, 1949; s. William St. Germaine and Ina Margaret (Lobermier) Valliere; children: Spencer Charles, Aimy Dixon. Student, SUNY, Buffalo, 1967-68, Syracuse U., 1969. Polit. writer Am. Indian Movement, 1972-79, Mpls., 1979—. Free-lance photographer, 1976—; co-hose, prodr. radio program: Living on Indian Time, KPFA, Berkeley, Calif., 1976-77; founder, editor Bay Area Indian News, Oakland, 1976-77; contbr. articles to profl. jours. Cadre mem. Am. Indian Movement, 1972-79; mem. Met. Opera Guild; tribal mem. Lac du Flambeau Band of Lake Superior Chippewa, Wis. With U.S. Army, 1971-72, Korea. Mem. Acad. Polical Sci., Nat. Audobon Soc., Nature Conservancy. Avocations: wildlife and environmental preservation, astronomy, classical music, Shakespearean drama, N.E. Asian political history. Home: 2535 11th Ave S #1 Minneapolis MN 55404-4502 E-mail: nativerealist@aol.com.

SAINT-GIRARD, CHRISTIAN, theatre director, choreographer, actor, educator, theater producer; b. N.Y.C., May 29, 1954; s. Victoria J. Walter. Student, U. Oslo, 1972, Fordham U., 1972-74, Stella Adler Conservatory, N.Y.C.; studied with Uta Hagen and H. Berghof, HB Studios, N.Y.C.; studied dance, Joffrey Ballet; student dance, Am. Ballet Theatre; also others. Dir. Merry-Go-Round Playhouse, Auburn, N.Y., 1990-92; dir. edn. Polka Dot Playhouse, Bridgeport, Conn., 2002; artistic dir. Playhouse-on-the-Green, Bridgeport, Conn., 2002. Mem. bd. advisors Actor's Outlet Theatre Ctr., N.Y.C., 1981-85, chmn. steering com., 1982-83; pres., producing artistic dir. Prodrs.' Assn. Real Theatre for Youth, Darien, Ct., 1986-87; tchr. workshops and classes; guest instr. acting and auditioning for mus. theatre and dance at profl. studios, including Actor's Outlet Theatre, Manhattan Theatre Workshop, N.Y.C., Studio at Once Upon a Time Prodns., Inc., N.Y.C., Phil Black's Dance Studio, N.Y.C., Darien Dance Ctr., Darien Arts Coun., Conn. Conservatory for Performing Arts, Workshop Prodns., Inc., Stratford (Conn.) Acad. Dance, Conn. Dance, Newtown (Conn.) Ctr. for Performing Arts, Showbiz Kids, Conn.; performer on Broadway in A Chorus Line, Grease, Shenandoah; on nat. tours in Camelot, A Light Night Music, Oliver!, title role in Pippin; performer in stock and dinner theatre in Funny Girl, Hello Dolly!, The King & I, Cabaret; also appeared in TV pilots, feature films, comml. and operas. Author: (with Viveca Lindfors) (play) Three Boards and A Passion, 1981; librettist (mus. play) Alice in Wonderland, 1985, (ballet) The Red Shoes, 1987; dir., choreographer Singin' in the Rain, She Loves Me, 42d Street, Cabaret, Mame, Into the Woods, Camelot, Applause, My Fair Lady, Unsinkable Molly Brown, Hello, Dolly!, Shenandoah, Music Man, Gypsy, Forty Carats, Chicago, On the Town, Twelfth Night, Cinderella, A Touch of Spring, West Side Story, Annie, Snow White, Pinocchio, Hansel and Gretel, Sleeping Beauty, The Magic Flute, Arsenic and Old Lace, Babes in Toyland, also others; choreographer Paint Your Wagon, Oklahoma, South Pacific, Fame Mem. SAG, AFTRA, Actors Equity Assn., Cath. Actors Guild. Republican. Roman Catholic. Avocations: painting, sketching, tennis. E-mail: CSGDirchor@aol.com.

ST. GOAR, HERBERT, retired food corporation executive; b. Hamburg, Germany, Apr. 7, 1916; came to U.S., 1938, naturalized, 1943; s. Otto and Thekla St.G.; m. Maria Karsch, Sept. 3, 1954; children: Edward, Elisabeth. Student schs., Hamburg, Germany; LL.B., Chattanooga Coll. Law, 1943. With Internat. Harvester Co., Hamburg, Germany, 1936-38; with Dixie Saving Stores, Inc., Chattanooga, 1938—, pres., 1969-98, chief exec. officer, 1969-98, pres. emeritus, 1998-99; ret., 1999. Author: Autobiography: Taking Stock of My Life, 2000. Bd. dirs. Chattanooga Opera Assn., Jr. C. of C., 1945-54; mem. Hamilton County Juvenile Ct. Commn. Served with Intelligence Sect., U.S. Army, World War II. Decorated Bronze Star, Legion of Merit.; Named Disting. Citizen Chattanooga, 1979 Mem. Southeastern Food Coop. Assn. (past pres.), Tenn. Wholesale Grocers Assn. (bd. dirs. 1988-91), Retailer-Owned Food Distrbrs. Assn. (bd. dirs. 1988-98), NGA Retailer-Owned Exec. Coun., Asparagus Club. Home: 1502 Hixson Pike Chattanooga TN 37405-2431

SAINT-JACQUES, BERNARD, linguistics educator; b. Montreal, Que., Can., Apr. 26, 1928; s. Albert and Germaine (Lefebvre) Saint-J.; m. Marguerite Fauquenoy. MA, Sophia U., Tokyo, 1962; MS, Georgetown U., 1964; Doctorat es Lettres and Scis. Humaines, Paris U., 1975. Asst. prof. linguistics U. B.C., Vancouver, Canada, 1967—69, assoc. prof., 1969-78, prof., 1978-90, prof. emeritus, 1991—; prof. Aichi U., Japan, 1990—2003. Mem. U.S. Citizen Amb. Program. Author: Structural Analysis of Modern Japanese, 1971, Aspects sociolinguistiques du bilinguisme canadien, 1976, Language and Ethnic Relations, 1979, Japanese Studies in Canada, 1985, Studies in Language and Culture, 1995; editor: Intercultural Communication Studies, 1998; co-editor: Contrasting Political Institutions, 1997, (with M. Iwasaki) Democratic Viability in Politics, 2000. Leave fellow Can. Council, 1974; profl. fellow Japan Found., 1981; research fellow French Govt., 1982, Ohira Programme, Japan, 1983 Fellow Royal Soc. Can. Acad., Internat. Acad. Intercultural Rsch.; mem. Linguistic Soc. Am., Can. Soc. Asian Studies, Can. Linguistics Assn., Sietar Japan. E-mail: bsaintj@telus.net.

ST. JAMES, MARGARET JEAN, not-for-profit developer; b. Bellingham, Wasn., Sept. 12, 1937; s. George Lawrence St. James and Dorothy Evelyn Wellman; m. Donald Frank Sobjack (div.); 1 child, Donald Bryon Sobjack; m. Paul Stuart Avery, Feb. 14, 1992 (dec. 2000); 2 stepchildren. Student, Lincoln Law Sch., 1964—65. Cert. pvt. investigator Calif. Founder COYOTE: Call Off Your Old Tired Ethics, San Francisco, 1973—, St. James Infirmary, San Francisco, 1998—; pres. emeritus Occupation, Health and Safety Clinic for Sex Workers/San Francisco Dept. Health. Prodr. Hooker's Ball, San Francisco, 1974—79; mem. Drub Adv. Bd., San Francisco, 1995—98; archivist Radcliff-Scheckinger Women's Libr., Cambridge, 1973—86. Editor: (newspaper) Coyote Howls, 1974—79; co-author: (anthology) Vindication of the Rights of Whores, 1988. Founding mem. Sex Workers Caucus/Harvey Milk Dem. Club, 1995; candidate San Francisco Bd. Suprs., 1996. Recipient Lifetime Achievement, Northridge Dept. Human Sex, Irvine, Calif., 1997, Recognition Resolution, Calif. Sen. Milton Marks, 1995. Democrat. Achievements include subject of documentaries Hookers, 1974, Ain't Nobody's Business, 1975, Hardwork 25, 1976. Avocations: gardening, painting, reading, movies, dance. Home: 2205 Henry St Bellingham WA 98225 Fax: 360-376-7010. E-mail: Paul_Avery26@yahoo.com.

ST. JOHN, ADRIAN, II, retired army officer; b. Ft. Leavenworth, Kans., Nov. 16, 1921; s. Adrian and Marie (McMahon) St John; m. Petronella Elizabeth Durham, Jan. 19, 1943 (dec. 1982); children: Adrian III, Brian; m. Florence Tucker Parrish, Jan. 29, 1998. BS, U.S. Mil. Acad., 1943; MA, U. Va., 1951; MPA, Am. U., 1981; postgrad., Army War Coll., 1960, U. Hawaii, 1963, Am. U., 1977-82. Commd. 2d lt. U.S. Army, 1943, advanced through grades to maj. gen., 1969; co. comdg. officer 15th Cav. U.S. Army, Europe, 1943—45; intelligence staff officer U.S. Army, Berlin, 1945—47, China desk officer gen. staff Washington, 1951—53, bn. comdg. officer 3d Bn., 31st Inf. Regt. Korea, 1954, comdr. 73d Tank Bn. Korea, 1955; mem. faculty Command and Gen. Staff Coll., Ft. Leavenworth, 1956—59; faculty adviser Iranian Def. Coll., 1959; S.E. Asia plans officer G3, U.S. Army-Pacific, 1960—64; long range plans br. Strategic Div., Orgn. Joint Chiefs of Staff, Washington, 1964—66; chief Surface P & O Div. J3, USMACV, Vietnam, 1966—67; comdg. officer 14th Armored Cav. Regt., Germany, 1967—69; asst. div. comdr. 4th Armored Div., Europe, 1969-70; chief Strategic Plans and Policy Div. J5, Orgn. Joint Chiefs of Staff, Washington, 1970-71; dir. plans gen. staff U.S. Army, Washington, 1971-72; comdg. gen. 1st Armored Div., Europe, 1972-74; vice dir. joint staff Joint Chiefs of Staff, 1974-76; ret., 1976; mem. adv. council on internat. security affairs Republican Nat. Com., 1977-80; del. Va. State Rep. Conv., 1980, 81; sr. mil. adv. U.S. Negotiating Del. Mut. Balanced Force Reductions, Vienna, 1982—87; Joint Chiefs of Staff rep. U.S. Del. Conventional Stability Talks, Vienna, 1987-88, negotiations on Conventional Armed Forces, Europe, 1989-92. Del., presenter Congress Arms Control Mid. East, Delphi, Greece, 1994; U.S. del. World Helicopter Championships, Moscow, 1994, Oreg., 1996; chmn. operational working group internat. conf. on arms control in Mid. East, Jordan, 1994; mem. advance party OSCE to prepare for elections, Bosnia, 1997; presenter plaques signed by Sec. of Def. to Australian authorities in 6 cities during ceremonies commemorating VJ Day, 1995; supr. parliamentary elections, Bosnia, 1997. Co-chmn. orchestral benefit ball Austrian Embassy, 1993, 1994; supr. Mcpl. Election Commn., Bosnia, 2000; participant in Conf. on Application European Arms Control Negotiations to Pakistan-India Situation, U.K., 2001; election supr. Kosovo, 2001. Decorated D.S.M. with oak leaf cluster, Silver Star, Legion of Merit with 3 oak leaf clusters, Bronze Star with V device, Joint Svc. Commendation medal, Army Commendation medal with oak leaf cluster, Joint Meritorious Unit award, French Croix de Guerre with silver star, Vietnamese Gallantry Cross with palm; recipient European Comdr. in Chief's Individual Project partnership award, 1968, Presdl. award Disting. Citizen, 1993, Dept. State Superior honor award, 1989, 91, Sec. of Def. medal for disting. pub. svc., 1992, medal as disting. grad. U.S. Mil. Acad., 1998. Mem. Am. Security Coun., Am. Fgn. Affairs Coun., Heritage Found., World Affairs Coun. Roman Catholic. Office: 9110 Belvoir Woods Pkwy Apt 118 Fort Belvoir VA 22060-2717 E-mail: sinjenii@att.net. *There are no limits to the heights man can reach so long as he cares not who gets the credit.*

ST. JOHN, BILL DEAN, diversified equipment and services company executive; b. Wewoka, Okla., 1931; BBA, So. Meth. U., 1952. Asst. treas. Seaboard Oil Co., 1954-58; auditor Alford Merony & Co., 1958-60; v.p. fin. Can. Refractories Ltd., 1968; with Dresser Industries Inc., Dallas, 1960-96; treas. Ideco div. Dresser Industries, Dallas, 1961-63, fin. contr. Dresser Industries Inc., Dallas, 1970-73, staff v.p. fin. svcs., 1975-76, v.p. acctg., 1976-80; exec. v.p. adminstrn. Dresser Industries, Inc., Dallas, 1980-92, vice chmn., 1992-96, vice chmn., CFO, 1993-96; mng. dir. SMG Mgmt. L.L.C., Dallas, 1997-2000; ret., 2000. With U.S. Army, 1952-54. Mem. AICPA.

ST. JOHN, BRIDGETTE ALAYNE, secondary school educator; b. New Orleans, Aug. 26, 1958; d. William Armand St. John Sr. and Patricia Meynier St. John. BA in Secondary Edn., La. Tech. U., 1981; MS in Math., Loyola U., New Orleans, 1991. Educator St. Rita's Sch., Harahan, La., 1981—85, Livaudais Jr. High, Terrytown, La., 1985—93, East Jefferson H.S., Metairie, La., 1994—. Ninth grade class sponsor Livaudais Jr. High, Terrytown, La., 1986—94; key club faculty advisor East Jefferson H.S., Metairie, 1994—, sophmore/jr. class sponsor, 1996—2000. Mem.: Dawn Busters Kiwanis Club. Office: East Jefferson HS 400 Phlox Ave Metairie LA 70001

ST. JOHN, DAVID A. actor; b. NYC, Sept. 10, 1956; s. Adam and Mary Ramirez. Grad, Garden State Theatre Acad., 1974—75, Acad. of Dance, 1976—86, Wiest Barron Sch. of TV, 1993. Actor/singer/dancer C.C. and Co., 1992—; actor Murder on Cue Mystery Co., Shrewsbury, NJ, 1997—, Kathy Reed Prod., 1997—, Nat. Coll. Comedy Tour, 1999—; actor/singer/dancer, 2002—. Actor: (TV miniseries, soap opera) Loving, 1993; (films) Jeffrey, 1994, Summer of Sam; (TV series) 100 Centre St, 2001; (plays) Bucks County Playhouse, 1991 Bd. mem. Oldwyck Players, 1992—93. Mem.: AFTRA, The Actors Fund, The Drama League. Avocations: travel, boating, cooking, interior decorating.

ST. JOHN, DONALD J. lawyer; b. Bridgeport, Conn., Mar. 1, 1934; s. Milton Francis and Mary (Byrne) St. John; m. Bette Noelle Tolli, Feb. 22, 1969; children: Christopher Michael, Jennifer Noelle. BS history, Fairfield U., 1960; JD, U. Conn., Hartford, 1963; MBA, U. Bridgeport, 1971. Bar: Conn. 1963, US Dist. Ct. Conn. 1964, US Ct. Appeals (2d cir.) 1964, US Supreme Ct. 1965, US Ct. Claims 1967, US Tax Ct. 1967. Staff legal rschr. US atty., Bridgeport, 1962; trial counsel law firm, 1963—71; staff counsel Dorr Oliver Corp., Stamford, Conn., 1971—74; div. legal counsel Buel div. Envirotech, Lebanon, Conn., 1974—77; assoc. counsel Peabody Internat. Corp., Stamford, Conn., 1977—82, v.p., gen. counsel, sec., 1982—86; Rep. Town Council Trumbull, Conn., 1972—73; chmn., 1973. Staff sgt. USAF, 1953—57. Mem.: Westchester Fairfield County Corp. Counsel Assn., ABA, Bridgeport Bar Assn., Aspetuck Valley Country (Weston, Conn.), K.C. Democrat. Roman Catholic.

ST. JOHN, EDWARD P. social sciences educator; b. Napa, Calif., July 11, 1950; s. Wesley V. and Gladys L. St. John; m. Angela Collins, Feb. 21, 1981; children: Denis W., Liam E. BS, U. Calif., Davis, 1972, EdM, 1974; EdD adminstrn., planning, and soc. policy, Havard Grad. Sch. of Edn., Cambridge, Mass., 1977. Prof., edn. leadership and policy studies Ind. U., Bloomington, Ind., 1998—; prof. of edn. U. of Dayton, Dayton, Ohio, 1996—97. Dir. Ind. Edn. Policy Ctr., Bloomington, Ind., 1998—2002. Author: (more than 100 articles and chapters) Refinancing the Coll. Dream (J. H. Univ. Press), Reinterpreting Urban Sch. Reform (Louis Miron, SUNY Press), 2002. Recipient Leadership Award, Assn. for the Study of Higher Edn., 2002, Robert P. Huff Golden Quill Award, Nat. Assn. of Student Fin. Aid Administrators, 1993; grantee Studies of State Fin. Indicators in Higher Edn., Lumina Found. for Edn., Postsecondary Pathways Project, Ind. Commn. for Higher Edn. and Lumina Found. for Edn., 2002—. Mem.: Assn. for the Study of Higher Edn. (bd. mem. 2001—03). Roman Catholic. Achievements include research that has examined the impact of federal and state education policies on changes in educational opportunity. Office: Ind Univ Sch of Edn 201 Rose Ave Bloomington IN 47405-1006

ST. JOHN, EVERT EUGENE, insurance company executive; b. Ft. Worth, Nov. 20, 1926; s. Warren Evert and Madeline Emily (Mount) St. J.; m. Mary Frances Wilson, June 23, 1953; children: Mary Madeline Whittinghill, James Warren, Paul Eugene. BA with hons., U. Tex., 1947. CFP, CLU, ChFC. Dir. agys. Prudential, Houston, 1960-69; v.p., founding dir. Sysco Corp., Houston, 1969-75; gen. agent Prin. Life, Des Moines, 1975—. Pres. bd. dirs. Goodwill Industries, Ft. Worth, 1998-2001, immediate past pres., bd. dirs., 2001—. Lt. USNR, 1944-69. Mem. Rotary. Republican. Baptist. Avocations: creative writing, golf. Office: St John Rigg Inc Carter Burgess Plz 777 Main St Ste 760 Fort Worth TX 76102-5353

ST. JOHN, HENRY SEWELL, JR., utility company executive; b. Birmingham, Ala., Aug. 18, 1938; s. H. Sewell and Carrie M. (Bond) St. J.; m. J. Ann Morris, Mar. 7, 1959; children: Sherri Ann, Brian Lee, Teresa Lynn, Cynthia Faye. Student, David Lipscomb Coll., 1956—58, U. Tenn., 1958—59, U. Ala., 1962—64. Engring. aide Ala. Power Co., Enterprise, 1960-62, Birmingham, 1962-66; asst. chief engr. Riviera Utilities, Foley, Ala., 1966-71, sec.-treas., gen. mgr., 1972—2001. Deacon Foley Ch. of Christ, 1975-82, elder, 1983-; chmn. Baldwin County unit Am. Cancer Soc., 1977; treas. Christian Care Ctr. Inc., 1981—; bd. dirs. AGAPE of Mobile, 1977—80; bd. dirs., pres. South Baldwin Civic Chorus, 1979—82; bd. dirs. Baldwin County Econ. Devel. Alliance, 1997—2001, exec. com., 1999—2001, sec., 1998—99, treas., 1999—2000, chmn., 2000—01. Mem.: IEEE (life), Chevrolet Nomad Assn. (bd. dirs. 1991—2002, v.p. 1993—2002), South Baldwin C. of C. (dir. 1972—75, pres. 1974, dir. 1981—90, 1992—95, amb. 2002—), Pub. Gas Assn. Ala. (bd. dirs. 1987—88), Am. Pub. Power Assn. (com. legis. and resolutions 1972—2001, chmn. State of Ala. mem. com. 1982—2001, com. on coms. 1997—2000, bd. dirs. 1997—2001, exec. com. 1999—2000, chmn. nat. membership com. 1999—2000, chmn. bylaws com. 2000—01, Kramer-Preston Pub. Svc. award 2002), United Mcpl. Distbrs. Group (bd. dirs. 1972—2001), Electric Cities Ala. (bd. dirs., exec. com. 1989—2001, vice chmn. 2000—01, chmn. 2001), Ala. Mcpl. Electric Authority (vice chmn. 1981—83, bd. dirs. 1981—2001, chmn. 1984—2001), Mcpl. Electric Utility Assn. Ala. (exec. com., dir. 1971—85), Ala. Consumer-Owned Power Distbrs. Assn. (chmn. 1974—75, sec.-treas. 1980, vice chmn. 1981, chmn. 1982—83), South Ala. Power Distbrs. Assn. (chmn. 1973—74), S.E. Electric Reliability Coun. (assoc.), Nat. Corvette Mus., Nat. Corvette Owners Assn., Azalea City Classic Chevy (bd. dirs., exec. com. 1989—99, v.p. 1991—92, 1996—99), Gulf Shores Golf (dir. 1974—75), Foley Quarterback (sec.-treas. 1984—85), Classic Chevy, Internat. (life). Home: PO Box 1817 Foley AL 36536-1817 Business E-Mail: stjohn@gulftel.com.

ST. JOHN, JOHN, food company executive; b. Battle Creek, Mich., Aug. 8, 1921; s. Raymond Martin and Hazel (Eastman) St. J.; m. Lorraine Margaret McCarthy, Feb. 27, 1943 (dec. Dec. 1991); 1 dau., Shannon Elaine; m. Betty Stewart Hill, Aug. 11, 1998. BA, Mich. State U., 1943. With Minute Maid Co. (and predecessors), 1949—, fin. v.p., 1963-65, pres., 1965-69; v.p. finance and ops. Citrus Central, Inc., Orlando, Fla., 1969-71, exec. v.p., 1971-87, mgmt. cons., 1987—. Dir., chmn. Farm Credit Capital Corp., Kansas City, Mo., 1985-87; bd. dirs., chmn. Fed. Farm Credit Banks Funding Corp., N.Y., 1983-88; asset mgr. Treasure Coast Citrus, Inc., Ft. Pierce, Fla., 1989—. Past pres., bd. dirs. Central Fla. unit Am. Cancer Soc. Served with USAAF, 1943-46. Mem. Country Club of Orlando, Interlachen Country Club, Univ. Club (Lansing, Mich.). Episcopalian. Home: 910 Pace Ave Maitland FL 32751-5768 Office: 1920 Boothe Cir Ste 200 Longwood FL 32750-6774

ST. JOHN, JULIE, mortgage company executive; BA in English, U. Mich.; MBA, Fla. State U. CPA, Fla. Prin. Arthur Young & Co.; v.p. info. sys. Residence Inn divsn. Marriott; sr. v.p. transaction processing and mgmt. sys. Fed. Nat. Mortgage Assn., Washington, 1990—. Office: Fed Nat Mortgage Assn 3900 Wisconsin Ave NW Washington DC 20016-2806

ST. JOHN, KATHERINE IVA, artistic director, dance educator; b. St. Paul, Nov. 18, 1948; d. Arthur E. and Lillian Faye (Teetsell) Tester; m. Curtis St. John (div.). BA, U. Utah, 1989; MA, Brigham Young U., 1994, U. Utah, 1994; postgrad., U. Calif., Riverside. Instr. U. Utah, Salt Lake City, 1989-94; dir. Ea. Arts, Salt Lake City, 1989—; artistic dir. Internat. Dance Theatre, Salt Lake City, 1993—. Author, choreographer: Radif E Raos; author: Afghan Dance: A Cultural and Historical Study; contbr. articles to profl. publs. Vol. Salt Lake Ethnic Arts Coun.; bd. chair Assn. Students Univ. Utah, 1992; speaker Utah Humanities Coun. Grantee Utah Arts Coun., Salt Lake City Arts Coun. Mem. Internat. Orgn. of Folk Arts, Mid. East Studies Assn., Soc. Ethnomusicology, Congress on Rsch. in Dance, Dance and the Child Internat., Phi Kappa Phi. Home: PO Box 526362 Salt Lake City UT 84152-6362 Office: Eastern Arts Ethnic Dance Co PO Box 526362 Salt Lake City UT 84152-6362

ST. JULIEN, THAIS MARY, soprano, musician; d. George W. St. Julien Jr. and Rosemary Gloria Bourda. Pvt. vocal studies, Charles Paddock, New Orleans, 1973—81, Virginia Mac Watters, Bloomington, Ind., 1978—81, Norma Newton, Houston, 1981—88, Andrea von Ramm, New Orleans, 1986; pvt. recorder studies, Milton G. Scheuermann, Jr., 1975—80; apprentice, Des Moines Metro Opera Festival, Indianola, Iowa, 1987; Opera Workshop, Loyola U., New Orleans, 1977—78; Baroque performance practice, Skip Sempe, 1995. Asst. season ticket sales mgr. New Orleans Opera Guild, 1974—77; ensemble singer New Orleans Musica da Camera, 1974—78, principle vocal soloist, 1978—, asst. music dir., 1980—91, asst. instrument builder, 1981—, co-artistic dir., 1991—, founder/dir. Vox Feminae (women's vocal ensemble), 1994—, chief adminstr., 1999—; mgr. single ticket sales New Orleans Philharm. Orch., 1977—79; founder, soloist Banquette Opera, New Orleans, 1979—84; founding mem., calligrapher Scriptease Calligraphy, New Orleans, 1980—92; founding mem., soloist Ezcudantza (voice/guitar duo), New Orleans, 1982—85; part- time libr. technician Tulane U., Maxwell Music Libr., New Orleans, 1989—. Musical advisor Hermann Grima Ho. Mus., New Orleans, 1980—84; sec., adv. bd. Entergy Arts Bus. Ctr., New Orleans, 1997—2002; adv. bd. New Orleans Internat. Music Colloquium, 1998—; musical advisor Musica Antiqua, Albany, Oreg., 1998—; founding dir. music series Belle Alliance Hist. Plantation, Donaldsonville, La., 2002—; bd. pres. New Orleans Musica da Camera, New Orleans; instr. vocal masterclass S.W. Mo. State U.; presenter in field; founding dir. Concert Series, New Orleans Bot. Garden, 2003—. Soloist, codirector, New Orleans Musica da Camera: recording; Centaur Records Satires, Desires and Excesses: Songs from the Carmina Burana, Natus Est: A Christmas Celebration, The Cross of Red: Music of Love and War from the Time of the Crusades, Maiden, Mother, Muse: The Women of the Cantigas of Alfonso X, Les Motets d'Arras: Songs and Dances of Medieval Arras, cd rom The Play of Robin and Marion, other A Christmas Offering, aired on National Public Radio (Early Music Am./Millenium of Music Nat. Radio Competition, 1996), editor, contbr.: newsletter The Cypher (Am. Guild Organists, New Orleans), solist, dir.: recording, Newport Classic Medee, soloist: recording, Clark Constructions Circles, Moonrise; co-host/prodr. (radio program) Continuum-WWNO, New Orleans, Continuum aired on WBPS, Portland, Oreg.; soloist, codirector, new orleans musica da camera: public radio international special Natus Est, aired in 1994 and 1995, Nat. Pub. Radio Christmas special Now Make We Mirthe, soloist, host; codirector n.o. musica da camera: Am. Pub. Radio special Alone of All Her Sex, soloist: Am. Pub. Radio special A Voice Still Heard, Early Jewish Music, Praises from the Heart, Nat. Pub. Radio special Tristan et Iseult, on Cathedral, Court and Countryside Series aired in 1981 and 1984, Nat. Pub. Radio special- The Sunday Show The Garden of Love, recitals, opera, orchestra, concert series, festivals, etc. Performances throughout the U.S.; contbr. articles to profl. jours.; hist. music adv. (films) Interview with the Vampire; soloist: nat. pub. radio spl. Creole Cameos: Music of New Orleans Creoles of Color. Founding mem., pres. bd. dirs. St. Charles Ave. Com., New Orleans, 1972—75. Named Vis. Artist in Residence with Musica da Camera, The Hist. Nat. Shrine of Our Lady of Prompt Succor, New Orleans, 1989—; recipient Lifetime Achievement award, Gambit Newspaper, Tribute to the Classical Arts, 1997, Pioneer in Preservation Honor award, Hist. Dist. Landmarks Commn., 1997, Cert. of Appreciation in Thankfulness for Contributions to the City, City of New Orleans, 2001. Mem.: Soc. Am. Magicians, Soc. Am. Magicians, La. Partnership for the Arts, Southeastern Medieval Assn., Entergy Arts Bus. Ctr., Am. Musicological Soc., Internat. Brotherhood of Magicians, MENSA. Avocations: magic, reading, drawing, photography. Office: New Orleans Musica da Camera 1035 Eleonore St New Orleans LA 70115 E-mail: mdc@nomdc.org.

ST. LIFER, JANE M. art appraiser; b. N.Y.C., Apr. 19, 1956; d. Martin R. and Marcia (Simon) St. L. BFA, Syracuse U., 1978; postgrad., The New Sch. Social Rsch., 1979, Ariz. State U., 1980, MA, N.J. City U., 1996; cert. in appraisal studies, George Washington U., 2002. Dir. print dept. Trail Side Galleries, Jackson, Wyo., 1978—79, Scottsdale, Ariz., 1978—79; gallery dir., Phoenix Art Press, 1980-81; dir. print dept. Hammer Galleries, N.Y.C., 1981-86; sales mgr. Gallery Urban, N.Y.C., 1986-88; dir., owner, pres. St. Lifer Art, Inc., N.Y.C., 1988—; asst. dir. Grand Ctrl. Art Galleries, N.Y.C., 1991-92; dir., cur. Digital Sandbox Network Gallery, 1999—2000. Lectr. Parsons Sch. Design, N.Y.C. Mem. Am. Soc. Appraisers (assoc.), Auctioneers Assn. (sec., v.p. 1990—), Nat. Mus. Women in Arts, Internat. Found. Art Rsch., Dog Fanciers Club, Nat. Arts Club. Avocations: culinary arts, dog fancier, theater. Office: St Lifer Art Inc 140 Riverside Blvd # 323 New York NY 10069 Office Phone: 212-580-2102.

ST. LOUIS, MARTIN, professional hockey player; b. Laval, Que., Can., June 18, 1975; m. Heather St. Louis; 1 child. Grad., U. Vt., 1997. Profl. hockey player Cleve. Lumberjacks (IHL), 1997—98, Calgary Flames, 1998—2000, Tampa Bay Lightning, 2000—. Mem. Team Can., World Cup of Hockey, 2004. Named to, NCAA East First All-Am. Team, 1995—97, NHL All-Star Team, 2003, 2004; recipient Lester B. Peterson award, 2004, Hart Meml. Trophy, 2004. Achievements include member of Stanley Cup Champion Tampa Bay Lightning, 2004; mem. World Cup Champion Team Can., 2004. Office: c/o Tampa Bay Lightning 401 Channelside Dr Tampa FL 33602*

ST. PATRICK, MATTHEW, actor; b. Phila., Mar. 16, 1979; Actor: (TV series) General Hospital, 1997, All My Children, 1998—2000, Six Feet Under, 2001—; TV appearances include NYPD Blue, 1996, 1998, Beverly Hills 90210, 1997, Mad TV, 2002, 2003. Office: c/o HBO 1100 Avenue of the Americas New York NY 10036*

ST. PAUL, ALEXANDRA DE LA VERGNE, lawyer; b. New Orleans, Apr. 12, 1955; d. Hugh De La Vergne and Laurie (Monte) St. P.; m. David K. Deitrich, Nov. 2, 1990. BS in Econs., U. Pa., 1977; JD, Loyola U., New Orleans, 1984. Bar: Fla. 1985, U.S. Dist. Ct. (ctrl. dist.) Fla. 1988, La. 1989; cert. cir. ct. mediator, Fla. Atty. Dye, Scott & Deitrich, P.A., Bradenton, Fla., 1985-89, Phelps, Dunbar, Marks, Claverie & Sims, New Orleans, 1989-90, Deitrich & St. Paul, P.A., Bradenton, 1990-98, Dye, Deitrich, Prather, Petruff & St. Paul, P.L., Bradenton, 1998—. Dir. Sarasota-Manatee (Fla.) Lawyer Referral Svc., Inc., 1991-95, v.p., 1991-93, pres., 1993-95; dir. Gulf Coast Legal Svcs., Inc., 1991-95; mem. 12th Judicial Cir. pro bono com., 1993-94. Dir. Women's Resource Ctr. Manatee, 1994-95, v.p., 1995; bd. trustees Loyola U., Law Sch. vis. com., 1993-98; dir. Manatee Players, Inc., 1986-88, v.p., 1987-88; sec. Manatee County Head Start Adv. Coun., 1993-98, chmn., 1998-99; v.p. Tidy Island Condominium Assn., Inc., 1998-01. Recipient Tobias Simon Pro Bono Svc. award, Chief Justice of Fla. Supreme Ct., 1991. Mem. Fla. Bar Assn. (grievance com. 1991-94, vice-chair 1992-93, chair 1994-95; mem. real property, and probate sects.), Manatee County Bar Assn. (dir. 1987-89, 90-91, treas. 1988-89; mem. real property, and probate sects.), Fla. Assn. Women Lawyers (dir. Manatee County chpt. 1987-88, 91-98, 1st v.p. 1995-96, pres. 1992-93, 2d v.p. 1987-88), Bar Assn. Legal Aid Soc., Inc. (dir. 1991-94, v.p. 1992-93), Jr. League Manatee County, Inc. (dir. 1991-94, League atty. 1988-90, asst. treas. 1991-92, treas. 1992-93, chair pub. affairs com. 1993-94, nom. com. 1994-95), Leadership Manatee (class of 1993-94). Republican. Office: Dye Deitrich Prather Petruff & St Paul PL 1111 3d Ave West Ste 300 Bradenton FL 34205 Office Phone: 941-748-4411. E-mail: astpaul@dyefirm.com.

ST. PIERRE, GEORGE ROLAND, JR., materials science and engineering administrator, educator; b. Cambridge, Mass., June 2, 1930; s. George Rol and Rose Ann (Levesque) St. P.; m. Roberta Ann Hansen, July 20, 1956; children: Anne Renee, Jeanne Louise, John David, Thomas George; m. Mary Elizabeth

Adams, Dec. 11, 1976; m. Gretchen Ann Butrick, June 29, 2001. BS, MIT, 1951, ScD, 1954; DSc (hon.), Ohio State U., 1998. Rsch. metallurgist Inland Steel Co., 1954-56; faculty Ohio State U., 1956—, prof. metall. engring., 1957-88, assoc. dean Grad. Sch., 1964-66, chmn. metall. engring., 1983-88, chmn. mining engring., 1985-92; dir. Ohio Mineral Rsch. Inst., 1984-92, prof., chmn. material sci. and engring., 1988-92, Presdl. prof., 1988-92, chmn., disting. u. prof. emeritus, 1992—; chief scientist Materials Directorate, Wright-Patterson AFB, 1995-96. Cons. in field; vis. prof. U. Newcastle, NSW, Australia, 1975; adv. com. materials sci. MIT, 1990-97; adv. bd. Argonne Nat. Lab., 1994-99. Editor: Physical Chemistry of Process Metallurgy, Vols. 7 and 8, 1961, Advances in Transport Processes in Metallurgical Systems, 1992, Transactions Iron and Steel Soc., 1994—; contbr. articles to profl. jours. Bd. dirs. Edward Orton Jr. Ceramic Found., 1989-92. With USAF, 1956-57. Recipient Milton (Mass.) Clarence Boylston Sci. prize, 1947; MacQuigg award, 1971; Alumni Disting. Tchr. award, 1978; named Disting. scholar Ohio State U., 1988, Presdl. prof. Ohio State U., 1988. Fellow Minerals, Metals & Materials Soc., AIME (bd. dirs. 1988-91, 93-96, Educator award 1996), Am. Soc. Materials Internat. (Bradley Stoughton Outstanding Tchr. award 1961, Gold medal 1987, Albert E. White award 1997); mem. Am. Inst. Mining Metall. and Petroleum Engrs. (Mineral Industry Edn. award 1987), Iron and Steel Soc. (Elliott lectr. 1994), Am. Contract Bridge League (gold life master), Faculty Club (pres. 1990-92), Sigma Xi. Home: 4906 Stonehaven Dr Columbus OH 43220 Office: Ohio State U Dept Materials Sci/Engring 2041 N College Rd Columbus OH 43210-1124 Office Phone: 614-893-5287. Personal E-mail: gstpierr@columbus.rr.com.

SAINT-PIERRE, GUY, engineering executive; b. Windsor Mills, Que., Can., Aug. 3, 1934; s. Armand and Alice (Perra) Saint-P.; m. Francine Garneau, May 4, 1957; children: Marc, Guylaine, Nathalie. B in Applied Sci. in Civil Engring, Laval U., 1957; diploma, Imperial Coll., London, 1958; MSc, U. London, 1959; LLD (hon.), Concordia U., 1992; hon. degree, Coll. Militaire Royal de Saint-Jean, 1993; DSc (hon.), Laval U., 1992; hon. degree Applied Sci., Sherbrooke, 1994; DSe (hon.), Montreal U. Registrar, Corp. Engrs. Que., 1964-66. V.p. Acres Que., 1967-70; minister of edn. Govt. Que., 1970-72, of industry and commerce, 1972-76; asst. to pres. John Labatt Ltd., Montreal, 1977-80, sr. v.p.; pres., chief operating officer Ogilvie Mills Ltd., Montreal, 1977-80; pres., chief exec. officer, bd. dirs. The SNC-Lavalin Group Inc., 1989-96; chmn. bd. The SNC-Lavalin Group, Inc., 1996—2002, Royal Bank of Can., 2001—04. Dir. GM of Can., Alcan Inc., Inst. Rsch. Public. Policy; chmn. Bus. Coun. Nat. Issues, 1995—97. Gov. Conseil du Patronat de Que. Served as officer C.E. Can. Army, 1959—64. Decorated companion Order of Can.; named Canada's CEO of Yr., 1994, Canada's Internat. Exec. of Yr., 1996; recipient Sir John Medal, 1993, Can. Engrs. Gold Medal award Can. Coun. Profl. Engrs., 1996; Engring. Inst. of Can.; inducted into Can. Bus. Hall of Fame, 2001. Mem.: Order Engrs. Que., Can. Mfrs. Assn. (chmn. bd., pres. 1987), Engring. Inst. Can., Montreal C. of C., Coun. Can. Unity (v.p.), Loxahatchee Club, Hermitage Club, Mt. Bruno Club, Mt. Royal Club, Can. Club Montreal (adv. com.). Liberal. Roman Catholic. Office: Royal Bank of Canada 1 Pl Ville Marie PO Box 6001 Montreal QC H3C 3A9 Canada E-mail: guy.saint-pierre@rbc.com.

ST. PIERRE, MICHAEL A. lawyer; b. Great Falls, Mont., May 29, 1955; BA magna cum laude, Boston Coll., 1977; JD, Suffolk U., 1980. Bar: R.I. 1980, Mass. 1980, U.S. Dist. Ct. R.I. 1981, U.S. Ct. Appeals (1st cir.) 2001, U.S. Supreme Ct. 1988. Law clk. to Chief Justice, R.I. Supreme Ct., 1980—81; asst. town solicitor Town of North Kingstown, 1980—84; atty. Revens, Revens & St. Pierre, Warwick, RI. Mem. Workers Compensation Bench Bar Com., 1991—, chmn., 1994—97; mem. disciplinary bd. R.I. Supreme Ct., 1997—. Mem.: ABA, R.I. Bar Assn. (Ho. of Dels. 1993—, meetings com. 1993—, exec. com. 1997—, pres. 2002—03), R.I. Trial Lawyers Assn. (young lawyers adv./clerkship com. 1987—92), Assn. Trial Lawyers Am., Fed. Bar Assn. Office: Revens Revens and St Pierre 946 Centerville Rd Warwick RI 02886

SAINT-PIERRE, MICHAEL ROBERT, funeral director, consultant; b. Indpls., July 12, 1947; s. Robert Ross and Gaile Russell (Cousins) S.; m. Betty Carolyn Wilhoit, Jan. 14, 1967; children: Michelle René, Paul Christopher. Student, Milligan Coll., 1965-67, Butler U., 1966; BS, East Tenn. State U., 1969; diploma, Ind. Coll. Mortuary Sci., 1970; postgrad., Nat. Found. Funeral Svc., Ind. U., Indpls., 1977; DLitt, Cin. Coll. Mortuary Sci., 1994. Cert. funeral svc. practitioner. Intern Hamlett-Dobson, Kingsport, Tenn., 1967-69; pres. J.C. Wilson & Co., Inc., Indpls., 1969—; evaluator, practitioner rep. Am. Bd. Funeral Svc. Edn., 1980—; prof., trustee Ind. Coll. Mortuary Sci., 1971-76; prof. Nat. Found. Funeral Svc., 1987—2000, trustee, chmn., 1995-96. Bd. advisors Nat. Bank Greenwood, Inc., 1978-80. Contbr. articles to profl. jours. Mem., sec. Johnson County (Ind.) Sheriff's Merit Bd., 1989—; bd. dirs. Ctrl. Ind. Better Bus. Bur., Indpls., 1982—86, Adult/Child Mental Health Ctr., Indpls., 1982—85, Allied Meml. Coun., Indpls., 1979—2001, Greater Johnson County Cmty. Found., chmn., 1996—99, 2002—03; pres. Ind. DeMolay Found., 2002—04; mem. Crossroads of Am. coun. Boy Scouts Am.; past mem., treas., bd. dirs. Consumer Info. Bur., Inc.; past bd. dirs. Ctr. for Life/Death Edn., Indpls.; elder Greenwood Presbyn. Ch., 1976—84; treas. Ind. Masonic Home Found. Recipient Disting. Svc. awards Ind. Coll. Mortuary Sci., 1978, Mid Am. Coll. Funeral Svc., 1982. Fellow: Ind. Funeral Dirs. Assn. (former bd. dirs., pres.), Acad. Profl. Funeral Svc. Practice, Nat. Funeral Dirs. Assn. (exec. bd. 2001—03), Associated Funeral Dirs. Internat. (pres. 1981), Nat. Found. Funeral Svc., Selected Ind. Funeral Homes (bd. dirs. 1988—93, pres. 1991—92); mem.: Marion County Funeral Dirs. Assn. (pres. 1974), Skyline Club, Rotary (pres. 1978—79, Paul Harris fellow), Shriner (past potentate), Scottish Rite (33d degree), York Rite, Masons (master 1989), Order Eastern Star, Nat. Eagle Scout Assn. Republican. Presbyterian. Office: Wilson St Pierre Funeral Svc PO Box 147 Greenwood IN 46142-0147

ST. PIERRE, RONALD LESLIE, medical and public health educator, university administrator; b. Dayton, Ohio, Feb. 2, 1938; s. Leslie Frank and Ruth Eleanor (Rhoten) St.P.; m. Joyce A. Guilford, Apr. 1, 1961; children: Michele Christine, David Bryan. BS, Ohio U., 1961; M.Sc., Ohio State U., 1962, PhD, 1965. Instr. anatomy Ohio State U., Columbus, 1965-67, asst. prof., 1967-69, assoc. prof., 1969-72, prof., 1972—2002, chmn. dept. anatomy, 1972-81, assoc. v.p. health scis., 1981-83, sr. assoc. v.p. health scis. and acad. affairs, 1983—2002, assoc. dean Coll. Medicine and Pub. Health, 1987-96, vice dean Coll. of Medicine and Pub. Health, 1996-2000, exec. vice dean, 2000—02, interim dean pub. health, 1999—2002, assoc. v.p., prof. emeritus, 2002—, spl. asst. to sr. v.p. health scis., 2002—; assoc. dir. Cancer Rsch. Ctr., 1974-78. Vis. research asso. Duke U., 1966-67; cons. Battelle Meml. Inst., Columbus. Contbr. articles to profl. jours. Chmn. Ohio Gov.'s Com. on Employment of Handicapped, 1970-78; mem. state exec. com. Presdl. Comm. Employment of Handicapped, 1970-78, chmn., 1971-72; mem. planning and adv. council White House Conf. on Handicapped Individuals, 1975-78; mem. Columbus Mayor's Com. on Internat. Yr. of Disabled. Recipient Lederle Med. Faculty award, 1968-71; prize for basic research South Atlantic Assn. Obstetricians and Gynecologists, 1968; Outstanding Individual award Ohio Rehab. Assn., 1969; Gov.'s award for community service, 1973 Mem. Am. Assn. Anatomists, Am. Assn. Immunologists, Soc. Exptl. Biology and Medicine, Sigma Xi (pres. Ohio State chpt. 1979-80) Republican. Presbyterian. Home: 8586 Button Bush Ln Westerville OH 43082-8675 Office: Ohio State U 218 Meiling Hall 370 W 9th Ave Columbus OH 43210-1238 Office Phone: 614-247-7205.

SAISSELIN, REMY GILBERT, fine arts educator; b. Moutier, Bern, Switzerland, Aug. 17, 1925; came to U.S., 1938, naturalized, 1944; s. Paul A. and Jeanne (Nydegger) S.; m. Nicole M. Fischer, May 31, 1955; children: Anne, Juliet, Peter. BA, Queens Coll., 1951; MA, U. Wis., Madison, 1952, MA in French, 1953, PhD, 1957. Asst. prof. French Western Res. U., Cleve., 1956-59; asst. curator publs. Cleve. Mus. Art, 1959-65; prof. French lit. U. Rochester, N.Y., 1965-70, prof. fine arts, 1970-87; prof. humanities Hobart & William Smith Coll., 1987-90. Asst. editor: Jour. Aesthetics and Art Criticism, 1959-62; author: Taste in Eighteenth Centruy France, 1965, Rule of Reason and Ruses of the Heart, 1970, Literary Enterprise in XVIII Century France, 1979, The Bourgeois and the Bibelot, 1984, The Enlightenment Against the Baroque, 1992; exhbns. landscapes, still lifes, and abstractions in France, 1997. Served with U.S. Army, 1944-46. Guggenheim fellow, 1972-73 Mem. Phi Beta Kappa. Home: Route de Sancerre 18220 Saint Ceols France

SAITO, FRANK KIYOJI, import and export firm executive; b. Tokyo, Feb. 28, 1945; s. Kaoru and Chiyoko S.; m. Elaine Tamami Karasawa, Feb. 22, 1975; children: Roderic Kouki, Lorine Erika. LLB, Kokugakuin U., 1967. With import dept. Trois Co. Ltd., Tokyo, 1967-68; founder import/export dept. Three Bond Co., Ltd., Tokyo, 1968-71; sales mgr. Kobe Mercantile, Inc., San Diego, 1971-76; pres. K&S Internat. Corp., San Diego, 1976-97, K&S Techs., Inc., San Diego, 1997—. Office: 9710 Scranton Rd Ste 150 San Diego CA 92121-1771

SAITO, ROBERT SHUNICHI, writer, poet; b. Alameda, Calif., Sept. 9, 1933; s. Sam Shunji Saito and Yayeko Umegawa; m. Naida Cervantes, Dec. 7, 1966. Cert., Coronado Sch. Fine Arts, 1980. Enlisted USN, 1955, advanced through grades to chief petty officer, 1971; pers. officer USS Camden, 1972-75, ret., 1975. Pres. Mega Travel Inc., La Mesa, Calif., 1983-84. Author of poetry, short stories. Recipient 1st Pl. award for Batik, Coronado Art Assn., 1977. Roman Catholic. Avocations: batik art, photography, fishing, walking, tai-chi.

SAITO, SHUZO, electrical engineering educator; b. Nagoya, Aichi, Japan, Jan. 12, 1924; s. Sukesaburo and Masa Saito; m. Yoko Nakane, Mar. 26, 1953; children: Jun'ichiro, Ken'jiro. BSEE, Nagoya U., 1948, MSEE, 1953, PhD, 1962. Mem. tech. staff Elec. Com. Lab. NT&T, Tokyo, 1953-64, chief rsch. sect., 1964-75, dir. rsch. dept., 1975-79; prof. speech sci. U. Tokyo, 1979-84; prof. elec. engring. Kogakuin U., 1984-92; prof. info. sci. Hokkaido Info. U., 1992-98. Mem. tech. staff Japanese Patent Agy., Tokyo, 1963; tech. specialist Japanese Ministry Transp., Tokyo, 1982. Author: Fundamental Speech Signal Processing, 1979; contbr. articles to profl. publs.; inventor PARCOR speech synthesis. Recipient Meritorious award Min. Sci. & Tech., Japan, 1977, Promotion award Asahi Newspaper Co., 1981, Nat. Rising Sun medal of 4th Grade of merit, 2000. Fellow: The Inst. of Electronics, Info. and Comm. Engrs. Japan (adviser speech rsch. com., pattern recognition com. 1983, paper award 1970, 1971, 1979, achievement award 1973), Acoustical Soc. Am., IEEE (chmn. acoustics, speech and signal processing Tokyo chpt. 1986—88, chmn. tech. program com. internat. conf. on acoustics, speech 1986); mem.: Acoustical Soc. Japan (exec. coun. 1969—83, Sato paper award 1972, meritorious award 1994), Audio and Visual Rsch. Group (hon.; pres. 1985—88). Avocations: golf, photography. Home: 2-40-3 Sakuragaoka Tama Tokyo 206-0013 Japan E-mail: ssaito@pep.ne.jp.

SAITO, WILLIAM HIROYUKI, software company executive; b. L.A., Mar. 23, 1971; s. Toshiyuki and Yoko S.; m. Yuko Saito; 2 children. BS in Biochemistry, U. Calif., Riverside, 1992; postgrad., U. Calif., 1996, 97. Cert. EMT. Programmer Merrill Lynch, Burbank, Calif., 1986-89; instr. Calif. Poly. U., Pomona, 1985-87; staff cons. computer sci. dept. U. Calif., Rancho Cucamonga, Tokyo, 1988-92; ptnr. I/O Software, Walnut, Calif., 1987-90, pres., CEO, co-founder Riverside, Calif., 1991—; CEO Japan I/O Software, Tokyo, 1994-97. Cons. IBM, Riverside, 1986-87, Japan IBM, Tokyo, 1988-90, Japan NEC, Tokyo, 1987-89, ASCII, Tokyo, 1988-90; guest lectr. U. Calif. Anderson Sch. Bus., Riverside, 1995—; judge Ernst and Young Entrepreneur of Yr. program, 1999; keynote spkr., mem. panels, chair groups at numerous confs. including Comdex, Internet Security Conf., 1999, CardTech/Secure Tech, Washington, 1998, Cbgo., 1999, Software Coun. So. Calif., San Bernardino, 1999, Nat. Info. Sys. Security Conf., Arlington, Va., 1999, Software Pubs. Assn., 1997, Assn. for Biometrics, 1998, IQPC, London, 1999, Biometrics Summit, Washington, 1999, Miami, 2000, Global Patent Strategy Briefings, London, 1999, RSA Conf., San Jose, Calif., 2000, NAFE, Peter F. Drucker Grad. Sch. Bus., Claremont, Calif., 2000, Security Industry Assn., Amelia Island, Fla., 2000, among others. Vol. medical asst. Kaiser Permanent, Riverside, 1989-92; bd. dirs. Riverside Arts Found., 1995-97, Higher Edn./Bus. Coun. City Riverside, 1998—, Riverside Cmty. On-Line, 1999—; bd. trustee UCR Found., 1998—; mem. adv. bd. Coll. Bus. San Francisco State U., 1998—, Marlan and Rosemary Bourns Coll. Engring., 1998—. Named Ernst & Young Entrepreneur of the Yr., 1998, Point of View Mag. America's 50 Top Up & Comers, 1998, one of Top 100 Computer Cos., Computer World. Mem. IEEE, AMA, AAAS, Am. Nat. Stds. Inst., Internat. Stds. Orgn., Nat. Inst. Stds. and Tech., Mensa. Republican. Roman Catholic. Avocations: fishing, tennis, skiing, stamp collecting/philately, classical music. Office: 10 Software Inc 3403 10th St Ste 200 Riverside CA 92501-3654

SAIZAN, PAULA THERESA, oil company executive; b. New Orleans, Sept. 12, 1947; d. Paul Morine and Hattie Mae (Hayes) Saizan; m. George H. Smith, May 26, 1973 (div. July 1976). BS in Accts. summa cum laude, Xavier U., 1969. CPA Tex. Systems engr. IBM, New Orleans, 1969-71; acct., then sr. acct. Shell Oil Co., Houston, 1971-76, sr. fin. analyst, 1976-77, fin. rep., 1977-79, corp. auditor, 1979-81, treasury rep., 1981-82, sr. treasury rep., 1982-86; asst. treas. Shell Credit Inc., Shell Leasing Co., Shell Fin. Co., Houston, 1986-88, sr. pub. affairs rep., 1988-89, sr. staff pub. affairs rep., 1990-91, program mgr., 1991-96, sr. program mgr., 1996-97, mgr. constituent rels. and edn. support, 1997-2000, mgr. nat. and cmty. outreach, 2000—03, mgr. stakeholder mgmt., 2003—04, sr. advisor corp. affairs, 2004—. Bd. dirs. Houston Downtown Mgmt. Dist., Greater Houston Conv. and Visitors Bur., United Negro Coll. Fund, Xavier U.; vice-chair Nat. Coun. Negro Women, Inc.; found. adv. coun. Links, Inc.; adv. bd. Sch. Engring, Tex. So. U.; del. White House Conf. on small bus., 1995. Mem. AICPA, NAACP (life, bd. dir., spl. contbn. fund, trustee), Tex. Soc. CPAs, Leadership Houston, Greater Inwood Partnership, LWV of Houston, Xavier U. Alumni Assn., Nat. Coun. LaRaza, Nat. Assn. Black Accts., Links Inc., Nat. Coun. Garden Clubs (life), Nat. Congress of Black Women, Alpha Kappa Alpha, Phi Gamma Nu, Kappa Gamma Pi. Roman Catholic. Home: 5426 Long Creek Ln Houston TX 77088-4407 Office: Shell Oil Co PO Box 2463 Houston TX 77252-2463 E-mail: paulusinv@aol.com., paula.saizan@shell.com.

SAJAK, PAT, television game show host; b. Chgo., Oct. 26, 1947; m. Lesly Brown, Dec. 31, 1990. Newscaster WEDC-Radio, Chicago, IL; disk jockey WNBS-Radio, Murray, KY; staff announcer, public affairs program host, weatherman WSM-TV, Nashville; weatherman, host The Sunday Show, 1977-81; host Wheel of Fortune, 1981—, The Pat Sajak Show, 1989-90. Film appearances include: Airplane II: The Sequel, 1982, Jack Paar is Alive and Well, 1987; NBC television specials, host, The Thanksgiving Day Parade, The Rose Parade. Served with U.S. Army, Vietnam. Office: Wheel of Fortune 3400 W Riverside Dr Burbank CA 91505-4669

SAKAC, SISTER ANN, college administrator. Pres., Mount St. Mary Coll., Newburgh, N.Y. Office: Mt St Mary Coll Office of the President Powell Ave Newburgh NY 12550-3494

SAKAGUCHI, TAKEHIRO, healthcare educator, researcher; b. Tokyo, July 1, 1947; s. Takeichi and Kimiko (Aota) Sakaguchi; m. Sanae Sakaguchi, Mar. 21, 1974. M of Hygiene, Kitasato U., Tokyo, 1972; D Med. Sci., St. Marianna U. Sch. Medicine, Kawasaki, Japan, 1985. Lectr. dept. pub. health Kitasato U., 1972-80; asst. prof. dept. hygiene St. Marianna U. Sch. Medicine, 1980-96, assoc. prof. dept. hygiene, 1996-97; prof. dept. life sci. Kawamura Coll., Tokyo, 1997-2000; prof. dept. human environment Kawamura Gakuen Woman's U., Abiko, Japan, 2000—. Lectr. Chuo U., Tokyo, 1988-97, Shizuoka (Japan) U., 1997-99, Nippon Dental U., Tokyo, 1998—. Contbr. articles Toxicology & Environmental Health and others. Mem. AAAS, Japanese Soc. Hygiene (councilor 1987—), Japan Soc. Occupl. Health (councilor 1990-96), Japanese Soc. Pub. Health (councilor 1993-96, 2002--), Japanese Assn. Infectious Diseases (councilor 1997—), Japanese Soc. Bacteriology, N.Y. Acad. Scis. Avocation: travel. Office: Kawamura Gakuen Woman's Univ 1133 Sageto Abiko Chiba 270-1138 Japan E-mail: t.sakagu@kgwu.ac.jp.

SAKAI, HIROKO, trading company executive; b. Nishiharu, Aichi-ken, Japan, Jan. 9, 1939; came to U.S., 1956; d. Kichiya and Saki (Shiraishi) S. BA, Wellesley Coll., 1963; MA, Columbia U., 1967, PhD, 1972. Journalist Asahi Evening News, Tokyo, 1963-65; escort interpreter Dept. State, Washington, 1967-68; econ. analyst Port Authority N.Y. and N.J., N.Y.C., 1968-69; sr. cons. Harbridge House, Inc., Boston, 1970-84, Quantum Sci. Corp., White Plains, N.Y., 1984-87; corp. planner ITOCHU Internat. Inc., N.Y.C., N.Y., 1988-92, dir. bus. devel., 1993-94, dir. venture and investment, 1995—. Interpreter Govt. Mass., Boston, 1974. Wellesley Coll. fellow, 1960-63, Columbia U. fellow, 1965-68; Columbia U. grantee, 1969. Mem. Regional Sci. Assn., Assn. Am. Geographers. Buddist. Avocations: piano, painting, tennis. Office: ITOCHU Internat Inc 335 Madison Ave New York NY 10017-4605 Home: 280 Commonwealth Ave Apt 306 Boston MA 02116-2422

SAKAI, KIYOKO, artist; b. Osaka, Japan, Oct. 24, 1938; Osaka, Japan, m. Keizo Sakai, Nov. 7, 1965; children: Miyako, Alisa. BA, Doshisha U., Kyoto, Japan, 1961; postgrad., Art Students League, N.Y.C., 1973—78. Exhibited in one woman shows at Cottage Gallery, N.J., Move 21, Osaka, Japan, Kanner Kurzan Mus., N.Y., Myung Sook Lee Gallery, N.Y., Osaka Prefecture Comtemporary Art Ctr., Japan, Drew U., N.J., Permanent Collection: Deloitte, Haskins and Sells, N.J., The Zen Studies Soc., N.Y., The New York Stock Exchange, N.Y.; group exhbn. Bergen Mus. of Art and Sci., N.J., Instituto Superiore Per Industrio Artistiche, Urbino, Italy, Newark Mus. Recipient award Bergen Mus. Juried Show, Ramapo Coll. Juried Show, Art Showcase award, Manhattan Art Internat., Manhattan Art Internat.; Kenneth Hayes Miller Meml. scholar Art Student League of N.Y. Life mem. Art Student League of N.Y. Avocations: music, dance, literature. E-mail: ksakai807@hotmail.com.

SAKAI, RICHARD, motion picture and television executive, producer; b. San Francisco, Jan. 28, 1954; s. Hisasi Quintus and Jean Misako S.; children: Benjamin, Timothy, Reilly. BA, UCLA, 1977, MFA, 1980. Pres. Gracie Films, Culver City, Calif., 1984—. Prodr. (film) Jerry Maguire, Bottle Rocket, As Good As It Gets, (TV) Simpsons. Mem. Acad. TV Arts and Scis. (6 Emmys), Acad. Motion Picture Arts and Scis. (nomination), PGA, ACLU. Office: Gracie Films 10202 Washington Blvd Culver City CA 90232-3119

SAKAKEENY II, GEORGE J. music educator, musician; b. Chgo., Ill., Jan. 8, 1956; s. George Joseph and Julia Sakakeeny; m. Jian D. Dong, June 26, 1993; 1 child, Nicholas L. Sakakeeny. MusB, Eastman Sch. Music, Rochester, NY, 1974—78. Prin. bassoon New Japan Philharm. Orch., Tokyo, 1979—83; prof. bassoon Oberlin Conservatory Music, Ohio, 1989—; guest prof. Ctrl. Conservatory Music, Beijing, 2001—. Prin. bassoon Promusica Chamber Orch. Columbus, Ohio, 1990—. Musician: (albums) IDRS 25th Anniversary CD, Blechinger Faggottkonzert. Mem.: Internat. Double Reed Soc. Office: Oberlin Conservatory Music 77 West Coll St Oberlin OH 44074 Business E-Mail: george.sakakeeny@oberlin.edu.

SAKALL, DANIEL, education educator; b. Mt. Clemens, Mich., Nov. 26, 1925; s. Basil and Juliana Bese Sakall; m. Melanie Lee Hollifield, July 17, 1971; children: William Jeffrey, Theodore Lee, Daniel Gregory; m. Mildred Louise Wells, Mar. 18, 1952 (div. Nov. 1962). BA, Alma Coll., 1959; BTh, William Tyndale Coll., 1959; MPA, U. Ariz., 1962. Supply pastor United Presbyn. Ch., Mich., 1952—61; sr. probation officer Superior Ct., Tucson, 1962—76; hist. home restorations Family Co., Prescott, Ariz., 1978—86; lectr. U. Ariz., 1963—80; prof. Cochise Coll., Douglas, Ariz., 1965—76, Yavapri Coll., Prescott, 1980—85; ret. Author: (book) Love and Evil, Casebook, 1974, 100 Words to God from Genesis, 2000, 100 Words in Dialogue with Holy Spirit, 2003. Mem. Assn. for Psychiatric Offenders Internat., 1969—77; pres. ADD Pub. Admin. Assn., Tuscon, 1964—76; treas. So. Ariz. Mental Health Assn., 1970—76. Recipient Verbi Domini Ministers, Ministers for Competency in Bible, 2001, Presdl. Commn. Citation award, 1975, Most Articulate Spkr., Western Interstate Conf. on Higher Edn., 1975. Mem.: Stephan Ministry St. Andrews Presbyn. Ch., Tucson Chaplain's Assn. Republican. Presbyn. Achievements include first to bring professional rehabilitation of offenders to Ariz. Avocations: writing, christian counselling. Home: 11372 No Sawtooth Rd Tucson AZ 85737 Personal E-mail: mlsakall@aol.com.

SAKAMOTO, GORDON, newspaper editor; Bur. chief AP, 1993—. Office: PO Box 2956 Honolulu HI 96802-2956

SAKAMOTO, NORMAN LLOYD, state legislator, civil engineer; b. Honolulu, May 22, 1947; s. Shuichi and Fusa (Hayashi) S.; m. Penelope A. Hayasaka, July 12, 1970; children: David H., Gregory F., Katherine E. BSCE, U. Hawaii, 1969; MSCE, U. Ill., 1970. Registered profl. engr., Calif., Hawaii; lic. spl. inspector, Hawaii; lic. contractor, Hawaii. Engr. storm drain City of L.A., 1970-71, engr. streets and frwys., 1972-73; engr. hydrology C.E., 1971-72; v.p. S & M Sakamoto, Inc., Honolulu, 1973-85; pres. SC Pacific Corp., Kapolei, Hawaii, 1985—; mem. Hawaii Senate, Dist. 16, Honolulu, 1996—. Bd. dirs. Bldg. Industry Assn., Honolulu, spl. appointee, 1991-92, pres.-elect, 1993, pres., 1994; bd. dirs. City Contractors Assn., Honolulu; trustee Home Builders Inst., 1993-96; del. White House Conf. on Small Bus., 1995; co-chair Hawaii Congress on Small Bus. Scoutmaster Honolulu area Boy Scouts Am., 1989-92, asst. scoutmaster, 1993—; elected to Hawaii State Senate, Dist. 15, 1996—; mem. Aliamanu Clubhouse adv. bd. Boys and Girls Club; mem. Edn. Commn. of the States. Named Remodeler of Month Bldg. Industry Assn., 1990, 91, 96, Remodeler of Yr., 1991, Legislator of Yr., Bldg. Industry Assn., 2003, Legislator of Yr., Friends of the Libr., 2003. Mem. ASCE, Nat. Assn. Home Builders, Internat. Fellowship Christian Businessmen, Nat. Fedn. Ind. Bus. (Guardian of Small Bus. award 1999), Constrn. Industry Legis. Assn., C. of C. Evangelical. Office: SC Pacific Corp 91-178 Kalaeloa Blvd Kapolei HI 96707-1819

SAKER, JOSEPH J. supermarket company executive; b. 1929; married. Chmn., pres., chief exec. officer, dir. Foodarama Supermarkets, Inc., Freehold, N.J., 1958—. Office: Foodarama Supermarkets Inc Bldg 6 Ste 1-922 Hwy 33 303 W Main St Freehold NJ 07728-4832

SAKIC, JOE (JOSEPH STEVE SAKIC), professional hockey player; b. Burnaby, B.C., Canada, July 7, 1969; m. Debbie Sakic. Capt. Que. Nordiques, 1991—95; with Colo. Avalanche, 1995—. Mem. Team Can., World Cup of Hockey, 1996, 2004, Team Can., Olympic Games, Nagano, Japan, 1998, Salt Lake City, 2002. Named to NHL All-Star game, 1990—94, 1996, 1998, 2000—02, 2004; recipient Conn Smythe Trophy, 1996, Hart Trophy, 2001, Lester B. Pearson Award, 2001, Lady Byng Trophy, 2001, MVP Award, NHL All-Star game, 2004. Achievements include mem. Stanley Cup Champion Colorado Avalanche, 1996, 2001; mem. Gold medal Canadian Hockey Team, Salt Lake City Olympic Games, 2002; mem. World Cup Champion Team Can., 2004. Office: c/o Colo Avalanche 1000 Chopper Cir Denver CO 80204-5809*

SAKIEWICZ, NICK, professional sports team executive; b. Passaic, N.J. m. Isabel Sakiewicz; 1 child, Nick Jr. Grad., U. New Haven. Soccer player F.C. Nantes, French 1st Divsn., 1982, N.Y. Arrows, Major Indoor Soccer League, 1983, F.C. Belenenses, Portuguese 1st Divsn., 1984; sales mgr. TIF Instruments, Miami, Fla., 1985-90; zone mgr. Agy. Svcs., Inc., Atlanta, 1990, dir. sales Tampa, Fla., v.p. sales & mktg. Balt.; asst. coach, goalkeeper coach Coll. Boca Raton (Fla.), 1987; goalkeeper coach Southeast Region, Olympic Devel. Program, 1985-89, Fla. Youth Soccer Assn., 1985-89; dir., then v.p. Providian Bancorp, San Francisco, 1995; past v.p. corp. sales Major League Soccer; pres., gen. mgr. Tampa Bay Mutiny, Major League Soccer, 1996-2000; gen. mgr. N.Y.-N.J. Metro Stars, Major League Soccer, East Rutherford, N.J., 2000—. Office: NY-NJ Metro Stars 3rd Fl 1 Harmon Plz Fl 3 Secaucus NJ 07094-2803

SAKIHAMA, DEAN SHO, communications educator; b. Torrance, Calif., Feb. 1978; s. Edward and Louise Sakihama. Student in Asian Am. Studies, U. Calif., Santa Barbara, 1996—2000. Instr. English Village of Sanwa, Japan, 2000—03; accounts coord. Jackson Dawson Comm., Torrance, Calif., 2003—. Editor: (student literary journal) Kalifornia Rollin.

SAKODA, FUTOSHI, executive; b. Mar. 12, 1932; V.p. Mainichi Shimbun, Chiyoda-ku, Japan. Office: Mainichi Shimbun 1-1-1 Hitotsubashi Choyoda-ku 100 Japan

SAKODA, ROBIN (SAK SAKODA), government official; b. Chgo., Apr. 3, 1956; s. Tom K. and Harumi Sakoda; m. Hannah Sakoda; children: David, Elliott, Leah, Thomas. BA, The Citadel, 1978; MA, U.S. Naval Postgrad. Sch., 1988. Sr. dir. for Japan Office of the Sec. of Def., Washington, 1994—99; pres. Sakoda Assocs., Arlington, Va., 1999—2002; sr. assoc. AALC, Ltd. Co., Arlington, 1999—2002; chief of staff to dep. sec. of state Dept. of State, Washington, 2003—. Sr. assoc. Pacific Forum, Ctr. for Strategic Internat. Studies, 1999—; assoc. Ctr. for Strategic and Internat. Studies, 2001—; adj. faculty U.S. Naval Postgrad. Sch., Monterey, Calif., 2000—. Lt. col. U.S. Army, 1978-99. Avocations: Judo, fishing. Office: Dept State Office of Dep Sec Washington DC 20520

SAKS, ERIC MAURICE, film producer, film director; Prodr., dir. Wipe Out, 1981, Insomnia, 1982, Suddenly I Burst into Another: The Life of Henry Tanner, 1983, Automatic, 1984, 4 Songs, 1986, Designated Shooting Area, 1987, Forevermore: Biography of Leach Lord, 1989, Don From Lakewood, 1989, You Talk/I Buy, 1990, Hide, 1990, Big Pixel Theory, 1990, I Will Testify: The Porter Wagoner Story, 1991, Gun Talk, part 1, 1991, part 2, 1995, Vote PSA, 1991, Cappy Peeper Trailers, 1991, This Summer PSA, 1991, KNBR, 1993, Copper Connection, 1993, Straight Talk About Deserts, 1994, Encrypts PSA, 1994, Friar-fr-kinds, 1994, Like I, Media Bust, 1994, Oceania: 10 years of lounge, tiki and exotica wanderings, 1995, Neglectosphere, 1995, Touch Tone, 1995, Fax Attack, Creosote, 1996, Smooth Warming, 2000, Love Machine, 2001, Dust, 2001. Annenberg grantee, Guggenheim fellow, 1997.

SAKS, GENE, theater and film director, actor; b. N.Y.C. Began career as an actor off-Broadway at Provincetown Playhouse and the Cherry Lane Theatre; played in: Auden's Dog Beneath the Skin, E.E. Cummings' Him, Molière's The Bourgeois Gentilhomme; appeared on Broadway in Mr. Roberts, South Pacific, Middle of the Night, The Tenth Man, A Shot in the Dark, Love and Libel, A Thousand Clowns; debut as dir. on Broadway Enter Laughing, 1963; dir. stage plays Nobody Loves an Albatross, 1964, Half a Sixpence, 1964 (Tony nominee Best Dir. Musical), Generation, 1965, Mame, 1966 (Tony nominee Best Dir. Musical), Same Time, Next Year, 1975 (Tony nominee Best Dir. Play), California Suite, 1972, I Love My Wife (best dir. of Musical award Drama Desk, Tony), 1977, Brighton Beach Memoirs (best dir. award, Tony), 1983, Biloxi Blues (best dir. of play award, Tony), 1985, The Odd Couple (female version), 1985, Broadway Bound, 1986, A Month of Sundays, 1987, Rumors, 1988, Lost in Yonkers, 1991 (Tony nominee Best Dir., Outer Critics Cir. award), Jake's Women, 1992, Barrymore, 1997, Mr. Goldwyn, 2001, Remembering Tennessee, 2001; dir. films Barefoot in the Park, The Odd Couple, Cactus Flower, Last of the Red Hot Lovers, Mame, Brighton Beach Memoirs, A Fine Romance; dir. TV movie Bye, Bye Birdie, 1995; appeared in films including a Thousand Clowns, Prisoner of Second Aveneue, Lovesick, The One and Only, The Goodbye People, 1986, Nobody's Fool, 1994, IQ, 1994. Recipient George Abbott award for lifetime achievement in the theatre, 1990; elected to Theatre Hall of Fame, 1991. Mem. Stage Dirs. and Choreographers (pres.).

SAKS, JUDITH-ANN, artist; b. Anniston, Ala., Dec. 20, 1943; d. Julien David and Lucy-Jane (Watson) S.; m. Haskell Irvin Rosenthal, Dec. 22, 1974; 1 child, Brian Julien. Student, Tex. Acad. Art, 1957-58, Mus. Fine Arts, Houston, 1962, Rice U., 1962; BFA, Tulane U., 1966; postgrad., U. Houston, 1967. Curator student art collection U. Houston, 1968-72; artist Am. Revolution Bicentennial project Port of Houston Authority, 1975-76. Solo shows include Alley Gallery, Houston, 1969, 2131 Gallery, Houston, 1969; group shows include Birmingham (Ala.) Mus., 1967, Meinhard Galleries, Houston, 1977, Galeire Barbizon, Houston, 1980, Park Crest Gallery, Austin, 1981; represented in permanent collections including L.B. Johnson Manned Space Mus., Clear Lake City, Tex., Harris County Heritage Mus., Windsor Castle, Smithsonian Instn.; commns. include Pin Oak Charity Horse Show Assn., Roberts S.S. Agy., New Orleans, Cruiser Houston Meml. Rm., U. Houston. Recipient art awards including 1st prize for water color Art League Houston, 1969, 1st prize for graphics, 1969, 1st prize for sculpture, 1968, Nat. 1st place award for original print DAR/Am. Heritage Com., 1987, Nat. 1st place award for acrylic painting, DAR, 2000, Tex. award for Acrylic, 2003, Nat. 3rd place award for painting, 2003, Tex. State 1st prize for drawing DAR, 2002, Shofar award, 2003. Outstaind Svc. awrd Boy Scout Troop 806, 2002. Mem. Art League Houston, Houston Mus. Fine Arts, DAR (Lady Washington chap., curator 1983-85, 93-95, contbr. Tex. sesquicentennial drawing for DAR mag., recording sec. 2001-03, libr. 2003—, Tex. Best Chpt. Chmn. award 2003, Tex. award for art 2003, Tex. State 1st prize acrylic 2004), Daus. Republic of Tex., Magna Charta Dames.

SAKURADA, YUTAKA, chemist; b. Kyoto, Jan. 1, 1933; s. Ichiro and Chiyoko (Okumura) S.; m. Keiko Sugimoto, May 10, 1960; children: Kazuhiro, Akihiro. BS, Kyoto U., 1956, MS, 1958, PhD, 1966. Rsch. fellow Cen. Rsch. Lab. Kuraray Co. Ltd., Kurashiki, Japan, 1958-62, 64-66; internat. fellow Stanford Rsch. Inst., Menlo Pk., Calif., 1962-64; tech. rep. N.Y. Office Kuraray Co. Ltd., N.Y.C., 1968-71; mgr. Med. Bus. Devel. Div. Kuraray, Osaka, Japan, 1974-77, gen. mgr. Med. Products Div., 1977-88, gen. mgr. Corp. Rand D Div., 1988-89; mng. dir. Kuraray Plastics Co. Ltd., Osaka, 1989-91. Bd. dirs. Haemonetics Corp., USA; vice chmn. Japanese Soc. for Biomaterials, Tokyo, 1987—96; pres. Haemonetics, Japan, 1991—2001, chmn., CEO, Japan, 2001—; pres. Haemonetics Japan/Asia, 2003—. Recipient Technology award The Soc. Polymers, 1984, Japanese Chem. Soc., 1985. Achievements include development of ethylene vinyl alcohol copolymer hollow fiber for hemo-dialyzer; development of dental adhesives. Home: GM Ebisunomori 1304 4-23-6 Ebisu Shibuya-ku Tokyo 150-0013 Japan Office Phone: 81-3-3237-7226.

SAKURAI, MOTOATSU, manufacturing executive; Grad., Tokyo U.; MBA, INSEAD, Fontainebleau, France, 1975. Joined Mitsubishi Corp., 1968—; with World Bank, Internat. Fin. Corp., Washington, 1978—81; various positions including gen. mgr. Mitsubishi Internat. Corp., N.Y.C., Washington, 1984—95; gen. mgr. corp. planning and devel. and coordination Mitsubishi Corp., 1995—2000; exec. v.p., COO Mitsubishi Internat. Corp., 2000—. Office: Mitsubishi Internat Corp 520 Madison Ave New York NY 10022-4223

SAKUTA, MANABU, neurologist, educator; b. Ichikawa, Japan, Oct. 31, 1947; s. Jun and Shizuko (Tsuji) Sakuta; m. Yuko Fukushi, June 17, 1973; children: Akiko, Junko, Ken-Ichi. MD, U. Tokyo, 1973, PhD, 1978; MS in Neurology, U. Minn., 1981. Diplomate Japanese Bd. Neurology, Japanese Bd. Internal Medicine. Asst. dept. neurology U. Tokyo, 1980, lectr. dept. neurology, 1984—; rsch. fellow dept. neurology U. Minn., Mpls., 1980-81, asst. prof., 1981-82; head dept. neurology Japanese Red Cross Med. Ctr., Tokyo, 1982-2000; prof. Japanese Red Cross Women's Coll. Sch. Nursing, Tokyo, 1983-85, instr., 1986-88; lectr. dept. medicine U. Kobe, 1990—; prof. dept. neurology Kyorin U., Tokyo, 2000—, chmn., 2000—, chmn. 1st internal medicine, 2002—. Cons. Nakayama Hosp., Ichikawa, Japan, 1980—. Contbr. articles to profl. jours. Fellow: Royal Soc. Medicine (London); mem.: AAAS, Am. Acad. Neurology, Japanese Soc. Autonomic Nervous Sys. (coun.), Japanese Soc. Sarcoidosis (coun.), Japanese Soc. Cerebrovascular Disease (coun.), Japanese Soc. Clin. Neurophysiology, Japanese Soc. Diabetology, Japanese Soc. Neurology (mem. coun. 1985—, mem. coun. Kanto br. 1984—, pres. Kanto br. 1984, mem. editl. bd. 1988—), Japanese Soc. Internal Medicine (pres. Kanto br. 1992), N.Y. Acad. Sci., Tetsumon Club, U. Minn. Alumni Club, Chevalier du Tastevin (Burgundy), Chevalier Club (pres. internat. com. 1995—), Clin. Neurology Club. Democrat. Buddhist. Office: Kyorin U Dept Neurology 6-20-2 Shinkawa Mitaka Tokyo 181-8611 Japan Office Phone: 81 0422 47 5511. Office Fax: 0422 47 5931. E-mail: sakuta@shimkei.jp.

SAKUTA, MASAAKI, engineering educator, consultant; b. Kagoshima, Japan, Feb. 16, 1929; s. Masanori and Haruko (Oozato) S.; m. Akiko Shimomura, Nov. 4, 1956; children: Shigeru, Mitsuru. B of Engring., Tokyo Inst. Tech., 1952; postgrad, MIT, 1959-60; DEng, Tokyo Inst. Tech., 1966. Cert. oceanic architect, architect-engr., Japan. Rschr. Taisei Constrn. Co. Ltd., Tokyo, 1956-58, chief rschr., 1960-69; mng. dir. Fuyo Ocean Devel. and Engring. Co. Ltd., Tokyo, 1969-77; advisor Taisei Corp. Co. Ltd., Tokyo, 1978-79; prof. Nihon U., Tokyo, 1977-99, prof. emeritus, 1999—; pres. Tsuruga Coll., Fukui, Japan, 2002—. Councilor Archtl. Inst. Japan, Tokyo, 1975-76, dir., 1989-91; vice dean Coll. Sci. and Tech., Nihon U., 1978-94; vice chmn., life mem. Pacific Congress on Marine Sci. and Tech., Japan, 1990—. Author: Transportation in Ocean Space, 1975, Construction Method of Marine Structures, 1976, Introduction of Ocean Development, 1977; patentee in field of Marine structure system with soft-touched basement. Mem. Visualization Soc. Japan, Inc. (hon., pres. 1991-92, Merit award 1992), Rotary (sr., charter). Mem. Liberal Dem. Party. Buddhist. Avocations: hiking, tennis, ping pong/table tennis, painting, reading. Home: 39-723 2chome2 Jingumae Shibuya-ku Tokyo 150-0001 Japan Office: 9-1004 1 chome 43 Kameido koutou-ku Tokyo 136-0071 Japan Office Phone: 03-3636-2206.

SALA, LUIS FRANCISCO, surgeon, educator; b. N.Y.C., Dec. 13, 1919; s. Luis and Josefina (Goenaga) S.; m. Judith Colon, June 5, 1943; children: Luis E., Francisco A., Jorge P., Jose M. BS cum laude, Georgetown U., 1939, MD, 1943; M.Sc. in Surgery, U. Pa., 1951. Diplomate: Am. Bd. Surgery. Intern, resident Presbyn. Hosp., San Juan, P.R., 1943-45, resident, 1944-45; chief resident Grad. Hosp. U. Pa., 1947-51, instr. surgery, 1950-51; clin. asst. surgery Med. Coll. Pa.; practice medicine, specializing in surgery Ponce, P.R., 1951-91; chmn. dept. surgery Damas Hosp., Ponce, 1955-88, dir. residency tng., 1955-85; prof. surgery U. P.R. Sch. Medicine, 1968-88; pres., dean, prof. surgery Ponce Sch. of Medicine, 1988-94. Del. P.R. Med. Assn., 1960-93, pres., 1965-66. Author: Consideraciones Basicas para la Acreditacion de Hospitales, 1978; founder, editor: Sci.-Ciencia, 1973; contbr. chpts. to books, articles to profl. jours. Active Boy Scouts Am., 1955-74; pres. adv. com. to pres. Cath. U. P.R., 1963-72; bd. dirs. Boys Home of Ponce, 1966-76; bd. regents Amigos Museo de Arte de Ponce, 1968-73, Cath. U., 1972-93; pres. bd. regents Ponce Med. Sch. Found., 1980-92. Served with M.C. U.S. Army, 1945-47. Recipient Silver Beaver award, 1965, Acad. Médica, Dto. Sur, 1st. Dr. Luis F. Sasa medal, 1995; named lt. P.R. Equestrian Order of Holy Sepulchre of Jerusalem, 1982—. Fellow ACS (gov. for P.R. 1965-74, Disting. Svc. award 1989), Internat. Soc. Surgery, P.R. Med. Assn. (so. dist., Dr. Pila medal for disting. svc. 1991), Indsl. Med. Coun. of SIF (apptd. pres. by Gov. of P.R. 1993-95), P.R. Mfrs. Assn. (Profl. of Yr. in area of svcs. 1994), C. of C. (Profl. of Yr. 1990), State Med. Examining Bd. (appt. by Gov. of P.R. 1995-99). Republican. Roman Catholic. Home: 6 Almena Alhambra Ponce PR 00731 Office: 43 Calle Concordia Ponce PR 00717-4984 E-mail: lsala_98@yahoo.com.

SALA, MARTIN ANDREW, biophysicist, inventor; b. Buffalo, N.Y., Sept. 6, 1957; s. Paul and Adrienne (Williams) Zahm; m. Erie Anne Wagner-Sala, Nov. 23, 1986; 1 child, Rebeckah. BA in Biophysics, SUNY, Buffalo, 1981. Dir. clin. engring. Buffalo Columbus Hosp., 1982-85; lab. inst. designer Roswell Park Cancer Inst., Buffalo, 1985-89; v.p. for R&D MBS Foundry, Brook's Grove, N.Y., 1989-96; pressetter applications engr. Nationwide Precision Prods., Henrietta, N.Y., 1996-97; sr. rsch. scientist sci. and tech. divsn. Corning, NY, 1997—. Cons. Lotus Link Found., Buffalo, 1990—, West N.Y. Clin. Engring. Assn., Buffalo, 1989—; guest lectr. Woods Hole Oceanog. Instn., Autonomous Med. Sch., Monterrey, Mexico; instr. authentic sci. rsch. Campbell Savona H.S. Author: Theory & Design of Core Memory, 1979, Purely Natural Causes, 1999; editor various periodicals, 1970—; inventor, developer Retrospex Sys. for large vehicles. With USN, 1976-81. Grantee NIH, 1990. Mem. Am. Inst. Physics, Instrument Soc. Am., AAAS, Internat. Soc. Magnetic Resonance in Medicine, Soc. for Advancement Med. Instrument Design, SPIE. Mem. Anglican Ch. Achievements include patents pending for new surgical measuring tool, facsimile design, canine surgical tool; invention of various novel scientific instruments, Retrospex Rear Vision System, patented vehicular safety devices, microscopic MRI analysis. Office: Corning Sp Td 01 Corning NY 14831-0001

SALACUSE, JESWALD WILLIAM, lawyer, educator; b. Niagara Falls, NY, Jan. 28, 1938; s. William L. and Bessie B. (Buzzelli) S.; m. Donna Booth, Oct. 1, 1966; children: William, Maria. Diploma, U. Paris, 1959; AB, Hamilton Coll., 1960; JD, Harvard U., 1963. Bar: N.Y. 1965, Tex. 1980. Lectr. law Ahmadu Bello U., Nigeria, 1963-65; assoc. Conboy, Hewitt, O'Brien & Boardman, N.Y.C., 1965-67; assoc. dir. African Law Ctr., Columbia U., N.Y.C., 1967-68; prof., dir. Rsch. Ctr., Nat. Sch. Adminstrn., Zaire, 1968-71; Mid. East regional advisor on law and devel. Ford Found., Beirut, 1971-74, rep. in Sudan, 1974-77; vis. prof. U. Khartoum, Sudan, 1974-77; vis. scholar Harvard Law Sch., 1977-78; prof. law So. Meth. U., Dallas, 1978-86, dean, 1980-86; dean, prof. internat. law Fletcher Sch. Law and Diplomacy, Tufts U., Medford, Mass., 1986-94, Henry J. Braker prof. comml. law, 1994—. Fellow Inst. Advanced Legal Studies, U. London, 1995; vis. prof. Ecole Nat. Ponts et Chaussées, Paris, 1990-95, Inst. Empressa, Madrid, 1995, U. Bristol, U. London Sch. Oriental and African Studies, 1995—; cons. Ford Found., 1978-82, 93, U.S. Dept. State, 1978-80, UN Ctr. on Transnat. Corps., 1988—, Harvard Inst. Internat. Devel., 1990—, Asia Found., 1992, Harvard Law Sch./World Bank Laos Project, 1991-93; with Sri Lanka fin. sector project ISTI/U.S. AID, 1993-94; lectr. Georgetown U. Internat. Law Inst., 1978-94, Panam. U., Mexico City, 1981; chmn. com. on Mid. Ea. law Social Sci. Rsch. Coun., 1978-84; chmn. Coun. Internat. Exch. Scholars, 1987-91; bd. dirs. Boston World Affairs Coun., 1988-95, Emerging Markets Income Funds. I & II, Inc., Global Ptnrs. Income Fund, Inc., Salomon Bros. Worldwide Income Fund, Inc., Asia Tigers Fund, Inc., India Fund, Inc., Emerging Markets Floating Rate Fund, Inc., Mcpl. Ptnrs. Funds I & II, Salomon Bros. High Income Funds I & II, Salomon Bros. 2008 Worldwide Dollar Govt. Term Trust, Mcpl. Ptnrs. Funds I & II; trustee Southwestern Legal Found., 1992—, Am. U. Paris, 1993-97; pres. Internat. Third World Legal Studies Assn., 1987-91; chmn. Inst. Transnat. Arbitration, 1991-93; pres. Assn. Profl. Schs. Internat. Affairs, 1988-89; Fulbright disting. chair in comparative law, Italy, 2000; pres. Internat. Ctr. for Settlement Investment Disputes Arbitration Tribunal, 2004— Author: (with Kasunmu) Nigerian Family Law, 1966, An Introduction to Law in French-Speaking Africa, Vol. I, 1969, Vol. II, 1976, (with Steng) International Business Planning, 1982, Making Global Deals-Negotiating in the International Marketplace, 1991, The Art of Advice, 1994, (video course) Negotiating in Today's World, 1995, The Wise Advisor, 2000, The Global Negotiator, 2003; contbr. articles to profl. jours. Mem. ABA, Dallas Bar Found. (trustee 1983-86), Coun. on Fgn. Rels., Am. Law Inst., Am. Soc. Internat. Law, Cosmos Club (Washington). Home: 220 Stone Root Ln Concord MA 01742-4755 Office: Tufts U Fletcher Sch Law-Diplomacy Medford MA 02155 Office Phone: 617-627-3633. Business E-Mail: jeswald.salacuse@tufts.edu.

SALAH, JOSEPH ELIAS, research scientist, educator; b. Jerusalem, Feb. 27, 1944; came to U.S., 1961; s. Elias and Souraya (Nesnas) S.; m. Marie Shintani, Jan. 30, 1965; 1 child, Anthony. BSEE, U. Ill., 1965, MSEE, 1966; PhD, MIT, 1972. Staff mem. Lincoln Lab., MIT, Lexington, 1966-76, group leader, 1977-83, sr. lectr. dept. earth, atmospheric and planetary scis. Cambridge, 1983—, prin. rsch. scientist, 1983—, dir. Haystack Obs. Westford, 1983—. Mem. adv. com. for astron. scis. NSF, Washington, 1985-88, mem. steering com. Coupling, Energetics and Dynamics of Atmospheric Regions, 1987-90, 96—; mem. com. on solar terrestrial rsch. NRC-NAS, Washington, 1986-89. Contbr. articles on physics of earth's upper atmosphere and ionosphere to sci. jours. Mem. Am. Geophys. Union, Am. Astron. Soc., Am. Meteorol. Soc., Internat. Union Radio and Sci., Internat. Assn. for Geomagnetism and Aeronomy. Office: MIT Haystack Obs RR 40 Westford MA 01886

SALAH, SAGID, retired nuclear engineer; b. Seoul, Sept. 2, 1932; came to U.S., 1954; s. Galim and Faiza (Sultan) Salahutdin; m. Ravile Almakay, Apr. 2, 1966; children: Shamil, Kamil, Safiye. BChemE, U. Fla., 1958, MS in Nuclear Engring., 1960, PhD in Nuclear Engring., 1964. Nuclear engr. AEC, Bethesda, Md., 1964-66; sr. design engr. Westinghouse Astronuclear Lab., Large, Pa., 1966-70; sr. sys. engr. Westinghouse Nuclear Energy Sys., Pitts., 1970-73; mem. sys. safety engring. staff U.S. Nuclear Regulatory Commn., Bethesda, 1973-93; ret., 1993. Nuclear engring. cons. Oak Ridge (Tenn.) Inst. Nuclear Studies, 1963, 64; instr. U. Md., College Park, 1973-76. Contbr. articles to Nuclear Sci. and Engring. Youth coach Nat. Capital Soccer League, Vienna, Va., 1975-85. Mem. Am. Nuclear Soc. (emeritus, reviewer trans. papers 1972), Sigma Tau. Moslem. Achievements include measurements of neutron energy spectra in heterogeneous media using differential and integral methods, neutron energy spectra measurements and analysis in intermediate spectra reactors, three-dimensional transient analysis of boron dilution in PWR reactors. Home: 9302 Kilport Ct Vienna VA 22182-3426 E-mail: srsalah@cox.net.

SALAHUDDIN, AHMAD, civil engineer, educator; b. Anbala, India, Sept. 19, 1941; arrived in Zimbabwe, 1987; s. Ahmad Chaudhary Shamsuddin and Sultanta Mahmuda. BSCE, Panjab U., Lahore, Pakistan, 1961; MSc in Civil Engring., Columbia U., 1967; PhD in Structural Engring., Concordia U., Montreal, Can., 1971. Design engr. cons. industry, Pakistan, 1961-65; rsch. assoc., asst. prof. Concordia U., Montreal, 1971-73, 77-81; specialist cons. Can., 1973-76, 81-83; assoc. prof. U. Bahrain, 1983-85; dir. Can. Inst. Tech. Edn., 1985-87; prof. engring. U. Zimbabwe, Harare, 1987—. Editor specifications draft Standards Assn. Zimbabwe, 1993—; coord. Indsl. cons. Civil Engring. U. Zimbabwe, 1994—; mem. sci. com. Internat. Symposium Design of Structures, Germany, 1996; mem. African Structural Engring. Edn. Forum, Johannesburg, South Africa, 1996. Contbr. articles to profl. jours. Fulbright-Hays fellow, Washington, 1965-67. Mem. ASCE, Internat. Assn. Shell and Spatial Sturctures, Internat. Assn. Bridge and Structural Engring. Avocations: scientific reading and writing, listening to music, computer technology. Home: 6 Montagu Ct 142 Josiah Chinamano Ave Harare Zimbabwe Office: U Zimbabwe Civil Engring Dept PO Box MP167 Mount Pleasant Harare Zimbabwe Office Phone: 263-4-303211 ext. 1387. E-mail: salahuddin@eng.uz.ac.zw., ahmadzw@yahoo.com.

SALAM, DEBERA JEAN, accounting company executive; b. Milw., Apr. 1, 1957; d. Leonard John Stadler and Joanne (Allen) Huberty; 1 child, Anthony Robert Ellington. Student, Marquette U., 1974-76, U. Houston, 1985-86. Cert. payroll profl. Payroll adminstr. Vetco Offshore, Houston, 1979-80; payroll mgr. Oncor Corp., Houston, 1980-83, Waukesha-Pearce Corp., Houston, 1983-87; mgmt. cons. Automatic Data Processing, Roseland, N.J., 1987-90; pres., owner Payroll Support Assocs., Houston, 1990—97; sr. mgr. Ernst & Young LLP, Houston, 1997—. Bd. advisors Warren Gorham & Lamont, Alexandria, Va., 1990—; pub. speaker on payroll compliance and adminstrn. matters; expert witness FMC vs. U.S., 1994. Author: Principles of Payroll Administration, 18th edit., 2003, Payroll Practitioners Compliance Handbook, 13th edit., 2003, (home study course) Mastering Payroll, 12th edit., 2003; editor-in-chief Propub. Publs., 1989-98. Mem. Am. Soc. Payroll Mgmt. (dir. fed. compliance 1990-95), Am. Payroll Assn. (pres. Houston chpt. 1986-87, spl. achievement award 1987, cert.), Am. Inst. Profl. Bookkeepers (mem. bd. advisors 1988—). Office: 1401 McKinney Houston TX 77010

SALAMA, C. ANDRE TEWFIK, electrical engineering educator; b. Heliopolis, Egypt, Sept. 27, 1938; arrived in Can., 1957; s. Tewfik and Sarine (Bigio) S.; m. Rhoda R. Kurtz, Dec. 19, 1974. BASc with honours, U. B.C., Vancouver, Can., 1961, MASc, 1963, PhD, 1966. Registered profl. engr., Ont. Mem. sci. staff Bell No. Rsch., Ottawa, Ont., Can., 1966-67; asst. prof. elec. engring. U. Toronto, Ont., 1967-70, assoc. prof., 1970-77, prof., 1977-92, univ. prof., 1992—. Chmn., bd. dirs. Can. Microelectronics Corp., Kingston, Ont., 1984—; program leader, bd. dirs. Micronet, Toronto, 1990—. Mem. editorial bd. Solid State Electronics, 1982—; contbr. over 200 articles to sci. jours. Recipient Izaak Walton Killam Meml. prize, 1994; Info. Tech. Assn. Can. and Natural Scis. and Engring. Rsch. Coun. fellow U. Toronto, 1989-90. Fellow IEEE (assoc. editor Trans. on Cirs. and Systems 1987-89, Millenium medal 2000), Royal Soc. Can.; mem. Electrochem. Soc., Assn. Profl. Engrs. Ont. Avocations: swimming, sailing, scuba diving, horseback riding, reading. Office: U Toronto Dept Elec Engring Toronto ON Canada M5S 1A4

SALAMAN, MAUREEN KENNEDY, writer, nutritionist; b. Glendale, Calif., Apr. 4, 1937; d. Ted and Elena (Peters) Kennedy; 1 child, Sean. With Making Healthy Choices, 1980—; hostess Le Sea Broadcasting, Sky Angel Satellite Worldwide Direct TV with Maureen Kennedy Salaman; pres. Nat. Health Fedn., Monrovia, Calif., 1982—. Cons., lectr., rschr. on cancer rsch. and metabolic medicine, nutrition; lobbyist for freedom of choice. Author: Foods That Heal, Nutrition: The Cancer Answer, 1983, 2d edit., The Diet Bible, The Light at the End of the Refrigerator, All Your Health Questions Answered, Naturally I and II, Achieving Super Immunity, How to Renew You; editor: Nosy News, Health Freedom News, 1982—2004; contbr. articles to profl. jours. Office: Nat Health Fedn PO Box 688 Monrovia CA 91017-0688 also: Maureen Kennedy Salaman Inc 1259 El Camino Real Ste 1500 Menlo Park CA 94025-4227

SALAMEH, SAMER FADI, communications executive; b. Beruit, Lebanon, Sept. 19, 1964; came to U.S., 1984; s. Souhad Boulos and Marie Kattar Salameh; m. Alexandra Salem-Slim, Nov. 15, 1997; 1 child, Natasha. BS in Mgmt. and Tech. Transfer, Polytech. U. of N.Y., 1988; M in Internat. Bus., The Fletcher Sch., 1991. Sales mgr. Nouvelles Frontiers, N.Y.C., 1985-86; legal asst. Curtis, Mallet-Prevost, N.Y.C., 1987-88; sr. legal asst. Carter Led Yard & Milburn, N.Y.C., 1988-89; strategic mktg. mgr. MCI Telecomms., Petagon City, Va., 1991-93, product mgr. internat. card, 1994; v.p. fin. Merl Industries, Bethesda, Md., 1993; dir. long distance divsn. SBC Comms., Mexico City, Mex., 1994—. Spl. advisor to CEO Telefonos de Mex., Mexico City, 1996—. Jabarra scholar Jacobs Industries, 1986-88, Citicorp-Wriston scholarship Citibank, 1990-91. Mem. Harvard Club. Roman Catholic. Avocations: padi scubadiving, skiing. Office: Prodigy Comms Inc 44 S Broadway Ste Ll3 White Plains NY 10601-4422

SALAMON, LESTER MILTON, political science educator; b. Pitts., Jan. 11, 1943; s. Victor William Salamon and Helen (Sanders) Weiss; m. Lynda Anne Brown, June 27, 1965; children: Noah, Matthew. BA in Econs. and Pub. Policy, Princeton U., 1964; PhD in Govt., Harvard U., 1971. Instr. dept. polit. sci. Tougaloo (Miss.) Coll., 1966-67; asst. prof. Vanderbilt U., Nashville, 1970-73; assoc. prof. policy scis. and polit. sci. Duke U., Durham, N.C., 1973-80, dir. Ctr. for Urban and Regional Devel., 1973—77; dep. assoc. dir. U.S. Office Mgmt. and Budget, Washington, 1977-79; dir. Ctr. for Governance and Mgmt. Rsch., Urban Inst., Washington, 1980-86; prof., dir. Inst. for Policy Studies, Johns Hopkins U., Balt., 1987-97, dir. Ctr. Civil Soc. Studies, 1997—. Author: America's Nonprofit Sector: A Primer, 1992, The Emerging Sector: Nonprofit Organizations in Comparative Perspective, 1994, Partners in Public Service: Government Nonprofit Relations in the Modern Welfare State, 1995, Defining the Nonprofit Sector: A Cross-National Analysis, 1996, International Guide to Nonprofit Law, 1997; editor: Beyond Privatization, 1989, Human Capital and America's Future, 1991, Global Civil Society, 1998, The Tools of Government, A Guide to The New Governance, 2002, The State of Non-Profit America, 2002, The Resilient Sector, 2003; mem. editl. bd. Adminstrn. and Soc., 1985—, Voluntas, 1988—, Nonprofit and Voluntary Sector Quar., 1990—, Pub. Adminstrn. Rev., 2000—. Mem. Balt. City Planning Commn., 1987-95; mem. Chesapeake Cmty. Found.; mem. adv. com on voluntary fgn. aid USAID. Recipient Laverne Burchfield award Am. Soc. Pub. Adminstrn., 1977, Disting. Book award Assn. of Rschrs. on Nonprofit Orgns. and Vol. Action, Disting. Book award Ind. Sector, 2002, Disting. Achievement award Assn. Rschrs. on Nonprofit Orgns. and Vol. Action, 2004. Mem. Internat. Soc. Third Sector Rsch. (vice chmn. 1991-95), Nat. Acad. Pub. Adminstrn., Social Sci. Rsch. Coun. (nonprofit field com.), Md. Assn. Nonprofit Orgns. (bd. dirs.). Avocations: tennis, swimming, carpentry, sailing. Home: 903 Lynch Dr Arnold MD 21012-1504 Office: Johns Hopkins U Inst Policy Studies 3400 N Charles St Baltimore MD 21218-2680 E-mail: lsalamon@jhu.edu.

SALAMON, LINDA BRADLEY, English literature educator; b. Elmira, N.Y., Nov. 20, 1941; d. Grant Ellsworth and Evelyn E. (Ward) Bradley; divorced; children: Michael Lawrence, Timothy Martin. BA, Radcliffe Coll., 1963; MA, Bryn Mawr Coll., 1964, PhD, 1971; Advanced Mgmt. Cert., Harvard U. Bus. Sch., 1978; D.H.L., St. Louis Coll. Pharmacy, 1993. Lectr., adj. asst. prof. Eng., Dartmouth Coll., Hanover, N.H., 1967-72; mem. faculty lit. Bennington Coll., Vt., 1974-75; dean students Wells Coll., Aurora, N.Y., 1975-77; exec. asst. to pres. U. Pa., Phila., 1977-79; assoc. prof. English, Washington U., St. Louis, 1979-88, prof., 1988-92, dean Coll. Arts and Scis., 1979-92; prof. English, George Washington U., Washington, 1992—; dean Columbian Coll. Arts and Sci., Washington, 1992-95; interim v.p. for acad. affairs George Washington U., Washington, 1995-96. Mem. faculty Bryn Mawr Summer Inst. for Women, 1979-99. Author, co-editor: Nicholas

Hilliard's Art of Limning, 1983; co-author: Integrity in the College Curriculum, 1985; contbr. numerous articles to literary and ednl. jours. Bd. dirs. Assn. Am. Colls., vice chmn., 1985, chmn., 1986; bd. dirs. Greater St. Louis council Girl Scouts U.S.A.; trustee Coll. Bd., St. Louis Coll. Pharmacy. Fellow Radcliffe Inst., 1973-74, Fulbright fellow, Taiwan, 2003, Ringler fellow Huntington Libr, 2004; Am. Philos. Soc. Penrose grantee, 1974; fellow Folger Shakespeare Libr., 1986, NEH Montaigne Inst., 1988. Mem. MLA, Renaissance Soc. Am., Cosmos Club, Phi Beta Kappa. Office: George Washington U Dept of Eng Rome Hall 760 801 22D St NW Washington DC 20052-0001

SALAMON, MICHAEL JACOB, psychologist, health care and psychology educator, media consultant; b. Bklyn., Oct. 18, 1951; s. Milton and Bessie (Kessler) S. BA, Queens Coll., 1974, MA, 1977, Hofstra U., 1981, PhD, 1983. Project dir. Nat. Coun. Sr. League, Far Rockaway, N.Y., 1974-78; dir., founder Adult Devel. Ctr., Hewlett, N.Y., 1978—; dir. rsch. Gustave Hartman YM-YWHA, Far Rockaway, 1978-82; asst. prof. psychology L.I. U., 1981-83; gerontology cons. St. Johns Hosp., Far Rockaway, 1980-83; adult devel. cons. CSE, Far Rockaway, 1980-83, N.Y. State Dept. of Labor, Far Rockaway, 1978-80; dir. rsch. divsn. Hebrew Home for Aged at Riverdale, 1983-85; dir. psychology St. John's Home and Hosp., 1986-88; dir. rsch., clin. supr. New Hope Guild Ctrs., Bklyn., 1989—. Vis. scholar Brookdale Found., Jerusalem, 1985; TV, radio, print media cons. on psych. issues. Author: Adult Assessment Scale, 1982; textbooks on gerontology, nursing homes, marriage and family, child and adolescent develop.; editor: Jour. Clin. Gerontology; reviewer Jour. Cons. and Clin. Psychology; contbr. articles to profl. jours. Assoc. bd. dirs. Dem. Club of Rockaways, 1981; bd. dirs. Young Israel of Woodmere, 1982; mem. bd. edn., exec. bd. Hebrew Acad. of the Five Towns and Rockaways, 1991, chmn., 1995-97; mem. bd. edn. PTACH Ctrs. for Learning Disabilities, 1991, chmn. 2000—. Bruner Found. grant, 1979, N.Y. State Dept. Social Svcs. grant, 1982. Fellow: APA, Prescribing Psychologists Register, Gerontol. Soc. Am. (rsch. fellow 1983, fellow behavior and soc. scis. sect. 1998); mem.: Am. Psychiat. Assn., Assn. Jewish Scientists, Psychologists in Long-Term Care Network (bd. dirs., chair steering com. 1993—98), Northeastern Gerontol. Soc. Democrat. Jewish. Office: Adult Devel Ctr 1728 Broadway Hewlett NY 11557-1601 Office Phone: 516-596-0073.

SALAMON, MIKLOS DEZSO GYORGY, mining engineer, educator; b. Balkany, Hungary, May 20, 1933; came to U.S., 1986; naturalized, 1993; s. Miklos and Sarolta (Obetko) S.; m. Agota Maria Meszaros, July 11, 1953; children: Miklos, Gabor. Diploma in Engring., Polytech U., Sopron, Hungary, 1956; PhD, U. Durham, Newcastle, England, 1962; doctorem honoris causa, U. Miskolc, Hungary, 1990. Rsch. asst. dept. mining engring. U. Durham, 1959-63; dir. rsch. Coal Mining Rsch. Controlling Coun., Johannesburg, South Africa, 1963-66; dir. collieries rsch. lab. Chamber of Mines of South Africa, Johannesburg, 1966-74, dir. gen. rsch. orgn., 1974-86; disting. prof. Colo. Sch. Mines, Golden, 1986-98, disting. prof. emeritus, 1998—, head dept. mining engring., 1986-90; dir. Colo. Mining and Mineral Resources Rsch. Inst., 1990-94; pres. Salamon Cons. Inc., Arvada, Colo., 1995—. 22d Sir Julius Wernher Meml. lectr., 1988; hon. prof. U. Witwatersrand, Johannesburg, 1979-86; vis. prof. U. Minn., Mpls., 1981, U. Tex., Austin, 1982, U. NSW, Sydney, Australia, 1990, 91-96; mem. Presdl. Commn. of Inquiry into Safety and Health in South African Mining Industry, 1994-95. Co-author: Rock Mechanics Applied to the Study of Rockbursts, 1966, Rock Mechanics in Coal Mining, 1976; contbr. articles to profl. jours. Mem. Pres.'s Sci. Adv. Council, Cape Town, South Africa, 1984-86, Nat. Sci. Priorities Com., Pretoria, South Africa, 1984-86. Recipient Nat. award Assn. Scis. and Tech. Socs., South Africa, 1971. Fellow South African Inst. Mining and Metallurgy (hon. life, v.p. 1974-76, pres. 1976-77, gold medal 1964, 85, Stokes award 1986, silver medal 1991, 99), Inst. Mining and Metallurgy (London), Hungarian Acad. Scis. (external), 1998; mem. AIME, Internat. Soc. Rock Mechanics. Roman Catholic. E-mail: mdg_salamon@msn.com.

SALAMON, MYRON BEN, physicist, educator, dean; b. Pitts., June 4, 1939; s. Victor William and Helen (Sanders) S.; m. Sonya Maxine Blank, June 12, 1960; children— David, Aaron. BS, Carnegie-Mellon U., 1961; PhD, U. Calif., Berkeley, 1966. Asst. prof. physics U. Ill., Urbana, 1966-72, assoc. prof., 1972-74, prof., 1974—, program dir. Materials Research Lab., 1984-91, assoc. dean. Coll. Engring., 2000—. Vis. scientist U. Tokyo, 1966, 71, Tech. U. Munich, Fed. Republic Germany, 1974-75; cons. NSF; Disting. Vis. Prof. Tsukuba (Japan) U., 1995-96. Editor: Physics of Superionic Conductors, 1979; co-editor: Modulated Structures, 1979; divisional assoc. editor: Phys. Rev. Letters, 1992-96; contbr. sci. papers to profl. jours. Recipient Alexander von Humboldt Sr. U.S. Scientist award, 1974-75; NSF coop. fellow, 1964-66; postdoctoral fellow, 1966; A.P. Sloan fellow, 1972-73; Berndt Matthias scholar Los Alamos Nat. Lab., 1995-96; visiting scientist CNRS and Inst. Laue-Langevin Grenoble, France, 1981-82. Fellow Am. Phys. Soc. Office: U Ill Coll Engring 1308 W Green St Urbana IL 61801-9013 Office Phone: 217-333-2152.

SALAMON, RENAY, real estate broker; b. N.Y.C., May 13, 1948; d. Solomon and Mollie (Friedman) Langman; m. Maier Salamon, Aug. 10, 1968; children: Mollie, Jean, Leah, Sharon, Eugene. BA, Hunter Coll., 1969. Licensed real estate borker, N.J. Mgr. office Customode Designs Inc., N.Y.C., 1966-68; co-owner Salamon Dairy Farms, Three Bridges, N.J., 1968-86; assoc. realtor Max. D. Shuman Realty Inc., Flemington, N.J., 1983-85; pres., chief exec. officer Liberty Hill Realty Inc., Flemington, N.J., 1985—. Cons. Illva Saronna Inc. (Illva Group), Edison, N.J. 1985—; real estate devel. joint venture with M.R.F.S. Realty Inc. (Illva Group), 1986—; bd. dirs. Anderson House. Mem. Readington twp. Environ. Commn., Whitehouse Sta., N.J., 1978-87, N.J. Assn. Environ. Commrs., Trenton, 1978—; fundraiser Rutgers Prep. Sch., Somerset, N.J., 1984-95; bd. dirs. Hunterdon County YMCA, 1987-95, Anderson House, 2000-; mem. N.J.-Israel Commn., 1998—; bd. trustees Rutgers Prep. Sch., 2000—; chair Hunterdon County Bd. Social Svc., 2002-; vice-chair Hunterdon County Health and Human Svcs. Commn., 2002-. Named N.J. Broker Record, Forbes Inc., N.Y.C. 1987. Mem.: Realtors Land Inst. Republican. Jewish. Office: Liberty Hill Realty Inc 415 US Highway 202 Flemington NJ 08822-6021

SALAMONE, JOSEPH CHARLES, polymer chemistry educator; b. Bklyn., Dec. 27, 1939; s. Joseph John and Angela (Barbagallo) S.; children: Robert, Alicia, Christopher. BS in Chemistry, Hofstra U., 1961; PhD in Chemistry, Poly. Inst. N.Y., 1967. NIH postdoctoral fellow U. Liverpool, England, 1966-67; rsch. assoc., Horace H. Rackham postdoctoral fellow U. Mich., Ann Arbor, 1967-70, adminstrv. sec., 1968-70; asst. prof., then assoc. prof. chemistry U. Mass., Lowell, 1970-76, prof., 1976-90, prof. emeritus, 1990—, dean Coll Sci., 1978-84, Disting. Rsch. fellow, 1984-90, chmn. dept. chemistry, 1975-78. Pres. Optimers Inc., Lowell, 1985-99; bd. dirs. Rochal Industries, Inc., Boca Raton, Fla.; cons. editor CRC Press, Inc., Boca Raton, 1992-97; v.p. chem. rsch. Bausch and Lomb, 1997-2000, v.p. rsch., 2000—. Author 2 books, 2 encys.; mem. editl. bd. Polymer, 1976-94, Jour. Macromolecular Sci.-Chemistry, 1985-2003, Progress of Polymer Sci., 1987-2002, ChemTech, 1995-99; adv. bd. Jour. Polymer Sci., 1974—; editor-in-chief Polymeric Materials Ency., 1993-97; contbr. over 167 articles to profl. jours.; holder 41 U.S. and internat. patents. Recipient Disting Alumnus award, Poly. Inst. N.Y., 1984. Mem. Am. Chem. Soc. (chmn. divsn. polymer chemistry 1982, Indsl. Chemistry award 2004), Polymer Sci., Am. Acad. Ophthalmology (assoc.), Pacific Polymer Fedn. (sec., treas. 1988-90, dep. v.p. 1991-92, v.p., 1993, pres. 1994-95). Office: Bausch & Lomb 1400 N Goodman St PO Box 30450 Rochester NY 14603-0450 Office Phone: 585-338-0042. Business E-Mail: joe_salamone@bausch.com.

SALAMOUN, PETER V. retired manufacturing executive; b. Jirice, Czechoslovakia, Sept. 6, 1926; came to U.S., 1956; s. Charles and Helen Salamoun; m. Mildred B. Bohac, June 3, 1950; children: Dashie Schouten, Peter C. Diploma in Bus., Acad. of Commerce, Czechoslovakia, 1946; Diploma in Indsl. Engring., Indsl. Engring. Coll., Chgo., 1959; Diploma in Bus., Al Hamilton Exec. GRP Program, Chgo., 1964. Cert. mfg. engr. Supt. plastics, castings Bell & Howell Co., Chgo., 1959-66, mgr. mfg., 1966-78, divsn. mgr. mfg., 1978-81, ops. mgr., 1981-85, internat. project mgr., 1985-87, ops. mgr., v.p. ops. Documail Systems, 1987-92. V.p., team leader total quality mgmt. Bell & Howell Documail Systems Comp., Chgo., 1992-93; internat. mfg. cons. Bell & Howell, Brazil, Australia, 1985-87, Internat. Exec. Svc. Corps, Stamford, Conn., 1992—. Author productivity and quality tech. papers in field. Chmn. referendum Niles (Ill.) Park Dist.; planning com. Save Open Space Referendum Project, Niles, 1974. Mem. Czechoslovak Nat. Coun. (chpt. chmn. 1988), Soc. Plastic Engrs. (sr. mem.) Republican. Roman Catholic. Avocations: snowskiing, traveling, langs., tree planting. Home: 2826 Pawnee Cir Glenview IL 60025-7301

SALAND, LINDA CAROL, anatomy educator, neuroscience researcher; b. NYC, Oct. 24, 1942; d. Charles and Esther (Weingarten) Gewirtz; m. Joel S. Saland, Aug. 16, 1964; children: Kenneth, Jeffrey. BS, CCNY, 1963, PhD in Biology, 1968; MA in Zoology, Columbia U., 1965. Rsch. assoc. dept. anatomy Columbia U. Coll. Physicians and Surgeons, N.Y.C., 1968-69; sr. rsch. assoc. dept. anatomy Sch. Medicine U. N.Mex., Albuquerque, 1971-78, asst. prof. anatomy, 1978-83, assoc. prof., 1983-89, prof., 1989-97, prof. dept. neuroscis., 1997—. Ad hoc reviewer study sect. NIH, 1994, 95, 97, 2000, mem. site visit team. Mem. editl. bd. Anat. Record, 1980-98; contbr. articles to profl. jours. Recipient Khatali Tchg. Excellence award, U. N.Mex. Med. Class of 2001; fellow NDEA, 1966—68. Mem. AAAS, Soc. for Neurosci., Women in Neurosci. (chmn. steering com. 1991-93). Office: U New Mex Sch Medicine Dept Neurosci MSC 084740 Albuquerque NM 87131-0001 Business E-Mail: lsaland@salud.unm.edu.

SALANS, CARL FREDRIC, lawyer; b. Chicago Heights, Ill., Mar. 13, 1933; arrived in France, 1972; s. Leon and Jean (Rudnick) Salans; m. Edith Motel, Sept. 26, 1956; children: Eric Lee, Marc Robert, Christopher John. AB, Harvard U., 1954; BA, Cambridge (Eng.) U., 1956, MA, 1958, LLB, 1958; JD, U. Chgo., 1957. Bar: Ill. 1958, D.C. 1973, U.S. Supreme Ct. 1972, (admitted in France as conseil juridique) 1972, (admitted in France as avocat) 1992. With State Dept., 1959-72, dep. legal adviser, 1966-72; practice law Paris, 1972—; ret. ptnr. Salans & Assocs., Paris, 1978—. Legal adviser U.S. del. Vietnam Peace Talk, Paris, 1968—71; vice-chmn. ICC Internat. Ct. Arbitration; arbitrator internat. cases; arbitrator U.S.-Iran Claims Tribunal, The Hague; mem. editl. bd. ICC Arbitration Bulletin. Mem.: ABA (chmn. com. East-West trade and investment 1975—82), Chartered Inst. of Arbitrators (U.K), Am. Arbitration Assn. (panel arbitrators), Am. Soc. Internat. Law, Am. C. of C. in France (bd. dirs. 1977—87, chmn. laws and pub. affairs com. 1980—85). Home: 18 Ave Raphael 75016 Paris France Office: Salans & Assocs 9 Rue Boissy d'Anglas 75008 Paris France Office Phone: 33 1 42 68 48 00. E-mail: csalans@salans.com.

SALANS, LESTER BARRY, physician, scientist, educator; b. Chicago Heights, Ill., Jan. 25, 1936; s. Leon K. and Jean (Rudnick) S.; m. Lois Audrey Kapp, Dec. 21, 1958; children: Laurence Eliot, Andrea Eileen. BA, U. Mich., 1957; MD with honors, U. Ill., 1961. Internal medicine intern Stanford U. Med. Ctr., 1961, resident, 1962-64; USPHS postdoctoral and spl. fellow Rockefeller U., 1964-67, asst. prof., 1967-68; asst. prof. medicine Dartmouth Coll., 1968-70, assoc. prof., 1970-77; assoc. dir. diabetes, endocrinology, metabolism, also chief lab. cellular metabolism and obesity Nat. Inst. Arthritis, Metabolism and Digestive Diseases, NIH, Bethesda, Md., 1976-81; adj. prof. Dartmouth Coll., 1978-79; dir. Nat. Inst. Arthritis, Diabetes, Digestive and Kidney Diseases, NIH, 1981-84; adj. prof. Rockefeller U., 1984—; v.p., head preclin. rsch. Sandoz Rsch. Inst., 1985-92; dean Mt. Sinai Sch. Medicine, 1984, prof. internal medicine, 1984-85, clin. prof. medicine, 1987—; v.p. scientific and acad. affairs Sandoz Rsch. Inst., 1993-97; pres. LBS Advisors, Inc., 1997—; prin. BioPharmAnalysis LLC, 2001—, Biopharmanalysis, LLC, 2001. Adj. prof. Rockefeller U., 1985—2001; vis. prof. U. Geneva, Switzerland, 1974—75; dir. Forest Labs., 1998—; mem. adv. bd. Naomi Berrie Diabetes Ctr., Columbia-Presbyn. Hosp., 1999—; vis. prof. dept. medicine Columbia U. Sch. Health Scis. Contbr. articles on insulin, diabetes mellitus, obesity to profl. jours., textbooks. Recipient NIH Rsch. Career Devel. award, 1972-76, NIH Dir. award, 1980, Juvenile Diabetes Fedn Pub. Svc. award, 1979 Fellow ACP; mem. AAAS, Am. Soc. Clin. Investigation, Am. Fed. Clin. Rsch., Am. Diabetes Soc., Am. Diabetes Assn. (Charles H. Best award 1985), Endocrine Soc., Assn. Am. Physicians, Am. Soc. Clin. Nutrition. Office: 767 Fifth Ave Ste 11-64 11th fl New York NY 10153

SALANT, DAVID JOHN, medical educator, nephrologist; b. Johannesburg, May 8, 1944; m. Anne Salant; children: Alon, Talya, Nira. MB BCh, U. of Witwatersrand, Johannesburg, 1969. Diplomate Am. Bd. Internal Medicine, Am. Bd. Nephrology. Cons. nephrologist Johannesburg Gen. Hosp., 1974-77; rsch. fellow Boston U. Med. Ctr., 1977-78, asst. prof. medicine, 1979-83, assoc. prof. medicine, 1983-88, prof. medicine, 1988—, chief renal sect., 1987—; prof. pathology and lab. medicine Boston U. Sch. Medicine, 1992—. Vis. prof. Stanford U., Calif., 1995; mem. study sect. NIH, Bethesda, Md., 1989-93. Contbr. articles to profl. jours., chpts. to books. Mem. sci. adv. bd. Nat. Kidney Found., N.Y.C., 1996-2002. Recipient Established Investigator award Am. Heart Assn., 1985-90. Mem. Am. Soc. Clin. Investigation, Am. Assn. Physicians, Am. Bd. Internal Medicine (bd. examiners neph. 1992-2002, bd. dirs. 1998-2002). Office: Boston U Med Ctr Evans Biomed Rsch Ctr 650 Albany St Fl 5 Boston MA 02118-2518 Fax: 617-638-7326. E-mail: djsalant@acs.bu.edu.

SALANT, RICHARD FRANK, mechanical engineer, educator; b. N.Y.C., Sept. 4, 1941; s. Joseph and Augusta (Dick) S.; m. Barbel Lang, Sept. 9, 1962; children: Scott M., Stephanie. BS, MS, MIT, 1963, DSc, 1967. Registered profl. engr., Ga. Asst. prof. U. Calif. Berkeley, 1966-68; asst. prof., assoc. prof. MIT, Cambridge, 1968-72; mgr. fluid mech. and heat transfer Borg-Warner Rsch. Ctr., Des Plaines, Ill., 1972-87; prof., chair tribology rsch. group Ga. Inst. Tech., Atlanta, 1987—, Ga. Power Disting. prof., 2001—. Cons. fluid sealing tech., Atlanta, 1987—. Assoc. editor Jour. Tribology, 1993-99, Jour. Fluids Engring., 1984-87; contbr. articles to profl. jours.; patentee in field. Fellow ASME (Henry R. Worthington medal 1996, Machine Design award 2003), Soc. Tribologists and Lubrication Engrs. (Edmond E. Bisson award 2000, Frank P. Bussick award 2002). Home: 1138 Manning Farms Ct Dunwoody GA 30338-2648 Office: Ga Inst Tech Sch Mech Engring Atlanta GA 30332-0405 Business E-Mail: richard.salant@me.gatech.edu.

SALAS, MAX, pediatrician, educator; MD, Nat. U. Mex., Mexico City, 1964. Diplomate Am. Bd. Pediats., 1969, Am. Bd. Pediatric Endocrinology, 1986. Rotating intern St. Luke's Hosp., St. Paul, 1963—64; resident in pediat. Children's Hosp., Boston, 1965—67, Sheffield, England, 1967—68; fellow in pediatric endocrinology Pitts. Children's Hosp., 1977—79, North Shore Univ. Hosp., Manhasset, NY, 1979—80; assoc. prof. pediat. UMDNJ/Robert Wood Johnson Med. Sch., New Brunswick, NJ, 1980—. Office: St Peters Univ Hosp 254 Easton Ave New Brunswick NJ 08901-1977 Office Phone: 732-745-8574.

SALAS, RANDALL NOUEL, automotive company executive; b. Willemstad, Curazao, Venezuela, Oct. 20, 1945; s. Herbert and Claire (Nouel) S.; m. Silvia M. Mago, Feb. 16, 1974; children: Maria Silvia, Claudia Isabella. Student, Santiago de León, Caracas, Venezuela, 1965; BS in Indsl. Engring., Cath. U., Caracas, 1971, BA in Journalism, 1976. Pilots coordinating engr. Gen. Motors de Venezuela, Caracas, 1971-73, methods engr., 1973-76, gen. supply products facilitator, 1976-78, products facility mgr., 1978-80, prodn. mgr., 1980-81, dir. personnel, 1981-86, dir. personnel and pub. govtl. relations, v.p., 1987-97; human resources and pub. rels. v.p. Orinoco Iron-Sivensa, Caracas, 1997—. Bd. dirs. Camara Automotriz de Venezuela, Caracas. Named to Labor Merit Order 1st Degree, Ministry of Labor, 1987. Mem. Coll. Engrs. Venezuela, Assn. Venezolana de Ejecutivos, Nat. Assn. Indsl. Relations Execs. Clubs: Lagunita Country (Caracas). Roman Catholic. Avocation: reading. Office: Sivensa Av Venezuela Torre America Piso 14 Bello Monte Caracas 1060 Venezuela Address: c/o SDP (OI) 14505 Commerce Way Ste 700 Miami Lakes FL 33016-1514

SALAT, CRISTINA, writer; b. N.Y.C. Student, L.I. U. Freelance editor, 1987—; author, editor, manuscript cons., workshop facilitator, 1985—. Author: Living in Secret, 1993, Alias Diamond Jones, 1993, Min Mors Koereste hedder Janey, 1995, Defending the Dreamcatchers, 1999, Robin, Romeo & Juliette, 1999, Peanut's Emergency, 1999; contbr. to anthologies including Sister/Stranger, 1993, Am I Blue, 1994, Once Upon A Time, 1996; contbr. to popular publ. Home: PO Box 13214 Pahoa HI 96778

SALATHE, JOHN, JR., retired manufacturing executive; b. Montreal, Sept. 25, 1928; s. John and Ida (Schenk) S.; m. Harriet Edith Styles; children: Linda Paul, Craig. BSME, San Jose State U., 1950. Gen. mgr. Indsl. Steel Tank & Body Co., Berkeley, Calif., 1958-62; project mgr. Pacific Foundry div. PACCAR Inc., Renton, Wash., 1962-66, prodn. mgr., 1966-70, asst. gen. mgr., 1970-71, gen. mgr., 1971-79; asst. v.p. PACCAR Inc., Bellevue, Wash., 1979-81, v.p., 1981-90; ret., 1991. Bd. dirs. Jr. Achievement, Seattle, 1979-85; mem. adv. bd. Seattle Pacific U., 1985-95. Sloan fellow Stanford U., 1970. Mem. Soc. Mfg. Engrs. (sr.), Am. Soc. Quality Control (sr.). Avocations: gardening, boating, reading.

SALATKA, CHARLES ALEXANDER, retired archbishop; b. Grand Rapids, Mich., Feb. 26, 1918; s. Charles and Mary (Balun) Salatka. Student, St. Joseph's Sem., Grand Rapids, 1932—38; MA, Cath. U. Am., 1941; JCL, Inst. Civil and Canon Law, Rome, 1948. Ordained priest Roman Catholic Ch., 1945. Instr. St. Joseph's Sem., Grand Rapids, 1945; assigned chancery office Diocese of Grand Rapids, 1948—54, vice chancellor, 1954—61; aux. bishop, 1961; vicar gen., 1961; consecrated bishop, 1962; pastor St. James Parish, Grand Rapids, 1962—68; titular bishop of Cariana and aux. bishop Diocese of Grand Rapids, 1962—68; bishop of Diocese of Marquette, 1968—77; archbishop of Diocese of Okla. City, 1977—92; ret., 1992. Mem.: Canon Law Soc. Am. Roman Catholic.

SALAVERRIA, HELENA CLARA, retired language educator; b. May 19, 1923; d. Blas Saturnino and Eugenia Irene (Loyarte) S. AB, U. Calif., Berkeley, 1945, secondary tchg. cert., 1946; MA, Stanford U., 1962. H.S. tchr., 1946-57; asst. prof. Luther Coll., Decorah, Iowa, 1959-60; prof. Spanish Bakersfield (Calif.) Coll., 1961—83, chmn. dept., 1973-80; ret., 1983. Mem. srs. adv. group edn. Cuesta Coll. Cmty. Svcs. Mem. AAUW (edn. com.), NEA, Calif. Fgn. Lang. Tchrs. Assn. (dir. 1976-77), Kern County Fgn. Lang. Tchrs. Assn. (pres. 1975-77), Union Concerned Scientists, Natural Resources Def. Coun., Calif. Tchrs. Assn. (chpt. sec. 1951-52), Yolo County Coun. Retarded, Soc. Basque Studies in Am., RSVP, Amnesty Internat., Common Cause, Sierra Club, Prytanean Alumnae, U. Women of Cambria, U. Calif. Alumni Assn., Stanford U. Alumni Assn., Friends of the Cambria Libr. Democrat. Home: PO Box 63 Cambria CA 93428-0063

SALAZAR, JOHN PAUL, lawyer; b. Albuquerque, N.Mex., Feb. 6, 1943; s. Henry Houghton and Anita (Chavez) Salazar; m. Terri J. Bestgen, June 12, 1967; children: Monique Michelle, John Paul, Stephen Houghton. BA, U. N.Mex., 1965; JD, Stanford U., 1968. Bar: N.Mex. 1968, U.S. Dist. Ct. N.Mex. 1968, U.S. Ct. Appeals (10th cir.) 1968, U.S. Supreme Ct. 1979. Dir. Rodey, Dickason, Sloan, Akin & Robb, P.A., Albuquerque, 1968—, mem. exec. com., 1984—86, mng. dir., west side office, 1985—88, chmn., environ. law sect., 1989—92, mem. exec. com., 1992—93, chair, environ. and natural resources dept., 1992—95, mem. exec. com., 1999—, chair, bus. dept., 2000—. Bd. visitors Stanford U. Law Sch., Calif., 1973—76; state campaign chmn. Jeff Bingaman for Atty. Gen., 1978, Jeff Bingaman for U.S. Sen., 1982, 84, 94; mem. presdl. search com. U. N.Mex., 1989—90; mem. Albuquerque Econ. Forum, past mem. bd. dirs., past chair, gov. affairs com., past vice chair; former hon. Cmdr. Field Command Def. Nuc. Agy., Kirtland AFB. Sr. editor N.Mex. Environ. Law Handbook, 1990, 2d edit., 1991, 3d edit., 1993. Former bd. dirs. N.Mex. Symphony Orch.; mem. Easter Seal Soc.; vice chmn. City of Albuquerque Charter Revision com., 1970—71; mem. Albuquerque Unity, 1971—73; chmn. N.Mex. Disting. Pub. Svc. Awards Coun., 1986, 1987; chmn. city affairs com. Albuquerque C. of C., 1972, v.p. govtl. affairs, 1973, pres.-elect, 1974, pres., 1975, chmn. nominating com., 1977; mem. Presbyn. Hosp. Ctr. Assocs.; bd. dirs. Albuquerque Hispano C. of C., 2000—. Mem.: ABA (environ. aspects of real estate transactions com., land use regulation com., Real Property, Probate & Trust Law sect., land use com., Urban, State and Local Govt. sect.), Albuquerque Armed Forces Adv. Assn., U. N.Mex. Alumni Assn. (pres. 1983—84, exec. com. 1982—85, bd. dirs. 1979—85), N.Mex. Chpt. Nat. Assn. Indsl. and Office Parks (past mem. N.Mex. border commn., past chair com. border devel. and internat. trade, mem. exec. com., Gov.'s Bus. Adv. Coun.), N.Mex. State Bar Assn. (former mem. jud. selection com., former sec.-treas. Young Lawyers sect., mem. Real Property, Probate and Trust sect., mem. Pub. Law sect., mem. Natural Resources, Energy and Environ. Law sect.), Albuquerque Bar Assn. (former mem. jud. selection com., former dir.), Nat. Resources, Energy & Environ. Law Sect. Roman Catholic. Office: PO Box 1888 Albuquerque NM 87103-1888

SALAZAR, KENNETH L. state attorney general; b. Mar. 2, 1955; s. Henry and Emma Salazar; m. Hope Hernandez; children: Melinda, Andrea. BA in Polit. Sci., Colo. Coll., 1977, LLD (hon.), 1993; JD, U. Mich., 1981. Bar: Colo. 1981, U.S. Dist. Ct. Colo. 1981, U.S. Ct. Appeals (10th cir.) 1981, U.S. Supreme Ct. 1999. Farmer, rancher, Conejos County, Colo.; law clk. Colo. Atty. Gen., 1979; assoc. Sherman & Howard, Denver, 1981—86; chief legal counsel Office of Gov., Denver, 1986—90; exec. dir. Colo. Dept. Natural Resources, Denver, 1990—94; dir. Parcel, Mauro, Hultin & Spaanstra, Denver, 1994—98; atty. gen. State of Colo., 1999—. Gov.'s rep. State Bd. Equalization, Denver, 1990. Mem. Israel Friendship League, 1986—89; chair Great Outdoors Colo., Denver, 1993—94, Rio Grande Compact Commn., 1995—97, Sangre de Cristo Land Grant Commn., 1993—95; mem. Colo. Water Conservation Bd., Denver, 1990—, City and County of Denver Ethics Panel, 1993; gov.'s rep. State Bd. on Property Tax Equalization, 1987—91; del. Soviet-Am. Young Leadership Dialogue, 1984; mem. adv. com. Colo. U. Sch. Law Natural Resources Law Ctr., 1989—92; mem. Western Water Policy Rev. Adv. Commn., 1995—97; bd. dirs. Denver Cmty. Leadership Forum, 1988, Servicios de la Raza HUD 202 Project, 1985—89, chair, 1986. Scholar Juan Tienda. Mem.: ABA, Am. Judicature Soc., Hispanic Bar Assn. (ABA task force on opportunities for minorities in legal profession, bd. dirs. 1986—87), Denver Bar Assn. (2d v.p. 1989, chair policy-cmty. rels. subcoms. 1982—84), Colo. Bar Assn. (bd. govs. 1989—90, task force to assess the legal profession 1986). Democrat. Avocations: basketball, outdoor activities, politics. Office: State Colo Dept Law 1525 Sherman St 7th Floor Denver CO 80203-1700 E-mail: attorney.general@state.co.us.

SALAZAR, OMAR MAURICIO, radiation oncologist, educator; b. Havana, Cuba, Sept. 22, 1942; came to U.S., 1959; naturalized, 1970; s. Aramis Victor and Nelida Raquel (Acosta) S.; m. Margarita Cristina Pedraza, July 7, 1979; children: Omar M.II, Sofia M. BS in Biology, Georgetown U., 1965; MD, U. P.R., 1969; MS, U. Rochester, 1974. Diplomate Am. Bd. Radiology. Intern U. Hosp. U. P.R., Rio Piedras, 1969—70, radiotherapy resident, 1970—73, chief resident, 1972-73; instr., fellow U. Rochester, NY, 1973-74, asst. prof., 1974-78, assoc. prof., 1978-81; prof., chmn. dept. radiation oncology U. Md., Balt., 1981-95; dir. radiation oncology La. State U. Med. Ctr., New Orleans, 1995-99; dir. dept. radiation oncology, dir. Cancer Ctr. Excellence Oakwood Health Sys., Dearborn, Mich., 1999—; pres. Assoc. in Radiation Oncology, PC, 2000—. Mem. CCIRC Nat. Cancer Inst., Bethesda, Md., 1980-84; prof. clin. oncology Am. Cancer Soc., 1989-1993; coord. USA, Circulo Radioterapeutas Ibero-Latino-Americanos-L.Am. Assn. Radiation Therapy, 1981-98, v.p., 1998-2000, pres. elect, 2000-2002, pres. 2002-; expert cons. internat. Atomic Energy Agy., Vienna, Austria, 1996—; examiner Am. Bd. Radiology, Phila., 1983-93; chmn. site cancer visit Nat. Cancer Inst., Bethesda, 1983, site visitor, 1982; co-investigator Whitaker Found., 1983; prof. clin. oncology Am. Cancer Soc., 1989-94. Author: Moments of Decision/Primary Brain Tumors, 1979, Bronchogenic Carcinoma, 1981, Unveiling Mysteries to Create Miracles, 2002; contbr. articles to profl. jours. Arthur A. Ward Trust grantee, 1981; Am. Cancer Clin. Fellowship award, 1984-86. Fellow: Am. Coll. Radiation Oncology (past pres., past chmn. bd. dirs., chancellor, Gold medal), Am. Coll. Radiology; mem.: AMA, Am. Assn. Cancer Edn., Am. Radiol. Soc., Radiol. Soc. Am., Md. Radiol. Soc., Med. Chirurgical Soc., Tex. Radiol. Soc., Ea. Coop. Oncology Group (chmn. brain and lung com. 1979—80), Radiation Therapy Oncology Group, Mask and Bauble Dramatic Soc., Big Five Club. Roman Catholic. Office Phone: 313-593-5852. E-mail: salazaro@oakwood.org.

SALAZAR, RAMIRO S. library administrator; b. Del Rio, Tex., Mar. 3, 1954; s. Jesus and Juanita (Suarez) S.; m. Cynthia Castillo, Dec. 19, 1976 (div. 1990); children: Ramiro Orlando, Selinda Yvette. BA, Tex. A&I U., 1978; MLS, Tex. Woman's U., 1979. Asst. libr. dir. Val Verde County Libr., Del Rio, 1975-76; libr. Robert J. Kleberg Pub. Libr., Kingsville, Tex., 1977-78; libr. dir. Eagle Pass (Tex.) Pub. Libr., 1980-84; dir. Main Libr. San Antonio Pub. Libr., 1984-90; dir. librs. El Paso Pub. Libr., 1991-93, Dallas Pub. Libr., 1993—. Chmn. Tex. State Libr. Planning Task Force, 1991-92; active Tex. Women's U. Sch. Libr. and Info. Studies Adv. Bd., 1993—, Alliance for Higher Edn. Libr. Dirs. Coun., 1993—. Trustee AMIGOS Bibliographic Coun.; bd. advs. U. N. Tex. Sch. Lib. and Info. Scis., 1993, Booker T. Washington H.S. of Performing and Visual Arts, 1995-96. Chair customer svc. steering com. City of Dallas, 1993—; chair coupon book/resident privilege card task force City of Dallas, 1995-96; active home instrn. program for presch. children Nat. Coun. Jewish Women, 1996—. Recipient H.W. Wilson Staff Devel. award jury, 1995-96. Mem. ALA, Coun., 1996-2000 (mem. nominations com. 1997—), Libr. Adminstrn. and Mgmt. Assn. (bldg. and equipment sect., arch. for pub. libr. com. 1993-95, cultural diversity com. 1995—, pres.'s programs com. 1996—), Tex. Mcpl. League (resolutions com. 1995—), Tex. Mcpl. Libr. Dirs. Assn. (Libr. Dir. of the Yr. 1996), Pub. Libr. Adminstrs. North Tex., Reforma (exec. bd. dirs.), Tex. Libr. Assn. (chmn. pubs. com. 1992-93, legis. com. 1993-95, ad hoc com. value of pub. librs. 1995—, awards com. 1995—), Jaycees. Democrat. Roman Catholic. Home: PO Box 15031 Dallas TX 75201-0031 Office: Dallas Pub Libr 1515 Young St Dallas TX 75201-5499

SALAZAR, STEVE, lawyer; b. Dallas, Aug. 3, 1965; s. Pedro and Catherine Salazar; m. Glenda Salazar; 1 child, Esteban Glen. BA in History, U. Tex., Arlington, 1986; JD, U. Houston, 1988. Assoc. Garcia Alonzo & Garcia, Dallas, 1988-90; pvt. practice Dallas, 1990—. Trustee Dallas County C.C. Dsit., 1992—; pres. Tex. Latino Trustee Assn., Austin, 1993-95; mem. Dallas City Coun., 1995—. Democrat. Avocation: marathons. Office: 238 W 12th St # A Dallas TX 75208-6611

SALAZAR-CARRILLO, JORGE, economics professor; b. Jan. 17, 1938; came to U.S., 1960; s. Jose Salazar and Ana Maria Carrillo; m. Maria Eugenia Winthrop, Aug. 30, 1959; children: Jorge, Manning, Mario, Maria Eugenia. BBA, U. Miami, 1958; MA in Econs., U. Calif., Berkeley, 1964; cert. in econ. planning, U. Calif., 1964, PhD in Econs., 1967. Sr. fellow, non-resident staff mem. Brookings Instn., Washington, 1965—. Dir., mission chief UN, Rio de Janeiro, 1974—80; prof. econs. Fla. Internat. U., Miami, 1980—, chmn. dept. econs., 1980—89; dir. Ctr. Econ. Rsch. & Edn.; former mem. coun. econ. advisors State of Fla.; advisor USIA; former advisor, contbg. editor Libr. of Congress, Washington; chmn. program com. Hispanic Profs. of Econs. and Bus.; cons. econs. AID, Washington, 1979—; former coun. mem. Internat. Assn. Housing, Vienna, 1981—; former exec. bd. Cuban Am. Nat. Coun., Miami, 1982—; bd. dirs., pres. Fla. chpt. Insts. of Econ. and Social Rsch. of Caribbean Basin, 1983—, U.S.-Chile Coun., Miami, 1984—, Fla.-Brazil Inst. Co-author: Trade, Debt and Growth in Latin America, 1984, Prices for Estimation in Cuba, 1985, The Foreign Debt and Latin America, 1983, External Debt and Strategy of Development in Latin America, 1985, The Brazilian Economy in the Eighties, 1987, Foreign Investment, Debt and Growth in Latin America, 1988, World Comparisons of Incomes, Prices and Product, 1988, Comparisons of Prices and Real Products in Latin America, 1990, The Latin American Debt, 1992, International Comparisons of Prices, Output and Productivity, 1996, Capital Markets, Growth and Economic Policy in Latin America, 1999, Growth in Latin America in the 1990s, 2000, Macroeconomics, 2001, Social Christian Doctrine and Econ. Devel., 2002; author: Wage Structure in Latin America, 1982, Oil and Development of Venezuela During the Twentieth Century, 1994. Fellow Brit. Coun., London, 1960, Georgetown U., Washington, 1961-62, OAS, Washington, 1962-64, Brookings Instn., Washington, 1964-65. Mem.: Collegium of Cuban Economists (1st v.p.), Cuban Banking Study Group (dir.), Assn. for Study Cuban Economy (former mem. exec. com.), Nat. Assn. Forensic Economists, Internat. Assn. Energy Economists, Nat. Assn. Cuban Am. Educators (exec. com.), N.Am. Econs. and Fin. Assn., Econometric Soc. Latin Am., Am. Econ. Assn., Knights of Malta. Roman Catholic. Home: 1105 Almeria Ave Coral Gables FL 33134-5503 Office: Fla Internat U Tamiami Campus Dm 319-B Miami FL 33199-0001 Office Phone: 305-348-3283. Business E-Mail: salazar@fiu.edu.

SALBEC, PATRICIA R. emergency medical technician; Emergency physician. Co-author: (book) the Physician's Guide to Domestic Violence: How to ask the right questions and recognize abuse. Mem. Atty. Gen.'s Policy Coun. on Violence Prevention; pres. Physicians for a Violence-free Soc., San Francisco. Mem.: Am. Coll. Emergency Physicians (chpt. pres.). Office: Physicians for a Violence-Free Soc 160 14th St San Francisco CA 94103

SALCEDO, JOSE RODOLFO, nephrologist; b. Guadalajara, Jal, Mex., June 15, 1945; came to U.S., 1971; s. Rodolfo Salcedo-Moreno and Sara (Contreras) Moya; m. Uma T. Salcedo, Nov. 8, 1974; children: Nicholas A., Jonathan E. BA, U. Guadalajara, 1964, MD, 1970. Diplomate Am. Bd. Pediatrics, Pediatric Nephrology. Resident Martland Hosp., Newark, 1971-74; fellow Children's Hosp., Washington, 1974-76, acting dir. pediatric nephrology, dir. dialysis unit, 1976-87; dir. pediatric nephrology divsn. N.J. Med. Sch., Newark, 1987-96; chief pediat. nephrology St. Joseph's Children's Hosp., Paterson, N.J., 1996—. Contbr. chpts. in books and articles to profl. jours. Office: St Joseph's Children's Hosp 703 Main St Paterson NJ 07503-2621

SALCEDO-DOVI, HECTOR EDUARDO, anatomist, educator, surgeon; b. Cordoba, Argentina, Nov. 9, 1958; s. Domingo and Rosa (Dovi) Salcedo; m. Adriana Gomez, Apr. 3, 1993; children: Camila, Marianna. MD, U. Nat. Cordoba, 1984; DO, N.Y. Coll. Osteopathic Medicine, 1995. Asst. prof. anatomy, histology N.Y. Coll. Osteo. Medicine, Old Westbury, 1990—93, prof. anatomy, physiology, 1993; chief intern Good Samaritan Hosp., 1996—, chief resident surgery, 2000. Fellow critical care/trauma, 2001—03. Mem.: ACS, Soc. CCM, Am. Coll. Chest Physicians, Am. Osteopathic Assn., Am. Med. Student Assn. Roman Catholic. Avocations: soccer, bicycling, tennis. Home: 2 Manchester Rd Huntington NY 11743-5532

SALCH, STEVEN CHARLES, lawyer, mediator, arbitrator; b. Palm Beach, Fla., Oct. 25, 1943; s. Charles Henry and Helen Louise (Alverson) S.; m. Mary Ann Prim, Oct. 7, 1967; children: Susan Elizabeth, Stuart Trenton. BBA, So. Meth. U., 1965, JD, 1968. Bar: Tex. 1968, U.S. Tax Ct. 1969, U.S. Dist. Ct. (so. dist.) Tex. 1969, U.S. Dist. Ct. (ea. dist.) Tex. 1972, U.S. Ct. Appeals (5th cir.) 1969, U.S. Ct. Appeals (fed. cir.) 1982, U.S. Ct. Fed. Claims, 1982. Assoc. Fulbright & Jaworski, Houston, 1968-71, participating assoc., 1971-75, ptnr., 1975—. Mem. panel of disting. neutrals CPR Inst. Co-author: Tax Practice Before the IRS, 1994; contbr. articles to legal jours. Pres. Tealwood Owners Assn., 1982—83, Meml. H.S. PTA, 1985—86; hon. life mem. Tex. PTA, 1986—; mem. devel. bd. U. Tex. Med. Br., Galveston, 2002—; adv. dir. 1894 Grand Opera House Soc., 2002—. Mem.: ABA (coun. dir. 1985—88, vice chair tax sect. 1988—91, chair tax sect. 1996—97, co-chmn. adv. bd. 2004—), Houston Bar Found., Am. Bar Found., Internat. Fiscal Assn., Am. Coll. Tax Counsel (regent 5th cir. 1999—), Am. Law Inst., Fed. Bar Assn., Houston Bar Assn., State Bar Tex., Theodore Tannenwald Foundation (trustee 2000—), Colonial Williamsburg Found., Menard Soc., Pelican Club Galveston, Yacht Club, Houston Downtown Club, Galveston County Club, Order of Coif, Phi Delta Phi, Phi Eta Sigma, Beta Alpha Psi. Presbyterian. Office: Fulbright & Jaworski 1301 Mckinney St Fl 51 Houston TX 77010-3031 Home: 4600 Caduceus Pl Galveston TX 77551-5719 Office Phone: 713-651-5433. E-mail: ssalch@fulbright.com. *Set goals for yourself. Unless you know where you are and where you want to be in life, you will not be able to map a plan to accomplish your goals.*

SALCUDEAN, MARTHA EVA, mechanical engineer, educator; b. Cluj, Romania, Feb. 26, 1934; arrived in Can., 1976, naturalized, 1979; d. Edmund and Sarolta (Hirsch) Abel; m. George Salcudean, May 28, 1955; 1 child, Septimiu E. BEng, U. Cluj, 1956, postgrad., 1962; PhD, U. Brasov, Romania, 1969; DSc (hon.), U. Ottawa, Ont., Can., 1992, U. B.C., Can., 2001. Mech. engr. Armatura, Cluj, 1956-63; sr. rsch. officer Nat. Rsch. Inst. Metallurgy, Bucharest, 1963-75; part-time lectr. Inst. Poly., Bucharest, 1967-75; sessional lectr. U. Ottawa, 1976-77, from asst. prof. to assoc. prof. to prof., 1977-85; prof., head dept. mech. engring. U. B.C., Vancouver, 1985-93, assoc. v.p. rsch., 1993-96, acting v.p. rsch. pro-tem, 1995, Weyerhausen Indsl. Rsch. chair computational fluid dynamics, 1996—2002, prof., Weyerhausen indsl. chair emerita dept. mech. engring., 2002—. Mem. grant selection com. for mech. engring. Natural Scis. and Engring. Rsch. Coun. Can.; mem. Nat. Adv. Panel to Min. Sci. and Tech. on advanced indsl. materials, Can., 1990; mem. governing coun. NRC; mem. def. sci.e adv. bd. Dept. Nat. Def.; chair Sci. Coun. B.C. Contbr. numerous articles to profl. jours. Decorated Order of B.C., 1998; recipient Gold medal B.C. Sci. Coun., Killam Rsch. prize U. B.C.; Rsch. Coun. Can. grantee, 1978—, Commemorative medal 125th anniversary Can. Confederation, 1993, Julian C. Smith medal Engring. Inst. Can., 1994-95, Meritorious Achievement award Assn. Profl. Engrs. & Geoscientists B.C., 1996, Killam Meml. prize engring., 1998. Fellow CSME, Can. Acad. Engring., Royal Soc. Can.; mem. ASME, Assn. Profl. Engrs. Ont., Order of Can. (apptd. officer 2004). Home: 1938 Western Pkwy Vancouver BC Canada V6T 1W5 Office Phone: 604-822-2732. Business E-Mail: msal@mech.ubc.ca.

SALDIN, DILANO KERZAMAN, physicist, educator; b. Colombo, Sri Lanka, Aug. 26, 1949; arrived in U.S., 1988; s. Hamlin Mesrur and Muzeena Saldin. BA, U. Oxford, 1971, DPhil, 1975. Jr. rsch. fellow Wolfson Coll., Oxford, England, 1976—81; lectr. Brasenose Coll., Oxford, 1979—81; rsch. fellow Imperial Coll., London, 1981—88; from asst. prof. to prof. U. of Wis., Milw., 1988—96, prof., 1996—, chair physics dept., 2000—01, 2002—. Contbr. articles over 100 to profl. jours. Grantee, Petroleum Rsch. Fund, 1990—94, NSF, 1994—, U.S. Dept. of Energy, 2001—; scholar Alice and Edith Hamer Major scholarship, U. of Manchester, Eng., 1968; Open Exhibition in Physics, Univ. Oxford. Mem.: Am. Physical Soc. Office: University of Wisconsin Milwaukee Physics Dept PO Box 413 Milwaukee WI 53201 Personal E-mail: dksaldin@uwm.edu. Business E-Mail: dksaldin@uwm.edu.

SALDIVAR, ENRIQUE, bioengineer, researcher; b. Mexico City, May 10, 1960; s. Pedro Saldivar Cadena and Alicia Salazar Flores; m. Adrienne Jane Sardella, Nov. 7, 1992; children: Cassandra Lane, Evan Valentine. MD, Universidad La Salle, 1983; MS, Universidad Autonoma Metropolitana, 1987; PhD, U. Calif., San Diego, 1992. Asst. prof. The Scripps Rsch. Inst., La Jolla, Calif., 1998 , sr. rsch. assoc., 1995—98, rsch. assoc., 1993—95; sr. scientist La Jolla Bioengring. Inst., 2003—. Mem. Whitaker Inst. Biomed. Engring., La Jolla, 1997—; vis. scholar U. Calif., San Diego, 2001—; founder Rainmaker Tech., Santee, Calif., 2001—. Contbr. articles to profl. jours. Recipient Nat. Instrumentation prize, Mexican Soc. Physiol. Scis., 1987, U. Merit medal, Universidad Autonoma Metropolitana, Mex., 1987; scholar, CONACYT, 1985—87, 1988—91, UCSD, 1991—92, Short-Term Invitation fellow for Rsch. in Japan, Japan Soc. for the Promotion of Sci., 1998, grantee, NIH, 1998—2003. Achievements include description and analysis of platelet interaction with surface bound proteins under flow; development of currently worldwide used tecnique to measure forming thrombus volume based on confocal microscopy. Office: La Jolla Bioengring Inst 505 Coast Blvd S La Jolla CA 92037 E-mail: enrique@ljbi.org.

SALE, DAVID TODD, lawyer; b. LI, NY, July 3, 1968; s. Jon A. and Beth K. Sale. B of Polit. Sci., Gettysburg Coll., 1990; JD, Nova Southeastern U., 1993. Bar: Fla. 1994, U.S. Dist. Ct. (so. dist.) Fla. 1994. Intern to spkr of house U.S. Ho. of Reps., Washington, 1988; asst. atty. gen. Fla. Atty. Gen.'s Office, Hollywood, 1994-95; asst. state atty. Broward County State Atty., Ft. Lauderdale, Fla., 1994-97; sole practitioner Ft. Lauderdale, Fla., 1997—. Mem. Com. to Re-elect Atty. Gen. Butterworth, 1992, Com. to Re-elect Judge Gary Cowart, 1997. Mem. Broward County Bar Assn., Broward Assn. Criminal Def. Lawyers (treas. 2001-02). Avocations: politics, history, basketball, golf, tennis. Office: 400 SE 9th St Fort Lauderdale FL 33316 E-mail: defendingd@aol.com.

SALE, GEORGE EDGAR, pathologist; b. Missoula, Mont., Apr. 18, 1941; s. George Goble and Ruth Edna (Polleys) S.; m. Joan M. Sutliff, 1989; children: George Gregory Colby, Teo Marie Jonsson. AB, Harvard U., 1963; MD, Stanford U., 1968. Intern U. Oreg., Portland, 1968-69; sr. asst. surgeon USPHS, Albuquerque, 1969-71; resident in pathology U. Wash., Seattle, 1971-75, instr. pathology, 1975-78, asst. prof., 1978-81, assoc. prof., 1981-88, prof., 1988—. Asst. mem. faculty clin. divsn. Hutchinson Cancer Ctr., Seattle, 1975-88, assoc. mem., 1988-91, mem., 1991—. Author, editor: Pathology of Bone Marrow Transplantation, 1984, Pathology of Transplantation, 1990. Mem. AAAS, Internat. Acad. Pathology, Coll. Am. Pathologists, Am. Assn. Investigative Pathologists, Physicians for Social Responsibility. Office: Fred Hutchinson Cancer Rsh Ctr G1-309 1100 Fairview Ave N Seattle WA 98109-4417 E-mail: gsale@fhcrc.org.

SALÉ, JAMIE, Olympic athlete, ice skater; b. Calgary, Alta., Can., Apr. 21, 1977; Profl. ice skater, Canada. Recipient (with David Pelletier) 2d pl. pairs, Can. Nat. Championships, 1999, 1st pl., 2000, 2001, 2002, ISU Four Continents, 2000, 2001, Skate Am., 2000, 2001, Skate Can., 2000, 2001, Sears Figure Skating Open, 2000, ISU Grand Prix Final, 2001, 2002, World Championships, 2001, Gold medal, 2002 Olympic Games, (with David Pelletier) Ptnrs. of the Yr. award, 30th Ann. Can. Sports awards, 2003. Office: Skate Canada 865 Shefford Rd Gloucester ON K1J 1H9 Canada

SALE, LLEWELLYN, III, lawyer; b. St. Louis, May 19, 1942; s. Llewellyn Jr. and Kathleen (Rice) S.; m. Cynthia Jean Bricker, Aug. 17, 1968 (div. Apr. 1995); children: Allyson J., Eryn E. AB cum laude, Yale U., 1964; LLB cum laude, Harvard U., 1967. Bar: Mo. 1967, U.S. Dist. Ct. (ea. dist.) Mo. 1967, U.S. Tax Ct. 1982, U.S. Ct. Claims 1985. From assoc. to ptnr. to mng. ptnr. Husch & Eppenberger, St. Louis, 1967-88; ptnr. Bryan Cave LLP, St. Louis, 1988—. Bd. dirs. Washington U. Child Guidance Clinic, St. Louis, 1978-80, Mental Health Assn. St. Louis, 1988-89. Mem. ABA, Bar Assn. Met. St. Louis (chmn. law econs. subcom. 1982), Media Club, Noonday Club. Avocations: spectator sports, jogging. Office: Bryan Cave 211 N Broadway Ste 3600 Saint Louis MO 63102-2733 Office Phone: 314-259-2649. Business E-Mail: lsale@bryancave.com.

SALE, MERRITT, classicist, comparatist, educator; b. New Haven, Nov. 27, 1929; s. William Merritt and Helen (Stearns) S.; m. Marilyn Mills, June 13, 1953 (div. Oct. 1967); children: Elizabeth, David; m. Anne Perkins, May 18, 1991. BA, Cornell U., 1951, MA, 1954, PhD, 1958. Engr. U.S. Metals Co., Carteret, N.J., 1951-52; instr. in classics Yale U., New Haven, 1957-58; asst. prof., assoc. prof. Washington U., St. Louis, 1958-75, chmn. classics dept., 1961-69, prof. classics and comparative lit., 1975—, chmn. comparative lit. dept., 1981-90. Author: Sophocles' Electra: Commentary with Introduction and Translation, 1970, Existentialism and Euripides, 1977, Homer and the Roland, 1993, The Government of Troy, 1995. Recipient Founder's Day award for Excellence in Teaching Washington U., 1978 Mem. Am. Philol. Assn., London Inst. for Classical Studies Home: 2342 Albion Pl Saint Louis MO 63104-2524 Personal E-mail: aperkins@midwest.net.

SALE, TOM S., III, financial economist; b. Haynesville, La., July 27, 1942; s. Thomas and Mary Belle (Fagg) S.; divorced; children: Jennifer Elizabeth, Sarah Elaine. BA, Tulane U., 1964; MA, Duke U., 1965; PhD, La. State U., 1972. CFA. Faculty mem. La. Tech. U., Ruston, 1965—75, prof. econs., 1975—98, ret., 1998. Head dept. econs. and fin. La. Tech. U., 1974-86, 90-95, dir. grad. studies Coll. Adminstrn and Bus., 1988-89; fin. cons. Contbr. articles to profl. jours. Mem. Southwestern Fin. Assn. (pres. 1985-86), Assn. Investment Mgmt. and Rsch. (exam. com. 1983-92, curriculum com. 1993—), SW Fedn. Adminstrv. Disciplines (v.p. 1988-89, pres. 1989-90), Dallas Assn. Fin. Analysts, Omicron Delta Kappa, Omicron Delta Epsilon. Episcopalian. Home: PO Box 1365 Ruston LA 71273-1365 E-mail: tomsale3@tcainternet.com.

SALEEBA, DAVID A. federal agency administrator; b. Hazleton, PA. BA in History, Pa. State U., 1971. Police officer, detective organized crime bur. Metro-Dade County Police Dept., Miami, Fla., 1972—75; with U.S. Secret Svc., Washington, N.Y.C., Miami, N.Mex., 1975—2001, spl. agt. in charge of district Albuquerque, 1990—95; asst. adminstr. for security mgmt. and safeguards NASA, Washington, 2001—. Office: NASA Hdqrs Mail Code X 300 E St SW Washington DC 20546

SALEEM, KADHARBATCHA S, neurobiologist, research scientist; b. Madras, India, Jan. 18, 1960; s. Kadharbatcha S and Najmunnisa B; m. Asiyabegum Abdulhasan, June 8, 1989; children: Farzana, Rizwana. BSc, Madras U., 1981, MSc, 1983, PhD, 1990. Rsch. scholar Post Grad. Inst. of Basic Med. Sciences, U. of Madras, Madras, India, 1985—90; rsch. scientist Frontier Rsch. Program, Riken Inst., Wako-shi, Japan, 1990—96, Riken Brain Sci. Inst., Wako-shi, Japan, 1996—97, staff scientist, 1997—2001, vis. scientist, 2001—; rsch. assoc. Wash. U., St. Louis, 2001—. Fellow Frontier Rsch. fellowship, Frontier Rsch. Program, 1990—96, Rsch. fellowship, Riken Brain Sci. Inst., 1996—97, Brain Sci. and Tech. Rsch. Found., Japan, 1997—2001. Mem.: Internat. Brain Rsch. Orgn., Japanese Neurosci. Soc., Soc. for Neurosci. (corr.). Achievements include research in MRI visualization of neuronal circuitry in the macaque monkey; anatomical and functional interactions between the higher visual cortical areas and prefrontal and medial temporal lobe areas in macaque monkeys. Home: 7561 Byron Pl 1W Saint Louis MO 63105 Office: Washington U Sch Medicine Dept Anatomy and Neurobiology 660 S Euclid Ave Saint Louis MO 63110 E-mail: saleemk@wustl.edu.

SALEH, ALI-ABDULLAH, state official; b. Beit al-Ahmer, Sanáa, Yemen, 1942; married; several children. Student, NCO Sch. Armed Forces, 1960; grad., Armor Sch., 1964; M in Mil. Sci. (hon.), 1989. With Yemen Armed Forces, 1958, advanced through ranks to marshal, 1997, dir. Armor Corps Arsenal, sgt., promoted to warrant officer, then to second lt., colonel, 1963, commandant various squadrons, battalions, brigades; commandant Taiz Governorate; mem. provisional Republican Coun.; dep.-in-chief, chief of staff Armed Forces, 1978; pres. Republic of Yemen, 1978—, 83, 94, lt. gen., 1990, chmn. Presdl. Coun., 1990, 93; pres. Armed Forces, 1978, 83, comdr.-in-chief, 1978, 88; dir. Armor Corps Arsenal; comdt. Armor Squadron, Armor Co., Armor battalion; comdt. armor brigade, mil gov. Bab El-Mandab region. Founder modern state of Yemen based on Dem. basis, polit. pluralism and freedom of the press, respect for Human Rights and the peaceful transfer of power; sec.-gen. People's Gen. Congress, 1982; chmn. Presdl. Coun. of Republic of Yemen, 1990—; ofcl. rep. to country both alone and as leader of dels. to several friendly and brotherly countries. Republican award People's Constituent Assembly for efforts and sacrifices in serving the country, 1979. Achievements include the rebuilding of Mareb great dam, extraction of oil and gas, and the establishment of the free-zone in Aden. Office: Embassy of Republic Yemen 2600 Virginia Ave NW Ste 705 Washington DC 20037-1905 Fax: 202-337-2017.

SALEH, BRIAN BEHROOZ, aerospace executive; b. Tehran, Iran, Apr. 25, 1939; came to U.S., 1959; m. Farideh Navidi, May 12, 1983. BSEE, Northrop U., Ingelwood, Calif., 1967; MBA, Golden Gate U., San Francisco, 1973; instr. credential, Calif. Design engr. radio frequency cirs. Space Systems/Loral, Palo Alto, Calif., 1970—, mgr. GOES Comm. Subsys., 1974-76, program engr. NATO-III Satellite, 1976-79, mgr. Insat Program Engring., 1979-85, mgr. GOES Spacecraft Engring., 1985-91, mgr. GOES Spacecraft, 1991-92, dir. GOES Prodn. Program, 1992-95, dir. Telstar Program, 1995-97, sr. dir. Fixed Svc. Satellite Programs, 1997-98, sr. dir. common products and planning, 1998, sr. exec. dir. CD Radio Program, 1998-99, v.p. program mgmt., 1999—2002; pres. Aerospace Tech., San Jose, Calif., 2002—.

SALEH, DAVID JOHN, lawyer; b. Buffalo, Apr. 24, 1953; s. Donald Thomas and Joan Barbara (Labaki) S.; m. Elizabeth Catherine Abdella, July 2, 1976; children: Anthony Donald, Amy Madeline, Anne Teresa, Andrew David. BA, SUNY, Buffalo, 1975, JD, 1978. Bar: N.Y. 1979, U.S. Dist. Ct. (we. dist.) N.Y. 1980. Assoc. Jeffrey D. Oshlag, Esq., Batavia, N.Y., 1978-82; ptnr. Oshlag, Saleh & Earl, L.L.P., Batavia, 1982—; chief counsel, sec. Am. Real Time Svcs., Inc., N.Y.C., 1988-91; atty. Town of Stafford, NY, 1994—2003; town atty. Town of Darien, NY, 2000—03, Town of Batavia, NY, 2002—03; corp. counsel, v.p. bus. support ventures Inlighten, Inc., 2003—. Prosecutor Village of Corfu, NY, 1997—; legal counsel City of Batavia Housing Authority, 1982—2003; atty. Village of Corfu, NY, 1981-2003, Pembroke Ctrl. Sch. Dist., 1985-90; chief counsel Intelligent Quotation Sys. Inc., Norwalk, Conn., 1987-93, Network Two Comm. Group, Inc., 1997-99; prosecutor Town of Pembroke, 1988-2003; chief counsel, dir., treas. GB's Country Corners Inc., 1991-93; v.p., chief counsel Marine Ptnrs. Funding, Inc., 1994-2002; counsel Corfu Fire Dist., 1995-2003, Weston Info. Techs. Inc., others. Mem. staff Buffalo Law Rev., 1976-78. Active Pembroke Vol. Fire Dept., 1976-79, Corfu Vol. Fire Dept., 1979—; bd. dirs. Corfu Area Bus. Assn., 1986-87; del. Rep. Caucus; trustee Corfu Free Libr. Assn., 1991-2002, pres., 1993-96; bd. dirs. St. Jerome Hosp. Found., 1992-98, treas., 1994-98; treas. Genesee Mercy Healthcare Found., Inc., 1996-98; parliamentarian Genesee County Rep. Com., 2000—. Mem. ABA, ATLA, N.Y. Defenders Assn., N.Y. State Bar Assn., Genesee County Bar Assn. (treas. 2003—, mem. jud. nominations com. for 8th jud. dist. N.Y., chmn. criminal def. com. 1995-2003), Erie County Bar Assn., N.Y. State Housing Renewal Ofcls., U. Buffalo Alumni Assn. (bd. dirs., v.p. fin. 1997-99, exec. v.p., pres.-elect 1999-2000, pres. 2000-02), Lions (pres. 1987-88, 2003-). Republican. Roman Catholic. Home: 54 E Main St Corfu NY 14036-9601 Office: Inlighten Inc 3370 Walden Ave Depew NY 14043 E-mail: dsaleh@rochester.rr.com.

SALEH, JOHN, lawyer; b. O'Donnell, Tex., June 29, 1928; s. Nahum and Arslie S. BBA, U. Tex., 1950, JD with honors, 1952; cert. U.S. Army Judge Advocate Sch., U. Va., 1953. Bar: Tex. 1952, U.S. Ct. Mil. Appeals, 1953, U.S. Tax Ct. 1954, U.S. Dist. Ct. (no. dist.) Tex. 1956, U.S. Ct. Appeals (5th cir.) 1960, U.S. Supreme Ct. 1961, D.C. 1982. Pvt. practice, Lamesa, Tex., 1954—. Tchg. instr. legal rsch. writing U. Tex. Sch. Law, 1950-52. Mem. editl. bd. Tex. Law Rev., 1951-52. Mem. ABA, ATLA, Tex. Law Rev. Assn. (life), Tex. Bar Assn. (spl. com. to study rev. code criminal procedure 1969-71), D.C. Bar Assn., Tex. Trial Lawyers Assn., Tex. Bar Found., Order of the Coif, The Million Dollar Advocates Forum, Phi Delta Phi. Home: 605 Doak Odonnell TX 79351 Office: 502 N 1st St Lamesa TX 79331-5406 Office Phone: 806-872-2171. Personal E-mail: bigjohn@pics.net.

SALEH, PAUL N. telecommunications industry executive; BS, MS, MBA, Univ. Mich. Various leadership positions Honeywell, 1985—96; sr. v.p., treas., CFO Walt Disney Co., 1997—2001; exec. v.p., CFO Nextel Commn., 2001—. Office: Nextel Comm Inc 2001 Edmund Halley Dr Reston VA 20191

SALEM, GEORGE RICHARD, lawyer; b. Jacksonville, Fla., Dec. 24, 1953; s. Kamel Abraham and Margaret Virginia (Bateh) S.; m. Rhonda M. Ziadeh, June 28, 1980; children: James George, Jihan Camille, Laila Suad, Sarah Rose. BA, Emory U., 1975, JD, 1977; LLM, Georgetown U., 1984. Bar: Ga. 1978, Fla. 1979, D.C. 1981. Ptnr. Thompson, Mann & Hutson, Washington, 1977-85; dep. solicitor U.S. Dept. Labor, Washington, 1985-86, solicitor of labor, 1986-89; ptnr. Akin, Gump, Strauss, Hauer & Feld, Washington, 1990—. Bd. dirs. Overseas Pvt. Investment Corp. Contbr. articles to profl. jours. Nat. exec. dir. ethnic voters div. Reagan Bush '84; bd. dirs. United Palestinian Appeal, Inc., 1981-85, 86—; mem. Arab Am. Inst., Jan.-Mar., 1985, Dec. 1986—, chmn. bd. dirs., 1999—; chmn. Arab-Ams. for Bush-Cheney, 2000; mem. Am. Arab Anti-Discrimination Com.; chmn. Arab-Ams. for Bush-Quayle '88, '92; adv. bd. Search for Common Ground in the Mid. East, 2001—; exec. adv. bd. Mid. East Inst., 2002—; bd. dirs. Am. Com. on Jerusalem, 1995—, Emory Law Sch. Coun., 2000-2002, Emory Bd. Govs., 1997-2001. Recipient Ellis Island Medal of Honor, 1992. Mem. ABA (labor and employment law sect.), Ga. Bar Assn. (labor rels. div.), Fla. Bar Assn. (labor rels. div.), D.C. Bar Assn. (labor rels. div.), Nat. Assn. Arab Ams. (bd. dirs. 1987, pres. 1992-94), Am. Ramallah Club (pres. D.C. chpt. 1984, Wash. rep. 1982-84), Am. Ramallah Fedn. (chmn. human rights com., Washington rep. 1982-84), Arab Am. Rep. Fedn. (chmn. 1985), Century Club Nat. Rep. Heritage Groups Coun., Delta Theta Phi, Omicron Delta Kappa. Mem. Eastern Orthodox Christian Ch. Office: Akin Gump Strauss Hauer & Feld 1333 New Hampshire Ave NW Washington DC 20036-1511

SALEM, KAREN E. information technology executive; BS in indsl. engring., Penn. State U.; MBA, U. Cin. Sr. cons. Anderson Consulting; dir. bus. solutions Burger King; v.p. info. tech. Rexall Sundown; IT head AFC Enterprises; sr. v.p. and CIO Corning Cable Sys., Winn-Dixie Stores, Inc., Jacksonville, Fla., 2002—. Office: Winn Dixie Stores Inc 5050 Edgewood Ct Jacksonville FL 32254-3699

SALEM, RIAD, radiologist, consultant; b. Montreal, Quebec, Canada, July 18, 1968; s. Faez Salem and Hala Sergie. MD, McGill U., Montreal, Canada, 1989—93; MBA, George Wash. U., Washington, DC, 1996—98. Lic. Physician Ill., 2003. Interventional radiologist Beaumont Hosp., Royal Oak, Mich., 2000—03, Northwestern Meml. Cancer Ctr., Chicago, Ill., 2003—. Med. dir. MDS Nordion, Ottawa, Ontario, Canada, 2003—. Recipient Gold Medal, McGill U. Faculty Med., 1993, Internal Medicine award, 1993. Mem.: Soc. Interventional Radiology. Office: Northwestern Meml Hosp 676 N St Clair St Suite 800 Chicago IL 60611 Office Phone: 312-695-6371. Home Fax: 312-695-5645; Office Fax: 312-695-5645. E-mail: r-salem@northwestern.edu.

SALEM, RICHARD ALLEN, mediator; b. N.Y.C., Aug. 15, 1930; s. Louis H. and Catherine (Levy) S.; m. Greta Waldinger, June 26, 1955; children: Susanne, Peter, Erica. BA in Sociology, Antioch Coll., 1953; MS in Journalism, Columbia U., 1957. Reporter Washington Post, 1957-59; editor, publ. Washington SBIC Newsletter, 1960-62; spl. asst. to dep. dir. for investment Small Bus. Adminstrn., Washington, 1963-64, assoc. dir. Office of Equal Opportunity, 1964-67, regional dir., 1967-68; Midwest dir. Cmty. Rels. Svc. U.S. Dept. Justice, Chgo., 1968-82; pres. Conflict Mgmt. Initiatives, Evanston, Ill., 1982—. Adj. prof. Loyola U., Chgo., 1986-90; mediator Wounded Knee Takeover, 1972, Skokie-Nazi Conflict, 1980. Co-author: Students Guide to Mediation and Law, 1987, Ctr. for Pub. Resources award, 1987; mem. editl. bd. Chgo. Reporter, 1996-2004; editor: Witness to Genocide - the Children of Rwanda, 2000; contbr. articles to profl. jours. Bd. dirs. Housing Options for Mentally Ill, Evanston, 1997—, Found. Self-Sufficiency Ctrl. Am., 2000—; sec. World Mediation Forum, 1997-2002. With U.S. Army, 1953-55. Recipient Outstanding Performance award U.S. Sr. Exec. Svc., 1980. Mem. Soc. Profls. in Dispute Resolution (2d v.p. 1988, bd. dirs. 1982-89, Mary Parker Follett award 1993). Home and Office: 1225 Oak Ave Evanston IL 60202-1220

SALEM, SUSANNE FRANCES, consulting executive; b. San Francisco, Mar. 25, 1945; d. Edward L. and Mary F. (Adams) Ledinski; m. Lee C. Salem, July 14, 1979. BS, Ariz. State U., 1979. Ins. agt. Atlantic Mut. Ins. Co. and Harris & Assocs., Los Angeles, 1964-73; ptnr. Acero Enterprises, Sierra Vista, Ariz., 1973-77; lease account mgr. Truck Leasing, Phoenix, 1979-80; sales and cons. Internat. Transp., Phoenix, 1980; owner Corp. Directions Cons. & Recruiting, Phoenix, 1980-86; v.p., bd. dirs. The Prism Group, Inc., Cons., Tempe, Ariz., 1987-94; human resource leader W.L. Gore & Assocs., 1994-95; cons. Salem & Assoc., 1986—99; human resources mgr. Silterra, 1999—. Guest speaker in field; bd. dirs. Southeastern Ariz. Drug Abuse Coun., 1975-77, The Ariz. Partnership, 1989-90, adv. bd. dirs. Maricopa Skill Ctr., 1989-91, Oreg. Literacy Orgn., 2000—. Contbr. articles to profl. jours. Mem. Am. Trucking Assns. (bd. dirs., scholar 1977-79, outstanding transp. grad. 1979), Ariz. C. of C. E-mail: ssalem@sprintmail.com.

SALEMBIER, VALERIE BIRNBAUM, publishing executive; b. Teaneck, N.J. d. Jack and Sara (Gordon) Birnbaum; m. Paul J. Block, Dec. 9, 1990. BA, Coll. New Rochelle, 1973. Advt. dir. Ms. Mag., N.Y.C., 1976-79, assoc. pub., 1979-81; pub. Inside Sports Mag., N.Y.C., 1982; sr. v.p. advt. USA Today, 1983-88; pub. TV Guide, Radnor, PA, 1988-89; pres. N.Y. Post, N.Y.C., 1989-90; pub. Family Circle Mag., N.Y.C., 1991-93; v.p. advt. N.Y. Times, 1993-95; v.p., pub. Esquire Mag., 1996—2003; sr. v.p., pub. Harper's Bazaar, N.Y.C., 2003—. Lectr. in field. Author: (book) Rotissereie League Baseball, 1982; freelance mag. writer:. Vice chair N.Y.C. Police Found.; bd. dirs., past pres. Nat. Alliance Breast Cancer Orgns., former bd. dirs.; bd. dirs., past pres. Beneficial Orgn. Aid Ex-Fighters; former trustee Ctrl. Synagogue, Coll. New Rochelle; trustee N.Y.C. Sports Devel. Corp. Mem.: Women in Comm., Com. 200, Womens Forum. Office: Harpers Bazaar 1700 Broadway New York NY 10019

SALEMI, JOSEPH SALVATORE, classics and humanities educator, poet, writer; b. N.Y.C., Feb. 1, 1948; s. Salvatore Joseph and Liberty Luce (Previti) S.; m. Helen Louise Palma, June 1, 1991. BA, Fordham U., 1968; MA, NYU, 1970, PhD, 1986. Permanent cert. English tchr., N.Y. Prof. composition and lit. Pace U., N.Y.C., 1977-84; prof. English, Nassau C.C., Westbury, N.Y., 1984-86, Fordham U., Bronx, N.Y., 1988-89; prof. classics Bklyn. Coll., CUNY, 1993-2000, Hunter Coll., CUNY, N.Y.C., 1989—; prof. humanities NYU, N.Y.C., 1983—. Author: Formal Complaints, 1997, Nonsense Couplets, 1999, Masquerade, 2003; poems and translations published in over seventy jours.:, book reviewer, essayist: Expansive Poetry and Music Online, assoc. editor: Iambs and Trochees; contbr. Expasive Poetry and Music On-Line. Recipient award Classical and Modern Lit. Jour., 1993; Musurillo scholar CUNY Grad. Ctr., 1975; sr. fellow NEH, 1982, Lane Cooper fellow NYU, 1983-84. Mem. Nat. Assn. Scholars, Am. Lit. Translators Assn., Renaissance Soc. Am. Roman Catholic. Avocation: military research. Home: 220 9th St Brooklyn NY 11215 Office: CUNY Hunter Coll Classics Dept 695 Park Ave New York NY 10021

SALEMI, MICHAEL KERRY, economist, educator; b. Chgo., Mar. 30, 1946; s. Michael and Helen Hill S.; m. Carrie Frances Benoit, Dec. 27, 1967 (div. July 1989); children: Benjamin, Caitlin; m. Ariana Pancaldo, Aug. 18, 1990; 1 child, Chiara. BA, St. Mary's Coll., Winona, Minn., 1968; MS, Purdue U., 1969; PhD, U. Minn., 1976. Asst. dir. Ctr. for Econ. Edn./U. Minn., Mpls., 1973-76; asst. prof. econs. U. N.C., Chapel Hill, 1976-82, assoc. prof. econs., 1982-87, prof. econs., 1987—; rsch. assoc./vis. prof. Grad. Inst. Internat. Studies, Geneva, 1982-83. Bd. editors Jour. of Econ. Edn., 1995—; contbr. articles to profl. jours. Adv. bd. The Econ. Literacy Project of Fed. Res. Bank, Mpls., 1999; bd. dirs. N.C. Coun. Econ. Edn., Raleigh, N.C., 1999-2000; chair rev. com. Vol. Nat. Content Stds. in Econs. Project, N.Y., 1996-97; bd. founders Nat. Coun. on Econ. Edn., N.Y., 1995—. Recipient Bower medal in econ. edn. Nat. Coun. Econ. Edn., N.Y., 1998, Erskine fellowship Canterbury U., Christchurch, New Zealand, 1998, Zachary Smith Professorship U. N.C., Chapel Hill, 1993-96, Bowman and Gordon Gray Professorship for Excellence in Undergrad. Tchg., 1987-90, Villard award for rsch. in econ. edn. Am. Assn. Econ. Educators, 2001. Mem. Am. Econ. Assn. (chair com. econ. edn. 1995-2000), Econometric Soc., Soc. Econ. Educators. Avocations: squash, photography, fishing. Office: Dept Econs Cb 3305 Gardner Hl Chapel Hill NC 27599-3305 E-mail: Michael_Salemi@unc.edu.

SALENTINE, THOMAS JAMES, pharmaceutical company executive; b. Milw., Aug. 8, 1939; s. James Edward and Loretta Marie S.; m. Susan Anne Sisk, Apr. 16, 1966; children: Anne Elizabeth, Thomas James Jr. BS in Acctg., Marquette U., Milw., 1961. CPA, Ind., Wis. Sr. audit mgr. Price Waterhouse, Milw., 1961-74; dir. corp. acctg. Ward Foods Inc., Wilmette, Ill., 1974-78; corp. contr. Johnson Controls Inc., Milw., 1984-85; v.p., contr. Stokely Van Camp Inc., Indpls., 1978-87; exec. v.p., CFO Bindley Western Industries Inc., Indpls., 1987—2001, also bd. dirs.; ptnr. Bindley Capital Ptnrs., LLC, 2001—. Bd. dirs. Priority Healthcare Corp., Nat. Refrigeration Svcs. Inc. Chmn. com. United Way, Indpls., 1989-90. Lt. USN, 1962-65. Mem. AICPA, Fin. Execs. Inst. Republican. Roman Catholic. Home: 13540 Brentwood Ln Carmel IN 46033-9488 Office: Bindley Capital Partners LLC 8909 Purdue Rd Indianapolis IN 46268-3146 Office Phone: 317-704-4154.

SALERNO, AMY, state legislator; m. Joe Armeni. BA, Youngstown State U., 1979; JD, Ohio State U., 1982. Bar: Ohio. Lawyer, small bus. owner, Columbus, Ohio; mem. Ohio Ho. of Reps., Columbus. Past chmn. Italian Village Commn; former mem. bd. dirs. St. Mark's Comty. HealthCtr.; former mem. Victorian Village Commn., Downtown Housing Task Force, Columbus. Recipient Appreciation cert. Italian Village Commn, Victorian Village Commn., Columbus City Coun., Outstanding Orgn. award Short North Bus. Assn.

SALERNO, CHERIE ANN (C. S. MAU), artist; b. Chgo., Nov. 21, 1948; d. Henry Jasper and Helen (Polyak) Mau; m. Kenneth Daniel Salerno; children: Nick Anthony, Brittney Ann. AAS in Advertising, Triton Coll., 1985; BFA, Art Inst. Chgo., 1999. Freelance comml. artist, Chgo., 1986-90, 2000—; artist Chgo. Fine Arts Exch., 1994-98; artist, owner C.S. Mau Studio, River Grove, Ill., 1992—; art dir., bd. dirs. Harrison St. Coop. Gallery, Oak Park, Ill., 1999—2002; art tchr. grades 3-7, 2000—03, Bethlehem Luth. Sch., River Grove, Ill., 2002—. Designer Centennial Quilt, River Grove Libr., 1988; logo designer, River Grove Sch., 1984. Designer stained glass window Bethlehem Luth. Ch., River Grove, Ill., 1999, Celebrating Diversity art exhibit, Chgo., 2002; cover designer Louie Records, Corvallis, Oreg., 1998-99, MSS Pub., Jefferson, Oreg., 2002, A440 Music Group, Chgo., for Henry Johnson and Nancy Wilson, 2003; cover artist Aim Mag., 2003-04. Vol. tchr. art Bethlehem Luth. Sch., River Grove, Ill., 1996-2002; vol. ElderCare, 1990-94. Fellow: West Suburban Art League (Excellences honor 1990—2004, excellences awards 1990—), Glenview Art League (Excellence award 1996), Chgo. Artist Coalition; mem.: Oak Park Art League (bd. dirs. 1989—, arts and stds. judge 1991—93, sch. bd. 1993—94, active fundraising 1994, stds. judge 2000—, juror of artist stds., Excellences merit 1990—94). Lutheran. Avocations: Japanese patio gardening, reading, aerobics and weight-lifting, sewing, gourmet cooking. Personal E-mail: cheriesart@salerno.com.

SALERNO, FREDERIC V. retired telecommunications company executive; b. N.Y.C., June 28, 1943; m. Patricia Van Arsdale; 3 children. BSEE, Manhattan Coll., 1965; MBA, Adelphi U.; postgrad. in mgmt., Pace U. With N.Y. Telephone (NYNEX Co.), N.Y.C., 1965—, various positions including staff asst. corp. hdqrs., installation and repair foreman, mgmt. positions, 1965-78, gen. mgr., 1978-83, v.p. transition, 1983-84, v.p. customer service, 1984-85, exec. v.p., chief operating officer New Eng. Telephone sub., 1985-87, pres., chief exec. officer, 1987-91, vice chmn., pres. worldwide svcs., 1991-94, vice chmn. fin. and bus. devel., 1994-97; now sr. exec. v.p., CFO Verizon Communications, Inc.(formerly Bell Atlantic), 1997—2000; vice chmn., CFO Verizon Communications, Inc., 2000—02. Bd. dirs. Akamai Technologies, Inc., The Bear Stearns Companies, Inc., Consolidated Edison, Inc., Gabelli Asset Mgmt., Popular, Inc. Past nat. vice chmn. YWCA; bd. dirs. L.I. Philharmonic. Mem. Ave of Americas Assn.

SALERNO, SISTER MARIA, nursing educator, adult and gerontological nurse; b. Syracuse, N.Y. d. Joseph and Josephine (Ostrowski) S. Diploma in nursing, St. Joseph's Hosp., Syracuse, 1962; BSN summa cum laude, Cath. U. Am., 1974, MS in Nursing, 1976, D of Nursing Sci., 1981; cert. nurse practitioner, U. Rochester, 1984. RN, N.Y., Md., Washington; cert. adult, geriatric nurse practitioner ANCC; joined Sisters of Third Franciscan Order, Roman Cath. Ch., 1963. Staff nurse St. Joseph Hosp. Health Ctr., Syracuse, 1962-63; sr. charge nurse ICU, gen. med. and surg. units St. Elizabeth Hosp., Utica, NY, 1965-66, head nurse pediat. unit, 1966-69; head nurse ECF Loretto Geriatric Ctr., Syracuse, 1969-72; lectr. Cath. U. Am., Washington, 1977—78, 1980—81, asst. prof. nursing, 1978-79, 81-92, assoc. prof., 1992—, dir. primary care adult/geriatric nurse practitioner programs, 1984—, co-dir. FNP program, 1994-97. Contbr. chpts. to books; contbr. articles to profl. jours. Vol. nurse practitioner Cmty. of Hope, Washington; instl. animal care and use com. George Washington U., 1996-, Cath. U. Am. 2000-, Veteran's Adminstrn. Med. Ctr., 2004-; scholarship com. Franciscan Found. for the Holy Land, 1996-. Grantee NIH, 1984-89, Cath. U. Am., 1989-90. Mem.: AAUP, ANA, D.C. League for Nursing (bd. dirs. 1995—97, 1999—), D.C. Nurse Practitioners Assn., N.Y. Acad. Scis., Nat. League for Nursing, Nat. Orgn. Nurse Practitioner Facilities, Nat. Gerontol. Nurses Assn., Am. Coll. Nurse Practitioners, Am. Acad. Nurse Practitioners, Am. Assn. for History of Nursing, Cath. U. Am. Nursing Alumni Assn. (pres. 1986—87, chpt. exec. bd. 1992—2003, treas. 1998—2003), Nat. Italian Am. Found. (assoc.), Sigma Theta Tau (grad. counselor Kappa chpt. 1985—87, awards com. 1987—89, grad. counselor Kappa chpt. 1991—97, eligibility com. 1991—97, 2002—03). Fax: 202-319-6485. Office Phone: 202-319-6545. E-mail: salerno@cua.edu.

SALERNO-SONNENBERG, NADJA, violinist; b. Rome, Jan. 10, 1961; came to U.S., 1969; d. Josephine Salerno-Sonnenberg. Grad., Curtis Inst. Music, 1975, Juilliard Sch., 1982; doctorate (hon.), N.Mex. State U., 1999. Profl. debut with Phila. Orch., 1971; appearances include Am. Symphony Orch., Balt., Chgo., Cin., Detroit, Houston, Indpls., Milw., Montreal, N.J., Pitts. symphonys, Boston Symphony Orch., Cleve., L.A. Chamber, Phila., Minn. orchs., New Orleans, N.Y., L.A. philharms.; festival appearances include Mostly Mozart Festival, Ravinia, Blossom, Meadow Brook, Gt. Woods, Caramoor, Aspen, Hollywood Bowl; internat. orchestral appearances include Vienna, Munich, Stuttgart, Frankfurt, Geneva, Rotterdam, Lisbon, Tokyo; featured on 60 Minutes, CBS, CBS Sunday Morning, NBC Nat. News, PBS Live from Lincoln Ctr., CNN Newsstand, Charlie Rose Show, Sesame Street; numerous appearances on The Tonight Show with Johnny Carson; rec. artist Capitol Classics and Jazz Records, 1987—, Nonesuch, 1996—; subject of documentary: Speaking in Strings, 1999 (film nominated for Oscar 2000). Recipient 1st prize Naumburg Violin Competition, N.Y.C., 1981; Avery Fisher Career grantee., N.Y.C., 1983, Avery Fisher prize, N.Y.C., 1999. Mem. AFTRA, Screen Actors Guild. Office: care M L Falcone Pub Rels 155 W 68th St Ste 114 New York NY 10023-5808

SALES, EUGENIO DE ARAUJO CARDINAL, archbishop emeritus; b. Acari, Brazil, Nov. 8, 1920; s. Celso Dantas and Josefa de A. Sales Student, Sem. Fortaleza City. Ordained priest Roman Cath. Ch., 1943, consecrated bishop, 1954, elevated to cardinal, 1969. Sede Plana apostolic adminstr., Natal, 1962, Salvador, 1964; archbishop Sao Salvador, 1968-71, Rio de Janeiro, 1971—. Editor: The Pastors Voice. Roman Catholic. Address: Rua Visconde de Piraja 339 22410-003 Rio de Janeiro Brazil

SALES, JAMES BOHUS, lawyer; b. Weimar, Tex., Aug. 24, 1934; s. Henry B. and Agnes Mary (Pesek) Sales; m. Beuna M. Vornsand, June 3, 1956; children: Mark Keith, Debra Lynn, Travis James. BS, U. Tex., 1956, LLB with honors, 1960. Bar: Tex. 1960. Practiced in, Houston, 1960—; head litig. dept. Fulbright & Jaworski, 1979—99, sr. ptnr., 1960—2000, of counsel, 2000—. Author: Products Liability in Texas, 1985; co-author: Texas Torts and Remedies, 6 vols., 1986; assoc. editor: Tex. Law Rev., 1960; contbr. articles to profl. jours. Trustee South Tex. Coll. Law, 1982—88, 1990—, A.A. White Dispute Resolution Ctr., 1991—94; cir. chair for membership The Supreme Ct. Hist. Soc., 1998—2001; trustee Tex. Supreme Ct. Hist. Soc., 2003—; chair commrs. Tex. Access to Justice Commn., 2004—; bd. dirs. Tex. Resource Ctr., 1990—97, Tex. Bar Hist. Found., 1990—2001. Named among Best Lawyers in Am., 1989—. Fellow: Houston Bar Found. (chmn. bd. 1982—83, sustaining life), Tex. Bar Found. (trustee 1991—95, vice-chmn. 1992—93, chmn. 1993—94, chair adv. bd. for planned giving 1994—, sustaining life mem.), Am. Bd. Trial Advocates, Am. Bar Found. (state chmn. 1993—98, sustaining life), Internat. Acad. Trial Lawyers, Am. Coll. Trial Lawyers (state chmn. 1993—96); mem.: FBA, ABA (ho. of dels. 1984—2003, mem. Commn. on IOLTA 1995—97), Bar Assn. 5th Fed. Cir., Gulf Coast Legal Found. (bd. dirs. 1982—85), Houston Bar Assn. (bd. dirs. 1970—79, pres.-elect 1979—80, pres. 1980—81), Tex. Law Rev. Assn. (bd. dirs. 1996—, pres. 1999—2000), Tex. Assn. Def. Counsel (v.p. 1977—79), State Bar Tex. (bd. dirs. 1983—88, chmn. bd. 1985—86, pres. 1988—89), So. Tex. Coll. Trial Advocacy (dir. 1983—87), So. Conf. Bar, Nat. Conf. Bar Pres. (coun. 1989—92), Internat. Assn. Def. Counsel, The Forum, Order of Coif, Inns of Ct. (bd. dirs. 1981—84), Westlake Club (bd. govs. 1980—85). Roman Catholic. Home: 10803 Oak Creek St Houston TX 77024-3016 Office: Fulbright & Jaworski 1301 McKinney St Houston TX 77010-3095 E-mail: jsales@fulbright.com.

SALESSI, JORGE, language educator, writer; b. Buenos Aires, Mar. 17, 1946; s. José Salessi and María Villanueva. PhD, MPhil, MA, Yale U., New Haven, Conn., 1980—90, U. of Calif. - Irvine, 1978—80, BA, 1978—90; MA (hon.), U. of Pa., Phila., 1995. Lectr. Yale U., 1985—90; assoc. prof. U. of Pa., 1990—95, undergraduate chair - romance languages, 1995—2001, dir. latin am. cultures program, 1996—2000. Editor - Hispanic Rev. U. of Pa., 1990—; editor - Jour. of the History of Sexuality U. of Chgo., 1994—98. Author: (essay of cultural analysis) Médicos maleantes y maricas (Argentine Book of the Yr., 1995), Medicos maleantes y maricas (1996 Selection of Books that made a mark); painting, Work table (selected 2nd Prize - Salón Nacional de Pintura, 1975). Recipient Membership, Phi Betta Kappa - Art History, 1980, Sigma Delta Phi, 1980. Mem.: Am. Assn. of Coll. Professors (life). Avocations: teaching, flying, travel, hikking, weightlifting. Home: 250 S 13thg St Apt 13A Philadelphia PA 19107 Office: University of Pennsylvania 510 Williams Hall Philadelphia PA 19104 Office Phone: 215-898-7429. Business E-Mail: jsalessi@sas.upenn.edu.

SALETTA, MARY ELIZABETH (BETTY SALETTA), sculptor, rancher; b. Miami, Fla., Sept. 30, 1941; d. Earl Robert and Alta Florence Cotner; m. Albert Michael Saletta, July 1, 1959; children: Tia Suzanne, Kamber Ann. Graphic artist Moore Bus. Forms Inc., Modesto, Calif., 1960-67, Live Oak Pub. Co., Oakdale, Calif., 1977-80; freelance artist U.S. Forest Svc., Modesto Irrigation Dist., Stanislaus Schs., New Don Pedro Dam Project, Calif., 1967-77; sculptor Saletta Sculpture, Oakdale, 1980—. Mem. adv. bd. Calif. State U. Coll. Arts, Letters and Sci., Turlock, 1999-2002; charter mem., dir. Downtown Arts Project, Modesto, 1992-96. One-woman shows City of Oakdale Redevel. Agy., 1990, Modesto C. of C., 1996; group shows include Calif. State U. Stanislaus, Turlock, 1986, Cowboy Artist Am. Mus., Kerrville, Tex., 1988, Benson Park Sculpture Garden, Loveland, Colo., 1989, 90, 93, Danada Sculpture Garden, Chgo., 1991, 93, Tucson Mus. Art, 1995; represented in permanent collections Tucson Mus. Art, Buckaroo Hall of Fame, cities of Modesto, Oakdale, Ripon, Calif., Stockton, Calif.; sculptures include life-size pub. sculptures Yesterday Is Tomorrow, 1991, Am. Graffiti, 1997, Stockton Firefighters Meml., 1998, World War II Meml., 1999, Nursing, the Finest Art, 2001, Chief Estanislao, 2001, Firefighter Sculpture produced at Laguna Beach Pageant of the Masters, 2002. Recipient Excellence in Fine Art award Bank Am., Stockton, Calif., 1959, Best of Show award Western Art Roundup, Winnamucca, Nev., 1987, 88, Excellence in Visual Arts award Stanislaus Arts Coun., Modesto, 1999. Mem. Nat. League Am. Pen Women, Ctrl. Calif. Art League (advisor 1991, Best of Show award 1987), Rotary (bd. dirs. Oakdale 1997-99). Democrat. Avocations: horses, skiing, mountain climbing, fishing. Home: 4255 Wellsford Rd Oakdale CA 95361-7930 Fax: 209-572-4089. E-mail: salettasculpture@aol.com.

SALGADO, LYNN ENZA GRANT, secondary school educator; b. Columbus, Ga., Oct. 21, 1950; d. Ninan Edward and Bessie Enza (Martin) Grant; m. Sal Salgado, July 3, 1999; children: Thomas Grant, Matthew Edward. BS, Vanderbilt U., 1973; MEd, Columbus U., 1984. Cert. elem. edn., spl. educator behavior disorders, Ga. Tchr. Dodson Elem. Sch., Hermitage, Tenn., 1973-75, Milford (Ohio) Village, 1975-77, Winterfield Elem. Sch., Columbus, Ga., 1980-81; spl. edn. tchr. Shaw H.S., Columbus, 1981-83; behavior specialist Lincoln Jr. H.S., Naperville, Ill., 1984-87; behavior specialist, dept. chair Severely Emotionally Disturbed, Broward County, Fla., 1987-97; behavior specialist Stoneman Zone, Broward County, 1998—2003; area behavior specialist Broward County Schs., 2003—. Creator, implementer spl. edn. program Forest Acad., Margate, Fla., 1988; facilitator Coop. Learning Insvc. for Tchrs., Broward County, 1989; tchr., trainer Broward Schs., 1998, North Area Broward Schs., 1998; lectr. in field; chair Sch. Improvement Team Goal #3 student performance, 1994; dept. chair, Cross Creek, Broward County Schs., 1994. Co-author: (trainer's manual) N. Area Broward County Functional Behavioral Assessment. Mgr. Coral Springs boys' soccer club, 1989-90; participant Supt.'s Ann. Planning Conf. Broward County Schs., 1989-90. Named Young Outstanding Educator, Milford Jaycees and Milford Bd. Edn., 1976, Cross Creek Tchr. of Yr., Broward County Schs., 1991; recipient award for Project H.E.L.P., Broward County Bd. Edn., 1989, 91, 93, 96-97. Mem. Broward Tchrs. Union (faculty coun. rep. at Cross Creek), So. Assn. Colls. and Schs. (chair 1990-91), Ramblewood Club Assn. (bd. dirs. 1998—, sec.), Kappa Delta Pi, Kappa Delta Epsilon. Republican. Methodist. Avocations: reading, writing, soccer, horseback riding.

SALGADO, SUSANA, musicologist, researcher, consultant; b. Montevideo, Uruguay, June 14, 1927; d. Juan Andres Salgado, Amelia Gomez-Eirin; m. Roberto O. Morassi. Musicologist, School of Humanities (Dept. of Musicology), Montevideo, Uruguay, 1954—65. Chair Uruguayan Music Rsch. Sch. Humanities, Dept. Musicology, Montevideo, Uruguay, 1965—71; cons., music divsn. Libr. Congress, Washington, 1994—. Mem. bd. advisors Garland Publishing for Opera performances, New York, 1992—; lectr. in field. Author: (Scholarly Book) The Teatro Solis, 150 Years of Opera, Concert and Ballet in Montevideo, 2003, Breve Historia de la Musica Culta en el Uruguay, Montevideo, 1971, 1980; contbr. 5 Grove Dictionaries including Opera; Music and Musicians; Women Composers, Am. Composers; Encyclopedia of Latin-American History and Culture and many others., articles to profl. jours. N/A. N/A. Mem.: Women National Book Association. Avocations: travel, swimming, walking. E-mail: saisalgado@aol.com.

SALGO, PETER LLOYD, internist, writer, anesthesiologist, journalist, commentator; b. N.Y.C., Nov. 9, 1949; s. Michael Nicholas and Ruth F. Salgo. BA, Columbia U., 1971, MD, 1975. Diplomate Am. Bd. Internal Medicine, Am. Bd. Anesthesiology; lic. physician, N.Y., Calif., Mass.; instrument rated comml. pilot. Internal medicine intern Columbia Presbyn. Med. Ctr., N.Y.C., 1975-76, resident in internal medicine, 1976-78; vis. faculty fellow intensive care medicine and anesthesiology, dept. anesthesiology Columbia U., N.Y.C., 1979-81; lectr. Harvard Med. Sch., Boston; clin. prof. medicine and anesthesiology Columbia P&S; mem. staff in anesthesia and medicine Mass. Gen. Hosp., Boston; attending in anesthesia and internal medicine Presbyn. Hosp., N.Y.C., assoc. vice chmn. dept. anesthesiology, chmn. inter-I.C.U. com., assoc. dir. surg. ICU. Host syndicated TV broadcast Healthcare 2000; aviation med. examiner FAA; comml. pilot. instrument Rated; host nat. radio med. program Sta. PRN, 1979—81; writer, producer, host med. info. broadcast Sta. WCBS-TV, N.Y.C., 1980—; med. corr. Sta. WCBS News, 1981—; corr. CBS Network Radio News, 1982—92; host. Healthtalk, 1982—88; med. corr. Sta. CNBC, 1989—, CNBC TV Network, 1989—93; host The Doctor Is In, Eyada.com, 2000—01; cons. to networks on med. content of TV programs; corr. Patient Info. Network, 1989—; anchor Americas Vital Signs, CNBC TV Network, Med. Crossfire, 2001—; lectr. in field.; expert guest on John F. Kennedy, Jr., crash NTSB Report Discovery Network, 2002; expert guest, med. cons. Fox News, 2001—02; host Second Opinion PBS, 2002—. Author: The Heart of the Matter, 2004. Recipient Leonard Pullman award Columbia U., 1971, Blakesley award Am. Heart Assn., Journalism award Medic-alert Found., Honorable Mention in Journalism, UPI, Alumni Assn. medal Columbia U. P&S, 1975, Emmy award for excellence in broadcast journalism, Journalism award Lions Eye Found. Fellow ACP; mem. AAAS, AMA, AFTRA, N.Y. State Med. Soc., N.Y. County Med. Soc., Am. Soc. Anesthesiologists. Office: Presbyn Hosp Dept Anesthesiology New York NY 10032 Office Phone: 212-305-6494. E-mail: pls1@columbia.edu.

SALHANY, LUCILLE S. broadcast executive; Formerly with Paramount Pictures; pres. Paramount Domestic Television, from 1985; chmn. Twentieth Television, a unit of Fox Inc., 1991-92, Fox Broadcasting Co., Beverly Hills, Calif., 1993-94; pres. United ParamountNetwork, 1994-97; pres., CEO JH Media, Boston, 1998—, HJ Media. Office: JH Media 34 Strawberry Hill St Dover MA 02030-2250

SALIBA, GEORGE, Maltese government official; b. Jan. 27, 1944; Pub. relations officer Kuwait Embassy, Malta, 1974—76; non-resident amb. to Saudi Arabia Riyadh, 1985—87; resident amb. to Libya Tripoli, 1987—93; rep. to UN Govt. of Malta, 1997-99; amb. of Malta to U.S., 1999—; high commr. for Malta to Can., 2000—; amb. of Malta to Mex., 2000—. Office: Embassy of Malta 2017 Connecticut Ave NW Washington DC 20008-6195 E-mail: george.b.saliba@gov.mt.

SALIBA, JACOB, manufacturing executive; b. East Broughton, Que., Can., June 10, 1913; s. Said and Nazira (David) S.; m. Adla Mudarri, May 31, 1942; children: John, Thomas, Barbara. BS, Boston U., 1941. Sr. supervising engr. Thompson and Lichtner Co., Boston, 1944-49; pres. Kingston Dress Co., Boston, 1949-51, Indsl. & Mgmt. Assocs., Inc., Boston, 1951-54, Maine Dress Co., Cornish, 1948-61; exec. v.p., mem. exec. com. Cortland Corp., Inc. (formerly Brockway Motor Co., Inc.), N.Y.C., 1954-59; exec. v.p. Sawyer-Tower, Inc., Boston, 1955-56, pres., 1956-59; v.p. Farrington Mfg. Co.; exec. v.p. Farrington Packaging Corp., 1959-61, Farrington Instruments Corp.; pres. N.E. Industries, Inc., from 1961, also bd. dirs.; pres. Fanny Farmer Candy

Shops, Inc., 1963-66, W.F. Schrafft & Sons Corp., 1967-68; pres. frozen foods divsn. W.R. Grace & Co., 1966-68; pres. Katy Industries, Inc., Elgin, Ill., 1969-88, chmn., CEO, 1988-94. Chmn. bd. dirs. Schon & Cie; bd. dirs. Dresdner RCM Europe Fund NYSE, Katy Industries, NYSE; spl. cons. Air Material Commmand, USAF, Dayton, Ohio, 1942-43; cons. to chief air staff USAF, 1952-54; co-chmn. Air Force Spare Study Group, 1953. Mem. corp. Mass. Gen. Hosp., Mus. Sci. Mem. Union League Club, Bridgton Club, Highlands Country Club, Palm Beach Yacht Club. Methodist. E-mail: salibagido@earthlink.com.

SALIBA, PHILIP E. archbishop; b. Abou-Mizan, Lebanon, 1931; came to U.S., 1956, naturalized, 1961; s. Elias Abdallah and Salema (Saliba) S. BA, Wayne State U., 1959; MDiv, DD, St. Vladimir's Sem., N.Y., 1964; DHL, Wayne State U., 1986. Became sub-deacon, deacon Antiochian Orthodox Christian Ch., 1945-49, ordained deacon, 1949-59, priest, 1959-66, consecrated archbishop, 1966, now met. and primate. Chmn. Standing Conf. Am.-Middle Eastern Christian and Moslem Leaders; chmn. Orthodox Christian Edn. Commn.; vice chmn. Standing Conf. Canonical Orthodox Bishops in Ams. Vice-chmn. St. Vladimir's Orthodox Theol. Sem. Mem. Antiochian Orthodox Christian Ch. Address: 358 Mountain Rd Englewood NJ 07631-3727 Office Phone: 201-871-1355. E-mail: archdiocese@antiochian.org.

SALIGMAN, HARVEY, retired consumer products and services company executive; b. Phila., July 18, 1938; s. Martin and Lillian (Zitin) S.; m. Linda Powell, Nov. 25, 1979; children: Martin, Lilli Ann, Todd Michael, Adam Andrew, Brian Matthew BS, Phila. Coll. Textiles and Sci., 1960. With Queen Casuals, Inc., Phila., 1960-88, v.p., 1966-68, pres., chief exec. officer, 1968-81, chmn., 1981-88; pres., chief operating officer Interco Inc., St. Louis, 1981-83, chief exec. officer, 1983-85, 1985-89, chmn., 1989-90; ret. Bd. dirs. Ameren Corp. (formerly Union Electric). Trustee Washington U., St. Louis, John Burroughs Sch., St. Louis, Nantucket Hist. Assn. Mem. St. Louis Club, Masons.

SALIMENA, KATHLEEN ELIZABETH, investor, writer; b. Phila., Sept. 25, 1948; d. Arthur M. Salimena and Rose Mercante. BS, Georgetown U., 1970; MA, U. Pa., 1973. Cert. tchr. State of NJ., 1971. Tchr. Spanish, French Lenape Regional HS, Medford, NJ, 1971—86, Haddonfield Meml. HS, 1986—87; corp. computer sales MBI Bus. Sys., Phila., 1987—88; self-employed investor, writer NJ, 1990—2001, Austin, Tex., 2001—. Contbr. to European mags.; SYGMA - internat. photo syndicator. Mem.: Nat. Press Club, Rotary (instr. English Mex. exch. group 2002, chair cluster meetings 2004). Roman Catholic. Achievements include development of Images That Inspired A King, United States Copyright Office 2002 (Proposed book). Office: PO Box 340074 Austin TX 78734 Personal E-mail: ksalimena@yahoo.com.

SALINAS, BARUJ, artist, architect; b. Havana, Cuba, July 6, 1935; came to U.S., 1959; s. Moises and Regina (Algazi) S.; 1 child, Shari Regina. BArch, Kent State U., 1958. Chief draftsman Calif. Exploration Co., Coral Gables, Fla., 1961-64; draftsman Stresscon, Miami, Fla., 1964-66; chief draftsman Pillsbury Co., Miami, Fla., 1966-70; artist Miami and Barcelona, Spain, 1970—. Instr. Winchester Sch. Art, Barcelona, 1992, 93, N.Y. Sch. Visual Arts, Barcelona, 1993; instr. art. Miami Dade Cmty. Coll. interam. campus, 1998-. Vol. Amnesty Internat., Paris, 1989-90; art coord. Internat. Com. for Human Rights, Miami, 1993-94, 95-96, 97, 98, 2000, 02, 03. Fellow Cintas Found., 1969, 70, Internat. Com. Human Rights, 2000, 02; Recipient 1st prize Ft. Lauderdale Mus. Art, 1969, 1st prize Cultura P.R., 1983. Democrat. Jewish. Avocations: travel, reading, music, sports. Home: 2740 SW 92nd Ave Miami FL 33165-3119

SALINAS, MARTHA F. manufacturing executive; b. Santa Maria, Calif., Aug. 6, 1972; d. Panfilo and Faustina Salinas. BA in Bus. Adminstrn., U. Tex., Austin, 1994, MBA, 1996. Fin. mgr., mktg. mgr. Chase Manhattan Bank, Houston, 1996—99; database mktg. mgr. Compaq Computer Co., Houston, 2000—. Mem.: Nat. Soc. Hispanic MBAs (exec. v.p. Houston 1998—99, pres. 1999—, Nat. Edn. Chair 2002—). Avocations: reading, community svc. Mailing: 10801 Legacy Park Dr #415 Houston TX 77064

SALINGER, ANTHONY WILSHIRE, educator, organization consultant; b. N.Y.C., Dec. 4, 1938; s. Alan Bijur Salinger and Frances (Wilshire) Riordan; m. Nina Lois Popick, Feb. 20, 1965 (div. 1981); children: Kerri Rae, Beth Kendra; m. Joan Marie Kelleher, Jan. 15, 1983; 1 child, Victoria Lucy. AB, U. N.C., 1965; MBA, Colo. State U., 1995. Staff mgr. AT&T Long Lines, N.Y.C., 1970-72, planning engr., 1972-74, dist. engr. White Plains, N.Y., 1974-76, staff supr. Bedminster, N.J., 1976-82, AT&T Planning and Design, Bedminster, N.J., 1982-83; venture mgr. AT&T Mktg. Devel., Basking Ridge, N.J., 1983-87; staff mgr. AT&T Mktg. Info. Systems, Basking Ridge, 1987-88; sr. tng. cons. AT&T Corp. Edn. Ctr., Basking Ridge, 1988-89, product mgr., 1989-91, sales ops. mgr., 1991-92, orgn. devel. mgr., 1993-94; quality dir. AT&T Phone Ctr., Parsippany, N.J., 1992-94; quality mgr. fin. dept. AT&T Consumer Products, Parsippany, 1994-96; mgr. strategic planning Lucent Technologies Consumer Products, Parsippany, 1996-97; skills devel. mgr. Lucent Technologies Human Resources, Parsippany, 1997; mng. ptnr. Alexis Gill, Inc., 1998-99; cons. M.F. Smith & Assocs., Inc., 1988—; ptnr. Wilshire Mgmt. Ptnrs., 2003—. Adj. prof. NYU Stern Sch. Bus., 1988-2001; mem. faculty U. Phoenix Online Campus, 1996-2001, George Rothman Inst. Enterpreneurial Studies, Fairleigh Dickinson U., 1997-2000; examiner N.J. Quality Achievement award, 1994, 98; accredited exec. assoc. Inst. Ind. Bus., 2003—, Svc. Corps Ret. Execs., 2003—; online tchg. asst. BrainMass, 2003-; mem. Independent Consultation Assn., 2004-. Author: Enhancing Communications Between Users and DP Staff, 1983, (with others) American Management Association Handbook, 4th edit., 1994, Strategy, Quality and Information Technology, 1997, (with others) Handbook of Business Strategy. Mem. faculty Quality Assurance Inst., Orlando, Fla., 1982-85; mem. Pingel Design Group, 1995; mem. adv. bd. Jointure for Cmty. Adult Edn., 1987-90; mem. Strategic Leadership Forum, 1996. Served with U.S. Army, 1961-64. Recipient Oliver Innovation award AT&T Long Lines, 1973, Capitol award Nat. Leadership Coun., 1991. Mem. IEEE, Soc. for Info. Systems Quality (pres. 1987), Data Processing Mgmt. Assn. (pres. 1982-85, Individual Performance award 1985), Nat. Spkrs. Assn., Internat. Platform Assn., Internat. Biog. Assn., ASTD, Am. Soc. Quality (sr. mem., chair annual svc. quality conf. 1994, 95), Assn. Systems Mgmt., Assn. for Quality and Participation, Toastmasters (award 1983). Republican. Episcopalian. Home and Office: 32 Oak Ridge Rd Bernardsville NJ 07924-1878 Office Phone: 908-766-0283. E-mail: salinger@att.net.

SALINGER, CHARLES, dermatologist; b. N.Y.C. s. Ernest and Mae (Brenner) S.; m. Donna Marcia Gafford, May 14, 1974 (div. 1992); children: Jennifer, Jeffrey. BS, U. Wis., 1965; MD, SUNY, Syracuse, 1968. Lic. M.D., Calif. Intern Charity Hosp., La. State U., New Orleans, 1968-69, resident in dermatology, 1969-72; chief of dermatology USAF Maxwell Hosp., Montgomery, Ala., 1972-74; pvt. practice, dermatology La Mirada, Calif., 1974—. Chief med. staff La Mirada (Calif.) Cmty. Hosp., 1987-88; clin. assoc. prof. dermatology, Coll. Osteo. Medicine, Pomona, Calif., 1977—; trustee Med. Ctr. La Mirada, 1985-90. Major USAF, 1972-74. Fellow Am. Acad. Dermatology, Am. Soc. Dermatologic Surgery, Internat. Soc. Dermatologic Surgery, Pacific Dermatologic Assn., L.A. Met. Dermatologic Soc. (pres. 1994-95, bd. dirs. 1987-90); mem. AMA, Calif. Med. Assn., L.A. County Med. Assn. Jewish. Avocations: downhill skiing, Little League baseball (mgr.), quarter-horses, billfishing. Home: 5440 Emerywood Dr Buena Park CA 90621-1635 Office: 12675 La Mirada Blvd La Mirada CA 90638-2200

SALINGER, J(EROME) D(AVID), author; b. N.Y.C., Jan. 1, 1919; s. Sol and Miriam (Jillich) S.; m. Claire Douglas, 1953 (div. 1967); children: Margaret Ann, Matthew; m. Colleen. Student, Valley Forge Mil. Acad., Columbia U., Ursinus Coll. Author: Catcher in the Rye, 1951, Nine Stories, 1953, Franny and Zooey, 1961, Raise High the Roof Beam, Carpenters; and Seymour: An Introduction, 1963; contbr. stories to New Yorker mag. Sgt. AUS, 1942-46. Address: care Harold Ober Assocs 425 Madison Ave New York NY 10017-1110

SALINGER, MICHAEL ALVIN, economist, educator; b. Cin., Aug. 24, 1956; s. James Alvin and Joyce (Joslin) S.; m. Julie Landsman, July 6, 1985; children: Philip Landsman, David Herbert, Nicholas Andrew. BA, Yale U., 1978; PhD, MIT, 1982. Asst. prof. Grad. Sch. Bus. Columbia U., N.Y.C., 1982-87, assoc. prof., 1987-90, Boston U., 1990—, faculty dir. undergrad. program, 1999-2000, chmn. dept. fin. and econ., 2000—, prof., 2001—. Economist FTC, Washington, 1985—86; acad. advisor Princeton Econs. Group, 1989—94; spl. cons. Nat. Econ. Rsch. Assocs., 1994—; vis. assoc. prof. MIT, 1997—98. Contbr. articles to profl. publs.; assoc. editor: Jour. Indsl. Econs., 1996—2002, mem. editl. bd.; 2002—, Rev. of Ind. Orgn., 2002—. Vol. The Alumni Fund, New Haven, 1978—. NSF fellow, 1979-82. Mem. Am. Econ. Assn. Jewish. Avocations: tennis, skiing. Office: Boston U Sch Mgmt 595 Commonwealth Ave Boston MA 02215-1704 E-mail: salinger@bu.edu.

SALINGER, PIERRE EMIL GEORGE, journalist; b. San Francisco, June 14, 1925; s. Herbert and Jehanne (Bietry) Salinger; m. Renee Laboure, Jan. 1, 1947; children: Marc(dec.), Suzanne, Stephen; m. Nancy Brook Joy, June 28, 1957; m. Nicole Helene Gillmann, June 18, 1965 (div. June 1988); 1 child, Gregory; m. Nicole Beauvillain de Menthon, June 17, 1989. BS, U. San Francisco, 1947. Reporter, night city editor San Francisco Chronicle, 1946—55; guest lectr. journalism Mills Coll., 1950—55; West Coast editor, contbg. editor Collier's mag., 1955—56; investigator select com. to investigate improper activities in labor or mgmt. field U.S. Senate, 1957—59; press sec. U.S. Senator Kennedy, 1959—60, Pres. Kennedy, 1961—63, Pres. Johnson, 1963—64; U.S. Senator from Calif., 1964; v.p. Nat. Gen. Corp., 1965; v.p. internat. affairs Continental Airlines, Inc. and Continental Air Services, Inc. (subsidiary), 1965—68; pres. Gramco Devel. Corp., 1968—; dep. chmn. Gramco (U.K.) Ltd., 1970—71; sr. v.p. AMROP Inc., 1969; with L'Express, Paris, 1973—78; contbg. corr. ABC for Europe, 1977—, Paris bur. chief, 1979—87, sr. editor, 1988—90, ABC News, 1988—93; vice chmn. Burson Marsteller, Washington, 1993—96. Ind. pub. rels. profl., 1996—. Author: (book) With Kennedy, 1966, On Instructions of My Government; editor: A Tribute to John F. Kennedy, 1964, A Tribute to Robert F. Kennedy, 1968, Je Suis un Americain, 1975, La France et le Nouveau Monde, 1976, America Held Hostage - The Secret Negotiations, 1981, the Dossier, 1984, Mortal Games, 1988, Secret Dossier - The Hidden Agenda Behind the Gulf Crisis, 1991, PS-A Memoir, 1995, John F. Kennedy Commander in Chief, 1997. Press officer Calif. Stevenson for Pres. Campaign, 1952, Richard Graves for Gov. Calif. Campaign, 1954; trustee Robert F. Kennedy Meml. Found.; chmn. bd. trustees Am. U. in Paris, 1978—88, hon. chmn., 1988—. With USNR, WWII. Decorated officer Legion of Honor France; recipient Ellis Island Medal of Honor, 1992. Mem.: Nat. Press Club. Home: La Bastiderose 99 Cherin Des Croupieres Lethor France

SALINS, PETER D. academic administrator; b. Berlin, June 15, 1938; came to U.S., 1939; s. Irwin and Ilse Daisy (Lessler) S.; m. Rochelle Chensky, Apr. 4, 1971; children: Jessica Elizabeth, Jonathan Andrew. BArch, Syracuse U., 1961, M in Regional Planning, 1968, PhD, 1969. Registered architect, Mass. Chmn. dept. urban affairs and planning Hunter Coll., CUNY, N.Y.C., 1973-93, 96-97, prof. dept. urban affairs and planning, 1980-97, dir. grad. program in urban planning, 1993-95, dir. urban rsch. ctr., 1995-97; provost, vice chancellor acad. affairs SUNY Sys. Adminstrn., Albany, 1997—. Sr. fellow Manhattan Inst. Policy Rsch., N.Y.C., 1985—; mem. Planning Accreditation Bd., Chgo., 1990—; Catherine Bauer Wurster lectr. U. Calif., Berkeley, 1993; dir. SUNY Rsch. Found., 1997—; prof. dept. polit. sci. U. Stony Brook, 1998. Author: The Ecology of Housing Destruction, 1980, Assimilation, American Style, 1997; co-author: Scarcity by Design, 1992; editor: Housing America's Poor, 1987, New York Unbound, 1988; co-editor Jour. of Am. Planning Assn., 1988-93 (Excellence award 1992, Journalism award 1994). Mem. planning com. Am. Acad. Sci., Washington, 1971-72; mem. adv. panel White House Domestic Policy Unit, Washington, 1977; dir. Citizens Housing and Planning Coun., N.Y.C., 1988—; trustee Lavanburg Found., N.Y.C., 1987—, Village of Baxter Estates, Nassau County, N.Y., 1992-99; mem. mayor's adv. commn. N.Y.C. Health and Hosps. Corp., 1995-96. Fellow: Am. Inst. Cert. Planners; mem.: ASPA (v.p. 1982—84, Luther Gulick award for outstanding acad. 1994), Am. Planning Assn. (v.p. 1986—88, policy bd. mem. 1986—, N.Y. met. chpt.), Lambda Alpha. Avocations: golf, reading, hiking. Office: SUNY Suny Plz Albany NY 12246-0001 E-mail: salinspd@syadm.suny.edu.

SALISBURY, ALAN BLANCHARD, information systems executive; b. Newark, Jan. 21, 1937; s. Lloyd Wade and Elizabeth Barry (Blanchard) S.; m. Florence Dorothy Conrad, May 21, 1971; children: Katherine Anne, Barbara Lynn. BS with distinction, U.S. Mil. Acad., 1958; MSEE, Stanford U., 1964, PhD, 1973; postgrad., Indsl. Coll. of Armed Forces, Washington, 1978. Commd. 2d lt. Signal Corps U.S. Army, 1958, advanced through grades to Maj. Gen., ret., 1987; asst. prof. U.S. Mil. Acad., West Point, N.Y., 1964-67; chief of data communications 1st Signal Brigade, Republic of Vietnam, 1968-69; tech. adv. Directorate of Mgmt. Info., Washington, 1970-71; dir. U.S. Army Ctr. for Tactical Computer Sci., Ft. Monmouth, N.J., 1975-77; project mgr. Operations Tactical Data Systems, Ft. Monmouth, N.J., 1978-82; program mgr. Joint Tactical Fusion Program, Washington, 1982-84; comdr. U.S. Army Info. Systems Engrng., Ft. Belvoir, Va., 1984-87; pres. Contel Technology Ctr., Fairfax, Va., 1987-91; exec. v.p. Microelectronics & Computer Tech. Corp., Austin, Tex., 1991-93; pres. Learning Tree Internat. USA, Inc., Reston, Va., 1993-99; ind. cons., 1999—. Bd. dirs. Sybase, Dublin, Calif., Challenger Ctr. for Space Sci. Edn., Alexandria, Va.; trustee Mitretek Systems, Inc., McLean, Va., Assn. Grads. U.S. Mil. Acad.; chmn. Ctr. for Nat. Software Studies; bd. visitors Software Engrng. Inst. Carnegie Mellon U., 1988-2002, Coll. of Engrng. U. Md., 1993-2001. Author: Microprogrammable Computer Architectures 1976, numerous articles in profl. jours.; founding editor Journal of Systems & Software, 1979-85. Decorated Bronze Star (2), 1969, D.S.M., 1987. Mem. Inst. for Elec. & Electronic Engrs. (sr.), Assn. for Computing Machinery, Armed Forces Communications & Electronics Assn. (chpt. pres. 1981-82), Phi Kappa Phi, Soc. of the Sigma Xi. Office: PO Box 2910 Reston VA 20195-0910 E-mail: abslsbry@aol.com.

SALISBURY, ALICIA LAING, state senator; b. N.Y.C., Sept. 20, 1939; d. Herbert Farnsworth and Augusta Belle (Marshall) Laing; m. John Eagan Salisbury, June 23, 1962; children: John Eagan Jr., Margaret Salisbury La Rue. Student, Sweet Briar Coll., 1957-60; BA, Kans. U., 1961. Mem. Kans. Senate, 1985—, v.p., chmn. commerce com., telecomm. stragegic planning, 1995, vice chmn. ways and means com., mem. utilities com., jt. com. on econ. devel., mem. orgn. and calendar rules com., mem. jt. com. corrections and juvenile justice, mem. confirmations oversight com. Elected mem. State Bd. Edn., Topeka, 1981-85, Kans.; past pres. Jr. League of Topeka; trustee Leadership Kans., 1982-89; bd. dirs. Topeka Cmty. Found., 1983—, Topeka Pub. Sch. Found., 1985-89, Capitol Area Pla. Authority, 1989—, Kans. Inc., 1996—, Mid-Am. Mfg. Tech. Ctr., 1994-96, mem. workers' compensation fund oversight com., 1993— Stormont-Vail Hosp. Aux.; mem. adv. commn. Juvenile Offenders Program, Kans., 1985-95; mem. adv. bd. Topeka State Hosp., Kans. Action for Children, 1982—, Kans. Ins. Edn. Found., 1984-95, Youth Ctr. at Topeka, 1987—; steering com. One Stop Career Ctr., 1996, Interstate Cooperation Com. Coun. State Govts.; mem. Nat. Fedn. Rep. Women; past bd. mem. United Way Greater Topeka, ARC, Family Svc. and Guidance, Topeka, Shawnee County Mental Health Assn., Florence Crittenton Svcs., Topeka, Topeka City Commn. Govtl. Adv. Com.; chmn. Topeka State Hosp. Grounds Adv. Com.; mem. Kans. Workforce Investment Partnership Coun. Recipient Woman of Yr. award Topeka Panhellenic Coun., 1997. Mem. Nat. Conf. State Legislators (exec. com.), Nat. Rep. Legislators' Assn. (Nat. Rep. Legislator of Yr. 1993, Gold Rose award 1992, Bus. Guardian award 1990, 99, Outstanding Individual Legis. Achievement award 1989), Shawnee County Rep. Women, Kans. State Hist. Soc. (exec. com.), Kappa Kappa Gamma. Episcopalian. Avocations: tennis, downhill skiing, water sports, horseback ridng, gardening. Office: Kans State Senate State Capital Topeka KS 66612

SALISBURY, DALLAS L. research institute executive; BA, U. Wash., 1970; MBA in Pub. Policy and Adminstrn., Syracuse U., 1973. Employee benefit security adminstrn. U.S. Dept. Labor, 1975—78; with U.S. Dept. Justice, 1974, Wash. State Legislature, 1971-72, Employee Benefit Rsch. Inst., Washington, 1978—, pres., CEO, mem. bd. trustees. Bd. dirs. The Health Project; mem. adv. bd. Nat. Acad. on Aging; lectr. in field; cons. in field. Mem. editl. adv. bd. Benefits Quar., Employee Benefits Jour., Healthplan; contbr. articles to profl. jours. Mem. ERISA adv. coun. Sec. of Labor; pres.'s adv. coun. PBGC. Fellow Nat. Acad. Human Resources. Office: Employee Benefit Research Inst 2121 K St NW Ste 600 Washington DC 20037-1800

SALISBURY, EUGENE W. lawyer, justice; b. Blasdell, N.Y., Mar. 20, 1933; s. W. Dean and Mary I. (Burns) S.; m. Joanne M. Salisbury, July 14, 1950; children: Mark, Ellen, Susan, David, Scott. BA in History and Govt. cum laude, U. Buffalo, 1959, JD cum laude, 1968. Bar: N.Y. 1960, D.C. 1973, U.S. Dist. Ct. (we. and no. dists.) 1961, U.S. Ct. Appeals (2d cir.) 1970, U.S. Ct. Appeals (D.C. cir.) 1973, U.S. Supreme Ct. 1973. Ptnr. Lipsitz, Green, Fahringer, Roll, Salisbury and Cambria, Buffalo, 1960—. Justice Village of Blasdell, 1961-2001; lectr. N.Y. Office Ct. Adminstrn., N.Y.C., 1961—; mem. N.Y. State Commn. on Jud. Conduct, 1989-2001, chmn., 2000-2001. Author: Manual for N.Y. Courts, 1973, Forms for N.Y. Courts, 1977. Capt. U.S. Army, 1949-54, Korea. Decorated Bronze Star, Purple Heart; recipient Citizen of Yr. award Indsl. Rels. Rsch. Assn., 2000; named Jurist of Yr., Erie County Judges and Police Conf., 2001, Magistrate of Yr., Erie County Magistrates Assn., 2001. Mem. ABA (del. spl. ct. sect. 1988-2001), D.C. Bar Assn., Erie County Bar Assn., N.Y. State Bar Assn., World Judges Assn., N.Y. State Magistrates Assn. (pres. 1973, Man of Yr. 1974), N.Y. State Jud. Conf., Upstate N.Y. Labor Adv. Coun., 1995—. Office: Lipsitz Green Fahringer Roll Salisbury and Cambria 42 Delaware Ave Ste 300 Buffalo NY 14202-3857 Office Phone: 716-849-1333. Business E-Mail: esalisbury@lipsitzgreen.com.

SALISBURY, FAYANN (ANNIE), elementary school educator; b. Milw., Wis., Sept. 28, 1953; d. James and Anita Katherine Salisbury. BS, U Wis., Oshkosh; MS, Emporia State U; MPSA, U Wis.; MF, Delta State U. Cert. tchg. Wis.,Ill.,Kans., D.C.,La. Tchr. Annunciation Cath. Elem. Sch., Washington, 1995—96, Shephard Elem. Sch., Washington, 1997—99, LacCourte Orilles Ojibwe Sch., Hayward, Wis., 1999—2000, Winter (Wis.) Sch. Dist., 2000—01; subsitute tchr. Drummond (Wis.) Sch. Dist., 2000—01; tchr. North Chgo. (Ill.) Dist. #187, 2001—02, Lake Villa (Ill.) Sch. Dist., 2002—03. Author: The Earth Gets Its Price, When Life Was a Song, 2003; songwriter: Hilltop Records. Mem.: Heart Assn., Ill. Assn. Phys. Edn., Health, Recreation and Dance, Ill. Tchr. Fedn., Nat. Tchr. Fedn., U.S. Tenis Assn. (assoc.). Avocations: writing, singing, dance, drama, sports.

SALISBURY, FRANK BOYER, plant physiologist, educator, author; b. Provo, Utah, Aug. 3, 1926; s. Frank M. and Catherine (Boyer) S.; m. Lois Marilyn Olson, Sept. 1, 1949; children: Frank Clark, Steven Scott, Michael James, Cynthia Kay, Phillip Boyer (dec.), Rebecca Lynn, Blake Charles; m. Mary Thorpe Robinson, June 28, 1991. BS, U. Utah, 1951, MA, 1952; PhD, Calif. Inst. Tech., 1955. Asst. prof. botany Pomona Coll., Claremont, Calif., 1954-55; faculty Colo. State U., Ft. Collins, 1955-66, prof. plant physiology, 1961-66; plant physiologist Expt. Sta., 1961-66; prof. plant physiology Utah State U., Logan, 1966-97, disting. prof. Agr., 1987-97, prof. emeritus, 1997—, head dept. plant sci., 1966-70; tech. rep. plant physiology AEC, Germantown, Md., 1973-74. Vis. prof. U. Innsbruck, Austria; Lady Davis fellow Hebrew U. Jerusalem, 1983; mem. aerospace medicine adv. com. NASA, 1988-93, life scis. adv. com., 1986-88, chmn. NASA Controlled Ecol. Life Support System Discipline Working Group, 1989-94; leader of project to grow wheat through a life cycle in Russian space station, Mir, 1990-97. Author: The Flowering Process, 1963, Truth by Reason and by Revelation, 1965, The Biology of Flowering, 1971, The Utah UFO Display, 1974, The Creation, 1976; co-author: (with R.V. Parke) Vascular Plants, Form and Function, 2d edit., 1970, (with C. Ross) Plant Physiology, 1969, 4th edit., 1992; (with W. Jensen) Botany: An Ecological Approach, 1972, Botany, 2d edit., 1984, (with others) Biology, 1977; editor Jour. Plant Physiology, Ams. and the Pacific Rim, 1989-96; editor, contbr.: Units, Symbols, and Terminology for Plant Physiology, 1996. Trustee Colo. State U. Rsch. Found., 1959-62; leader People to People bot. del. to South Africa, 1984, to China, 1988, Soviet Union, 1990; fin. sec. Ohio Columbus Mission LDS Ch., 1997-99. NSF sr. postdoctoral fellow Germany and Austria, 1962-63. Fellow AAAS; mem. Am. Soc. for Gravitational and Space Biology (Founders award 1994), Am. Soc. Plant Physiologists (editorial bd. 1967-92), Am. Inst. Biol. Scis. (governing bd. 1976-79), Bot. Soc. Am. (merit award 1982), Sigma Xi, Phi Kappa Phi. Mem. Lds Ch. Home: 2250 Bryan Cir Salt Lake City UT 84108-2711 *This is an extremely exciting time to live! Science has provided marvelous insight into the cosmos, the earth, and the nature of life. The fact that mankind exists and can contemplate it all cries out that it has purpose and direction. My life is full to overflowing because God's revelation of Himself adds the final capstone to this beautiful structure.*

SALISBURY, HELEN HOLLAND, education educator; b. Bedford, Ind., Dec. 15, 1923; d. Deward Julius and Zella (Kinser) Holland; m. Charles Jackson Salisbury, Jan. 10, 1942; children: Creggie Helen Salisbury Henderson, Andrew Jackson Salisbury Henderson. BS in Home Econs., Ind. U., 1957; MEd, U. Va., 1967; EdD, Temple U., 1979. Plating chemist Curtiss-Wright, Indpls., 1943; supr. sch. lunch program Charlottesville Pub. Sch., Va., 1963—65; dir. Harcum Jr. Coll. Lab. Sch., Bryn Mawr, Pa., 1966—68, prof. edn., 1965—73; tchg. assoc. Temple U., Phila., 1974; early childhood cons., 1979—. Prof. edn. Harcum Jr. Coll., 1982—94, dir. infant devel. practice, 1982—94; early childhood cons. Head Start, 1965; instr. Child Care Tng. Project, Pa., 1992—94. Co-author: Diagnosing Individual Needs for Early Childhood Education, 1975. Mem.: DAR, ASCD, Orgn. Mondiale pour L'Education Prescolaire, Delaware Valley Assn. Edn. Young Children, Nat. Assn. Edn. Young Children, Kappa Alpha Theta. Episcopalian. Home: 3915 Nimit Dr Bloomington IN 47401-8964 Office: Harcum Jr Coll Montgomery Ave Bryn Mawr PA 19010

SALISBURY, HOLLY BUCKNER, university arts director; b. Paris, Ky., Apr. 29, 1945; d. Catlett Lockhart and Marjorie Witherspoon (Routt) Buckner; m. William Benson Salisbury III, Aug. 24, 1967 (div. 1980); children: Leila Witherspoon, Brent Buckner. Student, L'Acad. de Belle Arte, Florence, Italy, 1965-66; BA, George Washington U., 1967. Art tchr. Charles County (Md.) Pub. Schs., 1967-70, Pks. and Recreation Dept., Prince George County, Md., 1970-73; dir. Singletary Ctr. for Arts U. Ky., Lexington, 1979—. Pres. Cen. Ky. Youth Orch., Lexington, 1986-88; site coord. Gov's. Sch. for Arts Lexington, 1988—. Editor (booklet) Artworks, 1983. Active Lexington Forum, 1986—; bd. dirs. Lexington Arts and Cultural Coun., 1989-90, Opera Cen. Ky., 1989—, Ky. Citizens for Arts, 1989—. Mem. Am. Bus. Women's Assn., Assn. Performing Arts Presenters (membership com.), U. Ky. Faculty Club, Lexington Arts Cultural Coun., Jr. League Lexington. Episcopalian. Avocation: painting. Home: 30 Mentelle Park Lexington KY 40502-1512

SALISBURY, ROBERT HOLT, political science educator; b. Elmhurst, Ill., Apr. 29, 1930; s. Robert Holt and Beulah (Hammer) S.; m. Rose Marie Cipriani, June 19, 1953; children: Susan Marie, Robert Holt, Matthew Gary. AB, Washington and Lee U., 1951; MA, U. Ill., 1952, PhD, 1955. Mem. faculty Washington U., St. Louis, 1955-65, prof., 1965-97, prof. emeritus, 1997—, chmn. dept. polit. sci., 1966-73, 86-92, dir. Center for Study Pub. Affairs, 1974-77, Sidney W. Souers prof. govt., 1982-97. Vis. prof. SUNY, Buffalo, 1965, So. Ill. U., Edwardsville, 1975; affiliated scholar Am. Bar Found., 1981-95; cons. U.S. Conf. Mayors, 1965, Hartford (Conn.) C. of C., 1964, NSF, 1973. Author: Interest Groups Politics in America, 1970, Governing America, 1973, Citizen Participation in the Public Schools, 1980, Interests and Institutions, 1992, The Hollow Core, 1993; contbr. articles to profl. jours. Mem. St. Louis County Charter Commn., 1967, Gov.'s Commn. on Local Govt., 1968-69. Guggenheim fellow, 1990; Rockefeller Ctr. scholar, 1990. Mem. Mo. Polit. Sci. Assn. (pres. 1964-65), Am. Polit. Sci. Assn. (exec. council 1969-71, v.p. 1980-81), Midwest Polit. Sci. Assn. (pres. 1977-78), Pi Sigma Alpha. Democrat. Methodist. Home: 709 S Skinker Blvd Saint Louis MO 63105-3225 Office: Washington U Dept Polit Sci Saint Louis MO 63130 E-mail: rhsalisb@artsci.wustl.edu.

SALISBURY, TAMARA PAULA, foundation executive; b. N.Y.C., Dec. 14, 1927; d. Paul Terrance and Nadine (Korolkova) Voloshin; m. Franklin Cary Salisbury, Jan. 22, 1955; children: Franklin Jr., John, Elizabeth, Elaine, Claire. BA, Coll. Notre Dame, 1948; postgrad., Am. U., George Washington U.

Chemist depts. pathology and chemotherapy NIH Cancer Inst., Bethesda, Md., 1946-52; asst. to chief of Chemistry Br. Office of Naval Rsch., Bethesda, 1953-55; v.p., COO Nat. Found. Cancer Rsch., Bethesda, 1973—. Mem. Assn. Internat. Cancer Rsch., 1995. Decorated d'Officier De L'Ordre De Leopold II; outstanding contbns. award Internat. Soc. Quantum Biology, 1983, award of appreciation Beth Israel Hosp., Harvard Med. Sch., Brigham & Women's Hosp., 1993. Mem. AAAS, Am. Chem. Soc., N.Y. Acad. Scis., Inst. Phys. and Chem. Biology (fgn.), Krebforschung Internat., Nat. Liberal Club. Home: 10811 Alloway Dr Potomac MD 20854-1504 Office: Nat Found Cancer Rsch 4600 E West Hwy Ste 525 Bethesda MD 20814-6900

SALIT, GARY, lawyer; Corp. counsel Bell Howell Co., Skokie, Ill. Office: Bell & Howell 3400 W Pratt Ave Lincolnwood IL 60712-ND

SALITERMAN, RICHARD ARLEN, lawyer; b. Aug. 3, 1946; s. Leonard Slitz and Dorothy (Sloan) S.; m. Laura Shrager, June 15, 1975; 1 child, Robert Warren. BA summa cum laude, U. Minn., 1968; JD, Columbia U., 1971; LLM, NYU, 1974. Bar: Minn. 1972, D.C. 1974. Legal staff subcom. on antitrust and monopoly U.S. Senate, Washington, 1971-72; acting dir., dep. dir. compliance and enforcement divsn. Fed. Energy Office, N.Y.C., 1974; mil. atty. Presdl. Clemency Bd., White House, Washington, 1975; pres. Saliterman & Siefferman, PC, Mpls., 1975—. Adj. prof. law Hamline U., 1976-81. Author: Advising Minnesota Corporations and Other Business Organizations, 4 vols., 1975; chmn. Hennepin County Bar Jour., 1985-87. Trustee, sec. Hopkins Edn. Found.; trustee W. Harry Davis Found., 1990-96; pres. Twin Cities Coun.; mem. nat. bd. dirs. Navy League U.S., Washington, 1997—, nat. judge adv., 2001-02; bd. dirs., sec. The Pavek Mus., 1992—. lt. USN, 1972-75, res., 1975—. Office Phone: 612-339-1400. Business E-Mail: rsaliterman@saliterman-law.com.

SALIZZONI, FRANK L. finance company executive; b. 1938; m. Sarah Salizzoni; 3 children. BS, Pa. State U.; MBA, George Washington U. V.p., CFO TWA, 1984-87; exec. v.p., CFO USAir, Inc., 1990-94, pres., COO, 1994-96; pres. H&R Block, Kansas City, Mo., 1996-99, CEO, 1999—. Office: H&R Block 4400 Main St Kansas City MO 64111-1812

SALKIND, ALVIN J. electrochemical engineer, biomedical engineer, educator, dean; b. N.Y.C. s. Samuel M. and Florence (Zins) S.; m. Marion Ruth Koenig, Nov. 7, 1965; children: Susanne, James. B.Ch.E., Poly. Inst. N.Y., 1949, M.Ch.E., 1952, D.Ch.E., 1958; postgrad. and mgmt. courses, Pa. State U., 1965, Harvard U., 1976. Registered profl. engr., N.Y., N.J. Chem. engr. U.S. Electric Mfg. Co., N.Y.C., 1952-54; sr. scientist Sonotone Corp., Elmsford, NY, 1954-56; research assoc. Poly. Inst. N.Y., 1956-58, adj. prof. chem. engring., 1960-70; with ESB-Ray OVAC Co., Yardley, Pa., 1958-79, dir. tech., 1971-72, v.p. tech., 1972-79; pres. ESB Tech. Co., 1972—79; prof., chief bioengring. divsn., dept. surgery UMDNJ-Robert Wood Johnson Med. Sch., Piscataway, NJ, 1970—2004, prof. emeritus, 2004—; prof. biomed. engring. and chem. and biochem. engring Rutgers U., Piscataway, NJ, 1985—2002, assoc. dean Coll. Engring., 1989—2001, emeritus prof., 2004—. Vis. prof. and exec. officer Case Ctr. for Electrochem. Sci., 1981—82; vis. prof. U. Miami, 2003—04; bd. dirs., cons. various cos., rsch. instns. and govt. orgns.; mem. rev. panels Nat. Rsch. Coun., NIH. Author (with S.U. Falk): Alkaline Storage Batteries, 1969; author: (with Herbert T. Silverman and Irving F. Miller) Electrochemical Bioscience and Bioengineering, 1973; editor (with E. Yeager): Techniques of Electrochemistry, 1971, vol. 2, 1973, vol. 3, 1978, History of Battery Technology, 1987; editor: (with F. McLarnon and V. Bogatzky) Rechargeable Zinc Electrodes, 1996; contbr. over 200 articles to profl. jours. Served with USNR, 1945-46. Recipient Alumnus citation Poly. Inst. N.Y., 1975, award Internat. Tech. Exch. Soc., 1992, Frank Booth award Internat. Power Sources Symposium Eng., 1999; Case Centennial scholar Case-Western Res. U., 1980. Fellow Acad. Medicine of N.J., Am. Coll. Cardiology, AAAS; mem. Electrochem. Soc. (past chmn. new tech. com., past chmn. battery div.), Assn. Advancement Med. Instrumentation, Indsl. Rsch. Inst. (emeritus 1979), N.Y. Acad. Scis., Sigma Xi, Phi Lambda Upsilon. Home: 51 Adams Dr Princeton NJ 08540-5401 also: UMDNJ-Robert Wood Johnson Med Sch 675 Hoes Ln Piscataway NJ 08854-5627 Office Phone: 732-235-4799. Business E-Mail: salkinaj@umdnj.edu. E-mail: asalkind@verizon.net.

SALKIND, MICHAEL JAY, science administrator, metallurgical engineer; b. N.Y.C, Oct. 1, 1938; s. Milton and Esther (Jaffe) S.; m. Miriam E. Schwartz, Aug. 16, 1959 (div. 1979); children: Michael Jay, Elizabeth Jane, Jonathan Hillson, Joshua Isaac; m. Carol T. Gill, Dec. 23, 1990. B in Metall. Engring., Rensselaer Polytech. Inst., 1959, PhD, 1962. Chief advanced metallurgy United Techs. Rsch. Labs., East Hartford, 1964-68; chief structures and materials Sikorsky Aircraft div. United Techs. Corp., 1968-75; dir. product devel. Avco Systems div., 1975-76; mgr. structures NASA, 1976-80; dir. aerospace scis. Air Force Office of Sci. Rsch., 1980-89; pres. Ohio Aerospace Inst., 1990—2003, Business Tech Network, 2003—; prin. KSG Alliance, 2003—. Adj. faculty metallurgy Trinity Coll., Hartford; adj. faculty aerospace U. Md., 1982-85; adj. faculty materials Johns Hopkins U., 1985-89; chair Ohio Math. and Sci. Coalition. Cons. editor Internat. Jour. Fibre Sci. and Tech.; editor Applications Composite Materials, 1973; contbr. to profl. jours. and textbooks. Evaluator Accreditation Bd. Engring. and Tech., 1989—; mem. Daniel Guggenheim Medal Bd. Awards, 1984-90; mem. Spirit of St. Louis Medal Bd., 1984-89; bd. dirs. Citizens' Acad. Charter Sch., Cleve. Internat. Program, NCCJ. Capt. U.S. Army, 1962-64. Recipient Disting. Leadership award, Cleve. Tech. Socs. Coun., 2002. Fellow AAAS, AIAA (assoc.), ASM Internat.; mem. ASME (Disting. lectr. 1989-93), ASTM (chmn. com. D-30 on high modulous fibers and their composites 1968-74), Am. Helicopter Soc., AIME, Brit. Inst. Metals, Rsch. Soc. Am., Plansee Soc., India Ohio C. of C., Cosmos Club, Union Club, 50 Club, Leadership Cleve., Sigma Xi, Alpha Sigma Mu. E-mail: michaelsalkind@adelphia.net.

SALL, JOHN, information technology executive; married; 4 children. BS, Beloit Coll.; MS, No. Ill. U. Co-founder, exec. v.p. SAS Inst., Cary, NC. Office: SAS Inst 100 SAS Campus Dr Cary NC 27513-2414

SALLAH, MAJEED (JIM SALLAH), retired real estate developer; b. Boston, Aug. 5, 1920; s. Herbert K. and Rose (Karem) Sallah; m. Aline C. Powers, Apr. 10, 1970; children: Christopher M., Melissa Rose. Pres., dir. Glo-Bit Fish Co., Gloucester, Mass., 1947—48, Live-Pak of Ohio, Inc., 1947—51, Cape Ann Glass Co., Gloucester, 1950—72, Marias Restaurant, 1960—, Cape Ann Realty Co., 1961—. Pres., treas., dir. Gloucester Hot-Top Constrn. Co., Goucester, 1967—75; pres., bd. dir. SGF Corp., 1983—85, SALFAD, Inc., Rossford, Ohio; pres., treas. Points East, Inc.; trustee Christopher Investment Trust; bd. dir. Lustal, Inc.; bd. dir., ptnr. Barsal, Inc., Toledo, Hamsal, Inc. Pres. Lebanese-Am. Bus. Men's Club; treas. Lebanese-Maronite Soc. With U.S. Army, 1942—45. Decorated Bronze Star. Mem.: Gloucester Assoc., Cape Ann Investment Corp., Gloucester Fraternity Assn., Lions, Am. Legion, Amvets, Loyal Order of Moose, Elks, Ky. Cols. (hon.). Roman Catholic. Home and Office: 56 Hilltop Rd Gloucester MA 01931-0078

SALLAH, MICHAEL D. journalist; Grad., U. Toledo. Joined The Blade, Toledo, 1989; nat. affairs writer Block News Alliance (The Blade and The Pitts. Post-Gazette). Named Best Reporter, Ohio Soc. Profl. Journalists, 2002; recipient Touchstone Newsie award, Press Club Toledo, 2002, 2 Crystal awards, Toledo Profl. Chptr., Women Comm., 2002, Medal winner, Investigative Reporters and Editors, Inc., 2004, Pulitzer Prize for investigative reporting, 2004. Office: The Blade 541 N Superior St Toledo OH 43660*

SALLAN, STEPHEN E. pediatrician; b. Detroit; MD, Wayne State U., 1967. Cert. pediat. Intern Boston Floating Hosp., 1967-68; resident in pediatrics Children's Hosp., Phila., 1968-69, Hosp. Sick Children, London, 1969-70; fellow in pediatric oncology Children's Hosp. Med. Ctr./Harvard U., Boston, 1973-75; mem. med. staff Dana Farber Cancer Inst., Boston, 1975—, chief of staff, 1995—; prof. pediatrics Harvard Med. Sch., Boston. Mem. AMA, AACR, ASCO, ASH, SPR. Office: Dana Farber Cancer Inst 44 Binney St Boston MA 02115-6084

SALLEE, MARGUERITE, association executive; m. Knox Sallee; 4 children. Grad., Duke U. Commr. Tenn. Dept. Hunan Svcs.; co-chmn., co-founder, pres., CEO CorporateFamily Solutions; co-chmn. Bright Horizons Family Solutions (formerly CorporateFamily), Cambridge, Mass. Dir. MagneTek, Inc., Bank Am., Tenn. and Ky., Ladies Profl. Golf Assn. Mem. Acad. Women of Achievement (Corp. Leadership award), Nashville Area C. of C. (chair). Office: Bright Horizons Family Solutions One Kendall Sq Bldg 200 Cambridge MA 02139

SALLEE, MARY LOU, state legislator; Mem. Mo. State Ho. of Reps. Dist. 144. Home: PO Box 128 Ava MO 65608-0128 Office: Mo Ho of Reps State Capitol Building Jefferson City MO 65101-1556

SALLEO, FERDINANDO, former Italian diplomat; b. Messina, Oct. 2, 1936; s. Carmelo and Maria Carla Stagno d'Alcontres; m. Anne Marie Riegler; children: Carmelo, Alberto. LLD, U. Rome, 1959. Enlisted Italian Fgn. Svc., Washington, 1960—; appt. to Paris, N.Y., Prague, Washington and Bonn, Germany; dep. dir. then. dir. gen. of devel. cooperation Ministry Fgn. Affairs, 1981-86; dir. gen. of econ. affairs Ministry of Fgn. Affairs, 1988; amb. OECD, Paris, 1986-88; amb. Soviet Union, 1989-93; dir. gen. polit. affairs Ministry of Fgn. Affairs, 1993, sec. gen., 1994-95; amb. of Italy to the U.S. Washington, 1995—2003. Vis. prof. U. Florence, 1982-84; prof. Rome U. LUISS, 1985-87. Recipient Grand Cross of Order of Merit of Italian Republic, 1993.

SALLER, RICHARD PAUL, classics educator; b. Ft. Bragg, N.C., Oct. 18, 1952; s. George E. and Arthea E. (North) S.; m. Carol Joann Fisher, Jan. 12, 1974 (div. Apr. 18, 2002; children: John E., Benjamin T.; m. Tanya M. Luhrmann, Jan. 4, 2003. BA in Greek and History, U. Ill., 1974; PHD in Classics, U. Cambridge, Eng., 1978. Asst. prof. Swarthmore (Pa.) Coll., 1979-84; assoc. prof. U. Chgo., 1984-89, prof., 1990—, dean of social scis., 1994—2001, provost, 2002—. Author: Personal Patronage, 1982, Patriarchy, Property and Death in the Roman Family, 1994; co-editor: Economy and Society in Ancient Greece, 1981; co-author: Roman Empire, 1987; editor Classical Philology, 1991-93. Rsch. fellow Jesus Coll., U. Cambridge, 1978-79; Ctr. for Adv. Study fellow, Stanford U., 1986-87; Trinity Coll., U. Cambridge fellow commoner, 1991. Mem. Am. Philol. Assn., Am. Hist. Assn. Office: U Chgo Dept History 1126 E 59th St Chicago IL 60637-1580 Office Phone: 773-702-8810.

SALLEY, JOHN JONES, retired academic administrator, oral pathologist; b. Richmond, Va., Oct. 29, 1926; s. Thomas Raysor and Kathryn (Josey) S.; m. Jean Gordon Cunningham, Dec. 21, 1950; children: Katharine Gordon, John Jones, Martha Cunningham. DDS, Med. Coll. Va., 1951; PhD, U. Rochester, 1954; DSc, Boston U., 1975. Research fellow U. Rochester, 1951-54; from instr. to prof., chmn. dept. oral pathology Med. Coll. Va., 1954-63, prof. emeritus, 1991—; prof. pathology, dean Sch. Dentistry U. Md., 1963-74, dean emeritus Sch. Dentistry, 1977—, ret., 1991; v.p. research and grad. affairs Va. Commonwealth U., Richmond, 1974-85; acting pres. Va. Ctr. for Innovative Tech., 1985, v.p., 1985-87. Cons. div. research grants NIH, 1962-66; cons. U.S. Naval Dental Sch., Bethesda, Md., 1966-75; spl. cons. Nat. Inst. Dental Research, NIH, 1957-64; cons. USPHS Hosp., Balt., 1963-74, U.S. Naval Hosp., Portsmouth, Va., VA Hosp., Balt., 1964-74; dental health div. USPHS; mem. Md. Adv. Council Comprehensive Health Planning, 1968-74, Nat. Health Council, 1970-71; pres. Am. Assn. Dental Schs., 1971-72, Conf. So. Grad. Schs., 1983-84; sr. program cons. Robert Wood Johnson Found., 1978-84; mem. career devel. rev. com. VA, 1974-78; mem. com. health care resources in VA, NRC, 1974-77; cons. WHO, 1969-75; mem. Va. Gov.'s Task Force Sci. and Tech., 1982-83, sci. advisor to Gov. of Va., 1984-86; mem. research com. Va. State Council Higher Edn., 1974-84; chmn. task force Council Grad. Schs. in U.S., 1979-82. Conbtr. articles in field; editorial rev. bd.: Jour. Dental Edn, 1974-78. Bd. dirs. Md. divsn. Am. Cancer Soc., 1963-70, Am. Fund Dental Health, Rappahannock C.C. Found., 1999—; bd. dirs. Nat. Found. Dentistry for the Handicapped, 1986, pres., 1992-94; mem. adv. bd. Va. Inst. for Devel. Disabilities, 1987-91; bd. trustees Middlesex County Pub. Libr., 1994-98, pres., 1995-97. With USAAF, 1944-46. Recipient Outstanding Civilian Service medal Dept. Army, 1961, Disting. Citizenship award State Md., 1974. Fellow AAAS, Am. Coll. Dentists; mem. ADA, Nat. Conf. Univ. Research Adminstrs., Am. Acad. Oral Pathology, Internat. Assn. Dental Research (Novice award 1953), Internat. Med. Informatics Assn. (chmn. working group 1989-92), Sigma Xi, Sigma Zeta, Omicron Kappa Upsilon. Episcopalian (vestryman). Home and Office: PO Box 838 Urbanna VA 23175-0838 E-mail: salleyj@oonl.com.

SALLIS, JAMES, writer; b. Helena, Ark., Dec. 21, 1944; s. Chappelle Horace and Mildred Clodine (Liming) S. Student, Tulane U., 1961-63, U. Tex., 1985-87. Tchr. intensive writing workshops Clarion (Pa.) Coll., U. Wash., Tulane U., Loyola U.; guest lectr. modern poetry, European lit., art; writer short stories, essays, poetry and trans. Editor New Worlds 1966-68; editor: (anthologies) The War Book, 1972, The Shores Beneath, 1973; features writer, reviewer, columnist Tex. Jazz, 1980-83, lead book reviewer Dallas Morning News, 1981-83; book reviewer Washington Post Book World, L.A. Times, 1993—; columnist Mag. of Fantasy and Sci. Fiction, Web Del Sol, Boston Globe, 2000—; author: A Few Last Words, 1972, The Guitar Players, 1982, 94, Jazz Guitars, 1984, The Long-Legged Fly, 1992, Saint Glinglin (translator), 1993, Difficult Lives, 1993, Moth, 1993, Black Hornet, 1994, Limits of the Sensible World, 1994, Renderings, 1995, The Guitar in Jazz, 1996, Ash of Stars: On the Writings of Samuel R. Delany, 1996, Death Will Have Your Eyes, 1997, Eye of the Cricket, 1997, Bluebottle, 1999, Gently into the Land of the Meateaters, 2000, Chester Himes: A Life, 2000, Time's Hammers, 2000, Sorrow's Kitchen, 2000, Ghost of a Flea, 2001, Cypress Grove, 2002.

SALLQUIST, GARY ARDIN, minister, non-profit executive; b. Sioux City, Iowa, July 7, 1938; s. Hal Thurston and Rosemary (Daggett) S.; m. Joyce Darleen Casey, June 10, 1960; children: Susan L. Rail, Steven P. BA, U. Nebr., Omaha, 1960; MDiv, Princeton Theol. Sem., 1993; D of Ministry, La. Bapt. U., 1997; D, Am. Coll. ChFC, CLU. Ptnr. Sallquist-Wilkinson Inc., Omaha; pres. Planned Giving Sys., Cin., 1987—90; min. adult edn. Coll. Hill Presbyn. Ch., Cin., 1993—95; dir. planned giving Promise Keepers, Denver, 1995—98; v.p., divsn. higher edn. PhilanthroCorp, Woodland Park, Colo., 1998—2000; headmaster Miami Valley Christian Acad., Cin., 2001—. Author: A Seminary Journey, 1995, The Counsel of Many, 1999, Classroom Classics, 2003. Pres. Omaha Jaycees, 1966-67; dirs. Creighton-St. Joseph Hosp., Omaha, 1975-81, Leadership Cin. Alumni Assn., 1987-89. Recipient Golden Key award Nebr. Jaycees, 1975. Mem. U. Nebr. Omaha Alumni Assn. (pres. 1968-70, Outstanding Alumnus award 1977), Pi Kappa Alpha (nat. pres. 1970-72). Avocations: basketball, running, tennis, reading, public speaking. Home: 5300 Barony Pl Cincinnati OH 45241 Office: Miami Valley Christian Acad 6830 School Rd Cincinnati OH 45244 E-mail: mvcaheadmaster@hotmail.com.

SALMANS, CHARLES GARDINER, banker; b. Washington, Apr. 23, 1945; s. Marion K. and Agnes A. (Gardiner) S.; m. Robin Elizabeth Wakeman, June 8, 1986; children: Jonathan, Peter, Charles II. BS, Northwestern U., 1967; MBA in Fin., Columbia U., 1970. Account supr. Burson-Marsteller, N.Y.C., 1970-74; v.p. Bankers Trust Co., N.Y.C., 1974-84; sr. v.p., divsn. head Chem. Bank, N.Y.C., 1984-96; global bank mng. dir. Chase Manhattan Bank (merger with Chem. Bank 1996), N.Y.C., 1996; sr. v.p., head of corp. comm. and investor rels. Quick & Reilly/Fleet Securities Inc., N.Y.C., 1996—98; sr. v.p. corp. comms. FleetBoston Fin. (merger), N.Y.C., 1998—2004, Bank of Am. (merger), N.Y.C., 2004—. Mem. editl. adv. bd. Grad. Sch. of Bus., Columbia U., N.Y.C., 1984—; chmn. bus. adv. com. Guggenheim Mus., N.Y.C., 1994—. Home: 6 Red Rose Cir Darien CT 06820-4928 Office: Bank of America Mailstop NY1-040-31-03 40 W 57th St 31st Fl New York NY 10019 Office Phone: 646-313-8631. E-mail: Charles.Salmans@bankofamerica.com.

SALMASSI, SADEGH, family practice physician; b. Baghdad, Iraq, Aug. 14, 1946; s. Jafar and Kobra (Alavi) S.; m. Tahereh Ali Nazari, Jan. 17, 1970; children: Ali (dec.), Nahal. BS, Pahlavi U., 1966, MD, 1973. Diplomate Am. Bd. Pathology, Am. Bd. Gen. Practice in Medicine and Surgery. Instr. pathology U. Ill. Sch. Medicine, Chgo., 1975-80; asst. prof. pathology, assoc. chmn. dept., dir. blood bank U. Mo., Kansas City, 1980-84; chmn. family practice Delano (Calif.) Regional Med. Ctr., 1984-86; pres. Delano Regional Med. Group, 1989-96. Chief of staff Delano Regional Med. Ctr., 1989. Fellow Am. Coll. Internat. Physicians, Coll. Am. Pathologists, Am. Acad. Family Physicians; mem. AMA, Am. Acad. Gen. Physicians, Calif. Med. Assn. Office: Sadegh Salmassi MD & Assocs Urgent Care Ctr 719 Main St Delano CA 93215-2935 also: Salmassi Cosmetic and Med Inst 719 Main St Delano CA 93215-2935 E-mail: mdfcap@aol.com.

SALMELA, DAVID DANIEL, architect; b. Wadena, Minn., Mar. 28, 1945; s. Laurie Fredrick and Lempi Christine (Matti) S.; m. Gladys Elaine Hanka, June 23, 1967; children: Cory, Chad, Tia, Kai, Brit. Grad. high sch., Sebeka, Minn. Registered profl. architect, Minn., Wis. Draftsman McKenzie Hague & Gilles, Mpls., 1965-66, A.G. McKee, Hibbing, Minn., 1966, ABI Contracting, Virginia, Minn., 1966-69, Archtl. Resources, Hibbing, 1969-70; designer, arch. Damberg Scott Peck & Booker, Virginia, 1970-89; arch. Mulfinger Susanka, Duluth, Minn., 1989-90; prin. Salmela Fospick Ltd., Duluth, 1990-94, Salmela, Arch., Duluth, 1994—. Fellow: AIA (WRCL/AIA award 1994, Record Houses award 1998, Honor award for architecture 1998, AIA/PIA award 2000, Louise Bethune award 2000, ASLA award 2001, 14 Minn. Honor awards, 5 Wood Design awards). Office: Architect 852 Grandview Ave Duluth MN 55812-1170 E-mail: ddsalmela@charter.net.

SALMELA, LYNN MARIE, clinical nurse specialist; b. Albert Lea, Minn., Mar. 29, 1960; d. Melvin Raymond and Patricia Lou (Bushey) Salmela. BSN, Winona State U., 1982; MA, Coll. St. Scholastica, 2000; compliant documentation mgmt. course, J.A. Thomas & Assocs., 2000; cert. emergency dept. electronic med. record tng., Epic Sys. Corp., 2004. RN Minn., Wis., cert. pub. health nurse, Minn., intravenous therapy nurse, in ambulatory electronic med. record application, Epic Sys. Corp., 2004. Staff nurse Milw. Children's Hosp. (now Children's Hosp. of Wis.), 1982—83, Mpls. Children's Hosp., 1983—86, St. Mary's Duluth (Minn.) Clinic, 1986—2001; adj. faculty mem. Coll. of St. Scholastica, Duluth, 1998—99; compliant Documentation Mgmt. Coord. St. Luke's Hosp., Duluth, 2000—03; clin. informatics analyst St. Mary's Duluth Clinic Health Sys., 2003—. Author: (newsletter) Volunteer Link, St. Mary's Grief Support Ctr., 1993, 1995—96; contbr. articles to profl. publs. and newspapers. Vol. presch. screening programs, Winona, Minn., 1981—82; vol. blood screening clinic, Milw., 1982; vol. med. staff Grandma's Marathon, Duluth, 1989; vol. St. Mary's Grief Support Ctr., Duluth, 1993—97. Recipient 1st Pl. award, Amateur Still Life Category, photography contest, 2001, 1st Pl. award portrait category, Photography Contest, 2002; scholar Presdl. scholar, Winona State U., 1978. Mem.: Nat. Assn. Clin. Nurse Specialists, Sigma Theta Tau. Republican. Avocations: walking, music, photography, writing, cooking, camping. Home: 110 S 58th Ave E Duluth MN 55804 Office Phone: 218-786-6253.

SALMI, MIKA, information technology executive; Student, U. Wis. Founder, CEO AtomFilms, San Francisco. Office: Atomshockware ShockwareCom 114 Sansome St #FL10 San Francisco CA 94104-3803

SALMOIRAGHI, GIAN CARLO, physiologist, educator; b. Gorla Minore, Italy, Sept. 19, 1924; came to U.S., 1952, naturalized, 1958; s. Giuseppe Carlo and Dina (Rinetti) S.; m. Eva Tchoukourlieva, Dec. 5, 1970; 1 child, George Charles MD, U. Rome, 1948; PhD, McGill U., 1959; DSc (hon.), Hahnemann U., 1995. Sr. med. officer Internat. Refugee Orgn., Naples, Italy, 1949-52; research fellow Cleve. Clinic Found., 1952-55; lectr. dept. physiology McGill U., Montreal, Que., Can., 1956-58; from neurophysiologist to dir., div. spl. mental health research NIMH, Washington, 1959-73; assoc. commr. research N.Y. State Dept. Mental Hygiene, Albany, 1973-77; assoc. dir. for research Nat. Inst. Alcohol Abuse, HHS, Bethesda, Md., 1977-84; prof. neurology and physiology Hahnemann U., Phila., 1984—94, vice provost for research affairs, 1984-85, chmn. dept. physiology, asst. v.p sci. affairs, 1986-94; clin. prof. psychiatry George Washington U., 1966-73. Contbr. articles to profl. jours. Recipient Superior Service award HEW, 1970 Fellow Am. Coll. Neuropsychopharmacology; mem. AAAS, Am. Physiol. Soc., Am. Soc. Pharmacology and Exptl. Therapeutics, Internat. Brain Research Orgn., Internat. Soc. Psychoneuroendocrinology, Am. Psychiat. Assn., Soc. Neurosci., Royal Soc. Medicine, Soc. Biol. Psychiat., Assn. Research Neurol. and Mental Disease, Research Soc. Alcoholism, Assn. Chmn. Dept. Physiology, Sci. Research Soc., Sigma Xi. Clubs: Cosmos (Washington). Home: 8216 Hamilton Spring Ct Bethesda MD 20817-2714

SALMON, BETH ANN, magazine editor in chief; b. Syracuse, N.Y., Oct. 1, 1969; d. Richard George and Sharon Dian (Clark) S. BFA, Emerson Coll., 1991. Editl. asst. Let's Live mag., L.A., 1994, asst. editor, 1994-95, editor in chief, 1995—. Author: (screenplays) Postcards, 1994, Watch Me, 1995. Office: Lets Live Magazine 11050 Santa Monica Blvd Los Angeles CA 90025-3594

SALMON, EDWARD LLOYD, JR., bishop; b. Jan. 30, 1934; s. Edward Lloyd Sr. and Helen Bernice (Burley) S.; m. Louise Hack, 1972; children: Catherine, Edward III. BA, U. of the South, 1956; BD, Va. Theol. Seminary, 1960. Ordained to deaconate Episc. Ch., 1960, to priesthood, 1961. Vicar St. Andrew's Ch., Rogers, Ark., rector, 1963-68; vicar St. James Ch., Eureka Springs, Ark., St. Thomas Ch., Springdale, Grace Ch., Siloam Springs; assoc. St. Paul's Ch., Fayetteville, 1968, rector, 1968-78, Ch. St. Michael and St. George, St. Louis, 1978-90; elected bishop Diocese S.C., 1990—. Pres. province IV Episcopal Ch.; chmn. bd. dirs. Speak, Inc., The Anglican Digest, Voorhees Coll., Denmark, S.C.; trustee, regent Univ. of South; pres. Nashotah House Seminary; pres. Kanuga Confs., Inc.; chmn. Anglican Inst. Chmn. bd. trustees Voorhees Coll. Episcopalian. Office: PO Box 20127 Charleston SC 29413-0127 E-mail: elsalmon@dioceseofsc.org.

SALMON, JOHN HEARSEY MCMILLAN, historian, educator; b. Thames, New Zealand, Dec. 2, 1925; came to U.S., 1969; s. John Hearsey and Elizabeth (McMillan) S. Grad., Royal Mil. Coll., Duntoon, Australia, 1946; MA, U. New Zealand, 1951; M.Litt., Cambridge (Eng.) U., 1957; Litt.D., Victoria U., 1970. Prof. history U. New S. Wales, Sydney, Australia, 1960-65; prof. history, dean humanities U. Waikato, New Zealand, 1965-69; Marjorie Walter Goodhart prof. history Bryn Mawr Coll., 1969-91, prof. emeritus, 1991—. Author: The French Religious Wars in English Political Thought, 1959, A History of Goldmining in New Zealand, 1963, Cardinal de Retz, 1969, Society in Crisis - France in The 16th Century, 1975, Renaissance and Revolt: Essays in the Intellectual and Social History of Early Modern France, 1987, Ideas and Contexts in France and England from the Renaissance to the Romantics, 2000; editor: The French Wars of Religion, 1967; co-editor: Francogallia by François Hotman, 1972, Historians and Ideologues, 2001; translator: The Muskets of Gascony by Armand Daudeyos, 2000; contbr. to hist. jours. Served as capt. New Zealand Forces, 1947—48, Japan. Fellow Royal Hist. Soc. Home: 1853 County Line Rd Villanova PA 19085-1729 E-mail: jhmsalmon@earthlink.net.

SALMON, JOSEPH THADDEUS, lawyer; b. Auburn, Ala., Nov. 13, 1927; s. William Davis and Helen (Bowman) S.; m. Mabel Marie Groves, July 7, 1951; children: Joseph Thaddeus Jr., Bruce Groves. BS, Auburn U., 1949; JD, U. Ala., 1951. Bar: Ala. 1951. Practice in, Montgomery, 1953-93; sec., gen. counsel Alfa Mut. Ins. Co., Alfa Mut. Fire Ins. Co., Alfa Mut. Gen. Ins. Co., Alfa Corp., Alfa Ins. Corp., Alfa Gen. Ins. Corp., Alfa Life Ins. Co.; ret., 1993. Served with USNR, 1946-47; to 1st lt. USAF, 1951-53. Mem. Internat. Assn. Def. Counsel, Ala. Def. Lawyers Assn., Montgomery County Bar Assn., Phi Alpha Delta, Kappa Sigma. Episcopalian. Home: 2731 Lansdowne Dr Montgomery AL 36111-1741

SALMON, MARLA E. nursing educator, dean; b. Vermillion, S.D., May 2, 1949; d. Everett Lloyd and Marceline Louise (Adamson) S.; m. Jerry Steven Anderson, Aug. 1, 1984; children: Jessica Louise White, Matthew Lawrence White. BA cum laude, U. Portland, 1971, BSN cum laude, 1972; MSN, 1999; ScD, Johns Hopkins U., 1977; DSc (hon.), UNMC, 2003. Dir. patient advocacy program Johns Hopkins U., Balt., 1974-75, instr., 1975-78; asst. prof. U. Minn., Mpls., 1978-82, asst. dir. PRONA, 1978-79, acting dir. PRONA, 1978-80, dir. pub. health nursing programs, 1980-85, assoc. prof.,

1982-86; prof. pub. health nursing, chmn. dept. U. N.C., Chapel Hill, 1986-92; dir. nursing div., Bureau Health Professions HHS, Rockville, 1991-97; prof., dean Grad. Sch. Nursing U. Pa., Phila., 1997-99, dir. grad. studies; dean, prof. Nell Hodgson Woodruff Sch. Nursing Emory U., 1999—. Trustee Robert Wood Johnson Found., 2002—; mem. Presdl. Task Force Health Care Reform, Washington, 1993; U.S. del. WHO, Geneva, 1995; cons. in field. Co-editor News Outlook, 1989-91; contbr. articles to profl. jours. Fulbright scholar, 1972-73; W.K. Kellogg fellow, 1984-87, Reflective Leadership fellow, 1985-86; Rsch. grantee, 1975-78; recipient Recognition award Assn. State Territorial Dirs. of Nursing, 1993, Achievement award Nat. Black Nurses Found., 1994, Presdl. award for meritorious exec. The White House, 1995. Mem. ANA (v.p. coun. community health nursing, 1988—, task force credentialing 1989), Am. Acad. Nursing, Am. Pub. Health Assn., Am. Tae Kwon Do Assn., Nat. League Nursing, N.C. League Nursing, N.C. Pub. Health Assn., N.C. Nurses Assn., Assn. Community Health Nurses Educators, Women's Health Leadership Trust, Sigma Theta Tau, Sigma Xi, Delta Omega. Avocations: athletics, gardening. Office: Emory U Nell Hodgson Woodruff Sch 1520 Clifton Rd Ste 402 Atlanta GA 30322-4207 Business E-Mail: msalmon@emory.edu.

SALMON, MATT, former congressman, communications company executive; b. Salt Lake City, Jan. 21, 1958; s. Robert James and Gloria (Aagard) S.; m. Nancy Huish, June, 1979; children: Lara, Jacob, Katie, Matthew. BA in English Lit., Ariz. State U., 1981; MA in Pub. Adminstrn., Brigham Young U., 1986. Mgr. pub. affairs U.S. West, Phoenix, 1988-94; mem. Ariz. State Senate, Mesa, 1990-94, U.S. Congress from 1st Ariz. dist., Washington, 1995-2001; mem. internat. rels. and sci. coms., asst. major whip; exec. v.p. APCO Worldwide, Scottsdale, Ariz., 2001—. Bd. dirs. Mesa United Way, 1990—, Ariz. Sci. Mus., 1992—. Recipient Outstanding Svc. award Ariz. Citizens with Disabilities, 1991, Excellence in Govt. award Tempe Ctr. for Handicapped, 1992; named Outstanding Young Phoenician, Phelps Dodge/Phoenix Jaycees, 1990, Outstanding Legislator, Mesa United Way, 1991. Republican. Mem. Lds Ch. Avocations: tennis, racquetball, bicycling. Office: 5800 N Kiva LN Paradise Valley AZ 85253-5944

SALMON, THOMAS PAUL, lawyer, academic administrator; b. Cleve., Aug. 19, 1932; s. Thomas Aloysius and Lucy Moylan (Conlon) S.; m. Madeleine Salmon, Aug. 16, 1958 (div. 1983); children: Marguerite M., Anne Marie, Thomas M., Caroline M.; m. Susan J. Bisson, 1984. AB in History and Govt., Boston Coll., 1954, JD, 1957, hon. degree, 1975; LLM in Taxation, NYU, 1958; hon. degree, U. Vt., Burlington, 1980. Bar: Vt. Clk. Ryan, Smith and Carbine, Rutland, Vt., 1958-59; assoc. Robert J. Crotty, Bellows Falls, Vt., 1959; pvt. practice, Bellows Falls, 1960-72; gov. State of Vt., Montpelier, 1973-77; sr. ptnr. Salmon & Nostrand, Bellows Falls, 1977-91; interim pres. U. Vt., Burlington, 1991-93, pres., 1993—. Judge Mcpl. Ct., Bellows Falls, 1963-65; chmn. bd. dirs. Green Mountain Power Corp., Burlington; bd. dirs. Vt. Electric Co., Rutland, Banknorth Group, Burlington, Union Mut. Life Ins. Co., Montpelier, Ctrl. Vt. Railroad, St. Albans; chmn. Jud. Conduct Bd., Montpelier, 1984-88. Mem. Vt. Ho. of Reps., 1965-70, minority leader, 1969-71. Mem. AMA, Vt. Bar Assn., Windham County Bar Assn. Office: Green Mountain Power 163 Acorn Ln Colchester VT 05446

SALMON, TIMOTHY JAMES, professional baseball player; b. Long Beach, Calif., Aug. 24, 1968; Outfielder Anaheim Angels (formerly Calif. Angels), Anaheim, 1992—. Named Minor League Player of Yr. The Sporting News, 1992, Am. League Rookie of Yr., 1993, Pacific Coast League MVP, 1992, Am. League Rookie of Yr. Baseball Writer's Assn. of Am., 1993. Office: Anaheim Angels 2000 Gene Autry Way Anaheim CA 92806-6100

SALMON, WILLIAM COOPER, mechanical engineer, engineering academy executive; b. N.Y.C., Sept. 3, 1935; s. Chenery and Mary (Cooper) S.; m. Josephine Stone, Sept. 16, 1967; children: William Cooper, Mary Bradford, Pauline Alexandra. SB in Mech. Engring., MIT, 1957, SM in Mech. Engring., 1958, Mech. Engr., 1959, SM in Mgmt. Sci., 1969. Registered profl. engr., Mass. Research and teaching asst. MIT, Cambridge, 1957-59; sr. engr. Microtech, Cambridge, 1959-60; 1st lt. U.S. Army Ord. C., Aberdeen, Md., 1960; asst. sci. advisor U.S. Dept. State, Washington, 1961-74, sr. advisor for sci. and tech., 1978-86; counselor for sci. and tech. Am. embassy, Paris, 1974-78; exec. officer Nat. Acad. Engring., Washington, 1986-99, exec. officer emeritus, advisor to pres., 1999—2001; sec., treas. Internat. Coun. Acad. Engring. and Technol. Scis., Inc., 2000—. Recipient Superior Honor award Dept. State, 1984, Meritorious Svc. award Pres. U.S., 1968, Kenneth A. Roe award Am. Assn. Engring. Socs., 1996; Sloan fellow MIT, 1969. Fellow: ASME; mem.: NSPE, Jr. Engring. Tech. Soc. (pres. 1998—2001), Soc. Colonial Wars, Cosmos Club, Masons. Episcopalian. Home and Office: 3601 N Peary St Arlington VA 22207-5345 E-mail: wsalmon@nae.edu., caets@nae.edu.

SALMONSON, MARTY LEE, stockbroker, consulting engineer; b. Wellsville, N.Y., Sept. 23, 1946; s. John William and Alice May (Olson) S.; Gail White, Sept. 17, 1971; children: René, Marci. AS in Engring. Sci., SUNY, Alfred, 1970; postgrad., SUNY, Buffalo, 1971; BS in Sci. and Bus. Mgmt., Empire State Coll., 1979. Engr. Dresser-Rand, Olean, N.Y., 1974-90, Petro-Marine, Gretna, La., 1990-91; stockbroker Franklin Lord, Scottsdale, Ariz., 1992, Charles Schwab, Phoenix, Ariz., 1993—. Cons. engr., Phoenix, 1994—. With U.S. Army, 1967-69, Vietnam. Mem. NSPE, ASME, VFW, Moose, Elks. Episcopalian. Achievements include development of state of the art programs for centrifugal compressors. Home: PO Box 26601 Phoenix AZ 85068-6601

SALNY, ABBIE FEINSTEIN, psychologist; b. N.Y.C., July 3, 1926; d. Carl and Edith (Cooperman) Feinstein; m. Jerome E. Salny, July 12, 1973. BA, NYU, 1949; MA, Montclair State U., 1953; EdD, Rutgers U., 1966. Lic. psychologist, N.J.; diplomate Am. bd. Profl. Psychology. Sch. psychologist Bd. of Edn., Parsippany, N.J., 1959-66; prof., dep. chair, acting chair psychology dept. Montclair State U., 1966-79; supervisory psychologist Am. and Internat. Mensa, 1979—; trustee Mensa Edn. and Rsch. Found., 1971-96. Chmn. scholarship com. Mensa Edn. and Rsch. Found., 1973-82, dir. sci. and edn. Am. Mensa com., 1983-87, dir. rsch. rev. com., 1984-88. Co-author: Mensa Genius Quiz Book, 1981, Mensa Genius Quiz Book II, 1983, Mensa Think Smart Book, 1985; author: Quiz-A-Day Book, 1986, Book of Literary Quizzes, 1988, Page-A-Day Puzzle Calendar, 1995—, others; contbr. articles to profl. jours. Fellow Am. Acad. of Sch. Psychologists; mem. Am. Psychol. Assn., N.J. Psychol. Assn., British Psychol. Soc., Am. Soc. of Journalists and Authors, Am. Mensa Ltd. Avocations: travel, cooking. Home and Office: 407 Breckenridge Wayne NJ 07470-4072

SALOM, ROBERTO, financial executive; b. Bogota, Colombia, July 12, 1944; came to U.S., 1966; m. Estell Kathleen Millard; children: David Andres, Robert W.A. Student, U. Andes, Bogota, 1965; BS, San Francisco State U., 1969, MBA, 1972; postgrad., U. Calif., Berkeley, 1973; PhD in Econs., NYU, 1977. Rsch. assoc. Fed. Res. Bank San Francisco, 1968-70, fin. analyst, 1970-73; mem. staff UN Devel. Program/Fund for Population Activities, N.Y.C., 1973-82, dep. chief program planning, 1982-83, dep. chief fin. br., 1983-87, chief fin. br., 1987-94; sr. officer UN Adv. Com. on Adminstrv. and Budgetary Questions, 1995—. Presenter seminars in field. Home: 5 Elmwood Ave Rye NY 10580-3401 Office: United Nations UN Plaza New York NY 10017 E-mail: salom@un.org.

SALOMAN, ORA FRISHBERG, musicologist, educator; b. N.Y.C. d. Naphtali Zvi and Lena Nidel Frishberg; m. Edward Barry Saloman, July 1, 1968. AB, Barnard Coll., 1959; MA, Columbia U., 1963, PhD, 1970. Asst. prof. music Baruch Coll., CUNY, N.Y.C., 1972—76, assoc. prof. music, 1977—81, prof. music, 1982—, chair, dept. music, 1978—84; prof. music Grad. Ctr., CUNY, N.Y.C., 1996—. Vis. scholar in residence Queen's U., Kingston, Ont., Canada, 1999. Author: Beethoven's Symphonies and J.S. Dwight: The Birth of American Music Criticism, 1995; contbr. chapters to books, articles to profl. jours. Fellow NEH, 1989. Mem.: Am. Musicol. Soc., Soc. Am. Music (editl. adv. bd. jour. 1995—97). Achievements include scholarship connecting European and American 19th century music criticism and reception history, particularly of music by Ludwig van Beethoven and by Hector Berlioz. Office: Baruch Coll CUNY Dept Fine and Performing Arts Box B7-235 One Bernard Baruch Way New York NY 10010-5585 Office Phone: 646-312-4055. E-mail: ora_saloman@baruch.cuny.edu.

SALOMON, DARRELL JOSEPH, lawyer; b. Feb. 16, 1939; s. Joseph and Rosalie Rita (Pool) S.; m. Christine Mariscal, Apr. 25, 1992; 1 child, Camilla Lind Mariscal. Student, Georgetown U., 1957-59; BS, U. San Francisco, 1965, JD, 1966. Bar: Calif. 1970, U.S. Dist. Ct. (cen. and no. dists.) Calif. 1970, U.S. Supreme Ct. 1971. Assoc. Offices of Joseph L. Alioto, San Francisco, 1970, 1973; dep. city atty. City of San Francisco, 1972; pvt. prac., 1973—84; ptnr. Hill, Farrer & Burrill, L.A., 1984-87, Arter & Hadden, L.A., 1987-94; dir. of litigation Keck, Mahin & Cate, San Francisco, 1994-96; chmn. Commerce Law Group A Profl. Corp., 1996-99; chief asst. dist. atty. City of San Francisco, 2000; gen. counsel San Francisco Examiner, 2001—03; chmn. Salomon & Assoc., PC, 2004—. Lectr. law Santa Clara U. Polit. columnist San Francisco Ind., 1999—2003. Mem. Human Rights Commn. City and County of San Francisco, 1975; mem., past pres. Civil Svc. Commn., San Francisco, 1976-84; trustee San Francisco War Meml. and Performing Arts Ctr., 1984-88; bd. dirs. L.A. Symphony Master Chorale, 1985-87, Marin Symphony Assn., 1995-97. Recipient Disting. Svc. citation United Negro Coll. Fund, 1975; D'alton-Power scholar Georgetown U., 1957. Mem. ABA, Consumer Attys. of Calif. (bd. govs. 1977), Soc. Calif. Pioneers, Chit Chat Club, San Francisco Lawyers Club. Office: 50 California St #1500 San Francisco CA 94111 E-mail: dsalomon@salomonlegal.com.

SALOMON, FRANK ERNEST, classical music administrator; b. N.Y.C., Apr. 2, 1936; s. Albert and Anna Theresa (Lobbenberg) S.; m. Martha Laredo, June 1, 1961; children: Lisa Ana, Yana Elena. Student, NYU, N.Y.C., 1953-58. Asst. mgr. Symphony of the Air, N.Y.C., 1959-61; adminstrv. dir. New Sch. Concerts, N.Y.C., 1959—; founder N.Y. String Orch. Seminar, N.Y.C., 1969—; co-adminstr. Marlboro (Vt.) Music Sch. Festival, 1960—; mgr. Peoples' Symphony Concerts, N.Y.C., 1972—; pres. Frank Salomon Assocs., N.Y.C., 1968—, Internat. Arts Found., N.Y.C., 1990—. Cons. Tokyo Opera City, 1995-98, Pablo Casals Hall, Tokyo, 1986-87; co-chair music panel, profl. tng. Nat. Endowment for Arts, Washington, 1970's-80's. Mgr. 1st U.S. tours Sir Simon Rattle City of Birmingham (Eng.) Symphony Orch., 1988, Sergiu Celibidache Munich Philharmonic, 1989, John Adams Ensemble Modern, Frankfurt, Germany, 1996, Masaaki Suzuki Bach Collegium Japan, 2003, 1st inter-disciplinary project in conjunction with Orch. Tour Sir Simon Rattle CBSO, 1992. With N.Y. Nat. Guard, 1955-59. Mem. Assn. Performing Arts Profls., Internat. Soc. Performing Arts (Patrick Hayes award 2000), Nat. Assn. Performing Arts Profls. Office: 201 W 54th St Apt 1C New York NY 10019-5520 E-mail: salomonf@aol.com., frank@franksalomon.com.

SALOMON, ROGER BLAINE, English language educator; b. Providence, Feb. 26, 1928; s. Henry and Lucia Angell (Capwell) S.; m. Elizabeth Helen Lowenstein, June 14, 1950; children— Pamela, Wendy. BA, Harvard, 1950; MA, U. Calif. at Berkeley, 1951, PhD, 1957. Instr. Mills Coll., Oakland, Calif., 1955-57; instr., then asst. prof. Yale U., New Haven, 1957-66; mem. faculty Case Western Res. U., Cleve., 1966—, prof. English, 1969—, Oviatt prof. English, 1990, chmn. dept., 1974-80, part-time prof. English, 1994-99; Oviatt prof. English emeritus, 1999—. Mem. adv. screening com. Am. lit. Sr. Fulbright-Hayes Program, 1973-76, chmn., 1975; mem. grants-in-aid selection com. Am. Council Learned Socs., 1976-78 Author: Twain and the Image of History, 1961, Desperate Storytelling: Post-Romantic Elaborations of the Mock-Heroic Mode, 1987, Mazes of the Serpent: An Anatomy of Horror Narrative, 2002. Served to 1st lt. USAF, 1952-53. Morse fellow, 1960-61; Guggenheim fellow, 1972-73 Mem. AAUP, MLA. Home: 2830 Coventry Rd Cleveland OH 44120-2231 Office: Case Western Reserve U Dept English Cleveland OH 44106

SALOMONE, JEFFREY PAUL, surgeon, educator; b. Reno, Nev., Dec. 6, 1961; s. Joseph Anthony and Peggy Ruth (Crompton) S. BS, U. Nev., 1983, MD, 1990. Diplomate Am. Bd. Surgery; cert. surg. critical care. Resident Tulane U. Med. Ctr., New Orleans, 1990-95, fellow in critical care, 1995-96; asst. prof. Emory U., Atlanta, 1996—2001, assoc. prof., 2001—. Cons. Nat. Registry of EMTs, Columbus, Ohio, 1996—. Fellow ACS; mem. AMA, Nat. Assn. Emergency Med. Svcs. Physicians, Am. Assn. for the History of Medicine, Soc. for Critical Care Medicine, Phi Kappa Phi. Avocations: gourmet cooking, photography, theater. Office: Emory U Dept Surgery TK Glenn Bldg Rm 312A 69 jesse Hill Jr Dr SE Atlanta GA 30303-3033 Office Phone: 404-616-7320. Business E-Mail: jsalomo@emory.edu.

SALOMONE, WILLIAM GERALD, lawyer; b. Flushing, N.Y., Apr. 14, 1948; s. Harry and Mary (Tartaro) S.; m. Mary Jo Piano, July 22, 1978; children: Jennifer Ann, Julie Marie, Joseph William. BCE, Manhattan Coll., 1970; MSCE, UCLA, 1971; PhD in Civil Engring., Purdue U., 1978; JD, U. Fla., 1985. Bar: Fla., U.S. Dist. Ct. (mid. dist.) Fla.; registered profl. engr., N.Y., N.J., Ill., Fla., Md., Ga. Rsch. fellow UCLA, 1970-71; project engr. Dames & Moore, Cranford, N.J., 1971-75; rsch. asst. Purdue U., West Lafayette, Ind., 1975-78; project mgr. Woodward-Clyde Cons., Chgo., 1978-80; prin. geotech. engr. Fluor Power Svcs., Chgo., 1980-81; v.p., dir. geotech. engring. Bromwell Engring, Inc., Lakeland, Fla., 1981-82; atty. Sarsota, Fla., 1986—. Cons. William G. Salomone, Lakeland, 1982—86; pvt. practice cons., 1986; adj. prof. bus. law U. Fla., 1985—86; adj. prof. U. South Fla., 1985, 1990—97, St. Leo U., 2000—01, 2001—02; pvt. mediator, Sarasota, 1987—; mediator Fla. Cir. Ct., 1991—, U.S. Dist. Ct. (mid. dist.) Fla., 1996—; spl. master code enforcement Sarasota County, Fla., 1991—92; water and wastewater regulation, 1999; spl. master stormwater, Cape Coral, Fla., 97; hearing officer Water and Wastewater Franchise Regulation, Hillsborough County, Fla., 1999—2003; gen. counsel Code Enforcement Bd., City of Northport, 1999—2001. Author: Salomone on Mediation: A Practice and Procedure Handbook, 1992, Earth and Its People: How We Can Prosper, 1994, Madam President, 2000, The Presidential Papers, 2000. Judge Lakeland Regional H.S. Sci. Fair, 1993, NFL Sunshine Debate Tournament Nat. Forensic League, Sarasota, 1991, Incarnation Sch. Sci. Fair, 1996, 98; chmn. citizens adv. com. Sarasota-Manatee Met. Planning Orgn., 1991-92; vice chmn. citizens adv. com. Sarasota Bay Nat. Estuary Program, 1992-93. NDEA Title IV fellow UCLA, 1970-71; recipient Letters of Commendation, Mayor of Lakeland, Sheriff of Bartow, Fla., Dept. Army C.E. Mem. ASCE (Young Civil Engr. of Yr 1982, letter of commendation, bd. county commrs.), NSPE (coll. scholarship com. 1983), Am. Arbitration Assn., Inc. (panel arbitrators and mediators), Fla. Engring. Soc. (Young Engr. of Yr. 1983, Journalism award 1992), Fla. Conflict Resolution Consortium (Excellence in Conflict Resolution award 2002) Chi Epsilon, Tau Beta Pi. Office: PO Box 15 Sarasota FL 34230-0015

SALONEN, ESA-PEKKA, conductor; b. Helsinki, Finland, June 30, 1958; Student, Sibelius Acad., Helsinki; studies with, Rautavaara and Panula. Prin. condr. Swedish Radio Symphony Orch., 1985—95; prin. guest condr. Philharmonia Orch., London, 1985—94, Oslo Philharm. Orch., 1985—90; artistic advisor Stockholm Chamber Orch., 1986—; music director L.A. Philharm. Orch., 1992—. Office: Columbia Artists Mgmt Inc 165 W 57th St New York NY 10019-2201 also: Los Angeles Philharm Orch 135 N Grand Ave Los Angeles CA 90012-3013

SALONER, GARTH, management educator; b. Johannesburg, Jan. 18, 1955; came to U.S. 1978; s. Max and Rachel (Aronowitz) S.; m. Marlene Shoolman, Dec. 26, 1978; children: Amber, Romy, Kim. B in Comm., U. Witwatersrand, 1976, MBA, 1977; MS in Stats., Stanford (Calif.) U., 1981, MA in Econs., PhD, Stanford (Calif.) U., 1982. Asst. lectr. U. Witwatersrand, 1977-78; asst. prof. econs. MIT, Cambridge, 1982-86, assoc. prof. econs. and mgmt., 1986-89, prof., 1990; vis. assoc. prof. bus. adminstrn. Harvard Bus. Sch., Boston, 1989-90; vis. asst. prof. Stanford U., 1986-87, prof. strategic mgmt. and econs. Grad. Sch. Bus., 1990—, Robert A Magowan prof., 1993-99, dir. rsch. and curriculum devel., 1993-96, assoc. dean for acad. affairs, 1994-96, co-dir. Ctr. Elec. Bus. & Commerce, 1999—, Jeffrey S. Skoll prof., 2000—. Bd. dirs., chmn. Quick Response Svcs., Inc.; chmn. Synthean, Aplia; rsch. assoc. Nat. Bur. Econ. Rsch., 1991—; mem. adv. bd. eOneGlobal, Spoke Software, Fiber Tower, It's The Content, ShareALot. Author: Strategic Management, 2001, Creating and Capturing Value, 2001; assoc. editor Rand Jour. Econs., 1986-88, co-editor, 1988-95; assoc. editor Internat. Jour. Indsl. Orgn., 1988-95, Econs. of Innovation and New Tech., 1988-95, Strategic Mgmt. Jour., 1991-94; contbr. articles to profl. jours. Nat. fellow, Hoover Inst., 1986-87, Sloan fellow, 1987-89; grantee, NSF, 1982, 85, 88. Mem. Am. Econ. Assn., Acad. Mgmt. Jewish. Avocations: bicycling, photography. Home: 4151 Amaranta Ave Palo Alto CA 94306-3903 Office: Stanford U Grad Sch Bus Stanford CA 94305

SALONGA, LEA, actress, singer; b. Manila, Feb. 22, 1971; d. Feliciano Genuino and Maria Ligaya (Imutan) S. Attended, Ateneo De Manila U., 1988-89. Actress, singer The King and I, Manila, 1978, Annie, Manila, 1980, The Rose Tattoo, Manila, 1980, The Bad Seed, Manila, 1981, The Goodbye Girl, Manila, 1982, Paper Moon, Manila, 1983, The Fantasticks, Manila, 1988, Miss Saigon, London, 1989-90 (Outstanding Performance by Actress in Musical Olivier award 1990), Broadway, 1991-92 (Best Actress in Musical Tony award 1991, Best Actress in Musical Drama Desk award 1991, Best Actress in Musical Outer Critics Circle award 1991, Outstanding Debut Theatre World award 1991), Les Miserables, Broadway, 1993, My Fair Lady, Manila, 1994, Into the Woods, Singapore, 1994, Les Miserables, London, 1996, 3rd nat. tour, 1996, also The Sound of Music, Manila, Fiddler on the Roof, Manila, Cat on a Hot Tin Roof, Philippine films include Bakit Labis Kitang Mahal?, Dear Diary, Pik Pak Boom, Captain Barbell, Ninja Kids, Like Father, Like Son, Tropang Bulilit; Philippine TV: (host) Kulit Bulilit, Love Lea, Naku, Ha!, Sunday Special, Iba Ito!, That's Entertainment!, This is It!, (co-host) Patok Na Patok!; opening act for Stevie Wonder, Menudo; concerts: The Filipinos of Miss Saigon, A Miss Called Lea, Lea Salonga in Concert, L.A., San Francisco, Les Miserables 10th Anniversary Concert, London, 1995; recs. include Small Voice, 1981 (gold record), Lea, Happy Children's Club, Christmas Album, We are the World, (debut album) Lea Salonga, 1993, Miss Saigon original London cast rec. (gold record), The King and I, Aladdin, 1992 (singing voice Princess Jasmine, motion picture soundtrack), Les Miserables 10th Anniversary Concert Album, 1996, Royal Couyabyab: The Silver Album, 1996, The Little Tramp, (singing voice) Mulan, 1998, (Broadway) Flower Drum Song, 2002; TV films include: Redwood Curtain, 1998, (TV series) As the World Turns, 2001, 03. Recipient AWIT award outstanding svc. Philippings Recording Industry, 1993, ASEAN Industry award performing arts, 1992, Ten Outstanding Young Men award outstanding debut, 1991, AWIT award outstanding performer, 1990, Presdl. Award of Merit Pres. Aquino, 1990, Laurence Olivier award best actress musical, 1990, Cecil award best recording by a child, 1984, Tinig award one of 10 outstanding singers, 1983, 92, 94, 92, ALIW award best child performer, 1980, 81, 82; named Outstanding Manilan by Govt. City of Manila, 1990. Mem. AFTRA, Actors' Equity Assn., Screen Actors' Guild. Roman Catholic. Avocations: music, reading, collecting raised-trunk elephants, collecting swatches, working on computers. Office: c/o Jeff Hunter 1325 Avenue Of The Americas New York NY 10019-6026 Address: 205 W 54th St Apt 9C New York NY 10019-5532

SALOOM, JOSEPH A., III, diplomat; b. Urbana, Ill., Apr. 8, 1948; s. Joseph A. and Barbara (Bombard) S.; m. Anne Elizabeth Mayer, Jan. 22, 1972; children: Elizabeth, Shahin, Ilyas. BA in Econs., Georgetown U., 1970; MS, MIT, 1973. Joined Fgn. Svc.; comml. officer AM. Consulate Gen., Dusseldorf, Germany, 1974-76; econ. officer Am. Embassy, Rabat, Morocco, 1976-78, fin. economist Jidda, Saudi Arabia, 1978-80, econ. counselor Kinshasa, Zaire, 1983-87, dep. chief mission Niamey, Niger, 1987-90, U.S. amb. to Guinea Conakry, Guinea, 1993-96; transp. economist Dept. State, Washington, 1980-83, dir. office monetary affairs, 1990-91, dep. asst. sec., 1991-93, dir. econ. policy African-Affairs bureau, 1996-97; min.-counselor for econ. affairs Am. Embassy, Berlin, 1997—2001; sr. examiner Bd. of Examiners, Alexandria, Va., 2001—. Home: 6104 Fort Hunt Rd Alexandria VA 22307 E-mail: saloomja@state.gov.

SALOOM, KALISTE JOSEPH, JR., lawyer, retired judge; b. Lafayette, La., May 15, 1918; s. Kaliste and Asma Ann (Boustany) S.; m. Yvonne Adelle Nassar, Oct. 19, 1958; children: Kaliste III, Douglas James, Leanne Isabelle, Gregory John. BA with high distinction, U. La., 1939; JD, Tulane U., 1942. Bar: La. 1942. Atty. City of Lafayette, 1948—52; judge City and Juvenile Ct., Lafayette, 1952—93; ret., 1993; of counsel Saloom & Saloom, Lafayette, 1993—; Eminent Scholar endowed chair in polit. sci. U. La., Lafayette, 2001. Mem. jud. coun. La. Supreme Ct., 1960-64; bd. dirs. Nat. Ctr. for State Cts., Williamsburg, Va., 1978-84, adv. coun., 1984—, mem. assocs. com., 1986—; judge pro tempore La. Ct. Appeal 3d Cir., 1992; tech. adviser Jud. Adminstrn. of Traffic Cts. mem. adv. com. Nat. Hwy. Traffic Safety Adminstrn., U.S. Dept. Transp., 1977-80, Nat. Com. on Uniform Traffic Laws, 1986; mem. expert panel Drunk Driving Protection Act U.S. Congress, 1989-91. Mem. editl. bd. Tulane Law Rev., 1941; contbr. articles to profl. jours. Active Boy Scouts Am., Evangeline Area coun. With U.S. Army, 1942-45. Recipient Civic Cup, City of Lafayette, 1965, Pub. Svc. award U.S. Dept. Transp., 1980, Disting. Jurist award Miss. State U. Pre-Law Soc., 1987, Disting. Svc. award Nat. Ctr. State Cts., 1988, Disting. La. Jurist award La. State Bar Found., 1992, U.S. Supreme Ct. Chief Justice Warren E. Burger Soc. award, 1999. Mem. ABA (Benjamin Flaschner award 1981, vice chair JAD com. on traffic ct. program 1989-2002), Am. Judges Assn. (William H. Burnett award 1982), Nat. Coun. Juvenile Ct. Judges, La. City Judges Assn. (past pres., panel drafting La. children's code 1989-91), La. Juvenile Ct. Judges Assn. (past pres.), Order of Coif, Equestrian Order of Holy Sepulchre (knight comdr.), Oakbourne Country Club, Rotary (Paul Harris fellow), KC. Democrat. Roman Catholic. Home: 502 Marguerite Blvd Lafayette LA 70503-3138 Office: 211 W Main St Lafayette LA 70501-6843

SALOSCHIN, ROBERT L. lawyer; b. N.Y.C., Jan. 15, 1920; s. Bruno Benedix and Edna Saloschin; m. Neita L. Saloschin, Dec. 10, 1949; children: Mary Ann, Joan Janelle. BA, Columbia Coll., 1940; JD, Columbia Law Sch., 1947. Bar: N.Y. 1947, D.C. 1960, Md. 1980, U.S. Supreme Ct. 1956. Pers. adminstr. USN, Washington, 1941-43; atty. Cahill, Gordon, Reindel, N.Y.C., 1947-49, Housing & Home Fin. Agy., Washington, 1950-52, Civil Aeronautics Bd., Washington, 1952-58; atty. Office of Legal Counsel, dir. Office Info. Law U.S. Dept. Justice, Washington, 1958-81; of counsel Lerch Early & Brewer, Bethesda, Md., 1981—. Cons. standing com. on law and nat. security ABA, Washington, 1981-91; developed legal strategy for ending racial segregation in interstate bus transp., ICC; mediator for Am. athletics orgns. Olympic Games. Patentee air navigation device; editor: A Short Guide to the Freedom of Information Act, annually, 1974—; editor law rev. Columbia Law Sch., 1947. Organizer, pres. Citizens for Quality Civilization, Inc., Bethesda, 1990—; pres. West Fernwood Citizens Assn., Bethesda, 1962-65; officer North Bethesda Congress of Citizens Assocs., Bethesda, 1965-75. Lt. comdr. USN, WWII. Decorated Air medal with oak leaf cluster. Mem. Ret. Officers Assn., Herring Bay Yacht Club, Phi Beta Kappa. Avocations: coastal cruising, flying, reading, bridge, lecturing in schools. Home: 6603 Lone Oak Dr Bethesda MD 20817-1649

SALOTTI, KATHRYN E. marriage and family therapist; d. Peter Arthur Floros and Henrietta Judith Albers; m. Richard Vincent Salotti, June 28, 1969; 1 child, Cara Dominique; m. Thomas Lee Moreland (div.); 1 child, Thomas Michael. AA, Pierce Jr. Coll., Calif., 1980; BA in Sociology cumma sum laude, Calif. State U., Northridge, 1983, M Ednl. Psychology, 1986. Lic. marriage and family therapist Calif. Bd. Behavioral Sci., 1989. Marriage and family therapist internship Exceptional Children's Found., Van Nuys, Calif., 1986—87, Tarzana Treatment Ctr., Calif., 1988—89; rschr., writer, editor, tchr. Gerry Grossman Seminars, Santa Monica, Calif., 1989—90; family therapist Crestwood Manor, San Jose, 1990—93; family therapist, treatment coord. Oakview Youth, Santa Barbara, 1993—94; program dir. Sanctuary Psychiatric of Santa Barbara, 1994—98, County of Santa Barbara Children's Svcs., 1998—. Recipient Academic Excellence award, Phi Kappa Phi, 1983. Mem.: Calif. Assn. of Marriage and Family Therapists. Republican. Avocations: writing, genealogy, dance, reading. Home: 1102 Bel Air Dr Santa Barbara CA 93105 E-mail: katcardi_8@msn.com.

SALOW, GLEN, diversified financial services company executive; m. Rosemary Salow. BSc in Acctg., Richard Stockton Coll.; MBA, Monmouth U. Acct. Amerada Hess Corp., 1977; various sr. level positions Consco Enterprises, Lehman Brothers; CIO Aetna Retirement Svcs.; from sr. v.p. tech. ops.

to exec. v.p., CIO American Express Co., N.Y., 1997—2000, exec. v.p., 2000—, CIO, 2000—. Mem. found. bd. Richard Stockton Coll., NJ. Office: American Express Company World Financial Ctr 200 Vesey St New York NY 10285

SALPETER, EDWIN ERNEST, physical sciences educator; b. Vienna, Dec. 3, 1924; came to U.S., 1949, naturalized, 1953; s. Jakob L. and Frieder (Horn) S.; m. Miriam Mark, June 11, 1950 (dec. 2000); children: Judy Gail, Shelley Ruth. MS, Sydney U., 1946; PhD, Birmingham (Eng.) U., 1948; DSc, U. Chgo., 1969, Case-Western Reserve U., 1970, U. Sydney, 1994, U. New South Wales, Sydney, 1996. Research fellow Birmingham U., 1948-49; faculty Cornell U., Ithaca, N.Y., 1949-97, now J.G. White prof. phys. scis. emeritus. Mem. U.S. Nat. Sci. Bd., 1979-85 Author: Quantum Mechanics, 1957, 77; mem. editorial bd. Astrophys. Jour, 1966-69; assoc. editor Rev. Modern Physics, 1971-92; contbr. articles to profl. jours. Mem. AURA bd., 1970-72. Recipient Gold medal Royal Astron. Soc., 1973, J.R. Oppenheimer Meml. prize U. Miami, 1974, C. Bruce medal Astron. Soc. Pacific, 1987, A. Devaucouleurs medal, 1992, Dirac Meml. medal U. New South Wales, 1996, Crafoord laureate Royal Swedish Acad. Scis., 1997, H. A. Bethe Prize, Am. Phys. Soc., 1999. Mem. NAS, Am. Astron. Soc. (v.p. 1971-73), Am. Philos. Soc., Am. Acad. Arts and Scis., The Royal Soc. (fgn.), Australian Acad. Sci., Deutsche Akademie Leopoldina. Home: 116 Westbourne Ln Ithaca NY 14850-2414 Office: Cornell U 612 Space Science Bldg Ithaca NY 14853-6801 E-mail: ees12@cornell.edu.

SALSBERG, ARTHUR PHILIP, publishing company executive; b. Bklyn., Aug. 28, 1929; s. Solomon William and Rae (Miller) S.; m. Rhoda Gelb, Sept. 11, 1960; children: Charles Martin, Solomon William. BBA, CCNY, 1951. Mng. editor Ojibway Press, N.Y.C., 1957-64; advt. and promotion mgr. RCA Corp., Harrison, N.J., 1965-67; editor N.Am. Pub. Co., Phila., 1967-70; v.p., gen. mgr. Lawyers World, Inc., Phila., 1970-72; editorial dir. Ziff-Davis Pub. Co., N.Y.C., 1973-83; editor, assoc. pub. CQ Communications, Inc., Hicksville, N.Y., 1984—. Mag. and newspaper pub. cons.; electronics instr.; local campaign publicist, speech writer for town mayor, town coun., libr. bd., sch. bd. Author: Complete Book of Video Games, 1977, Collier's Ency. Yearbook, 1977, 78, 79, 80, 81, 82, First Book of Modern Electronics Fun Projects, 1986, Second Book of Modern Electronics Fun Projects, 1986; editor: Audio Mag, 1967-70, Lawyers World, 1970-72, Popular Electronics, 1973-83, Comm. Handbook, 1973-83, Stereo Directory, 1973-83, Tape Recorder Directory, 1973-83, Citizens Band Handbook, 1976-83, Invitation to Electronics, 1972-83, Modern Electronics, 1984-91, Computer Craft, 1992-93, MicroComputer Jour., 1994-96; assoc. pub.: Amateur Radio Equipment Buyers Guide, 1988, 89, 90, 91, 92, Amateur Radio Antenna Buyers Guide, 1989, 90, 91-92. Publicity chmn. Nassau coun. Boy Scouts Am., 1975; mem. adv. com. Bramson OR Tech. Inst., 1975. With AUS, 1951-53, Korea. Recipient Indsl. Mktg. Mag. award, 1959 Home: 7844 Lexington Club Blvd Apt A Delray Beach FL 33446-3426

SALSBURY, MICHAEL H. lawyer; b. 1949; BA, Dartmouth Coll.; JD, U. Va. Bar: D.C. 1975. Gen. counsel MCI Comm. Corp., Washington; exec. v.p. & gen. coun. MCI; ptnr. Jenner & Block Law Firm. Office: MCI Comms Corp 1801 Pennsylvania Ave NW Washington DC 20006-3606

SALT, ALFRED LEWIS, priest; b. Hackensack, N.J., Apr. 30, 1927; s. Alfred John and Lily (Tittle) S.; m. Elizabeth May Loveland, June 18, 1949; children: Richard John, Michael Rob, Christopher William, Katharine Anne. BA with honors, Bishop's U., Lennoxville, Can., 1949, MA in History, 1951, BD, 1960; grad. advanced mgmt. program, Harvard U., 1970; D Ministry, Grad. Theol. Found., 1988. Ordained to ministry Episcopal Ch. as deacon, 1951, as priest, 1952. Incumbent St. Philip's, Sawyerville, Canada, 1951—52, St. John the Evangelist, Portneuf, 1952—54; rector Christ Ch., Stanstead, 1954—62, St. Michael's Ch., Sillery, 1962—72, All Saints Ch., Millington, NJ, 1972—93; hon. asst. Grace Ch., Port Huron, Mich., 1993—98, Trinity Ch., Lexington, Mich., 1998—2001, St. Monica's Ch., Naples, Fla., 2002—03, St. John's Ch., Naples, 2004—. Bishop's chaplain Diocese of Que., 1962, hon. canon, 1970; pres. Morris Convocation. Morris County, N.J., 1974-78, retreat condr., 1979—; with Victorious Ministry Through Christ, Orlando, Fla., 1981-92, dir., 1986-92, v.p., 1989-92; dir. VMTC Can., 1995-2002. Author: Compass Book on Healing, 1996; contbr. articles to religious jour. Mem. Superior Coun. Edn., Que., 1964-70; commr. Que. Protestant Sch. Bd., 1970-72; trustee Heath Village, Hackettstown, N.J., 1974-76; mem. Passaic Twp. Welfare Bd., Millington, 1977-78, 82. With USAAC Res., 1944-45; with USN, 1945-46. Mem. Naples Deanery Clericus, Order St. Luke (chaplain), Harvard Club of Naples. Home: 4822 Martinique Way Naples FL 34119 also: North Hatley 190 Chemin du Lac Quebec QC Canada JOB 2CO Personal E-mail: alemsalt@comcast.net. *The more I come to know Jesus, the more I come to know myself. The more I submit myself to Him, the less I depend upon myself.*

SALTARELLI, MICHAEL A. priest; b. Jersey City, N.J., Jan. 17, 1933; s. Angelo Michael and Caroline (Marzitello) Saltarelli. BA, Seton Hall U., 1956; MA, Manhattan Coll., 1975. Ordained to ministry Cath. Ch., 1960. Assoc. pastor Holy Family Ch., Nutley, NJ, 1960—77; pastor Our Lady of Assumption, Bayonne, 1977—82; exec. dir. Archdiocesan Pastoral Svcs., Newark, 1982—85; pastor St. Catherine Of Siena Ch., Cedar Grove, 1985—90; aux. bishop Archdiocese of Newark, 1990—96; bishop Diocese of Wilmington, Del., 1996—. Vicar for priests Archdiocese of Newark, 1987—. Office: 1925 Delaware Ave Ste 1-a Wilmington DE 19806-2301

SALTEN, DAVID GEORGE, academic administrator; b. N.Y.C., Aug. 23, 1913; s. Max Elias and Gertrude (Brauer) S.; m. Frances Claire Brown (div. 1983); children: Phoebe, Cynthia, Melissa; m. Adrienne O'Brien, 1989. ScB, Washington Sq. Coll., N.Y.C., 1933; AM, Columbia U., 1939; PhD, NYU, 1944; LLD (hon.), Lynn U., 1976; L.H.D., Nova U., Ft. Lauderdale, Fla., 1983; Sc.D. (hon.), N.Y. Inst. Tech., 1984; LHD (hon.), Hofstra U., 1996. Registered psychologist, N.Y. Chemist Almay Cosmetics, 1934-35, City of New York, 1938-40; tchr., chmn. dept., high sch. prin. N.Y.C. Bd. Edn., 1940-50; assoc. prof. Hunter Coll. Grad. Program, 1947-63; supt. of schs. City of Long Beach, N.Y., 1950-62, City of New Rochelle, N.Y., 1962-65; exec. v.p. Fedn. of Jewish Philanthropies, N.Y.C., 1965-69; exec. v.p., provost N.Y. Inst. Tech., Old Westbury, 1969-90; chmn. Nassau County Indsl. Devel. Agy., Mineola, NY, 1985—2002; exec. dir. Nassau County Tax Relief Commn., 1990-93. Mem. White House Conf. on Edn., 1955, White House Conf. on Youth, 1960; U.S. resource person on edn. World Mental Health Congress, Paris, 1961; mem. Bd. Edn., Hawthorne, Cedar Knolls, N.Y., 1963-65; mem. adv. council Columbia U. Sch. of Social Work, 1967-69; chmn. adv. council NYU Sch. Edn., 1963-65; chmn. adv. council to Select Com. on Higher Edn. N.Y. Legislature, 1971-73. Author: Mathematics: A Basic Course, 1957. Editor instructional software. Contbr. articles on edn. and ednl. adminstrn. to profl. publs. Vice chmn. N.Y. State Mental Health Council, Albany, 1965-72; pres. N.Y. State Citizens Council, 1957; pres. Nat. Council on Aging, Washington, 1975-77; chmn. Nassau County Local Devel. Agy., 1982—, Nassau County Local Devel. Corp., N.Y., 1982—, pres., 1992—; chmn. Nassau County Cultural Devel. Bd., 1980—94; bd. dirs. NAACP Legal Def. Fund, 1964-74; chmn. bd. trustees The Hewlett Sch., 1991—. Recipient citation U.S. Navy, 1947, Mental Health Assn., Nassau County, N.Y., 1955, Long Beach Edn. Assn., N.Y., 1962, Council of City of New Rochelle, N.Y., 1965, Council of Town of Islip, N.Y., 1982. Fellow AAAS, Am. Orthopsychiat. Assn.; mem. Princeton Club (N.Y.C.). Avocations: opera, ballet, international travel, photography. Office: Office of the President Hoffstra University Hempstead NY 11549

SALTER, CHRISTOPHER LORD, geography educator; BA, Oberlin Coll., 1961; MA, U. Calif. Berkeley, 1968, PhD, 1970. Tchr. Tunghai U., Taiwan, 1961; prof. Dept. Geography UCLA, 1968—87; coord. Alliance Network Nat. Geog. Alliance, 1987—89; prof. geography U. Mo., Columbia, Mo., 1989—2002, chmn. Dept. Geography, 1989—2002, prof. emeritus, 2002—. Founder Calif. Geog. Alliance, 1983—87. Editor: The China Geographer, 1975—78; author: Social Studies for the 21st Century; editor; author (and editor): over 20 books. Recipient George J. Miller award Nat. Coun. for Geog. Edn., 1992, Disting. Geography Educator award Nat. Geog. Soc., 1990, Disting. Tchg. Achievement award Nat. Coun. for Geog. Edn., 1999, Disting. Faculty award U. Mo. Alumni Assn., 1999. Mem.: Mo. Geog. Alliance, Geography Edn. Proram, Nat. Geog. Soc., Nat. Coun. Geog. Edn. (pres. Calif. chpt. 1975—76, Outstanding Educator award Calif. chpt. 1981), Am. Geog. Soc., Assn. Am. Geographers. Office: Univ Mo Dept Geography Dept Geography 3 Stewart Hall Columbia MO 65211-6170

SALTER, EDWIN CARROLL, retired physician; b. Oklahoma City, Jan. 19, 1927; s. Leslie Ernest and Maud (Carroll) S.; m. Ellen Gertrude Malone, June 30, 1962; children— Mary Susanna, David Patrick BA, DePauw U., 1947; MD, Northwestern U., 1951. Intern Cook County Hosp., Chgo., 1951-53; resident in pediatrics Children's Meml. Hosp., Chgo., 1956-58, Cook County Hosp., Chgo., 1956-58; practice medicine specializing in pediatrics Lake Forest, Ill., 1958-97; attending physician Lake Forest Hosp., 1958—, pres. med. staff, 1981-82. Attending physician Children's Meml. Hosp., Chgo.; clin. faculty mem. dept. pediatrics Northwestern U. Med. Sch. Served to capt. M.C., U.S. Army, 1954-56 Mem. AMA, Ill. State Med. Soc., Lake County Med. Soc. (pres. 1984), Phi Beta Kappa Republican. Methodist. Home: 19 N Maywood Rd Lake Forest IL 60045-3233

SALTER, KEVIN THORNTON, lawyer; b. N.Y.C., Oct. 21, 1947; s. Hershel Fletcher and Elizabeth (Thornton) S.; m. Eleanor Raftery, Aug. 28, 1982. BA, Iona Coll., 1973; JD, St. John's U., 1977. Bar: N.Y. 1978, U.S. Dist. Ct. (so. and ea. dists.) N.Y., 1978. Atty. Nat. Coun. on Compensation Ins., N.Y.C., 1978-80; coun. James G. Barron, N.Y.C., 1980-81; assoc. St. Regis Paper Co./ Champion Internat., N.Y.C. and Stamford, Conn., 1981-88; sr. ptnr. Kroll & Tract, N.Y.C., 1988-94; ptnr. Peterson & Ross, N.Y.C., 1994-98, Querrey & Harrow, 1998—. With U.S. Army, 1967-69. Mem.: N.Y. State Bar Assn. Office: Querrey & Harrow 120 Broadway Ste 2800 New York NY 10271-3699 Office Phone: 212-233-0130.

SALTER, LESTER HERBERT, lawyer; b. Waterbury, Conn., Apr. 26, 1918; s. Nathan M. and Eva G. (Levy) S.; m. Nina P. Scheftel, Sept. 15, 1951; 1 child, Ellen Lee. BS in Econs, U. Pa., 1940, LLB, 1948. Bar: R.I. 1948. Trial atty. Office of Chief Counsel, IRS, Newark and Boston, 1949-53; pvt. practice Providence, 1953-57; partner Salter & McGowan, Providence, 1957-70, Salter, McGowan, Arcaro & Swartz, Providence, 1970-74; pres. Salter, McGowan, Swartz & Holden, Inc., Providence, 1974-95, Salter, McGowan & Swartz, Inc., Providence, 1995-97, Salter, McGowan, Swartz & Sylvia, Inc., Providence, 1997-99, Salter, McGowan, Sylvia & Leonard, Inc., Providence, 2000—. Lectr. Northeastern U., 1955-56; chmn. U. R.I. Fed. Tax Inst., 1972-77; chmn. disciplinary bd. Supreme Ct., R.I., 1975-81; mem. R.I. Adv. Commn. Jud. Appts., 1978-82, ethics adv. panel Supreme Ct., R.I., 1987-92. Assoc. editor: R.I. Bar Jour, 1961-68. Served with F.A. AUS, 1941-46. Decorated Bronze Star. Fellow: ABA, Am. Bar Found; mem.: Am. Judicature Soc., New Eng. Bar Assn. (pres. 1996—97), Am. Law Inst. (life), R.I. Bar Assn. (pres. 1986—87), ABA (ho. of dels. 1987—2000, bd. govs. 1999—2000). Home: 75 Blackstone Blvd Providence RI 02906-5413 Office: 321 S Main St Providence RI 02903-7108 Office Phone: 401-274-0300.

SALTER, MARY JO, poet; b. Grand Rapids, Mich., Aug. 15, 1954; d. Albert Gregory and Lornina (Paradise) S.; m. Brad Leithauser, 1980; children: Emily Salter, Hilary Garner. BA cum laude, Harvard U., 1976; MA, Cambridge U., 1978. Instr. Harvard U., 1978-79; instr. English conversation Japan, 1980-83; lectr. English Mt. Holyoke Coll., South Hadley, Mass., 1984—, Emily Dickinson sr. lectr. in humanities, 1995—. Staff editor Atlantic Monthly, 1978-80; poet-in-residence Robert Frost Place, 1981; poetry editor The New Republic, 1992-95. Author: Henry Purcell in Japan, 1985, Unfinished Painting, 1989 (Lamont prize in poetry 1988), The Moon Comes Home, 1989, Sunday Skaters: Poems, 1994 (Nat. Book Critics Circle award nomination 1994), A Kiss in Space: Poems, 1999, Open Shutters: Poems, 2003; co-editor: Norton Anthology of Poetry, 4th edit., 1996; contbr. to periodicals including New Yorker, New Republic, Kenyon Rev. Amy Lowell scholar, 1995; recipient Discovery prize Nation, 1983; Nat. Endowment for Arts fellow, 1983-84, Guggenheim fellow, 1993. Mem. Internat. P.E.N. Office: care Alfred A Knopf Inc 1745 Broadway New York NY 10019 E-mail: njsalter@mtholyoke.edu.

SALTERS, KISHA DEANDREA, organization management professional; d. Reuben Harold and Theresa Yvonne Salters. BA in Psychology, NYU, 1997; MA in Human Resources Devel., George Washington U., 1999. Corp. intern Tiffany & Co., N.Y.C., 1995—96; human resources intern Dickstein, Shapiro, Morin LLP, Washington, 1997, Hogan & Hartson LLP, Washington, 1998; orgn. and human performance cons. Accenture (formerly Andersen Consulting), Reston, Va., 1999—2003; sr. orgn. change mgmt. practitioner Orizon, Inc., Rockville, Md., 2003—. Alumnae assn. class agt. The Madeira Sch., McLean, Va., 1993—, chair centennial planning com., 2003—. Scholar, Advt. Women of N.Y., 1996—97, Leopold Schepp Found., 1996—99. Roman Catholic. Avocations: travel, gourmet dining, volunteering.

SALTERS, RICHARD STEWART, engineering company executive; b. St. Johns, Mich., Apr. 4, 1951; s. Stewart Arthur and Mary Ann (Eiseler) S.; m. Patricia Lynn Shumsky, Oct. 23, 1971 (div. Mar. 1982); children: Tiffani, Destiny; m. Marilyn L. DeVille, Sept. 5, 1998 (div. Aug. 2002); children: Wyatt, Madison; m. DeAnna Griffith, July 2003. BS in Engring., Purdue U., 1974. Field engr. Henkels & McCoy, Inc., Blue Bell, Pa., 1972-77; area mgr. engring. dept. Harris McBurney Co., Inc., Jackson, Mich., 1977-81; project engr. Lambic Telcom, Inc., Ridgewood, N.J., 1981-82; pres. S & H Assocs., Inc., Lafayette, La., 1982—. Mem. Engring. Soc. of Detroit, City Club of Lafayette. Roman Catholic. Avocations: racing thoroughbred horses, skiing, golf, tennis. Office: S & H Assocs Inc PO Box 52721 Lafayette LA 70505-2721 also: Seattle WA

SALTHE, STANLEY NORMAN, retired theoretical biology educator; b. N.Y.C., Oct. 16, 1930; s. Christian and Ruth (Idland) S.; m. Barbara May Salthe, May 23, 1959; children: Eric Peter, Rebecca May. BS, Columbia U., 1959, MA, 1960, PhD, 1963. Asst. prof. Bklyn. Coll. CUNY, 1965, assoc. prof. biology, 1971, prof., 1973—; prof. emeritus Bklyn. Coll., CUNY, 1991—; vis. scientist in biol. scis. Binghamton (N.Y.) U., 1992—. Author: Evolutionary Biology, 1972, Evolving Hierarchical Systems, 1985, Development and Evolution, 1993. With USAF, 1950-54 Woodrow Wilson fellow, 1959; rsch. grantee NSF, 1966-70, CUNY, 1970-73. Mem. Gen. Evolutionary Rsch. Group, Washington Evolutionary Systems Soc., Internat. Soc. for History, Philosophy and Social Studies Biology, Am. Soc. Naturalists, Phi Beta Kappa. Business E-Mail: ssalthe@binghamton.edu.

SALTMARSH, SARA ELIZABETH, lawyer; b. Jacksonville, Fla., Nov. 15, 1956; d. Ernest Olmstead and Anne (Frankenberg) S. Student, Randolph-Macon Woman's Coll., 1974-76; BA in English with honors magna cum laude, Fla. State U., 1978; postgrad., Iowa State U., 1980-81; JD, U. Tex., 1986. Bar: Tex. 1987; cert. family law. Assoc. Ausley & Slaikeu, P.C., Austin, Tex., 1987-90, Law Offices of Edwin J. Terry, Jr., Austin, 1990-92; pvt. practice law Austin, 1992—. Mem. security com. Travis County Commr.'s Ct., 1991-93; mem. Ctrl. Tex. Collaborative Law Family Practice Group, Inc., 2002-. Editor: Reference Guide to Travis County Practice, 1991, 92, 93, 95, 96, 97. Bd. dirs. Faith Home for Children with AIDS, 1997-98. Givens Disting. scholar, 1974, Lyndon Baines Johnson Meml. scholar, 1976; recipient Am. Jur. award Wills and Estates, 1986, Marital Relations and Divorce, 1986. Fellow: Austin Young Lawyers' Assn. Found., Tex. Bar Found.; mem.: Austin Young Lawyers' Assn. (co-chmn. It's the Law com. 1990—91), Tex. Ctr. Legal Ethics Professionalism, Travis County Women Lawyers' Assn., Williamson County Bar Assn., Travis County Bar Assn. (sec.-treas. family law sect. 1989—90, v.p. 1990—91, pres. 1991—92, bd. dirs. 1991—92, chair mentor program com. 1993—94, chair mentor program com. 1996—98), Tex. Exes, Tex. Acad. Family Law Specialists, Am. Inns of Ct. (barrister 1996—99), ABA, Sierra Club, Fla. State Univ. Alumni Assn. (life), Lambda Iota Tau, Phi Beta Kappa. Democrat. Avocations: irish dance, skiing, ice skating, in-line skating, windsurfing, basketry. Office: 160 Garden Gate DR Ponte Vedra Beach FL 32082-3668

SALTSMAN, JOHN B. former political party executive, commissioner; BS, MBA, Christian Bros. U. V.p. strategic planning McKenzie Mgmt. Co., Cleveland, Tenn.; West Tenn. field rep. Pres. Bush Re-election Campaign, 1992; with Office of Congressman Don Sundquist; campaign field dir. Don Sundquist Gubernatorial Campaign, 1994; adminstrv. asst. Office of Gov. Sundquist; exec. dir. Tenn. Rep. Caucus, 1996; chmn. Tenn. Rep. Party, Nashville; commr. transp. State of Tenn., Tenn., 1995—. Mem. state fin. com. Gov. Sundquist's Re-election Campaign, 1998. Office: James K Polk Bldg 505 Deaderick St Nashville TN 37243 Fax: 615-292-9619.

SALTYKOV, BORIS GEORGIEVICH, economist, politician; b. Moscow, Dec. 27, 1940; s. Georgy N. and Evdokia M. (Pukaleva) Saltykov; m. Lubov N. Clochkova; 2 children. Student, Moscow Inst. Physics & Tech. Rschr., chief engr. Ctrl. Econ. Math. Inst. USSR Acad. Scis., Moscow, 1967—73, sr. rschr., 1973—86, head dept. Inst. Econ. Forecasting, 1986—91, vice dir. Analytical Rsch. Ctr. on Problems Social, Econ. and Sci. Tech. Devel., 1991—96; min. for sci. and tech. policy, pub. affairs chmn. commn. to UNESCO, vice premier of Russian govt. Russian Fedn., 1992—93; mem. Russian Parliament, 1993—95. Pres. Russian House for Internat. S & T Coop., 1996—. Contbr. over 70 articles to profl. jours. Mem.: Am. Acad. Arts and Scis. (fgn.). Avocation: yachting. Office: Russian House for Interna S&T Coop Brusov per 11 125009 Moscow Russia E-mail: bsaltykov@minstp.ru.

SALTZ, HOWARD JOEL, newspaper editor; b. Bronx, N.Y., Apr. 11, 1960; s. Fred Raymond and Sheila Lois (Goldberg) S. BA in Liberal Arts, SUNY, Stony Brook, 1983. Reporter Greenwich Time, So. Conn. Newspapers divsn. Times Mirror, 1983-85; with MediaNews Group, 1985—, N.J. Advance, Dover, 1985-87, editor, 1987-88, Hamilton (Ohio) Jour.-News, 1988-89, Fremont (Calif.) Argus, 1989-91; editor Johnstown Tribune-Democrat, 1991; dep. bus. editor Denver Post, 1996-98, dep. mng. editor features, 1998-2000, multimedia editor, 2000—02, assoc. editor/new media & strategic devel., 2002—. Adv. com. dept. journalism Ohlone Coll., Fremont, Calif., 1990-91. Bd. dirs. YMCA, Fremont-Newark, Calif., 1990-91, Johnstown Area Heritage Assn., 1991-93. Mem. Greater Johnstown C. of C. (bd. dirs. 1991-96), Soc. Profl. Journalists (bd. dirs. Northern Calif. chpt. 1990-91). Avocations: skiing, travel, scuba. Address: 535 Garfield St Denver CO 80206-4513 Office: Denver Post 1560 Broadway Denver CO 80202-5177 E-mail: hsaltz@denverpost.com.

SALTZBERG, EUGENE ERNEST, emergency physician, educator; b. Chgo., Feb. 2, 1947; s. Samuel and Florence (Weiner) S.; m. Roberta Rice, Apr. 28, 1984; children: Noah Edward, Evan Hale, Paige Erica. BA in Psychology cum laude, U. Ill., 1968; MD, Chgo. Med. Sch. U. Health Scis., 1972. Diplomate Am. Bd. Emergency Medicine, Am. Bd. Med. Examiners. Resident Children's Meml. Hosp., Chgo., 1974; health officer Pitkin County, Aspen, Colo., 1975-79; clin. instr. dept. medicine Northwestern U., Chgo., 1981—; chief of staff Condell Med. Ctr., Libertyville, Ill., 1996-97; med. dir. The Lambs Farm, Libertyville, 1986—. Asst. clin. prof. U. Health Sci., Chgo. Med. Sch., 1988—; chmn. instnl. rev. bd. Cornell Med. Ctr., 2002—; expert witness in field. Fellow: Am. Acad. Emergency Medicine; mem.: ACP, Coalition and Ctr. for Ethical Med. Testimony (charter), Am. Coll. Forensic Medicine, Physicians for Social Responsibility, Soc. for Critical Care Medicine, Univ. Assn. for Emergency Medicine. Jewish. Avocation: golf. Home: 265 Ravine Dr Highland Park IL 60035

SALTZBURG, STEPHEN ALLAN, law educator, consultant; b. Phila., Sept. 10, 1945; s. Jack Leonard and Mildred (Osgood) Adelman; m. Susan Lee, March 10, 1990; children: Mark Winston, Lisa Marie, Diane Elizabeth, David Lee Mussehl. AB, Dickinson Coll., 1967; JD, U. Pa., 1970. Bar: Calif. 1971, D.C. 1972, Va. 1976. Law clk. U.S. Dist. Ct. (no. dist.) Calif., San Francisco, 1970-71, U.S. Supreme Ct., 1971-72; asst. prof. law sch. U. Va., Charlottesville, 1972-74, assoc. prof., 1974-77, prof., 1977-87, Class of 1962 prof., 1987-90; Howrey prof. trial advocacy, litigation and profl. responsibility George Washington U. Law Sch., Washington, 1990—2004, Wallace and Beverley Woodbury univ. prof., 2004—. Reporter Alaska Rules of Evidence, 1976-77, Alaska Civil Jury Instrns., 1979-81, Adv. Com. on Rules of Criminal Procedure, 1984-89, Va. Rules on Evidence, 1984-85, Civil Justice Act Adv. Group, U.S. Dist. Ct. D.C., 1992-93, chmn., 1994-99; dep. asst. atty. gen. criminal divsn. U.S. Dept. Justice, 1988-89; mem. adv. com. on Fed. Rules of Criminal Procedure, 1989-95, on Fed. Rules of Evidence, 1992-95; mediator dispute resolution program U.S. Ct. Appeals, 1993—. Author: Evidence in America, 1987, American Criminal Procedure, 7th edit., 2004, Criminal Law: Cases and Materials, 1994, 2d edit., 2000, Evidence: The Objection Method, 1997, 2d edit., 2000, Federal Rules of Evidence Manual, 1975, 8th edit., 2002, Federal Rules of Evidence Trial Book, 1998, A Modern Approach to Evidence, 2d edit., 1982, Military Rules of Evidence Manual, 5th edit., 2004, Basic Criminal Procedure, 1994, 3d edit., 2003, Military Evidentiary Foundations, 1994, 2d edit., 2000, Trying Cases to Win: Anatomy of a Trial, 1999, Trying Cases to Win: Evidence: Weapons for Winning, Vol. 1, 2000, Vol. 2, 2002, Vol. 3, 2004, California Federal Evidence Trial Book, 1999, Ohio Rules of Evidence Trial Book, 1999, Washington Evidence Trial Book, 1999. Mem.: ABA (chmn. com. on trial advocacy criminal justice sect. 1992—96, co-chmn. task force on civil trial stds. litig. sect. 1996—97, task force on Ind. Counsel Act litig. sect. 1997—99, mem. criminal justice sect. coun. 2000—, task force on terrorism and the law 2001—02, litigation sect. coun. 2001—04, ho. of dels. 2001—, task force on gatekeeper regulation and the profession 2002—, task force on enemy combatants 2002—, chair ABA Justice Kennedy Commn. 2003—), Am. Law Inst. Office: George Washington U Law Sch 2000 H St NW Washington DC 20052 Office Phone: 202-994-7089.

SALTZMAN, BARRY, actor; b. Chgo., Nov. 1, 1961; s. Bernard William and Cynthia Iris (Gordon) Saltzman. BA in Theatre and Drama, Ind. U., 1983. Mem. entertainment legal MGM Studios, 2001—. Actor: (plays) Rosencrantz and Guilderstern are Dead, 1984, On the Verge, 1986, The Skin of Our Teeth, 1987, The Magic Barrell and Other Stories, 1988, Vampire Lesbians of Sodom, 1990, The Little Prince, 1990, Broadway Bound, 1991, The Merry Widow, 1991, The Miser, The Liar, Green Stockings, 1992, Julius Ceasar, 1992, The Real Live Brady Bunch, 1993, Beachwood Palace Jubilee, 1994—95, Theft, 1994, The Smell of Ennui, 1995, The Big Time Jubilee, 1995—96, Lysistrata, The Shadow Box, 2004, others; (TV films) Bradymania, 1993, others. Adminstr., fundraiser Hunger Project, 1986—88; fundraiser Youth at Risk, 1988, AIDS Walk Chgo., 1990; group discussion leader, fundraiser Stop AIDS Chgo., 1987—90; various adminstrv. and enrollment roles Werner Erhard and Assocs., Chgo., 1986—90; mem. Human Rights Campaign Fund, 1990—94; adminstrv. vol. Gore-Liberman, 2000. Recipient medallion for Acting Excellence, Amoco Cos./Am. Coll. Theatre Festival, Kennedy Ctr., Washington, 1982. Mem.: AFTRA, AEA. Personal E-mail: bjsaltzman@yahoo.com.

SALTZMAN, IRENE CAMERON, consumer products company executive; b. Cocoa, Fla., Mar. 23, 1927; d. Argyle Bruce and Marie T. (Neel) Cameron; m. Herman Saltzman, Mar. 23, 1946 (dec. May 1986); children: Martin Howard (dec.), Arlene Norma Hanly. Owner Irene Perfume and Cosmetics Lab., Jacksonville, Fla., 1972—. Mem. Cummer Mus. Art, Jacksonville, 1972-. Mem. Ret. Judge Advocates Assn. of USAF (hon.), Mil. Officers Assn. Am., Aircraft Owners and Pilots Assn., Trade, Cosmetic, Toiletry and Fragrance Assn., Ret. Officers Assn., Ponte Vedra Club. Democrat. Episcopalian. Avocations: aviation, painting, travel, swimming, golf. Home: 2701 Ocean Dr S Jacksonville Beach FL 32250 E-mail: irene@ireneparfums.com.

SALTZMAN, JOSEPH, journalist, producer, educator; b. LA, Oct. 28, 1939; s. Morris and Ruth (Weiss) S.; m. Barbara Dale Epstein, July 1, 1962; children: Michael Stephen Ulysses, David Charles Laertes. BA, U. So. Calif., 1961; MS, Columbia U., 1962. Freelance writer, reporter, prodr., 1960—; reporter Valley Times Today, LA, 1962-64; editor Pacific Palisades Palisadian Post, 1964; sr. writer, prodr. CBS-TV, LA, 1964-74; freelance broadcast cons. LA, 1974—; prof. journalism U. So. Calif., LA, 1974—; assoc. dir. Sch. Journalism U. So. Calif. Annenberg, 1996-99; assoc. dean Annenberg Sch. for Comm., 1999—2003; sr. prodr. investigative unit Entertainment Tonight, 1983; dir. Image of the Journalist in Popular Culture project Norman Lear Ctr., Annenberg Sch. Comm., U. So. Calif., 2001—. CFO The Jester & Pharley

Phund. Author: Frank Capra and the Image of the Journalist in American Film, 2002; prodr.(writer): (documentaries) Black on Black, 1968, The Unhappy Hunting Ground, 1971, The Junior High School, 1971, The Very Personal: Death of Elizabeth Schell-Holt-Hartford, 1972, Rape, 1972, Why Me?, 1974, Entertainment Tonight, 1983; editor (columnist): USA Today, 1983—; King Features Syndicate, 1983—92; contbg. editor: Emmy Mag., 1986—90, Roberts Reviewing Svc., 1964—95, others. Recipient AP cert. of excellence and merit, 1968, 72, 73, 74, 75, Edward R. Murrow awards for disting. achievements in broadcast journalism, 1969, 72, Alfred I. duPont-Columbia U. award in broadcast journalism, 1973-74, Silver Gavel award ABA, 1973, Ohio State award Am. Exhbn. Ednl. Radio-TV Programs and Inst. for Edn. by Radio-TV Telecom. Ctr., 1974, Broadcast Media awards San Francisco State U., 1974, 75, Media award for excellence in comm. Am. Cancer Soc., 1976, Disting. Alumni award U. So. Calif., 1992; Seymour Berkson fellow, 1961; Robert E. Sherwood fellow, 1962; alt. Pulitzer traveling fellow, 1962-63. Mem. NATAS (regional Emmy awards 1965, 68, 74, 75), Radio-TV News Assn. (Golden Mike awards 1969, 71, 73, 75), Writers Guild Am., Greater LA Press Club (awards 1968, 74, 75), Columbia U. Alumni Assn., U. So. Calif. Alumni Assn., Skull and Dagger, Blue Key, Phi Beta Kappa, Sigma Delta Chi, Pi Sigma Alpha, Alpha Epsilon Rho. Home: 2116 Via Estudillo Palos Verdes Peninsula CA 90274-1931 Office: U So Calif Annenberg Sch Journalism Univ Park Los Angeles CA 90089-0001 Office Phone: 213-740-3918. E-mail: saltzman@usc.edu.

SALTZMAN, PHILIP, television writer, producer; b. Sonora, Mexico, Sept. 19, 1928; came to U.S., 1929, naturalized, 1948; s. Louis and Vanya (Liberman) S.; m. Caroline Veiller, Jan. 24, 1960; children: Jennifer, Daniel, Anthony. BA, UCLA, 1951, MA, 1953. Free lance writer, 1958-68. Pres. Woodruff Prodns., Inc. Writer: TV shows Alcoa Goodyear Theater, 1959, Richard Diamond, 1959, Rifleman, 1961, Perry Mason, 1964, Dr. Kildare, 1964, Fugitive, 1964, Twelve O'Clock High, 1966; producer, writer: TV shows Felony Squad, 1966-69, F.B.I, 1969-73, Barnaby Jones, 1973-77; producer, writer, creator Intertect, 1973; producer: TV movie The FBI vs. Alvin Karpis, 1974, Attack on Terror: The FBI vs. the KKK in Mississippi, 1975, Brinks: The Great Robbery, 1976; co-writer: feature film The Swiss Conspiracy, 1975; creator, writer, producer TV movie Crossfire, 1975; exec. producer: TV shows Barnaby Jones, 1978-80, Escapade, 1978, Colorado C-I, 1978, A Man Called Sloane, 1979, The Aliens Are Coming, 1979, Freebie and the Bean, 1980; producer: TV shows Bare Essence, 1982; supervising producer-writer Partners in Crime, 1984; producer, writer Crazy Like a Fox, 1985; producer, co-writer TV movie That Secret Sunday, 1986; exec. supervising producer The New Perry Mason movies, 1987-88; exec. supervising producer, writer Jake and The Fatman, 1987-88; supervising producer Columbo, 1989-90; creator, writer The Caller, 1991. Mem. dean's coun. Coll. Letters and Sci., UCLA, Friends of English, UCLA. Mem. Writers Guild Am., West, Caucus for Writers, Producers, Dirs., Acad. TV Arts and Scis., PEN Ctr. USA West. Personal E-mail: cpsaltzman@aol.com.

SALTZSTEIN, SUSAN L. lawyer; b. N.Y., 1965; BA, U. Pa., 1987; JD magna cum laude, Columbia U., 1991. Bar: N.Y. 1992. Atty. Skadden, Arps, Slate, Meagher & Flom LLP, N.Y., 1992—. Office: Skadden Arps Slate Meagher & Flom LLP Four Times Sq New York NY 10036

SALUSTRO, LARRY J. lawyer; b. 1947; BA in English and Am. Lit., George Washington U., 1969; JD with honors, U. Mich. Law Sch., Ann Arbor, 1974. Spl. asst. atty. gen. State of Minn., 1974—83; comml. and regulatory atty. AT&T, 1983—95, regional v.p., law and govt. affairs, 1995—97; sr. v.p., gen. counsel Wis. Energy Corp., Milw., v.p., legal, regulatory, and govtl. affairs, 1997—2004, exec. vp., gen. counsel, 2004—. Office: Wis Energy Corp PO Box 2949 Milwaukee WI 53201*

SALVA, LAWRENCE J. communications executive; 2 children. BA summa cum laude, Rowan U., 1977. CPA Pa. With Coopers & Lybrand, Phila., 1977—87; ptnr. PricewaterhouseCoopers, 1988—2000; sr. v.p. Comcast Corp., Phila., 2000—, controller, 2000—. Mem. Fin. Execs. Internat. Com. Corp. Reporting. Mem.: AICPA, Pa. Inst. CPA. Office: Comcast Corp 1500 Market St Philadelphia PA 19102

SALVADOR, RICHARD ANTHONY, pharmaceutical executive; b. Albany, N.Y., May 19, 1927; s. Domenico and Irma Ida Salvador; m. Carole Snarski, Sept. 17, 1966; children: Barbara, Diana. BS in Chemistry-Biology, Siena Coll., 1951; AM in Pharmacology, Boston U., 1953; PhD in Pharmacology, George Washington U., 1956. Rsch. fellow Boston U. Sch. Medicine, 1951-53, George Washington U. Sch. Medicine, Washington, 1953-57; postdoctoral fellow NIH, Bethesda, Md., 1957-58; rsch. instr. Sch. U. Wash. U., St. Louis, 1958-60; sr. pharmacologist Burroughs Wellcome & Co., Tuckahoe, N.Y., 1960-69; group chief biochem. nutrition Hoffmann-La Roche Inc., Nutley, N.J., 1970-73, sect. head pharmacology, 1973-75, asst. dir. pharmacology, 1975-79, dir. exptl. therapeutics, 1979-83, asst. v.p. exptl. therapeutics, 1983-85, v.p. preclin. devel., 1985-94, v.p. internat. preclin. devel., 1984-96; ret.; sci. advisor Crummy, Del Deo, Dolan, Griffinger & Vecchlone, 1997—2000; pres., CEO AngioGenex, Inc., 2001—. Bd. dirs. Suntory Pharm. Rsch. Labs.; sr. advisor Axonyx Inc., 1997—2002; cons. in field. With U.S. Army, 1945-47. Mem. AAAS, Am. Assn. Pharmaceutics Scientists, Am. Soc. Pharmacology and Exptl. Therapeutics, Am. Soc. Clin. Pharmacology and Therapeutics, N.Y. Acad. Sci.

SALVANESCHI, LUIGI, real estate and development executive, business educator; b. Casale, Italy, 1929; came to U.S., 1959; s. Ernesto and Carolina (Bassignana) S.; m. Lenore M. Rickels, Aug. 20, 1958; 1 child, Margherita Lina. Classical Maturity, Valsalice, Torino, Italy, 1950; PhD, Vatican U., Rome, 1958; cert. in real estate, UCLA, 1965. Restaurant mgr. McDonalds Co., Chgo., 1959-61, restaurant mgr. and supr. Los Angeles, 1961-63, real estate mgr., 1964-68, v.p. real estate Oakbrook, Ill., 1969-83; sr. v.p. real estate and constrn. Kentucky Fried Chicken, Louisville, 1983-88; pres., COO, dir. Blockbuster Entertainment, Ft. Lauderdale, Fla., 1988-91; disting. adj. prof. Barry Univ., 1991—. Adj. prof. Sch. Bus. U. Louisville, 1987; dir. Fla. Fun-Train subs. First Am. Rwys., Hollywood, Fla. Author: Location, Location, Location, 1997, Renaissance 2000: Liberal Arts Essentials for Tomorrow's Leaders, 1998. Dir. Ft. Lauderdale Internat. Movie Festival. Served as 2d lt. in Italian Infantry, 1945-46. Recipient Outstanding Italo-Am. award Italian Am. Fedn., 1991; named Colonel of the Commonwealth of Ky., 1984. Mem. Nat. Assn. Real Estate Execs. (co-founder, bd. dirs.). Roman Catholic. Avocations: reading classics in latin and greek, mountain hiking. Office: Barry Univ Sch of Bus 11300 NE 2nd Ave Miami FL 33161-6695

SALVATI, EUGENE PHILIP, retired surgeon; b. Pursglove, W.Va., Sept. 7, 1923; MD, U. Md., 1947. Diplomate Am. Bd. Surgery. Intern Muhlenberg Hosp., Plainfield, N.J., 1947-49, med. staff; resident in surgery St. Vincent Hosp., Indpls., 1949-50, Indpls. VA Hosp., 1950-51, Ind. U. Med. Ctr., 1953-54; fellow in colorectal surgery Allentown Gen. Hosp.; clin. prof. surgery R.W. Johnson Sch. Medicine, U. Medicine and Dentistry N.J.; pvt. practice Plainfield. Fellow ACSI mem. AMA, Am. Soc. Colon & Rectal Surgeons. Office: Assoc ColoRectal Surg 3900 Park Ave Ste 101 Edison NJ 08820-3032 Office Phone: 732-494-6640.

SALVATIERRA, OSCAR, JR., transplant surgeon, urologist, educator; b. Phoenix, Apr. 15, 1935; s. Oscar and Josefine S.; m. Pamela Moss; children: Mark, Lisa Marie. BS, Georgetown U., 1957; MD, U. So. Calif., 1961. Intern, resident in surgery and urology U. So. Calif.-Los Angeles County Med. Ctr., 1961-66; practice medicine Pomona, Calif., 1968-72; chief staff Casa Colina Hosp., 1972; post doctoral fellow in transplantation U. Calif.-San Francisco, 1972-73, asst. prof. surgery and urology, 1973-75, assoc. prof., 1975-81, prof., 1981-91, chmn. transplant service, 1974-91; attending surgeon and urologist Moffitt Hosp., 1973—; exec. dir. Pacific Transplant Inst., 1991-94; prof. surgery/pediatrics, dir. pediat. renal transplantation Stanford U. Med. Ctr., 1994—, attending surgeon, urologist and pediat. Chair faculty senate Stanford U. Sch. Medicine, 2002—; study sect. NIH, 1981-85, nat. adv. bd., 1986-92, chmn. nat. adv. bd. 1990-92, chmn. spl. study sect., 1997, 99. Contbr. over 270 articles and chpts. to med. lit.; mem. editl. bd. Transplantation and Immunology, 1984—, Transplantation, 1987—, Transplantation Procs., 1990—, Pediat. Transplantation, 1998—; assoc. editor Am. Jour. Kidney Diseases, 1987-89. Nat. bd. advisors Agent Orange Class Assistance Program, 1988-96. With M.C., U.S. Army, Vietnam, 1966-68. Decorated Army Commendation medal, Grand Ufficiale of Italian Rep. with title His Excellency award; named Oscar Salvatierra Transplantation Fellows Symposium in his honor, 2001; recipient Chancellor's award for pub. svc., U. Calif., 1986, Commendation resolution, Calif. State Legislature, 1990, Presdl. medal and Diploma of Honor, Argentina, 1999, Rambar-Mark award, Stanford U., 1999, Franklin Ebaugh award, 2003, Pioneer award, Nat. Kidney Found., 2004; grantee, NIH, 1974—76, 1980—83, 1988—90, 2003—, USPHS, 1986—89. Fellow ACS (bd. govs. 1986-92); mem. Am. Surg. Assn., Am. Soc. Transplant Surgeons (bd. dirs. 1977-85, pres. 1983-84, chmn. adv. com. on issues 1984-87), Soc. Univ. Surgeons, Soc. Univ. Urologists, N.Y. Acad. Scis., Am. Soc. Nephrology, Internat. Transplantation Soc. (bd. dirs. 1984—, pres.-elect 1996-98, pres., 1998-2000), Soc. Pediatric Urology, Am. Urol. Assn., Nat. Kidney Found., Renal Physicians Assn. (bd. dirs. 1984-87), Pacific Coast Surg. Assn., San Francisco Surg. Soc., United Network Organ Sharing (bd. dirs. 1984-88, pres. 1985-86), Internat. Soc. for Organ Sharing (bd. dirs. 1991—, pres. 1993-95), Am. Soc. for Minority Health and Transplant Profls. (pres. 1992-94), Natziger Surg. Soc. Achievements include being the principle lay figure in passage and enactment of National Organ Transplant Act, 1984; introduction of Pope John Paul II to the 18th International Transplantation Congress for Encyclical on Organ Transplantation, 2000. Office: Stanford U Med Ctr 703 Welch Rd Ste H2 Palo Alto CA 94304-1708 Business E-Mail: osalvatierra@stanfordmed.org.

SALVATORE, DIANE J. editor-in-chief; BA in Journalism, Pa. State U.; MA in English and Creative Writing, NYU. Rschr., reporter The Soho News, NYC; editl. asst. Met. Home, NYC, Cosmopolitan, NYC; sr. assoc. editor Ladies' Home Jour., NYC, 1985—88; articles assoc. editor Glamour, NYC, 1988—89; sr. editor Redbook, NYC, 1989—94; dep. editor Good Housekeeping, NYC, exec. editor, 1994—99; editor in chief YM, NYC, 1998—2002; exec. dir. Marie Claire, 2001; editor in chief Ladies Home Jour., NYC, 2002—. Contbr. articles and short stories in various nat. periodicals. Mem.: Am. Soc. Mag. Editors.

SALVATORE, RICHARD JOHN, cinematographer, company executive; b. Bklyn., May 25, 1950; s. Peter Louis and Julia (Stampano) S. AA, Los Angeles Valley Coll., 1972. Artist George Whiteman & Assocs., Hollywood, Calif., 1968-72; ind. cinematographer Hollywood, 1976—; founder RJS Motion Picture and TV, Northridge, 1991—; co-founder RJS Promotions, 1993—. Tchr. Prodrs. Assn., Hollywood, 1975—, Am. Film Inst., Beverly Hills, Calif., 1984—; CEO Omnicom Sys., Canoga Park, Calif., 1981—; co-owner Norman Borines World Bruce Lee Mus., Las Vegas, 1992—; founder RJS Comms., 1995—; bd. dirs., cinematographer Davidson Design Prodns., San Diego; cons. entertainment mktg. and advt. spl. projects (tie-ins and global exposure), 1991—; creative cons. for programming JM Entertainment, Hollywood, Calif., 1997-98. Photographer: Solace, 1968 (Memorable mention Los Angeles County Fair 1968), Night Wind Dragon, 1971. Pres. Robert F. Kennedy campaign com., L.A., 1967, Gun Control Act of 1968, L.A.; dist. leader/area leader Muscular Dystrophy Assn., Los Angeles County, 1966-70. Recipient fin. grant U. Calif., 1972. Mem. Soc. Operating Cameramen (assoc.), Acad. TV Arts and Scis. (assoc.). Avocations: Kung Fu, collecting old movies. E-mail: rjs4000@core.com.

SALVATORELLI, JOSEPH J. engineer, consultant; b. Oct. 22, 1924; s. Luigi and Agnes (D'Amario) S.; m. Dolores A. Biello, Aug. 11, 1946; 1 child, Joel Girard. Diploma in civil engring., Drexel U., 1954, BSCE, 1956. Registered profl. engr., N.J., Pa., Md., Va., Del., N.Y., Nebr.; lic. sewage/water treatment plant operator; registered land surveyor. With Albright & Friel, Inc., Phila., 1946-59, ptnr., 1959-62, v.p., dir., 1962-71; sr. assoc. Taylor Wiseman Taylor, Mt. Laurel, N.J., 1971-75, v.p., ptnr., 1975-85; ret., 1985. Cons. in field, 1986—; mem. rsch. adv. coun. P.S.E.G. Rsch. Corp., 1986-89. Contbr. articles to profl. publs. Pres. Island House Unit Owners, 1974-76, 79-84; pres. Island House Condominium Assn., Margate, N.J., 1976-77. Sgt. U.S. Army, 1943-46, PTO. Recipient Alumni Achievement award Drexel U., 1959, named Alumnus of Yr., 1976. Mem. NSPE (life), ASCE (life, dir. Phila. sect., chmn. san. engring. divsn. 1968-69), Am. Acad. Environ. Engrs. (diplomate, life), Am. Water Works Assn. (life), N.J. Water Environment Assn. (life), N.J. Waterworks Assn. (Svc. award 2002), Pa. Mcpl. Authorities Assn., N.J. Assn. Environ. Authorities (dir. 1972-74, hon. life), Environ. Assessment Assn. (cert. environ. inspector), Franklin Inst., Pa. Water Environ. Assn. (life, pres. 1971-72, High Hat award 1975, Hazeltine award 1980), Water Environ. Fedn. (life, dir. 1973-76, Arthur Sidney Bedell award 1973, Svc. award 1976), Ea. Pa. Water Pollution Control Operators Assn. (life, Svc. award 1973, Bolenius-Wiest Clean Streams award 1983), Alpha Sigma Lambda (ETA chpt.), Yeadon, Pa. Kiwanis (sec. 1968-70, pres. 1972, dir.). Roman Catholic.

SALVATY, BENJAMIN BENEDICT, lawyer; b. Chgo., Dec. 22, 1940; s. Benjamin Benedict and Marion Therese (Ryan) S.; m. Patircia Louise Recor, Aug. 29, 1964; children: Paul Benedict, Kathleen Anne. BBA, U. Notre Dame, 1962; JD, U. So. Calif., 1965. Bar: Calif. 1966, U.S. Dist. Ct. (no., cen., ea. and so. dists.) Calif., U.S. Ct. Appeals (9th cir.), U.S. Tax Ct., U.S. Supreme Ct. Sr. trial atty. Calif. Dept. Transp., 1966-79; gen. atty. The Atchison, Topeka and Santa Fe Railway Co., 1980-89; sr. ptnr. Hill, Farrer & Burrill, Los Angeles, 1990—. Mem. ABA (litigation sect. urban, state and local govt. law com. on condemnation, zoning and planning com.), Am. Bd. Trial Advs., Am. Judicature Soc., Internat. Right Way Assn., Irish Am. Bar Assn. (bd. dirs. 1985—, treas. 1991, sec. 1992, v.p. 1992-93, pres. 1993-94), Italian Am. Lawyers Assn., State Trial Attys. Assn. (pres. 1975-79), Calif. State Bar (chmn. condemnation com. 1987-88, vice chmn. 1986-87), Pasadena Bar Assn., L.A. County Bar Assn. (condemnation and land valuation com.). Office: Hill Farrer & Burrill LLP One California Plz 37th Fl 300 S Grand Ave Los Angeles CA 90071-3109 Fax: 213-624-4840. Office Phone: 213-621-0865.

SALVENDY, GAVRIEL, industrial engineer, educator; b. Budapest, Hungary, Sept. 30, 1938; came to U.S., 1968; s. Paul and Katarina (Brown) S.; m. Catherine Vivien Dees, Apr. 1, 1966; children: Laura Dorit, Kevin David. MSc in Engring. Prodn, U. Birmingham, Eng., 1966, PhD, 1968; Doctorate (hon.), Academia Sinica, 1995, Chinese Acad. Scis., 1995. Asst. prof. indsl. engring. SUNY, Buffalo, 1968-71; mem. faculty Purdue U., 1971—, prof. indsl. engring., chmn. human factors program, 1977, Fulbright distinguished prof., 1979-80, 81-82, NEC prof. indsl. engring., 1984-99; chair, prof., head dept. indsl. engring. Tsinghua U., China, 2001—. Chmn. Internat. Commn. on Human Aspects in Computing, Switzerland, 1986-91. Co-author: Prediction and Development of Industrial Work Performance, 1973, Human Aspects of Computer Aided Design, 1987; sr. editor: Machine-Pacing and Occupational Stress, 1981, Social, Ergonomic and Stress Aspects of Work with Computers, 1987, Designing and Using Human-Computer Interfaces and Knowledge Based Systems, 1989; editor: Handbook of Industrial Engineering, 1982, 3d edit., 2001, Human Computer Interaction, 1984, Handbook of Human Factors, 1987, 2d edit., 1997, Cognitive Engineering in the Design of Human Computer Interaction and Expert Systems, 1987; founding editor: Internat. Jour. on Human-Computer Interaction, Internat. Jour. Human Factors in Mfg.; co-editor: Work with Computers: Organizational Management, Stress and Health Aspects, 1989, Human Computer Interaction: Software and Hardware Interfaces, 1993, Human-Computer Interaction: Applications and Case Studies, 1993, Design of Work and Development of Personnel in Advanced Manufacturing, 1994, Organization and Management of Advanced Manufacturing, 1994, Advanceds in Applied Ergonomics, 1996, Handbook of Human Factors and Ergonomics, 2d edit., 1997, Design of Computing Systems (2 vols.), 1997, Ergonomics in Manufacturing, 1998, Handbook of Industrial Engineering, 3d edit., 2001; contbr. articles to profl. jours., chpts. to books. Pres. Lafayette Jewish Sunday Sch., 1980-81. Fellow APA, Inst. Indsl. Engrs. (sr., Phil Carroll award 1973), Human Factors and Ergonomics Soc. (past officer), Ergonomics Soc. (hon., life mem.); mem. NAE. Office: Purdue U Sch Indsl Engring West Lafayette IN 47907 Office Phone: 765-494-5426. Business E-Mail: salvendy@ecn.purdue.edu.

SALVESEN, MAGDA ABERCROMBY, art historian, garden historian; b. Edinburgh, Scotland, June 20, 1944; came to US, 1976; d. Harold Keith and Marion Eleanora (Cameron) S.; m. Jon R. Schueler, July 29, 1976 (dec. Aug. 1992). MA, U. St. Andrews (Scotland), 1966, U. London, 1968; Cert. in Secondary Edn., Moray House Coll. Edn., Edinburgh, 1976. Asst. Richard Demarco Gallery, Edinburgh, 1968; exhibn. officer Scottish Arts Coun., Edinburgh, 1969-71; tchr. middle sch. The Day Sch., N.Y.C., 1976-81; ESL tchr. Berlitz Sch. Langs., N.Y.C., 1983-85; exec. adminstr. Archs./Designers/Planners for Social Responsibility, N.Y.C., 1985-88; lectr. art history New Sch. U., N.Y.C., 1988—; lectr. garden history and theory N.Y. Botanical Garden, Bronx, 1990—. Lectr. in field. Editor: (manuscript by Jon Schueler) The Sound of Sleat: A Painter's Life, 1999; dir., exec. prodr.: (video) Jon Schueler: A Life in Painting, 1999. Bd. mem. Queens (N.Y.) Bot. Garden. Democrat. Avocations: museuming, reading, travel, gardening. Address: 40 W 22nd St New York NY 10010 E-mail: msalvesen@earthlink.net.

SALVESON, MELVIN ERWIN, business executive, educator; b. Brea, Calif., Jan. 16, 1919; s. John T. and Elizabeth (Green) S.; m. Joan Y. Stipek, Aug. 22, 1944; children: Eric C., Kent Erwin. BS, U. Calif. at Berkeley, 1941; MS, Mass. Inst. Tech., 1947; PhD, U. Chgo., 1952. Cons. McKinsey & Co., N.Y.C., 1947—48; asst. prof., dir. mgmt. sci. research U. Calif. at Los Angeles, 1948—54; mgr. advanced data systems, cons. strategic planning Gen. Electric Co., Louisville and N.Y.C., 1954-57; pres. Mgmt. Scis. Corp., L.A., 1957-67; group v.p. Control Data/CEIR, Inc., 1967-68; pres. Electronic Currency Corp., 1964—; chmn. OneCard Internat., Inc., 1983-92, UniCard Sys. Inc., 1992—; founder and pres. So. Calif. Econ. Alliance, 1992-96, also bd. dirs.; founding chair Am. Soc. for Edn. and Econ. Devel., 1996-98, also bd dirs.; exec. dir. Am. Found. for Edn. and Econ. Devel. Bd. dirs. Diversified Earth Scis., Inc., Eco Rx Inc., Eexcel Enterprise Inc., Veritas et Justus Inc., Algeran, Inc., Electronic Currency Corp.; founder MasterCard System, L.A., 1966; chmn. Corporate Strategies Internat.; prof. bus. Pepperdine U. 1972-85; adj. prof. U. So. Calif., Webster U., U. Phoenix, 1972-; adviser data processing City of L.A., 1962-64; futures forecasting IBM, 1957-61; adviser strategic systems planning USAF, 1961-67; info. systems Calif. Dept. Human Resources, 1972-73, City L.A. Automated Urban Data Base, 1962-67; tech. transfer NASA, 1965-70, others; mem. bd. trustees, Long Beach City Coll., 1990-95. Contbr. articles to profl. jours. Served to lt. comdr. USNR, 1941—46. Named to Long Beach City Coll. Hall of Fame; recipient Dist. Alumnus 1992 award Calif. Coll. System, 1992. Fellow: AAAS, Inst. Mgmt. Sci. (founder, past pres.), Inst. for Ops. Rsch. and Mgmt. Scis.; mem.: CSSP Alumnus, Calif. Yacht Club, Founders Club (L.A. Philharm. Orch.). Republican. Office: 515 Ocean Ave # 405 S Santa Monica CA 90402-2623 Office Phone: 310-917-1911. Personal E-mail: mesalveson@aol.com.

SALVO, JOSEPH ALDO, lawyer; b. N.Y.C., Feb. 20, 1933; s. Charles A. and Marietta (Mancuso) S.; m. Joan Del Vecchio, May 30, 1959; children: Joseph C., John, Joanne. BBA, St. John's U., 1960, LLB, 1962. Bar: N.Y. 1962, U.S. Dist. Ct. (ea. and so. dists.) N.Y., U.S. Supreme Ct. Spl. agt. U.S. Treasury Dept.; pvt. practice Douglaston, N.Y., 1962—; counsel Italian Charities Am., Inc., Elmhurst, N.Y., 1975—. Chmn. Columbian Lawyers Scholarship Corp. With U.S. Army, 1954-56. Mem. Queens County Bar Assn. (chmn. law office mgmt. com. 1983—), Columbian Lawyers Assn. (pres. 1978-79, historian), Nat. Italian Am. Bar Assn. Democrat. Roman Catholic. Avocations: music, sports, arts. Home: 1333 137th St College Point NY 11356-2006 Office: 42-24 Douglaston Pky Douglaston NY 11363-1528

SALWEN, MARTIN J. pathologist, educator; b. Bklyn., Sept. 21, 1931; s. David Simon and Rose (Hittner) S.; m. Jane Stafford, July 21, 1979; children: Jennifer Artis, Zachary David; children by previous marriage: John Duncan, Jonathan M. BS, CCNY, 1953; MD, SUNY, Bklyn., 1957. Intern Hosp. of St. Raphael, New Haven, 1957-58; resident Yale-New Haven Hosp., 1958-59; fellow Yale U. Sch. Medicine, New Haven, 1959-61; attending pathologist Yale-New Haven Hosp., 1961-67; asst. prof. pathology Yale U., New Haven, 1965-71; prof. pathology Hahneman Med. Coll., Phila., 1971-79; clin. prof. pathology SUNY Health Sci. Ctr., Bklyn., 1979-93, disting. svc. prof., 1993—; dir. labs. U. Hosp. of Bklyn., 1986—97. Dir. pathology Kings County Hosp. Ctr., Bklyn., 1979-97, co-dir. residency tng. program, 1982-97, dir. labs. Monmouth Med. Ctr., Long Branch, N.J., 1967-78; chief Med. Lab. Ctr., USAF Hosp., Tachikawa, Japan, 1964-66; Jean Redman Oliver master tchr., 1992. Pres. Prospect Park South Assn., Bklyn., 2001-04. Capt. USAF, 1964-66, Japan. Fellow Coll. Am. Pathologists, Am. Soc. Clin. Pathologists, Assn. Clin. Scientists, N.Y. Acad. Medicine, SUNY Alumni Assn. (pres. 1996-7, chmn. bd. trustees 2000-02, Disting. Svc. award 2002), Alpha Omega Alpha. Home: 934 Albemarle Rd Brooklyn NY 11218-2708 Office: SUNY Health Sci Ctr Bklyn 450 Clarkson Ave Brooklyn NY 11203-2056 Business E-Mail: martin.salwen@downstate.edu.

SALYER, KENNETH E. surgeon; b. Kansas City, Kans., Aug. 18, 1936; s. Everett A. and Laurene S.; m. Luci Lara-Salyer; children: Kenneth E. Jr., Leigh Green-Salyer. BS, U. Mo., 1958; MD, U. Kans., 1962. Intern Parkland Meml. Hosp., Dallas, 1962-63, resident in gen. surgery, 1963-67; fellow in surgery U. Tex. SW Sch. Med., Dallas, 1965-67, founder, dir. residency tng. program, 1969-78; prof. surgery, chair plastic surgery, 1969-78; resident in plastic surgery U. Kans. Sch. Med., Kansas City, 1967-69; founder, dir. Internat. Craniofacial Inst., Dallas, 1986—. Editl. bd. mem. Annals of Plastic Surgery, 1977-79, Jour. of Speech and Hearing Disorders (editl. cons.) 1982, Tex. Medicine (editl. cons.) 1981-85, Jour. of Craniofacial Surgery, 1990—, Italian Jour. Craniomaxillofacial Surgery, 1990—, Argentinian Jour. Plastic Surgery (internat. consultative coun. 1995—). Author: Techniques in Aesthetic Craniofacial Surgery, 1989, Cleft Lip and Palate Treatment Center: A Booklet for Parents, 1994, (with J. Bardach) Surgical Techniques in Cleft Lip and Palate, 1987, 2d edit. 1991, (with others) The Atlas of Craniomaxillofacial Surgery, 1982; editor: Symposium on Plastic Surgery in the Orbital Region, 1976; author various book chpts. Recipient Nat. Inst. Health award public health svc., sr. clin. traineeship Cancer Control Program 1967-69, Plastic Surgery Resident Program Participation award 2nd place 1967-69, scholar. competition (hon. mention) Edn. Found. Am. Soc. Plastic and Reconstructive Surgeons, 1972, Rsch. Grant award Ednl. Found. Am. Soc. Plastic and Reconstructive Surgeons 1975-76, Hektoen Gold medal for original investigation "Spectrum of Rsch. and Clin. Mgmt. of Craniofacial Anomalies" exhibit at AMA, San Francisco 1977, selected hon. mem. Japanese Soc. Craniofacial Surgery 1993, selected chmn. med. adv. bd. Children's Craniofacial Assn. 1993; grantee Internat. NIH Microvascular Surg. Rsch. 1969, Vets. Admin. Hosp. Maxillofacial Rsch. 1972-78, Sid Richardson Found. med. rsch. 1975-76, Gen. Electric Found. for Craniofacial Deformities 1985-87; recipient various awards for videos. Mem. AMA (mem. various coms.), Am. Acad. Pediat. (exec. com. section on plastic surgery, founding mem., sec.-treas. 1987-90, chmn. 1991—), Am. Assn. of Pediat. Plastic Surgery (founding mem., chmn. 1991—), Am. Assn. Plastic Surgery (mem. various coms.), Am. Burn Assn., Am. Cleft Palate Assn. (mem. various coms.), Am. Coll. Surgeons, Am. Soc. for Aesthetic Plastic Surgery, Am. Soc. Maxiofacial Surgery (mem. various coms.), Am. Soc. Plastic and Reconstructive Surgery (mem. various coms.), Am. Soc. for Reconstructive Microsurgery, Argentine Soc. of Plastic Surgery, Children's Craniofacial Assn. (chmn. med. adv. bd.), Chirugio Soc., Craniofacial Biology Group, Dallas County Med. Soc., Dallas Soc. Plastic Surgery, Euro. Assn. for Craniomaxillofacial Surgery, Internat. Coll. Surgeons, Internat. Confederation for Plastic Reconstructive Surgery (founding mem.), Internat. Craniofacial Club, Internat. Craniofacial Travel Club, Internat. Soc. Clin. Plastic Surgery, Internat. Soc. Cranofacial Surgery (hon. mem.), Lipoplasty Soc. of N.A., Inc., McKorkle Soc., Pan-Pacific Surg. Assn., Physicians Art Assn., Plastic Surgery Rsch. Coun., Soc. for Biomaterials, Soc. Craniofacial Genetics, Soc. Head and Neck Surgery, So. Med. Assn., Southwestern Med. Found., Tex. Soc. Plastic Surgery (mem. various coms., pres.-elect 1982-83, pres. 1983-84), Tex. State Med. Assn., Wound Healing Soc. Avocations: skiing, running, travel. Office: Internat Cranio Inst 7777 Forest Ln Ste C717 Dallas TX 75230-2550

SALYER, STEPHEN LEE, media executive; b. Lexington, Ky., July 20, 1950; s. Ralph Conley Salyer and Margaret Miles; children: Samuel Wilmot, Duncan Davis, Clara Josephine. BA, Davidson Coll., 1972; MPA, Harvard U., 1975. Pres. Citizens' Com. on Population and the Am. Future, Washington,

1972-73; cons. Rockefeller Family Assocs., N.Y.C., 1973-75; assoc. pub. issues program Population Coun., N.Y.C., 1977-79; asst. to the pres. Ednl. Broadcasting Corp., Sta. WNET TV, N.Y.C., 1975-76, v.p. corp. affairs, 1979-80, v.p. program devel. and mktg., 1981-82, sr. v.p. edn. divsn., 1982-86, sr. v.p. mktg. and comm., 1986-88; pres., CEO Pub. Radio Internat., Mpls., 1988—, also bd. dirs. Chmn. bd. dirs. Pub. Interactive, LLC, 1999—; bd. dirs. McPhail Ctr. for Music, Philanthropic Rsch., Inc. Guidestar, 2001—, Davidson Coll., 2004—; mem. nat. adv. com. Nat. Peace Found., 1991—. Co-author: (with James J. Bausch) Toward Safe, Convenient and Effective Contraceptives, 1978. Fellow Japan Soc. U.S.-Japan Leadership, 1996; mem. Nat. Commn. on Population Growth and the Am. Future, Washington, 1970-72. Root-Tilden scholar NYU Sch. Law, 1976-79; Brit.-Am. Program fellow, 1990. Mem. Harvard Club (N.Y.C.). Office: Pub Radio Internat 100 N 6th St Ste 900 A Minneapolis MN 55403-1516 Home: 1981 Sheridan Ave Minneapolis MN 55405

SALYERS, LARRY G. airport terminal executive; Dir., mgr. Tri-State Airport, Huntington, W.Va. Office: Tri-State Airport Ferguson Field 1449 Airport Rd Unit 1 Huntington WV 25704

SALZBERG, RUSS, sportscaster; b. N.Y. m. Vikki Salzberg; 2 children. Sports radio personality Sta. WFAN, Astoria, N.Y., 1993—; sportscaster Sta. WWOR-TV UPN 9 News, Secaucus, N.J. Sports anchor Sta. WOR-TV; former real estate salesman. Office: WFAN-AM Infinity Broadcasting Kaufman Astoria Studios 34-12 36th St Astoria NY 11106 also: Care Sta Wwor-Tv Upn 9 News 9 Broadcast Plz Secaucus NJ 07094-2913

SALZBERG, STEVEN, research scientist; BA in English cum laude, Yale U., 1980, MS in Computer Sci., 1982, MPhil in Computer Sci., 1984, PhD in Computer Sci., 1989. Rsch. asst., sr. knowledge engr. Applied Expert Sys., Inc., 1985—87; assoc. in rsch. Harvard Bus. Sch., 1988—89; asst. prof. dept. computer sci. Johns Hopkins U., 1989—96, assoc. prof., 1996—99, rsch. prof., 1999—; investigator Inst. for Genomic Rsch., Rockville, Md., 1997—, sr. dir. bioinformatics, 1998—. Contbr. articles to profl. jours. Achievements include development of first computational gene-finding systems for the human genome. Office: Inst for Genomic Rsch 9712 Medical Center Dr Rockville MD 20850

SALZINGER, KURT, psychology educator; b. Vienna, Nov. 15, 1929; came to U.S., 1940; AB in Psychology, NYU, 1951; AM in Psychology, Columbia U., 1952, PhD in Psychology, 1954. Cert. psychologist, N.Y. Research psychologist Linden Hill Sch. for Disturbed Adolescents, Hawthorne, 1954—56; assoc. project dir. N.Y. State Psychiatric Inst., 1956—67, prin. rsch. scientist, 1967—91; rsch. assoc in med. psychology Columbia U., N.Y.C., 1961—; assoc. prof. psychology Polytech. U., Bklyn., 1964—68, prof., 1968—92, head dept. social scis., 1981—84; prof. psychology, dir. grad. program clin./sch. psychology Hofstra U., Hempstead, NY, 1992—2001, prof. psychology emeritus, 2003—, sr. scholar in residence, 2003—. Exec. dir. Sci. Am. Psychol. Assn., 2001-03; vis. investigator Roscoe B. Jackson Meml. Lab., Bar Harbor, Maine, 1959, 60 (summers); lectr. psychology dept. Columbia U., N.Y.C., 1959-70, grad. seminar in abnormal psychology Rutgers U., 1960; vis. prof. in learning theory CUNY, 1971; program officer Applied Exptl. Psychology Sect. NSF, 1979-81; mem. numerous editorial bds. for profl. jours. Author: Psychology: the Science of Behavior, 1969, Schizophrenia Behavioral Aspects, 1973; editor: Psychology in Progress: Annals of the New York Academy of Sciences, 1976; co-editor: Research in Verbal Behavior and Some Neurophysiological Implications, 1967, Studies in Verbal Behavior, 1973, The Roots of American Psychology: Historical Influences and Implications for the Future, 1977, others; contbr. numerous articles to profl. jours. and chpts. to books; consulting editor, reviewer profl. jour. Recipient Sustained Superior Performance award, NSF, 1981. Fellow AAAS, APA (divs. 1, 3, 9, 12, 25, numerous offices and coms.), Am. Psychopathol. Assn. (Stratton award 1964), N.Y. Acad. Scis. (pres., numerous offices), Behavior Therapy and Rsch. Soc. (clin. fellow); mem. Sigma Xi, Psi Chi. Home: 161 W 75th St New York NY 10023-1801 Office: Hofstra U Hempstead NY 11550 Office Phone: 516-463-5638.

SALZMAN, ARTHUR GEORGE, architect; b. Chgo., June 20, 1929; s. Russell Harvey Salzman and Mildred Olive (Olsen) Erickson; m. Joan Marie Larson, Aug. 16, 1952; children: Lisa Jo Salzman Braucher, David Ralph. BS in Archtl. Engring., U. Ill., 1952; MArch, Ill. Inst. Tech., 1960. Registered architect, Ill., Mich., Nat. Coun. Archtl. Registration Bds. Architect Skidmore, Owings & Merrill, Chgo., 1960, Mies van der Rohe, Arch., Chgo., 1960-69; assoc. The Office of Mies Van Der Rohe, Chgo., 1969-81; v.p. FCL Assocs., Chgo., 1981-86; exec. v.p. Lohan Assocs., Chgo., 1986-91; pvt. practice Evanston, Ill., 1992—. Bldg. code restructuring com. City of Chgo., 1994-96, bldg. code electronic version com., 1997, bldg. code rev. com., 1998-2004. V.p. Chgo. area Unitarian-Universalist Coun., Chgo., 1974—76; bd. dirs. Savoy-aires, Evanston, Ill., 1985—88, 1990—93, pres., 1992—93; active Chgo. Com. on High Rise Bldgs. Cpl. U.S. Army, 1952—54. Mem. AIA (bd. dirs. Chgo. chpt. 1992-96, sec. 1994-96, Ill. region bd., alt. del. 1997-98, del. 1999-2000, Disting. Svc. award for profl. excellence 2003), Am. Soc. Testing and Materials Internat., Constrn. Specifications Inst., Internat. Code Coun. (profl.), Precast-Prestressed Concrete Inst., Cliff Dwellers Club, North Shore Musicians Club. Avocations: acting, singing. Home: 1018 Greenwood St Evanston IL 60201-4212 Office: 1603 Orrington Ave Ste 1060 Evanston IL 60201-5041 Personal E-mail: salzmanagev@att.net.

SALZMAN, DAVID ELLIOT, entertainment industry executive; b. Bklyn., Dec. 1, 1943; s. Benjamin and Rose Harriet (Touby) S.; m. Sonia Camelia Gonsalves, Oct. 19, 1968; children: Daniel Mark, Andrea Jessica, Adam Gabriel. BA, Bklyn. Coll., 1965; MA, Wayne State U., 1967. Dir. TV ops. Wayne State U., 1966-67; producer Lou Gordon Program, 1967-70; program mgr. Sta. WKBD-TV, Detroit, 1970-71, Sta. KDKA-TV, Pitts., 1971-72, gen. mgr., 1973-75; program mgr. Sta. KYW-TV, Phila., 1972-73; chmn. bd. Group W Prodns., N.Y.C and Los Angeles, 1975—; founder, pres. United Software Assocs., 1980-81; creator News Info. Weekly Service, 1981; exec. v.p. Telepictures Corp., 1980-84, vice chmn., 1984; pres. Lorimar Telepictures Corp. (merger Telepictures and Lorimar, Inc.), 1985-90, Lorimar TV, 1986-90; creator Newscope: Nat. TV News Cooperative, 1983; pres., CEO David Salzman Entertainment, Burbank, Calif., 1990-93; co-CEO Quincy Jones-David Salzman Entertainment (QDE), 1993—; exec. prodr. Jenny Jones Show, 1991—2003. Exec. prodr. Mad-TV, The Rerun Show, Jumble, In the House, 68th Ann. Acad. awards, Concert of the Americas, 1995, Vibe-TV, 1997-98, Steel, 1997; CEO David Salzman Enterprises, 1998—; co-owner Vibe Mag., 1995—, Spin Mag., 1995—, Sta. WNOL-TV, 1995—, Sta. WATL-TV, 1995—, Sta. KCWE-TV, 1995, Sta. WGRB-TV, 1998; bd. dirs. Broadwave USA, Digital Express; guest lectr. at schs.; bd. govs. Films of Coll. and Univ. Students; co-prodr. (Broadway shows) Urinetown, The Dinner Party, 2001, Into the Woods, 2002. Contbr. articles to Variety and numerous comms. trade publs. Bd. dirs. Pitts. Civic Light Opera, Am. Blood Bank, Pitts., Hebrew Inst., Jewish Community Ctr., Harrison, N.Y., Temple Etz Chaim, USC Sch. Cinema-TV, Emory U. Ctr. for Leadership, Emory Bus. Sch., Bklyn. Coll. Found., HELP group. Recipient award Detroit chpt. Am. Women in Radio and TV, 1969, award Golden Quill, 1971, award Golden Gavel, 1971, local Emmy award, 1972, award AP, 1974, Gold medal Broadcast Promotion Assn., 1983, Lifetime Achievement award Bklyn. Coll., 1990, Disting. Alumnus award, Golden Plate award Am. Acad. Achievement, 1995; BPME Gold medal San Francisco Film Festival, 1984, N.Y., 1985, Chgo., 1986, Tree of Life award Jewish Nat. Fund, 1988. Mem. Acad. TV Arts and Scis., Nat. Assn. TV Program Execs., Radio-TV News Dirs. Assn., Am. Mgmt. Assn., Am. Film Inst., Brooklyn Coll. Found. Office: Mad TV Hollywood Ctr Studios 2d Fl 1040 N Las Palmas Bldg 2 Hollywood CA 90038 E-mail: Davids@madtv.com. *"We know what we are but not what we may be."*.

SALZMAN, ERIC, composer, writer; b. N.Y.C., Sept. 8, 1933; s. Samuel and Frances (Klenett) S.; m. Lorna Jackson, Dec. 24, 1955; children: Eva, Stephanie. BA in Music with honors, Columbia U., 1954; MFA, Princeton U., 1956. Music critic N.Y. Times, N.Y.C., 1958-62; dir. music Sta. WBAI-FM, N.Y.C., 1962—63, 1968—72; music critic N.Y. Herald Tribune, N.Y.C., 1963-66; asst. prof. Queens Coll. CUNY, Queens, 1966-68; artistic dir. Quog Music Theater, N.Y.C., 1970-80; co-founder, artistic dir. Am. Music Theater Festival, Phila., 1982-94; asst. artistic dir. Contemporary Opera, 1999—. Mem. guest faculty NYU, Yale U., Banff Ctr. for Arts, Can., Conservatoire Nationale, Lyon, France; assoc. artistic dir. Ctr. Contemporary Opera, 2000—; founder, artistic dir. Electric Ear, Electric Circus, N.Y.C., 1967-68, New Image of Sound, Hunter Coll., N.Y.C., 1968-71, Free Music Store, N.Y.C., 1968-72. Prin. works include (compositions) String Quartet, 1955, Sonata for Flute and Piano, 1956, Night Dance for Orch., 1957, Whitman Songs for Voice and Piano, 1955—57, Partita for Violin, 1958, Cummings Set for Voice and Piano, 1958, Inventions for Orch., 1957, In Praise of the Owl and the Cuckoo for Soprano, Guitar, Violin, and Viola, 1963, Foxes and Hedgehogs, Verses and Cantos for 4 Voices, two Instrumental Groups with Sound Sys., 1964, Queens Collage, An Acad. Festival Overture for Tape, 1966, Larynx Music, Verses for Soprano, Guitar, and 4 track Tape, 1966, Helix, 1971, Fantasy on Lazarus, 1974, Accord, 1975, Variations on Sacred Harp Tunes, 1982, and numerous others, (radio opera) Voices, 1971, (mime-dance prodn.) The Peloponnesian War, 1967, (multimedia participatory work) Feedback, 1968, The Nude Paper Sermon, 1969, (multimedia environ. work) Can Man Survive?, 1969—71, (media poem) Ecolog, 1972, (musical theater prodn.) Saying Something, 1972, Biografitti, 1972, Lazarus, 1973, (with Michael Sahl) The Conjurer, 1974, Stauf, 1974, Noah, 1978, The Passion of Simple Simon, 1979, Boxes, 1982 (Seagram Prodn. award), (opera buffa) Civilization and its Discontents, 1980 (Prix Italia award Assn European Broadcasters), (with Ned Jackson) Big Jim and the Small-time Investors, 1986, (with Valeria Vasilevski) The True Last Words of Dutch Schultz, 1996, (with Michel Rostain) La Prière du Loup (Wolfman Prayer), 1997, (adaptations) Strike Up the Band, 1984, Love Life, 1990, The Silent Twins, 1992, prodr., dir (with Teresa Stratas) The Unknown Kurt Weill, (with Joel Grey and N.Y.C. Opera) Silverlake, Civilization and its Discontents, The Tango Project (Record of Yr. award Stereo Rev.), Two to Tango, The Palm Court, The Waltz Project, Moore's Irish Melodies, A Portrait Album, Notebooks of Anna Magdalena Bach, An Old-Fashioned Christmas, Revelation in the Courthouse Park, Casino Paradise, recs. include Civilization and its Discontents, Wiretap, The Nude Paper Sermon, Noah, Accord; author: 20th Century Music: An Introduction, 1967, (4th edit.), 2001, (translated into Spanish, Portuguese, Hungarian, and Japanese); editor: Musical Quar., 1984—91; contbg. editor, critic Stereo Rev., N.Y.C., 1970—99; contbr. N.Y. Times, New York Herald-Tribune, N.Y. Mag., others; composer: (commns., premiers) Can., 1995, France, 1997, The Netherlands, 1997; composer: (with Francois Godin) Abel Gance à New York, 1999—; composer: music for La Bonne Ame de Jetchouan (Bertolt Brecht), 2003—04; with Eva Salzman Cassandra, 2001, with Valeria Vasilevski The Jukebox in the Tavern of Love, 2002; arranger French version: commns., premiers Strike Up the Band, 2000. Fulbright scholar St. Cecilia Acad., 1956-58, Darmstadt Ferienkurse, 1957; recipient Armstrong, Prix Italia radio awards, Sang prize for criticism. Mem. South Fork Nat. History Soc. (mem. coun.). Avocations: natural history, ornithology. Home: 29 Middagh St Brooklyn NY 11201-1339 E-mail: esalzman@aba.org.

SALZMAN, ROBERT JAY, accountant; b. Bklyn., Dec. 7, 1941; s. Irving and Sydelle (Feingold) S.; m. Constance A. Freeman, Sept. 16, 1990. BA, Allegheny Coll., Meadville, Pa., 1962; MBA, U. Pa., 1965; JD, N.Y. Law Sch., 1972. Bar: N.Y. 1973; CPA, N.Y. Acct., N.Y.C., 1965—; pvt. practice Robert J. Salzman, CPA, P.C., N.Y.C., 1970—. Home: 10 E End Ave New York NY 10021-1106 also: 82 Sycamore Dr East Hampton NY 11937-1482 also: 2801 NE 183rd St Miami FL 33160-2100 Office Phone: 212-744-2860. E-mail: rsalzman@rjspc.com.

SAM, DAVID, federal judge; b. Hobart, Ind., Aug. 12, 1933; s. Andrew and Flora (Toma) S.; m. Betty Jean Brennan, Feb. 1, 1957; children: Betty Jean, David Dwight, Daniel Scott, Tamara Lynn, Pamela Rae, Daryl Paul, Angie, Sheyla. BS, Brigham Young U., 1957; JD, Utah U., 1960. Bar: Utah 1960, U.S. Dist. Ct. Utah 1966. Sole practice and ptnr., Duchesne, Utah, 1963-76; dist. judge State of Utah, 1976-85; judge U.S. Dist. Ct. Utah, Salt Lake City, 1985-97; chief judge U.S. Dist. Ct., Salt Lake City, 1997—99, sr. judge, 1999—. Atty. City of Duchesne, 1963-72; Duchesne County atty., 1966-72; commr. Duchesne, 1972-74; adv. com. Codes of Conduct of Jud. Conf. US, 1987-91, Jud. Coun. of 10th Cir., 1991-93; mem. US Del. to Romania, Aug. 1991. Chmn. Jud. Nomination Com. for Cir. Ct. Judge, Provo, Utah, 1983; bd. dirs. Water Resources, Salt Lake City, 1973-76. Served to capt. JAGC, USAF, 1961-63. Named Judge of Yr., Utah State Bar, 1999. Mem. Utah Bar Assn., Supreme Ct. Hist. Soc., Am. Inns of Ct. VII (counselor 1986-89), A. Sherman Christensen Am. Inn of Ct. I (counselor 1989-98), Utah Jud. Conf. (chmn. 1982), Utah Dist. Judges Assn. (pres. 1982-83), Order of Coif (hon. Brigham Young U. chpt.); J. Ruben Clark Law Soc. Salt Lake Chpt., (adv. bd. 2002—), Utah Valley State Coll. (adv. bd. legal studies dept., 2003-). Mem. Lds Ch. Avocations: beekeeping, reading, sports. Office: US Dist Ct US Courthouse 350 S Main St Ste 441 Salt Lake City UT 84101-2180 Office Phone: 801-524-6190. Business E-Mail: davidsam@utd.uscourts.gov.

SAMAHA, ELIE, producer, film company executive, business owner; b. Beirut; came to U.S., 1981; Bouncer Studio 54; owner Celebrity Cleaners, Los Angeles, 1982—; ptnr. club Roxbury, 1990—; CEO, chmn. Franchise Pictures, Burbank, Calif. Producer, exec. producer over 40 films. With Lebanese Christian Army. Office: Sound of Thunder Franchise Pix 8228 Sunset Blvd #308 Los Angeles CA 90046

SAMANT, VIJAY B. biotechnology company executive; BS Chem. Engring., U. Bombay, 1975; MS Chem. Engring., Columbia U., 1977; MBA, MIT, 1983. Numerous pos., including CEO vaccine divsn. Merck & Co., Inc., 1977—2000; pres., CEO, dir. Vical Inc., San Diego, 2000—. Adv. coun. Ctr. Advanced Study of India U. Pa.; dean's adv. engring. coun. sch. engring. & applied sci. Columbia U., vis. com. chem. engring. Office: Vical Inc 10390 Pacific Center Ct San Diego CA 92121-4340

SAMARTINI, JAMES ROGERS, retired appliance company executive; b. Cleve., Apr. 13, 1935; s. Leonard Henry and Grace Rogers (Tully) S.; m. Irene Ann Kurnava, Sept. 16, 1961 (dec. June 1994); m. Julia S. Rubin, Sept. 8, 1996; children: David L., James F., Patrick R. AB, Dartmouth Coll., 1957; MBA, Harvard U., 1961. Fin. supr. Ford Motor Co., Dearborn, Mich., 1966-72; v.p. fin. and adminstrn. Thonet Industries Inc., York, Pa., 1972-74; from asst. controller to v.p., CFO Mead Corp., Dayton, 1974-86; CFO Whirlpool Corp., 1986-91, exec. v.p., chief adminstrv. officer, 1991-95; ret., 1995. Bd. dirs. Peoples State Bank, St. Joseph, Mich., 1987-95. Trustee Troashron Marvelwood Sch., 2004—, The Marvelwood Sch., 2004—; mem. adv. bd. Salvation Army; chmn. bd. trustees Whirlpool Found., 1993—95; trustee Dayton Opera Assn., 1977—86, pres., 1985—86; bd. dirs. Epilepsy Assn. We. Ohio, 1986, S.W. Mich. Symphony Orch., 1991—93; mem. bd. fin. Town of Kent (Conn.), 1999—, mem. zoning bd. appeals, 2001—. Mem.: Kent. Libr. Assn. (bd. dirs., treas. 2002—), Fin. Execs. Inst. (bd. dirs. 1983—86). Home: PO Box 129 South Kent CT 06785-0129

SAMBERG, ARTHUR (ART) J. investment company executive; BS, MIT; MS, Stanford U.; MBA, Columbia U. Bd. mem. Coll. Summit's Nat. Bd. Dirs. Mem.: MIT Corp.*

SAMBOL, DAVID, diversified financial services company executive; BBA in Acctg., Calif. State U., 1982. CPA. Acct. Ernst & Whinney; with Countrywide Fin. Corp., Calabasas, Calif., 1985—94, mng. dir. capital markets, 1994—2000, sr. mng. dir., chief prodn., 2000—02, exec. mng. dir. loans & capital markets, 2003—. Bd. dirs. Countrywide Home Loans, Inc., Balboa Life & Casualty, Countrywide Fin. Holding Co., Inc. Office: Countrywide Fin Corp 4500 Park Granada Calabasas CA 91302-1613

SAMBUR, MARVIN, federal agency administrator; B in Elec. Engring., CCNY, 1968; M in Elec. Engring., MIT, 1969, PhD in Elec. Engring., 1972. Tech. staff mem. Bell Labs., Murray Hill, NJ, 1968—77; sr. v.p. ITT Def. Comms., Nutley, NJ, 1977—88; pres., gen. mgr. electron tech. divsn. ITT, Easton, Pa., 1988—91, pres., gen. mgr. aerospace/comms. divsn. Ft. Wayne, Ind., 1991—98; pres., CEO ITT Def., McLean, Va., 1998—2001; asst. sec. for acquisition/svc. acquisition exec. Dept. Def., USAF, Washington, 2001—. Recipient Golden Apple award, 1999, Outstanding Leadership award, Inst. Environ. Mgmt. and Assessment, 1994. Mem.: IEEE (Centennial award), Acoustical Soc. Am., Eta Kappa Nu, Tau Beta Pi. Office: Dept of Def Asst Sec AF 1060 Air Force Pentagon Washington DC 20330-1060

SAMBURG, A. GENE, security company executive; b. Indpls., Apr. 25, 1941; s. A. George and Hermine (Wittgenstein) S.; m. Lorrie Silverman, June 26, 1966; children: Kimberly Jill, Thomas Blair. BEE, Cornell U., 1964; OPM, Harvard U., 1985. Engr. Westinghouse Corp., 1964-72; founder, pres. and CEO Kastle Systems, Inc., 1972—. Adv. on bus. programs Cornell U.; lectr. on entrepreneurship Georgetown U.; spl. lectr. for numerous profl. and ednl. courses in field. Patentee in field. Named E&Y Master Entrepreneur of Yr., Washington, 1999. Mem. IEEE, ASME, CPP, Am. Soc. Indsl. Security, Woodmont Country Club, City Club (Washington), Tower Club (McLean, Va.). Home: 1401 N Oak St Arlington VA 22209 Office: Kastle Systems Inc 1501 Wilson Blvd Arlington VA 22209-2403 E-mail: gene@kastle.com.

SAMEK, EDWARD LASKER, service company executive; b. N.Y.C., Oct. 26, 1936; s. Richard E. and Jane L. Samek; m. Marthann Lauver, June 26, 1960; children: Anne, Margaret, Elizabeth. BS in Commerce and Fin., Bucknell U., 1958; MBA, Columbia U., 1960. Brand mgr. Procter & Gamble Co., Cin., 1960-62; dir. new products Johnson & Johnson, New Brunswick, NJ, 1962-67; v.p., gen. mgr. Avon Products Inc., N.Y.C., 1967-75; pres., CEO Childcraft Edn. Corp., Edison, NJ, 1975-78, also dir.; pres. Hudson Pharm. Corp., West Caldwell, 1978-82; CEO, chmn. bd., pres. Secrephone Ltd., Ft. Washington, Pa., 1982-94, exec. v.p., 1994-95; chmn., pres., CEO Medifax SecrePhone, Atlanta, 1995-96; chmn., CEO The MRC Group, Cleve., 1996-98; vice chmn. Medquist Inc., Marlton, NJ, 1998—. Bd. dir. A. Gary Shilling & Co., MedPlus, Inc., Cin., VeriText LLC, Alliance Imaging, Inc., Anaheim, Calif., Third Millenniam Healthcare, Atlanta, N.Am. Mgmt. Corp., Boston. Pres. bd. trustees Hartridge Sch., Plainfield, NJ, 1969-76; v.p. bd. trustees Wardlaw-Hartridge Sch., Plainfield and Edison, 1975—; trustee, v.p. bd. Plainfield Symphony, 1976-86; trustee Friends of Acadia, 2003—. Served with Ordinance Corps, U.S. Army, 1958-59. Mem. Young Pres. Orgn., Princeton Club, World Pres. Orgn. Home and Office: 1717 Woodland Ave Edison NJ 08820-1039

SAMELSON, JUDY, editor; Editor Playbill, N.Y.C., 1993—. Office: Playbill 52 Vanderbilt Ave Fl 11 New York NY 10017-3870

SAMER, BILL FRED CARL, illustrator, writer, multimedia designer; b. Elizabeth, NJ, Sept. 2, 1953; s. Fred Carl and Myrtle Edith (Levey) Samer. BA, Concordia Coll., Bronxville, N.Y., 1994; MA, Kean U. N.J., Union, 1980; AA in multimedia design, Union Coll., Cranford, N.J., 2004. Editor Top of the Stairs; founder Gracevine, 1975—. Author: Moongate, 2003, UK, for Mother, 2003. Walker CROP, Clifton, NJ, 1978; vol. I Found It TV campaign, NY, 1976; active Interfaith Hospitality Network, 2003, Am. Cancer Soc., 2004, William Samer Activist Orgn., 1987, Am. Leukemia Soc, 2004; del. to conv. Luth. Ch.-Mo. Synod, Ridgewood, NJ, 1976. Mem.: TV and Film Prodn. Club (dir.). Avocations: hiking, volleyball, cd's, Open mic poetry reading. Home and Office: Gracevine/WHAT 936 Louisa St Union NJ 07083-6725

SAMET, DEE-DEE, lawyer; b. Greensboro, N.C., Sept. 18, 1940; BA, U. Ariz., 1962, JD, 1963. Bar: Ariz. 1964. Ptnr. Samet & Gage, P.C., Tucson, 2001; pvt. practice Tucson, 2001—. Arbitrator U.S. Dist. Ct. Ariz., Gender Equality Task Force, 1993; judge pro tem Pima County Superior Ct., 1985—; Ninth Cir. Lawyer rep., 1990-93; mem. Jud. Performance Rev. Commn., 1996-99; pres. Casa de los Ninos, 2003-04. Mem. State Bar Ariz. (family law sect., workers compensation sect., trial law sect., co-chair worker's compensation sect. 1988-89, gender bias task force, bd. govs. 1994-97, pres.-elect, pres. 1999-2000), Nat. Panel Arbitrators, Am. Arbitration Assn. (com. on exams., supreme ct. state Ariz. 1984-91), Pima County Bar Assn. (bd. dirs. 1994—), Nat. Assn. Coun. for Children, Ariz. Assn. Coun. for Children, So. Ariz. Fed. Bar Assn. (exec. com. 1995—, v.p. Tucson chpt. 2003-04, pres. 2004), So. Ariz. Women Lawyers Assn. (bd. dirs. 1990, pres. 1994-95, treas. alt. dispute resolution sect. 2003-04, chmn.-elect 2004), Nat. Orgn. Social Security Claimants' Reps. Office: Dee-Dee Samet PC 717 N 6th Ave Tucson AZ 85705-8304 Office Phone: 520-624-8595. Business E-Mail: deedee@samet.psemoil.com.

SAMET, JACK I. lawyer; b. N.Y.C., Aug. 6, 1940; s. William and Tillie (Katz) S.; m. Helen Ray, Feb. 12, 1967; 1 son, Peter Lawrence. BA, Columbia U., 1961; JD, Harvard U., 1964. Bar: N.Y. 1964, Calif. 1973. Assoc. Whitman & Ransom, N.Y.C., 1966-69, Hall, Casey, Dickler & Howley, N.Y.C., 1969-73; ptnr. Ball, Hunt, Hart, Brown & Baerwitz, L.A., 1973-81, Buchalter, Nemer, Fields & Younger, L.A., 1981-94, Baker & Hostetler, L.A., 1994—, mem. policy com., 1997-98; ptnr.-in-charge L.A., 1997-98. Arbitrator Nat. Assn. Securities Dealers, L.A., 1976—; speaker, panelist Calif. Continuing Edn. of Bar, 1988. Named a So. Calif. Superlawyer, 2004. Mem. ABA, Sports Club/L.A., Million Dollar Advocates Forum, Am. Bd. Trial Advocates. Avocations: exercise, reading. Home: 2741 Aqua Verde Cir Los Angeles CA 90077-1502 Office: 333 S Grand Ave Los Angeles CA 90071-1504 E-mail: jsamet@bakerlaw.com.

SAMET, JONATHAN MICHAEL, epidemiologist, educator; b. Va., Mar. 26, 1946; AB in Chemistry and Physics, Harvard Coll., 1966; MD, U. Rochester, 1970; MS in Epidemiology, Harvard Sch. Pub Health, 1977. Diplomate Am. Bd. of Internal Medicine, Nat. Bd. Med. Examiners. Intern in medicine U. Ky. Med. Ctr., Lexington, 1970-71; asst. resident in medicine U. N.Mex. Affiliated Hosps., Albuquerque, 1973-74, sr. resident, 1974-75; rsch. fellow in clin. epidemiology Channing lab. Harvard Med. Sch., Boston, 1975-78, rsch. assoc. in medicine, 1978-83; epidemiologist Cancer Rsch. and Treatment Ctr. U. N.Mex., Albuquerque, 1980-87, asst. prof. medicine, 1978-82, assoc. prof. medicine, 1982-88, assoc. prof. family, cmty., and emergency medicine, 1985-88, prof. family, cmty., and emergency medicine, 1986-94, prof. medicine, 1988-94, clin. prof. medicine, 1994—; prof., chmn. dept. epidemiology The Johns Hopkins U., Balt., 1994—, co-dir. risk scis. and pub. policy inst., 1995—. Chief pulmonary divsn. U. N.Mex. Hosp., Albuquerque, 1985-94, chief pulmonary and critical care divsn. dept. medicine, 1986-94; mem. indoor air quality and total human exposure com., sci. adv. bd. U.S. EPA, 1987-95; chmn. biol. effects of ionizing radiation VI com. NRC, 1994-98, mem. bd. environ. studies and toxicology, 2002, chmn., 2003; Inst. Medicine, 1997; chmn. com. on rsch. priorities for airborne particulate matter, NRC, 1998-2004; chmn. epidemiology and disease control study sect. 2 NIH, 2002. Editor pro tem Am. Jour. of Epidemiology, 1991—92; editor: Am. Jour. of Epidemiology, 1992—98; assoc. editor Tobacco Control: An Internat. Jour., 1991—; editor: Epidemiologic Revs., 1994—2002, Epidemiology, 2002—. With U.S. Army, 1971-73. Recipient Clinton P. Anderson award Am. Lung Assn. N.Mex., 1988, Surgeon Gen.'s medallion, 1990, Award for Excellence in Environ. Health Rsch. The Lovelace Inst., 1996, Inst. of Medicine, Nat. Acad. Scis., 1997. Fellow: AAAS, Am. Coll. Epidemiology (pres. 2000—01); mem.: Md. Thoracic Soc., Internat. Soc. of Indoor Air Quality and Climate, Internat. Epidemiol. Assn., N.Mex. Thoracic Soc. (sec.-treas. 1982—83, v.p. 1983—84, pres. 1984—85), Am. Thoracic Soc. (long range planning com. environ. and occupational health assembly 1992—, program com. behavioral scis. sect. 1994—95), Soc. for Epidemiol. Rsch. (pres.-elect 1988—89, pres. 1989—90, exec. com. 1988—91), Delta Omega Alpha, Alpha Omega Alpha. Office: Dept Epidemiology The Johns Hopkins U 615 N Wolfe St Ste W6041 Baltimore MD 21205-2103 Office Phone: 410-955-3286. Business E-Mail: jsamet@jhsph.edu.

SAMET, KENNETH ALAN, hospital administrator; b. Bklyn., Mar. 17, 1958; married. BA, Old Dominion U., 1990; MA, U. Mich., 1982. Adminstrv. intern Mt. Vernon Hosp., Fairfax, Va., 1981; adminstrv. resident Washington Hosp. Ctr., 1982-83, pres., 1991—; asst. to pres. Washington Health Care Corp., 1983-85, dir. system devel., 1985-86; v.p. system devel. Medlantic Health Care Group, Washington, 1986-88, exec. v.p. systems, bus. devel., 1988-91; pres. Medlantic Enterprises, Washington, 1988-91; exec. v.p., COO

Medlantic Health Care Group, 1991—. Mem. D.C. Hosp. Assn., Md. Hosp. Assn., Va. Hosp. Assn. (bd. dirs.). Home: 9041 Holly Leaf Ln Bethesda MD 20817-2657 Office: Washington Hosp Ctr 110 Irving St NW Rm 2a2 Washington DC 20010-2975

SAMFORD, YETTA GLENN, JR., lawyer, director; b. Opelika, Ala., June 8, 1923; s. Yetta Glenn and Mary Elizabeth (Denson) S.; m. Mary Austill, Sept. 6, 1949; children: Mary Austill Lott, Katherine Park Alford, Yetta Glenn III (dec.). BS, Ala. Poly. Inst., 1947; LLB, U. Ala., 1949, LLD (hon.), 1995; DHL (hon.), U. Mobile, 2001. Bar: Ala. 1949, U.S. Dist. Ct. (mid. dist.) Ala. 1950, U.S. Ct. Appeals (5th cir.) 1961, U.S. Ct. Appeals (11th cir.) 1981. Since practiced in, Opelika; ptnr. Samford, Denson, Horsley, Pettey, Bridges & Hughes (& predecessors), 1949—. Mem. Ala. Senate from Lee and Russell counties, 1958-62; mem. State of Ala. Bd. of Corrections, 1969-75; mem. adv. bd. State Docks, 1987-2000. Trustee U. Mobile, 1963-92, life trustee, 1992—, trustee U. Ala., 1972-93, trustee emeritus, 1993—. Mem. Ala. Law Inst. Coun., Ala. Acad. of Honor, Masons, Phi Delta Phi, Omicron Delta Kappa, Alpha Tau Omega. Republican. Baptist. Home: 615 Terracewood Dr Opelika AL 36801-3850 Office: Samford Denson Horsley Pettey Bridges & Hughes PO Box 2345 Opelika AL 36803-2345 E-mail: sdhpb@mindspring.com.

SAMIOS, NICHOLAS PETER, physicist; b. N.Y.C., Mar. 15, 1932; s. Peter and Niki (Vatick) S.; m. Mary Linakis, Jan. 12, 1958; children: Peter, Gregory, Alexandra. AB, Columbia U., 1953, PhD, 1957. Instr. physics Columbia U., N.Y.C., 1956-59; asst. physicist Brookhaven Nat. Lab., Upton, NY, 1959-62, assoc. physicist, 1962-64, physicist, 1964-68, sr. physicist, 1968—, group leader, 1965-75, chmn. dept. physics, 1975-81, dep. dir. for high energy and nuclear physics, 1981, dir., 1982-97, dep. dir. RIKEN/BNL Rsch. Ctr., 1998—. Adj. prof. Stevens Inst. Tech., 1969-75, Columbia U., 1970—; dep. dir. RIKEN BNL Rsch. Ctr. Contbr. articles in field to profl. jours. Bd. dirs. Stony Brook Found., 1989, L.I. Assn., 1989. Recipient E.O. Lawrence Meml. award, 1980, award in physics and math. scis. N.Y. Acad. Scis., 1980; named AUI Disting. Scientist, 1992, W.K.H. Panofsky prize, 1993. Fellow Am. Phys. Soc. (chmn. divsn. of particles and fields 1975-76, chmn. PEP exptl. program com. 1976-78); mem. Internat. Ctr. Future Acceleration, Akademia Athenon (corr.). Achievements include being an expert in field of high energy particle and nuclear physics. Office: RIKEN/BNL Rsch Ctr Bldg 510A, Physics Dept Brookhaven Natl Lab Upton NY 11973-5000 E-mail: samios@bnl.gov.

SAMMARCO, PAUL WILLIAM, ecologist, researcher; b. Hackensack, N.J., Oct. 18, 1948; s. Giacomo and Esther (Galanti) S.; m. Jean Sogioka, May 29, 1971 (div. 1996); children: Mimi Cecile, Dustin Paul, Jack Isao; m. Donna M. Melancon, Aug. 12, 1998; stepchildren: Lindsay Claire, Ben Charles. BA, Syracuse U., 1970, postgrad., 1970—71; cert., Marine Biology Lab., Woods Hole, Mass., 1971; cert. Fairleigh Dickinson U., W.I. Lab., U.S.V.I., 1972; PhD, SUNY, Stony Brook, 1977. Teaching asst. Syracuse (N.Y.) U., 1970-71; teaching asst. Discovery Bay Marine Lab. SUNY-Stony Brook Overseas Acad. Program, Jamaica, 1974; teaching asst. SUNY, Stony Brook, 1971-77; asst. prof. Clarkson U., Potsdam, N.Y., 1977-79; vis. asst. prof. tropical ecology in St. Croix, V.I., SUNY Potsdam, 1979; sr. rsch. scientist Australian Inst. Marine Sci., Townsville, Queensland, 1979-89; coord. Shelf Seas Rsch. Program, 1985-86; dir. environ. rsch. of Resource Assessment Commn. Prime Minister's commn. on natural resources, Canberra, Australia, 1989-91; exec. dir. La. Univs. Marine Consortium, Chauvin, 1991-95, prof., 1995—. Adj. prof. La. State U., U. La. at Lafayette, U. New Orleans, Nicholls State U., U. Campinas-Brazil, 1997-99, Ctrl. Queensland U., Australia, 1997-2002, U. Maine at Orono, 2001—03; pres. Endless Shores Music Pubs.; pres. P&J Records, LLC. Composer, arranger, prodr. popular and sacred music; former mem. Australian Chamber Choir, Wesley Choir, Canberra; editor (with M.L. Heron) The Bio-Physics of Marine Larval Dispersal, 1994, Marine Biology (Berlin), 2000—; contbr. numerous articles to profl. jours.; editl. advisor Marine Ecology Progress Series, 1985-93; co-editor Proceedings 6th Internat. Coral Reef Symposium, 1988, Procs. 8th Internat. Coral Reef Symposium. Mem. chancel choir First United Meth. Ch., Houma, La. Recipient Internat. Sci. Exch. award, 1988-89. Mem. ASCAP, Australian Marine Scis. Assn. (keynote spkr. 1981, counselor 1984-89, chmn., organizer nat. conf. 1987, chmn. Australia Acad. Sci. Boden Conf. 1990), Internat. Soc. Reef Studies (counselor 1997-2000), Australian Coral Reef Soc., Sigma Xi. Home: 200 Greenwood St Houma LA 70364-4542 Office: La Univs Marine Consortium 8124 Highway 56 Chauvin LA 70344-2110 Office Phone: 985-851-2876. Business E-Mail: psammarco@lumcon.edu.

SAMMET, JEAN E. computer scientist; b. N.Y.C. d. Harry and Ruth S. BA, Mt. Holyoke Coll., Sc.D. (hon.), 1978; MA, U. Ill. Group leader programming Sperry Gyroscope, Great Neck, N.Y., 1955-58; sect. head, staff cons. programming Sylvania Electric Products, Needham, Mass., 1958-61; with IBM, 1961-88; adv. program mgr. Boston, 1961-65; program lang. tech. mgr. IBM, 1965-68; programming tech. planning mgr. Fed. Systems div., 1968-74, programming lang. tech. mgr., 1974-79, software tech. mgr., 1979-81, div. software tech. mgr., 1981-82, programming lang. tech. mgr., 1983-88; programming lang. cons. Bethesda, Md., 1989—. Chmn. history of computing com. Am. Fedn. Info. Processing Socs., 1977-79; mem. exec. com. Software Patent Inst., 1991—, edn. com., 1992—, chair edn. com., 1992-93; bd. dirs. Computer Mus., 1983-93. Author: Programming Languages: History and Fundamentals, 1969; editor-in-chief: Assn. Computing Machinery Computing Revs, 1979-87; contbr. articles to profl. jours. Fellow Assn. for Computing Machinery, 1994, (charter, pres. 1974-76, Disting. Svc. award 1985), Computer History Mus.; mem. NAE, Upsilon Pi Epsilon. Home and Office: 3124 Gracefield Rd Apt 311 Silver Spring MD 20904-5818

SAMMIS, ANNE MIMI, sculptor, artist; b. Pitts., July 9, 1940; d. Jesse Fleet and Anne Candler (Baker) S.; m. Lee W. Patterson, Feb. 14, 1960 (div. 1969); m. Avery Rockefeller, Jr., Mar. 3, 1971 (dec. Dec. 1979). Grad. high sch., Middlebury, Conn. One-woman shows include Wally Findlay Gallery, N.Y.C., 1980, UN, N.Y.C., 1998, 2001, Capitol Bldg., Madison, Wis., 1999, Newport (R.I.) Art Mus., 2002, U. R.I., Kingston, 2003; exhibited in group shows, including The Hague, The Netherlands, 1998, Nat. Sculpture Soc., N.Y.C., 2002, Prague Am. Embassy, Czech Republic, 2003-2004; represented in over 400 pub. and pvt. permanent collections in Am. and Europe, including Aspen (Colo.) Chapel, Rio Grand Trail, Aspen, Brockton (Mass.) Hosp., Unity Sch. Christianity, Unity Village, Mo., Women and Infants Hosp., Providence, Dance Aspen, Children's Mus., Providence, Town of Narragansett, R.I., Archbishop Canterbury Lambeth Palace, Eng.; prin. works in bronze range from 1 to 22 feet, incorporating fountains and moveable figures, including R.I. Women Vets. Meml., Exeter, R.I., Embrace of Life II, Rainbow of Souls, Three Dancing Children, Dancing on the World, Visitation, Dance of Peace. Recipient Artist of Merit award Courthouse Ctr. for Arts, Kingston, R.I., 2000. Studio: PO Box 335 Narragansett RI 02882 Office Phone: 401-682-2389. E-mail: mimisammis@yahoo.com.

SAMMON, WILLIAM JOSEPH, historian, consultant; b. Cleve., May 6, 1966; s. Martin Joseph and Abigail Clare Sammon; life ptnr. BS in History, U. Notre Dame, 1988, MA in Internat. Peace Studies, 1992; MA in Area Studies S.E. Asia, U. London, 1994; postgrad. in History, U. Hawaii, 1997—. Cert. fed. legal rschr. Congl. Rsch. Svc. Congl. rsch. asst. Senator John Glenn, U.S. Senate, Washington, 1993; mng. dir. Cortech Ohio, Cleve., 1994-96; v.p. Asian Ops., Advanced Gaming Technologies, Inc., Manila, 1996-98; U. Hawaii doctoral fellow Bangkok, 1999-2001; mng. ptnr. b2b Consulting, Bangkok, 2001—. Vol. U.S. Peace Corps, Samut Prakarn, Thailand, 1988-90; Dem. party campaign advisor 10th Congl. Dist., Cleve, 1994. John. J. Gilligan fellow in internat. peace studies, Joan Kroc Inst. Internat. Peace Studies, 1991-92, Congl. fellow LBJ Found., 1993, Asia Pacific fellow, U. Hawaii Found., 1998; Fgn. Lang. Area Studies grantee Sch. Hawaiian, Asian and Pacific Studies, 1999-2001. Mem. Siam Soc., Ancient Soc. Cogers (London, sec. 1993-94). Libertarian. Roman Catholic. Avocations: cooking, reading, travel. Office: b2b Consulting Unit 15C 1867/73 Charoen Nakorn Rd KLNGSRN Bangkok 10660 Thailand

SAMMONS, ELAINE D. manufacturing executive; m. Charles A. Sammons (dec. 1988). Chmn. Sammons Enterprises, Inc., Dallas, 1988—. Chmn. bd. Sammons Ctr. for the Arts, Dallas, 1988—. Office: Sammons Enterprises Inc 5949 Sherry Ln Ste 1900 Dallas TX 75225-8015

SAMMONS, MARY F. retail executive; b. Portland, Oreg., Oct. 12, 1946; d. Lee W. and Ann (Cherry) Jackson; m. Nickolas F. Sammons, Sept. 12, 1967; 1 child, Peter. BA, Marylhurst Coll., 1970. Buyer Fred Meyer Inc., Portland, 1975-80, v.p., merchandiser, 1980-85, sr. v.p., softgoods div. mgr., from 1986, sr. v.p., apparel & home electronics group, 1996, exec. v.p., apparel, home & home electronics group, 1997—98; pres. Fred Meyer Stores, Portland, 1998, pres., CEO, 1999; pres., COO Rite Aid Corp., Camp Hill, Pa., 1999—2003, pres., CEO, 2003—. Chmn. Nat. Assoc. Chain Drug Stores. Named Woman of Achievement, YWCA, Portland, 1987. Mem. Am. Mgmt. Assn. Office: Rite Aid Corp 30 Hunter Ln Camp Hill PA 17011*

SAMO, AMANDO, bishop; b. Moch Island, Federated States of Micronesia, Aug. 16, 1948; s. Benito and Esiper Samo. BA in Psychology, Chaminade U., 1973; diploma in religious edn., EAPI, Manila, Philippines, 1982. Ordained priest Roman Cath. Ch. Parish priest Cath. Ch., Truk, Afghanistan, 1977—87; aux. bishop Diocese of the Carolines and Marshalls, Truk, 1987—95, bishop, 1995—. Founder, bd. dirs. Marriage Encounter-Carolines-Marshalls, Truk, 1982—88, dir. ch. leadership tng. programs, 1986—; mem. Bishop's Conf. Oceania, 1988; pontificial commn. Cor Unum, Rome, Rome, 1995. Chmn. Chmn. Bishop's commn. justice and devel., 1995. Roman Catholic. Home: PO Box 939 Chuuk FM 96942-0939 Office: Diocese Caroline Is PO Box 250 Chuuk FM 96942-0250

SAMOJLIK, EUGENIUSZ, medical educator, clinical researcher; b. Kuchmy-Bialystok, Poland, Aug. 20, 1933; s. Michael and Anastazia S.; m. Anna Morozewicz, Apr. 10, 1965; children: Dorothy, Michael. BS in Biomedicine, U. Warsaw, 1958, PhD in Reproductive Endocrinology, 1964. Rsch. asst. Maternity Inst. Dept. Pharmacology, Warsaw, 1958-62, sr. asst., 1962-66; asst. prof., chief reproductive pharmacology & toxicology Inst. Pharmacy Dept. Pharmacology, Warsaw, 1966-70; assoc. prof., chief hormone rsch. lab. Med. Acad. Dept. Clin. Endocrinology, Warsaw, 1970-73; staff rschr. II Syntex, Inc. Rsch. Divsn., Palo Alto, Calif., 1974-75; asst. prof. physiology, dir. radioimmunoassay lab. Milton S. Hershey (Pa.) Med. Ctr., Divsn. Endocrinology, 1975-80; staff endocrinologist VA Med. Ctr. Dept. Medicine, Sect. Endocrinology, East Orange, N.J., 1980-82; dir. endocrine lab. Newark Beth Israel Med. Ctr., Dept. Medicine, 1982-92; assoc. prof. medicine divsn. endocrinology U. Medicine & Dentistry-N.J. Med. Sch., Newark, 1982—; chief endocrine lab. dept. Labs. NBIMC, 1994-96. Vis. researcher UCLA Sch. Medicine, Torrance, Calif., 1973; vis. scientist Nat. Inst. Child Health Human Devel., Reproductive Br., Bethesda, Md., 1973-74; lectr. in field. Mem. internat. adv. bd. Jour. Assisted Reproductive Tech. and Andrology, mem. editorial bd., 1996; contbr. articles to profl. jours. Grantee WHO, 1973-74, Ciba-Geigy, 1982-83, Nat. Cancer Inst., 1983-86, 85-88; tng. program fellow Worcester Found. Experimental Biology, Shrewsbury, Mass., 1967-69. Mem. AAAS, Am. Soc. Andrology, Am. Assn. Clin. Chemistry, Nat. Acad. Clin. Biochemistry, Acad. Medicine N.J., Endorcine Soc. Home: 73 Sykes Ave Livingston NJ 07039-1318 Fax: 973-972-5185. E-mail: samojleu@umdnj.edu.

SAMONS, SANDRA LEA, psychotherapist; b. Ann Arbor, Mich., Dec. 20, 1934; d. Warren Earl and Opal Marie (Lillie) Fowler; m. Doyle Vernon Samons, Aug. 29, 1955; children: Jerry, David, James. MSW, U. Mich., 1976; PhD, Inst. for Advanced Study of Human Sexuality, 2001. Cert. social worker. Therapist, sr. social worker Maurice Spear Campus, Adrian, Mich., 1977—83; pvt. practice mental health therapist Homestead Cons. Ctr., Ann Arbor, 1985—; therapist Saline (Mich.) Cmty. Hosp.-Greenbrook, 1984—87, McAuley Mental Health, Ann Arbor, 1987—89; lead mental health therapist U. Mich.-CG-SP, Ann Arbor, 1993—2000. Part-time lectr. Ea. Mich. U., Ypsilanti, 1988—90; social work field instr. Siena Heights Coll., Ea. Mich. U., U. Mich. Sch. Social Work; spkr. in field. Contbr. articles to profl. jours., chpt. to book. Mem.: NASW, Nat. Assn. Cognitive/Behavioral Therapists, Am. Assn. Marriage and Family Therapy, Henry Benjamin Internat. Gender Dysphoria Assn., Internat. Found. for Gender Edn., Am. Assn. Sex Educators, Counselors and Therapists, Nat. Assn. Alcoholism and Drug Abuse Counselors, Mich. Alcohol and Addiction Assn., Mich. Assn. Alcoholism and Drug Abuse Counselors. Avocations: creative writing, travel, reading, movies, cats. Home: 1480 Shevchenko Dr Ann Arbor MI 48103-9001 Office: Homestead Counseling Ctr 1480 Shevchenko Dr Ann Arbor MI 48103-9001 E-mail: SLSamons@umich.edu.

SAMOREK, ALEXANDER HENRY, electrical engineer, mathematics and technology educator; b. Detroit, Feb. 14, 1922; s. Walter and Gladys (Kurys) S.; m. Deloris Gehrig 1944 (dec. Mar. 1948); 1 child, David A.; m. Matilda Louise Dusincki, May 10, 1952 (dec. Dec. 1998). Student, U. Detroit, 1946-49; BSEE, Detroit Inst. Tech., 1961. Electronics instr. Radio Electronic and TV Sch., Detroit, 1946-49; electronics inspector USAF Procurement Office, Detroit, 1950-53; chief technician Wayne Engring. and Rsch. Inst., Wayne State U., Detroit, 1954-57; elec. engr. Control Engring. Co., Detroit, 1957-60; chief engr., engring. mgr. Weltronic Co. subs. Ransburg Corp., Clare, Mich., 1960-84; electronic instr. Redford High Sch., Redford Twp., Mich., 1966; instr. math. and elec./electronics Mid. Mich. Community Coll., Clare, 1984-95. With USAAF, 1942-46. Mem. (life) IEEE, Soc. Automotive Engrs. E-mail: samorek@quik.com.

SAMOYLOVA, TATIANA I. biochemist, researcher; d. Ivan A Zayets and Lidiya R Torzhinskaya; m. Alexander M Samoylov, Mar. 1, 1981; 1 child, Alexei A Samoylov. MS, Kyiv State U., 1982, PhD, 1991. Postdoctoral rsch. assoc. Inst. of Plant Genetics and Crop Plant Rsch., Gatersleben, Germany, 1995—96; assoc. rsch. prof. Scott-Ritchey Rsch. Ctr., Coll. of Vet. Medicine, Auburn U., Ala., 1996—. Author: (book chpt.) Genetic Library Construction and Screening: Advanced Techniques and Applications; contbr. scientific papers. Fellow, Muscular Dystrophy Assn., 1998—99; Biogrant fellow, Auburn U., 2000—02. Achievements include patents for methods and compositions for targeting compounds to muscle; methods and compositions for targeting compounds to brain; patents pending for ligand sensor device and uses thereof; peptides for recognition and targeting of glial cell tumors; design of anti-cancer drug and treatment of individual tumors; research in identification of object-specific peptide ligands for novel gene/drug delivery systems and detection systems; preservation of biological materials. Office: Auburn University CVM Scott-Ritchey Rsch Ctr Auburn AL 36849 Office Phone: 334-844-5569. E-mail: samoiti@vetmed.auburn.edu.

SAMPAS, DOROTHY MYERS, retired government official; b. Washington, Aug. 24, 1933; d. Lawrence and Anna Cornelia (Henkel) Myers; m. James George Sampas, Dec. 8, 1962; children: George, Lawrence James. AB, U. Mich., 1955; postgrad., U. Paris, 1955-56; PhD, Georgetown U., 1970; cert., Nat. War Coll., Washington, 1987, Naval Post Grad. Sch., 1993. Registered lobbyist State Legis. Mich., 1954—55; with Bur. Pub. Affairs Dept. State, Washington, 1958-60, analyst Bur. of Adminstrn., 1973-75, div. chief, dep. chief Office of Position and Pay Mgmt., 1979-83, div. chief Office of Mgmt., 1983-84, dir. Office of Mgmt., 1984-86; vice consul Am. Consulate Gen., Hamburg, Fed. Republic Germany, 1960-62; cons. Trans Century Corp., Washington, 1972; gen. svcs. officer Am. Embassy, Brussels, 1975-79, embassy minister-counselor Beijing, 1987-90; minister-counselor U.S. Mission to UN, N.Y.C., 1991-94; Am. ambassador to Islamic Republic of Mauritania, 1994-97; ret., 1998. Mem.: Cosmos Club. Presbyterian.

SAMPER, JOSEPH PHILLIP, retired photographic products company executive; b. Salt Lake City, Aug. 13, 1934; s. Juan M. and Harriet (Howell) S.; m. Gail Samper; children: Joaquin P., Christopher F. With Eastman Kodak Co., Rochester, N.Y., 1961—; asst. to gen. mgr. mktg. div. Eastman Kodak Co. (U.S. and Can. photog. div.), 1976-77; asst. v.p., asst. gen. mgr. mktg. div. Eastman Kodak Co. (U.S. and Can. photographic div.), 1977-79; v.p., gen. mgr. mktg. div. Eastman Kodak Co., 1979—, exec. v.p., gen. mgr. photographic div., 1983-86, vice chmn., exec. officer, 1986-90; chief exec. officer, pres. Kinder-Care Learning Ctrs., Inc., 1991-92; pres., CEO Sun Microsystems Computer Co., 1994-95; chmn., CEO Cray Rsch., Inc., Eagan, Minn., 1995-96, Quadlex, Inc., Fremont, Calif., 1996-97; pres., CEO Avistar Systems Corp., Palo Alto, Calif., 1997—, chmn., 1998—; founding ptnr. Gabriel Venture Ptnrs., Redwood Shores, Calif., 1998—. Bd. dirs. Interpub. Group, N.Y.C. With USN, 1952-56. Recipient Alfred Knight award Am. Grad. Sch. Internat. Mgmt., 1961, Barton Kyle Young award, 1961; Sloan fellow, MIT, 1972-73 Roman Catholic.

SAMPLE, FREDERICK PALMER, former college president; b. Columbia, Pa., May 22, 1930; s. William Walter and Erna Rebecca (Roye) S.; m. Mary Jane Drager, Aug. 19, 1951; children: Jeffrey Lynn, Roger Lee. AB, Lebanon Valley Coll., 1952; MEd, Western Md. Coll., 1956; DEd, Pa. State U., 1968; D in Pedagogy, Albright Coll., 1968. Tchr. Annville (Pa.) High Sch., 1952-53; tchr. Red Lion Area (Pa.) High Sch., 1953-57, prin., 1957-59, supervising prin., 1959-64; supt. Manheim Twp. Sch. Dist., Neffsville, Pa., 1964-68; pres. Lebanon Valley Coll., Annville, Pa., 1968-83; supt. Bellefonte (Pa.) Area Sch. Dist., 1987-92. Ednl. cons.; adminstr. Bucknell U., 1985-87. Mem. Phi Delta Kappa. Republican. Home: 2205 James Buchanan Dr Elizabethtown PA 17022-3173 E-mail: fps0522@dejazzd.com. *Despite failures, difficulties, and disappointments I have tried to find the honorable, responsible, productive, true, and humane solutions to problems and make decisions for progress.*

SAMPLE, JOSEPH SCANLON, foundation executive; b. Chgo., Mar. 15, 1923; s. John Glen and Helen (Scanlon) S.; m. Patricia M. Law, Dec. 22, 1942 (div.); children: Michael Scanlon, David Forrest, Patrick Glen; m. Miriam Tyler Willing, Nov. 19, 1965. BA, Yale U., 1947. Trainee, media analyst, media dir. Dancer-Fitzgerald-Sample, Inc., advt. agy., Chgo., 1947-50, v.p., media dir., 1952-53; pres. Mont. Television Network KTVQ, Billings, KXLF-AM-TV, Butte, Mont., KRTV, Great Falls, Mont., KPAX-TV, Missoula, Mont., 1955-84; dir., prodr. Yellowstone Pub. Radio KEMC, Billings, 1993—. Chmn. Wheeler Ctr. Mont State U., 1988—. Served with AUS, 1943-46. With U.S. Army, 1950-52. Mem. Rotary, Yellowstone Country Club, Port Royal Club, Hole in The Wall Golf Club, Hilands Golf Club, Naples Yacht Club. Home: 606 Highland Park Dr Billings MT 59102-1909 Office: 14 N 24th St Billings MT 59101-2422 Office Phone: 406-256-5667. Personal E-mail: scatman01@msn.com.

SAMPLE, LISA L. education educator; d. William C. and Dorothy A. Edgar; m. David S. Sample, Nov. 10, 1990. AA, St. Charles County CC, Mo., 1994; BS, U. Mo., 1996, MA, 1998, PhD, 2001. Asst. prof. U. Nebr., Omaha, 2001—. Bd. dirs. Local Coord. Coun., Omaha. Contbr. articles to profl. jours. Grantee, Nat. Inst. Justice, 2001—04, NE Dept. Correctional Svcs., 2003. Office: Univ Nebr DSC 2 Criminal Justice Dept Omaha NE 68182 Business E-Mail: lsample@mail.unomaha.edu.

SAMPLE, STEVEN BROWNING, university executive; b. St. Louis, Nov. 29, 1940; s. Howard and Dorothy (Cunningham) Sample; m. Kathryn Brunkow, Jan. 28, 1961; children: Michelle Sample Smith, Elizabeth Ann. BS, U. Ill., 1962, MS, 1963, PhD, 1965; DHL (hon.), Canisius Coll., 1989; LLD (hon.), U. Sheffield, Eng., 1991; EdD (hon.), Purdue U., 1994; DHL (hon.), Hebrew Union Coll., 1994; DL (hon.), U. Nebr., 1995. Sr. scientist Melpar Inc., Falls Ch., Va., 1965—66; assoc. prof. elec. engring. Purdue U., Lafayette, Ind., 1966—73; dep. dir. Ill. Bd. Higher Edn., Springfield, 1971—74; exec. v.p. acad. affairs, dean Grad. Coll., prof. elec. engring. U. Nebr., Lincoln, 1974—82; prof. elec. and computer engring. SUNY, Buffalo, 1982—91; pres. U. So. Calif., LA, 1991—, prof. elec. engring., 1991—, Robert C. Packard pres.'s chair, 1995—. Bd. dirs. Santa Catalina Id. Co., UNOVA, William Wrigley Jr. Co., Advanced Bionics, AMCAP/Am. Mut. Fund, Inc., Keck Sch. Medicine; vice-chmn. Western NY Tech. Devel. Ctr., Buffalo, 1982—91; chmn. bd. dirs. Calspan-UB Rsch. Ctr., Inc., Buffalo, 1983—91; mem. Calif. Coun. Sci. and Tech., Irvine, Calif., L.A. Bus. Advisors, Nat. Acad. of Engring., 1998—; cons. in field; chmn. Pacific-10 Conf., 1997—; bd. dirs. Galaxy Inst. Edn., 1991—94; mem. Knight Commn. on Intercoll. Athletics, 2003—. Author: Contrarian's Guide to Leadership, 2001; contbr. articles to profl. jour. Timpanist St. Louis Philharm. Orch., 1955—58; chmn. Western NY Regional Econ. Devel. Coun., 1984—91; trustee U. at Buffalo Found., 1982—91, Studio Arena Theatre, Buffalo, 1983—91, Western NY Pub. Broadcasting Assn., 1985—91; chmn. Gov.'s Conf. on Sci. and Engring. Edn., Rsch. and Devel, 1989—91; sr. warden Ch. of Our Savior, 1996—98; mem. Calif. Bus.-Higher Edn. Forum (CBHEF), 1995—97; trustee LEARN, 1991—; mem. bd. dir. 1st Interstate Bancorp, 1991—96, Galaxy Inst. Edn., 1991—94, Niagara Mohawk Power Corp., 1988—91; vestry Ch. of Our Savior, 1996—2001; mem. bd. gov. LA Annenberg Met. Project (LAAMP), 1994—2000; mem. bd. dir. Western Atlas, Inc., 1994—97, The Presley Co., 1991—; bd. dir. Buffalo Philharm. Orch., 1982—91, Regenstrief Med. Found., Indpls., 1982—, Rsch. Found. SUNY, 1987—91; bd. dir. LA chpt. World Affairs Coun., Hughes Galaxy Inst. Edn., Calif., 1991—94; bd. dir. Rebuild LA Com., Coalition of 100 Club, L.A.; mem. bd. dir. Dunlop Tire Corp., 1987—91, Greater Buffalo C. of C., 1985—91, United Way Buffalo and Erie County, 1985—91; bd. dir. U. So. Calif. Keck Sch. Medicine. Named Engr. of Yr., NY State Soc. Profl. Engrs., 1985; recipient Disting. Alumnus award, U. Ill., 1980, Alumni Honor award, U. Ill. Coll. Engring., 1985, citation award, Buffalo Coun. on World Affairs, 1986, Outstanding Elec. Engr. award, Purdue U., 1993, Humanitarian award, Nat. Conf. Christians and Jews, 1994, Hollzer Meml. award, Jewish Fedn. Coun. Greater L.A, 1994, Eddy award, LA County Econ. Devel. Corp., 2000; fellow, Sloan Found., 1962—63, Grad. fellow, NSF, 1963—65, Am. Coun. Edn. fellow, Purdue U., 1970—71. Mem.: NAE, IEEE (Outstanding Paper award 1976), Knight Commn. on Intercollegiate Athletics, Am. Acad. Arts and Sci., Assn. Pacific Rim Univ. (co-founder, chmn. 1997—2002), Coun. on Fgn. Rels., Nat. Assn. State Univ. and Land-Grant Coll. (ednl. telecomms. com. 1982—83, chmn. coun. of pres. 1985—86, edn. and tech. com. 1986—87, exec. com. 1987—89), Assn. Am. Univ. (exec. com. 1995—2000, vice-chmn. 1997—98, tenure com. 1997—2001; chmn. 1998—99, assessing quality of univ. edn. and rsch. com. 2000—, co-chair task force on rsch. accountability 2001—02, internationalization com. 2002—). Episcopalian. Achievements include patents in field. Office: U So Calif Office of Pres University Park Adm 110 Los Angeles CA 90089-0012

SAMPLES, JERRY WAYNE, military officer, educator; b. July 18, 1947; s. Wilmer Clark and Nellie Virginia (Price) Samples; m. Kathleen Miller, Nov. 2, 1969; children: Christopher John, Steven Wayne. BS, Clarkson Coll., 1969; MS, Okla. State U., 1979, PhD, 1983. Registered profl. engr., Va. Lab. asst. Columbia Ribbon & Carbon, Glenn Cove, NY, 1969—70; asst. prof. mech. engring. US Mil. Acad., West Point, NY, 1979—82, assoc. prof. mech. engring., 1985—87; assoc. prof. dept. civil and mech. engrs. U. Pitts., Johnstown, Pa., 1989—96, prof. engring, dir. engring. tech., 1996—; commd. 2d lt. US Army, 1969; with Air Command and Staff Coll. Maxwell AFB, Ala., 1983; exec. officer 10th Engr. Bn., 1983—85; bn. comdr. 10th engr. bn. 3d inf. divsn., 1987—89; advanced through grades to col., 1991. Pres. Tchg. the Tchrs., Inc. Author (with others): (book) Fundamentals of Engineering Examination, 1991, The Best EIT Review for the Fundamentals of Engineering Exam, 1995, GRE Engineering, 1996. Decorated Legion of Merit, Meritorious Svc. Medal, Army Commendation Medal. Mem.: SAE (Ralph R. Teetor award 1994), ASEE, ASME (bd. dirs. ASME Found.), AIAA, Phi Kappa Phi. Home: 108 Laurlis Ln Johnstown PA 15904-1742 Office: Univ Pitts at Johnstown Dept Engineering Technology Johnstown PA 15904 E-mail: samps2@twd.net.

SAMPLINER, RICHARD EVAN, physician; b. Cleve., Apr. 14, 1941; m. Linda Sampliner. BA, Yale U., 1963; MD, Case Western Res. U., 1967. Diplomate Am. Bd. Internal Medicine, Am. Bd. Gastroenterology. Intern Univ. Hosps., Cleve., 1967-68; resident New England Med. Ctr., Boston, 1970-71; sr. resident Boston City Hosp., 1971-72; chief of gastroenterology VA Med. Ctr., Tucson, 1980—; prof. medicine U. Ariz., Tucson, 1990—. Contbr. 250 articles to profl. jours. With USPHS, 1968-70. Fellow: Am Gastroenterology Assn.; mem.: Am. Soc. Gastroent. Endoscopy, Am. Coll. Gastroenterology. Office: SAVAHCS 111G1 3601 S 6th Ave Tucson AZ 85723-0001 E-mail: samplinr@email.arizona.edu.

SAMPRAS, PETE, retired professional tennis player; b. Washington, Aug. 12, 1971; s. Sam and Georgia Sampras. Mem. U.S. Davis Cup team., named to Olympic Team Atlanta, 1996 Chairman ATP Tour Charities program, 1992. Winner tournaments including Phila., 1990, Manchester, 1990, U.S. Open, 1990, 1993, Grand Slam Cup, 1990, L.A., 1991, Indpls., 1991, Lyon, 1991, IBM/ATP Tour World Championship-Frankfurt, 1991, 94, U.S. Pro Indoor, 1992, Lipton Internat., 1993, Wimbledon, 1993, 94, 95, 97, 98, 99, 2000; Australian Open, 1994, 97, Italian Open, 1994, U.S. Open, 1990, 93, 95, 96, 2002, San Jose Open, 1996, Memphis Open, 1996, ATP Tour World Championship/Hannover, Germany, 1996, Australian Open Wimbledon, 1997, Advanta Championships, 1998; ranked # 1 during 1993, 94 season, finalist Australian Open, 1995; retired, 2003 Achievements include 1st male to win the U.S Open, Wimbledon, and the Australian Open in succession, mem. U.S. Davis Cup Team, 1991, became only the fourth player to finish as No. 1 three (or more) consecutive years, 1st player to surpass $5 million in a season, all-time leader in career earnings, named ATP Tour Player of the Year, 1993-94, Jim Thorpe Tennis Player, 1993. Office: ATP Tour 420 W 45th St New York NY 10036-3503

SAMPSON, DAVID ALLAN, federal agency administrator; b. Washington, Ind., July 2, 1957; s. Beryl Harrel and Laura Evelyn (King) S.; m. Karen Ann Nichols, Dec. 10, 1978. BA, David Lipscomb Coll., Nashville, 1978; MDiv, New Orleans Bapt. Theol. Sem., 1982. Minister Westchurch Ch. of Christ, Hammond, Ind., 1978-82; sr. minister Park Row Ch. of Christ, Arlington, Tex., 1982—; pres., CEO Arlington (Tex.) C. of C.; chmn. Tex. Coun. on Workforce and Econ. Competitiveness; asst. sec. for econ. devel. Dept. Commerce, Washington, 2001—. Bd. dirs. emergency chaplain program Arlington Community Hosp., 1985—; adv. bd. Arlington Meml. Hosp., 1985—; bd. dirs. Neo-natal Bioethics Review Bd., 1986—. Contbr. articles to profl. jours. Mem. United Way; bd. dirs. Arlington Ind. Sch. Dists, Communications Bd., 1985—. Named Arlington's Minister of Yr., Kiwanis, 1985. Mem. Arlington C. of C. (bd. dirs. 1985—, chmn. emergency preparedness com. 1985—), Arlington Ministerial Assn. (pres. 1985-86), Soc. Biblical Lit., Internat. Ch. Soc. (chmn. North Tex. chpt.), Phi Alpha Theta. Lodges: Rotary. Republican. Avocations: travel, tennis. Office: Dept Commerce Econ Devel Adminstrn 14th & Constitution Ave NW Washington DC 20230

SAMPSON, DAVID SYNNOTT, lawyer; b. Troy, N.Y., Oct. 2, 1942; s. Stephen Hastings and Ruth (Hall) S.; m. Arlene Mernit, July 1, 1967; children: Christopher Hastings, Jamie Everett. BA, St. Lawrence U., 1965; JD, Albany Law Sch., 1973. Bar: N.Y. 1975, D.C. 1977, U.S. Ct. Appeals (D.C. cir.) 1977. Reporter Troy Record, 1965-67; newsman AP, 1967-70; spl. asst. N.Y. State Dept. Environ. Cons., Albany, 1972-74; panel dir. Com. on Critical Choices for Ams., N.Y.C., 1974-75; chief legis. asst. U.S. Rep. H.J. Heinz, Washington, 1975-77; assoc. Boasberg, Hewes, Finkelstein & Klores, Washington, 1977-79; exec. dir. Am. Land Forum, Washington, 1978-79; ptnr. Pattison, Sampson, Ginsberg & Griffin, Troy, N.Y., 1979-87; exec. dir. Hudson River Valley Assn., Troy and Cold Spring, N.Y., 1987-89, Hudson River Valley Greenway Coun., Albany, 1989-2000; of counsel Martin, Shudt, Wallace, DiLorenzo & Johnson, Troy, 2001—; postgrad. in geology and planning U. Albany, 2001—. Adj. prof. Columbia U. Grad. Sch. Arch., Planning and Preservation, 2000—. Contbr. book revs., articles to profl. jours. Pres. Samaritan Hosp. Found., 1985-87; bd. dirs. Samaritan Hosp., Troy, 1985-88, St. Gregorys Sch., Loudonville, N.Y., 1982-87, Troy Pub. Libr. Found., 1991—, Scenic Hudson, Poughkeepsie, N.Y., 1982-92, 93-99; mem. Scenic Hudson Land Trust, 1996-01, Husdon River Found., 1999—, Hudsonia, 2001—; mem. adv. bd. Preservation League N.Y., Albany, 1989; mem. N.Y. State Freshwater Wetlands Appeals Bd., 1980-94, chmn., 1984-94; active U.S./UK Countryside Stewardship Exch., Eng., 1989; founder Czech-Hudson Greenway Project, 1992; bd. dirs. Hudson River Found., 1997—. Recipient Greenway award DuPont Corp., 1994, Environ. Alumni award Albany Law Sch., 1997. Mem. Am. Conservation Assn. (bd. dirs. 1987—), N.Y. Pks. and Conservation Assn. (founding dir. 1986-94), N.Y. State Bar Assn. (chmn. hist. preservation com. 1980-85, exec. com. 1985—, chmn. environ. law sect. 1990-91, Bar Assn. City of N.Y. Avocation: bicycling. E-mail: dvsampson@aol.com.

SAMPSON, EARLDINE ROBISON, education educator; b. Russell, Iowa, June 18, 1923; d. Lawrence Earl and Mildred Mona (Judy) Robison; m. Wesley Claude Sampson, Nov. 25, 1953; children: Ann Elizabeth, Lisa Ellen. Diploma, Iowa State Tchrs. Coll., 1943, BA, 1950; MS in Edn., Drake U., 1954; postgrad., No. Ill. U., Iowa State U., 1965-66, 74. Cert. tchr., guidance counselor, Iowa. Tchr. elem. sch. various pub. sch. sys., 1943-48; cons. speech and hearing Iowa Dept. Pub. Instrn., Des Moines, 1950-52; speech therapist Des Moines Pub. Schs., 1952-54, 55; lectr. spl. edn. No. Ill. U., DeKalb, 1964-65; tchr. of homebound Cedar Falls (Iowa) Pub. Schs., 1967-68; asst. prof. edn. U. No. Iowa, Cedar Falls, 1968; asst. prof., counselor Wartburg Coll., Waverly, Iowa, 1968-70; instr. elem. edn., then head of advising elem. edn. Iowa State U., Ames, 1972-82; field supr. elem. edn. U. Toledo, 1988, 89; ind. cons. Sylvania, Ohio, 1989—. Cons. Des Moines Speech and Hearing Ctr., 1958-59; cons. Sartori Hosp., Cedar Falls, 1967-69. Fellow, NDEA, 1965. Methodist. Avocations: public speaking on preservation of prose and poetry, reading, music, photography. Home: 4047 Newcastle Dr Sylvania OH 43560-3450 *My creed is based on the words of Edwin Markham: "There is a destiny that makes us brothers; none goes his way alone. All that we send into the lives of others comes back into our own." Just reward came from a former student who stated "I have never known you to compromise your principles".*

SAMPSON, FRANKLIN DELANO, minister; b. Houston, Jan. 31, 1947; s. Harry Burney and Annie Belle (Lenzia) S.; m. Fannie Marie Iles, Mar. 12, 1972; children: De Anza Michelle, Franklin Delano, Jr., Frederick Dwayne. BA, U. Houston, 1970; D of Ministries (hon.), Mt. Hope Bible Coll., 1978. Ordained to ministry Nat. Bapt. Conv., 1969. Pastor Friendship Missionary Bapt. Ch., Houston, 1972—; moderator Unity Missionary Bapt. Gen. Assn., Houston, 1985-94; chmn. Minister's Conf. of Missionary Bapt. Gen. Conv., Dallas, 1987—, Commn. on Orthodoxy of Nat. Bapt. Conv. of Am., Inc., Shreveport, La., 1987—; chief exec. officer Visions of Faith Ministries, Inc., Houston, 1985—. Mem. Bapt. Mins. Assn. of Houston and Vicinity (v.p. 1990—), Unity Missionary Bapt. Gen. Assn. (Houston, moderator 1985-93), Masons. Democrat. Home: 12947 Wincrest Ct Cypress TX 77429-2001 Office: Friendship Missionary Bapt Ch 4812 Bennington St Houston TX 77016-7003

SAMPSON, HUGH ALBERT, JR., medical educator; b. Winnipeg, Man., Can., 1948; BA, Hamilton Coll., 1971; MD, SUNY, Buffalo, 1975. Diplomate Am. Bd. Pediats., Am. Bd. Allergy and Immunology. Intern Children's Meml. Hosp.-Northwestern U., Chgo., 1975-76, resident, 1976-79; fellow in allergy and immunology-pulmonary medicine Duke U. Med. Ctr., Durham, N.C., 1978-80, mem. staff Balt., 1980-86; prof. pediat. Johns Hopkins U., Balt., 1986—97; prof., pediat. Mt. Sinai Sch. of Medicine, NYC, 1997—. Mem. staff Johns Hopkins Hosp., Balt. Co-author: Intestinal immunology and Food Allergy, 1995, Food Allergy: Adverse Reactions to Foods and Food Additives, 1991, Pediatric Allergy: Principles and Practice, 2003 Mem. Am. Acad. Allergy and Immunology, Am. Assn. Immunologists, Soc. Pediat. Rsch., Sigma Xi, Inst. Medicine, 2004. Office: Mt Sinai Sch Medicine One Gustave L Levy Pl Box 1198 New York NY 10029 Office Phone: 212-241-5548. Business E-Mail: hugh.sampson@mssm.edu.

SAMPSON, JEROME MARK, pulmonologist; b. Houston; BA in Chemistry, So. Meth. U., 1977; MD, U. Tex., 1981, pulmonary fellow; MSA, Ctrl. Mich. U., 1998. Diplomate Am. Bd. Internal Medicine; cert. Am. Bd. Quality Assurance and Utilization Rev. Physicians, Am. Bd. Managed Care Medicine, Am. Coll. Physician Execs. Pv. practice, W. Palm Beach, Fla., 1986-92; staff physician VA Med. Ctr., Prescott, Ariz., 1992-93, chief of medicine Alexandria, La., 1994-2000, chief of staff, pulmonologist, 2001—. Office: VA Med Ctr PO Box 69004 Alexandria LA 71306-9004 Home: 5136 NW 62nd St Gainesville FL 32653-4075

SAMPSON, JOHN EUGENE, consulting company executive; b. Feb. 25, 1941; s. Delbert John and Mary Etta (Dodrill) S.; m. Mary Margaret Treanor, Aug. 14, 1965; children: J. Mark, Sharon. AB with distinction, Nebr. Wesleyan U., 1963; MBA, Ind. U., 1964. Mgmt. asst., exec. trainee Office Sec. Def., Washington, 1963—64; mem. staff Com. Econ. Devel., Washington, 1964—69; coord. environ. planning Gen. Mills Inc., Mpls., 1969—72, mgr. devel. planning, 1972—74; dir. corp. planning Cen. Soya Co. Inc., Ft. Wayne, Ind., 1974—76, v.p. corp. planning, 1976—80, v.p. corp. planning and devel., 1980—82, v.p. corp. devel., corp. sec., 1982—84; v.p. corp. planning and devel. Internat. Multifoods, Inc., 1984—96; pres. Sampson Assocs., Edina, Minn., 1996—. Author: How to Sell Your Business and Get the Best Price For It, 2003. Mem. bd. govs. Nebr. Wesleyan U., 1974-80; chmn. bd. trustees St. Joseph United Meth. Ch., Ft. Wayne, 1984; bd. dirs., treas. North Ind. United Meth. Found., 1981-84; lay mem. North Ind. Ann. Conf. United Meth. Ch., 1980-84; bd. dirs. Anthony Wayne coun. Boy Scouts Am., 1984; lay mem. Minn. Ann. Conf. United Meth. Ch., 1985-91, 97-00; chmn. conf. bd. devel. Minn. United Meth. Conf., 1986-91; chmn. bd. trustees Hennepin Ave. United Meth. Ch., Mpls., 1990-92, chair adminstrv. coun., 1993-95, lay leader, 1995-98; chair exec. com. North Naples (Fla.) United Meth. Ch., 2002—, co-chmn. bldg. com., 2002—. Mem. Ind. U. Sch. Bus. Alumni Assn. (pres. 1984-85), Interlachen Country Club, Country Club of Naples (bd. dirs. 2004—). Home: 6612 Gleason Ter Edina MN 55439-1131 also: Unit 1701 4451 Gulf Shore Blvd N Naples FL 34103 Office: Sampson Assocs 5200 Willson Rd Ste 404 Edina MN 55424-1345 Office Phone: 952-928-0800.

SAMPSON, ROBERT NEIL, natural resources consultant; b. Spokane, Wash., Nov. 29, 1938; s. Robert Jay and Juanita Cleone (Hickman) S.; m. Jeanne Louise Stokes, June 7, 1960; children— Robert W., Eric S., Christopher B., Heidi L. BS in Agr, U. Idaho, 1960; M.Public Adminstrn., Harvard U., 1974. Soil conservationist Soil Conservation Service, Burley, Idaho, 1960-61, work unit conservationist Orofino, Idaho, 1962-65, agronomist Idaho Falls, Idaho, 1967-68, info. specialist Boise, 1968-70, area conservationist, 1970-72, land use specialist Washington, 1974-77, dir. environ. services div., 1977; land use program mgr. Idaho Planning and Community Affairs Agy., Boise, 1972-73; exec. v.p. Nat. Assn. Conservation Dists., Washington, 1978-84, Am. Forestry Assn., Washington, 1984-95; sr. fellow Am. Forests, Washington, 1995-2000; affiliate prof. Dept. Forest Resources U. Idaho, 1997—. Instr. soils and land use Boise State U., 1972; F.K. Weyerhaeuser vis. fellow in comml. forestry Yale Sch. Forestry and Environ. Studies, 2001; pres., The Sampson Group, Inc., 1996—, Vision Forestry LLC, 2000—; rsch. scientist, Yale Sch. Forestry and Environ. Studies, 2001—. Author: Farmland or Wasteland: A Time To Choose, 1981, For Love of the Land, 1985; contbr. articles to profl. and popular publs. Pres. Orofino Golf Assn., 1966, Clearwater County Search and Rescue Unit, 1966-67; chmn. Nat. Commn. on Wildfire Disasters, 1992-94. Recipient President's citation Soil Conservation Soc. Am., 1978; named Boise Fed. Civil Servant of Year Boise Fed. Bus. Assn., 1972 Fellow Soil and Water Conservation Soc. (Hugh Hammond Bennett award 1992); mem. Soc. Am. Foresters. Presbyterian. Office Phone: 703-924-0773. E-mail: rneilsampson@cs.com.

SAMPSON, SAMUEL FRANKLIN, sociology educator; b. Malden, Mass., Sept. 22, 1934; s. Samuel Daniel and Margaret Louise (Grimes) S.; m. Patricia Katherine Driscoll, Apr. 8, 1972. BA, U. Okla., 1960, MA, 1961; PhD, Cornell U., 1968. Asst. prof. dept. sociology SUNY, Binghamton, 1965-66; research assoc. dept. sociology Cornell U., Ithaca, N.Y., 1966-67; lectr., chmn. bd. tutors and advs. Harvard U., Cambridge, Mass., 1967-72; assoc. prof. dept. urban studies and planning MIT, Cambridge, 1971-72; prof. sociology U. Vt., Burlington, 1972-2000, chmn. dept. sociology, 1972-76, 90-96, prof. emeritus, 2000—. Research and policy cons. Public & Community Agys. and Orgns., 1969— Gen. editor: Bobbs-Merrill Studies in Sociology, 1970-77; contbr. articles to profl. jours. Served with USAF, 1954-58. Mem. AAUP, AAAS, Internat. Sociol. Assn., Am. Sociol. Assn., Am. Acad. Arts and Scis., Ea. Sociol. Soc., Soc. Study Social Problems, New Eng. Sociol. Assn., Soc. Sci. Study Religion, Internat. Sociol. Assn. Home: 215 S Cove Rd Burlington VT 05401-5445 Office: Univ Vt Dept Sociology 31 S Prospect St Burlington VT 05405-1704 E-mail: lhcarew@zoo.uvm.edu.

SAMPSON, WILLIAM ROTH, lawyer; b. Teaneck, NJ, Dec. 11, 1946; s. James and Amelia (Roth) S.; 1 child, Lara; m. Drucilla Jean Mort, Apr. 23, 1988; stepchildren: Andy, Seth. BA in History with honors, U. Kans., 1968, JD, 1971. Bar: Kans. 1971, Mo. 2004, US Dist. Ct. Kans. 1971, US Ct. Appeals (10th cir.) 1982, US Ct. Claims 1985, US Ct. Appeals (8th cir.) 1992. Assoc. Turner & Balloun, Great Bend, Kans., 1971; ptnr. Foulston & Siefkin, Wichita, Kans., 1975-86, Shook, Hardy & Bacon, Overland Park, Kans., 1987—. Adj. prof. advanced litig. U. Kans., 1994; mem. faculty trial tactics inst. Emory U. Sch. Law, 1994-97; mem. merit selection panel US Dist. Ct. Kans., 1999; lectr., presenter in field. Author: Kansas Trial Handbook, 1997; mem. Kans. Law Rev., 1969-71, editor, 1970-71; contbr. articles to profl. jours. Chmn. stewardship com. Univ. Friends Ch., Wichita, 1984-86; bd. dir. Friends U. Retirement Corp., Wichita, 1985-87; chmn. capital fund drives Trinity Luth. Ch., Lawrence, Kans., 1990-93, mem. ch. coun., 1990-92, stewardship com. Trinity Episcopal Ch., 2002—; bd. dir. Lied Ctr. of Kans., 1994-97. Lt. USNR, 1971-75. Fellow: Kans. Bar Found., Am. Bar Found.; mem.: ABA, Lawyers for Civil Justice (bd. dirs. 2003—04), Am. Inn Ct. (Judge Hugh Means chpt. Master of Bench), Kans. U. Law Soc. (bd. govs. 1993—96), Kans. Assn. Def. Counsel (pres. 1989—90, legis. coun. 1991, 1993, William H. Kahrs Disting. Achievement award 1994), Def. Rsch. Inst. (Kans. state rep. 1990—98, nat. bd. dirs. 1998—2000, nat. pres. 2003—04, Exceptional Performance citation 1990), Internat. Assn. Def. Coun. (faculty mem. trial acad. 1994), Am. Bd. Trial Advs. (pres. Kans. chpt. 1990—91, nat. bd. dir. 1990—91), Wichita Bar Assn. (bd. dirs. 1985—86), Johnson County Bar Assn. (bench-bar com. 1989—, Boss of Yr. award 1990), Douglas County Bar Assn., Kans. Bar Assn. (chmn. Kans. coll. advocacy 1986, CLE com. 1987—88, long-range planning), Assn. Def. Trial Attys., Club at Porto Cima, Order of Coif, Omicron Delta Kappa, Phi Alpha Theta, Delta Sigma Rho. Republican. Episcopalian. Avocations: jogging, golf, skiing, travel, reading. Office: Shook Hardy & Bacon 2555 Grand Ave Kansas City MO 64108-2613 Office Phone: 816-474-6550. E-mail: wsampson@shb.com.

SAMRA, NICHOLAS JAMES, bishop; b. Paterson, N.J., Aug. 15, 1944; s. George H. and Elizabeth L. (Balady) S. BA, St. Anselm Coll., 1966; BD, St. John Sem., Brighton, Mass., 1970. Ordained priest Melkite-Greek Cath. Ch., 1970, bishop Melkite-Greek Cath. Ch., 1989. Assoc. pastor St. Anne Ch., North Hollywood, Calif., 1970—78; pastor Holy Cross Ch., Anaheim, Calif., 1973—78, St. John The Bapt. Ch., Northlake, Ill., 1978—81, St. Michael Ch., Hammond, Ind., 1978—81, St. Anne Ch., West Paterson, NJ, 1981—89; aux. bishop Diocese of Newton, Mass., 1989—. Chaplain Police Athletic League Supporters, North Hollywood, 1970; vicar gen., corp. v.p., and regional bishop of Midwest region Diocese of Newton; transl. articles on Melkite subjects; mem. Ecumenical Commn., L.A., 1974—78. Mem.: Cath. Archives Assn. Home and Office: 158 Pleasant St Brookline MA 02446-5239

SAMS, JAMES FARID, real estate development company executive; b. Bay City, Mich., Apr. 21, 1932; s. James and Adele Sams; m. Betty Suham Hamady, Aug. 17, 1957; children: James Karl, Alicia Diane, Victoria Saab. BA, Northwestern U., 1954; JD, U. Mich., 1957; LLM, Harvard U., 1959. Com. counsel ABA spl. com. World Peace/Law, Washington, 1960-63; ptnr. Reeves, Harrison, Sams & Revercomb, Washington, 1964-69, Brown & Sams, Washington, 1969-71, Kirkwood, Kaplan, Russin, Veechi & Sams, Beirut, 1971-74; owner, prin. Am. Devel. Services Corp., Washington, 1978—. Rep. U.S. State Dept. Ams. Abroad, Washington, 1965; del. UN Com. on Internat. Trade Law, N.Y.C., 1970; adv. bd Ctr. for Internat. and Comparative Law, U. Mich. Law Sch. Contbr. articles to profl. jours. Co-founder, dir. Am. Near East Refugee Aid, Washington, 1968-92; mem. adv. bd. Georgetown U. Ctr. for Arab Studies; mem. visitors com. U. Mich. Law Sch.; mem. adv. bd. Ctr. Internat. and Comparative Law; former chmn., dir. Grameen Found. USA, Washington. Served to lt. U.S. Army, 1957-58. Mem. ABA, Bar Assn. of Washington, Am. Soc. Internat. Law, Cosmos Club. Home: 8907 Fernwood Rd Bethesda MD 20817-3015 Home Fax: 301-365-5655. E-mail: adsc@erols.com.

SAMSON, ALLEN LAWRENCE, investor, bank executive; b. Milw., Nov. 16, 1939; s. Harry E. and Rose (Landau) S.; m. Vicki Faye Boxer, July 3, 1977; children: Daniel, Rachel; children from previous marriage: Nancy, David. BS, U. Wis., 1962, LLB, 1965. Bar: Wis. 1965. Asst. dist. atty. Milw. County Dist. Attys. Office, 1965-67, dep. dist. atty., 1968-70; assoc. Samson & Nash, Milw., 1967-68; ptnr. Samson, Friebert, Sutton and Finerty, Milw., 1970-73; v.p., sec. Am. Med. Svcs., Inc., Milw., 1973-83, exec. v.p., chief exec. officer, 1983-86, chmn., chief exec. officer, 1986-90; cons. nursing homes Samson Med. Mgmt. Co., Milw., 1990-93; pres. Liberty Bank, Milw., 1994—2001; vice chmn. State Fin. Bank, 2001—03; trustee State of Wis. Investment Bd., 2003—. Pub. mem. State of Wis. Investment Bd., 2003—; pub. mem. nursing home study Wis. Legis. Bur., 1988-89; mem. bd. visitors U. Wis. Law Sch., 1992—; mem. health policy adv. coun. Med. Coll. Wis., 1992-96. Bd. dirs. Nat. Found. Jewish Culture, 1996—98; trustee Milw. Ballet, 1982—89, Milw. Art Mus., 2001—, pres. bd. trustees, 1992—95; bd. dirs. Milw. Symphony Orch., 1995—2002, treas., 1996—2000; bd. dirs. Wis. Womens Bus. Initiative, War Meml. Corp., 1993—95, Jewish Fedn., 1985—, pres., 2000—02; bd. dirs. Milw. Jewish Home, 1992—96, Jewish Cmty. Ctr., 1985—96; pres. Milw. Parks Found., 1998—; gen. chmn. Wis. Israel Bond Campaign, 1993—94, chmn., 1996—98, bd. dirs., exec. com., 1986—; gen. chmn. ann. camp Milw. Jewish Fedn., 1990—91; pres. Jewish Vocat. Svc., 1976—78; Alexis de Tocqueville's leadership chmn. United Way campaign, 1995. Recipient Kaplan prize for econ. devel. Govt. of Israel, 1986, United Way Fleur de Lys award, 1996, Israel Bonds Star of David award, 1999. Avocations: tennis, skiing, golf. Office: State Fin Bank 815 N Water St Milwaukee WI 53202-3529

SAMSON, ALVIN, former distributing company executive, consultant; b. N.Y.C., May 2, 1917; s. Morris and Jennie (Buitekant) S.; m. Ann Carol Furmansky, Aug. 15, 1942; children: Leslie Joan, Marla Adriane. Br. mgr. U.S. Hardware and Paper Co., 1947-51; mdse. mgr. U.S. Servateria, 1951-57; dir. purchasing U.S. Consumer Products, Los Angeles, 1959-64, v.p. ops., 1964-66, pres., 1966-72, 1966-72, Zelman Co., Los Angeles, San Francisco and Las Vegas, 1968-72, Triple A Corp., Los Angeles, 1966-72, U.S. Consumer Products-Wesco Mdse., Los Angeles, 1972-74; v.p. APL Corp., N.Y.C., 1967-74; pres. USCP-WESCO, 1974-85; cons. A. Samson Cons., Beverly Hills, 1985-92; retired, 1992. Active USCG Aux., 1981-02, divsn. capt., 1992—. With USAAC, 1942-45. Named Man of Year Housewares Club So. Calif., 1965 Mem. Nat. Assn. Service Merchandisers (dir. 1982-85)

SAMSON, CHARLES HAROLD, JR., (CAR SAMSON), retired engineering educator, consultant; b. Portsmouth, Ohio, July 12, 1924; s. Charles Harold and Gertrude (Morris) S.; m. Ruth Aileen Baumbach, Sept. 12, 1947; children: Peggy Aileen, Charles Harold III. BS, U. Notre Dame, 1947, MS, 1948; PhD, U. Mo., 1953. Registered profl. engr., Tex., Ind. Asst. field rep. Loebl, Schlossman and Bennett (archs. and engrs.), Chgo., 1948-49; structures engr. Convair Aircraft, Ft. Worth, 1951-52, sr. structures engr., 1952-53, project aerodynamics engr., 1956-58, project structures engr., 1958-60; asst. prof. civil engring. U. Notre Dame, 1953-56; office engr. Wilbur H. Gartner & Assocs., South Bend, Ind., 1954; grad. lectr. civil engring. So. Meth. U., Dallas, 1952-53, 56-60; prof. structural engring. and mechanics, depts. aerospace and civil engring. Tex. A&M U., College Station, 1960-64, prof. civil engring., 1964-94, prof. emeritus, 1994—, head dept., 1964-79, assoc. head dept., 1989-92, constrn. area engring. leader, dir. ctr. constrn. edn., 1992-93; rsch. engr. Tex. Transp. Inst., Tex. A&M U., 1960-62, head structural rsch. dept., 1962-65, acting pres., 1980-81, v.p. planning, 1981-82. Pres. S.W. Athletic Conf., 1979-81; v.p. NCAA, 1981-83, mem. coun., 1983-85; cons. systems engring. and quality mgmt.; Tex. Quality Award examiner, 1998-99, sr. examiner, 2000. Contbr. articles to profl. jours. Served to ensign USNR, 1943-46. Recipient Gen. Dynamics-Ft. Worth Excellence in Tchg. award, 1962, Engring. hon. award U. Notre Dame, 1982. Fellow ASCE (life), Nat. Inst. Engring. Mgmt. and Systems (pres. 1989-90), NSPE (past v.p., chmn. profl. engrs. in edn., pres. 1987-88, award 2000)); mem. Am. Soc. Engring. Mgmt., Am. Soc. Engring. Edn., Tex. Soc. Prof. Engrs. (past nat. dir., pres. 1973-74, Tex. Engring. Dream Team 2000), Nat. Assn. Parliamentarians, Internat. Soc. Systems Sci., Order of the Engr. (chmn., bd. govs. 1989-91), Am. Soc. for Quality, Internat. Coun. on Systems Engring., Sigma Xi, Sigma Gamma Tau, Tau Beta Pi, Phi Kappa Phi, Chi Epsilon. Home: 810 Dogwood Ln Bryan TX 77802-1144 Office Phone: 979-779-0424. Personal E-mail: samson@cox-internet.com.

SAMSON, DUKE STAPLES, neurosurgeon; b. Odessa, Tex., Jan. 16, 1943; s. Horace Stanford and Ruby Sue (Nicholson) S.; m. Patricia Celine Bergen, July 15, 1989; children: Lorne Daniel, Gabriel Stanford. BA, Stanford U., 1965; MD, Washington U., St. Louis, 1969. Diplmate Am. Bd. Surgery, Am. Bd. Neurosurgery. Intern Duke U. Med. Ctr., Durham, N.C., 1969-70; neurosurg. resident U. Tex. S.W. Med. Sch., Dallas, 1970-75; fellow Ctr. Medico U. Hosp., Paris, France, 1972-73; vis. fellow dept. neurosurgery Katonspital U. Zurich, Switzerland, 1973; asst. prof. dept. surgery U. Tex. Health Sci. Ctr., Dallas, 1975-80, assoc. prof. dept. surgery, 1981-84, prof., chmn. divsn. neurosurgery, 1984-86, Clark prof. and chmn. divsn. neurosurgery, 1985-95, Lois C.A. and Darwin E. Smith disting. chair neurol. surgery, 1983—. Hosp. appts. VA Med. Ctr., Parkland Meml. Hosp., Children's Med. Ctr., Dallas, 1977—, Zale Lipshy U. Hosp., St. Paul Med. Ctr., Dallas, 1989—; cons. neurosurgery svc. Walter Reed Med. Hosp., Washington, 1982—; mem. editl. bd. Surg. Neurology, Neurosurgery. Contbr. over 110 articles and abstracts to profl. jours., over 36 chpts. to books; author: (for symposium) Neurological Conflicts and Concerns, 1977. Honored visitor Royal Australian Coll. of Surgeons, Disting. Vis. Prof. U. Buenos Aires, Argentina, 1996; grantee: Miles Labs., 1984-85, NIH, 1986-89, 89. Mem. Am. Assn. Neurol. Surgeons (Donaghy Lectureship 1997), Congress of Neurol. Surgeons (Honored Guest 1999), Soc. Neurol. Surgeons, Acad. Neurol. Surgery, Kason Rsch. Soc., Neurosurg. Rsch. Soc. Avocations: creative writing, handgun shooting, horses. Office: U Tex SW Med Ctr Dept Neurol Surgery 5323 Harry Hines Blvd Dallas TX 75390-7208 E-mail: samson@utsw.swmed.edu.

SAMSON, LEONA D. biological engineering educator, research center director, researcher; BSc in Biochemistry, Aberdeen (Scotland) U., 1974; PhD, London U., 1978. Postdoctoral rschr. U. Calif., San Francisco, Berkeley; from asst. prof. to full prof. dept. molecular and cellular toxicology Harvard Sch. Pub. Health, 1983—2001; prof. biol. engring. and toxicology MIT, 2001—, dir. MIT Ctr. for Environ. Health Scis., MIT Toxicogenomics Rsch. Program, 2001—. Mem. exec. com. Computational and Systems Biology Initiative MIT; mem. bd. sci. counselors NIEHS; mem. coun. for extramural grants ACS. Named Am. Cancer Soc. Rsch. Prof., 2001; recipient Burroughs Wellcome Toxicology Scholar award, 1993, Charlotte Friend Women in Cancer Rsch. award, 2000. Mem.: Inst. Medicine, 2004. Office: Ctr for Environ Health Scis MIT Bldg 56-235 Cambridge MA 02139 Business E-Mail: lsamson@mit.edu.

SAMSON, RICHARD MAX, theater director, investment company executive; b. Milw., June 13, 1946; s. Harry E. and Rose (Landau) Samson; m. Nancy K. Pinter; children: Gina Shoshana, Alayna Tamar 1 stepchild, Christopher P. BA, U. Wis., 1968. Dir., owner Puppet Co., Jerusalem, 1972-73; pres. Century Hall, Inc., Milw., 1974-75; dir. purchasing Am. Med. Svcs., Inc., Milw., 1973-74, v.p., 1974-82, exec. v.p., 1982-86, pres., 1986-90, Samson Investments, Milw., 1990—2002. Bd. dirs. Liberty Bank, Milw.; sec. Super Sitters, Mequon, Wis., 1987—2004. Co-prodr., dir.: (plays) Loss of Breath: The Unfinished Life and Death of Edgar Allan Poe, 1999; Stones of Wisdom, 2003; co-creator, dir. Einstein: Hero of the Mind, 2002; The Apollo of Bellac, 2004. Pres. bd. dirs. Theatre X, Milw., 1982, Holton Youth Ctr., Milw., 1994, Children's Outing Assn., 1996, Jewish Found. Econ. Opportunity, 1996—2004; v.p. bd. dirs. ArtReach, Milw., 1987; mem. funding bd. Wis. Cmty. Fund, 1989—93; dir. Mask and Puppet Co. Milw., 1992—; treas. nat. bd. dirs. Am. for Peace Now, 2002—04; bd. dirs. Bnai Or Religious Fellowship, 1988—93, Milw. Jewish Coun., 1992—94. Recipient Humanitarian Peace award, Ecumenical Refugee Coun., 1989, Social Justice award, Wis. Cmty. Fund, 1997, Human Rels. award, Wis. region NCCJ, 1998, Cmty. Svc. Human Rels. award, Wis. chpt. Am. Jewish Com., 2000. Avocations: chess, comic book collecting, puppetry. Office: Samson Investments 100A E Pleasant St Milwaukee WI 53212-3975

SAMSOT, ROBERT LOUIS, newspaper editor, consultant; b. New Orleans, July 20, 1943; s. Robert Desposito and Mary Helen (Dohan) S.; m. A. Michael Newton, June 9, 1965; children: Kathleen Anderson Samsot English, Robert Dohan Samsot. BA in Journalism, U. N.C., Chapel Hill, 1965; cert. in Bus.

Adminstrn., Rockhurst Coll., 1982. Reporter Rocky Mountain News, Denver, 1965-67, The Comml. Appeal, Memphis, 1967-72; reporter, editor Newsday, L.I., N.Y., 1972-80; Gannett profl.-in-residence U. Kans., Lawrence, 1980-81; met. editor The Kansas City (Mo.) Times, 1981-84; city editor The Plain Dealer, Cleve., 1984-87; lifestyle editor, dep. editor N.J., dep. editor nat. The Phila. Inquirer, 1987-97; regional editor Balt. Sun, 1997-98; nat. editor USA Today, 1998-2000; asst. city editor The Washington Post, 2000—. Cons. W.K. Kellogg Nat. Fellowship, Battle Creek, Mich., 1984-93; freelance writer, 1965—. Youth soccer coach Northport, N.Y., 1976-80, dir., 1979-80, Shaker Heights, Ohio, 1984-87, Swarthmore (Pa.) Recreation Assn., 1987-88; coach Johnson County (Kans.) Soccer League, 1983-84, U. Kans. Women's Soccer Club, 1980-81; bd. dirs. Suffolk County Heart Assn., L.I., 1974-75. Mem. Nat. Assn. Hispanic Journalists, Investigative Reporters and Editors. Democrat. Roman Catholic. Avocations: travel, fishing, outdoor sports. Home: 10413 Breckinridge Ln Fairfax VA 22030-3417 Office: The Washington Post 1150 15th St NW Washington DC 20071-0002

SAMUEL, CARREN C. hospital administrator; b. Jan. 7, 1959; arrived in U.S., 1977, d. George A. and Ira P. Dundas; m. Boysing Samuel, Sept. 17, 1984; children: Boysing Jr., Michael C. AS, N.Y.C. Tech. Coll., Bklyn., 1981; BS, L.I. U., Bklyn., 1984, MPA, 1991. Cert. RRT Nat. Bd. for Respiratory Care. Respiratory therapist Kingsbrook Jewish Med. Ctr., Bklyn., 1983—86, asst. dir., respiratory care, 1986—94, dir., respiratory care, 1994—2001, adminstrv. dir., cardiopulmonary svcs., 2001—. Mem.: Am. Assn. for Respiratory Care. Office: Kingsbrook Jewish Med Ctr 585 Schenectady Ave Brooklyn NY 11203

SAMUEL, GEORGE, healthcare information company executive; b. Tiruvalla, Kerala, India, May 25, 1958; came to U.S., 1980; s. VC and Elizabeth Samuel. BS, Kerala U., 1979; AAS, Lehigh Coll., 1980; MBA, So. Calif. U., 1995. Programmer, analyst Knowledge Data Sys., San Antonio, 1982-85, tech. mgr., 1985-87, dir. mgmt. info. sys. Cin., 1987-88, v.p., acct. mgr. Detroit, 1988-89, Larkspur, Calif., 1989-91, v.p., R & D products divsn., 1991-93; pres., CEO Healthcare Media Enterprises Inc., Novato, Calif., 1993—. Vol. Project Open Hand, Oakland, Calif., 1992—, Big Bros. and Sisters. Mem. Am. Mgmt. Assn., Toastmasters Internat. Avocations: tennis, skiing, car racing.

SAMUEL, PAUL, retired cardiologist, educator; b. Janoshaza, Hungary, Jan. 17, 1927; came to U.S., 1954, naturalized, 1960; s. Adolf and Magda (Zollner) S.; m. Gabriella R. Zeichner, Mar. 27, 1954; children: Robert Mark, Adrianne Jill. Baccalaureat, Kemeny Zsigmond Gymnasium, Budapest, Hungary, 1945; MD, U. Paris, 1953. Intern Queens Hosp. Ctr., N.Y.C., 1954-55; resident L.I. Jewish Med. Ctr., New Hyde Park, N.Y., 1959-61; adj. prof. Rockefeller U., N.Y.C., 1971-81; adj. prof. medicine Cornell U., N.Y.C., 1979—; pvt. practice, Forest Hills, N.Y., 1961—; ret. Clin. prof. medicine Albert Einstein Coll. Medicine, Bronx, N.Y., 1981—; dir. Arteriosclerosis Rsch. Lab., L.I. Jewish-Hillside Med. Ctr., New Hyde Park, 1962—; chmn. N.Y. Lipid Rsch. Club, Rockefeller U., 1977-78. Contbr. articles to med. jours. Fellow Am. Coll. Cardiology; mem. ACP, Am. Heart Assn. (fellow coun. on arteriosclerosis, Disting. Achievement award), Am. Fedn. Clin. Rsch., Harvey Soc. Home: 25 Nassau Dr Great Neck NY 11021-2163

SAMUEL, RALPH DAVID, lawyer; b. Augusta, Ga., May 8, 1945; s. Ralph and Louise Elizabeth (Wurreschke) S.; m. Lynn Christel Malmgren, June 12, 1971; children: Lynn Britt, Ralph Erik. AB, Dartmouth Coll., 1967; JD, Dickinson Sch. of Law, 1972. Bar: Pa. 1972, U.S. Dist. Ct. (ea. dist.) Pa. 1972, U.S. Ct. Appeals (3d cir.) 1973, U.S. Supreme Ct. 1976. Law clk. to hon. judge John P. Fullam U.S. Dist. Ct. (ea. dist.) Pa., Phila., 1972-74; assoc. MacCoy, Evans & Lewis., Phila., 1974-76; ptnr. Samuel and Ballard, P.C., Phila., 1976-98; pres., CEO Ralph D. Samuel & Co., P.C., Phila., 1998—. Established Samuel Poetry Fellow Dartmouth Coll., Hanover, N.H., 1994. Contbr. articles to profl. jours., poetry to publs. Trustee The George Sch., Newtown, Pa., 1983-90; chmn. bd. dirs. Stapeley in Germantown, 1985-90; mem. Chase Fund Com., 2000; chmn. budget com. Phila. Yearly Meeting of Friends, 1991-93; bd. dirs., mem. fin. com. Phila. Ranger Corps., 1992-94; pres. Cedar Park Neighbors, Phila., 1975-78, West Mt. Airy Neighbors, Phila., 1981-82. Mem. Pa. Soc., Athenaeum of Phila., Sunday Breakfast Club. Mem. Soc. Of Friends. Avocations: music, writing, squash, tennis. Office: PO Box 35185 Philadelphia PA 19128-0185 Fax: (215) 701-1085. Office Phone: 215-893-9992. E-mail: RalphSamuel@RalphSamuel.com.

SAMUEL, ROBERT THOMPSON, optometrist; b. Kansas City, Mo., June 27, 1944; s. Manlius Thompson and Helen Evelyn (Syverson) S. BA, William Jewell Coll., 1966; postgrad., U. Mo., Kansas City, 1967; MS, U. Mo., 1968; DOptometry, U. Tenn., Memphis, 1971; postgrad., U. Mo., St. Louis, 1995, Northeastern State U., 1998. Cert. optometrist, Mo. Buyer Recco, Inc., Kansas City, Mo., 1963-67; histology lab. instr. William Jewell Coll., Liberty, Mo., 1965-66; pvt. practice optometry Gladstone, Mo., 1972—; staff doctor O.H. Gerry Optical Clinics, 1996—. Panel doctor Ford Motor Co., Claycomo, Mo., 1985—, Union Pacific R.R., Kansas City, 1985—, TWA Airlines, 1990, Union Carbide, 1990. Publicity coord. Rep. Party, Kansas City, Mo., 1975-76; chmn. Save Your Vision Week, Kansas City, 1977; mem. Theatre League of Kansas City, 1976—, Kansas City Mus., 1986—, Friends of Art, 1985, Friends of Mo. Town 1955, 1980—. Recipient Outstanding Young Men of Am. award Jaycees, 1978, Good Citizens award DAR, 1962. Mem. Am. Optometric Assn., Mo. Optometric Assn., Optometric Soc. Greater Kansas City, Heart of Am. Contact Lens Congress, Am. Acad. Sports Vision, Vol. Optometric Svcs. for Humanity, Smithsonian Assocs., Lions (exec. bd. dir. Lions Eye Clinic 1974-84, bd. dirs. 1982—, Outstanding Svc. award 1973, 74, editor Lions Optometric Ctr. Quar. 1974-84), Kappa Alpha Order (treas. 1966). Republican. Lutheran. Avocations: photography, music, piano, swimming, travel. Home: 6325 N Monroe Ave Kansas City MO 64119-1923 Office: 1170 W 152 Hwy Liberty MO 64068-2035 also: 5601 NE Antioch Rd Kansas City MO 64119-2302

SAMUEL, ROGER D. newspaper publishing executive; Dir. advt. The Flint (Mich.) Jour., 1991—96, pub., 1996—. Office: The Flint Jour 200 E 1st St Flint MI 48502-1911

SAMUEL, STEVEN A. cardiologist; b. N.Y.C., Feb. 23, 1951; BS, Duke U., 1973; MD, Albert Einstein Coll. Medicine, 1978. Diplomate Nat. Bd. Med. Examiners, Am. Bd. Internal Medicine, Am. Bd. Cardiovasc. Disease. Resident in family practice Southside Hosp., Bay Shore, NY; resident in internal medicine Univ. Hosp. and VA Med. Ctr.; resident in internal medicine, chief resident in internal medicine, fellow in cardiology SUNY, Stony Brook, attending physician dept. medicine, divsn. cardiology, 1984—85; pvt. practice Moorestown (N.J.) Med. Assocs., 1985—87, Trenton (N.J.) Cardiology Cons., 1987—. Tchg. assoc. dept. medicine, divsn. cardiology Cooper Hosp./Univ. Med. Ctr., Camden, NJ, 1986—87; mem. active staff dept. medicine, sect. cardiology St. Francis Med. Ctr., Trenton, 1987—, sect. chief cardiology, 1994—96; mem. active staff dept. medicine, sect. cardiology Robert Wood Johnson Univ. Hosp. at Hamilton, Trenton, 1994—. Named one of Top Drs. 2003, N.J. Montly Mag.; recipient Founders' award, Women's Heart Rsch. Fund, 1995, Good Guys award, Women's Polit. Caucus of N.J., 1998. Fellow: Am. Coll. Cardiology; mem.: AMA, ACP, Mercer County Med. Soc., Med. Soc. N.J. Office: 1235 Whitehorse Mercer Rd # 317 Trenton NJ 08619-3810

SAMUELI, HENRY, electrical engineering educator, entrepreneur; b. Buffalo, N.Y., Sept. 20, 1954; s. Aron and Sala (Traubman) S.; m. Susan Faye Eisenberg, Aug. 22, 1982; children: Leslie Pamela, Jillian Meryl, Erin Sydney. BS, UCLA, 1975, MS, 1976, PhD, 1980. Staff engr. TRW Inc., Redondo Beach, Calif., 1980-83, section mgr., 1983-85; asst. prof. UCLA, 1985-90, assoc. prof., 1990-94, prof., 1994—. Cons. TRW, Inc., Redondo Beach, 1985-89; co-founder, chief scientist PairGain Techs., Inc., Tustin, Calif., 1989-94; co-founder, chief tech. officer Broadcom Corp., Irvine, Calif., 1991—. Named one of Top 20 Entrepreneurs of 1997, The Red Herring Mag., 1997, one of Top 50 Cyber Elite, Time Digital Mag., 1997. Mem.: NAE. Republican. Jewish. Avocations: skiing, basketball. Office: Broadcom Corp PO Box 57013 Irvine CA 92619-7013

SAMUELS, ABRAM, stage equipment manufacturing company executive; b. Allentown, Pa., Sept. 15, 1920; s. Irving and Ann (Friedman) S.; m. Harriet Ann Goodman, Sept. 1, 1945; children: Margaret A. Samuels Berger, Katherine E., Sally R. Samuels Slifkin, John A., Dorothy M. Samuels Lampl, Caroline J. Samuels Bagli. BS, Lehigh U., 1942; auditor philosophy, Princeton U., 1962-65. Pres. Automatic Devices Co., Allentown, 1946-75, chmn. exec. com., 1987-92, chmn. bd., 1975-87, 93—, Mchts. Bank, 1981-85, chmn. exec. com., 1985-91. Past guest lectr. Cedar Crest Coll., 1969-71, 84, Muhlenberg Coll., 1977-82, 92. Author: Where the Colleges Rank, 1973. Pres. Samuels Family Found., 1959—; past pres. Pa. Soc. for Crippled Children and Adults, 1957-58; past pres., hon. bd. dirs. Lehigh County Crippled Children's Soc., 1949-51; past pres. Lehigh County Humane Soc., 1960-64, Cedar Crest Coll. Assocs., 1968-70; bd. dirs. Allentown Hosp., 1977-88, chmn. bd., 1987; vice chmn. Allentown Hosp.-Lehigh Valley Hosp. Ctr., 1988; pres. Lehigh County Hist. Soc., 1976-78; past bd. dirs. Nat. Soc. for Crippled Children and Adults, Pa. Mental Health Assn., Merchants Bank, 1965-91, Lehigh County Indsl. Devel. Corp., Pa. Stage Co., 1983-84, Health East, Inc., 1985-91, Nightingale Awards of Pa., 1989-91; trustee St. Augustine's Coll., 1970-77, 92-95, Allentown YWCA, 1977-83, Cedar Crest Coll., 1996—; hon. doctorate, 2003; bd. dirs. Fund to Benefit Children and Youth of Lehigh Valley Inc., 1992-2003, Lehigh County Hist. Soc., 1999-2003. With AUS, 1942-46. Recipient Benjamin Rush award Lehigh County Med. Soc., 1954, Allentown Human Relations award, 1979; named Outstanding Young Man of Year Jr. C. of C., 1954. Mem. Hon. First Defenders, C. of C. (past v.p. 1960), Pa. German Soc., Am. Soc. Psychical Rsch. (trustee 1985-91, treas. 1990), Princeton Club (N.Y.C.), Rotary (pres. Allentown club 1955-56, dist. gov. 1964-65). Republican. Office: 2121 S 12th St Allentown PA 18103-4751

SAMUELS, BARRY IVAN, radiologist, medical educator; b. Detroit, Oct. 31, 1940; s. Alex and Ida Samuels; m. Carole Paulette Samuels, June 20, 1964; children: Marc, Craig. BA, Wayne State U., 1961; MD, U. Mich., 1965. Lic. physician, Tex., Mich., Calif., La., Ariz. Assoc. prof. radiology U. Tex. M.D. Anderson Cancer Ctr., Houston, 1989—2002, prof. radiology, 2002—. Sr. asst. surgeon USPHS, 1966-68. Mem. Am. Coll. Radiology, Am. Inst. Ultrasound, Tex. Radiol. Soc., Tex. Med. Assn., Houston Radiol. Soc. Avocations: walking, reading, music, art, travel.

SAMUELS, DONALD L. lawyer; b. Washington, May 8, 1961; s. Jack Donald Samuels and Francis Diane (Katcher) Yeoman; m. Sherri Tubin Samuels. AB, Brown U., 1983; JD, Columbia U., 1986. Bar: Calif. 1986, U.S. Dist. Ct. (cen., no., ea. and so. dists.) Calif. 1988, U.S. Ct. Appeals (9th cir.) 1989, Colo. 1996, U.S. Ct. Appeals (7th cir.) 1996, U.S. Dist. Ct. Colo. 1997, U.S. Ct. Appeals (10th cir.) 1997, Tex. 1998. Law clk. Hon. William D. Keller, L.A., 1986-87; assoc. Sidley & Austin, L.A., 1987-94, ptnr., 1994-95, Samuels & Samuels, L.A., 1995-97; officer, dir., shareholder Ireland & Stapleton, Denver, 1997—2002; ptnr. Holme, Roberts & Owen, LLP, Denver, 2002—. Mem. ABA, Calif. Bar Assn., Colo. Bar Assn., Tex. Bar Assn., Phi Beta Kappa. Home: 5692 S Florence St Greenwood Village CO 80111-3713 Office: Holme Roberts & Owen LLP Ste 4100 1700 Lincoln St Denver CO 80203-4541 Office Phone: 303-866-0548. Business E-Mail: donald.samuels@hro.com.

SAMUELS, FERN JACQUELINE, artist, educator; b. Chgo., Feb. 16, 1931; d. Noah S. and Ann (Zager) Andrews; m. Howard Stanley Samuels, Sept. 17, 1950; children: Mitchell, Paul, David. BFA, Loyola U., 1973; MFA, Sch. Art Inst. Chgo., 1983. Instr.-coord. Mundelein Coll., Chgo., 1976-83; faculty Columbia Coll., Chgo., 1978-2000. Instr. workshops Field Mus., Chgo., 1976, Lake Forest Coll., Chgo., 1976, Lincoln Park Cultural Ctr., Chgo., 1973, Ill. Inst. Tech., Chgo., 1980—, Latin Sch., Chgo., 1976; juror St. Louis Arts Guild, 1998. One-women shows include Northwestern U., 1988, Ea. Ill. U., Chgo., 1989, Countryside Gallery, 1988, Upstart Gallery, 1990, Soho 20, N.Y.C., 1993, Loyola U., 1995, Morraine Valley Coll., 1995, McDonough Mus. Art, 1997, Fyr Place Gallery, 2000, Gallery on Azeele, 2000, Mos Art Gallery, Lake Park, Fla., 2004, Cornell Mus., Del Ray, Fla., 2004; exhibited in group shows including Smithsonian Air and Space Mus., 1983, Freeport Mus., 1995, Rockford Mus., 1996, Butler Inst. Am. Art, 1998, Lafayette Mus., 1999, Columbus Mus. Art, 2000, So. Ohio Mus., 2000, South Bend Regional Mus., 2000, Univ. Mus. S.D., 2001, Gallery 228, N.Y., N.Y., 2003. Mem. LWV, Chgo., 1969—; founding mem. Alternative Fibers, Chgo., 1982; chairperson, coord. Seven Ethnic Museums, Chgo., 1986; membership chmn. ARC Gallery, Chgo., 1983-86, pres. 1988-90; bd. dirs. Artist Book Works, Chgo., 1992-93. Recipient Best of Show award Women in the Visual Arts, Boca Raton, Fla., 2001, Judges Recognition award, Boca Raton, 2001, 2nd prize Boca Mus. Artists Guild, 2001, 1st prize, 2002, 1st prize Women in Visual Arts, Del Ray, Fla., 2002, Mus. Exhibits, 2002, Jewish Mus., Miami, Norton Mus., West Palm Beach, Fla., 2002, 2004, Cornell Mus. of Art and Sci., Del Ray, 2002, Art Club Chgo., 2003, Permanent Collection, Rutgers U., 2003, 1st prize Northwood U., West Palm Beach, Fla., 2003, 1st prize Boca Mus. Artist Guild, 2003; grantee Columbia Coll., 1981; Fern Samuels Scholarship Fund est. Columbia Coll., Chgo., 1st prize Milagro Art Ctr., Del Ray Fla., 2003, 1st prize Boca Mus. Artist Guild, 2003. Mem. Nat. Assn. Women Artists, Internat. Soc. Exptl. Artists, Nat. Collage Soc., Arts Club Chgo., Chgo. Soc. Arts, City of Hope (Bobby Blechman chpt. founding mem.), Sch. Art Inst. Chgo. Alumni (2d prize 2002). Democrat. Avocations: reading, music, theater, exercise. Home: 84 Saint James Ct Palm Beach Gardens FL 33418 E-mail: ucars1@aol.com.

SAMUELS, JANET LEE, lawyer; b. Pitts., July 18, 1953; d. Emerson and Jeanne (Kalish) S.; m. David Arthur Kalow, June 18, 1978; children: Margaret Emily Samuels-Kalow, Jacob Richard Samuels-Kalow, Benjamin Charles Samuels-Kalow. BA with honors, Beloit Coll., 1974; JD, NYU, 1977. Bar: N.Y. 1978, D.C. 1980. Staff atty. SCM Corp., N.Y.C., 1977-80, corp. atty., 1980-83, sr. corp. atty., 1983-85, assoc. gen. counsel Allied Paper div., 1983-86, corp. counsel, 1986, Holtzmann, Wise & Shepard, 1986-88. Mem. N.Y. State Bar Assn., Mortar Board, Phi Beta Kappa. E-mail: JanetLSamuels@yahoo.com.

SAMUELS, JOHN M., JR., industrial engineer; B in Indsl. Engring., GM Inst.; M in Indsl. Engring., PhD in Indsl. Engring., Penn. State U. Assoc. prof. indsl. engring. Penn. State U.; numerous positions GM; with Conrail, 1978—96, Norfolk (Va.) So. Corp., 1998—, sr. v.p. ops. planning and support, 1998—. Mem. exec. com. Transp. Rsch. Bd., 1998-2003, past chmn. exec. com., 2001. Chmn. Accreditation Bd. Engring. and Tech., 2004; chmn. adv. bd. Old Dominion U. Coll. Engring., 2004. Fellow Inst. Indsl. Engrs. (sr. mem.), World Acad. Productivity Sci.; mem. NAE, Am. Rlwy. Engring. Assn. (sr. mem.), Alpha Pi Mu, Tau Beta Pi, Sigma Xi. Office: Norfolk So Corp 3 Commercial Pl Norfolk VA 23510-9237

SAMUELS, JOHN STOCKWELL, III, mining company executive, financier; b. Galveston, Tex., Sept. 15, 1933; s. John Stockwell and Helen Yvonne (Poole) S.; children: Evelyn Kathleen, John Stockwell, Ainlay Leontine, Peter Ashton Hayes. AB, SM, Tex. A&M U., 1954; JD, Harvard U., 1960. Bar: N.Y. 1961. With Chadbourne, Parke, Whiteside & Wolff, N.Y.C., 1960-73; pres. Internat. Carbon & Minerals, N.Y.C., 1973-78, Carbomin Group, Inc., N.Y.C., 1978—, U.S. Reduction Inc., 1996—. Chmn. bd. J.S. Samuels & Co. Bd. dirs. City Center Music and Drama, Inc., N.Y.C.; chmn. bd. dirs. N.Y.C. Ballet, N.Y.C. Opera, 1976-81, Lincoln Ctr. Theatre, N.Y.C., 1979-81, Lincoln Ctr., N.Y.C. With U.S. Army, 1954-57. Mem. Century Assn. Democrat. Episcopalian. Office Phone: 212-838-2004. E-mail: jss@usr-inc.com.

SAMUELS, LESLIE B. lawyer; b. St. Louis, Nov. 10, 1942; s. Joseph E. and Dorothy J. (Bernstein) S.; m. Judith B. Thorn, June 19, 1966 (div. Aug. 1976); children: Colin T., Polly B.; m. Augusta H. Gross, Nov. 8, 1980. BS in Econs., U. Pa., 1963; LLB magna cum laude, Harvard U., 1966; postgrad., London Sch. Econs., 1966-67. Bar: N.Y., 1969, U.S. Dist. Ct. (so. dist.) N.Y. 1973, U.S. Tax Ct., 1980, U.S. Supreme Ct. 1994; CPA. Tax analyst Gulf Oil Co., London, 1967-68; assoc. Cleary, Gottlieb, Steen & Hamilton, N.Y.C., 1968-75, ptnr., 1975-93, 96—; asst. sec. for tax policy U.S. Dept. Treasury, Washington, 1993-96; vice-chair com. fiscal affairs OECD, 1994-96. Mem. Pres.'s Com. on the Arts and the Humanities, Washington, 1994-96. Editor Law Rev.; contbr. articles to profl. jours. Dir. Lower Manhattan Cultural Coun., N.Y.C., 1981-93, Roy Lichtenstein Found., N.Y.C., 1999—; active Carter-Mondale Transition Planning Group, Washington, 1976-77. Fulbright fellow London Sch. Econs., 1966-67. Mem. N.Y. State Bar Assn., Assn. of Bar of City of N.Y., Harvard Club (N.Y.C.). Democrat. Office: Cleary Gottlieb Steen & Hamilton One Liberty Plaza New York NY 10006 E-mail: lsamuels@cgsh.com.

SAMUELS, LESLIE EUGENE, marketing and management consultant; b. St. Croix, V.I., Nov. 12, 1929; s. Henry Francis and Annamartha Venetia (Ford) S.; m. Reather James, Oct. 24, 1959; children: Leslie Jr., Venetia, Yvette, Philip. MusB, NYU, 1956; JD, Blackstone Sch. Law, 1975; MBA, Columbia Pacific U., 1984, PhD, 1985. Concert soloist Van Dyke Studios, N.Y.C., 1956-65; dir. Housing, Preservation and Devel., N.Y.C., 1966—; bandmaster N.Y. State Dept. Rehab. and Recreation, N.Y.C., 1967-76; pres., CEO Samuels and Co., Inc., N.Y.C., 1986—, Coll. Philosophy and Edn., 1998—; exec. dir., CEO Samuels Inst. Hist. Rsch. of Christian Prins., 1991—. Cons. in field., 1984—; mem. N.Y., N.J. Minority Bus. Purchasing Coun., Inc., Nat. Minority Bus. Coun., Inc., Internat. Trade divsn.; evangelist, lectr. Principles of the Christian Faith; adj. prof. St. Martin's Coll. and Sem., 1995; dir. pvt. sch. state edn. dept., 1996. TV apperances include: Bill Slibert's Rev., 1953, Ladies Day, 1953; Author: Redemption, 2000. Mem. chmn. congrl. coun. of the Virgin Island, 1960-64, Bronx County Com., 1969; dist. leader Bronx 86th Assembly Dist., 1969; advisor Astor Home for Children, Bronx, 1973, Bronxville C. of C., Bklyn., 1975; charter mem. Rep. Presdl. Task Force, 1989; exec. dir. Samuels Inst. Hist. Rsch. Christian Principles, 1991—; mem. Nat. Rep. Senatorial Com., 1992. With U.S. Army, 1951-53. Mem. Maison Internationale des Intellectuels, Am. Mgmt. Assn., Nat. Black MBA Assn., Harvard Bus. Rev., Sloan Mgmt. Rev., Calif. Mgmt. Rev., Columbia Pacific U. Alumni Assn., Internat. Platform Assn., Smithsonian Assocs., Ind. Citizen's Club (pres. Bronx 1967-77). Republican. Avocation: sports. Home: 2814 Bruner Ave Bronx NY 10469-3403 E-mail: samuelsinstitut@webtv.net.

SAMUELS, MARC, health care consultant; b. Bethesda, Md., Feb. 8, 1968; s. Monica (Leiter) Samuels; 1 child, Jeb. BA cum laude, U. Mich., 1989; MPH in Policy and Adminstrn., Yale U., 1992; JD, U. Tex., 1996. Staff asst. McManis Assocs., Health Care Consultants, Washington, Law Offices of Deborah L. Steelman, Washington, Office of Policy Devel., The White House, Washington, VP's Domestic Policy Office, Washington; health care cons., legis. asst., health law sect. Jenkens & Gilchrist PC, Austin, Tex.; asst. to Gov. for Health Policy, Office of Gov. George W. Bush, Austin, Tex.; personal asst. to commr. Tex. Health and Human Svcs. Commn., Austin, Tex.; prin. Samuels Health Strategies, Austin, Tex. Mem. adv. bd. U. Houston Health Law and Policy Inst.; advisor Tex. Lifescience Found., Austin. Co-author: The Managed Care Answer Book, 1996, 4th edit., 1999, Risk Contracting and Capitation Answer Book, 1998, 2d edit., 1999; contbr. articles to profl. jours. Dep. rsch. dir. Kay Bailey Hutchison for U.S. Senate, 1993; health care policy advisor George W. Bush for Gov., 1994, Jeb Bush for Gov., 1998, Bush for Pres. Campaign Exploratory Com., 1999; chmn. A Policy Forum for Young Am., 1996. Spencer Scholar Risk & Ins. Mgmt. Soc., 1996; recipient Baker and Botts prize, 1996. Business E-Mail: msamuels@hillcopartners.com.

SAMUELS, SANDOR E. diversified financial services company executive; Grad., Princeton, 1974; JD, U. Calif., L.A., 1977. Law clk. U.S. Dist. Judge Irving Hill, 1977—79; atty. Munger, Tolles and Olson, 1979—83, First Interstate Bancorp, 1984—88, sr. v.p., asst. gen. counsel, 1988; sr. v.p., gen. counsel Fox Inc., 1989—90; sr. v.p., gen. counsel, sec. Countrywide Fin. Corp., Calabasas, Calif., 1990—91, mng. dir., legal, gen. counsel. sec., 1991—2000, sr. mng. dir., legal, gen. counsel, sec., 2001—03, sr. mng. dir., chief legal advisor, sec., 2003—. Bd. dirs. U. Judaism, Bet Tzedek Legal Svcs., Adat Ari El Synagogue. Mem.: Mortgage Bankers Assn. Am. (chair legal issues com.). Office: Countrywide Fin Corp 4500 Park Granada Calabasas CA 91302-1613

SAMUELS, WILLIAM MASON, physiology association executive; b. Dover, Ohio, Jan. 17, 1929; s. William Mason and Anne Frieda (Fankhauser) S.; m. Joanne Gorenflo, Oct. 2, 1971; children: Robert Lee, Ann Frances. AB, U. Ky., 1951; postgrad., Georgetown U., 1952. Mng. editor for Ind., Courier-Jour. & Times, Louisville, 1955-65; dir. office of v.p. U. Ky. Med. Center, Lexington, 1965-70; exec. dir. Am. Soc. Allied Health Professions, Washington, 1973—78; assoc. Schs. Allied Health Professions, 1970—73; exec. dir. Am. Assn. Blood Banks, Washington, 1978-80, Nat. Soc. Med. Research Washington, 1980-84, Am. Physiol. Soc., Bethesda, Md., 1984-92; retired, 1992—. Contbr. articles to profl. jours. Mem. secretariat Nat. Commn. Health Certifying Agys.; v.p. Coalition Health Funding; cons. to fed. agys.; vol. Habitat for Humanity, Boca Raton. With USAF, 1951-53, USAFR, 1954-76, lt. col. ret. Named Ky. Man of Yr. Sigma Phi Epsilon, 1968 Mem.: AMA (coun. on allied health edn. accreditation), Washington Soc. Assn. Execs., Health Staff Soc., Am. Hosp. Assn. (coun. on edn.), Am. Optometric Assn. (coun. on edn., coun. on optimetric clin. care, nat. commn. on paraoptometric cert.), Am. Soc. Assn. Execs., Pinehurst (NC) Country Club, Lions. Presbyterian. Home: 6055 S Verde Trail H-120 Boca Raton FL 33433-4406

SAMUELSON, CECIL O. academic administrator; b. 1942; BS, MS, MD, U. Utah. V.p. health scis. U. Utah, Salt Lake City, 1970-90; sr. v.p. Intermountain Health Care, Inc., Salt Lake City, 1990—; dean IHC Hosps. Inc., Salt Lake City, 1990—; pres. BYU, Provo, Utah, 2003—. Office: Office of the Pres Brigham Young U Provo UT 84602

SAMUELSON, CYNTHIA, information technology executive; b. N.C. m. Lawrence Samuelson. BA in Math., Hampton U.; MS in Computer Sci., Fairleigh Dickinson U.; postgrad., U. So. Calif. Mathematician Westinghouse R&D Ctr., Pitts.; with FTC, Washington, U.S. Dept. Commerce, Washington, Nat. Edowment for the Arts; info. resource mgmt. dir. Dept. of Transp.; prin. dir. info. mgmt. Office of the Asst. Sec. of Def. for Command, Control, Comm. and Intelligence, Washington; bus. devel. dir. Lucent Technologies Govt. Solutions (now Avaya), Basking Ridge, NJ, v.p. mktg., telesales and svcs. Mem. Aero. and Space Engring. Bd., NAS. Bd. dirs. Sch. Engring., Hampton U.; mentor Boy Scouts Am.; mentor various pub. and pvt. sector orgns. Named one of Fed. Computer Week's Top 100 Fed. Info. Tech. Execs.; recipient Bronze medal, Dept. Transp., Medal for Meritorious Civilian Svc., Dept. of Def., Exceptional Civilian Svc. award, Tech. award, Black Engr.'s Women of Color. Mem.: Armed Forces Comm. and Electronics Assn. (bd. dirs.). Office: Avaya 211 Mount Airy Rd Basking Ridge NJ 07920

SAMUELSON, DERRICK WILLIAM, lawyer; b. Mpls., July 24, 1929; s. Oscar W. and Ruth (Hill) S.; m. Diana L. Webster, Aug. 10, 1957; children: David W., Deirdre S. Columbia. BS, U.S. Mil. Acad., 1951; LL.B., Harvard U., 1957. Bar: N.Y. 1958. Assoc. firm Lowenstein, Pitcher, Hotchkiss, Amann & Parr, N.Y.C., 1957-60; staff atty. internat. div. Warner-Lambert Pharm. Co., Morris Plains, N.J., 1960-63; counsel internat. div. Olin Mathieson Chem. Corp., N.Y.C., 1964-65; v.p., gen. counsel ITT World Communications Inc., N.Y.C., 1965-70, ITT Asia Pacific, Inc., N.Y.C., 1970-81; sr. counsel ITT Corp., N.Y.C., 1981-87, asst. gen. counsel, asst. sec., 1987-92; of counsel Mulvaney, Kahan & Barry, San Diego, 1993—. Mem. panel neutrals and internat. panel Am. Arbitration Assn., 1995—; mem. bd. arbitrators Nat. Assn. Securities Dealers, Inc., 1996—. Pres. Am-Indonesian C. of C., 1976-79, Smoke Rise Club, 1976-77, 88-89; chmn. Am. ASEAN Trade Coun., Inc., 1978-92. With U.S. Army, 1951-54. Office: First Nat Bank Bldg 401 W A St San Diego CA 92101-7901 E-mail: dsamuelson@prodigy.net.

SAMUELSON, DONALD B. former state legislator; b. Brainerd, Minn., Aug. 23, 1932; s. Walter H. and Ellen (Gallagher) S.; m. Nancy O'Brien, 1952; children: Stephen, Laura, Paula, Christine. Chmn. 6th Dist. Com. on Polit. Edn. State of Minn., 1960-66; mem. Minn. Ho. of Reps., St. Paul, 1969-76, 1981-82, Minn. Senate from 12th dist., St. Paul, 1982—; pres. Minn. Senate, St. Paul, 2001—. Chmn. Health & Human Svc. Fin. Div. Com., mem. Commerce and Consumer Protection, mem. Family Svc. Com., mem. Fin. and Health Care Com.; former foreman Bor-Son Construct Co.; union bus. mgr. Chmn. 6th Dist. Com. on Polit. Edn., Minn., 1960-66; mem. State Ctrl. Com.

Dem-Farmer-Labor Party, 1964-66, former chmn. Crow Wing County. Mem. Housing and Redevel. Authority, Minn. AFL-CIO, Bricklayers Union, Elks, Eagles, Moose. Democrat. Home: 1018 Portland Ave Brainerd MN 56401-4133

SAMUELSON, DOUGLAS ALAN, information systems company executive; b. Reno, Nev., July 27, 1948; s. Norman Harold and Shirley (Leder) S.; m. Francine Ruth Kimel, Jan. 7, 1979; children: Andrew, Diane. BA, U. Calif., Berkeley, 1969; MS, George Washington U., 1981, DSc, 1990. Computer systems analyst Bank of Am., San Francisco, 1972-73; cons. San Rafael, Calif., 1973-75; ops. rsch. analyst U.S. Govt., Washington, 1975-82; analyst, v.p. Micro-Zeit/Internat. Telesystems Corp., Reston, Va., 1983-88; asst. prof. Memphis State U., 1990-92; pres. InfoLogix, Inc., Annandale, Va., 1988—; prin. scientist Puma Sys., Inc., Falls Church, Va., 1997-98; chief statistician FMAS Dyncorp., Columbia, Md., 2000; sci. advisor ITT Rsch. Inst., 2001. Vis. rsch. scholar George Washington U., 1993—95, mem. nat. adv. coun. Sch. Engring. and Applied Sci., 1996—2000, adj. prof. lectr., 1997—; adj. assoc. prof. George Mason U., Fairfax, Va., 1994—96, external rsch. prof. Krasnow Inst. for Advanced Study, 2001—; adj. assoc. prof. U. Pa., Phila., 2001—. Co-editor, author (with others): Human Rights and Statistics: Getting the Record Straight, 1992, Health Information and Ethics: Protecting Fundamental Human Rights, 1997; author (column) The ORacle, 1986—; contbr. articles to profl. jours. Bd. dirs. George Washington U. Engr. Alumni Assn., 1994—, v.p., 1996-98, pres., 1998-2000. Mem. AAAS, Washington OR/MS Coun. (pres. 1989-90, 96-97), Am. Statis. Assn. (chair com. on scientific freedom and human rights 1985-88), Inst. for Ops. Rsch. and Mgmt. Sci. (bd. dirs. 1998-2000). Democrat. Jewish. Achievements include patent for systems for regulating arrivals of customers to servers. Office: InfoLogix Inc 8711 Chippendale Ct Annandale VA 22003-3807 E-mail: samuelsondoug@netscape.net.

SAMUELSON, JOAN BENOIT, professional runner; b. Cape Elizabeth, Maine, May 16, 1957; d. André and Nancy Benoit; m. Scott Samuelson; children: Abigail, Anders. Student, Bowdoin Coll., N.C. State U. Long-distance coach Boston U.; runner; Runner 10K L.L. Bean Run, July 4, 1997. Bd. dirs. Gulf of Maine Aquarium, Found. for Advancement Edn., Internat. Amateur Athletic Fedn. Coun.; active Maine Lung Found., Natural Resources Coun. Main, Alzheimer's Found., Multiple Sclerosis Soc., Spl. Olympics. Recipient Gold medal Olympic Games, 1984 (set world record); won Boston Marathon, 1983 (set world record). Office: Edwin P Whittemore 114A Massachusetts Ave Arlington MA 02474-8624 also: Roadrunners Club of America 1150 S Washington St Ste 205 Alexandria VA 22314-4493

SAMUELSON, KENNETH LEE, lawyer; b. Natrona Heights, Pa., Aug. 22, 1946; s. Sam and Frances Bernice (Robbins) Samuelson; m. Marlene Ina Rabinowitz, Jan. 1, 1980; children: Heather, Cheryl. BA magna cum laude, U. Pitts., 1968; JD, U. Mich., 1971. Bar: Md. 1972, DC 1980, U.S. Dist. Ct. (trial bar) Md. 1984. Assoc. Weinberg & Green, Balt., 1971-73, Dickerson, Nice, Sokol & Horn, Balt., 1973; asst. atty. gen. State of Md., 1973-77; pvt. practice Balt., 1978; ptnr. Linowes and Blocher, Silver Spring, Md., 1979-93, Semmes, Bowen & Semmes, Balt. and Washington, 1993—95, Wilkes Artis, Chartered, Washington, 1995—2001, Deckelbaum Ogens & Raftery, Washington, 2001—, Bethesda, Md., 2001—. Spkr. in field telecom., fin. and real estate. Bd. govs. Washington Bldg. Congress, 1998—2001; bd. dirs. DC Assn. Retarded Citizens, Inc., 1986—2001. Mem.: ABA (co-chair tech. com. 1999—, coun. mem. sect. real property, probate and trust law 2000—, moderator various programs), Montgomery County Bar Assn. (mem. jud. selections com. 1988—90), Internat. Coun. Shopping Ctrs. (organized co-faculty program "univ." 1988, NAFTA 1992, condemnations 1994, leasing 1997, high tech. effects 1998, pub./pvt. partnerships 1999), E. Coast Builders Conf., Apt. and Office Bldg. Assn. Met. Washington, Civil Code Drafting Com. Russian Legis., Nat. Assn. Corp. Real Estate Execs., Washington Assn. Realtors, Inc., DC Bldg. Industry Assn., Am. Arbitration Assn. (arbitrator, mediator 1995—2003), Md. Inst. Continuing Profl. Edn. Lawyers, Md. Bar Assn. (litig. sect. 1982—84, real property, planning and zoning sect., chmn. comml. trans. com.), DC Bar (mem. comml. real estate com., chmn. legal opinions project), Am. Coll. Real Estate Lawyers (moderator various programs), Lambda Alpha, Phi Beta Kappa. Office: Deckelbaum Ogens & Raftery Chartered # 165 2020 Pennsylvania Ave NW Washington DC 20006 Office Phone: 301-347-3469. Personal E-mail: ksamuelson@bigfoot.com.

SAMUELSON, M. KRISTIN, music educator, vocalist; b. Milw., May 11, 1951; d. Albert C. and Jeanlyn C. (Gunderson) S.; m. Edward Allen Joffe, May 22, 1982 (div. Oct. 1996); 1 child, Janine Kirsten Joffe. BA, Denison U., 1973; MMus, New Eng. Conservatory Music, 1976; EdD, Columbia U., 1999. Acad. advisor Dean's Office New Eng. Conservatory, Boston, 1976-79; singer/soloist Nat. Opera Co., Raleigh, N.C., 1980, Boston Symphony Orch., 1976, Enchanted Circle Concerts, Boston, 1979, 84, Banff Festival, Canada, 1978—79, N.Y. Choral Soc., 2002; singer/voice tchr. Montanea Festival, Leukerbad, Switzerland, 1989-90; singer/soloist Sixth Internat. Congress of Women in Music, N.Y.C., 1990; instr. Columbia U., N.Y.C., 1994-98, N.Y.U./Lee Strasberg Theatrical Inst., N.Y.C., 1997—2002; singer, dir. Am. Voices Chamber Ensemble, 2000—; asst. prof. voice, dir. opera, musical theatre Jacksonville (Fla.) U., 2002—. Adj. asst. prof. Franklin & Marshall Coll., Lancaster, Pa., 1985-2002; lectr. in field; workshop leader Symposium for Care of Profl. Voice, 1999, 2003, Fla. Theatre Conf., 2003, Fla. Music Tchrs. Assn., 2003, Nat. Assn. Tchrs. of Singing (North Fla.), 2003. Contbr. articles to profl. jours. Recipient Frances Yeend's Instr. scholarship Chautauqua Inst., N.Y., 1973, Florence C. Rowe Meml. scholarship New Eng. Conservatory, Boston, 1975-76. Mem.: The Voice Found., Nat. Assn. Tchrs. of Singing, N.Y. Singing Tchrs. Assn. Avocations: bicycling, travel, langs., playing piano. Office Phone: 904-256-7347. E-mail: ksamuel@ju.edu.

SAMUELSON, PAMELA ANN, law educator; b. Seattle, Aug. 4, 1948; d. Peter David and Margaret Susanne (Green) S.; m. Robert J. Glushko, May 7, 1988; 1 child, Robert M. BA in History, U. Hawaii, 1971, MA in Polit. Sci., 1972; JD, Yale U., 1976. Bar: N.Y. 1977, U.S. Dist. Ct. (so. dist.) N.Y. 1977. Rsch. assoc. Vera Inst. of Justice, N.Y.C., 1976-77; assoc. Willkie Farr & Gallagher, N.Y.C., 1977-81; prin. investigator Software Engring. Inst., Pitts., 1985-86; asst. prof. Law Sch. U. Pitts., 1981-84, assoc. prof. Law Sch., 1984-87, prof. Law Sch., 1987-96; prof. law and info. mgmt. U. Calif. Law Sch./Sch. Info. Mgmt. and Sys., Berkeley, 1996—. Bd. dirs. Berkeley Ctr. for Law and Tech./U. Calif., Berkeley; vis. prof. Emory Law Sch., Atlanta, 1989-90, Cornell Law Sch., Ithaca, 1995-96; mem. Nat. Rsch. Coun. Study Com. on Intellectual Property Rights and Info. Infrastructure, 1998-2000. Contbr. articles to profl. jours. Bd. dirs. ACLU Greater Pitts., 1983-88, Electronic Frontier Found., 2000—. John D. and Catherine T. MacArthur Found. fellow, 1997, Pub. Policy fellow Electronic Frontier Found., 1997—; recipient Disting. Alumni award U. Hawaii, 2000. Mem. ABA (sci. and tech. sect.), Am. Intellectual Property Law Assn. (subcom. chair 1988-89), Assn. Am. Law Schs. (intellectual property sect.). Democrat. Avocations: gardening, reading. Office: U Calif Berkeley Sch Info Mgmt and Sys 102 South Hall #4600 Berkeley CA 94720-4600 E-mail: pam@sims.berkeley.edu.

SAMUELSON, PAUL ANTHONY, economist, educator; b. Gary, Ind., May 15, 1915; s. Frank and Ella (Lipton) Samuelson; m. Marion E. Crawford, July 2, 1938 (dec.); children: Jane Kendall, Margaret Wray, William Frank, Robert James, John Crawford, Paul Reid; m. Risha Eckaus, 1981; 1 stepchild, Susan Miller. BA, U. Chgo., 1935; MA, Harvard U., 1936, PhD (David A. Wells prize 1941), 1941; LLD (hon.), U. Chgo., Oberlin Coll., 1961, Boston Coll., 1964, Ind. U., 1966, U. Mich., 1967, Claremont Grad. Sch., 1967; LLD (hon.), Seton Hall U., 1971, U. N.H., 1971; LLD (hon.), Keio U., 1971, Widener Coll., 1982; LLD (hon.), Cath. U. at Riva Aguero U., Lima, Peru, 1980, Harvard, 1972; LLD (hon.), Gustavus Adolphus Coll., 1974, U. So. Calif., 1975; LLD (hon.), U. Pa., 1976; LLD (hon.), U. Rochester, 1976, Emmanuel Coll., 1977, Stonehill Coll., 1978; LLD (hon.), Indiana U. of Pa., 1993; DLitt (hon.), Ripon Coll., 1962; DLitt (hon.), No. Mich. U., 1973; DLitt (hon.), Valparaiso U., 1987, Columbia U, 1988; LHD (hon.), Williams Coll., 1971; DSc (hon.), U. Mass., 1972; DSc (hon.), U. R.I., 1972, Tufts U., 1988, East Anglia U., Norwich, Eng., 1966; DSc (hon.), Rensselaer Poly. Inst., 1998; D (hon.), U. Catholique de Louvain, Belgium, 1976, City U., London, 1980, New U. Lisbon, 1985, Univ. Nat. de Educacion a Distancia, Madrid, 1989, Univ. Politecnica de Valencia, Spain, 1991. Prof. econs. MIT, 1940—65, inst. prof., 1966, prof. emeritus, 1986; mem. staff Radiation Lab., 1944—45; prof. internat. econ. relations Fletcher Sch. Law and Diplomacy, 1945; cons. Nat. Resources Planning Bd., 1941—43, WPB, 1945, U.S. Treasury, 1945—52, 1961—74, Bur. Budget, 1952, RAND Corp., 1948—75, Fed. Res. Bd., 1965—; council Econ. Advisers, 1960—68; econ. adviser to Pres. Kennedy; sr. adviser Brookings Panel on Econ. Activity; mem. spl. commn. on social scis. NSF, 1967—68; cons. Congl. Budget Office, Federal Reserve Bd., 1965—; Gordon Y Billard Fellow MIT, Boston, 1986—; vis. prof of polit. econ. Ctr. Japan-U.S. Bus. and Econ. Studies, NYU, 1987—. Stamp Meml. lectr., London, 1961; Wicksell lectr., Stockholm, 62; Franklin lectr., Detroit, 62; Carnegie Found. reflective year, 1965—66; John von Neumann lectr. U. Wis., 1971; Gerhard Colm Meml. lectr. New Sch. for Social Rsch., N.Y.C., 1971; Sulzbacher Meml. lectr. Columbia Law Sch., N.Y.C., 1974; J. Willard Gibbs lectr. Am. Math. Soc., San Francisco, 1974; John Diebold lectr. Harvard, 1976; Alice E. Blurneuf lectr. Boston Coll., 1981; Horowitz lectr. Jerusalem and Tel Aviv, 1984; Marschak Meml. lectr. UCLA, 1984; Tennenbaum lectr. Ga. Inst. Tech., 1985; Julis Steinberg Meml. lectr. Wharton Sch., 1986; Godkin lectr. Harvard, 1986; Woodward lectr. U. B.C., 1987; lectr. Harvard 350 Symposium Harvard U., 1986; Olin lectr. U. Va., 1989; Commemorative lectr. Stonehill Coll., 1990; Lionel Robbins Meml. lectr. Claremont Coll., 1991; mem. nat. adv. com. Inst. for Rsch. on Poverty. Author: Foundations of Economic Analysis, 1947, Foundations of Economic Analysis, enlarged edit., 1983, Economics, 1948—95, Readings in Economics, 1955—73; author: (with R. Dorfman and R.M. Solow) Linear Programming and Economic Analysis, 1958; author: Collected Scientific Papers, 5 vols., 1966, 1972, 1978, 1986; co-author: numerous other books; columnist: Newsweek, 1966—81, assoc. editor: Jour. Pub. Econs., Jour. Internat. Econs., Jour. Fin. Econs., Jour. Nonlinear Analysis, adv. bd.: Challenge Mag., mem. editl. bd.: Proces NAS; contbr. articles to profl. jours. Chmn. Pres.'s Task Force Maintaining Am. Prosperity, 1964; mem. Nat. Task Force on Econ. Edn., 1960—61; econ. adviser to Pres. John F. Kennedy, 1959—63; mem. adv. bd. Nat. Commn. Money and Credit, 1958—60. Recipient David A. Wells prize, Harvard U., 1941, John Bates Clark medal, Am. Econ. Assn., 1947, Alfred Nobel Meml. prize, 1970, medal of Honor, U. Evansville, Ill., 1970, Albert Einstein Commemorative award, 1971, Alumni medal, U. Chgo., 1983, Britannica award, 1989, Gold Scanno prize, Naples, Italy, 1990, Paul A. Samuelson Professorship established in his name, MIT, 1991, Nat. Medal of Sci., Washington, 1996; fellow hon. fellow, London Sch. Econs. and Polit. Sci., Guggenheim, 1948—49, rsch. fellow, Ford Found., 1958—59. Fellow: Econometric Soc. (v.p. 1950, pres. 1951), Am. Philos. Soc., Am. Econ. Assn. (hon.; pres. 1961), Brit. Acad. (corr.); mem.: NAS, AAAS, Nat. Assn. Investment Clubs (Disting. Svc. award in Investment Edn. 1974), Leibniz-Akademie der Wissenschaften und der Literatur (corr.), Internat. Econ. Assn. (pres. 1966—68, hon. pres.), Com. Econ. Devel. (commn. on nat. goals, rsch. adv. bd. 1959—60), Club of Econ. and Mgmt. (medal, hon. Valencia, Spain 1990), Omicron Delta Epsilon (trustee), Phi Beta Kappa. Office: MIT E52 # 383C Dept Econs 50 Memorial Dr Cambridge MA 02142 Office Phone: 617-253-3368.

SAMUELSSON, MARCUS, food service executive; Degree, Culinary Inst. Göteborg, Switzerland. Chef Aquavit, N.Y.C., 1991, worked under Jan Sendel, exec. chef, 1995—, opened Mpls.; chef Georges Blanc, Lyon, France. Chosen to cook for Sweden's royal family; chosen to cook at gala dinner honoring the late Patrick Clark at Tavern on the Green; launched new line of traditional Swedish prepared foods. Featured Gourmet, USA Today, Food and Wine, N.Y. Times, Australian Vogue Entertaining, appeared CNN, Discovery Channel, ABC's Good Morning Am., (numerous local N.Y. TV programs). Named Best Rising Star Chef, James Beard Found., 1999; named one of Great Chefs Am., Culinary Inst. Am.; recipient three-star restaurant rev. for Aquavit, N.Y. Times, four-star rating, Forbes, three and a half-star rating, Crain's. Avocations: museums, art galleries. Office: Aquavit 13 West 54th St New York NY 10019

SAN, NGUYEN DUY, psychiatrist, educator; b. Langson, Vietnam, Sept. 25, 1932; arrived in Can., 1971, naturalized, 1977; s. Nguyen Duy and Tran Tuyet, Quyen (Trang) San; m. Eddie Jean Ciesielski, Aug. 24, 1971; children: Thuan Le, Megan Thuloan, Muriel Mylinh, Claire Kimlan, Robin Xuanlan, Baodan Edward. MD, U. Saigon, 1960; postgrad, U. Mich., 1970. Intern Cho Ray Hosp., Saigon, 1957—58; resident Univ. Hosp., Ann Arbor, Mich., 1968—70, Lafayette Clinic, Detroit, 1970—71, Clarke Inst. Psychiatry, Toronto, Canada, 1971—72; chief of psychiatry S. Vietnamese Army, 1964—68; sr. psychiatrist Queen St. Mental Health Ctr., Toronto, 1972—74; unit dir. Homewood San., Guelph, 1974—80; cons. psychiatrist Guelph Gen. Hosp., Guelph, 1974—80, St. Joseph's Hosp., Guelph; practice medicine specializing in psychiatry Guelph, 1974—80; unit dir. inpatient svc. Royal Ottawa Hosp., Canada, 1980—84, dir. psychiat. rehab. program, 1985—87; asst. prof. psychiatry U. Ottawa Med. Sch., 1980—85; assoc. prof. psychiatry, 1985—87; bd. dir. Hong Fook Mental Health Svc., Toronto, 1987—; dir. East-West Mental Health Ctr., Toronto, 1987—; chmn., bd. dir. Access Alliance Multicultural Health Ctr., Toronto, 1988—; cons. UN High Commr. for Refugees, 1987—. Author: Etude du Tetanos au Vietnam, 1960, Psycholsomatic Medicine: Theoretical, Clinical, and Transcultural Aspects, 1983, Uprooting, Loss and Adaptation, 1984—87, S.E. Asian Mental Health, 1985, Ten Years Later: Indochinese Communities in Can., 1988, Refugee Resettlement and Well-Being, 1989; co-author: The Psychology and Physiology of Stress, 1969. Served, 1953—68, Army Republic of Vietnam. Mem.: NY Acad. Sci., Internat. Soc. Hypnosis, Am. Soc. Clin. Hypnosis, Am. Psychiat. Assn., Can. Psychiat. Assn., Can. Med. Assn. Buddhist. Office: 2238 Dundas St W Ste 306 Toronto ON Canada M6R 3A9

SAN AGUSTIN, JOE TAITANO, political organization worker, educator; b. Agana, Guam, Oct. 15, 1930; s. Candido S. and Maria P. (Taitano) San A.; m. Carmen Santos Shimizu, June 18, 1955; children: Mary, Ann, Joe, John. BA, George Washington U., 1954, MA, 1956. Chief budget and mgmt. Office of Govt. Guam, Agana, 1966-68; dir. dept. adminstrn. Govt. Guam, Agana, 1968-74; senator Guam Legislature, Agana, 1977—95; asst. v.p. Bank of Guam. Minority leader 16th Guam Legislature, 1981-82, vice-speaker 17th and 18th Guam Legislature, 1983-86, chmn. com. on ways and means 17th and 18th Guam Legislatures, 1983-86, chmn. com. on health, edn. and welfare 19th Guam Legislature, 1987, chmn. com. on edn., 1991, econ. com.; speaker 20th, 21st, 22nd Guam Legislature, 1989-95, chmn. econ. com. Guam Legis., 1975. bd. dirs. Bank of Guam, Agana; chmn. bd. dirs. Guam Greyhound, Inc., Guam Aqua Rsch. Inc.; chmn. Guam Dem. Party; adj. instr. U. Guam. Democrat. Roman Catholic. Office: 155 Hessler Pl Agana GU 96910-5004

SANANMAN, MICHAEL LAWRENCE, neurologist; b. Bklyn., Oct. 11, 1939; s. Jack and Sarey (Bykofsky) S.; m. Elisa Joan Freeman, Apr. 12, 1964; children: Amy, Peter. AB, Swarthmore Coll., 1960; MD, Columbia U., 1964. Diplomate Am. Bd. Psychiatry and Neurology. Intern U. Hosp., San Francisco, 1964-65; resident in neurology N.Y. Neurol. Inst., N.Y.C., 1966-69; practice medicine specializing in neurology Elizabeth, N.J., 1972—. Cons. neurologist Rahway (N.J.) Hosp., Trinitas Hosp., N.J., Union Hosp., N.J.; instr. neurology Columbia U., N.Y.C., 1971-75; assoc. clin. prof. neurology U. Medicine and Dentistry N.J., Newark, 1975—. Lt. comdr. M.C., USNR, 1969-71. Mem. AMA, Am. Acad. Neurology, Am. Epilepsy Soc., N.J. Acad. Medicine, Am. Eastern EEG Socs., Am. Assn. EMG and Electrodiagnosis. Office: 700 N Broad St Elizabeth NJ 07208-2310 Office Phone: 908-354-3994. Personal E-mail: Mikesan48@aol.com.

SANBORN, ANNA LUCILLE, pension and insurance consultant; b. Bklyn., Mar. 29, 1924; d. Peter Francis and Matilda M. (Stumpp) Galligen; 1 son, Dean Sanborn. BA, Bklyn. Coll., 1945. Head dept. benefit and estate planning Union Ctrl. Life Ins. Co., N.Y.C., 1949-51; adminstr. employee benefits Seaboard Oil Co., N.Y.C., 1952-56; with Frank J. Walters Assocs., Inc., N.Y.C., 1957—, pres., 1970—. Bd. dirs. Archdiocesan Svc. Corp. Mem. Am. Acad. Actuaries. Republican. Roman Catholic. Home and Office: Frank J Walters Assocs 58-13 Seabury St Flushing NY 11373-4825 Personal E-mail: fjwainc@aol.com.

SANBORN, DOROTHY CHAPPELL, retired librarian; b. Apr. 26, 1920; d. William S. and Sammie Maude (Drake) Chappell; m. Richard Donald Sanborn, Dec. 1, 1943; children: Richard Donald, William Chappell. Asst. cataloger El Paso (Tex.) Pub. Libr., 1954-55, 57-59, Stanford Rsch. Inst., Menlo Park, Calif., 1955-57; libr. Auburn (Calif.) Pub. Libr., 1959-62; cataloger Sierra Coll., Rocklin, 1962-64; reference libr. Sacramento (Calif.) City Libr., 1964-66; county libr. Placer County (Calif.), Auburn, 1966-89, ret., 1989. Chmn. Mountain Valley Libr. Sys., 1970-71, 75-76, 1984-85; cons. county libr. Alpine County Libr., Markleeville, Calif., 1973-80. Pres. Auburn Friends of Libr., 1995-97; vol. Peace Corps., Thailand, 1991-93. With WAVES, 1944-46. Mem. AAUW (pres. chpt. 1982-84), Calif. Libr. Assn., Soroptimists. Democrat. Mem. United Ch. Christ. Home: 135 Midway Ave Auburn CA 95603-5415 *Personal philosophy: To strive to make a continuing contribution.*

SANBORN, GEORGE FREEMAN, JR., genealogist; b. Laconia, N.H., Jan. 18, 1944; s. George Freeman and Charlotte (Dearborn) S.; m. Melinde Laura Lutz, Mar. 30, 1984 (div.); children: Ruth Alice, Lowell Freeman. AB, Boston U., 1967; AM, U. Ill., 1968; MEd, U. N.H., 1981. French tchr. Souris (P.E.I., Can.) Regional H.S., 1968-69; French and occupational studies tchr. Massey-Vanier H.S., Cowansville, Que., Can., 1969-70; French and English tchr. Kings Coll. Sch., Windsor, N.S., Can., 1970-71; translator, revisor Province of N.B., Fredericton, 1971-73; sr. govt. revisor Province of Ont., Toronto, 1973-75; French and Spanish tchr. Tilton (N.H.) Sch., 1978-80; living unit coord. Laconia (N.H.) State Sch., 1982-83; ref. libr. New Eng. Hist. Geneal. Soc., Boston, 1983-85, acquisitions libr., dir. libr. ops., 1985-95, publs. asst., 1996-2000, ref. libr., 2000—. Editor The N.H. Geneal. Record, 1990-93; compiler Vital Records of Hampton, N.H., 1992, 98; contbr. articles to profl. jours. Fellow Am. Soc. Genealogists, Soc. Antiquaries Scotland; mem. Soc. of the Cin. in the State of N.H., Soc. of Mayflower Descendants in the State of N.H., New Eng. Hist. Geneal. Soc., P.E.I. Geneal. Soc., N.H. Soc. Genealogists (pres. 1988-95), Geneal. Soc. Vt. (chair publs. com. 1992-96). Democrat. Presbyterian. Avocations: gardening, bantam raising, Scottish Gaelic language, antique glass and china. Home: 24 Thornton St Derry NH 03038-1628 Office: New Eng Hist Geneal Soc Libr 99 Newbury St Boston MA 02116-3007 Office Phone: 617-536-5740.

SANBORN, KATHY, career planning administrator, consultant; BA in Psychology, Calif. State U., Sacramento, 1989. Founder Life and Career Coaching, Sacramento, 2001. Keynote spkr., trainer, workshop presenter in field. Author: (book) Grow Your Own Love, 2001, The Seasons of Your Career, 2003; singer (composer): (CD) Critical Mass, 1996; contbr. articles to profl. jours.; columnist: various web sites. Mem.: Golden Key Honor Soc. (life). Office: Life and Career Coaching PO Box 215664 Sacramento CA 95821 Office Phone: 916-502-5770. Business E-Mail: kathy@lifeandcareercoaching.com.

SANCHEZ, BEATRICE RIVAS, art institute executive, artist; b. San Antonio, June 17, 1941; MFA, U. Mass., 1975. Artist in residence Trinity U., San Antonio, 1976; coord. fine arts program Fla. Sch. Art, Palatka, 1976-78; acad. dean, assoc. dean Md. Coll. Art & Design, 1978-82; dean Cranbrook Acad. Art, 1982-87; pres. Kansas City Art Inst., 1987—. Exhibited in group shows Women's Nat. Exhbn., Washington, 1980, Montgomery County (Md.) Regional Juried Exhbn., 1981, Greater Reston (Va.) Art Ctr., 1981, Alternative Space Gallery, Kansas City, Mo., 1991. Trustee Native Am. and Alaskan Indian Culture Inst., Santa Fe. Mem. Nat. Assn. Schs. of Art and Design (bd. dirs.). Office: Kansas City Art Inst Office of the President 4415 Warwick Blvd Kansas City MO 64111-1820

SANCHEZ, BERNADETTE M. state senator; BA in Psychology, MA in Counseling and Family Studies, U. N.Mex. Clin. mental health and sch. counselor; Dem. senator dist. 26 N.Mex. State Senate. Mem. edn. com. N.Mex. State Senate, vice chair corps. and transp. Home: 7712 Ranchwood NW Albuquerque NM 87120 Office: NMex State Senate State Capitol Mail Rm Dept Santa Fe NM 87503 E-mail: senate@state.nm.us.

SANCHEZ, FAUSTO H. advertising agency executive; b. Camaguey, Cuba, Oct. 21, 1953; came to U.S., 1966; s. Fausto Rene and Eloisa (Aparicio) S. AA, Miami (Fla.) Dade Community Coll., 1976; BA, U. Miami, 1979; postgrad., UCLA, 1980-82. Dir., newswriter, anchor Sta. KMEX-TV, Hollywood, Calif., 1980-82; producer, dir. Brighton Communications, Hollywood, 1982-84; dir. mktg. Edward J. DeBartolo Corp., Miami, 1984-86; chmn., pres., creative dir. Sanchez & Levitan Advt., Miami, 1986—. Author: Hispanic Market, 1982. Mgr. advt. Aida Levitan for Commr. Campaign, Miami, 1988. Recipient Media award Calif. N.G., 1983, award of excellence Nat. Addy, 1989, Best of Show, 1988, 2 1st place Gold Addy awards, 1987, Am. Advt. Fedn., 4th Dist., 1st place radio Se Habla Espanol Awards, 1988, Addy award, 1988. Mem. Advt. Fedn. of Greater Miami. Democrat. Avocations: films, tennis, sailing. Office: Sanchez & Levitan Advt Inc 3191 Coral Way Ste 510 Miami FL 33145-3220

SANCHEZ, HAZEL, reporter; BA in Broadcasting and Electronic Comm., Marquette U. Asst. prodr., news anchor Sta. WISN-TV, Milw.; host, moderator Teen Connection Wis. Pub. TV, Green Bay; reporter, weekend anchor Sta. WBAY-TV; gen. assignment reporter Sta. WCBS-TV, N.Y.C., 2000—. Recipient Golden Eagle, 1997, CINE award, 1997, award, Wis. Broadcast Assn., 1997, Midwest Emmy, 1997. Office: CBS 524 W 57th St New York NY 10019

SANCHEZ, LEONEDES MONARRIZE WORTHINGTON (HIS ROYAL HIGHNESS DUKE DE LEONEDES OF SPAIN SICILY GREECE), fashion designer; b. Flagstaff, Ariz., Mar. 15, 1951; s. Rafael Leonedes and Margaret (Monarrize) S. BS, No. Ariz. U., 1974; studied, Fashion Inst. Tech., N.Y.C., 1974-75; AA, Fashion Inst. D&M, L.A., 1975; lic., La Ecole de la Chambre Syndical de la Couture Parisian, Paris, 1976-78; certificate, La Mason de Couture, Paris, 2000. Lic. in designing. Contract designer/asst. to head designer House of Bonnet, Paris, 1976—; dress designer-in-residence Flagstaff, 1978—; mem. faculty No. Ariz. U., Flagstaff, 1978-80; designer Ambiance, Inc., L.A., 1985—; designer Interiors by Leonedes subs. Studio of Leonedes Couturier, Ariz., 1977, 1978, 1978, Rome, 1987, Milan, Spain, 1989, Palazzo de Leonedes, 1998, designer Liturgical Vesture subs.; CEO Leonedes Internat., Design Consortium, Leonedes Internat. Ltd., 1999—; designer El Casillo de Nuevo Espana, Santa Fe, N.Mex., La Maison de Couture, Paris, 2000, La Maison de Couture de Leonedes Internat., Paris, 2001. Owner, CEO, designer Leonedes Internat., Ltd., London, Milan, Paris, Spain, Ambian Ariz, Calif., Appolonian Costuming, Ariz., London, Milan, Paris, El Castillo de Leonedes, Sevilla, Spain, Villa Apollonian de Leonedes, Mykonos, Greece, Palazzo de Leonedes Internat., Sicily; cons. House of Bonnet, Paris, 1976—, Bob Mackie, Studio City, Calif., 1974-75; CEO, designer artistical dir., Leonedes internat.; appointee commn. on religious antiquities Congregation on the Arts, The Vatican, Italy, 1998. Bd. dirs. Roman Cath. Social Svcs., 1985-86, Northland Crisis Nursery, 1985—; bd. dirs., chmn. Pine Country Transit, 1986-88; pres. Chicanos for Edn.; active master's swim program ARC, Ariz., 1979—; eucharistic min., mem. art and environ. com., designer liturgical vesture St. Pius X Cath. Ch.; vol. art tchr., instr. St. Mary's Regional Sch., Flagstaff, 1987-90, vol. art dir.; mem. Flagstaff Parks and Recreation Commn., 1994-96, citizens' adv. com. master plan, 1994-96; mem. cmty. bd. adv. com. Flagstaff Unified Sch. Dist., 1995; active Duke de Leonedes Found. de Nuevo Espana, Santa Fe, Duke de Leonedes Found. de Neuvo Espana, Santa Fe; prin. chair Duke de Leonedes Found., The Netherlands, 1995; de neuvo espana Duke de Leuedes Found., Santa Fe, N.Mex., 1996. Decorated Duke de Leonedes (Spain), 1994, His Royal Highness (Spain, Greece, Sicily), 1998; recipient Camellian Design award 1988, Atlanta. Mem. AAU (life, chairperson swimming Ariz. 1995, vice chairperson physique, mem. citizen adv. bd. parks and recreation, chairperson state of Ariz. physique, swimming, adv. to Olympic inquiry com., advisor to internat. Olympic com. on physique), Am. Film Inst., Am. Assn. Hist. Preservation, Costume Soc., Am. Nat. Physique Com., Internat. Consortium Fashion Designers, Nat. Cath. Edl. Assn., La Legion de Honour de la Mode Parisienne, Social Register Assn., Phi Alpha Theta (historian 1972-73, pres. 1973-74), Pi Kappa Delta (pres. 1972-73, historian 1973-74). Republican.

Avocations: body building, swimming. Office: El Castillo de Leonedes Seville Spain also: El Castillo de Nuevo Espana Santa Fe NM 87501 also: Villa de Apollonian de Leonedes Mykonos Greece

SANCHEZ, LINDA T. congresswoman; b. Orange, Calif. m. Mark Sanchez. BA in Spanish Lit., U. Calif., Berkeley; JD, UCLA, 1995. Bar: Calif. 1995. Clk. to Hon. Chief Justice Terry Hatter, Jr. Ctrl. Dist. Ct., Calif.; compliance officer Nat. Elec. Contractors Assn. and Internat. Brotherhood Elec. Workers, 1998—2002; mem. from 39th Calif. dist. U.S. Ho. of Reps., 2003—; mem. judiciary com.; mem. govt. reform com., small bus. com. Lectr. Nat. Assn. Elected and Apptd. Ofcls., 1998—. Exec. sec.-treas. Orange County ctrl. labor coun. AFL-CIO; campaign worker Loretta Sanchez for U.S. Congress, 1996, 1998. Mem.: Internat. Brotherhood Elec. Workers (Local 441). Democrat. Office: 1007 Longworth Bldg Washington DC 20515 also: 4007 Paramount Ste 106 Lakewood CA 90712

SANCHEZ, LORETTA, congresswoman; b. Lynnwood, Calif., Jan. 7, 1960; BA, Chapman U., 1982; MBA, Am. U., 1984. With Orange County Transp. Authority, 1984-87, Fieldman Rolapp & Assocs., 1987-90; strategic mgmt. cons. Booz Allen & Hamilton; owner, operator AMIGA Advisors Inc.; mem. U.S. Congress from 47th Calif. dist., 1997—; former mem. edn. and the workforce com., mem. armed svcs. com.; mem. House Select Com. on Homeland Security, House Blue Dogs. Mem. Anaheim Rotary Club. Democrat. Office: US Ho of Reps 1230 Longworth Ho Office Bldg Washington DC 20515-0001 Office Phone: 202-225-2965. E-mail: loretta@mail.house.gov.

SANCHEZ, MARY ANNE, retired secondary school educator; b. Galesburg, Ill., Aug. 4, 1939; d. Stephen Mingare and M. Margaret Kennedy; m. J. Manuel Sanchez, Dec. 26, 1980. BS in Edn., Western Ill. U., 1961; MA, Ill. State U., 1970. Tchr., Stanford, Ill., 1962-64, Titusville, Fla., 1964-66, Montgomery County Bd. Edn., Chevy Chase, Md., 1969-72, Hillsborough County Bd. Edn., Tampa, Fla., 1972-96; ret., 1996. Mary Anne Sanchez Young Woman scholarship named in her honor by Social Studies Dept. Leto Comprehensive H.S., 1999. Mem. Nat. Coun. for Social Studies, Fla. Coun. for Social Studies, Adult Edn. Assn. Home: 2715 W Ivy St Tampa FL 33607-1922

SANCHEZ, PAULINE STELLA, artist; MFA, UCLA. Artist and mem. faculty Art Ctr. Coll. of Design, 1989—. One-woman shows include Rosamund Felsen Gallery, Angeles Gallery, ACME, Ace Gallery, Marc Jancou Galerie, Zurich, Froment y Putman Galerie, Paris, exhibited in group shows at MOCA, Santa Monica Mus., The Drawing Ctr., N.Y., Galerie Krinzinger, Vienna, Monash U. Gallery, Australia, Kulturzentrum bein den Minoriten, Austria, New Langton Arts, San Francisco, Fotouhi Cramer Gallery, N.Y., Auckland Art Mus., New Zealand, Los Angeles Contemporary Exhibitions, Museu de Arte de Sao Paulo, Brazil. Recipient Credac Artist award, France-Europe;, John Simon Guggenheim Meml. Found. fellow, 2003, Foundation Cartier pour l'Art fellow, Nat. Endowment of Arts fellow. Office: Art Ctr Coll of Design 1700 Lida St Pasadena CA 91103

SANCHEZ, RAYMOND G. former state legislator; b. Albuquerque, Sept. 22, 1941; s. Gillie and Priscilla S.; 1 child, Raymond Michael. BA, U. N.Mex., 1964, JD, 1967. Bar: N. Mex. 1967. Ptnr. Sanchez, Mowrer & Desiderio, P.C., Albuquerque; mem. N.Mex. Ho. of Reps., 1970—; speaker N. Mex. Ho. of Reps., 1983—84, 1987—88, 1992—2000; mem. judiciary com., rules and order of bus. com., voters and elections com.; interim mem. workers compensation, legis. reform study coms., legis. coun.; pres. Naleo Educational Fund, Albuquerque, 2001. Bd. dirs. New Mex. Amigos, N.Mex. Diamond Jubilee/U.S. Constl. Bicentennial Commn., New Mex. First, Albuquerque Com. Fgn. Rels., N. Valley Neighborhood Assn. Mem. Nat. Assn. Latino Elected and Apptd. Ofcls. (bd. dirs.), Alameda Optimist Club (bd. dirs., charter mem.), U. N.Mex. Sch. Law Alumni Assn. (bd. dirs.), Elks Club, Sigma Xi. Democrat. Avocations: handball, scuba diving, swimming, spectator sports. also: PO Box 1966 Albuquerque NM 87103-1966

SANCHEZ, RICARDO S. career military officer; b. Rio Grande City, Tex. B in Math. and History, Tex. A&I U.; M in Ops. Rsch. and Sys. Analysis Engring., Naval Postgrad. Sch. Commd. officer U.S. Army, 1973, advanced through ranks to lt. gen., 2003, platoon leader 4th Bn., 68th Armor, 82nd Airborne Divsn., aide-de-camp to the asst. divsn. comdr. 82nd Airborne Divsn., action control officer Office of the Sec. of the Joint Staff, U.S. Forces Korea/Eighth U.S. Army, ops. officer and exec. officer 3rd Bn., 8th Cavalry, 3rd Armored Divsn., dep. ops. officer 3rd Armored Divsn. Frankfurt, Germany, comdr. 2nd Bn., 69th Armor, 197th (Separate) Inf. Brigade Ft. Benning, Ga., investigator Office U.S. Army Insp. Gen. Agy. Washington, comdr. 2nd Brigade, 1st Inf. Divsn. Ft. Riley, Kans., dep. chief staff U.S. So. Command Miami, Fla., dir. ops. U.S. So. Command, asst. divsn. comdr. for support 1st Inf. Divsn., dep. chief staff ops. U.S. Army Europe, commdg. gen. V Corps 1st Armored Divsn., 2001—03, commdg. gen. Coalition Ground Forces (Combined Joint Task Force 7), 2003—04, commdg. gen. V Corps, 2003—04, 2004—; commdr. Multi-Nat. Force-Iraq, 2004. Decorated Def. Superior Svc. medal, Legion of Merit, Bronze Star with V device and oak leaf cluster, Joint Svc. Commendation medal, Army Commendation medal, Meritorious Svc. medal with four oak leaf clusters, Army Achievement medal with oak leaf cluster, Liberation of Kuwait medals, S.W. Asia Campaign medal. Office: USAREUR V Corps 09111 Heidelburg Germany*

SANCHEZ, ROBERT FRANCIS, journalist; b. Bradenton, Fla., Jan. 1, 1938; s. Robert and Frances Alice (Thompson) S. BS in English Edn., Fla. State U., 1959, MS, 1962, postgrad., 1971-74. Mem. faculty Fla. State U., Tallahassee, 1962-67; mem. faculty Fla. A&M U., Tallahassee, 1968-71; writer, editor Tallahassee Democrat, 1965-74; editl. writer Miami Herald, 1974-2000. Co-recipient Pulitzer Prize, 1983 Mem. Phi Delta Kappa, Sigma Delta Chi Republican. Methodist. Home: 2324 Williams Rd Tallahassee FL 32311 Office: Fla Dept Hwy Safety & Motor Vehicles 2900 Apalachee Pkwy Tallahassee FL 32399-0509

SANCHEZ, SONIA, English literature educator; Laura Carnell prof. English, Temple U., Phila., chmn. women's studies program. Lectr. on black culture and lit., women's rights and social justice at over 500 univs. colls. in U.S.; reader her poetry worldwide. Author 16 books, including We A BaddDDD People, Under a Soprano Sky, Homegirls and Handgrenades (Am. Book award 1985), Like the Singing Coming Off the Drums, 1999; contbg. editor Black Scholar, Jour. African Studies; editor 2 books black lit. Bd. dirs. MADRE. Recipient Lucretia Mott award, 1984, cmty. svc. award Nat. Black Caucus State Legislators; Pew fellow in arts, 1992-93. Mem. Women's Internat. League for Peace and Freedom (sponsor, Peace and Freedom award 1989). Office: Temple U Dept English 10th Fl Anderson Hall 1114 W Berks St Philadelphia PA 19122-6007

SANCHEZ, WALTER MARSHALL, lawyer; b. Lake Charles, La., July 3, 1959; s. John Augustine Sanchez and Louise Page Dugas Meyer; m. Frances E. Morgan, Oct. 18, 1986; children: Clare, Madeline, Kate, John. BS, La. State U., Baton Rouge, 1981, JD, 1984. Bar: La. 1984, U.S. Supreme Ct. 1984; bd. cert. family law specialist, La. Bd. of Legal Specialization. Assoc. Godwin, Painter, Roddy, Lorenzi & Watson, Lake Charles, 1985-86; ptnr. Godwin, Roddy, Lorenzi Watson & Sanchez, Lake Charles, 1986-90, Lorenzi, Sanchez & Palay, LLP, Lake Charles, 1990—. Vice chmn. La. Indigent Defender Bd., New Orleans, 1994-96; chmn. 14th Jud. Dist. Indigent Defender Bd., Lake Charles, 1987-96; mem. faculty trial advocacy tng. program La. State U. Law Ctr., 1993—; mem. Joint Legis. Com. for Study Indigent Def. Sys., 1996-97; mem. spl. com. to study reinstatement of fault in divorce La. State Law Inst., 1998-2001; apptd. judge pro tempore City Ct. of Sulphur, 1999—. Mem. La. Assn. Criminal Def. Attys. (bd. dirs. 1990—, pres. 1997-98) La. Task Forse on Indigent Defense Svc., 2004—; Am. Mensa., Order of St. Charles. Democrat. Roman Catholic. Office: Lorenzi Sanchez & Palay LLP PO Box 3305 Lake Charles LA 70602-3305

SANCHEZ DE LEON, ROBERTO J. physician, educator, writer; b. Caracas, Venezuela, Sept. 21, 1949; s. Pablo and Alicia (Santander) Sanchez de L.; m. Imperia Brajkovich, Feb. 14, 1975 (div.); m. Morella H. Ferrero; children: Vanessa, Michelle, Lorena, Geraldine, Giselle. MD, U. Caracas, Venezuela, 1972. Intern, resident in internal medicine Maternity Hosp., Caracas, Venezuela, 1972-78; resident in intensive care U. Hosp., Caracas, 1978-80; asst. prof. U. Caracas, 1981-85; resident pulmonology and chest clinic Hammersmith Hosp. London U., 1982-84; resident in intensive care Manheim Hosp. Heidelberg U., Germany, 1984-85; assoc. prof. U. Caracas, 1985-90, prof., 1990—, head dept., 1999—. Author: (children's lit.) Papa's Stories, 1999, (poetry) Yo En Ti, 1997, Basics in Pulmonary Physiology. Fellow Royal Coll. Chest Physicians; mem. Am. Coll. Chest Physicians, Am. Thoracic Soc. (associated, regular prof.), L.Am. Thoracic Soc. Avocations: swimming, diving, art. Office: PO Box International 281 Miami FL 33102 E-mail: rsanchez@ven.net.

SANCHEZ-WAY, RUTH DOLORES, health services administrator; b. N.Y.C., Aug. 8, 1940; d. Manuel and Cruz Maria (Rivera) Sanchez; m. Harley Milton Dirks, Feb. 9, 1974 (dec. Aug. 1986); stepchildren: Timothy, Darcy Kimmel, Marcine Thomas, James, David, Dale; m. David Vincent Way, Apr. 16, 1988. BS, St. John's U., 1962; MSW, Fordham U., 1965; PhD, NYU, 1978; postgrad., Emory U., Geroge Washington U. Cert. social worker, Md. Spl. asst. to dir. Nat. Inst. Alcohol Abuse and Alcoholism, U.S. Dept HEW, Rockville, Md., 1971-79; assoc. dep. adminstr. EEO Office Asst. Sec. Health, U.S. Dept. HEW, 1979-83; dep. dir. Office Adolescent Pregnancy Programs HHS, Washington, 1983-91; assoc. adminstr. minority health concerns Substance Abuse & Mental Health Svcs. Adminstrn., HHS, Rockville, 1993-96, divsn. dir. Ctr. for Substance Abuse Prevention, 1991-96, acting dep. dir. Ctr. for Substance Abuse Prevention, 1997, acting dir., 1997—2000, dir., 2000—02; assoc. dir. Ctr. for Faith-Based and Cmty. Initiatives, HHS, 2002—03; v.p. health and cmty. initiatives Mgmt. Scis. for Devel., 2003—. Bd. dirs. Nat. Health Coun., Washington, 1987-94, Nat. Coun. on Alcoholism and Drug Dependence, N.Y.C., 1979-91, Nat. orgn. ADOL Pregnancy Parenting and Prevention, Washington, 1991-93. Vol. Girl Scouts U.S.A., N.Y.C., 1996—. Recipient Excellence in Govt. Svc. award Mex.-Am. Legal Def. and Ednl. Fund, 2000, Presdl. Meritorious Exec. Rank award SES, 1998, Sec.'s award for disting. svc. HHS, 2001; primary care policy fellow USPHS. Mem. NASW, APHA, Chesapeake Crusing Multihull Assn. (past commodore, Kilmon award 1996). Roman Catholic. Avocations: sailing, skiing, jazzercise. Office: 4455 Connecticut Ave NW Ste A100 Washington DC 20008 Office Phone: 202-537-7410. Personal E-mail: rsanchez@msdglobal.com.

SAND, JOHN HALVDAN, obstetrician, gynecologist; b. San Diego, May 7, 1951; MD, U. Calif., Davis, 1976. Diplomate Am. Bd. Ob-Gyn. Intern USPHS, San Francisco, 1976-77; resident in internal medicine Mercy Hosp. Med. Ctr., San Diego, 1978-79; resident in ob-gyn. U. N.Mex., Albuquerque, 1979-81, Gallup Indian Med. ctr., Ellensburg, Wash., 1981-83; mem. staff Tucson Med. Ctr., 1986-89, Univ. Med. Ctr., Tucson, 1989-92, St. Joseph's Hosp., Tucson, 1989-92; pvt. practice, Ellensburg, 1992—. Mem. staff Kittitas Valley Cmty. Hosp., Ellensburg, 1983-86, chief OBG, 1992—. Fellow ACOG; mem. AMA, Am. Assn. Gynecol. Laparoscopists, Am. Inst. for Ultrasound in Medicine. Office: 611 S Chestnut St Ste B Ellensburg WA 98926-4815

SAND, LEONARD B. federal judge; b. N.Y.C., May 24, 1928; BS, NYU, 1947; LL.B., Harvard, 1951. Bar: N.Y. 1953, U.S. Supreme Ct. 1956, D.C. 1969. Clk. to dist. ct. judge, N.Y., 1952-53; asst. U.S. atty. So. Dist. N.Y., 1953-54; asst. to U.S. Solictor Gen., 1956-59; mem. firm Robinson, Silverman, Pearce, Aronsohn Sand and Berman, N.Y.C., 1960-78; judge U.S. Dist. Ct. So. Dist. N.Y., 1978—, now sr. judge. Adj. prof. law NYU. Note editor: Harvard Law Rev, 1950-51. Del. N.Y. State Constl. Conv., 1967; v.p., treas. Legal Aid Soc. Fellow Am. Coll. Trial Lawyers; mem. ABA, Assn. Bar City N.Y. (v.p.), N.Y. State Bar Assn., Fed. Bar Coun. Office: US Dist Ct US Courthouse 500 Pearl St New York NY 10007-1316

SAND, SEAWARD ALWYN, geneticist, researcher; b. Lockport, NY, Sept. 20, 1922; s. Seaward Alwyn Sr. and Gertrude Morris Sand; m. Mavis Hawthorne Gillette, Aug. 15, 1948; children: Beverly Vail, Valerie Waite, Kimberly Warner, Natalie Waugh, Kevin Gillette, Bryan Morris. *Parents raised five children in Lockport and Niagra Falls, NY. Mother, Gertrude, 1898-1995, taught thirty years in Niagra Falls elementary schools. Paternal grandfather, Reuben W. Sand, 1863-1930, early American professional photographer, apprenticed his sons. Austin W.W. Sand, 1891-1945, became official photographer, Lightning Division, U.S. Army, 1917-1919. His glass-plate negatives are filed, Naval & Servicemen's Park, Buffalo, NY. Father, Seaward, 1895-1997, became leading portrait photographer in Lockport, serving Professional Photographers Society of New York as President at age 31, for six years as Secretary or Treasurer, and four years as Chairman. Recognized as Master Photographer and Craftsman, his career-portraiture of 67 years is organized and researchable in Lockport Public Library.* Student, Kans. State Coll., 1943—44, Cornell U., 1941—43, student, 1946—47, AB in Physics, 1947, MS in Sci. Edn., 1948, PhD in Genetics, 1955. H.S. tchr. physics, chemistry and biology, Horseheads, NY, 1948—50; grad. asst. plant breeding dept. NY State Coll. Agr., Cornell U., Ithaca, 1950—54; asst. then assoc. geneticist Conn. Agrl. Exptl. Sta., New Haven, Windsor and Mt. Carmel, 1954—64; assoc. cancer rsch. scientist basic nicotiana genetic rsch. NY State Dept. Health, Roswell Park Meml. Inst., Orchard Park and Buffalo, 1964—84; ret., 1984. Vis. assoc. prof. biology SUNY, Stony Brook, 1962—63; Fulbright lectr. genetics dept. Trinity Coll., Dublin, 1963; rsch. collaborator, guest assoc. geneticist biology dept. Brookhaven Nat. Lab., Upton, NY, 1962—69; mem., contbr. Gordon Rsch. Confs., Andover, NH, 1979, Andover, 81; participant internat. congresses in field; participant Sackler Colloquium (epigenics) NAS, Washington, 2002. *Career benefits accrued from the sponsorship and Nicotiana materials of Harold H. Smith; from institutional freedoms, colleagues' discussions, and my wife's constancy. Appreciation of McClintock's seminal maize investigations stimulated study of mutable-genes. Resulting are thesis and eleven publications, 1955-76, nine in genetics. Connecticut tobacco research contributed five papers, 1955-61 (genetic ozone-resistance), and two Station Bulletins. DNA-code excitement inspired analytical reviews (epigenetics and differentiation) published in American Naturalist (1961 & 1965). A definitive interspecific-hybridization, retaining alien chromosomes, gave first genetic evidence that cytoplasmic-chromosomal interactions may alter floral morphology (Science, 1960; Journal of Heredity, 1973). Four collaborations (Hicks, Gerstel, Chen, Johnson & Bonnett) employed these unique plants, advancing seven significant publications, 1977-82. Eighteen abstracts, 1954-79, summarize presentations at Genetics Society annual meetings.* Contbr. articles to profl. jours. Life mem. Rep. Nat. Com., Washington, 2004—; spkr. Geneal. Soc. Program, Niagara County, 2004, Niagara County N.Y. Genealogical Soc. Program (San Lineage & Father's Photog. Career), Lockport, 2004; platinum mem. Rep. Presdl. Task Force, Washington, 2001—. With U.S. Army, 1943—46. Grantee, Cornell U., 1941—43, 1946—47, Employers' State Budgets, Conn. and NY, 1954—84; scholar, NY State Bd. Regents, 1941—43, 1946—47. Fellow: AAAS; mem.: Am. Genetic Assn., Genetics Soc. Am. (jour. referee). Methodist. Avocations: travel, equity investing, national and international policy, science, university relations. Home: 420 Fillmore Ave East Aurora NY 14052-1707

SAND, THOMAS CHARLES, lawyer; b. Portland, Oreg., June 4, 1952; s. Harold Eugene and Marian Anette (Thomas) S.; m. Rhonda Diane Laycoe, June 15, 1974; children: Kendall, Taylor, Justin. Student, Centro des Artes y Lenguas, Cuernavaca, Mex., 1972; BA in English, U. Oreg., 1974; JD, Lewis and Clark Coll., 1977. Bar: Oreg. 1977, U.S. Dist. Ct. Oreg. 1977, U.S. Ct. Appeals (9th cir.) 1984. Assoc. Miller, Nash, LLP, Portland, 1977-84, ptnr., 1984—, mng. ptnr., 1999—. Mem. Oreg. State Bar Com. on Professionalism, 1989, chmn., 1990; dir. young lawyers divsn. Multnomah County Bar Assn., 1980; spl. asst. atty. gen. Wasco County 1983 Gen. Election; spkr. in field. Contbr. articles to legal jours. Mem. U.S. Dist. Ct. of Oreg. Hist. Soc., 1990—; bd. dirs. Portland Area coun. Camp Fire, Inc., 1978-90, pres., 1984-86; bd. dirs. Oreg. Indoor Invitational Track Meet, Inc., 1982-84. Recipient Boss of the Yr. award Portland Legal Secs. Assn., 1989, Disting. Grad. award Lewis and Clark Law Sch., 2004. Mem. ABA (securities litig. com., subcom. on broker-dealer litig.), Oreg. Bar Assn., Multnomah Bar Assn. (bd. dirs. task force on structure and orgn. 1989, chmn. com. on professionalism 1988, nominating com. 1986, participating atty. in N.E. legal clin. Vol Lawyers project, award of merit for svc. to profession 1988), Securities Industry Assn. (compliance and legal divsn.), Northwestern Sch. of Law, Lewis and Clark Coll. Alumni Assn. (bd. dirs. 1992, pres. 1997), Valley Comm. Presbyterian Ch., Multnomah Athletic Club, Portland Golf Club. Avocations: golf, guitar, camping, river rafting, children's sports. Office: Miller Nash LLP 111 SW 5th Ave Ste 3500 Portland OR 97204-3699 Office Phone: 503-224-5858. Business E-Mail: tom.sand@millernash.com.

SANDAGE, ALLAN REX, astronomer; b. Iowa City, June 18, 1926; s. Charles Harold and Dorothy (Briggs) S.; m. Mary Lois Connelley, June 8, 1959; children: David Allan, John Howard. AB, U. Ill., 1948, DSc (hon.), 1967; PhD, Calif. Inst. Tech., 1953; DSc (hon.), Yale U., 1966, U. Chgo., 1967, Miami U., Oxford, Ohio, 1974, Graceland Coll., Iowa, 1985; LLD (hon.), U. So. Calif., 1971; D (hon.), U. Chile, 1992. Astronomer Mt. Wilson Obs., Palomar Obs., Carnegie Instn., Washington, 1952—; Peyton fellow Princeton U., 1952; asst. astronomer Hale Obs., Pasadena, Calif., 1952-56; astronomer Obs. Carnegie Instn., Pasadena, Calif., 1956—; sr. rsch. astronomer Space Telescope Sci. Inst. NASA, Balt., 1986—; Homewood Prof. of physics Johns Hopkins U., Balt., 1987-89. Vis. lectr. Harvard U., 1957; mem. astron. expdn. to South Africa, 58; cons. NSF, 1961—64; Sigma Xi nat. astronomer U. Basel, 1985, 92, vis. prof., 94; vis. rsch. astronomer U. Calif., San Diego, 1985—86; vis. astronomer U. Hawaii, 1986; Lindsey lectr. NASA Goddard Space, Durham, England, 1992; Grubb-Parsons lectr. U. Durham, England, 1992. Assoc. editor: Ann. Rev. Astronomy and Astrophysics, 1990—. Recipient Helen Warner prize, Am. Astron. Soc., 1960, Pope Pius XI Gold medal, Pontifical Acad. Sci., 1966, Rittenhouse medal, 1968, Russell prize, 1973, Adon medal, Obs. Nice, 1988, Crafford prize, Swedish Royal Acad. Scis., 1991, Tomalla Gravity prize, Swiss Phys. Soc., 1993, Peter Gruber Found. prize for cosmology, 2000; scholar Fulbright-Hays scholar, 1972. Mem.: Astron. Soc. Pacific (Gold medal 1975), Royal Soc. London (fgn.), Am. Philos. Soc., Franklin Inst. (Elliott Cresson medal 1973, Gruber Cosmology prize 2000), Royal Astron. Soc. Can., Royal Astron. Soc. (Eddington medal 1963, Gold medal 1967), Lincei Nat. Acad. (Rome), Phi Beta Kappa. Home: 8319 Josard Rd San Gabriel CA 91775-1003 Office: 813 Santa Barbara St Pasadena CA 91101-1232

SANDAGE-MUSSEY, ELIZABETH ANTHEA, retired market research executive; b. Larned, Kans., Oct. 13, 1930; d. Curtis Carl and Beulah Pauline (Knupp) Smith; m. H.L. Danner, 1948 (div. 1956); children: Dianna Louise Danner Wilson, David Alan Danner; m. Charles Harold Sandage, July 18, 1971; m. Robert D. Mussey, Oct. 21, 2000. BS, U. Colo., 1967, MA, 1970; PhD in Comms., U. Ill., 1983. Pub. rels. rep., editor Martin News Martin Marietta Corp., Denver, 1960-63, 65-67; retail advt. salesperson Denver Post, 1967-70; instr. advt. U. Ill., 1970-71, vis. lectr. advt., 1977-84; v.p., corp. sec., dir. Farm Rsch. Inst., Urbana, Ill., 1984-95; ret., 1995. Editor: Advertising as a Social Force: Selected Speeches and Essays by Charles H. Sandage, 1998, Occasional Papers in Advertising, 1971, The Sandage Family Cookbook, 1976, 3d edit., 2002, The Inkling (Carle Hosp. Aux. Newsletter), 1975-76. Bd. dirs. U. Ill. Libr. Friends, 1991-95; exec. dir. Sandage Charitable Trust, 1986—. Mem. U. Ill. Alumni Assn. (pres.'s coun.), Champaign Social Sci. Club, The Book Club, Moneymakers Investment Club, Kappa Tau Alpha.

SANDAHL, BONNIE BEARDSLEY, human services administrator, educator; b. Washington, Jan. 17, 1939; d. Erwin Leonard and Carol Myrtle (Collis) Beardsley; m. Glen Emil Sandahl, Aug. 17, 1963; children: Cara Lynne, Cory Glen. BSN, U. Wash., 1962, MN, 1974; cert. pediat. nurse practitioner, 1972. Dir. Wash. State Joint Practice Commn., Seattle, 1974-76; instr. pediatric nurse practitioner program U. Wash., Seattle, 1976, course coord. quality assurance, 1977-78; pediatric nurse practitioner/health coord. Snohomish County Head Start, Everett, Wash., 1975-77; clin. nurse educator (specialist), nurse mgr. Harborview Med. Ctr., Seattle, 1978-97, dir. child abuse prevention project, 1986-97; mgr. Children's Ctr., Providence Health Sys. Northwest, 1997-2000; v.p. clin. svcs. and ops., COO Seattle Children's Home, 2000—03, exec. dir., 2003—. Spkr. legis. focus on children, 1987; clin. assoc. dept. pediatrics U. Wash. Sch. Medicine, 1987—; clin. faculty U. Wash. Sch. Nursing, 1987—97; mgr. Providence Gen. Children's Ctr., Everett, 1997—2000; gov. appointee State Interagy. Coord. Coun., 1998—, gov. appointee chair, 2004. Interim chair nat. coun. health planning and devel. HHS, 1980—87; mem. task force pharmacotherapeutic courses Puget Sound Health Sys. Agy., 1975—88, pres., 1980—82; mem. task force pharmacotherapeutic courses Wash. State Bd. Nursing, 1985—86; mem. child devel. project adv. bd. Mukiteo Sch. Dist., 1984—85; mem. parenting adv. com. Edmonds Sch. Dist.; chmn. hospice-hom health task force Snohomis County Hospice Program, Everett, 1984—85, bd. dirs. hospice, 1985—87, mem. adv. com., 1986—88; mem. Wash. State Health Coordinating Coun., 1977—82, chmn. nursing home bed projection methodology task force, 1986—87; mem. adv. com. uncompensated care Wash. State Legislature, 1983—84; mem. joint select com. Tech. Adv. Com. Managed Health Care Sys., 1984—85; pres. Alderwood Manor Cmty. Coun., 1983—85; treas. Wash. St. Women's Polit. Caucus, 1983—84; mem. com. examine changes in Wash. State Criminal Sex Law, 1987; appointee county needs assessment com. Snohomish County Govt. United Way, 1989, 1994; chair human svcs. adv. coun. Snohomish County Human Svcs. Dept., chmn. adv. com., 1998—; gubernatorial appointee state interagency coordinating coun. Health Svcs. Adv. Com. Wash. State, 1995—97. Recipient Golden Acorn award, Seattle-King County PTA, 1973, Katherine Rickey Vol. Participation award, 1987. Mem.: ANA (chair com. examiners maternal-child nursing practice 1988—90), King County Nurses Assn. (1st v.p. 1992—96, pres. 1996—97, Nurse of the Yr. 1985), Wash. State Nurses Assn. (chair healthcare reform task force 1992—96, Hon. Leadership award 1981), Sigma Theta Tau. Home: 1814 201st Pl SW Lynnwood WA 98036-7060 Office: Seattle Childrens Home Seattle WA 98119-2899

SANDBERG, IRWIN WALTER, electrical and computer engineering educator; b. N.Y.C., Jan. 23, 1934; s. Ben and Estelle (Hornick) S.; m. Barbara A. Zimmerman, June 15, 1958; 1 dau. Heidi L. Ed., CCNY, 1951-53; B.E.E., Poly. Inst. Bklyn., 1955, M.E.E., 1956, D.E.E., 1958. Tech. aid Bell Telephone Labs., Inc., Murray Hill, N.J., summer 1954, mem. tech. staff, 1958-67, head systems theory research dept., 1967-72, mem. math. and statis. research ctr., 1972-86; prof. elec. and computer engring. U. Tex., Austin, 1986—, now holder Cockrell Family Regents Chair in Engring.; engr. Wheeler Labs., Great Neck, N.Y., summer 1955. Vis. prof. U. Calif.-Berkeley, 1965; U.S. del. Union Radio Scientifique Internationale, Munich, Germany, 1966; U.S. nat. inst. rep. Advanced Study Inst. on Network and Signal Theory, NATO, Bournemouth, Eng., 1972; lectr. study inst. NATO (Knokke), Belgium, 1966, Copenhagen, 1970; disting. invited spkr. Asilomar Conf., 1973-74; main lectr. European Conf. on Circuit Theory and Design, The Hague, 1981; advisor Inst. Electronics, Info. and Comm. Engrs., Tokyo; advisor Am. Men and Women of Sci., 1993. Patentee (in field). Recipient Best Paper award Asilomar Conf., 1970, Achievement award IEEE Circuits and Systems Soc., 1986, Classic Paper citation ISI press, 1984, Outstanding Alumnus award Poly. U., 1993. Fellow IEEE (life, adminstrv. com. group circuit theory 1969-70, vice chmn. group circuit theory 1971-72, Centennial medal, Millennial medal, Cirs. and Sys. Soc. Golden Jubilee medal, Cirs. and Sys. Soc. disting. lectr.), AAAS; mem. NAE, Soc. for Indsl. and Applied Math., Eta Kappa Nu, Sigma Xi, Tau Beta Pi Home: 8505 Hickory Creek Dr Austin TX 78735-1527 Office: Univ Tex Dept Elec Comp Engr Austin TX 78712 E-mail: sandberg@ece.utexas.edu.

SANDBERG-MORGAN, BARBARA, retired communication and women's studies educator; b. McAllen, Tex., Dec. 19, 1934; d. Dean M. and Katherine (Hurlbert) Baer; m. Robert Morgan, July 31, 1976 (dec. Nov. 1994); 1 chld, Allison Morgan. BS, Ind. U., 1959; MA, Columbia U., 1963, EdD, 1974. Registered drama therapist. Prof. William Paterson U., Wayne, N.J., 1963-2000, prof. emerita, 2000—. Instr. Tchrs. Coll./Columbia U., N.Y.C., 1971-77; drama therapist, 1979—; mem. adv. bd., drama cons. Jersey Shore Arts Ctr., Ocean Grove, N.J., 1996—; dir. edn. Inner City Ensemble, Paterson, N.J., 1984-89; dir. Washington St. Gallery, Paterson, 1989-93. Dir. Paterson Bicentennial Pageant, Hist. Commn., 1992; dir. Washington St. Cultural Activities Assn., Paterson, 1990-93. Recipinet Heritage Citizen award Pater-

son, 1993, citation for tchg. excellence William Paterson U., 1994; named Woman of Yr., World of the Arts-Girl Scout Coun., 1995. Mem. Nat. Assn. for Drama Therapy (founding; bd. dirs.). Avocations: acting, directing, gardening. Home: 400 Deal Lake Dr Apt 2J Asbury Park NJ 07712-5174 E-mail: millik@sedona.net.

SANDBLOM, STEVEN KIRK, lawyer; b. Des Moines, Nov. 26, 1951; s. Donald Dean and Jane (Moffet) S.; m. Sally Anne McKlveen, June 24, 1972; children: Sarah J., Scott T. BA, Drake U., 1973, JD, 1975. Bar: Iowa 1976, U.S. Dist. Ct. (no. and so. dists.) Iowa 1976, U.S. Tax Ct. 1976, U.S. Ct. Appeals 8th cir.) 1976. Ptnr. Baker, Johnsen & Sandblom, Humboldt, Iowa, 1976—. Asst. atty. gen. State of Iowa, Des Moines, 1976; rsch. asst. Supreme Ct. Adminstr., Des Moines, 1972-75; Humboldt County magistrate Iowa Dist. Ct., Humboldt, Iowa, 1977-83, 85-96; juvenile ct. referee Iowa Dist. Ct., Humboldt, Wright and Pocahontas counties, 1982-89. Bd. dirs., chmn. Congregational Ch., Humboldt, 1978-82; bd. dirs. Humboldt Homes Ltd., 1982-88, Humboldt Workshop, 1984-99, Humboldt County Meml. Hosp. Found., 1997—. Mem. ABA, Iowa State Bar Assn. (mem. juvenile law com. 1983-90, bd. govs. 1990-2000, chair Gen. Practice Sect., 2001-03), Humboldt County Bar Assn. (pres. 1984-85), Jud. Dist. 2B Bar Assn. (sec. 1979-84, pres. 1986-87), Kiwanis (pres. 1986-87). Home: 13 Woodland Dr Humboldt IA 50548 Office: Baker Johnsen & Sandblom PO Box 337 Humboldt IA 50548-0337 Office Phone: 515-332-1157. E-mail: ssandblom@humboldtlaw.com.

SANDBORG, MARIANNE M. voice educator, musician; d. Lloyd and Dorothy Miller; m. Dr. Jeffrey R. Sandborg. MusM, Voice, U. of Ill., Champaign-Urbana, 1977—81; BS, Voice, Old Dominion U., Norfolk, Va., 1973—77. Resident artist/tchg. assoc., voice Roanoke Coll./Fine Arts Dept., Salem, Va., 1987—; organist and soloist Second Presbyn. Ch., Roanoke, Va., 1988—. Recipient Semi-finalist, N.Y. Oratorio Competition, 1990, Excellence in the Arts, Perry F. Kendig Found., 1998, Semi-finalist and finalist, Yrjo Kilpinen Internat. Voice Competition, 1999, Best Vocalist, 2000, Roanoker Mag., 2000, First-Prize Winner, Diana Barnhart/Phila. Cathedral Voice Competition, 2003. Mem.: Am. Guild of Organists, Nat. Assn. of Teachers of Singing. debuting world premieres of compositions written by several composers; collaborating with contemporary composers of note, including Gunther Schuller, Margaret Brower, Daniel Pinkham, Gordon Marsh and Aaron Garber. Office: Roanoke College/Fine Arts Dept 221 College Ave Salem VA 24153 Office Phone: 540-375-2214. E-mail: msandbor@roanoke.edu.

SANDBORN, VIRGIL ALVIN, civil engineer, educator; b. Conway Springs, Kans., Apr. 30, 1928; s. Kenneth Arthur and Mamie Una (Durham) S.; m. Virginia Ruth Cerny, June 12, 1955; children: Peter Alan, Patricia Marie. B in Aero. Engring., U. Kans., 1950; M in Aero. Engring., U. Mich., 1953. Aero. research scientist NACA-NASA, Cleve., 1951-62; cons. scientist AVCO R&AD, Wilmington, Mass., 1962-63; from prof. to prof. emeritus Colo. State U., Ft. Collins., 1963—. Vis. scientist NASA-Ames Research Ctr., Moffett Field, Calif., 1972-73, Navy Underwater Ctr., Newport, R.I., 1984-85. Author: Resistance Temperature Transducers, 1972, Classnotes for Experimental Methods in Fluid Mechanics, 1981. Mem. AIAA, Sigma Xi. Home: 917 Cheyenne Dr Fort Collins CO 80525-1559 E-mail: v.sandborn@comcast.net.

SANDBURG, HELGA, author; b. Maywood, Ill., Nov. 24, 1918; d. Carl and Lilian (Steichen) S.; m. George Crile, Jr., Nov. 9, 1963; children by previous marriage: John Carl Steichen, Paula Steichen Polega. Student, Mich. State Coll., 1939-40, U. Chgo., 1940. Dairy goat breeder, also personal sec. to father, 1944-51; sec. manuscripts div., also for keeper of collections Library of Congress, 1952-56; adminstrv. asst. for papers of Woodrow Wilson, 1958-59; writer, lectr., 1957—. Author: (novels) The Wheel of Earth, 1958, Measure My Love, 1959, The Owl's Roost, 1962, The Wizard's Child, 1967; (non-fiction) Sweet Music, A Book of Family Reminiscence and Song, 1963; (with George Crile, Jr.) Above and Below, 1969; (poetry) The Unicorns, 1965; To A New Husband, 1970, The Age of the Flower, 1994; (young adult novels) Blueberry, 1963; Gingerbread, 1964; (juveniles) Joel and the Wild Goose, 1963; Bo and the Old Donkey, 1965, Anna and the Baby Buzzard, 1970; Children and Lovers: 15 Stories by Helga Sandburg, 1976; (biography) A Great and Glorious Romance: The Story of Carl Sandburg and Lilian Steichen, 1978; "...Where Love Begins", 1989, (recorded poems) From in the Dream: Helga Sandburg Reads her Poems, 2001; also numerous short stories; rep. in collections.; contbr.short stories, poems, articles to popular mags. including Seventeen. Recipient Va. Quar. Rev. prize for best short story, 1959, Borestone Mountain poetry award, 1962, Poetry award Chgo. Tribune, 1970; 2d prize 7th Ann. Kans. Poetry Contest, Florence Roberts Head Ohioana Book award, 1990; grantee Finnish Am. Soc. and Svenska Inst., 1961 Mem. Authors Guild, Poetry Soc., Am. Milk Goat Record Assn., Am.-Scandinavian Found., Nat. Nubian Club, Coun. Save the Dunes, Am. Luxembourg Soc., Acad. Am. Poets. Address: 2060 Kent Rd Cleveland Heights OH 44106-3339 E-mail: helgacrile@aol.com.

SANDDAL, NELS DODGE, foundation executive, consultant; b. Salt Lake City, Feb. 17, 1949; s. James Wesley and Charlotte Jean (Ewer) S.; m. Brenda Kay Lille Griffin, Sept. 27, 1970 (div. June 1990); m. Theresa Louise Knipe, Oct. 10, 1992; 1 child, Jami. BA in English, Carroll Coll., 1966-70; MS in Psychology, Mont. State U., 1996. In-svc. trainer Boulder (Mont.) River Sch. and Hosp., 1974-75; group home mgr. REACH, Inc., Bozeman, Mont., 1975-76; community home trainer Devel. Disabilities Tng. Inst., Helena, Mont., 1976-77; tng. coord. emergency med. svcs. bureau State Dept. Health and Environ. Scis., Helena, 1977-82; cons., lead staff Nat. Coun. State Emergency Med. Svcs. Tng. Coords., Inc., Lexington, Ky., 1981-86; account exec., lead staff Nat. Assn. Emergency Med. Techs., Clinton, Miss., 1986-87; pres., CEO Assn. Mgmt. and Cons., Inc., Boulder, 1983-89; writer, prodr., dir. North Country Media Group, Great Falls, Mont., 1990-91; chief conf. planner S.O.S. Conf. Planning Consortium, Great Falls, 1991-92; exec. dir. Critical Illness & Trauma Found., Bozeman, Mont., 1986-91, pres., CEO, 1991—. Season course leader Nat. Outdoor Leadership Sch., Lander, Wyo., 1966—74; mem. exec. com. Nat. Coun. State EMS Tng. Coords., 1977—82, chmn., Ky., 1979—81; mem. adv. com. pediatric emergency med. svcs. tng. project Children's Hosp. Nat. Med. Ctr., Wash., 1985—88, pediatrics emergency instr., 1986—90; mem. grant peer rev. com. divsn. injury epidemiology Ctrs. for Disease Control, Atlanta, 1986—87; cons. Emergency Med. Svcs. Bureau, Helena, 1977, Devel. Disabilities Tng. Inst., Helena, 1977—78; mem. injury prevention profls. New Eng. Network to Prevent Childhood Injuries, Newton, Mass., 1988—95; mem. core faculty devel. trauma sys. tng. program U.S. Dept. Transp., Wash., 1989—; tech. assistance team mem. EMS, 1991—93; EMS instr. and program coord. Great Falls Vocat. Tng. Ctr., 1991—93; rsch. asst. inst. for cmty. studies U. Mo., Kansas city, 1983—95; assoc. rsch. prof. psychology Mont. State U., 1999—; asst. clin. prof. surgery U. Nev. Sch. Medicine, 1999—; exec. com. Intermountain Regional EMS Children Coord. Coun., Bozeman, Mont., 1994—2002; site reviewer Commn. for Accreditation of Ambulance Svcs., Glenview, Ill., 1997—; firefighter/EMS trainer Gallatin Gateway Vol. Fire Dept., Gallatin Gateway, Mont., 1998—2001; asst. chief Gallatin Gateway Fire Dept., 2001—; bd. dirs. Five Rivers chpt. ARC, Bozeman, Mont., 1998—2001; med. officer Gallatin River Ranch, 2001—. Editor and tech. cons.: Workbook for Prehospital Care and Crisis Intervention, 4th edit., 1992, 5th edit., 1993, Instructor Resource Manual for Prehospital Care and Crisis Intervention, 4th edit., 1992, Workbook for First Responder, 1990; contbg. editor Jour. of Prehospital Care, 1984-85, The EMT Jour., 1980-81; edit. cons. Am. Acad. Orthopaedic Surgeons, 1980-81; contbr. numerous articles to profl. jours.; video prodr. and presenter in field. Mem. Park County DUI Task Force, Livingston, 1993-96; inaugural coord. Mont. Safe Kids Coalition, Big Timber, 1988-90; adv. com. Nat. Significance Project for Respite Care, 1977-78; mem. basic life support com. of Mont., Mont. Heart Assn., 1977-82. Recipient Golden award for humanity ARC, 1976, 500 Hour award, 1976, Outstanding Svc. award Nat. Coun. State EMS Tng. Coords., 1979, Leadership award, 1981, Charter Membership award, 1984, J.D. Farrington award for excellence Nat. Assn. Emergency Med. Technicians, 1981, Jeffrey S. Harris award, 1985, Outstanding Svc. award Am. Heart Assn., 1982, Appreciation cert. for paramedic emergency care U.S. Dept. Transp., 1984, appreciation awards Colo. Trauma Inst., 1993, Healthy Mothers/Healthy Babies, Helena, Mont., 1997, Kans. Bd. of EMS, Topeka, 1996, 98, Intermountain Regional EMS for Children Coordinating Coun., Inc., 1998. Mem. Nat. Registry EMTs (20 yr. recognition), Mont. Bd. Med. Examiners. Democrat. Avocations: mountain climbing, hiking, sailing, golf, skiing. Home: 115 Lay Pass Manhattan MT 59741 Office: 115 Lay Pass Rd Manhattan MT 59741-8032 E-mail: nsanddal@citmt.org.

SANDE, THEODORE ANTON, architect, educator, foundation executive; b. New London, Conn., Nov. 21, 1933; s. Lars Anton and Viola (Edgcomb) S.; m. Solveig Inga-Maj Imselius, Aug. 6, 1960; children: Susanne Ingrid, Lars Michael. BSc in Architecture, R.I. Sch. Design, 1956; MArch, Yale U., 1961; PhD, U. Pa., 1972; grad. Cultural Instns. Mgmt. Program, Mus. Collaborative, 1983; postgrad., Attingham (Eng.) Summer Sch., 1980. Vis. prof. history of architecture Rensselaer Poly. Inst., fall 1973-74, U. Pa., 1976-77; adj. prof. Am. studies and history Case-Western Res. U., 1981—92. Vis. lectr. in historic preservation Cleve. State U., summer 1994, spring 1998; lectr. art Williams Coll., 1972-75; attended teleconfs. non-profit orgn. mgmt. Drucker Found., 1992. Designer, Arkitekt, Hakon Ahlberg, SAR, Arkitekt, Stockholm, 1960, designer, Washburn, Luther & Rowley, Architects, Attleboro, Mass., 1961-62, Barker & Turoff, Architects, Providence, 1962-63, jr. partner, Turoff Assocs., Architects, 1964-67, partner, Turoff & Sande, Architects, Providence, 1968-70, prin. Ted Sande, Architect, Cranston, R.I., 1970, Cleve., 1993—, emeritus architect, R.I., 2004— author: Industrial Archaeology: A New Look at the American Heritage, 2d edit, 1978; contbg. author: Guidebook to Philadelphia Architecture, 1974; editor: New England Textile Mill Survey, 1971; co-editor: Historic Preservation of Engineering Works, 1981; contbr. articles to profl. jours.; two-man show drawings, Providence Art Club, 1970. Dir. profl. svcs. office hist. properties Nat. Trust Hist. Preservation, Washington, 1975—77, dir. planning and devel., 1977—78, acting v.p. office hist. properties, 1978—79, v.p., 1979—80; mem. Old Georgetown Bd. Nat. Commn. Fine Arts, 1979—81; co-chmn. Conf. Indsl. Archeology Smithsonian Instn., 1971; active Shaker Heights Landmark Commn., 1982—84, Cleve. Landmarks Commn., 1985—2004; mem. archtl. bd. rev. Village of Hunting Valley, Ohio, 2000—; mem. Leadership Cleve. Class 86/87, Ohio Gov.'s Commn. on Bicentennials the NW Ordinance and U.S. Const., 1986—89, Cleve. Bicentennial Commn., 1992—94, Stan Hywet Hall and Gardens, Akron, Ohio, trustee, 1997—; chmn. Schweinfurth Trust, 1999—; mem. vis. com. Mandel Sch. Scis., Case We. Res. U., 1993—2003; trustee Universal Circl Inc., 1981—93, Nat. Rock and Roll Mus. and Hall of Fame, mem. exec. bdlg. com., 1993—95; instnl. rep. Cleve. Arts Consortium, 1987—93. Fellow: We. Res. Hist. Soc. (life; exec. dir. 1981—93, exec. dir. emeritus 1993—); mem.: SAR, AIA (com. hist. resources 1972—74), Cleve. Restoration Soc. (pres. 1994—97, trustee, hon., life trustee), Ohio Mus. Assn. (trustee 1982—87), Am. Assn. Mus., Internat. Com. for Conservation of Indsl. Heritage (chmn. bd. dirs. 1978—81), Soc. Archtl. Historians (preservation com. 1972—74), Soc. Indsl. Archeology (co-founder, 1st pres. 1971—72, dir. 1973—76, project supr. handbook on adaptive use of indsl. bldgs., gen. chmn. 15th ann. conf.), Philos. Club Cleve. (past pres.), Rowfant Club (past pres. 2002—03, coun. of fellows). Episcopalian. Home: 13415 Shaker Blvd Cleveland OH 44120-1586

SANDEFER, G(EORGE) LARRY, lawyer; b. Washington, Mar. 2, 1950; s. George Hall and Mary Gray (Babers) S. BS, Auburn U., 1972; JD, U. Fla., 1978. Bar: Fla. 1978, U.S. Dist. Ct. (mid. dist.) Fla. 1978, U.S. Ct. Appeals (5th and 11th cirs.) 1981, U.S. Supreme Ct. 1982; cert. in criminal trial law Fla. Bar. Asst. state atty., criminal divsn., lead trial atty. State of Fla., Clearwater, 1977-86; sole practice Clearwater, 1986-88; assoc. Kimpton, Burke and White, P.A., Clearwater, 1988-90; pvt. practice, Clearwater, 1991—. Mem. Indian Rocks Civic Assn., 1994-2000, Leadership Pinellas; city commr. Indian Rocks Beach, 1994-00. 1st lt. USAF, 1973-75. Mem. ATLA, Pinellas County Trial Lawyers Assn., Fla. Assn. Criminal Def. Attys., Colo. Bar Assn., Fla. Bar Assn., Clearwater Bar Assn., St. Petersburg Bar Assn., Kiwanis. Avocations: tennis, skiing, boating. Address: 111 N Belcher Rd Ste 202 Clearwater FL 33765-3259

SANDEFUR III, JAMES, publishing executive; children: Jasmine K. Sandefur, Amiah B. Sandefur. A in bus. mngmt., Profl. Career Devel. Inst., 2004. Corr. reporter Speakin' Out News, Huntsville, Ala., 1995; chief organizer The Writer's Regime, Athens, Ala., 2001—. List owner Nat. Writers Union, N.Y.C., 2002. Supporter Dem. Nat. Com., 2003. Labor. Achievements include development of diverse literary firm. Avocations: organizing for labor unions, demonstrations for civil liberty, jogging, hiking, exploring. Home: PO Box 542 Athens AL 35612 Office: The Writer's Regime PO Box 542 Athens AL 35612-0542 Office Phone: 256-412-0949.

SANDELMAN, JON, investment banker; Bachelor's Degree, Adelphia U.; JD, Cardozo Sch. Law. Dep. head global equities, mng. dir. equity derivatives Salomon Bros.; head equity fin. products NationsBank (now Bank Am. Securities), N.Y.C., 1998—2002; head equities Banc Am. Securities LLC, N.Y.C., 2002—04, pres., 2004—, head debt and equities, 2004—. Office: Bank of Am Securities LLC 9 W 57th St New York NY 10019*

SANDER, ALISON BISHOP, international consultant; b. Boston, July 28, 1959; d. Frank E.A. and Emily (Jones) S. BA, U. Chgo., 1983; JD cum laude, MBA, Harvard U., 1987. Assoc. Goldman Sachs, N.Y.C., 1987—89; pres., CEO Cambridge Transnat. Assocs., Boston, 1990—97; mgr., globalization topic leader Boston Cons. Group, 1997—. Mem. bd. mgrs. N.E. Yearly Meeting of Friends, Boston, 1992-94; bd. dirs. Lisle Fellowship, Mich., 1990-94, Harvard Coop., Cambridge, Mass., 1984-87, Boston Ctr. for Internat. Visitors, 1993-94; overseer Boston Sci. Mus., 1998-; globalization commr. State of World Forum, 1998-. Recipient Perry S. Herst prize U. Chgo., 1981. Mem. UN Assn. N.Y. (panel), Coun. Fgn. Rels., Asia Soc., World Affairs Coun., Harvard Bus. Sch. Club of Boston, Phi Beta Kappa. Avocations: running, ballet, playing the dulcimer. Home: 74 Buckingham St Cambridge MA 02138-2229 Office: Boston Cons Group Exch Pl Boston MA 02109

SANDER, DOROTHY E. manufacturing executive; V.p. adminstrn. and benefits Hanson Industries, 1984-95; assoc. dir. Hanson PLC, 1993-95; v.p. adminstrn. U.S. Industries, Inc., Iselin, NJ, 1995—98, sr. v.p. adminstrn., 1998—, West Palm Beach, Fla., 2000—. Mem. adv. bd. Bank of N.Y. Bd. editors HR-Law and Practice mag., Feminist Press. Office: US Industries Inc 777 S Flagler Dr Ste 1112 West Palm Beach FL 33401

SANDER, FRANK ERNEST ARNOLD, law educator; b. Stuttgart, Germany, July 22, 1927; came to U.S., 1940, naturalized, 1946; s. Rudolf and Alice (Epstein) S.; m. Emily Bishop Jones, Apr. 26, 1958; children: Alison Bishop, Thomas Harvey, Ernest Ridgway Sander. AB in Math. magna cum laude, Harvard U., 1949, LLB magna cum laude, 1952. Bar: Mass. 1952, US Supreme Ct. 1952. Law clk. to Chief Judge Magruder U.S. Ct. Appeals, 1st Cir., 1952-53; law clk. to Justice Frankfurter, U.S. Supreme Ct., 1953-54; atty. tax divsn. Dept. Justice, 1954-56; with firm Hill & Barlow, Boston, 1956-59; mem. faculty Harvard Law Sch., 1959—, prof. law, 1962—, Bussey prof., 1981—, assoc. dean, 1987-2000. Spl. fields fed. taxation, family law, welfare law, dispute resolution; chmn. Coun. on Role of Cts.; mem. panels Am. Arbitration Assn., Fed. Mediation and Conciliation Svc.; chmn. Coun. on Legal Edn. Opportunity, 1968—70; cons. Dept. Treasury, 1968; treas. Harvard Law Rev., 1951—52; mem. dispute resolution standing com. Mass. Supreme Jud. Ct., 1994—2004; drafting com. Uniform Mediation Act, 1998—2001. Author: (with Westfall and McIntyre) Readings in Federal Taxation, 2d edit., 1983, (with Foote and Levy) Cases and Materials on Family Law, 3d edit., 1985, (with Gutman) Tax Aspects of Divorce and Separation, 4th edit., 1985, (with Goldberg, Rogers and Cole) Dispute Resolution, 4th edit., 2003. Mem. tax mission Internat. Program Taxation to Republic of Colombia, 1959; mem. com. on civil and polit. rights President's Commn. on Status of Women, 1962-63; trustee Buckingham Browne and Nichols Sch., 1969-75; chmn. Mass. Welfare Adv. Bd., 1975-79. With AUS, 1945-46. Recipient Whitney North Seymour medal Am. Arbitration Assn., 1988, spl. award for disting. svc. to dispute resolution Ctr. for Pub. Resources Inst. for Dispute Resolution, 1990. Mem. ABA (chmn. standing com. dispute resolution 1986-89, Kutak medal 1993, D'Alemberte-Raven award 1999), Boston Bar Assn., Phi Beta Kappa. Home: 74 Buckingham St Cambridge MA 02138-2229 Office: Harvard U Sch of Law Cambridge MA 02138 Office Phone: 617-495-3184.

SANDER, SUSAN BERRY, environmental planning engineering corporation executive; b. Walla Walla, Wash., Aug. 26, 1953; d. Alan Robert and Elizabeth Ann (Davenport) Berry. BS in Biology with honors, Western Wash. U., 1975; MBA with honors, U. Puget Sound, 1984. Biologist, graphic artist Shapiro & Assocs., Inc., Seattle, 1975-77, office mgr., 1977-79, v.p., 1979-84, pres., owner, 1984—, also bd. dirs. Named Employer of Yr., Soc. Mktg. Profl. Svcs., 1988, Small Bus. of Yr., City of Seattle, Environ. Cons. of Yr., King County, Bus. Person of Yr., Washington State, 2003; recipient merit scholar, Overlake Svc. League, Bellevue, Wash., 1971, scholar, Wester Wash. U. Bellingham, 1974—75, U. Puget Sound, 1984, Identity award, PEMA Corp., 1996, Mktg. award, Soc. Mktg. Svc. Profls., 2000, 2001, Woman of the Yr., Washington State, 2002, Diamond award, 2003. Mem.: WTS, Am. Coun. Engring. Cos., Student Conservation Assn. (bd. dirs.), Portland C. of C., Seattle C. of C. Avocation: Avocations: swimming, hiking, travel, painting. Office: 101 Yesler Way Ste 400 Seattle WA 98104-3425 E-mail: ssander@shap.com.

SANDERBECK, RANDE PAUL, music educator, musician; b. Greensburg, Pa., Oct. 26, 1953; s. William Leo and Vella Mae Sanderbeck; m. Lori Suzanne Chisholm, Oct. 28, 1980. MusB, W.Va. U., 1978, MusM, 1985; D in Musical Arts, U. Ky., 1997. Prof. percussion East Tenn. State U., Johnson City, 1985—. Arranger Percussion Ensembles, Johnson City, Tenn., 1985—2004; percussion performance Jazz Quartets, Johnson City, 1985—. Composer: Homage to Max; contbr. articles to profl. jours. Scholar, W.Va. U., 1974—78, U. Ky., 1990—91. Mem.: Percussive Arts Soc. Avocations: performing music, travel. Home: 1801 Todd Dr Johnson City TN 37604 Office: East Tenn State Univ PO Box 70661 Johnson City TN 37614 Personal E-mail: r.sanderbeck@worldnet.att.net. E-mail: sanderbe@mail.etsu.edu.

SANDERCOX, ROBERT ALLEN, college official, clergyman; b. Akron, Ohio, May 20, 1932; s. Monroe J. and Elverda (Arnold) S.; m. Nancy Lee Wertz, Sept. 13, 1958; children— Alison Grace, Megan Louise, Robert Philip BA, Bethany Coll., W. Va., 1954; M.Div., Yale U., 1957; postgrad., U. Buffalo, W.Va. U.; LittD, Bethany Coll., 1989. Ordained to ministry Christian Ch. (Disciples of Christ). Asst. minister Park Ave Christian Ch., N.Y.C., 1954-57; asst. provost Bethany Coll., 1957-60, v.p., dean students, 1960-75, v.p., dir. devel., 1975-79, interim pres., 1979-80, v.p., provost for coll. advancement, 1980-89, sr. v.p., 1989-95, cons. to the pres., 1995-97, sr. v.p. emeritus, 1997—. Trustee Bethany Coll., 2004—. Trustee Christian Ch. Disciples of Christ in W.Va., Parkersburg, 1984-88; chmn. Brooke County Landmarks Commn., 1988-98, Brooke County Mus. Bd., 1995-98. Recipient Alumni Disting. Service award Bethany Coll., 1982 Mem. Coun. for Advancement and Support Edn., Duquesne Club (Pitts.), Order of Symposiarch, Rotary, Kiwanis (pres. 1967), Alpha Sigma Phi (nat. treas. 1982-84, v.p. 1984-86, grad. sr. pres. 1986-88, bd. dirs., trustee Ednl. Found. 1982-95, chmn. Ednl. Found. 1994-95, Delta Beta Xi svc. award 1960). Republican. Home: 4557 Middleton Park Cir E Jacksonville FL 32224-6609 Address: 715 Buckwood Ln Lititz PA 17543 Personal E-mail: r.sandercox@prodigy.net.

SANDERLIN, TERRY KEITH, counselor; b. Ashland, Oreg., Aug. 5, 1950; s. Calvin Carney and Myrtle Estell (Cope) S.; m. Theresa Emma Garcia, Jan. 19, 1969 (div. Feb. 1976); 1 child, Sean Eric; m. Margaret Lillian Lutz, Dec. 26, 1987. B in Bus., U. N.Mex., 1982, M in Counseling, 1983, EdD, 1993. Diplomate Am. Psychotherapy Assn.; lic. clin. mental health, N.Mex., sch. counselor, N.Mex.; cert. hypnotherapist Internat. Assn. Counselors and Therapists; pvt. pilots lic.; glider lic.; keelboat cert. Unit supr. Bernalillo County Juvenile Detention Ctr., Albuquerque, 1978-80; counselor Independence Halfway House, Albuquerque, 1980-81; mental health worker Bernalillo County Mental Health Ctr., Albuquerque, 1981-82; probation parole officer N.Mex. Probation/Parole, Albuquerque, 1982-87, dist. supr. Gallup, 1987-88; vocat. counselor Internat. Rehab. Assn., Albuquerque, 1989-91; counseling psychologist VA, Albuquerque, 1991-98; owner, dir. Counseling and Tng. Specialist, Albuquerque, 1988—. Counselor Albuquerque (N.Mex.) Counseling Specialist, 1983-86; guest lectr. sociology dept. U. N.Mex., Albuquerque, 1992; presenter 5th Annual S.W. Substance Abuse Conf., Albuquerque, 1992; presenter N.Mex. Corrections Dept., Santa Fe, 1993. Author: (video tapes) Breathing Free & Good, 1991, Understanding Adolescent Satanism, 1991, (manual) Social Skills and Anger Management, 1993, Anger Management Intervention with Offender Populations, 1998, The Impulsivity Factor in Offender Behavior, 1999; contbr. articles to profl. jours. Vol. counselor Adult Misdemeanor Probation, Albuquerque, 1974-76; panel mem. Cmty. Corrections Selection Panel, Albuquerque, 1987-90. With U.S. Army, 1969-72, Vietnam. Recipient Outstanding Citizenship, Albuquerque Police Dept., 1974; N.Mex. Dept. Pub. Safety rsch. grantee, 1995. Mem.: Am. Psychotherapy Assn. Democrat. Avocations: scuba diving, martial arts, canoeing, flying, sailing. Office: Counseling & Tng Specialist 127 Bryn Mawr Dr SE Ste E Albuquerque NM 87106-2209 Office Phone: 505-550-0145. E-mail: TK.4@juno.com.

SANDERMAN, MAURICE, construction company executive; b. 1940; Acct. Shepard, Schwartz & Harris, Chgo., 1961-68; with Kaufmann Broad Homes, Oak Brook, Ill., 1968-74, B.A. Storms Cons., Chgo., 1974-76; pres. Northbrook (Ill.) Devel. Corp., 1976-86; chmn. bd. dirs., CEO, pres. Sundance Homes Inc., Schaumburg, Ill., 1981—. Office: Sundance Homes Inc 70 E Lake St Ste 1600 Chicago IL 60601-5917

SANDERS, AARON PERRY, radiation biophysics educator; b. Phoenix, Jan. 12, 1924; s. DeWitt and Ruth (Perry) S.; m. Betty Mae Gelein, Aug. 11, 1944 (div.); children: Merle Sanders Ireland, Julie Sanders Mitchel, James DeWitt; m. Georgia Anne Bullock, Nov. 26, 1972 (div.); 1 child, Kai Marie; m. Vallie E. Flint. BS, U. Tex., El Paso, 1950; MS (AEC fellow), U. Rochester, 1952; PhD, U. N.C., 1964. Diplomate: Am. Bd. Health Physics. Baggage clk., ticket agt. Greyhound Bus Lines, Phoenix, 1942, dispatcher, ticket agt. El Paso, Tex., 1946-50; asso. health physicist Brookhaven Nat. Lab., Upton, N.Y., 1951-53; instr. physics, radiol. safety officer N.C. State Coll., 1953; instr. radiology Duke Med. Center, Durham, N.C., 1953-56, dir. radioisotope lab., 1953-65; asso. in radiology Duke Med. Ctr., 1956-57, asst. prof., 1957-64, assoc. prof., 1964-65, assoc. prof., dir. div. radiobiology, 1965-70, prof., dir. div. radiobiology, 1970-83, prof. emeritus, 1983—; chmn. Biomed. Physics Dept. King Faisal Specialist Hosp., Riyadh, Saudi Arabia, 1984-86. Fulbright sr. lectr. radiol. physics, Argentina, 1958-59; cons. N.C. Bd. Health, 1961-76; mem. N.C. Radiation Protection Commn., 1976-83, chmn., 1978-79 Contbr. articles to profl. jours. Served with USNR, 1942-45. Mem. AAAS, Am. Assn. Physicists in Medicine, AAUP, Soc. Exptl. Biology and Medicine, Health Physics Soc., Soc. Nuclear Medicine, Biophys. Soc., Radiation Research Soc., Undersea Med Soc., Sigma Xi, Sigma Pi Sigma. Office Phone: 480-891-0308. *Each individual has an obligation to himself and society to pursue an education to his maximum capability. This capability should then be used in his career in an effort to contribute to society as much, or more, than he receives. In work and personal relations you must never deny a man the dignity of his work by ridicule or denigration, and you must never use people.*

SANDERS, ADRIAN LIONEL, educational consultant; b. Paragould, Ark., Aug. 3, 1938; s. Herbert Charles and Florence Theresa (Becherer) S.; m. Molly Jean Zecher, Dec. 20, 1961. AA, Bakersfield Coll., 1959; BA, San Francisco State U., 1961; MA, San Jose State U., 1967. 7th grade tchr. Sharp Park Sch., Pacifica, Calif., 1961-62; 5th grade tchr. Mowry Sch., Fremont, Calif., 1962-64; sci. tchr. Blacow Sch., Fremont, Calif., 1964-76; 5th grade tchr. Warm Springs Sch., Fremont, 1977-87, 5th grade gifted and talented edn. tchr., 1987-94; edn. cons., 1994—. Mem. San Diego Hist. Soc., 1999, Alzheimer's Family Relief Program, Rockville, Md., 1986; vol. 7 km. Race for Alzheimer's Disease Willow Glen Founders Day, San Jose, 1988-92. Named Outstanding Young Educator, Jr. C. of C., Fremont, Calif., 1965. Mem. Zoolog. Soc. San Diego, Calif. Ctr. for the Arts (Escondido). Avocations: photography, travel, visiting presidents' birthplaces, collecting license plates, collecting matchbooks worldwide. Home and Office: 1437 Stoneridge Cir Escondido CA 92029-5514

SANDERS, BARRY, retired football player; b. Wichita, July 16, 1968; s. William and Shirley Sanders. Student, Okla. State U., 1986—89. With Detroit Lions, 1989—99; ret., 1999. Named NFL Rookie of Yr., 1990, NFL Offensive Player of the Yr., 1997, 1994, NFL Player of the Yr., 1991, 1997; named to

Sporting News Coll. All-Am. team, 1987, 1988, Pro Bowl, 1989—98; recipient Heisman Trophy award, 1988. Achievements include holds NCAA single season record in rushing yards (2,628); led NFL in rushing, 1990, 94, 96, 97; #3 all-time on NFL rushing list (15,269); inducted into NFL Hall of Fame, 2004.

SANDERS, BARRY R. lawyer; b. Oak Park, Ill., July 21, 1957; s. Eugene Haze and Muriel Efty Sanders; m. Diane Gaffney Sanders, Dec. 28, 1985; 1 child, Mattie Maria Murielle. BA, U. Va., 1979, Cambridge U., 1981; LLM, U. Tex., 1983; MA, Cambridge U., 1986. Bar: Calif. 1984, Ariz. 1985, U.S. Dist. Ct. (no. dist.) Calif. 1984, U.S. Dist. Ct. (ea. dist.) Calif. 1985, U.S. Dist. Ct. Ariz. 1987, U.S. Ct. Appeals (9th cir.) 1989, U.S. Supreme Ct. 1996, U.S. Ct. Appeals (8th cir.) 2001. Shareholder Pohlman & Sanders, PA, Phoenix, 1989—91, Ryley, Carlock & Applewhite, PA, Phoenix, 1991—99, Allen, Price, Padden & Sanders PC, Phoenix, 1999—. Recipient Henry prize in Moral Philosophy, U. of Aberdeen, Scotland, 1978. Mem.: State Bar Ariz. (chair antitrust sect. 1998—99, 2002—03). Avocation: golf. Office: Allen Price Padden & Sanders PC 3131 E Camelback Rd Ste 110 Phoenix AZ 85016

SANDERS, BERNARD (BERNIE SANDERS), congressman; b. Brooklyn, Sept. 8, 1941; s. Eli and Dorothy (Glassberg) S.; m. Jane O'Meara, 1988; children: Levi, Heather, Carina, David. BA, U. Chgo., 1964. Freelance writer, carpenter, youth counselor, 1964-76; with Govt. Vt., 1965-66; dir. Am. People's Hist. Soc., Burlington, Vt., 1976-81; mayor of Burlington, 1981-89; mem. (at large) U.S. Congress from Vt., 1991—. Mem. progressive caucus, mem. com. fin. svcs., com. on govt. reform. Author filmstrips and articles on social, hist. and polit. subjects. Chmn. Vt. Liberty Union Party, 1975-76, candidate for gov., 1972, 76, 86, U.S. Senate, 1971, 74. Independent. Jewish. Office: US Ho of Reps 2233 Rayburn Ho Office Bldg Washington DC 20515-4501

SANDERS, CHARLES ADDISON, retired physician; b. Dallas, Feb. 10, 1932; s. Harold Barefoot and May Elizabeth (Forrester) Sanders; m. Elizabeth Ann Chipman, Mar. 6, 1956; children: Elizabeth, Charles Addison, Carlyn, Christopher. MD, U. Tex., 1955. Intern, asst. resident Boston City Hosp., 1955—57, chief resident, 1957—58; clin. and rsch. fellow in medicine Mass. Gen. Hosp., Boston, 1958—60, chief cardiac catheterization lab., 1962—72, gen. dir., 1972—81, physician, 1973—81, program dir. myocardial infarction rsch. unit, 1967—72; exec. v.p. E.R. Squibb and Sons, 1981—84, Squibb Corp., 1984—88, vice chmn., 1988—89; chief exec. officer Glaxo Inc., Research Triangle Park, NC, 1989—94, chmn., 1992—95; assoc. prof. medicine Harvard U. Med. Sch., 1969—80, prof., 1980—83; candidate U.S. Senate, 1996. Chmn. Commonwealth Fund N.Y.C., Nat. Found. for Biomed. Rsch. Mem. editl. bd.: New Eng. Jour. Medicine, 1969—72. Mem. Pres.'s Coun. Advisors on Sci. and Tech.; chmn. Project Hops; trustee U. N.C., Chapel Hill. Capt. USAF, 1960—62. Mem.: ACP, Mass. Med. Soc., Am. Heart Assn. Office: 100 Europa Dr Ste 170 Chapel Hill NC 27517-2310

SANDERS, CHARLES F. dean; DDS Dental-Orthodontics, Howard U., 1968. Dentist. Office: 600 W St NW Washington DC 20059

SANDERS, CHARLES FRANKLIN, management and engineering consultant; b. Louisville, Dec. 22, 1931; s. Charles Franklin and Maragret Rhea (Timmons) S.; m. Marie Audrey Galuppo, Dec. 29, 1956; children: Karen Lynn, Craig Joseph, Keith Franklin. B.Chem. Engring., U. Louisville, 1954, M.Chem. Engring., 1958; PhD, U. So. Calif., 1970. Research engr. Exxon Research and Engring. Co., Linden, N.J., 1955-62; asst. prof. engring. Calif. State U., Northridge, 1962-68, assoc. prof., 1968-71, prof., 1971-82, chmn. dept., 1969-72, dean Coll. Engring. and Computer Sci., 1972-81; pres., chief exec. officer, dir. Rusco Industries, Los Angeles, 1981-82; exec. v.p. Energy Systems Assocs., Tustin, Calif, 1982-89, Energeo, San Francisco, 1989-95, also bd. dirs.; v.p. tech. Smith-Bellingham Capital, San Francisco, 1989-91. Bd. dirs. Catalyst Air Tech., Inc. Bd. dirs. San Fernando Valley Child Guidance Clinic, 1979-81. Served to 1st lt. U.S. Army, 1956-57. NSF fellow, 1965-67 Mem. AIChE, NSPE, Calif. Soc. Profl. Engrs., Am. Soc. for Engring. Edn., Combustion Inst. Republican. E-mail: cfs@cox.net.

SANDERS, DALE R. lawyer; b. N.Y.C., Feb. 1, 1946; m. Jo-Ann Sanders, Dec. 25, 1967; 1 child. Bar: Fla. 1970, Wyo. 1991, U.S. Dist. Ct. (so. dist.) Fla. 1971, U.S. Tax Ct. 1972. Atty. Kirsch & Druck, P.A., Ft. Lauderdale, Fla., 1970-71, Kirsch, Digiulian, Druck et al, Ft. Lauderdale, Fla., 1971-72, Digiulian, Spellacy, Lyons, Ft. Lauderdale, Fla., 1972-77, Lyons & Sanders, Chartered, Ft. Lauderdale, Fla., 1977—. With USAR, 1969-75. Mem.: Broward County Trial Lawyers Assn. (pres. 1980), Broward County Bar Assn. (pres. 1990), Fla. Bar (bd. govs. 1991—95, mem. 17th cir. jud. nominating commn. 1992—96, vice chair 1996—2002, mem. State of Fla. jud. qualifications commn.). Office: Lyons and Sanders Chartered 600 NE 3rd Ave Fort Lauderdale FL 33304-2618

SANDERS, DANIEL S. oil industry executive; BSME, U. S.C., 1961. Engr. Exxon Chem. Co., Baton Rouge, 1961, v.p. olefins, 1971—88; exec. v.p. Exxon Chem. Ams., 1971—88, Exxon Chem. Asia Pacific, 1971—88; exec. asst. to chmn. Exxon Corp., N.Y.C., 1988—90, exec. asst. to pres., 1988—90; sr. v.p. Exxon Co. U.S.A., 1990—92; worldwide pres. basic chem. group Exxon Chem. Co., 1992—94; v.p. human resources Exxon Corp., 1994—98; pres. Exxon Chem. Co., 1999—; v.p. Exxon Corp, 1999—. Bd. mem. Chem. Mfrs. Assn., exec. com., chmn. CHEMSTAR policy com.; bd. mem. Am. Plastics Coun., Chlorine Chem. Coun. Bd. mem. YMCA of Met. Dallas, exec. com.; bd. mem. Houston YMCA. Office: 13501 Katy Fwy Houston TX 77079

SANDERS, DEION LUWYNN, professional football player; b. Ft. Myers, Fla., Aug. 9, 1967; Student, Fla. State U. Baseball player N.Y. Yankees, 1988—90, Atlanta Braves, 1991—94, Cin. Reds, 1994—95, 1997, 2001; football player Atlanta Falcons, 1989—94, San Francisco 49ers, 1994, Dallas Cowboys, 1995—99, Washington Redskins, 2000, Baltimore Ravens, 2004—; TV Analyst CBS NFL Today, 2001—04. Mem. Championship team Super Bowl XXIX, 1994, Championship team Super Bowl XXX, 1995. Named to Sporting News Coll. All-Am. football team, 1986—88, Sporting News NFL All-Pro football team, 1991, 1992, 1994, Pro Bowl team, 1991—94, 1996—99; recipient Jim Thorpe award, 1988. Office: c/o Baltimore Ravens 1101 Russel st Baltimore MD 21230*

SANDERS, EDWIN PERRY BARTLEY, judge; b. Madisonville, Ky., July 12, 1940; s. Virgil Perry and Eunice Jane (Denton) S.; m. Kathryn Walker, Jan. 28, 1967; children: Christopher Charles, Carroll Denton. BS in Bus., Stetson U., 1965, JD, 1968. Bar: Fla. 1968. Ptnr. Ford, Wren and Sanders, 1968-69; mem. Landis, Graham, French, Husfeld and Ford, PA, DeLand, Fla., 1970-83; prof. real estate Stetson U. Sch. Bus. Adminstrn., 1980-83; judge 7th Jud. Cir. Ct. Volusia County, DeLand, Fla., 1983—. With U.S. Army. Mem. Fla. Bar Assn., Volusia County Bar Assn., Lake Beresford Yacht Club, Rotary. Democrat. Episcopalian. Home: 340 Washington Oaks Dr Deland FL 32720-2760 Office: Volusia County Courthouse 101 N Alabama Ave Ste D443 Deland FL 32724 also: PO Box 611 Deland FL 32721-0611 Office Phone: 386-736-5946.

SANDERS, ELIZABETH ANNE WEAVER (BETSY SANDERS), management consultant; b. Gettysburg, Pa., July 25, 1945; Student, Gettysburg Coll., 1963—65; BA in German Lang. and Linguistics, Wayne State U., 1967; MEd, Boston U., 1970; postgrad., U. Wash., 1976—78. Prin. The Sanders Partnership, Sutter Creek, Calif., 1971-90; founder, dir. Nat. Bank So. Calif., 1971-90; v.p., gen. mgr. Nordstrom Inc. Bd. dirs. Wal Mart Stores, Inc., Washington Mut., Wellpoint Health Sys., Inc., Wolverine Worldwide, Inc., Denny's Inc., H.F. Ahmanson Co., Carl Karcher Enterprises, Sport Chalet, St. Joseph Health Sys. Author: Fabled Service. Trustee Gettysburg Coll. Recipient Woman of Achievement in Bus. award YWCA South Orange County, Director's Choice award, 1997; named Woman of Yr. Bus. and Industry YWCA North Orange County, Humanitarian of Yr. NCCJ, Author of Yr., 1996, Dir. of Yr., Corp. Gov. Forum for Corp. Dirs., 2002. Mem. Internat. Women's Forum. Office: The Sanders Partnership PO Box 14 Sutter Creek CA 95685-0014 E-mail: betsanders@aol.com.

SANDERS, FRANKLIN D. retired insurance company executive; b. Newton, Mass., Apr. 24, 1935; s. Franklin and Ethel Shriner (Dulaney) S.; m. Jane Gray Collier, June 18, 1960; children— Cynthia, Franklin D., Nancy, Carolyn AB, Amherst Coll., 1957; MBA, Harvard U., 1959. With 1st Boston Corp., N.Y.C., 1960-86, mng. dir., 1976-86; pres. Aegis Ins. Services Inc., Jersey City; ret. Treas., bd. dirs. Assoc. Electric & Gas Ins. Services, Ltd., Hamilton, Bermuda, 1986-97. Chmn. Republican Exec. Com., Bernardsville, N.J., 1965-72, Bernardsville Zoning Bd. of Adjustment, 1966-99. Mem. Harvard Club (N.Y.C.). Episcopalian. Avocations: sailing, skiing, golf.

SANDERS, GARY HILTON, physicist; b. N.Y.C., Aug. 27, 1946; s. Sidney Simon and rose (Kershner) S.; m. Marjorie Clark King, June 9, 1973; children: David Ethan, Laurie Kate. AB, Columbia U., 1967; PhD, MIT, 1971. Rsch. asst. MIT, Cambridge, 1967-71; rsch. assoc. Princeton U., 1971—78, asst. prof., 1971—78; mem. staff Los Alamos (N.Mex.) Nat. Lab., 1978-94; project mgr., dep. dir. laser interferometer gravitational wave obs. Calif. Inst. Tech., Pasadena, 1994—. Guest physicist DESY, Hamburg, Germany, 1968-71; guest scientist Brookhaven Nat. Lab., Upton, N.Y., 1971-75, 84-89; vis. scientist Fermi Nat. Accelerator Lab., Batavia, Ill., 1977-79. Contbr. articles to profl. jours. Chmn. N.Mex. Conservation Voters Alliance, 1983-90, Govs. Task Force on Water Resources, N.Mex., 1984-85; bd. dirs. N.Mex. Citizens for Clear Air and Water, 1979-94. Mem. Am. Phys. Soc. Democrat. Home: 572 Alta Vista Way Laguna Beach CA 92651-4039 Office: Calif Inst Tech Mail Code 18 34 Pasadena CA 91125-0001 E-mail: sanders@ligo.caltech.edu.

SANDERS, GERALD HOLLIE, communications educator, educator; b. Mt. Vernon, Tex., Dec. 10, 1924; s. Elmer Hugh and Velma Mae (Hollowell) S.; m. Mary Dean Crew, July 18, 1947, children: Michael Dwaine, Rose Ann, Susan Kathleen, Randall Wayne. BA, Southeastern Okla. U., 1947; MA, Tex. Tech U., 1969; PhD, U. Minn., 1974. Program dir. Sta. WEWO, Laurenburg, N.C., 1947-49; sports dir. Sta. KFYO, Lubbock, Tex., 1949-50; gen. mgr. Sta. KLVT, Levelland, Tex., 1950-51, 53-54; sports dir. Sta. KCUL, Ft. Worth, 1954-55; asst. mgr. Sta. KDAV, Lubbock, 1955-57; mgr. Sta. KCBD, Lubbock, 1957-58; owner Sta. KSEL, Lubbock, 1958-67, Sta. KBUY, Amarillo, Tex., Sta. KERB, Kermit, Tex., Sta. KBEK, Elk City, Okla., Sta. KZZN, Littlefield, Tex.; lectr. communications The Coll. of Wooster, Ohio, 1967-68, asst. prof., 1968-75, assoc. prof., 1975-81, chmn. dept. communication, 1974-81, Miami U., Oxford, Ohio, 1981-92, prof. emeritus comm., 1992—. Disting. lectr. Jinan U., Zhong Shan U., Fudan U., Nanjing U., Beijing U., China, 1989; cons. in field, Oxford, 1982—; polit. and trial cons., 1996—. Author: Introduction to Contemporary Academic Debate, 1983; also articles. Active Political Campaigns. Served to col. USMC, 1943-46, PTO, 1951-53, Korea. Recipient Disting. Svc. award Delta Sigma Rho-Tau Kappa Alpha, 1991, Am. Forensic Assn., 1991. Mem. Am. Forensic Assn. (pres. 1978-82), Speech Communication Assn., Speech Communication Assn. of Ohio (pres. 1976-77), Disting. Svc. award 1978), Am. Inst. Parliamentarians, Soc. Trial Cons. Presbyterian. Avocations: sports, political campaigns. Home: 200 Country Club Dr Oxford OH 45056-9050 Office: Advocacy Unltd PO Box 457 Oxford OH 45056-0457 E-mail: gsanders@one.net.

SANDERS, HAROLD BAREFOOT, JR., judge; b. Dallas, Tex., Feb. 5, 1925; s. Harold Barefoot and May Elizabeth (Forrester) S.; m. Jan Scurlock, June 6, 1952; children— Janet Lea, Martha Kay, Mary Frances, Harold Barefoot III. BA, U. Tex., 1949, LLB, 1950. Bar: Tex. bar 1950. U.S. atty. No. Dist. Tex., 1961-65; asst. dep. atty. gen. U.S., 1965-66; asst. atty. gen., 1966-67; legis. counsel to President U.S., 1967-69; partner firm Clark, West, Keller, Sanders & Butler, Dallas, 1969-79; U.S. dist. judge for No. Dist. Tex., Dallas, 1979—, chief judge, 1989-95. Mem. Tex. Ho. of Reps., 1952-58; Dem. nominee U.S. Senate, 1972. Lt. (j.g.) USNR, World War II. Mem. ABA (chmn. nat. conf. fed. trial judges 1988-89), Fed. Bar Assn. (Disting. Svc. award Dallas 1964), Dallas Bar Assn., State Bar Tex. (jud. conf. U.S. 1989-92, jud. panel on multidistrict litigation 1992-2000, jud. conf. com. to rev. cir. coun. conduct and disability orders 2001—), Blue Key, Phi Delta Phi, Phi Delta Theta. Methodist. Office: US Courthouse 1100 Commerce St Dallas TX 75242-1016

SANDERS, IRWIN TAYLOR, sociology educator; b. Millersburg, Ky., Jan. 17, 1909; s. Robert Stuart and Lucy (Taylor) S.; m. Margaret Rydberg, June 23, 1934 (dec. Feb. 1997); children: Gerda S. (Groff), Robert Stuart (dec. Sept. 1998); m. Mary Ann Hawkes, Nov. 1, 1997. Student, Tenn. Mil. Inst., 1920-25; AB, Washington and Lee U., 1929; student, Theol. Sem., Princeton, 1932-33; PhD, Cornell U., 1938; D.Pedagogy (hon.), R.I. Coll., 1981; Litt.D. (hon.), Washington and Lee U., 1981. Instr. American Coll., Sofia, Bulgaria, 1929-32, dean, 1934-37; asst. prof. sociology Ala. Coll., 1938-40; successively asst. prof., asso. prof., prof., head dept. sociology, distinguished univ. prof. U. Ky., 1940-56; lectr. sociology Harvard Sch. Pub. Health, 1958-62; chmn. dept. sociology and anthropology Boston U., 1960-63, 69-72, prof. sociology, 1972-77, Univ. lectr., 1973-74, also co-dir. community sociology tng. program. Research dir. Assos. Internat. Research, Inc., Cambridge, Mass., 1956-60; asso. dir. Internat. Tng. and Research Program, Ford Found., 1962-66; v.p. Edn. and World Affairs, 1967-69; social science analyst Bur. Agrl. Econ., U.S. Dept. Agr., summer 1943; sr. social scientist Bur. Agrl. Econ., U.S. Dept. Agr. (Office Fgn. Agrl. Relations), 1943; social sci. Bur. Agrl. Econ., U.S. Dept. Agr. (Extension Service), summer 1944; agrl. attaché Am. Embassy, Belgrade, Yugoslavia, 1945-46; research assoc. Harvard, 1952-53; cons. rural welfare division FAO Author: Balkan Village, 1949, The Community, 1958, 3d rev. edit., 1975, Rainbow in the Rock, People of Rural Greece, 1962, Rural Society, 1977; co-author: Alabama Rural Communities, 1940, Sociological Foundations of Education, 1942, Kentucky: Designs for Her Future, 1944, Farmers of the World, 1945, Making Good Communities Better, 1950, Bridges to Understanding: International Programs at U.S. Colleges and Universities, 1970; Editor: Societies Around the World, 1953, Collectivization of Agriculture in Eastern Europe, 1958, The Professional School and World Affairs, 1968; series editor: Social Movements: Past and Present, 1980-95. Bd. dirs. Am. Farm Sch., Thessaloniki, Greece, Sofia Am. Schs., Inc., Assn. for Study Southeastern Europe, Bucharest, Rumania; mem. corp. bd. Mass. Half-Way Houses, Inc., 1988—. Decorated Royal Order of Phoenix Greece). Mem. Am. Sociol. Soc. (disting. cmty. sect. award 1983), Eastern Sociol. Soc., So. Sociol. Soc. (pres. 1955-56), Rural Sociol. Soc. (pres. 1956-57, Disting. Rural Sociologist 1993), New Eng. Sociological Assn. (Apple award 1993), Am. Assn. Advancement Slavic Studies, Bulgarian-Am. Studies Assn. (hon. pres.), Modern Greek Studies Assn. (council), Am. Assn. for S.E. European Studies (pres. 1980), Société European de Culture (Venice), Rumanian Studies Soc. (council), Bulgarian Acad. Scis. (fgn. mem.), Am. Assn. for Promotion Bulgarian Culture (hon. pres.), Cornell Club (N.Y.), Phi Beta Kappa, Omicron Delta Kappa, Kappa Phi Kappa, Delta Sigma Rho, Delta Upsilon. Democrat. Presbyterian. Home: 99 Norumbega Rd #11 Weston MA 02493-2495 Office: 96 Cummington St Boston MA 02215-2407

SANDERS, JACK FORD, physician; b. St. Louis, Mich., July 16, 1918; s. Ford and Viva (Marvin) S.; m. Gretchen A. Jellema, Feb. 2, 1945; children: Karen Jean, Vicki Leigh, Mary Beth, Donald Curtis, Wendy Lynn BS summa cum laude, Alma Coll., Mich., 1939; MD, U. Mich., 1945; LL.D., Northwood U. Diplomate Am. Bd. Internal Medicine; cert. flight instr. aircraft and instruments, airplane single and multi-engine land and sea; flight safety counselor FAA; CAP check pilot; sr. aviation med. examiner. Intern Henry Ford Hosp., 1945-46, resident in internal medicine, 1947-50; practice medicine specializing in internal medicine Alma, Mich.; sr. attending physician internal medicine Butterworth Hosp., Blodgett Hosp., Grand Rapids, Mich.; cons. St. Mary's Hosp., Grand Rapids, Ferguson-Droste-Ferguson Hosp.; med. dir. Mich. Masonic Home, Alma, 1940—91; med. dir. rehab. div., chmn. dept. medicine, chief staff Gratiot Community Hosp.; chmn. dept. medicine Tri-County Hosp., Edmore, Mich.; clin. assoc. prof. medicine Coll. Human Medicine, Mich. State U. Mem. Com. on Aging, Gov's Adv. Coun. on Heart Disease, Cancer and Stroke; del White Ho. Conf. on Aging; bd. dirs. Mich. Masonic Home and Hosp.; chmn. bd. Cen. Mich. Wendy's, Inc.; sec., treas. Gratiot Aviation, Inc. Contbr. articles to profl. jours. Chmn. bd. govs. Mich.; bd. dirs. Northwood U., Gratiot Cmty. Airport Bd. Instr. ACTS, U.S. Air Corps and lt. (j.g.) M.C., USNR, WWII. Fellow ACP, Am. Geriatrics Soc.; mem. AMA, Mich. State Med. Soc., Gratiot Med. Soc., Kent Med. Soc., Gratiot-Isabella-Clare County Med. Soc. (pres. 1965), Am. Diabetes Assn., Am. Heart Assn., Am. Multiple Sclerosis Soc., Mich. Crippled Children and Adults Soc., East Ctrl. Mich. Health Svc. Assn., Mason (33d degree), Rotary, Phi Sigma Pi (hon.). Office: Mich Masonic Pathways Alma MI 48801-2174 Home: 1200 Wright Ave Ste 107 Alma MI 48801-1133 Business E-Mail: jsanders@masonicpathways.com.

SANDERS, JACK THOMAS, religious studies educator; b. Grand Prairie, Tex., Feb. 28, 1935; s. Eula Thomas and Mildred Madge (Parish) S.; m. M. Patricia Chism, Aug. 9, 1959 (dec. Oct. 1973); 1 son, Collin Thomas; m. Susan Elizabeth Plass, Mar. 3, 1979. BA, Tex. Wesleyan Coll., 1956; M.Div., Emory U., 1960; PhD, Claremont Grad. Sch., 1963; postgrad., Eberhard-Karls U., Tuebingen, Germany, 1963-64. Asst. prof. Emory U., Atlanta, 1964-67, Garrett Theol Sem., Evanston, Ill., 1967-68, McCormick Theol. Sem., Chgo., 1968-69; assoc. prof. U. Oreg., Eugene, 1969-75, prof., 1975-97, head dept. religious studies, 1973-80, 85-90, prof. emeritus, 1997—. Author: The New Testament Christological Hymns, 1971, Ethics in the New Testament, 1975, 2d edit., 1986, Ben Sira and Demotic Wisdom, 1983, The Jews in Luke-Acts, 1987, Schismatics, Sectarians, Dissidents, Deviants: The First One Hundred Years of Jewish-Christian Relations, 1993, Charisma, Converts, Competitors: Societal and Sociological Factors in the Success of Early Christianity, 2000; editor: Gospel Origins and Christian Beginnings, 1990, Gnosticism and the Early Christian World, 1990; mem. edit. bd. Jour. Bibl. Lit., 1977-83. Mem. policy bd. Dept. Higher Edn. Nat. Council Chs., N.Y.C., 1971-73. NDEA grad. study fellow, 1960-63; Fulbright Commn. fellow, 1963-64; Am. Council Learned Socs. travel grantee, 1981; NEH fellow, 1983-84 Mem. Studiorum Novi Testamenti Soc., Assn. for Jewish Studies, Soc. Bibl. Lit. (regional sec. 1969-26, sabbatical rsch. award 1976-77), Soc. for Sci. Study of Religion, Assn. for Sociology Religion. Democrat. Home: 704 NW 3d Dr Pendleton OR 97801-1411 Office: U Oregon Dept Religious Studies Eugene OR 97403 E-mail: jsanders@oregon.uoregon.edu.

SANDERS, JACQUELYN SEEVAK, psychologist, educator; b. Boston, Apr. 26, 1931; d. Edward Ezral and Dora (Zoken) Seevak; 1 child, Seth. BA, Radcliffe Coll., 1952; MA, U. Chgo., 1964; PhD, UCLA, 1972. Counselor, asst. prin. Orthogenic Sch., Chgo., 1952—65; rsch. assoc. UCLA, 1965—68; asst. prof. Ctr. for Early Edn., L.A., 1969—72; assoc. dir. Sonia Shankman Orthogenic Sch., U. Chgo., 1972—73, dir., 1973—93, dir. emeritus, 1993—; curriculum cons. day care ctrs. L.A. Dept. Social Welfare, 1970—72; instr. Calif. State Coll., L.A., 1972, lectr. dept. edn. U. Chgo., 1972—80, sr. lectr., 1980—93, clin. assoc. prof. dept. psychiatry, 1990—93, emeritus, 1993—; instr. edn. program Inst. Psychoanalysis, Chgo., 1979—82. Cons. Osawatomie State Hosp. (Kans.), 1965—68; reading cons. Foreman H.S., Chgo.; treas. Chgo. Inst. Psychoanalysis, 2003—. Author: Greenhouse for the Mind, 1989; editor (with Barry L. Childress): Psychoanalytic Approaches to the Very Troubled Child: Therapeutic Practice Innovations in Residential & Educational Settings, 1989; editor: Severely Disturbed Children and the Parental Alliance, 1992; editor: (with Jerome M. Goldsmith) Milieu Therapy: Significant Issues and Innovative Applications, 1993; editor: The Seevak Family, The Zoken Family; contbr. articles to profl. jours. Mem. vis. com. univ. sch. rels. U. Chgo.; bd. dirs. KAM Isaiah Israel Congregation, 1997—2001, Chgo. Inst. for Psychoanalysis. Recipient Alumna award, Girls' Latin Sch., Boston, Bettelheim award, Am. Assn. Children's Residential Ctrs., Disting. Svc. award, Radcliffe Assn., 2002; scholar Radcliffe Coll. scholar, 1948—52; Univ. fellow, UCLA, 1966—68. Mem.: Chgo. Inst. for Psychoanalysis, Assn. Children's Residential Ctrs. (past pres.), Harvard Club (bd. dirs. 1986—2001, Chgo.), Radcliffe Club (sec.-treas. 1986—87, pres. 1987—89, Chgo.). Home: 5842 S Stony Island Ave Apt 2G Chicago IL 60637-2033 E-mail: jsand09@attglobal.net.

SANDERS, JAMES ALVIN, minister, religious studies educator; b. Memphis, Nov. 28, 1927; s. Robert E. and Sue (Black) S.; m. Dora Cargille, June 30, 1951; 1 son, Robin David. BA magna cum laude, Vanderbilt U., 1948, BD with honors, 1951; student, U. Paris, 1950-51; PhD, Hebrew Union Coll., 1955; DLitt, Acadia U., 1973; STD, U. Glasgow, 1975; DHL, Coe Coll., 1988, Hebrew Union Coll., 1988, Hastings Coll., 1996, Calif. Luth. U., 2000. Ordained teacher Presbyn. Ch., 1955; instr. French Vanderbilt U., 1948-49; faculty Colgate Rochester Div. Sch., 1954-65, assoc. prof., 1957-60, Joseph B. Hoyt prof. O.T. interpretation, 1960-65; prof. O.T. Union Theol. Sem., N.Y.C., 1965-70, Auburn prof. Bibl. studies, 1970-77; adj. prof. Columbia, N.Y.C., 1966-77; prof. Bibl. studies Sch. Theology and Grad. Sch., Claremont, Calif., 1977-97; vis. prof. Union Theol. Seminary and Columbia U., 1997-98, Yale Divinity Sch., 1998, Jewish Theol. Seminary, 2001. Ann. prof. Jerusalem Sch. of Am. Schs. Oriental Rsch., 1961-62; fellow Ecumenical Isnt., Jerusalem, 1972-73, 85; Ayer lectr., 1971, 79, Shaffer lectr., 1972, Fondren lectr., 1975, Currie lectr., 1976, McFadin lectr., 1979, Colwell lectr., 1979; guest lectr. U. Fribourg, Switzerland, 1981, 90, Hebrew Union Coll., 1982, 88, Oral Roberts U., 1982, Tulsa U., 1982, Ind. U., 1982, Coe Coll., 1983, Garrett Sem., 1984, Pepperdine U., 1985, Western Sem., 1985, Bethany Sem., 1986; lectr. Union Sem. Sesquicentennial, 1987, U. Wis., 1987, U. Chgo., 1987; Gray lectr. Duke U., 1988; guest lectr. Notre Dame U., Georgetown U., Tex. Christian U., 1989, Alexander Robertson lectr. U. Glasgow, 1990-91, Gustavson lectr. United Theol. sem., 1991; assoc. program lectr. Smithsonian, 1990, Am. Bible Soc. Sesquicentennial, 1991, U. N.Mex., 1992, 94, 97, Am. Interfaith Inst., 1992, Georgetown U., 1992; Lily Rosmen lectr. Skirball Mus., 1992; vis. prof. U. N.Mex., 1992, Southwestern U., 1992, Calif. Luth. U., 1992, 94, Willamette U., 1993, Peter Craigie lectr. U. Calgary, 1993, U. So. Ariz., 1993; Samuel Iwry lectr. John Hopkins U., 1993; lectr. San Diego State U., 1994, Creighton U., 1995, The Mercantile Libr., N.Y.C., 1995, U. Heidelberg, Germany, 1995, U. Mich., 1995; session chair, Internat. Congress for Fiftieth Anniversary of Dead Sea Scrolls, Jerusalem, 1997; Womack lectr. The Methodist Coll., 1996; Purcell lectr. Barton Coll., 1997, Vatican Symposium, 1999, Temple Emanu-El, 1999, Hebrew Union Coll., 2001; mem. internat. O.T. text critical com. United Bible Socs., 1969—; mem. nat. adv. acad. bd. Hebrew Union Coll., 1997—; co-founder, exec. officer Ancient Bibl. Manuscript Ctr. for Preservation and Rsch., 1977-80, pres., 1980-2003, vis. prof. Jewish Theol. Sem., 2001—; chmn. bd. Shepherd U., L.A., 2002—. Author: Suffering as Divine Discipline in the Old Testament and Post-Biblical Judaism, 1955, The Old Testament in the Cross, 1961, The Psalms Scroll of Qumran Cave 11, 1965, The Dead Sea Psalms Scroll, 1967, Near Eastern Archaeology in the Twentieth Century, 1970, Torah and Canon, 1972, 74, Identité de la Bible, 1975, God Has a Story Too, 1979, Canon and Community, 1984, From Sacred Story to Sacred Text, 1987, Luke and Scripture, 1993; editor: Paul and the Scriptures of Israel, 1993, Early Christian Interpretation of the Scriptures of Israel, 1997, The Function of Scripture in Early Jewish and Christian Tradition, 1998, The Canon Debate, 2002; contbr. over 280 articles to profl. jours.; mem. editl. bd. Jour. Bibl. Lit., 1970-76, Jour. for Study Judaism, Bibl. Theology Bull., Interpretation, 1973-78, New Rev. Standard Version Bible Com.; 2 vols. of essays: A Gift of God in Due Season, 1996, The Quest for Context and Meaning, 1997 pub. in honor of Sanders' retirement. Trustee Am. Schs. Oriental Research. Fulbright grantee, 1950-51, Lilly Endowment grantee, 1981, NEH grantee, 1980, 91-92; Lefkowitz and Rabinowitz interfaith fellow, 1951-53, Rockefeller fellow, 1953-54, 85, Guggenheim fellow, 1961-62, 72-73, Human Scis. Rsch. fellow, 1989. Mem. Soc. Bibl. Lit. and Exegesis (pres. 1977-78), Phi Beta Kappa, Phi Sigma Iota, Theta Chi Beta. Home: PO Box 593 Claremont CA 91711-0593 Office: Ancient Bibl Manuscript Ctr 1325 N College Ave Claremont CA 91711-3154 E-mail: SandersJA@aol.com.

SANDERS, JAMES F. lawyer; b. Johnson City, Tenn., Mar. 3, 1945. B.A., Vanderbilt U., 1967, J.D., 1970. Bar: Tenn. 1970, Wash. 1972. Practice, Nashville; mem. Neal and Harwell. Mem. Tenn. Bar Assn., Wash. State Bar Assn., ABA, Am. Judicature Soc., Phi Delta Phi. Mem. Nat. Moot Ct. Competition, 1969-70. Office: Neal and Harwell 8th Floor Third Nat Bank Bldg Nashville TN 37219

SANDERS, JAMES GRADY, biogeochemist; b. Norfolk, Va., June 10, 1951; s. Allen Buford and Maple Seretha (Myers) S.; m. Dorothea L. Palmer, 2001. BS in Zoology, Duke U., 1973; MS in Marine Scis., U. N.C., 1975, PhD in Marine Scis., 1978. Postdoctoral investigator Woods Hole (Mass.) Oceanog. Instn., 1978-80; vis. scientist Chesapeake Biol. Lab. U. Md., Solomons, 1980-81; asst. curator Estuarine Rsch. Ctr., Md. Acad. Natural Scis., 1981-85, assoc. curator, 1985-89, curator, 1989-99, dir., 1983-99, v.p., 1999; chair dept.

ocean, earth and atmospheric scis. Old Dominion U., Norfolk, 1999-2001; dir. Skidaway Inst. Oceanography, Savannah, Ga., 2001—. Cons. EPA Sweden, Stockholm, 1985-90; mem. Md. Sea Grant Adv. Com., College Park, 1983-90, Environ. Commn., Calvert County, Md., 1981-88; mem. environ. biology panel Office R & D EPA, Washington, 1986-95, sci. adv. bd., ecol. processes and effects com., 2003--; regional rep. Coastal Resources Adv. Commn., Md., 1983-86; bd. dirs. Am. Chestnut Land Trust; mem. bd. govs. Consortium for Oceanog. Rsch. and Edn., 1999—, exec. com., 2003--. Assoc. editor Estuaries, 1996-99; mem. editl. bd. Environ. Toxicology and Chemistry, 2000-03; contbr. more than 70 articles to sci. jours. Grantee NOAA, EPA, NSF. Mem. AAAS, Am. Geophys. Union, Am. Soc. Limnology and Oceanography, Soc. for Environ. Toxicology and Chemistry, Estuarine Rsch. Fedn. (treas. 1993-97), So. Assn. Marine Labs. (pres. 2004--). Achievements include first identification of relationships between algal growth and chemical transformations of arsenic in aquatic systems. Office: Skidaway Inst Oceanography 10 Ocean Science Cir Savannah GA 31411 Home: 11 Wesley Crossing Savannah GA 31411 Office Phone: 912-598-2400. E-mail: sanders@skio.peachnet.edu.

SANDERS, JERRY, social services executive; b. San Pedro, Calif., July 14, 1950; m. Rana Sampson; children: Jamie, Lisa. AA, Long Beach City Coll., 1970; BA in Pub. Adminstrn., Nat. U., 1988; student, San Diego State U. Cert. P.O.S.T mgmt. Police officer San Diego Police Dept., 1973-93, chief of police, 1993-99; pres. United Way San Diego, 1999—. Bd. dirs. The Nat. Conf., San Diego State U. Cmty. Adv. Bd., Children's Initiative, Youth Econ. Enterprise Zones; mem. cmty. leaders adv. bd. ElderHelp of San Diego. Recipient Headliner of Yr. award San Diego Press Club, 1984, 93, Exceptional Performance citation for SWAT leadership, 1986. Office: United Way 4699 Murphy Canyon Rd San Diego CA 92123-5371

SANDERS, JIMMY DEVON, public administration and health services educator; b. Montgomery, Ala., Nov. 6, 1945; s. Harold Wright Sanders and Elsie M. (Huett) Harris; m. Linda Ruth Sweatt, Mar. 25, 1966; children: Richard Devon, Robert Pearson. B Gen. Studies, U. Nebr., Omaha, 1968; MPA, U. Okla., 1973, U. So. Calif., 1988, D Pub. Adminstrn., 1989. Commd. officer USAF, 1964, advanced through grades to lt. col., 1985, various health svc. adminstrv. positions, 1964-83, dir. base med. svcs., 1980-83; sr. health policy analyst Dept. Def., Washington, 1983-88; ret., 1988; assoc. prof. mgmt. and healthcare mgmt. Marymount U., Arlington, Va., 1988-91; dir. Atlantic region Troy State U., Norfolk, Va., 1991-94; dir. Fla. region Troy State U., Ft. Walton Beach, 1995-96, assoc. prof. pub. adminstrn., 1996—. Health care cons. various hosps. and cities, 1987—, Ret. Officers Assn., Arlington, 1988-90. Fellow Am. Coll. Health Care Execs.; mem. Assn. Mgmt./Internat. Assn. Mgmt. (pres. 1996-97), Internat. Soc. Rsch. in Healthcare Fin. Mgmt., 2000—. Republican. Lutheran. Avocations: walking, reading, golf. Home: 10850 US Highway 331 Montgomery AL 36105-6105 Office: Troy State U PO Box 2829 Fort Walton Beach FL 32549-2829

SANDERS, JOE MAXWELL, JR., pediatrician, association administrator; b. Hartsville, S.C., July 5, 1940; m. Dorothy Garvin, June 6, 1963; children Joe M. III, Eric T. BS, The Citadel, 1962; MD, Med. U. S.C., 1967. Diplomate Am. Bd. Pediatrics. Rotating intern, resident in pediatrics Letterman Army Med. Ctr., San Francisco, 1967-70; fellow in adolescent medicine San Francisco Children's Hosp., 1970-71; chief adolescent medicine svc. Fitzsimmons Army Med. Ctr., 1971-86; dir. adolescent medicine svc. Med. Coll. Ga., 1986-88; assoc. exec. dir. Am. Acad. Pediatrics, Elk Grove Village, Ill., 1988-93, exec. dir., 1993—. Asst. clin. prof. pediatrics U. Colo. Health Scis. Ctr., 1971-76, assoc. clin. prof., 1976-83, clin. prof. 1983-86; assoc. prof. pediatrics Med. Coll. Ga., 1986-88; clin. prof. pediatrics, U. Chgo., 1991—; cons. for adolescent medicine Surgeon Gen. Army, 1976-86; mem. med. com. Rocky Mt. Planned Parenthood, 1981-86; vis. prof. dept. pediatrics U. Kansas (Wichita), 1984, 87, dept. pediatrics and family practice, E. Tenn. State U., Johnson City, 1985, U. Fla., Gainesville, 1987, Fitzsimmons Army Med. Ctr., Denver, 1989, U. Chgo., 1991, Baylor Coll., Houston, 1994, others. Contbr. numerous articles and abstracts to profl. jours., chpts. to books; mem. editl. bd. Jour. Current Adolescent Medicine, 1979-81, Substance Abuse: A Guide for Profls., 1985-88; reviewer Pediatrics, 1984—, Jour. Pediatrics, 1986—, Jour. Adolescent Health, 1986—, Am. Jour. Diseases of Children, 1987—, Jour. Am. Med. Assn., 1987—; guest lectr., speaker at many sci. confs. and med. soc. meetings. Mem. teenage coord. coun. Richmond County Health Dept., 1986-88, head start health adv. com. CSRA Econ. Opportunity Authority, Inc., 1986-88; med. cons. Alexian Bros. Med. Rels. Com. Decorated Legion of Merit, U.S. Army, 1987; recipient Adele Hoffman award, Sect. on Adolescent Health, 1988. Fellow Am. Acad. Pediatrics (com. on adolescence 1980-87, chmn. 1983-87, chmn. uniformed svcs chpt. 1981, 84, mem. exec. com. mil. pediatrics sect. 1976-79, sec.-treas. 1976-77, chmn. 1977-79, mem. steering com. to establish non-geographic mil. dist. chpt., mem sect. on adolescent health 1979—, program com. 1981-83, task force on substance abuse, chmn. 1984-85, cons. 85-87, task force on sch. based clinics, 1987—), Soc. Adolescent Medicine (edn. com., ambulatory care com., 1975-80, chmn. nominating com. 1978, exec. coun. 1980-83, chmn. awards com. 1990-93, pres. 1987-88, past pres's. coun. 1988—, Outstanding Achievement award 1994); mem. AMA (mem. planning com. nat. coalition on adolescent health, rep. Am. Acad. Pediatrics, Soc. Adolescent Medicine to Coalition 1987—, chmn. working group on rsch. agenda 1987-88, adv. com. on unintentional injuries 1987), Ambulatory Pediatric Assn., So. Soc. for Pediatric Rsch., Soc. Med. Cons. to Armed Forces, Order Mil. Med. Merit, Sigma Xi. Home: 449 W Rosiland Rd Palatine IL 60074-1098 Office: Am Acad Pediatrics 141 Nortwest Point Blvd Elk Grove Village IL 60007

SANDERS, KEITH PAGE, journalism educator; b. Ashland, Ohio, Sept. 25, 1938; s. Merwin Morse and Phyllis Pearl (Snyder) S.; m. Jane Carmel Adams, June 11, 1966; children: Paige Ann, Kevin Scott. BS in Journalism, Bowling Green State U., 1960; MS in Journalism, Ohio U., 1964; PhD in Mass. Comm., U. Iowa, 1967. Sports editor Ashland (Ohio) Times Gazette, 1960-61, Dover (Ohio) Daily Reporter, 1961-62; instr. journalism Bowling Green (Ohio) State U., 1963-64, U. Iowa, Iowa City, 1965-67; prof. journalism U. Mo., Columbia, 1967—2001, assoc. dean grad. studies Sch. Journalism, 1986-87, 90-91, O.O. McIntyre disting. prof., 1993, prof. emeritus, 2002—. Cons. in field. Contbr. articles to profl. jours. including Journalism Quar., Mass Media Rev., Jour. Broadcasting, Electronic Jour. of Comm.; assoc. editor Mass Comm. Rev., 1981-92, mem. editl. bd., 1972-98; mem. editl. bd. Journalism Monographs, 1973-80, Mass Comm. and Soc., 1998—. Recipient Award for Outstanding Achievement U. Mo. Alumni Assn., 1986; Joyce Swan Disting. Faculty award U. Mo., 1973; inducted into Columbia Bowling Hall of Fame, 1999. Mem. Internat. Soc. for Sci. Study of Subjectivity (treas. 1990-95), Assn. for Edn. in Journalism/Mass. Comm. (Trayes Prof. of Yr. 1987), Soc. Profl. Journalists, Mo. State Bowling Assn. (bd. dirs. 2000—), Kappa Tau Alpha (exec. dir. 1991—), Omicron Delta Kappa. Avocations: bowling, golf, fishing. Home: 6551 N Creasy Springs Rd Columbia MO 65202-8093 Office: Univ of Missouri Sch Journalism Columbia MO 65211-1200

SANDERS, MARION YVONNE, retired geriatrics nurse; b. St. Petersburg, Fla., Dec. 4, 1936; d. Ira Laurey and Maude Mae Cherry Sanders; children: Dwayne Irwin, Princess Charrie. BS, Fla. A&M U., 1959; MS, Nova U., Ft. Lauderdale, Fla., 1992. RN, Fla. Staff nurse Lantana (Fla.) TB Hosp., 1960-61, Mercy Hosp., St. Petersburg, 1961; gen. duty nurse VA, Tuskegee, Ala., 1961-62; staff nurse John Andrews Hosp., Tuskegee, 1962-63; gen. duty staff nurse Brewster Meth. Hosp., Jacksonville, Fla., 1963-65, Duval Med. Ctr., Jacksonville, 1965-66; pvt. duty nurse Dist. 2 Registry, Jacksonville, 1966-70; supr. Eartha White Nursing Home, Jacksonville, 1970; staff nurse Bapt. Hosp., Jacksonville, 1971-73, City-County Methadone Clinic, Jacksonville, 1976-78; pvt. duty nurse Home Nursing, Jacksonville, 1982-86, pvt. duty geriatric nursing and gerontology specialist, 1995—2001, Sr. Companion Svc. Corp., 1997-98; ret., 2001. Respite and relief sr. companion vol. Urban Jacksonville Cathedral Found., 1996-98. Mem. Ideas for Am.'s Future, 1997, 1998, NAACP, 1997—98; vol. shelter mgr. ARC, Miami, Fla., 1992—94; vol. cmty. activist, 1994; vol. Jacksonville Cmty. Rels. Bd., 1996, Jacksonville Inc. Cathedral Found., 1997—; sr. companion Svc. Corp., 1997—98, 1999; mem. Brewseter's and Cmty. Nurses Alumni, 1998—2000, 2001—02; vol. Rep. Senatorial Com., 1999; vol. cmty. svcs., elem. grades tutor, polit. campaigns, tchr. health edn.; vol. Rep. Nat. Com., 1997—2000, 2001—02, Rep. Com. Fla., 1997—98, Northside Rep. Club, 1997, 1998, 1999; active St. Stephen AME Ch., Jacksonville, tch. Bible studies for youth, advocate for poor, homeless and prisoners. Recipient Cert. of Recognition, Rep. Party, Fla. and Wash., 1990, Rep. Congl. Orgn., 1988, 90, 91. Mem. ANA (mem. polit. action coms.), Fla. Nurses Assn., Women's Missionary Soc. (life). Republican. Methodist. Avocations: reading the holy bible, teaching sunday school, volunteer work. Home: 4832 N Main St Apt 14 Jacksonville FL 32206-1458

SANDERS, MARLENE, anchor, journalism educator, news correspondent; b. Cleve., Jan. 10, 1931; d. Mac and Evelyn (Menitoff) Sanders; m. Jerome Toobin, May 27, 1958 (dec. Jan. 1984); children: Jeff, Mark. Student, Ohio State U., 1948—49. Writer, prodr. Sta. WNEW-TV, N.Y.C., 1955-60, P.M. program Westinghouse Broadcasting Co., N.Y.C., 1961-62; asst. dir. news and pub. affairs Sta. WNEW, N.Y.C., 1962-64; anchor, news program ABC News, N.Y.C., 1964-68, corr., 1968-72, documentary prodr., writer, anchor, 1972-76, v.p., dir. TV documentaries, 1976-78; corr. CBS News, N.Y.C., 1978-87; host Currents Sta. WNET-TV, N.Y.C., 1987-88; host Met. Week in Rev., 1988-90; host Thirteen Live Sta. WNET-TV, 1990-91; prof. dept. journalism NYU, N.Y.C., 1991-93, adj. prof. journalism, 1996—; adj. prof. journalism, adminstr. Columbia U. Grad. Sch. Journalism, N.Y.C., 1994-95. Profl.-in-residence Freedom Forum Media Studies Ctr., 1997-2000; freelance broadcaster, narrator; chmn. bd. womensenews.org, chair RSVP, Inc., 1997-. Co-author: Waiting for Prime Time: The Women of Television News, 1988. Mem. N.Y.C. Commn. on Women's Issues, 2003—. Recipient award N.Y. State Broadcasters Assn., 1976, award Nat. Press Club, 1976, Emmy awards, 1980, 81, others. Mem. Am. Women in Radio and TV (Woman of Yr. award 1975, Silver Satellite award 1977), Women in Comm. (past pres.), Coun. Fgn. Rels. Personal E-mail: sanders110@aol.com.

SANDERS, MARY ELIZABETH, author, historian; b. Baton Rouge, May 25, 1923; d. Jared Young and Mary (Briggs) S. BA, La. State U., 1944, MA, 1955. Adminstrv. asst. Congressman J.Y. Sanders, Washington, 1942-43, Sanders, Miller, Downing, Rubin & Kean, Baton Rouge, 1946-48; librarian, archivist New Orleans Pub. Libr., 1955-57. Appeared on Restore Am.-La. program Home & Garden TV, 1999. Author: Avoca Plantation Receipts and Other Family Favorites, 1995; editor: Letters of a Southern Family, 1816-1941, 2001, Diary in Gray: Civil War Journal of J. Y. Sanders, 1994; compiler Records of Attakapas District, La., 1739-1811, 1962, Records of Attakapas District, La., Vol II: St. Mary Parish, 1811-1860, 1963, Records of Attakapas District, La., Vol. III: St. Martin Parish, 1808-1860, 1974, St. Mary Parish, Louisana, Heirship Series: Vol. I—Annotated Abstracts of the Successions, 1811-1834, 1972, Vol. II—Selected Annotated Abstracts of Marriage Book 1, 1811-1829, 1973, Vol. III—Selected Annotated Abstracts of Court Records, 1811-1839, 1978. Mem. La. Hist. Records Adv. Commn., Baton Rouge, 1981-85; charter mem., pres. La. Genealogy and Hist. Soc., 1954-56, editor, 1957-58; hon. mem. Morgan City (La.) Arch. Commn., 1985—; co-trustee J. Y. Sanders Found., Baton Rouge, 1988—; pres. La. Archives Found., Baton Rouge, 1988-96, Young-Sanders Ctr. Found., Morgan City, 1998—; mem. La. State U. Found., Baton Rouge, 1988-92; mem. nat. bd. Coun. Conservative Citizens, St. Louis, 1997—; hon. chmn. La. Sovereingty Party, Baton Rouge, 1999. Named Hon. Citizen Morgan City, La., 1985; recipient award of commendation La. State Dept. Archives, Records Mgmt. and History, 1988, cert. of appreciation Coun. Conservative Citizens, 1996, cert. of honor Jud. Watch, 1999. Mem. DAR (registrar La. soc. 1983-86, nat. vice chmn. flag com. 1986-89, corr. sec. 1992-95), United Daus. of the Confederacy (divsn. corr. sec. 1989-91, divsn. pres. 2000-2002, Gen. Grave Markers com. 2002-), Jefferson Davis medal 1989, cert. of merit 1998), Huguenot soc. of Founders of Mamakin in Colony of Va. (nat. registrar 1979-85), Colonial Dames Am. Republican. Christian Scientist. Avocations: genealogy, preservationist, cooking. Home: 2332 Wisteria St Baton Rouge LA 70806-5352

SANDERS, MELANIE, newscaster; b. Dayton, Ohio; m. Troy Carter Sr.; 2 children. Grad. in Journalism, Ohio U. Reporter WTVY, Panama City, Fla., weekend anchor Dothan, Ala.; noon anchor WKRG, Mobile, Ala.; news anchor WDSU News Channel 6, New Orleans, 1997—. Active Links, House of Ruth, Soc. for Prevention of Cruelty to Animals. Office: WDSU News Channel 6 846 Howard Ave New Orleans LA 70113

SANDERS, NANCY IDA, writer; b. Everett, Pa., May 17, 1960; d. Richard J. and Phyllis (Harden) Hershberger; m. Jeffrey L. Sanders, May 23, 1982; children: Daniel M., Benjamin L. Freelance writer, 1985—. Editor TCC Manuscript Svc.; contbg. editor The Christian Communicator, 1992-2000; asst. editor Trails 'N Treasure, Christian Mag. for Kids, 1998-99; leader Chino Hills Writers Critique Group. Author: Favorite Bible Heroes: Activities for Ages 4 and 5, 1993, Bible Crafts on a Shoestring Budget for Grades 3 and 4, 1993, Amazing Bible Puzzles: Old Testament, 1993, Amazing Bible Puzzles: New Testament, 1993, Jumbo Bible Bulletin Boards: More Bible Stories for Preschool and Primary, 1994, Jumbo Bible Bulletin Boards: Fall and Winter, Preschool and Primary, 1994, Jonah: Six Fun Surprises, 1994, Moses: Six Fun Surprises, 1994, My Book About Ben and Me, 1994, My Book About Sara and Me, 1994, Cents-ible Bible Crafts, 1995, The Fall into Sin, 1995, Jesus Walks on the Water, 1995, WA-A-A-AY COOL Bible Puzzles, 1996, Red Hot Bible Puzzles, 1996, Marshal Matt and the Slippery Snacks Mystery, 1996, Marshal Matt and the Case of the Secret Code, 1996, Marshal Matt and the Topsy-Turvy Trail Mystery, 1996, Marshal Matt and the Puzzling Prints Mystery, 1997, Marshall Matt and the Case of the Freezing Fingers, 1997, Archy's Adventures with Colors, 1998, Archy's Adventure with Numbers, 1998, Archy's Alphabet Adventure, 1998, Unforgettable Edible Bible Crafts, 1999, Old Testament Days, 1999, Bible Crafts and More, 1999, Lost and Found, 2000, Hidden Treasure, 2000, Comet Campout, 2000, Moon Rocks and Dinosaur Bones, 2000, 15 Irrestible Mini-Plays for Teaching Math, 2000, Can't Catch Me!, 2000, Off to the Fair, 2000, Cooks, Cakes, and Chocolate Milkshakes, 2000, The Super Duper Seed Surprise, 2000, A Kid's Guide to African American History, 2000, Just Right Science Plays for Emergent Readers, 2001, (with Jeff Sanders) American History Mini-Books, 2001, 25 Read and Write Mini-Books That Teach Word Families, 2001, Fresh and Fun: November, 2001, The Pet I'll Get, 2001, My Many Hats, 2001, Kingdom Kidz: Noah, 2001, Kingdom Kidz: Solomon, 2001, Kingdom Kidz: Zacchaeus, 2001, Kingdom Kidz, Martha and Mary, 2001, To Follow Yahweh's Plan, 2001, 15 Easy to Read Mini-Book Plays, 2002, Math Mystery Mini-Books, 2002, Munch and Learn Math Story mats, 2002, 15 Easy and Irresistible Math Mini-Books, 2002, Holiday and Seasonal Plays, 2002. Mem. Soc. Children's Book Writers and Illustrators. Home: 15212 Mariposa Ave Chino Hills CA 91709-2703

SANDERS, RANN V. systems administrator, consultant; b. Snoqualmie, Wash., Oct. 29, 1966; s. Vernon Albert and Theresa Rae Sanders; m. Samol Pha, July 20, 2002; 1 child, Nyah Ashley. Degree in Computer Acctg. Specialist, Cascade Bus. Coll., 1988. Cert. MCP Microsoft, 2000, CCA Citrix, 2002, MCSE Microsoft, 2003, MCSA, Messaging Microsoft, 2003. Sr. lan adminstr. Mktg. One Inc., Portland, Oreg., 1997—98; network engr. DaVita, Inc., Tacoma, 1999—2000; desktop tech. support Frank Russell Corp., Tacoma, 2001; network info. sys. engr. City of Lakewood, Wash., 2002—03; customer engr. Siemens, Seattle, 2002—03; network mgr. Lee Smart Cook Martin & Patterson, PS, Inc., Seattle, 2003—. Pres. 5th Corner PC Users Group, Bellingham, Wash., 1993—96; cons. Winsys Cons., Bellingham, Wash., 1993—96. Conservative. Avocations: pool, fishing. Office: Lee Smart Cook Martin & Patterson PS 1800 One Convention Pl 701 Pike St Seattle WA 98101 Office Phone: 206-624-7990. Personal E-mail: rann@engineer.com. Business E-Mail: rvs@leesmart.com.

SANDERS, RICHARD BROWNING, judge; b. Tacoma, Wash. 1 child: Laura. BA, U. Wash., 1966, JD, 1969. Assoc. Murray, Scott, McGavick & Graves, Tacoma, Wash., 1969, Caplinger & Munn, Seattle, 1971; hearing examiner State Wash., Olympia, 1970; pvt. practice Wash., 1971-95; justice Wash. Supreme Ct., Olympia, 1995—. Adj. prof. U. Wash. Sch. Law; lectr. in field. Contbr. articles to profl. jours. Office: Supreme Court of Washington Temple of Justice PO Box 40929 Olympia WA 98504-0929 Fax: (360) 357-2092. E-mail: j_r.sanders@courts.wa.gov.

SANDERS, RICHARD HENRY, lawyer; b. Chgo., Apr. 10, 1944; s. Walter J. and Marian (Snyder) Sikorski; m. Sharon A. Marciniak, July 8, 1967 (div. Oct. 1979); 1 child, Douglas Bennett. BS, Loyola U., Chgo., 1967; JD, Northwestern U., 1969. Bar: Ill. 1969, Ind. 1990, D.C. 1990, U.S. Dist. Ct. (no. dist.) Ill. 1970, U.S. Dist. Ct. (no. and so. dists.) Ind. 1990, U.S. Ct. Appeals (7th cir.) 1990, U.S. Supreme Ct. 1990. Assoc. Vedder, Price, Kaufman & Kammholz, Chgo., 1969-76, ptnr., 1976—, mem. exec. com., 1991-93, health law area leader, 1989-91, 93-95, 2001—04. Adj. prof. Sch. of Law Northwestern U., 1994—; mem. svc. dispute resolver panel Am. Health Lawyers Assn. Alt. Dispute Resolution, 2000—. Mem. ABA, Ill. Bar Assn. (chmn. health sect. 1989-90), Chgo. Bar Assn., Ind. Bar Assn., D.C. Bar Assn., Am. Health Lawyers Assn., Ill. Assn. Health Attys., Univ. Club, Evanston Golf Club (Skokie). Avocations: skiing, diving, photography, golf. Office: Vedder Price Kaufman & Kammholz 222 N La Salle St Ste 2600 Chicago IL 60601-1100 Office Phone: 312-609-7644. Business E-Mail: rsanders@vedderprice.com.

SANDERS, RICHARD KINARD, actor; b. Harrisburg, Pa., Aug. 23, 1940; s. Henry Irvine and Thelma S. BFA, Carnegie Inst. Tech., 1962; postgrad. (Fulbright scholar), London Acad. Music and Dramatic Art, 1962-63. Pres. Blood Star, Inc. Mem. various acting cos., Front St., Memphis, Champlain Shakespeare Festival, Vt., Center Stage, Balt., N.Y. Shakespeare Festival, N.Y.C., Chelsea Theater Center, N.Y.C., Mark Taper Forum, Los Angeles, Arena Stage, Washington; appeared on: (Broadway) Raisin; (TV series) Les Nessman on WKRP in Cincinnati and The New WKRP in Cincinnati, Paul Sycamore in You Can't Take It With You, Mr. Beanley in Spenser; writer of many episodes of WKRP and other situation comedies; writer NBC movie Max and Sam; numerous TV and film appearances. Vol. Peace Corps, Northeastern Brazil, 1966-69. Recipient Buckeye Newshawk award, 1974-79, Silver Sow award, 1979 Mem. Writers Guild Am., Screen Actors Guild, AFTRA, Actors Equity Assn. Office: PO Box 1644 Woodinville WA 98072-1644

SANDERS, RICHARD LOUIS, executive editor; b. Rockville Centre, N.Y., July 14, 1949; s. Louis Chadrone and Grace Marie (Clarke) S.; m. Laurie Anne Miroff, July 24, 1970. BFA in Film, NYU, 1976. Sr. editor Us mag., N.Y.C., 1978-83, exec. editor, 1983-85; sr. editor People mag., N.Y.C., 1985-91; gen. editor Entertainment Weekly, N.Y.C., 1991-92, assistant mng. editor, 1993-95, exec. editor, 1995—. Office: Entertainment Weekly 1675 Broadway New York NY 10019-5820

SANDERS, ROBIN RENEE, diplomat; b. Hampton, Va., July 5; d. Robert M. and Geneva (Machoney) Sanders. B.A., Hampton Inst.; M.A., Ohio U., 1979, M.S., 1979. Broadcast lic. FCC 3d class. Editoral assts. Essence Mag., N.Y.C., 1974-76, Fgn. Broadcast Info. Service, Washington, 1976-77; intern account exec. Burson-Marsteller Co., N.Y.C., 1977-78; pub. relations assoc. Seventeen mag., N.Y.C., 1979-80; polit. and counselor officer Am. embassy, Dominican Republic, 1980-83, consular officer Am. consulate, Oporto, Portugal, 1983-86, dep. polit. sect. chief Am. Embassy Khartoum, Sudan, 1986-88; spl. asst. AF Bur., 1988-89; dir. for pub. diplomacy for Africa, State Dept.; dir. for Africa, Nat. Security Coun. at the White House, 1988-89, 97-99; spl. asst. for L.Am., Africa and internat. crime for the under sec. for polit. affairs Dept. State, Washington; chief of staff, sr. fgn. policy Mem. Ho. Internat. Rels. Com.; U.S. amb. to Republic of Congo, 2002—; cons. Profl. Women's Seminar, 1983, 84; speaker U. Oporto, 1983; researcher dept. internat. relations Ohio U., 1978; TV producer dept. gerontology Hampton Inst., 1976-77. Recipient 1st place award for painting Two Faces, Scholastic Art Bd., 1981, Dept of State Meritorious award, 1989, three State Dept. Superior Honor awards, three State Dept. Meritorious Honor awards; journalism scholar Syracuse U, 1970. Dir. Nat. Security Coun., 1989; political Econ. Officer Namibia, 1989. Mem. Women in Communications, Pub. Relations Soc. Am., Am. Fgn. Service Assn., Nat. Council Negro Women, Black Caucus, Mus. African Art, Coun. on Fgn. Rels., D.C. C. of C.; Alpha Kappa Alpha, Alpha Kappa Mu. Consular Corps (Oporto); Diplomatic (Santo Domingo), Thursday Luncheon Group, Capital Press (Washington). Home: 110 E Bloomfield St Rome NY 13440-4339 Address: Embassy Republic of the Congo 310 Avenue des Aviateurs Kinshasa Gombe Republic of the Congo

SANDERS, RODGER, construction executive; Pres. Highland Homes, Dallas, 1987—. Office: Highland Homes 12850 Hillcrest Rd Ste 200 Dallas TX 75230-1509

SANDERS, STEPHANIE KENYATTA, music educator; b. Anderson, Ind., Apr. 20, 1970; d. Lola Sanders Redmond and Saadiq Saajad. MusB in edn., Jackson State U., 1988—92; MusM, U. of Houston, 1993—95; Further Study, Regent U., 2001. Teacher's Cert. Tex., 1993. Pvt. lesson instr. - saxophone, flute and bassoon Houston Ind. Sch. Dist., Houston, 1993—97, Ft. Bend Ind. Sch. Dist., Mo. City, Tex., 1993—97; asst. band dir. MacArthur H.S., Houston, 1995—97; asst. dir. of bands / instr. of music Alcorn State U., Alcorn State, Miss., 1997—2000; jazz ensemble dir. Prairie View A&M U., Prairie View, Tex., 1998—99; asst. prof. of music / jazz ensemble dir. / asst. dir. of bands Norfolk State U., Norfolk, Va., 2000—. Cons. Norfolk Pub. Schools, Norfolk, Va., 2000. Musician: (solo performer) Va. Symphony. Adv. bd. for flute faire Old Dominion U., Norfolk, Va., 2001. Recipient Faculty Devel., Norfolk State U., 2000, 2001, 2002, 2003. Mem.: Music Educators Nat. Conf., Internat. Assn. Of Jazz Educators, Coll. Band Directors Nat. Assn., Am. Fedn. of Musicians - Local 125, Phi Delta Kappa, Order of Ea. Star, Alpha Kappa Alpha Sorority, Inc., Kappa Kappa Psi Hon. Band Frat. (hon.), Tau Beta Sigma Hon. Band Sorority (hon.). Democrat-Npl. United Ch. Of Christ. Avocations: reading, performing, dining, conversationalist, travel. Home: PO Box 10647 Norfolk VA 23513-0647 Office: Norfolk State University 700 Park Ave Norfolk VA 23504 Personal E-mail: sksanders18@msn.com. E-mail: sksanders@nsu.edu.

SANDERS, SUMMER, Olympic athlete, news correspondent, newscaster; b. 1972; d. Bob and Barbara Sanders. Olympic swimmer, Barcelona, 1992; ret. from profl. swimming, 1993; host game show for children Figure It Out Nickelodeon, 1997—; broadcaster WNBA Lifetime TV, 1997—98; co-host NBA Inside Stuff, 1998—. Recipient Gold medal, 200m Butterfly, Barcelona Olympic Games, 1992, Silver medal, 200m Individual Medley, 1992, Bronze medal, 400m Individual Medley, 1992. Office: care Nickelodeon/Figure It Out 1515 Broadway Fl 38 New York NY 10036-8901 also: NBA Inside Stuff care NBA Entertainment Inc 450 Harmon Meadow Blvd Secaucus NJ 07094-3618

SANDERS, WALLACE WOLFRED, JR., civil engineer; b. Louisville, June 24, 1933; s. Wallace Wolfred and Mary Jane (Brownfield) S.; m. Julia B. Howard, June 9, 1956; children— Linda, David. B.C.E., U. Louisville, 1955; MS, U. Ill., Urbana, 1957, PhD, 1960; M.Engring., U. Louisville, 1973. Research asst., then research assoc. U. Ill., 1955-60, asst. prof., 1960-64; mem. faculty Iowa State U., Ames, 1964-98, prof. civil engring., 1970-98, assoc. dir. engring. research, 1980-91, assoc. dean research, 1988-91, interim asst. vice provost for research and advanced studies, 1991-92. Cons. to govt. and industry. Contbr. numerous papers to profl. jours. Bd. dirs. Northcrest Retirement Cmty., Ames, 1976-82, 92-98, pres., 1987-91, 96-2003; bd. dirs. Am. Bapt. Homes of the Midwest, Mpls., 1998—. Mem. ASCE (R.C. Reese research prize 1978), Am. Welding Soc. (Adams Meml. membership award 1971), Am. Ry. Engring. Assn., Am. Soc. Engring. Edn. Baptist. Home and Office: 1924 Northcrest Cir Ames IA 50010-5113 Business E-Mail: wsanders@iastate.edu.

SANDERS, WALTER JEREMIAH, computer company executive; BSEE, U. Ill., 1958. From sales mgr. to group dir. mktg. Semiconductor divsn. Fairchild Camera and Instrument Corp., 1967—69; sales and mktg. mgr. Motorola Semiconductor; engr. Douglas Aircraft Co.; co-founder Advanced Micro Devices, Inc., Sunnyvale, Calif., 1969, CEO, 1969—2002, chmn., 1969—. Office: Advanced Micro Devices Inc 1 AMD Pl Sunnyvale CA 94086

SANDERS, WAYNE R. paper products manufacturing executive; b. Chgo., July 6, 1947; s. Ralph G. and Bernice F. (Swanson) S.; m. Kathleen E. Lessard, Aug. 22, 1970; children: Tracy, Amy, Megan. BCE, Ill. Inst. Tech., 1969;

MBA, Marquette U., 1972. Fin. analyst Ford Motor Co., Dearborn, Mich., 1972-75; sr. fin. analyst Kimberly-Clark Corp., Neenah, Wis., 1975, dir. bus. planning internat., 1976-80, dir. bus. planning U.S. consumer bus., 1980-81; v.p. strategic planning Kimberly-Clark of Can., Toronto, Ont., 1981-82, pres., 1982 85; sr. v.p. Kimberly-Clark Corp., Dallas, 1986, pres. infant care sector Neenah, Wis., from 1987, former pres. personal care div., pres., chief oper. officer world consumer, nonwovens and svc. and indsl. ops., 1990—, pres., CEO, 1990-91, chmn., CEO, 1991—2002. Elected mem. Neenah Sch. Bd., 1980-81; nat. trustee Boys and Girls Clubs Am., 1994; trustee Marquette U., Milw. Roman Catholic.

SANDERS, WILLIAM EUGENE, marketing executive; b. Asheboro, N.C., Nov. 16, 1933; s. Arthur Ira and Picola (Loftin) S.; m. Velna Elizabeth Sumner, June 8, 1957; children: William Eugene Jr., George Herbert Sumner. AB in Polit. Sci., U. N.C., 1956, postgrad. in Law, 1956-57. Marketing rep. Encyclopaedia Britannica, Greensboro, N.C., 1957-60, Am. Pubs., Chgo., 1960-66; pres. S&W Distbrs., Inc., Greensboro, 1966—. Little league coach Civitans, Greensboro, 1967-68. With U.S. Army Res., 1957-63. Named Hon. Amb. Dept. of Labor, Ky., 1976, Ky. Col., 1976, Hon. Mem. La. Lt. Gov. Staff, 1984; recipient Cert. Appreciation Jefferson Davis Parish Libr., Jennings, La., 1986, Top Sales award Am. Media. Corp., 1996, Marshall Cavendish Top Prodn. award, 1990-91, Mktg. award Am. Media, 1995, Gold Cir. award Penworthy Books, 1999, 2000, 01, Marshall Cavendish quota Prodn. award, 1999, 2000, Rosen Prodn. award, 2002. Mem.: Gen. Alumni Assn. (co-chmn. Greensboro chpt. 1979—80, Rosen Prodn. award 2001—02), State Libr. Assn. S.C., State Libr. Assn. N.C., State Libr. Assn. La., State Libr. Assn. W.Va., State Libr. Assn. Va. Democrat. Methodist. Office: S&W Distbrs Inc 1600 E Wendover Ave # H Greensboro NC 27405-6854 Office Phone: 336-272-7394.

SANDERS, W(ILLIAM) EUGENE, JR., internist, educator; b. Frederick, Md., June 25, 1934; s. W(illiam) Eugene and E. Gertrude (Wilburn) S.; m. Christine Culp, Feb. 22, 1974. AB, Cornell U., 1956, MD, 1960. Diplomate: Am. Bd. Internal Medicine. Intern Johns Hopkins Hosp., Balt., 1960-61, resident, 1961-62; instr. medicine Emory U. Sch. Medicine, Atlanta, 1962-64; chief med. resident, instr. U. Fla. Coll. Medicine, Gainesville, 1964-65, asst. prof. medicine and microbiology, 1965-69, asso. prof., 1969-72; prof., chmn. dept. med. microbiology, prof. medicine Creighton U. Sch. Medicine, Omaha, 1972-95, prof. emeritus, 1995—. Cons.-in-research Fla. Dept. Health and Rehab. Services, 1966— Editor: Am. Jour. Epidemiology, 1974-95; contbr. sci. articles to profl. jours. Served as med. officer USPHS, 1962-64. Recipient NIH Research Career Devel. award, 1968-72; John and Mary R. Markle scholar in acad. medicine, 1968-73 Mem. Am. Soc. for Microbiology, Infectious Diseases Soc. Am., Soc. for Epidemiol. Research, Am. Lung Assn., Thoracic Soc., N.Y. Acad. Scis., Phi Beta Kappa, Sigma Xi, Phi Kappa Phi. Achievements include patent on enocin antibiotic and RBE limonene and perrilyl alcohol. Home: 1901 Pennsylvania Ave Englewood FL 34224 E-mail: ecsanders@gls3c.com. *Each day provides more challenges and more opportunities than the preceding. No individual can possibly cope with each of these in any given day. Success depends upon establishing priorities and maintaining them. Fight only those battles and pursue with fervor only those opportunities that improve both one's self and one's fellow man.*

SANDERS, WILLIAM JOHN, research scientist; b. Detroit, July 10, 1940; s. John William and Charlotte Barbara (Linsday) Steele; m. Gary Roberts, Sept. 12, 1961; children: Scott David, Susan Deborah. BS, U. Mich., 1962; MSEE, U. Calif., Berkeley, 1964. Sr. rsch. scientist Stanford (Calif.) U., 1967-97; pres. Sanders Data Systems, 1991—. Pres. Computers in Cardiology, 1990-93, dir., 2000—, dir. info. svcs., 2001—. Inventor cardiac probe; contbr. articles to profl. jours. Mem. IEEE Computer Soc., Assn. Computing Machinery. Avocations: bicycling, wind surfing. Office: Sanders Data Sys 3980 Bibbits Dr Palo Alto CA 94303-4531 E-mail: bill@sandersdata.com.

SANDERS-HALL, PATRICIA E. health facility administrator; d. Lloyd M. and Marguerite E. Sanders; m. Steven W. Hall, Dec. 6, 1986; children: Kahliah Aisha-Brown Hall, Rashaad Zahkee-Lloyd Hall. BA, U. Mo., Kansas City, 1972; MA, U. Denver, 1974. Cert. health scis. adminstrn. U. Colo. Health Scis. Ctr., 1988. Dir. speech therapy Hope Ctr., Denver, 1974—76; dir.speech pathology Easter Seal Rehab. Ctr., Lakewood, Colo., 1976—80; mgr. speech and audiology Mercy Med. Ctr., Denver, 1980—88; dir. rehab. medicine U. Colo. Health Scis. Ctr., Denver, 1988—99; v.p. Kans. U. Med. Ctr., Kansas City, 1999—. Pvt. practice mgmt. trainer, Overland Park, Kans., 1990—. Author (performing artist): (poetry & storytelling) A Women's Inalienable Writes (Mayor Award of Excellence in the Arts, 1997). Pres. PTO, Aurora, Colo., 1987—89; v.p. Jack & Jill of Am., Inc., Denver, 1994—96; bd. mem. Denver Black Arts Festival, 1988—98, Colo. Donor Alliance, Denver, 1997—99. Recipient Golden Poet award, World of Poetry, 1988, 1991, 1994; fellow, U. Denver, 1972—74; Curator's Academic scholar, U. Mo., 1968—72. Mem.: NAFE, Assn. Healthcare Execs., Am. Hosp. Assn., Nat. Storytellers Assn., Alpha Kappa Alpha. Democrat. Methodist. Avocations: party/event planning, desktop publishing, cooking. Office: Univ Kans Med Ctr 3901 Rainbow Blvd Kansas City KS 66160 E-mail: psanders@kumc.edu.

SANDERSON, ARTHUR CLARK, engineering educator; b. Providence, Oct. 23, 1946; s. Robert Leroy and Julia Ayer (Oldham) S.; m. Susan Rita Walsh, Aug. 14, 1971; children: Angeline Mirada, Andrew McWain. BS, Brown U., 1968; MS, Carnegie-Mellon U., 1970, PhD, 1972. Rsch. engr. Westinghouse Electric Corp., Pitts., 1968-70; vis. rsch. scientist Delft (The Netherlands) U. Tech., 1972-73; prof. Carnegie-Mellon U., Pitts., 1973-87, co-dir. robotics inst., 1981-87; rsch. dir. Philips Rsch. Labs., Briarcliff Manor, N.Y., 1985-87; prof., dept. chmn. Rensselaer Poly. Inst., Troy, N.Y., 1987—; divsn. dir. elec. & comm. systems NSF, Arlington, Va., 1998-2000; v.p. rsch. Rensselaer Poly. Inst., 2000—. Vis. prof. Univ. Iberoamericana, Mexico City, 1975-77, Inst. Info. Sci. & Elecs., U. Tsukuba, Japan, 1996-97. Contbr. 3 books, over 250 articles to profl. jours. Fellow AAAS, IEEE (pres. robotics and automation soc. 1989, 90); mem. AIAA (mem. space automation and robotics tech. com.), Am. Assn. Artificial Intelligence, Soc. Mfg. Engrs. Home: 26 Riverwalk Way Cohoes NY 12047-3335 Office: Rensselaer Poly Inst 110 8th St Troy NY 12180-3522 E-mail: sandea@rpi.edu.

SANDERSON, DAVID R. physician; b. South Bend, Ind., Dec. 26, 1933; s. Robert Burns and Alpha (Rodenberger) S.; divorced, 1978; children: David, Kathryn, Robert, Lisa; m. Evelyn Louise Klunder, Sept. 20, 1980. BA, Northwestern U., 1955, MD, 1958. Cons. in medicine Mayo Clinic, Rochester, Minn., 1965-87, chmn. dept. thoracic disease, 1977-87, cons. in medicine Scottsdale, Ariz., 1987—2000, chmn. dept. internal medicine, 1988-96, vice chmn. bd. govs., 1987-94. Assoc. dir. Mayo Lung Project, Nat. Cancer Inst., Rochester. Contbr. articles to profl. jours. Recipient Noble award Mayo Found., Rochester, Chevalier Jackson award Am. Bronchoesophagologic Assn., 1990. Fellow ACP, Am. Coll. Chest Physicians (gov. for Minn. 1981-87); mem. Am. Bronchoesophagologic Assn., World Assn. for Bronchology, Internat. Bronchoesophagologic Assn., Internat. Assn. Study of Lung Cancer, AMA, Sigma Xi, Sigma Chi (Significant Sig award 1989). Presbyterian. Home: 10676 E Bella Vista Dr Scottsdale AZ 85258-6086 Office: Mayo Clinic Scottsdale 13400 E Shea Blvd Scottsdale AZ 85259-5499 E-mail: dsanderson958@md.northwestern.edu.

SANDERSON, DOUGLAS JAY, lawyer; b. Boston, Apr. 21, 1953; s. Warren and Edith S. Sanderson; m. Audrey S. Goldstein, June 6, 1982; children: Scott M.G., Phoebe H.G. BA, Trinity Coll., Hartford, Conn., 1974; JD, George Washington U., 1977. Bar: Va. 1977, D.C. 1978, U.S. Dist. Ct. (ea. dist.) Va. 1978, U.S. Ct. Appeals (4th cir.) 1978. Assoc. Bettius, Rosenberger & Carter, P.C., Fairfax, Va., 1977-82; ptnr. Bettius & Sanderson, P.C. and predecessor firms, Fairfax, 1982-86; prin. Miles & Stockbridge P.C., Fairfax, 1986-95; br. head Miles & Stockbridge, Fairfax, 1989-91; co-owner McCandlish & Lillard, P.C., Fairfax, 1995—. Trustee Cambridge Ctr. Behavioral Studies, Cambridge, 1981-90. Editor: Consumer Protection Reporting Svc., 1976-77. Bd. dirs. Legal Svcs. No. Va., Inc., 1991-97, pres., 1993-95; vol. counsel Arts Coun. of Fairfax County, Inc., 1991-. Mem. ABA, Va. Bar Assn., Fairfax Bar Assn., Ctrl. Fairfax C. of C. (bd. dirs. 1988-93). Avocations: sports, reading. Office: McCandlish & Lillard 11350 Random Hills Rd Ste 500 Fairfax VA 22030-6044

SANDERSON, GEOFF, professional hockey player; b. Hay River, N.W.T., Can., Feb. 1, 1972; Hockey player, Hartford, 1990—97, Carolina Hurricanes, 1997—98, Vancouver Canucks, 1998, Buffalo Sabres, 1998—2000, Columbus Blue Jackets, 2000—. Office: Columbus Blue Jackets 150 E Wilson Bridge Rd Columbus OH 43085-2328

SANDERSON, JAMES RICHARD, retired naval officer, planning and investment company consultant; b. Selma, Calif., Dec. 27, 1925; s. Charles Maxwell and Edith (Wente) S.; m. Betty Lee Bradley, Sept. 19, 1947. Student, U. Calif.-Berkeley, 1943-44, U. Wash., 1944, U. Willamette, 1944-45; grad., USNR Midshipman Sch. at Columbia U., 1945, Nat. War Coll., 1966; student, Gen. Line Sch., Monterey, Calif., 1953, Sr. Officers Ship Material Mgmt. Course, Idaho Falls, Idaho, 1979; BA in Internat. Affairs, George Washington U., 1968. Served as enlisted man U.S. Naval Res., 1943-45; commd. ensign USN, 1946, advanced through grades to vice adm., 1980; gunnery officer U.S.S. Mansfield, 1946-47, U.S.S. Bausell, 1947-48; flight trainee Naval Air Sta., Pensacola, Fla., 1949, Corpus Christi, Tex., 1950; served in Attack Squadron 195, Alameda, Calif., 1950-52; flight instr. Naval Air Sta., Pensacola, 1953-55; served in Attack Squadron 16, 1955-57; air ops. officer on staff Comdr. Carrier Div. Four, U.S.S. Forrestal, 1957-60; ops. officer Attack Squadron 43, Naval Air Sta., Oceana, Va., 1960-62; comdg. officer Attack Squadron 76, 1962-63; comdr. Attack Carrier Air Wing Three in U.S.S. Saratoga, 1963-65; spl. support plans officer, Pacific Area Strategic Plans and Policy Div., Office of Chief of Naval Ops., Washington, 1966-67; exec. asst. and sr. aide to dep. chief. naval ops., 1967-69; comdg. officer U.S.S. Ranier, 1969-70; dep. chief of staff for ops. and plans U.S. Sixth Fleet, 1970-71; comdg. officer U.S.S. Saratoga, 1971-73; dep. comdr. Naval Striking and Support Forces, So. Europe, Naples, Italy, 1973-76; vice dir. ops. Joint Chiefs of Staff, Washington, 1976-77; asst. dep. chief naval ops. for plans, policy and ops., 1977-79; comdr. Task Force Sixty, U.S. 6th Fleet, 1979-80, Carrier Group Two, 1979-80, Battle Force Sixth Fleet, 1979-80, Carrier Striking Force So. Region, 1979-80; dep. and chief staff, comdr. in chief Atlantic/U.S. Atlantic Fleet, Norfolk, Va., 1980-83; ret., 1983; exec. cons. Exec. Planning & Investment Co., Inc., Virginia Beach, Va., 1983-85; sr. v.p. for corp. ops. Computer Dynamics, Inc., 1984-86; asst. to pres. Eastern Computers, Inc., 1986—; cons., prin. Exec. Planning and Investment Co., Inc., 1986-94; sr. fellow joint and combined warfare course Armed Forces Staff Coll., 1994—. Decorated 21 campaign medals, including D.S.M., Legion of Merit with 3 gold stars, D.F.C., Meritorious Service medal, Air medal with 4 gold stars, Navy Commendation medal with combat distinguishing device. Mem. NRA, KT, U. Calif. Alumni Assn., George Washington U. Alumni Assn., Nat. War Coll. Alumni Assn., Naval Acad. Athletic Assn., Assn. Naval Aviation, Tailhook Assn., The Golden Eagles, Smithsonian Assn., Nat. Eagle Scout Assn. (regent, Disting. Eagle Scout award 1994), Nat. Skeet Shooting Assn., KT Eye Found., Nat. Assn. Individual Investors, Nat. Wildlife Assn., Order of Daedalians, Army Navy Country Club (Arlington, Va.), Masons (33d degree), Shriners, Sojourners, Royal Order of Scotland. Clubs: Army Navy Country (Arlington, Va.). Lodges: Masons (33 degree), Shriners, Knight Templer, Sojourners.

SANDERSON, JANET A. ambassador; b. Tucson, Ariz., Apr. 1955; Diploma, Coll. of William and Mary, 1977; MA in Nat. Security Studies, Naval War Coll., 1993. Econ. officer U.S. Fgn. Svc., 1978; various govt. positions, including energy and petroleum advisor Bur. of European Affairs (OECD), 1986—88; various state dept. positions to dept. econ. counselor to min./counselor for econ. affairs U.S. Embassy, Cairo, dept. chief of mission Amman, Jordan, 1997—2000; U.S. amb. to Algeria, 2000—. Recipient Herbert A. Salzman award for Internat. Econ. Performance, U.S. Dept. of State, 1996, numerous honor awards. Address: care Dr Mike Sanderson 111 7 Dartmouth Pl Davis CA 95616

SANDERSON, JEROME ALAN, retired statistician, accountant; b. Nashville, Oct. 18, 1945; s. Bernard and Anna Sanderson; m. Rhona J. Flehinger, Oct. 5, 1990. BSBA, U. Tenn., 1968; MS in Tech. of Mgmt., Am. U., 1974. CPA, Md. Survey statistician Bur. of Census, Washington, 1968-80, U.S. Dept. Energy-Energy Info. Adminstrn., Washington, 1980—2004; ret., 2004. Chief minerals & metals sect. Bur. of Census Fgn. Trade Divsn., Washington, 1977-80. Mem. Hexagon, Inc., Washington, 1984—, Camelot Community Neighborhood Watch, Annandale, Va., 1993—. Mem. Greater Washington Soc. of CPAs, Md. Assn. CPAs, Alpha Epsilon Pi. Avocations: amateur radio, stamp collecting/philately. Home: 8309 Grand Messina Cir Boynton Beach FL 33437-7106

SANDERSON, KIMBERLY LEA, dancer, educator, small business owner; b. Wichita, Kans., May 14, 1967; d. Kenneth Leroy and Karyn Elizabeth Woodward; m. John Scott Sanderson, Oct. 2, 1992; children: Cheyenne, Garrett, Lilliana. AA in Early Childhood, BCCC, 1988. Cons. Kreative Kids Consulting, Viola, Kans., 1988—2003; prin., owner Kreative Kids, Inc., Conway, Kans., 1993—; tchr. Loved-A-Lot Christina Acad., Viola, 2000—03; prin., owner Jazz-For-Jesus Dance Troupe, Wichita, Kans., 2001—. Author: Laurens Love, 2000. Illustrator Three Trees, Wichita, 1998. Mem.: Childcare Assn. (From Chaos To Calm award 2003). Republican. Avocations: gardening, art, teaching, family. Home and Office: Kreative Kids Consulting 25200 WK 42 Viola KS 67149

SANDERSON, MARY LOUISE, medical association administrator; b. Fairmont, W. Va., Oct. 29, 1942; d. Lawrence Oliver and Frances Evelyn (Shuttleworth) Shingleton; m. William W. Olmstead III, Dec. 1966 (div. June 1974); children: William W. IV, Happy; m. Lester F. Davis, III, Oct. 1979 (div. Dec. 1986); m. David S. Sanderson, Sept. 1992. Student, Vassar Coll., 1960-62, Carnegie Mellon, 1962-63. Real estate broker, N.C. Exec. sec. Creative Dining, Raleigh, N.C., 1980-83, Sea Pines Plantation Co., Hilton Head, S.C., 1973-79; adminstr. Am. Bd. Neurological Surgery, Houston, 1983—. Vol. Interact, Raleigh, 1984-86, M.D. Anderson Cancer Ctr./Camp Star Trails, 1994—; docent Mordecai House Hist. Preservation, Raleigh, 1981-83; mem. Reach to Recovery, 1995—. Recipient Vol. award N.C. State Gov., 1986. Mem. Am. Soc. Assn. Execs. Democrat. Episcopalian. Office: Am Bd Neurol Surgery 6550 Fannin St Ste 2139 Houston TX 77030-2718*

SANDERSON, RITA MARYE, history educator; b. West Palm Beach, Fla., Dec. 16, 1935; d. Joseph Nicholas and Marie Emma (Dore) Lavan; m. Glenn Smith Sanderson, Nov. 18, 1954; children: Patricia, Shannon, Siena, Keith. BA, Fla. Atlantic U., 1973, MA. Tchr. Northeast High Sch., Oakland Park, Fla., 1967-84; tchr., dept. head Ft. Lauderdale (Fla.) H.S., 1984-99; ret.; instr. Broward C.C. Life mem. Ctr. Study Presidency, Washington, 1983—; patron Met. Opera. Mem.: Ret. Educators Assn., The Heritage Found., Opera Soc. Republican. Roman Catholic. Home: 1629 NE 1st Ave Fort Lauderdale FL 33305-2923

SANDHU, HARVINDER SINGH, spinal surgeon, educator; b. Jalandhar, Punjab, India, Mar. 18, 1962; s. Jagtar singh and Shivtej Kaur Sandhu; m. Sonia Kaur Chattha, May 25, 1997; 1 child, alexi. BS, Northwestern U., 1982, MD, 1987; MBA, Columbia U., 2001. Diplomate Am. Bd. Orthopedic Surgery, Nat. Bd. Med. Examiners. Attending spine surgeon UCLA, 1994-97, Hosp. for Spl. Surgery, N.Y.C., 1997—. Pres. Sandhu Cons., Scarsdale, N.Y., 1999—. Recipient Outstanding Sci. Exhibit award Internat. Soc. for Study of the Lumbar spine, 1999, Volvo award for Lumbar Spine Rsch., 2002. Mem. Am. Acad. Orthopedic Surgery (biologic implants com. 2000—), Orthopedic Rsch. Soc., N.Am. Spine Soc. (Outstanding Sci. Exhibit award 1996), Scoliosis Rsch. Soc., Beta Gamma Sigma. Office: Hosp for Spl Surgery 535 E 70th St New York NY 10021 Fax: (212) 774-2600. E-mail: sandhuh@hss.edu.

SANDIFER, KEVIN WAYNE, archival services executive; b. Shreveport, La., Sept. 5, 1956; s. Glenn Eugene and Beverly Sue (Mauritzen) S. BS in Libr. Sci., La. State U., Shreveport, 1985, BA in History, 1987; M in Spl. Libr. Instrn., U. Arlington, 1989. Pub. Red River Press, Blanchard, La., 1985-87; pres., CEO Archival Svcs., Inc., Blanchard, La., 1988—. Author: Layman's Look at Starting a Religious Archive, 1982 (Disting. Writing award 1983), Complete Document Restoration Manual, 1986, Introduction to Religious Archival Science, 1988. 2d edit., 1998, Public Relations are an Asset for the Museum and Archives, 1986, 2d edit., 1998, Photography Simplified for the Archivist, 1990, 2d edit., 1995, Christianityn and the Ark of the Covenant, 1998, others; editor: (textbook) Oral History, 1985. Archivist Grandstone Bluff Mus., 1985-90. Named Outstanding Historian Northwest La., Shreveport Jour., 1982, Expert Archivist Shreveport Times, 1983. Fellow Soc. Am. Archivists; mem. Am. Assn. State and Local History, La. Hist. Soc., North La. Hist. Assn. Southern Baptist. Avocations: reading, writing, running track. Home and Office: 3900 Roy Rd Apt 37 Shreveport LA 71107-9631

SANDITEN, EDGAR RICHARD, investment company executive; b. Okmulgee, Okla., Feb. 1, 1920; s. Herman and Anna (Sanditen) S.; m. Isabel Raffkind, Jan. 26, 1945; children: Linda Caryl, Judith Marie, Ellen Jane, Michael Jay. Student, Western Mil. Acad., 1934-37; BS in Bus., Okla. U., 1941. With Otasco, Inc., Tulsa, 1941-87, v.p., 1970, pres., 1974-77, chmn., chief exec. officer, 1977-83, chmn. employees retirement trust, 1983-87; prin., chmn. Sanditen Investments, Ltd., Tulsa, 1987—. Fin. advisor Bank of Okla., 1978-84. Chmn. Tulsa Charity Horse Show, 1969-71, 80-84; bd. dirs. Tulsa Opera, 1979—, chmn., 1979-81, 83-85, v.p., 1989 (Champion Fundraiser, 1989-96); bd. dirs. Tulsa Ballet Theatre (Dimedici award 1989), Tulsa Philharm. 1990—, Tulsa Hist. Soc., 1995-99, Fenster Mus., 1983-85, Ret. Sr. Vols., 1997—; mem. B'nai Emunah Synagogue; pres. Temple Israel, 1968-70; chmn., pres. Children's Med. Ctr., 1979-81; bd. dirs. NCCJ, 1983—, pres., 1985-87; mem. adv. bd. dirs. U. Okla. Coll. Bus. Adminstrn., 1986—; hon. chmn. Ronald McDonald House, 1991; bd. dirs. St. John Med. Ctr., 1978-87, chmn., 1978-81. With USAAF, 1943-46. Recipient Nat. Humanitarian award Nat. Jewish Hosp., 1987, Brotherhood award NCCJ, 1991, Alfred Aaronson Cmty. Rels. award, 1993; named Boss of Yr., Am. Bus. Women's Assn., 1976; named to Tulsa Hall of Fame, 1996. Mem. Tulsa Jr. C. of C. (honor award 1943), Tulsa C. of C. (v.p. 1978 79), Quarter Century Club Automotive Industry, So. Hills Country Club (bd. dirs. 1990-96, fin. chmn., exec. com., v.p. 1992, pres. 1995). Office: Sanditen Investments Ltd 3314 E 51st St Ste 207K Tulsa OK 74135-3527

SANDLER, ADAM, actor; b. 1964; Student, NYU. Film appearances include Remote Control, 1987, Shakes the Clown, 1992, Coneheads, 1993, Mixed Nuts, 1994, Airheads, 1994, Billy Madison, 1995, Happy Gilmore, 1996, Bullet Proof, 1996, The Wedding Singer, 1998, The Water Boy, 1998, Big Daddy, 1999, Punch Drunk Love, 2002, Mr. Deeds, 2002, Anger Management, 2003, 50 First Dates, 2004; tv appearances include Saturday Night Live: The Best of Chris Farley, 1998, Saturday Night Life: The Best of Mike Myers, 1998, Saturday Night Live: The Best of Phil Hartman, 1998, Little Nicky, 2000, Big Daddy, 1999; actor, writer Saturday Night Live (Emmy award nomination for writing 1991, 92); appeared on TV programs ABC Afterschool Special, 1990, Saturday Night Live Mother's Day Special, 1992, MTV Music Video Awards, 1994, Saturday Night Live Presents president Bill Clinton's All-Time Favorites, 1994, The 37th Annual Grammy Awards, 1995, The ESPY Awards, 1996; co-writer screenplays, Billy Madison, 1995, Happy Gilmore, 1996, The Water Boy, 1998; rec. artist album They're All Gonna Laught at You!, 1993; writer, actor: Little Nicky, 2000, Eight Crazy Nights, 2002. Recipient People's Choice award, 2000. Office: Agy for Performing Arts 888 7th Ave Ste 602 New York NY 10106-0699

SANDLER, BERNICE RESNICK, women's rights specialist; b. N.Y.C., Mar. 3, 1928; d. Abraham Hyman and Ivy (Ernst) Resnick; children: Deborah Jo, Emily Maud. BA cum laude, Bklyn. Coll., 1948; MA, CCNY, 1950; EdD, U. Md., 1969; LLD (hon.), Bloomfield Coll., 1973, Hood Coll., 1974, R.I. Coll., 1980, Colby-Sawyer Coll., 1984; LHD (hon.), Grand Valley State Coll., 1974; Dr. Pub. Service (hon.), North Adams State Coll., 1985; LLD (hon.), Goucher Coll., 1991; LHD (hon.), Plymouth State Coll., 1992, Wittenberg U., 1993, Ripon Coll., 1998. Research asst., nursery sch. tchr., employment counselor, adult edn. instr., sec.; psychologist HEW, 1970; tchr. psychology Mt. Vernon Coll., 1970; head Action Com. for Fed. Contract Compliance, Women's Equity Action League, 1970-71; edn. specialist U.S. Ho. Reps., Washington, 1970; dep. dir. Womens Action program, HEW, Washington, 1971; dir. project on status and edn. of women Assn. Am. Colls., Washington, 1971-91; sr. assoc. Ctr. for Women Policy Studies, 1991-94; sr. scholar in residence Nat. Assn. Women in Edn., Washington, 1994—2000; sr. scholar Women's Rsch. and Edn. Inst., 2000—. Cons., 1991—; expert witness, 1990—; writer, 1971—; vis. lectr. U. Md., 1968-69; adv. bd. Women's Equity Action League Ednl. and Legal Def. Fund, 1980—, trustee, 1974-80, Women's Equity Action League, 1971-78; adv. com. Math./Sci. Network, 1979, Wider Opportunities for Women, 1978-85, Women's Legal Def. Fund, 1978-84; Nat. Coun. for Alternative Work Patterns Inc., 1978-85, Women's Hdqs. State Nat. Bank for Women's Appointments, 1977-78, and others. Mem. adv. bd. Jour. Reprints Documents Affecting Women, 1976-78, Women's Rights Law Reporter, 1970-80; editor: (newsletters) On Campus With Women, 1971-91, About Women on Campus, 1991-99; contbr. articles. Mem. bd. overseers Wellesley Coll. Ctr. for Rsch. on Women, 1975-87; bd. dirs. Ctr. for Women's Policy Studies, 1972-75; mem. exec. com. Inst. for Ednl. Leadership, 1982-87, mem. program adv. com., 1987-88, chair bd. dirs., 1981, chair adv. com., 1975-81; mem. affirmative action com., task force on family, nat. affairs commn. Am. Jewish Com., 1978, bd. dirs. D.C. chpt.; tech. adv. com. Nat. Jewish Family Ctr., 1980-89; adv. coun. Ednl. Devel. Ctr., 1980-85; adv. bd. Urban Inst., 1981-85, Women Employed Inst., 1981-84, Ex-New Yorkers for N.Y., 1978-79; mem. adv. com. Arthur and Elizabeth Schlesinger Libr. History of Women in Am., 1981-85; nat. adv. com. Shelter Rsch. Inst., Calif., 1980-82; chair adv. panel project on self-evaluation Am. Insts. for Rsch., 1980-82; bd. dirs. Equality Ctr., 1983, Evaluation and Tng. Inst., Calif., 1980, Inst. for Studies in Equality, 1975-77; exec. v.p. Bd. Women for Women, 1997—. Recipient Athena award Intercollegiate Assn. Women Students, 1974, Elizabeth Boyer award Women's Equity Action League, 1976, Rockefeller Pub. Svc. award Princeton U., 1976, Women Educators award for activism, 1987, Anna Roe award Harvard U., 1988, Readers Choice honors Washington Woman Mag., 1987, Woman of Distinction award Nat. Assn. Women in Edn., 1991, Georgina Smith award AAUP, 1992, Woman of Achievement Turner Broadcasting System, 1994; named one of 100 Most Powerful Women Washingtonian Mag., 1982, one of the nation's 100 Most Important Women, Ladies Home Jour., 1988, Leadership Matters award Inst. Ednl. Leadership, 1997, Medal of Honor, Vet. Feminists, 2001, Donna Shavlik award Am. Coun. Edn., 2003, Mary Keetz award Women's Consortium Pa. State Sys. Higher Edn. Mem. Assn. for Women in Sci. Found. (bd. dirs. 1977—), Am. Soc. Profl. and Exec. Women (adv. bd. 1980). Avocations: birding, music, swimming, hiking. Office: Women's Rsch and Edn Inst 1350 Connecticut Ave NW Ste 850 Washington DC 20036-1740

SANDLER, DEBORAH, performing company executive; married; children: Shira, Benjamin. Degree, Temple U.; MA in Musicology, NYU. Exec. dir. Opera Festival N.J., Princeton, NJ, 1981—92, gen. dir., 1992—98, Ky. Opera, Louisville, 1998—. Office: Kentucky Opera 101 S Eighth St Louisville KY 40202

SANDLER, GERALD HOWARD, computer science educator, company executive; b. N.Y.C., Sept. 17, 1934; s. Irving and Sally S.; m. Ann Sandler; children: Eric, Steven. BS, CUNY, 1956, MS, 1957. With Grumman Aerospace, 1963-83; past pres. Grumman Data Systems & Svcs., Bethpage, N.Y., 1983-95; pres. GHS Enterprises, 1995—; prof. computer sci. Poly. U., Farmingdale, N.Y., 1995—. Author: System Engineering, 1963. Home: 46 Bonnie Dr Westbury NY 11590-2804

SANDLER, HERBERT M. savings and loan association executive; b. N.Y.C., Nov. 16, 1931; s. William B. and Hilda (Schattan) S.; m. Marion Osher, Mar. 26, 1961. BSS, CCNY, 1951; JD, Columbia U., 1954. Bar: N.Y. 1956. Asst. counsel Waterfront Commn. N.Y. Harbor, 1956-59; ptnr. firm Sandler & Sandler, N.Y.C., 1960-62; pres., dir., mem. exec. com. Golden West Savs. & Loan Assn. and Golden West Fin. Corp., Oakland, Calif., 1963-75; co-chmn. bd., co-CEO, dir., mem. exec. com. World Savs. & Loan Assn. and Golden West Fin. Corp., Oakland, 1975—. Charter mem. Thrift Instns. Adv. Coun., to Fed. Res. Bd., 1980-81; former chmn. Legis. and Regulation Com. Calif. Savs. and Loan League; former mem. bd. dirs. Fed. Home Loan Bank, San Francisco. Pres., trustee Calif. Neighborhood Services Found.; chmn.

Urban Housing Inst.; mem. policy adv. bd. Ctr. for Real Estate and Urban Econs. U. Calif., Berkeley. With U.S. Army, 1954-56. Office: Golden West Fin Corp 1901 Harrison St Oakland CA 94612-3588*

SANDLER, IRVING HARRY, art critic, art historian; b. N.Y.C., July 22, 1925; s. Harry and Anna (Robin) S.; m. Lucy Freeman, Sept. 4, 1958; 1 child, Catherine Harriet. BA, Temple U., 1948; MA, U. Pa., 1950; PhD, NYU, 1976. Instr. in art history NYU, 1960-71; prof. emeritus art history SUNY, Purchase; art critic N.Y. Post, N.Y.C., 1960-65. Author: The Triumph of American Painting: A History of Abstract Expressionism, 1970, The New York School: Painters and Sculptors of the Fifties, 1978, Alex Katz, 1979, Al Held, 1984, American Art of the 1960s, 1988; editor (with Amy Newman) Defining Modern Art: Selected Writings of Alfred H. Barr Jr., 1986, Mark di Suvero at Storm King Art Ctr., 1996, Art of Postmodern Era: From Late 1960s to Early 1990s, 1996, Natvar Bhavsar, 1998, Stephen Antonakos, 1999, A Sweeper-Up After Artists: A Memoir, 2003. John Simon Guggenheim fellow, 1965; Nat. Endowment for Arts fellow, 1977. Mem. Coll. Art Assn., Internat. Assn. Art Critics. Home: 100 Bleecker St New York NY 10012-2202

SANDLER, KENNETH BRUCE, advertising executive; b. Newark, July 24, 1942; s. Ralph M. and Mae (Ness) S.; m. Denise Ann Brooks, May 8, 1973 (div. 1988); children: Todd, Brooke. BS in Pharmacy, BS in Chemistry, Rutgers U., 1967, MBA, 1970. Registered pharmacist, N.J. Mgr. mktg. research E.R. Squibb and Sons, Princeton, N.J., 1970-73; account exec. Deltakos div. J. Walter Thompson, N.Y.C., 1973-75, exec. v.p., 1982-84; v.p., account group supr. Rolf Werner Rosenthal Inc., N.Y.C., 1975-82; pres. Sandler Comm. Inc., N.Y.C., 1984—2002, Sandler & Recht Comm., Durham, NC, 1991—2002, Sandler Pub. Rels., N.Y.C., 1996—2002. Mem. Am. Pharm. Assn., Am. Mktg. Assn., Nat. Assn. Retail Druggists, Am. Soc. Hosp. Pharmacists. Home: 45 Sutton Pl S Apt 6H New York NY 10022

SANDLER, LUCY FREEMAN, art history educator; b. N.Y.C., June 7, 1930; d. Otto and Frances (Glass) Freeman; m. Irving Sandler, Sept. 4, 1958; 1 child, Catherine Harriet. BA, Queens Coll., 1951; MA, Columbia U., 1957; PhD, NYU, 1964. Asst. prof. NYU, 1964-70, assoc. prof., 1970-75, prof. fine arts, 1975-86, Helen Gould Sheppard prof. art history, 1986—2003, chmn. dept., 1975-89; editorial cons. Viator, UCLA, 1983-97; Helen Gould Sheppard prof. emerita, 2003—. Author: The Peterborough Psalter in Brussels, 1974, The Psalter of Robert De Lisle in the British Library, 1983, new edit., 1999, Gothic Manuscripts 1285-1385, 1986, 'Omne Bonum': A Fourteenth-Century Encyclopedia of Universal Knowledge, 1996, The Ramsey Psalter, 1999, Der Ramsey-Psalter (Glanzlichter der Buchkunst 12), 2003, Der Bestiarium aus Peterborough/The Peterborough Bestiary, 2003, The Lichtenthal Psalter and the Patronage of the Bohun Family, 2004; editor: Essays in Memory of Karl Lehmann, 1964, Art the Ape of Nature: Studies in Honor of H.W. Janson, 1981, Coll. Art Assn. Monograph Series, 1970-75, 86-89, Gesta, 1991-94; asst. editor Art Bull., 1964-67, mem. editl. bd., 1994; mem. editl. bd. Jour. Jewish Art, 1978, Speculum, 1994. Trustee Godwin-Ternbach Mus., Queens Coll., 1982-94; chair dels. exec. com. Am. Coun. Learned Socs., 2002-04. NEH fellow, 1967-68, 77; fellow Pierpont Morgan Library; Guggenheim fellow, 1988-89. Fellow Medieval Acad. Am. (councillor 2002—), Soc. Antiquaries (London); mem. AAUP, Coll. Art Assn. (pres. 1981-84), Internat. Ctr. Medieval Art (adv. bd., bd. dirs. 1976-80, 84-87, 89-92, 1995-2001). Home: 100 Bleecker St Apt 30A New York NY 10012-2207 Office: NYU Dept Fine Arts New York NY 10003 Office Phone: 212-998-8181.

SANDLER, MARION OSHER, savings and loan association executive; b. Biddeford, Maine, Oct. 17, 1930; d. Samuel and Leah (Lowe) Osher; m. Herbert M. Sandler, Mar. 26, 1961. BA, Wellesley Coll., 1952; postgrad., Harvard U.-Radcliffe Coll., 1953; MBA, NYU, 1958; LLD (hon.), Golden Gate U., 1987. Asst. buyer Bloomingdale's (dept. store), N.Y.C., 1953-55; security analyst Dominick & Dominick, N.Y.C., 1955-61; sr. fin. analyst Oppenheimer & Co., N.Y.C., 1961-63; sr. v.p., dir. Golden West Fin. Corp. and World Savs. & Loan Assn., Oakland, Calif., 1963-75, vice chmn. bd. dirs., CEO, mem. exec. com., dir., 1975-80, pres., co- chief exec. officer, dir., mem. exec. com., 1980-93, chmn. bd. dirs., CEO, mem. exec. com., 1993—; pres., chmn. bd. dirs., CEO Atlas Assets, Inc., Oakland, 1987—, Atlas Advisers, Inc., Oakland, 1987—, Atlas Securities, Inc., Oakland, 1987—. Mem. adv. com. Fed. Nat. Mortgage Assn., 1983-84. Mem. Pres.'s Mgmt. Improvement Coun., 1980, Thrift Insts. Adv. Coun. to Fed. Res. Bd., 1989-91, v.p., 1990, pres., 1991; mem. policy adv. bd. Ctr. for Real Estate and Urban Econs. U. Calif., Berkeley, 1981—, mem. exec. com. policy adv. bd., 1985—; mem. ad hoc com. to rev. Schs. Bus. Adminstrn. U. Calif., 1984-85; vice chmn. industry adv. com. Fed. Savs. and Loan Ins. Corp., 1987-88, Ins. Corp., 1987-88; bd. overseers NYU Schs. Bus., 1987-89; mem. Glass Ceiling Commn., 1992-93. Mem. Phi Beta Kappa, Beta Gamma Sigma. Office: Golden W Fin Corp 1901 Harrison St Fl 6 Oakland CA 94612-3588*

SANDLER, MICHAEL DAVID, lawyer; b. Los Angeles, Feb. 27, 1946; AB, Stanford U., 1967; JD, Yale U., 1972. Bar: Calif. 1973, D.C. 1973, Wash. 1985. Assoc. Steptoe & Johnson, Washington, 1972-75, 77-79, ptnr., 1980-85; spl. asst. to legal adviser Dept. of State, Washington, 1975-77; ptnr. Foster, Pepper & Shefelman, Seattle, 1985-97, Sandler Ahern & McConaughy PLLC, Seattle, 1997—. Adj. prof. law Georgetown U., Washington, 1979, 81-82, U. Wash., Seattle, 1985-92. Vol. Peace Corps, Ethiopia and Ghana, 1968-70. Mem. ABA (chair 1995-96 sect. internat. law and practice). Office: Sandler Ahern & McConaughy PLLC 1200 5th Ave Ste 1900 Seattle WA 98101-3135 E-mail: mike@sandlaw.com.

SANDLER, NORMAN, communications executive; Formerly dir. pub. rels. Motorola, Inc., Schaumburg, Ill., now dir. global strategic issues. Office: Motorola Inc 1303 E Algonquin Rd Schaumburg IL 60196-1079

SANDLER, RICHARD H. lab administrator, gastroenterologist; MD, Mich. State U. Coll. Human Medicine. Resident, pediatrics Mich. State U., Lansing; fellow, pediatric gastroenterology, hepatology, and nutrition Harvard Med. Sch., Boston Children's Hosp.; fellow, human metabolism and nutrition Mass. Gen. Hosp., Boston; asst. in medicine, instr., divsn. of gastroenterology and nutrition The Children's Hosp., Harvard Med. Sch., Boston, 1989—90; dir. Biomed. Acoustics Rsch. Group, Evanston, Ill., 1990—, pres., CEO, 1997—; assoc. prof., pediatrics Rush Med. Coll., Chgo., 1990—; adj. assoc. prof., biomed. engrng. U. Ill., Chgo., 2002—. Office: Rush Univ Med Ctr 1725 W Harrison St Chicago IL 60612 Address: 1725 W Harrison St Ste 946 Chicago IL 60612 Office Phone: 312-942-2889.

SANDLER, ROBERT MICHAEL, insurance company executive, actuary; b. N.Y.C., Apr. 20, 1942; s. Albert and Ruth (Marcus) S.; m. Annette L. Marchese, Aug. 18, 1963; children— David, Glenn BA in Math., Hofstra U., 1963. Various actuarial positions Met. Life, N.Y.C., 1963-68; various actuarial positions Am. Internat., N.Y.C., 1968-80; v.p., casualty actuary American Internat. Group, Inc., N.Y.C., 1980-84, sr. v.p., sr. actuary, sr. claims officer, 1984-95, exec. v.p., 1995—, dir. various subs. Mem. Casualty Acturial Soc. (assoc.), Am. Acad. Actuaries, Internat. Actuarial Assn., Am. Internat. Underwriters (chmn. 1994—). Republican. Office: Am Internat Group 70 Pine St New York NY 10270-0002*

SANDLER, ROSS, law educator; b. Milw., Jan. 31, 1939; s. Theodore T. and Laurette (Simons) S.; m. Alice R. Mintzer, Sept. 15, 1968; children: Josephine, Jenny, Dorothy. AB, Dartmouth Coll., 1961; LLB, NYU, 1965. Bar: N.Y. 1965, Fla. 1965. Assoc. atty. Cahill Gordon Reindel & Ohl, N.Y.C., 1965-68; asst. U.S. atty. So. Dist. N.Y., 1968-72; assoc. atty. Trubin Sillcocks Edelman & Knapp, N.Y.C., 1972-75; sr. staff atty. Natural Resources Def. Coun., N.Y.C., 1975-81, 83-86; spl. advisor to mayor City of N.Y., 1981-82; exec. dir. Hudson River Found., N.Y.C., 1983-86; commr. N.Y.C. Dept. Transp., 1986-90; ptnr. Jones Day Reavis & Pogue, N.Y.C., 1991-93; law prof. N.Y. Law Sch., 1993—, dir. Ctr. for N.Y.C. law, 1993—; pres. N.Y. Legis. Svc., 1998—. Mem. N.Y.C. Procurement Policy Bd., 1994—; vis. lectr. Yale Law Sch., New Haven, 1977; adj. prof. law NYU Law Sch., 1976-94; chair, mem. N.Y.C. Taxi and Limousine Commn., 1980-90. Co-author: A New Dirction in Transit, 1978, Democracy by Decree, 2003; columnist Environ. Mag., 1976—80; editor: (jour.) City Law; contbr. chapters to books, articles. Trustee Woods Hole (Mass.) Rsch. Ctr., 1983—; mem. exec. com. Hudson River Found., 1986-96; mem. adv. coun. Ctr. Biodiversity and Conservation Am. Mus. Nat. History, 1996—. Recipient Pub. Interest award NYU Law Alumni, 1987, Louis J. Lefkowitz award Fordham Law Sch. Urban Law Jour., 1989, Lifetime Achievement award N.Y. State Bar Assn., 1998. Mem. City Club of N.Y. (chair 1992-93, trustee). Office: NY Law Sch 57 Worth St New York NY 10013-2959

SANDLER, STANLEY IRVING, chemical engineering educator; b. N.Y.C., June 10, 1940; s. Murray C. and Celia M. (Kamenetsky) S.; m. Judith Katherine Ungar, June 17, 1962; children: Catherine Julietta, Joel Abraham, Michael Howard. BChemE, CCNY, 1962; PhD, U. Minn., 1966. Chartered engr., European Union. NSF postdoctoral fellow Inst. Molecular Physics, U. Md., College Park, 1966-67; successively asst. prof., assoc. prof., prof. dept. chem. engrng. U. Del., Newark, 1967-82, H.B. du Pont prof., 1982-2000, chmn. dept., 1982-86, dir. Ctr. for Molecular and Engrng. Thermodynamics, 1992—, interim dean Coll. of Engrng., 1992, H.B. duPont chair, 2000—. Vis. prof. Imperial Coll., London, 1973—74, U. Nat. del Sur, Bahia Blanca, Argentina, 1985, Tech. U., Berlin, 1981, Berlin, 1988—89, U. Queensland, Brisbane, Australia, 1989, Brisbane, 96, U. Calif., Berkeley, 1995, U. Melbourne, Australia, 2003; cons. maj. oil and chem. cos. Author: Chemical and Engineering Thermodynamics, 1977, 3d rev. edit., 1998, Modeling Vapor-Liquid Equilibrium, 1998; editor: Fluid Properties and Phase Equilibria, 1977, Chemical Engineering Education in a Changing Environment, 1989, Kinetic and Thermodynamic Lumping of Multicomponent Mixtures, 1991, Models for Thermodynamic and Phase Equilibria Calculations, 1993, AI Chem E Jour., 2000—; mem. adv. bd. Jour. Chem. Engrng. Data, Chem. Engrng. Edn., Indsl. Engrng. Chem. Rsch., Indian Chem. Engr., Engrng. Sci. and Tech. (Malaysia); also numerous articles. Mem. adv. bd. chem. engrng. La. State U., Carnegie-Mellon U., Princeton U. Recipient U.S. sr. Scientist award Alexander von Humboldt Found., 1988, Francis Alison award U. Del., 1993, Ashton Cary award Ga. Tech. U., 1994, Phillips Lecture award Okla. State U., 1993, Rossini Lectureship award Internat. Union Pure Applied Chemistry, 1998; Miegunyah fellow U. Melbourne, Australia, 2003, hon. professorial fellow, 2004-2009, Hikal Chemcon Dist. Spkr. award, Indian Inst. Chem. Engrs., 2004. Fellow Inst. Chem. Engrs. (Britain), AIChE (jour. adv. bd., editor 2000—, Profl. Progress award 1984, Warren K. Lewis award 1996, Del. Soc. award 1998, Founders award, 2004), U.S. Nat. Acad. Engring., Am. Chem. Soc. (award Del. sect. 1989, E.V. Murphree award 1997), Am. Soc. Engrng. Edn. (lectr. chem. engrng. div. 1988), Cosmos Club (Washington). Jewish. Avocations: jogging, stamp collecting/philately. Home: 202 Sypherd Dr Newark DE 19711-3627 Office: U Del Dept Chem Engrng Newark DE 19716 Office Phone: 302-831-2945. E-mail: sandler@udel.edu.

SANDLER, THOMAS R. accountant; b. Mt. Kisco, N.Y., Dec. 16, 1946; s. Louis and Susan (Rosen) S.; m. Alison G. Corneau, Aug. 26, 1972; children— Justin C., Shawn A. BS summa cum laude, Ithaca Coll., 1968; MS, SUNY-Binghamton, 1972. C.P.A., N.Y., Colo. 1982. Asst. acct. KPMG Peat Marwick, White Plains, N.Y., 1972, mgr. Phoenix, 1975, sr. mgr. N.Y.C., 1978, ptnr. Denver, 1981-92, ptnr. in-charge corp. recovery svcs. N.Y.C., 1993-94; mng. ptnr. BDO Seidman, Denver, 1994-95; CFO, treas., sec. Samsonite Corp., Denver, 1995-98; pres. Samsonite Am., Denver, 1998—. Contbr. articles to profl. jours. Past trustee, past pres. Colo. Children's Chorale; treas., past pres., gov., mem. exec. com., committeeman Colo. Golf Assn.; committeeman U.S. Golf Assn. bd. dirs. Pacific Coast GOlf Assn.; chmn. Travel Goods Assn. Mem. AICPA, Colo. Soc. CPAs (chmn. real estate and govt. acctg. com.), Bear Creek Golf Club, Country Club at Castle Pines. Home: 896 Anaconda Ct Castle Rock CO 80108-9044 Office: Samsonite Corp Corp Bldg 11200 E 45th Ave Denver CO 80239-3000 E-mail: tom_sandler@Samsonite.com.

SANDLER, TODD MICHAEL, economist, political scientist, educator; b. Mt. Kisco, N.Y., Dec. 16, 1946; s. Louis and Susie Sandler; m. Jean Marie Murdock, June 28, 1985; 1 child, Tristan Jon. BA, SUNY, Binghamton, 1968, MA, 1969, PhD, 1971. Asst. prof. Ariz. State U., Tempe, 1971-76; assoc. prof. U. Wyo., Laramie, 1976-79, prof., 1979-85, U. S.C., Columbia, 1985-86; prof. econs. and polit. sci. Iowa State U., Ames, 1986-2000, Disting. prof., 1995—2001; Dockson prof. U. So. Calif., L.A., 2000—. Author: Collective Action: Theory and Applications, 1992, Global Challenges, 1997, Economic Concepts for the Social Sciences, 2001, Global Collective Action, 2004; co-author: The Theory of Externalities, Public Goods and Club Goods, 1986, The Economics of Defense, 1995, (book) The Theory of Externalities, Public Goods and Club Goods, 2d edit., 1996, International Terrorism in 1980s, 1989, The Political Economy of NATO, 1999, The Future of Development Assistance: Common Pools and International Public Goods, 1999, Regional Public Goods: Typologies, Provision, Financing, and Development Assistance, 2002; co-editor: Defense Economics, 1989—94, Handbook of Defense Economics, 1995; assoc. editor: Jour. Environ. Econs. and Mgmt., 1988—89, Jour. Pub. Econ. Theory, 1999—, mem. editl. bd.: Social Sci. Quar., Pub. Fin. Rev., Fiscal Studies, Bull. Econ. Rsch., Internat. Studies Quar.; mem. editl. bd. Jour. Conflict Resolution, 2004— (Editl. award Terrorism and Polit. Violence); spl. adv. editor: Def. and Peace Econs., 2000—. Co-recipient Rsch. Related to Prevention of Nuc. War award, Nat. Acad. of Scis., 2003; fellow NATO postdoctoral, 1977, 1998—2000, Australian Nat. U., 1981, 1994, Sr., Inst. Policy Reform, 1990—91, 1992—94, Hon., U. Wis.-Madison, 1990; grantee NSF, 1989, 1993. Mem.: Pub. Choice Soc., So. Econ. Assn., Assn. Environ. and Resource Econs., Royal Econ. Soc., Am. Econ. Assn., Internat. Def. Econs. Assn. (exec. bd.). Office: U So Calif Sch Internat Rels Los Angeles CA 90089 Office Phone: 213-740-9695. E-mail: tsandler@usc.edu.

SANDLIN, ANATHALEE GRAY, writer, music company owner; b. Hastings, Nebr., Nov. 12, 1945; d. Lloyd Vern and Elizabeth Powers Gray; m. John Everett Sandlin, Jr.; children: Leigh Ellen Cauthen, Kristin Ann Spain, Heidi Anathalee Wilson. Columnist Nat. Skeet Shooters Review, 1982-83; bus. mgr. Ducktape Music Prodns., Decatur, Ala., 1984—; prin., owner Rockin Rabbit Music Other Ducks Music, Decatur, 1986—, AGS Publishing, Decatur, 1997—. Artist-media liason various tv award shows and benefit concerts, Southeast, U.S., 1986-96; bd. dirs. Tenn. Valley Homeless Shelter, Ala.; lectr. in field. Author: When Grandma Was Really Cooking, 1989, The Decatur Daily Cookbook, 1993, The Rosary-A Treasure of Graces, 1997. Mem. ASCAP, BMI, North Ala. Songwriters Assn. (bd. dirs., chmn. 1984-86). Avocations: painting, cooking, full time grandmother. Office: PO Box 2854 Decatur AL 35602-2854

SANDLIN, DOROTHY, artist; b. Chgo., Feb. 20, 1930; d. Clarence L. and Mary E. Sehnert; m. Henry L. Sandlin, July 18, 1953 (div. Mar. 1973); children: Lee Henry, Neil Bryan; m. Michael C. Lazich, Jan. 18, 1985. AA, North Park Coll., 1949; student, Ariz. State U., 1950, 52, Art Inst. Chgo., 1955-65, Am. Acad. Art, 1994-96. Legal sec. Sidley & Austin, Chgo., 1975-94. Represented by Weatherburn Gallery, Naples, Fla., 2000—. One woman shows include Elmhurst (Ill.) Art Mus., 1996, Strawn Gallery, Jacksonville, Ill., 1998, 2001, Tall Grass Gallery, Park Forest, Ill., 1997, 2000, Deer Path Gallery, Lake Forest, Ill., 2000; featured in Best of Pastel, 1996, Landscape Inspirations, 1997. Recipient 1st place in various art festivals, Springfield, Ill., Wilmette, Ill.,Woodstock, Ill., Glenview, Ill., Evanston, Ill., Top 200 award Arts for the Parks nat. competition, Jackson Hole, Wyo, 1998. Mem. Pastel Soc. Am. (signature mem.), Midwest Pastel Soc. (signature mem., Hon. Mention 1994), Oil Painters Am., Chgo. Artists Coalition, Art Inst. Chgo. Alumni Assn. Home: 11560 Tea Tree Ln Frankfort IL 60423 Studio: 218 Forest Blvd Park Forest IL 60466

SANDLIN, MAX ALLEN, JR., congressman; b. Texarkana, Ark., Sept. 29, 1952; s. Max Allen and Margie Beth (Barnett) S.; children: Hillary, Max III, Emily, Christian. BA, Baylor U., 1975, JD, 1978. Bar: Tex. Assoc. Huffman & Palmer, Inc., Marshall, Tex., 1978-82; ptnr. Sandlin & Buckner, Marshall, 1982-96; judge County of Harrison, Marshall, 1986-89, county ct. judge, 1989-96; v.p., gen. counsel Howell & Sandlin, Inc., 1990-96; mem. Congress from 1st Tex dist., 1997—; mem. ways & means com. Mem. exec. com. Tex. Supreme Ct. Jud. Edn. Com., Austin, 1987—; bd. dirs. Security State Bank, Elysian Fields, Tex., East Tex. Legal Svcs., Nacogdoches; bd. dirs., treas. East Tex. Housing & Fin. Corp., Marshall, 1990—. Chairman Harrison County Dem. Party, Marshall, 1982-88; mem. exec. com. Marshall-Harrison County Industries, Marshall, 1986-89; founder, sponsor, mem. Michelson-Reves Mus. Art; post supr. Boy Scouts Am., 1982-86; mgr. Marshall Youth Baseball, 1980. Recipient Appreciation award Tex. Dept. Human Resourcs, 1985. Mem. Harrison County Bar Assn. (pres. 1982-84), Baylor U. Alumni Assn. (bd. dirs.), Marshall Symphony Soc. (bd. dirs. 1988-90), Marshall Rotary. Democrat. Baptist. Avocations: politics, hunting, fishing, baseball, classical cars. Office: 324 Cannon Washington DC 20515-0001

SANDLOW, LESLIE JORDAN, gastroenterologist, educator; b. Chgo., Jan. 7, 1934; s. Harry H. and Rose (Ehrlich) S.; m. Joanne J. Fleischer, June 16, 1957; children: Jay, Bruce, Lisa. BS, U. Ill., 1956; MD, Chgo. Med. Sch., 1960. Intern Michael Reese Hosp. and Med. Ctr., Chgo., 1961, med. resident, rsch. fellow gastrointestinal rsch., 1961-64, physician-in-charge clin. gastroenterology lab., 1963-74, asst. attending physician, 1964-67, assoc. attending physician, 1967-72, vice chmn. divsn. gastroenterology, dir. ambulatory medicine, 1968, dir. ambulatory care, 1969-76, attending physician, 1972—, assoc. med. dir., 1972-73; clin. asst. Chgo. Med. Sch., 1963-68, clin. instr., 1966; asst. prof. dept. medicine Pritzker Sch. Medicine, U. Chgo., 1973-76, assoc. prof., 1976-85, prof., 1985-90; prof. clin. medicine and med. edn. U. Ill. Coll. Medicine, Chgo., 1990-91, prof. medicine and med. edn., 1992—, sr. assoc. dean for grad. and continuing med. edn., 1993—, head dept. med. edn., 1993—, sr. assoc. dean for med. edn. affairs, 1994—. Dep. v.p. profl. affairs Michael Reese Hosp. and Med. Ctr., 1973-78, dir. Office Ednl. Affairs, 1976-81, assoc. v.p. acad. affairs, 1978-82, dir. quality assurance program, 1981-91, v.p. planning, 1982-83, v.p. profl. affairs and planning, 1983-88, dir. divsn. internal medicine, 1986-93, v.p. profl. and acad. affairs, 1988-91, med. dirs. acad. and med. affairs, 1992-94; med. dir. Michael Reese Health Plan, Inc., 1972-74, interim exec. dir., 1976-77; cons. gastroenterologist Ill. Ctrl. Hosp., 1978-80; vis. prof. Pontifica U. Catolica Rio Grande do Sul, Brazil, 1978, U. Fed. Espirito Santo, Brazil, 1978, Nordic Fedn. for Med. Understanding, Akureyri, Iceland, 1978, Seoul Nat. U. Sch. Medicine, 1981, Coll. Physicians and Surgsons, Kharachi, Pakistan, 1994, U. Tex., Ft. Worth, 1977, U. Ariz., Tucson, 1977, Loyola U. Med. Sch., Maywood, Ill., 1979; cons. in field; coord. Health Scis. Librs. in Ill.; mem. Midwest Med. Libr. Network; mem. subcom. on delivery of ambulatory med. care Inst. Medicine Chgo.; mem. cmty. resources task force Interinstnl. Cardiovascular Ctr.; chmn. steering grp Ill. Regional Med. Program; past co-chmn. curriculum com. U. Chgo. Reviewer Rsch. in Med. Edn./Assn. Am. Med. Colls., 1985—, Acad. Medicine/Assn. Am. Med. Colls., 1989; contbr. numerous articles to profl. publs. Mem. Skokie (Ill.) Bd. Health, 1973-85, chmn., 1976-85; bd. dirs. Group Health Assn. Am., 1976-78, Portes Ctr., 1980—; bd. dirs. Good Health Program Skokie Valley Hosp., 1978-80; bd. dirs., exec. com. Rsch. and Edn. Found. of Michael Reese Hosp. Med. Staff, 1992—; pres.-elect Inst. Medicine Chgo., 2002-. Recipient numerous grants, including NIH, 1988, Michael Reese Hosp. Found., 1994-95, Chgo. Cmty. Trust, 1994-95. Fellow Am. Coll. Gastroenterology; mem. N.Y. Acad. Scis., Inst. Medicine, Assn. Am. Med. Colls., Am. Coll. Physician Execs. (co-chair resource mgmt. com. of quality assurance forum), Soc. Dirs. Med. Coll. Continuing Med. Edn., Soc. Dir. Rsch. in Med. Edn. Home: 2314 N Lincoln Park W Chicago IL 60614-3455 Office: U Ill Coll Medicine Med Edn MC 784 1819 W Polk St Chicago IL 60612-7331

SANDMAN, DAN D. lawyer; BA, Ohio State U., 1970, JD, 1973. Bar: Ohio 1973, Pa. 1995. Gen. counsel, sec. Marathon Oil Co., 1986-92, USX Corp., Pitts., 1992—. Office: USX Corp 600 Grant St Ste 6172 Pittsburgh PA 15219-2805

SANDMAN, JAMES JOSEPH, lawyer; b. Albany, N.Y., June 16, 1951; s. Edgar A. and Margaret M. (Dugan) S.; m. Elizabeth D. Mullin, June 2, 1985; children: Joseph M., Elizabeth D. AB summa cum laude, Boston Coll., 1973; JD cum laude, U. Pa., 1976. Bar: Pa. 1976, D.C. 1977, U.S. Supreme Ct. 1980, Colo. 1982. Law clk. to judge U.S. Ct. Appeals (3d cir.), Wilkes-Barre, Pa., 1976-77; assoc. Arnold & Porter, Washington, 1977-82, ptnr., 1991—, mng. ptnr., 1996—, assoc. Denver, 1982-83, ptnr., 1984-91. Exec. editor U. Pa. Law Rev., 1975-76. Bd. govs. D.C. Bar; mem. bd. overseers U. Pa. Law Sch.; trustee Wilkes U.; bd. dirs. Washington Performing Arts Soc. Mem. ABA, Order of Coif, Phi Beta Kappa. Democrat. Office: Arnold & Porter 555 12th St NW Washington DC 20004-1206 Office Phone: 202-942-5758. Business E-Mail: james.sandman@aporter.com.

SANDMAN, KIMBERLY SUE ADAMS, newswriter; m. Christopher Bruce Sandman, Oct. 28, 1995; 1 child, Joseph Grant. BS in Home Econs., U. Tex., 1987. Reporter North Lake Travis LOG, Lago Vista, Tex., 1998—2000; freelance writer, 2000—; pres. Creative Concepts, Inc., 2003—; humor columnist. Author: (humor column) Mommy Moments. Sec. Lago Vista Area C. of C., Tex., 2000—01; worship com. chmn. Ascension Luth. Ch. Coun., Austin, 2000—01. Mem.: Nat. Soc. Newspaper Columnists, Nat. Newspaper Assn., Writer's League Tex. Lutheran. Avocations: gardening, sewing, reading. Office: Creative Concepts Inc PO Box 4686 Lago Vista TX 78645 E-mail: ks-cci@austin.rr.com.

SANDMAN, PAUL WILLIAM, lawyer; b. Albany, N.Y., June 21, 1947; s. Edgar Augustus and Margaret Mary (Dugan) S.; m. Mary Elizabeth O'Brien, Aug. 28, 1971; children— Katherine M., Margaret M., William A. AB, Boston Coll., 1969; JD, Harvard U., 1973. Bar: Mass. 1973, U.S. Dist. Ct. Mass. 1974, U.S. Ct. Appeals (1st cir.) 1974. Assoc., Goodwin, Procter & Hoar, Boston, 1973-81; corp. counsel Wang Laboratories, Inc., Lowell, Mass., 1981-84, v.p., corp. counsel, 1984—92, sr. v.p., gen. counsel, sec., 1992-93, sr. v.p., gen. counsel, sec., Boston Scientific Corp. 1993-. Bd. dirs. AMC of Mass. Bay, Boston, 1987—. Mem. Am. Corp. Counsel Assn. (bd. dirs. 1987—). Office: Boston Scientific Corp One Boston Scientific Pl Natick MA 01760-1537

SANDMAN, PETER M. risk communication consultant, speaker; b. N.Y.C., Apr. 18, 1945; s. Howard Edwin and Gertrude Leah (Orgel) S.; m. Susan Marie Goertzel, June 18, 1967 (div. 1975); m. Jody Sue Lanard, June 10, 1990; children: Alison, Jennifer; 1 stepchild, James Sachs. BA in Psychology, Princeton U., 1967; MA in Comm., Stanford U., 1968, PhD, 1971. Reporter Toronto (Ont.) Star, Can., 1966; stringer Time, 1966-67; instr. comm. Stanford (Calif.) U., 1968-70; instr. journalism Calif. State Coll., Hayward, 1970; sr. editor The Magazine, 1970; asst. prof. Ohio State U., Columbus, 1971-72; asst. prof. natural resources, journalism U. Mich., Ann Arbor, 1972-75, assoc. prof. natural resources, 1975-77; assoc. prof. comm., coord. Cook Coll. comm. program Rutgers U., New Brunswick, N.J., 1977-83, prof. journalism, 1983-94, prof. dept. human ecology, 1992-94; adj. prof., 1994—. Adj. prof. TV, radio Ithaca (N.Y.) Coll., 1976, grad. program in pub. health Rutgers U., 1986—, dept. environ. and cmty. medicine Robert Wood Johnson Med. Sch., Rutgers U., 1987—; adv. com. environ./occupl. health info. program 1984-89; founder, dir. environ. comm. rsch. program N.J. Agrl. Exptl. Sta., Rutgers U., 1986-92; vis. scholar urban and environ. policy Tufts U., Medford, Mass., 1990-91; rsch. prof. George Perkins Marsh Inst., Clark U.; comm. coun. Environ. Def. Fund, 1985—; bd. advisors grad. program in tech. and sci. comm. Drexel U., Phila., 1988—; cons. on comm. ACP, 1976-79, The Cousteau Soc., 1977-79, Pres. Com. on the Accident at Three Mile Island; specialist in comm. coop. ext. svc. U.S. Dept. Agr., 1977-86; cons. risk commn. office policy analysis EPA, 1986-88; exec. com. Sci. Writing Educators Group, 1978-81; cons. ARCO Chem., Boise Cascade, Chevron, Ciba-Geigy, Consumers Power, Dow, Du Pont, Johnson and Johnson, Johnson Wax, Procter and Gamble, Union Carbide, others. Cons. editor Random House, 1982-89, McGraw-Hill, 1989-94, Holt, Rinehart and Winston, 1978-81; contbg. editor Apt. Life, 1971-75; freelance writer, 1966—; editl. bd. Pub. Rels. Rsch. Ann., 1981-91, Jour. Pub. Rels. Rsch., 1991-94; editl. adv. bd. Environ. and Behavior, 1976-86; contbr. articles to profl. jours. Bd. dirs. N.J. Environ. Lobby, 1984-90, Nuclear Dialogue Project, 1985-90, pres. 1986-90; pub. info. com. N.J. chpt., Am. Cancer Soc., 1981-86, vice-chmn., 1983-86; comm. coord. N.J. Campaign for a Nuclear Weapons Freeze, 1982-85; socioeconomic subcom., com. on biotechnology agr. divsn. Nat. Assn. State Univs. and Land Grant Colls., 1988-90; bd. advisors Environ. Scientists for Global Survival, 1988-91; sci. review panel, radium/radon adv. bd. N.J. Dept. Environ. Protection, 1987-88; com. to survey the health effects mustard gas

and lewisite Inst. Medicine, NAS, 1992. Mem. AAUP, ACLU (bd. dirs. N.J. chpt. 1984-87), Environ. Def. Fund, Nat. Assn. Profl. Environ. Communicators, Sci. Writing Educators Group, Soc. for Risk Analysis, Soc. Environ. Journalists, Internat. Assn. Pub. Participation Practitioners, Sigma Delta Chi. Home: 59 Ridgeview Rd Princeton NJ 08540-7601 Fax. 609-683-0566. Office Phone: 609-683-4073. E-mail: peter@psandman.com.

SANDOR, GYORGY, pianist; b. Budapest, Hungary; came to U.S., 1938, naturalized, 1943; s. Ignac and Zsenka (Czipszer) S.; 1 child, Michael. Student, Liszt Ferenc Acad., Budapest, 1927-33; studied piano with, Bela Bartok; composition with, Zoltan Kodaly. Mem. piano faculty Juilliard Sch., 1982—. Made concert debut, Budapest, 1931; toured, Europe, 1931-38, Am. debut Carnegie Hall, N.Y.C., 1939, touring throughout U.S., Mexico, Can., W.I., North Africa, C.Am., S.Am., Europe, Australia, Far East, New Zealand; rec. with N.Y. Philharm. and Phila. orchs., also solo rec. (Grand Prix du Disque for rec. entire piano repertory of Bela Bartok's works 1964); rec. entire solo piano repertory of Prokofiev, 1967, Kodály, 1973; author: On Piano Playing, 1981; world premiers include Bartok's 3d Piano Concerto, Ormandy and Phila. Orch., 1946, Dance Suite piano version, Carnegie Hall, 1945, Concerto for Orch., piano version by Bartok, 1990, Sony Classical, Vox Candide Turnabout, Columbia Records, Trio, Phillips Records, Brahms 2d Piano Concerto, Chopin 1st Concerto, De Falla Nights in the Gardens of Spain. Named to Order of Arts and Letters, French Govt., 2003.

SANDORSEN, CASSIOPEIA, public health service officer; b. East Chicago, Ind., July 30, 1958; Health info. mgmt. cons. Wash. U. Sch. Medicine, St. Louis, 2001—; clin. analyst cons. Sisters Saint Mary DePaul Health Ctr., Bridgeton, Mo., 2002—. Clin. analyst cons. Gateway Health Info. Mgmt. Project, St. Louis, 2002—. Audio tape and cd series, Sound of Poetry, poetry, Half-Dimension, anthology, Essence of a Dream, Diamonds and Pearls, The Fourth Dimension, New Dawnings, Dreams Gone By, Theatre of The Mind, 2003, Autumn Necklace, Best Poems and Poets of 2003, 2004. Founder Nat. Law Enforcement Mus., Washington, 2003—03; mem. Republican Presdl. Task Force, 2003—04. Recipient Poetic Achievement award, Creative Arts and Sci. Enterprises, 1997, Amherst Soc., 1998, Malcolm Baldridge Nat. Quality award, Bush Adminstrn., 2002, award, Robert Wood Johnson Found., 2003; scholar, Esperanto League of N.Am., 2003. Mem.: Am. Acad. Poets, Internat. Soc. Poets, Mo. Bot. Garden, St. Louis Art Mus., Mo. Hist. Soc., Am. Mus. Natural History, St. Louis Symphony Orch. Vivaldi Soc. Republican. Avocations: nature walks, gardening, fiber arts, travel.

SANDOVAL, AMADA, education program director; Interim dir. women's ctr. Princeton U., NJ. Mem.: Modern Lang. Assn. Am. (exec. coun. 2002—). Office: Princeton Univ 243 Frist Campus Ctr Princeton NJ 08544-2142 E-mail: sandoval@princeton.edu.

SANDOVAL, ARTURO ALONZO, art educator; b. Espanola/Cordova, N.Mex., Feb. 1, 1942; s. Lorenzo Sandoval and Cecilia Eulalia (Archuleta) Harrison; (div. Sept. 1982); 1 child, Avalon Valentine Galaglorial. Student, U. Portland, 1959; BA, Calif. State Coll., L.A., 1964, MA, 1969; MFA, Cranbrook Acad. Art, Bloomfield Hills, Mich., 1971. Designer, illustrator Western Lighting Corp., L.A., 1964-66; advt. designer, adult edn. instr. spl. svcs. USN, Yokosuka, Japan, 1966; interior design asst. Walter B. Broderick & Assocs., La Mesa, Calif., 1967; asst. prof. art dept. U. Ky., Lexington, 1974-76, assoc. prof., 1976-86, full prof., 1986—, dir. art dept. Barnhart Gallery, 1976—, curator, 1979—. Teaching asst. Calif. State Coll., L.A., 1969, Cranbrook Acad. Art, Bloomfield Hills, 1969-71; fiber art demonstrator Mus. Art, Grand Rapids, Mich., 1970; batik and tie-dye demonstrator Gwynn's Fabric Shop, Birmingham, Mich., 1970; instr. Calif. State Coll., L.A., 1970, So. Ill. U., Carbondale, 1971, Edwardsville, 1971, 72, 73, asst. prof., 1971-73; presenter various lectures and workshops throughout the U.S., 1973—; juror Mo. Women Festival Arts, St. Louis, So. Ill. U., East St. Louis, 1974, Paramount Arts Assn., Ashland, Ky., 1975, Ind. Weavers Guild, Indpls., 1979, Fed. Corrections Inst., Lexington, 1979, Hawaii Craftsman Hui and Art Dept. U. Hawaii, Manoa, Honolulu, 1982, art dept. Va. Intermont Coll., Bristol, 1982, Arrowmont Sch. Arts and Crafts, Gatlinburg, Tenn., 1984, Ctr. Contemporary Art, U. Ky., Lexington, 1984, Guild Greater Cin.,Carnegie Art Ctr., Covington, Ky., 1989, S.C. Arts Commn., Charleston, 1990, Adams Art Gallery, Dunkirk, N.Y., 1994; visual arts cons. Ky. Arts Commn., Frankfort, 1977; curator Visual Arts Ctr. Alaska, Anchorage, 1982, Ky. Art and Crafts Found., Inc., Louisville, 1985; mem. artist adv. panel Ky. Art and Crafts Found., Louisville, 1986, 87, 92-2000; visual arts cons. Arts Midwest, 1987; artistic advisor Ky. Guild Mktg. Bd., Berea, 1988, 91, 92, 93; bd. trustees Ky. Guild 1995-98, Am. Craft Coun., N.Y.C., 1996—; vis. artist/critic Allen R. Hite Inst., U. Louisville, 1992; vis. artist Coll. Human Environ. Scis., U. Ky., Lexington, 1993; vis. artist/ lectr. fiber dept. Cranbrook Acad. Art, Bloomfield Hills, Mich., 1994, Art. Dept. St. Louis Comm. Coll.-Florissnat Valley, 2001, U. Arizona, 2001; curator, Art Wuilts 2001, River Oaks Square Art Ctr., Louisiana, 2001. Exhibited in group shows at Yeiser Art Ctr., Paducah/Paramount Arts Ctr., Ashland/S.E. Cmty. Coll., Cumberland, 1994, Textile Arts Centre, Chgo., 1994, Winnipeg (Man., Can.) Art Gallery, 1994, Riffe Gallery, Ohio Arts Coun., Columbus, 1994, Royal Hiberian Acad., Gallagher Gallery, Dublin, Ireland, Cooper Gallery, Barnsley, South Yorks, Gt. Britain, Shipley Art Gallery, Gateshead, Gt. Britain, 1994, Grand Rapids (Mich.) Art Mus., 1994, Whatcom Mus. History and Art, Bellingham, Wash., The Rockwell Mus., Corning, N.Y., Mus. Art, Washington State U., Pullman, The Hyde Collection, Glen Falls, N.Y., 1994, U. Art Galleries, U. S.D., Vermillion, 1994, Barnhart Gallery, U. Ky., Lexington, 1994, Sawtooth Ctr. Visual Art, 1994, Santa Fe Gallery, Santa Fe Cmty. Coll., Gainesville, Fla., 1994, Liberty Gallery, Louisville, 1994, Asahi Shimbun Gallery, Tokyo, Takashimaya Gallery, Osaka, 1994, Minn. Mus. Art, Landmark Ctr., St. Paul, 1994, S.C. State Mus., Columbia, 1994, Galbreath Gallery, Lexington, 1994, U.K. Art Mus., 1998, Giles Gallery, Richmond, Ky., 2004, Ky. Mus. of Art and Design, 2004, Ronald Barr Gallery, New Albany, Ind., 2004, City Gallery, S.C., 2004, Tuska Gallery, Ky., 2004, Pres. Room. Ky., 2004, numerous others; represented in permanent collections at Wabash Coll., Crawfordsville, Ind., Greenville County Mus. Art, Greenville, S.C., Mus. Modern Art, N.Y.C., St. Mary's Coll., Notre Dame, Ind., Coll. St. Rose, Albany, N.Y., Bowling Green (Ohio) StateU., U. Notre Dame, Transylvania U., Lexington, U. Ky. Mus. Art, Lexington, Mid-Am. Rare Coin Auction Galleries, Lexington, Henry Luce Found., N.Y.C., Lexington Ctrl. Libr., UK Art Mus., 1998, Nat. Mus. Am. Art, Renwick Gallery, 1999, J.B. Speed Art Mus., Louisville, 2000; Linda Schwartz Gallery, 2000, Tuska Gallery, 2000, President's Room, KY, 2000, Shands Gallery, 2001, Friedman Gallery, 2001, KGAG Offices, 2001, Actor;s Theater, 2001, Ronald Barr Gallery, 2001, Opera House Gallery, 2001. Recipient Alexandra Korsakoff Galston Meml. prize St. Louis Artist's Guild, 1971, Mus. Merit award Mus. Arts and Scis., Evansville, 1972, Creative Rsch. Grant So. Ill. U.-Edwardsville Rsch. Found., 1972, Craftsman fellowship Nat. Endowment for Arts, Washington, 1973, Friend of Mus. award Mus. Arts and Scis., Evansville, 1973, Clay Eugene Jordan ann. bequest prize for crafts St. Louis Artist's Guild, 1973, Teaching Improvement grant U. Ky. Rsch. Found., 1974, Travel grant U. Ky. Rsch. Found., 1977, Judges Choice award Berea (Ky.) Coll., 1978, Handweaver's Guild Am. award, 1978, Fiber award LeMoyne Art Found., Tallahassee, 1981, Elise Strout Merit award Mus. Arts and Scis., Evansville, 1981, Handweavers Guild Am. award, 1983, Martha Ryan Merit award Mus. Arts and Scis., Evansville, 1984, Best of Show award Gayle Willson Galleries, Southampton, 1984, Juror's merit award Brenau Coll., Gainesville, Ga., 1985, Installation Grant Ind. Arts Commn., Ft. Wayne, 1985, All Smith fellowship Ky. Arts Coun., Frankfort, 1987, Merit award Spotlight '88 Am. Craft Coun. Southeast Conf., Tuscaloosa, Ala., 1988, Merit award Mus. Arts and Scis., Evansville, 1989, Design Grant, Arts and Cultural Coun. for O.A. Singletary Ctr. for Arts, Lexington, 1990, Visual Arts fellowship Nat. Endowment for Arts, Washington, 1992, Hon. award Ky. Crafts Mktg. Bd., Frankfort, 1994, Rude Osolnik Craftsman award Ky. Crafts Mktg. & KAC Fund, 1998, 1st pl. Lexington Art League, Reverse Raffle, Lexington, 1999, Art-in-Arch. Program commn. Gen. Svcs. Adminstrn., London, Ky., 2002; NEA vis. artist grantee Pyramid Atlantic Press, Riverdale, Md., 1996; Gen. Svcs. Adminstrn., Art-in-Architecture, London, Ky., 2002, Artist award Ky. Gov.'s award in the arts, 2003. Mem. Lexington Fiber Guild Inc., Louisville Visual Arts Assn., Ky. Art and Craft Found., Inc., Ky. Guild Artists and Craftsmen, Am. Craft Coun., Friends of U. Ky. Mus. Art, Friends of Fiber Art, Surface Design Assn. Home: PO Box 25153 Lexington KY 40524-5153 Office: U Ky Dept Art 207 Fine Arts Bldg Lexington KY 40506-0022 Office Phone: 859-257-8149.

SANDOVAL, ISABELLE MEDINA, education educator; b. Laramie, Wyo., Sept. 30, 1948; d. John Ben and Ida Medina Sandoval; 1 child, Tomas Andres Duran. BA, U. N.Mex., 1970; MA, U. Mo., 1976; EdD, U. Wyo., 1982. Cert. Spanish, reading, English, adminstrn. Tchr. Spanish and English Menaul Sch., Albuquerque, 1971-73; tchr. bilingual edn. and reading Kansas City, Mo., 1973-78; tchr. title I Sch. Dist. #60, Pueblo, Colo., 1978-83, adminstr., 1983-88, Acad. Dist. 20, Colorado Springs, Colo., 1988-95; human resources coord. Harrison Dist. 2, Colorado Springs, 1995-98; prof. education Coll. of Santa Fe, N.Mex. V.p. Hispano Crypto Jewish Resource Ctr., Denver. Author numerous poems. Pres. South Holman Domestic Water Assn. Mem. Geneal. Soc. Hispanic Am., Hispanic Geneal. Rsch. Ctr. N.Mex., Mana del Norte, Olibama Lopez Tushar Hispanic Legacy Rsch. Ctr., N.M. Jewish Hist. Soc. (bd. dirs.), N.Mex. Acequia Assn., N.Mex. Land Grant Forum, Soc. for Crypto Judaic Studies, Nat. Assn. Sephardic Artists, Writers and Intellectuals, LaSallian Leadership (bd. dirs.), Phi Kappa Phi, Kappa Delta Phi, Phi Delta Kappa. Jewish. Avocations: poetry, researching family history and hispano jewish materials. Home: 4358 Lost Feather Santa Fe NM 87507-2580 Office: Coll of Santa Fe 1600 Saint Michaels Dr Santa Fe NM 87505-7615

SANDOVAL, JONATHAN HOUGH, education educator; b. Hayward, Calif., Oct. 5, 1942; s. John Starbird and Marian Hough Sandoval; m. Susan Irene Beecher, Aug. 21, 1982; 1 child, Marian Beecher. BA, U. Calif., Santa Barbara, 1964, MA, U. Calif., Berkeley, 1966, PhD, 1969. Lic. psychologist Calif., 1979, sch. psychologist Calif., 1969. Sch. psychologist Richmond (Calif.) Sch. Dist., 1969—72; lectr. U. Calif., Berkely, 1969—73, prof. Davis, 1973—, chair grad. group in edn., 1990—98, dir. divsn. edn., 1995—2001. Editor: (nonfiction book) Test Interpretation and Diversity: Achieving Equity in Psychological Assessment, 1998, Crisis Counseling, Intervention and Prevention in the Schools, 1998, 2001; author: Suicidal Youth: School-based Intervention and Prevention, 1991, Preparing for Crises in the Schools: A Manual for Building School Crisis Response Teams, 1996, 2001. Recipient Sandra Goff Meml. award for Disting. and Exemplary Svc. to the Assn. and to the Profession of Sch. Psychology, Calif. Assn. Sch. Psychologists, 2000. Fellow: APA (com. and bd. chair counsel reps. 1987—, Jack Bardon Disting. Svc. award divsn. sch. psychology 2002), Am. Orthopsychiatric Assn. (life); mem.: NASP, Am. Ednl. Rsch. Assn., Soc. for the Study Sch. Psychology. Independent. Achievements include research in school psychology. Avocations: travel, gardening, collectable automobiles, aviation. Office: Sch Edn Univ Calif Davis 1 Shields Ave Davis CA 95616-8579

SANDOVAL, PAULA E. state senator; m. Paul Sandoval; 5 stepchildren. BA in Comm., MPA. State sen., dist. 34 Colo. Senate, Denver, 2002—. Mem. Finance Com. Bd. govs. Colo. State U.; mem. Denver Welfare Reform Bd.; bd. mem. Greenway Found.; mem. Hispanic Edn. Adv. Coun., Colo. Healthy Kids Coalition. Democrat. Office: State Capitol 200 E Colfax Ave Denver CO 80203

SANDOVAL IÑIGUEZ, JUAN CARDINAL, archbishop; b. Yahualica, Mar. 28, 1933; Created cardinal Roman Cath. Ch., 1994, ordained priest Roman Cath. Ch., 1957. Co-adjuctor bishop, Cuidad Juarez, Mexico, 1988—92; bishop, 1992—94; archbishop Guadalajara, Mexico, 1994—. Office: Arzobispado Guadalajara Apartado Postall 1-331 Liceo 17 Guadalajara 44100 Mexico

SANDQUIST, GARY MARLIN, engineering educator, researcher, consultant, writer; b. Salt Lake City, Apr. 19, 1936; s. Donald August Sandquist and Lillian (Evaline) Dunn; m. Kristine Powell, Jan. 17, 1992; children from previous marriage: Titia, Julia, Taunia, Cynthia, Carl; stepchildren: David, Michael, Scott, Diane, Jeff. BSME, U. Utah, 1960; MS in Engring. Sci., U. Calif., Berkeley, 1961; PhD in Mech. Engring., U. Utah, 1964, MBA, 1995. Registered profl. engr., Utah, N.Y., Minn., Calif.; cert health physicist, quality auditor; diplomate Am. Acad. Environ. Engring. Staff mem. Los Alamos (N.Mex.) Sci. Lab., 1966; postdoctoral fellow MIT, 1969-70; rsch. prof. surgery Med. Sch., U. Utah, Salt Lake City, 1974—85, prof., dir. nuc. engring. dept. mech. engring., 1975—, acting chmn. dept., 1984-85, adj. prof. civil engring., 1996—; expert in nuc. sci. Internat. Atomic Energy Agy., UN, 1980—; chief scientist Rogers and Assocs. Engring. Corp., Salt Lake City, 1980—90, sr. nuclear engr., 1998—; sr. health physicist URS Corp., 1990—; mgr., owner Applied Sci. Profls., LLC, Salt Lake City, 1999—. Vis. scientist MIT, Cambridge, Mass., 1969-70; advisor rocket design Hercules, Inc., Bachus, Utah, 1962; sr. nuc. engr. Idaho Nat. Engring. Lab., Idaho Falls, 1963-65; cons. nuc. sci. State of Utah, 1982—; vis. prof. Ben Gurion U., Beer Sheva, Israel, 1985, U.S. Mil. Acad., West Point, N.Y., 2003-; affiliate faculty Idaho State U., 1998—; cons. various cos.; spkr. Nuc. Energy Inst., 1990—. Author: Geothermal Energy, 1973, Introduction to System Science, 1985. Comdr. USNR, 1954-56, Korea; ret. Recipient Glen Murphy award in nuc. engring. Am. Soc. Engring. Edn., 1984. Fellow ASME, Am. Nuc. Soc.; mem. Am. Soc. Quality (sr.), Am. Health Physics Soc., Am. Soc. Engring. Edn., Alpha Nu Sigma, Sigma Xi, Tau Beta Pi, Pi Tau Sigma. Republican. Mem. Lds Ch. Home: 40 C Wilson Rd West Point NY 10996 Office: U Utah 2110 Merrill Engring Bldg Salt Lake City UT 84112 E-mail: gms@asp-llc.com.

SANDRICH, JAY H. television director; b. L.A., Feb. 24, 1932; s. Mark R. and Freda (Wirtschafter) S.; m. Nina Kramer, Feb. 11, 1952 (div.); children: Eric, Tony, Wendy; m. Linda Green Silverstein, Oct. 4, 1984. BA, UCLA, 1953. Prodr. (TV show) Get Smart, 1965; dir. (TV shows) He and She, 1967, Mary Tyler Moore Show, 1970-88, Soap, 1977-79, Cosby Show, 1984-92; dir. (films) Seems Like Old Times, 1980, For Richer, For Poorer (HBO), 1992, Neil Simon's London Suite (NBC), 1996. Served to 1st lt. Signal Corps U.S. Army, 1952-55. Mem. Dirs. Guild Am. (award 1975, 85, 86), TV Acad. Arts and Scis. (Emmy award 1971, 73, 85, 86). Office: care Andy Elkin Creative Artists Agy 9830 Wilshire Blvd Beverly Hills CA 90212

SANDRIDGE, DONALD OTIS, music educator; b. Waynesboro, Va., Aug. 31, 1950; s. Otis Chester and Lucille Spitler Sandridge. Mus EdB, James Madison U., Harrisonburg, Va., 1973; MS in Edn., Old Dominion U., Norfolk, Va., 1983; Advanced Cert., Westminster Choir Coll., Princeton, N.J., 1986. Min. of music Bethany United Meth. Ch., Gloucester Point, Va., 1975—82, Orcutt Bapt. Ch., Newport News, Va., 1983—85, First Presbyn. Ch., Newport News, Va., 1988—94; dir. of choral activities Gloucester County Pub. Schs., Va., 1973—. Chmn. fine arts dept. Gloucester H.S., Va., 1973—; chairperson Gloucester County Parks and Recreation Commn., 1999—; bd. dir. Hampton Rds. Educators Credit Union. Concert chmn. Mid. Peninsula Cmty. Concert Assn., Gloucester, Va., 1975—2001; state sponsor Nat. Beta Club (Va. chpt.). Recipient Freedom Goode award, Gloucester County, Youth Adv. award, 30 Yr. Sponsor award, Nat. Beta Club. Mem.: Abingdon Ruritan Club (bd. dir. 2001—). Presbyn. Home: PO Box 1271 7736 Points Pl Gloucester Point VA 23062 E-mail: dotissinger@aol.com.

SANDRIDGE, WILLIAM PENDLETON, JR., lawyer; b. Winston-Salem, N.C., Jan. 27, 1934; m. Jane Carolyn Yeager, Dec. 10, 1966; children: Jane, William. AB, U. N.C., 1956; LLB, U. Va., 1961. Bar: N.C. 1961. Mem. Womble Carlyle Sandridge & Rice, PLLC, Winston-Salem, 1962—. Chmn., bd. dirs. Horizons Residential Care Ctr., 1980, Food Bank N.W. N.C., Inc., 1988-89, Data Max Corp., 1996. Office: Womble Carlyle Et Al One W Fourth St Winston Salem NC 27101 Office Phone: 336-721-3503.

SANDROK, RICHARD WILLIAM, lawyer; b. Evergreen Park, Ill., July 8, 1943; s. Edward George and Gertrude Jeanette (Van Stright) Sandrok; m. Rebecca Fitzz, June 19, 1973; children: Richard William, Jr., Alexander Edward, Philip Robert, Erika Joy. BA, Wheaton (Ill.) Coll., 1965; JD, U. Ill., 1968. Bar: Ill. 1968, U.S. Dist. Ct. (no. dist.) Ill. 1971. Assoc. Hinshaw Culbertson Moelmann Hoban & Fuller, Chgo. and Wheaton, 1971-75, ptnr. Wheaton, 1976-89, Lisle, Ill., 1989—2001; sole practice Glen Ellyn, Ill., 2001—. Reviewer: Legal Checklists. Capt. U.S. Army, 1969—71. Mem.: ABA, Def. Rsch. Inst., Assn. Def. Trial Attys., DuPage County Bar Assn. (chmn. med./legal com. 1978—79), Am. Arbitration Assn. (arbitrator), Chgo. Bar Assn., Ill. Bar Assn. Home: 818 Revere Rd Glen Ellyn IL 60137-5537 Office: Richard W Sandrok Atty at Law 818 Revere Rd Glen Ellyn IL 60137 E-mail: RWS283@aol.com.

SANDS, CHRISTINE LOUISE, English educator; b. Johnstown, Pa., Oct. 13, 1947; d. Joseph and Margaret (Kocsis) Migut; m. Angelo Joseph Sands, Dec. 28, 1968 (div. Nov. 1989); children: Vincent, Linda. BS in German, Indiana U. Pa., 1969, BS in English, 1975; postgrad., Slippery Rock U., 1971-76. Tchg. cert. Pa. Educator New Castle (Pa.) Schs., 1969—. Student advisor, judge Forensics, New Castle, 1981-96, Youngstown (Ohio) Reading Festival, 1981-95. Pres. New Castle City Coun., 1996; parish coun. St. Vitus Ch., New Castle, 1986-92; basketball referee PIAA, Mechanicsburg, Pa., 1972-91; coach New Castle H.S. Bowling, 1986-97. Democrat. Roman Catholic. Avocations: reading, travel, sports, cooking, politics. Home: 819 E Hillcrest Ave New Castle PA 16105-2256 Office: New Castle HS 230 N Jefferson St New Castle PA 16101-2274

SANDS, DEANNA, editor; Mng. editor Omaha World Herald, 95—. Office: Omaha World-Herald World-Herald Sq Omaha NE 68102-1138

SANDS, DOLORES S. dean; BSN, MSN, Wayne State U.; PhD, Ariz. State U. Prof., dir. Ctr. Health Care Rsch. and Evaluation U. Tex., Austin, 1984-89, dir. grad. program nursing adminstrn., 1989—, former acting dean, asst. dean rsch. and resources, asst. dean baccalaureate program, now dean, Laura Lee Blanton chair in nursing, also now Joseph H. Blades Centennial Meml. prof. in nursing. Mem. nursing sci. rev. com. Exploratory Rsch. Ctr. Grants; mem. adv. coun. on nurses edn. and practice divsn. nursing Health Resources and Svcs. Adminstrn. U.S. Dept. Health and Human Svcs., 1991 93, co-chair adv. coun., 1993-95, mem. adv. group nat. task force for workforce projections of nurse practitioners and nurse-midwives, 1993, now mem. joint coun. primary care workforce workgroup; active Nat. Ctr. for Nursing Rsch., NIH. Contbr. articles to profl. jours. Grantee USPHS, 1986-89; recipient Alumni Achievement award Ariz. State U., 1987. Mem. ANA, Coun. Nurse Rschrs., Soc. Rsch. in Nursing Edn., Phi Kappa Phi, Sigma Theta Tau. Office: U Tex Austin Sch Nursing Office Dean 1700 Red River St Austin TX 78701-1412

SANDS, HAROLD WINTHROP, banker, financial adviser; b. N.Y.C., Aug. 25, 1926; s. Harold Aymar and Muriel Winthrop Sands; m. Joan Hodges Baker, Sept. 6, 1961; children: Harold, Serena. Student, CBS-NBS Tellers' Acad., 1950—52, Am. Inst. Banking, 1967-69; postgrad., Miami Dade U., 1968-71. V.p., devel. officer, regional mgr. S.E. Banks, Miami, London, Europe, Caribbean, 1967-79; v.p. Marine Midland Bank N.V., London, 1979-85; sr. cons., fin. adviser Sun Life Assurance Soc., London, 1985-87; U.K. rep. Wright Investment Svc., London, 1987-92; v.p. Kreditbank Global Mgmt., Miami, 1993-94; dir., trustee Kapok Bermuda Ltd., London, 1994-96; gen. ptnr. The Winthrop Group L.P., Newport, RI, 1996-2001; assoc. v.p. Pre-paid Legal Svcs., Inc., Newport, RI, 2001—; gen. mgr. Peace Mgmt. Group LLC, Newport, RI. Founder Lorimex Internat., N.Y.C., 1952-60; CEO acctg., sales Paramount Pictures Corp., N.Y.C., 1950-52; founder, CEO Distbrs. for Mexico Rex Chain Belt, Ampudia A.S. Mex., 1960-67. Chairperson N.Am. com. London C. of C., 1985-88, chmn. Caribbean com., 1988-91; hon. treas. European Atlantic Group, 1980—; mem. Rep. Com.; mem. Woolnoth Soc. Coun., City of London, 1980-93; trustee La Farge Restoration Fund of Newport, 1996—; trustee Preservation Soc. Newport, mem. fin. and edn. coms., 1994-2000; com. mem. Tall Ships Salute, 1995; bd. dirs. Newport Hist. Soc., 2001—. Master sgt. U.S. Army, 101st Armed Calvery, 1949-54. Decorated Imperial House of David, 1995, Comdr. of Most Revered Order of the Star of Ethiopia. Mem.: SAR (Newport chpt.), Order of Founders and Patriots, The Guild of Internat. Bankers London, Order of 1st Families of R.I., Soc. Colonial Wars (Providence and Boston chpts.), RAC Club London, Ida Lewis Club (Newport, R.I.), Clambake Club, Reading Rm. Club, Ends of the Earth Club London, Broad St. Ward Club London, Rotary Internat., Pilgrim's London. Avocations: sailing, tennis, skiing, boating, chess. Home: 10 Cherry Creek Rd Newport RI 02840 E-mail: hss6518@aol.com.

SANDS, HARRY, psychologist, health administrator, researcher; b. N.Y.C., Jan. 6, 1917; s. Morris and Lena Sandrowitz; m. Helene Purl, June 24, 1945; children: Jeffrey, Richard. AB, NYU, 1941, PhD in Psychology, 1952. Diplomate Am. Bd. Profl. Psychology; lic. psychologist, N.Y. Rsch. fellow dept neurology Neurol. Inst./Columbia U. Phys. and Surg., N.Y.C., 1941-42, rsch. chief psychophysiologist Head Injury Project, 1942-44; assoc. dir., chief psychologist Baird Found. Clinic for Children with Epilepsy/Beth David Hosp., N.Y.C., 1944-46; instr. Washington Sq. Coll./NYU, 1947-50, Bklyn. Coll., 1950-52; exec. dir. Com. Pub. Understanding of Epilepsy, N.Y.C., 1952-53, United Epilepsy Assn. Am., N.Y.C., 1953-56; dir. and clin. psychologist Psychol. Lab., Inc., N.Y.C., 1955-61; dir. Epilesy Asn. N.Y., Epilepsy Found. Am., N.Y.C., 1956-68; dir. program planning and evaluation Epilepsy Found. Am., Washington, 1972-74; assoc. staff adult therapy clinic Postgrad. Ctr. for Mental Health, N.Y.C., 1962-66, assoc. staff supervision therapeutic process, 1971-73, assoc. supr., sr. supr. psychoanalysis, psychotherapy, 1974—85, tng. analyst, pyschoanalysis, psychotherapy, 1993-98, exec. v.p., CEO, 1979—87, exec. dir., CEO, 1987—88. Pvt. practice psychoanalysis and psychotherapy, N.Y.C., 1952-98; cons. divsn. resource devel. Nat. Inst. on Drug Abuse, Rockville, Md., 1978-79, Commn. for Control of Epilepsy and its Consequences, HEW, Washington, 1977, legal and protective svcs. project, Harvard U. Sch. of Pub. Health, Boston, 1974, cons. classification exceptional children, adequacy of classification for physically and sensorially handicapped, Vanderbilt U., Knoxville, 1974, bd. trustees, exec. com., 1988—; bd. dirs. Postgrad. Ctr. Residences, I, II, and III, N.Y.C., 1991-96, sec., 1991-2000, 2002—, pres. Editor: (book) Epilepsy: A Handbook for the Mental Health Professional, 1982 (Book of Yr. award ANA, 1982); co-author: (books) Epilepsy Fact Book, 1979, Education and Training Beyond the Doctoral Degree, 1995, Impact of Managed Care on Psychodynamic Treatment, 1996, The Guide to Pastoral Counseling and Care, 2000; contbr. chpts. in books, articles to profl. jours. Mem. tech. adv. com. on epilepsy N.Y. Dept Health, N.Y.C., 1945, planning com. advisory com on epilepsy, N.Y. State Dept. Mental Hygiene, Albany, 1952, joint legis. com. of State of N.Y. on program of pub. health, medicaid and compulsory health and hosp. ins., Albany, 1953; mem com. on Neurol. Disorders in Industry and com. on Emergency Med. Identification, AMA, Chgo., 1953, com. of info. svcs. and employment com., handicapped sect., Comty. Coun. of Greater N.Y., N.Y.C., 1954, joint legis. com. on mental retardation and physical handicaps, State of N.Y., Albany, 1956. Recipient fellowship Internat. Rehab. Rsch. Program of Social and Rehab. Svcs., HEW, Washington, 1972, Gold medal award for lifetime achievement in practice of psychology, Am. Psychol. Found., Washington, 1995; grantee Social Rehab. Svcs, HEW, Washington, 1968, 78. Fellow APA (bd. govs. coll. profl. practice 1994-99, co-chair nat. conf. on postdoctoral edn. and tng., Washington, 1992-94, bd. govs. coll. profl. practice, 1994-99, coun. reps. 1988-91, 1994, treas. com. for advancement profl. practice, practice directorate, 1992-94, cons. 1995, Karl F. Heiser Presdl. award 1993, Disting. Psychologist award Divsn. Psychotherapy 1995); mem. Am. Acad. Psychology, N.Y. State Psychol. Assn. (pres. 1978-79, 1985-86, coun. of reps. 1957-60, 1986-91, Allen J. Williams Jr. Meml. award 1993), Postgrad. Psychoanalytic Soc., Nat. Acad. of Practices (Disting. Practitioner in Psychology 1995), Psi Chi, Sigma Xi. Democrat. Jewish. Avocations: travel, theater, music, ballet. Home and Office: 219 E 69th St Apt 7 D New York NY 10021-5455

SANDS, JEROME D. investment company executive; Chmn. bd. dirs., Robinson-Humphrey Co. LLC, Atlanta. Office: Robinson-Humphrey Co 3333 Peachtree Rd NE Atlanta GA 30326-1070

SANDS, MATTHEW LINZEE, physicist, researcher; b. Oxford, Mass., Oct. 20, 1919; m. Freya Kidner, 1978; children: Michael, Richard, Michelle. BA, Clark U., 1940; MA, Rice U., 1941; PhD, MIT, 1948. Physicist U.S. Naval Ordnance Lab., 1941-43, Los Alamos Sci. Lab., 1943-46; research asso., then asst. prof. physics Mass. Inst. Tech., 1946-50; sr. research fellow, asso. prof., prof. physics Calif. Inst. Tech., 1950-63; prof., dep. dir. Linear Accelerator Center, Stanford, 1963-69; prof. physics U. Calif.-Santa Cruz, 1969-85, prof. emeritus, 1985—, fellow Kresge Coll.; vice chancellor for sci., 1969-72; pres.

Sands-Kidner Assocs., Inc., 1986-90. Vis. prof. U. Paris-Sud, spring 1976; mem. Commn. Coll. Physics, 1960-66, chmn., 1964-66; cons. Office Sci. and Tech., ACDA, Inst. Def. Analyses, 1962-67; mem. Pugwash Conf. Sci. and World Affairs, 1960-63; cons. on accelerator physics, 1975-93. Author: (with W.C. Elmore) Electronics-Experimental Techniques, 1948, (with R.P. Feynman and R.B. Leighton) The Feynman Lectures on Physics, 3 vols, 1965, (with others) Physical Science Today, 1973; also articles.; Mem. editorial bd.: Il Nuovo Cimento, 1972-85. Fulbright scholar Italy, 1952-53 Fellow Am. Phys. Soc. (Robert R. Wilson prize 1998); mem. Am. Assn. Physics Tchrs. (Disting. Service award 1972), Fedn. Am. Scientists, AAAS. Achievements include special research electronic instrumentation for nuclear physics, cosmic rays, accelerators, high-energy physics, science education, science and public affairs, electron storage rings. Home: 160 Michael Ln Santa Cruz CA 95060-1704 Business E-Mail: sands@scipp.ucsc.edu.

SANDS, RICHARD E. food products executive; b. Canandaigua, N.Y., Mar. 3, 1951; s. Marvin Sands and Marilyn Alpert; m. Sharon Gillick, Apr. 1991. BA in Psychology, U. Vt.; postgrad., U. Calif.; M, PhD, U. N.C. Teaching rsch. asst. psychology dept. U. N.C., Chapel Hill, 1974-79; exec. trainee Canandaigua Wine Co. Inc., 1979-82, exec. v.p., 1982-86, pres., chief oper. officer, 1986—; now CEO Canadaigua Wine Co. Inc., 1993—. Office: Canandaigua Wine Co Inc 116 Buffalo St Canandaigua NY 14424-1086 Address: Canandaiqua Brands 300 Willowbrook Ofc Park Fairport NY 14450

SANDS, ROBERT, food products executive; Gen. counsel Constellation Brands, Inc., Fairport, NY, 1986, exec. v.p., gen. counsel, CEO, internat., 1998—2000, group pres., 2000—02, pres., COO, 2002—. Office: Constellation Brands Inc 300 Willowbrook Office Park Fairport NY 14450*

SANDSTEAD, HAROLD HILTON, medical educator; b. Omaha, May 25, 1932; s. Harold Russel and Lula Florence (Hilton) S.; m. Kathryn Gordon Brownlee, June 6, 1959 (dec. May 13, 1989); m. Victoria Regan Liddle, Feb. 14, 1990 (div. Oct. 1993); children: Eleanor McDonald, James Brownlee, William Harold. BA, Ohio Wesleyan U., 1954; MD, Vanderbilt U., 1958. Diplomate Am. Bd. Internal Medicine, 1967, Am. Bd. Nutrition, 1967, Am. Bd. Physician Nutrition Specialists, 2001; lic. physician Tex. Intern, asst. resident in internal medicine Barnes Hosp. Washington U., St. Louis, 1958-60; asst. resident in pathology Vanderbilt Hosp., Nashville, 1960-61; asst. surgeon USPHS U.S. NAMRU 3, Cairo, 1961-63; asst. resident in internal medicine Thayer VA Hosp. Vanderbilt, Nashville, 1963-64; chief resident in internal medicine Vanderbilt Hosp., Nashville, 1964-65; instr. internal medicine, asst. prof. biochemistry Med. Sch. Vanderbilt U., Nashville, 1965-70, asst. prof. internal medicine, assoc. prof. nutrition, 1970-71; dir. USDA-ARS Human Nutrition Rsch. Ctr., Grand Forks, N.D., 1971-84; adj. prof. biochemistry and internal medicine Sch. Medicine U. N.D., Grand Forks, 1971-84; dir. USDA-ARS Human Nutrition Rsch. Ctr. on Aging, Boston, 1984-85; prof. nutrition Tufts U., Medford, Mass., 1984-85; prof. preventive medicine and community health U. Tex. Med. Br., Galveston, 1985—; chmn. preventive medicine and community health Med. Br. U. Tex., Galveston, 1985-90, prof. internal medicine, human biol. chemistry and genetics, 1986—. Cons. NAS, FNB, NIH, WHO, USDA; Joseph Goldberger vis. prof. AMA, 1976, Ellen Swallow Richards Meml. lectr., 1984; W.O. Atwater lectr. USDA, 1984; Sam E. and Mary F. Roberts lectr., 1985, Raymond Ewell Meml. lectr., 1985; Welcome prof. in basic sci. Fedn. Am. Socs. Exptl. Biology, 1988. Mem. editl. bd. Jour. Nutrition, Am. Jour. Clin. Nutrition, Jour. Lab. Clin. Medicine, Biol. Trace Element Rsch., Nutrition Rsch., Nutritinal Rsch. Internat., Trace Elements Medicine Biology, Jour. Trace Elements Exptl. Medicine, Jour. Am. Coll. Nutrition, Cancer Prevention, Cancer Prevention Internat., Annual Rev. Nutritional Rsch., Nutrition Rsch. Newsletter; contbr. chpts. to books; contbr. over 300 articles to profl. jours. Med. dir. USPHS reserves U.S. Army, 1963. Recipient Future Leader award Nutrition Found., 1968-70, Hull Gold medal AMA, 1970, Recognition award USDA, 2004. Fellow ACP, Am. Soc. Nutrition Scis. (Mead Johson award 1972, fellow 1998); mem. Am. Soc. Clin. Nutrition (various office including pres.), Am. Soc. Nutrition Scis., ACP, Internat. Soc. for Trace Element Rsch. in Humans (pres. 2002-04), Sigma Xi, Alpha Omega Alpha. Avocations: gardening, fishing, reading. Office: U Tex Med Br Ewing Bldg Galveston TX 77555-1109 Office Phone: 409-772-4661. Business E-Mail: hsandste@utmb.edu.

SANDSTROM, DALE VERNON, state supreme court justice; b. Grand Forks, ND, Mar. 9, 1950; s. Ellis Vernon and Hilde Geneva (Williams) S.; m. Gail Hagerty, Mar. 27, 1993; children: Jack, Carrie, Anne. BA, N.D. State U., 1972; JD, U. N.D., 1975. Bar: N.D. 1975, U.S. Dist. Ct. N.D. 1975, U.S. Ct. Appeals (8th cir.) 1976. Asst. atty. gen., chief consumer fraud and antitrust div. State of N.D., Bismarck, 1975-81, securities commr., 1981-83, pub. svc. commr., 1983-92, pres. commn., 1987-91, justice Supreme Ct., 1992—. Chair N.D. Commn. on Cameras in the Courtroom, 1993—, Joint Procedure Com., 1996—; mem. exec. com. N.D. Jud. Conf., 1995—, chair-elect, 1997-99, chair, 1999-2001; mem. Gov.'s Com. on Security and Privacy, Bismarck, 1975-76, Gov.'s Com. on Refugees, Bismarck, 1976; chmn. Gov's Com. on Comml. Air Transp., Bismarck, 1983-84. Mem. platform com. N.D. Reps., 1972, 76, exec. com., 1972-73, 85-88, dist. chmn., 1981-82; former chmn. bd. deacons Luth. Ch.; mem. ch. coun., exec. com., chmn. legal and constl. rev. com. Evang. Luth Ch. Am., 1993—; mem. exec. bd. dirs., No. Lights Coun., dist. chair Boy Scouts Am., 1998-2000. Named Disting. Eagle Scout, Boy Scouts Am., 1997. Mem. ABA, N.D. Bar Assn., Big Muddy Bar Assn., Nat. Assn. Regulatory Utility Commrs. (electricity com.), N.A. Assn. Securities Adminstrs., Order of De Molay (grand master 1994-95, mem. Internat. Supreme coun., Legion of Honor award), Nat. Eagle Scouts Assn. (regent for life), Shriners, Elks, Eagles, Masons (33d degree, chmn. grand youth com. 1979-87, Youth Leadership award 1986), Bruce M. VanSickle Am. Inn of Court (pres. 1999-2001). Office: State ND Supreme Ct Judicial Wing 1st Fl 600 E Boulevard Ave Bismarck ND 58505

SANDSTROM, JAMES E. military career officer; b. Minn., Apr. 1, 1949; m. Jeannie; children: Bret, Kelly. BS in Aero. Engring., USAF Acad., Colo. Springs, 1971; M in Aeronautics and Astronautics, Purdue U., W. Lafayette, Ind., 1972; attended, Squadron Officer Sch.; grad., Air Command & Staff Coll., Maxwell AFB, Ala., 1983, Indsl. Coll. Armed Forces, Fort Lesley J. McNair, Wash. DC, 1988; postgrad., Syracuse U., 1997, Johns Hopkins U., 1997. Commd. 2nd lt. USAF, 1971, student, undergraduate pilot tng., 1972—73, student, F-4 pilot tng., 20th Tactical Fighter Squadron George AFB, Calif., 1973, F-4 pilot and weapons officer, 421st Tactical Fighter Squadron Udorn Royal Thai AFB, Thailand, 1974—75, weapons officerand OV-10 flight comdr., 21st Tactical Air Support Squadron Shaw AFB, SC, 1975—76, F-104 fighter weapons instr. and weapons officer, 69th Tactical Fighter Tng. Squadron Luke AFB, Ariz., 1976—80, F-16 weapons officer and flight comdr., 34th Tactical Fighter Squadron Hill AFB, Utah, 1980—82, project officer, tactics and test directorate, later, chief of standardization and evaluation, 57th fighter weapons wing Nellis AFB, Nev., 1983—85, comdr., 430th Tactial Fighter Squadron, 1985—87, chief current ops. (J31) Hdqrs. US Pacific Command Camp H.M. Smith, Hawaii, 1988-90, dep. comdr. for ops. Tactical Tng. Wing Luke AFB, Ariz., 1990-91, dir. Fighter Tng. and Tactical Hdqrs. Tactical Air Command Langley AFB, Va., 1991-92, comdr. 388th Fighter Wing Hill AFB, Utah, 1992-94, comdr. 23rd Wing Pope AFB, N.C., 1994-95, comdr. 4404th Composite Dhahran, Saudi Arabia, 1994-96, dep. for theater air def., dep. chief plans and ops. hdqrs. Washington, 1996-97, dir. command and control task force, dep. chief staff, 1997, dep. dir. command and control, dep. chief of staff, 1997, dir. command and control, dep. chief of staff air & space, 1997-98, prin. asst. dep. undersec. Air Force for Internat. Affairs, Pentagon, 1998, comdr., 19th Air Force Randolph AFB, Tex., 2002—04, ret., 2004; dir. ops. US Ctrl. Command, MacDill AFB, Fla., 1998—2001, chief of staff, Operation Enduring Freedom, 2001—02; spl. asst. to comdr. Air Edn. anf Tng. Command, Randolph Air Force Base, Tex., 2001—02. Decorated Legion of Merit with oak leaf cluster, Def. Meritorious Svc. medal, Meritorious Svc. medal with oak leaf cluster, Air Force Commendation medal with two oak leaf clusters.*

SANDU, ADRIAN, mathematician, computer scientist, educator; b. Bucharest, Romania, Nov. 28, 1965; came to U.S., 1992; s. Gheorghe and Marioara Sandu; m. Corina S., June 20, 1992; children: Andreea, Monica. BS, MS, Tech. U. Bucharest, 1990; MS, PhD, U. Iowa, 1997. Instr. Tech. U. Bucharest, 1990-92; rsch. assoc. Courant Inst. Math. Scis., N.Y.C., 1997-98; asst. prof. computer sci. Mich. Technol. U., Houghton, 1998—2003, Va. Poly. Inst. and State U., Blacksburg, 2003—. Contbr. articles to profl. jours. Mem. Am. Math. Soc., Soc. Indsl. and Applied Math. Avocations: skiing, rollerskating, camping. Home: 316 Cedar Hill Dr Blacksburg VA 24060 Office: Va Poly Inst and State U Dept Computer Sci Blacksburg VA 24060 Business E-Mail: asandu@cs.vt.edu.

SANDUM, HOWARD E. literary agent; b. Devils Lake, N.D., July 7, 1929; s. Howard E. Sandum and Gladys I. Lien; m. Evangeline M. Olson, May 12, 1955 (dec. Feb. 1972); children: Kyrie L. (dec.), Beret S. Canakes, Rachel S. Tune, Joseph H., Marn S. Turley; m. Marta R. Enebuske, July 28, 1975. BA, St. Olaf Coll., Northfield, Minn., 1951; postgrad., U. Minn., 1954-56, 60-62. Editor trade religion The Macmillan Co., N.Y.C., 1962-63, editor-in-chief Collier Books divsn., 1963-71; editor-in-chief Adult Trade divsn. The World Pub. Co., N.Y.C., 1971-73; dir. office for comm. Luth. Ch. in Am., N.Y.C., 1973-76; editl. dir. The Saunders Press (W.B. Saunders Co.), Phila., 1979-81; editl. dir. Harvest Books Harcourt Brace Jovanovich, N.Y.C. and San Diego, 1982-83; mng. dir. Sandum & Assocs. Lit. Agy., N.Y.C., 1987—. Founder, dir. The Pub. Inst., U. Pa., Phila., 1980-82; dir. pub. info. The Am. Luth. Ch., Mpls., 1960-62; night editor AP, Boise, Idaho, 1956-60. Editor Scandinavian Rev., 1976-78. Lay reader, usher Ch. of Holy Trinity, N.Y.C., 1990—; planning chmn. New St. Peters Lutheran Ch. at Citicorp Ctr., N.Y.C., 1970-78. Capt. USMC, 1952-54, res. Recipient Disting. Alumnus award St. Olaf Coll., 2000. Mem. Met. Mus. Art (sustaining), N.Y. Soc. Libr. Episcopalian. Avocations: cooking, museums, urban walking. Home and Office: Sandum & Assocs a Lit Agy 144 E 84th St New York NY 10028-2004

SANDVIG, SALLY, state legislator; m. Henry David Sandvig; 3 children. Student, N.D. State U. Sales rep. Avon; rep. Dist. 21 N.D. Ho. of Reps., mem. human svc. and govt. and vet. affairs coms. Precinct chmn., dist. sec. Dist. 21, Cass, N.D.; 4-H leader; client coun. mem. LAND; mem. Dem. Women. Soroptimist Internat. Tng. Awards scholar, 1988. Mem. Avon Pres.'s Club. Office: ND Ho of Reps State Capitol Bismarck ND 58505 Address: 201 11th St N Fargo ND 58102-4652

SANDVIK, HELVI, state agency administrator; BS Econs., Kalamazoo Coll.; MBA, U. Alaska. From transportation planner to dep. commr. State of Alaska Dept. Transportation; bd. dirs. Alaska Indsl. Devel. & Export Auth.; pres. NANA Devel. Corp. Office: AIDEA 813 W Northern Lights Blvd Anchorage AK 99503

SANDWEISS, JACK, physicist, researcher; b. Chgo., Aug. 19, 1930; s. Charles Ray and Florence (Hymovitz) S.; m. Letha Ann Boeck, Jan. 16, 1956; children: Daniel Howard, Anne Florence, Benjamin Lewis. Student, UCLA, 1948-50; BS, U. Calif., Berkeley, 1952, PhD, 1957. Research assoc. Radiation Lab., U. Calif., Berkeley, 1957; instr. Yale U., New Haven, 1957-59, asst. prof., 1959-62, assoc. prof., 1962-64, prof. physics, 1964—, Donner prof. physics, 1980—, former chmn. dept. physics. Cons. Brookhaven Nat. Lab., Fermi Nat. Accelerator Lab.; chmn. high energy physics adv. panel Dept. Energy-NSF, 1982-86. Editor Phys. Rev. Letters, 1988—; contbr. articles to profl. jours. Fellow Am. Phys. Soc. (chmn. div. particles and fields 1980); mem. NAS, AAAS. Home: 248 Ogden St New Haven CT 06511-1221 Office: Yale Univ Physics Dept Sloane Physics Lab PO Box 2081-21 New Haven CT 06520-8121 E-mail: sandweiss@hepmail.physics.yale.edu.

SANDWEISS, MARTHA A. author, American studies and history educator; b. St. Louis, Mar. 29, 1954; d. Jerome Wesley and Marilyn Joy (Gilk) S. BA magna cum laude, Radcliffe Coll., 1975; MA in History, Yale U., 1977, MPhil in History, 1981, PhD, 1985. Smithsonian-Nat. Endowment Humanities fellow Nat. Portrait Gallery, Washington, 1975-76; curator photographs Amon Carter Mus., Ft. Worth, 1979-86; adj. curator photographs, 1987-89; dir. Mead Art Mus. Amherst Coll., 1989-97, adj. assoc. prof. of fine arts and Am. studies, 1989-94, assoc. prof. Am. studies, 1994-97, assoc. prof. Am. studies and history, 1997-2000, prof. Am. studies and history, 2000—. Author: Carlotta Corpron: Designer with Light, 1980, Masterworks of American Photography, 1982, Laura Gilpin: An Enduring Grace, 1986, (catalogue) Pictures from an Expedition: Early Views of the American West, 1979, Print the Legend: Photography and the American West, 2002; co-author: Eyewitness to War: Prints and Daguerreotypes of the Mexican War, 1989; editor: Historic Texas: A Photographic Portrait, 1986, Contemporary Texas: A Photographic Portrait, 1986, Denizens of the Desert, 1988, Photography in Nineteenth Century America, 1991; co-editor: Oxford History of the American West, 1994. Fellow Ctr. for Am. Art and Material Cultures, Yale U., 1977-79, NEH, 1988, 2000-01, Am. Coun. Learned Socs., 1996-97, Weatherhead, 2000-2001. Office: Amherst Coll Am Studies Dept Box 2225 Amherst MA 01002-5000

SANDY, JOHN A. political organization administrator, state legislator; b. Twin Falls, Idaho, June 8, 1948; m. Robin Sandy; 1 child, Alex McConnell. BS in Agr., U. Idaho. Farmer; apptd. senator, dist. 22 Idaho Senate, Boise, 1995-98, elected senator, dist. 22, 1998—. Mem. agrl. affairs, state affairs, edn., and transp. coms. Idaho state Rep. 1st vice chair, 1992-98; chmn. Idaho Republican Party, 2002-. Republican. Methodist. Office: State Capitol PO Box 83720 Boise ID 83720-3720

SANDY, LEWIS GORDON, physician, healthcare executive; b. Detroit, July 18, 1958; s. William Haskell and Marjorie Mindel (Mazor) S.; m. Kathleen Anne Morgan, June 17, 1984; children: Matthew, Natalie, Jonah. BS, U. Mich., 1979, MD, 1982; MBA, Stanford U., 1988. Diplomate Am. Bd. Internal Medicine, Nat. Bd. Med. Examiners. Intern Beth Israel Hosp., Boston, 1982-83, resident, 1983-85; Robert Wood Johnson clin. scholar U. Calif., San Francisco, 1985-86, clin. fellow in medicine, 1986-88; instr. Harvard Med. Sch., 1988-91; assoc. chief internal medicine Harvard Community Health Plan, Boston, 1988-89, dir. Health Ctr., 1989-91; v.p. Robert Wood Johnson Found., Princeton, NJ, 1991—96, exec. v.p., 1997—2003, United Healthcare, Edina, Minn., 2003—; clin. assoc. prof. medicine U. Medicine and Dentistry NJ/Robert Wood Johnson Med. Sch., 1991—. Cons. Kaiser Found. Health Plan, Oakland, Calif., 1987-88. Fellow ACP; mem. APHA, AMA, Am. Coll. Physician Execs., N.J. Med. Soc., Middlesex County Med. Soc., N.J. Acad. Medicine, Soc. Gen. Internal Medicine, Alpha Omega Alpha. Office: 5901 Lincoln Dr Edina MN 55436 Home: 6711 Indian Hills Rd Edina MN 55439-1069

SANDY, ROBERT EDWARD, JR., lawyer; b. Libertyville, Ill., Feb. 16, 1943; s. Robert Edward and Elizabeth Ann (Carroll) S.; m. Joan Mary Phillips, Apr. 19, 1969; children: Mary Rosanne Phillips-Sandy, John Robert Phillips-Sandy. AB, Harvard U., 1965; JD, U. Chgo., 1968. Bar: Mass. 1969, Maine 1972, U.S. Dist. Ct. Mass. 1970, U.S. Dist. Ct. Maine 1972, U.S. Ct. Appeals (1st cir.) 1994, U.S. Supreme Ct. 1980. Atty. Boston Redevel. Authority, 1969-72; ptnr. Sandy and Sandy, Waterville, Maine, 1972-83, Sherman and Sandy, Waterville, 1983-87; sr. ptnr. Sherman & Sandy, Waterville, 1987—. Mem. Waterville Bar Assn., Maine Bar Assn., Maine Trial Lawyers Assn., ABA. Avocations: boating, skiing, community theater, Maine Internat. Film Festival,. Home: 9 Cleveland Pl Waterville ME 04901 Office: Sherman & Sandy 74 Silver St Waterville ME 04901-6524 Office Phone: 207-872-7727. E-mail: info@shermanandsandy.com.

SANDY, STEPHEN, writer, educator; b. Aug. 2, 1934; s. Alan Francis and Evelyn Brown (Martin) S.; m. Virginia Scoville, 1969; children: Nathaniel Merrill, Clare Scoville. AB, Yale U., 1955; AM, Harvard U., 1958, PhD, 1963. Instr. Harvard U., 1963-67; vis. prof. U. Tokyo, 1967-68; asst. prof. Brown U., Providence, 1968-69; mem. faculty Bennington (Vt.) Coll., 1969—2002; McGee prof. writing Davidson (N.C.) Coll., 1994. Lectr. U. R.I., 1969; prof. Summer Sch. Harvard U., 1986, 87, 88; poetry workshop dir. Chautauqua Instn., 1975, 77, Johnson (Vt.) State Coll., 1976, 77, Bennington Coll., 1978-80, 89, Bennington Writing Seminars Program, 1994-96, Wesleyan Writers Conf., 1981. Author: Stresses in the Peaceable Kingdom, 1967, Roofs, 1971, End of the Picaro, 1977, The Hawthorne Effect, 1980, The Raveling of the Novel: Studies in Romantic Fiction from Walpole to Scott, 1980, Riding to Greylock, 1983, To a Mantis, 1987, Man in the Open Air, 1988, The Epoch, 1990, Thanksgiving Over the Water, 1992; translator: Seneca's Hercules Oetaeus, 1995, Vale of Academe A Prose Poem for Bernard Malamud, 1996, Marrow Spoon, 1997, Aeschylus's Seven Against Thebes, 1998, The Thread, New and Selected Poems, 1998, Black Box, 1999, Surface Impressions:A Poem, 2002. Councillor English Harvard Grad. Soc. Coun., 1969-74. With U.S. Army, 1955-57. Recipient Fulbright postdoctoral award, 1967-68; Dexter fellow, 1961, Yaddo fellow, 1963-68, 76, 93, 97, 98, 00, 02, Invited Poetry fellow Breadloaf Writers Conf., 1968, Ingram Merrill Found. fellow, 1985, MacDowell Colony fellow, 1986, 93, Blue Mt. Ctr. fellow, 1985, 88, Creative Writing fellow Nat. Endowment Arts, 1988, Vt. Coun. Arts fellow, 1988—, Sr. fellow Provincetown Fine Arts Work Ctr., 1998, Rockefeller Found. residency Bellagio Study and conf. ctr., 2001, Huber Found. grantee, 1973, Vt. Coun. Arts grantee, 1974; nominee for Pulitzer Prize, 1971; named Phi Beta Kappa Poet, Brown U., 1969, Yale U., 2003. Mem. Signet Soc., Elizabethan Club.

SANDY, WILLIAM HASKELL, training and communication systems executive; b. N.Y.C., Apr. 28, 1929; s. Fred and Rose S.; m. Marjorie Mazor, June 15, 1952; children: Alan, Lewis, Barbara. AB, U. Md., 1950, JD, 1953; postgrad. Advanced Mgmt. program, Harvard Bus. Sch., 1970-71. Bar: Md. 1953. From planner-writer to acct. supr. Jam-Handy Orgn., Detroit, 1953-64, v.p., 1964-69, sr. v.p., 1969-71; pres. Sandy Corp., Troy, Mich., 1971-88, chmn., 1988-96; pres. Rudgate Corp., Bloomfield Hills, Mich., 1996—. Author: Forging the Productivity Partnership, 1990. Bd. govs. Northwood Inst., 1976-80; bd. dirs. Cranbrook Sci. Inst., Met. Ctr. High Tech., 1993, Birmingham (Mich.) Cmty. House, 1997-2003, Mich. Opera Theatre; pres. Graphic Arts Coun., 1992-93; trustee Detroit Inst. Arts, 1992-93; v.p. nat. exec. coun. Harvard Bus. Sch., 1985-89; mem. Bloomfield Hills Zoning Bd., Walsh Coll. Leader in Residence, Pres.'s Adv. Coun.; mayor City of Bloomfield Hills, 1996-97; mem. Troy Downtown Devel. Authority, 1996-99; Inst. for Humanities trustee U. Mich.; adv. bd. U. Mich. Mem. ASTD, Am. Mktg. Assn. (pres. Detroit chpt. 1975), Nat. Found. Am. Mktg. Assn (bd. dirs. 1998), S.E. Mich. BBB (bd. dirs. 1999), Adcraft Club, Nat. Assn. Ednl. Broadcasters, Harvard Bus. Sch. Club (pres. Detroit chpt. 1983-85), The Hundred Club. Home: 596 Rudgate Rd Bloomfield Hills MI 48304-3355 Home (Winter): 535 Sanctuary Dr B404 Longboat Key FL 34228-3852 E-mail: sandyfamily@aol.com.

SANETO, RUSSELL PATRICK, pediatric neurologist, epileptologist, neurobiologist; b. Burbank, Calif., Oct. 10, 1950; s. Arthur and Mitzi (Seddon) S.; m. Kathleen D. Saneto. BS with honors, San Diego State U., 1972, MS, 1975; PhD, U. Tex. Med. Br., 1981; DO, U. Osteo. Medicine and Surgery, 1994. Tchg. asst. San Diego State U., 1969-75; substitute tchr. Salt Lake City Sch. Dist., 1975; tchg. and rsch. asst. U. Tex. Med. Br., 1976-77, NIH predoctoral fellow, 1977-81, postdoctoral fellow, 1981; Jeanne B. Kempner postdoctoral fellow UCLA, 1981-82, NIH postdoctoral fellow, 1982-87; asst. prof. divsn. neurosci. Oreg. Regional Primate Rsch. Ctr., Beaverton, 1987-89; asst. prof. dept. cell biology and anatomy Oreg. Health Scis. U., Portland, 1988-90, U. Osteo. Medicine and Surgery, 1991-94, Cleve. Clinic, 1994-2001; asst. prof. neurology and pediatrics U. Wash. Children's Hosp. and Regional Med. Ctr., Seattle, 2001—. Lectr. rsch. methods Grad. Sch., 1982; vis. scholar in ethics So. Bapt. Theol. Sem., Louisville, 1981; sci. advisor United Mitochondrial Disease Found. Contbr. articles to profl. jours. Recipient Merit award Nat. March of Dimes, 1978; named one of Outstanding Young Men in Am., 1979, 81, one of Men of Significance, 1985. Mem. AAAS, Am. Acad. Pediats., Am. Acad. Neurology, Am. Epilepsy Soc., Bread for World, Winter Confs. Brain Rsch., Neuroscis. Study Program, N.Y. Acad. Scis., Am. Soc. Neurochemistry, Soc. Neurosci., Sigma Sigma Phi. Democrat. Mem. Evangelical Free Ch. Office: Childrens Hosp and Regional Med Ctr Neurology 5D-4 4800 Sand Point Way NE Seattle WA 98105 E-mail: russ.saneto@seattlechildrens.org.

SANETTI, STEPHEN LOUIS, lawyer; b. Flushing, N.Y., June 25, 1949; s. Alfred Julius Sanetti and Yolanda Marie (DiGioia) Boyes; m. Carole Leighton Koller, Sept. 21, 1974; children: Christopher Edward, Dana Harrison. BA in History with honors, Va. Mil. Inst., 1971; JD, Washington and Lee U., 1974. Bar: Conn. 1975, U.S. Ct. Mil. Appeals 1975, U.S. Dist. Ct. Conn. 1978, U.S. Ct. Appeals (2d cir.) 1979, U. S. Supreme Ct. 1980. Litigation atty. Marsh, Day & Calhoun, Bridgeport, Conn., 1978-80; gen. counsel Sturm, Ruger & Co., Southport, Conn., 1980—, v.p., 1993-2000, also bd. dirs., 1998-2000, vice chmn., sr. exec. v.p., 2000—03, pres., COO, 2003—. Dir. Product Liability Adv. Coun., 1988-2002; tech. advisor Assn. Firearm and Toolmark Examiners; chmn. Legis. and Legal Affairs com. Sporting Arms and Ammunition Mfrs. Inst., 1993-2001; bd. govs. Nat. Shooting Sports Found., 2002-. Served to capt., chief criminal law 1st Cavalry Div. Staff Judge Advocate, U.S. Army, 1975-78. Mem. Am. Acad. Forensic Sci., Def. Rsch. Inst. Republican. Roman Catholic. Office: Sturm Ruger & Co Inc 1 Lacey Pl Southport CT 06490-1241

SANFELICI, ARTHUR H(UGO), editor, writer; b. Haledon, N.J., May 23, 1934; s. Hugo and Anna (Schilder) S.; m. Betty Louise Van Riper, Aug. 10, 1957; children: Brian Arthur, Amy Elizabeth, Gary Hugh, Bruce Richard. Attended, Lehigh U., 1952-55. Assoc. editor Flying Mag., N.Y.C., 1961-64; mng. editor Am. Aviation Mag., Washington, 1964-68; dist. sales mgr. Gates Learjet Co., N.Y.C., 1969-71; exec. editor Airport World Mag., Westport, Conn., 1971-74; spl. project editor Aircraft Owners & Pilots Assn., Washington, 1974-75, mng. editor Pilot mag., 1975-79, editor AOPA Newsletter, AOPAirport Report, Gen. Aviation Nat. Report, 1979-88; pub. cons., 1989-90; sr. editor Flight Safety Found., Washington, 1989-92; editor S-Cubed divsn. Maxwell Labs., Alexandria, Va., 1992-95; comms. dir. Helicopter Assn. Internat., Alexandria, 1996-97; editor Shooting Sports USA, 1997-98. Editor, compiler: Yesterday's Wings; Editor Aviation History Mag., Leesburg, Va., 1990—; author: 135 Ways to Get Even With Your Kids, 2003. Pilot USAF, 1955—60. Mem. Nat. Aeronautic Assn., Aero Club of Washington, Soc. Aerospace Comms. Home: 5 Oak Shade Rd Sterling VA 20164-1163

SANFELIPPO, PETER MICHAEL, cardiac, thoracic and vascular surgeon; b. Milw., Nov. 1, 1938; s. Michael L. and Genevieve M. (Gagliano) S.; m. Cecelia Monica Reuss, May 25, 1968. MD, Marquette U., Milw., 1965; MS in Surgery, U. Minn., 1976. Diplomate Am. Bd. Surgery, Am. Bd. Thoracic Surgery, Am. Bd. Gen. Vascular Surgery. Intern Sacred Heart Hosp., Spokane, Wash., 1965-66; gen. surgery fellow Mayo Grad. Sch. Medicine, Rochester, Minn., 1966, 69-73; residency in thoracic surgery USAF Med. Ctr., Lackland AFB, Tex., 1973-75; thoracic surgeon USAF Med. Corps, various locations, 1966-78; pvt. practice cardiac, thoracic and vascular surgery Ohio Heart & Thoracic Surgery Ctr., Columbus, 1978-91; prof. cardiothoacic and vascular surgery U. Tex. Health Ctr., Tyler, Tex., 1991—. Contbr. articles to profl. jours. Lt. col. USAF, 1966-78. Decorated Air Force Commendation medal. Fellow ACS, Am. Coll. Cardiology, Am. Coll. Angiology, Am. Coll. Chest Physicians; mem. AMA. Avocations: scouting, camping, photography, gardening.

SANFILIPPO, ALFRED PAUL, dean, medical educator, pathologist; b. Racine, Wis., Aug. 30, 1949; s. Paul Joseph and Therese (Rhode) Sanfilippo; m. Janet Lee Thompson, 1973; children: Lisa, Joseph. Student, Max Planck Inst. Exptl. Medicine, Gottingen, Germany, 1966—68; BA in Physics, MS in Physics, U. Pa., 1970; PhD in immunology, Duke U., 1975, MD, 1976. Diplomate Am. Bd. Pathology, lic. physician NC, Md. Intern in anatomic pathology Duke U. Hosp., 1976—77, resident in anatomic and clin. pathology, 1977—79, postdoctoral rschr. divsn. tumor virology dept. surgery, 1976—79; asst. prof. pathology and exptl. surgery, lectr. immunology Duke U., 1979—84, from assoc. prof. to prof. pathology, 1984—93, from assoc. prof. to prof. exptl. surgery, 1985—93, prof. immunology, 1990—93; attending pathologist Duke U. and Durham VA Hosps., 1979—93; staff mem. Duke Surg. Pvt. Diagnostic Clinic, 1979—93; dir. Transplantation Lab Durham VA Hosp., 1979—93; dir. immunopathology Duke U. Med. Ctr., 1982—93, exec. com. dept. pathology, 1989—91; Baxley Prof. and chair pathology dept. John's Hopkins U., Balt., 1993—2000; pathologist-in-chief Johns Hopkins Hosp., Balt., 1993—2000; sr. v.p. health scis., dean. coll. medicine & pub. health Ohio State U., Columbus, 2000—, exec. dean health scis., 2004—. Mem. Duke Comprehensive Cancer Ctr., 1979—93; dir. rsch. Johns Hopkins Comprehensive Transplant Ctr.; mem. Third Frontier Commn. Adv. Bd., Ohio, 2004—; cons. Battelle Human Affairs Rsch. Ctrs., Seattle, 1985—93, NSF of

Switzerland, 1992—93, numerous US govt. adv. coms.; mem. editl. bd. Transplantation, 1985—, Pathobiology, 1989—, Transplantation Now, Japan, 1989—, Pathology, Rsch. and Practice, 1990—, Human Immunology, 1992—, Lab. Investigation, 1993—, Xeno, 1994—, Virchows Archiv, 1998—, Transplant Immunology; reviewer Am. Jour. Kidney Diseases, Am. Jour. Ophthalmology, Am. Jour. Pathology, New Eng. Jour. Medicine, Jour. of AMA, Jour. Am. Soc. Nephrology, Jour. Clin. Investigation, Jour. Leukocyte Biology, Kidney Internat., others; contbr. numerous articles to prof. jours.; speaker and presenter in field. Bd. trustees Omeris, Columbus, Ohio, 2004—. Recipient Kermit G. Osserman Award, Myasthenia Gravis Found., 1976, Wiley D. Forbus Award, NC Soc. Pathologists, 1979, Reach for Sight Physician Investigator Award, 1990; grantee numerous, NIH. Fellow: Am. Soc. Clin. Pathologists (coun. on edn. and rsch. 1994—96); mem.: Southeastern Organ Procurement Found. (exec. com 1992—97, sec. 1992—93, treas. 1993—94, v.p. 1994—95, pres. 1995—96), Assn. for Rsch. in Vision and Ophthalmology, Am. Soc. Nephrology, Am. Soc. Transplant Physicians (pres. 1985—86), Am. Soc. Histocompatibility and Immunogenetics, Transplantation Soc., US-Can. Acad. Pathology, Am. Assn. Med. Colls., Am. Assn. Immunologists, AMA, Am. Soc. Investigative Pathology (pres. 2002—03), Intersociety Pathology Coun., Assn. Pathology Chairs (sr. fellow), Am. Soc. Transplantation (past pres.), Alpha Omega Alpha. Office: Office Dean Ohio State U Coll Medicine 370 W 9th Ave 200 A Meiling Columbus OH 43210*

SANFILIPPO, JOSEPH SALVATORE, physician, reproductive endocrinologist, educator; b. Bklyn., Feb. 21, 1948; s. Joseph Philip and Elena Teresa (Canepa) S.; m. Patricia M. Cantwell, June 21, 1974; children: Angela, Andrea, Luke. BS, St. John's U., NYC, 1969; MD, Chgo. Med. Sch., 1973. Diplomate Am. Bd. Ob-Gyn., spl. qualification in reproductive endocrinology. Intern Mil. County Gen. Hosp.; resident in ob-gyn. SUNY Upstate Med. Ctr., Syracuse; instr. dept. ob-gyn. U. Louisville Sch. Medicine, 1977—79, asst. prof., 1979—83, assoc. prof., 1983—89, prof., 1989—97, dir. divsn. reproductive endocrinology, 1993—97; James and Marilyn Gilmore prof. ob-gyn. MCP Hahnemann Sch. Medicine, 1998—2001; vice chmn. reproductive sci. Magee-Women's Hosp., Pitts., 2001—; chmn. ob-gyn. Alleghney Gen. Hosp., 1998—2001; prof. ob-gyn. and reproductive sci. U. Pitts. Sch. Medicine, 2001—. Pres. med. staff Alliant Health System/Norton Hosp. and Alliant Med. Pavilion, Louisville, 1994—; dir. gynecology Kosair-Children's Hosp., Louisville, 1979—. Editor: Risk Management for Healthcare Professionals, 2001, MBA Handbook for Healthcare Professionals, 2002; editor-in-chief: Jour. Pediat. Adolescent Gynecology, 1989—. Named Disting. Alumnus, Chgo. Med. Sch., 1990. Fellow: N.Am. Soc. for Pediat. Adolescent Gynecology (exec. dir.), Am. Soc. for Reproductive Medicine (v.p.); mem.: ACOG (chair gynecol. prolog fifth edit.). Avocations: jogging, boating, fishing, amateur radio. Office: Univ Pitts Sch Medicine Dept Ob-gyn and Reproductive Scis 300 Halket St Pittsburgh PA 15213-3180 Office Phone: 412-641-1204. Business E-Mail: jsanfilippo@mail.magee.edu.

SANFILIPPO, MARY HELENA, nun; b. Buffalo, N.Y. BA in History, San Francisco Coll. Women, 1957; MA in History, U. San Francisco, 1967; PhD in History, U. Notre Dame, 1972. Cert. tchr. Calif. Tchr. various elem. and h.s., Calif., 1950-66; governing coun. Sisters of Mercy, Burlingame, Calif., 1972-74, archivist, 1977-87; acad. dean Russell Coll., Burlingame, 1974-82; educator King Coll., Bristol, Tenn., 1988-90, Va. Intermont Coll., 1989-90; founder, exec. dir. Tri-County (Free) Health Clinic, Richlands, Va., 1989-95; educator U. San. Francisco, 1996, Chabot/Los Positas C.C. Dist., Hayward/Livermore, Calif., 1996—; devel. dir. Mercy Retirement and Care Ctr., Oakland, Calif., 1997—2002. Author: Inward Wealth and Outward Splendor: New England Transcendentalists View the Roman Catholic Church, 1987. Bd. dirs. Cath. Healthcare West-S.W., 1995—, Tri-County Health Clinic, Richlands, Va., 1991-95, Assn. Free Clinics, Va., 1993-95, Mercy Hosp. and Med. Ctr., San Diego, 1982-88, St. Rose Hosp., Hayward, Calif., 1981-87, Soc. Calif. Archivists, 1981-85, Mercy H.S., Burlingame, Calif., 1980-84, St. Mary's Hosp. and Med. Ctr., San Francisco, 1974-77, Mercy Retirement & Care Ctr., Oakland, Calif., 1974-77; bd. dirs. United Way of S.W. Va., Lebanon, 1993-95; cmty. outreach vol. SHARE, HelpLine, Mercy Project, Food Bank, Meals on Wheels, Water Project of Clinch Valley, Va., 1987-95. Recipient Outstanding Vol. Svc. award, Appalachian Agy. Sr. Citizens, 1995, Disting. Citizen of Yr. award, Richlands Area C. of C., 1994, Outstanding Citizen award, Woodmen of the World, 1994, Cmty. Builder's awards, Masons, 1992, 93, Gov.'s Gold award for volunteering excellence, Commonwealth of Va., 1992. Mem. Orgn. of Am. Historians. Roman Catholic. Avocations: volunteering, travel, crossword puzzles, reading, choral singing. E-mail: helenarsm@yahoo.com.

SANFILIPPO, STEPHEN NICHOLAS, retired secondary school educator; b. Bklyn., Sept. 27, 1948; s. Niccolo Sanfilippo and Ottilie Fredericka Nalbach; m. Susan Margaretha Joyce, June 20, 1970. BS in Edn. and History, Northeast Mo. State U., 1970; postgrad., Old Dominion U., 1971-74; MA in Liberal Studies, SUNY, Stony Brook, 1997, MA in History, 2002. Tchr. history Longwood Sr. H.S., Mid. Island, NY, 1974—2003; ret., 2003. Advisor Colonial-Am. Music, East Hampton (N.Y.) Hist. Soc., 1996—; interpreter music of the Whitman era, Walt Whitman Birth Place Assn., Huntington, N.Y., 1988—. Host Sta. WUSB-FM, Stony Brook, N.Y., 1980—. With USN, 1970-74. Mem. L.I. Coun. Social Studies, L.I. Traditional Music Assn. (pres. 1981-83), Suffolk County Hist. Soc., SUNY Italian Cultural Studies Ctr. Democrat. Roman Catholic. Avocations: bird watching, camping, canoeing, folk music and folk musical instruments, hand puppeteer. Home: 113 Woodlot Rd Ridge NY 11961-1938 Office: Longwood Sr HS 100 Longwood Rd Middle Island NY 11953 E-mail: ssanfili@longwoodcsd.com.

SANFORD, BILL R. medical products executive; BS, Kans. State U. Pres., CEO Steris Corp., Mentor, Ohio, 1987—, also chmn. bd. dirs. Bd. dirs. Key Corp., Cleve. Clinic Found., Edison Biotechnology Ctr., Primus Ventur Ptnrs., neuroControl Corp., BIOMEC, Inc., Cleve. Tomorrow, Case Western Res. U., Health Industries Mfrs. Assn. Office: 5960 Heisley Rd Mentor OH 44060-1834 Fax: 440-639-4457.

SANFORD, BRUCE WILLIAM, lawyer; b. Massena, N.Y., Aug. 5, 1945; s. Doris (Suhrland) Sanford; m. Marilou Green, May 17, 1980; children: Ashley Anne, Barrett William. BA, Hamilton Coll., 1967; JD, NYU, 1970. Bar: N.Y. 1970, Ohio 1971, D.C. 1981, Md. 1985. Staff reporter Wall St. Jour., 1966-67; assoc. Baker and Hostetler, Washington, 1971-79, ptnr., 1979—. Author: Sanford's Synopsis Law of Libel and Privacy, rev. edit., 1991, Libel and Privacy, 2nd edit., 1991, Don't Shoot the Messenger: How Our Growing Hatred of the Media Threatens Free Speech for All of Us, 1999. Trustee Nat. Symphony Orch. Assn.; bd. dirs. Thomas Jefferson 1st Amendment Ctr., U. Va., Charlottesville; pres. Washington Nat. Cathedral Assn., 2002--. Mem. ABA (governing bd., forum com. on communication law, chmn. defamation torts com. 1985-86). Office: Baker & Hostetler LLP 1050 Connecticut Ave NW Washington DC 20036-5304

SANFORD, DAVID BOYER, writer, editor; b. Denver, Mar. 4, 1943; s. Filmore Bowyer and Alice Irene (Peterson) S. BA with honors, U. Denver, 1964; MS in Journalism with honors, Columbia U., 1965. With New Republic mag., Washington, 1965-76, mng. editor, 1970-76, Politics Today (formerly Skeptic), Santa Barbara, Calif., 1976-78, contbg. editor, 1978-79; editorial writer Los Angeles Herald Examiner, 1978-79; mng. editor Harper's mag., N.Y.C., 1979-80; editor Wall St. Jour. mag., 1980-81; sr. spl. writer Wall Street Jour., 1981—. Syndicated columnist, 1970-71; commentator Can. Broadcasting Corp., 1967-76; judge Heywood Broun award Newspaper Guild, 1971; mem. print screening com. Champion-Tuck awards, 1985, 86, Judge Wuxtry award, 1990. Author: Who Put the Con in Consumer?, 1972, Me and Ralph, 1976; editor, co-author: Hot War on the Consumer, 1970. Recipient Sackett Law prize, Columbia, 1965, Eckenberg prize, 1965, Gold award, N.Y. Art Dirs. Club, 1977, Wuxtry award for disting. achievement in headline writing, Internat. Soc. for Gen. Semantics, 1989, Pulitzer prize, 1997, Sci.-in-Soc. award, Nat. Assn. Sci. Writers, 1997; Centennial scholar, 1960—64, N.Y. Newspaper Guild fellow, 1964—65. Mem. Phi Beta Kappa, Omicron Delta Kappa. Democrat. Home: 118 Prospect Park W Brooklyn NY 11215-4270 E-mail: david.sanford@wsj.com.

SANFORD, DAVID HAWLEY, philosophy educator; b. Detroit, Dec. 13, 1937; s. Hawley Seager and Alice Katherine (Brown) S.; m. Anne Irene Zeleney, July 10, 1965; children: Daria Margaret, Katherine Eugenia. Student, Oberlin Coll., 1955-57; BA, Wayne State U., 1960; PhD, Cornell U., 1966. Instr., asst. prof. philosophy Dartmouth Coll., Hanover, N.H., 1963-70; assoc. prof. Duke U., Durham, N.C., 1970-78, prof., 1978—, chmn. dept., 1986-89. Vis. faculty U. Oreg., U. Mich., Dalhousie U. Author: If P, then Q: Conditionals and the Foundations of Reasoning, 1989, paperback edit., 1992, 2d edit., 2003; contbr. articles to profl. jours. Samuel S. Fells fellow, 1962-63, NEH fellow, 1974-75, 82-83, 89-90, Nat. Humanities Ctr. fellow, 1989-90 Mem. Am. Philos. Assn. (exec. com. Eastern div. 1979-81), N.C. Philos. Soc. (pres. 1983-85), Soc. for Philosophy and Psychology, Phi Beta Kappa. Home: 2227 Cranford Rd Durham NC 27705-1007 Office: Duke Univ Dept Philosophy PO Box 90743 Durham NC 27708-0743 Address: PO Box 575 Truro MA 02666-0575 E-mail: dhs@duke.edu.

SANFORD, ERIC, lawyer; b. Potsdam, N.Y., July 11, 1951; s. Gerald Ernest Sanford and Annabelle Esther Slater; m. Janis Desmond, Oct. 9, 1977 (div. Feb. 1984); 1 child, Janine. BS in Econ., Ariz. State U., 1993; JD, Stanford U., 1996. Bar: N.Y. 1997. Co-owner Redwood Constrn. Inc., Phoenix, 1986-88; legal asst. Charles P. Franklin, P.C., Tempe, Ariz., 1990-91; rsch. asst. Econ. Analysis Corp., Tempe, 1992-93; summer assoc. Comptroller of Currency, Washington, 1994; assoc. Cadwalader, Wickersham & Taft, N.Y.C., 1996-99, Milbank, Tweed, Hadley & McCloy LLP, N.Y.C., 1999—. Exec. editor Stanford Law Rev., 1995-96. Student Found. Leadership scholar Ariz. State U. Student Found., 1992; Turken Found. scholar Sam and Ida Turken Found., 1992. Mem. ABA, Phi Beta Kappa. Avocations: bicycling, travel, computers, skiing, reading. Office: 1 Chase Manhattan Plz New York NY 10005-1401

SANFORD, GLENDA LEVONNE, educational administrator; b. Mpls., Apr. 3, 1935; d. Robert Emmanuel and Stella Glendora (Larson) Carlson; m. Reed Ellis Sanford, June 17, 1955 (div. June 1979); children: Kenneth, Paul, Sheryl Sanford Vanscoy; m. Vernon Edward Almlie, Aug. 12, 1995; stepchildren: Jurgan, William, Ann Almlie Iglehart. AA, U. Minn., 1955; BA, Moorhead (Minn.) State U., 1979; MS, N.D. State U., 1986. Bus. office mgr. U. Minn. Health Svc., Mpls., 1955-58; office mgr. Reed E. Sanford Inc., Fargo, 1958-77; exec. dir. YWCA of Fargo-Moorhead, 1979-85; owner, mgr. farm and rental properties, Fargo, 1981-89; pres. Sanford Money Mgmt. Inc., Fargo, 1987—; program coord. Early Childhood Tracking Sys. State of N.D., Bismarck, 1989-98; spl. pub. adminstr. Cass County, Fargo, 1988-89; tax preparer H&R Block, Fargo, 1999—. Spkr. Women in Leadership N.D. State U. and KFME, Fargo, 1975-76; advisor N.D. Office Vol. Svcs., Bismarck, 1984-86. Mem. bds. YWCA, LWV, AAUW, Fargo, 1989-92; pres., treas. Jr. League Fargo-Moorhead, 1971-75; pres., bd. mem. Hot Line, Inc., Fargo, 1970-76, United Way of Cass County, Fargo, 1983, N.D. Dental Aux., Fargo, 1975-77; del. White House Conf. on Family, L.A., 1981. Recipient Women Helping Women award Soroptimist Internat., Moorhead, 1984. Mem. AAUW, LWV (treas. 1990-92), Women's Polit. Caucus (fundraising chair 1989-94), N.D. Mental Health Assn. Republican. Lutheran. Avocation: reading. Home and Office: 2101 10th St S Fargo ND 58103-5307

SANFORD, JAMES KENNETH, public relations executive; b. Clyde, N.C., Jan. 23, 1932; s. James Edward S. and Bernice (Crawford) Peebles; m. Judith Bullard Longshore, 2001; children: Timothy, Scott, Jeannette. AA, Mars Hill (N.C.) Coll., 1952; AB, U. N.C., 1954, MA, 1958. Pub. rels. officer Asheville (N.C.) United Appeal, 1954; reporter, copy editor Winston-Salem (N.C.) Jour., 1957-59, asst. state editor, 1959-61, news editor, 1961-63, editorial writer, 1963-64; dir. pub. info. and publs. U. N.C., Charlotte, 1964-94; pub. rels. cons. Charlotte, N.C., 1994—. Cons. Commn. on Future of Mars Hill Coll., 1990-91, City of Charlotte, 1991. Author: Charlotte and UNC Charlotte: Growing Up Together, 1996, Building Future From the Past: The History of Gaston College 1964-99, 1999; co-author: Fifty Favored Years, 1972; contbg. author: The North Carolina Century: Tar Heels Who Made a Difference, 1900-2000, 2002; contbr. numerous articles to mag. and newspapers. Mem. attractions com. Charlotte Conv. and Visitors Bur., 1994; pres. elect Internat. House, 2001-2002, adv. com. Sta. WTVI Pub. TV, Charlotte, 1986-94; chmn. bd. deacons local ch., 1994-95; mem. gen. bd. Bapt. State Conv. of N.C., 2000-2003; mem. Coun. on Christian Higher Edn., 2000-2003; pres. Mars Hill Coll. Nat. Alumni Bd., 2001. Elected to N.C. Pub. Rels. Hall of Fame, 1995; recipient Alumnus by Choice award U. N.C. at Charlotte, 1996. Fellow Pub. Rels. Soc. Am. (chmn. S.E. dist. 1991); mem. Coll. News Assn. Carolinas (Lewis Gaston award 1982), Charlotte Pub. Rels. Soc. (pres. 1974, Infinity award 1986), Coun. for Advancement and Support Edn. (asst. dist. chmn. 1975-76), Phi Kappa Phi. Baptist. Avocations: writing, hiking, photography. Home and Office: 74 Fairway Rdg Lake Wylie SC 29710-9209 Office Phone: 803-831-2999.

SANFORD, JAMES L. science administrator; BA in Indsl. Mgmt., Mich. State U.; MBA, Utah State U. Mgr. contracts and pricing B-2 divsn. Northrop Grumman Corp, LA, 1985—88, asst. treas., corp. dir. banking and internat. fin., 1988—96, v.p. contracts and pricing, 1996—2003, corp. v.p., treas., 2003—. Bd. vis. Def. Acquisition U. Mem.: Treasury Mgmt. Assn. (cert. cash mgr.), Aerospace Industries Assn. (chmn. procurement and fin. exec. com.). Office: Northrop Grumman Corp 1840 Century Park E Los Angeles CA 90067-2199

SANFORD, JO ANNE, state agency administrator; b. Laurinburg, N.C., Oct. 18, 1950; m. William E. Brewer, Jr.; 1 child, Charlotte Brewer. BA Polit. Sci., N.C. State U., 1972; JD, U. N.C. Sch. Law, 1975. Spl. deputy atty. gen. N.C. Atty. Gen.'s Office, 1975—95; chair N.C. Utilities Commn., Raleigh, 1995—2001; bd. dirs. USAC, 2001—. Apptd. to N.Am. Numbering Coun. FCC; bd. dirs. Nat. Regulatory Rsch. Inst. Master: N.C. Bar Assn.; mem.: Women Execs. in State Govt., Wake County Bar Assn. Office: 4325 Mail Svc Ctr Raleigh NC 27699-4325

SANFORD, JOHN JOSEPH, lawyer, director; b. Providence, Sept. 24, 1944; s. Albert C. and Helen (Regan) S.; m. Claire Louise Hosinski, July 19, 1969; children: Ellen, Mary, Martha, Anna. BS, USAF, 1966; JD cum laude, Suffolk U., 1973. Bar: Maine 1973, Mass. 1973, U.S. Dist. Ct. Maine 1973. Ptnr. Harmon, Jones, Sanford & Elliott, Camden, Maine, 1973—. Vis. lectr. Law Sch., Harvard U., Cambridge, Mass., 1978—; dir. Wayfarer Marine Corp., Camden, Maine, 1997—. Chmn. bd. trustees Camden Cmty. Hosp., 1983-84, N.E. Health, Rockport, Maine, 1984-86; trustee Camden Area YMCA, 1975-78, Camden Pub. Libr., pres., 1996-2001. Capt. USAF, 1966-70, Vietnam. Mem. ABA, ATLA, Maine Bar Assn., Maine Trial Lawyers Assn., Camden Squash Club. Roman Catholic. Home: Harbor Rd Camden ME 04843 Office: Harmon Jones Sanford & Elliott 20 Mechanic St Camden ME 04843-1707 E-mail: jsanford@mint.net.

SANFORD, KENNETH RICHARD, small business owner; b. Sparta, Wis., June 15, 1951; s. Richard Allen Sanford and Janet May Perry. Cert. artorist Internat. Soc. Arboriculture. Engr. C.D.I. Corp., Silicon Valley, Calif.; owner Ken's Tree Svc. and Landscaping, Mercer Island, Wash. Author: Legion's Riddle, The Journey Home, 2003. Home: PO Box 920 Mercer Island WA 98040

SANFORD, MARSHALL (MARK SANFORD), governor, former congressman; b. Ft. Lauderdale, Fla., May 28, 1960; m. Jenny Sullivan; 4 children. BA, Furman U., 1983; MBA, U. Va., 1988. With Goldman Sachs, 1988, CRC Realty, 1988-89; prin. Southeastern Ptnrs., 1989—, Norton & Sanford, 1993—95, 2001—02; mem. U.S. Congress from 1st Dist. S.C., 1995-2001; mem. govt. reform and oversight com., internat. rels. com., sci. com., joint econ. com.; gov. of S.C., 2003—. Republican. Office: Office of the Governor PO Box 12267 Columbia SC 29211

SANFORD, RICHARD CHARLES, writer; b. Detroit, Feb. 25, 1950; s. Charles Edward Sanford and Margaret Mary Mathieu; m. Renee Shechtman Sanford, Feb. 27, 1983; 1 child, Sara. BA, New Coll., Sarasota, Fla., 1972. Writer self employed, San Francisco, 1983—92, The Boeing Co., Seattle, 1992—. Author: The Calling, 1990, Roadkill, 1995, Long Time Gone, 2002; artist in residence (sch. program) The Art of Citizenship, Issaquah (Wash.) Sch. Dist., 1991. Grantee, Pomegranate Found., 1991. Mem.: Soc. for Tech. Comm. (sr.).

SANFORD, RICHARD D. computer company executive; b. 1944; With Arthur Andersen Co., N.Y.C., 1968-77; exec. v.p. Commodore Internat. Ltd., 1977-81; chmn., CEO, former pres. Intelligent Electronics Inc., Exton, Pa., 1982-98; chmn. Brinton Group, Chadds Ford, Pa., 1998—. With USMC, 1964-68. Office: Brinton Group 1653 Brinton Bridge Rd Chadds Ford PA 19317-9451

SANFORD, SARAH J. healthcare executive; b. Seattle, July 20, 1949; d. Jerome G. and Mary L. (Laughlin) S. BS in Nursing, U. Wash., 1972, MA in Nursing, 1977. Cert. in advanced nursing adminstrn. Critical care staff nurse Valley Gen. Hosp., Renton, Wash., 1972-75, Evergreen Gen. Hosp., Kirkland, Wash., 1975-76; instr. nursing Seattle Pacific U., 1977-79; with Overlake Hosp. Med. Ctr., Bellevue, Wash., 1979-88, critical care coord., 1979-80, dir. acute care nursing, 1980-82, assoc. adminstr., 1982-83, sr. v.p. patient care, 1983-88; exec. dir. AACN, Aliso Viejo, Calif., 1988-90, CEO, 1990-99. Bd. dirs. Partnership for Organ Donation, Boston, Am. Soc. of Assn. Execs. Found., Washington. Co-editor: Standards for Nursing Care of the Critically Ill, 1989; contbr. articles to books and jours. Fellow Am. Acad. Nursing; mem. AACN (pres. 1984-85, bd. dirs. 1981-83), ANA, Am. Coll. Healthcare Execs., Soc. for Critical Care Medicine, Am. Orgn. Nurse Execs., Sigma Theta Tau.

SANFTLEBEN, KURT ALLEN, career officer; b. St. Louis, Oct. 28, 1952; s. George P. and Betty J. (Zimmer) S.; m. Gail Elizabeth Miller, Dec. 13, 1980; 1 child, Amy Elizabeth. BA, Mich. State U., 1974; MA, Calif. State U., 1989; EdD, Coll. of William and Mary, 1993. Cert. postgrad. tchr., phys. distbn. mgmt. profl. Commd. med. svc. corps U.S. Army, 1974, advanced through ranks to lt. col., 1992, platoon leader 7th inf. divsn., 1974-76; logistics officer U.S. Army Hosp., Fort Stewart, Ga., 1976-80; company comdr. 3rd Inf. Divsn., Aschaffenburg, Germany, 1981-83; logistics officer Walter Reed Army Med. Ctr., Washington, 1983-86; bat. exec. officer 2d Armored Divsn., Fort Hood, Tex., 1986-88; logistics officer U.S. Army III Corps Surgeon's Office, Fort Hood, Tex., 1988-90; chief med. plans and ops. U.S. Atlantic Command, Norfolk, Va., 1990-93; prof. mil. medicine Uniformed Svcs. Univ. of the Health Scis., Bethesda, Md., 1993-94, ret., 1994; dep. dir. Va. Commonwealth Challenge, 1994-97. Dir. USMC Rsch. Ctr., 1998—; mem. Sch. Edn. Deans Coun., Coll. William and Mary, mem. sch. edn. devel. bd., mem. bd. dirs. The Assoc. of 1775. Author: Meeting the Challenge: A Successful Dropout Recovery Program, 1997, The Unofficial Joint Medical Officer's Guide, 1995; contbg. author: Planning for Health Service Support, 1993, Postal History of the American Expeditionary Force, 1917-1921, 1990. Decorated Legion of Merit, Def. Meritorious Svc. medal, Expert Field Med. badge; recipient Pres.'s award Mich. State U., 1974. Mem. ASCD, ALA, ASTD, Am. Assn. Higher Edn., Assn. Mil. Surgeons of U.S., Nat. Eagle Scout Assn., Kappa Delta Pi. Libertarian. Unitarian Universalist. Home: 4928 Breeze Way Dumfries VA 22026-1253 Office: Marine Corps Rsch Ctr MCCDC 2040 Broadway St Quantico VA 22134-5139 E-mail: sanftlebenka@tecom.usmc.mil., kurt@sanftleben.com.

SANGER, EILEEN, artist; b. Far Rockaway, N.Y., Mar. 24, 1952; d. Edward Herbert and Gladys Minerva Sanger; m. Freddy Profit, May 28, 1989; 1 child, Kristen. Student, Roslyn Sch. Painting, 1975—77. Accounts receivable supr. Kwik Kopy Printers, Inc., N.Y.C., 1978-82; acctg. supr. Insul-lite Window Mfg., Inc., Garden City, N.Y., 1984-89; ptnr., owner Sweet'ms, Rocky Point, N.Y., 1991-93, Bellport (N.Y.) Lane Art Gallery, 1994-98. Exhibited in group shows at Mills Pond House Gallery, St. James, N.Y., 1993—94, Vanderbilt Mus., Northport, N.Y., 1993—94, Guild Hall, East Hampton, N.Y., 1993—95, 1997, Gallery North, Setauket, N.Y., 1993—95, 1997, 1998, 1999, B.J. Spoke Gallery, Huntington, N.Y., 1994, Stony Brook (N.Y.) Mus., 1999, Represented in permanent collections Neo-Futurarium Hall of Pres., Chgo., Port Jefferson (N.Y.) Free Libr. N.Y. Found. for Arts spl. opportunity grant, 1994, 96; Stu-Art Oils award Suburban Art League, 1993, Grumbacher Oils award Wet Paint Studio Group, 1994-97. Mem. Nat. League Am. PEN Women, Smithtown Twp. Arts Coun., Southbay Arts Assn. (1st pl. 1995, 2d pl. 1996), East Ends Arts Coun., Brookhaven Arts Coun., Long Island Plein Air Painters Soc. (founding mem.). Avocation: gourmet cooking. Home: 49 Rolling Rd Miller Place NY 11764-2223

SANGER, FREDERICK, retired molecular biologist; b. Rendcomb, Gloucestershire, Eng., Aug. 13, 1918; s. Frederick and Cicely Sanger; m. Joan Howe, 1940; children: Robin, Peter Frederick, Sally Joan. BA, St. John's Coll., Cambridge U., 1940, PhD, 1943; D.Sc. (hon.), Leicester U., 1968, Oxford U., 1970, Strasbourg U., 1970, Cambridge U. Beit Meml. Med. Research fellow U. Cambridge, 1944-51, research scientist dept. biochemistry, 1944-61, research scientist, div. head Med. Research Council Lab. of Molecular Biology, 1962-83. Contbr. articles in field to sci. jours. Recipient Nobel prize for chemistry, 1958, 80; Gairdner Found. ann. award, 1971, 79, William Bate Hardy prize Cambridge Philos. Soc., 1976, Copley medal Royal Soc., 1977; fellow King's Coll., Cambridge U., 1954. Mem. Am. Acad. Arts and Scis. (hon. fgn. mem.), Am. Soc. Biol. Chemists (hon.), Fgn. Assn., NAS. Two time Nobel Prize winner in chemistry for work on amino acids and gene sequencing. Home: Far Leys Fen Ln Swaffham Bulbeck Cambridge CB5 ONJ England

SANGER, JOSEPH WILLIAM, cell biologist; s. Joseph James and Mary Jackson S.; m. Jean McGilvray, Sept. 12, 1964; children: John McGilvray, Matthew Kernan. BS, Manhattan Coll., 1962; PhD, Dartmouth Coll., 1968; MA (hon.), U. Pa., 1976. Assoc. in anatomy U. Pa. Sch. Medicine, Phila., 1971-72, asst. prof., 1972-76, assoc. prof., 1976-85, prof., 1985—; chair, cell biology grad. program U. Pa., Phila., 1990-95, interim chmn. Dept. Cell and Devel. Biology, 2003—. Exec. trustee Marine Biol. Lab., Woods Hole, Mass., 1991-93, trustee, 1990-93, Bermuda biol. St., Saint George's Bermuda, 1977-82. Editor: (video) Cell Motility and the Cytoskeleton, 1991-98; editl. bd. cell motility and cytoskeleton Wily-Liss, N.Y.C., 1986—; contbr. articles to profl. jours. Humboldt fellow Humboldt Found., 1979-80. Fellow AAAS (nominating com. 2000-2003). Office: U Pa 1051 BRB II/III 421 Curie Blvd Philadelphia PA 19104-6058 Office Phone: 215-898-6919. Business E-Mail: sangerj@mail.med.upenn.edu.

SANGER, STEPHEN W. consumer products company executive; b. 1945; With Gen. Mills, Inc., Mpls., 1974—, v.p., gen. mgr. Northstar Divsn., 1983, v.p., gen. mgr. new bus. devel., 1986, pres. Yoplait USA, 1986, pres. Big G Divsn., 1988, sr. v.p., 1989, vice chmn. bd., 1992-96, pres., 1993-95, CEO, chmn. bd., 1995—. Bd. dirs. Donaldson Co., Inc., Mpls. Treas. Guthrie Theatre Found., Mpls. Office: Gen Mills Inc One General Mills Blvd Minneapolis MN 55426

SANGIOVANNI, JOHN PAUL, ophthalmic epidemiologist, eye and vision researcher; s. John Paul and Marie SanGiovanni; m. Brigitte SanGiovanni. BA, Boston Coll., 1988; MA, Brandeis U., 1993; MS, Harvard U., 1994, DSc, 1999. Neuroanatomy rsch. asst. Harvard Med. Sch./McLean Hosp., Belmont, Mass., 1988—91; study coord. Children's Hosp./Harvard Med. Sch., Boston, 1993—95; rsch. cons. Harvard Med. Sch./Children's Hosp., Boston, 1996—2000; rsch. asst. UN U., Boston, 1996—97; rsch. assoc. Internat. Nutrition Found., Boston, 1999—2000; rsch. cons. Harvard Sch. Pub. Health/Coll. Alcohol Study, Boston, 1999—2000; rsch. fellow Nat. Eye Inst., NIH, Bethesda, Md., 2000—04, staff scientist, 2004—. Rep. fellows' com. NIH, 2001—02; mem. faculty student-adminstrn. liaison com. Harvard U. Sch. Pub. Health, Boston; chairp disting. clin. tchr.'s award com. NIH, Bethesda, 2001—02. Contbr. manuscripts to sci. publs. Recipient Albert Schweitzer Urban fellowship, 1996—97, Chateaubriand scholarship, French Nat. Govt. Mission of Sci. and Tech., 2000, NAS/Sigma Xi grant in aid of rsch., NAS, 1997; scholar, Teagle Found., 1994—99. Mem.: Assn. for Rsch. in Vision and Ophthalmology (mem. profl. edn. and devel. com. 2001—). Achievements include research in role of dietary long-chain polyunsaturated fatty acids in pathogenesis of retinal disease; nutritional factors associated

with age-related eye disease; novel method of measuring visual acuity in infants; risk factors for pediatric cataract. Office: Nat Eye Inst NIH MSC 2510 31 Center Dr Bethesda MD 20892-2510

SANGIOVANNI, MARY ELIZABETH, writer, freelance manager; b. Orange, N.J., Jan. 28, 1976; d. Michael Louis and Suzanne Kathleen SanGiovanni; 1 child, Adam Joseph. BA in English, Fairleigh Dickinson U., 1998. Asst. editor Marquis Who's Who, New Providence, NJ, 1998—99, from freelance coord. to freelance supr., 1999—2001, freelance mgr., 2002—. Author: (short stories) Under Cover of Night, 2002; contbr. short stories to various periodicals, articles to various periodicals. Mem.: Garden State Horror Writers (v.p. 2001, pres. 2002—03), Horror Writers Assn. (internet mailer editor 2003—), Mid Atlantic Horror Profls., Nat. Assn. Women Writers. Roman Catholic. Avocations: reading, movies, model building, video games, computer art. Office: Marquis Whos Who 630 Central Ave New Providence NJ 07974

SANGIULIANO, BARBARA ANN, tax consultant; b. Bronx, N.Y., Dec. 28, 1959; d. Patrick John and Mildred (Soell) Gallo; m. John Warren Sangiuliano, Aug. 28, 1982. BA, Muhlenberg Coll., 1982; MST, Seton Hall U., 1989, JD, 1997. Bar: N.J. 1997; CPA, N.J., 1987; CMA. Sr. tax mgr. KPMG Peat Marwick, Short Hills, N.J., 1988-92; sr. tax analyst Allied Signal, Morristown, N.J., 1992-93; tax mgr. AT&T, Morristown, 1993-96, Lucent Techs., Morristown, 1996-97; tax atty. Witman, Stadtmauer & Michaels, Florham Park, NJ, 1997-98; tax cons. Ernst & Young LLP, Iselin, NJ, 1998—2003, Deloitte & Touche, Parsippany, NJ, 2003—. Mem. AICPA, ABA, N.J. Soc. CPAs (past pres. Union County chpt.), N.J. Bar Assn., Inst. Mgmt. Accts., Mensa, Omicron Delta Epsilon, Phi Sigma Iota. Republican. Roman Catholic. Avocations: reading, bicycling, fencing. Home: 340 William St Scotch Plains NJ 07076-1430 Office: Deloitte & Touche Two Hilton Ct Parsippany NJ 07054-4410 Personal E-mail: pudd__bear@msn.com.

SANGMEISTER, GEORGE EDWARD, lawyer, consultant, former congressman; b. Joliet, Ill., Feb. 16, 1931; s. George Conrad and Rose Engaborg (Johnson) S.; m. Doris Marie Hinspeter, Dec. 1, 1951; children: George Kurt, Kimberley Ann. BA, Elmhurst Coll., 1957; LLB, John Marshall Law Sch., 1960, JD, 1970. Bar: Ill. 1960. Ptnr. McKeown, Fitzgerald, Zollner, Buck, Sangmeister & Hutchison, 1969-89; justice of peace, 1961-63; states atty. Will County, 1964-68; mem. Ill. Ho. of Reps., 1972-76, Ill. Senate, 1977-87, 101st-103rd Congresses from 4th (now 11th) Dist. Ill., 1989-95; ret., 1995; cons. McKeown, Fitzgerald, Zollner, Buck, Hutchison, Ruttle and Assocs., 1990—. Chmn. Frankfort Twp. unit Am. Cancer Soc., Will County Emergency Housing Devel. Corp.; past trustee Will County Family Svc. Agy.; past bd. dirs. Joliet Jr. Coll. Found., Joliet Will County Ctr. for Econ. Devel., Silver Cross Found., Silver Cross Hosp. With inf. AUS, 1951-53. Mem. ABA, Ill. Bar Assn., Assn. Trial Lawyers Am., Am. Legion, Frankfort (past pres.), Frankfort C. of C., Old Timers Baseball Assn., Lions. Home: 20735 Wolf Rd Mokena IL 60448-8927

SANGREE, WALTER HINCHMAN, social anthropologist, educator; b. N.Y.C., June 15, 1926; s. Carl Michael and Constance (LaBoiteaux) S.; m. Mary Lucinda Shaw, June 14, 1952 (div. Jan. 1986); children: Margaretta Elizabeth, Mary Cora; m. Ilse Michaelis, Dec. 31, 1988. AB, Haverford Coll., 1950; MA, Wesleyan U., 1952; PhD, U. Chgo., 1959. Asst. prof. anthropology U. Rochester, N.Y., 1957-64, assoc. prof., 1964-73, prof., 1973-95, prof. emeritus, 1995—, chmn. dept. anthropology, 1974-77, acting chmn. dept., 1990; vis. scholar dept. anthropology Harvard U., 1979-80. Vis. scholar Ctr. for Population Studies, Harvard U., 1986-87; rsch. fellow Ctr. for African Studies, Boston U., 1998—. Author: Age, Prayer & Politics in Tiriki, Kenya, 1966; contbr. articles to profl. jours. Co-clk. Rochester Friends Meeting, 1977-79. Fulbright scholar U.K. and Kenya, 1954-56; NSF research fellow Nigeria, 1963-65 Mem. Am. Anthrop. Assn., African Studies Assn., Sigma Xi. Democrat. Mem. Soc. Of Friends. Home and Office: PO Box 1290 65 Meadow View Dr Nantucket MA 02554-2717 Office Phone: 508-228-4195. Personal E-mail: sangree@comcast.net.

SANI, ROBERT LEROY, chemical engineering educator; b. Antioch, Calif., Apr. 20, 1935; m. Martha Jo Marr, May 28, 1966; children: Cynthia Kay, Elizabeth Ann, Jeffrey Paul. BS, U. Calif.-Berkeley, 1958, MS, 1960; PhD, U. Minn., 1963. Postdoctoral researcher dept. math Rensselaer Poly. Inst., Troy, N.Y., 1963-64; asst. prof. U. Ill., Urbana, 1964-70, assoc. prof., 1970-76; prof. chem. engring. U. Colo., Boulder, 1976—; co-dir. Ctr. for Low-g Fluid Mechanics and Transport Phenomena, U. Colo., Boulder, 1986-89, dir., 1989—. Assoc. prof. French Ministry Edn., 1982, 84, 86, 92, 94, 95, 96, 97; cons. Lawrence Livermore Nat. Lab., Calif., 1974-84. Contbr. numerous chpts. to profl. publs.; co-author three books; mem. editorial bd. Internat. Jour. Numerical Methods in Fluids, 1981—, Revue Européenne des Éléments Finis, 1990—, Internat. Jour. Computational Engring. Sci., 1998—, Internat. Jour. Computational & Numerical Analysis & Applications, 2000-. Guggenheim fellow, 1970 Mem. AICE, Soc. for Applied and Indsl. Math., World User Assn. in Applied Computational Fluid Dynamics (bd. dirs.). Democrat. Office: U Colo Dept Chem & Biol Engring UCB 424 Boulder CO 80309-0424 Office Phone: 303-492-5517. Business E-Mail: sani@pastis.colorado.edu.

SAN JOSE, ANGEL MOLINA, surgeon; b. Manila, Dec. 9, 1939; came to U.S., 1966; MD, Far Ea. U., Manila, 1965. Diplomate Am. Bd. Surgery. Intern to resident in gen. surgery Mt. Sinai Hosp., Cleve., 1966-67, 67-71; pvt. med. practice, 1973—. Attending physician Ingalls Meml. Hosp., Harvey, Ill., South Suburban Hosp., Hazel Crest, Ill., Miller County Hosp., Colquitt, Ga., 2003—. Fellow ACS; mem. Ill. Surg. Soc., Am. Soc. Gen. Surgeons. Office: 210 W Main St Ste 4 Colquitt GA 39837

SANKOVITZ, JAMES LEO, retired development director, lobbyist; b. St. Paul, July 3, 1934; s. John L. and Mabel A. (Hanrahan) S.; m. Margaret E. Mathews, Aug. 3, 1957; children: Richard, Therese, Patrick, Margaret, Katherine. BS in Journalism, Marquette U., 1956; MA in Speech, U. Denver, 1963. Dir. pub. rels. Coll. of St. Mary of the Wasatch, Salt Lake City, 1956-57; dir. pub. info. Colo. Sch. of Mines, Golden, 1957-63; assoc. dir. devel. Marquette U., Milw., 1963-66, dir. alumni fund, 1966-67, dir. alumni rels., 1967-69, asst. v.p. univ. rels., 1969-70, v.p. univ. rels., 1970-78, v.p. govtl. rels., 1978-86, v.p. govtl. and community affairs, 1986-97; ret., 1997. Contbr. articles to profl. jours. Founding dir. Univ. Nat. Bank, Milw., 1971-74; bd. dirs. St. Coletta Sch., Jefferson, Wis., 1970-76, 86-93, chair, 1974-76. Mem. Nat. Assn. for Ind. Colls. and Univs. (bd. dirs. Washington 1986-90), Disting. Svc. award 1986), Assn. Jesuit Colls. and Univs. (fed. affairs cons. Washington 1974-90), Assn. Cath. Colls. and Univs. (fed. affairs cons. Washington 1974-85, Blue Key, Alpha Sigma Nu. Roman Catholic. Avocations: woodworking, reading. Home: 4057 N Prospect Ave Milwaukee WI 53211-2121 E-mail: jsankovitz@wi.rr.com.

SANKS, ROBERT LELAND, environmental engineer, emeritus educator; b. Pomona, Calif., Feb. 19, 1916; s. John B. and Nellie G. (Church) S.; m. Mary Louise Clement, May 16, 1946 (dec. Oct. 1994); children: Margaret Nadine, John Clement; m. Edith Millen Harrington, Dec. 2, 1999. Registered profl. engr.; Mont. Draftsman City of La Habra Calif., 1940; asst. engr. Alex Morrison cons. engr., Fullerton, Calif., 1941; jr. engr. U.S. Army Engrs., Los Angeles, 1941-42; asst. research engr. dept. civil engring. U. Calif.-Berkeley, 1942-45; structural engr. The Austin Co., Oakland, Calif., 1945-46; instr. dept. civil engring. U. Utah, Salt Lake city, 1946-49, asst. prof. Salt Lake City, 1949-55, assoc. prof., 1955-58; structural engr. The Lang Co., Salt Lake City, 1950; instrument man Patti McDonald Co., Anchorage, 1951; checker Western Steel Co., Salt Lake City, 1952; structural engr. Moran, Proctor, Meuser and Rutledge, N.Y.C., 1953, F.C. Torkelson Co., Salt Lake City, 1955; soils engr. R.L. Sloane & Assocs., Salt Lake City, 1956; prof., chmn. dept. civil engring. Gonzaga U., Spokane, Wash., 1958-61; prof. dept. civil engring.-engring. mechanics Mont. State U., Bozeman, 1966-82, prof. emeritus, 1982—; vis. prof. U. Tex.-Austin, 1974-75; part-time sr. engr. Christian, Spring, Sielbach & Assoc., Billings, Mont., 1974-82. Cons. engr., 1945—; lectr. at pumping sta. design workshops, 1988—; assoc. specialist San. Engring. Research Lab., 1963-65, research engr., 1966. Author: Statically Indeterminate Structural Analysis, 1961; co-author: (with Takashi Assano) Land Treatment and Disposal of Municipal and Industrial Wastewaters, 1976, Water Treatment Plant Design for the Practicing Engineer, 1978; editor-in-chief: Pumping Station Design, 1989 (award Excellence profl. & scholarly pub. div. Assn. Am. Pubs. 1989), 2d edit., 1998; contbr. articles on civil engring. to profl. publs. Mem. Wall of Fame, Fullerton High Sch., 1987; NSF fellow, 1961-63 Mem. ASCE (life, chmn. local qualifications com. intermountain sect. 1950-56, pres. intermountain sect. 1957-58), Am. Water Works Assn. (pres. Mont. sect. 1981-82, George Warren Fuller award), Mont. Water Environ. Fedn., Assn. Environ. Engring. Profs., Rotary, Sigma Xi, Chi Epsilon. Home: 411 W Dickerson St Bozeman MT 59715-4538

SAN MIGUEL, LOLITA, artistic director; Student, Sch. Am. Ballet. Performer Robert Joffrey Co., Benjamin Harkarvy Co., Slavenska-Franklin Ballet; soloist Met. Opera Ballet; founder Puerto Rican Dance Theatre, N.Y., 1970; artistic dir., founder Ballet Concierto de P.R., Santurce, 1978—. Tchr., ballet mistress Ballet Hispánico, N.Y.; tchr. Dance Theatre Harlem, Performing Arts H.S., Adelphi Coll., Hofstra U., L.I. U., Clark Ctr., Met. Opera. Office: Ballet Concierto de PR PO Box 13245 San Juan PR 00908-3245*

SAN MIGUEL, MANUEL, painter, historian, composer, poet, art collector; b. Guayama, P.R., Sept. 29, 1930; s. Manuel and Luisa (Griffo) San M.; m. Sandra Bonilla, July 12, 1969; children: Manuel, Ana. Student, U. P.R., 1947-51, U. Pa., 1966-68, Arts Students League, N.Y.C., 1968-69. Historian San Juan Nat. Historic Site, Nat. Park Svc., 1953-63; exec. sec. Acad. Arts and Scis., San Juan, 1963-64. Founder of mus. and study collection El Morro Castle San Juan Nat. Hist. Site; painter, writer, musician, 1964—; co-founder Caribbean Art Gallery, San Juan, PR, Galeria Campeche, N.Y.C.; cons. in field. Exhibited in U. P.R., 1958, 62, Ateneo de P.R., 1962, Pan-Am. Union, Washington, 1963, Bienal Mex., 1972, Bienal Rio de Janeiro, 1976, Orange County Schs. Mus. Art, Orlando, Fla., 1992, Mus. Modern Art, Paris, 1994, Expo of the Americas, Orlando, 1996, 98, Galeriá Santiago, San Juan, P.R., 2000, Galeria Campeche, San Juan, P.R., 2001, Simon Bolivar Gallery, Caracas, 2001, Galerie Santiago, 2003, numerous other nat. and internat. exhbns.; contbr. monographs on historical work in San Juan Nat. Historic Site to U.S. Nat. Archives, Washington; contbr. poetry to anthologies including Anthology of Latin American Poets, vol. III, 1987; rec. artist popular music of P.R.; soloist U. P.R. choir, Carnegie Hall, N.Y.C., 1949. Capt. U.S. Army, 1951-53, Korea. Decorated Bronze Star with valor clasp and oak leaf cluster, Purple Heart, Combat Infantryman Badge, others; named One of Ten Outstanding Hispanic Men, Orlando, Fla., 1991; recipient Recognition award for contbns. to Hispanic Am. Culture, Govt. P.R., 1996, Hispanic Heritage Found., medal Painters & Designers 20th Century, Cambridge, Eng., 2000; Coqui de Oro award for contbns. to Puerto Rican arts Casa de P.R., Inc., 1999. Mem. AAAS, VFW (life), Disabled Am. Vets. (life), Am. Legion, Ateneo de P.R. (bd. govs. 1959-60), Am. Biog. Inst. (bd. advisors, life mem. bd. govs.), Am. Philatelic Soc. (postal commemorative soc.), Inst. P.R. Culture (cons.), P.R. Philatelic Assn. (charter), Internat. Platform Assn., Lions (Lion of Yr. 1962-63). Achievements include documentary research in the restoration of Castillo San Marcos, St. Augustine, Fla., Castillo San Felipe de Barajas, Colombia, South Am., and restoration of San Juan fortifications and city walls. Home: 1214 Howell Creek Dr Winter Springs FL 32708

SAN MIGUEL, SANDRA BONILLA, social worker; b. Santurce, P.R., May 23, 1944; d. Isidoro and Flora (Carrero) Bonilla; m. Manuel San Miguel, July 12, 1969. BA, St. Joseph's Coll., 1966; MS in Social Work, Columbia U., 1970. Cert. social work mgr., sch. social work specialist. Case worker Dept. Labor, Migration Divsn., N.Y.C., 1966-68; clin. social worker N.Y.C. Housing Authority, N.Y.C., 1968-69, Children's Aid Soc., N.Y.C., 1969-71; sr. social worker Traveler's Aid Soc., San Juan, P.R., 1971-74; coord., supr. Dept. Addiction Control Svcs., San Juan, P.R., 1974-77; substance abuse div. dir. Seminole County Mental Health Ctr., Altamonte Springs, Fla., 1978-81; cons. pvt. practice Hispanic Cons. Svcs., Winter Springs, Fla., 1982—; adj. prof. Seminole C.C., Lake Mary, Fla., 1986-90; sch. social worker Seminole County Pub. Schs., Sanford, Fla., 1986-91, lead sch. social worker, 1991—. Pres.'s minority adv. coun. U. Ctrl. Fla., 1982—, vice-chair, 1982-86, chair, 1986-90; bd. regents EEO adv. com. State U. Sys. Fla., 1985-89; bd. dirs. Seminole Cmty. Mental Health Ctr., 1986-94, 95-2001, v.p., 1988-90, pres., 1990-91; adv. bd. Nat. Devereux Found. Ctrl. Fla., 1993-98, women's adv. bd. South Seminole Hosp., Fla., 1994-96; mem. multicultural cmty. adv. com. Seminole County Pub. Schs., 1993—; mem. Fla. Consortium on Tchr. Edn. for Am. Minorities, 1990-96; mem. local com. Hispanic Info. and Telecomms. Network, 1990; mem. Seminole County (Fla.) Juvenile Justice Coun., 1993—; mem. statewide student svcs. adv. com. Dept. Edn. Fla., 1993-96, student svcs. adv. group, 1996-97. Named Ednl. Support Ctr. Tchr. of Yr., Seminole County Pub. Schs., 2000; recipient Pres.'s Outstanding Svc. award, UCF, 1991, Ponce de Leon Hispanic Cmty. award, 1992, Bd. Svc. Recognition Plaque, Seminole Cmty. Mental Health Ctr., 1991, Outstanding Contribution to Student Svcs. cert., Fla. Dept. Edn., 1995, Manuel Martinez award for Outsanding Contbns. to Puerto Rican Cmty. in Ctrl. Fla., La Casa de Puerto Rico, 1999. Mem.: NASW (appt. nat. sch. social work credential com. 1996—99), Nat. Network Social Work Mgrs., Collegiate Social Workers P.R., Fla. Assn. Student Svcs. Adminstrs., Sch. Social Work Assn. Am. (founding mem.), Fla. Assn. Sch. Social Workers (co-founder minority caucus 1988, columnist quar. newsletter article Minority Corner 1988—92, bd. dirs. 1989—, website article From the Gallery 2001—, sec. 1990—92, v.p. 1992—93, pres. 1993—94, Leadership Plaque 1994, Adminstr. of Yr. 1999), Nat. Network Social Work Mgrs., St. Joseph's Coll. Alumni Assn., Columbia U. Alumni Assn. (nat. bd. dirs. 1997—). Office: PO Box 195933 Winter Springs FL 32719-5933 E-mail: sanmiguel1969@earthlink.net.

SANNA, RICHARD JEFFREY, lawyer; b. N.Y.C., July 20, 1949; s. Francis and Ann (Bryant) S.; m. Rosemarie A. Lagnena, Nov. 21, 1971; children: John, Kristin, Michele, Elisabeth. BA, St. Johns U., Jamaica, N.Y., 1971; JD, Del. Law Sch., 1975. Bar: N.Y. 1977, U.S. Dist. Ct. (so. dist.) N.Y. 1978, U.S. Dist. Ct. (ea. dist.) N.Y. 1979, U.S. Ct. Appeals (2d cir.) 1979, U.S. Supreme Ct. 1980. Assoc. McKay, King, Castricone & Piazza, Queens, N.Y., 1978-80; sr. ptnr. Sarisohn, Sarisohn, Thierman, Carner & LeBow, Commack, N.Y., 1980-82; ptnr. Migliore, Sanna & Infranco P.C., Commack, 1982-85; sole practice Hauppauge and Commack, N.Y., 1985; sr. counsel Eagle Funding, Natl., Jericho, N.Y., 1990—. Mem. adv. council St. Martins of Tours Ch., Bethpage, N.Y., 1983—; atty. Bethpage Civic Assn., 1985—. Mem. N.Y. State Bar Assn., Suffolk County Bar Assn. (chmn. fee dispute com. 1984-86, recipient I.U.J.H. F.D. Roosevelt award for meritorious svc. AFL-CIO, 1992), Assn. Trial Lawyers Am., N.Y. Trial Lawyers Assn., Columbian Lawyers Assn. Lodges: K.C. Republican. Roman Catholic. Home: 91 Sycamore Ave Bethpage NY 11714-2226

SANNER, GEORGE BRADLEY, bank executive; b. Balt., Sept. 20, 1953; s. George E. and Marjorie (Hohman) S.; m. Ann Margaret Tehan, Aug. 31, 1991 (div.); children: Anne, Meredith, Kimberly. BA, U. Va., 1974; MBA, Loyola Coll., Balt., 1978. Asst. v.p. Union Trust Co., Balt., 1974-82; v.p. Am. Security Bank, Washington, 1982-86; sr. v.p. Bank of Md., Towson, 1986-87; mng. dir. Provident Bank of Md., Balt., 1987-94; sr. v.p. FCNB Bank, Frederick, Md., 1994-95; pres./CEO Regal Bancorp, Owings Mills, Md., 1995—; also bd. dirs. Bd. dirs. Md. Bank Svcs., Inc., Chesapeake Bus. Fin. Corp.; pres., CEO Regal Bank and Trust, 1995—. Airman USAF, 1973-75. Mem. Md. Bankers Assn. (bd. dirs. 2001—), Alpha Sigma Nu. Republican. Methodist. Avocations: golf, tennis, amateur radio. Office: Regal Bancorp 10123 Reisterstown Rd Owings Mills MD 21117-3814 E-mail: bsanner@regalbankandtrust.com.

SANNER, JOHN HARPER, retired pharmacologist; b. Anamosa, Iowa, Apr. 29, 1931; s. Lee Michael and Helen (Grace) S.; m. Marilyn Joan Eichorst, Dec. 28, 1958; children: Linda Leigh, Steven Bradley. BS, U. Iowa, 1954, MS, 1961, PhD, 1964. Rsch. investigator G.D. Searle & Co., Skokie, Ill., 1963-69, sr. rsch. investigator, 1969-75, rsch. fellow, 1975-86, ret., 1986—. Conducted pioneering rsch. in prostaglandin antagonists; contbr. articles to profl. jours. Mem. Deerfield (Ill.) Cable and Telecomm. Commn. 1st lt. USAFR, 1955-57. Mem. Am. Soc. for Pharmacology and Exptl. Therapeutics (ret.), Ill. Videomakers Assn. Democrat. Avocation: video photography and production. Office: Sanner Video Svc PO Box 199 Deerfield IL 60015-0199 Office Phone: 847-945-4351. Personal E-mail: johnsanner@aol.com.

SANNER, KRISTIN NOELLE, language educator; b. Connellsville, Pa., Dec. 14, 1968; d. Kenneth Eugene and Barbara Lee (Dixon) Sanner; m. William Bentley Walker, Oct. 1, 1994; 1 child, Isaac Sanner Walker. BA, Pa. State U., 1991; MA, U. Scranton, Pa., 1998; PhD, SUNY, Binghamton, 2003. Environ. educator Shaver's Creek Environ. Ctr., Huntingdon, Pa., 1992—93; libr. Susquehanna County Libr., Montrose, Pa., 1993—98; tchg. asst., adj. instr. Binghamton U., 1999—2003. Adj. instr. Keystone Coll., La Plume, Pa., 1998—99, U. Scranton, 1998—99, Luzerne County C.C., Nanticoke, Pa., 1996—; lectr. U. Scranton, Pa., 2003—04; asst. prof. Mansfield U., 2004—. Contbr. articles to profl. jours. Bd. dirs. Woodbourne Nature Preserve, Dimock, Pa., 1998—; com. mem. Grad. English Orgn., Binghamton, 2000—01. Recipient O'Hara award, U. Scranton, 1997, Grad. Student award for Rsch. Excellence, 2003; fellow Dissertation Yr. fellow, Binghamton U., 2002—03. Mem.: MLA. Avocations: snow shoeing, gardening, hiking, skiing.

SANO, EMILY JOY, museum director; b. Santa Ana, Calif., Feb. 17, 1942; d. Masao and Lois Kikue (Inokuchi) S. BA, Ind. U., 1967; MA, Columbia U., 1970, MPhil, 1976, PhD, 1983. Lectr. Oriental Art Vassar Coll., Poughkeepsie, N.Y., 1974-79; curator Asian Art, asst. dir. programs Kimbell Art Mus., Ft. Worth, 1979-89; dep. dir. collections and exhbns. Dallas Mus. Art, 1989-92; dep. dir., chief curator Asian Art Mus., San Francisco, 1993-95, dir., 1995—. Author: Great Age of Japanese Buddhist Sculpture, 1982; editor: The Blood of Kings, 1986, Weavers, Merchants and Kings, 1984, Painters of the Great Ming, 1993. Active Assn. Art Mus. Dirs.; vis. com. Harvard U. Art Mus. Woodrow Wilson Fellow, 1966-67; grantee Carnegie, 1963-64, Fulbright-Hays, 1977-78. Office: Asian Art Museum 200 Larkin St San Francisco CA 94102-4734 E-mail: esano@asianart.org.

SANO, KEIJI, neurosurgeon, educator; b. Shizuoka Prefecture, Japan, June 30, 1920; s. Takeo and Haru (Sase) S.; m. Yaeko Sano. MD, U. Tokyo, 1945, PhD, 1951. Asst. U. Tokyo, 1945-56, lectr., chief out patient clinic, 1956-57, assoc. prof. neurosurgery, 1957-62, prof. neurosurgery, 1962-81, emeritus prof., 1981—; prof. neurosurgery Teikyo U., 1981-96; dir. Fuji Brain Inst., 1986—. Pres. 5th Internat. Congress Neurol. Surgery, 1973; pres. Internat. Conf. on Cerebral Vasospasm, 1990; chmn., dir Nat. Com. for Brain Rsch., Sci. Coun. of Japan, 1987-91. Mem. Japan Neurosurg. Soc. (pres. 1965), Japanese Assn. Rsch. in Stereo-ancephalotomy (pres. 1966), Asian and Australasian Soc. Neurol. Surgeons (pres. 1967-71, hon. life pres. 1971—), World Fedn. Neurosurg. Socs. (pres. 1969-73, hon. life pres. 1973—), Japanese Soc. CNS CT (pres. 1978—), Am. Assn. Neurol. Surgeons (hon.), Deutsche Gesellschaft für Neurochirurgie (hon.), Academia Eurasiana Neurochirurgie (hon.), Academia Eurasiana Neurochirurgica (pres. 1986), Soc. Neurol. Surgeons (hon.), Am. Acad. Neurol. Surgery (hon.), Congress Neurol. Surgeons (hon.), Scandinavian Neurosurg. Soc. (corr.), Am. Surg. Assn. (sr.), Am. Neurol. Assn. (corr.), ACS (hon.). Achievements include research on treatment of brain tumors, aneurisms, stereo-encephalotomy, vascular lesions. Home: 4-22-6 Den-en-chofu Ota-ku Tokyo 145 0071 Japan

SANOFF, ALVIN PAUL, education consultant, writer; b. NYC, July 1, 1941; s. Harry and Sema (Kravitz); m. Jane O. Blakely, Aug. 25, 1968; children: Geoffrey L., Scott L., Michael B. AB cum laude in Sociology, Harvard Coll., 1963; MS in Journalism, Columbia U., 1964. Reporter Washington Star, 1965; editor Newhouse Newspapers Washington Bur., 1965-66; pub. info. officer Sm. Bus. Adminstrn., Washington, 1966-67; reporter Balt. Sun, 1967-71; editoral page editor Dayton (Ohio) Jour. Herald, 1971-77; from assoc. editor to asst. mng. editor U.S. News & World Report Mag., Washington, 1977-98, mng. editor Guides to Am.'s Best Colls. and Grad Schs., 1992-98. Sr. v.p. Maguire Assocs., Bedford, Mass., 1998-2000; dir. Schs. Edn. Rsch. Project, Tchrs. Coll., Columbia U., 2000—. Creator, series editor: Authors' America TV Series, 1992-95; contbg. editor Prism Mag., 2000—, Washingtonian Mag., 2004—. Recipient Best Editl. Writing award Ohio AP, 1974; NEH Fellow, 1974-75. Jewish. Avocations: reading, music, walking, travel. Office: 5510 Johnson Ave Bethesda MD 20817-3518 E-mail: apsanoff@erols.com.

SANSALONE, WILLIAM ROBERT, biochemist, educator, biomedical researcher; b. Vineland, N.J., Feb. 16, 1931; s. Fortunato and Rosa (Pelle) Sansalone; m. Alice E. Koury, June 25, 1960; 1 child, Catherine. *William Sansalone's parents left Gerace, a historic cathedral town in Calabria, Italy, for Philadelphia in 1913. In 1916, they purchased a parcel of woodland in Malaga, a small community in southern New Jersey. They cleared 35 acres and established themselves in produce farming; it was here they reared eight children and spent their last years. All of their 44 descendants were born in the United States.* BS, Rutgers U., 1953, PhD, 1961; MS, U. N.H., 1955. Biochemistry rsch. asst. U. Conn., Storrs, 1955-56; instr. biochemistry SUNY Downstate Med. Ctr., Bklyn., 1961-64, asst. prof. biochemistry, 1964-70, assoc. prof., 1970-71; project scientist NIH, Bethesda, Md., 1971-72, sr. project scientist, 1972-73, exec. sec. biochemistry study sect., 1973-74, program dir. rev., 1974-83, assoc. dir. sci. program ops., 1983-87, dir. office of program planning and evaluation, 1987-96; sr. fellow Georgetown U., Washington, 1999—2002, adj. prof. biochemistry, 2002—. Vis. assoc. prof. physiology and biophysics Med. Coll. Pa., Phila., 1970. *After retiring from the National Institutes of Health in 1996, William Sansalone launched a writing career, having completed the Certificate Program in Editing and Publications at Georgetown University, Washington, DC, in 1997. His publications from 1997-98 include a history of St. Mary's Church in Malaga, New Jersey, founded in 1922, and a biography of distinguished Cornell University biochemist Harold H. Williams (1907-91). In 1999, Dr. Sansalone was appointed senior fellow at the Georgetown University Center for Food and Nutrition Policy, where he was a writer-editor. In 2001, he transferred to Georgetown University Medical Center.* Contbr. articles to profl. jours. Served to 1st lt. USAF, 1956—58. Mem.: AAAS, Soc. Exptl. Biology and Medicine, Am. Soc. Nutritional Scis., Biophys. Soc., Harvey Soc., Sigma Xi, Alpha Gamma Rho (chpt. treas. 1968—70). Roman Catholic. Home: 6835 Old Stage Rd Rockville MD 20852-4359 Office Phone: 202-687-2891. Personal E-mail: ws31@prodigy.net. Business E-Mail: ws23@georgetown.edu.

SANSBURY, OLIN BENNETT, JR., retired university/orchestra administrator; b. Florence, S.C., Dec. 10, 1937; s. Olin Bennett and Gladys Ruth (Snipes) S.; m. Helen Cecile Hyman, Aug. 24, 1963; 1 child, Olin Bennett, III. BA in History, Wofford Coll., 1959; PhD in Internat. Studies, U. S.C., 1972. Reporter, editorial writer WBTW-TV, Florence, 1963-64, 1966-67; asst. dir. student affairs U. S.C., Florence, 1969-70, dean students, Francis Marion Coll. Columbia, 1970-71, asst. vice provost, asst. prof. govt. and internat. studies, 1971-73, chancellor, assoc. prof. govt. and internat. studies Spartanburg, 1973-93, chancellor emeritus, 1993—; exec. dir. Greenville Symphony Assn., 1994-99; ret. Bd. dirs. S.C. Coun. Econ. Edn., 1977-94, S.C. Coun. for the Humanities, 1986-96, Am. Coun. Edn. Commn. Govtl. Rels., 1991-93, S.C. Arts Alliance, 1996-99; rep. Pres.' Commn. Divsn. II NCAA, 1991-93; founding com. bd. regents Leadership, Spartanburg, 1980-85. With U.S. Army, 1960-63. H.B. Earhart fellow, 1965-66, 69 Mem. Am. Assn. State Colls. and Univs. (bd. dirs. 1989-92).

SANSEVERINO, RAYMOND ANTHONY, lawyer; b. Bklyn., N.Y., Feb. 16, 1947; s. Raphael and Alice Ann (Camerano) S.; m. Karen Marie Mooney, Aug. 24, 1968 (dec. 1980); children: Deirdre Ann, Stacy Lee; m. Victoria Vent, June 6, 1982 (div. 1995); m. Kimberley Frank, May 11, 2002. AB in English Lit., Franklin & Marshall Coll., 1968; JD cum laude, Fordham U., 1972. Bar: N.Y. 1973, U.S. Dist. Ct. (so. and ea. dists.) N.Y. 1973, U.S. Ct. Appeals (2d cir.) 1974, U.S. Supreme Ct. 1986. Assoc. Rogers & Wells, N.Y.C., 1972-75, Corbin & Gordon, 1975-77; ptnr. Corbin Silverman & Sanseverino LLP, 1978—2001, mng. ptnr., 1985—2001; ptnr. Brown Raysman Millstein Felder & Steiner LLP, 2001—, chair comml. real estate leasing group, 2001—, mem. exec. com., 2003—. Contbr. articles to profl. jours.; articles editor Fordham Law Rev., 1971-72. Recipient West Pub. Co. prize, 1972. Mem. ABA, Assn. Bar City of N.Y., N.Y. State Bar Assn., Twin Oaks Swim and Tennis Club (bd. dirs. 1981-2002, pres. 1993-2001), Alumni Assn. Franklin and Marshall Coll. (bd. dirs. 2001—, chair devel. and philanthopy com. 2003-04, treas. 2004—,

mem. exec. com. 2004—) Republican. Roman Catholic. Office: Brown Raysman et al 900 3d Ave New York NY 10022 Office Phone: 212-895-2910. E-mail: rsanseverino@brownraysman.com.

SANSOM, WILLIAM B. consumer products executive; BS in Civil Engring., The Citadel. Commr. transp., commr. fin. and adminstrn. Tenn. State Govt., 1979—83; CEO H.T. Hackney Co., Knoxville, 1983—, also chmn. bd. dirs. Dir. Martin Marietta Materials, NC, 1994—, First Tenn. Nat. Corp. Address: PO Box 238 Knoxville TN 37901-0238 Fax: 423-456-1291.

SANSONE, PAUL J. automotive executive; b. 1955; CEO, gen. mgr. Sansone Auto Network, Avenel, N.J., 1980—. Office: 100 Route 1 N Avenel NJ 07001-1630

SANSONETTI, THOMAS L. federal agency administrator; Grad., MBA, U. Va.; JD, Washington and Lee U. Chief of staff, legis. dir. Congressman Craig Thomas; assoc. solicitor on energy and natural resources Dept. Interior, solicitor, 1990; ptnr. Holland and Hart, Cheyenne, Wyo., 1993—2001; asst. atty. gen. Environment and Natural Resources Divsn. U.S. Dept. Justice, Washington, 2001—. Chmn. rules com. Rep. Nat. Com., 1996—2000; mem. Wyo. Rep. State Com. Republican. Office: US Dept Justice Environment and Natural Resources Divsn 950 Pennsylvania Ave NW Washington DC 20530-0001

SANSTEAD, WAYNE GODFREY, school system administrator; b. Hot Springs, Ark., Apr. 16, 1935; s. Godfrey A. and Clara (Buen) S.; m. Mary Jane Bober, June 16, 1957; children: Timothy, Jonathan. BA in Speech and Polit. Sci, St. Olaf Coll., 1957; MA in Pub. Address, Northwestern U., 1966; Ed.D., U. N.D., 1974. Tchr., Luverne, Minn., 1959-60; dir. forensics Minot (N.D.) High Sch., 1960-71, tchr. social sci., 1960-78; mem. N.D. Ho. of Reps., 1965-70, 83-85, N.D. Senate, 1971-73; lt. gov. N.D. Bismarck, 1973-81; supt. pub. instrn. N.D., Bismarck, 1985—. Served with AUS, 1957-59. Recipient Disting. Alumnus award St. Olaf Coll., 1991; named Outstanding Freshman Senator A.P., 1971, Outstanding Young Educator, N.D. Jr. C. of C., 1967, Outstanding Young Man, Minot Jr. C. of C., 1964; Coe Family Found. scholar, 1963, Eagleton scholar Rutgers U., 1969. Mem. N.D. Edn. Assn., NEA (legis. com. 1969—), Central States Speech Assn., Am. Forensic Assn., Jr. C. of C., Sons of Norway, Elks, Toastmasters. Democrat. Lutheran (Chmn. We. Nd Rsch. And Social Action Com 1962-68). Home: 1120 Columbia Dr Bismarck ND 58504-6514 Office: Dept Pub Instrn 600 E Boulevard Ave Dept 201 Fl 9,10,11 Bismarck ND 58505-0660

SANSWEET, STEPHEN JAY, journalist, author, marketing executive; b. Phila., June 14, 1945; s. Jack Morris and Fannie (Axelrod) S. BS, Temple U., 1966. Reporter Phila. Inquirer, 1966-69; reporter Wall Street Jour., Phila., 1969-71, Montreal, Que, Can., 1971-73, L.A., 1973-84, dep. bur. chief, 1984-87, bur. chief, 1987-96; dir. speciality mktg. Lucasfilm Ltd., San Rafael, Calif., 1996-97, dir. content mgmt. and fan rels., 1997—; sr. editor Star Wars Galaxy Mag., 1996-2000; columnist Star Wars Insider, 1994—. Lectr. bus. journalism U. So. Calif., L.A., 1984-87. Author: The Punishment Cure, 1976, Science Fiction Toys and Models, 1981, Star Wars: From Concept to Screen to Collectible, 1992, Tomart's Price Guide to Worldwide Star Wars Collectibles, 1994, 2d edit., 1997, The Quotable Star Wars, 1996, Star Wars Scrapbook: The Essential Collection, 1998, Star Wars Encyclopedia, 1998, Star Wars Collectibles: A Pocket Manual, 1998, Anakin Skywalker: The Story of Darth Vader, 1998, Star Wars: The Action Figure Archive, 1999; cons. editor: Star Wars Galaxy card sets, 1993, 2d series, 1994, 3d series, 1995; editor: Star Wars Trilogy Spl. Edn. card sets, 1997. Recipient award for best fire story Phila. Fire Dept., 1968, Pub. Svc.-Team Mem. award Sigma Delta Chi, 1977; finalist Loeb award, 1990. Mem. Soc. Profl. Journalists. Avocation: collecting toys and movie memorabilia. Office: Lucasfilm Ltd PO Box 10228 San Rafael CA 94912-0228

SANT, JOHN TALBOT, lawyer; b. Oct. 7, 1932; s. John Francis and Josephine (Williams) S.; m. Almira Steedman Baldwin, Jan. 31, 1959; children: John Talbot Jr., Richard Baldwin, Frank Williams. AB, Princeton U., 1954; LLB, Harvard U., 1957. Bar: Mo. 1957. Assoc. Thompson, Mitchell, Douglas & Neill, St. Louis, 1958-60; atty. McDonnell Aircraft Co., St. Louis, 1960-61; asst. sec., 1961-62; sec., 1962-67, McDonnell Douglas Corp., St. Louis, 1967-76; asst. gen. counsel, 1969-74; corp. v.p. legal, 1974-75; corp. v.p., gen. counsel, 1975-88; bd. dirs., 1978-82; sr. v.p., gen. counsel, 1988-91; ptnr. Bryan Cave, 1991-96; of counsel, 1997. Vestry of St. Michael and St. George, St. Louis, 1979-82, 87-90, 93-95; bd. dirs. Grace Hill Neighborhood Svcs., Inc., St. Louis, 1987-93; pres. Grace Hill Settlement House, 1996-97; mem. transition task force Supt. Elect. of St. Louis Pub. Schs., 1996, found. dir. St. Louis Pub. Schs. Found., chair Partnership For Youth, Inc., 2001—. Mem. ABA (pub. contracts sec., coun. 1987-91), Mo. Bar Assn., St. Louis Bar Assn. Home: 9 Ridgewood St Saint Louis MO 63124-1849 Office: Bryan Cave 1 Metropolitan Sq Ste 3600 Saint Louis MO 63102-2750

SANT, ROGER W. energy executive; Masters, Harvard U. Instr. corp. fin. Stanford U. Grad. Sch. Bus.; founder several businesses; dir. Mellon Inst.'s Energy Productivity Ctr.; co-founder AES Corp., Washington, 1981, CEO, 1981—93, chmn. bd., 1981—2003, chmn. emeritus, 2003. Mem. bd. dirs. The Summit Found. (chmn.), World Wildlife Fund (chmn. 1994-2000), Marriott Internat., Inc.; regent, Smithsonian Inst. Author: The Least-Cost Energy Strategy; co-author: Creating Abundance-America's Least-Cost Energy Strategy; contbr. articles to profl. jours.

SANTA-COLOMA, BERNARDO, secondary school educator, counselor; b. N.Y.C., May 31, 1934; s. Bernardo Santa-Coloma Sr. and Belma Remotti; m. Sofia A. Santa-Coloma, Dec. 22, 1981; childen: Ananda, Anita. BA in Humanistic Psychology, U. Calif., Santa Cruz, 1973; MA in Integral Counseling Psychology, Calif. Inst. Integral Studies, San Francisco, 1976; MEd in Secondary Edn., U. Nev., Las Vegas, 1979; 3 level cert., Feuerstein's Instrumental, Enrichment Program; postgrad., U. Sarasota and U. Houston. Cert. secondary edn. tchr. ESL, history, English Tex., guidance counselor Tex. Edn. Agy., nat. counselor, lic. marriage and family therapist Tex., profl. counselor Tex. Mem. tchr. corps., vol. VISTA, Las Vegas, Nev., 1976-79; family counselor, English tutor Diocese of Matamoros and Valle Hermoso Tamps, Mexico, Cath. Family Svcs. and Vol. Ednl. and Social Svcs., Amarillo, Tex., 1980-82; grad. asst. Pan Am. U., Brownsville, Tex., 1983-84; at-risk program, low-level reading instr. Brownsville Ind. Sch. Dist., 1984-94; basic skills instr. James Pace High Sch., Brownsville; pres. Alternative Edn. Ctr./Brownsville Ind. Sch. Dist., 1994—. Counselor and psychotherapist Family Effectiveness and Devel. Program, Kids in Crisis, Teenage Crisis Hotline, La Casa Esperanza Home for Boys; basic adult reading instr. Southmost Coll.; ESL, lang. arts tchr. Alternative Ctr.; at-risk tchr., pvt. practice counselor, Brownsville Ind. Sch. Dist. Family Ctrs., 1994—1998; part-time counselor Holistic Mind and Health Inst., Brownsville, 1998; counselor, psychotherapist, contract worker, counselor supr., chem. dependency counselor Recovery Ctr., Cameron County Housing Authority, 1999-2001, Citadel Group, 2003—; medicaid provider, approved supr. LPC interns, LMFT assocs.; supr. Weslaco, Deer Oaks Mental Health Assocs., 2002—2004, Bd. Prisons, Tex. Commn. Alcohol/Drug Prevention prog. counselor, recovery ctr., 2004—. Contbr. articles to profl. jours. in U.S. and Mex. including Integracion Integral, Journey in Matamoros. Vol. VISTA, 1976-79, VISTA Tchr. Corps, Las Vegas, Peace Corps, Thailand, 1979, Vol. Edn./Soc. Svc., Tex., Mex., 1980-82. With USN, 1952-56, medic neuropsychiatric wards San Diego and Guam. Recipient scholarship U. Calif.-Santa Cruz, 1971-73, U. Nev. tchr. corps scholar, 1977-79; named grad. asst. Calif. Inst. Integral Studies, 1974-76. Home: PO Box 3941 Brownsville TX 78523-3941 also: Country Club 2009 Madero Dr Brownsville TX 78526-1734 Fax: 956-548-0028. Office Phone: 956-982-3843., 956-548-0028. E-mail: bsantacoloma@rgv.rr.com. *Waking up is really the seed of perfection, of personal and transpersonal realization - involution precedes evolution! To be is to do and to do IS. In the final analysis, final judgment, what shall we - yes, you and I contribute to our fellowman, to posterity? - we often die before giving birth to ourselves - truly to be reborn is not easy; we create, instead, an intense paradox, toward life, toward our destiny (i.e., a paradoxical process of self denial instead of one of genuine self interest, self-realization,-actualization, ad infinitum, in tune with spirit, the cosmos...'Like trees', we begin with a seed. Some do not develop at all. Some die young. And some grow into towering heights with many flourishing branches).*

SANTAMARINA, RODRIGO, surgeon, researcher; s. Fernando Santamarina and Yolanda Novella; m. Regina Echeverria, Apr. 8, 2000; children: Daniella, Gabriel. BS, Francisco Marroquin U., Guatemala, 1993, MD, 1995. Resident in gen. surgery Francisco Marroquin U., 1995—98; rsch. fellow Plastic Surgery Ctr. Md., Balt., 1998—99; intern in gen. surgery Berkshire Med. Ctr., U. Mass., Pittsfield, 1999—2000, resident in gen. surgery, 2001—03, chief resident in gen. surgery, 2003—04; fellow in hand surgery U. Mass. Hosp., Worcester, 2004—. Mem. faculty, instr. anatomy Balt. Workshop Plastic Surgery, 2003; presenter, instr. in anatomy, endoscopic facial surgery, Taiwan, 1999. Contbr. articles to profl. jours. Mem.: ACS, Mass. Med. Benevolent Soc., NY Acad. Scis., Mass. Med. Soc. Avocation: photography. Office: 281 Lincoln St Worcester MA 01605-2192

SANTANA, CARLOS, guitarist; b. Autlan de Navarro, Mexico, July 20, 1947; Guitarist Santana Mgmt., San Rafael, Calif., 1987—, Prin. Guts and Grace Records, 1993. Played guitar in Tijuana nightclubs, recorded with Mike Bloomfield and Al Kooper's Super Session, founder, guitarist rock band Santana, 1966—, appeared at Woodstock Festival, 1969, rec. artist Columbia Records, 1969—97, albums include Santana, 1968, Abraxas, 1970, Santana III, Caravanserai, 1972, Welcome, 1973, Greatest Hits, 1974, Barboletta, 1974, Lotus, 1975, Amigos, 1976, Festival, Moonflower, 1977, Inner Secrets, 1979, Marathon, 1979, Swing of Delight, 1980, Zebop, 1981, Shango, 1982, Havana Moon, 1983, Beyond Appearances, 1985, Freedom, 1987, Viva Santana!, 1988, Doin' It, 1990, Spirits Dancing In the Flesh, 1990, Milagro, 1992, Brothers, 1994, Sacred Fire: Live in South America, 1995, Dance of the Rainbow Serpent, 1995, Supernatural, 1999, solo albums include Devadip Carlos-Oneness: Silver Dreams, Golden Reality, 1979, Blues for Salvador, 1987, appeared in film Soul to Soul, 1971, Love and Music, 1971, Fillmore, 1972, Dominoes: An Uncensored Journey Through the 60s, The All-Star Reggae Session, 1988, Santana: Viva Santana (A Conversation with Carlos), 1989, Carlos Santana: Sacred Fire: Live in Mexico, 1993, History of Rock 'N' Roll, Vol. 6, History of Rock 'N' Roll, Vol. 7, 1995, Blue Note-A Story of Modern Jazz, 1996, Ricky Martin: One Night Only, 1999, 1999, world-wide concert tours with Santana Band, performed and recorded with Buddy Miles, Herbie Hancock, McCoy Tyner, John McLaughlin, Jose Feliciano, Wayne Shorter and Alice Coltrane, Aretha Franklin, Olatunji; rec. artist: Arista Records. Named to Rock and Roll Hall of Fame, 1998; recipient Gold Medal award, 1977, Grammy award, 1989, 1999, Century award Billboard Mag., 1996, Spl. Achievement award ALMA, 1999. Office: Santana Mgmt PO Box 10348 San Rafael CA 94912-0348 *Keep an open heart, focus on the positive, be true to your innermost feelings, but most of all make time to visit the Lord within.*

SANTANA, NIURKA MARIBEL, psychologist, educator; b. N.Y., N.Y., Dec. 5, 1969; d. Angel M. and Idalia L. Santana. BA, Fla. Internat. U., 1991; MS, Miami Inst. of Psychology, 1993; PhD, Carlos Albizu U., 2000. Adj. faculty Carlos Albizu U., Miami, Fla., 1997—; case mgr. United Behavorial Health, Miami, 2001—03; lic. psychologist Pinecrest Rehab Hosp., Delray Beach, Fla., 2002—; neuropsychologist Rehab without Walls, Ft. Lauderdale, 2003—. Author: (poster) Capgras Syndrome: A Case Study, 2003, (presentation) Development of a Consumer Satisfaction Scale. Mem.: Am. Psychological Assn. Cath. Avocations: writing, dance, poetry.

SANTANGELO, GASPARE CHARLES, education educator, retired principal; b. N.Y.C., June 1, 1937; s. Joseph and Rose Santangelo; m. Josephine A. Gaulli, June 29, 1980; children: Christina, Robert De Lia Jr. children: Steven, Robert, Joseph, Philip. BS, St. Francis Coll., N.Y.C., 1958; MS, SUNY, New Paltz, 1966; PhD, Pacific Western U., L.A., 1990. Cert. tchr. N.Y., supt. schs. Calif., sch. dist. adminstr. N.Y. Tchr. and asst. prin. South Huntington (N.Y.) Schs., 1959—68; adminstrv. asst. to the supt. of schs. San Diego City Schs., 1968—71; tchr. and prin. South Country Schools, Bellport, NY, 1971—92; assoc. prof. edn. Dowling Coll., Oakdale, NY, 1992—. Dir. Ctr. for Human Interaction, East Patchogue, NY, 1982—99. Author: (training manual) A Rational Approach to Stress Management, 1984, (instructional manual) A Nation in Crisis AIDS: Identifying the Risks, 1988. Achievement in Sci. fellow, Nat. Inst. Sci., 1966. Personal E-mail: gcsant@aol.com.

SANTANGELO, JOSEPH ANTHONY, corporation executive; b. Norristown, Pa., Apr. 13, 1954; s. Anthony Charles and Grace (Bonfiglio) S.; m. Susan Eldred, Sept. 16, 1978; children: Jenifer, Mark. BS in Acctg., Drexel U., 1977. CPA, Pa. Staff acct. to sr. mgr. Price Waterhouse, Phila., 1977-87; treas. FPA Corp., Huntingdon Valley, Pa., 1987—94; CFO Orleans Homebuilders, 1994—. Mem. Mt. Laurel, N.J. Newcomers Orgn. Mem. Am. Inst. CPA's, Pa. Inst. CPA's, Pi Kappa Phi (bd. dirs. 1978-81). Republican. Roman Catholic. Avocations: basketball, golf, softball, volleyball. Home: 59 Horseshoe Dr Mount Laurel NJ 08054-3055 Office: Orleans Homebuilders Inc One Greenwood Square 3333 Street Rd Ste 101 Bensalem PA 19020

SANTANGELO, MARIO VINCENT, dentist; b. Youngstown, Ohio, Oct. 5, 1931; s. Anthony and Maria (Zarlenga) S. Student, U. Pitts., 1949-51; DDS, Loyola U., Chgo., 1955, MS, 1960. Instr. Loyola U., 1957-60, asst. prof., 1960-66, assoc. prof., 1966-70, chmn. dept. radiology, 1962-70, dir. dental aux. utilization program, 1963-70, chmn. dept. oral diagnosis, 1967-70, asst. dean, 1969-70; pvt. practice, Chgo., 1960-70. Cons. Cert. Bd. Am. Dental Assts. Assn., 1967-75, VA Rsch. Hosp., 1969-75; counselor Chgo. Dental Assts. Assn., 1966-69; mem. dental student tng. adv. com. divsn. dental health USPHS, HEW, 1969-71; cons. dental edn. rev. com. NIH, 1971-72; cons. region IV, USPHS, HEW, Atlanta, 1973-76, region V, Chgo., 1973-77; mem. Commn. on Dental Edn. and Practice, Fedn. Dentaire Internat., 1984-92; mem. bd. visitors Washington U. Sch. Dental Medicine, St. Louis, 1974-76. Contbr. articles to dental jours. 1st Lt. USAF, 1955—56, Capt. USAF, 1956—57. Recipient Dr. Harry Strusser Meml. award NYU Coll. Dentistry, 1985. Fellow Am. Coll. Dentists (life); mem. ADA (life, asst. sec. coun. dental edn. 1971-81, acting sec. 1981-82, sec. 1982-90, dir. 1990-92, asst. sec. commn. on dental accreditation 1975-81, acting sec. 1981-82, sec. 1982-90, dir. 1990-92, acting sec. commn. continuing dental edn. 1981-82, sec. 1982-90, dir. 1990-92), Ill. State Dental Assn. (life), Chgo. Dental Assn. (life), AMA (edn. work group 1982-86), Assembly Specialized Accrediting Bodies (coun. on postsecondary accreditation 1981-92, award of merit 1992), Am. Assn. Dental Schs., Odontographic Soc. Chgo. (life), Am. Acad. Oral Pathology, Am. Acad. Dental Radiology, Can. Dental Assn. (commn. on dental accrediation award of merit 1992), Am. Acad. Oral Medicine, Am. Assn. Dental Examiners (hon.), Blue Key, Omicron Kappa Upsilon, Xi Psi Phi. Home: 1440 N Lake Shore Dr Chicago IL 60610-1626

SANTANIELLO, ANGELO GARY, retired state supreme court justice; b. New London, Conn., May 28, 1924; s. Samuel C. and Katie Santaniello; m. Catherine A. Driscoll, June 1948 (dec.); children: Samuel Gary, Lisa Mary; m. Catherine M. Cooper, Sept. 27, 1968; 1 child, Maria Roberta. BA, Coll. Holy Cross, 1945; JD, Georgetown U., 1950. Bar: Conn. 1950, U.S. Dist. Ct. Conn. Sole practice, New London, 1950-53; sr. ptnr. Santaniello & Satti, 1953-61, Santaniello Satti Wilensky & Schwartz, 1962-65; judge Conn. Cir. Ct., 1966-71, Conn. Ct. Common Pleas, 1971-73, Conn. Superior Ct., 1973-85, adminstrv.judge, 1978-85, chief adminstrv. judge, civil divsn., 1979-85; assoc. justice Conn. Supreme Ct., Hartford, 1985-87, sr. assoc. justice, 1987-94; chief mediator State-Fed. ADR, Inc., 1993-95; mediator Conn. Superior Ct. Annexed Mediation Program, 1996—. Asst. pros. atty. New London Police Ct., 1951-55; bd. dirs. New London Fed. Savs. and Loan. Trustee New London Pub. Libr., Lawrence and Meml. Hosp.; bd. dirs. Am. Cancer Soc.; chmn. New London Rep. Party, 1956-65; nat. committeeman Conn. State Young Reps., 1959-61; legal counsel Conn. State Senate Rep. Minority, 1961-65; campaign mgr. for gubernatorial candidate, 1962; mem. athletic coun. Holy Cross Coll., 1971-77, chmn., 1972-73; trustee Mitchell Coll., 1976-89, chmn., 1988-91. Served to lt. (j.g.) USNR, 1942-46. Recipient Columbus award Italian-Am. Civic Assn., 1964, In Hoc Signo award Holy Cross Coll., 1976, 1st Humanitarian award Eastern Conn. chpt. March of Dimes, 1983, Conn. Supreme Ct. Law Day award, 1999. Mem. Conn Bar Assn. (Henry J. Naruk award 1999), New London Bar Assn., Am. Justinian Soc., Holy Cross Alumni Assn. (bd. dirs., pres. 1981-82), Conn. Trial Lawyers Assn. (Jud. award). Roman Catholic. Home: 25 Shirley Ln New London CT 06320-2929 Office: 70 Huntington St New London CT 06320-6113

SANTAS, ARISTOTELIS, philosophy educator, massage therapist; b. Lefkas, Greece, July 10, 1961; s. Constantine and Mary Santas; m. Patricia Ann McDonald, Oct. 23, 1982; children: Alethea Day Santas-McElwain, Michael Andrew, Aris Caddell. PhD, Fla. State U., 1989. Cert. massage therapist NCBTMB, 2002. Prof. Valdosta State U., Ga., 1990—. Massage therapist Golden Pyramid, Valdosta, Ga. Contbr. articles to profl. jours. V.p. People's Tribunal, Valdosta, Ga., 1999—2002; mem. Valdosta Project Change, Ga., 1996—98. Recipient Ron Brown award for corp. leadership, US Govt., 1998. Mem.: AAUP, Can. Soc. for Study of European Ideas, Ga. Philos. Soc., Southeastern Philosophy of Edn. Soc. Avocation: martial arts. Office: Valdosta State Univ Dept Philosophy Valdosta GA 31698 Office Phone: 229-333-5949. Business E-Mail: asantas@valdosta.edu.

SANTEE, DALE WILLIAM, lawyer, air force officer; b. Washington, Pa., Mar. 28, 1953; s. Robert Erwin and Elsbeth Emma (Bantleon) S.; married; 1 child, Enri De'Von; m. Junko Mori, June 2, 1992. BA, Washington & Jefferson Coll., 1975; MA, U. No. Ariz., 1982; JD, U. Pitts., 1978. Bar: Pa. 1978, U.S. Ct. Mil. Appeals 1979, Calif. 1989. Floor mgr., commn. salesman J.C. Penney Co., Washington, Pa., 1971-76; asst. mgr. Rach Enterprises, Charleroi, Pa., 1977-78; legal intern Washington County Pub. Defender; commd. 2d lt. USAF, 1979, advanced through grades to col., 2001; from asst. staff judge advocate to area def. counsel Luke Air Force Base, Ariz., 1979-81; claims officer 343 Combat Support Group/Judge Advocate, Eielson AFB, Alaska, 1981-83; sr. staff legal adviser Dept. Vet. Affairs, Washington, 1983-89; asst. staff judge advocate Mil. Justice div. Air Force Judge Advocate Gen.'s Office, Washington, 1986-89, 63CSG/Judge Advocate, Norton Air Force Base, Calif., 1989-91; dep. pub. defender Juvenile div. San Diego County, 1990-93, dep. alt. pub. defender, 1993-98; asst. staff judge advocate 452 AMW, March Air Res. Base, Calif., 1991-99, staff judge advocate, 1999-2001; supervising dep., alt. pub. defender Conflict Parent-Child Office, 1998-2001, dep. alt. pub. defender, 2001—; sr. IMA 21 AF/JA, Mc Guire AFB, NJ, 2001—03, HQ Air Res. Pers. Ctr., Denver, 2003—04, HQ PACAF/JA, Hickam AFB, 2004—. V.p. Neuer Enterprises, Nanjemoy, Md., 1983-89; participant Mgmt. Devel. Seminar, 1988. Mem. San Diego County Rep. Party; pres., co-chmn. legis. com. PTA Zamorano Elem. Sch., San Diego, chmn. SITE com.; mem. San Diego County Child Abuse Coord. Coun., San Diego County Commn. on Children and Youth, San Diego County Juvenile Ct. Mental Health Task Force, San Diego County Unified Sch. Dist. Parent Adv. Coun.; bd. dirs. San Diego County Youth Ct. Program, Pub. Defenders Assn., Train Ct. Apptd. Spl. Advocates for Voices for Children, McGill Ctr. Creative Problem Solving Youth Curriculum Com. Decorated Air Force Commendation medal, 1981, 89, Air Force Meritorious Svc. medal, 1991, 96, 99, 2001, 2003, Air Force Achievement medal, 2000; named Outstanding Young Man of Am., U.S. Jaycees, Montgomery, Ala., 1981; acad. scholar Washington & Jefferson Coll., 1971-75, Beta scholar Washington & Jefferson Coll., 1974, Pa. Senatorial scholar Pa. Senate, 1975-78; named Juvenile Justice Commn. Atty of Yr., 1997; recipient Clara Shortridge Foltz award ABA/Nat. Legal Aid and Defender Assn., 1999, Judge Advocates Assn. Outstanding Career Armed Svcs. Atty. award, 2000. Mem. Pa. Bar Assn., Calif. Bar Assn., San Diego County Bar Assn., San Diego County Psych-Law Soc. Avocations: swimming, softball, stamp and coin collecting, foreign travel. Office: 8525 Gibbs Dr Ste 201 San Diego CA 92123 Office Phone: 858-974-5819. E-mail: Dale.Santee@sdcounty.ca.gov.

SANTELLE, JAMES LEWIS, prosecutor; b. Milw., Sept. 10, 1958; s. James Nathaniel and Carol Jean (Hasley) S. BA, Marquette Univ., 1980; JD, Univ. Chgo., 1983. Bar: Wis. 1983, U.S. Dist. Ct. (ea. and we. dist.) 1983, U.S. Ct. Appeals (7th cir.) 1983. Clerk Hon. Judge Robert W. Warren, Milw., 1983-85; asst. U.S. atty. Ea. Dist. Wis., Milw., 1985—, civil divsn. chief, 1993—99, interim U.S. atty., 2001—02; prin. dep. dir. Exec. Office U.S. Attys., U.S. Dept. Justice, Washington, 1999—2001, exec. asst. U.S. atty., 2002—03; chief civil divsn. Western Dist. Mich., Grand Rapids, 2003—. Profl. responsibility com., investigator Wis. Bd. of Attys., 1993-99, Ea. dist. of Wis. Bar Assn. (sec. 2001-.). Editor: The Milw. Lawyer, 1986-92. Bd. dirs. Waukesha County Coun. Alcoholism and Other Drug Abuse, 1993-99; citizen counselor Badger Boys State, 1986—; coach Wis. Bar Found. High Sch. Mock Trial Tournament, 1986-99. Avocations: running, swimming. Office: US Atty Office 517 E Wisconsin Ave Rm 530 Milwaukee WI 53202-4580

SANTER, BENJAMIN, atmospheric scientist, meteorologist; b. Washington, June 3, 1955; BS Environ. Scis. with 1st class honors, U. East Anglia, Norwich, Eng., 1976; NATO Rsch. Studentship, U. East Anglia, 1977, PhD in Climatology, 1987. Jr. rsch. assoc. Sch. Environ. Scis. U. East Anglia, Norwich, Eng., 1978-79, rsch. assoc. climatic rsch. unit, 1983-87; project engr. dept. new techs., air pollution and Dornier Sys. GmbH, Friedrichshafen, Germany, 1980-83; postdoct., rsch. scientist Max-Planck Inst. Meteorologie, Hamburg, Germany, 1987-92; physicist earth and environ. scis. directorate Lawrence Livermore Nat. Lab., Livermore, Calif., 1992—. Expert witness German Bundestag Enquete Commn. Hearings on Greenhouse-Gas-Induced Climate Change, Bonn, Germany, 1992; cons. Battelle Pacific Northwest Lab., 1992-93, mem. sci. adv. panel climate change, data and detection program NOAA, 1995—; mem. Climate Variability and Predictability Numerical Experimentation Group, 1995—; participant numerous confs., workshops; lectr. in field. Co-author: Proceedings of NATO Advanced Study Institute on Physically-Based Modelling and Simulation of Climate and Climatic Change, 1988, Science and Engineering on Supercomputers, 1990, Supercomputer '90, Greenhouse-Gas-Induced Climate Change: A Critical Appraisal of Simulations and Observations, 1991, Global Warming: Concern for Tomorrow, 1993, Agricultural Dimensions of Global Climate Change, 1993, Dahlem Workshop on Global Changes in the Perspective of the Past, 1993, Climate Change int the Intra-American Sea, 1993, Communicating About Climate: the Story of the Model Evaluation Consortium for Climate Assessment, 1997; mem. editl. bd. Climatic Change, 1996—; contbr. numerous articles to profl. jours., chpts. to books. MacArthur fellow John D. and Catherine T. MacArthur Found., 1998; Ford Travel scholar, 1974; recipient Outstanding Scientific Paper award U.S. Dept. Commerce Environ. Rsch. Lab. Nat. Oceanic and Atmospheric Adminstrn., 1997, Norbert Gerbier-MUMM Internat. award World Meteorol. Orgn., 1998, E.O. Lawrence award U.S. Dept. Energy, 2002. Mem. Am. Geophys. Union. Achievements include research in climate modeling and greenhouse-gas effects supporting the hypothesis that human activity contributes to global warming. Office: Lawrence Livermore Nat Lab PCMDI PO Box 808 L-264 Livermore CA 94551-0808 Home: 2160 Goldenrod Ln San Ramon CA 94583-5555 Fax: (925) 422-7675. E-mail: santer1@llnl.gov.

SANTI, DANIEL V. biotechnology company executive; BS in Pharmacy, SUNY; MD, U. Calif., San Francisco; PhD in Medicinal chemistry, SUNY. Founder, chmn. bd. Parnassus Pharms.; founder, chmn. bd. dirs. Protos, a subsidiary of Chiron Corp., 1988; co-founder, chmn. bd. dirs. Kosan Bioscis., Inc., Hayward, Calif., chmn., CEO, 1998—; prof. biochemistry and biophysics, pharm. chemistry U. Calif., San Francisco, 1974—2001. Mem. sci. adv. bd. Chiron Corp., Mitotix, Inc.; cons. in field. Contbr. over 275 articles to profl. jours. Achievements include patents for in combinatorial chemistry and other areas. Office: Kosan Biosciences Inc 3832 Bay Center Pl Hayward CA 94545

SANTIAGO, BENITO RIVERA, professional baseball player; b. Ponce, P.R., Mar. 9, 1965; m. Bianca Santiago; 1 child, Benny Beth. Baseball player San Diego Padres, 1986-92, Florida Marlins, 1993-94, Cin. Reds, 1995, 2000—, Philadelphia Phillies, 1996, Toronto Blue Jays, 1997-98; catcher Chgo. Cubs, 1999. Named Nat. League Rookie of Yr. Baseball Writers' Assn. Am., 1987, Sporting News All-Star Team, 1987, 89, 91, 92; recipient Gold Glove award, 1988-90, Silver Slugger award, 1987-88, 90-91; holder maj. league rookie record for most consecutive games batted safely. Office: Cin Reds 100 Cinergy Fld Cincinnati OH 45202-3543

SANTIAGO, MIKE, communications executive; Pres. Creators Syndicate, L.A., 1997—. Office: Creators Syndicate 5777 W Century Blvd Ste 700 Los Angeles CA 90045-5675

SANTILLI, ANTHONY J., JR., investment company executive; Chmn., CEO, pres. Am. Bus. Fin. Svcs., Bala Cynwyd, Pa., 1988—.

SANTINA, DALIA, nutritionist, writer, skin care specialist; b. Amman, Jordan, Sept. 24, 1954; d. Mahmoud Dauod Abbasi, Widad Abbasi; m. Mohammed Shafiq Santina. BA in English Lit., U. Riyadh, Saudi Arabia, 1977; diploma in computer programming, Western Bus. Coll., 1980; diploma in Skin Aesthetics, Career Acad. Beauty, 1989; PhD in Holistic Nutrition, Clayton Coll. Natural Health, 1994. Cert. paramedical acne 1990, glycolic acid services 1991, mgmt. aging and sun-damaged skin 1992, natural pharmacology 1992, aesthetic peeling 1992, oxygenation of the skin 1993, lymphatic drainage massage techniques 1994, homeopathic esthetiocology 1994, iridology diploma 1995, cert. chem. peels 1996, hydrotherapy 1997, glycolic treatments 1998, diploma in iridology 2003, cert. in herbology 2003. Exec. asst. to v.p. Am. Health Ctr., Newport Beach, Calif., 1988—89; skin care co. Skinclub, Huntington Beach, Calif., 1991—96; lectr. holistic nutrition/skin health issues, 1999—. Translator computer sys. tng. manuals, Dallas, 1983—84; tech. translator England and No. Ireland, 1984. Author: Holistic Skin Is...In, 2001, Super Supplements for Skin, Body & Mind, 2004; contbr. articles to profl. jours. Recipient Gold medal in Table Tennis, Sports Bd., Kuwait, 1972. Avocations: horseback riding, reading, antiques. Personal E-mail: dalia4skin@msn.com.

SANTINI, DANILO JOHN, energy economist, urban systems engineer; b. Louisville, Mar. 10, 1945; s. Danilo Gene Santini and Mary Margaret (Dink) Brown; m. Tomma Jean Trent, Dec. 28, 1969; children: Laura Trent, Danilo Thomas. BArch, MIT, 1968; MS in Bus. and Econs., Ill. Inst. Tech., 1972; PhD Urban Systems/Pub. Policy Analysis, Northwestern U., 1976. High sch. tchr. math. and sci. George Washington High Sch., Charleston, W.Va., 1968-70; asst. scientist Argonne (Ill.) Nat. Lab., 1974-79, scientist, 1980-92; sect. mgr., 1993—. Archtl. draftsman Bowman & Assocs., Vecellio and Kreps, Charleston, Va., 1963-70, Teng & Assocs., Chgo., 1971-72; lectr. in econs. U. Ill. at Chgo., 1983, Lewis U., Romeoville, Ill., 1984; mem. alternative fuels com. Transp. Rsch. Bd., Washington, 1989—96, chmn., 1996-91. Contbr. chpts. to books, articles to profl. jours. Trustee, mem. bldg. com. Friendship United Meth. Ch., Bolingbrook, Ill., 1991—; asst. coach Pony-Colt Baseball, Bolingbrook, 1984-86; active Am. Field Svcs., 1989-90. Northwestern U. fellow, 1972-74, Ill. Inst. Tech. fellow, 1970. Mem. Am. Econs. Assn., Internat. Assn. Energy Economists (chpt. pres. 1985-86), Internat. Inst. Forecasters, Regional Sci. Assn., Sigma Iota Epsilon. Avocations: bowling, walking. Office: Argonne Nat Lab 9700 Cass Ave Lemont IL 60439-4803

SANTINI, DEBRAH ANN, art educator, artist; BFA in Painting, U. Mass., 1983, MFA in Printmaking, 1994; postgrad., Pratt Inst., 1983-84; MEd in Printmaking, U. Hartford, 1988. Cert. tchr. 5-12, Mass., K-12 (provisional), Conn. Art tchr. Granby (Conn.) Meml. H.S., 1989-90, Suffield (Conn.) H.S., 1990-91; tchr. U. Mass, Amherst, 1991-93; asst. prof. State U. West Ga., Carrollton, 1994—. Artist-in-residence Bridgeport Mus. Art, Sci. and Industry, 1988, Lit. Showcase, Bristol, R.I., 1990, Connecticut Loves to Read, Windsor, Conn., 1991, Internat. Reading Assn., San Antonio, 1993, Am. Book Sellers Assn., Chgo., 1995, 96, Southeastern Book Sellers Assn., Nashville, 1996, So. Festival Books: Tenn. Humanities Coun., 1996, Westside Magnet Sch., LaGrange, Ga., 1997, 5th Annual Children's Storytelling Festival, Mableton, Ga., 1997; adj. prof. U. Hartford, Conn., 1991-92; lectr. in field. One-woman shows include Josoloff Gallery, U. Hartford, 1987, Springfield (Mass.) Ctrl. Gallery, 1988, Western New England Coll., Springfield, 1989, Fitchburg (Mass.) Mus. Fine Arts, 1993, Am. Internat. Coll., Springfield, 1993; group shows include Taipei Mus. Arts, 1988, 90, New Britain (Conn.) Mus. Art, 1989, U. Wis., Kenosha, 1991, Okla. State U., Stillwater, 1991, Associated Artists, Winston-Salem, N.C., 1992, San Jacinto Coll., Houston, 1993, Print Club Albany, Schenectady, N.Y., 1995, Arno Maris Gallery, Westfield, Mass., 1995, Artlink, Fort Wayne, Ind., 1996, Rolling Stone Press, Atlanta, 1996, 97, Appalachian State U., Boone, N.C., 1997, Rutgers U., New Brunswick, N.J., 1997, Cultural Ctr. Recoleta, Buenos Aires, 1997, Cultural Ctr. Trapalanda, Rio Cuarto, Cordoba, 1997, Contemporary Art Ctr., Mendoza, 1997, U. Minn., Mpls., 1998, Woman Made Gallery, Chgo., 1998, Visual Arts Alliance Nashville Am. Pop Culture Gallery, 1998, Museao Emilio Caraffa, Cordoba, 1998, Nat. U. Chaco, 1998, Columbus (Ga.) Mus., 1998; represented in permanent collections Gardiner Art Gallery, Okla. State U., Agawam (Mass.) Pub. Libr., Smith Coll. Rare Book Room, Neilson Libr., Northampton, Mass., Cultural Arts Ctr., Douglasville, Ga., Ga. Coll., Milledgeville, Chattahoochee Valley Art Mus., LaGrange; illustrator: The Baby Who Would Not Come Down, 1989, Santa's Secret Helper, 1990, Tulips, 1992, 96, Cinderella, 1994, The Last Dance, 1996, Wishing, 1996, When Young Melissa Sweeps, 1998, Oh, Georgia, Too!, 1998, (mags.) US KIDS, 1991, CRICKET, 1991, READ, 1993, POCKETS, 1998, 99. Recipient Purchase award Cimarron Nat. Works on Paper, 1991, Douglas County Regional Juried Fine Arts Show, 1994, Pressed & Pulled IV, 1995, XIX LaGrange Nat. Biennial Exhbn., 1996, Merit award Springfield Art League 76th Nat. Exhbn., 1995, Overall Excellence award Southeastern Libr. Assn., 1996; Don Freeman Meml. grantee Soc. Children's Book Writers Illustrators, 1987, Mass. Arts Lottery grantee, 1988, Nat. Endowment Arts/Southern Artists Fedn. grantee, 1996.

SANTINI, GINO, marketing professional; Pres. SERM and skeletal products; pharm. dir. Lilly affiliate, Belgium, 1990, gen .mgr., 1991, area dir. to v.p. corp. strategy and bus. devel., 1994—95; pres. Am. ops. and global mktg. Eli Lilly and Co., 1999—. Office: Eli Lilly and Co Lilly Corp Ctr Indianapolis IN 46285

SANTINI, JORGE, mayor; b. San Juan, P.R., 1960; BA, U. P.R.; law degree cum laude, Interam. U. Ptnr. Miranda Cardenas & Córdova, 1986; legal advisor Gov. of P.R., 1994—96; mem. Sen. of P.R.; mayor City of San Juan, 2001—. Chmn. Sen. Jud. Com.; vice-chmn. Govt. and Fed. Affairs Com., Banking, Consumer Affairs, and Pub. Corps. Com. Lt. col. Puerto Rico Nat. Guard. New Progressive Party. Office: PO Box 9024100 San Juan PR 00902-4100

SANTISTEBAN, JOSEPH HENRY, human resources specialist; b. N.Y.C., July 15, 1946; s. Mario Santisteban and Antonia (dec.) Rivera; m. Evangelista Pilapil, Oct. 26, 1969 (dec. Dec. 1998); children: Jason, Damien. BA, Chapman U., 1972—74; BS, U. of Nebr., 1982—84; MA, Embry-Riddle Aero. U., 1986—90; PhD, U. of the Philippines, 1988—90. Cert. tchr. Ariz. State Bd. Edn., 1993. Chief master sgt. USAF, 1963—94; sr. staff recruiter Swift Transp. Co., Phoenix, Ariz., 1993—99; recruiting and tng. mgr. ATC Leasing Co. Inc., Kenosha, Wis., 1999—2000; human resources dir. Ill. Auto Truck Co. Inc., Des Plaines, 2000—. Chief enlisted mgr. U.S. Air Force, Phoenix, 1963—93; coll. instr. Embry-Riddle Aero. U., Phoenix, 1990—93. Translator. Leader Boy Scouts of Am., 1979—2003, CAP, 1986—92, 2003—. Decorated Bronze Star Medal w/V Dept. of Def.; recipient Outstanding Cmty. Svc. Award, Ariz. C. of C., 1992, Outstanding Svc. Award, Mayor of Mayaguez, PR, 1998, Presdl. Humanitarian Award, Republic of the Philippines, 1970, Outstanding Leader of the Yr., CAP, 1992, Cert. of Recognition, U.S. Sec. of Def., 1994. Mem.: VFW, Air Force Security Police Assn., Air Force Assn., Shriners, Masons. Home: 2465 Forest View Rd Lindenhurst IL 60046-8720 Office: Illinois Auto Truck Co Inc 1669 Marshall Dr Des Plaines IL 60018-1840 Personal E-mail: joesandy@att.net.

SANTMAN, LEON DUANE, lawyer, former federal government executive; b. Phila., July 29, 1930; s. Elmer William and Anna Mary (Moffitt) S.; m. Juliet Gloria Peacock, June 16, 1952; 1 dau., Lorri Leigh Santman Myers. BS, U. S., COAST Guard Acad., 1952; LLB, U. Houston, 1953; LLM, George Washington U., 1968. Bar: Tex. 1963, Md. 1974. Commd. ensign U.S. Coast Guard, 1952, advanced through grades to comdr., 1967, ret., 1972; assoc. gen. counsel Cost of Living Council, Washington, 1972-74; asst. gen. counsel U.S. Dept. Transp., Washington, 1974-77, dir. Materials Transp. Bur., 1977-85; dir. ship ops. Maritime Adminstrn., 1985-88. Episcopalian.

SANTOMERO, ANTHONY M. bank executive, public policymaker; b. N.Y.C., Sept. 29, 1946; s. Camillo and Jean (Oddo) S.; m. Marlena Belviso, Aug. 21, 1971; children: Jill Renee, Marc Anthony. AB, Fordham U., 1968; PhD, Brown U., 1971; EDhe (hon.), Stockholm Sch. Econs., 1992; LHC, U. Rome, 2003. Successively asst. prof., assoc. prof., prof. fin. Wharton Sch., U. Pa., Phila., 1972-84, R.K. Mellon prof. fin., 1984—2002, R.K. Mellon prof. emeritus of fin., 2002—, vice dean, dir. grad. div., 1984-87, dep. dean, 1990-94; dir. Wharton Fin. Instns. Ctr., 1995-2000; pres. Fed. Reserve Bank, Phila., 2000—. Asst. prof. econs. Baruch Coll., CUNY, 1971-72; vis. prof. European Inst. Advanced Studies in Mgmt., Brussels, 1977-78, Stockholm Sch. Econs., 1989-90, U. Rome, Tor Vergata, 1994-97, Ecole Superieure des Sciences Economiques et Commerciales, France, 1977-78. Author: Financial Markets, Instruments and Institutions, 1997, 2001, Challenges for Modern Central Banking, 2001; adv. editor Jour. Banking and Fin., 1978—, assoc. editor Jour. Money, Credit and Banking, 1980—2002, Jour. Fin. Svc. Rsch., 2000—, bd. editors Jour. Econs. and Bus., 1979—, European Fin. Mgmt., 1996—, Advances in Internat. Banking and Fin., 1993—, founding co-editor Brookings-Wharton Papers on Fin. Svcs., 1997—2000, adv. bd. European Banking Report, 1994—, Jour. Internat. Econ. Law, 1997—, editl. bd. Open Econs. Rev., 1990—, mem. faculty adv. bd. Jour. Internat. Econ. Law, 1997—, mem. bd. advisory editors Advances in Fin., Investment and Banking, 1992, editl. adv. bd. Jour. Fin. Stability, 2003—; contbr. articles to profl. jours. Mem.: Am. Econs. Assn., Am. Fin. Assn. Roman Catholic. Home: 310 Keithwood Rd Wynnewood PA 19096-1224 Office: Fed Reserve Bank Phila Ten Independence Mall Philadelphia PA 19106-1574 E-mail: santomero@phil.frb.org.

SANTONA, GLORIA, lawyer; b. Gary, Ind., June 10, 1950; d. Ray and Elvira (Cambeses) S.; m. Douglas Lee Frazier, Apr. 12, 1980. BS in Biochemistry, Mich. State U., 1971; JD, U. Mich., 1977. Bar: Ill. 1977. Atty. McDonald's Corp., Oak Brook, Ill., 1977-82, dir., 1982-86, assoc. gen. counsel, 1986-92, asst. v.p., 1989-93, v.p., sec., dep. gen. counsel, 1996-99, v.p., U.S. gen. counsel, sec., 1999-2001, sr. v.p., gen. counsel, sec., 2001—03, exec. v.p., gen. counsel, sec., 2003—. Mem. ABA, Chgo. Assn., Am. Corp. Counsel Assn., Am. Soc. Corp. Secs. Office: McDonalds Corp 1 Mcdonalds Plz Oak Brook IL 60523-1911

SANTONI, RONALD ERNEST, philosophy educator; b. Arvida, Que., Can., Dec. 19, 1931; s. Fred Albert and Phyllis (Tremaine) S.; m. Marguerite Ada Kiene, June 25, 1955; children: Christina, Marcia, Andrea, Juanita, Jonathan, Sondra. BA, Bishop's U., Lennoxville, Que., 1952; MA, Brown U., 1954; PhD, Boston U., 1961; postgrad., U. Paris-Sorbonne, 1956-57. Asst. prof. philosophy U. Pacific, Stockton, Calif., 1958-61; postdoctoral rsch. fellow Yale U., New Haven, 1961-62; asst. prof. philosophy Wabash Coll., Crawfordsville, Ind., 1962-64; faculty Denison U., Granville, Ohio, 1964—, prof. philosophy, 1968—2002, chmn. dept., 1971-73, 82-84, 92, Maria Theresa Barney chair in philosophy, 1978—, prof. emeritus, 2002—. Peace lectr. Bethel Coll., 1985; vis. scholar in philosophy Cambridge U., Eng., 1986, 90, 94, 97, 99, 2001, vis. lectr. in philosophy, 1990; vis. fellow Clare Hall, Cambridge U., 1986; vis. fellow in philosophy Yale U., 1975, 81, 93-94, 97; keynote speaker 2d Internat. Conf. on Nuclear Free Zones, Cordoba, Spain, 1985; Internat. Studies Assn., London, 1989, speaker and U.S.A. co-chair Internat. conf. Internat. Philosophers for Prevention of Nuclear Omnicide, Moscow, 1990; del. and raporteur UN meeting of Peace Messenger Orgns., Dagomys, Sochi, USSR, 1991; invited participant Colloquium on Technological Risks to Environment, Montreal, 1993; invited spkr. U. Paris (Sorbonne), 2004; spkr. in field. Contbg. author: Current Philosophical Issues: Essays in Honor of C.J. Ducasse, 1966, Towards an Understanding and Prevention of Genocide, 1984, Nuclear War: Philosophical Perspectives, 1985, Genocide: A Critical Bibliographic Review, 1988, Just War, Nonviolence and Nuclear Deterrence: Philosophers on War and Peace, 1992, The Institution of War, 1991, Violence and Human Co-Existence, 1994, Hiroshima's Shadows, 1998, The Encyclopedia of Genocide, 1999, Human Coexistence and Sustainable Development, 2001, Das Sein und das Nichts, 2003, Global Studies Encyclopedia, 2003; author: Bad Faith, Good Faith and Authenticity in Sartre's Early Philosophy, 1995, Sartre on Violence: Curiously Ambivalent, 2003; editor, contbr. Religious Language and the Problem of Religious Knowledge, 1968; co-editor Social and Political Philosophy, 1963; contbg. editor Internet on the Holocaust and Genocide; mem. editl. bd. Jour. Peace and Justice Studies; contbr. over 130 articles to profl. jours. V.p. NAACP, Licking County, 1967; co-organizer Crawfordsville (Ind.) Human Rels. Coun., 1962-64; nat. exec. com. Episcopal Peace Fellowship, 1968-78; internat. coun. Internat. Inst. on the Holocaust and Genocide, 1985—; nat. coun. Fellowship of Reconciliation, 1988-89; trustee Margaret Hall Sch., Versailles, Ky., 1972-74; nat. bd. dirs. Promoting Enduring Peace, 1982—. Canadian Govt. Overseas fellow Royal Soc. Can., 1956-57; Church Soc. for Coll. Work faculty fellow, 1961-62; Yale postdoctoral rsch. fellow, 1961-62; Danforth assoc., 1963-64; Soc. for Religion in Higher Edn. postdoctoral fellow, 1972—; Yale rsch. fellow, 1975; guest fellow Berkeley Coll., Yale U., 1975, 81, 93-94, 97, elected assoc. fellow, 1994—; vis. fellow in philosophy Yale U., 1981, 93-94, 97; Robert C. Good faculty fellow Denison U., 1985-86, 2000-01, Robert C. Good faculty fellow, 1993-94; elected life mem. Clare Hall, Cambridge (Eng.) U., 1986; elected mem. High Table, King's Coll., Cambridge U., 1999; recipient Mellon award for disting. faculty Denison U., 1972, Crossed Keys Faculty of Yr. award Denison U., 1986-87; Philosophy, Freedom and Action Conf. held in his honor, 2002. Mem. Am. Philos. Assn., Ch. Soc. for Coll. Work, Soc. for Phenomenology and Existential Philosophy, Internat. Philosophers for Peace (v.p. 1983-85, v.p. cen. div. 1990-91, internat. pres. 1991-96, internat. exec. com. 1996—), Sartre Soc. of N.Am. (exec. com. 1994—), Sartre Circle (coord. 1997—), le groupe d'Etudes Sartriennes, Gandhi-King Soc., Union of Bi-Nat. Profls. Against Omnicide (v.p. 1978—), Concerned Philosophers for Peace (founding 1980—, pres. 1996-97), Fellowship of Reconciliation, Amnesty Internat., ACLU. Episcopalian. Home: 500 Burg St Granville OH 43023-1005 E-mail: santoni@denison.edu. *Gratitude for what one has been given, commitment to personal growth and integrity, some "gracious gall", listening to the world's humiliated, and a recognition that genuine success is a gift of grace, never fully deserved.*

SANTOPIETRO, ALBERT ROBERT, lawyer; b. Providence, R.I., Oct. 18, 1948; s. Alfred and Marie (Epifanio) Santopietro; m. Linda Stuart, 1994; children: Hope, Spencer, Anna. BA, Brown U., 1969; JD, U. Va., 1972. Bar: R.I. 1973, Conn. 1983, Mass. 1997, U.S. Dist. Ct. R.I. 1973, Ill. 1974, U.S. Dist. Ct. Mass. 1997. Atty. Met. Life Ins. Co., Oak Brook, Ill., 1974—75, Seligman Group, N.Y.C., 1975—76, Mut. Benefit Life Ins. Co., Newark, 1976—78, asst. counsel, 1978—81, counsel, 1982—; assoc. counsel Conn. Mutual Life Ins. Co., Hartford, 1981—82, counsel, 1995—; 2d v.p. and assoc. gen. counsel Mass. Mutual. Home: 142 Pond Brook Rd Huntington MA 01050-9620 Office: 1500 Main St Ste 2800 Springfield MA 01115 Office Phone: 413-226-1068. Office Fax: 413-226-2068. E-mail: asantopietro@massmutual.com.

SANTORO, ANTHONY RICHARD, history professor; b. Feb. 2, 1939; m. Carol Lynne; 1 child, Melissa. AB, Coll. of the Holy Cross, 1960; MA, U. Calif., 1962; PhD, Rutgers U., 1978. Instr. history Monmouth Coll., West Long Branch, N.J., 1963-67; v.p. for adminstrn., chair depts history and philosophy, registrar Briarcliff Coll., Briarcliff Manor, N.Y., 1967-77; v.p. Devel. and Coll. Rels. Ladycliff Coll., Highland Falls, NY, 1977—78; pres. St. Joseph's Coll., Standish, Maine, 1979-87, Christopher Newport U., Newport News, Va., 1987-96, pres. emeritus, disting. prof. history, 1996—. Author: Theophanes Chronographia: A Chronicle of 8th Century Byzantium, 1982; co-author: An Eyewitness to History: The Short History of Nikephoros the Patriarch of Constantinople, 1991, (4-track DVD) Triumph of the Will (Leni Riefenstahl), 2001. Office: Christopher Newport U McMurran Hall 217 1 University Pl Newport News VA 23606-2998 Office Phone: 757-594-7709. Office Fax: 757-594-7718. Business E-Mail: santoro@cnu.edu.

SANTORO, CHARLES WILLIAM, investment banker; b. NYC, Apr. 20, 1959; s. Dino and Dorice (Gillick) S.; m. Vanessa Lee Bishop; 1 child, Olivia Charlotte. BA in Econs., Columbia U., 1982; MBA, Harvard U., 1984. With Morgan Stanley & Co., N.Y.C., 1984-88; sr. v.p., coord. officer European mergers and acquisitions Morgan Stanley Internat., London, 1989-90; mng. dir., head internat. investment banking, bd. dirs. Smith Barney, Inc., N.Y.C., 1991-93, head investment banking new bus. group, 1993-95; mng. dir., head. indsl. corp. finance Paine Webber Inc., N.Y.C., 1995-96, vice chmn. investment banking, 1996-2000; co-founder, mng. gen. ptnr. Sterling Investment Ptnrs. LP, Westport, Conn., 1999; co-founder, mng. ptnr. Sterling Investment Advisors LLC, 1999—, Sterling Investment Ptnrs. Mgmt. LLC, 1999—; chmn. US Maintenance, Inc. Bd. dirs. Interline Brands, Inc. (formerly Wilmar Industries, Inc.), Washington Inventory Svc., Inc., Marine Corp Law Enforcement Found. Recipient fellowship Harvard Bus. Sch., 1983. Mem. Harvard Club of N.Y., N.Y. Athletic Club, Columbia Coll. Alumni Assn. (co-chmn. class of '82 com. 1982—), Kings Crown Rowing Assn. of Columbia U. (trustee). Republican. Roman Catholic. Home: 3 Alden Ter Greenwich CT 06831-4422 Office: 276 Post Rd W Westport CT 06880-4703 E-mail: santoro@sterlinglp.com.

SANTORO, FRANK ANTHONY, lawyer; b. Plainfield, N.J., Dec. 14, 1941; s. Frank V. and Nancy M. (Scavuzzo) S.; m. Patricia Ferrante, Oct. 10, 1964; children— Frank, Jennifer. B.S. in Chemistry, Seton Hall U., 1963, J.D., 1970. Patent atty. Exxon Corp., Linden, N.J., 1970-73; sole practice, South Plainfield, N.J., 1973—; atty. Planning Bd. Borough South Plainfield, 1971-73; mcpl. prosecutor Borough South Plainfield, 1972. Councilman Borough South Plainfield, 1977-79, mcpl. atty., 1985-93; mcpl. chmn. South Plainfield Republican Orgn., 1981-84. Mem. Middlesex County Bar Assn., UNICO Nat. Roman Catholic. Office: 129 S Plainfield Ave PO Box 272 South Plainfield NJ 07080-0272

SANTORO, MILÉNA, education educator; d. Bruce Alfred and Rolande Andrews; m. Robert Andrew Santoro, July 10, 1993. PhD, Princeton U., 1988—94. Assoc. prof. of french Georgetown U., 1996—. Sec. Am. Coun. for Qué. Studies, 1999—2003; book rev. editor Women in French Studies, 2002—; sec./treas. Assn. for Can. Studies in the US, 2003—. Rsch.: book Mothers of Invention: Feminist Authors and Experimental Fiction in France and Que., 2002. Recipient French Govt. Scholar, The Govt. of France, 1991-1992; fellow Grad. Fellowship, Princeton U., 1988-1991, 1992-1993, Doctoral Fellowship, Social Sciences and Humanities Rsch. Coun. of Can., 1991-1993. Mem.: Société des Professeurs Français et Francophones d'Amérique, AAUP, Am. Assn. of Teachers of French, Conseil Internat. d'études Francophones, Women in French, Assn. Internationale d'études québécoises, Modern Languages Assn., Assn. for Can. Studies in the US, South Atlantic Modern Languages Assn., Am. Coun. for Qué. Studies (sec. 1999—2003). Avocations: travel, gardening, cooking, singing, tai chi. Office: French Dept Georgetown U 37th and 'O' Sts Washington DC 20057-1047

SANTORUM, RICK, senator; b. Winchester, Va., May 10, 1958; s. Aldo and Catherine (Dughi) S.; m. Karen Garver, June 2, 1990; children: Elizabeth Anne, Richard John Jr., Daniel James, Sarah Maria, Peter Kenneth. BA in Polit. Sci., Pa. State U., State College, 1980; MBA, U. Pitts., 1981; JD, Dickinson Sch. Law, 1986. Bar: Pa. 1986. Adminstrv. asst. State Sen. Doyle Corman, Harrisburg, Pa., 1981-86; exec. dir. local govt. com. Pa. State Senate, Harrisburg, 1981-84, exec. dir. transp. com., 1984-86; assoc. atty. Kirkpatrick and Lockhart, Pitts., 1986-90; mem. 102nd-103rd Congresses from 18th Pa. dist., Washington, D.C., 1991-95; U.S. Senator from Pa., 1995—. Mem. Agr. Com., Armed Svcs. Com., Rules and Adminstrn. Com., Spl. Com. on Aging, Com. on Banking. Bd. dirs. Mt. Lebanon Extended Day Program, 1987-91; mem. Child Advocacy Project, 1987-91. Mem. KC, Italian Sons and Daus. Assn. Republican. Roman Catholic. Avocations: golf, racquet sports. Office: US Senate 511 Dirksen Senate Bldg Washington DC 20510-0001 also: Widener Bldg One South Penn Sq Ste 960 Philadelphia PA 19107

SANTOS, ADELE NAUDE, architect, educator; b. Cape Town, South Africa, Oct. 14, 1938; came to U.S., 1973; d. David Francois Hugo and Aletta Adèle Naudé. Student, U. Cape Town, South Africa, 1956-58; diploma, Archtl. Assn., London, 1961; MArch in Urban Design, Harvard U., 1963; MArch., M in City Planning, MArch, U. Pa., 1968. Registered arch., Pa., Mass. Pvt. practice architecture with Antonio de Souza Santos, 1966-73; ptnr. Interstudio, Houston, 1973-79; assoc. prof. architecture Rice U., Houston, 1973-78, prof., 1979; prof. architecture and urban design, dept. architecture U. Pa., Phila., 1981-90; founding dean Sch. Architecture U. Calif., San Diego, 1990-94; pvt. practice architecture and urban design Adele Naude Santos, Arch., Phila., 1979-90, Adele Naude Santos and Assocs., San Diego and Phila., 1991—2002; prof. architecture Coll. Environ. Design U. Calif., Berkeley, 1994—2003; dean Sch. Architecture and Planning, MIT, 2004—. Project dir., co-filmmaker for 5 part series, 1979-80; works include Albright Coll. Ctr. for the Arts, Reading, Pa., 1991, Franklin-LaBrea Housing, Hollywood, Calif., 1995, Inst. of Contemporary Art, Phila., 1991, Yerba Buena Gardens, San Francisco, 1998. Wheelwright Travelling fellow, Harvard U., 1968; NEA grantee, 1976, Tex. Com. for Humanities grantee, 1979; recipient (with Hugo Naudé) Bronze medal for House Naudé Capt. Inst. South African Architects, 1967, award for public TV program So. Ednl. Communications Assn., 1980, 3d place award Inner city Infill Competition, 1986; winner Internat. Design Competition, Hawaii Loa Coll., hon. mention Cin. Hillside Housing Competition and City Visions, Phila., 1986; winner competition for Franklin/La Brea Affordable Housing Project Mus. Comtemporary Art and Community Redevel. Agy. City L.A., 1988, Pa. Soc. Architects design award for Franklin/La Brea Multi-Family Housing, 1988; winning entry collaborative competition for amphitheater, restaurant and natural history mus., Arts Pk., La., 1989; winner competition for 24-unit residential devel., City of Camden, N.J., 1989, for New Civic Ctr., City of Perris, Calif., 1991, children's mus. The Zeum, 1998, child care facility Yerba Buena Gardens, San Francisco, 1998, Please Touch Mus., Phila., 1998, winner design competition ChildCare Ctr. U. Pa., 1999. Fellow Am. Inst. Archs.; mem. Pa. Soc. Archs., Archs. Registration Coun. (U.K.). Office: 2527 South St Philadelphia PA 19146-1037 also: Santos Prescott & Assocs 33 Zoe St San Francisco CA 94107-1709

SANTOS, ARTHUR MAGNO, thoracic cardiovascular surgeon; b. Pasay City, Philippines, May 15, 1946; BS in Pre-medicine, Far Eastern U., Manila, Philippines, 1967; MD, U. of the East, 1972. Diplomate Am. Bd. Surgery, Am. Bd. Thoracic Surgery. Intern St. Francis Gen. Hosp., Pitts., 1973-74, resident in gen. surgery, 1974-77; resident McKeesport (Pa.) Hosp., 1977-79; resident in thoracic and cardiovascular surgery Shadyside Hosp., Pitts., 1979-81; pvt. practice Assn. of Thoracic Surgeons, Pitts., 1981—. Fellow ACS. Office Phone: 412-469-7030.

SANTOS, CHARLES DANIEL, cultural organization administrator; b. San Antonio, July 17, 1960; s. John Joseph and Lucille (Lopez) Santos. BS in Sociology, U. Tex. Prin. dancer, tour mgr. Sharir Dance Co., 1981—92; info. systems adminstr. Tex. Gen. Land Office/Vets. Land Bd., 1987—95; assoc. prodr. The Juliet Hollister Awards/UN, 1996, 1998; prodr., founder, artistic dir. Austin Festival of Dance, NY, 1991—2001; mng./devel. dir. Eos Music, Inc., N.Y.C., 1995—98; producing dir. Dancers Responding to AIDS, N.Y.C., 1997—2000; prodr., mng. dir. Lower Manhattan Cultural Coun., N.Y.C., 2000—01; exec. dir. TITAS, Dallas, 2001—. Steering com. Human Rights Campaign Austin, 1994—96; chmn. Triangle On Stage, Austin Lyric Opera, 1995; project coord. BodyCount, Day Without Art/World AIDS Day, 1993—95; cultural arts panelist City of San Antonio, 2002; dance panelist Nat. Endowment for the Arts, 2003; numerous others; nat. adv. bd. African Am. Dance Ensemble, 2000—, Estate Project, 1999—, Eos Orch., 2001—; bd. dirs. Sharir Dance Co., 1995—97, Christopher House, 1994—95, AIDS Svcs. Austin, 1992—94, Ronald K. Brown/Evidence Dance Co., 2001, Dance Coun., 2001—, TITAS, 2001—. Named Master of Ceremonies, Christopher House for outstanding achievement in Austin cmty., 1994; recipient Outstanding Cmty. Event/Cmty. Svc. award, Tex. Human Rights Found., 1994, Leadership Austin, 1995, J. Blanton Belk Founders award of Outstanding Achievement, UWP Internat. Alumni Assn., 2000. Home: 3016 Thomas Ave Apt A Dallas TX 75204-2709 Office Phone: 214-775-1232.

SANTOS, EDWIN J. auditor; BS, Bryant Coll., 1981. Gen. auditor United Bank, Conn., 1987—91, Fleet Bank, Conn., 1991—93, regional gen. auditor, 1993—95, dir. corp. audit, 1995—99; dir. audit FleetBoston Fin. Corp.,

1999—2002, chief auditor, 2002—. Bd. mem. Roger Williams Hosp.; vice chmn, bd. dirs. Travelers Aide of RI; founding mem. Fleet Corp. Diversity Coun.; vice chmn. bd. trustees Bryant Coll. Office: FleetBoston Fin Corp 100 Federal St Boston MA 02110

SANTOS, KAREY MICHALE, elementary school educator; b. Paramus, N.J., Oct. 3, 1956; d. Donald James Keeney and Barbara Jean (Wilson) Alderman; m. Joseph Karl Santos, Aug. 28, 1976; children: Sonya Rae, Donald Wesley. BA, U. S.C., Aiken, 1989, Interdisciplinary MA in Natural Sci., 1995. Math./sci. specialist Millbrook Elem. Sch., Aiken, SC, 1989—. Tchr., sponsor math. and sci. acad. teams, 1992—; mem. State Curriculum Standards Revision Team and Assessment Coms., 1999—. Recipient Sci. Scope award NASCO, 1992, Palmetto Cablevision Tchr. of Yr., 1992, Am. Nuclear Soc. Achievement award, Nat. Presdl. award for excellence in math. and sci. tchg., 2000; grantee Westinghouse, 1992-2002 EIA, So. Bell, Project Wild, Bryan Foods, Am. Chem. Soc. Mem. NSTA (Optical Data Corp. Videoisk award 1992, 93), S.C. Coun. Tchrs. Math., Soc. Elem. Pres. Awardees, S.C. Marine Edn. Assn., Environ. Edn. Assn. S.C. Home: 13 Normandy Ln Aiken SC 29801-2852 Office: Millbrook Elem Sch 225 E Pine Log Rd Aiken SC 29803-7613

SANTOS, LEONARD ERNEST, lawyer; b. Caracas, Venezuela, Aug. 5, 1946; s. Paul Joseph and Frieda (Epstein) S.; m. Jeannie Bernadette Niedermeyer, Oct. 28, 1978; children: Jonathan, Matthew, Andrew. BA cum laude, Tufts U., 1967; JD, NYU, 1971. Bar: Ariz. 1972, D.C. 1972, U.S. Dist. Ct. D.C. 1972, U.S. Ct. Appeals (9th and 5th cirs.) 1972, U.S. Supreme Ct. 1972. Law clk. to cir. judge U.S. Ct. Appeals (9th cir.), San Francisco, 1971-72; assoc. Hogan & Hartson, Washington, 1972-76; sr. atty. internat. affairs U.S. Dept. Treasury, Washington, 1976-83; internat. trade counsel U.S. Senate Fin. Com., Washington, 1983-87; ptnr. Verner, Liipfert, Bernhard, McPherson & Hand, Washington, 1987-89, Perkins Coie, Washington, 1989-98, World Mae, Washington, 1998-99, Santos Family Found., Washington, 2000—; pres. Martin Santos Properties, LLC, 2001—, JMA Properties, LLC, 2003—, THAPROP LLC, 2003—. Note and comment editor NYU Law Jour., 1970; contbr. legal publs.; editor ABA Compendium of Foreign Trade Remedy Laws, 1998. Exec. dir. Dole for Pres. campaign, Washington, 1988, 96. Mem. NAFTA (chpt. 19 dispute settlement panels) Republican. Roman Catholic. Avocations: architecture, economics. Office: Martin Santos Prop LLC 900 Seventeeth St NW Ste 900 Washington DC 20006 Office Phone: 202-833-2559. Personal E-mail: santlen@aol.com.

SANTOS, LISA WELLS, critical care nurse; b. Richardson, Tex., Oct. 25, 1963; d. Malcolm R.N. and Maitland Anne (MacIntyre) Wells; m. Ignacio Santos, Jr., Dec. 17, 1988. Cert. med. asst., x-ray-lab. technician, Tex. Coll. Osteopathy, 1983; ASN, El Centro Coll., 1988; postgrad., U. North Tex.; BS in Bus. Mgmt., Le Tourneau U., 1993; postgrad., U. Phoenix, 1995—. RN, Tex.; cert. in CPR; cert. case mgr., cert. profl. health care quality, advanced competency certification in continuity of care Nat. Bd. Competency in Continuity of Care; assoc. cert. mgr. Inst. Cert. Profl. Mgrs.; cert. disability analyst, fellow Am. Bd. Disability Analysts. Med. technologist Family Med Ctr., Dallas, 1984-85, Beltline Med. Clinic, Dallas, 1985-86; nurse, lab. technician Primacare, Dallas, Plano, Richardson, Tex., 1986-88; charge nurse telemetry unit NME Hosp.-RHD Meml. Hosp., Denton, Tex., 1988-89; nurse ICU Denton (Tex.) Regional Med. Ctr.; nurse Angel Touch, Dallas, 1989; nurse cons. Travelers Ins., Richardson, Tex., 1990-91; med. rev. specialist Nat. Group Life, Las Colinas, Tex., 1991-94, mgr. coordinated care, 1994-95; pres. San Cal Health Care Options, Lewisville, Tex., 1994-95; clin. dir. PRN Associated Care/ Am. Care Source, Dallas, 1995-97; quality health mgr., utilization review mgr. Mutual of Omaha, Dallas, 1997; with Cigna Integrated Care, 1998—2002; case mgr., team leader The Hartford, 2002—; owner Monitos, 1997—; realtor New Castle Properties, 2002—. Contbr. articles to profl. jours. Mem. AACN, NAFE, Nat. Assn. Health Care Quality (cert.), Nat. Assn. Quality Assurance Profls., Assn. Nurses in AIDS Care, Case Mgmt. Soc. Am., Am. Assn. Law Ethics and Medicine, Am. Assn. Continuity of Care, Alpha Epsilon Delta, Alpha Beta Kappa, Gamma Beta Phi.

SANTOS, RICHARD J. association administrator; m. Linda Lee Perry; children: Betsy Lee, Lee, Steffen. Ins. claim rep.; nat. comdr. Am. Legion, Indpls., 2001—. Commr. Md. Vets. Commn., Md. Mil. Monuments Commn. With USNR. Mem.: Am. Legion (life; mem. vets. affairs and rehab. commn., citizens flag alliance, policy coordination and action group, vets. planning and coord. com., legis. commn., NEC liaison to V&AR commn., chmn. pub. rels. commn.). Office: American Legion PO Box 1055 700 N Pennsylvania St Indianapolis IN 46206

SANTOS, SHARON LEE, parochial school educator; b. Perth Amboy, N.J., June 23, 1955; d. John Anthony Santos and Dolores Estelle Barrett. BA in History, Kean U., 1978, MA in Guidance and Counseling, 1985; MA in Systematic Theology, Seton Hall U., 1998. Religious sr. Franciscan of Our Lady of Guadalupe; cert. tchr. K-12, guidance counelor N.J., religion tchr. Diocese of Metuchen, N.J. Tchr. Archdiocese of Newark, Diocese of Metuchen, Perth Amboy, Fords, NJ, Woodbridge, NJ; dir. religious edn. Vicariate of Perth Amboy, St. Mary Parish, New Monmouth, NJ. Guest spkr. on biblical and doctrinal topics various cities in N.J., 1993—; adv. bd. on evangelization Diocese of Meetuchen, 1999. Mem.: Fellowship of Cath. Scholars, St. Edith Stein Guild (life), Kappa Delta Phi. Avocations: astronomy, gardening. Office: St Mary Cath Ch 26 Leonardville Rd New Monmouth NJ 07748 Home: 355 Carr Ave Keansburg NJ 07734-1419

SANTOSO, IRENE, art director, graphics designer; b. Surabaya, Indonesia, Mar. 13, 1974; d. Bing Santoso and Soezana Djohan-Lie. AAS, Fashion Inst. Tech., 1994; BFA, Parsons Sch. Design, 1996. Sr. art dir. Tribal DDB, N.Y.C., 2001—02; creative dir. Hooloo.com, N.Y.C., 2001, USWeb/CKS Cornerstone, N.Y.C., 1997—2000; graphic artist Polo Ralph Lauren, N.Y.C., 1996—97. Design book, Shift Japan Website, 2000 (IMS SRC 100); author: (poetry) Am. Poetry Soc., 1999; website, Pixel Surgeon, 2001 (Outstanding Female Designer, 2001). Recipient Student award, Typographic Dir.'s Club, 1996, Am. Graphic Design award, Mag. Graphic Design: USA, 2000. Avocation: fluent in spoken and written Mandarin, Cantonese, Japanese, Bahasa Indonesia. Personal E-mail: irene@irenesantoso.com.

SANTSCHI, PETER HANS, marine sciences educator; b. Bern, Switzerland, Jan. 3, 1943; came to U.S., 1976; s. Hans and Gertrud (Joss) S.; m. Chana Hoida, Mar. 28, 1972; children: Rama Aviva, Ariel Tal. BS, Gymnasium, Bern, 1963; MS, U. Bern, 1971, PhD summa cum laude, 1975; Privatdozent, Swiss Fed. Inst. Tech., Zurich, Switzerland, 1984. Lectr. chemistry Humboltianum Gymnasium, Bern, 1968-70; teaching rsch. asst. U. Bern, 1970-75; rsch. scientist Lamont-Doherty Geol. Obs., Columbia U., Palisades, N.Y., 1976-77; rsch. assoc. Lamont-Doherty Geol. Obs. Columbia U., Palisades, N.Y., 1977-81; sr. rsch. scientist Lamont-Doherty Geol. Obs., Columbia U., Palisades, N.Y., 1981-82, Swiss Inst. Pollution Control, Zurich-Duebendorf, Switzerland, 1982-88; prof. oceanography Tex. A&M U., College Station, 1988—, prof. marine scis. Galveston, Tex., 1988—, sect. head chem. oceanography dept. oceanography College Station, 1990—. Head isotope geochemistry and radiology sect. Swiss Inst. Water Resources and Water Pollution Control, Zurich, 1983-88; mem. rev. panel on chem. oceanography NSF, 1990-91. Contbr. articles to profl. jours. Cpl. Swiss Army, 1964-65. Mem. AAAS, Am. Chem. Soc., Am. Geophys. Union, Oceanography Soc., Am. Soc. Limnology and Oceanography. Avocation: swimming. Office: Tex A&M U Oceanography Dept Galveston TX 77553-1675 E-mail: santschi@tamug.tamu.edu.

SANTULLI, RICHARD T. air transportation executive; BS in Applied Math, MS in Applied Math, MS in Operations Rsch., Bklyn. Polytechnic Inst. Investment banker Goldman Sachs & Co., 1969—80; chmn., CEO NetJets (name changed from Exec. Jet Aviation, Inc. in 2002), Columbus, Ohio and Woodbridge, NJ, 1984—. Office: NetJets Inc 581 Main St Woodbridge NJ 07095

SANTUZZI, ALECIA MARIE, psychologist, educator, researcher; b. Cleve., 1976; d. Paul Anthony and Darlene Mary Santuzzi. MS, Tulane U., 1998; BA in Psychology, Ohio U., 1998. Adj. faculty Tulane U., New Orleans, 2000—. Recipient Predoctoral Nat. Rsch. Svc. award, NIH/Nat. Inst. Mental Health, 2000—03. Mem.: APA, Soc. for Indsl. and Orgnl. Psychology, Soc. for Personality and Social Psychology, Am. Psychol. Soc., Acad. Mgmt., Phi Beta Kappa. E-mail: asantuz@tulane.edu.

SANWICK, JAMES ARTHUR, corporate financial executive; b. Balt., Feb. 15, 1951; s. Alfred George and Catherine Anne (von Sas) S.; m. Brenda Julia Tietz, Sept. 20, 1980; children: Luke Graham, Sierra Catherine. AS, Catonsville (Md.) C.C., 1975; BS, U. No. Colo., 1976; M in Pub. Administn., U. Alaska S.E., 1985. Lic. tchr. Dr. Edward deBono Thinking Skills Courses; cert. sr. profl. in human resources. Recreation therapist Md. Sch. for the Blind, Balt., 1974; dir. camp New Horizon United Cerebral Palsy Md., Balt., 1975; sub-dist. mgr. Nat. Park Svc., various, 1976-82; freelance mgmt. cons. Juneau, Alaska, 1982-84; regional mgr. div. labor standards Alaska Dept. Labor, Juneau, 1983-88; adj. faculty sch. bus. and pub. administrn. U. Alaska S.E., Juneau, 1985-93; mgr. Alaska Productivity Improvement Ctr., Juneau, 1989-93; mgr. human resources and pub. affairs Greens Creek Mining Co., Juneau, 1989-93; mgr. human resources, security and pub. affairs Rawhide Mining Co., Fallon, Nev., 1993-98; founder Ctr. for Innovation and Comm., Truckee, Calif., 1997—; v.p. Mgmt. Resources Cons., Truckee, 1998—; prin. and exec. v.p. Sierra High Tech. Ventures, 2001—; pres. Pvt. Wealth Mgmt. Group, 2003—; gen. mgr. Global Art Ptnrs. LLC, 2003—. Owner Sierra Bldg. Alternatives, 1995—; bd. dirs. Gov.'s Com. on Employment Disabled Persons, Alaska Acad. Decathalon Inc.; chmn. Job Svc. Employer Com., Alaska, 1989-93; bd. advisors Inst. Mine Tng. U. Alaska S.E., 1989-93; bd. dirs. Sierra High Tech. Group. Co-author: (info. phamphlet) Blue Water Paddling in Alaska, 1980; editor: (film) Green's Creek Project, 1990; photographic editor: Inside Passage Mag., 1982, 83; photographer: (book) Death Valley, 1977. Patrolman Nat. Ski Patrol System, Juneau, 1978—83; instr., trainer ARC, Alaska, 1979—82, 1979—82, 1979—82; v.p. bd. dirs. Alaska Acad. Decathlon; mem. Reno Exec. Roundtable, 1995—; v.p. strategic devel. Sierra High Tech. Group, 2000—. Recipient Nat. New Svc. award United Cerebral Palsey, 1975; named Candidate of Yr. Nat. Ski Patrol System, 1979. Mem. ASTD, Am. Creativity Assn., Nev. Mining Assn. (human resources com. 1993—), Soc. Human Resources Mgmt., Juneau Ski Club. Avocations: skiing, hiking, scuba diving, guitar, tennis. Office: PO Box 1793 Truckee CA 96160-1793 Office Phone: 775-782-8133. E-mail: jsanwick@pumg.us.

SANYOUR, MICHAEL LOUIS, JR., diversified financial services company executive; b. Richmond, Va., Aug. 24, 1930; s. Michael Louis, Sr. and Betty (Toobert) Sanyour; m. Therese Marie McCarthy, June 1, 1951 (dec. Sept. 25, 2002); children: Jeffrey, Mark, Jennifer, Florence, Norman, Ned. AA, Union Coll., 1952; SB, Rutgers U., 1954, postgrad., 1978-82; MBA, Harvard U., 1956; postgrad., Am. Coll., 1987-92. CLU; ChFC. V.p. Harbridge Ho., Inc., Boston, 1956-63, also dir.; corp. v.p. mktg. Volkswagen Am., Inc., Englewood Cliffs, NJ, 1963-70; pres., CEO Subaru Am., Pennsauken, NJ, 1970-75, also dir., Wofac Co., Bridgewater, NJ, 1975-82; exec. v.p., dir. Sci. Mgmt. Corp., 1975-82; pres., CEO, dir. Metrologic Instruments Inc., Blackwood, NJ, 1982-85; pres., COO, dir. Avant-Garde Computing, Inc., Mt. Laurel, NJ, 1985-86; prin., dir. CMS Cos., Phila., 1986—. Bd. dirs. CSS Industries, Inc. Co-author: (book) Chief Executive's Handbook, 1975, Am. Mgmt. Assn.'s Publs., 1990. Trustee W. Jersey Chamber Mucis Soc., 1983—, pres., 1987—88; councilman Moorestown, NJ, 1988—; dep. mayor, 1999—2002; mayor, 2003—; bd. dirs. Meml. Health Alliance, 1992—97, ARC Burlington County, 1989—94, Coriell Inst. Med. Rsch., 1992—, v.p., 2002—; bd. dirs. World Affairs Coun., Phila., 1992—98, Moorestown Cmty. Ho., 2000—, Phila. Pres.'s Orgn., 1994—97, vice chmn., 1992—93, chmn., 1993—94; class sec. HBS Class of '56, 1986—96. With USNG, 1948—56. Decorated knight of St. John's of Jerusalem; recipient Alumni award, Rutgers U., 1954, award, Am. Cancer Soc., 1978—79. Mem.: World Affairs Coun. Phila., Automotive Orgn. Team, World Pres.'s Orgn., South Jersey C. of C. (v.p., dir.), Am. Mensa Ltd., Harvard Club (N.Y.C.), Union League (Phila.) (bd. dirs. 1993—97), Harvard Bus. Sch. Club (Phila.) (pres. 1980—81, chmn. 1983—84, dir. 1984—), Rotary (pres. Moorestown 1987—88, bd. dirs.), Legatus, Delta Sigma Pi, Beta Gamma Sigma. Home: 201 E Maple Ave Moorestown NJ 08057-2011 Office: 1926 Arch St Philadelphia PA 19103-1444 Office Phone: 215-246-3009. E-mail: mlsanyour@aol.com, mls@cmsco.com.

SANZ, LUIS E. gynecologist, educator; b. Camaguey, Cuba; m. Miriam D. Sanz; 1 child, Monica G. MD, Georgetown U., 1976. Uro-gynecology and vaginal reconstruction surgery dept. ob-gyn. Georgetown U., Washington, 1980, prof., vice-chmn. dept. ob-gyn. Sch. Medicine, 1980—. Author: Gynecologic Surgery, 1995; contbr. over 40 articles to profl. jours., chapters to books. Served with U.S. Army, 1966—68, Vietnam. Decorated Vietnam Campaign medal U.S. Army. Fellow: ACOG (assoc.; memberr). Roman Catholic. Avocations: biking, reading, travel, weightlifting. Office: Georgetown U Sch Medicine 5530 Wisconsin Ave #645 Chevy Chase MD 20815

SANZONE, DONNA S. publishing executive; b. Bklyn., Apr. 4, 1949; d. Joseph J. Seitz and Faye (Brooks) Rossman; m. Charles F. Sanzone, Jan. 2, 1972; children: Danielle, Gregory. BA magna cum laude, Boston U., 1970; MA, Northeastern U., 1979. Grad. placement specialist Inst. Internat. Edn., N.Y.C., 1970-72; adminstr. AFS Internat. Scholarships, Brussels, 1972-74; editor Internat. Ency. Higher Edn., Boston, 1974-76, G.K. Hall & Co., Pubs., Boston, 1977-81, exec. editor, 1981-91, editor-in-chief, 1991-96; v.p. Oryx Press, Boston, 1996-2000; editor-in-chief Grolier Acad. Reference, Danbury, Conn., 2000—. Contbg. author: Access to Power, 1981. Mem.: ALA, Libr. and Info. Tech. Assn., Assn. Coll. and Rsch. Librs., Soc. for Scholarly and Profl. Pub., Assn. Am. Pubs. Office: Grolier Acad Ref 18 Pine St Weston MA 02493-1116

SAON, GEORGE A. computer scientist, researcher; b. Brasov, Romania, Oct. 6, 1970; s. Elena Florina Tripsa and Stelian Saon. PhD in Computer Sci., Henri Poincare U., Nancy, France, 1997. Asst. lectr. Academie de Nancy-Metz, Nancy, 1997—98; rschr. IBM, Yorktown Heights, NY, 1998—. Contbr. articles to profl. jours. Recipient 1st prize at regional final Alsace-Lorraine, Internat. French Math Problem Solving Championship, 1998. Mem.: AAAS. Avocations: reading, skiing. Home: 10 Brookside Dr Apt LD Greenwich CT 06830 Office: IBM TJ Watson Rsch Ctr Rt 134 Yorktown Heights NY 10598 Business E-Mail: saon@watson.ibm.com.

SAPARETO, FRANK VINCENT, II, investment advisor, state legislator; b. Haverhill, Mass., Jan. 12, 1960; s. Frank Vincent and Alice Lambert S.; children: Frank V. III, Justin John. BS, U. Mass., 1982. Cert. IAFP; registered investment adviser; lic. ins. profl., Mass., N.H., securities regulation profl., Mass., N.H.; cert. fund specialist. Fin. planner Eastcorp., Inc., Springfield, Mass., 1989-93; pres. FVS Fin., Inc., Derry, N.H., 1993—; state rep. dist. 13, mem. gen. ct. N.H. Ho. of Reps., Concord, 1997—2002; state senator N.H. Sen., Concord, 2003. Vice-chmn. Derry Taxpayers Assn., 1994-96, chmn., 1995-96; mem. zoning bd. Town of Derry, 1994-96. Mem. several profl. orgns. Avocations: Porsche Club of Am., kayaking, scuba diving, skydiving, chess. Home: 14 Oxbow Ln Derry NH 03038-4533 Office: FVS Financial Inc 14 Oxbow Ln Derry NH 03038-4533

SAPARIUC, IOAN, mathematician, researcher; b. Botosani, Romania, Aug. 24, 1974; s. Gheorghe and Ana Vasilica Sapariuc; m. Florentina Voroneanu, July 30, 2000. BS in Math. and Mechanics, Alexandru Ioan Cuza U., Iasi, Romania, 1997; MS in Applied Math., Rensselaer Poly. Inst., 2002, PhD grad. student in math., 1999—. Tchr. math. Mihai Eminescu H.S., Botosani, 1997—98, Electrocontact H.S., Botosani, 1998—99. Grantee, NSF, 2001, 2003. Mem.: Soc. Indsl. and Applied Math. (assoc.).

SAPEGA, ALEXANDER A. sports medicine physician, orthopedic surgeon; BS with distinction, Cornell U., 1975; MD, Temple U., 1980. Diplomate Am. Bd. Orthopaedic Surgery; lic. physician, Phila., N.J. Intern, residency, fellowship U. Pa. Sch. of Medicine, Phila., 1982-85; fellow in sports medicine Temple U., Phila., 1985-86; asst. instr. orthopaedic surgery U. Pa. Sch. Medicine, Phila., 1982-85; clin. instr. orthopaedic surgery Temple U. Sch. Medicine, Phila., 1985-86; asst. prof. U. Pa. Sch. Medicine, Phila., 1986-92; asst. prof., clin. educator Hosp. U. Pa., Phila., 1992-95, assoc. prof., clin. educator, 1995—; dir. post-grad. fellowship Knee Surgery Program Hosp. U. Pa., Phila., 1995—; chief sports medicine svc. Hosp. U. Pa., Phila., 1995—. Faculty lectr. for symposia and ednl. groups; invited lectr. to med. and sci. meetings. 1983—; clin. rsch. assoc. Inst. of Sports Medicine and Athletic Trauma, 1975-76; attending surg. staff Dept. Orthopaedic Surgery, Temple U., Phila., 1985-86; attending staff dept. orthopaedic surgery Hosp. Univ. Pa., Phila, 1986—, dept. orthopaedic surgery The Grad. Hosp., Phila, 1986—; chief of sports medicine svc., Phila. VA Hosp., 1986-92; attending staff dept. orthopaedic surgery, Mt. Sinai Hosp., Phila., 1989—, dir. U. Pa. Sports Medicine Ctr., Phila., 1995. Contbr. about 40 articles to profl. jours. including Am. Jour. Bone and Joint Surgery, Am. Jour Sports Medicine, Jour. Orthopaedic Rsch.; also revs., monographs and chpts. in books; mem. edtl. bd. Am. Jour. Knee Surgery, 1988-95. Post Grad. Advances in Sports Medicine, 1988-91; cons. reviewer Medicine and Sci. in Sports and Exercise, 1983-86, The Am. Jour. of Bone and Joint Surgery, 1988-95, Jour. of Orthopaedic Rsch., 1988-91; mem. edtl. bd. for rsch. Am. Jour. Bone and Joint Surgery, 1990-99; inventor: Apparatus for Reconstructive Knee Ligament Surgery, 1988, Method for Reconstructive Knee Ligament Surgery, 1990. Recipient N. Am. Traveling fellowship Am. Orthopaedic Assn.; grantee: NIH, 1982-85, VA, 1985-86, 88-90. Advanced Tech. Ctr. S.E. Pa., 1986. Fellow Am. Acad. Orthpaedic Surgeons (Elizabeth Winston Lanier award 1986); mem. Orthopaedic Rsch. Soc., Arthroscopy Assn. N.Am., Herodicus Soc. Office: NJ Knee and Shoulder Ctr 1288 Rte 73 S Ste 100 Mount Laurel NJ 08054

SAPER, CLIFFORD BAIRD, neurobiology and neurology educator; b. Chgo., Feb. 20, 1952; s. Julian and Susan Menkin S.; m. Barbara Susan Farby, Aug. 26, 1973; children: Rebecca Michelle, Leah Danielle, Sean Zachary. BS, MS, U. Ill., 1972; MD, PhD, Washington U., 1977. Diplomate Am. Bd. Psychiatry and Neurology. Intern Jewish Hosp., St. Louis, 1977-78; resident New York Hosp., N.Y.C., 1978-81; asst. prof. Washington U., St. Louis, 1981-84, assoc. prof., 1984-85, U. Chgo., 1985-88, prof., 1988-92, chmn. com. on neurobiology, 1987-92; James Jackson Putnam prof. neurology and neurosci. Harvard Med. Sch., 1992—; chmn. dept. neurology Beth Israel Deaconess Med. Ctr., Boston, 1992—. Editor-in-chief Jour. of Comparative Neurology, 1994—; contbr. articles to profl. jours. Fellow: Royal Coll. of Physicians (London); mem.: Soc. for Neurosci., Am. Physiol. Soc., Am. Acad. Neurology, Am. Neurol. Assn. Office: 330 Brookline Ave Boston MA 02215-5400

SAPERSTEIN, DAVID, novelist, screenwriter, film director; b. Bklyn. s. Louis and Celia S.; m. Ellen Mae Bernard; children: Ivan, Ilena. Student, CCNY Film Inst., CCNY. With CBS-TV Ed Murrow Show-Person To Person; writer, prodr., dir. Skyline Films, Inc., 1963-83. Asst. prof. film NYU Grad. Sch., Tisch Sch. Arts, 1992-93; instr. screenwriting Manhattan Marymount Coll., 1996-99, N.Y. Film Acad., 1997. Lyricist 90 pub. songs; theatrical prodns. include musicals Blue Planet Blue, Clowntown; author: Cocoon, 1985 (bestseller), Fatal Reunion, 1987 (Book of the Month selection), Metamorphosis, 1988, Red Devil: The Book of Satan, 1989, Funerama, 1994, Dark Again, 1999, Retribution, 2003, A Christmas Visitor, 2004, Green Devil: The Book of Belail, 2004; movies include Cocoon (Best Original Story for Screen 1985, 2 Acad. awards); writer, dir. My Sister's Keeper, Personal Choice (Beyond the Stars), Hearts & Diamonds; writer Torch, Sara Deri, Queen of America, Italian Ices, Joshua's Golden Band, Roamers, Vets, Do Not Disturb, Snatched, Jack in the Box, (with Joe Cacaci) SchoolHouse, Point of Honor, Roberto!, The John Gill Story: In Defense of Ivan the Terrible, Joshua's Golden Band, Fighting Back, Babs' Labs, Silyan, (nonfiction) Woman in the Year 2000, 1975; writer, prodr. Hallmark channel (with George Samerjan) A Christmas Visitor, 2002; writer, dir. music videos Dr. Bill, Teenage Mutant Ninja Turtles, Fallow Angel, Wowii; segment prodr. for Northstar Ent./PBS Reppies; dir. over 300 TV commls.; writer dir. over 200 documentaries, corp. and indsl. films, videos including Dance of the Athletes (Emmy nomination), Explorers in Aqua-Space, Rodeo: A Matter of Style; creator first interactive internet publishing at www.darkagain.com. Recipient Cine Golden Eagle award, N.Y. Film Festival award, San Francisco Film Festival award, Venice Film Festival award, Melbourne Film Festival award, N.Y. Art Dirs. award, Chgo. Film Festival award, Townsend Harris medal CCNY, 1998. Mem. Writer Guild Am., Dir. Guild of Am., BMI, Nat. Honor Soc. Office: Ebbets Field Prodns Ltd Wykagyl Station PO Box 42 New Rochelle NY 10804-0042

SAPERSTEIN, LEE WALDO, mining engineering educator; b. N.Y.C., July 14, 1943; s. Charles Levy and Freda Phyllis (Dornbush) S.; m. Priscilla Frances Hickson, Sept. 16, 1967; children: Adam Geoffrey, Clare Freda. BS in Mining Engring., Mont. Sch. Mines, 1964; DPhil in Engring. Sci., Oxford U., 1967. Registered profl. engr., Ky., Mo., Pa. Laborer, miner, engr. The Anaconda Co., Butte, Mont., and N.Y.C., 1963-64; asst. prof. mining engring. Pa. State U., University Park, 1967-71, assoc. prof., 1971-78, prof., 1978-87, sect. chmn., 1974-87; prof., chmn. dept. mine engring. U. Ky., Lexington, 1987-93; dean Sch. Mines and Metallurgy U. Mo., Rolla, 1993—2004, prof. mining engring., 1993—. Chmn. engring. accreditation comm., 1989-90, bd. dirs. Accreditation Bd. for Engring. and Tech., 1992-2001, sec. of bd., 1995-98, pres.-elect, 1998-99, pres. 1999-2000, ABET fellow. Contbr. articles to refereed jours. Rhodes scholar Oxford U., 1964-67; recipient Linton E. Grinter Disting. Svc. award, 2004. Mem. NSPE, ASEE, Soc. Mining, metallurgy and Exploration, Inc. (disting. mem. AIME-Soc. Mining Engrs.), Am. Assn. Rhodes Scholars. Home: 801 Laurel Dr Rolla MO 65401-3841 Office: U Mo 305 V H Mc Nutt Hl Rolla MO 65409-0810 Office Phone: 573-341-4153. E-mail: saperste@umr.edu., saperste@rollanet.org.

SAPERSTEIN, MARC ELI, religious studies educator, rabbi; b. NYC, Sept. 5, 1944; s. Harold Irving and Marcia Belle (Rosenblum) S.; m. Roberta Shapiro, June 17, 1970; children: Sara Michal, Adina Ruth. AB, Harvard U., 1966, PhD, 1977; student, Pembroke Coll., U. Cambridge, Eng., 1966-67; MA, Hebrew U., Jerusalem, 1971, Hebrew Union Coll., N.Y.C., 1972. Ordained rabbi, 1972. Lectr. in Hebrew lit. Harvard U., Cambridge, Mass., 1977-79; lectr. in Jewish studies Harvard U. Divinity Sch., 1979-81, asst. prof. Jewish studies, 1981-83, assoc. prof., 1983-86; Gloria M. Goldstein prof. Jewish history and thought Washington U., St. Louis, 1986-97, chmn. program Jewish and Near Eastern Studies, 1989-97; rabbi Temple Beth David, Canton, Mass., 1973-86; Charles E. Smith prof. of Jewish history George Washington U., Washington, 1997—, dir. Judaic studies, 1997—. Mem. exec. bd. Cen. Conf. Am. Rabbis, 1985-87. Author: Decoding the Rabbis, 1980, Jewish Preaching, 1200-1800, 1989, Moments of Crisis in Jewish-Christian Relations, 1989, Your Voice Like a Ram's Horn, 1996, also articles; editor: Essential Papers on Messianic Movements and Personalities in Jewish History, 1992, Witness from the Pulpit, 2000. Fellow Charles and Julia Henry Fund, 1966-67, Am. Coun. Learned Socs., 1983-84, Inst. Advanced Studies Hebrew U., Jerusalem, 1989, Am. Acad. for Jewish Rsch., 1994—, Ctr. for Judaic Studies, U. Pa., 1995-96; Danforth Found. Kent fellow, 1973-77. Mem. Assn. Jewish Studies (bd. dirs. 1983-99, book rev. editor 1997-2002), Am. Acad. Jewish Rsch. (exec. bd. 2000—), Phi Beta Kappa. Jewish. Office: George Washington U Dept History 2142 G St NW Washington DC 20037-2721 E-mail: msaper@gwu.edu.

SAPHIR, RICHARD LOUIS, pediatrician; b. N.Y.C., May 1, 1933; s. Samuel and Grace (Greenberg) Saphir; m. Judith Schwartz, Dec. 6, 1958; 1 child, Steven. BA, NYU, 1954; MD, SUNY, NYC, 1958. Diplomate Nat. Bd. Med. Examiners, Am. Bd. Pediat. Asst. attending pediatrician Mt. Sinai Hosp., NYC, 1965—71, asst dir., pediat. acute care clinic, 1970—78, 1971—82, assoc. clin. prof. pediat., 1982—88, attending pediatrician, 1982—; chief, pediatric svcs. U.S. Naval Hosp., Newport, RI, 1967—69; clin. prof. pediat. Mt. Sinai Sch. Medicine, NYC, 1988—. Bd. dirs. Mt. Sinai Children's Ctr. Found., N.Y.C., 1987—. Contbr. articles to profl. jours. Chmn. cmty. and adv. com. N.Y.C. Info. and Counseling Program for Sudden Infant Death Syndrome, 1979—81; med. bd. YMHA, N.Y.C., 1982—86. Comdr. USNR, 1967—69. Fellow: N.Y. County Med. Soc. (vice chmn. com. child welfare 1974—85), N.Y. Pediat. Soc. (pres. 1978—79), Am. Acad. Pediatrics (com. sci. meetings 1985—97, chmn. prep course 1991—96, edtl. adv. bd. Continuing

Med. Edn. audiotapes 1991—2001, ednl. program rep. ambulatory care quality improvement program 1992—2002, ednl. advisor proficiency testing program 1996—99, editl. bd. Pediat. in Rev. 1997—2003, ednl. adv. Uniformed Svcs. pediat. seminar 1997—, mem. super cont. med. edn. planning com. 2000—, chmn. super cont. med. edn. planning com. 2002—, Com. on Continuing Med. Edn. 2002—), N.Y. Acad. Medicine (treas. 1987—89). Office: BSM Pediatrics PC 55 E 87th St New York NY 10128-1043 Office Phone: 212-722-4950. Business E-Mail: richard.saphir@verizon.net.

SAPIENZA, TONY, public relations executive; With Hewlett-Packard; sr. counsel Miller/Shandwick, Boston, pres. Office: Miller/Shandwick Technologies 101 Main St Cambridge MA 02142-1519

SAPIN, BURTON MALCOLM, political science educator, foreign policy analyst; b. N.Y.C., Dec. 14, 1926; s. Julius Sidney and Selma (Greifer) S.; m. Barbara Miller Piane, Dec. 11, 1960 (div. Aug. 1984); children: Julia Elizabeth, David Ralph; m. Judith Leitner, Sept. 12, 2001. AB, Columbia U., 1945, AM, 1947; PhD, Princeton U., 1953. Rschr. Brookings Instn., Washington, 1958-60; asst. prof. MIT, Cambridge, Mass., 1960-61; policy ofcl. U.S. Dept. State, Washington, 1961-65; prof. polit. sci. U. Minn., Mpls., 1965-69; dean Sch. Internat. Affairs George Washington U., Washington, 1969-83, prof. polit. sci. and internat. affairs, 1969-94, prof. emeritus, 1994—. Cons. Rand, Washington, 1994-97; vis. prof. Kansai U., Osaka, Japan, summer, 1991, Internat. U. Japan, Niigata, Japan, 1985, Hopkins-Nanjing Program, Nanjing, China, 1987-88. Author: Foreign Policy Decision Making, 1954, 2002, Making of U.S. Foreign Policy, 1966; contbr. articles to profl. jours. With USN, 1945-46. Democrat. Jewish. Home: 5500 Friendship Blvd Apt 1816N Chevy Chase MD 20815-7267

SAPINSKY, JOSEPH CHARLES, magazine executive, photographer; b. N.Y.C., Dec. 13, 1923; s. Simon Moses and Janet (Charles) S.; m. Jane Tomney, Oct. 21, 1970; children— Michael Joseph, Jane Anne, Laura Alexandra. Certificate illustration, Pratt Inst., 1943; certificate advt. design, 1947; postgrad., Colgate U., 1943, Cornell U., N.C. U. Art dir. Today's Living, N.Y. Herald Tribune, N.Y.C., 1960-63; art dir. N.Y. Mag., N.Y.C., 1963-65; asso. art dir., dir. photography Sat. Evening Post, N.Y.C., 1965-67; dir. publs. I.O.S., Geneva, 1967-69; art dir. This Week, N.Y.C., 1969, Jock N.Y. mag., N.Y.C., 1970; dir. publs. I.I.G., London, 1970; art dir. Woman's Day mag., N.Y.C., 1971-83; exec. art dir. Woman's Day Spls., N.Y.C., 1983-92; comml. photographer, 1992—. Cons. art dir. Infinity mag., N.Y.C., 1971-73; instr. dept. photography Sch. Visual Arts, N.Y.C., New Sch., N.Y.C. Served with USNR, 1943-46; capt. Res. ret. Recipient numerous art dir. awards. Mem. Am. Soc. Mag. Photographers, Soc. Illustrators, Am. Soc. Mag. Editors, Am. Inst. Graphic Arts, Soc. Publ. Designers, Mil. Officers Assn. Home: 242 Campbell Rd Box 207 Cherry Valley NY 13320-0207 Office Phone: 607-264-3080. E-mail: snipas@telenet.net.

SAPIRIE, STEPHEN ALAN, public health administrator; b. Milw., June 17, 1938; s. Samuel Ralph and Florence Katheryn (Canatsey) Sapirie; m. Manana Gagua; children: Mark, Nicholas. BSc, U. Tenn., 1960; MBA, Am. U., Washington, 1968; D in Pub. Health, U. N.C., 1980. Chief mgmt. sys. Naval Command Sys., Washington, 1966-68; computer sys. analyst WHO, Geneva, 1968-70, health sys. analyst, 1970-74, health planner Burma, Thailand, 1974—75, program mgmt. officer New Delhi, 1978-85, scientist family health divsn. Geneva, 1985—90, chief strengthen county health info., 1990—98. Dir. INFORM Mgmt. Scis. for Health, Boston, 1999—. Co-author: Health Project Management, 1974. Lt. USN, 1960-66. Avocation: tennis. Office: Mgmt Scis Health 891 Centre St Boston MA 02130 Business E-Mail: ssapirie@msh.org.

SAPIRO, GUILLERMO, engineering educator, consultant; b. Montevideo, Uruguay; s. Jacob Sapiro and Miriam Schwartz; m. Daila Gheiler, Dec. 17, 1994; children: Eitan, Nahdav. PhD, Technion U., Israel, 1993. Postdoctoral assoc. MIT, Cambridge, Mass., 1993-94; mem. tech. staff HP Labs., Palo Alto, Calif., 1994-97; assoc. prof. U. Minn., Mpls., 1997—. Cons. HP, Motorola, Summus, Optibase. Author: Goemetric PDE's and Image Analysis, 2001. Recipient award PECASE White House, Young Investigator award ONR, Career award NSF. Office: U Minn 200 Union St SE Minneapolis MN 55455 Fax: 625-625-4583. E-mail: guille@ece.umn.edu.

SAPOFF, MEYER, retired electronics executive; b. NYC, June 2, 1927; s. Benjamin and Mary (Charney) Sapoff. Student, Mohawk Coll., 1946—48; BSEE magna cum laude, Poly. Inst. Bklyn., 1950, postgrad., 1952—53, MIT, 1951, U. Pa., 1951—52; MSEE, Drexel Inst. Tech., 1952. Rsch. engr. Franklin Inst. Labs., Phila., 1950-52; rsch. fellow sr. grade Poly. Inst. Bklyn., 1952-53; dir. rsch. Victory Engring. Corp., Springfield, NJ, 1953-57, dir. engring., 1957-63, v.p., 1963-69; cons., sr. staff scientist Keystone Carbon Co., St. Mary's, Pa., 1969-70; pres. Thermometrics, Inc., Edison, NJ, 1970-86, chmn. bd. dirs., 1986-93, sr. staff cons., 1993-96; pres. MS Cons., Princeton, NJ, 1993—96; ret., 1996. Chmn. E20 temperature com. 6th Symposium Temperature, Measurement and Control in Sci. and Industry; U.S. del. to tech. com. 65th Internat. Electrotech. Commn.; cons. in field. Contbr. articles to profl. jours.; patentee in field. Active West Orange (NJ) PTA, 1960—76, Citizens League West Orange, 1962—75; trustee George St. Playhouse, New Brunswick, NJ, 1993—2001; bd. dirs. Jewish Ctr., Princeton, 1995—98, fin. chmn., 1995—96, v.p. fin., 1996—98; bd. dirs. United Jewish Fedn. Princeton Mercer Bucks, 1998—, treas., 2001—03. Recipient Indsl. Rsch. IR-100 award, 1974; fellow, Poly. Inst. Bklyn., 1953; scholar, NYU, 1948—50. Mem.: AAAS, ASTM (1st vice-chmn. E20 com. temperature measurement 2000—, award of merit 1998), IEEE, Am. Ceramic Soc., Poly. Inst. Bklyn. Alumni Assn., Tau Beta Pi, Eta Kappa Nu. Home: 1137 Stuart Rd Princeton NJ 08540-1216

SAPOLSKY, HARVEY MORTON, political scientist, educator; b. Haverhill, Mass., Feb. 21, 1939; s. Abraham and Anne Betty (Selig) S.; m. Karen P. Stenbo, Aug. 27, 1966. BA, Boston U., 1961; MPA, Harvard U., 1963, PhD, 1967. Mem. faculty MIT, 1966—, prof. polit. sci., 1977—, dir. comm. forum, 1987-95, dir. security studies program, 1989—; dep. dir. Univ. Health Policy Consortium, 1978-83, assoc. chmn. faculty, 1981-83. Vis. prof. U. Mich., 1971-72; cons. Artificial Heart Assessment Panel Nat. Heart and Lung Inst., Washington, 1972-73; mem. Ethics and Health Policy Panel Hastings (N.Y.) Ctr., 1979-80; mem. com. on Fed. Rsch. on Effect of Ionizing Radiation NRC, Washington, 1980-81; mem. com. on Risk Perception and Comm. NRC, 1987-88, mem. com. on tech. alternatives to anti-pers. mines, 1999-2001; mem. Sec. of Energy's Task Force on Alternative Futures for Dept. of Energy Labs., 1994-95. Author: The Polaris System Development, 1972, (with D. Altman and Richard Greene) Health Planning and Regulation, 1981, (with A. Drake, S. Finkelstein) The American Blood Supply, 1982, Science and the Navy, 1990; editor: Consuming Fears: The Politics of Product Risks, 1986; co-editor: Federal Health Programs, 1981, (with S. Altman), 1981, (with R. Crane, W.R. Newman and E. Noam) The Telecommunications Revolution, 1992; also articles. Mem. AAAS (sec. sect. social and econ. scis. 1968-73), Am. Polit. Sci. Assn., Nat. Acad. Social Ins., Coun. on Fgn. Rels. Home: 37 Edgemoor Rd Belmont MA 02478-3916 Office: MIT Security Studies Program E38-600 Cambridge MA 02139

SAPORTA, JACK, psychologist, educator; b. N.Y.C., Oct. 21, 1927; s. David and Victoria (Fils) S.; m. Judith Hammond, May 28, 1967 (div. 1979); children: David J., Victoria Johnson. AB cum laude, Adelphi U., 1951; PhD, U. Chgo., 1962. Diplomate Am. Bd. Profl. Psychology; lic. clin. psychologist. Pvt. practice, 1962-99; supt. Tinley Park (Ill.) Mental Health Ctr., 1975-78; chief manpower tng. and devel. Ill. Dept. Mental Health, Chgo., 1978-82; dean, prof. Forest Inst. Profl. Psychology, Des Plaines, Ill., 1982-85; coord. studies Fielding Grad. Inst., Santa Barbara, Calif., 1984—; mem. faculty Ill. Sch. Profl. Psychology, Chgo., 1985-97. Mem. adj. faculty psychology Lake Forest Grad. Sch. Mgmt., 1987-97; mem. Ill. State Clin. Psychology Lic. and Disciplinary Com., Springfield, 1984-93; profl. staff Forest Hosp., Des Plaines, 1977-96; mem. attending doctoral profl. staff Luth. Gen. Hosp., Park Ridge, Ill., 1986-2000, emeritus, 2000—. Served with U.S. Army, 1946-47, Germany. Named Educator of Yr., Forest Inst., 1982, Outstanding Faculty Mem. Lake Forest Grad. Sch. Mgmt. Fellow Acad. Clin. Psychology, NTL-Inst. (faculty); mem. APA (accreditation site vis. team), Ill. Psychol. Assn., Chgo. Psychol. Assn. (cert. recognition 1999, mem. exec. bd.). Avocations: tennis, computers, do-it-yourself home projects. Home: 13077 Stone Creek Court Huntley IL 60142

SAPOSNIK, IRA STEPHEN, physician, historian; b. Chgo., Dec. 16, 1952; s. Matthew Marvin and Harriet (Robinson) Saposnik. AB History cum laude, Loyola U., Chgo., 1974, MD with honors, 1980; JD, Nashville Sch. Law, 1997; PhD in History summa cum laude, Imperial War Mus./Thornewood U., London, 2001. Diplomate Am. Bd. Ophthalmology. Clin. assoc. prof. U. Va., Charlottesville, 1985—88; pvt. practice ophthalmology Roanoke, Va., 1985—88; dept. head ophthalmology U.S. VA, Salem, Va., 1985—86; pvt. practice Omega Healthcare, Knoxville, 1988—90, med. dir., 1990—93; clin. instr. Vanderbilt U., Nashville, 1993—2000; med. dir. N.Am. Biols., Nashville, 1993—98; pvt. practice Nashville Chronic Care, 1999—2000; multiple sclerosis rsch. Nashville, 2000—. Dir. Med. Legal Cons., Nashville, 1997—. Actor: (films) Glory, 1989, Gettysburg, 1993, Gods and Generals, 2002; singer: (Operas) The Mikado, 2001; composer: (TV films) The Doctor Is In, 2000, Symphony # 1 in C Minor, The Doctor Has Returned, 2002, Symphony # 2 in D Minor, Ode to America. Recipient Citizen award medal, City of Chgo., 1987, cert. Appreciation, Chgo. Police Dept., 1987, N.Y. City Fire Dept. & EMS, 2001, award for med. assistance for 9/11, City of N.Y. Trustees, 2001. Republican. Jewish. Achievements include discovery that multiple sclerosis is genetically related and acts as a viral type trigger mechanism rather than a true autoimmune disease. Avocations: fishing, skiing, astronomy, electronics. Home and Office: 320 Lauderdale Nashville TN 37205 E-mail: mdatty@aol.com.

SAPP, A. EUGENE, JR., former electronics executive; b. Winston-Salem, N.C., 1933; married. BEE, Ga. Inst. Tech., 1959. With Tex. Instruments Inc., 1959—62, SCI Systems Inc., Hunstville, Ala., 1962—73, from v.p. to pres., COO, 1973—99, pres., CEO, 1999—2002. Bd. dirs. SCI Systems, Inc. Office: SCI Systems Inc 2101 Clinton Ave W Huntsville AL 35805-3093 also: 500 Civic Ctr Dr Augusta GA 04330

SAPP, DONALD GENE, retired minister; b. Phoenix, Feb. 27, 1927; s. Guerry Byron and Lydia Elmeda (Snyder) Sapp; m. Anna Maydean Nevitt, July 10, 1952 (dec.); m. Joann Herrin Mountz, May 1, 1976; children: Gregory, Paula, Jeffrey, Mark, Melody, Cristine. AB in Edn., Ariz. State U., 1949; MDiv, Boston U., 1952, STM, 1960; D Ministry, Calif. Grad. Sch. Theology, 1975. Ordained to ministry Meth. Ch., 1950. Dir. youth activities Hyde Park (Mass.) Meth. Ch., 1950-52; minister 1st Meth. Ch., Peabody, Mass., 1952-54, Balboa Island (Calif.) Cmty. Meth. Ch., 1954-57, Ch. of Foothills Meth., Duarte, Calif., 1957-63; sr. minister Aldersgate United Meth. Ch., Tustin, Calif., 1963-70, Paradise Valley (Ariz.) United Meth. Ch., 1970-83; dist. supt. ctrl. w. dist. Desert S.W. Conf. United Meth. Ctr., Phoenix, 1983-89; ret., 1989. Editor: Wide Horizons, 1983—89; contbr. articles to profl. jours. Trustee Plz. Cmty. Ctr., LA, 1967—70; bd. dirs. Orange County Human Rels. Coun., Calif., 1967—70, Interfaith Counseling Svc. Found., 1982—89, Wesley Cmty. Ctr., Phoenix, 1983—89; pres. Met. Phoenix Commn., 1983—85; chaplain City of Hope Med. Ctr., Duarte, 1957—63; bd. dirs. Coun. Chs., LA, 1963—67; del. Western Jurisdictional Conf. United Meth. Ch., 1984, 1988; gen. conf. United Meth. Ch., 1988; corp. mem. Sch. Theology Claremont, Calif., 1972—80. With USN, 1945—46. Mem.: Bishops and Exec. Roundtable, Ariz. Ecumenical Coun., Rotary (pres.), Tau Kappa Epsilon, Kappa Delta Pi. Democrat. Avocation: overseas travel. Home: 7316 E Krall St Scottsdale AZ 85250-4518

SAPP, JOHN RAYMOND, lawyer; b. Lawrence, Kans., June 18, 1944; s. Raymond Olen and Amy (Kerr) S.; m. Linda Lee Tebbe, July 3, 1965; children: Jeffrey, Jennifer, John. BA, U. Kans., 1966; JD, Duke U., 1969. Bar: Wis. 1969, U.S. Dist. Ct. (ea. dist.) Wis. 1969, U.S. Ct. Appeals (7th cir.) 1974, U.S. Ct. Appeals (4th cir.) 1984, U.S. Supreme Ct. 1974. Assoc. Michael, Best & Friedrich, Milw., 1969-76, ptnr., 1976-90, mng. ptnr., 1990—. Dir. Roadrunner Freight Systems, Milw., 1992—, J.J. Keller Co., 2003—. Bd. dirs. Milw. Symphony, 1981-95, mem. exec. com., 1993-95; bd. dirs. Boy Scouts Am., Milw., 1986—, pres. 1990-92; mem. Milw. Arts Bd., 1990, Greater Milw. Com.; bd. dirs. Zool. Soc., 1995—, v.p., 2000—; bd. dirs. Lex Mundi, 1997-2000, mem. exec. com., 1997-2001; bd. dirs. Jr. Achievement Greater Milw., 2001—. Avocations: golf, curling, print collecting. E-mail: jrsapp@mbf-law.com.

SAPP, WALTER WILLIAM, lawyer, energy company executive; b. Linton, Ind., Apr. 21, 1930; s. Walter J. and Nona (Stalcup) S.; m. Eva Kaschner, July 10, 1957 (dec.); children: Karen Elisabeth, Christoph Walter. AB magna cum laude, Harvard, 1951; JD summa cum laude, Ind. U., 1957. Bar: Ind. 1957, N.Y. 1959, Colo. 1966, U.S. Supreme Ct. 1972, Tex. 1977. Pvt. practice, N.Y.C., 1957-60, 63-66; practice in Paris, 1960—63; assoc. atty. Cahill, Gordon, Reindel & Ohl, Paris, 1960-63, N.Y.C., 1957-60, 63-65, ptnr., 1966; gen. counsel Colo. Interstate Corp., 1966-76, v.p., 1968-76, sec., 1971-76, sr. v.p., dir., exec. com., 1973-75, exec. v.p., 1975-76; v.p. Coastal States Gas Corp., 1973-76; sr. v.p., gen. counsel Tenneco, Inc., Houston, 1976-92, sec., 1984-86; pvt. practice Houston, 1992—. Editor-in-chief Ind. U. Law Jour., 1956-57. Trustee Houston Ballet, 1982-85, Awty Internat. Sch., 1989-98, 99—, vice-chmn., 1994-97, pres. 1997-98, chmn., 1999-2002, pres., 2002-03; bd. dirs. Harris County Met. Transit Authority, 1982-84, Houston Internat. Protocol Alliance, 1992-94, Houston Symphony, 1989—, v.p., 1991-94, 2001-03; adv. bd. Inst. for Internat. Edn. S.W. region, 1987-2003, chmn., 1992-94, Internat. and Comparative Law Ctr. Southwestern Legal Found., 1976-92. Lt. USNR, 1951-54. Recipient Chevalier, Ordre Nat. du Mérit, France. Mem.: ABA, Houston Bar Assn., Assn. Bar City of N.Y., Tex. Bar Assn., N.Y. State Bar Assn., Alliance Française Houston (bd. dirs. 1989—2001, v.p. 1991—94, 1998—2001), French-Am. C. of C. (bd. dirs. 1987—92), Order of Coif. Mem. United Ch. of Christ. Office: 1111 Hermann Dr Unit 8B Houston TX 77004-6928

SAPP, WARREN CARLOS, professional football player; b. Orlando, Fla., Dec. 19, 1972; m. Jamiko, 1998; 1 child, Mercedes. Student, U. Miami. Defensive tackle Tampa Bay Buccaneers, 1994—2003, Oakland Raiders, 2004—. Named NFL Defensive Player of the Yr., 1999; named to Pro-Bowl, 1997—2003. Achievements include mem. of Super Bowl XXXVII Champion Tampa Bay Buccaneers, 2002. Avocation: swimming. Office: c/o Oakland Raiders 1220 Harbor Bay Pkwy Alameda CA 94502*

SAPPINGTON, SHARON ANNE, retired school librarian; b. West Palm Beach, Fla., Sept. 15, 1944; d. A.D. and Laura G. (Jackson) Chambless; m. Andrew Arnold Sappington III, June 11, 1966; children: Andrew Arnold IV, Kevin Sean. Student, Fla. So. Coll., 1962—64; BA in Edn., U. Fla., 1966; media specialist, U. Ala., 1980. 5th grade tchr. Tates Creek Elem., Lexington, Ky., 1966-68; 4th grade tchr. Sadieville (Ky.) Elem., 1968-69; libr. media specialist A.H. Watwood Elem., Childersburg, Ala., 1980-98; ret., 1998. Guest storyteller Young Author's Conf., Winterboro, Lincoln, Sylacauga, and Fayetteville, Ala., 1982-94; vis. com. mem. Southeastern Accreditation Assn.; program presenter Internat. Reading Assn., Birmingham, Ala., 1983; guest spkr. rare children's books "By the Way" TV talk show, 1983; pres. Tale Tellers of St. Augustine, 2003-; chmn. RSVP Read Aloud Program, 2002-. Creator, presenter: (slide presentation) Tellers of Tales and Sketchers of Dreams, 1983, (multimedia programs) Dinosaurs, Teddy Bears, and Wild Things, 1990, Shanghaied in the Beijing Airport, 1994. Circle chmn., Sunday tchr. Grace United Meth. Ch., Birmingham, 1973, 92-95; delivery mem. Meals on Wheels, Birmingham, 1975-76; radio reader for the blind WBHM Pub. Broadcasting, Birmingham, 1980; guest spkr., program presenter Jaycees, Kiwanis, and C. of C., Childersburg, 1993-94. Title I grantee, 1991, Stutz Bearcat grantee, 1992. Mem. AAUW, ALA, Internat. Platform Assn., Am. Assn. Sch. Librs., Ala. Libr. Assn. (children's and sch. divsn. publicity chmn. 1991-93, chmn. Nat. Libr. Week in Ala. 1993-94, Outstanding Youth Svcs. award 1989), People to People Internat. (libr. del. to China 1993), Kappa Delta Pi. Democrat. Methodist. Avocation: collector of 19th century illustrated children's literature. Home: 5131 Shore Dr Saint Augustine FL 32086-6473

SAPRA, SUNIL K. economics professor; b. New Delhi, July 15, 1953; came to the U.S., 1979; s. Chaman and Usha Sapra; m. Santosh Baghat, Jan. 16, 1986. MA in Econs., Delhi Sch. Econs., 1976; PhD in Econs., Columbia U., 1983. Asst. prof. dept. econs. SUNY, Buffalo, 1983-91; assoc. prof. dept. econs. and stats. Calif. State U., L.A., 1991-94, prof. dept. econs. and stats., 1994—. Cons. Argonne Nat. Labs., 1984-87; statis. cons. Barksdale, Inc., L.A., 1994; presenter in field. Referee Econometrica, Econometric Revs., Jour. Econometrics, Jour. Applied Econometrics, Jour. Royal Statis. Soc., Explorations in Econ. History, Jour. Quantitative Econs., Jour. Bus. and Econ. Stats., Bull. Econ. Rsch., Rev. Internat. Econs., Procs. Far Ea. Econometric Soc., NSF, Acad. Internat. Bus.; contbr. articles to profl. jours.; mem. editl. bd. InterStat, Bus. Functions and Applications. Grantee NSF, 1989-90 Mem. Am. Statis. Assn., Indian Econometric Soc., Western Econ. Assn. (instnl. rep.). Avocations: solving mathematical and statistical puzzles, playing cricket. Office: Calif State Univ Dept Econs 5151 State University Dr Los Angeles CA 90032-4226 Office Phone: 323-343-2941. Business E-Mail: ssapra@calstatela.edu.

SAPSOWITZ, SIDNEY H. entertainment and media company executive; b. N.Y.C., June 29, 1936; s. Max and Annette (Rothstein) Sapsowitz; m. Phyllis Skopp, Nov. 27, 1957; children: Donna Dawn Chazen, Gloria Lynn Aaron, Marsha Helene Gleit. BBA summa cum laude, Paterson State U. (N.J.), 1980. Various fin. and oper. systems positions Metro Goldwyn Mayer, Inc., N.Y.C., 1957-68; exec. v.p., dir. Penta Computer Assoc. Inc., N.Y.C., 1968-70, Cons. Actuaries Inc., Clifton, N.J., 1970-73; exec. v.p., CFO Am. Film. Theatre, N.Y.C., 1973-76, Cinema Shares Internat Distrb. Corp., N.Y.C., 1976-79; sr. cons. Solomon, Finger & Newman, N.Y.C., 1979-80; exec. v.p., CFO Met. Goldwyn Mayer, L.A., 1980-82; various positions leading to exec. v.p. fin. and adminstrn., CFO MGM/UA Entertainment Co., Culver City, Calif., 1982-86, also bd. dirs.; fin. v.p.; chief bus. and ops. officer, Office of Pres., dir. United Artists Corp., Beverly Hills, Calif., 1986-87; chmn. bd., CEO MGA/UA Telecommunications Corp., Beverly Hills, 1986-89; sr. exec. v.p., dir., mem. exec. com. MGA/UA Communications Co., 1986-89; chmn., CEO Sid Sapsowitz & Assocs., Inc., 1989—. Pres., Wayne Conservative Congregation, N.J., 1970-77. Mem. Am. Mgmt. Assn., Am. Film Inst., Acad. Motion Picture Arts and Scis., Fin. Exec. Inst., TV Acad. Arts and Scis., KP (chancellor comdr.).

SAPULICH, JOSEPH M. art director; b. Chgo., Ill. s. George and Barbara Sapulich; m. Cathy Chevalier, Oct. 10, 1987; children: Joshua, Sarah. AA in design and fine art, Am. Acad. of Art, 1980—83. Art dir./film Big Idea Productions, Chgo., 1995—2003. Author: (book) The Touch of Glory, 2000, Beyond Sight, 1998; films, Jonah: A Veggie Tales Movie, 2002. Pastor Freedom in Christ, Chgo.; prison chaplain Stateville Corrections, Joliet, Ill.; pres. Freedom in Christ, Inc., Chgo., 2000—03. Recipient Ministry of the Yr., Stateville Corrections, 2000. Home: 8931 Glenshire Tinley Park IL 60477 Office: Freedom in Christ, Inc P O Box 9214 Lombard IL

SARABANDI, KAMAL, science administrator; b. Tehran, Iran, Nov. 4, 1956; s. Abbas-Ali S. and Fatemeh Jaleh Hooshi; m. Shiva Goltalab-Rad, Aug. 10, 1985; 1 child, Arya Joseph. MSE in Elec. Engring., U. Mich., 1986; MS in Maths., PhD in Elec. Engring., 1989. Microwave engr. Iran's Telecomms. Rsch. Ctr., Tehran, 1980-84; asst. rsch. scientist U. Mich., Ann Arbor, 1989-92, asst. prof., 1992—96, assoc. prof., 1996—2001, dir. Radiation Lab., 2000—, prof., 2001—. Contbr. articles to profl. jours.; patents for multifunction compact planar antenna, 1998, plannar antenna including a superstatic lens with effective diploelectric constant, 1998. Recipient HP Equipment award Hewlett-Packard Co., 1997, Disting. Lectr. award German-Am. Coun. Found., 1999. Fellow IEEE (chmn. awards com. geosci. and remote sensing 1998-2002, mem. ADCOM geosci. and remote sensing 1998-2002, mem. TAB award coun. 2000-02, assoc. editor AP and sensor jour. 2000—, v.p. geosci. and remote sensing 2002—, 1st Prize Paper Contest with Daniel Lawrence 2000); mem. Electromagnetics Acad., USNC/URSI Comm. F. Office: U Mich 1301 Beal Ave Ann Arbor MI 48109-2122 E-mail: saraband@eecs.umich.edu.

SARACEVIC, TEFKO, information science educator; married; 2 children. MS in Libr. Sci., Case Western Reserve U., 1962, PhD in Info. Sci., 1970. Assoc. dean, prof. comm., info. and libr. studies Rutgers U., New Brunswick, NJ. Editor-in-chief: Info. Processing and Mgmt., 1985—. Avocations: reading, skiing. Office: Rutgers U Sch Comm Info & Libr Studies 4 Huntington St New Brunswick NJ 08901-1071 Office Phone: 732-932-7500 x 8500. E-mail: tefko@scils.rutgers.edu.

SARACHIK, MYRIAM PAULA MORGENSTEIN, physics educator; b. Antwerp, Belgium, Aug. 8, 1933; came to U.S., 1947; d. Solomon and Sarah (Segal) Morgenstein; m. Philip Sarachik, Sept. 6, 1954; 1 child, Karen Beth. AB, Barnard Coll., 1954; MS, Columbia U., 1957, PhD, 1960. Rsch. assoc. IBM Watson Labs., Columbia U., N.Y.C., 1960-61; mem. tech. staff Bell Telephone Labs., Murray Hill, N.J., 1962-64; asst. prof. physics CCNY, 1964-67, assoc. prof., 1967-70, prof., 1971—, Disting. prof., 1995—. Advisor NSF, NRC. Contbr. articles to profl. jours. Recipient N.Y.C. Mayor's award for excellence in sci. and technology, 1995, Sloan Pub. Svc. award, 2004. Fellow AAAS, Am. Phys. Soc. (v.p. 2001, pres.-elect 2002, pres. 2003), N.Y. Acad. Scis.; mem. NAS, Am. Acad. Arts and Scis. Office: CCNY Physics Dept Convent Ave and 138 St New York NY 10031 Office Phone: 212-650-5618. E-mail: sarachik@sci.ccny.cuny.edu.

SARAF, DILIP GOVIND, career and management consultant; b. Begaum, India, Nov. 10, 1942; s. Govind Vithal and Indira Laxman (Divekar) S.; m. Mary Lou (Arnold), July 25, 1970; one child, Rajesh Dilip. B in Tech.(hon.), Indian Inst. Tech., Bombay, 1965; MSEE, Stanford Univ., 1969. Sr. mgmt. trainee Delhi Cloth and Gen. Mills Co., India, 1965—68; sr. rsch. engr. SRI Internat., Menlo Park, Calif., 1969—78; project dir. Kaiser Electronics, San Jose, Calif., 1978—87; sr. engring. mgr. Varian Assoc., Santa Clara, Calif., 1987—90; pres. Total Quality, 1990—94; sr. cons. QI Internat., St. Paul, 1994—98; dir. Louis Allen Assoc., San Jose, Calif., 1998—99; sr. cons. Pers. Decisions Internat., San Francisco, 1999—2001; pvt. practice mgmt., orgnl. cons., and exec. coach, 2001—. Cons. tchg. Univ. Santa Clara, 1972, 73; counselor, Career Transitions Unlimited Author: The 7 Keys to a Dream Job: A Career Nirvana Playbook, 2004; contbr. articles to profl. jour.; patentee in field. Bd. dir. Peninsula Children's Ctr., Palo Alto, Calif. Mem. IEEE, Am. Inventors, Am. Soc. Quality Control, Speaker's Bur. Home and Office: 33106 Lake Champlain St Fremont CA 94555-1217 Business E-Mail: dilip@7keys.org.

SARAI, DARSHAN SINGH, environmentalist, entomologist; b. Jandesarai, India, Jan. 9, 1932; s. Kartar Singh and Gurdev Kaur Sarai; m. Mohinder Kaur Arora, June 7, 1959; children: Sumandeep, Bina, Nina. BSc with honors, Punjab U., 1954, MSc, 1956; PhD, U. of Alberta, 1966. Sr. rsch. fellow Govt. of India, 1957—59; asst. prof. Khalsa Coll., Amritsar, India, 1957—63; grad. tchg. asst. U. Alberta, Canada, 1963—66; entomologist Mo. State, 1967—69; chmn., environ. sciences Water and Waste Water Tech. Sch., Neosho, Mo., 1969—78; lab. dir. and quality control Water Dist. #1 of Johnson Cty., Mission, Kans., 1978—99; freelance author, 1999—. Mem.: Am. Water Works Assn., Kiwanis Club (pres. 1996—97). Home: 1360 Heathbrook Circle Asheville NC 28803

SARAKATSANNIS, LEONIDAS NICHOLAS, musician, concert pianist, music educator, composer, conductor; b. Newport, Ky., May 30, 1929; s. Nicholas Demetrius Sarakatsannis and Melanthia Leonidas Kazangi; m. Frances Charles Nicholas, Jan. 22, 1956; children: Demetrius Leonidas, Nicholas Leonidas, Melanie Leonidas. MusB, Coll. Music, 1951; MusM, Coll.-Conservatory of Music, 1956; D in Musical Arts, U. Cin., 1968; postgrad., U. Mich., 1964. Cert. piano Ohio, 1949. Chmn. piano dept. U. Fla., 1959—63; dir. piano program So. Ill. U., Edwardsville, 1964—65; tchg. asst. U. Cin. Coll. Conservatory Music, 1965—68; chmn. dept. music U. Ctrl. Fla., Orlando, 1968—72; dir. applied music No. Ky. U., Highland Heights, Ky., 1972—77; pianist in residence Bloomsburg (Pa.) U., 1979—80; pianist, prof. music, chmn. music dept. U. Guam, Mangilao, 1981—93; adj. prof. music Manatee C.C., Bradenton, Fla., 1994—. Coll. recital chmn. Fla. State Music

Tchrs. Assn., 1962; adjudicator chmn. World Piano Competition, Cin., 1981—88; condr. Guam Symphony Orch., Mangilao, GM, 1981—85. Composer: (musical composition) Twelve Excursions For The Young Pianist, (voice and piano composition) A Communion Hymn; One Is Holy, (piano composition) Six Guam Sketches for Piano, (various compositions) Sonata for Piano, (musical composition) Hymns for Voice and Piano Entitled Praise the Lord, One is Holy, Yia Tin Photini, Six Guam Sketches for Piano; musician: (solo) Fla. Symphony, (piano soloist) Three performances with the Cincinnati Symphony Orchestra under Eric Kunzel and Thor Johnson, North Port (Fla.) Orchestra, Delius Festival in Jacksonville, Asolo Theater, Sarasota, Fla., Taft Mus., Cin., Manatee C.C., Saipan, Guam, Hawaii, and 5 Concerts in Japan, Carnegie Libr. Recitals, Xavier U., Coll. Mount Joseph, others, North Port Orchestra. Bd. dirs. Guam Symphony Orch., Mangialo, 1982—86, Ctrl. Fla. Civic Music Assn., Orlando, 1968—72; v.p. Ctrl. Fla. Music Tchrs. Assn., Orlando, 1970—72. Acting sgt. U.S. Army, 1951—53. Recipient Composition award, Fla. Composers League, 1962, Musical Contbn. to the Cultural Life of our Cmty. award, U. Guam, 1983. Mem.: Coll. Music Soc., Pi Kappa Lambda (hon.), Phi Mu Alpha Sinfonia (recital chmn. 1950—56). Home: 4539 Hamlets Grove Dr Sarasota FL 34235

SARANDON, SUSAN ABIGAIL, actress; b. N.Y.C., Oct. 4, 1946; d. Phillip Leslie and Lenora Marie (Criscione) Tomalin; m. Chris Sarandon, Sept. 16, 1967 (div. 1979); children: Eva Maria Livia Amurri, Jack Henry Robbins, Miles Guthrie Robbins. BA in Drama and English, Cath. U. Am., 1968. Actress: (plays) include An Evening with Richard Nixon, 1972, A Coupla White Chicks Sittin' Around Talkin', 1980-81, A Stroll in the Air, Albert's Bridge, Private Ear, Public Eye, Extremities, 1982, (films) Joe, 1970, Lady Liberty, 1972, The Rocky Horror Picture Show, 1975, Lovin' Molly, 1974, The Front Page, 1974, The Great Waldo Pepper, 1975, Dragon Fly, 1976, Crash, 1976, The Other Side of Midnight, 1977, The Last of the Cowboys, 1978, Checkered Flag or Crash, 1978, Pretty Baby, 1978, King of the Gypsies, 1978, Something Short of Paradise, 1979, Loving Couples, 1980, Atlantic City, 1980 (Prix Genie Best Fgn. Actress award 1981, Acad. award nominee 1981), Tempest, 1982 (Best Actress award Venice Film Festival 1982), The Hunger, 1983, Buddy System, 1984, Compromising Positions, 1985, The Witches of Eastwick, 1987, Bull Durham, 1988, Sweet Hearts Dance, 1988, A Dry White Season, 1989, The January Man, 1989, White Palace, 1990, Thelma and Louise, 1991 (Acad. award nominee for best actress 1992, Golden Globe award nominee 1992), The Player, 1992, Light Sleeper, 1992, Bob Roberts, 1992, Lorenzo's Oil, 1992 (Acad. award nominee 1993), The Client, 1994 (Acad. award nominee for best actress), Little Women, 1994, Safe Passage, 1994, Dead Man Walking, 1995 (Golden Globe award nominee for best actress 1996, Acad. award for best actress 1996), James and the Giant Peach (voice), 1996, 187 (voice), 1997, Illuminata, 1998, Twilight, 1998, Stepmom (also producer), 1998, Joe Gould's Secret, 1999, Baby's in Black, 1999, Cradle Will Rock, 1999, Anywhere But Here, 1999, (voice) Rugrats in Paris: The Movie - Rugrats II, 2000, Moonlight Mile, 2002 (also exec. prodr.), The Banger Sisters, 2002, Igby Goes Down, 2002, Ice Bound, 2003, Moonlight Mile, 2003; TV appearances The Haunting of Rosalind, 1973, F. Scott Fitzgerald and The Last of the Belles, 1974, Who Am I This Time, 1982, A.D., 1985. Mussolini: The Decline and Fall of Il Duce, 1985, Earthly Possessions, 1999, (TV series) A World Apart, 1970-71, Search for Tomorrow, 1972-73; TV appearances: Friends, 2001 (Emmy nominee), Malcolm in the Middle, 2002 (Emmy nominee). Mem. AFTRA, Screen Actors Guild, Actors Equity, Acad. Motion Picture Arts and Scis., NOW, MADRE, Amnesty Internat., ACLU Office: Internat Creative Mgmt care Samuel Cohen 40 W 57th St New York NY 10019-4001*

SARANTAKOS, LYNELL MOSS, agricultural products executive; b. Greenville, Pa., July 13, 1942; d. Silas Frederick Moss and Nell Thompson Ullery. Student, U. SC, 1961—62; grad., John Robert Powers Modeling Sch. Asst. Gelio/Agra Internat., Inc., Bonham, Tex., 1996—99; CEO, owner Agrl. Rsch. Technologies Internat., Inc., Bonham, 1999—. Mem.: BBB, NAFE, Organic Trade Assn., Pi Beta Phi. Office: Agricultural Research Technologies Intl 400 S Center Street Bonham TX 75418 Personal E-mail: lsarantakos@yahoo.com. E-mail: lsarantakos@yahoo.com.

SARASTE, JUKKA-PEKKA, conductor; b. Heinola, Finland, 1956; Doctorate(hon.), York U., Toronto, Ont., 1995. With Finnish Radio Symphony Orch., 1978—, prin. condr., 1987—, music dir., 1987—2001; prin. condr. Scottish Chamber Orch., 1987-91; music dir. The Toronto Symphony Orch., 1994—2001. Recipient 1st prize, Scandinavian Conducting Competition, 1981. Office: care CAMI Berlin Albrechtstrasse 18 D-10118 Berlin Germany

SARASWAT, KRISHNA, electrical engineering educator; married; 2 children. BE in Electronics, Birla Inst. Tech. and Sci., India, 1968; MSEE, Stanford U., 1969, PhD in Elec. Engring., 1974. Product engr. Tex. Instruments, Dallas, 1963—70; rsch. assoc. Integrated Cirs. Lab. Stanford (Calif.) U., 1974—78, sr. rsch. asoc. Integrated Cirs. Lab., 1978—83, dir. rsch. program on mfg. sci. for VLSI, CIS, 1985—93, prof. elec. engring., 1983—. Dir. Integrated Cirs. Lab. Stanford U., 1996—97, dir. NSF/SRC Engring. Rsch. Ctr. for Environmentally Benign Semicondr. Mfg., 1999—; mem. tech. com. Internat. Workshop on Statis. Metrology, 1995—97; mem. Joint Indo/U.S. Com. on Microelectronics to Advise Govt. of India, 1986—88; sec. Internat. Symposium on Physics of VLSI, 1984. Contbr. numerous tech. papers to profl. jours. Recipient Inventor Recognition award, Semicondr. Rsch. Corp., 1987. Fellow: IEEE (mem. tech. com. internat. reliability physics symposium 1997—98, mem. tech. com. internat. interconnect tech. conf. 1997, mem. fellow evaluation com. 1994—, assoc. editor Transactions on Electron Device 1988—90, mem. tech. com. internat. device rsch. conf. 1985—88, chmn. device tech. group internat. electron devices meeting 1984, Best Paper award 1984, 1985, 1990); mem.: Materials Rsch. Soc., Electrochem. Soc. (Thomas D. Callinan award 2000). Achievements include research in physics and technology of silicon VLSI devices and interconnects. Office: Stanford U Elec Engring CISX 326 Stanford CA 94305

SARAVOLATZ, LOUIS DONALD, epidemiologist, physician educator; b. Detroit, Feb. 15, 1950; s. Samuel and Saya Betty (Chonich) S.; m. Yvette Susanne Braymer, Oct. 6, 1990; children: Samuel Francis, Louis Donald II, Stephanie Nicole. BS, U. Mich., 1972, MD, 1974. Fellow Am. Coll. Epidemiology. Intern Henry Ford Hosp., Detroit, 1974-75, 1975-77, fellow, 1977-79, dir. hosp. epidemiology, 1979-82, divsn. head infectious diseases, 1982-96, dir. infectious diseases rsch. lab., 1982-96; prof. medicine Case-Western Res. U., 1993-96, Wayne State U. Sch. Medicine, Detroit, 1996—. Clin. prof. medicine U. Mich. Med. Sch., Ann Arbor, 1986-96; mem. AIDS clin. drug devel. com. NIH, 1990-95; chmn. dept. internal medicine St. John Hosp. and Med. Ctr., 1996—. Contbr. over 140 articles to profl. pubs. Active Blue Ribbon Com. on AIDS State of Mich., Detroit, 1990; chmn. physician com. on AIDS Greater Detroit Health Coun., 1989. Master: ACP, Am. Coll. Physicians; fellow: Royal Soc. Medicine (London), Infectious Diseases Soc. Am. (chmn. antimicrobial use and clin. trials com. 2000—03). Office Phone: 313-343-3362. Business E-Mail: louis.saravolatz@stjohn.org.

SARAYA, NUSSHY, physician, education educator; b. Benyghazi, Libya, June 14, 1973; arrived in U.S., 1999; s. Ibrahim Saraya; m. Lisa Dawn Alonso, Feb. 1, 1999; 1 child, Maya Elizabeth. MD, Cairo Univ., Cairo, Egypt, 1997. Cert. gen. cert. edn. London Univ., Eng., 1988. Adj. prof. Metropolitan Coll., N.Y., 2002—, Touro Coll., N.Y., 2002—, Coll. of New Rochelle, N.Y., 2003—. Mem.: AAUP, Am. Scholar Assn. Avocations: reading, literature, fishing, political science.

SARAZIN, CRAIG LEIGH, astronomer; b. Milw., Aug. 11, 1950; s. Valley V. and Martha V. (Gustafson) S.; m. Jane Curry, June 12, 1971; children: Stephen N., Andrew T. BS in Physics, Calif. Inst. Tech., 1972; MA in Physics, Princeton U., 1973, PhD in Physics, 1975. Millikan fellow Calif. Inst. Tech., Pasadena, 1975; mem. Inst. Advanced Study, Princeton, N.J., 1975-77; asst. prof. U. Va., Charlottesville, 1977-79, assoc. prof. dept. astronomy, 1979-86, prof., 1986-96, W.H. Vanderbilt prof. astronomy, 1996—, chmn. dept., 1992-95. Vis. asst. prof. U. Calif., Berkeley, 1979; vis. scientist Nat. Radio Astronomy Obs., Charlottesville, 1977-82; vis. prof. physics Inst. Advanced Study, 1981-82, Joint Inst. Lab. Astrophysics vis. fellow U. Colo., Boulder, 1985-86; mem. com. on Space Astronomy Astrophysics, Washington, 1984-86, mem. x-ray astronomy working group, 1989-99, mem. Heineman prize com., 1995-98; chmn. Chandra users com., 1993-01, Advanced Satellite for Cosmology and Astrophysics users com., 1995-2000; mem. High Energy Astrophysics from Space Panel, 1999-2000; chmn. USRA Sci. Coun., 2000—. Author: X-ray Emission from Clusters of Galaxies; contbr. numerous articles to profl. jours. NSF grantee, 1981-86, NASA grantee, 1979-82, 86—; recipient Haren Fischer Physics prize Calif. Inst. Tech., 1971. Mem. Am. Astron. Soc., Internat. Astron. Union. Home: 664 Courtyard Ct Charlottesville VA 22903-7876 Office: Leander J McCormick Obs Dept of Astronomy U of Va PO Box 3818 Charlottesville VA 22903-0818 Office Phone: 434-924-4903. Business E-Mail: sarazin@virginia.edu.

SARBANES, PAUL SPYROS, senator; b. Salisbury, Md., Feb. 3, 1933; s. Spyros P. and Matina (Tsigounis) S.; m. Christine Dunbar, June 11, 1960; children— John Peter, Michael Anthony, Janet Matina. AB, Princeton, 1954; BA (Rhodes scholar), Oxford (Eng.) U., 1957; LL.B., Harvard, 1960. Bar: Md. bar 1960. Law clk. to judge Morris Soper U.S. Ct. Appeals (4th cir.), 1960-61; asso. Piper & Marbury, Balt., 1961-62; adminstrv. asst. Walter W. Heller; chmn. Council Econ. Advisers, 1962-63; exec. dir. Charter Revision Commn., Balt., 1963-64; asso. Venable, Baetjer & Howard, Balt., 1965-70; mem. Md. Ho. of Dels., 1967-71, 92d Congress from 4th Dist. Md., 93d-94th congresses from 3rd Dist. Md.; U.S. senator from Md., 1977—. Mem. banking com. U.S. Senate, 1977—, mem. fgn. rels. com., 1977—, mem. joint econ. com., 1979—, mem. budget com., 1993—. Democrat. Greek Orthodox. Office: US Senate 309 Hart Senate Bldg Washington DC 20510-0001 also: Tower 1 Ste 1710 100 S Charles St Baltimore MD 21201-2725

SARD, SUSANNAH ELLEN, non-profit executive; b. Boston, May 10, 1944; d. Russell Ellis and Miriam Clark Sard. AB, Bryn Mawr Coll., 1966. Devel. adminstr. Ky. Ednl. TV, Lexington, 1978—88; dir. found. and corp. rels. Sarah Lawrence Coll., Bronxville, NY, 1991—96; dir. devel. The Town Hall, N.Y.C., 1998—2002; exec. dir. Women's City Club of N.Y., 2002—04; program officer R.J. & S.H. Kaplan Family Found., N.Y.C., 2004—. Alumni bd. Rippowam Cisqua Sch. Mem.: Women in Devel., Blue Hill Troupe. Office: Kaplan Family Found 866 UN Plz Ste 306 New York NY 10017 E-mail: owlkap@aol.com.

SARDO, SANFORD, music educator; b. New York, NY, Aug. 29, 1969; s. Joan Marie and Joseph James Smith(Stepfather); m. Jennifer Lynn McKenna, July 3, 1999. BA, SUNY, Stony Brook, NY, 1992; MSc in Edn., CUNY-Queens Coll., 1998. Cert. Tchr. N.Y., 1993, Music Edn. Orff-Shulwerk, 1995. Tech. dir. Broadhollow Theaters, Lindenhurst, NY, 1989—93; dir. choral activities Calhoun High School Choral Pgm., 1993—. Music counselor MapleWood Sch. Day Camp, Wantagh, NY, 1991—94. Singer: (performance) Back-up Choir @ Kenny Rogers Christmas Show, 1998; dir., dir.: Choir Performance @ Disney's Magic Music Days, 1998, 2000. Recipient Choral Soc. Award in Music Edn., CUNY- Queens Coll., 1993, Music Educator of the Yr., Long Island Musicians Assn., 1995, Tchr. Recognition Award, Kiwanis Club of Merrick, 1998, Legis. Citation, Nassau County Legis., 1998, 2003, Cert. of Recognition, Merrick C. of C., 2002, Nassau County Legis., 2002. Mem.: Nassau Music Educators Assn., NY State Sch. Music Assn., Music Educators Nat. Conf., Am. Fedn. Tchrs., NY Congress of PTAs (life). R-Consevative. Roman Catholic. Home: 89 Charles St Lindenhurst NY 11757 Office: Calhoun HS Choral Program 1786 State St Merrick NY 11566 Personal E-mail: sardomus@aol.com. E-mail: chschoir@aol.com.

SAREMBOCK, IAN JOSEPH, internist; b. Cape Town, Republic of South Africa, June 9, 1951; m. Ghita Marueen Sarembock; children: Craig Murray, Kerri Lauren. MD, U. Cape Town, 1975, PhD, 1988. Diplomate Am. Bd. Internal Medicine, Am. Bd. Cardiovasc. Medicine, Am. Bd. Interventional Cardiology. Sr. house officer dept. internal medicine U. Cape Town and Groote Schuur Hosp., Cape Town, 1979-80, resident in internal medicine, 1980-83, sr. registrar Cardiac Clinic, 1985-86; Velva Schrire meml. rsch. fellow Cardiac Clinic Groote Schur Hosp., 1983-85; postdoctoral rsch. assoc. divsn. cardiology Yale U., New Haven, 1986-88; attending cardiologist divsn. cardiology VA Ctr., West Haven, Conn., 1987-88; asst. prof. internal medicine cardiovasc. divsn. U. Va. Health Scis. Ctr., Charlottesville, 1988-93, assoc. prof. internal medicine cardiovasc. divsn., 1993-99, dir. coronary care unit, 1988—, prof. internal medicine cardiovasc. divsn., 1999—; interventional cardiologist, 1988—; cardiology cons. Salem (Va.) VA Med. Ctr., 1988—. Lectr., presenter in field; invited prof. Heart-Lung Inst., Utrecht, Netherlands, 1992; mem. faculty restenosis summits, Cleve. Clinic, 1992, 93, 97. Contbr. articles to profl. publs. Mem. policy working com., house staff supervision Commonwealth of Va., 1990—. Grantee U. Va. Sch. Medicine, 1989, Beecham Labs., 1989-90, Am. Heart Assn., 1989-91, 91-92, 95-98, NIH, 1991-94, 2000—. Fellow ACP, Coll. Physicians South Africa, Am. Coll. Cardiology (allied health profls. com. 1993—), Coun. Thrombosis Atherosclerosis and Vascular Biology; mem. AAAS, Am. Heart Assn. (bd. dirs. Charlottesville/Albermarle divsn. 1991—, mem. Va. affiliate rsch. peer rev. subcom. 1992—, thrombosis coun. 1987, fellow coun. on clin. cardiology 1989), South African Med. and Dental Coun. Office: U Va Health Sys Cardiovasc Div Box 800158 Charlottesville VA 22908-0158 Fax: 434-982-0901. E-mail: ijs4s@virginia.edu.

SARETZKY, GARY D. archivist; s. Simon Saretzky and Hannah Westermann; m. Kathlinda Girard, Aug. 2, 1980; children: Alexander, Nicholas, Anya. BA, U. Wis., 1968, MA, 1969. Cert. archivist Acad. Cert. Archivists. Archivist Ednl. Testing Svc., Princeton, NJ, 1969—93, Monmouth County, Manalapan, NJ, 1994—. Adj. faculty Mercer County C.C., Trenton, NJ, 1977—, Rutgers U., New Brunswick, NJ, 1993—; photographer, conservator, 1975—. Contbr. articles to profl. jours.; more than 100 exhibits. Pres. Colonial Hts. Civic Assn., Lawrenceville, NJ, 1986—; mem. adv. bd. N.J. State Hist. Records, 1981—96. Recipient Recognition award, N.J. Hist. Commn., 1999, Arline Custer award, Mid-Atlantic Regional Archives Conf., 2001. Mem.: Mid-Atlantic Regional Archives Conf. (N.J. caucus chair 1998—2002, co-chair program com. 2002—03), Soc. of Am. Archivists, Am. Inst. for Conservation. Office: Monmouth County Archives 125 Symmes Dr Manalapan NJ 07726

SAREYAN, ANDY, publishing executive; m. Nancy Marshall; children: Alex, Eliza. Graduated summa cum laude in Econ., Middlebury Coll.; MBA, Stanford U. Various consumer mktg. positions Time Inc., 1987—91; consumer mktg. dir., Can. and Latin Am. Time Internat., 1991—93; v.p., consumer mktg. and develop. Entertainment Weekly, 1993—97; v.p., assoc. pub. In Style, 1997—99; founding pub. Real Simple, 1999; pres. Parenting Group, 2001—02, Entertainment Weekly, NY, 2002—. Office: Entertainment Weekly 1675 Broadway New York NY 10019*

SARFATY, WAYNE ALLEN, insurance agent, financial planner; b. Rochester, NY, Apr. 18, 1951; s. Benjamin and Grace (Rowan) S.; m. Karen Nugent, July 12, 1957 (div. Apr. 2004); children; Melissa A., Gabrielle M. Student, Parsons Coll., 1971-74. Cert. ins. agt. Sales rep. Met. Life, Rochester, N.Y., 1979-81; register rep. Prudential Fin. Svcs., Rochester, 1981-92; owner, broker Wayne A. Sarfaty & Assocs., Rochester, 1992—. Dir. tng. films. Mem. Eagle Club. Recipient Nat. Quality award Nat. Assn. Life Underwriters, 1982-90; named to Million Dollar Round Table, NALU, 1987. Mem.: Eagle Club, Am. Legion. Avocations: camping, auto racing, darts. Home: 8 Rosencrans St Cohocton NY 14826-0182 E-mail: was2@frontiernet.net.

SARGEANT, ERNEST JAMES, lawyer, educator; b. Spokane, Wash., Sept. 26, 1918; s. Ernest Edward and Louise (McWhinnie) S.; m. Helene Sophie Kazanjian, Jan. 29, 1944 BA cum laude, Harvard U., 1940, LL.B. magna cum laude, 1947. Bar: Mass. 1947. Assoc. Ropes & Gray, Boston, 1947, 52-56, ptnr., 1956-90, of counsel, 1991—. Lectr. law Harvard U. Law Sch., Cambridge, Mass., 1961-62, 65-92; adj. prof. Boston Coll. Law Sch., 1990-98. Grad. treas. Harvard Law Rev., Cambridge, 1971-98. Capt. U.S. Army, 1942-46, 51-52. Mem. Am. Law Inst. (council), ABA, Boston Bar Assn. Clubs: Union (Boston); Country (Brookline, Mass.). Home: 24 Highgate Wellesley Hills MA 02481-1420 Office: Ropes & Gray 1 International Pl Boston MA 02110-2624

SARGEANT, THOMAS, real estate company executive; Grad. magna cum laude, U. S.C. CPA. With Arthur Andersen & Co.; contr. Trammell Crow Residential, 1986, CFO, 1989, group fin. officer N.E. group, Mid-Atlantic group and Midwest group, 1992; treas., v.p. adminstrn. AvalonBay Communities, Inc., Alexandria, Va., CFO, 1995 , exec. v.p., 2000 . Mem.: Phi Beta Kappa. Office: AvalonBay Communities INc Ste 300 2900 Eisenhower Ave Alexandria VA 22314*

SARGENT, CAROLE FUNGAROLI, publishing executive; d. Michael and Betty Foley. BA, George Mason Univ., 1990; MA, Univ. Va., 1992, PhD, 1994. Radio host, announcer WUNC-FM, Chapel Hill, NC, 1994—97; vis. scholar U. NC, Chapel Hill, NC, 1994—97; instr. Duke U. Adult Edn., Durham, NC, 1995—96; English prof. Georgetown U., Wash., DC, 1997—2003; pres. Aword in Time, Inc., 2003—. Author: Traditional Degrees for Nontraditional Students, The Slam and Scream, (book reviews) The News & Observer. Recipient Outstanding English Maj. award, George Mason U., 1989; Smith fellow, 1988, 1989, Dupont fellowship, U. Va., 1992. Mem.: Bibliographical Soc. of the Univ. Va., Authors Guild, Nat. Pres. Club, U. Va. Alumni Assn. (life), Alpha Chi. Independent. Avocation: standard poodles. Office: A Word in Time Inc 2308 Mt Vernon Ave #813 Alexandria VA 22301 E-mail: carole@awordintime.com.

SARGENT, CHARLES LEE, manufacturing executive; b. Flint, Mich., Mar. 22, 1937; s. Frank T. and Evelyn M. (Martinson) S.; m. Nancy Cook, June 9, 1962; children: Wendy L., Joy A., Candace L. B ME, GM Inst., 1960; MBA, Harvard U., 1962. Reliability engr. AC Spark Plug div. GM, Flint, 1962-63; with Thetford Corp., Ann Arbor, Mich., 1962-95, pres., chmn. bd. dirs., 1974-95, Thermassan Corp., 1969-72; pres., owner Quality Boat Lifts, Inc., Fort Myers, Fla., 1996—. Trustee Lincoln Cons. Schs., 1973-77, Ketterine U., 1989, chmn. 1995-97. Patentee in field. Elder Presbyn. Ch. Recipient Entrepreneurial Achievement award GMI, 1989; named Entrepreneur of the Yr., Harvard Bus. Sch. Club of Detroit, 1981, Engring. Achievement award Kettering U., 1999. Mem. Barton Hills Country Club (bd. dirs. 1985-87, pres. 1987), Harvard Bus. Sch. Club of Detroit (bd. dirs. 1983-93). Avocations: travel, golf. Home: 27701 Marina Point Dr Bonita Springs FL 34134-0762 Office Phone: 239-432-9110.

SARGENT, DAVID JASPER, academic administrator; b. Manchester, N.H., Aug. 5, 1931; s. Merton Jasper and Marguerite (Riley) S.; m. Shirley Woodbury Swift, Dec. 21, 1951. Student, U. NH, 1949-51; JD magna cum laude, Suffolk U., Boston, 1954; LLD (hon.), Suffolk U., 1978. Bar: NH 1954, Mass. 1954, US Supreme Ct. 1978. Assoc. Kowal and Sargent, Boston, 1954-57; asst. prof. Suffolk U. Law Sch., Boston, 1955—58, assoc. prof., 1958—62, prof., 1962—, dean, 1972—89; pres. Suffolk U., Boston, 1989—. Chmn. Mass. Supreme Ct. Commn. on the Future of the Cts., 1989-; cons. Am. Trial Lawyers Assn., 1957-81; mem. Mass. Jud. Selection Com., 1974-77, Nat. Bd. Trial Advocacy, 1978—. Contbr. articles to legal publications. Bd. trustees Anatolia Coll., Thessaloniki, Greece. Recipient Nat. Svc. award Am. Trial Lawyers Assn., 1968, Outstanding Alumnus award Suffolk U. Law Sch., 1978; hon. mem. Minn. Bar. Mem. ABA, Am. Law Inst., Mass. Bar Assn., NH Bar Assn., Masons. Episcopalian. Office: Suffolk U President's Office 25th Fl 8 Ashburton Pl Boston MA 02108-2770*

SARGENT, ERIC WINSLOW, otolaryngologist, surgeon; MD, U. of Mich., Ann Arbor, Mich., 1982—86. American Board of Otolaryngology - Head & Neck Surgery Am. Bd. of Otolaryngology, 1993. Otologist Mich. Ear Inst., Farmington Hills, Mich., 2001—; assoc. prof. St. Louis U. Sch. of Medicine, St. Louis, 1993—2001. Office: Michigan Ear Institute 30055 NW Hwy #101 Farmington Hills MI 48334

SARGENT, HERB, writer, television producer; b. Phila., July 15, 1923; m. LeGrand Council Mellon. Student, Pa. State U., 1941—43, U. Calif., L.A., 1946—48. Writer (TV series) Broadway Open House-NBC, 1950-51, Colgate Comedy Hour (Fred Allen)-NBC, 1951-52, Victor Borge Show-NBC, 1953, Tonight Show (Steve Allen)-NBC, 1954-58, Steve Allen Sunday Show-NBC, 1958-61, Tonight Show (Johnny Carson)-NBC, 1962-63, The Perry Como Show-NBC, 1963-64, That Was the Week That Was-NBC, 1964-65, The Corner Bar-ABC, 1972-73, Ivan the Terrible-CBS, 1976, The News is the News-NBC, 1983, (TV spls.) The Steve Allen Show with Peter Ustinov, Louis Armstrong and Van Cliburn-NBC, 1959, Music from Shubert Alley-NBC, 1959, Bing Crosby Special-ABC, 1961, Milton Berle Special-NBC, 1962, 9 Perry Como Spls.-NBC, 1963-64, Annie: The Women in the Life of a Man-CBS, 1970, 3 Burt Bachrach Spls., 1970-71, (Sammy Davis Spl.) Sammy, 1972, (Paul McCartney spl.) James Paul McCartney, 1973, Lily-CBS, 1973, The Best of Saturday Night Live-NBC, 1979, The 40th Annual Emmy Awards-Fox, 1988, Diet America Challenge-CBS, 1989, Time Warner Presents: The Earth Day Special-ABC, 1990, The 43rd Annual Primetime Emmy Awards Presentation-Fox, 1991, Saturday Night Live: All the Best of the Mother's Day-NBC, 1992, The 2nd Annual Saturday Night Live Mother's Day Special-NBC, 1993; writer, script cons. Saturday Night Live-NBC, 1975-95, NBC 75th Anniversary, 2002; prodr. (TV series) That Was the Week That Was-NBC, 1964-65, The News is News, 1983, (TV spls.) The Wonderful World of Aggravation, 1972, Alan King Looks Back in Anger-A Review of 1972, 73, Lily-CBS, 1973, The George Segal Show, 1974, Happy Endings, 1975, Love, Life, Liberty, and Lunch, 1976, (radio) NPR's Backfire!, 1992—, (screenplay) Bye Bye Braverman, 1968; co-creator (TV series) The Corner Bar-ABC, 1972-73, Ivan the Terrible-CBS, 1976, others. Writer People for the Am. Way, 1970—. Sgt. U.S. Army Air Corps, 1943-46. Recipient 6 Emmy awards, 6 Writers Guild awards. Mem. NATAS (bd. govs.), Writers Guild Am. East (coun. mem. 1985-91, pres. 1991—), Dramatists Guild, Songwriters Guild Am. Office: Writers Guild Am East 555 W 57th St New York NY 10019-2925 Office Phone: 212-767-7800.

SARGENT, JOHN, psychiatrist; MD, U. Rochester, 1973. Diplomate in psychiatry, child and adolescent psychiatry Am. Bd. Psychiatry and Neurology; diplomate Am. Bd. Pediats.; approved clin. supr. Am. Assn. Marriage and Family Therapy. Intern and resident pediat. U. Wis., Madison, 1973-77; resident child and adolescent psychiatry Phila. Child Guidance Ctr., 1978-80; resident gen. psychiatry Hosp. U. Pa., Phila., 1984-87; dir. child and adolescent psychiatry U. Pa. Med. Sch., 1989-97, dir. adult residency program, 1989-97; mem. staff Children's Hosp. Phila., Phila. Child Guidance Ctr., 1980-97; dir. edn. and rsch., dean Karl Menninger Sch. Psychiatry & Mental Health Svcs., Topeka, 1997—2001; prof. psychiatry Baylor Coll. Medicine, Houston, 2001—; dir. child and adolescent psychiatry Ben Taub Hosp., Houston, 2001—. Assoc. prof. psychiatry and pediat. U. Pa. Med. Sch., 1987-97; Pfeiffer/Adams prof. psychiatry Karl Menninger Sch. Psychiatry. Mem. editl. bd. Jour. Am. Acad. Child and Adolescent Psychiatry; co-author: Madness, Chaos and Violence: Therapy with Families at the Brink; co-editor: Primary Care Pediatrics; contbr. over 60 articles to profl. jours. Faculty, organizer Eastern European Child Abuse and Child Mental Health Program, Soros Found. and Children's Mental Health Alliance. Office: Baylor Coll Medicine One Baylor Plaza BCM 350 Houston TX 77030 Office Phone: 713-798-7889. Business E-Mail: asargent@bcm.tmc.edu.

SARGENT, JOSEPH DENNY, insurance executive; b. West Hartford, Conn., Sept. 11, 1929; s. Thomas Denny and Elizabeth (Owen) S.; m. Mary A. Tennant, June 25, 1955; children: Robert Tennant, Thomas Denny II, Mary Diane, Suzanne Davis. BA, Yale U., 1952. Ptnr. Conning & Co., Inc., Hartford, Conn., 1957-86, mng. ptnr., 1986-92; chmn., CEO Conning & Co., Hartford, Conn., 1986-91, chmn., 1992, vice-chmn., 1993-95; chmn. Conning Internat., London, 1986-92; vice chmn. Conning & Co., 1993-95; chmn. Bradley, Foster & Sargent, 1995—2002. Bd. dirs. Beekley Corp., Bristol, Conn., Tenwick Reins., Stamford, Conn.; past trustee MMI Co., Chgo., Mut. Risk, Bermuda, Policy Mgmt. Sys., Columbia, S.C.; chmn. Conn. Surety Corp., Hartford, 1993-97, Bradley, Foster & Sargent, Hartford, Beazley Furlonge Holdings, Ltd., London; trustee McLean Fund; chmn., treas. SKI Ltd, 1956-96. Past trustee Wadsworth Atheneum, Children's Svcs. of Conn.; trustee Hartford Hosp. Mem. Yale Club (Hartford), Hartford Club, Hartford Golf Club. Home: 25 Colony Rd West Hartford CT 06117-2215 Office: City Place II 185 Asylum St Hartford CT 06103-3408

SARGENT, PAMELA, writer; b. Ithaca, N.Y., Mar. 20, 1948; BA, SUNY, Binghamton, 1968, MA, 1970. Mng. editor, Binghamton, 1970-73; asst. editor, 1973-75; Am. editor Bull. Sci. Fiction Writers Am., Johnson City, NY, 1983-91. Author: Cloned Lives, 1976, Starshadows, 1977, The Sudden Star, 1979, Watchstar, 1980, The Golden Space, 1982, The Alien Upstairs, 1983, Earthseed, 1983, Eye of the Comet, 1984, Homesmind, 1984, Venus of Dreams, 1986, The Shore of Women, 1986, The Best of Pamela Sargent, 1987, Alien Child, 1988, Venus of Shadows, 1988, Ruler of the Sky, 1993 (Nebula best novelette award 1992, Locus best novelette award 1993, Electric Sci. Fiction award 1993), Climb the Wind: A Novel of Another America, 1999, (with Ron Miller) Firebrands: The Heroines of Science Fiction and Fantasy, 1998, Child of Venus, 2001, Behind the Eyes of Dreamers and Other Short Novels, 2002, The Mountain Cage and Other Stories, 2002, Eye of Flame: Fantasies, 2003; editor: (anthology) Women of Wonder, 1975, Bio-Futures, 1976, More Women of Wonder, 1976, The New Women of Wonder, 1978, (with Ian Watson) Afterlives, 1986, Women of Wonder, The Classic Years, 1996, Women of Wonder, The Contemporary Years, 1995, Nebula Awards 29, 1995, Nebula Awards 30, 1996, Nebula Awards 31, 1997, Conqueror Fantastic, 2004. Office: care Richard Curtis Assocs Inc 171 E 74th St New York NY 10021-3221

SARGENT, ROBERT GEORGE, engineering educator; b. Port Huron, Mich., June 14, 1937; s. George O. and Marie L. (Roome) S.; m. Dorothy Baum, 1970; 1 dau., Tiffany. BSE, U. Mich., 1959, MS, 1963, PhD, 1966. Elec. engr. Hughes Aircraft Co., Culver City, Calif., 1959-61; faculty mem. Syracuse U., 1966—, asst. prof., 1966-70, assoc. prof., 1970-81, prof. indsl. engrng. and ops. research, 1982-96, chmn. dept., 1982-85, prof. elec. and computer engrng., 1994-96, prof. elec. engrng. and computer sci., 1996—. Vis. faculty Cornell U., 1981-82, Ctr. Econ. Rsch. Tilburg U., 1996; bd. dirs. Winter Simulation Conf., 1974-84, chmn. bd., 1979-81, gen. chmn., 1977, TIMS Coll. on Simulation and Gaming, 1978-80; pres. WSC Found., 2003-. Dept. editor: Communications of Assn. Computing Machinery, 1980-85; editorial adv. bd. ACM Transactions on Modeling and Simulations, 1989-98; contbr. articles to profl. jours. Recipient Svc. award Winter Simulation Conf., 1984. Mem. Assn. Computing Machinery (nat. lectr. 1985-89, Svc. award 1985), Inst. Ops. Rsch. and Mgmt. Scis. (Disting. Svc. award for Simulation 1988, Lifetime Profl. Achievement award 2002), Inst. Indsl. Engrs. (Svc. award 1985), Soc. Computer Simulation (bd. dirs. 1984-87), Computer Soc. IEEE (mem. exec. com. simulation 1985-99). Office: Syracuse U Dept Elec Engrng and Computer Sci Syracuse NY 13244-0001

SARGENT, RONALD L. retail office and business products executive; BS, MBA, Harvard U. Various mgmt. and planning positions with Kroger Co., 1974-89; regional v.p. ops. Staples Inc., 1989, pres., COO, 1998—2002, pres., CEO, 2002—. Bd. dir. Aramark Corp., Yankee Candle Corp., Mattel Inc. Office: Staples Inc PO Box 9265 Framingham MA 01701-9265*

SARGENT, THOMAS ANDREW, retired political science educator; b. Indpls., Apr. 24, 1933; s. Thomas Edward and Inez (Secrest) S.; m. Cecily Constance Fox-Williams, 1965 (dec.); children: Sarah Beatrice, Andrew Fox; m. 2d Frances Petty, 1987. BA, DePauw U., Greencastle, Ind., 1955; MA, Fletcher Sch. Law and Diplomacy, Tufts U., 1959, MA in Law and Diplomacy, 1968, PhD, 1969. With First Nat. City Bank, N.Y.C., 1959-64, asst. accountant, 1963-64; asst. sec. Irving Trust Co., N.Y.C., 1964-66; mem. faculty Ball State U., Muncie, Ind., 1969-89, dir. London Ctr., 1973-74, chmn. polit. sci. dept., 1977-80, prof. polit. sci., 1979-89, prof. emeritus, 1989—, acting asst. to dean Coll. Scis. and Humanities, 1981-82, assoc. dean Coll. Scis. and Humanities, 1982-85, dir. spl. programs Minnetrista Ctr., 1985-87; dir. E.B. Ball Ctr., Muncie, 1987-89, dir. emeritus, 1989—. Contbg. editor Ripon Forum, 1973-78. Bd. dirs., exec. v.p. Ea. Ind. Cmty. TV, Muncie, 1974-76, pres., 1976-77; mem. nat. bd. govs. Ripon Soc., Washington, 1976-84; mem. Indpls. Com. Fgn. Rels., 1977—; bd. dirs. Hist. Muncie, Inc., 1979-85, pres., 1980; bd. dirs. Muncie Civic Theatre Assn., 1978-81, 90-96, 1st v.p., 1992-96; exec. dir. Ind. Consortium for Internat. Programs, 1982-88; mem. Ind. Real Estate Commn., 1983-91; trustee DePauw U., 1983—; bd. dirs. Muncie Symphony Orch., 1985-95, pres., 1991-93; mem. bd. govs. Minnetrista Cultural Ctr., Muncie, 1989-94, chmn., 1992-94; trustee Malpas Trust, 1990—, pres., 1997—; bd. dirs. Arts Ind., Inc., 1992-99, Muncie Children's Mus., 1994-2000, v.p., 1996-97, pres. 1997; trustee Ind. Colls. Ind., 1996—, United Meth. Meml. Home, Warren, Ind., 1997—. 1st lt. USAF, 1955-58. Named Sagamore of Wabash, 1988. Mem. Am. Polit. Sci. Assn., Delaware County Hist. Alliance (bd. dirs. 1980-86, 87-95, pres., 1987-91), Soc. Profl. Journalists, Delaware County Club, Columbia Club (Indpls.), Maxinkuckee Yacht Club (Culver, Ind.), Rotary, Phi Delta Theta. Republican. Methodist. E-mail: tsarg123@aol.com.

SARGENT, WALLACE LESLIE WILLIAM, astronomer, educator; b. Elsham, Eng., Feb. 15, 1935; s. Leslie William and Eleanor (Denniss) S.; m. Anneila Isabel Cassells, Aug. 5, 1964; children: Lindsay Eleanor, Alison Clare. B.Sc., Manchester U., 1956, M.Sc., 1957, PhD, 1959. Research fellow Calif. Inst. Tech., Pasadena, 1959-62; sr. research fellow Royal Greenwich Obs., 1962-64; asst. prof. physics U. Calif., San Diego, 1964-66; mem. faculty dept. astronomy Calif. Inst. Tech., 1966—, prof., 1971-81, Ira S. Bowen prof. astronomy, 1981—, dir. Palomar Obs., 1997-2000. Miller prof. U. Calif., Berkeley, 1993; Thomas Gold lectr. Cornell U., Ithaca, NY, 1995; Sackler lectr. Harvard U., Cambridge, Mass., 1995, U. Calif., Berkeley, 1996; Icko Iben lectr. U. Ill., 2002. Contbr. articles to profl. jours. Alfred P. Sloan fellow, 1968-70. Fellow Am. Acad. Arts and Scis., Royal Soc. (London); mem. Am. Astron. Soc. (v.p. 2004—, Helen B. Warner prize 1969, Dannie Heineman prize 1991, Henry Norris Russell lectr. 2001), Royal Astron. Soc. (George Darwin lectr. 1987, assoc. 1998), Astron. Soc. Pacific (Bruce Gold medal 1994), Internat. Astron. Union. Clubs: Athenaeum (Pasadena). Home: 400 S Berkeley Ave Pasadena CA 91107-5062 Office: Calif Inst Tech Astronomy Dept 105-24 Pasadena CA 91125-0001 Office Phone: 626-395-4055.

SARGENT, WILLIAM WINSTON, retired anesthesiologist; b. Oshkosh, Wis., Feb. 28, 1933; s. Sprague Spencer and Lila Jane (Gjermundson) S. BS in Medicine, U. Ill., Chicago, 1955, MD, 1957; MS in Anesthesiology, U. Minn., 1967. Diplomate Am. Bd. Anesthesiology. Staff anesthesiologist St. Anthony Hosp., Rockford, Ill., 1960-61, Swedish Am. Hosp., Rockford, 1960-61; instr. anesthesiology U. Minn., Mpls., 1967-74, asst. prof. anesthesiology, 1974-80; staff anesthesiologist St. Luke's Hosp., Duluth, Minn., 1980-95, ret., 1995. Contbr. articles to profl. jours. Capt. USAF, 1961-64, France. Fellow Am. Coll. Anesthesiologists; mem. AMA, Am. Soc. Anesthesiologists, Minn. Soc. Anesthesiologists, Minn. State Med. Assn., St. Louis County Med. Soc. Presbyterian.

SARGUS, EDMUND A., JR., judge; b. Wheeling, W.Va., July 2, 1953; s. Edmund A. Sr. and Ann Elizabeth (Kearney) S.; m. Jennifer L. Smart, Jan. 7, 1978; 2 children. AB with honors, Brown U., 1975; JD, Case Western Res. U., 1978. Bar: Ohio 1978, U.S. Dist. Ct. (so. dist.) Ohio 1979, U.S. Dist. Ct. (no. dist.) Ohio 1981, U.S. Ct. Appeals (6th cir.) 1985, U.S. Dist. Ct. (no. dist.) W.Va. 1988, U.S. Ct. Appeals (4th cir.) 1988. Assoc. Cinque, Banker, Linch & White, Bellaire, Ohio, 1978-79, Stanley C. Burech, St. Clairsville, Ohio, 1980-82; ptnr. Burech & Sargus, St. Clairsville, 1983-93; U.S. Atty. Dept. of Justice, Columbus, Ohio, 1993-96; dist. judge U.S. Dist. Ct. (so. dist.) Ohio, Columbus, 1996—. Spl. counsel Ohio Atty. Gen., Columbus, 1979-93. Solicitor Village of Powhattan Point, Ohio, 1979-93; councilman City of St. Clairsville, 1987-91. Mem. ABA, Ohio Bar Assn. Office: US Dist Ct 85 Marconi Blvd Columbus OH 43215-2823

SARHAN, MANSOOR MOHAMED, library director; b. Nuwidrat, Bahrain, Jan. 1, 1945; s. Mohamed Abdulla and Sukainah Ahmed (Ismail) S.; m. Zahra Abul Kassim Dashti, Aug. 22, 1971; children: Nazha, May, Mohamed. BA in History, Beirut (Lebanon) Arab U., 1972; B in Libr. Sci., U. Bombay, India, 1980; MA in Librarianship, Leeds (Eng.) Poly., 1985; diploma exec. mgmt., U. Bahrain, Isa Town, 1990; PhD in Hist. Documentary Studies, Universal Acad., London, 2003. Tchr. for English lab. Ministry of Edn., Manama, Bahrain, 1963-73, libr. Manama (Bahrain) Pub. Libr., 1973-82, head pub. librs., 1982-88, dir. pub. librs., 1989—. Gen. organizer Bahrain Internat. Book Fair, Manama. Author: The Book and the Libraries, 1983, Cultural Movement in Bahrain 1940-1990, 1993, Bahrain National Bibliography, 1995, Libraries in Islamic Dynasties, 1997, Survey of Cultural Movement in Bahrain during Twentieth Century, 2000, Pioneers of Bookshops in Bahrain, 2000, Libraries in Bahrain, 2001, in Memory of Ebrahim Al-arrayed, 2002, Selections from Ebrahim Al-arrayed's Poetry, 2002, The Education in Bahrain Kingdom, 2003, Shaikh Ahmed Mohamed Al-khalifa: The Poet of Nature and Beauty, 2003. Lectr. schs., clubs and assns., Bahrain, 1975—; gen. organizer yearly piano concert Ministry of Edn., Bahrain, 1988—. Mem. Bahrain Libr. Assn. (pres. 1994—), Arab Fedn. for Librs. and Info., Nuwidrat Club (pres. 1966—). Avocations: reading, music, tennis, chess. Home: House 46 Rd 4301 Nuwidrat 643 Bahrain Office: Ministry of Edn PO Box 43 Manama Bahrain E-mail: mansoorsarhan@hotmail.com.

SARI, MOUNA, language educator; BA with hon. in English Lang. and Lit., Hassan II U., Casablanca, Morocco, 1988; MA in English with honors, S.E. Mo. State U., 1994; MA in Applied Linguistics, So. Ill. U., Carbondale, 1997; MA in Gen. Linguistics, U. Ill., Urbana-Champaign, 2001, postgrad., 2003—. Grad. tchg. asst. S.E. Mo. State U., 1991—93; ESL instr. U. Ark. Spring Internat. Lang. Ctr., 1993—94; from grad. tchg. asst. to computer lab attendant So. Ill. U., Carbondale, 1994—97; ESL instr. Murray State U. Inst. for Internat. Studies, 1997—98; grad. tchg. asst. linguistics dept., engring. dept., religious studies program U. Ill., Urbana-Champaign, 1998—. Grad. rsch. asst. Ctr. for African Studies, Urbana, 2003; grad. tchg. asst. U. Ill., Urbana, 2001, Urbana, 03, Arabic lang. examiner, Springfield, 1999—2000. Fellow, U. Ill., 1999—2003, Fulbright-Hays, 2001, Nat. African Lang. Resource Ctr., 2002, Mich. State U., 2002; scholar, Moroccan Govt., 1984—88, U. Ill., 2002. Mem.: TESOL, Mid-Am. TESOL, African Lang. Tchrs. Assn.

SARI, ROBERT, retail executive; V.p., legal affairs Thrify PayLess, 1994—97; assoc. gen. counsel Rite Aid Corp., 1997—2000, sr. v.p., dep. gen. counsel and sec., 2000—02, sr. v.p., gen. counsel and sec., 2002—. Office: Rite Aid Corporation 30 Hunter Lane Camp Hill PA 17011

SARIDIS, GEORGE NICHOLAS, electrical, computers and system engineering educator, robotics and automation researcher; b. Athens, Greece, Nov. 17, 1931; arrived in U.S., 1961, naturalized, 1971; s. Nicholas and Anna (Tsofa) S.; m. Panayota Dimarogona, Apr. 10, 1985. Diploma in Mech. and Elec. Engring., Nat. Tech. U., Athens, 1955; MSEE, Purdue U., 1962, PhD, 1965. Instr. Nat. Tech. U., 1955-63, Purdue U., West Lafayette, Ind., 1963-65, asst. prof., 1965-70, assoc. prof., 1970-75, prof., 1975-81; prof. elec., computer and sys. engring. Rensselaer Poly. Inst., Troy, N.Y., 1981-96, dir. Robotics and Automation Lab., 1982-96, prof. emeritus, 1997—. Dir. NASA Ctr. for Intelligent Robotic Systems for Space Exploration, 1988-92; engring. program dir. NSF, Washington, 1973; hon. prof. Huazhong U., Wuhan, China. Author: Self-Organizing Control of Stochastic Systems, 1977, Stochastic Processes Estimation and Control, 1995, Entropy in Control Engineering, 2001, Hierachically Intelligent Machines, 2002; co-author: Intelligent Robotic Systems: Theory and Applications, 1992, Reliable Plan Selection by Intelligent Machines, 1996, Design of Intelligent Control System Based on Hierarchical Stochastic Automata, 1996; contbr. articles to profl. publs.; co-author: Intelligent Robotic Sys.; co-editor, contbg. author: Fuzzy Automata, 1977, editor, contbg. author: Advances in Automation and Robotics, Vol. 1, 1985, Advances in Automation and Robotics, Vol. 2, 1990. Recipient Ktesibios award, Med. Control Assn., 2003. Fellow IEEE (founding pres. robotics and automation coun. 1981-84, Centennial medal 1984, Third Millennium medal 2000, Disting. Mem. award Control Sys. Soc. 1989, MCA Ktesibios award 2003); mem. ASME, Soc. Mfg. Engrs./Robotics Internat.-Machine Vision Assn. (sr.), Am. Soc. Engring. Edn., N.Y. Acad. Scis., Acad. Athens (Greece). Home: 38 Loudonwood E Loudonville NY 12211-1465 Office: Rensselaer Poly Inst Dept Electrical Computer & Sys Engring Sch of Engring Troy NY 12180-3590

SARINO, EDGARDO FORMANTES, radiologist, physician; b. Laoag City, Ilocos Norte, Philippines, Nov. 6, 1940; came to U.S., 1965, naturized, 1983; s. Epafrodito Cruze and Esperanza Raval Formantes S.; m. Milagros Felix Ona, Dec. 6, 1965; chldren: Edith Melanie, Edgar Michael, Edenn Michele. MD, U. of the East, 1964; MBA in Healthcare Svcs. Mgmt. Emphasis, W.Va. U., 1999, . Diplomate Am. Bd. Radiology. Rotating intern St. Clare's Hosp., N.Y.C., 1965-66; resident in anatomical pathology Coney Island Hosp, N.Y.C., 1966; resident in gen. surgery Manhattan VA Hosp., N.Y.C., 1966-67, U. Bellevue Med. Ctr., N.Y.C., 1967-68; resident in radiology Manhattan VA Hosp., N.Y.C., 1968-71; fellow in diagnostic radiology, 1968-71; staff radiologist Mercer Med. Ctr., Trenton, N.J., 1973-83; chief nuclear medicine svc. Louis Johnson VA Med. Ctr., Clarksburg, W. Va., 1983-93, acting chief radiology svc., 1988-92, chief imaging svc., 1993—, assoc. chief staff imaging, 1998—; clin. assoc. prof. radiology U. W.Va. Sch. Med., 1989—; teaching asst. gen. surgery N.Y.U.-Bellevue Med. Ctr., N.Y.C., 1967-68. Contbr. articles to med. jours. Recipient Cert. of Merit Mallinkrodt Pharm., 1969. Mem. Am. Coll. Physician Execs., Soc. Nuclear Med., Am. Coll. Radiology, Radiol. Soc. N.Am., Harrison County Med. Soc., W. Va. Radiol. Soc., Assn. Phillipine Practicing Physicians in Am. Philippine Radiol. Soc. Am. Office: Louis Johnson VA Med Ctr Clarksburg WV 26301 Home: 12 Canoa Hills Dr Henderson NV 89052-6634 E-mail: efsarino@msn.com.

SARIS, PATTI BARBARA, federal judge; b. 1951; BA magna cum laude, Radcliffe Coll., 1973; JD cum laude, Harvard U., 1976. Law clerk to Hon. Robert Braucher Mass. Supreme Judicial Ct., 1976-77; atty. Foley Hoag & Eliot, Boston, 1977-79; staff counsel U.S. Senate Judiciary Com., 1979-81; atty. Berman Dittmar & Engel, Boston, 1981-82; chief civil divsn. U.S. Atty.'s Office, 1984-86; U.S. magistrate judge U.S. Dist. Ct. Mass., 1986-89; assoc. justice Mass. Superior Ct., 1989-94; dist. judge U.S. Dist. Ct. Mass., 1994—. Bd. overseers, chair com. on defender svcs. judicial conf. Harvard. Bd. trustees Beth Israel Hosp.; active Wexner Heritage Found. Recipient award Haskell J. Cohn Disting. Jud. Svc. award Boston Bar Assn.; Nat. Merit scholar, 1969. Mem.: Phi Beta Kappa. Office: US Courthouse Courthouse Way Ste 6130 Boston MA 02210

SARKAR, ARINDAM, information technology executive; b. Guwahati, Assam, India, Sept. 30, 1970; s. Amit and Reba Sarkar; m. Monica Mallick, Sept. 10, 1970; 1 child, Amisha. BA with honors, Delhi U., 1991; MBA, Modern Inst. Mgmt., New Delhi, 1994. Pres. Interactive Group, Fremont, Calif., 1995—99; chmn., CEO YBE Info Sys., Inc., Foster City, Calif., 1999—2001; CEO, pres. IG2000 Info Sys., Inc., Fremont, 2001—. Mem.: Fedn. Indo-Am. Assns. of No. Calif. (sr. v.p. 2001—02). Hindu. Avocations: travel, sports, photography, outdoors. Office: IG2000 Info Sys Inc 47550 Kato Rd Fremont CA 94538 Business E-Mail: ary@ig2000systems.com.

SARKAR, INDRA NEIL, medical informatician; b. Framingham, Mass., June 23, 1977; s. Basu Deb and Mahamaya S. BS, Mich. State U., 1999; MPhil, Columbia U., 2002. Tchg. asst., rsch. asst. Mich. State U., East Lansing, 1995-99; rsch. asst. Am. Mus. Natural History, N.Y.C., 2000—; tchg. asst. Columbia U., 2001—02, chmn., grad. student adv. coun., 2002—03. Dir. Mosaic Data Sys., Bedford, Mass., 1995—. Mem. Am. Med. Informatics Assn., AAAS, N.Y. Acad. Scis., Union Concerned Scientists., Am. Inst. Biol. Scis. Avocations: reading, cooking, soccer, programming, writing. Office: Columbia Presbyn Med Ctr Vanderbilt Clin 5 622 W 168th St New York NY 10032

SARKAR, SIDDHARTHA, pathologist; b. Khargpur, India, Aug. 9, 1936; s. Sailabala and Manmatha Nath S.; m. Patricia French, Apr. 6, 1963; children: Jayashri. BS, Calcutta U., 1956; MS, Cornell U., 1957; GVS, Vet. Coll., Calcutta, 1956; PhD, MIT, 1963. Mem. WHO, Geneva, 1975-77; clin. prof. SUNY Upstate Med. U., Syracuse, N.Y., 1999—. Dir. SUNY Ob/Gyn Andrology Svc., Syracuse, 1989—. Patentee in field. Durnham fellow oncology, Am. Cancer Soc., 1966-71.

SARKIS, ZIAD JOSEPH, private equity executive; b. Beirut, July 8, 1968; arrived in France, 1975; s. Nicolas Ata and Claude (Moussalli) Sarkis; m. Elisabeth Kalman, June 21, 1997; 3 children. BAS in Anthropology, Econs. and Math. with distinction and honors, MS in Engring. and Mgmt., Stanford U., 1990; PhD in Econs., Oxford U., Eng., 1998. Cons. McKinsey & Co., San Francisco, 1990, N.Y.C., 1991—92, Paris, 1992; ptnr. AT Kearney, N.Y.C., London, Paris, 1992—94; co-founder, sr. ptnr., bd. dirs. Mitchell Madison Group, N.Y.C., London, Paris, 1992—2000; ptnr. PAI Ptnrs. (formerly Paribas Affaires Industrielles), London, Paris, 2001—. Bd. dirs. Yoplait, JBB Santé. Greek Catholic. Office: PAI Ptnrs 28 Old Brompton Rd #320 London SW7 3SS England

SARKISIAN, CHERILYN See **CHER**

SARKISIAN, PAMELA OUTLAW, artist; b. Spokane, Sept. 26, 1941; d. Willard Clinton and Frances (Montieth) Outlaw; m. Ronald Edward Sarkisian, Nov. 11, 1960; children: Ronald Abraham, Michelle Suzanne. Grad. h.s., Stockton, Calif. Art student, Oceanside, Calif., 1972-80; founder Palette 'N Easel Studio, Oceanside, 1980—, operator, mgr., 1980—, art tchr. in residence, 1985—; ret., 2004. Publisher greeting cards Polytint, Ltd., Eng., 1995, 96; fine art prints pub. by Bentley House, Ltd., Walnut Creek, Calif., 1994-97. Designer collector plate series Danbury Mint/MBI, Inc., gift items Enesco Internat. Gift Co.; represented by Casay Gallery, Kailau, Kona, Hawaii, 1991, Galeria Jean Lammelin, Paris, 1991, 2d St. Gallery, Encinitas, Calif., 1991, Blondes Gallery, San Diego, 1992, Valentine-Owens Gallery, Santa Monica, Calif., 1992, Sodarco Gallery, Montreal, 1993, Surtex, 1993, Jacob G. Javity Conv. Ctr., NYC, 1993, Laura Larkin Gallery, Del Mar, Calif., 1993-94, Charles Hecht Galleries, Tarzana and Palm Desert, Calif., 1993-96, Lou Martin Gallery, Laguna Beach, Calif., 1994, Charles Hecht Gallery, La Jolla, Calif., 1995-96, Calif. Art Gallery, Laguna Beach, 1996, Hunter Gallery, Tucson, 1996, Cottage Gallery at Carmel, Calif., 1996, Dy'ans-Branham Gallery, Laguna Beach, 1997-99, Aka'mai Gallery, Del Mar, 1998-99, Gallery Adrienne, La Jolla, 1998, Cosmopolitan Gallery, La Jolla, 1998-99, The Lillian Berkley Collection, Escondido, Calif., 1999-2003, Waters Edge Gallery, Rancho Mirage, Calif., 2003; one-woman shows include AKA Mai Gallery, 1999, Lillian Berkeley Collection, 2001, Four Seasons-Aviara, La Costa, Calif., 2001, Waters Edge Gallery, Rancho Mirage, 2003. Pres. Zonta Internat., Oceanside, 1980-81; mem. Emblem Club #177, Oceanside, 1971-2003; princess Daughters of the Nile, San Diego, 1974; bd. dirs. Oceanside Girls Club, 1980. Recipient 1st Pl. award San Dieguito Art Guild, 1978, 85, 2nd Pl. award, 1983, 89, 3rd Pl. award, 1983, 1990; winner People's Choice award Internat. Show of Women Artists of the West, Las Vegas, 1992. Mem. North County Art Assn. (founder), Carlsbad Oceanside Art League, 1978, San Dieguito Art Guild, Fallbrook Art Assn., San Diego Art Inst., Assn. pour Promotion Artiste Français, Artisphere. Avocations: ceramics, sculpture, swimming. Office: Palette 'N Easel Studio 1021 S Coast Hwy Oceanside CA 92054-5004 Office Phone: 760-722-9444. E-mail: pamiwigle@msn.com.

SARLE, CHARLES RICHARD, health facility executive; b. Saratoga Springs, N.Y., Sept. 21, 1944; s. John Robert and Marjorie Elizabeth (Swick) S.; m. Marion D. Wallace, June 21, 1968; children: Richard Charles, Robert Edmond. BBA cum laude, Northea. U., 1968; MBA, Babson Coll., 1973. CPA, Mass., Vt. Staff acct. Price Waterhouse & Co., Boston, 1968-70, George Kanavich, CPA, Wellesley, Mass., 1970-72; controller Human Resource Inst., Boston, 1972-73, adminstr., 1973-77; controller Brattleboro (Vt.) Retreat, 1977-78, dir. adminstrn., 1978-85, v.p., 1985-88, chief exec. officer, 1988-97; pres., CEO Carrier Found., Belle Mead, N.J., 1997—. Speaker in field. Mem. commn. Vt. Health Bldg. Fin. Agy., 1978-90; trustee Austine Sch. for Deaf and Hard of Hearing, 1990-97, pres., 1994-97; trustee Winston Prouty Ctr. for Child Devel., 1982-97, treas., 1983-90, sec., 1991-97; trustee Health Rsch. and Edn. Trust N.J., 1998-99, N.J. Hosp. Assn., 1999—, policy devel. com., 1998-01, fin. com., 2000—; bd. govs. NCCJ, 1998-2003, exec. com., 1999-2003. Recipient recognition award Brattleboro C. of C., 1985. Fellow AICPA, Mass. Soc. CPA, Am. Coll. Healthcare Execs. (regent Va. br. 1991-95); mem. Am. Hosp. Assn. (del.-at-large 1988-92, del.-at-large to regional policy bd.), Nat. Assn. Pvt. Psychiat. Hosps. (bd. dirs. polit. action com. 1983-93, trustee 1998-2000), Nat. Psychiat. Alliance (trustee 1989-96, pres. 1994-96), Vt. Soc. CPA (Cmty. Svc. award 1984), Hosp. Fin. Mgmt. Assn. (hosp. cost com. 1985-96), Rescue, Inc. (trustee 1982-83), New Eng. Healthcare Assembly (trustee 1995-97). Avocations: skiing, fishing, tennis, photography. Home: PO Box 840 Belle Mead NJ 08502-0840 Office: Carrier Foundation Rt 601 Belle Mead NJ 08502 Office Phone: 908-281-1000. E-mail: rsarle@carrierclinic.com.

SARLES, H. JAY, bank executive; Vice chmn. Fleet Fin. Group Inc., Boston. Office: Fleet Fin Group Inc 1 Federal St Boston MA 02110-2012

SARLES, HARVEY B. humanities educator; b. Buffalo, July 12, 1933; s. Leonard and Hattie (Rosen) S.; m. Janis Marie Hardy, Nov. 18, 1956; children: Amy Sarles Oakes, Stefan Hardy. BA, SUNY, Buffalo, 1954, MA, 1959; PhD, U. Chgo., 1966. Mathematician Cornell Aero. Lab., Buffalo, 1955-57; asst. prof. anthropology U. Pitts., 1962-66; from assoc. prof. to prof. anthropology U. Minn., Mpls., 1966-86, prof. cultural studies, comparative lit., 1986—. Adj. faculty Humanist Inst., N.Y.C., 1986—; dir. Ctr. Comparative Thought, Mpls., 1980-86. Author: Language and Human Nature, 1985, Teaching As Dialogue, 1993, Nietzsche's Prophecy, 2001. Mem. MLA. Avocation: playing violin. Home: 1225 Lasalle Ave Minneapolis MN 55403-2361 Office: Univ Minn CSCL-350 Folwell Minneapolis MN 55455 E-mail: sarle001@umn.edu.

SARMA, RADHA J. cardiologist, educator; arrived in U.S., 1968; m. Jonnalagedda S.M Sarma; 1 child, Srinivas J. MBBS, Andhra Med. Coll., Visakhapatnam, India, 1966. Diplomate Am. Bd. of Internal Medicine, 1977, Am. Bd. of Internal Medicine, 1977, Cardiovascular Diseases Am. Bd. of Internal Medicine, 1979. Asst. prof. of medicine USC Sch. of Medicine, Los Angeles, Calif., 1975—77; dir., noninvasive cardiology Rancho Los Amigos Med. Ctr., Downey, Calif., 1978—81; dir. noninvasive cardiology King-Drew Med. Center-UCLA, Los Angeles, Calif., 1981—87; chief of cardiology USC Rancho Los Amigos Med. Ctr., Downey, Calif., 1987—96; med. dir. of cardiology & critical care Northridge Hosp. Med. Ctr., Northridge, Calif., 1996—98; assoc. prof. of medicine USC Keck Sch. of Medicine, Los Angeles, Calif., 1998—; dir. cardiac exercise lab. LACUSC Med. Ctr; assoc. dir. echocardiography lab. LACUSC Med. Ctr. Contbr. articles to profl. jour. V.p. Fedn. of Indo-American Assn., L.A., Calif., 1996—97; v.p., planning Fedn. of IndoAmerican Assn. (F.I.A.), L.A., Calif., 1996—97; vice-chair Vedic Edn. and Social Cultural Orgn. (VESCO), L.A., Calif., 2000; coord. 11th tana conf. Telugu Assn. of N.Am. (TANA), Anaheim, Calif., 1995—96; web master Calif. Chpt. of Am. Coll. of Cardiology, Anaheim, Calif., 2001; mem. & regional faculty Am. Heart Assn., L.A., Calif., 1998; pres. Telugu Assn. of So. Calif., L.A., Calif., 1994—95; regional faculty, task force mem. Am. Heart Assn., L.A., Calif., 1998. Grantee Grant in Aid, Am. Heart Assn., 1980-1982. Fellow: ACP, Am. Heart Assn., Am. Coll. of Cardiology. Avocations: computers and electronics, music, dance. Office: USC Keck Sch of Medicine LACUSC Medc 1200 N State St Rm 7440 Los Angeles CA 90033 E-mail: sarma@usc.edu.

SARNA, JONATHAN DANIEL, history professor; b. Phila., Jan. 10, 1955; m. Ruth Langer; children: Aaron Yehuda, Leah Livia. B of Hebrew Lit. with honors, Hebrew Coll., 1974; BA in Judaic Studies and History summa cum laude with highest honors, Brandeis U., 1975; MA in History, Yale U., 1976, MPhil in History, 1978, PhD in History, 1979. Vis. lectr. Hebrew Union Coll.-Jewish Inst. Religion, 1979-80, from asst. prof. to assoc. prof. to prof. Am. Jewish History, 1980-90; Joseph H. & Belle R. Braun prof. Am. Jewish History Brandeis U., Waltham, Mass., 1990—, chmn. dept., 1992-95, 98-01. Cons. Am.-Holy Land Project, 1978—, rschr., 1975-77; abstractor, cons. ABC-CLIO, 1981—; core constituency mem. Conf. on Religion and Life of Nation, Indpls., 1983-85; adv. bd. Maurice Amado Found., 1990-95; mem. grad. fellowship com. Wexner Found., 1989-93; adj. com. Ctr. for Study of N.Am. Jewry, Ben-Gurion U., Israel, 1991—, Ctr. for Am. Jewish History, Temple U., 1991—; dir. Am. Jewish Experience Curriculum Project, 1982—, Boston Jewish History Project, 1992-95, Ctr. for Study Am. Jewish Experience, 1986-90, acad. advisor, 1981-84, acad. directory, 1984-86; asst. in Am. history Yale U., 1978; vis. assoc. prof. Hebrew U., Jerusalem, 1986-87; vis. asst. prof. Judaic studies U. Cin., 1983-84; chmn. bd. Hebrew-Judaic Online Network in Jewish Studies; chair acad. adv. and editl. bd. Jacob-Rader Marcus Ctr. of Am. Jewish Archives; dir. Gralla Fellowship Program for Journalists in

the Jewish Press, Bernard and Rhoda Sarnat Ctr. for the Study of Anti-Jewishness; chief historian Nat. Mus. Am. Jewish History, Celebrate 350, the 350th Anniversary of Am. Jewish Life; lectr. in field. Author: Jacksonian Jew: The Two Worlds of Mordecai Noah, 1981, The American Jewish Experience: A Reader, 1986, rev. edit., 1997, JPS: The Americanization of Jewish Culture (A History of the Jewish Publication Soc. 1888-1988), 1989, (with Alexandra S. Korros) American Synagogue History: A Bibliography and State-of-the-Field Survey, 1988, (with Janet Liss) Yahadut Amerika: American Jewry: An Annotated Bibliography of Publications in Hebrew, 1991, (with Nancy H. Klein) The Jews of Cincinnati, 1989, (with Ellen Smith) The Jews of Boston, 1995, (with David G. Dalin) Religion and State in the American Jewish Experience, 1997 (Choice Outstanding Acad. Book of 1998); editor, translator People Walk on Their Heads: Moses Weinberger's Jews and Judaism in New York, 1982; co-editor: Jews and the Founding of the Republic, 1985; editor: (with Daniel J. Elazar and Rela Geffen Monson) A Double Bond: The Constitutional Documents of American Jewry, 1992, (with Henry D. Shapiro) Ethnic Diversity and Civic Identity: Patterns of Conflict and Cohesion in Cincinnati Since 1820, 1992, (with Lloyd Gartner) Yehude Artsot Ha-Berit, 1992, (with Mark A. Raider and Ronald W. Zweig) Abba Hillel Silver and American Zionism, 1997, (with Pamela S. Nadell) Women and American Judaism: Historical Perspectives, 2001; editor: Observing America's Jews (Marshall Sklare), 1993, Minority Faiths and the American Protestant Mainstream, 1997, (with A. Mittleman and R. Licht) Jewish Polity and American Civil Society, 2002, (with Mittleman and Licht) Jews and the American Public Square, 2002; editor (with Eli Lederhendler) America and Zion: Essays and Papers in Memory of Moshe Davis, 2002, American Judaism: A History, 2004. Acting asst. libr. Am. Jewish Hist. Soc., 1973-75, chmn. acad. coun., 1992-95; v.p. Cin. chpt. Am. Jewish Com., 1985-88, bd. dirs., 1982-84, 88-90; dir. Cin. Coun. for Soviet Jews, 1986—, chmn. adv. bd., 1987 90; leadership coun. Cin. Jewish Fedn., 1981-88, edn. planning and budgeting com., 1982-84, strategic planning com., 1985-86; bd. dirs. Congregation B'nai Tzedek, chmn. adult Jewish edn., 1981-86; bd. dirs. U. Cin. Hillel Found., 1981-86, New Jewish H.S.; active Am. Hist. Assn., Can. Jewish Hist. Soc. Recipient Benjamin J. Shevach Meml. prize for disting. leadership in Jewish edn., 2000, Sklare award for a Career of Disting.Rsch., 2002; Hebrew Free Loan Assn. fellow Am. Jewish Hist. Soc., 1974-75, Charles Andrew fellow Yale U., 1976-77, Howard F. Brinton fellow Yale U., 1977-78, Loewenstein-Wiener fellow Am. Jewish Archives, 1977, fellow Nat. Found. for Jewish Culture, 1977-79, Meml. Found. for Jewish Culture, 1977-79, 82, 83, Lady Davis Endowment, 1986-87, 2001, Bernard and Audre Rapoport fellow Am. Jewish Archives, 1979-80; PEW endowment grantee, 1991-94, Lilly Endowment grantee, 1984-93. Mem. Am. Acad. Religion, Assn. for Jewish Studies, Orgn. Am. Historians, Am. Hist. Assn., Am. Jewish Hist. Soc., Phi Beta Kappa. Office: Brandeis UDept Near Eastern & Judaic Studies MS 054 Waltham MA 02454 Fax: (781) 736-2070. E-mail: sarna@brandeis.edu.

SARNAT, BERNARD GEORGE, plastic surgeon, educator, researcher; b. Chgo., Sept. 1, 1912; s. Isadore M. and Fanny (Silverman) S.; m. Rhoda Elaine Gerard, Dec. 25, 1941; children: Gerard, Joan. SB, U. Chgo., 1933, MD, 1937; MS, DDS, U. Ill., 1940. Diplomate Am. Bd. Plastic Surgery, 1947. Intern Los Angeles County Gen. Hosp., 1936-37; resident oral and plastic surgery Cook County Hosp., Chgo., 1940-41; asst. to Dr. Marshall Davison (gen. surgery) Univ. Hosp., Chgo., 1942-43; asst. to Drs. Vilray P. Blair and Louis T. Byars (plastic and reconstructive surgery), St. Louis, 1943-46; practice medicine specializing in plastic surgery Chgo., 1946-56, Beverly Hills, Calif., 1956-91; asst. histology U. Ill. Coll. Dentistry, 1937-40, prof., head dept. oral and maxillofacial surgery, 1946-56; asst. dept. surgery, divsn. plastic surgery Washington U. Sch. Medicine, St. Louis, 1944-46; prof., dir. dept. oral and plastic surgery St. Louis U. Coll. Dentistry, 1945-46; clin. asst. prof. surgery (plastic surgery) U. Ill. Coll. Medicine, 1949-56; adj. prof. oral biology Sch Dentistry UCLA, 1969—, mem. Dental Rsch. Inst., 1974-95, adj. prof. plastic surgery Sch. Medicine, 1974—; attending staff Cedars-Sinai Med. Ctr., L.A., 1956-91, emeritus, 1991—, mem. staff, sr. rsch. scientist, chief plastic surgery, 1961-81. Cons. in gen., plastic and maxillofacial surgery VA Regional Office, Chgo., until 1956; lectr. in field. Sr. author: (with Dr. Isaac Schour) Oral and Facial Cancer, 2nd edit., 1957, (with Dr. Daniel Laskin) Surgery of the Temporomandibular Joint, 1964; editor: (with Daniel Laskin) The Temporomandibular Joint A Biological Basis for Clinical Practice, 4th edit., 1991, (with Andrew D. Dixon) Factors and Mechanisms Affecting Growth of Bone, 1982, Normal and Abnormal Bone Growth: Basic and Clinical Research, 1985, Fundamentals of Bone Growth: Methodology and Applications, 1991; contbr. chpts. to textbooks, articles to surg. and sci. jours., other pubs. Co-winner Joseph A. Capps prize for med. rsch. Inst. Medicine, Chgo., 1940, Frederick B. Noyes prize, 1940; recipient Kerbs award for rsch. plastic and reconstructive surgery, 1950, 1st prize, sr. award Found. Am. Soc. Plastic and Reconstructive surgeons, 1957, Beverly Hills Acad. of Medicine award, 1959, Nat. Achievement award medicine Phi Epsilon Pi, 1964, 1st prize Am. Rhinologic Soc., 1980, medal Hebrew U., Jerusalem, 1985, medal Tel Aviv U., 1985, Disting. Svc. Alumni award U. Chgo. Pritzker Sch. Medicine, 1987, hon. award Am. Soc. Maxillofacial Surgeons, 1990, Dallas B. Phemister Profl. Achievement award Dept. Surgery U. Chgo., 1993, Disting. Alumnus award U. Ill. Coll. Dentistry, 1994, Craniofacial Biology Rsch. award Internat. Assn. for Dental Rsch., 1995, Disting. Scientist award, Pioneer in Medicine award Cedars-Sinai Med. Ctr., L.A., 1999, Profl. Achievement citation U. Chgo. Alumni Assn., 2003, citatioon of excellence in rsch. Plastic Surgery Ednl. Found., 2003, Profl. Achievement award U. Ill. Alumni Assn., 2004. Fellow ACS, AAAS, Am. Assn. Plastic Surgeons (hon. award 1993); mem. Calif. Med. Soc., L.A. Med. Soc., Am. Soc. Plastic and Reconstructive Surgeons, Plastic Surgery Rsch. Coun. (founding mem. 1955, chmn. 1957), Calif. Soc. Plastic Surgeons, Beverly Hills Acad. Medicine (pres. 1962-63), Internat. Assn. Craniofacial Biology, Am. Assn. Pediat. Plastic Surgeons (hon. 2000), Am. Assn. Phys. Anthropologists, Internat. Assn. Study Dento-Facial Abnormalities (hon.), Sigma Xi, Omicron Kappa Upsilon, Zeta Beta Tau, Phi Delta Epsilon, Alpha Omega (Internat. Achievement medal 1988). Home: 1875 Kelton Ave Apt 301 Los Angeles CA 90025-8505 E-mail: bsarnat@earthlink.net.

SARNELLE, JOSEPH R. electronic publishing specialist, magazine and newspaper editor; b. Bklyn., Aug. 24, 1951; s. Alphonse Louis and Julie Lena (Mingarelli) S.; m. Ruth Patricia Cullen, Aug. 5, 1982 (dec.); children: Cullen Joseph, D'Arcy Emilie. BA, Cornell U., 1973; postgrad., Sch. Visual Arts, N.Y.C., 1976—77, The New Sch., 1979—80. Graphic artist Lewahl KC Graphics, N.Y.C., 1974-76; editor United Bus. Publs., N.Y.C., 1976-79; mng. editor Lebhar-Friedman Inc., N.Y.C., 1979-88; assoc. mng. editor Home-Owner Mag., N.Y.C., 1988-90; mgr. online sys. devel. Info. Builders Inc., N.Y.C., 1990—. Cons. video Markham-Novelle Pub. Rels., N.Y.C., 1988-89; cons. Best info. Family Media, N.Y.C., 1990-91. Author, dir. (videos) J. Roland Pepe's Guide to New York City, 1980, Underground Roundup, 1981. McMullen scholar, Cornell U., Regents scholar, State of N.Y., 1969; recipient Best Headline of Yr. award Lebhar-Friedman Inc., 1982. Office: Info Builders Inc 2 Penn Plz New York NY 10121 E-mail: joe_sarnelle@ibi.com.

SARNO, PATRICIA ANN, biology educator; b. Ashland, Pa.; d. John Thomas and Anna (Harvest) S. BS, Pa. State U., 1966, MEd, 1971; postgrad. Bucknell U., 1967, Bloomsburg U., 1970. Programmer planetarium, tchr. sci. Pottsville (Pa.) High Sch., 1967; tchr. biology Schuylkill Haven (Pa.) Area High Sch., 1967-91, sci. chmn., coord. dist., 1973-91; lead tchr. sci. Pa. Acad. Suprs. and Curriculum Devel. Dist. Pa. Sch., 1991—; cons. Contbr. to profl. jours. Pa. Edn. Dept., career program Pottsville Hosp. Dow Chem. Co. grantee, 1971. Mem. AAAS, AAUW, NEA, Pa. Edn. Assn. (exec. bd.), Nat. Assn. Biology Tchrs., Nat. Tchrs. Assn., Pa. Assn. Supervision and Curriculum Devel., N.Y. Acad. Scis., Pa. Tchrs. Assn., Am. Inst. Biol. Scis., Pa. Acad. Scis., Pa. State U. Alumni Assn., Schuylkill Haven Edn. Assn., Phi Sigma, Delta Kappa Gamma. Discoverer spider species Atypus snetzingeri, 1973. Home: 49 S Balliet St Frackville PA 17931-1703 Office: Schuylkill Haven HS Schuylkill Haven PA 17972

SARNOFF, JOSEPH C. academic administrator; b. Bronx, N.Y., Apr. 3, 1946; s. Philip and Jeannette (Seiden) S.; divorced; children: Allison, Philip, Julie. BA, Northland Coll., 1968; MS, U. Wis., Milw., 1969, Clarkson U., 1978. Lectr. biology Bronx Cmty. Coll., 1970; from assoc. dir. student union to dir. student union, activities and volunteerism SUNY, Potsdam, 1970—. Acting village justice Village of Potsdam, 1986, 89—, chair zoning bd., 1988-90, co-chair com. to rewrite zoning codes, 1989. Recipient Pres. award for excellence in pub. svc. SUNY, Potsdam, 1992, Point of Excellence award Kappa Delta Pi, 1995. Mem. Assn. Colls. & Univs. Internat., Nat. Assn. Coll. Activities, N.Y. State Magistrates Assn., SUNY Coll. Union Profls., Points of Light Found. Avocations: long distance running, biking, refinishing antique furniture. Office: SUNY Potsdam 44 Pierrepont Ave Potsdam NY 13676-2294

SARNOFF, LILI-CHARLOTTE (LOLO SARNOFF), artist; b. Frankfurt, Germany (as Swiss citizen), Jan. 9, 1916; arrived in U.S., 1940; d. Willy and Martha (Koch von Hirsch) Dreyfus; m. Stanley Jay Sarnoff, 1948; children: Daniela Martha Bargezi, Robert L. Grad., Reimann Art Sch., Germany, 1936, U. Berlin, 1938; student, U. Florence, Italy, 1948-54; DFA (hon.), Corcoran Coll. Art & Design, 2003. With Red Cross Swiss Motor Corps, 1939—40; Red Cross nurse Bellevue Hosp., N.Y.C., 1942—47; rsch. asst. Harvard Sch. Pub. Health, 1950-54; rsch. assoc. cardiac physiology Nat. Heart Inst., Bethesda, Md., 1954-59; pres. Rodana Rsch. Corp., Bethesda, 1959—61; v.p. Catrix Corp., Bethesda, 1959—61; prin., owner Dara's Sr. Pets for Srs., 2003. Inventor Flolite light sculptures under name Lolo Sarnoff, 1968—; one-woman shows include Agra Gallery, Washington, 1969, Corning (N.Y.) Glass Ctr. Mus., 1970, Gallery Two, Woodstock, Vt., 1970, Gallery Marc, Washington, 1971, 1972, Franz Bader Gallery, 1976, Gallery K, 1978, 1981, 1985, 1987, 1991, Retrospective Show, 1995, Alwin Gallery, London, 1981, Galerie von Bartha, Basel, Switzerland, 1982, La Galerie L'Hotel de Ville, Geneva, 1982, Pfalzgalerie, Kaiserslautern, Germany, 1985, Galerie Les Hirondelles, Geneva, 1988, Represented in permanent collections. Founder, pres. Arts for Aging, Inc., Bethesda, 1988—; pres. Dara's Canine Found., Inc., 1999—. Recipient Golda Meir award, 1995, Life Commitment to Arts award, Swiss Am. Cultural Exch., 1999, Path of Achievement award for Arts and Humanities, Montgomery County, Md., 2000, Outstanding Citizen award, Iona Sr. Citizen Svcs., Washington, 2002. Home: 7507 Hampden Ln Bethesda MD 20814-1331 E-mail: lolos@erols.com.

SARNOFF, THOMAS WARREN, television executive; b. N.Y.C., Feb. 23, 1927; s. David and Lizette (Hermant) S.; m. Janyce Lundon, May 21, 1955; children: Daniel, Timothy, Cynthia. Grad., Phillips Acad., 1939-43; student, Princeton, 1943-45; BS in Elec. Engring., Stanford U., 1948, postgrad. Sch. Bus. Adminstrn., 1948-49; D.H.L., Columbia Coll. Engaged in prodn. and sales with ABC, Inc., 1949-51; prodn. Metro-Goldwyn-Mayer, 1951-52; with NBC, 1952-77; v.p. prodn. and bus. affairs NBC (Pacific div.), 1956-60, v.p. adminstrn. West Coast, 1960-62, v.p. charge West Coast, 1962-65, staff exec. v.p. West Coast, 1965-77; pres. NBC Entertainment Corp., 1972-77, Sarnoff Internat. Enterprises, 1977-81, Sarnoff Entertainment Corp., 1981—; exec. v.p. Venturetainment Corp., 1981-87, pres., 1987—. Bd. dirs. Multimedia Games, Inc., 1998—, chmn. bd., 2004—. Exec. producer Bonanza: The Next Generation, 1987, Bonanza: The Return, 1993, Back to Bonanza Retrospective, 1993, Bonanza: Under Attack, 1995. Mem. Calif. Commn. for Reform Intermediate and Secondary Edn. Pres., Research Found., St. Joseph Hosp., Burbank, 1965-73, Permanant Charities Com. of Entertainment Industries, 1971-72; nat. trustee Nat. Conf. Christians and Jews. Served with Signal Corps AUS, World War II. Mem. Acad. TV Arts and Scis. (chmn. bd. trustees 1972-74, chmn. past pres.'s coun. 1989-92), Acad. TV Arts and Scis. Found. (pres. 1990-99, chmn., CEO 1999—), The Caucus for Prodrs., Writers and Dirs. Office: 2451 Century Hl Los Angeles CA 90067-3510 Office Phone: 310-203-9234.

SARPKAYA, TURGUT, mechanical engineering educator; b. Aydin, Turkey, May 7, 1928; came to U.S., 1951, naturalized, 1962; s. Hasip and Huriye (Fetil) S.; m. Gunel Ataisik, Aug. 26, 1963. BS in Mech. Engring, Tech. U. Istanbul, 1950, MS, 1951; PhD in Engring, U. Iowa, 1954. Research engr. MIT, Cambridge, 1954-55; asst. prof. U. Nebr., 1957-59, assoc. prof., 1959-62, prof. mech. engring., 1962, distinguished prof., 1962-66; research prof. U. Manchester, Eng., 1966-67, U. Gottingen, Fed. Republic of Germany, 1971-72; prof. mech. engring., chmn. dept. mech. engring. U.S. Naval Postgrad. Sch., Monterey, Calif., 1967-71, 72—, Disting. prof. mech. engring., 1975—. Cons. aerospace industry, 1967—, petroleum industry, 1976—. Author: Mechanics of Wave Forces on Offshore Structures, 1981; mem. editorial bd.; Zentralbaltt fur Mathematik; editor: Procs. Heat Transfer and FLuid Mechanics Inst., 1970; contbr. chpts. to many books and over 200 papers on fluid dynamics. Served with C.E. AUS, 1955-57. Fellow Royal Instn. Naval Architects, AIAA, ASME (Lewis F. Moody award 1967, exec. bd. fluids engring. fivsn., chmn. review com., Freeman Scholar award 1988, Engring. award 1991, Fluids Engring. award 1990, Collingwood prize 1957, Offshore Mechanics and Arctic Engring. award 1993, Turning Goals into Reality award, NASA, 2002); mem. Heat Transfer and Fluid Mechanics Inst. (chmn., Am. Inst. Aeros. and Astronautics, Am. Soc. Engring. Edn. Achievements include patent for fluidic elements. Home: 25330 Vista Del Pinos Carmel CA 93923-8804 Office: Naval Postgrad Sch Mech Engring Code ME SL 700 Dyer Rd Monterey CA 93943-5000 E-mail: sarp@nps.navy.mil.

SARRAF, SHIRLEY A. secondary school educator; BA in polit. sci., U. Calif., Davis, 1968; MEd, Idaho State U., 1976, postgrad., 1976—. Cert. Educator Nat. Bd. Edn., 2001. Asst. psychometrist U. Wash., 1969-72; asst. prof. dept. fgn. lang. Farah Pahlavi U., Teheran-Vanek, Iran, 1978-79; tchr. presch. program T.L.C. Child Care Ctr., Pocatello, Idaho, 1980-82; dir. of curriculum for English as a second lang. Idaho State U., Pocatello, Idaho, 1982-85; tchr. English, Math, History, Computers Highland High Sch. Sch. Dist. 25, Pocatello, Idaho, 1986—2001; tchr. English Folsom H.S., Folsom, Calif., 2001—. Infant and child stimulation workshops Idaho State U. Pocatello, Idaho, adj. prof. U. Teheran, Iran, 1978-79. Recipient Tchr. of the Year award State of Idaho, 1994-95. Home: PO Box 6001 Folsom CA 95763-6001

SARREALS, SONIA, data processing consultant; b. NYC, Sept. 17, 1938; d. Espriela and Sadie Beatrice (Scales) Sarreals; m. Waldro Lynch, Sept. 18, 1981 (div. Oct. 1983). BA in Langs. summa cum laude, CCNY, 1960; cert. in French, Sorbonne, Paris, 1961. Systems engr. IBM, N.Y.C., 1963-69; cons. Babbage Systems, N.Y.C., 1969-70; project leader Touche Ross, N.Y.C., 1970-73; sr. programmer McGraw-Hill, Inc., Hightstown, N.J., 1973-78; staff data processing cons. Cin. Bell Info. Systems, 1978-89; sr. analyst AT&T, 1989-92; lead tech. analyst Automated Concepts Inc., Arlington, Va., 1992-96; tech. cons. Teksystems, Reston, Va., 1996—. Elder St. Andrew Luth. Ch., Silver Spring, 1992-96. Downer scholar CUNY, 1960; Dickman Inst. fellow Columbia U., 1960-61. Mem.: Assn. for Computing Machinery, Phi Beta Kappa. Democrat. Avocations: needlecrafts, sewing. Home: 13705 Beret Pl Silver Spring MD 20906-3030 Office: Teksystems 12343 Sunrise Valley Dr Reston VA 20191 Business E-Mail: ssarreals@teksystems.com.

SARRING, KEVIN LEE, architect, archaeologist; b. Berwyn, Ill., Apr. 17, 1953; s. Ernest James Sarring and Grace Luceille Thiele. Cert., Magdalen Coll., 1970; BSc, U. of Ill., 1976; MS, Columbia U., 1978. Lic. State of Ill., DC. Conservator intern ICOMOS, Union RempArt, Paris, 1976; arch., v.p. Harry Weese and Associates, Chgo., 1978—89; arch. Joseph Pell Lombardi, N.Y.C, 1977—78; intern Municipality of NY Bur. of Bldg. Design, N.Y.C, 1977—78; project mgr. Cloister Investment Pte. Ltd., Singapore, 1991—92; ceo Kevin Lee Sarring Arch., Chgo., 1992—; arch. US Dept of State, Washington, 1995—; draughtsman John Vincent Anderson Arch., Woodstock, Ill. Editl. asst. Inland Arch., Chgo., 1983—94; instr. Art Inst., Chgo., 1994; arch. World Monuments Fund, Angkor, Siem Reap, Cambodia, 1994—95, Hasbrouck Peterson Zimoch Sirirattumrong, Bangkok, 1994; arch. project mgr. Bldg. Blocks/ Broady -Campbell, Ind., 1994. Am. legis. Seoul restoration planning, Grand Central Terminal, restoration, Auditorium Theatre Chicago, Horatio Wilson (Allen) residence Libertyville, 59 th Street Bridge Restoration Chicago, Raffles Hotel Singapore, Field Museum of Natural History, Ebway International Headquarters, Circle City Storefronts, Forum of Trajan Rome. V.p. and bus. mgr. Up With People Sing Out Chgo., Chgo., 1968—71. Recipient Cert. of Appreciation, Sec. of State, 1998, Recognition Dars es Salaam, Fgn. Buildings Office US Dept. of State, 1998, Citation of Merit Chgo. Field Mus., Chgo. Chpt. of Constrn. Specifications Inst., 1988, Franklin award, Sec. of State, 2003. Mem.: Assn. for Preservation Tech. (life). Home: 214 South Virginia Ave Falls Church VA 22046-4128 Office: Oveseas Buildings Operations OBO/PE/DE/ADB Washington DC 20522-0602

SARRIS, ANDREW GEORGE, film critic; b. Bklyn., Oct. 31, 1928; s. George Andrew and Themis (Katavolos) S.; m. Molly Clark Haskell, May 31, 1969. AB, Columbia, 1951. Film critic Village Voice, N.Y.C., 1960-89, N.Y. Observer, 1989—. Editor-in-chief Cahiers du Cinema in English; instr. Sch. Visual Arts, 1965-67; asst. prof. N.Y. U., 1967-69; assoc. prof. films Columbia Sch. Arts, N.Y.C., 1969-81, prof., 1981— Author: The Films of Josef Von Sternberg, 1966, Interviews with Film Directors, 1967, The Film, 1968 The American Cinema, 1968, Confessions of a Cultist, 1970, The Primal Screen, 1973, The John Ford Movie Mystery, 1976, Politics and Cinema, 1978. Served with Signal Corps AUS, 1952-54. Guggenheim fellow, 1969 Mem. Am. Film Inst. (dir.), Soc. Cinema Studies, Nat. Soc. Film Critics, N.Y. Film Critics. *I keep on working toward that last deadline.*

SARROS, P. PETER, diplomat, consultant; b. Greece, Aug. 20, 1935; (parents Am. citizens); s. Basil and Helen Sarros. BA summa cum laude, Hobart Coll., 1957; M Pub. and Internat. Affairs, Princeton U., 1959, PhD, 1964. U.S. fgn. svc. officer Dept. of State, Washington, 1960-92, sr. fgn. affairs cons., 1993—2003. Spl. amb. to the Vatican, 1978; charge U.S. Mission to The Vatican, 1975—80; acting dep. asst. sec. for Human Rights, 1980—82; dir. Regional Polit. Affairs for Latin Am., 1985—92; adj. prof. diplomacy George Mason U., 1992—93; diplomatic assignments in Venezuela, Dominican Republic and Iceland, 1961—67; diplomat in residence Johns Hopkins Sch. Advanced Internat. Studies, 1972—73. W. Wilson fellow Princeton U., 1957-60. Mem. Am. Fgn. Svc. Assn., Ft. Myer Officers Club, Phi Beta Kappa. Avocation: bibliophile. Home: 1200 N Nash St Arlington VA 22209-3616 Office: Dept of State IRM/OPS Washington DC 20520

SARRY, CHRISTINE, ballerina; b. Long Beach, Calif., May 25, 1946; d. John and Beatrice (Thomas) S.; 1 child, Maximilian Sarry Varriale. With Joffrey Ballet, 1963—64, Am. Ballet Theatre, 1964—68, prin. dancer, 1971—74; leading dancer Am. Ballet Co., 1969—71; ballerina Eliot Feld Ballet, 1974—81. Dir. faculty Ballet Tech., N.Y.C., also freelance guest tchr. Performed ballets for Agnes DeMille, Antony Tudor, Jerome Robbins, Eliot Feld; appeared at White House, 1963, 67; U.S. Dept. State tours include, Russia, 1963, 66, S.Am., 1964, 76, various tours of N.Am., Orient, Europe, various appearances U.S. nat. TV; partnered by Mikhail Baryshnikov.

SARSON, JOHN CHRISTOPHER, television producer, director, writer; b. London, Jan. 19, 1935; s. Arnold Wilfred and Annie Elizabeth (Wright) S.; m. Evelyn Patricia Kaye, Mar. 25, 1963; children: Katrina May, David Arnold BA with honors, Trinity Coll., Cambridge, Eng., 1960, MA, 1963. Dir. Granada TV, Manchester, Eng., 1960-63; producer, dir. Sta. WGBH-TV, Boston, 1963-73; pres. Blue Penguin, Inc., Boulder, Colo., 1974—; v.p. TV programming Sta. WYNC-TV, N.Y.C., 1989-90. Dir. Pub. Broadcasting Assocs., Newton, Mass.; cons. to numerous pub. TV stations Creator, producer MAsterpiece Theatre, PBS, 1970-73, Zoom, PBS, 1971-73; producer Live From the Met, PBS, 1977-79, Kid's Writes, Nickelodeon, 1982-83, American Treasure, a Smithsonian Journey, 1986, Spotlight Colorado, 1991, Parenting Works, 1993, 95-97, Club 303, 1994. Served with Royal Navy, 1956-57 Recipient Emmy award, 1973, 74, Peabody award Ohio State U., 1978, Internat. Emmy award, 1983, Nat. Acad. TV Arts and Scis. Gov.'s award, 1991. Mem. Dirs. Guild Am., Nat. acad. TV Arts and Scis. (gov. Heartland chpt.), Windows on the Rockies User Group (pres.). Avocations: music, cooking, gardening, travel, computers. Home and Office: 3031 5th St Boulder CO 80304-2501 E-mail: csarson123@hotmail.com.

SARTAIN, JAMES EDWARD, lawyer; b. Ft. Worth, Feb. 9, 1941; s. James F. and May Belle (Boaz) S.; m. Barbara Hardy, Aug. 17, 1962; 1 child, Bethany Sartain Hughes. BA, Tex. A&M U., 1963; LLB, Baylor U., 1966. Bar: Tex. 1966, U.S. Ct. Mil. Appeals, 1971, U.S. Dist. Ct. (no. dist.) Tex. 1974. Staff atty. Dept. Justice, Washington, 1970-72; staff atty. to U.S. Sen. William L. Scott Fairfax, Va., 1972; pvt. practice Ft. Worth, 1973—2001, Abilene, Tex., 2001—. Bd. dirs. Ft. Worth Boys Club, 1980-89, Oakwood Cemetery, Ft. Worth, 1979-84; adv. dir. Grady McWhinney Rsch. Found., Abilene, Tex., 12th Armored Divsn. Meml. Mus., Abilene. Capt. arty. U.S. Army, Vietnam. Fellow Coll. State Bar Tex.; mem. ABA, NRA, VFW, Abilene Bar Assn., Baylor Law Alumni Assn., Masons, Phi Delta Phi. Republican. Presbyterian. Home: PO Box 450 Abilene TX 79604-0450 Office Phone: 915-676-2492.

SARTOR, DANIEL RYAN, JR., lawyer; b. Vicksburg, Miss., June 2, 1932; s. Daniel Ryan and Lucy Leigh (Hubbs) S.; m. Olive Guthrie Moss, Oct. 12, 1957; children— Clara M., Daniel Ryan, Walter M. BA, Tulane U., 1952, LL.B., 1955. Bar: La. 1955. Instr. Tulane U., New Orleans, 1955-56, asst. prof., 1956-57; ptnr. Snellings, Breard, Sartor, Inabnett & Trascher, Monroe, La., 1957—. Contbr. articles to profl. jours. Fellow Am. Coll. Trust and Estate Counsel, Am. Bar Found., La. Bar Found.; mem. La. State Law Inst. (mem. council 1969—, sec. civil law sect. 1969-97, sr. officer 1997—), La. State Bar Assn. (chmn. sect. on trust estate, probate and immovable property 1973-74, bd. govs. 1974-75), Lotus Club, Bayou DeSaird Country Club. Democrat. Methodist. Home: 2405 Pargoud Blvd Monroe LA 71201-2326 Office: Snellings Breard Sartor 1503 N 19th St Monroe LA 71201-4960 Office Phone: 318-387-8000. Business E-Mail: rsartor@snellingslawfirm.com.

SARTORELLI, ALAN CLAYTON, pharmacologist, educator; b. Chelsea, Mass., Dec. 18, 1931; m. Alice C. Anderson, July 7, 1969. BS, New Eng. Coll. Pharmacy Northeastern U., 1953; MS, Middlebury (Vt.) Coll., 1955; PhD, U. Wis., 1958; MA (hon.), Yale U., 1967. Rsch. chemist Samuel Roberts Noble Found., Ardmore, Okla., 1958—60, sr. rsch. chemist, 1960—61; mem. faculty dept. pharmacology Yale Sch. Medicine, New Haven, 1961—, prof., 1967—, head devel. therapeutics program Comprehensive Cancer Ctr., 1974—90, chmn. dept. pharmacology, 1977—84, 1998—2000, dir. Comprehensive Cancer Ctr., 1984—93, Alfred Gilman prof. pharmacology, 1987—, prof. epidemiology, 1991—97. Head devel. therapeutics program Comprehensive Cancer Ctr., 1974—90, chmn. dept. pharmacology, 1977—84, 1998—2000, dep. dir., 1982—84, dir., 1984—93, Alfred Gilman prof. pharmacology, 1987—; Charles B. Smith vis. rsch. prof. Meml. Sloan-Kettering Ctr., 1979; William N. Creasy vis. prof. clin. pharmacology Wayne State U., 1983; Mayo Found. vis. prof. oncology Mayo Clinic, 1983; Walter Hubert lectr. Brit. Assn. Cancer Rsch., 1985; Pfizer lectr. in clin. pharmacology U. Conn. Health Ctr., 1985; William N. Creasy vis. prof. clin. pharmacology Bowman Gray Sch. Medicine, 1987; Wellcome vis. prof. basic sci. U. Pitts. Sch. Medicine, 1990; sci. adv. bd. ImmunoGen, Inc., 1981—90, U. Ind. Cancer Ctr., 1992, Cancer Inst. N.J., 1993—, Cell Pathways, Inc., 1993—2003; chmn. cancer sci. adv. bd. ViraChem., Inc., 1986—93, The Liposome Co., 1986—2001, Vion Pharms., 1993—, bd. dirs., chmn. sci. adv. bd.; chmn. vis. sci. adv. com. Columbia U. Comprehensive Cancer Ctr., 1986—99; chmn. pres.'s cancer adv. bd. Fox Chase Cancer Ctr., 1992—; clin. investigation rev. com. Nat. Cancer Inst., 1968—72, mgmt. cons. to dir. divsn. cancer treatment, 1975—77, bd. sci. counselors, divsn. cancer treatment, 1978—81, chmn. com. to establish nat. coop. drug discovery groups, 1982—83, chmn. spl. rev. com. Outstanding Investigator grant applications, 1992, chmn. ad hoc contracts tech. rev. group, 93; instnl. rsch. grants com. Am. Cancer Soc., 1971—76, coun. analysis and projection, 1978—79; cons. in biochemistry U. Tex. M.D. Anderson Hosp. and Tumor Clinic, Houston, 1970—76; cons. Sandoz Forschungs-Institut, Vienna, 1977—80; mem. exptl. therapeutics study sect. NIH, 1973—77, working cadre nat. large bowel cancer project, 1973—76; adv. com. cancer Rsch. Ctr., Washington U. Sch. Medicine, 1971—75, SLSB Ptnrs., L.P., 1992—96; sci. adv. com. U. Iowa Cancer Ctr., 1979—83; external adv. com. Wis. Clin. Cancer Ctr., 1978—79, Duke Comprehensive Cancer Ctr., 1983—94; external adv. bd. U. Ariz. Cancer Ctr., 1982—92, U. So. Calif. Cancer Ctr., 1983—93, Clin. Cancer Rsch. Ctr., Brown U., 1980—86; nat. program com. 13th Internat. Cancer Congress, 1979—81; cons. Bristol-Myers Co., 1982—93, selection com. prize in cancer rsch., 1977—85, chmn., 1979—81, chmn. selection com. award for disting. achievement in cancer rsch., 1989—92; bd. advisors Drug and Vaccine Devel. Corp. (Ctr. for Pub. Resources), 1980—81, Specialized Cancer Ctr., Mt. Sinai Med. Ctr.,

1981—90, Grace Cancer Drug Ctr., Roswell Park Meml. Inst., 1986—89; med. and sci. adv. com. grants rev. subcom. Leukemia Soc. Am., 1983—88; program planning com. Mary Lasker-Am. Cancer Soc. Conf., 1986; external sci. rev. com. Massey Cancer Ctr., 1989—94; bd. visitors Moffit Cancer Ctr. U. South Fla., 1989—92; dep. dir. Cancer Prevention Rsch. Unit for Conn., 1989—93, acting dir., 1991—93; nat. bd. Look Good...Feel Better program Cosmetic Toiletry and Fragrance Assn., 1989—91; organizing com. Conf. on Bioreductive Drug Activation, 1993—94; chmn. bd. spl. cons. Inst. for Cancer Therapeutics, 1993; scientific adv. bd. U. Ill. Cancer Ctr., 2001; chmn. sci. adv. bd. Celator Technologies Inc., 2002—. Regional editor Am. Continent Biochem. Pharmacology, 1968—2003, exec. editor, 1993—2003, editor-in-chief Cancer Comm., 1969—93, Oncology Rsch., 1993—; editor: Handbuch der experimentellen Pharmakologie vols. on antineoplastic and immunosuppressive agts., series on cancer chemotherapy Am. Chem. Soc. Symposium, 1976; founder, exec. editor Pharmacology and Therapeutics, 1975—2003, editl. bd. Internat. Ency. Pharmacology and Therapeutics, 1972—94, Seminars in Oncology, 1973—83, Chemico-Biol. Interactions, 1975—78, Jour. Medicinal Chemistry, 1977—82, Cancer Drug Delivery, 1982—85, Jour. Enzyme Inhibition, 1984—2002, Jour. Liposome Rsch., 1986—92, In Vivo, 1990—2002, Cancer Biotherapy, 1992—97, Cancer Rsch., Therapy and Control, 1993—97, Oncology Reports, 1995—, Molecular and Cellular Differentiation, 1996—, mem. adv. bd. Advances in Chemistry Series, ACS Symposium Series, 1977—80, editl. adv. bd. Cancer Rsch., 1970—71, assoc. editor, 1971—78, Current Awareness in Biol. Scis., Current Advances in Pharmacology and Toxicology, 1983—88, Cancer Cells, 1989—91, Jour. Exptl. Therapeutics and Oncology, 1995—, exec. adv. bd. Ency. of Human Biology, 1987—90, Dictionary of Sci. and Tech., 1989—91, editl. cons. Biol. Abstracts, 1984—88; contbr. articles to profl. jours. Bd. dirs. Schubert Performing Arts Ctr., 1992—2001, Schubert Opera Bd., 1991—2000, chmn., 1993—. Recipient Outstanding Alumni award, Northeastern U., 1987, Mike Hogg award, M.D. Anderson Cancer Ctr., U. Tex., 1989, Alumni Achievement award, Middlebury Coll., 1990, AACR-Bruce F. Cain Meml. award, 2001, Drug Discovery and Devel. award, Glaxo SmithKline, 2002. Fellow: AAAS, N.Y. Acad. Scis.; mem.: Coun. Biology Editors, Conn. Acad. Sci. and Engring., Inst. Medicine NAS (com. on govt. industry collaboration in biomed. rsch. and edn. 1989, mem. Forum on Drug Devel. and Regulation 1989—93), Assn. Am. Cancer Insts. (v.p. 1986, liaison rep. to Nat. Cancer Inst. 1986, bd. dirs. 1986—89, pres. 1987—88, chmn. bd. dirs. 1989), Am. Soc. Pharmacology and Exptl. Therapeutics (award com. 1988, chmn. 1992, award in exptl. therapeutics 1986, Otto Krayer award 2002), Am. Soc. Cell Biology, Am. Soc. Biochemistry and Molecular Biology, Am. Soc. Microbiology, Am. Chem. Soc., Am. Assn. Cancer Rsch. (dir. 1975—78, chmn. publs. com. 1981—88, dir. 1984—87, v.p. 1985—86, fin. com. 1985—88, exec. com. 1985—89, pres. 1986—87, chmn. exec. com. 1987, chmn. awards com. 1987, chmn. nominating com. 1993—95, mem. devel. com. 1995—97). Home: 4 Perkins Rd Woodbridge CT 06525-1616 Office: Yale U Dept Pharmacology 333 Cedar St New Haven CT 06520-8066 Office Phone: 203-785-4533. E-mail: alan.sartorelli@yale.edu.

SARU, GEORGE, artist; b. Checea, Timis, Romania, Mar. 1, 1920; s. George and Zorca (Pavlov) S.; m. Semizaliana Brinzan, Aug. 31, 1945; children: Dorian, Horia. BFA, Acad. Fine Arts, Jassy, Romania, 1944; MFA, Acad. Fine Arts, Bucharest, Romania, 1948; Diplomate, Acad. Di Belle Arti, Perugia, Italy, 1963. Editor-in-chief Arta Mag., Bucharest, 1950-64; dep. chancellor Inst. Fine Arts, Bucharest, 1966-67, prof., 1948-82. Exhibited in group shows at Biennale di Venezia, 1954, 56, Mus. of Modern Art, Sczecin, Poland, 1965, 75, Vienna, Austria, 1956, Moscow, 1958, Geneva, 1961, Berlin, 1963, Paris, 1968, Leningrad, 1972, Orly, France, 1972, San Sebastian, Spain, 1973, Washington, 1973, Cairo, Egypt, 1974, Quebec, 1975, Prague, Czechoslovakia, 1979; one-man shows include Dalles Art Gallery, Bucharest, 1956, 70, 77, 81, Pushkin Mus., Moscow, 1960, LeMire Gallery, New Orleans, 1983, Alex Gallery, Washington, 1987, Morin Miller Gallery, N.Y.C., 1988, 89, 90, Dome Gallery, N.Y.C., 1991, The York Sq. Gallery, New Haven, 1995, Romanian Cultural Ctr., 1997, N.Y. Gallery @49, N.Y., 1999; represented in permanet collections The Weisman Mus. Art, Mpls., Nat. Mus. Art Romania. Recipient Nat. award for Painting, Bucharest, 1950, Laureat of the State prize Bucharest, 1951, Internat. award for Painting, 1953, Gold medal Laureat or Triennial, Sofia, Bulgaria, 1976, Aachen, Germany, 1996; named Internat. Man of Yr. Internat. Biog. Ctr. Cambridge, Eng., 1995-96. Mem. UNESCO, Fine Arts Guild of Romania, Internat. Assn. Fine Arts, Assn. Internat. Arts Plastiques. Avocations: music, sculpture, etching, travel. Home and Office: 560 Main St Apt 446 New York NY 10044-0014 E-mail: compur@aol.com.

SARVAS, MARK GERALD, writer; b. N.Y.C., Sept. 26, 1964; s. Michael and Eva Sarvas; m. Susan Dana Einbinder, Dec. 21, 2002. Student, NYU, 1982—86. Lit. editor: The Elegant Variation; contbr. lit. jours. Mem.: PEN. Democrat. Achievements include development of www.elegvar.com, one of the earliest and leading literary weblogs. Personal E-mail: info@marksarvas.com.

SARVELA, PAUL D. health facility administrator, educator; BA in Psychology, U. Mich., 1981, MS in Ednl. Psychology, 1983, PhD in Health Edn., 1984. With Ford Aerospace and Comms. Corp., 1984—86; from asst. prof. to prof. health edn., family and cmty. medicine U. Ill., Carbondale, Ill., 1986—92, prof. health edn., family and cmty. medicine, 1992—, chmn. dept. Health Care Professions, 1999—, interim dean Coll. Applied Scis. and Arts, 2002—. Dir. Ctr. Rural Health and Social Svc. Devel., 1993—2000; cons. in field. Contbr. numerou articles to jours. in field. Mem.: Am. Coun. Edn., Am. Coll. Healthcare Execs., Am. Acad. Health Behavior. Office: So Ill Univ Coll Applied Scis and Arts Carbondale IL 62901-6604 E-mail: psarvela@siu.edu.

SARVIS, ELAINE MAGANN, retired assistant principal; b. Conway, S.C., May 11, 1947; d. John Thomas and Gloria (Winkler) Duckett; m. John Wesley Magann, Aug. 2, 1969 (dec. Nov. 1975); children: Christiane, James Wesley; m. Francis Mack Sarvis, Dec. 18, 1982. BA in Elem. Edn., U. S.C., 1969, MEd in Early Childhood, 1976, postgrad., 1990. Cert. elem. adminstrn. tchr., S.C. Tchr. Southside Elem. Sch., Augusta, Ga., 1969-70, Homewood Elem. Sch., Conway, 1970-71, Timmerman Sch., Columbia, S.C., 1972-73, South Conway Elem. Sch., Conway, 1973-74, 1975-76, instructional specialist, 1976-80, tchr., 1980-90, Horry County Gifted and Talented Program, Conway, 1990-91. Mem. com. Horry County Tchr. Incentive Program, Conway, 1989-91; bd. dirs. Horry County Sick Leave Bank Program, 1990-92. Mem. First Bapt. Ch., Conway, 1958-99, Ocean Dr. Presbyn. Ch., 1999—, North Myrtle Beach High Parent Tchr. Orgn., 1990; neighborhood chmn. Am. Heart Assn., Conway, 1978. Named Tchr. of Yr. County of Horry, 1990. Republican. Baptist. Avocations: reading, decorating, gardening, movies, travel. Office: 4317 Turtle Ln Little River SC 29566 E-mail: emsarvis@yahoo.com.

SARWARK, JOHN FRANCIS, orthopaedic surgeon, educator; b. Aurora, Ill., Jan. 24, 1954; m. Maria Panico Sarwark; children: John, Robert, Annie. BS, U. Ill., Champaign, 1975; MD, Northwestern U., 1979. Resident in orthop. surgery Northwestern U., 1979—84; attending pediat. orthop. surgeon Childrens Mercy Hosp., Kansas City, Mo., 1985—88, Childrens Meml. Hops., Chgo, 1988, interim divsn. head pediat. orthop. surgery, 1997—; asst. prof. orthop. surgery Northwestern U. Med. Sch., Chgo, 1988—94, assoc. prof. orthop. surgery, 1994—2001; med. dir. ctr. childhood safety Childrens Meml. Hosp., Chgo., 1997—; prof. orthop. surgery Northwestern U. Med. Sch., Chgo., 2001—. Faculty Med. Ethics and Humanities Program, Northwestern U. Med. Sch., Chgol, 1996-99. Contbr. articles to profl. jours. V.p. Pathways Awareness Found., Glenview, 1993—. Recipient Berkheiser award, Inst. Medicine, Chgo., 1990. Fellow: Pediat. Orthop. Soc. N.Am. (mem.-at-latge 1992—93, mem.-at-large 2002—04, bd. dirs.), Scoliosis Rsch. Soc. (edn. com. 1996—2000, fellow com. 2000—), Am. Acad. Pediat. (exec. com. orthopedic sect. 1997—, chair 2002—04), Am. Acad. Orthop. Surgeons (faculty chmn. com. on pub. edn. 1998—2001, assoc. editor Orthopedic Monthly Online 2003—), Am. Orthop. Assn., Alpha Omega Alpha. Avocations: fines arts, travel. Office: Divsn Pediat Orthopaedic Surgery Childrens Meml Hosp 2300 N Childrens Plz Box #69 Chicago IL 60614-3394 E-mail: jsarwark@childrensmemorial.org.

SARWER-FONER, GERALD JACOB, psychiatrist, educator; b. Volkovsk, Grodno, Poland, Dec. 6, 1924; arrived in Can., 1932, naturalized, 1935; s. Michael and Ronia Sarwer-F.; m. Ethel Sheinfeld, May 28, 1950; children: Michael, Gladys, Janice, Henry, Brian. BA, Loyola Coll. U., Montreal, 1945, MD magna cum laude, 1951; DPsychiatry, McGill U., 1955. Diplomate Am. Bd. Psychiatry and Neurology. Intern. Univ. Hosps. U. Montreal Sch. Medicine, 1950-51; resident Butler Hosp., Providence, 1951-52, Hosps. Western Res. U., Cleve., 1952-53, Queen Mary Vets. Hosp., Montreal, 1953-55; cons. psychiatry, dir. psychiatric rsch., 1955-61; lectr. psychiatry U. Montreal, 1953-55; lectr., asst. prof., assoc. prof. McGill U., 1955—70; dir. dept psychiatry Queen Elizabeth's Hosp, Montreal, 1964-71; prof. psychiatry U. Ottawa, Ont., 1971-89, prof., chmn. psychiatry, 1974-86, prof., 1989—; dir. dept. psychiatry Ottawa Gen. Hosp., 1971-87; dir. Lafayette Clinic, Detroit, 1989-92; prof. psychiatry and behavioral Neurosciences Wayne State U., Detroit, 1989—. Cons. in psychiatry Ottawa Gen. Hosp., Royal Ottawa Hosp., Children's Hosp. of Eastern Ont., Ottawa, Windsor (Ont.) Western Hosp. Ctr., Ottawa Sch. Bd.; Z. Lebensohn lectr. Silbey Meml. Hosp. Cosmos Club, Washington, 1991; disting. lectr. XI World Congress Psychiatry, Hamburg, 1999, XII World Congress Psychiatry, Yokohama, Japan, 2002; mem. test com. Nat. Bd. Med. Examiners, 1975-81; pres. Que. Psychiat. Assn., 1966-68; mem. adv. panel on psychiatry Def. Rsch. Bd. Can., Dept. Nat. Def., 1958-62. Editor: Dynamics of Psychiatric Drug Therapy, 1960, Research Conference on the Depressive Group of Illnesses, 1966, Psychiatric Crossroads-the Seventies, Research Aspects, 1972, Social Psychiatry in the Late 20th Century, 1993; founder, editor in chief Psychiat. Jour. U. Ottawa, 1976-90, emeritus editor in chief, 1990—; mem. editorial bds. of numerous internat. and nat. profl. jours.; editor numerous audio-video tapes; contbr. to more than 200 articles to profl. jours. Bd. govs. Queen Elizabeth Hosp., Montreal, 1966-71; life gov. Queen Elizabeth Hosp. Found.; cons. Protestant Sch. Bd., Westmount, Que., 1966-71; advisor Com. on Health, City of Westmount, 1969-71. Served to lt. col. Royal Can. A Med. Corps, 1949-62. Fulbright fellow, 1951-53; recipient Sigmund Freud award Am. Assn. Psychoanalytic Physicians, 1982, William V. Silverberg Meml. award Am. Acad. Psychoanalysis, 1990, Poca award Assn. Psychiat. Out Patient Ctrs. Am., 1990; Simon Bolivar lectr. Am. Psychiat. Assn., New Orleans, 1981; Can. Forces Decoration; decorated Knight of Malta. Fellow: AAAS, Am. Assn. Social Psychiatry (v.p. 1987—89, pres.-elect 1990, pres. 1992—94), World Psychiat. Assn. (v.p. sect. on edn. 1989—, mem. internat. adv. com. 9th World Congress Rio de Janeiro 1993, disting. lectr. 1996, XI World Congress Hamburg 1999, dist. lectr. XII World Congress Hokohama 2002, organizing com. sci. com. X World Congress in Madrid, mem. nominating com.), Benjamin Rush Soc. (founding mem., councillor), Am. Coll. Psychiatrists (bd. regents 1978—80, pres. com. long range planning and policy 1986—89, emeritus), Am. Psychopath. Assn., Collegium Internat. Neuropsychopharmacology, Internat. Psychoanalytical Assn. (mem. program com. 31st congress NY 1979), Royal Coll. Psychiatry (Found. fellow), Can. Psychiat. Assn. (life; bd. dirs. 1958—62, founder, chair com., sect. psychotherapy 1962—64), Am. Acad. Psychiatry and the Law (sr.; pres. 1977, Silver Apple award), Am. Coll. Neuropsychopharmacology (life), Can. Coll. Neuropsychopharmacology (life; hon. found. 1958—), Am. Psychiat. Assn. (life; chair sci. program com., VI World Congress of Psychiatry, Honolulu 1974—77, chair com. psychiatry, law 1975—77, chair task force model commitment code 1976—80, v.p., chmn. sci. program com. 1974—77, VI World Congress of Psychiatry Honolulu 1974—77), Am. Coll. Psychoanalysts (life; pres.-elect 1983, pres. 1984—85, chair by-laws and constn. com. 1994—2001, Henry Laughlin award 1986), Am. Coll. Mental Health Adminstrn. (life), Royal Coll. Physicians and Surgeons (exec. sec. test psychiat. com. 1987—89), Internat. Coll. Psychosomatic Medicine (sec.-gen. 1979—83); mem.: Am. Psychoanalytic Assn. (mem. program com. 1972—76), Alliance for Mental Health Svcs. (pres. 1999—2000), Mich. Psychoanalytic Soc., Soc. Biol. Psychiatry (sr.; pres. 1983—84, H. Azima Meml. lectr. 1963, George M. Thompson award 1997), Can. Assn. Profs. Psychiatry (pres. 1976—77, 1982—86), Can. Psychoanalytic Soc. (pres. 1979—81), Royal Can. Mil. Inst. Club, Cosmos Club. Home and Office: 3220 Bloomfield Shr Dr West Bloomfield MI 48323-3300 Office Phone: 248-855-9080. Office Fax: 248-855-8321. Personal E-mail: sarwfon@aol.com.

SASAHARA, ARTHUR ASAO, cardiologist, educator, researcher; b. Del Rey, Calif., May 11, 1927; s. Harold Hango and Blanche (Takayama) S.; m. Alice Ann Guenther, Apr. 2, 1955; children: Ann Mariko, Claire Michiko, Ellen Reiko, Karen Hideko, Mark Tadao. AB, Oberlin Coll., 1951; MD, Case Western Res. U., 1955; AM (hon.), Harvard U., 1987. Diplomate Am. Bd. Internal Medicine. Intern Boston City Hosp., 1955-56; jr. asst. med. resident Mass. Gen. Hosp., Boston, 1956-57; fellow in cardiology West Roxbury VA Med. Ctr., Mass., 1957-58, Children's Hosp. Med. Ctr., Boston, 1958-59; sr. resident in medicine Yale-New Haven Med. Ctr., 1959-60; asst. chief med. svc., dir. cardiopulmonary lab., dep. chmn. rsch. and edn. com. VA Hosp. West Roxbury, 1960-70, chief cardiopulmonary sect., 1971-74, assoc. chief staff for rsch. and edn., 1970-76, chief med. svc., 1974-82, West Roxbury-Brockton VA Hosp., 1982-87; prof. medicine Harvard Med. Sch., Boston, 1974-93, prof. emeritus, 1993—; cons. cardiovascular-pulmonary diseases Boston, 1965-87; cons. pediatric cardiology Children's Hosp. Med. Ctr., Boston, 1976-86; physician Brigham and Women's Hosp., Boston, 1979-82, sr. physician, 1982—. Dir. thrombolytics rsch. pharm. products divsn. Abbott Labs., Abbott Park, Ill., 1987—95, sr. med. dir., 1995—97; sr. physician cardiovascular divsn. Brigham and Women's Hosp., 1998—. Author-editor: Pulmonary Embolic Disease, 1965, Pulmonary Emboli, 1975, New Therapeutic Agents in Thrombosis and Thrombolysis, 1997, 2d edit., 2002; contbr. articles to profl. jours.; designer constant infusion med. pump, Harvard Apparatus Co., 1973; editorial bd. Jour. Nuclear Medicine, 1981-83, Am. Jour. Medicine, 1971-72, Circulation, 1973-78, VASA, 1978-85, Jour. Cardiovascular Medicine, 1980-86, Primary Cardiology, 1986-89. With U.S. Army, 1945-47. NIH grantee, 1963-82; VA grantee, 1961-87. Fellow ACP, Am. Coll. Chest Physicians, Am. Coll. Cardiology; mem. AAAS, Internat. Soc. Fibrinolysis and Thrombolysis, Am. Fedn. Clin. Rsch., Internat. Soc. Thrombosis and Hemostasis, Am. Heart Assn., Alpha Omega Alpha. Democrat. Episcopalian. Home: 1115 Beacon St # 12 Newton MA 02461-1154

SASAKI, CLARENCE TAKASHI, surgeon, educator; b. Honolulu, Jan. 24, 1941; s. Tsutomu and Carla Harumi (Mirikitani) S.; m. Carolyn Elizabeth Lindahl, June 26, 1967; children: Peter Gordon, John Eric. BA, Pomona Coll., 1962; MD, Yale U., 1966. Diplomate: Am. Bd. Otolaryngology. Intern San Francisco Hosp., U. Calif., 1966-67; resident in surgery Dartmouth Med. Sch., 1967-68; resident in otolaryngology Yale U. Med. Sch. Hosps., New Haven, 1970-73, faculty mem., 1973—, assoc. prof., 1977-82, prof. surgery, 1982—, chief sect. otolaryngology, 1981—, Charles Ohse prof. surgery, 1988—, vice chmn. dept. surgery, 1996. Author: Surgery of the Skull Base, Head and Neck Surgery, Vol. 1 Atlas Otolarynogology, Vocal Fold Physiology, Laryngeal Function in Phonation and Respiration, Neurological Diseases of the Larynx; mem. editl. bd. profl. jours. Served to maj. M.C. U.S. Army, 1968-70. Recipient award Fowler Triological Soc., 1979. Mem. Am. Acad. Otolaryngology (1st prize clin. rsch.), Am. Soc. Head and Neck Surgery (coun.), Assn. Rsch. Otolaryngology, Am. Laryngol. Rhinol. and Otol. Soc. (coun., sec. ea. sect. 1990, v.p. 1998), New Eng. Otolaryngology Soc. (pres. 1987, coun.), Assn. Acad. Depts. Otolaryngology (coun.), Am. Laryngol. Assn. (Casselberry award 1999), Pan Pacific Surg. Assn., Soc. for Neurosci., Soc. Neurovascular Surgery, Soc. for Head and Neck Surgeons, Am. Neurotolog. Soc., Pan Am. Assn. Oto-rhino-laryngology and Bronchoesophagology, Conn. Med. Soc., N.Y. Acad. Scis., Soc. Univ. Otolaryngologists, Collegium ORLAS, Cartesian Soc. (co-dir.), Am. Bronchoesophagological Assn. (mem. coun., treas. 2003, Broyles-Maloney award 2004), N.Am. Skull Base Soc., Laryngeal. Cancer Assn. (Padua), Am. Otol. Soc., Dysphagia Rsch. Soc. (treas., pres.), Lawn Club, Mory's Assoc., Yale Club, Phi Beta Kappa, Sigma Xi. Office: Yale U Med Sch Dept Surgery PO Box 208041 333 Cedar St New Haven CT 06520-8041 Office Phone: 203-785-2592.

SASAKI, JOHN ERIC, art company executive, artist; b. New Haven; s. Clarence and Carolyn S. BFA, Pepperdine U., 1994. Supr. Cinesite Digital Studios, Hollywood, Calif., 1994-95, composite supr., 1995-96; compositor Digital Domain, Venice, Calif., 2000—02; composite supr. Manex Visual Effects, Alameda, L.A., 1998-2000; compositor Sony Pictures Imageworks, 2001—02. CEO John E Sasaki Inc., Pacific Palisades, Calif., 1998—. Visual effects credits include (films) Titanic, The Matrix, The Fifth Element, Armageddon, Sphere, Space Jam, Waterworld, Deep Blue Sea, Almost Famous, Crouching Tiger, Hidden Dragon, How the Grinch Stole Christmas. Vol. Rep. Party, L.A., 1990—. Mem. Pepperdine Alumni. Salisbury Sch. Alumni (class agt.). Home and Office: Apt 207 10651 Eastborne Ave Los Angeles CA 90024-8500 E-mail: johnesasaki@hotmail.com.

SASAKI, TSUTOMU (TOM SASAKI), real estate company executive, international trading company executive, consultant; b. Tokyo, July 28, 1945; came to U.S., 1979; s. Tsuneshiro and Kimiko (Fujiwara) S.; m. Yoko Katsura, Feb. 21, 1971; children: Mari, Tomoko. BA, Sophia U., Tokyo, 1969. Plant export adminstrn. Ataka & Co., Ltd., Osaka, Japan, 1969-76; officer Seattle-First Nat. Bank, Tokyo, 1976-79, AVP bus. mgr., 1982-84, AVP Japan mgr. Seattle, 1979-82, v.p. Japan mgr., 1984-90; owner, pres. BBS Internat., Inc., Seattle, 1990—. Bd. dirs. InterPac Devel. Inc., BBS Bus. Svc., Inc., The Japanese Cmty. Svcs. Seattle. Bd. dirs. Adopt-a-Stream Found., Everett, Wash., 1987-2002; bd. trustees N.W. Sch., Seattle, 1987-2002, internat. adv. to bd. trustees, 2002-. Am. Field Svc. scholar, 1963-64. Mem. Japan Am. Soc. Wash. (chmn. membership com. 1988, bd. dirs. 1997—), British Am. Bus. Coun., Fairwood Golf & Country Club, Wash. Athletic Club. Avocations: golf, gardening, music, photography. Home: 4625 136th Ave SE Bellevue WA 98006-3007 Office: BBS Internat Inc 2819 Elliot Ave #201 Seattle WA 98121 Office Phone: 206-623-5714. E-mail: sasaki@bbsint.com.

SASAKI, Y(ASUNAGA) TITO, engineering executive; b. Tokyo, Feb. 6, 1938; arrived in U.S., 1967; s. Yoshinaga and Chiyoko Sasaki; m. Janet L. Cline; 1 child, Heather N. Diploma in indsl. design, Royal Coll. Art, London, 1962; MS in Ekistics, Athens (Greece) Tech. Inst., 1965. Cert. planner, Am. Inst. Cert. Planners. Tech. officer London County Coun., 1962-63; sr. rschr. Inst. Battelle, Geneva, Switzerland, 1965-67; planning dir. Golden Gate Bridge, San Francisco, 1970-74; pres. Visio Internat., Inc., San Francisco, 1974-85, Quantum Mechanics Corp., Sonoma, Calif., 1981—. Mem.: AIAA, ASME, Am. Welding Soc., Am. Vacuum Soc. Achievements include co-developer of the world's most sensitive helium leak detector; co-developer of the world's lowest out-gasing stainless steel. Home: PO Box 200 Vineburg CA 95487-0200 Office: Quantum Mechanics Corp 21885 8th St E Sonoma CA 95476-9797 E-mail: TitoSasaki@attglobal.net.

SASARAN, LAURA JEANNE, humanities educator; b. Trenton, N.J., Oct. 16, 1945; d. Lewis and Jeanne Rose Sasaran. MA in Humanities, San Francisco State U, 1970. Prof. Humanities Coleman Coll., Lamesa, Calif., chair Gen. Edn. and Tech. Mem.: Calif. Humanities Assoc. (assoc.), Cmty. Coll. Humanities Assoc. (assoc.), Coll. Art Assoc. (assoc.). Home: 1333 8th Ave San Diego CA 92101 Office Phone: 619-465-3990. E-mail: lsasaran@coleman.edu.

SASEK, GLORIA BURNS, English language and literature educator; b. Springfield, Mass., Jan. 20, 1926; d. Frederick Charles and Minnie Delia (White) Burns; m. Lawrence Anton Sasek, Sept. 5, 1960. BA, Mary Washington Coll. of U. Va., 1947; student, U. Paris, 1953, U. Stranieri, Perugia, Italy, 1955; MA, Radcliffe Coll., 1954; EdM, Springfield Coll., 1955. Tchr., head dept. jr. and sr. hs English, Pub. Schs., Somers, Conn., 1947—59; tchr. English, Winchester (Mass.) Pub. Schs., 1959—60; mem. faculty La. State U., Baton Rouge, 1961—, asst. prof. English, 1971-96, chmn. freshman English, 1969-70. Named La. State U. Yearbook Favorite Prof., 1978; recipient George H. Deer Disting. Tchg. award, La. State U., 1977, Disting. Undergrad. Tchg. award, Amoco Found., 1994, commendation, La. Ho. of Reps., 1996. Mem. MLA, AAUP (chpt. v.p. 1981-84), South Ctrl. MLA, South Ctrl. Renaissance Soc., South Ctrl. Conf. on Christianity and Lit. Office: 1458 Kenilworth Pkwy Baton Rouge LA 70808 E-mail: glsasek@worldnet.att.net.

SASENICK, JOSEPH ANTHONY, animal health and food safety company executive; b. Chgo., May 18, 1940; s. Anthony E. and Caroline E. (Smicklas) S.; m. Barbara Ellen Barr, Aug. 18, 1962; children: Richard Allen, Susan Marie, Michael Joseph. BA, DePaul U., 1962; MA, U. Okla., 1966. With Miles Labs., Inc., Elkhart, Ind., 1963-70; product mgr. Alka-Seltzer, 1966-68, dir. mktg. grocery products divsn., 1968-70; with Gillette Corp., Boston, 1970-79, dir. new products/new ventures, personal care divsn., 1977; v.p. diversified cos. and pres. Jafra Cosmetics Worldwide, 1977-79; mktg. dir. Braun AG, Kronberg, W. Ger., 1970-73; chmn. mng. dir. Braun U.K. Ltd., 1973-77; with Abbott Labs., North Chicago, 1979-84, corp. v.p., pres. consumer products divsn., 1979-84; pres., CEO, Moxie Industries, 1984-87; pres., CEO Personal Monitoring Technologies, Rochester, N.Y., 1987; pres. Bioline Labs., Ft. Lauderdale, Fla., 1988; mng. dir., ptnr. Vista Resource Group, Newport Beach, Calif., 1988-90; pres., CEO, Alcide Corp., Redmond, Wash., 1991-92, chmn., CEO, 1992—, 2001—. Mem. Columbia Tower Club, El Niguel Club, Wash. Athletic Club, Tech. Alliance, Rainier Club. Home: 1301 Spring St Apt 24J Seattle WA 98104-1353 Office: Alcide Corp PO Box 89 Redmond WA 98073-0089

SASHIN, DONALD, pet physicist, radiological physicist, educator; b. N.Y.C., Dec. 11, 1937; s. David and Pearl (Taub) S.; m. Kathleen Flaherty, July 24, 1967; children: Deirdre Moira, Courtenay Aileen. BS in Physics, MIT, 1960; MS in Physics, Carnegie Inst. Tech., 1962; PhD in Physics, Carnegie Mellon U., 1968. Instr. radiology and radiation health U. Pitts., 1967-70, asst. prof. radiology, 1970-74, asst. prof. indsl and environ. health, 1970-77; asst. prof. radiation health, 1977-87; assoc. prof. radiology U. Pitts., 1974—, assoc. prof. radiation health, 1987-89, assoc. prof. environ. and occupl. health, 1989-2000. Contbr. articles to profl. jours., patentee in field. Recipient Cum Laude award sci. exhibit Radiol. Soc. N.Am., 1977, cert. of merit sci. exhibit, 1979. Mem. IEEE, AAAS, Am. Phys. Soc., Am. Assn. Physicists in Medicine, Soc. Nuclear Medicine, Health Physics Soc., Sigma Xi. Democrat. Roman Catholic. Avocations: golf, fishing, swimming, sailing. Home: 4360 Centre Ave Pittsburgh PA 15213-1403 Office: PET Facility B938 PUH/UPMC 200 Lothrop St Pittsburgh PA 15213-2546 Office Phone: 412-647-0713.

SASIDHARAN, VINOD, travel and tourism educator, researcher; b. Attingal, Kerala, India, Oct. 14, 1972; arrived in U.S., 1996; s. Sasidharan Nair and Radhamony Sasidharan. Postgrad. diploma in hotel adminstrn., Inst. Hotel Mgmt., India, 1994; MSc in Tourism Policy and Mgmt., U. Birmingham, Eng., 1996; PhD in Leisure Studies, Pa. State U., 2001. Grad. asst., grad. student rep., instr., rsch. asst., project dir. dept. leisure studies Pa. State U., University Park, 1996—2001; asst. prof. dept. recreation parks and tourism San Diego State U., 2001—. Presenter in field. Guest editor: journal Leisure Sciences, 2002; contbr. chapters to books, articles to profl. jours. Grantee, USDA Nat. Forest Svc., 1999—2001, 2002, U.S. Dept. Interior Nat. Pk. Svc., 2000—01, Office Internat. Programs, San Diego State U., 2001, 2003; Albert Kligman fellow, Pa. State U., 2000—01. Mem.: Calif. Pk. and Recreation Soc., Calif. Soc. Pk. and Recreation Educators (treas. 2001), Nat. Recreation and Pk. Assn., Travel and Tourism Rsch. Assn. Office: San Diego State U 5500 Campanile Dr PSFA 447 San Diego CA 92182-4531 Office Phone: 619-594-4726. E-mail: vinod.sasidharan@sdsu.edu.

SASKO, NANCY ANN, insurance agent; b. Camp Lejuene, NC, Nov. 22, 1956; d. George Michael Jr. and Margaret (Simons) S. BA in English Lit., Ind. U., 1981. Customer svc. rep. Apple Computer, Inc., Denver, 1982—89; owner Monitor Systems, Inc., Denver, 1992—; long term care ins. sales rep. Sr. Ins. Svs., 2003—. Substitute tchr. Ft. Wayne (Ind.) Cmty. Schs., 2003—. Avocations: classical music, art, reading, gardening, cooking. Address: 2427 Loganberry Cove Fort Wayne IN 46818 Personal E-mail: nancysasko@aol.com.

SASMAN, IRENE DEAK HANDBERG, educational publishing executive; b. Jamaica, N.Y. d. Paul and Irene (Dyroff) Deak; children: Roger B. Handberg III, Ryan Paul Handberg; m. Timothy Carl Sasman. BS, Fla. State U.; MEd, U. N.C., 1970. Cert. tchr. in reading and math., N.C. Lead tchr., reading specialist Chapel Hill (N.C.) City Schs., 1966-69; dir. learning lab. Seminole Community Coll., Sanford, Fla., 1974-78; basic skills cons. EDL/McGraw-Hill Book Co., Orlando, Fla., 1978-82; regional dir. EDL/Arista Pub., Orlando, 1982-84; mktg. mgr., product mgr. Arista/Regents/EDL-Hachette, N.Y.C., 1984-85; v.p. mktg. and sales Raintree Pubs., Milw., 1985, gen. mgr., pub., 1985-87; dir. spl.

projects Simon & Schuster, Englewood Cliffs, N.J., 1987-88, v.p. corp. devel. N.Y.C., 1988-90, sr. v.p., 1990-91; chmn. Irene Handberg Internat., N.Y.C., 1991—; pres. The Learning Connection, New York, N.Y., 1991—. Co-author: EDL/McGraw-Hill Teacher's Guide. Elected precinct woman com. Dem. County Com., Fla.; capt. Nat. Cancer So., Fla., chmn. Sch. Adv. Com., Fla. NSF fellow U. N.C., 1969; recipient Svc. award Jr. Achievement. Mem. Chief Exec. Officers Group (coun. small bus. execs.), Sales and Mktg. Execs., Profl. Dimensions, Chief Exec. Officers Club. Lutheran. Avocations: spectator sports, art, music, skiing. Office: The Learning Connection 300 E 93rd St Apt 29C New York NY 10128-6109

SASMOR, JAMES CECIL, publishing representative, educator; b. N.Y.C., July 29, 1920; s. Louis and Cecilia (Mockler) S.; 1 child from previous marriage, Elizabeth Lynn; m. Jeannette L. Fuchs, May 30, 1965. BS, Columbia U., 1942; MBA, Calif. Western U., 1977, PhD, 1979. Fellow, Diplomate Am. Bd. Med. Psychotherapists, Am. Assn. Sex Educators, Counselors and Therapists; lic. healthcare risk mgr., Am. Inst. Med. Law; diplomate Am. Bd. Sexology, Am. Bd. Disability Analysts (sr. analyst); cert. tchr. health scis. Registered rep. Nat. Assn. Security Dealers, 1956—57; founder, owner J.C. Sasmor Assocs., Pub.'s Reps., N.Y.C., 1959—89; co-founder, pres., dir. adminstrn. Continuing Edn. Cons., Inc., 1976—. Pub. cons., 1959—; clin. assoc. U. So. Fla. Coll. Medicine, 1987-89, mem. adj. faculty Coll. Nursing, 1980-89; dir. Ednl. Counseling Comprehensive Breast Cancer Ctr., U. So. Fla. Med. Ctr., 1984-89, client librn. mental health inst., 1979-89; lectr. divsn. allied health nursing and pub. svc. Yavapai Coll. Author: Economics of Structured Continuing Education in Selected Professional Journals, Perception May Be Reality Vols. I and II; contbr. chpts. to Childbirth Education: A Nursing Perspective; contbr. articles to profl. jours. Team tchr. childbirth edn. Am. Soc. Childbirth Educators; bd. dirs. Tampa chpt. ARC; pres. Sedona (Ariz.) unit Am. Cancer Soc., 1995—, co-chmn. adult edn. com., founder Am. Cancer Soc. edn. dept. Sedona Med. Ctr.; bd. dirs. Ariz. divsn., mem. pub. edn. com.; county nursing ednl. cons. ARC, chmn. instrnl. com. on nursing and health, 1979-85; founding mem. coun. trustees Ariz. Nurses Found., 1998. With USN, 1942-58, PTO; lt. USNR ret. Recipient cert. of appreciation ARC, 1979, Am. Fgn. Svc. Assn., 1988, Dept. Health and Rehab. Svcs. award for Fla. Mental Health Inst. Svc., 1980; Internat. Coun. Sex Edn. and Parenthood fellow Am. U., 1981, Accomplished Elder award Ariz. Coun. of Govts. Mem. NAACOG (bd. dirs. Tampa chpt.), Nat. Assn. Pubs. Reps. (pres. 1965-66), Am. Soc. Psychoprophylaxis in Obstetrics (dir. 1970-71), Am. Soc. Childbirth Educators (co-founder, dir. 1972—), Internat. Coun. Women's Health Issues (chmn. resources com.), Health Edn. Media Assn., Nursing Educators Assn. Tampa, Lions (bd. dirs. Found. Ariz. 1991-2000, past pres. Sedona club, bd. dirs., chair sight, hearing, and scholarship coms.), Phi Theta Kappa (Honors scholar 2000-03, hon., advisor chpt. Beta Gamma Pi). Home: 235 Arrowhead Dr Sedona AZ 86351-8900 Office: PO Box 2282 Sedona AZ 86339-2282 Office Phone: 928-284-9897. E-mail: jsasmor@iglide.net.

SASS, NEIL LESLIE, toxicologist; b. Balt., Oct. 24, 1944; s. Samuel and Blanche (Radoon) S.; m. Anita Paige Hoswell, June 29, 1984. BS, Wake Forest Coll., 1966; MS, W.Va. U., 1969, PhD, 1971; MS, Johns Hopkins U., 1984. Commd. officer USPHS, 1966, advanced through grades to capt., 1988, comdr. Preventive Medicine unit, 1989; served as rsch. toxicologist med. labs. U.S. Army, Edgewood Arsenal, Md., 1971-74; chief clin. investigations William Beaumont Army Med. Ctr., El Paso, Tex., 1974-77; toxicologist Bur. of Foods FDA, Washington, 1977-82; spl. asst. to dir. Ctr. for Food Safety and Applied Nutrition, FDA, Washington, 1982-99; dir. divsn. toxicological rsch. Ctr. for Food Safety and Applied Nutrition, Washington, 1996-99; chief toxicologist, chem. lab. dir., state counterterrorism coord., chem. lab. dir. Ala. Dept. Pub. Health, Montgomery, 1999—. Jewish. Office: Ala Dept Pub Health The RSA Tower 201 Monroe St Ste 1450 Montgomery AL 36104-3735 Home: 2160 Woodley Rd Montgomery AL 36111-1013 Office Phone: 334-206-5973. Business E-Mail: nsass@adph.state.al.us.

SASS, RONALD LEWIS, biology and chemistry educator; b. Davenport, Iowa, May 26, 1932; s. Erwin Leese and Flora Alice (Puck) S.; m. Joyce R. Moorhead, 1951 (div. 1968); children: Dennise, Andria; m. Margaret Lee Macy, Apr. 4, 1969; children: Hartley, Dennis. BA, Augustana Coll., Rock Island, Ill., 1954; PhD, U. So. Calif., L.A., 1957. Chemist U.S. Army, Rock Island (Ill.) Arsenal, 1951-54; asst. prof. Rice U., Houston, 1958-62, assoc. prof., 1962-66, HC & OK Wiess prof., 1966—, chmn. biology, 1981-87. Co-dir. Rice Ctr. for Edn., Houston, 1988—; chair Rice Earth Sys. Inst., Houston, 1990—, Ecology and Evolutionary Biology, 1995—; cons. EPA, Washington, 1990—, Coll. Bd., N.Y.C., 1988-96. Contbr. articles on chemistry, biology and biochemistry to profl. jours. NSF predoctoral fellow U. So. Calif., 1954-57, fellow AEC, 1957-58, Guggenheim fellow, 1965, sr. rsch. fellow NRC, 1988. Mem. Internat. Geospher-Biosphere Program (com. chair 1990—). Avocations: tennis, fishing. Office: Rice U Ecology & Evolutionary Biology Mail Stop 170 Houston TX 77251 E-mail: sass@rice.edu.

SASS, STEPHEN LOUIS, education educator; b. N.Y.C., Mar. 11, 1940; s. Abraham Silver and Betty (Gelb) S.; m. Karen Rae Sande Sass, Feb. 19, 1966; children: Adam Joshua Sass, Erik Nathaniel Sass. BChe, CCNY, 1961; PhD, Northwestern U., Evanston, Ill., 1966. Asst. prof. Cornell U., Ithaca, N.Y., 1967-73, assoc. prof., 1973-79, prof., 1979—. Mem. NSF Adv. Bd., Sci. Unit, Lehrer Newshour, 2003— Author: The Substance of Civilization, 1998; contbr. more than 180 papers in field. Named Stephen H. Weiss Presdl. fellow, Cornell U.; recipient Outstanding Paper award, Scripta Metallurgica, 1984, Acta Metallurgica, 1996. Fellow: Am. Phys. Soc., Am. Soc. Materials. Home: 1025 Highland Rd Ithaca NY 14850-1447 Office: Bard Hall Dept Materials Sci/Engring Cornell U Ithaca NY 14853 E-mail: sls7@cornell.edu.

SASSA, SCOTT M. Internet company executive; Formerly with Rogers & Cowan Pub. Rels. Agy.; past v.p. new bus. devel. Ohlmeyer Comm. Co.; past v.p. network mgmt. Fox Broadcasting Co.; dir. sales promotion, then v.p./gen. mgr. Cable Music Channel Turner Broadcasting Sys., exec. v.p. Turner Network TV, then pres. Turner Entertainment Group, bd. dirs., mem. exec. com., 1988—97; past pres. Andrews Group; past CEO Marvel Entertainment; pres. TV Stations divsn. NBC, 1997—98, pres. Entertainment divsn., 1998—99, pres. West Coast, 1999—2002, cons. strategic projects, 2002; CEO Friendster, 2004—. Office: Friendster Inc 415 N Mary Ave Ste 112-280 Sunnyvale CA 94085 Office Phone: 650-618-2638. Office Fax: 650-618-2527.*

SASSAN, DENNIS DONALD, lawyer; b. Chgo., Apr. 16, 1942; s. John Joseph and Grace Elizabeth (Gendusa) S.; m. Carol Jo Krejci, Aug. 22, 1964 (div. Oct. 1994); children: Anthony J., Dino J. JD, DePaul U., 1965. Bar: Ill. 1965, U.S. Dist. Ct. (no. dist.) Ill. 1965. Trust adminstr. Ctrl. Nat. Bank, Chgo., 1964-65; estate tax atty. U.S. Dept. Treasury, Chgo., 1965-70; pvt. practice Chgo., Oakbrook Terrace and Niles, Ill., 1970—. Mem. FBA, Ill. State Bar Assn., Chgo. Bar Assn. Home: 9042 N Cumberland Ave Niles IL 60714 Office: Sassan and Sassan 7788 N Milwaukee Ave Niles IL 60714 E-mail: legal@callero.com.

SASSER, CHARLES WAYNE, journalist, educator, writer; b. Sallisaw, Okla., Jan. 3, 1942; s. Ben Garland and Mary Louise Sasser; m. Dianne Carol Reilly, Oct. 8, 1965 (div. 1978); children: David, Michael; m. Katherine Renee, Feb. 2, 1979 (div. Oct. 1986); 1 adopted child, Joshua Dale; m. Donna Sue Baker, Oct. 7, 1995; stepchildren: DeAnn, Darren, Michael. AA, Miami (Fla.)-Dade Jr. Coll., 1968; BA, Fla. State U., 1969; postgrad., Okla. State U., 1977-78. Police officer Miami Police Dept., 1965-68; detective Tulsa Police Dept., 1970-79; coll. instr. Tulsa Jr. Coll., 1976—; freelance journalist, 1979—. Horse rancher, trainer, Mannford, Okla., 1971-78, Chouteau, Okla., 1996—; dir. criminal justice program Am. Christian Coll. Tulsa, 1974-78; profl. rodeo clown Profl. Rodeo Cowboy Assn., Okla., 1984-86; pres., CEO Fly High Inc., 2000—. Author: No Gentle Streets, 1984, The Girl Scout Murders, 1989, The Walking Dead, 1989, One Shot-One Kill, 1990, Homicide!, 1990, The 100th Kill, 1992, Always a Warrior, 1994, Shoot to Kill, 1994, Last American Heroes, 1994, In Cold Blood: Oklahoma's Most Notorious Murders, 1994, Smoke Jumpers, 1996, First Seal, 1997, Doc: Platoon Medic, 1998, Fire Cops, 1998, At Large, 1998, Arctic Homestead, 2000, Liberty City, 2000, Operation No Man's Land, 2000, Taking Fire, 2001, The War Chaser, 2001, The Return, 2001, Detachment Delta: Punitive Strike, 2002, Raider, 2002, The Encyclopedia of Navy Seals, 2002, Detachment Delta: Iron Weed, 2003, Magic Steps to Writing Success, 2003, Hill 488, 2003, Going Bonkers: The Wacky World of Cultural Madness, Detachment Delta: Operation Deep Steel, Crosshairs on The Kill Zone; editor Keystone Sportsman Mag., 1975-78; contbr. articles to periodicals; actor Wagoner (Okla.) Playhouse Dinner Theater, 1997—. Pres. Keystone Crossroads Hist. Assn., Mannford, 1977; del. Creek County Reps., Sapulpa, Okla., 1977-78, Sequoyah County Reps., Sallisaw, Okla., 1984-85. With U.S. Army Spl. Forces, 1966-67, 72-83; 1st sgt. USAR, 1991-97, ret.; with USN, 1960-64. Recipient Tulsa Author's award, City of Tulsa, 1992. Mem. Okla. Writers Fedn., Tulsa Nightwriters (Nightwriter of the Yr. 1990, 96, 2002). Avocations: martial arts, steer roping, scuba diving, parachuting, horses. Home and Office: 30934 E 660 Rd Rt 1 Box 288 Chouteau OK 74337-9617 Office Phone: 918-476-6189.

SASSER, GARY, trucking executive; Student, U. Tenn. Pres., CEO Averitt Express Inc., Cookeville, Tenn., 1971—. Served with USMCR. Office: Averitt Express Inc PO Box 3166 Cookeville TN 38502-3166*

SASSER, ROBERT, retail buyer; From various positions to sr. v.p. Roses Stores, Inc., sr. v.p. merchandise and mktg., 1997—99; v.p., gen. merchandise mgr. Michaels Stores, Inc., 1994—96; COO Dollar Tree Stores, Inc., Chesapeake, Va., 1999—, pres., 2001—. Office: Dollar Tree Stores Inc 500 Volvo Pkwy Chesapeake VA 23320*

SASSO, ELEANOR CATHERINE, state senator; b. Fall River, Mass., Dec. 9, 1934; d. Robert Charles and Ellen (O'Hare) Ashworth; m. Louis Anthony Sasso, 1957; children— Ellen Marie, Ann Marie, Robert. BS, Immaculata Coll., Pa., 1957. Mem. R.I. State Senate, 1979—; researcher Bur. Nat. Affairs, from 1978. Chmn. Cranston Recycling Commn., 1972-73; mem. Cranston Transvan Com., from 1973; mem. Spl. Gov.'s Commn. To Study Entire Election Process, 1977-78. Mem. LWV, Met. Nursing and Health Assn. (bd.), Common Cause, Save the Bay. Democrat. Roman Catholic. Home: 60 Glenmere Dr Cranston RI 02920-6148 Office: Senate Chamber State House Providence RI 02903

SASSO, JOHN, advertising and public strategies executive; BA, Boston U. Chief of staff Gov. Michael Dukakis, Mass., 1983—87; sr. v.p. Hill, Holliday, Connors, Cosmopulos, Inc., Advt., Boston, 1988—90; pres. Advanced Strategies, 1990—. Mgr. Geraldine Ferarro v.p. campaign, 1984; advisor Dukakis pres. campaign, 1988; bd. dirs. Fannie Mae Found., 1993—; gen. election mgr. of the DNC then sr. advisor Kerry-Edwards pres. campaign, 2004—. Bd. dirs. Heller Sch. Social Policy at Brandeis U. Office: Kerry Edwards 2004 Inc PO Box 34640 Washington DC 20043

SASSOON, ANDRE GABRIEL, lawyer; b. Cairo, Apr. 13, 1936; arrived in U.S., 1959; s. Gabriel and Sarine (Tawil) S.; m. Barbara Dee Freedman, Aug. 15, 1965 (div. 2001); children: Daniel, Gabriel, Sarina. GCE, Oxford U., Cambridge U., Eng., 1953; JD, Villanova U., 1969; LLM, Harvard U., 1970. Bar: Pa. 1969, NY 1970. Product mgr. Rohm & Haas Co., Phila., 1960-66; law clk. Dist. Atty.'s Office, Phila., 1968; assoc. Weil, Gotshal & Manges, NYC, 1970-73; pvt. practice NYC, 1973—; pres., CEO Sterimed Internat., Inc., 1999—. Dir. elem. Youth in Distress, NYC, 1982—; v.p., dir. internat. Anti-Drug Abuse Found., NYC, 1987—; v.p., dir., mem. exec. com. Hebrew Immigrant Aid Soc., NYC, 1977—; internat. sec., gov. bd. internat. govs. World Sephardi Fedn., NYC, 1988—; co-pres., chmn., U.S. com., dir. internat. Jewish Com. for Sephardi '92, NYC, 1989—; mem. NY State Christopher Columbus Quincetenary Commn., Statewide Outreach Com., 1991—. Editor Villanova Law Rev.; contbr. articles to profl. jours. Chmn. bd. Sloan's Auctioneers & Appraisers, 2001—03, chmn., 1953—, Sloans and Kenyon, 2003—. With USAR, 1960—66. Recipient Israel Trade award Govt. of Israel, 1985. Mem. ABA, Am. Arbitration Assn. (panel mem. 1971—), Am. Soc. Internat. Law, Order of Coif, 0840 Internat. Pvt., 0860 Internat. Pub. Home: 641 Fifth Ave Apt 30H New York NY 10022 Office: 600 Madison Ave New York NY 10022-1615 E-mail: AndreSassoon@aol.com.

SASTROWARDOYO, TERESITA MANEJAR, nurse; b. Iloilo, Philippines; came to U.S., 1960; d. Timoteo and Monica (Casianan) Manejar; m. Sumarsongko H. Sastrowardoyo, June 8, 1962; children: Timoteo, Daniel (dec.), Benjamin. BSN, Ctrl. Philippine U., Iloilo, 1957; cert. operating rm. and surgical nursing, St. Luke's Hosp Ctr., N.Y.C., 1960-61. Head nurse med. unit Emmanuel Hosp., Roxas City, Philippines, 1957-58; supr. oper. rm. Brent Hosp., Zamboanga City, Philippines, 1958-60; staff nurse oper. rm. Jewish Meml. Hosp., N.Y.C., 1961-62; evening staff nurse oper. rm. Flower and Fifth Ave Hosp., N.Y.C., 1963-65; staff nurse oper. rm., charge nurse night shift St. Lukes Hosp. Ctr., N.Y.C., 1966-76; staff nurse oper. rm. South Side Hosp., Bayshore, N.Y., 1976—, asst. head nurse operating room, 2003—. Mem.: N.Y. State Nurses Assn., Ctrl. Philippine U. Alumni Assn. N.Y., N.J. and Conn. (bd. dirs. 1994—95, 1995—97). Baptist. Avocations: gardening, reading.

SASTRY, SRIN, scientist, researcher, educator; b. Eluru, India, Mar. 1, 1953; s. S.B.R. Murthy and Vasundhara Devi; m. Nora L. Linderoth, July 12, 1986; 1 child, Olivia. PhD, Madurai U., India, 1983; postgrad., U. Calif., Berkeley, 1983-93. Fellow Louis B. Mayer Found., N.Y.C., 1993-96; asst. prof. Rockefeller U., N.Y.C., 1993—. Grantee Hewlett-packard Found., Cancer Rsch. Inst., 2000; recipient Postdoctoral Trainee award NIH, 1990-93; rsch. fellow Indian Coun. Agrl. Rsch., 1979-83; merit scholar Indian Coun. Agrl. Rsch., 1970-72. Mem. AAAS, Am. Chem. Soc., Am. Soc. Biochemistry and Molecular Biology, Am. Soc. Photobiology. Office: Rockefeller U Box 174 1230 York Ave New York NY 10021 E-mail: sastrys2000@yahoo.com.

SATA, LINDBERGH SABURO, psychiatrist, educator; b. Portland, Oreg., Jan. 6, 1928; s. Charles Kazuo and Ito (Kojima) S.; m. Yuriko Kodama, Aug. 19, 1956; children: Roberta, Camille, Holly, John. BS, U. Utah, 1951, MD, 1958, MS, 1964. Intern U. Utah Coll. Medicine, Salt Lake Gen. Hosp., 1958-59, resident in psychiatry, 1959-62, chief resident in psychiatry, 1961-62; adminstrv. chief resident neurology U. Utah Coll. Medicine, VA Hosp., Salt Lake City, 1960-61; fellow Inst. for Mental Retardation, Letchworth Village, Thiells, N.Y., 1962; intern Behavioral Sci. Intern Program Nat. Tng. Labs., Bethel, Maine, 1966; instr. U. Utah, 1962-64; asst. prof. The Psychiat. Inst. U. Md., Balt., 1964-67, assoc. prof., 1967-68, U. Wash., Seattle, 1968-77, asst. dean, 1969-70, prof., 1977-78; prof., chmn. St. Louis U. Sch. Medicine, 1978-94, prof. emeritus, chmn. emeritus, 1994—. Fellow Am. Coll. Psychiatrists, Am. Psychiat. Assn., Pacific Rim Coll. Psychiatrists (founding); mem. Am. Assn. for Social Psychiatry. Office: 1606 Riverview Dr NE Auburn WA 98002-3054

SATAN, MIROSLAV, professional hockey player; b. Topolcany, Slovakia, Oct. 22, 1974; Left wing Edmonton Hockey Team, Buffalo Sabres, 1997—. Mem. Slovakian Nat. Team World Championships, 1996. Office: Buffalo Sabres Marine Midland Arena One Seymour H Knox III Plz Buffalo NY 14203

SATCHER, CLEMENT MICHAEL, elementary school educator; b. L.A., Aug. 21, 1939; s. Dexter Getzwiller and Vera Janette (Laney) S.; m. Brenda Susan McMonigle, Oct. 1972 (div. Dec. 1980); children: Monica, Catherine. AA, Santa Monica Coll., 1972; BA, Calif. State U., Northridge, 1975; cert., Calif. State U., San Bernardino, 1997. Cert. tchr. Sr. elec. draftsman Hughes Telecomm., El Segundo, Calif., 1969—73, elec. designer, 1973—76; illustrator, film and sound operator U.S. Army Engr. Sch., Fort Belvoir, Va., 1961-63; lighting design engr. Epcot, Walt E. Disney Enterprises, Glendale, Calif., 1981-82, elec. designer Disneyland, Anaheim, Calif., 1987-88; lighting technician Theater Vision Inc., North Hollywood, Calif., 1984; elec. engr. Tippetts-Abbett-McCarty-Stratton, L.A., 1984-85; architect Azarak Corp., Westlake Village, Calif., 1985-87, Ward Investment Co., Costa Mesa, Calif., 1988; portrait photographer DeSpain Portrait Svc., Milford, Iowa, 1989-90; caretaker Looking Glass Enterprises, Yucca Valley, Calif., 1990-92; caretaker Dusty Rose Ranch, Desert Hot Springs, Calif., 1992-94; chem. dependency technician Betty Ford Ctr., Rancho Mirage, Calif., 1994. Architect Dept. Water Resources, State Calif., Santa Barbara, 1990; poet, painter, cartoonist; substitute tchr. various sch. dists., 2004. Author: Out of the Flock, 1965, 72; poetry included in anthologies; paintings represented in permanent collections ACLU Headquarters, L.A., Archbiship Office, L.A. With U.S. Army, 1961-63. Recipient Golden Poet award World of Poetry, 1989-90, Best Poets award Nat. Libr. Poetry, 1995 96. Mem. Internat. Soc. Poets, 521 Studio Washington. Home: 34560 Judy Ln Cathedral City CA 92234-6309 Personal E-mail: Sikematcher@aol.com.

SATCHER, DAVID, former public health service officer; b. Anniston, Ala., Mar. 2, 1941; s. Wilmer and Anna Satcher; m. Nola Satcher; children: Gretchen, David, Daraka, Daryl. BS, Morehouse Coll., 1963; MD, PhD, Case Western Reserve U., 1970; recipient of many honorary degrees and numerous disting. honors. Resident and fellow Strong Mem. Hosp., U. Rochester, UCLA, and King Drew; former faculty UCLA Sch. Medicine and Pub. Health; faculty, chair dept. family medicine King-Drew Med. Ctr., LA, interim dean, 1977—79; dir. King-Drew Sickle Cell Rsch. Ctr.; prof., chmn. dept. cmty. and family medicine Morehouse Sch. Medicine, Atlanta, 1979—82; pres. Meharry Med. Coll., Nashville, 1982—93; dir. Ctrs. for Disease Control and Prevention, Atlanta, 1993—98; adminstr. Agy. for Toxic Substances and Disease Registry, 1993—98; asst. sec., surgeon gen. HHS, Washington, 1998—2002; sr. vis. fellow Kaiser Family Found., Washington, 2002—; dir. Nat. Ctr. for Primary Care at Morehouse Sch. Medicine, Atlanta, 2002—. Apptd. mem. Coun. of Grad. Med. Edn., 1986, chmn.; former Robert Wood Johnson Clin. Scholar; former Macy Faculty Fellow. Named Nashvillian of Yr., 1992; recipient Watts Grassroots award for cmty. leadership, 1978, Nat. Conf. Christians and Jews awards, 1985, Black Achievment award, Ebony Mag., 1994, Brewslow award in pub. health, 1995, Dr. Nathan B. Davis award, AMA, 1996, Lifetime Achievement award, NY Acad. Medicine, 1997, Bennie Mays Trailblazer award, Nat. Found. for Infectious Diseases, Jimmy and Roslyn Carter award. Fellow: Am. Acad. of Family Physicians; mem.: Inst. Medicine NAS, Alpha Omega Alpha, Phi Beta Kappa. Focuses on promoting healthly lifestyles and ending disparities in healthcare. Office: Kaiser Family Foundation Ste 250 1450 G St NW Washington DC 20005 also: Nat Ctr for Primary Care at Morehouse Sch Medicine 720 Westview Dr SW Atlanta GA 30310 Office Phone: 404-756-5740. Office Fax: 404-756-5767. Business E-Mail: ncpc@msm.edu.*

SATHER, GLEN CAMERON, professional hockey team executive, coach; b. High River, Alta., Canada, Sept. 2, 1943; m. Ann Sather; 2 children. Former professional hockey player; coach Edmonton Oilers, Nat. Hockey League, Alta., Can., 1977-89, gen. mgr., 1981—2000, pres., 1982—2000, alt. gov., 1990—2000; pres., gen. mgr. NY Rangers, 2000—, head coach, 2003—04. Head coach, Stanley Cup Champions, 1984, 1985, 1987, 1988. Recipient Jack Adams Award for NHL Coach of the Yr., 1986. Office: c/o New York Rangers 2 Pennsylvania Plaza New York NY 10121

SATHYAMOORTHY, MUTHUKRISHNAN, engineering researcher, educator; b. Sathanur, Tamil Nadu, India, Feb. 21, 1946; s. Kuppusamy and Visalakshi Muthukrishnan; m. Chitra Subbiah, May 26, 1971; children: Mohanakrishnan, Kumaran. B in Civil Engring., U. Madras, India, 1967; M in Engring. Mechanics, Indian Inst. of Tech., Madras, India, 1969, PhD in Aero. Engring., 1973. Lectr. Indian Inst. of Tech., Madras, India, 1969-74; rsch. fellow U. Birmingham, Eng., 1974-76; asst. prof. Clarkson U., Potsdam, NY, 1979-82, assoc. prof., 1982-92, assoc. prof., exec. officer, 1992-94, prof., exec. officer, 1994-97, prof., chair, 1997-2001; dean engring. W.Va. Univ. Inst. Tech., 2001—. Vis. rsch. faculty U. Calgary, Can., 1977-79. Contbn. author: Handbook of Civil Engineering Practice, 1988; editor: Material Nonlinearity in Vibrations, 1985; author: Nonlinear Analysis of Structures, 1998. Recipient Appreciation cert. U.S. Army, 1990, Outstanding Advisor award Clarkson U., 1993, Tau Beta Pi Faculty award, 1997, Disting. Tchg. award Clarkson Univ., 2001. Fellow ASME (mem. nat. student sect. com. 1992-94, mem. gen. awards com. 1994-99, Nat. Faculty Advisor award 1993, Dedicated Svc. award 1999); AIAA (assoc.), Aero. Soc. India. Avocations: overseas travel, camping, photography, fishing. Office: Office of Dean of Engring W Va Univ Inst Technology Montgomery WV 25136 Home: 321 2nd Ave Montgomery WV 25136-2403 Office Phone: 304-442-3161. Business E-Mail: msathy@wvutech.edu.

SATIN, CLAIRE JEANINE, sculptor, book artist; b. Bklyn., Jan. 9, 1942; BA, Sarah Lawrence Coll., 1956; MFA, Pratt Inst., 1968. Instr. art edn. dept. edn. Bklyn. Mus., 1958-59; instr. dept. edn. and dept. Fine Arts Broward Cmty. Coll., Ft. Lauderdale, Fla., 1971-83; dir. Broward Cmty. Coll. Gallery, Ft. Lauderdale, 1975-76. Artist rep. Vorpal Gallery, Soho, N.Y.C., Jan van der Donk Gallery, Chelsea, N.Y.C. Collections include Victoria and Albert Mus., London, Getty Ctr. Hist. Art and Humanities, L.A., Mus. Modern Art, N.Y.C., Mus. Art, Ft. Lauderdale, King Stephen Mus., Szekesfeherdr, Hungary, Ruth and Marvin Sackner Archive of Concrete and Visual Poetry, others; commd. works include: Chapman Chronicles, State of Alaska, U. Alaska, Fairbanks, 1992, Alphawalk, New Tampa Regional Libr., Hillsborough County, Tampa, Fla., 1997 (catalog); Alphastory, Pembroke Pines Libr., Pembroke Pines, Fla., Broward County Art in Pub. Places Program (brochure), Am. Ctrs., New Delhi, Bombay, India. Bd. dirs. Broward County Cultural Affairs Coun., Ft. Lauderdale, 1975-83, hon. chair, 1981—. Recipient S. Fla. Cult Consortium award Miami Art Mus., Fla., 1997-98; So. Arts Fedn./NEA Regional Visual Arts fellow, 1996; Fla. State Individual Artist fellow Statewide Exhbn., 1978, 97-98; Cult Consortium fellow Miami Art Mus., 1997-98; Tiffany Found. grantee, 1968-69, Meml. Found. for Jewish Culture, 2001-02. Mem. Internat. Sculpture Ctr., Am. Craft. Coun., Ctr. Book Arts, Fonteneda Soc. (bd. dirs. 1997—). Office: care ARTWORKS/ARTSPACE 101 SW 1st St Dania FL 33004-3628

SATIN, JOSEPH, language professional, university administrator; b. Phila., Dec. 16, 1920; s. Reuben Philip and Harriet (Price) Satin; m. Selma Rosen (dec. 1978); children: Mark, Diane; m. Barbara Jeanne Dodson (dec. 1987); m. Terrye Sagan, 1992. BA, Temple U., 1946; AM, Columbia U., 1948, PhD, 1952. Instr. integrated studies W.Va. U., Morgantown, 1952-54; prof. English and Comparative Lit. Moorhead (Minn.) State U., 1954-63; chmn. dept. English and Journalism Midwestern U., Wichita Falls, Tex., 1963-73; dean Sch. Arts and Humanities Calif. State U., Fresno, 1973-89. Mgr concert series Moorhead State Univ, 1956—61; mem nat bd consult NEH, Washington, 1979—; dir London semester Calif State Univ, Fresno, 1982—92; dir Frank Lloyd Wright Auditorium Project. Author: (book) Ideas in Context, 1958, The 1950's: America's "Placid" Decade, 1960, Reading Non-Fiction Prose, 1964, Reading Prose Fiction, 1964, Shakespeare and His Sources, 1966, Reading Literature, 1968, The Humanities Handbook (2 vols), 1969, (poems) The Journey Upward, 1999, Poems on the Internet (www.Poetry.com), 2000; editor: (book) Frank Lloyd Wright-Letters to Apprentices, 1982, Letters to Architects, 1984, Letters to Clients, 1986, Treasures of Taliesin, 1985, The Guggenheim Correspondence, 1986, Frank Lloyd Wright: His Living Voice, 1987, Frank Lloyd Wright, The Crowning Decade, 1989; translator: Federico Fellini, Comments on Film, 1987; contbr. Encyclopedia Int Educ, 1978; dir: Univ Press, Calif State Univ, 1982—92. With U.S. Army, 1943—46, ETO. Named Nat Grand Prize Winner, Nat Library Poetry N Am Ann Poetry Contest, 1998. Jewish. Avocations: creative writing, music. Home: 65 Maywood Dr San Francisco CA 94127-2007 E-mail: tewilder@juno.com.

SATINE, BARRY ROY, lawyer; b. N.Y.C., July 25, 1951; s. Norman S. and Fay (Mekles) S.; m. Janice Bea Halfond, Aug. 4, 1974; children: David, Leah. BA, CCNY, 1972; JD, George Washington U., 1975. Bar: N.Y. 1976, D.C. 1977, U.S. Dist. Ct. (so. dist.) N.Y. 1978, U.S. Supreme Ct. 1979, U.S. Dist. Ct. (ea. dist.) N.Y. 1982, U.S. Ct. Appeals (2d cir.) 1989. Trial atty. U.S. Civil Svc. Commn., Washington, 1975—78; atty. AT&T, N.Y.C., 1978—81, N.Y. Tel. Co., N.Y.C., 1981—82; mem. assoc. Surrey & Morse, N.Y.C., 1982—84, ptnr., 1985, Jones Day, 1986—. Mem.: Assn. of Bar of City of N.Y. Office: Jones Day 222 East 41st Street New York NY 10017 Office Phone: 212-326-3904. Business E-Mail: barrysatine@jonesday.com.

SATINOVER, JEFFREY B. physicist, psychiatrist, writer; b. Chgo., Sept. 4, 1947; s. Joseph and Sena (Rotman) Satinover; m. Julie Rachel Leff, June 10, 1982; children: Sarah Katherine, Anne-Rebecca, Jenny Leigh. BS, MIT, 1971; EdM, Harvard U., 1973; MD, U. Tex., 1982; Diplomate, C.G Jung Inst.,

Zurich, Switzerland, 1976; MS, Yale U., 2002. Diplomate Am. Bd. Psychiatry and Neurology, Am. Bd. Geriat. Psychiatry. Fellow dept. psychiatry and child psychiatry Yale U., New Haven, 1982-86; founder, exec. dir. Sterling Inst., Stamford, Conn., 1985-92; med. dir. Temenos Inst., Westport, Conn., 1984—; pvt. practice Westport, 1992—. William James lectr. psychology and and religion Harvard U., 1975; mem. catchment area coun. S. W. Regional Mental Health Bd., 1988—92; mem. Lower Fairfield County Regional Action Coun. Against Substance Abuse, 1990—92; with relativistic heavy ion group dept. physics Yale U., New Haven, 1999—2001, with condensed matter theory group, 2001—03, with theoretical condensed matter physics group, 2002—03; dir. rsch. VKRA Quantitative Fin., 2003—; mem. condensed matter physics group U. Nice, France, 2003—; vis. lectr. dept. politics Princeton U., 2004—. Co-author: Jungian Psychotherapy, 1984, Science and the Fragile Self, 1990, Jungian Analysis, 1993; author: Homesexuality and the Politics of Truth, 1994, The Empty Self: Gnostic Foundations of Modern Identity, 1994, Feathers of the Skylark, 1996, Cracking the Bible Code, 1997, The Quantum Brain, 2001; contbr. articles to profl. jours. Active nat. physician's resource coun. Focus on Family, 1994—97; pres. C. G. Jung Found., NY, 1988—92; founder, mem. exec. bd. com. Save Our Schs., 1994—; bd. dirs. Toward Tradition; bd. advisors Family Inst. Conn., 1996—; bd. dirs. Klingberg Family Ctrs., 1994—96. Capt. N.G. USAR, 1989—94, maj. USAR, 1995—. Recipient Seymour Lustman Residency Rsch. 2d pl. award, Yale U. Psychiatry Dept., 1983, 1985. Mem.: Internat. Assn. Analytical Psychology, Am. Psychiat. Assn. (Burroughs-Wellcome fellow 1983—85), Aspetuck Valley Country Club, Alpha Omega Alpha. Republican. Jewish. Avocations: tennis, harpsichord, jazz keyboard. Business E-Mail: jsatinov@princeton.edu.

SATINSKY, BARNETT, lawyer; b. Phila., June 17, 1947; s. Alex and Florence (Talsky) S.; m. Fredda Andrea Wagner, June 17, 1973; children: Meagen, Sara Beth, Jonathan. AB, Brown U., 1969; JD, Villanova U., 1972. Bar: Pa. 1972, U.S. Dist. Ct. (ea. dist) Pa. 1975, U.S. Dist. Ct. (mid. dist.) Pa. 1975, U.S. Ct. Appeals (3d cir.) 1981. Law clk. Phila. Ct. Common Pleas, 1972-73; dep. atty. gen. Pa. Dept. Justice, Harrisburg, 1973-75; 1st asst. counsel Pa. Pub. Utility Commn., Harrisburg, 1975-77, chief counsel, 1977; assoc. Fox, Rothschild, O'Brien & Frankel, LLP, Phila., 1978-81; ptnr. Fox Rothschild LLP, Phila., 1981—. Children Svcs. Rev. com., United Way Southeast Pa., 1984-86; bd. dirs. ACLU, Harrisburg, 1973-74, Voyage House, Inc., 1994-96. Mem. ABA (pub. utility, labor and employment law sects., employee benefits com. 1984—), Pa. Bar Assn. (labor rels., pub. utility law sects. 1980—, pub. utility law com., governing coun. 1991-93), Phila. Bar Assn. (labor law com. 1980—, chmn. pub. utility law com. 1988-91), Nat. Assn. Coll. and Univ. Attys., Nat. Assn. Regulatory Commrs. (staff subcom. law 1977), Soc. for Human Resource Mgmt., Louis D. Brandeis Law Soc. Democrat. Jewish. Office: Fox Rothschild LLP 2000 Market St Philadelphia PA 19103-3291 E-mail: bsatinsky@frof.com.

SATIR, BIRGIT H. medical educator, medical researcher; b. Copenhagen, Mar. 22, 1934; Magistra in Biochemistry, U. Copenhagen, 1961. Rsch. assoc. dept. zoology U. Chgo., 1962-66; asst. rsch. physiologist U. Calif. Dept. Physiology-Anatomy, Berkeley, 1967-74, assoc. rsch. physiologist, 1974-76, adj. assoc. prof., 1976-77; sci. dir. Analytical Ultrastructure Ctr., Cancer Rsch. Inst. Albert Einstein Coll. of Medicine, Bronx, N.Y., 1977-84, prof. dept. anatomy and structural biology, 1977—. Rschr. Phys.- Chem. Inst. Copenhagen, 1956-57, Biol. Inst., Copenhagen, 1958-61; mem. Cellular and Molecular Basis of Disease Rev. Com., Nat. Inst. Gen. Med. Scis., 1977-79; vis. prof. divsn. biology Calif. Inst. Tech., 1984-85. Mem. editl. bd. Jour. Ultrastructural Rsch., 1975-80, Jour. Cell Biology, 1979-81, Modern Cell Biology, 1980-90, Jour. Eukaryotic Microbiology, 1989-95. Rsch. fellow U. Geneva, 1965-66, Spl. fellow USPHS, 1972-73; recipient Outstanding Women Scientist award N.Y. chpt. Assn. Women in Sci., 1990, Rsch. award Am. Diabetes Assn., 1995. Fellow AAAS, Royal Danish Acad. Sci. and Letters; mem. Am. Soc. Cell Biology (coun. 1975-78, minority affairs com. 1987-90, fin. com. 1993—), Am. Assn. Anatomists, Am. Soc. Biochemistry and Molecular Biology, Electron Microscopy Soc. Am. (program vice-chairperson 38th Meeting 1980, program chairperson 39th Meeting 1981), NYSEM (pres. 1979-80), N.Y. Acad. Sci., Biophys. Soc. Office: Albert Einstein Coll of Medicine Dept Anatomy & Structural Biology 1300 Morris Park Ave Bronx NY 10461-1926

SATITPUNWAYCHA, PON, surgeon; b. Bangkok, 1936; MD, Chulalongkorn Hosp. U., Bangkok, 1962. Intern Passavant Meml. Hosp., Chgo., 1963; resident Northwestern U. Med. Sch., Chgo., 1964-69; surgeon Cypress Fairbanks Med. Ctr. Hosp., Houston. Mem. ACS (life; Disting. Philanthropy award 2001), AMA (life), Soc. Am. Gastrointestinal Endoscopic Surgery, Soc. Laparascopic Surgery, Am. Soc. Colo-rectal Surgeons, S.W. Surg. Congress. Office: 11301 Fallbrook Dr Ste 101 Houston TX 77065-4269 Office Phone: 281-890-9146.

SATLOFF, ROBERT B. think-tank executive; BS, Duke U.; MS, Harvard U.; PhD in Oriental Studies, Oxford U. Staff Washington Inst. for Near East Policy, 1985—, exec. dir. Author, editor: The Politics of Change in the Middle East, 1993, From Abdullah to Hussein: Jordan in Transition, 1994, and Troubles on the East Bank: Challenges to the Domestic Stability of Jordan, 1986; frequent commentator on the Middle East in major Am. newspapers including the Washington Post, N.Y. Times, Wall St. Jour. and L.A. Times; has appeared on various TV and radio programs to offer his analysis of events in the Middle East. Office: The Washington Inst for Near East Policy 1828 L St NW Ste 1050 Washington DC 20036-5128

SATO, EUNICE NODA, former mayor, consultant; b. Livingston, Calif., June 8, 1921; d. Bunsaku and Sawa (Maeda) Noda; m. Thomas Takashi Sato, Dec. 9, 1950; children: Charlotte Patricia, Daniel Ryuichi and Douglas Ryuji (twins). AA, Modesto Jr. Coll., 1941; BA, U. No. Colo., 1944; MA, Columbia U., 1948. Pub. sch. tchr. Mastodon Twp. Schs., Alpha, Mich., 1944-47; ednl. missionary Reformed Ch. Am., Yokohama, Japan, 1948-51; coun. mem. City of Long Beach, Calif., 1975-86; mayor, 1980-82. Sec. corp. bd. Los Angeles County Health Systems Agy., 1978-79 Monthly contbr. articles to 2 neighborhood papers, 1975-86. Bd. dirs. Long Beach chpt. ARC, 1975-2000, mem. exec. com., 1978-91, 93-99, past pres. and v.p., mem. Calif. state svc. coun., A.R.C., 1995-2001; bd. dirs. Goodwill Industries, 1978-82; trustee St. Mary's Bauer Med. Ctr., 1977—; pres. Industry Edn. Coun., Long Beach, 1984-86, mem. exec. bd., 1984—; bd. dirs. Industry Edn. Coun. of Calif.; treas. So. Calif. Consortium of I.E.C., 1984-86, pres., 1988-89; mem. State Adv. Group on Juvenile Justice and Delinquency Prevention, 1983-91, Calif. Coun. Criminal Justice, 1983-92, legis. com. Girl Scout coun. Calif., 1986-92, chair, 1991-92; bd. dirs. Long Beach coun. Girl Scouts U.S., 1986-92, Region III United Way, 1974-88; mem. Asian Pacific adv. com. Calif. Dept. Rehab., 1985-87, recreation commn. City of Long Beach, 1985-86, pub. safety policy com. League Calif. Cities, 1981-86, cmty. econ. and housing devel. com. So. Calif. Assn. Govts., 1976-86, Calif. Task Force to Promote Self-Esteem and Personal and Social Responsibility, 1987-90; Long Beach chpt. pres. NCCJ, 1987-88; pres. Internat. Cmty. Coun., 1986-87, bd. dir. 1986-2001, pres. Japanese Am. Reps., 1987, 88, exec. bd. mem. 1987-2003; presdl. appointee Nat. Adv. Coun. Ednl. Rsch. and Improvement, 1991-94; pres. Aux. to Sch. Theology, Claremont, 1990-91, exec. bd. 1989-91, nat. selective svc. sys. local bd. 138, 1990-2001, SCA Edison Co. Equal Opportunity adv. coun., 1990-94; chair selection com. Leadership Long Beach, 1990-91, sec. exec. bd., 1991-92; chair adv. bd. AIESEC, 1990-92; chmn. Long Beach Area Rep. Party, 1990-92; asst. sec. cen. com., L.A, 1990-92; sec.-gen. coun. on fin. and administrn. United Meth. Ch., 1992-2000; appointed by Gov. to commn. on tchr. credentialing State Calif., 1994, L.A. coun. svc. coun. A.R.C., 1995-99; chair adminstrv. bd. Leisure World Cmty. Ch., 1996-2002; rep. to South Coast Ecumenical Coun., 1993-2002, chair pastor parish rels. com., 2000; chair Parents Day Festival com. greater L.A. county, 1996-2000, Blue Ribbon Com. for Effective Parenting in Long Beach, 1997-99. Recipient Outstanding Svc. award Long Beach Coord. Coun., 1969, Mother of Yr. award Silverado United Meth. Ch., 1973, Hon. Svc. award Calif. PTA, 1963, Continuing Svc. award, 1974, hon. life membership award Nat. PTA, 1974, Outstanding Laywoman of Yr. award Long Beach Area Coun. Chs., 1976, Woman of Yr. award State Women's Coun.-C. of C., 1979, Long Beach Internat. Bus. and Profl. Women's Club, Nat. Merit award DAR, 1982, Citizen of Yr. award Los Altos YMCA, 1982, Calif. Cmty. Pool for Handicapped, 1982, Outstanding Citizen award Torch Club of Long Beach, 1983, W. Odie Wright award Industry Edn. Coun., 1990, Humanitarian award NCCJ, 1992, Vol. of Yr. award ARC, 1995, 1st Life Membership award Long Beach chpt. UN Assn., Kunsho award of Order of the Sacred Treasure, Gold Rays with rosette from Japanese Govt., 1996, Sr. Vol. of Yr. Long Beach C.C., 1999, Al Taucher Rep. of Yr. award, 2001. Mem. Industry Edn. Coun. Long Beach (hon. life), Long Beach C. of C. (Dewey Smith cmty. svc. award), Lions (hon. life), Soroptimist Internat. (Woman of Distinction in Econ. and Social Devel. 2001), Alpha Iota. Republican. Presbyterian. Home: Bixby Village 551 Pittsfield Ct Unit 101 Long Beach CA 90803-6355

SATO, GLENN KENJI, lawyer; b. Honolulu, Jan. 6, 1952; s. Nihei and Katherine (Miwa) S.; m. Donna Mae Shiroma, Apr. 4, 1980 (dec. Aug. 1985); m. Nan Sun Oh, Mar. 27, 1987 (dec. Nov. 1997); children: Gavan, Allison, Garrett; m. Sandra K. Kumagai, Nov. 21, 1999. BBA, U. Hawaii, 1975; JD, U. Calif., San Francisco, 1977. Bar: Hawaii 1978, U.S. Dist. Ct. Hawaii, 1978, U.S. Ct. Claims 1990. Assoc. Fujiyama, Duffy & Fujiyama, Honolulu, 1978-80, 83-87, ptnr., 1987-95; stockholder Law Offices of Glenn K. Sato, Honolulu, 1980-82; pres. ISL Svcs., Inc., Honolulu, 1983; ptnr. Sato & Thomas, Honolulu, 1995-98; pvt. practice Honolulu, 1998—. Vice chmn. Pattern Jury Instrn. Com., State of Hawaii, Honolulu, 1993. Treas. Polit. Action Com., Honolulu, 1993. Mem. Platform Assn., Beta Gamma Sigma. Avocations: golf, hunting, target shooting, surfing. Office: 220 S King St Ste 600 Honolulu HI 96813-4585

SATO, JUNICHI STEVEN, musician, music educator; MusB, DePaul U., 1995; MusM, Ind. U., 1998. Pvt. music tchr., Chgo., 1991—; assoc. instr. Ind. U., Bloomington, 1998—2000; owner, music pub., engraver J.S. Sato Music Edits., Chgo., 1995—; piano instr. Music Makers, Western Springs, Ill., 2001—. Lectr. DePaul U. Sch. Music, Chgo., 2004—; piano instr. DePaul U. Cmty. Music Divsn., 2003—; soloist, chamber pianist, 1978—; adjudicator internat. music competitions, 2000—. Composer (for piano solo): Gray Mass, 1998; composer: (for piano and cello) Variations on a Japanese Air, 2002; arranger: (for piano) Passacaglia and Fugue (Bach), 2000, Psalm XIII (Liszt), 1997; appearances on TV and radio., Dolores Kohl Edn. Found. scholar, 1991, Japanese Am. Citizens League scholar, 1995. Mem.: ASCAP, Chgo. Area Music Tchrs. Assn. (tech. com. 2002—, composition festival 2003—, co-chair Roberta Savler Piano Contest 2003—), Nat. Music Pubs.' Assn. Avocations: chess, flight simulation, computer programming. Home and Office: 707 W Waveland Ave Apt 311 Chicago IL 60613-4112

SATO, KAZUYOSHI, pathologist; b. Shibata, Niigata, Japan, Apr. 3, 1930; came to U.S., 1968; s. Katsueita and Kyo (Sakagawa) S.; m. Ann Marie Farrenkopf, July 5, 1964 (dec. Aug. 1983); children: P.T. Sachiko, P. Miyoko, Michael T., Phillip K. Student, Niigata U., Japan, 1954, MD, 1958. Diplomate Am. Bd. Pathology, Anatomic and Clin. Pathology. Intern USAF Hosp., Tachikawa, Japan, 1958-59, Ellis Hosp., Schenectady, N.Y., 1959-60, asst. resident in pathology, 1960-61; resident in pathology Free Hosp. for Women, Brookline, Mass., 1961-62, The Children's Hosp. Med. Ctr., Boston, 1962-63, resident in neuropathology, 1963-64; resident fellow in pathology Mayo Grad. Sch. Medicine, Rochester, Minn., 1968-70; dir. labs. Falmouth (Mass.) Hosp., 1972-96; dir. Falmouth Hosp. Service Lab., Sandwich, Mass., 1986-93. Pathologist and rsch. assoc. Atomic Bomb Casualty Commn., Nagasaki, Japan, 1964-68; pathologist, chief of pathology USPHS Hosp., Norfolk Va., 1970-72, Falmouth (Mass.) Hosp., 1972-97. Recipient Fulbright scholarship, 1959. Fellow Coll. Am. Pathologists, Am. Soc. Clin. Pathologists; mem. Assn. Mil. Surgeons U.S. Home: 88 Two Ponds Rd Falmouth MA 02540-2225

SATO, PAUL HISASHI, pharmacologist; b. Mt. Vernon, N.Y., Mar. 22, 1949; s. Yoshio and Lury (Shiogi) S.; m. Jeanne Ellen Courville, June 29, 1996. BS, Jamestown Coll., 1971; MS, NYU, 1972, PhD, 1975. Rsch. assoc. Roche Inst. Molecular Biology, Nutley, N.J., 1975-77; assoc. prof. Mich. State U., East Lansing, 1977—. Office: Mich State U Dept Pharmacology/Toxicol East Lansing MI 48824 E-mail: sato@msu.edu.

SATO, RICHARD MICHIO, consulting engineering company executive; b. Paia, Maui, Hawaii, Dec. 30, 1934; s. Shinichi and Namie (Hanazawa) S.; m. Althea Reiko Ouye; children: Janice Muraoka, Kelvin. BSCE, U. Hawaii, 1956. Registered civil/structural engr., Calif., Hawaii, Guam. Civil and structural engr. Dalton Dalton Assocs., L.A., 1960-62; structural engr. William M. Taggart, SE, L.A., 1962-67; project coord. Office of Univ. Planning U. Hawaii, Honolulu, 1967-69; project engr. T.Y. Lin Hawaii, Honolulu, 1969; pres. Sato & Assocs., Inc. (formerly Richard M. Sato & Assoc. & Sato & Kuniyoshi, Inc.), Honolulu, 1969—. 1st lt. U.S. Army, 1957-59. Mem. Am. Concrete Inst., Prestressed Concrete Inst., Structural Engrs. Assn. Hawaii (pres. 1976), Consulting Engrs. Coun. Hawaii, Hui Kokua Kinipopo (pres. 1993—), U. Hawaii Pres.'s Club, U. Hawaii Alumni Assn., Chi Epsilon. Avocations: golf, sports fan. Office: Sato & Assocs Inc 2046 S King St Honolulu HI 96826-2219

SATOH, YUKO, music educator; b. Ichinomiya, Aichi, Feb. 8, 1967; s. Naohiro Nakata and Kimiko Satoh. BA, Tokyo Nat. U. of Fine Arts and Music, 1990, MA, 1993, Washington U., St. Louis, 2001. Editor, translator Shogakukan, Tokyo, 1990—91; asst. editor Musicol. Soc. Japan, Tokyo, 1993—94; rsch. assoc. Washington U., St. Louis, 2000—01; asst. dir. JUST Inst., Columbus, Ohio, 2001—. Mem.: Am. Translators Assn. Office: JUST Inst 5295 Olentangy River Rd Columbus OH 43235 E-mail: yukosatoh777@hotmail.com.

SATRE, PHILIP GLEN, casino entertainment executive, lawyer; b. Palo Alto, Calif., Apr. 30, 1949; s. Selmer Kenneth and Georgia June (Sterling) S.; m. Jennifer Patricia Arnold, June 30, 1973; children: Malena Anne, Allison Neal, Jessica Lilly, Peter Sterling. BA, Stanford U., 1971; JD, U. Calif.-Davis, 1975; postgrad. sr. exec. program, MIT, 1982. Bar: Nev. 1975, Calif. 1976. Assoc. Vargas & Bartlett, Reno, 1975-79; v.p., gen. counsel, sec. Harrah's, Reno, 1980-83, sr. v.p., 1983-84; pres. Harrah's East, Atlantic City, 1984; pres., CEO Harrah's Hotels and Casinos, Reno, 1984-91; dir., sr. v.p. Gaming Group The Promus Cos., Inc., Memphis, 1988-91, dir., pres., COO, 1991-94, dir., pres. CEO, 1994-95; pres., CEO Harrah's Entertainment, Inc., Memphis, 1995—, chmn., pres., CEO, 1997—; dir. JDN Realty Co., Memphis, 1999—. Dir., treas. Nat. Jud. Coll., Reno. Active The Stanford Athletic Bd., 1996—. Mem. ABA, Nev. Bar Assn., Calif. Bar Assn., Order of Coif, Phi Kappa Phi, Stanford Alumni Assn. (pres. Reno chpt. 1976-77), Young Pres. Orgn., The Bus. Roundtable. Office: PO Box 29526 Las Vegas NV 89126-9526 also: 5100 W Sahara Ave Las Vegas NV 89146

SATTER, LARRY DEAN, nutritionist; b. Madelia, Minn., July 30, 1937; m. 1966; 3 children. BS, S.D. State U., 1960; MS, U. Wis., 1962, PhD in Biochemistry and Dairy Sci., 1964. Asst. prof. to assoc. prof. dairy sci. U. Wis., Madison, 1964-73, prof., 1973-81; mem. staff U.S. Dairy Forage Rsch. Ctr., U. Wis., USDA, Madison, 1981-87, dir., 1987-98, rsch. dairy scientist, 1998—. Recipient Am. Feed Mfrs. award, 1977. Mem. Am. Dairy Sci. Assn., Am. Soc. Animal Sci., Am. Inst. Nutrition. Office: U Wis USDA Dairy Forage Rsch Ctr 1925 Linden Dr W Madison WI 53706-1108 E-mail: ldsatter@facstaff.wisc.edu., lsatter@dfrc.wisc.edu.

SATTER, RAYMOND NATHAN, judge; b. Denver, Oct. 19, 1948; s. Charles Herbert and Muriel Vera (Tuller); m. Suzanne Elizabeth Ehlers, May 28, 1977. BA, U. Denver, 1970; JD, Cath. U., 1973. Bar: Colo. 1973, U.S. Dist. Ct. Colo. 1973, U.S. Ct. Appeals (10th cir.) 1973, U.S. Supreme Ct. 1976, U.S. Tax Ct. 1981. Assoc. Wallace, Armatas & Hahn, Denver, 1973-75; ptnr. Tallmadge, Wallace & Hahn, Denver, 1975-77; pvt. practice Denver, 1978-87; Denver County judge, 1987—; presiding judge Denver County Ct., 2001—. Gen. counsel Satter Dist., Denver, 1977-78; assoc. mcpl. judge City of Englewood, Colo., 1985-86; com. on civil rules Colo. Supreme Ct., 1988-2003. Pres. Young Artists Orch. Denver, 1985-87; sec. Denver Symphony Assn., 1985-86. Mem. Colo. Bar Assn. (ethics com.), Denver Bar Assn. (bd. trustees 1998-2001, Jud. Excellence award 1992, 95). Avocations: sailing, opera, classical music, fishing, bridge. Office: Denver County Ct 108 City & County Bldg 1437 Bannock St Denver CO 80202-5337 Business E-Mail: rsatter@ci.denver.co.us.

SATTERFIELD, CHARLES NELSON, chemical engineer, educator; b. Dexter, Mo., Sept. 5, 1921; s. Charles David and Hermine (Weber) S.; m. Anne Pettingell, July 6, 1946; children: Mark Edward, Joye. BS cum laude, Harvard U., 1942; MS, MIT, 1943, Sc.D., 1946. Registered profl. engr., Mass. Asst. prof. chem. engring. Mass. Inst. Tech., Cambridge, 1946-53, asso. prof., 1953-59, prof., 1959-92; emeritus prof., 1992—. Lectr. indsl. chemistry Harvard, 1948-57; cons.on rocket propellants Dept. Def., 1952-60; mem. com. chem. kinetics NRC, 1960-66; chmn. ad hoc panel on abatement nitrogen oxide emissions from stationary sources Nat. Acad. Engring., 1970-72; indsl. cons. to major cos. in petroleum and chem. industries; lectr. in field Euorpe, U.S. Co-author: Thermodynamic Charts for Combustion Processes, 1949, Hydrogen Peroxide, 1955 (translated into Russian 1957), Role of Diffusion in Catalysis, 1963; author: Mass Transfer in Heterogeneous Catalysis, 1970 (translated into Russian 1976), Heterogeneous Catalysis in Practice, 1980 (translated into Russian 1984), repub. as Heterogeneous Catalysis in Industrial Practice, 1991, also more than 140 tech. papers; mem. editl. adv. bd. Indsl. and Engring. Chemistry, 1966-68, Advances in Chemistry Series, 1971-73, 82-86, Energy and Fuels, 1990-95, Applied Catalysis, 1995-2001; patentee in field. Named Top Scientist in the World in CHem. Engring., Univ. Leiden, 1987. Fellow Am. Acad. Arts and Scis.; mem. Am. Chem. Soc., Am. Inst. Chem. Engrs. (Wilhelm award 1980), Sigma Xi, Tau Beta Pi. Home: 38 Tabor Hill Rd Lincoln MA 01773-2906 Office: Dept Chem Engring Mass Inst Tech Cambridge MA 02139

SATTERFIELD, JOHN ROBERTS, JR., retired college president and music educator; b. Danville, Va., Dec. 4, 1921; s. John Roberts and Sara Elise Council Satterfield; m. Carolyn Talley, Dec. 18, 1948; children: John Roberts III, Kenneth Scott, Keith Charles, Jean Council. BA, U. N.C., 1949, MusM, 1950, MA, 1955, PhD, 1962. Asst. prof. music Davidson (N.C.) Coll., 1953-60; assoc. prof. music Fla. Prebyn. Coll., St. Petersburg, 1960-63, prof. music, 1963-67, prof. humanities and music, 1967-68; v.p. acad. affairs, prof. humanities and music Elmira (N.Y.) Coll., 1968-70; asst. dir. N.C. Bd. Higher Edn., Raleigh, 1970-72; asst. v.p. acad. affairs U. N.C. Gen. Adminstrn., Chapel Hill, 1972, dir. Ctr. Continuing Renewal of Higher Edn., 1972; provost Kalamazoo (Mich.) Coll., 1972-75, exec. v.p., 1973-75; pres. Wagner Coll., Staten Island, N.Y., 1975-81; ret., 1981; part-time instr. music Durham (N.C.) Tech. C.C., 1997. Vis. prof. music U. Ky., Lexington, 1964, U. Tex., Austin, 1966; cons. Fla. State Dept. Edn., N.Y. State Depts. Edn. and Civil Svc., U.S. Office Edn., N.C. Bd. Higher Edn., Siena Coll., Coll. St. Benedict, U. Dayton, Davidson Coll., Ohio U. Editor: Christopher Tye: The Latin Ch. Music, Part I: The Masses, 1973, Part II: The Shorter Latin Works, 1973; translator: The Technique of My Musical Language (Olivier Messaien), 2 vols., 1956; chief author: Private Higher Education in North Carolina: Conditions and Prospects, 1971, (video) Myth and Symbol: An Occasional Lecture, 2000; contbr. numerous articles and revs. to profl. jours. and newspapers, short stories and verse to quars., chpts. to books; composer music; keyboardist (movie) The Handmaid's Tale, 1990. Bd. mem., Empire State Found. Ind. Liberal Arts Colls., N.Y.C., 1975-81, United Meth. City Soc., N.Y.C., 1975-81. Capt., USAF, 1942-45. Decorated Bronze Star, Presdl. Citation with Cluster, Belgian Fourragère, Croix de Guerre; recipient Composers award N.C. Symphony Soc., 1951, Harbison award, the Danforth Found., 1965-66. Mem. The Melville Soc. Avocations: reading, travel, cooking. Home: 1401 Brigham Rd Chapel Hill NC 27517-3403

SATTERTHWAITE, CAMERON B. physics educator; b. Salem, Ohio, July 26, 1920; s. William David and Mabel (Cameron) S.; m. Helen Elizabeth Foster, Dec. 23, 1950 (div. July 1979); children: Mark Cameron, Tod Foster, Tracy Lynn, Keith Alan, Craig Evan (dec.). BA, Coll. Wooster, 1942; postgrad., Ohio State U., 1942-44; PhD, U. Pitts., 1951. Chemist Manhattan dist. project Monsanto Chem. Co., Dayton, Ohio, 1944-47; research chemist DuPont, Wilmington, Del., 1950-53; researcher, adv. physicist Westinghouse, Pitts., 1953-61; asso. prof. physics U. Ill., Urbana, 1961-63, prof., 1963-79, prof. emeritus, 1979—; prof. physics Va. Commonwealth U., Richmond, 1979-85, prof. emeritus, 1985—, chmn. dept. physics, 1979-82. Program dir. NSF, 1975-76; field sec. Friends Com. on Nat. Legis., 1988-90. Contbr. articles to profl. jours.; patentee in field. Sch. dir., Monroeville, Pa., 1959-61; trustee, mem. fin. com. Southeastern Univs. Research Assn., 1980-85; Democratic nominee for U.S. Congress, 1966; del. to Dem. Nat. Conv., 1968, 72, 2000; sec. Urbana Free Libr. Found., 1998-2002. Fellow Am. Phys. Soc.; mem. Fedn. Am. Scientists (chmn. 1968). Home: 308 E Colorado Ave Urbana IL 61801-5918 E-mail: csatter@uiuc.edu.

SATTERTHWAITE, GEORGE, II, security firm executive; b. San Jose, Costa Rica, Apr. 18, 1935; s. Livingston Lord andAdelaide (Bristol) S.; m. Helen Marie McCann, June 28, 1958 (div. July 1982); children: Patricia Ann, Livingston Lord, Frank Lord; m. Deanna Marie Kelliher, Apr. 30, 1983; 1 child, Kelley Elizabeth. BA in Internat. Rels., U. Pa., 1957; MA in History, Johns Hopkins U., 1965. Commd. 2d lt. U.S. Army, 1957, advanced through grades to col., 1979, retired, 1987; chief indsl. security Planning Rsch. Corp., McLean, Va., 1987-89; corp. dir. security PRC Inc., McLean, Va., 1989-96; cons., 1996-98; cons., contracts officer SSI Inc., McLean, Va., 1998—2000, photography and security cons., 2000—. Mem. County Bd. Elections, Fort Washington, 2003—; mem. admissions coun. U. Pa., 2002—. Mem.: Am. Soc. Indsl. Security. Republican. Roman Catholic. Avocations: photography, music, volks marching, travel. Home and Office: 513 Holly Rd Fort Washington MD 20744-6606 Personal E-mail: GS2nd@aol.com.

SATTERTHWAITE, HELEN FOSTER, retired state legislator; b. Blawnox, Pa., July 8, 1928; d. Samuel J. and Lillian (Schreiber) Foster; m. Cameron B. Satterthwaite, Dec. 23, 1950 (div. July 1979); children: Mark Cameron, Tod Foster, Tracy Lynn, Keith Alan, Craig Evan (dec.). BS in Chemistry, Duquesne U., 1949. Biol. technician USDA, 1967-68; lab. technician U. Ill. Coll. Agr., 1968-70; rsch. asst. Iowa State U. Coll. Agr., 1971, Gulf R & D, Harmarville, Pa., 1950; rsch. chemist E.I. duPont de Nemours & Co., Wilmington, Del., 1951-53; technician Nat. Sci. Lab., U. Ill. Coll. Vet. Medicine, 1971-74; rep. Ill. Ho. of Reps., Springfield, 1974-92, majority leader, 1991-92, mem. sch. fin. task force, 1990-92, chmn. com. on higher edn., 1983-91, vice chmn. elem. and secondary edn., 1983-91; ret., 1993. Mem. Commn. on Mental Health and Devel. Disabilities, 1975-85, mem. exec. com., 1977-85, vice chmn., 1979-85; mem. Commn. to Visit and Examine State Instns., 1977-85; mem. Task Force on Global Climate Change, 1991-96; treas. LWV, 1995-98, sec., 1998-2001; treas. Bus. and Profl. Women's Club, 1993-94, sec., 1994-95; bd. dirs. East Ctrl. Ill. Health Sys. Agy., 1977-79, Champaign County Mental Health Ctr., 1993-2002, Univ. YWCA, U. Ill., 1987—, Girls Inc., 1992-96; bd. dirs. Champaign County United Way, 1970-74, mem. budget com., 1973-74, mem. joint rev. com. on funding Champaign County mental health programs, 1973; co-chmn. task force on mental retardation Champaign County Mental Health Bd., 1973; mem. Ill. Devel. Disability Advocacy Authority, 1977-85, vice chmn., 1979-80; chmn. Ill. House Dem. Study Group, 1979-81; mem. Edn. Commn. on States, 1985-92, Nat. Conf. State Legis. Commn. on Labor and Edn., 1985-92; bd. govs. U. YMCA, 1995-2003. Recipient Freshman Legislator of Yr. award Ill. Edn. Assn., 1975, commndation Ill. State's Attys. Assn., 1975, Best Legislator award Ind. Voters Ill., 1976, 78, 80, 82, 84, 86, 88, 90, cert. of honor Assn. Student Govts., 1977, Disting. Svc. cert. AMVETS, 1977, Environ. Legislator of Yr. award Ill. Environ. Coun., 1977, 79, 81, 83, Meritorious Svc. award Champaign County Coun. on Alcoholism, 1978, Ill. C.C. Trustees ASsn., 1986, Perfect Voting Record award Ill. Credit Union League, 1979, Ill. Wildlife Fedn., 1979, cert., of spl. recognition Ill. Women's Polit. Caucus, 1979, 80, Pub. Svc. award Izaak Walton League, 1980, Friend of Edn. award Ill. Bd. Edn., 1985, cert. of appreciation Champaign County Urban League, 1987, Resolution of Honor, Ill. Libr. Assn., 1987, 100 Percent award Ill. Coun. Sr. Citizens Orgns., 1989, Dare To Be Great award Ill. Women Adminstrs., 1989; named Person of Yr., Champaign County Mental Health Assn., 1981, Pub. Citizen of Yr., Illino Dist. and Ill. chpt. NASW, 1981, Legislator of Yr., Ill. Assn. Sch. Social Workers, 1989. Mem. Ill. Conf. Women Legislators (co-convenor 1981-83), Nat. Order Women Legislators (bd. dirs.

region IV 1982, treas. 1983-84), State Univs. Annuitants Assn. (exec. com. U. Ill. Urbana Champaign chpt. 2003—), Champaign County League Women Voters, Delta Kappa Gamma. Mem. Soc. Of Friends.

SATTERWHITE, MARC, music educator, composer; b. Abilene, Tex., Mar. 11, 1954; s. E.C. and Charlou Thomas Satterwhite; m. Rebecca Jemian, May 22, 1988. MusB, Mich. State U., 1976; MusM, Ind. U., 1984, Mus D, 1991. Asst. prin. double bass Mexico City Philharm. Orch., 1980—82; asst. prof. music Western Mich. U., Kalamazoo, 1985—87, Lamar U., Beaumont, Tex., 1990—94; asst./assoc. prof. music U. Louisville, 1994—. Composer: (symphony) Goyescas Negras: Symphony no 1 in Three Movements, Black Fugatos: Symphony no. 2 in Two Movements, (work for symphonic wind ensemble) Llanto por Cristina Gómez. Mem., treas. Bloomington Com. for Democracy in L.Am., 1987—90; composition chair Ky. Music Teachers Assn., 1998—2000; mem., moderator Ars Femina, Louisville, 1984—2000. Mem.: ASCAP, Am. Composers Forum, Am. Music Ctr., Soc. of Composers, Inc., Phi Eta Sigma, Phi Kappa Phi, Pi Kappa Lambda, Phi Mu Alpha Sinfonia. Avocations: travel, ethnic cooking, Spanish language and literature.

SATTERWHITE, ROBERT LEE, library director; b. Oil city, Pa., July 16, 1941; s. Robert Linwood and Mettie Elizabeth S.; m. Mary Willis Woodruff, Aug. 12, 1972; childre; Benjamin, Elizabeth. BA in English, Hiram Coll., 1965; MA in English, U. Mich., 1966; MLS, U. Pitts., 1973. Instr. English W.Va. Inst. Tech., Montgomery, 1966-71; supr. ref. dept. Northwest Regional Libr. System, Panama City, Fla., 1973-77; regional ref. libr. Florence (S.C.) County Libr., 1977-80, dir. Vienna (W.Va.) Pub. Libr., 1980 89, Hopkinsville (Ky.) - Christian County Pub. Libr., 1989—. Recipient Pub. Svc. award Hopkinsville Human Rels. Commn., 1998. Mem. Ky. Libr. Assn.(treas. pub. libr. sect. 1994-95, sec. pub. libr. sect. 1995-96, mem. legis. com. 1996-97), Hopkinsville Civitan Club (sec. 1998-99). Avocations: creative writing, reading, guitar. Office: Hopkinsville-Christian County Pub Libr 1101 Bethel St Hopkinsville KY 42240-2051

SATTIN, ALBERT, psychiatry and neuropharmacology educator; b. Cleve., Oct. 5, 1931; s. Sam and Edith Sattin; m. Renee Schnider, Dec. 16, 1962; children: Rebecca Lee, Michael M. BS, Western Res. U., 1953, MD, 1957. Diplomate Am. Bd. Psychiatry and Neurology. Intern Washington U., St. Louis, 1957-58; resident in psychiatry Case-Western Res. U., Cleve., 1958-62; fellow dept. biochemistry U. London., 1965-66; instr., sr. instr. Case-Western Res. U. Sch. Medicine, 1965-70, asst. prof. psychiatry and pharmacology, 1970-77; assoc. prof. psychiatry Ind. U. Sch. Medicine, Indpls., 1977-84; assoc. prof. psychiatry and neurobiology Ind. U. Grad. Sch., 1984-91; assoc. prof. psychiatry and biobehavioal scis. UCLA, 1991—. Chief Antidepressant Neuropharmacology Lab, West L.A. and Sepulved VA Med. Ctrs., 1991—; mem. Brain Rsch. Inst., UCLA, 1997—. Contbr. articles to profl. jours. Grantee NIMH, NSF, VA. Fellow Am. Psychiat. Assn. (life, disting. fellow); mem. Soc. for Neurosci. Soc. Biol. Psychiatry, Internat. Soc. Neurochemistry. Office: West LA VA Med Ctr PO Box 84122 11301 Wilshire Blvd Los Angeles CA 90073-1003

SATTLER, BRUCE WEIMER, lawyer; b. South Gate, Calif., July 30, 1944; s. LeRoy Edward and Mary Beth (Weimer) S.; m. Earle Martha Ross, July 22, 1972. BA, Stanford U., 1966, JD, 1969. Bar: Colo. 1969, U.S. Dist. Ct. Colo. 1969, U.S. Dist. Ct. Mont. 1982, U.S. Dist. Ct. (no. dist.) Tex. 1989, U.S. Ct. Appeals (10th cir.) 1969, U.S. Ct. Appeals (9th cir.) 1984. Assoc. Holland & Hart, Denver, 1969-75, ptnr., 1975-87; supervising trial atty. Equal Employment Opportunity Commn., Denver, 1973; ptnr. Morris, Lower & Sattler, Denver, 1987-90, Faegre & Benson, Denver, 1990—. Bd. dirs. ACLU of Colo., Denver, 1975-80, 88-94, Colo. Legal Svcs., Legal Aid Soc. of Metro Denver, 1976—, Colo. Lawyers Com., Denver, 1990-94, Children's Legal Clinic, Denver, 1989-91, Colo. Women's Employment and Edn., Denver, 1986-89. Fellow Am. Coll. Trial Lawyers, Coll. Labor and Employment Lawyers; mem. ABA, Denver Bar Assn., Colo. Bar Assn. Office: Faegre & Benson 3200 Wells Fargo Ctr 1700 Lincoln St Denver CO 80203 E-mail: bsattler@faegre.com.

SATTLER, ROLF, retired plant morphologist, educator; b. Göppingen, Germany, Mar. 8, 1936; arrived in Can., 1962; s. Otto and Emma Sattler; m. Liv Hamann, May 1, 1963 (div. 1985). PhD, U. Munich, 1961; DSc (hon.), Colombo U. Asst. prof. McGill U., Montreal, Que., Can., 1964-69, assoc. prof., 1969-77, prof., 1977-97, emeritus prof., 1997—. Author: Organogenesis of Flowers, 1973 (Lawson medal 1974), Biophilosophy, 1986; editor: Theoretical Plant Morphology, 1978, Axioms and Principles of Plant Construction, 1981; contbr. articles to profl. jours. NATO fellow, 1962-64. Fellow Royal Soc. Can., Linnean Soc. London; mem. Can. Bot. Assn., Sci. and Med. Network.

SATULOFF, BARTH, accounting executive, dispute resolution professional, investment strategist, publisher; b. Buffalo, Dec. 13, 1945; s. Bernard and Annette (Lurie) S.; m. Gail Lois Seid Jaffe, Aug. 23, 1992. BBA in Acctg., U. Miami, 1967, MBA, 1969. CPA, Fla., N.Y., Ill., La.; registered securities arbitrator, NYSE, AMEX, NASD; cert. state ct. arbitrator, Fla.; Spl. Master, Fla. pvt. property and land use cases; cert. comml. arbitrator Am. Arbitration Assn.; appt. spl. arbitrator Prudential Ins. remediation cases, Fla. Staff acct. Price Waterhouse, Miami, Fla., 1969-71; tax specialist Laventhol & Horwath, Miami, 1973-74; mng. dir. Barth Satuloff, CPA, Miami, 1974-99; chief investment officer, pres., chmn. bd. dirs. Caddis & Co., Inc., Reno, 1998—. Pres., bd. dirs. Satuloff Bros., Inc., Buffalo, 1974-94, Miami, 1994-97. Satuloff Bros. Nev., Inc., Reno, 1997—; CEO, dir. Papillon Press, Inc., Miami, 1998—. Mem. Ctr. for the Arts, Vero Beach, Fla., Met. Mus. Art, N.Y.C.; mem. Fla. state com. Nat. Mus. Women in the Arts, Washington. With Fla. N.G., 1970—76. Mem.: AICPA (mem. small bus. taxation com. of tax divsn. 1993—96, mem. fed. tax forms com. of tax divsn. 1997—99), Am. Arbitration Assn. (nat. panel arbitrators and mediators), Fla. Inst. CPA, Idaho Rivers United, Nature Conservancy, Audubon Soc., Miami Country Day Sch. Alumni Assn. (sec. 1987—93, bd. dirs. 1987—, treas. 1994—), Ducks Unltd., Rocky Mountain Elk Found. (life; founder Indian River chpt., Fla. state chmn.), Nat. Wild Turkey Fedn., Trout Unltd. (life), Safari Club Internat., Antique Automobile Club Am., Cadillac-LaSalle Club, Am. Rivers. Avocations: hunting, fishing, photography, antique automobiles. Home and Office: 23 Seagull Pl Vero Beach FL 32960

SATZ, JEFFREY S. telecommunications industry executive, consultant; b. Jackson Heights, NY, Feb. 10, 1973; s. Robert L. and Linda J. Satz; m. Elizabeth Stacy Panzer, Dec. 27, 1997; children: Zachary C., Madeline R. BS/ME, Rensselaer Poly. Inst., 1995. Engr. Nortel Networks, Richardson, Tex., 1995—98, sr. engr., 1998—2000, mgr., 2000—. Recognition from Am. Registry of Outstanding Profls. Mem.: IEEE, NY Acad. Scis., Mensa. Avocations: home repair, reading, walking. Home: 4456 Big Sky Dr Plano TX 75024

SATZ, LOUIS K. publishing executive; b. Chgo., Apr. 28, 1927; s. Harry Addison and Faye (Pollen) S.; m. Janet Maas, Jan. 2, 1952 children: Jay, Jonathan. BS in Mktg, U. Ill., 1949. Circulation dir. Pubs. Devel. Corp., Chgo., 1953, Guns mag., Jr. Arts and Activities, 1961; wholesaler sales mgr., then v.p., dir. sales Bantam Books, Inc., N.Y.C., 1962-80, sr. v.p., dir. diversified markets, 1980-84; pub. Passport Books, Lincolnwood, Ill., 1985-88; pres. Louis K. Satz Assocs., Pub. Cons., N.Y.C., 1988-91; ptnr. Scott/Satz Group, Pub. Cons., Walnut Creek, Calif., 1991—. Guest lectr. Sarah Lawrence Coll.Pub. Sch., Pace U.; faculty Hofstra U., Denver Pub. Inst.; cons. World Book Encyclopedia, 1995—; bd. dirs. N.Y. is Book Country, Brandeis U. Pub. Scholarship Fund, Oscar Dystel Fellowship NYU. Served with AUS, World War II, ETO. Mem. Am. Assn. Pubs. (chmn. small books mktg. div. 1975) Office: Scott Satz Group 558 Monarch Ridge Dr Walnut Creek CA 94597 Office Phone: 925-934-2919. E-mail: louksatz@aol.com.

SAUBERT, WALTER E. (WALLY SAUBERT), trucking and transportation company executive; b. Seattle; m. Alicejo Saubert. BS in Econs., U. Wash. Joined Am. Red Ball Internat., 1972, various mgmt. and exec.-level positions, v.p., gen. mgr., 1983; co-founder Red Ball Corp., 1985, CEO, 1989; chmn., CEO Atlas World Group, 1996—. With USMC, 1965-68, Vietnam.

SAUCEDA, AUGUSTINA JO, pre-school educator; b. Denver, Colo., Nov. 21, 1970; d. Edward Cardenas and Gloria Marta Estrada; m. Ritchie Martin Sauceda, Apr. 7, 1970; children: Ritchie Martin Jr., Chloe Sophia-Maria. Childcare provider Augustina's Childcare, Thornton, Colo., 1997—99; pre-school tchr. Upper Room Christian Acad., Fed. Heights, Colo., 1998—99, Step By Step Child Devel. Ctr., Thornton, Colo., 1999—2001, Augustina's Childcare-Preschool, Henderson, Colo., 2001—. Newsletter writer USDA Forest Svc., So. Platte Dist., Lakewood, Colo., 1989—90, Denver's Most Wanted Dance Co., Brighton, Colo., 2003—04. Author: (book) Miracles of a Family, 2001; co-author: (book series) Lovito, 2003; author: (poetry collection) Inspired Thoughts, 1997. Youth group leader Upper Room Christian Ctr., Fed. Heights, 1999—2000; nursery ministry Harvest Worship Ctr., Fed. Heights, 1999—. Recipient Leadership Award, Student to Work Action Program/Thornton, Colo., 1988. Mem.: Harvest Worship Ctr., Colo. Wildlife Fed. (hon.). Republican. Christian. Achievements include advising local childcare providers to begin their own in-home childcare business; offering profl. resume preparation. Home and Office: Augustina's Childcare-Preschool 11770 East 114th Place Henderson CO 80640

SAUCIER, BONNIE L. dean, pediatrics nurse; b. Alton, Ill., Oct. 12, 1945; d. Robert E. and Laura L. (Rice) Powers; children: Michelle Marie, Kent Lawrence. Diploma, St. Johns Hosp. Sch. Nursing, Springfield, Ill., 1966; BA, Stephens Coll., 1976; MEd, U. Mo., 1977; MSN, U. Mo., Kansas City, 1983; PhD in nursing, Tex. Womans U., 1986. RN, Calif., Tex. Pedriatric staff nurse St. Johns Hosp., St Louis, 1966-69; asst. head nurse pedriatrics North Kansas City (Mo.) Meml. Hosp., 1969-71; instr. nursing Trenton (Mo.) Jr. Coll., 1974-81; asst. prof. Mo. Western State Coll., St. Joseph, Mo., 1981-84; Inst. Cook County Coll., Gainesville, Tex., 1984-85; dir. health scis. Midwestern State U., Wichita Falls, Tex., 1986-92; prof., chair dept. nursing Calif. State U., Bakersfield, 1992—. Adj. inst. U. Tex., Arlington, 1985-86; bd. dirs. ARC. Wichita Falls, 1988-92; adv. bd., cons. Vernon (Tex.) Regional Jr. Coll., 1987-92, trustee Red River Hosp. Wichita Falls, 1989 92. Contbr. articles to profl. jours. Adv. bd. Care Team Healtha Care Svcs. Wichita Falls, 1991-92; bd. dirs. March of Dimes, 1989, Nat. Kidney Found., 1989-90; mem. Midwestern Div. Tex. Hosp., 1987-92; Tex. Orgn. of Baccalaureate Nursing Programs, 1989-92, Tex. Outstanding Rural Scholars Adv., 1989-92, Tex. Nurses Edn. Adv., 1989-90. Profl. Nursing Shortage grant, Office of Gov., 1991, Profl. Nursing Retention grantee Coordinating Bd., 1991; named to Women's Hall of Fame, Mayors Commn., 1991. Mem. Tex. Nurses Assn. (coun. edn. 1991-92), Tex. Nurses Assn. #11 (pres. 1990-91, bd. dirs. 1991-92), Calif. Nurses Assn. (state adv. com. for nursing manpower study 1992), Calif. Assn. Colls. of Nursing (health care adv. com., MSA program 1992-93, acad. senator), Tex. League for Nursing (bd. dirs. 1985-92), So. Coun. on Collegiate Edn., Sigma Theta Tau. Republican. Roman Catholic. Avocations: walking, travel, racquetball, reading. Office: Calif State U 9001 Stockdale Hwy Bakersfield CA 93311-1022

SAUCIER, GENE DUANE, retired state legislator; b. Dallas, Sept. 25, 1931; s. Albert L. and Myrtle Irene (West) S.; m. Marilyn Emmy Cox, Dec. 27, 1952 (div. Sept. 1980); children: Alan, Steve, Renee; m. Giulia Riga LaCagnina, Nov. 28, 1981. BS in Agronomy Soils, Miss. State U., 1953; MS in Counseling, U. So. Miss., 1970, EdD in Adult Edn., 1978. Builder, developer Saucier Co., Hattiesburg, Miss., 1957-70; dir. admissions U. So. Miss., Hattiesburg, 1970-74, dean spl. acad. svcs., 1974-84, asst. v.p. bus. and fin., 1984-93; mem. Miss. Ho. of Reps., Jackson, 1993-99; ret., 1999. Mem. Fed. Land Coun., 1997—2003; scoutmaster Boy Scouts Am., 1960—70, chmn. camping and activities Pine Burr area, 1970; bd. dirs., founder Hub Coun., 2000; bd. dirs. Miss. Wild Turkey Fedn., Pine Burr chpt., 2000. 1st lt. pilot USAF, 1953—56. Named Forest County Tree Farmer of Yr., 1996, Miss. Tree Farmer Yr., 1996; recipient Forestry award Miss. Wildlife Fedn., 1997, Legislator of Yr. Coastal Conservation Assn., 1997. Mem. So. Assn. Collegiate Registrars and Admissions Officers (bd. dirs. 1981, local arrangements chmn. 1981, v.p. admissions and fin. aid 1982-83, pres. 1985-86), Miss. Assn. Collegiate Registrars and Admissions Officers, Miss. Forestry Assn. (exec. bd. dirs. 1992-94, bd. dirs. 1992-94), Soc. Am. Foresters (cert. rev. bd. 2003), Miss. Nature Conservancy, Forrest/Lamar Forestry Assn. (pres. 1989-92), Audobon (v.p. Forest County chpt. 2004), Sigma Chi, ODK, Phi Delta Kappa, Omicron Delta Kappa.

SAUCIER, GUYLAINE, corporate director; b. Noranda, Que., Can., June 10, 1946; d. Gérard and Yvette (Thiffault) S. Chartered acct., École Hautes Etudes Commls., Montreal, Can., 1971. Formerly chair Joint Com. on Corp. Governance. Bd. dirs. Petro-Can., Axa Assurances Inc., Bank Montreal, Nortel Networks Corp., Tembec Inc., Altran Techs.; mem. Commn. Inquiry Unemployment Ins. Fellow Inst. Chartered Accts., Inst. Corp. Dirs.; mem. Order Can. Avocation: tennis. Office Phone: 514-397-5494. E-mail: gusauci@gsaucier.com.

SAUCIER LUNDY, KAREN, nursing educator; b. Hattiesburg, Miss., Oct. 7, 1954; d. William Marshall and Ruth (Landers) S.; m. Joel Christopher Lundy, Dec. 27, 1986; 1 child, Marshall Parker. BSN, U. So. Miss., 1975; MS in Cmty. Health Nursing, U. Colo. Health Scis. Ctr., 1978; MA in Sociology, PhD in Sociology, U. Colo., 1987. RN. Clin. nurse U. Miss. Med. Ctr., Jackson, 1976-77; clin. specialist HEW, USPHS, Atlanta, 1978-80; clin. instr. U. Miss. Med. Ctr. and Med. Sch., 1980-81; asst. prof. Loretto Heights Coll., Denver, 1983-85; instr. U. Colo., Boulder, 1982-85; prof., dean sch. nursing Delta State U., Cleveland, Miss., 1985-90; assoc. prof. U. So. Miss. Coll. Nursing, Hattiesburg, 1990—2001, prof., 2001—. Mem. Miss. Bd. Nursing, 1990-94. Author: Community Health, 1987, nursing text, 1991, Family and Community Health Nursing, 1991 (AJN Book of the Year 1991), Community Health Nursing, 2001 (AJN Book of the Yr. 2001). Vol. Spl. Olympics, Miss., Fla., 1979-80; mem. ARC, 1978—; cons. Sierra Club, Denver, 1977-78, Headstart, Tampa, Fla., 1978-79; bd. dirs. March of Dimes, Jackson, 1979-81, Am. Cancer Soc., 1985—. Am. Coll. Test Merit scholar 1972-75; USPHS fellow, 1977; named Educator Nurse of Year Miss. Nurses' Assn., 1989. Fellow Am. Acad. Nursing; mem. ANA, APHA, Assn. Cmty. Health Nurse Educators, Am. Sociol. Assn., So. Sociol. Assn., Am. Assn. Colls. Nursing (accreditation site evaluator 2000—), Nat. League Nursing (accreditation site visitor 1988—), Kappa Delta. Democrat. Avocation: photography. Home: 89 James Switzer Rd Purvis MS 39475-3036 Office: U So Miss Coll Nursing 118 College Dr #5095 Hattiesburg MS 39406-0001 Fax: 601-794-9369. E-mail: karen.lundy@usm.edu., kslundy@msn.com.

SAUDEK, CHRISTOPHER D. medical educator; b. Bronxville, N.Y., Oct. 8, 1941; s. Robert and Elizabeth (Koch) S.; m. Susan Saudek; children: Mark S., Deborah M., Christina A., Anthony C. AB, Harvard U., 1963; MD, Cornell U., 1967. Resident in medicine Presbyn. St. Luke's Hosp., Chgo., 1967-69, Boston City Hosp., 1969-70; fellow in metabolism Thorndike Lab, Harvard U., Cambridge, Mass., 1970-72; asst prof. Cornell U., Ithaca, N.Y., 1973-80; assoc. prof. Johns Hopkins U., Balt., 1981-91, prof., 1991—; former pres. American Diabetes Assoc. Author Johns Hopkins Guide to Diabetes, 1997; co-author (with Sandra Woodruff) The Complete Diabetes Prevention Plan, 2004. Named Outstanding Clinician in Diabetes, Am. Diabetes Assn., 1991. Office: Johns Hopkins U Med Sch Osler 576 600 N Wolfe St Baltimore MD 21287-0005*

SAUDER, MAYNARD, manufacturing executive; b. Feb. 15, 1932; CEO Sauder Woodworking, Archibald, Ohio.

SAUDER, RANDY JAMES, state legislator, lawyer; b. Dubois, Pa., June 6, 1954; s. Harvey Louis and Dorothy Lee S.; children: Michael Louis, Angela Lynn. BA in Theology, Andrews U., 1979; JD, Detroit Coll. of Law, 1987. Bar: Ga. 1989, U.S. Dist. Ct. Ga. 1989, U.S. Ct. Appeals, 1989. Dean of staff New Friends Youth Camp, Ontario, Canada, 1977; minister Seventh Day Adventist Ch., Canada, 1979-87; law clk. Vandeveer, Garzia, Tomkin, Detroit, 1985-86; assoc. Cochran, Camp & Snipes, Smyrna, Ga., 1987-94; pres. Am. Investment Corp., Atlanta, 1987—; mem. Ga. Ho. of Reps., Smyrna, 1995—; pres. Atlanta Spinal Therapeutic Systems, Smyrna, Ga., 1993. Editor Marietta (Ga.) Rotary Metroliner, 1990-92. Vice chmn. Cascade Adventist Elem. Sch. Bd., Atlanta, 1987-91; vol. Am. Cancer Soc., Cobb County, Ga., 1990, 91; trustee, vice chmn. Smyrna Hosp. Found., 1992, chmn., 1993. Named Ga. 2000 statesman of Yr. Smyrna Moose Lodge. Mem. ABA, Ga. Bar Assn. (real estate, corp. banking sects.), Cobb County Bar Assn., Cobb C. of C., Smyrna C. of C., Marietta Metro Rotary Club (sec. 1992-93, Disting. Svc. award 1990-91). Avocations: golf, tennis, computers. Office: 248 Roswell St NE Marietta GA 30060-2064

SAUER, BRAD T. manufacturing executive, mechanical engineer; BS in Mech. Engring., U. Minn.; MBA, St. Thomas U. Joined 3M Co., 1981, gen. mgr., med. solutions bus., Imation Corp., 1997—99, new bus. devel. dir., commercial graphics divsn., 1999, mng. dir., 3M Korea Ltd., 1999—2001, exec. dir., Six Sigma, 2001—02, exec. v.p., electro and comm. bus., 2002—. Office: 3M Co 3M Ctr Saint Paul MN 55144

SAUER, BRIAN, molecular geneticist, researcher; b. Columbus, Wis., Sept. 18, 1949; s. Alan and V.E. Sauer. BS, U. Wis., 1972; PhD, U. Calif., Berkeley, 1979. Staff scientist Frederick (Md.) Cancer Rsch. Facility, 1982—84; prin. investigator DuPont Co., Wilmington, Del., 1984—90; sr. rsch. scientist DuPont-Merck Co., Wilmington, 1991—93; expert NIH, Bethesda, Md., 1993—96, sr. staff fellow NIDDK, 1996—98; mem./head devel. biology, dir. Transgenic Core Facility Okla. Med. Rsch. Found., Oklahoma City, 1998 2001; dir. transgenic tech. Stowers Inst. for Med. Rsch., Kansas City, Mo., 2001—. Vis. asst prof. Hood Coll., Frederick, 1983; adj. prof. cell biology U. Okla., 2000—01; prof. biochemistry U. Kans. Med. Ctr., 2002—; mem. faculty Okla. Ctr. for Neurosci., 2000—01. Mem. editl. bd. Analytical Biochemistry, 1994—, Nucleic Acids Rsch., 2001—; patentee in field. Damon Runyon-Walter Winchell Cancer Fund postdoctoral fellow Stanford U., 1979. Mem.: AAAS, Genetics Soc. Am., Am. Soc. for Microbiology, Sierra Club. Office: Stowers Inst 1000 E 50th St Kansas City MO 64110 Office Phone: 816-926-4432.

SAUER, DAVID ANDREW, librarian, technical writer; b. Urbana, Ill., Feb. 25, 1948; s. Elmer Louis and Frances (Hill) S. BA, Northwestern U., 1970; MS, Simmons Coll., 1975. Reference libr. Boston U., 1976-78, bibliographer, 1978-84, sci. bibliographer, 1984-88, founder and head libr. Stone Sci. Libr., 1988-94; v.p. info. svcs. CyberHelp, Inc., 1995-98; sr. tech. editor Qualcomm, Inc., 1997-2000, 2003—; tech. pubs. supr. QCP Inc., 2000—01, staff tech. writer/libr., 2001—02; librarian San Diego Maritime Mus., 2002—03. Co-author of 12 books including: Access for Windows 95: The Visual Learning Guide, 1995, Windows NT 4.0 Visual Desk Reference, 1997, Discover Netscape Communicator, 1997. Mem. S.W. Corridor Project, Boston, 1977-87, Forest Hills Neighborhood Improvement Assn., Boston, 1977-90, Forest Hills/Woodbourne Neighorhood Group, 1991-94. Mem. ALA, IEEE, Spl. Librs. Assn., Soc. Tech. Comm., Hillside Colony Homeowners Assn. Democrat. Home: 2340 29th St San Diego CA 92104

SAUER, ELISSA SWISHER, nursing educator; b. Williamsport, Pa., Jan. 9, 1935; d. Oliver S. and Emily Louisa (Gehron) Swisher; m. Raymond James Sauer, Nov. 27, 1964. Diploma, Reading (Pa.) Hosp. Sch. Nursing, 1957; BS, Albright Coll., Reading, 1958; MSN, U. Pa., 1964. Instr. Reading Hosp. Sch. Nursing, 1957—60, 1964—66, 1969—70, Abington Meml. Hosp. Sch. Nursing, 1960—63; nurse Cmty. Health and Civic Assn., Ardmore, Pa., 1966-67; pub. health coord. Albert Einstein Med. Ctr., 1967-68; pvt. duty nurse, 1968-73; clin. faculty Schuylkill County AVTS, 1973-74; prof. nursing Reading Area C.C., 1975-80; oncology nurse adminstr.-educator Comprehensive Cmty. Cancer Ctr., Allentown, Pa., 1981-85; exec. dir. Holy Family Home Health Care, Orwigsburg, Pa., 1985-89; dir. nursing programs, asst. dean health svcs. Reading Area C.C., 1989-2000, asst. dean emerita, 2001—. Cons. nursing edn. and continuing edn.; evaluator for nat. nurse aide cert. assessment program, 2000—. Author: Procedure Manual to accompany Fundamentals of Nursing: Human Health and Function, 3d edit., 2003. Mem.: Sigma Theta Tau. Home: 1114 Pepper Ridge Dr Reading PA 19606-3803 E-mail: esauer@ptd.net.

SAUER, GORDON CHENOWETH, retired dermatologist, educator; b. Rutland, Ill., Aug. 14, 1921; s. Fred William and Gweneth (Chenoweth) S.; m. Mary Louise Steinhilber, Dec. 28, 1944; children: Elisabeth Ruth, Gordon Chenoweth, Margaret Louise, Amy Kieffer.; m. Marion Green, Oct. 23, 1982. Student, Northwestern U., 1939-42; BS, U. Ill., 1943, MD, 1945. Diplomate Am. Bd. Dermatology and Syphilology. Intern Cook County Hosp., Chgo., 1945-46; resident dermatology and syphilology N.Y.U.-Bellevue Med. Center, 1948-51; dermatologist Thompson-Brumm-Knepper Clinic, St. Joseph, Mo., 1951-54; pvt. practice Kansas City, Mo., 1954—; mem. staff St. Luke's, Research, Kansas City Gen. hosps.; assoc. instr. U. Kans., 1951-56, vice-chmn. sect. dermatology, 1956-58, assoc. clin. prof., 1960-64, clin. prof., 1964-93; clin. prof. emeritus, 1993—; head sect. dermatology U. Kans., 1958-70. Clin. assoc., acting head dermatology sect. U. Mo., 1955-59, cons. dermatology, 1959-67, clin. prof., 1967—; cons. Munson Army Hosp., Ft. Leavenworth, Kans., 1959-68; dermatology panel, drug efficacy panel Nat. Acad. Sci.-FDA, 1967-69. Author: Manual of Skin Diseases, 1959, 7th edit., 1995, Teen Skin, 1965, John Gould Bird Print Reproductions, 1977, John Gould's Prospectuses and Lists of Subscribers to His Work on Natural History: With an 1866 Facsimile, 1980, John Gould The Bird Man, 1982, John Gould The Bird Man: Associates and Subscribers, 1995, John Gould The Bird Man: Bibliography 2, 1996, John Gould The Bird Man: Correspondence, Vol. 1 through 1838, 1998, vol. 2 through 1841, 1998, vol. 3, 1842-45, 1999; editor Kansas City Med. Bull., 1967-69; contbr. articles to profl. jours. Bd. dirs. Kansas City Area coun. Camp Fire Girls Am., 1956-59, Kansas City Lyric Theatre, 1969-74, Kansas City Chamber Choir, 1969-74, Chouteau Soc., 1985-97, U. Mo.-Kansas City Friends of Libr., 1988-92; bd. dirs. Mo. br. The Nature Conservancy, 1984-91. Sr. asst. surgeon USPHS, 1946-48. Named Dermatology Found. Practitioner of Yr., 1992; recipient Soc. for History of Natural History Founders' award, London, 2001. Fellow Am. Acad. Dermatology and Syphilology (dir. 1975-79, v.p. 1980); mem. Mo., Jackson County med. socs., Mo. Dermatol. Soc. (pres. 1974-75), Dermatology Found. (trustee 1978-83), Am. Ornithol. Union, Wilson Ornithol. Soc., Royal Australasian Ornithologists Union, Soc. Bibliography Natural History, Am. Dermatol. Assn., Alpha Delta Phi, Nu Sigma Nu. Presbyterian. Office: 422 E 55th St Kansas City MO 64110-2454

SAUER, HAROLD JOHN, physician, educator; b. Detroit, Dec. 1, 1953; s. Peter and Hildegard (Muehlmann) S.; m. Kathleen Ann Iorio, Sept. 4, 1982; children: Angela Karin Ferrante, Peter Rolf Jan Muehlmann, Josef Andrew John Iorio. BS, U. Mich., 1975; MD, Wayne State U., 1979. Diplomate Am. Bd. Ob-Gyn. Resident in ob-gyn William Beaumont Hosp., Royal Oak, Mich., 1979-83, fellow in reproductive endocrinology and infertility, 1983-85; asst. prof. dept. ob-gyn and reproductive biology Mich. State U., East Lansing, 1985-91, assoc. prof. ob.-gyn, 1991—, chmn. group practice clinicians coun., 1995—, interim chmn., 1996-98, 2002—, dept. vice chair, 1996—. Mem. staff St. Lawrence Hosp., Lansing, Mich., 1985—98, Sparrow Hosp., Lansing, 1985—; cons. Mich. Dept. Social Svcs., Lansing, 1985—; mem. Mich. Bd. Medicine, 1992—2000, chmn., 1994—97, mem., 2003—; bd. dirs. Fedn. State Med. Bds.; examer Am. Bd. Ob-gyn., 1998—; mem. Bd. of Medicine, 2003—. Fellow Am. Coll. Ob.-Gyn. (sec. Mich. sect. 1990-96, treas. 1996-99, vice-chmn. 1999-2002, chmn. 2002—); mem. AMA, Ingham County Med. Soc., Lansing Ob-Gyn. Soc., Am. Soc. Reproductive Medicine, Am. Assn. Gynecol. Laparoscopists, Wayne State U. Med. Alumni Assn., Mich. Soc. Reproductive Endocrinology (sec.-treas. 1991-93). Roman Catholic. Avocations: classical piano, microcomputers, skiing. Home: 2601 Creekstone Trl Okemos MI 48864-2455 Office: Mich State U Dept Ob-Gyn Reproductive Biology 1200 E Michigan Ave Ste 730 Lansing MI 48912-1895 E-mail: sauerh@msu.edu.

SAUER, HARRY JOHN, JR., mechanical engineer, educator, academic administrator; b. St. Joseph, Mo., Jan. 27, 1935; s. Harry John and Marie Margaret (Witt) S.; m. Patricia Ann Zbierski, June 9, 1956; children: Harry John, Elizabeth Ann, Carl Andrew, Robert Mark, Katherine Anne, Deborah Elaine, Victoria Lynn, Valerie Joan, Joseph Gerard. BS, U. Mo., Rolla, 1956, MS, 1958; PhD, Kans. State U., 1963. Instr. mech. engring. Kans. State U., Manhattan, 1960-62; sr. engr., cons. Midwest Rsch. Inst., Kansas City, Mo., 1963-70; mem. faculty dept. mech. and aerospace engring. U. Mo., Rolla, 1957—, prof., 1966—, assoc. chmn., 1980-84, dean grad. study, 1984-92. Cons. in field; mem. Gov.'s Commn. on Energy Conservation, 1977; mem. Mo. Solar Energy Resource Panel, 1979-83; mem. Accreditation Bd. for Engring. and Tech. Co-author: Environmental Control Principles, 1975, 4th edit., 1985, Thermodynamics, 1981, Heat Pump Systems, 1983, Engineering Thermodynamics, 1985, Principles of Heating, Ventilating and Air Conditioning, 1991, 4th edit., 2001; contbr. articles to profl. jours. Pres. St. Patrick's Sch. Bd., 1970-72, St. Patrick's Parish Council, 1975-76. Recipient Ralph R. Teetor award Soc. Automotive Engrs., 1968; Hermann F. Spoehrer Meml. award St. Louis chpt. ASHRAE, 1979; also E. K. Campbell award of merit, 1983; Louise and Bill Holladay disting. fellow, 1999. Mem. ASME, ASHRAE (disting. svc. award 1981, exceptional svc. award 2001), NSPE, Soc. Automotive Engrs., Am. Soc. Engring. Edn., Mo. Soc. Profl. Engrs., Mo. Acad. Sci. (Most Disting. Scientist award 2003), Sigma Xi. Roman Catholic. Home: 10355 College Hills Dr Rolla MO 65401-7726 Office: Dept of Mech Engring U Mo Rolla MO 65401 Office Phone: 573-341-4143. Business E-Mail: sauer@umr.edu.

SAUER, MARY JULIA, special education educator; b. Pitts., Oct. 10, 1949; d. Edward Henry and Julia Ann (Polkabla) Sauer; 1 child, Jason Michael Sauer; m. John Harold Moore, Oct. 27, 1990 (div.); 1 adopted child, Jocelyn Quan. BS in Art Edn., Edinboro State Coll., 1971; MS in Spl. Edn., Clarion State Coll., 1980; postgrad, U. Pitts., 1988—. Cert. art tchr., spl. edn. tchr. for mentally retarded. Tchr. Polk (Pa.) State Sch. & Hosp., 1971-72; vol. VISTA, Bath, N.Y., 1972-73; tchr. Polk Ctr., 1973-80, program specialist, 1980-92; residential svc. supr., qualified mental retardation profl. Polk (Pa.) Ctr., 1992—. Lectr., speaker, video on local TV on history of Polk Ctr., 1987. Patentee beer bottle shaped cake pan; cakes displayed in TV videos and in various mags.; creator history video Polk Ctr., Some Leaky Boot Statues, Polk Center--100 Years; creator video A Century of Care-The History of the Evolution of Institional Care of the Devlopment Disabled. Past vol. Big Bros./Big Sisters. Democrat. Roman Catholic. Avocations: cake decorating, reading. Home: PO Box 97 Franklin PA 16323

SAUER, PETER WILLIAM, electrical engineer, educator; b. Winona, Minn., Sept. 20, 1946; s. Alfred von Rohr and Eleanor Francis (Sawyer) S.; m. Sylvia Louise Stenzel, Aug. 23, 1969; children: Katherine Dora, Daniel Alfred. BSEE, U. Mo., 1969; MSEE, Purdue U., 1974, PhD, 1977. Registered profl. engr., Va., Ill. Design engr. Langley AFB, Hampton, Va., 1969-73; asst. prof. elec. engring. U. Ill., Champaign-Urbana, 1977-82, assoc. prof., 1982-85, prof., 1985—, Grainger prof., 1998—. Elec. engr. Chanute AFB, Rantoul, Ill., 1983-89, res. dir. engring. ops., 1989-93; chief engring. programs, East HQ AMC, Scott AFB, Ill., 1993-98. Author: Power System Dynamics and Stability; contbr. articles to IEEE Transactions on Power Apparatus, IEEE Transactions on Power Systems, IEEE Transactions on Cirs. & Systems. Pres. Trinity Luth. Ch., Urbana, 1990-93, treas., 1994—. Maj. USAF, 1989-96, lt. col., 1996. Named Outstanding Young Coll. Educator, Champaign-Urbana Jaycees, 1982. Fellow IEEE (chpt. chmn. Ctrl. Ill. sect. 1982-83, chmn. power engring. 1988-2002, outstanding power engr. 1997), Nat. Acad. Engring. Lutheran. Achievements include development of systematic dynamic model reduction techniques for electric machines and power systems, explaining the relationship between power system stability and steady-state solutions. Office: U Ill 1406 W Green St Urbana IL 61801-2918 Office Phone: 217-333-0394.

SAUER, TIMOTHY DUWAYNE, mathematician, educator; b. Valley City, N.D., May 21, 1956; s. DuWayne Morris and Phyllis Jeannine (Jansen) S.; m. Kathleen Tongue Alligood, Oct. 21, 1987; 1 child, Katherine Anne. BS in Math., Mich. State U., 1977; PhD in Math., U. Calif., Berkeley, 1982. Lectr. Mich. State U., East Lansing, 1982-85; asst. prof. George Mason U., Fairfax, Va., 1985-90, assoc. prof., 1990-96, prof., 1996—, disting. prof. Coll. Arts and Scis., 1999—. Co-author: Chaos: An Introduction to Dynamical Systems, 1996; co-editor: Coping with Chaos, 1994. Mem. Am. Math. Soc., Soc. Indsl. and Applied Mathematicians. Office: Math Sci Dept George Mason Univ Fairfax VA 22030

SAUERBREY, ELLEN ELAINE RICHMOND, diplomat; b. Balt., Sept. 9, 1937; d. Edgar Arthur and Ethel Frederika (Landgraf) Richmond; m. Wilmer John Emil Sauerbrey, June 27, 1959. AB summa cum laude in Biology and English, Western Md. Coll., 1959. Biology instr., chmn. sci. dept. Baltimore County Sch. System, 1959-64; dist. mgr. Baltimore County U.S. Census, 1970; Md. Ho. of Dels., Annapolis, 1978-94, minority leader, 1986-94; radio talk show host Sta. WBAL, Balt., 1996; U.S. rep. com. status women UN, 2002—; amb. to UN Commn. on the Status of Women, 2002—. Rep. nominee for Gov., 1994, 98; bd. dirs. BBB; U.S. del. commn. human rights UN, 2001, 03; head U.S. del. Baltic states conf., 03; U.S. del econ. commn. Latin Am. and Caribbean, 04; mem. adv. commn. women in svcs. Def. Dept., 2004—. Nat. chmn. Am. Legis. Exec. Coun., 1990—91; trustee Md. Coun. Econ. Edn., Franklin Sq. Hosp.; founder United Citizen's for Md.'s Future; bd. advisors Yorktown University; Rep. Nat. Com. Woman Md., 1996—2003; Rules com., 1996; del. Rep. Nat. Convs., 1968, 1976, 1984, 1988, 1992, 1996, 2000, platform com., chmn. subcom. on economy, 1977; nat. adv. bd. Nat. Conservative Campaign Fund; mem. credentials com. Rep. Nat. Convs., 1984; vice chmn. Rep. State Ctrl. Com. of Balt. County, 1966—71; state chmn. Md. chpt. George W. Bush for Pres., 1999—2000. Recipient Pvt. Property award Greater Balt. Bd. Realtors, 1984; named Legislator of Yr., Md. Assn. Builders and Contractors, 1982, Am. Legis. Exec. Coun., 1986, Western Md. Coll. Alum of Yr., 1988, Outstanding Legis. Leader, Am. Legis. Exec. Coun., 1992, Rep. Woman of Yr., Md. Rep. Party, 1995, Nat. Fedn. Ind. Bus., Guardian of Small Bus. award, 1989, Lifetime Svc. award Baltimore County Rep. Party, 2003, Md. State of Mind award, 2004; named one of top 100 Md. Women, The Daily Record, 1998. Mem. DAR, Nat. Fedn. Rep. Women (Margaret Chase Smith award 1995, Lifetime Svc. award Balt. chpt., 2003, Md. State of Mind award 2004), Md. Fedn. Rep. Women, Am. Legis. exch. Coun. (chmn. emeritus), Md. Farm Bur., Md. Conservative Union, Beta Beta Beta, Phi Beta Kappa. Presbyterian. Avocations: gardening, travel. Personal E-mail: Ellen99@erols.com.

SAUERHAFT, STAN, public relations executive, consultant; b. N.Y.C. s. Al and Rae S.; m. Rosalie Cynthia Tolkin; children: Richard Craig, Douglas Clark, Robert James. BA, U. Mich., 1948, MA, 1949. Editor, scriptwriter Paramount News, 1950-51; scriptwriter Hearst Metrotone News, N.Y.C., 1951-52; editor Food Bus. Mag., N.Y.C., 1952-53; acct. supr. Selvage, Lee & Chase, N.Y.C., 1953-55; v.p., mem. creative plans bd. Comm. Counselors, Inc. McCann-Erickson, N.Y.C., 1955-59; pres. Chase and Sauerhaft Assocs., N.Y.C., 1959-65; exec. v.p., dir., mem. mgmt. com. Hill & Knowlton, Inc., N.Y.C., 1965-86; vice chmn. bd., dir. Burson-Marsteller, U.S., 1987-88; vice chmn., dir. Burson-Marsteller Internat., 1988—. Instr., lectr. Columbia U. Grad. Sch., 1962-65, Wharton Grad. Sch., 1968, U. Mich. Bus. Sch., 1969, NYU Grad. Bus. Sch., 1984-87; initiated pub. rels. course NYU Grad. Bus. Sch. Author: The Merger Game, 1971, Handbook of Strategic Public Relations and Integrated Communications, 1998, (novel) End Game, 2004; co-author: Image Wars, 1989; contbr. numerous bus. articles and chpts. to anthologies. Chmn. West Point Civilian Pub. Affairs Adv. Com., 1986-2003; mem. exec. com. of bd. Inst. for Pub. Rels. Rsch. and Edn., 1984-87; mem. bd. visitors LS&A Coll. of U. Mich., 1990-95. Staff sgt. AUS, 1945-46. Mem. Pub. Rels. Soc. Am. (Coll. of Fellows; nat. accreditation bd. 1981-83), Pub. Rels. Soc. N.Y. (pres. 1983-85), Soc. Profl. Journalists, Authors Guild Inc., Pub. Affairs Coun. (bd. dirs.), Am. Platform Tennis Assn. (v.p.), U. Mich. Alumni Club, Union League Club N.Y. (chmn. pub. affairs com. 1980-84, bd. visitors U. Mich.), Burning Tree Country Club (Greenwich, Conn.), Windmill Club (Armonk, N.Y.), Seabrook Island Club (S.C.), Sigma Delta Chi. Republican. Avocations: golf, platform tennis, bridge. Office Phone: 914-273-8849. Personal E-mail: rosauerh@aol.com. *A father's advice to his sons: If you can't outthink them, outwork them. But better yet, try to do both. Also, the best luck seems to befall the hardest workers.*

SAUERS, WILLIAM DALE, lawyer, playwright; b. Santa Cruz, Calif., June 18, 1926; s. Myrl Melvin and Helen (Fightmaster) S.; m. Barbara Gean Cole, May 9, 1945; children: Kathleen McCarty, Deborah Nelson, Susan Reeves. AB, Fresno State U., 1949; JD, Stanford U., 1952. Bar: Calif. 1953, U.S. Dist. Ct. (no. dist.) Calif. 1953, U.S. Ct. Appeals (9th cir.) 1953, U.S. Supreme Ct. 1964. Asst. sec. State Bar of Calif., San Francisco, 1952-55; dep. dist. atty. County of Santa Clara, San Jose, Calif., 1955-58; ptnr. Finch, Sauers et al., Palo Alto, Calif., 1958-88; pvt. practice law Palo Alto and San Jose, Calif., 1988—. Playwright: A Rainbow on Mt. Olympus and San Jose, 1993, Did Not I Dance with You?, 1994, A Fork in the Road, 1995, What'll We Do With Mama, 1996, Reluctant Strangers, 1997, Lynch Mob Hunt, 1998. Sec. Urban Coaliton of Palo Alto, 1969-72; chmn. ARC chpt. Palo Alto, 1973-76, Family Svc. Assn., 1973-76, Sr. Corp. Affiliates, Palo Alto, 1981-85, Oreg. Stage Works, Ashland, 2002-; chmn. bd. trustees Menlo Coll., Atherton, Calif., 1984-88;, dir. Oreg. Shakespeare Festival, Ashland, 1989-95; pres. San Jose Repertory Theatre, 1989-91; chmn. San Francisco Shakespeare Festival, 1994-98. Mem. ABA, Calif. State Bar Assn., Phi Delta Phi. Republican. Episcopalian. Avocations: skiing, tennis, golf, fly fishing, back packing. Office: Mount & Stoelker Riverpark Tower Ste 1650 333 W San Carlos San Jose CA 95110-2711 E-mail: wsauers@mount.com.

SAUFLEY, LEIGH INGALLS, judge; m. William Saufley; 2 children. Grad., Maine Sch. Law. Pvt. practice, Ellsworth; asst. counsel U.S. VA; asst., then dep. atty. gen. Maine, 1981-90; judge Maine Dist. Ct., 1990—93; justice Maine Superior Ct, 1993—97; assoc. justice Maine Supreme Judicial Ct., 1997—2001, chief justice, 2001—. Office: Cumberland County Courthouse PO Box 368 142 Federal St Portland ME 04112-0368 E-mail: amanda.j.martin@state.me.us.

SAUFLEY, WILLIAM EDWARD, banker, lawyer; b. Washington, Mar. 7, 1956; s. Franklin Dewit and Ruth Constance (Wright) S.; m. Leigh Ingalls, Jan. 3, 1981. BA, Dartmouth Coll., 1977; JD, U. Maine, 1980. Bar: Maine 1980, U.S. Dist. Ct. Maine 1980. Of counsel Maine Legislature, Augusta, 1981-84; v.p. counsel Maine Savs. Bank, Portland, 1984-88, gen. counsel, sec., 1988-91; corp. sec. The One Bancorp, Portland, 1984-91, gen. counsel, 1989-91; sr. v.p., gen. counsel Fleet Bank of Maine, Portland, 1992-94; of counsel Monaghan, Leahy, Hochadel & Libby, Portland, 1995-96; sr. v.p. Atlantic Bank N.A., Portland, 1996-97; sr. v.p., gen. counsel Coastal Bank, Portland, 1999—. Trustee 75 State St Home for Elderly, Portland, 1986-92; pres. Christmas in April Greater Portland, 1997-99. Mem. ABA, Maine Bar Assn. (chmn. consumer and fin. instns. law sect. 1996-97). Democrat. Roman Catholic. Avocations: photography, computers, skiing. Office: Coastal Bank PO Box 8550 Portland ME 04104-8550 E-mail: wsaufley@coastalbankme.com.

SAUL, APRIL, photographer; b. Bklyn., May 27, 1955; children: Amy, Nicholas. BA in English, Tufts U.; MA in Mass Comm., U. Minn. Staff photographer Balt. Sun, 1980, Phila. Inquirer, 1981—. Co-recipient Pulitzer Prize for exploratory journalism, 1997; named Photography of the Yr., Soc. Newspaper Design, 1994; recipient Robert F. Kennedy Journalism award, 1983, Budapest award, World Press Photo, 1991, Gold medal, best in show award, Soc. Newspaper Design, 1994; Nikon/NPPA Documentary Sabbatical grantee, 1985. Office: Phila Inquirer PO Box 8263 Philadelphia PA 19101-8263

SAUL, B. FRANCIS, II, bank executive, director; b. Washington, Apr. 15, 1932; s. Andrew Maguire and Ruth Clark (Sheehan) S.; m. Elizabeth Patricia English, Apr. 30, 1960; children: Sharon Elizabeth, B. Francis III, Elizabeth Willoughby, Andrew Maguire II, Patricia English. Grad., Georgetown Prep. Sch., 1950; BS, Villanova U., 1954, DCS (hon.), 1989; LLB, U. Va., 1957; LLD (hon.), Nat. U. Ireland, 1998. Bar: D.C. 1959. Chmn., pres. B.F. Saul Co., Chevy Chase, Md., 1957—; chmn., trustee B.F. Saul Real Estate Investment Trust Co., Chevy Chase, 1964—; with Chevy Chase Bank, F.S.B., 1969—, chmn., CEO, founder; chmn. Fin. Gen. Bankshares, Inc., 1978-82; chmn., CEO, trustee Saul Ctrs., Inc., 1993—. Chmn. bd. dirs. 1st Am. Bankshares, Inc., Washington, 1978—85; dir. Colonial Williamsburg Hotel Properties, Inc., 1983—96. Honors com. John F. Kennedy Ctr. Performing Arts, 1995—; trustees coun. Nat. Gallery of Arts, 1995—; dir. bd. visitors and govs. Washington Coll., 1995—; hon. trustee Brookings Inst., 1993—; dir. Nat. Sporting Libr., 1998—; trustee Fed. City Coun., Nat. Geog. Soc., 1985—, Suburban Hosp., 1972—76, Johns Hopkins Med. Bd., 2000—01, Corcoran Gallery ARt, Washington, 1972—90; bd. dirs. Wadsworth Preservation Trust, 1983—91; vis. com. Sch. Arch. U. Va., Greenway, 1985—90, Portsmouth (R.I.) Abbey Sch., 1979—84, United World Coll. of Am. West, Montezuma, N.Mex., 1982—85, D.C. Fund for Creative Space, 1980—82, D.C. chpt. ARC, 1964—86, Cork U. Found., 1997—; mem. Ea. Shore Land Conservancy, 2002—, James Madison Coun., 1997—; archdiocese fin. coun. for Archbishop of Washington, 1990—. Mem. Mortgage Bankers Assn. Met. Washington (pres. 1968), Nat. Assn. Real Estate Investment Truste (pres. 1973-74), Internat. Coll. Auditors Prefecture Econ. Affairs Holy See, Alfalfa Club, Alibi Club, Met. Club, Knights of Malta, Chevy Chase Club, Burning Tree Club, Friendly Sons of St. Patrick (pres. 1992), Wianno Club, The Brook Club, Bohemian Club, Md. Club, White's Club (London). Roman Catholic. Home: 1 Quincy St Chevy Chase MD 20815-4226 Office: BF Saul Co 7501 Wisconsin Ave Bethesda MD 20814

SAUL, IRVING ISAAC, lawyer; b. July 9, 1929; s. Israel Jacob and Jennie (Green) S.; m. Lita Brown, Dec. 29, 1950; children: Joanne Ilene, Sandra Lynn. BA, Washington and Jefferson Coll., 1949; LLB, U. Pitts., 1952; postgrad., Georgetown U., 1949, Ohio State U., 1951. Bar: Ohio 1952, U.S. Dist. Ct. (so. dist.) Ohio 1954, U.S. Supreme Ct. 1961, U.S. Ct. Appeals (6th cir.) 1966, U.S. Dist. Ct. (no. dist.) Ohio 1967, U.S. Dist. Ct. (ea. dist.) Wis. 1973, U.S. Ct. Appeals (7th cir.) 1978, U.S. Ct. Appeals (4th cir.) 1978, U.S. Ct. Appeals (fed. cir.) 1991. Pvt. practice, Dayton, Ohio, 1952—. Cons. in antitrust litigation; bd. advs. Fed. Civil Practice Abstracts, 1986-88, Ohio Dist. Ct. Rev., 1988—; adj. prof. complex litigation Sch. of Law U. Dayton, 1996-98; lectr. in field. Contbr. articles to profl. jours. James Gillespie Blaine scholar, 1948. Mem. Ohio Bar Assn. (chmn. fed. cts. and practice com. 1977-79, chmn. pvt. enforcement com. 1979-92, bd. govs. antitrust sect. 1982-94), Dayton Bar Assn. (chmn. fed. ct. practice com. 1976-77, 78-80, chmn. com. on judiciary 1987-88), Am. Judicature Soc., Masons (Shriner), Phi Beta Kappa. Jewish. Office: 113 Bethpolamy Ct Dayton OH 45415-2512

SAUL, J. PHILIP, pediatrician, educator; b. Atlanta, Aug. 17, 1956; s. Ralph L. Saul and Phyllis Cohen; m. Amy M. Davis, Jan. 3, 1954; children: Andrew Davis, Lillian Margaret. BS, Duke U., 1978, MD, 1982. Diplomate Am. Bd. of Pediat., 1987, Am. Bd. of Pediat., Subboard on Pediatric Cardiology, 1988. Internship Children's Hosp., Boston, 1982—83; residency Med. U. S.C. Children's Hosp., 1983—84; chief pediatric cardiology Med. U. of SC., Charleston, SC, 1997—, prof. of pediat., 1997—; med. dir. Children's Hosp. at Med. U. S.C., Charleston, 2001—. Author: Arrhythmias in Children, and Young Adults with Congenital Heart Disease, 2001; contbr. more than 300 articles to profl. jours. Grantee Randomized Clin. Trials for Pediatric Heart Disease, NIH, 2001-2006. Mem. Soc. for Pediat. Rsch., Heart Rythem Soc., Am. Heart Assn., Am. Coll. of Cardiology, North Am. Soc. of Electrophysiology. Achievements include patents in field. Office: Medical University of South Carolina 165 Ashley Avenue PO Box 250915 Charleston SC 29425

SAUL, JOHN WOODRUFF, III, writer; b. Pasadena, Calif., Feb. 25, 1942; s. John Woodruff and Adeline Elizabeth (Lee) S. Student, Antioch Coll., 1959-60, Cerritos Coll., 1960-61, Mont. State U., Missoula, 1961-62, San Francisco State Coll., 1963-65. In various positions, primarily in L.A. and San Francisco, 1965-76. Author: Suffer The Children, 1977, Punish the Sinners, 1978, Cry for the Strangers, 1979, Comes the Blind Fury, 1980, When the Wind Blows, 1981, The God Project, 1982, Nathaniel, 1984, Brainchild, 1985, Hellfire, 1986, The Unwanted, 1987, The Unloved, 1988, Creature, 1989, Second Child, 1990, Sleep Walk, 1990, Darkness, 1991, Shadows, 1992, Guardian, 1993, The Homing, 1994, Black Lightning, 1995, The Blackstone Chronicles, 1997, The Presence, 1997, The Right Hand of Evil, 1999, Nightshade, 2000, The Manhattan Hunt Club, 2001, Midnight Voices, 2002; also other novels under pseudonyms; creator computer game "John Saul's Blackstone Chronicles," 1998. Bd. dirs. Seattle Theatre Arts, 1978-80; bd. govs. Tellurian Communities, Inc., Madison, Wis.; v.p. Chester Woodruff Found., N.Y.C. Mem. Authors Guild. Democrat. Swedenborgian. Office: care Jane Rotrosen 318 E 51st St New York NY 10022-7803 *For a writer, the education of experience is without doubt the best education.*

SAUL, JULIAN, retail executive; b. 1940; CEO, pres. Queen Carpet, Dalton, Ga., 1962—; pres. Shaw Industries, Dalton, 1999—. Office: PO Box 1527 Dalton GA 30722-1527

SAUL, MARK E. mathematics educator, consultant; b. NYC, June 17, 1948; s. Sidney and Shura Saul; m. Carol Portnoy, June 26, 1968; children: Susanna, Michael, Peter. BA, Columbia U., 1969; MS, Courant Inst. Math. Scis., NYU, 1975; PhD, NYU, 1987. Tchr. math. and computer sci. Bronx High Sch. Sci., NY, 1969—85; tchg. fellow Adm. Hyman H. Rickover Found., 1985; tchr. Bronxville Schs., NY, 1985—2003; project dir. NSF, 2003—; dir. for curriculum rsch. and innovation Gateway Project, CUNY Rsch. Found., 2003—. Dir. Rsch. Sci. Inst. Ctr. Excellence in Edn., McLean, Va., 1987, San Diego, 90, Cambridge, Mass., 1992—99; cons. computer graphics 1984 Olympics ABC-TV, N.Y.C., 1983—84; pres. N.Y.C. Interscholastic Math. League, N.Y.C., 1979—89, Am. Regions Math. League, 1989—2000; dir. ARML-Soviet Student Exch., 1991—96; cons. Ednl. Testing Svc., Princeton, NJ, 1980—82; panelist/cons. LaGuardia HS Performing Art, N.Y.C., 1977—86; tchr. trainer N.Y.C. Bd. Edn., 1981; tchr.-coord. computer sci. Hollingworth Ctr. for Gifted, Tchrs. Coll., Columbia U., 1984; instr. Lehman Coll., 1984—92, Johns Hopkins U. Ctr. Talented Youth, 1986, Sophie Davis Biomed. Ctr. CCNY, 1986—94, Sarah Lawrence Coll., 1987—94; mem. U.S. del. to Internat. Congress Math. Educators, Budapest, 1988, Quebec, 92, Seville, 96, Tokyo, 2000. Co-author: Science/Mathematics Research Programs in the High School, 1982, The New York City Problem Book, 1986, Read the Question: A Thinking Student's Guide to the SAT's, 1992; co-author: (with I.M. Gelfand) Trigonometry, 2001; author: Enrichment Problems in Leadership Manual for High School Supervisors in Mathematics, 1982; assoc. editor edn. Notices of Am. Math. Soc., 1996—2002, math. field editor Quantum, 1991—2001, mem. editl. bd. Mathematics and Informatics Jour., 1991—, Math. Horizons Jour., 1992—96, mem. editl. panel MAA Anneli Lax New Math. Libr., 1996—. Judge Internat. Math. Olympiad, Washington, 1981, chief guide, 2001; author contest questions Mass. Math. League Ann. Contest, 1981; mem. authors' com. Educating Teachers of Science, Mathematics, and Technology: New Practices for the New Millennium, 1998—2000. Recipient Presdl. award for Excellence in Teaching Math., NSF, 1984, Paul Erdos award, World Fedn. Nat. Math. Competitions, 1998; Tandy Tech. scholar, 1994, Gabriela and Paul Rosenbaum Found. fellow, 1995. Mem.: Nat. Coun. Tchrs. Math. (bd. dirs. 2001—04), Am. Math. Soc., Math. Assn. Am. (mem. com. on high sch. contests 1981—92), Assn. Tchrs. Math. (exec. bd. mem. 1980—85). Avocation: chamber music. Home: 711 Amsterdam Ave Apt 27K New York NY 10025-6929 Office Phone: 703-292-5092. Business E-Mail: msaul@nsf.gov.

SAUL, NORMAN EUGENE, history educator; b. LaFontaine, Ind., Nov. 26, 1932; s. Ralph Odis and Jessie (Neff) S.; m. Mary Ann Culwell, June 27, 1959; children: Alyssa, Kevin, Julia. BA, Ind. U.- Bloomington, 1954; MA, Columbia U., 1959, PhD, 1965; postgrad., Leningrad State U. (USSR), 1960-61. Asst. prof. Brown U., 1965-68; vis. assoc. prof. Northwestern U., 1969-70; assoc. prof. U. Kans., Lawrence, 1970-75, prof. history, 1975—, chmn. dept. history, 1981-89. Inst. Advanced Study, Princeton U., 2000. Author: Russia and the Mediterranean 1797-1807, 1970, Sailors in Revolt, 1978, Distant Friends: The United States and Russia, 1763-1867, 1991, Concord and Conflict: The United States and Russia, 1867-1914, 1996, War and Revolution: The United States and Russia, 1914-1921, 2001; editor: Russian-American Dialogue on Cultural Relations, 1776-1914, 1997. Fulbright scholar, London, 1954-55, Helsinki, 1968-69, Soviet Am. Exch. scholar Internat. Rsch. and Exch. Bd., Moscow, 1973-74, 91-92; fellow Ford Found., 1957-59, Hall Ctr. for Humanities, 1989, 95; recipient Byron Caldwell Smith Book award for Distant Friends Hall Ctr. for Humanities, 1993, Robert H. Ferrell book award for concert and conflict Soc. Historians Am. Fgn. Rels., 1997, Pub. Scholar award Kans. Humanities Coun., 1997, Higuchi Rsch. award U. Kans., 1997, Steeples award for Svc. to Kans., 2000, Herbert Hoover Libr. Assn. award, 2001, Franklin and Eleanor Roosevelt Inst. award, 2002. Mem. Am. Assn. Advancement of Slavic Studies, Kans. State Hist. Soc. Home: 1002 Crestline Dr Lawrence KS 66049-2607 E-mail: nsaul@ku.edu.

SAUL, RALPH SOUTHEY, financial service executive; b. Bklyn., May 21, 1922; s. Walter Emerson and Helen Douglas (Coutts) S.; m. Bette Jane Bertschinger, June 16, 1956; children: Robert Southey, Jane Adams. BA, U. Chgo., 1947; LL.B., Yale U., 1951. Bar: D.C. 1951, N.Y. 1952. With Am. Embassy, Prague, Czechoslovakia, 1947-48; assoc. Lyeth & Voorhees, N.Y.C., 1951-52; asst. counsel to gov. State of N.Y., 1952-54; staff atty. RCA, 1954-58; with SEC, 1958-65, dir. divsn. trading and markets, 1963-65; v.p. corporate devel. Investors Diversified Services, Inc., Mpls., 1965-66; pres. Am. Stock Exch., N.Y.C., 1966-71; co-chief exec., chmn. mgmt. com. 1st Boston Corp., 1971-74; chmn., CEO. INA Corp., Phila., 1975-82, CIGNA Corp., Phila., 1982-84. Trustee Com. for Econ. Devel., Brookings Inst. With USNR, 1943-46, PTO. Mem. ABA, N.Y. Stock Exch. (regulatory adv. com.), Union League, Merion Golf Club, Links Club. Office: Cigna Corp One Logan Square PO Box 7716 18th and Cherry Sts Philadelphia PA 19192

SAUL, STEPHANIE, journalist; b. St. Louis, Jan. 28, 1954; d. Elmer William and Nancy (Cromer) Saul; m. Walt Bogdanich, Jan. 2, 1982; children: Nicholas Walter Bogdanich, Peter Eric Bogdanich. BA, U. Miss., 1975. Reporter New Albany (Miss.) Gazette, 1974, Clarion-Ledger, Jackson, Miss., 1975—80, The Plain Dealer, Cleve., 1980—84; nat. corr. Newsday, Melville, NY, 1984—. Adj. prof. journalism Columbia U., N.Y.C., 1999—. Named Journalist of Yr., Times Mirror Co.; recipient Silver Gavel award, ABA, 1980, George Polk award for regional reporting, 1981, Nat. Press Club award, 1990, IRE award, Investigative Reporters and Editors, 1995, Headliner award, Atlantic City Press Club, 1995, Roy Howard award, Scripps Howard Found., 1995, Pulitzer Prize for investigative reporting, 1995, Golden Typewriter award for pub. svc. journalism, N.Y. Press Club, 1995, Silver Em Miss. Scholastic Press Assn., 1997, N.Y. Assn. of Black Journalists award, 1998, James Aronson award for social justice journalism, Hunter Coll., N.Y., 1999. Office: Newsday 235 Pinelawn Rd Melville NY 11747-4250

SAUL, WILLIAM EDWARD, civil engineering educator; b. N.Y.C., May 15, 1934; s. George James and Fanny Ruth (Murokh) S.; m. J. Muriel Held Eagleburger, May 11, 1976. BSCE, Mich. Tech. U., 1955, MSCE, 1961; PhD in Civil Engring., Northwestern U., 1964. Registerd profl. engr., Wis., Idaho, Mich., profl. structural engr., Idaho. Mech. engr. Shell Oil Co., New Orleans, 1955-59; instr. engring. mechanics Mich. Tech. U., Houghton, 1960-62; asst. prof. civil engring. U. Wis., Madison, 1964-67, assoc. prof., 1967-72, prof., 1972-84; dean, prof. civil engring. U. Idaho Coll. Engring., Moscow, 1984-90; prof. civil engring. Mich. State U., East Lansing, 1990—2000, chmn. dept. civil and environ. engring., 1990-95, chmn. emeritus, prof. emeritus, 2000. Cons. engr., 1961—; vis. prof. U. Stuttgart, Germany, 1970-71. Co-editor Conf. of Methods of Structural Analysis, 1976. Bd. dirs. Idaho Rsch. Found., 1984-90. Fulbright fellow 1970-71; von Humboldt scholar, 1970-71. Fellow ASCE (pres. Wis. sect. 1983-84), Mich. Soc. Profl. Engrs., NSPE (Steinman award 2003); mem. Internat. Assn. Bridge and Structural Engrs., Am. Concrete Inst., Am. Soc. Engring. Edn., Sigma Xi, Phi Kappa Phi, Tau Beta Pi, Chi Epsilon. Avocations: hiking, reading, travel, gadgets. Home: 1971 Cimarron Dr Okemos MI 48864-3905 Office: Mich State U 3546 Engring Bldg E East Lansing MI 48824 Business E-Mail: saul@egr.msu.edu.

SAULINO, MICHAEL FRANCIS, physiatrist; b. Philadelphia, Pa., Mar. 16, 1964; MD, PhD, Hershey Med. Ctr., Pa., 1986—93. Cert. Phys. Medicine and Rehab. Am. Bd. PM&R, 1998, Spinal Cord Injury Am. Bd. PM&R, 2000. Attending physician Magee Rehab. Hosp., Phila., 1998—; residency program dir. Thomas Jefferson U. Hosp., Phila., 2001—. Consulting physician Thomas Jefferson U., Phila., 1998—. Recipient AMA Physician Recognition Award, AMA, 2001-2004. Mem.: Assn. Am. Colls., Nat. Stroke Assn., Physiatric Assn. Sports, Spine, and Orthop. Rehab., Am. Coll. Sports Medicine, Internat. Soc. Phys. and Rehab. Medicine, Am. Coll. Physician Execs., Am. Acad. Phys. Medicine and Rehab., Am. Assn. Neurol. Surgeons (assoc.). Office: Magee Rehab Hosp 1513 Race St Philadelphia PA 19102 Business E-Mail: msaulino@mageerehab.org.

SAUNDERS, AUDREY JAYNE, federal official; b. Cin. d. Robert James and Margaret Ann (Philpot) Saunders. BA, U. Cin., 1971; MS, Xavier U., Cin., 1975; postgrad., Lehman Coll., Bronx, 1990—92. Tchr. N.Y.C. Bd. Edn., 1985—94; with IRS, Cin., 1995—97, tax examining asst., 1997—2003, Holtsville, NY, 2003—. Adult basic edn. tchr. Gen. Edn. Devel. Program Math, 1974—77. Author children's books. With U.S. Army, 1977—81. Methodist. Home: 646 West End Dr Medford NY 11763

SAUNDERS, BARRY WAYNE, state official; b. Roxboro, N.C., June 9, 1944; s. Charlie Clifton and Mary Louise (Mooney) S.; m. Brenda Kaye Bell, Oct. 18, 1987; children: Dara Louise Saunders Lockamy, Erin Elissa (dec.). BA, Campbell u., 1971; MEd, U. N.C., 1974; EdD, N.C. State U., 1990. Tchr. Granville County Sch. System, Oxford, N.C., 1966-69; mental health counselor Vocat. Rehab., Henderson, N.C., 1971-75; staff devel. specialist John Umstead Hosp., Butner, N.C., 1975-82; trainer, asst. mgr., mgr. tng. N.C. Dept. Transp., Raleigh, 1982—; mgr. tng. (on loan from N.C. Dept. Transp.) Gov.'s Office of Quality Improvement, 1995-96; mgr. tng. N.C. Dept. Transp., Raleigh, 1996-2000; ret., 2000. Pres. Omicron Cons., Mill Spring, NC, 1982—. Contbr. articles to profl. jours., poems to N.C. Poetry Soc., 1981. Sec. Dem. Party, Person County, N.C., 1980-84. Mem. Nat. Mgmt. Assn. (bd. dirs. state govt. chpt. 1992-95, v.p. 1997-98), Triangle Quality Coun. (bd. dirs. 1995-96), Nat. Transp. Tng. Dirs. Assn. (v.p. 1997-2000). Methodist. Home: 121 Canoe Dr Mill Spring NC 28756

SAUNDERS, CHARLES ALBERT, lawyer; b. Boulder, Colo., Jan. 18, 1922; s. Charles and Anna (Crouse) S.; m. Betti Friedel, Oct. 18, 1946; children— Melanie, Stephen, Cynthia, Shelley. BA, U. Houston, 1942; LLB, U. Tex., 1945. Bar: Tex. bar 1945. Since practiced in, Houston; partner firm Fulbright & Jaworski, L.L.P., 1959—. Editor: How To Live-and Die-With Texas Probate, 8 vols., 1968, Texas Estate Administration, 1975. Bd. dirs. Houston Symphony Soc., 1964—; bd. dirs. Am. Lung Assn., San Jacinto, 1965—, pres., 1972-73; past mem. bd. govs. U. Houston. Recipient Leon Jaworski award for cmty. svc. Houston Bar Assn., 1997, U. Tex. Law Sch. Disting. Alumnus award in Cmty. Svc., 1999. Mem. ABA, State Bar Assn., Houston Bar Assn., Am. Coll. Trust and Estate Coun. (regent 1972-80, pres. 1978-79), Internat. Acad. of Estate and Trust Law, Assn. Cmty. TV (bd. dirs. 1970—). Republican. Presbyterian. Home: 19 Willowron Dr Houston TX 77024-7618 Office: Fulbright & Jaworski 1301 Mckinney St Ste 5100 Houston TX 77010-3031 E-mail: csaunders@fulbright.com.

SAUNDERS, CHARLES BASKERVILLE, JR., retired association executive; b. Boston, Dec. 26, 1928; s. Charles Baskerville and Lucy (Carmichael) S.; m. Margaret MacIntire Shafer, Sept. 9, 1950; children— Charles Baskerville III, George Carlton, Margaret Keyser, Lucy C., John R. Grad., St. Mark's Sch., 1946; AB, Princeton, 1950. News reporter, polit. columnist Ogdensburg (N.Y.) Jour., 1950-51; edn. reporter Hartford (Conn.) Times, 1951-53; asst. dir. pub. relations Trinity Coll., Hartford, 1953-55; asst. dir. pub. info. Princeton, 1955-57; legis. asst. Sen. H. Alexander Smith, 85th Congress, 1957-58; asst. to asst. sec. for legislation HEW, 1958-59; asst. to sec. Arthur S. Flemming, 1959-61, dep. asst. sec. for legislation, 1969-71; asst. to pres. Brookings Instn., 1961-69; dep. commr. of edn. for external affairs U.S. Office Edn., 1971-72; dep. asst. sec. for edn. HEW, 1973-74; dir. govt. relations Am. Council on Edn., 1975-78, v.p. for govt. relations, 1978-87, sr. v.p., 1987-92. Author: Brookings Institution: A Fifty-Year History, 1966, Upgrading the American Police, 1970, Four Centuries in America, 2000. Mem. Montgomery County Bd. Edn., 1966-70, Md. Higher Edn. Commn., 1989-2002 (chmn. 1994-95, vice chmn. 1995-2002); chmn. bd. dirs. Md. Higher Edn. Loan Corp., 1994-95. Mem. Jamestowne Soc. Democrat. Presbyterian. Home: 7622 Winterberry Pl Bethesda MD 20817-4848

SAUNDERS, DEBRA J. columnist; b. Newton, Mass., Dec. 8, 1954; BA in Latin and Greek, U. Mass., Boston, 1980. Asst. dir. Arnold Zenker Assocs., 1982-83; writer/rschr., account exec. Todd Domke Assocs., Sacramento, 1983-84, Russo Watts & Rollins, Sacramento, 1985-86; asst. to Rep. Leader Calif. Assembly, Sacramento, 1987-88; columnist, editl. writer L.A. Daily News, 1988-92; columnist San Francisco Chronicle, 1992—. Leader study group on polit. speechmaking Harvard U., Cambridge, Mass., 1984; tchr. editl. and column writing UCLA Ext., 1992. Published in Wall St. Jour., Nat. Review, Weekly Std., Reason mag.; syndicated nationally via Creators Syndicate; appeared on Politically Incorrect, CNN and BBC radio. Office: San Francisco Chronicle 901 Mission St San Francisco CA 94103-2905

SAUNDERS, DONALD LESLIE, hotel owner, real estate investor; b. Brookline, Mass., Jan. 28, 1935; s. Irving M. Saunders and Shirley Brown; m. Liv. Ullmann, 1985; children: Lisa M., Pamela R. AB in Econs., Brown U., 1957; grad., Inst. Real Estate Mgmt., 1963; LLB, 1989. Cert. property mgr. Inst. Real Estate Mgmt., Ill. Chmn., pres., CEO D.L. Saunders Real Estate Corp., Boston, 1957—; CEO, chmn. D.L. Saunders Cos., Boston; co-owner Boston (Mass.) Pk. Plz. Hotel & Towers, 1976—, chmn., 1976—, CEO, 1976—; gen. ptnr. SaunStar Land Co.; ptnr. 20 & 50 Park Plaza Complex, LLC. Bd. dirs. Park Sch. Corp., Brookline, Mass., Carlton House Condominium, Brown U. Comml. Real Estate Devel. Co.; mem. real estate subcom. Brown U.; pres. Farview Inc., 1976—; trustee emeritus Brown U., 1972—; bd. govs. John Carter Brown Libr. of Americana at Brown U. Mem. Nat. Assn. Realtors, Ea. Point Resident's Assn., Ocean Reef Club, Ocean Reef Yacht Club, Racquet Club, Brown U. Club, Lotos Club, The Players, Union League Club, Hope Club, Boston Tennis and Racquet Club, Ea. Point Yacht Club, Belmont Country Club, Univ. Club, Providence, R.I., Union Club, Charles River Yacht Club, The Worcester (Mass.) Club, Boston (Mass.) Coll. Club, Harvard Club, Confrerie Chaine des Rotisseurs, N.Y.C. Office: DL Saunders Cos 20 Park Plz Boston MA 02116-4399

SAUNDERS, ELMO STEWART, librarian, historian; b. Bradenton, Fla., Apr. 3, 1936; s. Warren Sawyer and Mary Irene Saunders; m. Margaret Overholt, Dec. 27, 1969; children: Lawrence Sawyer, Matthew Augustus, Emily S. Summers. BA, DePauw U., 1959; MA, Ball State U., 1962, Ind. U., 1964; PhD, Ohio State U., 1980. Sr. reference librn. Ohio State U. Librs., Columbus, 1964—77; collections coord. Purdue U. Librs., Lafayette, Ind., 1978—. Cons. U.S. AID, Washington, 1984—90. Contbg. author, editor: The Sun King: Louis XIV and the New World, 1984, Treaties of the War of the Spanish Succession, 1995; contbr. articles to profl. jours. Pvt. 1st class U.S. Army, 1961. Mem.: Soc. for French Hist. Studies. Independent. United Methodist. Avocations: remodeling a Victorian house, raising livestock, book collector. Home: 3703 Dayton Rd Lafayette IN 47905 Office: Purdue Univ Humanities Libr 504 West State St West Lafayette IN 47907 Office Phone: 765-494-2829. E-mail: ssaunder@purdue.edu.

SAUNDERS, GEORGE LAWTON, JR., lawyer; b. Mulga, Ala., Nov. 8, 1931; s. George Lawton and Ethel Estell (York) S.; children: Kenneth, Ralph, Victoria; m. Terry M. Rose. BA, U. Ala., 1956; JD, U. Chgo., 1959. Bar: Ill. 1960. Law clk. to chief judge U.S. Ct. Appeals (5th cir.), Montgomery, Ala., 1959-60; law clk to Justice Hugo L. Black U.S. Supreme Ct., Washington, 1960-62; assoc. Sidley & Austin, Chgo., 1962-67, ptnr., 1967-90; founding ptnr. Saunders & Monroe, Chgo., 1990—. With USAF, 1951-54. Fellow: Am. Coll. Trial Lawyers; mem.: Law Club, Quadrangle Club, Point-O-Woods Club, Chgo. Club, Order of the Coif, Phi Beta Kappa. Democrat. Baptist. Home: 179 E Lake Shore Dr Chicago IL 60611-1306 Office: Saunders & Monroe Ste 1302 33 N Dearborn St Chicago IL 60602

SAUNDERS, GEORGE WENDELL, management consultant, retired government official; b. Hubbard, Ohio, Oct. 17, 1917; s. Phillip and Mary (Shafer) S.; m. Audrey Edna Bogue (dec. Nov. 1979); children: Wayne George, Wendy Jean; m. Virginia Hutson Baker, June 25, 1987; stepchildren: John Milton Jr., Kathee Eloise. B in Acctg., Rider Coll., 1937; postgrad, Harvard U., 1943; grad., Indsl. Coll. Armed Forces, 1955, Fgn. Service Inst., Naval War Coll.; student, Grad. Sch. Dept. Agr., Dept. Def. Computer Inst. Auditor, acct. U.S. Rubber Co., N.Y.C., 1937-39; acct., office mgr. S. King Fulton, Inc., Washington, 1939-40; with War Dept. and Civil Aero. Adminstrn., Washington, 1940-41; adminstrv. asst., sr. investigator Bur. Fed. Supply Treas. Dept., Washington, 1941-47; ops. planning analyst, orgn. and methods examiner, supply specialist Fed. Supply Services GSA, Washington, 1957-55, dep. dir. stores mgmt. div., 1955-61, dir. supply distbn. div., acting asst. dir. nat. buying div., 1956-61, dir. distbn. programs div., 1961-64, asst. commr. supply distbn., 1964-71, asst. commr. trans. and pub. utilities, 1971-73, dep. commr., 1973-75; v.p. Washington Mgmt. Group, Washington Mktg. Group, 1975-79; pvt. practice cons., 1979—. Mem. Fed. Safety Council, Fed. Fire Council and Nat. Def. Trans. Bd., 1970-75 Contbr. to govt. publs. Chmn. bd. dirs., past pres. North Chevy Chase Swimming Pool Assn., 1960; vestryman, treas. Episc. Ch., Silver Spring, Md., 1950. Served with USN World War II, PTO, ATO, comdr. Res. ret., 1975. Recipient Adminstrs. Exceptional Service award GSA, 1975. Mem. Ret. Officers Assn., Am. Legion (exec. bd. Thad Dulin chpt. 1986-87, adj. 1988, vice comdr. 1989-91, comdr. 1991-95), Leisure World Golf Club, Kenwood Country Club, Montgomery Village Golf Club, Lions (pres. Rossmoor Club Silver Spring, 1988-89), Fireside Forum (v.p., bd. dirs.), Leisure World. Republican. Avocations: golf, travel, aviation, swimming. Home and Office: 15107 Interlachen Dr Apt 812 Silver Spring MD 20906-5633

SAUNDERS, HAROLD HENRY, foundation administrator; b. Phila., Dec. 27, 1930; s. Harold Manuel Saunders and Marian Elizabeth Weihenmayer; m. Barbara Mc Garrigle, May 4, 1963 (dec. Oct. 1973); children: Catherine Elizabeth, Mark Harril; m. Carol Eleanor Jones Cruse, June 2, 1990. AB, Princeton U., 1952; PhD, Yale U., 1956; LittD, New England Coll., 1999; D of Internat. Rels., Dickinson Coll., 2004. With CIA, Washington, 1959-61; sr. staff Nat. Security coun., Washington, 1961-74; dir. intelligence and rsch., asst. sec. Near East and South Asian affairs Dept. of State, Washington, 1974-81; fellow Am. Enterprise Inst. Brookings Inst., Washington, 1981-91; professorial lectr. Johns Hopkins U. SAIS, George Mason U., 1984—91; dir. internat. affairs Kettering Found., Washington, 1991—; pres. Internat. Inst. Sustained Dialogue, 2002—. Author: The Other Walls: Arab-Israeli Peace Process in Global Perspective, 1985, 91, A Public Peace Process: Sustained Dialogue to Transform Racial & Ethnic Conflicts, 1999. Trustee Princeton U., 1996—2000; pres. Class of '52, 2002—; ruling elder Lewinsville Presbyn. Ch., McLean, Va., 1971—; bd. dirs. East-West Inst., N.Y.C., 1981—89, Ptnrs. Dem. Change, San Francisco, 1995—, InterNews, Arcata, Calif., 1999—2001. Lt. USAF, 1957—59. Recipient Disting. Fed. Civilian Svc. award Pres. U.S., 1978, Disting. Honor award Dept. of State, 1981, First Disting. Achievement award Germantown Acad., Phila., Lifetime Achievement award Search for Common Ground, 2004. Mem. Internat. Sc. Polit. Psychology (gov. coun. 1991-94), Coun. on Fgn. Rels., Princeton Club N.Y., Phi Beta Kappa. Avocation: writing. Home: 2101 Lorraine Ave Mc Lean VA 22101 Office: Kettering Found 444 N Capitol St NW Washington DC 20001

SAUNDERS, HEATHER MARIE, air transportation executive; b. Lubbock, Tex., May 28, 1977; d. Kathy A. Wimmer. BS in Human Factors, Embry-Riddle Aero. U., Daytona Beach, Fla., 2000; MS in Aero. Sci., Embry-Riddle Aero. U., Houston, 2003. Human factors support engr. Illgen Simulation Techs., Inc., Washington, 2001—02; asst. ctr. dir. Embry-Riddle Aero. U., Houston, 2002—03; mem. airport ops. staff City of Houston Airport Authority, 2003—. Vol. Susan G. Komen Breast Cancer Found. Mem.: Women in Aviation (assoc.), Aircraft Owners and Pilots Assn. (assoc.), Human Factors and Ergonomics Soc. (assoc.). Avocations: diving, travel. Home: 715 FM 1959 Rd # 1103 Houston TX 77034 Office: City of Houston Airport Authority Houston TX 77032 Personal E-mail: hsaunders25@aol.com.

SAUNDERS, J. FARRELL, historic site director; b. Albermarle, N.C., Nov. 11, 1935; BA, Elon Coll., 1968. Supt. Russell Cave Nat. Monument, Bridgeport, Ala., 1991-94, Little River Canyon Nat. Park, 1991-94, Cowpens Nat. Battlefield, Chesnee, S.C., 1994—. Office: Cowpens Nat Battlefield PO Box 308 Chesnee SC 29323-0308*

SAUNDERS, JAMES ROBERT, English educator; b. Richmond, Va., Apr. 4, 1953; s. Marjorie Charlotte (Wilson) S.; m. Renae Nadine Shackelford, July 6, 1982; 1 child, Monica. BA, U. Va., 1975, MA, 1981; JD, Harvard U., 1978; PhD, U. Mich., 1986. Instr. U. Va., Charlottesville, 1973-74, 80-82; lectr. Mary Washington Coll., Fredericksburg, Va., 1981-82; instr. U. Toledo, 1985-86, asst. prof., 1986-90, assoc. prof., 1990-96, prof., 1996-97, Purdue U., West Lafayette, Ind., 1997—. Vis. scholar U. Mich., 1996-97. Author: The Wayward Preacher in the Literature of African American Women, 1995, Tightrope Walk: Identity, Survival and the Corporate World in African American Literature, 1997; co-author (with Renae Nadine Shackelford): Urban Renewal and the End of Black Culture in Charlottesville, Virginia: An Oral History of Vinegar Hill, 1998, (with Monica Renae Saunders) Black Winning Jockeys in the Kentucky Derby, 2003; reader Jour. Soc. for Study of Multi-Ethnic Lit. of U.S., 1996-99; editor: (with Renae Nadine Shackelford) The Dorothy West Martha's Vineyard: Stories, Essays and Reminiscences by Dorothy West Writing in the Vineyard Gazette, 2001; contbr. essays to Gloria Naylor: Critical Perspectives Past and Present, Readings on Native Son, The Critical Response to Gloria Naylor; mem. editl. bd. Modern Fiction Studies; contbr. articles to profl. jours. including So. Lit. Jour., Hollins Critic, Langston Hughes Rev., Lit. of U.S., Modern Fiction Studies, Obsidian II, Coll. Lit. Dir. Vinegar Hill Oral History Project, Charlottesville, 1980. Faculty rsch. fellow U. Toledo, 1988, 90, 95; recipient Cert. of Excellence Options, Inc., 1996, Somia Soul award 2001. Avocations: basketball, reading, hiking, pet collecting, attending plays. Office: Purdue U Dept English 1356 Heavilon Hall Dept English West Lafayette IN 47907-1356

SAUNDERS, JANET MCGEE, small business owner, healthcare administrator; b. Portsmouth, N.H., June 11, 1958; d. John P. and Louise (Flynn) McG.; m. Peter C. Saunders. AA in Recreation Leadership, Colby-Sawyer Coll., New London, N.H., 1979; AS in Natural Scis., Colby-Sawyer Coll., 1980, BS in Health Records Adminstrn., 1981; Cert. in Health Records Adminstn., US Pub. Health Svc. Hosp., Balt., 1981. Registered record adminstr., Am. Health Info. Mgmt. Assn.; lic. real estate agt., Ga. Med. record technician, supr. patient accounts U.S. Pub. Health Svc. Hosp., 1981-82; chief fin. counselor Champus HBA Wyman Pk. Health System Inc. (formerly USPHS), 1981-82; claims specialist Blue Cross/Blue Shield, Atlanta, 1982-83; health record adminstr., quality control mgr. Computer Health Corp., Atlanta, 1983-84; sales assoc. Ernst Resort Devel., Atlanta, 1984-86; owner Errands Etc., Atlanta, 1984-87; sales mgr. Am. Svc. Life Ins. Co., Atlanta, 1988-92; health benefits cons., 1988—; healthcare practice mgmt. cons., 1988—; founder, owner Pet Med. Info. Bur., 1992—; prin. Saunders Auctioneers & Appraisers, N.H. and Mass., 1997—, Antiques, Arts & Books @ Sign of Mermaid, Kingston, N.H., 1999—; property mgr.; lic. broker, owner Saunders Real Estate. Cons. health benefits mgmt. for small businesses and individuals, S.E., U.S., 1989—. Contbr. articles to prof. jours., manuals. Counselor to delinquent youths Youth Svcs., USA, 1975-76. Gov's. funded program Commn. on Crime and Delinquency, 1976-77; mem. Nat. Right to Life Com., 1985-90; chmn. Summerfest-MDA fundraiser, Atlanta, 1989; coord., fundraising and devel. N.H. Soc. Prevention of Cruelty to Animals, 1992-93; chair charity events MDA. Mem. U.S. Pub. Health Svc. Officers Club (Balt., sec.-treas. 1980-82), Am. Vet. Health Info. Mgmt. Assn., Nat. Auctioneers' Assn., Alpha Chi, Phi Theta Kappa. Roman Catholic. Avocations: books, literature, history and preservation, dance, horseback riding. Home and Office: PO Box 360 2 King Pine Way Kingston NH 03848 Office Phone: 603-234-0682. E-mail: jsaunders@jmacofnh.com.

SAUNDERS, JOSEPH ARTHUR, office products manufacturing company executive; b. Creston, Mont., July 9, 1926; s. Albert Henry and Edith Margaret (Rhodes) S.; m. Lois Evelyn White, June 19, 1948 (dec. Oct. 1986); children: Albert Henry II, Margaret Jean; m. Eva Homor, July 18, 1987; stepchildren: Rodney, Charmaine. Educated pub. schs., Youngstown, Ohio and Winthrop, Maine. With Saunders Mfg. Co. Inc., doing bus. as Saunders, Winthrop, 1947—, exec. v.p., 1967-77, pres., 1977-88, CEO, 1967-96, chmn. bd., 1988—. Chmn. Saunders Internat. B.V., Netherlands, Graphic Utilities, 1999—, RhinoSkin, Inc., 2000—; co-founder, sec., bd. dirs. Dirigo Bank and Trust Co., Augusta, Maine, 1969-86; co-founder, dir. Cushnoc Bank and Trust Co., Augusta, Maine, 1988-94. Chmn. jour. ADL Torch of Liberty Award, 1997. With U.S. Army, 1945-47. Recipient ADL Torch of Liberty award, 1998. Mem. Maine C. of C. and Industry (bd. dirs. 1976-81, chmn. mfg. coun. 1978-82), Maine Metal Products Assn. (bd. dirs. 1983-84), Soc. Mfg. Engrs. (cert. new product engr.), Internat. Bus. Forms Industries (chmn. assocs. 1976-77, co-chmn. exhibits com. 1978-82), Order of the Black Leaf, Document Mgmt. Industries Assn., Bus. Products Industry Assn., Office Products Mfrs. Assn. (bd. govs. 1988-94, v.p. 1990), Am. Legion, Masons, Shriners, others. Achievements include patentee in field. Home: PO Box 123 Readfield ME 04355-0123 Office: Saunders Mfg & Mktg PO Box 243 Winthrop ME 04364-0243

SAUNDERS, JOSEPH W. financial services company executive; Head credit card svcs. Household Credit Svcs.; chmn. & CEO Fleet Credit Card LLC, 1997—2001; chmn. bd, CEO & pres. Providian Fin. Corp., 2001—. Office: 201 Mission St San Francisco CA 94105

SAUNDERS, LONNA JEANNE, lawyer, newscaster, talk show host; b. Cleve. d. Jack Glenn and Lillian Frances (Newman) Slaby. Student, Dartmouth Coll.; AB in Polit. Sci. with honors, Vassar Coll.; JD, Northwestern U., 1981; cert. advanced study in Mass Media, Stanford U., 1992. Bar: Ill. 1981. News dir., morning news anchor Sta. WKBK-AM, Keene, NH, 1974-75; reporter Sta. KDKA-AM, Pitts., 1975; pub. affairs dir., news anchor Sta. WJW-AM, Cleve., 1975-76; helicopter traffic reporter WERE-AM Radio, Cleve., 1976-77; morning news anchor Sta. WBBG-AM, Cleve., 1978; talk host, news anchor Sta. WIND-AM, Chgo., 1978-82; atty. Arvey, Hodes, Costello & Burman, Chgo., 1981-82; host, "The Stock Market Observer", news anchor WCIU-TV, Chgo., 1982-85; staff atty. Better Govt. Assn., Chgo., 1983-84; news anchor, reporter Sta. WBMX FM, Chgo., 1984-86; pvt. practice Chgo., 1985—; news anchor Sta. WKQX-FM, Chgo., 1987. Instr. Columbia Coll., Chgo., 1987-90; guest talk host Sta. WMCA, N.Y.C., 1983, Sta. WMAQ, Chgo., 1988, Sta. WLS, Chgo., 1989, Sta. WWWE, Cleve., 1989, Sta. KVI, Seattle, 1994, WCBM-AM, Balt., 1996, WRC-AM, Wash., D.C., 1997; host, prodr. The Lively Arts, Cablevision Chgo., 1986; talk show host The Lonna Saunders Show, Sta. KIRO-AM, Seattle, 1995-96; news anchor, WTOP-AM Radio, Washington, D.C., 1996-97; talk host, "Today and Tomorrow show", WMAL-AM radio, Washington, D.C., 1997, freelance reporter, CBS Radio Network, N.Y.C., 1975—; writer, General Media, N.Y.C., 1996—; atty. Lawyers for Creative Arts, Chgo., 1985-91; guest columnist Gainesville (Fla.) Sun Newspaper, 1998-99, Rockford (Ill.) Register Star Newspaper, 1998—; freelance writer Indians Ink mag., 1998—. Columnist Chgo. Life mag., 1986—; editl. bd. Jour. Criminal Law and Criminology, 1979-81; contbr. articles to profl. jours.; creator pub. affairs program WBBM-AM, Chgo., 1985. Mem. women's action coun. Amnesty Internat., 2000—. Recipient Akron Press Club award for best pub. affairs presentation, 1978; grantee Scripps Howard Found., 1978-81; AFTRA George Heller Meml. scholar, 1980-81. Fellow Am. Bar Found.; mem. ABA (mem. exec. coms. Lawyers and the Arts, Law and Media 1986-92, chmn. exec. com. Law and Media 1990-91, 91-92, Young Lawyers divsn. liaison to Forum Com. on Comm. Law 1991-93, Commn. for Partnership Programs 1993-94, regional divsn. chair Forum on Comm. Law 1995-96). Roman Catholic. Avocations: theater, piano, baseball.

SAUNDERS, MARTIN WESLEY, music educator; b. Goldsboro, NC, Apr. 11, 1969; s. James (Jim) Wesley and Nancy Martin Saunders; m. Regina Lee Hoblit, July 19, 1994; children: Brayden James, Trevin Reid. MusM, Wright State U., Dayton, Ohio, 1992—94; MusB Edn., Winthrop U., Rock Hill, SC, 1987—92; Dr. of Musical Arts (In Progress), U. of Okla., Sch. of Music, Norman, Okla., 2001—03. Prof. of trumpet and jazz Marshall U. Dept. of Music, Huntington, W.Va., 2002—; usaf trumpeter USAF Heartland of Am. Band, Omaha, 1994—2001. Musical dir. USAF Heartland of Am. Jazz Ensemble, the Noteables, 1999—2001. Musician: (musical recording) Out of the Blue (CD Album), Heartland Sketches (CD album), Holiday Joy (CD Album), Always and Forever (CD Album), 'Tis the Season (CD Album). Choir dir. Thanksgiving Luth. Ch., Bellevue, Nebr., 1999—2000. Sr. airman USAF, 1994—2001, Offutt AFB, Omaha, Nebr. Decorated Achievement Medal USAF; recipient Artist Faculty, Nat. Trumpet Competition, 2003, Adjudicator, Internat. Trumpet Guild, 2000, Guest Clinician, U. of Wis., Eau Clare Jazz Festival, 1999, Ohio Chpt. Internat. Trumpet Guild, 1996. Mem.: Am. Fedn. of Musicians (assoc.), Internat. Assn. for Jazz Edn. (assoc.), Internat. Trumpet Guild (assoc.). Methodist. Home: 1739 Woodward Terrace Huntington WV 25705 Office: Marshall University Department of Music One John Marshall Drive Huntington WV 25755 Personal E-mail: mgbtsaunders3@wmconnect.com. E-mail: m.saunders@marshall.edu.

SAUNDERS, MARY L. career officer; BS in Social Work, Tex. Woman's U., 1970; grad., Squadron Officer Sch., 1973; MA in Guidance and Counseling, Rider Coll., 1978; grad., Air War Coll., 1993; nat. security leadership course, Johns Hopkins U., 1997. Commd. 2d lt. USAF, 1971, advanced through grades to brigadier gen., 1997; air terminal ops. officer 610th Mil. Airlift Support Squadron, Yokota Air Base, Japan, 1973-75; dep. comdr., comdr. Mil. Air Traffic Coordinating Office Mil. Traffic Mgmt. Command, McGuire AFB, N.J., 1976-79; chief of transp. 6168th Combat Support Squadron, Taegu Air Base, South Korea, 1982-83; comdr. 475th Transp. Squadron, Yokota Air Base, Japan, 1983-84; transp. staff officer Joint Deployment Agy., MacDill AFB, Fla., 1986-88, J-5, U.S. Transp. Command, Scott AFB, Ill., 1988-90; chief contingency plans divsn. J-5, U.S. So. Command, Quarry Heights, Panam, 1990-92; chief logistic plans Hdqs. Air Force Res., Robins AFB, Ga., 1993-96; dir. transp. Office Dep. Chief Staff Installations/Logistics Hdqs. USAF, The Pentagon, Washington, 1996-98; comdr. Def. Supply Ctr. Columbus Def. Logistics Agy., Columbus, Ohio, 1998—. Decorated Legion of Merit, Def. Meritorious Svc. medal with oak leaf cluster, Meritorious Svc. medal with 2 oak leaf clusters. Mem. AAUS, NAFE, Air Force Assn., Nat. Def. Transp. Assn. Office: Def Supply Ctr Columbus PO Box 3990 Columbus OH 43216-5000

SAUNDERS, MYRA KATHLEEN, dean, law librarian, educator; b. San Francisco, 1950; BA, U. Calif., Berkeley, 1972; MLS, U. So. Calif., 1973; JD, U. San Diego, 1979. Law libr. U. San Diego, Whittier Coll. Sch. Law, U. Calif., Berkeley; assoc. law libr. for pub. svcs. UCLA, 1983—89, law libr., prof. law in residence, 1989—, assoc. dean Hugh and Hazel Darling Law Libr., 1989—. Contbr. articles to profl. jours. Office: 1112 Law Bldg 405 Hilgard Ave Los Angeles CA 90095-1458

SAUNDERS, PAUL CHRISTOPHER, lawyer; b. N.Y.C., NY, May 21, 1941; s. John Richard and Agnes Grace (Kelly) Saunders; m. Patricia Newman, Aug. 14, 1968; children: Dr. Paul Christopher, Michael Eagan. AB, Fordham Coll., 1963; JD, Georgetown U., 1966; Certificat, Institut d'Études Politiques, Paris, 1962. Bar: NY 1966, DC 1967, US Supreme Ct 1969. Assoc. Cravath, Swaine & Moore LLP, N.Y.C., 1971-77, ptnr., 1977—; disting. visitor from practice Georgetown U. Law Ctr., 2003—. Mem ed bd: Georgetown Law Jour, 1965—66; editor (editor-in-chief): The Advocate, 1969—70. Trustee Fordham U., 1991—96; bd. regents Georgetown U., bd. visitors Law Ctr., 1996—97; trustee, vice-chmn Fordham Prep. Sch., 1986—94; v.p., bd. dirs. Legal Aid Soc., 1983—88; bd. dirs., trustee Lawyers Com. Civil Rights Under Law, 1985—, co-chair, 1995—97; v.p., trustee Vols. Legal Svc., Inc., 1999—; bd. dirs. Office of the Appellate Defender, 1999—; mem. N.Y. State Judicial Inst. on Professionalism in the Law, 2000—; chmn. bd. dirs. Constitution Project, 2000—. Capt JAGC U.S. Army, 1967—71. Decorated Meritorious Svc. medal; recipient John Carroll medal, Georgetown U., 1995, Whitney N. Seymour award, Lawyers Com. Civil Rights Under Law, 2000.

Fellow: Am. Bar Found., Am. Coll. Trial Lawyers; mem.: ABA, London Ct. Internat. Arbitration, Assn. Bar City N.Y., NY State Bar Assn., Westchester Country Club (Rye, NY), Apawamis Club (Rye, NY), Phi Beta Kappa, Pi Sigma Alpha. Democrat. Roman Catholic. Home: 1220 Park Ave New York NY 10128-1733 also: 455 Polly Pk Rd Rye NY 10580-1960 Office: Cravath Swaine & Moore LLP Worldwide Plz 825 8th Ave Fl 39 New York NY 10019-7475 E-mail: psaunders@cravath.com.

SAUNDERS, PETER PAUL, investor; b. Budapest, Hungary, July 21, 1928; emigrated to Can., 1941, naturalized, 1946; s. Peter Paul and Elizabeth (Halom) Szende; m. Nancy Louise McDonald, Feb. 11, 1956; children: Christine Elizabeth McBride, Paula Marie McMullen. Student, Vancouver Coll., 1941-44; B.Com., U. B.C., 1948. Acct. Canadian Pacific Rly. Co., 1948-50; founder, pres. Laurentide Fin. Corp., Ltd., 1950-66, vice chmn., 1966-67; chmn., pres. Coronation Credit Corp. Ltd., Vancouver, B.C., Can., 1968-78, Versatile Corp. (formerly Coronation Credit Corp. and Cornat Industries Ltd.), Vancouver, B.C., Can., 1978-87; prin., pres. Saunders Investment Ltd., Vancouver, 1987—. Past pres. Vancouver Symphony Soc., 1968-70, Can. Cancer Soc., B.C. and Yukon Region, 1975-77, Vancouver Art Gallery Assn., 1981-83; chmn. Vancouver Opera Round Table, 1984-92. Mem. Vancouver Club, Shaughnessy Golf and Country Club, Royal Vancouver Yacht Club, Thunderbird Country Club (Rancho Mirage, Calif.). Avocations: golf, skiing, hunting, boating. Home: 3620 Alexandra St Vancouver BC Canada V6J 4B9 Office: Saunders Investment Ltd PO Box 49352 Bentall Ctr Vancouver BC Canada V7X 1L4

SAUNDERS, PHILIP D. professional basketball coach; b. Cleve., Feb. 23, 1955; m. Debbie Saunders; children: Ryan, Mindy, Rachel and Kimberly (twins). Student, U. Minn. Asst. coach U. Minn Golden Golphers, 1982-86, U. Tulsa, 1986-88; head coach Continental Basketball Assn. Rapid City (S.D.) Thrillers, 1988-89, La Crosse (Wis.) Catbirds, 1989-94, gen. mgr., 1991-93, team pres., 1991-94; head coach Continental Basketball Assn. Sioux Falls (S.D.) Skyforce; gen. mgr., head coach Minn. Timberwolves, 1995—. Named CBA Coach of the Yr., 1989, 92. Office: Minn Timberwolves 600 1st Ave N Minneapolis MN 55403-1416

SAUNDERS, ROBERT SAMUEL, venture capital executive; b. Akron, Ohio, Dec. 3, 1951; s. Samuel Robert and Rose Saunders; m. Heidi Ruth Fulkerson, Mar. 18, 1978. AB with distinction, Stanford U., 1973; MSc with distinction, London Sch. Econs., 1974; diploma, U. Stockholm, 1976; MA, Harvard U., 1978. Cons. World Bank, Washington, 1975—77; sr. cons. Boston Cons. Group, 1978—82; dir. competitive strategy analysis Bain and Co., Boston, 1982—86; sr. v.p., chief planning officer Krupp Cos., Boston, 1986—88. Chmn. Saunders Capital Group, Boston, 1988—94; mng. dir. Providian Capital Mgmt., Louisville, 1993—97; sr. mng. dir. Chrysalis Ventures, Louisville, 1997—; vice chmn. Telemics, Inc., Louisville; chmn. Internat. Mktg. Concepts, Louisville; fin. com. chmn. Pub. Radio Partnership, Louisville, 1996—; chmn. Venture Club Louisville, 1995—; investment com. chmn. African Am. Venture Capital Fund, 1993—; chmn. adv. bd. dept. computer engring. and computer sci. U. Louisville; bd. dirs. Metacyte, Inc., Louisville, Constrn. Software Tech., Inc., Cin., Ygnition, Inc., Seattle, bCatalyst, LLC, Louisville, Tech Skills LLC, Austin, Compliance & Ethics Learning Solutions, Chgo., Actor's Theater, Louisville, Tech. Enterprise Network, Louisville; dev. com. chmn. Walden Theater, Louisville; with Compliance & Ethics Learning Solutions, Inc., Chgo., CWK, Inc., Atlanta. Editor: Stanford Quar. Rev., 1973. Del. Mass. Dem. Nat. Conv., San Francisco, 1984; co-founder Weston Conservation Trust, Mass., 1988. Marshall scholar, 1973-75; NEH fellow, 1978; Swedish Govt. Fulbright grantee, 1975, U.S. Congress Profl. Devel. grantee, 1976. Mem. Am. Econ. Assn., Internat. Union for Sci. Study of Population. Unitarian Universalist. Home: PO Box 99252 Louisville KY 40269-0252 Office: Chrysalis Ventures Ste 1650 National City Tower, 5th St Louisville KY 40202

SAUNDERS, RON, lawyer, former state legislator; b. Key West, Fla., Oct. 30, 1954; s. Jack and Edith (Hill) S. BS with high honors, U. Fla., 1976, JD, 1979. Bar: Fla. 1979. Pvt. practice, Key West, 1979-94, Tallahassee, 1995—; mem. Fla. Ho. of Reps., 1986-94, chmn. appropriations com., 1990-92, chmn. cmty. affairs com., 1992-94. Mem. Fla. Tax and Budget Reform Commn., 1993-94. Pres. Key West Jaycees, 1981-82; chmn. bd. trustees Fla. Keys C.C., 1983-86; pres. Fla. Keys Land and Sea Trust, 1990-91. Named Outstanding Chpt. Pres., Fla. Jaycees, 1982, Outstanding Young Floridian, 1993, Most Effective Mem., Fla. Ho. of Reps., 1991, 92. Mem. Fla. Bar Assn. (bd. govs. young lawyers sect. 1982-86). Democrat. Episcopalian. Office: Bryant Miller & Olive 201 S Monroe St Ste 500 Tallahassee FL 32301-1879 Address: 1207 11th St Key West FL 33040-4097

SAUNDERS, SALLY LOVE, poet, educator; b. Bryn Mawr, Pa., Jan. 15, 1940; d. Lawrence and Dorothy (Love) S. Student, Sophia U., Tokyo, Japan, 1963, U. Pa., Columbia; BS, George Williams Coll., 1965. Tchr. Shipley Sch., Bryn Mawr, 1962-65, Agnes Irwin Sch., Wynnewood, Pa., 1964-65, Montgomery County Day Sch., Wynnewood, 1962, Miquon (Pa.) Sch., Waldron Acad., Merion, Pa., 1965-66, Phelps Sch., Malvern, Pa., 1965-70, Frankford Friends Sch. Phila., 1965-66, Haverford (Pa.) Sch., 1965-66, Friends Sem. Sch., N.Y.C., 1966-68, Ballard Sch., N.Y.C., 1966-67, Lower Merion Sch., Ardmore, Pa., nights 1967-71, Univ. Settlement House, Phila., 1961-63, Navajo Indian Reservation, Fort Defiance, Ariz., 1963, Young Men's Jewish Youth Center, Chgo., 1964-65, Margaret Fuller Settlement House, Cambridge, Mass., 1958-61; poetry therapist Pa. Hosp. Inst., 1969-74, also drug rehab. house; poet in residence Tyrone Guthrie Ctr., Newbliss, Ireland, Aug. 1988; poetry workshop leader Pendle Hill Quaker Ctr., Wallingford, Pa., Apr. 1988; poetry week leader Ferry Beach, Saco, Maine, summer 1988. Pioneer in poetry therapy. Poet, 1946—; poems pub. in periodicals including others; author: Past the Near Meadows, 1961, Pauses, 1978, Fresh Bread, 1982, Random Thoughts, 1992, Patchwork Quilt, 1993, Quiet Thoughts and Gentle Feelings, 1996, Word Pictures, 1998; contbr. poems to newspapers. Mem. Acad. Am. Poets, Nat. Fedn. State Poetry Socs., Am. Poetry League, Nat. League Am. Pen Women, Poetry Therapy Assn. (v.p.), Avalon Orgn., Authors Guild, Nat. Writers Club, Pen and Brush Club, N.H., Pa. poetry socs., Cath. Poetry Soc. (asso.), Fla. State Poetry Soc. (asso.) Episcopalian. Home: 2030 Vallejo St Apt 501 San Francisco CA 94123-4854 Office: 609 Rose Hill Rd Broomall PA 19008-2254 Office Phone: 610-356-0849. E-mail: slovesndrs@aol.com. *So often during my life I have found great comfort and strength in writing and reading poetry. With my poetry I want to help others to get in touch with their own powers. Poetry, to me, is a rare and beautiful freedom and this is what I want to share with others.*

SAUNDERS, STEVEN R. corporate communications specialist; s. Lawrence J. and Sara (Leinoff) Saunders; m. Maureen Collins, May 28, 1977; children: Keira, Erin, Burke. BA, Washington & Lee U., 1968. Dep. mayor Town of Oyster Bay, NY, 1970—74; staff asst. NY State Legis., Albany, 1974—75; legis. dir. US Rep. Norman F. Lent, Washington, 1975—77; comm. dir. Nat. Rep. Senatorial Com., Washington, 1977—79; staff dir. Rep. Conf. of the US Senate, Washington, 1979—81; asst. US trade rep. Exec. Office of the Pres., Washington, 1981—82; pres. Saunders & Co., Alexandria, Va., 1982—. Pres. N.Am.-Mongolia Bus. Coun., Alexandria, 1998—. Editor: Japan Hands: Who's Who in US-Japan Relations in the US Government, 1990. Pres. Zorig Found. USA, Alexandria, 2000—; co-chmn. Am. Coun. Young Polit. Leaders, 1982—89. Recipient Businessman for Liberty award, Liberty Ctr., 2001, Investment Envoy of the Yr. award, Govt. Mongolia-Ulaanbaatar, 2002. Mem.: Am. Mgmt. Assn. (internat. coun. 1995—), Theodore Roosevelt Assn. (trustee 1970—). Republican. Avocation: art. Office: Saunders & Co 1015 Duke St Alexandria VA 22314 Office Phone: 703-549-1555.

SAUNDERS, SYLVIA CHRISTIE, biologist, educator; arrived in U.S.A., 1958; d. Zachariah and Cleodine Christie; m. Hermon Saunders, June 24, 1971; children: Reeka, Eric. BSc, NYU, 1962, MSc, 1965, PhD, 1969. From asst. prof. to prof. CUNY, N.Y.C., 1966—75, prof., 1975—, asst. dean, 1966—75. Founder and coord. Cleo & Zack Project CUNY, 2000—. Nominee Chase Nat. Prof. of Yr.; grantee, NIH, 1970—, NSF, 1970—. Mem.: AAAS, N.Y. Acad. Scis. Avocations: gardening, writing, reading, mentoring. Office: Borough of Manhattan Cmty Coll 199 Chambers St New York NY 10007

SAUNDERS, TERRY ROSE, lawyer; b. Phila., July 13, 1942; d. Morton M. and Esther (Hauptman) Rose; m. George Lawton Saunders Jr., Sept. 21, 1975. BA, Barnard Coll., 1964; JD, NYU, 1973. Bar: D.C. 1973, Ill. 1976, U.S. Dist. Ct. (no. dist.) Ill. 1976, U.S. Ct. Appeals (7th cir.) 1976, U.S. Supreme Ct. 1983. Assoc. Williams & Connolly, Washington, 1973-75, Jenner & Block, Chgo., 1975-80, ptnr., 1981-86, Susman, Saunders & Buehler, Chgo., 1987-94; pvt. practice Law Offices of Terry Rose Saunders, Chgo., 1995—2002; ptnr. Saunders & Doyle, Chgo., 2002—. Author: (with others) Securities Fraud: Litigating Under Rule 10b-5, 1989. Recipient Robert B. McKay award NYU Sch. Law. Mem. ABA (co-chair class actions and derivative suits com. sect. litig. 1992-95, task force on merit selection of judges, co-chair consumer and personal rights litig. com. sect. litigation 2000-02), Chgo. Bar Assn., Order of Coif, Union League Club. Office: 33 N Dearborn St Chicago IL 60602 E-mail: trsaunders@saundersdoyle.com.

SAUNDERS, WARD BISHOP, JR., retired aluminum company executive; b. Gilroy, Calif., Nov. 26, 1919; s. Ward Bishop and Lamira (Doan) S.; m. Elaine McDermott, Oct. 11, 1942; children: Douglas L., Myra K., Leslie J. BS, U. Calif., Berkeley, 1942; JD, Stanford U., 1948. Bar: Calif. 1948, U.S. Dist. Ct. (no. dist.) Calif. 1948, U.S. Supreme Ct. 1956. Atty. Kaiser Aluminum & Chem. Corp., Oakland, Calif., 1951-65, div. v.p., 1965-71, v.p., 1971-84. Dir. Volta River Authority, Accra, Ghana, Aluminium Bahrain, Manama, Bahrain, Hindustan Aluminium Co., Bombay, India; mng. dir. Volta Aluminium Co. Ltd., Tema, Ghana, 1971-84. Served to lt. USNR, 1942-46. Mem. Kaiser Aluminum Salaried Retirees Assn. (bd. dirs. 1988-94, pres. 1992-93, v.p. 1995-98), Commonwealth Club of Calif. Republican. Unitarian Universalist. Home: 6123 Estates Dr Oakland CA 94611-3117

SAUNDERS, W(ARREN) PHILLIP, JR., economics educator, consultant, author; b. Morgantown, W.Va., Sept. 3, 1934; s. Warren Phillip and Thelma Marie (Dotson) S.; m. Nancy Lee Trainor, June 16, 1956; children: Kathleen M., Kevin W., Keith A., Kent T., Kristine A. BA, Pa. State U., 1956; MA, U. Ill., 1957; PhD, MIT, 1964. Instr. econs. Bowdoin Coll., Brunswick, Maine, 1961-62; rsch. assoc., from asst. to assoc. prof. econs. Carnegie-Mellon U., Pitts., 1962-70; prof. econs. Ind. U., Bloomington, 1970—; assoc. dean Coll. of Arts and Scis. Ind. U., Bloomington, 1974-78, chmn. dept. econs., 1988-92. Cons. Agy. for Instructional Tech., Bloomington, 1976-78, 81-84, 92-93. Author: (books) Political Dimension of Labor-Management Relations, 1986; author, editor: Framework for Teaching Basic Economic Concepts, 1995; (Workbooks) Introduction to Macroeconomics (18th edit.), 1998, Introduction to Microeconomics (18th edit.), 1998; contbr. articles to Am. Econ. Rev., 1964—. Chmn. staff-parish rels. com. First United Meth. Ch., Bloomington, 1982-94. Recipient Vilard award for disting. rsch., Nat. Assn. Econ. Educators, N.Y.C., 1986, Leavey award for edn. Freedoms Found., Valley Forge, Pa., 1986, Disting. Svc. award. Nat. Coun. Econ. Edn., 1995. Mem. Am. Econ. Assn., Midwest Econ. Assn. (1st v.p. 1988-89), Soc. Econs. Educators (pres. 1992-93). Home: 3725 E Brownridge Rd Bloomington IN 47401-4209 Office: Ind Univ Dept Econs Bloomington IN 47405 E-mail: saunders@indiana.edu.

SAUNDERS, WILLIAM HUNDLEY, JR., retired chemist, educator; b. Pulaski, Va., Jan. 12, 1926; s. William Hundley and Vivian (Watts) S.; m. Nina Velta Plesums, June 25, 1960 (dec. June 1982); children: Anne Michele, Claude William; m. Barbara Andrews, Apr. 27, 2002. BS in Chemistry, Coll. William and Mary, 1948; PhD in Organic Chemistry, Northwestern U., 1952. Rsch. assoc. MIT, 1951-53; instr. U. Rochester, 1953-56, from. asst. prof. to assoc. prof., 1956-64, prof. chemistry, 1964-91, faculty sr. assoc., 1991-95, chmn. dept., 1966-70, prof. emeritus, 1996—. Author: Ionic Aliphatic Reactions, 1965; (with A.F. Cockerill) Mechanisms of Elimination Reactions, 1973; (with L. Melander) Reaction Rates of Isotopic Molecules, 1980; contbr. numerous articles to profl. jours. With U.S. Army, 1944-45, ETO. Guggenheim fellow, 1960-61; Sloan Found. fellow, 1961-64; NSF sr. postdoctoral fellow, 1970-71 Mem. Am. Chem. Soc., Royal Soc. Chemistry, Phi Beta Kappa, Sigma Xi, Phi Lambda Upsilon. Democrat. Unitarian Universalist. Avocations: bicycling, cross country skiing, travel. Home: 15 Parkwood Ave Rochester NY 14620-3401 Office: U Rochester Dept Chemistry River Sta Rochester NY 14627 Office Phone: 585-275-4235. Business E-Mail: saunders@chem.rochester.edu.

SAUSMAN, KAREN, zoological park administrator; b. Chgo., Nov. 26, 1945; d. William and Annabell (Lofaso) S. BS, Loyola U., 1966; student, Redlands U., 1968. Keeper Lincoln Park Zoo, Chgo., 1964-66; tchr. Palm Springs (Calif.) Unified Sch., 1968-70; ranger Nat. Park Svc., Joshua Tree, Calif., 1968-70; zoo dir. The Living Desert, Palm Desert, Calif., 1970—. Natural history study tour leader internat., 1974—; part-time instr. Coll. Desert Natural History Calif. Desert, 1975-78; field reviewer conservation grants Inst. Mus. Svcs., 1987—, MAP cons., 1987—, panelist, 1992—; internat. studbook keeper for Sand Cats, 1988-2001, for Cuvier's Gazelle, Mhorr Gazelle, 1990-2000; co-chair Arabian Oryx species survival plan propogation group, 1986-95; spkr. in field. Author Survival Captive Bighorn Sheep, 1982, Small Facilities- Opportunities and Obligations, 1983; wildlife illustrator books, mags, 1970—; editor Fox Paws newsletter Living Desert, 1970—, ann. reports, 1976—; natural sci. editor Desert Mag., 1979-82; compiler Conservation and Management Plan for Antelope, 1992; contbr. articles to profl. jours. Past bd. dirs., sec. Desert Protective Coun.; adv. coun. Desert Bighorn Rsch. Inst., 1981-85; bd. dirs. Palm Springs Desert Resorts Convention and Visitors Bur., 1988-94; bd. dirs., treas. Coachella Valley Mountain Trust, 1989-92. Named Woman Making a Difference Soroptomist Internat., 1989, 93, 97, Woman of Distinction, Riverside Bus. Press, 2000. Fellow Am. Assn. Zool. Parks and Aquariums (bd. dirs., accredation field reviewer, desert antelope taxon adv. group, caprid taxon adv. group, felid taxon adv. group, small population mgmt. adv. group, wildlife conservation and mgmt. com., chmn. ethics com. 1987, mem. com., internat. rels. com., ethics task force, pres'. award 1972-77, outstanding svc. award 1983, 88, editor newsletter, Zool. Parks and Aquarium Fundamentals 1982); mem. Internat. Species Inventory System (mgmt. com., policy adv. group 1980-96), Calif. Assn. Mus. (v.p. 1992-96), Calif. Assn. Zoos and Aquariums, World Assn. Zoos and Aquariums (coun. 2002-, governing coun. 2002-, pres.-elect 2003), Western Interpretive Assn. (so. Calif. chpt.), Am. Assn. Mus., Arboreta and Botanical Gardens So. Calif. (coun. dirs.), Soc. Conservation Biology, Nat. Audubon. Soc., Jersey Wildlife Preservation Trust Internat., Nature Conservancy, East African Wildlife Soc., African Wildlife Found., Kennel Club Palm Springs (past bd. dirs., treas. 1978-80), Scottish Deerhound Club Am. (editor Scottish Deerhounds in N.A., 1983, life mem. U.K. chpt.), Internat. Bengal Cat Soc. (pres. 1994-96). Avocations: pure bred dogs, cats, dressage, painting, photography. Office: The Living Desert 47 900 Portola Ave Palm Desert CA 92260 E-mail: kastld@aol.com.

SAUTE, ROBERT EMILE, drug and cosmetic consultant; b. West Warwick, RI, Aug. 18, 1929; s. Camille T. and Lea E. (Goffinet) S.; m. Arda T. Darnell, May 18, 1957; children: Richard R., Steven N., Allen K. BS, RI Coll. Pharmacy, 1950; MS, Purdue U., 1952, PhD, 1953. Registered pharmacist. Tech. asst. to pres. Lafayette (Ind.) Pharmacal, 1955-56; sr. rsch. and devel. chemist H.K. Wampole Denver Chem. Co., Phila., 1956-57; supt. Murray Hill (NJ) plant Strong Cobb Arner Inc., 1957-60; adminstrv. dir. rsch. and devel. Avon Products Inc., Suffern, NY, 1960-68; dir. rsch. and devel. toiletries divsn. Gillette Co., Boston, 1968-71; group v.p. Dart Industries, LA, 1972-75; pres. Saute Cons., Inc., LA, 1975—. Bd. dirs. Joico Labs., Inc., Cosmetics Enterprises, Ltd. Contbr. to books; patentee in field. With U.S. Army, 1953-55. Named Old Master, Disting. Alumnus, Purdue U. Fellow Soc. Cosmetic Chemists (bd. dirs. 1987-89, 94-96, chmn. Calif. chpt. 1986); mem. AAAS, N.Y. Acad. Scis., Soc. Investigative Dermatology, Am. Assn. Pharm. Scientists, Purdue U. Alumni Assn. (old master, disting. alumnus), Sigma Xi, Rho Chi. Avocations: travel, art, music, cooking, wine. Office Phone: 818-896-1444.

SAUTER, JOHNNY, race car driver; Race car driver Richard Childress Racing, Welcome, NC. Named Champion, Rookie of Yr., Am. Speed Assn., 2001, 10 Time winner. Office: c/o Richard Childress Racing PO Box 1189 236 Industrial Dr Welcome NC 27347

SAUTER, MICHAEL JOSEPH, real estate company executive; b. Cleve., Oct. 10, 1957; s. Harry Albert and Carmel Ann Sauter; m. Carol Ann Sauter, Sept. 6, 1988; children: Ryan, Rory, Mary Colleen. BA, Seattle U., 1981. Cert. real property adminstr. Bldg. Owners & Mgmt. Inst., lic. real estae broker Wash., Ariz. With asset mgmt. divsn. Corp. Cath. Archdiocese, Seattle, 1979—89; asst. mgr. Portland, Oreg., 1989—92; v.p. Jones & Murphy, Inc., Seattle, 1992—2001; CEO S-J Mgmt. LLC (formerly Jones & Murphy, Inc.), Seattle, 2001—. Mem.: Comml. Brokers Assn., Rental Housing Assn. Puget Sound, Master Builders Assn., Wash. Multi-Housing Assn., Nat. Multi Housing Coun. Avocations: sports, coaching, running, travel. Office: S J Mgmt LLC 2150 N 107th Ste 440 Seattle WA 98133 Office Phone: 206-365-7900. Office Fax: 206-361-2105. Business E-Mail: msauter@sjm.biz.

SAUTTER, CHESTER ARTHUR, physicist, educator; b. Scotia, Nebr., Nov. 16, 1933; s. Henry Edward and Edna Emma Sautter; m. Shirley D'Anne Gaston; children: Gregory, Lorraine, Britta, Rachel. BA, Nebr. Wesleyan U., 1955; MA, U. Nebr., 1958, PhD, 1963. Postdoctorate rschr. Physics Inst. U. Aarhus, Denmark, 1963—64; from asst. prof. to prof. emeritus Concordia Coll., Moorhead, Minn., 1964—97, assoc. prof., 1997—. Guest rsch. prof. U. Wash. State, Pullman, Wash., 1974—75; cons. N.Mex. coun. Chs., Window Rock, Ariz., 1981—82; vis. prof. History of Sci. U. Minn., Mpls., 1988—89; vis. rsch. prof. Nuclear Radiation Ctr. Wash. State U., 1975—76; vis. rsch. prof. Los Alamos (N.Mex.) Nat. Lab., 1984; vis. prof. and rschr. Idaho Nat. Engring. Lab., Idaho Falls, Idaho, 1989—91. Contbr. articles to profl. jours. Grantee, Fulbright Internat. Exchange Coun., 1963—64. Mem.: Soc. Preservation and Encouragement of Barbershop Quartet Singing in Am., Sigma Pi Sigma, Sigma Xi. Avocations: reading, travel, canoeing, picture framing, barbershop singing. Home: 1 Cooper Lane Bella Vista AR 72714

SAUVAGEAU, YVON, application developer; b. Montreal, Que., Can., Dec. 10, 1961; s. Yvon Sauvageau and Huguette Bergeron. BSc in Computer Sci., McGill U., Montreal, 1986. Cert. Java developer Sun Microsystems. Software engr. NSK Technologies, Paris, 1997—99, Merrimac Interactive Media, Cocoa, Fla., 1999—2000, Cisco Systems, Inc., San Jose, Calif., 2000—. Mem.: IEEE. Achievements include patents pending for method and apparatus for drawing line graphs; development of compression algorithm for the Java language binaries; software tool for the evaluation of binary compatibility between Java language binaries; graphical user interface of network topology maps. Office: Cisco Systems Inc 3550 Cisco Way SJC19/3/3 San Jose CA 95134

SAUVÉ, CAROLYN OPAL, writer, journalist, poet; b. Columbus, N.C., Apr. 30, 1934; d. Anthony Floyd and Nina Morris Pittman; m. Joseph Ernest Sauvé, Mar. 31, 1953; children: Floyd, Kenneth, Timothy. Student, Spartanburg Meth. Coll., 1952—53; AAS, Isothermal C.C., 1976. Editor, author, photographer: History of Polk County, 1983; author, photograph APP Jour., 1999; author: Spirit of the Age, 1996. Trustee Isothermal C.C., Spindale, N.C., 1985-93; bd. dirs. Area Mental Health Bd., Spindale, 1985-91; v.p., sec., edn. chmn. Am. Cancer Soc., Polk County, N.C., 1975-79; bd. dirs. Juvenile Justice Bd., Rutherfordton, N.C., 1978-82; chmn. Polk County Commn., Columbus, 1978-82; chmn. Polk County Rep. Party, Columbus, 1984-86, 95-98; vice chmn., dist. chmn. N.C. Rep. Women's Club, Raleigh, 1975-79; chmn. World Missions Com., 1994-2000; chmn. bd. Polk County Dept. Social Svcs., 2003—. Mem. Polk County Hist. Assn. (pres. 1984-86, v.p. 1996-2000). Presbyterian. Avocations: creative writing, boating, cake decorating, grandchildren. Home: 165 Landrum Rd Columbus NC 28722-9545

SAVAGE, CHRISTINE R. state legislator; b. Union, Maine, Aug. 5, 1931; m. Elmer Savage, four children. Town ofc. mgr. Town of Union, 1975-90, acting mgr., municipal mgmnt., 1990-91, town mgr., 1991-95; mem. Dist. 60 Maine Ho. of Reps., Augusta, 1994-99; mem. Dist. 12 Maine Senate, Augusta, 2000—. Home: 504 Barrett Hill Rd Union ME 04862 Office: Maine Senate 3 State House Station Augusta ME 04333

SAVAGE, ELDON PAUL, retired environmental health educator; b. Bedford, Iowa, Apr. 4, 1926; s. Paul and Nora (Arthur) S.; m. Ella May, June 5, 1948; children: Steven P., Michael D. BS, U. Kans., 1950; MPH, Tulane U., 1958; PhD, Okla. U., 1968. Coord. environ. sanitation demonstration projects USPHS, Kans., Iowa and Pa., 1950-64; chief state aids sect. pesticide ctr. Ctr. for Disease Control, Atlanta, 1964-70; chief chem. epidemiology sect. Inst. Rural Environ. Health, Colo. State U., Ft. Collins, 1970-84, prof., dir. environ. health divsn., 1984-85, head dept. environ. health, 1985-90, dir. environ. health svcs., 1987-93, prof. emeritus, 1993—. Contbr. articles to profl. jours. Mem. Am. Acad. Sanitarians (sec., treas., diplomate), Nat. Environ. Health Assn., Sigma Xi, Gamma Sigma Delta. Home: Savage EE Arabian Horses 5220 Apple Dr Fort Collins CO 80526-4302 Office: Colo State U Inst Rural Envrion Health Fort Collins CO 80523-0001

SAVAGE, FRANK, investment executive; b. Rocky Mount, N.C., July 10, 1938; s. Frank and Grace Vivian (Pitt) S.; B.A., Howard U., 1961; M.A., Sch. Advanced Internat. Studies, Johns Hopkins U., 1964; m. Lolita Valderrama, Apr. 19, 1980; children— Eric, Brett, Mark, Antoine, Grace, Frank Jr. Officer overseas div. Citibank, N.Y.C., 1964-70; v.p., then pres. Equico Capital Corp., N.Y.C., 1970-73; exec. v.p. TAW Internat. Leasing, N.Y.C., 1973-75; mem. staff of chmn. bd., v.p. Equitable Life Assurance Soc. U.S., N.Y.C., 1975-76, then v.p., investment officer, then exec. v.p., dep. to chief exec. officer; now chmn. Equitable Capital Mgmt. Corp. subs. Equitable Life Assurance Soc. U.S., sr. v.p. Equitable Life Assurance Soc. U.S.; bd. dirs. Lockheed, Essence Communications, Equico Capital Corp., United Mut. Life Ins. Co.; former chmn. bd. Freedom Nat. Bank of N.Y. Chmn. bd. Ops. Crossroads Africa, 1980; mem. task force White House Conf. on Small Bus., 1978—; trustee Johns Hopkins U., 1977—; bd. dirs. Essence Communications, N.Y. Philharm. Mem. Coun. Fgn. Rels., N.Y.C. Pvt. Industry Coun. (former chmn.). Recipient Blackafrica award, 1977, Harlem Commonwealth Coun. Banking award, 1979, Outstanding Alumni award Howard U., 1982. Presbyterian. Office: Equitable Capital Mgmt 19th Fl 1285 Avenue Of The Americas fl 19 New York NY 10019-6028

SAVAGE, JAMES FRANCIS, editor; b. Boston, July 23, 1939; s. James and Hanora (Enright) S.; m. Sharon Kaye Base, May 29, 1965; 1 son, Sean. AA, Boston U., 1959, BS, 1961. Reporter Quincy (Mass.) Patriot Ledger, 1961-63; reporter Miami (Fla.) Herald, 1963-67, investigative reporter, 1967-78, investigations editor, 1978-84, assoc. editor investigations, 1984—. Investigative reporter Boston Herald Traveler, 1967 Served with AUS, 1962. Recipient Nat. Headliners award, 1969, Fla. Press Assn. award, 1972, George Polk Meml. award for investigative reporting, 1973, 80, Pub. Service award Nat. A.P. Mng. Editors, 1974, 80, award Fla. Soc. Newspaper Editors, 1974, 75, Nat. Disting. Service award Sigma Delta Chi, 1979, 87, Pulitzer Prize Staff award for Nat. Reporting, 1987, Outstanding Investigative Reporting award Investigative Reporters and Editors, 1988, Disting. Alumni award Boston U. Coll. Communications, 1990, Pulitzer Prize Staff Pub. Svc. award, 1993; Profl. Journalism fellow Stanford, 1974-75 Home: 1004 Orange Is Fort Lauderdale FL 33315-1651 Office: 1 Herald Plz Miami FL 33132-1609

SAVAGE, JOHN EDMUND, computer science educator, researcher; b. Lynn, Mass., Sept. 19, 1939; s. Edmund J. and Eldora A. (Guay) S.; m. Patricia Joan Landers, Jan. 29, 1966; children: Elizabeth, Kevin, Christopher, Timothy ScB, ScM, MIT, 1962, PhD, 1965. Mem. tech. staff Bell Telephone Labs., Holmdel, N.J., 1965-67; prof. computer sci. Brown U., Providence, 1967—, chmn. dept. computer sci., 1985-91. Vis. prof. U. Paris, 1980-81, Warwick U., Eng., 1991-92; mem. dept. vis. com. elec. engring. and computer sci. MIT, 1991—; cons. in field. Author: The Complexity of Computing, 1977; (with others) The Mystical Machine, 1986, Models of Computation: Exploring the Power of Computing, 1998; editor: (with Thomas Knight) Advanced Research in VLSI and Parallel Systems, 1992; chmn. editl. bd. Computing Rsch. News, 1990-96; mem. editl. bd. Jour. Computer and Sys. Scis., 1993—; patentee data scrambler, 1970, means and methods for generating permutation of a square, 1976. Mem. MIT Corp. vis. com. dept. elec. engring. and computer sci., 1991-2002. Fulbright-Hays grantee, 1973; NSF fellow, 1961, Guggenheim fellow, 1973 Fellow AAAS, IEEE, Assn. Computing Machinery; mem.

Computing Rsch. Assn. (bd. dirs. 1990-96), Sigma Xi, Tau Beta Pi. Avocations: reading, bicycling, walking. Office: Brown U Dept Computer Sci 115 Waterman St Providence RI 02912-9016 Office Phone: 401-863-7642. E-mail: john_savage@brown.edu.

SAVAGE, JOHN WILLIAM, lawyer; b. Seattle, Oct. 11, 1951; s. Stanley and Jennie Sabina (Siggstedt) S.; m. Rebecca Lee Abraham, Oct. 1, 1983; children: Bennett William, James Oliver. Student, Lewis and Clark Coll., 1969-71, JD Northwestern Sch. Law, 1977; BA, U. Wash., 1973. Bar: Oreg. 1977, Wash. 2002, U.S. Dist. Ct. Oreg. 1977, U.S. Ct. Appeals (9th cir.) 1977, U.S. Ct. Appeals (fed. cir.) 1998, U.S. Supreme Ct., 1985. Pvt. practice law, Portland, Oreg., 1977-79; ptnr. Bailey, Olstad, Rieke, Geil & Savage, P.C., Portland, 1979-80; ptnr., shareholder Rieke, Geil & Savage, P.C., Portland, 1980-95; shareholder Rieke & Savage, P.C., Portland, 1995—. Mem. Oreg. Literacy Inc., Portland, 1979-85; mem. standing com. City Club, Portland, 1984-88, chmn. law and pub. safety standing com. 1986-87. Recipient award of merit, Gerry Spence's Trial Lawyers Coll., 1999. Mem. ABA (chairperson young lawyers sect. Nat. Cmty. Law Week 1983-84, inmate grievance com. 1984-88), Assn. Trial Lawyers Am., Trial Lawyers for Pub. Justice, Oreg. Trial Lawyers Assn. (edn. com. 2002—), Oreg. Bar Assn. (def. of indigent accused com. 1985-89), Oreg. Criminal Def. Lawyers Assn. (bd. dirs. 1984-86), Multnomah Bar Assn. (v.p. young lawyers sect. 1980, pres.-elect 1981, pres. 1982, Disting. Svc. award, bd. dirs. 1989-92, task force chair 1992-93, jud. selection com. 1998-99, cir. ct. liaison com. 2002—, Award of Merit 1994). Home: 397 Furnace St Lake Oswego OR 97034-3957 Office: STE 200 820 SW 2ND Ave Portland OR 97204-3087 E-mail: jwsavage@rieke-savage.com.

SAVAGE, JOSEPH GEORGE, hospital administrator; b. Bklyn. s. Joseph George Jr. and Eileen (Schnell) S.; m. Lynn Ann Campbell; children: Kimberly, Patricia, Joseph IV. BA, Oswego Coll., 1977; postgrad., Seton Hall U., 1985. Pub. affairs dir. L.I. chpt. Nat. Multiple Sclerosis Soc., N.Y.C., 1977-79, exec. dir. Conn. chpt., 1979-80; dir. devel., mktg. Clara Mass Meml. Med. Ctr., Belleville, N.J., 1980-81; exec. dir. Found. of St. Joseph's Hosp. Med. Ctr., Paterson, N.J., 1981-89; sr. v.p. St. Francis Hosp. Heart Ctr., Roslyn, N.Y., 1989-92; v.p. St. Vincents Hosp. and Med. Ctr., N.Y.C., 1992-98, Cathedral Health Care Sys., Newark, 1998—. Commr. health City of Clifton, 1990-94; bd. dirs. N.Y. Heart Coun., 1989-93, Cath. Family and Cmty. Svcs., 1992—, Osweo Coll. Alumni, 1992—, St. Mary's Hosp., Passiac, N.J., 1993—, v.p., 1998—. Fellow Nat. Assn. Hosp. Devel. (communication chair 1982-85, edn. chair 1985-86, bd. dirs., regional dir. 1988-89), Friendly Sons of St. Patrick, Ancient Order of Hibernians, Rotary (past pres. Clifton Club, Paul Harris fellow, Walter Head fellow). Roman Catholic. Avocations: swimming, golf. Office: Cathedral Health Care Sys 219 Chestnut St Newark NJ 07105-1558 Home: 14 Limonite Rd Hackettstown NJ 07840-4821

SAVAGE, JOSEPH SCOTT, physician; b. Malden, Mass., Dec. 30, 1958; s. Jospeh Edward and Arlene Barbara S.; m. Gwendolyn Kieko Uezo, July 4, 1979 (div); m. Terri Armstrong, Apr. 2, 1998; 1 child, Colin Eric. BA, Wheaton Coll., 1983; DO, Osteopath, Medicine, Kirksville Coll., 1987. Diplomate Am. Bd. Osteopathic Med. Examiners, Am. Bd. Emergency Medicine. Coomd. maj. USAF, 1988; coord. EMS svcs. Wright Patterson AFB, Dayton, Ohio, coord. disater svcs.; attending physician USAF hosp., Lakenheath, Eng., 1988-91, asst. dir. emergency dept., 1990-91; dir. emergency tng. we. Europe divsn. USAF RAF, Lakenheath, Eng., 1990-91; flight surgeon USAF Hosp. Holloman AFB, N. Mex., 1991-92; flight surgeon Space Shuttle contigency opers. USAF, Holloman AFB, N. Mex., 1991-92; resident physician Wright State U./USAF, Dayton, 1992-95; staff physician, instr. tactical medicine USAF Hosp., Wright Patterson AFB, 1995-97, EMS dir., 1996-97; clin. instr. emergency medicine Wright State U., 1996—; clin. tng. in mind-body medicine The Mind-Body Med. Inst., Deaconess-Beth Israel Hosp., Boston, 1997; staff physician New Century Physicians, Dayton, 1997—. Med. dir. Ohio Acad. Holistic Health, Dayton, 1998-99, Ohio Wellness Ctr., 1998-99; spl. asst. Dept. Health and Human Svcs., Rockville, Md., 1986; health policy fellow U.S. Senate, Wash., 1988; chief cons. Dayton, SWAT Team, 1994-96; keynote spkr. Ohio State EMS, Columbus, 1995; Ohio Holistic Health Expo, 1998; spl. lectr. mind-body medicine, Ohio Wellness Ctr.; keynote spkr. Ohio Holistic Health Expn., 1998; guest lectr. grand rounds Good Samaritian Hosp., 1998; Spl. lectr. Unitarian Universalist Ch., Oakwood, Ohio, 1993; guest lectr., Rotary Club, 1999. Contr. Chpt: (textbook) Emergency Medicine Reference Book, 1999. Decorated Commendation medal USAF, 1993, 97, Meritorious Svc. medal, 1991, recipient Dir's award USPHS U.S. Surgeon Gen., 1987; named to Internet Book of Honor, 1999. Fellow Internat. Biog. Assn. (life), mem. Am. Coll. Emergency Physicians. Avocations: fine arts, athletics. Home: 1211 W Main St Bldg 1205 Troy OH 45373-2564

SAVAGE, MARK RANDALL, lawyer; b. Chicopee, Mass., Mar. 10, 1959; m. Lucia Clara Savage; children: David, Ryan. BA, U. Calif., Berkeley, 1982; JD, Stanford U., 1988. Bar: Calif. Jud. law clk. to Judge James Holden, North Bennington, Vt., 1988-89; mng. atty. Pub. Advs., Inc., San Francisco, 1989—2003; sr. atty. Consumers Union of U.S., Inc., San Francisco, 2003—. Gen. counsel Cmty. Tech. Found. Calif., San Francisco, 1998—; bd. dirs. Family Bridges, Inc., Oakland, Calif. Contbr. articles to profl. jours. Bd. dirs. Inst. for Civic Arts and Pub. Spaces, Inc., Albuquerque, 1996—2001. Recipient Drum Maj. award So. Christian Leadership Conf., 1998, Diversity, Innovation and Reform in Edn. award, 1995, El Fuego Nuevo award Assn. Mex. Am. Educators, 1999, Leadership Recognition award Calif. Primary Care Assn., 1999, Screaming Eagle award Calif. Reinvestment Coalition, 2004. Office: Consumers Union 1535 Mission St San Francisco CA 94103-2566 Office Phone: 415-431-6747. Business E-Mail: MarkSavage@igc.org.

SAVAGE, MICHAEL PAUL, medicine educator, interventional cardiologist; b. Wilkes-Barre, Pa., Jan. 25, 1955; s. Peter J. and Olga J. (Sekerchak) S.; m. Kathleen A. Gallagher, June 1989; children: Katherine, Andrew. BA, Wesleyan U., Middletown, Conn., 1976; MD, Jefferson Med. Coll., 1980. Diplomate Am. Bd. Internal Medicine, Am. Bd. Cardiovascular Disease Interventional Cardiology, Nat. Bd. Med. Examiners. Intern, then resident New Eng. Deaconess Hosp.-Harvard U. Med. Sch., Boston, 1980-83; fellow Jefferson Med. Coll., Phila., 1983-86, asst. prof. medicine, 1986-91, assoc. prof., 1991—, dir. cardiac catheterization, 1990—, dir. interventional cardiology sect., 1996—. Cons. Johnson & Johnson Interventional Sys. Co., Warren, N.J., Scimed/Boston Scientific, Maple Grove, Minn., GlaxoSmithKline, Phila.; lectr. coronary angioplasty and cardiac catheterization. Contbr. articles to profl. jours. including New Eng. Jour. Medicine, Circulation, Am. Jour. Cardiology, Jour. Am. Coll. Cardiology, JAMA, Lancet, chpts. to books. Fellow Am. Coll. Cardiology, Soc. Cardiac Angiography and Interventions, Pa. Med. Soc., Am. Heart Assn., Am. Fedn. for Clin. Rsch. Roman Catholic. Achievements include rsch. in interventional cardiology concerning new techniques in treatment of coronary artery disease, culminating in international, prospective trials demonstrating superiority of implantable coronary stents over conventional balloon angioplasty. Office: Jefferson Heart Inst 925 Chestnut St Philadelphia PA 19107-5001 Office Phone: 215-955-6478.

SAVAGE, MURRAY, engineering executive; Various fin., mgmt., and strategic planning roles, including CFO Profl. Svc. Industries Inc., Lombard, Ill., pres., 1998—2000, CEO, 2000—. Office: PSI Corp Hdqs Ste 400 1901 S Meyers Rd Oakbrook Terrace IL 60181

SAVAGE, R. BRUCE, computer company executive; b. 1949; With sales and mktg. CIBA-Geigy; with Dendrite Internat. Inc., Morristown, N.J., pres. internat. divsn., exec. v.p., COO internat. ops. Office: Dendrite Internat Inc 1200 Mt Kemble Ave Morristown NJ 07960

SAVAGE, RANDALL ERNEST, journalist; b. Commerce, Ga., Mar. 3, 1939; s. Ernest Kyle and Sara Beatrice (Collins) S.; m. Joyce Carol Martin, Nov. 26, 1964 (div. May 1984); children: Kimberly Dawn, Bradley Kyle; m. Mary Elizabeth Hallmark, Aug. 4, 1984; children: Brock Morgan, Laura Marie, Shaw Hamilton. Student, U. Md.-European Div., RAF Bentwaters, Eng., 1967-69; BA in Journalism, U. Ga., 1972. Service sta. worker Collins Service Sta., Commerce, Ga., 1958; billing clk. Benton Rapid Express, Atlanta, 1958-61; truck driver So. Oil Co., High Point, NC, 1964-65; reporter Commerce News, Ga., 1972; sr. spl. projects reporter Macon Telegraph and News, Ga., 1972—, polit. and investing reporter. Served with U.S. Army, 1961-64; with USAF, 1966-69. Recipient 3rd place in news AP, Atlanta, 1976, 2nd place in news AP, Atlanta, 1976, 1st place in sports AP, Atlanta, 1984, 2d place in news Green Eyeshades award, 1976; Pulitzer prize, 1985, Outstanding Alumnus award Henry W. Grady Coll. of Journalism and Mass Communication, U. Ga., 1989. Baptist. Avocations: jogging, softball, fishing, free-lance writing. Home: 985 Chads Ford Ct Macon GA 31210-1572 Office: WMAZTV 1314 Gray Hwy 31211 Macon GA 31201

SAVAGE, ROBERT HEATH, advertising executive; b. Chillicothe, Ohio, Nov. 24, 1929; s. Russell Heath and Frances (Hunt) S.; m. Lorna Dale, May 2, 1970. BA, Principia Coll., 1951; MBA, Harvard U., 1956. Brand mgr. Procter & Gamble, Cin., 1956-60; sr. v.p., mgmt. supr., dir. Ogilvy & Mather, Inc., N.Y.C., 1960-71; mktg. mgr. personal products div. Lever Bros., N.Y.C., 1971; exec. v.p. Botsford Ketchum, Inc., San Francisco, 1972, pres., 1972-78, chmn., 1978-81; pres. KM&G Internat., Inc., 1978-81, Saatchi and Saatchi Compton, Inc., N.Y.C., 1981-83; mng. dir. Henson Assocs., N.Y.C., 1983-86; ptnr. CMA Assocs., Southport, Conn., 1987—. Mngt. cons., sports and video mktg. cons., 1987—; chmn. Flying Rhinoceros, Inc., 1996—. With USMCR, 1951-54. Mem. Gipsy Trail Club, Colliers Reserve Country Club, Brooklawn Country Club. Home and Office: 273 Harbor Rd Southport CT 06490-1320 E-mail: rsavage881@aol.com.

SAVAGE, STEPHEN MICHAEL, lawyer; b. Norwich, Conn., Apr. 23, 1946; s. Alfred and Iva (Allen) S.; m. Lois Palestine, July 4, 1968; children: Meredith, William, Sam. BA, U. Pa., 1968, JD, Harvard U., 1973. Bar: Ariz. 1973, U.S. Dist. Ct. Ariz. 1973. With Fennemore Craig, Phoenix, 1973—, chmn. mgmt. com., 1988—. Mem. Greater Phoenix Leadership; bd. dirs. Ariz. Diabetes Assn., Phoenix, 1983-87; chmn. bd. trustees Ariz. Sci. Ctr., Phoenix; chmn. bd. dirs. All Saints' Episcopal Day Sch., Phoenix, 1988; comdr., pres. Mounted Sheriff's Posse Maricopa County, Phoenix, 1992-93. Mem. ABA, State Bar Ariz. (chmn. sect. corp., banking and bus. law 1983-84), Maricopa County Bar Assn., Phoenix Country Club, Forest Highlands Country Club. Avocations: team roping, golf. Office: Fennemore Craig 3003 N Central Ave Ste 2600 Phoenix AZ 85012-2913

SAVAGE, SUSAN M. state official, former mayor; b. Tulsa, Okla., 1936; married; 2 children. Student, U. Aix-Marseilles, Aix-en-Provence, France, 1969, City of London Poly., Eng., 1972; BA in Sociology with honors, Beaver Coll., 1974. Pre-trial rep. Phila. Ct. Common Pleas, 1974-75; criminal justice planner Montgomery County Criminal Justice Unit, 1975-77; exec. dir. Met. Tulsa Citizens Crime Com., 1977-87; vol. coord. Vote Yes For Tulsa, 1987; chief of staff to mayor City of Tulsa, 1988-92, mayor, 1992—2002; sec. of state State of Okla., Oklahoma City, 2003—. Active Lee Elementary Sch. PTA; bd. dirs., treas. Okla. Crime Prevention Assn.; bd. dirs. Youth Svcs. of Tulsa County, 1984-88, pres., 1986-87; co-chair Safe Streets/Enhanced 911 Steering Com., 1987; mem. C. of C. Task Force/Community Edn. Network, 1983. Mem. U.S. Conf. Mayors (chmn. com. energy and environment). Office: State Capitol Rm 101 Oklahoma City OK 73105 Home: 224 NW 33rd St Oklahoma City OK 73118-8614 Business E-Mail: susan.savage@sos.state.ok.us.

SAVAGE, TERRY, television personality, journalist, stockbroker; Grad., U. Mich. Registered investment advisor stocks and commodity futures. Founding mem., 1st woman trader Chgo. Bd. Options Exch.; mem. Internat. Monetary Market; columnist Chgo. Sun Times, Chgo.; personal fin. columnist Barron's Online; featured columnist MSN Money website; columnist pvt. website www.TerrySavage.com. Bd. dirs. Devon Energy, Broadway Stores, Chicago Mercantile Exchange; former bd. mem. McDonald's Corp., Pennzoil-Quaker State Corp.; former co-editor Options Trading Strategies newsletter; spkr. in field. Host Money Talks; author: Terry Savage's New Money Strategies for the 90s, 1993, Terry Savage Talks Money: The Common-Sense Guide to Money Matters, 1999, The Savage Truth on Money, 1999; columnist Chgo. Sun-Times. Dir. Chgo. Mus. Sci. and Industry, Northwestern Meml. Hosp. Found., Econ. Club Chgo., Execs. Club Chgo., Jr. Achievement Ill., Ill. Coun. on Econ. Edn., Women's Bus. Devel. Ctr. Recipient Outstanding Consumer Journalism award Nat. Press Club, 1987, Dir.'s Choice award, 1994, 2 Emmy awards, Outstanding Personal Finance Columnist award, Northwestern U.; Woodrow Wilson fellow in Am. history and econs. Mem. Phi Beta Kappa. Office: Chgo Sun-Times Hollinger Inc 401 N Wabash Ave Chicago IL 60611-5642 also: Terry Savage Productions 676 N Michigan Ave Ste 3610 Chicago IL 60611 E-mail: savage@suntimes.com.

SAVAGE, TERRY RICHARD, information systems executive; b. St. Louis, Oct. 21, 1930; s. Terry Barco and Ada Vanetta (Cochran) S.; m. Gretchen Susan Wood, Sept. 26, 1964; children: Terry Curtis, Christopher William, Richard Theodore. AB, Washington U., St. Louis, 1951, MA, 1952; PhD, U. Pa., 1954. Mgr. system software IBM Rsch., Yorktown Heights, N.Y., 1956-63; dir. data processing Documentation Inc., Bethesda, Md., 1963-64; mgr. info. systems Control Data Corp., Rockville, Md., 1964-67; dir. rsch. Share Rsch. Corp., Santa Barbara, Calif., 1967-68; computer-aided acquisition and logistic support program mgr. TRW, Redondo Beach, Calif., 1968-92; ret., ind. cons. pvt. practice, 1992—. Expert witness for various coms. U.S. Congress, 1981, 84, 88, 89. Contbr. articles to profl. jours. Bd. dirs. ABC-Clio Press, Santa Barbara, 1970-75, Help the Homeless Help Themselves, Rancho Palos Verdes, Calif., 1988-94, ChorusLiners, Rancho Palos Verdes, 1983—, Savage Info. Svcs., Inc., Torrance, Calif., 1992—. Mem.: Cosmos Club. Home and Office: 30000 Cachan Pl Rancho Palos Verdes CA 90275-5412 E-mail: terrysavage@cox.net.

SAVAGE, THOMAS JOSEPH, executive development company executive, priest; b. Medford, Mass., Oct. 28, 1947; s. Frank James and Viola Augustine (Ballou) S. B.A. summa cum laude, Boston Coll., 1971; M. City Planning, U. Calif.-Berkeley, 1973; M. Pub. Policy, Harvard U., 1982, EdD, 1985. Assoc. Cheswick Ctr., Boston, 1973, dir., 1984—; assoc. Instl. Strategies Assocs., Cambridge, Mass., 1975-87; asst. acad. v.p. Fairfield (Conn.) Univ., 1986-88; pres. Rockhurst Coll., Kansas City, Mo., 1988-96, pres. Nat. Seminars Group., Shawnee Mission, Kans., 1991—; sr. cons. William M. Mercer, Inc., San Francisco, 1998—; adj. faculty Lesley Coll., Cambridge, 1982-85; cons. Lilly Endowment, Indpls., 1983-87; chmn. planning com. Jesuits New Eng. Province, Boston, 1985-88. Author: Seven Steps to a More Effective Board, 1994, The Goverance of Catholic Health Care Institutions, Catholic Health Assn., Spring, 1988; also articles. Del. Bridges for Peace, Soviet Union, 1985; Trustee Regis U., 1989-97, U. Detroit Mercy, 1995—, St. Louis U., 1991—, Loyola Marymount, 1994—; bd. dirs. Valentine-Radford Comm., 1992—, Preferred Health Profls., 1992-97, Kauffman Found., 1993—, Menning er Clinic, 1993—; co-chair FOCUS (Comprehensive Strategic Plan for Kansas City), 1992-97; founding chmn. Brush Creek Ptnrs., 1994-96. Mellon fellow, 1971-73. Mem. Am. Planning Assn., Nat. Policy Assn., AAAS, Assn. Jesuit Colls. and Univs. (bd. dirs. 1989-96), World Future Soc., Bostonian Soc., Phi Beta Kappa. Roman Catholic. Club: Harvard. Office: William M Mercer Inc Three Embarcadero Ctr San Francisco CA 94111

SAVAGE, TOY DIXON, JR., lawyer; b. Norfolk, Va., Oct. 12, 1921; s. Toy Dixon and Hildreth Gatewood S.; m. Mary Hunter Hankins, Oct. 19, 1946; children: Tracy G., Toy D. III. BA in Econ., U. Va., 1943, LLB, 1948; LittD (hon.), Ea. Va. Med. Sch., 1995. Assoc., ptnr. Willcox & Savage PC, Norfolk, 1948—. Mem. ho. of dels. Gen. Assembly Va., 1954-63; bd. dirs. Sentara Health Sys., United Cmty. Fund, 1968-73; chmn. Norfolk Found. Distribution Com., Hampton Rds. Areawide Coop. Com., 1963-64, 76-78; trustee Chrysler Mus., Va. Found. for Ind. Coll., Camp Found., North Shore Found., Va. Hist. Soc., Ea. Va. Med. Sch. Found., Va. Mus. Fine Arts, 1975-85; trustee, deacon Freemason St. Bapt. Ch.; mem. Govs. Adv. Bd. on Indsl. Devel., 1983-92; chmn. task force on health care Govs. Commn. on Future of Va., 1984-85; pres. Old Dominion U. Ednl. Found., 1972-73, Med. Ctr. Hosps., 1966-68; vice-chmn. Ea. Va. Med. Authority, 1964-66. Home: 3100 Shore Dr Virginia Beach VA 23451

SAVAGE, WILLIAM EARL, savings and loan executive, religious educator; b. Wilmore, Ky., Feb. 5, 1918; s. Earl Wilson and Mary Nell (Jones) S.; m. Dorothy Jane Dorrycott, Dec. 28, 1939; children: Sue Ann, William Earl II, Carolyn. AB, Asbury Coll., Wilmore, Ky., 1939; LHD, Asbury-Theol. Sem., 1995. V.p. Pinciand Coll., Deland, Fla., 1939-42; bus. mgr. Ky-Wesleyan Coll., Owensboro, 1942-44; v.p. bus. adminstrn. Asbury Theol. Sem., 1946-76; pres. First Fed. Savs. and Loan, Lexington, Ky., 1982-85, vice chmn. bd. dirs., 1982—; ret. Mem. United Meth. Bd. Global Ministries, 1960-72; mem. adminstrv. bd. Park United Meth. Ch., Lexington, 1960—; mem. World Meth. Coun., 1961—, exec. com., 1975—; bd. dirs. Asbury Theol. Sem., Wilmore, 1945—; lay leader Ky. Conf. United Meth. Ch., 1964-68; treas. bd. dirs. Ky. Meth. Found., 1982-88. Trustee Cardinal Hill Children's Hosp., Lexington, 1954-60, Good Samaritan Hosp., Lexington, 1964-92; bd. dirs. Lexington Coun. Arts, 1980-86. Mem. Ky. Savs. Loan League, Nat. Assn. Cert. Revenue Appraisers, U.S. Savs. League, Ky. Crippled Children's Soc. Democrat. Home: 132 Wesley Dr Wilmore KY 40390-9795

SAVAGE, WILLIAM WOODROW, JR., historian, consultant, social sciences educator; b. Richmond, Va., Oct. 13, 1943; s. William Woodrow and Margaret (Clarke) Savage, m. Sheila Bobalik, July 30, 1983; 1 child, William Woodrow III. BA in Journalism, U. S.C., 1964, MA in History, 1966; PhD in History, U. Okla., 1972. Instr. Coll. Gen. Studies U. S.C., Columbia, 1966; vis. lectr. history Iowa State U., Ames, 1970; asst. editor U. Okla. Press, Norman, 1972-75; from asst. prof. to assoc. prof. history U. Okla., Norman, 1974—89, prof., 1989—. Tech. adviser Korine-Dunlap Prodns., Nashville, 1982—83; adviser Am. Frontier Project, N.Y.C., 1982—85; bd. cons. editors Popular Culture Librs., Binghamton, NY, 1991—99. Author: The Cherokee Strip Live Stock Association, 1973, The Cowboy Hero, 1979, Singing Cowboys and All That Jazz, 1983, Comic Books and America, 1945 54, 1990; editor: Indian Life, 1977, Cowboy Life, 1993; co-editor: The Frontier, 1979; editor (newsletter): Comparative Frontier Studies, 1975—86, Norman and Cleve. County Hist. Mus., 1975; co-prodr., host (TV series) Norman Cable TV, 1986—88; columnist: Okla. Gazette, 1993—95; contbr. articles to profl. jours. Recipient Spl. Recognition award, Okla. Jazz Hall of Fame, 1993. Mem.: Western History Assn., So. Hist. Assn., Okla. Hist. Soc., Sigma Delta Chi. Avocations: panelology, mixed media and collage. Office: U Okla Dept History 455 W Lindsey Rm 424 Norman OK 73019

SAVARD, DENIS JOSEPH, former professional hockey player, coach; b. Pointe Gatineau, Que., Can., Feb. 4, 1961; With Chgo. Black Hawks, 1980-90, 96-97; ret., 1997; asst. coach devel. Chgo. Black Hawks, 1997—; with Montreal Canadiens, 1990-93, Tampa Bay Lightning, 1993-96. Mem. Stanley Cup championship team 1983; player NHL All-Star games, 1982-84, 86, 88, 91. Recipient Michel Briere trophy, 1979-80. Office: Chgo Blackhawks 1901 W Madison St Chicago IL 60612-2459

SAVARI, SERAP AYSE, engineering educator, researcher; b. Astoria, NY, Nov. 4, 1968; d. Aykut and Sirin Savari. MS, MIT, 1991, PhD, 1996. Mem. tech. staff Bell Labs., Lucent Techs., Murray Hill, 1996—2003; acad. guest faculty computer sci. and comm. sys. Swiss Fed. Inst. Tech., 2003; assoc. prof. dept. elec. engring. and computer sci. U. Mich., Ann Arbor, 2003—. Program com. Data Compression Conf., 2000—04. Contbr. articles to profl. jours. Mem.: IEEE (program com. Internat. Symposium on Info. Theory 2001—02, assoc. editor Source Coding IEEE Transactions on Info. Theory 2002—, program com. Internat. Symposium Info. Theory 2004), Toastmasters, Tau Beta Pi, Phi Beta Kappa. Home: 3070 Whisperwood Dr Apt 431 Ann Arbor MI 48105 Office: 4225 EECS Bldg 1301 Beal Ave Ann Arbor MI 48109 Business E-Mail: savari@eecs.umich.edu.

SAVAS, EMANUEL S. public management and public policy educator; b. N.Y.C., June 8, 1931; s. John and Olga (Limbos) S.; m. Helen Andrew, Dec. 25, 1955; children: Jonathan, Stephen. BA, U. Chgo., 1951, BS, 1953; MA, Columbia U., 1956, PhD, 1960; PhD (hon.), U. Piraeus, Greece, 2000. Control systems cons. IBM, Yorktown Heights and White Plains, N.Y., 1959-65; urban systems mgr. N.Y.C., 1966-67; 1st dep. city adminstr. Office of Mayor of N.Y.C., 1967-72; chmn. Mayor's Urban Action Task Force, 1969-72; prof. pub. mgmt. Columbia U., N.Y.C., 1972-83, dir. Center for Govt. Studies, 1973-83, assoc. dir. Center for Policy Rsch., 1973-81; asst. sec. for policy devel. and rsch. HUD, Washington, 1981-83; prof. mgmt. Baruch Coll., CUNY, 1981-94, prof. public policy, 1994—, dir. public policy program, 1994-97, chm. dept. mgmt., 1986-93; dir. Privatization Rsch. Orgn., 1986—. Cons. NSF, HUD, Dept. Transp., Dept. Energy, World Bank, AID, U.S. Dept. State, Pres.'s Commn. on Privatization, UN, UN Devel. Program, ILO, UNIDO, USIA, also others; mem. voting bd. Blue Cross and Blue Shield Greater N.Y., 1976-79, bd. dirs., 1979-81; mem. Pres.-Elect's Urban Affairs Task Force, 1980, N.Y. State Senate Adv. Commn. on Privatization, 1990-95; mem. Gov. Pataki privatization coun., N.Y., 1995-2000; dir. U.S.-USSR Joint Project on Mgmt. of Large Cities, 1973-81; advisor on privatization Govt. Poland, 1990-92, Govt. Lesotho, 1992, Govt. Ukraine, 1993, N.Y.C. mayor, 1994-98, Govt. South Africa, 1996, Govt. Botswana, 1996, Govt. Philippines, 1997, others. Author: Computer Control of Industrial Processes, 1965, Organization and Efficiency of Solid Waste Collection, 1977, Privatizing the Public Sector, 1982, Moscow's City Government, 1985, Privatization, 1987, Privatization and Public-Private Partnerships, 2000, 21 fgn. edits., others; editor: Alternatives for Delivering Public Services, 1977, Privatization for New York, 1992; co-author The New Public Management, 2002; mem. editorial bd. Urban Affairs Quar., Privatization Report, Privatization Watch, State and Local Govt. Rev.; contbr. 115 articles to profl. jours. Mem. N.Y.C. Mayor-elect Giuliani transition team, 1993, N.Y. Gov.-elect Pataki transition team, 1994; mem. Tenafly (N.J.) Borough Coun., 1996. With U.S. Army, 1953-54, Korea. Recipient Systems Sci. and Cybernetics award IEEE, 1968, Louis Brownlow award Am. Soc. Public Adminstrn., 1970, Honor award Templeton Found., 1989, Leadership award Nat. Coun. Pub.-Private Partnerships, 1993, Outstanding Acad. award Am. Soc. Pub. Adminstrn., 1996. Mem. Sigma Xi, Psi Upsilon. Clubs: City of N.Y. (trustee 1974-77, Richard Childs award 1979). Greek Orthodox. Office: CUNY Baruch Coll Box C-305 17 Lexington Ave New York NY 10010-5518 Office Phone: 212-802-5909. Personal E-mail: prisect@aol.com.

SAVEDGE, ANNE CREERY, artist, photographer; b. Richmond, Va., Jan. 29, 1947; d. Leslie Roy Jr. and Dorothy (Rakes) C.; m. Edwin Clement Savedge Jr., Aug. 11, 1967; 1 child, Ross Alan. BS, James Madison U., 1969; M in Art Edn., Va. Commonwealth U., 1977. Art instr. Colonial Heights HS, Va., 1969-78; instr. Va. Mus. Robinson House, Richmond, Va., 1983-86; vis. artist Office of Youth and Cmty. Svc., Dinwiddie, Va., 1986-87; artist-in-residence Richmond Children's Mus., 1987-88; instr. Shenandoah Photographic Workshops, 1988; adj. faculty Va. Mus. of Fine Arts, 2000—. Adj. faculty U. Richmond, 1978-2000—; artist-in-residence Va. Mus. of Fine Arts, Richmond, 1984-86, Richmond Children's Mus., 1987-88; curator Bedford Gallery Photoshow Longwood Coll., Farmville, Va., 1985, Light Images Gallery Photoshow James Madison U., Harrisonburg, Va., 1985, 1708 East Main Gallery Photoshow, Richmond, 1987, 90, New Realities/Digital Transformations show, 1997, pub. in Intro. to Digital Photography, 2002 by Joe Ciaglia (p65), Exploring Color Photography, 1989 by Robert Hirsch (p 135); artist Fay Gold Gallery, Atlanta, 1985-87, Nat. Copier Art Show; artist-in-edn. gifted program Dinwiddie, Va., 1988; instr. Chesterfield Tech. Ctr., 1989—. One-woman shows include Marsh Gallery, U. Richmond, 1986, 1708 Gallery, 1994, Baton Rouge, 1991, "Pinholes & Pixels" 1912 Gallery, 2000, "Veils of Water", Bishop Gallery, Longwood Ctr. for the Visual Arts, Farmville, 2003, Cultural Arts Ctr. at Glen Allen, 2002; exhibited in group shows Pleiades Gallery, NYC, 1989, Martin Gallery, Washington, 1989, Midwest Invitational, 1993-94, Mars Gallery, Ariz., 1994, Bloom Gallery, Milan, 1995, Longwood Ctr. for Visual Arts, 1997, Chrysler Mus., 1999, Art Mus. Western Va., 2002, Cultural Arts Ctr. Glen Allen, 2002; represented in permanent collections Polaroid Internat. Collection, Fed. Res. Bank, Chrysler Mus., Valentine Mus., Longwood Ctr. for Visual Arts, Va., Art Mus. Western Va.; pub. in Magic Wand, 1st and 2nd edits., 1998. Adv. coun. Richmond Arts Coun.; evaluation com. Partners-in-Arts; master tchr. Va. State T&I Skills USA Nat. Conf.; chmn. 1708 Gallery Exhbns., 1995-96. Named Art Tchr. of Yr., Chesterfield County, 1997-98, Art Educator of Yr., Va. Art Edn. Assn., 1999, hon. mention Excellence in Photographic Tchg. award Santa Fe Ctr. for the Visual Arts;

individual artist fellow Va. Commn. for Arts, 1999, profl. fellow Va. Mus. Fine Arts. Mem. Nat. Art Edn. Assn. (presenter Chgo. chpt. Nat. Conf. 1998, Chgo. chpt. Washington Nat. Conf. 1999, Southeastern Art Educator of Yr. 2000), Richmond Artists Assn. (pres. 1978-80, cert. distinction 1980), Soc. for Photographic Edn., Va. Soc. for Photographic Arts (steering com. 1976—, fundraising chmn. 1978—, mem. chmn. 1980-86). Methodist. Home: 5318 Verlinda Dr Richmond VA 23237-3307 E-mail: asavedge@savedge.com.

SAVEDRA, JEANNINE EVANGELINE, artist, art educator; b. Montebello, Calif., Dec. 21, 1965; d. Robert Anthony Savedra and April Elizabeth (Sanchez) Baroth. Student, Pasadena C.C., Calif., 1985-87, Otis Art Inst./Parsons Sch., 1987-88; BA in Studio Art, Calif. State U., L.A., 1991; postgrad., 1992-93; MA in Art/Humanities, Calif. State U., Dominguez Hills, 1999; postgrad. IMMEX Inst., UCLA, 1999; postgrad., Getty Edn. Inst. for Arts. Cert. art tchr., Calif. Children's counselor Salvation Army, Pasadena, Calif., 1987-88; graphic artist Calif. State U., L.A., 1989; pvt. investigator Larry J. Larsen Investigations and Trial Preparations, L.A., 1990-93; art instr. Pasadena Unified Sch. Dist., 1994-95; studio art instr. Visual Arts and Design Acad., Pasadena, 1995—, coord./lead tchr., 1999—2000. Supr. mural Pasadena Playhouse Improvement Assn., 1995-96; mentor Puente program U. Calif., Berkeley, 1995—; educator Nat. Conf. Human Rels., Temescal Canyon, Calif., 1996, Annenberg Inst. Sch. Reform, Brown U., 1998—; apptd. to ednl. adv. com. Jack Scott, mem. Assembly, Calif. State Legislature, 1997—; apptd. to Sierra Madre Arts Commn., 1999; artist exch. program Cultural Min., Havana, Cuba, 2000. Co-author interactive multi-media ednl. CD-ROM. Appt. to Sierra Madre Downtown Improvement Com., 2000; founding mem. Nat. Campaign for Tolerance, Montgomery, Ala. Calif. Partnership Acad. grantee, 1996—; recipient Excellence in Visual Arts award Calif. State U., 1990. Mem. Nat. Art Edn. Assn., L.A. County Mus. Art, Mus. Contemporary Art, Nat. Soc. Women Artists, Mus. Tolerance, Pasadena Armory Ctr. for Arts, Armand Hammer Art Mus.

SAVELKOUL, DONALD CHARLES, retired lawyer; b. Mpls., July 29, 1917; s. Theodore Charles and Edith (Lindgren) S.; m. Mary Joan Holland, May 17, 1941; children: Jeffrey Charles, Jean Marie, Edward Joseph. BA magna cum laude, U. Minn., 1939; JD cum laude, William Mitchell Coll. Law, 1951. Bar: Minn. 1951, U.S. Dist. Ct. Minn. 1952, U.S. Ct. Appeals (8th cir.) 1960, U.S. Supreme Ct. 1971. Adminstrv. work various U.S. govt. depts., including Commerce, War, Labor, Wage Stblzn. Bd., 1940-51; mcpl. judge Fridley, Minn., 1952-53; pvt. practice law Mpls., St. Paul, Fridley, 1951-96; ret., 1997. Chmn. bd. Fridley State Bank, 1962-95; pres. Banrein, Inc., 1962-95, Babbscha Co., 1962-95; mem. faculty William Mitchell Coll. Law, 1952-59, corp. mem., 1956-99; sec. Fridley Recreation and Svc. Co., 1955-97; mem. Minn. Legislature, 1967-69. Mem. Gov.'s Com. Workers Compensation, 1965-67, Gov.'s Adv. Coun. on Employment Security, 1957-60, 62-63; gen. counsel Minn. AFL-CIO Fedn. Labor, 1952-71. 1st lt. AUS, 1943-46. Decorated Bronze Star; recipient Disting. Alumni award, Coll. Liberal Arts U. Minn., 1995, Hon. Ronald E. Hachey Outstanding Alumna/us award, Wm. Mitchell Coll. of Law Alumni Assn., 1997. Mem. ABA, Minn. Bar Assn. (chmn. 1957-58, bd. dirs. 1958-62, 68-69, labor law sect.), Justice William Mitchell Soc., Am. Legion, U. Minn. Pres.'s Club, Phi Beta Kappa. Roman Catholic. Office: 916 Moore Lake Dr W Fridley MN 55432-5148

SAVELL, EDWARD LUPO, lawyer; b. Atlanta, Apr. 29, 1921; s. Leon M. and Lillian (Lupo) S.; m. Bettie Patterson Hoyt, Oct. 11, 1944; 1 dau., Mary Lillian Savell Clarke. BBA, Emory U., 1947, LL.B., 1949. Bar: Ga. 1948, U.S. Dist. Ct. (mid. and no. dist.) Ga.; mediator and arbitrator, Ga. Assoc. A.C. Latimer, Atlanta, 1948-53; ptnr. Carter, Latimer & Savell, Atlanta, 1953-56, Woodruff, Latimer & Savell (and successor firms), Atlanta, 1956-87; of counsel Savell & Williams, Atlanta, 1987—. Instr. John Marshall Law Sch., 1951-55; dir. Legal Aid Soc., 1955-58; investigator Fulton county Judges Grievance Com. Contbr. articles to legal jours. With USAF, 1942-45, CBI. Fellow Internat. Acad. Trial Lawyers (pres. 1978-79, Dean of Acad. 1976); mem. Atlanta Bar Assn. (sec.-treas. 1953-54), ABA, State Bar Ga., Ga. Def. Lawyers Assn. (founder, v.p.), Internat. Assn. Ins. Counsel, Atlanta Claims Assn., Lawyers Club Atlanta, Cherokee Town and Country Club, Commerce Club, Univ. Yacht Club (past commodore), Chi Phi, Phi Delta Phi (past pres.). Presbyterian. Office: Savell and Williams 1500 Equitable Bldg 100 Peachtree Atlanta GA 30303

SAVELL, POLLY CAROLYN, lawyer; b. N.Y.C., Oct. 24, 1960; d. Joel Morton and Elsie Rhea (Crane) S. BA, U. Md., 1982; diploma, Internat. Comp. Law Inst., Paris, 1983; JD, NYU, 1985. Bar: N.Y. 1986. Assoc. corp. and entertainment divsn. Battle Fowler, N.Y.C., 1986-87; atty. Columbia Pictures Entertainment Inc., N.Y.C., 1987-89; counsel Turner Broadcasting Sys. Inc., Atlanta, 1989-91; sole practice Atlanta, 1991-93; asst. gen. counsel WorldCom Inc., N.Y.C., 1993—2001; pvt. practice N.Y.C., 2001—. Bd. dirs. Eviction Intervention Svcs., Homelessness Prevention, Inc. Mem. ABA, Fed. Comm. Bar Assn., Am. Corp. Counsel Assn., Assn. of Bar of City of N.Y. (telecomm. law com.), Task Force Internat. Legal Studies. Democrat. Methodist. Office: 410 Park Ave Ste 1530 New York NY 10022

SAVERCOOL, SUSAN ELISABETH, elementary school educator; b. La Grande, Oreg., Aug. 1, 1947; d. Edwin Gilbert and Francis Gwynne Kirby; m. Niles Seymour Duncan, June 21, 1971 (div. Sept. 1976); m. Lawrence Yeldham Savercool, Aug. 6, 1983; 1 child, David R. BA in Theater/English, Calif. State U., Northridge, 1969; MA in Elem. Edn., No. Ariz. U., 1988. Cert. elem. tchr. Calif., Ariz. Elem. tchr. St. Catherine of Siena Sch., Reseda, Calif., 1969—71; presch. tchr. La Palma E. Preschool, Anaheim, Calif., 1973—74; elem. tchr. Egremont Sch., Encino, Calif., 1977—80, Ganado Intermediate, Ariz., 1980—84, Blue Ridge Elem., Lakeside, Ariz., 1986—98; freelance writer Penn Yan, NY, 2000—03. Presenter poetry for tchrs. workshop Blue Ridge Elem., Lakeside, 1991—96; instr. elem. lang. arts No. Ariz. U., Flagstaff, 1992. Editor: (books) Mountains of Time, vols. 1-5, 1992—97, Saint Bobo and Other Contemporary Short Stories, 1994. Actress, make-up head Theater Mountain, Lakeside, 1993—97; contbg. author Oliver House Mus., Penn Yan, 2000—03; contbr. Internat. Libr. Poetry. Scholar, Arts Coun., 1968. Mem.: Nat. Acad. Songwriters, Nat. Homer Poet Famous Poets Soc. (outstanding poet/contrb., internat. libr. poetry editions 2004), Phi Kappa Phi. Democrat. Roman Catholic. Achievements include development of Ars Poetica and Photo Lit. Posters gift lines; freelance writing (as Glenn MacCauley). Avocations: reading, fishing, community chorus, community theater, writing.

SAVEROT, PIERRE-MICHEL, nuclear waste management company executive; b. Charnay les Macon, France, Aug. 30, 1952; m. Francoise Solamito; children: Cyprien, Luc, Scott-Eugene. MS, Northwestern U., 1977. Formerly with SGN, Sybelpro, Cogema Inc., Numatec, West Valley Nuclear Svcs., NUSYS; sr. cons., asst. to pres. JAI Corp., Fairfax, Va., 1994—. Mem. Inst. Nuclear Waste Mgmt. (chmn. 1996—). Home: 3112 White Daisy Pl Fairfax VA 22031-1463 Office: JAI Corp 2750 Property Ave Fairfax VA 22031-4312 Office Phone: 703-645-0440. Office Fax: 703-645-0445.*

SAVETH, EDWARD NORMAN, history educator; b. N.Y.C., Feb. 16, 1915; s. Isidor and Eva (Vasa) S.; m. Harriet Obstler, June 22, 1975; 1 child by previous marriage, Henry. BSS., CCNY, 1935; MA, Columbia U., 1937, PhD, 1946. Prof. history Grad. Faculty New Sch. for Social Research, N.Y.C., 1960-63; Fulbright prof. Kyoto U., Kyoto, Japan, 1964-65; prof. Dartmouth Coll., 1965-66; Disting. vis. prof. Tex. Lutheran Coll., Seguin, 1966-67; Disting. prof. SUNY-Fredonia, 1967-85; adj. prof. SUNY, Buffalo, 1987—; lectr. USIA, Nepal, 1965, Morocco, 1977; Fulbright prof. Hebrew U., Jerusalem, 1981. Vis. prof. U. Rochester, 1972; lectr. Beijing Tchrs. Coll., 1989. Author: American historians and European Immigrants, 1947; author, editor: Understanding the American Past, 1954, Henry Adams, 1963, American History and the Social Sciences, 1964; revisions editor: Ency. Americana, 1962; contbr. numerous articles to mags. Mem. Am. Hist. Assn., Orgn. Am. Historians Home: 50 Stahl Rd Apt 201 Getzville NY 14068-1552

SAVIA, ALFRED, conductor; b. Livingston, NJ; Asst. condr. Omaha Symphony, 1976-78, Fla. Symphony Orch., 1978-78, assoc. condr., 1979-86, prin. guest condr., 1986-87; asst. condr. Colo. Philharm., 1979-81; resident condr. New Orleans Symphony, 1986-88, assoc. condr., 1988-89; resident condr. Philharm. Orch. Fla. (now Fla. Philharm. Orch.), 1987-89; music dir. Evansville (Ind.) Philharm., 1989—; assoc. condr. Indpls. Symphony Orch., 1990-96, artistic dir., prin. condr. summer season, 1991-96. Guest condr. Indpls. Symphony, New Orleans Symphony, Kitchener-Waterloo Symphony, Can., Presdl. Symphony Ankara, Turkey, Aalborg Symphony, Denmark, Korea Philharm., San Antonio Symphony, Alabama Symphony, Hudson Valley Philharm., Fla. Symphony Orch., Colo. Philharm., Denver Chamber Orch., Lubbock Symphony, Nebr. Chamber Orch., Miami Ballet, Orlando Opera Co., St. Louis Symphony, R.I. Philharm., Nat. Repertory Orch., Ill. Symphony, Grant Park Symphony, Osnabruck Symphony Orch., others. Recipient High Fidelity Musical Am. Young Artist award, 1985. Office: Evansville Philharm Orch PO Box 84 Evansville IN 47701-0084 also: Parker Artists 382 Central Park W Apt 9G New York NY 10025-6032

SAVIGNON, SANDRA J. linguistics educator; d. Harold Frederick Koepke and Joy Louise Delhaye; m. Gabriel M. Savignon, June 11, 1961; children: Daniel, Catherine Joy Doyle, Julie Marie. BA, U. Ill., 1961, MA, 1962, PhD, 1971. Prof. of French U. of Ill., Urbana-Champaign, 1971—97; prof. of applied linguistics Pa. State U., State College. Recipient Woodrow Wilson Nat. fellowship, Woodrow Wilson Found., 1961, Robert J. Ludwig Nat. Disting. Fgn. Lang. Leadership award, N.Y. State Assn. of Fgn. Lang. Tchrs., 1984, Land of Lincoln Leadership award, Ill. Fgn. Lang. Tchrs.' Assn., 1988, Disting. Prof., Internat. TESOL Summer Inst., Teachers of English to Speakers of Other Languages, 1990, Pres., Am. Assn. for Applied Linguistics, 1992—93, Convenor, Sci. Commn. on LanguageTeaching and Lang. Tchr. Edn., Internat. Assn. for Applied Linguistics, 1996—2004. Office: 305 Sparks University Park PA 16802 Personal E-mail: sjsavignon@psu.edu.

SAVILLE, DERRIC JAMES, lawyer; b. Ft. Madison, Iowa, Oct. 2, 1964; s. Jacob Abraham and Brenda K. (Lawrence) S.; m. Jeannene Irene Abbott, Mar. 21, 1987. BS, U. Iowa, 1987; M of Studies in Law, JD cum laude, Vt. Law Sch., 1991. Bar: Minn. 1991, U.S. Dist. Ct. Minn. 1995, Upper Sioux Comty. Tribal Ct. 1996. Atty. Saville Law Office, Mpls., 1991—98; with Saville Title Svcs., Inc., Plymouth, Minn. Chair subcom. Dist. Planning Adv. Commn. #279, Maple Grove, Minn., 1994-96. Articles editor Ferae Naturae, 1991. State del. Reform Party, Maple Grove, 1996; chair mental health adv. bd. Hennepin County Commitment Def. Project, 1998-2002. Mem.: Brain Injury Assn. Minn. (bd. dirs., chair-elect 1996—, chair 1998—99), Minn. Head Injury Assn. (bd. dirs. 1995—96). Avocations: fishing, hiking, orienteering. Office: Saville Title Svcs Inc 505 Hwy 169 N Ste 230 Plymouth MN 55441 Home: 1340 cobblestone Rd N Champlin MN 55316 Office Phone: 763-398-0377.

SAVILLE, DUDLEY ALBERT, chemical engineering educator; b. Lincoln, Nebr., Feb. 25, 1933; s. George A. and Alta (Goddard) S.; m. Joy Wagner, Mar. 7, 1959; children: Alexander, Andrea. BS, U. Nebr., 1954, MS, 1959; Ph.D, U. Mich., 1966. Engr. Carbide & Carbon Chem. Co. (Institute), W. Va., 1954-55; research engr. Chevron Research Corp. (Richmond), Calif., 1959-61, Shell Devl. Co., Emeryville, Calif., 1966-68; asst. prof. Princeton U. (N.J.), 1968-71, assoc. prof., 1971-77, prof. dept. chem. engring., 1977, Stephen C. Mocaleer prof. Engring. and Applied Sci., 2001. Assoc. editor Jour. Physico-Chem. Hydrodynamics, 1980-87; mem. adv. bd. Jour. Colloid Interface Sci., 1992-94; contbr. articles to profl. jours. Served to 1st lt. USAF, 1955-58. Recipient Alpha Chi Sigma award for chem. engring. rsch. AIChE, 1997. Mem. NAE, AIChE, Am. Chem. Soc., Am. Phys. Soc. Office: Princeton U Dept Chem Engring Princeton NJ 08544-0001

SAVILLE, KATHLEEN JO, instructional technologist; b. Clifton Forge, Va., Nov. 18, 1955; d. Leon Hunter and Elizabeth Pignato Saville. BS, James Madison U., 1978, MEd, 1982. Sch. libr. Clarksville (Va.) Primary Sch., 1979; sch. libr., media specialist Woodstock (Va.) Mid. Sch., 1979-82; instr. No. Mich. U., Marquette, 1982—. Mem. Assn. Ednl. Comm. and Tech. (sec., treas. 1999—). Office: No Mich U 1401 Presque Isle Ave Marquette MI 49855 Fax: 906-227-1333. E-mail: ksaville@nmu.edu.

SAVILLE, PAUL C. financial executive; Sr. v.p. fin., CFO, treas. NVR Inc., McLean, Va., 1993—2002, exec. v.p., 2002—. Office: NVR Inc 7601 Lewinsville Rd Ste 300 Mc Lean VA 22102-2827*

SAVILLE, ROYCE BLAIR, lawyer; b. Cumberland, Md., Aug. 5, 1948; s. E. Blair and Audrey (Cosner) S.; m. Sharon Ann Brinkman, Apr. 3, 1981; children: Melissa Anne, Lauren Ashley, Meagan Elizabeth, Philip Clarke. BA, W.Va. U., 1970, JD, 1974. Bar: W.Va. 1974, U.S. Dist. Ct. (so. and no. dists.) W.Va. 1974. Assoc. William J. Oates, Jr. Atty. at Law, Romney, W.Va., 1974—75; ptnr. Oates & Saville Attys. at Law, Romney, 1975—78; pvt. practice Romney, 1978—99; mng. ptnr. Saville and Davis, PLLC, 1999—2001, Saville and Stewart, PLLC, 2001—. Pres. Potomac Land Co., 1975—; mental hygiene commr. Hampshire County, Romney, 1976—; mcpl. judge City of Romney, 1980-90. Mem. W.Va. Jud. Hearing Bd., Hampshire County Devel. Authority, Romney, Hampshire County Farm Bur., Nat. Trust for Hist. Preservation; dir. Potomac Highlands Travel Coun., Elkins, W.Va., 1984-88; mem. adv. bd. Peterkin Conf. Ctr. of Renewal, Romney, 1988-90; del. W.Va. Dem. Conv., Charleston, 1984; vestryman St. Stephen's Episcopal Ch., Romney, 1984-86, Bd. of Trustees, Indian Mound Cemetery 2003-. Mem. ABA, ATLA, NRA (life), W.Va. Bar Assn., South Br. Valley Bar Assn. (pres. 1996-97), W.Va. Trial Lawyers Assn., Waterfowl U.S.A. (life), N.Am. Hunting Club (life), Hampshire Camp 284 SCV (judge adv.), Civil War Preservation Trust, W.Va. Law Sch. Assn. (life), W.Va. U. Alumni Assn. (life), Masons (Clinton Lodge #86), Scottish Rite of Freemasonry, USA Valley of Martinsburg, Orient of W.Va., Osiris Temple AAONMS, Romney chpt. #84 OES, Rotary (Paul Harris fellow), Phi Alpha Delta (life). Democrat. Episcopalian. Avocations: gun collecting, antique collecting, local history. Home: Liberty Hall 276 E Main St Romney WV 26757-1821 also: Mill Island Moorefield WV 26836 Office: 95 W Main St PO Box 2000 Romney WV 26757-2000 also: 113 Winchester Ave Moorefield WV 26836 Office Phone: 304-822-3875.

SAVILLE, THORNDIKE, JR., coastal engineer; b. Balt., 1925; s. Thorndike and Edith Saville; m. Janet Foster, Aug. 28, 1950; children: Sarah, Jennifer, Gordon. AB, Harvard U., 1947; MS, U. Calif., Berkeley, 1949. Rsch. asst. U. Calif., Berkeley, 1947-49; hydraulic engr. Beach Erosion Bd. and Coastal Engring. Rsch. Ctr., Washington, D.C. and Ft. Belvoir, Va., 1949-81, chief rsch. divsn., 1964-71, tech. dir., 1971-81; cons., 1981—. Contbr. more than 85 articles to engring. and sci. publs. With U.S. Army Air Corps., 1943—46. Recipient Meritorious Civilian Svc. award, Dept. Army, 1981, Comdr.'s award, 1998. Fellow: ASCE (Huber award 1963, Moffatt-Nichol award 1979, Internat. Coastal Engring. award 1991), AAAS, Wash. Acad. Scis.; mem.: Am. Shore and Beach Preservation Assn. (bd. dirs. 1976—97, v.p. 1988—95, M. P. O'Brien award 1997), Permanent Internat. Assn., Navigation Congresses (hon.; U.S. commr. 1971—78, U.S. commr. emeritus 1987—, U.S. rep. PTC II 1991—98), Nat. Acad. Engring., Am. Geophys. Union, Cosmos Club (Washington). Home and Office: 5601 Albia Rd Bethesda MD 20816-3304

SAVIN, RONALD RICHARD, chemicals executive; b. Cleve., Oct. 16, 1926; s. Samuel and Ada (Silver) Savin; m. Gloria Ann Hopkins, Apr. 21, 1962; children: Danielle Elizabeth, Andrea Lianne. BA in Chemistry and Lit., U. Cin., 1944-46; BA in Chemistry and Literature, U. Mich., 1948; postgrad., Columbia U., 1948-49, Sorbonne, Paris, 1949-50; grad., Air War Coll., 1975, Indsl. Coll. Armed Forces, 1976. Pres., owner Premium Finishes, Inc., Cin., 1957-91. Cons. aerospace and anti-corrosive coatings; inventor, owner Hy-erpseal, Inc. Contbr. articles to profl. jours. With USAF, 1948—55, World War II, Korea, col. USAFR, 1979—96. Mem.: Fedn. Coatings Tech., Fedn. Paint Techs., Nat. Assn. Corrosion Engrs., Steel Structures Painting Coun., Res. Officers Assn., Air Force Assn., Army Navy Club. Achievements include patents in field. Avocations: scientific development, photography, tennis.

SAVINELL, ROBERT FRANCIS, engineering educator; b. Cleve., May 26, 1950; s. Robert D. and Lotte R. Savinell; m. Coletta A. Savinell, Aug. 23, 1974; children: Teresa, Robert, Mark. BSChemE, Cleve. State U., 1973; MS, U. Pitts., 1974, PhD, 1977. Registered profl. engr., Ohio. Rsch. engr. Diamond Shamrock Corp., Painesville, Ohio, 1977-79; assoc. prof. U. Akron, Ohio, 1979-86; prof. Case Western Reserve U., Cleve., 1986—, dir. Ernest B. Yeager Ctr. for Electrochem. Scis., 1991—, assoc. dean engring., 1998—, interim dean of engring., 2000, dean engring., 2001. Divsn. editor Jour. Electrochem. Soc., 1988-91; N.Am. editor Jour. Applied Electrochemistry, 1991-97; contbr. articles to profl. jours. Named Presdl. Young Investigator, NSF, Washington, 1984-89, Outstanding Engring. Alumnus, Cleve. State U., 1984. Fellow Electrochem. Soc., AIChE (program chmn. 1986-92); mem. Electrochem. Soc. (divsn. officer 1992—), Internat. Soc. Electrochemistry (v.p. 1995-98). Avocations: sailing, skiing. Office: Case Sch Engring CRWU-500 Nord Hall Cleveland OH 44106-7220 Office Phone: 216-368-4436. Business E-Mail: rfs2@case.edu.

SAVING, THOMAS ROBERT, economics educator, consultant; b. Chgo., Dec. 27, 1933; s. Harold John and Frances Josephine (Fillipino) Saving; m. Barbara Jean Sorby, Aug. 22, 1959; children: Jason Lee, Nicole Aline. BA in Econs., Mich. State U., 1957; MA in Econs., U. Chgo., 1958, PhD in Econs., 1960. Asst. prof. U. Wash., Seattle, 1960—61, Mich. State U., East Lansing, 1961—63, assoc. prof., 1965—66, prof., 1966—68; prof. econs. Tex. A&M U., 1968—89, head dept. econs., 1985—91, disting. prof. econs., 1989—, dir. Pvt. Enterprise Rsch. Ctr., 1991—. Pres. RRC, Inc., College Sta., 1979—89, chmn. bd., 1989—; pub. trustee The Bd. of Trustees of Social Security and Medicare Trust Funds, 2000—; mem. bipartisan commn. to strengthen Social Security Pres. Commn., 2001. Author: Money, Wealth, Economic Theory, 1966. Mem.: Mont Pelerin Soc., Econometric Soc., Western Econs. Assn. (pres. 1971—72), So. Econ. Assn. (pres. 1981—82), Am. Econ. Assn. Home: 1402 Post Oak Cir College Station TX 77840-2322 Office: Tex A&M U Pvt Enterprise Rsch Ctr College Station TX 77843-4231 Office Phone: 979-845-7559.

SAVIO, FRANCES MARGARET CAMMAROTTA, music educator; b. Phila., Oct. 2, 1936; d. Frank Cammarotta and Margaret Eleanor Cammarotta Parilla; m. Savio, Sept. 12, 1959; 1 child, Margaret Mary. B Music Edn., Immaculata Coll., 1958; M Music Edn., Trenton State U., 1976. Music and English tchr. East Lansdowne (Pa.) schs., 1958—59; music tchr. Mary Calcott Elem. Sch., Norfolk, Va., 1959—61; music and English tchr. Northside Jr. High, Va., 1961—63; kindergarten tchr. Bar H. Crocker Country Day Sch., Oceanside, NY, 1965—68; gen. music tchr. K-8, drama dir. St. Bartholomew Sch., NJ, 1968—. Leader Girl Scouts U.S.A.; music dir., counselor, music coord. summer camps, Pa., N.J., Va.; organist, pastoral musician St. Bartholomew Ch., East Brunswick, 1968—90; mem. curriculum com. Diocese of Trenton, 1977; organist adult choir, dir. folk group St. Bartholomew Ch., East Brunswick, NJ; mem. profl. day com., mem. com. for outstanding Cath. educator Metuchen Diocese; mem. Altar Rosary Soc. Named Tchr. of Excellence, Diocese of Metuchen, 1995. Mem.: Nat. Music Honor Soc., Pi Kappa Lambda. Home: 14 Hershey Rd East Brunswick NJ 08816

SAVITS, BARRY SORREL, surgeon; b. Phila., Feb. 14, 1934; s. Frank and Sophia (Cohen) S.; children: George, Frank, Alexander. BA, Princeton U., 1955; MD, U. Pa., 1959; cert. surg. residency, Mt. Sinai Hosp., N.Y.C., 1965. Prof. surgery Project Hope, Ecuador, 1965-66; instr. surgery Albert Einstein Med. Coll., Bronx, N.Y., 1966-67; surgeon LaGuardia Med. Group, Queens, N.Y., 1970-72; dir. surgery St. Mary's Hosp., Bklyn., 1973-91, Kingsbrook Jewish Med. Ctr., Bklyn., 1991-2000; attending N.Y. Meth. Hosp., 2000—, N.Y. Cmty. Hosp., 2001—. Vis. surgeon Hope-Ecuador, 1965-66, Care-Medico, Afghanistan, 1976. Comdr. USN, 1967-69. Fellow ACS (gov. 1991-97); mem. Soc. Am. Gastrointestinal Endoscopic Surgeons, Assn. Acad. Surgery, Assn. Surg. Program Dirs., Bklyn. Surg. Soc. (pres. 1992-93). Jewish. Avocations: reading, children. Office: 263 7th Ave Ste 4E Brooklyn NY 11215 Fax: 718-369-8121. Office Phone: 718-369-8110. E-mail: bsavits@aol.com.

SAVITSKY, DANIEL, engineer, educator; b. N.Y.C., Sept. 26, 1921; s. Maxim and Anna (Oleksiw) S.; m. Mary Wysocki; children: Jean, James, Anne. BCE, CCNY, 1942; MSc, Stevens Inst. Tech., 1952; PhD, NYU, 1971. Registered profl. engr., N.Y. Structural engr. EDO Corp., College Point, N.Y., 1942-44; aero. rsch. scientist Nat. Adv. Com. for Aero., Langley Field, Va., 1944-47; prof. emeritus Stevens Inst. Tech., Hoboken, N.J., 1947—. Chmn. high speed vehicle com. Internat. Towing Tank Conf., 1978-88; cons. Naval Studies Bd., Nat. Rsch. Coun. Author: (with others) Yearbook of Science and Technology, 1987; patentee hydrofoil controls. Fellow Soc. Naval Architects and Marine Engrs. (hon. mem., Adm. Cochrane award 1967, Davidson medal 1996), Am. Soc. Naval Engrs., Niantic Bay Yacht Club (Conn.), Sigma Xi. Roman Catholic. Avocations: sailing, skiing, tennis. Home: 597 Delcina Dr Westwood NJ 07675-6111 Office: Davidson Lab 711 Hudson St Hoboken NJ 07030-5953 Office Phone: 201-216-5307. E-mail: dsavitsk@stevens.edu.

SAVITT, SUSAN SCHENKEL, lawyer; b. Bklyn., Aug. 21, 1943; d. Edward Charles and Sylvia (Dlugatch) S.; m. Harvey Savitt, July 2, 1969 (div. 1978); children: Andrew Todd, Daniel Cory. BA magna cum laude, Pa. State U., 1964; JD, Columbia U., 1968. Bar: N.Y. 1968, U.S. Dist. Ct. (so. and ea. dists.) N.Y. 1973, U.S. Tax Ct. 1973, U.S. Ct. Appeals (2d cir.) 1981, U.S. Supreme Ct. 1980, U.S. Dist. Ct. (we. dist.) N.Y. 1996. Atty. Nassau County Legal Svcs., Freeport, N.Y., 1973-74; asst. corp. counsel City of Yonkers, 1977-78; from assoc. to ptnr. Epstein, Becker & Green, P.C., N.Y.C., 1978-94; ptnr. Winston & Strawn, N.Y.C., 1994—. Adj. prof. Elizabeth Seton Coll., Yonkers, 1982-83; mem. NYU exec. coun. Met. Ctr. for Ednl. Rsch. Devel. and Tng., 1987-90; mediator Vol. Mediation Panel, U.S. Dist. Ct. (so. dist.) N.Y., 1997—, U.S. Dist. Ct. (ea. dist.) N.Y., 1999—. Mem. Hastings-on-Hudson (N.Y.) Sch. Bd., 1984-93, v.p., 1986, 87-88, pres., 1989-90, 92-93; bd. dirs. Associated Blind, 1993-95, Nat. Child Labor Com., 2001-2004, Liberal Arts Alumni Coun., Pa. State U., 2001—; bd. dirs., 2003-, Search for Change, 1996—2002, sec., 1998—2002; bd. dirs. Pa. State Profl. Women's Network of N.Y., 1996-2003, pres., 1998-2000. Mem. ABA (internat. law sect., litigation, dispute resolution and labor law sect.), N.Y. State Bar Assn. (labor law sect., comml. litigation sect.), Women's Bar Assn., Fed. Bar Coun., Pa. State Alumni Club (v.p. Westchester County 1985-87), Phi Beta Kappa, Alpha Kappa Delta, Phi Gamma Mu, Pi Kappa Phi. Office: Winston & Strawn 200 Park Ave New York NY 10166-0005 Office Phone: 212-294-4772. Business E-Mail: ssavitt@winston.com. E-mail: sssavitt@aol.com.

SAVITZ, FRED, education educator; b. Phila., Sept. 2, 1946; m. Jill Lynn, Dec. 21, 1968; children: Ryan, Ian. BA, Ursinus Coll., 1968; EdM, Temple U., 1970, EdD, 1977. Asst. prof. St. Joseph's U., Phila., 1980-86; divsn. chairperson Neumann Coll., Aston, Pa., 1986-92, prof., 1992—. Motivational spkr. Chester (Pa.) Edn. Found. Author (curriculum): Odyssey of the Mind; contbr. articles to profl. jours. Chaplain Neumann Coll. Men's Lacrosse Team. Mem. Pa. Assn. of Colls. and Tchr. Educators (bd. dirs. 2000—). Avocations: running, music. Home: 1532 Willowbrook Ln Villanova PA 19085

SAVITZ, MARTIN HAROLD, neurosurgeon; b. Boston, Jan. 20, 1942; s. Nathan and Bernice Beatrice (Segal) S.; m. Susan Rayna Gordon, June 23, 1968 (div. Sept. 1977); 1 child, Sean Isaac; m. Harmony Gwynne Keys, Oct. 28, 1979; 1 child, Ariel Austryn. AB, Harvard U., 1963; MD, Hahnemann U., 1969; MS in Psychology, Calif. Coast U., 1998; PhD in Med. Ethics, MCh, Am. Internat. U., 2003. Diplomate Am. Bd. Neurol. Surgery, Am. Bd. Clin. Neurol. Surgery, Nat. Bd. Med. Examiners, Am. Bd. Forensic Medicine, Am. Bd. Minimally Invasive Spinal Surgery, Am. Bd. Neurol. Imaging. Intern Boston City Hosp., 1969—70; resident in neurosurgery Mount Sinai Hosp., N.Y.C., 1970—74; clin. instr. dept. neurosurgery Mt. Sinai Sch. Medicine, N.Y.C., 1974—82, asst. clin. prof., 1982—86, assoc. clin. prof., 1986—97. Vis. prof. neurosurgery Med. Coll. Pa.-Hahnemann Sch. Medicine, 1998-99, adj. prof. bioethics Drexel U. Coll. Medicine, 1998-2004; provost, dean surg. rsch. Am. Internat. U., 1999—; adj. prof. pain mgmt. U. N.Mex. Sch. Medicine, 2002-03; adj. prof. surgery U. Health Scis., Antigua, 2001-02; attending neurosurgeon Nyack (N.Y.) Hosp., 1974-99, Good Samaritan Hosp., Suffern, N.Y., 1974-99, Cmty. Hosp., Dobbs Ferry, N.Y., 1995-99, Westchester Med. Ctr., Valhalla, N.Y., 1998-99; mem. pres.'s coun. Harvard Coll.,

1991-99, marshal of commencement, 1993—, admissions and fin. aid com., 1978—; mem. alumni bd. trustees Hahnemann U., 1991-94; head exam com. Am. Bd. Clin. Neurosurgery, 1995-99; lectr. in field. Contbg. editor Mt. Sinai Jour. Medicine, 1976-90, asst. editor, 1990—; mem. editl. bd. Jour. Orthopaedic Neurol. Medicine and Surgery, 1991-99; exec. editor Minimally Invasive Global Update, 1999—2002; editor-in-chief Jour. Minimally Invasive Spinal Technique, 2000—; asst. editor Jour. Royal Coll. Physicians and Surgeons, 2000—; contbr. chpts. to textbooks, articles to profl. jours. Fellow: ACS, Am. Back Soc., Am. Acad. Minimally Invasive Spinal Medicine and Surgery (exec. dir. 1999—), Internat. Biog. Ctr. (Man of Yr. 1994), Murphy Ctr. for Codification of Human Orgnl. Law, Am. Acad. Neurol. Orthopaedic Surgeons (bd. dirs. 1994—99, Lifetime Achievement award 1998), N.Y. Acad. Medicine, Am. Biog. Inst. (Man of Yr. 1995), Royal Coll. Physicians and Surgeons (U.S., exec. dir. 2000—01, vice chancellor 2002—, prof. minimally invasive spinal surgery), Internat. Coll. Surgeons (exec. com. 1994, chmn.-elect 1995, chmn. 1996, bd. regents 1997—2003, v.p. 1998—2000), Phila. Coll. Physicians, Am. Forensic Examiners Coll. (ethics com. 1995—2000); mem.: AAAS, AMA, N.Y. Acad. Scis., Hastings Ctr., Internat. Soc. Minimal Intervention in Spinal Surgery, Internat. Fedn. of Surg. Colls., N.Y. State Neurosurg. Soc., Congress Neurol. Surgeons, N.Y. Soc. Neurosurgery, Am. Coun. Bd. Certification (exec. dir. 2001—), Am. Fedn. Med. Accreditation (vice-chmn. 1997, chmn. 1998—99), Am. Assn. Neurol. Surgeons, John Harvard Soc., Phi Delta Epsilon, Alpha Omega Alpha. Jewish. Avocations: travel to all 7 continents, photography of rare fauna and flora, archeology. Home: Hobbit Holw New City NY 10956 Office: 30 Old Phillips Hill Rd New City NY 10956-2108 Fax: 845-634-5075. Office Phone: 845-634-5075. Personal E-mail: drbcasey@aol.com.

SAVITZ, MAXINE LAZARUS, aerospace company executive; b. Balt., Feb. 13, 1937; d. Samuel and Harriette (Miller) Lazarus; m. Sumner Alan Savitz, Jan. 1, 1961; children: Adam Jonathan, Alison Carrie. BA in Chemistry magna cum laude, Bryn Mawr Coll., 1958; PhD in Organic Chemistry, MIT, 1961. Instr. chemistry Hunter Coll., N.Y.C., 1962-63; sr. electrochemist Mobility Equipment Rsch. and Devel. Ctr., Ft. Belvoir, Va., 1963-68; prof. chemistry Federal City Coll., Washington, 1968-72; program mgr. NSF, Washington, 1972-74; dir. FEA Office Bldgs. Policy Rshc. U.S. Dept. Energy, Washington, 1974-75, dir. div. indsl. conservation, 1975-76, from dir. div. bldgs. and community systems to dep asst sec., 1975-83; pres. Lighting Rsch. Inst., 1983-85; asst. to v.p. engring. Ceramic Components div. The Garrett Corp., 1985-87; gen. mgr. ceramic components divsn. AlliedSignal Inc., Torrance, Calif., 1987-99; gen. mgr. tech. partnerships Honeywell, Torrance, Calif., 1999—2001, ret., 2001; prin. Washington Adv. Group. Bd. dirs. Am. Coun. for Energy Efficient Economy, Draper Corp.; bd. dirs. divsn. engring. and phys. sci. NRC; cons. State Mich. Dept. Commerce, 1983, N.C. Alternative Energy Corp., 1983, Garrett Corp., 1983, Energy Engring. Bd., Nat. Rsch. Bd., 1986—93, Office Tech. Assessment, U.S. Congress Energy Demand Panel, 1987—91; nat. materials adv. bd. NRC, 1989—94, adv. bd. on energy and environ. systems, divsn. of engring. and physical sci., 2002—; chmn. U.S. Advanced Ceramic Assn., 1992; adv. com. divsn. ceramics/materials ORNL, 1989—92, adv. com. dir., 1992—96; mem. lab. adv. com. Pacific N.W. Nat. Lab., 2000—; adv. bd. Sec. Energy, 1992—2002; mem. Def. Sci. Bd., 1993—96; vis. com. adv. tech. Nat. Inst. Stds. and Tech., 1993—98, Nat. Sci. Bd., 1999—2004; mem. bd. on energy and environ. sys. NRC, 2002—, mem. divsn. on engring. and phys. sci., 2003—. Editor Energy and Bldgs.; contbr. articles to profl. jours. Mem. policy com. NAE, 1994-98. NSF postdoctoral fellow, 1961, 62, NIH predoctoral fellow, 1960, 61. Mem. Nat. Acad. Engring. E-mail: maxinesavitz@aol.com.

SAVITZ, SAMUEL J. actuarial consulting firm executive; b. Phila., Dec. 23, 1936; s. Paul and Ann (Gechman) S.; m. Selma Goldberg, June 15, 1958; children: Jacqueline Beverly, Steven Leslie, Michelle Lynn. BS in Adminstrn., Temple U., 1958; postgrad., 1965, U. Pa., 1960-62. Pension analyst provident Mut. Life Ins. Co., Phila., 1958-61; v.p. The Wirkman Co., Phila., 1961-64; pres. Samuel J. Savitz & Assoc., Inc., Phila., 1964-86; sr. prin. Laventhol & Horwath, Phila., 1986-90; chmn. Savitz Orgn., Inc., Phila., 1990—. Vis. lectr. U. Pa., Phila., 1960, La. State U., 1972-74; faculty Villanova U., 1971-75; cons. in field. Contbr. articles to profl. jours. Mem. pension com. Fedn. JewishAgys., Phila., 1960; bd. dirs. Am. com. Weizmann Inst. Sci., 1984-85, Phila. All-Star Forum, 1987-95, Mann Music Ctr., 1992—; trustee Fgn. Policy Rsch. Inst., 1996—, Pa. Acad. Fine Arts, 1998—, Nat. Liberty Mus. and Edn. Ctr., 1999—, Am. Interfaith Inst., 1999—, Encore Series, Inc., 1999—; pres. Philly Pops, 1999—, Florentine Festivals USA, Inc., 2000-2002, Regional Performing Arts Ctr., 2002—, Kimmel Ctr. for the Performing Arts, 2002—, Nat. Mus. of Am. Jewish History, 2002—. With USAR, 1954-62. Mem. Am. soc. Pension Actuaries (dir. 1969-75), Union League Phila. Jewish. Home: 470 Conshohocken State Rd Bala Cynwyd PA 19004-2639 Office: 1845 Walnut St Philadelphia PA 19103-4708

SAVNER, DAVID A. lawyer; b. Chgo., Mar. 15, 1944; BA, Northwestern U., 1965, JD magna cum laude, 1968. Bar: Ill. 1968. Ptnr. Jenner & Block, Chgo.; sr. v.p., gen. counsel, sec. Gen. Dynamics Corp., Falls Church, Va., 1998—99, sr. v.p. law, sec., 1999—. Editor Northwestern U. Law Review, 1967-68. Mem. ABA, Chgo. Bar Assn., Chgo. Coun. Lawyers, Order of Coif. Office: Gen Dynamics Corp 3190 Fairview Park Dr Falls Church VA 22042-4523*

SAVOIA, MARIA CHRISTINA, vice dean; BA with highest honors, Wellesley Coll., 1972; MD, Harvard U., 1976. Diplomate Am. Bd. Internal Medicine. Med. intern U. Calif., San Diego, 1976-77, med. resident, 1977-79, fellow divsn. infectious diseases, 1980-84, clin. instr. medicine, 1980-84, asst. adj. prof. medicine, 1984-90, acting vice-chair dept. medicine, 1987-89, assoc. prof. clin. medicine, 1990-96, assoc. dean curriculum and student affairs sch. medicine, 1990—2003, vice dean med. edn., 2003—, acting dir. office learning resources sch. medicine, 1991-95, acting assoc. dean admissions sch. medicine, 1991, chief acad. officer sch. medicine, 1994—, prof. clin. medicine, 1996—; sr. fellow in med. edn. Harvard Macy Inst., Boston, 1996-97; assoc. investigator VA Med. Ctr., San Diego, 1981-84, asst. chief to acting chief med. svc., 1984-90, 87-89. Author: (with others) Medical Microbiology and Infectious Diseases, 1986, Infectious Disease, 1986, Principles and Practice of Infectious Diseases, 1989, Infections in Urology, 1990, Medical Complications During Pregnancy, 1995, and others; contbr. numerous articles and abstracts to profl. jours. Recipient Calif. Women in Govt. award, 1987; NSF grantee, 1972; Durant scholar Wellesley (Mass.) Coll., 1968-72. Fellow Infectious Diseases Soc. Am.; mem. Am. Soc. Microbiology. Office: Univ Calif Sch Medicine Assoc Dean Student Affairs 9500 Gilman Dr La Jolla CA 92093-0606

SAVOIE, LEONARD NORMAN, transportation company executive; b. Manchester, N.H., Aug. 8, 1928; s. Joseph Peter and Angelina (Desmarais) S.; m. Elsie Anne Berscht, June 9, 1951; children: Deborah Anne, Judith Lynn, Andrew Peter. BS, Queen's U., 1952; MBA, U. Detroit, 1955. Indsl. engr. Kelsey-Hayes Can. Ltd., Windsor, Ont., Can., 1952-60; mgmt. cons. P.S. Ross & Partners, Toronto, Ont., 1960-64; pres., gen. mgr. Kelsey-Hayes Can. Ltd., 1964-70; pres., chief exec. officer Algoma Central Ry., Sault Ste. Marie, Ont., 1970-93, vice-chmn., 1993-96. Bd. dirs. Can. Gen. Ins. Co., E-L Fin. Corp. Ltd., Empire Life Ins. Co., Newaygo Forest Products Ltd., Gt. Lakes Power Ltd. Bd. dirs. United Appeal. Mem. Profl. Engrs. Ont., Engring. Inst. Can., Canadian, Sault Ste. Marie chambers commerce. Clubs: Rotary, Toronto, Toronto Ry, Sault Ste. Marie Golf. Office: 517 Conservation Dr Brampton ON Canada L6T 3S1 E-mail: lens@sprint.ca.

SAVOIE, PAUL-ANDRÉ, information technology executive; BA in Commerce, Concordia U. Pres., tech. dir. R.A.N.K.I.N. Techs.; pres. Datacom Wireless Corp., Laval, Canada, 1999—. Gov. Le Portage; bd. dirs. Fondation Roméo Dallaire, Ambulance St.-Jean. Named one of Top 40 Under 40, 2002. Office: Datacom Wireless Corp 440 Armand-Frappier Blvd Ste 350 Laval QC Canada H7V 4B4

SAVOPOULOS, MARIOS A. architect, director; BArch with hons., U. Tex. Lic. Calif. From sr. assoc. to prin., dir. design, entertainment-related projects Perkowitz & Ruth, Newport Beach, Calif., 1993—99, prin., 1999—, dir. design, entertainment-related projects, 1999—. Mem.: AIA, Internat. Coun. Shopping Ctrs., Urban Land Inst. Office: Perkowitz & Ruth 15 Corporate Plaza Ste 200 Newport Beach CA 92660

SAVOY, DOUGLAS EUGENE, bishop, religious studies educator, explorer, writer; b. Bellingham, Wash., May 11, 1927; s. Lewis Dell and Maymie (Janett) S.; m. Elvira Clarke, Dec. 5, 1957 (div.); 1 son, Jamil Sean (dec.); m. Sylvia Ontaneda, July 7, 1971; children: Douglas Eugene, Christopher Sean, Sylvia Jamila. Student, U. Portland, 1947-8; DST, D Canon and Sacred Law, Jamilian U. of the Ordained, 1980. Ordained to ministry Internat. Community of Christ Ch., 1962, bishop, 1971. Head bishop Internat. Community of Christ Ch., 1971—; lectr. in ministerial tng. studies, 1972—; pastor Univ. Chapel, Reno, 1979—; founder Jamilian Parochial Sch., 1976; chancellor, founder Sacred Coll. of Jamilian Theology; pres., founder Jamilian U. of the Ordained, 1980; pres. Advs. for Religious Rights and Freedoms; chmn. World Coun. for Human Spiritual Rights, 1984—; head Jamilian Order of Patriarchs, 1990—; engaged in newspaper pub. West Coast, 1949-56; began explorations in jungles east of Andes in Peru to prove his theory that high civilizations of Peru may have had their origin in jungles, 1957; pres., founder Andean Explorers Found & Ocean Sailing Club, Reno. Expedition dir. Grand Ophir Sea Expedition; capt. Feathered Serpent III-Ophir, 1997-98. Author: Antisuyo, The Search for Lost Cities of the High Amazon, 1970, Vilcabamba, Last City of the Incas, 1970, The Cosolargy Papers, vol. 1, 1970, vol. 2-3, 1972, The Child Christ, 1973, Arabic edit., 1976, Japanese edit., 1981, The Decoded New Testament, 1974, Arabic edit., 1981, Millenium Edition, 1983, On The Trail of The Feathered Serpent, 1974, Code Book and Community Manual for Overseers, 1975, Prophecies of Jamil, First Prophecy to the Americas, vol. 1, 1976, Second Prophecy to the Americas, 1976, The Secret Sayings of Jamil, The Image and the Word, vol. 1, 1976, vol. 2, 1977, Project X— The Search For the Secrets of Immortality, 1977, Prophecy to the Races of Man, Vol. 2, 1977, Solar Cultures of The Americas, 1977, Dream Analysis, 1977, Vision Analysis, 1977, Christoanalysis, 1978, The Essaei Document: Secrets of an Eternal Race, 1978, Millennium edit., 1983, The Lost Gospel of Jesus: Hidden Teachings of Christ, 1978, Millennium edit., 1983, Secret Sayings of Jamil, vol. 3., 1978, vol. 4, 1979, Prophecy to The Christian Churches, vol. 3, 1978, The Sayings, vol. 4, 1979, Solar Cultures of Oceania, 1979, Prophecy of The End Times, vol. 4, 1980, Solar Cultures of Israel, vols. 1 and 2, 1980, Solar Cultures of China, 1980, Christotherapy, 1980, Christophysics, 1980, Christodynamics, 1980, Code Book of Prophecy, 1980, The Sayings, vol. 5, 1980, vol. 6, 1981, Solar Cultures of India, 1981, Prophecy on the Golden Age of Light and the Nation of Nations, Vol. 5, 1981, Solar Cultures of Israel, vol. 3, 1981, The Counsels, 1982, Prophecy of the Universal Theocracy, vol. 6, 1982, Prophecy of the New Covenant, vol. 7, 1982, The Book of God's Revelation, 1983, Miracle of the Second Advent, 1984, Clerical Studies in Theology, Book I, Book II, Book III, Book IV, Transformative Theology: The School of Revelation, Transformative Theology: The School of Prophecy, Liturgical Theology: Preparation for Advanced Degrees, 1993; over 400 audio tape rec. lectures, 1974—, numerous others.; dir. documentary film Adventure: Trail of the Feathered Serpent, 1970, Lost City of the Andes, 1987; wrote, dir. videos Royal Roads to Discovery, Mystery of the Essenes of Old Israel, Secrets From the High Andes of Peru, 1993, The Gran Vilaya Expeditions, 1996; contbr. articles on Peruvian cultures to mags., also articles on philosophy and religion; discoverer lost city of Incas at Vilcabamba Cuzco, numerous ancient cities in Amazonia including Gran Pajaten, Gran Vilaya, Monte Peruvia, Twelve Cities of the Condor, Gran Saposoa. Trustee in Trust Head Bishop Internat. Community of Christ. Served with AS USNR, 1944-46. Decorated Order of the Grand Cross Senate of Peru, 1989; recipient Participant's medallion Seawanhaka Yacht Club, 1977; Gold medal Ministry Industry and Tourism Peru, Silver Hummingbird, 1987; Silver medal and scroll City of Ica, Peru; honored with Gene Savoy Day by City of Reno, 1996, numerous exploring awards. Mem. Geog. Soc. Lima, Andean Explorers Found., Ocean Sailing Club (Explorer of the Century 1989, Flag awards), World Coun. for Human Spiritual Rights, Advs. for Religious Rights and Freedoms, Authors Guild, Explorers Club (N.Y.C., Flag awards), L.A. Yacht Club. Home: 2025 La Fond Dr Reno NV 89509-3025 Office: 643 Ralston St Reno NV 89503-4436 E-mail: gene@savoy.reno.nv.us. *One who makes dreams come true is that person who gets an idea, figures out how to make it work and then throws all of his energy into the project, stopping at nothing.*

SAVOY, SUZANNE MARIE, advanced practice nurse; b. NYC, Oct. 18, 1946; d. William Joseph and Mary Patricia (Moclair) S. BS, Columbia U., 1970; M in Nursing, UCLA, 1978; PhD in Nursing, Loyola U. RN, cert. clin. nurse specialist, cert. critical care nurse. Staff nurse MICU, transplant Json Meml. Hosp., Miami, 1970-72; staff nurse MICU Boston U. Hosp., 1972-74, VA Hosp., Long Beach, Calif., 1974-75; staff nurse MIRU Cedars-Sinai Med. Ctr., L.A., 1975-77; critical care clin. nurse specialist Anaheim (Calif.) Meml. Hosp., 1978-81; practitioner, instr. Rush-Presbyn.-St. Luke's Med. Ctr. Coll. Nursing, Chgo., 1982-88; rsch. assoc. dept. neurosurgery Rush U., 1984-88; clin. rsch. assoc. Medtronic, Inc. Drug Adminstrn. Sys., Mpls., 1988-91; staff nurse crit. care Harper Hosp., Detroit, 1992-93; clin. nurse specialist, surg./trauma crit. care Detroit Receiving Hosp., 1993-95; clin. instr. Wayne State U. Coll. of Nursing, Detroit, 1991-96, adj. faculty staff, 1996-98. Program coord. Crit. Care ACNP-CC MSN, Wayne State U., 1993-96; adult crit. care clin. nurse specialist Saginaw Gen. Hosp., 1996-98; card. clin. nurse specialist Covenant Healthcare Sys., Saginaw, 1998—; neurosci. clinician acute stroke unit Harper Hosp., Detroit, 1989; edn. cons. Crit. Care Svcs., Inc., Orange, Calif., 1979-81. Co-author articles for profl. jours. Mem. Am. Assn. Neurosci. Nurses (treas. Ill. chpt. 1983-85, pres. 1986-87, SE Mich. chpt. 1992-98, bd. dirs., treas., program chair), Am. Assn. Crit. Care Nurses (bd. dirs. Long Beach chpt. 1981-82, treas. NEMC chpt. 1999-2001), Assn. Healt Care Quality (treas. 2002—, Am. Assn. Spinal Cord Injury Nursing (mem. rsch. com. 1993-95), Lambda and Gamma Phi (bd. dirs. 1994-96), Sigma Theta Tau. Roman Catholic. Office Phone: 989-583-6532. Personal E-mail: cardiopn@aol.com. Business E-Mail: ssavoy@chs-ml.com.

SAVRIN, LOUIS, lawyer; b. Phila., Jan. 20, 1927; s. William Philip and Anna (Sass) S.; m. Barbara J. Schwimmer, Jan. 16, 1954; children: Jonathan Eric, Philip Wade, Daniel Scott. BS, N.Y. U., 1948; JD, U. Pa., 1951. Bar: N.Y. 1952. Atty. tax dept. Arthur Young & Co. (C.P.A.'s), N.Y.C., 1951-55; pvt. practice N.Y.C., 1955—. Gen. counsel, sec. Pickwick Internat., Inc., N.Y.C., 1965-77 Assoc. editor: U. Pa. Law Rev, 1949-51. Mem. sch. bd. Dist. 21, Bklyn., 1962-68; docent Whitney Mus. Am. Art. With AUS, 1945-46. Mem. N.Y. State Bar Assn., N.Y. County Lawyers Assn., Real Estate Tax Rev. Bar Assn.; mem. B'nai B'rith (pres. lodge 1957-59, named to lodge Hall of Fame 1967, Torch of Freedom award Anti-Defamation League 1982). Home: 50 Park Ave Apt 17H New York NY 10016-3082 Office: 60 E 42nd St New York NY 10165-0006 Office Phone: 212-682-7030.

SAVUKOV, IGOR M. physicist, researcher; m. Oksana V. Savukova. BS in Physics and Applied Math., Moscow Inst. of Physics and Tech., 1992; PhD, U. Notre Dame, 2002. Rsch. worker Inst. Applied Optics, Kiev, 1992—96; tchg. and rsch. asst. U. Notre Dame, Ind.; rsch. assoc. Princeton (NJ) U., 2002—. Mem.: Am. Phys. Soc. Achievements include discovery of large negative-energy contributions; research in formulation of gauge-invariant many-body perturbation theory; accurate calculations of complex atoms; precision measurements of transition rates. Office Phone: 609-258-0154. E-mail: isavukov@princeton.edu.

SAVULICH, ANDREW MICHAEL, photographer; b. Wilkes Barre, Pa., Sept. 16, 1949; s. Michael Andrew Savulich and Mary Yaremko; m. Mary Jo Downing, Sept. 16, 1992. BS in Landscape Arch., Rutgers U., 1971. Landscape arch. Carol Johnson Assoc., Cambridge, Mass., 1971—72, John Crowe Assoc., Belmont, Mass., 1972—75; freelance photographer N.Y.C., 1977—93; staff photographer N.Y. Daily News, N.Y.C., 1993—. One-man shows include Internat. Ctr. Photography, N.Y.C., 1994, Casa dos Crivos, Encontros da Imagen, Braga, Portugal, 2000, Journées Photographiques, Bienne, Switzerland, 2001, Musée de la Photographie, Charleroi, Belgium, 2002, periodical, Spy "It's a Wonderful Town", 1991—93, Granta Issue #46 Crime, 1994, book, City of Chance - New York Spot News & Street Photography, 2002. Recipient 1st pl. spot news, Nat. Press Photographers Assn., 1997; Fellowship grant in photography, NEA, 1986, Ernst Hass Photographer Work grantee, 1992. Office Phone: 212-210-1510.

SAWABINI, WADI ISSA, retired dentist, educator; b. Jaffa, Palestine, Jan. 14, 1917; s. Issa J. and Julia C. (Malak) S.; m. Harriet Colgate Abbe Lack, Aug. 6, 1949; children— Wadi' Issa, Frederick Lack, Stuart John, Julia Malak. Student, College des Ecoles Chrétiennes, 1924-32; D.D.S., Am. U. Beirut, 1940. Grad. study Forsyth Dental Infirmary, 1940-41; intern Med. Center Hosp. Vt. (formerly DeGoesbriand Meml. Hosp.), Burlington, 1941-42; attending staff; assoc. pvt. practice Dr. Charles I. Taggart, 1942-51; pvt. practice Burlington, 1951-88, ret.; instr. oral pathology U. Vt., 1951-58; dir. U. Vt. (Sch. Dental Hygiene), 1953-72; asst. prof. oral hygiene U. Vt. (Coll. Medicine), 1958-72; chief dental staff Mary Fletcher Hosp., 1958-68, assoc. prof. dept. allied health scis., 1969-72. Mem. adv. bd. Vt. Pub. Health Dept.; mem. Vt. Bd. Health, 1980-86; v.p. bd. dirs. Overlake Day Sch., 1962-63; mem. Ethan Allen Homestead Fundraising Com., 1990—. Paul Harris fellow Burlington Rotary. Fellow Internat. Coll. Dentists (mem. exec. council 1950-54), Am. Coll. Dentists; mem. Vt. Dental Soc. (pres. 1956-57, mem. bd. rev., Disting. Service award 1972), New Eng. Dental Soc., Champlain Valley Dental Soc., C. of C., ADA, Fedn. Dentaire Internat. Republican. Episcopalian (vestryman). Clubs: Mason (Shriner), Rotary (dir. 1955-56, pres. 1961-62), Ethan Allen (Burlington). Home: 512 Acorn Ln Gardenside Shelburne VT 05482-7316 E-mail: wsawabini@iopener.net. *I attribute my life's happiness to my alma mater, The American University of Beirut. It gave me technical expertise and love to seek knowledge, international understandings, and service to fellowman without regard to color nationality or religion.*

SAWAI, DAHLEEN EMI, language educator; b. Honolulu, Mar. 13, 1954; d. Kiyoto and Aiko Sawai. BA, U. Hawaii, Manoa, 1975, diploma in elem. edn., 1977, diploma in secondary edn., 1981, MEd, 1984. Cert. tchr. Hawaii. English tchr. Tokyo Family Court, 1977—78; Japanese tchr. Kailua H.S., Honolulu, 1978—80; English tchr. Family Ct. Probation Officer Tng. Sch., Tokyo, 1983—84; Japanese tchr. W. R. Farrington H.S., Honolulu, 1985—; educator Consortium for Tchg. Asia and the Pacific in the Schs., Honolulu, 1989—95; tchr. Family Court Probation Officer Training Sch., Tokyo, 1995—. Instr. Sch. Cmty. Based Mgmt., Honolulu, 2000—; interpreter Star Tanjo, 1976; chmn. Dept. World Langs. W.R. Farrington H.S., Honolulu, 2001—. Dir. Moanalua Gardens Cmty. Assn., Honolulu, 1976—77, sec., 1978—80. Scholar, Keio Gijuku Daigaku, 1982—84. Mem.: Nat. Coun. Japanese Lang. Tchrs., Farrington Alumni and Cmty. Found., Japanese Cultural Ctr. Hawaii, Alliance Drama Edn., Temari Ctr. for Asian and Pacific Arts, Pi Lambda Theta.

SAWALLISCH, WOLFGANG, conductor; b. Munich, Aug. 26, 1923; s. Wilhelm and Maria (Obermeier) Sawallisch; m. S. Mechthild. Ed., Wittelsbacher Gymnasium, Munich, Musikalische Ausbildung; pvt. music studies; D (hon.), Curtis Inst. of Music, Westminister Choir Coll. of Rider U., Villanova U. Condr., Augsburg, Germany, 1947-53; musical dir. Aachen, Germany, 1953-58, Wiesbaden, Germany, 1958-60, Cologne Opera, 1960-63; condr. Hamburg Philharm. Orch., 1960-73, hon. mem., 1973—; music dir. Phila. Orch., 1993—2003. Prin. condr. Vienna Symphony Orch., 1960—70, hon. mem.; prof. Staatliche Hochschule fur Musik, Cologne, 1960—63; musical dir. Bayerische Staatsoper Munich, 1971—92; dir. Staatsoper Munich, 1982—92, hon. mem., 1992—; permanent condr. Teatro alla Scala, Milan. Decorated Osterreichisches Ehrenkreuz fur Kunst und Wissenschaft, Bundesverdienstkrenz, Bayerischer Verdienstorden, Grosses Bundesverdienstkreuz mit Stern Fed. Republic Germany, Order of Rising Sun Japan; recipient Accademico Onorario Santa Cecilia, 1975, Toscanini Gold Baton, La Scala, 1993, Bruckner-Ring, Vienna Symphony Orch., 1980, Bayerisches Maximilians-order fur Wissenschaft und Kunst, 1984, Chevalier dans L'ordre Nat. de la Legion d'Honneur de France, 1991, Pa. Gov. Disting. Artist award, Avatar award for artistic excellence, Arts and Bus. Coun., Phila. Mem.: Richard Strauss Gesellschaft Munich (pres. 1976). Office: Phila Orch 260 S Broad St Fl 16 Philadelphia PA 19102-5002

SAWAYA, RAYMOND, neurosurgeon; b. Latakia, Syria, May 5, 1949; s. Emile and Josephine (Boulos) S.; m. Kristin Tveit; children: Marc-Emile, Corinne Marguerite. MD, St. Joseph U., Beirut, 1974. Diplomate Am. Bd. Neurol. Surgery. Intern Beeckman-Downtown Hosp., N.Y.C., 1974-75; resident in surgery SUNY, Syracuse, 1975-76; resident in neurosurgery U. Cin., 1976-80, Johns Hopkins Hosp., Balt., 1981; vis. scientist NIH, Bethesda, Md., 1981-82; assoc. prof. U. Cin., 1983-90, dir. div. neuro-oncology, 1983-90; neurosurgeon Mayfield Neurol. Inst., Cin., 1983-90; prof., chmn. dept. neurosurgery U. Tex. M.D. Anderson Cancer Ctr., Houston, 1990—. Contbr. numerous articles on neurosurgery to profl. jours. Research Adv. Group grantee VA Med. Ctr., 1984. Mem. Am. Radium Soc., Tex. Med. Assn., Am. Assn. Neurol. Surgeons, Congress of Neurosurgeons, Soc. Surg. Oncology, Houston Neurol. Soc. (pres.), Johns Hopkins Alumni Assn. Roman Catholic. Avocations: music, bridge, swimming. Office: 1515 Holcombe Blvd # 64 Houston TX 77030-4009

SAWCZUK, IHOR S. urologist; b. N.Y.C., Oct. 5, 1952; s. Stefan and Stefania (Mruczkewycz) S. BA, NYU, 1974; MD, Med. Coll. of Pa., 1979. Diplomate Am. Bd. Urology. Chief Allen Pavilion Urology Columbia-Presbyn. Med. Ctr., N.Y.C., 1988—99; prof. urology Columbia U., N.Y.C., 1993—, vice chmn. Dept. of Urology, 1994—2001; chmn. urology Hackensack (NJ) U. Med. Ctr., 2001—, chief urologic oncology Cancer Ctr. Adv. bd. Kidney Cancer Assn., 1994—, Kidney and Urology Found., 2002—; dep. dir. Internat. Coop. Urological Edn. Project, 1994-96. Co-editor: (book) Urologic Clinics of North America, 1993. Bd. dirs. Children of Chernobyl, Short Hills, N.J., 1992-98. Recipient Young Investigator award Nat. Kidney Found., 1987, Alpha Omega Alpha Vol. Clin. Faculty award N.J. Med. Sch., 2003. Mem. ACS, Am. Urological Assn. (scholar 1986), N.Y. Acad. Scis., Soc. Internat. de Urologie, Soc. Urologic Oncology, European Acad. Scis. Office Phone: 201-336-8090.

SAWDEI, MILAN A. lawyer; b. Bakersfield, Calif., Aug. 23, 1946; BA, U. Calif., Long Beach, 1969; JD, W.S.U., 1975. Bar: Calif. 1975, U.S. Dist. Ct. (ctrl. dist.) Calif. 1975. House counsel Sanyo Electric, Inc., 1975-77; assoc. counsel Brown Co. (Gulf & Western), 1978-80; divsn. counsel Petrolane, Inc., 1980-83; sr. counsel Bergen Brunswig Corp., Orange, Calif., 1983-90, v.p., chief legal officer, 1990-92, exec. v.p., chief legal officer, sec., 1992—. Mem. ABA, Am. Corp. Counsel Assn., Am. Soc. Corp. Secs., L.A. County Bar Assn. Office: Bergen Brunswig Corp 4000 Metropolitan Dr Orange CA 92868-3510

SAWHILL, ISABEL VAN DEVANTER, economist; b. Washington, Apr. 2, 1937; d. Winslow B. and Isabel E. Van Devanter; m. John C. Sawhill, Sept. 13, 1958; 1 son, James W. BA, NYU, 1962, PhD, 1968. Asst. prof. econs. Goucher Coll., Balt., 1969—73; sr. rsch. assoc. Urban Inst., 1973—77, program dir., sr. fellow, 1980—93; dir. Nat. Commn. Employment Policy, Washington, 1977—79; program assoc. dir. Office Mgmt. and Budget, 1993—95; sr. fellow and Arjay Miller chair in pub. policy Urban Inst., 1995—97; sr. fellow Brookings Instn., Washington, 1997—2003, v.p., dir. econ. studies, 2003—. Vis. prof. Georgetown U. Law Ctr., 1990-91; chairperson rsch. adv. bd. Com. for Econ. Devel., 1995-98. Author: Getting Ahead, 1998, Updating America's Social Contract, 2000, Restoring Fiscal Sanity, 2004. Bd. dirs. Manpower Demonstration Res. Corp.; pres. Nat. Campaign Prevent Teen Pregnancy, 1996—. Mem. Am. Econ. Assn., Assn. Pub. Polit. Analysis and Mgmt. (pres. 1988), Phi Beta Kappa. Office: Brookings Inst 1775 Massachusetts Ave NW Washington DC 20036-2103

SAWICK, KAREN ANN, real estate agent; b. Elizabeth, N.J., Apr. 6, 1947; d. Florian Albert and Janet Gloria (Anthony) Smiles; m. Richard Henry Sawick, July 6, 1996; children: Robert Richard, Jeffrey Christopher. Student, Fairleigh Dickinson U. Lic. real estate salesperson, N.J. Dental asst. Dr. Ferrec, Ramsey, N.J., 1965-67; office mgr. Dr. Walter Stocker, Basking Ridge, N.J., 1974-76; sec.-treas. N.E. Atlantic Airlines, Somers Ct., Westfield, Mass., 1971-76; real estate salesperson Schlott Realtors, Better Homes and Gardens, Chester, N.J., 1976-80. Poet/author: Diamonds and Pearls, 1997. Vol. Morristown Meml. Hosp., 1974; mem. Chaplain's Conf. Somerset County, 1974;

active vol. Red Cross, 1976, C. of C., Marion/Ocala. Mem. Suncoast Better Bus. Fedn., Ocala/Marion C. of C., Bd. Realtors of Hunterdon County and Somerset County. Presbyterian. Avocations: writing, humane animal societies. Home: 8919 SW 204th Cir Dunnellon FL 34431-5726

SAWKO, FELICJAN, civil engineering educator; b. Wilczuki, Poland, May 17, 1937; s. Czeslaw and Franciszka (Nawrot) S.; m. Genowefa Stefania Bak, Apr. 18, 1960; children: Andrew, Barbara, Piotr, Ryszard, Paul. BSc, Leeds (Eng.) U., 1958, MSc, 1960, DSc, 1973. Chartered engr. Civil enr. Rendel, Palmer & Tritton, Eng., 1959-62; lectr. Leeds U., 1962-67; prof. Liverpool (Eng.) U., 1967-86; prof., head dept. civil engring. Sultan Qaboos U., Oman, 1986-95; ret., 1995. Cons. in civl engring., 1962-86. Editor: Developments in Prestressed Concrete, 1978, Computer Methods for Civil Engineers, 1984; contbr. articles to profl. jours. Fellow Instn. Civil Engrs. Roman Catholic. Avocations: bridge, photography, coin collecting/numismatics, travel. Home: 23 Floral Wood Liverpool L17 7HU England

SAWOROTNOW, PARFENY PAVLOVICH, mathematician, educator; b. Ust Medveditskaya, Russia, Feb. 20, 1924; came to U.S., 1949, naturalized, 1965; s. Pavel Ivanovich and Anna Davidovna (Soloview) S.; student U. Graz (Austria), 1946-49; MA (Peirce scholar), Harvard U., 1951, PhD (Shattuck fellow), 1955. Teaching fellow Harvard U., 1953-54; instr. math. Cath. U. Am., Washington, 1954-57, asst. prof., 1957-62, assoc. prof., 1962-67, prof., 1967-96, prof. math. emeritus, 1997—. NSF grantee, 1967, 70; with Georgetown U. and George Washington U., 1971-77. Mem. Am. Math. Soc., Math. Assn. Am., Calcutta Math. Soc., N.Y. Acad. Scis., Sigma Xi. Mem. Eastern Orthodox Ch. Contbr. articles to and referred papers for math. rsch. jours. Home: 6 Avon Pl Hyattsville MD 20782-3328 Office: Cath U Am Dept Math 4th And Michigan Ave NE Washington DC 20064-0001

SAWTELLE, CARL S. psychiatric social worker; b. Boston, July 14, 1927; s. Carl Salvador and Martha (Bellamacina) S.; BA, Suffolk U., Boston, 1951; MSW, Simmons Sch. Social Work, 1953; m. Thelma Florence Ramsay, Aug. 20, 1950; children: Tracy Lynn, Lisa June. Social worker Tewksburry (Mass.) State Hosp., 1952; psychiat. social worker, head psychiat. social worker, dir. clin. social work Taunton (Mass.) State Hosp., 1953-74; 1st dir. clin. social work, Plymouth, Mass., 1974-78; co-founder, v.p. 1st legally established War On Poverty program Triumph, Inc., Taunton; co-founder 1st Greater Taunton Coun. on Alcoholism, 1972. With USCG, 1944-46. 1st lic. social worker in Mass., 1980. Mem. Nat. Assn. Social Workers (co-founder Southeast Mass. chpt. 1957, pres. 1957, Spl. Mass. Chpt. award 1978), Acad. Cert. Social Workers (chmn. 1962-72), Am. Legion, Mass. Mental Health Social Workers Assn. (co-founder, pres. 1972-74, other offices). Created innovated programs, resources, opportunities, svcs. to state mental hosp. patients and their families; mentor to young social workers; contbr. advancement of knowledge, practice quality and standards of psychiat. social work; father of licensing and registration of Social Workers in Mass. Home: 9 Tracywood Rd Canton MA 02021-3501

SAWYER, CHARLES HENRY, anatomist, educator; b. Ludlow, Vt., Jan. 24, 1915; s. John Guy and Edith Mabel (Morgan) S.; m. Ruth Eleanor Schaeffer, Aug. 23, 1941; 1 dau., Joan Eleanor. BA, Middlebury Coll., 1937, DSc honoris causa, 1975; student, Cambridge U., Eng., 1937-38; PhD, Yale, 1941. Instr. anatomy Stanford, 1941-44; assoc., asst. prof., assoc. prof., prof. anatomy Duke U., 1944-51; prof. anatomy UCLA, Los Angeles, 1951-85, prof. emeritus, 1985—, chmn. dept., 1955-63, acting chmn., 1968-69, faculty research lectr., 1966-67. Editorial bd.: Endocrinology, 1955-59, Proc. Soc. Exptl. Biology and Medicine, 1959-63, Am. Jour. Physiology, 1972-75; Author papers on neuroendocrinology. Mem. Internat. Brain Research Orgn. (council 1964-68), AAAS, Am. Assn. Anatomists (v.p. 1969-70, Henry Gray award 1984), Am. Physiol. Soc., Am. Zool. Soc., Neurosci. Soc., Endocrine Soc. (council 1968-70, Koch award 1973), Am. Acad. Arts and Scis., Nat. Acad. Scis., Soc. Exptl. Biology and Medicine, Soc. Study Reprodn. (dir. 1969-71, Hartman award 1977), Internat. Neuroendocrine Soc. (council 1972-76), Hungarian Soc. Endocrinology and Metabolism (hon.), Japan Endocrin Soc. (hon.), Phi Beta Kappa, Sigma Xi. Home: 466 Tuallitan Rd Los Angeles CA 90049-1941 Office: U Calif Sch Medicine Dept Neurobiology Los Angeles CA 90095-1764

SAWYER, CHARLES HENRY, art educator, art museum director emeritus; b. Andover, Mass., Oct. 20, 1906; s. James Cowan and Mary Pepperrell (Frost) S.; m. Katharine Clay, June 28, 1934. BA, Yale U., 1929, MA, 1947; student, Harvard Law Sch., 1929-30; student of Fine Arts, Harvard U. Grad. Sch., 1930-32; LHD, Amherst Coll., 1950; DFA, U. New Hampshire, 1951; LHD, Clark U., 1953. Dir. Addison Gallery of Am. Art, art instr. Phillips Acad., Andover, Mass., 1930-40; dir. Worcester (Mass.) Art Mus., 1940-46; dir. divsn. of the arts, prof. history of art Yale U., New Haven, Conn., 1947-56; master Timothy Dwight Coll. Yale U., New Haven, 1947-53; dean Sch. of Architecture and Design, Yale U., New Haven, 1947-56; dir. mus. of art U. Mich., Ann Arbor, 1957-72, prof. history of art, 1957-76, dir. emeritus mus. of art, 1973—, prof. emeritus history of art, 1977—. Mem. art adv. commn. Harvard U., 1940-58, Cambridge,, Amherst (Mass.) Coll., 1948-60, Smith Coll., Northampton, Mass. 1948-55, U. Notre Dame, Ind., 1973-82, Smithsonian Art Commn., Smithsonian Instn., Washington, 1953-80; trustee Corning (N.Y.) Mus. of Glass, 1950-75. Author: (book) Art in English Public Schools, 1936; author various articles, exhibition catalogues etc., 1931—. Mem. Art Commn. State of Mass., Boston, 1940-44, Historic Sites Commn., State of New Hampshire, Concord, 1948-58, Arts Coun., State of Mich., Lansing, 1964-72. Named Hon. Mem. NMAA Commn. Washington, 1985—. Fellow Am. Acad. Arts and Scis.; mem. Assn. Art Mus. Dirs. (hon. mem. 1973—), Century Assn. N.Y., Am. Antiquarian Soc. Episcopalian. Avocations: hist. rsch., gardening. Home: 801 W Middle St Apt #172 Chelsea MI 48118

SAWYER, CHARLES S. environmental engineer, engineering educator; b. Jan. 8, 1959; s. Joshua S. Sawyer, Regina S. George; m. Marvel A. Cole; 1 child, Marvin. BSME, U. Sierra Leone, 1980; MS in Chem. Engring., Va. Poly. Inst. and State U., Blacksburg, 1987; PhD in Environ. Engring., U. Conn., 1992. Lic. profl. engr., Conn.; diplomate qualified environ. prof. Pres., prin. engr. Bryxx Engring. Inc., North Haven, Conn., 2001—; prof. U. Conn., Storrs, 1992—2002. Bd. dirs. Amistad Am. Inc, 2001—. Contbr. articles to profl. jours. Fellow: ASCE; mem.: Conn. Soc. Civil Engrs. (chmn. water resources com. 1995—2000, newsletter editor 2001—02, treas. 2002—), Am. Geophys. Union. Home and Office: 15 Patten Rd North Haven CT 06473-2828 Personal E-mail: csswayer@aol.com. Business E-Mail: csawyer@bryxx.com.

SAWYER, DAVID JONATHAN, educator; b. Fayetteville, N.C., Aug. 26, 1927; s. Noah Devon and Mary Woodie (Jackson) S.; m. Margaret T. Sawyer, June 16, 1950 (dec.); 1 child, Phyllis (dec.); m. Carolyn Gertrude Sawyer, June 29, 1975; children: Phyllis, Lois. Grad. H.S., Fayetteville. Prodn. operator Glidden Chem. Co., Balt.; paraprofl. Balt. City Sch. With U.S. ARmy, 1946. Mem. Homeless Children Balt. (bd. mem., transport rep. 1997—). Democrat. Baptist. Avocations: writing, playing pool, travel. Home: 3524 Elmora Ave Baltimore MD 21213 Office: 1220 E 20th St Baltimore MD 21218-6314 E-mail: sawyerdj73@aol.com.

SAWYER, DIANE (L. DIANE SAWYER), newscaster, journalist; b. Glasgow, Ky., Dec. 22, 1945; d. E. P. and Jean W. (Dunagan) Sawyer; m. Mike Nichols, Apr. 29, 1988. BA, Wellesley Coll., 1967. Reporter Sta. WLKY-TV, Louisville, 1967—70; adminstr. press office White House, 1970—74; rschr. Richard Nixon's memoirs, 1974—78; gen. assignment reporter, then Dept. State corr. CBS News, 1978—81; co-anchor Morning News CBS, 1981—, co-anchor Early Morning News, 1982—84; corr., co-editor 60 Minutes CBS-TV, 1984—89; co-anchor Prime Time Live (now known as 20/20) ABC News, 1989—; co-anchor Day One, 1995, Turning Point, 1996, Good Morning Am. ABC News, N.Y.C., 1999—. Named to TV Hall of Fame, 1997; recipient 2 Peabody awards for pub. svc., 1988, Robert F. Kennedy award, 13 Emmy awards, 2 Dupont awards (one Spl.), IRTS Lifetime Achievement award. Office: Good Morning America Fl 10 147 Columbus Ave New York NY 10023-5900

SAWYER, DOLORES, motel chain executive; b. Shreveport, La., Oct. 16, 1938; d. Orlan B. Greer and Doris Lucile (Sanders) Eckman; m. Raymond Lee Sawyer Jr., June 11, 1960; children: Lisa Kay, Linda Faye. BSN, Northwestern State Coll., 1960; MSN, Tex. Woman's U., 1975. Supr. obstetrics dept. Highland Hosp., Shreveport, La., 1962-64; head nurse (3-11 shift) Scott and White Meml. Hosp., Temple, Tex., 1966-71, dir. of nursing edn., 1975-76; sch. nurse Temple Ind. Sch. Dist., 1971-72; instr. Mary-Hardin Baylor Coll., Belton, Tex., 1972-74; asst. prof., clin. specialist U. Tex. Arlington, 1976-86; v.p. Budget Host Internat., Arlington, Tex., 1986-96, sr. v.p., 1996—, also bd. dirs. Recipient Amoco Outstanding Tchg. award, 1981. Mem. Sigma Theta Tau. Republican. Methodist. Avocations: reading, tole painting, gardening, crafts, piano. Office: Budget Host Internat Ste B 2307 Roosevelt Dr Arlington TX 76016-5865 Office Phone: 817-861-6088. Personal E-mail: rsawyerl@airmail.net. Business E-Mail: dsawyer@budgethost.com.

SAWYER, DONALD E. urologist; b. Cambridge, Mass., Sept. 11, 1944; m. Anne Ross, June 30, 1968. BA, U. Vt., 1966; MD, N.Y. Med. Coll., 1970. Diplomate Am. Bd. Urology. Intern N.Y. Med. Coll., 1970-71, resident, 1971-72, Lahey Clinic, 1972-75; urologist in pvt. practice, Long Beach, Calif., 1979-99, Los Alamitos, Calif., 1979-99, Ocean Springs, Pascagoula, Miss., 1999—2001, VA Med. Ctr., Jackson, 2001—. Asst. prof. urology U. Miss. Med. Ctr., 2001—. Contbr. articles to profl. jours. Served as lt. comdr. USN, 1975-79. Avocations: travel, walking, physical fitness. Office: VA Med Ctr 1500 E Woodrow Wilson Dr Jackson MS 39216 Office Phone: 601-364-1358. Business E-Mail: Donald.Sawyer@med.va.gov.

SAWYER, DONALD T. retired chemistry professor; b. Pomona, Calif., Jan. 10, 1931; s. Donald T. and Lilas S. Sawyer; m. Shirley S. Scott, June 21, 1952; children: Sharon L, Robert S, Andrew T. BS, Univ. Calif., L.A., 1953, PhD, 1956. Prof. chemistry Univ. Calif., Riverside, 1956—; disting. prof. chemistry Tex. A&M U., College Station, 1985—; adj. prof. of chemistry U. Ky., Lexington, 2002—. Cons. Shell Devel. Corp, Houston, 1972—92; sci. advisor U.S. Food & Drug Adminstrn., Los Angeles, Calif., 1975—82; dean, coll. phys. sciences Univ of Calif., Riverside, 1970—74; mem., adv. com. Rsch. Corp., New York, NY, 1978—82; cons. Philip Morris Corp, Richmond, Va., 1968—92. Author: (book) Electrochemistry for Chemists, 2nd ed, (textbook) Chemistry Experiments for Instrumental Methods. Mem. Riverside Symphony Assn., 1968—72. Recipient Tolman Award, So. Calif Sect. of Am. Chem. Soc., 1982; grantee Guggenheim Fellowship, John Simon Guggenheim Meml. Found., 1962-1963, AAAS Fellow, 1978, Fellowship, Japan Soc. for Promotion Sci., 1983. Home: 1545 Player Dr Lexington KY 40511 Personal E-mail: sawyerd9@insightbb.com.

SAWYER, HOWARD JEROME, physician; b. Detroit, Nov. 17, 1929; s. Howard C. and Dorothy M. (Risley) S.; m. Janet Carol Hausen, July 24, 1954; children: Daniel William, Teresa Louise BA in Philosophy, Wayne State U., 1952, MD, 1962, postdoctoral, 1969-72. Diplomate Am. Bd. Preventive Medicine in Occupational and Environ. Medicine. Intern William Beaumont Hosp., Royal Oak, Mich., 1962-63, resident in surgery, 1963-64; chief physician gen. parts div. Ford Motor Co., 1964-66; med. dir. metall. products dept. Gen. Electric Co., Detroit, 1966-73, chem. and metal div., 1972-73; staff physician Detroit Indsl. Clinic, Inc., 1973-74; pres., med. dir. OccuMed Assocs., Inc., Farmington Hills, Mich., 1974-84; dir. OccuMed div. Med. Service Corp. Am., Southfield, Mich., 1984-86; dir. occupational, environ. and preventive medicine Henry Ford Hosp., 1987-91; pres. Sawyer Med. Cons., P.C., 1991—. Adj. asst. prof. occupational and environ. health scis. Wayne State U., 1974—, lectr. occpl. and environ. medicine Sch. of Medicine, 1998—; lectr. Sch. Pub. Health, U. Mich., Ann Arbor, 1977-88; cons. med. dir. St. Joe Minerals Corp., 1976-87, Chesbrough Pond's Inc., 1979-83; cons. Anaconda, Bendix, Borg Warner Chems., Fed. Mogul, Gen. Electric, Gt. Lakes Chems., other corps. Contbr. articles to profl. jours., chpts. to textbooks. Fellow Am. Coll. Preventive Medicine, Am. Occupational and Environ. Med. Assn., Mich. Occupational and Environ. Med. Assn. (pres. 1986), Am. Acad. Occupational Medicine; mem. AMA, Detroit Occupational Physicians Assn. (pres. 1984), Mich. State Med. Soc., Oakland County Med. Soc., Am. Indsl. Hygiene Assn., Mich. Indsl. Hygiene Soc. E-mail: buzsaw@mediaone.net.

SAWYER, JAMES, lawyer; b. N.Y.C., Feb. 18, 1946; s. Jules and Florence Barbara (Wishnew) S.; m. Margot Peretz, June 8, 1995; children: Kim, Caryn. BA, Adelphi U., 1967; JD, St. Johns U., 1969. Bar: N.Y. 1970, U.S. Dist. Ct. (so. and ea. dist.) N.Y. 1971, U.S. Tax Ct. 1972, U.S. Ct. Appeals (2d cir.) 1972, U.S. Ct. Appeals (1st cir.) 1975, Fla. 1981, U.S. Supreme Ct. 1981. Ptnr. Martin, Van De Walle & Sawyer, Great Neck, N.Y., 1970-81, Hession, Halpern, Bekoff & Sawyer, Mineola, N.Y., 1982-87, Sawyer, Halpern and Demetri, Garden City, NY, 1987—. Pres. Temple Or-Elohim, Jericho, N.Y., 1987-89; active Nassau County Med. Malpractice Panel, 1982-86. Mem. ABA, N.Y. State Bar Assn., Nassau County Bar Assn. Address: Sawyer Davis & Halpern and Demetri Esq 666 Old Country Ste 701 Garden City NY 11530-2010 E-mail: jsawyeresq@aol.com.

SAWYER, JAMES S. manufacturing executive; BS in Geology, Wesleyan U.; MBA, MIT. V.p. Praxair, treasurer, 1992—2000, CFO, 2000—. Office: Praxair 39 Old Ridgebury Rd Danbury CT 06810-5113

SAWYER, JOHN EDWARD, management educator; b. Florence, Ariz., July 26, 1954; s. Almus Wilmore and Betty (Mossman) S.; m. Dana Lee Strandberg, Aug. 5, 1989; children: Adrian John, Alexander Lyn, Jordan Estelle. BA in Psychology, Calif. State U., Long Beach, 1977; MA in Counseling Edn., Calif. State U., Fresno, 1979; AM in Indsl./Orgnl. Psychology, U. Ill., 1985, PhD of Indsl./Orgnl. Psychology, 1987. Project dir. Youth Svc. Bur., Modesto, Calif., 1979-81; counselor Horizons Youth Svc. Bur., Livermore, Calif., 1981-82; lectr., tchg. asst. U. Ill., Urbana, 1982-87; asst. prof. Tex. A&M U., College Station, 1987-91; asst. prof. mgmt. U. Del., Newark, 1991-95, assoc. prof., 1995—2003, mgmt. area head, 1998—2001, chair dept. bus. adminstrn., 2001—, prof., 2003—. Human resources rschr. Xerox Corp., Rochester, N.Y., 1985-86; orgnl. cons. Mercy Hosp., Urbana, 1983, Tex. Dept. Mental Health, San Antonio, 1989-90; trainer, cons. DuPont Merck Pharm. Co., Wilmington, 1994, Hercules, Wilmington, 1996. Mem. editl. bd. Jour. Mgmt.; contbr. chpt. in book and articles to profl. jours. Grantee Tex. Engring. Experiment Sta., 1989, Tex. Higher Edn. Coordinating Bd., 1990, Gen. Univ. Rsch. Program, 1993, Ctr. for Info. Sys. Mgmt. Edn. and Rsch., 1994. Mem. APA, Acad. Mgmt. (invited guest editl. bd.), Judgment and Decision Making Soc., Soc. Indsl. and Orgnl. Psychology. Home: 214 Cullen Way Newark DE 19711-6112 Office: Univ Delaware Dept Bus Adm Newark DE 19716 E-mail: sawyerj@lerner.udel.edu.

SAWYER, LEONARD SYLVESTER, retired lawyer; b. Lincoln, N.H., June 14, 1925; s. Howard Symmes and Rose Veronica (Eagan) S.; m. Caroline Eldora Smith, Sept. 7, 1960; children: Edward M., Charles L. BA, U. N.H., 1947; LLB, Boston U., 1950. Bar: N.H. 1950. Ptnr. Edes & Sawyer, Woodsville, N.H., 1954-56; pvt. practice Plymouth, N.H., 1956-94; ret., 1994. Justice Plymouth Dist. Ct., 1965-85. Selectman Town of Plymouth, 1963-65; moderator Plymouth Water and Sewer Dist., 1974-2004;del. N.H. Constl. Conv., 1984; mem. N.H. Audubon Soc., Plymouth Hist. Soc., New Hampton Hist. Soc., Upper Pemi Valley Hist. Soc.; local coord. FISH program, 1994—; vol. Plymouth Regional Sr. Ctr., Quincy Bog Natural Area. Served with U.S. Army, 1950-54. Mem. N.H. Bar Assn., Am. Judicature Soc., Lions (past pres. Plymouth chpt.), Grange (master, treas.), Am. Legion. Democrat. Roman Catholic. Avocations: hiking, swimming, reading. Home: 13 Cummings St Plymouth NH 03264-1106

SAWYER, LINDA, advertising executive; married; 2 children. Avrett, Free & Ginsberg; SSC&B; Ted Bates Worldwide; Goldberg Marchesano Washington; exec. v.p., group acct. dir. Deutsch, Inc., NYC, gen. mgr., 1997—2001; mng. ptnr., COO Interpublic Group Deutsch, Inc., NYC, 2001—. Bd. dir. Advt. Ednl. Found. Named one of Women to Watch, Advt. Age Mag., 2002. Office: Deutsch Inc 111 Eighth Ave New York NY 10011*

SAWYER, MALCOLM JAMES, JR., religious studies educator; b. Farmington, Maine, Oct. 31, 1951; s. Malcolm James and Bertha Brindley Sawyer; m. Kay Lynn Fuqua, Dec. 15, 1973; children: James Daniel, Jonathan David, Joel Nathaniel, Joshua William. BA, Biola U., 1973; ThM, Dallas Theol. Sem., 1978, PhD, 1987. Asst. prof. Simpson Coll., San Francisco, 1984—89; prof. Western Sem., Los Gatos, Calif., 1989—. Bd. mem. Bay Cities Bible Inst., Oakland, Calif., 1995—97; mem. adv. bd. Christian Counseling Internat., Scott's Valley, Calif., 1999—2002. Author: Charles Augusts Briggs and Tensions in Late Nineteenth Century America Theology, 1994, Taxonomic Charts on Biblical and Theological Studies, 1999; contbr. articles to profl. jours. Mem.: Am. Acad. Religion, Soc. for Bibl. Lit., Evang. Theol. Soc. (far west pres. 2001—02). Home: 16485 Severn Rd San Leandro CA 94578 Office: Western Seminary 16330 Los Gatos Blvd Los Gatos CA 95032

SAWYER, MILDRED CLEMENTINA, retired real estate agent; b. Boston, Nov. 19, 1928; d. Joseph Felix and Assunta (Malone) Volpe; m. Frederick Myles Sawyer, June 15, 1957 (dec. Jan. 1995); children: Frederick G., Bernard G. Grad. h.s., Brockton, Mass. Clk. Prudential Ins. Co., Brockton, Mass., 1947-57, Clark Bros., Olean, N.Y., 1957-58; typist N.J., R.I., 1958-87; real estate sales rep. JLC & Home Realty, Chepachet, No. Scituate, 1984-97; ins. sales agt. Mass. Indemnity Life Ins. Co., Cranston, R.I., 1984-89; security sales rep. First Am. Nat. Securities, Cranston, 1986-89; ret., 1995. Author: A Lifetime of Hints for Everyday Living, 1996, The Path Into Vietnam: An Historical Reflection, 2002; author numerous poems. Sec. Cold Springs Harbor Heights Civic Assn., Huntington, L.I., N.Y., 1961-63, Save All Foster's Environ., Foster, R.I., 1969-87, Students for a Dem. Soc., Warwick, 1970-72. Mem. Soc. of Children's Books, Writers and Illustrators, Soc. of Childrens Books Writers and Illustrators of New England, Noetic Sci. Avocations: reading, exercising, gardening, cooking, sewing. Home: 49A Mount Hygeia Rd Foster RI 02825-1923

SAWYER, NELSON BALDWIN, JR., credit union executive; b. Jacksonville, Fla., Nov. 11, 1948; s. Nelson Baldwin and Nancy (Watson) S.; m. Carla Lee Dowden, Aug. 9, 1986. BA, U. North Fla., 1974. Program cons. State of Fla., Jacksonville, 1974-81; product mgr. Qualified Plan Designs, Inc., Jacksonville, 1981-83, Associated Gen. Contractors, Jacksonville, 1983-86; membership mgr. Calif. Credit Union League, Pomona, 1986-87, comm. mgr., 1987-90; sr. v.p., COO Calif. League Svcs. Corp., Pomona, 1990-93; sr. v.p. Wescorp, San Dimas, Calif., 1994-97; v.p. Travis Fed. Credit Union, Vacaville, Calif., 1997-2000; pres., CEO Chevron Valley Credit Union, Bakersfield, Calif., 2000—. Chmn. bd. dirs. Calif. Ctr. Credit Union, 1996-97, Product Rsch. Orgn. for Credit Unions. Bd. dirs. Jacksonville C. of C., 1983-84, Taft Coll. Found., 2001—, Am. Heart Assn., Bakersfield, 2002—; mem. assembly of dels. Calif. Credit Union, 2002—. Mem. U.S. Jaycees (pres. Jacksonville 1983-84, chmn. bd. '84-85, senator, U.S., 1984—, internat. senator 1984—, Outstanding Young Man Am. 1983), Rotary Club of Bakersfield, Fla. Yacht Club. Republican. Episcopalian. Office: Chevron Valley Credit Union 8200 Granite Falls Dr Bakersfield CA 93312-5592

SAWYER, PAMELA Z. state legislator; b. Providence; BA, U. R.I. Mem. Bolton (Conn.) Bd. Edn., 1981-93; justice of peace City of Bolton, 1983—; mem. Conn. Ho. of Reps., Hartford, 1993—, asst. minority leader, 1997—. Mem. Edn. Transp. Exec. Nominations coms. Office: Legis Office Bldg 300 Capitol Ave Hartford CT 06106-1553

SAWYER, RAYMOND LEE, JR., motel chain executive; b. New Orleans, Oct. 7, 1935; s. Raymond Lee Sawyer and Eloise Falvy (Searcy) Easley; m. Dolores Jean Young, June 11, 1960; children: Lisa Kay, Linda Faye. BA, Northwestern State U., 1959. Art dir., advt. mgr. Natural Food and Farming Mag., Atlanta, Tex., 1959-66, editor, 1963-66; asst. editor, editor Tourist Court Jour./Southwest Water Works Jour., Temple, Tex., 1966-73, editor, 1973-75; founding ptnr., sr. v.p. Budget Host Inns, Ft. Worth, 1975-83, pres., chief exec. officer, 1983—. Named Man of Yr. Motel Brokers Assn. Am., 1974; recipient Bob Gresham Meml. award Nat. Innkeeping Assn., 1975. Mem. Am. Automobile Assn. (mem. lodging adv. panel 1990—). Methodist. Avocations: photography, writing.

SAWYER, RAYMOND TERRY, lawyer, consultant, theater producer; b. Cleve., Oct. 1, 1943; s. R. Terry and Fanny Katherine (Young) S.; m. Katherine Margaret Schneider, Aug. 5, 1972; children: Margaret Young, John Terry. BA, Yale U., 1965; LLB, Harvard U., 1968. Bar: Ohio 1969, U.S. Dist. Ct. (no. dist.) Ohio 1970, prin., Sawyer LLC, 2002-. Assoc. Thompson Hine LLP, Cleve., 1968-76, ptnr., 1976—83, 1986—2001, chmn. bus. transactions and org. dept., 1998—2001; exec. dir. Ohio Housing Fin. Agy., Columbus, 1983-84; counsel to gov. State of Ohio, Columbus, 1984, chief of staff, 1985-86, chmn. Gov.'s commn. on housing, 1989-90; prin. Sawyer LLC, Cleve., 2002—. Bd. dirs. Premix, Inc., North Kingsville, Ohio. Assoc. prodr.: Frankie and Johnny in the Clair de Lune, 2002—03; Match, 2004—. Vol. VISTA, East Palo Alto, Calif., 1968—69; mem. Tech. Leadership Coun., 1987—95, Leadership Cleve., 1986—87, Cleve. Found. Study Commn. on Med. Rsch. Edn., 1991—92, George W. Codrington Charitable Found., 1989—, chmn., 1989—2003; mem. Ohio Bd. Regents, Columbus, 1987—96, chmn., 1992—93; trustee Cleve. Ballet, 1987—2000, Cleve. Orch., 1993—, sec., exec. com., 1997—; mem. exec. com. MetroHealth Sys., 1998—; mem. Juilliard Coun. Juilliard Sch.; mem. pres.'s adv. coun. Case Western Res. U. Named Man of Yr. Womanspace, 1982. Mem. Ohio State Bar Assn. (chair corp. law com. 1993-95), Yale U. Alumni Assn. (pres. Cleve. chpt. 1980-81), Assn. Yale Alumni (del. 1996-99). Democrat. Presbyterian. Office: Sawyer LLC 3900 Key Ctr Cleveland OH 44114-1216

SAWYER, ROBERT MCLARAN, history educator; b. St. Louis, Nov. 12, 1929; s. Lee McLaran and Harrie (Alcock) S.; m. Patricia Ann Covert, Nov. 23, 1955; children— Ann Marie, Lee McLaran, Gail Louise. BS, S.E. Mo. State Coll., 1952; MA, U. Ill., 1953; PhD, U. Mo., 1966. Tchr. Rolla (Mo.) Public Schs., 1955; asst. prof., then asso. prof. history U. Mo., Rolla., 1956-67; mem. faculty U. Nebr., Lincoln, 1967—, prof. history of edn., 1969—, chmn. dept. history and philosophy of edn., 1975-81; mem. council U. Nebr. (Coll. Arts and Scis.), 1979—. Vis. prof. Ark. State U., Jonesboro, summer 1966; proposal reviewer Nat. Endowment Humanities, 1979 Author: The History of the University of Nebraska, 1929-1969, 1973, The Many Faces of Teaching, 1987, The Art and Politics of College Teaching, 1992, The Black Student's Guide to College Success, 1993, The Handbook of College Teaching, 1994; also articles, revs. Served with AUS, 1953-55. Mem. Orgn. Am. Historians, History Edn. Soc., Am. Ednl. Studies Assn., Soc. Profs. Edn., Phi Alpha Theta, Phi Delta Kappa. Home: 2640 S 35th St Lincoln NE 68506-6623 Office: Univ Nebr 29 Henzlik Hall Lincoln NE 68588

SAWYER, THOMAS C. former congressman; b. Akron, Ohio, Aug. 15, 1945; m. Joyce Handler, 1968; 1 child, Amanda. BA, U. Akron, 1968, MA, 1970. Pub. sch. tchr., Ohio; adminstr. state sch. for delinquent boys; legis. agt. Ohio Pub. Utilities Commn.; mem. Ohio House Reps., Columbus, 1977-83; mayor City of Akron, 1984-86; mem. U.S. Congress from 14th Ohio dist., Washington, 1987—2003; mem. energy and commerce com. Democrat.

SAWYER, THOMAS EDGAR, management consultant; b. Homer, La., July 7, 1932; s. Sidney Edgar and Ruth (Bickham) S.; m. Joyce Mezzanatto, Aug. 22, 1954; children: Jeffrey T., Scott A., Robert J., Julie Anne. BS, UCLA, 1959; MA, Occidental Coll., 1969; PhD, Walden U., 1990. Project engr. Garrett Corp., LA, 1954-60; mgr. devel. ops. TRW Systems, Redondo Beach, Calif., 1960-66; spl. asst. to gov. State of Calif., Sacramento, 1967-69; prin., gen. mgr. Planning Rsch. Corp., McLean, Va., 1969-72; dep. dir. OEO, Washington, 1972-74; assoc. prof. bus. mgmt. Brigham Young U., 1974-78; pres., chmn. bd. Mesa Corp., Provo, Utah, 1978-82; pres., dir. Sage Inst. Internat., Inc., Provo, 1982-88; chmn. bd., CEO Pvt. Telecom. Networks, Inc. (name changed to Nat. Applied Computer Techs, Inc.), Orem, Utah, 1988-98; chief tech. officer GST Telecom. (formerly Greenstar Telecom., Inc.), San Francisco, 1993-98, also bd. dirs. Vancouver, Wash., 1995-98; chmn. bd. NeTrue Comm., Inc., Fullerton, Calif., 1998—2002; chmn. bd., CEO Telecom, Inc., Salt Lake City, 2002—; sr. dir. Econ. Rsch. Inst., MMG Holdings, Tokyo, 2003—; consul gen. for Republic of Liberia Monvoria, 2004—; dir.

ops. First European Investment Found., Fruitland Park, Fla., 2004—. Bd. dirs. Intechna Corp., HighTech Corp., Indian Affiliates, Inc., Greenstar USA, Inc., San Francisco, 1994-98, GST Global Comm., Inc., Vancouver, Can., 1998-2002, Highpoint Telecom., Inc., Vancouver, 1998-2001, World Wide Wireless Comm., Inc., Salt Lake City, 1998-2000, Columbia Hosp., Orem, 1998—; sr. dir. Econ. Rsch. Inst., MMG Holdings, Ltd., Tokyo, 2003-; consul gen. for Republic of Liberia, Monrovia, Liberia, 2004-. Author: Assimilation Versus Self-Identity: A Modern Native American Perspective, 1976, The Promise of Funding a New Educational Initiative Using the Microcomputer, 1988, Computer Assisted Instruction: An Inevitable Breakthrough, Current Challenges of Welfare: A Review of Public Assistance as Distributive Justice, 1989, New Software Models for Training and Education Delivery, 1989, New Organizations: How They Deviate from Classical Models, 1989, Increasing Productivity in Organizations: The Paradox, 1989, An Introduction and Assessment of Strategic Decision Making Paradigms in Complex Organizations, 1989, The Future of Technology in Education, 1989, Impact of Failure by Senior Executives to Receive Accurate Critical Feedback on Pervasive Change, 1990, The Influence of Critical Feedback and Organizational Climate on Managerial Decision Making, 1990. Chmn. Nat. Adv. Coun. Indian Affairs, Utah State Bd. Indian Affairs, So. Paiute Restoration Com., Utah Cmty. Mediation Ctrs., 2002—; trustee Utah Valley State Coll., Orem, 2000—, Coll. Ea. Utah, Price, 2001—; mem. Utah Dist. Export Coun., Utah dist. SBA Coun.; mem. adv. coun. Nat. Bus. Assn.; mem. Utah Job Tng. Coordinating Coun. Served with USMC, 1950-53. Mem. ASPA, Am. Mgmt. Assn., Utah Coun. Small Bus. (dir.), Utah State Hist. Soc. (bd. dirs. 1993-99), Masons. Republican. Mem. Lds Ch. Home: 548 W 630 S Orem UT 84058-6154 Office Phone: 801-944-4090.

SAWYER, THOMAS HARRISON, health, physical education and recreation director; b. Apr. 5, 1946; s. Harrison Donald and M. Daughn (Geer) Sawyer; m. Kathleen Ann Daly, July 5, 1969; children: Shawn Thomas, Meghan Daly. BS, Springfield Coll., 1968, MPE, 1971; EdD, Va. Polytech Inst., 1977. Instr. health, phys. edn., recreation Va. Mil. Inst., Lexington, 1969—72, asst. prof., 1972—75, assoc. prof., 1975—79; dir. recreation ctr. U. Bridgeport, 1979—81; assoc. prof. head dept. Mont. Tech. Inst., Butte, 1981—84; prof., chmn. phys. edn. dept. Ind. State U., Terre Haute, 1984—89, prof., 1984—, coord. sport mgmt. programs, 1984—. Cons. Mont. Fitness, Butte, 1981—84, ARC, Mont., 1981—83, Wellness-Pillsbury Co.; pres. Ind. Ctr. Sport Edn., Inc., 1995—. Mem. edtl. bd.: Jour. Employee Health and Fitness, Mag. Health Mgrs., 1984—89; contbr. articles to profl. jours. Bd. dirs. YMCA, Butte, 1981—84; mem. Sch. Bd. Dist. 1, Butte, 1982—84; bd. dirs. Vocation Edn. Coun. Mont., 1983—84; chair Task Force for Encouragement of Quality, Daily Phys. Edn. Programs for Ind. Pub. Schs., 1987—88, Phys. Edn. Adv. Task Force, 1988—91; dir. Ctr. Coaching Edn., 1988—94, Ind. PACE, 1984—99, Ind. LANSE, 1999—. Recipient Founder's award, Alcohol Svcs., Buena Vista, Va., 1979, Red Triangle, YMCA, Butte, 1982; scholar, NDEA, 1968; N.Am. fellow, Health, Phys. Edn., Recreation, Sport, and Dance, 2000. Mem.: ARC (bd. dirs. Terre Haute chpt. 1985—87, 1988—94, state svc. coun. 1993—99, chair 1994—97, bd. dirs. Terre Haute chpt. 1996—2000, 2002—, state svc. coun. 2002—, Vol. Safety award 1981), Soc. Study of Legal Aspects of Sport and Phys. Activity (treas. 1994—96, exec. dir. 1997—2001, editor Jour. Legal Aspects of Sports 1995—2000, Hon. award 2003), Coun. Facilites and Equipment (chair 1995—97, Prof. Recognition award 2002, Hon. award 2002), Am. Assn. Active Lifestyles and Fitness (pres.-elect 1996—97, pres. 1997—2000, Hon. award 2003), Employee Svcs. Mgmt. Assn., Assn. Fitness in Bus., Nat. Assn. Sports Offcls., Ind. Assn. Phys. Edn., Recreation and Dance (editor jour and newsletter 1987—, conv. coord. 1992—2000), Am. Alliance for Health, Phys. Edn., Recreation and Dance (editl. bd. 1991—95, chair 1993—95, hon. award 2004). Office: Dept Recreation and Sport Mgmt Terre Haute IN 47809-0001 Personal E-mail: pmsawyr@aol.com.

SAWYER, TIMOTHY KENNETH, music educator; b. Minneapolis, Minn., June 20, 1960; s. Lester Joseph and Lolita Eileen Sawyer; m. Heidi Kahl, Dec. 30, 1989; children: Erika Lynn, Emily Anne. BA, Bethel Coll. St. Paul, 1983; MusM, U. Minn., 1994—94. Dir. choral activities Northwestern Coll., St. Paul, 1995—, coord. vocal studies, asst. dir. choral activities, 1989—95; artistic dir. and coord. Two Rivers Chorale, 2004—. Assoc. condr. Minn. Chorale, Mpls., 1997—2004; choir dir. Colonial Ch. of Edina, Edina, Minn., 1995—; artistic staff U. Toronto Bach Festival. Bd. dirs. Sixth World Choral Symposium, Minneapolis, Minn., 1998—2002. Named Oustanding Young Men of Am., 1996. Mem.: Music Educators Nat. Conf., Chorus Am., Nat. Assn. Tchrs. Singing (state treas. 1992—94, Winner grad. divsn. 1986, Winner undergrad. divsn. 1983), Internat. Fedn. Choral Music, Am. Choral Dirs. Assn. (chair repertoire and stds. coms. 1992—2002), Phi Kappa Phi, Phi Kappa Lambda. Conservative. Achievements include extensive touring, choral performances and recordings with Dale Warland Singers, Plymouth Music Series, Montana Chorale, SDG Cantorum; Oregon Bach Festival Chorus; performances with Minnesota Opera New Music Theatre Ensemble, American Composers Forum; jingles and commercial recordings. Avocations: home repair, cooking, calligraphy. Home: 2809-29th Ave NE Minneapolis MN 55418 Office: Northwestern College 3003 Snelling Ave N Saint Paul MN 55113 Office Phone: 651-631-5252.

SAWYER, WILLIAM C. lawyer; b. Bangor, Maine, Aug. 26, 1929; s. Frank S. and Linda M. (Makanna) S.; m. Mary A. Eaton (div.); m. Joan N. Gardner; children: William D., Constance, Faith. AB cum laude, Harvard Coll., 1951, JD, 1954. Bar: Mass., U.S. Dist. Ct. Mass., U.S. Ct. Mil. Appeals, U.S. Supreme Ct. Assoc. Palmer & Dodge, Boston, 1958-61; ptnr. Sawyer, Burlingham, Tucker & Salloway, Boston, 1961-85, Dicara, Selig, Sawyer & Holt, Boston, 1985-90, Clarkin, Sawyer & Phillips, P.C., Boston, 1990—. Bd. dirs. Jones & Vining, Inc., Ayer Sales, Inc., Applied Geographics, Inc., Applied Tech., Inc., others. Contbr. articles to profl. jours. Bd. trustees Mass. Conv. Ctr. Authority, 1991-97; pres., treas., chmn. Metro. Area Planning Coun., 1975-87; pres. Mass. Assn. Regional Planning Agys., 1980, 87; bd. dirs. Nat. Assn. Regional Couns., 1980-86; mem. Mass. Selectman's Assn., 1975—; bd. selectman Town of Action, 1967-75, chmn., 1969, 75; Rep. candidate Mass. Atty. Gen., 1990; pres. New Eng. Rep. Coun.; mem. Rep. State Com.; Rep. candidate Congress, 5th Congl. Dist., Mass., 1980. 1st lt. U.S. Army, 1955. Recipient Regional Leadership award Planning Commns. and Couns. New Eng., 1987, and others. Mem. ABA, Mass. Bar Assn., Boston Bar Assn. Avocations: golf, painting, reading. Office: Clarkin Sawyer & Phillips PC 1 Center Plz Ste 240 Boston MA 02108-1801

SAWYER, WILLIAM CURTIS, pest control company executive; b. Lockport, N.Y., Jan. 25, 1933; s. Fletcher D. and Mildred R. (Schnurstein) S.; m. Noreen T. Doran, Aug. 8, 1959 (div. 1987); children: Curtis P., Todd T.; m. Gail P. Mangan, 1988. Student, Cornell U., 1950-52. Technician McLeod Indsl. Fumigators, Buffalo, 1949-50; v.p. Sawyer's Exterminating, Rochester, N.Y., 1958-76, pres., 1976—. Sgt. USMC, 1952-56. Mem. Nat. Pest Control Assn. (bd. dirs. 1981-88), Empire Pest Control Assn. (treas. 1981-85, bd. dirs. 1978-85), N.Y. State Pest Control Assn. (bd. dirs. 1981-85), Small Bus. Assn. Rochester (bd. dirs. 1981-85), Meml. Art Gallery, Rochester Area C. of C., Rochester Club, Masons, Shriners, Rochester Rotary. Republican. Avocations: flying, ballroom dancing, scuba diving. Home: 3126 Brockport Rd Spencerport NY 14559-2164

SAWYER, WILLIAM DALE, physician, educator, university dean, foundation administrator; b. Roodhouse, Ill., Dec. 28, 1929; s. Cloyd Howard and Eva Collier (Dale) S.; m. Jane Ann Stewart, Aug. 25, 1951; children: Dale Stewart, Carole Ann. Student, U. Ill., 1947-50; MD cum laude, Washington U., St. Louis, 1954; ScD (hon.), Mahidol U., Bangkok, 1988; DPH (hon.), Chiang Mai U., Thailand, 1993, Chulalongkorn U., 1998. Intern Washington U.-Barnes Hosp., 1954-55, resident, 1957-58, fellow, 1958-60; asst. prof. microbiology Johns Hopkins U., Balt., 1964-67; prof., chmn. dept. microbiology Rockefeller Found.-Mahidol U., Bangkok, 1967-73, Ind. U. Sch. Medicine, Indpls., 1973-80; prof. depts. medicine, microbiology and immunology Wright State U., Dayton, Ohio, 1981-87, dean Sch. Medicine, 1981-87; pres. China Med. Bd. N.Y., Inc., 1987-97. Adj. prof. biology Ball State U., Muncie, Ind., 1978-80; hon. prof. microbiology Sun Yat Sen U. Med. Sci., 1987; hon. prof. Peking Union Med. Coll., 1989; hon. advisor Beijing Med. U.; cons. U.S. Army Med. R & D Command, WHO Immunology Ctr., Singapore, 1969-73; mem. bd. sci. advisers Armed Forces Inst. Pathology, 1975-80, chmn., 1979-80; adj. prof. medicine and microbiology and immunology N.Y. Med. Coll., Valhalla, 1990-96; hon. prof. China Med. U., 1995, West China U. Med. Sci., 1995, Zhejiang Med. U., 1995, Jiujang Med. Coll., 1995, Hunan Med. U., 1996, Xian Med. U., 1996, Shanghai Med. U., 1996. Contbr. numerous articles to profl. jours. Mem. Lobund adv. bd. U. Notre Dame; dir. Georgetown Area Cmty. Found., 1998-2002, pres. 1999; mem. exec. com. Georgetown Cmty. Resource Ctr., 2000-03. Served to maj. M.C., USA, 1955-64. Recipient Gold medal of merit Airlangga U., Indonesia, 1992, Pub. Health Recognition award Asia-Pacific Acad. Consortium Pub. Health, 1993, China Health medal, 1996, White Magnolia award, 1996. Fellow ACP; mem. AAAS, Am. Soc. Microbiology (br. pres. 1976), Sci. Rsch. Soc. Am., Am. Fedn. Clin. Rsch., Ctrl. Soc. Clin. Rsch., Infectious Diseases Soc. Am., Soc. Exptl. Biology and Medicine, Am. Acad. Microbiology, Am. Assn. Pathologists, Assn. Am. Med. Colls. (coun. deans 1980-87), Phi Beta Kappa, Sigma Xi, Alpha Omega Alpha. Home: 124 Poppy Hills Cv S Georgetown TX 78628-1179 E-mail: wllmsawyer@aol.com.

SAWYER-MORSE, MARY KAYE, nutritionist, educator; b. Ft. Stockton, Tex. BA in Psychology, S.W. Tex. State U., 1978; MS in Nutrition, Incarnate Word Coll., 1987; PhD, U. Tex., 1997. Lic. dietitian. Nutrition svcs. con. Christian Sr. Svcs., 1985-87, exec. dir., 1987-90; nutrition svcs. cons. Alternative Adult Day Care Ctr., 1989-90; pvt. cons. dietitian, 1990—; cmty. dietitian Health Enhancement Ctr. Humana Hosp. Met., 1990-91; assoc. prof., dietetic program dir. U. Incarnate Word, San Antonio, 1991—. Presenter Innovative Nutrition Svc. Model S.W. Tex. Gerontol. Soc. Ann. Meeting, 1988, Diabetic Homebound Svcs. Nat. Conf. Meals-On-Wheels Am., 1989; spkr. in field. Contbr. articles to profl. jours. Named Tex. Dietetic Educator, 2003; recipient Disting. Rsch. award, 1977, 1978, Acad. Excellence award, 1978, Women's Leadership award, YWCA, 1988, Creative Tchg./Rsch. award, 1994; grantee, U.S. Dept. Edn., 1997—2000; Carnation Corp. scholar, 1995. Mem.: Nat. Spkrs. Assn. (devel. dir. 2000—01, Tex. Dietetic Educator of the Yr. 2003), San Antonio Dist. Dietetic Assn., Tex. Dietetic Assn., Am. Dietetic Assn. (sec. 1990—92, mem. nominating com. 1993—94, dietetic educators practice group). Office Phone: 210-829-7597. Personal E-mail: marykaye@thecenterforsuccess.com.

SAWYERS, ELIZABETH JOAN, librarian, administrator; b. San Diego, Dec. 2, 1936; d. William Henry and Elizabeth Georgiana (Price) S. AA, Glendale Jr. Coll., 1957; BA in Bacteriology, UCLA, 1959, M.L.S., 1961. Asst. head acquisition sect. Nat. Library Medicine, Bethesda, Md., 1962-63, head acquisition sect., 1963-66, spl. asst. to chief tech. services div., 1966-69, spl. asst. to assoc. dir. for library ops., 1969-73; asst. dir. libraries for tech. services SUNY-Stony Brook, 1973-75; dir. Health Scis. Library Ohio State U., Columbus, 1975-90, spl. asst. to dir. Univ. librs., 1990—. Mem. Assn. Acad. Health Scis. Library Dirs. (sec./treas. 1981-83, pres. 1983-84), Med. Library Assn., Am. Soc. for Info. Sci., Spl. Libraries Assn., ALA Office: Ohio State Univ Librs 1858 Neil Ave Columbus OH 43210-1225

SAX, DANIEL SAUL, neurologist, educator; b. Balt., Jan. 27, 1935; s. Benjamin and Miriam (Helfgott) S.; m. Joan Atherton Bond, Mar. 25, 1962; children: Karen Bond, John Derek, Diana Atherton. AB, Johns Hopkins U., 1955; MD, U. Md., 1959. Diplomate Am. Bd. Psychiatry and Neurology. Intern Boston City Hosp., 1959—60, resident in neurology and neuropathology neurologic unit, 1961—64; resident in neurology N.E. Med. Ctr., Boston, 1961; asst. prof. neurology Northwestern U., Chgo., 1966-67; assoc. prof. neurology Albert Einstein Med. Sch., N.Y.C., 1967-69, Boston U. Sch. Med., 1969-76, prof. neurology, 1976-2000, prof. emeritus neurology, 2000—. Chief neurology svcs. Boston VA Outpatient Clinic, 1974-90; EEG lab. dir., cons. Gifford Med. Ctr., Randolph, Vt., 1977—, neurologist, 1977—; cons. neurology Boston VA Med. Ctr., 1991-2000, hon. staff, 2002. Clin. adv. com. Vt. divsn. Nat. MS Soc., 2001, clin. adv. com. ctrl. N.E. chpt., 1977—. Lt. comdr. USNR, 1964-66. Fellow: Am. Acad. Neurology; mem.: AMA, Internat. Soc. Women Health and Sexuality, Huntington's Study Group, Huntington's Dx Soc. (mem. adv. bd. Mass. chpt. 1980—2000, clin. adv. bd. 2001—), Multiple Sclerosis Soc. (clin. adv. bd. 1977—), Boston Soc. Neurology and Psychiatry (pres. 1982—83, exec. com. 1985—, Vt. bd. med. practice 2002—), Mass. Med. Soc., Am. Soc. Neuroimaging, Am. Assn. for Study of Headache, Am. Neurol. Assn. Avocations: tree farmer, oenology, music. Office: Gifford Med Ctr Neurology 44 S Main St Randolph VT 05060 also: 258 W Cummings Park Woburn MA 01801 E-mail: dsax@giffordmed.org., dssax@adelphia.net.

SAX, JOSEPH LAWRENCE, lawyer, educator; b. Chgo., Feb. 3, 1936; s. Benjamin Harry and Mary (Silverman) S.; m. Eleanor Charlotte Gettes, June 17, 1958; children: Katherine Elaine Dennett, Valerie Beth, Amber Sax Rosen. AB, Harvard U., 1957; JD, U. Chgo., 1959; LLD (hon.), Ill. Inst. Tech., 1992. Bar: D.C. 1960, Mich., 1966, U.S. Supreme Ct. 1969. Atty. U.S. Dept. Justice, Washington, 1959-60; pvt. practice law Washington, 1960-62; prof. U. Colo., 1962-65, U. Mich., Ann Arbor, 1966-86; dep. asst. sec. and counselor U.S. Sec. Interior, Washington, 1994-96; prof. U. Calif. Law Sch., Berkeley, 1986—. Fellow Ctr. Advanced Study in Behavioral Scis., 1977-78, Order of the Coif Disting. Visitor, 2004. Author: Waters and Water Rights, 1967, Water Law, Planning and Policy, 1968, Defending the Environment, 1971, Mountains Without Handrails, 1980, Legal Control of Water Resources, 3rd edit., 2001, Playing Darts with a Rembrandt, 1999. Fellow: AAAS. Office Phone: 510-642-1831. Business E-Mail: saxj@law.berkeley.edu.

SAX, KENNETH J. bank executive; BA, MBA, U. Memphis. Examiner in charge BankBoston, 1996—98, gen. auditor, 1998—99; v.p. operational assurance FleetBoston Fin. Corp., Boston, 1999—2002, chief credit officer, 2002—03, chief risk officer, sr. v.p., 2003. Mem.: Risk Mgmt. Assn., Inst. Internal Auditors. Office: FleetBoston Fin Corp 100 Federal St Boston MA 02110

SAX, MARY RANDOLPH, speech and language pathologist; b. July 13, 1925; d. Bernard Angus and Ada Lucile (Thurman) TePoorten; m. William Martin Sax, Feb. 7, 1948. BA magna cum laude, Mich. State U., 1947; MA, U. Mich., 1949. Cert. clin. competence in speech and lang. pathology. Supr. speech correction dept. Waterford Twp. Schs., Pontiac, 1949-69; lectr. Marygrove Coll., Detroit, 1971-72; pvt. practice in speech and lang. pathology Wayne and Oakland Counties, Mich., 1973—. Co-investigator Support Pers. Profl. Practice of Speech-Lang. Pathology; mem. stroke com. Mich. Heart Assn., 1982—99; counselor to divsn. stroke liaisons Am. Heart Assn. Mich.; stroke advisor for Midwest affiliate Am. Heart Assn., 1999—, advocacy com. for Midwest affiliate of Ill., Ind. and Mich., 1999—; liaison between Am. Heart Assn. of Mich. and Am. Heart Assn., Dallas, 1996—98; adj. speech pathologist, Southfield, Mich.; lectr. on stroke Mich. Spkrs. Bur., Am. Heart Assn., 1990—; pub. spkg. coach, 1989—; mem. adj. faculty SS Cyril and Methodius Sem., Orchard Lake, Mich., 1989—90; adj. St. Mary's Prep. Sch., Orchard Lake, 1990—; mem. Met. Detroit Operation Stroke com. Am. Stroke Assn., 1999—, mem. med. subcom. to move area hosps. to become primary stroke ctrs. with acture stroke teams, 2001—; founder, mem. Stroke Project Task Force for Detroit, 1993—98; com. mem. Charette, study Arch. and Design for phys. restructuring Franklin, Mich., 1993; invited speech pathology del. Internat. Health Programs People to People Citizen Amb. Program, 1996; mem. sci. coun. on stroke Am. Heart Assn., 1980—2002; invited U.S. rep. speech and lang. pathology (cancelled because of 9/11) Med. People to People Amb. Program, neurol. ctrs., Czech Republic, Hungary and Austria. Contbr. articles to profl. jours. including Lang. and Lang. Behavior Abstracts, Lang. Speech and Hearing Svcs., Speech Lang. Hearing Jour. Active Franklinites for Responsible Govt. Recipient Svc. Recognition award Coll. Edn. Mich. State U.; grantee Inst. Articulation and Learning, 1969, others; Christian svc. commn. St. Owen, Birmingham co-chmn. blood dr. Red Cross, Franklin, Mich., 1991—. Mem.: Am. Stroke Assn. (Metro Detroit Operation Stroke com.), Founders Soc. of Detroit Inst. Arts, Franklin Found. (mem. natural resources adv. coun. 1991—99, bd. dirs. 1994—98), Pvt. Practitioners Speech-Lang. Pathology (co-founder), Internat. Assn. Logopedics and Phoniatrics (Switzerland), Am. Heart Assn. Mich. (mem. stroke awareness seminars, continuing edn. for physicians and other profls., planning and operation edn.), Mich. Speech-Lang.-Hearing Assn. (pvt. practitioner liaison 1991—, developer structural parameters for State Clin. Svc. award 1999—, com. comty. and hosp. svcs., mem. state award selection com.), Am. Speech-Lang.-Hearing Assn. (clin. competence cert.), Mich. Humane Soc., Gamma Phi Beta, Kappa Delta Pi, Phi Kappa Phi, Theta Alpha Phi. Achievements include research in language and speech acquisition in children in reference to the development of and prediction of biological speech change; research interests in developmental phonatory voice disorders, and in adult acquisition of language and speech relative to central and autonomic nervous systems. Office: 31320 Woodside Dr Franklin MI 48025-2027

SAX, ROBERT EDWARD, food service equipment company executive; b. Phila., Nov. 2, 1938; s. Sam and Jessie (Sirisky) S.; m. Rochelle E. Sax, Jan. 11, 1959; children: Nathan, Beverly. Student, U. Pa., 1960-66; diploma, Xerox Sys., Chgo., 1987. Pres. Robert E. Sax Assocs., Inc., Blackwood, N.J., 1965-79; sr. sales mgr. Household Internat., Inc., Veron Hills, Ill., 1979-90; v.p. nat. accounts True Food Svc. Equipment, O'Fallon, Mo., 1990—. Author: It's Yours Just Ask, 1975. Pres. Assn. Representing Children Handicaps, Berlin, N.J., 1971. Named Man of Yr. Sta. WPEN-AM, Camden, N.J., 1969. Mem. Nat. Hot Rod Assn., Rolls Royce Owner's Club, Masons. Office: 317 Cobble Creek CIR Cherry Hill NJ 08003-1839 Fax: 856-751-0035.

SAXBE, WILLIAM BART, lawyer, former government official; b. Mechanicsburg, Ohio, June 24, 1916; s. Bart Rockwell and Faye Henry (Carey) S.; m. Ardath Louise Kleinhans, Sept. 14, 1940; children: William Bart, Juliet Louise Saxbe Blackburn, Charles Rockwell. AB, Ohio State U., 1940; LL.B., 1948; hon. degrees, Central State U., Findlay Coll., Ohio Wesleyan U., Walsh Coll., Capital U., Wilmington Coll., Ohio State U., Bowling Green State U. Bar: Ohio 1948. Practiced in, Mechanicsburg, 1948-55; partner Saxbe, Boyd & Prine, 1955-58; mem. Ohio Gen. Assembly, 1947-48, 49-50; majority leader Ho. Reps., 1951-52, speaker, 1953-54; atty. gen. Ohio, 1957-58, 63-68; partner Dargusch, Saxbe & Dargusch, 1960-63; mem. U.S. Senate from, Ohio, 1969-74; atty. gen. U.S., 1974; ambassador to, 1975-77; partner firm Chester, Saxbe, Hoffman & Wilcox, Columbus, Ohio, 1977-81; of counsel firm Jones, Day, Reavis & Pogue, Cleve., 1981-84, Pearson, Ball & Dowd (merger Pearson, Ball & Dowd and Reed, Smith & McClay), Washington, 1984-93; ind. spl. counsel Central States Teamsters Pension Fund, 1982—; of counsel Chester Willcox & Saxbe, Columbus, Ohio, 1994—. Served with 107th Cav. AUS, 1940-42; Served with 107th Cav. USAAF, 1942-45; col. Res. Mem. Am., Ohio bar assns., Am. Judicature Soc., Chi Phi, Phi Delta Phi. Clubs: Mason (33d degree) (Columbus), University (Columbus), Columbus Athletic (Columbus), Columbus (Columbus), Scioto Country (Columbus); Urbana (Ohio) Country; Burning Tree Country (Bethesda, Md.); Country of Fla. (Boynton Beach). Republican. Episcopalian. Home: 1171 N Ocean Blvd Gulf Stream FL 33483-7273 Office: 16 S Main Mechanicsburg OH 43044

SAXBERG, BORJE OSVALD, management educator; b. Helsinki, Finland, Jan. 25, 1928; came to U.S., 1950, naturalized, 1966; s. Oskar Valdemar and Martha (Granberg) S.; m. A. Margrete Haug; children: Bo Erland Haug, Bror Valdemar Haug. BA, Swedish Sch. Bus. and Econs., 1950; BS, Oreg. State U., 1952; MS, U. Ill., 1953, PhD, 1958. Teaching asst., instr. U. Ill., 1953-57; prof. dept. mgmt. and orgn. U. Wash., 1957—; asso. dean U. Wash. (Bus. Sch.), 1967-70, chmn. dept. mgmt. and orgn., 1972-76, chmn. faculty senate, 1980-81, chmn. dept. mgmt. and orgn., 1989-93; dir. program in entrepreneurship and innovation, 1989-95. Cons. in field. Author: (with R. Joseph Monsen) The Business World, 1967, (with H.P. Knowles) Personality and Leadership Behavior, 1971, (with R.A. Johnson) Management, Systems and Society, 1976, (with B. Mar) Managing High Technology, 1985. Ford Found. fellow, 1960-61 Mem. Am. Sociol. Assn., Rainier Club, Swedish Club (Seattle). Home: 7336 58th Ave NE Seattle WA 98115-6257 Office: Univ Wash Grad Sch Bus 353200 Seattle WA 98195-3200

SAXE, DEBORAH CRANDALL, lawyer; b. Lima, Ohio, July 23, 1949; d. Robert Gordon and Lois Barker (Taylor) Crandall; m. Robert Saxe, June 3, 1989; children: Elizabeth Sara, Emily Jane. BA, Pa. State U., 1971; MA, UCLA, 1973, JD, 1978. Bar: Calif. 1978, D.C. 1979, U.S. Dist. Ct. D.C. 1979, U.S. Dist. Ct. (ea. dist.) Calif. 1981, U.S. Dist. Ct. (ctrl. dist.) Calif. 1982, U.S. Dist. Ct. (no. and so. dists.) Calif. 1987, U.S. Ct. Appeals (4th and D.C. cirs.) 1979, U.S. Ct. Appeals (6th cir.) 1985, U.S. Ct. Appeals (8th and 9th cirs.) 1987, U.S. Ct. Appeals (2nd cir.) 1990, U.S. Supreme Ct. 1982, U.S. Dist. Ct. (no. dist.) Ill. 2001, U.S. Ct. Appeals (7th cir.) 2001. Assoc. Seyfarth, Shaw, Fairweather & Geraldson, Washington, 1978-83, Jones, Day, Reavis & Pogue, Washington, 1983-85, L.A., 1985-87, ptnr., 1988-97; shareholder Heller Ehrman White & McAuliffe LLP, 1997—. Judge pro tem, Small Claims Ct., L.A., 1985-88. Co-author: Advising California Employers, 1990, 2d edit., 1995; contbg. editor Employment Discrimination Law, 1989. Bd. dirs. Constitutional Rights Found., 1997—2002; chair Eisner Pediatric and Family Med. Ctr., L.A., 1996—98, bd. dirs., 1990—2003, Los Angeles County Bar Found., 1997—99. Fellow: Coll. Labor and Employment Lawyers; mem.: ABA (labor law sect. 1978—), L.A. County Bar Assn. (labor and employment law sect. 1985—, mem. exec. com. 1988—, chair 2002—03), Calif. Bar Assn. (labor law sect. 1985—), Phi Beta Kappa, Pi Lambda Theta. Office: Heller Ehrman White & McAuliffe 601 S Figueroa St Fl 40 Los Angeles CA 90017-5704 Fax: 213-614-1868. Office Phone: 213-689-0200. E-mail: dsaxe@hewm.com.

SAXE, STEVEN LOUIS, lawyer; b. San Francisco, May 28, 1942; s. Jules Irving and Marian (Adams) S.; m. Joanne Saxe, July 12, 1964; children: Julie Ann, Jeffrey Scott. BS, U. Calif., Berkeley, 1964; JD, U. San Francisco, 1967. Bar: Calif. 1967, U.S. Dist. Ct. (no. and ea. dist.) Calif. 1967. Clk. Calif. Ct. Appeals, San Francisco, 1967-68; assoc. Farella, Braun & Martel, San Francisco, 1968-69; sr. counsel Bank Am., San Francisco, 1969-80; ptnr. Boyden, Cooluris, Hauser & Saxe, San Francisco, 1980-91, Pillsbury, Madison & Sutro, San Francisco, 1991-2000, Boyden Cooluris Livingston & Saxe PC, Larkspur, Calif., 2000—. Dir. Ecumenical Assn. Housing, San Rafael, Calif., 1985-92; pres. Congregation Rodef Sholom, San Rafael, 1992-94; dir., pres. Fair Housing Marin, San Rafael, 1995—. Mem. ABA, Consumer Bankers Assn., Coll. Am. Consumer Fin. Svcs. Lawyers (regent). Office: Boyden Cooluris Livingston & Saxe PC 900 Larkspur Landing Cir Ste 155 Larkspur CA 94939-1723 E-mail: ssaxe@bclslaw.com.

SAXENA, AMOL, podiatrist, consultant; b. Palo Alto, Calif., June 5, 1962; s. Arjun Nath and Veera Saxena; m. Karen Ann Palermo, Aug. 11, 1985; children: Vijay, Tara Ann. Student, U. Calif., Davis, 1980-82; BA, Washington U., St. Louis, 1984; D in Podiatric Medicine, William Scholl Coll. Podiatric Medicine, 1988. Diplomate Am. Bd. Podiatric Surgery; lic. podiatrist, Calif., Ill. Resident in podiatric surgery VA Westside Br., Chgo., 1988-89; cons. Puma U.S.A., Inc., Framingham, Mass., 1986—; pvt. practice Mountain View, Calif., 1989-93; with dept. sports medicine Palo Alto Med. Found., 1993—. Dir. Puma Sports Medicine, Framingham; mem. podiatry team St. Frances/Gunn Los Altos (Calif.) High Sch., Palo Alto, 1989—, Stanford (Calif.) U., 1989—; mem. med. staff El Camino Hosp., 1989—, team podiatrist Stanford U., 1989—. Guest editor Lower Extremity; mem. editl. bd. Jour. Foot and Ankle Surgery; contbr. articles to profl. jours. Vol. coach Gunn High Sch. Track and Cross County, Palo Alto, 1989—; podiatrist U.S. Olympic Track and Field Trials, New Orleans, 1992, 1993. Fellow Am. Acad. Podiatric Sports Medicine, Am. Coll. Foot and Ankle Surgeons; mem. Am. Podiatric Med. Assn., Calif. Podiatric Med. Assn., Am. Med. Soccer Assn., Aggie Running Club. Republican. Avocation: running. Office: 1197 E Arques Ave Sunnyvale CA 94085-3904 also: 913 Emerson St Palo Alto CA 94301-2415

SAXENA, ARJUN NATH, physicist; b. Lucknow, India, Apr. 1, 1932; came to U.S., 1956, naturalized, 1976; s. Sheo and Mohan (Piyari) Shanker; m. Veera Saxena, Feb. 9, 1956; children: Rashmi, Amol, Varsha, Ashvin. BSc, Lucknow U., 1950, MSc, 1952, profl. cert. in German, 1954; post MS diploma, Inst. Nuc. Physics, Calcutta, India, 1955; PhD, Stanford U., 1963. Rsch. asst. Stanford U., 1956-60; mem. tech. staff Fairchild Semicondr. Co., Palo Alto, Calif., 1960-65; dept. head Sprague Electric Co., North Adams, Mass., 1965-69; mem. tech. staff RCA Labs., Princeton, NJ, 1969-71; pres., chmn. bd. Astro-Optics, Phila., 1972; pres. Internat. Sci. Co., Princeton Junction, NJ, 1973—. Disting. vis. scientist Centre de Récherches Nucléaires,

Strasbourg, France, 1973, 77; sr. staff scientist, mgr. engring. Data Gen. Corp., Sunnyvale, Calif., 1975-80; mgr. process tech. Signetics Corp., Sunnyvale, 1980-81; Gould AMI scientist, dir. advanced process devel. Gould AMI Semicondrs., Santa Clara, Calif., 1981-87; dir. Ctr. for Integrated Electronics, prof. dept. elec. and computer system engring. Rensselaer Poly. Inst., Troy, N.Y., 1987-96, emeritus prof., 1996—; disting. vis. scientist Inst. Microelectronics, Stuttgart, Germany, 1993-94. Contbr. articles to semicondr. tech., optics, nuc. and high-energy physics to sci. jours.; patentee in field. Treas. pack 66 Boy Scouts Am., West Windsor, N.J., 1970-74. Recipient Disting. Citizen award State of N.J., 1975. Mem. IEEE (life, sr.), Stanford U. Alumni Assn. (life). Home: 4217 Pomona Ave Palo Alto CA 94306-4312

SAXENA, BRIJ B. endocrinologist, biochemist, educator; PhD, India; DSc, U. Muenster, W.Ger.; PhD, U. Wis., 1961; DSc (hon.), Bundelkhand U., India, 2002. Asst. prof. biochemistry and endocrinology N.J. Coll. Medicine., 1966-74; assoc. prof. biochemistry Cornell U. Med. Coll., N.Y.C., 1974—, prof. biochemistry, 1974—, prof. endocrinology, 1981—, dir. div. reproductive endocrinology, Harold and Percy Uris endowed prof. reproductive biology, 2000—. Contbr. 200 articles to profl. jours. Recipient Career Scientist award N.Y.C. Health Research Council; Upjohn research award; Campoz da Paz award. Fellow Royal Soc. Medicine (London); mem. Am. Soc. Biol. Chemists, AAAS, Endocrine Soc., Harvey Soc., Am. Physiol. Soc., Am. Chem. Soc. Office: Cornell U Med Coll 515 E 71st St Ste 412 New York NY 10021-4805 Office Phone: 212-746-3067. Business E-Mail: brs2003@med.cornell.edu.

SAXENA, KAILASH N. writer, retired science educator; s. Devi Dayal and Yashoda Devi Saxena; m. Savitri Saxena, May 5, 1954; children: Renu, Sudhir. PhD, U. Allahabad, India, 1947—51. Prof. zoology U. of Delhi, India, 1968—82, head dept. zoology, 1976—79; vis. scientist, entomology lab Agrl. State U., Wageningen, Netherlands, 1975—75; vis. scientist, insect biochemistry sect. Max Planck Inst. for Biochemistry, Martinsried (Munich), Germany, 1982—83; program leader, crop pests rsch. Internat. Ctr of Insect Physiology & Ecology (ICIPE), Nairobi, Kenya, 1983—92, dy dir./dy dir. gen., 1992—95; cons. entomologist, bioscience writer/editor Fremont, Calif., 1996—. Editor of publications (biol. sciences) Indian Nat. Sciance Acad., New Delhi, 1976—79; assoc. editor / editor-in-chief, insect sci. & its application ICIPE Sci. Press, Nairobi, 1987—94; editor / editor-in-chief, arthropod mgmt. tests Entomol. Soc. of Am., Lanham, Md., 1997—2003. Contbr. more than 100 rsch. & rev. articles in profl. jours. Recipient Membership / Fellowship, Indian Nat. Sci. Acad., 1973, Hooker Award for 1974-75, Indian Agrl. Rsch. Inst., India, 1976. Mem.: Entomol. Soc. of Am. Achievements include research in Advanced knowledge on/developed approach to insect pest mgmt. by biologically intensive and environment-friendly methods for resource-limited farmers in Africa. Avocations: india's classical music, photography.

SAXENA, NARENDRA K. marine research educator; b. Agra, India, Oct. 15, 1936; came to U.S., 1969; s. Brijbasi Lal and Sarbati Saxena; children: Sarah Vasanti, Lorelle Sarita. Diploma Geodetic Engr., Tech. U., Hanover, Fed. Republic Germany, 1966; Dr. Tech. Sci., Tech. U., Graz, Austria, 1972. Research assoc. geodetic sci. Ohio State U., Columbus, 1969-74; asst. prof. U. Ill., Urbana, 1974-78, U. Hawaii, Honolulu, 1978-81, assoc. prof., 1981-86, prof., 1986—, dept. chmn., 1994-97, prof., dir. Pacific Mapping program SOEST, 1998—. Adj. rsch. prof. Naval Postgrad. Sch., Monterey, Calif., 1984-87; founding pres. Pacific Congress on Marine Sci. and Tech. Internat., Honolulu; pres. Pacon Internat. Inc., 1987-2002. Editor Jour. Marine Geodesy, 1976—. Mem. Neighborhood Bd., Honolulu, 1984. Fellow Marine Tech. Soc. (various offices 1974—); mem. Am. Geophys. Union, The Tsunami Soc. Office: U Hawaii Pacific Mapping Prog/SOEST 2525 Correa Rd HIG # 440 Honolulu HI 96822 E-mail: nsaxena@hawaii.edu.

SAXER, RICHARD KARL, metallurgical engineer, retired air force officer; b. Toledo, Aug. 31, 1928; s. Alexander Albert and Gertrude Minnie (Kuebeler) S.; m. Marilyn Doris Mersereau, July 19, 1952; children: Jane Lynette, Robert Karl, Kris Renee, Ann Luette. Student, Bowling Green State U., 1946-48; BS, U. S. Naval Acad., 1952; MS in Aero. Mechanics Engring., Air Force Inst. Tech., 1957; PhD in Metall. Engring., Ohio State U., 1962; grad., Armed Forces Staff Coll., 1966, Indsl. Coll. Armed Forces, 1971; disting. grad., Air Force Inst. Tech., 2003. Commd. 2d lt. U.S. Air Force, 1952, advanced through grades to lt. gen., 1976; electronics officer, mech. officer (4th Tactical Support Sqadron, Tactical Air Command), Sandia Base, N.Mex., 1953-54; electronics and mech. officer, spl. weapons assembly sect. supr. (SAC 6th Aviation Depot Squadron), French Morocco, 1954-55; project engr. mech. equipment br. Air Force Spl. Weapon's Center, Kirtland AFB, N.Mex., 1957-59; project officer Nuclear Safety div., 1959-60; assoc. prof. dept. engring. mechanics Air Force Inst. Tech., 1962-66; asso. prof., dep. dept. head USAF Acad., 1966-70; comdr., dir. Air Force Materials Lab., Wright-Patterson AFB, Ohio, 1971-74; dep. for Reentry System Space and Missile Systems Orgn., 1974-77; dep. for aero equipment Aero. Systems Div., 1977-80, dep. for tactical systems, 1980, vice comdr., 1981-83; aero. systems div. dir. Def. Nuclear Agy., 1983-85, ret., 1985; pres. R.K. Saxer & Assocs., 1985-91; CEO Universal Tech. Corp., Dayton, Ohio, 1991—96. Research and tech. com. materials and structures NASA, 1973-74; chmn. planning group aerospace materials Interagy. Council Materials, 1973-74; mem. Nat. Mil. Adv. Bd., 1971-74, NATO adv. group for research and devel., 1973-74 Contbr. articles to profl. jours. Decorated Def. Disting. Svc. medal, Legion of Merit, Meritorious Service medal USAF, D.S.M., Joint Svc. Commendation medal, Air Force Commendation medal with 3 oak leaf clusters, Army Commendation medal U.S., Def. Superior Service medal, Cross of Gallantry with palm Vietnam, Def. Meritorious Service medal; recipient Disting. award for systems mgmt. Air Force Assn., 1979; Disting. Alumnus award Ohio State U., 1986, Disting. Alumni award Air Force Inst. Tech., 2003. Mem. Air Force Assn., Am. Def. Preparedness Assn. (pres. Dayton 1977-78), Sigma Xi, Phi Lambda Epsilon, Alpha Sigma Mu, Masons, Shriners. Home: 215 Dalfaber Ln Springboro OH 45066-1571

SAXL, JANE WILHELM, state legislator; b. N.Y.C., Aug. 26, 1939; d. Seymour F. and Doris (Fuld) Wilhelm; m. Joseph Saxl, Nov. 17, 1957; children: Susan S., Ruth L., Mary-Anne, Michael V. BA, U. Ill., Springfield, 1973, MA, 1974. City councilor City of Bangor, Maine, 1987-93; mem. Maine Ho. Reps., Augusta, 1992—, chair banking and ins. com. Sec./treas. Penobscot Valley Coun. Govts., 1988-91. Mem. Bangor Sch. Bd., 1984-87, Family Planning Maine, Natural Resources Coun., Penobscot Dem. Com.; bd. dirs. Bangor Beautiful, Bangor Conv. and Visitors Bur.; past chmn. Bangor Recycling. Recipient 1st Maine Waste Mgmt. award, 1995, Toll Fellow Scholarship award, 1996. Mem. LWV (pres. Maine chpt. 1987-93), Nat. League State Legislators, E./W. Hwy Assn., Maine Women's Lobby, Friends of Bangor Pub. Libr., Spruce Run Assocs., Maine Audubon Soc. (award 1999), Tuesday Forum, Maine Women's Legis. Lobby. Democrat. Jewish. Avocations: bird watching, fly fishing. Office: Maine Legislature 2 State House Sta Augusta ME 04333-0002 Home: 196 Norway Rd Bangor ME 04401-5851

SAXMAN, ANNA ESTHER, lawyer; b. Latrobe, Pa., May 14, 1949; d. Harry Suydam and Eleanor Ruth S.; m. Robert Halpert, Feb. 18, 1989. BS magna cum laude, U. Vt., 1978, JD magna cum laude, 1985. Clk. to presiding justice Vt. Supreme Ct., Montpelier, 1985-86; assoc. Langrock, Sperry, Parker & Wool, Burlington, Vt., 1986—; atty. Vt. Defender Gen., dep. defender gen., 2000—. Mem. Task Force on Gender Bias in the Legal System, Montpelier, 1988—. Editor U. Vt. Law Rev. Pres., bd. trustees Vt. Assn. for Mental Health, Montpelier, 1989—. Mem. ABA, ATLA, Vt. Bar Assn. (chmn. women's sect. 1989—, chmn. com. on rights of the mentally and physically handicapped, 1988-89, pres. 2003-04). Office: Vermont Def Gen Office 120 State St Montpelier VT 05620-3301

SAXON, RANDALL LEE, pastor, author, educator; b. Waverly, N.Y., Oct. 28, 1947; s. Sherman Kenyon and Velma Marie (Dunning) S.; m. Diane Louise Kennedy, June 23, 1973 (div. Feb. 1985); children: Heather Marie, David Arthur; m. Anna Louise Clock, Mar. 15, 1986; children: Jennifer Elizabeth, Austin Todd. BA, Mansfield U., 1969; MDiv, Princeton Sem., 1973; certificate, Mansfield Coll., Oxford, Eng., 1980, Wadham Coll., Oxford, 2003; D of Ministry, Drew U., 1992. Ordained to ministry Presbyn. Ch. U.S.A., 1973. Asst. pastor United Meth. Ch., Flemington, N.J., 1970-71; intern pastor Wattsburg (Pa.) Presbyn. Ch., 1971-72, East Greene Presbyn. Ch., Erie, Pa., 1971-72; asst. pastor Fewsmith Presbyn. Ch., Bellville, N.J., 1972-73; assoc. pastor Presbyn. Ch., Gettysburg, Pa., 1973-78; sr. pastor 1st Presbyn. Ch., Southampton, N.Y., 1978-86, Presbyn. Ch. of the Covenant, Port Arthur, Tex., 1986-91, 1st Presbyn. Ch., Wilmette, Ill., 1991-94, Peoria, Ill., 1994—; instr. parish nursing program OSF St. Francis Med. Ctr., Peoria, Ill., 1995-99; instr. Inst. Learning in Retirement Bradley U., Peoria, Ill., 1995—; instr. social scis. Ill. Ctrl. Coll., East Peoria, Ill., 1999—. Nat. chaplain Sigma Theta Epsilon, Mansfield, Pa., 1968-72; permanent clk. Presbytery of Carlisle, Camp Hill, Pa., 1975-77, Synod of the Trinity, Camp Hill, 1977-78; jour. clk. Presbytery of L.I., Commack, N.Y., 1980-84; mem. Presbytery of Great Rivers. Author: Voices in the Wilderness, 1985, At the Ffeete of Christe and His Church, 1981, Developing A Ministry of Evangelism With Baby Boomers in A Suburban Setting, 1992, America's Debt to the Native American, 1999, Watch Your Mouth! A Brief History of Everyday Words and Phrases, 2003; editr: Special Prayers and Prose for Special People of God, 1998; author articles, poetry, hymns. Program dir. Camp Brule, Boy Scouts Am., Forksville, Pa., 1972; dir. Youth in Govt. Seminar, Harrisburg, Pa., 1977; v.p. Internat. Seamen's Ctr., Houston, 1987-89; chairperson City Task Force on Edn. Summit, Port Arthur, 1990-91; active Presbyn. Hist. Soc. Recipient cert. Shinnecock Indian Tribe, 1981; named an Outstanding Young Man of Am., Jaycees, 1971; Susquehanna Collegiate Inst. grantee, 1972. Mem. Acad. Parish Clergy, Am. Soc. Ch. History, Presbyn. Hist. Soc., Presbyn. Writers Guild, Scottish Soc. S.E. Tex. (pres. 1990-91), Ill. State Hist. Soc., The Co. of Pastors, The Lincoln Party, The Lincoln Project, Abraham Lincoln Assn., Rotary (pres. 1977-78). Democrat. Avocations: coin collecting/numismatics, canoeing, white-water rafting, travel, gardening. Home: 3628 N Breckenridge Ct Peoria IL 61614-8034 Office: United Presbyn Ch 2400 W Northmoor Rd Peoria IL 61614-3343 Office Phone: 309-693-2002. E-mail: rls@unitedpc.org.

SAXTON, CATHERINE PATRICIA, public relations executive; b. Sheffield, Eng., July 5, 1944; d. Clifford and Kate Ann Saxton. BA cum laude, Fordham U., 1978. Mgr. corp. comms. Westinghouse Broadcasting & Cable Co., N.Y.C., 1981-82; prin., pres. Saxton & Assocs., N.Y.C., 1983—; CEO Potter/Saxton Assocs., Inc., N.Y.C., 1985-90, The Saxton Group Ltd., 1990—, co-founder, co-chair A-List Strategic affiliate, 2003—. Prof. pub. speaking Katharine Gibbs Coll., N.Y.C., 1977—. Mem. exec. com. Mayor's Commn. for a Vietnam Vets. Meml., 1982-90. Roman Catholic. Home: 325 E 90th St New York NY 10128-5260

SAXTON, H. JAMES, congressman; b. Nicholson, Pa., Jan. 22, 1943; s. Hugh R. and Helen M. (Billings) Saxton; m. Helen Jean Gadomski, June 9, 1965; children: Jennifer, James Martin. BA, East Stroudsburg State Coll., 1965; postgrad. in elem. edn., Temple U., 1967-68. Tchr. Bordentown Pub. Schs., Bordentown, N.J., 1965-68; realtor Jim Saxton Realty Co., Bordentown, N.J., 1968-85; assemblyman N.J. State Assembly, Trenton, 1975-81; state senator N.J. State Senate, Trenton, 1981-84; mem. U.S. Congress from 3rd N.J. dist., Washington, 1985—; mem. armed svcs. com., resources com., chmn. wildlife subcom., chmn. joint econ. com. Mem. travel and tourism caucus, maritime caucus, congl. port caucus environ. and energy study conf., Rep. study com., Stripers Ltd. (99th Congress); sec. N.J. Congl. Del., Washington, 1985-89. Active Boy Scouts Am., Burlington Council. Bordentown C. of C. Clubs: Leadership Found. N.J. Lodges: Elks. Republican. Office: US Ho of Reps 339 Cannon House Office Bldg Washington DC 20515-3003

SAXTON, LLOYD, psychologist, writer; b. Loveland, Colo., Sept. 28, 1929; s. Oliver George and Alice Augusta (Andersen) S.; m. Nancy Alison Roberts, Dec. 17, 1955; children: Perry Brent, Jay Ronald, Barbara Jean. AB in English, U. Calif., Berkeley, 1950, BS in Psychology, 1954; MS in Psychology, San Francisco State U., 1955; PhD in Psychology, U. of the Pacific, Stockton, Calif., 1957. Diplomate Am. Bd. Forensic Examiners, lic. psychologist Calif. Intern in clin. psychology Children's Hosp., San Francisco, 1955-56; teaching fellow U. Pacific, San Francisco, 1955-57, instr. psychology, 1957-58, asst. prof. psychology, 1958-60; assoc. prof. psychology Am. Acad. of Asian Studies, San Francisco, 1960-62, prof. psychology, 1962-65; chmn. dept. psychology Coll. of San Mateo, Calif., 1965-75, prof. psychology, 1975-92; pvt. practice San Francisco/Larkspur, 1958—; emeritus, 1995. Author: Individual, Marriage and the Family, 1968, Individual, 9th edit., 1996; author/editor: A Marriage Reader, 1970, The American Scene, 1970. Mem. APA, AAAS, AAUP, Am. Assn. Marriage and Family Therapists, Western Psychol. Assn., Am. Coll. Forensic Examiners, Mensa, Am. Chess Fedn. Democrat. Avocations: chess, sailing, music, ballet, opera. Home and Office: 57 Hatzic Ct Larkspur CA 94939-1992

SAXTON, WILLIAM MARVIN, lawyer; b. Joplin, Mo., Feb. 14, 1927; s. Clyde Marvin and Lea Ann (Farnan) S.; m. Helen Grace Klinefelter, June 1, 1974; children: Sherry Lynn, Patricia Ann Painter, William Daniel, Michael Lawrence. AB, U. Mich., 1949, JD, 1952. Bar: Mich. Mem. firm Love, Snyder & Lewis, Detroit, 1952-53, Butzel, Long, Detroit, 1953—, dir., chmn., CEO, 1989-96, dir. emeritus, 1997—. Lectr. Inst. Continuing Legal Edn.; sec., bd. dirs. Fritz Broadcasting, Inc., 1983-97; mem. mediation tribunal hearing panel for 3d Jud. Dist. Mich., 1989—, 6th Jud. Dist., 1994—. Trustee Detroit Music Hall Ctr. Soc. for the Performing Arts, 1984-99; trustee Hist. Soc. U.S. Dist. Ct. (ea. dist.) Mich., 1992-95, pres., 1993-95. Recipient Disting. award Mich. Road Builders Assn., 1987. Master of Bench Emeritus Am. Inn of Court; fellow Am. Coll. Trial Lawyers, Am. Bar Found., Am. Coll. Labor and Employment Lawyers, Mich. Bar Found.; mem. ABA, FBA, Detroit Bar Assn. (dir. 1974-79, Goodnow Pres.'s award 1996), Mich. Bar Assn. (atty. discipline panel, Disting. Svc. award 1998, Champion of Justice award, 2003), Detroit Indsl. Rels. Rsch. Assn. (treas. 1980—, v.p. 1982, pres. 1984-85), Mich. Young Lawyers (pres. 1954-55), Am. Law Inst., Indsl. Rels. Rsch. Assn. Am. Arbitration Assn., U.S. 6th Cir. Ct. Appeals (life, mem. jud. conf., mem. bicentennial com.), Am. Inn Ct., Cooley Club, Renaissance Club, Detroit Golf Club (dir. 1983-89), Detroit Athletic Club. Office: Butzel Long 150 W Jefferson Ave Ste 100 Detroit MI 48226-4416 Office Phone: 313-225-7001. E-mail: saxton214@aol.com.

SAY, ALLEN, children's writer, illustrator; b. Yokohama, Japan, Aug. 28, 1937; arrived in U.S., 1953; s. Masako Moriwaki; m. Deirdre Myles, Apr. 18, 1974; 1 child, Yuriko. Weekend arts program, Chouinard Art Inst., L.A.; classes, Art Ctr. Coll. Design, L.A.; studied arch., U. Calif., Berkeley. Pub. EIZO Pr., Berkeley, 1968. Author, illustrator: Dr. Smith's Safari, 1972, Once Under the Cherry Blossom Tree: An Old Japanese Tale, 1974, The Feast of Lanterns, 1976, The Bicycle Man, 1982, A River Dream, 1988, The Lost Lake, 1989, Tree of Cranes, 1991, Grandfather's Journey, 1993 (Caldecott medal 1994, Boston Globe/Horn Book award 1994), The Stranger in the Mirror, 1995, Emma's Rug, 1996; author: The Innkeeper's Apprentice, 1989, El Chino, 1990, Home of the Brave, 2002; illustrator: A Canticle to the Waterbirds, 1968, Two Ways of Seeing, 1971, Magic and Night River, 1978, The Lucky Yak, 1980, The Secret Cross of Lorraine, 1981, How My Parents Learned to Eat, 1984 (Horn Book honor list 1984, Christopher award 1985), The Boy of the Three Year Nap, 1988 (Boston Globe/Horn Book award 1988, Caldecott honor book 1989), Allison, 1997; retrospective Japanese Am. Nat. Mus., L.A., 2000. Office: care Houghton Mifflin Children's Book Dept 222 Berkeley St Boston MA 02116-3748*

SAY, BURHAN, physician; b. Istanbul, Turkey, Feb. 26, 1923; came to U.S. 1951; s. Ethem Serif and Ayse Say; m. Elizabeth E. Jackson, Nov. 5, 1955; children: Ahmet Serif, Daniel Demir. MD, U. Istanbul, 1946. Diplomate Am. Bd. Pediatrics, Am. Bd. Med. Genetics. Asst. prof. pediatrics Hacettepe U., Ankara, Turkey, 1960-64, prof. pediatrics, 1964-73; clin. prof. of pediatrics U. of Okla./Tulsa Med. Coll., 1975—. Dir. H.A. Chapman Inst., Tulsa, 1982—; v.p. Children's Med. Ctr., Tulsa, 1988—. Contbr. articles to profl. jours. Pres. Am. Cancer Soc., Tulsa, 1980-90, Great Plains Genetics Soc., Tulsa, 1993. Lt. Turkish Army, 1946-48, Turkey. Fulbright scholar, Boston, 1966-68. Avocations: sports. Home: 6216 E 99th St Tulsa OK 74137-5503

SAY, CALVIN, state legislator; b. Feb. 1, 1952; m. Cora Say; children: Geoffrey, Jared. BEd, U. Hawaii at Manoa. Mem. state house State of Hawaii, 1976—; mgr. Kotake Shokai Ltd.; spkr. ho. State of Hawaii, 1999—. Chmn. fin. com. Sstate of Hawaii, mem. labor mgmt. com. Mem. Palolo Little League, Pop Warner, Hawaii Youth Symphony, Hawaii Sports Hall of Fame and Mus., Palolo Cmty. Coun., Honolulu Symphony Soc., Gov.'s Com. Commemorating the Chinese Bicentennial.; dir. Pacific Rim Found. Democrat. Office: Hawaii Ho Reps Hawaii State Capitol Rm 431 415 S Beretania St Honolulu HI 96813-2407

SAY, CARLOS C. physician, surgeon; b. Philippines, Aug. 4, 1940; came to U.S., 1964; s. Felipe and Teresa Chua S.; m. Loretta Young, May 31, 1969; children: Brian Patrick, Janice Charlene. AA, U. Santo Thomas, Manila, 1959, MD, 1964; MS in Pub. Health, U. Mo., 1973. Intern Cambridge (Mass.) City Hosp., 1964-65; resident in gen. surgery The Carney Hosp., 1965-68; fellowship in surg. oncology Boston U. Med. Ctr., 1970-71; postdoctoral trainee NIH-Nat. Cancer Inst., 1971-73; chmn. dept. of clin. oncology Oak Forest (Ill.) Hosp., 1973-75; pvt. practice Atwater, Calif., 1975—. Staff physician Mercy Hosp., Merced, Calif., 1975—, Merced Cmty. Med. Ctr., 1975—, Bloss Meml. Dist. Hosp., Atwater, 1975—, Meml. Hosp. of Los Banos, Calif., 1990—. Contbr. articles to profl. jours. Fellow Am. Acad. of Family Physicians, Internat. Coll. of Surgeons, Am. Soc. of Abdominal Surgeons, Am. Coll. Emergency Physicians; mem. Merced Mariposa Med. Soc., Calif. Med. Assn., Am. Soc. of Clin. Oncology, Am. Assn. for Cancer Rsch., Am. Soc. of Gastrointestinal Endoscopy Am. Burn Assn., Am. Soc. of Enteral and Hyperalimentation Assn., Am. Assn. for Cancer Edn., U. Mo. Med. Sch. Alumni, Calif. Thracic Soc., Am. Acad. of Family Practice, Soc. Surg. Oncology, N.Y. Acad. of Sci.

SAYDUN, YUDA, information technology executive; BA in Polit. and Diplomatic Sci., U. Libre de Bruxelles, Belgium, 1975; MBA, UCLA, 1982. Asst. gen. mgr. Contifinance, Panama, 1976—79; v.p. gen. mgr. Latin Am. Tech Data Corp., Clearwater, Fla., 1993—97, sr. v.p. gen. mgr., 1997—2000, pres., Latin Am. and Carribean divsn., 2000—. Office: Tech Data Corp 5350 Tech Data Dr Clearwater FL 33760-3122

SAYE, JOANNE M. research scientist, pharmacologist; b. Greenville, Ala., Aug. 28, 1948; d. Joe V. and Reba C. Majors; children: Nikki, William. BS, Auburn Univ., Auburn, Ala., 1970, MS, 1977; PhD, Univ. Va., Charlottesville, Va., 1992. Rsch. asst. Univ. Va., Charlottesville, Va., 1981—91; rsch. scientist DuPont Merck Pharm., Wilmington, Del., 1991—95; sr. rsch. scientist DuPont Merck/DuPont Pharm., Wilmington, Del., 1995—99; assoc. dir., gen. pharm. DuPont Pharm. Co., Wilmington, Del., 1999—2000, dir. gen. pharm., 2000—01; dir. metabolic diseases BMS/Dupont Pharm., Wilmington, Del., 2001; preclin. project dir. AstraZeneca Pharm, Wilmington, Del., 2002—. Editor: American Journal of Physiology, 1998—2000; contbr. articles pub. to numerous profl. jour., scientific papers, many presetations. Fundraiser Am. Heart Assn., March of Dimes, Diabetes Assn., 1991—. Scholar Gen. Motors Scholarship, 1966—70. Fellow: N. Am. Assn. for the Study of Obesity; mem.: Safety Pharmacology Soc., Gen. Pharmacology Dicussion Group (chair 1998—99), Biochemical Phamacology Discussion Group (exec. com., chair 1997—2001), Gamma Sigma Delta. Avocations: hiking, reading, photography. Office: AStra Zeneca Pharm 1800 Concord Pike Wilmington DE 19850-5437 Office Phone: 302-885-1370.

SAYERS, GALE, computer company executive, retired professional football player; b. Wichita, Kans., May 30, 1943; s. Roger Earl and Bernice (Ross) S.; m. Ardythe Elaine Bullard, Dec. 1, 1973; children: Gale Lynne, Scott Aaron, Timothy Gale, Gaylon, Guy, Gary. Student phys. edn., Kans. U., N.Y. Inst. Finance. Running back Chgo. Bears Profl. Football Team, 1965-72; then asst. to athletic dir. Kans. U.; athletic dir. So. Ill. U., to 1981; v.p. mktg. Computer Suppy by Sayers, Northfield, Ill., 1984-86; pres. Crest Computer Supply Co., Skokie, Ill., 1986—; now pres., ceo Sayers Computer Source, Mt. Prospect, Ill. Columnist Chgo. Daily News. Author: (with Al Silverman) I Am Third, 1970. Co-chmn. legal def. fund sports com. NAACP; co-ordinator Reach-Out program, Chgo.; hon. chmn. Am. Cancer Soc.; commr. Chgo. Park Dist. Recipient numerous awards for playing, also holder numerous Nat. Football League records; named to Pro Football Hall of Fame, 1977 Mem. Kappa Alpha Psi. Office: Sayers Computer Source 1150 Feehanville Dr Mount Prospect IL 60056-6007

SAYERS, MARTIN PETER, pediatric neurosurgeon; b. Big Stone Gap, Va., Jan. 2, 1922; s. Delbert Bancroft and Loula (Thompson) S.; m. Marjorie W. Garvin, May 8, 1943; children: Daniel Garvin Sayers, Stephen Putnam Sayers, Julia Hathaway Sayers Bolton, Elaine King Sayers Buck. BA, Ohio State U., 1943, MD, 1945; postgrad., U. Pa., 1948-51. Intern Phila. Gen. Hosp., 1945-46; resident in neurosurgery U. Pa. Hosps., Phila., 1948-51; practice medicine specializing in neurosurgery Columbus, Ohio, 1951—; mem. faculty Ohio State U., Columbus, 1951-87, clin. prof. neurosurgery, 1968-87, emeritus, chief dept. pediatric neurosurgery, 1960-87. Cons. Bur. Crippled Children Services Ohio.; Neurosurgeon Project Hope, Ecuador, 1964, Ceylon, 1968, Cracow, Poland, 1979 Served as lt. jr. grade M.C., USN, 1946-48. Mem. Am. Assn. Neurol. Surgeons (chmn. pediatric sect.), Congress Neurol. Surgeons (pres.), Neurosurg. Soc. Am. (pres.), Am. Soc. Pediatric Neurosurgery, Soc. Neurol. Surgeons. Office: 931 Chatham Ln Columbus OH 43221-2417

SAYKIEWICZ-SAJKIEWICZ, JAN NAPOLEON, marketing educator; b. Lublin, Poland, June 10, 1939; arrived in U.S., 1987; s. Jan Sajkiewicz and Ewa Komorowska; m. Elzbieta Katarzyna Przetacznik, Aug. 27, 1966; children: Jan Rafal, Olaf Xawery, Mateusz Konstanty. MS in Econs., Ctrl. Sch. Planning & Stats., Warsaw, Poland, 1962, PhD, 1969; diploma in African studies, U. Warsaw, 1968; diploma, U. Calif., Berkeley, 1972. Cert. internat. tourism profl. Rsch. assoc. U. Calif., Berkeley, 1972-73; asst., assoc. prof. Ctrl. Sch. Planning & Stats., Warsaw, 1962-75; lectr. in mktg. Exec. Tng. Ctrs., Warsaw, 1969-88; assoc. prof. U. Warsaw, 1974-88; lectr., prof. Warsaw Acad. Arts, 1980-87; prof. Duquesne U. Sch. Bus. Adminstrn., Pitts., 1987—, L. Kozminski Acad. Entrepreneurship and Mgmt., Warsaw, 1998—. Vis. prof. Fordham U., N.Y.C., 1978, Duquesne U., Pitts., 1981, No. Jiaotong U., Beijing, 1997; Fulbright prof., 2000-2001; expert Internat. Labor Orgn., Geneva, 1982; vice-chmn., bd. dirs. Consumer Cooperative Enterprises, Warsaw, 1982-88; mem. Inter-Polcom, Chamber of Industry, Commerce, Warsaw, 1984-86; sec. gen., chief treas. Polish Mktg. Assn., 1974-81, exec. bd., 1985-88. Author: Concentration of Commercial Activities, 1972, Marketing Concept in Business Management, 1975, 2nd edit., 1976, 3rd edit., 1977, Management Systems in Integrated Capitalist Business, 1975; contbr. articles to profl. jours.; transl. profl. lit. Active Solidarity Movement, Poland, 1980-81; social and econ. coun., The Capital City of Warsaw, Poland, 1987-88. Recipient Silver and Gold Crosses of Merit, Coun. of State, Poland, 1980, 1982, Individual award for pedagogical performance, Min. Edn., Poland, 1981, Golden Mermaid Hon. Decoration for svc., Capital City of Warsaw, 1985, Akdeniz Univ. award, Turkey, 2002, award, Fulbright Fgn. Scholarship Bd. and U.S. Dept. State, 2002; vis. scholar, U. Calif., Berkeley, 1972—73, Fordham U., N.Y., 1978, No. Jiaotong U., Beijing, 1997, fellow, Ford Found., 1972—73, rsch. grantee, U.S. Dept. Edn., 1993, 1994. Fellow: Am. Acad. Mktg. Sci.; mem.: Polish Inst. Arts and Scis. in Am. (bd. dirs. 1995—97, adv. coun. 2003—), Am. Mktg. Assn. (profl. and exec. mem.), Acad. Internat. Bus., Internat. Mgmt. Devel. Assn. (exec. v.p. 1997, pres. 2002, award 2001). Roman Catholic. Avocations: social studies, books, travel, cognac. Home: 5853 Douglas St Pittsburgh PA 15217-2101 E-mail: saykiewicz@duq.edu.

SAYLER, ROBERT NELSON, lawyer; b. Kansas City, Mo., June 1, 1940; s. John William and Roberta (Nelson) S.; m. Martha Leith, Aug. 1962; children: Christina, Bentley. BA, Stanford U., 1962; JD, Harvard U., 1965. Bar: U.S. Dist. Ct. D.C. 1966, U.S. Ct. Appeals (D.C. cir.) 1966, U.S. Supreme Ct. 1971, D.C. 1972, U.S. Ct. Appeals (2d cir.) 1977. From assoc. to ptnr. Covington & Burling, Washington, 1965—. V.p. Neighborhood Legal Services, Washington, 1980-82; pres. Legal Aid Soc., Washington, 1983-84. Fellow Am. Bar Found., Am. Coll. Trial Lawyers; mem. ABA (dir. programs, program chmn. 1981, 85, coun., chmn. litigation sect., mem. standing com. on fed. judiciary). Democrat. Office: Covington & Burling PO Box 7566 1201 Pennsylvania Ave NW Washington DC 20004-2401

SAYLES, CATHY A. lawyer; b. Kansas City, Mo., Sept. 8, 1960; d. Harold Richard and June A. Sayles. BA, U. Kans., 1982, JD, 1985. Bar: Kans. 1985, U.S. Dist. Ct. Kans. 1985, U.S. Ct. Appeals (8th and 10th cirs.) 1985. Assoc. Shamberg, Johnson, Bergman & Goldman, Overland Park, Kans., 1985-86, Couch & Pierce, Overland Park, 1986 89; sr. atty. for litigation Koch Industries, Inc., Wichita, Kans., 1989-95; legal cons., Kansas City, Mo., 1995-97; gen. counsel Ferrellgas, Inc., Liberty, Mo., 1997—. Mem. Phi Beta Kappa. Office: Ferrellgas Inc One Liberty Pla Liberty MO 64068

SAYLES, KRISTI RENEE, elementary school educator, writer, application developer; b. Galveston, Tex., Feb. 11, 1960; d. Elmer and Christimae Spitler, Betty Spitler(Stepmother); m. Terry Dwight Sayles, Dec. 17, 1994; children: Jarred, Jason Mangrum, Jacob Mangrum, Joseph(dec.). MA in reading edn., Murray State U., 1995. Tchr. Benton County Adult Edn. Ctr., Camden, Tenn., 1994—95, Camden Elem. Sch., 1995—. Tutor Tutor.com, 2001—. Author: (software) Instant Writer Software Collection, (e-book) Entrepreneur$ Tell All, The Day I Woke Up as an Ostrich-An Odd Collection. Ch. song leader True Gospel Mission Ch., Camden, Tenn., 1999—2003, ch. Sunday sch. tchr., 1999—2003. Master: West Tenn. Writing Project; mem.: NEA, Benton Country Reading Assn., Tenn. Edn. Assn., Internat. Reading Assn. Christian. Avocations: creative writing, reading, researching with internet, bible study. Home: 125 Mckelvy Rd Camden TN 38320 Office: Camden Elem Sch 208 Washington Avenue Camden TN 38320 Personal E-mail: kristisayles@yahoo.com.

SAYLES, LEONARD ROBERT, management educator, consultant; b. Rochester, N.Y., Apr. 30, 1926; s. Robert and Rose (Sklof) S.; m. Kathy Ripin; children: Robert, Emily. BA with highest distinction, U. Rochester, 1946; PhD in Econs. and Social Sci., MIT, 1950. Asst. prof. Cornell U., 1950-53, U. Mich., 1953-56; prof. emeritus Grad. Sch. Bus. Adminstrn., Columbia U., 1956-91, prof. bus. adminstrn., 1962—, head div. indsl. relations and orgnl. behavior, 1960-72; adviser to adminstr. NASA, 1966-71; sr. rsch. scientist Ctr. for Creative Leadership, Greensboro, N.C., 1988-94. Disting. vis. lectr. McGill U., 1974; bd. govs. Center for Creative Leadership, 1984-88. Author: (with G. Strauss) The Local Union, 1953, Managerial Behavior, 1964, Human Behavior in Organizations, 1966, (with E. Chapple) Measure of Management, 1961, Behavior of Industrial Work Groups, 1958, Individualism and Big Business, 1963, (with W. Dowling) How Managers Motivate, 1971, (with M. Chandler) Managing Large Systems; Organizations for the Future, 1971, 2d edit., 1993, (with G. Strauss) Personnel, 4th edit, 1980, Managing Human Resources, 2d edit, 1981, Leadership, 1979, (with R. Burgelman) Inside Corporate Innovation, 1985, Managing in Real Organizations, 1989, The Working Leader, 1993, (with K. Ripin) Insider Strategies for Outsourcing Information Systems, 1999; mem. editorial bd. Human Orgn., 1957-62 Trustee Seacrest Sch., 1996-97. Fellow Am. Anthropol. Assn.; mem. Phi Beta Kappa. Office Phone: 239-597-7840. E-mail: LRSayles@aol.com.

SAYLES, RONALD LYLE, computer executive; b. Waukesha, Wis., Oct. 12, 1936; s. Burton Lyall and Sophia (Lapaz) S.; m. Fumiko Soeda, Jan. 15, 1957. BS in Secondary Edn., U. Wis., Milw., 1978. Computer operator Mortgage Assocs., Milw., 1966-71, Kohl's Food Stores, Wauwatosa, Wis., 1971-83; supr. computer ops. Kohl's Dept. Stores, Menomonee Falls, Wis., 1983-86, prodn. coord., 1986-87, scheduling coord., 1987-98, ret., 1998. Contbr. articles on old time radio programs. Vol. Jim Moody for Congress, 1984, 86, 88, 90, Shirley Krug for State Assembly, 1984, 86, 88, 90, Tom Barrett for State Senate, 1990, 91, Tom Barrett for Congress, 1991, 92, 94-96, 98, 2000, Bill Clinton for Pres., 1992, 96, Al Gore for Pres., 2000, Tom Barrett of Gov. of Wis., 2000, Tom Barrett for Mayor Milw. With USN, 1954-57. Mem. Milw. Area Radio Enthusiasts (pres.), Soc. to Preserve and Encourage Radio Drama, Variety and Comedy, U. Wis.-Milw. Alumni Assn. (life), Nightmare Players. Democrat. Home: 4278 N 53rd St Milwaukee WI 53216-1343

SAYLOR, MARK JULIAN, newspaper editor; b. Wellsville, N.Y., Mar. 19, 1954; s. Richard Samuel and Naomi (Roth) S.; children: Samuel, Benjamin, Katie. BA cum laude, Harvard Coll., 1976. Staff writer Ark. Democrat, Little Rock, 1976-77, San Jose (Calif.) Mercury News, 1977-81, asst. met. editor, 1981-82, govt. and politics editor, 1982-85; asst. city editor San Diego County edit. LA Times, L.A., 1985-89, city editor San Diego edit., 1989-91, Calif. polit. editor, 1991-95; entertainment editor Business, 1995—. Avocation: chess master. Office: LA Times Times Mirror Sq Los Angeles CA 90053

SAYLOR, PETER M. architect; b. Phila., July 26, 1941; s. Harry T. and Dorothy (Johnson) S.; m. Caroline Metcalf, Apr. 4, 1970; children: Thomas S., Elizabeth B. BArch, U. Pa., 1963, MArch, 1965. Registered arch., Iowa, Pa., N.J., Ind., Wis., Conn., Ohio, Minn. Architect Mitchell-Giurgola, Phila., 1967-70; ptnr. Dagit-Saylor Architects, Phila., 1970—. Design critic, juror U. Pa., 1975—; bd. dirs. Found. for Architecture, Phila., 1980-90. Bd. dirs. Chestnut Hill Cmty. Assn., Phila., 1976—79, v.p., 1979; bd. dirs. All Saints Hosp., Wyndmoor, Pa., 1981—86, Cathedral Village Retirement Cmty., 1998—2001. Recipient various bldg. design award Fellow AIA (bd. dirs. Phila. chpt. 1973-82, chpt. pres. 1981-82); mem. Pa. Soc. Archs., Chestnut Hill Hist. Soc. (bd. dirs. 1988-95, pres. 1989-92), Phila. Soc. Preservation of Landmarks (bd. dirs. 1989-96, pres. 1993-94), Phila. Mus. Art (friends bd. dirs. 1990-93), Phila. Cricket Club (bd. dirs. 1985-91), Mask and Wig Club (pres. 1980-81, bd. dirs. 1970-84). Republican. Episcopalian. Office: Dagit-Saylor Archs 100 S Broad St Philadelphia PA 19110-1023 Office Phone: 215-972-0500. E-mail: psaylor@dagitsaylor.com.

SAYLOR, THOMAS G. state supreme court justice; b. Meyersdale, Pa., Dec. 14, 1946; BA in Govt., U. Va., 1969; JD, Columbia U., 1972; LLM, U. Va., 2004. Pvt. practice, 1972-82, 87-93; 1st asst. dist. atty. Somerset County, 1973-76; dir. Pa. Bur. Consumer Protection, 1982-83; 1st dep. atty. gen. Commonwealth of Pa., 1983-87; elected judge Superior Ct. Pa., 1993; elected justice Supreme Ct. Pa., 1997—. Contbr. articles to legal publications. Bd. overseers Widener U. Sch. Law. Mem. ABA, Am. Law Inst., Pa. Bar Assn., Cumberland County Bar Assn., Dauphin County Bar Assn., Appellate Judges Conf. Office: Fulton Bldg 16th Fl 200 N 3d St Harrisburg PA 17101

SAYRE, DAVID, physicist; b. N.Y.C., Mar. 2, 1924; s. Ralph E. and Sylvia (Rosenbaum) S.; m. Anne Bowns, Dec. 26, 1947. BS, Yale U., 1944; MS, Auburn U., 1948; PhD, Oxford (Eng.) U., 1951. Staff mem. radiation lab. MIT, Cambridge, 1943-46; rsch. assoc. U. Pa., Phila., 1951-55; mathematician IBM Corp., N.Y.C., 1955-59, corp. dir. programming, 1959-62; mem. rsch. staff IBM T.J. Watson Rsch. Ctr., Yorktown Heights, N.Y., 1962-90, ret., 1990. Cons. U.S. Office Naval Rsch., London, 1951; mem. U.S.A. Nat. Com. for Crystallography, 1952-55, 81-84, vice chmn., 1984-86; vis. fellow All Souls Coll., Oxford U., 1972-73; guest scientist dept. physics SUNY, Stony Brook, 1980—; guest rschr. Brookhaven Nat. Lab., Upton, N.Y., 1983—; disting. guest prof. dept. chemistry Rutgers U., 1996-98. Co-author: Waveforms, 1947; editor: Computational Crystallography, 1983; co-editor: Structural Studies on Molecules of Biological Interest, 1983, X-Ray Microscopy II, 1988; contbr. numerous articles to profl. jours. Trustee Village of Head-of-the-Harbor, L.I., N.Y., 1975-95. Named one of Most Notable 20th Century Crystallographers, Hist. Atlas Crystallography. Mem. Am. Crystallographic Assn. (treas. 1952-55, pres. 1983, Fankuchen award 1989) Episcopalian. Achievements include devel. of atomicity-based direct phasing method for x-ray crystallography, (with others) of first FORTRAN compiler and first virtual computer system; contbns. to x-ray microscopy; first observation (with others) of x-ray diffraction pattern from single biol. cell; extension of x-ray crystallographic methods into field of non-crystals.

SAYRE, EDWARD CHARLES, librarian, consultant; b. Longview, Wash., Aug. 15, 1923; s. Kenneth C. Sayre and Clare (Davis) Clingan; m. Virginia A. Hoy, June 9, 1951; children: Steven Anthony, Sabrina Karen. BA, Coll. of Gt. Falls, 1955; MA, U. Idaho, 1961; MLS, U. Md., 1968. Coord. libr. svcs. Thomas Nelson CC, Hampton, Va., 1968-69; dir. Roswell (N.Mex.) Pub. Libr., 1969-70; cons. N.Mex. State Libr., Santa Fe, 1970-72; dir. Ctrl. Colo. Libr. Sys., Denver, 1972-78, Serra Coop. Libr. Sys., San Diego, 1978-79, Los Alamos (N.Mex.) County Libr. Sys., 1979-88; county adminstr. Los Alamos County, 1988-89; cons., 1976—. Contbr. articles to profl. jours. Mem. state governing coun. Common Cause N.Mex. Home: 3 Timber Ridge Rd Los Alamos NM 87544-2317 E-mail: esayre4207@aol.com.

SAYRE, EDWARD VALE, chemist; b. Des Moines, Sept. 8, 1919; s. Edward Agnew and Audrey (Vale) S.; m. Virginia Nelle Rogers, Oct. 20, 1943. BS, Iowa State U., 1941; AM, Columbia U., 1943, PhD, 1949. Mgr. rsch. sect. Manhattan Dist. project Columbia U., 1942-45; rsch. chemist Eastman Kodak Rsch. Labs., Rochester, N.Y., 1949-52; sr. chemist Brookhaven Nat. Lab., Upton, N.Y., 1952-84; rsch. phys. scientist Smithsonian Instn., Washington, 1984—. Dir. rsch. Museum Fine Arts, Boston, 1975-80, sr. scientist, 1980-84; sr. scientist Alexander von Humboldt Found., 1980; vis. lectr. Stevens Inst. Tech., 1955-61; adj. prof. fine arts Inst. Fine Arts, N.Y. U., 1960-74; disting. vis. prof. Am. U. Cairo, 1970; Regents prof. U. Calif., Irvine, 1972; mem. sci. adv. coun. Winterthur Mus. Contbr. numerous rsch. articles to profl. jours.; assoc. editor Archaeometry, 1969-93, Art and Archaeology Tech. Abstracts, 1970-87, Jour. Archaeol. Sci., 1971-77. Guggenheim fellow, 1969; recipient U.S. sr. scientist award Alexander von Humboldt Found., 1980-81, George von Hevesy medal, 1984, Alumni Disting. Achievement citation Iowa State U., 1996, Pomerance award Archaeol. Inst. Am., 1999. Fellow Internat. Inst. for Conservation of Hist. and Artistic Works, Am. Inst. for Conservation of Hist. and Artistic Works; mem. Am. Chem. Soc. Clubs: Cosmos. Home: Apt 616 1330 Massachusetts Ave NW Washington DC 20005-4152

SAYRE, JOHN MARSHALL, lawyer, former government official; b. Boulder, Colo., Nov. 9, 1921; s. Henry Marshall and Lulu M. (Cooper) S.; m. Jean Miller, Aug. 22, 1943; children: Henry M., Charles Franklin, John Marshall Jr., Ann Elizabeth Sayre Taggart (dec.). BA, U. Colo., 1943, JD, 1948. Bar: Colo. 1948, U.S. Dist. Ct. Colo. 1952, U.S. Ct. Appeals (10th cir.) 1964. Law clk. trust dept. Denver Nat. Bank, 1948-49; asst. cashier, trust officer Nat. State Bank of Boulder, 1949-50; ptnr. Ryan, Sayre, Martin, Brotzman, Boulder, 1950-66, Davis, Graham & Stubbs, Denver, 1966-89, of counsel, 1993—; asst. sec. of the Interior for Water and Sci., 1989-93. Bd. dirs. Boulder Sch. Dist. 3, 1951-57; city atty. City of Boulder, 1952-55; gen. counsel Colo. Mcpl. League, 1959-63; prin. counsel No. Colo. Water Conservancy Dist. and mcpl. subdist., 1964-87, spl. counsel, 1987, bd. dirs. dist., 1960-64; former legal counsel Colo. Assn. Commerce and Industry. Lt. (j.g.) USNR, 1943-46, ret. Decorated Purple Heart; recipient William Lee Knous award U. Colo. Law Sch., 1999. Fellow Am. Bar Found. (life), Colo. Bar Found. (life); mem. ABA, Colo. Bar Assn., Boulder County Bar Assn. (pres. 1959), Denver Bar Assn., Nat. Water Resources Assn. (Colo. dir. 1980-89, 93-95, pres. 1984-86), Denver Country Club, Phi Beta Kappa, Phi Gamma Delta, Phi Delta Phi. Home: 355 Ivanhoe St Denver CO 80220-5841 Office: Davis Graham & Stubbs 1550-17th St Ste 500 Denver CO 80202 E-mail: john.sayre@dgslaw.com.

SAYRE, LINDA DAMARIS, human resources professional; b. Washington, Nov. 26, 1945; d. Wallace Stanley and Kathryn Louise (McKnight) S. BA in English, Wells Coll., 1967; MA in Sociology, U. Sussex, Brighton, Eng., 1969; EdD in Adult and Continuing Edn., Rutgers U., 2002. Human resources specialist N.Y.C. Human Resources Adminstrn., 1967-68; rsch. assoc. Presdl. Campaign Gov. Nelson Rockefeller, N.Y.C., 1968; ednl. coord. Isabella Geriat. Ctr., N.Y.C., 1970-72; rsch. assoc. N.Y.C. Mayor's Commn. on City Fins., 1973-75; project mgr. Urban Acad. for Mgmt., N.Y.C., 1976-80; internal and external tng. cons. Boston and N.Y.C., 1980-83; tng. cons. N.Y.C. Bd. of Edn., 1983-84; tng. and edn. dir. Gen. Hosp. Ctr., Passaic, N.J., 1984-87; dir. human rels. Bronx (N.Y.) Lebanon Hosp., 1987-90; external cons. Atlanta, N.Y.C., 1990-95; tng. & devel. mgr. BOC Gases, Murray Hill, N.J., 1995-99. Mem. steering com. Broadway Dems., N.Y.C., 1974-80, 93-96, pres., 1975, 77; coord. Carter Presdl. Campaign, N.Y. 20th Congl. Dist., 1976; bd. Westside Cares Food Voucher, N.Y.C., 1993-95. Mem.: ASTD (no. N.J. programs 1985—86, Atlanta chmn. nat. affairs 1991, nat. leadership design team), N.Y. ASTD (v.p. prof. edn. 1993, pres. 1994, past pres. 1995, co-chair adv. coun. 1996, nominating com. 1997—98, chair succession planning com. 1998, cmty. action team 1999). Democrat. Avocations: writing, community service. Home: 448 Riverside Dr New York NY 10027-6801

SAYRE, MATT MELVIN MATHIAS, lawyer; b. Seattle, Sept. 5, 1934; s. Melvin Edward and Ethyl Elizabeth (Mathias) Sayre; m. Sheri Teagle, Oct. 21, 1956; children: Jeffrey Mathias, Steven Michael, David Matthew. BA, U. Wash., 1956; JD, Gonzaga U., 1964. Bar: Wash. 1964, U.S. Dist. Ct. (we. dist.) Wash. 1964, U.S. Ct. Appeals (9th cir.) 1972, U.S. Supreme Ct. 1980, DC 1981. Law clk. to Hon. Robert T. Hunter, Olympia, Wash., 1964-65; asst. counsel Pacific Car & Foundry Co., Renton, Wash., 1965-66; ptnr. Mullavey, Hageman, Treece & Sayre, Seattle, 1966-69, McBride & Sayre, 1969-71; pvt. practice Seattle, 1971-94; sr. ptnr. Sayre Law Offices, 1994—. Judge pro tem King County Superior Ct., 1973—83, 1989—2003. Trustee King County Bar Found., 1985—88, 1992—98; bd. visitors Seattle U. Sch. Law, 1991—2002. Served to 1st lt. USAFR, 1957—60. Recipient Pro Bono Svc. award, 1988. Mem.: South King County Bar Assn., King County Bar Assn. (treas. 1982—85, trustee 1985—88, mem. bench-bar delay reduction task force 1987—89, 2d v.p. 1988—89, 1st v.p. 1989—90, pres. 1990—91, Geisness award 1977), Wash. Bar Assn. (spl. dist. counsel 1982—88, editor adv. bd. 1986—89, chair BAR-PAC 1991—94, chair pub. rels. com. 1992—93), Rainier C. of C. (pres. 1977—78), Seattle Yacht Club (staff judge adv. 2000—01), Wash. Athletic Club, Useless Bay Golf and Country Club, Lions, Phi Delta Phi, Beta Theta Pi. Office: Boren & Jefferson Bldg 1016 Jefferson St Seattle WA 98104-2435 Office Phone: 206-625-0092.

SAYRE, ROBERT FREEMAN, English language educator; b. Columbus, Ohio, Nov. 6, 1933; s. Harrison M. and Mary (White) S.; (divorced); children— Gordon, Nathan, Laura; m. Hutha Refle, May 7, 1988. BA, Wesleyan U., Middletown, Conn., 1955; PhD, Yale U., 1962. Instr. English U. Ill., Urbana, 1961-63; Fulbright lectr. Lund (Sweden) U., 1963-65; faculty U. Iowa, 1965-72, prof. English, 1972-98, prof. emeritus, 1998—. Dir. inter-profl. seminars NEH, 1978, 79; Fulbright lectr. Montpellier, France, 1984; exch. prof. U. Copenhagen, 1988-89; mem. adv. bd. Leopold Ctr. for Sustainable Agr., 1994—, chair, 1996—. Author: The Examined Self: Benjamin Franklin, Henry Adams and Henry James, 1964, Adventures, Rhymes and Designs of Vachel Lindsay, 1968; Thoreau and the American Indians, 1977; editor: A Week on the Concord and Merrimac Rivers, Walden, The Maine Woods, Cape Cod (H.D. Thoreau), 1985, Take This Exit: Rediscovering the Iowa Landscape, 1989, New Essays on Walden, 1992, American Lives: An Anthology of Autobiographical Writing, 1994, Recovering the Prairie, 1999, Take the Next Exit, 2000; contbr. articles to profl. jours. Guggenheim fellow, 1973-74.

SAYRE, ROBERT MARION, ambassador; b. Hillsboro, Oreg., Aug. 18, 1924; s. William Octavius and Mary Sayre; m. Elora Amanda Moyhihan, Dec. 29, 1951; children: Marian Amanda, Robert Marion, Daniel Humphrey. BA summa cum laude, Willamette U., 1949; JD cum laude (Alexander Welborn Weddell Peace prize 1956), George Washington U., 1956; MA, Stanford U., 1960; LLD, Willamette U., 1965. Bar: D.C. 1956, U.S. Ct. Appeals 1956, U.S. Supreme Ct. 1962. Joined U.S. Fgn. Service, 1949; econ. adviser on Latin Am., dir. Truman Point 4 Program, 1950-52; mil. adviser, 1952-57; officer charge inter-Am. security affairs, 1955-57; polit. counselor embassy, 1957-59; fin. attache embassy Havana, Cuba, 1960; exec. sec. Task Force Latin Am., State Dept., Kennedy's Alliance for Progress, 1961; officer charge Mexican affairs Task Force Latin Am., State Dept., 1961-63; dep. dir. Office Caribbean and Mexican Affairs, 1963-64; dir. Office Mexican Affairs, 1964; sr. advisor White House, 1964-65; sr. dep. asst. sec. Bur. Inter-Am. Affairs, Dept. State, 1965-68; acting asst. sec. Dept. State, 1968—; Am. ambassador to Uruguay, 1968-69, to Panama, 1969-74; sr. insp. Dept. State, 1974-75, insp. gen., 1975-78; ambassador to Brazil, 1978-81; chmn. U.S. Interdepartmental group on Terrorism, dir. Counter-terrorism and Emergency Planning Dept. State, 1981-84, sr. insp., 1985; ptnr. IRC Group, Inc., 1986-87; from adv. to U.S. rep. to under sec. for mgmt. Orgn. of Am. States, 1987-94; sr. assoc. Global Bus. Access, Ltd., Washington, 1995—; chair Open Forum Working Group on Internat. Econs. U.S. Dept. State, 1995-96. Sr. councilor Atlantic Coun. Washington Inst. Fgn. Affairs. Capt. AUS, WWII; col. Res., ret. Decorated Soc. Cross (Brazil); Cross of Balboa (Panama); recipient Outstanding Employee award Dept. State, 1952, Superior Honor awards, 1964, 75, Disting. Honor award, 1978, Outstanding Performance award, 1982-85, Presdl. Meritorious award, 1986, Fgn. Svc. Cup award, 1990, Sec.'s Cert. of Appreciation, U.S. Dept. State, 1996. Mem. Am. Acad. Diplomacy, Inter Am. Bar Assn., Inter Am. Dialogue, Atlantic Coun. Washington Inst. Fgn. Affairs, Cosmos Club, Dacor House, Blue Key, Phi Delta Theta, Phi Eta Sigma, Tau Kappa Alpha. Episcopalian. Home: 3714 Bent Branch Rd Falls Church VA 22041-1028 Office: Global Business Access Ltd 1825 I St NW Ste 400 Washington DC 20006-5415

SAYRE, WILLIAM O. geologist, educator; s. Ralph M. and Lois J. Sayre; m. Patricia Roberts, Apr. 21, 1989; 1 child, Adam. BS, Western Wash. U., 1976; PhD, U. Southampton, Eng., 1980. Lic. profl. geologist Fla. Geologist U.S. Geol. Survey, Flagstaff, Ariz., 1983—84; assoc. prof. Eckerd Coll., St. Petersburg, Fla., 1984—91, assoc. prof., chair, 1991—96, prof., 1996—99, asst. dean, 1999—2000; acting v.p. Coll. Santa Fe, 2000—01, prof., dir., 2001—. Mem., chair Fla. Bd. Profl. Geologists, Tallahassee, 1988—91. Mem.: N.Mex. Geol. Soc., Am. Geophys. Union, Geol. Soc. Am. Office: Coll Santa Fe 1600 St Michaels Dr Santa Fe NM 87505

SAYWARD, TERESA R. state representative; m. Kenneth Sayward; 4 children. Lic. Realtor N Y N.Y. state rep., 2002—. Apptd. Assembly Minority Task Force on State of N.Y. Agrl.; owned, operated Holstein Cattle Dairy Farm, Wilsboro; chairwoman Willsboro's Zoning Bd. of Appeals; town supr., Willsboro, NY; bd. of suprs. Essex County, chairwoman bd. suprs.; chairwoman Econ. Devel., Planning and Publicity Com., Essex County Bd. of Suprs. Legis. Com.; lobbyist in Albany for Essex County. Minority mem. Corrections Com.; standing com. Edn., Environ. Conservation and Tourism; chairwoman Inter-Govtl. Affairs Com. at N.Y. State Assn. of Counties, North County Adv. Coun. for N Y State Divsn. for Women; dir. Adirondack Assn. of Towns and Villages, Plattsburgh North Country Regional C. of C.; bd. dirs. Smith House Health Care Ctr., Cornell Coop. Ext. Soil and Water Conservation Dist., Adirondack North County Assn., Willsboro Devel. Corp.; mem. Corp. of the Champlain Valley Physicians Hosp. Med. Ctr. Avocations: gardening, art, golf. Office: 7559 Court St Rm 203 Elizabethtown NY 12932 Address: LOB 633 Albany NY 12248 E-mail: saywart@assembly.state.ny.us.

SAYWELL, WILLIAM GEORGE GABRIEL, business development and management consultant; b. Regina, Sask., Can., Dec. 1, 1936; s. John Ferdinand Tupper and Vera Marguerite S.; m. Helen Jane Larmer; children: Shelley Jayne, William James Tupper, Patricia Lynn. BA, U. Toronto, 1960, MA, 1961, PhD, 1968; LLD (hon.), U. B.C., 1994, Simon Fraser U., 1997. Asst. prof. dept. East Asian studies U. Toronto, 1963-69, asst. prof., 1969-71, assoc. prof., 1971-82, prof., 1982-83, chmn. dept., 1971-76; prof. dept. history, pres., vice chancellor Simon Fraser U., Burnaby, B.C., Can., 1983-93; pres., chief exec. officer Asia Pacific Found. of Can., Vancouver, B.C., 1993-99; vice chmn. Intercedent Ltd., 1999—; pres. William Saywell & Assocs., Vancouver, 1999—. Cons. in higher edn.; sinologist and 1st sec. Can. Embassy, Beijing, 1972-73; dir. U. Toronto-York U. Ctr. Modern East Asia, 1974-75; prin. Innis Coll., 1976-79; vice provost U. Toronto, 1979-83; dir. Tokyo-Mitsubishi Bank (Can.), Seashore Mineral Resources, Palcan Power, VLinx Ltd. Author articles and revs. on Chinese affairs to profl. jours. Decorated Order of Can. Order of B.C. Office: 701 2095 Beach Ave Vancouver BC Canada V6G 1Z3

SAZAMA, KATHLEEN, pathologist, lawyer; b. Sutherland, Nebr., May 8, 1941; d. Roger William and Esther Mary (Reitz) Paulman; m. Franklin Jed Sazama, Aug. 26, 1962; children: Clare Ann, Jill Patrice. BS, U. Nebr., 1962; MS, Am. U., 1969; MD, Georgetown U., 1976; JD, Cath. U. Am., 1990. Diplomate Am. Bd. Pathology; lic. pathologist Mich., Va., Md., D.C., Calif., Pa., Tex.; bar: Md. Intern and resident Georgetown U. Med. Ctr., Washington, 1976-78; resident NIH, Bethesda, Md., 1978-79; clin. asst. prof. pathology Uniformed Svcs. U. Health Scis., Bethesda, 1981-89; clin. affiliate Ferris State Coll., Big Rapids, 1985-86; chief lab. of blood bank practices FDA Ctr. for Biologics Evaluation and Rsch., Bethesda, 1986-89; cons. Ober, Kaler, Grimes & Shriver, Balt., 1989-90; assoc. med. dir. Sacramento (Calif.) Med. Found. Blood Ctr., 1990-92; asst. clin. prof. pathology U. Calif., Davis, 1990-92, assoc. prof., dir. clin. pathology, 1992-93; prof. pathology and lab. medicine Allegheny U. of the Health Scis., Phila., 1994—99; v.p. for faculty acad. affairs U. Tex./M.D. Anderson Cancer Ctr., Houston, 2000—02, prof. lab. medicine, 2000—. V.p. bd. Met. Washington Blood Banks, Inc., 1981-84; pres. bd. Am. Assn. Blood Banks, 2003-04; spkr. in field. Author: (with others) Stat: The Laboratory's Role, 1986; contbr. numerous articles to profl. jours. Comdr. USPHS, 1986-89. Fellow Coll. Am. Pathologists, Am. Soc. Clin. Pathologists; mem. AMA, ABA, Am. Assn. Blood Banks (bd. dirs.), Nat. Health Lawyers Assn., Phi Kappa Phi, Beta Beta Beta. Avocations: tennis, playing bridge. Address: Univ of Texas MD Anderson Cancer Center 1515 Holcombe Blvd # 800 Houston TX 77030-4009 Business E-Mail: ksazama@mdanderson.org.

SAZEGAR, MORTEZA, artist; b. Tehran, Iran, Nov. 11, 1933; s. Hassan Ali and Zahra (Frootan) S.; m. Patricia Jean Kaurich, July 13, 1959. BA, U. Tex., El Paso, 1955, BS, 1956; postgrad., Baylor U. Coll. Medicine, 1956-57, Cornell U., 1958-59. One man exhibitions include, Poindexter Gallery, N.Y.C., 1964, 67, 69, 71, 73, 75, 77, group exhibitions include, Detroit Inst. Arts, 1965, Chgo. Art Inst., 1965, Univ. Art Mus., U. Tex., Austin, 1965, 72, Whitney Mus. Am. Art, 1970, Cleve. Mus. Art, 1972, Corcoran Gallery Art, Washington, 1973, Tyler Sch. Art, Temple U., Phila., 1979; represented in permanent collections, Whitney Mus. Am. Art, N.Y.C., San Francisco Mus. Modern Art, Riverside Mus., N.Y.C., U. Mass., Amherst, Corcoran Gallery Art, Prudential Ins. Corp. Am., Mus. Contemporary Art, Tehran, Iran. Mem. Artists Equity Assn. Democrat. Address: 1223 Homeville Rd Cochranville PA 19330-1712

SAZIMA, HENRY JOHN, retired oral and maxillofacial surgery educator; b. Cleve., Dec. 25, 1927; s. Henry Charles and Frances (Masin) S.; m. Carol Ann Watson, Sept. 10, 1955; 1 child, Holly Ann Sazima Davani. BS, Case Western Res. U., 1948, DDS, 1953; grad. sch. medicine, U. Pa., 1956-57; grad. sch. edn., Chapman Coll., 1967-69. Diplomate Am. Bd. Oral and Maxillofacial Surgery. Chief maxillfacial div. Naval Support Act, Saigon, Vietnam, 1969—70; chmn. dental dept. Naval Med. Ctr., Phila., 1971—73, San Diego, 1979—80; spl. asst. dentistry Sec. Def. Health Affairs, Washington, 1973—77; comdg. officer Naval Dental Ctr., Parris Island, SC, 1977—79; dep. chief dental divsn. Bur. Medicine and Surgery, Washington, 1980—82; comdg. officer Nat. Naval Dental Ctr., Bethesda, Md., 1982—83; dir. resources divsn. Chief Naval Ops., Washington, 1983—84; dep. commdr. for readiness and logistics Naval Med. Command, Washington, 1984—87, ret. rear admiral, 1987; emeritus clin. assoc. prof. oral and maxillofacial surgery Georgetown U. Med. Ctr., 2003—; exec. dir. Acad. Dentistry Internat., 1988—2000, exec. dir. emeritus, 2000—. Cons., lectr., rschr. in field. Co-author: Management of War Injuries, 1977; contbr. articles to profl. jours. Recipient Residents award St. Vincent Charity Hosp., 1957, Hillenbrand award Acad. Dentistry Internat., 2000; named Disting. Alumnus, Case Western Res. U. Sch. Dentistry, 2002-03. Fellow Am. Coll. Dentists, Assn. Oral and Maxillofacial Surgeons, Internat. Assn. Oral and Maxillofacial Surgeons, Acad. Dentistry Internat. (Blue Cloud award 1995); mem. Brit. Soc. Oral and Maxillofacial Surgeons, European Assn. Maxillofacial Surgery, Case Western Alumni Assn. (Disting. Alumnus, 2002-03), Assn. Mil. Surgeons of U.S. (chmn. internat. com. 1984-86, Margetis award 1971), Internat. Coll. Dentists (dep. regent 1971-87), Hospitaller Order of St. John of Jerusalem, Hospitlar Knights of Malta, Omicron Kappa Upsilon, Delta Tau Delta, Psi Omega. Clubs: Mil. Order of CARABAO. Republican. Roman Catholic. Avocations: sports, tennis, music, travel. Home: c/o Cortese PO Box 21302 South Euclid OH 44121-0302 E-mail: sazimo@comcast.net.

SBAITY-KASSEM, FATIMA HASAN, political economist, researcher; b. Tripoli, Lebanon, Aug. 19, 1944; d. Hasan Abdelkader Sbaity and Asma Abdallah Karkanawi; m. Ziad Kassem Kassem, May 27, 1972 (dec. Mar. 1997); children: Hana, May, Ramzi. BBA, Am. U., Beirut, 1965, M in Devel. Adminstrn., 1970; M in Internat. Econs., Columbia U., 1991, MPhil in Internat. Rels., 1995, postgrad. Instr. Chweifat (Lebanon) Nat. Coll., 1965-69; chief women and devel. sect. UN-ESCWA/UNESOB, Beirut, 1970—90; trade expert, internat. economist, 1990—. Contbr. chapters to books. Bd. dirs. CAWTAR, Tunis, 1999—. Mem. Am. Polit. Sci. Assn., Acad. Polit. Scis.

Home: 10 Waterside Plz Apt 18F New York NY 10010 Office: UN Econ ESCWA Commn Western Asia PO Box 5749 New York NY 10163-5749 E-mail: kassemz@cyberia.net.lb., sbaity-kassem@un.org.

SBARBARO, ROBERT ARTHUR, banker; b. Bklyn., Jan. 24, 1933; s. John Vincent and Louise Olga (Perigone) S.; m. Kathleen Ann Noonan, Sept. 12, 1959; children— Robert, Paul, Nancy. BA, Wagner Coll., 1954, postgrad., 1977. CFP. Programming mgr. IBM, 1956-59; regional ops. mgr. Univac, 1959-65; asst. v.p., mgr. Computax Corp., N.Y.C., 1965-70; sr. v.p. Irving Trust Co., N.Y.C., 1970-89; pres. SPAR Cons., Manasquan, N.J., 1990—. Mem. Montvale (N.J.) Recreation Commn., 1979-80; treas. Pascack Hills High Sch. Parents Assn., 1978-79; trustee Wagner Coll.; pres. Allington Towers Condo Assn., Hollywood, Fla., 1998, treas., 1999. With USN, 1954-56. Recipient Alumni Achievement award Wagner Coll., 1987—. Mem. Data Processing Mgmt. Assn., Am. Banking Assn., Data Security Inst., Internat. Assn. for Fin. Planning, K.C. Republican. Roman Catholic. Avocation: sports. Home and Office: 1541 Tanner Ave Manasquan NJ 08736-2217 E-mail: sbarbaro1@att.net.

SCADDEN, DAVID THOMAS, hematologist, oncologist, research scientist; b. 1953; BA in English Lit., Bucknell U.; MD, Case Western Res. U., 1980. Diplomate Am. Bd. Internal Medicine. Intern Brigham-Women's Hosp., Boston, 1980-81, resident in internal medicine, 1981-83, fellow in hematology/oncology, 1983-86; staff Dana Farber Inst. Brigham & Women's Hosp., Boston, 1986—; prof. medicine Harvard U.; co-dir. Harvard Stem Cell Initiative, AIDS Rsch. Ctr. for Ptnrs. Health Care, Mass. Gen. Hosp., AIDS Rsch. Ctr., Brigham and Women's Hosp.; dir. Center for Regenerative Medicine and Tech., Mass. Gen. Hosp.; chief of hematologic malignancies Mass. Gen. Hosp. Contbr. publications in the field. Recipient Clin. Scientist award in Translational Rsch., 2002, Career award, Burroughs Wellcome Fund. Mem.: Internat. Congress of Cell Transplant Soc. Achievements include research in parathyroid hormone (PTH) stimulation of the production of stem cells; adult hematopoietic stem cells with emphasis on their interaction with the microenvironment and cell cycle control. Office: AIDS Rsch Ctr Mass Gen Hosp Fruit St Boston MA 02114 also: Ctr for Regenerative Medicine and Tech Mass Gen Hosp 13th St Bldg 149 Rm 5212D Boston MA 02129 Office Phone: 617-726-5615. Office Fax: 617-726-4691. Business E-Mail: scadden.david@mgh.harvard.edu.

SCAFETTA, JOSEPH, JR., lawyer; b. Chester, Pa., May 10, 1947; s. Giuseppe and Mary (Koslosky) S.; m. Teresa M. Talierco, July 4, 1986; 1 child, Joseph III. BS in Aero. Engring., Pa. State U., 1969; JD, U. Pitts., 1972; M in Patent Law, Georgetown U., 1973; MBA, George Washington U., 1983. Bar: Pa. 1972, U.S. Patent and Trademark Office 1973, D.C. 1978, Va. 1979, U.S. Supreme Ct. 1980, U.S. Ct. Appeals (fed. cir.) 1982. Legal rschr. Arent, Fox, Kintner, Plotkin et al, Washington, 1973; law clk. to presiding judge U.S. Dist. Ct. S.C., Columbia, 1973-74; assoc. Colton & Stone, Arlington, Va., 1975-77, Craig & Antonelli, Washington, 1977-78, Wigman & Cohen, Arlington, 1978-83, Wenderoth, Lind & Ponack, Washington, 1983-86, Cushman, Darby & Cushman, Washington, 1986-87; counsel Russell, Georges & Breneman, Arlington, 1987-91, Young & Thompson, Arlington, 1991-96; pvt. practice Arlington, 1996-98; counsel Oblon, Spivak, McClelland, Maier & Neustadt, Arlington, 1999—. Voting mem. Nat. Commn. for Social Justice, 1995-97. Author: Book Review Copyright Handbook, 1979, The Constitutionality/Unconstitutionality of the Patent Infringement Statute, 1979, (with others) Patents on Microorganisms, 1980; editor: An Intellectual Property Law Primer, 1975; contbr. articles to profl. jours. Mem. Consumer Affairs Commn., Alexandria, Va., 1985-87; charter mem. Christopher Columbus Quincentenary Jubilee Com., 1990-93; chair Va. chpt. Commn. for Social Justice, 1987—; mem. Fairfax County Dem. Com., Falls Church, 1987-89; parliamentarian City Dem. Com., Alexandria, 1985-87. Recipient Robert C. Watson award Am. Patent Law Assn., 1975. Mem.: Patent and Trademark Office Soc., D.C. Bar Assn., Am. Intellectual Property Law Assn. (mem. pub. info. com. 1983—2001), Va. Bar Assn., Am. Arbitration Assn. (mem. comml. panel), ABA, Avanti Italiani (pres. Alexandria chpt. 1981—83), Grand Lodge Va. (state pres. 1993—95), Sons of Italy. Office: 1755 Jeff Davis Hwy Ste 400 Arlington VA 22202-3530

SCAFFIDI, JUDITH ANN, academic administrator; b. Bklyn., Aug. 2, 1950; d. Anthony William and Rose Virginia (Nocera) S. BA, SUNY, Plattsburg, 1972, MS, 1973; postgrad., Einstein Coll. Medicine, 1983; PhD (hon.), Internat. U. Bombay, 1993; HHD (hon.), London Inst. Applied Rsch., 1993. Cert. secondary edn. English. VISTA mem. ACTION, N.Y.C., 1976-77; coord. cultural resources Learning Leaders, N.Y.C., 1977-80, tng. splst. in Bklyn., 1980—. Field supr., adj. faculty Coll. for Human Svcs., N.Y.C., 1984-86; adv. coun. chair Ret. Sr. Vol. Program in Bklyn., 1983-86; adv. bd. Ret. Sr. Vol. Program in N.Y.C., 1983-86. Acvive Am. Friends Svc. Com., 1994—. Recipient award for svcs. in promotion literacy Internat. Reading Assn. and Bklyn. Reading Coun., 1986, award for outstanding leadership Ret. Sr. Vol. Program, 1986, cert. of appreciation Mayor City of N.Y., 1991, cert. of appreciation for exceptional support and encouragement of volunteerism, 1998. Mem. NAFE, Cath. Tchrs. Assn. Bklyn. (del. sch. dist. 18, 1982-91), Internat. Platform Assn., World Found. Successful Women, Am. Biog. Inst. (rsch. bd. advisors 1992-93), Am. Biog. Inst. Rsch. Assn. (bd. govs. 1992—), Internat. Parliament for Safety and Peace (dep. mem. and diplomatic passport), Maisson Internat. de Intellectuels (Acad. MIDI), Cath. Alumni Club N.Y., Amnesty Internat. Roman Catholic. Avocations: foreign and domestic travel, reading, walking. Home: 2330 Ocean Ave Apt 3H Brooklyn NY 11229-3036 Office: Learning Leaders 352 Park Ave S Fl 13 New York NY 10010-1709

SCAFURO, LISA A. writer, journalist, poet; b. Ridgewood, N.J., Apr. 22, 1958; d. Angelo C. Scafuro and Barbara A. Purdy; m. Samuel C. Ilechuku, May 21, 1981 (div. Apr. 0, 2001); 1 child, Samantha Elise Ilechuku. BS in Design Scis., Ariz. State U., Coll. Architecture, 1981; student, Art Students League N.Y., 1975—76, student, 1987; postgrad., CCNY, 1988—89; student, Rudgewood Sch. Photography, 1977. Lic. realtor Ariz., 1998. Designer The Kling Partnership, Phila., 1981—83; project designer Ballinger Architects, 1983—85; project mgr., constrn. Columbia Presbyn. Med. Ctr., N.Y.C., 1987; project mgr., arch. NY Hosp./Cornell Med. Ctr., 1987—88; project mgr., constrn. Columbia U./Columbia Presbyn. Med. Ctr., 1988—90; archtl. cons. pvt. practice, Saddle River, NJ, 1990—. Student Paolo Soleri: arch./visionary/philosopher, Paradise Valley, Ariz., 1986—. Author (illustrator): (children's book - a series) Adventures at Cedar Hollow: Tigre Encounters the Great Horned Owl; author: (poetry contempory historical) George W. Bush & September. Team leader Rep. Re-election Com., Scottsdale, Ariz., 2000. Mem.: Am. Poets Soc. (assoc.). Liberal. Avocations: swimming, skiing, horseback riding, walking, auto restoration, jewlery design with shells/turquoise. Personal E-mail: lasarizona@aol.com.

SCAGGS, BOZ (WILLIAM ROYCE SCAGGS), musician; b. Ohio, June 8, 1944; m. Carmella Scaggs; children: Oscar, Austin. Student, U. Wis. Restaurateur Blue Light Café, San Francisco, 1984—. With Steve Miller's band The Marksmen, then Ardells band (also under name Fabulous Night Train), formed own rhythm-and-blues band The Wigs, rejoined Steve Miller, 1967, rec. 2 albums with (Steve Miller) Children of the Future and Sailor, solo albums include Boz, 1966, My Time, 1972, Slow Dancer, 1976, Down Two Then Left, 1977, Middle Man, Hits, 1980, Other Roads, 1988, Silk Degrees, 1990, The New York Rock and Roll Soul Review, 1991. Recipient Grammy award Best Rhythm and Blues Song for Lowdown, 1976. Office: care/ Slims 1790 Broadway Fl 6 San Francisco CA 94109-2466

SCAGLIONE, LOUIS, III, music educator, conductor; b. Berwyn, Ill., June 7, 1969; s. Louis F. and Sharon L. Scaglione. BS Music Edn., U. Ill., 1992; M Music, Temple U., 1996. Cert. K - 12 Instnl. I in Music Pa., 1998, Spl. K - 12 Tchg. in Music Ill., 1992. Artistic dir. Arts at Andalusia, Andalusia, Pa., 1995—; conductor Phila. Young Artists Orch., 1997—; assoc. conductor Phila. Youth Orch., 1998—, exec. dir., 2001—; mem. faculty Temple U. Music Preparatory Divsn., Phila., 1998—. Trustee Andalusia Found., Andalusia, Pa., 2000—; bd. trustees Youth Work Found., Union League Phila., 2002—. Mem.: Music Educators Nat. Conf., Am. Choral Drs. Assn., Coll. Music Soc., Am. Symphony Orch. League (dir. youth orch. divsn. 2000—), Union League of Phila. (mem. house com. 2000—), Pi Kappa Lambda, Phi Eta Sigma, Kappa Delta Pi, Golden Key Soc. Office: Phila Youth Orch PO Box 41810 Philadelphia PA 19101 Personal E-mail: louisscag@aol.com.

SCALA, JAMES, health care industry consultant, writer; b. Ramsey, N.J., Sept. 16, 1934; s. Edvigi and Lorene (Hendricksen) S.; m. Nancy Peters, June 15, 1957; children: James, Gregory, Nancy, Kimberly. BA, Columbia U., 1960; PhD, Cornell U., 1964; postgrad., Harvard U., 1968; LHD (hon.), Hofstra U., 1998. Cert. nutrition specialist. Staff scientist Miami Valley Labs., Procter and Gamble Co., 1964-66; head life scis., dir. fundamental rsch. Owens Ill. Corp., 1966-71; dir. nutrition T.J. Lipton Inc., 1971-75; dir. health scis. Gen. Foods Corp., 1975-78; v.p. sci. and tech. Shaklee Corp., San Francisco, 1978-85, sr. v.p. sci. affairs, 1986-87. Cons. Georgetown U. Med. Sch., U. Calif.-Berkeley ext. Author: Making the Vitamin Connection, 1985, The Arthritis Relief Diet, 1987, 2d edit., 1989, Eating Right for a Bad Gut, 1990, 2d edit., 1992, Eating Right for a Bad Gut, new edit., 1999, The High Blood Pressure Relief Diet, 1988, 2d edit., 1990, Look 10 Years Younger, Feel 10 Years Better, 1991, 2d edit., 1993, Prescription for Longevity, 1992, 2d edit., 1994, If You Can't/Won't Stop Smoking, 1993, The New Arthritis Relief Diet, 1998, 25 Natural Ways to Manage Stress and Avoid Burnout, 2000, 25 Natural Ways to Relieve Irritable Bowel Syndrome, 2000, 20 Natural Ways to Reduce the Risk of Prostate Cancer, 2001, 25 Natural Ways to Lower Blood Pressure, 2002; editor: Nutritional Determinants in Athletic Performance, 1981, New Protective Roles for Selected Nutrients, 1989; columnist: Dance mag.; contbr. articles to profl. jours. With USAF, 1953-56. Disting. scholar U. Miami, Fla., 1977, Fla. Atlantic U., 1977. Mem. AAAS, Am. Inst. Nutrition, Am. Coll. Nutrition, Brit. Nutrition Soc., Sports Medicine Coun., Am. Soc. Cell Biology, Inst. Food Technologists, Astron. Soc. Pacific (bd. dirs., chmn. devel. coun.), Am. Dietetic Assn., Olympic Club (San Francisco), Oakland Yacht Club, Sigma Xi. Republican. Personal E-mail: jscala2@comcast.net. *I am in awe of the incredible resiliency of living things, but most of all the human spirit.*

SCALES, FREDA S. dean, nursing educator; BSN, Okla. Bapt. U., 1965; MSN, Ind. U., 1970; PhD, Purdue U., 1977. Mem. staff faculty Sch. Nursing Ind. U., Inpls., 1970-82; dean Coll. Nursing Valparaiso (Ind.) U., 1982—. Mem. ANA, Am. Assn. Coll. Nursing, Nat. League Nursing. Office: Valparaiso U Coll Nursing Valparaiso IN 46383 Fax: 219-464-5425.

SCALES, JAMES LEONARD, orthopedic surgeon, health facility administrator; b. Sacramento, May 15, 1952; s. James Leonard and Ruth Marie S.; m. Donna Marie Coppola, Oct. 11, 1983; children: James, Steven, Kevin. AB, Harvard U., 1974; MS, Rutgers U., 1978; MD, U. Medicine and Dentistry N.J., 1979. Diplomate Am. Bd. Orthopedic Surgery. Resident in surgery U. Medicine and Dentistry N.J., Rutgers Med. Sch., Piscataway, 1979—80; resident in orthopaedic surgery U. Medicine and Dentistry N.J., N.J. Med. Sch., Newark, 1982—86; staff physician med. unit Meadowlands Sports Complex, East Rutherford, NJ, 1980—88; orthop. surgeon D'Ascoli Orthop. Surgery, Sparta, NJ, 1986—88; pres. Andover Orthop. Surgery & Sports Medicine Group, PA, Newton, NJ, 1988—. Cons. orthop. N.J. Cardinals, Augusta, 1997—; chief surgery Newton Meml. Hosp., 1994—96; chief orthop. surgery N. Jersey Surgery Ctr., Newton, 1998—; bd. dirs. Garden State Orthop. Network, Bridgewater, NJ, 1998—. Vol. physician U.S. Olympic Com., U.S. Olympic Tng. Ctr., Lake Placid, NY, 1997; Interviewer Harvard Club N.J., 1975—98. Fellow: Am. Acad. Orthopaedic Surgeons; mem.: AMA, Am. Coll. Sports Medicine, Am. Med. Soc., Pa. Med. Soc., N.J. Med. Soc., Pa. Orthopaedic Soc., N.J. Orthopaedic Soc. Avocations: running, music. Office: Andover Orthop Surgery 280 Newton-Sparta Rd Newton NJ 07860 Home: 59 Underrock Rd Sparta NJ 07871 Office Phone: 973-579-7443.

SCALES, JOHN THOMAS, state official; b. Cambridge, Mass., July 5, 1935; s. Frank and Louise Adelaide (Gifford) S. Cert.-qualified law libr. Libr. clk. Harvard U. Law Sch. Libr., Cambridge, Mass., 1955-58, Assn. Bar City N.Y., N.Y.C., 1958-60, NYU Sch. Law, N.Y.C., 1960-61; law libr. Paul, Weiss, Rifkind, Wharton & Garrison, N.Y.C., 1961-69, Kelley, Drye & Warren, N.Y.C., 1969-71; editl. asst. N.J. Law Jour., Newark, 1971; reference libr. Seton Hall U., Law Sch. Libr., Newark, 1971; asst. law libr. Essex County Law Libr., Newark, 1972-80; tech. asst. legal activities State N.J. Bd. Pub. Utilities, Newark, 1981—. Roman Catholic. Avocations: opera, professional sports, public affairs. Home: 628 Arnold Ave Point Pleasant Beach NJ 08742-2531 Office: Bd Pub Utilities State NJ 2 Gateway Ctr Newark NJ 07102-5003 E-mail: john.scales@bpu.state.nj.us.

SCALES, ROBERT H., JR., retired army officer; b. Gainesville, Fla., Aug. 5, 1944; m. Diana Weiss; children: Maria, Monica. BS, U.S. Mil. Acad., 1966; MS, PhD in History, Duke U. Commd. 2d lt. U.S. Army, 1966, advanced through grades to maj. gen.; dep. chief staff for base ops./dep. chief staff for doctrine Tng. and Doctrine Command, Ft. Monroe, Va., 60 1997; comdr. U.S. Army War Coll., Carlisle Barracks, Pa., 1997—2000; pres., CEO Walden Univ., 2000—02; sr. v.p. Sylvan Learning Sys., 2002—. Prin. author: Certain Victory: The U.S. Army in the Gulf War, 1993, Firepower in Limited War, 1995, Yellow Smoke: The Future of Land Warfare for America's Military, 2003. Decorated DSM, Silver Star, Legion of Merit with 4 oakleaf clusters, Bronze Star medl, Air medal, others. Office: Sylvan Learning Sys 1001 Fleet St Baltimore MD 21202

SCALES, WILLIAM CLINTON, SR., minister, small business owner; b. Charleston, W.Va., July 2, 1915; s. Edward F. and Zephyr Ivory Scales; m. Myra Elizabeth Mills, Mar. 7, 1934; 1 child, William Clinton Jr. Co-owner M. and S. Shoe Repair Co., Charleston, W.Va., 1936; pres. Scales Delicious Potato Chip Co., Cleve., 1938—41, Hal'Le-Lu'Jah Records Co., Cleve., 1941—45; min. Allegheny Conf. Seventh Day Adventist Ch., Pine Forge, Pa., 1945—81; founder, owner Real Truth Assoc. Inc., 1981—. Author: (book) Born to Win Souls, 1996, co-author various religious tracts, Bible lessons, manuals. Recipient Soulwinning Super Star award, Gen. Conf. Ministerial Assoc., 2001. Home: 3625 Shandwick Pl Birmingham AL 35242 Office: Real Truth Assoc Inc PO Box 381824 Birmingham AL 35242 E-mail: R.L.Truth@aol.com.

SCALETTA, PHILLIP JASPER, lawyer, educator; b. Sioux City, Iowa, Aug. 20, 1925; s. Phillip and Louise (Pelmulder) Scaletta; m. Helen M. Beedle; children: Phillip R., Cheryl D. Kesler. BS, Morningside Coll., Sioux City, Iowa, 1948; JD, U. Iowa, 1950. Bar: Iowa 1950, U.S. Dist. Ct. Iowa 1950, Ind., U.S. Supreme Ct. 1968. Ptnr. McKnight and Scaletta, Sioux City, Iowa, 1950—51; field rep. Farmers Ins. Group, 1951—54, sr. liability examiner Aurora, Ill., 1954—60, br. claims mgr. Ft. Wayne, Ind., 1960—66; prof. Purdue U., West Lafayette, 1966—. Dir. profl. masters programs Krannert Grad. Sch. of Mgmt. Purdue U., 1987—90; of counsel Mayfield & Brooks Attys. at Law, 1967—; arbitrator Panel of Arbitrators Am. Arbitration Assn. Co-author: Bus. Law and Regulatory Environments, 5th edit., 1996, Bus. Law Workbook, 5th edit., 1996, Foundations of Bus. Law and Legal Environment, 1986, 1997, Student Workbook and Study Guide, 1986, 1997; contbr. numerous articles to profl. jours. Mem. Ind. Gov.'s Commn. Individual Privacy, 1975. Recipient Best Tchr. of Yr. award, Standard Oil Ind. Found., 1972, Outstanding Tchr. award, Purdue U. Alumni Assn., 1974, Most Effective Tchr. award, Krannert Grad. Sch. Mgmt. Purdue U., 1991. Mem.: Midwest Bus. Adminstrn. Assn., Tri State Bus. Law Assn. (past pres.), Tippecanoe County Bar Assn., Am. Bus. Law Assn. (pres., Sr. Faculty Excellence award 1989), Beta Gamma Sigma (bd. govs.). Office: Purdue U 511 Krannert Bldg West Lafayette IN 47907 E-mail: scaletta@mgmt.purdue.edu.

SCALETTA, PHILLIP RALPH, III, lawyer; b. Iowa City, Iowa, Dec. 18, 1949; s. Phillip Jasper and Helen M. (Beedle) S.; m. Karen Lynn Scaletta, May 13, 1973; children: Phillip, Anthony, Alexander. BSIM, MS, Purdue U., 1972; JD, Ind. U., 1975. Bar: Ind. 1975, U.S. Dist. Ct. Ind. 1975, Ill. 1993. Assoc. Ice Miller Donadio & Ryan, Indpls., 1975-81, ptnr., 1981—. Contbr. articles to profl. jours. Chmn. Ind. Continuing Legal Edn. Found., Indpls., 1989; mem. Environ. Quality Control Water Com., 1988-98. Mem. Ind. Bar Assn., Indpls. Bar Assn., Def. Rsch. Inst., Internat. Assn. Def. Counsel, Gyro Club Indpls. (v.p. 1992-93, pres. 1993-94, bd. dirs. 1990—). Avocations: golf, skiing, tennis. Home: 7256 Tuliptree Trl Indianapolis IN 46256-2136 Office: Ice Miller 1 American Sq Indianapolis IN 46282-0020 Office Phone: 317-236-2330.

SCALETTAR, ELLEN, state legislator; b. N.Y.C. BA cum laude, CCNY; JD, U. Md. Hearing officer City of Woodbridge; mem. Conn. Ho. of Reps., Hartford, 1993-98; asst. treas. govtl., corp., and cmty. rels. Hartford, Conn., 1999—. Office: Office of the Treas 55 Elm St Hartford CT 06106-1746

SCALIA, ANTONIN, judge; b. Trenton, N.J., Mar. 11, 1936; s. S. Eugene and Catherine Louise (Panaro) Scalia; m. Maureen McCarthy, Sept. 10, 1960; children: Ann Forrest, Eugene, John Francis, Catherine Elisabeth, Mary Clare, Paul David, Matthew, Christopher James, Margaret Jane. AB, Georgetown U., 1957; student, U. Fribourg, Switzerland, 1955—56; LLB, Harvard U., 1960. Bar: Ohio 1962, Va. 1970. Assoc. Jones Day Cockley & Reavis, Cleve., 1961—67; assoc. prof. U. Va. Law Sch., 1967—70, prof., 1970—74; gen. counsel Office Telecomm. Policy, Exec. Office of Pres., 1971—72; chmn. Adminstrv. Conf. U.S., Washington, 1972—74; asst. atty. gen. U.S. Office Legal Counsel, Justice Dept., 1974—77; prof. law U. Chgo., 1977—82; judge U.S. Ct. Appeals (D.C. cir.), 1982—86; justice U.S. Supreme Ct., Washington, 1986—. Vis. prof. Georgetown Law Ctr., 1977, Stanford Law Sch., 1980—81; vis. scholar Am. Enterprise Inst., 1977. Editor: Regulation mag., 1979—82. Fellow Sheldon fellow, Harvard U., 1960—61. Office: US Supreme Ct Supreme Ct Bldg 1 First St NE Washington DC 20543-0001

SCALICE, JOHN A. nuclear energy executive; BS in Mech. Engring., Poly. Inst. Bklyn., 1970; MS in Nuclear Engring., Poly. Inst. N.Y., 1979. Lic. sr. reactor operator. From startup engr. to plant mgr. Shoreham Nuclear Power Sta., L.I. Lighting Co.; plant mgr. Watts Bar Nuclear Plant, TVA, Spring City, 1989-91, plant mgr. Browns Ferry Nuclear Plant, Athens, Ala., 1991-93, site v.p. Watts Bar Nuclear Plant, 1993-98; acting chief nuclear officer TVA Nuclear, Chattanooga, 1998, chief nuclear officer, exec. v.p., 1998—. Office: TVA Nuclear 1101 Market St Chattanooga TN 37402-2801 Fax: 423-751-8686.

SCALLEN, THOMAS KAINE, broadcast executive; b. Mpls., Aug. 14, 1925; s. Raymond A. and Lenore (Kaine) S.; m. Bille Jo Brice; children by previous marriage: Thomas, Sheila, Patrick, Eileen, Timothy and Maureen (twins). BA, St. Thomas Coll., 1949; JD, U. Denver, 1950. Bar: Minn. Asst. atty. gen. State of Minn., Mpls., 1950-55; sole practice Mpls., 1955-57; pres. Med. Investment Corp., Mpls., 1957—, Internat. Broadcasting Corp., Mpls., 1977—; owner Harlem Globetrotters. Pres., exec. producer Ice Capades; chmn. bd. dirs. Century Park Pictures Corp., Los Angeles, chmn. bd. dirs. Blaine-Thompson Co., Inc., N.Y.C; chmn. Apache Plastics, Inc., Stockton, Calif. Served with AUS. Mem. World Pres. Orgn., Minn. Club, Calhoun Beach Club, L.A. Athletic Club. Clubs: University (St. Paul, Mpls.), Rochester (Minn.) Golf and Country, Edina (Minn.) Country, Athletic (Mpls.). Home: Heron Cove Windham NH 03087 Office: Internat Broadcasting Corp 80 S 8th St Ste 4701 Minneapolis MN 55402-2207

SCALLY, MARK, diversified financial services company executive; b. Jan. 11, 1947; BBA, U of Iowa. CPA, Calif. From mem. staff to chmn. bd., mng. ptnr. McGladrey & Pullen, LLP, Bloomington, Minn., 1971-84, chmn. bd., mng. ptnr., 1984—. Office: McGladrey & Pullen LLP 3600 W 80 St Ste 500 Davenport IA 52801-1803

SCALZA, MARGARET T. publishing executive; b. Jersey City, May 27, 1936; d. Louis Patrick and Josephine M. (Cleary) Scalza; m. David Jenkins, Sept. 30, 1951 (div. 1962); children: Alison Brittain, Cynthia Higgins, Ann Jenkins Tunis Owner Towne House Restaurant, Hackettstown, N.J., 1963-65; pres. Kinsley Assocs., Inc., Hackettstown, N.J., 1966—. Pub. purchasing guides, sch. directories, N.J., N.Y., Calif., Ill. Co-chmn. Northwestern N.J. divsn. U.S. Postal Customer Coun., 1978—; trustee Trnanquility United Meth. Ch. Mem. NAFE, Nat. Assn. Sch. Bus. Ofcls., North Ctrl. Jersy Assn. Realtors, Hackettstown Trade Assn. (sec.-treas., bd. dirs. 1963). Republican. Avocations: cooking, sewing, reading, flower arranging, crabbing. Home: 9 House Wren Hackettstown NJ 07840-2815 Office: 4 Woodward Terr Hackettstown NJ 07840-4602

SCANDARY, E. JANE, special education educator, consultant; b. Saginaw, Mich., Sept. 12, 1923; d. Leonard William and Reva Charlotte (Smith) Leipprandt; m. Theodore John Scandary; children: John S., Robert G. BA, Mich. State U., East Lansing, 1945, EdS, 1963, PhD, 1968; MEd, Wayne State U., 1951. Cert. secondary and spl. edn. tchr., Mich. Therapist speech and lang. Ann J. Kellogg Sch., Battle Creek, Mich., 1945-47; supr. speech therapy programs Wayne County Schs., Detroit, 1948-52; supr. programs for phys., hearing and visually impaired Ingham Intermediate Schs., Mason, Mich., 1960-78; spl. edn. cons. Mich. Dept. of Edn., Lansing, 1978-87, Livingston Intermediate Schs., Howell, Mich., 1987—. Rsch. assoc. Mich. State U., East Lansing, 1965-66, adj. prof., 1969-75, 81-82; mem. adv. com. China-U.S. Sci. Exchange Program Spl. Edn.; guest lectr. seminars spl. edn. Australia, Eng., Iran, Israel, Aruba, Germany, Scotland. Editor Chronicles newsletter, 1987—; contbr. articles to profl. jours. Vol. Mich. Hist. Mus., 1995—, Meals-on-Wheels, 1998-2001, Salvation Army, 2000—; chair futures com. Mich. Dept. Edn., 1992, editor, chair Task Force Futuresin Spl. Edn. 2000 AD and Beyond, 1992; bd. dirs. Delta Dist. Libr., 1998—. 1st Chance Early Childhood grantee, 1972-78; recipient Resolution of Tribute Mich. State Senate, 1986, 3d Pl. award Mid-Mich. Spring Art Show, 1998; Scandary award for outstanding contbrs. early childhood edn. established in her name, 1990. Mem. Nat. Coun. Exceptional Children (field editor 1976-86, pres. div. physically handicapped 1982-83), Mid-Mich. Art Guild, World Future Soc., Capitol Area Quilt Guild. Avocations: painting, writing, reading, creative sewing.

SCANDURA, JOSEPH MICHAEL, cognitive scientist, software engineer; b. Bay Shore, N.Y., Apr. 29, 1932; s. Joseph and Lucy S.; m. Alice Baker, Aug. 13, 1960; children: Jeanne, Janette, Joseph, Julie. AB, U. Mich., 1953, MA, 1955; PhD, Syracuse U., 1962; postdoctoral, Stanford U., summer 1964, 68-69, U. Calif.-Berkeley, summer 1968, MIT, summer 1972; postgrad., U. Kiel, W.Ger., 1975, Inst. Edl. Tech., Italy, summer 1978. Tchr. math., sci. White Plains, Bay Shore, 1953-56; instr. math., head wrestling coach Syracuse U., N.Y., 1956-63; asst. prof. edn., math. SUNY-Buffalo, 1963-64; research asst. prof. math. edn. Fla. State U., Tallahassee, 1964-66; dir. instructional systems, structural learning U. Pa., Phila., 1966-96; Fulbright prof. U. Koblenz & Dresden, 1998-99. Founder, chmn. Intelligent Micro Systems, Narberth, Pa., 1978-2002; chmn. bd. sci. advisors MERGE Rsch. Inst., 1973-2002; prin. investigator NIST Advanced Tech. Program Project on Automating Supply Chain, 19677—; cons. U.S. Office Edn., NSF, NAS, Tex. Instruments, Borg-Warner, U.S. Army; organizer, lectr., participant profl. confs., 1963—; dir. NATO Advanced Study Inst. on Structural Process Theories of Complex Human Behavior, 1977; coach undefeated Ea. Intercollegiate Wrestling Championship Team, 1963. Author: Mathematics - Concrete Behavioral Foundations, 1971, (with others) An Algorithmic Approach to Mathematics - Concrete Behavioral Foundations, 1971, Structural Learning I - Theory and Research, 1973, Problem Solving - A Structural Process Approach with Instructional Implications, 1977, (with A.B. Scandura) Structural Learning and Concrete Operations - An Approach to Piagetian Conservation, 1980, Cognitive Approach to Software Development, 1988, Prodoc (comprehensive suite of software devel. and maintenance tools), 1989, Cognitive Approach to Software Engineering and Re-engineering, 1991, ongoing projects; Flexys-customizable reengineering automation, Autobuilder-automated specification and implementation component based software while guaranteeing correctness, intelligent tutor authoring of devel. sys. model IT and tutor IT, 1992—, NATO Advanced Study Inst., 1993, Automated Software Conversions and Re-engineering, 1993; contbr. 200 articles to profl. jours.; editor: Research in Mathematics Education, 1967, Structural Learning II - Issues and Approaches, 1976, (with C.J. Brainerd) Structural Process Models of Complex Human Behavior, 1978; developer, producer numerous computer-based instructional systems and software devel. systems; 4 software patents. Recipient Renssalaer award, 1949, Bausch and Lomb award, 1949, Nat. AAU Wrestling Champion

and Outstanding Wrestler award, 1955; Fulbright scholar, 1975-76, 1998-99; U.S. Office Edn. fellow, 1978-79. Fellow: APA (chmn. E.L. Thorndike award com. 1974—79), Structural Learning Soc. (sr.; chmn. 1969—80, editor in chief Jour. Structural Learning 1976—90, chmn. 1985—88, Jour. Structural Learning and Intelligent Systems 1990—2001, chmn. 1995—, founder, sr. advisor Tech., Instr., Cognition & Learning 2002—); mem.: IEEE, AAUP, Univ. Profs. for Acad. Order, Psychonomic Soc., Math. Assn. Am., Nat. Coun. Tchrs. Math. (past fed. funds com. chmn.), Am. Ednl. Rsch. Assn. (chmn. Structural Learning and Tech., Instrn., Cognition and Learning), Assn. Computing Machinery, Phi Delta Kappa, Phi Eta Sigma, Phi Kappa Phi. Home: 1249 Greentree Ln Narberth PA 19072-1219 Office: U Pa Instructional Systems Philadelphia PA 19104 E-mail: scandura@scandura.com. *Accomodation to -- as well as leadership of -- groups, institutions and/or societies is an essential ingredient of success in most walks of life. There are circumstances, however, which require inner direction, whether developing a new scientific paradigm or standing firm against political pressures. Although vindication is rarely complete and often delayed, following one's best instincts yields its own rewards— perhaps the satisfaction of ultimately being proven right but more often simply knowing one did what had to be done.*

SCANDURA, TERESA ANNE, management educator; b. Cin., Aug. 22, 1960; d. Alfred Joseph and Nevilyn Mae (Zobjeck) S. BBA, U. Cin., 1982, PhD, 1988. Data processing asst. U.S. EPA, Cin., 1980-82; intern GE Aircraft Engines, Cin., 1982; research, teaching asst. dept. mgmt. U. Cin., 1983-88; research asst. Nagoya (Japan) U., 1983-88; asst. prof. mgmt. dept. mgmt. U. Miami, Coral Gables, Fla., 1990—, asst. prof., 1990-93; assoc. prof., 1993—. Jour. reviewer; contbr. articles to profl. jours., chpts. to books. Bd. Big Bros./Big Sisters Greater Cin., Inc., 1987-88, United Way Miami, 1991-92, Rotary Internat. Exch., Sister Cities Program, Miami. Dissertation fellowship Am. Assembly Collegiate Schs., Bus., St. Louis, 1988, univ. dean. U. Cin., 1988, rsch. com. grantee U. Ky., 1989; U.S. Dept. Labor rsch. grantee. Mem.: APA, So. Mgmt. Assn. (best paper award com., track chair, pres.), Acad. Mgmt., Nat. Acad. Mgmt. (reviewer, jr. mem. nominating com. 1983—, careers divsn. exec. com., divsn. chair rsch. methods divsn., dissent award com.), Beta Gamma Sigma. Roman Catholic. Avocations: travel, exercise, music. Office: U Miami Coll Bus Adminstrn Dept of Mgmt 345C BE Bldg Coral Gables FL 33124 Office Phone: 305-284-3746.

SCANGOS, GEORGE A. medical company executive; BA in Biology, Cornell U.; PhD in Microbiology, U. Mass. Postdoctoral fellow Yale U., New Haven; faculty Johns Hopkins U., Balt.; pres. biotech. Bayer Corp., 1993—96; pres., CEO, dir. Exelixis, Inc., South San Francisco, Calif., 1996—. Bd. dirs. Onyx Pharms., Inc. Office: Exelixis Inc 170 Harbor Way South San Francisco CA 94083

SCANLAN, JAMES PATRICK, philosophy and Slavic studies educator; b. Chgo., Feb. 22, 1927; s. Gilbert Francis and Helen (Meyers) S.; m. Marilyn A. Morrison, June 12, 1948. BA, U. Chgo., 1948, MA, 1950, PhD, 1956. Research fellow Inst. Philos. Research, San Francisco, 1953-55; instr. Case Inst. Tech., Cleve., 1955-56; from instr. to assoc. prof. Goucher Coll., Balt., 1956-68; prof., dir. Slavic Ctr. U. Kans., Lawrence, 1968-70; prof. Ohio State U., Columbus, 1971-91, dir. Slavic Ctr., 1988-91, prof. emeritus, 1992—. Vis. rsch. scholar Moscow State U., 1964-65, 69, 98, Acad. Scis. USSR, Moscow, 1978, 93, Russian State U. for the Humanities, 1995; fgn. vis. fellow Slavic Rsch. Ctr., Hokkaido U., Sapporo, Japan, 1987-88. Author: Marxism in the USSR, 1985, Dostoevsky the Thinker, 2002; editor: Historical Letters by Peter Lavrov, 1967, Soviet Studies in Philosophy, 1987—92, Russian Studies in Philosophy, 1992—97, Technology, Culture and Development: The Experience of the Soviet Model, 1992, Russian Thought After Communism, 1994; co-editor: Russian Philosophy, 1965, Marxism and Religion in Eastern Europe, 1976. Served with USMC, 1945-46. Woodrow Wilson Internat. Ctr. fellow, 1982; recipient Translation award Nat. Translation Ctr., 1967, Faculty Rsch. award Fulbright-Hays, 1982-83. Mem. Am. Philos. Assn., Am. Assn. Advancement Slavic Studies, Phi Beta Kappa. Home: 1000 Urlin Ave Apt 206 Columbus OH 43212-3324 Personal E-mail: scanlan.1@osu.edu.

SCANLAN, JOHN DOUGLAS, foreign service officer, former ambassador; b. Thief River Falls, Minn., Dec. 20, 1927; s. Paul Douglas and Ruby (Bennes) S.; m. Margaret Anne Calvi; children: Kathleen, Michael, Malia, John. BA, U. Minn., 1952, MA in Russian Studies, 1955. Instr. U. Minn., 1955; Soviet research analyst U.S. Dept. State, Washington, 1956-58; third sec. Am. Embassy, Moscow, 1958-60, cultural attache Warsaw, 1961-65, second sec. Montevideo, 1966-67; prin. officer Am. Consulate, Poznan, Poland, 1967-69; sr. rep. to U.S. Dept. Defense, Washington, 1969-71; desk officer U.S.-Soviet bilateral relations, 1971-73; polit. counselor Am. Embassy, Warsaw, 1973-75; mem. state exec. seminar Washington, 1975-76; spl. asst. to Dir. Gen. of Fgn. Service, 1976-77; dep. dir. for Europe, USIA, 1977-79; dep. chief Mission in Belgrade, Yugoslavia, 1979-81; dep. asst. sec. of state for European affairs, 1981-82; fgn. affairs fellow Fletcher Sch. Law and Diplomacy, Tufts U., 1983-84; chmn. U.S. del. to Conf. on Security and Coop. in Europe, Cultural Forum Preparatory Conf., Budapest, 1984; amb. to Yugoslavia, Am. Embassy, Belgrade, 1985-89; dep. comdt. U.S. Army War Coll., Carlisle Barracks, Pa., 1989-91. Mem. exec. bd. Project on Ethnic Rels.; mem. Ctr. Strategic and Internat. Studies U.S.-European-Poland Action Commn. Mem. Planning Commn., Falls Church, Va., 1972-73, City Council, 1975-79. Recipient Presdl. Meritorious Service award for Diplomacy, 1984. E-mail: ambscan@earthlink.net.

SCANLAN, MICHAEL, priest, academic administrator; b. Far Rockaway, N.Y., Dec. 1, 1931; s. Vincent Michael and Marjorie (O'Keefe) S. BA, Williams Coll., 1953; JD, Harvard U., 1956; MDiv, St. Francis Sem., Loretto, Pa., 1975; LittD (hon.), Coll. Steubenville, 1972; LLD (hon.), Williams Coll., Williamstown, Mass., 1978; PdD (hon.), St. Francis Coll., Loretto, Pa., 1987; STM, 3d Order Regular of St Francis, 1996. Ordained priest Roman Catholic Ch., 1964; Cross Pro Ecclesia et Pontifice, 1990. Acting dean Coll. Steubenville, Ohio, 1964-66, dean, 1966-69; rector pres. St. Francis Major Sem., Loretto, Pa., 1969-74; pres. Franciscan U. Steubenville, 1974-2000, chancellor, 2000—. Pres. (FIRE) Cath. Alliance for Faith, Intercession, Repentence and Evangelism, 1984—. Author: The Power in Penance, 1972, Inner Healing, 1974, A Portion of My Spirit, 1979, The San Damiano Cross, 1983, Turn to the Lord-A Call to Repentance, 1989, The Truth About Trouble, 1989, What Does God Want: A Practical Guide to Making Decisions, 1996, (with James Manney) Let the Fire Fall, 1997, The Holy Spirit: Holy Desire, 1998, Rosary Companion with Luminous Mysteries, 2002; chmn. editl. bd. New Covenant mag., 1985-92. Mem. Diocese of Steubenville Ecumenical Commn., 1964-69; bd. dirs. Rumor Control Ctr., Steubenville, 1968-69, C. of C., Steubenville, 1976-79; bd. trustees St. Francis Prep. Sch., Spring Grove, Pa., 1969-74; vice-chmn., bd. trustees St. Francis Coll., Loretto, Pa., 1969-74; trustee United Way, Steubenville, 1975-80; chmn. nat. svc. com. Cath. Charismatic Renewal, 1975-78. Staff judge adv. USAF, 1956-57. Named Sacrae Theologiae Magister Third Order Regular St Francis, 1996. Roman Catholic. Avocations: tennis, golf, skiing. Office: Franciscan U Office of Chancellor 1235 University Blvd Steubenville OH 43952-1796 Office Phone: 740-283-6466. *If you are going to change something, you've got to live on vision, before you live on reality. You have to be so inspired by the vision, that you keep telling everybody until it gets in them, and they start living it with you.*

SCANLAN, THOMAS CLEARY, publishing executive, editor; b. Birmingham, Mich., May 18, 1957; s. Thomas Matthew and Emily (Cleary) S.; m. Sally Sachs, June 20, 1981; children: Bridget C., Thomas M., Patrick J. BS, St. Louis U., 1979. Salesman Walter Heller Co., Chgo., 1979-82; pub., editor Surplus Record, Inc., Chgo., 1982—. Office: Surplus Record Inc 20 N Wacker Dr Chicago IL 60606-2806

SCANLAN, THOMAS JOSEPH, college president, educator; b. NYC, Mar. 5, 1945; s. Thomas Joseph and Anna Marie (Schmitt) S. BA in Physics, Cath. U. Am., 1967; MA in Math., NYU, 1972; PhD in Bus. Adminstrn., Columbia U., 1978; LLD (hon.), Coll. Mt. St. Vincent. Prin. Queen of Peace HS, North Arlington, NJ, 1972-75; dir. fin., edn. NY Province, Bros. of Christian Sch., Lincroft, NJ, 1978-81; vice chancellor Bethlehem U., Israel, 1981-87; pres. Manhattan Coll., Bronx, NY, 1987—. Bd. dirs. Am. Coun. on Edn. Trustee Commn. on Ind. Colls. and Univs., 2002, Assn. Cath. Colls. and Univs., 1994—. Recipient Pro Ecclesia et Pontifice medal, Pope John Paul II, Vatican City, 1986. Mem. Bros. of Christian Schs., Am. Coun. Edn., Assn. Cath. Colls. and Univs. (trustee 1994—), Assn. Am. Colls., Nat. Cath. Edn. Assn., Nat. Asns. Ind. Colls. and Univs., Nat. Collegiate Athletic Assn. (exec. com. and divsn. 1), Metro Atlantic Athletic Assn., Equestrian Order of the Holy Sepulchre of Jerusalem, Phi Beta Kappa, Beta Gamma Sigma, Phi Beta Kappa Fellows. Avocations: golf, reading, movies. Office: Manhattan Coll Office of Pres Manhattan Coll Pky Bronx NY 10471-3913 Office Phone: 718-862-7301. Business E-Mail: thomas.scanlan@manhattan.edu.

SCANLON, CHARLES FRANCIS, retired army officer, defense consultant, writer, publisher; b. Nashville, Jan. 31, 1935; s. Francis James Gordon and Dorothy Rose (Compton) S.; m. Barbara Jean Schoen, Oct. 9, 1954; children: Teri, Brett, Ashlyn, Kellie. BA in Polit. Sci., U. Fla., 1960; grad., Command and Gen. Staff Coll., Ft. Leavenworth, Kans., 1970, Naval War Coll., Newport, R.I., 1977; MA in Am. Studies, U. Hawaii, 1974; postgrad., Pa. State U., 1982, Harvard U., 1984, 92. Commd. 2d lt. U.S. Army, 1960, advanced through grades to maj. gen., 1988; chief collection U.S. Army Europe, Heidelberg, Germany, 1977-78; comdg. officer 66th Mil. Intelligence Brigade, Munich, 1978-80; chief ops. U.S. Army Intelligence and Security Command, Arlington, Va., 1980-82; exec. officer Dept. Army Asst. Chief Staff Intelligence, Washington, 1982-83; dep. commdr. gen. U.S. Army Intelligence and Security Command, Arlington, 1983-85; dir. estimates Def. Intelligence Agy., Washington, 1985-86, dir. attaches, 1986-90; comdg. gen. U.S. Army Intelligence and Security Command, Ft. Belvoir, Va., 1990-93; ret., 1993; pres. Internat. Security Counterintelligence Cons. Svcs., Fairfax Station, Va., 1993—, Satellite Beach, Fla., 1993—99, Melbourne Beach, Fla., 1999—. Decorated Def. D.S.M., Army D.S.M., Nat. Intelligence D.S.M., Legion of Merit with 3 oak leaf clusters, Bronze Star with 2 oak leaf clusters; elected to U.S. Mil. Intelligence Hall of Fame, 1995. Mem. Assn. US Army, Nat. Mil. Intelligence Assn. (pres. 1974-76), 101st Airborne Divsn. Assn., Berlin US Military Vets. Assn., Def. Intelligence Alumni Assn., Sigma Nu. Baptist. Avocations: boating, scuba diving, racquetball, soaring, reading. Office: 3220 River Villa Way Ste 160 Melbourne Beach FL 32951-3039 Home: 3220 River Villa Way Apt 160 Melbourne Beach FL 32951-3039

SCANLON, DOROTHY THERESE, history professor; b. Bridgeport, Conn., Oct. 7, 1928; d. George F. and Mazie (Reardon) Scanlon. AB, U. Pa., 1948, MA, 1949, Boston Coll., 1953; PhD, Boston U., 1956; postdoctoral scholar, Harvard U., 1962—64, postdoctoral scholar, 1972. Tchr. history and Latin Marycliff Acad., Winchester, Mass., 1950—52; tchr. history Girls Latin Sch., Boston, 1952—57; prof. Boston State Coll., 1957—82, Mass. Coll. Art, Boston, 1982—95, prof. emerita, 1995—; lectr. Cape Mus. Fine Arts, Dennis, Mass., 1997—. Author: Instructor's Manual to Accompany Lewis Hanke, Latin America: A Historical REader, 1974; contbr. Biographical Dictionary of Social Welfare, 1986. Recipient Disting. Svc. award, Boston State Coll., 1979, Faculty award of excellence, Mass. Coll. Art, 1985, Faculty Disting. Svc. award, 1987. Mem.: AAUW, AAUP, History of Sci. Soc., Am. Assn. History of Medicine, Am. Studies Assn., Orgn. Am. Historians, Am. Hist. Assn., L.Am. Studies Assn., Pan-Am. Soc., Delta Kappa Gamma, Phi Alpha Theta. Home: 23 Mooring Ln Dennis MA 02638-2321 Office: Mass Coll Art Dept History 621 Huntington Ave Boston MA 02115-5801

SCANLON, JANE CRONIN, mathematics professor; b. N.Y.C., July 17, 1922; d. John Timothy and Janet Smiley (Murphy) Cronin; m. Joseph C. Scanlon, Mar. 5, 1953 (div.); children: Justin, Mary, Anne, Edmund. Student, Highland Park Jr. Coll., 1939-41; BS, Wayne State U., 1943; MA, U. Mich., 1945, PhD, 1949. Mathematician Air Force Cambridge Research Center, 1951-54; instr. Wheaton Coll., Norton, Mass., 1954-55; asst. prof. Poly. Inst. Bklyn., 1957-58, asso. prof., 1958-60, prof., 1960-65; prof. math. Rutgers U., New Brunswick, N.J., 1965-91, prof. emerita, 1991—. Cons. Singer-Kearfott Div., Naval Research Lab. Office Naval Research Fellow Princeton, 1948-49; Horace H. Rockham Postdoctoral fellow U. Mich., 1950-51, Rutgers Research Council fellow, 1968-69, 72-73; NSF vis. professorship for women Courant Inst., NYU, 1984-85. Author: Fixed Points and Topological Degree in Nonlinear Analysis, 1964, Advanced Calculus, 1967, Differential Equations: Introduction and Qualitative Theory, 1980, 2d edit., 1994, Mathematics of Cell Electrophysiology, 1980, Mathematical Aspects of Hodgkin-Huxley Neural Theory, 1987; editor: Analyzing Multiscale Phenomena Using Singular Perturbation Methods, 1999. Mem. Am. Math. Soc., Soc. for Indsl. and Applied Math., Internat. Soc. Chronobiology. Home: 110 Valentine St Highland Park NJ 08904-2106 Office: Rutgers U Dept Math New Brunswick NJ 08903 E-mail: croninscanlon@erols.com.

SCANLON, LAWRENCE EUGENE, English language educator; b. Montclair, N.J., Sept. 12, 1927; s. Leo Dudley and Margaret Gertrude (Kennedy) S.; m. Anne Maxwell Sherrerd, Aug. 23, 1952; children: Lawrence Francis, Neal Patrick, Heidi Anne. BA, Wesleyan U., 1951; MA, Rutgers U., 1952; PhD, Syracuse U., 1958. Asst. prof. English Mount Holyoke Coll., South Hadley, Mass., 1958-63; prof. Hartford (Conn.) Coll. for Women, 1963-92. Author: First Came Commodore Perry, 1969, A Memorial of Ebensee, 1994, The Story He Left Behind Him Paddy the Cope, 1994. Justice of the peace Town of East Granby, Conn., 1970-72; v.p. Capital Region Libr. Coun., Hartford, 1970-74. With U.S. Army, 1945-46. Fulbright grantee, Austria, 1952-53, Japan, 1964-65, West Germany, 1980-81, summer grantee NEH, 1974. Avocations: writing, travel, gardening, investing. Home: 101 Holcomb St East Granby CT 06026-9531

SCANLON, PAT H. lawyer; b. Houma, La., Aug. 4, 1936; s. Leo Joseph and Mary (Ezell) S.; m. Carlene Myers, June 10, 1961; children: Margaret, Pat, Jr., Cissy, John. BS in Geology, La. State U., 1957; LLB with distinction, U. Miss., 1960. Assoc. Satterfield, Shell, Williams & Buford, Jackson, Miss., 1960-62; ptnr. Young, Scanlon & Sessums, Jackson, 1962—95; with Scanlon, Sessums Parker & Dallas PLLC, 1995-2002; with Watkins & Eager PLLC, 2003—; chmn., commnr. Miss. Jud. Performance Commn., Jackson, 1980-83; instr. Jackson Sch. Law, 1963-66; chmn. Miss. Law Inst., Jackson, 1970. Mem. editorial bd. Miss. Law Jour., 1959-60; contbr. articles to profl. jours. Mem. vestry St. James Episcopal Ch., Jackson, 1972-75, 79-82). Served to capt. USAR. Fellow Am. Coll. Trial Lawyers, Internat. Soc. Barristers, Am. Bar Found., Miss. Bar Found. (pres. 1986-87, trustee 1980-83); mem. Miss. Bankruptcy Conf. (pres. 1984-85), Miss. Young Lawyers Assn. (pres. 1969-70), Miss. State Bar Assn. (2d v.p. 1970-71, pres. 1988-89), Hinds County Bar Assn. (pres. 1974-75), Fed. Bar Assn. (pres. Miss. chpt. 1972-73). Office: 2000 Deposit Guaranty Plz Jackson MS 39201

SCANLON, PAUL DAVID, pulmonologist, educator; b. Rochester, Minn., Oct. 31, 1952; s. Paul William and Jane Marie (Blomstrand) Scanlon; m. Margaret Ann Muirhead, Apr. 12, 1975; children: Luke Michael, Kelsey Lynn. BA, U. Minn., 1975; MD, Mayo Med. Sch., Rochester, 1978. Diplomate Internal Medicine, Pulmonary Medicine, Critical Care Medicine. Intern, resident in medicine Johns Hopkins U., Balt., 1978—81; fellow in pulmonary & critical care medicine Harvard U., Boston, 1981—84; assoc. cons. Mayo Clinic, Rochester, 1984, sr. assoc. cons., 1985—87, cons., 1988—. From asst. prof. to assoc. prof. medicine Mayo Med. Sch., 1984—2001, prof., 2001—; med. dir. Mayo Clinic Pulmonary Lab., 1988—, Mayo Pulmonary Svcs., 1991—, Mayo Clinic Pulmonary Clin. Rsch. Ctr., 1994—. Co-author: Interpretation of Pulmonary Functions Tests, 1997, 2d edit., 2003; contbr. articles to profl. jours. Dir. Rochester Montessori Sch. Bd., 1988—91, pres., 1988—89; dir. Rochester Pub. Sch. Bd., 1994—2002, pres., 1997; mem. Rochester Art Ctr. Bd., 1996—2002, chair edn. com., 2000—02; mem. Rochester Civic Music Bd., 2004—. Recipient Creative Initiative award, Com. Urban Design Environment, 2002; Lung Health Study grantee, Nat. Heart Lung & Blood Inst., 1993, 1994, 1997, Clin. Rsch. Network grantee, 2003, Lung Tissue Rsch. Consortium grantee, 2004. Fellow: ACP, Am. Coll. Chest Physicians (chair occupt. and environ. com. 1993—94); mem.: Am. Thoracic Soc. (chair membership com. 2003—). Avocations: bicycling, cross country skiing, art, local history. Office: Mayo Clinic 200 1st St SW Rochester MN 55905

SCANLON, PETER JOSEPH, priest; b. Worcester, Mass., Sept. 2, 1931; s. Peter and Julia (O'Sullivan) Scanlon. AB, STB, St. Mary's Sem. and U., 1953, licentiate in sacred theology, 1957. Ordained priest Roman Cath. Ch., 1957, cert. campus minister. Asst. pastor St. Mary's Parish, Southbridge, Mass., 1957-58; adminstr. St. Patrick's Parish, Rutland, 1958-61; Cath. chaplain Worcester Poly. Inst., 1961—; Bishop's vicar for coll. Roman Cath. Diocese Worcester, 1969—; fire chaplain City of Worcester Fire Dept., 1971—. Diocesan bd. edn. Roman Cath. Diocese Worcester, 1969—; trustee Becker Coll., Worcester, 1971—2002, Aquinas Assn. Phi Kappa Theta, Worcester, 1975—2000. Recipient award to hon. alumnus, Worcester Poly. Inst., 1985, award, Becker Coll., 1990. Mem.: Cath. Campus Ministry Assn., Nat. Assn. Diocesan Dirs. Campus Ministry. Home: 44 Westwood Rd Shrewsbury MA 01545 Office: Campus Ministry Diocese Worcester PO Box 903 Worcester MA 01613-0903 Office Phone: 508-757-6097. Business E-Mail: priest@wpi.edu. E-mail: priest@wpi.edu.

SCANLON, PETER REDMOND, accountant; b. N.Y.C., Feb. 18, 1931; s. John Thomas and Loretta Dolores (Ryan) S.; m. Mary Jane E. Condon, Mar. 7, 1953; children: Peter, Barbara, Mark (dec.), Brian, Janet. BBA in Acctg., Iona Coll., 1952, LLD (hon.), 1992. CPA, N.Y. Mem. profl. staff Coopers & Lybrand, N.Y.C., 1956-66, ptnr., 1966-91, vice chmn., 1976-82, chmn., chief exec. officer, 1982-91, ret. chmn., 1991—. Hon. ptnr. N.Y.C. Partnership, 1991. Mem. fin. coun. Diocese of Palm Beach, 1995-2002. Lt. USN, 1952-56. Decorated Knight of Malta, Knight Holy Sepulchre; recipient Arthur A. Loftus award Iona Coll., 1974, Trustee award, 1990, Crain's N.Y. All Star award, 1990, Best in Class award Conf. Bd. Youth Edn., 1991. Mem.: AICPA, NY State Soc. CPAs, Jupiter Inlet Beach Club, NY Athletic Club. Roman Catholic.

SCANLON, ROSEMARY, economist; b. Dec. 25, 1939; d. Donald Angus and Mary Agnes (MacDonald) MacLellan; m. Michael Scanlon, Apr. 24, 1965 (div. 1979); children: Sean Donald, Jennifer. AB, St. Francis Xavier U., N.S., 1959; MA (Ford Found. scholar), U. New Brunswick, 1960; PMD, Harvard Bus. Sch., 1981. Instr. econs. Coll. of William and Mary, Williamsburg, Va., 1960—63; asst. prof. Old Dominion U., Norfolk, Va., 1963—65; econ. analyst Port Authority of NY and NJ, 1969—93, sr. economist for regional rsch., 1977—80, mgr. econ. devel. planning, 1980—83, chief economist, 1983—. Asst. dir. Planning and Devel. Dept., 1985; apptd. dep. state comtr., NYC, 1993—97; vis. rsch. fellow London Sch. Econ., 1997—2000; cons. urban and regional econs., 2000—; assoc. prof. econs. Real Estate Inst. NYU, 2001—; bd. dirs. Emera, Inc. Author (with others): Cities in a Global Society, 1989; author: The Arts as an Industry, 1993, The Regional Economy, 1993; editor: (project) The London-NY Study, 2000; author: Bldg. for Growth, A development strategy, 2002. Recipient Outstanding Achievement award, Exec. Dirs. award, 1987, de Luca award for lifetime achievement in econ. devel., 1999, Disting. Alumnus award, St. Francis Xavier U., 2001. Mem.: Nat. Coun. for Urban Econ. Devel. (bd. dirs. 1982—88). Home: 10 Clinton St Apt 9T Brooklyn NY 11201-2710 Office: 11 W 42nd St New York NY 10036 Office Phone: 212-922-3250. E-mail: rosemaryscanlon@msn.com.

SCANLON, TERRENCE MAURICE, public policy foundation administrator; b. Milw., May 1, 1939; s. Maurice John and Anne (Hayes) S.; m. Judy Ball, June 14, 1969; children: Michael Mansfield, Justin Ball, Brendan Hayes. BS, Villanova U., 1961. Staff asst. The White House, Washington, 1963-67; with SBA, Washington, 1967-69, Dept. of Commerce, Washington, 1969-83, mem. office Minority Bus. Enterprise, 1969-80, with Internat. Trade Adminstrn., 1980-81, with Minority Bus. Devel. Agy., 1981-83; mem. Consumer Product Safety Commn., Washington, 1983-89, vice chmn., 1983-84, chmn., 1985, 86-89; v.p., treas. The Heritage Found., Washington, 1989-91, v.p. corp. rels., 1991-94; chmn., pres. Capital Rsch. Ctr., Washington, 1994—. Am. Polit. Sci. Assn. Congl. fellow, 1967-68 Mem. Sovereign Mil. Order of Malta, University Club. Home: 4510 Dexter St NW Washington DC 20007-1115 Office: Capital Rsch Ctr 1513 16th St NW Washington DC 20036-1401 E-mail: tscanlon@capitalresearch.org.

SCANNELL, HERB, broadcast executive; m. Sarah Scannell; 1 child, Caroline. BA in English and History, Boston Coll. Dir. program promotion Showtime/The Movie Channel; dir. programming Nickelodeon, N.Y.C., 1988—89, v.p. programming, 1989—90, sr. v.p. programming; exec. v.p. Nickelodeon/Nick at Nite Network and U.S. TV; pres. Nickelodeon/Nick at Nite/Nick at Nite's TV Land, 1996—. Office: NICKELODEON 1515 Broadway Rm 3882 New York NY 10036-8901

SCANNELL, JOHN R. publishing consultant; b. Dobbs Ferry, N.Y., Dec. 23, 1947; s. John Joseph and Veronica Rose (Hannigan) S.; m. Faye Naomi Snyder, July 11, 1969; children: Michelle, Amanda, Rebecca, Benjamin. BS in Edn., Kutztown (Pa.) State Coll., 1965; MA in Speech, U. Wash., 1974. Tchr. English Nazareth (Pa.) Sch. Dist., 1969-70, Upper Dauphin Sch. Dist., Elizabethville, Pa., 1970-72; tchr. Bellevue (Wash.) Sch. Dist., 1974-85; sales rep. Macmillan Pub., Seattle, 1985-88; sr. nat. cons. social studies and lang. arts McGraw-Hill Pub., Bothell, Wash., 1988—. Pres., Our Lady of Lake Parents Club, Seattle, 1981-83; dir. Our Lady of Lake Players, Seattle, 1980, 82, 84. Recipient Wilma Grimes award U. Wash., 1972; named DECA Tchr. of Yr., Nazareth H.S., 1970. Mem. Nat. Coun. Tchrs. English, Nat. Coun. for Social Studies, Nat. Hist. Soc. Democrat. Roman Catholic. Avocations: woodworking, reading. Home: 22627 7th Dr SE Bothell WA 98021-8274

SCANNELL, WILLIAM EDWARD, aerospace company executive, consultant, psychologist; b. Muscatine, Iowa, Nov. 11, 1934; s. Mark Edward and Catharine Pearson (Fowler) S.; m. Barbara Ann Hoemann, Nov. 23, 1957; children: Cynthia Kay, Mark Edward, David Jerome, Terri Lynn, Stephen Patrick. BA in Gen. Edn., U. Nebr., 1961; BS in Engring., Ariz. State U., 1966; MS in Systems Engring., So. Meth. U., 1969; postgrad. in law, Western State U., 1977, 81-82; PhD, U.S. Internat. U., 1991. Commd. 2d lt. USAF, 1956, advanced through grades to lt. col., 1972; B-47 navigator-bombardier 98th Bomb Wing, Lincoln Air Force Base, Nebr., 1956-63; with Air Force Inst. of Tech., 1963-65, 68-69; chief mgmt. engring. team RAF Bentwaters, England, 1965-68; forward air contr. 20th Tactical Air Support Squadron, Danang, Vietnam, 1970-71; program mgr. Hdqrs. USAF, Washington, 1971-74, staff asst. Office of Sec. Def., 1974-75, ret., 1975; account exec. Merrill Lynch, San Diego, 1975-77; program engring. chief Gen. Dynamics, San Diego, 1977-79, engring. chief, 1979-80, program mgr., 1980-83; mgr. integrated logistics support Northrop Corp., Hawthorne, Calif., 1984-88, mgr. B-2 program planning and scheduling Pico Rivera, Calif., 1988-91; pres. Scannell and Assocs., Borrego Springs, Calif., 1991—. Author: The Nature of Motivation in Aerospace Executives, 1991. Cpl. USNG, 1952-54. Decorated DFC with three oak leaf clusters, Air medal with 11 oak leaf clusters, Vietnamese Cross Gallantry with palm, Meritorious Svc. medal. Mem. APA, Psi Chi. Republican. Roman Catholic. Home: 6130 Center Point Rd Fredericksburg TX 78624 E-mail: william@scannell.net.

SCANTLAN, GEORGE WILLIAM, minister; b. Leasburg, Mo., Dec. 17, 1936; s. George Albert and Nina May (Kitchen) Scantlan; m. Betty Sue Pinnell, Oct. 20, 1956; children: Steven William, Brenda Ann Nagrone, Cheryl Lynn Tate. AA, Southwest Bapt. U., 1956; BA, Okla. Bapt. U., 1959; MDiv, So. Seminary, 1965. Pastor Friendship Bapt., Philpot, Ky., 1961—65, Fellowship Bapt., Baxter Springs, Kans., 1965—69, Ft. Wyman Bapt., Rolla, Mo., 1969—74; pastor asst. First Bapt., O'Falon, Mo., 1974—76; pastor Post Falls (Idaho) Bapt., 1976—85, Elgin (Oreg.) Bapt., 1985—89, Immanuel Bapt., Jefferson City, Mo., 1990—2002. Author: Poetry by George, 2004, composer numerous songs. Coach Baxter Little League, Baxter Springs, 1967—69, Elgin Little League, 1987—89. Recipient State Champion, Famous Poet Soc., Oreg., 2000. Avocations: poetry, composing songs, drawing, woodworking.

SCAPANSKI, GENE ALBERT, academic administrator, educator; s. Albert Ludwig and Mildred Gertrude Scapanski; m. Marilyn Jean Isaak, May 15, 1971; children: Nicole Michelle Gilbertson, Tanya Jeanne Piltingsrud. BA, St. Paul Sem., 1964; Licentiate in Sacred Theology, Cath. U. of Am., Washington, 1968; STD summa cum laude, Pontificia Universitas a S. Thoma in Urbe, Rome, 1988. Dir. adult religious edn. and youth ministry Ch. of St. Mark, McLean, Va., 1968—72; dir. religious edn. Ch. of St. Ann, Arlington, Va.,

1972—73; dir. adult edn. and youth ministry Diocese of Richmond, Va., 1973—75; founding dir. Ctr. for Religious Edn., U. of St. Thomas, St. Paul, 1975—86; dir. grad. programs in catechetics and liturgy U. St. Thomas, St. Paul, 1977—83, dean pastoral studies, 1983—86, St. Paul Sem. Sch. of Divsn., U. St. Thomas, St. Paul, 1988—94, assoc. prof. systematic and pastoral theology, 1994—99; dean sch. of continuing studies U. St. Thomas, St. Paul, 1998—2003; prof. systematic and pastoral theology St. Paul Sem. Sch. of Divsn., U. St. Thomas, St. Paul, 1999—; v.p. for mission U. St. Thomas, St. Paul, 2003—. Commn. mem. Ecumenical Commn., Archdiocese of St. Paul and Mpls., 1997—, Luth.-Cath. Covenant Commn., St. Paul, 2001—. Author: (chpt.) The Emergence of the Laity in Catholicism & Protestantism in the 20th Century, Vatican II - The Church as Communio: A Council of the Laity., (book reviewer) Records of the American Catholic Historical Society of Philadelphia, 1991; columnist Modern Ministries Mag.; editor: (proceedings) Conf. for Caregivers; contbr. articles to profl. jours. Bd. dirs. Macalester-Groveland Cmty. Coun., St. Paul, 1999, Life's Missing Link, Mpls., 2002. Bush Leadership fellowship, Bush Found., 1986. Office: Univ of St Thomas 2115 Summit Ave AQU104 Saint Paul MN 55105-1078 Business E-Mail: gascapanski@stthomas.edu.

SCARANGELLA, JESSICA RUTHANNE, music educator; b. Bethesda, Md., July 16, 1955; d. Ruth and Anthony J. Scarangella. MusB in Edn., East Carolina U., 1978; MusM in Piano Performance, West Chester U., 1980; EdD in Curriculum and Supervison, Vanderbilt U., 1993. Music instr. Belmont U. Sch. Music, Nashville, 1994—98; choral dir. Deep Creek Mid. Sch., Chesapeake, Va., 1998—. Dir. music Tidewater Dinner Theatre, Norfolk, Va., 1974—83. Recipient Academic award, Peabody Coll. of Vanderbilt U., 1991—93; fellow, Vanderbilt U., 1991—93; scholar, East Carolina U., 1974—78, West Chester U., 1978—80. Mem.: Nashville Songwriters Internat. (corr.), Music Educators Nat. Conf. (life), Kappa Delta Phi (life), Alpha Phi Gamma (life), Phi Kappa Lambda (life). Home: 2505 Dominion Ave Norfolk VA 23518 Office: Deep Creek Mid Sch 1955 Deal Dr Chesapeake VA 23323 Personal E-mail: jrsmus@aol.com.

SCARBOROUGH, ANN BARLOW, secondary school educator; Tchr. sci. Farmville (N.C.) Mid. Sch., South Ctrl. HS, Winterville, NC. Recipient Outstanding Earth Sci. Tchr. award, 1992. Mem.: N.C. Sci. Tchrs. Assn. (pres. 2003).

SCARBOROUGH, CHARLES BISHOP, III, broadcast journalist, writer; b. Pitts., Nov. 4, 1943; s. Charles Bishop and Esther Francis (Campbell) S.; m. Linda Anne Gross, Dec. 14, 1972; children: Charles Bishop IV, Elizabeth Anne; m. Anne Ford Uzielli, Oct. 2, 1982; m. Ellen Carol Ward, Sept. 25, 1994. BS, U. So. Miss., 1969. Prodn. mgr. Sta.-WLOX-TV, Biloxi, Miss., 1966-68; reporter, anchorman Sta.-WDAM-TV, Hattiesburg, Miss., 1968-69; reporter, anchorman, mng. editor Sta.-WAGA-TV, Atlanta, 1969-72; reporter, anchorman Sta.-WNAC-TV, Boston, 1972-74, NBC News, N.Y.C., 1974—. Author: (novels) Stryker, 1978, The Myrmidon Project, 1981, Aftershock, 1991. Served with USAF, 1961-65. Recipient awards for journalism AP (9), 1969-72, Emmy awards (28), 1974-2004, award Aviation/Space Writers Assn., 1977, 78, 88, UPI award for journalism N.Y. Press Club award, 1988, 89, Sigma Delta Chi award, Deadline Club award, Terry Anderson Journalism award Working Press Assn. N.J., 1992. Mem.: Phi Kappa Phi. Office: NBC News 30 Rockefeller Plz Rm 723 New York NY 10112-0036

SCARBOROUGH, JOE, former congressman; b. Atlanta, Apr. 9, 1963; children: Joey, Andrew. BA, U. Ala., 1985; JD, U. Fla., 1990. Atty., 1990—; mem. U.S. Congress from 1st Fla. dist., Washington, 1995—2001. Mem. govt. reform com., judiciary com., armed svcs. com.; chmn. civil svc. subcom.; co-chmn. New Federalists; bd. dirs. Emerald Coast Pediat. Primary Care, Inc. Publisher The Fla. Sun. Mem. Fellowship Christian Athletes, Navy League (bd. dirs.), Rotary, Republican.

SCARBOROUGH, JOHN SAMUEL, pharmacy, medicine and ancient history educator; b. St Louis, Sept. 3, 1940; s. William John and Irene (Parish) S.; m. Lysa Gunlefinger, May 18, 1972 (div. Sept. 1990); children: Anne Elise, Isaac McKean; m. Yasemin Er, Dec. 27, 1990; 1 child, Amber Dilara. AB, BS in Zoology and History, Baker U., 1961, DHL (hon.), 1993; MA in Byzantine Studies, U. Denver, 1963; PhD in Ancient History-History Medicine, U. Ill., 1967; MA in Classics and History of Medicine, Oxford (Eng.) U., 1981. Instr. W.Va. Wesleyan Coll., W.Va., 1964, N.E. Mo. State U., Mo., 1966; from asst. prof. to prof. U. Ky., Lexington, Ky., 1966-85; prof. history pharmacy-medicine, classics, ancient history U. Wis., Madison, Wis., 1985—. Author: Roman Medicine, 1969, 2d edit., 1976, Facets of Hellenic Life, 1976, Medical Terminologies: Classical Origins, 1992, 2d edit., 1998; editor, author: Symposium on Byzantine Medicine, 1985, Folklore and Folk Medicine, 1987; editor Studies in Ancient Medicine, 1990—; contbr. articles to Episteme, Pharmacy in History, Wis. Acad. Rev., others. Fellow Wolfson Coll., Oxford U., 1981. Mem. Soc. for Ancient Medicine (pres., newsletter editor Lexington 1976-85, Madison 1985-87), Am. Inst. History of Pharmacy (bd. dir., editor jour. 1985-87, Kremers award for hist. writing 1982), Byzantine Studies Conf. (governing bd. 1986-91), Am. Philol. Assn., Am. Assn. for History Medicine, Assn. Ancient Historians, Am. Inst. Archaeology, History of Sci. Soc., Internat. Acad. of History of Medicine, Internat. Acad. of History of Pharmacy, Welt-Gesellschaft fuer Geschichte der Veterinärmedizin. Avocations: woodcarving, science fiction, classical music. Home: 25 Coronado Ct Madison WI 53705 Office: U Wis Sch Pharmacy 777 Highland Ave Madison WI 53705

SCARBOROUGH, ROBERT HENRY, JR., enterpreneur; b. Hawkinsville, Ga., Mar. 12, 1923; s. Robert Henry and Janet Augusta (Burton) S.; m. Walterene Brant, July 1, 1946; children— Robert Henry, James Burton BS, U.S. Mcht. Marine Acad., 1944; BBA, U. Hawaii, 1969, MBA, 1971; MS, George Washington U., 1971, Armed Forces Staff Coll., 1963, Nat. War Coll., 1971. Commd. lt. (j.g.) USCG, 1949; advanced through grades to vice adm., 1978; chief Office of Ops. USCG, 1974-75, chief of staff, 1975-77, comdr. 9th Coast Guard Dist., 1977-78, vice comdt., 1978-82, ret., 1982; exec. dir. Navy League U.S., 1982-84; pres. Polaris Potomac Corp., 1985-96. Entrepreneur, 1996—. With USNR, 1942-49 Decorated DSM, Legion of Merit. Mem. Beta Gamma Sigma Office: 5357 37th St N Arlington VA 22207-1312

SCARBOROUGH, STEPHEN J. construction executive; Pres. Std. Pacific Corp., Costa Mesa, Calif., 1965—. Office: Std Pacific Corp 1565 W MacArtha Blvd Costa Mesa CA 92626

SCARBOROUGH, WILLIAM KAUFFMAN, historian, educator; b. Balt., Jan. 17, 1933; s. James Blaine and Julia Irene (Kauffman) Scarborough; m. Patricia Estelle Carruthers, Jan. 16, 1954; children: Catherine Krohn, William Bradley. AB, U. N.C., 1954; MA, Cornell U., 1957; PhD, U. N.C., 1962. Asst. prof. history Millsaps Coll., Jackson, Miss., 1961—63, N.E. La. U., Monroe, 1963—64; assoc. prof. history U. So. Miss., Hattiesburg, 1964—76, prof. history, 1976—, chair and prof. history, 1980—90, Charles W. Moorman Disting. Alumni Prof. in the Humanities, 1996—98. Author: (book) The Overseer: Plantation Management in The Old South, 1966, Masters of the Big House, 2003 (Landry award, 2003); editor: The Diary of Edmund Ruffin, 3 vols., 1972—89 (Landry award, 1989). Lt. (j.g.) USNR, 1954—56. Recipient Grand Marshal award, 2003, Wright Lit. Excellence award, 2004. Fellow: St. George Tucker Soc. (pres. 2002—03); mem.: AAUP (chpt. pres. 2002—03), The Hist. Soc., S.C. Hist. Soc., Agr. History Soc., Miss. Hist. Soc. (pres. 1979, Willie D. Halsell prize 1993), So. Hist. Assn., Phi Beta Kappa. Avocations: golf, gardening, football, basketball. Home: 1120 Estelle St Hattiesburg MS 39402 Office: Univ So Miss Dept History 118 College Dr # 5047 Hattiesburg MS 39406 Office Phone: 601-266-4336.

SCARBROUGH, ALLEN LEE, writer, philosopher; b. Albany, Oreg., Feb. 7, 1956; s. Grady Elmer Scarbrough and Grace Maxine Eilert; m. Debra Elaine Volz, Apr. 21, 2001; children: Ami Kodel Ontiveros, Nathan Daniel, Carolyn Knodel, Tyler James. BS, Oreg. State U., 1986. Author: (philosophy) The Spiritual Universe. Home: 12200 SW 126th Ave Tigard OR 97223 Personal E-mail: allens405@aol.com.

SCARBROUGH, FRANK EDWARD, government official; b. Knoxville, Tenn., Sept. 27, 1942; s. James L. and Anna Dale (Edwards) S.; 1 child, Elizabeth Anne. BS, U. Tenn., 1964; AM, Harvard U., 1966, PhD, 1971. Rsch. assoc. U. Bern, Switzerland, 1971-73; instr. U. Pa., Phila., 1973-76; chemist food additive rev. FDA, Washington, 1977-80, chief regulatory affairs staff, 1980-86, dep. dir. Office Nutrition, 1986-89, dir. Office Nutrition, 1989-92, dir. Office Food Labeling, 1992-97; U.S. mgr. dor codex alimentarius USDA, Washington, 1997—. Contbe. author: Food Labeling, 1994 Recipient award of merit FDA, 1985, Superior Svc. award USPHS, 1991, Disting. Svc. award HHS, 1993, Pres.'s Meritorious Exec. award, 2001. Mem. Am. Chem. Soc., Am. Soc. Clin. Nutrition, Inst. Food Technologists. Office: USDA 14th And Independence SW Washington DC 20250-0001 Personal E-mail: eds942@hotmail.com. Business E-Mail: ed.scarborough@fsis.usda.gov.

SCARBROUGH, SARA EUNICE, librarian, archivist, consultant; b. Houston, Jan. 8, 1933; d. George Washington Johnson and Frances Elizabeth Evans; m. Henry Lester Scarbrough Sr., July 5, 1953 (dec. Mar. 1993); children: Henry Lester Jr., Sarita. BA, Talladega Coll., 1953; MLS, U. Tex., 1968; PhD, Columbia State U., 1998. Cert. tchr., libr., media specialist, adminstr. Music tchr. Brazos County Pub. Schs., Bryan, Tex., 1954-58; English tchr. Edgewood Sch. Dist., San Antonio, 1958-62; head libr. Houston Ind. Sch. Dist., 1962-92; dir. Hope Resource Ctr., Houston, 1992—. Exec. bd. Friends of the Houston Pub. Libr., 1994-99. Author: History of a Black Family on the Brazos, 1998. Treas. West McGregor Civic Assn., Houston, 1995—96; pres. Women's Missionary Soc., Houston, 1994—97, pres. Sr. Adult Ministry, 1999. Named Churchman of the Yr., Good Hope Ch., Houston, 1993. Mem. AAUW, Tex. Libr. Assn., U. Tex. Alumni Assn., Order of the Ea. Star (worthy matron, Outstanding Contbn. award 1995), Zeta Phi Beta (Lambda Zeta chpt. exec. bd., sec., chmn. econ. devel. 1998, Outstanding Contbn. to Econ. Devel. award 1999). Avocations: music, travel, genealogical research, bibliotherapy. Home: 3901 Fernwood Dr Houston TX 77021-1521

SCARCELLA, VINCENT A. finance company executive; s. Santi and Maria Scarcella. BS, Wagner Coll., 1984, MBA, grad. asst., Wagner Coll., 1986. V.p., fin. contr. Merrill Lynch, N.Y.C., 1986—. Contbr. articles to profl. jours.; musician piano recitals. Ch. organist, vol. St. Joseph's Ch. Recipient Cert. of Appreciation, IRS, 1985 - 1986, Wall St. Jour. award, Wagner Coll., 1986; scholarship, 1980—86. Mem.: Delta Mu Delta. Office: Merrill Lynch New York NY

SCARDELLETTI, ROBERT A. labor union officer; Pres. Transp. Comms. Internat. Union, Rockville, Md. Office: Transp Comms Internat Union 3 Research Pl Rockville MD 20850-3279

SCARDINO, MARJORIE MORRIS, publishing company executive; b. Flagstaff, Ariz., Jan. 25, 1947; d. Robert Weldon and Beth (Lamb) Morris; m. Albert James Scardino, Apr. 19, 1974; children: Adelaide Katherine Morris, William Brown, Albert Henry Hugh. BA, Baylor U.; JD, U. San Francisco. Ptnr. Brannen Wessels & Searcy, Savannah, Ga., 1976-85; pub. Ga. Gazette Pub. Co., Savannah, 1978-85; pres. The Economist Newspaper Group, Inc., N.Y.C., 1985-93; chief exec. The Economist Group, London, 1993-97, Pearson P.L.C., London, 1997—. Non-exec. dir. Nokia Corp. Bd. dirs. Carter Ctr., The Bus. Coun.; trustee others, Victoria and Albert Mus. Office: Pearson PLC 80 Strand London WC2R ORL England

SCARF, HERBERT ELI, economics educator; b. July 25, 1930; s. Louis H. and Lena (Elkman) W.; m. Margaret Klein, June 28, 1953; children: Martha Anne Samuelson, Elizabeth Joan Stone, Susan Margaret Merrell. AB, Temple U., 1951; MA, Princeton U., 1952, PhD, 1954; LHD (hon.), U. Chgo., 1978. With RAND Corp., Santa Monica, Calif., 1954-57; asst., assoc. prof. stats. Stanford (Calif.) U., 1957-63; prof. econs. Yale U., New Haven, 1963-70, Stanley Resor prof. econs., 1970-78, Sterling prof. econs., 1979—. Vis. assoc. prof. Yale U., New Haven, 1959-60; dir. Cowles Found. Rsch. in Econs., Yale U., 1967-71, 1981-84, divsn. social sciences, 1971-72, 1973-74. Author: Studies in the Mathematical Theory of Inventory and Production, 1958, Computation of Economic Equilibria, 1973; editor: Applied General Equilibrium Analysis, 1984. Recipient Lanchester prize Ops. Rsch. Soc. Am., 1974, Von Neumann medal, 1983; named Disting. fellow Am. Econ. Assn., 1991. Fellow: INFORMS, Econometric Soc. (pres. 1983); mem.: NAS, Am. Philos. Soc., Am. Acad. Arts and Scis. Democrat. Jewish. Office: Yale U Cowles Found Rsch Econs PO Box 208281 New Haven CT 06520-8281 E-mail: herbert.scarf@yale.edu.

SCARF, MARGARET (MAGGIE SCARF), author; b. Phila., May 13, 1932; d. Benjamin and Helen (Rotbin) Klein; m. Herbert Eli Scarf, June, 1953; children: Martha Samuelson, Elizabeth Stone, Susan Merrell. BA, South Conn. State U., 1989. Contbg. editor New Republic, Washington, 1978—, Self Mag., N.Y.C., 1991—; writer-in-residence Jonathan Edwards Coll., 1995—. Assoc. fellow Jonathan Edwards Coll. Yale U., New Haven, 1979—; sr. fellow Bush Ctr. in Child Devel. and Social Policy, Yale U., 1991—; mem. adv. bd. Am. Psychiat. Press, Poynter Fellowship Journalism Yale U., 1995-96. Author: Meet Benjamin Franklin, 1968, Antarctica: Exploring the Frozen Continent, 1970, Body, Mind, Behavior, 1976 (Nat. Media award Am. Psychological Assn. 1977), Unfinished Business: Pressure Points in the Lives of Women, 1981, Intimate Partners: Patterns in Love and Marriage, 1987, Intimate Worlds: Life Inside the Family, 1996, Secrets, Lies, Betrayals: The Body/Mind Connection, 2004; contbr. numerous articles to jours. including N.Y. Times mag. and book rev., Psychology Today; TV appearances include: David Letterman Show, Oprah Winfrey Show, CBS News, Good Morning Am., Today Show, Phil Donahue, numerous others. Recipient Nat. Media award Am. Psychol. Found., 1971, 74, 77, Conn. UN award Outstanding Conn. Women, 1987, cert. commendation Robert T. Morse Writers Competition Am. Psychiat. Assn., 1997, Disting. Svc. award Am. Psychiat. Assn., 1999, cert. of recognition N.Y. State Soc. Clin. and Social Work, 1998; grantee Smith Richardson Found., 1991-94; Ford Found. fellow, 1973-74, Neiman fellow Harvard U., 1975-76, Ctr. Advanced Study in Behavioral Scis. fellow, 1977-78, 85-86, Alicia Patterson Found. fellow, 1978-79. Mem. Conn. Soc. Psychoanalytic Psychologists, Am. Psychiat. Press (mem. adv. bd. 1992), Lawn Club, Elizabethans, PEN Writer's Assn. Avocations: reading, hiking, swimming. Office: Jonathan Edwards Coll Yale U 68 High St New Haven CT 06511-6643 Business E-Mail: maggie.scarf@yale.edu.

SCARL, HILARI BROOKE, actress, writer, television producer; b. Phoenix, June 20, 1966; d. Eugene and Marilyn Scarl. Attended, U. Ga., 1986; BA, Ga. State U., 1988; attended, Am. Musical and Dramatic Acad., 1992. Founder, dir. Theatre Sprouts, Atlanta, 1988—90; actor Theatreworks, USA, N.Y.C., 1992—94, Nat. Theatre of the Deaf, Chester, Conn., 1994—95; founder, dir. Young Players Ensemble, Los Angeles, Calif., 1989—; TV prodr. Go/Voy Pictures, 2004, TLC Stone Stanley Entertainment, Fox/Rocket Sci. Labs. Playwrite The Girl From Nowhere, 1998, Cozenage, 2003. Vol. acting coach Hole in the Wall Gang Camp, Ashford, Conn., 1993; vol. interpreter Deaf West, Studio City, Calif., 1995—96; fundraiser, triathlete Leukemia & Lymphoma Soc., Los Angeles, 2003. Nominee Heideman award, Actors Theatre of Louisville; recipient Boss award for Best Actress, Neighborhood Playhouse, 1989; Writing scholarship, East West Players, 2004. Democrat. Jewish. Avocations: skiing, camping, travel, Am. Sign Lang., fire eating. Home: 1320 N Martel Ave 6 Los Angeles CA 90046 E-mail: hilariB@aol.com.

SCARLATA, PAUL ANTHONY, oral surgeon; b. McKeesport, Pa., Apr. 3, 1935; s. Joseph Mario and Josephine Gloria (Battaglia) S.; m. Mary Jane Parks, June 15, 1963 (dec. 1982); children: Stephanie, Anthony, Christopher, Matthew, Sarah; m. Darla K. Hosler, May 27, 1988 (div. 1994). BS, U. Pitts., 1957, DDS, DMD, U. Pitts., 1961. Resident in oral surgery Western Pa. Hosp., Pitts., 1962-63, St. Luke's Hosp., N.Y.C., 1963-64; practice gen. dentistry and oral surgery Chambersburg, Pa., 1967—; chief dental svc. Chambersburg Hosp., 1974-76, 82-84. Treas. Franklin County (Pa.) Heritage, 1971—, pres., 1977-78; fgn. student exch. host Youth for Understanding, appointed regional field dir. Capt., oral surgeon AUS, 1964—67, Mannheim, Germany. Recipient Buhl Planetarium Sci. award 1st prize Astronomy 6" Newtonian Reflector, 1952. Mem. ADA (life), Pa.Dental Assn., We. Pa. Assn., Gt. Lakes socs. oral surgeons, N.Y. Soc. Clin. Oral Pathologists, Am. Dental Soc. of Anesthetists, Cumberland Valley Dental Soc. (pres. 1982-83), Am. Legion (life), Chambersburg Club, Antique Studebakers Club, Antique Auto Assn. (life mem.), Univ. Club Pitts. Home: 3166 St Andrews Dr Chambersburg PA 17201-1465 Office: 421 Phoenix Dr Chambersburg PA 17201-2328 Office Phone: 717-263-9275. Personal E-mail: pars@pa.net. Business E-Mail: tooth@pa.net.

SCARLETT, P. LYNN, foundation administrator, writer; b. Pitts., Dec. 8, 1949; d. James Miles and Virginia (Young) S.; m. James R. Trotter, May 6, 1978; 1 child, Rachel Scarlett Trotter. BA, U. Calif., Santa Barbara, 1970, MA, 1972. Vis. lectr. U. Calif., Santa Barbara, 1980-81; book rev. editor Reason Mag., Santa Barbara, 1982-85; dir. rsch. Reason Found., Santa Monica, Calif., 1985-89, v.p. rsch., 1990—. Mem. task force Calif. Joint Legis. Com. on Surrogate Parenting, Calif., 1989-90; panel reviewer Project 88 Phase II, 1990; chmn. issues com. Citizens for Balanced Community, Santa Barbara, 1989—; bd. dirs. Laguna Blanca Sch., Santa Barbara. Author: (chpt.) Food Politics, 1982; contbr. articles to profl. jours. Chmn. Jim Trotter for City Coun., Carpinteria, Calif., 1990—; mem. parents aux. Laguna Blanca, 1986-88. Geneva Inst. of Internat. Studies fellow, 1974-75. Mem. Friends of Girls Club Corp. (2d v.p. 1986-87). Avocations: bird watching, illustrator, swimming. Office: Reason Found 3415 S Sepulveda Blvd Ste 400 Los Angeles CA 90034-6014

SCARLETT, PATRICIA LYNN, federal agency administrator; BA, MA in Polit. Sci., U. Calif., Santa Barbara. Joined Reason Pub. Policy Inst., 1979—, dir. rsch., 1985, mgr., 1989, exec. dir., v.p. rsch., pres., 2001—; asst. sec. policy, mgmt. and budget U.S. Dept. Interior, Washington, 2001—. Chair Inspection and Maintenance Rev. Com.; panelist Pay-as-You-Throw project EPA, 1995; tech. advisor N.Am. Integrated Waste Mgmt. Project Solid Waste Assn., 1995—96; bd. dirs. EarthShell Corp.; com. mem. Nat. Environ. Policy Inst.; sr. fellow Found. for Rsch. on Econs. and the Environment; environ. campaign advisor to George W. Bush; mem. Bush transition adv. team EPA. Contbr. articles to profl. jours. Bd. mem. Thoreau Inst. Republican. Office: US Dept Interior Policy Mgmt and Budget 1849 C St NW Washington DC 20240

SCARMINACH, CHARLES ANTHONY, lawyer; b. Syracuse, N.Y., Feb. 19, 1944; s. John Louis and Lucy (Egnoto) S.; children: John, Catherine, Karen, Charles, Robert. MA, U. Buffalo, 1965; JD, Syracuse U., 1968. Bar: N.Y. 1968, S.C. 1974. Gen. counsel Sea Pines Co., Hilton Head Island, S.C., 1973-78; sole practice Hilton Head Island, 1978-83; ptnr. Novit & Scarminach, P.A., Hilton Head Island, 1983-93, Novit Scarminach & Williams P.A., Hilton Head Island, 1993—2002, Novit, Scarminach & Akins, P.A., Hilton Head Island, 2003—. Bd. dirs. Nations Bank, Hilton Head Island. Chmn. bd. Sea Pines Montessori Sch., Hilton Head Island, 1979-83; bd. dirs. Hilton Head Preparatory Sch., 1984-93, chmn. bd. trustees 1986-93. Maj. U.S. Army, 1968-73. Mem. ABA, S.C. Bar Assn., N.Y. State Bar Assn., Hilton Head Island C. of C. (bd. dirs. 1996-99), Sea Pines Club. Roman Catholic. Home: 10 Wood Duck Ct Hilton Head Island SC 29928-3010 Office: Novit Scarminach & Akins PA PO Drawer 14 Hilton Head Island SC 29938-0014 Office Phone: 843-785-5850. E-mail: cscarminach@ns-lawfirm.com.

SCARNE, JOHN, game company executive; b. Steubenville, Ohio, Mar. 4, 1903; s. Fiorangelo and Maria (Tamburro) S.; m. Steffi Kearney, 1956; 1 son, John Teeko. Student pub. schs., Guttenberg, N.J. Pres. John Scarne Games, Inc., North Bergen, N.J., 1950—. Gaming cons. Hilton Hotels Internat. Magician stage, screen and television; Author: Scarne on Dice, 1945, Scarne on Cards, 1950, Scarne on Card Tricks, 1950, Scarne on Magic Tricks, 1952, Scarne's New Complete Guide to Gambling, 1962, The Odds Against Me, 1967, Scarne's Encyclopedia of Games, 1973, The Mafia Conspiracy, 1976, Scarne's Guide to Casino Gambling; Scarne's Guide to Modern Poker; Contbr. to: World Book Ency, 1970, Ency. Brit, 1975. Cons. to U.S. Armed Forces, 1941-45. Named Man of Year for Police Chiefs of U.S., 1960 Office: Unit 312 2581 Countryside Blvd Clearwater FL 33761-3521

SCAROLA, JOHN, lawyer; b. Bklyn., July 24, 1947; s. John Anthony and Grace Ellen (Turnbull) S.; m. Anita Helene Kargauer, Jan. 4, 1969; children: Kristen, John Michael, Janna, David, Cara. BA, Georgetown U., 1969, JD, 1973. Bar: Fla. 1973, U.S. Dist. Ct. (so. dist.) Fla. 1974, U.S. Ct. Appeals (5th cir.) 1976. Chief felony prosecutor State Atty.'s Office, 15th Jud. Cir., West Palm Beach, Fla., 1973-78; ptnr., dir., officer Searcy, Denney, Scarola, Barnhart & Shipley, P.A., West Palm Beach, 1978—. Spl. counsel Fla. Jud. Qualifications Commn., Tallahassee, 1981—; asst. spl. prosecutor Statewide Grand Jury, Fla., 1977-78; instr. Palm Beach Jr. Coll., Lake Worth, Fla., 1974-78. Candidate Fla. State Senate, Dist. 84, 1978; chmn. bd. The Lord's Place Inc., West Palm Beach, 1981—; bd. dirs. Children's Genetic Disease Found., Miami, Fla., 1982-87; pres. Serra Club of the Palm Beaches, West Palm Beach, 1980; bd. dirs. Fla. Rural Legal Svcs., 1997—. Served with USAR, 1966-72. Mem. ABA, Fla. Bar (bd. cert. civil trial practice and comml. and bus. litigation 1984, pres.'s pro bono award 1984), Acad. Fla. Trial Lawyers, Palm Beach County Bar Assn. (Cmty. Svc. award 1994), Palm Beach County Trial Lawyers Assn. (pres. 1989-92). Roman Catholic. Home: 107 Schooner Lane Jupiter FL 33407 Office: Searcy Denney Scarola Barnhart & Shipley PA 2139 Palm Beach Lakes Blvd West Palm Beach FL 33409-6601 Office Phone: 561-686-6300. Business E-Mail: jsx@searcylaw.com.

SCAROLA, JOHN MICHAEL, dentist, educator; b. N.Y.C., Nov. 18, 1934; s. Michael Fidelis and Filomena Mary (Turso) S.; m. Theodora Mary Marty, June 15, 1963; children: Michael A., John P., Stephen A., Robert M., Mary E. BS, Fordham Coll., 1956; DDS, Columbia U., 1960. Instr. Columbia Dental Sch., N.Y.C., 1962-68, asst. clin. prof., 1969-72, course dir. fixed partial dentures, 1969-72, assoc. clin. prof., 1973-86, course dir. prosthodontic elective, 1977-91, clin. prof., 1986—. Lectr., clin. prof. postgrad. prostodontics Columbia U., N.Y.C., 1986—, AEGD-Columbia U., N.Y.C., 1990-92, Luth. Med. Ctr., Bklyn., 1993—; cons. in prosthodontics Northport VA Hosp., East Northport, N.Y., 1970-91. Scoutmaster Boy Scouts Am., Port Washington, N.Y., 1976-78; chmn. spl. gifts Bishop's Annual Appeal, St. Peter's-Port Washington, 1977-78; Cath. Youth Orgn. sports coach St. Paul The Apostle, Brookville, N.Y., 1980-83; fundraising com. The Yard, Martha's Vineyard, Mass., 1990; concert com. Musician's Emergency Fund, N.Y.C., 1992. Lt. USNR, 1960-62. Fellow Am. Coll. Dentists (chmn. N.Y. sect. 1994, regent of Regency 1), N.Y. Acad. Dentistry (pres. 1989-90), Greater N.Y. Acad. Prosthodontics (dir. 1993-97); mem. Greater N.Y. Acad. Prosthodontics Found. (dir., pres. 1989-97), N.Y. Acad. Dentistry Endowment Fund (dir., pres. 1992-93). Republican. Roman Catholic. Avocations: golf, opera, classical music, gardening. Home: 83 Fruitledge Rd Glen Head NY 11545-3317 Office: 501 Madison Ave New York NY 10022-5602

SCARPA, A. MICHAEL, apparel executive, corporate financial executive; Degree in acctg., 1982. CPA 1982. Fin. analyst Krementz & Co.; from budget mgr. to CFO Liz Claiborne, N.Y., 1983—2000, CFO, 2000—, sr. v.p., 2002—. Office: Liz Claiborne 1441 Broadway New York NY 10018-1805

SCARPA, ANTONIO, medical educator, researcher, physiologist; b. Padua, Italy, July 3, 1942; s. Angelo and Elena (DeRossi) S. MD cum laude, U. Padua, 1966, PhD in Pathology, 1970; MA (hon.), U. Pa., 1978. Asst. prof. biochemistry, biophysics U. Pa., Phila., 1973-76, assoc. prof., 1976-80, prof., 1980-86, dir. biomed. instrumentation group, 1983-86; prof., chmn. dept. physiology and biophysics Case Western Res. U., Cleve., 1986—, dir. tng. ctr., program project, 1983—, prof. medicine, 1989—, D. and I. Myers prof., 1998—. Cons. study sect. NIH, Bethesda, 1984—, Am. Heart Assn., Dallas, 1986-91; pres., assoc. chair dept. physiology, 1993-94; vice chair Nat. Caucus Basic Sci. Presidents, Washington. Editor (books): Frontiers of Biological Energetics, Calcium Transport and Cell Function, Transport ATPases, Membrane Pathology, Membrane and Cancer Cells; editor (jours.) Archives Biochemistry and Biophysics, Cell Calcium, Biochemistry Internat., The Scientific Jour.; mem. editl. bd. Circulation Rsch., 1978-81, Biophys. Jour., 1979-82, Jour. Muscle Rsch., 1979—, Magnesium, 1982—, Physiol. Revs., 1982-90, FASEB Jour., 1987-92, Molecular Cellular Biochemistry, 1988—; contbr. numerous articles to profl. jours. Mem. Am. Soc. Physiologists, Am. Soc. Biol. Chemistry, Biophys. Soc. (exec. coun. 1980-83, 85-89, 94-97), U.S.

Bioenergetics Group (program chmn. 1974-75, 82, 83, exec. officer 1985-90, assoc. chmn. dept. physiology, pres. 1993-95), Biophys. Soc. (treas. 1998—), Assn. Am. Med. Colls. (adminstrv. bd., exec. coun.), Federated Am. Soc. Exptl. Biologists (bd. dirs.). Avocations: farming, sailing, painting. Office: Case Western Reserve Univ Dept Of Physiology Cleveland OH 44106

SCARPELLI, VITO, adult education educator, administrator; b. Passaic, N.J., July 17, 1946; s. Peter and Celia (Pignataro) S.; m. JoAnn Motti, Aug. 23, 1970; children: Anthony, Michele. BA in Acctg. and Edn., Montclair State Coll., 1968; MA, Kean Coll., 1984; postgrad., St. Peters, Jersey City State U., Seton Hall U., Kans. State U. Prin. Roselle Park Mid. Sch., 1996—; supr. P. Scarpelli & Sons, Nutley, N.J., 1968-84; bus. adminstr. John J. Baum, Inc., Wayne, N.J.; salesman Realty World-Monaco Realty, Nutley, 1980—; asst. track coach, tchr. jr. H.S. Belleville Bd. Edn., 1968-69; dir. adult edn. and summer programs Roselle Park (N.J.) Bd. Edn., 1984-96. Dir. Union County Summer Youth Employment and Tng., Roselle Park, 1986, asst. curriculum coord., 1992-96, dir. tech., 1993-96; adj. prof. Jersey City State Coll., 1993-96. Pres. Nutley Am. Little League, 1987-97; v.p. Nutley Basketball Assn.; past pres. Lincoln Sch. PTA. Mem. N.J. Prins. and Suprs. Assn., Nat. Assn. Secondary Sch. Prins., N.J. Bus. Edn. Assn., N.J. Edn. Assn., Roselle Park Edn. Assn., LERN, KC (grand knight 1976). Independent. Roman Catholic. Avocation: fishing. Home: 81 Milton Ave Nutley NJ 07110-3017 Office: Roselle Park Bd Edn 510 Chestnut St Roselle Park NJ 07204-1928

SCARPETTI, ANGELINA (LEE SCARPETTI), state legislator; b. Faeto Fogga, Italy; d. Carmine & Giovianina Capozziello, four children, four grandchildren. Grad., Bridgeport (Conn.) Ctrl. H.S. Restaurant cons., Trumbull, Conn.; mem. Conn. State Senate, 1985—. Mem. environ. com., housing com. and transp. com., asst. majority leader Conn. State Senate; mem. Rep. Town Com.; sec. Greater Bridgeport Transit Dist. Address: Senate Rep Ofc LOB Rm 3400 Hartford CT 06106 Office: 80 Hill Pkwy Middlebury CT 06762-3328

SCARPULLA, TERESA, artist; b. San Francisco, Oct. 30, 1964; d. Frank Scarpulla and Cecilia Amado. BFA with high distinction, Calif. Coll. Fine Arts, 1993—95; MFA, La. State U., 1998—2001. Instr. La. State U., 1999—2001. Ind. rsch. scholar Met. Mus. of Art, 2001—03, Am. Craft Libr., 2001—03; gallery cons., NYC, 2001—03; artist in residence Kala Inst., Berkeley, Calif., 1996, Vt. Studio Ctr., Johnson, Vt., 1999. Finalist Fulbright commn., Egypt, 2002. Mem.: Chronicle of Higher Edn., Coll. Art Assn. Avocation: sailing. Home: 1670 Wilson Ct Concord CA 94521 Office: Scarpulla Studios 1670 Wilson Ct Concord CA 94521

SCARR, SANDRA WOOD, retired psychology educator, researcher; b. Washington, Aug. 8, 1936; d. John Ruxton and Jane (Powell) Wood; m. Harry Alan Scarr, Dec. 26, 1961 (div. 1970); children: Phillip, Karen, Rebbecca, Stephanie; m. James Callan Walker, Aug. 9, 1982 (div. 1994). AB, Vassar Coll., 1958; AM, Harvard U., 1963, PhD, 1965. Asst. prof. psychology U. Md., College Park, 1964-67; assoc. prof. U. Pa., Phila., 1967-71; prof. U. Minn., Mpls., 1971-77, Yale U., New Haven, 1977-83; Commonwealth prof. U. Va., Charlottesville, 1983-95, chmn. dept. psychology, 1984-90; CEO, chmn. bd. dirs. KinderCare Learning Ctr., Inc., 1995-97; ret., 1997. Mem. nat. adv. bd. Robert Wood Johnson Found., Princeton, N.J., 1985-91; coord. coun. psychology SUNY Bd. Regents, N.Y.C., 1984-92; prof. Kerstin Hesselgren, Sweden, 1993-94. Author: Race, Social Class and Individual Differences in IQ, 1981, Mother Care/Other Care, 1984 (Nat. Book award APA 1985), Caring for Children, 1989; editor Jour. Devel. Psychology, 1980-86, Current Directions in Psychol. Sci., 1991-95. Fellow Ctr. for Advanced Studies, Stanford U., Calif., 1976-77; grantee NIH, NSF, others, 1967-95. Fellow AAAS, APA (chmn. com. on human rsch. 1980-83, coun. of reps. 1984-89, bd. dirs. 1988-90, Award for Disting. Contbn. to Rsch. on Pub. Policy 1988), Am. Psychol. Soc. (bd. dirs. 1992—, pres. 1996-97, James McKeen Cattell award 1993); mem. Am. Acad. Arts and Scis. (coun. mem. 1995-2000), Behavior Genetics Assn. (pres. 1985-86, exec. coun. 1976-79, 84-87, Dobzhansky award 2004), Soc. for Rsch. in Child Devel. (governing coun. 1974-76, 87-93, chmn. fin. com. 1989-91, pres. 1989-91), Internat. Soc. for Study of Behavioral Devel. (exec. bd. 1987-94). Avocations: dogs, gardening. Home: 77-6222 Kaumalumalu Dr Holualoa HI 96725-9757 Office Phone: 808-322-9445. Personal E-mail: sandrascar@aol.com.

SCARRITT, RICHARD WINN, lawyer; b. Enid, Okla., Dec. 13, 1938; s. Nathan Spencer and Rilla Fayette (Winn) S.; m. Gloria June Gaba, Nov. 7, 1966 (div. Nov. 1971); m. Deborah Louise Guillemot, Sept. 3, 1986; 1 child, Nathan Spencer IV; ward, Samantha Jo Wickizer. BA, Okla. U., 1960; JD, Harvard U., 1963. Bar: Mo. 1963, U.S. Dist. Ct. (we. dist.) Mo. 1964, U.S. Supreme Ct. 1971. Assoc. Spencer, Fane, Britt & Browne, Kans. City, Mo., 1963-68, ptnr., chmn. real estate sect., 1969—. Guest lectr. real estate law U. Mo. Extension Ctr., Independence, 1966-68; mem. panel of arbitrators Am. Arbitration Assn.; chmn. standard forms com., mem. govt. affairs, zoning law and legis. coms. Met. Real Estate Bd. Greater Kansas City; panelist Plaza West Assn., Kansas City, 1971-78. Co-author: Missouri Real Estate Forms and Practice, 1988, supplements, 1989-98. Mem. Clay County Econ. Devel. Coun.; dir. Brookside Roller Hockey League, Kansas City Jr. Blades Amateur Hockey Assn. Fellow Am. Coll. Real Estate Lawyers (attys.' opinions com.); mem. ABA (real property, probate and trust law sect., loan documentation, real estate financing and comml. fin. svcs., environ. law com. subcom. energy law and real property, corp., banking and bus. law sect., comml. fin. svcs. com.), Mo. Bar Assn. (property law com., adv. coun., energy law com.), Kansas City Met. Bar Assn. (real estate law com., chmn. com. coun.), Lawyers Assn. Kansas City, Mo. C. of C., Kansas City Club, SAR, Mensa, Phi Delta Theta. Republican. Episcopalian. Avocations: photography, collecting art, electronics, computers, youth sports. Home: 825 W 53rd Ter Kansas City MO 64112-2327 Office: Spencer Fane Britt & Browne 1000 Walnut St Ste 1400 Kansas City MO 64106-2140 Fax: 816-474-3216. E-mail: rws@spencerfane.com.

SCARRITT, THOMAS VARNON, newspaper editor; b. Tuscaloosa, Ala., Jan. 28, 1953; s. Charles Wesley and Valerie (Varnon) S.; m. Kathryn Rush Hubbard, Dec. 28, 1973; children: Sara Kathryn, Thomas Varnon Jr. BA in Journalism, U. N.C., 1974; MBA, Samford U., 1995. Reporter The Birmingham (Ala.) News, 1975-79, Washington corr., 1979-83, news editor, 1983-85, editl. page editor, 1986-89, exec. editor, 1989-97, editor, 1997—. Bd. dirs. Workshops Inc., Girls Inc. Ctrl. Ala., 2002-. Mem. Am. Soc. Newspaper Editors, Soc. Profl. Journalists, Kiwanis (Birmingham), Phi Beta Kappa. Episcopal. Home: 4240 Clairmont Ave S Birmingham AL 35222-3724 Office: The Birmingham News 2200 4th Ave N Birmingham AL 35203-3840 Office Phone: 205-325-2205. E-mail: tscarritt@bhamnews.com.

SCARSE, OLIVIA MARIE, cardiologist, consultant; b. Chgo., Nov. 10, 1950; d. Oliver Marcus and Marjorie Ardis (Olsen) S. BS, North Park Coll., 1970; MD, Loyola U., Maywood, Ill., 1973. Diplomate Am. Bd. Internal Medicine, Am. Bd. Cardiovascular Diseases. Surg. intern Resurrection Hosp., Chgo., 1974; resident in internal medicine Northwestern U., Chgo., 1974-77; cardiovascular disease fellow U. Ill., Chgo., 1977-80; dir. cardiac catherization lab. Cook County Hosp., Chgo., 1981; dir. heart sta. MacNeal Hosp., Berwyn, Ill., 1983; dir. electrophysiology Hines VA Hosp., Maywood, Ill., 1984-85; dir. progressive care Columbus Hosp., Chgo., 1985-88, pvt. practice, 1984—, Ill. Masonic Hosp., Chgo., 1989-96. Founder Physician Cons. for Evaluation of Clin. Pathways, Practice Parameters and Patient Care Outcomes, 1991—. Dir. continuous quality improvement Improvement Columbus, 1990-95; mem. presdl. ad hoc com. on prevention and treatment of domestic violence Chgo. Med. Soc., 1997—. Pillsbury fellow Pillsbury Fund, 1980. Fellow Am. Coll. Cardiology; mem. AMA, ACP, Chgo. Med. Assn., Ill. State Med. Assn., Am. Heart Assn. (coun. on clin. cardiology), Crescent Countries Found. for Med. Care, Physicians Health Network, Cen. Ill. Med. Rev. Orgn. Avocations: musician, ballet and tap dancer, actress, model, singer. Home and Office: 2650 N Lakeview Ave Apt 4109 Chicago IL 60614-1833

SCARTELLI, JOSEPH PAUL, music therapy educator, dean; b. Scranton, Pa., May 4, 1952; s. Joseph Anthony and Angela Rose Scartelli; m. Frances Marie DiMaggio, June 15, 1974; children: Nicole, Joseph. BS in Music, Mansfield U., 1974; MusM in Music Therapy, U. Miami, Fla., 1977, PhD in Music Edn., 1981. Cert. music therapist. Tchr. Dade County Pub. Schs., South Miami, Fla., 1976-77; grad. tchg. fellow U. Miami, 1979-80, instr. music therapy, 1980-81; asst. prof. music Radford (Va.) U., 1981-87, assoc. prof. music, 1987-89, prof. music, 1989—, dean Coll. Visual and Performing Arts, 1988—. Mem. editl. bd. Jour. Music Therapy, 1996-2004, Arts in Psychotherapy, 1984—. Author monograph: Music and Self-Management, 1989; contbr. articles to profl. jours., chpts. to book. Bd. dirs. Radford U. Found., 1990—; bd. commrs. renovation project Dumas Music Ctr., Roanoke, Va., 1998—; bd. dirs. Va. Arts, Richmond, Va., 1992—; mem. City of Radford Arts and Events Commn., 1996—. Recipient Outstanding Young Alumni award Mansfiled U., 1986, Music Alum Honor Roll, 1990, Resolution of Recognition, Va. State Bd. Edn., 1999, Educator of Yr. award Radford C. of C., 2001. Mem. Am. Music Therapy Assn. (award of merit 1998), Assn. Performing Arts presenters, Internat. Coun. Fine Arts Deans. Avocations: music performance, golf, martial arts, tennis, carpentry. Home: 501 Randolph St Radford VA 24141 Office: Radford U Coll Visual/Performing Arts Radford VA 24142 E-mail: jscartel@radford.edu.

SCARTH, BRUCE WORDEN, music educator; b. Silverton, Oreg., Sept. 16, 1953; s. William Osborne and Donna LaRae Scarth; m. Beth Kay Carlson, Oct. 2, 1976; children: Alyssa Katherine, Kyla Elisabeth, Brandon Micheal. AA, Clark Coll., 1973; BA in Music Edn., Ctrl. Washinton U., 1976. Dir. h.s. choral Lakeview H.S., Oreg., 1976—78, Sandy H.S., Oreg., 1978—. Mem.: NEA, Am. Choral Dirs., Music Educators Nat. Conf., Boy Scouts Am. (asst. scoutmaster 1981—2004). Independent. Avocations: travel, acting, handyman. E-mail: scarthb@ortrail.k12.or.us.

SCARWID, DIANA ELIZABETH, actress; b. Savannah, Ga. d. Anthony and Elizabeth Scarwid. Grad., Am. Acad. Dramatic Arts, 1975; degree in Theater Arts, Acting, Pace U., 1975. Appeared in films including Pretty Baby, Honeysuckle Rose, Inside Moves, (Oscar award nomination Best Supporting Actress), Mommie Dearest, Rumble Fish, Strange Invaders, Silkwood, Psycho III, Extremeties, Heat, Neon Bible, The Cure, Gold Diggers: The Secret of Bear Mountain, What Lies Beneath, The Angel Doll, A Guy Thing, 2002, Party Monster, 2002; TV films include Thou Shalt Not Kill, Studs Lonigan, Guyana Tragedy: The Story of Jim Jones, Desperate Lives, A Bunny's Tale, After the Promise, Night of The Hunter, Critical Choices, Bastard Out of Carolina, Angel of Pennsylvania Avenue, Truman (Emmy nomination 1996), If These Walls Could Talk, Ruby Bridges Story, also mini-series From the Earth to the Moon, Before He Wakes; theater prodns. include Key Exchange, Toronto, Can., A Thousand Clowns, Jupiter, Fla., Gethsamanie Springs, Mark Taper Forum, L.A., Spoon River Anthology, Ring 'round the Moon, N.Y.C., Nat. Shakespeare Conservancy, NY; (TV films) Down Will Come Baby, 1999, Dirty Pictures, 2000, Path to War, 2002 Avocations: reading, bicycle riding, crabbing from row boat, walking.

SCASTA, DAVID LYNN, forensic psychiatrist; b. Austin, Tex., Dec. 13, 1949; s. Albert Ray and Helen Pearl (Hennessy) S. BA, Baylor U., 1972, MD, 1977. Diplomate Am. Bd. Psychiatry and Neurology. Staff physician U. Houston, 1977-78; adminstr. Temple U. Med. Sch., Phila., 1982-83; resident in psychiatry Temple U. Hosp., 1982; dir. consultation svcs. Grad. Hosp., 1983-84; dir. outpatient programs Phila. Psychiat. Ctr., 1983-84; pvt. practice Grad. Hosp. Phila. Psychiat. Ctr., 1984-89; med. dir. Phila. Consultation Ctr., 1987-89; attending psychiatrist Hunterdon Med. Ctr., Flemington, NJ, 1989-98, chmn. dept. psychiatry, 1996-97; pvt. practice New Hope, Pa., 1989—; pvt. practice forensic psychiatry Princeton, NJ, 1998—; dir. emotional recovery unit, cons. Coordinated Med. Network, 2002—. Clin. assoc. prof. dept. psychiatry Temple U. Med. Sch., Phila., 1983—. Editor Jour. of Gay & Lesbian Psychotherapy, 1987-98. Dist. rep. Rep. Party of Tex., Houston, 1977, precinct sec., 1975-77; bd. dirs. Phila. Bapt. Assn., 1995-2003; mem. exec. com., 1996-2003. Named Ginsberg Fellow Group for Advancement of Psychiatry, 1980-82. Disting. Fellow Am. Psychiat. Assn. (disting., pres. Caucus of lesbian, gay and bisexual mems. 1996-97); mem. AMA, Assn. Gay and Lesbian Psychiatrists (pres. 1995-97, newsletter editor 1987-94), Am. Acad. Psychiatry and the Law, Am. Coll. Forensic Examiners. Republican. Avocations: skiing, antiques. Office: Ind Psychiat Svcs 115 Commons Way Princeton NJ 08540-1507

SCATENA, LORRAINE BORBA, retired rancher, women's rights advocate; b. San Rafael, Calif., Feb. 18, 1924; d. Joseph and Eugenia (Simas) de Borba; m. Louis G. Scatena, Feb. 14, 1960, dec. Nov. 1995; children: Louis Vincent, Eugenia Gayle. BA, Dominican Coll., San Rafael, 1945; postgrad., Calif. Sch. Fine Arts, 1948, U. Calif., Berkeley, 1956-57. Cert. elem. tchr., Calif. Tchr. Dominican Coll., 1946; tchr. of mentally handicapped San Anselmo (Calif.) Sch. Dist., 1946; tchr. Fairfax (Calif.) Pub. Elem. Sch., 1946-53; asst. to mayor Fairfax City Recreation, 1948-53; tchr., libr. U.S. Dependent Schs., Mainz am Rhine, Fed. Republic Germany, 1953-56; translator Portugal Travel Tours, Lisbon, 1954; bonding sec. Am. Fore Ins. Group, San Francisco, 1958-60; rancher, farmer Yerington, Nev., 1960-98. Hostess com. Caldecott and Newbury Authors' Awards, San Francisco, 1959; mem. Nev. State Legis. Commn., 1975; coord. Nevadans for Equal Rights Amendment, 1975-78, rural areas rep., 1976-78; testifier Nev. State Senate and Assembly, 1975, 77; mem. adv. com. Fleischmann Coll. Agr. U. Nev., 1977-80, 81-84; speaker Grants and Rsch. Projects, Bishop, Calif., 1977, Choices for Tomorrow's Women, Fallon, Nev., 1989. Poetry presenter World Congress on Arts and Comm., Lisbon, Portugal, 1999, Washington, 2000, St. John's Coll.-Cambridge U., 2001, Vancouver, B.C., Can., 2002. Trustee Wassuk Coll., Hawthorne, Nev., 1984-87; mem. Lyon County Friends of Libr., Yerington, 1971—, Lyon County Mus. Soc., 1978—; sec., pub. info. chmn. Lyon County Rep. Women, 1968-73, program v.p., 1973-75; mem. Lyon County Rep. Ctrl. Com, 1973-74, Marin County Soc. Artists, San Anselmo, Calif., 1948-53; charter mem. Eleanor Roosevelt Edn. Fund for Women and Girls, 1990, sustaining mem., 1992—; Nev. rep. 1st White House Conf. Rural Am. Women, Washington, 1980; participant internat. reception, Washington, 1980; mem. pub. panel individual presentation Shakespeare's Treatment of Women Characters, Nev. Theatre for the Arts, Ashland, Oreg., Shakespearean Actors local performance, 1977; mem. Nev. Women's History Project, U. Nev., 1996—; mem. pres.'s circle Dominican U. Calif., 1997-; mem. Bancroft Libr.'s coun. U. Calif., Berkeley, 2002-. Recipient Outstanding Conservation Farmer award Mason Valley Conservation Dist., 1992, Soroptimist Internat. Women Helping women award 1983, invitation to first all-women delegation to U.S.A. from People's Republic China, U.S. House Reps., 1979; Public Forum Travel grantee Edn. Title IX, Oakland, Calif., 1977; Internat. Biog. Ctr. (Cambridge) fellow World Lit. Acad., 1993. Mem. AAUW (life mem. nat. br. 1975—, Leaders Circle 1998-), Lyon County Ret. Tchrs. Assn. (unit pres. 1979-80, 84-86, v.p. 1986-88, Nev. State Outstanding Svc. award 1981, state conv. gen. chmn. 1985), Rural Am. Women Inc., AAUW (br. pres. 1972-74, 74-76, chair edn. found. programs 1983—, state conv. gen. chmn. 1976, 87, state sec. 1970-72, state legis. program chmn. 1976-77, state chmn. internat. rels. 1979-81, state pres. 1981-83, br. travelship, discovering women in U.S. history Radcliffe Coll. 1981, State Humanities award 1975, Future Fund Nat. award 1983, Lorraine Scatena endowment gift named in her honor for significant contbns. to AAUW Ednl. Found. 1997), Mason Valley Country Club, Italian Cath. Fedn. (pres. 1986-88), Uniao Portuguesa Estado da Calif., Nat. Mus. of Women in the Arts (charter mem., 1987, assoc., mem. mus. coun. 2000—). Roman Catholic. Avocations: writing, photography. Home: PO Box 247 Yerington NV 89447-0247

SCATES, ALICE YEOMANS, former government official, consultant; b. Pitts., Jan. 21, 1915; d. William E. and Georgiana L. (Lloyd) Yeomans. BS, State Tchrs. Coll., Glassboro, N.J., 1936; MEd, Duke U., 1949; EdD, George Washington U., 1963. Tchr. elem. sch., Haddon Heights, N.J., 1937-43; civilian personnel officer Sedalia Army Airfield, Mo., Greenfield Army Airfield, S.C., 1944-46; pers. tng. officer VA Ctr., Dayton, Ohio, 1947—48; rsch. assoc., dir. Am. Coun. on Edn. Staff for Office Naval Rsch. Projects, 1949-53; asst. dir. Nat. Home Study Coun., 1954; editor, rsch. asst. Office of Edn. HEW, 1955, rsch. analyst, coord. coop. rsch. program, 1956-64, program planning officer occupl. rsch. program, 1965-66, dir. basic rsch. br. secondary edn., 1967-69; program planning and eval. officer Nat. Ctr. Ednl. R & D, 1969-71; eval. specialist Office Program Eval., 1971-80; eval. officer Office of Mgmt. U.S. Dept. Edn., 1980-82, cons., 1982-91; mem. continuing care adv. com. Md. State Office on Aging, 1994-99. Contbr. articles to profl. jours.; editor: Life Line, 1998—. Mem. Nat. Continuing Care Residents Assn.; bd. dirs. Town Ctr. Cmty. Assn., Columbia, Md., 1997-2001. Capt. U.S. Army, 1943-46. Fellow AAAS; mem. LWV, Am. Sociol. Assn., Am. Ednl. Rsch. Assn., Adult Edn. Assn., Kappa Delta Pi, Phi Delta Gamma. Home and Office: Vantage House # 1006 5400 Vantage Point Rd Columbia MD 21044-2667 E-mail: ayscates@msn.com.

SCATES, ALLEN EDWARD, professional volleyball coach; BA, UCLA, 1961, MS, 1962. Coach volleyball UCLA, 1970—. Coached UCLA to 18 NCAA championships. Recipient All Time Great Coach awrd USA Volleyball, 1995, Alumnas of Yr. in Profl. Devel., UCLA, 2003; inducted Volleyball Hall of Fame, 1993, Calif. Beach Volleyball Hall of Fame, 1998, UCLA Hall of Fame, 2003; named Coach of Yr., 5 times, U.S. Olympic Com. Coach Yr., 1998. Office: UCLA Morgan Ctr PO Box 24044 Los Angeles CA 90024-0044 E-mail: ascates@athletics.ucla.edu.

SCATURRO, PETER K. investment banker; b. Mar. 15, 1960; m. Kathleen Scaturro; 2 children. Grad., Columbia U. Cash mgr. Chase Manhattan, 1981—86; with Bankers Trust/Deutsche Bank, 1986—97, ptnr., 1997—99; mng. dir. pvt. banking Citigroup, 1999—; mng. dir., head U.S. pvt. banking Citibank, 1999—2000; CEO Citigroup Pvt. Bank, 2000—; exec. v.p. Citicorp, 2000—. Mem. adv. bd. Columbia U.; mem. adv. coun. Am. Mus. Natural History; mem. corp. coun. Carnegie Hall; mem. adv. bd., Snowmass Inst.; mem. Internat. House and Mega Cities. Trsutee Inn-City Scholarship Fund, Caramoor. Mem.: Fgn. Policy Assn. (bd. mem.), Young Pres. Orgn., Econ. Club N.Y. Office: Citigroup Pvt Bank 475 Steamboat Rd Greenwich CT 06830-7144*

SCATURRO, PHILIP DAVID, investment banker, university chancellor; b. Newark, Dec. 8, 1938; s. Charles and Rose (Montino) S. BA, Williams Coll., 1960; JD, MBA, Columbia U., 1963. Analyst Ladenburg, Thalmann & Co., Inc., N.Y.C., 1964-67; v.p. Sellin, Forbes & Smith, N.Y.C., 1967, Allen & Co. Inc., N.Y.C., 1967-71, mng. dir., exec. v.p., 1977—; gen. ptnr. R&S Assocs., N.Y.C., 1972-76; pvt. investor, N.Y.C., 1976-77; chmn. bd. trustees New Sch. U., N.Y.C., 1999—. Bd. dirs. Wilmorite, Inc., Rochester, NY. Bd. dirs. Mass. Mus. Contemporary Art Found., Inc., North Adams; bd. dirs., mem. exec. com., chmn. fin. com., treas. N.Y.C. Opera, trustee, mem. exec. com.; trustee New Sch. U., 1989—. Mem. Univ. Club (N.Y.C.), Century Assn. Avocations: opera, music, theater, wine, fly fishing. Office: Allen & Co 711 Fifth Ave 9th Fl New York NY 10022-3111

SCAVARDA, DONALD ROBERT, composer, artist; b. Iron Mountain, Mich., June 18, 1928; m. Barbara Janet Regner, Nov. 13, 1965. MMus, U. Mich., 1953. Co-founder, organizer Once Festival Musical Premieres, Ann Arbor, Mich., 1960-65. Composer: Groups For Piano, 1959, Sounds for Eleven, 1961, (Haiku song cycle) In the Autumn Mountains, 1961, Matrix for Clarinetist (widely recognized as the pioneering work in discovery and development of clarinet multiphonics), 1962, (piano, clarinet, 8mm film) Landscape Journey, 1963, (film score for electronic realization) Greys, 1963, (multiple film projection and tape) Caterpillar, 1965; paintings include Chamber Music, 1997, Portrait of Helen P., 1998; video films: Blood of Christ, 2002, Marathon, 2002, Concerto for Orchestra, 2002; composed recordings named to Top 10 List, Art Forum Mag., 2003; boxed CD-set, Music From the Once Festival-1961-1966, 2003 Fulbright scholar, 1953; recipient 1st prize for Fantasy For Violin And Orchestra BMI Inc., 1954. Home: PO Box 1908 Ann Arbor MI 48106-1908

SCAVONE, EDMOND, retired surgeon; b. Italy, 1919; arrived in U.S., 1924, naturalized, 1941; s. Giacomino and Serafina (Guarino) S.; m. Jane Frances Kennedy, Jan. 10, 1946 (dec. June 1996); children: Michael, John, Lawrence, Mary Ann, Gregory (dec.). BS, Loyola U., 1941; MD, U. Md., 1944. Bd. cert. gen. surgery. Roman Catholic.

SCEARSE, PATRICIA DOTSON, nurse educator, college dean; b. Wabash, Ind., Sept. 4, 1931; d. Claude Richard and Lilly Etta (Colvill) D.; m. Vernon Quinton Scearse, June 26, 1955 (dec. Mar. 1990); 1 child, Victoria Lynn Lenderman. BS, Earlham Coll., 1955; MS, U. Colo., 1968; D in Nursing Sci., U. Calif., San Francisco, 1974. RN. Staff nurse Reid Meml. Hosp., Richmond, Ind., 1954-55; head nurse, instr. Hillcrest Bapt. Hosp., Waco, Tex., 1955-56; instr. Sch. Nursing Candler Hosp., Savannah, Ga., 1956-60; adminstrv. asst., edn. cons. Wyo. State Bd. Nursing, Cheyenne, 1964-68; asst. prof. San Diego State U., 1969, Ball State U., Muncie, Ind., 1969-71; assoc. prof., area chairperson U. Mich., Ann Arbor, 1974-80; prof., dean Coll. Nursing Tex. Christian U., Ft. Worth, 1980-95, emeritus dean, prof., 1995—. Pub. policy editor Jour. Profl. Nursing, Phila., 1986-89; editorial cons. Jour. Pub. Health Nursing, New Haven, 1984-89; contbr. articles to profl. jours. Recipient Outstanding Nurse award Sigma Theat Tau, Beta Alpha, Ft. Worth, 1986; Kennedy Inst. Ethics postdoctoral fellow, Georgetown U., 1978. Mem. ANA, APHA (bd. govs. 1976), Am. Assn. Colls. of Nursing (bd. dirs. 1982-84, 85-87), Nat. League for Nursing, Coun. Baccalaureate and Higher Degree Programs (bd. rev.), Assn. Community Health Nurse Educators (named Great 100 Nurses 1992). Home: 3818 Hunt Chase Dr Greensboro NC 27407-5472

SCEATS, D(ONALD) JAMES, JR., neurological surgeon; b. Pueblo, Colo., Aug. 15, 1956; s. Donald James Sr. and Marsha (Marsh) S.; m. Deborah Ann Jalowiec, May 22, 1988 (div. Dec. 1994); children: Lindsey Anne, Hunter James, Benjamin James; m. Kristin Britt Olsen, June 29, 1996. BA in Chemistry summa cum laude, Whitman Coll., Walla Walla, Wash., 1978; MD with honors, U. Colo., 1982. Diplomate Am. Bd. Neurol. Surgery, Nat. Bd. Med. Examiners. Intern U. Colo., Denver, 1982-83; resident in neurol. surgery U. Fla., Gainesville, 1989; neurol. surgeon Colorado Springs (Colo.) Neurol. Assoc., 1989—. V.p. Colo. Springs Neurol. Assoc. Contbr. articles to profl. jours. Recipient Analytical Chemistry award Am. Chem. Soc., 1977. Mem. Am. Assn. Neurol. Surgeons, Congress Neurol. Surgeons, Colo. Med. Soc., Colo. Neurosurg. Soc. (v.p. 2001—), El Paso County Med. Soc., Phi Beta Kappa. Republican. Avocations: hunting, snowshoeing. Office: Colorado Springs Neurol 175 S Union Blvd Ste 310 Colorado Springs CO 80910- Office Phone: 719-473-3272. E-mail: djsceats@usa.net.

SCEDROV, ANDRE, mathematics and computer science researcher, educator; b. Zagreb, Croatia, Aug. 1, 1955; came to U.S., 1977, naturalized, 1987; s. Oleg and Mira (Petric) S.; m. Bonnie Carol Hoke, July 23, 1983. BA, U. Zagreb, 1977; MA, SUNY, Buffalo, 1979, PhD in Math., 1981. T.H. Hildebrandt asst. prof. rsch. U. Mich., Ann Arbor, 1981-82; asst. prof. U. Pa., Phila., 1982-88, assoc. prof., 1988-92, prof., 1992—. Vis. scholar U. Milan, 1982, McGill U., Montreal, 1985, U. Sydney, Australia, 1986, U. Catholique de Louvain, Louvain-La-Neuve, Belgium, 1988, U. Paris 7, 1992, Rijksuniv Utrecht, The Netherlands, 1993, CNRS Lab. de Math. Discretes, Marseille, France, 1995, Stanford U., 1995, Isaac Newton Inst. for Math. Scis., Cambridge, Eng., 1995, IST, Lisbon, Portugal, 2002; vis. scientist Math. Scis. Inst. Cornell U., Ithaca, N.Y., 1987; vis. fellow SRI Internat., Menlo Park, Calif., 1995, Mittag-Leffler Inst., Stockholm, 2001; vis. assoc. prof. Stanford U., 1989-90; cons. Odyssey Rsch. Assocs., Ithaca, 1987, HP Labs., Palo Alto, 1990; vis. prof. Keio U., Tokyo, 1997; program chair IEEE Symposium on Logic in Computer Sci., Santa Cruz, Calif., 1992, mem. organizing com., 1992-97, mem. adv. bd., 1997—, mem. program com. Phila., 1990, Copenhagen, 2002, program co-chair Math. Founds. Programming Semantics, New Orleans, 1999, mem. program com., 2001; mem. program com. Logical Found. Computer Sci., Tver, Russia, 1992, St. Petersburg, Russia, 1994, Linear Logic Tokyo '96, 1996, Computer Sci. Logic '98, Brno, Czech Republic, 1998, Typed Lambda Calculi and Applications L'Aquila, Italy, 1999, Category Theory in Computer Sci., Edinburgh, Scotland, 1999, Theoretical Aspects of Computer Software, Japan, 2001, Internat. Symposium on Software Security, Tokyo, 2003, IEEE Computer Security Found. Workshop, N.S., Can., 2001, Asilomar, Calif., 2003, 2004, ACM Conf. on Computer and Comm. Security, Washington, 2004; plenary spkr. 2d Croatian Math. Congress, Zagreb, 2000; invited spkr. Math. Founds. Programming Semantics, Oxford (Eng.) U., 1992, U. Colo., Boulder, 1996, Computer Sci. Logic, San

Miniato, Italy, 1992, Internat. Summer Sch. Logic Computer Sci., Chambery, France, 1993, Proof and Computation, Marktoberdorf, Germany, 1993, Logic and Computer Sci. CIRM, Marseille-Luminy, France, 1994, Winter Sch. on Linear Logic and Applications, Lisbon, Portugal, 1995, 10th Internat. Congress on Logic, Philosophy and Methodology of Sci., Florence Italy, 1995, Linear Logic Meeting and Spring Sch., Tokyo, 1996, Linear Logic Workshop CIRM, Marseille-Luminy, France, 1998, Constructivism in Mathematics and Computing, The Netherlands, 1999, EEF summer sch. logical methods BRICS, Aarhus, Denmark, 2001, First Joint Meeting between Am. Math Soc and Soc. Math de France, Lyon, 2001; Second Internat. Workshop on Secure and Survivable Systems, Tokyo, 2001, Internat. Symposium on Software Security, Tokyo, 2002, Logic and Interaction Programme, CIRM, Marseille-Luminy, 2002, CONCUR 2003, Concurrency Theory, Marseille, France, 2003; invited panelist IEEE Computer Security Found. Workshop, Pacific Grove, Calif., 2003-04; Theory of Cryptography Conference, Boston, Mass., 2004. Author: (with P. Freyd) Categories, Allegories; editor Math. Structures in Computer Sci., 1989—, Annals Pure Applied Logic, 1993—, Perspectives in Mathematical Logic book series, 1997—; contbr. articles and rsch. papers to profl. publs. Recipient Young Faculty award Nat. Scis. Assn. U. Pa., 1987; Rsch. grantee NSF, 1985—, Office Naval Rsch., 1988—. Fellow Japan Soc. for Promotion Sci. (sr.); mem. AAAS, Am. Math. Soc. (Centennial rsch. fellow 1993-94, mem. 1st joint internat. meeting with Soc. Math of France, Lyon, 2001), Assn. for Symbolic Logic (editor jours. 1988-93, chair nominating com. 1993, program com. 1988-90, coun. 1990-96, coordinating editor jours. 1994-96 exec. com. 1998-2001, program chair ann. meeting 2001), Assn. for Computing Machinery, Math. Assn. Am. Office: U Pa Dept Math 209 S 33rd St Dept Math Philadelphia PA 19104-6317 Office Phone: 215-898-5983. E-mail: scedrov@cis.upenn.edu.

SCELFO, CHRIS, university football coach; b. Abbeville, La., Sept. 30, 1963; m. Nancy Caldwell; children: Sarah Beth, Joseph II. BS, N.E. La. U., 1986, MEd, 1988. Asst. coach River Oaks H.S., Monroe, La., 1986; asst. offensive line and tight ends coach N.E. La. U., 1986-87; offensive line grad. asst. coach U. Okla., Norman, 1988, receiver coach, 1989; offensive line coach Marshall U., 1990-95, offensive coord., 1993-95; asst. head coach, offensive line coach U. Ga., Augusta, 1996-98; head football coach Tulane U., New Orleans, 1998—. Office: Tulane U Dept Athletics 6823 Saint Charles Ave New Orleans LA 70118-5665*

SCELSA, JOSEPH VINCENT, sociologist, educator, university executive; b. N.Y.C., Dec. 7, 1945; s. Albert John and Katherine Mary S.; m. Joyce Ann Tisi, Nov. 13, 1981; 1 child, Jonathan. AA, LIU, 1966, BA, 1968; MA, CUNY, 1973, MSEd, 1978; MA, Columbia U., 1983, EdD, 1984. Cert. sch. counselor, N.Y. Counselor, tchr. N.Y.C. Bd. Edn., 1970-78, coord. career and occupational edn., 1979; coord. specialized counseling CUNY, 1979-81; pvt. practice counseling, N.Y.C., 1975—; lectr. grad. faculty Herbert H. Lehman Coll., CUNY, 1980—; dean Calandra Inst., CUNY, 1994—; prof. student pers. Queens Coll., CUNY, 1999, v.p., 2000. Consul gen. of Italy in N.Y. Active Coun. of 1000 nat. Italian-Am. Found.; past cive chair multi cultural adv. bd. N.Y.C. Bd. Edn., 1990-91; N.Y. State Mentoring Program Adv. Bd., 1990—; bd. dirs. Nat. Ethnic Coalition Orgns., 1990—, Coalition Italo-Am. Assn., 2000—; Italian Apostalate, N.Y., 1993. Decorated cavaliere Order of Merit Republic of Italy; recipient Disting. Alumni award LIU, 1985, Organizational Leadership award Coalition Italo-Am. Assns., Inc., 1988, Americus award Bronx Community Coll., 1989, Role Model award Club DaVinci, 1990, Inte I-A Student Assn. award, CUNY, 1991, Intergroup Rels. Chancellor's award, 1994, FIERI Leadership award, 1993, Philip Mazzei award, 1993, Ellis Island medal of honor, 1997, N.Y. State Govs. award for Excellence, 1999, Medal for 3d Millennium, 2000; named House of Savoy, 1997; Italian fellow John Jay Coll., 1993; inductee St. Lucy's Hall of Fame, 1996. Mem. Am. Counseling Assn., Am. Mental Health Counselors Assn. (cert. of recognition 1979, counselor of yr. 1983-84), Nat. Acad. Cert. Clin. Mental Health Counselors, Nat. Bd. for Cert. Counselors, Am.-Italian Hist. Assn., N.Y. State Mental Health Counselors Assn. (past pres., Outstanding Work award 1980), Ill. Club. Home: 41 Carwall Ave Mount Vernon NY 10552-1211 Office: CUNY 25 w 43rd St New York NY 10036-8003

SCHAAB, ARNOLD J. lawyer; b. Newark, 1939; s. Robert George and Pauline Schaab; m. Marcia Stecker, 1964 (div. 1978); children: Emily Diana, Genevieve; m. Patricia Caesar, 1981 (div. 1996); m. Susan McGlamery, 2000; one child: Robert George II. BA, New Sch. U., 1962; LLB, Harvard U., 1965. Bar: NY 1967, US Dist. Ct. (so. and ea. dists.) NY 1967. Assoc. Chadbourne & Parke, NYC, 1966-69; ptnr. Anderson, Kill & Olick, NYC, 1969-78; sr. ptnr. Pryor, Cashman, Sherman & Flynn LLP, NYC, 1978—. Chmn. Literacy Ptnrs., Inc. Fulbright scholar Law Faculty U. Paris. Fellow NY Bar Found., Am. Bar Found.; mem. ABA (vice chair internat. fin. transactions com., sections bus. law, sci. tech law, intellectual property law internat. law practice), NY State Bar Assn. (chmn. internat. law practice sect., chmn. spl. com. free trade Ams., ho. dels., fin. com., long range planning com., by-laws com.), Assn. Bar City NY (com. pvt. investment funds, com. internat. trade, com. fgn. comparative law), Computer Law Assn., Univ. Club (treas., chmn. fin. com., chmn. audit com.), Doubles, Archaeol. Inst. Am., Bibl. Archaeology Soc. Office: Pryor Cashman Sherman & Flynn 410 Park Ave New York NY 10022-4441

SCHAAL, BARBARA ANNA, evolutionary biologist, educator; BS in Biology with honors, U. Ill., Chgo., 1969; MPhil in Population Biology, Yale U., 1971, PhD in Population Biology, 1974. spkr. in field. Assoc. prof. biology Washington U., St. Louis, 1980-86, prof., 1986—; prof. genetics Wash. U. Sch. Medicine, Spencer T. Olin prof. biology in arts and scis., chair dept. biology, 1993-97, mem. various coms. Assoc. editor Molecular Biology and Evolution, Am. Jour. Botany, Molecular Ecology, Conservation Genetics. Trustee St. Louis Acad. Scis. Fellow AAAS; mem. NAS, Bot. Soc. Am. (pres. 1995-96, Merit award 1999), Nature Conservancy (trustee Mo. chpt.). Achievements include research on the evolutionary process within plant populations. Office: PO Box 1137 Saint Louis MO 63188-1137

SCHAAP, ALETTA JOHANNA, artist; b. Phila., June 20, 1948; d. Adolf and Ella Betsey Sanders S.; n. Patrick John Adrian Quinlan, July 4, 1982; children: Adriane, Alexander. AB with high honors, U. Mich., 1970; MFA, U. Puget Sound, 1973; MBA, UCLA, 1983. Assoc. dir. J. Paul Getty Trust, L.A., 1984-96; analyst FCA Am. Mortgage Corp., L.A., 1983; coun. mem. U.S. Holocaust Meml. Mus., Washington, 1997—. Mem. Am. Assn. Mus., Am. Crafts Coun., Internat. Coun. Mus. Democrat. Avocations: crafts, cultural events, exhibitions. Office: US Holocaust Meml Mus 100 Raoul Wallenberg Pl SW Washington DC 20024-2126

SCHACHMAN, HOWARD KAPNEK, molecular biologist, educator; b. Phila., Dec. 5, 1918; s. Morris H. and Rose (Kapnek) S.; m. Ethel H. Lazarus, Oct. 20, 1945; children— Marc, David. BSChemE, Mass. Inst. Tech., 1939; PhD in Phys. Chemistry, Princeton, 1948; DSc (hon.), Northwestern U., 1974; MD (hon.), U. Naples, 1990. Fellow NIH, 1946-48; from instr. to asst. prof. U. Calif., Berkeley, 1948-54, assoc. prof. biochemistry, 1954-59, prof. biochemistry and molecular biology, 1959-91, chmn. dept. molecular biology, dir. virus lab., 1969-76, prof. emeritus, dept. molecular and cell biology, 1991-94, prof. grad. sch., 1994—. Mem. sci. coun. and sci. adv. bd. Stazione Zoologica, Naples, Italy, 1988—; cons. bd. sci. Meml. Sloan-Kettering Cancer Ctr., 1988—97; mem. sci. adv. com. Rsch. ! Am., 1990—; William Lloyd Evans lectr. Ohio State U., 1988; Carl and Gerty Cori lectr. Washington U. Sch. Medicine, 1993; faculty rsch. lectr. U. Calif., Berkeley, 1994; Alta. Heritage Found. for Med. Rsch. vis. prof. U. Alta., 1996; Wellcome vis. prof. in basic med. scis., 1999—2000; Walter C. MacKenzie lectr. Sch. Medicine U. Alta., Edmonton, Canada, 2001. Author: Ultracentrifugation in Biochemistry, 1959. Mem. bd. sci. counselors Cancer Biology and Diagnosis divsn. Nat. Cancer Inst., 1989-92; ombudsman in basic scis. NIH, 1994—2002. Lt. USNR, 1945-47. Recipient John Scott award, 1964, Warren Triennial prize Mass. Gen. Hosp., 1965, Alexander von Humboldt award, 1990, Berkeley citation for disting. achievement and notable svc. U. Calif., 1993, Theodor Svedberg award, 1998; Guggenheim Meml. fellow, 1956. Mem.: NAS (chmn. biochemistry sect. 1990—93, panelist sci. responsibility and conduct of rsch. 1990—92), AAAS (mem. com. on sci. freedom and responsibility 1998—, Sci. Freedom and Responsibility award 2000), Acad. Nat. Dei Lincei (fgn. mem.), Fedn. Am. Socs. for Exptl. Biology (pres. 1988—89, pub. affairs exec. com. 1989—, pub. svc. award 1994), Am. Soc. Biochemistry and Molecular Biology (pres. 1987—88, chmn. pub. affairs com. 1989—2000, Merck award 1986, Herbert A. Sober award 1994, pub. svc. award established in his name 2001 2001), Am. Chem. Soc. (Calif. sect. award 1958, award in chem. instrumentation 1962). Achievements include development of the ultracentrifuge as a tool for studying macromolecules of biological interest; studies on structure and function of a regulatory enzyme: Aspartate transcarbamylase. Office: U Calif Berkeley Dept Molecular Cell Bio 229 Stanley Hall # 3206 Berkeley CA 94720-3206

SCHACHNER, LAWRENCE ALAN, pediatric dermatologist; b. Mar. 3, 1945; s. Alex and Sarah (Rosenberg) S.; m Janet Smallberg, Dec. 21, 1970; children: Hollis, Adam. BS, Bklyn. Coll., 1965; MD, U. Nebr., 1972. Diplomate Am. Bd. Pediat., Am. Bd. Dermatology. Intern in pediat. Montefiore Hosp. and Med. Ctr., Bronx, NY, 1972-73, resident in pediat., 1973-75, chief resident in pediat., 1975-76, resident in dermatology, 1976-77; chief resident in dermatology NYC Hosps., Albert Einstein Coll. Medicine, Yeshiva U., Bronx, 1977-78, Bronx Mcpl. Hosp. Ctr., 1977-78; from asst. prof. to assoc. prof. dermatology and pediat. U. Miami, Fla., 1978-89, prof. dermatology and pediat., 1989—, dir. M. Pediat. and M. Pediatric-Dermatology Confs., 1992—, interim chmn. dermatology, 2003—; chmn. U. Miami Med. Group, 1996—. Dir. divsn. pediat. dermatology U. Miami, 1978—; organizing com. Internat. Congress Pediatric Dermatology, 1989-92; cons. in field. Sr. editor: (with others) Pediatric Dermatology Textbook, 1987, 2d edit., 1995, 3d edit., 2003; contbr. articles to profl. jours. Mem. Am. Acad. Dermatology (task force on pediatric dermatology 1982-85), Am. Acad. Pediat. (bd. dirs. pediatric dermatology sect. 1987—, chmn. 1992-95), Am. Soc. for Pediatric Dermatology (exec. bd. dirs. 1982-83, 86-96), Soc. for Pediatric Dermatology (v.p. 1982-83, 86-87, pres.-elect 1988-89, pres. 1989-90), Internat. Soc. Pediatric Dermatology (v.p. 1998—), Am. Dermatol. Assn., Soc. for Investigative Dermatology, Inc., Miami Dermatol. Soc., Miami Pediat. Soc., Fla. Dermatology Soc., Fla. Pediat. Soc., Nat. Ichthyosis Assn. (med. advisor), Dystrophic Epidermolysis Bullosa Rsch. Assn. (med. advisor, bd. dirs.). Avocations: fishing, tennis, reading, poker, sports. Office: U Miami Sch Medicine 1600 NW 10th Ave # R-250 Miami FL 33136-1090 Office Phone: 305-243-6742. E-mail: LSchachn@med.miami.edu.

SCHACHT, HENRY BREWER, electronics executive, director; b. Erie, Pa., Oct. 16, 1934; s. Henry Blass and Virginia (Brewer) Schacht; m. Nancy Godfrey, Aug. 27, 1960; children: James, Laura, Jane, Mary. BS, Yale U., 1956, MA (hon.), 1988; MBA, Harvard U., 1962; DSc (hon.), DePauw U., 1982. Sales trainee Am. Brake Shoe Co., N.Y.C., 1956—57; investment mgr. Irwin Mgmt. Co., Columbus, Ind., 1962—64; v.p. fin. Cummins Engine Co., Inc., Columbus, 1964—66, v.p., cen. area mgr. internat. London, 1966—67, group v.p. internat. and subsidiaries, 1967—69, from pres. to CEO, 1969—94, chmn., 1977—95; CEO Lucent Techs., Murray Hill, NJ, 1995—97, consultant, 1998—99, interim CEO, 2000—02, chmn., 2002—03, dir., senior adv., 2003—. Bd. dirs. AT&T, 1981—95, Chase Manhattan Corp., Chase Manhattan Bank N.A., Alcoa, Rockefeller Found., Urban Inst., Nat. Exec. Svc. Corps. Trustee emeritus Culver Ednl. Found.; active Bus. Coun., Coun. Fgn. Rels., The Assocs., Harvard Bus. Sch., Bus. Enterprise Trust; hon. trustee Brookings Instn., Com. Econ. Devel., Yale Corp.; chmn. trustees Ford Found.; sr. mem. Conf. Bd. With USNR, 1957—60. Mem.: Tau Beta Pi. Republican. Office: Ford Foundation 320 E 43d St New York NY 10017-4890 also: Lucent Techs 600 Mountain Ave New Providence NJ 07974

SCHACHT, HENRY MEVIS, writer, consultant; b. Pasadena, Calif., Feb. 28, 1916; s. Henry and Amelia (Claussen) S.; m. Mary Joan Turnbull, Dec. 30, 1937; children: Henry John, Linda Joan. BA, U. Calif., Berkeley, 1936. Info. specialist U. Calif., Berkeley, 1936-42; dir. agr. NBC, San Francisco, 1942-59, ABC, San Francisco, 1959-60; agrl. columnist San Francisco Chronicle, 1959-93. Dir. agrl. info. U. Calif., 1961-65; v.p. corp. relations, corp. sec. Calif. Canners & Growers, San Francisco, 1965-81; freelance writer, 1936—; cons. radio-TV to FAO of UN, Cairo, 1963, Mexico City, 1965, Tokyo, 1966; dir. Calif. Co. for Internat. Trade; dir. Agrl. Issues Ctr., U. Calif. Pres. U.S. Fruit Export Coun., 1972-75; exec. sec. Commn. Calif. Agr. and Higher Edn., 1993-95; adv. bd. Agrl. Issues Ctr. U. Calif., 1990—2002. Mem. Pub. Rels. Soc. Am., Pub. Rels. Roundtable San Francisco, Nat. Assn. Farm Broadcasters, Agrl. Rels. Coun., Nat. Canners Assn. (dir. 1966-81) Home: 60 Hiller Dr Oakland CA 94618-2351

SCHACHT, JOCHEN HEINRICH, biochemistry educator; b. Königsberg, Fed. Republic Germany, July 2, 1939; arrived in U.S., 1969; s. Heinz and Else (Sprenger) S.; m. Helga Hildegard Seidel, Jan. 27, 1967; children: Miriam Helga, Daniel Jochen. BS, U. Bonn, Fed. Republic Germany, 1962; MS in Chemistry, U. Heidelberg, Fed. Republic Germany, 1965, PhD in Biochemistry, 1968. Asst. research chemist, Mental Health Research Inst. U. Mich., Ann Arbor, 1969-72, from asst. prof. to assoc. prof. biochemistry, Dept. Biol. Chemistry & Otolaryngology, 1973-84, prof., 1984—, chmn. grad. program in physiol. acoustics, 1981—; hon. prof. Med. Acad. of the Chinese PLA, Beijing, 1998. Vis. prof. Karolinska Inst., Stockholm, 1979-80; acting dir. Kresge Hearing Rsch. Inst., U. Mich., 1983-84, assoc. dir., 1989-99, dir., 2000—; mem. hearing rsch. study sect. USPHS, NIH, Nat. Inst. Neurol. and Communicative Disorders and Stroke, 1986-89, Task Force Nat. Strategic Rsch. Plan, Nat. Insts. Deafness and Communication Disorders, USPHS, NIH; hon. prof. Hunan Med. U., Changsha, China, 1999—, Tonghi Med. U., Wuhan, China, 1999—; guest prof. Fourth Mil. Med. U., Xian, China, 1999—. Mem. editl. bd. Hearing Rsch., 1990—; assoc. editor Audiology & Neuro-Otol., 1995—; contbr. more than 200 articles to profl. jours., book chpts., revs.; co-editor Neurochemistry of Cholinergic Receptors, 1974. Fogarty Sr. Internat. fellow NIH, 1979, Sen. J. Javitz Neurosci. investigator, 1984; recipient Chercheur Etranger rsch. award INSERM, Paris, 1986, 94, Animal Welfare award Erna-Graff Found., Berlin, 1987, Disting. Faculty Achievement award U. Mich., 1989, Employer of Yr. award Nat. Capital Assoc. Coop. Edn. and Gallaudet U., Washington. Mem. Am. Soc. Neurochemistry, Internat. Soc. Neurochemistry, Soc. for Neurosci., Assn. for Rsch. in Otolaryngology, Am. Soc. Biol. Chemists, Assn. Espanola de Audiologia Exptl. Avocations: photography, travel, birding. Office: U Mich Kresge Hearing Rsch Inst Ann Arbor MI 48109-0506 Office Phone: 734-763-3572. E-mail: schacht@umich.edu.

SCHACHT, RONALD STUART, lawyer; b. Stamford, Conn., Nov. 7, 1932; s. Saul Albert and Faye Dorothy (Gittleman) S.; m. Natalie Helene Goldman, June 17, 1956; children: Patti Ellen, Bonnie Anne, Cindy Joy. BS, U. Conn., 1954; LL.B., NYU, 1957, LL.M., 1960. Bar: N.Y. 1957, D.C. 1980. Tax atty. IRS, N.Y.C., 1957-62; assoc. Proskauer Rose, LLP, N.Y.C., 1962-69, ptnr., 1969—, mng. ptnr., 1981-84, mem. exec. com., 1985-95. Lectr. Practising Law Inst., NYU Inst. Fed. Taxation; adj. asst. prof. Sch. Continuing Edn., NYU, 1970-72. Bd. dirs. Congregation Agudath Shalom, Stamford, 1968-73; mem. com. Fedn. Jewish Philanthropies, N.Y.C., 1972-80. Mem. N.Y. State Bar Assn., Assn. of Bar of City of N.Y., N.Y. County Lawyers Assn. (bd. dirs. 1977-83, chmn. ins. com. 1975-85), Newfield Swim Club (bd. dirs. 1967-70, pres. 1979), Phi Kappa Phi, Gamma Chi Epsilon. Democrat. Jewish. E-mail: rss6945@yahoo.com.

SCHACHTEL, BARBARA HARRIET LEVIN, epidemiologist, educator; b. May 27, 1921; d. Lester and Ethel (Neiman) Levin; m. Hyman Judah Schachtel, Oct. 15, 1941 (dec. Jan. 1990); m. Louis H. Green, Feb. 26, 1995; children: Bernard, Ann Mollie. Student, Wellesley Coll., 1939-41; BS, U. Houston, 1951, MA in Psychology, 1967; PhD, U. Tex., Houston, 1979. Psychol. examiner Meyer Ctr. for Devel. Pediat., Tex. Children's Hosp., Houston, 1967-81; instr. dept. pediat. Baylor Coll. Medicine, Houston, 1967-81, asst. prof. dept. medicine, 1982—. Asst. dir. biometry and epidemiology Sid W. Richardson Inst. for Preventive Medicine, Meth. Hosp., Houston, 1981-88, dir. quality assurance, 1988-93; ret., 1993; mem. instl. rev. bd. for human rsch. Baylor Coll. Medicine, Houston, 1981-87, 97—; mem. devel. bd. U. Tex. Health Sci. Ctr., Houston, 1987-97; mem. dean's adv. bd. Sch. Arch., U. Houston, 1987-89. Contbr. articles to profl. jours. V.p., bd. dirs. Houston-Harris County Mental Health Assn., 1966—67; vice-chmn. bd. mgrs. Harris County Hosp. Dist., Houston, 1974—90, chmn., 1990—92, bd. dirs., 1970—93; trustee Inst. Religion in Tex. Med. Ctr., 1990—, vice chmn., 2000—; sec. Bo Harris County Hosp. Dist. Found. Bd., 1993—; bd. dirs. Congregation Beth Israel, 1993—95, Planned Parenthood of Houston, Inc., 1994—2000, Houston Ind. Sch. Dist. Found., 1993—2001, Crisis Intervention, 1994—96. Named Great Texan of Yr., Nat. Found. for Ilietis and Colitis, Houston, 1982, Outstanding Citizen, Houston-Harris County Mental Health Assn., 1985; recipient Good Heart award B'nai Brith Women, 1984, Women of Prominence award Am. Jewish Com., 1991, Mayor's award for outstanding vol. svc., 1994. Mem. APA, APHA, Wellesley Club of Houston (pres. 1968-70). Avocations: golf, tennis, books. Home: 2527 Glen Haven Blvd Houston TX 77030-3511

SCHACHTER, HINDY LAUER, public management educator; b. N.Y.C., May 8, 1945; d. George and Doris (Trenk) Lauer; m. Irving Schachter, Dec. 4, 1967; 1 child, Amanda. BA, Bklyn. Coll., 1966; MA, NYU, 1968; PhD, Columbia U., 1978. Asst. prof. Sch. Mgmt. N.J. Inst. Tech., Newark, 1979-85, assoc. prof. Sch. Mgmt., 1985-89, prof. pub. mgmt. Sch. Mgmt., 1989—. Trainer and workshop presenter in field. Author: Public Agency Communication, 1983, Frederick Taylor and The Public Administration Community, 1989, Reinventing Government or Reinventing Ourselves, 1997; sect. editor Pub. Adminstr. Quar., Pa., 1990—; mem. editl. bd. Pub. Adminstrn. Rev.; contbr. chpts. to books, articles to profl. jours. Recipient fellowship U.S. Office Edn., 1970-78, Lectr. Series grant GTE, 1984-85, Ednl. Devel. grants N.J. Dept. Higher Edn., 1985-87, 93, rsch. grant N.J. Dept. of Transp., 1995, 97, 2000, 02, 03, U.S. Dept. Transp., 2001. Mem. Am. Soc. for Pub. Adminstrn. (exec. com. sect. for profl. devel. 1980-89, 97, chair sec. for profl. devel. 1982, 2003), Am. Polit. Sci. Assn. Jewish. Avocation: bicycling. Office: NJ Inst Tech University Hts Newark NJ 07102

SCHACTER, BRENT ALLAN, oncologist, health facility administrator; b. Winnipeg, Man., Can., June 1, 1942; s. Irvin C. and Claire (Easton) S.; m. Sora Ludwig, Dec. 20, 1981; children: Isanne, Jennifer, Miriam. BSc, MD with honors, U. Man., 1965. Intern Winnipeg Gen. Hosp., 1965-66, jr. asst. resident, 1967-68; asst. resident in internal medicine Barnes Hosp., St. Louis, 1968-69; clin. fellow hematology Barnes Hosp. and Washington U., St. Louis, 1969-70; rsch. fellow, asst. in medicine U. Tex. Southwestern Med. Sch., Dallas, 1970-72; asst. prof. internal medicine U. Man., Winnipeg, 1972-77, assoc. prof. medicine, 1977-87, prof., 1987—; pres., CEO CancerCare Manitoba, Winnipeg, 1993—2003; CEO Can. Assn. Provincial Cancer Agys., 2003—. Lectr. in field; sci. officer grant panel C, Nat. Cancer Inst. Can., 1978, mem., 1979-82; mem. Man. Health Rsch. Coun. grant panel, 1982-84, 89-91, Coun. for Canadian Strategy for Cancer Contro, 2002-; adv. bd. Can. Porphyria Found., 1988—; mem. steering com. Can. Strategy For Cancer Control, 1999-2002, co-chair steering com., 2000-02, mem. coun., 2002—; mem. steering com. Can. Cancer Stats., 2000—; chair stds. task force Coun. for Can. Strategy for Cancer Control, 2002- . Contbr. numerous articles and abstracts to profl. jours. Bd. dirs. Nat. Cancer Inst. Can., 2000—. Recipient Med. Rsch. Coun. Can. Vis. Scientist award, 1986; fellow Muscular Dystrophy Assn., 1964, John S. McEachern Meml. fellow Can. Cancer Soc., 1969-70, Med. Rsch. Coun. Can. fellow, 1970-72, Nat. Cancer Inst. of Can. rsch. fellow, 1966-67; Isbister scholar, 1962, 63, Med. Rsch. Coun. Can. scholar, 1975-80. Fellow Royal Coll. Physicians; mem. AAAS, Royal Coll. Physicians and Surgeons of Can. (specialty com. in med. oncology 1985-94, bd. med. examiners in med. oncology 1987-90, specialty com. in hematology 1989-93, core com. mem. 1990-96, chmn. bd. examiners med. oncology 1990-93, mem. regional adv. com. Sask./Man. dist. 1992-97), Am. Fedn. for Clin. Rsch., Can. Soc. for Clin. Investigation (awards com. 1980-82, chmn. 1981-82), Am. Soc. Hematology, Can. Soc. Hematology, Am. Soc. Clin. Oncology, Can. Bone Marrow Transplant Group, Can. Assn. Provincial Cancer Agys., Can. Hemophilia Soc. (mem. clinic dirs. group 1990-93, sec-treas. 1991-93, Golden Jubilee medal Queen Elizabeth II 2002). Avocations: cross country skiing, scuba diving, model railroading. Home: 224 Lamont Blvd Winnipeg MB Canada R3P 0E9 Office: CancerCare Manitoba 675 McDermot Ave Winnipeg MB Canada R3E 0V9 E-mail: brent.schacter@cancercare.mb.ca.

SCHAD, THEODORE MACNEEVE, science research administrator, civil engineer, consultant; b. Balt., Aug. 25, 1918; s. William Henry and Emma Margaret (Scheldt) S.; m. Kathleen White, Nov. 5, 1944 (dec. Aug. 1989); children: Mary Jane, Rebecca Christina; m. Margot Cornwell, March 19, 1995. BSCE, Johns Hopkins U., 1939. Registered profl. engr., DC. Staff water resources engring. U.S. Army C.E., U.S. Bur. Reclamation, Md., Colo., Oreg., Wash., 1939-54; prin. budget examiner water resources programs U.S. Bur. Budget, Exec. Office of Pres., 1954-58; sr. specialist engring. and pub. works, dep. dir. Congl. Rsch. Svc., Libr. of Congress, 1958-68; staff dir. U.S. Senate Select Com. Nat. Water Resources, 1959—61; exec. dir. Nat. Water Commn., 1968-73; exec. sec. Environ. Studies Bd., 1973-77; dep. dir. Commn. Natural Resources, NAS, Washington, 1977-83; exec. dir. Nat. Ground Water Policy Forum, 1984-86; sr. fellow Conservation Found., Washington, 1986—; U.S. commr. Permanent Internat. Assn. Nav. Congresses, Brussels, 1963-70, commr. emeritus, 1987—. Cons. U.S. Senate Com. Interior and Insular Affairs, 1963, U.S. Ho. of Reps. Com. Sci. and Tech., 1962-65, U.S. Office Saline Water, 1965-67, A.T. Kearney, Inc., Alexandria, Va., 1979-80, Chesapeake Rsch. Consortium, 1984, Ronco Cons. Corp., 1986—, Gambia River Basin Devel. Commn., Dakar, 1986-87, Apogee Rsch. Corp., 1987—, Office Tech. Assessment, U.S. Congress, 1992-95. Contbr. articles to Ency. Brit. and profl. jours. Treas. Nat. Speleol. Found., 1961-65, trustee, 1965—; bd. dirs. Vets. Coop. Housing Assn., Washington, 1958-81, v.p., 1960-72. Recipient Meritorious Svc. award U.S. Dept. Interior, 1950, Icko Iben award Am. Water Resources Assn., 1978, Henry P. Caulfield medal, 1990, Woodrow Wilson award for disting. govt. svc. Johns Hopkins U., 1997. Fellow: ASCE (treas. Nat. Capital chpt. 1952—55, v.p. 1967, pres. 1968, Julian Hinds prize 1991); mem.: AAAS, U.S. Soc. on Dams, Internat. Commn. Irrigation and Drainage, Permanent Internat. Assn. Nav. Congresses (commr. emeritus), Nat. Acad. Pub. Adminstrn., Am. Acad. Environ. Engrs. (Gordon Maskew Fair award 2002), Am. Geophys. Union, Nat. Speleol. Soc., Am. Water Works Assn. (hon.), Am. Alpine Club, Seattle Mountaineers Club, Colo. Mountain Club (Denver), Cosmos Club, Potomac Appalachian Trail Club. Home: 4540 25th Rd N Arlington VA 22207-4102 Office: The Conservation Found 1260 24th St NW Washington DC 20037-1103

SCHADE, STANLEY GREINERT, JR., hematologist, educator; b. Pitts., Dec. 21, 1933; s. Stanley G. and Charlotte (Marks) S.; m. Sylvia Zottu, Mar. 24, 1966; children: David Stanley, Robert Edward. BA in English, Hamilton Coll., 1955; MD, Yale U., 1961. Diplomate Am. Bd. Internal Medicine, Am. Bd. Hematology, Am. Bd. Oncology. Intern, resident, hematology fellow U. Wis., Madison, 1962-66; chief hematology Westside VA Hosp., Chgo., 1971-77; prof. medicine, chief hematology U. Ill., Chgo., 1978—97. Contbr. articles to profl. jour. Served to maj. US Army, 1967-69. Fulbright fellow Tubingen, Fed. Republic of Germany, 1956. Fellow Am. Coll. Physicians; mem. Am. Soc. Hematology. Presbyterian. Avocation: medical ethics. Home: 189 N Delaplaine Rd Riverside IL 60546-2060 Office: Westside VA Med Ctr Dept Medicine MP111 820 S Damen Ave Chicago IL 60612-3728

SCHADOW, KAREN E. public speaking trainer/educator; b. Mar. 1949; 1 child, Kelby. BA in comm. and humanities magna cum laude, Fla. State U., 1971, MA in theatre magna cum laude, 1973. Previous cameraperson numerous programs, ABC TV, previous prodn. staff mem.; pres. The Voice of Success!, NYC. Adh. asst. prof. NYU, 1990—; instr. Bergen Cmty. Coll., NJ; creator, presenter various lectures and seminars for sch. and orgn. including Nat. Acad. TV Arts & Scis., NY Coalition Women in Arts and Media, high sch., nationwide. Mem.: Nat. Acad. TV Arts & Scis. (past mem. bd. govs., Emmy award 1984), Fla. State U. Theatre Project, New England Soc., Univ. Film & Video Assn., Screen Actors Guild, Actors' Equity, NY Women in Comm. (v.p. student affairs).

SCHADT, JAMES PHILLIP, investment and software executive; b. Saginaw, Mich., Aug. 7, 1938; s. Phillip Jr. and Jean D. (Cardy) S.; m. Barbara L. Soldmann, Aug. 16, 1959; children: Lauren C., Andrew F. BA, Northwestern U., 1960. With Procter & Gamble USA, 1960-65, Glendinning Cos., 1965-70, Squibb Corp., 1971-73, Pepsi Co., 1973-77, Sara Lee, 1977-80; pres., CEO

Cadbury Schweppes Inc., 1981-91; dir., pres., COO Reader's Digest Assoc. Inc., Pleasantville, N.Y., 1991-94, pres., CEO, 1994—97, chmn., pres., CEO, 1995-97; chair Dailey Capital Mgmt., L.P., Southport, Conn., 1997—; chmn. Mercator Software, Inc., Wilton, Conn., 2000—03. Trustee Northwestern U. Mem. Blind Brook Club (Purchase, N.Y.), Chgo. Club, Am. Enterprise Inst. (trustee), Country Club of Fairfield, Conn., John's Island Club, Lotos Club N.Y.C.*

SCHAECHTER, MOSELIO, microbiology educator; b. Apr. 26, 1928; children: Judy, John. Student, Cen. U., Ecuador, 1947-49; MA, U. Kans., 1952; PhD, U. Pa., 1954. Postdoctoral fellow State Serum Inst., Copenhagen, 1956-58; from instr. to asst. prof. to assoc. prof. U. Fla., Gainesville, 1958-62; from assoc. prof. to disting. prof. dept. microbiology Tufts U., Boston, 1962-95, prof. emeritus, 1995—. Adj. prof. San Diego State U., 1995—, U. Calif., San Diego, 2004—. Editor: Molecular Biology Bacterial Growth, 1985, Escherichia coli and Salmonella Typhimurium, 1987, 95, Mechanisms of Microbiol. Disease, 1989, 92; author: In the Company of Mushrooms, 1997. Mem. Am. Soc. Microbiology (pres. 1985-86, chmn. internat. activities), Am. Soc. Med. Sch. Microbiology Chmn. (pres. 1984-85, chair internat. activities 1986-94), Soc. Gen. Microbiology, Boston Mycol. Club, Sigma Xi. Avocations: field mycology, hiking. Business E-Mail: mschaech@sunstroke.sdsu.edu.

SCHAEDE, RICHARD EDWIN, retired family practice physician; b. Thomasboro, Ill., Aug. 28, 1927; s. Mayo William and Opal Mae (Hutchison) S.; m. Ila Marlene Coffey, June 13, 1949; children: Pamela, Janet, Mark. BS in chemistry, U. Ill., 1949; BS in Medicine, U. Ill., Chgo., 1951, MD, 1953. Diplomate Am. Bd. Family Practice. Chief dept. internal medicine, cardiology, Shilling AFB, 1955-57; physician Chanute AFB, Rantoul, Ill., 1954-55; founder, pvt. practice Rantoul Clinic, 1957-80; assoc. dean medicine U. Ill., Champaign, 1972-78, assoc. prof. clin. medicine, 1978-86; dir. Christie Clinic Satellite, Champaign, 1980-85; pvt. practice Marion, Ill., 1986—2003. Mem. faculty Parkland Coll., Champaign, 1970-72. Bd. dirs. Rantoul Elem. Sch. Bd., 1959-70; pres. Outlook T.B. Sanitorium Bd., 1959-69. Seaman first class USNR, 1945-46; capt. USAF, 1955-57. Fellow Am. Coll. Family Practice; mem. Rotary. Republican. Lutheran. Avocations: hunting, fishing. Home: 10242 Limb Branch Ln Marion IL 62959 6020

SCHAEDLER, RUSSELL WILLIAM, microbiologist, physician, educator; b. Hatfield, Pa., Dec. 17, 1927; s. Robert and Sophia Louise (Enz) S. BS, Ursinus Coll., 1949; MD, Jefferson Med. Coll., 1953. Intern Jefferson Med. Coll. Hosp., Thomas Jefferson U., Phila., 1953-54, prof., chmn. dept. microbiology, 1968-91, Plimpton-Pugh prof., 1985—2003, prof. emeritus, 2003—. Asst. Rockefeller Inst. for Med. Research, asst. physician Hosp. of Rockefeller Inst., 1954-57; asst. prof. Rockefeller Inst., resident asso. physician, 1957-62, asso. prof., physician to Hosp., 1962-68; asso. mem. Armed Forces Epidemiology Bd., Enteric Commn., 1967-72; mem. bacteriology and mycology study sect. NIH, 1970-74, chmn., 1973-74; mem. and chmn. NIH bacteriology and mycology AHR study sect., 1978-82 Mem. editorial bd. Jour. Bacteriology, 1965-69, Jour. Infection and Immunity, 1970-72; contbr. articles to sci. jours. Bd. dirs. Cardeza Found. Served with U.S. Army, 1946-47. Mem. Am. Assn. Immunologists, Am. Soc. Microbiology, Am. Gastroent. Assn., Infectious Disease Soc. Am., Coll. Physicians Phila., Harvey Soc., AAAS, J. Aitken Meigs Med. Assn., N.Y. Tb and Health Assn. (bd. dirs. 1965-68), Sigma Xi, Alpha Omega Alpha. Clubs: Vesper, Sydenham Coterie. Research in anaerobes and microecology of the gut. Home: 320 Delancey St Philadelphia PA 19106-4209

SCHAEFER, C. BARRY, railroad executive, lawyer, investment banker; b. Elizabeth, N.J., Feb. 23, 1939; s. Carl H. and Evelyn G. (Conk) S.; m. Carol Ann Craft, July 11, 1970; children: Sara Elizabeth, Susan Craft. BS in Engring., Princeton U., 1961; MS in Engring., U. Pa., 1962; LLB, Columbia U., 1965; MBA, NYU, 1970. Bar: N.Y. 1966, Nebr. 1972. With Kelley, Drye, Warren, N.Y.C., 1966-69; asst. gen. counsel Union Pacific Corp., N.Y.C., 1969-72; western gen. counsel Union Pacific R.R. Co., Omaha, 1972-74, v.p., western gen. counsel, 1974-77, v.p. law, 1977-82; sr. v.p. planning and corp. devel. Union Pacific Corp., N.Y.C., 1984-88, exec. v.p. Bethlehem, Pa., 1988; sr. advisor Dillon Read & Co. Inc., 1989-91; mng. dir. The Bridgeford Group, 1992-97, Beacon Group, 1997-01, The Bridgeford Group, 2001—. Nat. bd. dirs. Jr. Achievement, Colorado Springs, Colo., 1986-2004. Mem. Racquet and Tennis Club (N.Y.C.), Round Hill Club (Greenwich, Conn.), Desert Mountain Club (Scottsdale, Ariz.).

SCHAEFER, CHARLES JAMES, III, advertising agency executive, consultant; b. Orange, NJ, Dec. 17, 1926; m. Eleanor Anne Montville, Apr. 8, 1961; 1 child, Charles James IV. AB, Dartmouth Coll., 1948, M in Comml. Sci., 1949. Mgr. foods promotion Beech-Nut, 1949—52; v.p. Dickie-Raymond, 1952-67; sr. v.p. Metromedia, 1968-69; exec. v.p., treas. The DR Group, Boston and NYC, 1969-76, pres., 1976-87; exec. v.p., dir. Needham Harper Worldwide Inc., NYC, 1984-87; chmn. bd. Marcoa DR Group, Inc., NYC, 1987-88; cons. Rapp Collins Marcoa, NYC, 1989-92; advt. cons., 1992—. Pres. Dartmouth Class of 1948, 1998-2000; trustee, mem. exec. com. Direct Mktg. Ednl. Found., 1983-89; campaign chairperson United Way Millburn-Short Hills, 1994, 95, trustee, 1991-98, 2000—. With USN, 1945-46. Mem. Direct Mktg. Assn. (chmn. awards com. 1971-76, Hall of Fame com. 1978-81, ethics com. 1981-86), Assn. Direct Mktg. Agys. (pres. 1980-82, gen. chmn. Caples awards 1985, chmn. Direct Mktg. Days NY 1988, NY Direct Marketer of Yr. award 1987, Silver Apple award 1989, contbr. to jour.), Dartmouth Club of NY (pres. 1968-70), Lotos Club (bd. dirs. 1985-88, treas. 1987-88), Canoe Brook Country Club (Summit, NJ). Home and Office: 307 Hobart Ave Short Hills NJ 07078-2207

SCHAEFER, CHRISTINA KASSABIAN, writer, genealogist; b. Meriden, Conn., May 31, 1954; d. Levon Harry and Lareine Alice (Kinstler) Kassabian; m. Douglas Eric Schaefer, May 1, 1981; children: Eric, Alice. BA in English, So. Conn. State Coll., 1975. V.p. Blue Sales, Inc., Guilford, Conn., 1977-81. Dir. Family Hist. Ctr., Annandale, Va., 1994-97. Author: The Center: Guide to Research in the National Capital Area, 1996, Guide to Naturalization Records of the United States, 1997, The Great War: Guide to the Service Records of All the World's Fighting Men and Volunteers, 1998, Genealogical Encyclopedia of the Colonial Americas: A Complete Digest of the Records of All the Countries of the Western Hemisphere, 1998, The Hidden Half of the Family: A Sourcebook for Women's Genealogy, 1999, Instant Information on the Internet/ A Genealogist's No-Frills Guide to the 50 States and the District of Columbia, 1999, Instant Information on the Internet: A Genealogist's No-Frills Guide to the British Isles, 1999. Vol. Boys Scouts Am., Springfield, Va., 1991—. Recipient 1st pl. literary award Conn. Soc. Genealogists, 1997, 1998; Selected for inclusion in Authors' Room of Libr. Va., 2000. Mem.: Bd. Cert. Genealogists.

SCHAEFER, DALE W. physicist, researcher, administrator; b. Willoughby, Ohio, May 17, 1941; s. George Louis and Edna (Romig) S.; m. Arlene Tellgren, Aug. 25, 1962; children: Jeanne, Joel. BS, Wheaton Coll., 1963; PhD, MIT, 1968. Postdoctoral fellow NSF, 1968; rsch. assoc. dept. physics M.I.T., Cambridge, Mass., 1968—70; rsch. assoc. IBM Watson Rsch. Ctr., Yorktown Heights, NY, 1970—72; mem. tech. staff Sandia Nat. Labs., Albuquerque, 1972-80, supr., 1980—88, mgr., 1988—. Chmn. program. com. Nat. Ctr. for Small Angle Scattering, Oak Ridge, Tenn., 1980—85; vis. scientist Ctr. Theoretical Physics U. Calif., Santa Barbara, 1983. Contbr. 110 articles to profl. jour. Recipient Am. Inst. Chemists award, 1963, Rensselaer Sci. medal, 1959, Kodak prize, 1966, DOE-BES Outstanding Sustained Rsch. award, 1986, grantee NSF, 1964. Fellow Am. Phys. Soc., Am. Inst. Chemists, Am. Inst. Chemists; mem. Site Visit Com., Los Alamos Nat. Lab., Materials Rsch. Soc., Am. Ceramic Soc., Sigma Xi. Avocations: hunting, skiing, golf. Home: 3323 Westside Ave Cincinnati OH 45208 Office: U Cin Dept Chem and Materials Engring Cincinnati OH 45221-0012 Office Phone: 513-556-5431. E-mail: dale.schaefer@uc.edu.

SCHAEFER, DAN L. former congressman; b. Gutenberg, Iowa, Jan. 25, 1936; s. Alvin L. and Evelyn (Everson) S.; m. Mary Margaret Lenney, 1959; children: Danny, Darren, Joel, Jennifer. BA, Niagara U., 1961, LLD (hon.), 1986; postgrad., Potsdam State U., 1961-64. Pub. rels. cons., 1967-83; mem. Colo. Gen. Assembly, 1977-78, Colo. Senate, 1979-83, pres. pro tem, 1981-82, majority whip, 1983; mem. 98th-105th Congresses from 6th dist. Colo., Washington, 1983-98. Bd. dirs. Gen. Instruments Co-chair Nat. Retail Sales Tax Caucus, Congl. Oil and Gas Forum; mem. Spkrs. Task Force on Environ.; founder Nat. Trails Caucus, House Renewable Energy Caucus; pres. Foothills Recreation Bd., 1973-76; sec. Jefferson County Rep. Party, Colo., 1975-76. With USMCR, 1955-57. Recipient Colo. Park and Recreation citation, 1976; named Elected Ofcl. of Yr., Lakewood/South Jeffco C. of C., 1986, 88, 90, Leadership award U.S. Congl. Adv. Bd., Am. Security Coun. Found., Taxpayers Friend award Nat. Taxpayer's Union, 1985-86, 88, 90, 91, 92, 93, 94, 95, Golden Bulldog award Watchdog of Treasury, 1985-86, 87-88, 88-89, 89-90, 91-92, 93-94, 95-96, Spirit of Enterprise award U.S. C. of C., 1995, Nat. Health award Am. Assn. Nurse Anesthetists, 1996, Nat. Security Scorecare Perfect 100 award Ctr. for Security Policy, 1995, Friend of Taxpayer Perfect 100% award Ams. for Tax Reform, 1996; named Guardian of Small Bus., Nat. Fedn. Ind. Bus., 1996. Mem. C. of C., Rotary, Beta Theta Pi. Roman Catholic.

SCHAEFER, FRANK WILLIAM, III, microbiologist, researcher; b. Dayton, Ohio, Sept. 1, 1942; s. Frank William Jr. and Irene Josephine (Krouse) S. BA, Miami U., Oxford, Ohio, 1964; MS, U. Cin., 1970, PhD, 1973. Rsch. assoc. parasitologist U. Notre Dame, South Bend, Ind., 1973-78; U.S. EPA EPA, Cin., 1978— Mem. ASTM, AAAS, Am. Soc. Parasitology, Am. Soc. Microbiology, Am. Water Works Assn., Soc. Protozoologists, Sigma Xi. Home: 9948 McCauley Woods Dr Sharonville OH 45241-1489 Office: US EPA 26 Martin Luther King Dr Cincinnati OH 45268 Office Phone: 513-569-7222. Business E-Mail: schaefer.frank@epa.gov.

SCHAEFER, GEORGE A., JR., bank executive; b. Cincinnati, Ohio, 1945; BS Engineering, U.S. Mil. Acad., West Point, 1967; MBA, Xavier U., 1974. Joined as mgmt. trainee Fifth Third Bancorp, Cin., 1971, pres., CEO, 1990—. Bd. dirs. Fifth Third Bancorp, Fifth Third Bank, Anthem, Inc, Ashland, Inc, Greater Cin./N. Ky. Internat. Airport, Cin. Bus. Com. Chmn., bd. trustees U. Cin.; bd. dirs. Children's Hosp. Med. Ctr., Greater Cin. C. of C., Health Alliance Greater Cin. Served U.S. Army, 1967—70, Europe and Vietnam. Recipient Bronze Star. Office: Fifth Third Bancorp Fifth Third Center 38 Fountain Square Plz Cincinnati OH 45263-0001*

SCHAEFER, GEORGE W. SANDY, musician, educator; b. Rahway, NJ, June 21, 1948; s. George W. and Loraine S. Schaefer; m. Lana Sue Ferrell, June 21, 1969; children: Nicholson, Erin. BS, Ind. State U., Terre Haute, 1970; MMus, U. Colo., Boulder, 1977; DMus, Ariz. State U., Tempe, 1994. Lectr. Calif. State U., Fresno, 1977—83, U. Wis., Oshkosh, 1983—88, asst. prof., 1992—99; assoc. prof. Chadron State Coll., Nebr., 1999—. Pres. Percussive Arts Soc. Wis. Chpt., 1997—99; treas. Namm Affiliated Music Bus. Instns., 2003—; pres. Internat. Assn. of Jazz Educators Nebr. Unit, 2003 . Musician: (CD) Percussion From the List, 1997; author: (books) Here to Stay: Rock and Roll Through 1970s, 1997, A Student's Guide to the Drum Set, 2000. Sgt. NORAD Band, 1970—74. Avocation: music. Office: Chadron State Coll 1000 Main St Chadron NE 69337 Office Phone: 308-432-6378. Business E-Mail: sschaefer@csc.edu.

SCHAEFER, GORDON EMORY, food products executive; b. 1932; married. BS, Marquette U., 1956. With Peat, Marwick, Mitchell & Co., 1955-59; contr., sec. Wells Badger, Badger Carton Co., 1960—64; treas. Pabst Brewing Co., Milw., 1965-72, v.p. adminstrn., 1972-75, v.p. ops., 1975—80, exec. v.p. ops, 1980—85, dir.; pres., dir. Krier Foods Inc., Belgium, Wis., 1981-85, Corrs Beverages, Chgo., 1985-86; dir. bus. devel. Lakeside Packing Co., Manitowoc, Wis., 1989-92; mng. dir. Robertson Assocs., Mfg. Europe Ltd., Cardiff, Wales, 1993-94. Bd. dirs. Fox Fin. Co., Berg Industries, Inc.; fin. and ops. cons.; owner, operator Schaefer's Orchards. Home: N27 W6567 Alyce St Cedarburg WI 53012 E-mail: schaefer1@milwpc.com.

SCHAEFER, HEINRICH C. retired anesthesiologist; b. Berlin, 1917; MD, U. Innsbruck, 1944. Diplomate Am. Bd. Anesthesiology. Intern St. Luke's Meth. Hosp., Cedar Rapids, Iowa, 1952-54; resident in anesthesiology Detroit Receiving Hosp., 1954-56; pvt. practice Detroit; sr. staff Henry Ford Hosp., Detroit, 1991-96, Cottage Hosp., Grosse Pointe, Mich., 1976-96; ret., 1996. Mem. AMA, Am. Soc. Anesthesiologists.

SCHAEFER, HENRY FREDERICK, III, chemistry professor; b. Grand Rapids, Mich., June 8, 1944; s. Henry Frederick Jr. and Janice Christine (Trost) S.; m. Karen Regine Rasmussen, Sept. 2, 1966; children: Charlotte, Pierre, Theodore, Rebecca, Caleb. BS in Chem. Physics, MIT, 1966; PhD in Chem. Physics, Stanford U., 1969; Doctorate (hon.), U. Plovdiv, Bulgaria, 1998, U. Sofia, 1999, Beijing Inst. Tech., 1999, Huntington Coll., Ind., 2002. From asst. prof. to prof. chemistry U. Calif., Berkeley, 1969-87; Graham Perdue prof., dir. Ctr. for Computational Chemistry U. Ga., Athens, 1987—. Apptd. Professeur d'Echange U. Paris, 1977, Gastprofessor Eidgenossische Technische Hochshule, Zurich, 1994, 95, 97, 2000, 02, 04; Wilfred T. Doherty prof., dir. Inst. Theoretical Chemistry, U. Tex., Austin, 1979-80; lectr. in field. Author: Science and Christianity: Conflict or Coherence? 2003; contbr. more than 1000 articles to profl. jours. including The Electronic Structure of Atoms and Molecules: A Survey of Rigorous Quantum Mechanical Results, 1972, Modern Theoretical Chemistry, 1977, Quantum Chemistry, 1983, A New Dimension to Quantum Chemistry, 1994; editor Molecular Physics, 1991-94, editor in chief, 1995—. Recipient Pure Chemistry award Am. Chem. Soc., 1979, Leo Hendrik Baekeland award, 1983, Schrödinger Medal, 1990, Centenary medal Royal Soc. Chemistry, London, 1992, Gold medal Comenius U., Bratislava, Slovakia, 2000; Sloan fellow, 1972, Guggenheim fellow, 1976-77; named one of 100 Outstanding Young Scientists in Am., Sci. Digest, 1984, named 3rd Most Highly cited chemist in world Science Watch, 1992. Fellow AAAS, Am. Phys. Soc., Am. Sci. Affiliation, Am. Acad. Arts and Scis.; mem. Internat. Acad. Quantum Molecular Sci., Am. Chem. Soc. (chmn. divsn. phys. chemistry 1992, award in theoretical chemistry 2003, Ira M. Remsen award 2003), World Assn. Theoretically Oriented Chemists (pres. 1996—). Presbyterian. Office: U Ga Ctr Computational Chemistry Athens GA 30602 Office Phone: 706-542-2067. E-mail: hfsiii@uga.edu.

SCHAEFER, JAME, religious studies educator; d. William J. Ehegartner and Norma I. Eppler; m. Wendelin W. Schaefer, Dec. 22, 1962; children: Joseph W., Peter F., Laura E. Momcilovic, Gretchen C. BA in Polit. Sci., Marquette U., 1961, PhD in Religious Studies, 1994; MA in History, U. West Fla., 1974. Cons. pub. participation in energy and environment issues, Sheboygan, Wis., 1986—2002; prof. religion and sci. Marquette U., Milw., 1995—; dir. interdisciplinary minor in environ. ethics Coll. Arts and Sci., Marquette U., Milw., 2001—03. Numerous appts. to local, state and fed. govtl. positions, 1980—2002. Contbr. articles to profl. jours. Mem. Energy Task Force State Wis., 1980—81; chair Radioactive Waste Rev. Bd. State Wis., 1982—83, vice-chair, 1983—85, chair edn. com., 1985—89; mem. Spl. Com. Low-Level Radioactive Waste Mgmt., State Legislature, State Wis., 1983—84; chair Local Emergency Response Planning Com. Sheboygan County, Wis., 1987—94; mem. Low-Level Radioactive Waste Coun., State Wis., 1988—2000, Citizens Adv. Com., Sheboygan River and Harbor Remedial Action Plan, Wis., 1990—96. Recipient Quality and Excellence in Tchg. Sci. and Religion award, Ctr. Theology and Natural Sci., 1998, Religion and Sci. Course award, John Templeton Found., 1996; Rosamund Gifford scholar. Mem.: Coll. Theology Soc., Soc. Christian Ethics, Internat. Soc. Environ. Ethics, Cath. Theol. Soc. Am. (convenor Theology and Ecology Group 2001—), Am. Acad. Religion. Roman Catholic. Office: Marquette Univ Dept Theology 115 Coughlin Hall Milwaukee WI 53201-1881 Office Phone: 414-288-3742. Personal E-mail: jamesphd@wi.rr.com. E-mail: schaeferj@marquette.edu.

SCHAEFER, JOHN H. finance company executive, securities company executive; b. 1952; BS in Chemistry, Polytechnic Inst. of Brooklyn, 1955; PhD, U. Ill., 1958. Chief strategic and adminstrv. officer, exec. v.p. Morgan Stanley & Co., Inc., NYC, 1998—2000, pres., COO, individual investor group, 2000—. Office: Morgan Stanley & Co Inc 1585 Broadway New York NY 10036 Office Phone: 212-761-4000.

SCHAEFER, JOHN PAUL, chemist; b. N.Y.C., Sept. 17, 1934; s. Conrad and Meta (Rekelkamm) S.; m. Helen Marie Schwarz, May 18, 1958; children— Ann Marie, Susan Margaret. BS, Poly. Inst. Bklyn., 1955; PhD in Chemistry, U. Ill., 1958; fellow, Calif. Inst. Tech., 1958-59. Asst. prof. U. Calif. at Berkeley, 1959-60; mem. faculty U. Ariz., 1960—, prof. chemistry, head dept., 1968-70; dean Coll. Liberal Arts U. Ariz., 1970-71, pres., 1971-82, Rsch. Corp., 1982—, also bd. dirs.; chmn. bd. Rsch. Corp. Techs. Inc., 1988—. Bd. dirs. Olin Corp., Rsch. Corp. Techs. Bd. dirs. Tucson Airport Authority; bd. govs. U.S.-Israel Binat. Sci. Found., 1972-77. Mem. AAAS, Nat. Audubon Soc., Tucson Audubon Soc. (pres. 1961-65), Am. Chem. Soc., Ariz. Acad., Nature Conservancy, Newcomen Soc., Sigma Xi, Phi Lambda Upsilon, Phi Kappa Phi. Office: Rsch Corp 101 N Wilmot Rd Ste 250 Tucson AZ 85711-3361

SCHAEFER, MARILYN LOUISE, artist, writer, educator; b. Cedar Rapids, Iowa, Apr. 22, 1933; d. Henry Richard and Maria Augusta (Dickel) S. AA, Monticello Coll. for Women, 1953; BFA, Cranbrook Acad. Art, 1956, MFA, 1960; MA cum laude, U. Chgo., 1958; MA, St. John's Coll., Santa Fe, 1979. Rsch. asst. editor Encyclopaedia Britannica, Chgo., 1960-63; humanities editor Encyclopedia Americana, N.Y., 1964-68; acquisitions editor Litton Ednl. Pub., N.Y., 1968-70; from instr. to prof. emeritus art and advt. design dept. N.Y.C. Tech. Coll. CUNY, 1970—. Contbg. editor Encyclopedia Americana, 1979—, Coll. Teaching jour., 1979. Contbr. articles to profl. publs. including Art and Auction mag., Art and Antiques mag., Am. Artist mag., Encyclopedia Americana, 1970—. Luce Found. postgrad. study fellow St. John's Coll., 1976-79; Ingram Merrill Found. grantee, 1983-84. Mem. AAUW, CUNY Acad. Arts and Scis. Home: 306 W 76th St New York NY 10023-8065 Office: NYC Tech Coll CUNY 300 Jay St Brooklyn NY 11201-1909

SCHAEFER, MARY ANN, health facility administrator, consultant; b. Chgo., May 18, 1942; d. Joseph and Mary A. (Kozyra) Strosnik; m. Robert Earl Schaefer, May 18, 1963; children: Debra Ann, Robert Joseph. Diploma in nursing, St. Francis Hosp. Sch. Nursing, Evanston, Ill., 1962; BA, Nat. Coll. Edn., Evanston, 1980; MBA in Health Svc. Mgmt., Webster U., 1990; MJ in Health Law, Loyola U., Chgo., 1993. Med. and surg. nurse Resurrection Med. Ctr., Chgo., 1962-79, charge nurse labor and delivery, 1978-79; coord. maternal child care Humana, Hoffman Estates, Ill., 1979-81; nurse mgr. labor and delivery Resurrection Med. Ctr., Chgo., 1981-91; mgr. Family Birthplace Resurrection Med. Ctr., Chgo., 1991-98; cons., prin. M/B Assocs.-Consultants Perinatal Healthcare and Edn., Barrington, 1994-98; mgr. Maternal-Child Health Sherman Hosp., Elgin, Ill., 1998-00, dir. women's svcs., 2000—. Seminar leader on childbirth edn., legal issues in nursing. Contbr. to Motor Facilitation Handbook; editorial bd. Essentials publ., Resurrection Med. Ctr. Mem. Assn. Women's Health, Obstetric and Neonatal Nurses (cert. in inpatient obstetric nursing, instr. principles and practice electronic fetal monitoring), Nat. Perinatal Assn. Perinatal Assn. Ill. (exec. bd.). Home: 5806 Prairie Ridge Rd Crystal Lake IL 60014-4601

SCHAEFER, PATRICIA, librarian; b. Ft. Wayne, Ind., Apr. 23, 1930; d. Edward John and Hildegarde Hartman (Hormel) S. MusB, Northwestern U., 1951; MusM, U. Ill., 1958; AMLS, U. Mich., 1963; DLS (hon.), Ind. Inst. of Tech., 2003. With U.S. Rubber co., Ft. Wayne, 1951-52; sec. to promotion mgr. Sta. WOWO, Ft. Wayne, Ind., 1952, sec. to program mgr., 1953-55; coord. publicity and promotion Home Telephone Co., Ft. Wayne, 1955-56; sec. Fine Arts Found., Ft. Wayne, 1956-57; libr. asst. Columbus (Ohio) Pub. Libr., 1958-59; audio-visual libr. Muncie (Ind.) Pub. Libr., 1959-86, asst. libr. dir., 1981-86, libr. dir., 1986-95. Chmn. Ind. Libr. Film Cir., 1962-63; treas. Ind. Libr. Film Svc., 1969-70, 83-85; mem. trustee adv. coun. Milton S. Eisenhower Libr., Johns Hopkins U.; mem. presdl. counsellors Johns Hopkins U., 1994—; bd. dirs. Franklin Elec. Co., Inc., 1982-2004. Weekly columnist Libr. Lines, Muncie Evening Press, 1981-83; program annotator Muncie Symphony Orch., 1963-2003, Masterworks Chorale, 1982-2003; contbr. articles to profl. jours. Bd. dirs. Muncie Symphony Assn., 1964-74, 85-91, Ctrl. City Bus. Assn., 1986-92, Ind. Inst. Tech., Ind. Humanities Coun., 1996-2002, Sta. WIPB-TV, 1996-2002, Muncie Ctr. for the Arts, 1999-2001; adv. coun. Coll. Fine Arts, Ball State U.; adv. com., bookshop dir. Midwest Writers Workshop, 1976-77; sec. Del. County Coun. for the Arts, 1978-79, pres., 1979-81, bd. dirs., 1985-86; pres.'s coun. Berea Coll., 1990-2001; bd. dirs. Muncie YWCA, 1977-82, 85-89, 95-2001, treas. 1981-82, 88-89; bd. govs. Minnetrista Cultural Ctr., 1998-2001; gen. chmn. Ind. Renaissance Fair, 1978-79; pres. Muncie Matinee Musicale, 1965-67; past pres. Ind. Film and Video Coun.; adv. bd. Cmty. Found. Muncie and Delaware County; bd. dirs. Wapehani coun. Girl Scouts U.S., 1989-96, ARC Hoosier Heartland chpt., 1997-2003. Named Woman Achievement Pub. Svc., 1986; recipient Sagamore of the Wabash award Gov. State of Ind., Outstanding Libr. award Ind. Libr. Fedn., 1995, Cert. of Congrl. Recognition, 1995, Cert. of Achievement, Women's Coalition, 1996, Cert. of Appreciation, Masterworks Chorale, 1998. Mem. ALA, Ind. Libr. Assn. (pres. 1987-88), Nat. League Am. Pen Women (pres. Muncie br. 1974-78), Altrusa (pres. 1986-87, cmty. svc. award 2000), Art Students League, Del. Country Club, Delta Zeta, Mu Phi Epsilon. Republican. Roman Catholic. Home: 5400 W Deer Run Ct Muncie IN 47304-5775

SCHAEFER, PATRICIA ANN, retired librarian; b. Lebanon, Ohio, Jan. 22, 1933; d. Riley Ray and Louise Collette (Fraher) Freeze; m. William H. Schaefer, Aug. 11, 1956; children: Susan P., Nancy A., William H. III(dec.). BS, Miami U., Oxford, Ohio, 1954. Med. technologist Mercy Hosp., Hamilton, Ohio, 1954-58, Middletown (Ohio) Hosp., 1958-62; libr. Middletown City Schs., 1979-93; intermediate libr. McKinley Sch., 1982-93; ret., 1993. Hon. bd. dirs. Am. Cancer Soc., 1961—; chmn. legis. City Charter Rev. Com., 1970, charter revision com., 1989; active YMCA, pres., 1977—79; bd. dirs. Middletown Symphony, 1974—78, Arts in Middletown, 1983—, Middletown Symphony Women, 1992—, exec. bd., 1995—; residential chmn. United Way, 1976, residential-retiree chmn., 1990; chmn. Sch. Tax Levy, 1978; co-chmn. Luncheon Style Show, 1998—2003; mem. exec. com. Ohio-Ky.-Ind. Regional Coun., 1986—88; mem. Bicentennial Com., Middletown; pres. Middletown Needy Youth Bd.; mem. adv. bd. Manchester Tech. Ctr., Drug Task Force Bd., Middletown Schs.; bd. dirs. Citizens Adv. Bd. Manchester Tech. Ctr., Middletown Fine Arts, 1993—, Dental Emergency Fund Area Children, 1994—; exec. bd. Leadership Middletown; pres. Care View Home Health, 2000, 2003—; co-chmn. Mary Alice Mack City Golf Tournament, 1998; mem. Middletown City Commn., 1983—88; adminstrv. bd. Meth. Ch.; mem. fin. com., sec. bd. trustees 1st United Meth. Ch., 1999—; exec. bd. United Meth. Women; mem. citizen's adv. com. Miami U., Middletown, co-chair major capital campaign, 2003—. Named Outstanding Woman of Butler County, 1997, hon. chmn., Charity Ball, 1998, Woman of Distinction, Soroptomists Internat., 2000; recipient Stuart Ives Svc. to Youth award, 1980. Mem.: PEO (pres. 1995—, co-chair state conv. 1997), LWV (pres. 1962—63), Am. Bus. Women's Assn. (pres. 1961—62), Registry Med. Technologists, Am. Soc. Clin. Pathologists, Middletown C. of C., Browns Run Country Club, Sigma Sigma Sigma. Methodist. Home: 1909 Antrim Ct Middletown OH 45042-2901

SCHAEFER, PHILIP WILLIAM, mathematics educator, researcher; b. Balt., Feb. 16, 1935; s. John Herman and Caroline Ellen (Doran) S.; m. Patricia Elizabeth Kirby, Oct. 11, 1958; children: Daniel T., Barbara T., Michael C., Susan E. BS, John Carroll U., 1956, MS, 1957; PhD, U. Md., 1964. Instr. Loyola Coll., Balt., 1959-60; asst. prof. U. South Fla., Tampa, 1964-67; asst. prof. to assoc. prof. U. Tenn., Knoxville, 1967-77, prof., 1977—. Cons. Oak Ridge (Tenn.) Nat. Labs., 1967-68. Editor: Maximum Principles and Eigenvalue Problems in Partial Differential Equations, 1988, Spectral Theory and Computational Methods of Sturm-Liouville Problems, 1997; contbr. over 60 articles to profl. jours. 1st lt. U.S. Army, 1957—59.

Mem. Am. Math. Soc., Soc. Indsl. and Applied Maths. Roman Catholic. Home: 608 Coventry Rd Knoxville TN 37923-2454 Office: U Tenn Dept of Math Cumberland Ave Knoxville TN 37996-1300 E-mail: schaefer@math.utk.edu.

SCHAEFER, ROBERT WAYNE, banker; b. Balt., Feb. 28, 1934; s. Roland Elmer and Lillian (Reid) S.; m. Elaine Lennon, May 18, 1963; children: Linda, Karen. Student, Balt. City Coll., 1949-51; BS in Acctg., U. Balt., 1955; MBA in Fin., Loyola Coll., 1971. C.P.A., Md. With First Nat. Bank of Md., Balt., 1951-55, 59—, comptroller, 1961—, v.p., 1965-69, sr. v.p., 1969-73, exec. v.p., 1973-96; exec. dir. France-Merrick Founds., Balt., 1996—. Instr. accounting N.C. State Coll., 1956-58; instr. accounting, econs., taxes, credit Balt. chpt. Am. Inst. Banking, 1960-66, Investment Com. State of Md. Retirement System and Baltimore Fire, Police Retirement System. Mem. Balt. City Sch. Bd., 1973-75, Balt. City Bd. Fin.; bd. dirs., treas. Balt. Area United Fund, 1964-79; past bd. dirs. Balt. coun. Boy Scouts Am., Balt. chpt. ARC, Boys Latin Sch.; trustee, pres. Wesley Home for Aged; bd. dirs. Balt. City Aquarium, Roland Park Country Sch., Md. Gen. Hosp., Western Md. Coll., 1981-92, Lyric Theatre, 1985—, Enoch Pratt Libr., 1986-93, Ind. Coll. Fund Md., 1990—, Coun. on Econ. Edn., YMCA Ctrl. Md., 1992, U. Balt. 1st lt. USMCR, 1956-58. Mem.: Fin. Execs. Inst., Md. CPA Assn., Bank Adminstrn. Inst. (past pres., bd. dirs. Balt. chpt.), U. Balt. Found., U. Balt. Alumni Assn. (bd. dirs. 1972—), L'Hirondelle Club, Valley Country Club. Republican. Methodist (bd. dirs., mem. finance com.). Home: 5903 Meadowood Rd Baltimore MD 21212-2436 Office: France-Merrick Foundations 1122 Kenilworth Dr Ste 118 Baltimore MD 21204-2142 Personal E-mail: riosels@aol.com. Business E-Mail: rschaefer@france-merrickfdn.org.

SCHAEFER, STEVEN DAVID, head and neck surgeon, physiologist; b. L.A., Mar. 25, 1945; s. Glen Arthur and Alice (Malerstein) S.; m. Phyllis Lois Clark, July 1, 1977; 1 child, Jessica Leigh. BA, U. Calif., Berkeley, 1967; MD, U. Calif., Irvine, 1972. Diplomate Am. Bd. Otolarnyology. Asst. prof. U. Tex. Southwestern and U. Tex. Dallas, 1972-82, assoc. prof., 1982-86, prof., 1986-92; prof, dept. chmn. N.Y. Med. Coll., N.Y.C., 1992—, N.Y. Eye and Ear Infirmary, N.Y.C., 1992—. Author 5 books and 7 monographs; contbr. over 160 articles and abstracts to med. jours., chpts. to books. Dir. pub. edn. Tex. div., Am. Cancer Soc., Dallas, 1978-80. Named prin. investigator NIH, 1980-94. Fellow Am. Laryngol. Assn., Am. Acad. Otolaryngology (Honor award 1990), Am. Laryngol. Rhinol. and Otol. Soc.; mem. N.Y. Acad. Sci., Soc. Univ. Otolaryngologists (pres. 1992-93), NIH Divsn. Rsch. Grants. Office: NY Eye & Ear Infirmary 310 E 14th St New York NY 10003-4201

SCHAEFER, THEODORE PETER, chemistry educator, retired; b. Gnadenthal, Man., Can., July 22, 1933; s. Paul Jacob and Margarethe (Wiebe) S.; m. Nicola Caroline Sewell, Dec. 26, 1960; children: Catherine, Dominic, Benjamin. BS with Honors, U. Man., 1954, MS, 1955; D.Phil. (Shell scholar), Oxford (Eng.) U., 1958; D.Sc. (hon. causa), U. Winnipeg, 1982. Prof. chemistry U. Manitoba, Winnipeg, Can., 1958—, Univ. Disting. prof., 1982-97, sr. scholar, 1997-2000, ret., 2000; researcher NRC, Ottawa, Can., 1959, 62, Nat. Phys. Lab., Teddington, U.K., 1960, 65, Argonne Nat. Lab., Chgo., 1967, 68; sr. fellow, mem. grants com. NRC, Ottawa.; mem. council Nat. Scis. and Engring. Research Council, Ottawa., 1980-85. Contbr. articles on nuclear magnetic resonance to sci. jours. Recipient Herzberg award Spectroscopy Soc. Can., 1975. Fellow Chem. Inst. Can. (Noranda award 1973), Royal Soc. Can.; mem. Order of Can. Home: 210 Oak St Winnipeg MB Canada R3M 3R4 *Persistence can sometimes emulate perspicacity.*

SCHAEFER, WILLIAM DAVID, English language educator; b. Dighton, Mass., May 11, 1928; s. Louis and Elsie K. (Otterbein) S.; m. Josephine R. Lamprecht, Aug. 8, 1958; 1 dau., Kimberly. BA, NYU, 1957; MS, U. Wis., 1958, PhD, 1962. Mem. faculty UCLA, 1962-90, prof. English, 1970-90, chmn. dept., 1969-71, exec. vice chancellor, 1978-87. Author: James (BV) Thomson: Beyond the City, 1965, Speedy Extinction of Evil and Misery, 1967, Education Without Compromise: From Chaos to Coherence in Higher Education, 1990; contbr. articles to profl. jours., short stories to literary mags. Served with AUS, 1954-56. Fulbright fellow Eng., 1961-62 Mem. MLA (exec. dir. 1971-78). Home: 164 Stagecoach Rd Bell Canyon CA 91307-1044 Office: UCLA 405 Hilgard Ave Los Angeles CA 90095-9000 E-mail: wschae444@aol.com.

SCHAEFER, WILLIAM GOERMAN, lawyer; b. Kansas City, Mo., June 16, 1941; m. Sharon Saylor, Dec. 21, 1963; children: James, Kristen. BA, U. Kans., 1963; JD, Harvard U., 1966. Bar: Ill. 1966, D.C. 1978, Md. 1984. Ptnr. Sidley & Austin, Chgo. and Washington, 1966-74, 78-93; v.p., gen. counsel DeKalb Genetics Corp., Ill., 1974-77; spl. counsel Bechel Corp., Gaithersburg, Md., 1993-96; sr. v.p. corporate affairs Vertis, Inc., Balt., 1996-2000; cons., 2000—.

SCHAEFFER, BARBARA HAMILTON, retired rental leasing company executive, writer; b. Newton, Mass., Apr. 26, 1926; d. Peter Davidson Gunn and Harriet Bennett (Thompson) Hamilton; m. John Schaeffer, Sept. 7, 1946; children: Laurie, John, Peter. Student, Skidmore Coll., 1943-46; AB in English, Bucknell U., 1948; postgrad., Montclair State U., 1950-51, Bank St. Coll. Edn., 1959-61, Yeshiva U., 1961-62. Cert. primary, secondary tchr. N.J. Dir. Pompton Plains Sch., N.J., 1959-62; adviser Episcopal Sch., Towaco, N.J., 1968-70; v.p. Deltona-DeLand Trolley, Orange City, Fla., 1980-81; pres. Monroe Heavy Equipment Rentals, Inc., Orange City, 1981—; also Magic Carpet Travel, 1985-88. Cons., founder, pres. TLC Travel Club, Orange City, 1981-88; lectr. on children's art, 1959-70. Contbr. articles to profl. jours. Mem. Nat. Trust Historic Preservation. Episcopalian. Avocations: restoring old homes, painting, piano, writing. Home: 400 Foothill Farms Rd Orange City FL 32763-5502

SCHAEFFER, CHARLES PERRY, newswriter, editor; b. Cumberland, Md., Mar. 20, 1926; s. Charles Perry and Dorothy Frances Schaeffer; m. Eliza Ann Riggins, June 16, 1950; children: Sally Ann Canepa, John, Jennifer Bartell. BA, U. Md., 1950. Writer U.S. Info. Agy., Washington, 1950—53; news picture writer UPI, N.Y.C., 1953—54; reporter Balt. Evening Sun, Balt., 1954—55, Am. Aviation Publs., Md., 1955—61; science writer Newhouse Newspapers, Washington, 1961—65; writer, exec. editor Kiplinger Personal Fin. Mag. (formerly Changing Times) Kiplinger Washington Editors, Inc, 1966—89. Mem. profit sharing bd. Kiplinger Washington Editors. Author: (anthology) Esquire's World of Humor, 1964, Saturday Review's Phoenix Nest, 1965; contbr. articles to mags. Chmn. scout troop Walter Reed Army Med. Ctr., Silver Spring, Md., 1971—72; pres Neighborhood Civic Assn., Silver Spring, 1963—64; bd. dirs. Woodlin Elem. Sch., Silver Spring, 1963—64. EM 3/C U.S. Navy, 1943—46, Pacific Theater of Operations. Decorated Phillippine Liberation Ribbon, 2 Stars USN, Pacific Theater Ribbon, Six Stars, Victory medal; recipient Blakeslee Nat. Sci. Writing award, Am. Heart Assn., 1965. Mem.: Soc. Profl. Journalists, Nat. Assn. Sci. Writers (life), Nat. Press Club (1st pl. consumer journalism 1987). Home: 6036 Chatsworth Ln Bethesda MD 20814 E-mail: schaeffer528@cs.com.

SCHAEFFER, GLENN WILLIAM, casino corporate financial executive; b. Pomona, Calif., Oct. 11, 1953; s. William Donald and Mary Louise (Miller) S.; m. Deborah Lynn Helfer, Sept. 6, 1974 (div. Apr. 1981); m. Renee Sue Riebel, May 25, 1985 AB summa cum laude, U. Calif., Irvine, 1974, MA, 1975; MFA, U. Iowa, 1977. Fin. cons. Dean Witter, Los Angeles, 1977-78; assoc. Hill and Knowlton, Inc., Los Angeles, 1978-81; v.p. Ramada Inns, Inc., Phoenix, 1981-84; exec. v.p., chief fin. officer Circus Circus Enterprises, Inc., Las Vegas, Nev., 1984-91, pres., 1991-93, also bd. dirs.; ptnr. Gold Strike Resorts, Jean, Nev., 1993-95; pres. Mandalay Resort Group, 1995—. Wine grower and estate bottler, N.Z. Founder and patron Internat. Inst. Modern Letters. Pres. Hitch fellow U. Calif.-Irvine, 1973-74 Mem. Phi Beta Kappa. Avocations: reading, bicycling. Office: Mandalay Resort Group 3950 Las Vegas Blvd S Las Vegas NV 89119

SCHAEFFER, LEONARD DAVID, healthcare executive; b. Chgo., July 28, 1945; s. David and Sarah (Levin) Schaeffer; m. Pamela Lee Sidford, Aug. 11, 1968; children: David, Jacqueline. BA, Princeton U., 1969. Mgmt. cons. Arthur Andersen & Co., 1969—73; dep. dir. mgmt. Ill. Mental Health/Devel. Disability, Springfield, 1973—75; dir. Ill. Bur. of Budget, Springfield, 1975—76; v.p. Citibank, N.A., N.Y.C., 1976—78; asst. sec. mgmt. and budget HHS, Washington, 1978, adminstr. HCFA, 1978—80; exec. v.p., COO Student Loan Mktg. Assn., Washington, 1980—82; pres., CEO Group Health, Inc., Mpls., 1983—86; chmn., CEO Blue Cross of Calif., Woodland Hills, 1986—96, WellPoint Health Networks Inc., Thousand Oaks, Calif., 1992—. Bd. dirs. Allergan, Inc., Irvine, Calif., Amgen, Inc., Thousand Oaks; bd. councilors U. So. Calif. Sch. Policy, Planning & Devel., 1988—; bd. dirs., exec. com. Blue Cross-Blue Shield Assn., Chgo., 1986—; mem. Congl. Prospective Payment Assessment Commn., 1987—93, Pew Health Professions Com., Phila., 1990—93; chmn. bd. trustees Nat. Health Found., LA, 1992—2001; chmn. bd. dirs. Nat. Health Care Mgmt., 1993—; mem. Coun. on the Econ. Impact of Health Sys. Change, 1996—; co-chair adv. coun. dept. of health care policy Harvard Med. Sch., 1998—; founding chmn. Coalition for Affordable and Quality Healthcare, 2000. Bd. govs. Town Hall of Calif., LA, 1989; bd. trustees The Brookings Inst., Nat. Health Mus., 2000—; adv. coun. Dept. Econs. Princeton (NJ) U.; adv. group Coun. on Health Care Econs. and Policy. Recipient Citation for Outstanding Svc., Am. Acad. Pediat., 1981, Disting. Pub. Svc. award, HEW, Washington, 1980; fellow, Kellogg Found., 1981—89; Internat. fellow, King's Fund Coll., London, 1990—. Mem.: Nat. Inst. Health Care Mgmt. (chmn.), Am. Assn. Health Plans (bd. dirs. 2001—), Health Ins. Assn. Am. (chmn. 1999), Inst. Medicine of NAS, Regency Club, Princeton Club, Cosmos Club. Office: WellPoint Health Networks Inc 1 WellPoint Way Thousand Oaks CA 91362-3893

SCHAEFFER, REINER HORST, military officer, foreign language professional; b. Berlin, Lichterfelde, Fed. Republic Germany, Jan. 13, 1938; arrived in U.S., 1958; s. Immanuel Emil and Wilhelmine (Fahrni) Frei-Schaeffer; m. Cathy Anne Cormack, Apr. 6, 1966; 1 child, Brian Reiner. Nat. cert., Bus. Sch., Thun, Switzerland, 1957; BGS in Bus., U. Nebr., 1970; MPA in Orgnl. Behavior, U. Mo., 1972; PhD in Fgn. Lang. Edn., Ohio State U., 1979. Commd. officer USAF, 1958, advanced through grades to lt. col.; instr. German, French USAF Acad., Colorado Springs, Colo., 1975-77, assoc. prof., 1979-81, chmn. German, 1981, dir. librs., 1982-86, prof., 1986-92, dir. Acad. Librs., 1986-92. Bd. dirs. Friends of AF Acad. Librs.; pres. Fgn. Lang. Ctr., Inc., 1999—2001; cons. Fgn. Langs., 2001—. Named Disting. Grad., Air Force Inst. Tech., 1979; recipient 5 Meritorious Svc. medals, 5 Air Force Commendation medals. Mem.: Am. Assn. Tchrs. German, Aspen Creek Meadows Homeowners Assn. (pres. 2004—), Swiss Club (pres. Colorado Springs chpt. 1990—96, chmn.), Alpha Sigma Alpha, Pi Alpha Alpha. Republican. Avocation: Avocations: skiing, golfing, hiking, soccer. Home: 751 Babbling Brook Prescott AZ 86303 Personal E-mail: swiss13@juno.com.

SCHAFER, ALICE TURNER, retired mathematics educator; b. Richmond, Va., June 18, 1915; d. John H. and Cleon (Dermott) Turner; m. Richard Donald Schafer, Sept. 8, 1942; children: John Dickerson, Richard Stone. AB, U. Richmond, 1936, DSc, 1964; MS, U . Chgo., 1940, PhD (fellow), 1942. Tchr. Glen Allen (Va.) High Sch., 1936-39; instr. math. Conn. Coll., New London, 1942-44, asst. prof., 1954-57, asso. prof., 1957-61, prof., 1961-62; prof. math. Wellesley Coll., 1962-80, Helen Day Gould prof. math., 1969-80, Helen Day Gould prof. math. emerita, 1980—, affirmative action officer, 1980-82; prof. math. Marymount U., Arlington, Va., 1989-96; ret., 1996. Instr. U. Mich., Ann Arbor, 1945-46; lectr. Douglass Coll., New Brunswick, N.J., 1946-48; asst. prof. Swarthmore (Pa.) Coll., 1948-51, Drexel Inst. Tech., Phila., 1951-53; mathematician Johns Hopkins Applied Physics Lab., Silver Spring, Md., 1945; lectr. Simmons Coll., Boston, 1980-88, Radcliffe Coll. Seminars, Cambridge, Mass., 1980-85; U.S. chair postsecondary math. edn. U.S./China Joint Conf. on Edn., 1992, co-chair Citizen Amb. program People to People U.S. and China Joint Conf. on Women's Issues, 1995, session women in sci. and math. Contbr. articles on women in math. and other articles to math. jours. Recipient Disting. Alumna award Westhampton Coll., U. Richmond, 1977; NSF sci. faculty fellow Inst. for Advanced Study, Princeton, N.J., 1958-59. Fellow AAAS (math. sect. A nominating com. 1979-83, mem.-at-large 1983-86, chair-elect sect. A 1991, chair 1992, retiring chair 1993, Assn. for Women in Math. rep., 1993—), AAUP (chmn. nat. com. W 1980-83, mem. nat. coun. 1984-87), Am. Math. Soc. (chmn. postdoctoral fellowship com. 1973-76, affirmative action procedures com. 1980-82, chair com. on Human Rights of Mathematicians 1988-94), Soc. Indsl. and Applied Math., Am. Statis. Assn., Inst. Math. Stats., Nat. Coun. Tchrs. of Math. (chair com. on women 1976-81), Math Assn. Am. (adv. com. for Women and Math. program 1987-89, dir. fund raising 1989-92, lectr. 1982—, chair devel. com. 1988-92, Yueh-Gin Gung and Charles Y. Hu disting. svc. to math. award 1998), Internat. Congress Mathematicians (mem. fund raising com. 1986), Assn. for Women in Math. (pres. 1973-75, Alice T. Schafer Prize established 1989, chair fund raising com. 1992-94, leader math. del. women mathematicians to China 1990, Disting. Svc. award 1996), Emily's List (mem. majority coun.), Cosmos Club, Phi Beta Kappa, Sigma Xi, Sigma Delta Epsilon. Achievements include first study of singularities of space curves in projective differential geometry; research on undulation point of a space curve. Home: 1010 Waltham St Apt A404 Lexington MA 02421-8064

SCHAFER, CARL WALTER, investment executive; b. Chgo., Jan. 16, 1936; s. MacHenry George and Gertrude (Herrick) S.; 1 child, MacHenry George II. BA with distinction, U. Rochester, 1958. Budget examiner Budget Bur., Exec. Office Pres., Washington, 1961—64, legis. analyst, 1964-66, dep. dir. budget preparation, 1966-68, dir. budget preparation, 1968-69; staff asst. U.S. Ho. of Reps. Appropriations Com., 1969; dir. budget Princeton (N.J.) U., 1969-72, treas., 1972-76, fin. v.p., treas., 1976-87, lectr. indsl. adminstrn., 1975; prin. Rockefeller & Co., Inc., 1987-90; pres. Atlantic Found., Princeton, N.J., 1990—. Pres., CEO, Palmer Square Inc., 1979-81; trustee, treas. McCarter Theatre Co. Inc., 1974-76; co-chmn. N.J. Gov.'s Task Force on Improving N.J. Econ. and Regulatory Climate, 1982-83; chmn. investment adv. com. Howard Hughes Med. Inst., 1985-92; trustee Am. Bible Soc., 1987-92; trustee, dir. Frontier Oil Corp., Labor Ready, Inc., The UBS, Harding Loevner, European Investors and Guardian Groups of Mut. Funds, The Claremont Inst., Harbor Br. Inst. Inc., Hamilton and Co., The Johnson Atelier and Sch. Sculpture, The Banbury Fund; mem. internat. adv. coun. Wm. Sword & Co., Inc. Bd. dirs. Jewish Guild for the Blind, 1988-96; chmn., investment com., William H. Donner Found. and Donner Can. Found., Amnesty Internat. Leadership Group. With USN, 1958—61. Mem. Phi Beta Kappa. Office: 66 Witherspoon St Ste 1100 Princeton NJ 08542-3226 Office Phone: 212-969-0917.

SCHAFER, ELIZABETH DIANE, historian, writer; b. Opelika, Ala., Sept. 26, 1965; d. Robert Louis and Carolyn Louise (Henn) S. BA in History cum laude, Auburn U., 1986, MA in History of Sci. magna cum laude, 1988, PhD in History of Tech. magna cum laude, 1993; MA magna cum laude, Hollins Coll., 1996—2003. Archivist Lee County Hist. Soc. Mus., 1988—. Ind. scholar, 1993—; presenter in field. Author: Beacham's Sourcebooks for Teaching Young Adult Fiction: Exploring Harry Potter, 2000, Lake Martin: Alabama's Crown Jewel, 2002, Auburn: Plainsmen, Tigers and War Eagles, 2003, Auburn Football, 2004; co-author: Women Who Made A Difference in Alabama, 1995; cons. editor Ency. of Sci., 1998; freelance editor various tech. docs.; editl. asst. Proceedings of the We. Soc. for French History, 1988-91, Nat. Forum: The Phi Kappa Phi Jour., 1990-91; contbr. History News Svc.; contbr. articles to profl. jours., encys., mags., chpts. to books. Recipient hon. mention poetry Writer's Digest, 1994 hon. mention children's non-fiction, 1997, children's non-fiction and fiction, 1998, Writer's Digest, Shirley Henn Meml. award Critical scholar, Hollins Coll., 1998. Mem. AAAS, AAUW, Am. Hist. Assn., Orgn. Am. Historians, Soc. History Tech., History Sci. Soc., Women's History Network, N.Y. Acad. Scis., So. Hist. Assn., Soc. Children's Book Writers and Illustrators, Children's Lit. Network, Ala. Poetry Soc., Children's Lit. Assn., Ala. Writer's Forum, Assn. Gravestone Studies, Lancaster Mennonite Hist. Soc., Lee County Hist. Soc. (life mem.), Auburn U. Alumni Assn. (life mem.), Descendants Mexican War Vets., United Daus. of the Confederacy, DAR (chmn. Light Horse Harry Lee's geneal. records com.), Daus. of Union Vets., Phi Alpha Theta (history hon.). Home and Office: PO Box 57 Loachapoka AL 36865-0057 E-mail: Elizabeth_D_Schafer@yahoo.com.

SCHAFER, GLENN S, insurance company executive; b. St. Johns, Mich., Sept. 6, 1949; BS in Acctg. magna cum laude, Mich. State U., 1971; MBA in Fin. summa cum laude, U. Detroit, 1976. CPA, Mich.; registered fin. prin. With Peat Marwick Mitchell and Co., 1971-74; from asst. contr. to sr. v.p., CFO Alexander Hamilton Life Ins. Co., 1974-82; sr. v.p., CFO E.F. Hutton Life, 1982-86; v.p. corp. fin. Pacific Life, 1986-87, sr. v.p., CFO, 1987-91, exec. v.p., CFO, 1991-95, pres., 1995—, also bd. dirs. Bd. dirs. PIMCO Advisor L.P., Mich. State U. Grad. Sch. Bus. Adv. Bd., Ct. Apptd. Spl. Advs. Sgt. USAR, 1968-74. Fellow Life Mgmt. Inst.; mem. AICPA, Fin. Execs. Inst. Office: Pacific Life Ins Co PO Box 9000 Newport Beach CA 92658-9030

SCHAFER, JAMES ARTHUR, physiologist; b. Buffalo, Oct. 10, 1941; s. Joseph James and Gladys Leita (Lighty) S.; m. Margaret Anne Schiefer, Aug. 16, 1964; children: James Arthur Jr., Kirsten Ann. BS, U. Mich., 1963, PhD, 1968. Postdoctoral fellow Gustav-Embden Ctr., Frankfurt, Germany, 1968-69, Duke U., Durham, N.C., 1969-70; asst. prof. U. Ala., Birmingham, 1970-72, assoc. prof., 1972-76, prof., 1976—, sr. scientist Nephrology Rsch. and Tng. Ctr., 1980—. Editor Am. Jour. Physiology: Renal, 1983-89, mem. editl. bd., 2001—; assoc. editor News in Physiol. Scis., 1997-2003; cons. editor Jour. Clin. Investigation, 1998-2003; mem. editl bd. Jour. Gen. Physiology, 1979-97, adv. editor, 1998—; mem. editl. bd. Kidney Internat., 1990-95; contbr. numerous articles to sci. jours. Chmn. rsch. com. Nat. Kidney and Urol. Diseases Adv. Bd. U.S. Dept. HHS, 1987-90. Recipient Established Investigator award Am. Heart Assn., 1971-76, Robert F. Pitts. Meml. award Internat. Union Physiol. Scis., Sydney, Australia, 1983, Max Planck-Von Humboldt Rsch. award Govt. of Germany, 1994, Homer W. Smith award Am. Soc. Nephrology and N.Y. Heart Assn., 1993; Jane Coffin Childs Meml. fellow, 1968-69. Mem. Am. Physiol. Soc. (councilor 1992-95, pres.-elect 1995-96, pres. 1996-97, past pres. 1997-98, Carl W. Gottschalk award 2001, Robert W. Berliner award 2004), Am. Soc. Nephrology (sec.-treas. 1989-92, councilor 1992-95), Am. Soc. Clin. Investigation (hon.), Fedn. Am. Socs. Exptl. Biology (bd. dirs. 1995-99, exec. com. 1996-97, pub. affairs exec. com. 1997-99). Avocations: classical music, racquet sports, mountain hiking. Office: U Ala Dept Phys & Biophysics 834 MCLM Bldg 1918 University Blvd Birmingham AL 35294-0005 Office Phone: 205-934-7106. Business E-Mail: jschafer@uab.edu.

SCHAFER, JOHN FRANCIS, retired plant pathologist; b. Pullman, Wash., Feb. 17, 1921; s. Edwin George and Ella Frances (Miles) S.; m. Joyce A. Marcks, Aug. 16, 1947; children— Patricia, Janice, James BS, Wash. State U., 1942; PhD, U. Wis., 1950. Asst. prof. to prof. plant pathology Purdue U., 1949-68; head dept. plant pathology Kans. State U., 1968-72; chmn. dept. plant pathology Wash. State U., Pullman, 1972-80; integrated pest mgmt. coordinator sci. and edn. USDA, 1980-81, acting nat. research program leader plant pathology Agrl. Research Service, 1981-82, dir. cereal rust lab., 1982-87, biol. sci. collaborator, 1987-95; ret., 1995. Vis. rsch. prof. Duquesne U., 1965-66; adj. prof. plant pathology U. Minn., 1982-92. Contbr. articles to profl. jours., chpts. to books. With AUS, 1942-46. Phi Sigma scholar, 1942. Fellow AAAS, Ind. Acad. Sci., Am. Phytopathol. Soc. (past pres.); mem. Am. Soc. Agronomy, Crop Sci. Soc. Am., Coun. for Agrl. Sci. and Tech. Achievements include identification of increased resistance to wheat leaf rust by genetic recombination; demonstration of probabilities of virulence to genetic resistance combinations, of tolerance as a mechanism of disease control, and of use of cultivaral diversity for disease protection; bred (with others) over 30 disease resistant cultivars of cereal crops, including Arthur wheat. Home: 3585 Round Barn Blvd Apt 121 Santa Rosa CA 95403 E-mail: joyjac@msn.com.

SCHAFER, JOHN STEPHEN, poet; b. N.Y.C., Sept. 5, 1934; s. Stephen James and Siiri (Halmi) S.; m. Gertrud Rosa Fleischmann, June 14, 1958; children: Sylvia F., John Stephen, Karen D., Kristen H. BA, Rutgers U., 1956, MBA, 1963. Advt. research mgr. Union Carbide Corp., N.Y.C., 1959—65; rsch. mgr. Bus. Week, N.Y.C., 1965—66; v.p. Opinion Rsch. Corp., Princeton, NJ, 1966—80; pres. Am. Econ. Found., Cleve., 1981—2002, trustee, 1975—2002; v.p., dir. Ams. for Competitive Enterprise System, Phila., 1970-82. Editor Linde Electric Welding Progress, 1959-62, ORC Pub. Opinion Index, 1968-72, AEF Straight Talk, 1981-82, Bellcore Exch., 1993-94; works pub. in Famous Poems of the Twentieth Century, 1996, Perceptions in Harmony, 1998, The Communicator, 2000-04, Best Poems and Poets of 2003, 2004, others. Polit. pollster Ed Clark for U.S. Pres., 1980; chmn. N.J. Libertarian party, 1983; nat. dir. U.S. Jaycees, 1965-66, v.p. N.J., 1964-65. Served to 1st lt. U.S. Army, 1957-59. Mem. Jr. Chamber Internat. (hon. life), Philosophean Soc., Scabbard and Blade, Delta Phi Alpha Presbyterian. Home: 114 Walton Palm Rd Panama City FL 32413-7311

SCHAFER, MICHAEL FREDERICK, orthopedic surgeon; b. Peoria, Ill., Aug. 17, 1942; s. Harold Martin and Frances May (Ward) S.; m. Eileen M. Briggs, Jan. 8, 1966; children: Steven, Brian, Kathy, David, Daniel. BA, U. Iowa, 1964, MD, 1967. Diplomate Am. Bd. Orthopedic Surgery. Intern Chgo. Wesley Meml. Hosp., 1967-68; resident in orthop. surgery Cook County Program, Northwestern U., Chgo., 1968-72; asst. prof. orthop. surgery Northwestern U., 1977—; Reyerson prof. and chmn. dept. orthopedic surgery; asso. attending orthopedic surgeon Northwestern Meml. Hosp., 1974—. Adj. staff Children's Meml. Hosp., Chgo., 1974—; cons. VA Lakeside Hosp., 1974—; panelist Bur. Health Manpower, HEW, 1976; sec.-treas. Orthop. Rsch. and Edn. Found.; attending orthop. surgeon Northwestern Meml. Hosp., 1980—, exec. dir. Back and Neck Inst. Contbr. articles to profl. jours. Maj. U.S. Army, 1973-74. Fellow Am. Orthopaedic Assn., Am. Acad. Orthopaedic Surgeons; mem. AMA, Am. Orthopedic Soc. Sports Medicine, Ill. Med. Soc., Chgo. Med. Soc., Scoliosis Rsch. Soc. Roman Catholic. Home: 1815 Ridgewood Ln W Glenview IL 60025-2205 Office: Northwestern U Med School Ste 910 645 N Michigan Ave Chicago IL 60611-2876 E-mail: m-schafer@northwestern.edu.

SCHAFER, MILTON, composer, pianist, educator; b. N.Y.C., Sept. 24, 1920; s. Abraham and May (Meyerson) S.; div. 1974; 1 child, Nina Kathryn. Cert., Paris Conservatory, 1950; student, Am. Conservatory, Fontainbleu, France; pvt. study, Nadia Boulanger, Paris, 1949-50; BS, Juilliard Sch. Music, N.Y.C., 1952; MA, CCNY, N.Y.C., 1967; studied with, Alfred Mirovitch, Irwin Freundlich, Lonnie Epstein. Lectr. music CCNY, N.Y.C., 1954—56, prof. music John Jay Coll., 1976—96; asst. to Frank Loesser Frank Music Pub., N.Y.C., 1956—58; music. dir. Am. Theatre Wing, N.Y.C., 1962. Mem. So. Hampton Poetry Workshop, 1997—. Piano recitals at Am. Embassy, Paris, 1949, Quaker Ctr. Internat., Paris, 1949, Town Hall, N.Y.C., 1950, 54; composer, lyricist: (children's song cycle) Mommy Gimme a Drinka Water, 1957 (recorded by Danny Kaye and televised by Nathan Lane with Boston Pops 1999), (Broadway musicals) Bravo Giovanni, 1962 (Tony award nomination for score), Drat! The Cat!, 1965 (voted Best Score of Yr. by Walter Kerr, book, music and lyrics by Ira Levin), (two revivals) He Touched Me, 1965 (recorded by Barbara Streisand), songs recorded by Peggy Lee, Sarah Vaughn, Jerry Vale, Eddie Fisher, Ah!Camminare, Frank Pourcel, I'm Five (recorded by The Muppets), I Like Old People, Don't You (recorded by Michael Feinstein); author: Practical Technique for Popular Piano Playing, 1947; author, composer adaptation Kate Simon's Bronx Primitive 1990 (staged reading at ASCAP 1998); music critic High Fidelity, 1975, Music Jour., 1976-78; author: (children's book) Crazy Barbara, 2003, I'm Big, 2004, also numerous poems. Staff sgt. USAAF, 1942-46. Co-winner Nat. Guild Piano Tchrs. Competition, N.Y.C., 1948. Mem. ASCAP, Dramatists Guild, The Bohemians. Avocations: reading, yoga, swimming, travel, poetry. Home: 33 Riverside Dr New York NY 10023-8012 E-mail: mschafer@aol.com.

SCHAFER, OSCAR S. investment company executive; Bachelor's Degree, Harvard Coll.; MBA, Harvard U. Bd. mem. Parker Vision Inc.; dir. Global Healthcare Ptnrs. Office: OSS Capital Mgmt 605 3rd Ave Lobby New York NY 10158*

SCHAFER, ROBERT LOUIS, agricultural engineer, researcher; b. Burlington, Iowa, Aug. 1, 1937; s. Marion Louis and Pansy (Head) S.; m. Carolyn Louise Henn, Aug. 1, 1959; 1 child, Elizabeth Diane. BS, Iowa State U., 1959, MS, 1961, PhD, 1965. Agrl. engr. Agrl. Rsch. Svc., USDA, Ames, Iowa,

1959-64, Auburn, Ala., 1964-95. Co-author: Advances in Soil Dynamics, 1994; contbr. articles to profl. jours. Fellow Am. Soc. Agrl. Engrs. (McCormick Case Gold medal 1997). Home: PO Box 189 Loachapoka AL 36865-0189 E-mail: rls@laltek.com.

SCHAFER, RONALD WILLIAM, electrical engineering educator; b. Tecumseh, Nebr., Feb. 17, 1938; s. William Henry and Esther Sophia Schafer; m. Dorothy Margaret Hall, June 2, 1960; children: William R., John C. (dec.), Katherine L., Barbara Anne. Student, Doane Coll., Crete, Nebr., 1956-59; BEE, U. Nebr., 1961, MEE, 1962; PhD in Elec. Engring., MIT, 1968. Tech. staff Bell Labs., Murray Hill, N.J., 1968-74; John and Marilu McCarty prof. elec. engring. Ga. Inst. Tech., Atlanta, 1974—2004, Inst. prof., 1991—2004; disting. tech. Hewlett Packard Labs., 2004—. Chmn. bd. Atlanta Signal Processors Inc., 1983-2001. Co-author: Digital Signal Processing, 1974, Digital Processing of Speech Signals, 1979, Speech Analysis, 1979, Discrete-Time Signal Processing, 1989, 2d edit., 1999, Computer-Based Exercises for Signal Processing Using Matlab, 1995, DSP First: A Multimedia Approach, 1998, Signal Processing First, 2003. Recipient Class of 34 Disting. Prof. award Ga. Inst. Tech., 1985. Fellow IEEE (Emanuel R. Piore award 1980, Edn. medal 1992, 3rd millennium award 2000), Acoustical Soc. Am.; mem. IEEE Acoustics Speech and Signal Processing Soc. (soc. award 1982, edn. award 2000), Nat. Acad. Engring., Kiwanis. Democrat. Office: Ga Inst Tech Dept Elec Engring Atlanta GA 30332-0001

SCHAFERMEYER, ROBERT WILLIAM, emergency physician, educator; b. St. Louis, Jan. 9, 1948; s. William Jacob and Virginia Rose (Cumming) S.; m. An ping Yuan, May 12, 1973; children: Christina, David, Matthew, Joseph Student, St. Louis U., 1966-69; MD, U. Mo., 1973. Diplomate Am. Bd. Emergency Medicine, Am. Bd. Pediats., sub-bd. pediat. emergency medicine. Mem. dept. emergency medicine East Tenn. Children's Hosp., Knoxville, 1979-81, Carolinas Med. Ctr., Charlotte, N.C., 1981—; clin. assoc. prof. pediats. U. N.C. Sch. Medicine, Chapel Hill, 1981-85, clin. prof. emergency medicine and pediats., 1994; assoc. chair dept. emergency medicine Carolinas Med. Ctr., Charlotte, 1982—. Dir. E.D. Cons. and Lectrs., Charlotte, 90—. Assoc. editor: Pediatric Emergency Medicine Concepts and Clinical Practice, 1992; editor: Pediatric Emergency Medicine: A Comprehensive Study Guide, 1995; contbr. articles and revs. to profl. jours. including Annals Emergency Medicine Jour.; reviewer Pediat. Emergency Medicine, Acad. Emergency Medicine; past mem. editl. bd. Pediat. Emergency Med. Jour. Com. mem. MEMAC Adv., Mecklenberg County, 1991-93; mem. task force Drug Abuse for County Commrs., Mecklenberg, 1989-90. Lt. commdr. USPHS, 1974-76. EMS-C grantee Maternal and Child Health, 1992-94. Fellow Am. Coll. Emergency Physicians (bd. dirs. 1994-2002, pres.-elect 1999-2000, pres. 2000-01, past pres. 2001-02, Weigenstein Outstanding Leadership award 2004); mem. Am. Acad. Pediats., N.C. chpt. Am. Coll. Emergency Physicians (councillor 1984-94, bd. dirs. 1983-89, pres. 1986-88, Leadership/Svc. award 1988, George Podgorny Emergency Medicine Svc. award 1996). Roman Catholic. Avocations: tae kwan do, photography, skiing. Office: Carolinas Med Ctr 1000 Blythe Blvd Charlotte NC 28203-5812 Office Phone: 704-355-3181.

SCHAFF, MANYA, foundation administrator; b. Chgo., Mar. 12, 1931; d. Louis Lipkin and Allene Ewing; m. Jay Barash Schaff, Mar. 25, 1951 (div. Jan. 20, 1971); children: Pamela Beth, William Franz Kim, Elizabeth Aline Sloan; m. Dimitri Polonsky, PhD, June 27, 1971 (div. Dec. 14, 2000). MusB, Northwestern U., 1953. Tchr. Carnegie-Mellon U., Pitts., 1961—65, Chatham Coll., Pitts., 1964—71, Immaculate Heart Coll., LA, 1972—79; instr. UCLA, 1973—79; program dir. Performing Tree, Inc., LA, 1982—88; program officer The Ahmanson Found., Beverly Hills, Calif., 1988—; tchr., performer Shady Side Acad., Pitts., 1968—71. Panelist L.A. Cultural Affairs Dept., 1983—85, L.A. Ednl. Partnership, Small Grants to Teachers, 1988—98; sr. facilitator Inst. for the Arts, Pitts. Pub. Schs., Pitts., 1985; bd. dir. Vista Del Mar Child Care, LA, 1979—82. Editor: Piano for Two Directory. Bd. dirs. Chamber Music Soc. of L.A., 1990—95. Recipient drawing prize, Assoc. Artists of Pitts., 1963, Pennational Artists Annual, 1964, fiber art prize, Annual Ehrman Mansion Show, 1977. Mem.: Pi Kappa Lambda (life), Sigma Alpha Iota (life). Democrat. Home: 2139 Roscomare Rd Los Angeles CA 90077 Office: The Ahmanson Found 9215 Wilshire Blvd Beverly Hills CA 90210 E-mail: mschaff@theahmansonfoundation.org.

SCHAFFER, ARCHIE, III, food products executive; b. Ft. Smith, Ark., 1948; B in Natural Scis., U. Ark., 1970. Adminstrv. asst. Gov. Dale Bumpers, 1971—75, Senator Bumpers, 1975—77; adminstr. Greenhurst Nursing Home, Charleston, Ark.; owner Schaffer & Assocs., Little Rock; exec. dir. Ark. Bus. Coun., 1987—91; dir. media, pub. and govtl. affairs Tyson Foods Inc., Springdale, Ark., 1991—99, sr. v.p. external rels., 1999—. Mem. Ark. Leadership Acad.; mem. agrl. devel. coun. U. Ark.; mem. adv. bd. Ark. LWV. Mem.: Ark. Nature Conservancy (bd. mem.). Office: Tyson Foods Inc 2210 W Oakland Dr Springdale AR 72762-6999

SCHAFFER, BRYAN STUART, finance educator; b. West Orange, N.J., Sept. 17, 1965; s. George Schaffer and Barbara Wilcox; m. Alyssa Kennedy, Jan. 2, 2003; children: Nanette Kennedy, Chelsea Kennedy, Alexander Kennedy. BS in Bus. Adminstrn., U. Fla., Gainesville, 1983—87; MBA, Ga. State U., Atlanta, 1988—89; PhD, U. Ga., Athens, 1998—2003. Sales rep., account exec. Pillsbury, Charlotte, NC, 1990—92; warehouse supr. McMaster-Carr Supply Co., Atlanta, 1992—96, Avon Products, Inc., Suwanee, Ga., 1996—98; asst. prof., mgmt. U. N.C., Asheville. Contbr. chapters to books, articles to profl. jours. Mem.: So. Mgmt. Assn., Soc. for Indsl. and Orgnl. Psychology, APA, Acad. of Mgmt., Beta Gamma Sigma. Home: 187 Owenby Cove Rd Asheville NC 28803 Office: Univ NC One University Heights CPO #1850 Asheville NC 28804-8507 E-mail: bschaffer@unca.edu.

SCHAFFER, CANDLER GARELD, conductor, hornist, educator; b. Takoma Park, Md., June 2, 1950; s. Henry Louis and June Georgette (Schweitzer) S. MusB, U. Miami, 1972; MEd, U. Md., 1977; MFA, U. Iowa, 1991, D Mus. Arts, 1992. Dir. orchestral studies Oreg. State U., Corvallis, 1982-85, Tex. Christian U., Ft. Worth, 1985-90; music dir., condr. Fla. Space Coast Philharm., Cocoa, 1995-99, Fla. Space Coast Pops, Cocoa, 1996-99, Wichita Falls (Tex.) Symphony Orch., 1996—, Wichita Falls Chamber Orch., 1998—2002. Mem. classical music selection panel Oreg. Arts Commn., 1984-85; grant cons. Irving (Tex.) Arts Coun., 1998; founder, bd. dirs. Camerata Winds Melbourne, Fla., 1994-96; co-founder, prin. condr. North Tex. Wind Symphony, Wichita Falls, 1997; adj. instr. horn Midwestern State U., 1996—. Bd. dirs. Willamette Arts Coun., Corvallis, 1983-85; mem. cultural execs. com. Brevard Cultural Alliance, Brevard County, Fla., 1995-96; co-founder, bd. dirs. Century Concerts, Wichita Falls, 1997-2000. Mem.: Am. Fedn. Musicians, Am. Symphony Orch. League. Avocations: surfing, hiking, reading, yoga. bus. Home: 704 Greenwood Manor Cir West Melbourne FL 32904-1914 Office: Wichita Falls Symphony Orch Kemp Ctr for Arts 1300 Lamar Wichita Falls TX 76301 E-mail: schafferc1@aol.com.

SCHAFFER, DAVID EDWIN, retired management systems executive; b. Nov. 3, 1929; s. Karl and Jeanette (Gotthelf) S.; m. Ariel Williams Sullivan, May 3, 1951; stepchildren: Adrienne Sullivan Smith, James W. Sullivan. Student, Wharton Sch. of U. Pa., 1948-49; BA, New Sch. for Social Rsch., 1959. Spl. edn. tchr. of emotionally disturbed children various schs. and hosps., 1954-65; br. mgr. 1st Westchester Nat. Bank, New Rochelle, N.Y., 1965-66; v.p. Longines-Symphonette Inc.; spl. asst. to chmn. bd. Longines Wittnauer Inc., Larchmont, N.Y., 1966-72; pvt. practice mgmt. cons. Franconia, N.H., 1973-77; v.p., dir. ops. Carroll Reed Ski Shops, Inc., 1978-80; ret. Instr. econs. Am. Inst. Banking, 1965-66. Moderator, Town of Franconia, 1973—, co-chmn. Frost Pl. com., founder, 1975—; bd. dirs. White Mountain Community Svcs., 1973-77; bd. dirs., past pres. No. N.H. Mental Health Services, 1975-77. Prodr.: numerous record albums. Vol. Hospice of the Littleton Area; mem. com. St. Mathews Chapel, Sugar Hill, N.H. With Signal Corps, AUS, 1951-53. Mem. Direct Mail Credit Assn. Am. (founding mem.), Asso. Retail Credit Men of N.Y.C., Direct Mail Assn. Am. (past chmn. subcom. on consumer affairs and regulatory agys.), Profile Club (pres., dir.). Democrat. Episcopalian. Home: River Rd Franconia NH 03580

SCHAFFER, DAVID IRVING, lawyer; b. N.Y.C., Oct. 17, 1935; s. Frank and Edith (Montlack) S.; m. Lois Ann Warshauer, June 16, 1957; children: Susan Edith, Eric Michael. BA, U. Pa., 1956; LL.B., Harvard U., 1959. Bar: N.Y. 1960. Assoc. Shearman & Sterling, N.Y.C., 1960-65; sec., counsel Yale Express System, Inc., N.Y.C., 1965-66; sr. v.p., gen. counsel, sec. Avis, Inc., Garden City, N.Y., 1966-83; v.p., gen. counsel U.S. Surgical Corp., Norwalk, Conn., 1983-86; of counsel Meltzer, Lippe, Goldstein & Schlissel, LLP, Mineola, NY, 1986-89; ptnr. Meltzer, Lippe, Goldstein & Breitstone, LLP, Mineola, 1989—. Past pres. Nassau County Legal Aid Soc., 1984-86. Bd. dirs. United Cmty. Fund, Great Neck, N.Y., 1980, Great Neck Estates Civic Assn., 1998—, L.I. Venture Group, 1988-2003. With USAR, 1960. Mem. ABA, N.Y. State Bar Assn., Nassau County Bar Assn., L.I. Software Assn., Harvard Club. Democrat. Home: 31 Amherst Rd Great Neck NY 11021-2910 Office: Meltzer Lippe Et Al 190 Willis Ave Mineola NY 11501-2693 E-mail: dlefty35@optonline.net., david.schaffer@mlg.com.

SCHAFFER, JACK, former state senator; b. Chgo., Oct. 12, 1942; s. Raymond and Francis (Barter) S.; divorced; children: Neal, Todd, Ryan. BS, No. Ill. U., 1965. Plant mgr. Oak Mfg. Co., Crystal Lake, Ill., 1967-68; auditor McHenry County, Ill., 1968 72. Sgt. U.S. Army, 1965-67. Mem. Rotary Office: Cmty Bankers Assn Ill 901 Community Dr Springfield IL 62703-5184

SCHAFFER, MARVIN W. investor; b. N.Y.C., Feb. 14, 1925; s. Harry David Schaffer and Lena Willick; m. Shirley Ruth Bookbinder, Apr. 17, 1948; children: Neil, Bruce, Paul. BBA cum laude, CCNY, 1948. Acct. various orgns., N.Y.C., 1948-57; sr. account exec. Merrill Lynch, N.Y.C., 1957-73; v.p. Numismatic Funding Inc., Jericho, N.Y., 1973-74, First Coinvestors, Inc., Alberston, N.Y., 1974-79; pres. Prestige Rare Coins Inc., Hempstead, N.Y., 1979-85; pvt. practice investor N.Y.C., 1985—. Solicitor Jewish Fedn., Boca Raton, Fla., 1986—90. Sgt. U.S. Army, 1943—45. Decorated Bronze Star, Purple Heart. Mem.: Am. Numismatic Assn. (life), Townsend Harris Alumni Assn., CCNY Alumni Assn., Tennis Club (mem. nominating com. 1995—98, mem. budget com. 1996—2000, capt. Rain Berry Bay Tennis Team 2002—03), Beta Gamma Sigma. Jewish. Avocations: tennis, politics, reading, gin rummy, travel. Home: 3125 Riviera Ave Delray Beach FL 33445 E-mail: Mash214@yahoo.com.

SCHAFFER, ROBERT (BOB SCHAFFER), former congressman; b. Cin., July 24, 1962; s. Robert James and Florence Ann (Bednar) S.; m. Maureen Elizabeth Menke, Feb. 8, 1986; children: Jenniffer and Emily (twins), Justin, Sarah Mary. BA in Polit. Sci., U. Dayton, 1984; hon. doctorate in mgmt., Colo. Tech. U. Speechwriter republican caucus Ohio Gen. Assembly, 1984-85; legis. asst. State of Ohio, Columbus, 1985; majority adminstrv. asst. Colo. State Senate, Denver, 1985-87, mem., 1987-96, U.S. Congress from 4th Colo. dist., Washington, 1997—2003, mem. agr. com., edn. and workforce com., resources com. Mem. Rep. Policy Com., GOP Theme Team; commr. Colo. Advanced Tech. Inst., 1988—; proprietor No. Front Range Mktg. and Distbn., Inc. Mem. Mental Health Bd. Larimer County, 1986-87; mem. com. on human svcs. Nat. Conf. State Legislatures; campain co-chmn. Arnold for Lt. Gov.; Republican candidate for Lt. Gov. of Colo., 1994. Named Nat. Legislator of Yr., Rep. Nat. Legislators Assn., 1995, Taxpayer Champion, Colo. Union of Taxpayers, 1995, Bus. Legislator of the Yr. Colo. Assn. Commerce and Industry, Named Guardina Small Bus. Nat. Fedn. Ind. Bus.; recipient Spirit of Enterprise award U.S. C. of C. Mem. Jaycees (Mover and Shaker award 1989), KC. Republican. Roman Catholic. Avocations: backpacking, skiing, baseball, painting, reading. Home: 5027 Alder Ct Fort Collins CO 80525-5588 Office: US Ho Reps 212 Cannon Ho Office Bldg Washington DC 20515-0001

SCHAFFER, SETH ANDREW, lawyer; b. Bklyn., Jan. 7, 1942; m. Karen (Kiki) Cohn, Dec. 1, 1968; children: Amanda, Julia, James. BA in Econs. magna cum laude, Harvard U., 1963, LLB cum laude, 1967; postgrad., Cambridge (Eng.) U., 1964. Bar: N.Y. 1970, U.S. Dist. Ct. (so. dist.) N.Y. 1973, U.S. Ct. Appeals (2nd cir.) 1973, U.S. Supreme Ct. 1980. Tchr. math. and econs. York (Pa.) Country Day Sch., 1967-68; assoc. dir. Vera Inst. Justice, 1969-72; asst. U.S. atty. U.S. Dist. Ct. (so. dist.) N.Y., 1972-75; chief counsel Moreland Act Commn. on Nursing Homes, N.Y.C., 1975-76; of counsel Stanley S. Arkin, P.C., Attys. at Law, 1976-77; v.p., gen. counsel, sec. of univ. NYU, N.Y.C., 1977-93, sr. v.p., gen. counsel, sec., 1993—. Adj. prof. law NYU Sch. Law. Dir. Not for Profit Coordinating Com. N.Y., Nat. Ctr. Philanthropy and the Law, N.Y.C. Henry fellow Cambridge U., 1964. Mem. Nat. Assn. Coll. and Univ. Attys. (past pres.), Assn. of Bar of City of N.Y., Phi Beta Kappa. Home: 14 Washington Mews New York NY 10003-6608 Office: NYU 70 Washington Sq S New York NY 10012-1091 Office Phone: 212-998-2244. E-mail: andrew.schaffer@nyu.edu.

SCHAFFNER, BERTRAM HENRY, psychiatrist; b. Erie, Pa., Nov. 12, 1912; s. Milton and Gerta (Herzog) S. Student, Harvard U., 1928-29, 32-33; AB, Swarthmore Coll., 1932; MD, Johns Hopkins U., 1937; diploma, William Alanson White Inst., 1953. Diplomate Am. Bd. Psychiatry, Am. Bd. Neurology. Intern Johns Hopkins Hosp., Balt., 1937-38; resident in neurology Mt. Sinai Hosp., N.Y.C., 1938-39; resident in psychiatry Bellevue Hosp., N.Y.C., 1939-40, N.Y. State Psychiat. Inst., N.Y.C., 1946-47; pvt. practice psychiatry and psychoanalysis N.Y.C., 1947—. Lectr. Sch. Nursing Cornell U., N.Y.C., 1950-60; mem. faculty, clin. supr. in psychotherapy William Alanson White Inst. Psychoanalysis, 1960—, med. dir. HIV svc., clin. supr. psychoanalysis, 1993—; cons., editor confs. Josiah Macy Jr. Found., 1949, 50, 51; cons. U.S. Children's Bur., 1946-47, Bur. Mental Health, V.I., 1954-60, World Fedn. Mental Health, 1958-68, others; mem. N.Y. County dist. bd. Com. on Gay and Lesbian Issues; cons. WHO, 1960-67; founder, exec. dir. U.S.-Caribbean Aid to Mental Health, Inc., 1960-68; organizer Biennial Caribbean Confs. for Mental Health, 1959-65; organizer, cons. Caribbean Fedn. for Mental Health, 1959-65; mem. rsch. study Pre-Soviet Russian Family in the Research in Contemporary Cultures, Columbia U., 1949-51. Mem. editl. bd. Jour. of Gay and Lesbian Psychotherapy, 1987—; author: Father Land: A Study of Authoritarianism in the German Family, 1948; contbr. numerous articles to profl. publs. Mem. acquisitions com. The Bklyn. Mus. of Art, 1995—; trustee Bklyn. Mus. of Art. Recipient Adolf Meyer award for Disting. Svc. on Behalf of Improved Care and Treatment of the Mentally Ill in the Caribbean, 1961. Fellow AMA (life), Am. Psychiat. Assn. (chmn. 1983-86, mem. com. on AIDS N.Y. County dist. br. 1989-99, life), Am. Acad. Psychoanalysis (life), Caribbean Psychiat. Assn.; mem. Group for Advancement of Psychiatry (chair internat. rels. com. 1960-65, chair com. on human sexuality 1987-98), Internat. Acad. Sex Rsch. Avocation: collecting asian and indian art. Home and Office: 220 Central Park S New York NY 10019-1417 Office Phone: 212-265-5539. E-mail: bertschmd@aol.com.

SCHAFFNER, CAROLYN MARIE, research administrator, biologist; b. Clarkson, N.Y., Oct. 20, 1960; d. Michael Frank and Carolyn Gertrude Skill; m. Kurt Charles Klotzbuecher, Oct. 23, 1987 (div. May 1996); m. Paul Lawrence Schaffner, Sept. 23, 2000; children: William Elliott, Josephine Marte. AS, Alfred State Coll., 1980; BS, Delaware Valley Coll., 1983; Master's degree, Villanova U., 1993. Rsch. technologist Wyeth Labs., Great Valley, Pa., 1984-86; sr. rsch. technician Arbus Rsch. Labs., Horsham, Pa., 1986; biologist Merck & Co. Inc., West Point, Pa., 1986-88, staff biologist, 1988-90, assoc. med. program coord., 1990-94, med. program coord., 1994-95, sr. med. edn. specialist, 1995-96, mgr. outcomes rsch. and mgmt., 1996—. Rschr., presenter in field. Author, rsch., presenter: Guidelines for Diagnosis and Treatment of Osteoporosis, 1998. Mem. APHA, Nat. Osteoporosis Found., Ea. Pa. Osteoporosis Soc. (founding mem.), Older Womens League. Office: Merck & Co Inc Broad St and Sumneytown Pk West Point PA 19486

SCHAFFNER, CYNTHIA VAN ALLEN, writer, curator, lecturer; b. Washington, Jan. 28, 1947; d. James Alfred and Abigail Fifthian (Halsey) Van Allen; m. Robert Todd Schaffner, June 11, 1972; 1 child, Hilary Van Allen. BA, Western Coll., 1969; MAT, Simmons Coll., 1971; MA in History of Decorative Arts, Cooper Hewitt Smithsonian Instn., N.Y.C., 1999. Editor Mademoiselle mag., N.Y.C., 1972-79; dir. devel. Am. Acad. in Rome, N.Y.C., 1987-89; curator Phila. Antiques Show, 1997-98; rsch. asst. Metropolitan Mus. Art, New York, 1999—; curator Halsey House, Southampton, N.Y., 1999—. Author: Discovering American Folk Art, 1991; co-author: Folk Hearts, 1984, American Painted Furniture, 1997; contbr. articles to popular mags. Co-chair Fall Antiques Show, N.Y.C., 1979-93; trustee Mus. Am. Folk Art, N.Y.C., 1980-95. Lisa Taylor fellow, 1995-96; Smithsonian Instn. Grad. Student fellow, 1998. Mem. Coll. Art Assn., Decorative Arts Soc., Cosmopolitan Club, Victorian Soc., Lenox Hill Hosp. Aux., Southampton Hist. Mus. (trustee 1996-2002). Avocations: canoeing, gardening, antiquing. Home: 850 Park Ave New York NY 10021-1845 E-mail: cvanschaf@aol.com.

SCHAFFNER, KAREN ANN See FIELD, KAREN ANN

SCHAFFNER, ROBERTA IRENE, retired medical, surgical nurse; b. Vero Beach, Fla., Oct. 5, 1926; d. Robert Wesley and Harriett Louise (Davis) Routh; m. David Leonard Schaffner, Apr. 25, 1947 (div. July 1975; dec.); children: Penny Routh S. (dec. July 1999), David Leonard II (dec. Jan. 1999). Mem. cadet nurse corps, Charity Hosp., New Orleans, 1944-45; ADA, Montgomery County C.C., Blue Bell, Pa., 1978; BSN, Gwynedd (Pa.) Mercy Coll., 1982, MSN, 1984. RN Pa. Med.-surg. nurse Chestnut Hill Hosp., Phila., 1978-2000, ret., 2000. Mem. delegation to study health care delivery sys., Moscow, Tbilisi, Azerbeijan, Kiev, 1981, Shanghai, Beijing, Nanjing, Hong Kong, 1984, Milan, Pisa, Bologna, Florence, Rome, Sorento, Naples, 1985. Cadet U.S. Nurse Corps, 1945. Mem. Oncology Nursing Soc., Sigma Theta Tau. Republican. Home: 1600 Church Rd Apt A214 Wyncote PA 19095-1929 E-mail: robertars4@aol.com.

SCHAFFNER-IRVIN, KRISTEN, oil executive; b. Seattle; m. Jeff Irvin; 4 children. B. in public relations, Ariz. State U. Sales mgr., fuel distributor Petro Am., 1987—92; owner Team Petroleum (formerly Kristin Schaffner Petroleum), Huntington Beach, Calif., 1992—. Office: Team Petroleum PO Box 659 Huntington Beach CA 92648 0659

SCHAGH, CATHERINE, federal agency administrator; Dir. impact aid program US Dept. Edn., Off Elem. Secondary Edn., Wash., DC, 1995—; analyst US Dept. Edn., Budget Off., divsn. dir. to program dir. Team leader US Dept. Edn., Class-Size Reduction Program, 1998—2000; co-pres. Annandale Bus. and Profl. Women, Va. Mem.: Annandale Bus. and Profl. Women Investment Club (treas.). Office: US Dept Edn Elem Secondary Edn 400 Maryland Ave SW FB-6 Rm 3E105 Washington DC 20202

SCHAIBERGER, GEORGE ELMER, microbiologist educator; Prof. microbiology U. Miami, Coral Gables, Fla., also dir. undergrad. microbiology immunology dept. Recipient Disting. Tchr. award Carski Found., 1992. Office: Univ Miami Cox Sci Bldg 251 1301 Memorial Dr Coral Gables FL 33124

SCHAIBLE, SIEGFRIED, mathematician, educator; PhD in Applied Math., U. of Koeln, Germany, 1971; Habilitation in Ops. Rsch., U. of Koeln, 1978. Wissenschaftlicher assistent U. of Koeln, Germany, 1967—71, akademischer rat/oberrat, 1971—79; full prof. U. of Alta., Edmonton, Canada, 1979—87, U. of Calif., Riverside, 1987—. Co-author, co-editor: Handbook of Geralized Convexity and Generalized Monotonicity, 2004, author, co-author, co-editor: several books; mem. editl. bd. 8 internat. sci. jours.; contbr. over 100 articles to profl. jours. Fellow: AAAS; mem.: Gesellschaft fuer Ops. Rsch., Math. Programming Soc., Inst. for Ops. Rsch. and Mgmt. Scis. Office: University of California Grad Sch of Mgmt Riverside CA 92521

SCHAIBLE, STACIE, newscaster; m. Mike Schaible; 1 child, Cade Michael. Student, Poynter Inst. for Media Studies; grad., U. Minn. Anchor WDAY-TV, Fargo, ND, KDLH-TV, Duluth, Minn., KXAN-TV, Austin, Tex., WFLA-TV, Tampa, Fla., 2000—. Recipient Katie award for Best Major Market Newscast. Avocations: golf, reading, travel. Office: WFLA-TV PO Box 1410 Tampa FL 33601

SCHAICH, WILLIAM L. physics educator; b. Springfield, Mass., Oct. 15, 1944; s. Wilbur Allison and Lillian Luella (Halfaker) S.; m. Georgia Jeann Loebrich, Dec. 23, 1966; children: Amy C., Lucy B. BS, Denison U., 1966; MS, Cornell U., 1968, PhD, 1970. Post doctoral fellow, Bristol, U.K., 1970-71; research asst. U. Calif., LaJolla, Calif., 1971-73; asst. prof. Ind. U., 1973-76, assoc. prof., 1976-80, prof., 1980—. Contbr. articles to profl. jours. Fellow Am. Physical Soc. Office: Ind U Swain Hall W Bloomington IN 47405 E-mail: schaich@indiana.edu.

SCHAIE, K(LAUS) WARNER, human development and psychology educator; b. Stettin, Germany (now Poland), Feb. 1, 1928; came to U.S., 1947, naturalized, 1953; s. Sally and Lottie Luise (Gabriel) S.; m. Coloma J. Harrison, Aug. 9, 1953 (div. 1973); 1 child, Stephan; m. Sherry L. Willis, Nov. 20, 1981. AA, City Coll., San Francisco, 1951; BA, U. Calif., Berkeley, 1952; MS, U. Wash., 1953, PhD, 1956; DPhil (hon.), Friedrich-Schiller U., Jena, Germany, 1997; ScD (hon.), W.Va. U., 2002. Lic. psychologist, Calif., Pa. Fellow Washington U., St. Louis, 1956-57; asst. prof. psychology U. Nebr., Lincoln, Nebr., 1957-64, assoc. prof., 1964-68; prof. chmn. dept. psychology W.Va. U., Morgantown, W.Va., 1964-73; prof. psychology, dir. Gerontology Rsch. Inst., U. So. Calif., 1973-81; Evan Pugh prof. human devel. and psychology Pa. State U., University Park, 1981—, dir. Gerontology Ctr., 1985—2003. Devel. behavior study sect. NIH, Bethesda, Md., 1970-72, chmn., 1972-74, chmn. human devel. and aging study sect., 1979-84, mem. expert panel in comml. airline pilot retirement, 1981, data and safety bd. shep project, 1984-91. Author: Developmental Psychology; A Life Span Approach, 1981, Adult Development and Aging, 1982, 5th rev. edit., 2002, Chinese and Spanish edits., 2003, Intellectual Development in Adulthood: The Seattle Longitudinal Study, 1996; editor: Handbook of Psychology of Aging, 1977, 5th rev. edit., 2001, Longitudinal Studies of Adult Development, 1983, Cognitive Functioning and Social Structure over the Life Course, 1987, Methodological Issues in Research on Aging, 1988, Social Structure and Aging: Psychological Processes, 1989, Age Structuring in Comparative Perspective, 1989, The Course of Later Life, 1989, Self-Directedness: Cause and Effects Throughout the Life Course, 1990, Aging, Health Behaviors and Health Outcomes, 1992, Caregiving Systems: Formal and Informal Helpers, 1993, Societal Impact on Aging: Historical Perspectives, 1993, Adult Intergenerational Relations: Effects of Societal Change, 1995, Older Adults Decision Making and the Law, 1996, Impact of Social Structures on Decision Making in the Elderly, 1997, Impact of the Workplace on Older Persons, 1998, Handbook of Theories of Aging, 1999, Mobility and Aging, 2000, Evolution of the Aging Self, 2000, Effective Health Behavior in the Elderly, 2002, Mastery and Control in the Elderly, 2003, Influence of Technology on Successful Aging, 2003; Independent Aging: Living Arrangements and Mobility, 2003, Religious Influences on Health and Wellbeing in the Elderly, 2004; editor Ann. Rev. Gerontology and Geriat., vol. 7, 1987, vol. 11, 1991, vol. 17, 1997; contbr. articles to profl. jours. Recipient Lifetime Achievment award, Mensa, 2000. Fellow APA (coun. reps. 1976-79, 83-86, Disting. Contbn. award, 1992, Lifetime Career award 2000), Am. Psychol. Soc., Gerontol. Soc. (Kleemeier award 1987, Disting. Mentorship award 1996); mem. Psychometric Soc., Internat. Soc. Study Behavioral Devel., Mensa. Unitarian Universalist. Avocations: hiking, stamps. Home: 425 Windmere Dr Apt 3A State College PA 16801-7670 Office: Pa State U Gerontology Ctr 135 E Nittany Ave Ste 405 State College PA 16802 E-mail: kws@psu.edu.

SCHAITBERGER, HAROLD, protective services official, labor union administrator; From firefighter to lt. Fairfax County, Va., 1966, lt.; from head legis. programs to gen. pres. Internat. Assn. Fire Fighters, Washington, 1976—2000, gen. pres., 2000—. Chmn. bd. trustees Internat. Assn. Fire Fighters Burn Found.; bd. dir. Internat. Assn. Fire Fighter Meml., Nat. Fallen Fire Fighter Meml. Mem.: AFL-CIO (exec. coun., v.p. transp. trade dept., v.p. maritime trade dept.), Muscular Dystrophy Assn. (v.p.). Office: Federal Firefighters Assn 1750 New York Ave NW 3rd Fl Washington DC 20006*

SCHAKE, LOWELL MARTIN, animal science educator; b. Marthasville, Mo., June 6, 1938; s. Martin Charles and Flora Olinda (Rocklage) S.; m. Wendy Anne Walkinshaw, Sept. 11, 1959; children: Sheryl Anne, Lowell Scott. BS, U. Mo., 1960, MS, 1962; PhD, Tex. A&M U., 1967. Asst. prof. Tex. A&M U., College Station, 1965-67, assoc. prof., 1969-72, prof., 1972-84, asst. prof., area livestock specialist Lubbock, 1967-69; prof., head animal sci. dept. U. Conn., Storrs, 1984-92; prof., chmn. animal sci. dept. Tex. Tech. U.,

Lubbock, 1992-95. Developer applied animal ethology program Tex. A&M U., 1970, New Eng. Biotech Conf. series, 1990, S.W. Beef Forum, 1993; chmn. Am. Registry of Profl. Animal Scientist Com. on Profl. Stds., 1988; chmn. Nat. Com. Execs. Officers of Animal Vet., Dairy and Poultry Sci. Depts., 1992; cons. Alpart, Kingston, Jamaica, 1975, U.S. Feeds Grain Coun., 1970-73, A.O. Smith Products Inc., 1968-92, Humphrey Land & Cattle Co., Dallas, 1980-86; lectr. in field. Author: Growth and Finishing of Beef Cattle, A Class Handbook, 1982, La Charrette: Village Gateway to the American West, 2003; contbr. articles to profl. jours. Recipient Innovative Teaching award Tex. A&M U., 1978. Mem. Am. Soc. Animal Sci., Plains Nutrition Coun. (adv. bd. 1967-80, sec.-treas. 1994-95, founder), Nat. Assn. Colls. and Tchrs. Agr., Am. Registry Profl. Animal Scientists (dir. for Northeast 1987-89), Coun. for Agr. Sci. and Tech. World Conf. on Animal Prodn., Am. Soc. Dairy Sci., Tiger Club (College Station) (pres.), Gamma Sigma Delta. Republican. Avocations: genealogy, fishing, gardening. Home: 142 Five Dove Cir Port Aransas TX 78373 E-mail: wschake1@centurytel.net.

SCHAKOWSKY, JANICE, congresswoman; b. Chgo., May 26, 1944; d. Irwin and Tillie (Cosnow) Danoff; m. Harvey E. Schakowsky, Feb. 17, 1965 (div. 1980); children: Ian, Mary; m. Robert B. Creamer, Dec. 6, 1980; 1 stepchild, Lauren. BS, U. Ill., 1965. Cert. elem. tchr., Ill. Tchr. Chgo. Bd. Edn., 1965-67; organizer Ill. Pub. Action Coun., Chgo., 1976-85; exec. dir. Ill. State Coun. Sr. Citizens, Chgo., 1985-90; mem. Ill. Ho. Reps., 1990-98, U.S. Congress from 9th Ill. dist., 1999—; mem. banking and fin. svcs. com., 1999—2000; mem. govt. reform com., 1999—2000; ho. dem. leadership team-deputy whip; mem. Energy and Commerce Com. Bd. dirs. Ill. Pub. Action, 4 C's Day Care Coun., Evanston, Ill.; steering com. mem. Cook County Dem. Women, 1986-90; del. Nat. Dem. Conv., 1988; governing coun. Am. Jewish Congress, 1990—. Named Outstanding Legislator Interfaith Coun. for Homeless, 1993, Legislator of Yr. Ill. Nurses Assn., 1992, Ill. Assn. Cmty. Mental Health Agys., 1994, Coalition of Citizens with Disabilities and Ill. Coun. Sr. Citizens, 1993, Cmty. Action Assn., 1991, Champaign County Health Care Assn., 1992, Rookie of Yr. Ill. Environ. Coun., 1991. Mem. ACLU, NOW, Nat. Coun. Jewish Women, Ill. Pro-Choice Alliance, Evanston Mental Health Assn., Evanston Hist. Soc., Evanston Friends of Libr., Rogers Park Hist. Soc. Democrat. Jewish. Avocations: travel, horsebackriding, reading. Office: Ho of Reps 515 Cannon Ho Office Bldg Washington DC 20515-1309

SCHALER, JEFFREY ALFRED, psychologist, educator; b. Alexandria, Va., July 7, 1951; s. Otto-Gerhard Julius and Elizabeth (Schiltz) Schaler; m. Renee Royak-Schaler, Mar. 31, 1974; 1 child, Magda Elise Schaler-Haynes. BA, Antioch Coll., 1973; MEd, U. Md., 1986, PhD, 1993. Cons. psychologist, Silver Spring, Md., 1973—; adj. prof. justice, law and soc. Am. U., Washington, 1990—2003, asst. prof. justice law and soc., 2003—; faculty, psychology Johns Hopkins U., Balt., 1992—2003; adj. prof. psychology Montgomery Coll., Rockville, Md., 1992—99, Chestnut Hill Coll., Phila., 1997—99; faculty Inst. Humane Studies, Fairfax, Va., 1996—99. Series editor, Under Fire Open Ct. Pubs., Chgo., 2002—. Author: Addiction is a Choice, 2000; editor: Drugs: Should We Legalize, Decriminalize, or DeRegulate?, 1998, Szasz Under Fire-The Psychiatric Abolitionist Faces His Critics, 2004; co-editor: Smoking: Who Has the Right?, 1998. Chmn. adv. coun. Montgomery County Drug Abuse, Rockville, Md., 1987—88, mem. coun., 1982—88. Recipient Thomas Szasz Civil Liberties award, Ctr. Ind. Thought, N.Y.C., 1999. Mem.: Am. Polit. Sci. Assn., Internat. Acad. Law and Mental Health. Avocations: golf, martial arts, walking. Office Phone: 240-460-0987. E-mail: jeffschaler@attglobal.net.

SCHALIT, ROBERT EDWARD, advertising executive; b. Albany, N.Y., Nov. 19, 1954; s. Samuel and Ann Ethal S.; m. Margaret Foye, Aug. 26, 1989. BA in English Lit., SUNY, Binghamton, 1976. Sr. writer Fairbrother & Co. Advt., Valatie, NY, 1999—2000; sr. copywriter Rueckert Advt. Pub. Rels., Albany, NY, 2000—. Freelance advt. copywriter Robert Schalit Freelance Copywriter, Schenectady, NY, 1990—. Author: (numerous ads, tv and radio commls.) CDPHP (HMO) Advertising Campaign. Bd. mem. Ind. Living in the Capital Dist., Schenectady, NY, 1983—84; support group facilitator The Samaritans Suicide Prevention, Albany, NY, 1990—93; pres. Creative Club, Albany, NY, 1988—89. Recipient awards, NORI. Mem.: Am. Mktg. Assn. (Capital region chpt.), The Ad Club, Phi Beta Kappa. Democrat. Jewish. Avocations: reading, poetry, blues harmonica, fitness activities, ship model building. Home: 1133 Van Curler Ave Schenectady NY 12308 Office: Rueckert Advtsg Pub Rels 638 Albany-Shaker Rd Albany NY 12211

SCHALL, ALVIN ANTHONY, federal judge; b. N.Y.C., 1944; s. Gordon William and Helen Schall; m. Sharon Frances LeBlanc, Apr. 25, 1970; children: Amanda Lanford, Anthony Davis. BA, Princeton U., 1966; JD, Tulane U., 1969. Bar: N.Y. 1970, U.S. Dist. Ct. (so. and ea. dists.) N.Y. 1973, U.S. Ct. Appeals (2d crct.) 1974, D.C. 1980, U.S. Dist. Ct. D.C. 1991, U.S. Ct. Appeals (D.C. crct.) 1991, U.S. Ct. Fed. Claims 1982, U.S. Ct. Appeals (fed. crct.) 1987, U.S. Supreme Ct. 1989. Assoc. Shearman & Sterling, N.Y.C., 1969—73; asst. U.S. atty. ea. dist. N.Y. Borough of Bklyn., 1973—78, chief appeals divsn., 1977—78; trial atty. civil divsn. U.S. Dept. Justice, Washington, 1978—87, sr. trial counsel, 1986—87, asst. to atty. gen., 1988—92; ptnr. Perlman & Ptnrs., Washington, 1987—88; judge U.S. Ct. Appeals (fed. cir.), Washington, 1992—. Office: 717 Madison Pl NW Washington DC 20439-0002

SCHALL, CAROL MARIE, special education services professional; b. Pitts., Sept. 4, 1960; d. Stanley Schall and Rita Agnes Bazner; m. Mary Louise Townley, Feb. 10, 1996; 1 child, Emily Breese Schall Townley. BS in Edn., Duquesne U., 1982; MEd, James Madison U., 1987; PhD, Va. Commonwealth U., 2003. Tchr. Grafton Sch., Berryville, Va., 1982—85, adminstr., 1985—93; tchr. Chesterfield Pub. Schs., 1993—94; dir. cmty. support Va. Commonwealth U., Richmond, 1994—98; dir. Va. Autism Resource Ctr., 1998—. Adj. instr. Va. Commonwealth U., Richmond, 1999—. Office: Va Autism Resource Ctr 4100 Price Club Blvd Richmond VA 23236

SCHALL, JEFFREY D. psychology educator; Prof. psychology Vanderbilt U., Nashville. Office: Vanderbilt U Dept Psychology 301 Wilson Hl Nashville TN 37240-0001

SCHALL, LAWRENCE DELANO, economics educator, consultant; b. Los Angeles, Nov. 5, 1940; s. Lee and Lillian (Seltzow) S.; m. Betty Jane Kay, Aug. 6, 1982; children: Michael Kay, Adam Kent. BA, UCLA, 1962; MA in Econs., U. Chgo., 1967, PhD in Econs., 1969. CPA, Wash. Sec.-treas. Permco Inc., Los Angeles, 1959-61; acting asst. prof. econs. U. Wash., Seattle, 1968-69, asst. prof., 1969-72, assoc. prof., 1972-76, prof., 1976—. Author: (with C. W. Haley) The Theory of Financial Decisions, 1972, 2d edit., 1979, Introduction to Financial Management, 1977, 6th edit., 1991, (with K. Henderson and R. May) Evaluating Business Ventures, 1982; contbr. articles to profl. jours. Recipient Bank of Am. Excellence award, 1983, Burlington No. Found. award, 1986, First Interstate Bank award, 1990, Andrew V. Smith award, U. Wash., 1992. Mem. Am. Econ. Assn., Am. Fin. Assn., Fin. Mgmt. Assn., Fin. Execs. Inst. Office: U Wash Sch Bus Adminstrn 261 Mackenzie Hall Dj # 10 Seattle WA 98195-0001

SCHALLENKAMP, KAY, academic administrator; b. Salem, S.D., Dec. 9, 1949; d. Arnold B. and Jennie M. (Koch) Krier; m. Ken Schallenkamp, Sept. 7, 1970; children: Heather, Jenni. BS, No. State Coll., 1972; MA, U. S.D., 1973; PhD, U. Colo., 1982. Prof. No. State Coll., Aberdeen, S.D., 1973-88, dept. chair, 1982-84, dean, 1984-88; provost Chadron (Nebr.) State Coll., 1988-92, U. Wis., Whitewater, 1992-97; pres. Emporia (Kans.) State U., 1997—. Cons. North Ctrl. Assn., nursing homes, hosps. and ednl. instns. Contbr. articles to profl. jours. Commr. North Ctrl. Assn., 1995-99. Bush fellow, 1980; named Outstanding Young Career Woman, Bus. and Profl. Women's Club, 1976. Mem. NCAA (pres.'s coun. 2000—), Kans. C. of C. (bd. dirs. 2000—), Am. Speech and Hearing Assn. (cert.), Rotary. Avocation: martial arts. Office: Emporia State U 1200 Commercial St Emporia KS 66801-5087 E-mail: schallka@emporia.edu.

SCHALLER, ANTHONY JOSEF, technology management executive; b. Pitts., Nov. 17, 1957; s. Josef and Ruth Bridgette (Petschick) S.; m. Anna Marie Johnson (div. Nov. 1997); children: Kristofer, Derek. BS in Computer Sci. and Bus. Mgmt., U. Pitts., 1982; grad. degree computer sci., Carnegie-Mellon U., 1987. Mgr. sys. devel. Carnegie-Mellon U., Pitts., 1980-87; sr. mgr. applications engring. Ingres Corp., Alameda, Calif., 1988-91; dir. tech. mktg. MTI/SF2 Corp., Sunnyvale, Calif., 1991-92; dir. multidatabase sys. devel. MDL Info. Sys., Inc., San Leandro, Calif., 1992-93, dir. intersect project, 1993-94; pres., founder Intersect Software, Inc., Alameda, 1994-97; v.p. engring., chief tech. officer Open Object/Electric Classifieds, Inc., San Francisco, 1997-98; v.p. tech. Ticketmaster Online-CitySearch, Inc., Pasadena, Calif., 1998-99; sr. v.p. tech., chief tech. officer, COO RioPort.com, San Jose, Calif., 1999—. Bd. dirs. ZealMedia, Inc., L.A.; tech./mgmt. cons. Turnaround Mgmt. Assn., Alameda, 1998-99. Mem. Assn. for Computing Machinery (program devel. and spkr. liason/coord. Pitts. chpt. 1983-84, vice-chmn. Pitts. chpt. 1984-85, chmn. Pitts. chpt. 1985-86, Svc. Recognition award 1985, 86). Achievements include patent for system and methods for performing multi-source searches over heterogeneous databases. Home: 211 Encounter Bay Alameda CA 94502-7909 Office: RioPort com 2895 Zanker Rd San Jose CA 95134-2101 Fax: 707-221-1598. E-mail: tony@schaller.net.

SCHALLER, BARRY R. judge; BA, Yale U., 1960, JD, 1963. Bar: Conn. 1963, US Dist. Ct. Conn. 1963, US Ct. Appeals (2nd cir.) 1964, US Supreme Ct. 1966. Ptnr. Bronson & Rice, Atty., New Haven, 1963-74; judge Ct. of Common Pleas, Cir., Conn., 1974-78, Superior Ct., Conn., 1978-92, Appellate Ct., Conn., 1992—. Counsel to Ho. of Reps., 1969; bd. pardons State of Conn., 1971-74, chair, 1973-74; exec. com. Conn. Planning Com. on Criminal Adminstrn., 1972-74; chair Superior Ct. Benchbook Com., 1985-92; vis. lectr. Yale Coll., 1986, 88; clin. instr. evidence and trial practice Yale Law Sch., 1989—; adj. prof., Quinnipiac Law Sch., 2002; vis. lectr. Trinity Coll., 2003—, Wesleyan (Conn.) U., 2003-04; Trinity Coll., Vt. Law Sch., 2003-04; lectr. W.Va. Magistrates Conf., 1990, Vt. Jud. Coll., 1992, Fla. Jud. Coll., 1993-94, 96, 99, 2002, 04, Ohio Jud. Coll., 1999, 2002, Mo. Jud. Coll., 2002, hosp. ethics. com., others; faculty Nat. Jud. Coll. Conn. Judges Inst., 1987-90; mem. Superior Ct. Jury Instrn. Com., 1989-92; exec. com. Conn. Ctr. for Jud. Edn., 1989-92; active Superior Ct. Civil Case Mgmt. Task Force; jud. evidence code drafting com. Author: A Vision of American Law: Judging Law, Literature, and the Stories We Tell, 1997, A Legal Prescription for Bioethical Ills, Quinnipiac Law Review, 2002; contbr. articles to profl. jours. Assoc. fellow Branford Coll.; adminstrv. co-sec. Yale Class of 1960; mem. adv. com. Fair Haven Mediation Bd., 19980-82; bd. dir. Russian-Am. Rule of Law Project; mem. working groups Yale Bioethics Project, adv. com. Dongahue Found. Yale; vestry mem., tchr. Trinity Ch., Branford, St. Andrew's Ch., Madison. Recipient book award Quinnipiac Law Sch., 1997; Guggenheim fellow Yale Law Sch., 1975-76, 84, 85-86. Fellow Conn. Bar Found. (charter life, fellows adv. com.); mem. Conn. Bar Assn., Hartford County Bar Assn., New Haven County Bar Assn., Conn. Judges Assn. (dir. 1990-92), Am. Law Inst., Yale Law Sch. Assn. (exec. com. 1990-92), Am. Inns of Ct. (bencher 1989-90), Conn. Russian-Am. Rule of Law Program (founder), Phi Delta Phi. Office: Appellate Ct State Conn 95 Washington St Hartford CT 06106-4431

SCHALLER, GEORGE BEALS, zoologist; b. Berlin, May 26, 1933; s. Georg Ludwig S. and Bettina (Byrd) Iwersen; m. Kay Suzanne Morgan, Aug. 26, 1957; children: Eric, Mark. BS in Zoology, BA in Anthropology, U. Alaska, 1955; PhD in Zoology, U. Wis., 1962. Rsch. assoc. Johns Hopkins U., Balt., 1963—66; rsch. zoologist Wildlife Conservation Soc., Bronx, NY, 1966—. Rsch. assoc. Am. Mus. Natural History. Author: The Mountain Gorilla, 1963 (Wildlife Soc. award 1965), The Year of the Gorilla, 1964, The Deer and the Tiger, 1967, The Serengeti Lion, 1972 (Nat. Book award 1973), Golden Shadows, Flying Hooves, 1973, Mountain Monarchs, 1977, Stones of Silence, 1980, The Giant Pandas of Wolong, 1985, The Last Panda, 1993, Tibet's Hidden Wilderness, 1997, Wildlife of the Tibetan Steppe, 1998; co-editor (with E.Vrba) Antelopes, Deer and Relatives, 2000. Decorated Order of Golden Ark, Netherlands, 1978; recipient Gold medal World Wildlife Fund, 1980, Explorers medal Explorers Club, 1990, Cosmos prize Japan, 1996, Tyler Environ. prize, 1997; Ctr. Advanced Study in Behavorial Scis. fellow Stanford U., 1962, fellow Guggenheim Found., 1971. Office: Wildlife Conservation Soc Bronx Park Bronx NY 10460 Business E-Mail: asiaprogram@wcs.org.

SCHALLER, JANE GREEN, pediatrician; b. Cleve., June 26, 1934; d. George and May Alice (Wing) Green; children: Robert Thomas, George Charles, Margaret May. AB, Hiram (Ohio) Coll., 1956; MD cum laude, Harvard U., 1960. Diplomate Am. Bd. Pediat., Am. Bd. Med. Examiners. Resident in pediat. Children's Hosp.-U. Wash., Seattle, 1960-63; fellow immunology Children's Hosp. U. Wash., 1963-65; faculty U. Wash. Med. Sch., 1965-83, prof. pediat., 1975-83; head divsn. rheumatic diseases Children's Hosp., Seattle, 1968-83; prof., chmn. dept. pediat., pediatrician-in-chief Tufts U. Sch. Medicine/New Eng. Med. Ctr., 1983-98; Karp prof. pediat. Tufts U. Sch. Medicine, Boston, 1983—, disting. prof., 1995—. Vis. physician Med. Rsch. Coun., Taplow, Eng., 1971-72; adj. prof. diplomacy The Fletcher Sch. Law and Diplomacy, Tufts U., 1998-2000. Contbr. articles to profl. jours. Bd. dirs. Seattle Chamber Music Festival, 1982-85; trustee Boston Chamber Music Soc., 1985—; mem. Boston adv. coun. UNICEF, tech. advisor UN Study on the Impact of Armed Conflict on Children, 1995-97; chmn., adv. com. children's rights divsn. Human Rights Watch, 1995—; mem. adv. com. Middle East divsn., 1998—; exec. com. Women's Commn. for Refugee Women and Children Internat. Rescue com., 1989-94, adv. coun. 1994—. Mem.: AAAS, Royal Coll. Pediats. U.K., Internat. Women's Forum, Mass. Women's Forum, Harvard U. Med. Sch. Alumni Coun. (v.p. 1977—80, pres. 1982—83), Physicians for Human Rights (exec. com. 1986—, founding pres. 1986—89), Com. Health in So. Africa (exec. com. 1986—92), Assn. Med. Sch. Pediat. Chmn. (exec. com. 1986—89, rep. to coun. on govt. affairs and coun. acad. socs.), New Eng. Pediat. Soc. (pres. 1991—93), Am. Coll. Rheumatology, Internat. Pediat. Assn. (pres.-elect 1998—2001, pres. 2001—04), Am. Acad. Pediat. (exec. com. sect. on internat. child health, head children's rights program, rep. to UNICEF), Am. Pediat. Soc., Soc. Pediat. Rsch., Inst. Medicine of NAS, Saturday Club, Tavern Club, Aesculapian Club (pres. 1988—89). Office: Floating Hosp for Children 750 Washington St # 8683 Boston MA 02111-1526

SCHALLER-DEMERS, DEBRA SUSAN, education coordinator, health facility administrator; b. Bronx, N.Y., Feb. 12, 1956; d. Emanuel and Gloria (Rosenberg) Schaller; m. Richard Raymond Demers, Sept. 11, 1977; children: Jaeson Demers, Alexander Demers. BA cum laude, Queens Coll., N.Y., 1977; MS, Capella Univ., 2004—. Graphic artist Reproducta, Inc., N.Y., 1979—83; calligraphy instr. Forest Hills Adult Ctr., N.Y., 1989—95; program assoc. & parent group Educators for Social Responsibility, N.Y., 1992—2002; edn. coord., rsch. integrity Weill Med. Coll. Cornell Univ., N.Y., 2002—. Cons. in field. Mem. PTA, Forest Hills, 2003—; vol. Forest Hills Youth Athletic Assn., 1990—2002; founding. mem. Grand Ctrl. Pkwy. Players, 1993—99. Mem.: Pub. Responsibility in Medicine & Rsch., Responsible Conduct of Rsch. Edn. Consortium, Soc. Rsch. Adminstr. Internat. Avocations: art, parent/student education advocacy. Office: Weill Med Coll Cornell Univ 425 E 61 St Ste 301 New York NY 10021

SCHALLERT, WILLIAM JOSEPH, actor; b. Los Angeles, July 6, 1922; s. Edwin Francis and Elza Emily (Baumgarten) S.; m. Rosemarie Diann Waggner, Feb. 26, 1949; children: William Joseph, Edwin G., Mark M., Brendan C. BA, UCLA, 1946. Co-founder, owner Circle Theatre, Hollywood, Calif., 1947-50. Appeared in motion pictures, TV, stage, radio, 1947—; movies include Lonely Are the Brave, Heat of the Night, Charley Varrick, Red Badge of Courage, Teachers; starred in TV series Patty Duke Show, 1963-66, Nancy Drew Mysteries, 1977-78, Little Women, 1979, The New Gidget, 1986-88, The Torkelson's, 1991-92; starred as judge in stage play and film The Trial of the Catonsville Nine, N.Y.C., Los Angeles, 1971 (Obie award 1971); starred as Dr. Pangloss in Candide, L.A., 1995; recorded voice of Abraham Lincoln for permanent installation at Lincoln Mus., Springfield, Ill., 2004. Trustee Motion Picture and TV Fund, 1977—. With AUS, 1942-44; with USAAC, 1944-45. Fulbright fellow Brit. Repertory Theatre, 1952-53. Mem. ASCAP, SAG (pres. 1979-81, trustee pension and health plan 1983—, founder Com. for Performers with Disabilities 1981—, Ralph Morgan award 1993).

SCHALLY, ANDREW VICTOR, endocrine oncologist, researcher; b. Poland, Nov. 30, 1926; arrived in U.S., 1957; s. Casimir Peter and Maria (Lacka) Schally; m. Ana Maria Comaru, Aug. 1976. BSc, McGill U., Can., 1955, PhD in Biochemistry, 1957; 25 hon. doctorates. Research asst. biochemistry Nat. Inst. Med. Research, London, 1949—52; dept. psychiatry McGill U., Montreal, 1952—57; research assoc., asst. prof. physiology and biochemistry Coll. Medicine, Baylor U., Houston, 1957—62; assoc. prof. Tulane U. Sch. Medicine, New Orleans, 1962—67, prof., 1967—. Chief Endocrine Polypeptide and Cancer Inst. VA Med. Ctr., New Orleans; sr. med. investigator VA, 1973—99, disting. med. rsch. scientist, 1999—. Author several books; contbr. articles to profl. jours. Co-recipient Nobel prize for medicine, 1977; recipient Van Meter prize, Am. Thyroid Assn., 1969, Ayerst-Squibb award, Endocrine Soc., 1970, William S. Middletown award, VA, 1970, Ch. Mickle award, U. Toronto, 1974, Gairdner Internat. award, 1974, Borden award, Assn. Am. Med. Colls. and Borden Co. Found., 1975, Lasker Basic Rsch. award, 1975; fellow sr. rsch. fellow, USPHS, 1961—62. Mem.: AAAS, NAS, Royal Acad. Medicine Spain, Acad. Sci. Mex., Acad. Sci. Russia, Acad. Sci. Hungary, Acad. Medicine Poland, Acad. Medicine Venezuela, Nat. Acad. Medicine Brazil, Mex. Acad. Medicine, Soc. Internat. Brain Rsch. Orgn., Soc. Exptl. Biol. Medicine, Soc. Biol. Chemists, Am. Physiol. Soc., Endocrine Soc. Home: 5025 Kawanee Ave Metairie LA 70006-2547 Office: VA Hosp 1601 Perdido St New Orleans LA 70112-1207 Office Phone: 504-589-5230. Office Fax: 504-566-1625.

SCHALOW, FRANK HICKEY, philosopher, educator; b. Denver, Feb. 23, 1956; s. Berthold Erich and Frances Schalow. BA summa cum laude, U. Denver, 1978; MA, Tulane U., 1980, PhD, 1984. Vis. asst. prof. Loyola U., New Orleans, 1984-86, asst. prof., 1986-90, assoc. prof., 1990-92; lectr. Dillard U., New Orleans, 1993—; vis. assoc. prof. Xavier U., New Orleans, 1994-97, U. New Orleans, 1995—. Mem. editl. adv. bd. Auslegung U. Kans., Lawrence, 1983-97, Heidegger Studies U. Wis., LaCrosse, 2000—; mem. dissertation adv. bd. Union Inst., Cin., 1999—. Author: Imagination and Existence, 1986, Renewal of the Heidegger-Kant Dialogue, 1992, Language and Deed, 1998, Heidegger and the Quest for the Sacred, 2001; co-author: Traces of Understanding, 1990. Mem. Am. Philos. Assn., N.Am. Heidegger Conf. (sec. convenor 1992), S.W. Philosophy Soc. (exec. com. 1993), Phi Beta Kappa. Avocation: golf. Home: 7310 Freret St New Orleans LA 70118 Office: U New Orleans Lakefront Campus New Orleans LA 70148 E-mail: fschalow@uno.edu.

SCHAMBERGER, MARCUS S. pediatric cardiologist; b. Germany; MD, U. of Erlangen-Nuremberg, Germany. Diplomate Am. Bd. Pediat., Am. Bd. Pediatric Cardiology. Fellow in pediatric cardiology Ind. U., Indpls., 1996—99; asst. prof. clin. pediat. Ind. U.-Riley Children's Hosp., Indpls., 1999—. Fellow: Am. Acad. Cardiology. Office: Riley Children's Hosp 702 Barnhill Dr RR 104 Indianapolis IN 46202-5225 Office Phone: 866-864-0855.

SCHAMEL, DOUGLAS L. science educator, researcher; b. Balt., June 10, 1949; s. Edwin J. and Marian R. Schamel; m. Diane M. Tracy, May 29, 1975; children: Jay T., Juliann T. BS, Allegheny Coll., 1971; MS, U. Alaska, 1974; PhD, Simon Fraser U., Burnaby, B.C., Can., 2000. Asst. prof. biology U. Alaska, Fairbanks, 1994—2001, assoc. prof. biology and sci. edn., 2001—. Scientist-in-residence Denali Elem. Sch., Fairbanks, 1989—91; dir. Fairbanks dist. sci. fair Fairbanks Coun. PTAs, 1989—2004; Alaska membership chair Soc. for Coll. Sci. Tchrs., Athens, Ga., 1990—2004; co-dir. Alaska statewide H.S. sci. symposium U. Alaska, Fairbanks, 1990—98, dir. Alaska Summer Rsch. Acad., 2002—04. Bd. mem. Alaska Bird Obs., Fairbanks, 2000—03. Named Outstanding Undergraduate Sci. Tchr., Kendall-Hunt/SCST, 1996, Advisor of the Yr., Golden Key Nat. Honor Soc., 1998; recipient Hon. Life Membership, Alaska State PTA, 1990. Mem.: NSTA, Alaska Shorebird Working Group, Contraborealis (dancemaster 2002—03). Office: Univ Alaska Fairbanks PO Box 756100 Fairbanks AK 99775 Office Phone: 907-474-6297. Personal E-mail: ffdls@uaf.edu. E-mail: ffdls@uaf.edu.

SCHANDER, MARY LEA, retired protective services official, educator, consultant; b. June 11, 1947; d. Gerald John Lea and Marian Lea Coffman; m. Edwin Schander, July 3, 1971. BA, Calif. Luth. Coll., 1969; MA, UCLA, 1970. Staff aide City of Anaheim (Calif.) Police Dept., 1970-72, staff asst., 1972-78, sr. staff asst., 1978-80; with Resource Mgmt. Dept. City of Anaheim, 1980-82; asst. to dir. Pub. Safety Agy. City of Pasadena Police Dept., 1982-85, spl. asst. to police chief, 1985-88, adminstrv. comdr., 1988-92, police comdr., 1992—2002. Freelance musician; publisher Australian Traditional Songs, 1985, Songs in the Air of Early California, 1994; lectr. Calif. Luth. Coll.; instr. Calif. State U., Northridge; cons. City of Lodz, Poland, Internat. Assn. Chiefs of Police, Govt. and Adminstrn. of Justice; speaker, panelist League of Calif. Cities, Pasadena Commn. on Status of Women; mcpl. mgmt. asst. CLEARS; adj. faculty Pasadena City Coll., 2000—, Glendale C.C., 2002—; instr. or trainer Media Survival Group; auditor Ell and Assocs. Prodr.: (cable TV program) Traditional Music Showcase; contbr. articles in field to profl. jours. Bd. dirs. ARC, Rotary Club Pasadena, S.W. Chamber Music; instr. Bd. Corrections, State Chmn. Publ. Rels., Red Cross Recipient Police Chief's Spl. award City of Pasadena, 1987, Women at Work Medal of Excellence, 1988, 2d Century Leadership award YWCA, 1998; Augustana fellow Calif. Luth. Coll., 1969, Clara Barton award for excellence San Gabriel Valley chpt. ARC. Mem. Am. Fedn. Tchrs., Pasadena Arts Coun., S.W. Chamber Music Soc. Home and Office: PO Box 50151 Pasadena CA 91115-0151 Office Phone: 626-824-4523. E-mail: mschander@earthlink.net.

SCHANK, ROGER CARL, computer science and psychology educator; b. N.Y.C., Mar. 12, 1946; s. Maxwell and Margaret (Rosenberg) S.; children: Hana, Joshua. BS, Carnegie Inst. Tech., 1966; MA, U. Tex., 1967, PhD, 1969; MA (hon.), Yale U., 1976. Asst. prof. linguistics and computer sci. Stanford (Calif.) U., 1968-74; rsch. fellow Inst. Semantics and Cognition, Castagnola, Switzerland, 1973-74; assoc. prof. computer sci. Yale U., New Haven, 1974-76, prof. computer sci. and psychology, 1976-89, chmn. dept. computer sci., 1980-85; John Evans prof. computer sci., psychology and edn., founder Inst. for Learning Scis. Northwestern U., Evanston, Ill., 1989-2000, prof. emeritus, 2000—; chmn., chief tech. officer Cognitive Arts, N.Y.C., 1995—. Pres., chmn. bd. Cognitive Sys., Inc., New Haven, 1981-88; pres., chmn. Computeach, Inc., 1982-88. Author: Conceptual Information Processing, 1975, Dynamic Memory, 1982, (with others) Scripts, Plans, Goals and Understanding, 1977, Cognitive Computer, 1984, Explanation Patterns, 1986, The Creative Attitude, 1988, Tell Me A Story, 1990, reprinted with new forward, 1995, The Connoisseur's Guide to the Mind, 1991, Engines for Education, 1995, Virtual Learning: A Revolutionary Way to Build a Highly Skilled Workforce, 1997, Dynamic Memory Revisited, 1999, Coloring Outside the Lines, 2000, Scrooge Meets Dick and Jane, 2001, Designing World-Class E-learning, 2001; editor Cognitive Sci. Jour.; inventor computer programs. Recipient Disting. career prof., Carnegie Mellon U., Pitts., 2001. Mem. Cognitive Sci. Soc. (founder). Office: Cognitive Arts 1840 Oak Ave #4 Evanston IL 60201-3642 E-mail: schank@cognitivearts.com.

SCHANNEP, JOHN DWIGHT, brokerage firm executive; b. Newport News, Va., May 23, 1934; s. Dwight Bahney and Harriet Louise (Quinn) S.; m. Helen Ann Harris, June 21, 1958; children: John Barton, Dwight David, Timothy Michael, Marie Louise. BS, U.S. Mil. Acad., 1956. Commd. 1st lt. U.S. Air Force, 1956, resigned, 1960; acct. exec. Dean Witter Reynolds, Phoenix, 1960-68, v.p., resident mgr. Tucson, 1968-83, sr. v.p., 1983-89; ret. Pres. Tucson Stock/Bond Club, 1971-72; bd. dirs. SNEDCO. Author, pub. Schannep Timing Indicator and the Dow Theory Investment Timing Newsletter (available on Internet), 1980—. Pres. Big Bros. Tucson, 1972-74. Mem. Nat. Assn. Security Dealers (Ariz. committeeman and chmn. 1971-73), Tucson C. of C. (v.p. 1971), Pinetop Lakes Golf and Country Club (treas. 1990-91, pres. 1991-93), West Point Soc. (pres. 1967), Lions (pres. Phoenix chpt. 1966.) Republican. Home: 5191 E Hill Place Dr Tucson AZ 85712-1346

SCHAPIRO, DONALD, lawyer; b. N.Y.C., Aug. 8, 1925; s. John Max and Lydia (Chaitkin) S.; m. Ruth Ellen Goldman, June 29, 1952 (dec. Aug. 1991); m. Linda N. Solomon, Oct. 10, 1993; children: Jane G., Robert A. AB, Yale U., 1944, LL.B., 1949. Bar: N.Y. 1949. Assoc. Paul, Weiss, Rifkind, Wharton & Garrison, N.Y.C., 1949-51; asst. chief counsel subcom. ways and means com.

on adminstrn. revenue laws U.S. Ho. of Reps., Washington, 1951-52; assoc. Barrett, Smith, Schapiro, Simon & Armstrong, N.Y.C., 1952-55, partner, 1955-88; ptnr. Chadbourne & Parke, 1988—. Vis. lectr. law Yale U. Law Sch., 1949-78, 94-95, instr. law and econs., 1945-49. Mem. Order of Coif, Phi Beta Kappa, Phi Delta Phi. Home: 1035 5th Ave New York NY 10028-0135 Office: Chadbourne & Parke 30 Rockefeller Plz Fl 32 New York NY 10112-0129 E-mail: dschapiro@chadbourne.com.

SCHAPIRO, JAIME, architect; b. Santiago, Chile, July 10, 1939; came to U.S., 1970; s. Gregorio Schapiro and Eva (Reizin) Epstein; m. Rebeca Schapiro, Oct. 10, 1970; children: Vivian, Caroline. B in Math., Nat. Inst., Santiago, 1957; degree in architecture, U. Chile, Santiago, 1964. Registered architect Fla.; cert. architect Chile, Peru. Prin. Schapiro Asociados, Cons., Lima, Peru, 1967-70; head designer archtl. planning office Columbia U., N.Y.C., 1970-72; prin. Arkbild, Inc., Miami, Fla., 1972-75, Jaime Schapiro AIA & Assocs., Miami, 1975—. Pres. GIII H Corp., Miami, 1978—, Urban Design Internat., Miami, 1978—; featured in various archtl. jour. articles. Sec. Jewish Vocat. Svcs., Miami, 1989, bd. dirs. 1986-89; mem. Am. Jewish Com., Miami. Recipient Fame award Fla. Achievement and Mktg. 1983, Aurora award S.E. Bldg. Conf., 1983, Concrete Design award Fla. Concrete Mfg. Assn., 1986; rsch. grantee Kyoto (Japan) U., 1964-66. Mem. AIA, Chilean Coll. Architects, Peruvian Coll. Architects. Jewish. Avocations: fencing, music, painting. Home: 1025 NE 89th St Miami FL 33138-3445 Office: Jaime Schapiro AIA & Assocs 1150 Kane Concourse Fl 3 Miami FL 33154

SCHAPIRO, JEROME BENTLEY, chemicals executive; b. NYC, Feb. 7, 1930; s. Sol and Claire (Rose) Schapiro; m. Edith Irene Kravet, Dec. 27, 1953; children: Lois, Robert, Kenneth. B.Chem. Engrng., Syracuse U., 1951; postgrad., Columbia U., 1951-52. Project engr. propellents br. US Naval Air Rocket Test Sta., Lake Denmark, NJ, 1951-52; with Dixo Co., Inc., Rochelle Park, NJ, 1954—; pres., 1966—. Lectr. detergent stds., drycleaning, care labeling, consumers stds., orgns., U.S., 1968—; U.S. del. spokesman on drycleaning Internat. Stds. Orgn.,Newton, Mass., 1971, Burssels, 1972, U.S. del. spokesman on dimensional stability of textiles, Paris, 1974, Ottawa, Can., 1977, Copenhagen, 1981; chmn. U.S. del. com. on consumer affairs, Geneva, 1974, 75, 76, spokesman U.S. del. on textiles, Pairs, 1974, mem. U.S. del. on care labeling of textiles, The Hague, Holland, 1974, U.S. del., chmn. del. coun. com. on consumer policy, Geneva, 1978, 79, 82, Israel, 1980, Paris, 1981, observer Internat. Std. Orgn./Consumer Com. on Policy meeting, Kyoto, Japan, 2000, Oslo, 2001; leader U.S. del. com. on dimensional stability of textiles, Manchester, Eng., 1984; fed. govtl. appointee to Industry Functional Adv. Com. on Stds., 1980-81; legal expert drycleaning techniques and procedures. Mem. Montclair (N.J.) Sch. Study Com., 1968-69; co-founder Jewish Focus, Inc., 1991, pub. Catskill/Hudson Jewish Star, 1991-98; v.p., treas. synagogue. 1st lt. USAF, 1952-53. Fellow ASTM (chmn. com. D-12 Soaps and Detergents 1974-79, mem. standing com. on internat. stds. 1980-84, hon. mem. award com. D-13 textiles); mem. AIChE, Am. Nat. Stds. Inst. (vice-chmn. bd. dirs. 1983-85, exec. com. 1979-81, 83-85, bd. dirs. 1979-85, fin. com. 1982-85, chmn. consumer coun. 1976, 79, 80, 81, mem. steering com. to advise Dept. Comerce on implementation GATT agreements 1976 77, mem. exec. stds. coun. 1977-79, intenat. stds. coun., chmn. internat. consumer policy adv. com. 1978-86), Am. Assn. Textile Chemists and Colorists (mem. exec. com. on rsch. 1974-77, chmn. com. on dry cleaning 1976-88, vice-chmn. internat. test methods com. 1982-86), Am. Chem. Soc. (emeritus), Stds. Engring. Soc. (cert.), Internat. Stds. Orgn. (mem. internat. stds. steering com. for consumer affairs 1978-81), Nat. Small Bus. Assn. (assoc. trustee 1983-85), Masons. Jewish. Home: PO Box 42 Gardiner NY 12525 Office: 158 Central Ave PO Box 7038 Rochelle Park NJ 07662-7038

SCHAPIRO, MARY, federal agency administrator, lawyer; b. N.Y.C., June 19, 1955; d. Robert D. and Susan (Hall) S.; m. Charles A. Cadwell, Dec. 13, 1980. BA, Franklin and Marshall Coll., 1977; JD, George Washington U., 1980. Bar: D.C. 1980. Trial atty., 1980-81; counsel to chmn. Commodity Futures Trading Commn., 1981-84; sr. v.p. Futures Ind. Assn., 1984; gen. counsel Futures Industry Assn., 1984-88; commr. SEC, Washington, 1988-94; chmn. Commodity Futures Trading Commn. (CFTC), Washington, 1994-96; pres. Nat. Assn. Securities Regulation, Inc., Washington, 1996—; vice chmn., pres., regulatory policy oversight Nat. Assn. of Securities Dealers, 1996—. Mem. Tech. Com. and the Develop. Markets Com. of the Internat. Org. of Securities (IOSCO); chmn IOSCO Cons. Com., 2001—. Mem. bd. trustees, vice chmn. audit com. Franklin and Marshall Coll.; bd. dirs. Cinergy Corp., 1999—, Kraft Foods. Named Fin. Women's Assn. Pub. Sector Woman of the Yr., 2000. Office: Nat Assn Securities Regulation Inc 1735 K St NW Washington DC 20006-1516

SCHAPIRO, MORTON OWEN, university administrator; m. Mimi Schapiro; children: Matt, Alissa, Rachel. BA in economics, Hofstra U., 1975; PhD, U. Pa., 1979. Prof. economics, asst. provost Williams Coll., 1980—91; chair, dept. economics U. So. Calif., 1991—94, dean, Coll. Letters, Arts and Sciences, 1994—2000, v.p. planning, 1998—2000; prof. economics Williams Coll., 2000—, pres., 2000—. Commentator Pub. Radio Internat; expert witness on econ. issues in higher edn. U.S. Congress. Co-author (with Michael S. McPherson): Keeping College Affordable, 1991, Paying the Piper, 1993, The Student Aid Game, 1998; contbr. articles to profl. jours. Office: Office of the President Williams Coll PO Box 687 Williamstown MA 01267

SCHAPP, REBECCA MARIA, museum director; b. Stuttgart, Fed. Republic Germany, Dec. 12, 1956; came to U.S., 1957; d. Randall Todd and Elfriede Carolina (Scheppan) Spradlin; m. Thomas James Schapp, May 29, 1979. AA, DeAnza Coll., 1977; BA in Art, San Jose State U., 1979, MA in Art Adminstrn., 1985. Adminstrv. dir. Union Gallery, San Jose, Calif., 1979-82; from mus. coordinator to dep. dir. de Saisset Mus. Santa Clara (Calif.) U., 1982-92, dir., 1993—. Mem. San Francisco Mus. Modern Art; bd. dirs. Works of San Jose, v.p. 1983-85. Mem. Non-Profit Gallery Assn. (bd. dirs.). Democrat. Avocations: racquetball, walking, bicycling, camping. Office: De Saisset Mus Santa Clara U 500 El Camino Real Santa Clara CA 95050-4345

SCHAPPELL, ABIGAIL SUSAN, speech, language, hearing and massage therapist; b. York, Pa., May 25, 1952; d. Felix and Ann (Getty) DeMoise; m. Gery Mylan Schappell, Oct. 20, 1979; 1 child, Jonathan Michael. BS with Master's equivalency, Longwood Coll., 1974; postgrad., Bloomsburg U., 1975—77; cert., Lehmann Sch. Massage and Muscle, 1991, East-West Sch. Massage Therapy, 1995—. Lic. speech-lang. pathologist, Pa. Speech-lang.-hearing specialist dept. pub. welfare Hamburg (Pa.) Ctr., 1975—2004. Judge deaf posters and essays Virginville (Pa.) Grange, 1990—, judge Pa. State Grange Conv., 1997, tchr. emergency pers. on communicating with deaf and hard of hearing, 1991, 92; leader demonstrations and workshops on sign lang. and dysphagia, non-verbal comm., active listening to various orgns., 1978—; instr. ARC, 1999-2002; bd. dirs. Berks Deaf and Hard of Hearing Svcs., 2000-; presenter in field. Pub: (Boy Scouts Coun. manual), Scouting for the Handicapped, Hawk Mountain, 1981-82. Sign/del. to conf. Bible Sch. dir., mem. Zion's United Ch. of Christ, Windsor Castle, Pa., 1985—; rep. nat. triann. conv. Penn Laurel coun. Girl Scouts U.S., 1975; vol. residential monitoring project Berks County ARC, 1998-99. Named Virginville Grange Cmty. Citizen of Yr., 1994—95; named one of Outstanding Young Women of Am., 1984. Mem.: AAUW, Schuykill Haven Bus. and Profl. Women (Young Careerist local, dist. and state honors 1980—81, pres. 1983—84, asst. dir. dist. 9 Pa. 1997—99, dist. 9 dir. 1999—2001, state mentoring com. 2001—03, dist. 9 parliamentarian 2002—04, state edn. and svc. funds com. 2003—, involvement on dist. and state level, presenter local, dist. and state level workshops, Eleanor Briner award as dist. 9 dir. 2000), Pa. Speech and Hearing Assn., Am. Assn. Mental Retardation (mem. Region 9 core com. for speech 1976, presenter at state conf. 1994, regional conf. 1995), Tory Town chpt. DAR, Young Careerist Alumni Assn. (life), Hamburg Area Soccer Assn. (sec. 1989—94), Order Ea. Star (mem., chaplain Blue Mountain chpt. 1981, 1982). Republican. Avocations: massage, signing, music. Home: 531 S 4th St Hamburg PA 19526-1307

SCHAR, DWIGHT C. construction company executive; b. 1942; With Ryan Homes, Washington, 1986-77, NVLand, 1977—, NVR L P, 1980-86, pres., 1986—. Bd. dirs. NVCompanies Inc. Office: NVR L P 7601 Lewinsville Rd Ste 300 Mc Lean VA 22102-2835

SCHAR, STEPHEN L. lawyer; b. Chgo., Oct. 19, 1945; s. Sidney and Lillian (Lieberman) Schar; m. Jessica S. Feit, Aug. 17, 1980; children: Scott Andrew, Elizabeth Loren. BA, U. Chgo., 1967; JD, DePaul U., 1970. Bar: Ill. 1970, U.S. Dist. Ct. (no. dist.) Ill. 1970. Assoc. Aaron, Aaron, Schimberg & Hess, Chgo., 1970-77, ptnr., 1977-80, Aaron, Schimberg, Hess, Rusnak, Deutsch & Gilbert, Chgo., 1980-84, Aaron, Schimberg, Hess & Gilbert, Chgo., 1984, Aaron, Schimberg & Hess, Chgo., 1984, D'Ancona & Pflaum, Chgo., 1985-98; mem. D'Ancona & Pflaum LLC, Chgo., 1999—2003; ptnr. Seyfarth Shaw LLP, Chgo., 2003—. Instr. estate planning Loyola U., Chgo., 1978—79. Bd. dirs. Jewish Children's Bur. Chgo., 1982—2001, pres., 1996—98, hon. dir., 2001—; pres. Faulkner Condominium Assn., Chgo., 1980—82, Carl Sandburg Village Homeowners Assn., Chgo., 1981—82. Mem.: Chgo. Estate Planning Coun., Chgo. Bar Assn. (pres. probate practice divsn. III 1979), Ill. Bar Assn. Home: 2155 Tanglewood Ct Highland Park IL 60035-4231 Office: Seyfarth Shaw LLP 111 E Wacker Dr Ste 4200 Chicago IL 60603-4209 Office Phone: 312-781-8649. E-mail: sschar@seyfarth.com.

SCHARF, CHARLES W. bank executive; married; two children. B, Johns Hopkins U., 1987; MBA, N.Y. U. With Comml. Credit Corp., 1987-95; various sr. positions to CFO Smith Barney, 1995-98; CFO global corp. & investment bank Citibank, 1998-2000; exec. v.p., CFO Bank One Corp., Chgo., 2000—. Office: Bank One Corp 1 Bank One Plaza Chicago IL 60670

SCHARF, MARK EDWARD, playwright; b. New Albany, Ind., Sept. 21, 1956; s. Edward Willis and Jane Louise Scharf; children: James Edward, Eric Michael. BSc, Va. Commonwealth U., Richmond, 1978; MFA, U. Va., Charlottesville, Va., 1984. Author: (play) The Whispers of Saints (Best Play and Best Prodn., Balt. Playwrights Festival, 2002), Freefall (Best Prodn., 3rd Pl. Balt. Playwrights Festival, 2001), Beltway Roulette (New Works Theatre Outstanding Achievment in Playwriting Award, 1993), The Mean Reds (Best Prodn., Balt. Playwrights Festival, 1998), No Riders (The Montgomery Playhouse Lit. Prize, 1995), (Best Original Script, Md. Theatre Festival, 1995), Lizard Brains (Best Play, New Works Theatre One-Act Play Marathon, 1994), Slower Delaware (Md. State Arts Coun. Individual Artist Fellowship in Playwriting, 1993), Hired Gun (Md. State Arts Coun. Individual Artist Fellowship in Playwriting, 1989), Zelda (Clay E. Delauney Playwriting Award, 1982), (E. Roger Boyle Playwriting Award, 1982). Mem.: The Dramatists Guild (assoc.). Home: 303 Palmspring Drive #10 Gaithersburg MD 20878 Personal E-mail: markscharf@aol.com.

SCHARF, WILLIAM, artist; b. Media, Pa., Feb. 22, 1927; s. Lester William and Ebba (Anderson) S.; m. Diana Denny, Mar. 11, 1947 (div. 1951); 1 child, William Denny; m. Sally Kravitch, Mar. 25, 1956; 1 child, Aaron Anderson. Student, Barnes Found., 1946-47; cert. in painting, Pa. Acad. of Fine Arts, 1947. Instr. Mus. Modern Art, N.Y.C., 1964, Sch. Visual Arts, N.Y.C., 1963-73, San Francisco Inst. Fine Arts, 1963, 66, 69, 74, 89. One man shows include David Herbert Gallery, N.Y.C., 1960, 62, San Francisco Inst. Fine Arts, 1969, Neuberger Mus., Purchase, N.Y., 1976, High Mus., Atlanta, 1978, Armstrong Gallery, N.Y.C., 1987, U. Mich. Mus. Art, Ann Arbor, 1993, The Phillips Collection, Washington, 2000-01, Frederick R. Weisman Mus., Malibu, Calif., 2001, P.S.I., MOMA, Queens, 2002, Richard York Gallery, N.Y.C., 2004; exhibited in group shows at Guggenheim Mus., N.Y.C., 1982, Hirschl-Adler Gallery, N.Y.C., 1980, Smith-Anderson Gallery, Palo Alto, Calif., Nat. Mus. Am. Art, Washington, 1987, 91, 92, Am. Acad. and Inst. Arts and Letters, N.Y.C., 1989, 91, Richard York Gallery, N.Y.C., 2002, Nat. Acad. Design Mus., N.Y.C., 2003; represented in permanent collections Phila. Mus. Boston Inst. Contemporary Art, Bklyn Mus., Solomon R. Guggenheim Mus., N.Y.C., Newark Mus., Nat. Mus. Am. Art, Smith Coll. Mus., Northampton, Mass., Zimmerli Mus., Rutgers U., New Brunswick, N.J., U. Mich. Mus. art., Phillips Collection, Washington, The Neuroscis. Inst., San Diego, The High Mus., Atlanta, Colgate U., Telfair Mus. of Art, Savannah, Ga., Rose Art Mus., Brandeis U., Montgomery (Ala.) Mus. Art. Trustee Rothko Found., N.Y.C., 1979—87; instr. Art Student's League, NY, 1987—2003. With USAF, 1945—46. Emmlen Cresson fellow Pa. Acad. Fine Arts, 1948. Mem.: Nat. Acad. Design, Soc. of Illustrators, Artist Equity Assn.

SCHARF, Y. DAVID, lawyer; b. N.Y.C., Apr. 10, 1968; BS in Mktg., NYU, 1988; JD, Bklyn. Law Sch., 1991. Assoc. Graubard Mollen & Miller, 1992—96, McDermott, Will & Emery, N.Y.C., 1996—98, ptnr., 1998—2000, Morrison Cohen Singer & Weinstein, N.Y.C., 2000—. Contbr. articles to profl. jours. Founder, trustee, bd. dirs., pro bono counsel Lifetime Care for the Jewish Disabled, Inc.; sec. Coun. Jewish Orgns. of the West Side, N.Y.C. Named to, Crain's N.Y. Bus. "40 under 40", 2004; recipient Founder's award, Lifetime Care Found., 1998. Mem.: ABA, N.Y. State Bar Assn. Office: Morrison Cohen Singer & Weinstein 750 Lexington Ave New York NY 10022*

SCHARFENBERG, MARGARET ELLAN, retired elementary school educator; b. Lansing, Mich., Mar. 22, 1924; d. John Milton and Florence Lucille (Craig) Amiss; m. Howard Edward Scharfenberg, June 29, 1946; children: Ann Derr Scharfenberg White, Joan Carol Scharfenberg Anderson, John Howard Scharfenberg. Student, Oberlin Coll., 1942-44; BA, Mich. State U., 1946; MA in Teaching, Rollins Coll., 1966. Cert. tchr., elem. supr., Fla. Tchr. Hill Elem. Sch., Maitland, Fla., 1964-65, Cheney Elem. Sch., Orlando, Fla., 1965-66; reading lab. tchr. Richmond Heights Elem. Sch., Orlando, 1966-68; supr. perceptual planning, oral clinician Orange County Schs., Orlando, 1968-69; reading lab. tchr. Winter Park (Fla.) H.S., 1969-72; from perceptual trainer to exptl. reading lab. tchr. Gateway Sch., Orlando, 1972-74; tchr. of migrant children Zellwood (Fla.) Elem. Sch., 1974-93; ret., 1993. Pioneer white/black sch. staffing Richmond Heights Elem. Sch., 1966-68; dir. Learning Skills Profl. Ctr., Orlando, 1971-74; speaker, cons. in field. Author, editor (newsletter) Paper Meeting, 1968-69, (perception package) Patterns for a Purpose, 1968-69; producer films on perceptual tng., 1968-69. Chaplain, Oleander Garden Cir.; chaplain, past sec., Lakes and Hills Garden Club; past sec. Tangerine Garden Club; chaplain, historian, past v.p. and pres. Women's Soc., Tangerine Cmty. Ch.; vol. Women of Hospice, Hospice Hope Chest; mem. Humane Soc. U.S.A.; mem. Congl. Ch. of Mt. Dora. Named Tchr. of Yr., Zellwood Elem. Sch., 1993. Mem.: NEA, AAUW, Internat. Reading Assn. (sec. Orange County coun. 1965, pres. 1969), Rosicrucian Order (A.M.O.R.C.), Lions (staff mem. seminars on perception, recipient various certs. and plaques), Gamma Phi Beta (past pres. alumna group). Republican. Congregationalist. Avocations: reading, boating, gardening, animal study. Home: 6492 Dora Dr Mount Dora FL 32757-7064

SCHARFF, JOSEPH LAURENT, lawyer; b. New Orleans, Oct. 2, 1935; s. Joseph Roy and Celia Ray (Rosenhein) S.; m. Mary Susan Greulach, June 29, 1963; children: Catherine Elizabeth, Robert Laurent, Anne Victoria. BS in Journalism, Northwestern U., 1957; JD, Harvard U., 1964. Bar: D.C. 1965, U.S. Supreme Ct. 1970, U.S. Ct. Appeals (D.C. cir.) 1965, U.S. Ct. Appeals (2nd cir.) 1980, U.S. Ct. Appeals (5th cir.) 1973, U.S. Ct. Appeals (10th cir.) 1977, U.S. Ct. Claims 1965. From assoc. to ptnr. Pierson, Ball & Dowd, Washington, 1964-89; ptnr. Reed Smith Shaw & McClay, Washington, 1989-95, counsel, 1996. Mem. ABA (fair trial-free press com. 1973-76, com. reps. media 1985-95, co-chmn. 1989-92), Fed. Comm. Bar Assn., Soc. Profl. Journalists, Radio-TV News Dirs. Assn. (counsel 1965-95, Disting. Svc. award 1987, J. Laurent Scharff Legal Internship established 1996), Media Inst. (First Amendment Adv. Coun. 1993-2003). Home and Office: 12000 Turf Ln Reston VA 20191-2123

SCHARFF, MATTHEW DANIEL, immunologist, cell biologist, educator; b. N.Y.C., Aug. 28, 1932; s. Harry and Constance S.; m. Carol Held, Dec. 19, 1954; children: Karen, Thomas, David. AB, Brown U., 1954, DrMedSci (hon.), 1994; MD, NYU, 1959. House officer II and IV med. service Boston City Hosp., 1959—61; rsch. assoc. NIH, 1961—63; asst. prof. Albert Einstein Coll. Medicine, Yeshiva U., Bronx, NY, 1963—67, assoc. prof., 1967—71, prof. dept. cell biology, 1971—, chmn. dept., 1972—83, dir. div. biol. scis., 1975—81; assoc. dir. Cancer Ctr., 1975—86, dir., 1986—95, dep. dir., 1995—2002. Served with USPHS, 1961-63. Recipient Alumni Achievement award NYU Sch. Medicine, 1980, N.Y. Acad. Medicine medal, 1990, Commemorative award Albert Einstein Coll. Medicine, 1993, Mayor of NY Lifetime Achievement award in sci. and tech., 2003. Mem. Am. Assn. Immunologists (Mentoring Excellence award 1998), Am. Soc. Clin. Investigation, Nat. Acad. Scis., Am. Acad. Arts and Sci., Phi Beta Kappa, Sigma Xi, Alpha Omega Alpha. Office: Albert Einstein Coll Med Dept Cell Biology 1300 Morris Pk Ave Bronx NY 10461-1926

SCHARFF, ROBERT CAESAR, social sciences educator, writer, humanities educator; b. Chicago, Ill., Oct. 10, 1939; s. Heinz Caesar and Margot Hansen Scharff; m. Judith Lutzhoff, June 13, 1964; children: Michael Caesar, Adam Bayard, Sarah Elizabeth Champlin-Scharff. AB, U. of Ill., 1957—61; MA, Northwestern U., 1961—64, PhD, 1961—70. Instr. of philosophy U.S. Air Force Acad., Colorado Springs, Colo., 1966—68; vis. asst. prof. of philosophy U. of Okla., 1968—69; asst. prof. of philosophy U. of N.H., Durham, 1970—75, assoc. prof. of philosophy, 1975—89, prof. of philosophy, 1989—. Editor Continental Philosophy Rev., Dordrecht, Netherlands, 1995—. Author: (book) Comte After Positivism; editor: (anthology) Philosophy of Tech.: The Tech. Condition; author: (article) Comte and Heidegger on the Historicity of Science, Revue Internationale de Philosophie, 52/1, Heidegger's Appropriation of Dilthey Before Being and Time, Jour. of the History of Philosophy, 35/1. 1st lt. USAF, 1965—68. Mem.: Assn. of Philosophy Jour. Editors, North Am. Heidegger Conf. (sec.-convener 1983, 1996), Internat. Soc. for Hermeneutics and Sci., Soc. for Phenomenology and Existential Philosophy, Am. Philos. Assn. Office: U of NH Dept of Philosophy Durham NH 03824-3574 Office Phone: 603-862-1040.

SCHARFFE, WILLIAM GRANVILLE, academic administrator, educator; b. Saginaw, Mich., Mar. 12, 1942; s. William Edward and Marion Kittie (Granville) S.; m. Mary Jo Whitfield, Sept. 4, 1965; children: Sue L., William W. BA, Mich. State U., 1965, MA, 1969, PhD, 1977. Tchr. English Webber Jr. High Sch., Saginaw, 1965-66; tchr. speech Arthur Hill High Sch., Saginaw, 1966-68; staff asst. for pers. Saginaw City Schs., 1968-73, dir. pers., 1977-94, dir. employee devel. and media ops., 1994-99; prin. Zilwaukee Jr. High Sch., Saginaw, 1973-74; asst. prin. North Intermediate Sch., Saginaw, 1974-75, 1975 77; dir. policy svcs. Mich. Assn. Sch. Bds., Lansing, 1999—. Adj. asst. prof. Mich. State U., East Lansing, 1977; adj. lectr. Ctrl. Mich. U., Mt. Pleasant, 1987, Mich. State U., 1977, Saginaw Valley State U., 1991; cons. in field. Author: Elfred Alanzo & Santa's Surprise, 1987. Bd. dirs. Japanese Cultural Ctr. and Tea House, Saginaw, 1986-97, pres., 1993-95. Recipient Key Man award United Way Saginaw County, 1978, Outstanding Svc. award, 1978. Mem.: Am. Assn. State Policy Svcs. (pres. 2004—), Soc. For Human Resource Mgmt., Mich. Mid. Cities Pers. and Labor Rels. Task Force (pres. 1980—82), Mich. Assn. Sch. Pers. Assn. (sec., bd. dirs. 1988—90, pres., bd. dirs. 1992—93), Mich. State U Alumni Club (pres. Saginaw County chpt. 2002—04), Saginaw Club (pres. 1996—97), Exch. Club (Saginaw chpt. pres. 1981), Phi Delta Kappa. Republican. Episcopalian. Avocations: writing, golf, photography, public speaking. Home: 2812 Adams Blvd Saginaw MI 48602-3103 Office Phone: 517-327-5928. Business E-Mail: bscharffe@masb.org.

SCHARFSTEIN, SOL, publishing executive; b. Dinivetz, Russia, Sept. 15; arrived in U.S., 1921; s. Asher and Fannie Scharfstein; m. Edythe Scharfstein; children: Joel, Alan, Janet. BA, NYU. Pub., author, translator KTAV Pubs., N.Y.C., Jersey City and Hoboken, NJ, 1948—. Author: 30 juvenile books, 24 textbooks; 90 ednl. toys. Co-founder Jewish day sch. East Side Hebrew Inst. Office: KTAV Pub House 930 Newark Ave Jersey City NJ 07306-6316

SCHARLATT, HAROLD, management company executive; b. N.Y.C., Dec. 9, 1947; s. Bertram and Miriam Louise (Stone) S.; BEd, SUNY, 1969, MA in Liberal Studies, 1973; advanced cert. adminstrn. and supervision, Oxford U., 1975; m. Mary Moore, June 10, 1978. Tchr., in-service instr. N.Y., 1970-77; mgmt. devel. specialist Union Carbide Corp., N.Y.C., 1977, mgmt. devel. cons., 1978-80; regional dir. Vector Mgmt. Systems, Inc., Lexington, Ky., 1980-82; pres. Tng. and Devel. Assocs., Inc., Lexington, 1982—. Mem. Am. Soc. Tng. and Devel., Soc. Human Resource Mgmt. Office: 2220 Vinewood Rd Lexington KY 40515-1245

SCHARLAU, CHARLES EDWARD, III, natural gas company executive; b. Chgo., Apr. 24, 1927; s. Charles Edward II and Esther (Powell) S.; m. Clydene Yvonne Sloop, Aug. 13, 1960; children: Caryn, Robin, Greg, Charles, Marti. LLB, U. Ark., 1951. Bar: Ark. 1951, U.S. Dist. Ct. (western dist.) Ark. 1951, U.S. Supreme Ct. 1958. Atty. Ark. Western Gas Co., Fayetteville, 1951-61, v.p., 1961-68, pres., 1968-78; pres., chmn. S.W. Energy Co., Fayetteville, 1978—98. Bd. dirs. Ablest, Inc., Clearwater, Fla., Arvest Bank, S.W. Energy Co., Fayetteville. Chmn. U. Ark. Devel. Coun., 1989-97; trustee U. Ark., 1997—. With USMC, 1945-46. Mem. ABA, Ark. Bar Assn., So. Gas Assn., Nat. Assn. Mfrs. (bd. dirs. 1986-89), Am. Gas Assn. (bd. dirs. 1987-90), U. Ark. Alumni Assn. (pres. 1972-73), Ark. C. of C. (pres. 1977-79), Beta Gamma Sigma. Methodist. Avocations: reading, tennis, canoeing, sports. Home: 1506 Sunset Pl Fayetteville AR 72701-1627 Office: Southwestern Energy Co 1083 Sain St Fayetteville AR 72703-6206 Office Phone: 479-521-0472. E-mail: ccsharlau@aol.com.

SCHARLEMANN, ROBERT PAUL, religious studies educator, clergyman; b. Lake City, Minn., Apr. 4, 1929; s. Ernst Karl and Johanna Meta (Harre) S. Student, Northwestern Coll., Watertown, Wis., 1946-49; BA, Concordia Coll. and Sem., St. Louis, 1952; BD, MDiv, Concordia Coll. and Sem., 1955; Dr. theol., U. Heidelberg (Germany), 1957. Ordained to ministry, Lutheran Ch., 1960. Tchr. Luth. parochial sch., Mobridge, SD, 1949—50; instr. philosophy Valparaiso U., 1957-59; postdoctoral fellow Yale U., 1959-60; pastor Bethlehem Luth. Ch., Carlyle, Ill., 1960-62, Grace Luth. Ch., Durham, N.C., 1962-63; asst. prof. religion U. So. Calif., 1963-64, assoc. prof., 1964-66; assoc. prof. religion U. Iowa, Iowa City, 1966-68, prof., 1968-81; Commonwealth prof. religious studies U. Va., Charlottesville, 1981-97, prof. emeritus, 1997—. Fulbright-Hays prof. U. Heidelberg, 1975-76 Author: Thomas Aquinas and John Gerhard, 1964, Reflection and Doubt in the Thought of Paul Tillich, 1969, The Being of God, 1981, Inscriptions and Reflections, 1989, The Reason of Following, 1991, L'intemporel et l'eternel, 1993, Can Religion be Understood Philosophically?, 1995, The Mystical Correlate of Symbolic Appearing, 2001; editor Jour. of Am. Acad. Religion, 1980-85; contbr. articles to profl. jours. Fulbright scholar U. Heidelberg, 1955-57. Mem. Am. Acad. Religion, Am. Theol. Soc., Deutsche Paul-Tillich Gesellschaft, European Soc. Culture, Soc. for Philosophy of Religion. Lutheran.

SCHAROLD, MARY LOUISE, psychoanalyst, educator; b. Mar. 3, 1943; d. Walter John and Louise Helen (Hartmann) Baumgartner; m. William Ballew McCollum, Aug. 23, 1964 (div. 1981); m. Harry Karl Scharold, June 19, 1982; children: Margaret Louise, Walter Ballew. BA with highest distinction, U. Kans., 1964; MD, Baylor Coll. Medicine, 1968; postgrad., Topeka Inst. Psychoanalysis, 1981. Diplomate Am. Bd. Psychiatry and Neurology. Intern Meml. Bapt. Hosp., Houston, 1968-69; resident in psychiatry Baylor Coll. Medicine, Houston, 1969—72, chief resident, 1971-72; psychoanalyst Houston, 1972—. Asst. prof. Baylor Coll. Medicine, Houston, 1973-76, asst. clin. prof., 1981-84, assoc. clin. prof., 1984—; dir. Baylor Psychiat. Clinic, Houston, 1973-76; co-dir. Rice U. Psychiat. Svc., Houston, 1981-82; asst. clin. prof. U. Kans. Sch. Medicine, Kansas City, 1977-81; tchg. assoc. Topeka Psychoanalytic Inst., 1984-86; tchg. analyst, Houston-Galveston Psychoanalytic Inst., 1986-90, tng. and supervising analyst, 1990—, v.p., 1994-96, pres., 1996-2001, bd. dirs., 2001—. Adv. bd. Leavenworth (Kans.) Mental Health Assn., 1977-81. Watkins scholar U. Kans., 1961-64. Fellow Am. Psychiat. Assn. (disting., mem. com. quality assurance 1986-87, chair Tex. peer rev. 1984-88), Am. Coll. Psychoanalysts; mem. Am. Psychoanalytic Assn. (cert. 1982, peer rev. com. 1985-90, prof. ins. commn. 1986-93, bd. profl. stds. 1994-2001, CME com. 1994-96, exec. coun. 1994-96, cert. com. 1995-98, preparedness and progress com. 1998—, chair preparedness and progress com. 2000—, coordinating com. bd. profl. stds. 2000—, bylaws com. 2001—, fin. com. 2003—), Am. Group Psychotherapy Assn., Ctr. Advanced Psychoanalytic Studies, Houston Psychiat. Soc. (v.p. 1984-85, pres.-elect 1985-86, pres.

1986-87), Houston-Galveston Psychoanalytic Soc. (sec.-treas. 1984-86, pres.-elect 1986-88, pres. 1988-90, alt. councillor 1994-96), Houston Group Psychotherapy Soc. (adv. bd. 1984-85), Hilltoppers, Mortar Bd., Phi Beta Kappa, Delta Phi Alpha, Alpha Omega Alpha, Pi Beta Phi Alumni Assn. Republican. Lutheran. Office: 2301 Westheimer Rd Houston TX 77098-1317 Office Phone: 713-590-2302. E-mail: mlscharold@mindspring.com.

SCHARP, ROBERT CHARLES, mining engineer, energy company executive; b. Nebraska City, Nebr., Jan. 21, 1947; s. Hoyt Merwin and Betty Jane (James) S.; m. Cheryl P. Naas, Aug. 8, 1969; children: Paula Jean, Jacob Robert. Engr. of mines degree, Colo. Sch. Mines; Advanced Mgmt. Program, Harvard U., 1987. Mining engr. Phelps Dodge Corp., Morenci, Ariz., 1974-75; chief engr. Kerr-McGee Coal, Gillette, Wyo., 1975-80; mgr. Jacobs Ranch Mine Jacobs Ranch Mine, Gillette, Wyo., 1980-88; gen. mgr. Galatia Mine, 1988-90; v.p. ops. Kerr-McGee Coal, Oklahoma Ciy, 1990-91; pres. Kerr McGee Coal Corp., Oklahoma Ciy, 1991-95, sr. v.p., 1995-97; CEO Shell Coal Pty. Ltd., 1997-2000; dir. Horizon Natural Resources Co., Ashland, Ky., 2002, chmn. & acting CEO, 2002—. Dir. Nat. Coal Coun., Australian Coal Rsch. Ltd., Australian Inst. for Sustainable Devel. of Mineral Resources, Queensland Mining Coun.; dir.-elect Coal Industry Adv. Bd. Served with U.S. Army C.E., 1970-73, Germany; col. Wyo. N.G., ret. 1993. Fellow Australian Inst. Mining and Metallurgy; mem. Australian Coal Assn. (dir. rsch. project, dir. sustainable devel. program), Minerals Coun. Australia (mem. exec. com.), NSW Minerals Coun. (mem. exec. com.), Am. Inst. Mining Engring., King Coal Club (U.S.) (bd. dirs.), World Coal Inst. (bd. dirs.). Office: Horizon Natural Resources Co 2000 Ashland Dr Ashland KY 41101 E-mail: bob.scharp@anglocoal.com.au.

SCHARP-RADOVIC, CAROL ANN, choreographer, classical ballet educator, artistic director; b. Ypsilanti, Mich., Aug. 9, 1940; d. John Lewis and Mary Vivien (Alther) Keeney; m. Jack Laurel Scharp, July 28, 1958 (div. July 1970); children: Kathryn E., Mark A.; m. Srecko Radovic, Nov. 15, 1989. Studied with Pereslavic, Danilova; student, Harkness Ballet, N.Y.C., Joffrey Ballet, Eglevsky Ballet, Briansky Ballet, Darvesh Ballet, N.Y.C.; studied with Jurgen Schneider, Am. Ballet Theatre, 1983-93; studied with Janina Cunova, Luba Gulyeava, Australian & Kirov ballet cos., 1983-93; studied with Ninel Kurgapkina, Ludmila Synelnikova, Genhrich Mayorov, Kirov Ballet, 1987-89; studied with Ludmila Sakharova, Perm Ballet, 1993; studied with Ludmila Synelnikova, Bolshoi Ballet Sch., Moscow, 1989; studied with Inna Zubkhovskaya, Alex. Stiopin, Lydia Goncharova, Valentina Chistova and Mararita Zagurskaya, studied with Mdm. Trafimova, Nina Sakhrouskaya and Valentina Rumyantsema, Vaganova Ballet Acad., St. Petersburg, Russia, 1993. Ballet mistress Adrian (Mich.) Coll., 1982-84; founder, artistic dir. Ann Arbor (Mich.) Ballet Theatre, 1980—. Former regional field judge Nat. Ballet Achievement Fund; dir. seminars Marygrove Coll., Detroit. Choreographer Cinderella, 1980, Nightingale, 1980, Nutcracker, 1984, Carnival of the Animals, 1981, Carmen, 1983, Midsummer Nights Dream, 1982, Vivaldi's Spring, 1990, Opulence, 1984, La Boutique Fantasque, 1995, Handel's Alcina, 1985, Gymnopedie, 1985, Gershwin's Preludes, 1996, Ravel's Bolero, 1997, Dracula, 1997, others. Ruth Mott grantee for choreography, 1982. Mem. Mich. Dance Assn. Avocations: gardening, reading, writing. Home: 6476 Huron River Dr Dexter MI 48130-9796 Office: CAS Ballet Theatre Sch Ann Arbor Ballet Theatre 548 Church St Ann Arbor MI 48104-2563

SCHATKEN, NANCY LEAH, medical editor; b. N.Y.C., Jan. 7, 1938; d. Robert V. and Lillian Belle (Neff) S. BS, U.N.C., 1959; cert. med. tech., Albany Sch. Med. Tech., 1960. Med. tech., instr. various orgns., 1960-66; acting mng. editor med. jours. Harper & Row, N.Y.C., 1966-69; assoc. editor Med. World News-McGraw-Hill, N.Y.C., 1969-70; owner, founder Mostly Med., N.Y.C., 1970—, St. James, Barbados, 1978-98. Avocations: travel, reading, swimming, entertaining. Address: 2677 Parkview Dr Hallandale FL 33009 Office Phone: 954-455-0039. E-mail: schatken@bellsouth.net.

SCHATT, PAUL, newspaper editor; b. N.Y.C., Aug. 31, 1945; divorced; children: Suzannah, Andrew. BA with distinction Polit. Sci., English, Ariz. State U., 1967. Editor Ariz. Republic, 1964-66, reporter, 1965-74, urban affairs editor, 1974-75, asst. city editor, 1975-79, chief asst. city editor, 1979-82, asst. met. editor, 1985-86, met. editor, 1986-88, editor edit. pages, 1993—; asst. editor Ariz. Mag., 1981-82, editor, 1982-85; editor edit. pages Phoenix Gazette, 1988-93, The Ariz. Republic, 1993-97, assoc. editor, 1998—. Pres. 1st amendment coalition of Az., 1999; vis. lectr. Pub. Affairs Journalism, Ariz. State U., 1976—, instr. Mass. Comm. Dept., 1974-76; dir. Eugene C. Pulliam Fellowship. Phoenix program, 1990—; writing coach, 1989; del. Pre White House Conf. Librs., 1991, pres., Arizona Newspapers Assn., 2000—. V.p. Crisis Nursery, 1984-87, bd. dirs. 1980-87; exec. bd. Hospice of the Valley, 1980-87; pres. Friends of Phoenix Pub. Libr., 1985-86, bd. dirs. 1986—; bd. trustees 1st Amendment Congress, 1989—; bd. dirs. Ariz. Humanities Coun., 1999—; Dean's adv. bd., Arizona State U. Honors Coll., 1999—, adv. bd., Northern Arizona U. Sch. of Communications, 1999—, bd. dirs. Camelback Hosps. 1982-89, chmn. bd. dirs. 1986-87, Cactus Pine Coun. Girl Scouts Am., 1988-89, Sun Sounds Inc., 1982-89, Valley Leadership Inc., 1991—, alum. assn., 1985-89, Ariz. Zool. Soc., 1991—, Barrow Neurol. Found., 1991—, Kids Voting, 1991-93, Barry Goldwater Inst., 1991-93, Ariz. Club, 1991—. With Ariz. Nat. Guard, 1966-79. Recipient Montgomery award Outstanding Svc. to Community Friends of Phoenix Pub. Libr., 1989; profl. Journalism fellow Stanford U., 1970-71. Mem. Am. Soc. Newspaper Editors, Soc. Profl. Journalists (pres. Valley of Sun chpt. 1974-75, 83-84, exec. bd. 1988-92), Sigma Delta Chi (co-chair nat. convention 1974). Office: The Ariz Republic Editorial Dept 200 E Van Buren St Phoenix AZ 85004-2238 E-mail: paul.schatt@pni.com.

SCHATTSCHNEIDER, DORIS JEAN, retired mathematics educator; b. N.Y.C., Oct. 19, 1939; d. Robert W. Jr. and Charlotte Lucile (Ingalls) Wood; m. David A. Schattschneider, June 2, 1962; 1 child, Laura E. AB, U. Rochester, 1961; MA, Yale U., 1963, PhD, 1966. Instr. in math. Northwestern U., Evanston, Ill., 1964—65; asst. prof. U. Ill., Chgo., 1965—68; prof. Moravian Coll., Bethlehem, Pa., 1968—2002, prof. emerita, 2003—. Project dir. Fund for the Improvement of Post-Secondary Edn. U.S. Dept. Edn., 1991—93, 1995—97; vis. scholar U. V.I., 2004. Author (with W. Walker): (books and models) M.C. Escher Kaleidocycles, 1977, 1987; co-author: Visual Geometry Project, 1986—91; author: Visions of Symmetry, 1990, 2d edit., 2004; co-author: (videos and activities) A Companion to Calculus, 1995; editor: Geometry Turned On, 1997, M.C. Escher's Legacy, 2003. Exhbn. curator Allentown Art Mus., 1979, Payne Gallery, 1987. Grantee NEH rsch. grantee, 1988—90. Mem.: Assn. for Women in Math., Am. Math. Soc., Math. Assn. Am. (editor 1980—85, gov. 1980—89, 1st v.p. 1994—96, Allendoerfer award 1979, Meritorious Svc. award 1991, Dist. Math. Tchg. award 1993), Pi Mu Epsilon (councillor 1990—96). Mem. Moravian Ch. Office: Moravian College Math Dept PPHAC 1200 Main St Bethlehem PA 18018-6650 E-mail: schattdo@moravian.edu.

SCHATZ, IRWIN JACOB, cardiologist, educator; b. St. Boniface, Man, Can, Oct. 16, 1931; came to US, 1956, naturalized, 1966; s. Jacob and Reva S.; m. Barbara Jane Binder, Nov. 12, 1967; children: Jacob, Edward, Stephen and Brian (twins). Student, U. Man., Can.), Winnipeg, 1951, MD with honors, 1956. Diplomate: Am. Bd. Internal Medicine. Intern Vancouver (B.C.) Gen. Hosp., 1955-56; resident Hammersmith Hosp., U. London, 1957, Mayo Clinic, Rochester, Minn., 1958-61; head sec. peripheral vascular disease Henry Ford Hosp., Detroit, 1961-68; asso. prof. medicine Wayne State U., 1968-71, chief sect. cardiovascular disease, 1969-71; assoc. prof., asso. dir. sect. cardiology U. Mich., 1972-73, prof. internal medicine, 1973-75; prof. medicine John A. Burns Sch. Medicine, U. Hawaii, 1975—, chmn. dept. medicine, 1975-90, interim chmn. dept. medicine, 2003—. Author: Orthostatic Hypotension, 1986; contbr. numerous articles to med. jour. Mem. jud. coun. State of Hawaii Supreme Ct., 2000—. Rockefeller Found. scholar, 1991. Master ACP (bd. gov. 1984-89, Laureate award Hawaii chpt. 1992); fellow Am. Coll. Cardiology (bd. gov. 1980-84); mem. Am. Heart Assn. (fellow coun. cardiology), Am. Fedn. Clin. Rsch., Asian-Pacific Soc. Cardiology (v.p. 1987-91), Accreditation Coun. for Grad. Med. Edn. (chmn. residence rev. com. internal medicine 1989-95), Hawaii Heart Assn. (pres.), Western Assn. Physicians, Am. Autonomic Soc. (chmn. bd. gov., pres. 1996-98), Pacific Interurban Club. Jewish. Home: 4983 Kolohala St Honolulu HI 96816-5126 Office: 1356 Lusitana St Honolulu HI 96813-2421

SCHATZBERG, ALAN FREDERIC, psychiatrist, researcher; b. NYC, Oct. 17, 1944; s. Emanuel and Cila (Diamand) S.; m. Nancy R. Silverman, Aug. 27, 1972; children: Melissa Ann, Lindsey Diamand. BS, NYU, 1965, MD, 1968; MA (hon.), Harvard U., 1989. Diplomate Nat. Bd. Med. Examiners, Am. Bd. Psychiatry and Neurology. Intern Lenox Hill Hosp., NYC, 1968-69; resident in psychiatry Mass. Mental Health Ctr., Boston, 1969-72; clin. fellow in psychiatry Harvard Med. Sch., Boston, 1969-72, asst. prof. psychiatry, 1977-82, assoc. prof., 1982-88, prof., 1988-91; interim psychiatrist-in-chief McLean Hosp., Belmont, Mass., 1984-86, dir. depression rsch. facility, 1985—, svc. chief, 1982-84, 86-88; psychiatrist adv. panel Eli Lilly & Co., Indpls., 1986-93; clin. dir. Mass. Mental Health Ctr., Boston, 1988-91; Kenneth T. Norris, Jr. prof. psychiatry and behavioral scis. Stanford (Calif.) U., 1991—, chmn. dept. psychiatry and behavioral scis. Sch. Medicine, 1991—. Cons. AMA Videoclinics, Chgo., 1979-83; mem. AMA/FAA panel on health regulations, Chgo., 1984-86; mem. NIH Biol. Psychopathology and Clin. Neuroscis. Intitial Rev. Group, 1991-95, chmn., 1993-94. Co-author: Manual of Clinical Psychopharmacology, 1986, 4th edit., 2003; contbr. more than 300 articles to profl. publs., chpts. to books; co-editor: Depression: Biology, Psychodynamics and Treatment, 1978, Hypothalamic-Pituitary-Adrenal Axis, 1988, Textbook of Psychopharmacology, 1995, 2d edit., 1998, 3d edit., 2004; mem. editl. bd. McLean Hosp. Jour., 1975-88, Jour. Psychiat. Rsch., 1986—, co-editor in chief, 2000—, Harvard Rev. Psychiatry, 1992—, Archives of Gen. Psychiatry, 1995—, Psychoneuroendocrinology, 1995—, Am. Jour. Psychiatry, 2002—, Anxiety, 1993, Jour. Clin. Psychopharmacology, 1993—; assoc. editor-in-chief Depression, 1992—; translational field editor Neuropsychopharmacology, 2002—. Maj. USAF, 1972-74. Rsch. grantee NIMH, 1984-87, 94—, Poitras Charitable Found., 1985-93, Pritzker Found., 1997—; recipient Mood Disorders Rsch. award Am. Coll. Psychiatrists, 2002. Fellow APA (Rsch. award 2002), Am. Coll. Neuropsychopharmacology (coun. 1994-97, pres. 2000-01), Am. Psychopathological Assn., Am. Coll. Psychiatrists, Biol. Psychiatry (pres.-elect 2003-); mem. Mass. Psychiat. Soc. (coun. 1987-90), No. Calif. Psychiat. Soc. (v.p. 1997-99), Soc. Biol. Psychiatry (pres. elect, 2001). Avocations: travel, swimming, fine arts, theater, golf. Office: Stanford U Sch Medicine 401 Quarry Rd Rm 300 Stanford CA 94305-5717 Office Phone: 650-723-6811. Business E-Mail: afschatz@stanford.edu.

SCHATZKI, GEORGE, law educator; b. 1933; AB, Harvard U., 1955, LLB, 1958, LLM, 1965. Prof. law u. Tex., Austin, 1965-79; dean U. Wash. Sch. Law, Seattle, 1979-82, prof., 1979-84; dean U. Conn. Sch. Law, Hartford, 1984-90, prof., 1984—2000; prof. law Ariz. State U., Tempe, 2000—, acting dean, 2004. Vis. prof. law U. Pa., Phila., 1973-74, Harvard U., Cambridge, Mass., 1977-78; vis. lectr. law Yale U., New Haven, 1993, 96. Co-author: Labor Relations and Social Problems: Collective Bargaining in Private Employment, 1978, Labor and Employment Law, 1988, 3d edit., 2002. Fellow Tchg., Harvard U., 1963—65. Office: Ariz State U Coll Law PO Box 877906 Tempe AZ 85287-7906 Office Phone: 480-965-0746. Business E-Mail: george.schatzki@asu.edu.

SCHAUB, HARRY CARL, lawyer; b. Hazleton, Pa., Feb. 3, 1929; s. Harry J. and Lida M. (Fisher) S.; m. Kathryn Klindt Deans, Aug. 14, 1982; children: Lisa A., Irene Cannon, Christian K. BA, U. Pa., 1950; JD, Yale U., 1955; postgrad., Columbia U., 1962. Bar: Pa. 1955. Assoc. Montgomery, McCracken, Walker & Rhoads, Phila., 1955-62, ptnr., 1963-99, of counsel, 1999—; dean, CEO Consular Corps Coll., 1998—2004. Consul Republic of Austria to State of Pa., 1978-84, consul gen., 1984—. Dir. Concerto Soloista Phila., 1997-99, Franklin Inn, 1998-2001; contbr. articles to profl. jours. V.p., bd. dirs. Luth. Ch. of Holy Communion, Phila., 1975-88; bd. dirs. YMCA Cen., Phila., 1986-91. Capt. U.S. Army, 1951-53. Decorated Golden Medal of Honor 1st Class (Austria), Grand Cross of Honor 1st class Austria; recipient Johann Strauss award, City of Vienna, 1979. Mem.: John Peter Zenger Law Soc. (founder, bd. dirs., pres. 1994—96), Mil. Order Fgn. Wars, Austrian Soc. Pa. (v.p., bd. dirs. 1981—97), Am. Coun. on Germany, Athenaeum of Phila., The Penn Club, Rittenhouse Club, Union League of Phila., Pi Gamma Mu, Phi Beta Kappa. Lutheran. Home: 1420 Locust St Apt 7K Philadelphia PA 19102-4205 Office: Montgomery McCracken 123 S Broad St Fl 24 Philadelphia PA 19109-1099 Office Phone: 215-772-7348. E-mail: hschaub@mmwr.com.

SCHAUB, MARILYN MCNAMARA, religion educator; b. Chgo., Mar. 24, 1928; d. Bernard Francis and Helen Katherine (Skehan) McNamara; m. Thomas Schaub, Oct. 25, 1969; 1 child, Helen Ann. BA, Rosary Coll., 1953; PhD, U. Fribourg, Switzerland, 1957; diploma, Ecole Biblique, Jerusalem, 1967. Asst. prof. classics and Bibl. studies Rosary Coll., River Forest, Ill., 1957-69; prof. Bibl. studies Duquesne U., Pitts., 1969-70, 73-01. Participant 8 archeological excavations, Middle East; hon assoc Am Schs Oriental Research, 1966—67, trustee, 1986—89; Danforth assoc, 1972—80; admin dir expedition to the Southeast Dead Sea Plains, Jordan, 1989—. Author: (book) Friends and Friendship for St. Augustine, 1964; translator (with H Richter): Agape in the New Testament, 3 vols, 1963—65. Mem.: Am Acad Religion, Cath Biblical Asn, Soc Biblical Literature. Democrat. Home: 25 Mckelvey Ave Pittsburgh PA 15218-1452

SCHAUBERT, DANIEL HAROLD, electrical engineering educator; b. Galesburg, Ill., Feb. 15, 1947; s. Robert Harold and Carolyn Virginia (Dunkle) S.; m. Joyce Marie Conard, June 15, 1968; 1 child, Karen Louise. BSEE, U. Ill., 1969, MS, 1970, PhD, 1974. Rsch. engr. U.S. Army Harry Diamond Labs., Adelphi, Md., 1977-80; rsch. engr., program mgr. U.S. Bur. Radiol. Health, Rockville, Md., 1980-82; prof. elec. engring. U. Mass., Amherst, 1982—, dept. head elec. and computer engring., 1994-98. Patentee in field. 1st lt. U.S. Army, 1974-77. Fellow IEEE (Third Millennium medal), IEEE Antennas and Propagation Soc. (membership chair 1980-82, editor newsletter 1982-84, sec.-treas. 1984-88, v.p. 1998, pres. 1999). Office: U Mass Elec and Computer Engring Amherst MA 01003

SCHAUBLE, JOHN EUGENE, physical education educator; b. Paterson, N.J., Aug. 14, 1949; s. Charles Eugene and Rosemary (White) S.; children: Sarah, Angela. BA, Bemidji State U., 1973, BS, 1974; MA, U. Ala., 1984. Cert. tchr. health, phys. edn., K-12; cert. swimming coach/level 4; cert. aquatic mgr.; cert. pool operator, ARC water safety instr., lifeguard instr., waterfront lifeguard instr., lifeguard mgmt. instr., first aid instr., CPR instr., water safety instr. trainer, AED essentials instr., disease prevention instr., oxygen adminstrn. instr., safety tng. for swim coaches instr.; cert. U.S.A. Track & Field level II. Northeast area dir. Phys. Fitness Inst. of Am., Albany, N.Y., 1974-75; head swim coach Lake Forest (Ill.) Swim Club, 1975-78; asst. swim coach/grad. asst. U. Ala., Tuscaloosa, 1978-79; head swim coach Palm Springs (Calif.) Swim Team, 1979-80; asst. swim coach Ft. Lauderdale (Fla.) Swim Team, 1980-82; aquatic dir., head swim coach Briarwood of Richmond Aquatic Club, Richmond, Va., 1982-83; head swimming coach, intramural coord. William Rainey Harper Coll., Palatine, Ill., 1983-85; boys/girls asst. swim coach Sch. Dist. 211, Palatine, 1985-90; nat. coach Palatine Swim Team, 1983-92; head boys and girls swim coach Adlai E. Stevenson High Sch., Lincolnshire, Ill., 1990-96, aquatic coord., 1990—, asst. girls track and field coach, 1992-99, varsity cross-country coach, 1999—, boys distance track and field coach, 1999—. Head coach Patriot Aquatic Club, 1992-94, head coach sr. team, 1994-99; fund raising com. U.S. Swimming, Inc., Colorado Springs, Colo., 1990-94; coaches rep. Ill. Swimming, Inc., Aurora, 1990-94, bd. dirs., tech. planning com., others. Nominated Coach of Yr., Nat. Jr. Coll. Athletic Assn., Ft. Pierce, Fla., 1984; named Boys Sectional Coach of Yr., Ill. High Sch. Assn., 1992. Mem. Ill. Swimming Assn. (nominated Coach of Yr. coll. divsn. boys 1984), Nat. Interscholastic Swimming Coaches Assn., Am. Swimming Coaches Assn., Am. Coll. Sports Medicine, Nat. Strength and Conditioning Assn., Ill. Track and Cross Country Coaches Assn., AAPHERD, NEA. Republican. Roman Catholic. Avocations: computer, running, swimming, tennis, weight tng. Home: 608 Applegate Ln Lake Zurich IL 60047-2363 Office: 1 Stevenson Dr Lincolnshire IL 60069-2824 Office Phone: 847-634-4000 ext. 1226. E-mail: coachswim@aol.com.

SCHAUBROECK, JOHN MICHAEL, education educator, academic administrator; b. Aurora, Ill., Nov. 2, 1961; s. Melvin Paul and Carol Jean Schaubroeck; m. Lai Wan Ha, Apr. 22, 1987; children: Jack Michael, Joseph Michael. BB, Western Ill.Univ., Macomb, Ill., 1984; PhD, Purdue Univ., 1988. Asst. prof. Univ. Nebr., Lincoln, Nebr., 1988—91, assoc. prof., 1991—99; prof. City Univ. Hong Kong, Hong Kong, 1997—99, Drexel Univ., Phila., 1999—, head dept., 1999—2004. External academic advisor City Univ. Hong Kong, 1999—, Chinese Univ. Hong Kong, 2000—, Hong Kong U., 2003—; assoc. editor Organized Behavior and Human Decision Processes, 2004—. Contbr. articles to 49 profl. jour. Mem.: Acad. of Mgmt. Roman Catholic. Office: Drexel Univ Academic Bldg 33rd Arch St 3rd Flr Philadelphia PA 19104 E-mail: jms43@drexel.edu.

SCHAUDIES, JESSE P., JR., business executive; b. Knoxville, Tenn., Aug. 27, 1954; s. Jesse P. and Adele (Thompson) S.; m. Elizabeth D. Schaudies, Sept. 15, 1979; children: Jesse P. III, Frederick T., Deneen Adele. BA magna cum laude, Duke U., 1976; JD, Georgetown U., 1979. Ptnr. Troutman Sanders, Atlanta, 1979-94; mng. dir. gen. affairs, gen. counsel, sec. Randstad N.Am., 1994—2001; global v.p. e-commerce Manpower Inc., 2002—. Mng. editor Am. Criminal Law Rev., 1978-79; contbr. articles to profl. jours. Mem. ABA, Ga. State Bar Assn. (labor sect., litigation sect.), Authors Ct. Ga. (charter), Industry Trade Assn. (officer), Internat. Lab. Orgn. (del.). Republican. Presbyterian. Office Phone: 33 0 15699 2302. E-mail: schaudies@aol.com.

SCHAUER, FRANZ PETER, civil and nuclear engineer, educator; b. Mankato, Minn., Nov. 29, 1932; s. Albert Franz and Marie Petrich (Nielsson) S.; m. Joan Laurie; children: Marie, Barbara, Franz, Jr., Lisa, Jill. BS, U.S. Mil. Acad., 1955; MSCE, MS in Nuc. Engring., Iowa State U., 1961, PhD, 1969. Cert. civil engr. Commd. 2d lt. U.S. Army, 1955, advanced through grades to col., 1980, ret., 1989; engr. U.S. AEC, Germantown, Md., 1964-75; exec. U.S. Nuc. Regulatory Commn., Bethesda, Md., 1975-82; prof. Minn. State U., 1982-93; pres. ADU Engring. Assn., Bethesda, 1994—. Engring. cons. Tex-La Power, Stone and Webster, Boston, 1987, Burns and Roe, NYC, 1986, U.S. Army, Washington, 1984, Todd Shipbuilding, Washington, 1983. Author: Advances in Structural Dynamics, 1980. Trustee Christ Luth. Ch. Fellow ASCE (com. mem.); mem. IEEE Computer Soc., ASME (com.mem.), Phi Kappa Phi, Sigma Xi. Lutheran. Avocations: tennis, computers. Home: Unit 261 6860 Gulfport Blvd S Saint Petersburg FL 33707-2108 Office: PO Box 1423 Mc Lean VA 22101-1423 Office Phone: 703-401-5454. Personal E-mail: franzschauer1000@hotmail.com.

SCHAUER, FREDERICK FRANKLIN, law educator; b. Newark, Jan. 15, 1946; s. John Adolph and Clara (Balayti) S.; m. Margery Clare Stone, Aug. 25, 1968 (div. June, 1982); m. Virginia Jo Wise, May 25, 1985. AB, Dartmouth Coll., 1967, MBA, 1968; JD, Harvard U., 1972. Bar: Mass. 1972, U.S. Supreme Ct. 1976. Assoc. Fine & Ambrogne, Boston, 1972-74; asst. prof. law W.Va. U., Morgantown, 1974-76, assoc. prof., 1976-78, Coll. William and Mary, Williamsburg, Va., 1978-80, Cutler prof., 1980-83; prof. of law U. Mich., Ann Arbor, 1983-90; Frank Stanton prof. of 1st Amendment Kennedy Sch. of Govt., Harvard U., Cambridge, Mass., 1990—, acad. dean, 1997—2002, acting dean, 2001. Vis. scholar, mem. faculty law Wolfson Coll. Cambridge (Eng.) U., 1977-78; vis. prof. Law Sch., U. Chgo., 1990; vis. fellow Australian Nat. U., 1993, 98; William Morton Disting. Sr. fellow in humanities Dartmouth Coll., 1991; vis. prof. law Harvard Law Sch., 1996, 97, 2000, 04; Ewald Disting. vis. prof. law U. Va., 1996, vis. prof. govt. Dartmouth Coll., 1997; disting. vis. prof. law U. Toronto, 2000. Author: The Law of Obscenity, 1976, Free Speech: A Philosophical Enquiry, 1982 (ABA cert. merit 1983), Supplements to Gunther Constitutional Law, 1983-96, Playing by the Rules: A Philosophical Examination of Rule Based Decision-Making in Law and Life, 1991, The First Amendment: A Reader, 1992, 2d edit., 1995, The Philosophy of Law, 1995, Profiles, Probabilities and Stereotypes, 2003; editor: Legal Theory, 1995-2000; contbr. articles to profl. jours. Mem. Atty. Gen.'s Commn. on Pornography, 1985-86. Served with Mass. Army N.G., 1970-71. NEH fellow, summer 1980, Guggenheim fellow, 2001-02. Fellow Am. Acad. Arts and Scis., Radcliffe Inst. for Adv. Studies; mem. Am. Philos. Assn., Am. Soc. for Polit. and Legal Philosophy (v.p. 1996-99), Assn. Am. Law Schs. (chmn. sect. constl. law 1984-86). Office: Kennedy Sch of Govt Harvard U Cambridge MA 02138 Office Phone: 617-495-8737. Business E-Mail: fred_schauer@harvard.edu.

SCHAUER, JEFFREY EDWARD, surgeon; b. Milw., 1952; MD, U. Wis., 1977. Diplomate Am. Bd. Surgery. Intern U. Wis. Hosp., Madison, 1977-78, resident, 1978-82; pvt. practice Rockford., Ill., 1982—. Clin. asst. prof. surgery U. Ill. Coll. Medicine, Rockford, acting chmn., 2000—03; attending surgeon Rockford Med. Hosp. Mem. ACS, Midwest Surg. Assn. Office: 1235 N Mulford Rd Rockford IL 61107 Office Phone: 815-964-3333. E-mail: jschauer103@acordoc.com.

SCHAUER, RONALD L. executive; BSEE, S.D. State U. Pres., CEO Magnetic Data, Inc.; founder, corp. v.p., gen. mgt. Stolle Corp.; mgr. lab. engring., mfg., product/process devel. 3M; chmn., pres. CEO HMT Tech., Fremont, Calif., 1994—. Office: HMT Technology Corp 1055 Page Ave Fremont CA 94538-7342

SCHAUER, THOMAS ALFRED, insurance company executive; b. Canton, Ohio, Dec. 24, 1927; s. Alfred T. and Marie A. (Luthi) S.; m. Joanne Alice Fay, Oct. 30, 1954; children: Alan, John, David, Susan, William. BSc, Ohio State U., 1950. With Ind. Ins. Svc. Corp., 1964—, Ind. Benefit Svc. Corp., 1984—2003. Dir. Bank One, Akron, N.A., Ohio, 1991-97, mem. adv. bd., 1997-2000. Chmn. Joint Hosp. Blood Com., 1974; bd. dirs. McKinley Life Ins. Co., 1991-95; bd. dirs. Better Bus. Bur., Canton, 1970-81, chmn., 1979-80; bd. dirs. area YMCA, 1974-92, v.p., 1975-82, pres., 1982-84; trustee Canton Cemetery Assn., 1988-91, Stark County Blue Coats, 1987—; bd. dirs. Hosp. Bur. Cen. Stark City, 1972-78; vice chmn. bd. Aultman Hosp., 1981-84, chmn., 1984-87; chmn. Aultman Health Svcs. Assn., 1990-93; pres. Aultman Hosp. Found., 1987-90, trustee, 1971-98, trustee emeritus, 1998—; chmn. bd. JMS Found., 1968—; bd. dirs. United Way, 1974-84, pres., 1976-78; mem. distbn. com. Stark County Found., 1977-87, chmn. distbn. com., 1984-87, dir. Dime Bank, Canton, 1965-72, Ctrl. Trust Co. NE Ohio, N.A., 1972-91; adv. bd. Malone Coll., 1979-92; trustee Kent State U., 1980-88, trustee emeritus, 1988—, N.E. Ohio Univs. Coll. Medicine, 1983-88; past trustee Canton Urban League, Boys Village (Smithville, Ohio), Canton Art Inst., Buckeye Coun. Boy Scouts Am. Served with USNR, 1946-48. Recipient gold key award United Way Ctrl. Stark County, 1981, award of merit Canton C. of C., 1984, red triangle award Canton Area YMCA, 1985. Mem. Chartered Ins. Inst. London, Nat. Assn. Mfg., Am. Soc. CPCUs, Am. Soc. CLUs, Assn., Advanced Life Underwriters, Am. Risk and Ins. Assn., Am. Soc. Pension Actuaries, Stark County Accident and Health Underwriters (past pres.), Canton Club (past pres.), Brookside Country Club, Atwood Yacht Club. Home: 1756 Dunbarton Ave NW Canton OH 44708-1807 Office: Millennium Ctr 200 Market Ave N Ste 100 Canton OH 44702 E-mail: tomschauer@att.net.

SCHAUER, WILBERT EDWARD, JR., lawyer, manufacturing executive; b. Milw., Oct. 28, 1926; s. Wilbert Edward and Gertrude (Nickel) S.; m. Genevieve Stone, June 23, 1951; children— Jeffrey Edward, Constance Emily, Gregory Wilbert, Martha Ann, Jennifer Caroline. BBA, U. Wis., 1949, MBA, JD, U. Wis., 1950. Bar: Wis. 1950. Accountant Pub. Service Commn. Wis., 1950-52; with Rexnord, Inc., Milw., 1952-87, v.p. finance, treas., 1968-76, v.p. fin. and law, 1977-78, exec. v.p. fin. and adminstrn., 1978-86, vice chmn., 1986-87. Alderman, Brookfield, Wis., 1958-68; pres. Common Council, 1966-68. Mem.: Moorings Country Club, Westmoor Country Club (Brookfield, Wis.). Home: 3215 Gulf Shore Blvd N Ph 4 Naples FL 34103-3920

SCHAUF, VICTORIA, pediatrician, educator, infectious diseases consultant; b. N.Y.C., Feb. 17, 1943; d. Maurice J. and Ruth H. (Baker) Bisson; m. Michael Delaney; 2 children. BS in Microbiology with honors, U. Chgo.,

1965, MD with honors, 1969. Intern in pediat. U. Chgo. Hosp., 1969-70; resident in pediat. Sinai Hosp. of Balt., 1970-71; chief resident pediat. Children's Hosp. Nat. Med. Ctr., Washington, 1971-72; rsch. trainee NIH, Bethesda, Md., 1972; adj. prof. microbiology Rush Med. Coll., Chgo., 1972—74; prof. pediat., head pediatric infectious diseases U. Ill., Chgo., 1974-84; med. officer FDA, Rockville, Md., 1984-86; chmn. dept. pediat. Nassau County Med. Ctr., East Meadow, NY, 1986-90; prof. pediat. SUNY, Stony Brook, 1987-94. Vis. prof. Rockefeller U., 1990-92; mem. vis. faculty Chiang Mai (Thailand) U., 1978; mem. ad hoc com. study sects. NIH, Bethesda, 1981-82; bd. dirs. Pearl Stetler Rsch. Found., Chgo., 1982-84; cons. FDA, 1987-88, 93-95, Can. Bur. Human Prescription Drugs, Ottawa, 1990—, Biotech. Investors, 1993-95; course dir. pediat. infectious diseases rev. course Cornell U. Med. Coll., N.Y.C., 1994, faculty, 1995. Co-author: Pediatric Infectious Diseases: A Comprehensive Guide to the Subspecialty, 1997; prodr. radio and TV programs in field; contbr. articles to profl. jours., chpts. to books. Vol. physician Cook County Hosp., Chgo., 1974-84; mem. adv. com. Nat. Hansen's Disease Ctr., La., 1986, Nassau County Day Care Coun., N.Y., 1988-90; mem. adv. bd. Surg. Aid to Children of World, N.Y., 1986-90; commr., sec. Kern County Children and Families Commn., 1999-2002; sec., bd. dirs. Indian Wells Valley Cmty. Found., 2001-. Am. Lung Assn. grantee U. Ill., 1977; recipient contract NIH, U. Ill., 1978-81, grantee, 1979-84. Fellow Infectious Diseases Soc. Am.; mem. Pediatric Infectious Diseases Soc. (exec. bd.), Soc. Pediatric Rsch., Am. Pediatric Soc., AAAS, Am. Soc. Microbiology, Am. Acad. Pediat., Phi Beta Kappa, Alpha Omega Alpha. Avocation: walking. Office Phone: 760-371-2128. Business E-Mail: vschauf@pol.net.

SCHAUFUSS, PETER, dancer, producer, choreographer, ballet director; b. Copenhagen, Apr. 26, 1950; s. Frank Schaufuss and Mona Vangsaae S. Student, Royal Danish Ballet Sch. Apprentice with Royal Danish Ballet, 1965; soloist Nat. Ballet Can., 1967-68, Royal Danish Ballet, 1969-70; prin. with LFB, 1970-74, N.Y.C. Ballet, 1974-77, Nat. Ballet Can., 1977-83; artistic dir. London Festival Ballet (now English Nat. Ballet), 1984-90; ballet dir. Deutsche Oper Berlin, 1990-93, Royal Danish Ballet, 1994-95, Peter Schaufuss Balletten, 1997—; guest appearances in Can., Denmark, France, Germany, Italy, Japan, U.K., U.S.A., USSR, Austria, S.Am.; presented BBC TV series Dancer, 1984; numerous other TV appearances; created roles include Rhapsodie Espagnole, The Steadfast Tin Soldier (Balanchine), Phantom of the Opera (Petit), Verdi Variations, Orpheus (MacMillan); ballets produced include La Sylphide (London Festival Ballet, Stuttgart Ballet, Roland Petit's Ballet de Marseille, Deutsche Oper Berlin, Teatro Comunale Firenze, Vienna State Opera, Opernhaus Zurich, Teatro dell'Opera di Roma, Hessisches Staatstheater Wiesbaden, Ballet du Rhin, Royal Danish Ballet, Ballet West), Napoli (Nat. Ballet Can., Teatro San Carlo, Naples, English Nat. Ballet, formerly London Festival Ballet), Folktale (Deutsche Oper Berlin), Dances from Napoli (London Festival Ballet), Bournonville (Aterballetto), The Nutcracker (London Festival Ballet, Graz Opera Ballet, Deutsche Oper Berlin), Giselle (Deutsche Oper Berlin, Royal Danish Ballet), Tchiakovsky Trilogy (Deutsche Oper Berlin), Sleeping Beauty (Deutsche Oper Berlin), Swan Lake (Deutsche Oper Berlin); staging of Romeo and Juliet (Royal Danish Ballet); producer, choreographer (Royal Danish Ballet) Hamlet, 1996; new versions of Hamlet, Swan Lake, Sleeping Beauty, The Nutcracker, Romeo and Juliet (Peter Schaufuss Balletten); prodr., choreographer The King, Manden Der Onskede Sig En Havudsigt, 1999, Midnight Express (Peter Schaufuss Balletten), 2000, The 3 Presents (Kermessen in Bruges), 2000, Hans Christian Andersen, 2001. Decorated officer Order of the Crown (Belgium); recipient Solo award 2d Internat. Ballet Competition, Moscow, 1973, Star of the Yr. award Abendzeitung, Munich, 1978, Evening Std. award, 1979, Soc. of West End Theatres Ballet award (now Oliver), 1979, Manchester Evening News Theatre awards-dance, 1986, Lakerolprisen, Copenhagen, 1988, Berlin Co. award for best ballet prodn. Berlinerzeitung, 1991, Edinburgh Festival Critics prize, 1991,; named Knight of the Dannebrog, 1988. Office: Holstebro Hallen Ved Hallen 4 7500 Holstebro Denmark

SCHAUMBER, PETER C. government agency administrator; b. 1942; m. Kathleen Charbonnet; children: Kathleen, Drew, Alexandra. BA, Georgetown U., 1964; JD, Georgetown U. Law Ctr., 1968. Mem. Nat. Labor Relations Bd., 2002—05; adj. prof. of law Nat. Law Ctr George Washington U., Georgetown U. Sch. of Bus., MBA Program; of counsel Wickwire Gavin, 1987—93; partner, dir. litigation dept. Colton and Boykin, 1980—87. Office: Franklin Court Bldg 1099 14th St NW Washington DC 20570-0001

SCHAUMBURG, HERBERT HOWARD, neurology educator; b. Houston, Tex., Nov. 6, 1932; m. Joanna Jane Austin; children: Barnabas Paul, Kristin Elizabeth. AB cum laude, Harvard Coll., 1956; MD, Washington U., 1960. Instr. in neurology Albert Einstein Coll. of Medicine, N.Y.C., 1964-67, asst. prof. neurology, 1967-69, assoc. prof. neurology, 1972-76, prof., 1976—, vice chmn., 1977-84, acting chmn., 1984-86, chmn., 1986—; instr. pathology Harvard Med. Sch., Boston, 1969-71. Mem. Am. Acad. Neurology, Am. Assn. Neuropathologists, Am. Neurol. Assn., Soc. Toxicology, Soc. Neurosci. Home: 616 King Ave City Island Bronx NY 10464 Office: Albert Einstein Coll Medicine 1300 Morris Park Ave Bronx NY 10461-1926 Office Phone: 212-430-3166. E-mail: schaumb@aecom.yu.edu.

SCHAUSS, ALEXANDER GEORGE, psychologist, biomedical researcher; b. Hamburg, Germany, July 20, 1948; came to U.S., 1953; s. Frank and Alla S.; m. Laura Babin; children: Nova, Evan. BA, U. N.Mex., 1970, MA, 1972; PhD, Calif. Coast U., 1992. Cert. eating disorders specialist. State probation/parole officer 2nd Judicial Dist. Ct., Albuquerque, 1969-73; criminal justice planner Albuquerque/Bernalillo County Criminal Justice Planning Com., 1973-75; state asst. adminstr. dept. corrections State of S.D., Pierre, 1975-77; dir. Pierce County Probation Dept., Tacoma, 1977-78; tng. officer IV Wash. State Criminal Justice Tng. Commn., Olympia, 1978-79; dir. Inst. Biosocial Rsch. City Univ. Grad. Sch., Seattle, 1979-80; exec. dir. Am. Inst. Biosocial and Med. Rsch. Inc., Tacoma, 1980—, Am. Preventive Med. Assn., 1992-94, Citizens for Health, 1992-95; dir. Citizens for Health Edn., 1994-96; assoc. prof. behavioral scis. Nat. Coll. Naturopathic Medicine, Portland, 1996-97, clin. prof. natural products rsch. dept., 1998-99; assoc. prof. rsch. S.W. Coll. Naturopathic Medicine & Health Scis., Tempe, Ariz., 1995-96, rsch. dir., 1995-96, sr. dir. rsch. Scottsdale, Ariz., 1996-97; adj. rsch. prof. botanical medicine Nat. Coll. Naturopathic Medicine, 1999—. Pres. Campaign To Label Genetically Engineered Foods, 1999—; mem. study group on health promotion WHO, Copenhagen, 1985; vis. lectr. pediats. The John Radcliffe Hosp., Oxford U., Eng., summer 1985; sec. coun. on food policy Nat. Assn. Pub. Health Policy, 1990-94, chmn., 1994-96; vis. scholar Kans. C.C. Consortium, 1982; vis. lectr. McCarrison Soc. Conf. at Oxford U., 1983; advisor Ministry Pub. Health for Thailand, 2000—, Ministry of Health, Nat. Ctr. for Natural Products and Virology, NIH, Malaysia; mem. presdl. adv. bd. Bastyr U., 1979-2000, S.W. Coll. Naturopathic Medicine, 1993-97; mem. devel. planning com., Office of Dietary Supplements, Office of Disease Prevention, NIH, Bethesda, 1996-99, mem. alternative medicine adv. coun. Office Alternative Medicine, NIH, 1997-99; chmn. safety com., compliance labeling integrity com. Nat. Nutritional Foods Assn., 1992—, mem. ComPLI, 1992—; chmn. ad hoc BSE Com. (Mad Cow's Disease), NNFA, 2001—; chair Asian affairs sub-com., mem. Latin Am. affairs sub-com. Am. Herbal Products Assn./NNFA Internat. Com., 2002—, mem. Codex com., 2002-. Author: Orthomolecular Treatment of Criminal Offenders, 1978, Diet, Crime and Delinquency, 1980, rev., 1995, Nutrition and Behavior, 1986, Nutrition and Criminal Behavior, 1990, Minerals, Trace Elements and Human Health, 1995, rev. edit., 1999, 100 Useful Weight Loss Tips that Promote Weight Management, 2003, Feed My Brain, 2004; co-author: Zinc and Eating Disorders, 1989, Eating for A's, 1991, Anorexia and Bulimia, 1997, Cat's Claw (Una de Gato) Uncaria Tormentosa, 1996, 100 Useful Weight Loss Tips that Promote Weight Management, 2003, Useful Hints in Weight Management, 2003, Feed My Brain, 2004; editor-in-chief Internat. Jour. Biosocial and Med. Rsch., 1979—92 reviewer U.S. Pharmacopeia Informational Monographs, 1998-99, Am. Bot. Coun., 2004—; mem. editl. bd. 8 jours. Master arbitrator Tacoma/Pierce County Better Bus. Bur., Tacoma, 1986-97; mem. Pierce County N. Area Transp. Adv. Coun., Tacoma, 1991-92; trustee Pierce County Pub. Safety Task Team, 1993, Nat. Inst. for Naturopathic Medicine, 1993-2000. Recipient Rsch. award Wacker Found., 1983-85, 88; fellow Am. Coll. Nutrition, 2003—, Am. Orthopsychiat. Assn., 1980-95. Fellow N.Y. Acad. of Sci. (emeritus); mem. Am. Chem. Soc., Acad. Eating Disorders, Inst. Food Technologists, Am. Assn. Clin. Nutritionists, Consultants Assn. for Natural Products Industry (pres. 2000, bd. dirs.), Internat. Assn. Eating Disorders Profls. (co-chair cert. and accreditation com. 2002—), Am. Found. Preventative Medicine (treas. 1992-93, found.), Acad. Criminal Justice Scis., Am. Soc. Criminology, Brit. Soc. Nutritional Medicine (hon.), Soc. for Food Sci. and Tech., Inst. Food Technologists Soc. Food Scientists and Tech., Soc. Orthomolecular Health Medicine, Rotary (chmn. cmty. svcs. com. Tacoma chpt. 1989-90, chmn. civic affairs com. 1989-90, Vladivostok com. 1991-93, internat. exch. com. 1994-95, world cmty. svcs. com. 1996-97). Office: Am Inst for Biosocial and Med Rsch Inc Life Scis Divsn PO Box 1174 Tacoma WA 98401-1174

SCHAUT, JOSEPH WILLIAM, retired bank executive; b. Cleve., May 30, 1928; s. Francis Xavier and Emma Gertrude (Urmann) S.; m. Susan Stiver, Apr. 23, 1955; children: Deborah Anne Schaut Payne, Gregory F., Mary Theresa Schaut Bentley, Michael J. B in Social Sci. in Econs., Georgetown U., 1950, JD, 1953. Bar: D.C. 1953, U.S. Mil. Ct. Appeals 1953, U.S. Dist. Ct. D.C. 1953, U.S. Ct. Appeals (D.C. cir.) 1953, Ohio 1954. Tax analyst Republic Steel Corp., Cleve., 1953 60, asst. to sec., 1960-67, asst. sec., 1967-81, dir. corp. properties, 1976-84, corp. sec., 1981-84; bus. cons., 1984-85; sr. trust officer AmeriTrust Co. Nat. Assn., 1986-92, Soc. Nat. Bank, Cleve., 1992-93, v.p., 1993-96, Mellon Bank F.S.B., 1996-98; ret., 1998. Served to col. USAR, 1950-78. Recipient award Silver Beaver Greater Cleve. Coun., Boy Scouts Am., 1975. Mem. Am. Soc. Corp. Secs. (dir. 1976-79), Ohio State Bar Assn., Greater Cleve. Growth Assn., Delta Theta Phi, Pi Gamma Mu Roman Catholic.

SCHEAR, BETTY Z. engineering executive, consultant; b. Dayton, Ohio, Dec. 17, 1925; d. Jacob Zukerman and Esther (Groban) Litwack; m. Burt E. Schear, July 4, 1948; children: Abe, Martin, Edith, Jesse. BS in Engring., U. Cin., 1948; MBA, U. Dayton, 1968. Assoc. editor Gardner Pubs., Cin., 1948-50; adminstrv. mgr. Schear Family Practice, Dayton, 1952-85; cons. Dayton, 1985—. Cons. Health Power, Inc., Columbus, Ohio, 1984-2000. One woman show U. Dayton, 1972. Mem. NSPE, NAFE, Nat. Mus. Women in the Arts (charter), Soc. Women Engrs., Am. Mgmt. Assn. Avocations: reading, art, travel, theater, music. Home: 4300 N Ocean Blvd # 8AB Fort Lauderdale FL 33308-5944

SCHECHNER, RICHARD, theater director, author, educator; b. Newark, Aug. 23, 1934; s. Sheridan and Selma Sophia (Schwarz) S.; m. Carol Martin; children: Samuel MacIntosh, Sophia Martin. BA, Cornell U., 1956; postgrad., Johns Hopkins U., 1957; MA, State U. Iowa, 1958; PhD, Tulane U., 1962. Asst. prof. theatre Tulane U., 1962-66, assoc. prof., 1966-67; prof. performance studies NYU, 1967-91, Univ. prof., 1991—; co-founder, co-dir. New Orleans Group, 1965-67; founder, dir. Performance Group, N.Y.C., 1967-80; founder, artistic dir. East Coast Artists, 1991—; Andrew H. White prof.-at-large Cornell U., 1999—; sr. fellow Ctr. for Cultural Sociology, Yale U., 2004—. Hon. prof. Shanghai Theatre Acad., 1995—; prof. titular adj. Instituto Superior de Arte, Havana, Cuba; bd. dirs. Theatre Comms. Group, 1977-78; advisor Internat. Theatre Inst., 1975-77, Ctr. Performance Rsch., Aberwystwich, Wales, 1993-97; pres. Bunch of Exptl. Theatres, 1975, 77, Fulbright Theatre Discipline Com., 1988-91. Author: Public Domain, 1968, Environmental Theater, 1973 (with others) Theatres, Spaces, Environments, 1975, Essays on Performance Theory, 1977, 2d edit. 1988, 3d edit., 2003, (with others) Makbeth, 1977, The End of Humanism, 1982, Performative Circumstances, 1983, Betweeen Theater and Anthropology, 1985, (with Samuel MacIntosh-Schechner) The Engleburt Stories: North to the Tropics, 1987, The Future of Ritual, 1993, Performance Studies--An Introduction, 2002, (with others) Yokastas, 2003; editor: Dionysus in 69, 1970; adv. editor: Asian Theatre Jour., 1985-; co-editor: Free Southern Theater, 1968, Ritual, Play, and Performance, 1976, By Means of Performance, 1990; gen. editor: (series) Worlds of Performance, 1993—, (with Lisa Wolford) Grotowski Sourcebook, 1997; editor: The Drama Rev., 1962-69, 85—, contbg. editor, 1971-85; adv. editor Jour. Ritual Studies, 1987—; dir. Dionysus in 69, 1968, Macbeth, 1969, Commune, 1970, The Tooth of Crime, 1972, Mother Courage, 1975, The Marilyn Project, 1975, Oedipus, 1977, Cops, 1978, The Balcony, 1979, The Red Snake, 1981, Richard's Lear, 1981, The Cherry Orchard, 1983, Prometheus Project, 1985, Don Juan, 1987, Tomorrow He'll Be Out of the Mountains, 1989, Ma Rainey's Black Bottom, 1992, Faust/Gastronome, 1993, The Oresteia, 1995, Three Sisters, 1997, Hamlet, 1999, Waiting for Godot, 2002, Yokastas, 2003. Served with AUS, 1958-60. Recipient Modello prize, 1985, Contbns. to Theatre Spl. award New England Theatre Conf., 1991, Work in Theatre award Towson State U., 1991; grantee John D. Rockefeller 3d Fund, 1971-72, 76, Asian Cultural Coun., 1988, 95; Guggenheim fellow, 1976, Fulbright fellow, 1976, 83, N.Y. Inst. Humanities fellow, 1987-94, NEH sr. rsch. fellow, 1988, Humanities fellow Princeton U., 1992, Am. Inst. Indian Studies, 1997, Montgomery fellow Dartmouth Coll., 1998; Am. Coun. Learned Socs. fellow, 2005. Office: NYU 721 Broadway 6th Fl Washington Sq New York NY 10003 E-mail: rs4@nyu.edu.

SCHECHTER, ARTHUR LOUIS, lawyer; b. Rosenberg, Tex., Dec. 6, 1939; s. Morris and Helen (Brilling) S.; m. Joyce Proler, Aug. 26, 1965; children: Leslie Schechter Karpas, Jennifer Schechter Rosen. BA, U. Tex., 1962, JD, 1964; postgrad., U. Houston, 1964-65. Bar: Tex. 1964, U.S. Dist. Ct. (ea. and so. dists.) Tex. 1966, U.S. Ct. Appeals (5th cir.), U.S. Supreme Ct. 1976; cert. Tex. Bd. Legal Specialization to Personal Injury Trial Law, 1964-. Pres. Arthur L. Schechter P.C., Houston, 1992-94, Schechter & Marshall, Houston, 1994-96; amb. U.S. to Commonwealth Bahamas, 1998-2000; atty. Schechter, McElwee & Shaffer, LLP, Houston, 2001—. Spkr. Marine Law Sem., 1983; spkr. in field. Contbr. to Law Rev., 1984. Bd. dirs. Theatre Under the Stars, Houston, 1972—78, Congregation Beth Israel, Houston, 1972—84, pres., 1982—84; bd. mem. Inst. Internat. Edn., 1996—98, S.E.A.R.C.H., 1996—98; pres. Am. Jewish Com., Houston, 1982—84, chmn. fgn. rels. com., chmn. United Jewish Campaign exec. com., chmn., 1993—94; pres. Jewish Fedn. Ctr. Houston, 1994—96; mem. Deans Coun. U. Tex. Law Sch.; chmn. Houston Metro Bd., 2002—04; mng. trustee mem. fin. com. Dem. Nat. Com., 1992, fin. chmn. Tex. Clinton/Gore '96; vice chmn. Clinton/Gore Jewish Leadership Coun., 1996; v.p. exec. com. Nat. Jewish Dem. Coun., 1992, chmn., 2004—; mem. Leadership Ctr. Dem. Senatorial Campaign Com.; trustee mem. Kerry/Edwards and Dem. Nat. Com.; mem. fin. coun. Nat. Dem. Orgn., 1979; chmn. of the bd. Met. Transit Autority of Harris County, 2002—04; bd. dirs. U. Tex. Med. Sch. Named one of Houston's Most Fascinating Mems. of the Med. Cmty., 2003; recipient Career and Recovery Resources Barrier Breaker award, United Way Agy., 2003, Search's Outstanding Leadership award, 2003, Israel Bonds Nat. Leradership award, 2004. Home: 19A West Ln Houston TX 77019-1007 Office Phone: 713-757-7811.

SCHECHTER, DONALD ROBERT, lawyer; b. N.Y.C., Feb. 24, 1946; s. Joseph and Katherine (Beer) S.; m. Roberta Sharon Horowitz, July 3, 1968; children: Elizabeth Anne, Sarah Marilyn. BA, Queens Coll., 1967; JD, Bklyn Law Sch., 1971. Asst. dist. atty. Queens County, Kew Gardens, N.Y., 1971-73; asst. atty. gen. organized crime task force City of N.Y., 1973-74; sole practice Forest Hills, N.Y., 1974—. Legal counsel Centro Civico Colombiano, Jackson Heights, N.Y., 1978—, Fedn. of Merchants and Profls. of Queens, Spanish Orgn., Jackson Heights, 1978—; hearing officer Family Ct., Queens County, Jamaica, N.Y., 1977; consumer counsel Civil Ct., Queens County, 1980. Mem. ABA, N.Y. State Bar Assn., Queens County Bar Assn. (chmn. lawyer placement), Nassau County Bar Assn., Audobon Soc., Sierra Club. Clubs: Glass Soc. Corvette, N.Y. Mets Dream Week. Lodges: KP. Democrat. Jewish. Avocations: antique automobiles, baseball, history, antiques. Office: Ste 1030 80-02 Kew Gardens Rd Kew Gardens NY 11415-3600

SCHECHTER, GERALDINE POPPA, hematologist; b. N.Y.C., Jan. 16, 1938; d. Josif and Victoria (Nosi) P.; m. Alan Neil Schechter, Feb. 6, 1965; children: Daniele Malka, Andrew M.R. AB, Vassar Coll., Poughkeepsie, N.Y., 1959; MD, Columbia U., 1963. Diplomate Am. Bd. Internal Medicine (bd. dirs. 1990-95, mem. hematology com. 1985-91). Intern, then resident Presbyn. Hosp., N.Y.C., 1963-65; resident, fellow, rsch. assoc. VA Med. Ctr., Washington, 1965-70, staff physician, 1970-74, chief hematology, 1974—; asst., assoc. prof. medicine George Washington U., Washington, 1971-81, prof. medicine, 1981—. Residency rev. com. internal medicine Am. Coun. for Grad. Med. Edn., 1996—. Mem. editl. bd. Blood, 1985-89; contbr. articles to hematologic jours. Office: VA Med Ctr Hematology Sect 50 Irving St NW Washington DC 20422-0001

SCHECHTER, JOEL, magazine editor, writer, educator; b. Washington, June 21, 1947; s. Henry Bear and Ruth (Lindauer) S. BA, Antioch Coll., 1969; DFA, Yale U., 1973. Lit. advisor Am. Place Theater, N.Y.C., 1973-77; asst. prof. SUNY, Stony Brook, 1974-77; prof. Sch. Drama Yale U., New Haven, 1977—92; editor Theater Mag., New Haven, 1977—92; prof. theatre arts San Francisco State U., 1992—. Polit. satire columnist New Haven Independent, 1988-90. Author: Durov's Pig, 1985, Satiric Impersonations, 1994, The Congress of Clowns, 1998, The Pickle Clowns, 2001, Popular Theatre: A Sourcebook, 2003; (play) The Complete Aristophanes, 1988. State senate candidate New Haven Green Party, 1988, 90. Fox fellow Yale U., Moscow, 1991. Mem. Lit. Mgrs. & Dramaturgs Am. (v.p. 1989—), Am. Soc. Theatre Rsch., Workmen's Cir. Office: San Francisco State U Dept Theatre Arts 1600 Holloway Ave Dept Theatre San Francisco CA 94132-1722

SCHECHTER, PAUL, physicist, educator; AB, Cornell U., 1968; PhD, Caltech, 1974. Mem. faculty Harvard U.; mem. staff Kit Peak Nat. Obs., Mt. Wilson and Las Campanas Obs.; prof. MIT, Cambridge, 1988—, dir. magellan telescopes, William A.M. Burden prof. Mem.: NAS. Office: Astrophysics Div Dept Physics MIT Rm 37-664 G Cambridge MA 02139

SCHECHTER, ROBERT SAMUEL, chemical engineer, educator; b. Houston, Feb. 26, 1929; s. Morris S. and Helen Ruth Schechter; m. Mary Ethel Rosenberg, Feb. 15, 1953; children: Richard Martin, Alan Lawrence (dec.), Geoffrey Louis. BS in Chem. Engring, Tex. A&M U., 1950; PhD in Chem. Engring, U. Minn., 1956. Registered profl. engr., Tex. Asst. prof. chem. engring. U. Tex. at Austin, 1956-60, assoc. prof., 1960-63, prof., 1963—; adminstrv. dir. Ctr. Statis. Mechs. and Thermodynamics, 1968-72, chmn. dept. chem. engring., 1970-73, chmn. petroleum engring., 1975-78, E.J. Cockrell, Jr. prof. chem. and petroleum engring., 1975-81, Dula and Ernie Cockrell prof. engring., 1981-83, Getty prof. engring., 1984-85, Getty Oil Centennial chair in Petroleum Engring., 1985-89, W.A. (Monty) Moncrief Centennial Endowed chair in Petroleum Engring., 1989-97; prof. emeritus U. Tex., 1997. Vis. prof. U. Edinburgh, Scotland, 1965-66; Disting. vis. prof. U. Kans., spring 1968; vis. prof. U. Brussels, 1969; Disting. Lindsay lectr. Tex. A&M U., 1993; cons. in field. Author: Variational Method in Engineering, 1967, (with G.S.G. Beveridge) Optimization: Theory and Practice, 1970, Adventures in Fortran Programming, 1975, (with B.B. Williams and J.L. Gidley) Acidizing Monograph, 1979, (with D.D. Shah) Enhanced Oil Recovery by Surfactants and Polymers, 1979; (with Maurice Bourrel) Microemulsions and Related Systems, 1988, Oil Well Stimulation, 1991; contbr. (with D.D. Shah) numerous articles to profl. jours. Served to 1st lt., Chem. Corps AUS, 1951-53. Decorated Chevalier Order Palmes Academique, 1978; recipient Outstanding Teaching award U. Tex., 1969, Outstanding Paper award, 1973, Gen. Dynamics award for Excellence in Engring. Teaching, Gen. Dynamics Corp., 1987, Sr. Rsch. award Engring. Rsch. Coun. of Am. Soc. Engring. Educators, 1991. Mem. AIME (Industry Edn. award 1998), AIChE (Founders award 1998), Am. Chem. Soc., Soc. Petroleum Engrs. (John Franklin Carll award 1994, Improved Oil Recovery Pioneer 1996), Nat. Acad. Engrs., Sigma Xi, Tau Beta Pi. Achievements include developing methods of measuring surface viscosity and ultra low inter-facial tensions; discovering instability of thermal diffusion. Home: 4700 Ridge Oak Dr Austin TX 78731-4724 Office: U Tex Dept Petroleum & Geosystems Austin TX 78712

SCHECHTER, STEPHEN L. political scientist; b. Washington, Nov. 28, 1945; s. William J. and Blossom (Rapaport) S.; m. Stephanie A. Thompson, Feb. 16, 1993; 1 child, Sarah J.; 1 stepdaughter: Kelly Anne Fahed. BA, Syracuse U., 1967; PhD, U. Pitts., 1972. Acting dir. Ctr. for Study of Federalism/Temple U., 1973-76; asst. to full prof. polit. sci. Russell Sage Coll., Troy, N.Y., 1977—; exec. dir. N.Y. State Commn. on Bicentennial of U.S. Constitution, 1986-90. Dir. Coun. for Citizenship Edn. Russell Sage Coll., N.Y., 1990—, dir. MAT/social studies program; coord. We The People, 1992—; pres. N.Y. State Coun. on Social Edn., 1992-93; co-dir. civic edn. exch. program Civitas of Russia, 1994—; sr. rsch. advisor N.Y. State Commn. on the Capital Region, 1995-97; mem. Social Sci. Edn. Consortium, 1999; mem. adv. com. for participation in govt. N.Y. State Edn. Dept., 1999—. Co-editor: World of the Founders: New York Communities in the Federal Period, 1990, Contexts of the Bill of Rights, 1990, New York and the Union, New York and the Bicentennial, 1990; editor: Roots of the Republic: American Founding Documents Interpreted, 1990, others; contbr. articles to profl. jours., chpts. to books in field; editor: Social Sci. Record, 1993-96. Chmn. Rensselaer County Bicentennial Commn., 1991; commr. Albany City Charter Revision Commn., 1997-98; dir. Troy-Sage Homeownership Partnership. Mem. Nat. Coun. Social Studies (state del. 1991), Internat. Assn. Ctrs. for Fed. Studies (co-founder 1976), Am. Polit. Sci. Assn., N.Y. State Acad. Pub. Adminstrn. Office: Russell Sage Coll 45 Ferry St Troy NY 12180-4115

SCHECHTERMAN, LAWRENCE, private chef, business consultant; b. Elizabeth, N.J., June 23, 1943; s. Josef and Sylvia (Berger) S.; children: Jill Laura, Danielle Sara, Gregory Jared. BA, U. Miami, Fla., 1966; JD, Suffolk U., 1969; LLM, NYU, 1973; AS in Culinary Arts, Art Inst. Ft. Lauderdale, 2001. Tax assoc. Coopers & Lybrand, N.Y.C., 1969-70; assoc. Bendit, Weinstock & Sharbaugh, Newark, 1970-72; pvt. practice East Brunswick, N.J., 1972-81; gen. counsel Equinox Solar, Inc., Miami, 1981-83; mem. Lawrence Schechterman, P.A., Boca Raton, Fla., 1983-93; pres. Ocean Cons. Group divsn. Securities Arbitration Recovery, Inc., Boca Raton, 1993-97. Author: (books) In the Mood with Food, A Bachelor's Guide to Wooing Her with Food, 1998, 2000, 01; (poetry) New Dimensions: An Anthology of American Poetry, 1967, The Harmony of Silence, 2000, Touched by Grace, 1999, Touched by Love, 1999, Surrounded By Dreams, 1998, A Trusting Heart, 2000; contbr. articles to profl. jours. Mem. coun. Twp. of East Brunswick, NJ, 1976—80; pres. B'nai Torah Congregation of Boca Raton Inc., 1987—89, trustee, 1989—91. Mem.: B'nai B'rith Men's Lodge (co-founder Lodge 2935, charter pres. 1973—74). Office: 20889 Saint Andrews Blvd Apt 4 Boca Raton FL 33433-1710

SCHECK, BARRY C. legal association administrator, educator; BS, Yale U., 1971; JD, JD, U. Calif., Berkeley, 1974. Bar: N.Y. 1974. Staff atty. Legal Aid Soc. N.Y.C., 1974—77; prof. Law, dir. Clin. Legal Edn., Trial Advocacy Programs Cardozo Sch. Law, Yeshiva U., N.Y.C., 1977—, dir. Jacob Burns Ctr. for Study of Law and Ethics, 1977—, lawyer, dir. Innocence Project, 1992—. Former faculty mem. Nat. Inst. Trial Advocacy and Def. Coun.; tchr., organizer trial advocacy programs numerous pub. defender offices, bas assns. and law firms; lectr. in field. Co-author: Raising and Litigating Claims of Electronic Surveillance. Commr. N.Y. Forensic Sci. Rev. Bd.; founder Innocence Project, 1992. Mem.: Assn. Bar N.Y.C. (com. on criminal ct.). Office: Innocence Project Benjamin N Cardozo Sch Law 55 5th Ave New York NY 10003-4301

SCHECTER, ARNOLD JOEL, public health educator; b. Chgo., Dec. 1, 1934; s. Benjamin and Leonore Natalie (Lyon) S.; m. Martha-Jean Berenson, Feb. 14, 1964; children: Benjamin, David, Anna. BA in Liberal Arts, U. Chgo., 1954, BS in Physiology-Neurophysiology, 1957; MD, Howard U., 1962; MPH, Columbia U., 1975. Diplomate Am. Coll. Preventive Medicine; med. lic., Ky., N.Y., N.J., N.C. Postdoc. dept. anatomy Harvard Med. Sch., Boston, 1962—65; instr. dept. medicine Mass. Gen. Hosp., Harvard Med. Sch., Boston, 1964-65; intern Beth Israel Hosp., Boston, 1966; gen. practitioner, sr. aviation med. examiner West Point, Ky., 1969-70; dir. inpatient rehab. ctr., drug and alcohol rehab. program Region Eight Mental Health and Mental Retardation Bd., Inc., Louisville, 1971-72; asst. prof. dept. psychiatry, divisional drug and alcohol abuse SUNY Downstate Med. Ctr., Bklyn., 1973-75; clin. assoc. prof. dept. preventive medicine N.J. Med. Sch., Newark, 1975-79; prof. dept. preventive medicine SUNY, Binghamton, 1979-99; prof. environ. scis. U. Tex.-Houston Sch. Pub. Health, 1999—; pres. Zumwalt Inst. for Environ. Health Inc., 1996—. Spl. expert Nat. Inst. Environ. Health Scis. NIH, 1997—98; cons. U.S. EPA, Washington, 1985—86, Washington, 1999—2000, WHO, 1986—90; sci. peer reviewer dioxin U.S. EPA, 1995,

2000; peer reviewer A.T.S.D.R. of C.D.C., 1995—2000; dir. clin. rsch. in drug abuse, coord., faculty mem. Career Tchr. Tng. Ctr., SUNY Downstate, 1972—75; assoc. dir. office primary health care edn., office of the dean N.J. Med. Sch., 1976—79; advisor Environ. Def. Fund, 1991—92, Nat. Vets. Legal Svcs. Project, 1991—92; co-founder assoc. editor The Am. Jour. Drug and Alcohol Abuse, N.Y.C., 1973—78, editl. bd., 1978—86; editl. adv. bd. Substance and Alcohol Actions/Misuse, Elmsford, NY, 1979—85; adj. prof. epidemiology U. N.C. Sch. Pub. Health, 1998—2004; adj. prof. occupl. medicine Duke Med. Ctr., 1998—99. Editor: Rehabilitation Aspects of Drug Dependence, 1977, Treatment Aspects of Drug Dependence, 1978, Biomedical Issues in Drug Abuse, 1981, Sociological Issues in Drug Abuse, 1981; editor: (with H. Alksne, E. Kaufman) Drug Abuse: Modern Trends, Issues and Perspectives, 1978, Critical Concerns in the Field of Drug Abuse, 1978; editor: Dioxins and Health, 1994; sr. editor: Dioxins and Health, 2d edit., 2003; contbr. over 200 articles to profl. jours. including Am. Jour. Pub. Health, Chemosphere, Women & Health, Toxicology and Applied Pharmacology, Am. Jour. Physiology, Jour. Occupl. and Environ. Health, Occupl. and Environ. Health, Environ. Health Perspectives; environ. sect. editor: Maxcy Rosenau Last Public Health and Preventive Medicine, 14th edit., 1988. Maj. M.C., U.S. Army, 1967-69. Recipient Pacesetter award Commonwealth Mass., 1990. Fellow: ACP, Am. Coll. Occupl. and Environ. Medicine, Am. Coll. Preventive Medicine; mem.: AAAS, APHA (chair Vietnam caucus), Soc. Epidemiology Rsch., Tex. Pub. Health Assn., Soc. for Epidemiologic Rsch., Am. Occupl. Medicine Assn., Am. Coll. Epidemiology, Assn. Tchrs. Preventive Medicine. Achievements include discovery of dioxin contamination of body tissues of general population of the U.S; dioxin hot spots in Vietnam with current contamination of Vietnamese by contaminated food; that PCB transformer fires can lead to contamination of buildings by dioxins, elevated dioxin body burden from Agent Orange in Vietnamese and in American Vietnam Veterans; development of congener specific tissue dioxin analysis as biomarker for dioxin exposure; developed naltrexone, a narcotic antagonist in rehabilitation of opiate addicts; discovery of PBDE grominated flame retardant contamination in breast milk of all U.S. mothers tested, and that levels are highest in the world. Home: 16606 Loch Maree Ln Dallas TX 75248-1711 Office: U Tex Sch Pub Health 5323 Harry Hines Blvd Rm V8112 Dallas TX 75390-7208 Office Phone: 214-648-1096. Business E-Mail: arnold.schecter@utsouthwestern.edu. E-mail: ajschecter@aol.com.

SCHECTMAN, STEPHEN BARRY, pharmaceutical executive; b. Washington, Oct. 20, 1947; s. Samuel and Rae (Tarnef) S.; m. Barbara L. Butcher, Sept. 10, 1969 (div. May 1994); children: Christopher, Matthew. BS, Randolph Macon Coll., 1970; postgrad., U. Tenn., 1974. Pres., CEO Medvac Corp., N.Y.C., 1993-94; spl. cons. Medco Containment Svcs., Montvale, NJ, 1991-93; ptnr. Hudson BioCapital Corp., N.Y.C., 1993-96; sr. dir. Schering-Plough Pharms., Kenilworth, NJ, 1996—2003; v.p. Schering My Health Solutions, Inc., Kenilworth, 2000—03; sr. v.p. strategy CRI, L.A., 2003—; pres. NewHealth Solutions Group, N.J. and Calif., 2003; pres., COO Impact Med. Solutions, Inc., Tustin, Calif., 2004—. Author (with others) Biomedical Innovation, 1980. Fellowship NIMH, NIH, 1969-73, postgrad. fellowship dept. physiology Georgetown U. Sch. of Medicine, 1975-76. Mem. AAAS, N.Y. Acad. Sci., Beta Beta Beta. Jewish. Home: Ste 4D 609 S Orange Ave South Orange NJ 07079-1063 Office: Impact Med Solutions Inc 14841 Yorba St Ste 101 Tustin CA 92780 Office Phone: 714-730-6401. E-mail: cydney102047@yahoo.com.

SCHEDLER, JOHN THOMAS, JR., state legislator, bank executive; b. New Orleans, La., Jan. 24, 1950; s. John Thomas Sr. and Catherine (Valadie) S.; m. Stephanie Ann Gelé; children: Michelle Christine, Rachael Ann, Jennifer Ashley. BS in Mktg., U. Southwestern La., 1971. Lic. real estate broker, ins. agt. Dist. mgr. Allen Parker Co., Baton Rouge, 1971-73; regional mgr. Foremost Ins. div. Sebrite Corp., Baton Rouge, 1973-75; v.p. ops. La. Mobile Svc. Corp., New Orleans, 1975-78; pres., CEO J.T. Schedler Cos., New Orleans, 1978-84; pres., CEO, dir. Fontainebleau Fed. Savs. Bank, Slidell, La., 1984—; mem. La. Senate from 11th dist., Baton Rouge, 1996—. Pres. Fountain Estates Homeowners Assn., Slidell, 1984—; chmn. Slidell Bd. Zoning and Adjustments, 1984-90, chmn., 1984-86, vice chmn., 1986; bd. dirs. Fountain Estates Recreation Assn., 1985-86, Slidell Meml. Hosp., 1990—, Delgado Community Coll. North Shore Campus, 1989—; mem. Slidell Econ. Devel. Com., 1987, Olde Towne Renovation Commn., 1988-89; dir. Olde Towne Incremental Tax Dist., 1989; bd. dirs., sec.-treas. Olde Towne Incremental Devel. Corp., 1989-90; mem. Slidell City Coun., 1990—. Named Employer of Yr. Slidell Bus. and Profl. Club, 1986. Mem. Slidell C. of C., St. Tammany Home Builders Assn., St. Tammany Realtors Assn., Rotary, Phi Kappa Theta. Democrat. Roman Catholic. Home: 106 Fountain Dr Slidell LA 70458-1532 Office: State of La PO Box 1656 Slidell LA 70459-1656

SCHEEDER, LOUIS, theater producer, director, educator; b. N.Y.C., Dec. 26, 1946; s. Louis W. and Julia H. (Callery) S. BA in English Lit., Georgetown U., 1968; postgrad., Sch. of Arts, Columbia U., 1968-69; MA in Performance Studies, NYU, 1995, PhD in Performance Studies, 2004. Founder, dir. The Classical Studio NYU, 1991—; Master Tchr., Tisch Sch. of the Arts, NYU. Dir. NYU Tisch Sch. of the Arts, Shakespeare Ensemble, 1989-90; mem. adv. council Nat. Com. on Arts and Edn., 1977-82; mem. D.C. Commn. on Arts and Humanities, 1976-80; bd. advs. New Playwrights' Theatre of Washington, 1975-82; asst. stage mgr. Arena Stage, Washington, 1969-70; dir., producer Folger Theatre Group, Washington, 1973-81; cons. Ctr. for Renaissance and Baroque Studies U. Md., 1984-91; asst. dir. Royal Shakespeare Co. Stratford-Upon-Avon, Eng., 1988. Dir., prodr. plays including Creeps (Am. premiere), 1973, The Farm (Am. premiere), 1974, The Collected Works of Billy the Kid (Am. premiere), 1975, Henry V, 1976, The Fool (Am. premiere), 1976, Mummer's End (world premiere), 1977, Teeth 'n' Smiles (Am. premiere), 1977, Two Gentlemen of Verona, 1977, Mackerel (world premiere), 1978, Black Elk Speaks (tour), 1978, Richard III, 1978, Whose Life Is It Anyway? (Am. premiere), 1978, Richard II, 1978, As You Like It, 1979, Custer (Kennedy Ctr.), 1979, Charlie and Algernon (Kennedy Ctr.), 1980, Crossing Niagara (Am. premiere), 1981, Love's Labour's Lost, 1981; also dir. Broadway, Off Broadway, regional prodns. including (Broadway) Charlie and Algernon, 1980, (Off Broadway) Creeps, 1973, Passover, 1986, (Off-Off-Broadway) The Gettysburg Sound Bite, 1989, Brunch at Trudy and Paul's, 1990, The Christmas Rules, 1991, The Monkey Business, 1992; dir. All's Well That Ends Well, 1990; dance: dir. Near Ruins, Ruby, 1996, Let's Go Thundering, 1997, Give Us a Kiss, Johnny, 1998, Keeper, 1999; prodr. How I Got That Story (Off Broadway), 1982, Diamonds (Off Broadway), 1984, Today, I Am a Fountain Pen (Off Broadway), 1986; dir. Man. Theatre Ctr., 1982, 83, 84, Nat. Arts Ctr., Ottawa, Ont., Can., 1984, Hedda Gabler, Ctr. Stage, Toronto, 1985, Reg: Life in the Trees, GeVa Theatre, 1991; asst. dir. Broadway prodn. Carrie, 1988, Pacific Rep. prodn. Merchant of Venice, 2002; author: (with Shane Ann Younts) All the Words on Stage: A Complete Pronunciation Dictionary for the Plays of William Shakespeare, 2002. Recipient Dixon award Georgetown U., 1968, Alumni Achievement award Georgetown U. Alumni Club Met. Washington, 1981, Mayor's Arts award, D.C., 1982, Acad. Excellence award NYU, 1995. Mem. Soc. Stage Dirs. and Choreographers, Episc. Actors' Guild (life; coun. 1990-96, 2002—). Home: 7 Stuyvesant Oval New York NY 10009-1901 E-mail: louis.scheeder@nyu.edu., ls36@nyu.edu.

SCHEEL, NELS EARL, finance company executive, accountant; b. Spencer, Wis., Sept. 25, 1925; s. Roland Edward and Louise Ernestine Scheel; m. Elaine Marie Carlisle, Aug. 28, 1949; children: Thomas W., John E., Martha L., Mark A., Mary E. BA, Youngstown Coll., 1949; MBA, U. Pa., 1950. CPA, Ohio. Staff acct. Lybrand Ross Bros., Cleve., 1950-54; asst. controller Century Foods, Youngstown, Ohio, 1954-62; treas., controller The Bailey Co., Cleve., 1962-63, Golden Dawn Foods, Sharon, Pa., 1963-82; v.p., chief fin. officer Peter J. Schmitt Co., Sharon, 1982-89; cons. to industry Columbiana, 1989—. Part-time faculty Youngstown (Ohio) State U., 1954—94; bd. mem. Sovereign Cirs., Inc., North Jackson, Ohio, 1992—2001, bd. chmn., 1995—99, sec.-treas., 1999—2001. Pres. Crestview Bd. Edn., Columbiana, Ohio, 1970-81; trustee Columbiana Cmty. Found., 2002—. Staff sgt. AUS, 1943-46, PTO, hon. discharge. Mem. Am. Inst. CPA's, Ohio Soc. CPA's.

SCHEELE, NICHOLAS V. automotive executive; b. Jan. 3, 1944; married; 3 children. With Ford British and European Ops., 1978; pres. Ford of Mex., 1988; chmn., CEO Jaguar Cars Ltd., 1992—99; chmn. Ford Europe, 2000—01; group v.p. Ford N.Am., 2001—02; COO Ford Motor Co., 2001—04, pres., 2001—; also bd. dirs. Chancellor U. Warwick, 2002—; adv. bd. Coventry U., Fulbright Commn., Durham U.; Midland coun. mem. Inst. Dirs. Active Save the Children, St. Basil's Appeal for Homeless Children; adv. bd. British Am. C. of C.; chmn. Foresight 2020. Decorated knight British Queen, Order of St. Michael and St. George. Master: Nat. Soc. for the Prevention Cruelty to Children (life); mem.: Soc. Motor Mfrs. and Traders (exec. com.). Avocations: reading, music. Office: Ford Motor Co One American Rd Dearborn MI 48126-1899

SCHEELE, PAUL DRAKE, former hospital supply corporate executive; b. Elgin, Ill., Aug. 6, 1922; s. Arthur R. and Helen M. (Christiansen) S. BA, Coe Coll., 1944; MBA, Harvard, 1947. With Am. Hosp. Supply Corp., 1947—; pres. Harleco div., Phila., 1966-68; group v.p. Am. Hosp. Supply Corp., 1968-70, exec. v.p., also pres. internat. group, 1970-74, v.p., asst. to chmn. bd., 1974-81. Chmn. bd. trustees Coe Coll. Served to 1st lt., inf. AUS, 1943-46. Mem. Harvard Bus. Sch. Club, Harvard Club Fla., Econ. Club (Chgo.), Tau Kappa Epsilon, Pi Delta Epsilon.

SCHEELER, CHARLES, construction company executive; b. Balt., June 20, 1925; s. George F. and Catherine Louise (Seward) S.; m. Mary Katherine Scarborough, Aug. 22, 1953; children— Charles P., George D., Donald C. BS, U. Md., 1948, LL.B., 1952. Bar: Md. 1952; CPA, Md. With C. J. Langenfelder & Son., Inc., Balt., 1949—, exec. v.p., treas., 1974-77, pres., chief exec. officer, 1977-95. Chmn. bd. Rosedale Fed. Savs. & Loan Assn. Served with USN, 1943-46, PTO. Mem. AICPA, Md. Assn. CPAs. Office: 4940 Campbell Blvd Ste 100 Baltimore MD 21236-5910

SCHEELER, JAMES ARTHUR, architect; b. Pontiac, Ill., Dec. 20, 1927; s. Aman B. and Jane (Steele) S.; m. Barbara Jean Lloyd, Sept. 2, 1950; children: James Erich, Carl Aman, Orissa Jane Elizabeth. BS with highest honors, U. Ill., 1951, MS, 1952; postgrad., U. Liverpool, 1952-53. Grad. asst. U. Ill., Urbana, 1950-52; draftsman-designer Lundeen & Hilfinger, Bloomington, Ill., 1952-53; designer Skidmore, Owings & Merrill, Chgo., 1955-59; partner Richardson, Severns, Scheeler & Assos., Inc., Champaign, Ill., 1959-65, v.p., treas., 1965-71; vice chmn. bd., dir. Prodn. Systems for Architects and Engrs., Inc., 1973-81. Vis. critic U. Ill., 1959-60. Mem. Plan Commn., Champaign, 1966—71, chmn., 1969-71; mem. Champaign County Regional Planning Commn., 1967-71; bd. dirs. Nat. Center for a Barrier-Free Environment, 1978—81, pres., 1981. Served with USN, 1946-47. Recipient various archtl. awards.; Francis J. Plym fellow, 1953-54; Fulbright fellow, 1953. Fellow AIA (treas. Ctrl. Ill. chpt. 1967-68, sec. 1968-69, pres. 1970-71, nat. dep. exec. v.p. 1971-76, pres. corp. 1974-78, exec. v.p. 1977-78, program devel. group exec. 1976-85, sr. exec. 1985-88, v.p. design practice group 1989, resident fellow 1990—, Edward D. Kemper award 2000), Internat. Union of Archs. Profl. Practice Commn. (sec., co-dir. 1994-2003), Fedn. Colls. Archs. Republic Mex. (hon.), Royal Australian Inst. Architects; mem. Ill. Arts Coun. (archtl. adv. bd. 1966-71), Japan Inst. Architect (hon.), Montessori Soc. Champaign-Urbana (dir. 1964-66), Gargoyle, Scarab, Phi Kappa Phi, Lambda Chi Alpha, Lambda Alpha, Cosmos Club. Episcopalian. Address: 11179 Saffold Way Reston VA 20190-3824

SCHEER, JOSEPH H. artist, education educator; b. Heildeberg, Germany, Sept. 6, 1958; arrived in U.S., 1960; s. James H. and Kathleen M. Scheer. BFA, Alfred Univ., Alfred, NY, 1984; MA, Univ. New Mex., Albuqergue, New Mex., 1986, MFA, 1987. Artist ind., Los Nutrius, N.Mex., 1986—89; prof. print media Sch. Art Design Alfred Univ., Alfred, NY, 1989—; co-dir. Inst. Electronic Art Alfred Univ., Alfred, NY, 1997—. Author: Night Visions: Secret Designs of Moths, 2003, Night Flyers, 2003; one-man shows include over 30; contbr. articles pub. in over 50 profl. jour. Recipient Silver award, 16th Gold Internat., Chgo., 2003, Stiftung Bockkunst Best Book Design award, Frankfurt, Germany, 2003; grantee Project grant, NYSCA, 2001. Mem.: Entomol. Soc. Am., Lepidoptersit Soc., Phi Kappa Phi. Office: Sch of Art & Design Alfred Univ 2 Pine St Alfred NY 14802

SCHEER, MARK JEFFREY, lawyer; b. N.Y.C., Jan. 6, 1962; s. Morton Herbert and Joan Sylvia (Weiss) S.; m. Sheryl Lynn Weinberg, Oct. 24, 1987; children: Matthew Jordan, Danielle Nicole, Lindsay Gayle. BS in Acctg., U. Fla., 1983, M in Acctg., 1984, JD, 1987. Bar: Fla. 1987, U.S. Tax Ct. 1988, U.S. Dist. Ct. (so. dist.) Fla. 1991. Ptnr. Gunster, Yoakley, & Stewart, P.A., Miami, Fla., 1987—. Mem. ABA, AICPA, Fla. Bar Assn., Fla. Isnt. CPAs. Jewish. Office: 2 S Biscayne Blvd Miami FL 33131-1806 Office Phone: 305-376-6000. E-mail: mscheer@gunster.com.

SCHEER, R. SCOTT, physician; b. N.Y.C., Oct. 24, 1938; s. Leonard and Josephine (Holtschl) S.; m. Beverly Joan Henry Scheer, Dec. 27, 1940; children: Kirsten Leigh, Laura Lynn. AB, Cornell U., 1960; MD, SUNY, Buffalo, 1965. Diplomate Am. Bd. Radiology (cert.), Am. Bd. Nuc. Medicine (cert.), Nat. Bd. Med. Examiners (cert.). Intern Santa Barbara (Calif.) Cottage Hosp., 1965-66; resident Cornell Univ.-N.Y. Hosp., 1966, Phila. Gen. Hosp., 1968-71; staff radiologist Meth. Hosp., Phila., 1971-72; assoc. dir. radiology Coatesville (Pa.) Hosp., 1972-77; dir. dept. radiology Norristown (Pa.) State Hosp., 1973-93; dir., chief exec. officer Med. Imaging Svcs., Chester Springs, Pa., 1977—; dir. radiology Scranton (Pa.) Imaging Ctr., 1993-94; cons. radiologist Oxford Valley Imaging Ctr., 1992-95, mng. ptnr., 1995-97; dir. radiology Allied Med. Group, Phila., 1997—; dir. diagnostic imaging lab. Premier Rsch. Worldwide, Phila., 1998—; cons. radiologist Berwick (Pa.) Hosp., 2000—. Cons. radiol. expert, 1981—; attending radiologist Pottstown Meml. Med. Ctr., 1977-93; cons. in MRI, Fonar Corp., 1990-92; cons. radiologist U.S. Radiology Assocs., Bensalem, Pa., 1996-97; mem. med. bd. Foxexec. Health Exams. Internat., 2001—. Capt. U.S. Army Med. Corps, 1966-68. Recipient N.Y. State Regents Med. scholarship, 1961. Mem. AMA, Am. Coll. Radiology, Radiol. Soc. N.Am., Pa. Med. Soc., Pa. Radiol. Soc., Chester County Med. Soc., Am. Inst. of Ultrasound in Medicine, Pa. Coll. Nuclear Medicine, Union League of Phila., Valley Forge Mountain Racquet Assn. Republican. Presbyterian. Avocations: photography, gardening, tennis. Office: Med Imaging Svcs 1420 Conestoga Rd Chester Springs PA 19425-1901 Home: 711 Pondview Way Downingtown PA 19335-4573

SCHEERER, ERNEST WILLIAM, dentist; b. Wabash, Ind., May 18, 1932; s. Ernest William and Anna Lucille (Bahler) S.; m. Ingrid Elvy Yvonne, Sept. 28, 1973. BS, Purdue U., 1954; DDS, Ind. U., 1961. Intern The Queen's Hosp., Honolulu, 1961-62; assoc. Pvt. Dental Practice, Honolulu, 1963-65; owner Pvt. Solo Dental Practice, Honolulu, 1965-75; ptnr. Dental Adminstrn., Honolulu, 1975—; pres. Scheerer & West Dental Corp., Honolulu, 1978—. Chief Dept. Dentistry Queen's Hosp., Honolulu. Contbr. various clin. articles to profl. jours. Mem. Big Bros., Hawaii, 1968-74. Mem. Master Acad. Gen. Dentistry, Hawaii Acad. Gen. Dentistry (past pres.), Am. Coll. Dentists, ADA, Hawaii Dental Assn. (treas.), Internat. Acad. Gnathology, Pierre Fauchard Soc., Fedn. Dental Internat., Am. Equilibration Soc., Acad. of Osseointegration, Am. Acad. Esthetic Dentistry, Omicron Kappa Upsilon, Delta Sigma Delta, Hawaii Med. Libr. (sec.), Elks. Mem. United Ch. of Christ. Club: Pacific. Avocations: tennis, travel, hawaiian music. Office: Scheerer & West Inc 735 Bishop St Ste 211 Honolulu HI 96813-4884 E-mail: ewscheerer@aol.com.

SCHEETZ, SISTER MARY JOELLEN, English language educator; b. Lafayette, Ind., May 20, 1926; d. Joseph Albert and Ellen Isabelle (Fitzgerald) S. AB, St. Francis Coll., 1956; MA, U. Notre Dame, 1964; PhD, U. Mich., 1970. Tchr. English, Bishop Luers High Sch., Fort Wayne, Ind., 1965-67; acad. dean St. Francis Coll. (now U. St. Francis), Fort Wayne, 1967-68, pres. Ft. Wayne, Ind., 1970-93, pres. emeritus, English lang. prof., 1993—. Mem.: Delta Epsilon Sigma. Office: U St Francis 2701 Spring St Fort Wayne IN 46808-3939 E-mail: jscheetz@sf.edu.

SCHEFF, ALICE MELLORS, nuclear medicine physician; b. New Haven, Apr. 19, 1945; d. Robert Charles and Jane (Winternitz) Mellors; m. David Jonathan Schiff, Sept. 6, 1969 (div. 1974); 1 child, William. AB in Biology summa cum laude, Vassar Coll., 1967; MA in Immunology, Johns Hopkins U., 1972; MD, Pa. State U., 1978. Diplomate Am. Bd. Nuclear Medicine, Am. Bd. Radiology. Intern and resident diagnostic radiology and nuclear medicine Milton S. Hershey Med. Ctr., Hershey, Pa., 1978-82; staff radiologist and coord. nuclear medicine Reading Hosp. and Med. Ctr., 1982-86; clin. asst. prof. dept. diagnostic imaging sch. medicine Temple U., 1986-93; nuclear medicine physician dept. radiation Albert Einstein Med. Ctr., 1986-93; asst. prof. radiology dept. radiology Hosp. of Univ. Pa., Phila., 1994—. Vis. fellow in magnetic resonance imaging Long Beach (Calif.) Meml. Med. Ctr., 1993; lectr. in field. Author: (with others) Pathology Annual, Vol. 4, 1974, Herpes-virus and Cancer: Advances in Cancer Research, Vol. 19, 1974; contbr. articles to profl. jours. Grantee Einstein Soc., 1989-91, Einstein Soc. and Breast Cancer Support Com., 1990-93, R.W. Johnson Pharm. Rsch. Inst., 1992. Mem. AMA, Am. Coll. Nuclear Physicians, Am. Coll. Radiology, Radiol. Soc. N. Am., Pa. Med. Soc., Pa. Radiol. Soc., Phila. County Med. Soc., Phila. Roentgen Ray Soc., Soc. Nuclear Medicine (chmn. edn. com. greater N.Y. chpt. 1986-89, sec. 1989-91, pres. elect 1991-93, 94—, chmn. continuing edn. and course approval com. 1989-93, bd. dirs. brain imaging coun. 1990-92, sec. 1992—, exec. com. acad. coun. 1994—, bd. dirs. correlative imaging coun.), Soc. Magnetic Imaging, Phi Beta Kappa. Avocations: recreational sports, nature, art, music, theater. Office: U Pa Hosp Dept Radiology Divsn Nuc Medicine 3400 Spruce St Philadelphia PA 19104-4206

SCHEFFEL, DONNA JEAN, elementary school educator; b. Balt., Sept. 20, 1953; d. G. Donald Scheffel and Mary LaVerne (Perry) Jones; 1 child, Amanda Lynne. BS, Salisbury (Md.) State Coll.; Cert., Baldwin-Wallace Coll., Berea, Ohio, 1983. Tchr. Wadsworth (Ohio) city schs., 1984-85, Parma (Ohio) city schs., 1984-85; elem. tchr. St. Leo the Great Sch., Cleve., 1985-91. Mem. team Early Prevention Sch. Failure; faculty rep. bd. dirs. Parent Tchr. Unit. Parma city schs., 1997—; 1st aux. svcs. computer sci. tchr. Bethel Christian Acad., Parma. Named one of Outstanding Young Women of Am., 1986. Mem.: ASCD, PEA, NEA, NAFE, Ohio Edn. Assn., N.E. Ohio Edn. Assn. Office: Bethel Christian Acad 12901 W Pleasant Valley Rd Parma OH 44130-5702

SCHEFFEL, KENNETH PAUL, retired archivist; b. Cin., Aug. 18, 1937; s. Edwin Reuben and Ivy Catherine (Happel) Scheffel. AB, Columbia U., N.Y.C., 1959; MS, U. Wis., 1963. Archivist U. Mich., Ann Arbor, 1967—2003, archivist emeritus, 2003—. Mem.: So. Hist. Assn., Orgn. of Am. Historians. Methodist. Home: 7857 Harrison Ave Apt 4 Mount Healthy OH 45231-3151 E-mail: kenschef@umich.edu.

SCHEFFING, DIANNE ELIZABETH, special education educator; b. St. Louis, Mar. 17, 1963; d. Eugene Shibley Scheffing Jr. and Sarah Ann (Lukens) Scheffing. BS, Mo. Bapt. Univ., 1988; MA, Fontbonne Univ., St. Louis, 1999; postgrad., Webster U., St. Louis, 2002. Cert. elem. edn. grades 1-8 Mo., mild/moderate cross-category grades K-12 Mo., severely developmentally delayed 2002. Kindergarden tchr. asst. Andrews Acad., St. Louis, 1989—91; sci. tchr. edn. dept. St. Louis Sci. Ctr., 1994—96; tchr. asst. multi-handicapped Kehrs Mill Elem./Rockwood Sch. Dist., St. Louis, 1996—2000; tchr. spl. edn. Gateway/Hubert Wheeler State Sch. for Severely Handicapped, St. Louis, 2000—. Mem., sec. St. Louis Young Reps. Club, 1988—94; majority mem. Bethel #44 Internat. Order of Job's Daughters, Ballwin, 1978—84. Named Woman of Yr., St. Louis Young Reps. Club, 1992, 1994. Mem.: Am. Cancer Soc. Methodist. Avocations: Olympic supporter, bowling, travel. Office: Gateway/Hubert Wheeler State Sch 100 S Garrison Saint Louis MO 63103 Personal E-mail: applecore@prodigy.net.

SCHEFFLER, ECKART ARTHUR, publisher; b. Glauchau, Germany, June 8, 1941; arrived in U.S., 1963; s. Arthur Ernst and Marianne (Baltzer) S.; m. Hannelore Baustian, July 29, 1966; children: Thomas, Daniel. Bookseller Buchhändlerschule, Leipzig, Germany, 1955-58; bookstore mgr. Bücher-Binder, Stuttgart, Germany, 1959-62; v.p. Adler's Fgn. Books Inc., N.Y.C., 1963-72; v.p., gen. mgr. Walter de Gruyter, Inc., Hawthorne, NY, 1972—. Served with USAR, 1964-69. Mem. Am. Assn. Pubs., Internat. Group of Sci., Tech. and Med. Pubs., Scholarly Pubs. Assn., Rotary. Lutheran. Office: Walter de Gruyter 1 Inc 200 Saw Mill River Rd Hawthorne NY 10532-1523 Office Phone: 914-747-0110. E-mail: escheffler@degruyterny.com.

SCHEFFLER, ISRAEL, philosopher, educator, education educator; b. N.Y.C., Nov. 25, 1923; s. Leon and Ethel (Grünberg) S.; m. Rosalind Zuckerbrod, June 26, 1949; children: Samuel, Laurie. BA, Bklyn. Coll., 1945, MA, 1948; M.H.L., Jewish Theol. Sem., 1949; PhD (Ford fellow 1951), U. Pa., 1952; A.M. (hon.), Harvard U., 1959; D.H.L. (hon.), Jewish Theol. Sem., 1993. Mem. faculty Harvard U., 1952-92, prof. edn., 1961-62, prof. edn. and philosophy, 1962-64, Victor S. Thomas prof. edn. and philosophy, 1964-92, professor emeritus, 1992—, hon. research fellow in cognitive studies, 1965-66, co-dir. Philosophy Edn. Rsch. Ctr., 1983-98, dir. Philosophy Edn. Rsch. Ctr., 1998—2003; scholar-in-residence The Mandel Ctr., Brandeis U., 2003—. Fellow Center for Advanced Study in Behavioral Scis., 1972-73 Author: The Language of Education, 1960, The Anatomy of Inquiry, 1963, Conditions of Knowledge, 1965, Science and Subjectivity, 1967, Reason and Teaching, 1973, Four Pragmatists, 1974, Beyond the Letter, 1979, Of Human Potential, 1985, Inquiries, 1986, In Praise of the Cognitive Emotions, 1991, Teachers of My Youth, 1995, Symbolic Worlds, 1997; co-author: Work, Education and Leadership, 1995; editor: Philosophy and Education, 1958, 66; co-editor: Logic and Art, 1972, Visions of Jewish Education, 2003; contbr. articles to profl. jours. Recipient Alumni award of merit Bklyn. Coll., 1967, Disting. Svc. medal Tchrs. Coll., Columbia, 1980, Benjamin Shevach award Boston Hebrew Coll., 1995; Guggenheim fellow, 1958-59, 72-73; NSF grantee, 1962, 65. Mem. Am. Acad. Arts and Scis., Am. Philos. Assn., Philosophy Edn. Soc., Nat. Acad. Edn. (charter), Philosophy of Sci. Assn. (prs. 1973-75), Charles S. Peirce Soc. (pres. 1998). Address: 3 Woodside Rd Newton MA 02460

SCHEFFLER, LEWIS FRANCIS, pastor, educator, research scientist; b. Springfield, Ohio, Oct. 13, 1928; s. Lewis Francis and Emily Louise (Kloker) S.; m. Willa Pauline Cole, Aug. 9, 1949 (div. 1978); children: Lewis F. Fischer, Richard Thomas, Gary Arlen, Tonni Kay; m. Mary Lee Smith, Apr. 18, 1978; stepchildren: Kimberly McCollum, Jeffrey McIlroy, Kerry Buell. BA in Liberal Arts, Cin. Bible Seminary, 1950; AA in Bus., Jefferson Coll., 1989; MAT, Webster U., 1989. Quality assurance Tectum Corp., Newark, 1954-57; rsch. group leader Owens-Corning Fiberglas, Granville, Ohio, 1957-64; tech. asst. to v.p. R&D and Engring., 1960-63; pres. Ohio Glass Fibers Cons., 1962-68; rsch. adminstr. Modiglas Fibers Corp., Bremen, Ohio, 1965-68; dir. R & D Flex-O-Lite Corp., St. Louis, 1968-71; pastor Christian Ch., St. Louis, 1972-75; police commns. Brentwood (Mo.) Police Dept., 1975-87; pastor Christian Ch., Potosi, Mo., 1988-89, Slater (Mo.) Christian Ch., 1989-93, Clark (Mo.) Christian Ch., 1996-99; asst. prof. English lang. and lit. Mo. Valley Coll., Marshall, 1989-94; adj. prof. theology Mo. Sch. Religion, 1993-97; adj. prof. English Moberly Area C.C., 1996-98; min. Ctrl. Union Cmty. Ch., Vaudalia, Mo., 1998—. Organizing co-chmn. aerospace composite materials com. ASTM, 1961; mem. exec. bd. Northwest Area Christian Ch., 1989-93; mem. Coun. of Areas of Mid-Am. Region Christian Ch., 1990-93; cons. and lectr. in field. Contbr. articles to profl. jours. Patentee in field. Money raiser United Appeal, chaplaincy Blessing Hosp., Quincy, Ill., 1974; vol. Ill. Divsn. Children and Family Svcs., 1972-75; sec. exec. com. N.W. Area Christian Ch. (Disciples of Christ), 1992-94. Mem. Medieval Acad. Am., Mo. Philol. Assn. Avocation: philosophy and pomology. Home: PO Box 15 Rush Hill MO 65280 *Now and then, God has so touched people in such a way that, recognizing it, we think "So that's what God must be like!" and our ethical and moral sensitivities are heightened.*

SCHEFFLER, STUART JAY, lawyer; b. Phila., Oct. 9, 1950; s. Walter and Fritzy (Salkoff) S.; m. Barbara Jane Green, July 3, 1975. BA cum laude, Pa. State U., 1972, MPA, 1973; JD, Temple U., 1980. Bar: Pa. 1980, U.S. Dist. Ct. (ea. dist.) Pa. 1981, U.S. Ct. Appeals (3d cir.) 1983, U.S. Supreme Ct. 1986. Tchr. Sch. Dist. of Phila., 1974-75; claims authorizer Social Security Adminstrn., HEW, Phila., 1975-76, equal opportunity specialist Office of Civil Rights, 1976-77; paraprofessional Law Offices of Ronald A. Bell., Bala

Cynwyd, Pa., 1978-80; assoc. Law Office of Robert B. Mozenter, Phila., 1980-81, Gekoski & Bogdanoff, Phila., 1981-82; ptnr. Rubin & Scheffler, Phila., 1982-84; sole practice, Phila., 1984-94; of counsel Solomon, Berschler, Warren & Schatz, P.C., Norristown, Pa., 1994— . Councilman Bakers Bay Condominium Assn., Phila., 1982; bd. dirs. Key West Coun. on the Arts, 1999—. Fellow Acad. of Advocacy, mem. ABA (tort and ins. practice, sports and entertainment, civil litigation sects.), Pa. Bar Assn. (legis. liaison, medico-legal coms.), Phila. Bar Assn., Am. Trial Lawyers Assn., Phila. Trial Lawyers Assn., Pa. Trial Lawyers Assn., Drug Info. Assn., Internat. Platform Assn., Phi Beta Kappa, Delta Sigma Rho, Tau Kappa Alpha, Zeta Beta Tau. Democrat. Club: Hartikvah Basketball Assn. (Phila.) (v.p. 1974—). Office: 522 Swede St Norristown PA 19401-4834

SCHEFFMAN, DAVID THEODORE, economist, management educator, consultant; b. Milaca, Minn., Dec. 1, 1943; s. David Theodore and Fern Virginia (Maas) Scheffman; 1 child, Christopher. BA, U. Minn., 1967; PhD, MIT, 1971. Lectr. Boston Coll., 1970-71; from asst. prof. to assoc. prof. Univ. Western Ont., London, Can., 1971-81; sr. economist FTC, Washington, 1979 82, dep. dir., 1983-86; prof., dir Inst. Applied Econs. Concordia U., Montreal, Que., Can., 1982-83; dir., bur. econs. FTC, Washington, 1985-88; Justin Potter prof., prof. bus. strategy and mktg. Vanderbilt U., Nashville, 1989-99, prof. of bus. strategy and mktg., 1999—; dir. LECG, N.Y.C., 1993-2001, Bur. Econs., FTC, Washington, 2001—03, LECG, 2003—; prof. bus. strategy Cornell U., 2001—02. Adj. prof. Georgetown U. Law Ctr., Washington, 1986; cons. Ont. Econ. Coun., Toronto, 1973-81, GM, 1977, Ctrl. Oil Inquiry, Ottawa, Ont., 1982-84, Ctrl. Govt., Ottawa, 1979-81, Can. Competition Tribunal, 1987-89, Can. Bur. Competition Policy, 1988 91, U.S. Sentencing Commn., 1988-89, PepsiCo, 1989-2000, Kraft Gen. Food, 1989-2001, PacifiCorp, 1989-93, NERA, 1991-93, Boeing, 1992-96, Berwind Industries, Inc., 1993-95, Comm. Ctrl., Inc., Applied Innovation, Inc., TEC, 1995-98, Nortel, 1995, Coca Cola, 1996-98. Author: Speculation and Monopoly in Urban Development: Analytical Foundations, 1977, An Economic Analysis of Provincial Land Use Policies in Ontario, 1980, Social Regulation in Markets for Consumer Goods and Services, 1982, An Economic Analysis of the Impact of Rising Oil Prices on Urban Structure, 1983, Strategy, Structure, and Antitrust in the Carbonated Soft Drink Industry, 1992. Recipient Dissertation Fellowship award NSF, 1967-68; vis. scholar U. Minn., 1978. Mem. Am. Econ. Assn., Strategic Mgmt. Soc., Am. Mgmt. Assn., Am. Mktg. Assn. Office: Fed Trade Commn Bur Econs 6th and Pa Ave NW Washington DC 20580 also: LECG 1725 I St NW #800 Washington DC 20006 Office Phone: 202-973-6482. E-mail: dscheffman@lecg.com.

SCHEIB, GARRY L. hospital administrator; BS with honors, MBA, Lehigh U. V.p. network ops., mgr. rels. U. Pa. health sys., affiliated hosps.; with Am. Medicorp, Humana; pres. bus. group Mediq, Inc.; pres., grad. health sys. Rancocoas Hosp., 1990—93; pres. Rancocas Hosp., Zurbrugg Hosp., 1997; exec. dir. Hosp. U. Pa., 1999—; sr. v.p. hosp. ops. U. Pa. Health Sys., 2002—. Pres. Burlington C.ofC.; mem. bd. dirs. various cmty. orgns. Office: Hosp U Pa 800 Spruce St Philadelphia PA 19107-6192

SCHEIB, GERALD PAUL, fine art educator, jeweler, metalsmith; b. L.A., Dec. 26, 1937; s. Harry William and Olive Bauer (Cartwright) S.; m. Elizabeth Ann Galligan, Dec. 27, 1965 (div. 1978); children: Gregory Paul, Geoffrey Paul; m. Dedra Lynn True, Oct. 1, 1983; 1 child, Adam True. AA, East L.A. Jr. Coll., 1959; BA, Calif. State U., L.A., 1962, MFA, 1968. Cert. life teaching credential in fine arts, secondary and coll. tchr., Calif. Secondary tchr. art L.A. Unified Sch. Dist., 1963-77; prof. fine art L.A. Community Coll. Dist., 1977-2001; ret., 2001; pres. faculty senate L.A. Mission Coll., San Fernando, Calif., 1983-84. Bargaining unit rep., AFT Coll. Guild Local 1521; elected Arts and Letters chair L.A. Mission Coll., 1993; owner, mgr. Artificers Bench, Sylmar, Calif., 1976—; cons. to Edward H. Bohlin Co. Custom Silver Works, 1998. Mem. policy bd. The Calif. Arts Project, 1995-97; chair L.A. County Art Edn. Coun., 1997-98; plank owner U.S. Naval Meml., Washington; trustee L.A. Artcore, 2001. With USNR, 1955-97, ret. Recipient of tribute City of L.A., 1983, Citizen of Month award, Los Angeles County, 1983, Cold War Cert. of Recognition, Sec. of Def., 2000. Mem. Calif. Art Edn. Assn. (membership chmn. 1985-87, pres.-elect 1989-91, pres. 1991-93, Calif.'s Outstanding Art Educator in Higher Edn. 1994-95), San Fernando Active 20-30 Club (pres. 1981-82), Nat. Assn. Scholars, Sons of Union Vets of Civil War, U.S. Naval Cryptologic Vets. Assn., L.A. Artcore (bd. dirs. 2001–). Republican. Avocations: collecting antiques, Civil War reenacting, creating custom jewelry. Office: 13356 Eldridge Ave Sylmar CA 91342-3200 Office Phone: 818-364-7678.

SCHEIB, JOHN W. music educator, conductor; b. Madison, Wis., Dec. 3, 1967; m. Amy M. Ferkovich; children: Jackson J., Mya M. MusB cum laude, U. of Wisconsin-Whitewater, 1986—90; MusM, U. of Wisconsin-Madison, 1992—95, PhD, 1999—2002. Instrumental music tchr. Fontana K-8 Sch., Wis., 1990, Poynette H.S., Wis., 1991—99; supr. of instrumental music student tchg. U. of Wisc.-Madison, 1999—2002; asst. prof. of music edn. Ball State U., 2002—. Clinician/adjudicator Wis. Sch. Music Assn., 1991—2002. Recipient Richard G. Gaarder award, Wis. Music Educators Assn., 1990. Mem.: Soc. for Rsch. in Music Edn., Soc. for Music Tchr. Edn., Ind. Music Educators Assn., Coll. Music Soc., Music Educators Nat. Conf., Phi Mu Alpha Sinfonia. Home: 8413 W Ashford Ln Muncie IN 47304 Office: Ball State U Muncie IN Personal E-mail: jwscheib@comcast.net.

SCHEIBE, KARL EDWARD, psychology educator; b. Belleville, Ill., Mar. 5, 1937; s. John Henry and Esther Julia (Friesen) S.; m. Elizabeth Wentworth Mixter, Sept. 10, 1961; children: David Sawyer, Robert Daniel. BS, Trinity Coll., 1959; PhD, U. Calif.-Berkeley, 1963; MA (hon.), Wesleyan U., 1973. Faculty mem. Wesleyan U., Middletown, Conn., 1963—, prof. psychology, 1973—, chmn. dept., 1973-76, 79-81, 86-88; v.p. Stonington Inst., 1984-91; dir. Saybrook Counseling Ctr., 1990—; prof. DUXX, Monterrey, Mexico, 1995—2002. Vis. prof. U. So. Calif., 1974; dir. rev. panels NSF Sci. Profl. Devel. Program, 1975-81; cons. Am. Council Edn., 1975-81 Author: Beliefs and Values, 1970, Mirror, Masks, Lies and Secrets, 1979, Studies in Social Identity, 1983, Self Studies: The Psychology of Self and Identity, 1995, The Drama of Everyday Life, 2000. Trustee Trinity Coll., Hartford, Conn., 1977-83; moderator congregation First Ch. of Christ, Middletown, 1981-82. Woodrow Wilson fellow, 1959; NSF fellow, 1961; NIMH research grantee, 1964-68; Fulbright fellow Cath. U. Sao Paulo, Brazil, 1972-73, 84. Mem. Am. Psychol. Assn., Eastern Psychol. Assn., Conn. Acad. Arts and Scis., Phi Beta Kappa Congregationalist. Home: 11 Long Ln Middletown CT 06457-4046 Office: Wesleyan U Dept Psychology Middletown CT 06459-0001 E-mail: kscheibe@wesleyan.edu.

SCHEIBE, MARGARET HELEN, elementary school educator, librarian; b. Cloquet, Minn., July 26, 1946; d. Clarence E. and Elsie L. Scheibe. Diploma in edn., Lakehead U., 1970; BS, U. Wis., Superior, 1971, MEd, 1973; PhD, Walden U., 1989. Cert. tchr., Minn.; cert. media generalist, Minn. Asst. registrar U. Wis., Superior, 1979-84, counselor, fgn. student advisor, 1984-85; registrar Coll. St. Scholastica, Duluth, Minn., 1985-87, dir. media and tech. program, 1987-98; media dir. Proctor (Minn.) Pub. Schs., 1998—. Cons. Ind. Sch. Dist. 709, Duluth, 1996-98, mem. cmty. edn. bd., 1995-98; tchr. abroad St. Scholastica, Louisburg, County Mayo, Ireland, 1997; presenter Pictish Arts Soc., Dingwall, Scotland, 1994, Edinburgh, Scotland, 1995. Contbr. articles to profl. jours. Bd. dirs. WDSE Edn. Com., Duluth, 1995—. Fellow Blandin Found., 1995, Northland Found., 1996; grantee U.S. West, 1995-96. Mem. ALA, Minn. Ednl. Media Orgn., Internat. Soc. for Tech. in Edn., Phi Delta Kappa (historian 1996-98), Delta Kappa Gamma (past pres. 1994-96). Democrat. Avocations: reading, archeology, celtic harp. Office: Proctor Pub Schs 131 9th Ave Proctor MN 55810-2741 Home: 904 Madison Ave Duluth MN 55811-5932

SCHEIBEL, ARNOLD BERNARD, psychiatrist, educator, research director; b. N.Y.C., Jan. 18, 1923; s. William and Ethel (Greenberg) S.; m. Madge Mila Ragland, Mar. 3, 1950 (dec. Jan. 1977); m. Marian Diamond, Sept. 1982. BA, Columbia U., 1944, MD, 1946; MS, U. Ill., 1952. Intern Mt. Sinai Hosp., N.Y.C., 1946-47; resident in psychiatry Barnes and McMillan Hosp., St. Louis, 1947-48, Ill. Neuropsychiat. Inst., Chgo., 1950-52; asst. prof. psychiatry and anatomy U. Tenn. Med. Sch., 1952-53, assoc. prof., 1953-55, UCLA Med. Ctr., 1955-67, prof., 1967—, mem. Brain Rsch. Inst., 1960—, acting dir. Brain Rsch. Inst., 1987-90, dir., 1990-95. Cons. in field. Contbr. numerous articles to tech. jours, chpts. to books.; mem. editl. bd. Brain Rsch., 1967-77, Developmental Psychobiology, 1968—, Internat. Jour. Neurosci., 1969—, Jour. Biol. Psychiatry, 1968—, Jour. Theoretical Biology, 1980—; assoc. editor News Report, 1989—. Mem. Pres.'s Commn. on Aging, Nat. Inst. Aging, 1980—. Served with AUS, 1943-46; from lt. to capt. M.C. AUS, 1948-50. Guggenheim fellow (with wife), 1953-54, 59; recipient Disting. Svc. award Calif. Soc. Biomed. Rsch., 1998. Fellow Am. Acad. Arts and Scis., Norwegian Acad. Scis., Am. Psychiat. Assn. (life, Harriet and Charles Luckman Disting. Tchg. award 1997) AAAS; mem. Am. Neurol. Assn., Soc. Neurosci., Pyschiat. Rsch. Assn., Soc. Biol. Psychiatry, So. Calif. Psychiat. Assn. Home: 16231 Morrison St Encino CA 91436-1331 Office: UCLA Dept Neurobiology Los Angeles CA 90024 *Intense personal tragedy can embitter life and choke off further personal creativity. It may also offer the opportunity to open new doors in the discovery of self. I am more aware than ever of my good fortune in having the opportunity to teach, to continue investigative work in the structure and function of the brain, and to give love and care to those who need it. I am more than ever convinced that loving and being loved is the greatest good that we can know, the state in which we most nearly fulfill our roles as human beings.*

SCHEIBEL, KENNETH MAYNARD, journalist; b. Campbell, Nebr., May 17, 1920; s. G. Alfred and Rachel Christine (Koch) S.; m. Helen Schmitt, May 14, 1955 (div. Sept. 1977); children: Victor Warren Schmitt, William Becker Schmitt, Kenneth Jr., Sally. Student, George Washington U., 1938—41; BA, U. Va., 1947, MA, 1949. Mag. salesman Periodical Pubs. Svc. Bur., Inc., 1935-38; reporter Internat. News Svc., Washington, 1940-41, Wall St. Jour., Washington, 1949-51; Washington corr. Gannett Newspapers, 1951-63; syndicated columnist N.Am. Newspaper Alliance, 1963-64; chief Washington bur. Donrey Media Group, 1964-67; founder, bur. chief Washington Bur. News, 1967—; founder nat. syndicated column Washington Farm Beat, 1970-85. Washington corr. Wis. State Jour., 1963-66, LaCrosse (Wis.) Tribune, 1963-66, Billings (Mont.) Gazette, 1964-71, V.I. Network, 1966-67, Moline (Ill.) Daily Dispatch, 1967-68, Drovers' Jour., 1967-68, Newport News (Va.) Daily Press & Times Herald, 1969-71, Packer Pub. Co., 1964-74, Gasoline Retailer, 1966-67, Okla., Farmer Stockman; congl. corr. F-D-C Reports, 1975-77; Washington columnist Farm Jour., 1960-75; dir. Nat. Press Bldg. Corp., 1973, v.p. pres. club and bldg corp., 1974; covered nat. polit. convs., campaigns; v.p. Fraser Assocs. (pub. rels.), Washington, 1976-79; Congl. broadcast interviewer. Contbr. nat. mags., newspaper syndicates. Incorporator War Meml. of Korea, Washington, 1981; editor Nat. Ctr. Fin. and Econ. Info., U.S.-Saudi Arabian Joint Econ. Commn., Riyadh, 1985-86; mem. Nat. Com. Korean War Meml., 1981. Capt. AUS, 1941-46, 755th Tank Bn., 1942-45, Europe, N. Africa, Italy. Decorated Bronze star, U.S. Army Occupation medal, Combat Infantryman badge; co-recipient Croix De Guerre (France), Thoth award for excellence in pub. rels., 1980. Mem. Izaak Walton League Am., White House Corrs. Assn., Overseas Press Club of Am., Am. Radio Relay League, Nat. Press Club (Washington; fin. sec., gov. 1969-73, vice chmn. bd. 1971, v.p., pres., 1974), Sigma Chi. Presbyterian. Home: 1325 18th St NW Apt 302 Washington DC 20036-6505 E-mail: kenscheib@earthlink.com. *The greatest sins are timidity and self indulgence, the greatest virtue is to love. Live each day, don't fret about yesterday or tomorrow. Enjoy the senses, learn from others, and never forget that both love and hate are returned.*

SCHEIBER, HARRY N. law educator; b. 1935; BA, Columbia U., 1955; MA, Cornell U., 1957, PhD, 1961; MA (hon.), Dartmouth Coll., 1965; D.Jur.Hon., Uppsala U., Sweden, 1998. Instr. to assoc. prof. history Dartmouth Coll., 1960-68, prof., 1968-71; prof. Am. history U. Calif., San Diego, 1971-80; prof. law Boalt Hall, U. Calif., Berkeley, 1980—. Chmn. jurisprudence and social policy program, 1982-84, 90-93, assoc. dean, 1990-93, 96-99; The Stefan Riesenfeld prof., 1991—; vice chair Univ. Academic Senate, 1993-94, chair 1994-95; dir. Earl Warren Legal Inst., 2002-; Fulbright disting. sr. lectr., Australia, 1983, marine affairs coord. Calif. Sea Grant Coll. Program, 1989-2000; vis. rsch. prof. Law Inst. U. Uppsala, Sweden, 1995, hon. prof. DiTella U., Buenos Aires, 1999; cons. Calif. Jud. Coun., 1992-93; acting dir. Ctr. for Study of Law and Soc., 1999-2001; co-dir. Law of the Sea Inst., 2002—; Cassel lectr., Stockholm U., 2003—. Author: The Wilson Administration and Civil Liberties, 1960, Ohio Canal Era, 1970; co-author: American Law and the Constitutional Order, 1988, The State and Freedom of Contract, 1998; author: Inter-Allied Conflicts and Ocean Law (1945-1953), 2001; co-author: American Law and the Constitutional Order, 1978, Law of the Sea: The Common Heritage and Emerging Challenges, 2000, numerous others; editor: Yearbook of the California Supreme Court Historical Society, 1994—; contbr. articles to law revs. and social sci. jours., 1994. Chmn. Littleton Griswold Prize Legal History, 1985-88; pres. N.H. Civil Liberties Union, 1969-70; chmn. Project '87 Task Force on Pub. Programs, Washington, 1982-85; dir. Berkeley Seminar on Federalism, 1986-95; cons. judiciary study U.S. Adv. Commn. Intergovernmental Rels., 1985-88, Pew Oceans Commn., 2002-03, Nat. Rsch. Coun., 2002-03; dir. NEH Inst. on Constitutionalism, U. Calif., Berkeley, 1986-87, 88-91. Recipient Sea Grant Colls. award, 1981-83, 84-85, 86-2002; fellow Ctr. Advanced Study in Behavioral Scis., Stanford Calif., 1967, 71; Guggenheim fellow, 1971, 88; Rockefeller Found. humanities fellow, 1979, NEH fellow, 1985-86; NSF grantee 1979, 80, 88-89. Fellow AAAS, Am. Acad. Arts and Scis., U. Calif. Humanities Rsch. Inst., Am. Soc. for Legal History (hon., pres. 2003—), Japan Soc. for Promotion of Sci. (invitational fellow); mem. Am. Hist. Assn., Orgn. Am. Historians, Agrl. History Soc. (pres. 1978), Econ. History Assn. (trustee 1978-80), Law and Soc. Assn. (trustee 1979-81, 96-99), Nat. Assessment History and Citizenship Edn. (chmn. nat. acad. bd. 1986-87), Marine Affairs and Policy Assn. (bd. dirs. 1991-96), Ocean Governance Study Group (steering com. 1991—), Internat. Coun. Environ. Law, Calif. Supreme Ct. Hist. Soc. (bd. dirs. 1993—, v.p. 1997-98). Office: U Calif Berkeley Law Sch Boalt Hall Berkeley CA 94720-2150 Business E-Mail: scheiber@law.berkeley.edu.

SCHEIBER, STEPHEN CARL, psychiatrist; b. N.Y.C., May 2, 1938; s. Irving Martin and Frieda Olga (Schor) S.; m. Mary Ann McDonnell, Sept. 14, 1965; children: Lisa Susan, Martin Irving, Laura Ann. BA, Columbia Coll., 1960; MD, SUNY, Buffalo, 1964. Diplomate Am. Bd. Psychiatry and Neurology. Intern Mary Fletcher Hosp., Burlington, Vt., 1964-65; resident in psychiatry Strong Meml. Hosp., Rochester, N.Y., 1967-70; asst. prof. U. Ariz., Tucson, 1970-76, assoc. prof., 1976-81, prof., 1981-86; exec. sec. Am. Bd. Psychiatry and Neurology, Inc., Deerfield, Ill., 1986-89, exec. v.p., 1989—. Adj. prof. psychiatry Northwestern U., Chgo. and Evanston, 1986—, Med. Coll. Wis., Milw., 1986—. Co-editor: The Impaired Physician, 1983, Certification, Recertification and Lifetime Learning in Psychiatry, 1994, Core Competencies for Psychiatric Practice, 2003, Core Competencies for Neurologists, 2003; contbr. articles to profl. jours. Mem. med. adv. com. Casas de los Ninos, Tucson, 1974-86; mem. mental health adv. com. Tucson Health Planning Coun., 1974-75; med. student interviewer Office of Med. Edn., 1975; mem. Glenbrook (Ill.) North H.S. Boosters Club, 1988-91; treas. Robert E. Jones Found., 1988-96. Surgeon USPHS, 1965-67. Recipient Outstanding Tchr. award, U. Ariz., 1986, Lifetime Achievement award, SUNY, Buffalo, 1998; grantee Group Therapy Outcome Studies on Inpatient Svc., 1980, Dialysis and Schizophrenia Pilot Project, NIH, 1978. Fellow: Group for Advancement of Psychiatry (invited mem., chmn. mem. edn. com. 1987—91, bd. dirs., sec. 1993—97, pres.-elect 1997—99, pres. 1999—2001), Assn. Acad. Psychiatry (parliamentary sec. 1979—84, treas. 1984—88, pres.-elect 1988—89, pres. 1989—90, Lifetime Educator award 2002), Am. Assn. Dirs. Psychiat. Residency Tng. (pres. 1981—82), Am. Coll. Psychiatrists (bd. regents 1992—2001, treas. 1995—2001), Am. Psychiat. Assn. (life; chmn. impaired physician com. 1985—88, cons. 1988—92, Disting. Life Fellow 2002); mem.: Oracle Heights Club (pres. 1983—84). Democrat. Jewish. Office: Am Bd Psychiatry & Neurology 500 Lake Cook Rd Ste 335 Deerfield IL 60015-5635

SCHEID, LINDA J. state legislator; b. June 16, 1942; 2 children. BA, Coe Coll.; JD, William Mitchell Coll. Law. Bar: Minn. Mem. Minn. Ho. of Reps., 1976, 82-90; mem. 47th dist. Minn. Senate, St. Paul, 1996—. Home: 6625 81st Ave N Brooklyn Park MN 55445-2513 Office: 317 Capitol 75 Constitution Ave Saint Paul MN 55155-1601

SCHEID, STEVEN L. investment company executive; 3 children. BS in acctg., Michigan St. U. CFO The Charles Schwab & Co. Inc., 1996—99, vice-chmn., 1999—2002; CEO Charles Schwab Investment Mgmt., 1999—2002; pres. Schwab Retail Group, 2000—02; chmn., CEO Janus Capital Group, Denver, 2004—. Fed. Reserve Bank of San Francisco's representative Fed. Advisory Coun., 2001—02; bd. dirs. The PMI Group Inc., Auto Desk Inc. Avocations: piano, clarinet, running, wine collecting. Office: Janus Capital Group Inc 151 Detroit St Denver CO 80206-4923*

SCHEIDLINGER, SAUL, psychologist; b. Bielitz, Austria, July 25, 1918; arrived in U.S., 1938; s. Solomon Scheidlinger and Rose Tenzer Scheidlinger; m. Lucy Prince, June 1946 (dec. Dec. 1969); 1 child, David J.; m. Rosalyn Tauber, June 1984. BSS, CCNY, 1942; MS, Columbia U., 1944; PhD, NYU, 1951. Lic. psychologist NY. Emeritus prof. psychiatry Albert Einstein Coll. Medicine, Bronx, NY, 1962—; adj. prof. clin. psychology in psychiatry Cornell U. Med. Coll., N.Y.C., 1994—. Author: Psychoanalytic Group Dynamics, 1980, Focus on Group Psychotherapy, 1982, Group Treatment of Adolescents in Context, Outpatient, Inpatient and School, 2002; editor: Internat. Jour. Group Psychotherapy, 1970—80. Fellow: Am. Group Psychotherapy Assn. (disting. fellow). Home: 715 Bleeker Ave Mamaroneck NY 10538

SCHEIDT, STEPHEN SLATON, internist, cardiologist; b. N.Y.C., Mar. 7, 1940; MD, Columbia P&S, 1965. Diplomate in internal medicine and cardiovascular diseases Am. Bd. Internal Medicine. Intern Montefiore Hosp., N.Y.C., 1965-66; resident in medicine Bellevue Hosp. - Columbia P&S, N.Y.C., 1966-68; fellow in cardiology Cornell U., 1968-70; prof. clin. medicine N.Y. Hosp. - Cornell Med. Ctr. (now N.Y. Presbyn. Hosp.). Fellow: ACP, Am. Coll. Cardiology; mem.: Am. Heart Assn. Office: NY Hosp - Cornell MC 525 E 68th St New York NY 10021-4870

SCHEIDT, W. ROBERT, chemistry educator, researcher; b. Richmond Heights, Mo., Nov. 13, 1942; s. Walter Martin and Martha (Videtich) S.; m. Kathryn Sue Barnes, Aug. 9, 1964; children: Karl Andrew, David Martin. BS, U. Mo., 1964; MS, U. Mich., 1965, PhD, 1968; postdoctoral studies, Cornell U., 1970. Asst. prof. U. Notre Dame, Ind., 1970-76, assoc. prof., 1976-80, prof., 1980—, William K. Warren prof., 1999—. Vis. prof. U. Wash., Seattle, 1980, U. Paris (Orsay), France, 1991, U. Strasbourg, France, 1998; mem. review sect. Metallobiochemistry NIH, Bethesda, 1991-96. Contbr. articles to profl. jours. Fellow AAAS; mem. Am. Chem. Soc. (assoc. editor Chem. Revs. jour. 1980-85), Am. Crystallographic Assn., Biophys. Soc., Sigma X. Democrat. Office: U Notre Dame Dept Chemistry Notre Dame IN 46556 Business E-Mail: scheidt.1@nd.edu.

SCHEIGE, STEVEN SHELDON, lawyer; b. N.Y.C., Mar. 15, 1950; s. Manfred Herman and Liba (Miller) S.; m. Fortuna Faye Gorelick, July 8, 1973; children: Robert, Susan-Lisa. BA, Rutgers U., 1972; JD, Georgetown U., 1975. Bar: Md. 1975. From atty.-advisor to asst. chief counsel Occupl. Safety and Health Rev. Commn., Washington, 1975-85, sr. atty., 1985-2001, team leader, 2001—. Spl. project coord. PTA, Montgomery County, Md., 1984; bd. dirs. Temple Israel Congregation, 1994-96, v.p., 1996-97; v.p. Tikvet Israel Congregation, 1997-2001, bd. dirs., 2001—. Mem. ABA, Md. State Bar Assn., Phi Beta Kappa. Jewish. Office: Occupational Safety and Health Rev Commn 1120 20th St NW Ste 9 Washington DC 20036-3411

SCHEIMAN, EUGENE R. lawyer; b. Bklyn., July 15, 1943; BA, L.I. U., 1966; JD cum laude, Bklyn. Law Sch., 1969. Bar: N.Y. 1970, U.S. Dist. Ct. (so. and ea. dists.) N.Y. 1971, U.S. Ct. Appeals (1st cir.) 1972, U.S. Ct. Appeals (5th cir.) 1973, U.S. Ct. Appeals (4th cir.) 1974, U.S. Supreme Ct. 1976, U.S. Ct. Appeals (2nd cir.) 1977, U.S. Ct. Appeals (fed. cir.), U.S. Ct. Appeals (11th cir.) 1989, U.S. Ct. Appeals (3rd cir.) 1990. Shareholder Buchanan Ingersoll, N.Y.C. Rsch. editor Bklyn. Law Rev., 1968, editor-in-chief, 1969. Mem. ABA (sect. on individual rights and responsibilities, franchise forum), ATLA, N.Y. State Bar Assn., Assn. Bar. City of N.Y. (com. on profl. discipline), Philonomic Honor Soc. Office: Buchanan Ingersoll PC 140 Broadway New York NY 10005 E-mail: scheimaner@bipc.com.

SCHEIN, VIRGINIA ELLEN, psychologist, editor; b. June 23, 1943; d. Jacob Charles and Anne Schein; m. Rupert F. Chisholm; 1 child, Alexander Nikos. BA cum laude, Cornell U., 1965; PhD, NYU, 1969. Lic. psychologist, Pa. Sr. rsch. assoc. Am. Mgmt. Assn., N.Y.C., 1969-70; mgr. personnel rsch. Life Office Mgmt. Assn., N.Y.C., 1970-72; dir. personnel rsch. Met. Life Ins. Co., N.Y.C., 1972-75; assoc. prof. Sch. Mgmt. Case Western Res. U., Cleve., 1975-76; vis. assoc. prof. Sch. Orgn. and Mgmt. Yale U., New Haven, 1977-80; mgmt. cons. Va. E. Schein, PhD, P.C., 1975—; assoc. prof. psychology Bernard M. Baruch Coll. CUNY, 1982-85; prof. mgmt. and psychology Gettysburg Coll., Pa., 1986—, chair mgmt. dept., 1993-95. Co-author: Power and Organization Development, 1988; author: Working from the Margins, 1995; mem. editl. rev. bds. Women Mgmt. Rev., Acad. Mgmt. Execs.; contbr. articles to profl. jours. Bd. dirs. Family Planning Ctr., 1988-91, Pvt. Industry Coun., 1990-93, Keystone Rsch. Ctr., 1996-98, Women Cmty. Svc., 1997-2003; bd. dirs. Survivors, Inc., pres. bd. dirs., 1991-92, Adams County Children and Youth Adv. Bd., 2003—. Mem.: APA (coun.rep. 1978—80, com. women 1980—83), Internat. Assn. Applied Psychology (divsn. orgnl. psychology chair sci. program com. 1995—98, pres.-elect 1998—2002, pres. 2002—), Acad. Mgmt. (rep. orgn.devel. divsn. 1979—81, exec. com. women mgmt. divsn.), Met. Assn. Applied Psychology (pres. 1973—74), Psi Chi. Office: Gettysburg Coll Dept Mgmt Gettysburg PA 17325 Office Phone: 717-337-6653.

SCHEINDLIN, RAYMOND PAUL, Hebrew literature educator, translator; b. Phila., May 13, 1940; s. Irving and Betty (Bernstein) S.; m. Shira Ann Joffe, 1969 (div. 1981); children— Dov Baer, Dahlia Rachel; m. Janice C. Meyerson, 1986. BA, U. Pa., 1961; M.H.L., Jewish Theol. Sem., N.Y.C., 1963; PhD, Columbia U., N.Y.C., 1971. Ordained rabbi, 1965. Asst. prof. McGill U., Montreal, Que., Can., 1969-72; asst. prof. Cornell U., Ithaca, N.Y., 1972-74; assoc. prof. Jewish Theol. Sem. of Am., N.Y.C., 1974-85, prof. Hebrew lit., 1985—, provost, 1984-90; dir. Shalom Spiegel Inst. of Medieval Hebrew Lit., 1996—; rabbi Congregation Baith Israel Anshei Emes, Bklyn., 1979-82. Mem. publ. com. Jewish Publ. Soc., Phila., 1985-90; mem. internat. adv. com. Ctr. for Judaic Studies U. Pa., 1995—; mem. bd. acad. advisors Catalan Mus. Jewish Culture, Gerona, Spain, 1993—; mem. editl. com. Jewish Quar. Rev., 1995—. Translator: (novella) Of Bygone Days by Mendele Mokher Seforim, 1973, Jewish Liturgy: A Comprehensive History by Ismar Elbogen, 1993; author: Form & Structure in the Poetry of Al-Mu'tamid Ibn 'Abbad, 1974, 201 Arabic Verbs, 1978, Wine, Women, and Death: Medieval Hebrew Poems on the Good Life, 1986, The Gazelle: Medieval Hebrew Poems on God, Israel and the Soul, 1991, Chronicles of the Jewish People, 1996, The Book of Job, 1998, A Short History of the Jewish People, 1998, (libretto) Miriam and the Angel of Death, 1984; mem. editl. com. Prooftexts, 1988—, Edebiyat, 1992—, Studies in Muslim-Jewish Rels., 1992—; mem. editl. bd. Arabic and Mid. Ea. Lits., Medieval Iberia; co-editor The Literature of Al-Andalus, 2000. Recipient Jewish Cultural Achievement award Nat. Found. for Jewish Culture, 2004; Guggenheim fellow, 1988, Annenberg Inst. fellow, 1993; sr. assoc. fellow Oxford Centre for Postgrad. Hebrew Studies. Fellow: Am. Acad. Jewish Rsch. (mem. exec. com. 2003—); mem.: PEN Am. Ctr., Jewish Publ. Soc. (bd. dirs. 1987—93), Assn. Jewish Studies, World Union Jewish Studies, Soc. Judeo-Arabic Studies. Home: 420 Riverside Dr New York NY 10025-7773 Office: Jewish Theol Sem Am 3080 Broadway New York NY 10027-4650 E-mail: ibngabirol@aol.com.

SCHEINER, JAMES IRA, engineering company executive; b. Mpls., May 7, 1944; s. Samuel L. and Sally Scheiner; m. Kristin Scofield; children: Alec, Zachary, Meredith. BS in Civil Engring., U.S. Mil. Acad., 1965; MPA, MCE,

Princeton U., 1967. Registered profl. engr., Pa. Cons., prin. transp. consulting divsn. Booz-Allen and Hamilton, 1971-79; dep. sec. adminstrn. Pa. Dept. Transp., 1979-83; sec. revenue Commonwealth of Pa., 1983-87; v.p. Huth Engrs., Inc., 1987-88; pres. Stoner Assocs., Inc., 1988-91; pres., COO Benatec Assocs., Inc., 1991—. Contbr. articles to profl. jours. Vice chair area bd. Leadership Harrisburg; group chair 1993 campaign cabinet capital region United Way; mem. Pa. Chamber Bus. and Industry Bd.; mem. Harsco Bd.; trustee Harrisburg Area C.C. Capt. CE, U.S. Army, Vietnam, 1967-71. Decorated Bronze Star, Purple Heart; recipient Disting. Svc. award Nat. Gov.'s Assn., 1986. Office: Benatec Assocs Capital City 200 Airport Dr New Cumberland PA 17070-2467

SCHEINFELD, JAMES DAVID, travel agency executive; b. Milw., Nov. 11, 1926; s. Aaron and Sylvia (Rosenberg) S.; children from previous marriage: John Stephen, Shaina, Robert Alan; m. Elna Magnusson, 1994. BA in Econs. magna cum laude, U. Wis., 1949. With Manpower, Inc., 1948-78, salesman, Chgo., 1949-51, br. mgr., 1951-53, nat. sales mgr., Milw., 1953-56, dir. sales, corp. sec., 1956-59, v.p. sales, 1959-62, exec. v.p. mktg., 1962-65, exec. v.p. (sr.), chief ops. officer, 1965-76, v.p. spl. projects, 1976-78, mem. exec. com., bd. dirs., 1959-76, cons., 1978-84; exec. v.p., chief exec. officer, bd. dirs. Transpersonal, Inc., Any Task Inc., Manpower Argentina, Manpower Europe, Manpower Ltd. (U.K.), Manpower Australia, Manpower Japan, Manpower Germany GmbH, Manpower Norway, Manpower Denmark, Manpower Venezuela, 1966-76; pres. Travway Internat. Inc. - Funway Holidays, Funjet, 1976-81, Aide Svcs., Inc., Tampa, Fla., 1976-81; pres., chief exec. officer Travelpower Inc., 1976-84; sr. v.p. Carlson Travel Network, 1984—. Mem. Hickory Travel Systems Inc., 1977-85, bd. dirs., 1978-85, pres., 1980-82, pres. emeritus, 1982—. Contbr. articles to profl. jours. Chmn. Cancer Crusade Milwaukee County, 1970; bd. dirs. Sinai-Samaritan Med. Ctr., Better Bus. Bur. Milw., 1979-90, Found. for Santa Barbara City Coll., 1989—, pres., 1996-2000; trustee U. Wis. Milw. Found., 1981-91, emeritus trustee, 1991—; mem. bus. adv. bd. U. Wis.-Milw., 1987—; chmn. bus. adv. bd. Santa Barbara City Coll., 1988-92; dir. Santa Barbara Trust for Hist. Preservation, 1995—, v.p., 1998-2004, pres. 2004-; mem. Greater Milw. Com., 1984-97; bd. dirs. Sasum Santa Barbara Med. Found. Clinic, 1989—. With USNR, 1944-46. Mem. Nat. Assn. Temporary Svcs. (pres. 1975-76, bd. dirs. 1969-77), Univ. Club Milw., La Cumbre Country Club (Santa Barbara), Rotary Club of Montecito Calif. Home and Office: 129 Rametto Rd Santa Barbara CA 93108-2317 E-mail: jimscheinfeld1@cox.net. *I do not often walk or look back where my footprints are. I prefer to walk that part of the beach I have never walked before. I am a person who thinks more about tomorrow than yesterday . . . more about what can be done than what has been done . . . more about challenges than accomplishments. Looking back is helpful only if I can find a sign to help me in my future.*

SCHEINHOLTZ, LEONARD LOUIS, lawyer; b. Pitts., June 2, 1927; s. Bernard A. and Marie (Getzel) S.; m. Joan R. Libenson, Aug. 16, 1953; children: Stuart, Nancy, Barry. BA, U. Pa., 1948, MA, 1949; LLB, Columbia U., 1953. Bar: Pa. 1954, U.S. Ct. Appeals (3d cir.) 1959, U.S. Ct. Appeals (6th cir.) 1968, U.S. Supreme Ct. 1972, U.S. Ct. Appeals (4th cir.) 1973, U.S. Ct. Appeals (5th cir.) 1981, U.S. Ct. Appeals (11th cir.) 1991, U.S. Ct. Appeals (2d cir.) 1993. Assoc. Reed, Smith, LLP, Pitts., 1953—62, spl. ptnr., 1962—64, gen. ptnr., 1964—97, head labor dept., 1980—86, of counsel, 1997—. Dir. Am. Arbitration Assn., N.Y.C., 1980-96. Author: Exemption Under the Anti-Trust Laws for Joint Employer Activity, 1982, The Arbitrator as Judge and Jury: Another Look at Statutory Law in Arbitration, 1985. Vice-chmn. Pa. AAA Fedn., Harrisburg, 1982-85; chmn. W. Pa. AAA Motor Club, 1979-82; trustee Montefiore Hosp., Pitts., 1976-79, Jewish Healthcare Found., 2004—; bd. dirs. Nat. Aviary, 1999—, United Jewish Fedn. Pitts., 1997-2000, Jewish Chronicle, Pitts., 1997-2003. With USN, 1945-46. Mem.: ABA, Allegheny County Bar Assn., Pa. Bar Assn. Republican. Jewish. Home: 746 Pinoak Rd Pittsburgh PA 15243-1153 Office: Reed Smith LLP Mellon Sq 435 6th Ave Pittsburgh PA 15219-1886 Office Phone: 412-288-3178. E-mail: leolen@adelphia.net.

SCHEINMAN, A. DANIEL, computer system networks executive; b. 1963; BA, Brandeis U.; JD, Duke U. Atty. Gray, Carey, Ware & Freidenrich, Palo Alto, Calif.; with Cisco Sys. Inc., San Jose, Calif., 1992—97, v.p., legal and govtl. affairs, 1997—2002, sr. v.p., corp. devel., 2002—. Bd. visitors Duke U. Law Sch. Office: Cisco Sys Inc 170 W Tasman Dr San Jose CA 95134*

SCHEINMAN, STANLEY BRUCE, international financial executive, lawyer; b. N.Y.C., Nov. 13, 1933; s. Samuel and Sadie (Seiffer) S.; m. Susan L. Elstein (dec.); m. Janet L. Donnely, Dec. 30, 1975 (dec.); children: Catherine Amy, Anthony Paul, Sarah Jean, Norah Jane; m. Maria Shea Burke, Nov. 17, 2000. AB, Cornell U., 1954; MBA, CCNY, 1957; JD (Harlan Fisk Stone scholar), Columbia U., 1960. Bar: N.Y. 1960. Assoc. firm Cravath, Swaine & Moore, N.Y.C., 1960-62; capital projects officer, legis. programs staff coord. AID, Washington, 1962-64; sr. exec. officer Bur. Pvt. Enterprise, AID, 1982-83; v.p. fin. and adminstrn. svcs. industries div., also v.p., counsel internat. div. PepsiCo. Inc., 1965-70; v.p. fin. and adminstrn. pharm. divsn. Revlon, Inc., 1970-72; sr. v.p. MCI Comm., 1972-76; pres., COO FSC Corp., Pitts., 1976-81; pres. New Venture Capital Corp., Washington, 1984-85; prin. Re Venture Assocs., Salisbury, Conn., 1985-86; chmn., CEO Internat. 800 Telcom Corp., Geneva, 1987-88; pres., CEO Zurich Depository Corp., Manhasset, N.Y., 1988-89; exec. v.p. AMIF&S Ltd., N.Y.C., 1989-91; pres. IT Svc. Corp., Westport, Conn., 1991-92; v.p. ops. and bus. devel. EQ Corp., Westport, 1992-95; exec. v.p., CFO, Computer Products and Svcs. Inc., Wilton, Conn., 1995-96; pres., mng. dir. TTC Internat. Ltd., London, 1996—. Mem.: ABA, Internat. Execs. Assn., Fin. Execs. Inst., Inst. for Dirs. (U.K.), Assn. Bar City NY, Brit.-Am. Club, Cornell Club, Fgn. Svc. Club, Paris-Am. Club. Home: 350 E 79th St Apt 33B New York NY 10021 Office: 43 Benbow House 24 New Globe Walk London SE1 9DS England

SCHEINMAN, STEVEN JAY, medical educator; b. Monticello, N.Y., Oct. 22, 1951; 2 children. AB summa cum laude, Amherst Coll., 1973; MD cum laude, Yale U., 1977. Diplomate Am. Bd. Internal Medicine in Neprology, lic. physician N.Y., Conn. Resident internal medicine Yale-New Haven Hosp., 1977-80; chief resident internal medicine Upstate Med. Ctr., Syracuse, N.Y., 1980-81, fellow nephrology, 1981-83, Yale-New Haven Hosp., 1983-84; asst. prof. medicine SUNY Upstate Med. U., Syracuse, 1984-90, asst. prof. pharmacology, 1988-90, assoc. prof. medicine and pharmacology, 1990-94, prof. medicine and pharmacology, 1994—, chief nephrology divsn. dept. medicine, 1994—2004, exec. v.p., dean Coll. Medicine, 2004—. Vis. scientist MRC Molecular Medicine Group, Royal Postgrad. Med. Sch. Hammersmith Hosp., London, 1992, London, 95; vis. scholar dept. biochemistry U. Oxford, 1985; attending physician U. Hosp., Syracuse, Crouse-Irving Meml. Hosp., Syracuse, VA Med. Ctr., Syracuse; dir. Nephrology Fellowship Program, 1993—; spkr. seminars, confs., orgns. Assoc. editor: Neph SAP, 2002—; contbr. Recipient Lange award, Yale U. Sch. Medicine, 1976, Resident Merit award, ACP (Conn. chpt.), 1980, Nat. Rsch. Svc. award, NIH, 1981—83, Clin. Investigator award, 1985—90, Charles R. Ross Rsch. award, SUNY-Health Sci. Ctr., 1992, Pres.'s award for Excellence and Leadership in Rsch., SUNY Upstate Med. U., 2001, Chancellor's Rsch. Recognition award, SUNY, 2002; grantee, Nat. Inst. Arthritis Diabetes Digestive and Kidney Diseases, 1981—83, 1985—90, 1995—2002, 2000—04, 2003—, Am. Heart Assn., 1985, 1988—90, 1990—91, 1992—95, 1995—97, NATO, 1995—98. Mem.: Assn. Subspecialty Profs., Nat. Kidney Found., Am. Heart Assn. Coun. on Kidney, Am. Soc. Bone and Mineral Rsch., Am. Physiol. Soc., Internat. Soc. Nephrology, Am. Soc. Nephrology (mem. editl. bd. Jour. 2000—02), Am. Fedn. Med. Rsch., Am. Soc. Clin. Investigation, Phi Beta Kappa. Home: 528 Plum St # 404 Syracuse NY 13204 Office: SUNY Upstate Med U 750 E Adams St Syracuse NY 13210-1834 Office Phone: 315-464-9720.

SCHEIRER, CURRY M, metrologist; b. Reading, Pa., Nov. 12, 1974; s. Barry and Maureen Scheirer; m. Melissa Dubble, Oct. 5, 1996; children: Allison, Emily. BS in physics, Kutztown U., 2000. Metrology engr. Agere Systems, Orlando, Fla., 1998—.

SCHEIRER, WILLIAM KENNETH, economist, consultant; b. Bethlehem, Pa., Oct. 17, 1937; s. Kenneth Raymond Scheirer and Pansy Elinor Ruch; m. Rita Gertrud Aase Simmersbach; children: Nicola, Erik, Peter, Karl. AB, Princeton U., 1959; student, London Sch. Econs., 1959—60, MIT, 1960—63. Sr. economist U.S. Small Bus. Adminstrn., Wash., 1980—95. Cons. Lehigh Valley Techonomics, Bethlehem, Pa., 1995—2004. Mem. editl. bd. Jour. Small Bus. Econs., 1988—93; contbr. chapters to books. Life mem., past pres. Kalorama Citizens Assn., 1968—; life mem. Com. 100 on Fed. City, Wash., 1999—. Mem.: Am. Econ. Assn., Torch Club. Avocation: reading. Home and Office: Lehigh Valley Techonomics 1890 Eaton Ave Bethlehem PA 18018 Office Phone: 610-954-9997. Personal E-mail: bethlehembill@hotmail.com.

SCHEIRING, MICHAEL JAMES, college official; b. Canton, Ohio, Oct. 11, 1949; s. Robert J. and Madonna L. (Geisigi) S.; m. Marcia L. Young, May 13, 1972; children: Kristy L., Lauren M. BA, Kent State U., 1971, MPA, 1972. Sect. supr. N.J. Dept. Treasury, Trenton, 1974-78; policy analyst to gov. Trenton, 1978-80; dir. adminstrn. N.J. Dept. Community Affairs, Trenton, 1980-82; dir. corp. budgeting N.J. Transit Corp., Newark, 1982-83; v.p. adminstrn. and fin. Thomas A. Edison Coll., Trenton, 1983—; exec. dir. Gov. Mgmt. Rev. Com., Gov.'s Office, Trenton, N.J., 1990-93. Trustee N.J. Ednl. Computer Corp., 1984-90; trustee, comptroller Edison Found., Trenton, 1984—; mem. adv. bd. National Ctr. Productivity; pres. U.D. Dollars for Scholars Found.; chmn. Trenton Audit Commn.; mem. citizen's delegation to China; trustee Robert Wood Johnson U. Hosp. Hamilton. Contbg. author: N.J. Zero-Based Budgeting, 1979. Named Vol. of Yr. N.J. United Cerebral Palsy. Mem. ASPA (nat. coun., v.p. programs 1984, v.p. membership 1985, pres. 1987-89), Old Barracks Assn. (trustee, pres.), Rotary (pres.). Roman Catholic. Home: 2 Lotus Ln Trenton NJ 08648-3211 Office: Thomas Edison State Coll Trenton NJ 08625

SCHEKMAN, RANDY W. molecular biology administrator, biochemist; b. St. Paul, Dec. 30, 1948; married, 1973; 1 child. BA, UCLA, 1970; PhD in Biochemistry, Stanford U., 1975; PhD (hon.), U. Geneva, 1997. Fellow U. Calif., San Diego, 1974-76, from asst. to assoc. prof. Berkeley, 1976-83, prof., 1983—, head divsn. biochemistry and molecular biology, 1990-97, co-chair dept. molecular and cellular biology, 1997—. Fellow Woodrow Wilson Found., 1970, Cystic Fibrosis Found., 1974, John S. Guggenheim Found., 1982-83; recipient Research award in microbiology & immunology, Eli Lilly, 1987, Lewis S. Rosenstiel award in basic biomedical sci., 1994, Gairdner Found. Internat. award, 1996, Albert Lasker award for basic med. rsch., Albert and Mary Lasker Found., 2002, Louisa Gross Horwtiz prize, Columbia U., 2002; named Amgen award lecturer, Protein Soc., 1999, Berkeley Faculty Rsch. lecturer, U. Calif., 1999. Mem. Am. Soc. Microbiology, Am. Soc. Biochemists & Molecular Biologists, Am. Acad. of Arts & Sciences (elected 2000), NAS (elected 1992); hon. mem. Japanese Biochemical Soc.; foreign assoc. EMBO. Achievements include research on molecular mechanism of secretion and membrane assembly in eucaryotic cells. Office: U Calif Dept Molecular Cell Bio 401 Barker Hall Spc 3202 Berkeley CA 94720-3202*

SCHELAR, VIRGINIA MAE, chemistry consultant; b. Kenosha, Wis., Nov. 26, 1924; d. William and Blanche M. (Williams) S. BS, U. Wis., 1947, MS, 1953; MEd, Harvard U., 1962; PhD, U. Wis., 1969. Instr. U. Wis., Milw., 1947-51; info. specialist Abbott Labs., North Chgo., Ill., 1953-56; instr. Wright Jr. Coll., Chgo., 1957-58; asst. prof. No. Ill. U., DeKalb, 1958-63; prof. St. Petersburg (Fla.) Jr. Coll., 1965-67; asst. prof. Chgo. State Coll., 1967-68; prof. Grossmont Coll., El Cajon, Calif., 1968-80; cons. Calif., 1981—. Author: Kekule Centennial, 1965; contbr. articles to profl. jours. Active citizens adv. coun. DeKalb Consol. Sch. Bd.; voters svc. chair League Women Voters, del. to state and nat. convs., judicial chair, election laws chair. Standard Oil fellow, NSF grantee; recipient Lewis prize U. Wis. Fellow Am. Inst. Chemists; mem. Am. Chem. Soc. (membership affairs com., chmn. western councilor's caucus, exec. com., councilor, legis. counselor, chmn. edn. com., editor state and local bulletins). Avocations: swimming, folk dancing.

SCHELBERT, HEINRICH RUEDIGER, nuclear medicine physician; b. Wuerzburg, Germany, Nov. 5, 1939; MD, U. Würzburg (Germany), 1964. Diplomate Am. Bd. Nuclear Medicine. Intern Mercy Med. Ctr., Phila., 1966-67, resident, 1967-68, 70-71; resident in cardiology U. Dusseldorf, Germany, 1971-72; fellow in cardiology, resident in nuclear medicine U. Calif., San Diego, 1968-69, asst. rsch. cardiologist, 1972-75, assoc. rsch. radiologist, 1975-76; hosp. assoc. UCLA Med. Ctr., 1977—; prof. radiol. scis. UCLA Sch. Medicine, 1980-90, prof. pharmacol. and radiol. scis., 1993—. Editor-in-chief: Jour. Nuc. Medicine, 2004. Recipient Georg von Hevesy prize 2d Internat. Congress World Fedn. Nuclear Medicine and Radiation Biology, 1978, 3d Internat. Congress World Fedn. Nuclear Medicine and Radiation Biology, 1982. Fellow Am. Coll. Cardiology; mem. Am. Heart Assn. (disting. scientific achievement award 1989), Soc. Nuclear Medicine (Herrman L. Blumgart pioneer lectr. award 1989, George De Hevesy Nuclear Medicine Pioneer award 1998), German Soc. Nuc. Med. (hon.), Swiss Soc. Nuc. Medicine (hon.; editor-in-chief). Office: UCLA Sch Medicine Dept Molecular Med B2-985J Box 956948 Los Angeles CA 90095-6948

SCHELD, WILLIAM MICHAEL, internist, educator; b. Middletown, Conn., Aug. 15, 1947; s. William Herman and Lucille Laverne (Houchens) S.; m. Susan Ella Vaughan, June 14, 1969; 1 child, Sarah Walker. BS, Cornell U., 1969, MD, 1973. Diplomate Am. Bd. Internal Medicine. Intern, then resident U. Va. Sch. Medicine, Charlottesville, 1973-76, fellow in infectious diseases, 1976-79, asst. prof., 1979-82, assoc. prof., 1982-88, prof., assoc. chair dept. infectious diseases, 1988—. Chair Inter-sci. Conf. on Antimicrobial Agents and Chemotherapy. Editor: Infections of the Central Nervous System, 1991, 97; contbr. sci. articles to profl. publs., chpts. to books. Fellow ACP, Infectious Diseases Soc. Am. (pres. 2002-2003); mem. Am. Soc. Clin. Investigation, Nat. Found. Infectious Diseases (pres. elect), Alpha Omega Alpha. Achievements include research on meningitis and other central nervous system infections, bacterial endocarditis, sepsis, etc. Home: 2075 Earlysville Rd Earlysville VA 22936-9634 Office: U Va Health Systems Box 801392 Charlottesville VA 22908

SCHELER, BRAD ERIC, lawyer; b. Bklyn., Oct. 11, 1953; s. Bernard and Rita Regina (Miller) S.; m. Amy Ruth Frolick, Mar. 30, 1980; children: Ali M., Maddie H., Zoey B. BA with high honors, Lehigh U., 1974; JD, Hofstra U., 1977. Bar: N.Y. 1978, U.S. Dist. Ct. (so. and ea. dists.) N.Y. 1978. Assoc. Weil, Gotshal & Manges, N.Y.C., 1977-81; sr. ptnr., chmn. bankruptcy and restructuring practice Fried, Frank, Harris, Shriver & Jacobson, LLP, N.Y.C., 1981—. Contbg. author: Collier on Bankruptcy, 15th edit. revised, Annual Survey of Bankruptcy Law; rsch. editor Hofstra U. Law Rev., 1975-77. Treas., bus. mgr. Trustees of Gramercy Park, N.Y.C., 1979-87. Fellow Am. Coll. Bankruptcy; mem. ABA (bus. bankruptcy com. corp. banking and bus. law sect., creditors' rights com. litig. sect.), N.Y. State Bar Assn., Assn. Bar City of N.Y. (com. on bankruptcy and corp. reorgn. 1991-94), Sigma Alpha Mu (v.p. 1973). Jewish. Home: 94 Larchmont Ave Larchmont NY 10538-3723 Office: Fried Frank Harris 1 New York Plz Fl 23 New York NY 10004-1901 E-mail: Schelbr@ffhsj.com.

SCHELL, ALLAN CARTER, retired electrical engineer; b. New Bedford, Mass., Apr. 14, 1934; s. Charles Carter and Elizabeth Schell; m. Shirley T. Sardineer; children: Alice Rosalind, Cynthia Anne. BS, MSE.E., MIT, 1956, Sc.D., 1961; student, Tech. U. Delft, Netherlands, 1956-57. Research physicist Air Force Cambridge Research Labs., Bedford, Mass., 1956-76, Guenter Loeser Meml. lectr., 1965; dir. electromagnetics directorate Rome Air Devel. Ctr., Bedford, 1976-87; chief scientist Hdqrs. USAF Systems Command, 1987-92; chief scientist, dep. dir. sci. and tech. Hdqrs. USAF Materiel Command, 1992-94. Dir. Electro; vis. assoc. prof. MIT, 1974; chair dept. of elec. engring. adv. coun. U. Pa., 1992-94. Contbr. articles to profl. jours.; patentee in field (9). Lt. USAF, 1958—60. Recipient Fulbright award, 1956-57, Meritorious Exec. award U.S. Govt., 1989; NSF fellow, 1955-56, 60-61. Fellow IEEE (bd. dirs. 1981-82, editor IEEE Press 1976-79, Procs. of IEEE 1990-92), Antennas and Propagation Soc. of IEEE (pres. 1978, editor tran. 1969-71, John T. Bolljahn award 1966), Internat. Sci. Radio Union, Sigma Xi, Tau Beta Pi. E-mail: a.schell@ieee.org.

SCHELL, BRAXTON, lawyer; b. Raleigh, NC, Feb. 24, 1924; s. Marshall H. and Margaret (Newsom) S.; m. Ann Cooper Knight, Mar. 30, 1951 (div. 1982); children: Braxton, Richard Knight, James Gray (dec.); m. Mary Rehill, Apr. 16, 1983. Student, N.C. State Coll., 1942-43; BS, U. N.C., 1948, JD with honors, 1951. Bar: N.C. 1951. Since practiced in, Greensboro; assoc. Smith, Moore, Smith & Pope, Greensboro, 1951-56; ptnr. Smith Moore Smith Schell & Hunter, Greensboro, 1956-85, Smith, Helms, Mullis, and Moore, 1986-87, Schell, Bray, Aycock, Abel & Livingston, 1987—. Gen. counsel, dir. Flagler Sys. and The Breakers Palm Beach, Inc. Assoc. editor: N.C. Law Rev. 1950-51. Chmn. Special Liason Tax Com. Southeastern Region, 1960-61; bd. dirs. N.C. Outward Bound Sch., 1975-88, chmn., 1977-80; trustee Outward Bound, Inc., 1978-81; bd. dirs. William R. Kenan Funds for Pvt. Enterprise, Arts and Engring., Tech. and Sci. and Ethics. Pilot USAAF, 1943-45. Fellow Am. Bar Found.; mem. ABA, N.C. Bar Assn., Greensboro Bar Assn., Order of Coif, Figure Eight Island Yacht Club, Greensboro Country Club (pres. 1971-72), Greensboro City Club (dir. 1980—), Phi Beta Kappa. Presbyterian. Home: 422B Fisher Park Cir Greensboro NC 27401-1615 Office: Schell Bray Aycock Abel & Living 1500 Renaissance Pla Greensboro NC 27420 Business E-Mail: bschell@sbaal.com.

SCHELL, GEORGE AARON, lawyer; b. Waco, Tex., May 11, 1939; s. George Alvin and Jessie Lee S.; m. Anne, 1960 (div. 1973); 1 child, Michael. BA, Baylor U., 1961, MA, 1963; JD, Loyola U., 1977; MS, Calif. State U., 1990. Bar: Calif. Prof. speech, comm. & debate Loyola Marymount U., L.A., 1963-77; pub. defender Plumas County, Quincy, Calif., 1978-80; deputy city atty. City of L.A., 1977-78, 81—. Office: LA City Atty 6262 Van Nuys Blvd Ste 160 Van Nuys CA 91401-2647 E-mail: gschell@atty.lacity.org.

SCHELL, JAMES MUNSON, financial executive; b. Kalamazoo, Mich., Mar. 25, 1944; s. Frank John and Shirley I. S.; m. Susan O'Laughlin, Aug. 6, 1966; children: Karen, Michael, Ryan. BA, Vanderbilt U., 1966; MBA, Washington U., 1968. Dir. term and internat. financing Chrysler Fin. Corp., Troy, Mich., 1976-79, v.p., treas., 1980-81; v.p. domestic treasury Am. Express Co., N.Y.C., 1981-82; v.p. fin. resources Hertz Corp., N.Y.C., 1982-83; v.p., chief fin. officer Clabir Corp., Greenwich, Conn., 1983-84; v.p., treas. Fairchild Industries, 1985-87; ind. fin. cons., 1987—. Bd. dirs. Jackson-Jordan Corp., CTI Industries, Country Home Bakers. Republican. Roman Catholic. Home: 40 Stony Brook Rd Darien CT 06820-4326 E-mail: jmsschell@aol.com.

SCHELL, KRAIG LEE, psychologist, educator; b. Cortez, Colo., Sept. 26, 1970; s. Gary Lee and Diana Charlene Schell; m. Paulette R. Barnes-Schell; 1 child, Samantha Marie. BS in Psychology, Okla. Christian U., 1992; MS in Psychology, U. Ctrl. Okla., 1995; PhD in Psychology, U. Cin., 2000. Prof. psychology Angelo State U., San Angelo, Tex., 2000—. Cons. McKesson Pharm., Montreal, Quebec, Canada, 2001—. Editor: (continuing education modules) On-line Contg. Ed. Series for Pharmacy. Bd. dirs. Goodwill Industries, San Angelo, 2000—03. Grantee, Nat. Assn. Chain Drug Stores, 1999. Mem.: Soc. Indsl. Orgnl. Psychologists, Am. Psychol. Soc. Independent. Avocations: music, computers, sports. Office: Angelo State Univ ASU Station #10907 San Angelo TX 76909 Business E-Mail: kraig.schell@angelo.edu.

SCHELL, LAWRENCE M. education educator, biologist; PhD, U. of Pa, 1973—80; MA, Temple U., 1972. Writer Plimoth Plantation, Mass., 1971—72; prof. SUNY at Albany, 1979—, assoc. dean for rsch. Coll. Arts & Scis., 2003—. Editor: Urbanism, Health and Human Biology in Industrialised Countries, Urban Ecology and Health in the Third World. Grantee Mohawk culture, behavior, toxicant exposure and health., NIH, 2000-2005, PCB's and the well being of Mohawk children and youth, 1995-2000, Blood lead in pregnancy/infancy and infant devel., 1992-1998. Fellow: Soc. for Applied Anthropology, Human Biology Assn.; mem.: Internat. Assn. for Human Auxology (exec. bd. 1998—), European Anthrop. Assn. (local treas. (u.s.) 1994—2002), Soc. for Pediatric and Perinatal Reserach, Am. Assn. of Phys. Anthropologists, Soc. for the Study of Human Biology (north am. secretary-treasurer 1985—95). Achievements include research in Use of child growth monitoring for detection of community health effects from toxic exposures. Office: A&S 237 University at Albany, SUNY 1400 Washington Avenue Albany NY 12222 Office Phone: 518-442-5761. E-mail: l.schell@albany.edu.

SCHELL, NORMAN BARNETT, preventive medicine physician, consultant; b. N.Y.C., May 25, 1925; s. Jack and Ada Sylvia (Rosen) S.; m. Lila Barbara Mendelsohn, Aug. 27, 1950; children: Martin, Judith, Steven. AB cum laude, NYU, 1946, MD, 1950; MPH, Harvard U., 1971. Diplomate Am. Bd. Pediats., Am. Bd. Preventive Medicine, Nat. Bd. Med. Examiners; lic. physician, N.Y. Rotating intern Beth Israel Hosp., N.Y.C., 1950-51; asst. resident in pediats. Mt. Sinai Hosp., N.Y.C., 1951-52; clin. fellow in pediats. N.Y.-Cornell Med. Ctr., N.Y.C., 1952-53; pvt. practice Jericho and Hicksville, N.Y., 1956-69; pub. health physician Nassau County Health Dept., Mineola, N.Y., 1969-76, dep. commr., 1976-90. Asst. prof. preventive medicine SUNY, Stony Brook, 1974-90; pediat. cons. N.Y. State Health Dept., 1956-69, HEW Project Head Start, N.Y.C., 1968-75; emeritus pediat. staff Nassau County Med. Ctr. Author: Keys to Childhood Illnesses, 1992; contbr. articles to profl. jours. Lt. M.C., USN, 1953-55, capt. M.C., USNR, 1981-85. Recipient Physician Recognition award AMA, 1970, Grade 1A Health Officer N.Y. State Health Dept., 1973. Fellow Am. Acad. Pediats. (com. on sch. health 1971-77, citation com. on med. edn. 1977), Am. Coll. Preventive Medicine, N.Y. Acad. Medicine; mem. Am. Coll. Legal Medicine (assoc.), Nassau County Med. Soc. (chmn. sch. health com.), Harvard Club N.Y.C., West Point Club, Phi Beta Kappa. Avocations: photography, classical music, computer technology. Home and Office: 63 Birchwood Park Dr Jericho NY 11753-2238

SCHELL, PAUL E.S. former mayor; b. Fort Dodge, Iowa, Oct. 8, 1937; m. Pam Schell. BA, U. Iowa, 1960; JD, Columbia U., 1963. Pvt. practice, 1963-74; dir. dept. cmty. devel. City of Seattle, 1974-77, mayor, 1998—2001; pres., founder Cornerstone Columbia Devel. Co., 1979-87; commr. Port of Seattle, 1989-99, pres. commn., 1995-99; dean Architecture and Urban Planning U. Wash., 1992-95; strategic adv. & bus. developer NBBJ Archtl. Firm, Seattle, 2001—. Past bd. dirs. Intiman Theatre, A Contemporary Theater; past pres. Allied Arts; founder, active Cascadia Project; bd. dirs. Trade Devel. Alliance; mem. Friends of the Pike Place Market; sr. adv. & bd. mem. Columbia Hospitality, Seattle. Office: NBBJ 111 S Jackson St Seattle WA 98104: Columbia Hospitality 2205 Alaskan Way Seattle WA 98121

SCHELLENBERGER, ROBERT EARL, retired management educator and department chairman; b. Janesville, Wis., July 25, 1932; s. Ervin William and Adelaide Louise (Keller) S.; m. Linda Eula Todd, Dec. 30, 1961; children: Brian T., Keith W., Heidi L. BSBA, U. Wis., 1958, MBA, 1959; PhD, U. N.C., 1963. Personnel supr. Libby McNeill and Libby, Janesville, Wis., 1957-58; from asst. prof. to assoc. prof. chmn. div. stats. dept. bus U. Md., College Park, 1963-68; chair dept. mgmt. So. Ill. U., Carbondale, Ill., 1968-70, dir. planning Sch. Human Resources Devel., 1970-71, prof. mgmt., 1968-71; vis. prof., dir. program evaluation Babcock Grad. Sch. Mgmt., Wake Forest U., Winston-Salem, N.C., 1971-73; prof. dept. mgmt. Temple U., Phila., 1973-81, from chmn. dept. mgmt. to asst. to acad. vice chancellor, 1975-77; prof. decision scis. dept. East Carolina U., Greenville, N.C., 1981-2000, chmn. decision scis. dept., 1989-95; ret., 2001. Pres. Md. Rsch. and Cons., Hyattsville, 1964-67; v.p. Ea. Acad. Mgmt., 1967; cons. Comml. Credit Corp., Balt., 1966. Author: Managerial Analysis, 1967, Policy Formulation, 1978, 2d edit., 1982; co-editor Jour. of Econs. and Bus., 1976; developer (software package) MANYSYM, 1965, 68, 78, 82, 86. Chmn. Utilities Com., Carbondale, 1970-72. Title IV NDEA fellow U. N.C., 1960-62, Earhart Jr. fellow U. Wis. Mem. Assn. for Bus. Simulation, SE Decision Scis. Inst., Decision Scis. Inst. (bd. dirs. 1974-77), Beta Gamma Sigma.

SCHELLER, RICHARD H. physiologist, science educator; b. Milw., Oct. 30, 1953; BA in Biochemistry with honors, U. Wis., 1975; PhD in Chemistry, Calif. Inst. Tech., 1980. Postdoctoral fellow divsn. biology Calif. Inst. Tech., 1980—81; postdoctoral fellow in molecular neurobiology Columbia U. Coll. Physicians and Surgeons, 1981—82; asst. prof. dept. biol. scis. Stanford (Calif.) U., 1982—87, assoc. prof. dept. biol. scis., 1987—90, assoc. prof.

dept. molecular and cellular physiology, 1990—93, assoc. prof. dept. biol. scis. by courtesy, 1990—93, prof. dept. molecular and cellular physiology, 1993—, prof. dept. biol. scis., 1993; assoc. investigator Howard Hughes Med. Inst., Stanford U. Med. Ctr., 1990—94, investigator, 1994—. Mem. molecular, cellular and devel. neurobiology rev. com. NIMH, 1993—96; mem. sci. adv. bd. Hereditary Disease Found., 1995—96; mem. neurobiology adv. bd. Cold Spring Harbor Lab., 1995; mem. sr. rev. com. McKnight Endowment Fund, 1995; mem. Nat. Adv. Mental Health Coun., 1996. Mem. editl. bd. Jour. Neurosci., 1984—90, DNA, 1984—, Ann. Rev. Neurosci., 1985—90, Molecular Brain Rsch., 1985, Cellular and Molecular Neurobiology, 1986, Synapse, 1989—91, Neuron, 1990, Current Opinion in Neurobiology, 1990, sect. editor Jour. Neurosci., 1991—95, monitoring editor Jour. Cell Biology, 1991, assoc. editor Genes to Cells, 1995; contbr. articles to profl. jours. Recipient Basil O'Connor award, March of Dimes Found., 1983, Presdl. Young Investigator award, 1985, Alan T. Waterman award, NSF, 1989, Merit award, NIMH, 1992, W. Alden Spencer award, Columbia U., 1993, award in molecular biology, NAS, 1997; fellow, NIH, 1976—80, 1981—82, Alfred P. Sloan Found., 1984, Klingstein fellow in Neurosci., 1985; scholar, McKnight Found., 1983, Pew scholar in biomed. scis., 1986, Camile and Henry Dreyfus Tchr. scholar, 1986. Mem.: Soc. for Neurosci. (young investigator award selection com. 1996). Office: Stanford U Med Ctr Mailcode 5428 B 155 Beckman Ctr Stanford CA 94305-5345

SCHELLHAMMER, RICHARD CHARLES, historian; b. Hartford, Conn., Jan. 22, 1961; s. Charles and Patricia Schellhammer; m. Mary Lynn Sweetapple, Aug. 12, 1983; children: Mary, Rebecca, Patricia. BA, Pa. State U., University Park, 1981—84; MA, U. Chgo., 1984—85; PhD, U. S.C., Columbia, 1986—93. Assoc. prof., history U. W. Ala., Livingston, 1994—. Contbr. articles to profl. jours. Youth coord. Knights of Columbus, Tuscaloosa, Ala., 1997—2004. Sasakawa Fellowship, Am. Assn. State Colls. & Univs., 2002. Mem.: Am. Hist. Assn., So. Hist. Assn., So. Conf. on Brit. Studies, Sumter County Hist. Assn., Phi Alpha Theta (faculty advisor 2002—04). Office: Univ W Ala Station 22 Livingston AL 35470 E-mail: rcs@uwa.edu.

SCHELLING, THOMAS CROMBIE, economist, educator; b. Oakland, Calif., Apr. 14, 1921; s. John M. and Zelda M. (Ayres) S.; m. Corinne T. Saposs, Sept. 13, 1947 (div. 1991); children: Andrew, Thomas, Daniel, Robert; m. Alice M. Coleman, Nov. 8, 1991. AB, U. Calif., Berkeley, 1943; PhD, Harvard U., 1951. U.S. govt. economist, Copenhagen, Paris, Washington, 1948-53; prof. econs. Yale U., 1953-58, Harvard U., Cambridge, Mass., 1958-90; prof. econs. and pub. affairs U. Md., College Park, 1990—2003, disting. univ. prof., 1990—2003. Sr. staff mem. RAND Corp., 1958-59; chmn. rsch. adv. bd. Com. Econ. Devel., 1978-81, 84-85; mem. sci. adv. bd. USAF, 1960-64, def. sci. bd., 1966-70; mem. mil. econ. adv. panel CIA, 1980-85; trustee Aerospace Corp., 1984-93. Author: National Income Behavior, 1951, International Economics, 1958, The Strategy of Conflict, 1960, Arms and Influence, 1966, Micromotives and Macrobehavior, 1978, Choice and Consequence, 1984; co-author: Strategy and Arms Control, 1961. Recipient Frank E. Seidman Disting. award in polit. economy, 1977. Fellow Am. Acad. Arts and Scis., AAAS, Assn. for Pub. Policy Analysis and Mgmt., Am. Econ. Assn. (pres. 1991, Disting. mem. award); mem. NAS (rsch. award 1993), Inst. Medicine, Ea. Econ. Assn. (pres. 1996). Office: Univ Md Sch Pub Affairs College Park MD 20742-0001 E-mail: tschelli@mail.umd.edu.

SCHELLMAN, JOHN A. chemistry professor; b. Phila., Oct. 24, 1924; s. John and Mary (Mason) S.; m. Charlotte Green, Feb. 10, 1954; children: Heidi M., Lise C. AB, Temple U., 1948; MS, Princeton U., 1949, PhD, 1951, Chalmers U., Sweden, 1983, U. Padua, Italy, 1990. USPHS postdoctoral fellow U. Utah, 1951-52, Carlsberg Lab., Copenhagen, 1953-55; DuPont fellow U. Minn., Mpls., 1955-56, asst. prof. chemistry, 1956-58; assoc. prof. chemistry Inst. Molecular Biology, U. Oreg., Eugene, 1958-63, prof. chemistry, rsch. assoc., 1963—. Vis. Lab. Chem. Physics, Nat. Inst. Arthritis and Metabolic Diseases, NIH, Bethesda, Md., 1980; vis. prof. Chalmers U., 1986, U. Padua, 1987. Contbr. articles to profl. jours. Served with U.S. Army, 1943-46. Fellow Rask-Oersted Found., 1954, Sloan Found., 1959-63, Guggenheim Found., 1969-70. Fellow Am. Phys. Soc., Biophys. Soc.; mem. NAS, Am. Chem. Soc., Am. Soc. Biochemistry and Molecular Biology, Am. Acad. Arts and Scis., Phi Beta Kappa, Sigma Xi. Democrat. Home: 65 W 30th Ave #508 Eugene OR 97405-3373 Office: Univ Oreg Inst Molecular Biology Eugene OR 97403 Office Phone: 541-346-6093. Business E-Mail: john@molbio.uoregon.edu.

SCHELM, ROGER LEONARD, information systems specialist; b. Kingston, N.Y., July 29, 1936; s. Frederick G. and Elizabeth M. (Wojciehowski) S.; m. Gloria Mae Dutterer, June 13, 1958; children: Sandra Lee Kern, Theresa Jean Sollitto, Ginger Lisa Shah. BA in Polit. Sci., Western Md. Coll., 1958; MA in Pub. Adminstrn., Am. U., 1970; postgrad., U. Md., 1960-62. Analytic equipment programmer Nat. Security Agy., Ft. Meade, Md., 1958-60; computer cons. various cons. firms Balt., 1960-68, Washington, 1960—68; mgr. army plans and programs Informatics Inc., Bethesda, Md., 1968; mgr. def. programs Automation Tech. Inc., Wheaton, 1968-69; dir. advanced planning Genasys Corp., Washington, 1969-71; mgr. info. systems Ins. Co. North Am., Phila., 1971-72, sect. mgr. computing ops., 1972-74; mgr. tech. services INA Corp., 1974-75; mem. spl. tech. projects INA Corp. merger with Conn. Gen. Ins. Co. to form CIGNA Corp. 1982, 1975-76, asst. dir. tech. services, 1977, asst. dir. spl. tech. projects, 1977-78, asst. dir. adminstrn., 1978-79, asst. dir. resource mgmt., data ctr. design, contingency planning, 1979-80; dir. corp. info. tech. now CIGNA Corp., 1981-82, dir. planning and control ops. div., 1982-83, v.p. strategic planning, systems div., 1983-84, v.p. applied research/expert systems, systems div., 1984-92; co-founder, pres. Schelm Internat., Inc., Cherry Hill, NJ, 1992—2002. Mem. adj. faculty Camden Coll., N.J., 1978-82; mem. Camden County EDP Adv. Com., 1980-82; mem. faculty Drexel U., Phila., 1983-95. Author: Ednl. Computer mag., 1982; mem. editl. adv. bd., author Small Sys. World mag., 1982-84; mem. editl. adv. bd. Spang-Robinson Report, 1986-87, Machine Intelligence News, 1987-93, AI Expert mag., 1985-88; cons. editor Expert Sys. Jour., 1987-91. Tech. advisor various sch. bds., colls., univs. and non-profit orgns. Served to capt. U.S. Army, 1959. Mem. Am. Assn. Artificial Intelligence, Assn. Computing Machinery (founder Delaware Valley chpt. vice. chmn., program chmn. 1983-84, chmn. 1984-85, founder Del. Valley Spl. Interest Group in Artificial Intelligence, 1985, vice chmn. 1985-87), World Future Soc. Home: 506 Balsam Rd Cherry Hill NJ 08003-3202

SCHELP, RICHARD HERBERT, mathematics professor; b. Kansas City, Mo., Apr. 21, 1936; s. Herbert and Ida Louise Schelp; m. Billie Marie Schelp, Dec. 20, 1958; children: Lisa Marie Martin, Richard John. BS in Math. and Physics, Ctrl. Mo. U., 1959; MS in Math., Kans. State U., 1961, PhD in Math., 1970. Assoc. mathematician applied physics lab. Johns Hopkins U., 1961-66; instr. math. Kans. State U., 1966-70; asst. prof. math. U. Memphis, 1970-74, assoc. prof. math., 1974-79, prof. math., 1979—2001, prof. emeritus, 2001—. Chair spl. session Fifth Hungarian Combinatorics Conf., Keszthely, Hungary, 1976, First Japan Conf. Graph Theory and Application, 1986, First China-USA Conf. on Graph and Applications, 1986, Seventh Hungarian Combinatorics, Eger, 1987; chair session Probabilistic Workshop, Budapest, Hungary, 1998; vis. rschr. Hungarian Acad. Scis.-Math. Inst., 1985, 90, Lab. Rsch. and Info., U. Paris-Sud, 1993, Hungarian Acad. Scis.-Computer and Automation Inst., 1994; presenter in field. Mem. editl. bd. Jour. Graph Theory, 1981—, co-mng. editor, 1981-86; reviewer Math. Revs.; contbr. more than 130 articles to profl. jours. Named Outstanding Educators Am., 1975; recipient Disting. Alumnus award, Kans. St. U, 1999—2000, Bd. Visitors Eminent Faculty award, U. Memphis, 2001; fellow NSF, U. Mass., summer, 1968; grantee Internat. Rsch. and Exch. (travel), 1985, 1990, NSF, 1986—87, 1992—95, Nat. Security Agy., 1988—91. Mem. Am. Math. Soc. (organizer spl. session 1997), Math. Assn. Am., Inst. for Combinatorics and its Applications, N.Y. Acad. Sci. Home: 355 Leonora Dr Memphis TN 38117-2102 Office: Dept Math Scis Univ Memphis Memphis TN 38152-0001 E-mail: rschelp@memphis.edu.

SCHELSKE, CLAIRE L. limnologist, educator; b. Fayetteville, Ark., Apr. 1, 1932; s. Theodore J. and Ida S. S.; m. Betty Breukelman, June 2, 1957; children: Cynthia, John, Steven. AB, Kans. State Tchrs. Coll., Emporia, 1955, MS, 1956; PhD, U. Mich., 1961. Tchg. and rsch. asst. dept. biology Kans. State Tchrs. Coll., 1952-55, vis. instr., summer 1960; teaching fellow dept. zoology U. Mich., 1955-57; asst. prof. radiol. health dept. environ. health U. Mich. (Sch. Public Health); asst. research limnologist Gt. Lakes Research Div., Inst. Sci. and Tech., 1967-68, assoc. rsch. limnologist, 1969-71, rsch. limnologist, 1971-87; asst. dir. Gt. Lakes Research Div., Inst. Sci. and Tech. (Gt. Lakes Research Div.), 1970-72, acting dir., 1973-76, assoc. prof. limnology, dept. atmospheric and oceanic sci., 1976-87; assoc. prof. natural resources Sch. Natural Resources, 1976-86, prof., 1986-87; Carl S. Swisher prof. water resources U. Fla., Gainesville, 1987-2000, eminent scholar emeritus, 2001—. Research fellow Inst. Fisheries Research, Mich. Dept. Conservation, 1957-60; research assoc. U. Ga. Marine Inst., 1960-62; fishery biologist, supervisory fishery biologist, chief Estuarine Ecology Program, Bur. Comml. Fisheries, Radiobiol. Lab., Beaufort, N.C., 1962-66; adj. asst. prof. dept. zoology N.C. State U., Raleigh, 1964-66; tech. asst. Office Sci. and Tech., Exec. Office of Pres., Washington, 1966-67; cons. Ill. Atty. Gen., 1977-79; eminent scholar emer., 2001. Author: (with J.C. Roth) Limnological Survey of Lakes Michigan, Superior, Huron and Erie, 1973. Recipient Disting. Alumnus award Emporia State U. (formerly Kans. State Tchrs. Coll.), 1989, Edward S. Deevey Award for Outstanding Sci. Achievement, Fla. Lake Mgmt. Soc., 2000. Fellow: AAAS, Am. Inst. Fishery Rsch. Biologists (regional and dist. dir. South-Ctrl. Gt. Lakes chpt. 1977—80); mem.: Soc. Internat. Limnology (nat. rep. 1998), Internat. Assn. Gt. Lakes Rsch. (editl. bd. 1970—73, chmn. 20th Conf. 1977, assoc. editor 1984—93), Ecol. Soc. Am. (assoc. editor 1972—75), Am. Soc. Limnology and Oceanography (sec. 1976—85, v.p. 1987—88, pres. 1988—90, Ruth Patrick award for sci. problem solving 2003). Home: 2738 SW 9th Dr Gainesville FL 32601-9003 Office: Dept Geol Sci Land Use and Environ Change Inst PO Box 112120 Gainesville FL 32611 E-mail: schelsk@ufl.edu.

SCHEMAN, L. RONALD, lawyer, professional society administrator; b. Aug. 9, 1931; s. Mac and Eleanor (Minkowitz) Scheman; m. Lucy M. Duncan; children: Ann, Corinne, Jennifer, Daniel. BA with distinction cum laude, Dartmouth Coll., 1953; JD, Yale U., 1956. Bar: N.Y., 1956, D.C., 1979. Pvt. practice law, Hartford, Conn., 1957, N.Y.C., 1958-59; fellow Inter-Am. Cultural Conv., Brazil, 1959-61; atty. dept. legal affairs OAS, Washington, 1961-64, planning officer, 1968-70, asst. sec. gen. for mgmt., 1975-84; exec. dir. Pan Am. Devel. Found., 1964-68, pres. Porter Internat. Co., Washington, 1970-75; ptnr. Coudert Bros., Washington, 1984-85; exec. dir. Ctr. Advanced Studies of the Americas, 1985-87; ptnr. Kaplan, Russin and Vecchi, 1987-90, Heller, Rosenblatt and Scheman, 1990-93; U.S. exec. dir. Inter-Am. Devel. Bank, Washington, 1993-98; chmn. Internat. Fin. Group, Greenberg, Traurig, 1998-2000; secretariat Inter-Am. Commn. on Human Rights, 1961-64; dir. gen. Inter-Am. Agy. for Cooperation and Devel., 2000—. V.p. fin. Robert R. Nathan Assocs., 1974-75; pub. Soviet Bus. and Trade, 1973-75; dir. Vision mag., 1973-74; assoc. dir. Coun. of Ams., 1976—; adj. prof. internat. orgn. George Washington U., 1979-83. Author: (books) Foundations of Freedom, 1966, The Inter-Am. Dilemma, 1988, The Alliance for Progress, A Retrospective, 1989, Greater Am., 2003, (articles) on inter-Am. affairs to profl. jours.; bd. editors: Mng. Internat. Devel. quar. Trustee Inter-Am. Bar Found., 1967-74, trustee Pan Am. Devel. Found., 1987-94, pres., 1976-83; chmn. Mus. of Americas Found., 1998—, Federal City Coun., 1998—; pres. Uruguay—U.S. C. of C., 1999-2000; mem. exec. com. Am. Jewish Com. of Washington; bd. dirs. East-West Trade Coun., 1974-75, Ctr. for Advanced Studies of the Ams., 1984-87. Decorated Order Bernardo O'Higgins (Chile), 1967, Russian Fedn., 1992. Mem. Washington Fgn. Law Soc. (bd. govs. 1965-67, pres. 1968), Am. Fgn. Law Assn. (v.p. 1971), Cosmos Club, Georgetown Club, Phi Beta Kappa. Home: 5002 50th Pl NW Washington DC 20016-4380 Office: Inter-Am Agy for Cooperation and Devel 1889 F St NW Washington DC 20006-4413

SCHEMMEL, RACHEL ANNE, food science and human nutrition educator, researcher; b. Farley, Iowa, Nov. 23, 1929; d. Frederic August and Emma Margaret (Melchert) Schemmel. BA, Clarke Coll., 1951; MS, U. Iowa, 1952; PhD, Mich. State U., 1967. Dietitian Children's Hosp. Soc., L.A., 1952-54; instr. Mich. State U., East Lansing, 1955-63, from asst. prof. to prof. food sci., human nutrition, 1967—. Author: Nutrition Physiology and Obesity, 1980; contbr. articles to profl. jours. Recipient Disting. Alumni award Mt. Mercy Coll., 1971, Borden award, 1986, Outstanding Alumni award U. Iowa, 1996, Mich. State U., 2002, Outstanding Achievement award Clarke Coll., 1997. Fellow: Am. Soc. Nutrition Scis.; mem.: Soc. for Nutrition Edn., Brit. Nutrition Soc., Am. Diet Assn. (pres. Mich. 1976—77, pres. Lansing 1960, Outstanding Dietetic Educator award 1988), Inst. Food Technologists, Am. Assn. Family and Consumer Scis. (chair nutrition health and food mgmt. divsn. 1995—97, Outstanding Leader award 1998), Phi Kappa Phi (pres. 1994—95), Sigma Xi (pres. Mich. State U. chpt. 1983—84, Sr. Rsch award 1986). Roman Catholic. Home: 1341 Red Leaf Ln East Lansing MI 48823-1339 Office: Mich State U Dept Food Sci Nutrit East Lansing MI 48824 E-mail: schemmel@msu.edu.

SCHEMNITZ, SANFORD DAVID, wildlife biology educator; b. Cleve., Mar. 10, 1930; s. David Arthur Schemnitz; m. Mary Margaret Newby, July 8, 1958; children: Ellen Kay, Steven, Stuart. Student, U. Wis., 1948-50; BS in Wildlife, U. Mich., 1952; MS in Wildlife, U. Fla., 1953; PhD in Wildlife, Okla. State U., 1958. Cert. wildlife biologist. Conservation aide State of Mich. Dept. Conservation, Ann Arbor, 1951-52; game research biologist State of Minn. Dept. Conservation, St. Paul, 1958-59; asst. prof. wildlife Pa. State U., University Park, 1960-61; prof. wildlife resources U. Maine, Orono, 1962-75; dept. head fish and wildlife sci. N.Mex. State U., Las Cruces, 1975-81, prof. wildlife scis., 1981—97. Mem. resource adv. coun. Bur. Land Mgmt., N.Mex., 1996-99. Editor: Wildlife Management Techniques Manual, 1980; contbr. over 100 articles to profl. jours. Fulbright Prof. Council for Internat. Exchange Scholars, Kathmandu, Nepal, 1983, Kenya, 1990. Mem. Am. Soc. Mammalogists, The Wildlife Soc. (life, S.W. regional rep. 1979-80), Ecol. Soc. Am., Wilson Ornithol. Soc., N.Mex. Wildlife Fedn. (bd. dirs. 1983—), Sigma Xi. Home: 8105 Dona Ana Rd Las Cruces NM 88007-6305 Business E-Mail: sschemni@nmsu.edu.

SCHENCK, JACK LEE, retired electric utility executive; b. Morgantown, W.Va., Aug. 2, 1938; s. Ernest Jacob and Virginia Belle (Kelley) S.; m. Rita Elizabeth Pietschmann, June 7, 1979; 1 son, Erik. BSE.E., BA in Social Sci., Mich. State U., 1961; MBA, NYU, 1975. Engr. AID, Tunis, Tunisia, 1961, Detroit Edison Co., 1962-63; engr., economist OECD, Paris, 1963-70; v.p. econ. policy analysis Edison Electric Inst., N.Y.C. and Washington, 1970-81; v.p., treas. Gulf States Utilities Co., Beaumont, Tex., 1981-92, sr. v.p., CFO, 1992-94. Cons. on electric utility restructuring and privatization in the former Soviet Union, 1994—. Mem. Internat. Assn. Energy Econs., Triangle Club, Eta Kappa Nu. Republican. Office Phone: 281-360-3960. E-mail: schenck1@aol.com.

SCHENCK, JOHN FREDERIC, physician; b. Decatur, Ind., June 7, 1939; s. John C. Schenck and Mildred Blosser; m. Jane Stark, Oct. 12, 1962 (div. 1982); children: Brooke, Kimberly, David; m. Susan J. Kalia, Oct. 8, 1994; 1 stepchild, Tania. BS in Physics, Rensselaer Poly. Inst., 1961; PhD in Physics, 1965; MD, Albany (NY) Med. Coll., 1977. Staff scientist electronics lab. GE, Syracuse, NY, 1965-73; assoc. prof. elec. engring. Syracuse (NY) U., 1970-73; intern Albany Med. Ctr. Hosp., 1977-78; staff mem., sr. scientist GE Global Rsch., Schenectady, NY, 1973—; mem. med. staff Ellis Hosp., Schenectady, 1981—98. Adj. asst. prof. dept. radiology U. Pa., 1983-2000; adj. prof. neurology Albany Med. Coll., 2003-; chmn. Workshop on Advances in Magnetic Resonance Imaging Safety and Compatibility, McLean, Va., 1996; dir. Magnetic Resonance Imaging rsch. Neurosci. Rsch. Ctr., Albany Med. Ctr., 2001-. Contbr. articles to profl. jours; 17 patents in field of magnetic resonance imaging. Recipient S.S. Greenfield award Am. Assn. Physicists in Medicine, 1993; Nat. Merit scholar, 1957-61; NSF fellow, 1962-63, Coolidge fellow GE, 2003. Fellow Am. Phys. Soc.; mem. IEEE, AAAS, Internat. Soc. Magnetic Resonance in Medicine, NY Acad. Scis., Sigma Xi. Home: 22 E Claremont Dr Voorheesville NY 12186-9104 Office: GE Global Rsch Bldg K1 NMR Schenectady NY 12309 Office Phone: 518-387-6543. Business E-Mail: schenck@crd.ge.com.

SCHENDEL, DAN ELDON, management consultant, business educator; b. Norwalk, Wis., Mar. 29, 1934; s. Leonard A. and Marian T. (Koch) S.; m. Mary Lou Sigler, Sept. 1, 1956; children: Suzanne, Pamela, Sharon. BS in Metall. Engring., U. Wis., 1956; MBA, Ohio State U., 1959; PhD (Ford Found. fellow), Stanford U., 1963. With ALCOA, 1956, U.S. Civil Svc., 1959-60, SRI, 1963-65; prof. mgmt., dir. exec. edn. programs Purdue U., Lafayette, Ind., 1965-85, Blake Family endowed chair in strategic mgmt.; vis. prof. U. Mich., 1988-89, U. Chgo., 1990-91. Dean German Grad. Internat. Sch. Mgmt. and Adminstrn., Hannover, Germany; pres. Strat egic Mgmt. Assocs., Inc. Author: (with others) Strategy Formulation: Analytical Concepts, 1978, Divided Loyalties, 1980, Fundamental Issues in Strategy, 1994; editor: (with others) Strategic Management: A New View of Business Policy and Planning, 1979; founding editor Strategic Mgmt. Jour., 1980—. Served with USAF, 1956-59. Fellow Acad. Mgmt.; mem. Strategic Mgmt. Soc. (founding pres., exec. dir.), Lafayette Country Club, Univ. Club Chgo. Home: 1327 N Grant St West Lafayette IN 47906-2463 Office: Krannert Grad Sch Mgmt Purdue U West Lafayette IN 47907 Office Phone: 765-494-4386. Business E-Mail: schendel@mgmt.purdue.edu.

SCHENDEL, STEPHEN ALFRED, plastic surgery educator, craniofacial surgeon; b. Mpls., Oct. 10, 1947; s. Alfred Reck and Jeanne Shirley (Hagquist) S.; children: Elliott, Mélisande. BA, St. Olaf Coll., Northfield, Minn., 1969; BS with high distinction, U. Minn., 1971, DDS, 1973; diplome asst. etranger with high honors, U. Nantes, France, 1980; MD, U. Hawaii, 1983. Diplomate Am. Bd. Plastic Surgery, Nat. Bd. Med. Examiners, Nat. Bd. Dental Examiners, Am. Bd. Oral and Maxillofacial Surgery (adv. com., bd. examiner 1991-95). Intern, then resident in oral and maxillofacial surgery Parkland Meml. Hosp., Dallas, 1975-79; resident in gen. surgery Baylor U. Med. Ctr., Dallas, 1983-84, Stanford (Calif.) U. Med. Ctr., 1984-86, resident in plastic surgery, 1986-89, acting assoc. prof. surgery, 1989-91, assoc. prof., 1991-95, head divsn. plastic and reconstructive surgery, 1992—2002, dir. residency tng., 1992-98, chmn. dept. functional restoration, 1994—2001, prof. surgery, 1995—2002; head plastic surgery, dir. Craniofacial Ctr. Lucile Salter Packard Children's Hosp., Stanford, chief pediat. surgery, 1997—2002. Asst. to Dr. Paul Tessier, Paris, 1987-88; asst. dept. stomatology and maxillofacial surgery Centre Hospitalier Regional Nantes, 1979-80; med. bd. Lucile Salter Packard Children's Hosp. at Stanford, 1991—. Assoc. editor Selected Readings in Oral and Maxillofacial Surgery, 1989—; mem. editl. bd. Jour. Cranio-Maxillofacial Surgery; contbr. articles to profl. jours., chpts. to books. Recipient Disting. Alumnus award St. Olaf Coll., 1993; Fulbright fellow, Nantes, 1979-80, Chateaubriand fellow Govt. of France, 1987-88. Fellow ACS, Am. Acad. Pediat.; mem. Internat. Soc. Craniofacial Surgeons, European Assn. Cranio-Maxillofacial Surgeons, Am. Soc. Pediat. Plastic Surgeons, Am. Assn. Plastic Surgery, Soc. Baylor Surgeons (founding), Am. Cleft Palate-Craniofacial Assn., Am. Soc. Plastic Surgeons (sec. 1996—), Am. Soc. Maxillofacial Surgeons (sec., pres. 2000-01), Assn. Acad. Chairmen Plastic Surgery, Zedplast (bd. dirs. 1993—), Omicron Kappa Upsilon. Avocations: fly fishing, painting and sculpture. Office: Stanford U Med Ctr NC 104 Divsn Plastic Reconstr Surg Stanford CA 94305 Office Phone: 650-723-5824. Business E-Mail: sschendel@stanford.edu.

SCHENDEL, WILLIAM BURNETT, lawyer; b. 1948; BA, Swarthmore Coll., 1970; JD, Boston U., 1974. Bar: Alaska 1976, U.S. Dist. Ct. (9th cir.) Alaska 1976, U.S. Supreme Ct. 1984. Ptnr. Schendel & Callahan, Fairbanks, Alaska, 1981—2002; of counsel Winfree Law Office, Fairbanks, 2002—. Mem. ABA, Alaska Bar Assn. (pres. 1998-99). Office: Winfree Law Office 301 Cushman St Ste 200 Fairbanks AK 99701-4629

SCHENDEL, WINFRIED GEORGE, insurance company executive; b. June 19, 1931; came to U.S., 1952, naturalized, 1956; s. Willi Rudolf Max and Anna Margarete (Sassen) S.; m. Joanne Wiiest, Aug. 24, 1953; children: Victor Winfried, Bruce Lawrence, Rachelle Laureen. BS in Elec. and Indsl. Engring., Hannover-Stadthagen U., Hannover, Fed. Republic of Germany, 1952. Elec. draftsman Houston Lighting & Power Co., 1954-57; elec. draftsman, corrosion technician Transcontinental Gas Pipeline Co., Houston, 1957-59; elec. engr. Ken R. White Cons. Engrs., Denver, 1959-61; sales engr. Weco divsn. Food Machinery & Chem. Corp., various locations, 1961-64; ins. field underwriter N.Y. Life Ins. Co., Denver, 1964-66, asst. mgr., 1966-70, mgmt. asst., 1970-71, gen. mgr., 1971-77, mgr., 1979-85, field underwriter, 1985—; gen. agt. Woodmen Accident and Life Ins. Co., Ft. Collins, Colo., 1998—. Ind. gen. agt., Denver, 1978-79; ins. broker and adviser, 1979—; gen. agent Assurity Life Ins., Lincoln, Nebr. Instnl. rep., advancement chmn. Denver Area coun. Boy Scouts Am., Lakewood, Colo., 1968-72; precinct chmn. Rep. party, Jefferson County, Colo., 1976, 78; founder, life mem. Sister City Program, Lakewood, Colo.; chmn. adv. bd. ARC, Jefferson County, Colo., 1987-89; elder Presbyn. Ch.; lay min. First United Meth. Ch., Ft. Collins, Colo., 1999—. Recipient Centurion award, 1966, Salesman of Yr. award Jefferson County Salesman with a Purpose Club, 1983, Top awards ARC, 1988-89. Mem. Nat. Asn. Life Underwriters, Gen. Agts. and Mgrs. Assn. (Conf. Nat. Mgmt. award 1975), Colo. Life Underwriters Assn. (reg. v.p. Denver met. area 1989-90), Mile High Assn. Life Underwriters (pres. 1986-87, nat. com. 1988, 91), Lakewood C. of C. (pres. people-to-people, Trailblazer of Yr. award 1982, 83, Trail Boss of Yr. 1983), Lions, Edelweiss Club, Internat. Order Rocky Mountain Goats, N.Y. Life Star, Masons, Rotary (bd. dirs. Foot Hills chpt. 2002—, Paul Harris award 1995), Shriners. Home and Office: 925 Deerhurst Cir Fort Collins CO 80525-6919 Home Fax: 970-206-9082.

SCHENECK, CAROL ANN, lawyer, educator; b. Eatontown, N.J., May 13, 1952; d. Harold Matthew and Lenora Marie (Spidaliere) S. BA in Math., Montclair State U., 1974; JD, Seton Hall U., 1980. Bar: N.J. 1980. Sys. analyst N.J. Bell, Newark, 1974-82; assoc. Dolan & Dolan, Esqs., Newton, 1982-85; legal/computer cons. Crum and Forster Inc., Basking Ridge, 1985-86; sr. trial atty. Crum & Forster-Paul Seligman, Basking Ridge, 1986-87; assoc. McGuire & Wilson, Denville, 1987-94; pvt. practice, Randolph, 1994—. Adj. prof. computer sci. County Coll. Morris, Randolph, 1983—. Past leader Brownies, Girl Scouts USA, 1970-71; past confrat. Christian doctrine tchr., St. Therese Ch., Roxbury, 1976; pres., bd. dirs. Drakesville at Roxbury Condo Assn., Roxbury Twp., 1991—; co-chair Cable TV Com., Roxbury Twp., 1994-95; mem. Bd. Adjustment, Roxbury Twp., 1997-2000, vice chair, 1998-99; active Dem. Orgn., 1995—; elected councilwoman Ward 2, Roxbury Twp., 2000-04. Roman Catholic. Avocations: computer science, exhibiting purebred american curl cats. Home: 37 Drake Ln Ledgewood NJ 07852-9646 Office: 431 State Route 10 Randolph NJ 07869-2126

SCHENK, QUENTIN FREDERICK, retired social work educator, mayor, psychologist; b. Fort Madison, Iowa, Aug. 25, 1922; s. Fred Edward John and Ida (Sabrowsky) S.; m. Patricia J. Kelley, Aug. 6, 1946 (div. Apr. 1970); children: Fred W. (dec. 1972), Patricia, Karl, Martha; m. Emmy Lou Willson, May 23, 1970. BA, Willamette U., 1948; MS, U. Wis., 1950, MS in Social Work, PhD, U. Wis., 1953. Lic. ind. clin. social worker, Wis.; cert. longterm care, Ariz. Asst. prof. social work U. Wis.-Madison, 1953-55, prof., chmn. extension social work, 1961-63; prof., former dean Sch. Social Welfare, Milw., 1962-68, prof. emeritus, 1990—; assoc. prof. U. Mo., 1955-61; project specialist Ford Found., 1968-71. Spl. cons. on urban mission in Africa United Presbyn. Ch., 1971-, World Council Chs., 1971-; advisor to Haile Sellassie I U., Addis Ababa, Ethiopia, 1968-71; Alderman City of Cedarburg (Wis.), 1974-82, mayor, 1982-86. Author: (with Emmy Lou Schenk) Pulling Up Roots, 1978, Welfare Society and the Helping Professions, 1981; author sect. on Ethiopia, Welfare in Africa, 1987; contbr. articles, bulls., reports to profl. lit. Mem. Nat. Trust for Hist. Preservation, Wis. Hist. Preservation Negotiating Bd., 1975-76; chmn. bd. Guest House, Milw., 1987-89; mem. Sierra Club, Planned Parenthood, Unitarian Ch. S.E. Ariz. (v.p. 1999), ACLU, Dem. Party of Wis. Lt. USNR, 1942-46. Decorated Air medal with four gold stars, Disting. Flying Cross; recipient Presdl. citation Pres. Harry Truman, 1948; scholar Fulbright Found., 1959-60. Mem. DAV (life), Am. Assn. Ret. Persons, Aircraft Owners and Pilots Assn., Nat. Audubon Soc., Nature Conservancy. Home: 3443 E Wild Rabbit Rd Hereford AZ 85615-9653 Personal E-mail: schenk@myvine.com.

SCHENK, SUSAN KIRKPATRICK, nursing educator, consultant, small business owner; b. New Richmond, Ind., Nov. 29, 1938; d. William Marcius and Frances (Kirkpatrick) Gaither; m. Richard Dee Brown, Aug. 13, 1960 (div. Feb. 1972); children: Christopher Lee, David Michael, Lisa Catherine; m. John Francis Schenk, July 24, 1975 (widowed Apr. 1995). BSN, Ind. U., 1962; postgrad., U. Del., 1973-75. RN, PHN, BCLS; cert. community coll. tchr., Calif.; cert. vocat. edn. tchr., Calif. Staff nurse, then asst. dir. nursing Bloomington (Ind.) Hosp., 1962-66; charge nurse Newark (Del.) Manor, 1967-69; charge nurse GU Union Hosp., Terre Haute, Ind., 1971-72; clin. instr. nursing Ind. State U., Terre Haute, 1972-73; clin. instr. psychiatric nursing U. Del., Newark, 1974-75; psychiatric nursing care coord. VA Med. Ctr., Perry Point, Md., 1975-78; from nurse educator to cmty. rels. coord. Grossmont Hosp., La Mesa, Calif., 1978—91; dir. psychiat. svcs. Scripps Hosp. East County, El Cajon, Calif., 1991-97; nursing instr., adult edn. Grossmont Union H.S. Dist., La Mesa, 1996—. Tech. advisor San Diego County Bd. Supervisors, 1987; tech. cons. Remedy Home and Health Care, San Diego, 1988; expert panelist Srs. Speak Out, KPBS-TV, San Diego, 1988; guest lectr. San Diego State U., 1987. Editor: Teaching Basic Caregiver Skills, 1988; author, performer tng. videotape Basic Caregiver Skills, 1988. Mem. patient svcs. com. Nat. Multiple Sclerosis Soc., San Diego, 1986-89; bd. dirs. Assn. for Quality and Participation, 1989. Adminstrn. on Aging/DHHS grantee, 1988. Mem. Ind. U. Alumni Assn. (life), Calif. Coun. Adult Edn., Mensa, Sigma Theta Tau. Avocations: piano, gardening, reading. Home and Office: 9435D Carlton Oaks Dr Santee CA 92071-2582 E-mail: susansks@aol.com.

SCHENKEL, PETE, food company executive; CEO, chmn. bd. So. Foods Group, Dallas, 1999—; chmn. Dallas Methodist Hospitals Found. Office: Southern Foods Group PO Box 279000 Dallas TX 75227-9600

SCHENKEL, SUZANNE CHANCE, retired natural resource specialist; b. Phila., Mar. 12, 1940; d. Henry Martyn Chance II and Suzanne (Sharpless) Jameson; m. John Lackland Hardinge Schenkel, June 15, 1963 (div. 2002); children: John Jr., Andrew Chance. BS in Edn., Tufts U., 1962. Tchr. Roland Pk. Country Sch., Balt., 1962-65; exec. dir. Mass. Citizens' Com. for Dental Health, Springfield, 1981-83; pub., editor Women's Investment Newsletter, Longmeadow, Mass., 1985-89; pub. affairs officer USDA's Soil Conservation Svc., Amherst, Mass., 1990-93; resource conservationist conservation & ecosys. assistance divsn. USDA's Natural Resources Conservation Svc., Washington, 1993-97; ops. partnership liaison East Regional Office, Beltsville, Md., 1997—2002; ret., 2002. Staff Merchant Marine and Fisheries com. U.S. Ho. of Reps., Washington, 1993. Author Wetlands Protection and Management Act. Chmn. Longmeadow (Mass.) Conservation Commn., 1984-90; supr. Hampden County (Mass.) Conservation Dist., 1985-90; bd. dirs., v.p. League of Women Voters of Mass., Boston, 1974-85; exec. com. Water Supply Citizens' Adv. Com.; adv. bd. Water Resources Authority, Mass., 1979-90; bd. dirs. Alliance for Chesapeake Bay, 2001. Mem. Soil and Water Conservation Soc., Nat. Assn. Conservation Dists. Episcopalian. Avocations: golf, tennis, sailing. Home: 304 W Coral Trace Cl Delray Beach FL 33445

SCHENKENBERG, MARY MARTIN, principal; b. Oakland, Calif., Nov. 29, 1944; d. Leo Patrick and Florence Kathryn (Brinkoetter) Martin; m. Philip Rawson Schenkenberg III, Aug. 20, 1966; children: Philip Rawson IV, Amy Lynn, Stephen Patrick. BA in English, Fontbonne Coll., 1966; MA Teaching in English, St. Louis U., 1975, PhD in English, 1991. Cert. tchr., Mo. Asst. prof. Fontbonne Coll., St. Louis, 1978-85; English dept. chair Nerinx Hall High Sch., St. Louis, 1979-89; asst. prof. Webster U., St. Louis, 1986-89; co-prin. Nerinx Hall High Sch., St. Louis, 1989-92, prin., 1992—. Adj. prof. St. Louis U., 1985-89; advanced placement reader Ednl. Testing Svc., Princeton, N.J., 1986-89. Author: (with others) The English Classroom in the Computer Age, 1991. Bd. pres. Mary, Queen of Peace Sch., St. Louis, 1977. Mem. ASCD, Nat. Coun. Tchrs. English, Greater St. Louis Tchrs. English (bd. dirs. 1989—). Roman Catholic. Avocations: tennis, theater, travel. Office: Nerinx Hall High Sch 530 E Lockwood Ave Webster Groves MO 63119-3278

SCHENKER, ERIC, university dean, economist; b. Vienna, Feb. 24, 1931; came to U.S., 1939, naturalized, 1945; s. Adolph and Olga (Strauss) S.; m. Virginia Martha Wick, Apr. 14, 1963; children: David, Richard, Robert. BBA, CCNY, 1952; MS, U. Tenn., 1955; PhD, U. Fla., 1957. Asst. prof. Mich. State U., 1957-59; mem. faculty U. Wis.-Milw., 1959—, prof. econs., 1965—; dean U. Wis.-Milw. (Sch. Bus. Adminstrn.), 1976—, dean, prof. emeritus, 1997—; dir. Urban Research Center, 1974-76; asso. dir. Center Great Lakes Studies, 1967-74, sr. scientist, 1974—; assoc. dean Coll. Letters and Scis., 1963-69. Bd. dirs. Am. Med. Bldgs., Ampco Metal, Pressed Steel; cons. in field. Author: The Port of Milwaukee: An Economic Review, 1967; co-author: Port Planning and Development as Related to Problems of U.S. Ports and the U.S. Coastal Environment, 1974, The Great Lakes Transportation System, 1976, Port Development in the United States, 1976, Maritime Labor Organizations on the Great Lakes-St. Lawrence Seaway System, 1978, Great Lakes Transportation System in the 80s, 1986; also monographs and articles. Sr. mem. Milw. Bd. Harbor Commrs., 1960-72, chmn., 1965-68; chmn. panel on future port requirements of U.S., Maritime Transp. Research Bd., Nat. Acad. Scis., 1973-76, chmn. panel on reducing tankbarge pollution, 1980-81; mem. pilotage adv. bd. to U.S. sec. transp., 1972-75; trustee Mt. Sinai Med. Ctr, 1984-88; mem. Econ. Progress Authority of Milw. Met. Sewerage Dist., 1983-88, Marine Bd., NAS, 1982-83, Gov.'s Coun. on Econ. Issues, 1983—. Served with AUS, 1952-54. Mem. Am. Econs. Assn., So. Econs. Assn., Phi Kappa Phi, Alpha Kappa Psi, Beta Gamma Sigma, Beta Alpha Psi. Home: 6792 N Melissa Ct Glendale WI 53209-3473 E-mail: esconinc@aol.com., Schenker@uwm.edu.

SCHENKER, LEO, retired utility company executive; b. Vienna, Jan. 3, 1922; came to U.S., 1952, naturalized, 1959; s. Max and Selda Lea (Podhorcer) S.; m. Alda R. Tinson, Jan. 20, 1949; children: Michael Gregory, Deborah Anne. BS with first class honors, U. London, 1942; MA in Sci. (Can. Inst. Steel Constrn. fellow), U. Toronto, 1950; PhD, U. Mich., 1954. Mng. dir. METAG Ltd., London, 1945-48; asst. rsch. engr. Hydro-Electric Power Commn. of Ont. (Can.), Toronto, 1948-52; rsch. assoc. U. Mich., Ann Arbor, 1952-54; with Bell Telephone Labs., 1954-87, various positions, dir. mil. electronic tech., 1968-71; dir. Loop Maintenance Systems Lab., 1971-80, exec. dir. Central Office Ops. div., 1980-83, exec. dir. network system planning div., 1983-84, exec. dir. tech. info. div., 1984-87. Adj. prof. elec. engring. Cooper Union, N.Y.C., 1989-97. Patentee communications tech. field. Served with RAF, 1942-45. Recipient Duggan medal Can. Inst. Steel Constrn., 1950 Fellow IEEE, Sigma Xi, Phi Kappa Phi. E-mail: lschen6161@aol.com.

SCHENKER, MARC BENET, preventive medicine educator; b. L.A., Aug. 25, 1947; s. Steve and Dosella Schenker; m. Heath Massey; children: Yael, Phoebe, Hilary. BA, U. Calif., Berkeley, 1969; MD, U. Calif., San Francisco, 1973; MPH, Harvard U., Boston, 1980. Instr. medicine Harvard U., Boston, 1980-82; asst. prof. medicine U. Calif., Davis, 1982-86, assoc. prof., 1986-92, prof., 1992—, chmn. dept. epidemiology and preventive medicine, 1995—. Fellow ACP; mem. Am. Thoracic Soc., Am. Pub. Health Assn., Soc. Epidemiologic Rsch., Am. Coll. Epidemiology, Soc. Occupl. Environ. Health, Internat. Commn. Occupl. Health, Assn. Tchrs. Preventive Medicine, Phi Beta Kappa, Alpha Omega Alpha. Office: Dept Pub Health Scis One Shields Ave TB 168 Davis CA 95616-8638

SCHENKER, STEVEN, internist, educator; b. Poland, Oct. 5, 1929; came to U.S., 1943, naturalized, 1946; s. Alfred and Ernestyna S.; m. Sally Ann Wood, May 11, 1956; children: Julie C. Schenker Burn, Steven A., David S., Andrew G., Jennifer E. Schenker Campeggi; m. Jo Ann Neumann, Nov. 24, 1985. BA, Cornell U., 1951, MD, 1955. Intern Harvard Service-Boston City Hosp., 1955-56, resident in medicine, 1956-58; asst. prof. medicine U. Cin. Sch. Medicine, 1961-63; asst. prof. U. Tex., Southwestern Sch. Medicine, 1963-67, assoc. prof. medicine, 1967-70; prof. medicine, biochemistry, dir. div. gastroenterology Vanderbilt U. Sch. Medicine, Nashville VA Hosp., 1970-82; prof. medicine and pharmacology U. Tex. Sch. Medicine, San Antonio, 1982—, dir. divsn. gastroenteroloty, 1982—2001. Chmn. study sect. Nat. Inst. on Alcohol Abuse and Addiction, 1980-83; chmn. study sects. VA, 1985-88. Editor: Hepatology, 1985-90. Contbr. numerous articles in field to profl. jours. Recipient Markle award, 1963; Career Devel. award NIH, 1968; Jurzykowski Found. for Research in Medicine award, 1979, Alcoholism Research Soc. award 1987. Mem. Am. Assn. for Study of Liver Diseases (pres. 1980, Disting. Svc. award 1997), Am. Soc. Clin. Investigation, Assn. Am. Physicians, Am. Gastroent. Soc., Am. Soc. Pharm. and Exptl. Therapeutics, Am. Soc. Clin. Nutrition, Internat. Soc. for Study of Liver Diseases, Alpha Omega Alpha. Home: 26025 Mesa Oak Dr San Antonio TX 78255-3533 Office: U Tex Med Sch San Antonio TX 78284 E-mail: stvschenker@aol.com.

SCHENKKAN, ROBERT FREDERIC, writer, actor; b. Chapel Hill, N.C., Mar. 19, 1953; s. Robert Frederic Sr. and Jean (McKenzie) Schenkkan; children: Sarah Victoria, Joshua McHenry. BA in Theatre Arts, U. Tex., 1975; MFA in Acting, Cornell U., 1977. Author: (plays) Final Passages, 1981, The Survivalist, 1982 (best of the fringe award Edinburgh Festival, 1984), Tachinoki, 1987, Tall Tales, 1988 (Playwrights Forum award, 1988, Best One Act Plays, 1993), Heaven on Earth, 1989 (Julie Harris Playwright award Beverly Hills Theatre Guild, 1989), The Kentucky Cycle, 1991 (Pulitzer prize for drama, 1992, L.A. Drama Critics Circle Best Play award, 1992, Penn Ctr. West award, 1993, Best Play Tony award nominee, 1993, Best Play Drama Desk award nominee, 1993), Conversations with the Spanish Lady and Other One-Act Plays, 1993, The Dream Thief, 1998, Handler, 1999, The Marriage of Miss Hollywood and King Neptune,The Devil and Daniel Webster, 2002, Arturo & Katherine, 2004, (TV films) Crazy Horse, (TV miniseries) Spartacus, (films) The Quiet American, 2002. Grantee Vogelstein Found., 1982, Arthur Found., 1988, Fund for New Am. Plays, 1990, Calif. Arts Coun., 1991. Mem.: SAG, Actors Equity, Writers Guild, Ensemble Studio Theatre, Dramatists Guild.

SCHENKLER, BERNARD, lawyer; b. Trani, Italy, Aug. 25, 1948; s. Wolf and Nettie Schenkler; m. Ellen Haberman, Sept. 25, 1977; children: Alan, Sarah. BA, U. Pa., 1970; JD, Columbia U., 1973; diploma in mcpl. law, Rutgers U., 1991. Bar: N.Y. 1974, N.J. 1977, D.C. 1979, U.S. Ct. Appeals (2d cir.) 1975, U.S. Dist. Ct. (so. and ea. dists.) N.Y. 1975, U.S. Tax Ct. 1978, U.S. Ct. Mil. Appeals 1978, U.S. Ct. Appeals (3rd cir.), U.S. Dist. Ct. (no. and we. dists.) N.Y. 1980, U.S. Ct. Claims 1985, U.S. Ct. Internat. Trade 1985, U.S. Ct. Appeals (fed. cir.) 1990, U.S. Ct. Appeals (D.C. cir.) 1990, U.S. Ct. Appeals (4th cir.) 1991, U.S. Ct. Vets. Appeals 1990, U.S. Supreme Ct. 1980. Atty bus. law unit N.Y.C. Human Resources Adminstrn., 1973-76, exec. asst. to gen. counsel, 1977; assoc. Ravin, Sarasohn, Cook, Baumgarten & Fisch, West Orange, N.J., 1978-85; ptnr. Ravin, Sarasohn, Cook, Baumgarten, Fisch & Rosen, Roseland, N.J., 1986-2000; of counsel Orloff, Lowenbach, Stifelman & Siegal, P.A., Roseland, N.J., 2000—. Author: Bankruptcy Aspects of Municipal Real Estate Taxation, 1991, Death and Bankruptcy, How the Probate and Bankruptcy Processes Interact, 1994, Close Encounters With the Bankruptcy Code, 1997. Mem. Randolph Twp. (N.J.) Bd. of Ethics, 1978-80. Mem. ABA, N.Y. State Bar Assn., N.J. State Bar Assn., Supreme Ct. N.J. (mem. dist. ethics com. Essex County 2001—), Essex County Bar Assn., D.C. Bar. Clubs: White Meadow Temple Men's Club (Rockaway, N.J.). Jewish. Avocations: Karate (black belt), golf, astronomy. Office: Orloff Lowenbach Stifelman & Siegal PA 101 Eisenhower Pkwy Ste 29 Roseland NJ 07068-1082 E-mail: bs@olss.com.

SCHENKMAN, JOHN BORIS, pharmacologist, educator; b. N.Y.C., Feb. 10, 1936; s. Abraham and Theresa (Moses) S.; m. Deanna Owen, June 5, 1960; children: Jeffrey Alan, Laura Ruth. BA in Chemistry, Bklyn. Coll., 1960; PhD in Biochemistry, SUNY Upstate Med. Ctr., Syracuse, 1964. Postdoctoral fellow U. Pa. Johnson Found., Phila., 1964-67, Inst. Protein Research Osaka U., Japan, 1967-68, Inst. Toxicology Tübingen U., Germany, 1968; asst. prof. Yale U. Sch. Medicine, New Haven, 1968-71, assoc. prof., 1971-78; prof. pharmacology U. Conn. Health Ctr., Farmington, 1978-2000, head dept., 1978-87; dir. grad. program cellular and molecular pharmacology U. Conn., Farmington, 1995-99, prof. emeritus, 2000—. Assoc. editor Drug Metabolism and Drug Interactions, 1988—, Xenobiotica, 1990—; mem. editl. bds.; contbr. articles to profl. jours. Served as sgt. U.S. Army, 1953-55. Research grantee NIH, NSF; recipient Research Career Devel award NIH, 1971-76. Mem. Am. Soc. Biochemists and Molecular Biologists, AM. Soc. Pharmacology Exptl. Therapeutics, Am. Med. Sch. Pharmacologists (councilor 1987-88). Jewish. Avocations: fishing, botany, wine making. Office: U Conn Sch Medicine Dept Pharm Farmington CT 06030-0001

SCHENTAG, JEROME JOHN, pharmacy educator; b. St. Clair, Mich., Jan. 25, 1950; s. John and Rose Schentag; m. Rita R. Sloan, June 26, 1976; 1 child, Annie. BS in Pharmacy, U. Nebr., 1973; D. Pharmacy, Phila. Coll. Pharmacy, 1975. Postdoctoral fellow SUNY, Buffalo, 1975-76, asst. prof. of pharmacy, 1976-81, assoc. prof., 1981-86, prof., 1986—; CEO CPL assoc., LLC, 2001—. Dir. Clin. Pharmacokinetics Lab., Millard Fillmore Hosp., Buffalo, 1981-2000. Editor: Applied Pharmacokinetics, 1981, 4th edit., 2004; contbr. articles to profl. jours. Am. Coll. Clin. Pharmacy fellow, 1985; recipient Disting. Young Alumni award Phila. Coll. of Pharmacy, 1989. Fellow Am. Assn. Pharm. Scientists; mem. Am. Soc. Microbiology. Office: U Buffalo Sch Pharms 543 Hochstetter Hall Buffalo NY 14260 E-mail: Schentag@Buffalo.edu.

SCHEPARTZ, ALANNA, biochemist, educator; b. N.Y.C., Jan. 9, 1962; m. Thomas E. Schrader; 1 child, Abigail BS, SUNY, Albany, 1982; PhD in Chemistry, Columbia U., 1987. NIH fellow Calif. Inst. Tech., 1988; asst. prof. Yale U., New Haven, Conn., 1988-92, assoc. prof. chemistry, 1992-94, Milton Harris assoc. prof. chemistry, 1994-95, prof., 1995—. Contbr. numerous articles to profl. jours. Recipient Presdl. Young Investigator award NSF, 1991, Camille and Henry Dreyfus Teacher-Scholar award, 1993; David and Lucille Packard Found. fellow, 1991, Eli Lilly Biochemistry fellow, 1991, Alfred P. Sloan Rsch. fellow, 1994. Mem. Am. Chem. Soc. (Arthur C. Cope Scholar award 1995, Eli Lilly award 1997). Achievements include research in bioorganic chemistry.

SCHEPP, RICHARD D. lawyer, retail executive; BBA, U. Wis., Eau Claire. Atty. Quarles & Brady, Milw.; dir. legal affairs and asst. corp. sec. Shopko Stores, Inc., 1992—96, v.p. legal affairs and corp. sec., 1996—98, sr. v.p. and gen. counsel, 1998—2000; sr. v.p. Kohl's, 2000—01, gen. counsel and sec., 2000—, exec. v.p., 2001—. Office: Kohl's Corp N56W17000 Ridgewood Dr Menomonee Falls WI 53051-5660

SCHEPPS, VICTORIA HAYWARD, lawyer; b. Brockton, Mass., June 11, 1956; d. William George and Lucy Victoria (Mitcheroney) Hayward; m. Frank Schepps, Sept. 18, 1982; children: Frank IV, Lucia. BA, Suffolk U., 1977; JD, U. San Diego, 1981. Instr., Northeastern U., Boston, 1981-83; assoc. Hoffman & Hoffman, Boston, 1983-85, Mark J. Gladstone, P.C., 1985-87; Doktor, Hirschberg & Schepps, 1987-88, Schepps & Reilly, 1988-90; pvt. practice Law Office of Victoria Hayward Schepps, Stoughton, Mass., 1990—. Mem. Mass. Conveyancing Assn., Mass. Bank Counsel, Inc. Democrat. Roman Catholic. Office: 6 Cabot Pl Ste 9 Stoughton MA 02072-4625

SCHER, HOWARD DENNIS, lawyer; b. Ft. Monmouth, N.J., Apr. 23, 1945; s. George Scher and Rita (Eitches) Zar; children: Seth Micah, Eli David. BA, Brandeis U., 1967; JD, Rutgers U., 1971. Bar: Pa. 1971, U.S. Dist. Ct. (ea. dist.) Pa. 1971, U.S. Ct. Appeals (3rd cir.) 1971, U.S. Supreme Ct. 1975. Asst. city solicitor City of Phila., 1971-73; assoc. Goodis, Greenfield, Henry & Edelstein, Phila., 1973-77, Montgomery, McCracken, Walker & Rhoads, Phila., 1977-80, ptnr., 1980-2001; shareholder Buchanan Ingersoll P.C., Phila., 2001—, mng. ptnr., Phila. office, mem. exec. com. Trustee Fedn. of Jewish Ags. of Greater Phila., 1994—; dir. Akiba Hebrew Acad., Merion, Pa., 1996-98; mem. pres.'s coun. Brandeis U.; chair Jewish Employment and Vocat. Svcs., 1998-02; chmn. Com. of Seventy, 2002. Fellow Am. Coll. Trial Lawyers, Internat. Acad. Trial Lawyers; mem. ABA, Pa. Bar Assn. (ho. of dels.), Phila. Bar Assn. (chmn. fed. cts. com. 2001-02), Brandeis U. Alumni Assn. (v.p. 1983-87). Home: 2222 Locust St Philadelphia PA 19103-5511 Office: Buchanan Ingersoll PC 11 Penn Ctr Ste 14th Fl 1835 Market St Philadelphia PA 19103 Office Phone: 215-665-3920. Office Fax: 215-665-8760. Business E-Mail: scherhd@bipc.com.

SCHER, HOWARD S. oncologist; b. Indpls., June 20, 1951; MD, NYU, 1976. Diplomate Am. Bd. Internal Medicine, Am. Bd. Med. Oncology. Intern Bellevue Hosp. Ctr.-NYU Sch. Medicine, N.Y.C., 1976—77, resident, 1977—80; fellow Meml. Sloan-Kettering Cancer Ctr., 1980—83, genitourinary oncology; assoc. prof. medicine Cornell U., 1992—. Office: Memorial Sloan Kettering Cancer Ctr 1275 York Ave New York NY 10021-6007

SCHER, IRVING, lawyer; b. N.Y.C., July 22, 1933; s. Charles and Tillie (Ballenberg) S.; m. Amy Lynn Katz, June 8, 1985; 1 child, Sara Katz-Scher. BA, CCNY, 1955; JD, Columbia U., 1962. Bar: N.Y. 1963. Assoc. Weil, Gotshal & Manges, N.Y.C., 1962-69, ptnr., 1969—. Adj. prof. NYU Sch. Law, 1972—; co-chmn. ann. anti-trust law inst. Practicing Law Inst., N.Y.C., 1976—; adv. bd. Antitrust and Trade Regulation Reports, 1980—. Author: Living With the Robinson-Patman Act, 2002; editor: Columbia Law Rev., 1960—61; revs. editor:, 1961—62, editor, co-author: Antitrust Advisor, 4th edit., 2003. Served as lt. USNR, 1955-59. Recipient Nat. Scholarship award, Columbia Law Sch., 1961—62; Harlan Fiske Stone scholar, 1960—62, Gluck scholar, 1960—61. Mem.: ABA (chmn. antitrust law sect. 1988—89), N.Y. State Bar Assn. (chmn. antitrust law sect. 1980—81, Lifetime Achievement award 1998). Office: Weil Gotshal & Manges 767 5th Ave New York NY 10153-0119 E-mail: Irving.scher@weil.com.

SCHER, JORDAN MAYER, physician, psychiatrist, drug abuse specialist; b. Balt. s. Robert Samuel and Marye Kremen Scher; m. Jeanne Nonken, July 20, 1954 (div. June 1960); children: Jan. Jo, Jill, Gabhriel. BS, Wesleyan U., 1945; MD, U. Md., 1949; PhD, Neuropsychopharmacology, Northwestern U., 1957. Diplomate Am. Bd. Psychiatry and Neurology, Am. Bd. Med. Hypnosis, cert. addiction specialist Am. Acad. Health Care Providers in Addiction Disorders. Resident and fellow in psychiatry U. Md. Psychiat. Inst., Balt., 1953—55; fellow in psychiatry NIMH, Bethesda, Md.; fellow in medicine, hypertension studies Cleve. Clinic Found., 1950—51; project dir., rsch. psychiatrist NIMH, 1955-57; dir. narcotics project Cook County (Ill.) Jail and Criminal Ct., 1957—59; coor. undergrad. psychiatry Northwestern U. Med. Sch., 1957—60; pvt. practice psychiatry Chgo., 1957—79; cons. Sheriff's Office and Cook County Jail, 1958—63; from asst. to assoc. prof. dept. neurology and psychiatry Northwestern U. Med. Sch., Chgo., 1960—63; dir. Chgo. Psychiat. Found. and Ontoanalytic Inst., Chgo., 1960—70; prof. dept. neurology and psychiatry Northwestern U., 1963—65; dir. psychiat. svcs. Bd. of Health, 1963—65; exec. dir. Nat. Coun. Drug Abuse, Chgo., 1971—79; dir. sct. on psychiatry and religion Yeshiva Torat Israel, Jerusalem, 1972—74; exec. dir. Methadone Maintenance Inst., Chgo., 1972—79; advisor acupuncture Nat. Inst. Acupuncture and Herbal Medicine, Taiwan, 1974—; psychiatrist cons. Diaspora Yeshiva, Jerusalem, 1980—; pvt. practice psychiatry Jerusalem, 1982—. Vis. prof. psychiatry and drug abuse Hebrew U., 1982-89; cons. psychiatry, Israel and numerous orgns.; rschr. in field; dir. Jerusalem Inst. Drug Abuse, 1980-85, Jerusalem House, Israel, 1989—; dir. drug abuse unit Ezrat Nashim; advisor on drugs and alcohol Min. of Health, Israel; commn. on addiction, chmn. Adult Subcom. on Drug Abuse, City of Jerusalem. Author: Narcotic Detoxification as Acute Induced Panic Disorder: Neuropsychopharmacological Causes, Treatment, and Implications, A Monograph, 1992, (with L. Appleby, J. Cumming) Chronic Schizophrenia, 1959, Theories of the Mind, 1963, Drug Abuse in Industry: Growing Corporate Dilemma, 1973; co-editor: (with M. Segal): Drugs and the Law, vol. 1, Perspectives in Drug Abuse, 1989; founder, editor The Jour. Existential Psychiatry, 1959-70; cons. Am. Psychiat. Assn. Jour., 1963-70, Jour. AMA, 1964-71; mem. editl. bd. Psychosomatics Jour., 1965-67, Human Context Jour., 1970-72, Medica Judaica Jour., 1971-72; editor, founder Nat. Coun. Drug Abuse Drug/Health Alert, 1972-79; co-editor: Perspectives in Drug Abuse, 1989; contbr. numerous articles to profl. jours.; patentee in field. Co-chair bus. adv. coun. Nat. Rep. Congl. Com., 2002-03. Lt. USNR, 1949-57. Recipient Key to City of St. Louis, 1969, Wisdom award of honor, Wisdom Soc., 1972, Pawlowski Peace prize, 1974, Physician's Recognition award, AMA, 1975—2004, DeQuincey prize in addiction rsch., 1993, Cert. of Honor 50 Yrs. of Dedicated Svc. to Med. Profession, AMA, 2002. Fellow AAAS, Royal Soc. Medicine, Am. Acad. Psychosomatic Medicine (program com.), World Med. Assn. (hon.; U.S. com.), Comprehensive Medicine Assn., Am. Assn. Clin. and Exptl. Hypnosis, Nat. Acad. Religion and Mental Health, Am. Geriatric Soc., N.Y. Acad. Scis.; mem. AMA, Am. Coll. Forensic Psychiatry, Am. Acad. Psychiatry and Law, Am. Acad. Psychiatry in Alcohol and Drug Abuse, Am. Soc. Neuroimaging, Am. Soc. Addiction Medicine, Am. Soc. Addiction Psychiatry, Am. Ontoanalytic Assn. for Existential Psychiatry (founder), Am. Soc. Psychoanalytic Physicians, Inc., Am. Med. Soc. Alcoholism, Am. Acad. Orthomolecular Psychiatry, Am. Med. Record Assn., Am. Soc. Group Psychotherapy and Psychodrama, Chgo. Soc. Assn. Execs., Ill. Rehab. Assn., Nat. Rehab. Assn., Nat. Coun. Crime and Delinquency, Chgo. Assn. Commerce and Industry, Assn. Advancement of Psychotherapy, Am. Soc. Group Psychotherapy and Psychodrama, Am. Assn. Psychoanalytic Physicians, Internat. Soc. Med. Hypnosis, Internat. Assn. Group Psychotherapy, Am. Psychiat. Assn., Internat. Ontoanalytic Assn., Vienna Med. Psychol. Soc. (hon.), Assn. Am. Med. Colls., Am. Acad. Neurology, Washington Psychiat. Soc., Am. Humanistic Psychology Assn., Am. Acad. Psychotherapists, Am. Soc. Psychoanalytic Medicine, Am. Group Psychotherapy Assn., Psychosynthesis Rsch. Found., Soc. Advancement of Gen. Systems Theory, Soc. Sci. Study of Sex, Human Ecology Found., Soc. Biol. Psychiatry, Am. Soc. Photobiology, Ill. Med. Soc., Sigma Xi, Phi Delta Epsilon. Jewish. Avocations: Biblical/Jewish-Christian studies, archaeology, cosmology, paleoanthropological studies on the origin and evolution of human mind and communication. Office Phone: 212-245-9585.

SCHER, KAREN MARIA, illustrator, multimedia specialist, systems engineer; b. Summit, N.J., June 20, 1963; d. Anthony Carmen and Phyllis (Bursese) Dirienzo; m. David Brian Scher, May 15, 1993; children: Samuel Jude, Anya Marie. BA summa cum laude, Fairleigh Dickinson U., 1995. Silk screen designer Continental Screen Printing, N.Y.C., 1984; freelance illustrator, 1984—; graphic artist Bellcore, Piscataway, N.J., 1984-85; with NY Life Ins. Co., Lebanon, N.J.; programmer Prudential-Bache Securities, Edison, N.J., 1987-88; info. ctr. cons. Supermarkets Gen. Corp., Woodbridge, N.J., 1988-90; programmer, ops. analyst Bell Atlantic, Madison, N.J., 1990-93, 1990-93, multimedia specialist, tech. staff, 1993-97; sys. engr. NCR-Internet Solutions, Iselin, N.J., 1997-99, Telcordia Technologies, Piscataway, 1999—, Internat. Internet Solutions, 2000—. Facilitator, author course Intro. to Internet and Mosaic, 1994. Recipient Don Bitger Ednl. Tech. award Bell Atlantic Ctr. for Networked Multimedia, 1994. Mem. Soc. for Applied Learning Tech., Phi Zeta Kappa. Office: Telcordia Technologies 444 Hoes Ln Piscataway NJ 08854-4104

SCHER, LAURA SUSAN, financial company executive; b. Passaic, N.J., Jan. 18, 1959; d. Alan E. and Frances Scher; m. Ian H. Altman, May 28, 1984. BA in Econs., Yale U., 1980; MBA, Harvard U., 1985. Assoc. cons. Bain & Co., Boston, 1981-83; chief exec. officer Working Assets Funding Service, San Francisco, 1985—. Named Baker Scholar, Harvard U., 1985.

SCHER, ROBERT SANDER, instrument design company executive; b. Cin., May 24, 1934; m. Audrey Erna Gordon, Oct. 21, 1961; children: Sarahh, Alexander, Aaron. SB, MIT, 1956, SM, 1958, Diploma in Mech. Engring., 1960, ScD, 1963. Rsch. and teaching asst. MIT, Cambridge, Mass., 1957-62; control system engr. RCA, Hightstown, N.J., 1963-65; engring. mgr. Sequential Info. System, Elmsford, N.Y., 1965-71; tech. dir. Teledyne Gurley, Troy, N.Y., 1971-78, v.p. engring., 1978-86, pres., 1986-92, Encoder Design Assocs., Clifton Park, N.Y., 1993—. Co-author patent Linear Digital Readout, 1975. Mem. ASME, Optical Soc. Am. Jewish. Avocation: chamber music. Home: 2 Laurel Oak Ln Clifton Park NY 12065-4712 Office Phone: 518-383-4910. E-mail: bobscher@nycap.rr.com.

SCHER, STANLEY JULES, lawyer; b. Bklyn., Dec. 19, 1929; s. Leo A. and Frances (Goldman) S.; m. Susan Goldman, June 16, 1957; children— William Goldman, Peter Lawrence, Alison Hope. LL.B., Bklyn. Law Sch., 1952. Bar: N.Y. 1954, U.S. Dist. Ct. (so. and ea. dists.) N.Y. 1960, U.S. Supreme Ct. 1970. Ptnr. Tullman, Fisher & Scher, N.Y.C., 1954-62; founder, sr. ptnr. Garbarini & Scher, P.C., N.Y.C., 1962—; med.-legal lectr. physicians, hosps., health-related facilities, 1970—; mem. faculty N.Y. State Trial Lawyers Assn., 1975—; lectr. Nassau Acad. Law, 1984, N.Y. State Bar Assn., 1983. Pres.

Baker Hill Civic Assn., Great Neck, N.Y., past zone leader Great Neck North Dem. Com., mem. Nat. CIC Orgn., Great Neck. Served with U.S. Army, 1952-54. Mem. ABA, Assn. Trial Lawyers Am., Soc. Med. Jurisprudence, N.Y. State Bar Assn., N.Y. County Lawyers Assn., Queens County Bar Assn., Nassau County Bar Assn. Jewish. Club: Temple Israel Couples (Great Neck, N.Y.) (past pres.). Lodge: B'nai B'rith. Home: 59 Essex Rd Great Neck NY 11023-1535 Office: Garbarini & Scher PC Rm 3500 1114 Avenue Of The Americas New York NY 10036-7790

SCHER, STEVEN PAUL, literature educator; b. Budapest, Hungary, Mar. 2, 1936; came to U.S., 1957, naturalized, 1963; Diploma in piano, Bela Bartok Conservatory of Music, Budapest, 1955; BA cum laude, Yale U., 1960, MA, 1963, PhD, 1966. Instr. German, Columbia U., N.Y.C., 1965-67; asst. prof. German, Yale U., New Haven, 1967-70, assoc. prof., 1970-74; prof. German and comparative lit. Dartmouth Coll., Hanover, N.H., 1974—, chmn. dept., 1974-80, 93-96, acting chmn. dept., 1982-83, Ted and Helen Geisel 3d Century prof. humanities, 1984-89, Daniel Webster prof. German and comparative lit., 2000—. Vis. prof. U. Paderborn, Fed. Republic Germany, summer 1980, Karl-Franzens-U. Graz, Austria, summer 1984; grant reviewer Guggenheim Found., NEH, Am. Council Learned Socs., others; cons. univ. presses and scholarly jours.; lectr. throughout world Author: Verbal Music in German Literature, 1968; editor: (with Charles McClelland) Postwar German Culture: An Anthology, 1974, 2d edit., 1980, Interpretationen: Zu E.T.A. Hoffmann, 1981, (with Ulrich Weisstein) Literature and the Other Arts. Proc. of IXth Congress of Internat. Comparative Lit. Assn., Innsbruck, vol. 3, 1981, Literatur und Musik. Ein Handbuch zur Theorie und Praxis eines komparatistischen Grenzgebietes, 1984, Music and Text: Critical Inquiries, 1992 (with Walter Bernhart and Werner Wolf) Word and Music Studies: Defining the Field, 1999; contbr. articles and essays to scholarly jours. Morse fellow, 1969-70; Humboldt fellow, 1972-73; Yale Coll. scholar, 1957-60, grad. fellow, 1960-62; DAAD grantee U. Munich, 1964-65 Mem. MLA (chmn. bibliography com. of div. lit. 1972-86), Am. Comparative Lit. Assn., Internat. Comparative Lit. Assn., Internat. P.E.N. Club Home: 6084 Dartmouth Hall Hanover NH 03755-3511 Office: Dartmouth College Dept German Studies 6084 Dartmouth Hall Hanover NH 03755-3511 E-mail: steven.p.scher@dartmouth.edu.

SCHERAGA, HAROLD ABRAHAM, physical chemistry educator; b. Bklyn., Oct. 18, 1921; s. Samuel and Etta (Goldberg) S.; m. Miriam Kurnow, June 20, 1943; children: Judith Anne, Deborah Ruth, Daniel Michael. BS, CCNY, 1941; A.M., Duke U., 1942, PhD, 1946, Sc.D. (hon.), 1961, U. Rochester, 1988, U. San Luis, 1992, Technion, 1993. Teaching, research asst. Duke U., 1941-46; fellow Harvard Med. Sch., 1946-47; instr. chemistry Cornell U., 1947-50, asst. prof., 1950-53, assoc. prof., 1953-58, prof., 1958-65, Todd prof. chemistry, 1965-92, Todd prof. chemistry emeritus, 1992—, chmn. dept., 1960-67. Vis. assoc. biochemist Brookhaven Nat. Lab., summers 1950, 51, cons. biology dept., 1950-56; vis. lectr. div. protein chemistry Wool Rsch. Labs., Melbourne, Australia, 1959; vis. prof. Weizmann Inst., Israel, 1970-80, Soc. for Promotion Sci., Japan, Aug. 1977; Ramachandran prof., India, 2002; mem. tech. adv. panel Xerox Corp., 1969-71, 74-79; mem. biochemistry tng. com. NIH, 1963-65, reviewers res., 1995-98; mem. rsch. career award com. NIGMS, 1967-71, NIH BBCA study sect. mem., 1998-2002; commn. molecular biophysics Internat. Union for Pure and Applied Biophysics, 1965-69, mem. commn. macromolecular biophysics, 1969-75, pres., 1972-75, mem. commn. subcellular and macromolecular biophysics, 1975-81; adv. panel molecular biology NSF, 1960-62; Welch Found. lectr., 1962, Harvey lectr., 1968, Gallagher lectr., 1968, Lemieux lectr., 1973, Hill lectr., 1976, Venable lectr., 1981; co-chmn. Gordon Conf. on Proteins, 1963; mem. coun. Gordon Rsch. Confs., 1969-71. Author: Protein Structure, 1961, Theory of Helix-Coil Transitions in Biopolymers, 1970; co-editor Molecular Biology, 1961-86; mem. editl. bd. Physiol. Chemistry and Physics, 1969-75, Mechanochemistry and Motility, 1970-71, Thrombosis Rsch., 1972-76, Biophys. Jour., 1973-75, Macromolecules, 1973-84, Computers and Chemistry, 1974-84, Internat. Jour. Peptide and Protein Chemistry, 1982-96, Jour. Peptide Rsch., 1997—; corr. PAABS Revista, 1971-73; mem. editl. adv. bd. Biopolymers, 1963—, Biochemistry, 1969-74, 85—, Structural Chemistry, 1989-93, Jour. Computational Polymer Sci., 1991-95, Jour. Biomolecular NMR, 1991—, Computational and Theoretical Polymer Sci., 1996-2000, Jour. Biomed. Sci., 1994—, Jour. Am. Chem. Soc., 1995-2000. Mem. Ithaca Bd. Edn., 1958-59; Bd. govs. Weizmann Inst., Israel, 1970-97; mem. staff Naval Research Lab. Project, Air Force OSRD Project, World War II. Fulbright, Guggenheim fellow Carlsberg Lab., Copenhagen, 1956-57, Weizmann Inst., Israel, 1963; NIH Spl. fellow Weizmann Inst., 1970; Fogarty scholar NIH, 1984, 86, 88-91; recipient Townsend Harris medal CCNY, 1970, Chemistry Alumni Sci. Achievements award, 1977, Kowalski medal Internat. Soc. Thrombosis and Haemostasis, 1983, Linderstrøm-Lang medal Carlsberg Lab., 1983, Internat. Soc. of Quantum Chemistry and Quantum Pharmacology award in Theoretical Biology, 1993, Stein & Moore award Protein Soc., 1995; named Hon. mem. Soc. Polymer Sci. Japan, 1995. Fellow AAAS, Biophys. Soc. (coun. 1967-70); mem. NAS, Am. Peptide Soc. (hon.), Am. Chem. Soc. (chmn. Cornell sect. 1955-56, mem. exec. com. div. biol. chemistry 1966-69, vice chmn. divsn. biol. chemistry 1970, chmn. divsn. biol. chemistry 1971, Eli Lilly award 1957, Nichols medal 1974, Kendall award 1978, Pauling award 1985, Mobil award 1990, Repligen award 1990, IBM award for computers in chem. and pharm. rsch. 1997, Hirschmann award in peptide chem., 1999), Am. Soc. Biol. Chemists, Am. Acad. Arts and Scis., N.Y. Acad. Scis. (hon. life), Hungarian Biophys. Soc. (hon.), Phi Beta Kappa, Sigma Xi, Phi Lambda Upsilon. Home: 212 Homestead Ter Ithaca NY 14850-6220 E-mail: has5@cornell.edu.

SCHERBER, AMY, food service executive; Degree, N.Y. Restaurant Sch. Line cook, pastry cook Bouley Restaurant; bread baker Mondrian restaurant; pastry chef, owner Amy's Bread, N.Y.C., 1992—; owner 3 retail cafes, N.Y.C., store, N.Y.C., 2001—. Tchr. baking various local culinary schs.; bd. dirs. Bread Bakers Guild Am., Women Chefs and Restauranteurs. Author: (books) Amy's Bread cookbook; appeared (TV series) Food Network, guest appearances (numerous TV cooking shows). Named Amy's Bread one of top bread bakeries, N.Y. Times, N.Y. Mag., Time Out N.Y., Gourmet, Food and Wine, Amy's Bread 3rd in Top 100 Bangs for the Buck in N.Y.C., Zagat Survey Restaurants, 2001, Amy's Bread Top 100 favorite cafes and restaurants in N.Y., 2001, N.Y. Woman Bus. Owner of Yr., Nat. Assn. Women Bus. Owners, 1999, Woman of Yr., Profl. Women's Exchange, 2001, N.Y.'s Woman of Power and Influence, 2001; named one of 30 Rising Bus. Owners in Young Millionaires article, Entrepreneur Mag.; named to 40 Under 40 Rising Stars in Bus., Crain's N.Y. Bus., 1997. Office: Amy's Bread 75 Ninth Ave New York NY 10011

SCHERCH, RICHARD OTTO, minister, consultant; b. Balt., Nov. 21, 1926; s. Richard Leopold and Anna Elizabeth (Finger) S.; m. Janice Marie Halbgewachs, June 24, 1951; children: Richard Paul, Leslie Carol, Lisa Beth, Jeremy Thomas. BA, Gettysburg Coll., 1948; BD, Luth. Sch. Theology, Phila., 1951; PhD, Johns Hopkins U., 1959; D Ministry, Lancaster Theol. Sem., 1975; cert. in dispute resolution recognition, Capital U., 1993. Ordained to ministry Luth. Ch., 1951. Mission developer, Wichita, Kans., 1951-53; pastor Trinity Luth. Ch., Manhattan beach, Calif., 1953-57; asst. pastor 1st Luth. Ch., Balt., 1957-59; pastor St. Mark's Luth. Ch., Birdsboro, Pa., 1961-65, Zion Luth. Ch., Lebanon, Pa., 1965-71, Shiloh Luth. Ch., York, Pa., 1972-75, Christ Luth. Ch., Paramus, N.J., 1976-81; sr. pastor Emmanuel Luth. Ch., Venice, Fla., 1981-93; owner Bldg. Bridges Consultation Svcs., Sarasota, Fla., 1993—98; mission developer Kansas City, Mo., 1959-61. Lectr. Chautauqua (N.Y.) Inst., 1963, 64, 65; instr. Johns Hopkins U., Balt., 1957-58, U. Balt., 1958-59; dir. Consult, Inc., Lebanon, Pa.; adj. faculty mem. Luther Coll., Teaneck, N.J., 1977-78, Bergen C.C., Paramus, 1979; chmn. profl. support com. Fla. Synod Luth. Ch. Am., Tampa, Fla., 1982-87, ptnr. in evangelism, Chgo., 1985-91; cons. Fla.-Bahamas Synod, 1993—, Episcopal Diocese of S.W. Fla., 1993—; faculty Interim Ministry Tng. Network, 1997—; interim ministry cons. Tng. Network, 1997-98. Comdr. USNR, 1956-77. Mem. Internat. Transactional Analysis Assn., Rotary. Republican. E-mail: dickscherch@earthlink.net.

SCHERDIN, MARY JANE LISKOVEC, retired librarian, information professional, researcher; b. LaCrosse, Wis., Sept. 29, 1940; d. Ambrose John and Martha Marie (Borgmeier) Liskovec; m. Arthur William Scherdin, Apr. 15, 1961 (div. 1976); children: James William, Laurette Therese (dec.), Amy Lynn; m. William A. Wera, July 11, 1998. BS in Elem. Edn., U. Wis., LaCrosse, 1961; MS in Libr. Sci., U. Wis., Madison, 1972, PhD in Edn. Adminstrn., 1989; MEd Profl. Devel. in Audiovisual Media, U. Wis., Whitewater, 1980. Children's libr. LaCrosse Pub. Libr., 1961; sch. libr. LaCrosse Pub. Schs., 1961-64; media dir. Whitewater Pub. Schs., 1971-75; head learning matter ctr. U. Wis., Whitewater, 1979-86, supr. arts media ctr., 1975-79, instr., 1976-78, asst. dean Milw., 1986-88, collection access coord. Madison, 1988-92; libr. dir. Edgewood Coll., Madison, 1992—2004; ret., 2004. Rschr. The Highsmith Co., Ft. Atkinson, Wis., 1983, ALA, Chgo., 1991-96, Cons. Psychologists Press, Palo Alto, Calif., 1991-96; cons. Myers-Briggs Type Indicator, 1992—; vis. prof. U. Wis., Madison, 1992-98. Co-author: K-12 Library Curriculum, 1974; author of bio-bibliographies of Wis. authors, 1981-83; designer; instructional computer programs 1983, 87, 89; author,editor: Discovering Librarians: Profiles of a Profession, 1994; contbr. articles to profl. jours. Pres. Jefferson (Wis.) Jaycettes, 1968-69; state and internal exec. v.p. Wis. Jaycettes, 1969-71; edn. chair Nat. Found. March of Dimes, Jefferson, 1970-74; vol. Nat. Found. Sudden Infant Death, Wis., 1975-83. Mem. AAUW (v.p. Ft. Atkinson 1974-75), Assn. Coll. and Rsch. Librs. (task force chair 1991-93, coll. libr. sect. nominating com., 1996, chair appts. com. 1997-98), Libr. Adminstrv. and Mgmt. Assn. (pubs. and bibliography com. 1989-91), Wis. Health Sci. Libr. Assn. (long range planning com. 1990-92, bd. dirs. 1992-93), Wis. Libr. Assn. (lit. awards com. 1980-84, chair lit. awards com. 1983, bd. dirs. 1987-88, chair edn. sect. 1993), Wis. Assn. Acad. Librs. (chair conf. planning 1985, 96, chair publs. 1993, chair 1988, info. literacy com. 1996-2001, chair info. lit. nat. immersion conf. 2000-01, ACRL liaison 1997), U. Wis. Sch. Libr. and Info. Studies Alumni Assn. (sec. 1993-95, v.p. 1999-2001, pres. 2002, past pres. 2003), Wis. Fedn. Ind. Colls. (tech planning team 1997-2002), Coun. Wis. Librs. (del. 1994-96). Avocation: violinist. Home: 6111 Winnequah Rd Madison WI 53716-3459

SCHERE, JEAN, researcher; b. Paris, Dec. 5, 1947; s. Robert Eugene Schere and Marie Rose Graillat; m. Danielle A. Cosson, Dec. 31, 1986; children: Constance, Elizabeth. BA, U. Pa., 1969, MBA in Mktg., 1972, PhD in Mgmt., 1981; MA in Internat. Law, Fletcher Sch., 1995. Lectr. mgmt. Wharton Bus. Sch., Phila., 1974—82; asst. prof. mgmt. Phila. Coll. Textiles, 1982—84; venture capitalist Inter Hotel, Montreal, Canada, 1987—91; asst. prof. econs. Tufts U., Medford, Mass., 1995—97; rsch. assoc. Fletcher Sch., Medford, 1997—2001. Dir. Sage, Phila., 1995—. U.S. del. Dem. Liberale, Paris, 2000—. Recipient Heizer award for best dissertation, Heizer Corp., 1982, Chevalier de L'Ordre, Nat. du Merite, 1998. Mem.: Aleps, Gesellschaft der Freunde von Bayreuth. Dl. Roman Catholic. Avocations: opera, swimming, skiing. Home: Apt 2 11 Edison Ave Medford MA 02155-5829 Office: Can Lodge 2 Grange Ter GY1 2BQ Guernsey Channel Islands E-mail: jschere@wanadoo.fr.

SCHERER, FREDERIC MICHAEL, economics professor; b. Ottawa, Ill., Aug. 1, 1932; s. Walter King and Margaret (Lucey) Scherer; m. Barbara A. Silbermann, Aug. 17, 1957; children: Thomas, Karen, Christina. AB with honors, U. Mich., 1954; MBA with high distinction, Harvard U., 1958, PhD, 1963; D (hon.), Univ. Hohenheim, 1996. Asst. prof. Princeton (N.J.) U., 1963-66; prof. econs. U. Mich., Ann Arbor, 1966-72; chief economist FTC, Washington, 1974-76; prof. econs. Northwestern U., Evanston, Ill., 1976-82; Joseph Wharton prof. polit. economy Swarthmore (Pa.) Coll., 1982-89; Aetna prof. pub. policy and mgmt. Harvard U., Cambridge, Mass., 1989-2000, emeritus prof., 2000—. Vis. prof. Ctrl. European U., Prague, 1993—94; lectr. Princeton U., 2000—04; Arthur Andersen disting. visitor U. Cambridge, 1997; Ludwig Erhard vis. prof. U. Bayreuth, 2000. Author: The Weapons Acquisition Process, 1964, Industrial market Structure and Economic Performance, 1990, The Economics of Multi-Plant Operation, 1975, Innovation and Growth, 1984, International High-Technology Competition, 1992, Competition Policies for an Integrated World Economy, 1994, Industry Structure, Strategy and Public Policy, 1996, New Perspectives on Economic Growth and Technological Innovation, 1999, Quarter Notes and Bank Notes, 2004; co-author: Mergers, Sell-Offs and Economic Efficiency, 1987. Mem. adv. panel NSF, Washington, 1980—83, U.S. Office Tech. Assessment, 1989—93, U.S. Bur. of Census, 1997—2000. Recipient Lifetime Achievement award, Am. Antitrust Inst., 2002; grantee, NSF, 1970, 1979, 1982, Sloan Found., 1996; sr. rsch. fellow, Internat. Inst. Mgmt., 1972—74, Census fellow, Am. Stats. Assn., 1989—90, Baker scholar, Harvard U., 1957, Centennial Rsch. grantee, O'Melveny & Myers, 1989. Mem.: Indsl. Orgn. Soc. (pres. 1992), Am. Econ. Assn. (v.p. 1988), European Assn. for Rsch. in Indsl. Econs. (co-founder 1974). Roman Catholic. Avocations: listening to music, musicology. Home: 601 Rockbourne Mills Ct Wallingford PA 19086-6779 Office Phone: 610-872-2557. E-mail: fmscherer@comcast.net.

SCHERER, GEORGE F. construction executive; Exec. v.p., treas., CFO, McCarthy Bldg. Cos., St. Louis. Office: McCarthy Bldg Cos 1341 N Rock Hill Rd Saint Louis MO 63124-1441

SCHERER, GEORGE ROBERT, retired secondary school educator; b. Marion, Ill., Sept. 2, 1923; s. Herman Albert and Alice Madora (Bulliner) S.; m. Margaret Mary Brzozowski, Dec. 31, 1945; children: Marion, Anne Madora. BS in Piano, Juilliard Sch., N.Y.C., 1948; MMus in Piano, Roosevelt U., 1952; studied with Rudolph Ganz. Cert. elem. and secondary tchr., Ill. Tchr. Chgo. Bd. Edn., 1954-85. Profl. chorister Chgo. Symphony Orch. Chorus, 1965-70; instr. Fenger Jr. Coll., Chgo., 1971-73; Fenger H.S. Choir appeared 4 seasons with Chgo. Civic Symphony Orchestra, 1968-71. Composer music for chorus and piano; author: Scherer "A Genealogy", 1996. Recipient (with choir) 16 superior awards in city and state contests, 1960-75. Mem. Am. Guild of Music Artists, Juilliard Sch. Music Alumni Assn., Roosevelt U. Alumni Assn. Avocations: painting, genealogy, piano. Home: 17841 Anthony Ave Country Club Hills IL 60478-4724

SCHERER, HAROLD NICHOLAS, JR., electric utility company executive, engineer; b. Plainfield, N.J., Apr. 5, 1929; s. Harold Nicholas and Nora (McDonough) S.; m. Jane Neely, Sept. 6, 1952 (div.); children: Anne Scherer McConnell, Peter; m. Patricia Condon, May 4, 1974; stepchildren: James, John, Joseph, Jeffery Ludwig, Jean Ludwig Ransdell. BE, Yale U., 1951; MBA, Rutgers U., 1955. Registered profl. engr., N.J., Mass. Various engring. positions Pub. Svc. Electric and Gas Co., Newark, 1951-63, Am. Electric Power Svc. Corp., N.Y.C., 1963-68, asst. chief. elec. engr., 1968-69, chief elec. engr., 1969-73, v.p. elec. engr., 1973-82, sr. v.p. elec. engring. Columbus, Ohio, 1982-90, also dir., until 1990; pres. Commonwealth Electric Co., Wareham, Mass., 1990-93, Cambridge (Mass.) Electric Light Co., Canal Electric Co., Com/Steam Co., 1990-93. Bd. dirs. Commonwealth Electric Co., Cambridge Electric Light Co., Com/Steam Co., Commonwealth Svcs. Co., Canal Electric Co.; cons. utility mgmt. and engring., 1993—; mem. joint U.S.-USSR working group on power transmission, 1975-81, joint U.S.-Italy working group on power transmission, 1979-88; vice-chmn. Am. Nat. Stds., N.Y.C., 1985-87; v.p. U.S. Nat. Com., 1985-93, pres., 1993-99, chmn. U.S. tech. com. Internat. Conf. on Large High Voltage Electric Sys., 1985-91, internat. adminstrv. coun., 1988-99, internat. exec. com., 1993-99; mem. engring. rev. bd. Bonneville Power Adminstrn., 1984-94; chmn. elec. sys. and equipment com. Edison Electric Inst., 1989-90, pres. power engring. edn. found., 1992-96; chmn. blue-ribbon panel Pacific Coast Blackouts, Bonneville-Power Adminstrn., 1996-97; bd. dirs. N.Y. State Ind. Sys. Operator, 1998—. Contbr. articles to profl. jours. Pres. N.J. Jr. C. of C., 1960-61; councilman City of Plainfield, 1963-65; mem. Watchung (N.J.) Hills Regional H.S. Bd. Edn., 1970-72; pres. Woods at Josephinum Civic Assn., Worthington, Ohio, 1983-84; trustee, treas. Beech Leaf Landing Trust, 2001-. Recipient Clayton Frost award U.S. Jaycees, 1961, Young Man of Yr. award Plainfield Jaycees, 1963, Lifetime Achievement award T&D Mag., 1990. Fellow IEEE (v.p. power engring. soc. 1988-89, pres. 1990-91, William Habirshaw award for transmission and distbn. engring. 1986, Disting. Mem. award Internat. Conf. on Large High Voltage Electric Systems 1996, Hon. Mem. award Internat. Conf. on Large High Voltage Electric Systems 2000, Philip Sporn award U.S. nat. com. Internat. Conf. on Large High Voltage Electric Systems 2002); mem. NAE, Yale Club N.Y.C., Tau Beta Pi, Beta Gamma Sigma. Home and Office: 467 Bay Ln Centerville MA 02632-3352 Personal E-mail: schererhn@aol.com.

SCHERER, JAMES R. research scientist; b. Kansas City, Dec. 31, 1931; s. Oscar Jacob and Anne Marie Scherer. BS, St. Mary's Coll., 1953; PhD, U. Minn., 1958. Rsch. chemist Dow Chem. Co., Midland, Mich., 1958—63, Western Regional Rsch. Lab., USDA, Albany, Calif., 1963—87; sr. staf scientist U. Calif., Berkeley, 1989—. Contbr. articles to profl. jours. Fellow: Am. Inst. Chemists; mem.: Optical Soc. Am., Am. Chem. Soc. Avocation: fly fishing.

SCHERER, KARLA, foundation executive, venture capitalist; b. Detroit, Jan. 13, 1937; d. Robert Pauli and Margaret (Lindsey) S.; m. Peter R. Fink, Sept. 14, 1957 (div. July 1989); children: Christina Lammert, Hadley McKenzie Tolliver, Allison Augusta Scherer; m. Theodore Souris, Sept. 5, 1992. Student, Wellesley Coll., 1954-55; BA, U. Mich., 1957; MA, U. Chgo., 1999. Chmn. Karla Scherer Found., Chgo., 1989—. Advisor on shareholders' rights; speaker on corp. governance to various univs. and profl. assns.; condr. workshops in field; leader only successful proxy contest of maj. U.S. publicly held corp., 1988; bd. dirs. R.P. Scherer Corp. Mem. vis. com. U. Chgo., Sch. for Humanities; former mem. bd. dirs. Cottage Hosp., Univ. Liggett Sch., Music Hall, Detroit League for Handicapped, Eton Acad.; former mem. adv. bd. Wellesley Coll; former mem. Rep. Dennis M. Hertel's Candidate Selection Com. for Armed Svcs. Acads.; mem. U. Mich. Ctr. for Edn. of Women Leadership Coun.; bd. dirs. Chgo. Humanities Festival, The Cradle. Named Outstanding Woman Leader of Yr. Oakland U., 1990, one of Metro Detroit's Dynamic Women Women's Econ. Club, 1992; recipient Most Influential Women award Crain's Detroit Bus., 1997, Northwood Univ. 1997 Disting. Women award, Women of Achievements Courage award Mich. Women's Found., 1997. Mem. Am. Mgmt. Assn. (gen. mgmt. coun. for growing orgns.), Internat. Women's Forum, Chgo. Network, Country Club Detroit, Grosse Pointe Club, Arts Club of Chgo., Casino Club. Office: 737 N Michigan Ave Ste 2330 Chicago IL 60611-2680

SCHERER, RONALD CALLAWAY, voice scientist, educator; b. Akron, Ohio, Sept. 11, 1945; s. Belden Davis and Lois Ramona (Callaway) S.; children: Christopher, Maria. BS, Kent State U., 1968; MA, Ind. U., 1972; PhD, U. Iowa, 1981. Research asst. U. Iowa, Iowa City, 1979-81, asst. research scientist, 1981-83, adj. asst. prof., 1983-88, adj. assoc. prof., 1988—; adj. asst. prof. U. Denver, 1984-86; asst. adj. prof. U. Colo., Boulder, 1984-93, adj. assoc. prof., 1993-96; research scientist The Denver Ctr. for the Performing Arts, 1983-88, sr. scientist, 1988-96; lectr. voice and speech sci. Nat. Theatre Conservatory, Denver, 1990-94; asst. clin. prof. Sch. Medicine U. Colo., Denver, 1988-96; assoc. prof. Bowling Green State U., Ohio, 1996—2001, prof., 2001—. Adj. assoc. prof. U. Okla., 1992-96; affiliate clin. prof. U. No. Colo., 1993-96; Oberlin Coll. affiliate scholar, 1996—; mem. exec. and legis. bd. Nat. Ctr. for Voice and Speech, 1990-96; G. Paul Moore lectr., The Voice Found., 2002. Author: (with Dr. I. Titze) Vocal Fold Physiology: Biomechanics, Acoustics and Phonatory Control, 1983; contbr. articles to profl. jours. Nat. Inst. Dental Research fellow, 1972-76. Fellow: Internat. Soc. Phonetic Scis. (auditor 1988—91); mem.: Am. Assn. Phonetic Scis. (nominating com. 1985—87, counselor 2000—03, councelor 2000—03), Internat. Assn. Logopedics and Phoniatrics, Acoustical Soc. Am., Am. Speech-Lang.-Hearing Assn., Internat. Arts Medicine Assn., Collegium Medicorum Theatri, Sigma Xi, Pi Mu Epsilon (G. Paul Moore lectr.). Office: Bowling Green State U Dept Comm Disorders Bowling Green OH 43403-0001 Office Phone: 419-372-7189.

SCHERER, VICTOR RICHARD, physicist, computer scientist, consultant, musician; b. Poland, Feb. 7, 1940; came to U.S., 1941; s. Emanuel and Florence B. Scherer; m. Gail R. Dobrofsky, Aug. 11, 1963; children: Helena Cecile, Markus David. BS magna cum laude, CCNY, 1960; MA, Columbia U., 1962; PhD, U. Wis., 1974. Health physics asst. Columbia U., N.Y.C., 1961-63; rsch asst. physics. dep. U. Wis., Madison, 1967-74; project assoc., project mgr. Inst. for Environ. Studies, World Climate-Food Rsch. Group, 1974-78; specialist computer systems U. Wis. Acad. Computing Ctr., 1978—; coord., sr. cons. Divsn. Info. Tech. U. Wis., Madison; concert pianist; tchr.; promoter contemporary composers. Researcher in particle physics, agroclimatology, soil-yield relationships and computer graphics; cons. on computer sys., electronic mail, geographic analysis, help desk and supercomputing applications. Fellow AEC, 1960-61. Mem. AAAS, Am. Phys. Soc., Am. Meteorol. Soc., Am. Soc. Agronomy, Assn. Computing Machinery, Nat. Computer Graphics Assn., Phi Beta Kappa, Sigma Xi. Office: U Wis-Madison Divsn Info Tech 1210 W Dayton St Madison WI 53706-1613 Office Phone: 608-262-3570. Business E-Mail: scherer@doit.wisc.edu.

SCHERF, DIETMAR, publishing executive, artist, minister; b. Graz, Austria, June 12, 1961; came to US, 1990; s. Friedrich and Maria S.; m. Patricia Michaela Rech, Apr. 9, 1987; children: Alexander, Deborah, Daniel, David. Diploma, trade sch., Graz, 1979. CEO Handelshaus D. Scherf, Vienna, 1987-90; CEO, pres. Scherf, Inc., Las Vegas, Nev., 1990-2000, creative dir., 2001—03; pastor, founder Megagrace Christian Ctr., Las Vegas, 2003—. Author: Short Term Trading, 1990, (booklet) Ross Perot, 1992, I Love Me: Avoiding and Overcoming Depressions, 1998, (as Alec Donzi) The Consultant, 2000, (book)Bulli$h: The Stock Market, 2004; composer, producer, performer (CD) Nice to Meet Ya!, 1994. Avocations: movies, reading, contemporary art, bible studies, music. Office: Megagrace Inc PO Box 80180 Las Vegas NV 89180-0180 Business E-Mail: ds@scherf.com.

SCHERGER, JOSEPH EDWARD, family physician, educator; b. Delphos, Ohio, Aug. 29, 1950; m. Carol M. Wintermute, Aug. 7, 1973; children: Adrian, Gabriel. BS summa cum laude, U. Dayton, 1971; MD, UCLA, 1975. Family practice residency U. Wash., Seattle, 1975-78; clin. instr. U. Calif. Sch. Medicine, Davis, 1978-80, asst. clin. prof., 1980-84, assoc. clin. prof., 1984-90, clin. prof., 1990—, dir. predoctoral program, 1991-92; med. dir. family practice and community medicine Sharp Healthcare, San Diego, 1992-96; assoc. dean primary care, chair dept. family medicine U. Calif., Irvine, 1996—2001, prof. dept. family medicine, 1996—2001; dean Fla. State U., Coll. Medicine, Tallahassee, 2001—03; clin. prof. family and preventive medicine U. Calif., San Diego, 2003—. Recipeient Hippocratic Oath award UCLA, Calif. Physician of Yr. award Am. Acad. Family Physicians. Mem. NAS (mem. Inst. Medicine), Am. Acad. Family Physicians, Soc. Tchrs. Family Medicine. Home: 2658 Del Mar Heights Rd # 604 Del Mar CA 92014 Office Phone: 858-232-8858. Business E-Mail: jscherger@ucsd.edu.

SCHERICH, EDWARD BAPTISTE, retired diversified company executive; b. Inland, Nebr., Dec. 3, 1923; s. Clarence H. and Clara E. (Baptiste) S.; m. Hyacinth Rau, Aug. 11, 1945 (div. 1980); children: Carol, Eileen, John.; m. Antoinette Currera, 1981; 1 stepdau., Sylvia McNamara. BBA, Tulane U., 1948. Acct. Colo. Milling & Elevator Co., Denver, 1948-50; accountant, office mgr. Southdown, Inc., New Orleans, 1950-55, controller, 1955-69; v.p. finance, sec., treas. Southdown Sugars Inc., New Orleans, 1970-73; v.p., sec., treas. Southdown Land Co., New Orleans, 1971-75; sec.-treas. Southdown, Inc., Houston, 1975-78, v.p., sec., 1979-84, treas., 1980-83; ind. fin. cons., 1984—; pres. Valmax Inc., 1989—. Served in USNR, 1943-45. Mem. Beta Gamma Sigma. Home: 633 Brouilly Dr Kenner LA 70065-1101 Office: PO Box 641307 Kenner LA 70064-1307

SCHERICH, ERWIN THOMAS, civil engineer, consultant; b. Inland, Nebr., Dec. 6, 1918; s. Harry Erwin and Ella (Peterson) Scherich; m. Jessie Mae Funk, Jan. 1, 1947; children: Janna Rae Scherich Thornton, Jerilyn Mae Scherich Dobson, Mark Thomas. Student, Hastings Coll., 1937—39, N.C. STate Coll., 1943—44; BS, U. Nebr., 1948; MS, U. Colo., 1951. Registered profl. engr., Colo. Civil and design engr. U.S. Bur. Reclamation, Denver, 1948—84, chief spillways and outlets sect., 1974—75, chief dams br. divsn. design, 1975—78, chief tech. rev. staff, 1978—79; chief divsn. tech. rev. Office Asst. Commr. Engring. and Rsch. Ctr., 1980—84; cons., 1984—. Mem. U.S. Com. Internat. Commn. Large Dams. With U.S. Army, 1941—45.

Fellow: NSPE (nat. dir. 1981—87, v.p. southwestern region 1991—93), ASCE; mem.: Profl. Engrs. Colo. (pres. 1977—78), Jefferson County West C. of C. Republican. Methodist. Home and Office: 3915 Balsam St Wheat Ridge CO 80033-4449

SCHERMAN, CAROL E. human resources professional; married; three children. BS in Orgnl. Behavior, U. San Francisco. With Bergen Brunswig Corp., exec. v.p. human resources. CEO Medi-Mail, Inc. subs. Bergen Brunswig Corp., Las Vegas. Active Human Resources Exec. Forum of Orange County; mem. human resources adv. com. Chapman U., Orange. Office: Bergen Brunswig Corp 4000 W Metropolitan Dr Orange CA 92868-3510

SCHERMAN, SUSAN LOUISE, nurse; b. Hoboken, N.J., Apr. 20, 1953; d. Everett Harold and Louise Annetta (Becker) S.; m. John Alfred Pendenza, Oct. 6, 1979. Student, St. Mary Hosp. Sch. Nursing, 1974, Katharine Gibbs Secretarial Sch., N.Y.C., 1975; BA, Sch. Nursing and Health Edn. Jersey City Coll., 1978. RN N.Y.; lic. lic. real estate sales rep. N.J., 1994, cert. notary pub. N.J., 2002. Sr. staff NYU Med. Ctr., N.Y.C., 1974-78; nurse Christ Hosp., Jersey City, 1975-78; pub. health nurse Retarded Infants Svcs., Inc., N.Y.C., 1978-80; pub. health nursing supr. Hoboken Pub. Health Nursing Svc., 1980-83; nurse cons. N.Y. County Health Svcs. Rev. Orgn., N.Y.C., 1983-86; cons. risk mgmt. Bower & Gardner, N.Y.C., 1986-91; nurse cons. Group Health, Inc., 1992; risk mgr. Jersey City Med. Ctr., 1992; sch. nurse/health edn. tchr. T. Roosevelt Sch., NJ, 1992-95; realtor Ray Fiore Real Estate, Hoboken, NJ, 1994; nurse cons. McAloon & Friedman, P.C. Attys., N.Y.C., 1995-2000; pediatric staff nurse div. devel. disabilities U. Medicine and Dentistry N.J., Newark, 2000—02; nurse paralegal Kasowitz, Benson, Torres & Friedman, LLP, N.Y.C., 2002—. Real estate agt. P.J. Miller Assocs., Secaucus, N.J.; condr., gen. mgr. The Robert Lawrence Orch., 1996—, prodr. CD, video, 1997; condr., gen. mgr. Susan Scherman Swing Band. Author: Community Health Nursing Care Plans: A Guide for Home Health Care Professionals, 1984, 2d edit., 2000; patentee in field. Notary pub., NJ. Mem. N.J. Bd. Realtors, Nat. Assn. Realtors, Hudson County Bd. Realtors, Soc. Scribes, Intravenous Nurses Soc., N.J. Bd. Realtors. Roman Catholic. Achievements include patents for medical device for toilet training male toddlers; owner of trademark Wee Wee Willy. Avocations: calligraphy, swimming, music. Office: 1633 Broadway New York NY 10019-6799

SCHERMER, JUDITH KAHN, lawyer; b. N.Y.C., Feb. 28, 1949; d. Robert and Barbara Kahn; m. Daniel Woodrough Schermer; 1 child, Sarah Nicole. BA, U. Chgo., 1971; JD, William Mitchell Coll. Law, 1987. Bar: Minn. 1987, U.S. Dist. Ct. Minn. 1987. Advt. and promotion specialist U. Chgo. Press, 1971-75; systems analyst Allstate Ins. Co., Northbrook, Ill., 1975-78, Lutheran Brotherhood, Mpls., 1980-83; polit. aide Mpls. City Coun., 1986-87; ptnr. Schermer & Schermer, Mpls., 1987-99, Schermer & Guy, Mpls., 1999—2001, Judith K. Schermer PLC, 2001—. Assoc chair 5th Congl. dist., state exec. com. Dem. Farm Labor Party. Mem. ATLA, Minn. Trial Lawyers Assn. (bd. govs., chair legis. com., employment com. 1999—), Minn. State Bar Assn., Minn. Women Lawyers, Nat. Employment Law Assn. Home: 4624 Washburn Ave S Minneapolis MN 55410-1846 Office: Lumber Exch Bldg 10 S 5th St Ste 950 Minneapolis MN 55402-1006

SCHERMERHORN, KENNETH, music director; b. Schenectady, N.Y., Nov. 20, 1929; Music dir. Nashville Symphonic Orch., Nashville, 1983—. Office: Nashville Symphony Orch 2000 Glen Echo Rd Ste 204 Nashville TN 37215

SCHERR, ALLAN LEE, computer scientist, executive, consultant; b. Balt., Nov. 18, 1940; s. Morris and Sarah (Kratzmar) S.; m. Marsha Kahn, Sept. 2, 1962 (div. 1974); children: Elise A., Stephanie L.; m. Linda Martin, June 8, 1980; 1 child, Katherine M. B.E.E., M.E.E., MIT, 1962, PhD.E.E., 1965. Mgr. time sharing option (TSO) design System Devel. div. IBM, Poughkeepsie, N.Y., 1967-70, mgr. multiple virtual storage (MVS) project, 1971-74, mgr. distributed systems programming System Communications div., 1977-80, dir. communications programming, 1980-81, dir. communications and applications systems corp. staff, 1981-83, dir. engring. and programming systems products div. White Plains, N.Y., 1983-86, dir. integrated applications info. systems div. Milford, Conn., 1986-88, v.p. devel. and integration application systems div., 1988-89, application solutions dir. architecture and devel., Application Solutions Line Bus., 1990-91; v.p. tech. World Wide Cons. Practices IBM Cons. Group, Milford, Conn., 1991-93; ind. cons. bus. process engring., info. tech., tech. mgmt. Weston, Conn., 1993-94; sr. v.p. software engring. EMC Corp., Hopkinton, Mass., 1994-2000, sr. v.p. tech., new bus. devel., 2000—01; ind. cons., 2001—; chief tech. officer Mission Control Productivity, Inc., 2000—03. Seminar leader Werner Erhard & Assocs., N.Y.C., 1982-90. Author: An Analysis of Time-Shared Computer Systems, 1966 (Grace Murray Hopper award Assn. Computing Machinery 1975); patentee in field. Mem. The Hunger Project, San Francisco, 1977. IBM fellow, 1984 Fellow IEEE; mem. Sigma Xi, Tau Beta Pi, Eta Kappa Nu Democrat. Home and Office: 18 Wyndclyffe Ct Rhinebeck NY 12572 Office Phone: 845-876-0785. E-mail: scherr@alum.mit.edu.

SCHERR, BARRY PAUL, foreign language educator; b. Hartford, Conn., May 20, 1945; s. Joseph and Helen Lillian (Shapiro) S.; m. Sylvia Egelman, Sept. 8, 1974; children: Sonia, David. AB magna cum laude, Harvard U., 1966; AM, U. Chgo., 1967, PhD, 1973. From acting asst. prof. to asst. prof. U. Washington, Seattle, 1970-74; from asst. prof. to prof. Russian, Dartmouth Coll., Hanover, NH, 1974—, chmn. dept. Russian, 1981-90, 96-97, chmn. program linguistics and cognitive sci., 1989-96, assoc. dean for humanities, 1997—2001, assoc. provost, 2001, provost, 2001—. Co-organizer Internat. Conf. Russian Verse Theory, 1987, Internat. Conf. Anna Akhmatova and the Poets of Tsarskoe Selo, 1989, Internat. Conf. Eisenstein at 100: A Reconsideration, 1998. Author: Russian Poetry: Meter, Rhythm and Rhyme, 1986, Maxim Gorky, 1988; co-trans. The Seeker of Adventure, Alexander Grin, 1989; mem. editorial bd. Slavic and East European Jour., 1978-88; co-editor: Russian Verse Theory: Procs. of the 1987 Conference at UCLA, 1987, O RUS! Studia litteraria Slavica in honorem Hugh McLean, 1995, A Sense of Place: Tsarskoe Selo and Its Poets, 1993, Twentieth-Century Russian Literature, 2000, Eisenstein at 100: A Reconsideration, 2001; co-translator, co-editor Maksim Gorky: Selected Letters, 1997; contbr. articles to profl. jours. Scholar Harvard Coll., 1963-66; fellow NDEA, 1966-69; grantee Internat. Rsch. and Exch. Bd., 1969-70, NEH, 1987, 89, U.S. Dept. Edn., 1987-89, Dartmouth Coll. Sr. Faculty, 1988; summer rsch. grantee Grad. Sch., Inst. Comparative and Fgn. Area Studies U. Wash., 1973. Mem. MLA (mem. exec. com. assoc. dept. fgn. langs. 1983-85, del. assembly 1986-88), Am. Assn. Advancement Slavic Studies, Am. Assn. Tchrs. Slavic and East European Langs. (pres. 1987-88, founder, past pres. No. New Eng. chpt., numerous coms.). Office: Dartmouth Coll Russian Dept Reed Hall Hanover NH 03755-3506 Office Phone: 603-646-2070. E-mail: Barry.scherr@Dartmouth.edu.

SCHERR, LAWRENCE, internist, educator; b. NYC, Nov. 6, 1928; s. Harry and Sophia (Schwartz) S.; m. Peggy L. Binenkorb, June 13, 1954; children: Cynthia E., Robert W. AB, Cornell U., 1950, MD, 1957. Diplomate Am. Bd. Internal Medicine (bd. dirs., sec.-treas. 1979-86). Intern Cornell Med. divsn. Bellevue Hosp. and Meml. Ctr., 1957-58, asst. resident, 1958-59, rsch. fellow cardiorenal lab., 1959-60, chief resident, 1960-61, co-dir. cardiorenal lab., 1961-62, asst. vis. physician, 1961-63, assoc. vis. physician, 1963-65, dir. cardiology and renal unit, 1963-67, assoc. dir., 1964-67, vis. physician, 1966-68; physician to out-patients N.Y. Hosp., 1961-63, asst. attending physician, 1963-66, assoc. attending physician, 1966-71, attending physician, 1971-2000; asst. attending physician, cons. Sloan-Kettering Cancer Ctr., 1962—2000. Chmn. dept. medicine North Shore Univ. Hosp., 1967-2001, chmn. emeritus, 2001-, dir. acad. affairs, 1969-93, sr. v.p. med. affairs, 1993-2000; exec v.p. for med. and acad. affairs North Shore-L.I. Jewish Health Sys., 1998-2000, trustee, Betsey Cushing Whitney dean, chief acad. officer, sr. v.p. acad. affairs, 2000-04; asst. in medicine Med. Coll. Cornell U., 1958-59; rsch. fellow N.Y. Heart Assn., 1959-60; instr. medicine Cornell U. Med. Coll., 1960-63, asst. prof., 1963-66, assoc. prof., 1966-71, prof., 1971-96, assoc. dean, 1969-96; prof. medicine, assoc. dean NYU Sch. Medicine, 1996—; career scientist Health Rsch. Coun., N.Y.C., 1962-66; tchg. scholar Am. Heart Assn., 1966-67; pres. N.Y. State Bd. Medicine, 1974-75; chmn. Accreditation Coun. for Grad. Med. Edn., 1988, N.Y. State Coun. on Grad. Edn., 1987-92. Contbr. articles to profl. jours. Lt. USN, 1950—53. Fellow N.Y. Acad. Medicine, Am. Heart Assn. (coun. on clin. cardiology); master ACP (chmn. and gov. Downstate N.Y. region II 1975-80, regent 1980-86, chmn. bd. regents 1985-86, chmn. bd. regents emeritus, nat. pres.-elect 1986-87, pres. 1987-88, pres. emeritus, Alfred Stengel Meml. medal); mem. AMA, Am. Fedn. Clin. Rsch., Harvey Soc., N.Y. Med. Soc., Nassau County Med. Soc., Assn. Am. Med. Colls., Am. Clin. and Climatologic Assn. Office: N Shore Univ Hosp Manhasset NY 11030 Office Phone: 516-562-2940. Business E-Mail: scherr@nshs.edu.

SCHERRER, GEORGE M. electrical engineer; b. Shawneetown, Ill., Oct. 30, 1914; s. George Bernard and Susan Scherrer; m. Ruby Nance Scherrer; children: George M. Jr., Irene, Nancy, Joyce, Fred, Jamie BSEE, U. Ill., 1938; postgrad., Princeton U., 1944, MIT, 1945. Registered profl. engr. Farmer; ptnr. Scherrer Equipment Co., Inc.; mgr. Saline Valley Conservancy Dist.; tchr. physcis Washington U., St. Louis; prin. engr. Rural Electric Adminstrn., 1940-46; design and constrn. REA power lines A. Y. Taylor Co., 1938-40. Presenter in field. Bd. dirs. Ohio Valley Improvement Assn.; mem. Citizens Adv. Coun. Ohio Valley Commn., co-chmn.; chmn. bd. Cath. Shrine Pilgrimage, Inc., 1997-2000; bd. dirs. Camp Ondessonk, 1957—. Lt. (j.g.) USNR, 1943-46. Mem. IEEE, Am. Soc. Agrl. Engrs. (sr. mem., cert.), Nat. Cattlemens Assn., Ill. Farm Bur. Democrat. Roman Catholic.

SCHERRER, HELENE CHALIFOUR, Canada government official; b. Que., Can., July 6, 1950; 2 children. Grad., Sillery's Jesus-Marie Coll.; BA in Social Work, Laval U. Councillor for Sillery, 1990—94; mem. Can. Parliament, 2000—; min. Can. heritage Govt. Can., Gatineau, 2003—. Office: House of Commons Ottawa ON Canada K1A 0A6 also: Can Heritage Les Terrasses de la Chaudiere 12th Fl 15 Gatineau PQ Canada K1A 0M5

SCHETKY, LAURENCE MCDONALD, metallurgist, researcher; b. Baguio, The Philippines, July 15, 1922; s. Gerald Laurence and Ethyl Jane (McDonald) S.; m. Diane Heiskell, Dec. 12, 1977 (div. Feb. 1986); m. Karen Searles, July 12, 1986 (div. Oct. 1994); 1 child, Mark Christian; m. Margarita A. Smith, Oct. 27, 1995. BSChemE, Rensselaer Poly Inst., Troy, N.Y., 1943, MMetE, 1948, PhD, 1953. Registered profl. engr., Mass. Rsch. fellow MIT, Cambridge, 1953-59; v.p. rsch. Alloyd Electronics, Inc., Cambridge, 1959-63; dir. R & D Internat. Copper Rsch. Assn., Inc., N.Y.C., 1963-83; pres. Memory Metals, Inc., Stamford, Conn., 1983-86; v.p., chief scientist Memry Corp., Brookfield, Conn., 1987—. Editor: Beryllium Technology, 2 vol., 1966, The Metallurgy of Copper, 13 vols., 1966-83; author: (with others) Copper in Iron and Steel, 1982; contbr. over 100 articles to physics and metallurgy jours. With USN, 1944-46, PTO. Rsch. fellow Alcoa Corp., 1948-53. Fellow Am. Soc. Metals Internat. (life), Brit. Inst. Materials; mem. AIME (life). Democrat. Episcopalian. Achievements include 17 patents in Electron Beam Technology, Vapor Phase Deposition, Shape Memory Actuators, medical devices. Office: Memry Corp 3 Berkshire Blvd Bethel CT 06801-1037 E-mail: l.m_schetky@memry.com.

SCHETLIN, ELEANOR M. retired university official; b. NYC, July 15, 1920; d. Henry Frank and Elsie (Chew) Schetlin. BA, Hunter Coll., 1940; MA, Tchrs. Coll., Columbia U., 1942, EdD, 1967. Playground dir. Dept. Parks, N.Y.C., 1940-42; libr. Met. Hosp. Sch. Nursing, N.Y.C., 1943-44, dir. recreation and guidance, 1945-58, historian Alumnae Assn., 2000—04; coord. student activities SUNY, Plattsburgh, 1959-63, asst. dean students, 1963-64; asst. prof., coord. student personnel svcs. CUNY, Hunter Coll., 1967-68; asst. dir. student personnel Columbia U., Coll. Pharm. Scis., N.Y.C., 1968-69, dir. student personnel, 1969-71; assoc. dean students Health Scis. Ctr. SUNY, Stony Brook, 1971-73, asst. v.p. student svcs., 1973-74, assoc. dean students, dir. student svcs., 1974-85. Founding mem. Sea Cliff unit 300 Nassau County Aux. Police; founding mem. Nassau NOW Women of Color Task Force. Contbr. articles to profl. jours.; author: Myths of the Student Personnel Point of View. Recipient NOW Alliance PAC award, 1991, 1999, Lifetime Achievement award, Nassau NOW, 1992, Task Force Women of Color award, NOW, 1994. Mem.: So. Poverty Law Ctr., Wellesley Ctrs. Rsch. Women, Nat. Women's History Project, Women's Environment and Devel. Orgn., Nat. Women's Studies Assn., Nat. Assn. Women Edn., Nat. Mus. Women in the Arts. Home: 60 Hildreth Pl East Hampton NY 11937

SCHETZ, JOSEPH ALFRED, aerospace engineer, educator; b. Orange, N.J., Oct. 19, 1936; s. Alfred John and Teresa (Zappa) S.; m. Katherine Frances Giorgianni, Jan. 31, 1959; children: Holly, Joseph, Katherine, John. BS, Webb Inst. Naval Architecture, 1958; MS, MA, PhD, Princeton U. Sr. scientist Gen. Applied Sci. Lab., Westbury, N.Y., 1961-64; assoc. prof. aerospace engring. U. Md., 1964-69; Fred D. Durham chair aerospace and ocean engring. Va. Poly. Inst. and State U., Blacksburg, 1999—, chmn. dept., 1969-93. Cons. Applied Physics Lab., Johns Hopkins, 1964-96, Atlantic Rsch. Corp., Alexandria, Va., 1966-72, Du Pont Corp., Richmond, Va., 1980-85; guest prof. Inst. for Theoretical Gas Dynamics, Aachen, Germany, summer 1970; religious edn. tchr. St. John's Roman Cath. Ch., Colesville, Md., 1965-69; prin. H.S. religion St. Mary's Roman Cath. Ch., Blacksburg, 1970-71; vis. scholar Beijing Rsch. Lab., 1985; vis. scientist Wright Labs., Dayton, Ohio, 1993. Author books, chpts. and articles. Republican precinct chmn., Montgomery County, Md., 1965-69; mem. Rep. Exec. Com., 1973-86; faculty adviser Va. Poly. Inst. Rep. Club, 1973-76. Fellow AIAA (assoc. editor jour. 1975-77, publs. com. 1978-84, edn. com. 1978-81, air breathing propulsion tech. com. 1994-97, Pendray Aerospace Lit. award 1997, Air Breathing Propulsion Tech. award 1998, Aerospace Contbn. to Soc. award 1999, J. Leland Atwood award 2004), ASME (life); mem. Soc. Naval Architects and Marine Engrs., Sigma Gamma Tau, Tau Beta Pi, Sigma Xi. Home: 607 Rainbow Ridge Dr Blacksburg VA 24060-5535 Office Phone: 540-231-9056. E-mail: ptiger@vt.edu.

SCHEUCH, RICHARD, economist, educator; b. N.Y.C., July 15, 1921; s. William Allen and Marjorie (Tuller) S.; m. Fayette Van Alstyne Smith, Sept. 1, 1948; children: Evelyn Scheuch Lord, W. Allen II. AB, Princeton U., 1942, MA, 1948, PhD, 1952. Asst. in econs. Princeton U., 1946-50; mem. faculty dept. econs. Trinity Coll., Hartford, Conn., 1950-89, G. Fox and Co. prof. econs. emeritus, 1989—, vis. prof., 1990—93. Trustee Watkinson Libr. Served with USNR, 1942—46. Woodrow Wilson fellow, 1946-47 Mem. Am. Econ. Assn., Indsl. Rels. Rsch. Assn., Hartford Golf Club. Unitarian Universalist. Home: 80 Loeffler Rd G522-523 Bloomfield CT 06002

SCHEUERLE, ANGELA ELIZABETH, geneticist; b. Syracuse, N.Y., Aug. 13, 1962; d. William Howard and Jane Frances (Walker) S.; m. Alan Joseph Eynon. BS in Biology magna cum laude, U. of the South, 1984; MD, U. South Fla., 1988. Resident in pediatrics Children's Hosp. Med. Ctr., Cin., 1988-91; fellow Inst. for Molecular and Human Genetics Baylor Coll. Medicine, Houston, 1991-95; asst. prof. pediat. divsn. med. genetics U. Tex. Med. Sch., Houston, 1995-98; fellow U. Chgo. Ctr. for Med. Ethics, 1998-99; adj. faculty U. Tex. Sch. Pub. Health, Houston, 2000—. Clin reviewer Tex. Birth Defects Registry, 1994—; med. dir. Tex. Birth Defects Rsch. Ctr., 1998—; mem. ethics in sci. and medicine program U. Tex. Southwestern Med. Sch., 1999—. Vol. Big Bros./Big Sisters, Tampa, Fla., 1978-82, Girl Scouts Am., Dallas; trustee St. Mark's Episcopal Sch., 1995-98; bioethics com. Episcopal Diocese of Tex. Fellow Am. Acad. Pediatrics, Am. Coll. Med. Genetics; mem. Am. Soc. Human Genetics, Phi Beta Kappa, Sigma Xi, Alpha Epsilon Delta. Democrat. Avocations: horseback riding, photography, crossword puzzles.

SCHEUMANN, JOHN B. construction executive; BS, Ball State U. Chair, CEO Crossman Cmtys., Indpls., 1996—. Office: 92 N Meridian St Ste 300 Indianapolis IN 46204-3003

SCHEUSNER, RONALD L. music educator; b. Watertown, S.D., Aug. 12, 1950; s. William H. and Edna Scheusner; m. Marsha Kay Herther, May 26, 1973; children: Heidi, Geoffrey. BS in Edn., No. State U., 1972; MusM, Wichita State U., 1976. Dir. bands Milbank (S.D.) H.S., 1978—80; asst. prof. Trevecca Nazarene U., Nashville, 1980—82; instr. music Va. Intermont Coll., Bristol, Va., 1982—84; dir. bands Douglas Middle Sch., Rapid City, SD, 1986—97, S.D. Sch. Mines and Tech., Rapid City, 1994—97, Battle Ground Acad., Franklin, Tenn., 1999—. Recipient Wolf Trap Acad. award, Nat. Fedn. Music Clubs, Washington, 1972. Mem.: Middle Tenn. Band and Orch. Assn., Internat. Trumpet Guild. Avocations: driving, model trains. Home: 1502 Jewell Dr Columbia TN 38401-5212 E-mail: RonS@bgacademy.com.

SCHEVE, MAY E. state legislator, political organization worker; b. St. Louis, June 27, 1964; d. Robert Anthony and May Ellen (Braun) S. BA, St. Louis U., 1987; postgrad., Webster U. Rep. Mo. State Ho. Reps. Dist. 98, 1991—2002; adminstr. Dem. Party, Jefferson City, Mo., 2002—. Committeewoman Gravois Twp. Dem. Club; chair, Mo. Dem. Party, 2002-. Mem. Women Legislators, Third Congl. Women's Club (sec.), Women's Dem. Forum, Alpha Gamma Delta, Kappa Beta Phi. Democrat. Office: Mo Democratic Party 419 E High St PO Box 719 Jefferson City MO 65102

SCHEVILL, EDWARD, social services agency director; b. Boston, Jan. 16, 1948; s. William Edward Schevill and Barbara Lawrence. Student, Syraucse (N.Y.) U., 1965-68. Coord., dir. Epilepsy Self-Help, Tucson, 1977-88; dir., pres. Epilepsy Outreach Project, Inc., Tucson, 1988—. Awards com., chair Dianne Lynn Anderson Meml. Award, Tucson, 1990—. Home: 922 N Campbell Ave Tucson AZ 85719-4915 Office: Epilepsy Outreach Project Inc 922 N Campbell Ave Tucson AZ 85719-4915

SCHEVILL, JAMES ERWIN, poet, playwright; b. Berkeley, Calif., June 10, 1920; s. Rudolph and Margaret (Erwin) S.; m. Margot Helmuth, Aug. 2, 1966; children (by previous marriage): Deborah, Susanna. BS, Harvard U., 1942; MA (ad eundem), Brown U.; LHD (hon.), R.I. Coll., 1986. Mem. faculty San Francisco State Coll., 1959-68, prof. English, 1968, dir. Poetry Center, 1961-68; prof. Brown U., 1969-85, prof. emeritus, 1985—. Reader various univs., insts., and orgns. Author: New and Selected Poems, 2000. Served to capt. AUS, 1942-46. Ford Found. grantee, 1954, 60-61, R.I. Com. on Humanities grantee, 1975; Fund Advancement Edn., 1953-54, Office for Advanced Drama Research fellow, 1957, Rockefeller fellow, 1964, Guggenheim fellow, 1981, McKnight fellow, 1984; recipient Performance prize Nat. Theatre Competition, 1945, 2d prize Phelan Biography Competition, 1954, 2d prize Phelan Drama Competition, 1958, William Carlos Williams award, 1965, Roadsted Found. award, 1966, Gov.'s award R.I., 1975, Best Story of Yr. award Ariz. Quart., 1977; story selected for O. Henry Awards Prize Stories, 1978; award in lit. Am. Acad. Arts and Letters, 1991; work commd. by Nat. Council Chs., 1956-61, Fromm Found., 1959, Trinity Repertory Co., R.I. Hosp., 1986, Providence Coll., 1986, Magdalena Group, 1992. Home: 1309 Oxford St Berkeley CA 94709-1424 Office: Brown U Dept English Providence RI 02912-0001 E-mail: mschevill@aol.com.

SCHEWE, DONALD BRUCE, archivist, library director; b. Cleve., Oct. 28, 1943; s. Norman Edward and Theodora (Robinson) S.; m. Charlene R. Wenz, June 10, 1965; children: Amanda Marie, Ann Elizabeth. BA, U. Nebr., 1964, MA, 1968; PhD, Ohio State U., 1971. Archivist Franklin D. Roosevelt Library, Hyde Park, N.Y., 1972-77, supervisory archivist, 1977-79, asst. dir., 1979-81; dir. Carter Presdl. Materials Project, Atlanta, 1981-86, Jimmy Carter Library, Atlanta, 1986-99, Ga. Dept. Archives and History, 2000; pres. Pawnee Creek Enterprises, 1999—. Editor: Franklin D. Roosevelt and Foreign Affairs, 1981. With U.S. Army, 1964-66, Vietnam, ret. lt. col. Mem. Assn. Records Mgrs. and Adminstrs., Soc. Ga. Archivists, Orgn. Am. Historians, Inst. of Cert. Records Mgrs. (pres. 1996-2000). Lodges: Rotary. Episcopalian. E-mail: dschewe@mindspring.com.

SCHEWEL, ROSEL HOFFBERGER, education educator; b. Mar. 1, 1928; d. Samuel Herman and Gertrude (Miller) Hoffberger; m. Elliot Sidney Schewel, June 12, 1949; children: Stephen, Michael, Susan. AB, Hood Coll., 1949; MEd, Lynchburg Coll., 1974, EdS, 1982, EdD (hon.), 2000. Reading resource tchr. Lynchburg Pub. Schs., Va., 1967-75; adj. prof. edn. Lynchburg Coll., 1973-79, assoc. prof. edn., 1980-92. Cons., seminar leader Woman's Resource Ctr., Lynchburg, 1980-92. Trustee, chair bd. trustees Lynchburg Coll., Va., 1992-98, 99—; bd. dirs. Va. Found. for Humanities and Pub. Policy, 1985-90, New Vistas Sch., Lynchburg Human Rights Commn., 1992-2000, Lynchburg Youth Svcs., 1993-97; bd. dirs. Venture Enterprising Women, Planned Parenthood of the Blue Ridge; trustee Va. Mus. of Fine Arts, 1985-90; apptd. Commn. on Edn. for All Virginians, 1990; bd. dirs. Action Alliance for Virginia's Children and Youth, 1995-2002; trustee Amazement Sq. Children's Mus., 1996—; vol. Ct. Apptd. Spl. Advocate, Riverviews Art Space Bd., 2002—. Recipient Disting. Svc. award NCCJ, 1973, Outstanding Woman in Edn. award YWCA, 1988, Disting. Alumni award Lynchburg Coll., 1993. Mem. Phi Kappa Phi. Democrat. Jewish. Address: 4316 Gorman Dr Lynchburg VA 24503-1948

SCHEXNAYDER, BRIAN EDWARD, opera singer, voice educator; b. Port Arthur, Tex., Sept. 18, 1953; s. Leonard and Dorothy (Carrier) S.; m. Sherri Scallan, Oct. 2, 1976. BA in Music, U. Southwestern La., 1976; postgrad., Juilliard Sch. Music, 1976-80. Vocal instr. Brian Schexnayder Vocal Studio, N.Y.C., 1995-97, Plano, Tex., 1997—. Performances with Met. Opera, N.Y.C., Paris Opera Co., Edmonton (Alta., Can.) Opera Co., New Orleans Opera Co., Santiago (Chile) Opera, Winnipeg (Man., Can.), St. Petersburg (Fla.) Opera, Jackson (Miss.) Opera Co., San Francisco Opera, Frankfurt Opera, Hamburg Staatsoper Opera, Oper der Studt Bonn, Spoleto (Italy) Festival of Two Worlds, Cin. Opera, Fla. Grand Opera. Mem. Am. Guild Musicians. Avocations: computers, billiards, remote control airplanes.

SCHEXNAYDER, CHARLOTTE TILLAR, state legislator; b. Tillar, Ark., Dec. 25, 1923; d. Jewell Stephen and Bertha (Terry) Tillar; m. Melvin John Schexnayder Sr., Aug. 18, 1946; children: M. John Jr., Sarah Holden, Stephen. BA, La. State U., 1944, postgrad., 1947-48. Asst. editor La. Agrl. Extension, Baton Rouge, 1944; editor The McGehee (Ark.) Times, 1945-46, 48-53; editor, co-publisher The Dumas (Ark.) Clarion, 1954-85, pub., 1985-99; mem. Ark. Ho. of Reps., Little Rock, 1985-99, asst. speaker pro tem, 1995—. Pres. Ark. Assn. Women, 1955, Nat. Newspaper Assn., Washington, 1991-92, Ark. Press. Assn., Little Rock, 1982, Nat. Fedn. Press Women, Blue Springs, Mo., 1977-78, Litte Rock chpt. Soc. Profl. Journalists, 1973; mem. pres.'s coun. Winrock Internat., 1990—; chmn. Dumas Area Cmty. Found., 2000-02. Editor: Images of the Past, 1991. 1st woman mem. Ark. Bd. Pardons and Parole, 1975-80; mem. Ark. Legis. Coun., 1985-92; bd. dirs. Women's Found. Ark., sec. 1999—; bd. dirs. Chicot-Desha Port Indsl. Com.; v.p. Desha County Mus., 1989—; dir. Dumas Indsl. Found., 1986—; mem. exec. com. Ark. Ctrl. Radiation Therapy Inst., 1991-92; mem. adv. bd. Ark. Profl. Women Achievement, 1992—; vice chair Ark. Rural Devel. Commn., 1991-96, chair 1996-97; mem. Winrock Internat. Adv. Coun., 1991—; founding incorporator Ark. Waterways Commn., 1996—, bd. dirs.; bd. visitors Manship Sch. Comm., La. State U., 1998—; bd. dirs. Main Street Ark., Hist. Preservation Alliance Ark.; mem. Ark. Transitional Employment Coun., 1999—; sec. Dumas Area Cmty. Fund, 2000—; bd. dirs. Enterprise Corp. for the Delta, 1999-2002, Dumas Main St., v.p.; bd. dirs. Historic Preservation Alliance Ark, 2000—; mem. Ark. Transitional Employment Assistance Bd., 2000; outstanding bd. mem. Ark. Main St., 2002; outstanding bd. chair Ark. Cmty. Found., 2003. Named Disting. Alumnus Ark. A&M Coll., 1971, Woman of Achievement Nat. Fedn. Press Women, 1970, Outstanding Arkansan C. of C., 1986; recipient Ark. Profl. Women of Distinction award No. Bank, Little Rock, 1990, Emma McKinney award Nation's Top Cmty. Newspaper Woman, 1980, Journalist award Nat. Conf. of Christians and Jews, 1989, Lifetime Achievement award Nat. Fedn. Press Women, 1992, Outstanding Svc. award Ark. Assn. Elem. Prins., Disting. Svc. award Ark. Press Assn., 1993; named to La. State U. Alumni Hall of Distinction, 1994, Disting. Svc. award Internat. Soc. Weekly Newspaper Editors, 1996, Golden Svc. award Ark. Press Assn., 1996, State Leadership award Ark. Waterways Commn., 1996, Horizon award League Women Voters Ark., 1998; named one Top 100 Ark. Women, Ark. Bus., 1995, 96, 97, 98; named to Journalism Hall of Fame La. State U., 1998; named Outstanding Bd. Mem. of Yr., Main Street Ark., 2002, Outstanding Bd. Mem., Ptnrs. of Ark. Cmty. Found., 2003, honored Outstanding Svc. Women's Found. Ark., 2003. Mem.: Ark. Delta Coun. (chmn. emeritus, v.p. Dumas Main St., mem. Main St. Ark. adv. bd.), Pi Beta Phi (Crest award 1992). Democrat. Roman Catholic. Home: 322 Court St Dumas AR 71639-2718 Office: PO Box 160 Dumas AR 71639-0160 E-mail: cts@seark.net.

SCHEXNIDER, ALVIN J. academic administrator; b. Lake Charles, La., May 26, 1945; s. Alfred and Ruth Mayfield Schexnider; m. Virginia Y. Reeves. BA, Grambling State U., 1968; MA, Northwestern U., 1971, PhD, 1973. Asst. dir. pers. Owens-Ill. Inc., 1968; asst. prof. So. U., 1973-74, Syracuse U., 1974-77; sr. prof. Fed. Exec. Inst., 1977-79; assoc. dean Va. Commonwealth U., 1979-84, vice provost undergrad. studies, 1987-95; asst. vice chancellor U. N.C., Greensboro, 1984-87; chancellor, pres. Winston-Salem (N.C.) State U., 1996-00; dir. office health policy devel./sch. medicine Wake Forest U., 2000—. Fellow Inter-Univ. Seminar on Armed Forces and Soc., 1975—. Gov. commn. Va. Future, 1982-84; bd. visitors Va. State U., 1986-87; mem. Va. State Bd. Edn., 1990-94, N.C. econ. devel. bd., 1997-2000; bd. trustees Wachovia Funds; vice chair Gov.'s Adv. Commn. on Revitalization of Va.'s Cities. Sgt. AUS, 1968-70. Norman Wait Harris fellow, 1971-72, fellow Ford Found., 1972, Woodrow Wilson Found., 1973; named to Outstanding Young Men Am., U.S. Jaycees, 1978. Fellow Nat. Acad. Pub. Adminstrn.; mem. ASPA (pres. Va. chpt. 1983-84, J. Sargent Reynolds award 1980), Am. Polit. Sci. Assn., Nat. Conf. Black Polit. Sci., Alpha Phi Alpha, Sigma Pi Phi. Office: Wake Forest U Medical Ctr Blvd Winston Salem NC 27157-0001 E-mail: aschexni@wfubmc.edu

SCHIAFFINO, S(ILVIO) STEPHEN, retired medical society executive, consultant; b. Bklyn., Nov. 1, 1927; s. Stephen Anthony and Jane (DiDonato) S.; m. Josephine Rose Bovello, Apr. 25, 1954; children: Susan, Stephen. BS, Georgetown U., 1946, MS, 1948, PhD in Biochemistry, 1956. Rsch. biochemist divsn. nutrition FDA, Washington, 1948-50, asst. br. chief divsn., 1954-60; mgr. chemistry dept. Hazelton Labs., Vienna, Va., 1960-61; with NIH, 1961—; scientist adminstr. NIH (Nat. Cancer Inst.), 1961-64, asst. chief rsch. grants rev. br., 1964-69, chief., 1969-72, assoc. dir. for sci. rev., 1972-78, dep. dir. divsn. rsch. grants, 1978-86; sr. sci. advisor office of extramural rsch. and tng., office of dir. NIH, 1986-87; exec. officer, sci. officer Am. Soc. for Clin. Nutrition, Bethesda, Md., 1987-93; cons., 1993—. Cons. in field. Served with U.S. Army, 1950—53. Recipient Superior Svc. award FDA, 1960, Superior Svc. award NIH, 1969. Mem. AAAS, Am. Soc. for Clin. Nutrition., Am. Soc. for Nutritional Scis.

SCHIAVELLI, MELVYN DAVID, academic administrator, science educator, researcher; b. Chgo., Aug. 8, 1942; s. Gene James and Frances Elizabeth (Giacomo) S.; m. Virginia Farrell, Sept. 10, 1966; children Timothy, Karen BS in Chemistry, DePaul U., 1964; PhD in Chemistry, U. Calif., Berkeley, 1967. Rsch. assoc. Mich. State U., East Lansing, 1967-68; from asst. prof. to assoc. prof. chemistry Coll. William and Mary, Williamsburg, Va., 1968-80, prof. chemistry, 1980-94, chmn. dept. chemistry, 1978-84, dean Faculty Arts and Scis., 1984-86, provost, 1986-93, acting pres., 1992; prof. chem. and biochem., provost U. Del., Newark, 1994—. Contbr. articles to profl. jours., 1969— Grantee NSF Petroleum Rsch. Fund, 1969-90. Mem. Am. Chem. Soc., Royal Inst. Chemists, Sigma Xi. Roman Catholic. Office: U Del Office Provost 129 Hullihen Hall Newark DE 19716

SCHIAVO, PASCO LOUIS, lawyer; b. Hazleton, Pa., June 21, 1937; s. Louis and Josephine (Cortese) S. BA, Lafayette Coll., 1958; JD, U. Pa., 1962. Bar: Pa. 1962, U.S. Dist. Ct. (mid. dist.) Pa. 1965, U.S. Ct. Appeals (3d cir.) 1972, U.S. Supreme Ct. 1970. Assoc. Laputka, Bayless, Ecker & Cohn, Hazleton, 1963-65; asst. dist. atty. Luzerne County, Wilkes-Berre, Pa., 1963-65; pvt. practice Hazleton, 1965—. Mem. disciplinary bd. Supreme Ct. Pa., Harrisburg, 1977-83. Contbr. articles to profl. jours. Pres. Luzerne County Commn. Econ. Opportunity, Wilkes-Barre, 1966-68. Mem. ABA, ATLA, Pa. Bar Assn., Luzerne County Bar Assn., Pa. Trial Lawyers Assn., Am. Judicature Soc., Nat. Bd. Trial Advocacy (diplomate, cert. civil trial advocate). Office: 199 N Church St Hazleton PA 18201-5874

SCHIAZZA, GUIDO DOMENIC (GUY SCHIAZZA), educational association administrator; b. Phila., May 17, 1930; s. Guido and Claudina (DiPrinzio) S.; m. Irmgard Heidi Reissmueller, May 15, 1954. BA, Pa. State U., 1952; postgrad., St. Joseph's U., 1954-55, Villanova U., 1954-55, Temple U., 1955-58. Cert. tchr., Pa.; cert. clinician, ednl. specialist, instructional specialist, sch. psychologist, guidance counselor, reading specialist. Speech therapist, lang. arts instr. Commonwealth of Pa., Dept. Edn., 1956-59; founder, clinician, instr., dir., bd. pres. Communicative Arts Ctr., Inc., Drexel Hill, Pa., 1958, Comm. Skills, Cmty. Resources Ctr., Inc., Drexel Hill, Pa., 1958, 1964—; charter mem. exec. bd., bd. pres. United Pvt. Acad. Schs., Assn. of Pa., Drexel Hill, 1966—; exec. bd. govs., bd. chmn. The Accrediting Commn., Drexel Hill, 1971—. Charter mem. Pa. State Univ. Radio and TV Guild, University Park, Pa., 1951—; mem. legis. action com., Pa. State U., Univ. Park, 1988—; cons. communications skills, The Accrediting Commn., 1971—, United Pvt. Acad. Schs. Assn., Pa., 1966—. Founder, chmn., CEO Am. Ednl. Group, 1991—; chmn. CEO Internat. Ednl. Group, 1991—; CEO Cmty. Resources Ctr., Drexel Hill, 1991—, project coord. Energy Quest, 1992—; active Nat. Com. to Preserve Social Security and Medicare, Washington, 1986—; Am. Immigration Control Found., Monterey, Va., 1987—, English First, Springfield, Va., 1988—; mem. pres.'s coun. Rep. Nat. Com., 1989—, Nat. Rep. Senatorial Com., 1989—, Rep. Presdl. Task Force, 1989—; mem. Congrl. Legis. Agenda steering com. Empower Am., 1999. 1st Lt. Signal Corps, U.S. Army, 1952-54. Recipient Svc. award United Pvt. Acad. Sch. Assn. Pa., Monroeville, Pa., 1978, Disting. Achievement and Svc. award Bd. Govs. of the Accrediting Commn., Downington, Pa., 1980, Dr. Charles Boehm Edn. of Yr. award University Park, Pa., 1990, Loyal and Dedicated Svc. award The Accrediting Commn., 1974. Mem. NEA, Libr. Congress (chartered), Internat. Platform Assn., Pa. Edn. Assn., Jefferson Ednl. Found., World Affairs Coun. Phila., Heritage Found., Nat. Trust for Hist. Preservation, Nat. Congl. Club, Pa. State U. Nittany Lions Club, Pa. State U. Alumni Assn., Pa. State U. Football Lettermen's Club, Pa. State U. Varsity "S" Club. Republican. Roman Catholic. Avocations: music, home and garden design, automotive design, reading, golf. Office: The Accrediting Commn 436 Burmont Rd Drexel Hill PA 19026-3630

SCHICHLER, ROBERT LAWRENCE, English language educator; b. Rochester, N.Y., May 16, 1951; s. Alfred James and Elizabeth Johanna (Flugel) S. BA in English, SUNY, Geneseo, 1974, MA in English, 1978; PhD of English, Binghamton U., 1987. Writer, asst. adminstr. Artists-in-Residence Program, Rochester, N.Y., 1978-79; substitute tchr. City Sch. Dist., Rochester, 1980-82; instr. English Talmudical Inst. Upstate N.Y., Rochester, 1981-82, Binghamton (N.Y.) U., 1983-84; rsch. asst. Medieval and Renaissance Texts and Studies, Binghamton, 1985-86; adj. asst. prof. Rochester Inst. Tech., 1987-89; asst. prof. English Ark. State U., State University, 1989-94, assoc. prof., 1994-99, prof., 1999—. Adj. asst. prof. Monroe C.C., Rochester, 1987-89. Author: King of the Once Wild Frontier: Reflections of a Canal Walker, 1993; editor: Lady in Waiting: Poems in English and Spanish, 1994, Abstracts of Papers in Anglo-Saxon Studies, 1988-2003, Ctr. for Medieval and Early Renaissance Studies, Binghamton, 1986-94, Spillway Pubs., Rochester, 1992—; asst. editor: Old English Newsletter, 1986-87, Mediaevalia, Binghamton, 1988-89; contbr. articles to profl. jours. Mem. Internat. Soc. Anglo-Saxonists, Medieval Acad. Am., Am. Numismatic Assn. Home: Apt M1 726 Southwest Dr Jonesboro AR 72401-7045 Office: Ark State U Dept English and Philosophy State University AR 72467-1890 E-mail: rschich@mail.astate.edu., boonzither@hotmail.com.

SCHICK, EDGAR BREHOB, German literature educator; b. Phila., June 28, 1934; s. Claude Ernest and Martha Henrietta (Brehob) S.; m. Margaret Barbara Buehl, Feb. 12, 1938; children: Susanne, Christina. AB magna cum laude, Muhlenberg Coll., 1955; MA, Rutgers U., 1962, PhD, 1965. Asst. prof. German SUNY, Binghamton, 1963-68, asst. to pres. Albany, 1968-72, asst. prof., 1968-72; v.p. acad. affairs St. John Fisher Coll., Rochester, N.Y., 1972-78, exec. v.p., 1978-80, assoc. prof., 1972-80; pres. Nasson Coll., Springvale, Maine, 1980-83; provost, v.p. acad. affairs, prof. Eastern Ill. U., Charleston, 1984-87; exec. dir. Bd. Trustees, Md. State Univs. & Colls., Annapolis, 1987-88; vice chancellor for policy and planning U. Md. System, Adelphi, 1988-91; sr. fellow Am. Assn. State Colls. and Univs., 1991-94; cons. Assn. Governing Bds., 1993-95; interim v.p., dean St. Mary Coll., Lawrence, Kans., 1997-98; pres. Luther Inst., Washington, 1998—2003, pres. emeritus, 2003—. Chmn. visitation team Mid. States Assn. Colls. and Schs., Phila., 1975-79; cons. IBM, Yorkville, N.Y., 1968, Nat. Luth. Campus Ministry, 1968-85, USAID, 1992-95. Author: Metaphorical Organicism in the Early Herder, 1971, Shared Visions of Public Higher Education Governance: Structures and Leadership Styles That Work, 1992, The "Local Board" in Multi-Campus Public Universities, 1994; contbr. articles on German lit. and higher edn. to profl. jours. Bd. dirs. United Way, 1981-82, Maine Ind. Colls. Assn., 1981-93, Deaton Hosp., Balt.; v.p. Christ Luth. Ch. Found., Balt.; mem. Accreditation Bd. for Engring. Tech.; pres. Oakleigh Forest Civic Assn. Fellow Univ. fellow, Rutgers U., New Brunswick, N.Y., 1962—63; grantee, Carnegie Found. Mem. Am. Assn. Higher Edn., Am. Assn. Univ. Adminstrs., Am. Assn. Tchrs. German, Assn. for Instl. Rsch., Soc. for Coll. and Univ. Planning, Thomas Mann Soc., Nat. Soc. Fund-Raising Execs. Lutheran. Home: 106 Quinn Rd Severna Park MD 21146-3015 E-mail: ebschick@erols.com.

SCHICK, HARRY LEON, investment company executive; b. N.Y.C., Oct. 24, 1927; s. Martin and Sadie (Spitz) S.; m. Eleanor Alter, Oct. 17, 1982; m. Inge Nussbaum, Oct. 12, 1964 (div. Nov. 1971); 1 child, Susan. AB magna cum laude, Bklyn. Coll., 1947; MS, Columbia U., 1948; postgrad., NYU, 1948-52. Securities analyst Sutro Bros., N.Y.C., 1948-52; asst. to pres. Clairdale Enterprises, Inc., N.Y.C., 1953-66; mgr. arbitrage dept. First Manhattan Co., N.Y.C., 1966-69, gen. ptnr., 1969-91, ltd. ptnr., 1992—. Lectr. Donaldson Sch. Orgn. and Mgmt., Yale U., New Haven, 1978-88, NYU Grad. Sch. Bus. Adminstrn., N.Y.C., 1977; lectr. in field. Bd. overseers Libr. of Jewish Theol. Sem.; trustee Washington Inst. for Near East Policy. Mem. Inst. Chartered Fin. Analysts, Am. Fin. Assn., Am. Econ. Assn., N.Y. Soc. Security Analysts (bd. dirs. 1975-76), Beta Gamma Sigma. Jewish. Home: 215 E 68th St Apt 15Y New York NY 10021-5726 Office: First Manhattan Co 437 Madison Ave New York NY 10022-7001 Office Phone: 212-756-3350.

SCHICK, IRVIN HENRY, academic administrator, educator; b. Wilkes-Barre, Pa., Aug. 10, 1924; s. Irvin and Elizabeth (Valentine) S.; m. Marilyn Freeman, July 17, 1954 (dec. Aug. 1961); m. Marjorie Bletch Beach, Dec. 23, 1967; 1 child, Carolyn Patricia. Diploma, Bliss Elec. Sch., 1947; BEE with distinction, George Washington U., 1958; MSEE (NSF fellow), U. Md., 1961. Engring. asst. Jeddo-Highland Coal Co., Pa., 1942-43; instr. Bliss Elec. Sch., Washington, 1947-50; prof. math. and elec. engring., dept. head Montgomery Coll., Rockville, Md., 1950-65, dir. ext., 1965-67, dean adminstrn., 1967-75, adminstrv. v.p., 1975-78, prof. emeritus, adminstrv. v.p. emeritus, 1978—. Tchr., tutor, cons. indsl. cos., 1949—. Served with USAAF, 1943-46. Mem. AAUP, IEEE, Am. assn. Sch. Adminstrs., Internat. Platform Assn., Md. State Tchrs. Assn., Montgomery County Edn. Assn., Bliss Elec. Soc. (bd. govs., past pres.), Tent Troupe Theatrical Orgn. (bd. govs.), Theta Tau, Sigma Tau (past pres.), Sigma Pi Sigma, Tau Beta Pi. Home: 105 Fleetwood Ter Silver Spring MD 20910-5512

SCHICK, MICHAEL WILLIAM, public relations executive; b. San Antonio, July 17, 1956; s. Lawrence Martin and Jeanne Frances (McCuen) S.; m. Diana Lynn McGinty, Mar. 14, 1988; children: Tiffany Michele, Jessica Diane. B in Media Arts with honors, U. S.C., 1979. Dir. prodns., asst. v.p. S.C. Savs. & Loan League, Columbia, 1978-81; dep. press sec. to U.S. Sen. Strom Thurmond Washington, 1981-85; sr. assoc. Civic Svc. Inc., Washington, 1985-2000; COO Justice Fellowship, Washington, 2000—01; dir. comm. U.S. Chamber of Commerce Inst. for Legal Reform, 2001—03; sr. v.p. Porter Novelli Issue Advocacy, 2003—. Co-founder, chmn. First Monday Night, McLean, Va., 1981-94; Fourth Presbyn. Ch., Bethesda, Md., 1988—; chmn. Creative Living Internat., Reston, 1988—. C.S. Lewis fellow C.S. Lewis Inst., 1999-2000. Republican. Avocations: golf, tennis, soccer, guitar. Home: 11560 Brass Lantern Ct Reston VA 20194-1221 Office Phone: 202-419-3246. E-mail: mschick@aol.com.

SCHICK, PAUL K. hematologist; b. Bruno, Czechoslovakia, Oct. 12, 1932; arrived in U.S., 1939; s. Oskar and Vilma (Rushosky) Schick; m. Barbara G. Pinsley, June 30, 1962; children: Darryl Richard, Jessica Ellen. Student, Tufts Coll.; DDS, Balt. Coll., 1957; MD, Boston U., 1961. Intern Kings County Hosp., Bklyn., 1961-62, resident in internal medicine, 1963-64; pvt. practice Manchester, Conn., 1965-69; fellow in hematology Montefiore Hosp., Bronx, NY, 1969-71; from asst. prof. medicine to assoc. prof. biochemistry Med. Coll. Pa., Phila., 1971-83; from assoc. prof. medicine to prof. Temple U. Sch. Medicine, Phila., 1979-88, prof. thrombosis, 1983-88; prof. medicine Jefferson Med. Coll., Phila., 1988—98, prof. emeritus, 1998—. Mem. editl. bd. e-Medicine; contbr. articles to profl. jours. Docent Barnes Found., Merion Station, Pa. Fellow: ACP; mem.: Am. Soc. Hematology (emeritus). Avocations: environmental education, producing educational computer programs, art and imaging.

SCHICK, THOMAS, diversified financial services company executive; Sr. exec. v.p. Shearson Lehman Brothers, 1986—92; exec. v.p. pub. affairs and comms. Travel Related Svcs. sub. Am. Express, 1992—93, Am. Express Co., 1993—. Office: Am Express Co World Fin Ctr 200 Vesey St New York NY 10285

SCHICKELE, PETER, composer; b. Ames, Iowa, July 17, 1935; s. Rainer Wolfgang and Elizabeth (Wilcox) S.; m. Susan Sindall, Oct. 27, 1962; children: Karla, Matthew. BA, Swarthmore Coll., 1957; MS, Julliard Sch. Music, 1960; PhD (hon.), Swarthmore, 1980, NDSU, 1994, NEC, 1999. Composer-in-residence Los Angeles High Sch., 1960-61; faculty Swarthmore Coll., 1961-62, Juilliard Sch. Music, 1961-65, Aspen Festival Music, Colo., 1963. Composer: scores for films The Crazy Quilt, 1965, Funny Man, 1967, Silent Running, 1972, Where the Wild Things Are, 1988, several non-theatrical and TV films; arranger for: Joan Baez albums Noel, 1966, Joan, 1967, Baptism, 1968; composer mus. score for film at Tex. pavilion of Hemisfair, San Antonio, 1968; TV appearances include: Profile on the Arts, Camera Three, Bach 'N' Roll, 13 Stars for 13, Dick Cavett Show, Mike Douglas Show, David Frost Show, ABC Comedy News, Boston Pops, Tonight Show with Johnny Carson; recorded: Hornsmoke, Schickele on a Lark, Thurber's Dogs; comedian, recorded 10 P.D.Q. Bach albums on Vanguard and 7 on Telarc; mem., The Open Window, chamber-rock trio, 1967-71; composer and lyricist: Oh Calcutta; composer of numerous works for orch., chorus, piano, chamber music, band, organ, voice and instruments, 1953—; commissioned: Nat. Symphony, N.Y., Philharmonic, Cleveland Orchestra, St. Louis Symphany; creator, host Schickele Mix, Pub. Radio Internat., family concerts with Am. Symphony Orch., 1994-95; author: The Definitive Biography of P.D.Q. Bach. Recipient Gershwin Meml. award, 1959, Elizabeth Tow Newman Contemporary Music award, 1964, Grammy awards, 1990-93, 2000; Ford Found. grantee. Mem. ASCAP (Deems Taylor award 1993), Am. Music Ctr., Assn. Classical Music, Am. Fedn. Musicians. Avocation: crossword puzzles. Office: ICM Artists care Jason Bagdade 40 W 57th St Fl 16 New York NY 10019-4098

SCHIEBLER, GEROLD LUDWIG, pediatrician, educator; b. Hamburg, Pa., June 20, 1928; s. Alwin Robert and Charlotte Elizabeth (Schmoele) Schiebler; m. Audrey Jean Lincourt, Jan. 8, 1954; children: Mark, Marcella, Kristen, Bettina, Wanda, Michele. BS, Franklin and Marshall Coll., 1950; MD, Harvard U., 1954. Intern pediat. and internal medicine Mass. Gen. Hosp., Boston, 1954—55, resident, 1955—56; resident pediat. U. Minn. Hosp., Mpls., 1956—57, fellow pediatric cardiology, 1957—58, rsch. fellow, 1958—59; rsch. fellow sect. physiology Mayo Clinic and Mayo Found., 1959—60; from asst. prof. pediatric cardiology to prof. emeritus U. Fla., 1960—2001, prof. emeritus, 2001—. Dir. divsn. Children's Med. Svcs. State of Fla., 1973—74, area med. dir., 1974—2000, cons., 2001—. Author (with L.P. Elliott): The X-ray Diagnosis of Congenital Cardiac Disease in Infants, Children and Adults, 1968, 1979; author: (with L.J. Krovetz and I.H. Gessner) Pediatric Cardiology, 1979. Named Children's Med. Svcs. Pediatrician of Decade, Gov. Jeb Bush, 1999; recipient Lifetime Achievement award, Coll. Medicine, 2004. Mem.: AMA (Benjamin Rush award 1993), AASA, Fla. Med. Assn. (past v.p., bd. govs., pres. 1991—92), Fla. Heart Assn. (past pres.), Fla. Pediat. Soc. (exec. com.), Soc. Pediatric Rsch. (emeritus), Am. Coll. Cardiology, Am. Acad. Pediat. (Abraham Jacobi award 1993), Inst. Medicine NAS, Alpha Omega Alpha, Phi Beta Kappa. Home: 408 Beachside Villas Amelia Island Plantation Amelia Island FL 32034-6551

SCHIECK, FREDERICK W. federal agency administrator; m. Sara Schieck; 1 child, Sara. B Fgn. Svc., Georgetown U.; MBA, Harvard U. Bd. trustees, v.p. exec. com. Pan-Am. Devel. Found.; with USAID; deputy adminstr. Agy. Internat. Devel., Washington, 2002—. With USAR. Office: USAID 1300 Pennsylvania Ave NW Washington DC 20523

SCHIEFFER, BOB, broadcast journalist; b. Austin, Tex., Feb. 25, 1937; m. Patricia Penrose; children: Susan, Sharon. BA in Journalism, Tex. Christian U., 1959. Reporter Ft. Worth Star-Telegram; news anchorman Sta. WBAP-TV, Dallas-Ft. Worth; with CBS News, 1969—, Pentagon corr., 1970-74, White House corr., 1974-79, chief Washington corr., 1982—; anchorman CBS Sunday Night News, 1973-74, Saturday edit. CBS Evening News, 1976—96, Monday-through-Friday edits. Morning, 1979-80; co-anchorman CBS Morning News, from 1985; also participant CBS news spls. and spl. reports, including Peace and the Pentagon, 1974, Watergate-The White House Transcripts, 1974, The Mysterious Alert, 1974, 1976, Ground Zero, 1981; Democratic Nat. Conv., 1976; Republican Nat. Conv., Campaign '72; and mem. Emmy award-winning team CBS Evening News with Walter Cronkite, 1971; anchors Face the Nation CBS News, 1991—, chief Washington corr., 1975; co anchor CBS Weekend News/Sunday News, N.Y.C. Author: (with Gary Paul Gates) The Acting President, 1989. Recipient various awards Sigma Delta Chi, various awards Tex. Associated Broadcasters, various awards AP Mng. Editors; co-recipient Emmy awards. Office: FACE THE NATION with Bob Schieffer 2020 M St NW Washington DC 20036-3304

SCHIEFFER, JOHN THOMAS, ambassador, former professional baseball team executive; b. Ft. Worth, Oct. 4, 1947; m. Susanne Silber, Sept. 22, 1979; 1 child. BA, U. Tex., 1970, MA, 1972, JD. Mem. Tex. Ho. Reps., 1972—76; ptnr.-in-charge of ballpark devel. Texas Rangers Baseball Club, 1990—91, pres., 1991—99, gen. ptnr., 1994—98; pres. J. Thomas Schieffer Mgmt. Co., 2000—01; U.S. amb. to Australia U.S. Dept. State, Sydney, 2001—. Office: 4150 Sydney Pl Washington DC 20521-4150 also: Am Embassy Moonah Pl Yarralumla ACT Sydney 2600 Australia*

SCHIELE, PAUL ELLSWORTH, JR., education business owner, writer; b. Phila., Nov. 20, 1924; s. Paul Ellsworth Sr. and Maud (Barclay) S.; m. Sarah Irene Knauss, Aug. 20, 1946; children: Patricia Schiele Sommers, Sandra Schiele Kicklighter, Deborah Schiele Hartigan. AT, Temple U., 1949; BA, LaVerne U., 1955; MA, Claremont Grad. U., 1961; PhD, U.S. Internat. U., San Diego, 1970. Cert. sec. tchr., Calif. 1961. Tchr. sci. and math. Lincoln High Sch., Phila., 1956-57, Ontario (Calif.) Sch. Dist., 1957-65; math. and sci. cons. Hacienda La Puente U. Sch. Dist., Calif., 1965-75; asst. prof. Calif. State U., Fullerton, 1975-83; pres., owner Creative Learning Environments and Resources, Glendora, Calif., 1983—, cons. sci. curriculum, 1985—. Dir. title III project ESEA, 1974-75, cons. for project, 1975-77; cons. in field. Author: (student workbook) Beyond the Earth, 1969, Primary Science, 1972, 2d edit., 1976, (novel) Under Cover of Night, 1995, Chasing the Wild Geese, 1996, Deceptive Appearances, 1997; editor: A Living World, 1974, 2d edit., 1986; writer 9 sound filmstrips, model units for sci. and math. activity books, 10 sci. activities for L.A. Outdoor Edn. Program, 1980; editor 21 sci. and math. activity books, 1975-76; writer, co-dir. (TV) Marine Biology Series, 1970-71; contbr. numerous articles to profl. mags., 1960-85; writer and designer of 2 sci. ednl. games; designer in field. Apptd. adv. com. Sci. and Humanities Symposium Calif. Mus. Sci. and Industry, 1974; mem. State Sci. Permit Com., Tide Pools of Calif. Coast, 1974-75; mem. Friends of Libr., Friends Libr. Found. Mem. Internat. Platform Assn., Internat. Soc. Photographers, Glendora Hist. Soc., ABI Rsch. Assn. (bd. govs.), Calif. Elem. Edn. Assn. (hon.), Nat. PTA (hon.), Calif. Inter-Sci. Coun. (pres., chmn. 1971, 72), Elem Sch. Scis. Assn. (past pres., bd. dirs.), Paddlewheel Steamboating Soc. of Am., Phi Delta Kappa (chartered). Republican. Lutheran. Avocations: travel, etchings, art collecting, fencing. Home: 231 Catherine Park Dr Glendora CA 91741-3018

SCHIER, DONALD STEPHEN, language educator; b. Ft. Madison, Iowa, Sept. 10, 1914; s. Francis and Marcella (Kenny) S. BA, State U. Iowa, 1936; MA, Columbia U., 1937, PhD, 1941. Mem. faculty State Tchrs. Coll., Bemidji, Minn., 1939-41, 41-42, Ill. Inst. Tech., 1946; mem. faculty Carleton Coll., Northfield, Minn., 1946-80, prof. French, 1953-80. Vis. prof. U. Wis., 1964-65; Brown tutor in French U. of South, Sewanee, Tenn., 1980-81 Author: Louis-Bertrand Castel, 1942; editor: (with Scott Elledge) The Continental Model, 1960, 2d edit., 1970; (Bertrand de Fontenelle), Nouveaux Dialogues des morts, 1965, rev. edit., 1974; translator: Letter on Italian Music (Charles de Brosses), 1978. Mem. selection com. Young Scholar Program, Nat. Found. Arts and Humanities, 1966-67. Served to capt. AUS, 1942-46. Mem. MLA, Am. Assn. Tchrs. French, Am. Soc. Eighteenth-Century Studies Home: 750 Weaver Dairy Rd Apt 1106 Chapel Hill NC 27514-1441

SCHIERINGA, PAUL KENNETH, special education educator, entertainer; b. Holland, Mich., Mar. 28, 1934; s. Peter and Mary (Van Kampen) Schieringa; m. Patti Ann Poling, Dec. 27, 1987. BA in Bus. Adminstrn., Hope Coll., 1957; MDiv, Founding Ch., Washington, 1963. Cert. nursing home adminstr., Ill. Quality control officer U.S. R.R. Retirement Bd., Chgo., 1957—61; entertainer, 1961—; med. mgr. hosps., nursing homes, mental health agencies, Chgo. and Ionia, Mich., 1971—87; theater adminstr. Croswell Opera House, Adrian, Mich., 1987—88; tchr. music/spl. edn./career edn. Guam Dept. Edn., Hagatna, 1991—2001. Cons. various nursing homes, Chgo., 1977—83, Betty's Learning Ctr., Upper Tumon, Guam, 1997—2001; mem. diabetes policy adv. bd. Mich. Dept. Pub. Health, Lansing, 1983—88; chairperson Citizens' Adv. Coun. for Southgate (Mich.) Mental Health Ctr., 1984—88. Composer: (songs) Free As A Gull, 1964, 23rd Psalm, 1972, He Cared So Much For Me, 1991, Lo, He Comes, 1992, It Still Took Calvary, 1997, (Chaplains Verse for Navy Hymn) Eternal Father Strong to Save, 1992. Co-chair restoration adv. bd. Naval Air Sta., Hagatna, 1993—2001; bd. dirs. Friends of Guam Pub. Libr., Hagatna, 1996—2001. Named to Ancient Order of the Chamorri, Gov. of Guam, 2001. Avocations: writing childrens' books, World War II historian, organ, fishing. Home: 879 W 32d St Holland MI 49423

SCHIESER, HANS ALOIS, education educator; b. Ulm, Germany, July 15, 1931; arrived in U.S., 1965; s. Alois and Anna (Stegmann) S.; m. Margret H. Schröer, June 6, 1962; children: Peter, Elisabeth. BA, Kepler Gymnasium, Ulm, 1952; MA in Philosophy, U. Passau, Fed. Republic Germany, 1959; EdM, Pedagogic Acad., Weingarten, Fed. Republic Germany, 1962; PhD, Loyola U., Chgo., 1970. Head tchr. Pestalozzischule, Ulm, 1964-65; learning disabilities tchr. Jeanine Schultz Meml. Sch., Skokie, Ill., 1966-67; co-dir. Oak Therapeutic Sch., Evanston, Ill., 1967-70; from assoc. prof. to prof. edn. DePaul U., Chgo., 1969-91, prof. emeritus, 1991—. Cons. in field; program cons. Delphian Soc., L.A., 1977-90; rschr., tchr. in Germany, 1991-; active in tchrs. edn. Midwest Montessori Tchr. Tng. Ctr., Evanston, Ill.; guest prof. State U. Chelyabinsk, State Linguistic U., Irkutsk, Russia, 1998-; ord. prof., dean of studies Gustav-Siewerth-Akademie, Germany. Author chpts. in books; contbr. articles to profl. jours.; adv. bd. Ann. Edits. Sociology, Dushkin Pub. Group, 1985-91. Pres. N.Am. Family Svc. Found., Oak Lawn, Ill., 1974-91; bd. dirs. S.O.S. Children's Villages USA, Washington, 1986-94; pres. emeritus S.O.S. Children's Village Ill., inc., Chgo.; bd. govs. Invest-in-Am. Nat. Found., Phila., 1988-90. Rsch. grant DePaul U., 1985-86, Rsch. sabbatical, 1989. Mem. Am. Ednl. Studies Assn., Nat. Soc. for Study of Edn., Philosophy of Edn. Soc. U.S.A., Soc. Educators and Scholars (bd. dirs. 1984-90), Am. Montessori Soc., Thomas More Gesellschaft/Amici Mori Europe, Phi Delta Kappa (pres. Zeta chpt., Chgo. 1973-75). Home: Veilchenweg 9 D-89134 Bermaringen Germany also: 400 E Main/6B/DJURI Evanston IL 60202 Office: DePaul U 2320 N Kenmore Ave Chicago IL 60614-3210 E-mail: prof_schieser@hotmail.com.

SCHIESSLER, ROBERT WALTER, retired chemical and oil company executive; b. Honesdale, Pa., Oct. 2, 1918; s. Walter A. and Josephine (Herzog) S.; m. Betty Hartman, June 5, 1939; children— Lynn Alice, Dale Ann; m. Florence Cutler, Aug. 16, 1968. BS, Pa. State U., 1939, PhD, 1944; MS, McGill U., 1941. Research chemist Gen. Electric Co., Schenectady, 1941; from instr. to asso. Prof. chemistry and dir. Am. Petroleum Inst. Research Pa. State U., 1942-55; chemistry and physics cons., 1946-55; tech. dir. Central Research div. Mobil Oil Co., Paulsboro and Princeton, N.J., 1950-60, mgr. central research div., asst. gen. mgr. research dept., 1960-62, gen. mgr.

research dept., 1962-67; v.p. research Mobil Research & Devel. Corp., 1967-68; chmn., pres. Indsl. Reactor Labs., Inc., 1966-67; mgr. long-range planning Mobil Oil Corp., 1968-72, gen. mgr. real estate and land devel., 1972-83; chmn. Mobil Land Devel. Corp., 1972-83; pres. Sandvik, Inc., 1983-84. Chmn. bd. trustees Gordon Rsch. Conf., Inc., 1957; mem. bd. Am. Chem. Soc. Peroleum Rsch. Fund, 1955-59, 60-63; Rsch. chemist Can. govt., 1940-41. Co-Author: Chemistry of Petroleum Hydrocarbons, 1954; discoverer method for prodn. super-explosive used by U.S. and Can., World War II; identified hydrocarbon structure for super-lubricant Mobil 1. Recipient award in petroleum chemistry Am. Chem. Soc., 1953; named outstanding young man State Coll. of Pa., outstanding young man Jr. C. of C., 1952; recipient Wisdom award, 1970 Fellow Am. Inst. Chemists, AAAS (v.p. for chemistry, chmn. chemistry sect. 1960); mem. Am. Chem. Soc., AAUP, Sigma Xi, Phi Lambda Upsilon, Phi Eta Sigma. Home: 1500 Palisade Ave Fort Lee NJ 07024-5337

SCHIEVELBEIN, THOMAS CLAYTON, shipyard executive, sales executive; b. Ft. Lewis, Wash., July 4, 1953; s. Clayton Glenn and Helen Faye (Jensen) S.; m. Betty Jo DeMent, Aug. 22, 1976; children: Stacy Jo, Lisa Jeanne. BS in Marine Engring., U.S. Naval Acad., 1975; ME in Nuclear Engring., U. Va., 1976. Regional sales mgr. GE, Schenectady, N.Y., 1976-82, mgr. advanced tech. Washington, 1982-87; dir. field sales Newport News Shipbuilding, Arlington, Va., 1987-92, dir. naval mktg., 1992-93, v.p. strategy and naval prog. devel., 1993-94, v.p. human resources and adminstr., 1994-95, exec. v.p., 1995—2001; corp. v.p. Northrop Grumman Corp, 2001—; pres. Northrop Grumman Newport News, 2001—. Founding mem. Virginia Career Education Foundation. Mem. Assn. Naval Aviators, Naval Submarine League, NSIA (bd. trustees). Office: Norhtrop Grumman Newport News Shipbuilding 4101 Washington Ave Bldg 86 Newport News VA 23607-9700

SCHIFF, ADAM BENNETT, congressman, lawyer; b. Framingham, Mass., June 22, 1960; s. Edward Maurice and Sherrill Ann (Glovsky) S.; m. Eve Schiff; 2 children, Alexa Marion, Elijah Harris. BA, Stanford U., 1982; JD, Harvard U., 1985. Bar: Calif. 1986. Assoc. Gibson, Dunn & Crutcher, L.A., 1986; asst. U.S. atty. U.S. Atty.'s Office, L.A., 1987—96; mem. Calif. Senate, 1997—2001, U.S. Congress from 29th Calif. dist., Washington, 2001—; mem. judiciary com., internat. rels. com. Spl. assignment to Czechoslovakia, Justice Dept., Bratislava, 1992. Democrat. Avocation: writing fiction. Office: 326 Cannon HOB Washington DC 20515-0529 E-mail: congressman.schiff@mail.house.gov.

SCHIFF, CHARLENE, adult education educator; b. Horochow, Wolyn, Poland, Dec. 16, 1929; arrived in U.S., 1948; d. Simcha and Fruma Perlmutter; m. Erwin H. Schiff; 1 child, Stephen Frank. Student, Ohio State U., 1949—50. Cert. Ikebana Internat., Yokohama, Japan, 1959, Art of Chinese Cooking Benedictine Sisters of Peking, 1958, Le Cordon Bleu, 1972. Lectr. on the Holocaust, various locations/orgns., 1985—. Author: Echoes of Memory, 2003. Mem. Va. Planning Com. for Holocaust Days of Remembrance, 1987—; past coord. Holocaust Child Survivors Group, Washington; gray lady U.S. Army Hosp., Munich, 1952—54; past mem. adv. bd. U.S. HOLUS Holocaust Meml. Mus. Named One of Alexandria's Outstanding Citizens, 1993; recipient 2d Century award, Jewish Theol. Sem., 1997. Mem.: Survivors of the Holocaust and Friends of Greater Washington, McCosh Infirmary Aux. Princeton U. (life), U.S. Army Quartermaster Wives Club, Hadassah (life). Avocations: reading, foreign films, gourmet cooking. Home: 309 Yoakum Pkwy #815 Alexandria VA 22304

SCHIFF, DAVID TEVELE, investment banker; b. N.Y.C., Sept. 3, 1936; s. John Mortimer and Edith Brevoort (Baker) S.; m. Martha Elisabeth Lawler, May 11, 1963; children: Andrew Newman, David Baker, Ashley Reynolds. B.Engring., Yale U., 1958. Trainee Chem. Bank N.Y. Trust, N.Y.C., 1959-62; analyst Madison Fund, N.Y.C., 1962; assoc., then partner Kuhn, Loeb & Co., N.Y.C., 1963-77; vice chmn. Kuhn Loeb & Co. Inc., 1977; mng. dir. Lehman Bros. Kuhn Loeb Inc., N.Y.C., 1977-83, also dir.; mng. ptnr. Kuhn, Loeb & Co. (formerly KLS Enterprises), 1984—. Dir., vice chmn. Am. Crown Life Ins. Co., N.Y.C., 1981-95; bd. dirs. Crown Life Ins. Co., Toronto, 1971-92; mem. lower Manhattan adv. bd. Chem. Bank, 1977-85; bd. advisors Venture Capital Fund of Am., 1998—; mem. leadership coun. Yale Sch. Forestry and Environ. Studies, 2000—. Trustee, chmn. bd. Wildlife Conservation Soc.; trustee Met. Mus. Art, Citizens Budget Commn., N.Y.C., Greater N.Y. coun. Boy Scouts Am., 1965-91; trustee Beekman Downtown Hosp., 1966-82, chmn., 1975-79; trustee Brooks Sch., North Andover, Mass., 1972-90, treas., 1987-90; bd. govs. Yale U. Art Gallery, 1973-97, Fed. Hall Meml. Assn.; mem. adv. bd. dirs. Outward Bound, Inc., 1983-99; mem. Provident Loan Soc. N.Y.; bd. dirs. Am. Hosp. of Paris Found., N.Y.C., 1987. With U.S. Army, 1959. Mem. Econ. Club N.Y.C., Pilgrims U.S., Brook Club, Century Assn., River Club, Maroon Creek Club (Aspen, Colo.), Mill Reef Club (Antigua), Yale Club N.Y.C. Episcopalian. Home: 770 Park Ave New York NY 10021-4153 Office: 50 Rockefeller Plz 15th Fl New York NY 10020-1605

SCHIFF, DONALD WILFRED, pediatrician, educator; b. Detroit, Sept. 11, 1925; s. Henry and Kate (Boesky) S.; m. Rosalie Pergament; children: Stephen, Jeffrey, Susan, Douglas. Student, Wayne State U., 1943-44, Oberlin Coll., 1944-45; MD, Wayne State U., 1949. Diplomate Am. Bd. Pediatrics. Intern Detroit Receiving Hosp., 1949-50; resident in pediatrics U. Colo., 1954-55, chief resident in pediatrics, 1955-56; instr. U. Colo. Health Scis. Ctr., Denver, 1956-59, asst. clin. prof., 1959-69, assoc. clin. prof., 1969-78, clin. prof., 1978-87, prof., 1987—; pvt. practice Littleton (Colo.) Clinic, 1956-86, chmn. bd., 1973-79; med. dir. HMO Colo., Denver, 1980-86; med. dir. Child Health Clinic The Children's Hosp., Denver. Contbr. articles to profl. jours. Bd. dirs. Sch. Dist. VI, Colo., 1962; pres. Arapahoe Mental Health Clinic, Denver, 1968-70, bd. dirs., 1964-70; adv. coun. State of Colo. Medicaid, Denver, 1981—. With USN, 1944-46, USPHS, 1952-54, Turtle Mountain Indian Reservation, N.D. Recipient 25 Yrs. Teaching award U. Colo. Sch. Medicine, 1981. Mem. Am. Acad. Pediatrics (chmn. Colo. chpt. 1973-79, alternate dist. chmn. 1977-81, chmn. dist. 8 1981-86, nat. pres. 1988-89), Rocky Mountain Pediatric Soc., Colo. Med. Soc. Home: 600 Front Range Rd Littleton CO 80120-4052 Office: The Childrens Hosp Child Health Clinic Box BO32 1056 E 19th Ave Denver CO 80218-1088

SCHIFF, EUGENE ROGER, internist, gastroenterologist, educator; b. Cin., Jan. 3, 1937; s. Leon and Augusta (Miller) S.; m. Dana Kendall, Dec. 27, 1965; children: David, Lisa. BA, U. Mich., 1958; MD, Columbia U., 1962. Diplomate Am. Bd. Internal Medicine, Am. Bd. Gastroenterology, Nat. Bd. Med. Examiners. Intern and med. resident Cin. Gen. Hosp., 1962-64; med. resident Parkland Meml. Hosp., Dallas, 1966-67; USPHS postdoctoral fellow in gastroenterology Southwestern Med. Sch., U. Tex., Dallas, 1967-69; asst. prof. medicine U. Miami Sch. Medicine, Fla., 1969-74, assoc. prof., 1974-78, prof., 1978—, chief div. hepatology, 1971—, dir. Ctr. for Liver Diseases, 1982—. Chief hepatology sect. VA Med. Ctr., Miami, 1971-97; chmn. adv. com. on gastrointestinal drugs FDA, Rockville, Md., 1983-85, 88-92, mem. adv. com. on blood safety, 1997—2000. Co-editor: Diseases of the Liver, 1982, 1987, 1993, 1998, 2003, Liver Transplantation, 2000. Bd. dir. Am. Digestive Health Found., 1996-2001, chmn. digestive health initiative on viral hepatitis, 1996-2001. Lt. comdr. USPHS, 1964-66. Master: ACP (gov. Fla. chpt. 1984—88), Am. Coll. Gastroenterology; fellow: Royal Coll. Physicians; mem.: AMA, Am. Gastroenterology Assn. (chmn. Biliary disorders sect. 1993—95), Internat. Assn. for Study of Liver Diseases (councilor), Argentine Soc. Gastroenterology (hon.), Am. Bd. Internal Medicine (subsplty. bd. gastroenterology), Am. Assn. for Study of Liver Diseases (sec.-treas. 1991—96, councilor 1997—2002, pres.-elect 2000, pres. 2001). Jewish. Home: 9307 SW 123rd Ter Miami FL 33176-5060 Office: U Miami 1500 NW 12th Ave Ste 1101 Miami FL 33136-1052 E-mail: eschiff955@aol.com., eschiff@med.miami.edu.

SCHIFF, FRANK, investment company executive; BS magna cum laude, U. Colo.; JD cum laude, Cornell Law Sch. Ptnr. White & Case LLP, head corp. dept.; mng. dir. DB Capital Ptnrs.; ptnr. MidOcean Ptnrs. Bd. dirs. Celerity Group, Inc. Mem.: NY State Bar. Office: MidOcean Ptnrs 320 Park Ave Ste 1700 New York NY 10022

SCHIFF, GARY STUART, academic administrator, educator, consultant; b. Bklyn., Mar. 27, 1947; s. Jacob and Lillian (Grumet) S.; children: Jeremy Jay, Rina Joy. BA, Bin Hebrew Lit., Yeshiva U., 1968; MA, Columbia U., 1970, Cert. in Middle East Studies, PhD, Columbia U., 1973; DHL (hon.), Gratz Coll., 1997. Asst. prof. Jewish studies and polit. sci. CUNY, 1973-76; dir. Mid. East affairs Nat. Jewish Cmty. Rels. Coun., N.Y.C., 1976-78; exec. asst. to pres. Acad. for Ednl. Devel., N.Y.C., 1978-83; pres., prof. Middle East studies Gratz Coll., Melrose Park, Pa., 1983-97. Vis. prof. Balt. Hebrew U., 1997, Washington Coll., Md., 1999-2000, 2000-2001; vis. asst. prof. polit. sci. Yeshiva U., 1973-77. Author: Tradition and Politics: The Religious Parties of Israel, 1977, The Energy Education Catalog, 1981; contbr. articles to profl. jours. Grantee NEH, Ford Found., Danforth Found., Woodrow Wilson Found., William Penn Found., Pew Charitable Trusts. Mem. Assn. of Colls. of Jewish Studies (bd. dirs.), Assn. for Israel Studies (v.p.), Coun. for Jewish Edn. (bd. dirs.), Assn. for Jewish Studies, World Jewish Congress (governing bd.), Am. Jewish Com. (N.Y. chpt. bd. dirs., Phila. chpt. communal affairs commn.). Avocations: cantorial music, boating, cats. Home: 29182 Ricks Landing Rd Kennedyville MD 21645-3306 E-mail: garygrant@aol.com.

SCHIFF, GILBERT MARTIN, virologist, microbiologist, medical educator; b. Cin., Oct. 21, 1931; married, 1955; 2 children. BS, U. Cin., 1953, MD, 1957. Intern U. Hosp., Iowa City, 1957-58, resident internal medicine, 1958-59; med. officer lab br. Communicable Diseases Ctr., Ga., 1959-61; head tissue culture investigation unit, perinatal rsch. br. Nat. Inst. Neurol. Diseases and Blindness, 1961-64; dir. clin. virology lab. U. Cin., 1964-78, asst. prof. medicine and microbiology, 1964-67, asst. prof. microbiology, 1967-71, prof. medicine Coll. Medicine, 1971—; pres. James N. Gamble Inst. Medical Rsch., 1984—. Attending physician dept. medicine Emory U., Atlanta, 1959-61; cons. com. maternal health Ohio State Med. Assn., 1964-70, Hamilton County Neuromuscular Diagnostic Clinic, 1966, 75, Contract Immunization Status in U.S., 1975-77; mem. com. viral hepatitis among dental pers. VA; mem. immunization practice adv. com. Surgeon Gen., 1971-75; dir. Christ Hosp Inst. Med. Rsch., Cin., 1974-83, chairperson libr. com., 1974—, mem. com. cancer programs, 1979—, mem. com. human rsch., 1980—, chairperson search com., dir. radiotherapy, 1980-82; mem. com. infection control, 1981—, mem. com. univ. liaisons, 1982—; mem. subcom. antimicrobial agents U.S. Pharmacopeia, 1977-80; mem. study sect., adv. com., review com. NIH; mem. com. Rubella immunization Ohio Dept. Health; com. Rubella control Cin. Dept. Health. Trustee Children's Hosp. Med. Ctr., rsch. com., 1985—; community adv. com. Hoxworth Blood Ctr., 1991—. Recipient career rsch. devel. award Nat. Inst. Child Health and Human Devel., 1970-74; grantee USPHS, 1964-67, Nat. found., 1965-67. Fellow ACP; mem. AAAS, Am. Soc. Microbiology, Am. Fedn. Clin. Rsch. (sec.-treas. 1967-70), Am. Pub. Health Assn., Sci. Rsch. Soc. Am., Ctrl. Soc. Clin. Rsch. (sec.-treas. 1977-81, v.p. 1983, pres. 1984), Infectious Disease Soc. Am. Am. Soc. Clin. Investigation, Sigma Xi. Office: Dept Pediatrics U Cincinnati Coll Med 3333 Burnet Ave Cincinnati OH 45229-3026

SCHIFF, GUNTHER HANS, lawyer; b. Cologne, Germany, Aug. 19, 1927; came to U.S., 1938; s. Hans and Alice (Goldstein) S.; m. Katharine MacMillan, Jan. 27, 1950 (div. 1957); children: Eric Alan, Mary Alice; m. JoAnn R. Schiff; children: Jage, Hans Judson. BSFS., Georgetown U., 1949, JD, 1952. Bar: D.C. 1952, Calif. 1953. Assoc., ptnr., of counsel various firms, Beverly Hills, Calif., 1954-94; pvt. practice Beverly Hills, Calif., 1994—. Sec. Los Angeles Copyright Soc., Beverly Hills, 1975-76 Contbr. articles to profl. jours. Pres. Beverly Hills Civil Svc. Commn., 1984-85, 88-89; pres. Free Arts for Abused Children, 1993-94, dir.; chmn. Rent Control Rev. Bd., Beverly Hills, 1980-84; trustee Young Musicians Found. With USNR, 1945-46. Mem. ABA, Beverly Hills Bar Assn. (chmn. Resolutions Com. 1977-78), Los Angeles County Bar Assn., Los Angeles Copyright Soc., USCG Aux., Calif. Yacht Club. Avocations: sailing, skiing, golf. Office: 9430 W Olympic Blvd Beverly Hills CA 90212-4552 E-mail: hgschiff@pacbell.net.

SCHIFF, JOHN JEFFERSON, JR., finance company executive; BA, Ohio State U. Chmn., CEO John J. & Thomas R. Schiff & Co., Inc., 1983-96; pres., CEO Cin. Fin. Corp., 1986—, also chmn. bd. dirs. Trustee Am. Inst. Charatered Property Casualty Underwriters; dir. 5th 3d Bancorp, Cinergy Corp., Std. Register Co., Cin. Bengals, Inc. Office: Cin Fin Group PO Box 145496 Cincinnati OH 45250-5496

SCHIFF, LAURIE, lawyer; b. Newark, Apr. 24, 1960; d. Norman Nathan and Claire Jane (Schott) Schiff. BS in Law, Western State U., Fullerton, Calif., 1987, JD, 1988. Bar: Calif. 1989. Ptnr. Schiff Mgmt., Newport Beach, Calif., 1983-89; pvt. practice Schiff & Assocs., Irvine, Calif., 1989-91; ptnr. Schiff & Shelton, Newport Beach, 1991—, Attys. Equity Law Group, LLP, 2001—. Probation monitor State Bar Ct. Calif., 1991—97, spl. prosecutor, 1997—. Prodr.: (Albums) Boys Just Want to Have Sex, 1984. Bd. dirs. Jewish Family Svcs. Orange County, 1994—99. Mem.: Orange County Bar Assn. (arbitrator 1995—), Am. Quarterhorse Assn., Am. Mensa, Online Feline Fanciers (v.p. 1995—97, bd. dirs. 1997—), Internat. Cat Assn. (chair legis. com. 1995—97, 1998—99, legal counsel 1999—, lic. splty. judge 2001—), Am. Polocrosse Assn., Saddlebrook Polocrosse (treas. 1991), Tonks West (v.p. 1994—96, pres. 1996—97), Tonkinese Breed Assn., Internat. Politically Correct Cat Club (v.p. 1996—). Democrat. Jewish. Office: Schiff & Shelton 3700 Campus Dr Ste 202 Newport Beach CA 92660-2603 E-mail: lschiff@schiff-shelton.com.

SCHIFF, MARGARET SCOTT, newspaper publishing executive; V.p., controller, personnel adminstr. Washington Post. Office: The Washington Post 1150 15th St NW Washington DC 20071-0002

SCHIFF, MARLENE SANDLER, entrepreneur; b. Great Barrington, Mass. d. Jack and Lena Yetta (Klein) Sandler; m. Haskel Schiff (dec. Feb. 1967), 1 child, Melissa Robin. BA, U. Mass., 1970; OPM, Harvard U., 1985. Founder, chief exec. officer, chmn. Transceiver East Inc., N.Y.C., 1971-88; founder, CEO, pres. MSS Assoc., Inc., N.Y.C., 1995—. Founder, CEO, pres. MSS Assocs., Inc. Pub. Best of American Lifestyles mag./catalog, 1995-97. Eye adv. com. N.Y. Hosp./Cornell Med. Ctr., 1988—; adv. bd. dirs. Sol C. Schneider Entrepreneurial Ctr. of the Wharton Bus. Sch. U. Pa., 1989, chair, 1991-95; adv. bd. nutrition and fitness project Harvard U. Sch. Pub. Health. Mem. Com. of 200 (bd. dirs. 1989-91, N.E. regional chair 1989-91, C200 Found. bd. 1991-93), Am. Fedn. Arts (membership and spl. events com. 1990). Home: 950 5th Ave New York NY 10021-1741 Fax: 212-737-0100. E-mail: mssnyny@aol.com.

SCHIFF, MARTIN, physician, surgeon; b. Phila., July 16, 1922; s. Isidore and Cecelia (Miller) S.; m. Mildred Tepley, Jan. 5, 1946; children: Denise Schiff Simon, Michael, David BS, Pa. State U., 1943; MD, U. Calif.-Irvine, 1951. Intern L.A. County Gen. Hosp., 1950-51; gen. practice medicine specializing in bariatrics L.A., 1951—. Mem. staff Brotmam Meml. Hosp.; lectr. L.A. area community colls. Author: Eat & Stay Slim, 1972, Miracle Weight-Loss Guide, 1976, One-Day-At-A-Time Weight Loss Plan, 1980, (5 tapes) Weight Loss Plan for Health, Happiness & A Longer Life Span, 1982, The Thin Connection, 1986, Lose Unwanted Pounds Permanently Without Dieting/Trying/Playing Games, 1998, Weight Control-Fact or Fiction?, 1999, The Power of Your Will, 1999, Connections: Feelings and Emotions, 2000, YOU: A Guide to You and a Roadmap to Your Inner Being, 2002, Your Physical State; A Weight Control Guide to Your Physical State; A Weight Loss Plan to Shed Unwanted Pounds Permanently; A Mental Road Map to Your Inner Being, 2003. Lt. USN, 1943-45, PTO Mem. AMA, Calif. Med. Assn., L.A. Med. Assn., Am. Soc. Weight Control Specialists Home: 1220 Corsica Dr Pacific Palisades CA 90272-4016 Office: 12900 Venice Blvd Los Angeles CA 90066-3510 Office Phone: 310-391-6791.

SCHIFF, ROBERT, healthcare consulting company executive; b. N.Y.C., Jan. 7, 1942; s. Henry and Jeanette (Levine) S.; m. Adrianne Bendich, Aug. 16, 1964 (div. July 1979); children: Jorden, Debra; m. Joann McTaggart, Aug. 24, 1986. BS, CCNY, 1964; MS, Iowa State U., 1966; PhD, U. Calif., Davis, 1968. Asst. prof. anatomy Tufts U. Sch. Medicine, Boston, 1969-72; mgr. serology rsch. Hyland divsn. Baxter Labs., Costa Mesa, Calif., 1972-74; dir. R & D J.T. Baker Diagnostics, Bethlehem, Pa., 1974-77; dir. diagnostic R & D Hoffmann-LaRoche, Nutley, N.J., 1977-80; group v.p. Warner Lambert Co., Morris Plains, N.J., 1980-82; pres., CEO Schiff & Co., Inc., West Caldwell, N.J., 1982—. Del. Nat. Commn. for Clin. Lab. Stds., 1979-80; vice chmn. R & D Coun. N.J., 1980-82; bd. dirs. E.P.I. subs. E-Z-EM, Westbury, N.Y., 1991-98. Contbr. numerous articles to profl. jours.; patentee in field. Bd. dirs. Pharm. Tng. Inst., 2002. Post Doctoral fellow U. Calif., Davis, 1969; Aid to Cancer Rsch. grantee, Mass., 1970. Mem. N.Y. Acad. Sci., Regulatory Affairs Profl. Soc. (cert.), Am. Soc. Quality Control (cert. quality auditor), Am. Assn. Clin. Chemistry, Brit. Inst. Regulatory Affairs, Parenteral Drug Assn., Sigma Xi. Avocation: licensed pilot. Office: Schiff & Co 1129 Bloomfield Ave West Caldwell NJ 07006-7123 Office Phone: 973-227-1830. Personal E-mail: rschiff13@aol.com. Business E-Mail: schiffandcompany@aol.com.

SCHIFF, STACY, writer; b. Adams, Mass., 1960; BA, Williams Coll. Sr. editor Simon and Schuster. Author: Saint-Exupery: A Biography, 1994, Véra (Mrs. Vladimir Nabokov): Portrait of a Marriage, 1999 (Pulitzer prize for Biography, 2000); contbr. The New Yorker, The N.Y. Times Book Rev., The Times Literary Supplement, others. Fellow, Guggenheim Found., Nat. Endowment for the Humanities.

SCHIFFER, CLAUDIA, model; b. Germany; Model Guess? jeans, 1989—, Revlon cosmetics, Chanel; amb., internat. spokesperson L'Oréal. Ptnr. Fashion Cafe, N.Y.C., London, New Orleans, Barcelona, Jakarta, Manila, others; host World Music Awards with Luke Perry, Monte Carlo, 1995. Runway debut in Chanel fashion show, 1990; appeared on covers of Mademoiselle, Cosmopolitan, Vogue, and over 100 others; creator series of exercise videos (with Kathy Kaehler) Claudia Schiffer's Perfectly Fit, 1996; pub.: (pictorial book) Memories. Hon. bd. dirs. Dishes AIDS; spokesperson Nat. Breast Cancer Coalition.

SCHIFFER, LARRY PHILIP, lawyer; b. NYC; s. Jerry and Alma Schiffer; m. Gail Beverly Wachtelkonig, Aug. 19, 1978; children: Jessica, Jamie. BA magna cum laude, CUNY, Bklyn., 1976; JD, Union U., 1979. Bar: N.Y. 1980, U.S. Dist. Ct. (so. and ea. dists.) N.Y. 1980. Law asst. N.Y. Supreme Ct.-Appellate Divsn., Bklyn., 1979-81; assoc. Werner, Kennedy & French, N.Y.C., 1982-89; ptnr. Werner & Kennedy, N.Y.C., 1989-99, LeBoeuf, Lamb, Greene & MacRae, LLP, N.Y.C., 1999—. Expert commentator on reins. IRMI.com; spkr. in field. Contbr. articles to profl. jours. Exec. com. MDA's Wings Over Wall Street. Mem. ABA (tort and ins. practice sect., chmn. excess surplus lines and reins. com. 1994-95, editor ESLR com. newsletter 1991-93, vice-chmn., webmaster, listserv moderator 1997—, coord. regional meetings, CLE bd. 1998-2001, chmn. tech. com. 1997-99, comms. coord. group com. 1997-99, chair-elect electronic media coord. group 1998-99, litigation sect.), N.Y. State Bar Assn. (chmn. com. assn. ins. programs, comml. and fed. litigation sect., torts, ins. and compensation law sect.), Fedn. Def. and Corp. Counsel (vice-chair excess and surplus line reins. sect.). Home: 295 Waverly Ave East Rockaway NY 11518 Office: LeBoeuf Lamb et al 125 W 55th St New York NY 10019-5369 Personal E-mail: lpschiffer@yahoo.com. Business E-Mail: lschiffe@llgm.com.

SCHIFFER, LOIS JANE, lawyer; b. Washington, Feb. 22, 1945; d. Benjamin and Clara (Goldberg) S. BA, Radcliffe Coll., 1966; JD, Harvard U., 1969. Bar: Mass. 1969, D.C. 1971, U.S. Supreme Ct. 1973. Legal svcs. lawyer Boston Legal Assistance Project, 1969-70; ct. law clk. D.C. Circuit Ct., Washington, 1970-71; assoc. Leva, Hawes, Symington, Martin, Oppenheimer, Washington, 1971-74; lawyer Ctr. for Law and Social Policy, Washington, 1974-78; chief gen. litig. sect. Land and Natural Resources divsn. U.S. Dept. Justice, Washington, 1978-81, spl. litig. counsel, 1981-84; gen. counsel Nat. Pub. Radio, Washington, 1984-89; ptnr. Nussbaum & Wald, Washington, 1989-93; acting asst. atty. gen. environ. and natural resources divsn. U.S. Dept. Justice, Washington, 1993-94, asst. atty. gen. environ. and natural resources divsn., 1994-2001; sr. v.p. for pub. policy Nat. Audubon Soc., 2001—02; ptnr. Baach, Robinson & Lewis, Washington, 2002—. Adj. prof. environ. law Georgetown U. Law Ctr., Washington, 1986—; lectr. Harvard Law Sch., 2004. Bd. dirs. Women's Legal Def. Fund, 1975-86, Am. Rivers, 1989-93; bd. dirs. ACLU/NCA, 1982-93, pres., 1988-90. Fellow Am. Bar Found.; mem. ABA, Am. Law Inst., Keystone Ctr. (bd. dirs.), Am. Bar Assn., Phi Beta Kappa. Democrat. Jewish. Avocations: reading, movies, hiking. Home: 4640 Brandywine St NW Washington DC 20016-4449 Office Phone: 202-659-7866. Business E-Mail: lois.schiffer@baachrobinson.com.

SCHIFFER, RANDOLPH BRENTON, physician; b. Highland Park, Mich., May 25, 1948; s. Alfred Brenton and Dolores (Aspenson) S.; m. Lynn Scott Bickley, Sept. 18, 1982; children: Brenton B., Randolph T. BA, Yale U., 1969; MD, U. Mich., 1976. Diplomate Am. Bd. Psychiatry and Neurology. Asst. prof. psychiatry and neurology U. Rochester, N.Y., 1981-87, assoc. prof. psychiatry and neurology, 1987-92, prof. neurology psychiatry and environ. medicine, 1993-98; Vernon and Elizabeth Haggerton prof. neurology Tex. Tech U. Health Sci. Ctr., Lubbock, 1998—, chair dept. neuropsychiatry, 1998—. Author: The Medical Evaluation of Psychiatric Patients, 1988; co-editor: Neuropsychiatry, 1996, 2d edit., 2003. 1st lt. USMC, 1969-72, Vietnam. Mem. Am. Neuropsychiat. Assn. (bd. dirs. 1986-92), Am. Acad. Neurology, Am. Psychiat. Assn. (Falk fellow 1979-81). Home: 4515 11th St Lubbock TX 79416-4815 Office: Tex Tech U Health Scis Ctr Dept Neuropsychiat 3601 4th St Lubbock TX 79430-0001 Office Phone: 806-743-2249.

SCHIFFMAN, GERALD, microbiologist, educator; b. N.Y.C., May 22, 1926; s. Samuel and Mollie (Brookner) S.; m. Lillian Ebert, July 12, 1951; children: Stewart, Howard. BA cum laude, NYU, 1948, PhD, 1954. Asst. prof. and disting. prof. microbiology Coll. Physicians and Surgeons, Columbia U., N.Y.C., 1960-63; asso. prof. dept. research medicine and microbiology U. Pa., Phila., 1963-70; prof. SUNY Health Sci. Ctr., Bklyn., 1970-97, disting. svc. prof., 1995-97, prof. emeritus, 1997. Cons. Contbr. articles to profl. jours. Served in U.S. Army, 1943-45, ETO. Decorated Bronze Star; recipient Nichols award, 1947; Atomic Energy fellow, 1948-52; NIH grantee, 1974-94. Mem. Am. Assn. Immunologists, Am. Chem. Soc., Am. Soc. Microbiology, AAAS, Harvey Soc., Soc. Complex Carbohydrates, Sigma Xi, Phi Beta Kappa, Mu Chi Sigma, Pi Mu Epsilon. Jewish. Office: 450 Clarkson Ave Brooklyn NY 11203-2056

SCHIFFMAN, HAROLD FOSDICK, Asian language educator; b. Buffalo, Feb. 19, 1938; s. Merl and Mathilda (Keller) S.; m. Marilyn Gail Hornberg, June 10, 1978; 1 son, Timothy Marc Rajendran. BA, Antioch Coll., 1960; MA, U. Chgo., 1966, PhD, 1969. Lectr. anthropology U. Calif.-Davis, 1966-67; asst. prof. U. Wash., Seattle, 1967-73, assoc. prof., 1973-78, prof., 1978-95, chmn. dept. Asian langs., 1982-87; prof. South Asian studies U. Pa., Phila., 1995-2000, acad. dir. Penn Lang. Ctr., Luce prof. lang. learning, 1995-2000, rsch. dir. Penn Lang. Ctr., 2000—; dir. Consortium for Lang. Policy and Planning, 2001—; dir. Pedagogical Materials Project South Asia Lang. Resource Ctr., 2002—. Trustee Am. Inst. Indian Studies, Chgo., 1979-82; lang. dir. Southeast Asian Summer Studies Inst., 1992-93, mem. lang. adv. com., 1993-94. Author: A Grammar of Spoken Tamil, 1979, A Reference Grammar of Spoken Kannada, 1983, Linguistic Culture and Language Policy, 1996, A Reference Grammer of Spoken Tamil, 1999; co-editor: Dravidian Phonological Systems, 1975; co-author: Language and Society in South Asia, 1981. Pres. bd. dirs. Seattle Pro Musica (choral group), 1976-78; mem. Pacific Northwest Chamber Chorus, Seattle, 1983-87. Sr. fellow Am. Inst. Indian Studies, 1976, 78; grantee U.S. Office Edn., 1971, 74, 78, NEH, 1984-87, Smithsonian Inst., 1984-87, Fulbright Rsch., 1993-94. Mem. Assn. Asian Studies (S. Asia council 1982-85), Am. Inst. Indian Studies (trustee 1979-82), Soc. S. Indian Studies (sec.-treas. 1973-75), Internat. Assn. Tamil Research (v.p. 1987-89). Mem. Soc. Of Friends. Office: U Pa Dept South Asia Studies 820 Williams Hall Philadelphia PA 19104-6305 E-mail: haroldfs@ccat.sas.upenn.edn.

SCHIFFMAN, JACQUELYN LINDA, psychologist, consultant, artist; b. Detroit, Feb. 21, 1939; d. Max Sam and Amy Fried Klein; m. Carl H. Schiffman, Nov. 17, 1967. BA, U. Mich., Ann Arbor, 1961; MS, So. Conn. U., New Haven, 1967. Cert. psychol. examiner Conn. Clin. psychology rsch. Conn. Valley Hosp., Middletown, 1961—63; vocational counselor Cmty. Progress Inc., New Haven, 1964—66; psychol. examiner Bd. of Edn., Cheshire, Conn., 1967—76; develop. sec. Am. Mus. Natural History, N.Y.C.,

1981—83; sr. mgr., founds. United Negro Coll. Fund, N.Y.C., 1983—85; devel. dir. Franklin Furnace, N.Y.C., 1985—86, ednl. & devel. cons., 1986—94. Exhibitions include Washington Sq. East Galleries, N.Y.C., 1994, Artists' Space, 1995, White Columns, 1996, Pierogi, the flatfile, Bklyn., 1997, Williamsburg Art and Hist. Soc., N.Y., 1998, Exit Art, N.Y.C., 1999, Figureworks Gallery, Bklyn., 2000—04, Rome Arts, 2000, Represented in permanent collections Mus. Am. History, Washington, Smithsonian Inst. Grantee, NEA, 1983. Mem.: Art Students League of N.Y. (life). Avocations: cooking, ballet. Home: 63-35 78th St Middle Village NY 11379 Personal E-mail: cnjschiffman@msn.com.

SCHIFFMAN, LOUIS F. management consultant; b. Poland, July 15, 1927; s. Harry and Bertha (Fleder) S.; m. Mina R. Hankin, Dec. 28, 1963; children: Howard Laurence, Laura Lea. BChemE, NYU, 1948, MS, 1952, PhD, 1955. Rsch. engr. Pa. Grade Crude Oil Assn., Bradford, 1948-50; tchg. fellow dept. chemistry NYU, 1950-54; rsch. chemist E.I. DuPont de Nemours & Co., Wilmington, Del., 1954-56, Atlantic Refining Co., Phila., 1956-59; project leader, group leader, head corrosion sect. Amchem Products Inc., Ambler, Pa., 1959-70; pres. Techni Rsch. Assocs. Inc., Willow Grove, Pa., 1970—. Bd. dirs. Techno Ventures, Inc., Tecxchange.com; real estate developer: ptnr. Bay Properties Co., Bay Club Marina, Margate, N.J., Willow Grove (Pa.) Assocs.; pub., editor Patent Licensing Gazette, 1968—, World Tech., 1973—; panelist on forum patents and inventions Delaware Valley Industry, 1973; mem. adv. oversight com. NSF, 1975, moderator energy conf. ERDA, Washington, 1976, Las Vegas, 1977; mem. adv. group in small bus. R&D programs Dept. Def., 1980. Editor: (with others) Guide to Available Technologies, 1985; contbr. to Encyclopedia of Chemical Technology, 1967; contbr. articles to profl. jours.; patentee in field. Recipient Founders Day award NYU, 1956. Fellow Am. Inst. Chemists; mem. Am. Chem. Soc., N.Y. Acad. Scis., Lic. Execs. Soc., Tech. Transfer Soc., Assn. Univ. Tech. Mgrs., Assn. Small Rsch. Cos. (editl. contbr. newsletter), Sigma Xi, Phi Lambda Upsilon. Home: 1001 Easton Rd 206M Willow Grove PA 19090 Office: Techni Rsch Assocs Inc PO Box 1036 Willow Grove PA 19090-0922 E-mail: techniresearch@yahoo.com.

SCHIFFNER, CHARLES ROBERT, architect; b. Reno, Sept. 2, 1948; Robert Charles and Evelyn (Keck) S.; m. Iovanna Lloyd Wright, Nov. 1971 (div. Sept. 1981); m. Adrienne Anita McAndrews, Jan. 22, 1983. Student, Sacramento Jr. Coll., 1967-68, Frank Lloyd Wright Sch. Architecture, 1968-77. Registered architect, Ariz., Nev., Wis. Architect Taliesin Associated Architects, Scottsdale, Ariz., 1977-83; pvt. practice architecture Phoenix, 1983—. Lectr. The Frank Lloyd Wright Sch. of Architecture, 1994, 95. Named one of 25 Most Promising Young Americans Under 35, U.S. mag., 1979; recipient AIA Honor award Western Mountain Region, 1993, Western Home awards Sunset Mag., 1989, 91, AIA Ariz. Merit award, 1993 and numerous others. Home: 5202 E Osborn Rd Phoenix AZ 85018-6137 Office: 2944 N 44th St Ste 101 Phoenix AZ 85018

SCHIFFRIN, MILTON JULIUS, physiologist; b. Rochester, NY, Mar. 23, 1914; s. William and Lillian (Harris) S.; m. Dorothy Euphemia Wharry, Oct. 10, 1942; children: David Wharry, Hilary Ann. AB, U. Rochester, 1937, MS, 1939; PhD cum laude, McGill U., 1941. Instr. physiology Northwestern U. Med. Sch., Chgo., 1941-45; lectr. pharmacology U. Ill. Med. Sch., 1947-57, clin. asst. prof. anesthesiology, 1957-61; with Hoffmann-La Roche, Inc., Nutley, N.J., 1946-79, dir. drug regulatory affairs, 1964-71, asst. v.p., 1971-79; pres. Wharry Rsch. Assn., Seattle, 1979—. Chmn. Everglades Health Edn. Ctr., 1986—87. Author: (with E.G. Gross) Clinical Analgesics, 1955; editor: Management of Pain in Cancer, 1957. Bd. dirs. Univ. Adult Day Ctr., 1993—; mem. adv. bd. Regional Ombudsman Program, 1998—, Residents Coun. Washington, 1998—. Capt. USAAF, 1942-46. Mem. Am. Med. Writers Assn. (bd. dirs. 1967-70, pres. N.Y. chpt. 1967-68, nat. pres. 1972-73), Am. Physiol. Soc., Internat. Coll. Surgeons, Am. Therapeutic Soc., Coll. Clin. Pharmacology and Therapeutics, Am. Chem. Soc. Home and Office: Unit 308 4400 Stone Way N Seattle WA 98103-7486 Office Phone: 206-284-8809. E-mail: grampa@highstream.net.

SCHIFLETT, MARY FLETCHER CAVENDER, retired health facility executive, researcher, educator; b. El Paso, Sept. 23, 1925; d. John F. and Mary M. (Humphries) Cavender: 1 son, Joseph Raymond. BA in Econs. with honors, So. Meth. U., 1946, BS in Journalism with honors, 1947; MA in English, U. Houston, 1971. Writer, historian Office Price Administrn., Dallas, 1946-47; asst. editor C. of C. Publs., Dallas, 1947-48; bus. writer Houston Oil, 1948-49; market analyst Cravens-Dargan, Ins., 1949-52; bus. writer Bus. Week and McGraw-Hill Pub. Co., 1952-56; freelance writer in bus. econs., banking and ins., 1956-68; spl. projects coord. Ctr. for Human Resources, Houston, 1969-73; dir. publs. Energy Inst. U. Houston, 1974-78; sr. rsch. assoc. Inst. Labor and Indsl. Rels., 1973—80; mem. adj. faculty Coll. Agr. U. Houston, 1976—85; dir. Ctr. for Health Mgmt., Coll. Bus. Adminstrn., 1980—83; various positions in planning and pub. affairs Tex. Med. Ctr., Houston, 1984—98, v.p., 1998—. Author: (with others) Dynamics of Growth, 1977, Applied Systems and Cybernetics, 1981, The Ethnic Groups of Houston, 1984, Names and Nicknames of Places and Things, 1986. Bd. dirs. Friends of Hermann Park, 1995—2002, mem. exec. com., 1996—2001, sec. bd. dirs., 1997—2001, mem. adv. bd., 2001—; mem. vol. svcs. exec. bd. So. Region Inst. Internat. Edn., 2003—; pres. Houston Ct. Humanities, 1979—80; project dir. Houston Meets Its Authors I-IV, 1980—83; publicity program dir. Houston Internat. City, 1980—83; pres. Rotary Club of River Oaks, 2003—04; mem. Rotary Charitable Trust, 1999—2003; mem. editl. adv. bd. Greater Houston Partnership, 2002—. Named One of Houston's Women of Yr., YMCA, 1988; recipient Outstanding Rotarian of Yr., Rotary Internat., 1998; Paul Harris fellow, 1996—. Mem.: Nat. Assn. Bus. Econs., Tex. Folklore Soc., Mortar Bd., Kirkos, Downtown Club, Theta Sigma Phi, Alpha Theta Phi, Delta Delta Delta. Methodist. Office: Tex Med Ctr 406 Jesse H Jones Libr Bldg Houston TX 77030 Personal E-mail: mfcs@swbell.net.

SCHIFRIN, LALO, composer; b. Buenos Aires, June 21, 1932; Student, Juan Carlos Paz and Olivier Messiaen.; PhD (hon.), RISD, 1989. Tchr. composition UCLA, 1970-71; guest condr. Israel Philharm, L.A. Philharm, L.A. Chamber Orch., Indpls. Symphony, Atlanta Symphony. Argentinian rep., Internat. Jazz Festival, Paris, 1955, formed own jazz group; composer for stage, modern dance, TV; with Dizzy Gillespie's band, 1962; film and TV composer, Hollywood, Calif., 1964—; compositions: (for ballet) Jazz Faust, 1963, (for orch.) Piano Concerto # 1, 1986, Cantos Aztecas, 1989, Concerto for guitar and orch., 1986, Concerto for double bass and orch., 1987, Three tangos for flute, harp and strings, 1987, Dance concertantes for clarinet and orch., 1990, Impressions for trumpet and orch., 1990, La Nouvelle Orleans Woodwind Quintet, 1991, Concerto # 2, 1992, Cantares Argentinos, 1992, Symphony # 1 for orch., 1993, Symphonic Impressions of Oman (recorded by London Symphony), 2001, (opera) The Trial of Louis XVI, 1988; theme for TV series Mission: Impossible (2 Grammy awards); film scores include The Cincinnati Kid, 1965, Cool Hand Luke, 1967, The Fox, 1968; film scores include Kelly's Heroes, 1970, W.U.S.A., 1970, Bullit, 1970, Dirty Harry, 1971, THX-1138, 1971, The Beguiled, 1971, Magnum Force, 1973, Enter the Dragon, 1973, The Four Musketeers, 1975, The Eagle Has Landed, 1977, Voyage of the Damned, 1976, Rollercoaster, 1977, Telefon, 1977, Boulevard Nights, 1979, The Concorde-Airport '79, 1979, Competition, 1981, Sudden Impact, 1984, The Sting II, 1985, The Fourth Protocol, 1987, Tango, 1996, Rush Hour, 1998, Rush Hour 2, 2001; TV series The Young-Lawyers, Mannix, 'Mission Impossible', Starsky and Hutch; writer orchestration for Grand Finale medley for Carreras, Domingo and Pavarotti, Rome, 1990, Dodger Stadium, 1994, Eiffel Tower, 1998, Yokohama, Japan, 2002; commd. Steinway Found piano concerto The Americas, selected by Nat. Symphony Orch., 1992. Recipient 4 Grammy awards, 1967, 1969, 1986, 6 Acad. award nominations Acad. Motion Picture Arts and Scis., 1966, 67, 75, 77, 80, 82, Walk of Fame award Hollywood C. of C.; chevalier de l'Ordre des Arts et des Lettres French gov. Office: care Brad Simon Orgn 122 E 57th St New York NY 10022

SCHIFTER, RICHARD, lawyer; b. Vienna, July 31, 1923; came to U.S., 1938; s. Paul and Balbina (Blass) S.; m. Lilo Krueger, July 3, 1948; children: Judith, Deborah, Richard P., Barbara, Karen BS in Social Sci. summa cum laude, CCNY, 1943; LLB, Yale U., 1951; DHL (hon.), Hebrew Union Coll., 1992. Bar: Conn. 1951, D.C. 1952, U.S. Supreme Ct. 1954, Md., 1958. Assoc. Fried, Frank, Harris, Shriver & Jacobson, Washington, 1951-57, ptnr., 1957-84; dep. U.S. rep. with rank of ambassador UN Security Council, N.Y.C., 1984-85; asst. sec. of state for human rights and humanitarian affairs Dept. State, Washington, 1985-92; U.S. rep. UN Human Rights Commn., Geneva, 1983 86, 93; spl. asst. to pres., counselor Nat. Security Coun., Washington, 1993-97, spl. adviser to Sec. of State, 1997-2001. Head U.S. del. Conf. on Security and Cooperation in Europe Experts Meeting on Human Rights, Ottawa, Ont., Can., 1985, Dem. Insts., Oslo, 1991; bd. dirs. U.S. Inst. Peace, 1986-92; mem. Congl. Commn. on Security and Cooperation in Europe, 1986-92. V.p., pres. Md. Bd. Edn., Balt., 1959-79; chmn. Md. Gov.'s Commn. on Funding Edn. of Handicapped Children, 1975-77, Md. Values Edn. Commn., 1979-83, Montgomery County Dem. Cen. Com., Md., 1966-70; del. Dem. Nat. Conv., 1968; bd. govs. Am. Jewish Com., 1992-93, 2001—, mem. exec. com., 2001—; chmn. Internat. Rels. Commn., 2001—; chmn. bd. dirs. Ctr. for Democracy and Reconciliation in Southeastern Europe, 2002—; bd. dirs. Inst. for Christian and Jewish Studies, 2002—. With U.S. Army, 1943-46, ETO. Decorated Austrian Gt. Golden Decoration with star, comdr. Order of the Romanian Star, Bulgarian Stara Planina Order 1st class; recipient Disting. Svc. award, Sec. of State, 1992. Mem. Phi Beta Kappa. Democrat. Jewish. Home: 6907 Crail Dr Bethesda MD 20817-4723 E-mail: rschifter@aol.com.

SCHILD, RAYMOND DOUGLAS, lawyer; b. Chgo., Dec. 20, 1952; s. Stanley Martin and Cassoundra Lee (McArdle) S.; m. Ellen Arthea Carstensen, Oct. 24, 1987; children: Brian Christopher, Melissa Nicole. Student, U.S. Mil. Acad., 1970; BA summa cum laude, De Paul U., 1974, JD magna cum laude, 1982; M in Life Scis., Order of Essenes, 1996. Bar: Ill. 1982, U.S. Dist. Ct. (no. dist.) Ill. 1982, U.S. Ct. Appeals (7th cir.) 1982, Idaho 1989, U.S. Dist. Ct. Idaho 1989, U.S. Ct. Appeals (9th cir.) 1989, U.S. Supreme Ct. 1990. Assoc. Clausen, Miller, Gorman, Caffrey & Witous, Chgo., 1982-84; law clk. to chief judge law divsn. Cir. Ct. Cook County, Chgo., 1984-85; assoc. John G. Phillips & Assocs., Chgo., 1985-87, Martin, Chapman, Park & Burkett, Boise, Idaho, 1988-89; pvt. practice Boise, 1989-90; pres. Martin, Chapman, Schild & Lassaw, Chartered, Boise, 1990-96; mng. assoc. prelitigation divsn. Litster Law Offices, Boise, 2001—. Dir. Behavioral Mgmt. Ctrs.; bd. dirs. Image Concepts Internat., Inc., Boise; lectr. on legal edn. ICLE and NBI, 1993-98. Co-host legal radio talk show KFXD, 1994; legal columnist Idaho Bus. Rev., 1988-96. Mem. adv. bd. Alliance for the Mentally Ill, Boise, 1991—, Parents and Youth Against Drug Abuse, Boise, 1991-92, Bethel Ministries; fair housing adminstr. Sauk Village (Ill.) Govt., 1987-88; instr. Ada County Youth Ct., Boise, 1992—. Schmitt fellow DePaul U., 1974; recipient award of merit Chgo. Law Coalition, 1987. Mem. ATLA, Idaho Trial Lawyers' Assn., Ill. State Bar Assn., Idaho State Bar Assn., Boise Estate Planning Counsel, Shriners (temple atty. 1994—, liaison Crippled Children's Hosp.), Masons (jr. steward 1992). Avocations: tennis, trombone, writing, music. Office: 6550 W Emerald Ste 108 Boise ID 83704

SCHILDKNECHT, CATHERINE KOCH, secondary school educator; b. Columbus, Ohio, Jan. 11, 1952; d. Richard Edward and Mary Lou (Dotson) Koch; m. David Eric Schildknecht, Aug. 16, 1975; children: Calvin Edward, Margaret Grace, William Austin, Peter Evertt. BA History, Wittenberg Univ., Springfield, Ohio, 1974; MA History, Loyola Univ., Chgo., 1976. Tchr., dept. chair St. Gabriel's Sch., Charlette, NC, 1977—83, St. Vincent Pallotti H.S., Laurel, Md., 1985—86, Holy Redeemer Sch., Kensington, Md., 1987—93; tchr. Cin. Hebrew Day Sch., Cin., 1994—96; tchr., cafeteria mgr. Covington Latin Sch., Covington, Ky., 1996—2000; tchr., dept. chair All St. Sch., Cin., 2000—03; tchr. Mt. Notre Dame H.S., Cin., 2003—. Editor (contbr.): (curriculum) Archdiocese of Cin., 2003, author 2 lesson plans. Bd. dirs. Montgomery Swim & Tennis Club, Montgomery, Ohio, 2003—, So. Carrol Swim Club, Mt. Airy, Md., 1989—93; ofcl. swimming, diving Ohio H.S. Athletic Assn., Ohio, 2000—; ofcl. swimming U.S. Swimming Assn., Cin., 1993—, YMCA, Cin., 2002. Mem.: History Soc., Nat. Coun. of History Edn., Ogrn. of Am. Hist., Am. Hist. Assn., Great War Soc. Republican. Luth. Avocations: reading, cooking, swimming, gardening.

SCHILDKRAUT, JOSEPH JACOB, psychiatrist, educator; b. Bklyn., Jan. 21, 1934; s. Simon and Shirley (Schwartz) S.; m. Elizabeth Rose Beilenson, May 22, 1966; children: Peter Jeremy, Michael John. AB summa cum laude, Harvard U., 1955; MD cum laude, Harvard Med. Sch., 1959. Intern medicine U. Calif. Hosp., San Francisco, 1959-60; resident in psychiatry Mass. Mental Health Center, Boston, 1960-63, dir. neuropsychopharmacology lab., 1967—98, founding dir., 1998—2004, sr. psychiatrist, 1967—; research psychiatrist NIMH, Bethesda, Md., 1963-67, cons., 1967-68; asst. prof. psychiatry Harvard Med. Sch., Boston, 1967-70, assoc. prof., 1970-74, prof., 1974—. Dir. psychiat. chemistry lab. Mass. Mental Health Ctr., 1977-98, founding dir., 1998-2004. Author: over 200 publ. including, Neuorpsychopharmacology and the Affective Disorders, 1970; editor: Depression and the Spiritual in Modern Art: Homage to Miró, 1996, U.S. patent, 2002; editor-in-chief Jour. Psychiat. Rsch., 1982-92; mem. editorial bd. Psychophysiology, 1968-74, Jour. Psychiat. Rsch., 1968-82, Psychopharmacology, 1970-84, Sleep Revs., 1972-79, Communications in Psychopharmacology, 1974-81, Psychotherapy and Psychosomatics, 1974-91, Rsch. Communications in Psychology, Psychiatry and Behavior, 1976—, Jour. Clin. Psychopharmacology, 1980—, Integrative Psychiatry, 1982-89, 91—, others. Bd. dirs. Med. Found., Boston, 1991-97 chair clin. rsch. com., 1994-96; trustee Mind/Body Med. Inst. Deaconess Hosp., Harvard Med. Sch., Boston, 1988-2002, chair sci. adv. bd., 1988-95. Served as surgeon USPHS, 1963-65. Recipient Anna-Monika Found. prize, 1967, Hofheimer award Am. Psychiat. Assn., 1971, hon. mention award, 1968; McCurdy-Rinkel prize No. New Eng. Dist. br. Am. Psychiat. Assn., 1969; William C. Menninger award ACP, 1978; Neuropsychiatry Classics, 1995; Lifetime Achievement award Soc. of Biological Psychiatry, 1996; Award for Rsch. in Mood Disorders The Am. Coll. of Psychiatrists, 1999. Fellow: Am. Psychiat. Assn. (disting. life); mem.: AAAS, Soc. Neurosci., Collegium Internat. Neuropsychopharmacologicum, Assn. Rsch. in Nervous and Mental Disease, Group Without a Name, Am. Soc. Neurochemistry, Am. Soc. Pharmacology and Exptl. Therapeutics, Am. Coll. Psychiatrists, Am. Psychopath. Assn., N.Y. Acad. Scis., Soc. Biol. Psychiatry, Am. Psychosomatic Soc., Am. Coll. Neuropsychopharmacology, Psychiat. Rsch. Soc., World Psychiat Assn. (sec. sect. biol. psychiatry 1972—77), Phi Beta Kappa. Achievements include patents in field. Home and Office: 35 Jefferson Rd Chestnut Hill MA 02467-2341 Office Phone: 617-734-7489.

SCHILE, WAYNE, newspaper publishing executive; Pub. Billings (Mont.) Gazette, 1984-98. Address: PO Box 36300 Billings MT 59107-6300 Office: 401 N Broadway Billings MT 59101-1243

SCHILLER, ARTHUR A. architect, educator; b. N.Y.C., July 23, 1910; s. Valentine and Rose (Bayer) S.; m. Anne O'Donnell, June 12, 1937; children: Valerie Schiller Schaefer, Virginia Schiller Waicul, Eileen Schiller Toomey. BArch, NYU, 1933; diploma, Beaux Arts Inst. Design, N.Y.C., 1935; MArch, MIT, 1939. Registered profl. architect, N.Y. Architect U.S. Govt., Washington, 1936-38, N.Y.C. Dept. Parks, 1938-47; chief architect Bd. Higher Edn., N.Y.C., 1947-51, dir. architecture and engring., 1951-67; coord. campus planning Queens Coll., N.Y.C., 1967-73; adj. prof. N.Y. Inst. Technology, Old Westbury, 1973-91. Cons. Triboro Bridge Authority, N.Y.C., 1946; lectr. CCNY, 1957-67. Mayor Village of Plandome Manor, N.Y., 1965-87, trustee, 1960-65; trustee Sci. Mus. L.I. 1986—. Named Man of Yr. AARP, 1990, Sr. Citizen of Yr. Nassau County, State of N.Y., 1992 . Fellow AIA (pres. Queens chpt. 1957-58); mem. N.Y. State Assn. Architects (dir. 1959-60), Assn. Univ. Architects (emeritus), U.S. Power Squadron (comdr. 1961-62, budget dir. 1988-91), Elks (life). Avocations: boating, gardening, conducting defensive driving courses for older citizens. Home: 15 Luquer Rd Manhasset NY 11030-1015

SCHILLER, DANIEL TOBY, communications educator; b. NYC, July 10, 1951; s. Herbert Irving and Anita Louise (Rosenbaum) S.; m. Susan Gray Davis, July 23, 1978; children: Ethan Davis, Lucy Hazel. BA, U. Wis., 1972; MA, U. Pa., 1976, PhD, 1978. Rsch. scholar U. Leicester (Eng.) Ctr. for Mass Communication Rsch., 1978-79; asst. prof. radio-TV-film dept. Temple U., Phila., 1979-83, assoc. prof., 1983-86; assoc. prof. Grad. Sch. Libr. and Info. Scis. UCLA, LA, 1987—90; from assoc. prof. to prof. comm. dept. U. Calif., San Diego, 1990—2001; prof. Grad. Sch. Libr. and Info. Scis. U. Ill. Inst. Comm. Rsch., Champaign, 2001—. Author: Objectivity and the News, 1981, Telematics and Government, 1982, Theorizing Communication, 1996, Digital Capitalism, 1999; author: (with Vincent Mosco) Continental Order?, 2001. Gannett Ctr. for Media Studies fellow Columbia U., 1986-87. Office: Univ Ill Grad Sch Libr and Info Sci 501 E Daniel Champaign IL 61820-6211 Office Phone: 217-244-5369.

SCHILLER, DONALD CHARLES, lawyer; b. Chgo., Dec. 8, 1942; s. Sidney S. and Edith (Lastick) S.; m. Eileen Fagin, June 14, 1964; children—Eric, Jonathan Ed., Lake Forest Coll., 1960-63; JD, DePaul U., 1966. Bar: Ill. 1966, U.S. Dist. Ct. (no. dist.) Ill. 1966, U.S. Supreme Ct. 1972. Ptnr. Schiller, DuCanto & Fleck (formerly Schiller & Schiller and Schiller & DuCanto), Chgo., 1966—; lectr. in law U. Chgo. Law Sch., 2001—. Chair domestic rels. adv. com. Cir. Ct. Cook County, 1993—2001, co-chmn. rules revision com., 2003—; spkr. profl. confs. Contbr. chpts. and articles to profl. publs. Mem. steering com. on juvenile ct. watching, LWV, 1980-81. Recipient Maurice Weigle award Chgo. Bar Found., 1978, Disting. Alumni award, DePaul U., 1988, various certs. of appreciation profl. groups: named One of Am.'s Best Divorce Lawyers, Town and Country, 1985, 98, The Nat. Law Jour., 1987, The Best Lawyers in Am., 1987—, One of Chgo's. Best Div. Lawyers, Crain's Chgo. Bus., 1981, Today Chgo. Woman, 1985, Inside Chgo. mag., 1988, Chgo. Sun Times, 2000, Worth Mag., 2002. Fellow Am. Bar Found., Am. Acad. Matrimonial Lawyers (nat. chair continuing legal edn. 1993-94); mem. ABA (bd. govs. 1994-97, chmn. family law sect. 1985-86, Ill. State del. 1980-84, mem. Ho. of Dels. 1984-2003, editor-in-chief Family Law Newsletter 1977-79; mem. editorial bd., assoc. editor Family Adv. Mag. 1979-84, speaker at confs. and meetings), Ill. Bar Assn. (pres. 1987-88, chmn. family law sect. 1976-77, editor Family Law Bull. 1976-77, bd. govs. 1977-83, treas. 1981 84, v.p. 1984-86, chmn. various coms., lectr., incorporator and pres. Ill. State Bar Assn. Mutual Ins. Co., Inc. 1988-89), Chgo. Bar Assn., Am. Coll. Family Law Trial Lawyers (diplomate). Office: Schiller DuCanto & Fleck 200 N La Salle St Ste 2700 Chicago IL 60601-1098 Office Phone: 312-609-5560. Business E-Mail: dschiller@sdflaw.com.

SCHILLER, HARVEY W. risk management company executive; m. Marcia Schiller. BS in chemistry, The Citadel; MS in chemistry, PhD in chemistry, U. Mich.; PhD (hon.), The Citadel, No. Mich. U. V.p. sports programming Tuner Broadcasting Sys., Inc., 1994—99; chmn. YankeeNets, 2000—02, Assante US, 2002—03; chmn. bd. GlobalOptions, Inc., Washington, 2003—. Chmn. mgmt. com. NYC2012 Olympic Bid Com.; exec. dir., sec. gen. US Olympic Com., 1990—94. With USAF, 1962—86. Office: GlobalOptions Inc 1615 L St NW Ste 300 Washington DC 20036 Office Phone: 202-293-2490.

SCHILLER, JAMES JOSEPH, lawyer; b. Cleve., July 1, 1933; s. Jacob Peter and Helen Elizabeth (Tosh) S.; m. Sara Brooke Wilson, Oct. 24, 1964; children: Charles A., Brooke V.G., Kristan W. BS, Case Inst. Tech., 1955; JD, U. Mich., 1961. Bar: Ohio 1962. Assoc. Marshman, Hornbeck & Hollington, Cleve., 1961-68; ptnr. Marshman, Snyder & Seeley, Cleve., 1968-73, Zellmer & Gruber, Cleve., 1973-80, Weston, Hurd, Fallon, Paisley & Howley, Cleve., 1980-88, Porter, Wright, Morris & Arthur, Cleve., 1989-95, James J. Schiller & Assocs., Cleve., 1995—. Campaign mgr. John J. Gilligan for Gov. of Ohio, Cuyahoga County, 1970; campaign dir. U.S. Senator Howard M. Metzenbaum, Cleve., 1973; mem. Ohio Dem. Com., 1970-73; dep. registrar motor vehicles Dept. Hwy. Safety, Cuyahoga County, 1971-74; trustee Greater Cleve. Regional Transit Authority, 1985-87; vestryman Christ Episcopal Ch., Shaker Heights, Ohio, 1974-76, 90-93, clk., 1974-76, sr. warden, 1992-93; chmn. bd. suprs. ChristCh. Found., 1995—; trustee Recovery Resources, 1988—, chmn. bd. dirs., exec. com., 1994-96; trustee Ohio Ch. Orch., exec. com., 199-2001; trustee Cleve. Ballet, 1997-98; trustee Cuyahoga Valley Scenic Ry., 1996—, vice chmn., 2002-03, chmn., 2003—. Lt. j.g. USNR, 1955-58. Recipient Cert. Commendation Bd. County Commrs., 1987. Mem. ABA, Ohio State Bar Assn. (ethics com. 1986-88), Cleve. Bar Assn., Rowfant Club (fin. com. 1988, coun. Fellowes 1990-91, 95—, advocate 1992-95, 2002—, v.p. 1998-99, pres. 1999-2000), Union Club, Cleve. Skating Club. Avocations: sailing, skiing, restoring furniture. Home: 13415 Shaker Blvd Cleveland OH 44120-1586 Office: James J Schiller & Assocs 13224 Shaker Sq Ste 210 Cleveland OH 44120-2349 Office Phone: 216-283-7220. Personal E-mail: jjsleg@msn.com.

SCHILLER, JUSTIN GALLAND, antiquarian bookseller, researcher, editor; b. Bklyn., Sept. 10, 1943; s. S. Gary and Constance Audrey (Galland) S. BA in English Renaissance Lit., Ithaca Coll., 1965; postgrad., SUNY, Binghamton, 1965—66. Prin. Justin G. Schiller, Bklyn., 1960-69; pres. Justin G. Schiller, Ltd., N.Y.C., 1969—. Instr. hist. children's literature Rare Books Sch., Columbia U., 1984-89, U. Va., Charlottesville, 1996—; lectr. in field. Editor: (with A. Lurie) Garland's Classics in Children's Literature, 73 vols.; contbr. articles to Horn Book mag., Am. Book Collector, The Book Collector, others. Mem. coun. Bibliog. Soc. Am., 2001—. Mem Antiquarian Booksellers Assn. Am., Assn. Internat. de Bibliophilie, Am. Antiquarian Soc., Grolier Club. Home: 77 W Chestnut St Kingston NY 12401-5929 Office: Justin G Schiller Ltd Antiquarian Booksellers Ste 302 Rockefeller Ctr 1270 Ave of the Americas New York NY 10020-1702 E-mail: jgs@childlit.com.

SCHILLER, LAWRENCE JULIAN, writer, motion picture producer, director; b. N.Y.C., Dec. 28, 1936; s. Isidore and Jean (Liebowitz) S.; children: Suzanne, Marc, Howard, Anthony, Cameron. BA, Pepperdine Coll., 1958. Photojournalist Life mag., 1959-69, Paris Match, 1960-69, London Sun. Times, 1960-69. Producer, dir.; (films) Hey, I'm Alive, The Winds of Kitty Hawk, Marilyn, Raid on Short Creek, An Act of Love, The Executioner's Song (Emmy award), Peter the Great (Emmy award), By Reason of Insanity, Margret Brourke-White Story, Plot to Kill Hitler, Double Jeopardy, Perfect Murder, Perfect Town, American Tragedy, Master Spy: The Robert Hanson Story, Henry Lee Series; author: Cape May Court House, Into the Mirror, American Tragedy, Perfect Murder, Perfect Town, Marilyn; collaborator: (with Albert Goldman) Lenny Bruce (with Eugene Smith) Minamata, (with Norman Mailer) The Executioner's Song (Pulitzer prize 1980), Oswald's Tale; (with O.J. Simpson) I Want To Tell You. Chmn. bd. dirs. Am.-Soviet Film Initiative, 1988; Am. del. Moscow Internat. Forum on Peace, 1987; mem. USSR-USA Bi-Lateral Talks, 1988. Recipient numerous awards in photojournalism Nat. Press Photographers Assn., Acad. award for The Man Who Skied Down Everest, 1975 Mem. Nat. Press Photographers Assn., Calif. Press Photographers Assn., Dirs. Guild of Am., Acad. of Motion Picture Arts and Scis. Democrat. Jewish.

SCHILLER, PIETER JON, venture capital executive; b. Orange, N.J., Jan. 14, 1938; s. John Fasel and Helen Roff (Roberts) S.; m. Elizabeth Ann Williams, Nov. 20, 1965; children— Cathryn Ann, Suzanne Elizabeth. BA in Econs. with honors, Middlebury (Vt.) Coll., 1960; MBA, NYU, 1966. Fin. analyst Merck & Co., Inc., N.Y.C., 1960-61; fin. analyst, asst. div. controller, dir. auditing, then asst. controller Allied Chem. Corp., N.Y.C. and Morristown, N.J., 1961-75, treas., 1975-79, v.p. planning and devel., 1979-83; Allied Corp. exec. v.p. diagnostic ops. Allied Health & Sci. Products Co., 1983-86; pres. subs. Instrumentation Lab., Lexington, Mass., 1983-86; gen. ptnr. Advanced Tech. Ventures, Waltham, Mass., 1986—. Bd. dirs. HealthShare Tech., Acton, Mass., Endius, Inc., Plainville, Mass., CLC Tech., Inc., Tampa, Fla., CytoLogix Corp., Waltham, Mass., Ardais Corp., Lexington, Mass.; bd. advisors Fresh Tracks Capital, LLC, Middlebury, Vt. Chmn. bd. trustees Newark Boys Chorus Sch., 1976—78, pres. bd., 1974—76; trustee Colonial Symphony Soc., 1978—85, v.p., 1980—82, pres., 1982—83; active Morris Mus., Morristown, Concord (Mass.) Mus., 1994—96, v.p., 1996—2000, chmn. bd. trustees, 2002—; pres. Middlebury Coll. Alumni Assn., 1994—96; chmn. allocations com. United Way of Morris County, 1974—79, v.p. bd. dirs., mem. exec. com., 1979—80; trustee Morris Mus. Arts and Scis., 1980—83; bd. dirs. New Eng. Coun., Boston, 1983—86; v.p. Middlebury Coll. Alumni Assn., 1992—94. Mem. Fin. Execs. Inst. Republican. Episcopalian. Avocations: skiing, photography. Home: 18 S Meadow Rdg Concord MA 01742-3051 Office Phone: 781-290-0707. E-mail: pschiller@atvcapital.com.

SCHILLER, WILLIAM RICHARD, surgeon; b. Bennett, Colo., Jan. 14, 1937; s. Francis T. and Frances M. (Finks) S.; m. Beverlee Schiller; children from previous marriage: Julie, Lisa. BS, Drury Coll., Springfield, Mo., 1958; MD, Northwestern U., 1962. Diplomate Am. Bd. Surgery; cert. of added

qualifications in surg. critical care, 1987, recertified in surg. critical care, 1994. Intern Passavant Meml. Hosp., Chgo., 1962-63; resident Northwestern U. Clin. Tng. Program, Chgo., 1963-68; assoc. prof. surgery Med. Coll Ohio, Toledo, 1970-78; prof. surgery U. N.Mex, Albuquerque, 1978-83; dir. Trauma Ctr. St. Joseph's Hosp., Phoenix, 1983-89; dir. burn and trauma ctr. Maricopa Med. Ctr., Phoenix, 1989-98; prof. surgery So. Ill. U., Springfield, 1998—2002; ret., 2002. Clin. prof. surgery U. Ariz. Health Sci. Ctr.; prof. surgery Mayo Grad. Sch. Medicine, Rochester, Minn. Contbr. chpts. to books, articles to profl. jours. Served as maj. M.C. U.S. Army, 1968-70, Vietnam. Fellow ACS; mem. Am. Assn. Surgery of Trauma, Cen. Surg. Assn., Western Surg. Assn., Soc. Surgery of Alimentary Tract, Am. Burn Assn., Internat. Soc. of Surgery. Republican. Home: 784 Aspen Compound Santa Fe NM 87501 Personal E-mail: wrschiller@direcway.com.

SCHILLING, CURTIS MONTAGUE, professional baseball player; b. Anchorage, Alaska, Nov. 14, 1966; m. Shonda Schilling; 1 child, Gehrig. Student, Yavapai Coll., Ariz. Selected by Boston Red Sox, 1986—88; pitcher Balt. Orioles, 1988—91, Houston Astros, 1991—92, Phila. Phillies, 1992—2000, Ariz. Diamondbacks, 2000—03, Boston Red Sox, 2004—. Named to MLB All-Star game, 1997—99, 2001, 2002, 2004; recipient Lou Gehrig award, Phi Delta Theta, 1996, Nat. League Championship Series Most Valuable Player, 1993, co-World Series Most Valuable Player, 2001. Achievements include led Nat. League in strikeouts (319), 1997, (300), 1998; led Nat. League in wins (22), 2001. Office: c/o Boston Red Sox 4 Yawkey Way Boston MA 02215-3496*

SCHILLING, FREDERICK AUGUSTUS, JR., geologist, consultant; b. Phila., Apr. 12, 1931; s. Frederick Augustus and Emma Hope (Christoffer) S.; m. Ardis Ione Dovre, June 12, 1957 (div. 1987); children: Frederick Christopher, Jennifer Dovre. BS in Geology, Wash. State U., 1953; PhD in Geology, Stanford U., 1962. Registered geologist, Calif.; cert. engrng. geologist, Calif.; registered environ. assessor, Calif. Computer geophysicist United Geophys. Corp., Pasadena, Calif., 1955-56; geologist various orgns., 1956-61, U.S. Geol. Survey, 1961-64; underground engr. Climax (Colo.) Molybdenum Co., 1966-68; geologist Keradamex Inc., Anaconda Co., M.P. Grace, Ranchers Exploration & Devel. Corp., Albuquerque and Grants, N.Mex., 1968-84, Hecla Mining Co., Coeur d'Alene, Idaho, 1984-86, various engring. and environ. firms, Calif., 1986-91; prin. F. Schilling Cons., Canyon Lake, Calif., 1991—. Author: Bibliography of Uranium, 1976. Del. citizen amb. program People to People Internat., USSR, 1990-91. With U.S. Army, 1953-55. Fellow The Explorers Club; mem. Geol. Soc. Am., Am. Assn. Petroleum Geologists, Soc. Mining Engrs., Internat. Platform Assn., Adventurers' Club L.A., Masons, Kiwanis, Sigma Xi, Sigma Gamma Epsilon. Republican. Presbyn. Avocation: track and field. Office: F Schilling Cons 30037 Steel Head Dr Canyon Lake CA 92587-7460 also: 14661 Myford Rd Ste C Tustin CA 92780-7205 Office Phone: 714-731-8438. E-mail: faschill@pacbell.net.

SCHILLING, JAMES STANFORD, physicist, educator; b. Little Rock, Aug. 26, 1941; s. Henry Stanford Schilling and Tracy Virginia Madigan; m. Joan Margaret Shealer, June 5, 1965 (div. 1977); 1 child, Paul; m. Elke Karin Havenstein, Apr. 12, 1978; children: Martin, James. BS, Notre Dame U., Ind., 1963; MS, U. Wis., 1965; PhD, U. Wis., 1969; Habilitation, U. Bochum, Germany, 1979. Tchg./rsch. asst. U. Wis., Madison, 1963—69; postdoctoral rschr. Tech. U. Munich, 1969—72; sr. rsch. assoc. U. Bochum, Germany, 1972—83, extraord. prof., 1983—86; assoc. prof. physics U. Munich, 1986—90; prof. Washington U., St. Louis, 1990—. Editor: (book) Physics of Solids Under High Pressure, 1981; contbr. articles to profl. jours. Grantee Rsch. grantee, Deutsch Forschungsgemeinschaft, 1975—90, Bundesministerium, Germany, 1987—91, NSF, 1991—. Avocations: golf, radio-control airplanes, piano. Office: Washington Univ Dept Physics CB1105 One Brookings Dr Saint Louis MO 63130

SCHILLING, THOMAS HAROLD, education educator; b. Harrogate, Eng., Sept. 9, 1965; s. David Harold and Patricia Ann Schilling; m. Hildur Elizabet Halliday, Dec. 26, 1992; children: Cynthia Bryndis, Haley Elisabet, Solveig Hanna. BS in Psychology, Fitchburg (Mass.) State Coll., 1988; ALM in Psychology, Harvard U., 1990; PhD in Devel. Psychology, U. Mass., 1997. Instr. psychology U. Mass., Amherst, 1993—96; vis. asst. prof. psychology Franklin and Marshall Coll., Lancaster, Pa., 1996—98; asst. prof. Fitchburg State Coll., 1998—2003, assoc. prof., 2003—. Contbr. articles to profl. jours. NIMH predoctoral trainee, 1994—95. Mem.: AAAS, Soc. for Rsch. in Child Devel., Am. Psychol. Soc., Psi Chi. Avocations: cross country skiing, bicycling, photography. Office: Fitchburg State Coll Dept Behavioral Sci 160 Pearl St Fitchburg MA 01420 Office Phone: 978-665-3431.

SCHILLINGS, DENNY LYNN, retired history educator, educational and grants consultant; b. Mt. Carmel, Ill., June 28, 1947; s. Grady Lynn and Mary Lucille (Walters) S.; m. Karen Krek; children: Denise, Corinne. AA, Wabash Valley Coll., 1967; BEd, Ea. Ill. U., 1969, MA in History, 1972; MA in Adminstrn., Govs. State U., 1996; postgrad., Ill. State U., No. Ill. U. Grad. asst. dept. history Ea. Ill. U., Charleston, 1969; tchr. Edwards County High Sch., Albion, Ill., 1969-70, Sheldon (Ill.) High Sch., 1971-73, Homewood-Flossmoor (Ill.) High Sch., 1973—2003, tchr. history, grants and devel. mgr., 1994—2003; supr. history dept. Coll. Liberal Arts and Scis, No. Ill. U., Dekalb, 2003—; ret., 2003; adj. prof. Trinity Christian Coll., 2003—. Participant, con. Atlantic Coun. U.S. and NATO, Washington, 1986, Internat. Soviet-U.S. Textbook Project Conf., Racine, Wis., 1987; moderator Soviet-U.S. Textbook Study: Final Report, Dallas, 1987; chair history content adv. com. Ill. Tchr. Certification Requirements Com. 1986; mem. Ill. State Bd. Edn., Com. to Establish Learner Outcomes, 1984, Joint Task Force on Admission Requirements Ill. State Bd. on Higher Edn., 1986—; mem. adv. com. for Jefferson Found. Sch. Programs, 1987-90, Ill. State Bd. Edn.'s Goals Assessment Adv. Com., 1987-90; chair Ill. Learning Standards Project, 1996-97. Author: (with others) Economics, 1986, The Examination in Social Studies, 1989, Links Across Time and Place: A World History, 1990, Illinois Government Text, 1990, 99, 2003, Challenge of Freedom, 1990; author: The Living Constitution, 1991, 3d edit., 2002; co-editor: Teaching the Constition, 1987; reviewer, cons. for ednl. instns. and organizations; chair editorial bd. Social Edn., 1983; contbg. editor Social Studies Tchr., 1987-88. Mem. steering com. Homewood-Floosmoor High Sch. Found., 1983-84; elected bd. edn. Homewood Elem. Dist. 153, 1999—. Mem. NEA, Am. Hist. Assn. (James Harvey Robinson prize com. 1990-91), Ill. Coun. Social Studies (v.p. 1981, editor newsletter 1979-84, pres. 1983), Ill. Edn. Assn. (Gt. Lakes coord. com. 1982-83), Nat. Coun. Social Studies (publs. bd. 1983-86, bd. dirs. 1987-90, 94-96, exec. com. 1989-90, chair conf. com. 1989-90, pres. 1993-94, program planning com. 1989, 91), Phi Alpha Theta. Avocations: computers, reading. Home and Office: 18447 Aberdeen St Homewood IL 60430-3525 Office Phone: 630-886-0507. E-mail: dschillings1@comcast.net.

SCHILLOW, NED WILLIAM, mathematics educator; b. Skippack, Pa., Aug. 3, 1950; s. William James and Doris Elizabeth (Shaffer) S. BS, Ursinus Coll., Collegeville, Pa., 1972; MS, Rutgers U., 1974; MEd, Temple U., Phila., 1976. Sec. tchr. Cherry Hill (N.J.) Sch. Dist., 1974-76; prof. math. Lehigh County Community Coll., Schnecksville, Pa., 1976—. Assoc. editor the UMAP Jour., 1986—; asst. newsletter editor Pa. State Math. Assn. Two Yr. Colls., 1982-90; columnist Mo. Coun. Tchrs. Math. newsletter, 1985-90; contbr. articles to profl. jours. and chpts. to books. Recipient Faculty Appreciation award Student Govt. of Lehigh County C.C., 1987, George Elison Faculty Svc. award, 1988, Employee Recognition award, 1989, Pa. Outstanding Teaching award State Commn. for C.C., 1992, Faculty Excellence award, 2003. Mem. Math Assn. Am., Am. Math. Assn. of 2-Yr. Colls., Nat. Coun. Tchrs. Math. (rep. 1988—), Pa. State Math. Assn. of 2-Yr. Colls. (exec. bd. 1982—), Pa. Coun. Tchrs. Math (exec. bd. 1979-84, conv. publicity com. 1991-92), Ea. Pa. Coun. Tchrs. Math. (exec. bd. 1979—, pres. 1980-82). Republican. United Ch. of Christ. Avocations: reading, travel, crystal. Home: PO Box 539 Skippack PA 19474 Office: Lehigh County Community Coll 4525 Education Park Dr Schnecksville PA 18078-2510

SCHILSKY, RICHARD LEWIS, oncologist, researcher; b. N.Y.C., June 6, 1950; s. Murray and Shirley (Cohen) S.; m. Cynthia Schum, Sept. 24, 1977; children: Allison, Meredith. BA cum laude, U. Pa., Phila., 1971; MD with honors, U. Chgo., 1975. Diplomate Nat. Bd. Med. Examiners, Am. Bd. Internal Medicine (subspecialty med. oncology); lic. physician, Mo., Ill. Intern, resident medicine Parkland Meml. Hosp., Southwestern Med. Sch., Dallas, 1975-77; clin. assoc. medicine br. and clin. pharmacology br. Divsn. Cancer Treatment, Nat. Cancer Inst., Bethesda, Md., 1977-80, cancer expert clin. pharmacology br., 1980-81; asst. prof. dept. internal medicine U. Mo. Sch. Medicine, Columbia, 1981-84; asst. prof. dept. medicine U. Chgo. Pritzker Sch. Medicine and Michael Reese Med. Ctrs., 1984-86, assoc. prof. dept. medicine, 1986-89; assoc. dir. joint sect. hematology and med. oncology U. Chgo. and Michael Reese Med. Ctrs., 1986-89; assoc. prof. dept. medicine, assoc. dir. sect. U. Chgo. Pritzker Sch. Medicine, 1989-91, prof. dept. medicine sect. hematology-oncology, 1991—; dir. U. Chgo. Cancer Rsch. Ctr., 1991-99; chmn. Cancer and Leukemia Group B, Chgo., 1995—; assoc. dean clin. rsch. biol. scis. divsn. U. Chgo., 1999—. Vivian Saykaly vis. prof. oncology McGill U., 1992; sci. com. Internat. Congress on Anti-Cancer Chemotherapy, 2002; adv. panel on hematologic and neoplastic disease U.S. Pharmacopeial Conv., 1991-95; cancer ctr. support grant rev. com. Nat. Cancer Inst., NIH, 1992-95; expert panel on advances in cancer treatment, 1992-93; mem. Cancer Ctrs. Working Group, 1996-97; oncologic drugs adv. com. FDA, 1996-2000, chmn., 1999-2000; mem. NCI Clin. Trials Implementation com., 1997-98; bd. scientific advisors Nat. Cancer Inst., 1999—, mem. clin. trials working group, 2004—. Mem. editl. bd. Investigational New Drugs, 1988-95, Jour. Clin. Oncology, 1990-93, Contemporary Oncology, 1991-95, Jour. Cancer Rsch. and Clin. Oncology, 1991—, Seminars in Oncology, 1997—; assoc. editor Clin. Cancer Rsch., 1994—, Cancer Therapeutics, 1997-99, Cancer, 2000—; contbr. articles to profl. jours., chpts. to books. With USPHS, 1977-80. Recipient Spl. Advancement for Performance award VA, 1983, Fletcher Scholar award Cancer Rsch. Found., 1989; grantee VA, 1981-87, Am. Cancer Soc., 1983-86, 92-95, Ill. Cancer Coun., 1985-86, Michael Reese Inst. Coun., 1985-86, Nat. Cancer Inst., 1987, 88-90, Burroughs-Wellcome Co., 1987-88, NIH/Nat. Cancer Inst., 1988— Fellow ACP; mem. AAAS, Am. Soc. Clin. Oncology (chmn. pub. rels. com. 1994-96, bd. dirs. 2002-), Am. Assn. Cancer Rsch. (chmn. Ill. state legis. com. 1992—), Am. Fedn. Clin. Rsch. (senator Midwest sect. 1983-84, councilor 1983-86, chmn.-elect 1987-88, chmn. 1988-89), Am. Cancer Soc. (bd. dirs. Ill. divsn. 1997—), Am. Assn. Cancer Edn., Am. Soc. Clin. Pharmacology and Therapeutics, Ctrl. Soc. Clin. Rsch., N.Y. Acad. Scis., Assn. Am. Cancer Insts. (bd. dirs. 1995-99), Chgo. Soc. Internal Medicine, Sigma Xi, Alpha Epsilon Delta, Alpha Omega Alpha. Office: U Chgo Biol Scis Divsn 5841 S Maryland Ave Chicago IL 60637-1463 Office Phone: 773-834-3914. Business E-Mail: rschilsk@medicine.bsd.uchicago.edu.

SCHIMBERG, A(RMAND) BRUCE, retired lawyer; b. Chgo., Aug. 26, 1927; s. Archie and Helen (Isay) S.; m. Barbara Zisook; children: Geoffrey, Kate. PhB, U. Chgo., 1949, JD, 1952. Bar: Ohio 1952, Ill. 1955, U.S. Supreme Ct. 1987. Assoc. Paxton & Seasongood, Cin., 1952-55; ptnr. Schimberg, Greenberger, Kraus & Jacobs, Chgo., 1955-65, Leibman, Williams, Bennett, Baird & Minow, Chgo., 1965-72, Sidley & Austin, Chgo., 1972-92, counsel, 1993-94; ret., 1994. Lectr. U. Chgo., 1953-54; gen. counsel Comml. Fin. Assn., 1978-94; past mem. editl. bd. Lender Liability News. Mng. and assoc. editor U. Chgo. Law Rev., 1951-52; contbr. articles to legal jours. Bd. dirs. U. Chgo. Law Sch. Alumni Assn., 1969-72; dir. vis. com. U. Chgo. Law Sch., 1980-83. Recipient Homer Kripke Lifetime Achievement award for contbns. to comml. fin. law, 1998. Mem. ABA (chmn. subcom. and charter mem. comml. fin. svcs. com.), Am. Coll. Comml. Fin. Lawyers (pres. 1994-95, bd. regents), Ill. Bar Assn. (chair comml. banking, bankruptcy sect. 1972-73), Chgo. Bar Assn. (chair ucc com., 1966, bd. mgrs. 1968-70, chair judiciary com. 1971-72), Law Club Chgo., Mid-Day Club, Lake Shore Country Club. Home: 132 E Delaware Pl Apt 5002 Chicago IL 60611-4944 Office: Sidley & Austin 55 W Monroe St Ste 2000 Chicago IL 60603-5008

SCHIMBERG, BARBARA HODES, organizational development consultant; b. Chgo., Nov. 30, 1941; d. David and Tybe Zisook; children from previous marriage: Brian Hodes, Valery Lodato; m. A. Bruce Schimberg, Dec. 29, 1984. BS, Northwestern U., 1962. Ptnr. Just Causes, cons. not-for-profit orgns., Chgo., 1978-86. Cons. in philanthropy, community involvement, and organizational devel., 1987—; Chgo. cons. Population Resource Ctr., 1978-82. Mem. women's bd. dirs. Mus. Contemporary Art; bd. dirs., vice chmn. Med. Rsch. Inst. Coun., Michael Reese Med. Ctr.; bd. dirs., chmn. Midwest Women's Ctr.; trustee Francis W. Parker Sch.; bd. dirs. Women's Issues Network Found., 1991-98, pres., 1993-94; mem. adv. bd. Med. Rsch. Inst. Coun., Children's Meml. Hosp. Mem. ACLU (adv. com.), Women's Bd. U. Chgo. Office: 132 E Delaware Pl Apt 5002 Chicago IL 60611-4944

SCHIMEK, DIANNA RUTH REBMAN, state legislator; b. Holdrege, Nebr., Mar. 21, 1940; d. Ralph William and Elizabeth Julia (Wilmot) Rebman; m. Herbert Henry Schimek, 1963; children: Samuel Wolfgang, Saul William. AA, Colo. Women's Coll., 1960; student, U. Nebr., Lincoln, 1960-61; BA magna cum laude, U. Nebr., Kearney, 1963. Former tchr. and realtor; mem. Nebr. Legislature from 27th dist., Lincoln, 1989—; chmn. govt., mil. and vets. affairs com. Nebr. Legislature, Lincoln, 1993-94, 99—, vice chair urban affairs com., 1995-98. Dem. Nat. committeewoman, 1984-88; chmn. Nebr. Dem. Com., 1980-84, mem. exec. com., 1987-88; past pres., sec. bd. dirs. Downtown Sr. Ctr. Found., 1990-96; mem. exec. bd. Midwestern Legis. Conf., 1995—, co-chair health and human svcs. com., 1995-96; exec. dir. Nebr. Civil Liberties Union, 1985; former bd. dirs. Nebr. Repertory Theater, Exon Found., 1997-2000; mem. adv. bd. Martin Luther Home, 1997—; chair Midwestern Legis. Conf. Coun. of State Govts., 2000-01, co-chair com. on intergovtl. affairs; mem. Midwest Interstate passenger Rail Commn., 2001—; mem. exec. bd. Coun. State Govts., 2000—; chair NCSL Task Force on Initiative and Referendum, 2001-02. Toll fellow, 1999; recipient Outstanding Alumni award U. Nebr., 1989, Tribute award YWCA, 1992, Friend of Psychology award N.E. Psychol. Assn., 1998, Woman of Yr. award Nova Chpt. Bus. & Profl. Women, 1999, Disting. Svc. award Nat. Guard Assn., 2000, Woman of Distinction award Soroptimists, 1999, Legis. of Yr. award N.E. Dental Hygienists Assn., 2001, Disting. Svc. award N.E. League of Municipalities, 2002, Lincoln Interfaith Leadership award, 2003, Harold Steck award ARC of N.E., 2004, others. Mem. Nat. Conf. State Legislators Women's Network (bd. dirs. 1993-96, 1st vice chmn.), PEO, Soroptimists, Delta Kappa Gamma (hon.), Mortar Bd. (cmty. advisor 1998, hon.). Democrat. Unitarian Universalist. Home: 2321 Camelot Ct Lincoln NE 68512-1457 Office: Dist # 27 State Capital Lincoln NE 68509

SCHIMEL, RICHARD E. lawyer; b. Jersey City, Mar. 2, 1954; s. Albert Samuel and Rose (Schoenfeld) S.; m. Barbara Cheryl Mulitz, Aug. 7, 1983. AB in History, Princeton U., 1975; JD, George Washington U., 1978. Bar: Md. 1978, D.C. 1979, U.S. Dist. Ct. D.C. 1979, U.S. Dist. Ct. Md. 1979, U.S. Ct. Appeals (D.C. cir.) 1979, U.S. Ct. Appeals (4th cir.) 1982. Jud. law clk. Prince George's County Cir. Ct., Upper Marlboro, Md., 1978-79; assoc. Clancy and Pfeifer, Chevy Chase, Md., 1979-82, Budow and Noble PC, Bethesda, Md., 1982—. Home: 9719 Culver St Kensington MD 20895-3654 Office: Budow and Noble PC 7201 Wisconsin Ave Ste 600 Bethesda MD 20814-4849 E-mail: rschimel@budownoble.com.

SCHIMKE, DENNIS J. former state legislator; m. Olive Young, Dec. 1964 (dec. 1998); 3 children. BS, U. N.D., 1968, MS, 1972. Bison rancher, Coteau Hills, ND, 1987—; tchr. h.s. math. and physics LaMoure, N.D., 1975-2000; lectr. math. N.D. State U., 2001—; rep. Dist. 28 N.D. Ho. of Reps., 1991-93, rep. dist. 26, 1995-97, mem. edn. and agr. com., 1991—93, 1995—97. Founding bd. dirs. N.D. Buffalo Assn., 1991—95. Home: PO Box 525 Edgeley ND 58433-0525

SCHIMMELBUSCH, WERNER HELMUT, psychiatrist; b. Vienna, Nov. 16, 1937; came to U.S., 1954; s. Hans Mowgli and Anneliese Martha (Koeppe) S.; m. Faye Karina Wrangel, Dec. 29, 1958 (div. Mar. 1967); m. Jeanette Ramona Dyal, Mar. 26, 1971; children: Andre Curt, Anne Ramona. MD, U. Wash., Seattle, 1962; psychiatrist, Yale U., 1968; adult psychoanalyst, Seattle Inst. Psychoanalysis, 1977, child psychoanalyst, 1992. Instr. Dept. Psychiatry and Behavioral Sci. U. Wash., Seattle, 1968-69; pvt. practice Seattle, 1969—. Clin. prof. U. Wash., Seattle, 1984—; tng. and supervising psychoanalyst Seattle Inst. Psychoanalysis, 1990—. Capt. U.S. Army, 1963-65. Mem. AMA, Am. Psychiatric Assn., Am. Psychoanalytic Assn., Seattle Psychoanalytic Soc. (pres. 1979-80, 94-96). Avocations: skiing, hiking, sailing. Office: 4033 E Madison St Seattle WA 98112-3104

SCHIMMELPFENNIG, DAVID EVERETT, agricultural studies educator, researcher; b. Columbus, Ohio, May 25, 1959; s. Hal Schimmelpfennig; m. Robin Davis; children: Lars, Everett. PhD Economics, Mich. State U., East Lansing, MI, 1992. Program leader Resource Economics Divsn. (ERS-USDA), Wash., 1992—; faculty USDA - Grad. Sch., Wash., 1995—. Sr. fulbright scholar U. of Pretoria, Pretoria, Gauteng, South Africa, 2002. Contbr. numerous articles to profl. jours. and mags., chpts. to books. Recipient Honors in Economics, Purdue U., 1981. Mem.: Internat. Assn. of Agrl. Economists. Achievements include principal investigator for two Rockefeller Foundation grants and one for United States agricultural extension service. Office: Economic Research Service (USDA) 1800 M Street NW Room 4195 Washington DC 20036-5831 Office Phone: 202-694-5507. E-mail: des@ers.usda.gov.

SCHIMMENTI, JOHN JOSEPH, lawyer; b. NYC, Mar. 21, 1938; s. John Marcus and Mae M. (Miranti) S.; m. Mary Elizabeth Sleep, Apr. 18, 1964. BA, Columbia Coll., 1959; J.D., Georgetown U., 1962, LLM, 1964. Bar: DC 1962, NY 1964, Calif. 1965, U.S. Dist. Ct. (cen. dist.) Calif. 1965, U.S. Ct. Appeals (9th cir.) 1966, U.S. Supreme Ct. 1971. Trial atty. Anti-Trust divsn. U.S. Dept. Justice, Washington, 1962-64, Lands divsn., LA, 1965-67; trial atty. Santa Fe R.R., LA, 1968-70; ptnr. Schimmenti, Mullins & Berberian, El Segundo, Calif., 1971-. Mem. S.W. Dist. Bar Assn. (pres. 1983), LA Bar Assn. (condemnation com. 1983), Columbia U. Alumni of So. Calif. (pres. 1978). Republican. Roman Catholic. Club: El Segundo Rotary (pres. 1977). Office: Unit 303 5630 Ravenspur Dr Rancho Palos Verdes CA 90275-3535 Office Phone: 310-874-4801.

SCHINDEL, DONALD MARVIN, retired lawyer; b. Chgo., Jan. 5, 1932; s. Harry L. and Ann (Schiff) S.; m. Alice Martha Andrews, Apr. 24, 1960; children: Susan Yost, Judith Harris, Andrea Glickman. BS in Acctg., U. Ill., 1953; JD, U. Chgo., 1956. Ptnr. Sonnenschein, Nath & Rosenthal, Chgo., 1956-2000, ret., 2000. Author: Estate Administration and Tax Planning for Survivors, 1987, supplements, 1988-1996. Pres. United Way Highland Park-Highwood, Ill., 2000—03; v.p. campaign United Way of the North Shore, 2004—; pres. Congregation Beth Or, Deefield, Ill., 1983—85. Fellow Am. Coll. Trust and Estate Counsel; mem. Chgo. Estate Planning Coun. (Austin Fleming Disting. Svc. award 1999), ABA, Ill. Bar Assn., Chgo. Bar Assn. (chmn. probate practice com. 1981-82). Clubs: East Bank (Chgo.). Avocations: tennis, travel, bridge, carpentry, running. Home: 636 Rice St Highland Park IL 60035-5012

SCHINDERLE, ROBERT FRANK, retired hospital administrator; b. Mayville, Wis., Aug. 3, 1923; m. Elizabeth, June 23, 1949; children— David, Gary, Mary, Brian. BS, Marquette U., 1949; MS, Northwestern U., 1959. Asst. office mgr. Western Leather Co., Milw., 1949-51; mgr. bus. office St. Francis Hosp., Peoria, Ill., 1951-55; credit mgr. Mercy Hosp., Chgo., 1955-59, asst. to adminstr., 1957-58, controller, 1958-59, asst. adminstr., 1959-65, St. Joseph Hosp., Joliet, Ill., 1965-70, assoc. adminstr., 1970-71, adminstr., 1971-76, exec. dir., 1976-86; dir. corp. legis. affairs and devel. Franciscan Sisters Health Care Corp., Mokena, Ill., 1986-89, ret. Chmn. Areawide Hosp. Emergency Services Council. Bd. dirs. Region IX Health Systems Agy., Our Lady of Angels Retirement Home, Joliet, Joliet YMCA, St. Joseph Coll. Nursing, Joliet. Fellow Am. Coll. Health Care Execs. (life); mem. Am. Hosp. Assn., Ill. Hosp. Assn. (chmn. 1975-76), Ill. Hosp. Licensing Bd. (chmn. 1982-97, vice chmn. 1997-), Catholic Hosp. Assn. (dir.), Ill. Cath. Hosp. Assn. (chmn. 1972-73) Lodges: Rotary, Elks, KC. Roman Catholic. Home: 408 W Newkirk Dr Plainfield IL 60544-1838

SCHINDLER, ALBERT ISADORE, physicist, researcher; b. Pitts., June 24, 1927; s. Jonas and Esther (Nass) S.; m. Phyllis Irene Liberman, June 17, 1951; children— Janet Mae, Jerald Scott, Ellen Susan. BS, Carnegie Inst. Tech., 1947, MS, 1948, DSc, 1950. Research asst. Carnegie Inst. Tech., Pitts., 1947-50, research physicist, 1950-51; supervisory rsch. physicist Naval Rsch. Lab., Washington, 1951-75; assoc. dir. research for material sci. and component tech. Naval Research Lab., 1975-85; prof. materials engrng. and physics Purdue U., West Lafayette, Ind., 1985-92, cons., 1992-97, dir. Ind. Ctr. for Innovative Superconductor Tech., 1988-91, dir. Midwest Superconductivity Consortium, 1990-91; dir. div. materials rsch. NSF, Washington, 1988-90; chief scientist Office Naval Rsch., Arlington, Va., 1997-99; cons., 1999—. Cons. in field. Recipient E.O. Hulburt award Naval Research Lab., 1956, Nat. Capitol award for applied sci., 1962, Pure Sci. award Naval Research Lab.-Sci. Research Soc. Am., 1965, award Washington Acad. Scis., 1965, USN Disting. Achievement in Sci. award, 1975, Alumni Merit award Carnegie Mellon U., 1976, Sr. Exec. Service award Dept. Navy, 1983, Superior Pub. Svc. award Dept. Navy, 1999. Fellow Am. Phys. Soc., Wash. Acad. Scis.; mem. Sigma Xi. (dir.) Home: 6615 Sulky Ln Rockville MD 20852-4344

SCHINDLER, ANDREW J. tobacco company executive; b. Harrisburg, Pa., Aug. 1944; BA, Franklin and Marshall Coll; MBA, U. Pa. Dir. mfg. Nabisco Foods Co., Parsippany, N.J., 1987-88; with R.J. Reynolds Tobacco Co., Winston-Salem, NC, 1974—, nat. mgr., sales pers., 1976-78, mgr. orgn. and devel., 1979-82, plant mgr., 1982-87, v.p. pers., 1988-89, sr. v.p. ops., 1989-91, exec. v.p. ops., 1991-94, pres., COO, 1994-95, pres., CEO, 1995—, chmn., 1999—; chmn., CEO, R.J. Reynolds Tobacco Holdings, Inc., Winston-Salem, NC, 1999—2004; exec. chmn. Reynolds American Inc., Winston-Salem, NC, 2004—. Mem. adv. bd. Wachovia Bank N.C., N.A. Vice chmn. N.C. Emerging Tech. Alliance; bd. dirs. N.C. Sch. Arts Found., Winston-Salem Bus., Inc.; bd. visitors Wake Forest U. Bapt. Med. Ctr. Capt. U.S. Army, Vietnam. Office: RJ Reynolds Tobacco Holdings PO Box 2959 401 N Main St Winston Salem NC 27102-2866

SCHINDLER, LAURA ANN, piano teacher, accompanist; b. St. Louis, Aug. 17, 1943; d. Francis Joseph and Alice Binkley (Hurtgen) Schindler; m. John Charles Noto, Dec. 27, 1986. BM cum laude, Fontbonne Coll., St. Louis, 1970; MAT, Washington U., St. Louis, 1972; student, Ecole Normale de Musique, Paris, 1973-74. Nat. cert. tchr. of music; cert. Orff Schulwerk, Mozarteum Acad., Salzburg, Austria. Organist, choir dir. St. John's Basilica, St. Louis, 1971-73; piano tchr. Cmty. Music Sch., St. Louis, 1971-73, St. Louis Inst. Music, 1972-73; accompanist Robert McFerrin, Sr., N.Y.C., Chgo.,Springfield, St. Louis, 1974-77; piano tchr., Orff instr. St. Louis Conservatory, 1974-82; pvt. piano tchr. and accompanist St. Louis, 1982—. Vocal accompanist Affiliate Artist Program, St. Louis, 1977; accompanist MTNA West. Ctr. Divsn. Auditions, St. Louis, 1979, Forest Park C.C. Chorus, 1980-82, Ethical Soc. Chorus, 1980-83, Washington U. Music Sch., 1970-72; adjudicator piano competitions, Mo. and Ill., 1978—; clinician Piano Tchr. Workshops, Mo./Ill., 1979—. Contbr. articles to profl. jours.; performer Today Show, NBC, 1976, Capella Soloists Sunset concerts, 1976, Bicentennial Horizons of Am. Music, 1976, Rubinstein Music Club Meetings, 1997—, Benefit for Mo. Com. for Firearms Safety, 1982; performer, composer Am. Composers Concert, 1976. Recipient Mid-Am. Disting. Ind. Piano Tchr. award N.W., 1997, Disting. Piano Tchr. award Cedarhurst Chamber Music and Beethoven Soc., 1992; Acad. fellow Washington U., 1970-72. Mem.: Piano Tchrs. Round Table (pres. 1999—2001, exec. bd. mem. 2003—), Musical Diversions Soc. (bd. dirs. 1995—), St. Louis Area Music Tchrs. Assn. (v.p. for programs 1986—88, pres. 1988—92, chair nominating com. 1996—2000), Rubinstein Music Club. Democrat. Mem. Ethical Soc. Avocations: travel, walking, reading, eastern european folk dancing, ballroom dancing. Home: 7567 Lindbergh Dr Saint Louis MO 63117-2173

SCHINDLER, TERI, sports association executive; m. Mike Gorman, 1988. Grad. summa cum laude, U. Notre Dame, Ind., 1983. News/sports desk runner 1984 Summer Olympic Games, 1984; exec. prodr. women's basketball Conn. Pub. TV; mgr. Big East TV Network; dir. broadcasting NBA Entertainment, 1997—2004; v.p. programming, mktg. Nat. Basketball Assn. Entertainment,

N.Y.C., 2004—. Freelance writer specializing in women's and environ. issues. Contbr. articles to newspapers including the Boston Globe. Nominee 8 Emmy awards for basketball, football; recipient Emmy award (New Eng. region), 1993, Emmy award, NBC Sports, Olympics Sydney, 2000; scholar, Rotary scholar, 1983. Mem.: Phi Beta Kappa. Office: KTM Inc 323 W 74th St New York NY 10023

SCHINDLER, WILLIAM STANLEY, retired public relations executive, consultant; b. Detroit, Jan. 4, 1933; s. William Henry and Katherine (Schilling) S. Student, Wayne State U., 1950-53. Sr. v.p. Campbell-Ewald Co., Warren, Mich., 1968-85; v.p. pub. rels. Detroit Med. Ctr., 1985-92; interim v.p. Wayne State U., Detroit, 1993. Cons. to bus., univs., and founds.; v.p. Sandusky Pub. Co., Mich. Editor: Progress Report-New Detroit, Inc, 1969. Past mem. Detroit Hist. Commn., Detroit Fire Commn.; chmn. Detroit CSC; past pres. Detroit Hist. Soc., Hist. Soc. Mich.; mem. Gov.'s Sesquicentennial Commn., Peoria, Az. Fire Pension. Bd, Personnel Bd., Hist. Preservation Com.; bd. dirs. Adult Well-Being Svcs., Sacred Heart Rehab. Ctr., Brush Park Devel. Authority, Harper Hosp. Aux. With U.S. Army, 1954-56. Decorated Commendation Medal with pendant. Mem. Pub. Rels. Soc. Am., Adcraft Club Detroit, Detroit Press Club, Sons Whiskey Rebellion, Recess Club, Univ. Club, Detroit Athletic Club, Prismatic Club, Box 12 Club, Heard Mus. Coun. Home: 8741 W Wescott Dr Peoria AZ 85382-8773

SCHINE, CATHLEEN, writer; b. Westport, Conn., 1953; m. David Denby, 1981; children: Max, Thomas. Student, Sarah Lawrence Coll., Barnard U., U. Chgo. Author: Alice in Bed, 1983, To the Birdhouse, 1990, Rameau's Niece, 1993 (one of best books of 1993 N.Y. Times, Voice Literary Supplement, finalist Book prize L.A. Times 1992-93), The Love Letter, 1995, The Evolution of Jane, 1998; contbr. articles, reviews, columns to popular publs. including N.Y. Times Mag., N.Y. Times Book Review, Village Voice, Vogue. Office: care Candida Donadio Donadio & Ashworth Inc 121 W 27th St Ste 704 New York NY 10001-6207

SCHINK, FRANK EDWARD, electrical engineer; b. N.Y.C., May 14, 1922; s. Frank and Elizabeth (Kreps) S.; m. Barbara Jean McCally, Oct. 26, 1946; children: Stephen Frank, Thomas Ross. BEE, Bklyn. Poly. (now Poly. U. N.Y.), 1952, MEE, 1955. Registered profl. engr., N.Y., N.J. Elec. engr. George G. Sharp, Naval Architect, N.Y.C., 1940-43, 45, Anaconda Co., N.Y.C., 1946-59, Anaconda-Jurden Assocs., N.Y.C., 1959-61; sr. engr. M.W. Kellogg Co., N.Y.C., 1961-62, Port Authority of N.Y. & N.J., N.Y.C., 1962-77, cons. engr., 1977-84, chief elec. engr., 1984-89; pvt. practice elec. cons. Cranford, N.J., 1989—. Mem. various coms. ELECTRO Confs., 1976-96, past bd. dirs.; mem. adv. coun. N.J. Union County Transp., Westfield, 1977-79; mem. Port Authority Maintenance Improvement coun., N.Y.C., 1979-80; mem. com. IEEE Vehicular Tech. Conf., 1993; lectr. seminars Internat. Elec. Exposition and Congress, 1986, 87, Power Engring. Soc. Chpts. Cong., 1996. Author/editor: Environmental Impact Assessment, 1977; contbr. articles to profl. jours. Pres. Brookside Civic Assn., Cranford, 1960-62; chmn. Cub Scout and Boy Scouts Troops, Cranford, 1960-65; capt. United Fund, Cranford, 1962; tchr. Am. Coun. for Emigres, N.Y.C., 1975. With U.S. Army, 1943-45, ETO. Fellow IEEE (vice chmn. region I 1986-87; chmn. N.Y. sect. 1984-85, vice chmn. 1982-84, treas. 1981-82, editor N.Y. sect. Monitor 1989-90, life mem. com. 1994-97; also various coms.); mem. IEEE Power Engring Soc. (ad com. 1978-87, exec. com. 1983-87, chpts. rep. 1976-80, chmn. Winter Power Confs., N.Y. 1990-2002), IEEE Industry Applications Soc. (coun. mem. 1977-90), Tau Beta Pi, Eta Kappa Nu. Republican. Methodist. Home and Office: 316 Flagship Terr Tinton Falls NJ 07753

SCHINK, JAMES HARVEY, lawyer; b. Oak Park, Ill., Oct. 2, 1943; s. Norbert F. and Gwendolyn H. (Hummel) S.; m. Lisa Wilder Haskell, Jan. 1, 1972 (div. 1980); children— David, Caroline, Elizabeth; m. April Townley, Aug. 14, 1982. BA, Yale U., 1965, JD, 1968. Bar: Ill. 1968, Colo. 1982. Assoc. Sidley & Austin, Chgo., 1968; law clk. to judge U.S. Ct. Appeals, Chgo., 1968-69; assoc. Kirkland & Ellis, Chgo., 1969-72, ptnr., 1972—. Sustaining fellow Art Inst. Chgo. Mem. ABA, Ill. Bar Assn., Chgo. Bar Assn., Chgo. Club, Saddle and Cycle Club, Mid-Am. Club, Econ. Club of Chgo., Sonnenalp Golf Club, Vail Racquet Club, Yale Club of Chgo., Racquet Club Chgo., Game Creek Club. Republican. Presbyterian. Home: 1530 N State Pkwy Chicago IL 60610-1614 Office: Kirkland & Ellis 200 E Randolph St Ste 6100 Chicago IL 60601-6436

SCHIOWITZ, MARK F. surgeon; b. Wilkes-Barre, Pa., Oct. 30, 1952; s. Albert and Jean (Fuerth) S.; m. Therese Greenfield, Oct. 23, 1994. BA, Franklin and Marshall Coll., 1974; MD, Jefferson Med. Coll., 1978. Diplomate in gen. surgery and surg. critical care Am. Bd. Surgery. Intern Albert Einstein Med. Ctr., Phila., 1978-79, resident in surgery, 1979-83; pvt. practice Wilkes Barre. Dir. surg. ICU, Wilkes-Barre Gen. Hosp., 1991—, chief sect. gen. surgery, 1993—. Contbr. articles to profl. jours. Bd. dirs. EMS of N.E. Pa., Pittston, 1991—2003. Fellow ACS (liaison physician commn. on cancer 1997); mem. Soc. Critical Care Medicine, Am. Soc. for Parenteral and Enteral Nutrition, Am. Trauma Soc., Pa. Soc. Critical Care Medicine (exec. coun. 1999—2001). Office: Med Arts Bldg 35 W Linden St Ste 220B Wilkes Barre PA 18702-2619

SCHIRMEISTER, CHARLES F. retired lawyer; b. Jersey City, June 18, 1929; s. Charles F. and Louise P. (Schneider) Schirmeister; m. Barbara Jean Fredericks, Feb. 9, 1952; children: Pamela, Charles Bradford. BA, U. Mich., 1951; LLB, Fordham U., 1956. Bar: N.Y. 1956, U.S. Dist. Ct. (so. dist.) N.Y. 1961, U.S. Ct. Appeals (2d cir.) 1961, U.S. Supreme Ct. 1961. Asst. dist. atty. New York County, NY, 1956-61; assoc. Thelen, Reid & Priest, N.Y.C., 1961-71, ptnr., 1971-94; ret., 1994. Trustee Ocean Grove (N.J.) Camp Meeting Assn.; deacon Cmty. Congl. Ch., Short Hills, NJ. Capt. USMC, 1951—53. Mem.: Canoe Brook Country Club (Summit, N.J.), Univ. Club (N.Y.C.), Sigma Alpha Epsilon. Republican. Avocations: tennis, oenology, golf. Home: 15 Beechcroft Rd Short Hills NJ 07078-1648

SCHIRO-GEIST, CHRISANN, rehabilitation counselor; b. Chgo., Dec. 31, 1946; d. Joseph Frank and Ethel (Fortunato) Schiro; m. John J. Conway Sr., Oct. 26, 1985; children: Jennifer, Daniel; stepchildren: Patricia, Nicole, John Jr., Denise, Christine. BS, Loyola U., Chgo., 1967, MEd, 1970; PhD, Northwestern U., 1974. Registered psychologist, Ill.; Diplomate Am. Bd. Vocational Experts. Tchr. sci. Northbrook (Ill.) Jr. High Sch., 1967-70; dir. career counseling and placement Mundelein Coll., Chgo., 1972-74; counselor human devel. Regional Service Agy., Skokie, Ill., 1975-87; assoc. prof. psychology, rehab. counselor Ill. Inst. Tech., Chgo., 1975-87; full prof. rehab. U. Ill., Champaign-Urbana, 1987—, dir. Disability Rsch. Inst., 2000—, dir. disability and rehab. edn. and tng. office of vice-chancellor, 2003—. Co-author: Placement Handbook for Counseling Disabled Persons, 1982; author, editor: Vocational Counseling with Special Populations, 1990. Rsch. grantee Northwestern U., 1974; Region V Short-Term Tng. grantee Rehab. Svcs. Adminstrn., 1978-79, Long-Term Tng. grantee, 1983—, RSA grantee, 1988-91, 91-94, 93-96, 96—, 99—; Mary E. Switzer fellow NIDRR, 1989-90, VA, 1991-92, World Rehab. Fund fellow, 1993; co-grantee SSA, 2000—. Mem. APA, ACA, Nat. Rehab. Assn.(WF Faulkes award 2001), Nat. Coun. Rehab. Edn. (named Educator of Yr. 1987), Ill. Rehab. Counseling Assn. (pres. 1979-80), Coun. on Rehab. Edn. (pres. 1982-85, editor jour. 1986-92), Ill. Rehab. Assn. (pres. 1994), Kappa Beta Gamma Alumni Assn. (nat. officer). Office: U Ill Disability Rsch Inst 1207 S Oak St Champaign IL 61820-6901

SCHISGAL, MURRAY, playwright; b. N.Y.C., Nov. 25, 1926; s. Abraham and Irene (Sperling) S.; m. Reene Schapiro, June 29, 1958; children: Jane, Zachary. Student, Bklyn. Conservatory of Music, 1948, L.I. U., 1950; LLB, Bklyn. Law Sch., 1953; BA, New Sch. Social Research, 1959. Playwright, screenwriter and prodr. movies, TV and theatre. Author: The Typists and The Tiger, London, 1960, N.Y.C., 1963, Ducks and Lovers, London, 1961, Knit One, Purl Two, Boston, 1963, Luv (One of the Best Plays of 1964-65), London, 1963, N.Y.C., 1964, Fragments, Windows and other plays, 1965, Best Short Plays, 1981, 83, 85; contbr. to Best Short American Plays 1994-1995; original TV plays The Love Song of Barney Kempinski, 1966, Natasha Kovolina Pipishinski, 1976; off-Broadway Fragments, 1967, The Basement, 1967; Jimmy Shine, 1968, 69, Shooting Towards the Millinneum, 1997, Playtime, 1997; Broadway The Chinese, N.Y.C., 1970 (pub. in Best Short Plays of the World Theatre 1973), Dr. Fish, 1970, An American Millionaire, 1974, All Over Town, 1974 (pub. Best Plays 1974-75); screenplay The Tiger Makes Out, 1967, The Pushcart Peddlers, prod. off-off-Broadway, 1979 (pub. as The Pushcart Peddlers, The Flatulist and other plays); novel Days and Nights of a French Horn Player, 1980, Walter and the Flatulist; prod. off-Broadway The Downstairs Boys, 1980, The Songs of War, 1989; prod. regional theatre A Need for Brussels Sprouts, 1981, Play Time, Denver Ctr. Theatre, 1991, The Japanese Foreign Trade Minister, Cleve. Playhouse, 1992, 74 Georgia Ave., 1992, Circus Life, 1992; prod. Broadway Twice Around the Park, 1982; Other Plays, 1983, Closet Madness and Other Plays, 1984, Popkins, Paris, 1990, Play Time, 1991, The Songs of War, 1989; prod. Off Broadway The New Yorkers, 1984, Circus Life, 1995; prodr. Extensions, 1994; co-author: screenplay Tootsie (Winner Los Angeles Film Critics, N.Y. Film Critics, Nat. Soc. Film Critics, Writers Guild Am. award for best comedy); author Luv and Other Plays, 1983, The Rabbi and the Toyota Dealer, 1985, Jealousy, There are No Sacher Tortes in Our Society, 1985, Old Wine in a New Bottle, 1987, Road Show, 1987, Man Dangling, 1988, Oatmeal and Kisses, 1990, (with others) Best Short American Plays of 1991, 92-93, Sexaholics and Other Plays, 1995, Extensions, 1994, Circus Life, 1995, The Artist and The Model (Best Am. Short Play), 1994-95, Play Time (Published by Dramatists Play Svc., 1997), The Man Who Couldn't Stop Crying (Best Am. Short Plays, 1997-98), We Are Family, 2002, produced regional theaters and Berlin undertitle Warum Nicht and Prague, 2003; A Fugue For Four Seasons produced in Paris under title La Regard, 2002; 74 Georgia Ave. produced in regional theater, 2002; First Love (Best Am. Short Plays 1991-2000); prodr. feature films A Walk on the Moon, 1999, (cable TV) The Devil's Arithmetic, 1999, Boys and Girls, 2000, Clubland, 2000 (also exec. prodr.); exec. prodr. (cable TV) A Separate Peace, 2003. Recipient Vernon Rice award otustanding achievement off-Broadway Theatre, 1963; Outer Circle award Outstanding Theatre, 1963; named Outstanding Playwright, 1963. Office: care Arthur B Greene 101 Park Ave 26th Fl New York NY 10178-0002

SCHIZAS, JENNIFER ANNE, law association administrator; b. Grand Island, Nebr., Aug. 18, 1959; d. John Delano and Jacqueline May (Pieper) S. BJ, U. Nebr., 1982. Rschr. U.S. Senator Carl T. Curtis, Washington, 1978; pub. rels. dir. Nebr. Solar Office, Lincoln, 1979; reporter Sta. WOWT-TV, Omaha, 1980-83; bur. chief Sta. KHAS-TV, Hastings, Nebr., 1983-84; divsn. dir. March of Dimes, Lincoln, 1986-90; exec. dir. Lincoln Arts Coun., 1990-92, Nebr. Food Industry Assn., Lincoln, 1992-93; dir. comm. Nebr. Bar Assn., Lincoln, 1993—. Mem. editor's exch. adv. bd. West Pub. CO., Eagan, Minn., 1995. Mem. Am. Soc. Assn. Execs., Nat. Assn. Bar Execs. (pub. rels. cons. 1995), Nebr. Soc. Assn. Execs. Sertoma Club (v.p.). Democrat. Greek Orthodox. Avocations: running, painting, antique collecting and refinishing. Office: Nebr Bar Assn 635 S 14th St Lincoln NE 68508-2700 Home: 4 Lake Hill Dr Durham NC 27713-8954 E-mail: jschizas@nebar.com.

SCHIZER, ZEVIE BARUCH, lawyer; b. Bklyn., Dec. 19, 1928; s. David and Bertha (Rudavsky) S.; m. Hazel Gerber, Aug. 23, 1962; children: Deborah Gail, Miriam Anne, David Michael. *Son David M. Schizer is Dean of Columbia Law School. Daughter Miriam A. Landau is a pediatrician in Boston. Daughter Deborah G. Scott is a professor at Temple University teaching in the Intellectual Heritage Program.* BA magna cum laude, NYU, 1950; JD, Yale U., 1953. Bar: N.Y. 1954, U.S. Dist. Ct. (so. and ea. dist.) N.Y. 1959, U.S. Ct. Appeals (2d cir.) 1959, U.S. Supreme Ct. 1959. Assoc. Guzik & Boukstein, N.Y.C., 1953-54; teaching fellow NYU Sch. Law, 1954-55; assoc. Philips, Nizer, Benjamin & Krim, N.Y.C., 1955-56, Aranow, Brodsky, Einhorn & Dann, N.Y.C., 1956-57; asst. counsel jud. inquiry Appellate Divsn. 2nd Dept., Bklyn., 1957-62; assoc. Hays, Porter, Spanier & Curtis, N.Y.C., 1963-68, ptnr., 1968-85; sec. United Aircraft Products, Inc., Dayton, Ohio, 1970-83; ptnr. Schizer & Schizer, N.Y.C., 1985—. Trustee Bklyn. Pub. Libr., 1966—2003, pres., 1985—88, N.Y. Young Dem. Club, N.Y.C., 1960—61; trustee East Midwood Jewish Ctr., Bklyn., 1991—, pres., 2003—. Mem. N.Y. County Lawyers Assn. (mem. profl. ethics com., mem. com. on profl. discipline), Phi Beta Kappa. Democrat. Jewish. Home: 1134 E 23rd St Brooklyn NY 11210-4519 Office: Schizer & Schizer 3 New York Plz New York NY 10004-2442 Office Phone: 212-943-3340. E-mail: zschizer@msn.com.

SCHJERVEN, ROBERT E. manufacturing executive; With McQuay-Perfex Inc., Trane Co.; v.p. mktg. and engring. Heatcraft Inc. (subs. Lennox Internat. Inc.), 1986—88, v.p., gen. mgr., 1988—91; pres., COO Armstrong Air Conditioning Inc., 1991—95, Lennox Industries Inc. (subs. Lennox Internat. Inc.), 1995—2000; COO Lennox Internat. Inc., 2000—01, CEO, 2001—. Office: 2140 Lake Park Blvd Richardson TX 75080

SCHLACKS, STEPHEN MARK, lawyer; b. Pittsburg, Kans., Oct. 13, 1955; BA, Austin Coll., Sherman, Tex., 1978; MBA, U. Dallas, 1982; JD, Baylor U., 1986. Bar: Tex. 1987, U.S. Dist. Ct. (so. dist.) Tex. 1987, (no., ea. and we. dists.) Tex. 1988, U.S. Ct. Appeals (5th cir.) 1987, (8th cir.) 1989, U.S. Supreme Ct. 1990; bd. cert. personal injury trial law Tex. Bd. Legal Specialization, trial advocacy Nat. Bd. Trial Advocacy. In mgmt. Johnson & Johnson Products, Inc., Sherman, 1978-84; assoc. atty. Wetzel & Assocs., The Woodlands, Tex., 1986-92; ptnr. Hope, Causey & Schlacks, P.C., Conroe, Tex., 1992-96, Law Office of Stephen M. Schlacks, The Woodlands, Tex., 1996-99, Schlacks, Harrison & Cox PLLC, The Woodlands, 1999—2003; prin. The Schlacks Law Firm, PLLC, The Woodlands, Tex., 2003—. Leon Jaworski scholar, 1984, Harcourt Brace Jovanovich scholar, 1986. Mem. Montgomery County Bar Assn., Sigma Iota Epsilon, Pi Gamma Mu. Republican. Presbyterian. Home: 66 Racing Cloud Ct The Woodlands TX 77381-5203 Office: 2202 Timberloch Pl Ste 107 The Woodlands TX 77380-1163 Office Phone: 281-363-3977. E-mail: schlacks@shcpllc.com.

SCHLAFER, DONALD HUGHES, veterinary pathologist; b. Sidney, N.Y., July 15, 1948; s. Donald Hughes and Mildred (Gamewell) S., Jr.; m. Judith Ann Appleton, Aug. 2, 1980; children: Nathan James, Russell Matthew. BS, Cornell U., 1971, MS, 1975; DVM, N.Y. State Coll. Vet. Medicine, Ithaca, 1974; PhD, Coll. Vet. Medicine, Athens, Ga., 1982. Diplomate Am. Coll. Vet. Pathologists, Am. Coll. Theriogenologists (exec. com. 1993-96), Am. Coll. Vet. Microbiologists. Gen. practice vet. medicine Guilderland Animal Hosp., Altamont, NY, 1975-77; resident dept. vet. pathology U. Ga., Athens, 1977-79; rsch. pathologist USDA Plum Island Animal Disease Ctr., Greenport, NY, 1975-82; asst. prof. dept. vet. pathology Cornell U., Ithaca, 1982-88, assoc. prof., 1988-97, prof. comparative reproductive pathology, 1997—, dir. Bovine Rsch. Ctr., 1982-91. Vis. fellow Oxford (Eng.) U., 1990—91; vis. pathologist San Diego Zoo, 2003; vis. prof. U. Padua, Italy, 2004; cons. in field. Contbr. articles to profl. publs. Named Theriogenologist of Yr., 2004. Mem. AVMA, Soc. for Study of Reproduction, Soc. for Theriogenology (exec. com. 1993-96). Office: T6020 Coll Vet Medicine Cornell U Ithaca NY 14853 E-mail: dhs2@cornell.edu.

SCHLAFLY, HUBERT JOSEPH, JR., communications executive; b. St. Louis, Aug. 14, 1919; s. Hubert J. and Mary Ross (Parker) S.; m. Leona Martin, June 12, 1944. BSEE, U. Notre Dame, 1941; postgrad., Syracuse U., 1946—47; DHL (hon.), Sacred Heart U., 2003; LHD (hon.). Electronics engr. Gen. Electric Co., Schenectady, 1941-44, Syracuse, 1946-47; project engr. radiation lab. MIT, 1944-45; dir. TV rsch. 20th Century-Fox Film Corp., N.Y.C., 1947-51; founder, v.p. Teleprompter Corp., N.Y.C., 1951-74, pres., 1971-72, exec. v.p. tech. devel., 1972-74; pres. Transponder Corp., Greenwich, 1977-86; chmn., CEO Portel Services Corp., 1984-86; chmn., pres. Portel Services Network, Inc., 1987-91, chmn. bd., 1991-97, ret., 1998. Cons. in field; industry coord., chmn. exec. com., cable tech. adv. com. FCC, 1972—75; adviser com. telecomm. Nat. Acad. Engring.; adviser Sloan Commn. Cable Comms.; mem. engring. adv. coun. U. Notre Dame, 1977, vice chmn., 83, chmn., 84; bd. dirs., sec. Milbrook Corp., 1994—2001; lectr. in field. Author: Computer in the Living Room; patentee in field. Bd. govs. Milbrook Club, 1993-98. Recipient Engring. Honor award U. Notre Dame, 1976, Nat. Acad. TV Arts and Scis. Emmy award, 1992, 99, Sci. Initiative award Sacred Heart U., 1997, Discovery award, 2001, David Sarnoff Citation award, Radio Club Am., 2004. Fellow Soc. Motion Picture and TV Engrs.; mem. IEEE (life, Delmer Ports award 1979), Nat. Cable TV Assn. (chmn. standards com. 1965-69, chmn. domestic satellite com. 1971-73, chmn. future svcs. com. 1972, assns. com. 1981, Outstanding Tech. Achievements award 1974), Electronic Industries Assn. (chmn. broadband cable sect. 1971-73, founding chmn. broadband comm. com.), Soc. Cable TV Engrs. (sr.), Fairfield Found. (hon.); named Notre Dame alumni Man of Yr., 1992, Rotary (pres. Greenwich club 1991-92), Knights of Malta, Knight St. Gregory the Great. Roman Catholic. Home and Office: 27 Orchard Dr Greenwich CT 06830-6711 E-mail: hschlafly@aol.com.

SCHLAFLY, PHYLLIS STEWART, writer; b. St. Louis, Aug. 15, 1924; d. John Bruce and Odile (Dodge) Stewart; m. Fred Schlafly, Oct. 20, 1949; children: John F., Bruce S., Roger S., Phyllis Liza Forshaw, Andrew L., Anne V. BA, Washington U., St. Louis, 1944, JD, 1978; MA, Harvard U., 1945; LLD, Niagara U., 1976. Bar: Ill. 1979, DC 1984, Mo. 1985, U.S. Supreme Ct. 1987. Syndicated columnist Copley News Svc., 1976—. Broadcaster Spectrum, CBS Radio Network, 1973—78; commentator Matters of Opinion sta. WBBM-AM, Chgo., 1973—75, Cable TV News Network, 1980—83; pres. Eagle Forum, 1975—. Author, pub.: Phyllis Schlafly Report, 1967—; author: A Choice Not an Echo, 1964, The Gravediggers, 1964, Strike From Space, 1965, Safe Not Sorry, 1967, The Betrayers, 1968, Mindszenty The Man, 1972, Kissinger on the Couch, 1975, Ambush at Vladivostok, 1976, The Power of the Positive Woman, 1977, First Reader, 1994, Turbo Reader, 2001, Feminist Fantasies, 2003, The Supremacists, 2004, The Tyranny of Judges and How to Stop It, 2004; editor: (book) Child Abuse in the Classroom, 1984, Pornography's Victims, 1987, Equal Pay for Unequal Work, 1984, Who Will Rock the Cradle, 1989, Stronger Families or Bigger Government, 1990, Meddlesome Mandate: Rethinking Family Leave, 1991. Del. Rep. Nat. Conv., 1956, 1964, 1968, 1984, 1988, 1992, 1996, 2004, alt., 1960, 1980, 2000; 1st v.p. Nat. Fedn. Rep. Women, 1964—67; nat. chmn. Stop ERA, 1972—; mem. Ronald Reagan's Def. Policy Adv. Group, 1980, Commn. on Bicentennial of U.S. Constn., 1985—91, Adminstrv. Conf. U.S., 1983—86; pres. Ill. Fedn. Rep. Women, 1960—64; mem. Ill. Commn. on Status of Women, 1975—85. Named Woman of Achievement in Pub. Affairs, St. Louis Globe-Democrat, 1963; named one of 10 Most Admired Women in World, Good Housekeeping poll, 1977—90, 100 Most Important Women of 20th Century, Ladies Home Jour., 1998; recipient 10 Honor awards, Freedom Found., Brotherhood award, NCCJ, 1975. Mem.: DAR (nat. chmn. Am. history 1965—68, nat. chmn. bicentennial com. 1967—70, nat. chmn. nat. def. 1977—80, 1983—95), ABA, Ill. Bar Assn., Phi Beta Kappa, Pi Sigma Alpha. Office: Eagle Forum 7800 Bonhomme Ave Saint Louis MO 63105-1906 Office Phone: 314-721-1213. E-mail: phyllis@eagleforum.org.

SCHLAGEL, RICHARD H. philosophy educator; b. Springfield, Mass., Nov. 22, 1925; BS in Pre-Med cum laude, Springfield Coll., 1949; MA in Philosophy, Boston U., 1952, PhD, 1955. Instr. philosophy Coll. of Wooster, 1954-55; instr. Clark U., 1955-56; asst. prof. George Washington U., 1956-62, assoc. prof., 1962-68, prof., 1968—, chmn. dept., 1965-69, 70-71, 77-83, named Elton prof. philosophy, 1986, Elton prof. emeritus, 2001—. Sabbatical, Paris, with travel throughout Europe, 1962-63, 69-70, 76-77, 83-84, 90-91. Author: The Vanquished Gods: Science, Religion, and the Nature of Belief, 2001, From Myth to Modern Mind: A Study of the Origins and Growth of Scientific Thought, vol. 1, Theogony through Ptolemy, 1995, vol. 2, Copernicus through Quantum Mechanics, 1996; Contextual Realism: A Metaphysical Framework for Modern Science, 1986; contbr. articles and reviews to profl. jours. Borden Parker Browne fellow, 1953-54. Mem. AAUP, Am. Philos. Assn., Washington Philosophy Club (v.p. 1964-65, pres. 1965-66).

SCHLAGETER, ROBERT WILLIAM, museum administrator; b. Streator, Ill., May 10, 1925; s. Herman Pete and Ida (Ladtkow) S.; divorced; children— David Michael, Robert William Diploma, Karl Ruprecht Univ., Heidelberg, Fed. Republic Germany, 1950, BA, U. Ill., 1950, MFA, 1957. Asst. prof. U. Tenn., Knoxville, 1952-58; dir. Mint Mus. Art, Charlotte, N.C., 1958-66; assoc. dir. Downtown Gallery, N.Y.C., 1966, Ackland Art Ctr., U. N.C., Chapel Hill, 1967-76; dir. Cummer Gallery Art, Jacksonville, Fla., 1976-92, dir. emeritus, 1992—. Fine arts cons. corp. and pvt. collecting, 1993—. Author: (exhbn. catalogue) Winslow Homer's Florida, George Inness' Florida, Martin Johnson Heade Florida, Robert Henri-George Bellows. Served with U.S. Army, 1943-45, ETO Home: 5201 Atlantic Blvd Apt 2 Jacksonville FL 32207-2473

SCHLAIN, BARBARA ELLEN, lawyer; b. N.Y.C., May 28, 1948; d. William and Evelyn (Youdelman) S. BA, Wellesley Coll., 1969; MA, Columbia U., 1970; JD, Yale U., 1973. Bar: N.Y. 1974, U.S. Dist. Ct. (so. dist.) N.Y. 1974, U.S. Ct. Appeals (2d cir.) 1975, U.S. Dist. Ct. (ea. dist.) N.Y. 1977. Assoc. firm Donovan Leisure Newton & Irvine, N.Y.C., 1973-76, Graubard Moskovitz McGoldrick Dannett & Horowitz, N.Y.C., 1976-79; atty. McGraw-Hill, Inc., N.Y.C., 1979-80, asst. gen. counsel, 1980-86, v.p., assoc. gen. counsel, asst. sec., 1986—. Sec. proprietary rights com. Info. Industry Assn., 1982-83. Author: outlines Practicing Law Inst., 1983, 84, 85, 86, 88; contbr. numerous articles to profl. jours. Bd. dirs., v.p., sec. Dance Rsch. Found., N.Y.C., 1983-86, chmn., 1986-98. Phi Beta Kappa scholar, Durant scholar Wellesley Coll., 1967-69. Mem. ABA, Assn. Am. Pubs. (lawyers com. 1979—), Assn. Bar City N.Y. (comm. law com. 1985-88). Office: The McGraw-Hill Companies Inc 1221 Avenue Of The Americas New York NY 10020-1095

SCHLANG, DAVID, real estate company executive, lawyer; b. NYC, May 2, 1912; s. Alexander and Blanche (Cohen) S.; m. Arlene Roth, May 9, 1948. LLB, NYU, 1933. Bar: NY 1935, US Dist. Ct. (so. dist.) NY 1940. Individual practice law, 1935-42; sec., pres. Schlang Bros. & Co., Inc., NYC, 1945—. Trustee Brookdale Hosp., Bklyn., 1980—, vice chmn., 1983—, Linroc Nursing Home, 1993—; founding mem. US Congl. Adv. Bd.; bd. dirs., vice chmn. Samuel Schulman Inst. Nursing Rehab. Brookdale Hosp., 1973—; bd. dirs. Legion Meml. Sq., Inc., 1983—. With AUS, 1942—45. Decorated Croix de Guerre with palm (France); recipient Conspicious Svc. award State of NY, 1965. Mem.: ABA, Real Estate Bd. NY, NY County Lawyers Assn., NY State Bar Assn., Criminal Investigation Divsn. Agts. Assn., Met. Club, US Senatorial Club. Home: 737 Park Ave New York NY 10021-4256 Personal E-mail: schlang67@aol.com.

SCHLEEDE, GLENN ROY, energy market and policy consultant; b. Lyons, N.Y., June 12, 1933; m. Sandra Christine Klafehn, Dec. 27, 1958; children: Kristen M., Kimberly J., Kendall E. BA, Gustavus Adolphus Coll., 1960; MA, U. Minn., 1968; advanced mgmt. program, Harvard U., 1987. Research asst. Indsl. Relations Ctr., U. Minn., Mpls., 1960-61; mgmt. intern, then contractor personnel specialist AEC, Argonne, Ill. and Germantown, Md., 1961-65; asst. chief div. natural resources U.S. Office Mgmt. and Budget, Exec. Office of Pres., Washington, 1965-72, exec. assoc. dir., 1981; dep. assoc. dir. Office of Policy Analysis, AEC, Germantown, 1972-73; assoc. dir. energy and sci. Domestic Council, The White House, Washington, 1973-77; sr. v.p. Nat. Coal Assn., Washington, 1977-81; pres. New Eng. Energy Inc., Westborough, Mass., 1982-92, also bd. dirs.; v.p. New Eng. Power Service Co., Westborough, 1982-92, also bd. dirs.; v.p. New Eng. Electric System, Westborough, 1986-92; pres., CEO, dir. Energy Market and Policy Analysis, Inc., Reston, Va., 1992—. Author numerous speeches, papers and congl. testimony on various nat. energy policy issues. Recipient Disting. Alumni in Bus. award Gustavus Adolphus Coll. Alumni Assn., St. Peter, Minn., 1987. Republican. Lutheran. Avocations: reading, travel, carpentry. Home: 1414 Hemingway Ct Reston VA 20194-1241 Office: Energy Market and Policy Analysis Inc PO Box 3875 Reston VA 20195-1875 E-mail: empainc@aol.com.

SCHLEGEL, FRED EUGENE, lawyer; b. Indpls., July 24, 1941; s. Fred George and Dorothy (Bruce) S.; m. Jane Wessels, Aug. 14, 1965; children: Julia, Charles, Alexandra. BA, Northwestern U., 1963; JD with distinction, U. Mich., 1966. Bar: Ind. 1966. Assoc. lawyer Baker & Daniels, Indpls., 1966-72, ptnr., 1972—; vice chmn. Meridian St. Preservation Commn., Indpls., 1975-90. Contbr. articles to profl. jours. Chmn. Pub. Schs. Edn. Found., Indpls., 1988—90; pres. Festival Music Soc., 1974—75, 1979, 1986—87; bd. dirs. chmn. Indpls. Symphony Orch., 2002—; bd. dir. Arts Coun., Indpls.,

1996—2002. Mem. ABA, Ind. Bar Assn., Energy Bar Assn., Northwestern U. Alumni Club Indpls. (pres. 1992-94), Northwestern U. Alumni Assn. (bd. dirs. 2002-). Republican. Episcopalian. Office: Baker and Daniels 300 N Meridian St Ste 2700 Indianapolis IN 46204-1782 Office Phone: 317-237-1410. E-mail: feschleg@bakerd.com.

SCHLEGEL, JOHN FREDERICK, management consultant, speaker; b. Ogden, Utah, Dec. 18, 1944; s. Max Joseph and Mary Georgia (Whittaker) S.; m. Priscilla Mary Hecht, Sept. 8, 1967. BS in Pharmacy, U. Pacific, 1967; D of Pharmacy, U. So. Calif., 1972, MS in Edn., 1980; ScD in Pharmacy (hon.), Mass. Coll. Pharmacy, 1984, L.I. U., 1985. Lic. pharmacist, Calif., Nev.; cert. assoc. exec. Chief pharmacist U. So. Calif. Sch. Pharmacy, LA, 1967-73, postdoctoral fellow, 1972—73, dir. pharmacy admissions, 1973-75; dir. office student affairs Am. Assn. Colls. Pharmacy, Alexandria, Va., 1975-77, asst. exec. dir., 1977-81, exec. dir., 1981-84; CEO Am. Pharm. Assn., Washington, 1984-89; exec. v.p., CEO Am. Acad. Facial Plastic and Reconstructive Surgery, Washington, 1989-92; pres. Schlegel & Assocs., 1992—. Cons. in field. Contbr. over 100 articles on pharmacy, health care and assn. mgmt.; presenter in field. Nat. del. White House Conf. on Aging, Washington, 1981. Disting. alumnus U. So. Calif. Sch. Pharmacy, 1985, U. the Pacific Sch. Pharmacy, 1987. Fellow Am. Soc. Assn. Execs.; mem. Am. Assn. Med. Soc. Execs., Fla. Soc. Assn. Execs., Phi Delta Chi (charter, bd. counsellors). Avocations: tennis, classical music, gardening. Office: 3390 Highlands Bridge Rd Sarasota FL 34235-6859 Office Phone: 941-341-0434. Business E-Mail: jschlegel@comcast.net.

SCHLEGEL, JOHN P. academic administrator; b. Dubuque, Iowa, July 31, 1943; s. Aaron Joseph and Irma Joan (Hingtgen) S. BA, St. Louis U., 1969, MA, 1970; BDiv, U. London, 1973; DPhil, Oxford U., 1977. Joined Soc. of Jesus, 1963, ordained priest Roman Cath. Ch., 1973. From asst. prof. to assoc. prof. Creighton U., Omaha, 1976-79, asst. acad. v.p., 1978-82; dean Coll. Arts and Scis. Rockhurst Coll., Kansas City, Mo., 1982-84, Marquette U., Milw., 1984-88; exec. and acad. v.p. John Carroll U., Cleve., 1988-91; pres. U. San Francisco, 1991-2000, Creighton U., Omaha, 2000—. Cons. Orgn. for Econ. Devel. and Cooperation, Paris, 1975-76. Author: Bilingualism and Canadian Policy in Africa, 1979; editor: Towards a Redefinition of Development, 1976; contbr. articles to profl. jours. Mem. Milwaukee County Arts Coun., 1986—88, Mo. Coun. on Humanities, Kansas City, 1984; trustee St. Louis U., 1985—91, Loyola U., Chgo., 1988—2004, Loyola U. New Orleans, 1995—98, St. Ignatius H.S., Cleve., 1990—91, Loyola Coll. in Md., 1992—98, Xavier U., 1998—2003. Oxford U. grantee, 1974-76; Govt. of Can. grantee, 1977-78. Mem.: Am. Coun. Edn., Bohemian Club. Avocations: racquet sports, classical music, cooking, hiking. Office: Creighton U Office Pres 2500 Calif Plz Omaha NE 68178 Office Phone: 402-280-2770. Business E-Mail: jpschlegel@creighton.edu.

SCHLEGEL, PETER NILES, urologist and educator; b. Malden, Mass., Feb. 17, 1958; s. Niles Matthew and Mary Patricia (McIntyre) S.; m. Suzanne Marie Bozzo, Sept. 14, 1991; children: Andrew Peter, Lucy Filice, Nicholas Halloran. AB, Hamilton Coll., 1979; MD, U. Mass., 1983. Diplomate Am. Bd. Urology, Nat. Bd. Med. Examiners; lic. physician, N.Y. Intern in gen. surgery and resident Johns Hopkins Hosp., Balt., 1983-85, resident, chief resident in urology, 1985-89, instr. urology, 1989; fellow-in-residence The Population Coun., N.Y.C., 1989-91, staff scientist, 1991—; asst. attending surgeon New York Hosp., N.Y.C., 1991-96; assoc. attending surgeon N.Y. Hosp., N.Y.C., 1996—; assoc. vis. physician Rockefeller U., N.Y.C., 1991—; asst. prof. urology Cornell Med. Coll., N.Y.C., 1991-96, assoc. prof. urology, 1996—2004, prof., 2004—, vice chmn. urology, 1999-2001, acting chmn., 2001—03, chmn., 2003—. Vis. prof. Austria, Israel, Indonesia, Saudi Arabia, Brazil, others; vis. fellow Royal Coll. Surgeons, 1993; co-dir. Ctr. for Male Reproduction and Microsurgery, Cornell Inst. for Reproductive Medicine, 2000—; lectr. in field. Contbr. numerous articles, abstracts to profl. jours., chpts. to books. Recipient Edwin Beer Program award N.Y. Acad. Medicine, 1996-98, New Investigator award Am. Found. for Urol. Disease, 1993-95, fellow, 1989-91; fellow Am. Cancer Soc., 1986-87, NIH, 1989-91; established Clinician award ESHRE, 1996. Mem.: Soc. for Male Reproduction /Urology (pres.), Soc. for Study of Male Reprodn., Am. Urol. Assn., Soc. for Basic Urol. Rsch., Soc. for Study of Reprodn., Am. Soc. Andrology, Am. Soc. Reproductive Medicine, Alpha Omega Alpha. Roman catholic. Avocation: sailing. Office: New York Hosp Dept Urology 525 E 68th St Dept Urology New York NY 10021-4885 Office Phone: 212-746-5491. E-mail: pnschleg@med.cornell.edu.

SCHLEGEL, RICHARD LAMAR, advocate, writer; b. Berrysburg, Pa., Feb. 11, 1927; s. Roy Frederick and Margaret Annetta (Deibler) Schlegel. BA, Pa. State U., State College, 1943—49; MPA, The Am. U., Washington, D.C., 1949—54. Budget officer US Govt. Agys., Wash., Mich., Hawaii, 1951—61; dir. of fin. Pa. State Govt., Harrisburg, 1963—65; editor & pub. Gay & Lesbian Orgns., Washington, 1967—72; retail sales promotion Paul Brooker Sales Internat., Wichita, Kans., 1972—79; ret. Contbr. articles to profl. jours. and publs., archival material and interviews to books. Fin. benefactor, charitable endowment Schlegel-Deibler Meml. Endowment, Bucknell U., Pa., Richard L. Schlegel Lesbian-Gay-Bisexual-Transgender Awareness Endowment, Pa. State U., State College, Richard L. Schlegel Gay-Lesbian-Bisexual-Transgender-Allies Awareness Endowment Fund, Am. U., Washington; fin. benefactor for capital improvements Slifer House Mus., Lewisburg, Pa., 2003. Sgt. U.S. Army, 1946—47, Tex. & Fla. Mem.: Pa. State Alumni Assn. (life), Am. Legion (life), Delta Tau Delta (life). Democrat. Lutheran. Achievements include founding the Richard L. Schlegel National Gay-Lesbian-Bisexual-Transgender-Allies Legion of Honor Awards. Home: 1319 W Market St Lewisburg PA 17837-1373 Personal E-mail: rlsinpa@jdweb.com.

SCHLEGELMILCH, REUBEN ORVILLE, electrical engineer, consultant; b. Green Bay, Wis., Mar. 8, 1916; s. Raymond Adolf and Emma J. (Schley) S.; m. Margaret Elizabeth Roberts, Aug. 22, 1943; children: Janet R., Raymond J., Joan C., Margaret Ann. BS in Elec. and Agrl. Engring., U. Wis., 1938; MS in Elec. and Agrl. Engring., Rutgers U., 1940; postgrad. in elec. engring., Cornell U., 1940-41, Poly Inst. Bklyn., 1947-51, U. Ill., 1941-42; SM in Indsl. Mgmt., MIT, 1955; postgrad. in elec. engring., Syracuse U., 1956-59, Fed. Exec. Inst., 1982. Registered profl. engr., N.J. Dir. rsch. and devel. Rome Air (Elec.) Devel. Ctr., N.Y., 1955-59; tech. dir. def./space Westinghouse Elec. Corp. Hdqrs., Washington, 1959-63; mgr. adv. tech. and missiles Fed. Sys. IBM, Owego, N.Y., 1963-68; gen. mgr., pres. Schilling Industries, Galesville, Wis., 1968-71; mgr. sys. design U.S. Army Adv. Sys. Concepts Agy., Alexandria, Va., 1971-74; mgr. gun fire control sys. Naval Sea Sys. Command, Washington, 1974-80; tech. dir. office R&D U.S. Coast Guard Hdqrs., Washington, 1980-86. Cons. in field, 1986—; govt. cons. electronics, Dept. Def. R & D Bd., 1949-54; indsl. cons. missile/space Aerospace Industries Assn., 1959-63; chmn. profl. sci. com. Rome Air Devel. Ctr., 1956-59; mem. nat. com. Engring. Mgmt. Inst. Elec. Engring., N.Y.C., 1956-59. Author tech. reports and articles; patentee target position indicator. Vol. Annandale Christian Cmty. for Action (Va.), 1973—; mem. winterset Civic Assn., Annandale, 1971—99. Fellow Alfred P. Sloan Found. MIT, 1954-55. Mem. IEEE (sr. life, sec., vice chmn., chmn. 1956-59, Recognition award 1959), Am. Def. Preparedness Assn.(chmn. So. Tier Empire Post 1967-68, recognition award 1968), NSPE, N.Y. Acad. Scis., Soc. Sloan Fellows MIT, Mason, Rotary, Shriners.

SCHLEGER, PETER RALPH, corporate communications specialist, writer; b. N.Y.C., Apr. 7, 1944; s. Hans Emil and Susan Erna (Jacoby) S.; m. Batya Kahane, Apr. 29, 1975; children— Shane, Jesse. B.S. in Bus. Adminstrn., Boston U., 1965; M.B.A., Pace U., 1969; M.A., U. So. Calif., 1977. Bus. mgr. N.Y.C. Bd. Edn., Bronx, 1968-70; owner, operator Sandwich City, Tel Aviv, 1971-73; writer Baer/Joelson Prodns., 1975-76; dir. communications Barkers, Bronx, 1977-80; prin. Peter Schleger Co., N.Y.C., 1980—; prodn. mgr. Fraternity Row, 1975; presenter various confs. Author screenplays The Assignment, 1975, Stanik & Catherine, 1976, Bridges, 1980; novel Tammuz Web, 1982. Contbr. articles to Tng. News and Tng. and Devel. Jour., Employee Benefits Jour., 1980-92, newspapers. Mem. Am. Soc. Tng. and Devel. (Communicator of Yr. 1981, exec. com. media div. 1981-83), Tau Kappa Epsilon. Democrat. Jewish. Lodge: Masons. Home: 780 W End Ave New York NY 10025-5573

SCHLEICHER, DONALD, music director; Degree, U. Wis., Northwestern U.; studied with Gustav Meier, Simon Rattle, Seiji Ozawa, Maurice Abravanel, Roger Norrington, Joel Smirnoff, Leon Fleisher. Band dir. Williamsville (N.Y.) South High Sch., 1977-84; past mem. music faculty U. Wis., Stevens Point; past mem. conducting faculty U. Mich.; dir. orch. studies, condr. Univ. Symphony Orch., head grad. program in orch. conducting U. Ill.; music dir. Quad City Symphony Orch. Assn., Davenport, Iowa. Conducting fellow Tanglewood Music Ctr., 1993; music dir., prin. condr. Pine Mountain Music Festival, Mich., 1994—; condr. orchs. N.Y., Ala., Wis., Hawaii, R.I., Ill.; guest condr., resident Fla. State U., Ark. State U., U. Minn., U. Akron, Ohio U., U. Buffalo, Ithaca Coll., Ohio State U.; guest condr. orchs. Bridgeport, Conn., Tallahassee, Fla., Lansing, Mich., Ann Arbor, Mich., Southfield, Mich.past dir. Detroit Chamber Winds; guest condr. Chautauqua Festival, 1996, Taiwan Symphony Orch. Wind Ensemble; presenter conducting clinic at nat. convention Music Educators Nat. Conf., Kansas City, 1996. Condr. operas including La Boheme, Suor Angelica, Il Pagliacci, Susannah, The Barber of Seville, La Traviata, The Marriage of Figaro, Madama Butterfly, Carmen. Office: Quad City Symphony Orch PO Box 1144 Davenport IA 52805-1144

SCHLEIFER, JAMES THOMAS, history professor; b. Rochester, N.Y., Nov. 15, 1942; s. James E. Schleifer and Jeanette L. Kern; m. Alison Pedicord; children: Katharine, Margaret. Diploma, U. Paris, 1962-63; BA with honors, Hamilton Coll., 1964; MA, Yale U., 1966, MPhil, 1968, PhD, 1972. Grad. asst. in history Yale U., New Haven, 1966-68; instr. in history Coll. of New Rochelle, N.Y., 1969-73, asst. prof. history, 1973-76, assoc. prof. history, 1976-83, prof. history, 1983—, dir. Gill Libr., 1987-99, dean Gill Libr., 1999—. Vis. prof. Am. history U. Paris, 1986, Yale U., 1983-84, 95; vis. fellow history dept. Yale U., 1981-82; mem. French Nat. Commn. for Pub. of Complete Works of Alexis de Tocqueville, 1986— Author: The Making of Tocqueville's "Democracy in America", 1980, 2d edit. 2000, De la Démocratie en Amérique, 1992, The College of New Rochelle: An Extraordinary Story, 1994; contbr. chpts. to books, articles, revs. to profl. publs.; assoc. editor Tocqueville Rev./La Revue Tocqueville, 1985-95. Grantee Am. Philos. Soc., 1979, 85, Coll. New Rochelle, 1976, 81, 85, NEH, 1982-83; fellow Yale U., 1964-68, Am. Coun. Learned Socs., 1974-75, 81-82; recipient Merle Curti award Orgn. Am. Historians, 1981. Mem. ALA, Tocqueville Soc., Am. Hist. Assn., Orgn. Am. Historians, Westchester Acad. Libr. Dirs. Orgn. Home: 220 Alston Ave New Haven CT 06515-2038 Office: Coll of New Rochelle Castle Pl New Rochelle NY 10805

SCHLEIFER, STEVEN J, psychiatrist, educator; b. New York City, NY, 1950; s. Jack and Caroline Schleifer; m. Sarah L Rosenberg; children: Jonathan, Jason, Justin, Tara. MD, Mt. Sinai Sch. of Medicine, 1975; BA, Columbia Coll., 1971. Diplomate Am. Bd. of Psychiatry and Neurology (Psychiatry), 1980, Nat. Bd. of Med. Examiners, 1976. Asst. prof. of psychiatry Mt. Sinai Sch. of Medicine, New York, NY, 1982—87; assoc. prof. of psychiatry UMDNJ-New Jersey Med. Sch., Newark, 1987—92, prof. of psychiatry, 1992—, chair, dept. of psychiatry, 1992—2001. Cons. NIH, Bethesda, Md., 1984—, Hackensack U. Med. Ctr., NJ, 1988—, Veterans Adminstrn. Med. Ctr., East Orange, NJ, 1988—2002; chief of svc., dept of psychiatry UMDNJ-Univ. Hosp., Newark; chief of svc. UMDNJ-Univ. Behavioral Healthcare, Newark, 1992—2002. Contbr. rsch. articles to profl. jours. Grantee Rsch. and Ednl. Grants in Psychoneuroimmunology and Gen. Psychiatry, NIH and Pvt. Foundations, 1982—2002. Fellow: (dist.) Am. Psychiat. Assn.; mem.: Rsch. Soc. Alcoholism, Acad. Psychosmat Med., Am. Psychosomatic Soc., Soc. of Biol. Psychiatry, Psychoneuroimmunology Rsch. Soc. Avocations: opera, skiing. Office: UMDNJ-New Jersey Med Sch 183 South Orange Ave Newark NJ 07103 E-mail: schleife@umdnj.edu.

SCHLEIN, DOV C. banker; Former chmn. Republic N.Y. Corp., N.Y.C.; now sr. adv. group chmn. on Israel HSBC, N.Y.C. Office: HSBC 452 5th Ave Fl 25 New York NY 10018-2786

SCHLEIN, MICHAEL EDWARD, diversified financial services company executive; m. Lisa Jordan Tamagni. BS in Econs., MS in Polit. Sci., MIT, 1984. Assoc., pub. fin. investment banking divsn. Smith Barney; chief of staff N.Y.C. dep. mayor for fin. and econ. devel., U.S. SEC, 1994—97; sr. v.p., global corp. affairs, human resources, and bus. practices Citigroup, Inc., N.Y.C., 1997—. Mem.: Phi Beta Kappa. Office: Citigroup Inc 399 Park Ave New York NY 10043

SCHLEIS, THOMAS HENRY, music educator, organist; b. Green Bay, Wis., Dec. 13, 1949; s. Samuel Henry and Jeanette Mary (Hall) Schleis. MusB, Lawarence U., 1968—72; MusM, U. Wis., 1972—74. Organist St. John's Cath. Chapel, Champaign, Ill., 1975—; prin. coach Opera Program, U. Ill., Urbana, 1987—, mgr., prin. coach, 1999—; lectr., vocal music lit. U. Ill., Urbana, 1981—. Dir. music, dance divsn. Nat. Acad. Arts, Champaign, 1982—87. Author classical music program annotator. Recipient Fulbright scholar, George-August U., Gottingen, Germany, 1977—78. Mem.: Am. Guild Organists (dean-east ctrl. Ill. chpt. 1994—2004). Roman Catholic. Avocations: reading, travel, working out. Home: 807 W Illinois Apt 9 Urbana IL 61801 Office: Sch Music Univ Ill 1114 W Nevada Urbana IL 61801 Office Phone: 217-333-3206. E-mail: tschleis@uiuc.edu.

SCHLENDER, WILLIAM ELMER, management sciences educator; b. Sawyer, Mich., Oct. 28, 1920; s. Gustav A. and Marie (Zindler) S.; m. Lela R. Pullen, June 9, 1956 (dec. June 1983); m. Margaret C. Krahn, Mar. 3, 1987. AB, Valparaiso U., 1941; MBA, U. Denver, 1947; PhD, Ohio State U., 1955. With U.S. Rubber Co., 1941-43, 46; asst. prof., assoc. prof. bus. adminstrn. Bowling Green State U., 1947-53; asst. prof. bus. orgn., prof. Ohio State U., 1954-65, asst. dean, 1959-62; assoc. dean Ohio State U. (Coll. Commerce and Adminstrn.), 1962-63; prof. mgmt. U. Tex., 1965-68, chmn. dept., 1966-68; dean Cleve. State U. Coll. Bus. Adminstrn., 1968-75, prof. mgmt., 1975-76; Internat. Luth. Laymen's League prof. bus. ethics Valparaiso (Ind.) U., 1976-79, Richard E. Meier prof. mgmt., 1983-86, Richard E. Meier prof. emeritus, 1986—. Vis. assoc. prof. mgmt. Columbia U., 1957-58; vis. prof. mgmt. U. Tex., Arlington, 1981-82; cons. in field; bd. govs. Internat. Ins. Soc., 1972-90. Author: (with M.J. Jucius) Elements of Managerial Action, 3d edit, 1973, (with others) Management in Perspective: Selected Readings, 1965; Editor: (with others) Management in a Dynamic Society, 1965; Contbr. (with others) articles to profl. jours. Served with AUS, 1943-45. Decorated Bronze Star. Recipient Exec. Order Ohio Comodr. for outstanding contbn. to growth and devel. of state. Fellow Acad. Mgmt.; mem. Indsl. Rels. Rsch. Assn. (pres. N.E. Ohio chpt. 1971-72), Am. Legion, Tau Kappa Epsilon, Rotary, Beta Gamma Sigma, Sigma Iota Epsilon, Pi Sigma Epsilon, Alpha Kappa Psi, Phi Kappa Phi. Home: PO Box 446 Sawyer MI 49125-0446 Office: Coll Bus Adminstrn Valparaiso U Valparaiso IN 46383 Personal E-mail: bschlend@aol.com. *I resolved long ago that where I worked and what I did would be guided not by prestige considerations, but by the answers to three questions: (1) Will my work allow me to grow by discovering and developing my capabilities? (2) Will it make a significant contribution to my profession and to the community? (3) Will I enjoy doing it? My career, and my personal philosophy, have these underlying guidelines.*

SCHLENKER, BARRY RICHARD, psychologist, educator, researcher; b. Passaic, NJ, Feb. 21, 1947; s. Henry Walter Schlenker and Ruth Stephanie (Gammelin) Allis; m. Patricia Anne O'Rorke, July 22, 1972; children: David Richard, Kristine Anne. BA summa cum laude, U. Miami, Fla., 1969; MA, U.S. Internat. U., 1970; PhD, SUNY, Albany, 1972. Asst. prof. U. Fla., Gainesville, 1972-76, assoc. prof., 1976-80, prof. psychology, 1980—, dir. social-personality program, 1984-98, 2004—, prof. mktg., prof. clin. psychology, 1976—. Author: A Contemporary Introduction to Social Psychology, 1976, Impression Management, 1980; editor: Self and Social Life, 1985; cons. editor 5 psychology jours. Recipient Rsch. Scientist Devel. award NIMH, 1979-83; NSF rsch. grantee, 1977-80, predoctoral fellow, 1970-72. Fellow APA, Am. Psychol. Soc., Soc. for Psychol. Study of Social Issues; mem. Southeastern Psychol. Assn., Delta Theta Mu, Phi Kappa Phi, Phi Eta Sigma. Avocation: baseball. Home: 8817 NW 6th Pl Gainesville FL 32607-1405 Office: U Fla Dept Psychology Gainesville FL 32611 Office Phone: 352-392-0601 253. Business E-Mail: schlenkr@ufl.edu.

SCHLENSKER, GARY CHRIS, landscaping company executive; b. Indpls., Nov. 12, 1950; s. Christian Frederick and Doris Jean (Shannon) S.; m. Ann Marie Tobin, Oct. 27, 1979; children: Laura Patricia, Christian Frederick II. Student, Purdue U., 1969-71, 73; A Bus. Adminstrn., Clark Coll., 1979; cert. emergency med. technician, Ind. Vocat. Tech. Inst., Lafayette, 1974. Salesman Modern Reference, Indpls., 1971; orthopaedic technician St. Elizabeth Hosp., Lafayette, 1973-75, asst. mgr. ambulance service, 1975; sales asst. Merck, Sharpe & Dohme, Oakbrook, Ill., 1975-77; v.p. Turfco, Inc., Zionsville, Ind., 1977-84; pres. Turfscape, Inc., Zionsville, 1984—. Speaker Midwest Turf Conf., 1991; del. erosion and sediment control econ. summit Internat. Erosion Control Assn., New Orleans, 2000. With U.S. Army, 1971-73. Mem. ASTM (erosion control subcom.), BBB, Nat. Fedn. Ind. Bus., Midwest Turf Found., Ohio Turf Found., Internat. Erosion Control Assn. (bd. dirs. Gt. Lakes chpt. 1998-2002), U.S. C. of C., Ind. C. of C., Zionsville C. of C., Phi Kappa Psi. Presbyterian. Avocations: woodworking, golf.

SCHLESINGER, ARTHUR, JR., (ARTHUR MEIER SCHLESINGER), writer, educator, historian; b. Columbus, Ohio, Oct. 15, 1917; s. Arthur M. and Elizabeth (Bancroft) S.; m. Marian Cannon, 1940 (div. 1970); children: Stephen Cannon, Katharine Kinderman, Christina, Andrew Bancroft; m. Alexandra Emmet, July 9, 1971; 1 son, Robert Emmet Kennedy. AB summa cum laude, Harvard U., 1938, mem. Soc. of Fellows, 1939—42; postgrad. (Henry fellow) (hon.), Cambridge (Eng.) U., 1938—39; hon. degrees (hon.), Muhlenberg Coll., 1950, Bethany Coll., 1956, U. N.B., 1966, New Sch. Social Rsch., 1966, Tusculum Coll., 1966, R.I. Coll., 1969, Aquinas Coll., 1971, Western New Eng. Coll., 1974, Ripon Coll., 1976, Iona Coll., 1977, Utah State U., 1978, U. Louisville, 1978, Northeastern U., 1981, Rutgers U., 1982, SUNY-Albany, 1984, U. N.H., 1985, U. Oxford, 1987, Akron U., 1987, Brandeis U., 1988, U. Mass., Boston, 1990, Hofstra U., 1991, Adelphi U., 1992, Dominican Coll., 1992, Mt. Ida Coll., 1993, Middlebury Coll., 1994, Roosevelt U., 1995, Lynn U., 1996, No. Ill. U., 1996, City U. N.Y., 1999, Harvard U., 2001, U. S.C., 2001, Miami U., 2001, Pa. State U., 2002, Ohio State U., 2003, U. of the South, 2003, Whitman Coll., 2003. With OWI, 1942-43, OSS, 1943-45; assoc. prof. history Harvard U., 1946-54, prof., 1954-62; vis. fellow Inst. Advanced Study, Princeton, N.J., 1966; Schweitzer prof. humanities CUNY, 1966-95. Cons. Econ. Cooperation Adminstrn., 1948, Mutual Security Adminstrn., 1951-52; spl. asst. to Pres. of U.S., 1961-64; mem. jury Cannes Film Festival, 1964; mem. Adlai E. Stevenson campaign staff, 1952, 56; chmn. Franklin Delano Roosevelt Four Freedoms Found., 1983—; trustee Robert F. Kennedy Meml., Twentieth Century Fund.; adv. Arthur and Elizabeth Schlesinger Library. Author: Orestes A. Brownson, 1939, The Age of Jackson, 1945 (Pulitzer prize for history 1946), The Vital Center, 1949, (with R.H. Rovere) The General and the President, 1951, The Age of Roosevelt Vol. I: The Crisis of the Old Order 1919-1933, 1957 (Francis Parkman prize Soc. Am. Historians 1957, Frederic Bancroft prize Columbia U. 1958), The Age of Roosevelt Vol. II: The Coming of the New Deal, 1958, The Age of Roosevelt Vol. III: The Politics of Upheaval, 1960, Kennedy or Nixon: Does It Make Any Difference?, 1960, The Politics of Hope, 1963, (with John Blum) The National Experience, 1963, A Thousand Days, 1965 (Pulitzer prize for biography 1966, Nat. Book award 1966), The Bitter Heritage, 1967, The Crisis of Confidence, 1969, The Imperial Presidency, 1973 (Sidney Hillman Found. award 1973), Robert Kennedy and His Times, 1978 (Nat. Book award 1979), The Cycles of American History, 1986, The Disuniting of America, 1991, A Life in The 20th Century: I, Innocent Beginnings, 2000, War and the American Presidency, 2004; contbr. articles to mags. and newspapers; film reviewer: Show mag, 1962-64, Vogue, 1967-72, Saturday Rev., 1977-80, Am. Heritage, 1981-82; editor: Harvard Guide to American History, 1954, Guide to Politics, 1954, Paths to American Thought, 1963, The Promise of American Life, 1967, The Best and the Last of Edwin O'Connor, 1970, History of American Presidential Elections 1789-1972, 1971, 1972-1984, 1986, The Coming to Power, 1972, The Dynamics of World Power: A Documentary History of United States Foreign Policy 1945-1973, 1973, History of U.S. Political Parties, 1973, Congress Investigates, 1975, Running for President, 1994; screenwriter: (teleplay) The Journey of Robert F. Kennedy. Served with AUS, 1945. Decorated comdr. Order of Orange-Nassau, The Netherlands, Ordem del Libertador, Venezuela, Order of St. Michael and St George, Gt. Britain; recipient gold medal in history and biography, Am. Acad. Arts and Letters, 1967, award for history, Ohio Gov., 1973, award in edn., Eugene V. Debs, 1974, Fregen Prize for Lit., Italy, 1983, award for internat. understanding, U. Thant, 1998, medal, Nat. Humanities1998, 1998; fellow, Guggenheim, 1946; grantee, Am. Acad. Arts and Letters, 1946. Mem. Am. Hist. Assn., Orgn. Am. Historians, Soc. Am. Historians (pres. 1989-92), Am. Acad. Arts and Letters (pres. 1981-84, chancellor 1984-87), Am. Philos. Soc., Mass. Hist. Soc., Colonial Soc. Mass., Russian Acad. Scis., Franklin and Eleanor Roosevelt Inst. (co-chmn. 1983—), ACLU, Coun. Fgn. Rels., Ams. for Dem. Action (nat. chmn. 1952-54), Century Assn., Knickerbocker Club, Phi Beta Kappa. Democrat. Unitarian. Home: 455 E 51st St New York NY 10022-6474

SCHLESINGER, B. FRANK, architect, educator; b. N.Y.C., Sept. 17, 1925; s. Augustus and Ethel (Brower) S.; m. Draga A. Christy; children: Jeff, Nike, Katherine, Daniel, Christy Anna; 1 stepson, Frances L. Haley Jr. Student, Middlebury Coll., 1946—48; BS, U. Ill., 1950; MArch, Harvard U., 1954. Draftsman Hugh Stubbins Assocs., 1953-55, Marcel Breuer, 1955-56; pvt. practice architecture Princeton, N.J., 1956-59, Doylestown, Pa., 1959-69, Phila., 1969-71, Washington, 1971—. Instr. archtl. design U. Pa., 1957-60; vis. critic Columbia Sch. Architecture, 1962-63, U. Pa., 1965; prof. emeritus Sch. Architecture, U. Md., 1971, prof. architecture, 1971-2001. With USNR, 1943-46. Wheelwright fellow Harvard U., 1963; Disting. Designer fellow Nat. Endowment for the Arts, 1984; recipient Design awards Pa. Soc. Archs., 1960-65, 69, 84, Bronze medal, 1965, Silver medal, 1973, Design awards Progressive Arch., 1966-67, 69, 72, 74, Design awards Interfaith Forum on Religion, Art and Arch., 1987, 92, Design awards Philia. chpt. 1960-61, 1963-65, 1968-69, Design awards No. Va. chpt. 1975, 2001, Design awards Wash. chpt. 1990, 1992, 1995, 2002, Centennial medal Wash. chpt. 2001. Fellow: AIA; mem.: Associated Harvard Alumni (dir. 1972), Harvard Grad. Sch. Design Alumni Assn. (pres. 1971—73). Address: 1015 33rd St NW Apt 806 Washington DC 20007-3538

SCHLESINGER, CHRIS, food service executive; b. Richmond, Va., Dec. 30, 1955; Grad., The Culinary Inst. Am., 1977. With Blue Pete's Restaurant, Virginia Beach, Va.; sous chef The Harvest Restaurant, Cambridge, Mass.; cook Hyatt Hotel; founder, chef, owner East Coast Grill, Cambridge, 1986—; founder Jake and Earl's Dixie BBQ, Cambridge, 1989-96, The Blue Room, 1990. Spkr. in field. Co-author: Thrill of the Grill, Salsas, Sambals, Chutneys and Chowchows. Named Best Chef of the N.E., James Beard Found., 1996. Avocation: sleeping on the beach. Office: East Coast Grill 1271 Cambridge St Cambridge MA 02139-1338

SCHLESINGER, DEBORAH LEE, librarian; b. Cambridge, Mass., Sept. 13, 1937; d. Edward M. and Edith D. (Schneider) Hershoff; divorced; children: Suzanne, Richard. BA, U. Mass., 1961; MS, Simmons Coll., 1974; postgrad., U. Pitts., 1983. Reference librarian Bently Coll., Waltham, Mass., 1964-65; dir. Carnegie Library, Swissvale, Pa., 1973-77, South Park Twp. Library, Library, Pa., 1977-81, Monessen (Pa.) Library, 1981-82, Lewis & Clark Library, Helena, Mont., 1983-88, 89—; state librarian Mont. State Library, Helena, Mont., 1988-89. Vis. scholar Pitts. Regional Library Ctr., 1982-83. Editor Pa. Union List, 1982-83. Mem. exec. bd. Mont. Cultural Advocacy, 1983—. Mem. Mont. Library Assn. (chmn. legis. com. 1984-92, MLA lobbyist 1992—), Mont. Assn. Female Execs. (fin. com. 1986—), AAUW (exec. com. 1985-86). Clubs: Montana (Helena). Democrat. Avocations: flying, painting, reading, rafting, travel. Office: Lewis & Clark Libr 120 S Last Chance Gulch St Helena MT 59601-4165

SCHLESINGER, HARVEY ERWIN, judge; b. June 4, 1940; BA, The Citadel, 1962; JD, U. Richmond, 1965. Bar: Va. 1965, Fla. 1965, U.S. Supreme Ct. 1968. Corp. counsel Seaboard Coast Line R.R. Co., Jacksonville, Fla., 1968-70; chief asst. U.S. atty. Mid. Dist. Fla., Jacksonville, 1970-75, U.S. magistrate judge, 1975-91, U.S. Dist. judge, 1991—. Adj. prof. U. North Fla., 1984-91; mem. adv. com. on Fed. Rules of Criminal Procedure to U.S. Supreme Ct., 1986-93; mem. Jud. Conf. Adv. Com. on Adminstrn. of Magistrate Judges Sys., 1996-2003, chmn., 1998-2003; chmn. U.S. Dist. Ct.

Forms Working Group, Washington, 1983—, Jud. Ct. Ad hoc Com. on Long Range Planning, 1998-2003; Jud. Conf. Jud. Officers Resources Working Group, 1998-99; 11th Cir. Dist. Judges Assn., 1991—, sec., treas. 1996- 97, v.p. 1997-98, pres.-elect., 1999-2001, pres., 2001-02. Bd. dir. Pine Castle Ctr. for Mentally Retarded, Jacksonville, 1970-87, pres., 1972-74, chmn. bd. dirs., 1973-74; trustee Pine Castle Found., 1972-76; trustee Congregation Ahavath Chesed, Jacksonville, 1970—, v.p., 1975-80, pres., 1980-82; v.p. S.E. Coun. Union Am. Hebrew Congregations, 1984-88; asst. commr. for exploring North Fla. Coun. Boy Scouts Am., 1983-86, exec. com., 1986-98, adv. bd., 1998—; mem. Boy Scouts Am. Nat. Jewish Com. on Scouting, Irving, Tex., 1986-93; mem. Fla. Sesquicentennial Commn., 1995-96; trustee River Garden Home for Aged, 1982—, sec., 1985—; co-chmn. bd. gov. Jacksonville chpt. NCCJ, 1983—, presiding co-chmn. 1984-89; nat. bd. trustees, N.Y.C., 1986-93; trustee Jacksonville Cmty. Found., 2000—, vice-chair, 2003—. Capt. JAGC, U.S. Army, 1965-68. Recipient Silver Beaver award Boy Scouts Am., 1986; George Washington Medal of Honor, Freedoms Found., Valley Forge, Pa., 1987, Silver Medallion Humanitarian award NCCJ, 1992, Founders award, Fed. Magistrate Judges Assn., 1999, William Green award for profl. excellence U. Richmond Law Sch., 2000, Jurist of Yr. award Am. Bd. Trial Adv., 2001. Mem. ABA (fed. rules of evidence and criminal procedure com. 1979-98, Nat. Conf. Spl. Ct. Judges, 1975-90, conf. newsletter editor, 1988-90, Nat. Conf. Fed. Trial Judges, 1990—, chmn. legis. com., 1996-97, Flascher award 1989), Va. Bar Assn., Fla. Bar Assn., Fed. Judges Assn., Jacksonville Bar Assn.; Fed. Bar Assn. (pres. Jacksonville chpt. 1974, 75, 81-82), Am. Judicature Soc., Chester Bedell Am. Inns of Ct. (pres. 1992-96), Rotary (Paul Harris fellow, pres. S. Jacksonville club), Masons (past master, past venerable master, knights comdr. of Ct. Honour, 33 degree Scottish Rite bodies), Shriners. Office: 300 N Hogan St Ste 11-150 Jacksonville FL 32202-4246 Office Phone: 904-549-1990.

SCHLESINGER, IRWIN D. neurologist; b. Bklyn., Sept. 13, 1935; s. Edward Schlesinger and Eva Parkoff; m. Marcia Rubinstein; 1 child, Lisa. BS, Bklyn. Coll., 1956; MD, SUNY, Medical U., Syracuse, 1961. Diplomate Am. Bd. Psychiatry and Neurology, Am. Bd. Clin. Neurophysiology. Intern then resident in medicine Cornell med. div. Bellevue Hosp., N.Y.C., 1961—63; resident in neurology Albert Einstein Coll. Medicine Bronx Mcpl. Hosp., 1965—68; neurologist Neurol. Specialities of L.I., Manhasset, NY, 1968—. Attending neurologist N. Shore Univ. Hosp., Manhasset, 1968—; staff neurologist L.I. Jewish Med. Ctr., Glen Oaks, NY, 1969—; cons. neurologist St. Francis Hosp., Roslyn, NY, 1975—; clin. assoc. prof. neurology Cornell U. Med. Coll., N.Y.C., 1971—95, NYU Med. Sch., N.Y.C., 1995—. Capt. USAF, 1963—65. Fellow: ACP, Am. Acad. Neurology; mem.: AMA, Am. Clin. Neurophysiology Soc., Am. Assn. Electrodiagnostic Medicine, Alpha Omega Alpha. Office: Neurological Specialties Long Island 170 Great Neck Rd Great Neck NY 11021

SCHLESINGER, JAMES RODNEY, economist; b. N.Y.C., Feb. 15, 1929; s. Julius and Rhea (Rogen) S.; m. Rachel Mellinger, June 19, 1954; children: Cora K., Charles L., Ann R., William F., Emily, Thomas S., Clara, James Rodney. AB summa cum laude, Harvard U., 1950, A.M., 1952, PhD, 1956. Asst. prof., then assoc. prof. U. Va., 1955-63; sr. staff mem. RAND Corp., 1963-67; dir. strategic studies, 1967-69; asst. dir. Bur. Budget, 1969, acting dep. dir., 1969-70; asst. dir. Office Mgmt. and Budget, 1970-71; chmn. AEC, 1971-73; dir. CIA, Feb.-July 1973; sec. US Dept. Def., 1973-75; vis. scholar Johns Hopkins Sch. Advanced Internat. Studies, 1976-77; asst. to Pres., 1977; sec. Dept. Energy, 1977-79; counselor Ctr. for Strategic and Internat. Studies, Georgetown U., 1979—; sr. adv. Lehman Bros., 1979—. Cons. in field; mem., Homeland Security Adv. Coun., 2002-, Def. Policy Bd., chmn., ind. panel investigating abuses at Abu Ghraib prison, 2004. Author: The Political Economy of National Security, 1960, America at Century's End, 1989; co-author: Issues in Defense Economics, 1967. Frederick Sheldon prize fellow Harvard U., 1950-51 Mem. Phi Beta Kappa. Republican. Presbyterian. Office: Lehman Bros 800 Connecticut Ave NW Ste 1200 Washington DC 20006-2709

SCHLESINGER, LEONARD ARTHUR, retail executive; b. NYC, July 31, 1952; s. Joe and Edith (Smukler) S.; m. Phyllis Barbara Fineman, Dec. 23, 1972; children: Rebecca, Emily, Katharine. BA, Brown U., 1972; MBA, Columbia U., 1973; DBA, Harvard U., 1979. Mgr. Procter & Gamble, Green Bay, Wis., 1973-75; asst. prof., assoc. prof. bus. sch. Harvard U., Boston, 1978-85; exec. v.p., COO Au Bon Pain, Inc., Boston, 1985-88; prof. bus. adminstrn. Harvard U., Boston, 1988-98; sr. v.p. Brown U., 1998-99; exec. v.p., COO Limited Brands, 1999—2003, vice chmn., 2003—. Bd. dirs. GC Companies, Chestnut Hill, Mass., 1997-2000, Borders Group, Inc., Ann Arbor, Mich., 1995-00, Limited Brands, Columbus, Ohio, 1996—, Pegasystems, Inc., Cambridge, Mass., 1996-00. Editor: Human Resources Mgmt. Jour., Jour. Mgmt. Inquiry; contbr. 40 articles to profl. jours. Jewish. Avocations: travel, music, bicycling. Home: 12 Edge of Woods New Albany OH 43054 Office: Limited Brands 3 Limited Pkwy Columbus OH 43230-1467 Office Phone: 614-415-7125. Business E-Mail: lschlesinger@limitedbrands.com.

SCHLESINGER, MILTON J. virology educator, researcher; b. Wheeling, W.Va., Nov. 26, 1927; s. Milton J. and Caroline (Oppenheimer) S.; m. Sondra Orenstein, Jan. 30, 1955. BS, Yale U., 1951; MS, U. Rochester, 1953; PhD, U. Mich., 1959. Rsch. assoc. U. Mich., Ann Arbor, 1953-56, 59-60; guest rsch. investigator Inst. Superiore di Sanita, Rome, 1960-61; rsch. assoc. MIT, Cambridge, 1961-64; asst. prof. virology Washington U. Sch. Medicine, St. Louis, 1964-67, assoc. prof., 1967-72, prof., 1972-99, chmn. exec. coun. divsn. biol. and biomed. scis., 1992-94, emeritus prof., 1999—. Vis. scientist Imperial Cancer Rsch. Fund, London, 1974-75; vis. scholar Harvard U., Cambridge, 1989-90, 95-96; mem. adv. panels Am. Heart Assn., Dallas, 1975-78, NSF, Washington, 1978-82; mem. sci. adv. bd. Friedrich Miescher Inst., Basel, Switzerland, 1988—, chmn., 1992-98; nat. lectr. Sigma Xi, 1991-93. Editor: Heat Shock, 1982, Togaviridae and Flaviviridae, 1986, Lipid Modification of Proteins, 1992, (monographs) The Ubiquitin System, 1988, Stress Proteins, 1990; mem. editl. bd. virology, 1975-92, Jour. Biol. Chemistry, 1982-87, Molecular and Cellular Biology, 1983-92. Bd. dirs. ACLU, St. Louis, 1966-72, Coalition for Environ., St. Louis, 1989-92. Fellow AAAS; mem. Am. Biol. Chemistry and Molecular Biology, Am. Soc. Microbiology, Am. Soc. Virologists, Am. Chem. Soc. Office: Dept Molecular Micro 8230 Washington U Med Sch 660 S Euclid Ave Saint Louis MO 63110-1010

SCHLESINGER, SANFORD JOEL, lawyer; b. N.Y.C., Feb. 8, 1943; s. Irving and Ruth (Rubin) Schlesinger; children: Merideth, Jarrod, Alexandra. BS in Govt. with hons., Columbia U., 1963; JD, Fordham U., 1966. Bar: N.Y. 1966, U.S. Dist. Ct. (so. and ea. dists.) N.Y. 1967, U.S. Ct. Appeals (2d cir.) 1968, U.S. Ct. Internat. Trade 1969, U.S. Tax Ct. 1993, U.S. Supreme Ct. 1978. Assoc. Frankenthaler & Kohn, N.Y.C., 1966—67; asst. atty. gen. trusts and estates bur. charitable found. div. State of N.Y., N.Y.C., 1967—69; ptnr. Rose & Schlesinger, N.Y.C., 1969—81, Goldshmidt, Oshatz, Powsner & Saft, N.Y.C., 1981—85; ptnr., head trusts and estates dept. Shea & Gould, N.Y.C., 1985—93; ptnr., head wills and estates dept. Kaye Scholer LLP, N.Y.C., 1993—2004, ptnr. co-chair family owned bus. practice group, 1993—2004; founding ptnr. Schlesinger Gannon & Lazetera LLP, N.Y.C., 2004—. Adj. faculty Columbia U. Sch. Law, 1989-94; adj. prof. N.Y. Law Sch., 1978-2003; adj. prof. grad. program in estate planning U. Miami Grad. Sch. Law, 1995-2003, N.Y. State Bar Jour., 1995—; dir. N.Y. State Bar Found.; mem. estate planning adv. com. Practising Law Inst., 1990—; bd. advisors and contbrs. Jour. of S Corp. Taxation, 1989-96; lectr. in field; condr. workshops in field. Author: Estate Planning for the Elderly Client, 1984, Planning for the Elderly or Incapacitated Client, 1993; columnist, mem. editl. bd. Estate Planning mag., 1995—; contbr. articles to profl. jours. Mem. adv. bd. Inst. Fed. Taxation NYU, 1988-96, chmn., 1993-94; mem. legis adv. com. Scarsdale (N.Y.) Sch. Bd., 1981-83, mem. nominating com., 1979-82; pres. dist. 17 N.Y.C. Cmty. Sch. Bd., 1970-71; mem. fin. and estate planning adv. bd. Commerce Clearing House, 1988—; mem. adv. bd. Tax Hotline, 1997—. Fellow Am. Coll. Trust and Estate Counsel (chmn. Downstate N.Y. 2001—); mem. ABA (chmn. social security and other govt. entitlements com. 1990-91, chmn. probate and trust com.-estate planning, drafting charitable giving coms., 1992-94), Internat. Acad. Estate & Trust Law (Academician 1992—), Nat. Acad. Elder Law Attys., Bklyn. Bar Assn., Assn. of Bar of City of N.Y., N.Y. State Bar Assn. (treas. trusts and estates sect. 1991-92, sec. trusts and estates sect. 1992-93, chmn. trusts and estates sect. 1994-95, chmn. exec. com. 1st jud. dist. 1987-91, jour. bd. editors 1995—), N.Y. State Bar Found. Avocations: baseball, writing. Office: Schlesinger Gannon & Lazetera LLP 499 Park Ave New York NY 10022 Office Phone: 212-652-3777. E-mail: sschlesinger@sglllp.com.

SCHLESINGER, STEPHEN CANNON, think-tank executive; b. Boston, Aug. 17, 1942; s. Arthur Meier and Marian (Cannon) S.; m. Judith Barbara Elster, Mar. 18, 1984; 1 child, Sarah Elizabeth. BA in Am. History and Lit. cum laude, Harvard U., 1964, JD, 1968; cert. study in European History, Cambridge U., 1965. Legal asst. to pres. N.Y. State Urban Devel. Corp., 1968; founder, editor The New Dem., 1969-72; speechwriter Dem. Presdl. Candidate George McGovern, 1972; staff writer TIME Mag., 1974-78; editorial writer, chief polit. corr. N.Y. Post, 1978; spl. asst. to Gov. Mario Cuomo, 1983-90; dir. for internat. orgns. N.Y. State Dept. Econ. Devel., 1990—94; vis. scholar Taub Urban Rsch. Ctr. NYU, 1995-97; spl. advisor UN Ctr. for Human Settlements, 1995-97; dir. World Policy Inst. at New Sch. U., N.Y.C., 1997—. With Gore Presdl. Campaign, 2000; mem. internat. election observer teams Nat. Dem. Inst., 1993, 90; teaching fellow in English composition Harvard U., 1968; adj. prof. in Am. politics New Sch. U., 1976-77; lectr. Royce Carlton Agy, 1984-88. Author: The New Reformers, 1975, Bitter Fruit: The Untold Story of the U.S. Coup in Guatemala, 1982, Act of Creation: The Founding of the United Nations, 2003; contbr. numerous articles and book revs. to profl. jours., mags. and newspapers; columnist: Boston Globe, 1973-74. Mem. Coun. Fgn. Rels., Roosevelt Inst., PEN, Author's Guild, Overseas Press Club. Unitarian Universalist. Avocations: bicycling, jogging, skiing, swimming, tennis. Home: 500 W 111th St Apt 4A New York NY 10025-1905 Office: World Policy Inst 66 5th Ave Fl 9 New York NY 10011 Office Phone: 212-229-5808. E-mail: schlesis@newschool.edu.

SCHLESS, GUY LACY, endocrinologist; b. Phila., May 22, 1929; s. Robert A. (M.D.) and Bena Schless; m. Nancy Esther Halverson, July 19, 1952; children: Karina Halverson, Lauritis Halverson. BA, Stanford U., 1951; MD, Jefferson Med. Coll., Phila., 1955. Intern Meth. Hosp., Phila., 1955-56; resident and rsch. fellow in metabolism Pa. Hosp., Phila., 1956-58, asst. physician, 1959-68, assoc. physician, 1968-71, physician, 1971—, chief med. clinics, 1965-67, sr. Mellon fellow in medicine, 1962-63. Vis. fellow, hon. sr. registrar medicine Guy's Hosp., U. London, 1958-59, vis. rsch. fellow in medicine Med. Sch., 1962-70, hon. cons. in medicine, 1971-90, hon. vis. cons. in metabolic medicine, 1990—; instr. medicine U. Pa., 1962-64, assoc., 1964-68, asst prof. medicine, 1968-80, clin. assoc. prof. medicine, 1980-95, 97—; clin. assoc. prof. medicine Jefferson Med. Coll., Phila., 1995-97; fellow in medicine Am. Philos. Soc.; cons. in medicine 5th naval dist. U.S. Navy, 1965—; cons. in medicine U.S. Naval Regional Med. Ctr., Portsmouth, Va., 1965—; participant White House Conf. Food, Nutrition and Health, 1969. Contbr. articles on metabolism to profl. jours. Bd. dirs. Brit. Cathedrals and Hist. Chs. Found., Inc., v.p., 1997-2003. Served as lt. comdr. M.C., USNR, 1960-62. Fellow Royal Soc. Medicine (London), Phila. Coll. Physicians, Royal Soc. Health (London), Royal Soc. Arts (London) (Benjamin Franklin fellow), Am. Coll. Endocrinology; mem. ACP, Am. Diabetes Assn., Athenaeum of Phila., Victorian Soc. in Am. (dir., v.p. 1977, pres. 1984-90, pres. emeritus 1990—). Republican. Home: 3926 Henry Ave Philadelphia PA 19129-1008 Office: Pa Hosp 304 Duncan Bldg 700 Spruce St Philadelphia PA 19106-4022 Fax: 215-829-3532.

SCHLESS, PHYLLIS ROSS, investment banker; d. Lewis H. and Doris G. Ross; m. Aaron Backer Schless, July 7, 1970; 1 son, Daniel Lewis Ross. Cert., Neighborhood Playhouse Sch. of Theatre, 1962, N.Y. Sch. Interior Design, 1964; BA in Econs., Wellesley Coll., 1964; MBA, Stanford U., 1966. Cert. theater prodns. Am. League Theater Owners and Prodrs. Assoc. internat. fin. Kuhn Loeb & Co., N.Y.C., 1966-70; fin. cons., 1971-73; sr. fin. analyst Trans World Airlines, N.Y.C., 1974-75; corp. fin., mergers and acquisitions Lazard Freres & Co., 1976-79; dir. mergers and acquisitions Am. Can Co., Greenwich, Conn., 1979-82; v.p. mergers and acquisitions Bear, Stearns & Co., N.Y.C., 1982-84; sr. v.p. corp. acquisitions Integrated Resources, 1984-85; chmn., chief exec. officer Ross Fin. Svcs. Group Inc., 1985—; supervisory dir. Merrill Lynch HYTS Funds, 1991-96. Bd. dirs. Calvary Hosp. Fund Bd., 1990-2000, chair investment com., 1995-99; trustee A.R. Tinker Fund, 1993—; trustee Nat. Child Labor Com., 1981-95, chmn., 1992-94; trustee New World Found., 1986-92, chair fin. com., treas. 1988-92; bd. dirs. Stanford Bus. Sch. Assn., N.Y., 1994—; adj. asst. prof. NYU, 1996—, Columbia U. Sch. Bus., 2001—; bd. dirs. Nat. Found. Tchg. Entrepreneurship, 1998—, metro. N.Y. chair, 2000—. Pres. Greater Bridgeport Nat. Coun. Jewish Women, 1971-73, bd. dirs., 1974-75; bd. dirs. Girls Clubs Am., 1975-89, mem. exec. com., 1982-89, pres., 1984-86; bd. dirs. Pauline Koner Dance Co., 1979-81, So. Conn. Child Guidance Clinic, 1981-83, New Canaan United Way, 1981-83; treas. Wellesley Class '64, 1984-89. Mem. Univ. Club. Office: Ross Fin Svcs Group Inc 6th Fl 689 5th Ave Fl 6 New York NY 10022-3133 also: PO Box 1986 East Hampton NY 11937-0908

SCHLESSER, ETHAN MARC, music educator, musician; b. Bklyn., July 27, 1967; s. Melvyn Schlesser and Marilyn Reitman; m. Joanna Alexandra Perry, May 1, 2004. BCS in Music, Univ. of Miami, Coral Gables, Fla., 1989. Lic. tchr. secondary edn. NY. Mus. theatre specialist City Lights Youth Theatre, N.Y.C., 1999—; mus. dir. Bklyn Youth Vocal Ensemble, 2000—; mus. specialist LifeLines-Ctr. for Family Life, Bklyn, 2002—; tchg. artist Bklyn Arts Coun., Bklyn, 2000—; prodr. Eon88Keys Prodns., Bklyn; vocal/choral tchr. NYC Bd. of Ed / Roy H. Mann JHS IS78, Bklyn, NY. Asst. mus. dir. Pk. Slope Cmty. Choir, Bklyn, 2002—. Composer (writer): (musical) Harmony; musician: (musical direction) Ding Dong Witch is Dead - Remix (Selection of 5th grade students into Wizard of Oz @ Madison Sq. Garden, 1996); prodr.: (original soul music group) SoulDeep (Assoc. des Cotes de Fer of NY - for outstanding work developing musical talent in Youth, 2002); composer: (h.s. school fight song) Pine Crest HS Marching Band Fight Song. Mem. /activity planner for spl. events, including the jingle bell jamboree concert event Pk. Slope C. of C., Bklyn, 2001—03. Recipient Special citation for Jingle Bell Jam Concert, Bklyn Borough Pres. Office, 2003; grantee Cmty. grantee, Pk. Slope Civic Coun., 2001—02.

SCHLESSINGER, JOSEPH, pharmacology educator; BSc in Chemistry/Physics magna cum laude, The Hebrew U., Jerusalem, 1968, MSC in Chemistry magna cum laude, 1969; PhD, The Weizmann Inst. Sci., Rehovot, Israel, 1974. Postdoctoral assoc. dept. chemistry Sch. Applied Physics, Cornell U., 1974-76; vis. scientist immunology br. Nat. Cancer Inst., NIH, Bethesda, Md., 1977-78; sr. scientist dept. chem. immunology The Weizmann Inst. Sci., Rehovot, 1978-80, assoc. prof. dept. chem. immunology, 1980-84, prof. dept. chem. immunology, Ruth & Leonard Simon prof., 1984-91; dir. div. molecular biology Biotech. Rsch. Ctr. Meloy Labs., Inc., Rockville, Md., 1985-86, dir. Biotech. Rsch. Ctr., 1986-88; rsch. dir. Rorer Biotech., Inc., King of Prussia, Pa., 1988-90; prof., chmn. dept. pharmcology NYU Med. Ctr., N.Y.C., 1990—2001; prof., chmn. pharmcology Yale U. Sch. of Medicine, New Haven, 2001—. Mem. editorial bds. European Molecular Biology Orgn. Jour., Jour. Cell Biology, Cell Regulation, Cancer Rsch., Receptors, Growth Factors, Cell Crowth & Differentiation, Protein Engineering, Oncogenes and Growth Factor Abstracts; contbr. articles to profl. jours. Recipient Sara Leedy prize, Weizmann Inst. Sci., 1980, Hestrin prize, Biochem. Soc. Israel, 1983, Levinson prize, 1984, The Drew-Ciba prize (with G. Blobel and A. Levine), 1995, Antoine Lacassagne prize, 1995, Disting. Service award, Miami Nature Biotechnology, 1999, Taylor prize (with T. Hunter and T. Pawson), 2000. Mem. European Molecular Biology Orgn., NAS, Am. Academy of Arts and Sciences. Office: Yale U Sch Medicine Sterling Hall Medicine B-295 333 Cedar St New Haven CT 06520

SCHLESSINGER, LAURA, radio talk show host; b. Brooklyn, Jan. 16, 1947; d. Monroe and Yolanda Schlessinger; m. Lewis G. Bishop, 1982; 1 child, Deryk. BS in Biological Sciences, SUNY, Stonybrook; MS in Physiology, M Phil in Physiology, PhD in Physiology, Columbia U. Lic. in marriage and family therapy; cert. marriage, family and child counseling, U. So. Calif. Psychotherapist in private practice, Los Angeles, Calif., 1980—90; nat. syndicated radio talk show host The Dr. Laura Schlessinger Program, 1990—. Past mem. faculty U. So. Calif., Pepperdine U, instr. UCLA, UC Irvine; pres. Dr. Laura Schlessinger Foundation. Author: Ten Stupid Things Women Do to Mess Up Their Lives, 1994, How Could You Do That?! The Abdication of Character, Courage and Conscience, 1996, Ten Stupid Things Men Do To Mess Up Their Lives, 1997, The Ten Commandments: The Significance of God's Law in Everyday Life, 1998, Damsels, Dragons, and Regular Guys, 2000, Parenthood by Proxy; Don't Have Them If You Won't Raise Them, 2000, Ten Stupid Things Couples Do To Mess Up Their Relationships, 2002 The Proper Care & Feeding Of Husbands, 2004; books for children Why Do You Love Me?, 1999, But I Waaannt It!, 2000, Dr. Laura Schlessinger's Growing Up is Hard, 2001, I Hate My Life!, 2001, Dr. Laura Schlessinger's Where is God?, 2003; featured on The Oprah Winfrey Show, A&E Biography, Larry King Live, Lifetime's Intimate Portrait, 20/20, The Today Show, PBS, Hannity & Colmes, CBS This Morning, 48 Hours, Meet the Press with Tim Russert, Crier Today, Eye to Eye with Connie Chung, ABC This Week, Dateline; featured in Time, U.S. News and World Report, People, USA Today, The New York Times Magazine, The Los Angeles Times, The Wall Street Journal and others; featured spkr. Nat. Congressional Prayer Breakfast, Mus. Radio and Television, Claremont Inst., PBS, Nat. Religious Broadcasters, Country Radio Seminar. Recipient Marconi Award for Network/Syndicated Personality of the Yr., 1997, Genii Award, American Women in Radio & Television, 1998, Israel 50th Anniversary Tribute award, 1998, Crystal Cathedral Academy award, 1998, Love of a Child award, Childhelp USA, 1998, Chairman's award, Nat. Religious Broadcasters, 2000, Nat. Heritage award, Nat. Council of Young Israel, 2001, Conservative Leadership award, Clare Booth Luce Institute, 2001, Woman of the Yr. award, 2002. Mem.: AFTRA, SAG, Nat. Assn. At-Home Mothers (bd. adv.). Achievements include being broadcasted on approximately 300 stations with 12 million listeners; the second most popular talk show host in the country, show syndicated since June 1994, on air radio career for more than 25 years. Office: Premire Radio Networks 15260 Ventura Blvd Ste 300 Sherman Oaks CA 91403-5337

SCHLEUSE, WILLIAM, retired psychiatrist, psychoanalyst; b. Austin, Oct. 18, 1932; s. Louis W. and Oleta Vivian (Hedgpeth) S.; m. Virginia Walker, 1965 (div. 1977); children: Martin, Stuart, Paul; m. Doris Laird, Apr. 20, 1985. BA, U. Tex., 1953; MD, U. Tex. Med. Br., Galveston, 1957. Diplomate Am. Bd. Psychiatry and Neurology. Pvt. practice psychiatry and psychoanalysis, Houston, 1962-81, Austin, 1981—2000; pres. med. staff Hedgecroft Hosp., Houston, 1966; ret., 2000. Photography exhibited in numerous shows, 1993—. Pres. Houston Psychiat. Soc., 1967, Austin chpt. Am. Assn. Individual Investors, 1992. Fellow Am. Psychiat. Assn. (life); mem. San Antonio/Austin Psychoanalytic Soc. (pres. 1996-98), Austin Fine Art Photography Group (founding mem.), Houston Yacht Club, Phi Beta Kappa. Avocations: sailing, boating, fine-art photography. Home: 2803 Regents Park Austin TX 78746-7619

SCHLEUSENER, RICHARD AUGUST, college president; b. Oxford, Nebr., May 6, 1926; s. August William and Katherine Charlotte (Albrecht) S.; m. Elaine Emma Wilhelm, June 12, 1949; children: Kathryn Jeanne Schleusener Miller, Richard Dennis, Rand Lee, Debra Sue, Jeffrey Thomas. BS, U. Nebr., 1949, DSc (hon.), 1984; MS, Kans. State U., 1956; PhD, Colo. State U., 1958; postgrad., MIT, 1951-52. Rsch. engr. Colo. State U., 1958-64, dir. Inst. Atmospheric Sci.; prof., head dept. meteorology S.D. Sch. Mines and Tech., Rapid City, 1965-74, v.p., dean engring., 1974-75, acting pres., 1975-76, pres., 1976-86, Black Hills Regional Eye Inst. Found., 1987-96, ret., 1996. Cons. weather modification U.S. Dept. Interior, 1964—, U.S. Forest Svc., 1966—, UNESCO, 1971—, also pvt. firms. Contbr. articles to tech. jours. With USAF, 1950-55. Inductee S.D. Hall of Fame, 2000. Mem. Am. Meteorol. Soc., Am. Geophys. Union, Rotary, Sigma Xi, Beta Sigma Psi. Lutheran. Home: Unit 104 4120 Villa Ridge Ct Rapid City SD 57701 E-mail: dickelaine3@rushmore.com.

SCHLEY, WAYNE ARTHUR, political consultant; b. Hamilton, Mont., May 22; AA, Shasta Coll., 1960; BS, Sacramento State U., 1963; MS, Am. U., 1974; postgrad., U. Alaska, 1970, Harvard U. Cert. high sch. tchr. (lifetime), Calif. Dept. Edn. Tchr., admin. Placer H.S., Auburn, Calif., 1963-70; spl. asst. to Sen. Ted Stevens, Washington, 1971-77; staff dir. minority and majority subcom. civil svc. Post Office and Gen. Svcs., Washington, 1977-86; minority staff dir. Senate Com. on Rules and Adminstrn., Washington, 1987-92; commr. U.S. Postal Rate Commn., Washington, 1992-95; cons. on legis. and postal issues Washington, 1995—. Elected bd. dirs. Assn. Postal Commerce, 2003—; chmn. Calif. Teenage Reps., 1963-64; regional v.p. Calif. Young Reps., 1964-66, state sgt. at arms, 1966-67; mem. Placer County Rep. Ctrl. Com., 1965-70. Recipient Cert. of Achievement, JFK Sch. Govt. Harvard U., 1982. Home and Office: 614 Massachusetts Ave NE Washington DC 20002-6006 Office Phone: 202-675-3379. E-mail: waschley@ups.com.

SCHLEY, WILLIAM SHAIN, otorhinolaryngologist; b. Columbus, Ga., Sept. 21, 1940; s. Frances Brooking Schley and Susie (Smith) Mathews. BA, Emory U., 1962, MD, 1966. Intern mixed surg. The Roosevelt Hosp., N.Y.C., 1966-67, resident in surgery, 1967-68; resident in otorhinolaryngology N.Y. Hosp.-Cornell Med. Ctr., N.Y.C., 1970-73; clin. instr. otorhinolaryngology Cornell U. Med. Coll., 1972-75, clin. asst. prof., 1975-81, assoc. prof., 1982—, acting chmn. dept. otorhinolaryngology, 1988-94, chmn. dept. otorhinolarygology, 1994—. Otorhinolaryngologist to outpatients with pvt. patient privileges N.Y. Hosp., 1973-75, asst. attending otorhinolaryngologist with pvt. patient privileges, 1975-81, assoc. attending, 1992—, acting otorhinolaryngologist-in-chief, 1988-94, otorhinolaryngologist-in-chief, 1994—; assoc. asst. surgeon otolaryngology Manhattan Eye, Ear, Nose and Throat Hosp., 1988-99; v.p. and sec. med. bd. N.Y. Hosp., 1994-97, pres., 1998-99; pres., v.p. med. bd. The N.Y. and Presbyn. Hosp., 1998, pres., 1998-99, mem. ex officio bd. trustees, 1998-99; mem. co-chmn. vis. day com. The N.Y. Hosp.-Cornell Med. Ctr., 1995-98; pres. N.Y. Hosp.-Cornell Med. Coll. Alumni Coun., 1996-98; course dir. Salzburg Cornell Med. Seminars, 1996—, steering com., 1999—. Author: (with others) Pulmonary Diseases of the Fetus Newborn and Child, 1978; contbr. numerous articles to profl. publs. Vestry St. James Ch., N.Y.C., 1994-97; mem. ad hoc bd. visitors Emory U., 1994-95; bd. dirs. Health Advs. for Older People, 1997—, v.p., 2000—; mem. adv. bd. Sch. Medicine Emory U., 2000—, chmn. adv. bd., 2002--. Lt. comdr. USNR. Recipient The Emery medal, 2001. Fellow ACS (Manhattan dist. #2 com. on applicants 1991-97, Manhattan Credentials Com. 1991-99); mem. Am. Acad. Otolaryngology-Head and Neck Surgery, Med. Soc. State of N.Y., N.Y. State Soc. Otolaryngology-Head and Neck Surgery (exec. coun. 1974-80, dist. dir. 1980), County Med. Soc. N.Y., N.Y. Laryngol. Soc. (sec.-treas. 1981-84, v.p. 1984-85, pres. 1985-86), N.Y. Bronchoscopic Soc. (v.p. 1986-94, pres. 1994-97), N.Y. Clin. Soc. (v.p. 1998-99, pres. 1999-2000), Assn. Emory Alumni (bd. govs. 1990-97, pres.-elect 1993-94, pres. 1994-95), Omicron Delta Kappa. Episcopalian. Avocations: astronomy, ornithology. Home: 430 E 63d St Apt 5E New York NY 10021-7927 Office: D510 449 E 68th St New York NY 10021 Office Phone: 212-746-2223. E-mail: schley@med.cornell.edu.

SCHLEYER, WILLIAM T. cable company executive; b. Phila. BS in Mech. Engring., Drexel U.; MBA, Harvard Bus. Sch. Mgr. IBM, Abbott Labs.; from sys. mgr. to pres., COO US West Media Group Continental Cablevision, 1977-97; pres., COO MediaOne, Boston, 1997—2000; prin. Pilot House Ventures, LLC, 2001; pres., CEO, broadband services unit AT&T Corp., 2001—03; CEO Adelphia Communications, 2003—. Office: Adelphia Communications 1 N Main St Coudersport PA 16915

SCHLICHTING, CATHERINE FLETCHER NICHOLSON, librarian, educator; b. Huntsville, Ala., Nov. 18, 1923; d. William Parsons and Ethel Loise (Breitling) Nicholson; m. Harry Fredrick Schlichting, July 1, 1950 (dec. Aug. 1964); children: James Dean, Richard Dale, Barbara Lynn. BS, U. Ala., 1944; MLS, U. Chgo., 1950. Asst. libr. U. Ala. Edn. Libr., Tuscaloosa, summers 1944-45; libr. Sylacauga (Ala.) H.S., 1944-45, Hinsdale (Ill.) H.S., 1945-49; asst. libr. Centre for Children's Books, U. Chgo., 1950-52; instr. reference dept. libr. Ohio Wesleyan U., Delaware, 1965-69, asst. prof., 1969-79, assoc. prof., 1979-85, prof., 1985—, curator Ohio Wesleyan Hist. Collection, 1986—, student pers. libr., 1966-72. Author: Introduction to Bibliographic Research: Basic Sources, 4th edit., 1983, Checklist of Biographical Reference Sources, 1977, Audio-Visual Aids in Bibliographic

Instruction, 1976, Introduction to Bibliographic Research: Slide Catalog and Script, 1980; info. cons. (documentary) Noble Achievements: The History of Ohio Wesleyan 1942-1992, 1992, 150 Years of Excellence: A Pictorial View of Ohio Wesleyan University, 1992. Mem. adminstrv. bd. Meth. Ch., 1973-81, chmn. adminstrv. bd., 1985—, mem. coun. on ministries, 1975-81, chmn., 1975-77, trustee, 1999—2003. Recipient Algernon Sidney Sullivan award U. Ala., 1944, Hon. Alumna award Ohio Wesleyan U., 1997; Ohio Wesleyan U.-Mellon Found. grantee, 1972-73, 84-85; GLCA Tchg. fellow, 1976-77. Mem. ALA, Ohio Libr. Assn., Midwest Acad. Libr. Conf., Acad. Libr. Assn. Ohio (dir. 1984-86), AAUP (chpt. sec. 1967-68), United Meth. Women (pres. Mt. Vernon dist. 1994-97, newsletter editor 1998—), Ohio Wesleyan Woman's Club (exec. bd. 1969-72, 77-79, 81-84, pres. 1969-70, sec. 1977-78), History Club (pres. 1971-72, v.p. 1978-79, 2003-04) Fortnightly Club (pres. 1975-76, 87-88, 2003-04), Am. Field Svc. (pres. Delaware chpt. 1975-76), Kappa Delta Pi, Alpha Lambda Delta. Democrat. Home: 57 Willow Brook Way S Delaware OH 43015 Office: Ohio Wesleyan U La Beeghly Library Delaware OH 43015

SCHLICHTING, KIMBERLY SUE, psychologist, educator, health facility administrator; b. Petersburg, Va., Sept. 7, 1967; d. John Eakin and Maureen Elizabeth Aitken; m. Troy Richard Schlichting, June 10, 1995; children: Ryan Troy, Hayden Riley. BA in psychology and social work, Whittier (Calif.) Coll., 1989; MA in pre-clin. psychology, San Diego State U., 1991; PhD in sch. psychology, U. Denver, 1999. Therapist Daybreak - Princeton, Denver, 1992—93, Adams Creek Mental Health, Commerce City, Colo., 1992—99; sch. psychologist Cherry Creek Schools, Englewood, Colo., 1999—2001; adj. prof. U. Denver, 2000—; clin. dir. Think Smart Day Treatment, Lakewood, Colo., 2002—04. Clin. assessor Excelsior Day Treatment, Aurora, Colo., 2002—. Recipient Mamie Dodd Miller scholarship, U. Denver, 1996—97. Mem.: Am. Psychol. Assn., Colo. Soc. Sch. Psychologists, Nat. Assn. Sch. Psychologists. Avocations: reading, scrapbooks.

SCHLICHTING, WILLIAM HENRY, lawyer, writer; b. Austin, Minn., Jan. 24, 1944; s. John Frederick and Frances Amelia (Garbisch) Schlichting. BA, St. Olaf Coll., 1966; MS, U. Chgo., 1970; JD, Columbia U., 1973; LLM in Taxation, NYU, 1979. Bar: NY 1974, Minn. 1981, US Tax Ct. 1982. Assoc. Shea & Gould, NYC, 1973—76; editor Law Jour. Pub. Co., NYC, 1976—79; tax dept. Matthew Bender & Co., Inc., NYC, 1979—81; assoc. Peterson, Hanson, Schlichting & Davies, Albert Lea, Minn., 1981—83; gen. counsel, sec. Med. Venture, Inc., Mpls., 1983—89; writer Matthew Bender & Co., Inc., NYC, 1989—91; acquisitions editor, classifier West Group, Eagan, Minn., 1991—2002. Writer Butterworth Legal Pub., Mason divsn., St. Paul, 1983—84. Author, editor Banking Law, 1981, Clark's Digest-Annotator, 1976—79; contbr. articles to profl. jours. Mem.: Minn. Bar Assn., NY State Bar Assn., Sigma Pi Sigma, Phi Beta Kappa. Lutheran. Home: 5901 Laurel Ave #325 Golden Valley MN 55416-1075

SCHLICHTMANN, JAN R. lawyer; b. Framingham, Mass., Mar. 16, 1951; BA, U. Mass., 1973; JD, Cornell U., 1977. Bar: DC 1977, Mass. 1978, N.H. 1978, U.S. Dist. Ct. Mass. 1978, U.S. Ct. Appeals (1st cir.) 1978, U.S. Supreme Ct. 1990. Pvt. practice, Boston, 1978—. Staff atty. U.S. Ho. Reps., 1978—79; lectr. U. Wis., Nat. Judiciary Coll., 1990. Mem. com. revise Mass. hazardous waste statute Commonwealth of Mass., 1990—92. Mem.: ATLA, Mass. Acad. Trial Attys., Mass. Bar Assn., Phi Beta Kappa. Office: 175 Federal St Boston MA 02110 Business E-Mail: jschlichtmann@levinlaw.com.

SCHLICKAU, GEORGE HANS, cattle breeder, professional association executive; b. Haven, Kans., Nov. 2, 1922; s. Albert Rudulph and Florence Elsabe (Wittorff) S.; m. Lois Marie Ritthaler, Apr. 26, 1955; children: Bruce Alan, Susan Marie, James Darwin, Nancy Ann. Grad. high sch. Breeder registered Schlickau Hereford cattle, Haven, 1943—; pres. Reno County (Kans.) Hereford Assn., 1947-56, treas., 1956-58; dir. Reno County Cattleman's Assn., 1970-74, sec., 1970-71, treas., 1974; dir. Kans. Hereford Assn., 1955-71, 84-90, v.p., 1959, pres., 1960, 61; mem. organizing bd. Kans. Bull Test Sta., county committeeman Kans. Livestock Assn., 1960-75, bd. dirs., 1976-80, v.p. purebred coun., 1990-91, pres. purebred coun., 1992-93; bd. dirs. Am. Hereford Assn., 1969-75, v.p., 1973-74, pres., 1974-75; bd. dirs. Am. Nat. Cattleman's Assn., 1974-76; mem. fgn. trade com. Nat. Cattlemsn's Assn., 1990-93. Contbr. articles in field to profl. jours.; exhibitor, also winner numerous awards at major cattle shows across country; guest speaker, judge at numerous Hereford cattle events across country. Host ann. judging sch. and contest for Future Farmers Am. and 4-H youth, 1940-84; dir. Kans. Nat. Jr. Livestock Show, 1973—, sec., 1982-83, chmn., 1984-85, bd. govs., 1988—; bd. dirs. Haven State Bank, 1962—, Equus Beds Groundwater Mgmt. Dist. 2, 1975-79, Beef leader Haven 4-H Club, 1947-67; mem. Haven H.S. Bd., 1962-65, clk., 1964-65; mem. agrl. adv. com. Hutchinson (Kans.) Cmty. Jr. Coll., Kans., 1974-82; adv. Am. Jr. Hereford Assn., 1977-82; pres. Parent-Tchr. League Luth. Sch., 1979-80, 83-84; mem. zoning bd. City of Haven, 1985-88; bd. dirs. Ark Valley Electric Coop Assn., 1984-96, v.p., 1986-90, pres. 1990-93, Dist. IV Kans. Electric Coop., 1986-96, chmmn., 1992; bd. dirs. Kans. Coop. Coun., 1994-96; vice chmn. KACRE, 1992, chmn. 1993; adv. coun. mem. Arthur Capper Coop. Ctr., 1994-96. Recipient Am. Farmer Degree award Future Farmers Am., 1942, Reno County Outstanding Young Farmer award Hutchinson Jaycees, 1959, Kans. Hereford Herdsman of the Year award High Plains Jour., 1960, Soil Conservation award Kans. Bankers Assn., 1968, Hon. State Farmer Degree award Future Farmers Am., 1972, Kans. Hereford Breeder of Yr., 1976, Portrait Gallery Outstanding Livestock Breeder award Kans. State U. Block and Bridle Club, 1978, Reno County 4-H Family of Yr. award, 1987, Reno County Farm Focus Family award Hutchinson C. of C., 1989, Stockman of Yr. award Kansas Livestock and Meat Industry Coun., 1994; named Kans. Seedstock Producer of Yr. BIF, 1988; Kans Jr. Livestock Show dedicatory, 1991, Master Farmer, Master Farm Homemaker, 1991. Mem. Kans. Wheat Growers Assn., Kans. Farm Bur., Haven Industries, Inc., Kansas City (Kans.) Hereford Club, Kans. State U. Block and Bridle Club (hon. mem.), Haven Booster Club (sec. 1952-53, pres. 1954-56), Future Farmers Am. (mem. adv. com. Haven chpt. 1971—) Lutheran (mem. sch. bd. 1967-70, chmn. 1969-70; chmn. ch. bd. 8 yrs., chmn. congregation 1984-88, elder 1977-79). Home: 14506 S Victory Rd Haven KS 67543-7903

SCHLICKAU, LOIS MARIE, farmer; b. Arlington, Kans., Sept. 18, 1933; d. Otto W. and Maria Edna (Goering) Ritthaler; m. George Hans Schlickau, Apr. 26, 1955; children: Bruce, Susan Russell, James, Nancy Bernard. AA, Hutchinson C.C., 1953. Treas., v.p., pres. Kans. State Bd. Agr., 1986—93, Kans. State Fair Bd., 1986—94, pres., 1992; treas., v.p. women's exec. com. Kans. Electric Coop., 1991—95; mem. Kans. Value Added Ctr. Bd., 1994—96, vice-chmn., 1995—96, Kans. Fairs Assn. Bd., mem., 1994—96, v.p., 1995—96; mem. Cong. Sam Brownback's Agrl. Adv. Bd., 1995—97, Senator Sam Brownback's Agrl. Adv. Bd., 1997—99, Cong. Jerry Moran's Exec. Adv. Bd., 1996—, Reno County Ext. Coun. Bd., sec., Reno County Farm Bureau Bd.; mem. Nat. Cattle Women Bd.; mem. internat. agr. project adv. com. Kans. State U., mem. adminstrv. structure task force; mem. Kans. Vocat. Agr. Edn. Task Force. Charter mem., dir., parliamentarian, com. mem., v.p. Am. Hereford Aux. Bd., pres., 1980—81; charter mem., dir., com. mem., v.p., pres. Kans. Hereford Aux. Bd.; project leader Haven 4-H and Lucky H 4-H; past pres. Ladies of Congregation, past Sunday Sch. tchr., choir St. Paul's Luth. Ch.; former parent/tchr. league chmn. St. Paul's Luth. Sch.; local soc. pres. Luth. Women's Missionary League, 1994—96, local soc. sec., 2001—03, com. chmn., zone v.p., sec., state bd. mem., v.p., parliamentarian, nat. bylaws com., 1995—99; bd. dirs. Hutchinson Cmty. Found., 1996—2001, mem. exec. com., 1999—2001, chair grants com.; mem. Hutchinson C.C. Leadership Adv. Com., 1999—; bd. dirs. Bank Haven Adv. Bd., 2001—. Named Outstanding Woman, Am. Hfd. Aux., 1985, Friend of Extension, Kans. Extension Svc., 1993; named to Hall Fame, Kans. Fairs Assn., 1997, Wall of Hon., Hutchinson HS, 2004; recipient Outstanding Woman award, Kans. Hereford Aux., 1976, Achievement award, Kans. State Grange, 1993. Mem.: Kans. Agr. Women (pres. 1998—2000, v.p., parliamentarian, coms. mem., nat. legis. rep. 2001—), Am. Agri-Women (chmn. nat. conv. com. 1996, mem. com., Livestock Commodity Com., Leaven award), Hutchinson Hosp. Corp. Bd. (bd. mem. 1998—2003, chmn. 2002, 2003), Kans. Tech. Enterprise Corp. Bd. (bd. dir. 1989—91, vice chmn. 1990—91), Reno County Hist. Soc. (dir. 1985—90, pres. 1988, dir. 1996—, v.p., sec., dir. 2000—), Hutchinson/Reno County C. of C. (mem. agri-bus. com.). Avocations: reading, cooking, travel. Home and Office: 14506 S Victory Rd Haven KS 67543 Office Phone: 620-465-7749.

SCHLICKEISEN, RODGER OSCAR, non-profit environmental organization executive; b. Houston, Jan. 24, 1941; s. Oscar and Elvene Alice (Rennemo) S.; m. Susan Jane Culver, May 23, 1970; 1 child, Derek. BA, U. Wash., 1963; MBA, Harvard U., 1965; DBA, George Washington U., 1978. Loan officer Export-Import Bank of U.S., Washington, 1968-70; pres. Gryphon, Inc., Washington, 1970-74; group dir. com. on budget U.S. Senate, Washington, 1974-79; assoc. dir. econs. and govt. U.S. Office of Mgmt. and Budget, Washington, 1979-80; v.p. Craver, Mathews, Smith & Co., Falls Church, Va., 1980-81, CEO, 1981-87; chief of staff Office of U.S. Senator Max Baucus, Washington, 1987-91; pres., CEO Defenders of Wildlife, Washington, 1991—, Defenders of Wildlife Action Fund, Washington, 2001—. Bd. dirs. Partnership Project, Inc., Washington, League Conservative Voters, Washington, Keystone Ctr., Colo.; bd. advisors Environ. Comms. Orgn., L.A., 1992—, Environ. Media Assn., L.A., 1992—. Contbr. articles to profl. publs. Va. state chmn. Common Cause, 1971-74. Office: Defenders of Wildlife 1130 17th St NW Washington DC 20036

SCHLIEBS, CHARLES ALLAN, venture capitalist, lawyer; b. Kansas City, Mo., Dec. 3, 1950; s. Edgar Emil and Elsie Elizabeth (Rosher) S.; m. Melanie Emily Schuldis, Nov. 15, 1981. BA, BS Econ., U. Pa., 1972; JD, Vanderbilt U., 1975. Bar: Mo. 1975, U.S. Supreme Ct. 1979, Pa. 1984. Assoc. Blackwell Sanders Matheny Weary & Lombardi, Kansas City, 1975-79, ptnr., 1980-82, various corp. positons, 1982-88; ptnr. Jones, Day, Reavis & Pogue, Pitts., 1988-99; co-founder, mgn. dir. iNetworks LLC, Pitts., 1999—. Mem. adv. bd. U. Pitts. Sch. Law Ctr. Internat. Legal Edn., 1995—, mem. internat. adv. bd. U. Pitts. Grad. Sch. Pub. and Internat. Affairs, 1990—, Duquesne U., Palumbo Sch. Bus. Adminstrn., Pitts., 1990—; bd. dirs. ITXS Inc., Schwoo, Inc., Sunquest Info. Sys. Inc. Chmn. bd. dirs. LaRoche Coll. Ctr. Study Ethics, 1999—. Mem. ABA, Internat. Bar Assn., Pa. Bar Assn., Duquesne Club. Home: 10 Myrtle Hill Rd Sewickley PA 15143-8700 Office: iNetworks LLC Times Bldg 3d Fl 336 4th Ave Pittsburgh PA 15222

SCHLIEVE, HY C. J. school administrator; b. Mandan, N.D., Apr. 4, 1952; s. Calvin L. and Loretta L. (Johnson) S.; m. Terri Ann Hansen, Dec. 30, 1977; children: Derek, Aaron, Jessica. BA, N.D. State U., 1974, MS, 1984; EdD, Calif. Coast U., 1994. Tchr., coach Halliday (N.D.) Pub. Sch., 1974-75, Drake (N.D.) Pub. Sch., 1975-76, Montpelier (N.D.) Pub. Sch., 1976-81; prin. Unity Pub. Sch., Petersburg, N.D., 1981-83, Page (N.D.) Pub. Sch., 1983-85; supt. Wolford (N.D.) Pub. Sch., 1985-87, Garrison (N.D.) Pub. Schs., 1987-93; prin. Buhl Joint Sch. Dist. 412, Idaho, 1993-95, Oconto Falls Area Sch. Dist., Wis., 1995-99; supt. Ellendale (N.D.) Pub. Schs. #40, 1999—. Com. mem. NDASA Rsch. and Evaluation, Garrison, 1988-93; fiscal agt. Mo. Hills Consortium, McLean County, N.D., 1989-93; cons. asbestos Garrison Pub. Sch. Dist., 1987-93. Sec. Govtl. Affairs Com., Garrison, 1987-93; mem. Tourism Com., Garrison, 1988-92, Econ. Devel. Com., 1988-89. Recipient Nat. Superintendent of the Yr. awd., North Dakota, Am. Assn. of School Administrators, 1992. Mem. Nat. Assn. Secondary Sch. Prins. (prin. assessor tng. 1990), NSBA Fed. Policy Coords. Network. Avocations: golf, hunting, fishing, bowling, outdoor activities. Office: Ellendale Pub Schs PO Box 400 321 N 1st St Ellendale ND 58436 Home: 729 5th St S Wahpeton ND 58075-4803

SCHLINGER, WARREN GLEASON, retired chemical engineer; b. Los Angeles, May 29, 1923; s. William McKinley and Esther (Gleason) S.; m. Katharine S. Stewart, June 29, 1947: children: Michael S., Norman W., Sarah Lynne. BS, Calif. Inst. Tech., 1944, MS, 1946, PhD, 1949. Registered profl. engr., Calif. Instr. Calif. Inst. Tech., Pasadena, 1949-53; chem. engr. Texaco Inc., Montebello, Calif., 1953-61, supr. research, 1961-69, mgr., 1969-81, assoc. dir., 1981-87, ret. 1987; cons. 1987—. Contbr. numerous articles to profl. publs. Patentee in field. Fellow AIChE (Chem. Engring. Practice award 1981, So. Calif. sect. Tech. Achievement award 1976, Electric Power Rsch. Inst. Achievement award 1985, Lifetime Achievement award Gasification Tech. Coun. 2003); mem. NAE, Am. Chem. Soc., Jonathan Club (L.A.), Sigma Xi, Tau Beta Pi. Home: 3835 Shadow Grove Rd Pasadena CA 91107-2241

SCHLITT, LYN M. lawyer; Gen. counsel Internat. Trade Commn., Washington, 1978—. Office: Internat Trade Commn 500 E St NW Washington DC 20436-0003

SCHLOERB, PAUL RICHARD, surgeon, educator; b. Buffalo, Oct. 22, 1919; s. Herman George and Vera (Gross) S.; m. Louise M. Grimmer, Feb. 25, 1950; children: Ronald G., Patricia S. Johnson, Marilyn A. Hock, Dorothy S. Hoban, P. Richard. AB, Harvard U., 1941; MD, U. Rochester, 1944. Intern U. Rochester Med. Sch., 1944—45, asst. resident, 1947—48, instr. surgery, 1952; rsch. fellow, resident Peter Bent Brigham Hosp., Boston, 1948—52; faculty U. Kans. Med. Ctr., Kansas City, 1952—79, prof. surgery, 1964—79, 1988—, dean for rsch., 1972—79, dir. nutritional support svc., 1993—2002; prof. surgery U. Rochester (N.Y.) Med Ctr., 1979—88, adj. prof. surgery, 1988—90; surgeon Strong Meml. Hosp., 1979—88, dir. Surg. ICU, 1979—85, dir. surg. nutritional support service. Contbr. over 100 articles to profl. jours. Lt. (j.g.), M.C. USNR, 1944-45; to lt. 1953-55. Mem. AMA, ACS, AAAS, Am. Surg. Assn., Soc. U. Surgeons, Am. Physiol. Soc., Internat. Soc. Surgery, Ctrl. Surg. Assn., Am. Assn. for Surgery of Trauma, Am. Assn. Cancer Rsch., Biomed. Engring. Soc., Am. Inst. Nutrition, Am. Soc. Clin. Nutrition, Sigma Xi. Office: Dept Surgery U Kansas Med Ctr Kansas City KS 66160-0001 Office Phone: 913-588-7565.

SCHLOM, JEFFREY BERT, research scientist; b. N.Y.C., June 22, 1942; s. David and Anna S.; m. Kathleen; children: Amy Melissa, Steven Michael. BS (Pres.'s scholar), Ohio State U., 1964; MS, Adelphi U., 1966; PhD, Rutgers U., 1969. Instr. Columbia Coll. Phys. and Surg., 1969-71, asst. prof., 1971-73; chmn. breast cancer virus segment Nat Cancer Inst., NIH, Bethesda, Md., 1973-76, chief lab. tumor immunology and biology, 1983—, head exptl. oncology sect., 1976-83; prof. George Washington U., Washington, 1975—. Disting. lectr. Can. Cancer Soc., 1985 Mem. numerous editorial bds.; contbr. numerous articles to profl. jours. Recipient Dir.'s award NIH, 1977, 89, Tech. Transfer award NIH, 1994, 95, 96, Disting. Scientist award Turin U., 1996, others. Mem. Am. Assn. Cancer Rsch. (Rosenthal award 1985), Am. Soc. Cytology (Basic Rsch. award 1987). Office: Inst Health Bldg 10 Rm 8B09 Bethesda MD 20892

SCHLOSBERG, THEODORE K. music educator; b. New Brunswick, N.J., Sept. 1, 1936; s. Ralph Schlosberg and Renee Aronson Schlosberg Sosin; m. Kathryn Sell Levine, Sept. 25, 1982; children: Lindsey Levine, Stephanie Levine Harvey; m. Natalie Berkowski, Aug. 14, 1959 (div. Feb. 1982); children: Susan Schlosberg McWilliams, Gail Schlosberg Sokoloff. BA in Music Edn., MusM, Trenton State Coll.; EdD in Creative Arts, Rutgers U. Music tchr. Plainfield Pub. Schs., 1960—67, Westfield Pub. Schs., 1967—96; founder, exec. dir. N.J. Workshop for Arts, 1972—. Dir. fine arts Lanark Camp, Maine, 1960—63; dir. Plainfield Sch. Music, 1960—68; dir. Plainfield Summer Music Workshop, 1964—67, Summer Music Workshop, Plainfield, 1964—67, Plainfield, 1997—, Workshop for Arts, Greenbrook, NJ, 1995, Recreation Dept. Music Workshops, Fanwood, NJ, 1995, Saturday Music Workshop, Plainfield, 1999—. Westfield Cmty. Ctr. Sr. Citizens Music Workshop, 2002. Recipient Faith in Westfield award, Westfield C. of C., 1991, 2001, numerous grants. Home: 26 Scudder Rd Westfield NJ 07090 Office: NJ Workshop for Arts Inc 150-152 E Broad St Westfield NJ 07090

SCHLOSS, IRVING STEVEN, lawyer; b. N.Y.C., Feb. 3, 1945; s. Arthur and Bianca (Steinberger) S.; m. Christine Skeeles, June 28, 1970 (div. Mar. 1999); children: Tracy, David; m. Deborah V. Abildsoe, Nov. 21, 1999. AB magna cum laude, Harvard U., 1966; LLB, Yale U., 1970. Bar: Conn. 1972, U.S. Dist. Ct. Conn. 1972, U.S. Ct. Appeals (2d cir.) 1973, U.S. Tax Ct. 1985; cert. mediator, 2003. Law clerk for Judge Spottswood Robinson, III (D.C. cir.) U.S. Ct. Appeals, Washington, 1970-71; ptnr. Tyler, Cooper & Alcorn, LLP, New Haven and Madison, 1976—. Co-author: Understanding TIAA-CREF: Planning for a Secure and Comfortable Retirement, 2000; bd. editors Tax Mgmt. Estates, Gift & Trust Jour.; contbr. articles to profl. jours. Bd. dirs. Guilford (Conn.) Free Libr., 1986-92, Shoreline Found., Guilford, 1984-93, 97—, New Haven Symphony Orch., 1995-2001; vol. CPTV Auction, West Hartford, 1987-88; mem. Rep. Town Commn., Guilford, 1987-91. Recipient Man of Yr. award Guilford YMCA, 1990. Mem. ABA, Conn. Bar Assn. (chmn. sect. corps. and other bus. orgns. 1988-90, mem. exec. com. estates and probate sect. 1996—), Am. Coll. Trust and Estate Counsel (editor ACTEC Studies), New Haven Conn. Bar Assn., Mory's Assn., Quinnipiack Club. Office: Tyler Cooper & Alcorn PO Box 1936 New Haven CT 06509-0906 also: 23 Woodland Rd Madison CT E-mail: ischlos@attglobal.net., schloss@tylercooper.com.

SCHLOSS, NATHAN, retired economist; b. Balt., Jan. 14, 1927; s. Howard L. and Louise (Levi) S.; m. Rosa Montalvo, Mar. 1, 1958; children: Nina L., Carolyn D. BS in Bus., Johns Hopkins U., 1950. Buyer Pacific Coast gen. merchandise office Sears Roebuck & Co., Los Angeles, 1955-60; staff asst. econ. rsch. dept. Chgo., 1960-63; sr. market analyst corp. rsch. dept. Montgomery Ward & Co., Chgo., 1963-65; rsch. mgr. real estate dept. Walgreen Co., Chgo., 1970-72; v.p. rsch. and planning Maron Properties Ltd., Montreal, Que., Can., 1972-74; corp. economist, fin. analyst Real Estate Rsch. Corp., Chgo., 1974-88, sr. v.p., 1986-88, treas., chief fin. analyst, 1982-88; economist Office of Ill. Atty. Gen., Chgo., 1988-97. Cons. in field, 1965-97. Contbr. articles on fin. and market analysis of real estate to profl. jours. Mem. Plan. Commn., village of Wilmette, Ill., 1975-77, tech. adv. com. on employment and tng. data Ill. employment and Tng. Coun., 1979-82, tech. adv. com. Ill. Job Tng. Coordinating Council, 1983-87; mem. com. on price indexes and productivity fgn. labor Bus. Rsch. Adv. Coun. of Bur. Labor Stats, Dept. Labor, 1979-88, chairperson, 1985-86, com. on employment and unemployment. Recipient Commendable Svc. Citation, Bur. Labor Stats., Dept. Labor, 1987. Mem. Am. Mktg. Assn., Nat. Assn. Bus. Economists, Ill. Econ. Assn., Lambda Alpha. Home and Office: 115 Hollywood Ct Wilmette IL 60091-3122

SCHLOSS, SAMUEL LEOPOLD, JR., retired food service executive, consultant; b. Montgomery, Ala., Mar. 30, 1926; s. Samuel Leopold and Amelia (Strauss) S.; m. Burke Hart Klein; children: Stephen, Alyce, Adam. BS in Indsl. Engring., Ga. Inst. Tech., 1947; MS in Indsl. Engring., Columbia U., 1948. Sec. Schloss and Kahn Inc., Montgomery, 1948-56, pres., 1956-86, chmn., 1986-94. Pres. Montgomery Acad., 1979-80, bd. dirs. emeritus, 1982; control bd. Montgomery Com. of One Hundred, 1984-86; bd. dirs. YMCA Metro Bd., Ctrl. Ala. Red Cross, 1996; chmn. 1997-99; past chmn. Montgomery chpt. Ala. Soc. Crippled Children and Adults; bd. dirs. Montgomery County Hist. Soc., 2004. Capt. USAFR, 1960. Mem. Montgomery C. of C. (pres. 1983), Standard Club (pres. 1964), Capital City Club (bd. govs. 1977-80), Rotary (pres. 1972-73), Montgomery Country Club. Republican. Office: Regions Tower 60 Commerce St Ste 1210 Montgomery AL 36104-3562

SCHLOSSBERG, CAROLINE BOUVIER KENNEDY (CAROLINE KENNEDY), writer, lawyer; b. Nov. 27, 1957; d. John Fitzgerald and Jacqueline Bouvier; m. Edwin A. Schlossberg, July 19, 1986; children: Rose, Tatiana, John (Jack) Bouvier Kennedy. Grad., Radcliffe Coll. (now part of Harvard), 1979; JD, Columbia Law Sch. Intern NY Daily News, 1977, Metropolitan Mus. Art, 1980; pres. John F. Kennedy Libr. Found.; chief exec. NYC Dept. Edn. Office Strategic Partnerships, 2002—04. Author: In Our Defense- The Bill of Rights in Action, 1990; co-author: The Right to Privacy, 1995. Co-founder Profiles in Courage Awards, 1989; hon. chairwoman Am. Ballet Theatre.

SCHLOSSER, ANNE GRIFFIN, librarian; b. N.Y.C., Dec. 28, 1939; d. C. Russell and Gertrude (Taylor) Griffin; m. Gary J. Schlosser, Dec. 28, 1965. BA in History, Wheaton Coll., Norton, Mass., 1962; MLS, Simmons Coll., 1964; cert. archives adminstrn., Am. U., 1970. Head UCLA Theater arts Libr., 1964-69; dir. Louis B. Mayer Libr., Am. Film Inst., L.A., 1969-88, dir. film/TV documentation workshop, 1977-87; head Cinema-TV Libr. and Archives of the Performing Arts, U. So. Calif., L.A., 1988-91; dir. Entertainment Resources Seminar, 1990; dir. rsch. libr. Warner Bros., 1991—. Project dir. Motion Pictures, Television, Radio: A Union Catalogue of Manuscript and Special Collections in the Wesern U.S., 1977. Active Hollywood Dog Obedience Club, Calif. Recipient numerous grants for script indexing, manuscript cataloging, libr. automation. Mem. Soc. Calif. Archivists (pres. 1982-83), Theater Libr. Assn (exec. bd. 1983-86), Spl. Librs. Assn. Democrat. Episcopalian. Avocations: running, swimming, reading, dog obedience training. Office: Warner Bros Rsch Libr 5200 Lankershim Blvd Ste 100 North Hollywood CA 91601-3100

SCHLOSSER, HERBERT S. broadcasting company executive; b. Atlantic City, Apr. 21, 1926; s. Abraham and Anna (Olesker) S.; m. Judith P. Gassner, July 8, 1951; children: Lynn C., Eric M. AB summa cum laude, Princeton, 1948; LL.B., Yale, 1951. Bar: N.Y. 1952. Assoc. firm Wickes, Riddell, Bloomer, Jacobi & McGuire, N.Y.C., 1951-54, Phillips, Nizer, Benjamin, Krim & Ballon, N.Y.C., 1954-57; with NBC, 1957-78; v.p., gen. mgr. Calif. Nat. Prodns., Inc. sub. NBC, 1960-61, dir. talent and program adminstrn., 1961-62, v.p. talent and program adminstrn., 1962-66; v.p. programs West Coast NBC, 1966-72; exec. v.p. NBC-TV Network, 1972-73, pres., 1973-74, mem. bd. dirs., 1973-78; pres. NBC, Inc., 1974-78, CEO, 1977-78; exec. v.p. RCA, 1978-85; sr. advisor broadcasting and entertainment Schroder & Co., Inc., N.Y.C., 1986—2000; sr. advisor, ind. cons. comms. investment banking Citigroup Global Markets Inc., 2000—. Pres. RCA cable sub. RCA, RCA Internat. Audio Visuals, Inc.; ptnr. Arts and Entertainment Cable Network, RCA/Columbia Home Video. Trustee Internat. Radio and TV Found., 1972-74; former mem. govs. Ford's Theatre Soc.; former trustee Nat. Urban League; chmn. bd. Am. Mus. of the Moving Image; bd. dirs. Chamber Music Soc. of Lincoln Ctr. With USNR, 1944-46. Recipient Humanitarian award NCCJ, 1974, Gold Brotherhood award, 1978 Mem. ABA, Assn. Bar City N.Y., Coun. on Fgn. Rels., Acad. TV Arts and Scis., Advt. Coun. (past dir.), Yale Law Sch. Assn., Internat. Radio and TV Soc. (trustee 1973-74), Hollywood Radio and TV Soc. (trustee 1970-72), Century Assn., Princeton Club (N.Y.), Phi Beta Kappa (pres. alumni assn. So. Calif. 1970-72. Office: Citigroup Global Markets 388 Greenwich St New York NY 10013-2375

SCHLOSSMAN, JOHN ISAAC, architect; b. Chgo., Aug. 21, 1931; s. Norman Joseph and Carol (Rosenfeld) S.; m. Shirley Goulding Rhodes, Feb. 8, 1959; children: Marc N., Gail S. Mewhort, Peter C. Student, Grinnell Coll., 1949-50; BA, U. Minn., 1953, BArch, 1955; MArch, MIT, 1956. Registered architect, Ill. Archtl. designer The Architects Collaborative, Cambridge, Mass., 1956-57; architect Loebl Schlossman & Hackl and predecessors, Chgo., 1959-65, assoc., 1965-70, prin., 1970-98, cons. prin., 1998—. Bd. overseers Coll. Arch. Illinois Inst. Tech., Chgo.; adv. bd. Coll. of Arch. and Landscape Arch. Univ. Minn., 2003—; founding bd. dirs. Chgo. Archtl. Assistance Ctr., 1974-79 Chmn. Glencoe Plan Commn., Ill., 1977-82; trustee Com. for Green Bay Trail, Glencoe, 1970-77, Chgo. Arch. Found., 1971-75, Graham Found. for Advanced Studies in Fine Arts, 1995-99, pres. 1999-2001; bd. dirs. Merit Sch. of Music, Chgo., 1983-93, pres., 1988-90, hon. trustee 1996; governing mem. Chgo. Symphony Orch.; mem. founders coun. Field Mus., Chgo.; mem. zoning & planning com. Greater North Mich. Ave. Assn., Chgo., 2000-01; mem. Nat. Trust Coun., Nat. Trust for Hist. Preservation, Washington. Named dir. for life Young Men's Jewish Council, Chgo., 1971; Rotch travelling scholar, 1957; sustaining fellow Art Inst. Chgo. Fellow AIA (trustee ins. trust 1971-76, chmn. ins. com. 1974-75, v.p. Chgo. chpt. 1975, chmn. architects liability com. 1976, 80-82, hon. found. trustee 1995—), Tavern Club (gov. 1986-88, v.p. 1990), The Club at Symphony Ctr., The Arts Club, Alpha Rho Chi. Office: Loebl Schlossman & Hackl 232 Mary St Winnetka IL 60093-1522

SCHLOSSMAN, STUART FRANKLIN, physician, educator, researcher; b. NYC, Apr. 18, 1935; s. Abe and Pearl (Susser) Schlossman; m. Judith Seryl Rubin, May 25, 1958; children: Robert, Peter. BA magna cum laude, NYU, 1955, MD, 1958; MA, Harvard U., 1975. Intern in medicine med. divsn. III Bellevue Hosp., N.Y.C., 1958—59, asst. resident in medicine med. divsn. III,

1959—60; Nat. Found. fellow dept. microbiology Coll. Physicians Columbia U., N.Y.C., 1960—62; asst. physician med. svc. Vanderbilt Clinic, Coll. Physician USPHS, Washington, 1960—62; Ward hematology fellow dept. internal medicine Sch. Washington U., St. Louis, 1962—63; rsch. assoc. lab. biochemistry Nat. Cancer Inst. USPHS, Washington, 1963—65; clin. instr. in medicine Sch. of Medicine George Washington U., 1964—65; assoc. in medicine, dir. blood bank Beth Israel Hosp., Boston, 1965—66; instr. Med. Sch. Harvard U., Boston, 1966—68, asst. physician, 1967—68, chief clin. immunology, 1971—73; physician Beth Israel Hosp., Boston, 1968—; from asst. to assoc. prof. medicine Harvard Med. Sch., Boston, 1968—77, prof., 1977—, Baruj Benacerraf prof. medicine, 1990—, chief divsn. tumor immunology and immunotherapy, 1973—; sr. physician Brigham and Women's Hosp., Boston, 1976—. Mem. editl. bd. Jour. of Immunology, 1969—74, Cellular Immunology, 1970—, Human Immunology, 1979—84, Clin. Immunology and Immunopathology, 1979—, mem. editl. bd.Hybridoma Hybridoma, 1980—, Cancer Investigation, 1981—, Stem Cells, 1981—, Cancer Revs., 1984, Internat. Jour. of Cell Cloning, 1983—86, mem. adv. bd. Cancer Treatment Reports, 1976—80, assoc. editor Human Lymphocyte Differentation, 1980—82; contbr. articles to profl. jours. Recipient Solomon Berson Achievement award, 1984, Robert Koch prize and medal, 1984. Fellow: AAAS; mem.: NAS, Assn. Am. Physicians, Am. Soc. Clin. Investigation, Am. Soc. Immunologists, Am. Soc. Hematology, Inst. of Medicine of NAS, Alpha Omega Alpha. Office: Dana-Farber Cancer Inst Divsn Tumor Immunology 44 Binney St Mayer 557 Boston MA 02115-6084 Office Phone: 617-632-3325. Business E-Mail: stuart_schlossman@dfu.harvard.edu.

SCHLOSSTEIN, RALPH L. diversified financial services company executive; With White House, Washington, Treasury Dept., Washington; mem. staff U.S. Congress, Washington; with Lehman Bros.; co-founder, pres. BlackRock Inc., N.Y., 1988—. Bd. dirs. BlackRock Inc., PNC Asset Mgmt. Group Inc. Office: BlackRock Inc 40 East 52nd St New York NY 10022*

SCHLOTFELDT, ROZELLA MAY, nursing educator; b. DeWitt, Iowa, June 29, 1914; d. John W. and Clara C. (Doering) Schlotfeldt. BS, State U. Iowa, 1935; MS, U. Chgo., 1947, PhD, 1956; DSc (hon.), Georgetown U., 1972, Adelphi U., 1979, Wayne State U., 1983, U. Ill., Chgo., 1985, Kent State U., 1987, U. Cin., 1989, Case Western Res. U., 1996; LHD (hon.), Med. U. S.C., 1976. Staff nurse State U. Iowa, VA Hosp., 1935—39; instr., supr. maternity nursing (State U. Iowa), 1939—44; asst. prof. U. Colo. Sch. Nursing, 1947—48; asst., then asso. prof. Wayne State U. Coll. Nursing, 1948—55; prof., asso. dean Wayne State U. Coll. Nursing (Coll. Nursing), 1957—60; dean Frances Payne Bolton Sch. Nursing, Case Western Res. U., 1960-72, prof., 1960—82, prof., dean emeritus, 1982—95. Vis. prof. Rutgers U., 1984—89, 1990—95, U. Pa., 1985—86; spl. cons. Surgeon Gen.'s Adv. Group on Nursing, 1961—63; mem. nursing rsch. study sect. USPHS, 1962—66; mem. com. on nursing edn. facilities Nat. League for Nursing-USPHS, 1962—64; mem. com. on health goals Cleve. Health Coun., 1961—66; mem. Cleve. Health Planning and Devel. Commn., 1969—72; adv. com. divsn. nursing W.K. Kellogg Found., 1959—67; v.p. Ohio Bd. Nursing Edn. and Nurse Registration, 1970—71, pres., 1971—72; mem. Nat. Health Svcs. Rsch. Tng. Com., 1970—71; mem. supply and edn. panel Health Manpower Com., 1966—67; rev. com. Nurse Tng. Act, 1967—68, bd. visitors Duke U. Med. Ctr., 1968—70; mem. coun., exec. com. Inst. Medicine of NAS, 1971—75; mem. nat. adv. health svcs. coun. Health Svcs. and Mental Health Adminstrn., 1971—75; mem. def. adv. com. on women in svcs. Dept. of Def., 1972—75; bd. dirs., treas. Nursing Home Adv. and Rsch. Coun., 1975—96; mem. adv. panel Health Svcs. Rsch. Commn. on Human Resources, NAS, 1977—85; cons. Walter Reed Army Inst.; adv. coun. on nursing U.S. VA, 1965—69, chmn., 1966—69; mem. Yale U. Coun. Com. on Med. Affairs, 1981—86; mem. adv. bd. Scholarly Inquiry for Nursing Practice, 1987—96. Mem. editl. bd. Advances in Nursing Sci., Inquiry, 1982—85, Jour. Nursing Edn., 1982—91; contbr. articles to profl. jours. Bd. visitors Syracuse U., 1990—97. 1st lt. Nurse Corps U.S. Army, 1944—46. Named Living Legend, Am. Acad. Nursing, 1995; recipient Disting. Svc. award, U. Iowa, 1973, Case Western Res. U., 1991, N. Watts Lifetime Achievement award, 1995. Fellow: Nat. League Nursing, Am. Acad. Nursing (v.p. 1975—77); mem.: ANA (chmn. commn. on nurse edn. 1967—70, mem. com. for studying credentialling 1976—79, adv. com. W.K. Kellogg Nat. Fellowship program 1981—85), Sigma Theta Tau (nat. v.p. 1948—50, selection com., disting. lectr. program 1986—87, Founders award for creativity 1985, Henderson fellow 1985), Pi Lambda Theta. Home: Judson Manor 1089 E 107th St #318 Cleveland OH 44106

SCHLOTMAN, J. MICHAEL, food products executive; Joined Kroger, Cin., 1985—, v.p. financial services & control, 1995—2000, v.p., CFO, 2000—. Office: Kroger 1014 Vine St Cincinnati OH 45202

SCHLOW, MICHAEL, food service executive; b. Bklyn. Diploma, Acad. Culinary Arts N.J.; trained with Mark Straussman. Chef, owner Radius, Boston; chef Coco Pazzo, Le Madri; exec. chef Sapore di Mare, L.I., 75 Main; owner Ariel & Michael; chef, owner Radius, Boston, 1999—. Office: Radius 8 High St Boston MA 02110

SCHLUB, ROBERT LOUIS, plant pathologist, educator; b. Springfield, Ohio, Jan. 22, 1951; s. Carl Frederick and Arvella May Schlub; m. Joanne DiLucca Schlub, Apr. 3, 1954; children: Hala Kristine, Karl Anthony, Susanna Ruth. BS, Ohio State U., 1973, MS, 1975; PhD, Mich. State U., 1979. Post-doctoral rsch. pathologist USDA, Soilborne Diseases Lab., Beltsville, Md., 1979—80; ext. plant pathologist La. State U.; asst. dir., co-owner Our Children's House-Montessori Sch., Baton Rouge, 1984—95; ext. plant pathologist III U. of Guam, 1995—2000, ext. plant pathologist IV, 2000—04, ext. plant pathologist V, 2004—. IPM coord. for Guam USDA, CSREES, Washington. Editor: (crop prodn. guide) Guam Cucurbit Guide, Eggplant, Pepper, and Tomato Prodn. Guide for Guam. Grantee 156,000, USDA, T-STAR, 2002-2005, 16,000, USDA,SARE Western Region, 1999-2002. Mem.: Am. Phytopathological Soc. (assoc.).

SCHLUB, TERESA RAE, minister; b. Oak Park, Ill., July 11, 1946; d. Robert Carl and Shirley Rae (Listhartke) Grupe. BA, Westmar Teikyo U., 1971; MDiv, Garrett Evangel. Seminary, Evanston, Ill., 1974. Ordained deacon United Meth. Ch., 1973, elder, 1978. Asst. minister First United Meth. Ch., Morris, Ill., 1974-76; minister Leaf River (Ill.) German Valley United Meth. Ch., 1976-82, East Jordan United Meth. Ch., Sterling, Ill., 1982-86, Paw Paw (Ill.) United Meth. Ch., 1986-89, Community United Meth. Ch., LaMoille, Ill., 1989-95, Capron (Ill.) United Meth. Ch., 1995—2000, North Boone Coop. Ministries, Poplar Grove, Ill., 1998—2000. Mem. alumni coun., sec. Garrett Evangel. Theol. Seminary, Evanston, 1974-76; mem. Conf. Bd. of Evangelism, 1974-76, founder, Schlub Ministries. Bd. dirs. Green Hills coun. Girls Scouts U.S., Freeport, Ill., 1986-88, Lee County Red Cross, Dixon, Ill., 1986-89, Crossroads Counseling Ctr., Mendota, 1989-91; bd. dirs. Quad County Counseling Ctr., Princeton, 1991—, treas., 1993-94; mem. Ill. Home Extension Assn., Grundy, Ogle, Whiteside and Lee Counties, 1974-89; sec. DeKalb Dist. Com. Ordained Ministry; mem. Boone County Coun. Aging, 1997-2000, Boone County Planning Commn., 1998-2000; founder Schlub Ministries; cert. in spiritual formation United Meth. Ch., 2003. Home: 5813 Beechwood Dr Apt B Loves Park IL 61111-1543 *Life becomes meaningful when one is able to become vulnerable and be willing to take risks. This becomes possible when one has faith in God and confidence in the self. It also helps to know and experience the love of others.*

SCHLUETER, DAVID ARNOLD, law educator; b. Sioux City, Iowa, Apr. 29, 1946; s. Arnold E. and Helen A. (Dettmann) S.; m. Linda L. Boston, Apr. 22, 1972; children: Jennifer, Jonathan. BA, Tex. A&M U., 1969; JD, Baylor U., 1971; LLM, U. Va., 1981. Bar: Tex. 1971, D.C. 1973, U.S. Ct. Mil. Appeals 1972, U.S. Supreme Ct. 1976. Legal counsel U.S. Supreme Ct., Washington, 1981—83; assoc. dean St. Mary's U., San Antonio, 1984—89, prof. law, 1986—, Hardy prof. trial advocacy, dir. advocacy programs, 2000—; reporter Fed. Adv. Com. on Criminal Rules, 1988—. Chmn. JAG adv. coun., 1974-75. Author: Military Criminal Justice: Practice and Procedure, 1982, 6th edit., 2004; (with others) Military Rules of Evidence Manual, 1981, 5th edit., 2003, Texas Rules of Evidence Manual, 1983, 6th edit., 2002, Texas Evidentiary Foundations, 1992, 2d edit., 1998, Military Evidentiary Foundations, 1994, 2d edit., 2000, Military Criminal Procedure Forms, 1997, 2d edit., 2003, Federal Evidence Tactics, 1997, Texas Rules of Evidence Trial Book, 2000; editor-in-chief: Emerging Problems Under the Federal Rules of Evidence, 3d edit., 1998; contbr. articles to legal publs. Maj. JAGC, U.S. Army, 1972-81. Fellow Am. Law Inst., Tex. Bar Found. (life), Am. Bar Found. (life); mem. ABA (vice-chmn. criminal justice sect. coun. 1991-94, vice-chmn. com. on criminal justice and mil. 1983-84, chmn. standing com. on mil. law 1991-92, mem. standing com. on armed forces law, chmn. editl. adv. bd., Criminal Justice Mag., 1989-91, 2000-), Tex. Bar Assn. Republican. Lutheran. Office: St Marys U Sch Law 1 Camino Santa Maria St San Antonio TX 78228-8603

SCHLUETER, JUNE MAYER, English educator, author; b. Passaic, N.J., Nov. 4, 1942; m. Paul Schlueter. BA in English magna cum laude, Fairleigh Dickinson U., 1970; MA in English, Hunter Coll., CCNY, 1973; PhD in English and Comparative Lit., Columbia U., 1977. Asst. prof. Lafayette Coll., Easton, Pa., 1977-84, assoc. prof., 1984-91, prof., 1991-92, Charles A. Dana prof., 1992—, head English dept., 1992-93; asst. to provost, 1986-90; acting provost., 1993-94; provost Lafayette Coll., Easton, Pa., 1994—. Fulbright prof. Gesamthochschule Kassel Univ., Fed. Republic Germany, 1978-79; chmn. Shakespeare Seminar Columbia U., 1989-91, 2004—, exec. bd., 1989—; active NEH summer seminar for coll. profs., 1981, lectr. Commonwealth Partnership Summer Lit. Inst., 1985-87, dir. summer seminar for sch. tchrs., 1988, selection panel, 1989, 91, evaluator Instl. Grant Program, 1990. Author: Metafictional Characters in Modern Drama, 1979, The Plays and Novels of Peter Handke, 1981; (with James K. Flanagan) Arthur Miller, 1987; (with James P. Lusardi) Reading Shakespeare in Performance: King Lear, 1990, Dramatic Closure: Reading the End, 1995, editor: Feminist Rereadings of Modern American Drama, 1989, Modern American Drama: The Female Canon, 1990, Critical Essays: The Two Gentlemen of Verona, 1995; (with Paul Schlueter) The English Novel: Twentieth Century Criticism, Vol. 2: Twentieth Century Novelists, 1982, Modern American Literature, Supplement II, 1985, An Encyclopedia of British Women Writers, 1988; (with Enoch Brater) Approaches to Teaching Beckett's Waiting for Godot, 1991; co-editor Shakespeare Bull., 1983-2003; assoc. editor Stages, 1984-90; editl. bd. Studies in Am. Drama, 1945-Present, 1989—2000; editl. cons. Modern Drama, Theatre Jour., PMLA, Studies in Twentieth Century Lit., others; contbr. revs., essays to profl. jours. Bd. govs. Fairleigh Dickinson U., Rutherford, N.J., 1985-90, bd. dirs., Madison, N.J., 1997—; mem. adv. com. Lehigh Valley Ednl. Coop., 1988-90; selection panel German Acad. Exch. Svc., Bonn, 1979. Rsch. grantee Lafayette Coll., 1977-93, NEH summer rsch. grantee, 1990, DAAD summer rsch. grantee, 1991. Mem. MLA, Shakespeare Assn. Am., Internat. Shakespeare Assn., Coll. English Assn., Samuel Beckett Soc., AAUP, Columbia Shakespeare Seminar. Home: 123 High St Easton PA 18042-1609 Office: Lafayette Coll Lafayette College Easton PA 18042 Office Phone: 610-250-5066.

SCHLUNTZ, ROGER, architecture educator; BArch, U. Nebr.; MArch, U. Calif., Berkeley. Faculty mem. Calif. Poly. State U., San Luis Obispo, Calif., U. Nebr., 1969—77; dir. arch. program Ariz. State U., 1980—89; prof., dean arch. U. Miami, 1992—99, dean Sch. Arch. and Planning U. N.Mex., Albuquerque, 1999—. Mem. Nat. Register Peer Profls. U.S. Gen. Svcs. Adminstrn.; bd. mem. Nat. Archtl. Accrediting Bd., 2001—04. Co-author (with Tom Laging): The Nebraska Capitol and Environs Plan (First Honor award Progressive Arch. mag.). Fellow: AIA (exec. dir.); mem.: Assn. Collegiate Schs. Arch. Office: Univ NMex Sch Arch and Planning 2414 Central Ave SE Albuquerque NM 87131*

SCHLUTER, PETER MUELLER, electronics company executive; b. May 24, 1933; s. Fredric Edward and Charlotte (Mueller) S.; m. Jaquelin Ambler Lamond, Apr. 18, 1970 (div. June 1990); children: Jane Randolph, Charlotte Mueller, Anne Ambler; m. Christine Moon Van Ness, Feb. 7, 1998. BME, Cornell U., 1956; postgrad., Harvard U. Grad. Sch. Bus. Adm, 1982. Sr. engr. Thiokol Chem. Corp., Brigham City, Utah, 1958-59; assoc. Porter Internat. Co., Washington, 1960-65, v.p., pres., treas., dir., 1966-70; pres., treas., dir. Zito Co., Derry, N.H., 1970-72; internat. bus. cons. Washington, 1972-74; v.p., dir. Buck Engrng. Co. Inc. (now Lab-Volt Sys., Inc.), Farmingdale, N.J., 1975, pres., CEO, dir., 1975—. Mem. Rep. Inaugural Book and Program Com., 1969; mem. cmty. adv. bd. Monmouth (N.J.) coun. Girl Scouts U.S.; mem. adv. coun. Monmouth U. Sch. Bus. Adminstrn.; bd. dirs. United Way of Monmouth County; trustee Monmouth Med. Ctr.; N.Am. rep., mem. presidium WORLDDIDAC, Bern, Switzerland, v.p., 1996—. Recipient Golden Osprey award So. Monmouth County C. of C., 1995. Fellow City and Guilds of London Inst. (hon.); mem. World Assn. Mfrs. and Distbrs. of Ednl. Materials (N.Am. rep.), Met. Club Washington, Rumson Country Club, Pi Tau Sigma. Home: 4 Quaker Ln Little Silver NJ 07739-1806 Office: PO Box 686 Farmingdale NJ 07727-0686

SCHLUTER, ROBERT ARVEL, physicist; b. Salt Lake City, Aug. 27, 1924; s. Arvel R. and Florence (Leach) S.; 1 child, Jonathan R. BS, U. Chgo., 1947, PhD, 1954. Rsch. assoc. U. Chgo. Inst. for Nuc. Studies, 1954; from instr. to asst. prof. MIT Lab. for Nuc. Studies, Cambridge, 1955-60; assoc. physicist Argonne (Ill.) Nat. Lab., 1961-72; prof. physics and astronomy Northwestern U., Evanston, Ill., 1961-92, prof. emeritus, 1992—. Guest scientist Brookhaven (NY) Nat. Lab., 1955-70, Lawrence Radiation Lab., U. Calif., Berkeley, 1958-60; guest appointee Aspen Inst. for Humanities, 1967; adv. Northwestern Rev., Northwestern Chronicle, 1985-92. Contbr. chapters to books. Served with Los Alamos, Manhattan Project, C.E., U.S. Army, 1943-46. Grantee, AEC NSF, Dept. Energy, NASA. Mem.: Nat. Assn. Scholars, Am. Phys. Soc. Achievements include first to observe K-Mesic X-rays, measure lambda hyperon magnetic moment, 2d and 3d excited states of the proton; research in experimental hydrodynamics. Avocations: mountain climbing and exploration, history of science. Home: 241 N Vine St Apt 902E Salt Lake City UT 84103-1971 Office: Northwestern U Dept Physics and Astronomy 2145 Sheridan Rd Evanston IL 60208-0834 Business E-Mail: schluter@northwestern.edu.

SCHMALBECK, RICHARD LOUIS, university dean, lawyer; b. Chgo., Dec. 31, 1947; s. George Louis and Betty Jeanne Schmalbeck; m. Linda Michaels; children: Suzanne, Sabine. AB in Econs. with honors, U. Chgo., 1970, JD, 1975. Bar: Ohio 1975, D.C. 1977. Asst. to dir. and economist Ill. Housing Devel. Authority, Chgo., 1971-73; assoc. Vorys, Sater, Seymour & Pease, Columbus, Ohio, 1975-76; spl. asst. to assoc. dir. for econs. and govt. Office of Mgmt. and Budget, Washington, 1976-77; assoc. Caplin & Drysdale, Washington, 1977-80; assoc. prof. law Duke U., Durham, N.C., 1980-84, prof. law, 1984-90, 93—, vice chmn. acad. coun., 1984—85, 2001—02; dean U. Ill. Coll. Law, Champaign, 1990-93. Assoc. editor U. Chgo. Law Rev., 1974-75; contbr. articles to profl. jours. Mem. ABA (articles editor jour. 1977-80), Am. Law Inst., Phi Beta Kappa. Office: Duke University Sch of Law PO Box 90360 Durham NC 27708-0360

SCHMALENBERGER, JERRY LEW, pastor, religious studies educator; b. Greenville, Ohio, Jan. 23, 1934; s. Harry Henry and Lima Marie (Hormel) S.; m. Carol Ann Walthall, June 8, 1956; children: Stephen, Bethany Allison, Sarah Layton Wallace. BA, Wittenberg U., 1956, DDiv (hon.), 1984; MDiv, Hamma Sch. Theology, Springfield, Ohio, 1959, D of Ministry, 1976. Ordained to ministry Luth. Ch., 1959. Dir. Camp Mowana, Mansfield, Ohio, 1958-59; pastor 3d Luth. Ch., Springfield, 1959-61, 1st Luth. Ch., Bellefontaine, Ohio, 1961-66, sr. pastor Tiffin, Ohio, 1966-70, Mansfield, 1970-79, St. John's Luth. Ch., Des Moines, 1979-88; pres. Pacific Luth. Theol. Sem., Berkeley, Calif., 1988-96, prof. parish ministry, 1988-99. Co-dir. Iowa Luth. Hosp. Min. of Health Program, Des Moines, 1986—88; Roland Payne lectr. Gbarnga Sch. Theology, Liberia, 1987; lectr. Luth. Theol. Sem., Hong Kong, 1994, 1999—2003, The United Theol. Coll., Kingston, Jamaica, 1994, HKBP Sem., Sumatra, 2001—03; guest prof. The Augustana Hochschule, Germany, 1996, 99, 2001; guest lectr. Inst. Superior Evang. Theol. Studies Theol. Sem., Argentina, 1998; guest lectr. Ecumenical Ctr., Montevideo, Uruguay, 1998; vis. faculty Moravian Theol. Sem., Paramaribo, 1998. Author: Lutheran Christians' Beliefs Book One, 1984, Book Two, 1987, Iowa Parables and Iowa Psalms, 1984, Saints Who Shaped the Church, 1986, Stewards of Creation, 1987, Nights Worth Remembering, 1989, The Vine and the Branches, 1992, Call to Witness, 1993, Plane Thoughts on Parish Ministry, 1994, Invitation to Discipleship, 1995, The Preacher's Edge, 1996, Preparation for Discipleship, 1998, These Will Preach, 1999, The Parables of Jesus and Their Flip Side, 2000, The Miracles of Jesus and Their Flip Side, 2001, Dear Friends and Family, 2001, The Preacher's Workbook, Cycle A., 2001, Cycle B., 2002, Cycle C., 2003; columnist Rite Ideas, 1987-88. Bd. dirs. Grand View Coll., Des Moines, 1980-88, Wittenberg U., Springfield, Ohio, 1974-87, Luth. Social Services of Iowa, 1980-87, chmn. pre fund drive, 1988; bd. dirs. Planned Parenthood of Mid-Iowa, Des Moines, 1987-88; dir. Evang. Outreach/Luth. Ch. Am., 1983-85; mem. Iowa Luth. Hosp. Charitable Trust, 1986-88; chair Com. for Homeless Fund, Des Moines, 1986. Named Outstanding Alumni Wittenberg U., 1965, Young Man of Yr. Tiffin Jaycees, 1965, Man of Yr. Bellefontaine Jaycees, Disting. Alumni award Trinty Sem., Columbus, 1989. Mem. NAACP, Acad. Preachers, Acad. Evangelists (organizer 1986—), Kiwanis, Rotary. Lutheran. Avocations: historical research and writing, travel, boating. Home and Office: 162 Pelican Loop Pittsburg CA 94565-2004 E-mail: jlschmalen@aol.com. *Personal philosophy: Not perfect, but forgiven, we find real life in living ours for others.*

SCHMALENSEE, RICHARD LEE, dean, economist, former government official, educator; b. Belleville, Ill., Feb. 16, 1944; s. Fred and Marjorie June (Veigel) S.; m. Edeth Diane Hawk, Aug. 19, 1967; children: Alexander Clayton, Nicholas Hawk. SB, MIT, 1965, PhD in econs., 1970. Asst. prof. econs. U. Calif., San Diego, 1970—74, assoc. prof. econs., 1974—77; instr. Sloan Sch. Mgmt., MIT, Cambridge, Mass., 1967—69, asst. prof., 1970, assoc. prof. applied econs., 1977-79, prof., 1979—, prof. dept. econs., 1986—, Gordon Y Billard Prof. of Econs. and Mgmt., 1988-99, dep. dean, 1996—98, interim dean, 1998, dean, 1998—2000, John C Head III Dean, 2001—; dir. Ctr. for Energy and Environ. Policy Rsch. MIT, Cambridge, Mass., 1991-99. Vis. prof. Harvard Bus. Sch., 1985—86, U. Louvain, Belgium, 1985, vis. assoc. prof., rsch. fellow, Belgium, 1973—74; vis. scholar dept. econs. Harvard U., 1980—81; editl. bd. Jour. of Econs. and Mgmt. Strategy, 1992—98; assoc. editor Internat. Jour. Indsl. Orgn., 1982—89, Zeitschrift für Nationalökonomie, 1987—89, 1993—, Jour. Econ. Perspectives, 1992—98; bd. editors Am. Econ. Review, 1982—86; assoc. editor Jour. Indsl. Econs., 1977—81, bd. editors, 1981—89; founding editor Regulation of Econ. Activity, 1978—89, co-editor, 1989—; mem. Pres.'s Coun. Econ. Advisers, 1989—91; bd. dirs. Am. Coun. for Capital Formation Ctr. for Policy Rsch., 1991—, environ. policy fellow, 1997—98; rsch. assoc. Nat. Bur. Econ. Rsch., 1992—; Internat. Rsch. Fellow Kiel Inst. World Econs., 2001—; spl. cons. NERA Econ. Cons., 1981—89, 1991—; bd. dirs. Internat. Securities Exch., 2000—, MFS Investment Mgmt., 2002—. Author: The Economics of Advertising, 1972, Applied Microeconomics, 1973, The Control of Natural Monopolies, 1979; co-author: An Introduction to Applied Macroeconomics, 1973, Markets for Power, 1983, Economics, 1988, Paying with Plastic, 1999, Markets for Clean Air, 2000, Did Microsoft Harm Consumers? Two Opposing Views, 2000; co-editor: The Empirical Renaissance in Industrial Economics, 1987, Handbook of Industrial Organization, 1989, Management: Inventing and Delivering Its Future, 2003. NSF grant, 1975-77, 81-83; Co-recipient Edward A. Hewett Prize, Am. Assn. for the Advancement of Slavic Studies, 1995 Fellow: AAAS, Econometric Soc.; mem.: Internat. Acad. Mgmt., Am. Econ. Assn. (nominating com. 1987, exec. com. 1993—95). Office: MIT Sloan Sch Mgmt 50 Memorial Dr Rm E52-473 Cambridge MA 02142-1347*

SCHMALER, TRACY ALICE, newspaper journalist, writer; b. Morristown, N.J., Sept. 23, 1972; d. Wayne Charles and Diane Marie Schmaler. BS in Mass Comm., Emerson Coll., 1994. News intern Boston Phoenix, 1994; staff reporter Berkshire Record, Great Barrington, Mass., 1994-96, Brattleboro (Vt.) Reformer, 1996-98, news wire editor, 1997-98; staff reporter Rutland (Vt.) Daily Herald, 1998—. Mentor Brattleboro Union H.S. Program, 1997. Recipient Spot News award New Eng. Press Assn., 1995. Mem. Soc. Profl. Journalists. Avocations: reading, snowboarding, tennis. E-mail: snowwhite@tds.net.

SCHMALSTIEG, WILLIAM RIEGEL, retired Slavic languages educator; b. Sayre, Pa., Oct. 3, 1929; s. John William and Dorothy Augusta (Riegel) S.; m. Emily Lou Botdorf, Mar. 28, 1952; children: Linda, Roxanne. BA, U. Minn., 1950; postgrad., Columbia U., 1952; MA, U. Pa., 1951, PhD, 1956; PhD (hon.), Vilnius U., 1994. Instr. U. Ky., Lexington, 1956-59; asst. prof. Lafayette Coll., Easton, Pa., 1959-63; assoc. prof. U. Minn., Mpls., 1963-64; prof. Pa. State U., University Park, 1964—2002, head dept. Slavic langs., 1969-91. Mem. Internat. Commn. Balto-Slavic Linguistics, 1973—; appointed Edwin Erle Sparks prof. Slavic Lang., 1990. Author: (with L. Dambriunas and A. Klimas) An Introduction to Modern Lithuanian, 1966, 4th edit., 1990, 5th edit., 1993, reprinted as Beginner's Lithuanian, 1999, An Old Prussian Grammar, 1974, Studies in Old Prussian, 1976, Indo-European Linguistics, 1980, An Introduction to Old Church Slavic, 1976, 2d edit., 1983, A Lithuanian Historical Syntax, 1988; (with Warren Held and Janet Gertz) Beginning Hittite, 1988, A Student Guide to the Genitive of Agent in the Indo-European Languages, 1995, An Introduction to Old Russian, 1995, The Historical Morphology of the Baltic Verb, 2000; editor Gen. Linguistics, 1971-82; mem. editl. adv. bd. Jour. Indo-European Studies, Baltistica, Linguistica Baltica, Acta Linguistica Lithuanica, Archivum Lithuanicum, Lietuviu Kalbotyros Klausimai, Baltu Filologija. Served to 1st lt. U.S. Army, 1952-54. NEH grantee, 1978-79, Fulbright grantee and exch. scholar Acad. Scis., Vilnius, USSR, 1986; recipient Humanities medal Pa. State U., 1983, Friend of Lithuania award Knights of Lithuania, 1990, Lithuanian Govt. Mazvydas medal, 1997; named Disting. Alumnus Breck Sch., 1990. Mem.: Assn. Advancement Baltic Studies (pres. 1982—84). Episcopalian. Home: 814 Cornwall Rd State College PA 16803-1430 E-mail: emily@leanonemily.com.

SCHMALZ, CARL NELSON, JR., artist, educator, printmaker; b. Ann Arbor, Mich., Dec. 26, 1926; s. Carl Nelson and Esther Dorothy (Fowler) S.; m. Dolores Irene Tourangeau, Dec. 2, 1950; children: Stephen Theodore (dec.), Mathew Nelson, Julia Irene. AB, Harvard U., 1948, MA, 1949, PhD, 1958; MA (hon.), Amherst Coll., 1969. Teaching fellow in fine arts Harvard U., Cambridge, Mass., 1950-52; asst. prof. Bowdoin Coll., Brunswick, Maine, 1953-62; curator, asst dir. Walker Art Mus., 1953-62; asst. prof. Harvard U., 1960; prof. Amherst Coll., 1962-95, prof. emeritus, 1995—. Lectr. in field; workshop tchr. in field. Author: Watercolor Lessons from Eliot O'Hara, 1974, Watercolor Your Way, 1978, Finding and Improving Your Painting Style, 1986, paperback, 1992; co-author: Science Education in the United States: Issues, Crises and Priorities, 1990; author numerous essays and reviews; exhibited in one-man shows including Cambridge (Mass.) Art Assn., 1948, Laing Gallery, Portland, Maine, 1955, Amherst (Mass.) Coll., 1963, U. Mass., 1965, W.C. Rawls Mus., Va., 1972, Concord (Mass.) Art Assn., 1974, Govt. House, Hamilton, Bermuda, 1979, Jones Library, Amherst, Mass., 1979, The Arlington, Kennebunkport, Maine, 1980, Harmon-Meek Gallery, Naples, Fla., 1987, 91, 92, 98, Gallery at 6 Deering St., Portland, Maine, 1987, 91, Fretz Gallery, Portland, 1987-88; exhibited in group shows including Jordan Marsh Co., 1947, 48, 50, 71-73, Colby Coll., 1958, Carnegie Inst., Pitts., 1963, FAR Gallery, N.Y.C., 1964-68, Am. Watercolor Soc., 1966, 68, 70, Bowdoin Coll. Mus., 1973, Balt. Watercolor Soc., 1976, Boston Atheneum, 1979, Watercolor U.S.A. Honor Soc., 1989, 91, Maine Art Gallery, 1991, Rolly-Michaux Gallery, Boston, 1995; represented in permanent collections: Signet Soc., Walker Art Mus., Brunswick, Maine, Jones & Laughlin Steel Corp., Diners Club Am., Kalamazoo Art Center, Hampshire Coll., Zanesville Art Inst., Blue Cross/Blue Shield, Philharmonic Ctr. for the Arts, Naples, Fla., Springfield (Mo.) Art Mus., Amherst Coll., Bowdoin Coll., Hampshire Coll., Kalamazoo Art Inst., Signet Soc., Springfield (Mo.) Art Mus.; work published in various pubs. including The Artist's Guide for Using Color, 1992, The Artist's Mag., 1994, Splash 3: Ideas and Inspirations, 1994. Mem. exec. bd. Interfaith Housing Corp., Amherst, 1966-76; pres. bd. trustees Amherst Day Sch., 1966-69; mem. Pelham Arts Lottery Coun., 1984-90; v.p. bd. dirs. Portland Mus. Art, 1957-62. Bacon fellow, 1951; recipient 1st prize watercolor Cambridge Art Assn. Ann., 1947, 1st prize for traditional watercolor Virginia Beach Boardwalk Show, 1965, South Mo. Trust purchase award Watercolor U.S.A., 1970, 1st prize watercolor 30th Ann. Kennebunk River Club Show, 1985, Purchase prize Watercolor U.S.A., 1997. Mem.: Coll. Art Assn., The Signet Soc., Watercolor U.S.A. Honor Soc. Democrat.

SCHMALZ, DOUGLAS J. agricultural company executive; sr. v.p., CFO Archer Daniels Midland Co., Decatur, Ill., 2002—. Office: Archer Daniels Midland Co 4666 E Fairies Pkwy PO Box 1470 Decatur IL 62526

SCHMALZ, MATHEW NELSON, academic administrator; b. Holyoke, Mass., Nov. 18, 1964; s. Carl Nelson and Dolores Tourangeau Schmalz; m. Kristin Donna Steinmetz, July 25, 1998; children: Anna Teresa, Katherine Dolores. AB, Amherst Coll., Mass., 1983—87; MA, U. Chgo., 1994—95, PhD, 1995—98. Dir. asian studies Coll. of the Holy Cross, Worcester, Mass., 2001—03. Edward bennett williams fellow Coll. of the Holy Cross, Worcester, Mass., 1998—. Contbg. editor: (book) Riting Between the Lines: Popular Christianity in India, Notes from the Mandala: Essays in Honor of Wendy Doniger, Theology and the Social Sciences; contbr. articles. Homeless shelter mgr. My Bros.' Pl., New York, 1988—89; tchr. Glenmary Home Missions, Idabel, Okla., 1982—83; house asst. The Missionaries of Charity, Varanasi, India, 1984—85; tchr. Indian Missionary Soc., Kotwa-Narayanpur, India, 1994—96. Recipient Thomas J. Watson Fellowship, Thomas J. Watson Found., 1987—88, Summa Cum Laude, Amherst Coll., 1987, Mosely Prize, 1987, John Woodruff Simpson Fellowship, 1990, Nat. Resources Fellowship, US Dept. Edn., 1990-1991, George Stebbins Moses Fellowship, Amherst Coll., 1991, George A. Plimpton Fellowship, 1993, Distinction in Doctoral Examinations, U. Chgo., 1994, Jr. Rsch. Grant, Am. Inst. Indian Studies, 1996; fellow Fulbright Dissertation Rsch. Abroad, US Dept. Edn., 1994-1995; grantee, The Wabash Ctr. for Tchg. Theology and Religion, 2000-2002; scholar Century Fellowship, U. Chgo., 1989-1993. Mem.: Assn. Asian Studies, Bhojpuri Sahitya Akademi, Soc. Hindu-Christian Studies, Coll. Theol. Soc., Am. Acad. Religion, Phi Beta Kappa (v.p., historian 2002—04). Liberal. Roman Catholic. Home: 7 Birch St Paxton MA 01612 Office: Coll of the Holy Cross 1 College St Worcester MA 01610 Office Phone: 508-793-2557. Business E-Mail: mschmalz@holycross.edu.

SCHMALZ, ROBERT FOWLER, geology educator; b. Ann Arbor, Mich., May 29, 1929; s. Carl Nelson and Esther Dorothy (Fowler) S.; m. Barbara Ann Leetch, July 18, 1964; children: Timothy F., Dorothy L. AB with honors, Harvard Coll., 1951; AM, Harvard U., 1954, PhD, 1959. Cert. profl. geologist. Rsch. asst. Harvard/W.H.O.I., Cambridge, Mass., 1957-58; asst. prof. Pa. State U., University Park, 1958-63, assoc. prof., 1963-69, prof. of geology, 1969-91, chmn. geology, 1971-74, undergrad. coord., 1974-77, prof. of geology emeritus, 1992—. Trustee Bermuda Biol. Sta., 1967-79; mem. adv. com. Appalachian Compact Users Radio Isotopes, University Park. Editor: Science Education in the United States, 1991, Environmental Radon, 1990; contbr. articles to profl. jours. Vice-chmn., chmn. State College (Pa.) Borough Water Authority, 1978—98; vice-chmn. U. Area Joint Authority, 1998—. With U.S. Army, 1955—57. Recipient Wilson Teaching award Earth and Mineral Sci. Coll., 1969, Lindback Teaching award Pa. State U., 1970. Fellow AAAS, Geol. Soc. Am.; mem. Am. Assn. Petroleum Geologists (disting. lectr. 1977-78), Soc. Econ. Mineralogists and Petrologists, Pa. Acad. Sci., Explorers Club, Cosmos Club, Sigma Xi. Avocations: historical railroad operations, sailing. Home: 305 E Mitchell Ave State College PA 16803-3637 E-mail: rfs3@psu.edu.

SCHMALZRIED, MARVIN EUGENE, financial consultant; b. Dighton, Kans., Nov. 11, 1924; s. Carl D. and Marie M. (Bahm) S.; m. Jean Landino, Nov. 27, 1946; children— Darlene, Candace, Cynthia, Derek, Valerie, Rebecca. BBA, Northwestern U., 1949; LL.B., U. Conn., 1955. Bar: Conn. bar 1955; C.P.A., Conn. Acct. Webster, Blanchard & Willard, CPA's (named changed to Price Waterhouse & Co.), Hartford, Conn., 1950-55; contr., asst. treas. J.B. Williams Co., Glastonbury, Conn., 1955-57; treas., sec. Curtis 1000, Inc. (name changed to Am Bus. Products, Inc.), Atlanta, 1957-61; asst. to pres. Am. Home Products Corp., N.Y.C., 1961-63, comptroller, 1964-67, v.p., 1967-72, sr. v.p., 1972-84; pres. Venda Vid, Inc., N.Y.C., 1986-90; sr. v.p. View-Master Ideal Group, Inc., N.Y.C., 1987-90; exec. v.p. Strategics Inc., 1993-95. Recipient Gold medal Conn. Soc. C.P.A.'s, 1953 Mem. AICPA, ABA, Old Greenwich Friday Evening Reading Soc. (pres.) Clubs: Darien Country. Home and Office: 26 Cove Ave Norwalk CT 06855-2400

SCHMANDT, JURGEN A. public affairs educator; b. Mar. 2, 1929; PhD, U. Bonn, Germany, 1956. Prin. adminstr. sci. policy OECD, Paris, 1960-65; assoc. dir. program sci. and tech. Harvard U., Cambridge, Mass., 1965-71; prof. pub. affairs U. Tex., Austin, 1971—2001; dir. and sr. adviser Houston Advanced Rsch. Ctr., The Woodlands, Tex., 1985—. Author: Acid Rain and Friendly Neighbors, 1988, The Regions and Global Warming, 1992, Scarce Water, 1998, Navigating the Waters of the Paso del Norte, 1999, Sustainable Development, 2000. Home: 11 Hull Circle Dr Austin TX 78746-3709 Business E-Mail: jschmandt@harc.edu.

SCHMANDT-BESSERAT, DENISE, archaeologist, educator; b. Ay, France, Aug. 10, 1933; came to U.S., 1965, naturalized, 1970; d. Victor and Jeanne (Crabit) Besserat; m. Jurgen Schmandt, Dec. 27, 1956; children: Alexander, Christopher, Phillip. Ed., Ecole du Louvre, 1965. Rsch. fellow in Near Eastern Archaeology Peabody Mus. Harvard U., Cambridge, Mass., 1969-71; fellow Radcliffe Inst., Cambridge, 1969-71; asst. prof. Middle Eastern studies U. Tex., Austin, 1972-81, assoc. prof., 1981-88, prof., 1988—; acting chief curator U. Tex. Art Mus., 1978-79. Vis. assoc. prof. U. Calif., Berkeley, 1987-88; curator Legacy of the Middle East exhbn. Jeddah (Saudi Arabia) Hist. Preservation Dept. Author: Before Writing, 1992, How Writing Came About, 1996, History of Counting, 1999; adv. editor Tech. and Culture, 1978-92; editl. adv. bd. Archaeology Odyssey, 2003—; mem. editl. bd. Written Communication, 1993-95, Visible Lang., 1985—, Explorations in Media Ecology, 2001, Ancient Adminstrn., 2001; contbr. articles to profl. jours. Recipient Kayden Nat. U. Press Book award, 1992, Robert W. Hamilton Author award, 1998, Walter J. Ong award Media aEcology Assn., 2004; named in Am. Scientist, 1999; Wenner-Gren Found. grant, 1970-71, NEA grant, 1974-75, 77-78, ACLS grant, 1984, Deutscher Akademischer Austauschdienst grant, 1986, NEH grant, 1992; NEH fellow, 1979-80, U. Wis. Inst. for Rsch. in Humanities fellow, 1984-85, USIA, Am. Ctr. Oriental Rsch. fellow, 1994-95, 97, 2001, Malone fellow 1997, 99, Weeks fellow Humanities Rsch. Ctr. Stanford U., 2003—. Mem. Am. Oriental Soc., Archeol. Inst. Am. (governing bd. 1983-89), Am. Anthropol. Assn., Am. Schs. of Oriental Rsch., Centro Internat. Rsch. Archeologiche Anthropologiche e Storiche (Rome). Business E-Mail: dsb@mail.utexas.edu.

SCHMAUS, SIEGFRIED H. A. engineering executive, consultant; b. Muelheim/Ruhr, W. Ger., Dec. 23, 1915; s. Wilhelm Friedrich and Hedwig (Flader) S.; student Staatliche Ingineur Schule, Duisburg, W. Ger., 1940-41, Esslingen, W. Ger., 1945-46; m. A. Babette Schmid, Aug. 17, 1946. Apprentice-designer Demag A.G., Duisburg, 1930-36; designer/supr. Meissner, Cologne, W. Ger., 1936-38; designer aircraft engines Daimler-Benz A.G., Stuttgart, W. Ger., 1943-45; designer Fischer & Porter, Warminster, Pa., 1948-53, Ametek Inc., Sellersville, Pa., 1954-65; staff rsch. engr. Fischer & Porter, Warminster, 1966-80; pres. Sensor Devel. Inc., Broomall, Pa., 1977—, Sensor Rsch. Inc., Phila., 1980-90. Patentee in field. V.p. Friends Hist. Rittenhouse Town. Served with German Luftwaffe, 1938-42. Recipient Hess Ingenuity award, 1962. Mem. Franklin Inst. (sr., silver mem.), Instrument Soc. Am. (sr.), Am. Soc. Mfg. Engrs., German Soc. Pa. (v.p. 1984, Founders medal 1987, Officer's Cross of the Gov. of Germany 1988), Masons. Republican. Lutheran. Home and Office: 15 Spoonbill Rd Lantana FL 33462-4752

SCHMECHEL, DONALD E. medical educator; MD, Harvard U., 1974. Neurology staff Duke U. Med. Sch., Durham, NC, 1979—82, geriatrics staff, 1982—84, prof. medicine, assoc. prof. neurobiology, 1979—. Assoc. dir. ADRC, dir., 1997—. Contbr. articles to profl. jours. Achievements include research in application of animal models and chemical anatomical methods to the problem of abnormal development and aging; neurodegenerative disorders particularly Alzheimer's Disease, Parkinsonism and mixed system atrophies, and frontal lobe dementias. Address: Ste A230 2200 W Main St Durham NC 27705 Office: Duke Univ Med Ctr Dept Medicine Divsn Neurology Box 3503 Durham NC 27710

SCHMEHL MORLEY, SUSAN LINDA, fine arts educator, artist; b. Aug. 29, 1949; BFA, U. Mass., Amherst, 1971; postgrad., Studio Art Ctr. Internat., Florence, Italy, 1994—95; MFA in Painting, Md. Inst. Coll. Art, 2003. With Peace Corps, 1973-76; studio arts, Spanish tchr., 1976-97; chair of fine and performing arts Berkshire Sch., Sheffield, Mass., 1997-2000. Fellow Skidmore Coll., 1994. Recipient Scholastic Art and Writing award for Outstanding H.S. Tchr., 1998, 2000, Outstanding Nat. Sculpture Tchr. award, Internat. Sculpture Ctr., 2001, Internat. Artist Residency, Jingdezhen Sanbao Ceramic Art Inst., China, 2002; Fulbright Meml. Fund scholar, Japan, 2002. Mem.: Nat. Assn. Art Educators, Ind. Sch. Art Instrs. Assn. Home: 245 N Undermountain Rd Sheffield MA 01257 E-mail: slsmorley@yahoo.com.

SCHMELING, GARETH, classics educator; b. Algoma, Wis., May 28, 1940; married. BA, Northwestern Coll., 1963; MA (Knapp fellow), U. Wis., 1964, PhD (Knapp travelling grantee 1965-66, Univ. fellow 1967-68), 1968. Asst. prof. classics U. Va., 1968-70; assoc. prof. U. Fla., 1970-74, prof., 1974-93, chmn. classics, 1974—, chmn. humanities, 1974-76, dir. Center for Studies in Humanities, 1978-87, prin. investigator Humanities Perspectives on Professions, 1975-87, acting chmn. dept. philosophy, 1986-88, disting. prof., 1998—. Vis. prof. U. Colo., Boulder, 1992; panelist, research div. Nat. Endowment for Humanities, also mem. nat. bd. consultants; dir. writing programs, U. Fla., 2003—. Translator and author Introduction: Cornelius Nepos: Lives of Famous Men, 1971; author: Petronius' Satyricon, 1971, Ovid's the Art of Love, 1972, Chariton and the Rise of Ancient Fiction, 1974, Homer's the Odyssey, 1974, A Bibliography of Petronius, 1977, Xenophon of Ephesus, 1980, Historia Apollonii Regis Tyri, 1988, The Novel in the Ancient World, 1996, Qui Miscuit Utile Dulci, 1998; contbr. numerous articles, revs. to profl. jours.; editor: Newsletter Petronian Soc. 1970—; editorial com.: U. Fla. Press Humanities Monographs, 1978—. Named 1 of 5 Tchrs. of Yr. for Arts and Scis. U. Fla., 1973; recipient Rome prize Am. Acad., 1977-78; U. Va. faculty fellow, summer 1969, summer 1970; U. Fla. fellow, summer 1971, summer 1974; Nat. Endowment for Humanities fellow, 1973-74; Am. Council Learned Socs. summer fellow, 1974; Am. Philos. Soc. grantee, 1970, 71, 72, 77-78, 84-85; U. Fla. grantee, 1977-78 Fellow Am. Acad. in Rome; mem. Am. Philol. Assn., Am. Classical League, Vergilian Soc., Classical Assn. of Middle West and South (sec.-treas. 1975-82, pres. 1985-86) Home: 320 NW 30th St Gainesville FL 32607-2524 Office: U Fla Dept Classics Gainesville FL 32611 Office Phone: 352-392-2075.

SCHMELTZER, EDWARD, lawyer; b. N.Y.C., Aug. 22, 1923; s. Harry A. and Julia (Hoffman) S.; m. Elizabeth Ann Cooper, June 19, 1949; children: Henry Cooper, Elizabeth Sabine. BA, Hunter Coll., 1950; MA, Columbia U., 1951; JD, George Washington U., 1954. Bar: D.C. 1954, U.S. Supreme Ct 1958. Economist PHA, 1951-53; econ. cons., 1953-54; trial atty. Fed. Maritime Bd. Maritime Adminstrn., 1955-60; dir. bur. domestic regulation Fed. Maritime Commn., 1961-66, mng. dir., 1966-69; ptnr. Morgan, Lewis & Bockius, 1969-76, Schmeltzer, Aptaker & Shepard, 1976—; sr. v.p., gen. counsel Sea Star Line, Jacksonville, 1999—2001. U.S. rep. 12th Diplomatic Conf. on Internat. Maritime Law, Brussels, 1967, 13th Diplomatic Conf., Brussels, 1968 Mem. bd. editors: Jour. Maritime Law and Commerce; Contbr. articles to profl. jours. Served with USAAF, 1943-46. Recipient Fed. Maritime Commn.; Distinguished Service award, 1969 Mem. Maritime Adminstrv. Bar Assn. (pres. 1971-73) Clubs: Cosmos (Washington). Home: 10412 Buckboard Pl Potomac MD 20854-3805 Office: The Watergate Ste 1000 2600 Virginia Ave NW Washington DC 20037-1905 Office Phone: 202-333-8800. E-mail: es@saslaw.com.

SCHMELTZER, JOHN C. financial writer; b. Davenport, Iowa, Sept. 30, 1945; s. J. Howard and Virginia Marie (Smith) S. BA, Wartburg Coll., Waverly, Iowa, 1967; MA, No. Ill. U., 1974. Reporter Davenport Times-Democrat, 1967, Lynchburg (Va.) News, 1968-69; dir. pub. rels. Doane Coll., Crete, Nebr., 1967-68; news editor Belvidere (Ill.) Daily Rep., 1971-72; reporter Chgo. Tribune Co./The Trib, Hinsdale, Ill., 1973-76; area editor Suburban Trib, Hinsdale, 1976-82; reporter, asst. bur. chief Chgo. Tribune, 1982-88, bur. chief, 1988-91, fin. writer, 1991—. Instr. McHenry County Coll., Crystal Lake, Ill., 1970-74, Coll. of DuPage, Glen Ellyn, Ill., 1982-86. Recipient 1st place award for spot news photography Iowa AP, 1967, 1st place award for pub. svc. Ill. AP, 1984, Peter Lisagor award Bus. Journalism, 1993, 94, 2003, Pulitzer prize for Gateway to Gridlock, 2001; filanist Gerald Loeb award for Disting. Bus. and Family Journalism, 2003. Mem. Nat. Assn. Hispanic Journalists, Soc. Am. Bus. Editors and Writers, Wartburg Coll. Alumni Assn., Soc. Profl. Journalists, Chgo. Headline Club. Lutheran. Avocations: golf, fishing. Home: 33 W Huron St Chicago IL 60610-3753 Office: Chgo Tribune 435 N Michigan Ave Chicago IL 60611-4066

SCHMEMANN, SERGE, journalist; b. Paris, Apr. 12, 1945; arrived in U.S., 1951; s. Rev Alexander and Juliana (Ossorguine) Schmemann; m. Mary Schidlovsky, Sept. 13, 1970; children: Anne, Alexander, Nathalie. BA cum laude, Harvard U., 1967; MA, Columbia U., 1971; LittD (hon.), Middlebury Coll., 1995. Desk editor AP, N.Y.C., 1972—75, UN corr., 1975—77, South Africa corr., 1977—79, Moscow corr., 1979—80; Moscow bur. chief N.Y. Times, 1980—87, 1991—95, Bonn bur. chief, 1987—90, Jerusalem bur. chief, 1995—98, dep. fgn. editor, 1998—2001, UN bur. chief, 2001—02; editor, editl. page Internat. Herald Tribune, Paris, 2003—. Author: (book) Echoes of a Native Land: Two Centuries of a Russian Village, 1997; contbr. articles to profl. publs. With U.S. Army, 1968—70, Vietnam. Recipient Hal Boyle award, Overseas Press Club, 1986, Pulitzer Prize for coverage of German reunification, 1991, Emmy award for Outstanding Individual Achievement in a Craft, Nat. TV Acad., 2003. Mem.: Phi Beta Kappa. Avocations: carpentry, piano. Office: NY Times 229 W 43rd St New York NY 10036-3959 Office Phone: 33-1-41-439200. E-mail: serge@nytimes.com.

SCHMERLING, ERWIN ROBERT, counselor, retired physicist; b. Vienna, July 28, 1929; came to U.S., 1955, naturalized, 1962; s. Heinrich H. and Lily (Goldsmith) S.; m. Esther M. Schmerling, Apr. 5, 1957; children: Susan D., Elaine M. BA, Cambridge U., 1950, MA, 1954, PhD in Radio Physics, 1958; grad., Advanced Mgmt. Program, Harvard, 1969, Fed. Exec. Inst., 1975. Asst. prof. elec. engring. Pa. State U., University Park, 1955-60, assoc. prof., 1960-62, 63-64; staff scientist NASA-Hdqrs., Washington, 1962-63, program chief ionospheric physics, magnetospheric physics, space plasma physics, 1964-82; asst. dir. space and earth scis. Goddard Space Flight Ctr., NASA, Greenbelt, Md., 1984-86; chief data system scientist Office Space Science and Applications NASA Hdqrs., Washington, 1986-88; SAIS program scientist NASA, Washington, 1988-89; data system scientist solar system exploration div. NASA Hdqrs., Washington, 1989-90, program mgr. astrophysics data systems, 1991-94; counselor Svc. Corps of Retired Execs. (SCORE), 1995—. Mem. U.S. coms. III and IV Internat. Sci. Radio Union, 1985—, sec. U.S. Com. III, 1966-69, chmn., 1969-72; chmn. subcom. C1 Com. Space Rsch. (COSPAR), 1984-88; mem. Adv. Group Aerospace R&D, NATO, 1978-85; vis. scholar Stanford U., 1983; cons. RCA, Gen. Electric, 1959-62. Contbr. papers to profl. jours. Recipient medal for contbns. to internat. geophys. programs Soviet Geophys. Soc., 1985. Fellow IEEE (mem. wave propagation standards com.); mem. Am. Geophys. Union, AAAS, Sigma Xi. Home: 2101 Wind Ln Wilmington DE 19810 E-mail: erwinschmerling@comcast.net.

SCHMEROLD, WILFRIED LOTHAR, dermatologist; b. Munich, Dec. 30; arrived in U.S., 1956; s. Wilhelm and Frieda (Hinterwinkler) Schmerold; m. Perlette J. Joers, 1962 (dec. Feb. 2003); children: Klaus, John, Will, James, Susan, Paul, Carl, Mike, Tom, Marianne. Abiturient, Altes Realgymnasium, 1938; MD, U. Munich, 1945. Diplomate Am. Bd. Dermatology, Am. Bd. Dermatopathology. Intern U. Munich Med. Faculty, 1945-46; asst. UN Hosp., Munich, 1946-50, Max Plank Inst., Munich, 1951-52, U. Erlangen, Germany, 1952-53, U. Munich, 1953-56; intern Fairview Park Hosp., Cleve., 1956-57; asst. U. Ill., Chgo., 1957-60, instr., 1960-75, clin. asst. prof., 1975—. Pvt. practice in dermatology, Carol Stream, Ill., 1959—; dermatopathologist, Carol Stream, 1978—. Contbr. articles to profl. jours. Charter mem. founders club Ctrl. DuPage Hosp., Winfield, Ill., 1963. Fellow: AMA, Chgo. Dermatol. Soc., Ill. State Med. Soc., Ill. Dermatol. Soc., Am. Soc. Dermatopathology, German Dermatol. Soc. (life), Am. Acad. Dermatology (life). Roman Catholic. Avocations: opera, travel, anthropology, archaeology, history. Office: Mona Kea Med Park 507 Thornhill Dr # B Carol Stream IL 60188-2703

SCHMERTMANN, JOHN HENRY, civil engineer, educator, consultant; b. N.Y.C., Dec. 2, 1928; s. Johannes Conrad Schmertmann and Margaret Anna-Marie (Carstens) Schmertmann Ottesen; m. Pauline Anne Grange, Aug. 11, 1956; children: Carl, Gary, Neil, Joy. BSC.E., MIT, 1950; MSC.E., Northwestern U., 1954, PhD in Civil Engring., 1962. Registered profl. engr., Fla. Soils engr. Mueser Rutledge Cons. Engrs., N.Y.C., 1951-54; soils engr. C.E., U.S. Army, Wilmette, Ill., 1954-56; asst. prof. civil engring. U. Fla., Gainesville, 1956-62, assoc. prof., 1962-65, prof., 1965-79, adj. prof., prof. emeritus; prin. Schmertmann & Crapps, Inc., Gainesville, 1979-97, LoadTest Inc., Gainesville, 1991—, Office John H. Schmertmann Inc., Gainesville, 1997—. Postdoctoral fellow Norwegian Geotech. Inst., Oslo, 1962-63; vis. scientist div. bldg. research NRC Can., Ottawa Ont., 1971-72 Author numerous profl. papers Fellow ASCE (br. pres. 1972, Collingwood prize 1956, Norman medal 1971, State of the Art award 1977, Middlebrooks award 1981, Terzaghi lectr. 1989), Fla. Engring. Soc.; mem. Nat. Acad. Engring. Lutheran. Avocation: sport fishing. Office: Office John H Schmertmann Inc 4509 NW 23rd Ave Ste 19 Gainesville FL 32606-6570

SCHMERTZ, ERIC JOSEPH, lawyer, educator, commissioner; b. N.Y.C., Dec. 24, 1925; married; 4 children. AB, Union Coll., 1948, LL.D. (hon.), 1978; cert., Alliance Francaise, Paris, 1948; JD, NYU, 1954. Bar: N.Y. 1955. Internat. rep. Am. Fedn. State, County and Mcpl. Employees, AFL-CIO, N.Y.C., 1950-52; asst. v.p., dir. labor tribunals Am. Arbitration Assn., N.Y.C., 1952-57, 59-60; indsl. relations dir. Metal Textile Corp. subs. Gen. Cable Corp., Roselle, N.J., 1957-59; exec. dir. N.Y. State Bd. Mediation, 1960-62, corp. dir., 1962-68; labor-mgmt. arbitrator, N.Y.C., 1962—; mem. faculty Hofstra U. Sch. Bus., 1962-70; prof. Hofstra U. Sch. Law, 1970—, Edward F. Carlough disting. prof. labor law, 1981-98, dean Sch. Law, 1982-89, disting. prof. emeritus of law, 1998—; of counsel The Dweck Law Firm, N.Y.C., 1999—; commr. labor rels. City of N.Y., 1990-91. Scholar-in-residence Pace U. Sch. Law, 1998—; 1st Beckley lectr. in bus. U. Vt., 1981; bd. dirs. Wilshire Oil Co.; mem. N.Y. State Pub. Employment Rels. Bd., 1991-97; cons. and lectr. in field. Co-author: (with R.L. Greenman) Personnel Administration and the Law, 1978; contbr. chpts. to books, articles to profl. jours., to profl. law confs., seminars and workshops. Mem. numerous civic orgns. Served to lt. USN, 1943-46. Recipient Testimonial award Southeast Republican Club, 1969; Alexander Hamilton award Rep. Law Students Assn.; Eric J. Schmertz Disting. Professorship Pub. Law and Pub. Svc. established Hofstra Law Sch., 1993. Mem. Nat. Acad. Arbitrators, Am. Arbitration Assn. (law com., Whitney North Seymour Sr. medal 1984), Fed. Mediation and Conciliation Svc., N.Y. Mediation Bd., N.J. Mediation Bd., N.J. Pub. Employment Rels. Bd., Hofstra U. Club, Princeton Club. Office: The Dweck Law Firm 230 Park Ave Rm 416 New York NY 10169-0422 Office Phone: 212-687-8200. E-mail: schmertz@dwecklaw.com.

SCHMERTZ, MILDRED FLOYD, editor, writer; b. Pitts., Mar. 29, 1925; d. Robert Watson and Mildred Patricia (Floyd) S. B.Arch., Carnegie Mellon U., 1947; M.F.A., Yale U., 1957. Archtl. designer John Schurko, Architect, Pitts., 1947-55; assoc. editor Archtl. Record, N.Y.C., 1957-65, sr. editor, 1965-80, exec. editor, 1980-85, editor-in-chief, 1985-90. Vis. lectr. Yale Sch. Architecture, 1979— Editor, contbr.: New Life for Old Buildings, other books on arch. and planning; contbg. writer: Architectural Digest, 2000—. Bd. mgrs. Jr. League, City of N.Y., 1964-65; commr. N.Y. Landmarks Preservation Commn., 1988-91. Fellow AIA; mem. Mcpl. Art Soc. N.Y., Century Assn. (N.Y.C.) Home and Office: 310 E 46th St New York NY 10017-3002

SCHMETTERER, JACK BAER, federal judge; b. Chgo, Ill, Apr. 11, 1931; s. Samuel and Gertrude (Schiff) Schmetterer; m. Joan L. Ruther, Mar. 18, 1956 (dec.); children: Laura, Mark, Kenneth; m. Barbara Friedman, Sept. 2, 2001. BA, Yale U., 1952, JD, 1955. Bar: Ill. 1956. Instr. polit. sci. Yale U., New Haven, 1954-55, U. Ga., Ga., 1957-58; ptnr. Schmetterer & Schmetterer, Chgo., 1958-63; asst. U.S. atty. U.S. Dist. Ct. (no. dist.) Ill., Chgo., 1963-68, 1st asst. U.S. atty., 1968-70; ptnr. Freeman, Schmetterer, Freeman & Salzman, Chgo., 1970-71; 1st asst. states atty. State's Atty. of Cook County, Chgo., 1971-73; assoc., ptnr., head of litigation Gottlieb & Schwartz, Chgo., 1973—85; US bankruptcy judge US Bankruptcy Ct. (no. dist.) Ill., Chgo., 1985—. Vis. prof. dept. criminal justice U. Ill., Chgo., 1974-76. Bd. dir. Cook County Ct. Watchers, Inc., until 1985, Better Govt. Assn., until 1985; former mem. Northbrook Village Bd., North Shore Mass Transit Dist. Bd. With US Army, 1956-58. Mem.: John Howard Assn. (chairperson 1997—99, adv. bd.), Fed. Bar Assn. (pres. Chgo. chpt. 1993—94), Fed. Trial Judges Conf., ABA, Just the Beginning Found. (v.p.), Decalogue Soc., Mackey-Wigmore Inn of Ct., Lawyers Club of Chgo. Office: US Bankruptcy Ct # 600 219 S Dearborn St Apt 600 Chicago IL 60604-1702

SCHMETTERER, ROBERT ALLEN, advertising executive; b. NYC, Nov. 23, 1943; s. Robert Mayer and Rosalie (Fernandez) S.; children: Adam, Tyler; m. Stacy Lynn Chiarello, Sept. 26, 1987. BS, Fairleigh Dickinson U., 1967, MBA, 1970. Sales promotion mgr. Brit. Motor Corp., Leonia, N.J., 1963-68; market research dir. Volvo, Rockleigh, N.J., 1968-71; v.p. market rsch. Scali, McCabe, Sloves Inc., N.Y.C., 1971-73, sr. v.p. dir. account service, 1974-79, exec. v.p., chief oper. officer, mng. dir., 1979-84; pres., chief exec. officer/worldwide HCM, N.Y.C. and Paris, 1984-87; pres., ptnr. Messner Vetere Berger McNamee Schmetterer, N.Y.C., 1987—97; chmn., CEO Euro RSCG Worldwide, NYC, 1997—2004; pres., COO Havas, 2002—04. Bd. dirs. N.Y.C. Partnership, 1987—. Author: Leap: A Revolution in Creative Business Strategy, 2003. Mem. Advt. Club N.Y. (dir. 1983). Address: Euro RSCG Worldwide 350 Hudson St Fl 6 New York NY 10014-4504

SCHMETZER, ALAN DAVID, psychiatrist; b. Louisville, Sept. 3, 1946; s. Clarence Frederick and Catherine Louise (Wootan) Schmetzer; m. Janet Lynn Royce, Aug. 25, 1968; children: Angela Beth, Jennifer Lorraine. BA, Ind. U., 1968, MD, 1972. Diplomate Am. Bd. Psychiatry and Neurology, subsplty. cert. in addiction psychiatry; diplomate Am. Psychotherapy Assn., Am. Bd. Forensic Med. Examiners, Assn. Convulsive Therapy. Intern Ind. U. Hosps., Indpls., 1972-73, resident, 1972-75; dir. clinics PCI, Inc., Anderson, Beech Grove, Kokomo, Ind., 1975-79; psychiat. cons. Cmty. Addiction Svcs. Agy., Indpls., 1975-80; instr. psychiatry in primary care Family Practice Residency Programs St. Francis Hosp., St. Vincent's Hosp. and Ind. U. Hosps., Indpls., 1975-91; med. dir. Child Guidance Clinic of Marion County, Indpls., 1980-81; chmn. psychiatry dept. St. Francis Hosp., Beech Grove, 1980-82; med. dir. Crisis Intervention Unit Midtown Mental Health Ctr., 1980-90, dir., 1990-96, med. dir., 1996-98; coord. emergency psychiat. svcs. Ind. U. Med. Ctr., Indpls., 1980-90, asst. prof. psychiatry, 1975-94, assoc. prof. psychiatry, 1994—2002, prof. psychiatry, 2002—, coord. psychiat. edn. of med. students, 1989-95, asst. chmn. dept. psychiatry, 1993-96, dir. psychiat. edn., 1995-97, asst. chmn. edn. dept. psychiatry, 1997—, dir. psychiatry residency tng., 1998—, dir. addiction psychiatry residency tng., 1999—; chief psychiatry Wishard Meml. Hosp., 1990-98. Primary psychiat. cons. Ind. Dept. Mental Health and Addiciton, 1988-89; med. dir. Ind. Divsn. Mental Health, 2001—03; supt. Larue D. Carter Meml. Hosp., 2003—; examiner Am. Bd. Psychiatry and Neurology. Contbr. articles to profl. jours. Maj. Ind. N.G., 1972-79. Decorated Army Commendation medal; recipient Residents award for outstanding teaching, 1985, 90, 97, 2003, Roeske Excellence in Teaching award, 1992, Med. Student Psychiatry Clin. Tchg. award, 2000, Eugene E. Levitt svc. award in psychology, 2003, Exemplary Psychiatrist award NAMI, 2004. Fellow Am. Psychiat. Assn. (disting.), Am. Ortho-psychiat. Assn.; mem. AMA (Physicians Recognition award 1978—), Ind. Med. Assn., Indpls. Med. Soc., Ind. Psychiat. Soc. (pres. 1989-90, 97-98), Am. Orthopsychiat. Assn., Am. Acad. Clin. Psychiatry, Univ. Faculty Club Indpls. (v.p. 1999-2000, pres. 2000-01), Athenaeum Turnverein Club, Alpha Phi Omega, Phi Beta Pi, Psi Chi, Alpha Epsilon Delta. Presbyterian. Office: Dept Psychiatry 1111 W 10th St PB-A212 Indianapolis IN 46202-4800 Office Phone: 317-274-1224. E-mail: aschmetz@iupui.edu.

SCHMETZER, FRANCES MYERS, secondary school educator; b. State College, Pa., Sept. 25, 1922; d. Charles Everett Myers and Olive Gilman Spicer; children: Margaret Jane, Charles Roy, Ann Marie. BA, Glenville State Teachers Coll., 1943; MRE, Presbyterian Sch. of Christian Edn., 1944. Tchr. Normantown H.S., Normantown, W.Va., 1943; dir. of Christian edn. St. Anthony Pk. Congl. Ch., St. Paul, 1944—46; assoc. dir. children's work Minn.

Coun. of Churches, St. Paul, 1946—48; dir. of Christian edn. United Ch. of Christ, Ohio, Mass., 1948—52, Calif., 1964—67; substitute tchr. Pub. Sch. Systems, Calif., 1967—69, 1973—78; tchr. John M. Gandy Sch., Ashland, Va., 1970—73; index libr. Readers Digest Assn., Pleasantville, NY, 1978—90; retired, 1990; Elderhostel coord. Glenville State Coll., Glenville, W.Va., 1992—94. Bd. of governors Glenville State Coll., Glenville, W.Va., 2000—. Chmn. historic bridge com. for grants Benedum Found. and Hist. Landmarks, Glenville, W.Va., 1992—98; chmn. country store mus. W. Va. State Folk Festival, Glenville, W.Va., 1992—2003. Recipient Cmty. Svc. award, Glenville State Coll. Alumni Assn., 1997, Best life style columist, Press Assn. Better Newspaper Contest, 2003. Mem.: Gilmer County Hist. Soc. (newsletter editor 2000—), Elderhostel (ambassador (Boston) 1998—), Gilmer County Ret. Sch. Employees (v.p., pres., sec. publicity 1991—2003). Republican. Protestant. Home: 209 High St Glenville WV 26351 Personal E-mail: franschmetzer@hotmail.com.

SCHMID, CHARLES ERNEST, acoustical engineer, administrator; b. Jamaica, N.Y., Oct. 30, 1940; s. Edson Scofield Schmid and Agatha Sofia Zimmermann; m. Linda Dexter, June 18, 1966; children: Andrew, Jenny. BSEE, Cornell U., 1963; MSEE, U. Conn., 1968; PhD, U. Wash., 1977. Systems engr. Gen. Dynamics/Electric Boat, Groton, Conn., 1963-66; fellow Honeywell, Seattle, 1966-90; exec. dir. Acoustical Soc. Am., Woodbury, N.Y., 1990—. With physics vis. com. U. Wash., 1999—. Congl. Sci. Engring. fellow AAAS, Washington, 1985-86. Fellow Acoustical Soc. Am.; mem. Am. Inst. Physics (gov. bd. 1991—, exec. com. 1993-99, 2003—). Achievements include research in simulation and analysis of underwater sound. Office: Acoustical Soc of Am 2 Huntington Quadrangle Melville NY 11747-4501 E-mail: charles@aip.org.

SCHMID, FRANK ANDREAS, economist; b. Hermaringen, Germany, May 11, 1962; came to U.S., 1993; s. Hans Andreas and Margarethe Schmid; m. Irene Evelyn Hinz, July 19, 1985 (div. Nov. 1991). Dipl.-Volkswirt, U. Gottingen, Germany, 1988; Dr.rer.pol., U. Luneburg, Germany, 1991, Dr.habil., 1996. Asst. prof. U. Vienna, 1991-94; lectr. U. Luneburg, Germany, 1996—2002, prof. fin., 2002—; sr. economist Fed. Res. Bank, St. Louis, 1997—. Vis. prof. fin. U. Osnabruck, Germany. 1st lt. German Navy, 1981-83. Rsch. grantee Deutsche Forschungsgemeinschaft, Bonn, Germany, 1995-97; sr. rsch. fellow Fin. Inst. Ctr., U. Pa., Phila., 1995-97; vis. scholar U. Pa., Fin. Dept., 1993-94, postdoctoral scholar Free U., Berlin, Germany, 1994-95. Lutheran. Avocation: distance running. Office: Fed Res Bank 411 Locust St Saint Louis MO 63102 E-mail: mail@frankschmid.com.

SCHMID, HARALD HEINRICH OTTO, biochemistry educator, academic director; b. Graz, Styria, Austria, Dec. 10, 1935; Came to U.S., 1962; s. Engelbert and Annemarie (Kletetschka) S.; m. Patricia Caroline Igou, May 21, 1977. MS, U. Graz, 1957, LLD, 1962, PhD, 1964. Rsch. fellow Hormel inst. U. Minn., Austin, 1962-65, rsch. assoc., 1965-66, asst. prof., 1966-70, assoc. prof., 1970-74, prof., 1974—. Cons. NIH, Bethesda, Md., 1977—; acting dir. Hormel inst. U. Minn., 1985-87, exec. dir., 1987-01; faculty mem. Mayo Med. Sch., Rochester, Minn., 1990—. Mng. editor Chemistry and Physics of Lipids, Elsevier Sci. Publs., Amsterdam, The Netherlands, 1984-01; contbr. numerous articles to profl. jours. Rsch. grantee NIH, 1967—. Mem. AAAS, Am. Soc. Biochemistry and Molecular Biology, Am. Chem. Soc., The Oxygen Soc. Avocations: yacht racing, downhill skiing, classical music. Home: 2701 2nd Ave NW Austin MN 55912-1195 Office: U Minn Hormel Inst 801 16th Ave NE Austin MN 55912-3679

SCHMID, RUDI (RUDOLF SCHMID), internist, educator, academic administrator; b. Switzerland, May 2, 1922; arrived in U.S., 1948, naturalized, 1954; s. Rudolf and Bertha (Schiesser); m. Sonja D. Wild, Sept. 17, 1949. BS, Gymnasium Zurich, 1941; MD, U. Zurich, 1947; PhD, U. Minn., 1954. Intern U. Calif. Med. Ctr., San Francisco, 1948—49; resident medicine U. Minn., 1949—52, instr., 1952—54; rsch. fellow biochemistry Columbia U., 1954—55; investigator NIH, Bethesda, Md., 1955—57; assoc. medicine Harvard Med. Sch., 1957—59; asst. prof. Harvard U., 1959—62; prof. medicine U. Chgo., 1962—66, U. Calif., San Francisco, 1966—91, recall prof. medicine, 1991—2004, prof. emeritus, 2004—, dean Sch. Medicine, 1983—89, assoc. dean internat. rels., 1989—95. Cons. to U.S. Army surgeon gen. NIH; hon. prof. Peking Union Med. Coll., Shanghai Second Med. U., Xian U. of Med. Sci., Jillin U. Medicine. Mem. editl. bd.: Blood, 1962—75, Jour. Clin. Investigation, 1965—70, Gastroenterology, 1965—70, Jour. Investigative Dermatology, 1968—72, Annals Internal Medicine, 1975—79, Procs. Soc. Exptl. Biology and Medicine, 1974—84, Chinese Jour. Clin. Scis., Jour. Lab. Clin. Medicine, 1991—, Hepatology Rsch. (Japan), 1993—, World Jour. Gastroenterology (China), 2002—, cons. editor: Gastroenterology, 1981—86. With Swiss Army, 1943—48. Master: ACP; fellow: Royal Coll. Physicians, N.Y. Acad. Scis., Am. Acad. Arts and Scis.; mem.: NAS, German-Am. Acad. Coun. (exec. com. 1992—99), Leopoldina/German Acad. Sci., Swiss Acad. Med. Scis., Am. Assn. Study Liver Disease (pres. 1965), Am. Gastroenterol. Assn., Am. Soc. Hematology, Am. Soc. Biol. Chemistry and Molecular Biology, Am. Soc. Clin. Investigation, Assn. Am. Physicians (pres. 1986), Internat. Assn. Study Liver (pres. 1980—82), IOM (sr.). Achievements include research in biochemistry, metabolism of hemoglobin, heme, prophyrins, bile pigments, liver and muscle. Home: 211 Woodland Rd Kentfield CA 94904-2631 Personal E-mail: s.d.schmid@worldnet.att.net.

SCHMID, SIGI, professional soccer coach; b. Tuebingen, West Germany, Mar. 20, 1953; came to U.S., 1962; children: Erik, Kurt, Kyle. BS in Econs., UCLA, 1976; MA in Bus. Adminstrn., U. So. Calif. CPA, Calif. Coach UCLA Bruins, 1980-99; head coach L.A. Galaxy, 1999—. Office: L A Galaxy 18400 Avalon Blvd 200 Carson CA 90746-2172

SCHMIDER, MARY ELLEN HEIAN, American studies educator, academic administrator; b. Chippewa Falls, Wis., Apr. 17, 1938; d. A. Bernard and Ellen Dagmar (Gunderson) Heian; m. Michael Heaton Leonard, June 16, 1962 (div. Oct. 1969); 1 child, William Gunerius Leonard; m. Carl Ludwig Schmider, June 17, 1970; 1 child, Dagmar Heian (née Schmider) Meinders. BA in English Lit. magna cum laude, St. Olaf Coll., Northfield, Minn., 1960; MA in English Lit., U. So. Calif., 1962; PhD in Am. Studies, U. Minn., 1983. Mem. founding faculty in English, Calif. Luth. Coll., Thousand Oaks, Calif., 1961-64; instr. dept. English U. Vt., Burlington, Vt., 1964-70; instr. Univ. writing program U. RI, South Kingston, RI, 1973-77; grad. asst. dept. rhetoric U. Minn., Mpls., 1975-76; dir. continuing edn./cmty. svc. Moorhead State U., Minn., 1977-86, dean grad. studies and grad. faculty, 1983-95; US Fulbright lectr. Lanzhou U., China, 1997. Mem. bd. pensions Luth. Ch. in Am., Mpls., 1982—87; mem. bd. higher edn. and schs. Evang. Luth. Ch. in Am., Chgo., 1987—95; cert. coll. mgmt. Carnegie Mellon U., 1987; bd. dirs. Luth. Brotherhood, Mpls., 1988—2001; collegiate full prof. U. Md., U. Coll., Europe, Heidelberg, Germany, 2000—; mem. Am. Speakers Program, Cultural Sect., U.S. Embassy, China, 2004—. Author: (biog. sketches) Biog. Dictionary of Social Welfare, esp. Jane Addams; contbr. Mem. exec. comm. Minn. Humanities Commn., St. Paul, 1983-89, chair, 1987-88. Bush Leadership fellow, 1987. Mem. US Fulbright Assn., Am. Studies Assn., Phi Beta Kappa, Phi Kappa Phi. Lutheran. Avocation: swimming, design, music, internat. travel, family activities. Home: 7701 180th St Chippewa Falls WI 54729-6440 Personal E-mail: mehscls@yahoo.com.

SCHMIDHAUSER, JOHN RICHARD, political science educator; b. N.Y.C., Jan. 3, 1922; s. Richard J. and Gertrude (Grabinger) S.; m. Thelma Lorraine Ficker, June 9, 1952; children: Steven, Paul, Thomas, John C., Martha, Sara, Susan. BA with honors, U. Del., 1949; MA, U. Va., 1952, PhD, 1954. Instr. U. Va., 1952-54; prof. constl. law U. Iowa, 1954-64, prof. polit. sci., 1967-73, U. So. Calif., 1973-92, prof. emeritus, 1993—. Mem. 89th Congress 1st dist. Iowa.; research fellow Research Inst. on Jud. Process, Social Sci. Research Council, 1958; sr. fellow law and behavorial sis. U. Chgo. Law Sch., 1959-60; Talbot vis. prof. govt. U. Va., 1982-83. Author: The Role of Supreme Court as Final Arbiter in Federal-State Relations, 1789-1957, 1958, The Supreme Court; Its Politics, Personalities and Procedures, 1960, Constitutional Law in the Political Process, 1963, (with Berg) The Supreme Court and Congress, 1972, (with Berg and Hahn) American Political Institutions and Corruption, 1976, (with Totten) Whaling in Japan-U.S. Relations, 1978, Judges and Justices, 1979, Constitutional Law in American Politics, 1984, Comparative Judicial Politics, 1987; contbr. chpt. to book; also numerous articles in jours. Chmn. Citizens Action Com. for Fair Representation in Iowa Legislature, 1961; dist. chmn. Operation Support Pres. Kennedy and Johnson, 1961—; chmn. Johnson County Dem. Ctrl. Com., 1961-64; del. Iowa Dem. Convs., 1956, 58, 60, 62; mem. Dem. Nat. Com. Alumni Coun., 1986—; chmn. Santa Barbara, Calif. Dem. Ctrl. Com., 1991-92; mem. exec. com. Los Padres chpt. of the Sierra Club, 1992-96; sec. Santa Barbara Dem. League, 1993-96. With USNR, 1941-45, PTO. Recipient Raubenheimer award U. So. Calif., 1991, Golden Key award for Comparative Rsch, 1991. Mem. Iowa City Mgr. Assn. (bd. reps. 1956-59, chmn. handbook revision 1958), Internat. Polit. Sci. Assn. (chmn. research com. for comparative jud. studies 1980-88), Am. Polit. Sci. Assn., Western Polit. Sci. Assn. (v.p., program chmn. 1980-81, pres.-elect 1981-82), AAUP (sec.-treas. State U. Iowa 1958-59, mem. com. on relationship fed. and state govt. to higher edn., mem. exec. com. U. So. Calif. chpt. 1983-92), Humanities Soc., Raven Soc., Phi Beta Kappa, Phi Kappa Phi. Unitarian (chmn. Iowa City Soc. Men's Club 1960-61). Avocation: French horn. Home: 726 Arbol Verde St Carpinteria CA 93013-2508 *For the young today the opportunity for a good education puts them at the threshold of great opportunities. I encourage them to enjoy that with the same spirit that my generation experienced.*

SCHMIDLI, KEITH WILLIAM, vocational education administrator, educator, researcher; b. Niagara Falls, N.Y., Oct. 11, 1952; s. Duane Irving and Jennie Mary (Schultz) S.; m. Jaquline Barbara Irish, May 27, 1978 (div. Jan. 3, 1982). AA in Liberal Arts and Scis., Niagara County C.C., Sanborn, N.Y., 1972; journeyman cert. auto/diesel mechanics, Trott Vocat. Sch., 1982; BS in Vocat. Tech. Edn. summa cum laude, SUNY, Buffalo, 1992, MS in Edn. summa cum laude, 1993; PhD magna cum laude, U. Buffalo, 1999; MBA, DBA, Cambridge State U., 2000, 01. Cert. tchr., N.Y.; cert. career devel. facilitator; cert. coord. for diversified coop. work-study programs. Maintenance mechanic, operating engr., machinist Gt. Lakes Carbon Corp., Niagara Falls, N.Y., 1973-82; owner, mgr. Apt. Rental Units, Niagara Falls, 1975-88; mechanic Tracy-Luckey Co. Inc., Andalusia, Ala., 1984-85; mechanic, operating engr. Niagara Falls Country Club, Lewiston, N.Y., 1985-86; millwright Custom Maintenance, Buffalo, 1986-87; pipefitter John Martin Plumbing, Niagara Falls, 1987; engring. technician Precious Plate, Niagara Falls, 1987-90; grad. adminstrv. asst. SUNY Coll., Buffalo, 1993-94, asst. prof., 1999—; adminstr. Niagara County C.C., Sanborn, N.Y., 1995-96. Faculty selection com. Dept. Tech. SUNY, Buffalo, 1992-94; tchg./curriculum cons. LaSalle Sr. H.S., Niagara Falls, 1992—; grad. student selection com. U. Buffalo, 1994-95, rsch. symposium com., 1994-95, acad. stds. com., 1995-99. Author: Increasing Enrollment in Secondary Vocational Eduction Programs Through Teacher-Based Promotion, 1993, Career Education: Exploring the Unfinished Agenda of Providing Applied Practical Knowledge and Skills Needed in a Changing Economy, 1999, Career Readiness and Employers' Expectations, 2000; contbr. articles to profl. jours. Vol., donor Red Cross Western N.Y., Buffalo, 1991-95; vol. Am. Heart Assn., Buffalo, 1996, Dept. Comty. Edn./Resource Devel., Niagara Falls, 1992. Mem. ASCD, ASME, Assn. Study of Higher Edn., Coun. Exceptional Children, Am. Soc. Quality, Soc. Mfg. Engrs., Libr. Congress Assoc., Am. Mus. Natural History, Postal Commemorative Soc., Alpha Sigma Lambda (charter pres. 1993-94), Kappa Delta Pi. Avocations: guitar playing, songwriting, camping, hunting, home remodeling. Office: SUNY Coll at Buffalo 109 Bacon Hall Buffalo NY 14222 Home: 5165 Lewiston Rd Lewiston NY 14092-1930 E-mail: schmidkw@buffalostate.edu., schmidkw@juno.com.

SCHMIDLY, DAVID J. university president, biology educator; b. Levelland, Tex., Dec. 20, 1943; m. Janet Elaine Knox, June 2, 1966; children: Katherine Elaine, Brian James. BS in Biology, Tex. Tech U., 1966, MS in Zoology, 1968; PhD in Zoology, U. Ill., 1971. From asst. prof. to prof. dept. wildlife fisheries scis. Tex. A&M U., College Station, 1971-82, prof., 1982-96, head dept. wildlife, 1986-92, CEO, campus dean Galveston, 1992-96; chief curator Tex. Coop. Wildlife Coll., College Station, 1983-86; v.p. Tex. Inst. Oceanography, 1992-96; v.p. rsch. and grad studies, dean grad. sch., tech. transfer Tex. Tech U., Lubbock, 1996—, prof. biol. scis., 1996—, pres., 2000—. Cons. Nat. Park Svc., Wildlife Assocs., Walton and Assocs., Continental Shelf Assn., LGL; lectr. in field; press adv. com. Tex. A&M U., 1983-96; charter mem. Tex. A&M U. Faculty Senate, 1983-85, chmn. Scholarship Com., 1978-82. Author: The Mammals of Trans-Pecos Texas including Big Bend National Park and Guadalupe Mountains National Park, 1977, Texas Mammals East of the Balcones Fault Zone, 1983, The Bats of Texas, 1991, The Mammals of Texas, 1994, Texas Natural History: A Century of Change, 2002; contbr. articles to profl. jours. Trustee Tex. Nature Conservancy, 1991—; mem. adv. bd. Ft. Worth Zoo, 2000. Recipient Dist. Prof. award Assn. Grad. Wildlife and Fisheries Scis., 1985, Donald W. Tinkle Rsch. Excellence award Southwestern Assn. Naturalists, 1988, Diploma Recognition La Universidad Autonoma de Guadalajara, 1989, La Universidad Autonoma de Tamaulipas, 1990. Fellow Tex. Soc. Sci. (bd. dirs. 1979-81); mem. AAAS, Am. Soc. Mammalogists (life, editor Jour. Mammalogy 1975-78), Am. Inst. Biol. Scis. (bd. dirs. 1993—, coun. affiliate socs. 1989—), Am. Naturalist, Soc. Marine Mammalogy (charter mem.), Soc. Systematic Zoology, The Wildlife Soc. Soc. Conservation Biology, Nat. Geog. Sci. Soc., S.W. Assn. Naturalists (life mem., bd. govs. 1980-86, 91—, pres. 1981, trustee 1986—), Tex. Mammal Soc. (pres. 1985-86), Assn. Systematic Collections (bd. dirs.), Chihuahuan Desert Rsch. Inst. (v.p. bd. scientists 1982—, bd. dirs. 1991), Mexican Soc. Mammalogists, Sigma Xi (v.p. 1986-87, pres. 1987-88), Disting. Scientist award 1991), Coun. Pub. Univ. Pres. and Chancellors (exec. com. 2000), Golden Key, Beta Beta Beta, Phi Sigma, Phi Kappa Phi. Home: 4607 9th St Lubbock TX 79416 Office: Tex Tech U PO Box 42005 Lubbock TX 79409-2005 E-mail: david.schmidly@ttu.edu.

SCHMID-SCHOENBEIN, GEERT WILFRIED WILFRIED, biomedical engineer, educator; b. Albstadt, Baden-Wurttemberg, Germany, Jan. 1, 1948; came to U.S., 1971; s. Ernst and Ursula Schmid; m. Renate Schmid-Schoenbein, July 3, 1976; children: Philip, Mark, Peter. Vordiplom, Liebig U., Giessen, Germany, 1971; PhD in Bioengring., U. Calif., San Diego, 1976. Staff assoc. dept. physiology Columbia U., N.Y.C., 1976-77, sr. assoc., 1977-79; asst. prof. dept. applied mechs. & engring. scis. U. Calif., San Diego, 1979-84, assoc. prof., 1984-89, prof., 1989-94, prof. dept. bioengring., 1994—. Editor: Frontiers in Biomechanics, 1986, Physiology and Pathophysiology of Leukocyte Adhesion, 1994, Molecular Basis of Microcirculatory Disorders, 2002; author more than 250 rsch. reports. Recipient Melville medal ASME, 1990, Ratschow medal European Soc. Phlebology, 1999. Fellow Am. Inst. for Med. and Biol. Engring., Am. Heart Assn.; mem. Biomed. Engring. Soc. (pres. 1991-92), Am. Microcirculatory Soc. (pres. 2003—), N.Am. Soc. Biorheology (pres. 1989-99), European Microcirculatory Soc., Am. Physiol. Soc., Am. Mech. Engring. Soc. Achievements include bioengineering research on cardiovascular disease, microcirulation, bioengineering, and lymphology. Office: U Calif San Diego Dept Bioengineering Ailwan Dr 9500 0412 La Jolla CA 92093-0412

SCHMIDT, ARTHUR, film editor; Editor: (films) (with Jim Clark) Marathon Man, 1976, The Last Remake of Beau Geste, 1977, Coal Miner's Daughter, 1980 (Academy award nomination best film editing, 1980), The Escape Artist, 1982, Firstborn, 1984, The Buddy System, 1984, (with Harry Keramidas) Back to the Future, 1985, Fandango, 1985, (with Gib Jaffe) Ruthless People, 1986, Who Framed Roger Rabbit?, 1988 (Academy award best film editing 1988, 1988), (with Keramidas) Back to the Future II, 1989, Back to the Future III, 1990, (with Dov Hoenig) The Last of the Mohicans, 1992, Death Becomes Her, 1992, (with Jim Miller) Addams Family Values, 1993, Forrest Gump, 1994 (Academy award best film editing, 1994), The Birdcage, 1996, (with Hoenig, Mark Stevens, Don Broschu) Chain Reaction, 1996, Contact, 1997, Primary Colors, 1998, What Lies Beneath, 1999, Cast Away, 2000; editor: (with Craig Wood and Steve Tlivkin) Pirates of the Caribbean, 2003. Office: Motion Picture & Video Editors Guild Local 776 7715 W Sunset Blvd Ste 220 Los Angeles CA 90046-3912

SCHMIDT, BARNET MICHAEL, communications and electronic engineer; b. New Milford, N.J., June 30, 1958; s. Frank Lowell and Lee (Fishkin) S. BSEE, BS Computer Sci., Stevens Inst. Tech., 1980, MSEE, 1985, PhD, 2003. Cert. comml. pilot/instrument. Electronic engr. Cessna Aircraft Co., Boonton, N.J., 1980-81; sr. sys. engr. Timeplex Corp., Unisys Co., Woodcliff Lake, N.J., 1981-85; tech. staff, cons. AT&T Bell Labs., Holmdel, N.J., 1985-90; tech. staff Bell Comms. Rsch. (now Telcordia Technologies, Inc.), Piscataway, NJ, 1990—95; tech. staff network transmission sys. lab. Lucent Technologies Bell Labs., Holmdel, N.J., 1995-99; sr. tech. staff data arch. divsn. AT&T Corp. R&D, Middletown, NJ, 1999—2000; mem. tech. staff network ops. sys. engring. lab Lucent Tech., Middletown, 2000—02; project engr., comm. sys. analysis BAE Sys. Inc., Totowa, NJ, 2002—; pres. Schmidt and Assocs., PC, Cons. Comms. Engrs., Oradell, NJ, 1999—. Cons. engr. Computer Scis. Corp., El Segundo, Calif., 1986-90; prin. Schmidt & Assocs., PC Tech. Assocs., LLC Cons. Mem. IEEE (sr.). Achievements include invention of neural-network based intelligent systems for isolating hidden troubles in telecommunications networks; novel adaptive filter synthesis techniques, statistical signal identification methods, multiplanar image correlation, parallel image processing systems; development of optimal SONET network architectures and routing methods; robust fault tolerant optical transmission sys. and network surveillance sys., dense wavelength division multiplexing system developing; performance analysis and tuning of communications networks and operational support systems, wireless network modulation error correcting codes, speed-spectrum optimal modulation and systems engineerin; patents in field of 5 patents in field; development of spread spectrum/secuire wireless system. Office: BAE Sys Inc 18A40 150 Parish Dr Wayne NJ 07474-0975

SCHMIDT, CHAUNCEY EVERETT, banker, director; b. Oxford, Ia., June 7, 1931; s. Walter Frederick and Vilda (Saxton) S.; m. Anne Garrett McWilliams, Mar. 3, 1954; children: Carla, Julia, Chauncey Everett. BS, U.S. Naval Acad., 1953; MBA, Harvard U., 1959. With First Nat. Bank, Chgo., 1959-76, v.p., gen. mgr. br. London, Eng., 1965-68, v.p. for, 1968-69, sr. v.p., 1969-72, exec. v.p., 1972, vice chmn. bd., 1973, pres., 1974-76; chmn. bd., chief exec. officer, dir. Bank of Calif. N.A., San Francisco, 1976—; chmn. bd., pres., chief exec. officer, dir. BanCal Tri-State Corp., 1976—. Dir. Amfac, Inc., Honolulu; mem. Adv. Council Japan-U.S. Econ. Relations; adv. bd. Pacific Rim Bankers Program. Exec. bd. and pres. San Francisco Bay Area council Boy Scouts Am.; council SRI Internat.; bd. dirs. Bay Area Council; bd. govs. San Francisco Symphony; trustee U.S. Naval War Coll. Fedn., Newport, R.I. Served with USAF, 1953-56. Mem. Assn. Res. City Bankers, Am. Bankers Assn., Internat. Monetary Conf., Calif. Bankers Clearing House Assn. (dir.), Calif. Roundtable (dir.), Japan-Calif. Assn. Clubs: Comml. (Chgo.); Bankers (San Francisco), Bohemian (San Francisco). Home: 40 Why Worry Farm Woodside CA 94062-3654 Office: Ste 140 525 Middlefield Rd Menlo Park CA 94025

SCHMIDT, CLAUDE HENRI, retired research administrator; b. Geneva, May 6, 1924; came to U.S., 1935; s. Roger Auguste Schmidt and Lucette (Henriette) Wuhrman; m. Melicent Esther Hane, June 25, 1953; children—Valerie Lynn, Jeffrey Allan AB, Stanford U., 1948, MA, 1950; PhD, Iowa State U., 1956. With Agrl. Rsch. Svc., USDA, 1956-88; rsch. entomologist Orlando, Fla., 1956-62; project leader Fargo, N.D., 1964-67; br. chief Beltsville, Md., 1967-72; area dir. N. Cen. region Fargo, 1972-82; lab. dir., 1982 88; acting dir. Red River Valley Agrl. Rsch. Ctr., 1988; collaborator, 1988-94; with Cass County Vector Control Dist., 1994—2003; ret. Entomologist IAEA, Vienna, Austria, 1962-64; sec. Nat. Mosquito Fish and Wildlife Commn., Washington, 1968-72 Editor Leafy Spurge News, 1994—; contbr. articles to profl. jours. Mem. state legis. com. AARP, N.D., 2000-03; mem. Fargo Sr. Commn., 2001—, chmn., 2003—. With AUS, Signal Corps 1942-46, to 1st lt. Med. Service Corps, 1950-53. Fellow Washington Acad. Sci., AAAS; mem. Am. Mosquito Control Assn. (pres. 1981-82), Am. Chem. Soc., Entomol. Soc. Am., Nat. Assn. Ret. Fed. Employees (pres. N.D. fedn., 1988-89). Lodges: Elks. Republican. Home: 1827 3rd St N Fargo ND 58102-2335

SCHMIDT, CYRIL JAMES, librarian; b. Flint, Mich., June 27, 1939; s. Cyril August and Elizabeth Josephine S.; m. Martha Joe Meadows, May 22, 1965; children: Susan, Emily. BA, Cath. U. Am., 1962; MSLS, Columbia U., 1963; PhD, Fla. State U., 1974. Asst. bus. and industry dept. Flint Pub. Library, 1963-65; reference librarian Gen. Motors Inst., Flint, 1965; asso. librarian S.W. Tex. State U., San Marcos, 1965-67; head undergrad. libraries, asst. prof. Ohio State U., 1967-70; dir. libraries SUNY, Albany, 1972-79; also mem. faculty SUNY (Sch. Library and Info. Sci.); univ. librarian Brown U., Providence, 1979-81; exec. v.p. Rsch. Libraries Group, Stanford, Calif., 1981-89; prin. cons. Schmidt & Assocs., Palo Alto, Calif., 1989—; univ. prof. San Jose (Calif.) State U., 1992—. Author papers in field. Libr. Svcs. Act fellow, 1962-63, Higher Edn. Act fellow, 1970-72 Mem. ALA, ACLU, Pi Sigma Alpha, Beta Phi Mu. Home: 244 Forest Ave Palo Alto CA 94301-2510 Office: San Jose State U 1 Washington Sq San Jose CA 95192-0001 Office Phone: 408-924-2465. Business E-Mail: jim_schmidt@sjsu.edu.

SCHMIDT, DANIEL EDWARD, IV, lawyer, commercial arbitrator; b. NYC, Dec. 17, 1946; s. Daniel Edward III and Mary (Mannion) S.; m. Gail Kennedy, Sept. 5, 1980; children: Kathryn Kennedy, Michael Kennedy. BA, St. Lawrence U., 1971; postgrad., New Sch., 1972; JD, St. John's U., 1975. Bar: N.Y. 1976; cert. arbitrator. From asst. counsel to assoc. gen. counsel Prudential Property & Casualty, Holmdel, N.J., 1975-81, assoc. gen. counsel, divsn. head, 1981-82; v.p., assoc. gen. counsel, asst. sec. Prudential Reins Co., Newark, 1982-84; dir., v.p., gen. counsel, corp. sec. Scor U.S. Group, N.Y.C., 1984-86, dir., sr. v.p., gen. counsel, corp. sec., 1986-89; dir., exec. com., sr. v.p., gen. counsel, corp. sec. Sorema N.A. Group, N.Y.C., 1989-94, dir., exec. com., exec. v.p., group gen. counsel, 1995-99, dir. exec. com., group exec. v.p., chief legal officer, 1999-2000; dep. gen. mgr., gen. counsel, corp. sec. Sorema Internat. Holding, N.V., Netherlands, 1993-96; U.S. counsel Groupama, France, 1996-2000; cons. Sorema NA Group, 2000—03. Pvt. practice comml. arbitrator, umpire, Little Silver, N.J., 1987—; reins. lectr., 1986—; founding dir., 1994-2003; pres., 1999-2002, chmn. 2002-2003, bd. dirs. ARIAS (U.S.), N.Y.C. Assoc. editor Arias-U.S. Quar. Presiding judge Ecclesiastical Trial Ct., 1999—2000, Episcopal Diocese of N.J., 1997—; bd. dirs., exec. com. ARC, Monmouth County, Shrewsbury, NJ, 1981—84. With U.S. Army, 1967—70. Mem. ABA, Am. Arbitration Assn. (panel comml. arbitrators, roster of umpires), N.Y. Bar Assn., Assn. Internat. Droit des Assureurs (U.S. chpt.), Bamm Hollow Country Club, Desert Mountain Club. Episcopalian. Avocations: bicycling, golf, skiing. Home and Office: Dispute Resolution Svcs Internat 628 Little Silver Point Rd Little Silver NJ 07739-1737 Office Phone: 732-741-3646. E-mail: dschmidt4@comcast.net.

SCHMIDT, DEREK, state legislator; b. Independence, Kans., Jan. 23, 1968; m. Jennifer Shaw, May 23, 1998. Student, Independence C.C.; B, Kans. U., 1990; M in Internat. Politics, U. Leicester, Eng., 1992; JD, Georgetown U., 1996. Bar: Kans. 1996, D.C. 1996, U.S. Supreme Ct. 2003. Mem. legis. staff Senator Nancy Kassebaum, 1992—96; gen. counsel, legis. dir. Senator Chuck Hagel, 1996—98; asst. atty. gen. State of Kans., 1999; legis. liaison, spl. counsel to Kans. Gov. Bill Graves, 2000; pvt. practice Scovel, Emert, Heasty & Chubb, Independence, 2000—; mem. Kans. Senate from 15th dist., Topeka, 2001—, chmn. agr. com., chmn., post audit com. Bd. dirs. Independence Industries, Inc. Grad. Leadership Kans., 1999; trustee, ea. Kans. br. Nat. Multiple Sclerosis Soc.; active Am. Coun. Young Polit. Leaders. Ralph Kirchner scholar U. Leicester; fellow Bowhay Inst. for Legis. Leadership Devel.; Henry Toll fellow, 2002. Mem.: Kans. State Hist. Soc., Inc. (bd. dirs.), Rotary. Republican. Office: State Capitol, Rm 143-N Topeka KS 66612

SCHMIDT, DIANE ELLEN, political scientist; b. St. Louis, Dec. 6, 1954; d. Ausby DeWitt Brown and Marjorie Caroline Landie; m. Alan George Schmidt, Sept. 16, 1952; children: Casey Alan, Jonathan Ausby. BA in Polit. Sci., U. of Mo., St. Louis, 1980; M.Econs., U. of Mo., 1982; PhD in Polit. Sci., Washington U., St. Louis, 1988. Cert. in European studies U. of Tilburg, The Netherlands, 1980. Assoc. prof. of polit. sci. Calif. State U., Chico, 1998—; assoc. dir. Survey Rsch. Ctr., Chico, 2000—02; adminstrv. coord. U. of Mo. Stock Market Project, St. Louis, 1981—82. Policy analyst, cons., Chico, 1998—. Author: (book) Writing in Political Science; contbr. book The American Democracy; author: (book) Expository Writing in Political Sciene; contbr. articles to profl. jours. Recipient Honored for Tchg. Excellence, Who's

Who Among America's Teachers, 1994, Thorstein Veblen award for best paper, U. of Mo., St. Louis, 1982; fellow JFK Inst. fellow, U. of Tilberg, The Netherlands, 1982; scholar Sri Lanka scholar, Expt. in Internat. Living, 1980. Mem.: Am. Polit. Sci. Assn., Pi Sigma Alpha, Phi Kappa Phi. Achievements include development of self-test software to accompany expository writing in political science. Avocations: singing, music. Office: California State University Chico Political Science Dept Chico CA 95929-0455 Personal E-mail: dschmidt@csuchico.edu. E-mail: dschmidt@csuchico.edu.

SCHMIDT, DONALD J. councilman, educator; b. Logansport, Ind., Mar. 11, 1937; s. Donald Betcher and Helen Louise Schmidt; m. Pamela Jean Atkins, Jan. 24, 1965; children: Jason Kurt, Justin Kraig. BS in Mech. Engring., Purdue U., Lafayette, Ind., 1960, MS in Edn., 1961. Asst. plant engr. Rea Magnet Wire, Lafayette, Ind., 1960; math tchr. N. Ctrl. H.S., Indpls., 1961—62; admissions counselor Western Mich. U., Kalamazoo, 1962—64; asst. prof., mech. engring. Purdue U., Fort Wayne, Ind., 1964—; councilman City of Fort Wayne, Ind., 1971—, pres., council, 1991, 1995, 1996, 2000, 2001, 2002. Arbitrator Better Bus. Bur., Fort Wayne, Ind., 1987—; bd. dirs. Allen County Solid Waste Dist., Fort Wayne, Ind., 1996—, Materials Processing Inc., Logansport, Ind., 1997—. Recipient Local Elected Offical Award, Ind. Pub. Health Assn., 1999. Mem.: Shrine, Scottish Rite, Mason. Republican. Avocations: golf, tennis, sailing. Home: 2110 Forest Park Fort Wayne IN 46805 Office: Purdue Univ 2101 Coliseum Blvd Fort Wayne IN 46805 E-mail: donjschmidt@comcast.net.

SCHMIDT, EDWARD CRAIG, lawyer; b. Pitts., Nov. 26, 1947; s. Harold Robert and Bernice (Williams) Schmidt; m. Elizabeth Lowry Rial, Aug. 18, 1973; children: Harodl Robert II, Robert Rial. BA, U. Mich., 1969; JD, U. Pitts., 1972. Bar: Pa. 1972, U.S. Dist. Ct. (we. dist.) Pa. 1972, U.S. Ct. Appeals (3d cir.) 1972, U.S. Ct. Appeals (DC cir.) 1975, U.S. Supreme Ct. 1981, U.S. Ct. Appeals (9th and 4th cirs.) 1982, U.S. Ct. Appeals (6th cir.) 1987, U.S. Ct. Appeals (2d cir.) 1992. Assoc. Rose, Schmidt, Hasley & Di Salle, Pitts., 1972-77, ptnr., 1977-90, Jones, Day, Reavis & Pogue, Pitts., 1990—2001, Thompson Coburn LLP, Washington, 2002—. Mem. adv. com. Superior Ct. Pa., 1978—80; NITA instr. Duquesne U., 1998—99. Asst. editor: Antitrust Discovery Handbook, 1980; co-editor: Antitrust Discovery Handbook-Supplement, 1982; contbr. articles to profl. jours. Bd. dirs. Urban League, Pitts., 1974—77. Mem.: Acad. Trial Lawyers Allegheny County (bd. govs. 1980), Internat. Acad. Trial Lawyers, Allegheny County Bar Assn. (mem. pub. rels. com. coun. civil litig. sect. 1977—80), DC Bar Assn., Pa. Bar Assn., Supreme Ct. Hist. Soc., Western Res. Acad. Alumni Assn. (trustee 1998—2000), Country Club Woodmore (Md.), Longue Vue Club (Pitts.), Duquesne Club (Pitts.), Rolling Rock Club (Lignonier, Pa.). Republican. Office: Thompson Coburn LLP 6th Fl 1909 K St NW Washington DC 20006-1167 Home: 110 Duke St Alexandria VA 22314 Office Phone: 202-585-6902. E-mail: eschmidt@thompsoncoburn.com.

SCHMIDT, ERIC EMERSON, information technology executive; b. Washington, Apr. 27, 1955; BSEE, Princeton U., 1976; MS in Engring., U. Calif., Berkeley, 1979, PhD in Computer Sci., 1982. Research intern Xerox Parc, Palo Alto, Calif., 1979-80, mem. research staff, 1980-83; software mgr. Sun Microsystems, Mountain View, Calif., 1983-84, software dir., 1984-85, v.p., gen. mgr. software products div., 1985-88; v.p. gen. systems group Sun Microsys., Mountain View, Calif., 1988-91; pres. Sun Tech. Enterprises, Inc., Mountain View, 1991-94; chief tech. officer Sun Microsys., Mountain View, 1994—97; chmn. & CEO Novell, Inc., Provo, Utah, 1997—2001; chmn., CEO Google, Inc., Mountain View, Calif., 2001—. Patentee in field. Mem. IEEE, Assn. Computing Machinery, Sigma Xi. Office: Google Inc 1600 Amphitheatre Pkwy 41 Mountain View CA 94043-1351*

SCHMIDT, FRANK BROAKER, executive recruiter; b. Shamokin, Pa., Aug. 8, 1939; s. Frank Wilhelm and Doris (Maurer) S.; children by previous marrage: Susan E., Tracie A.; m. Elizabeth Mallen, Mar. 18, 1989; children: Alexandra M., Frank W.M., Drake M. BS, U. Pa., 1962; MBA, Case Western Res. U., 1969; cert. brewmaster, Siebel Inst. Brewing Tech., Chgo., 1964. With Carling Brewing Co., Cleve., 1964-69, mgr. sales and advt. div., brand mgr., 1969-70; advt. and merchandising mgr. The Pepsi-Cola Co., Purchase, N.Y., 1970-73, dir. mktg. programs, then dir. mgmt. devel., 1973-74; dir. sales and mktg. The Olga Co., Van Nuys, Calif., 1974-75; mng. dir. Stanton Chase Internat., 1995—2001; pres. F.B. Schmidt, Internat., L.A., 1975—95, 2001—. Chmn. Mediterranean Properties, 1994—. Author: Draft Beer Manual, 1967, Assn. Nat. Advertisers Computerized Media System, 1970. Chmn. Morrison Ranch Estates Homeowners Assn., 1993-96. Mem. Calif. Exec. Recruiters Assn., Wharton Alumni Assn., Personnel Cons. Am. (region chmn. 1981-83, chmn. 92-95), Am. Mktg. Assn. Republican. Avocations: sports cars, flying, marathon bicycling, racing. Office: FB Schmidt Internat 5737 Kanan Rd Agoura Hills CA 91301-1601

SCHMIDT, GEORGE, physicist, educator; b. Budapest, Hungary, Aug. 1, 1926; s. Laszlo Schmidt and Katalin Wellisch; m. Katalin Varkonyi, June 26, 1955; children: Franklin R., Ronald W. Diploma in Elec. Engring., Tech. U., Budapest, 1950; PhD in Physics, Hungarian Acad. Scis., Budapest, 1956; M in Engring., Stevens Inst. Tech., 1961. Sr. lectr. Israel Inst. Tech., Haifa, Israel, 1957-58; asst. prof. Stevens Inst. Tech., Hoboken, N.J., 1959-61, assoc. prof., 1961-63, prof. physics, 1963-83, George Meade Bond prof. physics and engring. physics, 1983-92, prof. emeritus, 1992—. Vis. prof. U. Wis., 1965, UCLA, 1972-73; vis. scientist Culham Labs., Culham, Eng., 1965, Ecole Polytechnique, Paris, 1979-80; cons. Sci. Applications Inc., Washington, 1981—, Poly. U. of N.Y., 1984—, Berkeley Assocs., Washington, 1985. Author: Physics of High Temperature Plasmas, 1966, 2nd rev. edit., 1979; contbr. sci. articles to profl. jours. Recipient Research award Stevens Inst. Tech., 1961. Fellow Am. Phys. Soc.; mem. N.Y. Acad. Scis. Office: Stevens Inst of Tech Dept Of Physics Hoboken NJ 07030 E-mail: gschmidt@stevens.edu.

SCHMIDT, GLENN NORBERT, special education educator; b. LaCrosse, Wis., Sept. 19, 1949; s. Norbert John and Arlene Louise Schmidt; m. Kristine Kay Hoover, Jan. 15, 1972; 1 child, John Charles. BA, U. Wis., Madison, 1971; MS in Edn., U. Wis., LaCrosse, 1976. Tchr. LaCrosse Home for Children, 1974—77; spl. edn. tchr. Sun Prairie (Wis.) Pub. Schs., 1977—. Mem. adv. panel on spl. edn. State Supt. of Schs., Madison, Wis., 1998—2001; Dem. Nat. Conv. L.A., 2000. Grantee Fulbright Meml. Fund, Japan, 1998. Mem.: NEA (alt. dir., Washington 2001—, del. Edn. Internat. Gen. Assembly, Costa Rica, Stockholm and Washingto 1989—98), Wis. Edn. Assn. Coun. (bd. dirs. 1995—), Sun Prairie Edn. Assn. (pres. 1990—). Democrat. Avocations: golf, travel, writing for periodicals. Home: 227 North St Sun Prairie WI 53590 Office: Sun Prairie Pub Schs 230 W Klubertanz Dr Sun Prairie WI 53590

SCHMIDT, GORDON PEIRCE, artistic director; Former dancer; resident choreographer Ballet Chgo., 1990-95; artistic dir. Grand Rapids (Mich.) Ballet, 1999—. Office: Grand Rapids Ballet Co 341 Ellsworth Ave Grand Rapids MI 49503-4045

SCHMIDT, HARVEY MARTIN, economic forecaster, educator, financial consultant; b. Sept. 15, 1925; s. Joseph David and Dorothy Schmidt; m. Barbara Bebe Bloom, Nov. 25, 1961; children: Ellen Louise, Jay Stephen, Gregg Arthur. Student, U. So. Calif., 1943; BA magna cum laude, Woodbury U., 1947. Assoc. prof. bus. Woodbury U., 1947—48; pvt. practice acctg. L.A., 1948—80; cons. mgmt., taxes and fins., 1965—82; econ. forecaster, internat. lectr., investment lectr. on audiotapes, 1989—. Investment lectr. on internat. cruise ships, 1992; fin. cons., Pacific Palisades, 1982—; pres. Harvey Schmidt Mgmt. Inc., 1983—, Med-Plan Operators, 1969—89, Kit Travel, 1987—. Contbr. articles to profl. jours. With USCG, 1943—44. Master: U.S. Contact Bridge League (life); mem.: Internat. Platform Assn., Bruin Athletic Club of UCLA, Exch. Club (pres. local chpt. 1953—56).

SCHMIDT, HERMAN J. former oil company executive; b. Davenport, Iowa, Feb. 26, 1917; s. Herman and Lillian (Beard) S.; m. Eileen Carpenter, Dec. 20, 1967; children: Paul David, Sarah Louise. AB, U. Iowa, 1938; JD, Harvard U., 1941. Bar: N.Y. 1943. With Cravath, Swaine & Moore, 1941-44, 47-51; tax counsel Socony Mobil Oil Co. Inc. (now Mobil Corp.), N.Y.C., 1951-55, adminstrv. asst. to gen. counsel, 1955, assoc. gen. counsel, 1955-56, gen. counsel, 1956-59, exec. v.p., 1959-74, vice chmn., 1974-78, dir., 1957-78; pres. Mobil Internat. Oil Co., 1959-63. Former chmn. bd. trustees Am. Enterprise Inst.; hon. life trustee U. Iowa Found. Served to 1st lt. M.I. Corps, AUS, 1944-47. Mem. Harvard Law Rev. Assn., Blind Brook Club (Ryebrook, N.Y.), Phi Beta Kappa, Phi Gamma Delta. Home: 15 Oakley Ln Greenwich CT 06830-3025

SCHMIDT, JAMES CRAIG, retired bank executive, savings and loan association executive; b. Peoria, Ill., Sept. 27, 1927; s. Walter Henry and Clara (Wolfenbarger) S.; m. Jerrie Louise Bond, Dec. 6, 1958; children: Julie, Sandra, Suzanne. Student, Ill. Wesleyan U., 1945, 48-50, Ph.B. in Bus. Adminstrn, 1952; postgrad., U. Ill. Coll. Law, 1950-52; JD, DePaul U., 1953. Spl. agt. Fidelity & Deposit Co., Chgo., 1956-58; with Home Fed. Savs. & Loan Assn., San Diego, 1958-67; asst. sec. bus. and transp. State of Calif., 1967-69; vice-chmn., pres. Gt. Am. Bank, San Diego, 1969-88. Pres. Conf. Fed. Savs. and Loans of Calif., 1974-75; mem. Calif. Toll Bridge Authority, 1969-74; mem. Calif. State Transp. Bd., 1972-78; past chmn. San Diego Bd. Commn. Task Force. Pres. San Diego Holiday Bowl Football Game, 1986; bd. dirs. San Diego Internat. Sports Coun., San Diego Hwy. Devel. Assn.; pub. mem. San Diego County Sunset Adv. Bd.; mem. City-County Re-Investment Task Force; mem. Valle De Oro Planing Group. Mem. Calif. Bar Assn., Ill. Bar Assn., Calif. League Savs. Instns. (chmn. 1986-87), Calif. C. of C. (bd. dirs. 1987-90), U.S. Savs. Instn. League (exec. com. 1983-86), San Diego East County C. of C. (bd. dirs. 1993), Catfish Club, Sigma Chi, Phi Delta Phi. Office: 8383 Center Dr Ste J La Mesa CA 91942-2913

SCHMIDT, JEAN, state representative; b. Cin., Nov. 29, 1951; married; 1 child. BS in Polit. Sci., BA in Social Studies-Secondary Edn., U. Cin. State rep. dist. 66 Ohio Ho. of Reps., Columbus, vice chair, human svcs. subcom., mem. banking pensions and securities, fin. and appropriations, human svcs. and aging, and pub. utilities coms. Chair, founder Sauls Found. 5K Race; mem. exec. com., econ. devel. com., 2001 com. Clermont County Ctrl. Com., Ohio; bd. trustees Clermont County Libr.; bd. dirs. Clermont County Mercy Hosp. Mem.: Milford-Miami Twp. Coalition on Aging, Coalition of Large Ohio Urban Twps., Clermont County and Southwest Twp. Assns., Clermont County Agrl. Soc., Ohio Twp. Assn., Clermont County LWV, Clermont County and Milford Miami Twp. Cs. of C., Leukemia Soc. Team in Tng., Clermont Northwest Rotery, Clermont and Hamilton Counties Rep. Clubs. Republican. Office: 77 S High St 11th fl Columbus OH 43215-6111

SCHMIDT, JOANNE (JOSEPHINE ANNE SCHMIDT), language educator; b. N.Y.C., June 7, 1950; d. Joseph William and Maria Esther (Morazzani) S. BA, Chestnut Hill Coll., Phila., 1972; MA, U. Va., 1974, PhD, 1980. Tchg. asst. U. Va., Charlottesville, 1973-76, Lycée Marie Curie, Sceaux, France, 1976-77; lectr. U. Va., Charlottesville, 1977-79; asst. prof. Cedar Crest Coll., Allentown, Pa., 1981-84, Calif. State U., Bakersfield, 1984-88, assoc. prof., 1988-94, prof., 1994—, chair dept., 1998—. Freelance translator, Bklyn., 1979-81, Allentown, Pa., 1981-84, Bakersfield, Calif., 1984—. Author: (book) If There Are No More Heroes There Are Heroines: A Feminist Critique of Corneille's Heroines, 1987, (jour.) San Jose Studies, 1987, (poetry book) (author as Teresita Bosch) Portraits, 1991; assoc. editor: (jour.) Coll. Tchg., 1985-89. V.p. Women, Inc., Allentown, 1983-84; pub. spkr. Alliance Against Family Violence, Bakersfield, Calif., 1985-90. Fulbright Hays grantee Fed. Govt., 1976-77, Affirmative Action grantee Calif. State U., 1985, 87, 91. Mem. MLA, NOW, Am. Assn. Tchrs. of French, Nat. Women's Studies Assn., Calif. Lang. Tchrs. Assn., Delta Kappa Gamma. Democrat. Avocations: carpentry, golf, creative writing, family history, oral history. Office: Calif State U Modern Langs & Lit Dept 9001 Stockdale Hwy Bakersfield CA 93311-1022

SCHMIDT, JOHN CHARLES, music educator; b. Kenedy, Tex., Feb. 19, 1941; s. Bruno Carl and Frances Mae (Schuessler) Schmidt; m. Jacqueline Sue Yetter, June 16, 1973. PhD in Musicology, NYU, N.Y.C., 1978; M. Sacred Music, Union Theol. Sem., N.Y.C., 1963; MusB, Southwestern U., Georgetown, TX, 1961. Instr. NYU, Bronx, 1969—73; prof. Tex. State U., San Marcos, 1976—; organist Covenant Presbyn. Ch., Austin, 1998—. Author: The Life and Works of John Knowles Paine; editor: (scholarly edition) John Knowles Paine Complete Piano Music, John Knowles Paine: Three Chamber Works for Piano and Strings, John Knowles Paine: Vocal Chamber Music, John Knowles Paine: The Nativity, Op. 39; contbr. articles to profl. jours. Fellow: Am. Guild Organists (S. Lewis Elmer award 2002); mem.: Am. Musicological Soc., Soc. for Am. Music, Coll. Music Soc. (life), Phi Mu Alpha (chpt. faculty advisor 1991—2002, Orpheus Award 1995), Kappa Sigma Frat. Presbyterian. Home: P O Box 1373 San Marcos TX 78667-1373 Office: Tex State Univ Sch Music 601 University Dr San Marcos TX 78666-4616 Personal E-mail: js26@txstate.edu. E-mail: js26@txstate.edu.

SCHMIDT, JOHN FREDERICK, III, government agency administrator, consultant; b. Natchez, Miss., May 13, 1949; s. John Frederick Schmidt, Jr. and Dorothy Eugenia Schmidt Swann; m. Joyce Evelyn Jones, Feb. 14, 1992 (div. Nov. 1994); 1 child, Nickolas Andrew. BS in Fin., La. State U., 1971. Mgmt. trainee La. Nat. Bank, Baton Rouge, 1971—72; prof. golfer Natchez, 1972—74; golf course mgr. Bayou Bend Country Club, Sumner, Miss., 1974—77; sales rep. Healthco, Miss., Jackson, 1977—78; grant mgr. North Delta Planning, Clarksdale, Miss., 1978—81; exec. dir. North Delta Regional Housing Authority, Clarksdale, Miss., 1981—. Bd. mem. Delta Workforce Investment Bd., Clarksdale, Miss., 2000—, vile chmn. Mem.: Pi Tau Pi, Phi Kappa Phi. Episcopal. Avocations: golf, reading, hunting. Office: North Delta Regional Housting Auth PO Box 1148 # 4 E Second St Clarksdale MS 38614 Office Phone: 662-627-9627. E-mail: 1ndrha@clarksdale.com.

SCHMIDT, JOHN RICHARD, agricultural economics educator; b. Madison, Wis., July 3, 1929; s. Oscar John and Alma Theodora (Ula) S.; m. Rosemary Pigorsch, Oct. 7, 1951; children: Janet, Deborah, Allen. BS, U. Wis., 1951, MS, 1953; PhD, U. Minn., 1960. Asst. prof. agr. econs. U. Wis., Madison, 1956-61, assoc. prof., 1961-65, prof., 1965-95, prof. emeritus, 1995—, chmn. dept., 1966-70; mng. dir. North Ctrl. Computer Inst., 1963—85; owner, mgr. JRS Computing Svcs., Madison, 1995—. Farm mgmt. cons. Am. Farm Bur. Fedn., Chgo., 1962; cons. Banco de Mexico, 1972-84, IBRD (World Bank), 1973-94, Agrl. Devel. Bank Iran, 1974-76; adv. bd. Internat. Devel. Inst., 1983; faculty Salzburg Seminar, 1983, 85. Contbr. articles to tech. jours., also monographs, bulls. Bd. dirs. U. Wis. Credit Union, 1968-77, pres., 1969-75; mem. com. Wis.-Upper Mich. Synod Sem., 1972-75, ch. coun. 1967-69, 72-75, pres. 1974-75. Mem. Rotary (pres. Madison West 1994-95), Delta Theta Sigma (nat. sec. 1962-64), Gamma Sigma Delta (pres. Wis. chpt. 1975). Lutheran. Home: 106 Frigate Dr Madison WI 53705-4426 Office: JRS Computing Svcs 6601 Grand Teton Plz Ste 4 Madison WI 53719-1049 E-mail: jrschmi1@facstaff.wisc.edu.

SCHMIDT, JOSEPH DAVID, urologist; b. Chgo., July 29, 1937; s. Louis and Marian (Fleigel) S.; m. Andrea Maxine Herman, Oct. 28, 1962. BS in Medicine, U. Ill., 1959, MD, 1961. Diplomate Am. Bd. Urology. Rotating intern Presbyn. St. Luke's Hosp., Chgo., 1961-62, resident in surgery, 1962-63; resident in urology The Johns Hopkins Hosp., Balt., 1963-67; faculty U. Iowa Coll. Medicine, Iowa City, 1969-76, U. Calif., San Diego, 1976—, prof., head divsn. urology, 1976—, vice-chmn. dept. surgery, 1985-97. Cons. U.S. Dept. Navy, San Diego, 1976—; attending urologist Vets. Affairs Dept., San Diego, 1976—; assoc. dir. for clin. rsch. U. Calif. San Diego Cancer Ctr., 1997-98. Author, editor: Gynecological and Obstetric Urology, 1978, 82, 93. Capt. USAF, 1967-69. Recipient Francis Senear award U. Ill., 1961. Fellow ACS; mem. AMA, Am. Urol. Assn. Inc., Alpha Omega Alpha. Avocations: collecting antique medical books, manuscripts. Office: U Calif Med Ctr Divsn Urology 200 W Arbor Dr San Diego CA 92103-8897 Office Phone: 619-543-5904. Office Fax: 619-543-6573. Business E-Mail: planeige@ucsd.edu.

SCHMIDT, JULIUS, sculptor; b. Stamford, Conn., June 2, 1923; s. Louis Frank and Susie (Koment) S.; m. Carolyn Marsha Wolf (div.); children: Ania J., Ianos; m. Mary Katherine Powers, 1981 (div.); 1 child, Araan J. Student, Okla. A&M U., 1950-51; BFA, Cranbrook Acad. Art, 1952, MFA, 1955; student, Ossip Zadkine, Paris, 1953, Accademia di Belle Arti, Florence, Italy, 1954. Chmn. sculpture dept. Kansas City Art Inst., 1954-59, R.I. Sch. Design, 1959-60, U. Calif.-Berkeley, 1961-62, Cranbrook Acad. Art, 1962-70, U. Iowa, Iowa City, 1970-93; ret., 1993. Exhibited in 40 one-man shows 1953—; group shows include Allen Meml. Art Mus., Oberlin, Ohio, 1958, Arts Club of Chgo., Mus. Modern Art, N.Y.C., 1960, Whitney Mus., 1960-63, Gallerie Claude Bernard, paris, 1960, Guggenheum Mus., 1962, San Francisco Mus. Art, 1962, Phila. Art Alliance, 1963, Battersea Park, London, 1963, Sai Paolo Bienal, Brazil, 1963, White House Festival of Arts, Washington, 1965, Bienale Middleheim, Belgium, 1971; represented in permanent collections Nelson Gallery-Atkins Mus., Kansas City, Mo., Art Inst., Chgo., Mus. Modern Art, N.Y.C., Mus. U. Nebr., Whitney Mus. Art, N.Y.C., Krannert Art Mus., Urbana, Ill., Washington, U., Walker Art Center, Mpls., Albright-Knox Mus., Buffalo, Detroit Inst. Art, U. Calif. Art Mus., Cranbrook Acad. Art, Mich., Princeton Mus. Art, Hirschhorn Mus., Washington, Numerous others. Served with USNR, World War II. Decorated Air medal (2); recipient Lifetime Achievement award in sculpture edn. Internat. Sculpture Ctr., 1998; Guggenheim fellow, 1963-64. Address: 5 Highview Knl NE Iowa City IA 52240-9149 E-mail: jfeschmidt@earthlink.net.

SCHMIDT, KAREN LEE, marketing professional, sales executive; b. Milw., Oct. 14, 1953; d. Walter K. and Marilyn V. Schmidt. BSBA, Colo. State U., 1975; postgrad., U. Louisville, 1978-79. Fin. analyst FICB of Louisville, 1975-79; sales rep. STSC, Inc., Chgo., 1979-81; regional software sales mgr. Xerox, Chgo., 1981-85; cen. region mgr. Datext, Inc., Chgo., 1985-87; regional mgr. Systems Software Assocs., Chgo., 1987-88; dir. bus. devel. Andersen Cons., Chgo., 1988-94; nat. dir. mktg. fin. svcs. KPMG, Chgo., 1994-95; chief mktg. officer Quantra Corp., Chgo., 1995-97; ptnr. in charge mktg. and sales BDO Seidman, Chgo., 1997—2000; exec. v.p. markets Land America, Richmond, Va., 2001—. Bd. trustees Theatre Va., 2002—. Home: 358 Maple St Glen Ellyn IL 60137-3812

SCHMIDT, KARL A. lawyer; b. Stockton, Calif., Sept. 18, 1947; BS, U. Calif., Berkeley, 1969, JD, 1974. Bar: Calif. 1974. Mem. Parker, Milliken, Clark, O'Hara & Samuelian, L.A. Contbr. Retaliation Matters. to L.A. Daily Jour. Ann. Employment Update, 1997, USC TAx Inst. 2003: Exec. Terminations. Mem. ABA. Office: Parker Milliken Clark O Hara & Samuelian 333 S Hope St Ste 2700 Los Angeles CA 90071-1449

SCHMIDT, KARL M., JR., political science educator; b. Utica, N.Y., Mar. 19, 1917; s. Karl Marx and Jennie Christina (Greenia) S.; m. Josephine Ruth Leighton Smith, Mar. 7, 1934 (div. Dec. 1942); 1 child, Karl Michael; m. Mary Erma Murphy, Apr. 3, 1943; children: Jill Sheryl Fowler, Glen Mark. AB, Colgate U., Hamilton, N.Y., 1948; MA, Johns Hopkins U., Balt., 1950, PhD, 1951. Asst. prof. govt. and econs. Union Coll., Schenectady, 1951-57; vis. prof. polit. sci. U. Hawaii, Honolulu, 1964-65; assoc. prof. polit. sci. Syracuse (N.Y.) U., 1957-70, prof. polit. sci. and pub. adminstrn., 1971-85, prof. emeritus, 1985—. Sr. resident adviser Pakistan Adminstrv. Staff Coll., Lahore, Pakistan, 1960-62, 67; rsch. cons. N.Y. State Dept. Audit and Control, Albany, 1956-57. Author: Henry A. Wallace: Quixotic Crusade, 1948, 1960; editor: American National Government in Action, 1965, Am. State and Local Government in Action, 1966, American Government in Action: National State and Local, 1967. Pres. Camillus (N.Y.) Dem. Club, 1964, 66; Co-chmn. Onon County McGovern for Pres., Syracuse, 1972, Profs. and Physicians for Humphrey, Syracuse, 1968; chmn. Town Planning Bd., Clayton, N.Y., 1988-90. With USCG, 1942-46. Mem. AAUP, Am. Polit. Sci. Assn., Am. Soc. Pub. Adminstrn., N.Y. State Polit. Sci. Assn., Sigma Nu. Democrat. Unitarian Universalist. Avocations: boating, apple-growing, grape-growing. Home: 16643 Rainbow Shores Dr Clayton NY 13624-2153

SCHMIDT, KLAUS DIETER, management consultant, university administrator, marketing and management educator; b. Eisenach, Germany, May 8, 1930; came to U.S., 1949, naturalized, 1952; s. Kurt Heinrich and Louise (Kruger) S.; m. Lynda Hollister Wheelwright, June 29, 1950; children: Karen, Claudia. BA in Econs., U. Calif., Berkeley, 1951; MBA, Stanford U., 1953; PhD in Bus. Adminstrn., Golden Gate U., 1978. Buyer, jr. mdse. mgr. Broadway Hale, 1952-54; sales mgr. Ames Harris Neville Co., 1954-56, ops. mgr., 1956-57; gen. mgr. Boise Cascade Corp., 1957-60; pres., chmn. bd. Kimball-Schmidt Inc., San Rafael, Calif., 1960-73, chmn. subs. Kalwall Pacific, 1962-67, chmn. subs. AFGOA Corp., 1966-69; asst. prof. mgmt. and mktg. San Francisco State U., 1970-75, assoc. prof. mgmt., 1975-80, prof. mgmt. and mktg., 1989-85, chmn. dept., 1979-85, prof. emeritus, 1989—, assoc. dean emeritus Sch. Bus., 1985-88; chmn. Schmidt Cons. Group, Brooklin, Maine, 1988—. Dir. Ctr. for World Bus., 1976-88, dir. U.S.-Japan Inst., 1981-88, editor-in-chief Sch. Bus. Jours., 1980-88; U.S. negotiator for Pres. Carter White House on Afghanistan issue, 1980-88; mem. Dept. Commerce Dist. Export Council, 1982-88; rsch. cons. SRI Internat. Author: (20 booklet series) Doing Business In ..., Stanford Rsch. Inst., 1978-80, A Spy For Life, 2004. Mem. Univ. Club (San Francisco), Alpha Delta Phi, Beta Gamma Sigma. Republican. Office: PO Box 269 Brooklin ME 04616-0269

SCHMIDT, KLAUS FRANZ, advertising executive; b. Dessau, Germany, May 25, 1928; came to U.S., 1951; naturalized, 1957; s. Franz and Elfriede (Klamroth) S.; m. Gisela Garbrecht, June 19, 1954; children: Dagmar Schmidt Etkin, Ena Schmidt Reynen. Student, Coll. of Journalism, Aachen, Germany, 1947-48, Sch. of Design and Printing, Bochum, Germany, 1948-50; BA, Wayne State U., 1956. Printer, compositor, 1948-56; type dir. Mogul Williams & Saylor, N.Y.C., 1956-59, Doyle, Dane, Bernbach, N.Y.C., 1959-61, Young & Rubicam, N.Y.C., 1961-68, v.p., dir. print ops., 1968-75, v.p., dir. creative support, 1975-85, sr. v.p., mgr. prodn. svcs., 1985-91; advt./graphic arts cons., 1991—. Co-organizer Vision Congress Internat. Ctr. for Communications Arts & Scis., N.Y.C., 1965, 67, 69, 77; chmn., bd. trustees Internat. Ctr. Typographic Arts, N.Y.C. 1969-70. Author: Signs of the Times, 1997; Am. editor Der Druckspiegel, 1957-64; contbg. editor Print Mag., 1968-01, The Dunn Report, 1991-95. Recipient Typomundus award, 1964, Internat. Book Exhbn. award, Leipzig, Germany, 1965. Mem. Print Advt. Assn. (chmn. N.Y. chpt. 1969-71, nat. sr. v.p. 1971-75), Am. Assn. Advt. Agys. (chmn. subcom. on phototypography 1969-75), Digital Distbn. of Advt. to Publ. Assn. (vice chmn. 1991-95), N.Y. Type Dirs. Club (pres. 1984-86, awards 1962, 64-66, 68, 69), N.Y. Art Dirs. Club (v.p. 1984-86), Advt. Prodn. Club (pres. 1982-84), Gravure Advt. Coun. (chmn. 1970-72). Home and Office: 549 Munroe Ave Sleepy Hollow NY 10591-1333

SCHMIDT, LEWIS A. retired music educator; b. Ridgeway, Pa., June 7, 1936; s. Clarence Leroy and Mary Caroline Schmidt; m. Geraldine Ann Matzinger, June 7, 1958; children: Lynn Ann, Laurie Jean, Scott Alan. BA in Music Edn., Lakeland Coll., Sheboygan, Wis., 1958; MusM Edn., Vandercook Coll. of Music, Chgo., 1963, Dr. of Musical Arts (hon.), 1992. Cert. tchng. Wis. Music tchr. Weston Schools, Cazenovia, Wis., 1958—59, Spring Green Schools, Wis., 1959—62; dept. chair, HS band dir. River Valley Sch. Dist., Spring Green, 1962—82; prof. music, condr. of bands Lakeland Coll., 1982—98. Cons. and adjudicator Wis. Sch. Musical Assn., Madison, 1970—. Cmty. band rep., bd. dirs. Nat. Band Assn., 1984—98; bd. dirs. Lions,Int., Spring Green, 1965—88. Recipient Outstanding Bandmaster Award, Phi Beta Mu, Citation of Excellence, Nat. Band Assn., Disting. Svc. Award, Wis. Music Edn. Assn., Sudler Scroll Award, Diploma of the Order of Merit, Historical Roll of Honor, John Philip Sousa Found. Mem.: Assn. of Concert Bands, Coll. Band Dir. Nat. Assn., Nat. Band Assn., Wis. Bandmasters Assn., Wis. Music Educators Assn., Music Educators Nat. Conf., Phi Beta Mu. Protestant. Achievements include serving as condr. of the Kiel Municipal Band, Wis; holding a place on the Ted Lins Wall of Fame for Disting. Svc. to the Cmty. (Spring Green, Wis.) and the River Valley Sch. Dist. Avocations: golf, fishing, reading. Home: N8371 Rhine Road Elkhart Lake WI 53020 Personal E-mail: laschmidt@excel.net.

SCHMIDT, LYNDA WHEELWRIGHT, psychotherapist; b. Beijing, July 29, 1931; came to the U.S., 1931; d. Joseph Balch and Jane Byers (Hollister) Wheelwright; m. Klaus Dieter, May 8, 1930; children: Karen Calley, Claudia Lewis. BA, U. Calif., Berkeley, 1965, MSW, 1968. Cert. Jungian analyst; bd. cert. diplomate Am. Bd. Examiners Clin. Social Work. Staff psychiat. social worker Pacific Med. Ctr., San Francisco, 1968-71; pvt. practice psychotherapy

and Jungian analysis San Francisco, 1971-87, Brooklin, Maine, 1985—. Tng. analyst CG Jung Inst., San Francisco, 1978—; mem. certifying com. CG Jung Inst., San Francisco, 1980-84; cons. and lectr. in field. Author: Time Out of Mind, Trekking the Hindu Kush, 1978, The Long Shore, A Psychological Experience of the Wilderness, 1991; contbr. articles to profl. jours. Fellow Calif. Soc. Clin. Social Workers; mem. NASW, Acad. Cert. Social Workers, Inc., CG Jung Inst. (chair certifying com. 1980-84), Alpha Phi Sorority. Democrat. Avocations: reading, horseback riding, travel, music. Home and Office: PO Box 269 Brooklin ME 04616-0269

SCHMIDT, MAARTEN, astronomy educator; b. Groningen, Netherlands, Dec. 28, 1929; came to U.S., 1959; s. Wilhelm and Antje (Haringhuizen) S.; m. Cornelia Johanna Tom, Sept. 16, 1955; children: Elizabeth Tjimkje, Maryke Antje, Anne Wilhelmina. BSc, U. Groningen, 1949; PhD, Leiden U., Netherlands, 1956; ScD, Yale U., 1966. Sci. officer Leiden Obs., The Netherlands, 1953-59; postdoctoral fellow Mt. Wilson Obs., Pasadena, Calif., 1956-58; mem. faculty Calif. Inst. Tech., 1959-95, prof. astronomy, 1964-95, exec. officer for astronomy, 1972-75, chmn. div. physics, math. and astronomy, 1975-78, mem. staff Hale Obs., 1959-80, dir. Hale Obs., 1978-80, emeritus prof. astronomy, 1996—. Co-winner Calif. Scientist of Yr. award, 1964 Fellow Am. Acad. Arts and Scis. (Rumford award 1968); mem. Am. Astron. Soc. (Helen B. Warner prize 1964, Russell lecture award 1978), NAS (fgn. assoc., recip. James Craig Watson Medal, 1991), Internat. Astron. Union, Royal Astron. Soc. (assoc., Gold medal 1980) Office: Calif Inst Tech 105 24 Robinson Lab Pasadena CA 91125-0001

SCHMIDT, MARTHA BUBECK, social sciences educator; b. Cadott, Wis., Sept. 28, 1912; d. Karl Christian and Lydia Sarah (Keller) Bubeck; m. Eugene Milton Schmidt, Sept. 11, 1943; children: Eugene Karl, Fredric John. BS, U. Wis., Stout, 1934; MPhil, U. Wis., Madison, 1947, M in Psychology and Behavioral Studies, 1959. Tchr. home econs. Barron (Wis.) High Sch., 1934-37; supr. student teaching U. Wis., Stout, 1937-38; state supr. home econs. edn. Wis. State Bd. Vocat. Edn., Madison, 1938-48; instr. adult evening sch. Madison Area Tech. Coll., 1949-69; guidance counselor Madison Met. Schs., 1959-79; coord. AARP and Wis. Ret. Tchrs. Assn., Madison, 1986-90; state chmn. health/long term care action group AARP, Wis., 1990-99, coord. health advocacy svcs., 1991-2001. Founder Future Homemakers of Am., 1943, past advisor; condr. fgn. study programs, Europe, Asia, Australia, 1971-88. Bd. dirs. Madison Oakwood Retirement Ctr., 1983-89, mem. resident care com., 1992—; com. mem. Wis. Legis. Study Elderly Abuse, 1985-88. Recipient Disting. Educator award, U. Wis., Stout, 1998. Mem.: AAUW, AARP, Mental Health Assn./Wis. Coalition Aging Groups (regional bd.), Valparaiso U. Guild (state pres. 1981—85), Luth. Women Missionary League, Nat. Honor Soc. Home Econs., Wis. Ret. Tchrs. Assn. (rec. sec. 1983—89, bd. dirs. 1990—2002), Madison Civics Club, Rotary (Sr. Svc. award 1998). Lutheran. Avocation: volunteering.

SCHMIDT, MICHAEL FRANCIS, lawyer; b. Detroit, Oct. 5, 1949; s. Carl Howard and Evelyn (Johnson) S.; m. Suzanne Lynn Sofian, June 10, 1977; children: Leslie Marie, Caroline Marie. BS summa cum laude, U. Detroit, 1971, JD magna cum laude, 1975. Bar: Mich. 1975, U.S. Dist. Ct. (ea. dist.) Mich. 1975, U.S. Dist. Ct. (we. dist.) Mich. 1978, U.S. Ct. Appeals (6th cir.) 1981. Assoc. Harvey, Kruse, P.C., Detroit, 1975-79, ptnr., 1979—. Mem. Pres.'s Cabinet, U. Detroit, 1981—, bd. dirs., treas. 1986—. Served with U.S. Army, 1971-77. Mem. Mich. Assn. Def. Counsel, State Bar Mich., Oakland County Bar Assn., Sorin Soc., Xavier Soc., Oakland Hills Country Club, Indianwood Golf Club, Beta Gamma Sigma, Alpha Sigma Nu. Roman Catholic. Office: 1050 Wilshire Dr Ste 320 Troy MI 48084-1526 E-mail: mschmidt@harveykruse.com.

SCHMIDT, NANCY ANNE, psychotherapist; b. Jersey City, July 18, 1958; d. William John Lawrence and Ruth Martha (Morant) S. BA summa cum laude, Fordham U., 1986; MA summa cum laude, N.J. City State U., 1990; cert. pastoral counselor, World Christianship Ministries, 1994. Cert. social worker, criminal justice specialist, hypnotherapist, addiction counselor, eating disorders specialist; cert. domestic violence counselor, cert. crisis counselor. Adj. prof. N.J. City State U. (formerly Jersey City State Coll.), 1988-91, adj. prof. psychology, 1990-94; pvt. practice West New York, 1990—; counselor Substance Abuse Treatment Ctr., Union City, N.J., 1994-96; substance abuse program dir. Sr. Treatment and Edn. Program, Union City, 1994-96; staff psychotherapist North Hudson Cmty. Action Corp. Mental Health Ctr., West New York, 1996-98, dir. mental health, addictive svcs., social work, psychiatry, 1998—. Bd. dirs. Hudson Health Care Partnership, Jersey City; bd. dirs. Hudson County Healthy Families 2000, mem. Hudson County Task Force on Women & Addiction, co-dir. Union City Police Dept./NHCAC Domestic Violence Outreach Program, Union City Police Dept. stress reduction cons.; presenter in field. Mem. APA, Am. Counseling Assn., Am. Assn. Family Counselors (cert.), Nat. Assn. Alcohol and Drug Abuse Counselors, Am. Assn. Christian Counselors, Am. Psychotherapy Assn., Alpha Sigma Lambda, Phi Kappa Phi, Psi Chi. Avocations: swimming, walking, reading, writing, poetry. Office: North Hudson Cmty Action Corp Mental Health Addictive Svc 5301 Broadway West New York NJ 07093-2622

SCHMIDT, PAUL JEFFREY, federal government official; b. Hinsdale, Ill., Feb. 2, 1960; s. Robert Herman and Shirley Ann Schmidt; m. Brenda Sue Schmidt, May 28, 1983; children: Brandon, Kelly. BS in Acctg., So. Ill. U., 1982, MBA, 1983. CPA, Ill. Asst. dir. U.S. GAO, Chgo., 1983—. Mem. Met. Planning Coun., 1999—. Mem. AICPAs, Ill. Soc. CPAs. Avocations: power lifting, reading, family. Office: US GAO 200 W Adams Ste 700 Chicago IL 60606 E-mail: schmidtpj@gao.gov.

SCHMIDT, PAUL JOSEPH, physician, educator; b. N.Y.C., Oct. 22, 1925; m. Louise Kern Fredericks, June 18, 1953; children: Damien, Matthew, Thomas, Maria. BS, Fordham U., 1948; MS, St. Louis U., 1952; MD, NYU, 1953. Diplomate Am. Bd. Pathology, Nat. Bd. Med. Examiners. Intern St. Elizabeth's Hosp., Boston, 1953-54; staff assoc. Nat. Microbiol. Inst., Bethesda, Md., 1954-55; chief blood bank dept. NIH, Bethesda, Md., 1955-74, asst. chief clin. pathology dept., 1963-65; sr. asst. surgeon USPHS, 1954, advanced through grades to med. dir., 1964-74; assoc. clin. prof. pathology, then clin. prof. Georgetown U., Washington, 1965-75; dir. S.W. Fla. Blood Bank, Inc., Tampa, 1975-90, pres., 1987-90; head transfusion medicine Transfusion Medicine Acad. Ctr., 1991—; prof. pathology U. South Fla., Tampa, 1975—. Cons. com. on Blood, AMA, 1964-69; tech. adv. Blood Transfusion Rsch. div. US Army, 1966-74; res. adv. com. Blood Program, ARC, 1967-73; com. Human Rsch. ARC, 1968-74; council on Immunohematology, Am. Soc. Clin. Pathologists, 1968-74; com. Anticoagulant Solutions, NRC-Nat. Acad. Sci., 1968-70; com. Plasmapheresis, NRC-Nat. Acad. Sci., 1969-70; com. Blood Bank Programs, N.Y.C., 1969-70; com. Component Therapy, NRC-Nat. Acad. Sci., 1969; com. standards, Am. Assn. Blood Banks, 1970-85 (chmn. 1981-85); Task Force on Blood Banking, Dept. HEW, 1972-73; adv. com. Blood Diseases and Resources, Nat. Heart Lung Blood Inst., 1975-79; cons. to surgeon gen. U.S. navy, 1976; dir. clin. svcs. ARC Blood Svcs., San Juan, P.R., 1993-95; clin. prof. pathology U. P.R., 1993-2001, Koppisch lectr., 1994; Molthan Meml. lectr. Pa. Assn. Blood Banks, 1995; DeGowin lectr. U. Iowa, 1997. Editor: Progress in Transfusion and Transplantation, 1972; mem. editl. bd. Transfusion, 1968—2003, Annals Clin. Lab. Sci., 1971-74, Blood, 1976-77; contbr. articles to profl. jours.; described etiology of renal failure after hemolytic blood transfusion reactions, 1967, Rh null disease, 1967. Mem. svc. and rehab. com. Fla. div. Am. Cancer Soc., 1976-84; bd. dirs. ARC, Tampa, 1978-83 (v.p. 1980); com. Transfusion Medicine, Coll. Am. Pathologists, 1981-92; bd. dirs. Am. Blood Commn., 1985-87; adv. com. Blood Products, FDA, 2000—03. Served with U.S. Army, 1944—46. Recipient Jour. Club Rsch. award NYU, 1952, Silver medal Spanish Red Cross, 1960, Emily Cooley award Am. Assn. Blood Banks, 1974, John Elliott award, 1993. Fellow Coll. Am. Pathologists (emeritus); mem. Am. Assn. Blood Banks (pres. 1987-88), Internat. Soc. Blood Transfusion, Fla. Assn. Blood Banks (pres. 1980-81), Cosmos Club, Rotary. Roman Catholic. Office: Fla Blood Svcs 10100 9th St N Saint Petersburg FL 33716 E-mail: pauljschmidt@aol.com.

SCHMIDT, PAUL WICKHAM, lawyer; b. Milw., June 25, 1948; s. Edmund Julian and Barbara (Wickham) S.; m. Cathryn Ann Piehl, June 27, 1970; children: Thomas Wickham, William Piehl, Anna Patchin. BA cum laude, Lawrence U., 1970; JD cum laude, U. Wis., 1973. Bar: Wis. 1973, U.S. Dist. Ct. (we. dist.) Wis. 1973, U.S. Supreme Ct. 1982, D.C. 1988. Atty. advisor Bd. Immigration Appeals, Washington, 1973-76; gen. atty. office of gen. counsel Immigration and Naturalization Service, Washington, 1976-78, acting gen. counsel, 1979-81, 86-87, dep. gen. counsel, 1978-87; assoc. Jones, Day, Reavis & Pogue, Washington, 1987-89, ptnr., 1990-92; mng. ptnr. Fragomen, Del Ray & Bernsen, PC, Washington, 1993-95; chmn. Bd. of Immigration Appeals, Falls Church, Va., 1995-2001, mem., 2001—03; judge Arlington (Va.) Immigration Ct., 2003—. Mem. ABA, Internat. Assn. Refugee Law Judges, D.C. Bar Assn., Wis. Bar Assn., Fed. Bar Assn. (immigration sect.). Avocations: crew volunteer, gardening, camping, history. Home: 711 S View Ter Alexandria VA 22314-4923 Office: Arlington Immigration Ct 901 N Stuart St Ste 1300 Arlington VA 22203 E-mail: paul.schmidt@usdoj.gov.

SCHMIDT, PETER GUSTAV, shipbuilding industry executive; b. Tumwater, Wash., Dec. 3, 1921; s. Peter G. and Clara Louise (Muench) S.; m. Elva Mary Ingalls, Dec. 3, 1945; children: Mimi Schmidt Fielding, Jill Schmidt Crowson, Janet Schmidt Mano, Hans. BSME, U. Wash., 1948; MS in Naval Architecture and Marine Engring., U. Mich., 1950. Naval architect Nat. Steel Shipbldg. Corp., San Diego, 1950-52, Carl J. Nordstrom/P. Spaulding, Seattle, 1952-53; pres. Marine Constrn. & Design Co., Seattle, 1953—, Astilleros Marco Chilena Ltd., Santiago, Chile, 1960—, Marco Peruana S.A., Lima, Peru, 1965—, Campbell Industries, San Diego, 1979-99, Campbell Ship Design & Engring., Seattle, 2000—. Author papers on fishing gear and vessels. Served to lt (j.g.) USN, 1942-45, PTO. Recipient Puget Sound's Maritime Man of Yr. award Puget Sound Press Assn., 1975, Naval Arch. and Marine Engring. Merit award U. Mich., 1996. Mem. Soc. Naval Architects and Marine Engrs., Wash. State Boatbuilders Assn. (pres. 1956-58), Alpha Delta Phi. Avocations: competitive sailing, classical music. Office: Marine Constrn & Design 2300 W Commodore Way Seattle WA 98199-1226 Office Phone: 206-285-3200.

SCHMIDT, RAYMOND PAUL, military officer, historian, diplomat; b. Western, Nebr., Sept. 14, 1937; s. Reuben Edward and Angeline Agnes (Kudlik) Schmidt; m. Roberta Ruth Schrom, June 11, 1961; 1 child, Douglas Craig. B in Edn., History and Social Sci., U. Nebr., 1958; postgrad., U. Md., 1960-62, The Am. U., 1975-81; M in History, U. Wis., 1966. Instr. math. and social sci. Sr. High Sch., Bellevue, Nebr., 1958-59; history instr. James Madison Meml. High Sch., Madison, Wis., 1966-68; ensign USN, 1959, historian, archivist Naval Security Group Command, 1968-81, advanced through grades to capt., 1981, sr. congl. security policy rev. officer, Naval Intelligence, 1981-82, sr. res. forces advisor Dept. Def., 1982-88, head Navy info. security policy, 1988-98, mgr. declassification program, 1998-00; cons., 2000—. Mem. Nat. Disclosure Policy Com. Team, Japan, 1989, Thailand, 89, Germany, 91, leader, Albania, 95. Author (with others): Naval Officers Guide, 1983, And I Was There, 1985; contbr. articles to profl. jours. Pres. North Ashburton Citizens Assn., Bethesda, Md., 1982—; merit badge counselor Boy Scouts Am., 1974—93; info. officer U.S. Naval Acad., Annapolis, Md., 1978—93; spkr. Pearl Harbor Symposium Adm. Nimitz Found., Tex., 1991, symposium moderator, 1992; active Montgomery County Planning Bd. Citizens Adv. Com., Md., 1989—94; ret. pers. adv. coun. Naval Dist. Washington. Named Hon. Adm. Great Navy, State of Nebr., 1983. Mem.: DAV (life), U.S. Naval Cryptologic Vets. Assn., Naval Intelligence Profls., Am. Hist. Assn., Nat. Trust Hist. Preservation, Nat. Classification Mgmt. Soc. (editor Viewpoints 1991—96), Nat. Assn. Ret. Fed. Employees, Naval Res. Assn. (life; sec./treas. 1966—68), Mil. Officers Assn. Am. (life), Res. Officers Assn. (life), Nat. Assn. Uniformed Svcs. (life), U.S. Naval Inst. (life; contbr.), Phoenix Soc., Colonial Williamsburg Found., U. Nebr. Alumni Assn. (life). Unitarian. Home: 6205 Lone Oak Dr Bethesda MD 20817-1743

SCHMIDT, RICHARD MARTEN, JR., lawyer; b. Winfield, Kans., Aug. 2, 1924; s. Richard M. and Ida (Marten) S.; m. Ann Downing, Jan. 2, 1948; children: Eric, Gregory, Rolf (dec.), Heidi. AB, U. Denver, 1945, JD, 1948. Bar: Colo. 1948, D.C. 1968. Dep. dist. atty., City and County of Denver, 1949-50; mem. firm McComb, Zarlengo, Mott & Schmidt, Denver, 1950-54; ptnr. Schmidt & Van Cise (and predecessor), Denver, 1954-65; gen. counsel USIA, 1965-68; of counsel Cohn and Marks, Washington, 1969—. Counsel spl. agrl. investigating subcom. Counsel Am. Soc. Newspaper Editors, 1968—; mem. Gov.'s Coun. Local Govt., Colo., 1963-64; chmn. Mayor's Jud. Adv. Com., Denver, 1963-64, Gov.'s Supreme Ct. Nominating Com., 1964-65; mem. Gov.'s Oil Shale Adv. Com., 1963-65, Colo. Commn. on Higher Edn., 1965. Life trustee U. Denver; bd. dirs. Nat. Press Found., 1993-2003. Mem. ABA (chmn. standing com. on assn. comms. 1969-73, chmn. forum com. on comms. 1979-81, co-chmn. nat. conf. lawyers and reps. of media 1984-89, mem. commn. on lawyer advt. 1964-68), Colo. Bar Assn. (gov.), Denver Bar Assn. (pres. 1963-64), D.C. Bar Assn., Cosmos Club (Washington). Episcopalian. Home: 1920 N St NW Ste 300 Washington DC 20036-1622 Office: Cohn and Marks 1920 N St NW Ste 300 Washington DC 20036-1622 Office Phone: 202-452-4837. Business E-Mail: richardschmidtjr@cohnmarks.com.

SCHMIDT, ROBERT, retired mechanics and civil engineering educator; b. Reshetylivka, Ukraine, May 18, 1927; arrived in U.S., 1949, naturalized, 1956; s. Alfred and Aquilina (Konotop) S.; m. Irene Hubertine Bongartz, June 10, 1978; children: Ingbert, Robert. Student, UNRRA-Univ., Munich, 1946—47, Technische Hochschule Karlsruhe, Germany, 1947—49, Vorpruefung; BS, U. Colo., 1951, MS, 1953; PhD, U. Ill., 1956. Tech. draftsman, Kalisch, Poland, 1943-45; rsch. asst. U. Ill., Urbana, 1953-56, asst. prof. mechanics, 1956-59; assoc. prof. U. Ariz., Tucson, 1959-63; prof. mechanics and civil engring. U. Detroit, 1963-99, chmn. civil engring. dept., 1978-80; ret., 1999. Lectr. Oakland U., 1997-98; rschr. in linear and nonlinear theory of elasticity, theories of arches, plates, and shells, and approximate methods of analysis. Editor: Indsl. Math., 1969—; book reviewer Applied Mechanics Rev., Indsl. Math. Jour.; contbr. numerous articles to profl. jours. With C.E., U.S. Army, 1951-52. Grantee NSF 1960-78. Mem. AAUP, ASCE, ASME (cert. recognition 1972), Am. Acad. Mechanics (founder), Indsl. Math. Soc. (pres. 1966-67, 81-84, 1st Gold award 1986), Sigma Xi. Avocations: biosophy, walking, bicycling, swimming.

SCHMIDT, ROBERT CHARLES, JR., finance executive; b. Oklahoma City, Apr. 2, 1942; s. Robert Charles and Francis Laura (Schiele) S.; m. Susan G. Dietz-Felbinger, Nov. 8, 1974; children: Laura Stewart, Elizabeth Berry Saldebar. BA, Westminster Coll., Fulton, Mo., 1964; postgrad., U. Okla., 1972, London Grad. Sch. Bus. Studies, 1974-76. Exec. trainee First Nat. Bank in St. Louis, 1967-68, comml. banker, 1968-74, v.p., mgr. client services div., 1974-76; v.p. treasury ops. Am. Express Co., N.Y.C., 1976-81, dep. treas., 1981-86; chmn. bd. Am. Express Export Credit Corp., 1982-86; group v.p., gen. mgr. Nat. Data Corp., Atlanta, 1986-88, exec. v.p., 1988-89, Capital Guaranty Corp., San Francisco, 1989-91; pres. Tampsco Enterprises, Inc., St. Louis, 1993; ptnr. The Whitelaw Group, St. Louis, 1994-96; pres. SCM Group, Inc., St. Louis, 1996—. Cons. City of N.Y., 1977 Loaned exec. United Fund, St. Louis, 1973; trustee Congl. Summer Assembly Edn. Fund, 1993—; Served with U.S. Army, 1965—67; dir. Crystal Lake Assn., The Endowment for Experimental Arch., Ltd. Decorated Army Commendation medal; recipient cert. of merit USO, 1966, Alumni Achievement award Westminster Coll., 1977 Mem. Treas. Group (chmn. 1982-83), Noonday Club (St. Louis), Crystal Downs Country Club (Frankfort, Mich.), Beta Theta Pi Republican. Episcopalian. Office: 230 S Bemiston Ave Ste 300 Saint Louis MO 63105-1907

SCHMIDT, ROBERT MILTON, physician, scientist, educator, administrator; b. Milw., May 7, 1944; s. Milton W. and Edith J. (Martinek) S.; children Eric Whitney, Edward Huntington. AB, Northwestern U., 1966; MD, Columbia U., 1970; MPH, Harvard U., 1975; PhD in Law, Medicine and Pub. Policy, Emory U., 1982; MA, San Francisco State U., 1999. Diplomate Am. Bd. Preventive Medicine, Am. Bd. Internal Medicine, Am. Bd. Hematology. Resident in internal medicine Univ. Hosp. U. Calif.-San Diego, 1970-71; resident in preventive medicine Ctr. Disease Control, Atlanta, 1971-74; commd. med. officer USPHS, 1971; advanced through grades to comdr., 1973; dir. hematology div. Nat. Ctr. for Disease Control, Atlanta, 1971-78, spl. asst. to dir., 1978-79, inactive res., 1979—; clin. asst. prof. pediatrics Tufts U. Med. Sch., 1974-86; clin. asst. prof. medicine Emory U. Med. Sch., 1971-81, clin. assoc. prof. community health, 1976-86; clin. assoc. prof. humanities in medicine Morehouse Med. Sch., 1977-79; attending physician dept. medicine Wilcox Meml. Hosp., Lihue, Hawaii, 1979-82, Calif. Pacific Med. Ctr., San Francisco, 1983—; dir. Ctr. Preventive Medicine and Health Rsch., 1983—, dir. Health Watch, 1983—; sr. scientist Inst. Epidemiol. and Behavioral Medicine, Inst. Cancer Rsch., Calif. Pacific Med. Ctr., San Francisco, 1983-88; prof. hematology and gerontology, dir. Ctr. Preventive Medicine and Health Rsch., chair health professions program San Francisco State U., 1983-99, prof. medicine, 1983—, prof. emeritus, Calif. State U. Sys., 1999—; founding dir. Health Watch Internat., 1994—, CEO, pres. Cons. WHO, FDA, Washington, NIH, Bethesda, Md., Govt. of China, Mayo Clinic, Rochester, Minn., Northwestern U., Evanston, Ill., Chgo., U. R.I., Kingston, Pan Am. Health Orgn., Inst. Pub. Health, Italy, Nat. Inst. Aging Rsch. Ctr., Balt., U. Calif., San Diego, U. Ill., Chgo., Columbia U., NYC, Harvard U., Johns Hopkins U., U. Chgo., UCLA, U. Calif. Berkeley, Brown U., Providence, U. Calif., San Francisco, Stanford U., Boston, Emory U., Atlanta, Duke U., NC, U. Tex., Houston, Ariz. State U., U. Hawaii, Honolulu, U. Paris, U. Geneva, U. Munich, Heidelberg U., U. Frankfurt, U. Berlin, Cambridge U., England, U. Singapore, others; vis. rsch. prof. gerontology Ariz. State U., 1989—90; mem. numerous sci. and profl. adv. bd., panels, com. Mem. editorial bd. Am. Jour. Clin. Pathology, 1976-82, The Advisor, 1988—, Generations, 1989—, Contemporary Gerontology, 1994—, Alternative Therapies in Health and Medicine, 1995—, Aging Today, 1997—; book and film reviewer Sci. Books and Films, 1988—, many other jours.; author: 17 books and manuals including Hematology Laboratory Series, 4 vols., 1979-86, CRC Handbook Series in Clinical Laboratory Science, 1976—; assoc. editor: Contemporary Gerontology, 1993 ; contbr. more than 300 articles to sci. jours. Alumni regent Columbia U. Coll. Physicians and Surgeons, 1980—. Northwestern U. scholar, 1964-66; NSF fellow, 1964-66; Health Professions scholar, 1966-70; USPHS fellow, 1967-70; Microbiology, Urology, Upjohn Achievement, Borden Rsch. and Virginia Kneeland Frantz scholar awards Columbia U., 1970; recipient Am. Soc. Pharmacol. and Exptl. Therapy award in pharmacology, 1970, Commendation medal USPHS, 1973, Meritorious Performance and Profl. Promise award, 1989, Student Disting. Teaching and Svc. award Pre-Health Professions Student Alliance, 1992, Leadership Recognition awards San Francisco State U., 1984-89, 91-96, Meritorious Svc. award, 1992. Fellow: ACPM, AAAS (med. scis. sect.), ACP (commentator ACP Jour. Club/Annals of Internal Medicine 1993—), Internat. Soc. Hematology, Am. Soc. Clin. Pathology, Am. Coll. Preventive Medicine (sci. com.), Am. Geriat. Soc., Royal Soc. Medicine (London), Gerontol. Soc. Am.; mem.: APHA, AMA, Emory Sch. Pub. Health, Calif. Coun. Gerontology and Geriat., Nat. Assoc. Adv. for Health Professions, Internat. Health Eval. Assn. (v.p. for Ams. 1992—94, bd. dirs. 1992—, pres. 1994—96), Calif. Med. Assn., San Francisco Med. Soc., NY Acad. Sci., Am. Soc. Aging (editl. bd. 1990—, Dychtwald Pub. Speaking award 1991), Am. Soc. Microbiology, Assn. Tchr. Preventive Medicine (edn. com., rsch. com.), Am. Coll. Occupl. and Environ. Medicine, Calif. Coun. Gerontology and Geriat., Am. Assn. Med. Info., Nat. Assn. Advisors for Health Professions (bd. dirs.), Am. Assoc. Blood Banks, Acad. Clin. Lab. Physicians and Scientists, Internat. Soc. Thrombosis and Hemostasis, Am. Soc. Hematology (hon.; emeritus), Internat. Commn. Standardization in Hematology, Am. Assn. Med. Info. (chair prevention and health evaln. informatics WG), Nat. Gallery of Art (Washington), Columbia U. Club No. Calif., Circle Club (Washington), Army and Navy Club, Golden Key (hon. faculty mem.), Harvard Club (NY and San Francisco), Northwestern U. Club. No. Calif., Cosmos Club (mem. art com. 1997—), Knights of Malta, Sigma Xi, Phi Beta Kappa. Home: Whaleship Plaza 25 Hinckley Walk San Francisco CA 94111-2303 Office: Health Watch Med Ctr Calif Pacific Med Ctr San Francisco CA 94120-7999 Office Phone: 415-956-5670. E-mail: rmschmidtmd@aol.com.

SCHMIDT, RONALD HANS, architect; b. Hoboken, N.J., Sept. 9, 1938. BArch., Syracuse U., 1961. Sr. designer Skidmore, Owings & Merrill, N.Y.C., 1963-68; ptnr., dir. archtl. design Grad. Partnership, Newark, 1968-81; pres., chief exec. officer Ronald Schmidt & Assocs., P.A., Englewood, N.J., 1981—. Chmn. Bergen County (N.J.) Econ. Devel. Corp.; mem. bd. regents Felician Coll.; mem. exec. com. Network of Opportunity. Recipient numerous awards. Office: 222 Grand Ave Englewood NJ 07631-4352 E-mail: rschmidt@RSAaia.com.

SCHMIDT, RUSSEL ALAN, II, sales executive; b. Stuttgart-Bad Canstatt, Germany, Nov. 18, 1953; arrived in U.S., 1954; s. Russell Allen and Phyllis (Coty) S.; m. Christie Ellen Duncan, Oct. 18 1975; children: Rachel Lea, Russell Alan III. BS, U. Minn., 1984. Lic. FCC gen. radiotelephone operator; cert. Motorola Effective Presentations, Successful Negotiator. Pres. Electronic Engring. Inds. Co., St. Paul, 1971-77, Dis-Com Inc., St. Paul, 1978-81; sales engr. Motorola Inc., Mpls., 1984-85, dist. sales engr., 1985-86, dist. sales mgr. (IBM), 1987-89, sr. account sales mgr. (IBM), 1989-93, sr. acct. sales mgr., 1993-95, market devel. mgr., 1995—2001; v.p. Essential Bus. Svcs. Roseville (Minn.), 1986—; pres. Forefront Devel. Inc., 2001—; chief mgr. RAC Schmidt Properties LLC, 2001—. Bd. dirs. Dis-Com Inc. 1978-81; chief TV engr. Renewal Internat. Inc., St. Paul, 1984-87; pres. Forefront Devel., Inc., 2001; chief mgr. R&C Schmidt Properties LLC; v.p. Essential Bus. Svcs. Roseville, 2001. Pub. (music CD) Living In Laodicea, 1999. Mem. Nat. SBA, St. Paul C. of C., North Suburban C. of C., Mpls. C. of C., North Oaks Golf Club. Republican. Lutheran. Avocations: small business or real estate ventures, non-fiction reading, computer programming, travel. Office: Motorola Semiconductor Products 5620 Smetana Dr Minnetonka MN 55343-9611 E-mail: russ2@spacestar.net.

SCHMIDT, RUTH ANN, retired academic administrator; b. Mountain Lake, Minn., Sept. 16, 1930; d. Jacob A. and Anna A. (Ewert) S. BA, Augsburg Coll., Mpls., 1952; MA, U. Mo., 1955; PhD, U. Ill., 1962; LLD, Gordon Coll., 1987. Asst. prof. Spanish Mary Baldwin Coll., Staunton, Va., 1955-58, SUNY-Albany, 1962-67, assoc. prof., 1967-78, dean of humanities, 1971-76; prof. and provost Wheaton Coll., Norton, Mass., 1978-82; pres. Agnes Scott Coll., Decatur, Ga., 1982-94, pres. emerita, 1994—. Interim pres. Lyon Coll., 1998; chair Women's Coll. Coalition, 1986-88. Author: Ortega Munilla y sus novelas, 1973, Cartas entre dos amigos del teatro, 1969. Trustee Gordon Coll., Wenham, Mass., 1980-86, Lyon Coll., 1993-2001; bd. dirs. DeKalb C. of C., 1982-85, Atlanta Coll. Art, 1984-94; mem. exec. com. Women's Coll. Coalition, 1983-88; v.p. So. Univ. Conf., 1993. Named Disting. Alumna Augsburg Coll., 1973 Mem. Assn. Am. Colls. (dir. 1979-82, treas. 1982-83), Soc. Values in Higher Edn., Am. Coun. Edn. (commn. on women in higher edn. 1985-88), AAUW, Assn. Pvt. Colls. and Univs. Ga. (pres. 1987-89), Internat. Women's Forum, Young Women's Christian Assn. Acad. Women Achievers. Democrat. Presbyterian. E-mail: ruthschmidt@mindspring.com.

SCHMIDT, SHEILA ELIZABETH, physician, writer; d. Carl Wilfred and Joyce Elizabeth Schmidt; children: Robert Chase Phelps, Hayden Elizabeth. MD, U. of Tex. @ Houston, Houston, Texas, 1989—93. Author: (inspirational/self-help) Pregnant and Blown Off (When Abortion is Not an Option). Recipient AOA, U. of Tex. @ Houston Med. Sch. Mem.: Brazoria County Med. Soc., Am. Med. Soc., Tex. Med. Soc. (mem.). Lutheran.

SCHMIDT, SHERI LYNN, band director; b. Kalamazoo, Mich., Dec. 21, 1969; d. Robert LaDuke and Judith LaDuke; m. Darin Schmidt, Mar. 29, 1993. B Music Edn., Western Mich. U., 1992; M Music Edn., VanderCook Coll. of Music, 1999. Cert. tchr. Asst. dir. bands Pennfield Schs., Battle Creek, Mich., 1992—98; dir. bands Shakamak Schs., Jasonville, Ind., 1998—2001; band dir. Lakeview Schs., Battle Creek, Mich., 2001—. Flute tchr., Battle Creek, 1985—2001. Mem.: Music Educator's Nat. Conf., Mich. Sch. Band and Orch. Assn. (treas. Dist. 8 1995—98). Presbyterian. Avocations: photography, yoga.

SCHMIDT, STANLEY ALBERT, editor, writer; b. Cin., Mar. 7, 1944; s. Otto Elliott William and Georgia (Metcalf) S.; m. Joyce Mary Tokarz, June 9, 1979. BS, U. Cin., 1966; MA, Case Western Res. U., 1968, PhD, 1969. Asst. prof. physics Heidelberg Coll., Tiffin, Ohio, 1969-78; freelance writer Lake Peekskill, N.Y., 1968—; editor Analog Sci. Fiction and Fact Dell Mags., N.Y.C., 1978—. Mem. bd. advisors Nat. Space Soc., Washington, 1982—.

Author: Newton and the Quasi-Apple, 1975, The Sins of the Fathers, 1976, Lifeboat Earth, 1978, Analog Yearbook II, 1981, Analog's Golden Anniversary Anthology, 1980, Analog: Readers' Choice, 1981, Analog's Children of the Future, 1982, Analog's Lighter Side, 1982, Analog: Writers' Choice, 1983, War and Peace: Possible Futures from Analog, 1983, Aliens from Analog, 1983, Writer's Choice, Vol. II, 1984, From Mind to Mind, 1984, Analog's Expanding Universe, 1986, Tweedlioop, 1986, Unknown, 1988, Unknown Worlds, 1989, Analog Essays in Science, 1990, Writing Science Fiction and Fantasy, 1991, Aliens and Alien Societies, 1995, Roads Not Taken, 1998, Which Way to the Future?, 2001, Generation Gap and Other Stories, 2002, Argonaut, 2002; contbr. stories to sci. fiction mags., articles to mags., chapters to books. Mem. Sci. Fiction Mus., Seattle, 2003—. Mem. Sci. Fiction and Fantasy Writers Am., Am. Assn. Physics Tchrs., Am. Fedn. Musicians, Heinlein Soc. Avocations: photography, hiking, linguistics, cooking, flying. Office: Analog Sci Fiction 475 Park Ave S New York NY 10016-6901

SCHMIDT, STANLEY EUGENE, retired speech educator; b. Harrington, Wash., Dec. 14, 1927; s. Otto Jacob and Ella Genevieve (Wilson) S.; m. Jayne Brown; children: Randall Lee, Stephen Douglas. BS in Edn., Beta Theta Pi, U. Idaho, 1956; MEd in Adminstrn., U. Oreg., 1958; MA in Speech, Wash. State U., 1975. Supt., tchr., coach Rose Lake (Idaho) Sch. Dist. #35, 1949-55; forensics coach, speech tchr., dir. forensics Jefferson H.S., Portland, Oreg., 1955-65; dir. forensics Portland C.C., 1965-93, lead speech instr., 1979-82, subject area chmn., 1986-90; adj. prof. speech U. Portland, 1987-93; ret., 1993. Parliamentarian faculty senate, 1975-80. Co-author anthology: The Literature of the Oral Tradition, 1963. Chmn., precinct committeeman Rep. Party, Kootenai County, Idaho, 1951-53; pres. Kootenai County Tchrs. Assn., 1953-54, North Idaho Edn. Assn., 1954-55, Oreg. Speech Assn., 1960-61, Oreg. C.C. Speech Assn., 1971-72. Recipient Excellence award U.S. Bank, Portland, 1993, Merit award N.W. Forensic Assn., 1992, Faculty Merit award Portland C.C., 1984. Mem.: N.W. Comm. Assn., Am. Forensic Assn., Oreg. Speech Assn. (pres.), Speech Comm. Assn., Western Speech Comm. Assn., Oreg. Ret. Tchrs. Assn, Am. Rose Soc., Portland Rose Soc. (Best Rose Garden in Portland Grand Sweepstakes award 2003), Scottish Rite 33 Degrees (comdr. multnomah coun. kadosh 1990—91), Royal Ark Mariners, York Rite Sovereign Coll., Royal Rosarian, Masons (worshipful master 1984—85, dist. dep. 1986—90, jr. grand deacon 1990—91, jr. grand steward 1991—92, grand orator 1992—93), Cryptic Masons of Oreg. (grand orator 1994—95, illustrious master 1997), Knights Templar (knight comdr. of temple of grand encampment), Order of Ea. Star (Worthy Patron 1953, 1970), Red Cross of Constantine (dir. of the work 1989—2001, recorder 1993—97, sovereign 2000—01, St. Laurence Conclave), Royal Order Scotland, Scottish Rite Found. (pres. 2002—), Benevolent and Protective Order of the Elks, Elks, Shriners (dir. of the work 1990—, group leader of the guides 1998—), Royal Arch Masons, Beta Theta Pi. Baptist. Avocations: rose gardening, stamps, coins, fishing, sports. Home: 5460 SW Palatine St Portland OR 97219-7259

SCHMIDT, TERRY L. health care executive; b. Chgo., Nov. 28, 1943; s. LeRoy C. and Eunice P. Schmidt; children: Christie Anne, Terry L. II. BS, Bowling Green State U., 1965; MBA in Health Care Adminstrn, George Washington U., 1971; Dr Health Adminstrn., Med. U. S.C., 2001. Resident in hosp. adminstrn. U. Pitts. Med. Center, VA Hosp., Pitts., 1968-69; adminstrv. asst. Mt. Sinai Med. Center, N.Y.C., 1969-70; asst. dir. Health Facilities Planning Council of Met. Washington, 1970-71; asst. dir. dept. govtl. relations A.M.A., Washington, 1971-74; contract lobbyist and govtl. rels. Wash. Reps. in Health, Washington, 1974-87; pres. Terry L. Schmidt Inc. Physician Svcs. Group, San Diego, 1987-99, Washington Actions on Health, 1975-79; partner Washington Coun. Medicine and Health, 1979-81; pres. Recreational Enterprises, Inc., Washington, 1977-78; v.p. Crisis Communications Corp. Ltd., 1982-90; pres. Med. Cons. Inc., 1983-84, Ambulance Corp. Am., La Jolla, Calif., 1984-87; exec. dir., chief operating officer Emergency Health Assocs. P.C., Phoenix, 1989-91, Charleston Emergency Physicians, Inc., S.C., 1990-94, Joplin Emergency Physican Assocs., 1991-92, Big Valley Med. Group, 1991-92, Blue Ridge Emergency Physicians, P.C., 1992-94, Berkeley Emergency Physicians, P.C., 1992-94; chmn., pres. Univ. Inst., 1992—; asst. dir. dept. emergency medicine Med. U.S.C., 1999—2001. Bd. dirs., Univ. Inst., 1997—, lectr., instr. dept. health svcs. adminstrn. George Washington U., 1969-83, preceptor, 1975-84; adj. prof. grad. sch. Pub. Health San Diego State U., 1996—, preceptor, 1989—, guest lectr. health care adminstrn. Nat. U. San Diego, 1992-93; guest lectr. Bus. Adminstrn. U.S. Internat. U., San Diego, 1994—; instr. Nat. Naval Sch. Health Care Adminstrn., 1971-73; faculty Civil Svc. Commn. Legis. Insts., 1972-76; fac. Am. Assn. State Colls. and U. Health Tng. Insts., 1975-78; mem. adv. com. ambulatory care standards Joint Commn. Accreditation of Hosps., 1971-72, pres., Recreational Enterprises, Inc., Wash., 1977-78, guest lectr. Med. U.S.C., 1998-99, preceptor, 1999—, assoc. prof. Coll. of Health, Med. U.S.C., 1999—. Author: Congress and Health: An Introduction to the Legislative Process and the Key Participants, 1976, A Directory of Federal Health Resources and Services for the Disadvantaged, 1976, Health Care Reimbursement: A Glossary, 1983; mem. editl. adv. bd. Nation's Health, 1971-73; contbr. articles to profl. jours. Bd. dirs. Nat. Eye Found., 1976-78. Mem. Med. Group Mgmt. Assn., Health Care Fin. Mgmt. Assn., Assn. Venture Capital Groups (bd. dirs. 1984-89), Amer. Coll. of Health Execs., Amer. Coll. of Med. Prac. Exec., Assn. of Univ. Progs. in Health Admin., San Diego Venture Group (chair 1984-87), Univ. Club (life), Natl. Rep. Club (life), Nat. Dem. Club (life), Capitol Hill Club (life), Alpha Phi Omega (pres. Bowling Green alumni chpt. 1967-70, sec.-treas. alumni assn. 1968-71). Office: Terry L Schmidt Inc Ste 113 611 7770 Regents Rd San Diego CA 92122-1967

SCHMIDT, THOMAS CHARLES, biomedical engineer, researcher; b. Jersey City, Feb. 21, 1947; s. Ernest J. and Shirley J. Schmidt; m. Marilyn I. Karcheski, Aug. 3, 1968; 1 child, Thomas M. B in Engring., Stevens Inst. Tech., 1968, M in Engring., 1973. Registered profl. engr., Fla., Calif. Vis. lectr. physiol. psychology Stevens Inst. of Tech., Hoboken, NJ, 1974—76; engr. Perry Techs., Riviera Beach, Fla., 1976—80; sr. rsch. engr., rsch. specialist, staff engr., sr. staff engr. Lockheed-Martin, San Diego, 1980—. Participant NASA Med-Ops. Task Group (Clin. Care Capability Project), Houston, 2000; chair ASME PVHO design sub-com., 2003—. Contbr. The Underwater Handbook: A Guide to Physiology and Performance for the Engineer, 1976, articles to profl. jours.; patentee in field. Dir., pub. safety chair Clairemont Town Coun., San Diego, 1997—; chair Balboa Ave. Citizens Adv. Com., San Diego, 1999—2003; mem. Cmty. Engagement Action Forum County Health and Human Svcs., San Diego, 1999—, participant strategic planning process, 1999—2003; mem. Clairemont-Mesa Planning Com., San Diego, 2000—. Recipient cert. of appreciation, State of Calif. (78th Assembly Dist.), 1999, cert. of recognition, 2000, 2001, cert. of appreciation, County of San Diego (3rd Dist. Supr.), 1999, County of San Diego (Asst Dir. Health and Human Svcs.), 2000, spl. commendation, City of San Diego (6th Dist. Councilmember), 1998, 1999, 2000, 2001, 2002, Cmty. Svc. award, City of San Diego (Dir. of Planning), 2001, 2002, commendation, Gov. of Calif., 2003, cert. of recognition, State of Calif. (76th Assembly Dist.), 2003, 2004, spl. commendation, City of San Diego (6th Dist. Councilmember), 2004, cert. of recognition, U. S. Congress (Calif. 50th Dist.), 2004, cert. of appreciation, ASME (Codes and Standards), 2004. Mem.: ASME (ANSI/ASME safety code com. - pressure vessels for human occupancy 1987—), Calif. Environ. Health Assn. (exec. bd. S.W. chpt. 2000—), Undersea and Hyperbaric Med. Soc. (submarine medicine com. 1984—, safety com. 1981—). Home: 5953 Castleton Dr San Diego CA 92117 Office: Lockheed-Martin 3929 Calle Fortunada San Diego CA 92123 E-mail: thomas.c.schmidt@lmco.com.

SCHMIDT, WALDEMAR ADRIAN, pathologist, educator; b. L.A., Aug. 22, 1941; s. Waldemar Adrian and Mary Charlotte (Parker) S.; m. Karmen LaVer Bingham, Feb. 1, 1963; children: Rebecca, Sarah, Waldemar, Diedrich. BS, Oreg. State U., 1965; PhD, MD, U. Oreg., 1969. Intern U. Oreg. Hosps. and Clinics, Portland, 1969-70, resident, 1970-73; pathologist LDS Hosp., Salt Lake City, 1973-77; prof. pathology U. Tex. Med. Sch., Houston, 1977-91, Oreg. Health and Scis. U., Portland, 1991—2003, prof. emeritus, 2003—; chief pathology and lab. medicine svc. Oreg. Health and Scis. U. and VA Med. Ctr., Portland, 1997—2001, vice chair pathology, 1997—2001; CEO Cascadia Placenta Registry, 1996—2002, dir., 2002—03. Author: Principles and Techniques of Surgical Pathology, 1982; editor Cytopathology Annual, 1991-94, Revs. in Pathology-Cytopathology, 1994-99. Asst. scoutmaster Boy Scouts Am., Houston, 1982-91. Maj. U.S. Army, 1970-76. Fellow Am. Soc. Clin. Pathologists, Coll. Am. Pathologists; mem. Internat. Acad. Cytology, Sigma Xi, Alpha Omega Alpha. Avocations: photography, silviculture, apiculture. Office: U Oreg Health and Scis U Sch Medicine Dept Pathology 3181 SW Sam Jackson Park Rd Portland OR 97201-3098

SCHMIDT, WAYNE WALTER, law association executive; b. St. Louis, Feb. 8, 1941; s. Warren W. and Geneva N. (Walker) S.; children: Andrew M., Nancy K. Diploma in English and comparative law, City of London Coll., 1963; BA, U. N.Mex., 1964; JD, Oklahoma City U., 1966; LLM, Northwestern U., 1974. Bar: N.Mex. 1966, Ill. 1968, D.C. 1970, N.Y. 1982. Dir. police legal advisor program Northwestern U., 1968-70; counsel Internat. Assn. Chiefs of Police, 1970-73; exec. dir. Am. for Effective Law Enforcement, Inc., Chgo., 1973—; pres. Pub. Safety Pers. Rsch. Inst., 1974—2002, Govt. Employment Rsch. Inst., Inc., 1986-89, Lauterbrunnen Properties, 1990-93; dir. Comprehensive Ensurers Market Syndicate, Inc., 1984-91, 93-94, Capital Exch. Mgmt., Inc., 1988-91. Cons. Uniform Code of Criminal Procedure. Co-author: Legal Aspects of Criminal Evidence, 1978, Introduction to Criminal Evidence, 1982, Introduction to Criminal Evidence and Court Procedure, 1987, 5th edit. 2003; editor Fire and Police Pers. Reporter, 1975—, Pub. Employment Health Law and Benefits, 1986-89, Fire and Police Am. Case Digest, 1984—. Served with U.S. Army, 1966-67. Mem. ABA (liaison to criminal justice coun. 1973—), Internat. Assn. Chiefs of Police (vice chair legis. com. 1988—). Office: Am Effective Law Enforcement Legal Ctr 841 W Touhy Ave Park Ridge IL 60068-3351 E-mail: aele@aol.com.

SCHMIDT, WILLIAM ARTHUR, JR., lawyer; b. Cleve., Oct. 2, 1939; s. William Arthur and Caroline (Jäger) S.; m. Gerilyn Pearl Smith, Sept. 30, 1967; children: Deborah, Dawn, Jennifer. BSBA, Kent State U., 1962; JD, Cleve. State U., 1968. Bar: Ohio 1968, Ill. 1990. Contract specialist NASA-Lewis, Cleve., 1962-66, procurement analyst, 1967-68; atty. Def. Logistics Agy., Alexandria, Va., 1968-73; assoc. counsel Naval Sea Sys. Command, Arlington, Va., 1973-75; procurement policy analyst Energy R & D Adminstrn., Germantown, Md., 1975-76; sr. atty. U.S. Dept. Energy, Germantown, 1976-78, counsel spl. projects Oak Ridge, Tenn., 1978-83; judge Agr. Bd. Contract Appeals, Washington, 1983-87; judge Bd. Contract Appeals HUD, Washington, 1987; chief legal counsel Fermilab, Batavia, Ill., 1987-92; gen. counsel Univ. Rsch. Assn., Inc., Washington, 1992—. Co-author: (NASA handbook) R & D Business Practices, 1968. Founder/dir. DOE Contractor Attys. Assn.; dir. Spotsylvania Crime Solvers. Mem. Fed. Bar Assn. (past pres. East Tenn. 1978-83, 25 Yr. Svc. award 1994), Ill. Bar Assn., Bd. Contract Appeals Judges Assn. (dir.-sec. 1986-88), Sr. Execs. Assn., Delta Theta Phi (dist. chancellor 1978-83), Sigma Chi. Republican. Lutheran. Avocations: classic cars, m-1 carbines. Home: 10611 King Elder Ct Spotsylvania VA 22553-3666 Office: Univ Rsch Assn Inc 1111 19th St NW Ste 400 Washington DC 20036-3627

SCHMIDT, WILLIAM C. retired chemicals executive; b. Niles, Mich., Sept. 27, 1938; s. Felix A. and Anna (Reifschneider) S.; m. Bethany Ann Boyd, Dec. 17, 1966; 1 child, Craig W. BBA, U. Mich., 1960, MBA, 1961. Cert. Mgmt. Acct. Various acctg. positions Dow Chem. Co., Midland, Mich., 1961-73; controller Dow Chem. Pacific Ltd., Hong Kong, 1973-78; area controller Dow Chem. Co., Midland, Mich., 1978-82, asst. corp. controller, 1982-98; v.p., chief fin. officer DowElanco, Indpls., 1989-98; chmn. bd. Wolverine Bank, F.S.B., 2004—. Bd. dir. Wolverine Bank FSB. Bd. dirs. Midland Hosp., 1982-89, 98—, chmn. bd., 1986-88, 2004—; bd. dirs. Mid-Mich. Health Corp., 1983-89, 2001—, chmn. bd., 1986-88; treas., bd. dirs. Indpls. Symphony Orch., 1992-98; dir. West Midland Family Ctr., 2000—; mem., vice chmn. Midland County Bldg. Authority, 2003—. Cpl. U.S. Army, 1962-64. Mem. Inst. Mgmt. Accts., Inst. Cert. Mgmt. Accts. (regent 1985-89), Am. Indsl. Health Coun. (treas. 1986-87), Ind. C. of C. (bd. dirs. 1992-98). Presbyterian. Home: 5908 Londonberrie Ct Midland MI 48640-6965

SCHMIDT, WILLIAM MAX, management consultant, business executive; b. Danville, Pa., Nov. 23, 1947; s. Frank Wilhelm and Doris Savilla (Maurer) S.; m. Marylea O'Reilly, Sept. 20, 1980. BS, U. Pa., 1969; MBA, Northwestern U., 1971. Mktg. specialist Moody's Investors Svc., Inc., N.Y.C., 1971-72; cons. William E. Hill & Co. Inc., N.Y.C, 1972-74; product supr. Internat. Paper Co., N.Y.C., 1974-79; dir. market analysis U.S. Industries, Inc., Stamford, Conn., 1979-82, mgr. corp. devel., 1982-84; dir. corp. mktg. Combustion Engring., Inc., Stamford, Conn., 1984-86, v.p. mktg., planning Union, N.J., 1986-91; pres. Pragmatics, Basking Ridge, NJ, 1991—2000; dir. global mktg. Gemplus Internat., Montgomeryville, Pa., 2000—. Author: (newsletter) Think Again, 1995. Bd. dirs. Curbing Hunger, Inc., Basking Ridge, N.J., 1995—; adv. Jr. Achievement, N.Y.C., 1976-78. Mem. TAPPI, Exec. Forum, Strategic Leadership Forum, Univ. Club, Sons of the Revolution, Wharton Club (N.Y.C.), Sigma Chi. Republican. Mem. United Ch. of Christ. Avocations: tennis, astronomy, canoeing, community service, coin collecting/numismatics. Home: 46 Quincy Rd Basking Ridge NJ 07920-2245 Office: Gemplus Corp 101 Park Dr Montgomeryville PA 18936 E-mail: billprag@worldnet.att.net.

SCHMIDT-NIELSEN, BODIL MIMI (MRS. ROGER G. CHAGNON), physiologist, educator; b. Copenhagen, Nov. 3, 1918; came to U.S., 1946, naturalized, 1952; d. August and Marie (Jorgensen) Krogh; m. Knut Schmidt-Nielsen, Sept. 20, 1939 (div. Feb. 1966); children: Astrid, Bent, Bodil; m. Roger G. Chagnon, Oct. 1968. DDS, U. Copenhagen, 1941, DOdont, 1946, DPhil, 1955; DS (hon.), Bates Coll., 1983; MD (hon.), U. Aarhus, Denmark, 1997. Mem. faculty Duke U., Durham, NC, 1952-64; prof. biology Case Western Res. U., Cleve., 1964-71, chmn. dept., 1970-71, adj. prof., 1971-74; trustee Mt. Desert Island Biol. Lab., Maine, rsch. scientist, 1971-86, exec. com., 1978-85, v.p., 1979-81, pres., 1981-85. Adj. prof. Brown U., Providence, 1971-75, dept. physiol. U. Fla., Gainesville, 1986—; mem. tng. grant com. NIGMS, 1965-71. Author: August and Marie Krogh, Lives in Science, 1995, Danish edit., 1997; editor: Urea and the Kidney, 1970; assoc. editor Am. Jour. Physiology: Regulatory, Integrative and Comparative Physiology, 1978-81. Trustee Coll. of Atlantic, Bar Harbor, Maine, 1972-92. Recipient Career award NIH, 1962-64, John Simon Guggenheim Meml. fellow, 1952-53; Bowditch lectr., 1958, Jacobaeus lectr., 1974. Fellow AAAS (del. coun. 1977-79), N.Y. Acad. Scis., Am. Acad. Arts and Scis.; mem. Am. Physiol. Soc. (coun. 1971-77, pres. 1975-76, Ray G. Daggs award 1989, Orr Reynolds award 1994, August Knogh lectr. 1994, Berliner award 1998), Soc. Exptl. Biology and Medicine (coun. 1967-71). Achievements include research, publications on biochemistry of saliva, water metabolism of desert animals, urea excretion, peristalsis of renal pelvis and concentrating mechanism, comparative kidney physiology, comparative physiology of excretory organs. Office: U Fla Dept Physiology Gainesville FL 32605 E-mail: Bodimi@aol.com.

SCHMIDT-NIELSEN, KNUT, physiologist, educator; b. Norway, Sept. 24, 1915; came to U.S., 1946, naturalized, 1952; s. Sigval and Signe Torborg (Sturzen-Becker) Schmidt-N. Mag. Scient., U. Copenhagen, 1941, Dr. Phil., 1946; Dr. Med. (hon.), U. Lund, Sweden, 1985; D in Philosophy (hon.), U. Tondheim, Norway, 1993. Research fellow Carlsberg Labs., Copenhagen, 1941-44, Carlsberg Labs. (U. Copenhagen), 1944-46; research assoc. zoology Swarthmore (Pa.) Coll., 1946-48; docent U. Oslo, Norway, 1947-49; research assoc. physiology Stanford U., 1948-49; asst. prof. Coll. Medicine, U. Cin., 1949-52; prof. physiology Duke U., Durham, N.C., 1952—, James B. Duke prof. physiology, 1963—; Harvey Soc. lectr., 1962; Regents' lectr. U. Calif. at Davis, 1963; Brody Meml. lectr. U. Mo., 1962; Hans Gadow lectr. Cambridge (Eng.) U., 1971; vis. Agassiz prof. Harvard, 1972. Wellcome vis. prof. U. S.D., 1988; mem. panel environmental biology NSF, 1957-61; mem. sci. adv. com. New Eng. Regional Primate Center, 1962-66; mem. nat. adv. bd. physiol. research lab. Scripps Instn. Oceanography, U. Calif. at San Diego, 1963-69, chmn., 1968-69; organizing com. 1st Internat. Conf. on Comparative Physiology, 1972-80; pres. Internat. Union Physiol. Scis., 1980-86, mem. U.S. nat. com. 1966-78, vice chmn. U.S. nat. com., 1969-78; mem. subcom. on environmental physiology U.S. nat. com. Internat. Biol. Programme, 1965-67; mem. com. on research utilization uncommon animals, div. biology and agr. Nat. Acad. Scis., 1966-68; mem. animal resources adv. com. NIH, 1968; mem. adv. bd. Bio-Med. Scis., Inc., 1973-74; chief scientist Scripps Instn. Amazon expdn., 1967. Author: Animal Physiology, 3d. edit, 1970, The Physiology of Desert Animals; Physiological Problems of Heat and Water, 1964, How Animals Work, 1972, Animal Physiology; Adaptation and Environment, 1975, 5th edit., 1997, Scaling: Why is Animal Size So Important?, 1984, The Camel's Nose: Memoirs of a Curious Scientist, 1998; sect. editor Am. Jour. Physiology, 1961-64, 70-76; editor Jour. Applied Physiology, 1961-64, 70-76; mem. editorial bd. Jour. Cellular and Comparative Physiology, 1961-66, Physiol. Zoology, 1959-70, Am. Jour. Physiology, 1971-76, Jour. Applied Physiology, 1971-76, Jour. Exptl. Biology, 1975-79, 83-86; cons. editor: Annals of Arid Zone, 1962—; hon. editorial adv. bd. Comparative Biochemistry and Physiology, 1962-63; chief editor News in Physiol Scis., 1985-88, cons. editor, 1988—; contbr. articles to sci. publs. Guggenheim fellow, 1953-54; grantee Office Naval Rsch., 1952-54, 58-61, UNESCO, 1953-54, Office Q.M. Gen., 1953-54, Office Surgeon Gen., 1953-54, NIH, 1955-86, NSF, 1957-61, 59-60, 60-61, 61-63; recipient Rsch. Career award USPHS, 1964-85, Internat. prize for biology Japan Soc. for the Promotion of Sci., 1992, Disting. Svc. medal Smithsonian Instn., Nat. Zool. Park, 1998; recipient N.C. award in sci., 1999. Fellow AAAS, N.Y. Acad. Sci., Am. Acad. Arts and Scis.; mem. NAS, N.C. Acad. Sci. (Poteat award 1957), Am. Physiol. Soc., Am. Soc. Zoologists (chmn. div. comparative physiology 1964), Soc. Exptl. Biology, Royal Danish Acad., Acad. Scis. (France) (fgn. assoc.), Royal Norwegian Soc. Arts. and Sci., Norwegian Acad. Scis. and Letters, Physiol. Soc. London (assoc.), Royal Soc. London (fgn.); hon. mem. Soc. Integrative & Comparative Biology, Harvey Soc., Zool. Soc. London, Deutsche Ornitologengesellshaft. Office: Duke U Dept Biology PO Box 90338 Durham NC 27708-0338

SCHMIDT-RINEHART, BARBARA COE, Spanish language educator; b. Delaware, Ohio, May 15, 1955; d. Robert E. and Ellen M. Schmidt; m. Kenneth L. Rinehart, May 29, 1987; children: Timothy Rinehart, Mark Rinehart. BA, Ohio U., 1977; EdM, Ashland Coll., 1986; PhD, Ohio State U., 1992. Tchr. Ontario HS, Ohio, 1977—85; Spanish prof. Ashland U., Ohio, 1986—. Contbr. articles various profl. jours. Named Cmty. Ambassador to Argentina, Delaware, Ohio, 1972; recipient Ed Allen award for Outstanding Coll. Fgn. Lang. Instr., Ohio Fgn. Lang. Assn., 1998. Mem.: Ohio Fgn. Lang. Assn., Am. Coun. on Tchg. Fgn. Lang., Am. Assn. of Tchrs. of Spanish and Portuguese. Office: Ashland U 401 Coll Ave Ashland OH 44805

SCHMIT, LUCIEN ANDRÉ, JR., structural engineer; b. N.Y.C., May 5, 1928; s. Lucien Alexander and Eleanor Jessie (Donley) S.; m. Eleanor Constance Trabish, June 24, 1951; 1 son, Lucien Alexander, III. BS, MIT, 1949, MS, 1950. Structures engr. Grumman Aircraft Co., Bethpage, N.Y., 1951-53; rsch. engr., aeroelastic and structures lab. MIT, 1954-58; asst. prof. engring. Case Inst. Tech., 1958-60, assoc. prof., 1961-63, prof., 1964-70; prof. engring. and applied sci. UCLA, 1970-91, Rockwell prof. aerospace engring. emeritus, 1991—. Sci. adv. bd. USAF, 1977-84. Contbr. articles on analysis and synthesis of structural systems, finite elements methods, design of fiber composite components and multidisciplinary design optimization to profl. jours. Fellow AIAA (Design Lecture award 1977, Structures, Structural Dynamics and Materials award 1979, Multidisciplinary Design Optimization award 1994, Walter J. and Angeline H. Crichlow Trust prize 1999), ASCE, Am. Acad. Mechanics; mem. NAE. Home: 545 3rd Ave S Edmonds WA 98020-4103 E-mail: schmit13@comcast.net.

SCHMIT, TIMOTHY BRUCE, musician; b. Oakland, Calif., Oct. 30, 1947; Band mem. Tim, Tom & Ron, the Contenders, New Breed, Glad, Poco, 1970—77, The Eagles, 1977—. Performed on albums with various artists including Warren Zevon, Robert Lamm, Dwight Yoakam, Ringo Starr, Tim McGraw, Jeff Larson, Dan Fogelberg, Elton John, The Wilsons, Don Henley, Beach Boys, Vince Gill, Eddie Money, Poison and many others. Musician: (albums) (solo) Playing it Cool, 1984, Timothy B., 1987, Tell Me the Truth, 1990, Feed the Fire, 2001, (with Poco) Poco, 1971, Deliverin', 1971, From the Inside, 1971, Good Feelin' to Know, 1972, Crazy Eyes, 1973, Cantamos, 1974, Seven, 1974, Head Over Heels, 1975, Very Best of Poco, 1975, Rose of Cimarron, 1976, Live, 1976, Indian Summer, 1977, Song of Richie Furay, 1979, Songs of Paul Cotton, 1979, Inamorato, 1984, Crazy Loving: The Best of Poco..., 1989, Forgotten Trail (1969-1974), 1990, (with The Eagles) Long Run, 1979, Eagles Live, 1980, Eagles Greatest Hits, Vol. 2, 1982, Hell Freezes Over, 1994, The Very Best of the Eagles, 1994, Selected Works: 1972-79, 2000, The Very Best of the Eagles, 2001, 2003. Named to with The Eagles, Rock and Roll Hall of Fame, 1998. Office: Lucan Records Ste 2D 8961 Sunset Blvd Los Angeles CA 90069*

SCHMITT, EDWARD A. manufacturing executive; Gen. mgr. ops. Ga. Gulf Corp., Atlanta, v.p. ops., 1993-97, exec. v.p., COO, 1997, CEO, pres., 1997—, also bd. dirs. Office: Ga Gulf Corp Ste 595 400 Perimeter Center Ter NE Atlanta GA 30346-1264

SCHMITT, GEORGE FREDERICK, JR., materials engineer; b. Louisville, Nov. 3, 1939; s. George Frederick and Jane Limbird (Hurst) S.; m. Ann Cheatham, July 31, 1965; 2 children. BS, U. Louisville, 1962, MS, 1963; MBA, Ohio State U., 1966. Chief integration and ops. divsn. Air Force Rsch. Lab. USAF Materials Directorate, Wright Patterson AFB, Ohio, 1966—; advanced engring devel. mgr. USAF Materials Lab., Wright Patterson AFB, Ohio, 1986-90, chief plans and programs br. Wright AFB, Ohio, 1989-90, asst. chief nonmetallic materials divsn., 1990-96. Guest lectr. U. Dayton, 1970, 95, Cath. U., 1973, U. Mich., 1975. Contbr. articles to profl. jours. Mem. Kettering (Ohio) Civic Band, 1965—, Affiliate Socs. Coun. Dayton, 1972-81; mem. Dayton Philharm Chorus, 1999—, Dayton Letter Carriers Band, 2000—, windjammers Circus Music Preservation Soc., 2001—. 1st lt. USAF, 1963-66. Named Fed. Profl. Employee of Yr., Dayton, 1972, One of Ten Outstanding Engrs., Engrs. Week, 1975; recipient Air Force Meritorious Civilian Svc. award, 1994, Burton award for svc., Playhouse South Cmty. Theater, 1998, Tech. Transfer award, Fed. Lab. Consortium, 2001, Internat. Program Supr. award, 2002. Fellow Soc. for Advancement Materials and Process Engrs. (Best Paper award 1973, nat. sec. 1975-76, nat. membership chmn. 1977-79, nat. v.p. 1979-81, nat pres. 1981-82, chmn. long-range planning com. 1983-87, trustee 1991—, chmn. Internat. SAMPE Symposium 1996, chmn. SAMPE Trophy com. 1998—, chmn. SAMPE Internat. conf., 2003), AIAA (assoc., materials tech. com.); mem. ASTM (rec. sec. 72-75, chmn. com. on erosion and wear 1976-79, chmn. liaison subcom. 1979-83, award of merit 1981), Am. Chem. Soc., Affiliate Socs. Coun. Dayton (chmn. 1978-79). Republican. Lutheran. Home: 1500 Wardmier Dr Dayton OH 45459-3354 Office: AFRL Materials and Mfg Directorate MLO Wright-Patterson AFB 2977 Hobson Way Bldg 653 Dayton OH 45433-7733 Office Phone: 937-656-9209. E-mail: george.schmitt@wpafb.af.mil.

SCHMITT, HOWARD STANLEY, minister; b. Waterloo, Ont., Can., Oct. 19, 1933; came to U.S., 1971; s. Delton Howard and Beulah (Weber) S.; m. Dorothy Jean West, May 20, 1960; children: Valerie Jean Schmitt Jones, Jeffrey Howard. B Theology, Toronto Bible Coll., Ont., Can., 1963. Ordained to ministry Mennonite Ch., 1963. Pastor Wanner Mennonite Ch., Cambridge, Ont., 1960-71, Calvary Mennonite Ch., Ayr, Ont., 1964-69, S. Union Mennonite Ch., West Liberty, Ohio, 1971-83; hosp. chaplain Mary Rutan Hosp., Bellefontaine, Ohio, 1983-85; dir. devel. Adriel Sch., West Liberty, Ohio, 1985-86; pastor Bay Shore Mennonite Ch., Sarasota, Fla., 1986-95, Sharon Mennonite Ch., Plain City, Ohio, 1995—2004; transitional pastor Oak Grove Mennonite Ch., West Liberty, Ohio, 2004—. Sec. Mennonite Conf. Ont., Cambridge, 1970-71; overseer Ohio Conf. Mennonites, West Liberty, 1972-78, 84-86; moderator Southeast Mennonite Conf., Sarasota, 1989-92; mem. Mennonite Ch. Gen. Bd., 1991-95. Vice chair Mary Rutan Hosp. Bd., 1978-83; sec. Plain City Ch. Fellowship, 1997—2002. Recipient 13 Yrs. Svc. award Vol. Chaplains Group, Mary Rutan Hosp., 1985. Mem. Sarasota Mennonite Mins. Fellowship (past sec., chmn.), Plain City Pastors' Fellowship, Ctrl. Ohio Mennonite Pastor Peer Group, Ohio Conf. Mennonites Coun. Mennonite. E-mail: howjean@prodigy.net.

SCHMITT, JOHANNA MARIE, plant population biologist, educator; b. Phila., Mar. 12, 1953; d. William Francis and Laura Belle (Wear) S.; m. Darrell Marion West, Aug. 6, 1983. BA, Swarthmore (Pa.) Coll., 1974; PhD, Stanford U., 1981. Postdoctoral rsch. assoc. Duke U., Durham, N.C., 1981-82; asst. prof. Brown U., Providence, 1982-87, assoc. prof. biology, 1987-94, prof.,

1994—. Mem. R.I. Task Force, New Eng. Plant Conservation program, 1991—; mem. regional advisory com. New Eng. Plant Conservation program, 2000-. Assoc. editor Evolution, 1990-92, Am. Naturalist, 2000-2001; contbr. articles to profl. jours. including Evolution, Ecology, Am. Naturalist, Genetics, Nature. Bd. dirs. Sojourner House, Providence, 1989-92. NSF grad. fellow, 1974, mid. career fellow, 1992-93; rsch. grantee, 1984—; recipient faculty award for women, 1991—. Mem. Soc. for Study of Evolution (coun. mem. 1990-92, exec. v.p. 1994-95, v.p. 1999), Bot. Soc. Am., Ecol. Soc. Am., Am. Soc. Naturalists (v.p. 1997, pres. 2002). Achievements include research on ecological genetics and genomics of natural plant populations: density-dependent phenomena, gene flow and population structure, inbreeding depression, the evolution of sex, maternal effects, seed ecology, natural selection, evolution of plasticity, adaptive significance of phytochrome, ecological risks of transgenic plants. Office: Brown Univ Dept Ecology & Evolution Providence RI 02912-0001

SCHMITT, JOHN K. army officer; b. Buffalo, July 17, 1949; m. Mee Ja; children: Charlene, Jeffrey. BS in Chemistry, St. Bonaventure U., 1971; MS in Sys. Mgmt., U. So. Calif. Commd. 2d lt. U.S. Army, 1971, advanced through grades to brig. gen.; dep. comdg. gen. Ft. Carson, Colo., to 1998; dep. chief of staff for ops. and plans, dir. Army Digitization Office, Pentagon, Washington, 1998—. Decorated Legion of Merit, Meritorious Svc. medal with 3 oak leaf clusters, Order Nat. Security Merit Samil medal (Korea), Def. Superior Svc. medal, Republic of Korea Order Nat. Security Merit Semil medal, Army Commendation medal, Nat. Def. Svc. medal with Svc. star, Expert Infantryman badge, Master Army Aviator badge, Sr. Parachutist badge, Ranger Tab, Dept. Army Staff Identification badge, Republic of Korea Army Hon. Aviator Wings. Office: Dep Chief Staff Operations and Plans 3A522 400 Army Pentagon Washington DC 20310-0400*

SCHMITT, JOHN PATRICK, lawyer; b. Hempstead, N.Y., Oct. 23, 1956; s. William Jude and Janet Patricia (Hurley) S.; m. Sylvia Yvonne Picard, Mar. 10, 1979; children: Emily, Patrick, Daniel, Peter. AB, Georgetown U., 1977; JD, Fordham U., 1980. Bar: N.Y. 1981. Assoc. Lord Day & Lord, N.Y.C., 1980-82, Patterson, Belknap, Webb & Tyler LLP, N.Y.C., 1983-88, ptnr., 1989—. Mem. ABA, N.Y. State Bar Assn., Assn. of Bar of City of N.Y. Democrat. Roman Catholic. Office: Patterson Belknap Webb & Tyler LLP 1133 Avenue Of The Americas Fl 22 New York NY 10036-6731 E-mail: jpschmitt@pbwt.com.

SCHMITT, KARL MICHAEL, retired political scientist; b. Louisville, Ky., July 22, 1922; s. Edward Peter and Mary Ann (Iula) S.; m. Grace Bernadette Leary, June 18, 1949; children: Karl, Edward, Barbara, William, Michael. BA, Cath. U. Am., 1947, MA, 1949; PhD, U. Pa., 1954. Teaching asst. U. Pa., 1948-50; instr. history Niagara U., 1950-54, asst. prof., 1954-55; research analyst U.S. Dept. State, 1955-58; asst. prof. dept. govt. U. Tex., 1958-63, assoc. prof., 1963-66, prof., 1966-91, prof. emeritus, 1991—, chmn., 1975-80. Vis. prof. U. Calif., Los Angeles, summer 1959, Nat. War Coll., 1970-71; vis. sr. fellow U. Manchester, Eng., 1988-89; cons. Dept. of State, 1962-70 Author: Communism in Mexico; A Study in Political Frustration, 1965, Mexico and the United States, 1821-1973: Conflict and Coexistence, 1974, others. Contbr. articles to profl. jours. Served with U.S. Army, 1943-45. Decorated Purple Heart. Mem. Tex. Cath. Hist. Assn. (pres. 1976-77). Roman Catholic. Home: 2603 Pinewood Ter Austin TX 78757-2136

SCHMITT, NATALIE CROHN, theater educator; b. Chgo., Aug. 10, 1936; d. Nathan N. and Lera Christina C. BA, U. Chgo., 1958, MA, 1961; PhD, Stanford U., 1968. Asst. prof. U. Ill., Chgo., 1968-72, assoc. prof. theatre, 1972-88, prof. theatre, 1988-99, prof. English, 1992-99, prof. emeritus, 1999—. Dir. theatre Brown U., Providence, 1961-63, U. Ill., 1968-98; founder Looking Glass Theater, Providence, 1962, dir., 1962-65; vis. assoc. prof. Stanford (Calif.) U., 1985. Author: Actors and Onlookers, 1990; contbr. articles to profl. jours. Sr. fellow Humanities Inst., U. Ill., 1983, NEH, 1984, 1996-97, assoc. fellow Stanford U., 1996-97. Mem.: Assn. Theatre Higher Edn. (chair theatre rsch. project 1973—74, dir. project, regional advisor 1975—78, conf. planner 1992), Assn. Soc. Theatre Rsch. (exec. com. 1999—2002, fin. com. 2000—02, treas. 2001—02). Avocation: ballet. Office: U Ill Dept Performing Arts 1040 W Harrison M/C 255 Chicago IL 60607 E-mail: nschmitt@uic.edu.

SCHMITT, RALPH GEORGE, manufacturing executive; b. Tarrytown, N.Y., Aug. 8, 1944; s. Alfons George and Otillie Lucie (Mehler) Schmitt; m. Kathleen OShaughnessy; children: Ralpha Scott, Carrie Lee, Kurt Ryan. BS, MIT, 1966, MS, 1967, U. Calif., 1970. Engr. McDonnell Douglas, Huntington Beach, Calif., 1967-70, Rockwell Internat., Downey, Calif., 1970-72; pres., chmn. bd. dirs. TPG Industries, LA, 1972-74; gen. mgr. Columbia Yacht divsn. Whittaker Corp., Chesapeake, Va., 1975-76; v.p. ops., dir. R&G Sloane Mfg. Co., LA, 1976-83; dir. mgr.-plastics Sweetheart Products Group Ft. Howard Paper Co., Wilmington, Mass., 1983-86; v.p., gen. mgr. PHI, City of Industry, Calif., 1986-90; v.p. ops. Dowty Aerospace, LA, 1991-93, Applied Sys. divsn. York (Pa.) Internat., 1993-96, v.p. product engring. and mfg. tech., 1996-99; v.p., gen. mgr. Airside Products, 1999-2000, Chillers, 2000—02; pres. Kysor//Warren, Columbus, Ga., 2002—. Mem.: Soc. Concurrent Product Devel. (adv. bd. dirs. 2002—), MIT Alumni Assn. (mem. nat. selection com. 1991—93, class v.p.), Sigma Xi, Sigma Alpha Epsilon, Sigma Gamma Tau, Tau Beta Pi. Home: 182 Burnt Hickory Way Fortson GA 31808-4468 Office Phone: 706-568-1514. E-mail: rschmitt@kysorwarren.com.

SCHMITT, ROBERT LEE, computer scientist; b. Astoria, NY, Oct. 1, 1948; s. Edward and Margaret Louise (Gleason) S.; m. Elsy Evagelene Burnett, June 1999; stepchildren: Eric Jason Marin, Alexis Michelle Marin. AAS in Data Processing, SUNY, Farmingdale, 1972; student, Hofstra U., 1972-73; BS in Computer Sci., SUNY, Stony Brook, 1974, MS in Computer Sci., 1975; postgrad., U. Md., 1979-80, 94-96; grad. diploma in strategic sci., U.S. Naval War Coll., 1991. Cert. computer programmer, data processor. Computer programmer U.S. Army Environ. Hygiene Agy., Aberdeen Proving Ground, Md., 1976; data sys. programmer Dept. Def., Ft. George G. Meade, Md., 1976—78, data sys. analyst, 1978—83, computer sys. analyst, 1983—85, sr. computer sys. analyst, 1985—86, computer scientist, 1986—89, mgr. sys. acquisition, 1989—94, dep. dir. for tech. fellow, 1994—95, sr. computer scientist, 1995—96, stds., tng. and verification engr., 1996—97, sys. engr., 1997—99, mgr. yr. 2000 compliance, 1999, sys. arch. implementation engr., 2000—01, sys. engr., 2001—02, dep. chief engring. divsn., 2002—03, acting dep. chief Sys. Engring Office, engr., 2003, lead sys. engr., 2003—. With Va. Summer Inst. for Math. Tchrs., 1995-96, dir. 1996-2000. With USNR, 1968-79. Home: 3002 Viburnum Pl Olney MD 20832-3073 Office: 9800 Savage Rd Fort George G Meade MD 20755-6000 Personal E-mail: robertleeschmitt@comcast.net.

SCHMITT, ROLAND WALTER, retired academic administrator; b. Seguin, Tex., July 24, 1923; s. Walter L. and Myrtle F. (Caldwell) S.; m. Claire Freeman Kunz, Sept. 19, 1957; children: Lorenz Allen, Brian Walter, Alice Elizabeth, Henry Caldwell. BA in Math, BS in Physics, U. Tex., 1947, MA in Physics, 1948; PhD, Rice U., 1951; DSc (hon.), Worcester Poly. Inst., 1985, U. Pa., 1985; DCL (hon.), Union Coll., 1985; DL (hon.), Lehigh U., 1986; DSc (hon.), U. S.C., 1988, U. Tech. De Compeigne, 1991; DL (hon.), Coll. St. Rose, 1992, Russell Sage, 1993, Hartford Grad. Ctr., 1995, Ill. Inst. Tech., 1996, Rensselaer Polytechnic Inst., 1997. With GE, 1951-88, R & D mgr. phys. sci. and engring., 1967-74, mgr. energy sci. and engring. R & D, 1974-78, v.p. corp. R & D, 1978-82, sr. v.p. corp. R & D, 1982-86, sr. v.p. sci. and tech., 1986-88, ret., 1988; pres. Rensselaer Poly. Inst., Troy, N.Y., 1988-93; ret., 1993. Bd. dirs. Blasch Precision Ceramics, GlobalSpec.com, Logical Net, Value Innovations; chair adv. bd. NYSTAR; bd. advisors LearnLinc, 1996-2000; tech. adv. bd. Chrysler Corp., 1990-93; tech. adv. coun. Mobil Corp., 1997-99; mem., past pres. Indsl. Rsch. Inst., 1978-88; energy rsch. adv. bd. U.S. Dept. Energy, 1977-83; mem. Nat. Sci. Bd., 1982-94, chmn., 1984-88; chmn. CORETECH, 1988-93; mem. Com. on Japan, NRC, 1988-90, Comml. Devel. Ind. Adv. Group, NASA, 1988-90; exec. com. Coun. on Competitiveness, 1988-93; chmn. NRC Panel on Export Controls, 1989-91; mem. Dept. Commerce Adv. Commn. on Patent Law Reform, 1990-92; adv. bd. Oak Ridge Nat. Lab., 1993-98; chair Rev. NATO Sci. program, 1998; mem. NRC panel rev. state dept. use sci. tech. and health, 1999—; chmn. Motorola's Sci. Adv. Bd., 1995-99; chmn. rsch. priority panel for NRC Future of Space Sci., 1994-95. Trustee N.E. Savs. Bank, 1978-84; bd. advisors Union Coll., Schenectady, 1981-84, Argonne Univs. Assn., 1979-82, RPI, 1982-88; bd. govs. Albany Med. Ctr. Hosp., 1979-82, 88-90; bd. dirs. Sunnyview Hosp. and Rehab. Ctr., 1978-86, Coun. on Superconductivity for Am. Competitiveness, 1987-89; mem. exec. com. N.Y. State Ctr. for Hazardous Waste Mgmt., 1988-89; chmn. Office of Tech. Assessment adv. panel on industry and environment; mem. Nat. Commn. Ill. Inst. Tech., 1993-94; chair NSF Acad. Rsch. Fleet Rev., 1998-99. With USAAF, 1943-46. Recipient RPI Community Svc. award, 1982, award for disting. contbns. Stony Brook Found., 1985, Rice U. Disting. Alumni award, 1985, IRI Medalist award, 1989, Royal Swedish Acad. of Engring. Sci., 1990, Arthur M. Bueche award Nat. Acad. of Engring., 1995, N.Y. State Bus. Coun.'s Corning award, 2001; named Fgn. Assn. of Engring. Acad. of Japan, U. Albany Found. Acad. Laureate, 1997; named to Jr. Achievement Capital Region Bus. Hall of Fame, 1996; inducted RPI Hall of Fame, 1999. Fellow AAAS, IEEE (Centennial medal 1984, Engring. Leadership award 1989, Founders medal 1992, Hoover medal 1993), Am. Phys. Soc. (Pake award 1993), Am. Acad. Arts and Scis.; mem. NAE (coun.), Am. Inst. Physics (chmn. 1993-98), Coun. Sci. Soc. Pres. (chair 1993-97), N.Y. Acad. Scis. (pres. coun. 1993—), Dirs. Indsl. Rsch., Rensselaer Alumni Assn. (Disting. alumni award 1993), Eta Kappa Nu (eminent mem.) Office: PO Box 240 Rexford NY 12148-0240 Office Phone: 518-384-0965. E-mail: roland@schmitt.org.

SCHMITT, STEPHEN RICHARD, electronics engineer; b. Phila., July 31, 1948; s. Robert Diehl and Janet Olive (Lawson) S.; m. Suzanne Marie Sachs, Oct. 9, 1981. BSc, Brown U., 1971; MSE, U. Pa., 1978. Registered profl. engr., Pa. Engr. Stone & Webster Engring. Corp., Cherry Hill, N.J., 1978-79, The Franklin Inst., Phila., 1980-81, Naval Air Devel. Ctr., Warminster, Pa., 1981-89; electronics engr. Hanscom AFB, 1989—. Served with USN, 1971-76. Mem.: Masons. Independent. Episcopalian. Home: 962 Depot Rd Boxboro MA 01719-1119 Office: AFSC/ESC/SR Hanscom AFB MA 01731 Office Phone: 781-377-5600. E-mail: srschmitt@att.net.

SCHMITT, WILLIAM ALLEN, lawyer; b. Louisville, Aug. 29, 1909; s. Michael Joseph and Naoma Katherine Schmitt; m. Dorothy S. Turner, June 12, 1936 (dec. Feb. 1998); 1 child, Selene S. Kaelin. Student, U. Louisville, 1933. Bar: Ky. 1936, U.S. Dist. Ct. (we. dist.) Ky. 1936, N.C. 1997. Pvt. practice law, Louisville, 1936—; assoc. atty. Schmitt & Schmitt, Louisville, 1936-60; judge Jefferson County Probate Ct., Louisville, 1962-70; alcohol beverage control adminstr. Jefferson County Govt., Louisville, 1962-70; law ptnr. Schmitt & Sandmann, Louisville, 1968-74; pvt. practice law Louisville, 1974—, Jamestown, N.C., 1997—. Author: Kentucky Probate, 1980, 2nd edit., 1997; contbr. articles to profl. jours. Election poll judge various gen. elections, Louisville; active Muir Chapel United Meth. Ch.; pres. Wildwood Country Club, 1964, Legal Aid Soc., Louisville, 1968. Lt. USN, 1944-46. Named to, Ky. Tennis Hall of Fame, 1993. Mem. ABA, ATLA, Am. Arbitration Assn. (arbitration panelist 1983—, cert. mediator 1985—), Nat. Assn. Securities Dealers (arbitration panelist 1990—, cert. mediator 1994—), Am. Coll. Trust and Estate Counsel (state chmn. 1978-83), Ky. Bar Assn. (life, spkr. at seminars and convs. 1960-80, pres. 1970-71, probate com. 1970-86, chmn. 1977-81, trustee 1971-86, chmn. 1978-86, clients indemnity fund), N.C. State Bar Assn., N.C. State Bar, Louisville Bar Assn. (spkr. at seminars 1960-80, pres. 1966, chmn. probate com. 1974-79, various meritorious svc. awards 1966-75). Avocation: tennis. Home: 109 Sagewood Rd Jamestown NC 27282-9489 Office: PO Box 997 Jamestown NC 27282-0997 also: 500 Ky Home Life Bldg 239 S 5th St Louisville KY 40202-3213 Office Phone: 336-887-1135.

SCHMITT, WOLF RUDOLF, consumer products executive; b. Koblenz, Germany, Mar. 12, 1944; s. Josef H. and M.H. (Baldus) S.; m. Toni A. Yoder, June 30, 1974. BA, Otterbein Coll., 1966; AMP, Harvard U. Bus. Sch., 1986. With Rubbermaid Inc., Wooster, Ohio, 1966—, pres., gen. mgr. housewares products div., 1984-91, exec. v.p., bd. dirs., 1987-91, pres., chief operating officer, 1991-92; chmn., CEO, 1993-99; ret., 1999. Bd. dirs. Parker Hannifin Corp., Kimberly-Clark Corp.; chmn. Value Am. Bd. dirs. Otterbein Coll., 1992—. Avocations: horticulture, tennis, sailing. Office: Trends 2 Innovation 105 E Liberty St Wooster OH 44691-4345

SCHMITTER, CHARLES HARRY, electronics manufacturing company executive, lawyer; b. Paterson, N.J., Feb. 4, 1928; s. Charles and Jennie (Schoe) S.; m. Margaret Ann Roose, Oct. 24, 1964 (dec. Dec. 1989). AB magna cum laude, Rutgers U., 1948; JD, Columbia, 1953. Bar: N.Y. bar 1956, Mich. bar 1960. Asso. atty. firm Cravath, Swaine & Moore, N.Y.C., 1955-59; asst. sec. Ford Motor Co., 1959-64; corp. sec. Sperry Rand Corp. (now Unisys Corp.), N.Y.C., 1964-87, ret., 1987. Served with AUS, 1953-55. Mem. Am. Bar Assn., Am. Soc. Corp. Secretaries, Phi Alpha Delta, Theta Chi. Clubs: Rockefeller Center Luncheon (N.Y.C.). Home: 420 E 51st St New York NY 10022-8014

SCHMITZ, ANDREW, agricultural studies educator; b. Central Butte, Saskatchewan, Canada, Oct. 5, 1940; s. Andreas and Katherine Schmitz; m. Helen Carole Anderson, July 16, 1966; children: Troy Gordon, Katrina Laur-Ayn Funk, Andre Lloyd, Evan Denis, Dean Michael. BSA, MSc, U. of Sask., 1963; PhD, U. Wis., 1968. D. of Letters-D.Lit. U. of Sask., 1999. Prof. U. of Calif. Dept. Agrl. and Resource Econs., Berkeley, Calif., 1968—94; rsch. prof. U. of Calif., 1986—; adj. prof. U. of Sask., Saskatoon, Canada, 1986—; chair U. of Calif. Dept. Agrl., Resource Econs., Berkeley, Calif., 1989—93; eminent scholar-ben hill griffin jr. endowed chair U. of Fla. Food and Resource Economics, Gainesville, Fla., 1994—; hon. chair U. Sask. Ctr. Study of Agrl., Law, Environment, Saskatoon, Canada, 2001. Project dir. Econ. Coun. Can., Saskatoon, SK, Canada, 1986—89; fellow Am. Agrl. Economics Assn., 1985—; rsch. dir. Turkish Agrl. Econs. Rsch. Inst., Ankara, Turkey, 1998—98; cons. various govt. agencies, various legal firms. Contbr. articles to prof. jours. Recipient Best Pub. Rsch., Western Agrl. Econs. Assn., 1980, Am. Agrl. Econs. Assn., 1981, Rsch. of Enduring Quality, 1984, 1987, Best Pub. Rsch., 1970, 1978, Quality of Comm., 1979, Lifetime Achievement award, So. Agrl. Econs. Assn., 2003, Enduring Rsch. Quality award, Am. Agrl. Econs. Assn., 2003. Fellow: Am. Agrl. Econs. Assn. Office: U Fla 1130A McCarty Hall Gainesville FL 32611-0240 Office Phone: 352-392-1845 415. E-mail: aschmitz@ifas.ufl.edu.

SCHMITZ, CLARENCE T. investment company executive; Exec. v.p., CFO Jefferies Group Inc., L.A.; mng. dir. Golenberg Schmitz Capital Ptnrs., LLC, L.A., 2000—. Office: Outsource Partners Internat Inc Ste 350 11150 Santa Monica Blvd Los Angeles CA 90025-3384

SCHMITZ, DENNIS MATHEW, English language educator; b. Dubuque, Iowa, Aug. 11, 1937; s. Anthony Peter and Roselyn S.; m. Loretta D'Agostino, Aug. 20, 1960; children— Anne, Sara, Martha, Paul, Matthew. BA, Loras Coll., 1959; MA, U. Chgo., 1961. Instr. English Ill. Inst. Tech., Chgo., 1961-62, U. Wis., Milw., 1962-66; asst. prof. Calif. State U., Sacramento, 1966-69, assoc. prof., 1969-74, prof., 1974-99; ret., 1999. Poet-in-residence, 1966-99. Author: We Weep for Our Strangeness, 1969, Double Exposures, 1971, Goodwill, Inc., 1976, String, 1980, Singing, 1985, Eden, 1989, About Night: Selected and New Poems, 1993, The Truth Squad, 2002. Recipient Discovery award Poetry Center, N.Y.C., 1968; winner First Book Competition Follett Pub. Co., 1969; di Castagnola award Poetry Soc. Am., 1986; Shelley Meml. award Poetry Soc. Am., 1987; NEA fellow, 1976-77, 85-86, 92-93, Guggenheim fellow, 1978-79. Mem. PEN, Assoc. Writing Programs. Roman Catholic.

SCHMITZ, DOLORES JEAN, primary education educator; b. River Falls, Wis., Dec. 27, 1931; d. Otto and Helen Olive (Webster) Kreuziger; m. Karl Matthias Schmitz Jr., Aug. 18, 1956; children: Victoria Jane, Karl III. BS, U. Wis., River Falls, 1953; MS, Nat. Coll. Edn., 1982; postgrad., U. Minn., Mankato, 1969, U. Melbourne, Australia, 1989, U. Wis., Milw., 1989, Carroll Coll., 1990, Cardinal Stritch Coll., 1990. Cert. tchr., Wis. Tchr. Manitowoc (Wis.) Pub. Schs., 1953-56, West Allis (Wis.) Pub. Schs., 1956-59, Lowell Sch., Milw., 1960-63, Victory Sch., Milw., 1964, Palmer Sch., Milw., 1966-84, 86-94, unit leader, 1984-86; ret., 1994. Co-organizer Headstart Tchg. Staff Assn., Milw., 1968; insvc. organizer Headstart and Early Childhood, Milw., 1969-92; pilot tchr. for Whole Lang., Hi-Scope and Math. Their Way, 1988-93; bd. dirs. Curriculum Devel. Ctr. of Milw. Edn. Ctr., 1993-94. Author: (curriculum) Writing to Read, 1987, Cooperation and Young Children (ERIC award 1982), Kindergarten Curriculum, 1953. Former supporter Milw. Art Mus., Milw. Pub. Mus., Milw. County Zoo, Whitefish Bay Pub. Libr., Riveredge Nature Ctr.; vol. fgn. visitor program Milw. Internat. Inst., 1966-94, holiday folk fair, 1976-94, Earthwatch, 1989; lobbyist Milw. Pub. Sch. Bd. and State of Wis., 1986-93; coord. comty. vols., 1990-94. Grantee Greater Milw. Ednl. Trust, 1989. Mem. NEA (life), ASCD, Milw. Kindergarten Assn. (rec. sec. 1986-93), Nat. Assn. for Edn. of Young Children, Tchrs. Applying Whole Lang., Wis. Early Childhood Assn., Milw. Tchrs. Ednl. Assn. (co-chmn. com. early childhood 1984-86), Assn. for Childhood Edn. Internat. (charter pres. Manitowoc chpt. 1955-56), Milw. Educating Computer Assn., Alpha Psi Omega. Roman Catholic. Avocations: bicycling, nature, world travel. Home: 1355 Pinellas Bayway S Apt 22 Tierra Verde FL 33715-2140 Personal E-mail: dolintv@aol.com. *Like a very old song said-Accentuate the POSITIVE, eliminate the negative,and don't mess with Mr. In-Between. Life is better for you and everyone around you if these "rules" are followed. Success=If it is to be, it is up to me. I can.*

SCHMITZ, EDWARD HENRY, retired distribution company executive; b. Glenbeulah, Wis., June 21, 1929; s. John Charles and Angeline Ann (Gundrum) S.; m. Janyth Lanier, Dec. 26, 1959; stepchildren: Janyth Lynn, Leslee; children: Robert, Ellen. BS in Bus. Adminstrn., Bryant Coll., 1955. Cert. purchasing mgr. Cons. engr. Alexander Proudfoot Co., Chgo., 1957—60; prod. inventory control mgr. Hills-McCanna co., Carpentersville, Ill., 1960—61; mgr. purchasing and traffic Hooker Glass Co., Chgo., 1961-65; materials mgr. API Industries, Chgo., 1965-71; purchasing mgr. G&W Electric Co., Blue Island, Ill., 1971-92; mgr. transp. svcs. Chgo. Tube and Iron Co., 1992-98, ret., 1998. Mem. First US Procurement Delegation to USSR, 1990; nation chief YMCA Indian Guide Youth Program, 1974—77; program dir. YMCA Trailblazer Youth Program, 1977—80. With U.S. Army, 1951—53. Apptd. adm. Gt. Navy of Nebr., 1977. Mem. Purchasing Mgmt. Assn. (bd. dirs. Chgo. chpt. 1971-73, 83-85), Nat. Assn. Purchasing Mgmt. (dist. chmn. 1980-90, asst. nat. chmn. 1989-91, nat. chmn. 1991-93), Am. Prodn. and Inventory Control soc., Traffic Men's Assn. of Chgo. (bd. dirs. 1994-98). Avocation: canoeing. Home: 1928 Calla Dr Joliet IL 60435-8522

SCHMITZ, JOHN, grain company executive; BS in Acctg., St. Cloud State U. CPA, Minn. With Harvest States (merged with Cenex, now Cenex Harvest States), Inver Grove Heights, Minn., 1974—, v.p., contr., 1986, sr. v.p., CFO, 1999, exec. v.p., CFO. Mem. AICPA, Nat. Soc. Accts. for Cooperatives, Minn. Soc. CPAs. Office: Cenex Harvest States 550 Cenex Dr Inver Grove Heights MN 55077

SCHMITZ, JOHN J. writer, educator; b. Fond du Lac, Wis., Mar. 9, 1937; s. John L. Schmitz and Josephine Knaus; children: David, Rebecca. BA, St. Francis Sem., 1963. CLU Am. Coll. Life Underwriters, 1975. Pres. John Schmitz Agy., Brookfield, Wis., 1992—; instr. Hondros Coll., Columbus, Ohio, 1994—. Cons. Bryant and Stratton Coll., Milw., 2003—04. Author: A Funny Thing Happened On My Way Out of Church, JoAnn: In Search of N.E.D. Bd. mem., officer Elmbrook Sch. Bd., Brookfield, Wis., 1988—92. Mem.: KC (assoc.; grand knight 1996—97). Achievements include development of Insurance Courses for Continuing Education. Avocations: writing, photography, travel. Home: 405 Lynnwood Lane Brookfield WI 53005-6134 Office: John Schmitz Agency 405 Lynnwood Lane Brookfield WI 53005-6134 Personal E-mail: jschmitz13@wi.rr.com. E-mail: jschmitz13@wi.rr.com.

SCHMITZ, JOHN PHILLIP, maxillofacial surgeon, researcher; b. Frankfurt, Germany, Germany, Jan. 3, 1953; s. Dorothy Budzein Schmitz; children: John Andrew, Anne Katherine, Kathleen Elizabeth Schmitx. PhD, Univ Tex. Health Sci. Ctr., 1996—96; DDS, Marquette U., 1978; MS, U. Maryland, 1987. Resident Univ. Hosp, San Antonio; prof. UTHSCSA, San Antonio, 2003—. Assoc. prof. UTHSCSA, 1993—2000. Mem. Leadership San Antonio, Tex., 2002—03. Ltc U.S. Army, 1972—2000. Achievements include first to develop edendoscopic Approaches For Mandibular Surgery In Children; developed and patented biodegradable bone repair substitutes. Office: San Pedro Facial Surgery 14500 San Pedro Ste 102 San Antonio TX Office Phone: 210-491-0015. Office Fax: 210-491-0352. Personal E-mail: schmitzjp@hotmail.com. E-mail: schmitzjp@hotmail.com.

SCHMITZ, ROBERT ALLEN, publishing executive, investor; b. Chgo., Jan. 19, 1941; s. John and Lee (Zeal) S.; m. Jenny Ann Quest, Aug. 23, 1969 (div.); m. Judith Mair Grey, Oct. 25, 1997; children: Alexander, Nicholas, Lara, Maximilian. BA with distinction, U. Mich., 1963; MBA, MIT, 1965. Asst. to pres. Lima (Peru) Light and Power Co., 1965-67; acquisition analyst W.R. Grace Co., N.Y.C., 1967-69; asst. to chmn. N.W. Industries, N.Y.C., 1969-70; prin. McKinsey & Co., Inc., N.Y.C., 1970-82; v.p. books Dow Jones & Co., N.Y.C., 1982-88; chmn., pres., chief exec. officer Richard D. Irwin, Inc., Homewood, Ill., 1983-89; pres., founder Quest Capital Ltd., 1989—; investment cons. Soros Fund Mgmt., 1990-92; mgn. dir., sr. ptnr. Trust Co. of the West, 1993-97; mng. dir., founder. Quest Turnaround Advisors, 1999—, COO, 2002—; chmn., founder Headline Media Group, 2001—. Mem. adv. bd. Coll. Commerce De Paul U., Chgo., 1985—; bd. dirs. Two Way Media, London, Premium TV Ltd., Cablecom GmBH, Zurich, Adams Rite Sabre, Inc., Glendale, Calif., Superior Fireplace Co., Fullerton, Calif., Houston Foods Co., Chgo., Archibald Candy Co., Chgo., US Media Group, Inc., Crystal City, Mo., Ctrl. Valley Publ., Merced, Hobby Products Co., Inc., Penrose, Colo., Automated Bar Controls, Vacaville, Calif., Spectran Techs., Inc., Sturbridge, Mass.; non-exec. chmn. PTV Ltd., London, 2 Way Media Ltd., London. Pres. Cultural Arts Ctr. Found., Homewood, Ill. Mem. Assn. Am. Pubs. (chmn. higher edn. divsn. 1989), Nature Conservancy (trustee N.Y. state chpt.). Office: Quest Capital Ltd 37 Purchase St Rye NY 10580 Office Phone: +44-7968285821. E-mail: bob.schmitz@ptvinc.com.

SCHMITZ, ROGER ANTHONY, chemical engineer, educator, academic administrator; b. Carlyle, Ill., Oct. 22, 1934; s. Alfred Bernard and Wilma Afra (Aarns) Schmitz; m. Ruth Mary Kuhl, Aug. 31, 1957; children: Jan, Joy, Joni. BSChemE, U. Ill., 1959; PhD in Chem. Engring., U. Minn., 1962. Prof. chem. engring. U. Ill., Urbana, 1962-79; Keating-Crawford prof. chem. engring. U. Notre Dame, Ind., 1979—, chmn. dept. chem. engring., 1979-81, dean engring., 1981-87, v.p., assoc. provost, 1987-95. Cons. Amoco Chems., Naperville, Ill., 1966—77; vis. prof. Calif. Inst. Tech., L.A., 1968—69. Contbr. articles to profl. jours. With U.S. Army, 1953—55. Fellow, Guggenheim Found., 1968. Mem.: AIChE (A.P. Colburn award 1970, R.H. Wilhelm award 1981), Am. Soc. Engring. Edn. (George Westinghouse award 1977), Nat. Acad. Engring. Roman Catholic. Home: 16865 Londonberry Ln South Bend IN 46635-1444 Office: U Notre Dame 301 Cushing Hall Notre Dame IN 46556 Office Phone: 574-631-7798. Business E-Mail: schmitz.1@nd.edu.

SCHMITZ, SHIRLEY GERTRUDE, marketing and sales executive; b. Brackenridge, Pa., Dec. 19, 1927; d. Wienand Gerard and Florence Marie (Grimm) S. BA, Ariz. State U., 1949. Tchr., guidance counselor Mesa HS, Ariz., 1949-51; area mgr. Field Enterprises Ednl. Corp., Phoenix, 1951-52, dist. mgr., 1952, regional mgr., 1953-55, br. mgr. Montreal, 1955-61, nat. supr. Chgo., 1961-63, asst. sales mgr., 1963-65, nat. sales mgr., 1965-70; v.p., gen. sales mgr. F.E. Compton Co. divsn. Ency. Brit., Chgo., 1970-71, exec. v.p., dir. sales, 1971-73; pres. CHB Port-A-Book Store, Inc., 1973-76; gen. mgr. Bobbs-Merrill Co., Inc., Indpls., 1976-82; v.p. sales U. S. Telephone Comms. of Midwest, Inc., Indpls., 1982-83; exec. v.p. sales and market devel. Entertainment Publ. Corp., Birmingham, Mich., 1983-89, sr. v.p. mktg. and sales Troy, Mich., 1989-92. Prin. S.G. Schmitz and Assocs., Chgo., 1992—; bd. adv., founder Ctr. Advancement Small Bus., Ariz. State U. W.P. Carey, Sch. Bus.; pres.'s cabinet capital fund raising campaign Ariz. State U. Bd. dirs., founder, pres. Shirley G. Schmitz Found., Inc. Recipient Elizabeth Cutter Morrow award Internat. Bd. YWCA, 1978, Disting. Achievement award Ariz. State U., 1995, Angel award Ariz. chpt. Nat. Assn. Women Bus. Owners, 1996,

Nat. Bus. Achievement award Beta Gamma Sigma, 1998, Impact for Enterprising Women award, 2001. Home: 11899 N 135th Way Scottsdale AZ 85259-3651 Office: SG Schmitz and Assocs Scottsdale AZ 85259-3651 E-mail: reysgs@aol.com.

SCHMITZ, STEPHEN E. mental health specialist, writer; s. Eugene J. and Evelyn K. Schmitz; life ptnr. Patricia A. Walker; children from previous marriage: Conzuelo Richman, Chia. BA in political sci., Colo. State U., 1971—76; MA in curriculum/instrn., U. Colo., 1990—93; PhD in found. edn., U. Fla., 1990—93. Asst. prof. edn. U. Guam, 1993—97; instr. Micronesian Lang. Inst., 1994—96; dir. chem. dependency svc. Cedar Crest Found., 1998—99; dir./chief adminstr. Cole Vocat. Svc., 2000; instr. writing, psychology, humanities ITT Tech. Inst., 2000—01; adj. instr. ESL Lyon Sch./Orangewood Children's Home, 2001—02, Orange Coast Coll., 2001—02; HIV case mgr. Orange County Health Care Agency, 2003—. Author: Gradebusters: How Parents Can Turn Underachievers Around, 1993, Strike Back! How Parents Can Bust the Teen Drug Culture, 1994; contbr. articles to profl. jours. Office: Orange County HCA Box 6099 Santa Ana CA 92702 E-mail: doctorschmitz@yahoo.com.

SCHMOKE, KURT L. dean, former mayor; b. Balt., Dec. 1, 1949; m. Patricia Schmoke; children: Katherine, Gregory. BA, Yale U., 1971; JD, Harvard U., 1976. Former assoc. Piper & Marbury; former pvt. practice; asst. U.S. atty; state's atty. Maryland, 1982-87; mayor City of Baltimore, 1987-99; ptnr. Wilmer Cutler Pickering LLP, Balt., 2000—03; dean Howard U. Sch. Law, Washington, 2003—. Apptd. mem. White House Domestic Policy Staff, 1977-78; former mem. Gov.'s Commn. on Prison Overcrowding; former mem. Md. Criminal justice Coord. Coun. & Task Force to Reform Insanity Def.; founder Balt. Community Devel. Financing Corp., 1988—. Office: Howard Univ Sch Law Office of the Dean 2900 Van Ness St NW Washington DC 20008*

SCHMOLKA, LEO LOUIS, law educator; b. Paris, Apr. 25, 1939; came to U.S., 1944; s. Francis and Irene S.; m. Lucille J. Schoenbaum, July 29, 1965; children— Andrew, Gregory. AB, Dartmouth Coll., 1960; LL.B., Harvard U., 1963; LL.M., NYU, 1971. Bar: N.Y. 1964. Assoc. Weil, Gotshal and Manges, N.Y.C., 1964-71, ptnr., 1971-81, of counsel, 1981—; adj. asst. prof. law NYU Sch. of Law, 1971-75; adj. assoc. prof. law NYU Law Sch., 1975-76, adj. prof., 1977-80, assoc. prof., 1981-84, prof., 1985—, mem. faculty, dir. IRS/NYU continuing profl. edn. program, 1987—. Cons. U.S. Treasury Dept. Office Tax Policy, Washington, 1994-95, Am. Law Inst., 1979-86, U. Miami (Fla.) Estate Planning Inst., 1976-80; vis. adj. prof. law U. Miami Sch. Law, 1977, 80, U. San Diego Sch. Law, 1999; vis. lectr. continuing legal edn. various univs. and tax insts., 1973—. Contbr. articles to legal jours. Fellow Am. Coll. Trust and Estate Counsel; mem. ABA, N.Y. State Bar Assn. (chmn. com. on income taxation estates and trusts 1973-75, estate and gift tax 1976-77, mem. exec. com. tax sect. 1978), Internat. Acad. Estate and Trust Law (academician). Office: NYU Sch Law 40 Washington Sq S Rm 430 New York NY 10012-1099 Office Phone: 212-998-6165. E-mail: schmolka@optonline.net.

SCHMOLL, HANS JOACHIM, internal medicine, hematology, oncology educator; b. Hannover, Germany, June 21, 1946; s. Johannes and Edeltraut (Schneider) S. MD, Med. U. Hannover, 1970, PhD, 1982. Rsch. assoc. Med. U., Hannover, 1971—84, prof. medicine and hematology-oncology, 1984—95; prof. medicine and hematology, chair hematology/oncology Martin Luther U., Halle-Wittenberg, Germany, 1996—. Author, editor: Kompendium Intern Onkologie, 1986, 4th edit., 2003; assoc. editor Cancer Rsch., 2002—; editor-in-chief Oncologie, 2001—; mem. editl. bd. European Jour. Cancer Annals of Oncology. Recipient German Cancer award, 2001, Sci. award, German Assn. Med. Oncologists, 1998. Mem.: German Assn. Med. Oncology (pres., chmn. 2001—). Home: Ludwig Barnay Strasse 9 D-30175 Hannover Germany Office: Martin Luther Univ Dept Hematol/Oncol Int Med IV D-06120 Halle Germany Office Phone: 00493455572924.

SCHMOLL, HARRY F., JR., lawyer, educator; b. Somers Point, N.J., Jan. 20, 1939; s. Harry F. Sr. and Margaret E. S.; m. Rita L. Miescier, Aug. 29, 1977. BS, Rider Coll., 1960; JD, Temple U., 1967. Bar: Pa., D.C. 1969, N.J. 1975. With claims dept. Social Security Adminstrn., Phila., 1960-67; staff atty. Pa. State U., State College, 1968-69, instr. criminal justice University Park, 1969-74; regional dir. Pa. Crime Commn., State College, 1969-70; campaign aide U.S. Senator Hugh Scott, Harrisburg, Pa., 1970; pvt. practice law State College, 1970-74, Manahawkin, NJ, 1975-96; prof. criminal justice, prof. emeritus bus. law Burlington County Coll., Pemberton, NJ, 1974—2002; assoc. Mattleman, Weinroth & Miller, P.C., Cherry Hill, NJ, 2003—. Judge mcpl. ct., Stafford Twp., 1982-85. Author: New Jersey Criminal Law Workbook, 1976, 2nd edit., 1979, Absecon Diary of Margie Roth, 1933-37, 2000. Former gen. counsel German Heritage Coun. N.J., Inc.; mem. Barnegat Twp. Rent Control Bd., 1991, Barnegat Twp. Zoning Bd., 1994; mem. fund distbn. com. United Way of Burlington County, N.J., 1987—; trustee H.B. Smith Indsl. Village Conservancy, 1988—; bd. trustees Holiday Village East Cmty. Svcs. Assn., 2003—; mem. Stafford Twp. Com., 1979-81; dep. mayor, 1979. Mem. Pa. Bar assn., N.J. Bar Assn., German-Am. Club So. Ocean County (past pres.), Tri-State Jazz Soc. (bd. dirs.). Office Phone: 856-429-5507. E-mail: HarrySchmoll2@comcast.net.

SCHMUKLER, SERGIO L. economist; arrived in U.S., 1992; PhD, U. Calif., Berkeley, 1997. Sr. economist World Bank, Washington, 1997—. Assoc. editor: Journal of Development Economics. Mem.: L.Am. and Caribbean Econ. Assn. (treas.). Office: World Bank 1818 H St NW Washington DC 20433 Office Phone: 202-458-4167.

SCHMULTS, EDWARD CHARLES, lawyer, corporate and philanthropic administrator, think-tank executive; b. Paterson, N.J., Feb. 6, 1931; s. Edward M. and Mildred (Moore) S.; m. Diane E. Beers, Apr. 23, 1960; children: Alison C., Edward M., Robert C. BS, Yale U., 1953; JD, Harvard U., 1958. Bar: N.Y. 1959, D.C. 1974. Assoc. White & Case, N.Y.C., 1958-65, ptnr., 1965-73, 77-81; gen. counsel Treasury Dept., Washington, 1973-74, undersec., 1974-75; dep. counsel to Pres. U.S., 1975-76; dep. atty. gen. of U.S. Dept. Justice, Washington, 1981-84; sr. v.p. external rels., gen. counsel GTE Corp., Stamford, Conn., 1984-94; sr. advisor Iraqi Ministry of Justice - Coalition Provisional Authority, 2004. Lectr. securities laws. Served to 1st lt. USMC, 1953-55; capt. USMCR. Mem. Am. Bar Assn., Assn. Bar City N.Y., Adminstrv. Conf. U.S. (council 1977-84), Sakonnet Golf Club, Met. Club.

SCHMUTZ, JOHN FRANCIS, lawyer; b. Oneida, NY, July 24, 1947; s. William L. and Rosemary S. Schmutz; m. H. Marie Roney, June 7, 1969; children: Gretchen, Jonathan, Nathan. BA cum laude, Canisius Coll., 1969; JD cum laude, Notre Dame U., 1972; LLM, George Washington U., 1975. Bar: Ind. 1972, DC 1975, Tex. 1993, U.S. Ct. Mil. Appeals 1972, U.S. Tax Ct. 1973, U.S. Supreme Ct. 1975. Legislation and maj. projects officer Office Judge Adv. Gen., 1972—74; appellate atty. U.S. Army Legal Svcs. Agy., 1974—75; assoc. Ice, Miller, Donadio & Ryan, Indpls., 1976—77; staff atty. Burger Chef Sys., Inc., Indpls., 1977—78, sr. atty., 1979, asst. chief legal counsel, 1978—80, chief legal counsel, 1980, v.p., gen. counsel, sec., 1981—91; v.p.-legal Hardee's Food Sys., Inc., 1983—91; v.p., gen. counsel Sbarro, Inc., 1991—92; v.p., gen. counsel, sec. La Quinta Inns, Inc., 1992—98, gen. counsel, sec., 1998—99; sr. v.p., gen. counsel, sec. Meditrust Cos., Inc., 2000—01, La Quinta Cos., Inc., 2001—02; founding prin. Turtle Creek Group, LLC, 2002—. Dir., v.p. Bursan Credit Union; dir. Food Svc. and Lodging Inst., RIX Sys., Inc., Burger Chef Distributive Corp.; v.p. Hardee's Food Sys., Inc. Exec. editor: Notre Dame Law Rev., 1971—72. Exec. bd. Boy Scouts Am.; bd. dirs. Blessed Sacrament Acad. Found. Mem.: ABA (dir. hospitality com., cmty. recreation and common interest devel. com.), Am. Corp. Counsel Assn. (bd. dirs.), Internat. Corp. Sec. Assn., Am. Hotel and Motel Assn. (gen. counsel com.), Nat. Restaurant Assn., Am. Assn. Corp. Counsel, San Antonio Bar Assn., Tex. Bar Assn., Indpls. Bar Assn., DC Bar Assn., Ind. Bar Assn., Fed. Bar Assn. Republican. Roman Catholic. Home: 17122 Eagle Star San Antonio TX 78248-1548 Office Phone: 210-240-3614. E-mail: jfschmutz@aol.com.

SCHMUTZHART, BERTHOLD JOSEF, sculptor, educator, art and education consultant; b. Salzburg, Austria, Aug. 17, 1928; came to U.S., 1958, naturalized, 1963; s. Berthold Josef and Anna (Valaschek) S. Student, Acad. for Applied Art, Vienna, Austria, 1956. Cert. fed. tchr., Austria. Prof. Werkschulheim Felbertal, Salzburg, 1951-58; sculptor Washington, 1959-60; tchr. Longfellow Sch., Bethesda, Md., 1960-63; prof., chmn. dept. sculpture Corcoran Sch. Art, Washington, 1963-94, prof. emeritus, 1994—; lectr. Smithsonian Instn., Washington, 1968-84. One-man shows include Fredericksburg Gallery Fine Art, Va., 1967-73, Franz Bader Gallery, Washington, 1978, 81, 83, 86, 88; group shows include Nat. Collection Fine Arts, Washington, 1961-70, High Mus. Art, Atlanta, 1965, Ark. Art Ctr., Little Rock, 1966, Birmingham Mus. Art, Ala., 1967, Hirschhorn Mus. and Sculpture Garden, Washington, 1981, Nat. Gallery Modern Art, New Delhi, 1990; represented in permanent collections Hirschhorn Collection; designer fountain, Gallery of Modern Art, Fredericksburg, 1967; author: The Handmade Furniture Book, 1981; contbr. articles to profl. jours. Fine arts panelist D.C. Commn. for Arts, 1973-79; chmn. bd. Market Five Gallery, Washington, 1978-82; bd. dirs. Franz Bader Gallery, Washington, 1981-86; trustee Arts for the Aging, Inc., Washington, 1990—98; chmn. Franz and Virginia Bader Fund, 2001—. Recipient 1st prize Washington Religious Arts Council, 1960, for sculpture, Little Rock, 1966, Louisville, 1968, Silver medal Audubon Soc., Washington, 1971 Mem. Guild for Religious Architects, Artists Equity Assn. (pres. D.C. chpt. 1973-75), AAUP, Am. Austrian Soc. (pres. 1968-70, exec. com.), Soaring Soc. Am. Home: 32 Layline Ln Fredericksburg VA 22406-4061 E-mail: bschmutzha@aol.com.

SCHNABEL, GARY A. health facility administrator, director; Compliance dir. Oreg. Bd. of Pharmacy, 1994-99, acting exec. dir., 1999, exec. dir., 1999—.

SCHNABEL, JULIAN, artist; b. 1951; B.F.A., U. Houston, 1972; postgrad., Whitney Mus. Ind. Study Program, N.Y.C., 1973-74. Exhibited one-man shows, Contemporary Art Mus., Houston, 1976, Galerie Dezember, Dusseldorf, West Germany, 1978, Mary Boone, N.Y.C., 1979, Daniel Weinberg Gallery, San Francisco, 1979, Bruno Bischofberger, Zurich, Switzerland, Young-Hoffman Gallery, Chgo., 1980, Mary Boone-Leo Castelli, N.Y.C., 1981, Stedelijk Mus., Amsterdam, Holland, 1982, Bruno Bischofberger, Zurich, Switzerland, 1982, Los Angeles County Mus. Art, 1982, U. Art Mus., Berkeley, Calif., 1982, The Tate Gallery, London, 1982, Mary Boone, N.Y.C., 1982, Bruno Bischofberger, Zurich, Switzerland, 1983, Leo Castelli, N.Y.C., 1983, Akron Art Mus., 1983, Leslie Waddington Gallery, London, 1983, Daniel Templon Gallery, Paris, 1983, Galerie Mario Diacono, Rome, 1983, Akira Ikeda Gallery, Tokyo, 1983, Donald Young Gallery, Chgo., Martine Hamilton Gallery, N.Y.C., Pace Gallery N.Y., 1984, Whitney Mus., 1988, San Francisco Mus. Modern Art, 1988, Mus. Fine Arts, Houston, 1988, Mus. Contemporary Art, Chgo., 1990, numerous others; group shows, Hidden Houston, U. St. Thomas, 1971, La. Gallery, Houston, 1972, W.I.S.P. Exhibition, Whitney Mus. Am. Art, N.Y.C., 1974, Holly Solomon Gallery, N.Y.C., 1977, Rennaissance Soc., U. Chgo., 1979, Daniel Templon, Paris, 1980, L'Amerique Aux Indepdendants, Grand Palais, Paris, 1980, Mary Boone, N.Y.C., 1980, La Biennale di Venezia, Venice, Italy, 1980, Indpls. Mus. Art, 1980, The Royal Acad., London, 1981, Whitney Mus. Am. Art, N.Y.C., 1981, Addison Gallery, Andover, Mass., 1981, Basel Kunstmuseum, Switzerland, 1981, Gayden Gallery, MIT, Cambridge, 1981, Kinsthallen, Goteborg, Sweden, 1981, Frankfurter Kunstverein, Frankfurt, West Germany, 1982, Inst. Contemporary Art, Boston, 1982, Whitney Mus. Am. Art, N.Y.C., 1982, Mus. Contemporary Art, LaJolla, Calif, 1982, Stedelijk Mus., Amsterdam, 1982, Art Inst. Chgo., 1982, la Biennale di Venezia, Venice, Italy, 1982, Fort Worth Art Mus., 1982, Milw. Art Mus., 1982, Stifelsen Karlsvik 10, Stockholm, 1983, Whitney Mus. Am. Art, N.Y.C., 1983, The Hirshhorn Mus., Washington, 1983, Nat. Mus. Art, Osaka, 1983, Bklyn. Mus., 1983, Mary Boone Gallery, N.Y.C., 1983, 64th Whitney Biennial, 1987, Pace Gallery, N.Y.C., 1990, Poche Gallery, Paris, 1991, Gian Ferrari Arte Contemporanea, Milan, 1993-94, Ramis Barquet Gallery, Mexico, 1995, Modern Art Gallery, Bologna, 1996-97, Thaddaeus Ropac, Salzburg, 1998-99, Galerie Forsblom, Helsinki, 2000; author: Nicknames of Maitre D's and Other Excerpts From Life, 1988; dir., screenwriter (film) Basquiat, 1996; writer, prodr. dir. (film) Before Night Falls, 2000. Office: Pace Gallery NY 32 E 57th St Fl 4 New York NY 10022-2530*

SCHNABEL, ROBERT VICTOR, retired academic administrator; b. Scarsdale, N.Y., Sept. 28, 1922; s. Frederick Victor and Louise Elizabeth (Frick) S.; m. Ellen Edyth Foelber, June 7, 1946; children: Mark F., Philip P. Student, Concordia Sem., St. Louis, 1943-45; AB, Bowdoin Coll., 1944; MS, Fordham U., 1951, PhD, 1955; LLD (hon.), Concordia Coll., 1988. Tchr. St. Paul's Sch., Ft. Wayne, Ind., 1945-49; prin. St. Matthew's Sch., N.Y.C., 1949-52; assoc. supt. edn. Central Dist., Luth. Ch.-Mo. Synod, 1952-56; asst. prof. philosophy Concordia Sr. Coll., Ft. Wayne, 1956-60, assoc. prof., 1960-65, prof., acad. dean, 1966-71; pres. Concordia Coll., Bronxville, N.Y., 1971-76; acad. v.p., dean Wartburg Coll., Waverly, Iowa, 1976-78; pres. Valparaiso (Ind.) U., 1978-88. Cons. Luth. Edn. Conf. N.Am., 1977-88. Contbr. articles to profl. jours. Mem. AAUP, Luth. Acad. Scholarship, Assoc. Colls. Ind., Nat. Assn. Ind. Colls. and Univs., Rotary, Phi Delta Kappa. Office: Valparaiso Univ 23 Huegli Hall Valparaiso IN 46383

SCHNABEL, ROCKWELL ANTHONY, ambassador; b. Amsterdam, Holland, Dec. 30, 1936; s. Hans and Wilhelmina S.; m. Marna Belle Del Mar, 1964; children: Mary Darrin, Christy Ann, Everton Anthony. BS in Bus. Adminstrn., Trinity Coll., The Netherlands, 1951-56; LLD (hon.), Pepperdine U. Pres. Unilife Assurance Group S.H. Luxembourg, 1974-78, Bateman Eichler Hill Richard Group, Los Angeles, 1981-83; U.S. amb. to Finland U.S. Dept. State, Helsinki, 1986—89; under sec. for travel and tourism U.S. Dept. Commerce, Washington, 1989-91, dep. sec., 1991-92, acting sec. of commerce, 1992-93; sr. ptnr. Trident Capital LLP Inc., L.A., 1992—2001; U.S. amb. to the European Union U.S. Dept. State, Brussels, 2001—. Bd. dirs. Internat. Game Tech., CSGystems Inc.; chmn. La.-Inc.; bd. trustees U. Calif. Bus. Sch. Past pres. L.A. Pension Bd., Calif., 1982; mem. L.A. Olympic Organizing Com., 1983-84. With Air N.G., 1958-64. Decorated comdr. Order of Good Hope, South Africa, Grand Cross of Lion of Finland; recipient Gold medal Dutch Govt., U.S. Dept. Commerce, medal of honor the Netherlands Olympic Com. Mem. L.A. Beach Club, Calif. Club, L.A. Country Club. Office: US Mission to the European Union Zinnerstraat 13 Rue Zinner B-1000 Brussels Belgium*

SCHNABEL, TIMOTHY BRIAN, writer, publishing executive; b. Elkhart, Ind., Mar. 2, 1963; s. John F. and Patsy J. Schnabel. BS, W.Va. U., Morgantown, 1985. Author: The Gift Giving Handbook For The Inept Man. Mem.: Publishers Mktg. Assn., Sigma Chi Frat. Lutheran. Office: Shanem Publishing 8491 Sunset Blvd #1700 West Hollywood CA 90069 Office Fax: 818-763-9166. Personal E-mail: tbs2000@aol.com. E-mail: shanempublishing@aol.com.

SCHNACK, HAROLD CLIFFORD, retired lawyer; b. Honolulu, Sept. 27, 1918; s. Ferdinand J. H. and Mary (Pearson) S.; m. Gayle Hemingway Jepson, Mar. 22, 1947 (dec. Feb. 24, 1998); children: Jerrald Jay, Georgina Schnack Hankinson, Roberta Schnack Poulin, Michael Clifford. BA, Stanford U., 1940, LLB, 1947. Bar: Hawaii 1947. Dep. prosecutor City and County Honolulu, 1947-48; gen. practice with father F. Schnack, 1948-60; pvt. practice, 1960—2001. Pres. Harcliff Corp., 1961—, Cedar Corp., 1964—, Schnack Indsl. Corp., 1969-73, Instant Printers, Inc., 1971-81, Koa Corp., 1964—, Nutmeg Corp., 1963-89, Global Answer Sys., Inc., 1972-78; pres., treas. Golden Rainbow, Inc. (Pasta Cafe), Reno, 2001-04. Pres. Goodwill Industries of Honolulu, 1971-72. Mem. Outrigger Canoe Club, Phi Alpha Delta, Alpha Sigma Phi. Office: 817 A Cedar St PO Box 3077 Honolulu HI 96802-3077

SCHNAITMAN, WILLIAM KENNETH, finance company executive; b. Talbot County, Md., May 12, 1926; s. William and Catherine Almeda (Cheezum) S.; m. Beverly June Marshall, July 13, 1963. Student, Strayer Bus. Sch., Balt., 1943. Clk. Comml. Credit Co., Balt., 1946-70, asst. sec., 1970-72, treas., 1972-75, dir. cash mgmt., 1976-87, ret., 1987. With AUS, 1944-46, ETO. Home: 12520 Wye Landing Ln Wye Mills MD 21679-2050

SCHNAKENBERG, DONALD G. financial administrator; b. Queens, N.Y., Dec. 6, 1939; s. Herman G. and Rose (Conte) S. BS in Acctg., Bklyn. Coll., 1960; MBA in Mgmt. with honors, Pace U., 1969. Acct. Rosen, Futterman & Berylson CPA's, N.Y.C., 1960-62; sr. acct. Fluhr, Massen & Light CPA's, N.Y.C., 1963; tax examiner N.Y. State Tax Commn., N.Y.C., 1963-65; acct. N.Y.C. Housing and Redevel. Bd., N.Y.C., 1965-67; sr. acct. N.Y.C. Bd. Edn., N.Y.C., 1967-68, N.Y.C. Housing and Redevel., N.Y.C., 1968; prin. budget examiner Bur. of Budget Office of Mayor, N.Y.C., 1968-76; fin. dir. N.Y.C. Coun., 1976-89; chief fin. officer Lower Eastside Svc. Ctr., N.Y.C., 1989-90, Promesa Inc., Bronx, 1990-91, cons., 1991-93; CFO Am. Chess Found., N.Y.C., 1993-94; cons., 1994—. Mem. Am. Mgmt. Assn., Govt. Fin. Officers Assn., JFK Dem. Club, Manhattan Chess Club. Democrat. Roman Catholic. Avocations: opera, classical music, chess, reading, football. Home: 12335 82nd Rd Apt 7K Kew Gardens NY 11415-1624 E-mail: donald.schnakenberg@yahoo.com.

SCHNAPP, ROGER HERBERT, lawyer, consultant; b. N.Y.C., Mar. 17, 1946; s. Michael Jay and Beatrice Joan (Becker) S.; m. Candice Jacqueline Larson, Sept. 15, 1979; 1 child, Monica Alexis. BS, Cornell U., 1966; JD, Harvard U., 1969; postgrad. Pub. Utility Mgmt. Program, U. Mich., 1978. Bar: N.Y. 1970, U.S. Ct. Appeals (2d cir.) 1970, U.S. Supreme, 1974, U.S. Dist. Ct. (so. dist.) N.Y. 1975, U.S. Ct. Appeals (4th and 6th cirs.) 1976, U.S. Ct. Appeals (7th cir.) 1977, U.S. Dist. Ct. (so. dist.) N.Y. 1975, U.S. Dist. Ct. (no. dist.) Calif. 1980, U.S. Ct. Appeals (8th cir.) 1980, Calif., 1982, U.S. Dist. Ct. (cen. dist.) Calif. 1982, U.S. Ct. Dist. (ea. dist.) Calif., 1984. Atty. CAB, Washington, 1969-70; labor atty. Western Electric Co., N.Y.C., 1970-71; mgr. employee rels. Am. Airlines, N.Y.C., 1971-74; labor counsel Am. Electric Power Svc. Corp., N.Y.C., 1974-78, sr. labor counsel, 1978-80; indsl. rels. counsel Trans World Airlines, N.Y.C., 1980-81; sr. assoc. Parker, Milliken, Clark & O'Hara, L.A., 1981-82; ptnr. Rutan & Tucker, Costa Mesa, Calif., 1983-84, Memel, Jacobs, Pierno, Gersh & Ellsworth, Newport Beach, Calif., 1985-86, Memel, Jacobs & Ellsworth, Newport Beach, 1986-87; pvt. practice Newport Beach, 1987—. Bd. dirs. Dynamic Constrn., Inc., Laguna Hills, Calif., 1986—; commentator labor rels. Fin. News Network; commentator Sta. KOCN Radio, 1990-91; commentator employment law Orange County Register; lectr. Calif. Western Law Sch., Calif. State U.-Fullerton, Calif. State Conf. Small Bus.; lectr. collective bargaining Pace U., N.Y.C.; lectr. on labor law Coun. on Edn. in Mgmt.; N.E. regional coord. Pressler for Pres., 1979-80; adv. bd. manufacturingzone.com.; dir. Orange County Bur. Jewish Edn., Friends of Fertility Found. Author: Arbitration Issues for the 1980s, 1981, A Look at Three Companies, 1982; editor-in-chief Indsl. and Labor Rels. Forum, 1964-66; columnist Orange County Bus. Jour., 1989-91; contbr. articles to profl. publs. Mem. Bus. Rsch. Adv. Coun. U.S. Dept. Labor; trustee Chapman U., 1991-95. Mem. Calif. Bar Assn. (chmn.), Labor Law Consulting Group, Calif. Bd. of Legal Specialization, Balboa Bay Club, The Ctr. Club (chmn. membership com.), Club 33. Republican. Jewish. Office: PO Box 9049 Newport Beach CA 92658-1049 E-mail: rhs@schnapp.com.

SCHNAUS, PETER, musical history educator; b. Berlin, Apr. 17, 1936; s. Kurt and Ilse (Grünbaum) S.; m. Ursula Grünbaum, Dec. 22, 1967; children: Christian, Andrea, Susanne. Assessor, Studienseminar Hannover, Germany, 1968; PhD, U. Freiburg, Germany, 1976. Tchr. Hannover H.S., 1966-70; asst., tchr. Musikhochschule, Hannover, 1970-82, prof. music history, 1982—2003; ret., 2003. Mem. Senat Musikhochschule, Hannover, 1979-99, spkr. dept. instrumental edn., 1979-2001, v.p., 1986-90. Author: E.T.A. Hoffmann als Beethoven—Rezensent der Allgemeinen Musikalischen Zeitung, 1977; editor, author: Europäische Musik in Schlaglichtern, 1990, Die Stimme der Mädchen, 2002; contbg. author: Kunst und Kultur, Vols. 3, 4 and 5, 1998-99; contbr. articles to profl. jours. Home: 4 Mendelssohnstrasse D-30173 Hannover Germany

SCHNECK, JEROME M. psychiatrist, medical historian, educator; b. NYC, Jan. 2, 1920; s. Maurice and Rose (Weiss) S.; m. Shirley R. Kaufman, July 24, 1943. AB, Cornell U., 1939; MD, SUNY, Bklyn., 1943. Diplomate Am. Bd. Psychiatry and Neurology, Am. Bd. Psychotherapy. Intern Interfaith Med. Ctr., 1943; psychiat. staff Menninger Clinic, Topeka, 1944-45; chief psychiatry and sociology dept. Fort Missoula, Mont., 1946, Camp Cooke, Calif., 1947; mem. psychiat. staff L.I. Coll. Hosp., 1947-48, Kings County Hosp., 1948-70, SUNY Hosp., Bklyn., 1955-70; assoc. vis. psychiatrist Kings County Hosp., 1949-70; mem. psychiat. staff State U. Hosp., Bklyn., 1955-70; pvt. practice N.Y.C., N.Y.C., 1947—; attending psychiatrist St. Vincent's Hosp. and Med. Ctr. N.Y., 1970—, hon. sr. psychiatrist, 1990—. Psychiat. cons. VA Regional Office, 1947-48, NY State Dept. Social Svcs., 1977-83, NY State Dept. Civil Svc., 1978-84, NY State Office Ct. Adminstrn., 1978-85, NY State Dept. Edn., 1981-83; dir. Mt. Vernon Mental Hygiene Clinic, 1947-52; assoc. chief psychiatrist Westchester County Dept. Health, 1949-50, cons., 1951-52; clin. instr. L.I. Coll. Medicine, 1947-50; clin. assoc. SUNY Coll. Medicine, Bklyn., 1950-53, asst. prof., 1955-58, assoc. prof., 1958-70; supervising psychiatrist Cmty. Guidance Svcs., 1955-70; cons. coun. on mental health AMA, 1956-58; cons. NBC, 1962, Ctr. Rsch. in Hypnotherapy, 1964-70; vis. lectr. N.Y. Med. Coll.-Met. Hosp., 1965; faculty, fellow Am. Inst. Psychotherapy and Psychoanalysis, 1970-85. Author: Hypnosis in Modern Medicine, 1953, 2d edit., 1959, Spanish lang. edit., 1962, 3rd edit., 1963, Studies in Scientific Hypnosis, 1954, A History of Psychiatry, 1960, The Principles and Practice of Hypnoanalysis, 1965 (Best Book award Soc. For Clin. and Exptl. Hypnosis 1965); editor: Hypnotherapy, Hypnosis and Personality, 1951; author over 400 med. and sci. publs., book chpts., articles; mem. bd. editors: Personality: Symposia on Topical Issues, 1960-61, Jour. Integrative and Eclectic Psychotherapy, 1986-89; contbg. editor Psychosomatics, 1961-75; mem. editorial bd. Voices—The Art and Science of Psychotherapy, 1965; features editor The Interne, 1942, co-editor, 1943. Lt. U.S. Army Field Arty. Res., 1939-42; capt. M.C. AUS, 1945-47. Recipient Shirley R. Schneck award to physician making significant contbns. to devel. of med. hypnosis, 1970, Clarence B. Farrar award for history of Am. psychiatry rsch. Clarke Inst. Psychiatry, U. Toronto, 1976, Roy M. Dorcus award for best clin. paper on hypnosis, 1981, Spl. Presdl. award for lifetime contbns. to lit. on sci. hypnosis, 1986. Fellow AAAS, APA (disting. life), Am. Med. Authors, Acad. Psychosomatic Medicine, Am. Psychiat. Assn. (disting. life), Am. Soc. Clin. Hypnosis (life), Soc. for Clin. and Exptl. Hypnosis (life, founder, founding pres. 1949-56, exec. coun. 1949—, assoc. editor jour. 1953—, Merit award 1955, Gold medal 1958, Bernard B. Raginsky award 1966, Shirley Schneck award 1970, Roy M. Dorcus award 1980, Spl. Presdl. award 1986), Am. Acad. Psychotherapists (co-founder, v.p. 1956-58), Am. Med. Writers Assn., Am. Soc. Psychoanalytic Physicians (hon., bd. dirs. 1958-62), Internat. Soc. Clin. and Exptl. Hypnosis (co-founder, bd. dirs. 1958-68, founding fellow), Internat. Acad. Eclectic Psychotherapists (charter); mem. AMA, NY Acad. Scis., Soc. Acad. Achievement (charter), Soc. Apothecaries London, Inst. Practicing Psychotherapists, Pan Am. Med. Assn. (v.p. sect. clin. hypnosis 1960-65, N.Am. v.p. 1966), NY Soc. Med. History (exec. com. 1956-62), Am. Bd. Med. Hypnosis (life, founder, pres. 1958-60, bd. dirs.), Inst. Rsch. in Hypnosis Inc. (bd. dirs., bd. editors 1957-70), Am. Assn. History Medicine, History of Sci. Soc., Assn. Advancement Psychotherapy (charter) Can. Med. History Assn., NY Soc. for Clin. Psychiatry (chmn. com. on history of psychiatry), Charles F. Menninger Soc., Internat. Soc. Hypnosis (hon. life), Brit. Soc. Med. Hypnosis (hon.), Internat. Soc. Hypnosis (hon. life), Sigma Xi. Address: 26 W 9th St New York NY 10011-8971

SCHNECK, STUART AUSTIN, retired neurologist, educator; b. N.Y.C., Apr. 1, 1929; s. Maurice and Sara Ruth (Knapp) S.; m. Ida I. Nakashima, Mar. 2, 1956; children: Lisa, Christopher. BS magna cum laude, Franklin and Marshall Coll., 1949; MD, U. Pa., 1953. Diplomate Am. Bd. Psychiatry and Neurology (bd. dirs., sec. 1990-91, v.p. 1991-92, pres. 1992-93). Intern Hosp. U. Pa., Phila., 1953-54; resident in medicine U. Colo. Med. Center, Denver, 1954-55, 57-58, resident in neurology, 1958-61; instr. neurology U. Colo. Sch. Medicine, 1959-61; instr. neuropathology Columbia U., N.Y.C., 1961-63; vis. fellow in neuropathology Columbia-Presbyn. Med. Ctr., N.Y.C., 1961-63; asst. prof. neurology and pathology U. Colo., 1963-67, assoc. prof., 1967-70, prof., 1970-95, assoc. dean clin. affairs Sch. Medicine, 1984-89, emeritus prof., 1996—. Cons. Fitzsimons Army Hosp., VA, Nat. Jewish Hosp.; pres. med. bd. Univ. Hosp., Denver, 1983-89, bd. dirs., 1989-90; mem. benefits adv. bd. U. Colo., 1999—, v.p. retired faculty assn. health sci. ctr., 1998-99, pres.,

1999-2001. Author (with Ida I. Nakashima) The Geezers' Guide to Colo. Hikes, 2002; contbr. articles to profl. jours. Served with USAF, 1955-57. USPHS fellow, 1961-63 Mem. Am. Acad. Neurology, Am. Assn. Neuropathologists, Am. Neurol. Assn., Univ. Srs. Assn. (chmn. bd. dirs. 1997-2002), Rocky Mountain Stroke Assn. (bd. dirs. 1998—), Ctr. for Personalized Edn. Physicians (bd. dirs. 1999—), Alpha Omega Alpha (bd. dirs. 1979-89, treas., pres. 1990-93, edit. bd. 1994—).

SCHNEEMAN, BARBARA OLDS, nutritionist, educator; m. Paul Schneeman; 1 child, Eric. BS in Food Sci. and Tech., U. Calif., Davis, 1970; PhD in Nutrition, U. Calif., Berkeley, 1974. NIH postdoctoral fellow gastrointestinal physiology Children's Hosp., Oakland, Calif., 1974-76; faculty mem. nutrition dept. nutrition and food sci. & tech. U. Calif., Davis, 1976—, prof. dept. internal medicine divsn. clin. nutrition, 1986—, assoc. dean Coll. Agrl. and Environ. Scis., 1985-88, chair dept. nutrition, 1988-93, dean Coll. Agrl. and Environ. Scis., 1993-99. Pres., bd. dirs. Dannon Inst., 1996—; vis. scientist Cardiovascular Rsch. Inst., U. Calif., San Francisco, 1991-92; lectr. women in sci. series Coll. St. Catherine, St. Paul, 1987; adv. dir. Blue Cross Calif., 1992-95; mem. dietary guidelines for Ams. adv. com. to Secs. of Agr., Health and Human Svcs., 1989-90, 94-95; mem. expert panel on food safety and nutrition Inst. Food Technologists, 1985-91; mem. external adv. bd. Post Ctr. for Nutrition and Health, 1989-90; councilor Soc. for Exptl. Biology and Medicine, 1988-91. Assoc. editor Jour. Nutrition, 1991-94; contbg. editor Nutrition Revs., 1982-90; editl. bd. Jour. Nutrition, 1982-87, Procs. for Soc. Exptl. Biology and Medicine, 1985-91, Acad. Press: Food Sci. and Nutrition, 1988-2001. Fellow NDEA, U. Calif., Berkeley; recipient Outstanding Cmty. Svc. award Tierra del Oro coun. Girl Scouts U.S., 1995, Future Leaders award for rsch. Nutrition Found., 1978-80, Samuel Cate Prescott award for rsch. Inst. Food Tech., 1985, Farma Food Internat. Fibre prize, Copenhagen, 1989, Ethel Austin Martin disting. lectr. on Human Nutrition, S.D. State U., 1999. Fellow AAAS; mem. Inst. Food Technologists (sec.-treas. nutrition divsn. 1988-89), Am. Physiol. Soc., Am. Inst. Nutrition (treas. 1989-92), Am. Heart Assn. (fellow arteriosclerosis coun.), Food and Nutrition Bd. IOM, 2001—. Office: U Calif Davis Dept Nutrition Davis CA 95616

SCHNEERSON, RACHEL, immunologist; Chief sect. Bacterial Disease Pathogensis and Immunity NIH, Bethesda, Md., 1983—. Co-editor: Coedited: Bacterial Vaccinnes, 1987. Recipient Albert Lasker Clin. Med. Rsch. award Albert and Mary Lasker Found., 1996. Achievements include development of first effective typhoid fever vaccine for children. Office: NIH 9000 Rockville Pike Rm 1a05 Bethesda MD 20892-0003

SCHNEEWIND, JEROME BORGES, philosophy educator; b. Mt. Vernon, N.Y., May 17, 1930; s. Jerome John and Charlotte (Borges) S.; m. Elizabeth G.R. Hughes, Feb. 23, 1963; children: Sarah, Rachel, Hannah. BA, Cornell U., 1951; MA, Princeton U., 1953, PhD, 1957. Instr. philosophy U. Chgo., 1957-60, Princeton U., 1960-61; asst. prof. Yale U., 1961-63; asso. prof. philosophy U. Pitts., 1964-68, prof., 1968-75, dean Coll. Arts and Scis., 1969-73; v.p., provost Hunter Coll., CUNY, 1975-81; prof. philosophy Johns Hopkins U., Balt., 1981—2003, chmn. dept., 1981-91, prof. philosophy emeritus, 2003—. Philosophy adviser Ency. Americana, 1967-98, mem. adv. bd. sci. tech. and values program NEH, 1975-78; mem. Coun. for Phil. Studies, 1975-80. Author: Backgrounds of English Victorian Literature, 1970, Sidgwick's Ethics and Victorian Moral Philosophy, 1977, The Invention of Autonomy, 1998; editor: Moral Philosophy From Montaigne to Kant, 1990; mem. editl. bd. Victorian Studies, 1968-75, The Monist, 1969-76, Am. Philos. Quar., 1975-77, Philos. Studies, 1975-78, Jour. of History Ideas, 1985—, pres. bd. dirs., 1988-2000; contbr. articles on ethics and history of ethics to publs. Served with Signal Corps, AUS, 1954-56. Mellon postdoctoral fellow, 1963-64; Guggenheim fellow, 1967-68; Am. Council Learned Socs. grantee, 1973; NEH sr. fellow, 1974, Ctr. for Advanced Study in the Behavioral Scis., 1992-93. Fellow AAAS; mem. Am. Philos. Assn. (exec. com. Ea. divsn. 1964-67, chmn. com. on teaching philosophy 1973-78, nominating com. 1986-88, v.p. Ea. divsn. 1994-95, pres. 1995-96, chmn. bd. officers, 1999-2002). Office: Philosophy Dept Johns Hopkins U Baltimore MD 21218 E-mail: jbs1@jhu.edu.

SCHNEIDER, ADELE GOLDBERG, librarian, educator; b. N.Y.C., May 13, 1924; d. Abraham and Anna (Levy) Goldberg; m. Noel Schneider, Jan. 1, 1950; children: Adam Matthew, Tracy Lynn. BA, Bklyn. Coll., 1945; MLS, Pratt Inst., 1965; MA, L.I. Univ., 1971. Field interview Gallup Poll, N.Y.C., 1941-48; social worker N.Y.C. Dept. Social Svcs., 1949-52; editor Bklyn. Coll. Alumni Quar., 1961-65; instr. Kingsborough C.C./CUNY, 1965-70, asst. prof. dept. libr., 1970-72, assoc. prof., 1972-88, prof., 1988-92, prof. emeritus, 1992—. Contbr. articles to profl. jours. Recipient lifetime achievement award Bklyn. Coll., 2000. Mem. ALA, Libr. Assn. CUNY, N.Y. Tech. Svcs. Librs., Beta Phi Mu. Home: 124 Oxford St Brooklyn NY 11235-2311 Office: 2001 Oriental Blvd Brooklyn NY 11235-2333 E-mail: lordduffy@msn.com.

SCHNEIDER, ADELE SANDRA, clinical geneticist; b. Johannesburg, Mar. 21, 1949; came to U.S., 1976, naturalized, 1981; d. Michael and Annette (Sive) S.; m. Gordon Mark Cohen, July 2, 1978; children: Jeffrey, Brian, Adrienne. MB, BChir, Witwatersrand U., Johannesburg, South Africa, 1973. Intern in internal medicine Baragwanath Hosp., Johannesburg, 1974, intern in gen. surgery, 1974; sr. house officer in pediatrics Coronation Hosp., Johannesburg, 1975; sr. house officer in radiation therapy Johannesburg Gen. Hosp., 1975-76; resident in pediatrics Wilmington (Del.) Med. Ctr., 1976-78; fellow in clin. genetics and metabolic diseases Children's Hosp. of Phila., 1978-81, staff physician Cystic Fibrosis Clinic, 1987-88; staff pediatrician Children's Rehab. Hosp., Phila., 1981-82, dir. pediatrics, 1982-87, acting med. dir., 1984-85; clin. instr. dept. pediatrics Jefferson Med. Coll., Phila., 1982-84, clin. asst. prof. dept. pediatrics, 1984—, clin. assoc. prof. pediats., 2002—; clin. geneticist Hahnemann Univ. Hosp., Phila., 1987-90, asst. clin. prof. dept. pediatrics and neoplastic diseases, 1987-90; clin. geneticist Albert Einstein Med. Ctr., Phila., 1990-92, acting dir. med. genetics, 1992-93, dir. clin. genetics program, 1993—. Mem. courtesy faculty Sch. Medicine Temple U., Phila., 1987; clin. geneticist St. Christopher's Hosp. for Children, Phila., 1987; genetics cons. dept. pediatrics Bryn Mawr (Pa.) Hosp.; genetics cons. Lankenan Hosp., Thomas Jefferson U. Hosp.; presenter, lectr. in field. Contbr. articles to profl. jours. Bd. dirs. Phila. Parenting Associates, 1986-93. Fellow Am. Coll. Med. Genetics; mem. Am. Soc. Human Genetics, Am. Chem. Soc. Office: Albert Einstein Med Ctr Dept Pediatrics 5501 Old York Rd Philadelphia PA 19141-3018

SCHNEIDER, ALLAN STANFORD, biochemistry, neuroscience and pharmacology educator, biomedical research scientist; b. N.Y.C., Sept. 26, 1940; s. Harry and Edith (Gonsky) S.; m. Mary-Jane Beekman Tunis, Dec. 14, 1968; children: Henry Seth, Joseph Benjamin B.Chem. Engring., Rensselaer Poly. Inst., 1961; MS, Pa. State U., 1963; PhD, U. Calif.-Berkeley, 1968. Chem. engr. E.I. du Pont de Nemours & Co. Exptl. Sta., Wilmington, Del., 1963-64; postdoctoral fellow Weizmann Inst. Sci., Rehovot, Israel, 1969-71; staff fellow NIH, Bethesda, Md., 1971-73; assoc. Sloan-Kettering Inst. Cancer Research, N.Y.C., 1974-80, assoc. mem., 1980-85; asst. prof. Cornell U. Grad. Sch. Med. Scis., N.Y.C., 1974-80, assoc. prof. biochemistry, 1981-83, assoc. prof. cell biology and genetic, 1983-85, chmn. biochemistry unit Sloan-Kettering div., 1982-83; assoc. prof. pharmacology and toxicology Albany (N.Y.) Med. Coll., 1985-86, prof. pharmacology and toxicology, 1986-94, prof. pharmacology and neurosci., 1995—, dir. grad. studies, 1987-91. Adjunct prof. Biomedical Sci., Sch. of Public Health, St. U. N.Y., Albany, 1987—; vis. prof. Weizmann Inst. Sci., Rehovot, Israel, 1987; vis. rsch. scholar U. Bergen, Norway, 1989, 95; vis. rsch. scholar, U. of Melbourne, Australia, 1998. Contbr. chpts to books, sci. articles to profl. jours. Rsch. grantee Am. Cancer Soc., 1980-83, Am. Heart Assn., 1977-82, 90-93, NIH, 1982-93, 2001—, NSF, 1977-79, 1997-2002, Cystic Fibrosis Found., 1980-82; established investigator Am. Heart Assn., 1977-82. Mem. Biophys. Soc., Soc. Neurosci., Soc. of Gen. Physiologist, Am. Heart Assn. (coun. on basic sci. 1977-95), Phi Lambda Upsilon, Tau Beta Pi (internat. com. for chromaffin cell biology 1987-93). Achievements include first isolation and characterization of chromaffin cells of the adrenal gland now widely used as a model neuronal cell culture system; determination of the relation between cytosolic calcium signals and neurohormone (adrenaline) secretion, relevant to cellular mechanism of hormone and neurotransmitter release; spectroscopic characterization of protein structure in situ in biomembranes and cells; theoretical and experimental analysis of optical activity spectra of turbid biological suspensions; research on neurochemistry of adrenal chromaffin cells, regulation of cell calcium and hormone and neurotransmitter release; mechanisms of nicotine dependence and fetal nicotine syndrome and effects of maternal smoking on fetal brain development. Office: Ctr for Neuropharmacology & Neurosci Albany Med Coll MC 136 Albany NY 12208 E-mail: schneia@mail.amc.edu.

SCHNEIDER, ANDREAS, education educator, researcher; b. Mannheim, Germany, Feb. 10, 1961; arrived in US, 1990; s. Heinz and Eleonore Stegerwald Schneider; m. Tanja Karp, 1999; children: Alina, Odin. Diploma in sociology, Mannheim U., 1991; PhD, Ind. U., Bloomington, 1997. Asst. instr. Ind. U., Bloomington, 1991—97; asst. prof. Tex. Tech. U., Lubbock, 1997—2003, assoc. prof., 2003—. Editor: Electronic Jour. Sociology, 1999—. Mem.: German Lebensrettungs Assn. Celtic. Achievements include invention of schneider scale. Avocation: auto restoration. Office: Tex Tech Univ Holden Hall PO Box 41012 Lubbock TX 79409-1012 Business E-Mail: andreas.schneider@ttu.edu.

SCHNEIDER, ARTHUR PAUL, retired videotape and film editor, author; b. Rochester, N.Y., Jan. 26, 1930; s. Mendell Phillip and Frieda (Bl) S.; m. Helen Deloise Thompson, June 5, 1954; children: Robert Paul, Lori Ann. Student, U. So. Calif., 1948. With NBC, 1951-68, film and videotape editor, 1953-60, developer double system method of editing video tape, 1958; pres. Burbank (Calif.) Film Editing, Inc., 1968-72, Electronic Video Industries Inc., 1977 79; supr. video tape editing Consol. Film Industries Inc., Hollywood, Calif., 1972-76, editorial supr., 1980-83; pvt. practice editing, 1983-88. Cons., lectr., author. Film and tape editor all: Bob Hope shows, 1951-67; supr. NBC kinescope and video tape editors (1966-67); video tape editor: Laugh-In Series, 1967-68; video tape editor: Comedy Shop Series, 1977-80; post-prodn. cons. to Video Systems and Broadcast Engring. mag.; video tape editor: TV series Sonny & Cher, 1973, Sonny Comedy Revue, 1974, Tony Orlando and Dawn, 1974, Hudson Bros., summer, 1974, Dean Martin Series, 1975-76, Mickey Mouse Club Series, Walt Disney Prodns., 1976, Redd Foxx Series, 1977; (author: Electronic Post Production and Videotape Editing, 1989 (pub. in Chinese 1995), Electronic Post Production Terms and Concepts, 1990; contbg. author: Association of Cinema and Video Laboratories (ACVL) Handbook, 5th edit., 1995, Focal Guide to Electronic Media CDRom Version, 1998, Jump Cut: Memoirs of a Pioneer Television Editor, 1997; oral history interview for Acad. TV Arts and Scis. Found. Archive of Am. TV First 50 Yrs., 2001; contbr. articles to publs. in field. Recipient Broadcast Preceptor award San Francisco State U., 1975; named hon. Ky. Col. Mem. Acad. Television Arts and Scis. (Emmy nominations and Emmy award for video tape editing 1966, 68, 73, 84, gov. 1977-80, sec. 1980-81), Am. Cinema Editors (life, Life Achievement award 1999), Soc. Motion Picture and TV Engrs., Delta Kappa Alpha (life). Home: 2586 Neptune Pl Port Hueneme CA 93041 Personal E-mail: art2586@earthlink.net.

SCHNEIDER, BENJAMIN, psychology educator, consultant; b. N.Y.C., Aug. 11, 1938; s. Leo and Rose (Cohen) S.; m. H. Brenda Jacobson, Jan. 29, 1961; children: Lee Andrew, Rhody Yve. BA, Alfred U., 1960; MBA, CUNY, 1962; PhD, U. Md., 1967. Lic. psychologist, Md. Asst. prof. adminstrv. scis. and psychology Yale U., New Haven, 1967-71; prof. psychology-mgmt. U. Md., College Park, 1971-79, prof. psychology and mgmt., 1982—2004; sr. rsch. fellow Pers. Rsch. Assocs., Inc., 2003—; John A. Hannah prof. orgnl. psychology Mich. State U., East Lansing, 1979-82. Vis. prof. Inst. Adminstrn. and Enterprise, U. Aix-Marseille, 1993, 99, 2001, Peking U., 1989, Tuck Sch. Bus. Adminstrn., Dartmouth Coll., 1999. Author: (with D.T. Hall) Organizational Climates and Careers, 1973, Staffing Organizations, 1976, 2d edit. (with N. Schmitt), 1986; (with F.D. Schoorman) Facilitating Work Effectiveness, 1988, Organizational Climate and Culture, 1990, (with D.E. Bowen) Winning the Service Game, 1995, (with S.S. White) Service Quality: Research Perspectives, 2004, (with D.B. Smith) Personality and Organizations, 2004; mem. editl. rev. bd. Jour. Applied Psychology, 1988-98, 2002—, Internat. Jour. Svc. Industry Mgmt., 1989—, Jour. Svc. Rsch., 1998—. Orgnl. Behavior and Human Decision Processes, 2002—, Cornell Quar., 2002—. Fulbright grantee, 1973-74 Fellow APA, Am. Psychol. Soc., Soc. for Indsl. and Orgnl. Psychology (pres. 1984-85, Disting. Sci. Contbns. award 2000, Scholarly Contbn. award 2004), Acad. Mgmt. (pres. orgnl. behavior div. 1982-83). Office: 1363 Caminito Floreo Ste G La Jolla CA 92037 Office Phone: 858-488-7594. E-mail: bschneider@pra-inc.com.

SCHNEIDER, CALVIN, physician; b. N.Y.C., Oct. 23, 1924; s. Harry and Bertha (Green) S.; m. Elizabeth Gayle Thomas, Dec. 27, 1967. AB, U. So. Calif., 1951, MD, 1955; JD, LaVerne (Calif.) Coll., 1973. Intern L.A. County Gen. Hosp., 1955-56, staff physician, 1956-57; pvt. practice medicine West Covina, Calif., 1957—. Staff Inter-Community Med. Ctr., Covina, Calif. With USNR, 1943-47. Republican. Lutheran.

SCHNEIDER, CARL EDWARD, law educator; b. Exeter, N.H., Feb. 23, 1948; s. Carl Jacob and Dorothy (Jones) S.; m. Joan L. Wagner, Jan. 6, 1976. BA, Harvard Coll., 1972; JD, U. Mich., 1979. Curriculum specialist Mass. Tchrs. Assn., Boston, 1972-75; law clk. to judge U.S. Ct. Appeals (D.C. cir.), Washington, 1979-80; law clk. Potter Stewart U.S. Supreme Ct., Washington, 1980-81; asst. prof. law U. Mich., Ann Arbor, 1981-84, assoc. prof. law, 1984-86, prof. law, 1986—, prof. internal medicine, 1998—, Chauncey Stillman prof. ethics, morality and practice of law; vis. prof. U. Tokyo, 1998. Author: The Practice of Autonomy: Patients, Doctors and Medical Decisions, 1998, (with Margaret F. Brinig) An Invitation to Family Law, 1996, (with Marsha Garrison) The Law of Bioethics, 2003; editor: (book) The Law and Politics of Abortion, 1980, Family Law in Action: A Reader, 1999 (with Margaret F. Brinig and Lee E. Teitelbaum), Law at the End of Life: The Supreme Court and Assisted Suicide, 2000; contbr. articles to profl. jours. Fellow Am. Council of Learned Socs., Ford Found., 1985, Hastings Ctr.; life fellow Clare Coll., Cambridge. Mem. Order of Coif. Office: U Mich Law Sch 801 Monroe St Ann Arbor MI 48109-1210

SCHNEIDER, CAROL GEARY, educational association administrator; B in History magna cum laude, Mount Holyoke Coll.; postgrad., U. London; PhD in History, Harvard U. Instr. U. Chgo., DePaul U., Chgo. State U., Boston U.; exec. v.p. Assn. Am. Colls. and Univs., Washington, 1988—98, pres., 1998—. Contbr. articles to profl. jours. Woodrow Wilson fellow, Harvard U., Kent fellow, Harvard Prize fellow, Mina Shaughnessy fellow, U.S. Dept. Edn., 1982. Mem.: Phi Beta Kappa. Office: Am Assn Colls and Univs 1818 R St NW Washington DC 20009

SCHNEIDER, CAROLYN ALICE BRAUCH, elementary school educator; b. N.Y.C., Dec. 15, 1946; d. Elliott David and Marie Alice (Giroux) B.; m. Thom J. Schneider, Aug. 3, 1978; children: Logan, Whitney, Brock. BS, U. Bridgeport, 1968. Tchr. phys. edn. Westview (Colo.) Elem. Sch., 1968-72, McElwain (Colo.) Elem. Sch., 1972-75; tchr. phys. edn., health Northglenn (Colo.) Mid. Sch., 1975—, coach gymnastics, 1975-84, coach track, 1975—2000, coach softball, 1998—2000, coach volleyball, 1975—96; coach xtreme competitve soccer, 1997—2003; coach explosion soccer, 1988—97. Coach North Area Soccer Assn., Thornton, Colo., 1995-96, 96-97 Rec. (competitive), 97— U-11B/Explosion White coach traveling competitive team, U-12B/Colo. XTreme competitive soccer team; instr., bldg. supr. Northglenn Recreation Dept., 1969-84, mem. sch. improvement team, rep. Dist. Sch. Improvement Team. Mem. NEA, AAHPERD (Colo. recipient Nat. Pathfinder award for Outstanding Leadership in Girls and Womens Sports, 2002), Colo. Edn. Assn., Am. Health Assn. Roman Catholic. Avocations: sports, reading, travel.

SCHNEIDER, CHARLES IVAN, newspaper executive; b. Chgo., Apr. 6, 1923; s. Samuel Hiram and Eva (Smith) S.; children: Susan, Charles I. Jr., Kim, Karen, Traci. BS, Northwestern U., 1944. Indsl. engr., sales mgr., v.p. mktg. and sales Curtis-Electro Lighting Corp., Chgo., 1945-54, pres., 1954-62, Jefferson Electronics, Inc., Santa Barbara, Calif., 1962-64; pres. 3 sub., v.p., asst. to pres. Am. Bldg. Maintenance Industries, Los Angeles, 1964-66; group v.p. Times Mirror Co., Los Angeles, 1966-88, ret.; pvt. investor and cons., 1988—. Bd. dirs. Jeppesen Sanderson, Inc., Denver, Graphic Controls Corp., Buffalo, Regional Airports Improvement Corp. Bd. regents Northwestern U., Evanston, Ill.; trustee, past pres. Reiss-Davis Child Study Center, L.A.; bd. govs., past pres. The Music Ctr.; trustee the Menninger Found.; pres. St. John's Hosp. and Health Ctr. Found., Santa Monica, Calif. Served with AUS, 1942-44. Mem. Chief Execs. Orgn. (past pres., bd. dirs.). Clubs: Standard (Chgo.); Beverly Hills Tennis (Calif.); Big. Ten of So. Calif. Avocations: tennis, squash, music, reading. Home: 522 N Beverly Dr Beverly Hills CA 90210-3318 *An individual's growth and success as a manager are in direct proportion to his or her ability to develop, motivate and lead able, capable people.*

SCHNEIDER, CHARLES M. healthcare provider company executive; Pres., founder Concordant Group, LLC; exec. v.p., COO HealthSource, 1990-97; pres., COO Oxford Health Plans, Inc., Trumbull, Conn., 2000—. Office: Oxford Health Plans Inc 418 Monroe Turnpike Trumbull CT 06611

SCHNEIDER, CYNTHIA PERRIN, art historian, educator; b. Pa., Aug. 16, 1953; m. Thomas J. Schneider; 2 children. BA in Fine Arts magna cum laude, Harvard U., 1977, PhD in Fine Arts, 1984. Asst. curator European paintings Mus. Fine Arts, Boston, unitl 1984; asst. prof. art history Georgetown U., Washington, 1984-90, assoc. prof., 1990—; amb. to The Netherlands Am. Embassy, The Hague, 1998-2001; dir., life sciences & society initiative Georgetown U., Washington, 2003—. Lectr. on Rembrandt and Dutch art in U.S. and Europe. Author: Rembrandt's Landscapes, 1990; organizer, writer (catalog) Rembrandts Landscapes: Drawings and Prints, Nat. Gallery Art, Washington, 1990; contbr. articles to profl. jours. Former vice-chmn. President's Com. on Arts and Humanities, mem. steering com. for Creative Am. and millenium planning group, also chmn. fed. design subcom.; corrd. arts policy Clinton-Gore Campaign, 1992; past bd. dirs. Nat. Mus. Women in Arts, Australian-Am. Leagership Dialogue. Office: Georgetown U Dept Art Music & Theatre 37th and O St NW Washington DC 20057 E-mail: cpschneider@restructassoc.com.

SCHNEIDER, DAN W. lawyer, consultant; b. Salem, Oreg., Apr. 28, 1947; s. Harold Otto and Frances Louise (Warner) S.; m. Nancy Merle Schmalzbauer, Mar. 29, 1945; children: Mark Warner, Edward Michael. BA cum laude, St. Olaf Coll., 1969; JD, Willamette U., 1974; LLM, Columbia U., 1975. Bar: Oreg. 1974, D.C. 1978, Ill. 1987. Trial atty. U.S. Dept. Justice Antitrust, Washington, 1975-79; dep. assoc. dir. U.S. SEC, Washington, 1979-86; gen. ptnr. Schiff Hardin & Waite, Chgo., 1986-95; name ptnr. Smith Lodge & Schneider, Chgo., 1995-98; ptnr. Hopkins & Sutter, Chgo., 1998-2000; internat. ptnr. Baker & McKenzie, Chgo., 2000—. Bd. dirs. NygaarArt, Northfield, Minn. Contbr. articles to profl. jours. Trustee, sec. Ill. Acad. Fine Arts, Chgo., 1990-98; mem. adv. bd. Steensland Art Mus., Northfield, 1990—; mem. adv. bd. Hallie Ford Mus. Art, Salem, Oreg., 1999—. Recipient 1st prize Nathan Burkan Law Essay Competition ASCAP, N.Y., 1974, Christie award Securities Transfer Assn., 1987. Mem. Met. Club. Chgo., Monroe Club, Plaza Club. Avocations: art collecting, art writing, music composition. Office: Baker & McKenzie 1 Prudential Plz 130 E Randolph St Ste 3700 Chicago IL 60601-6342 E-mail: dan.w.schneider@bakernet.com.

SCHNEIDER, DANIEL SCOTT, pediatric cardiologist; b. Mitchell, S.D., July 17, 1953; s. Robert George and Lois Irene (Theis) S.; m. Lisa Anne Magri, Oct. 22, 1988; children: Elizabeth, Emily, Luisa, Robert, Daniel. BS, Creighton U., 1975, MD, 1979. Diplomate Am. Bd. Pediat., Am. Bd. Pediat. Cardiology. Commd. ensign USN, 1979, advanced through grades to comdr., 1992; pediat. cardiologist Childrens Hosp. of the Kings Dau., Norfolk, Va., 1992—. Gen. bd. dirs. Cath. Charities of Hampton Rds., 1999—. Named Tchr. of Yr. Portsmouth Naval Hosp. Pediat. Residents, 1992; recipient Faculty Tchg. award Children's Hops. of Kings Daus., 2001. Mem. tidewater Down Syndrome Assn. (profl. adv. 1993—), Alpha Sigma Nu, Alpha Omega Alpha. Roman Catholic. Office: Childrens Hosp the Kings Daus 601 Childrens Ln Norfolk VA 23507-1910 Office Phone: 757-668-7587. E-mail: schneids@chkd.com.

SCHNEIDER, DENNIS RAY, microbiology educator and executive; b. Sinton, Tex., June 10, 1952; 2 children. BA with honors, U. Tex., 1974, PhD, 1978. Post-doctoral fellow Behringwerke AG, Marburg/Lahn, West Germany, 1978-79; postdoctoral fellow U. Mo. Med. Sch., Columbia, 1980-81; rsch. microbiologist New England Nuc., North Billerica, Mass., 1981-82; dir. R & D Austin (Tex.) Biol. Lab., 1982-88; adj. assoc. prof. U. Tex., Austin, 1986—; dir. R & D devel. Micro-Bac Internat., Austin, 1988-94, v.p. Round Rock, Tex., 1994—. Author: Bioremediation: A Desktop Manual for the Environmental Professional; contbr. chpt. to Microorganism Adaptation to Host Defense. Grantee NASA, 1988, 92, 93. Mem. AAAS, Am. Soc. for Microbiology, Mensa, Profl. Assn. Dive Instrs. Avocations: scuba diving, writing. Office: Micro-Bac Internat 3200 N I H 35 Round Rock TX 78681-2410 E-mail: drdiver@mail.utexas.edu.

SCHNEIDER, DONALD FREDERIC, banker; b. N.Y.C., Nov. 12, 1939; s. Charles and Lillian S.; m. Mary Patricia McCafferty, Sept. 7, 1963; children—Laurie, John. BS, Lehigh U., 1961; MBA, N.Y. U., 1968. Mgmt. trainee Marine Midland Bank, N.Y.C., 1961-65, asst. sec., 1965-68, asst. v.p., 1968-69, v.p., 1969-79, 1st Nat. Bank Chgo., 1979-87; fin. cons. Cigna Individual Fin. Svcs. Co., Chgo., 1987; v.p. Irving Trust Co./Bank of N.Y., 1987-90, Citibank N.A., N.Y.C., 1990-96; MMS Assocs., Inc., 1997-99; retired, 1999. Mem. corp. trust activities com. Am. Bankers Assn., fiduciary and securities ops. exec. com. Mem. Am. Soc. Corporate Secs. (pres. Chgo. region 1987), Securities Transfer Assn. Home and Office: 13 Linton Ct Pinehurst NC 28374-9751 E-mail: donschneider@nc.rr.com.

SCHNEIDER, DUANE BERNARD, English literature educator; b. South Bend, Ind., Nov. 15, 1937; s. William H. and Lillian L. (Pitchford) S.; m. Crystal J. Gips; children: Jeffrey, Eric, Lisa, Emily. BA, Miami U., Oxford, Ohio, 1958; MA, Kent State U., 1960; PhD, U. Colo., 1965. Instr. engring. English U. Colo., 1960-65; asst. prof. English Ohio U., Athens, 1965-70, assoc. prof., 1970-75, prof., 1975-98, chmn. Faculty Senate, 1981-83, chmn. dept. English, 1983-86, prof. emeritus, 1998—; dir. Ohio U. Press, 1986-95; part-time faculty New Sch. U., N.Y.C., 2000—. Editor, pub. Croissant & Co., 1968-2002. Author: (with others) Anais Nin: An Introduction, 1979. Mem. Thomas Wolfe Soc. (trustee, pres. 1979-81). Home: 72 Kakely St Albany NY 12208

SCHNEIDER, EDWARD LEE, botanic garden administrator; b. Portland, Oreg., Sept. 14, 1947; s. Edward John and Elizabeth (Mathews) S.; m. Sandra Lee Alfarone, Aug. 2, 1968; children: Kenneth L., Cassandra L. BA, Ctrl. Wash. U., 1969, MS, 1971; PhD, U. Calif., Santa Barbara, 1974. From asst. to assoc. prof. botany S.W. Tex. State U., San Marcos, 1974-84, prof., 1984-94, chmn. biology dept., 1984-89, dean sci., 1989-92; pres., CEO Santa Barbara (Calif.) Botanic Garden, 1992—. Author: The Botanical World, CEOs and Trustees--Building Working Partnerships; contbr. articles to profl. jours. Bd. dirs. Ctr. for Plant Conservation. Recipient Presdl. Rsch. award S.W. Tex. State U., 1986, Disting. Alumnus award Ctrl. Wash. U., 1996; grantee NSF, 1980, 90. Fellow Tex. Acad. Sci. (pres. 1992-93); mem. Internat. Water Lily Soc. (bd. dirs., sec. 1989-96, inducted into Hall of Fame, Award of Appreciation 1997), Bot. Soc. Am. (bd. dirs., Award of Merit 1998), Am. Assn. Bot. Gardens and Arboreta (bd. dirs.), Internat. Pollination Congress, Nat. Coun. Deans, Am. Assn. Mus. (assessment program adv. com.). Home: 1140 Tunnel Rd Santa Barbara CA 93105-2134 Office: Santa Barbara Botanic Garden 1212 Mission Canyon Rd Santa Barbara CA 93105-2126 E-mail: eschneider@sbbg.org.

SCHNEIDER, EDWARD LEWIS, medicine educator, research administrator; b. N.Y.C., June 22, 1940; s. Samuel and Ann S. BS, Rensselaer Poly. Inst., 1961; MD, Boston U., 1966. Intern and resident N.Y. Hosp.-Cornell U., N.Y.C., 1966-68; staff fellow Nat. Inst. Allergy and Infectious Diseases, Bethesda, Md., 1968-70; research fellow U. Calif., San Francisco, 1970-73; chief, sect. on cell aging Nat. Inst. Aging, Balt., 1973-79, assoc. dir., 1980-84,

dep. dir., 1984-87; prof. medicine, dir. Davis Inst. on Aging U. Colo., Denver, 1979-80; dean Leonard Davis Sch. Gerontology U. So. Calif., L.A., 1986—, exec. dir. Ethel Percy Andrus Gerontology Ctr., 1986—, prof. medicine, 1987—, William and Sylvia Kugel prof. gerontology, 1989—. Sci. dir. Buck Ctr. for Rsch. in Aging, 1989-98; cons. MacArthur Found., Chgo., 1985-93, R.W. Johnson Found., Princeton, N.J., 1982-87, Brookdale Found., N.Y.C., 1985-89. Editor: The Genetics of Aging, 1978, The Aging Reproductive System, 1978, Biological Markers of Aging, 1982, Handbook of the Biology of Aging, 1985, 95, 96, Interrelationship Among Aging Cancer and Differentiation, 1985, Teaching Nursing Home, 1985, Modern Biological Theories of Aging, 1987, The Black American Elderly, 1988, Elder Care and the Work Force, 1990, A Secure Old Age: Financing Long-Term Care, 1998, Ageless: Take Control of Your Age and Stay Youthful for Life, 2003. Med. dir. USPHS, 1968—. Recipient Roche award, 1964. Fellow Gerontology Soc., Am. Soc. Clin. Investigation; mem. Am. Assn. Retired Persons, U.S. Naval Acad. Sailing Squadron (coach 1980-86). Office: U So Calif Andrus Gerontology Ctr Los Angeles CA 90089-0001 E-mail: eschneid@usc.edu.

SCHNEIDER, EDWARD MARTIN, retired internist, medical educator; b. Cleve., May 12, 1922; s. Sol S. and Beatrice Hilda (Sicherman) Schneider; m. Jane H. Einstein, June 18, 1950 (dec. Aug. 2001); children: Douglas A., Robert S. 1 stepchild, Donald E. Deutsch. Student, Northwestern U., 1940-43; MD, U. Cin., 1946. Diplomate Am. Bd. Internal Medicine. Intern Mt. Sinai Hosp., Cleve., 1946-47, asst. resident medicine, 1947-48, sr. asst. resident medicine, 1950-51; fellow in medicine Cin. Gen. Hosp., 1951-52; asst. prof. of medicine U. Okla. Sch. Medicine, Oklahoma City, 1952-57; sr. physician gastroenterology Miner's Meml. Hosp. Assn., McDowell, Ky., Beckley, W.Va., 1957-61; chief of medicine Cameron Meml. Hosp., Bryan, Ohio, 1961-62; chief medical rsch. sect. Upjohn Co., Kalamazoo, Mich., 1962-67; pvt. practice Woodland Hills, Calif., 1968-81. Author 17 rsch. papers. Capt. M.C., AUS, 1948-50. Recipient Cert. of Recognition, Dept. Def. Fellow ACP, Am. Coll. Gastroenterologists; mem. Assn. Mil. Surgeons (life), Am. Assn. Study Liver Disease (emeritus), Sigma Xi. Avocations: amateur radio, music appreciation. Home: 1521 Lake Forest Dr Charlottesville VA 22901 E-mail: edwardmd@sprintmail.com.

SCHNEIDER, EDWIN KAHN, research scientist; b. Philadelphia, Pa., May 6, 1948; s. Abraham and Edna May Schneider; m. Penelope Lee Ganzel, Aug. 5, 1980; children: Andrew Ganzel, Thomas Schmidt. AB, Harvard U., 1970, PhD, 1975. Postdoctoral rsch. assoc. MIT, Cambridge, Mass., 1974—77, prin. rsch. scientist, 1984—84; NATO postdoctoral fellow Reading U., England, 1977—78; rsch. fellow, assoc. Harvard U., Cambridge, Mass., 1978—83; assoc., sr. rsch. scientist U. Md., College Park, Md., 1984—93; sr. rsch. scientist Ctr. for Ocean-Land-Atmosphere Studies, Calverton, Md., 1993—; prof. climate dynamics George Mason U., Fairfax, Va., 2002—. Author: (book chapter) Climate Change: An Integrated Perspective; contbr. (articles) Encyclopedia of Global Environmental Change; contbr. articles to profl. jours. Fellow, NSF, 1970—72; grantee, NSF, NOAA, NASA, DOE, EPRI, 1985—2002; Nat. Merit scholar, 1966—70. Fellow: Am. Meteorol. Soc.; mem.: Royal Meteorol. Soc., Am. Geophys. Union. Achievements include research in Hadley circulation, El Nino/Southern Oscillation, atmospheric and oceanic dynamics, climate change. Avocations: orchestral violinist, golf. Office: Center for Ocean-Land-Atmosphere Studies 4041 Powder Mill Rd Suite 302 Beltsville MD 20705

SCHNEIDER, ELAINE CAROL, lawyer, researcher, writer; b. Mpls., Aug. 28, 1957; d. Allan William and Deborah G. Schneider; m. William Mack Olivé, Oct. 10, 1987 (div. July 1996); 1 child, Vanessa Inez Olivè; m. G.R. Smith, Jan. 2, 2002. BA, U. Minn., 1979; JD, William Mitchell Coll. Law, St. Paul, 1982. Bar: N.Mex. 1984, Minn. 1998, D.C. 1999. Assoc. Settles, Kalamarides & Assocs., Anchorage, 1982, Dickson, Evans & Esch, Anchorage, 1982; legal rschr. John Hanson, Anchorage, 1983; acct. rep. Westlaw Svcs., Inc., Albuquerque, 1984, sales rep. New Orleans, 1985-86; libr. sales rep. West Pub. Co., Spokane, Wash., 1986-87, reference atty. St. Paul, 1988-97, product mgr., 1997-2001; pvt. practice Mpls.; CEO, mem. Coeur à Coeur Fashion Beauty Products, LLC, Minn., 2004. Ethics adv. bd. N.Mex. Bar, Albuquerque, 1984-85; midwest regional conf. com. Am. Immigration Lawyers Assn., 2000. Author: Substantive Judicial Law Outline of Habeas Corpus, 1984, What They Don't Teach You in the Bar Review Course, 1991, Challenging an Incredibility Finding on Appeal, An Incredibility Paradigm, 2001; mem. law rev. staff: William Mitchell Coll. Law, 1980—81. Atty. immigration and naturalization law Minn. Advocates for Human Rights, Refugee and Immigrant Project. Recipient Vol. Pro Bono Atty. award, 15th Ann. Minn. Advocates for Human Rights, 1999. Mem. Phi Beta Kappa. Avocations: ventriloquism, skiing, swimming, travel, languages. Office: 701 4th Ave S Ste 500 Minneapolis MN 55415-1810 Personal E-mail: avocatecs@aol.com.

SCHNEIDER, FRANK DAVID, family physician; b. Brookline, Mass., Aug. 12, 1961; s. Morris I. and Shirley R. (Freedman) S.; m. Peggy S. Lorton, Aug. 14, 1993; children: Michael, Brian, Daniel, Allison. BA, Boston U., 1983, MD, 1987; MS in Pub. Health, U. Mo., 1992. Diplomate Am. Bd. Family Practice; lic. physician N.C., Tex. Intern Duke U., Fayetteville, NC, 1987—88, resident in family practice, 1988—90; acad. fellow, clin. instr. dept. family and cmty. medicine U. Mo., Columbia, 1990—92; asst. prof. U. Tex. Health Sci. Ctr., San Antonio, 1992—98, dir. med. student edn. dept. family practice, 1993—99, assoc. prof., 1998—, residency dir., 1999—2002; co-dir. Ctr. Violence Prevention, 2004—. Mem. staff Univ. Hosp., San Antonio, 1992, U. Mo. Hosp. and Clinics, Columbia, 1990, Santa Rosa Hosp., 1997; lectr. in field. Contbr. articles on family violence and med. edn. to profl. jours. Am. Acad. Family Physicians Found. grantee, 1994, HHS grantee, 1995, 98, 2000; recipient Tex. Acad. Family Physicians Rsch. award, 1996. Mem.: AMA (nat. adv. coun. violence and abuse 2001—, chair edn. com.), Tex. Med. Assn., Bexar County Med. Soc., Tex. Acad. Family Physicians (pres. 2003—), Soc. Tchrs. Family Medicine (chmn. group on fellowship tng. 1991—93, chmn. group on violence edn. 1996—2000, edn. com. 1997—2001, family medicine curriculum project adv. com. 2001—04), Am. Acad. Family Physicians (commn. on pub. health 2001—), Assn. Am. Med. Colls. (group on ednl. affairs 1998—). Office: U Tex Health Sci Ctr Dept Family Practice 7703 Floyd Curl MSC 7794 San Antonio TX 78229-3900 Office Phone: 210-567-4555. E-mail: fschneider@uthscsa.edu.

SCHNEIDER, GERALD L. plastic surgeon; b. Mechanicsburg, Pa., Oct. 25, 1945; s. Gordon Henry and Pauline Emma (Rife) S.; 1 child, Ross Roberts. BS, No. Ariz. U., 1968; MD, U. Ariz., 1973. Intern Naval Regional Med. Ctr., San Diego, 1973-74; resident in gen. surgery U.S. Naval Hosp., San Diego, 1974-78, resident in plastic surgery Portsmouth, Va., 1978-80, staff surgeon divsn. plastic surgery San Diego, 1981-83, chief divsn. plastic surgery, 1983-84; pvt. practice Flagstaff, Ariz., 1984-90; staff surgeon La Jolla (Calif.) Cosmetic Surgery Ctr., 1990-91; surgeon Scripps Clinic & Rsch. Found., La Jolla, 1991—. Capt. USNR Fellow ACS; mem. Am. Soc. Plastic Surgeons. Avocation: golf. Office: Scripps Clinic & Rsch Found 10666 N Torrey Pines Rd La Jolla CA 92037-1092 Office Phone: 858-554-9606. Business E-Mail: gschneider@scrippsclinic.com.

SCHNEIDER, GISELA HELGA, medical technician; arrived in U.S., 1959; d. Bernhard Richard Hackstein and Martha Maria Bruckhoff-Hackstein; children: Hans, Sigfried, Gisela, Erika, Walter. Cert. histo-technologist ASCP; Bd. Registry Chgo. Histo-technologist Kaiser-Med. Group, Walnut Creek, Calif., 1964—74, C.C. County Hosp., Martinez, Calif., 1974—75, Alta Bates Hosp., Berkeley, Calif., 1975—83, Pathology Svcs., Inc., Berkeley, 1983—90, histo-pathology supr., 1983—90; histo-technologist U. Calif., San Francisco, 1990—2003. Avocations: reading, writing, travel, music, foreign languages. Home: 280 Tono Ln Walnut Creek CA 94597 Office Phone: 415-353-1610.

SCHNEIDER, GRETA, economist, speaker, author, real estate investor; b. Bklyn. Student, Bklyn. Conservatory of Music, 1961—66; BA, MA, CUNY, 1975, MA, 1976. Writer, cons., Pitts., 1972-73; cons. Flushing, N.Y., 1973-85; sr. writer, cons. Buck Cons. Inc., N.Y.C., 1985-86; chmn., CEO Schneider Cons. Inc., N.Y.C., 1986-90; pvt. cons. Greta Schneider Cons., N.Y.C., 1991—; prin. Schneider Consulting Group, 1996—. Lectr. The Learning Annex, 1995-96, 2002, Seminar Ctr., N.Y.C., 1998-, others; advisor Am. Women's Econ. Devel. Corp., 1988—; adv. bd. Women's Profl. Coun., 1998; guest mem. discussion Reuters Bus. Report, 1998; mem. Women's Econ. Round Table, 1998; mem. Profl. Women's Adv. Bd., 1998; spkr. in field. Author: Exploding the Bankruptcy Mystique, 1993, Holistic Bankruptcy, 1998, 2002. Mem. Little Theatre Group, Marathon Cmty. Ctr., Little Neck, N.Y., 1980-83; founder, pres. Bankruptcy Anonymous, 1996; mem. Bklyn. Conservatory of Music, 1961-66. Cambridge Biographical Inst. fellow, 1993. Mem. AFTRA, Nat. Assn. Women Bus. Owners, Nat. Assn. Bus. Communicators, Internat. Platform Assn. (spkr. 2001), Employee Assistance Profls. Assn., Soc. Human Resource Mgmt., U.S. C. of C., Writers Guild Am., Rotary. Avocations: chef, pilot, tennis, chess, speech coach. Office: c/o Manhasset Properties Inc 403 Main St #4 Port Washington NY 11050 Office Phone: 516-767-0012.

SCHNEIDER, HAROLD LAWRENCE, lawyer; b. N.Y.C., June 24, 1942; s. Milton and Florence (Haimowitz) S.; m. Sandra Berkowitz, Aug. 3, 1974; children: Mara Susan, Douglas Howard. BS, CCNY, 1964; JD, Fordham U., 1967; LLM, NYU, 1968. Bar: N.Y. 1967. Ptnr. Kirkpatrick & Lockhart LLP, N.Y.C. Lectr. continuing legal edn. programs and bus. seminars. Editor Fordham Law Rev., 1967; contbr. articles to profl. jours. Mem. ABA, N.Y. State Bar Assn., N.Y.C. Bar Assn. Jewish. Avocations: sports memorabilia, reading, music, antiquing. Home: 305 E 86th St Apt 4J New York NY 10028-4702 Office: Kirkpatrick & Lockhart LLP 599 Lexington Ave New York NY 10022-6030

SCHNEIDER, HOWARD, lawyer; b. N.Y.C., Mar. 21, 1935; s. Abraham and Lena (Pincus) S.; m. Anne Evelyn Gorfinkle; children: Andrea Rose, Jeffrey Winston. AB, Cornell U., 1956, JD with distinction, 1959. Bar: N.Y. 1960, D.C. 1976. Assoc., then ptnr. Stroock & Stroock, N.Y.C., 1959—75; gen. counsel Commodity Futures Trading Commn., Washington, 1975—77, Roseman & Colin (now Katten Muchin Zavis Rosenman), N.Y.C., 1977—. Contbr. articles to profl. jours. Served to capt. USAR, 1956-66. Mem.: ABA (chmn., com. on regulation of futures and derivative insts. 1997—2001), Assn. Bar City of N.Y. (chmn. com. 1982—86). Republican. Jewish. Home: 20 E 74th St New York NY 10021 Office: Katten Muchin Zavis Rosenman 575 Madison Ave New York NY 10022-2585 Office Phone: 212-940-8787. Business E-Mail: howard.schneider@kmzr.com.

SCHNEIDER, HOWARD STEWART, newspaper editor, educator; b. Bklyn., Oct. 10, 1945; s. Robert and Helen (Friedman) S.; m. Ilene Roberta Weinstein, July 3, 1967; children— Lara Joy, Scott Michael, Jillian Debra BA cum laude in Journalism and Psychology, Syracuse U., 1966; MS in Journalism, Columbia U., 1967. Co-editor, founder weekly newspaper Syracuse U., NY, 1965-66; editor-pub. Poor Howard's Wednesday Afternoon Post, Wellfleet, Mass., 1966-68; reporter Newsday, Long Island, NY, 1969-76, editor, 1976-85, sr. editor, 1985, mng. editor, 1986—2003, editor, exec. v.p., 2003—. Adj. prof. journalism SUNY-Stony Brook 1983-87. Author profiles on Luciano Pavarotti, Tom Seaver, Edward Albee, and Johnny Carson Recipient Nat. Hearst award Syracuse U., 1965; editor George Polk award-winning series, 1979, 1st pl. N.Y. State Pub.'s Assn., 1982, (supr. reporting and editing team) Pulitzer prize for local reporting, 1984 Jewish. Office: Newsday 235 Pinelawn Rd Melville NY 11747-4250

SCHNEIDER, JAMES M. computer company executive; b. 1950; B, Carroll Coll, 1973. Mgmt. to ptnr. Price Waterhouse; sr. v.p. fin. MCI Commns.; corp. planning, controller Dell Computer, sr. v.p., CFO, 2000—. Bd. dirs. Dell Fin. Svcs., Gen. Commn., Inc. Mem. Fin. Exec. Inst. Office: Dell Computer 1 Dell Way Round Rock TX 78682

SCHNEIDER, JAN, retired obstetrics and gynecology educator; b. Prague, Czechoslovakia, Dec. 10, 1933; came to U.S., 1963, naturalized, 1967; s. Evzen and Erika S.; m. Sandra Wilson, May 20, 1961; children— Hana, Donald, Kathryn, Jonathan. M.B., U. London, 1957; M.P.H., U. Mich., 1967. Prof. ob-gyn, chief obstetric service dept. ob-gyn U. Mich. Med. Sch., Ann Arbor, 1963-77; prof., chmn. ob-gyn. Med. Coll. Pa. and Hahnemann U. (now Drexel U. Coll. Medicine), Phila., 1978-97, assoc. dean, 1997-99, prof. and chmn. emeritus of ob-gyn., 1999—. Editor: (with R. J. Bolognese and R. H. Schwarz) Perinatal Medicine, 2d edit, 1981. Fellow Am. Coll. Obstetricians and Gynecologists, Soc. Perinatal Obstetricians, Am. Gynecol. and Obstet. Soc., Phila. Obstet. Soc. Presbyterian.

SCHNEIDER, JANET M. arts administrator, curator, painter; b. N.Y.C., June 6, 1950. d. August Arthur and Joan (Battaglia) S.; m. Michael Francis Sperendi, Sept. 21, 1985. BA summa cum laude, Queens Coll., CUNY, 1972; spl. study fine arts Boston U. Tanglewood Inst., 1971. With Queens Mus., Flushing, N.Y.C., 1973-89, curator, 1973-75, program dir., 1975-77, exec. dir., 1977-89. Collections arranged include: Sons and others, Women Artists See Men (author catalog), 1975, Urban Aesthetics (author catalog), 1976, Masters of the Brush, Chinese Painting and Calligraphy from the Sixteenth to the Nineteenth Century (co-author catalog), 1977, Symcho Moszkowicz: Portrait of the Artist in Postwar Europe (author catalog), 1978, Shipwrecked 1622, The Lost Treasure of Philip IV (author catalog), 1981, Michaelangelo: A Sculptor's World (author catalog), 1983, Joseph Cornell: Revisited (author catalog), 1992, Blueprint for Change: The Life and Times of Lewis H. Latimer (co-author catalog), 1995. Chmn. Cultural Instns. Group, N.Y.C., 1986-87; mem. N.Y.C. Commn. for Cultural Affairs, 1991-93; bd. dirs. N.Y.C. Partnership, 1987-88, Gallery Assn. N.Y. State 1979-81; exec. dir. Cultural Inst. Group, 1995—. Mem. Artists Choice Mus. (trustee 1979-82), Am. Assn. Mus., Phi Beta Kappa.

SCHNEIDER, JOAN, public relations company owner; BS, Boston U., 1972; postgrd., Harvard U. Pres. Schneider & Assocs., 1980—. Office: 240 Newbury St Boston MA 02116-3609

SCHNEIDER, JOANNE, artist; b. Lima, Ohio, Dec. 4, 1919; d. Joseph and Laura (Office) Federman; m. Norman Schneider, May 15, 1941; children— Melanie Schneider Tucker, Lois Schneider Oppenheim. BFA, Syracuse U., 1941. One-man shows John Heller Gallery, N.Y.C., 1954, 55, 57, 58, Tirca Karlis Gallery, Provincetown, Mass., 1963, Frank Rehn Gallery, N.Y.C., 1965, 66, 69, 72, 75, Elaine Benson Gallery, Bridgehamton, N.Y., 1972, 74, 79, 85, St. Mary's Coll., St. Mary's City, Md., 1978, Alonzo Gallery, N.Y.C., 1978, Discovery Art Gallery, Clifton, N.J., 1978; group shows include Whitney Mus., N.Y.C., Pa. Acad. Arts, Corcoran Galleries, Washington, Toledo Mus., U. Nebr., Everson Mus., Syracuse, N.Y.; represented in permanent collections Met. Mus. Art, N.Y.C., Colby Coll., Syracuse U., Butler Inst., St. Mary's Coll., U. Notre Dame, Guild Hall, East Hampton, N.Y. Recipient Audubon Artists Stanley Grumbacher Meml. award, 1972 Address: 35 E 75th St New York NY 10021-2761 *A life spent in pursuit of creative expression is a fuller, more satisfying life.*

SCHNEIDER, JOHN ARNOLD, investor; b. Chgo., Dec. 4, 1926; s. Arnold George and Anna (Wagner) S.; m. Elizabeth C. Simpson, Oct. 20, 1951; children: Richard Ward, William Arnold, Elizabeth Anne. BS, U. Notre Dame, 1948. Exec. assignments with CBS-TV in, Chgo. and N.Y.C., 1950-58; v.p., gen. mgr. sta. WCAU-TV, Phila., 1958-64; sta. WCBS-TV, N.Y.C., 1964-65; pres. CBS TV Network, 1965-66, CBS/Broadcast Group, 1966-69, 71-77; exec. v.p. CBS, Inc., 1969-71, sr. v.p., from, 1977; pres., chief exec. officer MTV Networks, Inc., 1979-84. Trustee, mem. exec. com. U. Notre Dame; trustee Com. for Econ. Devel. Served with USNR, 1943-46. Mem.: Indian Harbor Yacht. Roman Catholic. Home: 155 Clapboard Ridge Rd Greenwich CT 06831-3304

SCHNEIDER, KIRK J. psychologist, writer; b. Cleve., July 27, 1956; s. Murray Harold Schneider and Laura Siegal; m. Jurate Elena Raulinaitis, Sept. 17, 1989. BA in Psychology, Ohio State U., 1978; MA in Psychology, West Ga. Coll., 1979; PhD in Psychology, Saybrook Inst., 1984. Lic. psychologist Mass., Calif. Suicide prevention staff Columbus Mental Health Ctr., 1977—78; family therapy trainee Ohio State U., 1978—79; counseling intern West Ga. Coll., 1978—79, grad. tchg. asst., 1978; adv. psychology trainee N.E. Cmty. Mental Health Ctr./Fairhill Psychiat. Hosp., East Cleveland, Ohio, 1979—80; intern, supervisee InterLogue-James F.T. Bugental, PhD, Santa Rosa, Calif., 1980—83; post-doctoral trainee Massillon (Ohio) State Hosp., 1984—85; staff psychologist Human Resources Inst., Norton, Fall River, Mass., 1985—87; pvt. practice, founder Ctr. for Existential Therapy, San Francisco, 1987—. Staff psychologist Ctr. for Nutritional Rsch., Quincy, Mass., 1987—88; mem. crisis counseling team Merrill-Lynch & Co., Boston, 1988; staff psychologist South Shore Coun. on Alcohol, Quincy, 1988—89; instr. Existential-Humanistic Inst., San Francisco, 1997—; adj. faculty Lesley Coll., Cambridge, 1986—90, Bentley Coll., Waltham, Mass., 1989, Union Inst., Cin., 1989—90, Calif. Sch. Profl. Psychology, Berkeley, Alameda, 1990—96, The Profl. Sch. Psychology, San Francisco, 1992, Saybrook Grad. Sch., San Francisco, 1995—, Calif. Inst. Integral Studies, San Francisco, 1996—, clin. supr., 1990—; adj. faculty Ctr. for Humanistic Studies, Detroit, 2001—; spkr. in field. Author, editor: The Paradoxical Self: Toward an Understanding of Our Contradictory Nature, 1990, Horror and the Holy: Wisdom-teachings of the Monster Tale, 1993, The Psychology of Existence: An Integrative, Clinical Perspective, 1995, The Handbook of Humanistic Psychology: Leading Edges in Theory, Research, and Practice, 2001; contbr. chapters to books, articles to profl. jours. Pres. Existential-Humanistic Inst., San Francisco, 1999—. Fellow: APA; mem.: AAAS, Assn. for Humanistic Psychology. Office: Saybrook Grad Sch 450 Pacific St San Francisco CA 94133

SCHNEIDER, MAHLON C. lawyer; b. 1939; BA, U. Minn., 1962, LLB, 1964. Bar: Minn. 1965. Atty. Green Giant Co., 1968—80, Pillsbury, 1980-84, v.p., gen. counsel foods divsn., 1984-89; corp. atty. Geo. A. Hormel & Co., Austin, Minn., 1989-90, v.p., gen. counsel, 1990-99, sr. v.p. external affairs, gen. counsel, 1999—. Office: Hormel Foods Corp 1 Hormel Pl Austin MN 55912-3680

SCHNEIDER, MARK, political science educator; b. N.Y.C., Oct. 28, 1946; s. Irving and Ida (Schwartz) S.; m. Susan Roth, June 27, 1986; children: Johanna, Elizabeth. BA, Bklyn. Coll., 1967; PhD, U. N.C., 1974. vis. scholar Russell Sage Found., 1997-98. Asst. prof. polit. sci. U. Mich., Ann Arbor, 1973-74, SUNY, Stony Brook, 1974-78, assoc. prof., 1978-85, prof., 1985—2004, chmn. dept., 1986—2004, disting. prof., 2004—. Fulbright sr. lectr., India, 1980-81. Author: The Competitive City, 1989, Public Entrepreneurs, 1995, Choosing Schools, 2000; contbr. articles to profl. jours. Vis. scholar, Inst. Edn. Scis., 2004—. Mem. Am. Polit. Sci. Assn. (v.p. 2000-01), Midwest Polit. Sci. Assn. Office: SUNY Dept Polit Sci Stony Brook NY 11794-4392

SCHNEIDER, MARK LEWIS, government official; b. Newark, Dec. 31, 1941; s. Benjamin and Ruth (Kobran) S.; m. Susan Gilbert, June 20, 1965; children: Aaron Mitchell, Miriam Beth. AB in Journalism with honors, U. Calif., Berkeley, 1963; MA in Polit. Sci., San Jose State Coll., 1965; LLD (hon.), Am. U., 2000. Reporter UPI, San Francisco, 1963-64, San Francisco News Call Bull., 1965; vol. Peace Corps, El Salvador, 1966-68; reporter Washington Daily News, 1969-70; mem. staff U.S. Senate Judiciary Subcom., 1970-71; legis. asst. to Sen. Edward M. Kennedy, 1971-77, 80-81; dep. asst. sec. for human rights Dept. State, Washington, 1977-79; mem. del. UN Gen. Assembly, 1978, UN Human Rights Commn., 1979; coordinator policy planning, sr. advisor Pan Am. Health Orgn., 1981-93; adminstr. for Latin Am. and Caribbean U.S. AID, 1993-99; dir. The Peace Corps, 1999-2001; sr. v.p. Internat. Crisis Group, Washington, 2001—. Lectr. Kennedy Inst. Politics, Harvard U., 1976; adj. prof. Georgetown U., 1996. Bd. dirs. Internat. Human Rights Law Group, 1981-92. Fulbright fellow, 1976; Recipient George W. Eastman medal for pub. svc. U. Rochestor, 2000. Mem. Am. Polit. Sci. Assn., Latin Am. Studies Assn. Democrat. Jewish. Home: 3517 Tilden St NW Washington DC 20008-3122 Office Phone: 202-785-1601. E-mail: mschneider@icg.org.

SCHNEIDER, MARKUS, computer scientist, researcher; b. Morsbach, Germany, Mar. 1, 1963; s. Johann Josef and Christel Schneider; m. Annette Potthoff, Dec. 19, 1994; children: Florian Markus, Tim Christopher. D rerum naturalium, U. Hagen, Germany, 2001. Asst. U. Hagen, Germany, 1990—2001. Office: Univ Fla CISE Department E450 CSE Building Gainesville FL 32611-6120 E-mail: mschneid@cise.ufl.edu.

SCHNEIDER, MARY ETTA, finance company executive; m. John Beardsley. Grad. cum laude, SUNY, Oswego; grad., Coll. Europe, Brugge, Belgium, Center Latin Am. Studies, Mex. City. Mng. dir., head loan syndications BankBoston, 1996—97, mng. dir., investment bank, 1997—98; exec. VP, specialized fin. Bank Boston Corp.; exec. VP, corp. banking group FleetBoston Fin. Corp., exec. VP, capital markets, 2002—. Mem. adv. bd. Metropolitan Opera; bd. dirs. Boys & Girls Club Boston. Office: FleetBoston Fin Corp 100 Federal St Boston MA 02110

SCHNEIDER, MARY LEA, college administrator; Student, Cardinal Stritch Univ., 1960-63; BA in Theology and Philosophy, Marquette U., 1966, MA in Theology, 1969, PhD in Religious Studies, 1971. Asst. prof. dept. religious studies Mich. State U., 1971-79, assoc. prof., 1979-84, prof., 1984-90, acting chair dept. religious studies, 1988-90; pres. Cardinal Stritch Coll., Milw., 1990—. Vis. instr. theology dept. U. San Francisco, summer 1969, Creighton U., summers 1974-77; spkr., presenter papers, mem. seminars in field; cons. Lilly Endowment, 1988; various TV and radio interviews, 1985— Contbr. articles, revs. to profl. publs. Trustee Pub. Policy Forum, Mt. St. Clare Coll., Clinton, Iowa, 1995—; mem. program Peter Favre Forum; mem. Greater Milw. Com. NEH travel grantee, 1986-87, 1990, rsch. grantee Coll. Arts and Letters Mich. State U., 1987-88. Mem. Am. Acad. Religion (chair Thomas Merton consultation 1979-81), Coll. Theology Soc. (chair Detroit-Cleve. region 1975-77, mem. com. on membership and objectives 1977-79, program dir., chair ann. conv. 1981-84, 88, convenor ecclesiology sect. ann. conv. 1984-87, pres. 1988-90, bd. dirs. 1990-92), Cath. Theol. Soc. Am., Am. Cath. Hist. Soc., History of Women in Religious Network, Tempo (Greater Milw. com.), Wis. Assn. Ind. Colls. and Univs. (exec. com. 1995—, chair, 1997—). Home: 225 W Bradley Rd Milwaukee WI 53217-3154 Office: Cardinal Stritch Univ 6801 N Yates Rd Milwaukee WI 53217-3945

SCHNEIDER, MARY LOUISE, retired elementary education educator; b. Waterville, Wash., Oct. 17, 1918; d. John Steve and Alice Ray (Jones) S. BA in Edn., Holy Names Coll., 1940. Cert. elem. tchr. Wash., 1940. Tchr. Mud Springs/Douglas County, Mansfield, Wash., 1941-42; elem. tchr. Mansfield Sch. dist., Douglas County, Wash., 1942-43, Waterville (Wash.) Sch. Dist., Douglas County, Wash., 1943-49, Lewis and Clark Elem. Sch., Wenatchee, Wash., 1949-60; spl. reading tchr. H.B. Ellison Jr. High, Wenatchee, 1960-62, Orchard Jr. High, Wenatchee, 1962-67; lang. arts tchr. Pioneer Jr. High, Wenatchee, 1967-77; retired, 1977. Author lang. arts learning packages for students, 1967; co-author: Name on the Schoolhouse, 1989. Vol. Am. Heart Assn., Wenatchee, 1975-90, Am. Cancer Soc., Wenatchee, 1975-88. Recipient Cert. of Recognition, Wash. State Ct. Cath. Daus. of the Ams., 1970, 72, 74. Mem.: AAUW (treas. 1973—75), PEO (pres. 1980—82, 1988—90), Chelan-Douglas County Sch. Retirees Assn. (com. chmn. 1989—90), Cath. Daus. of the Ams. (state pres. 1984—86, nat. evangelization chmn. 1986—88, local ct. pres. 1958—60, 1999—2001, author Wash. State Ct. of Cath. Daus. 1988). Avocation: sewing.

SCHNEIDER, MATHIEU, professional hockey player; b. N.Y.C., June 12, 1969; Hockey player Montreal Canadiens Nat. Hockey League, 1990-95, hockey player N.Y. Islanders, 1995-96, hockey player Toronto Maple Leafs, 1996-98, defenseman N.Y. Rangers, 1998—. Mem. Stanley Cup championship team, 1993; played All-Star Game, 1996. Office: NY Rangers Madison Sq Garden 2 Penn Plz New York NY 10121-0101

SCHNEIDER, MATTHEW ROGER, lawyer; b. N.Y.C., Nov. 7, 1948; s. Theodore David Schneider and Rosalind (Schwartz) Werner; m. Marjorie Ann Friedlander, Mar. 6, 1976; children: Adam Benjamin, Emily Beth. BA, Cornell U., 1970; student, Georgetown U., 1971; JD, Cath. U., Washington, 1974. Bar: D.C. 1976, U.S. Dist. Ct. D.C., 1994. Staff asst. U.S. Senate Jud. Com.,

Washington, 1973-74; counsel U.S. Senate Govt. Ops. Com., Washington, 1974-77; spl. asst. Office of Sec. Def., Washington, 1977-79; dir. legis. affairs SEC, Washington, 1979-81, sr. counsel, divsn. corp. fin., 1981-82; chief of staff U.S. Senator Jeff Bingaman, Washington, 1983-85; prin. Law Office Matthew Schneider, Washington, 1985-87; ptnr. Willkie, Farr & Gallagher, Washington, 1987-95, Garvey Shubert Barer, Washington, 1996—98, mng. dir. D.C. office, 1998—, bd. dirs. Nat. Epilepsy Found., 2000—, mem. exec. com., 2001—; Bd. dirs Capitol Hill Hosp., Washington, 1987—95, chmn. govt. and legal affairs com., 1997—. Avocations: physical fitness training, singing, guitar. Office: Garvey Schubert Barer 5th Fl 1000 Potomac St NW Ste 5 Washington DC 20007-3501

SCHNEIDER, MICHAEL H. federal judge; b. San Antonio, Jan. 6, 1943; AA, Lon Morris Coll., 1963; BS, Stephen F. Austin State U., 1965; JD, U. Houston, 1970; LLM, U. Va., 2001. Asst. dist. atty. Harris County, 1971—75; of counsel Parks & Moss, 1975—76; atty. Dresser Industries, 1976—80; mcpl. judge City of West University Place, 1978—90; v.p., gen. counsel Bawden Drilling Inc., 1980—86; gen. solicitor Union Pacific R.R. Co., 1986—89; of counsel McFall & Sartwelle, 1989—90; presiding judge 157th Civil Dist. Ct. Harris County, 1990—96; chief justice Tex. 1st Ct. Appeals, Houston, 1996—2002; justice Tex. Supreme Ct., 2002—04; judge US Dist. Ct. (ea. dist.) Tex., 2004—. Tchr. Ball HS, Galveston, Tex. Named Trial Judge of the Yr., Tex. Assn. Civil Trial and Appellate Specialists, 1994, 2001. Mem.: ABA, Tex. Bar Found., Houston Bar Found., Houston Bar Assn., State Bar Tex. Methodist.*

SCHNEIDER, MICHELLE G. state representative; b. 1954; 2 children. Student, Ohio State U., U. Cin. Small bus. owner; mayor, 1997—99; state rep. dist. 35 Ohio Ho. of Reps., Columbus, 2000—, chair, human svcs. and aging com., mem. banking pensions and securities, health, and pub. utilities coms. Councilwoman Madeira City Coun., 1993—. Mem.: Am. Coll. Health Care Adminstrn. (Disting. Health Care Adminstr. Yr. 1989), Madeira Alumni Assn., Madeira Sch. Found. Office: 77 S High St 11th fl Columbus OH 43215-6111

SCHNEIDER, NANCY REYNOLDS, pathologist, educator; b. Schenectady, N.Y., July 27, 1942; d. Charles Philip Jr. and Ruth Louise (Taylor) Reynolds; m. John Stanley Schneider, July 13, 1968. BA, Ohio Wesleyan U., 1963; MA, U. Mich., 1964; MD, PhD, Cornell U., 1981. Diplomate Am. Bd. Pathology, Am. Bd. Med. Genetics; lic. Tex. Bd. Med. Examiners. Resident in pathology U. Tex. Southwestern Med. Ctr., Dallas, 1982-85, asst. instr. pathology, 1986, instr. pathology, 1986-87, asst. dir. hemotherapy dept., 1986-87, asst. prof. pathology, 1987-92, dir. cytogenetics lab., 1987—, assoc. prof. pathology, 1992-97, prof. pathology, 1997—. Attending staff physician Parkland Meml. Hosp., Dallas, 1986—. Contbr. articles to profl. jours. and chpt. to book. Mem. AMA, AAAS, Am. Soc. Clin. Pathologists, Am. Soc. Human Genetics, Tex. Genetics Soc., Coll. Am. Pathologists, Phi Beta Kappa. Office: Univ Tex Southwestern Med Ctr Dept Pathology 5323 Harry Hines Blvd Dallas TX 75390-7208

SCHNEIDER, NICHOLAS MCCORD, planetary scientist, educator, text-book author; b. Appleton, Wis., Dec. 17, 1956; s. Ben Ross Jr. and Mackay (McCord) S. BA in Physics and Astronomy, Dartmouth Coll., 1979; PhD in Planetary Sci., U. Ariz., 1988. Assoc. prof. lab. for atmospheric & space physics and dept. of astrophysical & planetary scis. U. Colo., Boulder, 1990—. Recipient Presdl. Young Investigator award NSF, 1991. Mem. Am. Astron. Soc. (divsn. for planetary scis.), Am. Geophys. Union, Internat. Astron. Union, Astron. Soc. of the Pacific. Office: U Colo Lab Atmospheric Space Physics 392 UCB Boulder CO 80309-0392

SCHNEIDER, PAM HORVITZ, lawyer; b. Cleve., Nov. 29, 1951; m. Milton S. Schneider, June 30, 1973; 1 child, Sarah Anne. BA, U. Pa., 1973; JD, Columbia U., 1976. Bar: N.Y. 1977, Pa. 1979. Assoc. White & Case, N.Y.C., 1976-78, Drinker Biddle & Reath LLP, Phila., 1978-84, ptnr., 1984-2001; founding ptnr. Gadsden Schneider & Woodward LLP, King of Prussia, Pa., 2001—. Contbr. articles to profl. jours. Fellow Am. Coll. Trust and Estate Counsel (past regent); mem. ABA (past chair, real property probate and trust law sect.), Internat. Acad. Estate and Trust Law (academician). Office: Gadsden Schneider & Woodward LLP The Merion Bldg 700 S Henderson Rd Ste 345 King Of Prussia PA 19406 E-mail: pschneider@gsw-llp.com.

SCHNEIDER, PAUL, writer; b. Passaic, N.J., Aug. 4, 1923; s. Solomon Peter and Rose (Levine) S.; m. Margaret Flood Perrin, Apr. 10, 1951; children: Peggy Lee, Peter Lincoln, Ann. BA, Harvard U., 1945. Writer, N.Y.C., Hollywood, Calif., 1954-91; staff writer Universal City Studios, North Hollywood, Calif., 1967-74; head writer Love of Life CBS Studios, N.Y.C., 1974-76. Writer: (TV) Star Trek, 1954-85, Bonanza, 1954-85, Marcus Welby, M.D., 1954-85, (movies) The Looters, 1957, Ride the Wind, 1966, (plays) Effigy, 1983, Acrimonious, 1962. Mem. Writers Guild Am. (chmn. violence com. 1980-81), Harvard Alumni Assn., Dems. for Action. Avocations: hiking, mountain trails, travel, zen. Home: PO Box 65 Idyllwild CA 92549-0065

SCHNEIDER, PETER, theater producer; m. Hope Schneider; 2 children. BA in Theater, Purdue U., 1972. Mng. dir. St. Nicholas Theater, Chgo., 1976-80; gen. mgr. Apollo Theater Prodns., London, 1980-83; dir. Olympic Arts Festival, L.A., 1984; with Walt Disney Studios, 1985—; pres. Walt Disney Theatrical Prodns. Walt Disney Pictures, Burbank, Calif., 1996-2000; chmn. Walt Disney Studios, Burbank, Calif., 2000—01; dir. Hyperion Theatricals, 2002—. Dir. plays The WPA, Playwrights Horizon, Circle Repertory Theater, N.Y.C. Office: Hyperion Theatricals 500 S Buena Vista St Burbank CA 91521-0006*

SCHNEIDER, PHYLLIS LEAH, writer, editor; b. Seattle, Apr. 19, 1947; d. Edward Lee Booth and Harriet Phyllis (Ebbinghaus) Russell; m. Clifford Donald Schneider, June 14, 1969; 1 child, Pearl Brooke. BA, Pacific Luth. U., 1969; MA, U. Wash., 1972. Fiction, features editor Seventeen Mag., N.Y.C., 1975-80; mng. editor Weight Watchers Mag., N.Y.C., 1980-81; editor YM mag., N.Y.C., 1981-86. Author: Parents Book of Infant Colic, 1990, Kids Who Make a Difference, 1993, Straight Talk on Women's Health: How to Get the Health Care You Deserve, 1993, Hot Health Care Careers, 1993, What Kids Like To Do, 1993; contbr. The Parents Answer Book, 1998; The Prose Reader, 2001, 2004. Recipient Centennial Recognition award Pacific Luth. U., 1990. Democrat. Episcopalian.

SCHNEIDER, RICHARD A. electronics company executive; BS in Acctg., MS in Acctg., U. Pa. CPA. With Reliance Group, Inc., Estee Lauder and Co., KPMG LLP; corp. contr. EDO Corp.; v.p., CFO NAI Technologies, Inc.; exec. v.p. fin., CFO DRS Technologies Inc., Parsippany, N.J., 1999—. Office: DRS Technologies Inc Five Sylvan Way Parsippany NJ 07054

SCHNEIDER, RICHARD GRAHAM, lawyer; b. Bryn Mawr, Pa., Aug. 2, 1930; s. Vincent Bernard and Marion Scott (Graham) S.; m. Margaret Peter Fritz, Feb. 15, 1958; children: Margaret W., Richard Graham Jr., John F. BA, Yale U., 1952; JD, U. Pa., 1957, MLA, 2001. Bar: Pa. 1958. Assoc. Dechert Price & Rhoads, Phila., 1957-66, ptnr., 1966-95; of counsel, 1995—. Case editor U. Pa. Law Rev., 1956-57. Trustee Baldwin Sch., Bryn Mawr, 1971-79, Episcopal Acad., Merion, Pa., 1976-83, Episcopal Cmty. Svcs., Phila., 2003—. 1st lt. USAF, 1952-54, PTO. Mem. ABA, Pa. Bar Assn., Phila. Bar Assn., Order of Coif, Merion Cricket Club, Merion Golf Club (sec. 1997-2002), Yale Club (pres. 1966-68). Republican. Presbyterian. Office: Dechert LLP 4000 Bell Atlantic Tower 1717 Arch St Lbby 3 Philadelphia PA 19103-2713 Personal E-mail: gladwyne@aol.com.

SCHNEIDER, RICHARD T(HEODORE), optics research executive, engineer; b. Munich, July 29, 1927; came to U.S., 1961; s. Wilhelm and Martha E. (Hofmann) S.; m. Lore M. Reinhard, May 16, 1950; children: Ursula M. Schneider Long, Richard W. Diploma in physics, U. Stuttgart, Fed. Republic of Germany, 1958, PhD, 1961. Registered profl. engr. Calif. Teaching asst. U. Stuttgart, 1958-61; sect. chief Allison div. Gen. Motors Corp., Indpls., 1961-65; assoc. prof. U. Fla., Gainesville, 1965-68, prof., 1968-88, prof. emeritus, 1988-90; pres. Eye Rsch. Lab., Inc., Alachua, Fla., 1984-90; chief scientist RTS Labs., Inc., Alachua, 1984-92. Cons. Allison div. Gen. Motors Corp., Indpls., 1965-67; IPA assignment Eglin AFB, Ft. Walton Beach, Fla., 1983; liaison scientist USN Office Naval Rsch., London, 1975. Editor: Uranium Plasmas, 1971; patentee in field; contbr. articles to profl. jours. Recipient Medal for Exceptional Sci. Achievement, NASA, 1975, Outstanding Tech. Achievement award, Fla. Engring. Soc., 1978. Mem. Internat. Soc. for Optical Engring., Sigma Xi, Tau Beta Pi (Eminent Engr. 1970). Avocation: flying airplanes. Home: 12903 NW 112th Ave Alachua FL 32615-6520 Office: Eye Rsch Lab 1663 Technology Ave Alachua FL 32615-9499 Office Phone: 386-462-2666. Personal E-mail: schneider-labs@worldnet.att.net.

SCHNEIDER, RICHARD WILLIAM, academic administrator; b. July 31, 1946; m. June 8, 1968. BS in Engring. cum laude, U.S. Coast Guard Acad., 1968; MA in Liberal Studies, Wesleyan U., 1972; PhD, U. Del., 1985. Ensign USCG, 1968, advanced through grades to RADM, 1993; navigator, gunnery officer, deck dept. head USCGC, Dallas, 1968-70; chief navigation sect. Officer Candidate Sch., Yorktown, Va., 1970-72; asst. dean academics, asst. prof. physics U.S. Coast Guard Acad., 1973-77; exec. officer Coll. Marine Studies U. Del., 1977-85; v.p. rsch. Drexel U., Phila., 1985, v.p., chief fin. officer, 1986, acting v.p. acad. affairs, 1986-88, sr. v.p., 1990-92; pres. Norwich U., Northfield, Vt., 1992—. Lectr. Paoli Tech. Enterprise Ctr., 1985, U. Del., 1984, Swarthmore Coll., 1984, meeting Nat. Coun. Univ. Rsch. Adminstrs., 1984, U. Del. Rsch. Park, 1982. Contbr. articles on total quality mgmt. to various publs. Recipient personal citation Joint Resolution Del. Legislature, 1980; named an Outstanding Young Man of Am., Jaycees, 1978. Office: Norwich U Office of Pres Northfield VT 05663

SCHNEIDER, RITA JOYCE, property management company executive, real estate broker, mortgage broker; b. Bklyn., June 22, 1932; d. Joseph George and Mary (Cohen) Rothkopf; m. Arthur B. Schneider, Oct. 18, 1953 (dec. Feb. 1995); children: Linda Ellen, Debra Carol. Degree in Comml. Art, Pratt Inst., 1953; BA in Acctg., Bklyn. Coll., 1954. Contr. Central Funding Co., Bklyn., 1973-80; owner, contbr. Riteway Mgmt. Inc., Coral Sprigns, Fla., 1980-86; realtor Riteway Internat. Realty Corp., Coral Sprigns, 1985-86, ERA Regal Internat. Realty Inc.; realtor, mortgage broker Regal Fin. Svcs. and LCAM Regal Assn Svcs., Coral Springs, 1986-94, mortgage broker, sr. loan officer contr., 1995—. Cons. in field. Active Cancer Soc., Bklyn., 1954-73, March of Dimes, Bklyn., 1960-70. Recipient 1st art award City of N.Y., 1950. Mem. Nat Bd. Realtors, North Broward Bd. Realtors, Fla. Assn. Mortgage Brokers, Nat. Real Estate Assn., Fla. Assn. Cmty. Mgrs. (lic), Cmty. Assn. Inst. Democrat. Jewish. Avocations: reading, dance, swimming. E-mail: reejay@aol.com.

SCHNEIDER, ROB, actor; Appeared in films Home Alone 2, 1992, Surf Ninjas, 1993, Demolition Man, 1993, The Beverly Hillbillies, 1993, Judge Dredd, 1995, The Adventures of Pinocchio, 1996, (tv series) Men Having Babies, 1995—, Men Behaving Badly (tv series), 1996, Down Periscope, 1996, Susan's Plan, 1998, Knock Off, 1998, 50 First Dates, 2004 Office: United Talent Agy 9560 Wilshire Blvd Fl 5 Beverly Hills CA 90212-2400

SCHNEIDER, ROBERT F. treasurer; b. 1961; With Kimball Internat., Inc., Jasper, Ind., corp. contr., 1990—, v.p., dir. acctg., 1992—, exec. v.p., CFO, asst. treas., 1997—. Office: Kimball Internat Inc 1600 Royal St Jasper IN 47549-1001

SCHNEIDER, ROBERT JAY, oncologist; b. Miami, Fla., May 31, 1949; s. Irving and Ethel (Pack) S.; m. Barbara Cunningham, June 1, 1974; children: Matthew, Kirsten. Student, Washington U., 1967-69; BA cum laude, Boston U., 1971; MD, Albert Einstein Coll. Medicine, N.Y.C., 1975. Diplomate Am. Bd. Internal Medicine, Am. Bd. Oncology; lic. physician, N.Y. Intern, jr. and sr. resident internal medicine Bronx Mcpl. Hosp., N.Y.C., 1975-78; fellow med. oncology Meml. Sloan-Kettering Cancer Ctr., N.Y.C., 1978-80, adj. attending physician/cons. dept. medicine, 1981—; asst. prof. medicine N.Y. Med. Coll., Valhalla, 1980-81. Clin. instr. medicine Cornell U. Med. Coll., 1978-80; jr. clin. faculty fellow Am. Cancer Soc., 1980-81; mem. N.Y. Met. Breast Cancer Group, 1990—; cons. cancer program No. Westchester Hosp. Ctr., Mt. Kisco, N.Y., 1981-82; mem. staff Westchester County Med. Ctr., Valhalla, N.Y., No. Westchester Hosp. Ctr., Mt. Kisco, Meml. Sloan-Kettering Cancer Ctr., N.Y.C. Contbr. articles to profl. jours. Mem. adv. bd. Cancer Care, Inc. Conn., 1997-99. Recipient Clin. Fellowship award Am. Cancer Soc., 1978-79. Mem. Am. Soc. Clin. Oncology, Westchester County Med. Soc., Soc. Integrative Oncology, Am. Soc. Breast Disease, N.Y. State Med. Soc., Woodway Country Club. Republican. Presbyterian. Achievements include research in detection and treatment of early breast cancer, the human spirit in the fight against cancer, salvage chemotherapy with etoposide, ifosfamide and cisplatin in refractory germ cell tumors. Office: 101 S Bedford Rd Ste 202A Mount Kisco NY 10549-3456

SCHNEIDER, SHARON M. systems administrator, information technologist; b. Detroit, Mar. 15, 1958; d. Peter and Mary S.; m. Wesley A. Comes, May 23, 1987. BS, Kutztown U., 1990; MS, MSIS, Drexel U., 1998. Reference and info. asst. Bucks County Free Libr., Doylestown, Pa., 1988-94; computer sys. tech. Cedar Crest & Muhlenberg Colls., Allentown, Pa., 1994-95; sys. adminstr., info. technologist Cedar Crest Coll., 1995—. Mem. Assn. Computing Machinery, World Future Soc.

SCHNEIDER, SOL, electronic engineer, consultant, researcher; b. N.Y.C., Feb. 24, 1924; s. David and Naomi F. Schneider; m. Rhoda B. Schneider, Apr. 16, 1950; children: Sandra E., Barry. BA, CUNY Bklyn. Coll., 1946; MS, NYU, 1949. Supervisory physicist U.S. Army Electronics Tech. and Devices Lab., Ft. Monmouth, N.J., 1948-80, chief pulse power and plasma devices, 1956-80; cons. Army Rsch. Office, 1980-85, U.S. Army Pulse Power Ctr., Ft. Monmouth, 1982-98, SRI, Internat., Menlo Park, Calif., 1983-91, Vitronics, Inc., Eatontown, N.J., 1987-96, Berkeley Rsch. Assocs., Springfield, Va., 1996—2002, U.S. Army Rsch. Lab., Adelphi, Md., 1997—2002. Adj. prof. Southwestern Ctr. for Elec. Engring. Edn., St. Cloud, Fla., 1980-86; mem. USN Pulsed Power Tech. Adv. Group, Washington, 1978-80, SDIO Pulsed Power Tech. Adv. Group, 1983-93, Adv. Group on Electronic Devices, Dept. Def., Washington, 1970-80. Contbr. articles to profl. jours.; holder 15 patents. With U.S. Army, 1942-46, ETO. Recipient award Sec. Army, 1963, U.S. Army R&D Achievement award Dept. Army, 1963, 78, Army Sci. award, 1978. Fellow: IEEE (life; chmn./editor symposium proc. 1957—80, chmn. emeritus internat. power modulator symposium 1981—2001, co-chmn. highvoltage workship 1989—90, exec. com. 1991—2001, mem. internat. sci. adv., awards com. internat. power modulator conf. 2001—, High Voltage award 1991, Germeshausen award 1992, Sol Schneider award created 2004); mem.: Am. Phys. Soc. (exec. com. gaseous electronics conf. 1961—66, sec. 1964, exec. com. electron and atomic physics divsn. 1965—66). Home: 100 Arrowwood Ct Red Bank NJ 07701-6717 E-mail: sols5017@yahoo.com.

SCHNEIDER, STANLEY SCOTT, biology professor; b. Lockhart, Texas, Jan. 22, 1953; s. Ernest O. and Marie Schneider; life ptnr. July 14, 1992. BS in Biology, S.W. Tex. State U., San Marcos, 1971—75, M in Sci., 1976; PhD, U. Calif., Davis, 1980—84. Lectr. S.W. Tex. State U., San Marcos, 1978—80; vis. lectr. U. Calif., Davis, 1984—85; prof. biology U. N.C., Charlotte, 1985—. Author: (over forty jour. articles) Animal Behavior, Behavioral Ecology and Sociobiology, Evolution, Ann. Rev. of Entomology, Ethology, Insects Sociaux, Apidologie, Jour. of Insect Behavior; editor: Jour. of Econ. Entomology, Jour. of Apidologie. Bd. mem. Time Out Youth, Charlotte, NC, 1992—97, pres., 1996—97. Grantee Fulbright Scholarship, 1987, Rsch. Grant, Whitehall Found., 1987, Nat Sci. Found., 1989, Rsch. Grants, U. S. Dept. of Agr., 1995—99. Mem.: Internat. Soc. for Behavioral Ecology, Internat. Union for the Study of Social Insects, Animal Behavior Soc. of Am., Entomol. Soc. of Am. Office: Dept of Biology U NC Charlotte NC 28223 Office Fax: 704-687-3128. Business E-Mail: sschnedr@email.uncc.edu.

SCHNEIDER, STEPHEN HARLEY, medical educator; b. Neptune, N.J., Apr. 1, 1948; s. Joseph and Edith (Himmelman) S.; m. Carole Robin Lowenstein, Aug. 31, 1981; children: Ari, Rachel. BA, MD, Boston U., 1972. Cert. in internal medicine and endocrinology, N.J. Rsch. assoc. Boston City Hosp., 1975-76, fellow divsn. diabetes and metabolism, 1976-77, asst. dir. diabetes clinic, 1976-77, dir. diabetes clinic, 1977-78, dir. diabetes and metabolism svcs., 1978-79; instr. medicine Boston Univ. Sch. Medicine, 1978-79; asst prof. medicine U. Medicine and Dentistry N.J.-Robert Wood Johnson Med. Sch., New Brunswick, N.J., 1979-85, assoc. prof. clin. medicine, 1985-88, assoc. prof. medicine, 1988-95, prof. medicine, 1995—. Mem. editl. bd. Diabetes Forcast Mag.; contbr. numerous articles to profl. jours. including Jour. Clin. Endo. & Nutr., New Eng. Jour. Medicine, Diabetes Care, Atherosclerosis, Japanese Heart Jour., Diabetologia, Metabolism. Bd. dirs. Juvenile Diabetes Assn., East Brunswick Jewish Ctr. Youth Com.; founding mem. affiliate Internat. Diabetic Athlete's Assn. Recipient McKeen Cattell award Am. Coll. Clin. Pharmacology, 1986; rsch. fellow Am. Heart Assn., 1976. Fellow ACP; mem. Am. Soc. Internal Medicine, Am. Coll. Sports Medicine, Am. Fedn. Clin. Rsch., Begg Soc., Phi Beta Kappa, Alpha Omega Alpha. Jewish. Avocations: football, soccer, history, theology, bicycling. Office: UMDNJ-Robert W Johnson Med Divsn Endocrinology PO Box 19 New Brunswick NJ 08903-0019 Office Phone: 732-235-7751. Business E-Mail: schneide@umdnj.edu.

SCHNEIDER, STEPHEN HENRY, climatologist, environmental policy analyst, researcher; b. N.Y.C., Feb. 11, 1945; s. Samuel and Doris C. (Swarte) S.; married, 1995; 2 children from previous marriage. BS, Columbia U., 1966, MS, 1967, PhD in Mech. Engring./Plasma Physics, 1971; DSc (hon.), N.J. Inst. Tech., 1990, Monmouth Coll., 1991. NAS, NRC rsch. assoc. Goddard Inst. Space Studies NASA, N.Y.C., 1971-72; fellow advanced study program Nat. Ctr. Atmospheric Research, Boulder, Colo., 1972-73, scientist, dep. head climate project, 1973-78, acting leader climate sensitivity group, 1978-80, head visitors program and dep. dir. advanced study program, 1980-87, sr. scientist, 1980-96, head interdisciplinary climate systems sect., 1987-92, prof. biol. scis. dept., sr. fellow Inst. Internat. Studies Stanford (Calif.) U., 1992—, prof. civil and environtl. engring. dept. (courtesy). Affiliate prof. U. Corp. Atmospheric Rsch. Lamont-Doherty Geol. Obs., Columbia, U., 1976-83; mem. Carter-Mondale Sci. Policy Task Force, 1976; Clinton-Gore sci. advisor, 1992, 96; sci. advisor, interviewee Nova Sta. WGBH-TV, Planet Earth, Sta. WQED-TV; mem. internat. sci. coms. climatic change, ecology, energy, environ. edn., food and pub. policy; expert witness congl. coms.; mem. Def. Sci. Bd. Task Force on Atmospheric Obscuration; lead author Intergovernmental Panel on Climate Change Working Group I, 1995-96; coord. lead author Working Group II, 1998—; mem. core writing team Synthesis Report, 2000—. Author: (with Lynne E. Mesirow) The Genesis Strategy: Climate and Global Survival, 1976; (with Lynne Morton) The Primordial Bond: Exploring Connections Between Man and Nature Through Humanities and Science, 1981, (with Randi S. Londer) The Coevolution of Climate and Life, 1984, Global Warming: Are We Entering the Greenhouse Century?, 1989; (with W. Bach) Interactions of Food and Climate, 1981; (with R.S. Chen and E. Boulding) Social Science Research and Climate Change: An Interdisciplinary Appraisal, 1983; (with K.C. Land) Forecasting in the Social and Natural Sciences, 1987; (with P. Boston) Scientists on Gaia, 1990; editor-in-chief: The Encyclopedia of Climate and Weather, 1996, Laboratory Earth: The Planetary Experiment We Can't Afford to Lose, 1997; editor: Climatic Change, 1976—; contbr. articles on theory of climate, influence of climate on soc., relation of climatic change to world food, population, energy, development and environ. policy issues, environ. aftereffects of nuclear war, carbon dioxide greenhouse effect, pub. understanding sci., environ. edn. Recipient Louis J. Battan Author's award Am. Meteorol. Soc., 1990, Mary B. Ansari Ref. Work award Geosci. Info. Soc., 1997; named one of 100 Outstanding Young Scientists in Am. by Sci. Digest, 1984; MacArthur Found. Prize fellow John D. and Catherine T. MacArthur Found., 1992. Fellow AAAS (Westinghouse award 1991), Scientists Inst. for Pub. Info.; mem. U.S. Assn. Club Rome, Am. Meteorological Soc., Am. Geophysical Union, Fedn. Am. Scientists, Soc. Conservation Biology, Soc. Ecol. Economics., Acad. Europae (fgn.), Ecol. Soc. Am., NAS (elected, 2002). Office: Stanford U Dept Biol Scis Stanford CA 94305-5020

SCHNEIDER, STEVEN L. company executive; BS, U of Kansas. Pres., CEO Trion, Inc., Sanford, N.C., 1993-99; sr. corp. v.p. & chmn., CEO Fedders Indoor Air Quality, Liberty Corner, NJ, 1999—. Office: Fedders Corp Westgate Corp Center 505 Martinsville Rd PO Box 813 Liberty Corner NJ 07938-0813

SCHNEIDER, STEVEN L. information company executive; Pres. Disclosure Inc., Bethesda, Md. Office: Disclosure Inc 1455 Research Blvd Rockville MD 20850-3194

SCHNEIDER, THOMAS PAUL, non-profit agency administrator; b. June 5, 1947; s. Milton and Gloria (Bocaner) S.; m. Susan G. Stein, May 31, 1987; children: Rachel Jenny, Daniel Joshua. BA with honors, JD, U. Wis., 1972. U.S. atty. U.S. Dist. Ct. (ea. dist.) Wis., Milw., 1993-2001; exec. dir. youth svcs. COA Youth & Family Ctrs., Milw., 2001—. Mem. Wis. Bar Assn. Democrat. Jewish. Office: COA Youth & Family Ctrs 909 E North Ave Milwaukee WI 53212 Office Phone: 414-263-8383. Business E-Mail: tomschneider@coa-yfc.org. E-mail: tomcoa@execpc.com.

SCHNEIDER, VALERIE LOIS, speech educator; b. Chgo., Feb. 12, 1941; d. Ralph Joseph and Gertrude Blanche (Gaffron) S. BA, Carroll Coll., 1963; MA, U. Wis., 1966; PhD, U. Fla., 1969; CAS, Appalachian State U., 1981. Tchr. English and history, dir. forensics and drama Montello (Wis.) H.S., 1963-64; instr. speech U. Fla., Gainesville, 1966-68, asst. prof. speech, 1969-70, Edinboro (Pa.) State Coll., 1970-71; assoc. prof. speech East Tenn. State U., Johnson City, 1971-76, prof. speech, 1976-97. Instr. newspaper course Johnson City Press Chronicle, 1979, Elizabethton Star, Erwin Record, Mountain City Tomahawk, Jonesboro Herald and Tribune, 1980; mem. investor panel USA Today, 1991-92. Editor East Tenn. State U. evening and off-campus newsletter, 1984-91; assoc. editor Homiletic, 1974-76; columnist Video Visions, Kingsport Times-News, 1984-86; book reviewer Pulpit Digest, 1986-90; contbr. articles to profl. jours. Chmn. AAUW Mass Media Study Group Com., Johnson City, 1973-74. Recipient Creative Writing award Va. Highlands Arts Festival, 1973, award Kingsport Times News, 1984, 85, Tri-Cities Met. Advt. Fedn., 1983, 84, hon. life mem. Tenn. Presbyn. Women, 2000; named Danforth assoc., 1977; finalist Money mag. contest, 1994, Writer's Digest contest, 2000. Mem.: AAUW (v.p. chpt. 1974—75, pres. 1975—76), Tenn. Basic Skills Coun. (pres. 1975—76, exec. bd. 1979—80, v.p. 1980—81), Religious Speech Comm. Assn. (Best Article award 1976), Tenn. Speech Comm. Assn. (exec. bd. 1974—77, publs. bd. 1974—78, pres. 1977—78), So. Speech Comm. Assn., Speech Comm. Assn. (Tenn. rep. to states adv. coun. 1974—75), Mensa, Presbyn. Women (hon.; life mem.), Johnson City Book Club (pres. 2001—03), Bus. and Profl. Women's Club (chpt. exec. bd. 1972—73, v.p. 1976—77), Pi Gamma Mu, Phi Delta Kappa, Tau Kappa Alpha, Delta Sigma Rho. Presbyterian. Home: 3201 Buckingham Rd Johnson City TN 37604-2775 Office: East Tenn State U PO Box 23098 Johnson City TN 37614-1310 E-mail: vlasastre@aol.com.

SCHNEIDER, WESLEY CLAIR, marketing communications company executive; b. Chgo., May 2, 1953; s. Clair A. and Ruth (Jenks) S.; m. Jeanie A. Tomaino, Nov. 23, 1990. BA magna cum laude, Ill. Wesleyan U., 1975. Sales rep. confectionery div. Am. Home Products, Chgo., 1975-77; midwest regional sales mgr. confectionery & snacks div. Beatrice Foods, Denver, 1977-78, mktg. analyst, 1978-80; product mgr. Tootsie Roll Industries, Chgo., 1980-85, mgr. internat. mktg., 1985-88; v.p., gen. mgr. Marden-Kane, inc., Chgo., 1988-91; pres., owner Creative Mktg. Comm., Inc., Chgo., 1991—. Bd. dirs. Wesleyan Co., Inc., Chgo.; speaker Inst. for Internat. Rsch. and Promotion Mktg. Assn. Am., N.Y.C., 1991. Patentee in field. Cubmaster Boy Scouts Am., Chgo., 1991; founder Silver Wicket Chairty Event; mem., chair candidates slating subcom. Kenilworth Citizens Adv. Com.; bd. dirs. Kenilworth Assembly Hall Soc., 2001—; chmn. Am. Leadership Fund., 2003; leadership coun. Ill. Wesleyan U.; asst. committeeman New Trier Rep. Orgn., 2003—, fin. chmn., 1998-2002; founder Christ The King Anglican Ch., 2004. Recipient Best Design award retail food category Nat. Flexible Packaging Assn., 1979, Indian statue Point of Purchase Advt. Inst., 1986, 87, U.S. Senatorial Medal of Freedom, 1999. Mem. Am. Def. Preparedness Assn.,

Exec. Club Chgo. (comms. com.) Internat. Platform Assn., Masons, Shriners, Sigma Chi. Anglican. Avocations: fishing, reading, politics. Office: Creative Mktg Comm Inc 980 N Mich Ave Ste 1400 Chicago IL 60611

SCHNEIDER, WILLIAM, JR., commissioner; PhD, NYU, 1968. Assoc. dir. for nat. security and internat. affairs Office Mgmt. Budget; under sec. state for security assistance, sci. and tech. U.S. Dept. Def., 1982—86, chmn. def. sci. bd.; pres. Internat. Planning Svcs., Inc.; commr., co-chair aerospace global issues Aerospace Commn. Chmn. Pres. Gen. adv. Com. on Arms Control and Disarmament, 1987—93; cons. in field. Office: Aerospace Commn Crystal Gateway One 1235 Jefferson Davis Hwy Ste 940 Arlington VA 22202-3283

SCHNEIDER, WILLIAM CHARLES, aerospace consultant; b. N.Y.C., Dec. 24, 1923; s. Charles J. and Margaret (Stoeffler) S.; m. Roseann Vasco, Oct. 6, 1964; children: Catherine M., Jeanne M., Robert J., Robert Sherer. BS, MIT, 1949; MS, U. Va., 1952; D in Engring., Cath. U. Am., 1976. Rsch. scientist NACA Langley Rsch. Ctr., Hampton, Va., 1949-55; asst. br. head Air-to-Air Missiles Bur. Aeros., Washington, 1955-60; dir. space vehicles USN Bur. Weapons, Washington, 1960-61; dir. space systems Internat. Tel. & Tel., Nutley, N.J., 1961-63; dep. dir. Gemini program Office Manned Space Flight NASA Hdqrs., Washington, 1963-65; dir., dep. dir. operations, mission dir. Office Manned Space Flight NASA Hdqrs. (Gemini program), 1965-66; dir. Apollo Applications Missions, 1966-67, Apollo Mission dir., 1967-68, dir. Skylab program, 1968-74, dep. assoc. adminstr. for space transp. systems, 1974-78, assoc. adminstr. for space tracking and data systems, 1979-80; v.p. mgmt. and product assurance Systems Group Computer Scis. Corp., Falls Church, Va., 1980-83, v.p. control systems, 1983-85, v.p. devel., 1985-90; cons., 1990—. Mem. life scis. strategic planning bd. NASA, life scis. div. working group, aerospace medicine adv. com. NASA, mem. space sta. adv. com.; mem. adv. space tech. com. NRC; bd. dirs. Spacetech Inc. Mem. bd. visitors Cath. U. Served with USNR, 1942-46. Recipient Exceptional Service medal NASA, 1965, Distinguished Service medal, 1968-73, Outstanding Leadership medal, 1980; Apollo Group Achievement award, 1969; Astronautics Engr. award, 1974; Robert J. Collier trophy, 1974; Am. Astronautical Soc. Space Flight award, 1974 Fellow AIAA, Internat. Acad. Astronautics, Planetary Soc., Am. Astron. Soc. (v.p.); mem. VFW, Armed Forces Comm. and Electronics Assn., Energy Mgmt. and Control Soc., NASA Alumni League (treas.), Brit. Interplanetary Soc. Home and Office: 16815 Centerfield Way Olney MD 20832-2000

SCHNEIDER, WILLIAM GEORGE, former life insurance company executive; b. Shenandoah, Iowa, Jan. 18, 1919; s. Fred M. and Abba F. (Ferguson) S.; m. Phyllis Welch, Mar. 28, 1943; children— Stephen F., Richard W. BA, State U. Iowa, 1940; postgrad., N.Y. U. With Met. Life Ins. Co., 1940-41, 45-46; with Bankers Life Co. (now named Prin. Fin. Group), Des Moines, 1946-84; sr. v.p. Bankers Life Co., 1970-82, exec. v.p., 1982-84, ret., 1984. Served with AUS, 1941-45. Fellow Soc. Actuaries; mem. Am. Acad. Actuaries, Des Moines Golf and Country Club, Phi Beta Kappa. Republican. Home: 3662 Ingersoll Ave Apt 414 Des Moines IA 50312-3422

SCHNEIDER, WILLIAM GEORGE, chemist, research consultant; b. Wolseley, Sask., Can., June 1, 1915; s. Michael and Phillipina (Krauschaar) S.; m. Jean Purves, Sept. 2, 1940; children: Judith Schneider Saunders, Joanne Schneider Spurrier. B.Sc., U. Sask., 1937, M.Sc., 1939, D.Sc., 1969; PhD, McGill U., 1941, D.Sc., 1970; D.Sc. (hon.), York U., 1966, Meml. U., 1968, McMaster U., 1969, Laval U., 1969, Moncton U., 1969, U. N.B., 1970, U. Montreal, 1970, Acadia U., 1976, U. Regina, 1976, Ottawa U., 1978; LL.D., U. Alta., 1968, Laurentian U., 1968. Head phys. chemistry sect., div. chemistry NRC Can., Ottawa, Ont., 1946-63, dir. div. pure chemistry, 1963-65, v.p., 1965-67, pres., 1967-80; research cons., 1980—. Author: (with J.A. Pople, H.J. Bernstein) High Resolution Nuclear Magnetic Resonance, 1959; contbr. articles to profl. jours. Decorated Order of Can., 1977 Fellow Royal Soc. Can. (Henry Marshall Tory medal), Royal Soc. London, Chem. Inst. Can. (medal 1969, Montreal medal 1973); mem. Internat. Union Pure and Applied Chemistry (pres. 1983-85) Office: 200 Rideau Terrace Ottawa ON Canada K1M 0Z3

SCHNEIDER, WILLYS HOPE, lawyer; b. N.Y.C., Sept. 27, 1952; d. Leon and Lillian (Friedman) S.; m. Stephen Andrew Kals, Jan. 21, 1979; children: Peter, Josefine. AB, Princeton U., 1974; JD, Columbia U., 1977. Bar: N.Y. 1978, U.S. Dist. Ct. (ea. and so. dists.) N.Y. 1978, U.S. Tax Ct. 1979. Law clk. to hon. Jack B. Weinstein U.S. Dist. Ct. (ea. dist.) N.Y., Bklyn., 1977-78; assoc. Paul, Weiss, Rifkind, Wharton & Garrison, N.Y.C., 1978-83, Kaye Scholer LLP, N.Y.C., 1983-87, 1987—. Contbr. articles to profl. jours. Mem. ABA, N.Y. State Bar Assn., Assn. of Bar of City of N.Y. Home: 320 W End Ave New York NY 10023-8110 Office: Kaye Scholer LLP 425 Park Ave New York NY 10022-3506 Office Phone: 212-836-8693. E-mail: wschneider@kayescholer.com.

SCHNEIDER-CRIEZIS, SUSAN MARIE, architect; b. St. Louis, Aug. 1, 1953; d. William Alfred and Rosemary Elizabeth (Fischer) Schneider; m. Demetrios Anthony Criezis, Nov. 24, 1978; children: Anthony, John and Andrew. BArch, U. Notre Dame, 1976; MArch, MIT, 1978. Registered architect, Wis. Project designer Eichstaedt Architects, Roselle, Ill., 1978-80, Solomon, Cordwell, Buenz & Assocs., Chgo., 1980-82; project architect Gelick, Foran Assocs., Chgo., 1982-83; asst. prof. Sch. Architecture U. Ill., Chgo., 1980-86; exec. v.p. Criezis Architects, Inc., Northfield, Ill., 1986—. Graham Found. grantee MIT, 1977, MIT scholar, 1976-78; Prestressed Concrete Inst. rsch. grantee, 1981. Mem. AIA, Chgo. Archtl. Club, Chgo. Women in Architecture, Am. Solar Energy Soc., NAFE, Jr. League Evanston, Evanston C. of C. Roman Catholic. Avocations: tennis, swimming. Office: 1775 Winnetka Ave Ste 100 Northfield IL 60093-3386

SCHNEIDMAN, BARBARA SUE, psychiatrist; b. Mpls., Jan. 18, 1944; d. Norman Reuben and MIldred (Roberts) S.; m. William McAllister. BA, U. Minn., Mpls., 1966, MD, 1970; MPH, U. Wash., 1974. Diplomate Am. Bd. Psychiatry and Neurology. Resident ob-gyn. U. Wash., Seattle, 1972-74, dir. gynecology, 1974-78, resident in psychiatry, 1978-81, cons. primary care, 1981-88; pvt. practice Seattle, 1981-93; cons. Sexual Assault Ctr., Seattle, 1981-93, Cen. Area Mental Health, Seattle, 1990-92; assoc. v.p. Am. Bd. Med. Specialties, Evanston, Ill., 1993-98; dir. divsn. of medical edn. liaison and outreach AMA, 1998—2002, v.p. med. edn., 2002—. Mem., chair Wash. State Bd. Med. Examiners, 1982-93; pres. Fedn. State Med. Bds., 1991-92. Mem. AMA, Am. Psychiat. Assn., Ill. Psychiat. Soc. Avocation: bicycling. Office: AMA 515 N State St # 7130 Chicago IL 60610-4325 Fax: 312-464-5830. Office Phone: 312-464-4804. Personal E-mail: barbara-schneidman@ama.aschiors.com.

SCHNEIER, EDWARD VINCENT, political science educator; b. Bronx, N.Y., May 25, 1939; s. Edward Vincent and Lillian (Buhr) S.; m. Janice Bernier, June 16, 1960 (div. Jan. 1974); children: Andrew, Katherine; m. Margrit Russenberger, May 13, 2000. BA, Oberlin Coll., 1960; MA, Claremont (Calif.) Grad. Sch., 1961, PhD, 1963. Rsch. fellow Brookings Instn., Washington, 1963; legis. asst. Senator Birch Bayh, Washington, 1963-64; asst. prof. The Johns Hopkins U., Balt., 1964-65, Princeton (N.J.) U., 1965-68; from asst. to assoc. prof. The City Coll., CUNY, 1968-93, prof., 2002, prof. emeritus, 2002—. Ptnr. Grassroots Tavern, N.Y.C., 1975—. Author: Congress Today, 1993, Legislative Strategy, 1993, Vote Power, 1974, Party and Constituency, 1970, New York Politics, 2001, Crafting Constitutional Democracies, 2003. State legis. dir. Am. for Dem. Action, Albany, 1992-2001; commr. Copake (N.Y.) Park Commn., 1991-2001; officer Downtown Ind. Dem., N.Y.C., 1975-90; candidate for Congress Dem. Primary, N.Y.C., 1976; lobbyist Com. for Equity in Edn., N.Y.C., 1994-2000. Rsch. fellow NEH, U. Chgo., 1978-80, Princeton, 1996, Fulbright Found., 1988-89, 2002. Mem. Am. Polit. Sci. Assn. Avocations: golf, skiiing, cooking. Home: 1284 Lake View Rd Copake NY 12516-1028 Office: Dept Polit Sci City College # 138th St New York NY 10031 E-mail: nedmarg@earthlink.net.

SCHNEIROV, ALLISON R. lawyer; b. Phila., 1966; BA magna cum laude, U. Pa., 1988; JD cum laude, NYU, 1991. Bar: N.Y. 1992. Atty. Skadden, Arps, Slate, Meagher & Flom LLP, N.Y., 1993—. Office: Skadden Arps Slate Meagher & Flom LLP Four Times Sq New York NY 10036

SCHNEITER, GEORGE MALAN, golfer, development company executive; b. Ogden, Utah, Aug. 12, 1931; s. George Henery and Bernice Slade (Malan) S.; m. JoAnn Deakin, Jan. 19, 1954; children: George, Gary, Dan, Steve, Elizabeth Ann, Michael. BS in Banking and Fin., U. Utah, 1955. With 5th Army Championship Golf Team, U.S. Army, 1955-56; assoc. golf pro Hidden Valley Golf Club, Salt Lake City, 1957; golf pro Lake Hills Golf Club, Billings, Mont., 1957-90, sec., 1957-61, pres., 1964-90, Schneiter Enterprises, Sandy, Utah, 1974—; developer Schneiter's Golf Course, 1973—, and subdiv., 1961—; player PGA tour, 1958-78, Sr. PGA tour, 1981—. Missionary So. State Mission, LDS Ch., 1951-52. Served with U.S. Army, 1955-56. Named winner, Utah sect. Sr. Championship, Wyo., Open Super Sr. Championshio, Salt Lake City Parks Tournament, Vernal Brigham Payson Open, Yuma Open, Utah Sr. PGA Chamption, Utah Super Sr. Championshio, World Pro Am., Kona, Hawaii, Ft. Carsopn Golf Champion; fellow Banking & Fin. fellow, First Security Bank Utah, 1953. Mem. PGA, Salt Lake City C. of C., Intermountain Golf Courst Supertaints Assn. Achievements include over 30 hole in ones. also: 8968 S 1300 E Sandy UT 84094 Office: 2009 Brassy Dr Las Vegas NV 89142-2033 Fax: (702) 457-7065.

SCHNELL, GEORGE ADAM, geographer, educator; b. Phila., July 13, 1931; s. Earl Blackwood and Emily (Bernheimer) S.; m. Mary Lou Williams, June 21, 1958; children: David Adam, Douglas Powell, Thomas Earl. BS, West Chester U., 1958; MS, Pa. State U., 1960, PhD, 1965; postdoctoral study, Ohio State U., 1965. Asst. prof. SUNY, New Paltz, 1962-65, assoc. prof., 1965-68, prof. geography, 1968-99, founding chmn. dept., 1968-94, prof. emeritus, 1999—. Adj. prof. SUNY, 2000—; vis. assoc. prof. U. Hawaii, summer, 1966; cons. cmty. action programming, 1965; manuscript reader, cons. to several pubs., 1967—; founder, founding bd. dirs., investigator Inst. for Devel., Planning and Land Use Studies, 1986-96; cons. Mid-Hudson Pattern for Progress, 1986, Open Space Inst., 1987, Mid-Hudson Regional Econ. Devel. Coun., 1989, Urban Devel. Corp., 1989-90, 93, Tech. Devel. Ctr., 1991, Catskill Ctr., 1991, Ednl. Testing Svc., 1993-94, 96, 97; cons. editor Exams Unltd., Albany, N.Y., 1995-99; ind. contracor and cons. Excelsior U., 2003—; founding mem. exec. bd. dirs. Hudson Valley Study Ctr., 1995-98; cons. several depts. geography, 1988—, Pa. Geog. Alliance, 1999; ind. contractor Excelsior U., 2003, cons., 2004; presenter in field. Author: (with others) The Local Community: A Handbook for Teachers, 1971, The World's Population, Problems of Growth, 1972; contbr. Pennsylvania Coal: Resources, Technology, Utilization, 1983, West Virginia and Appalachia: Selected Readings, 1977, Hazardous and Toxic Wastes: Technology, Management and Health Effects, 1984, Environmental Radon: Occurrence, Control and Health Hazards, 1990, Natural and Technological Disasters: Causes, Effects and Preventive Measures, 1992, Conservation and Resource Management, 1993, Medicine and Health Care into the 21st Century, 1995, Forests: A Global Perspective, 1996, (with M.S. Monmonier) Ecology of the Wetlands and Associated Systems, 1998, (with M.S. Monmonier) Renewable Energy: Trends and Prospects, 2002; co-author: (with M.S. Monmonier) The Study of Population: Elements, Patterns, Processes, 1983, Map Appreciation, 1988; editor, contbr.: (with G.J. Demko and H.M. Rose) Population Geography: A Reader, 1970; contbr. articles to profl. jours. Appt. mem. local bds. and coms. Town and Village of New Paltz, New Paltz Ctrl. Sch. Dist., 1965—; elder Reformed Ch. of New Paltz; Rep. committeeman Town of Gardner, Ulster County, N.Y., 2000-01. With AUS, 1952-54. Recipient Excellence award N.Y. State/United Univ. Professions, 1990; Disting. Alumnus award West Chester U., 1994. Mem. Assn. Am. Geographers, Pa. Geog. Soc. (mem. editl. bd. Pa. Geographer, Disting. Geographer award 1994), Pa. Acad. Sci. (assoc. editor jour. 1988—), Nat. Coun. for Geog. Edn., Paltz Club. Home: 29 River Park Dr New Paltz NY 12561-2636 Office: SUNY at New Paltz Dept Geography 75 S Manheim Blvd New Paltz NY 12561-2400 Personal E-mail: georgeschnell@msn.com.

SCHNELL, ROBERT LEE, JR., lawyer; b. Mpls., Sept. 20, 1948; s. Robert Lee and Dorothy Mae (Buran) S.; m. Jacqueline Irene Husak, Dec. 19, 1969 (div. Aug. 1988); children: Robert Lee III, Elizabeth Anne, Jennifer Irene; m. Julie Ann Bemlott, Sept. 29, 1989; children: Helen Bridget, Michael Henry. BA cum laude, Princeton U., 1970; JD magna cum laude, Harvard U., 1974. Bar: Minn. 1974, U.S. Dist. Ct. Minn. 1974, U.S. Ct. Appeals (8th cir.) 1975, U.S. Supreme Ct. 1990. Assoc. Faegre & Benson, Mpls., 1974-81, ptnr., 1982—. Bd. dirs. United Way of Mpls., 1992-93. Office: Faegre & Benson 2200 Wells Fargo Ctr 90 S St Ste 2200 Minneapolis MN 55402-1109

SCHNELL, ROGER THOMAS, small business owner, retired state official; b. Wabasha, Minn., Dec. 11, 1936; s. Donald William and Eva Louise (Barton) S.; m. Barbara Ann McDonald, Dec. 18, 1959 (div. Mar. 1968); children: Thomas Allen, d. Scott Douglas. A in Mil. Sci., Command and Gen. Staff Coll., 1975; A in Bus. Administn., Wayland Bapt. U., 1987. Commd. 2d lt. Alaska N.G., 1959, advanced through grades to col., 1975, shop supt., 1965-71, personnel mgr., 1972-74, chief of staff, 1974-87, dir. logistics, 1987; electrician Alaska R.R., Anchorage, 1955-61, elec. foreman, 1962-64; dir. support personnel mgmt. Joint Staff Alaska N.G., 1988-92, ret.; personnel mgr. State of Alaska, 1992, asst. commr. dept. mil. and vets. affairs, 1992-95, dep. commr. dept. mil. and vets. affairs, 1995-98, 2002—; owner RTS Enterprises, Anchorage, 1999—. Prin., owner RTS Enterprises, 1999—; adv. bd. state joint armed svc. com. State of Alaska, 2001—; dep. commr. dept. Mil. and Vet. Affairs, 2003—. Chmn. Alaska Nat. Guard Mus. Trust Fund, 2001—02; chmn. pastor parish rels. com. Meth. 1st Ch., 2001—02; bd. dirs. Meth. Trust Fund, 2002—. Mem. Fed. Profl. Labor Relations Execs. (sec. 1974-75), Alaska N.G. Officers Assn. (pres. 1976-78, bd. dirs. 1988—), Assn. U.S. Army (corp.), NG Assn. U.S. (life, retiree rep. from Alaska 1993—), Am. Legion, Amvets, Elks. Republican. Methodist. Avocations: travel, photography. Home and Office: Huntwood Park Estates 6817 Queens View Cir Anchorage AK 99504-5203 Office Phone: 907-428-6009. E-mail: rogertschnell@gci.net., rtschnellenterprises@gci.net., rogertschnell@gci.net.

SCHNELLE, KARL BENJAMIN, JR., chemical engineering educator, consultant, researcher; b. Canton, Ohio, Dec. 8, 1930; s. Karl Benjamin and Kathryn Emily (Hollingsworth) S.; m. Mary Margaret Dabney, Sept. 8, 1954; children: Karl Dabney, Kathryn Chappell. BS, Carnegie Mellon U., 1952, MS, 1957, PhD, 1959. Registered profl. engr., Tenn. Chem. engr., shift foreman Organics area Pitts. Plate Glass Co., New Martinsville, W.Va., 1952-54; asst. prof. chem. engring. Vanderbilt U., Nashville, 1958—61, prof. chem. and environ. engring., 1980—, assoc. prof., 1961—64, assoc. prof. environ. and air resources engring., 1967—70, prof., 1970—80, chmn. divsn. socio-tech. sys., 1972—75, chmn. environ. and water resources engring., 1975—76, chmn. environ. engring. and policy mgmt. dept., 1976—80, chmn. chem. engring. dept., 1980—88, prof. chem. and environ. engring., 1980—; Alexander Heard disting. svc. prof., 1995-96. V.p. ECCE, Nashville, 1983-88, pres., 1989—; mem. Air Pollution Control Bd., State Tenn., 1978-82, 82-87; Fulbright prof. U. Liege, Belgium, 1977; invited prof. Universite Catholique de Louvain, Belgium, 1982; vis. prof. chem. engring. Danish Tech. Inst., Lyngby, Denmark, 1988-89. Fellow AICE; mem. Air and Waste Mgmt. Assn., Instrument Soc. Am. (mgr. edn. and rsch. 1964-67), Am. Soc. Engring. Edn., Am. Soc. Environ. Engrs., Sigma Xi, Phi Kappa Phi, Tau Beta Pi. Office: Vanderbilt U VU Station B 351604 Nashville TN 37235-1604 Office Phone: 615-322-3370. Business E-Mail: schnelk2@ctrvax.vanderbilt.edu.

SCHNELLE, PHILLIP DAVID, electrical engineer, consultant; b. Orange, Tex., Feb. 29, 1952; s. Philip Davis and Mary (Lyons) Schnelle; m. Janie Lou Wilson, June 17, 1972; children: Brandy Glennon, Elisabeth, Phillip. MSEE, U. Del., Newark, 1975. Registered Profl. Engr., Tex., 1982. Cons. DuPont Engring. Project Group, Wilmington, Del., 1974—80; sr. cons. DuPont Engring. Services Divsn., Beaumont, Tex., 1980—85; prin. cons. DuPont Engring. Tech., Wilmington, Del., 1985—. Lyme disease activist London Britian Twp., Landenberg, Pa., 1990—. Recipient Engring. Excellence Award, DuPont Co., 2001. Mem.: Instrumental Soc. of Am. Achievements include research in dynamic modeling, advanced control applications (regulatory and MPC), data modeling (neural networks MVS and TSA)and interfaces between SPC and APC (Lab Feedback Control and Performance Monitoring). Avocations: fishing, sailing.

SCHNELLER, EUGENE STEWART, health administration and policy educator; b. Cornwall, N.Y., Apr. 9, 1943; s. Michael Nicholas and Anne Ruth (Gruner) S.; m. Ellen Stauber, Mar. 24, 1968; children: Andrew Jon, Lee Stauber. BA, L.I. U., 1967; AA, SUNY, Buffalo, 1965; PhD, NYU, 1973. Rsch. asst. dept. sociology NYU, N.Y.C., 1968-70; project dir. Montefiore Hosp. and Med. Ctr., Bronx, N.Y., 1970-72; asst. prof. Med. Ctr. and sociology Duke U., Durham, N.C., 1973-75; assoc. prof., chmn. dept. sociology Union Coll., Schenectady, 1975-79, assoc. prof., dir. Health Studies Ctr., 1979-85; prof., dir. Sch. Health Mgmt. and Policy, Ariz. State U., Tempe, 1985—91, assoc. dean rsch. and adminstrn. Coll. Bus., 1992-94; dir. L. William Seidman Rsch. Ctr., Tempe, 1992-94, counselor to pres. for health profl. edn., 1994-96; clin. prof. cmty. and family medicine U. Ariz., 1995-96, clin. prof. prevention, rsch., 1997—2002; prof., dir. Sch. Health Mgmt. and Policy W.P. Carey Sch. Bus. Ariz. State U., 1996—2002, prof. Sch. Health Mgmt. and Policy, 2002—. Vis. rsch. scholar Columbia U., N.Y.C., 1983-84; chmn. Western Network for Edn. in Health Adminstrn., Berkeley, Calif., 1987-92; commr. Calif. Commn. on the Future Med. Edn., 1996-97; mem. Ariz. Medicaid Adv. Bd., 1990-92, Ariz. Data Adv. Bd., 1989-91, Ariz. Health Care Group Adv. Bd., 1989; mem. health rsch. coun. N.Y. State Dept. Health, 1977-85; fellow Accrediting Commn. on Edn. for Health Svcs. Adminstrn., 1983-84, commr., 1999—. Author: The Physician's Assistant, 1980; mem. editorial bd. Work and Occupations, 1975-93, Hosps. and Health Svcs. Adminstrn., 1989-92, Health Adminstrn. Press, 1991-94; Health Mgmt. Review, 1996, Electronic Hallway, 1999; contbr. articles to profl. jours., chpt. to book. Trustee Barrow Neurol. Inst., Phoenix, 1989-95; chair nat. adv. com. Nat. Adv. Com. of the Investigator Awards in Health Svcs. Rsch. Robert Wood Johnson Found., 1993-96. Mem. APHA, Am. Sociol. Assn., Assn. Univ. Health Programs Health Adminstrn. (bd. dirs. 1990-96, chmn. bd. dirs. 1994-95), Pharm. and Therapeutics Soc. (trustee 1999—, sec. 1999—). Home: 11843 N 114th Way Scottsdale AZ 85259-2609 Office: Ariz State U Sch Health Mgmt and Policy WP Carey Sch of Bus Tempe AZ 85287 Office Phone: 480-965-6334. Business E-Mail: gene.schneller@asu.edu.

SCHNEPS, JACK, physics educator; b. N.Y.C., Aug. 18, 1929; s. Elias and Rose (Rephen) S.; m. Lucia DeMarchi, Mar. 11, 1960; children: Loredana, Melissa, Leila. BA, N.Y. U., 1951; MS, U. Wis., 1953, PhD, 1956. Asst. prof. physics Tufts U., 1956-60, asso. prof., 1960-63, prof., 1963—, chmn. dept. physics, 1980-89, Vannevar Bush chair, 1995—. Vis. scientist European Orgn. Nuclear Research, Geneva, Switzerland, 1965-66; lectr. Internat. Sch. Elementary Particle Physics, Yugoslavia, 1968; vis. research fellow Univ. Coll., London, Eng., 1973-74; vis. prof. Ecole Polytechnique, Palaiseau, France, 1982-83, The Technion, Haifa, Israel, 1989-90, Coll. de France, Paris, 1997; chmn. Internat. Neutrino Com., 2002—. Contbg. author: Methods in Subnuclear Physics, Vol. IV, 1970; editor Proc. of Neutrino 88, 1989; contbr. articles to profl. jours. NSF postdoctoral fellow U. Padua, Italy, 1958-59 Fellow Am. Phys. Soc.; mem. European Phys. Soc., AAUP, Phi Beta Kappa, Sigma Xi. Home: 3 Foxcroft Rd Winchester MA 01890-2407 Office: Dept Physics Tufts U Medford MA 02155 Office Phone: 617-627-3374. E-mail: jacob.schneps@tufts.edu.

SCHNESE, CARSTEN B. corporate financial executive; Fin. dir. STILL Material Handling Ltd, Bilston, England, 1999—2002; v.p. of fin., CFO Linde Lift Truck Corp, Summerville, SC, 2002—.

SCHNIEDERS, RICHARD J. food products executive; b. Remsen, Iowa; 2 children. BA Math., U. Iowa, 1970. With exec. devel. program SYSCO Corp., Memphis, 1982, dir. supplies and equipment, v.p. merchandising and exec. v.p., promoted to pres., CEO, 1988, chmn., sr. v.p. merchandising svcs. dept. Houston, 1992, responsible multi-unit sales, dir. corp., 1997, exec. v.p. food svc. ops., 1998, pres., COO, 2000—02, chmn., CEO, 2003—. Mem. Aviall Inc. (bd. dirs.). Office: SYSCO Corp 1390 Enclave Pkwy Houston TX 77077-2099*

SCHNIPPER, DON MARTIN, lawyer; b. Little Rock, Jan. 17, 1939; m. Mary Ann Evans, June 3, 1961; children: Caroline, Elizabeth. AB, U. Ark., 1963, JD, 1964. Bar: Ark. 1964, U.S. Supreme Ct. 1971. Ptnr. Wood, Smith, Schnipper & Clay, Hot Springs, Ark., 1964—. Spl. assoc. justice Ark. Supreme Ct., 1976-88. V.p. 1st United Meth. Ch., 1976-77, pres. 1977, vice chmn. bd. dirs. 1975-76; chmn. Ouachita Regional Counseling and Mental Health Ctr., 1977, pres. bd. dirs. 1970l bd. dirs. Hot Springs Childrens Home. Fellow Am. Bar Found.; mem. ABA, Ark. Bar Assn. (chmn. young lawyers sect. 1969-70, ho. of dels. 1973-76, exec. council 1976-79, chmn. exec. council 1980-81, pres. 1985-86), Garland County Bar Assn. (pres.), Hot Springs C. of C. (bd. dirs. 1966—, pres. 1977, Disting. Svc. award 1970), U. Ark. Alumni Assn. (bd. dirs. 1978-84, nat. pres. 1982-83). Home: 850 Quapaw Ave Hot Springs National Park AR 71901-3926 Office: Wood Smith Schnipper & Clay 123 Market St Hot Springs National Park AR 71901-5398 Office Phone: 501-624-1252.

SCHNITTMAN, EVAN RANDOLPH, publishing executive; b. Bklyn., May 29, 1963; s. Irvin and Johanna (Reinhardt) Schnittman; m. Stefanie Mia Silverman, Sept. 19, 1993; children: Emily Anya, David Philip. Degree, U. Iowa, 1985. Ednl. rep. F.A. Davis Pubs., Chgo., 1988—91, acquisitions editor, 1991—93; sr. editor Little, Brown & Co., Boston, 1993—95; editor-in-chief The Princeton Rev., N.Y.C., 1995—98, v.p., pub., 1998—2000, exec. v.p., 2000—02; v.p., sr. dir. Oxford U. Press, N.Y.C., 2002—. CEO Evan Schnittman, LLC, Montclair, NJ, 2000—02, Netpointments, Inc., Montclair, 2001—02; advisor The Smithereens, Scotch Plains and Carteret, NJ, 2000—. Mem. adv. bd. Montclair Econ. Devel. Commn., 1999—2003. Mem.: Am. Assn. Pubs. (profl. sci. pub.-electronic info. com. 2003—). Democrat. Office: Oxford U Press 198 Madison Ave New York NY 10016

SCHNITZER, MARTIN COLBY, economist, educator; b. Wilmette, Ill., Aug. 20, 1925; s. Leon Wendell and Homera Almeda (Portman) Schnitzer; m. Joan Hammet Brown, June 30, 1951; children: Melanie, Meredith, Marcy. Student, U. of South, 1944-46; BA, U. Ala., 1949, MBA, 1951; PhD, U. Fla., 1960. Asst. prof. bus. U. Ark., Fayetteville, 1955-58; asst. prof. U. Fla., Gainesville, 1958-60; prof. mgmt. Va. Tech., Blacksburg, 1960—2000, Va. Poly. Inst. and State U., Blacksburg, 1964—. Cons. Joint Econ. Com. U.S. Congress, 1968—75; mem. adv. bd. U.S. Sec. of Commerce, 1970—72; mem. U.S. East-West Trade Commn., 1974—75, Va. Indsl. Facilities Financing Commn., 1974—76, Fulbright Selection Com., 1976, Va. Gov.'s Bd. Economists, 1978—82, Va. Export Coun., 1982—; lectr. Inst. Econ. Planning and Rsch., Warsaw, 1985, Oskar Lange Acad. Econs., Wroclaw, Poland, Karl Marx U., Budapest, Hungary. Author: (book) Regional Unemployment and the Relocation of Workers, 1970, The Economy of Sweden, 1970, Comparative Economic System, 1971, 8th edit., 2000, Readings in Public Finance and Public Policy, 1972, East and West Germany: A Comparative Economic Analysis, Income Distribution, 1975, U.S. Business Involvement in Eastern Europe, 1980, Doing Business in Washington, 1981, Contemporary Goverment and Business Relations, 2d edit., 1983, 4th edit., 1990, International Business, 1984, Government, Business and the American Economy, 2001; editor: Va. Social Sci. Jour., 1964—68. Grantee, Resources for the Future, 1967; Am. Philos. Soc. grantee, 1963—64. Episcopalian. Home: 606 Rainbow Ridge Dr Blacksburg VA 24060-5536 *I have no prescription for success, but would suggest that a successful person is one who has touched the lives of others favorably. I think that this is the way in which immortality is attained.*

SCHNITZLER, BEVERLY JEANNE, designer, art educator, writer; b. Berkeley, Calif. children: Erich Gregory. BS, Ariz. State U., 1954; MA, Calif. State U., L.A., 1959; postgrad., Claremont Grad. Sch., 1956-59, Chouinard Art Inst., L.A., 1960-63. Spl. art tchr. and cons. Alhambra (Calif.) City Sch. Dist., 1958—60; prof. art Calif. State U., L.A., 1960—2002, prof. emeritus, 1998—. Cons. in art and creative fabric art Calif. State U., L.A., 1960—; lectr. in field; Calif. State U. del. for internat. acad. exch. guidelines to Yunnan Art Inst.,

Kunming, China, 1993. Author: New Dimensions in Needlework, 1978; project dir. and head designer heraldic banners Calif. State U., L.A., 1986-87; exhibiting artist in fiber art; exhibited at Regional Golden Thimble Exhbn., 1990 Participant student/prof. exch. program Kunming, 1993; lifetime sponsor Pasadena Fine Arts Club, sponsor student scholarship com., 1996-98, historian, 2003—. Calif. State U. L.A. instl. grantee, 1978, 79; AAUW Found. grantee, 1988; recipient Award for Outstanding Artistic Merit, Calif. State U. L.A. Assoc. Students, 1987; scholar conf. Spain and Portugal of the Navagators: The Age of Discovery to the Enlightenment, Georgetown U., 1990, scholar conf. participant Portugal and Spain of the Navigators: The Age of Exploration, George Washington U., 1992; recipient Emily Gates Nat. Alumna Achievement award Sigma Sigma Sigma, 1995. Mem. Nat. Surface Design Assn., Costume and Textile Coun. of L.A. County Mus., Internat. Designers Assn., Internat. World Conf. of Educators, AAUW, Costume Soc. Am., Fine Art Club of Pasadena. Office: Calif State U Art Dept 5151 State University Dr Los Angeles CA 90032-4226

SCHNOBRICH, ROGER WILLIAM, lawyer; b. New Ulm, Minn., Dec. 21, 1929; s. Arthur George and Amanda (Reinhart) S.; m. Angeline Ann Schmitz, Jan. 21, 1961; children: Julie A. Johnson, Jennifer L. Holmers, Kathryn M. Kubinski, Karen L. Holetz. BBA, U. Minn., 1952, JD, 1954. Bar: Minn. 1954. Assoc. Fredrikson and Byron, Mpls., 1956-58; pvt. practice Mpls., 1958-60; ptnr. Popham Haik, Schnobrich & Kaufman, Mpls., 1960-97, Hinshaw & Culbertson, Mpls., 1997—. Bd. dirs. numerous corps., Mpls. With U.S. Army, 1954-56. Mem. ABA, Minn. Bar Assn., Hennepin County Bar Assn., Order of Coif, Law Rev. Roman Catholic. Avocations: family, jogging, reading, golf. Home: 530 Waycliff Dr N Wayzata MN 55391-1385 Office: Hinshaw & Culbertson 3100 Campbell Mithun Tower 222 S 9th St Minneapolis MN 55402-3389 Office Phone: 612-334-2512. E-mail: rschnobrich@hinshawlaw.com.

SCHNOLL, HOWARD MANUEL, financial consultant, investment company executive; b. Milw., June 6, 1935; s. Nathan P. and Della (Fisher) Schnoll; m. Barbara Ostach, Dec. 3, 1988; children: Jordan, Terry, Jeffrey, Robert, Tammy, Daniel. BBA, U. Wis., 1958. CPA Wis.; cert. mgmt. cons., registered investment advisor. Mng. ptnr. Nankin, Schnoll & Co., S.C., Milw., 1966-86; mng. ptnr., bd. dirs. BDO Seidman, 1986-90; pres., COO Universal Med. Bldgs., L.P., Milw., 1990, also bd. dirs.; pres. Howard Schnoll & Assocs., Milw., 1991; mng. dir. Grande, Schnoll & Assocs., Milw., 1992-93; exec. mng. dir., COO Glaisner, Schilffarth, Grande & Schnoll, Ltd., Milw., 1993-98; exec. v.p., treas., bd. dirs. GS2 Securities, Inc., Milw., 1998-99; sr. v.p. B. C. Ziegler and Co., Milw., 1999—. Bd. dirs. Milw. World Festival, Inc., 1968—, pres., 2003—; bd. dirs. City of Festivals Parade, Milw., 1983—89, Aurora Health Care Ventures, Milw. Heart Rsch. Found., Milw., Milw. Heart Inst., Arthritis Found.; pres. Impact, 1993—, bd. dirs.; pres., treas. Am. Heart Assn., Milw., 1978—82; capt. United Way, Milw., 1985; mem. greater Milw. com. Nat. Found. Ileitis and Colitis. Served to sgt. U.S. Army, 1956—63. Mem.: AICPA, Acct. Computer Users Tech. Exchange, Wis. Inst. CPAs, B'nai Brith (pres. 1960—62), Boca Grove Golf and Tennis (bd. dirs. 2003—, treas. 2004—), Brynwood Country Club (pres. 1988—2000, bd. dirs., treas.). Jewish. Avocations: golf, tennis. Office: BC Ziegler & Co 250 E Wisconsin Ave Ste 2000 Milwaukee WI 53202-4298 E-mail: hschnoll@ziegler.com.

SCHNOOR, JEFFREY ARNOLD, lawyer; b. Winnipeg, Man., Can., June 22, 1953; s. Toby and Ray (Kass) S. BA, U. Man., 1974, LLB, 1977. Bar: Man. 1978. Assoc. McJannet Weinberg Rich, Winnipeg, 1977-84, ptnr., 1984-86; exec. dir. Man. Law Reform Commn., Winnipeg, 1986-97; dir. criminal justice policy Man. Dept. Justice, Winnipeg, 1998—2002, exec. dir. policy devel. & analysis, 2002—. Pres. Fedn. Law Reform Agys. Can., 1995-98; del. Uniform Law Conf. Can., 1986—, exec. com. 1996-2001, chair civil sect., 1996-97, v.p., 1998-99, pres., 1999-2000. Trustee United Way of Winnipeg, 1990-97, 99—, exec. com., 1990-97, 2001— treas., 1991-92, pres., 1994-95, cmty. rels. com. 1995-98, chmn. 1996-97, chair United Way 2005 com., 1997-98, hon. solicitor, 2001—, chmn. 211 implementation com., 2001—; mem. R&D 2000 steering com., United Way of Can., 1995-98; bd. dirs. Winnipeg Libr. Found., 1997-2001; Man. Voluntary Sector Coun., 2001—, U. Man. Winnipeg area study adv. group, 2001-. Named Queen's Counsel Govt. of Man., 1992; recipient Chair's award of distinction United Way of Can., 1997. Mem. Law Soc. Man. (lectr. bar admission course 1981-96), Man. Bar Assn. (life, governing coun. 1988-96, recipient Cmty. Svc. award 1999), Can. Bar Assn. (legis. and law reform com. 1994-2000, 01—03, vice-chair 1997-2000, chair 2001-03, nat mag. editl. bd. 2002—). Avocations: travel, languages, performing arts, exercise. Office: Policy Development & Analysis 1210-405 Broadway Winnipeg MB Canada R3C 3L6 Office Phone: 204-945-2900. E-mail: jschnoor@gov.mb.ca.

SCHNOOR, NEAL HENRY, music educator; b. Norfolk, Nebr., July 19, 1966; s. Walden Lowell and Ann Magdalene (Zach) Schnoor; m. Teresa Lynn Travis, Sept. 8, 1965; children: Rachel Ann, Graham Ronald. BFA in Edn., Wayne State Coll., 1990; MusM, U. Nebr., Lincoln, 1996, PhD, 1999. Cert. tchr. Nebr., 1990. Band dir. Wakefield Pub. Sch., Wakefield, Nebr., 1990—91; dir. of bands Kearney H.S., Kearney, Nebr., 1991—94; dir. bands Lincoln Northeast H.S., Lincoln, Nebr., 1996—97; assoc. prof. music and edn. U. of Nebr., Kearney, Nebr., 1997—. Bd. dirs. Nebr. Network for Ednl. Renewal, Kearney, Nebr., 2001—, Kearney, 2001—. Contbr. articles to profl. jours. Mem.: NEA, U. Nebr. Kearney Edn. Assn., Nebr. State Edn. Assn., Coll. Music Soc., Nebr. State Bandmasters Assn. (pres. elect 2004, Outstanding Young Band Dir. award 1994), Nebr. Music Educators Assn. (exec. bd. 2002—), Music Educators Nat. Conf., Phi Kappa Phi, Pi Kappa Lambda. Roman Catholic. Avocations: golf, private pilot, travel, reading. Office: U Nebr Kearney 905 W 25th Kearney NE 68845-4238 Business E-Mail: schnoorn@unk.edu.

SCHNUCK, CRAIG D. grocery store company executive; b. Apr. 20, 1948; BS, Cornell U., 1967, MBA, 1971. With Schnuck Markets, Inc., Hazelwood, Mo., 1971—, v.p., 1975-76, exec. v.p., sec., 1976-83, pres., chief exec. officer, 1983-91, also bd. dirs., 1991, chmn., CEO, 1991—. Office: Schnuck Markets Inc 11420 Lackland Rd Saint Louis MO 63146-3559

SCHNUCK, SCOTT C. grocery store executive; b. 1950; Pres., COO Schnuck Markets, Inc., St. Louis, 1992—. Office: Schnuck Markets Inc 11420 Lackland Rd Saint Louis MO 63146-3559

SCHNUCK, TODD ROBERT, grocery store company executive; CFO Schnuck Markets, Inc., St. Louis. Office: Schnuck Markets Inc 11420 Lackland Rd Saint Louis MO 63146-3559

SCHNUR, ROBERT ARNOLD, lawyer; b. White Plains, N.Y., Oct. 25, 1938; s. Conrad Edward and Ruth (Mehr) S.; children: Daniel, Jonathan. BA, Cornell U., 1960; JD, Harvard U., 1963. Bar: Wis. 1966, Ill. 1966. Assoc. Michael, Best & Friedrich, Milw., 1966-73, ptnr., 1973—. Chmn. Wis. Tax News, 1983-90; adj. prof. tax law U. Wis. Law Sch., 1988—. Capt. U.S. Army, 1963-65. Fellow Am. Coll. Tax Counsel; mem. ABA, Wis. Bar Assn. (chmn. tax sect. 1986-88), Milw. Bar Assn. Home: 3093 Timber Ln Verona WI 53593 Office: Michael Best Friedrich 100 E Wisconsin Ave Ste 3300 Milwaukee WI 53202-4108 E-mail: raschnur@mbf-law.com.

SCHOCHET, BARRY P. health care executive; b. N.Y.C., Mar. 13, 1951; s. George and Freda Schochet. BA in Zoology, U. Maine, 1973; MA in Health Care Adminstrn., George Washington U., 1975. Asst. adminstr. Doctors Hosp., Hollywood, Fla., 1975-76, Cypress Community Hosp., Pompano Beach, Fla., 1976-77, adminstr., 1977-78, exec. dir., 1978-79; asst. regional v.p. Nat. Med. Enterprises, St. Petersburg, Fla., 1979-80, asst. v.p. Los Angeles, 1980-81, v.p. ops. Tampa, Fla., 1981-83, sr. regional v.p., 1984-87, sr. divisional v.p., 1987-89, exec. v.p., 1989-91, sr. exec. v.p. and COO Santa Monica, Calif., 1991-93, pres., COO hosp. group, 1993-95; exec. v.p. operations Tenet Healthcare (formerly Nat. Med. Enterprises), Dallas, 1995—99; vice chmn. Tenet Healthcare, 1999—. Mem. Am. Hosp. Assn., Fedn. Am. Health Care Systems (bd. govs. 1985—, bd. dirs. 1989—, chmn. 2000), Am. Coll. Health Care Execs., Fla. League Hosps. (bd. dirs. 1981—, chmn. 1988-89), bd. dir. Healthcare leadership coun., 1999—. Office: Tenet Healthcare 3820 State St Santa Barbara CA 93105

SCHOCHOR, JONATHAN, lawyer, educator; b. Suffern, N.Y., Sept. 9, 1946; s. Abraham and Betty (Hechtor) S.; m. Joan Elaine Brown, May 31, 1970; children: Lauren Aimee, Daniel Ross. BA, Pa. State U., 1968; JD, Am. U., 1971. Bar: D.C. 1971, U.S. Dist. Ct. D.C. 1971, U.S. Ct. Appeals (D.C. cir.) 1971, Md. 1974, U.S. Dist. Ct. Md. 1974, U.S. Supreme Ct. 1986. Assoc. McKenna, Wilkinson & Kittner, Washington, 1970-74, Ellin & Baker, Balt., 1974-84; ptnr. Schochor, Federico & Staton, Balt., 1984—. Lectr. in law; expert witness to state legis. Editor-in-chief: Am. U. Law Rev., 1970—71. Mem. ABA, ATLA (state del. 1991, state gov. 1992-95), Am. Bd. Trial Advs. (membership com. 1994—), Am. Bd. Trial Advs., Am. Judicature Soc., Md. State Bar Assn. (spl. com. on health claims arbitration 1983), Md. Trial Lawyers Assn. (bd. govs. 1986-87, mem. legis. com. 1985-88, chmn. legis. com. 1986-87, sec. 1987-88, exec. com. 1987-92, v.p. 1987-88, pres.-elect 1989, pres. 1990-91), Balt. City Bar Assn. (legis com. 1986-87, spl com on tort reform 1986, medicolegal com. 1989-90, cir. ct. for Balt. City task force-civil document mgmt. sys. 1994-95), Bar Assn. D.C., Internat. Platform Assn., Phi Alpha Delta. Office: Schochor Federico & Staton PA 1211 Saint Paul St Baltimore MD 21202-2783

SCHOCK, ROBERT CHRISTOPHER, lawyer; b. New Rochelle, N.Y., Apr. 12, 1948; s. Carl Frederick and Elizabeth Woodbury (Slocomb) S. BA cum laude, Wake Forest U., 1970, JD, U. Tenn., 1973. Bar: Tenn. 1974, Ga. 1978, U.S. Dist. Ct. (no. dist.) Ga. 1978, U.S. Ct. Appeals (5th cir.) 1978, U.S. Ct. Appeals (11th cir.) 1982. Gen. atty. U.S. Dept. Justice Immigration Svc., Atlanta, 1974-80; sole practitioner Atlanta, 1980—. Contbg. author: Immigration Law, 1996, 2000, 2001. Mem. Am. Immigration Lawyers Assn. (Atlanta chpt. treas. 1992-93, sec. 1993-94, INS liaison chair 1995-96), Phi Alpha Theta. Presbyterian. Avocations: exercise, travel, gardening. Office: 235 Peachtree St NE Ste 400 Atlanta GA 30303-1400 Office Phone: 404-880-3302.

SCHOCK, ROBERT NORMAN, geophysicist; b. Monticello, N.Y., May 25, 1939; s. Carl Louis and Norma Elizabeth (Greenfield) S.; m. Susan Esther Benton, Nov. 28, 1959; children: Pamela Ann, Patricia Elizabeth, Christina Benton. BS, Colo. Coll., 1961; MS, Rensselaer Poly. Inst., 1963, PhD, 1966; postgrad., Northwestern U., 1963-64. Cert. Calif. state wine judge. Jr. geophys. trainee Continental Oil Co., Sheridan, Wyo., 1960; jr. geologist Texaco In., Billings, Mont., 1961; teaching asst. Rensselaer Poly. Inst., Troy, N.Y., 1961-63, research asst., 1964-66; research assoc. U. Chgo., 1966-68; sr. research scientist Lawrence Livermore Nat. Lab., U. Calif., 1968—, group leader high pressure physics, 1972-74, sect. leader geoscis. and engring., 1974-76, div. leader earth scis., 1976-81, head dept. earth scis., 1981-87, energy program leader, 1987-92, dep. assoc. dir. for energy, 1992-98, sr. fellow Ctr. Global Security Rsch., 1998—. Pres. Pressure Sys. Rsch. Inc.; mem. faculty Chabot Coll., 1969-71; dir. Alameda County Flood Control and Water Conservation Dist., 1984-86, chair, 1985; mem. adv. panel on geoscis. U.S. Dept. Energy, 1985-87; chair adv. com. U. Calif. Energy Inst., 1992-98, mem. rsch. adv. com. Gas Rsch. Inst., Chgo., 1995-2001; chmn. World Energy Coun., London, Study Group Energy Tech. in 21st Century, 1999—; mem. instrumentation and facilities rev. panel NSF, 2001—. Mem. editl. bd. Rev. Sci. Instruments, 1975-77; assoc. editor Jour. Geophys. Rsch., 1978-80; bd. assoc. editors 11th Lunar and Planetary Sci. Conf., 1980; mem. adv. bd. Physics and Chemistry of Minerals, 1983-97; rsch. and publs. on high pressure physics, solid state physics, physics of earth interior, rock deformation, energy R&D and energy policy. Fulbright sr. fellow U. Bonn (Germany), 1973; vis. research fellow Australian Nat. U. Canberra, 1980-81 Mem. AAAS, Am. Geophys. Union, Sigma Xi, Commonwealth of Calif. Club, Cosmos Club (Washington). Office: Lawrence Livermore Nat Lab PO Box 808 Livermore CA 94551-0808 E-mail: schock1@llnl.gov.

SCHOCK, TRISHA KAY, primary school educator; d. Delmas A. and Sandra Kay Schock. BA in edn., comm. arts, theater, Allegheny Coll., Pa., 1988; MEd, Ashland (Ohio) U., 1994. Cert. tchg. K-8 Ohio, Pa. Substitute tchr. Mentor (Ohio) Schs., 1988—89, kindergarten tchr., 1989—. Cons. phonics Saxon Publ., Norman, Okla., 1996—; cert. personal trainer Internat. Sports Sci. Assn., Santa Barbara, Calif., 2003—. Mem.: DEA, NEA (state delegate for Ohio), North East Ohio Edn. Assn., Ohio Edn. Assn., Mentor Tchr. Assn. Avocations: travel, reading, photography, gardening, cat lover. Home: 221 Harbor Ridge Ln Fairport Harbor OH 44077 Office: Mentor Village Schs Sterling Morton Elem 9292 Jordan Dr Mentor OH 44060 E-mail: schock@mentorschools.org.

SCHOCKAERT, BARBARA ANN, marketing professional; b. Queens, N.Y., Dec. 13, 1938; d. Lawrence Henry and Eleanor Veronica (Tollner) Grob; children: Donna Ann, Don. Grad., Ocean County Coll., Toms River, N.J., 1999. Cert. notary pub. V.p. ops. Am. Vitamin Products, Inc., Freehold, N.J., 1977-89, v.p. ops. Foods Plus div., 1990-94, sales coord., 1994—, product devel. mgr., 1996—, pvt. label mgr., DSD mgr., 1998—; assoc. Ocean County Realty, Toms River, N.J., 1987-90, Crossroads Realty, Toms River, 1990—. Contbg. author: Greatest Poems of the Western World, 1989 (Golden Poet award). Past pres. mayor's adv. coun., past pres. of help line Town of Jackson, N.J.; past bd. dirs. Big Bros. of Ocean County; speaker community svc. orgns. Named Woman of Yr., Jaycees, 1974; recipient Capitol award Nat. Leadership Coun., 1991, Silver Bowl award for 1st pl. poetry contest, 1996. Mem. N.J. Realtors Assn., Internat. Platform Assn., Alpha Beta Gamma. Home: 977 Fairview Dr Toms River NJ 08753-3064

SCHODEK, DANIEL L. architecture educator; BS in Archtl. Engring., U. Tex., MS in Archtl. Engring., 1966; MA (hon.), Harvard U., 1981; PhD in Civil Engring., MIT, 1971. With Brown and Root, Engrs. and Contractors, 1964, Boston Redevelopment Authority/Urban Sys. Lab., 1968; cons. Mass. Harbor Island Commn. Study, 1968; instr. Grad. Sch. Design Harvard U., Cambridge, Mass., 1969—70, asst. prof. arch. Grad. Sch. Design, 1970—77, assoc. prof. archtl. tech. Grad. Sch. Design, 1977—82, prof. archtl. tech. Grad. Sch. Design, 1982—92, asst. chmn. dept. arch., 1979—81, faculty dir. Lab. for Computer Graphics and Spatial Analysis, 1981—91, faculty dir. Lab. for Constrn. Tech., 1985—91; bridge design cons. Durbrow & Assocs., Engrs., Burlington, Vt., 1989—91; Kumagai prof. archtl. tech. Grad. Sch. Design Harvard U., 1992—; founding ptnr. World Wellness Environments, Inc., 1996—; with H. Steinkamp and Assocs., Consulting Engrs., Rosenberg, Tex., Foster-Miller, Inc., Waltham, Mass. Mem. adv. bd. Computer Graphics Conf., 1981, 82; dir. 1983 Computer Graphics Conf.: An Internat. Conf. Focusing on Computer Graphics in Environmental Planning and Design, Harvard, 1983. Author: Structures, 1980—2003, Landmarks in American Civil Engineering, 1987 (Abel Wolman award, Am. Inst. Graphic Artists award, 1995, Leipzig Book award, 1995), Structures in Sculpture, 1992; co-editor: Industrialization Forum, 1974—78; mem. editl. bd.: Building and Environment, 1986—. Mem.: ASCE, Boston Soc. Civil Engrs., Soc. Mfg. Engrs. Office: Harvard Grad Sch Design 48 Quincy St Cambridge MA 02138*

SCHODORF, JEAN, state legislator; b. Cherry Point, N.C., June 11, 1950; m. Richard Schodorf; children: Brian, Kelly, Kristin. BA, U. N.Mex., 1972, MS, 1973; PhD, Wichita State U., 1981. Mem. Kans. State Senate, 2000—. Active USD 259 Bd. Edn., 1989—. Republican. Methodist. Home: 3039 Benjamin Ct Wichita KS 67204 Office: State Capitol Rm 143-N Topeka KS 66612 E-mail: jschodor@swbell.net.

SCHOECK, RICHARD J(OSEPH), English and humanities scholar, poet; b. N.Y.C., Oct. 10, 1920; s. Gustav J. and Frances M. (Kuntz) S.; m. Reta R. Haberer, 1945 (div. 1976); children: Eric R., Christine C., Jennifer A.; m. Megan S. Lloyd, Feb. 19, 1977. MA, PhD, Princeton U., 1949. Instr. English Cornell U., 1949-55; from asst. prof. to assoc. prof. U. Notre Dame, 1955-61; prof. English U. Toronto, 1961-71; head dept. English St. Michael's Coll., 1965-70; prof. vernacular lit. Pontifical Inst. Mediaeval Studies, Toronto, 1964-71; dir. rsch. activities Folger Shakespeare Libr., also dir. Folger Inst. Renaissance and 18th Century Studies, 1970-74; adj. prof. English Cath. U. Am., 1972; prof. English, medieval and renaissance studies U. Md., 1974-75; prof. English and humanities U. Colo., Boulder, 1975-89, prof. emeritus, 1987—, chmn. dept. integrated studies, 1976-79; chmn. comparative lit., 1983-84; prof. Anglistik Univ. Trier, 1987-90, head dept. (Geschäftsführer), 1988-89; adj. prof. English U. Kans., Lawrence, 1990—2000. Vincent J. Flynn prof. letters Coll. St. Thomas, 1969; vis. prof. Princeton U., 1964, U. Dallas, 1985; vis. fellow Inst. Advanced Studies in Humanities, Edinburgh, 1984-85; vis. scholar Corpus Christi Coll., Oxford, 1994, Wolfson Coll., Oxford, 1997; fellow Assn. Advancement Edn., 1952-53, Yale U., 1959-60, Can. Coun. 1967-68, Ctr. for the Book, Brit. Libr., 1995-96; cons. NEH: bd. dirs. Natural Law Inst. U. Notre Dame; advisor Italian Acad. for Advanced Studies in Am., 1993. Author: The Achievement of Thomas More, 1976, Intertexuality and Renaissance Texts, 1984, Erasmus Grandescens, 1988, (poems) A Raging Against Chaos, 1989, The Eye of a Traveller, 1992, The Knights Book, 1993, My Hiroshima, 1997, (poems) Laurentian Codicil, 2002, rev. edit., 2004, (poems) Prairie Epiphanies, 2003, Childhood and Old Age, 2001; Erasmus of Europe, Vol. I, The Making of a Humanist, 1467-1500, 1990, Vol. II The Prince of Humanists, 1501-1536, 1993; contbr. numerous articles, papers, revs. to jours. and mags.; editor: Delehaye's Legends of the Saints, 1961, Editing 16th Century Texts, 1966, Roger Ascham: The Scholemaster, 1966, Shakespeare Quar., 1972-74, Acta Conventus Neo-Latini Bononiensis, 1985; gen. editor: The Confutation of Tyndale, 3 vols., 1973; co-editor: Voices of Literature, 2 vols., 1964, 66, Chaucer Criticism, 2 vols, 1960, 61, Style, Rhetoric and Rhythym: Essays by M.W. Croll, 1966, Acta Conventus Neo-Latini Torontonensis, 1991; former gen. editor: Patterns of Literary Criticism; spl. editor Canada vol. Rev. Nat. Literatures, 1977, Sir Thomas Browne and the Republic of Letters, 1982, A Special Number of English Language Notes, 1982; gen. editor (series) Renaissance Masters, 1992-99; mem. editl. bds. profl. jours. Served with U.S. Army, 1940-46. Guggenheim Found. fellow, 1968-69, Fulbright fellow, 1983; recipient Centennial medal U. Colo., 1976, Falconer Madan award Bibliographical Soc., London, 1997; co-recipient 1st prize Mellen Poetry Competition, 1997; grantee Can. Coun., UNESCO, Am. Coun. Learned Socs., U. Toronto, U. Colo. Fellow Royal Soc. Can., Royal Hist. Soc.; mem. Internat. Assn. Neo-Latin Studies (pres. 1976-79), MLA, Renaissance Soc. Am., PEN (N.Y.), Internat. Assn. U. Profs. English, HEH. Home: 1516 Fountain Drive Lawrence KS 66047 *More than a thousand years ago Bede summed up what are for me the principles of my professional career: I have always thought it fitting to learn and to teach and to write.*

SCHOELKOPF, R. GERALD, archivist, librarian; b. Reading, Pa., July 6, 1945; s. Russell Albert Schoelkopf and Stella M. Zarychta. BA, Villanova U., 1967; MLS, McGill U., Montreal, 1969. Circulation / reference libr. West Chester U., Pa., 1969—76, rare books libr. & Univ. archivist, 1976—. Author: (index) Centennial History of West Chester State College, 1992. Catholic. Avocations: photography, travel, horseback riding, kayaking, book binding. Home: 139 W Beidler Rd King Of Prussia PA 19406 Office: FHG Libary West Chester U High St West Chester PA 19383 Office Fax: 610-436-2251. E-mail: rschoelkopf@wcupa.edu.

SCHOELLER, DALE ALAN, nutrition research educator; b. Milw., June 8, 1948; s. Arthur B. and Anne Clare S.; m. Madeline Mary Juresh, Aug. 22, 1970; children: Nicholas Paul, Gregory Scott, Erica Lee. BS with honors, U. Wis., Milw., 1970; PhD, Ind. U., 1974. Postdoctoral fellow Argonne (Ill.) Nat. Lab., 1974-76; from asst. prof. to prof., also rsch. assoc. U. Chgo., 1976-91, assoc. prof., 1991—, prof., 1996; assoc. prof. U. Wis., Madison, 1997-98, prof., 1998—. Chmn. com. on human nutrition and nutritional biology U. Chgo., 1991-97. Author: (book chpt.) Obesity, 1992; co-author: (book chpt.) Annual Review of Nutrition, 1991. Mem. Am. Soc. Nutritional Scis. (v.p. elect 2001, Mead Johnson award 1987), Am. Soc. for Clin. Nutrition (Herman award 2000), Am. Soc. for Mass Spectrometry, N.Am. Soc. for Study of Obesity. Achievements include development of stable isotope methods for the study of human energy metabolism including first human use of doubly labeled water for measurement of free-living total energy expenditure. Office: U Wis Dept Nutrition 1415 Linden Dr Madison WI 53706-1527 E-mail: dschoell@nutrisci.wisc.edu.

SCHOEM, ALAN HOWARD, lawyer; b. Washington, Dec. 18, 1946; s. David and Lillian S.; m. Hazel Schoem, Jan. 4, 1970; children: Cara Beth, Scott Robert. BA, U. Md., 1968; JD, Am. U., 1972. Bar: D.C. 1972, Md. 1973, U.S. Ct. Appeals D.C. 1973, U.S. Supreme Ct. 1980. Atty. GAO, Washington, 1972-73; atty. Office of Gen. Counsel, Consumer Product Safety Commn., Washington, 1973-79, asst. gen. counsel Bethesda, Md., 1979-87, dir. div. adminstrv. litigation, 1987-94. Legis. fellow to U.S. Senator Paul Wellstone, Washington, 1992; atty., advisor to chmn. Ann Brown Consumer Product Safety Commn., 1994-96; exec. asst. Office of Compliance, 1996-97, dir., 1997—. Pres. Stonebridge Homeowners Assn., North Potomac, Md., 1985-86, Lakewood Elem. Sch. PTA, Rockville, Md., 1986-88; v.p. T.S. Wooton High Sch. PTSA, Rockville, 1988-91, cluster coord., 1989-91. Democrat. Jewish. Avocation: reading. Home: 14809 Rolling Green Way North Potomac MD 20878-4202 Office: Consumer Product Safety Com 4330 E West Hwy Bethesda MD 20814-4408 Office Phone: 301-504-7519. E-mail: aschoem@cpsc.gov.

SCHOEMEN, MICHAEL E. lawyer; Ptnr. Schoeman, Marsh, Updike & Welt, NYC. Office: Schoeman Marsh Updike & Welt 600 W 42nd St New York NY 10036-1909

SCHOEN, ALLEN HARRY, retired aerospace engineering executive; b. N.Y.C., Mar. 10, 1936; s. Harry Alfred and Dorothy Julia (Browne) S.; m. Patricia Alice O'Madigan, June 1, 1958 (div. 1989); children: Theresa Mary, James Allen, Karen Linda; m. Lauria Juliette Trahan, Feb. 14, 2001. SB in Aero. Engring., MIT, 1958, postgrad., 1989. Aerodynamicist Douglas Aircraft Co., Santa Monica, Calif., 1958-61, United Aircraft Co., Farmington, Conn., 1961-66; with Boeing Helicopters, Phila., 1966-98, tech. mgr., 1980-84, dir. tech., 1984-86, dep. tech. dir. V-22 Osprey joint program, 1986-88, dir. preliminary design, 1988-92, dir. devel. engring., 1992-95, dir. devel. program, 1995-98; ret., 1998. Aero. adv. com. NASA, Washington, 1985-90. Patentee propulsion sys.; contbr. articles to profl. jours. Fellow AIAA (assoc.), Am. Helicopter Soc. (hon., pres. Phila. chpt. 1983-84, v.p. Mideast region 1986-88, dir.-at-large 1988-90, Paul E. Haueter meml. award 1999). Republican. Episcopalian. Avocations: photography, gardening, woodworking, woodcarving.

SCHOEN, CHARLES JUDD, service executive; b. Owatonna, Minn., Sept. 6, 1943; s. John Nicholas and Dorothy Georgine (Jacobson) S.; m. Birgitta Marianne Haggren, Dec. 15, 1972; 1 child, Vanja Karina. BA, U. Minn., 1965. Stockbroker Harris, Upham and Co., Mpls., 1967-70; with Litton Industries, Sydney, Australia, 1970-71; gen. mgr. Westinghouse Electric, Mpls., 1971-77; pres. Westco Security, Wayzata, Minn., 1977—, Automatic Alarm Corp., Wayzata, Minn., 1986-95; pres., chmn. Westec Security Products, Laguna Beach, Calif., 1993—. Bd. chmn. SpyderNet, Minn., 1993—. Author (historian): History of Wayzata, 2004. Past pres. Wayzata Hist. Soc. With USN, 1966-67 Mem. Assn. Former Intelligence Officers. Office: Westco Security 401 Lake St E Wayzata MN 55391-1667

SCHOEN, REM, retired investment executive; b. NYC; s. Harry L. and Rita (Connors) S. BS, Trinity Coll., Burlington, Vt., 1951. Registered rep. Bache & Co., N.Y.C., 1956-61; instl. sales Gruntal & Co., 1961-65; v.p., ptnr., dir. instl. sales Pressman, Frohlich & Frost, Inc., N.Y.C., 1965-74; allied mem. N.Y. Stock Exchange; with Bernard Herold & Co., Inc., N.Y.C., 1974-77, Hamershlag, Kempner & Marks, N.Y.C., 1978-80; v.p. North East Securities, N.Y.C., 1980-82; sr. account exec. Smith Barney Harris Upham, N.Y.C., 1982-84, Gruntal & Co. (formerly Herzfeld & Stern), N.Y.C., 1984—2004; ret., 2004. Fin. adviser to banks in Paris, Milan, Geneva. Author: Childhood Poems, 1972. Vol. Lighthouse, N.Y. Assn. for Blind; fund chmn. ex-officio, trustee Trinity Coll. of Vt. Home: 225 E 70th St New York NY 10021-5211 Office: Gilford Securities 850 Third Ave New York NY 10022 Fax: 212-826-9738.

SCHOEN, RICHARD MELVIN, mathematics educator, researcher; b. Celina, Ohio, Oct. 23, 1950; s. Arnold Peter and Rosemary (Heitkamp) S.; m. Doris Helga Fischer-Colbrie, Oct. 29, 1983; children: Alan, Lucy. BS, U. Dayton, 1972; PhD, Stanford U., 1976. Lectr. U. Calif.-Berkeley, 1976-78, prof. math., 1980-85; asst. prof. Courant Inst. NYU, 1978-80; prof. math. U. Calif.-La Jolla, 1985-87, Stanford U., 1987—. Contbr. articles to profl. jours. Fellow NSF, 1972, Alfred P. Sloan Found., 1979, MacArthur Found. prize, 1983, Bôcher prize, 1989. Mem. Am. Acad. Arts and Scis., Am. Math. Soc., Nat. Acad. Sci. Democrat. Office: Stanford U Mathematics Dept Stanford CA 94305

SCHOEN, STEVAN JAY, lawyer; b. NYC, May 19, 1944; s. Al and Ann (Spevack) S.; m. Cynthia Lukens; children: Andrew Adams, Anna Kim. BS, U. Pa., 1966; JD, Cornell U., 1969; MPhil, Cambridge U. (Eng.), 1980. Bar: N.Mex. 1970, N.Y. 1970, U.S. Supreme Ct. 1976, U.S. Tax Ct. 1973, U.S. Ct. Internat. Trade 1982. Dir. Vista law recruitment OEO, Washington, 1970-71; atty. Legal Aid Soc. of Albuquerque, 1971-73; chief atty. N.Mex. Dept. Health and Social Svcs., Albuquerque, 1973-77; ptnr. Brennan, Schoen & Eisenstadt, 1979-88, Stevan J. Schoen PA, 1989—2001, Bingham, Hurst, Apodaca, Wile & Schoen, P.C., 2001—03; prin. Stevan J. Schoen, P.A., Placitas, N.Mex., 2003—; probate judge Sandoval County, 1990-98. Arbitrator NYSE; mem. N.Mex. Supreme Ct. Appellate Rules Com., 1982—92; chmn. rules com. Com. on Fgn. Legal Cons., 1993; chmn. N.Mex. Supreme Ct. Com., Probate Ct. Rules and Forms, 1998—2002, Jud. Edn. Planning com.; mem. state bd. Profl. Engrs. and Surveyors, 2003—; mem. state bd. to lic. engrs., 2004—. Mem. Mayor's Albuquerque Abd. Com. on Fgn. Trade Zone, 1992-94; v.p. Placitas Vol. Fir Dept., 1974-86; bd. edn. Bernalillo Pub. Sch. Dist., 1996-97; chair Sandoval County Dem. Party, 2001-03. Recipient Cert. for Outstanding Svc. to Judiciary, N.Mex. Supreme Ct., 1982, Outstanding Svc. award N. Mex. Supreme Ct., 1992, 2003, Cert. of Appreciation, N.Mex. Sec. of State, 1980, Pro Bono Pub. Svc. award, 1989, Cert. of Recognition Legal Aid, 1994, award Las Placitas Assn., 1996; named Outstanding Probate Judge, N.Mex State Senate, 1998. Mem. Am. Judges Assn. (ho. of dels. 1999-2002), Nat. Coll. Probate Judges, State Bar N.Mex. (past chmn. real property, probate and trust sect. 1989, Outstanding Contbn. award 1989, task force on regulation of advt. 1990-91, past chmn. appellate practice sect. 1991, past chmn. internat. law sect. 1991-92, commn. on professionalism 1992-95, organizing com. U.S.-Mex. law inst. 1992), N.Mex. Probate Judges Assn. (chmn. 1993-99, award 1998, N.Mex. state bar, chair sr. lawyers sect. 2003), Bench and Bar Com. (co-chair 2001-2002), Oxford-Cambridge Soc. N.Mex. (sec.), M.Mex. Assn. Counties (adv. bd. 1995-98). Home and Office: 4 Hillside Dr Placitas NM 87043 Office Phone: 505-867-2802. Business E-Mail: schoenlaw@comcast.net.

SCHOEN, WILLIAM JACK, financier; b. Los Angeles, Aug. 2, 1935; s. Jack Conrad and Kathryn Mabel (Stegmayer) S.; m. Sharon Ann Barto, Oct. 1, 1966; children: Kathryn Lynn, Karen Anne, Kristine Lea, William Jack. BS in Fin. magna cum laude, U. So. Calif., 1960, MBA, 1963. Mktg. mgr. Anchor Hocking Glass Co., 1964-68; v.p. sales and mktg. Obear-Nester Glass Co., 1968-71; pres. Pierce Glass Co., Port Allegheny, Pa., 1971-73; pres., chief exec. officer, dir. F.&M. Schaefer Brewing Co., N.Y.C., 1973-81; now chmn., pres. Wilshar Mgmt. Co. Inc., Naples, Fla., 1981—; chmn. Health Mgmt. Assocs. Inc., Naples, 1983—, also bd. dirs. Contbr. to indsl. publns. Founder Marine Corp. Heritage Found.; mem. Bus. Coun. of 100 of Fla.; bd. dirs. Internat. Coll. Found.; chmn. Schoen Found. Served with USMC, 1953-56, Korea. Mem. Naples Yacht Club, Port Royal Club, Quail Creek Country Club, Teton Springs Club, Phi Kappa Phi. Republican. Lutheran. Office Phone: 239-598-3175.

SCHOENBERG, APRIL MINDY, nursing administrator; b. Nassau, N.Y., June 2, 1955; d. Robert and Eleanor (Marks) Christian; m. Gerald Duggan, 1979 (div.); children: Lance, Craig, Danielle; m. Bruce Schoenberg; 1 child, Michael. BSN, Long Island U., 1978. Intravenous cert., 1994, cen. line intravenous cert., 1995; cert. Nassau Fire Commn. Head nurse Sunrise Manor Nursing Home, Bayshore, N.Y., 1982-87; unit coord. East Neck Nursing Ctr., Babylon, N.Y., 1987-89; dir. nursing svcs., asst. dir. nursing svcs. Oceanside (N.Y.) Care Ctr., 1988-91; PRI nurse, medicare nurse, rehab. coord., MDST coord. Ctrl. Island Health Care, Plainview, N.Y., 1993-95; reviewer, monitor restraints and psychoactive medications Quality of Care Mgmt., N.Y.C., 1995—2003; RN discharge planner Northshore Hosp. Plainview (N.Y.), 1995—. Asst. info. Tumor Registry Northshore Hosp., Manhasset, N.Y., 1975. Assoc. mem. Am. Mus. Natural History; sponsor Child Reach, 1984—. Mem. N.Y. State Nurses Assn., Multiple Sclerosis Soc., Nat. Trust Hist. Preservation, The Nature Conservancy Soc. Avocations: puzzles, bowling, racquetball, reading, speed walking. Office Phone: 516-719-2572.

SCHOENBERG, LAWRENCE JOSEPH, computer services company executive; b. N.Y.C., July 4, 1932; s. Samuel and Selma (Shapiro) S.; m. Barbara Brizdle, Sept. 15, 1990; children: Douglas, Eric, Julie. AB, U. Pa., 1953, MBA, 1956. Sr. systems analyst IBM, N.Y.C., 1956-59; asst. mgr. systems Litton, Orange, N.J., 1959-61; sr. cons. Computer Scis., N.Y.C., 1961-63; exec. v.p. Automation Scis., N.Y.C., 1963-65; chmn., chief exec. officer AGS Computers, Mountainside, N.J., 1966-91. Chmn. ITAA (formerly ADAPSO), Arlington, Va., 1983; bd. dirs. Penn-Am. Group, Inc., Merisel Inc., Sungard Inc., Cellular Tech. Svcs. Co., Inc.; chmn. Gov. Tech. Svcs., Inc. Contbr. articles to profl. jours. Trustee Charles Babbage Inst., Dickinson Coll. vice chmn. overseers U. Pa. Librs. Cpl. U.S. army, 1953-55. Mem. Software Industry Assn. (dir. 1976-91), Orange Lawn Tennis Club, Germantown Cricket Club, Longboat Key Club, Racquet Club of East Hampton. Office: GTSI Inc PO Box 8460 Longboat Key FL 34228-8460

SCHOENBERG, MARK GEORGE, government agency administrator; b. Bklyn., Nov. 22, 1947; s. Abraham Arthur and Ruth Millie (Dunn) S. BA, Columbia U., 1971, postgrad., 1972-73, N.C. State U., 1971-72. Research asst. NIMH-sponsored project at N.C. State U., Raleigh, 1971-72; asst. to pres. Key Electric Ltd., Glen Oaks, N.Y., 1973-76, gen. mgr. Los Angeles, 1976; asst. to pres. Kalsan Electric, Hempstead, N.Y., 1977; asst. mgr. Lincoln Inn, Rockville Ctr., N.Y., 1978; expert, cons. EPA, Washington, 1978; assoc. dir. U.S. Regulatory Council, Washington, 1979-82; exec. dir. Regulatory Info. Service Ctr., Washington, 1982-99; sr. advisor to dep. adminstr. Gen. Svcs. Adminstrn., 1999—. Avocations: healthy gourmet cooking, early music, wine collecting, travel. Office: US Gen Svcs Admin 1800 F St NW Washington DC 20405

SCHOENBERGER, JAMES EDWIN, retired federal agency administrator; b. Dayton, Ohio, Sept. 7, 1947; s. Harry Robert and Elizabeth Jane Schoenberger; m. Aura Victoria Montana, June 24, 1977; children: David, Eric. BSCE, Purdue U., 1969; MBA, Harvard U., 1971. V.p. ops. for midwestern housing developer Herman Devel. Group, Indpls., 1971-74; various positions New Communities Adminstrn. and with sec. HUD, Washington, 1974-77, assoc. dep. asst. sec., 1981-83; dir. land utilization Peabody Coal Co., St. Louis, 1977-81; sr. v.p. ops. The Investment Group, Washington, 1983-86; gen. dep. asst. fed. housing commr. HUD, Washington, 1987-89, assoc. gen., dep. asst. sec., 1990-97, ret., 1997. Roman Catholic. Avocations: computers, philanthropy.

SCHOENBERGER, STEVEN HARRIS, physician, research consultant; b. Cleve., Nov. 26, 1950; s. Stanford L. and Irene (Gold) S. BA, Tulane U., 1972; MD, U. Autonoma Guadalajara, Mex., 1976. Diplomate Am. Bd. of Urology. Asst. prof. Tulane U. Sch. Medicine, New Orleans, 1983—. Rsch. assoc. Delta Regional Primate Rsch. Ctr., Covington, La., 1983-85, chief section of urology Lawrence and Meml. Hosp., New London, Conn.; chmn. laser com., Lawrence and Meml. Hosp., New London, Conn., 1989—, chief sect. urology, 2003—; rsch. cons. Pfizer Med. Group, Groton, Conn., 1989—. Fellow ACS, Am. Soc. Laser Medicine and Surgery; mem. Soc. Univ. Urologists, N.Y. Acad. Scis., New Eng. Escadrille. Office: 3 Shaws Cv Ste 206 New London CT 06320-4968 Office Phone: 860-443-0622.

SCHOENBUCHER, BRUCE, health physicist; b. Dec. 15, 1943; s. Albert King and Alice Elizabeth (Thomson) S.; m. Patty Jo Parry, Feb. 3, 1965 (div. Feb. 1980); children: Teresa Marie Schoenbucher Abbey, Bonnie Lynn Schoenbucher Mendoza; m. Nancy Lippincott, Jan. 3, 1987; 1 child, Carly Cramer Cutler. BS in Radiation Protection Engring., Tex. A&M U., 1977, MS in Nuclear Engring., 1982. Lic. med. physicist, Tex.; cert. healthcare safety profl. Health physicist nuclear sci. ctr. Tex. A&M U., College Station, 1971-75, health physicist Coll. Vet. Medicine, 1977-79; mgr. radiation safety programs U. Tex. Med. Br., Galveston, 1980-88, asst. dir. environ. health and safety, 1984-88, radiation safety officer, dir. environ. health and safety, 1988—; radiation safety officer Burn Inst Shriners Hosp. for Crippled Children, Galveston, 1991—. Presenter in field. Contbr. articles to profl. publs. With USN, 1962-71. Mem. APHA, Health Physics Soc. (med. sect. exec. bd. 1993-96, mem. pub. info. com. 1981-84, chmn. 1982-84), South Tex. Chpt. Health Physics Soc. (chmn. ad hoc com. on licensure of med. physicists 1988-89, chmn. fin. com. 1986-88, treas. 1980-85, pres-elect 1985-86, pres. 1986-87), Am. Assn. Physicists in Medicine, Am. Biol. Safety Assn., Am. Soc. Safety Engrs., Laser Inst. Am., Nat. Fire Protection Assn., Tex. Safety Assn., Galveston C. of C., U.S. Coast Guard Auxilliary, Phi Kappa Phi, Sigma Nu Epsilon, Tau Beta Pi. Office: U Tex Med Br 301 University Blvd Galveston TX 77555-5302 E-mail: bschoenb@utmb.edu.

SCHOENE, KATHLEEN SNYDER, lawyer; b. Glen Ridge, N.J., July 24, 1953; d. John Kent and Margaret Ann (Bronder) Snyder. BA, Grinnell Coll., 1974; MS, So. Conn. State Coll., 1976; JD, Washington U., St. Louis, 1982. Bar: Mo. 1982, Ill. 1983. Head libr. Mo. Hist. Soc., St. Louis, 1976-79; assoc. Peper, Martin, Jensen, Maichel & Hetlage, St. Louis, 1982-88, ptnr., 1989-98, Armstrong Teasdale LLP, St. Louis, 1998—, exec. com., 2003—. Bd. dirs. Legal Svcs. of Eastern Mo. Author: (with others) Missouri Corporation Law and Practice, 1985, Missouri Business Organizations, 1998; contbr. articles to profl. jours. Trustee Grinnell (Iowa) Coll., ex officio voting mem., 1991-93; bd. dirs. Jr. League St. Louis, 1995-96, Leadership Ctr. Greater St. Louis, 1995-96, FOCUS St. Louis, 1996-2001, exec. com., 1997-99; active St. Louis Forum, 1997—, Herbert Hoover Boys and Girls Club, St. Louis, 1999—. Mem. ABA, Nat. Conf. Bar Founds. (trustee 1996-2000, pres. elect 1997-98, pres. 1998-99), The Mo. Bar (bd. govs. 1997-99, chair bus. law com. 2000-02), Ill. State Bar Assn., Bar Assn. Met. St. Louis (treas. 1991-92, sec. 1992-93, v.p. 1993-94, pres.-elect 1994-95, pres. 1995-96, chair small bus. com. 1987-88, exec. com. 1988-96, chair bus. law sect. 1988-89, mem. exec. com. young lawyers sect. 1988-90), St. Louis Bar Found. (bd. dirs. 1994-2000, v.p. 1995-96, pres. 1996-98). Home: 7824 Cornell Ave Saint Louis MO 63130-3701 Office: Armstrong Teasdale One Metropolitan Sq Saint Louis MO 63102 E-mail: kschoene@armstrongteasdale.com.

SCHOENER, THOMAS WILLIAM, zoology educator, researcher; b. Lancaster, Pa., Aug. 9, 1943; BA, Harvard Coll., 1965, PhD, 1969. Asst. prof. Harvard Coll., Cambridge, Mass., 1972-73, assoc. prof., 1973-75, U. Wash., Seattle, 1975-76, prof., 1976-80, U. Calif., Davis, 1980—, chairperson sect. evolution and ecology divsn. biol. scis., 1993-99. Mem. editl. bd. dirs. Oecologia, 1984-93; past mem. editl. bd. Evolution, Am. Naturalist, Sci., Acta Oecologia; contbr. chpts. to books, articles to profl. jours. Recipient MacArthur prize Ecol. Soc. Am., 1987; grantee NSF, 1975—, Nat. Geog. Soc.; jr. fellow Harvard U., 1969-72; Guggenheim fellow, 1992-93. Mem. NAS, Am. Acad. Arts and Scis., Am. Ornithologists Union (elective), Am. Soc. Naturalists, Ecol. Soc. Am., Am. Soc. Ichthyologists and Herpetologists, Cooper Ornithol. Soc., Am. Arachnological Soc., Soc. Study of Amphibians and Reptiles. Avocations: weight lifting; reading. Office: U Calif Sect Evolution Ecology Davis CA 95616

SCHOENFELD, DAVID ALAN, statistician, educator; b. Ft. Monmouth, N.J., Apr. 19, 1945; s. Robert Louis Schoenfeld and Helene Flapan; m. Ellen Maureen Beeks, Dec. 30, 1973; children: Heather, Elizabeth, Jonathan. BA, Reed Coll., 1967; MA, U. Oreg., 1968, PhD, 1974. Postdoctoral fellow Stanford (Calif.) U., 1974—75; rsch. asst. SUNY, Buffalo, 1975—77; from asst. to assoc. scientist Dana-Farber Cancer Inst., Boston, 1977—86; from asst. prof. to prof. dept. of biostats., Sch. Pub. Health Harvard U., Boston, 1977—, assoc. prof. to prof. dept. medicine, 1985—, assoc. prof. dept. medicine Med. Sch., 1985—88, prof. biostatistics, 1998—; dir. Biostatistics Ctr. Mass. Gen. Hosp., Boston, 1985—. Co-editor: (book) Aids Clinical Trials, 1995. Fellow: American Statis. Assn.; mem.: Assn. of GCRC Statisticians, Internat. Statis. Inst., Biometric Soc., Inst. of Math. Stats. Avocation: skiing. Home: 41 Brook Rd Sharon MA 02067 Office: Mass Gen Hosp 50 Staniford St Boston MA 02114 Personal E-mail: david@schoenfeld.com. E-mail: dschoenfeld@partners.org.

SCHOENFELD, HOWARD ALLEN, management consultant, lawyer; b. N.Y.C., Apr. 17, 1948; s. Irving and Muriel (Levy) S.; m. Paula Simon; 1 child, Haley Rebecca. BA, U. Pa., 1970; JD, Georgetown U., 1973. Bar: Md. 1973, U.S. Dist. Ct. Md. 1973, Wis. 1976, U.S. Dist. Ct. (ea. dist.) Wis. 1976, U.S. Dist. Ct. (we. dist.) Wis. 1987. Law clk. Md. Ct. Appeals, 1973-74; assoc. Gordon, Feinblatt, Rothman, Hoffberger & Hollander, Balt., 1974-76; ptnr. Trebon & Schoenfeld, Milw., 1976-85, Godfrey & Kahn, Milw., 1985—2002. Chmn. John Anderson Campiagn for Pres., Wis., 1980; pres. Milw. Jewish Coun., 1987-89, mem., 1983—. Recipient Young Leadership award Milw. Jewish Fedn., 1983. Mem. ABA, Wis. Bar Assn., Milw. Bar Assn. Office: DSC Advisors 5465 Grand Ave Ste 100 Gurnee IL 60031 Office Phone: 414-223-5712. E-mail: hasreorg@aol.com.

SCHOENFELD, LAWRENCE JON, real estate developer, asset lender; b. L.A., Nov. 30, 1945; s. Donald and Trudy Schoenfeld; m. Carol Sue Gard, Aug. 24, 1969. AA, L.A. Valley Coll., Van Nuys, Calif., 1963; BBA, Wichita State U., 1969, MSBA, 1970; grad., Army Med. Acad., 1976, US Army Command/Gen Staff Coll., Ft. Leavenworth, Kans., 1988. Cert. tchr., Calif.; life lic. jr. coll. tchg. credential, Calif.; lic. real estate broker (cert.) developer, Calif.; cert. hotel specialist, Marriott, 2003. Asst. treas. Advance Mortgage, L.A., 1970-72; v.p. ops. Unigem Internat., L.A., 1972-98; pres. C. & L. Schoenfeld Investments Inc., Manhattan Beach, Calif., 1998—. Bd. dirs. The Schoenfeld Constrn. Co., South Star Wours, Uniorr Corp., Execucentre-West, Schoenfeld & Co., Customer Ground Handling Svc. Corp.; co-developer Los-Osos Mini Storage Co., Los Osos, Calif., Bay Osos, 1984, Bay Osos Mini Storage Co., 1984, El Mercadero World Trade Show, Guatemala, 1986, 97, Santiago, 1987, Bahai, 1988, Paraguay, 1989, El Mercado, Costa Rica, 1990, Panama City, 1995, Manaus, 1996, Guayaquil, 1998, Los Osos Mini Storage Co., Quito, 1991, Santa Cruz, 1993, Ecuador, 1998, Uruguay, 1999, Punta del Este, 1999, Fortaleza, Brazil, 2000, San Jose, Costa Rica, 2002, Quilto, 2003, Iquasso Falls, Brazil, 2004; pres. Accents on Beverly Hills, 1991, Accents at the Biltmore, Santa Barbara, 1995, Accents on Newport Beach, 1996, Accents on San Francisco Travelers Centrury Club, 2001, The Regis, L.A. Mem. Improvement Commn., Hermosa Beach., Calif. 1976-78. Served to maj. Med. Svc. Corps, U.S. Army, 1970-72; lt. col. USAR, 1972—. Recipient Humanitarian award, Richstone Found., 2001. Mem. South Am. Travel Assn., World Trade Assn. (assoc.), Town Hall, Wichita State U. Alumni Assn. (nat. dist. rep., mem. coun. 1992—), Res. Officers Assn., Brit. Am. C. of C., Skal Internat., Travelers Century Club, Navy Golf Club, Palos Verdes Golf Club. Jewish. Office: 224 5th St Manhattan Beach CA 90266-5710 also: 8405 Pershing Dr Ste 301 Playa Del Rey CA 90293-7861 Office Fax: 310-318-7106. Personal E-mail: lccorp@earthlink.net.

SCHOENFELD, MICHAEL, academic administrator, education educator; b. Bklyn., June 11, 1962; s. Leon and Elaine Schoenfeld; m. Elizabeth Temple, Oct. 11, 1987; 1 child, Abigail. BA, Duke U., 1984; MS, SUNY, Stony Brook, 1986. Radio reporter, news anchor Voice of Am., Washington, 1986—88, pub. affairs and congl. liaison officer, 1988—90, chief of staff, exec. asst. to the dir., 1990—92; dir. tv program devel. Worldnet TV/USIA, Washington, 1992—93; dir. comm. Corp. for Pub. Broadcasting, Washington, 1993—94, sr. v.p. for policy and pub. affairs, 1994—97; vice chancellor for pub. affairs Vanderbilt U., Nashville, 1997—, lectr. in edn. and pub. policy, 2001—. Mem., nat. coun. Nat. Press Found., Washington, 1995—97; mem. steering com. Coll. is Possible Campaign Am. Coun. on Edn., Washington, 1998—2000; cons. on pub. affairs; dir. WPLN Nashville (Tenn.) Pub. Radio, 1997—, chmn. WPLN, 2000—03. Mem. task force on water and sewer rate reductaion Metro Nashville Govt.; chmn. cmty. com. Nashville Symphony; pres. NATAS, 2003—; chmn. transition comm. task force Mayor-elect Bill Purcell, Nashville, 1999—99; v.p., gov. NATAS, Nashville, 1997—2003; dir. Devel. Exch., Mpls., 2000—01, Our Kids, Nashville, 1998—2001, Opportunities Industrialization Ctr., Nashville, 1998—2000, Belcourt Theater, Nashville, Ctr. for Nonprofit Mgmt., Nashville; bd. dirs. Tenn. Repertory Theater, 2003—; chmn.-elect Nashville Shakespeare Festival, 2003—; bd. dirs. Families and Children's Svcs., 2004—; comm. com. Nat. Humanities Ctr., Research Triangle Park, NC, 2001; grad. Leadership Nashville, 1998—98, Leadership Music, 2004. Named 40 Under 40: Top Leaders Under the Age of 40, Bus. Nashville Mag., 2000, Best Media Spokesperson, Nashville Scene, 2000, 2001, Vol. of Yr., Nashville Area C. of C., 2004; recipient Superior Honor award, President's Adv. Bd. on Broadcasting to Cuba, 1991. Mem.: Pub. Rel. Soc. Am. (bd. dirs. 2003—), Assn. Am. Univs. (mem. pub. affairs com. 2000—), Nat. Assn. Coll. and U. Bus. Officers (bd. dirs. 2002—), Coun. for the Advancement and Support of Edn. (commn. on comm. 1998—2002), Nashville Com. on Fgn. Rels., Nat. Press Club, U. Club Nashville. Home: 3827 Richland Ave Nashville TN 37205 Office: Vanderbilt Univ 405 Kirkland Hall Nashville TN 37240 Personal E-mail: michael.schoenfeld@vanderbilt.edu. E-mail: michael.schoenfeld@vanderbilt.edu.

SCHOENFELD, MICHAEL P. lawyer; b. Oct. 17, 1935; s. Jack and Anne Schoenfield; m. Helen Schorr, Apr. 3, 1960; childrne: Daniel, Steven, Tracy. BS in Acctg., NYU, 1955; LLB, LLD, Fordham U., 1958. Bar: N.Y. 1959, U.S. Supreme Ct. 1963. Coun. Am. Home Assurance Co., N.Y.C., 1958-62; ptnr. Schoenfeld & Schoenfeld, Melville, N.Y., 1959—. V.p. Interstate Brokerage Corp., 1965-84, pres., 1984-90; ptnr. Melville Realty Co., 1977-90; legal adv. various bus. orgns. V.p., trustee Temple Beth David, Commack, N.Y., 1972-75; chmn. Cmty. Action Com. of Dix Hills and Commack, 1970-72, Dix Hills Planning Bd., 1972-74; treas. Dix Hills Rep. Club, 1976-80; mem. Huntington (N.Y.) Zoning Bd. Appeals, 1980-91, chmn., 1986-89. Recipient United Jerusalem award Israel Bond Drive, 1977, City of Hope Svc. award, George Bacon award Fordham Law Sch. Mem.: Suffolk County Bar Assn., NY State Bar Assn. Home: 14 Clayton Dr Dix Hills NY 11746-5517 Office: 999 Walt Whitman Rd Melville NY 11747-3007 Office Phone: 631-673-5004.

SCHOENFELD, ROBERT LOUIS, biomedical engineer; b. N.Y.C., Apr. 1, 1920; s. Bernard and Mae (Kizelstein) S.; m. Helene Martens, Jan. 22, 1944 (div. 1965); children: David, Joseph, Paul; m. Florence Moskowitz, Dec. 11, 1965 (dec. 1989); children: Nedda, Bethany; m. Shulamith Stechel, July 8, 1990. BA, Washington Square Coll., 1942; BSEE, Columbia U., 1944; MEE, Poly. Inst. Bklyn., 1949, DEE, 1956. Rsch. assoc. Columbia U. Med. Sch., N.Y.C., 1947-51; rsch. fellow Sloan Kettering Cancer Rsch. Inst., N.Y.C., 1951-56; assoc. prof. Poly. Inst. Bklyn., 1957—59; biomed. engr. Rockefeller U., N.Y.C., 1957—59, from asst. prof. to assoc. prof., 1957-90, prof. emeritus, 1990—. Contbr. articles to profl. jours. Lt. Signal Corps, U.S. Army, 1944-46, ETO. Fellow IEEE (mem. editl. bd. 1965-75, Centennial medal 1985), Am. Inst. for Med. and Biol. Engring. Democrat. Jewish. Achievements include pioneering application of computer automation to biological laboratory experiments. Office: Rockefeller U 1230 York Ave New York NY 10021-6399 E-mail: RLS@mail.rockefeller.edu.

SCHOENFELD, WALTER EDWIN, manufacturing executive; b. Seattle, Nov. 6, 1930; s. Max and Edna Lucille (Reinhardt) S.; m. Esther Behar, Nov. 27, 1955; children— Lea Anne, Jeffrey, Gary. BBA, U. Wash., 1952. Dir. Reading Railroad, 1964—68; Vice pres., dir. Sunshine Mining Co., Kellogg, Idaho, 1964-69, First N.W. Industries, Inc. (Seattle Super Sonics), 1968-79; chmn. bd., pres. Schoenfeld Industries, Inc. (diversified holding co.), 1968-93; vice chmn., acting pres., CEO, Vans, Inc., 1993-97, chmn., bd. dirs., 1997—. Ptnr. Seattle Mariners Baseball Club, 1977-81, Seattle Sounders Soccer Club, 1974-79; bd. dirs. Hazel Bishop Cosmetics. Bd. dirs. Wash. China Rels. Coun., 1980—, Sterling Recreation Orgn., 1985-90; chmn. Access Long Distance of Washington; bd. govs. Weizmann Inst. Sci., Rehovot, Israel, 1980—; trustee Barbara Sinatra Children's Ctr., Eisenhower Hosp., Rancho Mirage, Calif., 1990—. With AUS, 1952-55, Korea. Recipient various service awards. Mem. Chief Execs. Orgn. (v.p., bd. dirs. 1987-93), Rainier Club, Tamarisk Country Club (Rancho Mirage, Calif.), Mission Hills Country Club, Glendale Country Club (Bellevue, Wash.), Alpha Kappa Psi. Office: 999 3rd Ave Ste 3800 Seattle WA 98104-4023

SCHOENFELDER, LASKA, commissioner, farmer; m. Mike Schoenfelder; 5 children. Student, Dakota Wesleyan U. Formerly with Dept. Commerce, Bur. Pers., Office Hwy. Safety; registrar of deeds Davison County, S.D., 1973-82; mem. S.D. Pub. Utilities Commn., Pierre, 1982—. Farmer, nr. Mt. Vernon, S.D.; mem. FCC Fed-State Joint Bd. Mem. Nat. Assn. Regulatory Utility Commrs. (com. oncomm. 1991—). Republican. Office: SD Pub Utilities Comm Capitol Bldg 1st Fl 500 E Capitol Ave Pierre SD 57501-5070 Fax: 605-773-3809.

SCHOENFIELD, RICK MERRILL, lawyer; b. Chgo., July 21, 1951; s. Herbert and Bernice (Krichilsky) S. BA, Northwestern U., 1973, JD cum laude, 1976; cert., Nat. Inst. Trial Advocacy, Chgo., 1979. Bar: Ill. 1976, U.S. Dist. Ct. (no. dist.) Ill. 1977, U.S. Ct. Appeals (7th cir.) 1979, U.S. Ct. Appeals (4th cir.) 1984, U.S. Supreme Ct. 1984, U.S. Dist. Ct. (ea. dist.) Wis. 1987. Assoc. Ettinger & Lake, Chgo., 1976-79, Ettinger & Assocs., Ltd., Chgo., 1979-81; ptnr. Ettinger & Schoenfield, Chgo., 1981-92, Schoenfield, Swartzman & Massin, Chgo., 1992—2002, DiVincenzo Schoenfield Swartzman, Chgo., 2002—. Instr. De Paul Law Sch., Chgo., 1977-78, Chgo.-Kent Coll. Law, 1989—, U. Ill. Chgo., 1991-94. Co-author Legal Negotiations: Gettin Maximum Results, 1988, The McGraw Hill 26 Hour Negotiation Course, 1991. Recipient award for Pro Bono Litigation, Operation Lakewatch, Chgo., 1983. Mem. Nat. Resources Def. Council. Office: Di Vincenzo Schoenfield Swartzman 33 N LaSalle 29th Fl Chicago IL 60602 Office Phone: 312-334-4800 109. E-mail: rschoenfield@aol.com.

SCHOENHALS, KATHERINE VIOLA, social worker; b. Detroit, June 3, 1935; d. Anthony Andrew and Claire Elizabeth (Burkhardt) Fodell; m. Donald Eugene Schoenhals; children: Martin, Juliann. BA, U. Mich., 1957, MA, 1963, Oakland U., 1980, PhD, 1991. Cert. tchr. K-12 reading; secondary permanent tchg. cert.; sch. social work approval, Mich. Tchr. h.s. Berkley (Mich.) Schs., 1957-58, Romulus (Mich.) Schs., 1958-60; sch. social worker Bloomfield Hills (Mich.) Schs., 1960-61, 64-69, Walled Lake (Mich.) Schs., 1971-73, Birmingham (Mich.) Schs., 1978-96; tutor, counselor State of Mich. Rehab. Svcs., Pontiac, 1994—. Cons., rschr. Head Start/High Scope, Southfield, Mich., 1997; part-time faculty Schoolcraft C.C., Livonia, Mich., 1997-98; cons. Hamilton (Mich.) Pub. Schs., 1994-95, Bloomfield Hills Assn. for Gifted and Talented, 1978-81; curriculum planning cons. Birmingham Schs., 1984-94; rschr. Southfield (Mich.) Schs./Head Start, 1997; tutor, tchr., trainer, cons. Sarasota Literacy Coun., 1999; asst. artistic dir. Historic Spanish Point, 1999; presenter in field. Editor: (book) Shadows of Blackhawk, 1996. Vol. tutor, reading cons. Baldwin Ctr., Pontiac, 1995; advisor Maple Clinic Adv. Bd., Birmingham, Mich., 1986—; storyteller Birmingham Storytelling Guild, 1994—; pres. PTA, Bloomfield Hills, 1977-78; co-leader Girl Scouts of Am., Bloomfield Hills, 1973-74; mem., vol. Emily's List, Dem. Party, Episcopal Women's Club. Regents Alumni scholar U. Mich., 1953-57. Mem. AAUW (vol.), ACLU (vol.), NEA (Birmingham rep. pers. sect. 1961—), Internat. Reading Assn. (world conf. presenter 1992), Am. Ednl. Rsch. Assn., Sch. Social Workers Assn. of Am., Mich. Sch. Social Worker Presenters (state conf. presenter 1992), Mich. Edn. Assn., Birmingham Edn. Assn. Democrat. Episcopalian. Avocations: reading, needlework/crafts, golf, walking/exercise, gardening. Home: 9397 Midnight Pass Rd Apt 506 Sarasota FL 34242-2950

SCHOENHARD, WILLIAM CHARLES, JR., health care executive; b. Kansas City, Mo., Sept. 26, 1949; s. William Charles S. and Joyce Evans (Thornsberry) Bell; m. Kathleen Ann Klosterman, June 3, 1972; children: Sarah Elizabeth, Thomas William. BS in Pub. Adminstrn., U. Mo., 1971; M of Health Adminstrn. with honors, Washington U., St. Louis, 1975. V.p., dir. gen. svcs. Deaconess Hosp., St. Louis, 1975-78; assoc. exec. dir. St. Mary's Health Ctr., St. Louis, 1978-81; exec. dir. Arcadia Valley Hosp., Pilot Knob, Mo.,

1981-82, St. Joseph Health Ctr., St. Charles, Mo., St. Joseph Hosp. West, Lake St. Louis, 1982—86; exec. v.p., COO SSM Health Care, St. Louis, 1986—. Adv. bd. dirs. Firstar Bank, 1998-2001. Contbr. articles to profl. jours. Mem. Mo. Commn. on Patient Safety, 2003—04; mem. fin. com. Cath. Health Assn. U.S., 1999—2001; mem. adv. bd. St. Louis chpt. Lifeseekers, St. Louis, 1985—94; mem. bd. mgrs. Kirkwood-Webster (Mo.) YMCA, 1990—96, sec., 1996; mem. healthcare adv. bd. Sanford Brown Colls., 1992—94; del. Am. Hosp. Assn. Regional Policy Bd., 1999—; bd. trustees Mo. Hosp. Assn., 1999—, chmn., 2002; mem. Greater St. Louis divsn. bd. dirs. Am. Heart Assn., 2001—03; bd. dirs. St. Andrews Mgmt. Svcs., Inc., 1994—2002, Mid Am. Transplant Svcs., 1995—, Lindenwood U., 1997—, Civic Entrepreneurs Orgn., 1997—2000, Greater St. Louis Boy Scouts Am., 1997—, Benedictine Health Sys., 2002; pres. Shaw Neighborhood Improvement Assn., St. Louis, 1979—80. With USN, 1971—72, Vietnam. Fellow Am. Coll. Health Care Execs. (regent Mo.-Gateway area 1997-2001, bd. govs. 2002—); mem. VFW, Am. Legion, U.S. Navy League, Phi Eta Sigma, Pi Omicron Sigma, Delta Upsilon, Delta Sigma Pi. Roman Catholic. Avocations: reading, walking. Home: 420 Fairwood Ln Saint Louis MO 63122-4429 Office: SSM Health Care 477 N Lindbergh Blvd Saint Louis MO 63141-7832 Office Phone: 314-994-7810.

SCHOENHERR, BOB, communications educator, consultant; s. Roy and Mary Schoenherr. MS in ednl. tech., CSU Long Beach, 1988. Cert. Ccna Cisco Systems, INC, 2001; USTPR profl. Calif., 1987, Am. Coaches Certification Calif., 1989. Instr./ coach Mountain Vista Jr. High, Roswell, N.Mex., 1975—78; electro optical inspector Hughes Aircraft, Marina Del Rey, Calif., 1977—78; math instr. Alta Vista Jr. High, Carlsbad, N.Mex., 1978—79; instr./coach Tibbets Jr. H.S., Farmington, N.Mex., 1979—83; elementart instr. Konocti Unified Sch. Dist., Clearlake, Calif., 1982—86; tng. mgr. assoc. Indsl. Dynamic, Torrance, Calif., 1987—88; h.s. instr./coach Middletown Unified Schools, Middletown, 1988—98; prof. tech. and mass comm. Yuba Coll. Clear lake Campus, Clearlake, 1998—; cons. Cisco Systems, INC, San Jose, 2000—. Chairperson Calif. HS Network Project, Santa Rosa, Calif., 1997—98; nat. chairperson inter-networking SkillsUSA-VICA, Leesburg, Va., 2000—04; regional Cisco acad. mgr. Cisco Systems, INC, San Jose, Calif., 2000—04; coll. academic senate Yuba Coll., Marysville, Calif., 2003—. Prodr.: (web design) California League of High Schools (Best H.S. Website, 1997); author: (photography) Lighthouse of the West Coast. Bd. mem. P.E.G. Com., Clearlake, Calif., 2000—04; com. mem. BORT, Lakeport, Calif., 2000—04; regional coord. Calif. Assn. of SkillsUSA, Middletown, Calif. Recipient Educator of the Yr., CLHS, 1995, Mng. Program of the Yr., Cisco Systems, INC, 2002, Outstanding Career Program in Calif., CACCICE, 2004. Mem.: Ammerican Assn. of Professors, USTA, Phi Delta Kappa (life). Office: Yuba Coll Clear Lake Campus 15880 Dam Road Xt Clearlake CA 95422 Office Phone: 707-995-4811. Office Fax: 707-994-3553. E-mail: bschoenh@yccd.edu.

SCHOENHERR, JOHN (CARL), artist, illustrator; b. N.Y.C., July 5, 1935; s. John Ferdinand and Frances (Braun) S.; m. Judith Gray; children: Jennifer L., Ian G. BFA, Pratt Inst., 1956. Painter, illustrator Owl Moon, 1987 (Caldecott medal, 1988); exhibitions include Hiram Blauvelt Art Mus., 1997. Recipient World Sic. Fiction award, World Sci. Fiction Conv., London, 1965, Silver medal, Phila. Acad. Natural Sci., 1984, purchase award, Hiram Blauvelt Art Mus., 1994. Mem.: Soc. Animal Artists (medal 1979, 1985), Am. Soc. Mammalogists (emeritus). Home and Office: 135 Upper Creek Rd Stockton NJ 08559-1209

SCHOENHOLZ, DAVID A. diversified financial services company executive; CFO Household Internat. Inc., Prospect Heights, Ill. Office: Household Internat Inc 2700 Sanders Rd Prospect Heights IL 60070-2701

SCHOENHUT, FREDERICK W. stock exchange executive; Previously prin. owner Copia Trading Co., Ltd.; coffee trader, 1980—; vice chmn. NY Bd. Trade, 2002—03, chmn., 2003—. Mem.: NY Cotton Exchange (NYCE), Coffee, Sugar, and Cocoa Exchange (CSCE), Commodity Floor Brokers and Traders Assn. (CFBTA) (vice chmn. 2003—). Office: NY Bd Trade One N End Ave 13th Fl New York NY 10282 Office Phone: 212-748-4040. Office Fax: 212-748-4156.*

SCHOENING, RUTH IRENE, retired music educator, musician; b. Moline, Ill., Mar. 23, 1922; d. Karl John and Cora Irene (Reynolds) Wilhelmsen; m. Raymond Edward Schoening, Apr. 28, 1945; children: Stephen Ray, Carol Irene Haertel, John Edward. MusB Edn., U. Wis., 1945, MusM, 1979. Cert. music tchr. Pvt. piano instr., Racine, Wis., 1945—; music instr. Racine Christian Sch., 1960-75; workshop presenter Music Educators Nat. Confs., 1975-82; instr. music U. Wis.-Parkside, Racine, 1985-90, 95, 98. Author, editor: From Sound to Symbol, 1969, Can You Do This?, 1984, Shortcuts for the Older Beginner, 1987. Organist Luth. Ch. Resurrection, Racine, 1960—; accompanist Racine Symphonic Chorus, 1987-98; vol. accompanist Racine Pub. Schs., 1983-93, Park High Sch. Concert Choir, 1998—; active vol. Christian Coalition, Chesapeake, Va., 1990—, nat. and state Rep. coms., 1993—. Mem. Am. Guild Organists, Music Tchrs. Nat. Assn. Avocations: reading, walking, computers, entertaining. Home: 923 Illinois St Racine WI 53405-2223

SCHOENKE, MARILYN LEILANI, foundation administrator; b. Wahiawa, Hawaii; m. Donald N. Basham; children: Neil, Steven, Leilani. BB, Corpus Christi State U. Exec. dir. Moanalua Gardens Found., Hawaii, 1994—. Exec. dir. Lawyer's Care; vol. Am. Cancer Soc. Mem. Alzheimer's Assn. (support svcs. coord., vol.), Manu O Ke Kai Canoe Club, Native Hawaiian C. of C., U.S. Tennis Assn., Hawaii Pacific Tennis Assn. Office: Moanalua Gardens Found 1352 Pineapple Pl Honolulu HI 96819-1754

SCHOENL, WILLIAM JAMES, history professor; b. Buffalo, Feb. 15, 1941; s. William and Erma Osborne Schoenl; m. Linda Volker, May 14, 1966; children: Karen Schoenl Carpenter, Lauren Schoenl van Loon, Mark William. BS in Math., Canisius Coll., 1963; MA in History, Columbia U., 1964, PhD in History, 1968. Prof. humanities Mich. State U., East Lansing, 1968-89, prof. history, 1989—. Mem. com. on rsch. Am. Soc. Ch. History, Chgo., 1988-93. Author: Intellectual Crisis in English Catholicism, 1982, C.G. Jung, 1998; editor: Major Issues in Jung, 1996, New Perspectives on the Vietnam War, 2002; author of poetry; contbr. articles and revs. to profl. jours. Mem., chair disbursement com. for dire needs overseas St. John Student Parish, East Lansing, Mich., 1971—. Rsch. grantee Nat. Endowment for the Humanities, Washington, 1970, Am. Philos. Soc., Phila., 1975, global competence grantee Mich. State U., East Lansing, 1993. Mem. Am. Hist. Assn., Ctr. for Jung Studies Detroit (trustee 1991-94), Kiwanis Club Okemos (chair internat. iodine deficiency disorders project 1994-98, chair Salvation Army project 1996—, chair human and spiritual values com. 1999-2002. Avocations: fishing, walking, travel, reading mysteries, snowshoeing. Home: 2643 Roseland East Lansing MI 48823 Office: Mich State Univ Dept History East Lansing MI 48824 Office Phone: 517-355-7500.

SCHOENRICH, EDYTH HULL, internal and preventive medicine physician; b. Cleve., Sept. 9, 1919; d. Edwin John and Maud Mabel (Kelly) Hull; m. Carlos Schoenrich, Aug. 9, 1942; children: Lola, Olaf. AB, Duke U., 1941; MD, U. Chgo., 1947; MPH, John Hopkins U., 1971. Diplomate Am. Bd. Internal Medicine, Am. Bd. Preventive Medicine. Intern John Hopkins Hosp., Balt., 1948-49, asst. resident medicine, 1949-50, fellow medicine, 1950-51, chief resident, pvt. wards, 1951-52; asst. chief, acting chief dept. chronic and cmty. medicine Balt. City Hosp., Balt., 1963-66; dir. svc. to chronically ill and aging Md. State Dept. Health, Balt., 1966-74; dir. divsn. pub. health adminstrn. Sch. Pub. Health, John Hopkins U., Balt., 1974-77, assoc. dean acad. affairs, 1977-86, dir. part time profl. programs and dep. dir. MPH program, 1986—, prof. dept. health policy and mgmt., 1974—, joint appointment medicine, 1978—. Contbr. articles to profl. jours. Trustee Friends Life Care Cmty., 1984—, Kennedy-Krieger Inst., Balt., 1985—, Vis. Nurses Assn., 1990-95, Md. Home and Cmty. Care Found., 1995—. Recipient Stebbins medal John Hopkins U., 1989, Disting. Med. Alumna award, 1997. Fellow ACP, Am. Coll. Preventive Medicine; mem. APHA, Assn. Tchrs. Preventive Medicine, Med. and Chirurg. Soc. Md., Balt. City Med. Soc., Phi Beta Kappa, Alpha Omega Alpha, Delta Omega. Avocations: gardening, music, theater, swimming. Home: 1402 Boyce Ave Baltimore MD 21204-6512 Office: Johns Hopkins Univ Sch Pub Health 615 N Wolfe St Baltimore MD 21205-2103 Office Phone: 410-955-1291. E-mail: eschoenr@Jhsph.edu.

SCHOENWALD, MAURICE LOUIS, retired lawyer; b. N.Y.C., Mar. 30, 1920; s. Jacob and Gertrude (Maier) S.; m. Susan Zysman, Nov. 14, 1943; children: David, Beth, Robin. BA, NYU, 1943; JD, Case Western Res. U., 1947. Bar: N.Y. 1947, Fla. 1978, U.S. Dist. Ct. (so. dist.) N.Y. 1950, U.S. Dist. Ct. (ctrl. dist.) Fla. 1980, U.S. Ct. Appeals (11th dist.) Ga. 1986. Pvt. practice, N.Y.C., 1948-80. Founder New Alternatives Fund, Melville, N.Y; pres. Accrued Equities Inc., fin. advisor, since 1954; prin. broker dealer; mem. faculty Hofstra U., 1968-69. Author: Investment Contracts, 1982, (handbook) Wealth Management, 1974. Bd. dirs. ACLU, Sarasota, Fla., 1984-86. Lt. (j.g.) USN, 1942-45. Decorated Philippine Presidl. Unit citation, Philippine Liberation medal with Bronze star attachment. Fellow Acad. Matrimonial Lawyers, Sarasota Sailing Squadron. Democrat. Achievements include development of first nationally traded mutual fund investing solely in environ. concerned companies and alternative energy. E-mail: newalternativesfund@compuserv.com.

SCHOETTGER, THEODORE LEO, city official; b. Burton, Nebr., Sept. 2, 1920; s. Frederick and Louise Cecelia (Gierau) S.; m. Kathlyn Marguerite Hughey, June 3, 1943; children— Gregory Paul, Julie Anne. BS in Bus. Adminstrn. with Distinction, U. Nebr., 1948. C.P.A., Calif. Sr. acct. Haskins & Sells, Los Angeles, 1948-55; controller Beckman Instruments, Inc., Fullerton, Calif., 1955-58, corp. chief acct., 1958-60; treas. Docummun Inc., Los Angeles, 1960-77; fin. dir. City of Orange, Calif., 1977-93. Mem. fin. com., treas., bd. dirs. Childrens Hosp., 1975-98. Served to lt. USNR, 1942-45. Mem. Calif. Soc. CPA's (nat. dir., v.p., past pres. Los Angeles chpt.), Fin. Execs. Inst., Mcpl. Fin. Officers Assn., Beta Gamma Sigma, Alpha Kappa Psi. Clubs: Jonathan, Town Hall. Methodist. Home: 2235 Sunset Rdg Mckinleyville CA 95519-4095

SCHOETTLE, ENID C.B. government agency administrator; m. Herbert Stuart Okun, Dec. 27, 1990. BA, Radcliffe Coll.; PhD in Polit. Sci., MIT, Cambridge, Mass. Faculty polit. sci. U. Minn., Mpls., Swarthmore Coll.; staff mem. Ford Found., 1976—91, dir. internat. affairs program, 1981—91; sr. fellow Coun. on Fgn. Rels., 1991—93; nat. intelligence officer for global and multilateral issues Nat. Intelligence Coun., 1993—96; chief advocacy and external rels. unit UN Dept. Humanitarian Affairs, 1996—97; spl. advisor Nat. Intelligence Coun., Washington, 1997—. Office: Central Intelligence Agy Nat Intelligence Coun Washington DC 20505

SCHOETTLE, FERDINAND P. legal educator; b. Phila., Aug. 17, 1933; s. Ferdinand P. and Helen Louise (White) S.; m. E. Bok, Feb. 13, 1965 (div. 1976); m. D. Jean Thomson, Nov. 24, 1979 (div. 1982); children: Michael, Derek, Katy. BA in History, Princeton U., 1955; LLD, Harvard U., 1960, MA in Econs., 1978, PhD, 1983. Bar: Pa. 1961, Minn. 1968. Asst., U.S. Senator J.S. Clark, Washington, 1961-62; assoc. Morgan, Lewis & Bockius, Phila., 1963-67; prof. U. Minn. Law Sch., Mpls., 1967—; vis. prof. Harvard U., 1972-74, Uppsala U., Sweden, 1984; guest scholar Brookings Inst., Washington, 1992-93. Co-author: State and Local Taxes, 1974; author: State and Local Taxation: The Law and Policy of Multi-Jurisdictional Taxation, 2003; editor: Tax Policy Notes, 1993—; contbr. articles to profl. jours. Lt. USN, 1955-57. Mem. sailing U.S. Olympic Team, 1956, 60. Mem. ABA (chmn. taxes and revenue com. 1979-82), Am. Law Inst. Office: U Minn Sch Law Minneapolis MN 55455 Office Phone: 612-625-6047. Business E-Mail: schoe001@umn.edu.

SCHOETTLER, GAIL SINTON, former ambassador; b. Los Angeles, Oct. 21, 1943; d. James and Norma (McLellan) Sinton; children: Lee, Thomas, James; m. Donald L. Stevens, June 23, 1990. BA in Econs., Stanford U., 1965; MA in History, U. Calif., Santa Barbara, 1969, PhD in History, 1975. Businesswoman, Denver, 1975-83; exec. dir. Colo. Dept. of Personnel, Denver, 1983-86; treas. State of Colo., Denver, 1987—95, lt. gov., 1995—99; former chmn. bd. Fischer Imaging Corp. U.S. amb. World Radio Comm. Conf., Istanbul, 1999-2000; bd. dirs. AspenBio, Inc., CancerVax Corp, Air Gate PCS. Active Douglas County Bd. Edn., Colo., 1979-87, pres., 1983-87; trustee U. No. Colo., Greeley, 1981-87; pres. Denver Children's Mus., 1975-85; bd. dirs. Gunnison Ranchland Conservation Legacy, Colo. Conservation Trust. Decorated Chevalier, French Legion of Honor; recipient Disting. Alumna award U. Calif., Santa Barbara, 1987, Trailblazer award AAUW, 1997, Childrens Advocacy award Colo. Soc. Sch. Psychologists, 1997. Mem. Internat. Women's Forum (mem. bd. dirs. 1981-89, pres. 83-85), Women Execs. in State Govt. (bd. dirs. 1981-87, chmn. 1988), Leadership Denver Assn. (bd. dirs. 1987, named Outstanding Alumna 1985), Nat. Congress Lt. Govs., Stanford Alumni Assn. Democrat.

SCHOETZ, DAVID JOHN, JR., colon and rectal surgeon, educator; b. Milw., Oct. 29, 1948; s. David John and Beverly (Rogers) S.; m. Ruthanne Brennan, Mar. 25, 1972; children: Elizabeth Anne, David John III. BA, Coll. of Holy Cross, 1970; MD, Med. Coll. Wis., Milw., 1974. Diplomate Am. Bd. Surgery, Am. Bd. Colon and Rectal Surgery (sr. examiner 1996—). Resident in surgery Boston U. Med. Ctr., 1974-81; resident in colon/rectal surgery Lahey Clinic Med. Ctr., Burlington, Mass., 1981-82, staff colon-rectal surgeon, 1982—, chmn. dept. colon-rectal surgery, 1987—2002; prof. surgery Med. Sch. Tufts U., Boston, 1999—, chmn. dept. med. edn., 2000—. Fellow ACS (commn. on cancer 1998-2003), Am. Soc. Colon and Rectal Surgeons (sec. 1999-2002, pres.-elect 2002-03, pres. 2003—04). Office: Lahey Clinic Med Ctr 41 Mall Rd Burlington MA 01803-4521

SCHOEWE, THOMAS M. retail executive; BA, MBA, Loyola U. of Chicago. CFO Beatrice Consumer Durables; v.p. business planning The Black & Decker Corp., 1986—89, v.p. finance, 1989—93, senior v.p., CFO, 1993—99; CFO, exec. v.p. Wal-Mart Stores, Bentonville, 2000—. Office: Wal-Mart Stores 702 SW 8th St Bentonville AR 72716

SCHOFIELD, ANTHONY WAYNE, judge; b. Farmington, N.Mex., Mar. 5, 1949; s. Aldred Edward and Margueriete (Knudsen) S.; m. Rebecca Ann Rosecrans, May 11, 1971; children: Josie, Matthew Paul, Peter Christian, Addie, Joshua James, M. Thomas, Jacob L., Daniel Z. BA, Brigham Young U., 1973, JD, 1976. Bar: Utah 1976, U.S. Dist. Ct. Utah 1976, U.S. Ct. Appeals (7th and 10th cirs.) 1977. Law clk. to hon. judge A. Sherman Christansen U.S. Dist. Ct. Utah, Salt Lake City, 1976-77; assoc. Ferenz, Bramhall, Williams & Gruskin, Agana, Guam, 1977-79; pvt. practice American Fork, Utah, 1979-80; assoc. Jardine, Linebaugh, Brown & Dunn, Salt Lake City, 1980-81; mem., dir. Ray, Quinney & Nebeker, Provo, Utah; judge 4th Jud. Dist. Ct., Provo, 1993—. Bishop Mormon Ch., American Fork, 1985-88; commr. American Fork City Planning Commn., 1980-85; trustee American Fork Hosp., 1984-93. Mem. Ctrl. Utah Bar Assn. (pres. 1987, 91). Avocations: photography, music. Office: 125 N 100 W Provo UT 84601-2849 Office Phone: 801-429-1045. E-mail: awschofield@yahoo.com.

SCHOFIELD, BARBARA CURTRIGHT, retired school administrator; b. Paris, Mo., Dec. 24, 1942; d. W.L. and Karoline Curtright; m. Alan Otis Schofield, Apr. 28, 1967 (div. 1986); children: Dianna Kay, Nichol LaVaughn, Theresa Alana. BS, U. Mo., Columbia, 1964; MEd, U. Mo., St. Louis, 1978; Cert. Ednl. Specialist, Southeast La. U., 1986. Cert. ednl. adminstr., La. Tchr. phys. edn. Neal Jr. High Sch., North Chicago, Ill., 1964-66, Deerfield (Ill.) High Sch., 1966-67, Holy Child H.S., Waukegan, Ill., 1970-72; dean of girls Antioch (Ill.) High Sch., 1972-74; dean of students, extra-curricular activities Washington (Mo.) High Sch., 1974-78; phys. edn. tchr. Clearwood Jr. High Sch., Slidell, La., 1978-83; asst. prin. Boyet Jr. High Sch., Slidell, 1983-2000; prin. Washington Jr. HS, Mo., 2000—03. Elder 1st Presbyn Ch., Slidell, 1985—90, 1993—95, 1995—95, 1997—99, 2003—; Elder Presbyn. Ch. Wash. Mem. MSTA, NEA, Mid. Sch. Assn., La. Assn. Educators (mem. congrl. contact team dist. 1), La. Assn. Sch. Exec., St. Tammany Assn. Educators (legis. chmn. 1980-81, pres. 1981-83), St. Tammany Adminstrs. Assn. (sec. 1991-92), Alpha Delta Kappa (pres. 1990-92), Delta Kappa Gamma. Avocations: bridge, reading, golf, bicycling, walking.

SCHOFIELD, JAMES ROY, computer programmer; b. Reedsburg, Wis., Aug. 16, 1953; s. G. C. Schofield and Margaret (Collies) Tverberg. BA, Carleton Coll., 1976. Programmer Brandon Applied Systems, San Francisco, 1977-78, Rand Info. Systems, San Francisco, 1979-83; systems programmer IBM, San Jose, Calif., 1983-91; programmer Office of Instnl. Rsch./U. Calif., Berkeley, 1991-94, Datis Corp., San Mateo, Calif., 1994-95, Compuware Corp., Los Gatos, Calif., 1995-96, Pacific Bell, San Ramon, Calif., 1996—2001, SBC Comms., San Ramon, Calif., 2002. Mem. Assn. for Computing Machinery, Commonwealth Club Calif., Phi Beta Kappa. Avocations: guitar, reading, swimming. Home: PO Box 25143 San Mateo CA 94402-5143 Office: SBC Comms 2600 Camino Ramon San Ramon CA 94583-5099

SCHOFIELD, ROBERT E(DWIN), history educator, academic administrator; b. Milford, Neb., June 1, 1923; s. Charles Edwin and Nora May (Fullerton) S.; m. Mary-Peale Smith, June 20, 1959; 1 son, Charles Stockton Peale. AB, Princeton U., 1944; MS, U. Minn., 1948; PhD, Harvard U., 1955. Research asst. Fercleve Corp. and Clinton Labs., Oak Ridge, 1944-46; research assoc. Knolls Atomic Power Lab., Gen. Electric Co., 1948-51; asst. prof., then assoc. prof. history U. Kans., Lawrence, 1955-60; mem. faculty Case Western Res. U., Cleve., 1960-79, prof. history of sci., 1963-72, Lynn Thorndike prof. history of sci., 1972-79; prof. history Iowa State U., Ames, 1979-93, prof. emeritus, 1993—, dir. grad. program history tech. and sci., 1979-92. Mem. Inst. Advanced Study, 1967-68, 74-75; Sigma Xi nat. lectr., 1978-80 Author: The Lunar Society of Birmingham, 1963, Scientific Autobiography of Joseph Priestley: Selected Scientific Correspondence, 1966, Mechanism and Materialism: British Natural Philosophy in an Age of Reason, 1970, (with D.G.C. Allan) Stephen Hales: Scientist and Philanthropist, 1980, The Enlightenment of Joseph Priestley: A Study of His Life and Work from 1733 to 1773, 1997, The Enlightened Dr. Joseph Priestley,LLDFRS: A Study of His Life from 1773 to 1804, 2004. Served with AUS, 1945-46. Fulbright fellow, 1953-54; Guggenheim fellow, 1959-60, 67-68 Fellow Am. Phys. Soc., Royal Soc. Arts; mem. History of Sci. Soc., Soc. History Tech., Midwest Junto History of Sci., Am. Soc. 18th Century Studies, Acad. Internat. d'Histoire des Scis. (corr.) Home: 44 Sycamore Rd Princeton NJ 08540-5323

SCHOGGEN, PHIL H(OWARD), psychologist, educator; b. Tulsa, Aug. 28, 1923; s. Walter B. and Emma F. (Alexander) S.; m. Maxine F. Spoor, June 28, 1944; children: Leida, Christopher, Ann, Susan. AB in Psychology, Park Coll., 1946; MS, U. Kans., Lawrence, 1951, PhD in Psychology, 1954. Asst. prof. psychology U. Oreg., 1957-62, asso. prof., 1962-66; prof., chmn. dept. psychology George Peabody Coll., 1966-75; prof. York U., Toronto, Ont., Can., 1975-77; prof. human devel. and family studies N.Y. State Coll. Human Ecology, Cornell U., 1977-90, prof. emeritus, 1990—, chmn. dept., 1977-82. Author: (with R. G. Barker) Qualities of Community Life, 1973; Behavior Settings: A Revision and Extension of Roger G. Barker's Ecological Psychology, 1989. Served with USNR, 1944-46, 50-51. Mem. APA. Home: 121 Vossland Dr Nashville TN 37205-3617 Personal E-mail: schoggph@comcast.net.

SCHOLDER, FRITZ, artist; b. Breckenridge, Minn., Oct. 6, 1937; Student, Wis. State Coll., 1956-57; AA, Sacramento City Coll., 1958; BA, Sacramento State Coll., 1960; MFA, U. Ariz., 1963, DFA (hon.), 1985, Ripon Coll., Wis., 1984, Concordia Coll., Minn., 1986; HHD (hon.), Coll. Sante Fe; DFA (hon.), U. Wis., Superior, 1993. Teaching asst. art Univ. Ariz., 1962-64; instr. art history, advanced painting Inst. Am. Indian Arts, 1964-69; artist in residence Dartmouth Coll., 1973; guest artist Santa Fe Art Inst., 1987, Okla. Art Inst., 1980-81, 88, Am. U., Washington, 1990. One-man shows include Crocker Art Gallery, Sacramento, 1959, Coll. Santa Fe, 1967, Roswell (N.Mex.) Art Center, 1969, Tally Richards Gallery Contemporary Art, Taos, N.Mex., 1971, 73, 75, 78-79, St. John's Coll., Santa Fe, 1972, Cordier & Ekstrom, N.Y.C., 1972, 74, 76, 78, 90, Gimpel & Weitzenhoffer, N.Y.C., 1977, Graphics 1 and 2, Boston, 1977, Smith Andersen Gallery, Palo Alto, Calif., 1979, Scottsdale Center for Arts, 1981, Tucson Mus. Art, 1981, Weintraub Gallery, N.Y.C., 1981, ACA Galleries, N.Y.C., 1984, 86, Louis Newman Galleries, L.A., 1985, 87, 90-94, Schneider Mus. Art, Ashland, Oreg., 1990, Alexander Gallery, N.Y., 1991, Thorne-Sagendorph Art Mus. Keene, 1996, Phoenix Art Mus., 1997, Scottsdale Mus. Art, 1998; exhibited group shows at Carnegie Art Inst., Butler Inst. Am. Art, Calif. Palace of Legion of Honor, Houston Mus. Fine Arts, Dallas Mus. Fine Arts, San Francisco Mus. Art, Denver Art Mus., Ft. Worth Art Center, Basel Art 5, Linden Mus., Stuttgart, Philbrook Art Center, Oakland Art Mus., Tucson Art Center, N.Mex. Art Mus., Edinburgh Art Festival, Museo de Bellas Artes, Buenos Aires, Biblioteca Nacional, Santiago, Chile, Mus. voor Land-en-Volkenkunder, Rotterdam, Amerika Haus, Berlin Festival, Center for Arts of Indian Am., Washington, Yellowstone Art Center, Nat. Mus. Modern Art, Tokyo, Kyoto, Japan, others, Smithsonian tour, Bucharest, Berlin, London, Ankara, Madrid, Belgrade, Athens, 1972-73; represented in permanent collections: Mus. Modern Art, N.Y.C., Art Inst. Chgo., Center Culturel Americain, Paris, Art Gallery Toronto, NEA, Houston Mus. Fine Arts, Boston Fine Arts Mus., Milw. Art Mus., Portland (Oreg.) Art Mus., Dallas Mus. Fine Arts, Bur. Indian Affairs, Mus. N.Mex., Smithsonian Instn., Bklyn. Mus., Phoenix Art Mus., San Diego Fine Arts Gallery, Okla. Art Center, Brigham Young U., Heard Mus., Phoenix, Bibliotheque Nat., Paris, San Francisco Mus. Art, Hermitage Mus., Leningrad, others; Included in: American Prints and Printmakers; Subject of: (PBS film) Fritz Scholder, 1976, Fritz Scholder, An American Portrait, 1983, Fritz Scholder, Painting the Paradox, 1998; author: Fritz Scholder Lithograph, 1975, 1983, Scholder/Indians, Fritz Scholder, Rizzoli, Fritz Scholder, Paintings and Monotypes, Afternoon Nap, 1991, Live Dog/Evil God, 1992, Fritz Scholder, A Survey of Paintings, 1993, Remnants of Memory, 1993, Fritz Scholder's Book of Symbols for Children, 1994, Fritz Scholder, Thirty Years of Sculpture, 1994, Rot/Red, 1995, Flirting with Possessions, 1997, Icons & Apparations, 1997, Thoughts at Night, 2000, Last Portraits, 2001, Fritz Scholder Paintings, 2002, From the Cave, 2002; guest artist Santa Fe Art Inst., 1987, Taos Inst. Art, 1990, Am. U., Washington, 1990. Recipient Ford Found. purchase award, 1962, 1st prize W.Va. Centennial Exhbn., 1973, purchase prize 13th S.W. Print Drawing Show, 1963, Hallmark purchase award, 1965, 1st prize Scottsdale Indian Nat., 1966, Grand prize Washington Biennial Indian Show, 1967, Grand prize Scottsdale Indian Nat., 1969, jurors award S.W. Fine Arts Biennial, 1970, 71, 72, prize in painting Am. Acad. and Inst. Arts and Letters, 1977, award in painting AAAL, 1977, internat. prize in lithography Intergrafiks, Berlin, 1980, 90, N.D. Gov.'s award in arts, 1981, N.Mex. Gov.'s award, 1983, Societaire Salon d'Automne, Paris, 1983, Golden Plate award Am. Acad. Achievement, 1985, Third prize Intergrafiks, 1990, Laird Leadership award in the arts U. Wis., Stevens point, 1995, Visionary award Inst. Am. Indian Arts, Gov.'s Arts award, Ariz., 2002; named Artist of the Yr. Scottsdale Arts Coun., 1998; John Hay Whitney fellow, 1962-63. Address: 118 Cattletrack Rd Scottsdale AZ 85250 E-mail: fritzscholder@earthlink.net. *I Believe in Art, Love, and the Unknown.*

SCHOLEFIELD, PETER GORDON, health agency executive; b. Newport, Wales, June 26, 1925; emigrated to Can., 1947, naturalized, 1952; s. Tom and Margaret (Bithell) S.; m. Erna Mary Cooper, Sept. 29, 1951; children— David, John, Paul. B.Sc., U. Wales, 1944, M.Sc., 1946, D.Sc., 1960; PhD, McGill U., Montreal, Que., Can., 1949. From research fellow to prof. biochemistry McGill U., 1949-65, dir. cancer research unit, 1965-69; asst. exec. dir. Nat. Cancer Inst. Can., Toronto, 1969-80, exec. dir., 1980-91, spl. adviser to chief exec. officer, 1991-92; dir. grants and awards Alta. Heritage Found. for Med. Rsch., Edmonton, 1992-94; coord. acad. affairs Samuel Lunenfeld Rsch. Inst. Mt. Sinai Hosp., Toronto, 1994-99; mem. adv. bd. Inst. Neuroscis. Mental Health and Addiction Can. Insts. Health Rsch., 2001—. Chair rsch. policy com., bd. dirs. Alzheimer Soc. of Can., 1994-2000; mem. health adv. com. Alta. Heritage Found. Med. Rsch, 1994-99; mem. Ont. Neurotrauma Found., 1999—, sec., 2003-, bd. dirs., 2003-, rsch. com., 2003-. Home: 2010 Islington Ave # 1503 Etobicoke ON Canada M9P 3S8 Personal E-mail: peter.scholefield@sympatico.ca.

SCHOLER, MARGARET D. adult education educator; b. La Habra, Calif., June 14, 1920; d. James Robards Darling and Ula McWhorter; m. Emerson C. Scholar, 1964 (dec.); m. Philip Lynden Evans, 1941 (div. 1960); children: Lynden Anthony Evans, Conrad St. George Evans, Madelon Blythe Evans Mitchell. AB, U. Calif., Berkeley, 1942. Rsch. crew U. Calif., Berkeley, 1942—43; asst. Robert Johnson, Interiors, Oakland, Calif., 1948; libr. asst. Oakland Pub. Libr., 1960—62; asst. mgr. Fairyland Dutchess Caterers, Oakland, 1962—63; mgr. art gallery Bret Harte Board Walk, Oakland, 1962—63; lectr. Am. Antiques Normandale Coll., Mpls., 1969—90, Ohio State U. Continuing Edn., Columbus, 1990—97, Cuesta Coll. Continuing Edn., San Luis Obispo, Calif., 1998—99, Elderhostel, Calif. Poly. U., Cambria Pines, 2000—01. Acquisitions co-chair Godfrey Ho. Mus., Mpls., 1978—90; bd. dirs. decorative arts coun. Mpls. Inst. Arts, 1980—90; lectr., Mpls. and St. Paul, 1970—90. Mem.: AAUW (co-chair programs Morro Bay chpt. 2000—02, garden tour chair 2003). Democrat. Episcopalian. Home: 2751 Ironwood Ave Morro Bay CA 93442

SCHOLER, SUE WYANT, state legislator; b. Topeka, Oct. 20, 1936; d. Zint Elwin and Virginia Louise (Achenbach) Wyant; m. Charles Frey Scholer, Jan. 27, 1957; children: Elizabeth Scholer Truelove, Charles W., Virginia M. Scholer McCal. Student, Kans. State U., 1954-56. Draftsman The Farm Clinic, West Lafayette, Ind., 1978—79; assessor Wabash Twp., West Lafayette, 1979-84; commr. Tippecanoe County, Lafayette, Ind., 1984-90; state rep. Dist. 26 Ind. Statehouse, Indpls., 1990—. Asst. minority whip, 1992-94, Rep. whip, 1994-2000, asst. Rep. leader, 2001—; mem. Tippecanoe County Area Plan Commn., 1984-90; chmn. Midwestern legis. conf. CSG, 1998. Bd. dirs. Crisis Ctr., Lafayette, 1984-89, Tippecanoe Arts Fedn., 1990-99, United Way, Lafayette, 1990-93; mem. Lafayette Conv. and Visitors Bur., 1988-90. Recipient Salute to Women Govt. and Politics award, 1986, United Sr. Action award, Outstanding Legislator award, 1993, Small Bus. Champion award, 1995, Ind. Libr. Fedn. Legislator award, 1995, Disting. Legislator award Nat. Alliance for Mentally Ill, 1997,, 2003, West Ctrl. Ind. Advocate award, 2003, Friend of Cmty. Action award, 1999, Disting. Pub. Svc. award Am. Legion, 2004. Mem. Ind. Assn. County Commrs. (treas. 1990), Assn. Ind. Counties (legis. com. 1988-90), Greater Lafayette C. of C. (ex-officio bd. 1984-90), LWV, P.E.O., Purdue Women's Club (past treas.), Kappa Kappa Kappa (past pres. Epsilon chpt.)., Delta Delta Delta (past pres. alumnae, house corp. treas.). Republican. Presbyterian. Avocations: golf, needlecrafts, reading. Home: 807 Essex St West Lafayette IN 47906-1534 Office: Indiana Statehouse 200 W Washington Rm 3-7 Indianapolis IN 46204

SCHOLES, EDISON EARL, army officer; b. McCaysville, Ga., Aug. 16, 1939; s. Alvin L. and Marie (Plemmons) S.; m. Elva E. Bussey, June 4, 1961; children: Juana Kimberly Scholes, Tracy Michele Scholes Heller, Michael Lee. BS in Physics cum laude, No. Ga. Coll., 1961; MS in Ops. Rsch., Naval Postgrad. Sch., 1970; postgrad., Army War Coll., 1980, Harvard Def. Policy Seminar, 1991. Commd. 2d lt. U.S. Army, 1961, advanced through grades to maj. gen., 1991; comdr. A Detachment, 10th Spl. Forces Group U.S. ArmyEurope, 1963-66; comdr. Co. D, 2d Bn.(Abn.), 8th Cav., 1st Cav. Divsn. U.S. Army, Republic of Vietnam, 1967-68, sr. adv. I Corps. Ranger Commd., 1970—71, comdr. 1st Bn., 23d Inf., 2d Inf. Divsn., 1976-77, comdr. 2d Tng. Bn., Sch. Brigade, U.S. Army Inf. Sch., 1978-79, comdr. 1st Inf. Tng. Brigade, U.S. Army Infantry Tng. Ctr., 1983-85, dep. commanding gen. chief of staff 3d U.S. Army/U.S. Army Cen. Command Ft. McPherson, Ga., 1986-88, asst. divsn. comdr. 82d Airborne Divsn. Ft. Bragg, N.C., 1988-89, chief of staff XVIII Airborne Corps, 1989-90, chief of staff joint task force-south, Op. Just Cause, 1989-90, dep. commanding gen. XVIII Airborne Corps, Operation Desert Shield/Desert Storm, 1990-91, dep. commanding gen. XVIII Airborne Corps, 1991-93; dep. comdr. Allied Land Forces, S.E. Europe NATO, 1993-95; program gen. mgr. Saudi Arabia N.G. Modernization Program, Vinnell Arabia, 1996—2002; pvt. cons., 2002—. Decorated Dept. Def. Disting. Svc. medal, Army Disting. Svc. medal with oak leaf cluster, Silver Star, Legion of Merit with oak leaf cluster, Bronze Star with V device and 4 oak leaf clusters, Purple Heart with oak leaf cluster, 6 Air medals, Army Commendation medal with V device and oak leaf cluster, Armed Forces Expeditionary medal, Combat Infantryman badge, Expert Infantry badge; Cross of Gallantry with Silver and Bronze Stars and Palm (Republic of Vietnam); numerous other domestic and fgn. awards; inducted into North Ga.'s Coll. and State U. Hall of Fame. Mem. 82d Airborne Divsn. Assn., Spl. Forces Assn., U.S. Army Ranger Assn., Spl. Ops. Assn. Baptist. Avocations: reading, camping, fishing.

SCHOLES, MYRON S. financier, former law and finance educator; b. Timmins, Ont., Can., July 1, 1941; BA, McMaster U., 1959—62, MBA, 1962—64; PhD in finance, U. Chgo., 1964—69; D (hon.), U. Paris-Dauphine, 1989, McMaster U., 1990, U. Leuven, 1998. Rsch. assoc., Ctr. for Math. Studies in Bus. and Econs. U. Chgo., 1966—67, instr. in fin., grad. sch. bus., 1967—68, assoc. prof., 1973—74, prof., 1975—79, dir., Ctr. for Rsch. in Security Prices, 1975—81, Edward Eagle Brown prof. fin., 1979—82; asst. prof. in fin. MIT Mgmt. Sch., Cambridge, 1968—72, assoc. prof., 1972—73; prof. law Stanford U., Calif., 1983—96, Frank E. Buck prof. Grad. Sch. Bus., 1983—96, sr. rsch. fellow, Hoover Instn., 1988—96, Frank E. Buck prof. emeritus fin., 1996—; mng. dir., sr. advisor Salomon Bros., 1990—93; prin. Long-Term Capital Mgmt., Greenwich, Conn., 1994—98; chmn. Oak Hill Platinum Ptnrs., Rye Brook, NY, 1999—; mng. ptnr. Oak Hill Capital Mgmt., 1999—. Bd. trustees Math. Scis. Rsch. Inst.; bd. dirs. Chgo. Mercantile Exchange, 2000—, chmn. Competitive Markets Adv. Coun., 2004—; bd. dirs. Chgo. Mercantile Exchange Holdings, 2001—, Intelligent Markets, Am Century, FEP/Constellation, UNext Inc., Salomon Swapco Inc. Contbr. articles to profl. jours. Recipient Nobel Prize for econ. scis., 1997. Mem.: Am. Fin. Assn. (v.p. 1989, pres. 1990), Econometrics Soc. Office: Arbor Investors 2775 Sand Hill Rd Ste 220 Menlo Park CA 94025-7019 Address: Oak Hill Platinum Ptnrs Reckson Exec Park 1100 King St Bldg 4 Rye Brook NY 10573 E-mail: mscholes@pacbell.net.*

SCHOLES, ROBERT THORNTON, physician, research administrator; b. Bushnell, Ill., June 24, 1919; s. Harlan Lawrence and Lura Zolene (Camp) S.; m. Kathryn Ada Tew, Sept. 3, 1948; 1 child, Delia. Student, Knox Coll., 1937-38; BS, Mich. State U., 1941; MD, U. Rochester, 1950; postgrad., U. London, 1951-52, U. Chgo., 1953. Intern Gorgas Hosp., Ancon, C.Z., 1950-51; lab. asst. dept. entomology Mich. State U., 1940-41; rsch. asst. Roselake Wildlife Exptl. Sta., 1941; rsch. assoc. Harvard U., 1953-57; served to med. dir. USPHS, 1954-71; med. officer, dep. chief health and sanitation divsn. U.S. Ops. Mission, Bolivia, 1954-57, chief health and sanitation divsn., Paraguay, 1957—60; internat. health rep. Office of Surgeon Gen., 1960-62; br. chief, rsch. grants officer, acting assoc. dir. Nat. Inst. Allergy and Infectious Diseases, NIH, Bethesda, Md., 1962-71; co-founder, pres. The Bioresearch Ranch, Inc., Rodeo, N.Mex., 1977—. Cons. Peace Corps, 1961, Hidalgo County Med. Svcs., Inc., 1979-99, N.Mex. Health Sys. Agy., 1980-86, N.Mex. Health Resources, Inc., 1981-93, Luna County Charitable Found., 1993—. Contbr. articles to profl. publs. Capt. USAAF, 1942-45. Commonwealth Fund fellow, 1953. Mem. AAAS, AMA, APHA, Am. Ornithologists Union, N.Y. Acad. Sci., Sembot Hon. Soc. Achievements include research, writing and field test of first health survey indices detailing anthropological parameters; institution of first country wide malaria control project in Paraguay. Home and Office: PO Box 117 Rodeo NM 88056-0117 E-mail: scholes@vtc.net.

SCHOLIN, MARGO S. lawyer; b. Sioux Center, Iowa, Nov. 16, 1950; BSN with highest distinction, U. Iowa, 1973; MSN, Tex. Woman's U., 1980; JD summa cum laude, U. Houston, 1983. Bar: Tex. 1983; RN, Tex. Ptnr. Baker & Botts, LLP, Houston. Assoc. editor Houston Law Rev., 1982-83. Recipient U. Houston Law Found. Acad. Excellence award, 1983. Fellow Houston Bar Found.; mem. ABA, State Bar of Tex., Houston Bar Assn., Order of the Coif, Order of the Barons, Sigma Theta Tau. Office: Baker & Botts 1 Shell Plz Houston TX 77002

SCHOLL, KATHLEEN KAY, economist; b. Ind., May 19, 1950; m. John Daniel Scholl, Dec. 18, 1971 (dec. Nov. 25, 1990). PhD, Purdue U., 1976—78. Consumer economist USDA, Hyattsville, Md., 1980—87; sr. coord. Am. Assn. of Ret. Persons, Washington, 1987—90; consumer economist U.S. GAO, Washington, 1990—. Recipient Disting. Alumni Award, Consumer and Family Sciences, Purdue U., 1992, Women of Purdue, Purdue U., 1994. Mem.: Am. Econ. Assn., Soc. of Govt. Economists (pres. 1996—97). Office: US GAO 441 G St NW Rm 6K17E Washington DC 20548 E-mail: schollk@gao.gov.

SCHOLL, YVETTE MARGUERITE, elementary school educator, writer; d. Ronald and Astrid Scholl. BS in English Secondary Edn., Buffalo State Coll., 1990. Cert. English tchr. Tex. Tchr. English Deady Mid. Sch., Houston, 1994—98, Stevenson Mid. Sch., 1998—2001, League City Interemediate Sch., League City, 2001—. Author: The Inheritance. Fellow: Greater Houston Area Writing Project.

SCHOLLANDER, WENDELL, III, lawyer; b. Chattanooga, Tenn., Oct. 15, 1974; s. Wendell and Jayn Schollander. BA, U. NC at Chapel Hill, 1997; JD, Wake Forest Law Sch., 2001. Missionary Presbyn. Ch., Guatemala, 1998; lawyer Schollander Law Offices, Winston-Salem, NC, 2001—. Co-author: (book) Forgotten Elegance, 2001, Small Business Owner's Guide to Bankruptcy, 2002. Scoutmaster Boy Scouts of Am., Winston-Salem, 2002—. Recipient Point of Light award, Pres. George Bush, 1992, Chevron Conservation award, Chevron Award Program, 1992, Take Pride in Am. award, Dept. of Interior, 1991, 1992. Mem.: SAR (awards chair 2002—).

SCHOLLANDER, WENDELL LESLIE, JR., lawyer; b. Ocala, Fla., May 17, 1943; s. Wendell Leslie and Martha (Dent) Schollander; m. Jayn Cochran; 1 child, Wendell Leslie III. BS, U. Pa., 1966, MBA, 1968; postgrad., Stetson U., 1969-70; JD, Duke U., 1972. Bar: N.C. 1977, Tenn. 1972, Fla. 1987. With Container Corp. Am., Fernandina, Fla., 1968-69; assoc. Miller, Martin, Chattanooga, 1972-75; asst. counsel R.J. Reynolds Industries, Inc., 1975-78, assoc. counsel, 1978-79, sr. assoc. counsel, 1979-82, sr. counsel, 1982-85; gen. counsel RJR Archer, Inc., Winston-Salem, N.C., 1979-85; of counsel Finger, Parker & Avram, Winston-Salem, 1985-87; ptnr. Schollander, Winston-Salem, 1987—. Gen. counsel Splty. Tobacco Council, 1985-87. Mem. ABA, N.C. Bar Assn., Forsyth County Bar Assn., Mensa, SAR, Phi Delta Phi, Kappa Sigma. Presbyterian. Office: 2000 W 1st St Ste 308 Winston Salem NC 27104-4225

SCHOLLE, PETER ALLEN, geologist, researcher; b. N.Y.C., Sept. 12, 1944; s. Julian and Ilse Elisabeth Scholle; m. Dana Shirley Ulmer, Sept. 27, 1992; children: Peter Jr. Allen, David Michael, Steven Daniel. BS, Yale U., New Haven, Conn., 1965; PhD, Princeton U., N.J., 1970. Rsch. geologist Cities Svc. Oil Co., Tulsa, 1970—71; asst. prof. U. of Tex. at Dallas, 1971—74; geologist, br. chief of petroleum geology U.S. Geol. Survey, Denver, 1974—83; chief scientist for carbonate geology Gulf Oil Co. Rsch., Houston, 1983—85; Albritton prof. geology So. Meth. U., Dallas, 1985—99; dir., state geologist N.Mex. Bur. Geology and Mineral Resources, Socorro, 1999—. Contbr. articles to profl. jours.; author (editor) 8 books and 100 sci. papers. Fellow Vis. Erskine fellow, U. of Canterbury, Christchurch, N.Z, 1991. Fellow: Soc. Sedimentary Geology (hon.; pres. 1988—89); mem.: Am. Assn. Petroleum Geologists (Disting. lectr. 1975—76, Sproule Meml. award 1979, Pres.'s award 1980—81), Am. Geol. Inst. (treas. 2003—), Assn. Am. State Geologists (treas. 2002—04, pres.-elect 2004—). Achievements include research in carbonate sedimentology. Avocations: travel, photography. Office: Bureau of Geology & Mineral Resources NM Inst of Mining & Tech 801 Leroy Place Socorro NM 87801 Office Phone: 505-835-5302. Personal E-mail: pscholle@gis.nmt.edu.

SCHOLSKY, MARTIN JOSEPH, priest; b. Stafford Spring, Conn., Jan. 16, 1930; s. Sigmund Felix and Mary Magdalen (Wysocki) S. BA, St. John's Sem., 1952, MA in History, 1956; MA in Classical Greek, Cath. U. of Am., 1966. Ordained priest Roman Cath. Ch., 1956. Asst. pastor St. Peter's Ch., Hartford, Conn., 1956-61; prin. St. Peter's Sch., Hartford, 1956-58; instr. St. Thomas Sem., Bloomfield, Conn., 1961-67, admissions dir., 1965-67; vocations dir. Archdiocese of Hartford, 1967-78; chaplain Newington (Conn.) Children's Hosp., 1961-78; weekend asst. St. Mary's Ch., Newington, 1961-78; pastor St. Bartholomew Ch., Manchester, Conn., 1978-90; dean Manchester Deanery, 1989-91; spiritual dir. St. Thomas Aquinas High Sch., New Britain, Conn., 1991-92. Weekend asst. St. Francis of Assis Ch., South Windsor, Conn., 1991-92; instr. Holy Apostle's Sem. & Coll., Cromwell, Conn., 1988-94; pastor St. Mary's Ch., East Hartford, Conn., 1992—. Contbr. articles to profl. jours. Home: 36 Griswold St Manchester CT 06040-3928 Office: St Marys Ch East East Hartford CT 06108 *Conscience is not our own personal feelings about things; rather, it is our innate awareness of the rightness and wrongness of our deeds as God sees them, an awareness, often denied, that still remains the measure by which God will ultimately judge us all.*

SCHOLTEN, GARY P. finance company executive; Grad., U. No. Iowa, 1980. From asst. planning analyst to v.p. retail info. scs. Prin. Fin. Group, Des Moines, 1980—2002, sr. v.p., CIO, 2002—. Fellow: Life Office Mgmt. Inst. (chmn. ind. product sys. com.). Office: Prin Fin Group 711 High St Des Moines IA 50392

SCHOLTZ, ROBERT ARNO, electrical engineering educator; b. Lebanon, Ohio, Jan. 26, 1936; s. William Paul and Erna Johanna (Weigel) S.; m. Laura Elizabeth McKeon, June 16, 1962; children: Michael William, Paul Andrew. BSEE, U. Cin., 1958; MSEE, U. So. Calif., 1960; PhD, Stanford U., 1964. Co-op student Sheffield Corp., Dayton, Ohio, 1953-58; MS and PHD fellow Hughes Aircraft Co., Culver City, Calif., 1958-63, sr. staff engr., 1963-78; prof. U. So. Calif., L.A., 1963—. Vis. prof. U. Hawaii, 1969, 78; cons. LinCom Corp., L.A., 1975-81, Axiomatix Inc., L.A., 1980-86, JPL, Pasadena, 1985, Tech. Group, 1987-89, TRW, 1989, Pulson Comm., 1992-93, Colley-Godward, Palo Alto, 1994-97, Time Domain Corp., 2000-01. Co-author: Spread Spectrum Comm., 3 vols., 1984, Spread Spectrum Communications Handbook, 1994, Basic Concepts in Information Theory and Coding, 1994; contbr. articles to profl. jours. (recipient Leonard G. Abraham award 1983, Donald G. Fink award 1984, Sr. Paper award Signal Processing Soc. 1992, Comm. Soc. Fred Ellersick Paper award 1997, Mil. Comms. Conf. award 2001, S.A. Shelkunoff prize Antennas and Propagation Soc., 2003). Pres. South Bay Cmty. Concert Orgn., Redondo Beach, Calif., 1975—79. Fellow IEEE (bd. govs. info. theory group 1981-86, bd. govs. communication soc. 1981-83, chmn. fin. com. NTC 1977, program chmn. ISIT 1981). Office: U So Calif Comm Scis Inst Dept Elec Engring Los Angeles CA 90089-2565 E-mail: scholtz@usc.edu.

SCHOLZ, JANE, newspaper publisher; b. St. Louis, July 31, 1948; d. Robert Louis and Mildred Virginia (Hudgins) S.; m. Jay W. Johnson, June 1979 (div. Dec. 1981); m. Douglas C. Balz, Jan. 1, 1983 BA, Mich. State U., 1970; MBA, U. Miami, 1981. Reporter Jour.-Gazette, Fort Wayne, Ind., 1970-73, The Miami Herald, Fla., 1973-77, asst. city editor, 1977-80; advanced mgmt. devel. participant Knight-Ridder Inc., Miami, Fla., 1980-85; pres., pub. Post-Tribune, Gary, Ind., 1985-91; editor Knight-Ridder/Tribune News Svc., Washington. Bd. dirs. United Way of Lake county, Ind., Gary chpt. Urban League, Ind., NW Ind. Forum. Mem. Am. Newspaper Pubs. Assn., Ind. C. of C. (bd. dirs.), Inland Press Assn. (bd. dirs.), Sigma Delta Chi Office: 790 National Press Building Washington DC 20045-1701

SCHOLZ, JOHN KARL, economist, educator; BA in Econs. and Math., Carleton Coll.; PhD in Econs., Stanford U., 1988. Asst. prof. econs. dept. LaFollette Inst. Pub. Affairs U. Wis., Madison, 1988—95, prof. dept. econs., 1998—. Sr. staff economist Coun. Econ. Advisers Exec. Office of the Pres., Washington, 1990—91; faculty rsch. assoc. Nat. Bur. Econ. Rsch., 1991—; dep. asst. sec. Office Tax Analysis U.S. Treasury Dept., 1997—98; dir. Inst. for Rsch. on Poverty, 2000—; mem. panel to evaluate the USDA's methodology for estimating eligibility and participation for the WIC program NRC, 2001—03; sr. rsch. affiliate Mich. Nat. Poverty Ctr.; mem. bd. outside scholars Mich. Retirement Rsch. Ctr., 2003—. Contbr. articles to profl. jours.; co-editor: Jour. Human Resources, 1994—; mem. editl. bd.: Nat. Tax Jour., 1998—, The B.E. Jours. in Econ. Analysis and Policy, 2001—. Office: Univ Wis-Madison Dept Econs 1180 Observatory Dr Madison WI 53706-1397*

SCHOLZ, PETER M. surgeon; MD, U. Basel, Switzerland, 1970. Diplomate Am. Bd. Surgery, 1983, Am. Bd. Thoracic Surgery, 1985. Intern in Surgery Duke U. Med. Ctr., Durham, NC, 1974—75; resident gen. and thoracic surgery Duke U. Med. Ctr., Durham, 1975—83; physician divsn. thoracic surgery Robert Wood Johnson U. Med. Group, New Brunswick, NJ, 1983—. Office: Clin Acad Bldg Ste 4100 125 Paterson St New Brunswick NJ 08901-1977 Office Phone: 732-235-7642.

SCHOLZ, SALLY J. philosopher, educator; b. Eugene, Oreg., Apr. 5, 1968; d. Howard T. and Jean E. Scholz; m. Christopher P. Kilby, July 13, 1996; children: Tessa, Luke. BA, U. Portland, Oreg., 1989; MA, Purdue U., 1991, PhD, 1993. Asst. prof. philosophy Villanova (Pa.) U., 1994—2001, assoc. prof. philosophy, 2001—. Dir. grad. studies, dept. philosophy Villanova U., 2002—. Author: On de Beauvoir, 2000, On Rousseau, 2001; co-editor: Peacemaking: Lessons from Past, Vision for Future, 2000. Mem.: N.Am. Soc. Social Philosophy (exec. officer 1994—2003), Am. Philos. Soc. (editor newsletter on feminism and philosophy 2003—). Democrat. Avocations: reading, hiking. Office: Villanova U 800 Lancaster Ave Villanova PA 19085 Office Phone: 610-519-4099. E-mail: sally.scholz@villanova.edu.

SCHOM, ALAN MORRIS, historian, educator; b. Sterling, Ill., May 9, 1937; s. Irving and Matilda Grossman (Stoler) Schom; m. Juliana Leslie Hill, Sept. 6, 1963 (div. Apr. 1964); children: Sarah Elizabeth Rose, Emma Sofia Anne. AB, U. Calif., Berkeley, 1964; PhD, Durham U., Eng., 1968. Assoc. prof. history U. Calif., Riverside, 1968—69; asst. prof. French history So. Conn. State U., 1969—76; historian, author, 1976—. Founder, editor French Colonial Studies, 1974—76; hist. cons. Simon Wiesenthal Ctr., L.A., 1998—; lectr., interviewee in field. Author: Lyautey in Morocco, Protectorate Administration 1912-1925, 1970, Emile Zola, A Bourgeois Rebel, 1987, Trafalgar, Countdown to Battle, 1803-1805, 1990, One Hundred Days, Napoleon's Road to Waterloo, 1993, Napoleon Bonaparte, 1997, The Eagle and the Rising Sun, Vol. I (1941-1943), The Japanese-American War, 1941-1945, 2003. Fellow Am. Philos. Soc. fellow, 1971, 1973; grantee Rsch. grantee, The Hoover Instn., 1984. Mem.: U.S. Naval Inst., Internat. B'nai B'rith, Am. Hist. Assn., The Naval Club (London. Avocations: sailing, book collecting, farming, Scottish Terriers. Office: Jupeau Auzouer en Touraine 37110 Indre-et-Loire France

SCHOMMER, TRUDY MARIE, pastoral minister, religion education; b. Wayzata, Minn., May 18, 1937; d. Edward and Gertrude (Mergen) S. BA, Coll. St. Catherine, St. Paul, 1966; MA, Manhattanville Coll., 1971, Pacifica Grad. Inst., 1996. Joined Order of Franciscan Sisters of Little Falls, Minn., 1955. Dir. religious edn. St. Pius X, White Bear Lake, Minn., 1971-77; campus min., theology tchr. St. Cloud (Minn.) State Univ., 1977-81; pastoral min. St. Galls, St. Elizabeth, Milw., 1981-85; dir. religious edn. St. Alexander's, Morrisonville, N.Y., 1985-90; pastoral min. of religious edn. St. Mary's, Bryantown, Md., 1990-91; diocesan dir. religious edn. Diocese of New Ulm, Minn., 1991—. Exec. bd. mem. Nat. Assembly Religious Women, Chgo., 1974-78. Author: Easiest Gospel Stories Ever, 1993; book reviewer Sister's Today, 1988-91. Mem. Network, Washington, 1978—. Mem. Nat. Cath. Edn. Assn., Nat. Parish Coords. and Dirs. Democrat. Roman Catholic. Home and Office: 113 Saint Paul St NW Apt 13 Preston MN 55965-8906 *Life is an adventure: a time each of us is given to explore and discover the many ways Christ's life and love permeates the whole world. Life is a challenge: together as Christians we face the many challenges and difficulties of life.*

SCHOMP, LISA JULIANA, automotive industry executive; b. 1951; d. Ralph and Kay S.; m. Mark Wallace; children: Aaron, Tyler, Logan. From mini-maid to pres. Ralph Schomp Automotive, Littleton, Colo., 1970-88, pres., 1988—. Named 1993 Woman of Yr. Englewood (Colo.) Bus. and Profl. Women. Office: Ralph Schomp Automotive 5700 S Broadway Littleton CO 80121-8007

SCHON, STEVEN ELIOT, lawyer; b. Detroit, Jan. 29, 1951; s. William and Betty Ruth (Conn) S. BA with distinction, U. Mich., 1972, JD magna cum laude, 1976. Bar: Calif. 1977, U.S. Dist. Ct. (no. dist.) Calif. 1977, U.S. Ct. Appeals (7th and 9th cirs.) 1979. Law clk. to Hon. J. Edward Lumbard, U.S. Ct. Appeals (2d cir.), N.Y.C., 1976-77; assoc. Howard, Rice Nemerovski, Canady, Falk & Rabkin, San Francisco, 1977-82; mem. Howard, Rice Nemerovski, Canady, Robertson & Falk, San Francisco, 1982—, also dir. Articles editor U. Mich. Law Rev., 1975-76. Angell scholar U. Mich., Ann Arbor, 1979-82. Mem. ABA (litigation sect.), Calif. Bar, San Francisco Bar Assn., Order of Coif, Phi Beta Kappa, Phi Delta Phi. Office: Howard Rice Nemerovski 7th Fl 3 Embarcadero Ctr Ste 7 San Francisco CA 94111-4074 Office Phone: 415-434-1600. Business E-Mail: sschon@hrice.com.

SCHONBERG, ALAN ROBERT, management recruiting executive; b. N.Y.C., Oct. 23, 1928; s. Julius and Evelyn (Guzik) S.; m. Carole May Kreisman, Dec. 27, 1975; children: William, Evelyn, David, Jeffrey. Nat. sales mgr. Majestic Specialties, Inc., Cleve., 1953-63; pres. Internat. Personnel, Inc., Cleve., 1963-65; chmn. Mgmt. Recruiters Internat., Inc., Cleve., 1965-98, 1998—2000, chmn. emeritus, 2001—. Pres., bd. dirs. Jewish Vocat. Service, Cleve., 1983—; trustees Mt. Sinai Hosp. (now Mt. Sinai Found.), Cleve., bd. dirs. Cleve. Jewish News; gen. chmn. Welfare Fund Campaign; trustee Am. Jewish Comm., Mt. Sinai Med. Ctr., Hebrew Immigrant Aid Soc. Named one of Cleve.'s 86 Most Interesting People, Cleve. Mag., 1986, Man of Yr. local chpt. Orgn. through Rehab. and Tng., 1996, Entrepreneur of Yr. Inc. Mag., Merrill Lynch Ernst & Young, 1995; recipient Human Rels. award Cleve. chpt. Am. Jewish Com., 1998. Mem. Internat. Franchise Assn., Internat. Confederation Pvt. Employment Agys. Assns., Am. Mgmt. Assn., Assn. Human Resource Cons. (chmn. 1980—), Org. for Rehab. and Training (ORT), Assn. Am.-Israel C. of C. (pres.), Ohio Israel C. of C. (co-chmn.), Jewish Family Svcs. Assn. (v.p., pres. 1998-2002). Avocation: world travel. Personal E-mail: aschonberg@adelphia.net.

SCHONBRUN, MICHAEL K. senior housing developer and operator; b. N.Y.C., Jan. 26, 1948; s. Arnold Laurance and Madeline (Courland) Schonbrun; m. Michelle I. Fredson, June 6, 1971 (div. Dec. 1998); 1 child, Ethan F.; m. Susan E. Juroe, Feb. 17, 2001; children: Adam J., Theodore C. BA, Yale U., 1969; JD, U. Pa., 1973. Bar: Ohio 1973, Colo. 1975. Asst. to gov. Ohio Gov.'s Office, Columbus, 1973—74, Colo. Gov.'s Office, Denver, 1974—75; asst. dir. Colo. Dept. Health, Denver, 1976—78; pres., CEO Nat. Jewish Hosp., Denver, 1979—91; sr. v.p. Blue Cross/Blue Shield of Colo., Denver, 1991—93; exec. v.p. Vitas Healthcare Corp. Inc., Miami, Fla., 1994—95; pres. Schonbrun & assocs., Boulder, Colo., 1995—97; founder, pres., CEO Balfour Sr. Care, Boulder, 1997—. Chmn. Young Pres.'s Orgn. Healthcare Focus Forum, Dallas, 1999—2001; bd. dirs. Colo. Assn. Housing and Svcs., Denver, United Bank of Denver, 1985—91; mem. leadership coun. Assisted Living Fedn. Am., Washington, 1999—. Contbr. articles to profl. jours. Chmn. bd. dirs. Rocky Mountain Alzheimers Assn., 2002, Denver Met. Air Quality Coun., 1985—89, Internat. Med. Corp., L.A., 1996—2000; mem. Colo. 2002 Winter Olympic Games Com., 1988—90. Democrat. Jewish. Avocation: travel, running, tennis, reading fiction, movies. Home: 1020 Niwot Rd Longmont CO 80504 Office: Balfour Senior Care 1855 Plaza Dr Louisville CO 80027-2325

SCHÖNEMANN, PETER HANS, psychology educator; b. Pethau, Germany, July 15, 1929; arrived in U.S., 1960, permanent resident, 1965; s. Max Paul Franz and Hertha Anna (Kahle) S.; m. Roberta Dianne Federbush, Jan. 29, 1962; children: Raoul Dieter, Nicole Deborah. Vordiplom in Psychologie, U. Munich, 1956; Hauptdiplom in Psychologie, U. Goettingen, 1959; PhD, U. Ill., 1964. Thurstone postdoctoral fellow U. N.C., 1965-66; asst. prof., then assoc. prof. Ohio State U., 1966-69; postdoctoral fellow Ednl. Testing Service, Princeton, N.J., 1967-68; vis. prof. Technische Hochschule, Aachen, Fed. Republic Germany, 1981; mem. faculty Purdue U., 1969—, prof. psychology, 1971-2001, emeritus, 2001—. Vis. prof. Univs. Munich, Bielefeld and Braunschweig, 1984-85, Nat. Taiwan U., 1992, 96, 97. Author papers in field. Recipient Found. for the Advancement of Outstanding Scholarship award, Taiwan, 1996. Mem. Soc. Multivariate Exptl. Psychology. Office: Dept Psychol Scis Purdue U Lafayette IN 47907 Business E-Mail: phs@psych.purdue.edu.

SCHONFELD, GUSTAV, medical educator, researcher, administrator; b. Mukacevo, Ukraine, May 8, 1934; came to U.S., 1946; s. Alexander Schonfeld and Helena Gottesmann; m. Miriam Steinberg, May 28, 1961; children: Joshua Lawrence, Julia Elizabeth, Jeremy David. BA, Washington U., St. Louis, 1956, MD, 1960. Diplomate Am. Bd. Internal Medicine. Intern. Bellevue Med. Ctr. NYU, 1960—61, resident in internal medicine, 1961—63; chief resident in internal medicine Jewish Hosp., St. Louis, 1963—64; from NIH trainee in endocrinology & metabolism to Kountz prof. medicine Washington U., St. Louis, 1964—96, Busch prof., chair medicine, 1996—99, Samuel E. Schechter prof. medicine, 2002—; rsch. assoc. Cochran VA Hosp., St. Louis, 1965—66, clin. investigator, 1968—70, cons. in internal medicine, 1972—; rsch. flight med. officer USAF Sch. Aerospace Medicine, Brooks AFB, Tex., 1966—68; from asst. physician to physician Barnes Hosp., St. Louis, 1972—96; physician-in-chief Barnes Jewish Hosp., St. Louis, 1996—99; clin. instr. medicine Harvard U. Med. Sch., Boston, 1970—72; assoc. prof. metabolism and human nutrition, asst. dir. Clin. Rsch. Ctr. MIT, Cambridge, 1970—72. Mem. rsch. com. Mo. Heart Assn., 1978-80; expert witness working group on atherosclerosis Nat. Heart, Lung and Blood Inst., 1979, Nat. Diabetes Adv. Bd., 1979; mem. endocrinologic and metabolic drugs adv. com. USPHS, FDA, 1982-86; mem. nutrition study sect. NIH, 1984-88, spl. reviewer metabolism study sect.; mem. adult treatment guidelines panel Nat. Cholesterol Edn. Program, 1986; mem. Consensus Devel. Conf. on Triglyceride, High Density Lipoprotein and Coronary Heart Disease, 1992; cons. Am. Egg Bd., Am. Dairy Bd., Inst. Shortening and Edible Oils, Ciba-Geigy, Sandoz, Fournier, Parke-Davis, Bristol-Meyers Squibb, Monsanto/Searle. Past editor: Atherosclerosis, past mem. editl. bd.: Jour. Clin. Endocrinology and Metabolism, Jour. Clin. Investigation, Jour. Lipid Rsch., past assoc. editor: Circulation. Recipient Berg Prize in Microbiology, 1957, 58, Faculty/Alumni award Washington U., 1995; named Physician honoree Am. Heart Assn. Mo. Affiliate, 1995; grantee MERIT status NIH. Fellow ACP, AAAS; mem. Assn. Am. Physicians, Am. Soc. for Clin. Investigation, Am. Physiol. Soc., Am. Soc. Biol. Chemists, Am. Inst. Nutrition, Am. Diabetes Assn., Am. Heart Assn. (program com. coun. on atherosclerosis 1977-80, 86-88, nutrition com. 1980-84, pathology rsch. com. 1980-83, budget com. 1991, awards com. 1992), Endocrine Soc., Alpha Omega Alpha. Office: Washington U Sch Medicine Box 8046 660 S Euclid Ave Saint Louis MO 63110-1010 Office Phone: 314-362-7038. Business E-Mail: gschonfe@wustl.edu.

SCHONFELD, WILLIAM ROST, political science educator, researcher; b. N.Y.C., Aug. 28, 1942; s. William A. and Louise R. (Rost) S.; m. Elena Beortegui, Jan. 23, 1964; children: Natalie Beortegui, Elizabeth Lynn Beortegui. Student, Cornell U., 1960-61; BA cum laude with honors, NYU, 1964; MA, Princeton U., 1968, PhD, 1970. Research asst. Princeton U., 1966-69, research assoc., 1969-70, vis. lectr., 1970; asst. prof. polit. sci. U. Calif.-Irvine, 1970-75, assoc. prof., 1975-81, prof., 1981—, dean Sch. Social Scis., 1982—2002; sr. lectr. Fond. Nat. de Sci. Politique, Paris, 1973-74; researcher Centre de Sociologie des Organisations, Paris, 1976-78. Author: Youth and Authority in France, 1971, Obedience and Revolt, 1976, Ethnographie du PS et du RPR, 1985 Recipient Disting. Teaching award U. Calif.-Irvine, 1984, Disting. Faculty Lectureship award for tchg., 1998, Daniel G. Aldrich Disting. Univ. Svc. award, 2000 01; Fulbright fellow Bordeaux, France, 1964-65; Danforth grad. fellow, 1964-69; Fulbright sr. lectr. Paris, 1973-74; NSF-CNRS Exchange of Scientists fellow Paris, 1976-78; Ford Found. grantee France, Spain, 1978-79; finalist Prof. Yr. Council for Advancement and Support of Edn., 1984; Lauds & Laurels Extraordinarious award, U. Calif. Alumni Assn., 2002. Mem. Am. Polit. Sci. Assn., Assoc. Francaise de Sci. Pol., Phi Beta Kappa. Office: U Calif Sch Social Scis Irvine CA 92697-0001

SCHONHOLTZ, JOAN SONDRA HIRSCH, banker, civic worker; b. N.Y.C., Sept. 8, 1933; d. Joseph G. and Mildred (Klebanoff) Hirsch; m. George J. Schonholtz, Aug. 21, 1951; children: Margot Beth, Steven Robert, Barbara Ellen. Student, Vassar Coll., 1950-52; BA, Barnard Coll., 1954; postgrad., Am. U., 1963. Chmn. bd. dirs., founding mem. Grand Bank (formerly) 1st Women's Bank of Md., Rockville, 1976-2001. Chmn. FWB Bancorp, Rockville, 1982—98, Grand Bank Inc.; bd. dirs. Century Bank. Pres. Ft. Benning Med. Wives, Ga., 1962—63; sec. Montgomery County Women's Med. Aux., Md., 1968; bd. dirs. Svc. Guild of Washington, 1968—77, sec., 1969—70, pres., 1975—77; bd. dirs. Pilot Sch. for Blind Multiple Handicapped Children, Washington, 1968—77, Strathmore Hall Arts Ctr., North Bethesda, Md.; spl. gifts chmn. Montgomery County Cancer Soc., 1968, 1969; mem. Washington Adv. Coun. on Deaf-Blind Children, 1972—74; chmn. Friends of Washington Adventist Hosp., Takoma Park, Md., 1993—94. Recipient Outstanding Svc. award, Svc. Guild of Washington, 1969. Mem.: Barnard Club, Vassar Club. Republican. Jewish. Home: 32 Beman Woods Ct Potomac MD 20854-5481 E-mail: g.schonholtz@aol.com.

SCHONHORN, HAROLD, chemist, researcher; b. N.Y.C., Apr. 2, 1928; s. Benjamin and Dorothy (Gitlin) S.; m. Esther Matesky, Jan. 17, 1954; children: Deborah, Jeremy. BS, Bklyn. Coll., 1950; PhD, N.Y. Polytech. U., 1959. Mem. tech. staff Bell Labs., Murray Hill, N.J., 1961-84; v.p. R & D Polyken Tech. div. Kendall Co., Lexington, Mass., 1984-93; pres. Schonhorn Consultants, 1993—. Contbr. over 100 articles to profl. jours. Pres. B'nai B'rith Lodge, Summit, N.J., 1970. With U.S. Army, 1953-55, Korea. Mem. Am. Chem. Soc. Achievements include 15 patents. Office Phone: 617-738-4742. Office Fax: 617-738-4742.

SCHOOF, ROBERT NORMAN, music educator; b. Battle Creek, Mich., June 9, 1952; s. Robert Norman and Irene Jean Schoof; m. Meri Leone Jones, Aug. 10, 1974; children: Thomas, Andrew. MusB, Western Mich. U., 1974; MA, Ea. Mich. U., 1978. Cert. continuing edn. tchr. Mich. Tchr. Deerfield (Mich.) Pub. Schs., 1974—75, Tecumseh (Mich.) Pub. Schs., 1975—77, St. Mary Parish Sch., Monroe, Mich., 1978—80, Monroe Public Sch., 1980—2004. Contbr.: to book Cartoons and Comics in the Classroom, 1983. Pres. 4th Mich. Reenactors, Co. A, 2002, v.p., 2003. Mem.: NEA, Multi Lakes Assn. Civil War Studies, Music Educators Nat. Conf., Phi Kappa Phi, Phi Delta Kappa, Pi Kappa Lambda. Avocations: reading, golf, Civil War reenacting. Personal E-mail: bschoof2@comcast.net.

SCHOOLAR, JOSEPH CLAYTON, psychiatrist, pharmacologist, educator; b. Marks, Miss., Feb. 28, 1928; s. Adrian Taylor and Leah (Covington) S.; m. Betty Jane Peck, Nov. 2, 1960; children: Jonathan Covington, Cynthia Jane, Geoffrey Michael, Catherine Elizabeth, Adrian Carson AB, U. Tenn., Knoxville, 1950, MS, 1952; PhD, U. Chgo., 1957, MD, 1960. Diplomate Am. Bd. Psychiatry and Neurology. Chief drug abuse research TRIMS, Houston, 1966-72; assoc. prof. U. Tex. Grad. Sch. Biomed. Scis., Houston, 1968—; prof. psychiatry Baylor Coll. Medicine, Houston, 1975—, prof. pharmacology, 1974—2002, prof. emeritus pharmacology and psychiatry, 2003—, chief div. psychopharmacology, 1973-82; dir. Tex. Research Inst. Mental Scis., Houston, 1972-85. Mem. Nat. Bd. Med. Examiners' Task Force on Drug Abuse and Alcoholism, 1982-; mem. Drug Abuse Adv. Com., FDA, Washington, 1983-85, chmn., 1984; chmn. profl. needs planning task force Nat. Inst. Drug Abuse, Washington, 1977- Editor: Current Issues in Adolescent Psychiatry, 1973, Research and the Psychiatric Patient, 1975, The Kinetics of Psychiatric Drugs, 1979, Serotonin in Biological Psychiatry - Advances in Biochemical Psychopharmacology, 1982. Cons. Parents' League Houston, 1972-74; mem. coordinating com. Citizens Mental Health Service, Houston, 1976; mem. acad. com. for study of violence Houston Police Dept., 1979; bd. dirs. Can-Do-It, Houston, 1982-. Served with U.S. Army, 1945-47, to 1st lt. USAR, 1950-62. Recipient Eugen Kahn award Baylor Coll. Medicine, Houston, 1964, Alumni award for Disting. Svc., U. Chgo., 1995, Psychiat. Excellence award Tex. Soc. Psychiat. Physicians, 1995. Fellow Am. Psychiat. Assn. (disting. life), Am. Coll. Psychiatrists, Am. Coll. Neuropsychopharmacology, Collegium Internationale NeuroPsychopharmacologicum, Am. Soc. Pharmacology and Exptl. Therapeutics. Episcopalian. Home: 1111 Hermann Dr Unit 17E Houston TX 77004-6930 Office: Baylor Coll Medicine One Baylor Pla PO Box 66575 Houston TX 77265-6575 Office Phone: 713-524-9700. E-mail: jschoolar@pol.net.

SCHOOLER, SHIRLEY JEAN, writer; b. Canandaigua, NY, Jan. 2, 1937; d. Harold Carlyle and Helen Frances Belle Morris; m. William Henry Schooler, Feb. 14, 1991; m. Patrick Flanagan (dec.). Civil svc. clerical Monroe County, Rochester, NY, 1967—74; freelance writer Rochester, 1978—88; novelist, 1995—. Mem. Writers & Books, Rochester, 2003. Author: (novels) The Red Sea Place, 2003. Sponsor Christian Found. for Children & Aging, Kans. City, 1996—2004 Mem.: publishedauthors.net. Republican. Roman Catholic. Avocations: reading, cooking, travel, politics. Home: 5 Colonial Parkway #1 Pittsford NY 14534

SCHOOLEY, ROBERT T. medical educator; b. Denver, Nov. 10, 1949; s. Robert Enoch and Lelia Francis (Barnhill) S.; m. Constance Benson; children: Kimberly Dana, Elizabeth Kendall. BS, Washington and Lee U., 1970; MD, Johns Hopkins U., 1974. Diplomate Am. Bd. Internal Medicine. Intern Johns Hopkins Hosp., Balt., 1974-75, resident, 1975-76; clin. assoc. lab. clin. investigation Nat. Inst. Allergy & Infectious Disease, NIH, Bethesda, Md., 1976-77, chief clin. assoc. lab. clin. investigation, 1977-78, med. officer lab. clin. investigation, 1978-79; from instr. to assoc. prof. medicine Harvard Med. Sch., Boston, 1979-90; prof. medicine U. Colo., Denver, 1990—. Dir. Colo. Ctr. for AIDS Rsch., 2003—. Mem. editl. bd.: Antimicrobial Agts. and Chemotherapy, 1987—2000, Biotherapy, 1987—95, Jour. Acquired Immune Deficiency Syndromes, 1988—, Clin. and Diagnostic Lab. Immunology, 1992, assoc. editor: Clin. Infectious Diseases, 2002—; contbr. articles to profl. jours. Clin. and rsch. fellow Infectious Disease Unit, Mass. Gen. Hosp., Boston, 1979-81; rsch. fellow Medicine Harvard Med. Sch., 1979-81; recipient Bonfils-Stanton award for sci. and medicine. Fellow Infectious Disease Soc. Am.; mem. AAAS, Am. Assn. Immunologists, Am. Soc. Clin. Investigation, Assn. Am. Physicians, Omicron Delta Kappa. Office Phone: 303-315-7233. E-mail: robert.schooley@uchsc.edu.

SCHOOLS, CHARLES HUGHLETTE, banker, lawyer; b. Lansing, Mich., May 24, 1929; s. Robert Thomas and Lillian Pearl (Lawson) S.; m. Rosemarie Sanchez, Nov. 22, 1952; children: Charles, Michael. BS, Am. U., 1952, MA, 1958; JD, Washington Coll. of Law, 1973; LLD, Bethune-Cookman U., 1973. Dir. phys. plant Am. U., 1952-66, owner, 1957—, Gen. Security Co., Washington, 1969—. Chmn., pres. Consol. Ventures Ltd.; pres., chmn. bd. McLean Bank (Va.), 1974—, Instl. Environ. Mgmt. Services; chmn. bd. Harper & Co.; chmn., pres. Community Assos. of Va., Associated Real Estate Mgmt. Services; dir. Computer Data Systems Inc., DAC Devel. Ltd., Am. Indsl. Devel. Corp., Intercoastal of Iran; mem. Met. Bd. Trades. Pres. McLean Boys' Club; bd. dirs. D.C. Spl. Olympics, Nat. Kidney Found.; trustee Bethune Cookman Coll., Western Md. Coll., Randolph Macon Acad. With USAAF, 1946-47, USAF, 1947-48. Mem. Va. C. of C., Profl. Businessman's Orgn., Georgetown Club of Washington, Touchdown Club of Washington, Univ. of Washington Club, Washington Golf and Country Club, Pisces Club (Washington), Halifax Club (Daytona Beach, Fla.), Masons, Alpha Tau Omega. Democrat. Office: 1313 Dolley Madison Blvd Mc Lean VA 22101-3926 Home: 458 S Beach St Ormond Beach FL 32174-7034

SCHOOLWERTH, ANTON C. nephrologist, educator; b. Surabaya, Indonesia, Nov. 17, 1941; s. Anton and Helene J. Schoolwerth; m. Judith Ann Emery, Aug. 12, 1967; children: Pieter Emery, Sara Ann, Kate Robinson. AB, Princeton U., 1963; MD, Harvard U., 1967; MS in Health Adminstrn., Va. Commonwealth U., 1997. Diplomate Am. Bd. Internal Medicine (in nephrology). Chief renal divsn. Penn State U. Coll. Medicine, Hershey, Pa., 1974—85; prof., chmn. divsn. nephrology, dept. internal medicine Med. Coll. of Va., Va. Commonwealth U., Richmond, 1985—2003, vice chmn. dept. internal medicine, 1993—2003; sr. cons. Chronic Kidney Disease Ctrs. for Disease Control and Prevention, 2004—. Vis. prof., nephrology sect. Dartmouth-Hitchcock Med. Ctr., Lebanon, NH, 2003—. Mem. adv. bd. kidney diseases outcomes quality initiative Nat. Kidney Found., N.Y.C., 2002—03; pres. Nat. Kidney Found. Va., Richmond, 2001—02. Mem.: Am. Soc. Hypertension (specialist in hypertension). Office: Dartmouth-Hitchcock Med Ctr One Medical Dr Lebanon NH 03756

SCHOOMAKER, PETER J. US Army Chief of Staff; BS in Edn. Adminstrn., U. Wyo., 1969; MA in Mgmt., Cen. Mich. U.; grad., USMC Amphibious War Sch., U.S. Army Command/Gen. Staff, Nat. War Coll.; LLD (hon.), Hampden-Sydney Coll. Commd. 2d lt. U.S. Army, 1969, advanced through grades to gen., 1997; comdr. troop C, 1st Squadron, 2d Armored Cavalry Regiment U.S. Army Europe and 7th Army, Germany, 1973-74; assignment officer Officer Pers. Mgmt. Directorate U.S. Army Mil. Pers. Ctr., Alexandria, Va., 1976-78; comdr. 1st Spl. Forces Operational Detachment Ft. Bragg, N.C., 1978-81; exec. officer 2d Squadron, 2d Armored Cavalry Regiment U.S. Army Europe and 7th Army, Germany, 1982-83; spl. ops. officer J-3 Joint Spl. Ops. Command Ft. Bragg, N.C., 1984-85; comdr. Combat Applications Group, Ft. Bragg, 1989-92; asst. divsn. comdr. 1st Cavalry Divsn., Ft. Hood, Tex., 1992-93; dep. dir. ops., readiness and mobilization Office of Dep. Chief of Staff Ops. and Plans, U.S. Army, Washington, 1993-94; comdg. gen. Joint Spl. Ops. Command U.S. Spl. Ops. Command, Ft. Bragg, 1994-96, comdg. gen., 1996-97, comdg. in chief, 1997—2000; chief of staff US Army, Washington, 2003—. Decorated Disting. Svc. medal, Def. Superior Svc. medal with 3 oak leaf clusters, Legion of Merit with 2 oak leaf clusters, Bronze Star medal with oak leaf cluster, Def. Meritorious Svc. medal with oak leaf cluster, Meritorious Svc. medal with 2 oak leaf clusters. Office: Pentagon 200 Army Washington DC 20310

SCHOONE, ADRIAN PAUL, lawyer; b. Harrison, Wis., Dec. 5, 1935; s. Adrian M. and Agnes (Zuiker) S.; m. Sally A Hall, Apr. 24, 1986; children—Mary Jude, Elizabeth, Stephen, Amalia. B.S., Marquette U., 1957, LL.B. cum laude, 1959. Bar: Wis. 1959, U.S. Dist. Ct. (ea. dist.) Wis. 1959, U.S. Ct. Appeals, (7th cir.) 1973. Assoc. Wood, Brady, Tyrell, Milw., 1960-61; mem. LaFrance, Thompson, Greenquist, Evans & Dye, Racine, Wis., 1961-70; ptnr. Schoone, McManus, Hankel, Ware & Fortune, Racine, 1970—; lectr. in field. Pres., Racine Commn. on Human Rights, 1967; mem. Wis. Equal Rights Council, 1969-71; mem. exec. com., life mem. Pres. Council, Marquette U., 1977— . Mem. Racine County Bar Assn., ABA, State Bar Wis. (pres. 1983-84), Assn. Trial Lawyers Am., Wis. Acad. Trial Lawyers, Def. Research Inst., Ins. Trial Counsel Wis., State Wis. Jud. Commn., Woolsack Soc., Alpha Sigma Nu. Club: Kenosha Country. Contbr. articles to profl. jours. Address: PO Box 97 Racine WI 53401-0097

SCHOONHOVEN, RAY JAMES, retired lawyer; b. Elgin, Ill., May 24, 1921; s. Ray Covey and Rosina Madeline (Schram) (White) S.; m. Marie Theresa Dunn, Dec. 11, 1943; children: Marie Kathleen "Kamie", Ray James, Jr., Pamela Suzanne, John Philip, Rose Lynn. BSC., U. Notre Dame, 1943; JD, Northwestern U., 1948. Bar: Ill. 1949, U.S. Supreme Ct. 1954, D.C. 1973, U.S. Ct. Mil. Appeals 1954. Assoc. Seyfarth, Shaw Fairweather & Geraldson, Chgo., 1949-57; ptnr. Seyfarth, Shaw Fairweather & Geraldson now Seyfarth Shaw, Chgo., 1957-92; ret. Chief rulings and ops. br. Wage Stabilization Bd. Region VII, Chgo., 1951-52. Book rev. editor: Ill. Law Rev., 1948. Served to lt.comdr. USNR, 1942-62. Mem. ABA, Ill. State Bar Assn., Chgo. Bar Assn., D.C. Bar Assn., Chgo. Athletic Assn., Univ. Club. Chgo., Fed. Bar Assn., Order of Coif. Republican. Roman Catholic. Home: 1182 Lynette Dr Lake Forest IL 60045-4601 Office: Seyfarth Shaw 55 E Monroe St Ste 4200 Chicago IL 60603-5863 Office Phone: 312-346-8000. *I work hard to preserve our free enterprise system and, hopefully, to make such contribution to our society that it is better for my having been a part of it.*

SCHOONMAKER, SAMUEL VAIL, III, lawyer; b. Newburgh, N.Y., Sept. 1, 1935; s. Samuel V. Jr. and Catherine (Wilson) S.; m. Carolyn Peters, Sept. 18, 1965; children: Samuel V. IV, Frederick P. BA magna cum laude, Yale U., 1958, JD, 1961. Bar: Conn. 1961, U.S. Dist. Ct. Conn. 1961, U.S. Dist. Ct. (so. and ea. dist.) N.Y. 1964, U.S. Ct. Appeals (2d cir.) 1964, U.S. Supreme Ct. 1965. Assoc. Cummings & Lockwood, Stamford, Conn., 1961-70, co-mng. ptnr., 1987-90, mng. ptnr., 1990-94, chmn. exec. com., 1987-96; founder, pres. Schoonmaker George & Colin, P.C., Greenwich, Conn., 1996—. State trial referee Conn. Superior Ct., 1989; pres. Schoonmaker Family Assn., New Paltz, N.Y., 1975-77. Sr. topical editor Conn. Bar Jour., 1977-81; mem. editl. bd. Fairshare and Am. Jour. Family Law, 1992—; contbr. articles to profl. jours. Chmn. Conn. Child Support Commn., 1984-86; mem. Conn. Family Support Com., 1986-90; mem. Darien (Conn.) Rep. Town Com., 1974-76, rep. town meeting, 1990-98; pres. Youth Tennis Found. New Eng., Needham, Mass., 1975-77; pres. New Eng. Lawn Tennis Assn., 1977-79 (Man of Yr. award 1979); pres., trustee Huegenot Hist. Soc., 1999—. Fellow Am. Acad. Matrimonial Lawyers Conn. (bd. mgrs., Disting. Svc. award 1988), Internat. Acad. Matrimonial Lawyers, Am. Bar Found.; mem. ABA (chmn. family law sect. 1982-83), Conn. Bar Assn. (chmn. family law sect. 1971-74), Conn. Bus. and Industry Assn. (bd. dirs. 1993-98), S.W. Conn. Bus. and Industry Assn. (bd. dirs. 1990-97), Pub. Defenders Assn. (chmn.), Wee Burn Country Club (Darien, Conn., asst. sec.), Yale Club (N.Y.C.), Phi Beta Kappa. Avocations: tennis, platform tennis. Home: 231 Old Kings Hwy S Darien CT 06820-5931 Office: Schoonmaker George & Colin PC PO Box 5059 81 Holly Hill Ln Greenwich CT 06831-5059

SCHOONMAKER POWELL, THELMA, film editor; b. 1940; m. Michael Powell, 1984 (dec. 1990). Editor: (films) Who's That Knocking at My Door, 1968, Woodstock, 1970 (Academy award nomination best film editing 1970), Raging Bull, 1980 (Academy award best film editing 1980), The King of Comedy, 1983, After Hours, 1985, The Color of Money, 1986, The Last Temptation of Christ, 1988, New York Stories (Life Lessons), 1989, GoodFellas, 1990 (Academy award nomination best film editing 1990), Cape Fear, 1992, The Age of Innocence, 1993, A Personal Journey with Martin Scorsese Through American Movies, 1995, Casino, 1995 (Am. Cinema Editors nomination best film editing 1995), Kundun, 1997, Bringing Out The Dead, 1999, Il Mio Viaggio in Italia, 2000, Gangs of New York, 2002 (Am. Cinema Editors award best dramatic film editing 2003, Acad. Award Nomination best film editing 2003). Office: Sikelia Prodns 110 W 57th St New York NY 10019

SCHOONOVER, ALEXANDRA CHERI, special education educator; b. Stockton, Calif., Sept. 12, 1969; d. Patrick David and Doreen Rochelle (Walker) Schoonover. AA, Am. River Coll., 1991; BA, Calif. State U., 2000. Tchr. Stanislaus Office of Edn., Modesto, Calif., 2000—; instr. Howard tng. Ctr., Modesto, Calif., 2003—. Substitute tchr. Kelly Svcs., Modesto, 2003—. Active Rep. Party, Turlock, Calif., 1992—95. Republican. Greek Orthodox. Avocations: genealogy, bicycling, hiking, writing.

SCHOONOVER, BRENDA B. ambassador; BA, Morgan State U., Balt.; postgrad., Howard U. Vol. Peace Corps, Philippines, 1961, adminstr. Office Talent Search, assoc. dir., dir. sch. partnership program; affirmative action officer Govt. of Arlington County, Va.; with Fgn. Svc. U.S. Dept. State, Manila, Colombo, Sri Lanka, Tunis, Tunisia, with Bur. Near East and South Asia Washington, 1978-88, chief pers. Bur. European and Can. Affairs, 1988-91, mem. Sr. Seminar, 1996-97; adminstrv. officer, dept. dir. Office Joint Adminstrv. Svcs. Am. Embassy, Brussels, 1992-96; Capstone fellow Nat. Def. U., Washington, 1997; U.S. amb. to Togo Am. Embassy, Lome, 1998-2000; amb.-in-residence Chapel Hill, NC, 2000—01; chargé d'affairs, ad interim min. counselor Am. Embassy, Brussels, 2001—. Recipient Order of the Mono award, The Togolese Govt., 2000, Presdl. Meritorious award, U.S., 2003, Sec. of State Career Achievement award, 2004. Mem.: Zonta Internat. Office: 108 Ironwoods Dr Chapel Hill NC 27516 E-mail: RCSchoon2@aol.com.

SCHOONOVER, JACK RONALD, retired judge; b. Winona, Minn., July 23, 1934; s. Richard M. and Elizabeth A. (Hargeisheimer) S.; m. Ann Marie Kroez, June 18, 1965; children: Jack Ronald, Wayne J. Student, Winona State Coll., 1956-58; LLB, U. Fla., 1962. Bar: Fla. 1962. Atty. Wotitzky, Wotitzky & Schoonover, 1962-69, Schoonover, Olmsted & Schwarz, 1969-75; spl. asst. state's atty. State of Fla., 1969-72; city atty. City of Punta Gorda, Fla., city judge, 1973-74; judge 20th Jud. Cir. Ct., Ft. Myers, Fla., 1975-81, 2d Dist. Ct. Appeal, 1981-97, chief judge, 1990-92, ret., 1997. Atty. Charlotte County Sch. Bd., 1969-75, Charlotte County Zoning Bd., Charlotte County Devel. Authority; mem. unauthorized practice law com. 12th Jud. Cir., mem. grievance com. 20th Jud. Cir.; adj. prof. Edison C.C.; tchr. Charlotte County Adult Edn. Assn. Served with USAF, 1952-56. Home and Office: 14380 Olde Hickory Blvd Fort Myers FL 33912-0816

SCHOONOVER, JAMES A. lab administrator; Divsnl. v.p. Olsten Corp.; with Medtox Labs., 1997—2000, v.p., sales and mktg., chief mktg., 2000—. Office: Medtox Scientific Inc 402 W County Rd D Saint Paul MN 55112*

SCHOONOVER, JEAN WAY, public relations consultant; b. Richfield Springs, NY; AB, Cornell U., 1941. With D-A-Y Pub. Rels., Ogilvy & Mather Co., N.Y.C., 1949-91, D-A-Y Pub. Rels. Inc. and predecessor, N.Y.C., 1949—; owner, pres. Dudley-Anderson-Yutzy Pub. Rels. Inc. and predecessor, N.Y.C., 1970—, chmn., 1984-88; merger with Ogilvy & Mather, 1983; sr. v.p. Ogilvy & Mather U.S., 1984-91; vice chmn. Ogilvy Pub. Relations Group, 1986-91; ind. cons., 1992—; pres. YWCA of the City of N.Y., 1994-98. Historian, Pub. Rels. Seminar; mem. USDA Agribus. Promotion Coun., 1985-86. Trustee Cornell U., 1975-80; mem. Def. Adv. Com. on Women in Svcs., 1987-89. Named Advt. Woman of Yr. Am. Advt. Fedn., 1972, one of Outstanding Women in Bus. & Labor, Women's Equity Action League, 1985; recipient Matrix award, 1976, Nat. Headliner award, 1984, N.Y. Women in Comm., 1976, Leadership award Internat. Orgn. Women Bus. Owners, 1980, Entrepreneurial Woman award Women Bus. Owners N.Y., 1981, Women of Distinction award Soroptimists Internat. N.Y., 1995, Achievement award LWV of N.Y.C., 1997. Mem. Women Execs. in Pub. Rels. N.Y.C. (pres. 1979-80), Pub. Rels. Soc. Am., Pub. Rels. Soc. N.Y. (pres. 1979), Womens Forum, Women's City Club. Home and Office: 25 Stuyvesant St New York NY 10003-7505

SCHOONOVER, MARGARET See LEFRANC, MARGARET

SCHOONOVER, PHILIP, retail executive; m. Cindi Schoonover; 2 children. Degree in mktg. and fin., U. N.H.; postgrad., Boston Coll. Former sales and mktg. exec. Sony Corp. Am.; former exec. v.p., gen. merchandise mgr. TOPS Appliances; sr. v.p. digital tech. Best Buy Co., Inc., 1995—2001, exec. v.p. digital solutions, 2001—02, exec. v.p. bus. devel., 2002—. Active Anti-Defamation League, United Jewish Appeal, Chabad Ho., United Way, Wayzata (Minn.) Yacht Club Youth Sailing Program. Avocation: sailing. Office: Best Buy Co Inc 110 SE 6th St Fort Lauderdale FL 33301

SCHOPF, JAMES WILLIAM, paleobiologist, researcher, educator; b. Urbana, Ill., Sept. 27, 1941; s. James Morton and Esther Julie (Nissen) S.; m. Julie Morgan, Aug. 7, 1965 (div. 1979); 1 child, James Christopher; m. Jane Shen, Jan. 16, 1980. AB with high honors, Oberlin Coll., 1963; A.M., Harvard U., 1965, PhD (Harvard fellow, NSF fellow), 1968. Research chemist NASA Ames Research Center, Calif., 1967; mem. lunar sample preliminary exam. team Manned Spacecraft Center, Tex., 1968-71; asst. prof. dept. earth and space scis. UCLA, 1968-70, assoc. prof., 1970-73, prof., 1973—, mem. Inst. Evolutionary and Environ. Biology, 1970-76, mem. Inst. Geophysics and Planetary Physics, 1973—, dean honors div. Coll. Letters and Sci., 1983-85, dir. Ctr. for Study Evolution and Origin of Life, 1985—, Sigma Xi Disting. lectr., 1976, Rubey lectr., 1976, Golden Yr. Disting. lectr., 1980, Faculty Research lectr., 1984; Sigma Xi Disting. lectr. U. Cin., 1980; Disting. lectr. Buffalo Mus. Sci., 1982; J.A. Bownocker lectr. Ohio State U., 1982. Vis. lectr. Am. Inst. Biol. Scis. Vis. Biologists Program, 1969-72; M.W. Haas vis. disting. prof. geology U. Kans., 1979; extraordinary vis. prof. exobiology U. Nijmegen, Netherlands, 1980-81; C. O'Neal lectr. Ohio Wesleyan U., 1982; Sandia disting. lectr. U. N.Mex., 1985; Sigma Xi disting. lectr. U. Oreg., 1985; Du Pont disting. lectr. U. Ill., 1985; R. Stanier disting. lectr. U. Calif.-Berkeley, 1987; H.P. Mangelsdorf disting. lectr. U. N.C., 1987; mem. Bot. Soc. Am. del., People's Republic China, 1978; Academia Sinica vis. research scientist, People's Republic China, 1981, 82; mem. NASA Terrestrial Bodies Sci. Working Group, 1975-76, space program adv. council NASA Life Scis. Com., 1976-78, NASA Working Group on Origins of Life, 1978-79, NASA Space Sci. Adv. Com., 1979-82, mem. NASA Life Scis. Strategic Planning Study Com., 1985—; Alan T. Waterman Award com. NSF, 1978-81; mem. working group on precambrian biostratigraphy Internat. Geol. Correlation Program, UNESCO, 1975—; mem. Working Group on Cambrian-Precambrian Boundary, 1976—; mem. adv. com. USSR and Eastern Europe, Commn. Internat. Relations NRC, 1981-85, mem. bd. earth sci. Commn. Phys. Scis., Math. and Resources, 1982-85, mem. space sci. bd., 1983-86; mem . com. on guidelines for paleontol. collecting, 1984-86, sub.-com. on evolution and diversity Commn. on Life Scis., 1986; mem. com. space research Internat.

Council Sci. Unions Mem. editorial bd.: Origins of Life, 1973—, Precambrian Research, 1973—, Evolutionary Theory, 1973—, U. Calif. Press, 1973-82, Paleobiology, 1974-83, Geomicrobiology Jour., 1977—, Evolutionary Monographs, 1977—; contbr. articles to profl. jours. Bd. dirs. Brentwood Glen (Calif.) Assn., 1972-75; trustee UCLA Found., 1983-85. Recipient N.Y. Bot. Garden award Bot. Soc. Am., 1966; Group Achievement award NASA, 1969; Outstanding Paper award Jour. Paleontology, 1971; Charles Schuchert award Paleontol. Soc., 1974; Disting. Teaching award UCLA, 1977; Alan T. Waterman award NSF, 1977; G. Hawk award U. Kans., 1979; spl. recognition diploma NASA, 1979; Outstanding Vol. in Phys. Scis. award Am. Assn. Pubs., 1983; Mark Clark Thompson medal Nat. Acad. Scis., 1986; Guggenheim fellow, 1973; U.S. Nat. Acad. Scis. exchange scientist USSR, 1975 Fellow Geol. Soc. Am. (vice-chmn. Cordilleran sect. 1983-84, chmn. 1984-85); mem. Bot. Soc. Am. (com. on sci. liaison with People's Republic China 1978—), Paleontol. Soc. (mem. Schuchert Award com. 1978-82), Internat. Soc. Study of Origin of Life (treas. 1977-83, nat. meeting adv. com. 1980, 83, 86, councilor, 1983—), Geochem. Soc. (nominating com. 1980-82), Soc. Study of Evolution (edn. com. 1980-83), Am. Philos. Soc., Sigma Xi (treas. UCLA chpt. 1972-74, chpt. v.p. 1984-84, pres. 1984-85). Office: UCLA Dept Earth Space Scis Los Angeles CA 90095-0001

SCHOPP, DAVID L. music educator; b. Tyrone, Pa., Oct. 1, 1965; s. David A. and Lee A. Schopp; m. Beth L. Rogers, June 24, 2000; 1 child, Maxwell. BS in Music Edn., Pa. State U., 1987. Music tchr. Tredyfrin-Easttown, Devon, Pa., 1987—88; band dir. Norristown (Pa.) Area HS, 1988—99, Hatboro-Horsham (Pa.) HS, 1999—. Recipient Gift of Time award, Am. Family Inst., 1990, 1992. Mem.: Music Educators Nat. Conf., Pa. Music Educators Assn. Office: Hatboro Horsham HS 899 Horsham Rd Horsham PA 19044 E-mail: dschopp@hatboro-horsham.org.

SCHOPPA, ELROY, accountant, financial planner; b. Vernon, Tex., Aug. 25, 1922; s. Eddie A. and Ida S.; m. Juanita C. Young, Aug. 11, 1956 (div.); children: Karen Marie, Vickie Sue. BBA, Tex. Tech. U., 1943; postgrad. Law Sch., U. Tex., 1946-47; MA, Mich. State U., 1950. CPA, Tex., Calif.; cert. real estate broker; cert. ins. agt.; notary public. Mem. faculty Tex. Tech. U., Lubbock, 1943, U. Tex., Austin, 1946-47, Mich. State U., East Lansing, 1947-50; auditor GM Corp., 1950-56; dir. systems and procedures Fansteel Metall. Corp., 1956-59; gen. auditor Consol. Electro Dynamics Corp., 1959-60; auditor, sr. tax acct. Beckman Inst. Inc., Fullerton, Calif., 1960-70; pres. Elroy Schoppa Acctg. Corp., La Habra, Calif., 1960—. Fin. planner Nat. Assn. Stock Dealers; bd. dirs., chmn. Mexican Ventures, Inc. (dba Baja BUDs, Del Norte); cons. to bus. CEO, pres., founder The Schoppa Family Found., 1999—; treas. La Habra Devel. Corp.; organizer, pres., 4-H Club, Vernon, Tex.; adviser Jr. Achievement, Waukegan, Ill.; bd. dirs. Klein Ctr. for Prevention of Domestic Violence; asst. football and basketball coach, Manzanola, Colo.; coach Am. Girls Sport Assn., La Habra; notary pub., 2002—. Served with USN, 1942-46, USNR, 1946-62. Mem. Calif. Soc. CPAs, USS LSM/LSMR Orgn., Phoenix Club (Anaheim, Calif.), Alpha Phi Omega, Theta Chi. Republican. Lutheran. Avocations: hunting, fishing, camping, travel. Office: 801 E La Habra Blvd Ste B La Habra CA 90631-5531

SCHOPPMEYER, MARTIN WILLIAM, education educator; b. Weehawken, N.J., Sept. 15, 1929; s. William G. and Madeleine M. (Haas) S.; m. Marilyn M. Myers, Aug. 9, 1958; children: Susan Ann, Martin William. BS, Fordham U., 1950; EdM, U. Fla., 1955, EdD, 1962. Tchr. Fla. pub. sch., 1955-59; instr., then asst. prof. U. Fla., 1960-63; assoc. prof., then prof. edn. Fla. Atlantic U., Boca Raton, Fla., 1963-68, dir. continuing edn., 1965-67; mem. faculty U. Ark., Fayetteville, Ark., 1968—, prof. edn., 1971-93, Univ. prof., 1993—99, Univ. prof. emeritus, 1999—, program coord. for ednl. adminstrn., 1983-90. Mem. Nat. Adv. Coun. Edn. Professions Devel., 1973-76; exec. sec. Ark. Sch. Study Coun., 1976—; evaluator instructional tng. program Nat. Tng. Fund, 1978; bd. dirs. Women's Ednl. and Devel. Inst., 1977-80, Nat. Sch. Devel. Coun., sec., 1989-90, v.p. 1990, pres., 1990-92; mem. oversight com. South Conway (Ark.) County Sch. Dist.; mem. state commn. to study effect of Amendment 59 to Ark. Constn.; cons. Lake View V. Huckabee, 1994-2002. Author book, monographs, articles in field. Mem. president's coun. Subiaco Acad., 1984-90; chmn. Subiaco Sch. Bd., 1990-93, mem., 1993-97. With U.S. Army, 1951-53, Korea. Recipient numerous fed. grants. Mem. V.F.W., Ark. Edn. Assn. (past chpt. pres.), Ark. Assn. Ednl. Adminstrs., KC, Rotary, Kappa Delta Pi, Phi Delta Kappa, Delta Tau Kappa. Roman Catholic. Home: 2950 Sheryl Ave Fayetteville AR 72703-3542 E-mail: mschoppmeyer@cox.-internet.com. *The only really sound investment for a family, a community, or a society is that money spent for the education of its youth.*

SCHOR, JOSEPH MARTIN, pharmaceutical executive, biochemist; b. Bklyn., Jan. 10, 1929; s. Aaron Jacob and Rhea Iress (Kay) S.; children: Esther Helen, Joshua David, Gideon Alexander, Eric, Neil; m. Laura Sharon Strumingher, June 14, 1992. BS magna cum laude, CCNY, 1951; PhD, Fla. State U., 1957. Sr. rsch. chemist Armour Pharm. Co., Kankakee, Ill., 1957-59, Lederle Labs., Pearl River, N.Y., 1959-64; dir. biochemistry Endo Labs., Garden City, N.Y., 1964-70; head dept. biochemistry DuPont and Endo Labs., 1970-77; v.p. sci. affairs Forest Labs., N.Y.C., 1977-94, sr. v.p. sci. affairs emeritus, 1995—. Editor, contbr.: Chemical Control of Fibrinolysis-thrombolysis, 1970. Contbr. articles to profl. jours. Patentee in field. USPHS fellow, 1955-57. Fellow Am. Inst. Chemists (cert. prof. chemist); mem. Am. Chem. soc. (chmn. Nassau County subsect. 1971-72), Internat. Soc. on Thrombosis and Hemostasis, N.Y. Acad. Scis., AAAS, Phi Beta Kappa, Sigma Xi. Home: 28 Meleny Rd Locust Valley NY 11560-1221 E-mail: joseph.m.schor@verizon.net.

SCHOR, LAURA STRUMINGHER, historian; b. N.Y.C., June 24, 1945; d. David Charles and Esther Rachel (Pearl) Gross; children: Eric Alain, Neil Remy; m. Joseph Martin Schor, June, 1992. BA, Queens Coll., CUNY, 1967; MA, U. Rochester, 1970, PhD, 1974. Asst. prof. SUNY, Fredonia, 1973-79; assoc. prof., dir. women's studies U. Cin., 1979-85, prof., vice provost, 1985-89; prof., provost, v.p. acad. affairs Hunter Coll., CUNY, N.Y.C., 1989-98; exec. dir. Hadassah, The Women's Zionist Orgn. of Am., Inc., N.Y.C., 1998-2000; dean CUNY Honors Coll., 2001—. Author: Women and the Making of the Working Class, 1979, What Were Little Boys and Girls Made Of?, 1984, The Odyssey of Flora Tristan, 1988, Les Jolies Femmes d'Edouard de Beaumont, 1994. Mem. Internat. Soc. for Study European Ideas, Am. Hist. Assn., French Hist. Assn., Phi Beta Kappa.

SCHOR, LAURENCE, lawyer; b. Bklyn., May 3, 1942; s. Julius and Ruth (Zackowitz) S.; m. Susan Leslie Gurevitz, Dec. 26, 1965; children: Meredith Nan, Joseph Sanford, Wendy Claire, Samuel Julius. BBA, So. Meth. U., 1963; JD, U. Tex., 1966; LLM, George Washington U., 1972. Bar: Tex. 1966, D.C. 1971, Md. 1993.; U.S. Ct. Appeals (D.C., 4th, 5th, 11th cirs.). Atty. NASA, Huntsville, Ala., 1966-68; asst. gen. counsel NASA support U.S. Army C.E., Washington, 1968-70; assoc. Sellers, Conner & Cuneo, Washington, 1970-73; from assoc. to ptnr. Max E. Greenberg, Trayman, Cantor, Reiss & Blasky, Washington, 1974-80; ptnr. Schnader, Harrison, Segal & Lewis, Washington, 1981-91, ptnr.-in-charge, 1986-88; mem. Miller & Chevalier, Washington, 1991-93; ptnr. Smith, Somerville & Case, LLC, Washington, 1993-96, McManus, Schor, Asmar & Darden, LLP, Washington, 1997—. Lectr. George Washington U., others. Author: The Right to Stop Work, 1991; author: (manual) Delays, Suspensions and Acceleration, Workplace Safety and Health in the 1990's, 1992; author: Claims Against Bonding Companies, Construction Contractors' Handbook of Business and Law, 1992, How to File a Federal Contract Claim, 1998, 2003; co-author: Suing a Government: Special Considerations for Book Construction Disputes: Representing the Contractor, 3d edit., 2001; author, editor 50 State Lien and Bond Laws, 1993—2004, Vol. 3 Form Book rewrite, 2000, editor update, 2001—04; contbr. chapters to books, articles to profl. jours. Founder, pres. Manor Lake Civic Assn., Montgomery County, 1969-71; precinct chmn. Montgomery County Dems., 1972-76; mem. D.C. City Coun. Procurement Reform Task Force, 1995-96. Mem. ABA (chmn. region III pub. contract law sect., 1982-88, chmn. constrn. com. 1986-90, sect. budget and fin. 1990-95), D.C. Bar Assn. (chmn. divsn. 10 govt. contracts and litigation, 1981-85), Fed. Bar Assn., Am. Coll. Constrn. Lawyers (founder, bd. govs., treas. 1996-2000, pres. elect 2000, pres. 2001-02), B'nai B'rith Youth Orgn (adult adv. bd. 2001-02), Phi Alpha Delta (pres. T.C. Clark chpt. 1965-66). Jewish. Avocations: reading, travel. Home: 7021 Mountain Gate Dr Bethesda MD 20817-3913 Office: McManus Schor Asmar & Darden LLP 1301 Connecticut Ave NW Fl 6 Washington DC 20036-1815 Office Phone: 202-296-9260. Business E-Mail: lschor@msadlaw.com.

SCHOR, OLGA SEEMANN, mental health counselor, real estate broker; b. Havana, Cuba, Mar. 2, 1951; came to U.S., 1961; d. Olga del Carmen (Hernandez) S.; m. David Michael Schor, Apr. 22, 1979; 1 child, Andrew. AA, Miami Dade Community Coll., 1971; BA, U. Fla., Gainesville, 1973; M.Edn., U. Miami, Fla., 1976; Psy.D., Nova U., 1981. Cert. Bert Rodgers Sch. Real Estate, Miami, 1981, Gold Coast Sch. Real Estate, 1988; lic. real estate broker. Teaching asst. U. Fla., Gainesville, 1972-73; counselor U. Miami, 1974-79; assoc. psychotherapist Linda H. Jamrozy & Assocs., Miami, 1976-78, Interactive Systems, Miami, 1978-79; psychometrist Jackson Meml. Hosp., Miami, 1979-85, tony Ciminero & Assocs., Miami, 1985-86; lectr. U. Miami, 1976-78, Jackson Meml. Hosp. Sch. Nursing, Miami, 1976; real estate broker The Keyes Co. Realtor, Coral Gables, 1981-88, Keyes Asset Mgmt., Miami, 1988—; CEO My Co. Realty, Inc., 1997—. Sec./treas. bd. dirs. BODS Inc., Miami. Chmn. creative writing Jr. Orange Bowl competition. Recipient Assoc. of Quarter award Keyes Co. Realtors, 1986. Mem. Am. Psychol. and Guidance Assn., Keyes Comml. Roundtable, Keyes Inner Circle, Coral Gables Bd. Realtors, Guilliver Acad.'s Parents Bd., Dade County Mental Health Assn., Million Dollar Sales Club. Clubs: South Fla. Sailing Assn. (Miami). Avocations: sailing, diving, reading, running, theater, acting, tennis. Office: My Company Realty Inc 2050 Coral Way Ste 505 Miami FL 33145-2682 Home: 15000 Old Cutler Rd Miami FL 33158-2116 E-mail: artistme@aol.com.

SCHOR, STANLEY SIDNEY, mathematical sciences educator; b. Phila., Mar. 3, 1922; s. Joseph and Dorothy (Abrams) S.; m. Irene Sternberg, June 19, 1949; children— Mark, Robin, Randi. AB, U. Pa., 1943, AM, 1950, PhD, 1952; certificate, U. Cin., 1944. Instr. U. Pa., Phila., 1950-53, asst. prof. stats., 1953-58, assoc. prof., 1958-64, dir. Nat. Periodic Health Exam. Research Group, 1958-64; dir. dept. biostats. AMA, Chgo., 1964-66; prof. biostats. Chgo. Med. Sch., 1964-66; prof., chmn. dept. biometrics Temple U. Med. Sch., 1966-75, adj. prof., 1975-85. Vis. prof. Tel Aviv U., 1973-74, Med. Coll. Pa., 1979; exec. dir. Cbards, Merck Sharp & Dohme, West Point, Pa., 1975-91; clin. prof. Hahnemann Med. Sch., 1975-85; cons. in field. Author: Fundamentals of Biostatistics, 1968; mem. editorial staff Jour. Trauma, 1955-91, Jour. AMA, 1964-91, Chest, 1966-91; contbr. articles to profl. jours. Served with AUS, 1943-46. Recipient Career Achievement award Pharm. Rsch. and Mfrs. Am., 1996, Stanley S. Schor fellowship in biostatistics U. N.C. and Merck given in his honor. Fellow Am. Public Health Assn., Am. Statis. Assn. (Career Achievement award), Phila. Coll. Physicians; mem. AAUP, Biometric Soc., Royal Soc. Health, Pi Gamma Mu. Home: 3912 S Ocean Blvd Apt 1105 Highland Beach FL 33487-3336

SCHOR, SUZI, lawyer, psychologist; b. Chgo., Feb. 1, 1947; d. Samuel S. and Dorothy Helen (Hineline); 1 child, Kate. BSBA, Ind. U., 1964; JD, Northwestern U., 1970, U. Palmer's Green, London, 1971; PhD in Fine Arts (hon.), U. Nev., PhD in Clin. Psychology, 1989, Kensington U., 1989. Bar: Ill., 1971. Pvt. practice, L.A., 1971-80; v.p. legal affairs Little Gypzy Mgmt., Inc., Beverly Hills, Calif., 1980—; trust officer, pvt. fiduciary svcs. Bank of Am., L.A. Mem. Pres.'s Coun. on Alcoholism. Author: 13th Step to Death, 1995; contbg. author Wine and Dine Mag.; contbr. articles to profl. jours. Bd. dirs. Nat. Ctr. for Hyperactive Children, L.A., 1989-91, sec. Rainbow Guild Cancer Charity, L.A., 1985-89, ind. cons. Jewish Legal Aid, L.A., 1988—; campaign coord. advisor Dem. Nat. Campaign, L.A., 1990, 94, 2000; donor mem. L.A. Coun. on World Affairs. Recipient Poet of Yr. award Nat. Libr. and Assn. of Poetry, 1995, 98. Mem. ABA (criminal justice com. 1994), AAUW, NAADAC, CAADAC, L.A. Breakfast Club (chmn. entertainment 1988-90), Rotary, Mensa, Beverly Hills Bar Assn., Century City Bar Assn. Jewish. Avocations: singing, skiing, writing. Office: 5011 Balfour Ln Woodland Hills CA 91364-2802

SCHORER, SUKI, ballet teacher; b. Boston; d. Mark and Ruth (Page) S.; 1 child, Nicole. Studied with, George Balanchine. Dancer San Francisco Ballet, 1956-59, N.Y.C. Ballet, 1959-72; prin. dancer N.Y.C. Ballet Co., 1968-72, artistic assoc. lecture demonstration program, 1972-95; mem. faculty Sch. Am. Ballet, 1972—, Brown Found. sr. faculty chair, 1998—. Internat. guest tchr. and lectr. specializing in Balanchine tng. and technique; artist dir., tchr. on Balanchine Essays (videos). Author (monograph) Balanchine Pointework, 1995, Suki Schorer on Balanchine Technique, 1999 (de la Torre Bueno prize 2000); created roles in Balanchine's Harlequinade, Don Quixote, Midsummer Night's Dream, Jewels, La Source, Raymonda Variations; repertory included prin. roles in Apollo, Serenade, Concerto Barocco, Symphony in C, La Somnambula, Stars and Stripes, Tarantella, Valse Fantaisie, The Nutcracker, Brahams Schoenberg, La Valse, Western Symphony, Ivesiana, Divertimento # 15, Ballet Imperial, others. Recipient Disting. Tchr. in Arts award Nat. Found. Advancement in Arts, 1997, award Dance mag., 1998. Office: Sch of Am Ballet 70 Lincoln Center Plz New York NY 10023-6548 Office Phone: 212-769-6600.

SCHORLING, WILLIAM HARRISON, lawyer; b. Ann Arbor, Mich., Jan. 7, 1949; s. Otis William Schorling and Ruthann (Bales) Schorling Moorehead; m. Lynne Ann Newcomb, June 1, 1974; children: Katherine Pearce, Ann Oury, John Roberts. BA cum laude, Denison U., 1971; JD cum laude, U. Mich., 1975. Bar: Pa. 1975, U.S. Ct. Appeals (3d cir.) 1977, N.J. 1998, Del. 2001. Ptnr. Eckert, Seamans, Cherin & Mellott, Pitts., 1984-89, Klett Rooney Lieber & Schorling, PC, Pitts., 1989—. Lectr. Pa. Bar Inst., Harrisburg, 1983—. Comml. Law League, N.Y.C., 1984—, mem. exec. coun. bankruptcy sect., 2003—. Profl. Edn. Systems, Inc., Eau Claire, Wis., 1986—, Southwest Legal Found., Dallas, 1994—; founders' coun. Comml. Fin. Assn. Edn. Found., 1991—; bd. dirs. Consumer Bankruptcy Assistance Project. Contbr. articles to profl. jours. Trustee Pa. Acad. Fine Arts. Fellow Am. Coll. Bankruptcy, Am. Bar Found.; mem. ABA (bus. law section coun. 2000—, chmn. bus. bankruptcy com. 1996-99, lectr. 1988—), Am. Banker Inst. (lectr. 1994—), Phila. Bar Assn. (lectr. 1996—), E. Dist. Bankruptcy Conf., Pa. Bar Assn. (lectr. 1983—), Allegheny County Bar Assn. (chmn. bankruptcy and comml. law sect. 1991), The Com. of Seventy (chmn. 2003—), Longue Vue Club, Duquesne Club, Pyramid Club, Pa. Soc. Presbyterian. Home: 12 Scudder Ct Pennington NJ 08534-2325 Office: Klett Rooney Lieber & Schorling 2 Logan Sq Fl 12 Philadelphia PA 19103-2707

SCHORNACK, JOHN JAMES, accountant; b. Chgo., Nov. 22, 1930; s. John Joseph and Helen Patricia (Patrickus) S.; m. Barbara Anne Lelli, June 5, 1965; children: Mark Boyd, Anne Marguerite Schornack Trueman, Erin Keeley Schornack Dickes, Tracy Bevan Schornack Power. BS, Loyola U., 1951; MBA, Northwestern U., 1956; grad., Advanced Mgmt. Program, Harvard Bus. Sch., 1969. With Ernst & Young (formerly Arthur Young & Co.), 1955-91, partner, 1964-91; firm dir. personnel Ernst & Young LLP (formerly Arthur Young & Co.), N.Y.C., 1966-71, asst. mng. ptnr. N.Y.C. office, 1971-72, mng. ptnr., 1972-74, mng. ptnr. Chgo. office, 1976-85, mng. ptnr. Midwest region, vice chmn., 1985-91; mem. mgmt. com. Arthur Young & Co. Mgmt. com. Arthur Young & Co.; vice chmn., mng. ptnr. Midwest region Ernst & Young, 1989-91; bd. dirs., chmn. Ernst & Young Found., 1981-91; chmn., bd. dirs. North Shore Bancorp, Inc., 1992-, Wintrust Fin. Corp., 1996-. Pres. Chgo. Youth Ctrs., 1979-95; bd. govs. Chgo. Symphony, 1979-85, trustee, 1985-2003, life trustee; vol. United Way, 1975-92, dir., 1989-92; vis. adv. com. sch. accountancy DePaul U., 1980-83; mem. Loyola U. Citizens Bd., 1977-94, chmn., 1993-94; mem. adv. com. Northwestern U. Grad. Sch. Mgmt., 1967-91; coun. U. Chgo. Grad. Sch. Bus., 1982-91; bd. dirs. Met. Planning Coun., 1992-95; trustee Kohl Children's Mus., 1994—, Lyric Opera, 1984-92, Cath. Theol. Union, 1992-97, Graham Found., 1992-98; trustee Barat Coll., 1983-98, life trustee, 1999-2001, vice chmn., 1985-90, chmn., 1990-97; trustee St. Francis Hosp., 1986-97, vice chmn., 1991-94; trustee Night Ministry, 1998—2004 Recipient Order of the Sacred Treas., Emperor of Japan, 1999. Mem. AICPA, Am. Acctg. Assn., Ill. Soc. CPAs, Midwest-Japan Assn. (chmn. 1983-99), Japan Am. Soc., 410 Club, Chgo. Club, Glen View Club, Ocean Club, The Little Club. Home: 314 Regent Wood Rd Northfield IL 60093-2762 Office: Ernst & Young LLP Great Lakes Reg Office 233 S Wacker Dr Chicago IL 60606-6306

SCHORR, ALAN EDWARD, librarian, publisher; b. N.Y.C., Jan. 7, 1945; s. Herbert and Regina S.; m. Debra Genner, June 11, 1967; 1 son, Zebediah. BA, CUNY, 1966; MA, Syracuse U., 1967; postgrad., U. Iowa, 1967-71; MLS, U. Tex., 1973. Tchr., rsch. asst. dept. history U. Iowa, 1967-70; govt. publs. and map libr., asst. prof. Elmer E. Rasmuson Libr., U. Alaska, 1973-78; assoc. prof., dir. libr. U. Alaska, Juneau, 1978-84; prof., dean univ. libr. Calif. State U., Fullerton, 1984-86; pres. The Denali Press, Juneau, 1986—. Freelance indexer and bibliographer; vis. lectr. Birmingham (Eng.) Poly., 1981; mem. Alaska Ednl. Del. to China, 1975. Author: Alaska Place Names, 1974, 4th edit., 1991, Directory of Special Libraries in Alaska, 1975, Government Reference Books, 1974-75, 1976, 1976-77, 1978, Government Documents in the Library Literature 1909-1974, 1976, ALA RSBRC Manual, 1979, Federal Documents Librarianship 1879-1987, 1988, Hispanic Resource Directory, 1988, 3d edit., 1996, Refugee and Immigrant Resource Directory, 1990, 92, 94; editor: The Sourdough, 1974-75, Directory of Services for Refugees and Immigrants, 1987, 3d edit., 1993, Guide to Smithsonian serial publs., 1987; book reviewer, columnist: S.E. Alaska Empire, 1979-82, L.A. Times; contbr. articles to profl. jours. Mem. Auke Bay (Alaska) Vol. Fire Dept., 1978—81, Juneau Borough Libr. Adv. Com., 1981—82, Juneau Borough Cemetery Adv. Com., 1980—81, Am. Book Awards Com., 1980; chmn. program evaluation com., former chmn. facilities com., former chmn. policy com. to v.p. Juneau Bd. of Edn., 2000—; mem. Juneau Bd. Edn., 1991—94, 1995—97, 1997—2000, 2000—03, 2003—04; mem. citizens adv. coun. Juneau Empire Newspaper, 2003—. Mem. ALA (mem. reference and subscription books rev. com. 1975-86, mem. reference and adult svcs. divsn. publs. com. 1975-77, Nat. Assn. Hispanic Publs., Mudge citation commn. 1977-79, 84-86, Dartmouth Coll. Medal Commn., Governing Coun. 1977-84, mem. Dewey medal com. 1984-85, Denali Press award), Alaska Libr. Assn. (mem. exec. bd. 1974-75, mem. nominating com. 1977-79), Pacific N.W. Libr. Assn. (rep. publs. com. 1973-75), Assn. Coll. and Rsch. Librs. (mem. publ. com. 1976-80), Spl. Librs. Assn. (assoc. editor geography and map divsn. bull. 1975-76), Internat. Assn. Ind. Pubs (bd. dirs. 1990-92), True North Fed. Credit Union (bd. dirs. 1997-, treas. 2001-2002, vice chmn., 2002-04, chmn., 2004-), PEN Ctr. USA West, Explorers Club N.Y., Wash. Athletic Club (Seattle). Office: Denali Press PO Box 1535 Juneau AK 99802

SCHORR, BRIAN LEWIS, lawyer, business executive; b. N.Y.C., Oct. 5, 1958; s. Philip I. and Hannah Schorr; m. Amy B. Horowitz; 2 children. BA magna cum laude, MA, Wesleyan U., Middletown, Conn., 1979; JD, NYU, 1982. Bar: N.Y. 1983, D.C. 1985, U.S. Supreme Ct. 1988. Assoc. Paul, Weiss, Rifkind, Wharton & Garrison, N.Y.C., 1982-90, ptnr., 1991-94; exec. v.p., gen. counsel Triarc Cos., Inc., N.Y.C., 1994—. Mem. bd. advisors Jour. Ltd. Liability Cos., 1994-98; lectr. CLE programs. Author: Schorr on New York Limited Liability Companies and Partnerships, 1994; contbr. articles to legal jours. Bd. dirs. Bronx (N.Y.) HS Sci. Endowment Fund, Inc. Mem. ABA, N.Y. State Bar Assn., Assn. Bar City N.Y. (chmn. com. on corp. law 1993-96, co-chmn. joint drafting com. N.Y. ltd. liability co. law, mem. spl. com. on mergers, acquisitions and corp. control contests 1996—), Tri Bar Opinion Com., Bronx H.S. Sci. Alumni Assn. (trustee). Office: Triarc Cos Inc 280 Park Ave New York NY 10017-1216

SCHORR, DANIEL LOUIS, broadcast journalist, author, lecturer; b. NYC, Aug. 31, 1916; s. Louis and Tillie (Godiner) S.; m. Lisbeth Bamberger, 1967; children: Jonathan, Lisa. BSS, CCNY, 1939; hon. doctorate, Kalamazoo Coll., Columbia Coll., Chgo., Wilkes U., Nebr. Wesleyan U., L.I. U., Brandeis U., Spartus Coll., Bates Coll., Haverford Coll. Asst. editor Jewish Telegraphic Agy., 1934-41; news editor ANETA (Netherlands) News Agy. in N.Y., 1941-43; freelance corr. N.Y. Times, Christian Sci. Monitor, London Daily Mail, 1948-53; Washington corr. CBS News, also spl. assignments, 1953-55; reopened CBS Moscow Bur., 1955; roving assignments U.S. and Europe, 1958-60; chief CBS News Bur., Germany, 1960-66; Washington corr. CBS, 1966-76; Regents prof. U. Calif., Berkeley, 1977; columnist Des Moines Register-Tribune Syndicate, 1977-80; sr. Washington corr. Cable News Network, 1980-85; sr. analyst Nat. Pub. Radio, 1985—. Author: Don't Get Sick in America!, 1971, Clearing the Air, 1977, Forgive Us Our Press Passes, 1999, Staying Tuned, 2001. With U.S. Army, 1943-46, 47. Decorated officer Orange Nassau (The Netherlands), Grand Cross of Merit (Germany); recipient citations of excellence for radio-TV reporting Soviet Union Overseas Press Club, 1956, Best TV Interpretation of Fgn. News award 1963, ACLU and other awards for pub. suppressed Congsl. intelligence report, Emmy awards for coverage of Watergate, 1972, 73, 74, Peabody award for lifetime of uncompromising reporting of highest integrity, 1992, George Polk award for radio commentary L.I. U., 1994, Disting. Svc. award Am. Soc. Journalism and Mass Comm., 1994, Golden Baton award for lifetime achievement A.I. DuPont Columbia U., 1996; inducted in Hall of Fame Soc. Profl. Journalists, 1991, Comms. Hall of Fame CCNY, 1999. Mem. Am. Acad. Arts and Scis. (elected), Coun. on Fgn. Rels. N.Y.C., Nat. Press Club. Office Phone: 202-513-2277. E-mail: dschorr@npr.org. *Journalism, for more than 60 years, has been both profession and outlook on life. I have always felt myself the observer and nonparticipant, the quintessential outsider. I have pursued the sense of things behind the appearance of things, the meaning behind the manipulation. I have fought, with dubious success, against the blurring of the media line between reality and fantasy.*

SCHORR, LISBETH BAMBERGER, child and family policy analyst, author, educator; b. Munich, Jan. 20, 1931; d. Fred S. and Lotte (Krafft) Bamberger; m. Daniel L. Schorr, Jan. 8, 1967; children: Jonathan, Lisa. BA with highest honors, U. Calif., Berkeley, 1952; LHD (hon.), Wilkes U., 1991, U. Md., 1994, Bank St. Coll. Edn., 1999, Wheelock Coll., 2000, Lewis & Clark Coll., 2001, Whittier Coll., 2003. Med. care cons. U.A.W. and Community Health Assn., Detroit, 1956—58; asst. dir. Dept. Social Security AFL-CIO, Washington, 1958—65; acting chief CAP Health Svcs., OEO, 1965—66; chief program planning Office for Health Affairs, OEO, Washington, 1967. Cons. Children's Def. Fund, Washington, 1973—79; scholar-in-residence Inst. of Medicine NAS, 1979—80; chmn. Select Panel on Promotion Child Health, 1979—80; adj. prof. maternal and child health U. N.C., Chapel Hill, 1981—85; lectr. social medicine Harvard U. Med. Sch., 1984—; dir. project on effective interventions Harvard U., 1988—; founder www.PathwaysToOutcomes.org; nat. coun. Alan Gutmacher Inst., 1974—79, 1982—85; pub. mem. Am. Bd. Pediat., 1978—84; vice chmn. Found. for Child Devel., 1978—84, bd. dirs., 1976—84, 1986—94; mem. coun. Nat. Ctr. for Children in Poverty, 1987—96; mem. children's program adv. com. Edna McConnell Clark Found., 1987—97; bd. dirs. Pub. Edn. Fund Network, 1991—93; co-chair Roundtable n Cmty. Change, Aspen Inst., 1992—; mem. bd. on children and families NAS, 1993—95; mem. Nat. Commn. State and Local Pub. Svcs., 1992—94; mem. task force on young children Carnegie Corp., 1992—94; mem. sec.'s adv. com. Head Start quality and expansion, 1993—94; mem. nat. selection com. Ford Found./Kennedy Sch. Awards for Innovations in Am. Govt., 1998—. Author: Within Our Reach: Breaking the Cycle of Disadvantage, 1988, Common Purpose: Strengthening Families and Neighborhoods to Rebuild America, 1997. Co-chmn. Boundaries task force Harvard Children's Initiative, 1998—2000; mem. Brookings Children's Roundtable, 1999—2002; bd. dirs. Nat. Student Partnerships, 2001—03, Eureka Cmtys., 1995—, Civic Ventures, 1997—99. Recipient Dale Richmond Meml. award, Am. Acad. Pediat., 1977, 9th ann. Robert F. Kennedy Book award, 1989, Nelson Cruikshank award, Nat. Coun. Sr. Citizens, 1990, Porter prize, 1993, PASS award, Nat. Coun. on Crime and Delinquency, 1997, Marian F. Langer award, Am. Orthopsychiat. Assn., 1999, Empatheia award, Vols. of Am., 1999. Mem.: Nat. Acad. on Social Ins., Inst. Medicine NAS, Phi Beta Kappa. Home and Office: 3113 Woodley Rd NW Washington DC 20008-3449 Office Phone: 202-462-3071. E-mail: lisbeth_schorr@hms.harvard.edu.

SCHORR, MARVIN G. technology company executive; b. N.Y.C., Mar. 10, 1925; s. Samuel and Fannie (Smolen) S.; m. Rosalie Yorshis, Dec. 22, 1957; children: Eric Douglas, Susan Ellen. BS, Yale U., 1944, MS, 1947, PhD, 1949.

Rsch. asst., instr. Yale U., New Haven, 1946-47; project dir. physics and electronics divsn. Tracerlab, Inc., 1940-51; exec. v.p., treas. Tech/Ops., Inc., Boston, 1951-62, CEO, 1962-88, chmn., 1988—. Spl. cons. USAF, 1951-52; dir. Mass. Tech. Devel. Corp., 1973-76, chmn. bd., 1976-83, dir. Ealing Corp., 1965-76, Hysil Mfg. Co., 1965-78, Dynamics Research Corp., 1978-85, Helix Tech. Corp., Costar Corp. Mem. nuclear engring. adv. com. Lowell Inst. Tech., 1958-68; trustee Park Sch., 1974-80; trustee Am. Coll. Greece, 1970-82, chmn. exec. com., 1980-82, hon. trustee, 1982—; trustee New Eng. Deaconess Hosp., 1972—, vice chmn. bd., 1978-81, chmn., 1981-86. Served with U.S. Army, 1944-46. Fellow AAAS; mem. IEEE, Ops. Rsch. Soc. Am., Am. Phys. Soc., Young Pres. Orgn. (chmn. New Eng. chpt. 1967-68), Boston Com. Fgn. Rels., The Forty-Niners, World Bus. Coun., Chief Execs. Orgn., Internat. Bus. Ctr.-Chief Exec. Officers Round Table, Explorers Club, Cosmos Club (Washington), Harvard Club, St. Botolph Club, Union Club, Yale Club (Boston and N.Y.C.), Longwood Cricket Club (Brookline, Mass.). Home: 330 Beacon St Boston MA 02116-1153

SCHORR, S. L. lawyer; b. N.Y.C., Feb. 19, 1930; s. Charles and Clara (Lerech) S.; m. Eleanor Daru, Mar. 23, 1956; children: Lewis, Andrew, Emily, Roberta. Student, L.I. U., 1948-50; LLB, Bklyn. Law Sch., 1953. Bar: N.Y. 1955, Ariz. 1962, U.S. Dist. Ct. Ariz. 1962, U.S. Supreme Ct. 1979. Planning commr. Pima County, Tucson, 1959-62; asst. city mgr. Tucson, 1962-63; ptnr. Lewis and Roca, Tucson, 1988—. Co-chair Continuing Legal Edn. Seminar on Ballot Box Zoning, U. Ariz., 1991, Ariz. State Bar Continuing Legal Edn. Seminar on Land Use Regulation and Litigation, 1977, 86, 89, 95. Bd. dirs. Pima Coll., 1966-67, So. Ariz. Leadership Coun., 1997—; mem. Commn. on Improved Govtl. Mgmt., Tucson, 1974-77, Gov.'s Econ. Planning and Devel. Adv. Bd., Phoenix, 1983-85; chmn. Gov.'s Task Force on Seriously Mentally Ill, Phoenix, 1989-91, Ariz. State Transp. Bd., 2003—. Mem. Ariz. Bar Assn., Pima County Bar Assn. Democrat. Office: Lewis Roca 1 S Church Ave Ste 700 Tucson AZ 85701-1611 Office Phone: 520-622-2090.

SCHORR-RIBERA, HILDA KEREN, psychologist; b. N.Y.C., May 2, 1942; d. Leon and Rosa Schorr-Ribera; m. Ira Eli Wessler, Aug. 6, 1971; children: Mike, Daniel. BA, Hunter Coll., 1963; MEd, U. No. Fla., 1982; PhD, U. Pitts., 1988. Lic. psychologist, Pa.; diplomate Am. Bd. Forensic Examiners; diplomate, fellow Am. Bd. Med. Psychotherapists and Psychodiagnosticians; diplomate Am. Bd. Forensic Medicine, Am. Acad. Experts in Traumatic Stress; cert. in clin. hypnosis. Psychotherapist South Hills Interfaith Ministries, Bethel Park, Pa., 1989-92, Profl. Psychol. Assn. of Greater Pitts., 1992; pvt. practice psychologist Pitts., 1993—. Child therapist Forbes Hospice, 1993—; group facilitator of adult wellness group and children's support groups Burger King Cancer Caring Ctr., Pitts., 1989—, Allegheny Hospice, Pitts., 1994—96; psychol. evaluator Washington (Pa.) County Ct., 1993—, Allegheny County Ct., Pitts., 1995—98; cons. psychologist to sch. dists. Allegheny and Washington Counties. Author: (with others) Educating the Child With Cancer, 1993. Keynote spkr. on illness and bereavement to profl. assns., hosps., schs. and agys., Pitts., 1989—. Mem. APA, Internat. Soc. Hypnosis, Am. Soc. Clin. Hypnosis, Am. Acad. Experts in Traumatic Stress, Am. Counseling Assn., Am. Coll. Forensic Examiners, Pa. Psychol. Assn., Greater Pitts. Psychol. Assn. Avocations: music, bilingual activities, reading, walking, travel. Office: 117 Ridgeway Ct Pittsburgh PA 15228-1729 Office Phone: 412-344-0222. Personal E-mail: schorrribera@yahoo.com.

SCHORSCH, ISMAR, clergyman, Jewish history educator; b. Hannover, Germany, Nov. 3, 1935; m. Sally Korn; children: Jonathan, Rebecca, Naomi. BA, Ursinus Coll., 1957; MA, Columbia U., 1961, PhD, 1969; MHL, Jewish Theol. Sem. Am., 1962; LittD (hon.), Wittenberg U., 1989, Ursinus Coll., 1990, Gratz Coll., 1995, Russian State U., 1996, Tufts U., 2000. Ordained rabbi, 1962. Instr. Jewish Theol. Sem., N.Y.C., 1964-68; asst. prof. Jewish Theol. Sem. Am., N.Y.C., 1970-72, assoc. prof., 1972-76, prof., 1976—, dean Grad. Sch., 1975-79, provost, 1980-84; chancellor, 1986—; asst. prof. Jewish history Columbia U., N.Y.C., 1968-70. Bd. dirs. Leo Baeck Inst., 1976, mem. exec. com., 1980, pres., 1985-86, 90—, mem. editorial bd. of yearbook, 1987; participant symposium Spirit and Nature: Religion, Ethics and Environ. Crisis, Middlebury Coll.; organizer Nat. Religious Partnership for the Environment. Author: From Text to Context: The Turn to History in Modern Judaism, 1994, (monograph) Sacred Cluster: The Core Values of Conservative Judaism, 1995; contbr. articles to profl. publs. Chaplain U.S. Army, 1962—64. Recipient Clark F. Ansley award Columbia U. Press, 1969; NEH fellow, 1979-80 Fellow Am. Acad. Jewish Rsch. Jewish. Office: Jewish Theol Sem 3080 Broadway New York NY 10027-4650

SCHORSKE, CARL EMIL, historian, educator; b. N.Y.C., Mar. 15, 1915; s. Theodore A. and Gertrude (Goldschmidt) S.; m. Elizabeth Gilbert Rorke, June 14, 1941; children: Carl Theodore, Anne (Mrs. J. L. Edwards), Stephen James, John Simon, Richard Robert. AB, Columbia U., 1936; MA, Harvard U., 1937, PhD, 1950; DLitt (hon.), Wesleyan U., 1967; DLitt (hon.), Bard Coll., 1982, Clark U., 1983, New Sch. Social Rsch., 1986, Miami U., 1987, Monmouth Coll., 1994, Princeton U., 1997; DPhil (hon.), U. Salzburg, 1986, U. Graz, 1996. Prof. history Wesleyan U., Middletown, Conn., 1946-60; prof. history U. Calif.-Berkeley, 1960-69, Princeton U., 1969-80, emeritus, 1980—. Author: (with Hoyt Price) The Problem of Germany, 1947, German Social Democracy 1905-17, 1955, Fin-de-Siècle Vienna, 1980, Thinking with History, 1998. Lt. (j.g.) USNR, 1943-46; with OSS, 1941-46. Recipient Austrian Cross of Honor for arts and scis., 1979, Pulitzer prize for gen. nonfiction, 1981, Grand prize for cultural edn. City of Vienna, 1985, Harvard Centennial medal, 1999; named Officer, French Order Arts and Letters, 1987, Great Silver medal of Honor, Austria, 1996, Gold Cross of Honor, City of Vienna, 2000; MacArthur fellow, 1981-86. Fellow Royal Acad. Fine Arts Netherlands (hon.); mem. Am. Acad. Arts and Scis., Austrian Acad. Scis. (corr.), Am. Hist. Assn. (council 1964-68, Disting. Scholar award 1992), Ctr. Advanced Study Behavioral Sci., Inst. Advanced Study., Getty Ctr. Home: 106 Winant Rd Princeton NJ 08540-6738

SCHOTLAND, DONALD LEWIS, retired medical educator, neurologist; b. Orange, N.J., Sept. 21, 1930; s. Joseph Henry and Elsie (Block) S.; m. Marilyn Goldfeder, July 6, 1955 (dec. 1974); m. Estherina Shems, Jan. 11, 1976; children: John, Thomas, Peter. AB, Harvard U., 1952, MD, 1957; spl. student, MIT, 1955-56; MA (hon.), U. Pa., 1973. Diplomate Am. Bd. Psychiatry and Neurology 1964. Intern U. Ill. Research and Edn. Hosp., 1957-58; asst. resident in neurology Columbia Presbyn. Med. Center, N.Y.C., 1958-61, asst. neurologist, 1961-65, asst. attending neurologist, 1965-66; asst. in neurology Coll. Physicians and Surgeons, Columbia U., N.Y.C., 1960-61, vis. fellow in neurology, 1961-64, assoc. in neurology, 1964-66, asst. prof. neurology, 1966-67; assoc. prof. Sch. Medicine, U. Pa., Phila., 1967-72, prof., 1972-98, prof. emeritus, 1998—. Speaker profl. confs., U.S., Can., Italy, Japan, China, France, Israel, Finland; dir. Henry M. Watts, Jr. Neuromuscular Disease Rsch. Ctr., 1974-90. Editor: Diseases of the Motor Unit, 1982; contbr. articles, papers to profl. publs. Served to 1st lt. USAR, 1958-65. NIH postdoctoral fellow, 1961-64; recipient Research Career Devel. award, 1966-67, various grants NIH and Muscular Dystrophy Assn. Fellow Coll. of Physicians of Phila.; mem. Am. Acad. Neurology, Am. Neurol. Assn., Phila. Neurol. Soc., Muscular Dystrophy Assn. (sci. adv. com. 1974-86, chmn. fellowship com. 1974-86, chmn. 6th Internat. Conf. 1980). Home: 1310 Wyngate Rd Wynnewood PA 19096-2455 Office: Hosp of Univ Pa 3400 Spruce St Philadelphia PA 19104-4283

SCHOTT, JOHN ROBERT, international consultant, educator; b. Rochester, N.Y., Jan. 30, 1936; s. John and Ellen (Waite) S.; m. Diane Elizabeth Dempsey, June 19, 1963; children: Elizabeth Anne (dec.), Jennifer, Jared Reed, George Kermit Alexander. BA magna cum laude, Haverford Coll., 1957; postgrad., Oxford U., 1957-59; PhD, Harvard U., 1964. Resident tutor in govt. Eliot House, Harvard Coll., Cambridge, Mass., 1960-64; inst. polit. sci. Wellesley (Mass.) Coll., 1964-66; policy planning specialist AID, Washington, 1966-67; chief Title IX div. AID, Washington, 1967-68; vis. prof. polit. devel. Fletcher Sch. Law & Diplomacy, Tufts U., Medford, Mass., 1968-70; sr. v.p. Thunderbird Grad. Sch. Internat. Mgmt., Phoenix, 1970-71; cons. internat. affairs Francestown, N.H., 1971-74; pres. Schott & Assocs., Inc., Jaffrey Center, N.H., 1974-93. Mem. U.S. Del. World Assembly Internat. Secretariat for Voluntary Service, New Delhi, 1967; advisor Office Prime Minister Royal Thai Govt., Bangkok, 1978-80, Minister Cooperatives Govt. of Indonesia, Jakarta, 1983-84; research asst. spl. appointment The Brookings Inst., Washington, 1960-61 Author: Kenya Tragedy: European Colonization in East Africa, 1964, Frances' Town: History of Francestown, N.H., 1972, 98, A Five-Year Comprehensive Plan for Development of Agricultural Cooperatives in Thailand, 1979, Recana-Komprehensip Pengembangan Kud, Jakarta, Indonesia, 1985, also various govt. reports and articles in profl. jours. and regional publs.; editor: An Experiment in Integrated Rural Development, 1978. Mem. Bd. of Selectmen, Francestown, N.H., 1975-78; trustee Spaulding Youth Ctr., Tilton, N.H., 1971-82, 85-89, pres. bd. trustees, 1972-75; trustee Internat. Inst. Rural Reconstrn., N.Y.C., 1979-89, mem. exec. com., 1985-89, bd. trustees N.H. Pub. Radio, 1990-96, chmn., 1993-95; mem. spl. study commn. Coop. Extension Svc. State of N.H., 1980-81, also mem. scenic and cultural by-ways com., 1993-96; forestry rep. County Extension Coun., Hillsboro County, N.H., 1979-82; pres. N.H. Timberland Owner's Assn., 1989-90, bd. dirs., 1988-91; chmn. N.H. chpt. The Nature Conservancy, 1990-93, hon. trustee, 1993—, chmn. N.H. Timber-Tourism Coalition, 1990-94; vice-chmn, Foresters Lic. Bd. State of N.H., 1990-95; bd. trustees Cheshire Med. Ctr., 1992-94, RiverMead Retirement Cmty., Peterborough, N.H., 1992-2000, chmn., 1996-2000; mem. bd. overseers cmty. econ. devel. program So. N.H. U., 1997-2001, chmn., 1997-2000; trustee Sharon Arts Ctr., 2001-03; bd. dirs. Granite State Conservation Voters Alliance, 2004. Fellow Rotary Found., 1957-58, Coslett Found., 1958-59, Harvard Arts & Scis., 1959-60, Fulbright scholar, 1962-63; recipient The Haverford award Haverford (Pa.) Coll., 1999. Mem. Am. Forestry Inst. (cert. tree farmer). Home and Office: Schott & Assocs 15 Upper Troy Rd Fitzwilliam NH 03447

SCHOTT, JOHN WILLIAM, psychiatrist; b. LaSalle, Ill., July 2, 1940; s. Joseph William and Anne Marie Schott; m. Sarah Purdy, June 4, 1966; children: Anne Rutherford, Hannah Elizabeth, Lilly Hamilton. AB, Johns Hopkins U., 1962; MD, Harvard U., 1966. Clin. dir. Dorchester Mental Health, Boston, 1970-73, Westboro (Mass.) State Hosp., 1973-75; chmn. dept. psychiatry Leonard Morse Hosp., Natick, Mass., 1975-91, MetroWest Med. Ctr., Framingham & Natick, Mass., 1991—2004; clin. instr. Harvard Med. Sch., Boston, 1991—; portfolio mgr. Steinberg Global Asset Mgmt., Boston, 1993—. Treas. AEMS Corp., Natick, 1990—2000; pres. Cochituate Enterprises, Natick, 1991—2004 Author: Mind Over Money, 1998, From Behind the Couch, 1999; assoc. editor Jour. of Psychology and Fin. Markets, 2000-2002, Jour. Behavior Finance, 2003—; writer, publisher The Schott Letter, 1983—. Dir. Learning Ctr. Deaf Children, Framingham, 197-2004; chmn. bd. trustees Dover (Mass.) Ch., 1978-80. Mem. Am. Psychoanalytic Assn., Am. Psychiat. Assn., Mass. Med. Soc., Boston Psychoanalytic Soc. (treas. 1983-90, 2000-04, chmn. bd. trustees 1986-90), East Chop Tennis Club, East Chop Beach Club. Mem. United Ch. of Christ. Avocations: croquet, chess, gardening. Home: 132 E Chop Dr Oak Bluffs MA 02557

SCHOTTENFELD, DAVID, epidemiologist, educator; b. N.Y.C., Mar. 25, 1931; m. Rosalie C. Schaeffer; children: Jacqueline, Stephen. AB, Hamilton Coll., 1952; MD, Cornell U., 1956; MS in Pub. Health, Harvard U., 1963. Diplomate Am. Bd. Internal Medicine, Am. Bd. Preventive Medicine. Intern in internal medicine Duke U., Durham, NC, 1956-57; resident in internal medicine Meml. Sloan-Kettering Cancer Ctr., Cornell U. Med. Coll., N.Y.C., 1957-59; Craver fellow med. oncology Meml. Sloan-Kettering Cancer Ctr., 1961-62; clin. instr. dept. pub. health Cornell U., N.Y.C., 1963-67, asst. prof. dept. pub. health, 1965-70, assoc. prof. dept. pub. health, 1970-73, prof. dept. pub. health, 1973-86; John G. Searle prof., chmn. epidemiology sch. pub. health U. Mich., Ann Arbor, 1986—, prof. internal medicine, 1986—. Vis. prof. epidemiology U. Minn., Mpls., 1968, 71, 74, 82, 86; W.G. Cosbie lectr. Can. Oncology Soc., 1987. Editor: Cancer Epidemiology and Prevention, 1982, 2d edit., 1996; author 9 books; contbr. more than 250 articles to profl. jours. Served with USPHS, 1959-61. Recipient Acad. Career award in Preventive Oncology, Nat. Cancer Inst., 1980-85, Disting. Achievement award, Am. Soc. Preventive Oncology, 1992. Fellow AAAS, ACP, Am. Coll. Preventive Medicine, Am. Coll. Epidemiology (Abraham Lilienfeld award 2002), Armed Forces Epidemiology Bd.; mem. soc. Epidemiologic Rsch. (pres. 1998-99), Phi Beta Kappa. Office: U Mich Sch Pub Health Dept Epidemiology 109 Observatory St Ann Arbor MI 48109-2029 Home: 25 River Birch Ln Dalton MA 01226-2104 Business E-Mail: daschott@umich.edu.

SCHOTTENHEIMER, MARTIN EDWARD, professional football coach; b. Canonsburg, Pa., Sept. 23, 1943; m. Patricia Schottenheimer; children—Kristen, Brian BA, U. Pitts., 1964. Football player Buffalo Bills, NFL, 1965-68, Boston Patriots, 1969-70; real estate developer Miami and Denver, 1971-74; asst. coach World Football League, Portland, 1974, N.Y. Giants, 1975-77, Detroit Lions, 1978-79, Cleve. Browns, 1980-84, head coach, 1985-88, Kansas City Chiefs, 1989-99, Washington Redskins, 2001, San Diego Chargers, 2002—; tv analyst ESPN, 1999—2001. Mailing: San Diego Chargers PO Box 609609 San Diego CA 92160-9609 Office: San Diego Chargers 4020 Murphy Canyon Rd San Diego CA 92123*

SCHOTTENSTEIN, IRVING E. construction company executive; b. 1920; Apt. bldg. developer, 1966-73; pres., CEO M/I Schottenstein Homes Inc., Columbus, Ohio, 1973—; chmn. bd. dirs. M/I Real Estate Co., Inc., Columbus, Ohio; ptnr. Brothers Realty Co., Columbus, Ohio. Address: MI Schottenstein Homes 3 Easton Oval Ste 500 Columbus OH 43219-6011

SCHOTTENSTEIN, ROBERT H. construction executive; Pres., vice chair M/I Schottenstein Homes, Columbus, Ohio, 1997—. Office: M/I Schottenstein Homes 3 Eastern Columbus OH 43219

SCHOTTER, ANDREW ROYE, economics educator, consultant; b. N.Y.C., June 6, 1947; s. I. Harvey and Sara (Rothstein) S.; m. Anne Howland, June 7, 1970; children: Geoffrey, Elizabeth. BS, Cornell U., 1969; MA, PhD, NYU, 1974. Asst. prof. Syracuse (N.Y.) U., 1974-75, NYU, 1975-81, assoc. prof., 1981-86, prof., chmn. econs. dept., 1989-93, 96-99, chmn. C.V. Starr Ctr. for Applied Econs., 1986-89, dir. Ctr. for Experiential Social Sci., 2001—. Vis. asst. prof. Cornell U., Ithaca, 1974-75; vis. prof. U. Venice, 1993, U. Amsterdam; cons. Gulf & Western Corp., N.Y. 1987, Pegalis & Wachsman, Great Neck, N.Y., 1987-88, Nat. Econ. Rsch. Assocs., White Plains, N.Y., 1989—. Author: Economic Theory of Social Institutions, 1981, Free Market Economics: A Critical Appraisal, 1985, 2d edit., 1990, Microeconomics: A Modern Approach, 1993, 3d edit., 2000; mem. editl. bd.: Am. Econ. Rev., 1995—, Exptl. Econs., 1997; assoc. editor: Games and Econ. Behavior; spl. editor: Exptl. Econs. Grantee Office of Naval Rsch., 1980-85, NSF, 1988-90, 97—; recipient Kenan Enterprise award, 1993. Mem. Am. Econ. Assn., Econometric Soc., Econ. Sci. Assn. (pres.-elect 1997), Gane Theory Soc. Office: NYU Dept Econs 269 Mercer St New York NY 10003-6633

SCHOTTLAENDER, COLIN, electronics executive; BS, U. Houston. With Raytheon Co., 1977—, v.p., gen. mgr. tactical systems, electronic systems, 1998—2002, pres. network centric systems, 2002—. Office: Raytheon Co 2501 W University Mc Kinney TX 75071

SCHOU, LARRY BRIAN, music educator; b. Dekalb, Ill, Feb. 25, 1959; s. Frank Laverne and Florence Ilene Schou. MusB in organ performance, Northern Ill. U., 1981; MusM in organ performance, U. Mich., 1982, DMA in organ performance, 1988. Dir. music St. Colman's Ch., Farmington Hills, Mich., 1981—83, St. Mary's Ch., Wayne, Mich., 1983—88; organist Trinity Luth. Ch., Vermillion, SD, 1988—2000; prof. music U. SD, Vermillion, 1988—, chair music dept., 2001—. Author: (music reviews) The Diapason, 1998—2000; contbr. articles various profl. jours. Named Outanding Young South Dakotan, Jaycees of SD, 1988, Outstanding Young Man of Am., Outstanding Young Am., 1996, 1998; Sasakawa fellowship, Am. Assn. State Coll. and U., 2002. Mem.: Vermillion Area Arts Coun. (v.p. 1995—96), Midwest Hist. Keyboard Soc., Am. Guild of Organists, SD Chpt. (sub-dean 1992—93, dean 1993—95, dir. of acad. 1997—2000, regional coun. 1996—2002). Achievements include commissioned and performed new organ work by Andy Glowaty, 1988; commissioned organ work by Emma Lou Diemer, 1994; commissioned harpsichord work by Robert Marek and organ work by Charles Collahan, 1996. Avocations: tennis, golf, travel. Office: U of SD 414 E Clark St Vermillion SD 57069 Office Phone: 605-677-5275. E-mail: lschou@usd.edu.

SCHOULTZ, LARS, political scientist, educator; b. San Gabriel, Calif., Aug. 23, 1942; s. Ture Wilhelm and Bernice (Bowie) S.; m. Jane Volland, Jan. 18, 1969; children: Nils Gibson, Karina Anne. BA, Stanford U., 1964, MA, 1966; PhD, U. N.C., 1973. Prof. Miami U., Oxford, Ohio, 1973—77, U. Fla., Gainesville, 1977—79; William Rand Kenan Jr. prof. polit. sci. U. N.C., Chapel Hill, 1979—. Author: Human Rights and U.S. Policy Toward Latin America, 1981, National Security and U.S. Policy Toward Latin America, 1987, The Populist Challenge, 1983, Beneath the United States, 1998. Sgt. U.S. Army, 1966-67. MacArthur fellow in internat. peace and security MacArthur Found., 1990-91, Fulbright fellow, Rockefeller Found. fellow, Ford Found. fellow, Social Sci. Rsch. Coun., Woodrow Wilson fellow, 1994-95, Nat. Humanities Ctr. fellow, 1999-00. Mem. Latin Am. Studies Assn. (pres. 1991-92, v.p. 1990-91). Democrat. Home: 250 Glandon Dr Chapel Hill NC 27514-3816 Office: U NC Inst Latin Am Studies Chapel Hill NC 27599-0001 Office Phone: 919-962-0422. E mail: Schoultz@unc.edu.

SCHOUMACHER, BRUCE HERBERT, lawyer; b. Chicago, May 23, 1940; s. Herbert Edward and Mildred Helen (Wagner) S.; m. Alicia Wesley (Sanchez), Nov. 4, 1967; children: Liana Cristina, Janina Maria. BS, U. Ill., Northwestern, 1961; MBA, U. Ill., Chgo., 1963, JD, 1966. Bar: Nebr. 1966, U.S. Dist. Ct. Nebr. 1966, Ill. 1971, U.S. Dist. Ct. (no. dist.) Ill. 1971, U.S. Ct. Appeals (7th cir.) 1979, U.S. Supreme Ct. 1982, U.S. Ct. Fed. Claims 1986. Assoc. Luebs, Tracy, and Huebner, Grand Island, Nebr., 1966-67, McDermott, Will, and Emery, Chgo., 1971-76; ptnr. McDermott, Will,and Emery, Chgo., 1976-89, Querrey and Harrow, Ltd., Chgo., 1989—. Instr. bus. adminstrn., Bellevue Coll., Nebr., 1967-70; lectr., U. Md. Overseas Program, 1970. Author: Engineers and the Law: An Overview, 1986; contbg. author: Construction Law, 1986, Construction Law Handbook, 1999, Construction Business Handbook, 2004; co-author: Successful Business Plans for Architects, 1992; contbr. articles to profl. jour. Capt., USAF, 1967-71, Vietnam. Decorated, Bronze Star, 1971. Fellow Am. Coll. Constrn. Lawyers; mem. ABA, AIA (profl. affiliate), Nebr. Bar Assn., Ill. State Bar Assn. (ad hoc com. large law firms 1992-98), chmn. membership and bar activities com. 1988-89, coun. ins. law sect., 1986-91, mem. spl. com. on computerized legal rsch. 1986-87, Chgo. Bar Assn. (chmn. fed. civil procedure com. 1982-83), Def. Rsch. Inst., Ill. Assn. Def. Trial Counsel, Chgo. Bldg. Congress (bd. dirs. 1985—, sec. 1987-89, 95—, v.p. 1989-91), Soc. Ill. Constrn. Attys., Western Soc. Engr. (assoc.), The Lawyers Club of Chgo., Tower Club, Chgo., Univ. Club Chgo., Pi Kappa Alpha, Phi Delta Phi. Republican. Methodist. Office: Querrey & Harrow Ltd 175 W Jackson Blvd Ste 1600 Chicago IL 60604-2827 Office Phone: 312-540-7046.

SCHOUTENS, HANS, mathematician, educator; b. Leuven, Belgium, Feb. 22, 1961; s. Louis Schoutens and Jose Van Passel; m. Parvaneh Pourshariati, Oct. 15, 1993. BA in Math., BA in Math. Edn., Cath. U. Leuven, Belgium, 1983, PhD in Math., 1991. Vis. asst. prof. Wesleyan U., Middletown, Conn., 1997—99, Ohio State U., Columbus, 2001—03; asst. prof. Rutgers U., New Brunswick, NJ, 1999—2001, CUNY, N.Y.C., 2003—. Fulbright fellow Columbia U., N.Y.C., 1992—93; rsch. fellow Oxford (Eng.) U., 1994—96; vis. prof. Inst. des Hautes Etudes Scientifiques, Bures-sur-Yvettes, 1997, Ecole Normale, U. Paris VII, 2002. Rsch. grantee, NSF, 2001—04. Mem.: Am. Math. Soc. Achievements include research in non-standard tight closure; big Cohen-Macaulay algebras; rigid analytic flatificators. Office: NYC Coll Tech CUNY 300 Jay St Brooklyn NY 11201 Personal E-mail: hschoutens@citytech.cuny.edu.

SCHOVILLE, DENNIS A(RNOLD), lawyer; b. Richland Ctr., Wis., May 31, 1945; BS, U. Wis., 1967; JD with Distinction, Ill. Inst. Tech., 1973; LLM, Northwestern U., 1974. Bar: Wis. 1973, Ill. 1973, U.S. Dist. Ct. (no. dist.) Ill. 1973, Calif. 1974, U.S. Dist. Ct. (so. dist.) Calif. 1974, U.S. Ct. Appeals (9th cir.) 1985, U.S. Ct. Claims. Ptnr. Schoville & Arnell, LLP, San Diego. Capt. U.S. Army, 1968-73. Recipient Broderick award for professionalism, integrity and ethics, 1996; named Consumer Attys. San Diego Trial Lawyer of the Yr., 1995, 99. Mem. ABA, ATLA, Am. Coll. Trial Lawyers, Am. Bd. Trial Advocates (past pres. San Diego chpt.), Consumer Attys. San Diego (past pres.), Ill. State Bar Assn., State Bar Wis., State Bar Calif., San Diego County Bar Assn., San Diego Trial Lawyers Assn. (Outstanding Trial Advocacy award-civil 1984, 89, 94), Am. Inns of Ct. (master), Nat. Guard Coun., Disting. Flying Cross Soc. Office: Schoville & Arnell LLP 1230 Columbia St Ste 800 San Diego CA 92101-3571

SCHOW, TERRY D. state official; b. Ogden, Utah, Dec. 14, 1948; s. Hugh Stuart Sloan and Minnie Aurelia (Ellis) Mohler; m. June Hansen, Feb. 14, 1973; children: Amy, Jason. AD, Honolulu C.C., 1975; BA, Chaminade U., 1975. Cert. in mgmt., Utah. Spl. and criminal investigator State of Utah, Ogden, 1976-83, lead investigator, 1984-92; investigator Fed. Govt., Salt Lake City, Denver, 1983-84; mgr. State of Utah, Ogden, 1992—99, state dir. vets. affairs, 2001—. Active Gov.'s Coun. on Vets. Issues, 1989-2001, chmn., 1990-2001; active State of Utah Privatization Policy Bd., 1989-92; chmn. 1st Congressional Dist. Utah Rep. Party, 1982-83, state exec. com., 1982-83; chmn. legis. dist Weber County Rep. Party, Ogden, 1987-91, 93—; trustee Utah's Vietnam Meml., Salt Lake City, 1988-90; leader Boy Scouts Am., Ogden, 1985—; citizens' adv. com. Ogden City Neighborhood Redevel., 1996-2000. Sgt. U.S. Army, 1967-70, 72-76, Vietnam. Decorated Bronze Star, Combat Inf. Badge; recipient Championship Team Trophy Pistol U.S. Army, 1975. Mem. DAV (life, Weber chpt. 4, comdr. 1994, state comdr. 1995—), NRA (life), VFW, AL (comdr. Ogden post 9 1996-97, state comdr. 1999—), Utah Peace Officers Assn., Utah Pub. Employees Assn. (bd. dirs. 1988-89, v.p. 1989-92, pres. 1992-93, chmn. Ogden Valley dist.), Kiwanis (pres. Ogden chpt. 1992-93, homeless vets. fellow Ogden 1992-00, Weber County vets. meml. com. 1994—, pres. Layton chpt. 1985-86, lt. gov. divsn. 3 ut/ld dist. Kiwanis internat. 1995-96, Kiwanian of Yr. 1982-83). Republican. Mem. Lds Ch. Avocations: woodworking, photography, scouting. Home: 4045 Bona Villa Dr Ogden UT 84403-3203 Office: State Utah Divsn Vets Affairs 550 Foot Hill Dr # 202 Salt Lake City UT 84108 Office Phone: 801-326-2372. E-mail: tschow@utah.gov.

SCHOWALTER, JOHN ERWIN, child and adolescent psychiatry educator; b. Milw., Mar. 15, 1936; s. Raymond Phillip and Martha (Kowalke) S.; m. Ellen Virginia Lefferts, June 11, 1960; children: Jay, Bethany. BS, U. Wis., 1957, MD, 1960. Diplomate Am. Bd. Psychiatry and Neurology (com. on cert. in child psychiatry 1983-85, chmn. 1986-87, bd. dirs. 1993-2000, chmn. com. added qualifications forensic psychiatry 1993-97); cert. in adult and child psychiatry also psychoanalysis. Intern in pediat. Yale-New Haven Hosp., 1960-61; asst. resident in psychiatry Cin. Gen. Hosp., 1961-63; fellow in child psychiatry Yale U. Child Study Ctr., New Haven, 1963-65; psychiatrist Mental Hygiene Clinic U.S. Army, Ft. Ord, Calif., 1965-67; asst. prof. Yale U. Child Study Ctr., 1967-70, assoc. prof. Sch. Medicine, 1970-75, dir. tng., 1971-96, prof. pediat. and psychiatry, 1975-89, chief child psychiatry, 1982-90, dir. child psychiatry clin. svcs., 1990—2003, Albert J. Solnit prof. child psychiatry and pediat., 1989—2003, interim chmn., 2001—02, prof. emeritus, sr. rsch. scientist, 2003—. Mem. publ. com. Yale U. Press., 1992-97; mem. sci. adv. bd. Sophia Found. Med. Rsch., Rotterdam, The Netherlands, 1984-89; dir. mental health and substance abuse Yale Preferred Health Plan, 1995-99. Co-author: The Family Handbook of Adolescence, 1979; contbr. numerous articles, book revs.; mem. editl. bd. Pediatrics, 1976-81, Children's Health Care, 1977-2003, Jour. Am. Psychoanalytic Assn., 1978, Pediatrics in Rev., 1978-85; asst. editor: Jour. Am. Acad. Child and Adolescent Psychiatry, 1988-97; co-editor: Yearbook Psychiatry and Applied Mental Health, 1988-97. Capt. U.S. Army, 1965-67. Fellow Am. Acad. Child and Adolescent Psychiatry (sec. 1985-87, pres. 1989-91, Simon Wile award 1996, mem. fin. planning com. 2000—, chair governance com.), Am. Coll. Psychiatrists (chair Laughlin fellowship com. 2000-01, chair membership com. 2002—), Am. Acad. Pediat.; mem. Am. Pediatric Soc., Am. Psychoanalytic Assn. (cert. adult and child), Group for Advancement Psychiatry (life fellow, com. on child psychiatry 1981, bd. dirs. 1989-91, pres. 1993-95, chair life fellowship com. 2000—), Assn. for Care of

Children's Health (pres. 1984-86), AMA (residency rev. com. for psychiatry 1983-87, 89-94), Soc. Profs. Child Psychiatry (pres. 1984-86), Western New Eng. Inst. Psychoanalysis (mem. faculty in child psychoanalysis 1984—, pres. 1986-88), Conn. Med. Soc., New Haven Med. Soc., Conn. Coun. Child Psychiatrists (pres. 1979-81), Benjamin Rush Soc. (sec., treas. 1998-99, v.p. 1999-2000, pres. 2000-2002), Sigma Xi. Lutheran. Home: 256 Ives St Hamden CT 06518-2200 Office: Yale U Child Study Ctr PO Box 207900 230 S Frontage Rd New Haven CT 06520-7900

SCHOWALTER, WILLIAM RAYMOND, college dean, educator; b. Milw., Dec. 15, 1929; s. Raymond Philip and Martha (Kowalke) S.; m. Jane Ruth Gregg, Aug. 22, 1953; children: Katherine Ruth, Mary Patricia, David Gregg. BS, U. Wis., 1951; postgrad., Inst. Paper Chemistry, 1951-52; MS, U. Ill., 1953, PhD, 1957; PhD (hon.), Inst. Nat. Poly. Lorraine, France, 1996. Asst. prof. dept. chem. engring. Princeton U., 1957-63, assoc. prof., 1963-66, prof., 1966-86, Class of 1950 prof. engring. and applied sci., 1986-89, acting chmn. dept. chem. engring., 1971, chmn. dept. chem. engring., 1978-87, assoc. dean Sch. Engring. and Applied Sci., 1971-77, class of 1950 prof. engring. and applied sci. emeritus, 2000—; dean Coll. Engring. U. Ill., Urbana, 1989-2001, dean, prof. emeritus, 2001—; Mobil prof. chem. engring. Nat. U. Singapore, 1998, sr. advisor to pres., 2001—. Sherman Fairchild disting. scholar Calif. Inst. Tech., 1977-78; vis. fellow U. Salford, Eng., 1974; vis. sr. fellow Sci. Rsch. Coun., U. Cambridge, Eng., 1970; cons. to chem. and petroleum cos.; editl. adv. bd. McGraw-Hill Pub. Co., 1964-92; co-chmn. Internat. Seminar for Heat and Mass Transfer, 1970; vis. com. for chem. engring. MIT, 1979-87, Lehigh U., 1980-87; mem. vis. com. Sch. Engring., Stanford U., 1990-2001; evaluation panelist Ctr. Chem. Engring. Nat. Bur. Standards, 1982-88, chmn., 1986-88; mem. commn. engring. and tech. sys. NRC, 1983-88; engring. rsch. bd., 1984-86; adv. coun. chem. engring. Cornell U., 1983-91; adv. coun. Sch. Engring., Rice U., 1986-92; adv. com. Ill. Inst. Tech., 1992-97; adv. coun. Coll. Engring., U. Calif., Berkeley, 1997-2001, Coll. Engring. U. Mich., 1997-2001, Sch. Engring. and Applied Sci., Princeton U., 1998-2002, Carnegie Inst. Tech., 1999-2001; acad. adv. bd. Sematech Corp., 1992-2001; internat. adv. panel Nat. U. Singapore, 1996, 2002; Reilly lectr. in chem. engring. U. Notre Dame, 1985, Van Winkle lectr. in chem. engring. U. Tex., Austin, 1986, David M. Mason lectr. chem. engring. Stanford U., 1987; Bird Stewart and Lightfoot lectr. chem. engring. U. Wis., 2001; R.H. Wilhelm lectr. in chem. engring. Princeton U., 2002; mem. fellowship program Packard Found. Sci. Adv. Panel, 1998—. Author: Mechanics of Non-Newtonian Fluids, 1978; co-author: Colloidal Dispersions, 1989; mem. editl. com. Ann. Rev. Fluid Mechanics, 1974-80, Internat. Jour. Chem. Engring., 1974-94, Indsl. and Engring. Chemistry Fundamentals, 1975-78, Jour. Non-Newtonian Fluid Mechanics, 1976-2001, AIChE Jour., 1979-83; contbr. articles to profl. jours. Mem. Ill. Gov.'s Sci. Adv. Com., 1989-96. Served with U.S. Army, 1953-55. Decorated officier des Palmes Académiques (France), 1995; recipient Disting. Svc. citation Coll. Engring., U. Wis., Madison, 1983; Guggenheim fellow, 1987-88. Fellow AIChE (William H. Walker award 1982, bd. dirs. 1992-94), NAS (class membership com. 2000, 2002, class chm. 2002—), Am. Acad. Arts and Scis.; mem. Am. Soc. Engring. Edn. (Lectr. award chem. engring. divsn. 1971, exec. com. engr. deans coun. 1992-95, vice-chair, engring. deans coun. pub. policy com. 1998, chair engring. deans coun. pub. policy com. 1999-2001), NAE (awards com. 1986-88, chmn. 1987, acad. adv. bd. 1991-94, chmn. 1992-94, coun. 1994-2000, Draper Award com. 2001-03), Am. Chem. Soc., Soc. Rheology (exec. com. 1977-79, v.p. 1981-83, pres. 1983-85, Bingham medal 1988), Sigma Xi, Tau Beta Pi, Phi Lambda Upsilon, Phi Eta Sigma.

SCHRADE, ROLANDE MAXWELL YOUNG, composer, pianist, educator; b. Washington, Sept. 13; d. Harry Robert and Isabelle Martha (Maxwell) Young; m. Robert Warren Schrade, Dec. 21, 1949; children: Robelyn, Rhonda Lee, Rolisa, Randolph, Rorianne. Studied with, Harold Bauer, NYC, Vittorio Giannini; student, Manhatten Sch. Music, Juilliard Sch. Music. Debut as concert pianist Town Hall, NYC, 1953, Nat. Gallery, Washington, 1954; concert pianist Constitution Hall, Washington, 1972; founder, dir. ann. performances Sevenars Concerts, Inc., Worthington, Mass., 1968—, music dir., 1975—, also broadcasts, 1984, 85; recitalist Radio Sta. WGMS-FM, Washington; mem. music faculty Allen-Stevenson Sch., NYC, 1968-89; co-founder, v.p., treas. Sevenars Music House, Inc., NYC, 1968—. Concerts include Lincoln Ctr., Alice Tully Hall, 1980, 93, Sevenars Concerts, Inc., 1968—, Lincoln Ctr., 2000; Lifetime TV film Tour, New Zealand, 1982-84; featured NBC Today Show with Schrade family pianists, 1993; named to Steinway Piano Co. Global Artist List; appearances PM Mag., TV film, 1980-81; composer, pub., recs. of over 100 songs; albums include America 76, Original and Traditional Songs for Special Days, 1988; editor: songs of Carrie Jacobs Bond, Boston Music Co.; TV feature film with Schrade Family Pianists, 1997; performed in Schrade-James Family Concert Lincoln Ctr., NYC, 2000, Lifetime TV showing. Mem. ASCAP, DAR (Bicentennial award 1972), Mut. Artists Mgmt. Alliance (founder, bd. dirs.). Episcopalian. Home and Office: 30 East End Ave Ste 3A New York NY 10028-7053 Office: Sevenars Concerts Ireland St S at Rte 112 Worthington MA 01098

SCHRADER, DARYL LYNN, mathematician, educator; b. Akron, Ohio, Apr. 29, 1945; s. Wilfred and Mildred Schrader; m. Elizabeth Scott, Aug. 10, 1983; 1 child, Christine. AA, Manatee Jr. Coll., Bradenton, Fla., 1966; BA in Astronomy, U. South Fla., 1968, BA in Math., 1969, MA in Physics, 1973. Instr. math. Shorecrest Preparatory, St. Petersburg, Fla., 1975—76; prof. math. and astronomy St. Petersburg Coll., 1977—. Adj. instr. U. South Fla., various locations, 1971—; cons. Tampa Bay Skeptics, Tampa, Fla., 1996—, Pinellas County Sci. Ctr., St. Petersburg, 1996—. Co-author: America's Planetariums and Observatories, 1991; author: (column) Astronomy, St. Petersburg Times, 1990—. Coord. pub. events on astronomy for cmty., St. Petersburg, 1979—. Named Disting. Alumni, U. South Fla., 2000. Fellow: Brit. Interplanetary Soc., Royal Astron. Soc.; mem.: Fla. Acad. Scis. (sect. chair computers and math. 1989—98), Sigma Pi Sigma. Achievements include coordinate one of largest public Halley Comet watches in North America. Avocations: Aikido, Karate, science fiction. Office: Saint Petersburg College PO Box 13489 6605 5th Ave N Saint Petersburg FL 33733-3489 Office Phone: 727-341-4384. Business E-Mail: Schrader@spcollege.edu.

SCHRADER, KEN, race car driver; b. Fenton, Mo., May 29, 1955; m. Ann Schrader; 1 child, Dorothy; 1 child, Sheldon Bradley. Profl. race car driver, 1971—. Named Rookie of Yr., NASCAR, 1985, winner, Lakehill Speedway Track Championship, Hendrick Motorsports, 1988, 2-time winner, Busch Clash, winner 3 consecutive times, Daytona 500 Poles, winner, Al Pro Auto Parts 500, 1989, Budweiser 500, 1991, Motorcraft Quality Parts 500, 1991. Office: c/o NASCAR PO Box 2875 Daytona Beach FL 32120-2875 also: Andy Petree Racing 908 Upward Rd Flat Rock NC 28731-8799

SCHRADER, LAWRENCE EDWIN, plant physiologist, educator; b. Atchison, Kans., Oct. 22, 1941; s. Edwin Carl and Jenna Kathryn (Tobiason) S.; m. Elfriede J. Massier, Mar. 14, 1981 BS, Kans. State U., 1963; PhD, U. Ill., 1967; grad., Inst. Ednl. Mgmt., Harvard U., 1991. Asst. prof. dept. agronomy U. Wis., Madison, 1969-72, assoc. prof., 1972-76, prof., 1976-84; prof., head dept. agronomy U. Ill., Urbana, 1985-89; dean Coll. Agr. and Home Econs. Wash. State U., Pullman, 1989-94, prof. dept. horticulture, 1994—. Chief competitive rsch. grants office Dept. Agr., Washington, 1980-81; trustee, treas. Agrl. Satellite Corp., 1991-94. Contbr. chpts. to books, articles to profl. jours. Active Consortium for Internat. Devel., 1989-94, chair fin. com., vice chair exec. com., 1990-92, trustee 1989-94; mem. exec. com. Coun. Agrl. Heads of Agr., 1992-94. Capt. U.S. Army, 1967-69. Recipient Soybean Researchers Recognition award 1983, Disting. Service award in Agriculture Kansas State U., 1987; Romnes Faculty fellow U. Wis., 1979 Fellow AAAS (steering group sect. agr. 1991-95, chair-elect sect. on agr., food and renewable resources 1995-96, chmn. 1996-97, past chmn. 1997-98, coun. mem. 1997-98), Am. Soc. Agronomy, Crop Sci. Soc. Am.; mem. Internat. Soc. for Hort. Sci., Am. Soc. for Hort. Sci., Am. Soc. Plant Biologists (sec. 1983-85, pres.-elect 1986, pres. 1987), Am. Chem. Soc., Coun. for Agrl. Sci. and Tech., Blue Key, Sigma Xi, Gamma Sigma Delta (Outstanding Alumnus award, 2003), Phi Kappa Phi, Phi Eta Sigma, Alpha Zeta (named to Centennial Honor Roll 1997). Methodist. Home: 3504 Crestview Rd Wenatchee WA 98801-9668 Office: Wash State U Tree Fruit Rsch & Extension Ctr 1100 N Western Ave Wenatchee WA 98801-1230 Office Phone: 509-663-8181 x265. Business E-Mail: schrader@wsu.edu.

SCHRADER, MICHAEL EUGENE, columnist, editor; b. Jersey City, Apr. 3, 1938; s. Eugene Charles and Anne Veronica (Kane) S. BA in Latin, NYU, 1961, MA in English, 1963; postgrad., UCLA, 1965-67, 68-69, Trinity Coll., Dublin, 1967-68, U. Copenhagen, Denmark, 1970. Asst. editor Macmillan Co., N.Y.C., 1962-64; teaching asst. U. Ill., Urbana, 1964-65; teaching asst., rsch. asst. UCLA, 1965-67, 68-69; sr. copy editor Dell Pub. Co., N.Y.C., 1971-72; copy chief Sat. Rev. mag., N.Y.C., 1972-76, Penthouse mag., N.Y.C., 1976-82; assoc. editor Med. Econs. mag., Oradell, N.J., 1982; sr. copy editor Woman's World mag., Englewood, N.J., 1983-84; book reviewer, sr. copy editor Nation's Restaurant News, N.Y.C., 1985—. Columnist: From the Bookshelf, in Nation's Restaurant News, 1988—. Friend of Bobst Libr., Soc. of Torch, NYU, 1994—, established Anne Kane Schrader Cookbook and Nutrition Collection. Recipient Danish Marshall award U. Copenhagen, 1970; Fulbright scholar, 1967-68. Fellow James Beard Found. (judge food and beverage book awards 1991-94); mem. Soc. of the Torch (charter), Internat. Assn. Culinary Profls. Democrat. Roman Catholic. Avocations: reading fiction and poetry, growing house plants, travel, movies, theater. Home: 30 Waterside Plz Apt 33H New York NY 10010-2627 Office: Lebhar-Friedman Inc Nation's Restaurant News 425 Park Ave New York NY 10022-3549

SCHRADER, RICHARD ALLEN, engineering company executive; b. Mannington, W.Va., Jan. 23, 1950; s. Everett A. and Betty (Eger) S.; m. Eileen Joann Gilmartin, June 8, 1972; children: Allison, Susanne BS, U.S. M il. Acad., 1972; MA, John Hopkins U., 1976; MBA, L.I.U., 1983. Registered profl. engr., N.J. Commd. 2d lt. U.S. Army, 1972, served with 84th Engr. Battalion, 1973-74, served with 94th engr. battalion Darmstadt, Fed. Republic Germany, 1977-80, advanced though the grades to capt.; transferred as maj. USAR, 1983; instr. U.S. Mil. Academy, West Point, N.Y., 1980-81, asst. prof., 1982-83; asst. to pres. Parsons Brinckerhoff Inc., N.Y.C., 1983-86, v.p. corp. fin., 1986—. Pres. Parsons Brinckerhoff Devel. Corp, N.Y.C.; pres. bd. dirs. Boylston Place Assn., Boston. Author: (with others) American National Security, 1981, Industrial Capacity and Defense Planning, 1983; coeditor: Defense Manpower Planning, 1981. Area Coordinator U.S. Mil. Acad. Admissions, North Central N.J., 1984—; faculty sponsor West Point Glee Club, 1981-83, West Point Forum, 1981-82. Mem. Society of American Mil. Engrs. (bd. dirs. West Point chpt. 1982-83), Am. Soc. of Civil Engrs., West Point Soc. of N.Y., Phi Kappa Phi. Office: Parsons Brinckerhoff Inc One Penn Plaza New York NY 10119

SCHRADER, ROBERT WESLEY, judge; b. Cheyenne, Wyo., Feb. 3, 1944; s. Marvin Glen and Bertha Lorene (Winingar) S.; m. Betty Ann Pruter, June 14, 1964; children: Christina Lynn, Tashana Dee. AA in Mortuary Sci., San Francisco Mortuary Sci., 1965; BSBA, U. Wyo., 1967, JD, 1979. Bar: Wyo., 1978, U.S. Dist. Ct. Wyo., 1978 U.S. Ct. Appeals (10th cir.), 1979, U.S. Supreme Ct., 1991. Assoc. Omohundro & O'Brien, Buffalo, Wyo., 1978-80; pvt. practice Schrader Law Office, Buffalo, 1980-84; ins. commr. State Wyo., Cheyenne, 1984-86; pvt. practice Schrader Law Office, Cheyenne, 1986-92; dist. ct. commr. 1st Jud. Dist., Cheyenne, 1987—. Justice of the peace, Johnson County, Wyo., 1980-84; dist. ct. commr. 4th Jud. Dist., Johnson County, 1981-84; pres., bd. mem. Attention Homes, Inc., Cheyenne, 1983-98; pres. Scottish Rite Found., Cheyenne, 1992—. Heels, Cheyenne Frontier Days, 1979—; Wyo. races officer Wyo. Emergency Mgmt. Agy., Cheyenne, 1991-97. Capt. U.S. Army, 1967-70, Vietnam, lt. col. USAFR ret. 1994. Decorated three Meritorious Svc. medals USAF, Combat Med. badge U.S. Army, Vietnam, 1968. Mem. VFW Post 11454 (adv.), Burns Lodge 41 AF&AM (past master), Scottish Rite Bodies, York Rite Bodies, Korein Shrine (chief clown), Shrine Circus (sec.-treas.), Phi Epsilon Phi, Sigma Phi Epsilon. Republican. Episcopalian. Avocations: flying, raising quarter horses, clowning, hunting, amateur radio. Home: 607 Monte Carlo Dr Cheyenne WY 82009-2050 Office: First Jud Dist Ct Dist Ct 309 W 20th St Cheyenne WY 82001-3601

SCHRADER, WILLIAM L. communications executive; BS, Cornell U. Exec. dir., co-founder Cornell Theory Ctr.; founder, pres., CEO NYSERNet; dir., founder N.E. Paralle Archs. Ctr. Syracuse (N.Y.) U.; chmn., CEO, founder PSINet, Inc., Herndon, Va., 1989—. Participant panel discussions of industry trends CNN, CNBC, MSNBC, FNN, First Bur., TechnoPolitics. Office: PSI Networks 45969 Nokes Blvd Ste 150 Sterling VA 20166-6553

SCHRADY, DAVID ALAN, civilian military employee, educator; b. Akron, Ohio, Nov. 11, 1939; s. Marvin G. and Sheila A. (O'Neill) S.; m. Mary E. Hilt, Sept. 1, 1962; children: Peter, Patrick, Matthew. BS, Case Inst. Tech., 1961, MS, 1963, PhD, 1965. Prof., chmn. Naval Postgrad. Sch., Monterey, Calif., 1974-76, dean acad. planning, 1976-80, provost and acad. dean, 1980-87, prof. ops. rsch., 1988—. Disting. prof., ops. rsch. educator, 1995—. Vis. prof. Cranfield Inst. Tech./Royal Mil. Coll. of Sci., Shrivenham, Eng., fall 1987-spring 88. Contbr. articles to profl. jours. Recipient Goodeve medal Ops. Rsch. Soc., U.K., 1992. Fellow: Inst. for Ops. Rsch. and the Mgmt. Scis., Mil. Ops. Rsch. Soc., (pres. 1978—79, Wanner medal 1984); mem.: Internat. Fedn. Ops. Rsch. Socs. (hon. treas. 1988—97), Ops. Rsch. Soc. Am. (pres. 1983—84, Kimball medal 1994). Avocations: guitar, motor sports. Office: Naval Postgrad Sch Dept Ops Rsch Monterey CA 93943-5000 Business E-Mail: dschrady@nps.edu.

SCHRAG, ADELE FRISBIE, business education educator; b. Cynthiana, Ky., May 7, 1921; d. Shirley Ledyard and Edna Kate (Ford) S.; m. William Albert Schrag, Apr. 6, 1963; 1 stepchild, Marie Carol. BS, Temple U., 1942; MA, N.Y. U., 1944, PhD, 1961. Tchr. Manor Twp. High Sch., Millersville, Pa., 1942-43, Downingtown (Pa.) Sr. High Sch., 1943-50; instr., asst. prof. Temple U. Sch. Bus. and Pub. Administrn., Phila., 1950-60; prof. bus. edn. and vocat. edn. Coll. Edn., 1960-85, sr. prof. edn., 1985-88, prof. emeritus, 1988—. Vis. lectr. N.Y. U.; cons. Phila. Community Coll., 1967-82 Editor: Business Education for the Automated Office, 1964; author: (with Estelle L. Popham and Wanda Blockhus) A Teaching-Learning System for Business Education, 1975, How to Dictate, 1981, Office Procedures Update, 1982, (with Robert Poland) A Teaching System for Business Subjects, 1988; contbr. articles to profl. jours., chpts. to books. Trustee Meth. Hosp., 1981—85, Sun Cities Symphony Assn., 1988—93, Habitat for Humanity of West Valley, 1994—, co-pres., 1999—2001; trustee Habitat for Humanity Ariz., 1999—2003. Recipient Profl. Panhellenic award, 1963; Kensington High Sch. Alumnae award, 1972 Mem. Soc. Automation in Bus. Edn. (pres. 1969-73, dir. 1974), Nat. Assn. Bus. Tchr. Edn. (pres. 1983-84), Bus. Edn. Certification Council, Phi Gamma Nu (nat. treas. 1952-54, nat. sec. 1954-56), Delta Pi Epsilon (policy commn. for bus. and econ. edn. 1975-78, dir. research found. 1978-83, pres. research found. 1983). Home: 14515 W Granite Valley Dr # 644 Sun City West AZ 85375-6021 E-mail: afs107@earthlink.net.

SCHRAG, EDWARD A., JR., lawyer; b. Milw., Mar. 27, 1932; s. Edward A. and Mabel Lena (Baumbach) S.; m. Leslie Jean Israel, June 19, 1954; children: Amelia Marie Schrag Prack, Katherine Allison Schrag Roberts, Edward A. III (dec.). BS in Econs, U. Pa., 1954; JD, Harvard, 1960. Bar: Ohio 1961. Assoc., then firm partner, now of counsel Vorys, Sater, Seymour and Pease, Columbus, 1960—. Sec. Ranco Inc., 1972-87; trustee Lake of Woods Water Co., 1972-91; mem. Ohio div. Securities Adv. Com. Mem. Downtown Area Com., 1970-74. Served to lt. (j.g.) USNR, 1954-57. Mem. ABA, Ohio Bar Assn. (chmn. corp. law com. 1986-88, chmn. securities regulation subcom., spl. com. bus. cts., bd. govs., corp. counsel sect., chmn. 1991-93), Columbus Bar Assn., Columbus Area C. of C., Navy League, Alpha Tau Omega, Beta Gamma Sigma, Phi Sigma Alpha, Pi Gamma Mu. Clubs: Capital, Crichton, Ohio State U. Pres.'s. Episcopalian. Home: 9400 White Oak Ln Westerville OH 43082-9606 Office: Vorys Sater Seymour & Pease PO Box 1008 52 E Gay St Columbus OH 43216-1008

SCHRAG, PETER, editor, writer; b. Karlsruhe, Germany, July 24, 1931; arrived in U.S., 1941, naturalized, 1953; s. Otto and Judith (Haas) S.; m. Melissa Jane Mowrer, June 9, 1953 (div. 1969); children: Mitzi, Erin Andrew; m. Diane Divoky, May 24, 1969 (div. 1981); children: David Divoky, Benaiah Divoky; m. Patricia Ternahan, Jan. 1, 1988. AB cum laude, Amherst Coll., 1953. Reporter El Paso (Tex.) Herald Post, 1953-55; asst. sec., asst. dir. publs. Amherst Coll., 1955-66, instr. Am. Studies, 1960-64; assoc. edn. editor Sat. Rev., 1966-68, exec. editor, 1968-69; editor Change mag., 1969-70; editor at large Saturday Rev., 1969-72; contbg. editor Saturday Review/Education, 1972-73; editl. adv. bd. The Columbia Forum, 1972-75; editl. bd. Social Policy, 1971—; contbg. editor More, 1974-78, Inquiry, 1977-80, The Am. Prospect, 1995—; editl. page editor Sacramento Bee and McClatchy Newspapers, 1978-96, contbg. editor, 1996—. Vis. lectr. U. Mass. Sch. Edn., 1970-72; fellow in profl. journalism Stanford U., Palo Alto, Calif., 1973-74; lectr. U. Calif., Berkeley, 1974-78, 90—; Pulitzer Prize juror, 1988-89; vis. scholar U. Calif. Inst. Govtl. Studies, Berkeley, 1998—. Author: Voices in the Classroom, 1965, Village School Downtown, 1967, Out of Place in America, 1971, The Decline of the Wasp, 1972, The End of the American Future, 1973, Test of Loyalty, 1974, (with Diane Divoky) The Myth of the Hyperactive Child, 1975, Mind Control, 1978, Paradise Lost: California's Experience, America's Future, 1998, Final Test: The Battle for Adequacy in America's Schools, 2003; contbr. articles. Adv. com. Student Rights Project, NY Civil Liberties Union, 1970-72; mem. Com. Study History, 1958-72; trustee Emma Willard Sch., 1967-69; bd. dirs. Park Sch., Oakland, Calif., 1976-77, Ctr. for Investigative Reporting, 1979-81, Ed Source, 1998—; bd. adv. Pub. Policy Inst. Calif. Guggenheim fellow, 1971-72; Nat. Endowment for Arts fellow, 1976-77 Office: 5835 Colton Blvd Oakland CA 94611-2204 Business E-Mail: pschrag@sacbee.com.

SCHRAGE, ROSE, educational administrator; b. Montelimar, France, Apr. 15, 1942; came to U.S., 1947; d. Abraham and Celia (Silbiger) Levine; m. Samuel Schrage, Dec. 12, 1935 (dec. 1976); children: Abraham, Leon. BRE, Beth Rivkah Tchrs. Sem., Bklyn., 1968; Paralegal, Manpower Career Devel. Agy., Bklyn., 1973; MS, L.I. U., 1975; Advanced Cert. Ednl. Adminstrn., Bklyn. Coll., 1983. Cert. sch. dist. adminstr., guidance counselor, tchr., asst. prin. Sec., N.Y.C., 1964-68; police adminstrv. aide N.Y.C. Police Dept., 1974-75; coord. state reading aid program Sch. Dist. 14, Bklyn., 1977-78, project dir. Title VII, 1978-81, asst. dir. reimbursable fed. and state programs, 1981-85, dist. bus. mgr., 1985-94, asst. prin., 1994—99, spl. edn. instrn. specialist, adminstr., 1999—; ednl. adminstr. Ctrl. Liaison Office for Impartial Hearings, divsn. student support svcs. Dept. Edn., N.Y.C., 2001—. Chmn. N.Y.C. Bd. Edn. IMPACT Com., Bklyn., 1986—. Author (poem): Never Again, 1983; contbg. editor Chai Today; contbr. articles on current affairs and concerns to profl. jours. Del. Republican. Jud. Conf., 1968; founder, pres Concerned Parents, Bklyn., 1977; radio co-host Israeli War Heroes Fund-Radiothon, Bklyn.; family counselor local social agys., Bklyn.; co-founder cmty. vol. ambulance Hatzalah, 1977. Recipient Cert. of Appreciation as vol. regional coord. N.Y. State Mentoring Program N.Y. Gov. Cuomo, 1991, Proclamation, N.Y. City Coun., 2003, State of N.Y. Legis. Resolution Proclamation N.Y. State Senate, 2003, U.S. Congress Proclamation, 2003. Mem. Am. Assn. Sch. Adminstrs., Assn. Orthodox Jewish Tchrs. (v.p. exec. bd., Orgn. award 2003), N.Y. State Assn. Sch. Bus. Ofcls., N.Y.C. Assn. Sch. Bus. Ofcls., Coun. Suprs. and Adminstrs. Avocations: tennis, needlepoint, piano, reading, communal activities.

SCHRAM, MARTIN JAY, journalist; b. Chgo., Sept. 15, 1942; s. Marlo Joseph and Charleene Janice (Fidler) S.; m. Patricia Stewart Morgan, May 23, 1964; children— Kenneth Marlo, David Morgan. BA, U. Fla., 1964. Reporter The Miami (Fla.) News, 1964-65; reporter Newsday, Garden City, N.Y., 1965-67, mem. Washington bur., 1967-69, White House corr., 1969-73, chief Washington bur., sr. editor paper, 1973-79; writer on the presidency Washington Post, 1979-81, nat. affairs writer, 1981-86; assoc. editor, editor Sunday edits. Chgo. Sun-Times, 1986-87; asst. mng. editor, editor Sunday edits. Rocky Mountain News, Denver, 1987-88; commentator Cable News Network, 1988-98; nat. editor Washingtonian Mag., 1988-90; polit. columnist United Feature Syndicate, Newspaper Enterprise Assn., 1989-94, Scripps Howard News Svc., Washington, 1994—; news story edit., columnist Fox News, Washington, 1998-2000; mng. editor Avoiding Armageddon, PBS/Ted Turner Documentaries TV Series, 2001—03. Fellow Gannett Ctr. for Media Studies, Columbia U., 1985-86; guest scholar Woodrow Wilson Internat. Ctr., 1990-91. Author: Running for President, A Journal of the Carter Campaign, 1976, Running for President: 1976, The Carter Campaign, 1977; (with others) The Pursuit of the Presidency, 1980, The Great American Video Game: Presidential Politics in the Television Age, 1987, Speaking Freely, 1995; co-author: Cell Phonex: Invisible Hazards in the Wireless Age, 2001, Avoiding Armaegeddon: Our Future. Our Choice, 2003; co-editor: Mandate for Change, 1993. Recipient James Wright Brown Meml. award Sigma Delta Chi, 1965, Lowell Mellet award Pa. State U., 1988. Office: Scripps Howard News Svc 1090 Vermont Ave NW Ste 1000 Washington DC 20005-4906

SCHRAM, RONALD BYARD, lawyer; b. Detroit, Sept. 7, 1942; s. Byron Canby and Mary Louise (Byard) S.; m. Carol Lorraine Anderson, July 19, 1969; children: Laura Mary, Alison Leigh. BA, Dartmouth Coll., 1964; MA in Econs., Cambridge U., England, 1966; JD, U. Mich., 1969, LLM, 1970, SJD, 1971. Bar: Mass. 1970. Assoc. Ropes & Gray, Boston, 1970-78, ptnr., 1978—2002. Trustee Dartmouth Coll., Hanover, N.H., 1981-92, Dartmouth-Hitchcock Med. Ctr., Lebanon, N.H., 1983-93, New Eng. Sports Mus., Cambridge, Mass., 1984-1999, Derby Acad., Hingham, Mass., 1982-89, ctrl. New Eng. chpt., Nat. Multiple Sclerosis Soc., Waltham, Mass., 2002—; bd. visitors Rockefeller Ctr. of Pub. Policy, Dartmouth Coll., 2003—. Keasbey Found. fellow, Cambridge U., 1964-66; George M. Humphrey fellow in law econ. policy, U. Mich. Law Sch., Ann Arbor, 1969-70. Mem. Boston Bar Assn., Am. Acad. Hosp. Attys., Phi Beta Kappa. E-mail: cschram1@aol.com.

SCHRAM, SUSAN GALE, agriculturist, consultant; b. Grand Rapids, Mich., June 19, 1948; d. Paul Gerard and Dorothy Maxine (Putnam) S. BS, Mich. State U., 1970, MA, 1973; PhD, U.Md. Tchr. Lansing (Mich.) City Schs., 1970; mem. child care staff Hawthorn Ctr. Psychiat. Facility, Northville, Mich., 1971-72; rsch. asst. U. Mich., Ann Arbor, 1973; county extension agt. Grand Haven, Mich., 1975-76; state program leader Coop. Extension Svc., East Lansing, Mich., 1976-80; exec. sec. Joint Council on Food and Agrl. Scis. U.S. Dept Agr., Washington, 1980-82; sr. rsch. assoc. Ctr. for Policy Rsch., Bethesda, Md., 1982-83; dir. rsch. & devel. LBS Internat., Bethesda, Md., 1983-84; cons. Office Sec. Agr. for Pub. Liason, Washington, 1984; staff Office Internat. Programs U. Md., 1985-86; spl. asst. to assoc. v.p. for agrl., 1987-88; spl. asst. to vice chancellor, 1988-90; asst. dir. fed. rels. for internat. programs Nat. Assn. State Univs. and Land Grant Colls., 1990-92; food and agrl. coord., dep. dir. Wash. ops. Consortium for Internat. Earth Sci. Info. Network, 1992-99; dep. dir. Wash. ops., 1996-99; pres. TBR Internat., Inc., Washington, 1999—2001; exec. dir. Partnership to Cut Hunger in Africa, 2000-2001; v.p. ACDI/VOCA, 2001—. Author handbooks, books and papers in field. V.p. Potowmac Overlook Condominiums, Washington, 1985. Recipient Exemplary Svc. award Asst. Sec. of Agr. for Sci. and Edn., 1982; named Mich. Regional Young Career Woman of Yr., Bus. and Profl. Women, 1976; grantee rural devel. Title V, 1977. Mem. Assn. Internat. Agriculture and Rural Devel. (pres. 1997-98, Disting. Svc. award 1999), Nat. Policy Assn., Phi Kappa Phi, Omicron Nu, Kappa Alpha Theta. Congregationalist. Avocation: photography. Home: 1001 26th St NW Apt 708 Washington DC 20037-1604 Office: ACDI/VOCA 50 F St NW Ste 1075 Washington DC 20001

SCHRAMEK, TOMAS, ballet dancer, educator; b. Bratislava, Czechoslovakia, Sept. 11, 1944; emigrated to Can., 1968, naturalized, 1973; s. Hans and Valeria (Neudorfer) S. BFA, Acad. Mus. and Theatre Arts, Bratislava, 1968. Mem. Sluk, Slovakia folk dance ensemble, 1959-68, prin. dancer, 1964-68; dancer Nat. Ballet Can., 1969-71, soloist, 1971-73, prin. dancer, 1973-91, prin. character artist, ballet master, 1991—. Mem. Actors Equity Assn., Assn. Can. TV and Radio Artists. Home: 125 Rose Park Dr Toronto ON Canada M4T 1R6 Office: Nat Ballet Canada 470 Queens Quay West Toronto ON Canada M5V 3K4 E-mail: tomaschr@rogers.com.

SCHRAMM, BERNARD CHARLES, JR., retired advertising agency executive; b. Balt., Jan. 23, 1928; s. Bernard C. and Juliet Marie (Barranger) Schramm; m. Florence Mae Fangman, 1950; children: Stephanie Schramm McDaniel, Carol Schramm Molander, Bernard Charles III, Claudia Schramm Smith. Grad., Balt. Poly. Inst., 1946. Prodn. mgr. Van Sant, Dugdale & Co., Balt., 1946-52; media dir. AWL Advt., Balt., 1952-55; dir. prodn. Henry J. Kaufman Assocs., Washington, 1955-58; exec. v.p. Avalon Hill Co., Balt., 1958-64; v.p. Cargill, Wilson & Acree Advt., Richmond, Va., 1964-68; pres. William Cook Advt. Inc. (now William Cook Mktg. Comm.), Jacksonville, Fla., 1968-89, chmn. bd., 1989-97; ret., 1997. Chmn. Otis F. Smith Found., 1991—97. Mem. exec. com., v.p. United Way N.E. Fla., 1982-87, bd. dirs., 1982-93; bd. dirs. N.E. Fla. chpt. ARC, 1976-89, chmn., 1980-81; bd. dirs. Fla. C.C. Found., 1976-89. Mem.: Am. Assn. Advt. Agys. (chmn. Fla. coun. 1984—85, So. Region Bd. of Govs. 1988—92, chmn. 1989, nat. bd. dirs., agy. mgmt. com. 1989—92), Jacksonville Area C. of C., San Jose Club, Rotary Club. Republican. Roman Catholic. Avocations: golf, reading, spectator sports, hunting. Home: 12856 Bay Plantation Dr Jacksonville FL 32223-0784

SCHRAMM, GEOFFREY SAUNDERS, webmaster; s. Lyn K. Saunders and Donald Arthur Schramm. B.A., George Mason U., Fairfax, Virginia, 1989—93; M.A., U. of Md., College Park, Maryland, 1994—96. Web content editor Nat. Endowment for the Humanities, Washington, 2002—, webmaster, 2000—02; instr. of english languages and literatures U. of Md., College Park, Md., 1996—2000. Author: (essay) Jane Sexes It Up: True Confessions of Feminist Desire; author: (designer) (web-based academic project) Brothers in Arms: Masculinity in Whitman's Civil War; editor (editorial assistant): The Classroom Electric: Dickinson, Whitman, and American Culture; editor: (editorial assistant and designer) The Dickinson Electronic Archives. Co-chair Lesbian, Gay, Bisexual, and Transgender Students' Assn. for George Mason U., Fairfax, Va., 1992—93. Recipient Outstanding Tchr. Nominee, The Panhellenic Assn., Intrafraternity Coun., and the Panhellenic Coun., U. of Md., 1998; fellow Grad. Tchg. Fellowship, U. of Md., 1994-2000; grantee Block grant, Com. for Africa and the Americas, 2000, Goldhaber Travel grant, U. of Md. Grad. Sch., 2001, 1996. Mem.: MLA (del. assembly for mid. atlantic region 2001—).

SCHRAND, RICHARD HENRY, broadcaster, writer; b. Cin., Nov. 1, 1957; s. Edward August and Jane Marie (Scheib) S.; m. Deborah Fortner, 1979 (div. 1985); 1 child, Cynthia Lanette; m. Sharon Lynn Lassandro, Dec. 24, 1986; children: Courtney Lynne, Richard Jr., Brandon Ian. Student, Ohio State U., 1975-76, No. Ky. U., 1976-77. Intern Sta. WCPO-TV, Cin., 1971-75; producer Sta. WKRC-TV, Cin., 1975-79; pub. affairs dir., reporter, anchor Sta. WCSC-TV, Charleston, S.C., 1979-83; actor Phila. Experiment, L.A., 1984; asst. promotion dir. Sta. WLWT-TV, Cin., 1983-86; spl. projects coord. Sta. KXAS-TV, Dallas/Ft. Worth, 1986-87; mgr. media svcs. NBC TV Network, Burbank, Calif., 1987-89; pres. Cyn-Court Enterprises, Burbank, 1989-91; mktg. dir. Sta. WPTA-TV, Ft. Wayne, Ind., 1991-92; v.p., gen. mgr. Branson (Mo.) Broadcasting Corp., 1992-95; dir. spl. projects/nat. media, graphics and advt. creator Jim Owens & Assocs., 1995-98; gen. mgr. Jim Owens Radio, Inc., Nashville, 1995-98; pres. GRFX ByDesign, Nashville, 1996—2004, Broadsword Prod., 2002—; v.p. Komodo Studios, L.A., 1999-2000; instr. computer graphics and web design Nossi Coll. Art, Nashville, 2001—. Instr., spkr. Graphic Design Tour, 2000—; computer design Nossi Coll. Art, 2001—, edu. bd., 2002—, adv. bd., 2003—, instr.-graphic art and design, 2004—; demonstrator 3D software SigGraph, MacWorld, 2001—. Author: Canoma Visual Insight, 2000, 3D Creature Workshop vol. 2, 2000, Macromedia Web Design Handbook, 2000, Adobe Golive 5F/X & Design, 2000, Adobe Live Motion Visual Jumpstart, 2000, Adobe Photoshop 6 Visual Jumpstart, 2000, Poser 4 Pro Pack F/X & Design, 2001, Final Cut Pro 3: The Complete Reference, 2002; contbr.: Pixels: 3D Book, 1999, Mastering Pixels: 3D, 2001; webmaster Crook & Chase Theater, Middle Tenn. LightWave Users Group, Nossi Coll. of Art, Games Plus, Handshak Prodns. Bd. dirs. Project Graduation, Dallas/Ft. Worth, 1986-87; mem. Muscular Dystrophy Assn., Charleston, 1980-83; publicist Housing Now, L.A., 1988. Recipient Regional Emmy award NATAS, 1975, award Broadcast Promotion and Mktg. Exec., Seattle, 1992. Avocations: guitar, writing, singing, golf. Office Phone: 615-812-2705. Business E-Mail: rschrand@broadswordproductions.com.

SCHRANDT, CURTIS LEON, lawyer, securities analyst, financial advisor; b. Van Nuys, Calif., Nov. 21, 1957; s. Edward Leon and Ethel Jeannine (Thompson) S. BS in Bus. Mgmt. summa cum laude, U. Utah, 1992, BA in Bus. Fin., 1993; JD cum laude, Quinnipiac U. Sch. Law, 1996. Bar: Conn. 1996, N.Y. 1998, D.C. 1999; CFA. Owner Friends-Exotic Pets, Salt Lake City and Orem, Utah, 1978-89; mgr. ZCMI Dept. Stores, Salt Lake City, 1991-93; ptnr. Hersh & Fowler-Cruz, White Plains, N.Y., 1996-98; owner Law Offices of Curtis L. Schrandt, Bridgeport, Conn., 1988—, CLS Enterprises, Stratford, Conn., 1996—. Fin. chmn. Hersh & Fowler-Cruz, 1996-98. Mng. editor Quinnipiac Law Rev., 1995-96 (Disting. Svc. award 1996). Mem. ABA, Conn. Bar Assn., N.Y. Bar Assn., D.C. Bar Assn. Office: Law Offices Curtis L Schrandt 35 Courtland St Ste 5 Bridgeport CT 06604 Home: 3158 Main St Stratford CT 06614-4817 Office Phone: 203-345-2138. E-mail: cschrandt@lawyer.com.

SCHRAUTH, WILLIAM LAWRENCE, banker, lawyer; b. Bklyn., Apr. 25, 1935; s. William L. and Louise (Rowland) S.; m. Nancy T. Tollner, Dec. 26, 1959; children: Christopher W., Anne, Michael J., Catherine A. BA, St. Bonaventure U., Olean, N.Y., 1956; JD, Fordham U., 1960. Bar: N.Y. 1960. Ptnr. Evans, Severn, Bankert & Peet and predecessor firms, Utica, N.Y., 1962-73; v.p. The Savs. Bank of Utica, 1973-74, exec. v.p., 1974-77, pres., 1977—. Trustee RSI Retirement Trust. Bd. dirs. Cmty. Found. of Herkimer and Oneida Counties Inc. Republican. Office: The Savs Bank of Utica 233 Genesee St Utica NY 13501-2811

SCHREADLEY, RICHARD LEE, writer, retired newspaper editor; b. Harrisburg, Pa., Jan. 3, 1931; s. Harry Leroy and Flora Rebecca (McQuilken) S.; m. Doris Arlene Sheaffer, Dec. 18, 1952; 1 child, Rhys Leroy. BA, Dickinson Coll., 1952; MA, Tufts U., 1968, MAL.D., 1969, PhD, 1972. Reporter The News and Courier, Charleston, S.C., 1975; asso. editor The Evening Post, Charleston, 1975-76, editorial page editor, 1976-77, editor, 1977-81; exec. editor The Evening Post and The News and Courier, 1981-88; assoc. editor and sr. writer mil. and polit. affairs The News and Courier, 1989. Author: From the Rivers to the Sea, The United States Navy in Vietnam, 1992, Valor and Virtue, The Washington Light Infantry in Peace and in War, 1996. Chmn. Fgn. Affairs Forum of Charleston, 1987-88, mem. steering com., 1989. Served to comdr. USN, 1949-52, 56-73. Mem. Navy League, Ret. Officer Assn., Washington Light Infantry, German Friendly Soc. Charleston, Army-Navy Club of Washington, Country Club of Charleston. Home: 812 Clearview Dr Charleston SC 29412-4511 E-mail: rlschrea@bellsouth.net.

SCHRECK, RICHARD THOMAS, accountant; b. Waterloo, N.Y., USA, Apr. 27, 1930; s. George Leonard and Isabella Cowan Schreck; m. Virginia Doris Main Schreck, Aug. 13, 1994; m. Barbara Ann Walsh Schreck, June 25, 1960 (dec. Sept. 1990); children: Michael Joseph, James Edward, Mary Ann. M.S. Music Edn., Ithaca Coll., Ithaca N.Y., 1948—53; Post Grad. Acctg., Syracuse U., 1956—63. Pub. acct. G.L. Schreck Acctg. Firm, Waterloo, NY, 1955—56; pub. acct. pvt. practice Waterloo, NY, 1956—. Pub. acct. Nat. Soc. Acct., Waterloo, NY, 1961—. Author: Waterloo in 1858, 1969; co-author: The History and Origin of Meml. Day In Waterloo, New York, 1966; author: The Descendants of Michael And Mary Blind Schreck, 1978. Mem. Augusta (GA) Symphony Orch., 1954, 7th Army Symphony Orch., 1955, Waterloo Chamber of Commerce, 1956—68, pres., 1967—68; trustee Village of Waterloo, 1964—77; founder, rsch. chmn. Waterloo Meml. Day Centennial Com., 1965—66; trustee Waterloo Libr. and Hist. Soc., 1965—97; ch. historian St. Mary's Ch., Waterloo, NY, 1966—; co-chmn. Waterloo Ctrl. Sch. Centennial Comm., 1985—86. With U.S. Army, 1953—55. Democrat. Catholic. Achievements include Co-Founder: Waterloo Meml. Day Museum; Provided the concept for the artist's design of the official Meml. Day Emblem; Had a major role in obtaining official nat. recognition for Waterloo, N.Y., as the birthplace of Meml. Day through congressional legislation and Presidential Proclamation, 1966. Office: Richard T Schreck Pub Acct 75 Washington St Waterloo NY 13165-1703

SCHRECK, ROBERT, commodities trader; b. 1944; With Pillsbury Co., Mpls., 1968-93, v.p.; exec. v.p. Commodity Specialists Co., Mpls., 1993—. Office: Commodity Specialists Co 301 4th Ave S Minneapolis MN 55415-1015

SCHRECK, ROBERT A., JR., lawyer; b. Buffalo; BS in Bus. Adminstrn., Georgetown U., 1974; MBA, Northwestern U., 1975, JD, 1978. Bar: Ill. 1978. Ptnr. McDermott, Will & Emery, Chgo., 1978—. Mem. ABA. Office: McDermott Will & Emery 227 W Monroe St Ste 4400 Chicago IL 60606-5096 E-mail: rschreck@mwe.com.

SCHRECKINGER, SY EDWARD, advertising executive, consultant; b. Bklyn., Jan. 10, 1937; s. Robert and Bessie (Gable) S.; m. Linda Fiarman, Mar. 4, 1962; children: Jamie Fran, Jon Gary. B.F.A., Pratt Inst., 1958. Art dir. Sudler and Hennesey, N.Y.C., 1958-61; sr. art dir. Marschalk Co., N.Y.C., 1961-63; group supr. Grey Advt., N.Y.C., 1963-66; v.p., assoc. creative dir. Hicks & Greist, N.Y.C., 1966-69; sr. v.p., assoc. creative dir. Young & Rubicam Inc., N.Y.C., 1969-88; advt. and mktg. cons. Oceanside, NY, 1988—2002; advt.-mktg. dir. Magnificent Muffin Corp., 1995—. Recipient Lion Venice Internat. Film Festival, 1972, Andy Ad Club, N.Y., 1965, 86, award Internat. Bus. Assn., Best award Hollywood Radio & TV Soc., 1971, Clio Am. TV Comml. Festival, 1967, 72, 82, 85, Effy, 1985. Jewish.

SCHREIBER, ALAN HICKMAN, lawyer; b. Muncie, Ind., Apr. 4, 1944; s. Ephriam and Clarrisa (Hickman) S.; m. Phyllis Jean Chamberlain, Dec. 22, 1972; children: Jennifer Aline, Brett Justin. Student, DePauw U., 1962-64; BS in Bus., Ind. U., 1966, JD, 1969. Bar: Fla. 1971, U.S. Dist. Ct. (so. dist.) Fla. Asst. State Atty.'s Office, Ft. Lauderdale, Fla., 1971-76; pub. defender 17th Jud. Cir., Ft. Lauderdale, 1976—. Cons. Fla. Bar News on Criminal Law, 1982; lobbyist for indigent funding, Fla., 1980—; apptd. to Supreme Ct. Com. on Racial and Ethic Bias; co-chair Chiles-MacKay task force on criminal justice. Contbr. articles to profl. jours. Mem. Dem. Exec. Com., Ft. Lauderdale, 1980; mem. Plantation Dem. Club, 1983; campaign chmn. Goldstein for Atty. Gen. Fla., 1982. Named Young Dem. of Yr., Broward County Young Dems., 1980; Man of Yr., Jewish War Vets., 1982; recipient B'nai B'rith Pub. Servant award, 1990, Dem. of Yr. award 2000, Harry Galkin Meml. award 2002. Mem. Fla. Bar Assn., Broward County Bar Assn., ABA, Nat. Legal Aid Defenders Assn., Phi Alpha Delta. Home: 885 Orchid Dr Fort Lauderdale FL 33317-1221 Office: 201 SE 6th St Fort Lauderdale FL 33301-3303 Office Phone: 954-831-7662.

SCHREIBER, BERTRAM MANUEL, mathematics professor; b. Seattle, Nov. 4, 1940; s. Isador and Amy (Hurwitz) S.; m. Rita Ruth Stusser, June 30, 1963; children: Susannah M. Schreiber Bechhofer, Deborah H. Schreiber Shapiro, Abraham D., Elisabeth T. Schreiber Seigel. BA, Yeshiva U., 1962; MS, U. Wash., 1966, PhD, 1968. Asst. prof. Wayne State U., Detroit, 1968-71, assoc. prof., 1971-78, prof., 1978—, chair dept. math., 1987-90. Vis. prof. Hebrew U., Jerusalem, 1975, 2000, Mich. State U., East Lansing, 1982-83, Nat. U. Singapore, 1992, U. New South Wales, Australia, 1992, Indian Statis. Inst., 1993, Tata Inst. Fund Res., Bombay, 1993, Bar Ilan U., 1993, Tel Aviv U., 1993, U. Utrecht, The Netherlands, 1993, U. Wroclaw, Poland, 1993, U. Paris VII, 1999, U. Granada, Spain, 1999-2000, U. Wash., Seattle, 2000. Contbr. articles to profl. jours. NSF grantee, 1968-87; Sci. and Engring. Rsch. Coun. Gt. Britain fellow U. Edinburgh, Scotland, 1976. Mem. Am. Math. Soc., Math. Assn. Am., Israel Math. Union, Edinburgh Math. Soc. Achievements include research in the fields of harmonic analysis, topological groups, and probability theory. Office: Wayne State U Dept Math Detroit MI 48202 Office Phone: 313-577-8838. E-mail: berts@math.wayne.edu.

SCHREIBER, DAVID M. lawyer, judge; b. Kansas City, Mo., Aug. 13, 1937; s. William and Hinda Gold Schreiber; m. Adrienne Rennie Ehre, May 31, 1959; children: Beth F., Kathy L. JD, LLB, U. Ariz., 1962; cert. jud. devel. adminstrv. law, Nat. Jud. Coll., 1997. Bar: Ariz., 1962, Nev., 1968, U.S. Ct. Appeals (9th cir.), 1978, U.S. Dist. Ct., 1968, U.S. Supreme Ct., 1972. Pvt. practice, Tucson, 1962-64; hearings officer, referee Indsl. Commn. Ariz., Phoenix, 1964-67; asst. v.p., house counsel First Western Savings & Loan, Las Vegas, Nev., 1967-69; chief dep. pub. defender Clark County Pub. Defenders Office, Las Vegas, 1969-71; chief dep. dist. atty., counsel Nev. Juvenile Ct., Las Vegas, 1971-76; pvt. practice Las Vegas, 1976-92; adminstrv. law judge State of Nev., Dept. Motor Vehicles and Pub. Safety, Las Vegas, 1992—. Chmn. Cmty. Devel. Adv. com., Clark County, Nev., 1995-96. Recipient Law Enforcement Commendation medal Nat. Soc. Sons Am. Revolution, 1995 Mem. Nat. Assn. Adminstrv. Law Judges. Avocations: classical music, collecting art, politics. Home: 3310 Brookfield Dr Las Vegas NV 89120-1969 Office: State Nev Dept Motor Vehicles 2701 E Sahara Ave Las Vegas NV 89104-4119

SCHREIBER, EILEEN SHER, artist; b. Denver, 1925; d. Michael Herschel and Sarah Deborah (Tannenbaum) Sher; m. Jonas Schreiber, Mar. 27, 1945; children: Jeffrey, Barbara, Michael. Student, U. Utah, 1942-45, NYU ext., 1966-68, Montclair (N.J.) State Coll., 1975-79; also pvt. art study. Exhibited Morris Mus. Arts and Scis., Morristown, N.J., 1965-73, N.J. State Mus., 1969, Lever House, N.Y.C., 1971, Paramus (N.J.) Mus., 1973, Newark Mus., 1978, 1991-92, Am. Water Color Soc., Audubon Artists, N.A.D. Gallery, N.Y.C., Pallazzo Vecchio Florence, Italy, Art Expo 1987, 1988, India Mus., 1994, 95, Athens (Greece) Mus., 1996, 97, Gaelin Gallery, Whippany, N.J., 2004; represented in permanent collections Tex. A&M U., Telesoft Inc., Phoenix, State of N.J., Morris Mus., Seton Hall U., Bloomfield (N.J.) Coll., Barclay Bank of Eng., N.J., Somerset Coll., NYU, Morris County State Coll., Broad Nat. Bank, Newark, Ind. Cmty. Bank, Consulting Actuaries, Internat., IBM, Am. Tel. Co., RCA, Johnson & Johnson, Champion Internat. Paper Co., Sony, Mitsubishi, Celanese Co., Squibb Corp., Nabisco, Nat. Bank Phila., Data Control, Ind. Cmty. Bank, Sperry Univac, Ga. Pacific Co., Pub. Svc. Co. N.J., Diane Levine Gallery, Boston, S.W. Gallery, Long Beach Island, N.J., others; also pvt. collections. Recipient awards N.J. Watercolor Soc., 1969, 72, 1st award in watercolor Hunterdon Art Ctr., 1972, Best in Show award Short Hills State Show, 1976, Tri-State Purchase award Somerset Coll., 1977, Art Expo, N.Y.C., 1987, 88, numerous others. Mem. Nat. Assn. Women Artists (chmn. watercolor jury, Collage award 1983, Marian Halpren Meml. award 1995), Nat., N.Y. Artists Equity, Printmaker Coun. Visual Artists (1st award in printmaking 1996), Women Visual Artists (Fla.). Office Phone: 609-492-4011.

SCHREIBER, GEORGE RICHARD, association executive, writer; b. Ironton, Ohio, July 4, 1922; s. George Joseph and Marie Frances (Heitzman) S.; m. Veva Jeanette Hopkins, May 14, 1945; children— Susan (Mrs. Arlan Shorey), George, Ellen (Mrs. Norman Hodge). AB, St. Joseph's Coll., Rensselaer, Ind., 1943, L.H.D., 1974; MA, U. Chgo., 1944. Exec. editor Billboard mag., 1945-60; editor, pub. Vend mag., 1946-66; editorial dir. Billboard Publs., 1966-70; pres., chief exec. officer Nat. Automatic Mdsg. Assn., Chgo., 1970-88, pres. emeritus, 1988—; pres., chief exec. Sunrise Books, 1994—. Mem. staff and faculty U. Chgo., 1944-46 Author: Verses from the River Country, 1941, What Makes News, 1943, Automatic Selling, 1954, A Concise History of Vending in the U.S.A, 1965, revised 2d edit., 1990, Millenium edit., 1999, The Bobby Baker Affair— How to Make Millions in Washington, 1964, Vending For Investors-How to Spot Phony Deals, 1994, 2d edit., 1996; contbg. author: Handbook of Modern Marketing, 1986. Chmn. Glenview (Ill.) Plan Commn., 1962-64, mayor, 1964-67; chmn. Region 1, Chgo. Area Transp. Study Group, 1962-63; bd. dirs. Rockefeller Meml. Chapel, U. Chgo., 1944-45; trustee St. Joseph's Coll., 1964—, chmn., 1970-76, life trustee, 1978—. Recipient Jesse H. Neal award for editorial achievement, 1964; dedication of St. Joseph's Coll. (Ind.) G. Richard Schreiber Dept. Humanities, 1987. Mem. The Authors Guild Inc., Am. Bus. Press (editorial bd.), Assn. Econs. Council, Am. Soc. Assn. Execs., Tavern Club, Internat. Club, Tower Club. Home: 735 Ravine Ave Lake Bluff IL 60044-2625 E-mail: vevaj@aol.com.

SCHREIBER, HARRY, JR., management consultant; b. Columbus, Ohio, Apr. 1, 1934; s. C. Harry and Audrey (Sard) S.; m. Margaret Ruth Heinzman, June 12, 1955; children: Margaret Elizabeth Schreiber Yeager, Thomas Edward, Amy Katherine Schreiber Garcia. BS, MIT, 1955; MBA, Boston U., 1958. CPA, N.Y. Acct. truck and coach divsn. Gen. Motors Corp., Pontiac, Mich., 1955; instr. MIT, Boston, 1958—61; pres. Data-Service, Inc., 1960—64, Harry Schreiber Assocs., Wellesley, Mass., 1964; mgr., nat. dir. merchandising cons. Peat, Marwick, Mitchell & Co., N.Y.C., 1964—70, ptnr. Chgo., 1970-75; chmn. bd. Close, Martin, Schreiber & Co., 1975—83; ptnr. Deloitte Haskins & Sells, 1983-85; chmn. bd. Harry Schreiber & Assocs., Ltd., 1985—. Mem. staff Work Simplification Conf., Lake Placid, N.Y., 1959-60; Tobe retailing lectr. Harvard Bus. Sch., 1963; lectr. indsl. engring. Northeastern U., 1958-61; lectr. info. sys. Babson Coll., 1962; lectr. Bridgeport Engring. Ins., 1962, Western Mich. U., 1975. Pub., Retail Working Papers, 1991—. Treas. Emmanuel Episcopal Ch., Chestertown, 1999—2004. Mem. Am. Inst. Indsl. Enrs. (chmn. data processing divsn. 1964-66, chpt. v.p. 1961, 65, chmn. retail industries divsn. 1976-78), Com. Internat. Congress Transp.Confs., Assn. for Computing Machinery, Assn. for Sys. Mgmt., Inst. Mgmt. Scis., Retail Rsch. Soc., Retail Fin. Execs., Nat. Retail Fedn. (retail sys. specifications com., acctg. stds. com.), Food Distbn. Rsch. Soc. (dir. 1972-78, pres. 1974), Japan-Am. Soc. Chgo., MIT Faculty Club, Hidden Creek Country Club (Reston, Va.), Chester River Yacht and Country Club (Chestertown, Md.), Army and Navy Club (Washington), Plaza Club (Chgo.). Republican. Home: 105 High St Chestertown MD 21620-1515 Office: 105 High St Chestertown MD 21620-1515 Office Phone: 410-778-3842. Personal E-mail: sharryschreiber@cs.com.

SCHREIBER, JAMES RALPH, obstetrician, researcher; b. Rosebud, Tex., May 29, 1946; s. Lester B. and Jane Elinore (Hodges) Schreiber; m. Mary Celia Schmitt, Aug. 16, 1968; children: Lisa, Joseph, Laura, Cynthia. BA, Rice U., 1968; MD, Johns Hopkins U., 1972. Diplomate Am. Coll. Ob-gyn., Am. Bd. Reproductive Endocrinology. Intern, ob-gyn. U. So. Calif. Los Angeles County Hosp., 1972-73, resident ob-gyn., 1973-74, 76-78; fellow reproductive endocrinology NIH, Bethesda, Md., 1974-76; asst. prof. ob-gyn U. Calif., San Diego, 1978-82; assoc. prof. U. Chgo., 1982-87, prof., 1988-91; prof., chmn. dept. Washington U., St. Louis, 1991—. Contbr. articles to profl. jours. Grantee, NIH, 1978—. Mem.: Soc. Gynecologic Investigation. Home: 22 Frontenac Estates Saint Louis MO 63131-2600 Office: Washington U Sch Medicine Dept Ob-Gyn 4911 Barnes Hospital Plz Saint Louis MO 63110-1003 E-mail: schreiberj@msnotes.wustl.edu.

SCHREIBER, JOHN T. lawyer; b. N.Y.C., Mar. 30, 1960; s. Toby Schreiber and Morley Ann (Perrish) Clark; children: Zoe Cassandra Bloch Schreiber, Alana Nichole Perrish Schreiber. BA Politics, Brandeis U., 1982; JD, Santa Clara U., 1986. Bar: Calif. 1987(cert. specialist appellate law); U.S. Dist. Ct. (no. dist.) Calif. 1987; U.S. Dist. Ct. (ea. dist.) Calif. 1990; U.S. Ct. Appeals (9th cir.) 1989, U.S. Supreme Ct. 1998. Assoc. Law Offices of Wm. D. McHugh, San Jose, Calif., 1987-88, Hallgrimson, McNichols, McCann & Inderbitzen, Pleasanton, Calif., 1989-92; pvt. practice Walnut Creek, Calif., 1993—. Bd. dirs. East Bay Depot for Creative Re-use, Oakland. Field coord. Cen. Contra Costa County, Tom Bradley Campaign for Govs., Concord, Calif., 1982, Clinton-Gore Campaign, Walnut Creek, Calif., 1992; mem. Ask-A-Lawyer Program Contra Costa Legal Svcs. Found., Richmond, Calif., 1992-96; co-chair Clinton-Gore Contra Costa County, 1996. Mem. ABA, Contra Costa Bar Assn. (program dir. appellate sect. 1993-95, 2000—, pres. appellate sect. 1995-96, MCLE com. 1995—), Santa Clara Bar Assn., Am. Israeli Pub. Affairs Com. Avocations: reading, golf, softball, movies, exercising. Office: 2000 Ridgewood Rd Alamo CA 94507-1044

SCHREIBER, KURT GILBERT, lawyer; b. Milw., Aug. 22, 1946; s. Raymond R. and Mildred L. (Kleist) S.; m. Nelda Beth Van Buren, May 3, 1974; children— Katharine Anne, Matthew Edward AB in Econs., Cornell U., 1968; JD, U. Mich., 1971; MS in Divinity, Vanderbilt U., 2003. Bar: Wis. 1971, Tex. 1979, Tenn. 1997. Internat. atty. Tenneco Internat. Holdings Co., London, 1974-78; atty. Tenneco Inc., Houston, 1978-80; 2d v.p., asst. gen. counsel Am. Gen. Corp., Houston, 1980-83, v.p., gen. counsel, 1983-84, sr. v.p., gen. counsel, 1984-93, sr. v.p., corp. sec., 1993-94; pvt. practice Houston, 1994-96; exec. v.p., gen. counsel Direct Gen. Corp., Nashville, 1996-98, pres., 1998—2001. Bd. dir. Cumberland Trust and Investment Co., Urban Housing Solutions. Fellow Tex. Bar Found.; mem. ABA, Wis. Bar Assn., Tex. Bar Assn., Tenn. Bar Assn. Home: 524 Turtle Creek Dr Brentwood TN 37027-5617

SCHREIBER, LOLA F. former state legislator; m. Marion Schreiber; 2 children. Student, S.D. State U. Mem. S. D. Ho. Reps., to 1997, vice-chmn. edn. com., mem. state affairs com. Chmn. edn. com., mem. judiciary com., mem. tax com., chmn. legislators exec. bd., 1995, 96, chmn. edn. com. Nat. Conf. State Legislators; commr. Edn. Commn. States; mem. policy and priorities com.; mem. adv. bd. Policymakers Inst., Danforth Found.; mem. Fin. Project. Home: 30045 173rd St Gettysburg SD 57442-5301

SCHREIBER, MELVYN HIRSH, radiologist; b. Galveston, Tex., May 28, 1931; s. Edward and Sue Schreiber; m. Laurentina; children— William, Diane, Karen, Lori. MD, U. Tex. Med. Br., Galveston, 1955. Diplomate: Am. Bd. Radiology (trustee 1987—). Intern U. Tex. Med. Br., Galveston, 1955-56, resident, 1956-59, asst. prof. radiology, 1961-64, asso. prof., 1964-67, prof., 1967—, chmn. dept. radiology, 1976-91. Author: (novels) Old Dog, New Tricks, A Collection of Essays, 1995, Footprints, 2001. Served as capt. M.C. U.S. Army, 1959-61. Markle Found. scholar, 1963-68 Fellow Am. Coll. Radiology; mem. Assn. Univ. Radiologists (pres. 1974-75). Office: U Tex Med Br Dept Radiology Galveston TX 77555-0001

SCHREIBER, PAUL SOLOMON, lawyer; b. Krakow, Poland, Mar. 29, 1941; came to U.S., 1949; s. John and Betty (Silber) S.; m. Joan A. Perlmutter, Mar. 20, 1971; children: Douglas Arun, Stacey Lauren. BS, CCNY, 1963; LLB, NYU, 1966, LLM, 1967; postgrad., U. Paris, 1967-68. Bar: N.Y. 1966. Assoc. Marshal, Bratter, Greene, Allison & Tucker, N.Y.C., 1969-76, ptnr., 1976-82, Kramer, Levin, Naftalis, Nessen, Kamin & Frankel, N.Y.C., 1982-94, Shearman & Sterling, N.Y.C., 1994—. Bd. dirs. Harbor Trust Co., Hoboken, N.J., 1985-92. Editor: Annual Survey Am. Law; co-author articles, papers and revs. Trustee Park Ave. Synagogue, N.Y.C., 1985—, pres., 1998-2003, hon. pres., 2003–; bd. dirs. Am. Friends of the Rambam Med. Ctr., N.Y.C., 1989-99, N.Y.C. chpt. Nat. Multiple Sclerosis Soc., 1991—, Sch. for Strings, 1994-96; bd. overseers Rabbinical Sch. Jewish Theol. Sem., 1995-96. Arthur Garfield Hayes fellow; Ford Found. fellow. Democrat. Jewish. Office: Shearman & Sterling 599 Lexington Ave Fl C2 New York NY 10022-6069

SCHREIBER, ROY EDWARD, education educator, writer; b. Newark, Mar. 13, 1942; s. William and Beatrice (Robinson) Schreiber; m. Linda Chen, June 29, 1996; 1 child, Elise K Watts. BA in history cum laude, U. of Calif. at Los Angeles, 1962, MA in history, 1965; PhD in history, London U., 1967. Asst. prof. history Upsala Coll., NJ, 1967—68, Ind. U., 1968—75, assoc. prof. history, 1976—85, prof. history, 1986—. Presenter in field. Author: (book) The Political Career of Sir Robert Naunton, 1589-1635, 1981, The First Carlisle- Sir James Hay, 1st Earl of Carlisle, 1580-1636 as Courtier, Diplomat and Entrepreneur, 1984, The Fortunate Adversities of William Bligh, 1991; editor (also co-editor): Hardinge of Penshurst, A Study in the Old Diplomacy, 1980, A Protestant in Purgatory, Richard Whately, Archbishop of Dublin, 1981, Fragmenta Regalia, 2002; author: (plays) Captain Bligh Against the World, 1988, Mr. Christian's Revenge, 1992, Remembering, 1997, (short stories) Surviving Moriori, Living History, 1993, Wayward Souls, 1994, Triumphant Reason, 1994—95; contbr. articles; referee Jour. of Brit. Studies, 1980, Can. Jour. of History, 1981, Jour. of Excellence in Coll. Tchg., 1998. Fellow: Royal Hist. Soc., Inst. of Hist. Rsch.; mem.: Authors Guild, Dramatists Guild. Home: 3406 Hays Ct South Bend IN 46614 Office: Ind Univ 1700 Mishawaka Ave South Bend IN 46634 Office Fax: 574-520-4538. Business E-Mail: rschreib@iusb.edu.

SCHREIBER, SALLY ANN, lawyer; b. El Paso, Tex., July 23, 1951; d. Warren Thomas and Joyce (Honey) S.; children: Amanda Honey, Ryan Thorp Luther. BBA, U. N.Mex., 1973; JD, Stanford U., 1976. Bar: Calif. 1976, Tex. 1977. Assoc. Johnson & Swanson, Dallas, 1976-81, ptnr., 1981-89; mem. firm Johnson & Gibbs, P.C., Dallas, 1989-93; of counsel Cox & Smith, Inc., Dallas, 1993-94; shareholder Munsch Hardt Kopf & Harr, P.C., Dallas, 1994—. Spkr.

in field. Editor Stanford U. Law Rev., 1975-76; co-author paper Internat. Bar Assn., 1986. Bd. dirs. The Lyric Opera of Dallas, 1982-86, bd. trustees, 1986-90; mem. law sch. bd. vis. Stanford (Calif.) U., 1981-84, 2004—; dir. Tex. Bus. Law Found., 1989—, treas. 1994-96, sec. 1996-98, 2003—. Mem. ABA, Tex. Bar Assn. (corp. law com. 1981—, vice chair 1993-97, chair 1997-2001, ptnrship. law com. 1985—, ltd. liability company com. 1992—, opinion com. 1989-98, codification com. 1997—, bus. law sect. coun. 1996—, vice chmn. 2004—), Calif. Bar Assn., Dallas Bar Assn. Home: 2737 Purdue Ave Dallas TX 75225-7910 Office: Munsch Hardt Kopf & Harr PC 4000 Fountain Pl 1445 Ross Ave Ste 4000 Dallas TX 75202-2790 E-mail: sschreiber@munsch.com.

SCHREIER, BRADLEY, sales executive, marketing executive; b. Aug. 19, 1951; m. Marge St. Pierre; children: Ryan, Kyle. BS in Social Studies and Econs., Minn. State U., Mankato, 1973. Letterpress supr. Carlson Craft, Mankato, Minn., 1973-74, custom svc. supr., 1974-76, office mgr., 1976-79; v.p. sales and mktg. Taylor Corp., Mankato, 1980-85, pres., COO, 1985—2001, CEO, 2001—. Bd. dirs. Malto Meal Corp., Mpls. Bd. dirs. Mankato Area United Way, 1975-81, v.p., 1979, 80, pres. bd. dirs., 1981; bd. dirs. YMCA, 1983-92, chmn. fin. com., co-chair spl. gifts divsn. 1 million dollar bldg. expansion capital campaign; bd. dirs. Immanuel-St. Joseph's Hosp., 1984-94, treas., 1988, vice chmn., treas, 1989, chmn. med. office bldg. task force, 1990, vice chmn., 1990, chmn. bd. dirs., 1991, 92, mem. exec. com., 1993-94; bd. dirs. Mankato Area Cath. Sch. Found., 1988—; pres. parish coun., mem. coun. Holy Rosary Ch., 1988—, chmn. fin. com., mem. com., 1989—; mem. pers. com. Loyola Cath. High Sch., 1989-90, mem. sch. bd., 1989-90; chmn. Mankato Area Cath. Sch. Bd., 1990—; coach Mankato Area Youth Baseball Assn., 1986—, bd. dirs., 1991—; pres. Mankato Royals Baseball, 1989, 90, bd. dirs., 1989-93; Fitzgerald 7th and 8th grade basketball coach, 1988, mem. Loyola Booster Club; bd. dirs. Mankato Basketball Assn., 1989—, traveling team coach, 1989—; basketball team coach Holy Rosary. Recipient Book of Golden Deeds award for Outstanding Cmty. Svc., Mankato Exch. Club, 1994, Disting. Alumni award Minn. State U., Mankato, 1994. Mem. KC. Office: Taylor Corp 1725 Roe Crest Dr Mankato MN 56003-1807 Office Phone: 507-625-2828.

SCHREIER, KAREN ELIZABETH, judge; U.S. atty. U.S. Dept. Justice Sioux Falls, S.D., 1993-99; judge U.S. Dist. Ct., Rapid City, SD, 1999—. Office: US Dist Ct 515 9th St Rapid City SD 57701-2626

SCHREIER, PETER, tenor; b. Meissen, Germany, July 29, 1935; Ed., Dresden Hochschule für Musik, Germany. With Dresden State Opera, Germany, 1959-63, Berlin Staatsoper, Germany, 1963. Appearances include Vienna State Opera, Salzburg Festival, La Scala, Milan, Sadler's Wells, London, Met. Opera, N.Y.C., Teatro Colon, Buenos Aires; recital debut London, 1978; debut as conductor, 1969; has conducted recordings of several choral works by J.S. Bach and Mozart. Office: Kammersänger Calberlastr 13 D-01326 Dresden Germany

SCHREINER, ALBERT WILLIAM, physician, educator; b. Cin., Feb. 15, 1926; s. Albert William and Ruth Mary (Neuer) S.; m. Jean Tellstrom, Dec. 12, 1953; 1 child, David William. BS, U. Cin., 1947, MD, 1949. Diplomate Am. Bd. Internal Medicine, 1958. Clin. investigator VA Hosp., Cin., 1957-59, chief med. svc., 1959-68, dir. dept. internal medicine, 1968-93; dir. resident program internal medicine Christ Hosp., Cin., 1978-87; mem. faculty U. Cin. Coll. Medicine, 1955—, assoc. prof. medicine, 1962-67, prof. internal medicine, 1967-98, emeritus prof. internal medicine, 1998—; attending physician Cin. Gen. Hosp., 1957—95. Cons. to med. dir. Gen. Electric, 1987-96; med. dirs. United Home Care Hospice, 1993-99, United Home Care Agy.; chair instnl. rev. bd. The Christ Hosp., 1988—; subinvestigator Sterling Rsch. Group, 2003—. Contbr. articles to profl. jours. Bd. dirs., chmn. health com. Cmty. Action Commn., 1968-71; trustee Drake Meml. Hosp., 1975-78, Leukemia Found. Southwest Ohio, Cancer Control, Am. Cancer Soc., bd. dirs. Hamilton County unit, 1990; bd. dirs., chair profl. affairs com. United Home Care Agy., 1998; bd. dirs. Gamble Inst. Med. Rsch., Cin., 1991-96, Sign of the Cross Housing for the Homeless, 2001-. Fellow: ACP; mem.: Am. Soc. Clin. Rsch. Program Dirs. Internal Medicine, Assn. Program Dirs. Internal Medicine, Clin. Soc. Internal Medicine (pres. 1979—80), Ohio Soc. Internal Medicine (trustee 1978, sec.-treas. 1981—85, v.p. 1982—83, pres. 1984—85), Ohio Med. Assn., Am. Fedn. Clin. Rsch., N.Y. Acad. Scis., Am. Cancer Soc. (bd. dirs. Hamilton County unit 1990—92), Am. Leukemia Soc. (med. adv. exec. bd.), Phi Beta Kappa, Sigma Xi. Roman Catholic. Home: 8040 S Clippinger Dr Cincinnati OH 45243-3248 Office: 2139 Auburn Ave Cincinnati OH 45219-2906

SCHREINER, GREGORY LEE, music educator; b. Freeport, Ill., Mar. 9, 1948; s. Val Lavone Schreiner and Opal Jeanette Toepfer. BMus, Millikin U., 1970; MA, We. Ill. U., 1973; MFA, UCLA, 1983. Musical dir. U. South Fla., Tampa, 1974—79; staff accompanist UCLA, 1983—87; instr. Santa Monica Coll., Santa Monica, Calif., 1987—90, Cerritos Coll., Norwalk, Calif., 1990—. Prodr.: Star of Hollywood Revisited. Pres. Marilyn Monroe Fan Club, 1983—. Mem.: Art Deco Soc. L.A. (bd. dirs.). Avocations: bicycling, collecting movie memorabilia. Home: 1237 Carmona Ave Los Angeles CA 90019 Office: Cerritos College 11110 Alondra Blvd Norwalk CA 90650

SCHREINER, JOHN CHRISTIAN, economics consultant, software publisher; b. Los Angeles, Nov. 2, 1933; s. Alexander and Margaret S.; m. Marie Nielsen, June 19, 1967; children: Christian Alexander, Carl Arthur, Elizabeth, Nathan Alexander. BSM.E., U. Utah, 1958; MBA, Harvard U., 1960; PhD, UCLA, 1970. Chartered fin. analyst. Design engr. Eimco Corp., Salt Lake City and N.Y.C., 1957-59; credit exec. James Talcott, Inc., N.Y.C. and Boston, 1960-65; lectr. mgmt. U. Utah, 1965-66; mem. faculty Grad. Sch. Mgmt., U. Minn., Mpls., 1969-84, chmn. dept. fin. and ins., 1973-74, 76-81; pres. The Sebastian Group, Inc., 1984—. Cons. to corps. and govt. agys. Co-author: Executive Recruiting: How Companies Obtain Management Talent, 1960; contbr. articles to profl. jours. Mem. Fin. Execs. Inst., Fin. Analysts Fedn., Tau Beta Pi, Phi Kappa Phi. Republican. Mem. Ch. Jesus Christ of Latter-day Saints (missionary, Ger. 1953-56). Club: Harvard Bus. Sch. Minn. Office: The Sebastian Group Inc 5730 Duluth St Minneapolis MN 55422-4000

SCHRENK, GARY DALE, foundation executive; b. San Jose, Calif., Apr. 29, 1949; s. Robert Shepard and Katherine Mildred (Grant) S.; m. Rhonda Lynn King, Oct. 9, 1981 (div. Jan. 1989); children: Stephen, Kristen, James. BA in Comm., Am. U., 1970; M in Nonprofit Mgmt., Regis U., 2002. TV dir. WTOP (now WUSA), Washington, 1971-73, KBTV (now KUSA), Denver, 1973-75; with Denver Area Boy Scouts Am., 1975-80; regional dir. St. Jude Children's Rsch. Hosp., Memphis, 1980-83; dir. devel. Denver Art Mus., 1983-85; asst. dir. devel. The Children's Hosp., Denver, 1985-87; pres. North Colo. Med. Ctr. Found., Greeley, 1987—. Dir., instr. Fast Start Course, 1985—2001; pres. Monfort Children's Clinic, Greeley, Colo., 1994—2001. Pres. Vision Together, Weld County, Colo., 1994—95; chmn., founding dir. Weld Citizen Action Network, 1995—98, 2000—02; founding dir. First Steps Weld County, 1993—99; chmn. Weld Cmty. Health Coalition, 1992—98; bd. dirs. North Colo. Health Alliance, 2002—; chmn. pub. support com. Team Colo. ARC, 1997—2004; regional svc., area 2 public support com. ARC, 2004—, bd. dirs. Centennial chpt., 2003—. Recipient Disting. Citizen award Highlanders, Denver, 1974. Mem. Assn. Fundraising Profls. (nat. found. bd. 1998-2003, nat. assembly 1994-98, bd. dirs. Colo. chpt. 1979-2000, 2003-, pres. 1984, internat. bd. dirs. 2004—), Colo. Assn. Nonprofit Orgns. (founding dir. 1987-92), Rotary, Greeley Country Club, Tahosa Alumni Assn. (past pres., past chair). Methodist. Avocation: golf. Home: 4956 13th St Greeley CO 80634-2215 Office: North Colo Med Ctr Found 1801 16th St Greeley CO 80631-5154 Office Phone: 970-356-9020. Business E-Mail: gary.schrenk@bannerhealth.com.

SCHRENKO, LINDA C. former state agency administrator; b. July 24, 1949; m. Frank Schrenko; 1 child, Katherine. BA in Elem. Edn., Augusta Coll., 1972, EdS in Adminstrn. and Supervision, 1986; MEd in Counseling, Ga. So. U., 1982. Tchr. 7th grade Richmond County (Ga.) Schs., 1972-74; tchr. 5th grade South Columbia (Ga.) Elem., 1974-76, tchr. Title I grades 1-6, 1976-77, tchr. 2nd grade, 1977-81, asst. prin., 1984-86; tchr. gifted program grades K-3 Columbia County Schs., 1981-82; counselor Evans Middle Sch., Columbia County, 1982-84; prin. South Columbia (Ga.) Elem., 1986-90; tchr. gifted program grades K-3 Columbia County Schs., 1981-82; counselor Evans Middle Sch., Columbia County, 1982-84; mat. and internat. edn. cons., 1990-94; supt. schs. Ga. Dept. Edn., Atlanta, 1994—2003. Bd. dirs. Coun. Sch. Performance, Edn. Commn. of States, Ga. Child Care Coun., Ga. Pub. Telecomm. Commn.; lectr. in field. Author: Teaching in the Learner Centered School. Past pres. Ctrl. Savannah Regional Area Humane Soc.; mem. Columbia County Humane Soc.; past pres. Columbia County Fedn. Republican Women; mem. Ga. Republican Found., Women Who Win.; mem. Kiokee Bapt. Ch., Appling, Ga. Named one of 100 Most Powerful and Influential People in Ga., Ga. Trend Mag., 1995-96. Mem. ASCD, Profl. Assn. Ga. Educators, Ga. Assn. Elem. Sch. Prins., Phi Delta Kappa. Republican.

SCHREYER, JOHN Y. oil industry executive; CFO Amerada Hess Corp., N.Y.C. Office: Amerada Hess Corp 1185 Avenue Of The Americas New York NY 10036-2601

SCHREYER, LESLIE JOHN, lawyer; b. N.Y.C., Apr. 11, 1946; s. Oscar and Greta (Loebl) S.; m. Judith Camps, Sept. 25, 1994; 1 child, Gabrielle. BA, Columbia U., 1967; LLB, Yale U., 1970; LLM in Taxation, N.Y.U., 1977. Bar: N.Y. 1971. Assoc. Chadbourne & Parke, N.Y.C., 1970-78, ptnr., 1978-81, 83—; dep. internat. tax counsel U.S. Treasury Dept., 1981-83; gen. counsel GLG Ptnrs. Svcs. Ltd., 2000—, also bd. dirs. Adj. assoc. prof. law NYU, 1990-97; cons. Am. Law Inst., Fed. Income Tax Project on Internat. Aspects of U.S. Income Taxation, 1983-91. Author: (with others) Foreign Tax Credit, 1980; contbr. numerous articles to profl. jours. Mem. ABA, Internat. Bar Assn., Internat. Fiscal Assn., N.Y. State Bar Assn., Assn. of Bar of City of N.Y., Phi Beta Kappa. Republican. Home: 60 E End Ave New York NY 10028-7907 Office: Chadbourne & Parke 30 Rockefeller Plz Fl 31 New York NY 10112-0129 E-mail: lschreyer@chadbourne.com., les@glgpartners.com.

SCHREYER, WILLIAM ALLEN, retired investment firm executive; b. Williamsport, Pa., Jan. 13, 1928; s. William L. and Elizabeth (Engel) S.; m. Joan Legg, Oct. 17, 1953; 1 child, DrueAnne Frazier. BA, Pa. State U., 1948. With Merrill Lynch, Inc. and predecessors, N.Y.C., 1948-93; CEO Merrill Lynch & Co., N.Y.C., 1984-92, chmn., 1985-93, chmn. emeritus, 1993—. Trustee Ctr. for Strategic and Internat. Studies, Pa. State U., 1986—, chmn. bd. trustees, 1993-96. With USAF, 1955-56. Mem. Econ. Club N.Y., River Club, Links Club, Saturn Club, Springdale Golf Club, Bedens Brook Club, Eldorado Country Club, Georgetown Club, Met. Club, Old Baldy Club, Nassau Club, The Carnegie Club at Skibo Castle, Knights of Malta. Roman Catholic. Office: Merrill Lynch & Co Inc 800 Scudders Mill Rd Plainsboro NJ 08536-1606

SCHRIBMAN, SHELLEY IRIS, database engineer, consultant; b. Weehawken, NJ, July 29, 1944; d. George and Mildred (Kamen) Shulman; m. Marshall Melvin Schribman, Aug. 26, 1979. BFA cum laude, Art Inst. Chgo., 1966; MBA, Simmon Coll. Grad. Sch. Mgmt., 1982. Asst. dir. Advanced Inst. Devel. Am. Repertory Theatre, NYC, 1970-71; ptnr. Sir Charles Cleaning Co., Boston, 1982-83; owner SIS Internat., Boston, 1984-87; database developer (freelance) Boston, 1995—; sys. analyst Dept. Pub. Health, Boston, 2000—. Cons. Boston Computer Soc., 1995-96, Catchpole Corp., Wellesley, Mass., 1996-97, Ptnrs. In Home Care Inc., Missoula, Mont., 1996-97; designer, developer Shulman Bankruptcy Program, 1998-99 Pres. Orgn. for Rehab. Through Tng., Boston, 1986-88; mem. LWV, Boston (housing specialist 1989-91, pres. 1990-91, nat. credentials chairperson 1991-92). Mem. Belmont Dramatic Club, Alumni Theatre, Lexington Players. Jewish. Avocations: acting, composing music. Home: 8 Whittier Pl #23D Boston MA 02114-1402 Office: Dept Public Health 250 Washington St Fl 5 Boston MA 02108-4619 Personal E-mail: shelleyischribman@rcn.com. Business E-Mail: Shelley.Schribman@state.ma.us.

SCHRIEFFER, JOHN ROBERT, physics educator, science administrator; b. Oak Park, Ill., May 31, 1931; s. John Henry and Louise (Anderson) Schrieffer; m. Anne Grete Thomsen, Dec. 30, 1960; children: Anne Bolette, Paul Karsten, Anne Regina. BS, MIT, 1953; MS, U. Ill., 1954, PhD, 1957, ScD, 1974, Tech. U., Munich, 1968, U. Geneva, 1968, U. Pa., 1973, U. Cin., 1977, U. Tel Aviv, 1987, U. Ala., 1990. NSF postdoctoral fellow U. Birmingham, England, Niels Bohr Inst., Copenhagen, 1957—58; asst. prof. U. Chgo., 1958—59; asst. prof., then assoc. prof. U. Ill., 1959—62; prof. U. Pa., Phila., 1962—79, Mary Amanda Wood prof. physics, 1964—79; Andrew D. White prof. at large Cornell U., 1969—75; prof. U. Calif., Santa Barbara, 1980—91, Chancellor's prof., 1984—91, dir. Inst. for Theoretical Physics, 1984—89; Univ. prof. Fla. State U., Tallahassee, 1992—, Univ. Eminent Scholar prof., 1995—, chief scientist Nat. High Magnetic Field Lab., 1992—. Pres.'s com. Nat. Medal of Sci., 1996—98. Author: Theory of Superconductivity, 1964. Recipient Comstock prize, NAS, 1968, Nobel prize for Physics, 1972, John Ericsson medal, Am. Soc. Swedish Engrs., 1976, Alumni Achievement award, U. Ill., 1979, Nat. medal of Sci., 1984; fellow Guggenheim, Copenhagen, 1967, Los Alamos Nat. Lab., Exxon faculty, 1979—89. Fellow: Am. Phys. Soc. (v.p. 1994, pres.-elect 1995, pres. 1996, past pres. 1997, Oliver E. Buckley solid state physics prize 1968); mem.: NAS (coun. 1990—), Acad. Sci. USSR, Royal Danish Acad. Scis. and Letters, Am. Acad. Arts and Scis. Office: Fla State Univ NHMFL 1800 E Paul Dirac Dr Tallahassee FL 32310-3748

SCHRIER, ARNOLD, historian, educator; b. N.Y.C., May 30, 1925; s. Samuel and Yetta (Levine) S.; m. Sondra Weinshelbaum, June 12, 1949; children— Susan Lynn, Jay Alan, Linda Lee, Paula Kay. Student, Bethany Coll., W.Va., 1943-44, Ohio Wesleyan U., 1944-45; BS, Northwestern U., 1949, MA, 1950, PhD (Social Sci. Research Council fellow, Univ. fellow), 1956. Asst. prof. history U. Cin., 1956-61, assoc. prof., 1961-66, prof., 1966-95, dir. grad. studies history, 1969-78, Walter C. Langsam prof. modern European history, 1972-95; Walter C. Langsam prof. history emeritus, 1995—. Vis. asst. prof. history Northwestern U., Evanston, Ill., 1960; vis. assoc. prof. history Ind. U., Bloomington, 1965-66; vis. lectr. Russian history Duke U., 1966; disting. vis. prof. U.S. Air Force Acad., 1983-84; dir. NDEA Inst. World History for Secondary Sch. Tchrs., U. Cin., 1965; Am. del. Joint U.S.-USSR Textbook Study Commn., 1989. Author: Ireland and the American Emigration, 1958, reissued, 1970, paperback edit., 1997, The Development of Civilization, 1961-62, Modern European Civilization, 1963, Living World History, 1964, rev., 1993, Twentieth Century World, 1974, History and Life: the World and Its People, 1977, rev., 1993, A Russian Looks at America, 1979, Irish Immigrants in the Land of Canaan, 2003. Pres. Ohio Acad. History, 1973-74, Midwest Slavic Conf., 1980. Served with USNR, 1943-46, 52-54. Recipient Disting. Svc. award Ohio Acad. History, 1992; Am. Council Learned Socs. fgn. area fellow, 1963-64 Mem. World History Assn. (v.p. 1986-88, pres. 1988-90). Home: 10 Diplomat Dr Cincinnati OH 45215-2073 E-mail: arnsond@aol.com.

SCHRIER, ERIC, publishing executive; married; three children. BA, Brown Univ., 1973; MJ in journalism, Univ. Calif., 1976. Founder, editor Novus, 1977; co-founder Science, 1980-86, mng. editor, 1980-86; founder, editor-in-chief Health mag., 1987-95; editor-in-chief Time Inc. Ventures, 1990—95; pres., CEO Time Inc. Health, 1995—99; editor-in-chief Readers Digest, Pleasantville, NY, 2000—. Dir. Am. Soc. Mag. Editors; editor, Newton at the Bat. Office: Readers Digest PO Box 200 Pleasantville NY 10572-0200

SCHRIER, MORRIS M. consultant; b. NYC, Dec. 22, 1909; s. Frank and Sophie (Nesati) Schrier; m. Margie Rocamora, Nov. 11, 1939 (dec. Jan. 1975); children: Carol R. (Schrier) Katowitz, Daniel R. BS, NYU, 1931; JD, Columbia U, 1934. V.p., sec., gen. counsel MCA Inc., NYC, 1959—79, legal cons., 1979—. Mem.: Assn. Bar City NY, Rockefeller Inst., ABA, United Cerebral Palsy, Nat. Cancer Adv. Bd (bd. dir.), Nat. Cancer Inst., Friars NYC, Harmonie. Jewish.

SCHRIER, ROBERT WILLIAM, physician, educator; b. Indpls., Feb. 19, 1936; s. Arthur E. and Helen M. Schrier; m. Barbara Lindley, June 14, 1959; children: David, Debbie, Douglas, Derek, Denise. BA, Depauw U., 1957, DSc (hon.), 1991, U. Colo., 1996, Silesian Acad. Medicine, Katowice, Poland, 1997; MD, Ind. U., 1962; DSc (hon.), DePaul U., 2004. Intern Marion County (Ind.) Hosp., 1962; resident U. Wash., Seattle, 1963-65; asst. prof. U. Calif. Med. Ctr., San Francisco, 1969-72, assoc. mem., 1970-72, assoc. dir. renal divsn., 1971-72, assoc. prof., 1972; prof., head renal disease U. Colo. Sch. Med., Denver, 1972-92, prof., chmn. Dept. Medicine, 1976—2002. Editor 45 textbooks in internal medicine, geriat., drug usage, and kidney disease; contbr. over 800 sci. articles to profl. jours. Pres. Nat. Kidney Found., 1984-86. With U.S. Army, 1966-69. Recipient David Hume award Nat. Kidney Found., Torchbearer award, Mayo Soley award Western Soc. Clin. Investigation, Robert H. Williams award Assn. Profs. Medicine. Mem. ACP (master, John Phillips award), Am. Soc. Nephrology (treas. 1979-81, pres. 1983, John Peters award), Internat. Soc. Nephrology (treas. 1981-90, v.p. 1990-95, pres. 1995-97, Jean Hamburger award 2003), Am. Clin. and Climatol. Assn. (v.p. 1986), Assn. Am. Physicians (pres. 1994-95), Western Assn. Physicians (pres. 1982), Inst. of Medicine of NAS, Alpha Omega Alpha. Achievements include research contributions centered on the pathogenesis of acute renal failure, genetic renal disorders, mechanisms of cell injury, diabetic nephropathy and renal and hormonal control of body fluid volume; advancement of a unifying hypothesis of sodium and water regulation in health and disease which has stimulated world-wide interest in the medical science community. Office: U Colo Health Scis Ctr Dept Medicine PO Box B178 Denver CO 80262-0001 E-mail: Robert.Schrier@uchsc.edu.

SCHRIER, STANLEY LEONARD, hematologist, educator; b. N.Y.C., Jan. 2, 1929; s. Harry and Nettie (Schwartz) S.; m. Peggy Helen Pepper, June 6, 1953; children: Rachel, Leslie, David. AB, U. Colo., 1949; MD, Johns Hopkins U., 1954. Diplomate Am. Bd. Internal Medicine (chmn. subsplty. bd. hematology). Intern Osler Med. Service, Johns Hopkins Hosp., 1954-55; resident U. Mich., Ann Arbor, 1955-56, U. Chgo. Hosp., 1958-59; sr. asst. surgeon USPHS, 1956-58; instr. medicine Stanford Sch. Medicine, Calif., 1959-60, asst. prof. medicine, 1960-63, assoc. prof., 1963-72, prof. medicine, 1972-95, chief divsn. hematology, 1968-94. Vis. scientist Weizmann Inst., Rehovot, Israel, 1967-68; vis. prof. Oxford U., Eng., 1975-76, Hebrew U., Jerusalem, 1982-83 John and Mary Markle scholar, 1961; recipient Kaiser award Stanford U., 1972, Kaiser award Stanford U., 1974, 75, David Rytand award, 1982, Eleanor Roosevelt Union Internationale Contre le Cancer award, 1975-76, Albion Walter Hewlett award, 1996. Fellow ACP; mem. Am. Soc. Hematology (pres. 2004), Am. Physiol. Soc., Soc. Exptl. Biology and Medicine, Am. Soc. Clin. Investigation, Western Assn. Physicians, Assn. Am. Physicians. Democrat. Jewish. Office: Stanford U Sch Medicine CCSR 1155 269 Campus Dr Palo Alto CA 94305-5156 E-mail: sschrier@leland.stanford.edu.

SCHRIER-POLAK, CAROL, lawyer; BA, Brandeis U., 1967; postgrad., Wayne State U., 1967-68; MSW, SUNY, Buffalo, 1969; JD, Temple U., 1977. Bar: Va. 1983, Pa. 1977. Exec. dir. Coun. for Children, Inc., Atlanta, 1972-74, Support Ctr. for Child Advocates Inc., Phila., 1977-83; legal cons. ABA/Nat. Resource Ctr. for Child Advocacy and Protection, Washington, 1983-84; assoc. Sharon Lieblich, PC, Alexandria, Va., 1984-88; atty. Bean, Kinney & Korman, P.C., Arlington, Va., 1988—, ptnr., 1990—. Mediator, 1994—; faculty Va. State Bar, Va. Trial Lawyers and local bar assns.; mem. child support quadrennial rev. panel Commonwealth of Va., 1999. Co-editor: Making Financial Decisions when Divorce Occurs: A Virginia Guide, 1993; editor legal manuals; contbr. articles to profl. jours. Bd. dirs. Legal Svcs. No. Va., 1991-97,; Mental Health Assn. No. Va., 1989-92; mem. Fairfax, Inc., 1999; mem. adv. coun. Healthy Families, 2000—, chair, 2002—. Fellow Am. Acad. Matrimonial Lawyers (sec.-treas. Va. chpt. 1999-2001, v.p. 2001-03, pres. elect 2003—); mem. ABA, D.C. Bar Assn., Va. Bar Assn. (family law bd. govs. 1990-94, faculty professionalism course 1999-2002, bar coun., named Washingtonian Best Lawyers 1995, 2001, 2004), Fairfax Bar Assn. (bd. dirs., sec. 1995-96, pres. 1997-98), Fairfax Bar Found. (bd. dirs., named Best Lawyer Am. 1994—). Office: Bean Kinney & Korman 2000 14th St N Ste 100 Arlington VA 22201-2552

SCHRIESHEIM, ALAN, research administrator; b. N.Y.C., Mar. 8, 1930; s. Morton and Frances (Greenberg) Schriesheim; m. Beatrice D. Brand, June 28, 1953; children: Laura Lynn, Robert Alan. BS in Chemistry, Poly. Inst. Bklyn., 1951; PhD in Phys. Organic Chemistry, Pa. State U., 1954; DSc (hon.), No. Ill. U., 1991; Laureate, Lincoln Acad., 1996; PhD (hon.), Ill. Inst. Tech., Chgo., 1992, Pa. State U., 2001. Chemist Nat. Bur. Standards, 1954—56; with Exxon Rsch. & Engring. Co., 1956—83, dir. corp. rsch., 1975—79; gen. mgr. Exxon Engring., 1979—83; sr. dep. lab. dir., COO Argonne Nat. Lab., 1983—84, lab. dir., CEO, 1984—96, dir. emeritus, 1996—; prof. chemistry dept. U. Chgo., 1984—96, lectr. Bus. Sch., 1996—99; prin. Washington Adv. Group, 1996—. Karcher lectr. U. Okla., 1977; Hurd lectr. Northwestern U., 1980; Rosenstiel lectr. Brandeis U., 1982; Welsh Found. lectr., 87; com. svc. NRC, 1980—; vis. com. chemistry dept. MIT, 1977—82; mem. vis. com. mech. engring. and aerospace dept. Princeton (N.J.) U., 1983—87, mem. vis. com. chemistry dept., 1983—87; mem. Pure and Applied Chemistry Com.; del. to People's Republic of China, 1978; mem. Presdl. Nat. Commn. on Superconductivity, 1989—91, U.S.-USSR Joint Commn. on Basic Sci. Rsch., 1990—93; mem. U.S. nat. com. Internat. Union Pure and Applied Chemistry, 1982—85; mem. magnetic fusion adv. com. Divsn. Phys. Scis. U. Chgo. Magnetic Fusion adv. com. to U.S. DOE, 1983—86; mem. Dept. Energy Rsch. Adv. Bd., 1983—85, Congl. Adv. Com. on Sci. and Tech., 1985—96; mem. vis. com. Stanford (Calif.) U., U. Utah, Tex. A&M U., Lehigh U.; bd. govs. Argonne Nat. Lab., 1984—96; mem. adv. com. on space sys. and tech. NASA, 1987—93; mem. nuc. engring. and engring. physics vis. com. U. Wis., Madison; mem. Coun. Gt. Lakes Govs. Regional Econ. Devel. Commn., 1987—, rev. bd. Compact Ignition Tomamak Princeton U., 1988—91; advisor Sears Investment Mgmt. Co., 1988—89; bd. dirs. HEICO, Smart Signal Corp.; adv. bd. Batterson Venture Ptnrs., Influx, UHV Aluminum, Valley Indsl. Assn., Coun. on Superconductivity for Am. Competitiveness; mem. State of Ill. Commn. on the Future of Pub. Svc., 1990—92; co-chair Indsl. Rsch. Inst. Nat. Labs./Industry Panel, 1984—87; mem. Nat. Acad. Engring. Adv. Commn. on Tech. and Soc., 1991—92, Sun Electric Corp. Bd., 1991—92, U.S. House of Reps. subcom. on Sci.-Adv. Group on Renewing U.S. Sci. Policy, 1992—96, Chgo. Acad. Scis. acad. coun., 1994—; mem. adv. bd. Chemtech; mem. sr. action group on R&D investment strategies Ctr. for strategic and Internat. Studies, 1995; bd. vis. Astronomy and Astrophysics Pa. State U., 1995—; bd. overseers Fermi Nat. Lab., 2003—. Adv. bd.: Chemtech, 1970—85, editl. bd.: Rsch. & Devel., 1988—92, Superconductor Industry, 1988—95; patentee in field. Mem. spl. vis. com. Field Mus. of Natural History, Chgo., 1987—88; trustee The Latin Sch. of Chgo., 1990—92; adv. bd. WBEZ Chicagoland Pub. Radio Cmty., 1990—96; mem. Conservation Found. DuPage County, 1983—96, Econ. Devel. Adv. Commn. of DuPage County, 1984—88, Ill. Gov.'s Commn. on Sci. and Tech., 1986—90, Inst. for Ill. Coun. Advisors, 1988—, Ill. Coalition Bd. Dirs., 1989—, Inst. for Ill. Adv. Rev. Panel, 1986—88, NASA Sci. Tech. Adv. Com. Manpower Requirements Ad Hoc Rev. Team, 1988—91, Ill. Sci. and Tech. Adv. Com., 1989—, chmn., 1997, mem. U. Ill. Engring. Vis. com., Urbana-Champaign, 1986—95; trustee Tchrs. Acad. for Math. and Sci. Tchrs. in Chgo., 1990—96; bd. visitors astronomy and astrophysics Pa. State U., 1995—; bd. dirs. LaRabida Children's Hosp. and Rsch. Ctr., 1987—95, Children's Meml. Hosp., Children's Meml. Inst. for Edn. and Rsch. Recipient Outstanding Alumni Fellow award, Pa. State U., 1985, laureate, Lincoln Acad. Ill., 1996, Disting. fellow, Poly. U., 1989. Fellow: AAAS (coun. del. chem. sect. 1986—92, sci. engring. and pub. policy com. 1992, standing com. audit 1992, bd. dirs. 1992—96, selection com. to bring FSU scientists to ann. mtg. 1995—), N.Y. Acad. Scis.; mem.: AIChE (award com. 1992—), NAE (adv. com. tech. and soc. 1991—92, mem. program adv. com. 1992—94, chair study fgn. participation in U.S. R&D 1993—96, NRC com. on dual use tech. 1996—97, com. to assess policies and practices of Dept. of Energy to design, ma 1998—99), Natanas Common Innovation Models (chmn. 2004—), Ctr. Strategic and Internat. Studies (sr. action group 1995—96), Indsl. Rsch. Inst. (co-chmn. Nat. Labs. Indsl. Panel 1984—87, fed. adv. com. to Fed. Sci. and Tech. Com. 1992—96, sr. action group on R&D Investment Strategies), Am. Nuc. Soc., Am. Petroleum Inst. (rsch. coord. coun.), Nat. Conf. Advancement Rsch. (conf. com. 1985—, site selection com. 1994, conf. com. 50th ann. 1996), Am. Mgmt. Assn. (R&D coun. 1988—), Am. Chem. Soc. (joint bd. coun. on sci. 1983—87, chmn. petroleum divsn. 1983—91, councilor, com. on chemistry and pub. affairs 1983—91, petroleum chemistry award 1969, 1995—96), Econ. Club, Comml. Club, Cosmos Club, Carleton Club (bd. govs.

1992—), Phi Lambda Upsilon, Sigma Xi. Home: 1440 N Lake Shore Dr Apt 31ac Chicago IL 60610-5927 Office: Argonne Nat Lab 9700 S Cass Ave Argonne IL 60439-4803 Office Phone: 630-252-3872. E-mail: schriesheim@anl.gov.

SCHRIEVER, BERNARD ADOLPH, management consultant; b. Bremen, Germany, Sept. 14, 1910; came to U.S., 1917, naturalized, 1923; s. Adolph Niholaus and Elizabeth (Milch) S.; children: Brett Arnold, Dodie Elizabeth Schriever Moeller, Barbara Alice Schriever Allan. BS, Tex. A&M U., 1931; MSM.E., Stanford U., 1942; D.Sc. (hon.), Creighton U., 1958, Rider Coll., 1958, Adelphia Coll., 1959, Rollins Coll., 1959; D.Aero. Sci. (hon.), U. Mich., 1961; D.Eng. (hon.), Bklyn. Poly. Inst., 1961; LL.D. (hon.), Loyola U., Los Angeles, 1960. Commd. 2d lt. U.S. Army Air Force, 1938; advanced through grades to gen. U.S. Air Force, 1961; comdr. ICBM Program, 1954-59, AFSC, 1959-66; ret., 1966; chmn. bd. Schriever & McKee, Washington, 1971-87; cons. B.A. Schriever, 1987—. Decorated D.S.M., D.S.M. with oak leaf cluster, Legion of Merit, Air medal, Purple Heart; named to Aviation Hall of Fame, 1980; recipient Forrestal award, 1987, Nat. Air and Space Mus. Trophy Lifetime achievement award, 1996. Hon. fellow AIAA; mem NAE, Am. Astron. Soc., Air Force Assn. Clubs: Burning Tree. Home: 4501 Dexter St NW Washington DC 20007-1116 Office: 1101 30th St NW Ste 200 Washington DC 20007-3769

SCHRIEVER, FRED MARTIN, management consultant, financial investor; b. N.Y.C. s. Samuel and Sara S.; m. Cheri G. Spatt; children: Melissa Ann, Elizabeth Ellen. BME, Poly. U. N.Y., 1956, MME, 1958. Registered profl. engr., N.Y., Wash.; cert. mgmt. cons. Chief engr. divsn. Sperry Corp., N.Y.C., 1956-64; ptnr. Booz, Allen and Hamilton, N.Y.C. and Washington, 1964 71; chmn., pres. RCG Internat. Inc., N.Y.C., 1971—96. Investor and cons. in field; dir. Nat. Exec. Svc. Corps., 1998—, Hagler Bailly Inc., 1996-2000. Fellow Inst. of Dirs., Inst. Mgmt. Consultants U.K.; mem. ASME, Inst. Mgmt. Cons., Chemists Club. Home: PO Box 32 Westport CT 06881-0032

SCHROCK, DONALD E. communications executive; BSEE, U. Ill.; MSEE, degree in bus. adminstrn., Ariz. State U. Various positions Motorola Semiconductor; v.p., divsn. gen. mgr. Burr-Brown Corp.; past v.p. ops Applied Micro Circuit Corp.; past group v.p., divsn. mgr. Hughes Aircraft Co. Office: Corp Hdqs Qualcomm Inc 5775 Morehouse Dr San Diego CA 92121

SCHROCK, EDWARD L. (ED SCHROCK), congressman, former state senator; b. Middletown, Ohio, Apr. 6, 1941; m. Judith Schrock. BA, Alderson Broaddus Coll., 1964; MA, Am. U., 1975. Commd. ensign USN, 1964, advanced through grades to capt., retired, 1988; investment broker, 1989-95; mem. Va. State Senate, 1996-2001, mem. gen. laws com., mem. local govt. com., mem. privileges & elections com., mem. transp. com.; mem. U.S. Congress from 2d Va. dist., 2001—; mem. armed svcs. com., budget com., govt. reform com., small bus. com. Republican. Baptist. Office: Office Bldg 322 Cannon House Washington DC 20515

SCHROCK, RICHARD ROYCE, chemistry educator; b. Berne, Ind., Jan. 4, 1945; m. Nancy F. Carlson, 1971; children: Andrew, Eric. BA, U. Calif., 1967; PhD, Harvard U., 1971; postdoctorate, Cambridge U., Eng., 1971-72. Rsch. chemist E.I. du Pont de Nemours & Co., Wilmington, Del., 1972-75; asst. prof. MIT, Cambridge, 1975-78, assoc. prof., 1978-80, prof. chemistry, 1980-89, Frederick G. Keyes prof. chemistry, 1989—. Contbr. articles to profl. jours. Recipient Bailar medal, U. Ill., 1998, Sir Geoffrey Wilkinson medal, Royal Soc. Chemistry, 2002. Mem. AAAS, Am. Chem. Soc. (award organometallic chemistry 1985, Harrison Howe award 1990, Humboldt award 1994, award inorganic chemistry 1996, Arthur C. Cope Scholar award 2001), NAS. Office: MIT Dept Of Chemistry Cambridge MA 02139 E-mail: rrs@mit.edu.

SCHROCK, ROBERT D., JR., orthopaedic surgeon, educator; b. Omaha, Nebr., Aug. 6, 1938; s. Robert D. and Elizabeth Winslow (Wetherbee) S.; m. Carolyn Gorthy, May 30, 1964; children: Robert D. III, Suzanne Bartlett Schrock Kelley. AB, Princeton U., 1960; MD, Cornell U., 1964. Cert. Am. Bd. Orthopadic Surgery. Instr. dept. orthopaedics U. Wash. Sch. Medicine, Seattle, 1969-70; clin. asst. prof. dept. orthopaedics U. Rochester (N.Y.) Sch. Medicine and Dentistry, 1972—. Pres. Genesee Valley chpt. Arthritis Found., Rochester, 1989-91 (Nat. Vol. award 1991, Zaia award 1993), Rochester Acad. Medicine, 1991-92. Author: (with others) Operative Surgery, 1976; contbr. articles to profl. jours. Cub master, Webelos leader Cub Scouts, Pittsford, N.Y., 1973-78 (Long House award 1977); elder Third Presbyn. Ch., Rochester, 1984-87. Maj. U.S. Army, 1970-72. Fellow ACS Coll. Surgeon, Am. Acad. Orthopaedic Surgeons, Am. Acad. Cerebral Palsy and Devel. Medicine, Am. Orthopaedic Foot and Ankle Soc., Rochester Acad. Medicine (co-chair com.); mem. Med. Soc. State N.Y. (com. mem.). Presbyterian. Avocations: tennis, photography, sailing. Home: 8 Stonegate Ln Pittsford NY 14534-1914 Office: Greater Rochester Orthop 30 Hagen Dr Ste 220 Rochester NY 14625

SCHROCK, SIMON, retail executive; b. Oakland, Md., Dec. 28, 1936; s. Noah and Cora (Burkholder) S.; m. Eva Lena Yoder, June 7, 1959 (dec. Apr. 1962); m. Pauline Yoder, Sept. 29, 1963; children: Janice Yvonne, Eldon Laverne, Ivan Dale. With Eastern States Farm Supply Co., Oakland, Md., 1957-59, Children's Hosp., Washington, 1959-61, Copp Properties, Vienna, Va., 1961-75; pres. Choice Books of No. Va., Fairfax, Va., 1975—. Chmn. Lighthouse Lit., 1976-2001. Author: Get on With Living, 1976, Price of Missing Life, 1981, One-Anothering, 1986, Vow-Keepers Vow-Breakers, A Smoother Journey, 1994, What Shall The Redeemed Wear, 2001, Where Has Integrity Gone, 2001, Don't Throw In the Towel, 2003; contbr. articles to ch. jours. Bishop Faith Christian Fellowship, Catlett, Va., 1981—. Avocations: travel, writing, biking. Office: 10100 Piper Ln Bristow VA 20136 E-mail: schrocks@nva.choicebooks.org.

SCHROCK, THEODORE R. surgeon; b. Berne, Ind., Oct. 21, 1939; s. N.J. and M.A. Schrock; married. AB, U. Calif., San Francisco, 1961, MD, 1964. Diplomate Am. Bd. Surgery. Intern U. Calif. Hosps., San Francisco, 1964-65, resident, 1965-67, 69-71; fellow Mass. Gen. Hosp., Boston, 1967-69; chmn. dept. surgery U. Calif. San Francisco Med. Ctr., 1993-99, J. Englebert Dunphy prof. surgery, 1998—, assoc. dean clin. svcs., chief med. officer, 1999—. Fellow ACS; mem. Am. Gastroenterological Assn., Am. Soc. Colon and Rectal Surgery, Am. Soc. Gastroenterological Endoscopy, Am. Surg. Assn., Soc. Surgery Alimentary Tract. Office: UCSF Campus Box 0296 500 Parnassus Ave San Francisco CA 94143-0296

SCHRODER, DIETER KARL, electrical engineering educator; b. Lübeck, Germany, June 18, 1935; arrived in U.S., 1964; s. Wilhelm and Martha (Werner) S.; m. Beverley Claire (Parchment), Aug. 4, 1961; children: Mark, Derek. BS, McGill U., Montreal, Que., Can., 1962, MS, 1964; PhD, U. Ill., 1968. Sr. engr. rsch. and devel. sect. Westinghouse Electric Corp., Pitts., 1968-73; fellow engr. rsch. and devel. sect. Westinghouse Electric Corp., Pitts., 1973-77, adv. engr., 1977-79, mgr., 1979-81; prof. elec. engring. Ariz. State U., 1981—. Rsch. Inst. Solid State Physics, Freiburg, Fed. Republic Germany, 1978-79. Author: Advanced MOS Devices, 1987, Semiconductor Material and Device Characterization, 1998; patentee in electrical field; contbr. articles to profl. jour. Life Fellow IEEE (life, disting. nat. lectr. 1993-2003); mem. Electrochem. Soc., Sigma Xi, Eta Kappa Nu. Mem. Baha'i Faith. Home: 10572 E Firewheel Dr Scottsdale AZ 85255-1911 Office: Ariz State U Dept Elec Engring Tempe AZ 85287-5706 Office Phone: 480-965-6621.

SCHRODER, JACK SPALDING, JR., lawyer; b. Atlanta, July 10, 1948; s. Jack Spalding Sr. and Van (Spalding) S.; m. Karen Keyworth, Sept. 1, 1973; children: Jack Spalding III, James Edward. BA, Emory U., 1970; JD, U. Ga., 1973. Bar: Ga. 1973, U.S. Dist. Ct. (no. dist.) Ga. 1973, U.S. Ct. Appeals (11th cir.) 1982. Assoc. Alston & Bird, Atlanta, 1973-78, ptnr., 1978—2003, sr. counsel, 2004—. Author: Credentialing: Strategies for a Changing Environment/BNA's Health Law and Business Series, 1996; co-editor, contbg. author: Georgia Hospital Law manual, 1979, 84, 92. Bd. dirs. Rsch. Atlanta, 1996-2000, pres., 1999, co-chair bd. advisors, 2003—; participant Leadership Ga., Atlanta, 1986. United Way (chmn. legal divsn.), Atlanta, 1980. Mem. ABA (vice chmn. medicine and law com. 1989-90), Am. Health Lawyers Assn. (bd. dirs. 1994-99, chmn. med. staff and physician rels. com. 1991-94, vice chair hosps. and health systems law inst. 2001--), Ga. Acad. Healthcare Attys. (pres. 1981-82), State Bar Ga. (bd. govs. 1987-89), Atlanta Coun. Younger Lawyers (pres. 1977-78), Atlanta Bar Assn. (pres. 1982-83), Atlanta Bar Found. (pres. 1991-95). Office: Alston & Bird One Atlantic Ctr 1201 W Peachtree St NW Atlanta GA 30309-3424 Office Phone: 404-881-7685.

SCHRODER, RICK, actor; b. S.I., N.Y., Apr. 3, 1970; s. Dick and Diane Schroder; m. Andrea; children Luke William, Cambrie, Faith Anne. Actor: (films) The Champ, 1979 (Golden Globe award 1979), The Last Flight of Noah's Ark, 1980, The Earthling, 1981, There Goes My Baby, 1994, Crimson Tide, 1995, I Woke Up Early the Day I Died, 1998, Poolhall Junkies, 2002, Consequence, 2003, Face of Terror, 2003; actor, writer, dir. (films) Black Cloud, 2004; (TV series) Silver Spoons, 1982-86, NYPD Blue, 1998-2001; (TV movies) Little Lord Fauntleroy, 1980, Two Kinds of Love, 1983, A Reason to Live, 1985, Hansel and Gretel, 1982, Too Young the Hero, 1988, Terror on Highway 91, 1989, Lonesome Dove, 1989, Across the Tracks, 1991, There Goes My Baby, 1993, Call of the Wild, 1993, Return to Lonesome Dove, 1993, Texas, 1994, Crimson Tide, 1995, Ebenezer, 1997, What We Did That Night, 1999, Lost Battalion, 2001; (TV spls.) The Jimmy McNichol Special, Doug Henning's World of Magic, An Orchestra is a Team, Too, Walt Disney's Tenth Anniversary Special, Battle of the Network Stars, Circus of the Stars, Missing, Have You Seen this Person?, S.O.S., Secrets of Surviving. Office: c/o ICM 8942 Wilshire Blvd Beverly Hills CA 90211*

SCHROEDER, ALBERT JOHN, retired pediatrician; b. Mpls., Aug. 31, 1919; BA, U. Minn., 1941, BS, 1943, MD, 1944. Diplomate Am. Bd. Allergy and Immunology, Am. Bd. Pediats. Intern U.S.N.V.H., San Diego, 1944-45; resident in pediats. U. Minn. Hosp., Mpls., 1946-48; fellow in pediat. allergy Boston Children's Hosp., 1970-72; mem. staff Fairview Southdale Hosp., Edina, Minn.; clin. assoc. prof. pediats. Med. Sch. U. Minn., 1978-90; ret. Fellow Am. Acad. Allergy and Immunology, Am. Acad. Pediats., Am. Coll. Allergists and Immunologists, AMA. Home: 7220 York Ave S #212 Edina MN 55435-4462

SCHROEDER, ALFRED CHRISTIAN, electronics research engineer; b. West New Brighton, N.Y., Feb. 28, 1915; s. Alfred and Chryssa (Weishaar) S.; m. Janet Ellis, Sept. 26, 1936 (dec.); 1 child, Carol Ann Schroeder Castle.; m. Dorothy Holloway, Nov. 21, 1981. BS, MS, MIT, 1937. Mem. tech. staff Sarnoff, Inc., Princeton, N.J., 1937-2000; ret. Contbr. articles to profl. jours. Recipient RCA Lab. awards, 1947, 50, 51, 52, 57, 70 Fellow IEEE (Vladimir Zworykin award 1971); mem. AAAS, Optical Soc. Am., Soc. Motion Picture and TV Engrs. (David Sarnoff Gold medal 1965), Soc. Info. Display (Karl Ferdinand Braun prize 1989), Sigma Xi. Mem. Soc. Of Friends. Achievements include 75 patents for color TV products including shadow mask tube. Home: Pennswood Village Apt B-22 Newtown PA 18940-2401

SCHROEDER, ARNOLD LEON, mathematics professor; b. Honolulu, May 27, 1935; s. Arnold Leon and Wynelle (Russell) S.; m. Maybelle Ruth Walker, Nov. 9, 1956; children: Steven, Michael, Wendy. BS in Math., Oreg. State U., 1960, MS in Stats., 1962; postgrad., UCLA, 1964, U. So. Calif., 1965. Prof. emeritus math./stats. Long Beach (Calif.) C.C., 1962—. Computer cons. McDonnell-Douglas Corp., 1966-74, statis. researcher and tutoring on Soc. Sci., Bio-Med, and Bus. Mgmt. using SPSS, Minitab, and Lin. Prog. Applications; dir. Schroeder's Statis. Svcs. Author: statistics/Math Note's for Colleges, 1986—. Chmn. bd. elders Grace Bible Ch., South Gate, Calif., 1985-92. With USAF, 1953-57. Mem. Am. Bowlers Tour (life). Home and Office: 5481 E Hill St Long Beach CA 90815-1923 E-mail: alschroeder@charter.net.

SCHROEDER, BARBET G. director; b. Teheran, Iran, Apr. 26, 1941; Film critic Cahiers du Cinema, L'air de Paris, 1958-63; owner, prin. Films du Losange, 1963—; dir. CAA, 1991—. Film dir.: More, 1969, The Valley, 1972, General Idi Amin Dada, 1974, Maitress, 1975, Koko, Talking Gorilla, 1978, Cheaters, 1983, The Charles Bukowski Tapes, 1985, Barfly, 1987, Reversal of Fortune, 1990 (Acad. award nominee best dir. 1990, Golden Globe award nominee best dir. film 1990), Single White Female, 1992, Kiss of Death, 1995, Before and After, 1996, Desperate Measures, 1997; film prodr.: La Boulangerie de Monceau, 1962, La Carriere de Suzanne, 1963, Mediterrannee, 1964, Six in Paris, 1968, My Night at Maud's, 1968, The Collector, 1966, Claire's Knee, 1971, Chloe in the Afternoon, 1972, (with Tchalgadjieff), Out One, 1972, (with Pierre Cottrell) The Mother and the Whore, 1973, Celine and Julie Go Boating, 1974, Flocons d'or, 1975, Perceval, 1978, Improper Conduct, 1983, La Carriere de Suzanne, Mediterranee, Tu Imagines Robinson, Out One, The Marquise of O, 1975, Le Passe-Montagne, 1977, The Rites of Death, Le Navire Night, Le Pont du Nord; asst. to dir. Jean-Luc Goddard for The Soldiers, 1968; co-prodr.: Chinese Roulette, 1977, The American Friend, 1977; appeared in films The Soldiers, 1960, Six in Paris, 1965, The Mother and the Whore, 1973, Celine and Julie Go Boating, 1974, L'amour Par Terre, Roberte, 1978, The Golden Boat, 1990, Beverly Hills Cop III, 1994, La Reine Margot, 1994, Mars Attack!, 1997; screenwriter: (with Paul Gegauff) More, 1969, (with Gegauff) The Valley, 1972, Maitress, 1975, Cheaters, 1983. Office: Creative Artists Agy 9830 Wilshire Blvd Beverly Hills CA 90212-1804

SCHROEDER, CHARLES EDGAR, investment management executive; b. Chgo., Nov. 17, 1935; s. William Edward and Lelia Lorraine (Anderson) S.; m. Martha Elizabeth Runnette, Dec. 30, 1958; children: Charles Edgar, Timothy Creighton, Elizabeth Linton. BA in Econs., Dartmouth Coll., 1957; MBA, Amos Tuck Sch., 1958. Treas. Miami Corp., Chgo., 1969-78, pres., 1978-2001, pres. emeritus, 2001—; chmn., bd. dirs Blvd. Bank of Chgo., 1981-91; chmn. Blvd. Bancorp., Inc., 1991-94. Bd. dirs. Nat.-Standard Co., Niles, Mich. Trustee Northwestern Meml. Hosp., 1985-2000, Northwestern U., 1989—. Lt. (j.g.) USN, 1958-60. Mem. Chgo. Club, Glen View Club, Comml. Club. Office: Miami Corp 410 N Michigan Ave Ste 590 Chicago IL 60611-4252

SCHROEDER, DAVID J. DEAN, psychologist; b. Hutchinson, Kans., Mar. 21, 1942; s. D.J.W. and Louise (Wedel) S.; m. Nevonna Joyce Thomas, May 24, 1964; children: Taryn Dee Schroeder Dye, Anita Joy Fitch. BA, Tabor Coll., 1964; MS, Kans. State Tchrs. Coll., 1967; PhD, U. Okla., 1971. Lic. psychologist, Kans. Rsch. psychologist Civil Aerospace Med. Inst., Oklahoma City, 1970-72, clin. rsch. psychologist, 1980-89, supr., 1989-90, mgr. human factors rsch. lab., 1990-91, mgr. aerospace human factors rsch. divsn., 1991—; intern Norfolk (Nebr.) Regional Ctr., 1972-73; clin. psychologist VA Hosp., Murfreesboro, Tenn., 1973-75, Topeka, 1975-80. Co-author: FAA Employee Survey: National Report, 1984, 86, FAA Employee Survey: Regional/Center Reports, 1984, 86, FAA Job Satisfaction Survey National Report, 1988, FAA Job Satisfaction Survey: Regional/Center/Work Group Reports, 1988; mem. adv. editl. bd. Aviation Space and Environ. Medicine, 1993-95, 99-2001. Mem. senate adv. com. Tabor Coll., Hillsboro, Kans., 1987-89; Christian edn. com. chmn. So. Dist. Conf. Mennonite Brethren Ch., Hillsboro, 1989; Sunday Sch. tchr. Western Oaks Christian Ch., Oklahoma City, 1990—. Fellow APA, Aerospace Med. Assn. (chmn. sci. program com. 1990-91, mem. coun. 1992-95, v.p. 1996-97, v.p. edn. and rsch. 1999-2002, pres.-elect, 2002-03, pres. 2003-04, program com. chair APA divsn. applied exptl. and engring. psychology 1996-97, sec.-treas. 1998-2001, pres.-elect 2001-02, pres. 2002-03, chmn. aerospace human factors com. 1999-2002, Raymond F. Longacre award for outstanding accomplishmnts in psychol. and psychiat. aspects of aerospace medicine 1997), Aerospace Human Factors Assn. (pres. 1994-95, Henry L. Taylor Founders award 2001); mem. Okla. Psychol. Assn. (bd. dirs. 1988-89, pres.-elect 1991, pres. 1992), Internat. Acad. Avaition and Space Medicine. Democrat. Achievements include research in assessing the interactive effects of alcohol, age and drugs on dynamic tracking and cognitive performance, personality characteristics and training success of air traffic control students, biofeedback, anxiety and burnout in government employees, fatigue and shiftwork. Home: 2601 NW 23rd St Oklahoma City OK 73107-2209 Office: PO Box 25082 Oklahoma City OK 73125-0082 Office Phone: 405-954-4846. Personal E-mail: djschro@att.net.

SCHROEDER, DONALD PERRY, retired food products company executive; b. Danville, Ill., Nov. 2, 1930; s. Donald Joseph and Pauline Hannah Schroeder; m. Barbara Ann Engle, Jan. 6, 1951; children: Patricia Ann Schroeder Capizzi, Helen Schroeder Marrano, Jeffrey Joseph. Student, Purdue U., 1949, Stanford U., 1982. Mgr. Schroeders I.G.A. Supermarket, Danville, 1950-57; specialist retail meat J.M. Jones Co., Champaign, Ill., 1957-59, mgr. retail zone, 1959-62, dir. meat ops., 1962-67; dir. customer services Olean (N.Y.) Wholesale Grocery Co., 1967-70; nat. dir. meat Ind. Grocers Alliance, Chgo., 1970-74; dir. meat ops. Fleming Cos., Inc., Topeka, 1974-83, v.p. meat., produce ops. Oklahoma City, 1983-88, v.p. meat ops., 1988-89, ret., 1989. Chmn. meat council Ind. Grocers Alliance, Chgo., 1962-87. Bd. dirs. Big Bros./Sisters Greater Oklahoma City, 1984-87, North Side YMCA, Oklahoma City, 1988-90. Mem. Nat. Livestock and Meat Bd. (universal meat cut identity com. 1970-73), United Fresh Fruit and Vegetable (bd. dirs. 1984-87). Republican. Roman Catholic. Avocations: yard and garden work, golf, fishing. Home: 5 Charnela Ln Hot Springs National Park AR 71909-3030

SCHROEDER, DOUGLAS FREDRICK, architect; b. Omaha, June 12, 1935; s. Walter Elmer and Ellen Ruth (Niles) S.; m. Joanne Vlecides, July 5, 1980. B.Arch., U. Mich., 1959. Registered Architect, Ill., N.C., Mich. Designer, draftsman C.F. Murphy Assocs., Chgo., 1959-63; architect, sr. architect Skidmore, Owings & Merrill, Chgo., 1964-67; architect, ptnr. Schroeder, Yamamoto & Schreiber, Chgo., 1968-69; ptnr. Hinds & Schroeder, Ltd., Chgo., 1972-74; propr. Douglas Schroeder Assocs., Chgo., 1974-83, 93—; ptnr. Siegel & Schroeder, P.C., Chgo., 1983-91; dir. SGA Planning and Constrn. Cons. Co. div. Goforth Group, Chgo., 1991-93; v.p. Yacht Harbor Mgmt. Co., South Haven, Mich., 1983-88. Dir. Inland Architect Mag. Contbr. articles to profl. jours. Bd. dirs. Chgo. Archtl. Assistance Ctr., 1982-84; chmn. Mass. Transp. Crisis Com., Chgo., 1973, Ill. Futures Forum, 1976-77; pres. Ill. Planning and Conservation League, Chgo., 1971-74. Named Outstanding Alumnus Lake Superior State U., 1971. Fellow AIA; mem. Am. Arbitration Assn. (arbitrator) Clubs: Cliff Dwellers (dir. 1971-74). Unitarian Universalist. Home: 700 W Irving Park Rd Apt 4A Chicago IL 60613-3133 Office: Douglas Schroeder Assocs Arch & Planners 980 N Michigan Ave Ste 1277 Chicago IL 60611-4523 E-mail: dschroeder@dsa-architects.com.

SCHROEDER, EDMUND R. lawyer; b. N.Y.C., Feb. 6, 1933; s. Robert C. and Rose A. (Garramone) S.; m. Elaine P. Diserio, Jan. 21, 1961; children: Edmund Jr., Christopher, Elizabeth. AB cum laude, Harvard U., 1953, LLB, 1958. Assoc. Archibald R. Graustein, N.Y.C., 1958-61, Root, Barrett, Cohen, Knapp & Smith, N.Y.C., 1961-67; ptnr. Barrett Knapp Smith & Schapiro, N.Y.C., 1967-88, Lord Day & Lord/Barrett Smith, N.Y.C., 1988-94, Cadwalader, Wickersham & Taft, N.Y.C., 1994-2000, sr. counsel, 2000—. Mem. adv. com. Commodity Futures Trading Comm. on Definition and Regulation of Market Instruments, 1975-76. Contbr. articles to profl. jours. Bd. dirs. Orch. St. Luke's N.Y.C., 1987—, chmn. exec. com., 1993-95; trustee The United Way of Scarsdale-Edgemont, 1990-92; mem. Scarsdale Bd. Edn., 1976-79; co-founder, 1st chmn. Edn. Through Music, Inc., N.Y.C., 1991—; trustee Hoff-Barthelson Music Sch., Scarsdale, 1974—, chmn. bd., 1986-90, hon. chmn., 1990—; trustee The Nat. Guild Cmty. Schs. Arts, Englewood, N.J., 1992-96; bd. advisors Sacred Heart/Mt. Carmel Sch. for Arts, Mt. Vernon, 1995-97; arbitrator Am. Arbitration Assn., Nat. Futures Assn. Mem.: ABA (chmn. com. futures regulation 1981—85), N.Y. State Bar Assn. (com. comty. and futures law and regulation 1996—), Bar Assn. City of N.Y. (founder, 1st chmn. com. futures regulation 1976—). Office: Cadwalader Wickersham & Taft 100 Maiden Ln New York NY 10038-4818 E-mail: edmund.schroeder@cwt.com.

SCHROEDER, EDWIN MAHER, law educator; b. New Orleans, June 25, 1937; s. Edwin Charles and Lucille Mary (Maher) S.; m. Marietta Louise DeFazio, Aug. 1, 1936; children: Edwin Charles II, Jonathan David, Margaret Louise. AA, St. Joseph Sem., St. Benedict, La., 1957; PhB, Gregorian U., Rome, 1959; JD, Tulane U., 1964; MS, Fla. State U., 1970. Bar: Mass. 1964. Asst. prof. law U. Conn., 1965-68; asst. prof., asst. law libr. U. Tex., 1968-69; asst. prof. Fla. State U., 1969-71, assoc. prof., 1971-75, prof., 1975—2004, dir. Law Libr., 1969—2004, asst. dean Coll. Law, 1979-83, assoc. dean Coll. Law, 1983-93. Mem. ABA, Am. Assn. Law Librs. (v.p. Southwestern chpt. 1983-84, pres. 1984-85), Order of Coif, Beta Phi Mu. Roman Catholic. Home: 806 Middlebrooks Cir Tallahassee FL 32312-2439 E-mail: eschroed@law.fsu.edu.

SCHROEDER, FRED ERICH HARALD, humanities educator; b. Manitowoc, Wis., June 3, 1932; s. Alfred William and Sissel Marie (Lovell) S.; m. Janet June Knope, Aug. 21, 1954; 1 child, Erich Karl. BS, U. Wis., 1960; MA, U. Minn., 1963, PhD, 1968. Elementary sch. tchr. various locations, Wis., 1952-60; asst. prof. English U. Minn., Duluth, 1968-71, assoc. prof. English, 1971-74, prof. behavioral sci., 1977-82, prof. humanities, 1974-96, dir. Ctr. for Am. Studies, 1986-87, dir. Inst. Interdisciplinary Studies, 1987-90, dir. dept. humanities and classics, 1989-90, dir. grad. liberal studies, 1992-95, prof. emeritus, 1996—. Author: Joining the Human Race: How To Teach Humanities, 1972, Outlaw Aesthetics: Arts and the Public Mind, 1977, Front Yard America: The Evolution and Meanings of a Domestic Vernacular Landscape, 1993; co-author: Encyclopedia of Modern Everyday Inventions, 2003; editor Interdisciplinary Humanities (formerly Humanities Edn. jour.), 1983-95, assoc. editor, 1995—; editor 5000 Years of Popular Culture, 1980, 20th Century Popular Culture in Museums and Libraries, 1981; lectr., writer Nat. Humanities Series, 1969-71; adv. editor Guide to U.S. Popular Culture, 2001. Mem. Minn. Humanities Commn., 1985-90. Woodrow Wilson Nat. Found. fellow, 1960-61, dissertation fellow 1963; NEH scholar, 1969-70; Inst. for Human Values in Medicine fellow, 1976. Mem. Am. Culture Assn. (pres. 1984-87), Nat. Assn. Humanities Edn. (pres. 1987-89, exec. sec.-treas. 1989-96), Am. Assn. for State and Local History (seminar instr. 1978-82), Popular Culture Assn. Avocations: collecting art, woodworking, gardening. Home: 5756 N Shore Dr Duluth MN 55804-9660 E-mail: fschroed@d.umn.edu.

SCHROEDER, GERALD FRANK, state supreme court vice chief justice; b. Boise, Idaho, Sept. 13, 1939; s. Frank Frederick and Josephine Ivy (Lucas) S.; children: Karl Casteel, Erich Frank. BA magna cum laude, Coll. of Idaho (now Albertson Coll. of Idaho), 1961; JD, Harvard U., 1964. Bar: Idaho 1965. Assoc. Moffatt, Thomas, Barrett & Blanton, Boise, 1965—66; pvt. practice Boise, 1966—67; asst. U.S. atty. Dept. Justice, Boise, 1967—69; judge Ada County Probate Ct., Boise, 1969—71; magistrate State of Idaho, Boise, 1971—75; dist. judge U.S. Dist. Ct. (4th dist.) Idaho, 1975—95; justice Idaho Supreme Ct., 1995—. Instr.Boise Bar Rev. Boise Bar Rev., 1973—; adj. faculty law Boise State U., 1986—95; former mem. Gov. Coun. on Crime and Delinquency. Author: Idaho Probate Procedure, 1971, (Novel) Triangle of the Sons-Phenomena, 1983; contbr. chpt. to history text. Adminstrv. and dist. judge 4th dist. State of Idaho, 1985—95; Bd. dirs. Boise Philharm. Assn., 1979—81. Fellow Toll fellow, Nat. Coun. State Govt., 1990. Mem.: Idaho Bar Assn., Boise Racquet and Swim Club (pres. bd. dirs. 1991—93). Office Phone: 208-334-3324. Business E-Mail: gschroeder@isc.state.io.us.

SCHROEDER, HAROLD KENNETH, JR., US magistrate judge; b. Buffalo, Aug. 6, 1936; s. Harold Kenneth and Margaret Mary (Mescall) S.; m. Jean Louise Benbenek, Aug. 20, 1958; children: Mary Margaret, Mark, Keith, Kurt, Jennifer. BS, Canisius Coll., 1958; JD, U. Buffalo, 1961; ML, Georgetown U., 1962. Bar: N.Y. 1961, D.C. 1961, U.S. Dist. Ct. (we. dist.) N.Y. 1961, Fla. 1979, U.S. Ct. Appeals (2nd cir.) 1981. Trial atty. U.S. Dept. Justice, Washington, 1962-63; spl. asst. U.S. Atty. D.C. Washington, 1962-63; U.S. Atty. Western Dist. N.Y. U.S. Dept. Justice, Buffalo, 1969-72; ptnr. Hodgson, Russ, Andrews, Woods & Goodyear, Buffalo, 1963-69, sr. ptnr., 1972-2000; U.S. magistrate judge We. Dist. NY, 2000—. Chmn. fed. merit selection panel U.S. Magistrate Judge We. Dist. N.Y., 1989, 92, 94, 98; chmn. U.S. Pub. Defender Selection Com., 1991, 95. Author: (with others) Law and Tactics in Federal Criminal Cases, 1964. V.p. Orchard Park, N.Y. Ctrl. Sch. Dist., 1972-76, Buffalo Sem., 1972-88. E. Barrett Prettyman fellow Georgetown U., 1961; recipient Disting. Alumnus award U. Buffalo Law Sch., 1996. Fellow Am. Coll. Trial Lawyers; mem. Western N.Y. Def. Trial Lawyers Assn. (Def. Trial Lawyer of Yr. 1996), Erie County Bar Assn. Avocation: tennis. Home:

3872 Baker Rd Orchard Park NY 14127-2031 Office: US Courthouse 68 Court St Buffalo NY 14202-3405 Office Phone: 716-332-7870. E-mail: kenneth_schroeder@nywd.uscourts.gov.

SCHROEDER, HERMAN ELBERT, scientific consultant; b. Bklyn., July 6, 1915; s. Henry W. and Caroline (Schmidt) S.; m. Elizabeth Barnes, June 13, 1938 (dec. July 27, 2002); children: Nancy Schroeder Tarczy, Edward L., Peter H., Martha L. Schroeder Lewis. AB summa cum laude, Harvard, 1936, A.M., 1937, PhD, 1939. With E.I. du Pont de Nemours & Co., Wilmington, Del., 1938-80, asst. dir. R&D, 1957-63, dir. R&D, 1963-80; pres. Schroeder Sci. Svcs., Inc., 1980—. Sci. cons. Met. Mus. Art, N.Y.C., Smithsonian Instn., Winterthur Mus. Mem. Chester County Sch. Bd., Unionville, Pa., 1950-56; pres. Assn. Harvard Chemists, 1955-57; mem. vis. com. Harvard Chemistry Dept., 1960-72; mem. sci. adv. com. Winterthur Mus.; trustee, chmn. research com. U. Del. Research Found., 1976-84, former v.p. Recipient award Internat. Inst. Synthetic Rubber Producers, 1979, Lavoisier medal DuPont, 1992, Disting. Achievment award PolyPrep, N.Y.C., 1997. Mem. AAAS, Am. Chem. Soc. (Charles Goodyear medal 1984), N.Y. Acad. Scis., Phi Beta Kappa, Alpha Chi Sigma. Home and Office: 74 Stonegates 4031 Kennett Pike Greenville DE 19807-2033 Personal E-mail: her2schro@aol.com. *A life in industrial research has been for me both challenging and rewarding. Forces which impel me are largely the compulsion to look for the new, to change for the better, be it by finding better ways to do things or by inventing products to make the world function better. Gratifyingly, these often make the world aesthetically more pleasant and sometimes cleaner. I am concerned by the growing hostility of society to science and to developments that ensure a more comfortable life and safer food and energy than would otherwise be possible.*

SCHROEDER, HORST WILHELM, food products executive; b. Schwerin, Germany, May 5, 1941; m. Gisela I. Kammin; 1 child, Bernd; stepchildren: Ralph, Isabel Lange. MBA, U. Gottingen, Hamburg, Fed. Republic Germany, 1965. Sr. auditor Price Waterhouse, Hamburg, 1966-70; fin. contr. Kellogg Co. of West Germany, Bremen, 1970-71, dir. fin., 1971-76, mng. dir., 1976-81; pres., chief exec. officer Kellogg Salada Can., Toronto, 1981-83; pres. Kellogg Internat., Battle Creek, Mich., 1983-86, Kellogg N.A., Battle Creek, 1986-88; exec. v.p. Kellogg Co., Battle Creek, 1988, pres., chief oper. officer, 1988—. Mem. adv. bd. J.L. Kellog Grad. Sch.; Bd. of govs. St. Joseph Acad. of Food Mktg., Phila., 1986-88; mem. com. external affairs U. Ill., Chgo., 1987-88. Mem. Am. Health Found. (bd. dirs. 1987—), KC (pres. 1988—, bd. dirs. 1989—). Avocations: golf, tennis. Office: Am Italian Pasta Co 1000 Italian Way Excelsior Springs MO 64024

SCHROEDER, JAMES WHITE, retired lawyer; b. Elmhurst, Ill., Apr. 19, 1936; s. Paul W. and Thelma C. (White) S.; m. Patricia N. Scott, Aug. 18, 1962; children: Scott W. and Jamie C. BA, Princeton U., 1958; JD, Harvard U., 1964. Bar: Colo. 1964, U.S. Dist. Ct. Colo. 1964, U.S. Ct. Appeals (10th cir.) 1965, U.S. Supreme Ct. 1972, U.S. Dist. Ct. D.C. 1973, U.S. Ct. Appeals (D.C. cir.) 1974, U.S. Ct. Appeals (8th cir.) 1977, U.S. Ct. Appeals (3d cir.) 1981, U.S. Claims Ct. 1983, U.S. Ct. Appeals (fed. cir.) 1983. Ptnr. Moseley, Wells & Schroeder, Denver, 1965-72, Kaplan Russin & Vecchi, Washington, 1973-92; counsel Whitman & Ransom, Washington, 1992-93; dep. under sec. U.S. Dept. Agr., 1993-2001. Arbitrator Am. Arbitration Assn. Active Ams. for Democratic Action, Smithsonian Instn.; bd. trustees Orlando Opera, 2003—. Lt. USNR, 1958-64. Am. Field Svc. scholar 1953, NROTC scholar, 1954. Mem. ABA, Fed. Bar Assn., Denver Bar Assn., Colo. Bar Assn., D.C. Bar Assn., Cap and Gown Club, Lincoln's Inn Club, City Club Denver (pres. 1972), Princeton Club Washington (pres. 1982-84). Democrat. Home: 621 Nadine Pl Celebration FL 34747

SCHROEDER, JOHN H. university chancellor; b. Twin Falls, Idaho, Sept. 13, 1943; s. Herman John and Azalia (Kimes) S.; m. Sandra Barrow; children: John Kimes, Andrew Barrow. BA, Lewis and Clark Coll., Portland, Oreg., 1965; MA, U. Va., 1967, PhD, 1971. Instr. history U. Wis., Milw., 1970-71, asst. prof., 1971-76, assoc. prof., 1976-86, prof., 1986—, Am. Coun. on Edn. fellow, 1982-83, assoc. dean, 1976-82, asst. to vice chancellor, 1982-85, acting vice chancellor, 1985-87, vice chancellor, 1987-90, chancellor, 1990-98, U. Wis. sys. prof., 1998—. Louis M. Sears Meml. lectr. Purdue U., 1978. Author: Mr. Polk's War: American Opposition and Dissent, 1973, The Commercial and Diplomatic Role of the American Navy 1829-1861, 1985, Matthew C. Perry: Antebellum Sailor and Diplomat, 2001 (Theodore and Franklin Roosevelt Naval History prize 2002, John Lyman Naval History award 2002). V.p. bd. dir. John Michael Kohler Arts Ctr.; bd. dir. Wis. Hist. Soc. Recipient Edward and Rosa Uhrig award U. Wis.-Milw., 1974, Disting. Teaching award AMOCO/U. Wis.-Milw., 1975, John Lyman Book award, 2001, Theodore and Franklin Roosevelt prize for Haval History, 2002. Mem. Orgn. Am. Historians, Soc. for History of Early Republic, Soc. for History Am. Fgn. Rels. Office: U Wis Dept History PO Box 413 2310 E Hartford Ave Milwaukee WI 53211-3165 E-mail: jhs@uwm.edu.

SCHROEDER, JOHN R. state legislator, banker; b. July 19, 1951; m. Sue Schroeder; 1 child, Zachary. Grad., U. Del., 1975. Mem. Del. Ho. of Reps., Dover, 1988—, mem. agrl. and natural resources com.; v.p. 2d Nat. Fed. Savs. Bank. Mem. Del. Family Law Commn., Greenway Coun. Parent Early Edn. Ctr., Atlantic States Marine Fisheries Commn., Edn. Improvement Commn.; mem. adv. coun. Jr. Achievement; bd. dirs. Friends of Lewes Libr.; past chmn. Eastern Sussex Family YMCA. Mem. Rehoboth Beach C. of C. (past pres.). Home: 47 Edgewater Dr Lewes DE 19958-9747 Office: Del Ho of Reps Legislative Hall PO Box 1401 Dover DE 19903-1401

SCHROEDER, JOYCE KATHERINE, state agency administrator, research analyst; b. Moline, Ill., Apr. 1, 1951; d. Reinhold J. and Miriam May (Schroeder). BS Math., U. Ill., 1973, MA Ops. rsch., 1978. Underwriter, programmer, Springfield, Ill., 1973-76; ops. rsch. analyst Ill. Dept. Transp., Springfield, 1976-78, data analyst, 1978-80, team leader, fatal accident reporting sys., 1980-83, mgr. safety project evaluation, 1983-92, mgr. accident studies and investigation, 1992—. Sys. engring. del. to China,China Assn. for Sci. and Tech., 1986; mem. staff Driving While Intoxicated Adv. Coun. and Task Force, State of Ill., 1983-86, 89-92, Gov. Task Force on Occupant Protection, 1988-90; Ill. Traffic Safety Info. Sys. Coun., 1993-95. Vol. Animal Protective League, Springfield; leader bd., co-chairperson LPGA Rail Classic, Springfield, 1983-87; amb. of goodwill Lions of Ill. Found., 1993; trustee, 1995-99. Named to Pres.'s Coun., U. Ill., 2004; recipient Disting. Svc. award, Lions of Ill. Found., 2003; fellow, 1995; Melvin Jones fellow, Lions Clubs Internat., 1993, fellow Laureate, Lions of Ill. Found., 2002. Mem.: N. Am. Conf. of Lions Found. (ann. conf. steering com. 2001—03, bd. dirs. 2004—), Past Dist. Gov. Assn. (sec.-treas. 1993—), Lions of Ill. Endowment Fund (trustee 1998—99, coord. meml. and endowments 1999—), Lions Club (dist. Gov. Ill. 1992—93, state membership coord. 1994—96, Melvin Jones fellow 1993), Springfield Lincoln Land Lions Club (charter pres. 1988—90, treas. 1993—95, news editor 1995—, treas. 2002—), Lions of Ill. Found. (amb. goodwill 1993, trustee 1995—99, treas. found. bd. 1996—97, v.p. found. bd. 1997—98, chmn. long range planning com. 1997—, pres. found. bd. 1998—99, policy ad hoc com. 1999—, chmn. policy ad hoc com. 2002—), Kappa Delta Pi, Phi Kappa Phi. Avocations: travel, music, sports, dogs, humanitarian svc. Office: Ill Dept Transp 3215 Exec Pk Dr Springfield IL 62703-4514 Office Phone: 217-785-3021. E-mail: jks999@juno.com.

SCHROEDER, JULIAN IVAN, biology professor; b. Summit, N.J., June 11, 1958; s. Manfred Robert and Anny (Menschik) S.; m. Marion G. Spors, Aug. 9, 1991; children: Julia Sofia K., Nicola A.J. Dr. rer. nat., U. Gottingen, Max Planck Inst., 1987. Postdoctoral rschr. dept. physiology UCLA Sch. Medicine, 1988-90; from asst. to prof. dept. biology U. Calif. San Diego, La Jolla, 1990-2000, Novartis Endowed chair in plant scis., 2000—. Contbr. articles to profl. jours. Named Highly Cited Rschr., Inst. for Sci. Info., 2002; recipient Heinz Meier Leibnitz prize, Deutsche Forschungs Gemeinschaft, 1984, Presdl. Young Investigator award NSF, 1991, Blasker award in environ. sci. and engring., San Diego Found., 2001; Alexander von Humboldt fellow, 1988, 1996. Mem. Biophys. Soc., Am. Assn. Plant Biologists (Charles Albert Shull award 1997). Achievements include identification of ion channels in higher plant cells, characterization of their functions in membrane signal transduction; cloning and functional roles of mineral nutrient and heavy metal transporters in plants roots. Office: U Calif San Diego Div Biology Ctr Molec Gene 9500 Gilman Dr La Jolla CA 92093-0116 Office Phone: 858-534-7759. Business E-Mail: JISchroeder@ucsd.edu.

SCHROEDER, KENNETH L. electronics executive; b. 1946; BSEE, U. Wis.; MBA, U. Pa. Gen. mgr. constrn. sys. divsn. Spectra-Physics; ops. mgr. computer group Hewlett-Packard; pres., COO Genus, Inc.; various KLA-Tencor Corp., San Jose, Calif., pres., COO, 1991-99, CEO, 1999—. Bd. dirs. SEMI, GaSonics Internat. Office: KLA Tencor Corp 160 Rio Robles San Jose CA 95134 Fax: 408-875-3030.

SCHROEDER, MARY MURPHY, federal judge; b. Boulder, Colo., Dec. 4, 1940; d. Richard and Theresa (Kahn) Murphy; m. Milton R. Schroeder, Oct. 15, 1965; children: Caroline Theresa, Katherine Emily. BA, Swarthmore Coll., 1962; JD, U. Chgo., 1965. Bar: Ill. 1966, D.C. 1966, Ariz. 1970. Trial atty. Dept. Justice, Washington, 1965—69; law clk. to Hon. Jesse Udall Ariz. Supreme Ct., 1970; mem. Lewis and Roca, Phoenix, 1971—75; judge Ariz. Ct. Appeals, Phoenix, 1975—79, U.S. Ct. Appeals (9th cir.), Phoenix, 1979—2000, chief judge, 2000—. Vis. instr. Ariz. State U. Coll. Law, 1976—78. Contbr. articles to profl. jours. Mem.: ABA (Margaret Brent award 2001), Am. Judicature Soc., Am. Law Inst. (coun. mem.), Fed. Bar Assn., Ariz. Bar Assn. (James A. Walsh Outstanding Jurist award 2004), Soroptimists. Office: US Ct Appeals 9th Cir US Courthouse Ste 610 401 W Washington St SPC-54 Phoenix AZ 85003-2156 Fax: 602-322-7320. E-mail: mary_schroeder@ca9.uscourts.gov.

SCHROEDER, PATRICIA SCOTT, trade association administrator, retired congresswoman; b. Portland, Oreg., July 30, 1940; d. Lee Combs and Bernice (Lemoin) Scott; m. James White Schroeder, Aug. 18, 1962; children: Scott William, Jamie Christine. BA magna cum laude, U. Minn., 1961; JD, Harvard U., 1964. Bar: Colo. 1964. Field atty. NLRB, Denver, 1964-66; practiced in Denver, 1966-72; mem. faculty U. Denver, 1969-72, C.C. Denver, 1969-70, Regis Coll., Denver, 1970-72; hearing officer Colo. Dept. Personnel, 1971-72; mem. 93d-104th Congresses from 1st Colo. dist., Washington, 1973-96; co-chmn. Congl. Caucus for Women's Issues, 1976-96; dir. New Solutions for a New Century, Civil Society Inst.; prof. Woodrow Wilson Sch. of Pub. and Internat. Affairs Princeton U., 1997; pres., CEO Assn. Am. Pubs., Washington, 1997—. Mem. Ho. Reps., ranking minority mem. judiciary subcom. on the Constitution, Nat. Security Com.; dean Congl. Women; chair Ho. Select Com. Children, youth and Families, 1991—93. Author: (book) Champion of the Great American Family, 1989, 24 Years of House Work and the Place is Still a Mess: My Life in Politics, 1998. Bd. dirs. Marguerite Casey Found. Named to Nat. Women's Hall of Fame, 1995. Congregationalist. Office: Assn Am Publishers 50 F St NW Fl 4 Washington DC 20001-1530

SCHROEDER, RITA MOLTHEN, retired chiropractor; b. Savanna, Ill., Oct. 25, 1922; d. Frank J. and Ruth J. (McKenzie) Molthen; m. Richard H. Schroeder, Apr. 23, 1948 (div.); children— Richard, Andrew, Barbara, Thomas, Paul, Madeline. Student, Chem. Engring., Immaculate Heart Coll., 1940-41, UCLA, 1941, Palmer Sch. of Chiropractic, 1947-49; D. Chiropractic, Cleve. Coll. of Chiropractic, 1961. Engring.-tooling design data coordinator Douglas Aircraft Co., El Segundo, Santa Monica and Long Beach, Calif., 1941-47; pres. Schroeder Chiropractic, Inc., 1982-93; dir. Pacific States Chiropractic Coll., 1978-80, pres. 1980-81. Recipient Palmer Coll. Ambassador award, 1973. Parker Chiropractic Research Found. Ambassador award, 1976, Coll. Ambassador award Life West Chiropractic Coll. Mem. Internat. Chiropractic Assn., Calif. Chiropractic Assn., Internat. Chiropractic Assn. Calif., Assn. Am. Chiropractic Coll. Presidents, Council Chiropractic Edn. (Pacific State Coll. rep.), Am. Pub. Health Assn., Royal Chiropractic Knights of the Round Table. Home: 8701 N State Highway 41 Spc 18 Fresno CA 93720-1010 Office: Schroeder Chiropractic Inc 2535 N Fresno St Fresno CA 93703-1831 Personal E-mail: drritas@comcast.net.

SCHROEDER, STEPHEN ROBERT, psychology researcher; b. Leipsic, Ohio, Oct. 28, 1936; BA, Josephinum Coll., 1958; MA, U. Toledo, 1964; PhD, U. Pitts., 1967. Lic. psychologist, Ohio, N.C. Postdoctoral rsch. assoc. Learning Rsch. and Devel. Ctr., U. Pitts., 1967-68; clin. asst. prof. dept. psychology U. N.C., Chapel Hill, 1968-73, clin. assoc. prof. depts. psychology and psychiatry, 1973-77, rsch. assoc. prof. dept. psychology, 1977-87, rsch. sci. Biol. Scis. Rsch. Ctr., 1973-87, assoc. prof. dept. psychiatry, 1977-86, prof. dept. psychiatry, 1986-87; dir. psychology Murdoch Ctr., Butner, N.C., 1973-75, dir. rsch. and devel., 1975-77; prof. dept. psychology and psychiatry Ohio State U., Columbus, 1987-90, dir. The Nisonger Ctr., 1987-90; prof. dept. human devel. and family life U. Kans., Lawrence, 1990—, prof. dept. pharmacology and toxicology, 1990—, dir. Bur. Child Rsch., 1990—, dir. Schiefelbusch Inst. for Life Span Studies, 1990—. Mem. program com. Gatlinburg Conf. on Mental Retardation and Devel. Disabilities, 1977-92, program chmn., 1992—; mem. N.C. divsn. Mental Health and Mental Retardation Rsch. Grants Rev. Bd., 1977-86; mem. statewide lead screening com. N.C. Dept. Meternal and Child Health, 1979-86; founding chmn. Annie Sullivan Enterprises, Inc., 1982-89, active, 1989-92, chmn., 1992—; mem. rsch. grant rev. bd. Ont. Mental Health Found., 1984—; mem. internat. rsch. exch. subcom. for Rsch. in Ednl. Rehab. in U.S. and German Dem. Republic, 1984-90; gen. ad hoc mem. grant rev. bd. NIMH, 1984; mem. mental retardation study com. NICHD, 1989-90; rsch. cons. Am. Occupational Therapy Found., Inc.; cons. pediats. ward N.C. Meml. Hosp., 1977-86; cons. civil rights divsn. U.S. Dept. Justice, 1987—; cons. No. Va. Tng. Ctr., 1983-85, 91, Murdoch Ctr., Western Carolina Ctr., Caswell Ctr., 1977-89; bd. dirs. Corp. of Guardianship; active Ohio Devel. Disabilities Planning Coun., 1987-90, Kans. Planning Coun. on Devel. Disabilities Svcs., 1990—, Kans. Prevention Task Force, 1991—, Gov. Task Force on Respite Care, 1991—. Author, editor chpts. to books; editor Am. Jour. Mental Retardation, 1987—; co-editor Jour. Applied Rsch. in Mental Retardation, 1980-86, Rsch. in Devel. Disabilities, 1987—; mem. editl. bd. Jour. Applied Behaviour Analysis, 1973-74, Mental Retardation, 1977-93, Analysis and Intervention in Devel. Disabilities, 1981-82; guest reviewer Jour. Applied Behaviour Analysis, Pediat. Psychology, Am. Jour. Psychiatry, Jour. Autism and Childhood Scizophrenia, Child Devel., Sci., Perceptual and Motor Skills, Pediatrics, Neurotoxicology; contbr. articles, papers to profl. jours. Mem. adv. bd. Ohio United Cerebral Palsy, 1988-90; active Ohio Prevention Coalition, 1987-90. Recipient Karl Heinz Renker medallion for interdisciplinary sci. collaboration German Dem. Republic, 1989. Fellow APA (pres. divsn. 33 mental retardation 1986-87, Nicholas Hobbs award 1989); mem. AAAS, Am. Assn. Mental Retardation, Am. Acad. Mental Retardation, Assn. Advancement Behavior Therapy (task force on self-injurious behavior 1981-82), Assn. Behavior Analysis, N.Y. Acad. Scis., Sertoma Club. Office: U Kansas KS Ctr Rsch Mental Retardation 1052 Dole Human Devel Ctr Lawrence KS 66045-0001

SCHROEDER, STEVEN ALFRED, medical educator; b. N.Y.C., July 26, 1939; s. Arthur Edward and Norma (Scheinberg) Schroeder; m. Sally B. Ross, Oct. 21, 1967; children: David Arthur, Alan Ross. BA, Stanford U., 1960; MD, Harvard U., 1964; LHD (hon.), Rush U., 1994; DSc (hon.), Boston U., 1996, U. Mass. Med. Ctr., 1997, Georgetown U., 2000, Med. Coll. Wis., 2002; DHL (hon.), U. Medicine Dentistry NJ, 2003. Diplomate Am. Bd. Internal Medicine. Intern and resident in internal medicine Harvard Med. Svc., Boston City Hosp., 1964—66, 1968—70; asst. prof., then assoc. prof. George Washington Med. Ctr., Washington, 1971—76; vis. prof. St. Thomas' Hosp. Med. Sch., London, 1982—83; prof. medicine, chief div. gen. internal medicine, mem. Inst. Health Policy Studies U. Calif., San Francisco, 1976—90; pres., CEO Robert Wood Johnson Found., Princeton, NJ, 1990—2002; clin. prof. medicine U. of Medicine and Dentistry N.J., 1990—2002; disting. prof. health and health care U. Calif., San Francisco, 2003—, dir. smoking cessation leadership ctr., 2003—. Conv. various govtl. and philanthropic health orgns.; chair internat. adv. com. faculty medicine Ben Gurion U., Israel. Sr. editor: Current Med. Diagnosis and Treatment, 1987—93, mem. editl. bd.: New Eng. Mag.; contbr. numerous articles to profl. jours. Mem. U.S. Prospective Payment Assessment Comm., 1983—88; bd. overseers Harvard Coll., 2000—; mem. IOM Coun.; bd. dirs. Am. Legacy Found., 2000—, vice chair, 2001—03, chair, 2003—; bd. dirs. Save Ellis Island, 2002—; dir. James Irvine Found. Master: ACP; mem.: APHA, Soc. Gen. Internal Medicine (past pres.), Inst. Medicine (coun. mem.), Assn. Am. Physicians, Physicians for Social Responsibility, Harvard Med. Alumni Assn. (pres.), Alpha Omega Alpha, Phi Beta Kappa. Office: U Calif San Francisco 3333 California St Ste 430 San Francisco CA 94143-1211

SCHROEDER, VAN ACE, lawyer; b. Lincoln, Nebr., Feb. 8, 1952; s. Clark Eugene and Shirley Mae (Suddarth) S.; m. Ann Marie Wallace, Nov. 20, 1982; children: Stephen C., Michael W. B.A., U. Nebr.-Lincoln, 1974, J.D., 1977. Bar: Nebr. 1977, U.S. Dist. Ct. Nebr. 1977, U.S. Ct. Appeals (8th cir.) 1987, U.S. Supreme Ct. 1994. Assoc. atty. Weber Law Offices, Bellevue, Nebr., 1977-80, Pelton Law Offices, Bellevue, 1980-82; assoc. Pelton, Bertolini, Schroeder, Veith & Blount, Bellevue, 1982-89, ptnr. Bertolini, Schroeder & Blount, 1989—; atty. coach Nebr. Mock Trial Project, Omaha Bryan High Sch., 1983, Bellevue E. High Sch., 1984-92. Recipient Am. Jurisprudence award Bancroft-Whitney Co., 1977; named to Outstanding Young Men of Am., 1985. Mem. Nebr. Bar Assn., Nebr. Assn. Trial Attys., Nebr. 2d Jud. Dist. Bar Assn., Omaha Bar Assn., Sarpy County Bar Assn. Democrat. Lodge: Eagles. Office: Bertolini Schroeder & Blount 1620 Wilshire Dr Ste 250 Bellevue NE 68005-6600

SCHROEDER, WILLIAM ARTHUR, law educator; b. Chgo., Mar. 19, 1943; s. Arthur C. Schroeder; children: Elizabeth, Matthew, David, Sara, John. BA, U. Ill., Champaign, 1966, JD, 1969; LLM, Harvard U., 1977. Bar: Mass. 1972, Mo. 1990, U.S. Supreme Ct. 1978. Instr. law Boston Coll., 1970-71; practicing atty. various firms, Mass., 1972-80; assoc. prof. law U. Ala., Tuscaloosa, 1980-84; prof. law So. Ill. U., Carbondale, 1984—. Vis. prof. law U. Mo.-Columbia, 1983; Washington U. 1991, 99. Co-author: Alabama Evidence, 1987, 3d edit., 2000; author: Missouri Evidence, 1992, 2d edit., 1999, 2000, Missouri Courtroom Handbook, 1999, 2000, 01, 02, 03, 04, Illinois Courtroom Handbook, 2004; contbr. articles to profl. jours. Fulbright scholar, 2004. Mem.: ABA, Lions, Harvard Club of St. Louis. Home: 27 Pinewood Dr Carbondale IL 62901 Office: So Ill U Lesar Law Bldg Carbondale IL 62901 Office Phone: 618-453-8747.

SCHROEDER, WILLIAM JOHN, electronics executive; b. Havre de Grace, Md., June 9, 1944; s. William Martin and Dorothy Jeanne (McLaughlin) S.; m. Marilee Jane Alne, May 28, 1966; children: Kristen, Kari Britt, Kimberley. BSEE, Marquette U., 1967, MSEE, 1968; MBA, Harvard U., 1972. Devel. engr. Honeywell Inc., Mpls., 1968-70; mgmt. cons. McKinsey & Co., Los Angeles, 1972-76; mgr. product planning Memorex Corp., Santa Clara, Calif., 1976-78; pres. Priam Corp., San Jose, Calif., 1978-85, chmn., 1985-86; pres. Conner Peripherals, Inc., San Jose, 1986-89, vice chmn., 1989-94; CEO Arcada Software Inc., a Conner Co., 1993-94; pres., CEO Diamond Multimedia Systems, Inc., San Jose, Calif., 1994-99, CyberIQ Sys., Inc., San Jose, Calif., 2000. Bd. dirs. ShareWave Inc., El Dorado Hills, Calif., CNF, Inc., Palo Alto, Calif., AlphaSmart, Cupertino, Calif., RioPort.com, San Jose. Office: CyberIQ Sys Inc 225 Baypointe Pky San Jose CA 95134-1627 E-mail: billshradr@aol.com.

SCHROEDER, W(ILLIAM) WIDICK, religion educator; b. Newton, Kans., Nov. 12, 1928; s. William Fredric and Irene (Widick) S.; m. Gayle Eadie, Sept. 1, 1956; children: Scott David, Carla Gayle. BA, Bethel Coll., 1949; MA, Mich. State U., East Lansing, 1952; BDiv, Chgo. Theol. Sem., 1955, DD (hon.), 1995; PhD, U. Chgo., 1960. Ordained to ministry Congl. Christian Ch., 1955. Instr. Mich. State U., 1953-54, U. Chgo., 1958-60; from asst. prof. to prof. religion and society Chgo. Theol. Sem., 1960-94, prof. emeritus, 1994—. Vis. fellow Mansfield Coll., Oxford, Eng., 1966; vis. lectr. Yale U., 1970; vis. scholar Ctr. for Process Studies, Claremont, Calif., 1976; vis. lectr. in ethics and soc. Div. Sch. U. Chgo., 1967-71, 76; editor Rev. of Religious Rsch., 1964-69. Author: (with Victor Obenhaus) Religion in American Culture: Unity and Diversity in a Midwestern County, 1964; Cognitive Structures and Religious Research, 1970; (with Victor Obenhaus, Larry A. Jones and Thomas P. Sweetser) Suburban Religion: Churches and Synagogues in the American Experience, 1974; (with Keith A. Davis) Where Do I Stand? Living Theological Options for Contemporary Christians, 1973, rev. edit., 1975, 3d edit., 1978; Flawed Process and Sectarian Substance: Analytic and Critical Perspectives on the United Church of Christ General Synod Pronouncement, Christian Faith: Economic Life and Justice, 1990; Toward Belief: Essays in the Human Sciences, Social Ethics, and Philosophical Theology, 1996; co-editor: (with Philip Hefner) Belonging and Alienation: Religious Foundations for the Human Future, 1976; (with Gibson Winter) Belief and Ethics: Essays in Ethics, the Human Sciences and Ministry in Honor of W. Alvin Pitcher, 1978; (with John B. Cobb, Jr.) Process Philosophy and Social Thought, 1981; (with Perry LeFevre) Spiritual Nurture and Congregational Development, 1984, Pastoral Care and Liberation Praxis: Essays in Personal and Social Transformation, 1986, Creative Ministries in Contemporary Christianity, 1991; (with Franklin I. Gamwell) Economic Life: Process Interpretations and Critical Responses, 1988; co-editor Studies in Religion, Society and Personality, Center for the Scientific Study of Religion, 1972-2001. Mem. Religious Rsch. Assn., Soc. Christian Ethics. Home: 6315 Longwood Rd Libertyville IL 60048-9447 *The aims of existence are aesthetic satisfaction and intensity of feeling. In facilitating these aims, the Divine Reality is the locus of potentiality, the mediator of experience, the evoker of feeling and the ultimate recipient of all that has become.*

SCHROER, BERNARD JON, industrial engineering educator; b. Seymour, Ind., Oct. 11, 1941; s. Alvin J. and Selma A. (Mellencamp) S.; m. Kathleen Dittman, July 5, 1963; children: Shannon, Bradley. BSE, Western Mich. U., 1964; MSE, U. Ala., 1967; PhD, Okla. State U., 1972. Registered profl. engr., Ala. Mech. designer Sandia Labs., Albuquerque, 1962-63; engr. Teledyne Co., Huntsville, Ala., 1964-67, Boeing Co., Huntsville, 1967-70, Computer Sci. Corp., Huntsville, 1970-72; dir. Johnson Ctr. U. Ala., 1972-91, prof., 1991—, chmn. dept. indsl. and sys. engring., 1991-94, assoc. v.p. rsch., 1994—. Mem. adv. coun. Energy Dept., Montgomery, Ala., 1980-86; bd. dirs So. Solar Energy Ctr., Atlanta, 1980-83; mem. gov.'s cabinet State of Ala., Montgomery, 1982; exec. dir. Ala. Automotive Mfrs. Assn., 2000—; mem. So. Tech. Coun., 2000—. Author: Modern Apparel Manufacturing Systems and Simulation, 1991; contbr. articles to profl. jours. Named Outstanding Engr., Robotics Internat., 1986, Outstanding Engr., So. Tech. Coun., 1987; recipient summer traineeship NSF, 1971. Fellow: Inst. Indsl. Engrs. (pres. 1972, 1986, Outstanding Engr. 1973, 1977); mem.: Soc. Computer Simulation. Lutheran. Home: 716 Owens Dr SE Huntsville AL 35801-2034 Office: U Ala Huntsville AL 35899-0001 E-mail: schroerb@email.uah.edu.

SCHROER, EDMUND ARMIN, retired utility company executive; b. Hammond, Ind., Feb. 14, 1928; s. Edmund Henry and Florence Evelyn (Schmidt) S.; m. Lisa V. Strope; children: James, Fredrik, Amy, Lisa, Timothy, Suzanne. BA, Valparaiso U., 1949; JD, Northwestern U., 1952. Bar: Ind. 1952. Pvt. practice law, Hammond, 1952—; assoc. Crumpacker & Friedrich, 1952; ptnr. Crumpacker & Schroer, 1954-56; assoc., then ptnr. Lawyer, Friedrich, Petrie & Tweedle, 1957-62; ptnr. Lawyer, Schroer & Eichhorn, 1963-66; sr. ptnr. Schroer, Eichhorn & Morrow, Hammond, 1967-77; pres., CEO No. Ind. Pub. Svc. Co., Inc., Hammond, 1977-93; chmn. No. Ind. Pub. Svc. Co., Hammond, 1978-93, chmn., CEO, 1989-93, also bd. dirs.; chmn., pres., CEO NIPSCO Industries, Inc., 1987-93; cons. NIPSCO Industries Inc., Hammond, 1993-96; also bd. dirs.; ret. Asst. dist. atty., No. Ind., 1954-56; trustee Ill. Ins. Exch., 1993-95. Trustee Sch. Bd., Munster, Ind., 1969-71, pres., 1971; fin. chmn. Rep. Party, Hammond, 1958-62; del. Ind. Rep. Conv., 1958, 60, 64, 66, 68. Mem. Fed. Bar Assn., Am. Gas Assn. (chmn. 1986), Rotary (pres. Hammond club 1968). Lutheran. Home and Office: No Ind Pub Svc Co 5265 Hohman Ave Hammond IN 46320-1722

SCHROER, GENE ELDON, lawyer; b. Randolph, Kans., Aug. 29, 1927; s. Harry Edward and Florence Lillian (Schwartz) S.; m. Edith Grace Kintner, Apr. 7, 1956 (div.); children: Kenneth G., Rebecca J., Sonya J., Connie J.; m. Anne Oliver; 1 child, Edward G. AB, LLB, Washburn U., 1957. Bar: Kans. 1957, U.S. Dist. Ct. Kans. 1957, U.S. Ct. Appeals (10th cir.) 1970, U.S. Supreme Ct. 1983. Pvt. practice, Topeka, 1957-68; ptnr. Schroer, Rice, P.A., Topeka, 1968—, pres., 1970—, also bd. dirs. Contbr. articles to profl. jours. and chpts. to books. Supr. Shawnee County Soil Conservation Dist., Topeka, 1968-84. With U.S. Army, 1951-53. Mem. ABA, Kans. Bar Assn., Assn. Trial

Lawyers Am. (gov. 1976-79, seminar lectr. 1973—, chmn. tort sect. 1974-75, instr. Nat. Coll. Adv. 1978, 81-88), Kans. Trial Lawyers Assn. (gov. 1972—, seminar lectr. 1974—, pres. 1974-75), Nat. Bd. Trial Advocacy (sustaining founder), Am. Bd. Trial Advs. (sec., treas. Kans. chpt. 1990-91, pres. 1991-92), Civil Justice Found. (founding sponsor), Trial Lawyers for Pub. Justice (bd. dirs. 1982-96). Democrat. Methodist. Office: Schroer Rice PA 115 SE 7th St Topeka KS 66603-3901 E-mail: gschroer@schroerrice.com.

SCHROLL, EDWIN JOHN, retired secondary educator, stage director; b. Watertown, NY, Feb. 14, 1941; s. Clarence Edwin and Frances Lucille (Snyder) S. BS, Lyndon State Coll., 1966; MS, Oswego State U., 1971. Cert. tchr. N.Y. English tchr. jr. h.s. Watertown (N.Y.) Sch. System, 1966-67; English tchr. h.s. Belleville (N.Y.) Cen. Sch., 1967-71, Massena (N.Y.) Cen. Sch., 1971-96, drama and speech tchr., 1988-96, drama coach, 1975-96, forensics coach; ret., 1996. Engr., announcer, programmer Pathways to Peace program Sta. WNCQ, Watertown, 1967-92; dir. Family History Ctr., Watertown, N.Y. Cinematographer, writer, narrator, prodr. (documentaries) The United States: A Bicentennial Tour, 1976, Europe on $100 a Day, 1986; cinematographer: (TV) Wish You Were Here in Cape Vincent, 2000, Partying, 1989; co-author: Standard Operations Procedures and Duties of a Desk Clerk, 1963, Wish You Were Here in Cape Vincent, 2000; prodn. supr. (hist. pageant) 1,000 Seasons, 2001; dir. various high sch. prodns.; actor various community prodns. Bd. dirs. Youth in Action, 1993-94; active Nat. Family Opinion, 1991—; state advocate Ednl. Theatre Assn., 1996; del. Citizens Ambassador Program of People to People Internat. Theatre Edn. Delegation to China, 1996; active Cape Vincent Arts Coun., 1997—, Gravelly Point Players, 1997—, Breakwater Art Gallery, 1997— Mem. Nat. Geog. Soc., Ednl. Theatre Assn., Archaeology Inst. Am., Am. Film Inst., Nat. Trust Hist. Preservation, Cinerama Preservation Soc. Republican. Mem. Lds Ch. Avocations: stamp and coin collecting, gardening, historical research, genealogy, travel. Home: PO Box 216 143 S Murray St Cape Vincent NY 13618 Office: Massena Sch System Nightengale Ave Massena NY 13662-1901 E-mail: edschroll@tds.net.

SCHROM, ELIZABETH ANN, retired writer; b. Princeton, Minn, June 7, 1941; d. Raymond Alois and Grace Eleanor (Hayes) S. Student, U. Minn., 1960; BA, St. Scholastica Coll., Duluth, Minn., 1963; postgrad., Princeton U., 1965; MEd, Temple U., 1972; MLS, Drexel U., 1974; postgrad., NYU, 1981, Russian Temple U., 1983. Tchr. Strandquist HS, Minn., 1963-64, Hutchinson HS, Minn., 1964-65, Peace Corps, Ankara, Turkey, 1965 67, Phila. Sch. Dist., 1968-80; children's libr. Laurel Pub. Libr., Del., 1983; writer Ortonville (Minn.) Ind. Newspaper, 1983—2004. Mem. Jewish Com. on Middle East, Washington, 1988-90, 93, Nat. Coun. Returned Peace Corps. Vol., Washington, 1989-99, Nat. Taxpayers Union, Washington, 1988-92; mem. bd. policy Liberty Lobby, Washington, 1989-2000; mem. Arkadashlar, 2003-04. Populist. Roman Catholic. Avocations: writing, cooking, history, travel, sewing. Home: 1141 US Hwy 12 Lot 8 Ortonville MN 56278

SCHROPP, JAMES HOWARD, lawyer; b. Lebanon, Pa., June 20, 1943; Work e-mail: schroja@ffhsj.com. s. Howard J. and Maud E. (Parker) S.; m. Jo Ann Simpson, Sept. 4, 1965; children: James A., John C., Jeffrey M., Jeremy M. BA, U. Richmond, 1965; JD, Georgetown U., 1973. Bar: D.C. 1973, U.S. Supreme Ct. 1980. Asst. gen. counsel SEC, Washington, 1973-79; ptnr. Fried, Frank, Harris, Shriver & Jacobson, Washington, 1979—. Adj. prof. Georgetown U., Washington, 1982-86; mem. faculty Nat Inst. for Trial Advocacy. Mem. ABA (discovery com. litigation sect. 1984-86, tender offer litigation subcom. corp. banking and bus. law sect. 1985-86, task force on broker-dealer compliance supervisory procedures 1987-89). Office: Fried Frank Harris Shriver & Jacobson 1001 Pennsylvania Ave NW Washington DC 20004-2505

SCHROPP, TOBIN, lawyer; b. 1962; BS in Fgn. Svc., Georgetown U., 1984, JD, 1987, LLM in Taxation, 1991. Bar: 1987. Sr. v.p., gen. counsel Peter Kiewit Sons' Inc., Omaha. Office: Peter Kiewit Sons Inc 1000 Kiewit Plaza Omaha NE 68131

SCHROTE, JOHN ELLIS, retired government executive; b. Findlay, Ohio, May 6, 1936; s. Millard L. and Alberta (Ellis) S.; m. Rachel Daly, Mar. 2, 1957; children: LTC James D., Gretchen, Wade. BS in Agr., The Ohio State U., 1958; MBA, Xavier U., 1964. Buyer-expediter McGraw Constrn. Co., Middletown, Ohio, 1958-59; buyer Armco Corp., Middletown, 1959-66; adminstrv. asst. Congressman D.E. Lukens, Washington, 1967-71; prin. asst. to assoc. dir. OEO, Washington, 1971-72; spl. asst. to sec. USDA, Washington, 1972-77, nat. rep. congl. com., 1977-79; adminstrv. asst. Congressman F.J. Sensenbrenner, Jr., Washington, 1979—81; acting asst. sec. USDA, Washington, 1981-82; dep. dir. presdl. pers. office The White House, 1982-83; exec. v.p. Bishop Bryant & Assocs., Washington, 1983-84; adminstrv. asst. Congressman F.J. Sensenbrenner, Jr., 1984—89; asst. to sec. and dir. congl. affairs Dept. Interior, Washington, 1989, dep. asst. sec. policy mgmt. and budget, 1989-91, asst. sec. policy mgmt. and budget, 1991-93; retired, 1993. Mem. Nat. Policy Forum, The Environ. Policy Coun., 1994-96, NC Seafood Indsl. Park Authority, 1994-97; mem. Currituck County Econ. Devel. Bd., 1994—; mem. Currituck County Rep. Exec. Com., 1993—, 3d Dist. Rep. Exec. Com., 1994-97, NC State Rep. Exec. Com., 1994-97; Currituck County Ext. Svc. Adv. Leadership Coun., 1994-2000; bd. dir. Currituck County 4-H Found.; mem. Ocean Hills Property Owners Assn.,1994— (treas. 1997-2000, v.p., 1996-97, 2003-04); commr. Northeastern NC Regional Econ. Devel. Commn., 1997—. Mem. Reagan-Bush Alumni Assn., Bush-Quayle Alumni Assn. Episcopalian. Home: PO Box 209 Corolla NC 27927-0209

SCHROTH, PETER W(ILLIAM), lawyer, management and law educator; b. Camden, N.J., July 24, 1946; s. Walter and Patricia Anne (Page) S.; children: Laura Salome Erickson-Schroth, Julia James. AB, Shimer Coll., 1966; JD, U. Chgo., 1969; M in Comparative Law, U.Chgo., 1971; SJD, U. Mich., 1979; postgrad., U. Freiburg, Fed. Republic Germany, Faculté Internationale pour l'Enseignement de Droit Comparé; MBA, Rensselaer Poly. Inst., 1988; DHL, Shimer Coll., 2000; MSc, Sch. Oriental and African Studies, 2000. Bar: Ill. 1969, N.Y. 1979, Conn. 1985, Mass. 1990; solicitor Supreme Ct. England and Wales 1995. Asst. prof. So. Meth. U., 1973-77; fellow in law and humanities Harvard U., 1976-77, vis. scholar, 1980-81; assoc. prof. N.Y. Law Sch., 1977-81; prof. law Hamline U., St. Paul, 1981-83; dep. gen. counsel Equator Bank Ltd., 1984-87; v.p., dep. gen. counsel Equator Holdings Ltd., 1987-94, v.p., gen. counsel, 1994-2000. Adj. prof. law U. Conn., 1985-86, Western New Eng. Coll., 1988—, adj. prof. of mgmt. Rensselaer Poly. Inst., 1988-98, prof., 1999—, dir. Ctr. for Global Bus. Studies, 2000—. Author: Foreign Investment in the United States, 2nd edit., 1977; author: (with Stiefel) Products Liability: European Proposals and American Experience, 1981; author: Doing Business in Sub-Saharan Africa, 1991; bd. editors Am. Jour. Comparative Law, 1981—84, 1991—, mem. editl. bd. Conn. Bar Jour., 1988—, sr. editor, 1993—2000, editor-in-chief, 2000—, recent decisions editor N.Y. Internat. Law Rev., —, mem. editl. rev. bd. Jour. Bus. in Developing Nations, 1996—2000, editor-in-chief, 2000—, co-editor-in-chief Jour. Legal Studies in Bus. Treas., mem. bd. trustees Shimer Coll. Mem. ABA (editor in chief ABA Environ. Law Symposium 1980-82), Am. Soc. Comparative Law (bd. dirs. 1978-84, 91—), Am. Fgn. Law Assn., Internat. Bar Assn., Internat. Law Assn. (com. multinat. banking), Acad. Internat. Bus., Conn. Civil Liberties Union (bd. dirs. 1985-92), Environ. Law Inst. (assoc.), Columbia U. Peace Seminar (assoc.), Hartford Club (bd. govs. 1995-98), Am. Corp. Counsel Assn. (pres. Conn. chpt.1997-2000), Conn. Bar Assn. (chair sect. of internat. law 1997-2000). Office: Rensselaer Poly Inst Lally Sch Mgmt and Tech 275 Windsor St Hartford CT 06120-2910

SCHROTH, THOMAS NOLAN, editor; b. Trenton, N.J., Dec. 21, 1920; s. Frank David and Loretta (Nolan) S.; m. Colette Streit, May 1, 1948 (div. 1958); 1 child, Valerie; m. Patricia Wiggins, Sept. 27, 1958; children: Jennifer, Amy, Anne. Student, Tuck Sch. Bus. Adminstrn., 1942; AB, Dartmouth Coll., 1943. Reporter Time, Washington, 1946-47, UPI, Boston, 1947-48; reporter, news editor Bklyn. Eagle, 1948-51, mng. editor, 1951-55; editorial adviser Magnum Photos, Inc., N.Y.C., 1955; exec. editor, pub. Congl. Quar. Inc. and Editorial Research Reports, Washington, 1955-68; founder, editor Nat. Jour. Ctr. Polit. Rsch., Washington, 1969-70; communications adviser Pub. Broadcasting Environment Ctr., Washington, 1970-71; asst. dir. pub. affairs for communications EPA, Washington, 1970-71, cons., 1972; exec. editor The Ellsworth (Maine) American, 1972-77; co-pub.-editor (with Patricia Schroth) Maine Life Mag., Sedgwick, 1977-81; editorial cons. U. Maine, Bangor, 1976-90; mng. editor South-North News Svc., Hanover, N.H., 1987-91; co-pub. New Leaf Pubs., Sedgwick, Maine, 1990—. Mem. Am. Press Inst. Seminar for Mng. Editors, 1953, Regional Transp. Adv. Com., 1996-99. Editor: Congress and the Nation, 1946-64--A Review of Government and Politics in the Postwar Years; editor Improving the U. of Maine trustee's pamphlet. Elected selectman Town of Sedgwick, 1989-94, moderator 1995—; bd. dirs. Blue Hill (Maine) Meml. Hosp., 1978-93, Bangor Symphony Orch., 1981-87, Blue Hill Concert Assn., 1991-2003; bd. dirs., v.p. Island Nursing Home, Deer Isle, Maine, 1985—; mem. Maine State Dem. Com., Augusta, 1985-92, 97—; bd. dirs. Downeast Transp., Inc., 1993—; del. Maine Dem. Nat. Conv., 2000. 1st lt. Army Airways Comm. Sys., USAAF, WWII. Mem. Sigma Delta Chi. Avocations: gardening, walking, music. Home and Office: 50 Benjamin River Rd Sedgwick ME 04676-9729

SCHROTT, NORMAN, retired clinical social worker; b. N.Y.C., Jan. 26, 1938; s. Walter Quido Otto and Anna (Klein) S.; m. Janet Ann Cupolo, July 25, 1964. BA in Sociology, Cleve. State U., 1972; MS in Social Planning and Adminstrn., Case Western Res. U., 1976. Lic. ind. social worker, Ohio. Adminstrv. specialist div. social svcs. Cuyahoga County Welfare Dept., Cleve., 1972-74, foster care specialist, 1976-79, child abuse supr., 1979-80, protective svcs. supr., 1980-2000. With U.S. Army, 1962—65. Grantee State of Ohio, 1974-76. Mem. Acad. Cert. Social Workers, Nat. Geog. Soc., Greater Cleve. Orchid Soc., Westshore Orchid Soc., Nat. Audubon Soc., Am. Orchid Soc. (student judge Great Lakes Judging Ctr.), Kiwanis. Home: 25925 Lake Rd Cleveland OH 44140-2563

SCHROYER, MICHAEL KEVIN, critical care nurse and hospital administrator; b. Kewanee, Ill., Sept. 14, 1959; s. Jesse Wayne and Shirley Ann (Brown) S.; m. Joy Anne, June 20, 1987; children: Tiffany Marie, Rebecca Ann, Adam Michael. Diploma, Moline Pub. Hosp. Sch. Nursing, 1980; BSN, Loyola U., 1984; MSN, Seton Hall U., 1987; postgrad., Rush U., 1990-91. Cert. nursing adminstr., hosp. adminstr. Nurse mgr., CCU, ICU, PICU, CCFP Jersey Shore Med. Ctr., Neptune, NJ; assoc. dir., critical care nursing Hyde Park Hosp., Chgo.; adminstrv. dir., transplant svcs. Rush-Presbyn./St. Lukes Med. Ctr., Chgo.; adminstrv. coord., v.p. cardiovascular and med./surg. svcs. United Med. Ctr., Moline, Ill.; adminstrv. leader, v.p. Regional CardioLife Ctr., Tenet Brookwood Med. Ctr., Birmingham, Ala., 1993-96; v.p. clin. svcs. MedCath McAllen (Tex.) Heart Hosp., 1996-98, MedCath Dayton (Ohio) Heart Hosp., 1998-2000, interim CEO, 2000, v.p. ops./COO, 2000—01; pres. / CEO Okla. Heart Hosp., Oklahoma City, 2001—; cons. The Rielly Group, Denver, 2001—. Author: Emergency Nursing, 1989, Nursing Spectrum, 1989, Comprehensive Nursing Care Plans, 1995. Former bd. dirs. Rock Island County chpt. Am. Heart Assn. Mem.: AACN, Am. Heart Assn. (bd. dirs. Oklahoma City chpt.), Am. Assn. Med. Cardiovasc. Adminstrs., Am. Coll. Healthcare Execs., Sigma Theta Tau. Office: Okla Heart Hosp 4050 W Memorial Rd Oklahoma City OK 73120 Home: 14614 Canterbury St Leawood KS 66224-3904 Business E-Mail: mschroyer@okheart.com.

SCHRUM, JAKE BENNETT, university administrator; b. Greenville, Tex., Feb. 9, 1946; s. Jake M. and Julia (Bennett) S.; m. Mary Woodman, Dec. 28, 1968; children: Julia Elizabeth, Emily Katharine. BA, Southwestern U., 1968, MDiv, Yale U., 1973; postgrad., Harvard U., 1983. Ordained to ministry Meth. Ch., 1969. Devel. officer Yale U., New Haven, 1973-77; dir. devel. Muhlenberg Coll., Allentown, Pa., 1977-78; v.p. Tex. Wesleyan Coll., Ft. Worth, 1978-82; v.p. univ. rels. Southwestern U., Georgetown, Tex., 1982-85; v.p. Emory U., Atlanta, 1985-91; pres. Tex. Wesleyan U., 1991-2000, Southwestern U., Georgetown, Tex., 2000—. Chmn. CASE, 1995—96; vice chair Associated Colls. of the South, 2004—; mem. exec. com. Coun. Ind. Colls.; bd. mem. Am. Coun. on Edn.; mem. exec. com. Annapolis Group; chair Ind. Colls. & Univs. Tex., 2004—; vice cahir, higher edn. com. Austin Area Rsch. Orgn.; bd. dirs. First Tex. Bank. Author: Democracy's Last Stand: The Role of the New Urban University, 1999; editor: A Board's Guide to Comprehensive Campaigns, 2000, Justice for All, 2001. Mem. exec. com. Tex. Ind. Coll. Fund; bd. mem. Austin Urban League; dir. Georgetown Area Cmty. Found., Georgetown Project. Named Man of Yr., Bnai Brith North Tex., 1995. Mem. Coun. Advancement and Support Edn. (bd. dirs. Europe), Nat. Assn. Ind. Colls. and Univs. (bd. dirs., exec. com. 1995-98), Rotary. Avocations: golf, public speaking. Office: Southwestern U PO Box 770 Georgetown TX 78627-0770

SCHRUM, JANICE LYNN, social sciences educator; d. Norman C. McCandless and Joyce L. Vanderford; m. Richard N. Schrum; children: Crystal, Elizabeth. BA, Wichita State U., 1995; MA, U. Mo., Kansas City, 2000, MPA, 2001, PhD, 2002. Lectr. orgnl. behavior and leadership U. Mo., Kansas City, 1996—. Office: Univ Mo Kansas City 5110 Cherry Kansas City MO 64110

SCHTEINGART, DAVID EDUARDO, internist; b. Buenos Aires, Oct. 17, 1930; came to U.S., 1957; s. Mario and Flora (Garfunkel) S.; m. Monica Naomi Starkman, July 3, 1960; children: Miriam, Judith, M. Daniel. MD, U. Buenos Aires, 1955. Diplomate Am. Bd. Internal Medicine. Fellow Mt. Sinai Hosp., N.Y.C., 1957-58, Maimonides Hosp., Bklyn., 1958-59, U. Mich., Ann Arbor, 1959-62, instr., 1962-63, asst. prof., 1963-68, assoc. prof., 1968-72, prof., 1972—. Contbr. articles to profl. jours., books. Pres. Beth Israel Congregation, Ann Arbor, 1974-79, Hebrew Day Sch., Ann Arbor, 1984-86, Jewish Fedn. Washtenaw County, Ann Arbor. Recipient rsch. grants NIH, Bethesda, Md., 1985—. Fellow Am. Coll. Physicians; mem. Endocrine Soc., N.Y. Acad. Scis., Am. Soc. Clin. Nutrition, Cen. Soc. Clin. Rsch., Am. Fedn. Clin. Rsch. Jewish. Avocations: tennis, running, community activities. Office: U Mich Med Sch 1150 W Medical Center Dr Ann Arbor MI 48109-0726

SCHUB, CRAIG S. health science association administrator; BS in Bus. Adminstrn., Calif. State U.; postgrad., Calif State U. With Johnson & Johnson, Ethicon divsn., 1981-85; acct. supr. health care mktg., ad. agency; dir. corp. planning, devel. PacifiCare Health Systems, 1990-93, pres., Secure Horizons USA, 1993—. Bd. dirs. Orange County Chapt. Am. Red Cross; trustee Alliance Aging Rsch., Washington D.C. Office: PacifiCare Health Systems 3120 W Lake Center Dr Santa Ana CA 92704-6917

SCHUBEL, JERRY ROBERT, marine science educator, scientist, university dean; b. Bad Axe, Mich., Jan. 26, 1936; s. Theodore Howard and Laura Alberta (Gobel) S.; m. Margaret Ann Hostetler, June 14, 1958; children: Susan Elizabeth, Kathryn Ann. BS, Alma Coll., 1957; MA in Tchg., Harvard U., 1959; PhD, Johns Hopkins U., 1968; DSc (hon.), Mass. Maritime Acad., 1997. Rsch. assoc. Chesapeake Bay Inst., Johns Hopkins U., Balt., 1968-69, rsch. scientist, 1969-74, adj. rsch. prof., assoc. dir., 1973-74; dir. Marine Sci. Rsch. Ctr. SUNY, Stony Brook, 1974-83, dean, leading prof., 1983-94, acting dir. Waste Mgmt. Inst., 1985-87, provost, 1986-89, dir. COAST Inst., 1989, Disting. Svc. prof., 1994-95, prof. emeritus, 1995—; pres. emeritus, CEO New England Aquarium, Boston, 1994—2001; vis. prof. Wash. Coll., Chestertown, Md., 2002—, dir. Alternative Futures Forum, 2002—; pres., CEO Aquarium of Pacific, Long Beach, Calif., 2002—. Hon. prof. East China Normal U., Shanghai, 1985—; sec. exec. com. Commn. on Food, Environ. and Renewable Resources, 1993, chair steering com., 1994; mem. governing bd. Regional Marine Rsch. Program, Greater N.Y. Bight, 1993-94; v.p., founding dir. Gulf of Maine Ocean Observing Sys., 1998-2002; adv. panel Nat. Whale Conservation Fund Coumd., 2001—; mem. rev. panel Nat. Sea Grant, 2002—, chair, 2004; bd. dirs. Internat. Resources Group, 2002—, rev. panel Census of Marine Life, U.S. Nat. Com., 2003-, mem. NSF Edn. and Human Resources Adv. Com., 2003-, South Bay Salt Pond Restoration, Nat. Sci. Panel, 2003-. Author: The Living Chesapeake, 1981, The Life and Death of the Chesapeake Bay, 1 986; (with H.A. Neal) Solid Waste Management and the Environment, 1987, Garbage and Trash: Can We Convert Mountains Into Molehills?, 1992; editor: (with B.C. Marcy Jr.) Power Plant Entrainment, 1978; (with others) The Great South Bay, 1991; sr. editor Coastal Ocean Pollution Assement News, 1981-86; co-editor in chief Estuaries, 1986-88; mem. editl. bd. CRC Revs. in Aquatic Scis.; contbr. articles to profl. jours. Mem. adv. bd. Environ. Sci. Com. Outer Continental Shelf, Minerals Mgmt. Scs., 1984-86, chmn., 1986; bd. dirs. N.E. Area Remote Sensing Sys., 1983-85, L.I. Incubator Corp.; v.p. L.I. Forum for Tech., 1989-92; chair Mass. Outfall Monitoring Task Force, 1995-98; mem. sci. adv. bd. EPA, 1996-98; commr. Nat. Rsch. Coun.'s Commn. on Engring. Tech. Sys., 1996-2000; mem. vis. com. dept. ocean engring MIT, 1995-2002; trustee Natural Heritage Insts., 1995-2001; mem. Boston Artery Bus. Bd. Dirs., 1994-2001; mem. Boston Mcpl. Rsch. Bur. Bd. Dirs., 1994-2001; mem. Annenberg Challenge Adv. Com., 1995-2002; hon. trustee Sci. Mus. L.I., 2000-02. Recipient L.I. Sound Am. Environ. Edn. award, 1987, Stony Brook U. medal, 1989, Matthew Fontaine Maury award, 1990, Ben Gurion U. medal, 1993, sci. achievement award Sci. Mus. L.I., 2000; Alfred P. Sloan fellow, 1959; Wheaton Coll. Disting. fellow, 2000. Mem. NAS (mem. marine bd. 1989-94, 2002—, mem. exec. com. 1990, vice chair 1991-94, chair 1992-94, com. on Coastal Ocean 1989-93), NSF (mem. edn. and human resources adv. panel 2003—), NAt. Sci. Panel (mem. San Francisco South Bay salt pond restoration 2003—), Nat. Sea Grant (adv. panel, 2002—), Nat. Assn. State Univ. and Land Grant Colls. (bd. dirs. marine divsn., chmn. 1986-88), L.I. Environ. Coun., L.I. Marine Resources Adv. Coun. (chair 1990-94), L.I. Rsch. Inst. (bd. dirs. 1992-94), L.I. Environ.-Econ. Roundtable (co-chair 1991-92), Suffolk County Recycling Commn., (chmn. 1987-88), Estuarine Rsch. Fedn. (v.p. 1982-83, pres. 1985-87), N.Y. Sea Grant Inst. (chmn. governing bd. 1988-90, mem. gov.'s task force on coastal resources 1990-91), Census Marine Life (mem. U.S. nat. com. 2003—), The Nature Conservancy (trustee L.I. chpt. 1991-94), Franklin Electronic Pubs. (bd. dirs. 1991—), Taproot (bd. dirs. 1988-93, vice chair 1990-93), Internat. Resources Group (bd. dirs., 2002—), Sigma Xi, Phi Sigma Pi. Avocation: photography. Office: Aquarium of the Pacific 100 Aquarium Way Long Beach CA 90802 Business E-Mail: jschubel@lbaop.org.

SCHUBERT, BARBARA SCHUELE, retired performing company executive; b. Cleve., Feb. 21, 1939; d. William Edward and Mildred Marianne (Matousek) Schuele; m. John Dwan Schubert, June 15, 1963; children: William Edward, Christopher John, David Matthew. BS in Social Scis., John Carroll U, 1962, MA in English, 1967; MEd, 1980. Cert. secondary tchr., elem. remedial reading tchr., Ohio. Tchr. Sch. on Magnolia, Cleve., 1980-82, Ruffing Montessori, Cleve., 1982-83; tchr. English U. Sch., Chagrin Falls, Ohio, 1983-86; gen. mgr. Ohio Ballet, Akron, 1987-90, assoc. dir., 1990-99; ret. Bd. trustees Ohio Ballet, 1974-87, 91-99. Bd. dirs. John Carroll U., 1990—; trustee Boys Hope Girls Hope, 2001. Mem.: Cleve. Skating. Roman Catholic. E-mail: BJSchubert@earthlink.net.

SCHUBERT, BLAKE H. lawyer; b. Wheeling, W.Va., Apr. 21, 1939; s. John Arnold and Esther Elizabeth (Masters) Schubert; m. Carol Jean Cramp, Jan. 13, 1962; children: Cheryl Lynn, Charles Bradley, Elisabeth Anne. BA, Ohio Wesleyan U., 1961; JD, U. Chgo., 1964. Bar: Ill. 1964, U.S. Dist. Ct. (no. dist.) Ill. 1968, U.S. Tax Ct. 1994. Counsel Brunswick Corp., Chgo., 1964—68; asst. group counsel FMC Corp., Chgo., 1968—73; gen. counsel Dresser Tool Group, Chgo., 1973—79; chmn. Schubert Securities, Oak Park, Ill., 1979—84, Inter-Am. Investmemts, Inc., Oak Park, 1980—. Gen. ptnr. Investment Trust Ltd., St. Petersburg, Fla., 1981—91, Inter-Am. Fund, Oak Park, 1982—91, Inter-Am. Fund I, Oak Park, 1982—91, Inter-Am. Fund II, Oak Park, 1984—89; chmn. Compath Video Corp., Oak Park, 1984—85; lectr. Am. Inst. Banking, 1965, Chgo. Inst. Fin. Studies, 1984—85. Author: The Well-Kept Secrets of Investing, 1982. Chmn. Park Forest Co-op., Ill., 1966—70; mem. Chgo. Bd. Options Exch., 1979—83; chmn. 1st United Ch. Endowment Fund, Oak Park, 1975—80. Home and Office: 522 Linden Ave Oak Park IL 60302-1659

SCHUBERT, GUENTHER ERICH, pathologist; b. Mosul, Iraq, Aug. 17, 1930; s. Erich Waldemar and Martha Camilla (Zschitzschmann) Schubert; children: Frank, Marion, Dirk. MD, U. Heidelberg, Germany, 1957; pvt. docent in pathology, U. Tuebingen, Germany, 1966. Asst. med. dir. University Tuebingen, Fed. Republic of Germany, 1966-76; prof. pathology, 1972; head Inst. Pathology, Wuppertal, Fed. Republic of Germany, 1976-96; chair of pathology U. Witten-Herdecke, Fed. Republic of Germany, 1985-96. Co-author: Coloratlas of Cytodiagnosis of the Prostate, 1975, Pathologie, 1984, 1997, Endoscopy of the Urinary Bladder, 1989, Textbook of Pathology, 1981, 1987. Mem. Wissenschaftlicher Beirat, Bundesarztekammer, Bonn, Germany, 1976—85; pres. Medizinisch Naturwissenschaftliche Gesellschaft, Wuppertal, 1984—85, Onkologischer Schwerpunkt, Wuppertal, 1985—93, OSP Bergisch-Land, 1992—95, Bergische Arbeitsgemeinschaft fur Gastroenterologie, Wuppertal, 1987—88, 1990—91, 1994—95. Mem.: N.Y. Acad. Scis., Internat. Acad. Pathology, Deutsche Gesellschaft fur Urologie, Deutsche Gesellschaft fur Nephrologie, Deutsche Gesellschaft fur Pathologie, Lions. Avocations: music, diving, photography. Office: Inst Pathology Am Anschlag 71 42113 Wuppertal Germany

SCHUBERT, HELEN CELIA, public relations executive; b. Washington City, Wis. d. Paul H. and Edna (Schmidt) S. BS, U. Wis., Madison. Dir. pub. rels. United Cerebral Palsy, Chgo., 1961; adminstrv. dir. Nat. Design Ctr., Chgo., 1962-67; owner Schubert Pub. Rels., Chgo., 1967—. Bd. dirs. Fashion Group, Chgo., 1988—95; adj. prof. comm. Roosevelt U., 1992—. Mem. women's bd. Am. Cancer Soc., Chgo., 1988—, Art Resources in Tchg., Chgo., 1988-92. Recipient Comm. award Am. Soc. Interior Designers, Chgo., 1979, 83, 88, 94; named to Chgo. Women's Hall of Fame City of Chgo., 1990. Fellow Nat. Home Fashion League; mem. Women's Ad Club Chgo. (pres. 1981-83, Woman of Yr. award 1987), Women in Comm. (pres. 1969-70, Matrix award Lifetime Achievement 1996), Am. Advt. Fedn. (lt. gov. 1983-85). Lutheran. E-mail: schube@mail.com.

SCHUBERT, JEANNE, artist; b. Harlan, Ky., June 2, 1932; d. Lewis Marion and Bertha Faye (Paul) Conklin; m. Robert Breckenridge Stroup, Feb. 5, 1953 (dec. May 1954); 1 child, Robert Breckenridge; m. Robert Buxton (div. 1967); 1 child, Beverly Buxton; m. Robert Kenyon Schubert, Apr. 25, 1970. Student, Cumberland Coll., Williamsburg, Ky., 1951, Rollins Coll., Winter Park, Fla., 1974, Art Students' League, N.Y.C., 1984. Mortgage clk. Orlando (Fla.) Fed. Savs., 1962-76; real estate broker Orlando; co-owner, creator Art Works Orlando, 1993-96. Mem./exhibitor Orlando Mus. Art, 1972—. Dayton Beach Mus., 1972—, Arts on Douglas, New Smyrna Beach, Fla., 1995—, Albertson-Peterson Gallery, Winter Park, 1990-99. One woman shows include Lighthouse Gallery, Tequesta, Fla., Orlando Mus Art Assocs., Valencia C.C., Orlando, LeMoyne Ctr. for Visual Arts, Tallahassee, Melvin Gallery, Lakeland, U. Ctrl. Fla., Orlando, Vero Beach (Fla.) Ctr. for the Arts, Osceola Ctr. for Arts, Kissimmee, Fla., Gallery Contemporanea, Hot Springs, Ark., Brevard Art Ctr. and Mus., Melbourne, Fla., Melvin Gallery, Fla. So. Coll., Albertson-Peterson Gallery, First Union Tower, Orlando, Arts on Douglas, New Smyrna Beach; exhibited in group shows at Orlando Mus. Art, 1984, 87, 88, 92, Barbara Gilman Gallery, Miami, Miami-Dade Coll., 1986, North Miami Mus. Art, Salmagundi Club, N.Y., Fla. Gulf Coast Art Ctr., Belleaire, 1986, U. Ctrl. Fla., 1987, Harmon Gallery of Am. Art, Sarasota, Fla., Crealde Art Ctr. Gallery, Winter Park,, Mus. Arts and Sci., Daytona Beach, Daytona Beach Art Ctr., Epcot Ctr., Lake Buena Vista, 1994-2001, Soc. of the Four Arts, West Palm Beach, 1997-2001; works in permanent collections at Maitland Art Ctr., Rollins Coll., Valencia C.C., Mus. Arts and Scis., Walt Disney World, Flagship Banks, Melbourne, Gen. Mills Corp., Orlando, Hyatt Regency Corp., Orlando, City Hall, Orlando, Barnett Bank of Fla., Jacksonville, Orange County Courthouse, Shands Hosp., Gainesville, Mayo Clinic, Jacksonville, Baker & Hostetler, Orlando, Akerman, Senterfitt & Eidson, Orlando, Holland and Knight, Orlando, City Orlando Collections Orange County Collection, Suntrust Collection, Orlando, Fla., others. Bd. dirs. Maitland (Fla.) Art Ctr., 1972—. Art Svcs. Coun. Art grant. Mem. Fla. Watercolor Soc., Fla. Artist Group (area rep. 1985-2001). Home: 318 N Riverside Dr Edgewater FL 32132

SCHUBERT, RICHARD D. medical educator, physician; b. Mount Vernon, NY, Sept. 21, 1946; s. Uriel and Florette Roos Schubert; m. Geane Linz Schubert; children: Daniel, Katherine, Michael. AB, Franklin and Marshall Coll., 1968; MD, Downstate Med. Coll., N.Y.C., 1972. Clin. assoc. prof. medicine Georgetown U. Hosp., Washington; physician, treas. Foxhall Internists PC, Washington. Author: Chickering and Sons, 2003. Fellow: ACP, Am. Coll. Rheumatology; mem.: Washington Clin. Pathol. Soc. (pres. 2001—02). Avocations: entomology, music, piano, medieval philosophy, Renaissance art. Office: Foxhall Internists PC 3301 New Mexico Ave NW Washington DC 20016

SCHUBERT, RICHARD FRANCIS, consultant; b. Trenton, N.J., Nov. 2, 1936; s. Yaro and Frances Mary (Hustak) S.; m. Virginia Thomas Austin, Sept. 15, 2000; children: Robyn, David. BA cum laude, Eastern Nazarene Coll., 1958; LLB, Yale U., 1961. Bar: Pa. 1962, U.S. Supreme Ct 1972. Arbitration atty. Bethlehem Steel Corp., Pa., 1961-66, asst. mgr. labor relations, 1966-70; exec. asst. to undersec. labor Washington, 1970; gen. counsel labor, 1971-73; dep. sec. labor, 1973-75; asst. to v.p. indsl. relations Bethlehem Steel Corp., 1973, asst. v.p. public affairs, 1975-77, v.p. public affairs, 1977-79, pres., 1979-80, vice chmn., 1980-82; pres., CEO ARC, 1982-89, Points of Light Found., 1990-95. Bd. dirs. Internat. Ctr. for Religion and Diplomacy, Mgmt. Tng. Corp. Bd. dirs. Women in Cmty. Svc.; sr. v.p. EXCN; chmn. emeritus Internat. Youth Found., chmn., Nazarene Compassionate Ministries; vice chmn. Leader to Leader Inst.; chmn. Nat. Job Corps Assn. Mem.: Ctr. Excellence in Govt., Coun. on Fgn. Rels., Northampton County Bar Assn., Pa. Bar Assn., Ea. Nazarene Alumni Assn. (pres. 1969—73), Phi Alpha Delta. Mem. Ch. of Nazarene. Home: 6615 Madison McLean Dr Mc Lean VA 22101-2425 Office: Ste 701 Crystal Gateway 4 1213 Jefferson Davis Hwy Alexandria VA 22202 E-mail: rfs@iyfnet.org.

SCHUBERT, RUTH CAROL HICKOK, artist, educator; b. Janesville, Wis., Dec. 24, 1927; d. Fay Andrew and Mildred Wilamette (Street) Hickok; m. Robert Francis Schubert, Oct. 20, 1946; children: Stephen Robert, Michelle Carol. Student, DeAnza Coll., 1972—73; AA Scholarship, Monterey Peninsula Coll., 1974; BA with honors, Calif. State U., San Jose, 1979. Owner, mgr. Casa De Artes Gallery, Monterey, Calif., 1977—86; dir. Monterey Peninsula Mus. Art Coun., 1975—76; quick-draw artist So. Oreg. Pub. TV, KSYS; leader painting workshops; demonstrator, lectr., judge in U.S., B.C. Can., New Zealand and Loreto, Baja, Mexico. One-woman shows include Aarhof Gallery, Aarau, Switzerland, 1977, Degli Agostiniani Recolletti, Rome, 1977, Wells Fargo Bank, Monterey, 1975, 1978, 1979, Seaside (Calif.) City Hall Gallery, 1979, 1989, Village Gallery, Lahaina, Hawaii, 1983, 1986, 1989, 1994, Portola Valley Gallery, 1984, 1985, Rose Rock Gallery, Carmel, 1984—86, Taupo (N.Z.) Arts Soc., 1988, Geyserland Art Mus., Rotorua, N.Z., 1988, Wanganui (N.Z.) Art Soc., 1988, Hallei Brown Ford Gallery, Roseburg, Oreg., 1991, 1995, Collection of Ann Cunningham, Carmel, 1993—95, catalog nat. group juried shows include, Sierra Nev. Mus. Art, Reno, 1980, Bard Hall Gallery, San Diego, 1980, San Diego Nat. Watercolor Show, Mid-West Nat. Watercolor Show, Rahr-West Mus., Manitowoc, Wis., 1980, Rosicrucian Mus., San Jose, 1981, 1984, Calif. State Agri-Images, Sacramento, 1984, XVII Watercolor West, Brea Civic Cultural Ctr., 1985, Watercolor West XXIII, Grand Art Galleries, Glendale, Calif., 1991, Watercolor West XXV, Riverside (Calif.) Art Mus., 1993, Nat. Pen Women at Marjorie Evans Gallery, Carmel, 1986, Monterey County Juried Expo, Monterey Peninsula Mus. Art, 1986, 1987, Am. Artists Group Exhbn., 1993, 1994, 1995, Gallery Hirose, Tsukuba, Ibaragi, Japan, Internat. Art Show for End of World Hunger, Ashland, Oreg., 1990, biann. art exhbn. Sumner Mus., Washington, D.C., 1992, State of the Art, New Eng. Fine Arts, Boston, 1993, N.W. Wildlife, Nightingale Gallery, Ea. Oreg. Coll., La Grande, 1993, N.W. Visual Arts Ctr. 19th Ann., Panama City, Fla., 1993, NWWS Waterworks N.W. Julie Tolles Gallery, Mercer Island, Wash., 1994, Represented in permanent collections Rogue Valley Manor Spl. Svcs., Medford, Oreg., Monterey Calif. Peninsula Mus. Art, Nat. Biscuit Co. subs. RJR Nabisco, San Jose, Waikato Mus. Art, Hamilton, N.Z., Muscular Dystrophy Assn., San Francisco, Old Sch. Hous Mus., Qualicum Bay, Vancouver Island, B.C., USS George Washington Aircraft Carrier, Adm. Robert Sprigg, Pres. Bill Clinton, Barbara Bush, George Montgomery, Marilyn Horne, Alison Krauss, also numerous pvt. collections. Recipient 1st prize, Monterey County Fair, 1979, Jade Fon Watercolor award, Hall of Flowers, San Francisco, 1980, 1st Nat. Art Show, NY Am. Artist mag., 1980, Nat. Art Appreciation award, 1984, award, Norcal State Art Fair, 1985, Watercolor award, 25 Ann. Aqueous Media Show, Salem, Oreg., 1990, Watercolor Transparent award, NWWS, Mercer Island, 1994, NWWS Signature Artist Waterworks, Seattle, 1999, award, Calif. Watercolor Soc., 2001, numerous other awards for watercolor paintings. Mem.: Watercolor West (signature), Women Artists Registry N.Am., Nat. Mus. Women in Arts, Art Alumni San Jose State U., Nat. League Am. Pen Women (pres. 1983—84, 1986—87), Cen. Coast Art Assn. (pres. 1982—85), Mid-West Watercolor Soc., Arts Coun. So. Oreg. (Silver award 2000), Watercolor Soc., Monterey Peninsula Watercolor Soc., Rogue Valley Art Gallery (bd. officer), LaHaina Arts Soc., Watercolor Soc. Oreg., Artists Equity Assn., Nat. Watercolor Soc. (assoc.), Am. Watercolor Soc. (assoc.). Achievements include Artwork selected for inclusion in profl. pubs. including "Best of Watercolor" in Rockport Publr. and "The California Art Preview" in Les Krantz. Home: 3533 Southvillage Dr Medford OR 97504-9283 Office Phone: 541-772-0136.

SCHUBERT, SCOTT E. corporate financial executive; BS in Mgmt., Purdue U., 1975, MBA in Fin., 1976. With Amoco Corp., 1976—91, internat. contr. exploration and prodn., 1991—95, v.p. worldwide fin. svcs., 1995—98; CFO WilTel, 1999—2003, NTL, Inc., NYC, 2003—. Office: NTL Inc 110 E 59th St New York NY 10022

SCHUBERT, WILLIAM G. federal agency administrator; m. Gail Marlene Becker; 2 children. Grad., U.S. Maritime Acad. Unltd. master lic. any oceans USCG. Master/offshore installation mgr. Global Marine Drilling; pres. Internat. Trade and Transp., Inc., Houston; offshore industry expert to maritime adminstrn. U.S. Dept. Transp., Washington, 1986—90, regional rep. maritime adminstrn., 1990—95, adminstr. to maritime adminstrn., 2001—. Co-founder U.S. Exporters Competitive Maritime Coun., 1998. Commd. officer USNR. Office: US Dept Transp Maritime Adminstrn 400 7th St SW Washington DC 20590

SCHUBERT, WILLIAM HENRY, curriculum studies educator; b. Garrett, Ind., July 6, 1944; s. Walter William and Mary Madeline (Grube) S.; children by previous marriage: Ellen Elaine, Karen Margaret; m. Ann Lynn Lopez, Dec. 3, 1977; children: Heidi Ann, Henry William. BS, Manchester Coll., 1966; MS, Ind. U., 1967; PhD, U. Ill., 1975. Tchr. Fairmount, El Sierra and Herrick Schs., Downers Grove, Ill., 1967-75; clin. instr. U. Wis., Madison, 1969-73; tchg. asst., univ. fellow U. Ill., Urbana, 1973-75, asst. prof. Chgo., 1975-80, assoc. prof., 1981-85, prof., 1985—, coord. secondary edn., 1979-82, coord. instrnl. leadership, 1979-85, dir. grad. studies Coll. Edn., 1983-85, coord. grad. curriculum studies, 1985—, coord. edn. studies, 1990-94, 96—, chair area curriculum and instrn., 1990-94. Vis. assoc. prof. U. Victoria (B.C., Can.), 1981; disting. vis. prof. U. S.C., 1986; presenter in field. Author (with Ann Lopez Schubert): Curriculum Books: The First Eighty Years, 1980; author: Curriculum: Perspective, Paradigm and Possibility, 1986, with Edmund C. Short and George Willis, 1985; author: (with J. Dan Marshall and James T. Sears) Turning Points in Curriculum: A Contemporary American Memoir, 2000; author: (with Ann Lopez Schubert, Thomas P. Thomas, Wayne M. Carroll) Curriculum Books: The First Hundred Years, 2002; editor (with Ann Lopez): Conceptions of Curriculum Knowledge: Focus on Students and Teachers, 1982; editor: (with George Willis) Reflections from the Heart of Educational Inquiry: Understanding Curriculum Teaching Through the Arts, 1991; editor: (with William Ayers) Teacher Lore: Learning From Our Own Experience, 1992, re-pub., 2001; editor: (with George Willis, R. Bullugh, C. Kridel, J. Holton) The American Curriculum: A Documentary History, 1993; assoc. editor, mem. editl. bd. Ednl. Theory, mem. editl. bd. Catalyst: Voices of Chicago School Reform, Taboo: The Jour. of Culture and Edn., former mem. editl. bd. Ednl. Studies, former cons. editor Phenomenology and Pedagogy, adv. bd. Tchg. Edn., Pi Lamda Pubs., 1995—, Jour. Curriculum and Supervision, —, mem. editl. bd. Curriculum and Teaching, —, emeritus editl. bd. Jour. Curriculum Theorizing, 1999—; editor: (book series) Student Lore, 1990—; cons. editor Jour. Curriculum Discourse and Dialogue, —, mem. adv. bd. Jour. Critical Issues in Curriculum and Instrn., 2000—, contbr. over 200 articles to profl. jours., —, chpt. to books., —. Mem.: ASCD (steering com. curriculum com. 1980—83, publs. com. 1987—90, internat. polling panel 1990—), Soc. Profs. of Edn. (exec. bd. 1988—97, pres.-elect 2000—01, pres. 2001—02), John Dewey Soc. (bd. dirs. 1986—95, chair awards com. 1988—90, co-chair lectures commn. 1989—91, 1989—91, pres.-elect 1990—91, pres. 1992—93), Inst. Dem. in Edn., Nat. Soc. Study Edn., World Coun. Curriculum and Instr., Am. Ednl. Studies Assn. (Lifetime Achievement award in Curriculum Studies 2004), Am. Ednl. Rsch. Assn. (chmn. creation and utilization of curriculum knowledge 1980—82, program chmn. curriculum studies divsn. 1982—83, sec. divsn. B 1989—91, v.p. 2000—01), Am. Assn. Colls. Tchr. Edn., Soc. Study Curriculum History (sec.-treas. 1981—82, pres. 1982—83, founding mem.), Profs. of Curriculum (factotum 1984—85), Internat. Acad. Edn., Scottish Rite, Masons, Phi Kappa Phi (pres. U. Ill. Chgo. chpt. 1981—82), Phi Delta Kappa. Office: U Ill Coll Edn M/C 147 1040 W Harrison St Chicago IL 60607-7129 Business E-Mail: schubert@uic.edu.

SCHUBERT, WILLIAM KUENNETH, hospital medical center executive; b. Cin., July 12, 1926; s. Wilfred Schubert and Amanda Kuenneth; m. Mary Jane Pamperin, June 5, 1948; children: Carol, Joanne, Barbara, Nancy. BS, U. Cin., 1949, MD, 1952; LHD (hon.), Coll. Mt. St. Joseph, Cin., 1997. Diplomate Am. Bd. Pediat. Pvt. practice specializing in pediat., Cin., 1956-63; dir. clin. rsch. ctr. Children's Hosp. Med. Ctr., Cin., 1963-76; dir. divsn. gastroenterology Children's Hosp., Cin., 1968-79; prof. pediat. U. Cin., 1969-96, prof. emeritus, 1997—, assoc. sr. v.p. for children's hosp. affairs Coll. Medicine, 1993-96; chief of staff Children's Hosp. Med. Ctr., Cin., 1972-88; chmn. dept. pediat. U. Cin., 1979-93; dir. Children's Hosp. Rsch. Found., Cin., 1979-93; pres., CEO Children's Hosp. Med. Ctr., Cin., 1983-96, trustee, 1983—. V.p. Ohio Solid Organ Transplant Consortium, Columbus, 1986-87, pres., 1987-88, alt. trustee, 1988-96; trustee med. rsch. James N. Gamble Inst., Cin., 1989-95; bd. dirs. Choice Care Found., Health Found. of Greater Cin. Contbr. over 100 articles to profl. jours. Trustee Greater Cin. Hosp. Coun., 1986-96, Assn. of Ohio Children's Hosp., Columbus, 1986-96, The Children's Hosp. Found., 1990—, Springer Sch., Cin., 1994-2003, Children's Convalescent Hosp., 1997—, The Children's Hosp., 2001—; chmn. Greater Cin. Hosp. Coun., 1989; co-chmn. Citizen's Com. for Med. Ctr., Cin., 1980-81; chmn. Hosp. Divsn. 1988 Fine Arts Fund, Cin., 1987; hon. trustee Babies' Milk Fund, Children's and Prenatal Clinics, Cin., 1994-2002. Recipient Disting. Alumni award U. Cin., 1992, Donald Newkirk award Ohio Hosp. Assn., 1997, Health Care Heros Lifetime Achievement award Bus. Courier, Cin., 2003, Great Living Cincinnatian award, 2004. Fellow Am. Acad. Pediat. (Murray Davidson award sect. on gastroenterology/nutrition 2003); mem. Am. Pediatric Soc. (councillor 1986-93), Soc. Pediatric Rsch., Assn. Med. Sch. Pediatric Dept. Chmn., Cin. Acad. Medicine, AMA, Midwestern Soc. for Pediatric Rsch., Am. Assn. for Study of Liver Diseases, Ctrl. Soc. Clin. Rsch., Am. Gastroenterological Assn., N.Am. Soc. Pediatric Gastroenterology, Nat. Reye's Syndrome Found. (med. dir. 1976-87), Internat. Assn. Study Liver Diseases. Clubs: Queen City (Cin.). Office: Children's Hosp Med Ctr Cin ML 5005 3333 Burnet Ave Cincinnati OH 45229-3026 E-mail: william.schubert@cchmc.org.

SCHUCH, BEVERLY, anchor; Bachelor, Muskingum Coll., New Concord, Ohio; grad. student in comm., Simmons Coll., Boston. Anchor, reporter, Portland, Maine, Providence; corr. N.Y. gen. news unit CNN, N.Y.C., reporter Moneyline, host Pinnacle; co-anchor Biz Buzz, CNN Fin. News, N.Y.C., co-anchor Take It Personally. Office: CNN 5 Penn Plz Fl 20 New York NY 10001-1810

SCHUCH, CYNTHIA SILLECK, nurse; b. Oceanside, N.Y., Oct. 31, 1956; AAS, SUNY, Morrisville, 1976; cert. in Cardiovascular Nursing, Meth. Hosp., Houston, 1978; BS in Nursing, U. Ala., 1984, MS in Nursing, 1985. RN, N.Y., Va., Ala., Calif. Staff nurse, relief charge nurse, postoperative surgical nurse Meth. Hosp., Houston, 1976-77, staff nurse ICU, 1977-78, cardiovascular nurse specialist, 1978-79; staff nurse ICU U. Va. Hosp., Charlottesville, 1979; staff nurse, relief charge nurse U. Ala. Hosp., Birmingham, 1979-80, scrub nurse, circulating nurse, 1980-83, staff nurse CICU, 1983-84, charge nurse CICU, 1984-86; staff nurse CICU Sutter Meml. Hosp., Sacramento, 1986-89, clin. specialist cardiac surgery unit, 1989—. Vol. instr. cardiac maintenance YMCA Shades Valley Br., Birmingham, 1984; instr. family night CPR, Sacramento, 1987—, BCLS instr., 1986—, ACLS instr., 1988—. Mem. Am. Assn. Critical Care Nurses (Houston-Gulf chpt. 1976-79, Greater Birmingham chpt. 1985-86, Sacramento chpt. 1986—), Phi Theta Kappa, Phi Kappa Phi, Sigma Theta Tau.

SCHUCHMAN, PHILIP MELCHOR, education educator; b. St. Charles, Mo., Feb. 19, 1951; s. Philip Melchor Schuchmann and Pauline Eleanor Schuchman; m. Lynn Christine Stolte, Sept. 2, 1971; children: Cassandra Lynn, Philip Ezekiel. MA, U. of Mo., 1971—80. Grad. rsch. asst. U. of Mo., 1973, grad. tchg. asst., 1973—75; instr. Avila Coll., Kansas City, Mo., 1975—82, Donnelly Coll., Kansas City, Kans., 1976—78; exec. dir. Westport Free Health Clinic, Kansas City, Mo., 1980—86; instr. Johnson County C.C., Overland Park, Kans., 1986—87; sr. prof. DeVry U., Kansas City, Mo., 1987—. Spkr. Kans. City Profl. Devel. Coun., 1996—. Author: Test Bank to Accompany Corley/Reed The Legal Environment of Business: Briefed Case Edition, Test Item File Principles of Economics, PowerPoint Lectures to a Company Macionis Sociology, 9th edit. Adv. bd. Red Bridge YMCA, Kansas City, Mo. Recipient Governor's Award for Excellence in Tchg., Coordinating Bd. for Higher Edn., 1998. Mem.: AAUP, Am. Sociol. Assn. Democrat. Roman Catholic. Office: DeVry University 11224 Holmes Rd Kansas City MO 64131-3626 Business E-Mail: pschuchman@kc.devry.edu.

SCHUCK, THOMAS ROBERT, lawyer, farmer; b. Findlay, Ohio, Feb. 7, 1950; s. Robert Damon and Katherine Margaretta (Beynon) S. BA, DePauw U., 1972; MA, U. Kent, U.K., 1974; JD, Harvard U., 1976. Bar: Ohio 1976, U.S. Dist. Ct. (no. dist.) Ohio 1977, U.S. Dist. Ct. (so. dist.) Ohio 1979, Ariz. 1990, U.S. Ct. Appeals (6th cir.) 1978, U.S. Ct. Appeals (9th cir.) 1991, U.S. Ct. Appeals Armed Forces, 2000, U.S. Supreme Ct. 2001. Law clk. U.S. Dist. Ct., Cleve., 1976-79; assoc. Taft, Stettinius & Hollister, Cin., 1979-87, ptnr., 1987—; owner, operator Rural Hill Farm. Participant Ohio Bench Bar Conf., Columbus, 1990, 91, Glenmoor Justice Inst., 2000; barrister Am. Inn of Ct., 1986-87, LEAD Clermont, 1997-98; mem. bar exam com. U.S. Dist. Ct. (so. dist.) Ohio; merit panel for bankruptcy judge selection U.S. Ct. Appeals Sixth Cir., 1998, chair, 2002; life mem. Jud. Conf. of 6th Cir. Contbg. author: Aids and the Law, 2d edit. 1992; contbr. articles to profl. jours. Trustee Mental Health Svcs. East, Inc., Cin., 1985-91; sec. bd. trustees Joy Outdoor Edn. Ctr., Inc., 1999—; mem. Clermont County Mental Health Bd., Batavia, Ohio, 1992-2000, vice chair, 1997-2000; mem. Clermont County Mental Retardation Developmental Disabilities Levy Steering Com., 1996, trustee, 2000-02, vice chmn., 2002; mem. May Festival Assocs., Cin., 1984-86; spl. gifts com. Cin. Art Acad., 1987, Ohio Found. Ind. Colls., 1995—, bd. dirs., 2003—; mem. WGUC Radio Cmty. Bd., 1984-86. Rotary Internat. Found. grad. fellow, 1972, 73. Mem. FBA (pres. Cin. chpt. 1994-95, v.p. 6th cir. 1996-99, nat. membership chair 1997-99, nat. sec. 2001-2002, nat. treas., nat. v.p. 2002-03, nat. pres.-elect 2003-04, nat. pres. 2004—, govt. rels. com.), Potter Stewart Am. Inn of Ct. (barrister 1986-87), U.S. Rowing Assn. (asst. referee), Harvard Club Cin. (pres. 1995-96), Camargo Hunt Club, Ohio Soc. (sec. 2002-03, treas. 2004—), Soc. Bacchus Am., Masons, Scottish Rite (trustee Valley of Cin. 2003—), Phi Beta Kappa, Delta Chi, Phi Eta Sigma, Sigma Delta Chi. Republican. Methodist. Avocations: reading, photography. Home: PO Box 615 189 State Route 133 Felicity OH 45120 Office: Ste 1800 425 Walnut St Cincinnati OH 45202-3957 Office Phone: 513-381-2838.

SCHUCKMAN, GREGORY A. academic administrator; b. Elizabeth, NJ, June 10, 1969; s. Gerry and Debra Myrtle Schuckman; m. Pamela A. Vaupel, Apr. 22, 1995; children: Alexandra Katherine, Graham Albert Edward, Mason Gregory Christopher. BS in Advt. honors program, U. Fla., 1991; M in govt. admin., U. Pa., 1993. Dir. govt. rels. and media affairs Am. Assn. of Engring. Socs., Washington, 1996—98; dir. comm. and pub. awareness Am. Assn. of Engring. Societies, Washington, 1998—99; founding dir. The Engring. Alliance, 1998—99; dir. comm. and corp. rels. Southeastern U. Rsch. Assn., Washington, 1999—2000; dir. fed. rels. U. Ctrl. Fla., Orlando, Fla., 2000—, mem. coun. grad. schs. fed. rels. adv. com., 2003—. Pub. policy com. mem. Am. Soc. of Assn. Executives, Washington, 1998—2000; founding chair, govt. rels., pub. affairs track Coun. of Engring. and Sci. Soc. Exe., Washington, 1996—99; comm. sect. coun. mem. Am. Soc. of Assn. Execs., 1998—2000, mem. advance Am. com., 1998—2000; program chair Nat. Conf. Advancement Rsch., Orlando, Fla., 2000—02, chair, 2002—; bd. dirs. No. Va. C.C. Chair Alexandria Econ. Opportunities Commn., Alexandria, Va., 1994—96, Alexandria Human Services Coun., Alexandria, Va., 1995—96; founding pres. Lorton Sta. Civic Assn., Lorton, Va., 2001—04; v.p. Fedn. of Lorton Cmtys./South County Fedn., Lorton, Va., 2003—; commr. Fla. Postsecondary Edn. Planning Commr., Tallahassee, 1991—91; fellow Thomas C. Sorensen Inst. for Polit. Leadership, U. Va., Charlottesville, Va., 1998—98; bd. advisers Presdl. Classroom for Young Am., Alexandria, Va., 1997—2003; trustee, chmn. govt. rels. com. Nat. Multiple Sclerosis Soc. Mid Fla. Chpt., Orlando, Fla., 2002—03. Decorated Commander's award for pub. svc. Dept. U.S. Army; recipient Hon. Alumnus, Presdl. Classroom for Young Am., 1999, Inducted Mem., U. Pa, Philomathean Soc., 1992, Louis Armstrong award for excellence in jazz performance, 1986, Pres.'s award, Coun. Engring. and Sci. Soc. Execs., 1997; Fla. Regents Scholar. Mem.: AAAS, Alliance for Sci. and Tech. Rsch. in Am. (bd. of advisors 2001), Coun. for the Advancement and Support of Edn., Nat. Assn. of State U. and Land Grant Coll., The Sci. Coalition (hon.), Nat. Press Club. Avocation: jazz improvisation. E-mail: gregs@mail.ucf.edu.

SCHUCKMAN, NANCY LEE, retired principal; b. Bklyn., June 3, 1939; d. Abraham Benjamin and Sophie (Kalefsky) S. BA, Bklyn. Coll., 1961, MS, 1964, postgrad., 1965-69, Hofstra U., 1970-72, Columbia U., 1979-80. Tchr. N.Y.C. Bd. Edn., 1961-69, adminstr., 1969-77, prin., 1977-97; ednl. journalist East New Yorker, East N.Y. Devel. Corp., Bklyn., 1974-76, Starrett City Sun, Bklyn., 1975-76; co-owner Lanah Ednl. Toys, Bklyn., 1975-76. Mem. Thomas Jefferson Dem. Club, Bklyn., 1978—, Kings County Dem. Com., 1981-97; polit. campaign coord. John F. Kennedy Dem. Club, Bklyn., 1974-76, mem. exec. bd., 1974-75; mem. adv. bd. Prin.'s Ctr. at Bklyn. Coll., 1989-95. Recipient City Coun. proclamation N.Y.C. Coun., 1987, Legis. Resolution, N.Y. State Assembly/Senate, 1997, Congrl. Record Recognition, U.S. Congress, 1997. Mem. ASCD, Nat. Assn. Elem. Sch. Prins., Coun. Suprs. and Adminstrs. (Ednl. Leadership Recognition award N.Y.C. Dist. 19, 1997, conv. registration chmn. 1985-88), Adminstrv. Women in Edn., Am. Assn. Sch. Adminstrs., Nat. Assn. Elem. Sch. Prins., N.Y.C. Elem. Prins. Assn. (exel bd. 1984-97, Svc. Appreciation award 1997), N.Y. State Reading Coun., Bklyn. Reading Coun. Democrat. Jewish. Avocations: education law, journalism, painting, travel, sports. Home: 122 Crispell Rd Krumville NY 12461-5408

SCHUDER, JOHN CLAUDE, biomedical engineer, educator; b. Olney, Ill., Mar. 2, 1922; s. Charles Claude Schuder and Louise Ella Muench; m. Retha Elizabeth Sumner, July 23, 1946; children: Linda Lee Brown, Charles Wayne, Jonna Elizabeth. BSEE, U. Ill., 1943; MSEE, Purdue U., 1951, PhD, 1954. Jr. engr. Westinghouse Rsch., East Pittsburgh, Pa., 1943-44; from instr. to asst. prof. Purdue U., West Lafayette, Ind., 1949-56; assoc. prof. Doane Coll., Crete, Nebr., 1956-57; fellow, asst. prof. U. Pa., Phila., 1957-60; from assoc. prof. to prof. emeritus U. Mo. Sch. Medicine, Columbia, 1960—. Cons. Hewlett-Packard, Medtronics, GE, Physio Control, NIH, others. Mem. editl. bd. PACE, 1991—; contbr. articles to profl. jours. Peace activist, anti-death penalty activist Columbia Fellowship Reconciliation, 1960—. Grantee, NIH, Am. Heart Assn., Mo. Heart Assn., others. Mem.: AAUP, Am. Soc. Artificial Internal Organs, IEEE Engring. Medicine and Biology Soc. (life), Sigma Xi. Mem. Soc. Of Friends. Achievements include research in experimental rationale for waveforms used in cardiac defibrilators; development of transcutaneous energy transformer used with implanted artificial hearts. Home: 105 Manor Dr Columbia MO 65203-1727 Office: U Mo Cardiothoracic Surgery DC011 00 Columbia MO 65212-0001 Office Phone: 573-882-8068. Business E-Mail: schuderj@health.missouri.edu.

SCHUDER, RAYMOND FRANCIS, lawyer; b. Wickford, R.I., Dec. 27, 1926; s. Rollie Milton and Selma (Ball) S.; m. Betty Jo Williams, Mar. 14, 1948; children: Gregg Williams, Glen Arva. AB, Emory U., 1949, JD, 1951. Bar: Ga. 1951. With Trust Co. Ga., Atlanta, 1951-54; assoc. firm Wheeler Robinson & Thurmond, Gainesville, Ga., 1954-59; pvt. practice law Gainesville, 1959-70, 76-96; ptnr. Schuder & Brown, Gainesville, 1971-76. Mcpl. ct. judge Gainesville, 1956-60, 73-75; magistrate ct. judge, 1985-2000, sr. magistrate, 2001-03. Supr. Upper Chattahoochee Soil and Water Conservation Dist., 1971-74; CEO, bd. dirs. Charles Thompson Estes Found., Inc., Gainesville. Cpl. USMCR, 1944-50; 1st lt. USAR, 1950-56, ret. Mem. State Bar Ga. (gov. 1966-70), Gainesville-Northeastern Bar Assn. (pres. 1969-70), Am. Legion, VFW, Elks. Methodist. Home: 2224 Riverside Dr Gainesville GA 30501-1232 Office: 2224 Riverside Dr Gainesville GA 30501-1232 E-mail: xrfs@charter.net.

SCHUELE, DONALD EDWARD, physics educator; b. Cleve., June 16, 1934; s. Edward and Mildred (Matousek) S.; m. Clare Ann Kirchner, Sept. 5, 1956; children: Donna, Karen, Melanie, Judy, Rachel, Ruth. BS, John Carroll U., Cleve., 1956, MS, 1957; PhD, Case Inst. Tech., 1962. Instr. physics and math. John Carroll U., 1956-59; part-time instr. physics Case Inst. Tech., 1959-62, instr., asst. prof., assoc. prof., 1962-70; mem. tech. staff Bell Telephone Labs., 1970-72; assoc. prof. physics Case Western Res. U., 1972-74, prof., 1974—, dean undergrad. coll., 1973-76, chmn. dept. physics, 1976-78; vice dean Case Inst. Tech., 1978-83, v.p. for undergrad. and grad. studies, 1983-84, dean, 1984-86, prof. physics, 1986-88, dean math. and natural sci., 1988-89, Albert A. Michaelson prof. physics, 1989—, acting chmn. elec. engring. and applied physics, 1992-93. Cons. in field. Co-editor: Critical Revs. in Solid State Scis, 1969-84; contbr. articles to profl. jours.; patentee in field. Mem. adv. bd. St. Charles Borromeo Sch., 1970-72; pres. Seed Found., 1986-89; trustee St. Mary's Sem., 1980-93; mem. Olympic Sports Equipment and Tech. Com., 1982-93; trustee Newman Found., 1983—, Northeastern Ohio Sci. Fair, 1983—; mem. Diocesan Pastoral Coun., 1992-94; active Rep. Presdl. task force. Recipient Disting. Physics Alumnus award John Carroll U., 1983; NSF Faculty fellow, 1961-63; Sam Givelber fellow Case Alumni Assn., 2001. Mem.: North Coast Thermal Analysis Soc., Am. Assn. Physics Tchrs., Am. Phys. Soc. (vice chair Ohio sect. 1995—96, chair 1996—97), Newman Apostolate, Case Alumni Coun. (life; 3d v.p. 2001—02, 1st v.p. 2002—03, pres. 2003—04, treas. 1992), Tau Beta Pi, Sigma Xi, Alpha Sigma Nu. Republican. Roman Catholic. Achievements include patents fluid pressure device, impact wrench torque calibrator, detection of wear particles and other impurities in industrial fluids, electrical oil analysis instrument. Home: 4892 Countryside Rd Cleveland OH 44124-2513 Office: Case Western Res U 10900 Euclid Ave Cleveland OH 44106-1712 Office Phone: 216-368-4013. E-mail: des3@case.edu.

SCHUELER, GERALD JOSEPH, technical writer, systems analyst, counselor; b. Darby, Pa., Oct. 29, 1942; s. Charles Carroll and Bertha Julia (Fadgen) S.; m. Betty Jane Sherlin, Aug. 17, 1963; children: Diane Sue, Joseph Carroll, Andrew Tyson, Crystal Ann. BS, U. Md., 1965; MS in Adminstrn., Ctrl. Mich. U., 1991; PhD, Capella U., Minn., 1996, 98. Lic. profl. counselor, D.C. Test dir. U.S. Army Test and Evaluation Command, Aberdeen Proving Ground, Md., 1965-75, ops. rsch. analyst, 1975-94; tech. writer Harford Writers Group, Aberdeen, Md., 1984—; sys. analyst Quantum Rsch. Internat., Bel Air, Md., 1999—. Co-owner Shellay, Aberdeen, 1964-99, Creative Sales & Svc., Aberdeen, 1975—; cons. Compucats Computer Store, Aberdeen, 1982-1989. Author: Enochian Magic, 1984, Enochian Physics, 1988; co-author: Coming into the Light, 1989, Angels Message to Humanity, 1996. Leader/com. mem. Boy Scouts Am., Aberdeen, 1974-80; officer Friends of Harford County Libr., Aberdeen, 1975—; county leader Harford County 4-H Club, Aberdeen, 1978-95. Mem. Am. Counseling Assn., Internat. Assn. Transpersonal Psychology, Noetic Inst. Dem. Avocations: computers, reading, crafts. Personal E-mail: jerry@schuelers.com.

SCHUELER, JOHN R. newspaper executive; b. Grosse Point, MI; m. Linda Schueler; children: Tracie, Lindsey. BA, W. Mich. U. With Miami Herald, Miami, Fla.; pres. New England Newspapers; v.p. consumer mktg. & circulation The Orange County Register, Santa Ana, Calif., 1991—92, exec. v.p. & gen. mgr., 1992—95, pres., COO, 1995-98; publisher Star Tribune, Mpls., 1998—2001; pub. Los Angeles Daily News, 2001—04; pres., CEO Los Angeles Newspaper Group, 2004—. Office: Los Angeles Daily News 21221 Oxnard St PO Box 4200 Woodland Hills CA 91367*

SCHUELKE, JOHN PAUL, religious organization administrator; b. Benton Harbor, Mich., Nov. 5, 1934; s. Alwin E. and Martha M. (Schoeneberg) S.; m. Noreta H. Petersen, Sept. 9, 1956; children: Alvin, Mary, Sheryl, Brian. BS in Acctg., U. Wyo., 1957; LLD (hon.), Concordia U., Irvine, Calif., 1983. CPA. From acct. to sr. acct. Colo. Interstate Gas Co., Colorado Springs, 1957-63; staff acct. Arthur Anderson & Co., Denver, 1963-64; mgr. fin. control Colo.

Interstate Corp., Colorado Springs., 1964-67, dir. fin. control, 1967-71; adminstrv. v.p. mfg. divsn. Marsh Instrument Co. subs. Colo. Mfg. Corp., Skokie, Ill., 1971-72; exec. officer bd. dirs., CAO Luth. Ch.-Mo. Synod, St. Louis, 1972-98, ret., 1999. Former chmn. Concordia Asia Ednl. Found.; lectr. in field. Asst. scoutmaster Boy Scouts Am., Colorado Springs; former mem. governing bd., sec. Luth. Svcs. in Am.; former mem. governing bd. Luth. Coun.-USA, com. Luth. Coop.; mem. Faith Luth Ch., Woodland Park; mem. bd. for human care ministries Luth. Ch.-Mo. Synod. Recipient God and Country award Eagle Scout. Mem. Alpha Kappa Psi, Gamma Delta (former pres.). Lutheran. Avocations: travel, fishing, reading.

SCHUELLER, THOMAS GEORGE, lawyer; b. Budapest, Hungary, Oct. 4, 1936; came to U.S., 1938; s. Herbert H. and Edith (Geiringer) S.; m. Sandra Burke, Sept. 3, 1960 (div. Apr. 1982); children: Katherine, Matthew, John. AB cum laude, Amherst Coll., 1958; LLB, Harvard U., 1962. Bar: N.Y. 1963. Salesman Gen. Mills. Inc., Utica, N.Y., 1958-59; assoc. Hughes Hubbard & Reed, N.Y.C., 1962-69, ptnr., 1969—. Bd. dirs., sec. Ballet Hispanico, N.Y.C., 1987-2001. Mem. ABA, Assn. of Bar of City of N.Y., Phi Beta Kappa. Home: 335 W 70th St New York NY 10023-3525 Office: Hughes Hubbard & Reed LLP 1 Battery Park Plz New York NY 10004-1482 also: PO Box 562 108 Fairchild Rd Sharon CT 06069-2440 Office Phone: 212-837-6744. E-mail: schuelle@hugheshubbard.com.

SCHUEPPERT, GEORGE LOUIS, financial executive; b. Merrill, Wis., July 1, 1938; s. George Henry and Eleanor Natalie (Pautz) S.; m. Kathleen Kay Carpenter, May 6, 1967; children— Steven Andrew, Stephanie Roanne, Stenning Karl BBA, U. Wis., Madison, 1961; MBA, U. Chgo., 1969. Treas., controller Steiger-Rathke Devel. Co., Phoenix, 1964-65; various positions Continental Ill. Nat., Chgo., 1965-76, 1981-86; mng. dir. Continental Ill. Ltd., London, 1977-81; sr. v.p. Continental Ill. Nat. Bank, Chgo., 1982-86; ptnr. Coopers & Lybrand, Chgo., 1986-87; exec. v.p. fin. CBI Industries Inc, Oak Brook, Ill., 1987-95, also bd. dirs., 1987-95; exec. v.p., CFO Outboard Marine Corp., Waukegan, Ill., 1996-97. Bd. dirs. Wells Mfg. Co., Barrington Bank & Trust Co. Pres. Gt. Books Found.; chmn., bd. dirs. De Paul U. Gov. Asst. Program. Lt. (j.g.) USN, 1961-64. Recipient Herfurth award U. Wis., 1960 Mem. Econ. Club Chgo. (bd. dirs., chmn. membership com.). Republican. Avocations: history; civic affairs; architecture; travel; golf. Home: 97 Otis Rd Barrington IL 60010-5129 Office: Great Books Found 35 E Wacker Dr Ste 2300 Chicago IL 60601-2298

SCHUERHOLZ, JOHN BOLAND, JR., professional baseball executive; b. Baltimore, MD, Oct. 1, 1940; s. John Boland and Maryne (Wyatt) Schuerholz; m. Ellen Louise Lawson, June 21, 1963; 1 child, Regina Marie Reagan; m. Karen Louise Wiltse, Sept. 18, 1978; 1 child, Jonathan Lawrence. B.E., Towson State U., 1962; postgrad., Loyola Coll. (Md.), 1964—66. Tchr. various schs., 1962—66; adminstrv. asst. Balt. Orioles, 1966—68, Kansas City Royals, 1968—70, asst. farm dir., 1970—75, farm dir., 1975, dir. scouting and player devel., 1976—79, v.p. player personnel, 1979—81, exec. v.p., gen. mgr., 1981—90, Atlanta Braves, 1990—. With AUS, 1966—72. Lutheran. Office: Atlanta Braves PO Box 4064 Atlanta GA 30302-4064

SCHUESSLER, ISABELLE SWEENY, school administrator; b. Washington, May 12, 1934; d. Charles Amos and Barbara (Crosser) Sweeny; m. Donald Charles Schuessler, Aug. 8, 1953; children: Donald C. Jr., Janet L., Douglas P., David J. AA, AB, George Washington U., 1962. Dir. St. Patrick's Episcopal Day Sch., Washington, 1962-86; founding head Washington Episcopal Sch., Bethesda, Md., 1986—2001. Cons. St. Andrew's Episcopal Sch., Bethesda, 1976-79, St. James' Children's Ctr., Potomac, 1991-1996, Cadence Episcopal Sch., Washington, 1992-1995; v.p. Nat. Assn. Episcopal Schs., N.Y.C., 1981-84, pres., 1984-86; evaluator Middle States Assn. Colls. and Schs.; cons. to schs. and sch. founding groups, churches for fundraising. Democrat. Episcopal. Avocations: volunteering, crafts. Home and Office: 9 Orchard Way South Potomac MD 20854

SCHUESSLER, JOHN T. food service executive; BS, Spring Hill Coll. Mgr. trainee Wendy's franchise, Atlanta, 1974-76; joined Wendy's Internat., 1976; dist. mgr., dir. area ops., regional dir. various zones U.S., 1976-83; regional v.p. ea. divsn., 1983-84; zone pres., 1984-86; divsn. v.p., 1986-87; sr. v.p. N.E. region, 1987-95; exec. v.p. U.S. ops., 1995-97; pres., COO U.S. ops., 1997-2000; pres., COO Can., 1999-2000; pres., CEO, 2000—. Trustee Wendy's Nat. Advtsg. Program. Office: Wendy's Internat 4288 W Dublin-Granville Rd Dublin OH 43017

SCHUESSLER FIORENZA, ELISABETH, theology educator; b. Tschanad, Romania, Apr. 17, 1938; parents German citizens; d. Peter and Magdalena Schuessler; m. Francis Fiorenza, Dec. 17, 1967; 1 child, Chris. MDiv, U. Wuerzburg, Germany, 1962; Lic. Theol., U. Wuerzburg, 1963; DrTheol, U. Muenster, Germany, 1970. Asst. prof. theology U. Notre Dame, South Bend, Ind., 1970-75, assoc. prof., 1975-80, prof., 1980-84; instr. U. Muenster, 1966-67; Talbot prof. N.T., Episcopal Div. Sch., Cambridge, Mass., 1984-88; Krister Stendahl prof. Divsn. Scripture and Interpretation Harvard U., Cambridge, Mass., 1988—. Harry Emerson Fosdick vis. prof. Union Theol. Sem., N.Y.C., 1974-75; guest prof. U. Tuebingen, Federal Republic of Germany, 1987, Cath. Theol. Faculty Luzern, Switzerland, 1990; Stiftungs prof. Humboldt U., Berlin, 1997; Ernst Troeltsch prof. U. Heidelberg, Germany, 1999. Author: Der Vergessene Partner, 1964, Priester für Gott, 1972, The Apocalypse, 1976, Invitation to the Book of Revelation, 1981, In Memory of Her, 1983, Bread not Stone, 1984, Judgement or Justice, 1985, Revelation: Vision of a Just World, 1991, But She Said - Feminist Practices of Biblical Interpretation, 1992, Discipleship of Equals: A Critical Feminist Ekklesialogy of Liberation, 1993, Jesus: Miriam's Child and Sophia's Prophet, Critical Issues in Feminist Christology, 1994, Sharing Her Word, 1998, Rhetoric and Ethic The Politics of Biblical Studies, 1999, Jesus and the Politics of Interpretation, 2000, Wisdom Ways, 2001, Grenzen uberschreiten, 2004; editor: Searching the Scriptures, 2 vols, 1993, 94, The Power of Naming, 1996; founding co-editor Jour. Feminist Studies in Religion; also editor other works. Mem.: Am. Acad. Arts and Scis., Soc. Bibl. Lit. (past pres.), Am. Acad. Religion. Office: Harvard Div Sch 45 Francis Ave Cambridge MA 02138-1911

SCHUETT, CAROL ANN, travel industry business analyst; b. Columbus, Wis., May 12, 1967; d. Arnold Joseph and Marilyn Delores (Krejcsi) S. BA in Internat. Bus. with honors, Augsburg Coll., 1996; postgrad., U. St. Thomas, 1997—. Travel agt. AAA, Mpls., 1986-88, Am. Express, Mpls., 1988-91, team leader, 1991-97; bus. analyst Northwest Airlines, Mpls., 1997—. Mem. NAFE, AAUW, Delta Mu Delta. Avocations: travel, reading, hiking, writing. Home: 6833 Bloomington Ave Richfield MN 55423-2661

SCHUETTE, CHARLES A. lawyer; b. Columbus, Ind., Feb. 24, 1942; BBA, U. Okla., 1964, JD, 1967. Bar: Okla. 1967, Fla. 1970, U.S. Supreme Ct. 1979, U.S. Dist. Ct. (so. dist.) Fla. 1982, U.S. Dist. Ct. (mid. dist.) Fla. 1982. With Akerman & Senterfitt. Fellow Am. Bar Found.; mem. ABA, Fla. Bar, Okla. Bar Assn., Dade County Bar Assn. Office: Akerman & Senterfitt 1 SE 3rd Ave Fl Miami FL 33131-1700

SCHUH, FRANK JOSEPH, drilling engineering company executive, consultant; b. Columbus, Ohio, Feb. 3, 1935; s. Sebastian and Elizabeth (Zorn) S.; m. Alice Virgene Kasler, June 16, 1956; children: Dwain Joseph, Michael James, Barbara Ann. BS in Petroleum Engring., MS in Petroleum Engring., Ohio State U., 1956. Registered profl. engr., Ohio. Drilling and rsch. engr. Atlantic Refining Co., Tex., La., 1956-62; mem. drilling engring. staff, dir. engring. Atlantic Richfield Co., Dallas, 1962-82, mgr. drilling rsch., sr. advisor Plano, Tex., 1982-86; v.p. Enertech Engring. & Tech., Dallas, 1986-87; pres. Drilling Tech., Inc., Plano, 1987—; v.p. Supreme Resources Corp., Dallas, 1988-92. Founder, 1st pres. Drilling Engring. Assn., Dallas, 1983-85; mem. tech. adv. com. Internat. Ocean Drilling Program, 2002—. Author: Drilling Equations, 1975; patentee horizontal drilling, high pressure drilling system, continuous heavy oil production process, 31 other patents. Precinct, region chmn. Rep. Party, Dallas, 1964-74; vol. bldg. com. Mary Immaculate Ch., Dallas, 1965-66; mem. tech. engring. and devel. com. Ocean Drilling Program, Bryan, Tex., 1980—. Recipient outstanding achievement in field of engring. award Nat. Engrs. Coun., 1980, Robert Earl McConnell award Am. Inst. Mining Engrs., 1994, Ohio State Univ. Coll. of Engring. Benjamin G. Lamme Meritorious Achievement medel, 1995. Mem. NAE, Soc. Petroleum Engrs. (nat. bd. dirs. 1983-86, Drilling Engring. award 1986, Disting. Mem. award 1989), Am. Petroleum Inst. (chmn. com. 6, 1985-88, svc. citation 1986), Am. Assn. Drilling Engrs., Soc. Ind. Profl. Earth Scientists, Petroleum Engrs. Club (pres. 1974-75), Ohio State U. Alumni Club (pres. 1968-69), Dallas-Ft. Worth Oilman's Club (handicapper 1973-86). Avocations: golf, sailing. Office: Drilling Technology Inc 5808 Wavertree Ln Ste 1000 Plano TX 75093-4513

SCHUH, G(EORGE) EDWARD, university dean, agricultural economist; b. Indpls., Sept. 13, 1930; s. George Edward and Viola (Lentz) S.; m. Maria Ignez, May 23, 1965; children: Audrey, Susan, Tanya. BS in Agrl. Edn, Purdue U., 1952, DAgr (hon.), 1992; MS in Agrl. Econs., Mich. State U., 1954; MA in Econs, U. Chgo., 1958, PhD, 1961; prof. (hon.), Fed. U. Vicosa, Brazil, 1965; hon. doctorate, Purdue U., 1992. From instr. to prof. agrl. econs. Purdue U., 1959-79; dir. Center for Public Policy and Public Affairs, 1977-78; dep. undersec. for internat. affairs and commodity programs Dept. Agr., Washington, 1978-79, chair bd. for internat. food and agrl. devel., 1995—2002; prof. agrl. and applied econs., head dept. U. Minn., Mpls., 1979-84; dir. agr. and rural devel. World Bank, Washington, 1984-87; dean Humphrey Inst. for Pub. Affairs U. Minn., 1987—96; Orville and Jane Freeman Endowed chair Humphrey Inst. for Pub. Affairs, U. Minn., 1996—; regents prof. U. Minn., 1998—. Program advisor Ford Found., 1966-72; sr. staff economist Pres.'s Coun. Econ. Advisors, 1974-75; mem. bd. on agr. and natural resources NRC, 1998—2004; trustee Internat. Food Policy Rsch. Inst., 1997-2003, Internat. Potato Ctr., 2004—. Author, editor profl. books; contbr. numerous articles to profl. publs. Trustee Sasakawa Africa Assn., 1998—. Served with U.S. Army, 1954-56. Recipient 60 at 60 award, Internat. Insts. for Cooperation in Agr. Fellow: AAAS, Am. Agrl. Econs. Assn. (bd. dirs. 1977—80, pres.-elect 1980—81, pres. 1981—82, Thesis award 1962, Pub. Rsch. award 1971, Article award 1975, Policy award 1979, Publ. of Lasting Value award 1988), Am. Acad. Arts and Scis.; mem.: Brazilian Soc. Rural Econs., Brazilian Soc. Agrl. Economists, Am. Econ. Assn., Internat. Assn. Agrl. Econs. Office: Humphrey Ctr U Minn 301 19th Ave S Minneapolis MN 55455-0429 E-mail: geschuh@hhh.umn.edu.

SCHUH, JOHN HOWARD, higher education educator, academic administrator; b. Cleve., July 29, 1947; s. Howard John and Elfreide Marie (Wachcic) S.; m. Linda Kay Rezin, June 30, 1973; 1 child, Kimberly Chrisette. BA, U. Wis., Oshkosh, 1969; M in Counseling, Ariz. State U., 1972, PhD, 1974. Resident complex dir. Ariz. State U., Tempe, 1970-72, asst. dir. housing, adj. prof., 1972-78; dir. residence life Ind. U., Bloomington, 1978-82, asst. dean, assoc. prof., 1982-84, assoc. dean, assoc. prof., 1985-87, assoc. dean students, prof. edn., 1985-87; assoc. v.p. student affairs Wichita State U., 1987-97, prof. counseling and sch. psychology, 1987-97; prof. higher edn. Iowa State U., 1997—2003, disting. prof., 2003—, chair dept. ednl. leadership and policy studies, 1998—. Cons., presenter in field. Editor: Programming and Activities in College and University Residence Halls, 1977; (with G.S. Blimling) Increasing the Educational Role of Residence Halls, 1981, A Handbook for Student Group Advisers, 1984, Enhancing Relationships with the Student Press, 1986, A Handbook for Student Group Advisers, 2d edit., (with G.D. Kuh and E.J. Whitt) Involving Colleges, (with M.L. Upcraft) Assessment in Student Affairs, (with N.W. Dunkel) Advising Student Groups and Organizations, (with A.M. Hoffman and R.H. Fenske) Violence on Campus, (with E.J. Whitt) Creating Successful Partnerships Between Academic and Student Affairs, (with M.C. Upcraft) Assessment Practice in Student Afairs, (with B. Bender) Benchmarking in Higher Edn., (with F. Hamrick and N. Evans) Foundations of Student Affairs Practice; gen. editor New Directions for Student Svcs.; assoc. editor Jour. of Coll. Student Devel.; contbr. articles to profl. jours., chpts. to books. Bd. dirs. NASPA Found., 2002—. Served to maj. USAR, 1973. Recipient Outstanding Rsch. award, Am. Coll. Pers. Assn. Commn. III, 1983, 1984, Contbn. to Knowledge award, Annuit Coeptis award, Sr. Scholar award, Presdl. Svc. award, ACPA Diamond Honoree, 1999, Contbn. to Lit. or Rsch. award, NASPA, Pillar of the Profession award, 2001, S. Earl Thompson award, Assn. of Coll. and Univ. Housing Officers Internat., 1999; scholar Fulbright scholar, 1994. Mem. Assn. Coll. Housing Officers (exec. bd. 1977-81, 85-87, chmn. legis. issues 1983-85), Am. Coll. Pers. Assn. (mem. media editl. bd. 1979-87, media bd. 1985-88, govtl. rels. com. 1984-85, Commn. III dir. 1979-82, commn. XII directorate 1987—), Nat. Assn. of Student Pers. Adminstrs. (bd. dirs. 1992-93, 99-2000, chair ann. conf. 2000), North Ctrl. Assn. Cons. Evaluator Corps. Home: 1706 Amherst Dr Ames IA 50014-3927 Office: Iowa State U N243 Lagomarcino Hl Ames IA 50011-0001 Office Phone: 515-294-6393. E-mail: jschuh@iastate.edu.

SCHUHSLER, HELMUT, biotechnology company executive; PhD in social and Econ. Scis., U. Econs., Vienna, Austria. Bd. dirs. Medigene AG, GPC Biotech; with TVM Techno Venture Mgmt., 1990—, mng. ptnr., 1998—; chmn. bd. Sequenom, Inc., San Diego, 1996—. Office: Sequenom Inc 3595 John Hopkins Ct San Diego CA 92121-1331

SCHUISKI, LARRY LEROY, information scientist, consultant; b. LA, Calif., Jan. 5, 1950; s. Leroy Hillis Duitsman and Charleen Edna (Nelson) Sager; m. Larissa Schuiski, June 17, 1988. BS in Physics with honors, U. Washington, 1972. Architect Boeing Computer Svcs., Seattle, 1978-88; dir. Trident Sys., San Francisco, 1988-92, View Star Corp., Alameda, Calif., 1993-95; v.p. Moore Document Solutions, Lake Forest, Ill., 1995-97; sr. cons. The Concours Group, Kingwood, Tex., 1997-99; sr. v.p. Attachmate corp., Bellevue, Wash., 1999—2002; pres., CEO Agilean Corp., Bellevue, Wash., 2002—.

SCHUL, BILL DEAN, psychological administrator, author; b. Winfield, Kans., Mar. 16, 1928; s. Fred M. and Martha Mildred (Miles) S.; m. Virginia Louise Duboise, Aug. 3, 1952; children: Robert Dean, Deva Elizabeth. BA, Southwestern Coll., 1952; MA, U. Denver, 1954; PhD, Am. Internat. U., 1977. Reporter, columnist Augusta (Kans.) Daily Gazette, 1954-58, Wichita (Kans.) Eagle-Beacon, 1958-61; youth dir. under auspices Kans. Atty. Gen., 1961-65; state dir. 7th Step Found., Topeka, 1965-66; mem. staff Dept. Preventive Psychiatry, Menninger Found., Topeka, 1966-71; dir. cons. Ctr. Improvement Human Functining, Wichita, 1975—. Psychologist Ctr. Human Devel., Wichita; assoc. prof. Holos U. Grad. Seminary, 2002-. Mng. editor The Register, Oxford, Kans., 1988—; author: (with Edward Greenwood) Mental Health in Kansas Schools, 1965, Let Me Do This Thing, 1969, (with Bill Larson) Hear Me, Barabbas, 1969, How to Be An Effective Group Leader, 1975, The Secret Power of Pyramids, 1975, (with Ed Pettit) The Psychic Powre of Pyramids, 1976, Pyramids: The Second Reality, 1979, The Psychic Power of Animals, 1977, Psychic Frontiers of Medicine, 1977, Animal Immortality, 1990, Life Song, 1995, Synchronize Your Brain, 1997, Wayward Angel, 1988. Bd. dirs. Recreation Commn., Topeka, United Funds, Topeka, Acadic Inst., Trees for Life; v.p. Pegasus Way; pres. Intraface Corp., 1989—; mem. adv. bd. Clayton U. With USN, 1945-46. Recipient John H. McGinnis Meml. award Nonfiction, 1972, Am. Freedom Found. award, 1966, Spl. Appreciation award Kans. State Penitentiary, 1967. Mem. Acad. Parapsychology and Medicine, Kans. Coun. Children and Youth (pres. 1965-66), Assn. Strenghtening higher Realities and Aspirations of Man (pres. 1970-71), Smithsonian Instn., Lions (pores. 1957). Address: 7233 192d Rd Winfield KS 67156-9803 Office Phone: 620-221-1843. E-mail: schul@kcisp.net. *Personal philosophy: While the purpose of life may include joy and contentment, I believe that the primary goal of life is learning. Considering life as a school allows us to assign reason and direction to our successes and failures, that every experience can contribute to our growth as long as it is used to expand our awareness and increase our will.*

SCHULBERG, BUDD, author; b. N.Y.C., Mar. 27, 1914; s. Benjamin P. and Adeline (Jaffe) S.; m. Virginia Ray, July 23, 1936 (div. 1942); 1 dau., Victoria; m. Victoria Anderson, Feb. 17, 1943 (div. 1964); children: Stephen, David; m. Geraldine Brooks, July 12, 1964 (dec. 1977); m. Betsy Anne Langman, June 9, 1979; children: Benn Stuart, Jessica A. Student, Deerfield Acad., 1931-32; AB cum laude, Dartmouth Coll., 1936, LLD, 1960; LittD, Long Island U., 1983; DHL, Hofstra U., 1987, Five Points Coll., 2001. Boxing editor Sports Illustrated; pres., prodr. Schulberg Prodns. Founder, dir. Watts Writers Workshop, L.A., 1965—; founder, chmn. Frederick Douglass Creative Arts Ctr., N.Y.C., 1971—. Screenwriter, Hollywood, 1936-39; writer "The Schulberg Report", Newsday Syndicate; author: What Makes Sammy Run?, 1941, The Harder They Fall, 1947, The Disenchanted, 1950, Some Faces in the Crowd, 1953, Waterfront, 1955 (Christopher award 1955), Sanctuary V, 1969, The Four Seasons of Success, 1972, Loser and Still Champion: Muhammad Ali, 1972, Swan Watch, 1975, Everything that Moves, 1980, Moving Pictures: Memories of a Hollywood Prince, 1981, Writers in America Love, Action, Laughter and Other Sad Tales, 1990, Sparring with Hemingway: And Other Legends of the Fight Game, 1995, La Foret Interdite, including dialogue in Black and White with James Badwin, 1997; editor: From the Ashes: Voices of Watts, 1967; screenwriter: (films) (with Samuel Ornitz) Little Orphan Annie, 1938, (with F. Scott Fitzgerald) Winter Carnival, 1939, (with Dorothy Parker) Weekend for Three, 1941, (with Martin Berkeley) City without Men, 1943, (with Dudley Nichols) Government Girl, 1943, On the Waterfront, 1954 (Academy award best original story and screenplay 1954, N.Y. Critics award 1954, Fgn. Corrs. award 1954, Screen Writers Guild award 1954, Venice Festival award 1954), A Face in the Crowd, 1958 (German Film Critics award 1957), Wind Across the Everglades, 1958, (teleplays) The Pharmacist's Mate, 1951, Paso Doble, Memory in White, The Legen That Walks Like a man, A Question of Honor, A Table At Ciro's; playwright: The Disenchanted: A Play in Three Acts, 1958, What Make's Sammy Run?, 1959, (musical) Senor Discretion Himself, 1985, (play in 2 acts) The Disenchanted, 1999, On the Waterfront, 2001; contbr. to Sports Illustrated, Life, N.Y. Times Book Rev., Esquire, Newsday Syndicate, Los Angeles Times Book Rev., N.Y. Times Sunday Mag., Playboy, The New Yorker. Bd. dirs. Westminster Neighborhood Assn., L.A., 1965-68, Inner City Cultural Ctr., L.A., 1965-68; mem. nat. adv. commn. on black participation John F. Kennedy Ctr. for Performing Arts; trustee Humanitas Prize. Lt. (j.g.) USNR, 1943-46, assigned to OSS. Awarded Army Commendation Ribbon for gathering photog. evidence of war crimes for Nuremberg Trial, 1945-46; recipient Susie Humanitarian award B'nai B'rith, Image award NAACP, Journalism award Dartmouth Coll., Merit award Lotos Club., L.A. Community Svc. award, 1966, B'hai Human Rights award, 1968, spl. award for Watts Writers Workshop, New Eng. Theater Conf., 1969, Heritage award Deerfield Acad., 1986, Amistad award, award for work with black writers Howard U., Prix Literaire, Deauville Festival 1989, Westhampton Writers Lifetime Achievement award, 1989, World Boxing Assn. Living Legend award, 1990, Southampton Cultural Ctr. 1st Annual Literature award, 1992, Lifetime Achievement award Guild Hall, 2003; named to Internat. Boxing Hall of Fame, 2003. Mem. Dramatists Guild, ASCAP, Authors Guild N.Y.C. (mem. council), ACLU, Writers Guild East (mem. coun.), Boxing Writers Am. (A. J. Liebling award 1997), P.E.N., Sphinx (Dartmouth), The Players Club, Yale/Dartmouth Club, Phi Beta Kappa. Address: Mr Mickey Freiberg Acme Literary Agy 4727 Wilshire Blvd Los Angeles CA 90064 also: Ms Mirian Altshuler 53 Old Post Rd N Red Hook NY 12571 Office Phone: 631-288-0514. E-mail: bschul@optonline.net.

SCHULBERG, JAY WILLIAM, foundation official; b. N.Y.C., July 17, 1939; s. Perry and Esther (Eagle) S.; m. Kathryn Carmel Nicholson, Sept. 18, 1968. BS (Founder's Day award 1961), NYU, 1961. With Seagram's Inc., 1962, Grumman Aircraft Co., 1963-66, Foote, Cone & Belding Inc., 1967-68, Ogilvy & Mather, Inc., N.Y.C., 1968-87, exec. v.p., head creative dept., 1985-87, also mem. U.S. coun. dirs., 1988-99; vice chmn., chief creative officer, bd. dirs. Bozell Worldwide, N.Y.C., 1987—99; office of chmn., also bd. dirs. Bozell, N.Y.C., operating bd.; creative dir. Outdoor with Found. for A Better Life, 2000—. Bd. dirs. Ogilvy & Mather Worldwide, chmn., exec. com. Author: The Milk Mustache Book; creator advt. campaigns for Am. Express, Bahamas, TWA, Maxwell House Coffee, Country Time, Gen. Foods, Duracell, Hardees, Brit. Tourism, Hershey's, Huggies, Merrill Lynch, N.Y. Times, Excedrin, Milk "Mustache", Tyco, USAF, Mass. Mut., Vanity Fair, Vassrette, others. Developed Big Apple campaign, N.Y.C. With AUS, 1962. Recipient Art Dirs. Club awards, One Show awards, Andy awards, Addy awards, Cannes, Hollywood Festival awards, 6 David Ogilvy awards; named Creative Dir. of Yr. Adweek Mag., 1986. Mem. The One Club, Internat. Rescue Com. (bd. dirs.).

SCHULER, ALISON KAY, lawyer; b. West Point, N.Y., Oct. 1, 1948; d. Richard Hamilton and Irma (Sanken) S.; m. Lyman Gage Sandy, Mar. 30, 1974, (dec. Mar. 2002); 1 child, Theodore. AB cum laude, Radcliffe Coll., 1969; JD, Harvard U., 1972. Bar: Va. 1973, D.C. 1974, N.Mex. 1975. Assoc. Hunton & Williams, Richmond, Va., 1972-75; asst. U.S. atty. U.S. Atty.'s Office, Albuquerque, 1975-78; adj. prof. law U. N.Mex., 1983-85, 90, 98—; ptnr. Sutin, Thayer & Browne, Albuquerque, 1978-85, Montgomery & Andrews, P.A., Albuquerque, 1985-88; sole practice Albuquerque, 1988—. Bd. dirs. Intellite, Inc. Bd. dirs. Am. Diabetes Assn., Albuquerque, 1980—85, chmn. bd. dirs., 1984—85; bd. dirs. June Music Festival, 1980—95, pres., 1983—85, 1993—94; bd. dirs. Albuquerque Conservation Trust, 1986—90, N.Mex. Osteo. Found., 1993—96; chairperson Albuquerque Com. Fgn. Rels., 1984—85; mem. N.Mex. Internat. Trade and Investment Coun., Inc., 1986—; chartered org. rep. troop 444 Boy Scouts Am., 1997—, mem. nominating com., mem.-at-large dist. com. Sandia dist., 1998—, dist. vice chmn., 1999—2002, v.p. Great S.W. coun., 2001—; Great S.W. coun. wood badge Boys Scout Am., 2002—; wood badge course dir. Boy Scouts Am., 2002—; mem. adv. bd. Care Net Pregnancy Ctr. of Albuquerque, 2003—; mem. coun. St. Lukes Luth. Ch., 1976—80, 1982—84, 1991—96, v.p., 1978—80, 1982—84, pres., 1994—95. Recipient Award of Merit, Sandia Dist., 2000, Svc. award, Albuquerque Astron. Soc., 2002, Silver Beaver award, Gt. S.W. Coun., 2002. Mem. Fed. Bar Assn. (coord.), ABA, Va. Bar Assn., N.Mex. Bar Assn. (chmn. corp., banking and bus. law 1982-83, bd. dirs. internat. and immigration law sect. 1987-95, chmn. 1993-94), Albuquerque Astron. Soc. (Svc. award 2002), Harvard U. Alumni Assn. (mem. fund campaign, regional dir. 1984-86, v.p. 1986-89, chmn. clubs com. 1985-88, chmn. communications com. 1988-91), Radcliffe Coll. Alumnae Assn. Bd. Mgmt. (regional dir. 1984-87, chmn. comms. com. 1988-91), Harvard-Radcliffe Club (pres. 1980-84). Home: 632 Cougar Loop NE Albuquerque NM 87122-1808 Office: 2155 Louisiana Blvd NE Ste 8500 Albuquerque NM 87110-8401 Office Phone: 505-872-0800. Personal E-mail: akschuler@aol.com.

SCHULER, JAMES JOSEPH, vascular surgeon; b. Aurora, Ill., Feb. 12, 1946; s. Ella Schuler; m. Catherine Weller, 1969; children: James Jr., Matthew. BS, St. John's U., 1968; MD with hons., U. Ill., 1972, MS in Biochemistry, 1975. Diplomate Am. Bd. Surgery, Am. Bd. Vascular Surgery. Intern U. Ill., Chgo., 1972-73, resident, 1973-78, chief resident, 1978-79, instr., 1975-79, asst. prof., 1980-85, assoc. prof., 1985-92, prof. surgery, 1992—, chief divsn. vascular surgery, 1988—. Lectr. Cook County Grad. Sch., Chgo., 1991—; attending surgeon Cook County Hosp., Chgo., 1992—, West Side Vets. Hosp., Chgo., 1979—. Assoc. editor: Civilian Vascular Trauma, 1992; co-author numerous book chpts.; contbr. articles to profl. jours. Vascular Surgery fellow U. Ill., 1979-80; rsch. grantee numerous granting bodies, 1980—. Fellow ACS; mem. Am. Venous Forum, Soc. for Vascular Surgery, Western Surg. Assn., Internat. Soc. for Cardiovascular Surgery, Midwestern Vascular Surg. Soc., Alpha Omega Alpha. Republican. Roman Catholic. Avocations: hunting, fishing. Office: U Ill Hosp 1740 W Taylor St Ste 2200 Chicago IL 60612-7232

SCHULER, JAMES K. construction executive; Chmn., pres., CEO Schuler Homes, Inc., Honolulu, 1973—. Office: Schuler Homes Inc 828 Fort Street Mall Ste 400 Honolulu HI 96813-4321

SCHULER, NICO STEPHAN, musicologist; b. Rosslau/Elbe, Germany, May 5, 1970; s. Jurgen and Karin Schuler; m. Sunnie Ran Oh, May 22, 1999; 1 child, Julia Patricia Vogel. MA in Musicology, Ernst-Moritz-Arndt U., Germany, 1995; PhD in Music Theory, Mich. State U., 2000. Asst. prof. Ctrl. Mich. U., Mt. Pleasant, Mich., 1999—2001; asst. prof., coord. music theory Tex. State U., San Marcos, 2001—. Chair methodology of music rsch. interest group German Musicological Soc., Kassel, Germany, 1994—2000; co-dir. Internat. Ctr. for New Music, Mt. Pleasant, Mich., 2001—. Author: (rsch. monograph) Hanning Schroder, 1996, (rsch. book) Epistemology, Musicology, AI, and the Process, 1995, MUSANA 1.0 - A Music Analysis Program, 1994 (displayed at CeBit, Internat. Computer Exhbn., Germany), 1996; editor: Wolfgang Amadeus Mozart, 1992, On Inter-Regional Music Cultural Relations in the Baltic Area, 1993, Festschrift Kurt Schwaen for his 85th Birthday,

1995, On the Problem and on Methods of Music Analysis, 1996, Musica Balitca: Inter-Regional and Music-Cultural Relations in the Baltic Area, 1996, Musica Baltica: Music in the Cities of the Baltic Area in the 17th and 18th Century, 1996, Between Music and Society Systems, 1996, The Similarity of New or Old: Dietrich Erdmann-Life and Work, 1997, On Problems of Music Historiography of Heroes and Geniuses, 1998, Computer-Applications in Music Research: Concepts, Methods, Results, 2002; contbr. Musik Netz Werke, Musikkonzepte - Konzepte der Musikwissenschaft, Otto Laske: Navigating New Musical Horizons, Colloquium. Stadt und Region als Schauplätze des Musikgeschehens, Studien zur lokalen und territorialen Musikgeschichte Mecklenburgs und Pommerns I; editor: (rsch. book series) Greifswald Monographs on Musicology, 1995—2001, Methodology of Music Research, 2002—; mem. editl. review bd.: rsch. book series Greifswald Monographs on Musicology, 2001—; translator: (rsch. book article) Jewish Nietzscheanism, 1997; editor: (jour.) Chamber Music Today, 1991—93, South Ctrl. Music Bull., 2002—; contbr. encyclopedia Die Musik in Geschichte und Gegenwart, encyclopedia The New Grove Dictionary of Music and Musicians, music dictionary Lexikon zur Deutschen Musikkultur, music dictionary Komponisten der Gegenwart; editor: (music dictionary) On-Line Dictionary of Modern Music, 2003—; author: (music analysis software) MUSANA. A Music Analysis Program, 1994—96, (multi-media software) Musica Multicolore, 1998; composer: (music composition) Memories & Thoughts, 1997. Recipient Predl. award for excellence in scholarly and creative activities, Tex. State U., 2003; fellow, German Academic Exch. Svc., 1996—97, Rsch. in Belgium and Netherlands, Mich. State U., 1999, 2000; grantee Global Young Scholar, 1999, President's Rsch. Investment Fund, Ctrl. Mich. U., 2001, Rsch. Enhancement grant, State of Tex., 2002, 2004; scholar, German Nat. Academic found., 1992—96. Mem.: Umbrella Orgn. Musicology Students (assoc.), Musica Reanimata (assoc.), Soc. for Ethnomusicology (assoc.), Assn. for Tech. in Music Instrn. (assoc.), Am. Musicological Soc. (assoc.), Soc. for Music Theory (assoc.), Coll. Music Soc. (assoc.; bd. mem. south ctrl. chpt. 2002—), Tex. Soc. for Music Theory (assoc.; exec. bd. mem. 2002—), Phi Beta Delta (assoc.; sec. alpha alpha chpt. 1999—2001). Achievements include research in Perspectivism in music rsch., a music research methodology; Several new measurements of computer-assisted music analysis. Avocations: travel, photography, swimming, gardening. Office: Tex State Univ San Marcos Sch Music 601 University Dr San Marcos TX 78666 Office Phone: 512-245-3395. Personal E-mail: nico.schuler@txstate.edu.

SCHULER, ROBERT HUGO, chemist, educator; b. Buffalo, Jan. 4, 1926; s. Robert H. and Mary J. (Mayer) S.; m. Florence J. Forrest, June 18, 1952; children: Mary A., Margaret A., Carol A., Robert E., Thomas C. BS, Canisius Coll., Buffalo, 1946; PhD, U. Notre Dame, 1949. Asst. prof. chemistry Canisius Coll., 1949-53; asso. chemist, then chemist Brookhaven Nat. Lab., 1953-56; staff fellow, dir. radiation research lab. Mellon Inst., 1956-76, mem. adv. bd., 1962-76; prof. chemistry, dir. radiation research lab. Carnegie-Mellon U., 1967-76; prof. chemistry U. Notre Dame, Ind., 1976—, dir. radiation lab., 1976-95, dir. emeritus, 1995—, John A. Zahm prof. radiation chemistry, 1986—; Raman prof. U. Madras, India, 1985-86. Vis. prof. Hebrew U., Israel, 1980. Author articles in field. Recipient Curie medal Poland, 1992. Fellow AAAS; mem. Am. Chem. Soc., Am. Phys. Soc., Chem. Soc., Radiation Research Soc. (pres. 1975-76), Sigma Xi. Clubs: Cosmos. Office: U Notre Dame Radiation Lab Notre Dame IN 46556 Office Phone: 219-239-7502. E-mail: schuler.1@nd.edu.

SCHULER, ROBERT JORDAN, English educator, writer; b. San Mateo, Calif., June 25, 1939; s. Edward Peter and Georgia Ruth Schuler; m. Carol Florence Schuler, Sept. 7, 1963; children: Sally, Edward Anthony, Michael. BA in Polit. Sci. with honors, Stanford U., 1961; MA in Comparative Lit., U. Calif., Berkeley, 1965; PhD in English, U. Minn., 1989. Instr. English Menlo Coll., Menlo Park, Calif., 1965-67; instr. humanities Shimer Coll., Mt. Carroll, Ill., 1967-77; prof. English U. Wis.-Stout, Menomonie, 1978—. Hormel prof. U. Wis.-Stout, 1995-96. Author: Seasonings, 1978, Axle of the Oak, 1978, Where is Dancers' Hill?, 1979, Morning Raga, 1980, Origins, 1981, The Red Cedar Scroll, 1981, Music for Monet, 1985; Floating Out of Stone, 1982 (award Coun. Wis. Writers 1983), Grace, 1995, Red Cedar Suite, 1999, Journey Toward the Original Mind, 1995, (book of poems) In Search of Green Dolphin Street, 2004; contbr. numerous poems to lit. jours. Bd. dirs. Shimer Coll. Assn., Waukegan, Ill., 1997—; dir. film series Menomonie Pub. Libr., 1997—; mem. land use planning com. Twp. of Menomonie, 1999-2002, writer land use plan, 2002—; commr. Land Use Plan Com., Menomonie, 2002—. Pub. grantee Ill. Arts Coun., Chgo., 1976, 77, Nat. Endowment for the Arts, Washington, 1978; fellow Danforth Found., 1969-70, lit. fellow (poetry) Wis. Arts Bd., Madison, 1997; recipient New Works award Wis. Arts Bd., 1999. Mem. Phi Kappa Phi. Avocations: cross country skiing, hiking, gardening. Home: E4549 479th Ave Menomonie WI 54751 Office: Dept English U Wis-Stout Menomonie WI 54751 Office Phone: 715-232-1454. E-mail: schulerr@uwstout.edu.

SCHULER, ROBERT LEO, appraiser, consultant; b. Cin., June 15, 1943; s. Del D. and Virginia D. (Heyl) S.; m. Shelagh J. Moritz, Aug. 11, 1962; children: Robert C., Sherry L. V.p. Comprehensive Appraisal Service, Cin., 1977—. Bd. dirs. Hamilton County Regional Planning Commn., Cin., 1987-88; mem. exec. com., past pres. OKI Regional Coun. Govts., Cin., 1981-92. Councilman City of Deer Park, Ohio, 1979-86; trustee Sycamore Twp., 1988-92; Ohio state rep. 36th dist., 1993—2000; senator, 7th Dist., Ohio, 2003-; active Scarlet Oaks Bus. Adv. Coun. Mem. Cin. Bd. Realtors, Ohio Assn. Realtors, Jaycees (v.p.). Republican. Roman Catholic. Home: 3648 Jeffrey Ct Cincinnati OH 45236-1544 Office: 3648 Jeffrey Ct Cincinnati OH 45236-1544 Office Phone: 614-466-9737.

SCHULER, THEODORE ANTHONY, b. Louisville, July 1, 1934; s. Henry R. and Virginia (Meisner) S.; m. Jane A. Bandy, July 29, 1979; children: Marc, Elizabeth, Eric, Ellen. BCE, U. Louisville, 1957, M in Engring., 1973. Registered profl. engr., Tenn. Design constrn. engr. Brighton Engring. Co., Frankfort, Ky., 1960-65; design engr. Hensley-Schmidt Inc., Chattanooga, 1965-68, assoc. mem., 1969-73, sr. assoc. mem., 1973-75, prin., asst. v.p., head Knoxville office, 1975-81; chief planning engr. engring. dept. City of Knoxville, 1981-96, ret., 1996. Served to lt. (j.g.) USNR, 1957-60. Fellow ASCE. Home: 5907 Adelia Dr Knoxville TN 37920-5801 Personal E-mail: Tschu30447@aol.com.

SCHULER, WALTER E. lawyer; b. Memphis, Tenn., Sept. 8, 1962; s. James D. and Clare A. Schuler. BBA magna cum laude, U. Memphis, 1993; JD cum laude with cert. in health law with hons., St. Louis U., 1996. Bar: Tenn. 1996, U.S. Dist. Ct. (Western Dist.) Tenn. 1996, U.S. Ct. Appeals (6th cir.), 1998. Assoc. The Bogatin Law Firm, PLC, Memphis, Tenn., 1996—. Contbr. articles to profl. jours., chpt. to book. Sgt. (E-5), U.S. Army, 1985-90, staff sgt. (E-6) USAR, 1990-93. Recipient Commendation Medal-1st Oak Leaf Cluster, U.S. Army, 1989, Army Achievement Medal-2nd Oak Leaf Cluster, 1989, Nat. Def. Svc. Med., 1992. Mem. Am. Health Lawyers Assn., ABA, Tenn. Bar Assn., Memphis Bar Assn. Office: Bogatin Law Firm PLC Ste 300 International Place Dr Memphis TN 38120

SCHULHOF, MICHAEL PETER, electronics company executive; b. N.Y.C., Nov. 30, 1942; s. Rudolph B. and Hannelore (Buck) Schulhof; m. Paola Nissim, Apr. 17, 1969; children: David Kenneth, Jonathan Nissim. BA, Grinnell Coll., 1964, DSc (hon.), 1990; MS, Cornell U., 1967; PhD, Brandeis U., 1970. Lic. comml. pilot. Am. rsch. fellow Brookhaven Nat. Lab., Uptown, NY, 1969—71; asst. to v.p. mfg. CBS Records, Inc., N.Y.C., NY, 1971—73, exec. com., bd. dirs., 1987—88; from gen. mgr. bus. products divsn. to sr. v.p. Sony Corp., N.Y.C., NY, 1973—86; pres. Sony Industries, N.Y.C., NY, 1978—86; chmn. Digital Audio Disc Corp., Terre Haute, Ind., 1986—96; pres. Sony Software Corp., 1991—96; pres., CEO Sony Corp. Am., 1993—95. Chmn. bd. dirs. Quadriga Art Inc., 1980—, World On Line, 1998—99; bd. dirs. Sony Corp., Japan, Sony Corp. Am., Sony Pictures Entertainment, Materials Rsch. Corp., J2 Global Commn., 1997—, CBS/Sportsline; chmn. Sony Music Entertainment; former chmn. Comml. Electronics, 1998—; chmn., CEO Global Tech. Investments, 2001—; mem., coun. of fgn. rels. and investment; svcs. policy, adv. com. U.S. Trade Rep. Contbr. articles to profl. jours. Trustee Brandeis U., 1990—, Lincoln Ctr. for Performing Arts, Inc., N.Y.C., Brookings Instn., Washington; investment and svcs. policy adv. com. U.S. Trade Rep.; active Coun. Fgn. Rels.; bd. dirs. Ctr. on Addiction and Substance Abuse at Columbia U., N.Y.C., Am. Hosp. of Paris Found. Fellow, NSF, 1970. Master: Am. Phys. Soc. (bd. dirs. 1978); mem.: Am. Radio Relay League, Computer and Bus. Equipment Mfrs. Assn. (bd. dirs.), Whitney Mus., Guggenhiem Mus., Aircraft Owners and Pilots Assn., Atlantic Golf Club, Fenway Golf Club, Profile Club, East Hampton Tennis Club, Gipsy Trail Club, Harmony Club. Achievements include patents for audio disc apparatus. Office: 375 Park Ave New York NY 10152-0002

SCHULHOFER, STEPHEN JOSEPH, law educator, consultant; b. N.Y.C., Aug. 20, 1942; s. Joseph and Myrelle S.; m. Laurie Wohl, May 28, 1975; children: Samuel, Jonah. AB, Princeton U., 1964; LLB, Harvard U., 1967. Bar: D.C. 1968, U.S. Dist. Ct. (ea. dist.) Pa. 1973, U.S. Supreme Ct. 1973. Law clk. U.S. Supreme Ct., Washington, 1967-69; assoc. Coudert Freres, Paris, 1969-72; prof. law U. Pa., Phila., 1972-86; prof. U. Chgo., 1986-2001; prof NYU, 2001—. speedy trial reporter U.S. Dist. Ct., Wilmington, Del., 1975-80; cons. U.S. EPA, Washington, 1977-78, U.S. Sentencing Commn., Washington, 1987-94. Author: Unwanted Sex: The Culture of Intimidation and the Failure of Law, 1998; Prosecutorial Discretion and Federal Sentencing Reform, 1979, The Enemy Within: Law Enforcement and Civil Liberties in the Wake of September 11, 2002; Editor: Criminal Law and its Processes, 1983, 89, 95, 2001; contbr. articles to profl. jours. Trustee, Cmty. Legal Services, Inc., Phila., 1981-86. Walter Meyer grantee Am. Bar Found., 1984. Mem. ACLU (Ill. bd. dirs. 1993-97), Law and Soc. Assn. Office: NYU Law Sch 40 Washington Sq S New York NY 10012

SCHULIAN, JOHN (NIELSEN SCHULIAN), screenwriter, author; b. L.A., Jan. 31, 1945; s. John and Estella Katherine (Nielsen) S.; m. Paula Lynn Ellis, Aug. 20, 1977 (div. Oct. 1984). BA, U. Utah, 1967; MS, Northwestern U., 1968. Copy editor Salt Lake City Tribune, 1968; reporter Balt. Evening Sun, 1970-75; sportswriter Washington Post, 1975-77; sports columnist Chgo. Daily News, 1977-78, Chgo. Sun-Times, 1978-84, Phila. Daily News, 1984-86; staff writer Miami Vice, Universal City, Calif., 1986-87, story editor, 1987, The Slap Maxwell Story, North Hollywood, Calif., 1987-88; exec. story editor TV series Wiseguy, Hollywood, 1988-89; co-prodr. TV series Midnight Caller, Burbank, Calif., 1989-90, supervising prodr., 1990-91; co-exec. prodr. TV series Reasonable Doubts, Burbank, 1991-92; creative cons. TV series The Untouchables, L.A., 1992-93; co-exec. prodr. TV series Hercules, Universal City, Calif., 1994-96; co-creator Xena: Warrior Princess, Universal City, 1995; assoc. prodr. (documentary) Ben Johnson: Third Cowboy on the Right, 1996; co-exec. prodr. (TV series) Lawless, 1996-97; consulting prodr. (TV series) JAG, 1999-2000; exec. prodr. (TV series) The Outer Limits, Vancouver, Canada, 2000-01; culture columnist MSNBC.com, 2001—02; co-exec prodr. (TV series) Tremors, Universal City, 2002—03. Spl. contbr. Sports Illustrated, 1998—; profl. in residence U. Utah, 2004. Author: Writers' Fighters and Other Sweet Scientists, 1983; contbg. editor Panorama mag., 1980-81; syndicated columnist UP Syndicate; commentator Nat. Pub. Radio, 1985-86; cons. The Reader's Catalog, 1989; contbr. articles to N.Y. Times, Playboy, Gentlemen's Quar., Oxford Am.Mag., The National, L.A. Times; included in The Best Am. Sports Writing, 1994. Mem. Pacific Coast League Hist. Soc. With U.S. Army, 1968-70. Recipient Nat. Headliners Club award, 1980, Column Writing award AP Sports Editors, 1979, 82, Best Sports Stories award, 1983, 84, Nat Fleischer Excellence in Boxing Journalism award Boxing Writers Assn. Am., 1985. Mem. Writers Guild Am., Phi Beta Kappa. Office: Endeavor Talent Agy 9701 Wilshire Blvd 10th Fl Beverly Hills CA 90212 Personal E-mail: jschulian@aol.com.

SCHULKE, DAVID, medical association administrator; Mem. U.S. Congress; dir. Alliance Devel. and Regulatory Affairs Am. Pharma. Assn.; exec. v.p. Am. Health Quality Assn., Washington. Mem.: Am. Pharma. Assn. (hon.). Office: Am Health Quality Assn 1140 Connecticut Ave Ste 1050 Washington DC 20036

SCHULKIN, CARL ROGER, secondary school educator; b. Bklyn., Mar. 14, 1943; s. Melvin and Blanche Schulkin; m. Bonnie Belle Blitz, June 15, 1965; children: Todd, Andrew. AB in History, Brown U., Providence, 1964; MA in History, U. Calif., Berkeley, 1966, PhD in History, 1973. Acting instr. U. Calif., Berkeley, 1971—72; tchr., coll. counselor Pembroke Hill Sch., Kansas City, Mo., 1974—. Founder, pres. Schulkin Ednl. Ent., Westwood, Kans., 1983—; U.S. history cons. Advanced Placement Program, 1993—. Author: In Pursuit of Greatness: A History of Pembroke Country Day School, 1985; contbr. articles to profl. jours. Mem. bridge com. Temple B'nai Jehudah, Kansas City, Mo., 1994—99, mem. social action task force, 1992; Mandel tchr. fellow U.S. Holocaust Meml. Mus., Washington, 1997—98; coord. history team #1 Woodrow Wilson Nat. Fellowship Found., 1990—94; pres. Greater Kansas City Coun. for the Social Studies, 2003—04. Named Sosland Family Chair, Pembroke Hill Sch., 1992—93; recipient Award for Tchg. Excellence, Pembroke Country Day Sch., 1978—79; fellow, Fulbright fellow, 1969—70. Mem.: Nat. Coun. for the Social Studies, Orgn. Am. Historians. Reform Jew. Avocations: web page design, photography. Home: 4815 Booth Ave Westwood KS 66205 Office: Pembroke Hill Sch 5121 State Line Rd Kansas City MO 64112

SCHULL, WILLIAM J. geneticist, educator; b. Louisiana, Mo., Mar. 17, 1922; married, 1946. BS, Marquette U., 1946; PhD in Genetics, Ohio State U., 1949. Head dept. genetics Atomic Bomb Casualty Comsn., Japan, 1949-51; jr. geneticist Inst. Human Biology, U. Mich., 1951-53, asst. geneticist, 1953-56, from asst. prof. to prof. human genetics, med. sch., 1956-72, prof. anthropology, 1969-72; prof. human genetics U. Tex. Grad. Sch. Biomedical Sci., Houston, 1972—. Vis. fellow Australian Nat. U., 1969; cons. Atomic Bomb Casualty Comsn., 1954, 56, NIH, 1956—, chmn. genetics study sect., 1969-72; dir. Child Health Survey, Japan, 1959-60; vis. prof. U. Chgo., 1963, U. Chile, 1975; German Rsch. Assn. guest prof. U. Heidelberg, 1970; mem. com. atomic casualties Nat. Rsch. Coun., 1951, subcom. biology Com. Dentistry, 1951-55, com. on collaborative project Nat. Inst. Neurol. Disease and Stroke, 1957—, panel in genetic effects of radiation, WHO, 1958—, panel experts human heredity, 1961—, nat. adv. com. radiation USPHS, 1960-64, bd. sci. counselors Nat. Inst. Dentistry Rsch., 1966-69; dir. Radiation Effects Rsch. Found. and head dept. epidemiology and Japan, 1978-80; adv. Nat. Heart and Lung Inst.; mem. subcom. biology and medicine AEC, human biology coun. Soc. Study Human Biology. Recipient Centennial award Ohio State U., 1970. Mem. AAAS, U.S.Mex. Border Health Assn., Japanese Soc. Human Genetics (hon.), Peruvian Soc. Human Genetics (hon.), Genetic Soc. Chile (hon.), Sigma Xi. Achievements include research in biometry. Office: U Tex Sch of Pub Health Human Genetics Ctr PO Box 20186 Houston TX 77225-0334

SCHULLER, DAVID EDWARD, cancer center administrator, otolaryngologist; b. Cleve., Oct. 20, 1944; m. Carole Ann Hauss, June 24, 1967; children: Rebecca, Michael. BA, Rutgers U., 1966; MD cum laude, Ohio State U., 1970. Diplomate Am. Bd. Otolaryngology 1975. Intern dept. surgery U. Hosps. Cleve., 1970-71; resident dept. otolaryngology Ohio State U., Columbus, 1971-72; resident dept. surgery U. Hosps. Cleve., 1972-73; fellow head and neck surgery Pack Med. Found. with John Conley, N.Y.C., 1973; resident dept. otolaryngology Ohio State U. Hosps., Columbus, 1973-75; fellow head and neck oncology and facial plastic and reconstructive surgery U. Iowa, Iowa City, 1975-76; trustee Ohio Cancer Found, 1988—; from clin. instr. to prof. and chmn. dept. otolaryngology The Ohio State U., Columbus, 1971—; dir. Am. Bd. Otolaryngology, 1988—2000; dir. Comprehensive Cancer Ctr., Columbus, 1997—; prof. sect. oral biology, Coll. Dentistry The Ohio State U., 1990—; dir. Arthur G. James Cancer Hosp. & Richard J. Solove Rsch. Inst., Columbus, 1988—; chair dept. otolaryngology Ohio State U., Columbus, 1990—; pres. American Board of Otolaryngology, 2000—. Mem., chmn. various coms. Ohio State U. Hosps. and Coll. Medicine, 1976—; dir. CCC head and neck oncology program Ohio State U., 1977—, hosps. physician flr. coord. 10th flr., 1977-82, dir. laser-microsurgery teaching and rsch. lab., 1987-88; mem. various coms. Grant Hosp., 1980-84; mem. Accreditation Coun. for the Grad. Med. Edn. Residency Review Com. for Otolaryngology, 1985—, chmn., 1988—; vis. prof., lectr., ACS prof. clin. Oncology, 1989-94. numerous instns. Author: (books) (with others) Otolaryngology-Head and Neck Surgery-4 Vols., 1986, Textbook of Otolaryngology-7th Edit., 1988, Otolaryngology-Head and Neck Surgery-Update I, 1988, Musculocutaneous Flaps in Head and Neck Reconstructive Surgery, 1989, Otolaryngology-Head and Neck Surgery Update II, 1990, Otorinolaringologia-Cirugia de Cabeza y Culleo, 1991, Otolaryngology-Head and Neck Surgery-4 Vols., 1992; contbr. chpts. to books and articles to profl. jours.; mem. editorial bd. New Horizons in Otolaryngology/Head and Neck Surgery, 1982-87, The Laryngoscope, 1986—, Am. Jour. Otolaryngology, 1988—, Facial Plastic Surgery Internat. Quar. Monographs, 1992—; mem. rev. bd. Jour. Head and Neck Surgery, 1985—; mem. editorial rev. bd. Otolaryngology-Head and Neck Surgery, 1990—; reviewer New Eng. Jour Medicine, 1992—. Recipient Cert. of Appreciation, Scioto Meml. Hosp., 1982, Edmund Prince Fowler award Triological Soc., 1984; Henry Rutgers scholar Rutgers U., 1965-66; grantee Nat. Cancer Inst., 1980-88, 90-97, Bremer Found., 1982-83, 87-88, Photomedica Inc., 1986-89, Upjohn Co., 1986-90, others. Mem. AMA (mem. rev. panel Archives of Otolaryngology-Head and Neck Surgery 1984—), Am. Cancer Soc. (mem. instl. grant rev. com. 1980—, chmn. rehab. com. Franklin County unit 1981-82, mem. profl. edn. com. 1981—, chmn. 1982-85, v.p. 1982-83, pres. 1986, 87, trustee Ohio divsn. 1988—), Am. Assn. Cosmetic Surgeons, Am. Acad. Facial Plastic and Reconstructive Surgery (mem. rsch. com. 1977-82, chmn. residency rels. com. 1982-85, mem. program com. 1982-85, v.p. mid. sect. 1983-87, chmn. by-laws com. 1988-90, treas. 1988-90, Honor award 1989), Am. Coll. Surgeons, Am. Cleft Palate Assn., Assn. Am. Cancer Insts., Am. Soc. Head and Neck Injury, Am. Acad. Otolaryngology Head and Neck Surgery (mem. editorial bd. self-instructional package program 1982—, del. bd. govs. 1982-87, Honor award 1983), Am. Soc. Laser Medicine and Surgery, Am. Laryngological, Rhinological, Otological Soc., Inc., Am. Laryngological Assn., Am. Soc. Clin. Oncology (mem. program com. 1989—), Am. Assn. Cancer Researchers, Am. Soc. Head and Neck Surgery (mem. coun. 1983-86, chmn. scholastic and fellowship award com. 1984-86, mem. profl. rels. and pub. edn. com. 1989—), Southwest Oncology Group (chmn. head and neck com. 1983—), Collegium ORLAS, Ohio State Med. Assn. (pres. sect. otolaryngology 1987—), Ohio Soc. Otolaryngology (pres. 1985, 86, 87), Acad. Medicine of Columbus and Franklin County, Columbus E.E.N.T. Soc., Franklin County Acad. Medicine (mem. profl. rels. com. 1982—), Head and Neck Intergroup (vice-chmn. 1984-86, chmn. 1986-89), Assn. Rsch. Otolaryngology, Ohio State U. Med. Alumni Soc. (class rep. 1980—, v.p. 1987-88, pres. 1989-90), Med. Forum, Med. Review Club, Order of Hippocrates (charter), Alpha Omega Alpha. Office: 456 W 10th Ave Columbus OH 43210-1240 also: Ohio State Univ Comp Cancer Ctr 300 W 10th Ave Columbus OH 43210-1240*

SCHULLER, GUNTHER ALEXANDER, composer; b. N.Y.C., Nov. 22, 1925; s. Arthur E. and Elsie (Bernartz) Schuller; m. Marjorie Black, June 8, 1948; children: Edwin Gunther, George Alexander. Student, St. Thomas Choir Sch., N.Y.C.; MusD (hon.), Manhattan Sch. Music, 1987, Northeastern U., 1967, U. Ill., 1968, Colby Coll., 1969, Williams Coll., 1975, Cleve. Inst. Music, 1977, New Eng. Conservatory Music, 1978, Rutgers U., 1980, Manhattan Sch. Music, 1987, Oberlin Coll., 1989. Tchr. Manhattan Sch. Music, 1950—63; head composition dept. Tanglewood, 1963—84; pres. New Eng. Conservatory Music, 1967—77; artistic dir. Berkshire Music Ctr., Tanglewood, 1969—84, Festival at Sandpoint, 1985—. Founder, pres. Margun Music Inc., 1975, GM Recs., 1980. French horn player Ballet Theatre, then prin. horn player Cin. Symphony Orch., 1943—45, prin. French horn Met. Opera Orch., 1945—59, Concerto #1 for Horn, 1945; composer: Quartet for Four Double Basses, 1947, Fantasy for Unaccompanied Cello, 1951, Recitative and Rondo for Violin and Piano, 1953, Music for Violin, Piano and Percussion, 1957, Contours, 1958, Woodwind Quintet, 1958, Seven Studies on Themes of Paul Klee, 1959, Spectra, 1960, Six Renaissance Lyrics, 1962, String Quartet No. 2, 1965, Symphony, 1965, opera The Visitation, 1966, opera Fisherman and His Wife, 1970, Capriccio Stravagante, 1972, The Power Within Us, 1972, Tre Invenzioni, 1972, Three Nocturnes, 1973, Four Soundscapes, 1974, Concerto No. 2 for Orch., 1975, Triplum II, 1975, Horn Concerto No. 2, 1976, Violin Concerto, 1976, Diptych for organ, 1976, Sonata Serenata, 1978, Contrabassoon Concerto, 1978, Deaï for 3 orchs., 1978, Trumpet Concerto, 1979, Octet, 1979, Eine Kleine Posaunemusik, 1980, In Praise of Winds (Symphony for Large Wind Orch.), 1981, Symphony for Organ, 1982, Concerto Quaternio, 1983, Concerto for Bassoon and Orch., 1984, Farbenspiel (Concerto No. 3 for Orch.), 1985, On Light Wings (piano quartet), 1984; author: Horn Technique, 1962, Early Jazz: Its Roots and Development, 1968, Musings: The Musical Worlds of Gunther Schuller, 1985, The Swing Era, 1989; premier of Symphony for Brass and Percussion, Cin., 1950, Salzburg Festival, 1957; Dramatic Overture, N.Y. Philharm., 1956; String Quartet, Number 1 Contemporary Arts Festival, U. Ill., 1957, String Quartet Number 3, 1986, Concertino for Jazz Quartet and Orch., Balt. Symphony Orch., 1959, Seven Studies on Themes of Paul Klee, Ford Found., commn., Minn. Symphony, 1959, Spectra, N.Y. Philharm., 1960, Music for Brass Quintet, Coolidge Found., Libr. of Congress, 1961, Concerto No. 1 for Orch., Chgo. Symphony Orch., 1966, Triplum, N.Y. Philharm. commd. Lincoln Ctr., 1967, Aphorisms for Flute and String Trio commd., Carleton Coll. Centennial, 1967, Eine Kleine Posaunenmusik, 1980, In Praise of Winds, 1983, Concerto Quaternio, N.Y. Philharm., 1983, Duologue for Violin and Piano, Libr. of Congress, 1984, Farbenspiel, Berlin Philharm., 1985, Concerto for Viola and Orch., 1985, String Quartet No. 3, 1986, Chimeric Images, 1988, Concerto for String Quartet and Orchestra, 1988, Concerto for Flute and Orchestra, 1988, On Winged Flight: A Divertimento for Band, 1989, Chamber Concerto, 1989, Concerto for Piano Three Hands, 1989, Phantasmata for Violin and Marinba, 1989, 5 Impromptus Eng. Horn and String Quartet, 1989, Impromptus and Cadenzas, 1990, Hommage à Rayechla for 8 cellos/or multiples thereof, 1990, A Trio Setting for clarinet, violin, piano, 1990, Violin Concert No. 2, 1991, Sonata Fantasia for piano, 1992, Ritmica-Melodia-Armonia for orch., 1992, Of Reminiscences and Reflections for orch., 1993 (Pulitzer prize for music, 1994), Brass Quintet No. 2, 1993, The Past is in the Present for orch., 1994, Sextet for left hand piano and woodwind quintet, 1994, Concerto for organ and orch., 1994, Mondrian's Vision, 1994, Magnificat and Nunc Dimittis (choir), 1994, Headin Out, Movin In (jazz ensemble), 1994, Lament for M (jazz ensemble), 1994, Rush Hour an 23d St., 1994, Blue Dawn into White Heat (concert band), 1995, An Arc Ascending, 1996; composer: Bright and Sassy, 1997, Ohio River Reflections for Piano Trio and Horn, 1998, Sonata for Alto Saxaphone, 1999, Fantasie Impromptu for Flutet Hpschd, 2000, Quodlibet - Vln, Cello, Horn, and Harp, 2001, The Birth of the Cool Suite, 2001, String Quartet No. 4, 2002, Concerto da Camera No. 2, 2002, Duo Concertante for Cello and Piano, 2002, Encounters for Jazz Bankd and Large Symphony Orch., 2003, String Trio, 2003. Named Guggenheim fellow, 1962, 1963, MacArthur fellow, 1991, Composer of Yr., Mus. Am., 1995; named to Am. Classical Music Hall of Fame, 1998; recipient Creative Arts award, Brandeis U., 1960, Deems Taylor award, ASCAP, 1970, Alice M. Ditson Conducting award, 1970, Rodgers and Hammerstein award, 1971, Friedheim award, 1988, William Schuman award, Columbia U., 1989, Down Beat Lifetime Achievement award, 1993, BMI Lifetime Achievement award, 1994, Gold medal, Am. Acad. Arts and Letters, 1997, Order of Merit Cross, Fed. Republic of Germany, 1997, Max Rudolf award, 1998. Mem.: Am. Acad. Arts and Scis., Nat. Inst. Arts and Letters. Address: 167 Dudley Rd Newton Center MA 02459-2830

SCHULLER, ROBERT HAROLD, minister, writer; b. Alton, Iowa, Sept. 16, 1926; s. Anthony and Jennie (Beltman) Schuller; m. Arvella DeHaan, June 15, 1950; children: Sheila, Jeanne, Carol, Gretchen. BA, Hope Coll., 1947; BD, Western Theol. Sem., 1950; DD, Hope Coll., 1973; LLD, Azusa Pacific Coll., 1970, Pepperdine U., 1976; LittD, Barrington Coll., 1977. Ordained to ministry Reformed Ch. Am., 1950. Pastor Ivanhoe Ref. Ch., Chgo., 1950—55; founder, sr. pastor Garden Grove Cmry. Ch., Calif., 1955—; founder, pres. Hour of Power TV Ministry, 1970—; founder, dir. Robert H. Schuller Inst. for Successful Ch. Leadership, 1970—; chmn. nat. religious sponsor program Religion in Am. Life, N.Y.C., 1975—. Bd. dirs. Freedoms Found. Author: God's Way to the Good Life, 1963, Your Future Is Your Friend, 1964, Move Ahead with Possibility Thinking, 1967, Self Love, the Dynamic Force of Success, 1969, Power Ideas for a Happy Family, 1972, The Greatest Possibiloty Thinker That Ever Lived, 1973, Turn Your Scars into Stars, 1973, You Can Become the Person You Want To Be, 1973, Your Church Has Real Possibilities, 1974, Love or Loneliness - You Decide, 1974, Positive Prayers for Power-Filled Living, 1976, Keep on Believing, 1976, Reach Out for A

New Life, 1977, Peace of Mind Through Possibility Thinking, 1977, Turning You Stress Into Strength, 1978, Daily Power Thoughts, 1978, The Peak to Peek Principle, 1981, Living Positively One Day at a Time, 1981, Self Esteem: The New Reformation, 1982, Tough Times Never Last, But, Tough People Do!, 1983, Tough Minded Faith for Tender Hearted People, 1984, The Be-Happy Attitudes, 1985, Be Happy You Are Loved, 1986, Success is Never Ending, Failure is Never Final, 1988, Believe in the God Who Believes in You, 1989; co-author: The Courage of Carol, 1978. Founder Robert H. Schuller Corr. Ctr. Possibility Thinkers, 1976; bd. dirs. Religion in Am. Life; pres. bd. dirs. Christian Counseling Svcs. Named Headliner of Yr. in Religion, Orange County, 1977, Clergyman of Yr., Religious Heritage Am., 1977; recipient Ddisting. Alumnus award, Hope Coll., 1970, Prin. award, Freedoms Found., 1974. Mem.: AIA (bd. dirs. 1986—), Religious Guild Architects (hon.), Rotary. Office: Religion Am Life 12141 Lewis St Garden Grove CA 92840-4627

SCHULMAN, ALAN MICHAEL, small business owner; b. Chgo., Feb. 5, 1946; s. Aaron and Anne Schulman; m. Barbara Picard, May 27, 1984; 1 child, Jeffrey. BBA, Roosevelt U., 1968. Salesman Dictaphone Corp., Chgo., 1968-69; sales engr. Boston Gear, Chgo., 1969-70, mgr. Imperial Packaging, Chgo., 1970-71; owner A.M.S. Distbg., Skokie, Ill., 1971-77; owner, pres. Greater Distbn. Svcs., Glenview, Ill., 1977-90, The Battery Bank div. Jalco, Inc., Glenview, 1982-92, Glentronics Inc., Glenview, 1989—. Host TV gardening program. Author (newspaper column) Gardening Information, 1980; host numerous TV fishing programs; contbr. articles on battery to nat. mags.; patentee in field; subject of mag., newspaper articles; appearances in nat. radio program Home Improvement U.S.A.; inventor in field. Named to, Freshwater Fishing Hall of Fame for world record catch, U. Ill. Chgo. Entrepreneurship Hall of Fame, 2003. Mem. Entrepreneurs Network. Clubs: Men's Garden of North Shore (Highland Park) (pres. 1984-85). Achievements include inventing basement watchdog pumps, socklight drawer lights, timely lighting care, plant light. Office: 1150 Willis Ave Wheeling IL 60090-5817

SCHULMAN, HAROLD, obstetrician, gynecologist, perinatologist; b. Newark, Oct. 26, 1930; m. Rosemarie Vincenti; childrne: Stanley H., Sandra C., Gina M. BS, U. Fla., 1951; MD, Emory U., 1955. Diplomate Am. Bd. Ob-Gyn., Am. Bd. Maternal and Fetal Medicine; registered diagnostic med. sonographer. Intern Jackson Meml. Hosp., Miami, Fla., 1955-56, resident, 1958-61; instr. dept. ob-gyn. U. Miami (Fla.) Sch. Medicine, 1961; instr., asst. prof. dept. ob-gyn. Temple U. Sch. Medicine, Phila., 1961-65; asst. prof. dept. ob-gyn. Albert Einstein Coll. Medicine, Bronx, 1965-67, assoc. prof., 1968-71, prof., 1971—, acting dept. chmn., 1972-73, chmn., 1973-80; assoc. dir. dept. ob-gyn Bronx Mcpl. Hosp. Ctr., 1967-70, dep. dir., 1970-72; chmn. dept. ob-gyn. Winthrop U. Hosp., Mineola, N.Y., 1984-93; prof. ob-gyn SUNY, Stony Brook, 1984-93; chmn. dept. ob-gyn. Lawnwood Regional Med. Ctr., Ft. Pierce, FL, 1995-2000. Author: Tipping the Scales, 2004; contbr. articles to profl. publs. Served to capt. U.S. Army, 1956-58. Am. Cancer Soc. fellow, 1959-60; USPHS trainee, 1965-66 Fellow ACOG (vice chmn. Dist. II 1972-75); mem. Bronx County Obstet. Soc. (pres. 1974), AAAS, Obstet. Soc. (sec. 1978-80, pres. 1982-83), N.Y. Obstetrical Soc., Soc. Maternal Fetal Medicine, Am. Gynecologic and Obstetric Soc., Am. Gynecol. Obstetrics, N.Y. Obstetics Soc. (pres. 1982), Phi Beta Kappa, Alpha Omega Alpha; hon. mem. Miami Ob-Gyn. Soc., South Atlantic Obstetricians and Gynecologists Soc., Buffalo Gynecologic and Obstetric Soc. (E.G. Winkler meml. lectr.), Croatian Ultrasound Soc. (hon.). Democrat. Jewish.

SCHULMAN, HEIDI, broadcast executive; married; 1 child. BA in Govt., Barnard Coll., 1968. Corr. NBC News, L.A., 1978-90; programming cons. U.S. Info. Agys. Worldnet Television, Washington, 1993-96; dir. Corp. Pub. Broadcasting, Washington, 1996—. Writer, anchor UFWB and KPOL radio, L.A., KCBS Newsradio, San Francisco. Recipient Emmy award, 1994. Office: Corp Pub Broadcasting 901 E St NW Ste 300 Washington DC 20004-2012

SCHULMAN, JOSEPH DANIEL, physician, health company administrator, medical geneticist, reproductive biologist, educator; b. Bklyn., Dec. 20, 1941; s. Max and Miriam (Grossman) S.; m. Dixie A. King; children: Erica N., Julie K. BA, Bklyn. Coll., 1961; MD, Harvard U., 1966. Diplomate Am. Bd. Pediat., Am. Bd. Ob-Gyn., Am. Bd. Med. Genetics. Intern, then resident in pediat. Mass. Gen. Hosp., Boston, 1966-68; clin. assoc. Nat. Inst. Arthritis and Metabolic Diseases, 1968-70; resident in obstetrics and gynecology and fellow in pediatrics N.Y. Hosp.-Cornell Med. Ctr., 1970-73; Gilbert and Nat. Found. fellow Cambridge (Eng.) U., 1973-74; head sect. human biochem. genetics Nat. Inst. Child Health and Human Devel., NIH, Bethesda, Md., 1974-83; dir. med. genetics program NIH, Bethesda, 1979-1983; prof. ob-gyn., pediat., genetics George Washington U., 1983-84; CEO Genetics & IVF Inst., Fairfax, Va., 1984-98; chmn., med. dir. Genetics & IVF, Inc., Bethesda, Md., 1984—; prof. human genetics, pediat., ob-gyn. Med. Coll. Va., 1984—; with dept. ob-gyn. Fairfax Hosp., 1984—. Advisor to numerous govt. and private agys. Author 3 books; contbr. numerous articles to med. jours.; editorial bd. Molecular Human Reproduction, 1995—. With USPHS, 1968-70, 74-83. Fellow ACOG; mem. Soc. Pediat. Rsch., Soc. Gynecologic Investigation, Am. Soc. Clin. Investigation, Am. Soc. Human Genetics, Am. Fertility Soc., Harvard Club, Cosmos Club, Phi Beta Kappa, Sigma Xi. Office: 3020 Javier Rd Fairfax VA 22031-4609

SCHULMAN, MARK ALLEN, market research company executive; b. Phila., Nov. 15, 1945; s. Morris and Ida (Dunn) S. AB, Washington Coll., Chestertown, Md., 1967; MA, U. Wis., 1968; PhD, Rutgers U., 1980. Dir., div. experimental studies U. Md. Ea. Shore, Princess Anne, Md., 1972-75; sr. project dir. Eagleton Inst. Poll Rutgers U., New Brunswick, N.J., 1975-77; sr. v.p. Louis Harris and Assocs., Inc., N.Y.C., 1977-81; pres. Schulman, Ronca & Bucuvalas, Inc., N.Y.C., 1981—. Mem. bd. visitors and govs. Washington Coll., 1999—; bd. dirs. New Sch. Univ. Jazz Program, 1997—. Mem. Am. Assn. Pub. Opinion Rsch. (pres. N.Y. chpt. 1994-95, sec./treas. 1997-98, conf. chair 1999-2000, pres 2002—), Coun. of Am. Survey Rsch. Orgns. (bd. 2000—). Office: Schulman Ronca & Bucuvalas Inc 145 E 32nd St New York NY 10016-6055

SCHULMAN, ROBERT S. lawyer; b. N.Y.C., July 9, 1941; s. Donald Benedict and Edythe (Smythe) S.; m. Susan Jan Von Helbig, Sept. 18, 1974; children: Elizabeth Jane, Jennifer Lynn. BA, Rutgers U., New Brunswick, 1963; JD cum laude, Rutgers U., Newark, 1966. Bar: N.J. 1967, Calif. 1976, U.S. Dist. Ct. N.J. 1967, U.S. Supreme Ct. 1970, U.S. Dist. Cts. (ctrl., no., so., ea., dists.) Calif. 1976, U.S. Ct. Appeals (9th cir.) Calif. 1976. With Pitney, Hardin & Kipp, Newark, N.J., 1966-74; dept. atty. gen. Office of N.J. Atty. Gen., Trenton, N.J., 1974-75; assoc. Cox, Castle & Nicholson, L.A., 1976-80; ptnr. Zobrist, Garner & Garrett, L.A., 1980-83, Stephens, Berg, Lasater & Schulman, L.A., 1984-91, Crosby, Heafey, Roach & May, L.A., 1991—. Atty. Bd. of Edn., Fairview, N.J., 1972, Bd. of Adjustment, Fairview, N.J., 1971-73. Contbr. articles to profl. jours. Dir. Deafwest Theatre, L.A., Calif., 1991-97. Mem. State Bar of Calif., Calif. Club. Republican. Congregationalist. Home: 905 Wiladonda Dr La Canada Flintridge CA 91011-3825 Office: Crosby Heafey Roach & May 355 S Grand Ave 29th Fl Los Angeles CA 90071

SCHULMAN, RUTH MERYL ARONSON, development director; d. Robert Jack and Joan Rae (Ginsburg) Aronson; m. Michael Andrew Schulman, June 16, 1985; 1 child, Zachary David. BA, SUNY at Postdam, Potsdam, NY, 1977—81. Dir. of devel. Animal Protective Found., Scotia, NY, 2001—; dir. of resource devel. United Way of Schenectady County, Schenectady, NY, 2000—01; dir. of annu. giving United Jewish Fedn. of Northeastern NY, Latham, NY, 1996—99; asst. dir. of devel. Equinox, Inc., Albany, NY, 1999—2000; interim regional dir./asst. to the dir./interim edn. coord. Anti-Defamation League, NY State Regional Office, Albany, NY, 1987—96. Bd. dirs. So. Saratoga YMCA, 2004—. Mem.: Gift Planning Group of Northeastern NY, Women In Devel. of Northeastern NY (bd. mem. 2003—), Assoc. of Fundraising Professionals, Hudson-Mohawk Chpt. (v.p. of programming 2002—). Home: 51 Grant Hill Court Clifton Park NY 12065 Office: Animal Protective Foundation 53 Maple Ave Scotia NY 12302 E-mail: schulman@animalprotective.org.

SCHULMAN, SIDNEY, neurologist, educator; b. Chgo., Mar. 1, 1923; s. Samuel E. and Ethel (Miller) S.; m. Mary Jean Diamond, June 17, 1945; children— Samuel E., Patricia, Daniel. BS, U. Chgo., 1944, MD, 1946. Asst. prof. neurology U. Chgo., 1952-57, assoc. prof., 1957-65, prof., 1965-75, Ellen C. Manning prof., divsn. biol. scis., 1975-93, Ellen C. Manning prof. emeritus, 1993—. Served with M.C. AUS, 1947-49. Mem. Am. Neurol. Assn., U. Chgo. Med. Alumni Assn. (pres. 1968-69), Chgo. Neurol. Soc. (pres. 1964-65) Home: Apt 9-C 5000 S East End Ave Chicago IL 60615-3140 Office: U Chgo Divsn Biol Scis CLI L633 (MC 7080) 5841 S Maryland Ave Chicago IL 60637

SCHULTE, BRUCE JOHN, lawyer; b. Burlington, Iowa, June 27, 1953; s. James Andrew and Julia Germaine S.; m. Mary E. Guest, July 1984 (div. Feb. 1995); children: James, John; m. Catherine Tobben, 2001. BA in Am. Studies, U. Notre Dame, 1975; JD, U. Iowa, 1978. Bar: Iowa 1978, U.S. Dist. Ct. (so. dist.) Iowa 1979, U.S. Ct. Appeals (8th cir.) 1982, Minn. 1988, U.S. Dist. Ct. Minn. 1988, Ill. 1989. Law clk. Justice K. David Harris Supreme Ct. Iowa, Des Moines, 1978-79; ptnr. Dailey, Ruther, Bauer, Schulte & Hahn, Burlington, Iowa, 1979-87; atty. Bennett, Ingvaldson & McInerny, Mpls., 1988; gen. counsel Blackwood Corp., St. Paul, 1988-89; publs. editor Nat. Inst. for Trial Advocacy-U. Notre Dame, Ind., 1989-91; asst. dean pub. affairs Chgo. (Ill.) Kent Coll. Law, 1991-94; dep. dir. assoc. rels. West Pub., Eagan, Minn., 1995-97; dir. mktg., v.p. acad. consulting Performance Comm. Group, Chgo., 1997-2001; cons. BJS Assocs., Evanston, Ill., 2001—. Key person com. ATLA, 1984-88; mem. commn. on jud. dists. Supreme Ct. Iowa, 1987-88; cons. in field. Author: Persuasive Expert Testimony, 1990, Laser Disc Technology in the Courtroom, 1990; editor: Cases and Materials on Evidence, 1991, Modern State and Federal Evidence, 1991, Problems and Cases for Legal Writing, 1991. State ctrl. com. Iowa Dem. party, 1981-88; devel. com. Frances Xavier Ward Sch., Chgo., 1993-95; cmty. task force Chgo. (Ill.) Downtown Circulator Project, 1994-96; v.p. pub. affairs U. Notre Dame Alumni Class of 1975; mem. adv. coun. Coleman Ctr. Entrepreneurship DePaul U., 2003—; publs. com. Nat. Law Firm Mktg. Assn., 1993-94. Notre Dame scholar U. Notre Dame, Ind., 1971-72; recipient Spectra award Internat. Assn. Bus. Communicators, 1993, Silver Trumpet, Publicity Club Chgo., 1994. Mem. ABA (mem. tech. com. lawyers conf. jud. adminstrn. divsn. 1995-2000, vice chair task force on image of judiciary 2000-01), Ill. Bar Assn. (mem. standing com. legal edn. and admission to bar 1993-97), Chgo. Bar Assn. (mem. law office tech. com. 1995-97), Assn. Am. Law Schs., Chgo. Pub. Rels. Forum (treas. 1997), Notre Dame Club Chgo. (co-chair Hesburgh Forum com. 1993-98, trustee 1995-98, sec. 1997-98), Nat. Soc. Fundraising Profls. (cert. fundraising profl., Midwest conf. steering com. 1997-99), Execs. Club of Chgo. (co-chair standing com. on edn. and pub. svc.). Avocations: sailing, choir, gardening, skiing. Home: 816 Main St Evanston IL 60202-1706 Personal E-mail: brucejschulte@aol.com.

SCHULTE, DAVID MICHAEL, investment banker; b. N.Y.C., Nov. 12, 1946; s. Irving and Ruth (Stein) S.; m. Patricia Gordon, Sept. 5, 1999; children: Michael B., Katherine F. BA, Williams Coll., 1968; postgrad., Exeter Coll., Oxford (Eng.) U., 1968-69; JD, Yale U., 1972. Bar: D.C. 1973. Law clk. to Mr. Justice Stewart, U.S. Supreme Ct., 1972-73; spl. asst. to pres. N.W. Industries, Inc., Chgo., 1973-75, v.p. corp. devel., 1975-79, exec. v.p., 1979-80; sr. v.p. Salomon Bros., Chgo., 1980-84; mng. ptnr. Chilmark Ptnrs., Chgo., 1984—. Editor-in-chief: Yale Law Jour, 1971-72. John E. Moody scholar Exeter Coll., Oxford U., 1968-69. Mem. Washington Bar Assn., Chgo. Club, Racquet Club, Bryn Mawr Country Club, Vineyard Golf Club. Office: Chilmark Ptnrs 875 N Michigan Ave Ste 3460 Chicago IL 60611-1957

SCHULTE, FRANCIS B. retired archbishop; b. Phila., Dec. 23, 1926; Grad., St. Charles Borromeo Sem. Ordained priest Roman Cath. Ch., 1952. Apptd. titular bishop of Afufenia and aux. bishop of Phila., 1981—85; bishop Wheeling-Charleston, W.Va., 1985—88; archbishop New Orleans, 1989—2002. Office: c/o 7887 Walmsley Ave New Orleans LA 70125-3431

SCHULTE, FREDERICK JAMES, newpaper editor; b. Mpls., June 6, 1952; s. Philip William and Katherine Schulte. BA, U. Va., 1974. News reporter Internat. Med. News Group, Washington, 1976-78; med. writer, gen. assignment reporter Sun-Sentinel, Ft. Lauderdale, Fla., 1978-83, investigative team leader, 1983-88, asst. regional editor, 1988-90, investigations editor, 1990—. Author: Fleeced! Telemarketing Rip-Offs and How to Avoid Them., 1995. Recipient Excellence in Med. Journalism award Fla. Med. Assn., 1983, 1st Pl. Investigative Reporting award Fla. Press Club, 1983, 1st Pl. Sustained Coverage award Inland Daily Press Assn., 1983, Non-deadlin Reporting prize Sigma Delta Chi, 1983, Green Eyeshade award Sigma Delta Chi, 1983, 1st Pl. Pub. Svc. award Fla. Press Club, 1986, 87, 89, 90, Media Merit award Assn. Trial Lawyers Am., 1986, 1st Pl. award Big Bros./Big Sisters Am., 1987, 1st Pl. Pub. Svc. award Fla. Soc. Newspaper Editors, 1987, Children's Express Journalism award, 1987, 1st Pl. Investigative Reporting award Unity Awards in Media, 1987, Pulitzer Prize finalist, 1987, Worth Bingham Meml. Fund prize, 1989, 96, Freedom of Info. award AP Mng. Editors Assn., 1990, Lowell Thomas award, 1992, John Hancock award, 1992, Silver Gavel award ABA, 1992, Depth Reporting award Fla. Soc. Newpaper Editors, 1993, Pub. Affairs/Social Issues Reporting award Unity Awards in Media, 1993, George Polk award L.I. U., 1993, Gerald Loeb award U. Calif., 1994; Pulitzer prize finalist for beat reporting, 1996, investigative reporting, 1999; Alicia Patterson Found. fellow, 1997. Mem. Investigative Reporters and Editors (S.E. regional coord., Disting. Investigative Reporting award 1985). Office: Sun-Sentinel 200 E Las Olas Blvd Ste 1000 Fort Lauderdale FL 33301-2293

SCHULTE, JEFFREY LEWIS, lawyer; b. N.Y.C., July 24, 1949; s. Irving and Ruth (Stein) S.; m. Elizabeth Ewan Kaiser, Aug. 13, 1977; children: Andrew Riggs, Ian Garretson, Elizabeth Alexandra. BA, Williams Coll., 1971; postgrad., Harvard U., 1971-72; JD, Yale U., 1976. Bar: Pa. 1978, Ga. 1993. Law clk. to hon. John J. Gibbons U.S. Ct. Appeals (3d cir.), Newark, 1976-77; assoc. Schnader, Harrison, Segal & Lewis, Phila., 1977-84, ptnr., 1985-92, founding ptnr. Atlanta, 1992-98, exec. com., 1994-98; ptnr. Morris, Manning & Martin, Atlanta, 1998—. Nat. steering com. lawyers com. to end "Pay-to-Play."; bd. adv. Cole Sch. Bus. Kennesaw State U. Contbr. articles to profl. jours. Mem.: ABA, Bus. and Tech. Alliance, Atlanta Venture Forum, Atlanta Bar Assn. (chmn. comm. and media rels. com.), Phila. Bar Assn., State Bar Ga., Pa. Bar Assn., Weekapaug Tennis Club, Yale Club of Ga. (bd. dirs. 1996—2002, pres. 2000—01, chmn. of bd. 2001—02), Weekapaug Yacht Club R.I., Williams Club N.Y.C., Williams Club Atlanta, Merion Cricket Club, Phi Beta Kappa. Office: Morris Manning & Martin Atlanta Financial Center 3343 Peachtree Rd NE Ste 1600 Atlanta GA 30326-1044 E-mail: jls@mmmlaw.com.

SCHULTE, STEPHEN CHARLES, lawyer; b. Evanston, Ill., June 26, 1952; s. George John and Mary Ruth (Lamping) S.; m. Kathleen Ann O'Donnell, Sept. 4, 1982; children: Kate, Maureen, John. BA magna cum laude, St. Louis U., 1973, JD, 1976. Bar: Ill. 1976, U.S. Dist. Ct. (no. dist.) Ill. 1976, U.S. Ct. Appeals (7th cir.) 1991. Atty. Perz & McGuire, Chgo., 1976-83; ptnr. Winston & Strawn, Chgo., 1983—. Founder, bd. dirs. Greater Orgn. for Less Fortunate (GOLF), Chgo., 1982—; fundraiser for Maryville Acad.; mem. Glenview Park Dist. Commn., 1989—, v.p., 1991-92, 98-99, pres., 1992-93, 99-2000. Mem. ABA, Ill. State Bar Assn., Chgo. Bar Assn., Ill. Trial Lawyers Assn., Ill. Assn. Def. Trial Counsel, Chgo. Vol. Legal Svcs., Nat. Legal Aid Defender Assn., Phi Beta Kappa. Avocations: basketball, baseball, golf, music, travel. Home: 941 Club Cir Glenview IL 60025-3101 Office: Winston & Strawn 35 W Wacker Dr Ste 4200 Chicago IL 60601-1695 E-mail: sschulte@winston.com.

SCHULTESS, LEROY KENNETH, lawyer, consultant; b. Garrett, Ind., May 7, 1907; s. George Mathias and Elizabeth (Lehmbeck) S.; m. Sarah Mildred Atwater, Apr. 28, 1942. AB, Mich. U., 1929; JD, Northwestern U., 1932. Bar: Ind. 1933. Practice law, LaGrange, Ind.; pres. Creek Chub Bait Co., Garrett, Lure, Inc., Garrett; hon. dir. Farmers State Bank, LaGrange. Recipient Meritorious awards Farmers State Bank, VFW, Boy Scouts Am., Am. Lung Assn. Mem. U. Mich. Alumni Assn., LaGrange C. of C., ABA, Ind. Bar Assn. (Golden Anniversary award), LaGrange County Bar Assn. (Outstanding and Dedicated Svc. awards), Sigma Chi, Phi Delta Phi, Rotary (LaGrange) (pres. 1956-7), LaGrange Country. Lodges: Shriners, Masons. Office: Farmers State Bank Bldg 220 S Detroit St Lagrange IN 46761-1808

SCHULTHEIS, ADAM JOHN, music educator, consultant; b. Quebec City, Que., Canada, Apr. 23, 1962; s. August Thomas and Joan Helen Schultheis; m. Cynthia Anne Forcey, Dec. 14, 1995; children: Johnathon Michael Bohnet, Caroline Emily, Thomas Gabriel, Christopher Addison, Aidan Patrick. *Father, August Thomas Schultheis, and mother, Joan Helen Kunca, were both WWII Veterans. Father was a private First Class in the 5th Army during WWII who received the following decorations: Purple Heart, Bronze Star, European-African-Middle Eastern Campaign Medal, WWII Victory Medal, Army of Occupation Medal, Combat Infantryman Badge, and Marksman Badge with Rifle Bar. Father was one of the first Americans to liberate Rome, Italy. Mother was a Second Lieutenant Nurse stateside for the Army Air Corps. She received the WWII Victory Medal. Wife Cynthia has numerous poems that have been deeply influential.* MusB in Edn., U. Ariz., Tucson, 1980—86; MS, Nova U., Ft. Lauderdale, Fla., 1987—89. Cert. elem. tchr. Nev. Orch. tchr. McCall Elem. Sch., North Las Vegas, 1986—92, Orr Mid. Sch., Las Vegas, 1992—97, Boulder City H.S., Nev., 1997—. Music leader, cons. Boy Scouts of Am., Boulder City, Nev., 1998—; hon. composer Vincennes U., Ind., 2000—; advisor U.S. Jr. Congl. Leadership Conf., Washington, 2001—. *This 19-year teacher veteran was a music scholarship winner from the University of Arizona, 1980, founded the string program in Boulder City, NV (1997) with 37 students, peaking at 180 middle and high school students in 2003. Founder of Boulder City Hometown Fiddlers, a non-profit student fiddler organization that performs for patriotic events/parades. This fiddle group is one of a few in the U.S. that perform in parades on electrical string instruments. Schultheis has received presidential, senatorial, congressional, gubernatorial, and mayoral commendations/recognitions for his volunteer work with the fiddle group. Only Boulder City teacher to receive Disney's American Teacher Award, 1999.* Founder, dir. Boulder City Hometown Fiddlers, Nev., 1999—2004; vol. Make A Difference Day Found., Las Vegas, 1999—2004. Named to, Clark County Sch. Dist.'s Hall of Fame, Las Vegas, 2001; recipient Disney Am. Tchr. Honoree, Disney Corp., 1999, Music For 1000 Children Award, U. Hartford, Hart Sch. Music, 2002, Achievement in Edn award, Rotary Club, Boulder, City, Nev., 2001, Placed on Wall of Tolerance, San Francisco State U., 2004; grantee Arts in the Cmty., Target Edn. Found., 2002, 2003, 2004; Cuban Music fellow, San Francisco State U., 2001. Mem.: Sons of the Am. Legion, Am. String Tchr. Assn. (life; advisor, cons. 1986—2003), Music Tchr. Nat. Assn. (life), KC, Valley Forge Freedom Found. (hon. Past George Washington Honor Medal Winner 2001). Conservative. Achievements include being Nevada's only participant in the 2001 National Independence Day Parade, Washington, D.C; being Nevada's only music participant in National World War Two Memorial Dedication, Washington, 2004. Avocations: fiddling, woodworking, gardening, hiking. Home: 1327 Bayleaf Terr Ave Henderson NV 89014 Office: Boulder City HSl 1101 Fifth St Boulder City NV 89005 Office Phone: 702-799-8200. Personal E-mail: adamschultheis@cox.net.

SCHULTHEIS, EDWIN MILFORD, dean, business educator; b. N.Y.C., Apr. 15, 1928; s. Milford Theodore and Lillian May (Hill) S.; m. Joan Edna Bruckner, June 23, 1956. BS, Hofstra Coll., 1950; MBA, NYU, 1958, EdD, 1972. Officer mgr., sales rep. Topton Rug Mfg. Co., N.Y.C., 1950-54; area mgr., trainer Mobil Oil Co., N.Y.C., 1954-62; coord. distributive edn. North Babylon (N.Y.) Pub. Schs., 1962-88, chmn. bus. mktg. and indsl. edn. depts., 1988-91; prof. bus. adminstrn. SUNY, Farmingdale, 1970-91; asst. prof. edn. NYU, 1973—; dir. edn. Syracuse (N.Y.) U., 1973-78; chmn. dept. bus. adminstrn. Five Towns Coll., Seaford, N.Y., 1991-92, divsn. chmn. bus. and tech. Dix Hills, N.Y., 1992-98, dean instrn., 1993-98, dep. dean of faculty, 1993-98, assoc. dean, 1996-97, prof. emeritus, 1998—. Test writer, cons. N.Y. State Dept. Edn., Albany, 1965—; textbook reviewer McGraw-Hill Book Co., N.Y.C., 1967-69; cons. Cornell U., 1975; dist. adviser Distributive Edn. Clubs N.Y., 1970, bd. govs., trustee, 1975-78; mem. curriculum adv. coun. Suffolk County (N.Y.) Distributive Edn. Assn., 1967—. Author: Modern Petroleum Marketing, 1971, Content and Structure of Belief-Disbelief Systems, 1972. Elder Presbyn. Ch., U.S.A. Named N.Y. State Tchr. of Yr., 1976, Outstanding Tchr. in N.Y. State, 1978; recipient Outstanding Svc. award Distributive Edn. Clubs N.Y., Suffolk County Distributive Edn. Assn., Tchr. Excellence award N.Y. State, 1980, Citation for Excellence in Edn. Gov. Mario Cuomo N.Y., 1991, Citation Excellence in Teaching Babylon Twp., 1991. Mem. Acad. Mgmt., Am. Petroleum Inst., Am. Security Coun., Suffolk County Assn. Distributive Edn. Tchrs. (mem. exec. bd. 1962-74), N.Y. State (pres. 1975-78), L.I. Distributive Edn. Assns. (hon. life, exec. bd. 1972-75), N.Y. State Occupl. Edn. Assn. (v.p. 1975-78), L.I. Bus. Edn. Chmns. Assn. (hon. life, exec. bd. 1972-75), N.Y. State Occupl. Edn. Assn. (v.p. 1975-78), L.I. Bus. Edn. Chmns. Assn. (hon. life), Distributive Edn. Clubs Am. (regional leader 1972-75, hon. life 1991), Bellport (N.Y.) Golf Club, Phi Delta Kappa, Kappa Delta Pi, Sigma Alpha Lambda, Phi Sigma Eta. Presbyterian (ordained ruling elder). Home: 14 Thorn Hedge Rd Bellport NY 11713-2616

SCHULTIS, GAIL ANN, library director; b. Freeport, Ill., May 12, 1951; d. Richard C. and Ida G. Schultis. BA, Cornell Coll., 1973; MLS, U. Mo., 1976; MA, U. Tex., San Antonio, 1989. Reference libr. U. Tex., San Antonio, 1976-79, El Paso, 1979-84, 89, head access svcs., 1984-88; reference libr. Park U., Parkville, Mo., 1989-96, dir. libr. sys., 1996—. Co-author: Best Self-Help & Self-Awareness Books, 1995. Mem. ALA, Am. Hist. Assn., Orgn. Am. Historians. Home: 10307 NW 57th Ter Parkville MO 64152-3396 Office: Park Univ Libr 8700 NW River Park Dr Parkville MO 64152-4358 Office Phone: 816-584-6704. Business E-Mail: ann.schultis@park.edu.

SCHULTZ, ALBERT BARRY, engineering educator; b. Phila., Oct. 10, 1933; s. George D. and Belle (Seidman) S.; m. Susan Resnikov, Aug. 25, 1955; children: Carl, Adam, Robin BS, U. Rochester, 1955; M.Engring., Yale U., 1959, PhD, 1962. Asst. prof. U. Del., Newark, 1962-65; asst. prof. U. Ill., Chgo., 1965-66, assoc. prof., 1966-71, prof., 1971-83; Vennema prof. U. Mich., Ann Arbor, 1983-99. Contbr. numerous articles to profl. jours. Served to lt. USN, 1955-58 Rsch. Career award NIH, 1975-80; Javits Neurosci. Investigator award NIH, 1985-92 Mem. NAE, Internat. Soc. for Study Lumbar Spine (pres. 1981-82), ASME (chmn. bioengring. div. 1981-82, H.R. Lissner award 1990), Am. Soc. Biomechanics (pres. 1982-83, Borelli award 1996), U.S. Nat. Com. on Biomechanics (chmn. 1982-85), Phi Beta Kappa

SCHULTZ, ARTHUR JOSEPH, JR., retired trade association executive; b. Detroit, June 20, 1918; s. Arthur Joseph and Olive U. (Beauchesne) S.; m. Barbara Farnan, Aug. 20, 1942; children: Arthur, Robert, William, Barbara, John, Karen. Student, U. Detroit, 1937-39, Naval Line Sch., 1947-48, Naval War Coll., 1956-57, Brookings Inst., 1962. Commd. ensign USN, 1940, advanced through grades to capt., 1950, comdg. officer Com. Strike/S. NATO, 1959-61, comdg. officer Naval Air Sta. Grosse Ile, Mich., 1961-63, ret., 1963; pres. Chrysler Corps. subs., Highland Park, Mich., 1971-75; dep. adminstr. VA, Washington, 1975-77; pres. Steel Shipping Container Inst., Union, N.J., 1977-89; ret., 1989. V.p. Detroit Aviation Commn., 1968-77; bd. dirs. United Way Union County, Elizabeth, N.J., 1981-85, sec.-treas., 1983-85; chmn. Hazardous Materials Adv. Com., Washington, 1984-85. Decorated Navy Cross; recipient Meritorious Svc. award VA, 1977. Mem. Am. Soc. Assn. Execs., Soc. Automotive Engrs., Mil. Order World Wars, St. Andrew Soc. Sarasota (pres.), Boca Royale Golf and Country Club (Fla.). Republican. Roman Catholic. Home: 51032 Dequindre Rd Shelby Township MI 48317-1020

SCHULTZ, ARTHUR LEROY, clergyman, educator; b. Johnstown, Pa., June 14, 1928; s. Elmer Albert Robert and Alice Lizetta (Flegal) S.; m. Mildred Louise Stouffer, Nov. 29, 1948; children: Thomas Arthur, Rebecca Louise. BA, Otterbein Coll., 1949; MDiv, United Theol. Sem., 1952; MEd, U. Pitts., 1955, PhD, 1963. Sr. min. Albright United Meth. Ch., Pitts., 1952-56; dir. pub. rels. Otterbein Coll., Westerville, Ohio, 1956-65, adj. prof. religion and philosophy, 1990-98; pres. Albright Coll., Reading, Pa., 1965-77, Ashland (Ohio) Coll., 1977-80; exec. dir. Cen. Ohio Radio Reading Svc., Columbus, 1980-84; parish min. Ch. Master United Meth., Westerville, 1984-89; min. of visitation Ch. Messiah United Meth., Westerville, 1991—2002. Pres. Pa. Assn. Colls. & Univs., Harrisburg, 1974-75. Trustee Reading Hosp., 1967-77,

Wyoming Sem., Kingston, Pa., 1971-80; v.p. Found. for Ind. Colls. Pa., Harrisburg, 1972-73; pres. Pa. Coun. on Alcohol Problems, Harrisburg, 1968-76; pres. Westerville (Ohio) Hist. Soc., 1986-89, Westerville Area Ministerial Assn., 1992-93. Named Outstanding Young Man of the Year Jr. C. of C., Westerville, Ohio, 1960. Mem. Brookstone Cmty. Assn. (sec. bd. trustees 1994-99, v.p. 1999-2000), Rotary (charter pres. 1959, dist. gov. 1965-66, dist. sec.-treas. 1982-93), Masons, Shriners, Torch Club. Republican. Methodist. Avocations: collecting post cards, golf, tennis, travel. Home: 151 Sandstone Loop W Westerville OH 43081-4599

SCHULTZ, ARTHUR WARREN, communications company executive; b. NYC, Jan. 13, 1922; s. Milton Warren and Genevieve (Dann) S.; m. Elizabeth Carroll Mahan, 1949 (div. 1987); children: Arthur Warren, John Carroll (dec.), Julia Hollingsworth; m. Susan Keefe, 1988. Grad., U. Chgo.; DLitt (hon.), Rosary Coll. With Foote, Cone & Belding Comms., Chgo., 1948-82, v.p., 1957-63, sr. v.p., dir., 1963-69, exec. v.p., 1969, chmn. bd., CEO, 1970-81, chmn. exec. com., CEO, 1981-82; dir. Chgo. Sun-Times Co.; vice chmn. Chgo. Sun-Times Newspaper Co., 1989-94. Lectr. in field. Author: In Praise of America's Collectors, 1997; co-author: Valley Club of Montecito, 1999; editor Caring for Your Collections, 1992. Pres. Cook County Sch. Nursing, 1963-64, Welfare Coun. Met. Chgo., 1965-67; mem. bus. adv. coun. Urban League Chgo., 1971-82; chmn. Nat. Com. to Save Am.'s Cultural Collections, 1990-94; mem. Pres.'s Com. Arts and Humanities, 1984-93; bd. dirs. Chgo. Crime Commn., 1965-71, Cmty. Fund Chgo., 1966-67, Better Bus. Bur., 1970-78, Lyric Opera Chgo., 1967-77, Chgo. Coun. Fgn. Rels., 1977-86, Chgo. Pub. TV, 1978-82, Chgo. Central Area Com., 1978-82; mem. millennium Com. to Save Am.'s Treasures, 1998; trustee YWCA, 1962-74, Calif. Coll. Arts & Crafts, 1985-87; trustee Art Inst. Chgo., 1975-2002, chmn. bd., 1981-84; trustee U. Chgo., 1977—, Santa Barbara Mus. Art, 1988—, pres., 1989-92. 1st lt. USAF, 1943-45. Recipient Alumni Svc. award U. Chgo., 1986. Mem. Am. Assn. Advt. Agys. (dir. 1968-71, 74-76, chmn. Chgo. coun. 1964-65, chmn. Ctrl. region 1970-71), Comml. Club, Valley Club (Montecito, Calif.), Delta Kappa Epsilon. Roman Catholic. Home and Office: 2072 China Flat Rd Santa Barbara CA 93108-2211

SCHULTZ, CARL HERBERT, real estate management and development company executive; b. Chgo., Jan. 9, 1925; s. Herbert V. and Olga (Swanson) S.; m. Helen Ann Stevesson, June 6, 1948; children: Mark Carl, Julia Ann. BS in Gen. Engring., Iowa State U., 1948. With Schultz Bros. Co., 1948—, mdse. mgr. and store planner, 1962-70, v.p. Lake Zurich, Ill., 1968-72, pres., 1972-2000; chmn., 2000—; pres. Ill. Schultz Bros. Co., Ind. Schultz Bros. Co., Iowa Schultz Bros. Co., Wis. Schultz Bros. Co.; chmn. Schultz Bros. Co., 2000—. Mem. Lake Bluff (Ill.) Zoning Bd. Appeals, 1976-85, chmn., 1978-85. Served with U.S. Army, 1944-46. Mem. Lake Zurich Indsl. Coun. (sec. 1976), Assn. Gen. Mdse. Chains (dir. 1975-86, exec. com. 1983-86, chmn. nat. conv. 1982), Ill. Retail Mchts. Assn. (dir. 1984-89), Wis. Retail Fedn. (dir. 1981-89) Clubs: Bath and Tennis (Lake Bluff). Presbyterian. Home: 701 E Center Ave Lake Bluff IL 60044-2607 Office: 815 Oakwood Rd Unit I Lake Zurich IL 60047

SCHULTZ, CLARENCE JOHN, minister; b. Morris Twp., Wis., Aug. 4, 1937; s. Clarence John Sr. and Ella Mae (Feavel) S.; m. Doroland Kay King, Aug. 24, 1957 (dec. Jan. 1974); children: Sharon Kay Braun, Susan May Schultz Rogers; m. Martha Ann Aylor, Apr. 5, 1975. BS, Bryan Coll., 1960. Ordained to ministry Conservative Congl. Ch., 1961. Min. 1st Congl. Ch., Herreid, S.D., 1961-66, Immanuel Evang. Congl. Ch., Sheboygan, Wis., 1966-77, Hope Congl. Ch., Superior, Wis., 1977-83, Zion Evang. Ch., Scottsbluff, Nebr., 1983-89, 1st Congl. Ch., Buffalo Center, Iowa, 1989-92, Kenosha, Wis., 1992-98, St. Lucas Cmty. Ch., Lake Elmo, Minn., 1998—. Mem. Conservative Congl. Christian Conf. (rec. sec. 1973-82, v.p. 1994-96, pres. 1996-99, Rocky Mountain area rep. 1987-89, endorser of chaplains 1988-2000, mem. credentials com. 1988--), Rotary (ch. chaplain com. 1993-95). Avocations: amateur radio, golf. Home and Office: 1195 Manning Ave N Lake Elmo MN 55042-9607 Personal E-mail: clarence.j.schultz@comcast.net.

SCHULTZ, DAVID A. political science educator, editor, writer, lawyer; b. Binghamton, N.Y., June 28, 1958; s. Fred L. and Margaret (Schuh) S.; m. Helene Levy, Sept. 10, 1982. BA, SUNY, Binghamton, 1980, MA, 1986, Rutgers U., 1982; PhD, U. Minn., 1989, JD, 1998. Bar: Minn. 1998. Dir. code enforcement City of Binghamton, 1982-84; planner Opportunities for Broome, Binghamton, 1984-86; prof. Gustavus Adolphus Coll., St. Peter, Minn., 1989-91, Trinity U., San Antonio, 1991-94, U. Minn., Mpls., 1995; prof. polit. sci. U. Wis., River Falls, 1996-99; prof. Hamline U. Grad. Sch. Pub. Adminstrn., 1999—. Adj. prof. Sch. of Law U. Minn., 1999—; adj. prof. Sch. Law U. St. Thomas, 2002—; editor Peter Lang Pub., N.Y.C., 1994—; lobbyist Common Cause Minn., St. Paul, 1994-99, pres., 1994-99. Author, editor: Law and Politics: Unanswered Questions, 1994,: Leveraging the Law, 1998, The Politics of Civil Service Reform, 1998; author: Inventors of Ideas, 1997, Jurisprudential Vision of Justice Antonin Scalia, 1996, It's Show Time! Media, Politics and Popular Culture, 2000, Encyclopedia of American Law, 2002, Money, Politics and Campaign Finance Reform in the States, 2002, Social Capital: Critical Perspectives on Community and Bowling Alone, 2002; author, editor: Invfentions of Ideas, 2de edit., 2003, Encyclopedia of Public Administration and PUblic Policy, 2003. V.p. Minn. Civil Liberties Union, Mpls., 1995, South Tex. ACLU, San Antonio, 1993-94, Lights, Camera, CAmpaign, Media Politics and Advertising, 2004. Mem. AAUP (pres. chpt. 1993-94). Avocations: tennis, running, cooking, gardening. Home: 1120 Saint Clair Ave Saint Paul MN 55105-2846 Office: Hamline U Grad Sch Pub Adminstrn MS-A1740 Saint Paul MN 55104 Office Phone: 651-523-2858. E-mail: DSchultz@hamline.edu.

SCHULTZ, DOUGLAS GEORGE, art museum director; b. Oakland, Calif., Oct. 3, 1947; s. Leon H. and Teresa (deMonte) S. AB, U. Calif., Berkeley, 1969, MA in History of Art, 1972; grad., Inst. Arts Adminstrn., Harvard U., 1971. Summer intern Nat. Gallery of Art, Washington, 1970; curatorial intern Albright-Knox Art Gallery, Buffalo, 1972, asst. curator, 1973-75, asso. curator, 1975-76, curator, 1977-79, chief curator, 1980-83, dir., 1983—. Adj. prof. art history SUNY, Buffalo, 1975-79; mem. adv. bd. Arts Council of Buffalo and Erie County 1975— Office: Albright-Knox Art Gallery 1285 Elmwood Ave Buffalo NY 14222-1096

SCHULTZ, E. EUGENE, JR., computer engineer; b. Chgo., Sept. 10, 1946; s. Earl Eugene and Elizabeth Claire Schultz; m. Cathy Brown Schultz, Aug. 9, 1975; children: Sarah Ardelle, Rachel Elizabeth, Leah Brown. BA, UCLA, 1968; MS, Purdue U., 1973, PhD, 1977. Cert. info. sys. security prof. Internat. Info. Sys. Security Cert. Consortium, info. security mgr. Info. Sys. Audit and Control Assn. Project leader, engr. Lawrence Livermore (Calif.) Nat. Lab., 1986—92; prin. Eugene Schultz and Assocs., Livermore, 1992—93; prin. security engr. ARCA Sys., San Jose, Calif., 1993—94; sr. cons. SRI Internat., Menlo Park, Calif., 1994—98; rsch. dir. Global Integrity Corp., Reston, Va., 1998—2001; prin. engr. Lawrence Berkeley (Calif.) Nat. Lab., 2001—. Adj. prof. Purdue U., West Lafayette, Ind., 1998—2001; mem. adv. bd. Recourse Techs., Redwood City, Calif., 1999—2002, ArcSight Corp., Sunnyvale, Calif., 2001—, Secure Soft, Carlsbad, Calif., 2003—. Author: Internet Security for Business, 1996, Windows NT/2000 Network Security, 2000, Incident Response, 2001, Intrusion Detection and Prevention, 2004; editor-in-chief: Computers and Security, 2002— (Golden Page award, 2003); contbr. articles to profl. jours. Active Livermore (Calif.) Vision 2000, 2001. Recipient Tech. Innovation award, NASA, 1986. Mem.: Info. Sys. Audit & Control Assn., Computer Security Inst., Info. Sys. Security Assn. (Profl. Contbn. award, Hall of Fame). Achievements include development of decluttering method for visual displays; founding the Department of Energy's Incident Response Team. Avocations: bicycling, travel. Home: 2587 Pienza St Livermore CA 94550 Office: Lawrence Berkeley Nat Lab 1 Cyclotron Rd Berkeley CA 94720

SCHULTZ, EILEEN HEDY, graphic designer; b. Yonkers, N.Y. d. Harry Arthur and Hedy Evelyn (Morchel) S. BFA, Sch. Visual Arts, 1955. Staff artist C.A. Parshall Studios, N.Y.C., 1955-57; editorial art dir. Paradise of the Pacific, Honolulu, 1957-58; graphic designer Adler Advt. Agy., N.Y.C., 1958-59; art dir. Good Housekeeping Mag., N.Y.C., 1959-82, creative dir. advt. and sales promotion, 1982-86; creative dir. Hearst Promo, 1986-87; pres. Design Internat., N.Y.C., 1987—. Creative dir. The Depository Trust Co., 1987-99. Art dir., editor, designer, 50th Art Directors Club Annual, 1973; columnist: Art Direction, 1969—. Dir. Sch. Visual Arts, N.Y.C., 1978—; trustee Sch. Art League, 1978—; advisor Fashion Inst. Tech., 1979—; adv. commn. N.Y.C. Cmty. Colls., 1979—. Named Fashion Inst. Tech. Ambassador of Good Will to Netherlands, 1955; recipient Outstanding Achievement Sch. Visual Arts Alumni Soc., 1976, Sch. Art League Youth award, 1976. Mem. Art Dirs. Club (pres. 1975-77), Soc. Illustrators (pres. 1991-93), Joint Ethics Com. (chmn. 1978-80), Am. Inst. Graphic Arts, Soc. Publ. Designers, Type Dirs. Club.

SCHULTZ, FRANKLIN M. retired law educator; b. Cin., June 16, 1917; s. Max and Goldie (Wise) S.; m. Jean Carol Barnett, Apr. 5, 1946 (dec. 1981); children: William B., John M., Katherine, Caroline; m. Virginia B. Henderson, Sept. 4, 1983 BA, Yale U., 1939, LLB, 1942. Bar: Ohio 1947, D.C. 1954, Mass. 1985, U.S. Supreme Ct. 1954. Atty. Fed. Power Commn., 1946-47; assoc. prof. Sch. Law, Ind. U., Bloomington, 1947-53; with firm Purcell & Nelson, Washington, 1953-80, ptnr., 1957-80, Reavis & McGrath, Washington, 1980-85; lawyer-in-residence Sch. Law, Washington and Lee U., 1985, vis. prof., 1991-94, ret., 1994; vis. prof. Sch. Law, U. Iowa, 1986-90. Lectr. Sch. Law, George Washington U., 1958-59; vis. prof. Sch. Law, U. Va., 1975; mem. ednl. appeal bd. U.S. Dept. Edn., 1974-82. Contbr. articles to profl. jours. Trustee Nantucket Land Coun., 1992—. Served to capt. AUS, 1942-46. Decorated Bronze stars. Mem. ABA (mem. council adminstrv. law sect. 1966-69, chmn. 1970-71, del. ho. of dels. 1972-74), D.C. Bar (gen. counsel 1977-79, mem. legal ethics com. 1976-81), Am. Law Inst., Am. Bar Found., Adminstrv. Conf. U.S. (council 1980-82) Home: PO Box 2414 Nantucket MA 02584-2414 E-mail: sinneton12@aol.com.

SCHULTZ, FREDERICK HENRY, investor, former government official; b. Jacksonville, Fla., Jan. 16, 1929; s. Clifford G. and Mae (Wangler) S.; m. Nancy Reilly, Aug., 1951; children: Catherine G., Frederick H., Clifford G., John R. BA, Princeton U., 1951; postgrad., U. Fla. Sch. Law, 1954-56. With Barnett Nat. Bank, Jacksonville, 1956-57; owner, operator investment firm, from 1957; mem. Fla. Ho. of Reps., 1963-70, speaker of the house, 1968-70; chmn. bd. Barnett Investment Svcs., Inc.; dir. Barnett Banks Inc., to 1979; vice chmn. bd. govs. Fed. Res. System, Washington, 1979-82. Bd. dirs. Wickes Lumber Co. Served to lt. U.S. Army, 1952-54, Korea Decorated Bronze Star Roman Catholic. Office: PO Box 1200 Jacksonville FL 32201-1200

SCHULTZ, GERALD ALFRED (JERRY SCHULTZ), retired chemicals executive; b. Lockport, NY, Jan. 22, 1941; s. Alfred Henry and Lucy Vivian (Proctor) S.;m. Barbara Joan Beals, July 13, 1962; 1 child, Amy Lynn Schultz-Kessler. AAS, Erie County Tech. Inst., Buffalo, 1961; BA in Chemistry, SUNY, Buffalo, 1969; postgrad., Harvard U., 1979. Rsch. technician Occidental Chem. Corp., Niagara Falls, NY, 1961—63; rsch. engr. Nat. Gypsum Co. Inc., Buffalo, 1963-66; from chemist, devel. mgr., gen. mgr. to v.p. Akzo Chems., Burt, N.Y. and Chgo., 1966-86; CEO VanDeMark Inc. subs. Groupe SNPE, Lockport, NY, 1986—2003; ret., 2003. Contbr. articles to profl. jours; patentee in field. Fund raiser United Way, Newfane, N.Y., 1982-84; treas., bd. dirs. Newfane Intercommunity Meml. Hosp., 1980-84; bd. dirs. ARC, Lockport, N.Y., 1980-84, 97-2000; mem. United Way Ea. Niagara Allocations Com., 1994-97. Mem. Am. Chem. Soc., Soc. Plastic Engrs., Soc. Plastics Industry (bd. dirs. 1974-76), Organic Peroxide Prodn. Safety Divsn. (chmn. 1974-76), Synthetic Organic Chem. Mfrs. Assn. (bd. dirs. 1991-94), Soc. Plastics Engrs., NY State Bus. Coun., NY State Chem. Alliance, Lockport Indsl. Coun. (treas. 1991-98), Ea. Niagara C. of C. (bd. dirs. 1992-95), Lockport Town and Country Club (bd. dirs. 1995-96), Olcott Yacht Club (past commr. 1975), Gateway Golf and Country Club. Republican. Episcopalian. Avocations: golf, gardening, computers, boating. Home: 12141 Hidden Links Dr Fort Myers FL 33913-8164 E-mail: g.schultz@snpe.com.

SCHULTZ, HARLEY, consulting company executive; b. NYC; s. William and Rose Diane Schultz. MBA, NYU, 1981. Pres. Harley Schultz & Assocs., Cons. in Mktg., Mgmt. and Internet Bus. Devel., Scarsdale, NY, 1987—. Mem. various charitable orgns. Avocations: sailing, golf, French literature, 19th-century art, classical music. Office: Harley Schultz & Assocs 130 Garth Rd # 250 Scarsdale NY 10583-3750 E-mail: harleyschultz@consultant.com.

SCHULTZ, HARRY, health science organization administrator; Dir. St. Boniface Gen. Hosp. Rsch. Ctr., Winnipeg, MB, Canada; chief innovation officer Winnipeg Regional Health Authority, Winnipeg. Office: Winnipeg Regional Health Authority 1800-155 Carlton St Winnipeg MB Canada R3C 4Y1

SCHULTZ, HARRY PERSHING, chemistry researcher, retired educator; b. Racine, Wis., Mar. 9, 1918; s. Harry Carl and Agnes (Olson) S.; m. Pearle Marie Henriksen, Sept. 25, 1943; children: Stephanie Schultz Buehler, Tor, Alison Schultz Mohns. BS summa cum laude, U. Wis., 1942, PhD, 1946. Rsch. chemist Nat. Def. Rsch. Coun., 1942-45, Merck & Co., Inc., Rahway, NJ, 1946-47; mem. faculty U. Miami, Coral Gables, Fla., 1947-91, prof. chemistry, 1952-84, chmn. chemisty dept., 1972-84, prof. emeritus, 1984—; rsch. chem. topology Big Horn, Wyo., 1991—. Vis. lectr. U. Wis., Madison, summer 1958; vis. prof. Mich. State U., East Lansing, summers 1960, 62; mem. adv. bd. Jour. Chem. Info. and Computer Scis., Washington, 1995-99. Author: (with Popp) Organic Chemical Preparation, 1964, (with Schultz) Sir Isaac Newton, 1972, (with others) Topology in Chemistry, 2001; contbr. numerous articles to profl. jours. Mem. Planning Commn., South Miami, Fla., 1951-55; mem. bd. trustees Sheridan Pub. Libr., 2002—. Grantee NIH, Walter Reed Army Inst. Rsch., Phi Beta Kappa, Sigma Xi, Phi Lambda Upsilon, Phi Kappa Phi, among others. Mem. Am. Chem. Soc. (chmn. Fla. sect. 1964, gen. chmn. 153rd nat. conf. 1967, councilor 1974-77, Fla. award 1986), Lions Club. Avocations: swimming, civil war memorabilia. Home: PO Box 262 Big Horn WY 82833

SCHULTZ, HELEN WELKLEY, marriage and family therapist, minister; b. Rochester, N.Y., Apr. 29, 1939; d. Russell Edward Sr. and Helen Elizabeth (Mater) Welkley; m. Leroy Benjamin Schultz, June 16, 1963; children: Mary Beth, Leroi George, Helen Susan, Rachel Anne. BA, MacMurray Coll., 1961; MDiv, Asbury Theol. Sem., 1965; MA, Syracuse U., 1974. Min. Cheningo United Meth. Ch., Truxton, N.Y., 1965-80; asst. min. Christ Covenant Ch., Truxton, 1980—; marriage and family therapist Onondaga Pastoral Counseling Ctr., Syracuse, N.Y., 1972-82, St. Andrew's Episcopal Ch., Syracuse, 1982—, Meml. Bapt. Ch., Cortland, N.Y., 1982—. Workshop presenter in field. Troop leader Girl Scouts U.S.A., 1957—, mem. program com. Ctrl. N.Y. coun., mem. wider opportunities com., gold award com.; chaplain Boy Scouts Am., 1997—, unit comdr. Baden Powell coun., 1998—; mem. Gospel Crusade Ministerial Assn. Recipient Appreciation pin Ctrl. N.Y. Girl Scout Coun., Syracuse, 1994. Mem. Am. Assn. for Marriage and Family Therapy (clin.), Gospel Crusade Ministerial Assn. Republican. Avocations: quilting, sewing, backpacking-camping, canoeing, gardening. Home and Office: 5458 Dog Hollow Rd Truxton NY 13158-3163

SCHULTZ, HOWARD, entrepreneur, professional basketball team owner; b. 1952; married; 2 children. BS, No. Mich. U., 1975. Joined as saleman Xerox Corp.; v.p. Hammarplast; founder, chmn. Starbucks Corp., 1987—, CEO, 1987—2000, chief global strategist, 2000—; chmn. & owner Seattle Supersonics, 2001—. Bd. govs. Nat. Assn. of Securities Dealers, 1998—2001. Named Exec. of the Year, Restaurants and Institutions mag., 2000. Office: Seattle Supersonics 351 Elliott Ave W Ste 500 Seattle WA 98119*

SCHULTZ, JANET K. nursing consultant, business executive; b. Rochester, N.Y., Jan. 23, 1944; d. Charles T. and Madelyn (Daley) Schultz. BSN with distinction, Ind. U., Indpls., 1968; MSN, Ind. U., 1980. Chmn. operating rm. and allied areas nursing Ind. U. Hosps., Indpls., 1971-76; asst. dir. edn. Assn. Operating Rm. Nurses, Denver, 1976-81; dir. edn. and profl. svcs. Baxter Healthcare Corp., McGaw Park, Ill., 1981-88; v.p. profl. svcs. AMSCO, Pitts., 1988-96; pres. Jan Schultz & Assocs., Roswell, Ga., 1996—2002; v.p. program devel. Med Ascend, Inc., Atlanta, 1998-99; prodn. mgr. HealthStream, Inc., Denver, 2002—. Participant internat. consultation on health care associated infections in urology WHO, 1999-2000; lectr. in field; cons. in field. Editl. adv. bd. OR Manager, 1985-98, contbg. editor, 2001—; editl. adv. bd. OR Reports, 1992—; bi-monthly columnist OR Manager, 1997—; contbr.: Design of Special Care Facilities in Hospitals, 1981, Perioperative Patient Care, 1983, 3rd edit., 1994, Sterilization Technology for the Health Care Facility, 1993, 2d edit., 1997, Disinfection, Sterilization and Prservation, 5th edit., 2001, Perioperative Services, 2001. Mem. Nurse Cons. Assn. (pres. 1984-88, bd. dirs. 1989-91), ANA, Assn. Operating Rm. Nurses (mem. environ. issues com. and audiovisual com. 1995-96, nat. environ. liaison 1997-99, Jerry G. Peers award Disting. Svc. 1997), Assn. for Advancement of Med. Instrumentation (bd. dirs. 1991-98, mem. sterilization stds. com., co-leader U.S. del. 1994-98), Am. Hosp. Assn. (EPA task force on chlorofluorocarbon use in healthcare 1988-89), Health Industry Mfrs. Assn. (chmn. sterilization and packaging subcom. 1994-96), Sigma Theta Tau. Office: 2170 S Parker Rd Ste 140 Denver CO 80231 Home: 15937 Ledge Rock Dr Parker CO 80134-3517 E-mail: jsassoc@msn.com.

SCHULTZ, JEFFREY ERIC, optometrist; b. Cleve., Jan. 28, 1948; s. Albert I. and Lenore (Aster) S.; m. Jane Steinman; children: Brian David, Amy Robin. BS in Zoology, Ohio State U., 1970, OD, MS in Physiol. Optics, 1974. Lic. optometrist, Ohio, Fla. Rsch. asst. Ohio State U. Coll. Optometry, Columbus, 1970-74, clin. instr., 1974-75; gen. practice optometry Cleve., 1975—. Clin. investigator Contact Lens Solutions, 1973—. Contbr. articles to profl. jours. Nikon scholar. Mem. Ohio Optometric Assn. (continuing edn. com. 1976-2001, chmn. sports vision com. 1977-79, keyman com. 1984—, coord. zone 2 PAC 1989-94, peer rev. and quality assurance com. 1992-2002, Optometric Recognition award 1978), Fla. Optometric Assn., Am. Optometric Assn. (Optometric Recognition award 1980, 82—, charter mem. contact lens sect. 1982—, mem. sports vision sect. 1983—), Am. Acad. Optometry (v.p. Cleve. chpt. 1991—), Nat. Eye Rsch. Found., Coun. Sports Vision, Vision Conservation Inst., Better Vision Inst., Orthokeratoloy Acad. Am., Interlens Internat.Contact Lens Referal Group, Internat. Soc. Refractive Surgery, Ohio Contact Lens Soc., Cleve. Optometric Assn. (trustee 1985—, pres. 1989-91), Cmty. Eye Care Assocs. (pres. 1994-95, sec.-treas. 1995—), Masons, Beta Sigma Kappa, Phi Eta Sigma. Avocations: stamp collecting/philately, fine art collecting. Office: 5706 Turney Rd Cleveland OH 44125-3971 E-mail: info@myeyedoc.com.

SCHULTZ, JEROME SAMSON, biochemical engineer, educator; b. Bklyn., June 25, 1933; s. Henry Herman and Sally (Warburg) S.; m. Jane Paula Schwartz, Sept. 1, 1955; children: Daniel Stuart, Judith Nyquist, Kathryn Hubbard. BS in Chem. Engring., Columbia U., 1954, MS, 1956; PhD in Biochemistry, U. Wis., 1958. Group leader biochem. rsch. Lederle Labs., N.Y., 1958-64; asst. prof. dept. chem. engring. U. Mich., Ann Arbor, 1964-67, assoc. prof., 1967-70, prof., 1970-77, chmn., 1977-85; sect. head, emerging engring. techs. NSF, Washington, 1985-86, dep. dir. cross-disciplinary rsch., 1986-87; dir. Ctr. for Biotech. and Bioengring. U. Pitts., 1987—, prof. chem. engring., 1987—, prof. medicine, 1990—, dir. bioengring. program, 1991—, chmn. dept. bioengring., 1998—2002, Disting. prof. engring., 1999; sr. scientist NASA/AMES, 2001—02. Editor Biotechnology Progress, 1988—; contbr. articles to profl. jours.; patentee in field. NIH rsch. career devel. awardee, 1970-75. Fellow AAAS, Nat. Acad. Engring., Am. Inst. for Med. and Biol. Engring. (pres. 1995); mem. Am. Chem. Soc. (past chmn. biochem. tech. divsn., M.J. Johnson award 2000), AIChE (past chmn. food and bioengring. divsn., Bioengring. award 1984), Am. Soc. Artificial Internal Organs, Sigma Xi, Phi Lambda Upsilon, Tau Beta Pi. Home: 111 Bentley Dr Pittsburgh PA 15238-2501 Office: U Pitts Ctr Biotechnol & Bioengring 300 Technology Dr Pittsburgh PA 15219-3122 E-mail: jssbio@pitt.edu.

SCHULTZ, JOHN L. writer, educator; b. Columbia, Mo., July 28, 1932; s. Gerard Frederick William and Jennie Lee (Brumley) S.; m. Anne Bray, Dec. 10, 1963 (div. Nov. 1975); children: Timothy, Susan; m. Betty E. Shiflett, May 9, 1992. Student, U. Mo., 1950-51, U. Iowa, 1951-53, U. Chgo., 1955-56, 58-59. Direct mail mgr. U. Chgo. Press, 1959-60; dir. mail cons. Free Press, Chgo., 1960-62, Aldine Pub. Co., Chgo., 1962-65, Quadrangle Books, Chgo., 1965-67; story workshop classes Chgo., 1965-70; chair English and writing Columbia Coll., Chgo., 1967-86, chair fiction writing, 1986-95, prof. emeritus, 1995—. Pres. The Story Workshop Inst., Chgo., 1997—, F Mag., Inc., Chgo., 1967—; cons. John Schultz Assocs., Chgo., 1986—, Schultz Group, Inc., 2000—; pub. Ga. Rev., Ohio Rev., Chgo. Tribune Law Rev. Author: The Tongues of Men, 1969, No One Was Killed, 1969, The Chicago Conspiracy Trial, 1993, Writing From Start to Finish, 1982, 90, 97; contbg. editor Evergreen Rev., N.Y.C., 1969-73; featured in PBS prodn. Daley: The Last Boss, 1996, A&E prodn. The Chgo. Conspiracy Trial, 1994, BBC radio drama The Chgo. Conspiracy Trial, 1993, Court TV The Chicago Conspiracy Trial, 1999, Jury in Politicized Trials. Cpl., M.C., U.S. Army, 1953-55, Korea. Ill. Arts Coun. fellow, 1983-84. Mem. MLA, Assoc. Writing Programs, Nat. Coun. Tchrs. English, Coll. Composition and Comms. Avocations: running, hunting, archery, rock climbing, travel, theater. Office: Columbia Coll Chicago 600 S Michigan Ave Chicago IL 60605-1900 E-mail: jschu10054@aol.com.

SCHULTZ, KENNETH CARL, antiques dealer; b. Hoboken, NJ, July 16, 1938; s. Arthur Edgar and Edna Caroline S. BA, Jersey City State Coll., 1960. Tchr. fifth grade Bd. Edn., Union City, N.J., 1960-61; window display artist B. Altman & Co., N.Y.C., 1962-69; display dir. Fortunoff's, N.Y.C., 1969-73; self employed antiques dealer Hoboken, 1973—. Owner, pub., writer Steamship Catalogues, 1980—. Lutheran. Avocation: collecting motion picture costumes and memorabilia. Office: Box M 753 Hoboken NJ 07030

SCHULTZ, KENNETH ROBERT, nuclear engineer, researcher; b. San Francisco, June 9, 1942; s. Robert Louis Schultz and Thelma Ione Schultz (nee Knutson); m. Mary Lou Abbott, June 20, 1964; children: Robert Wilton, Elizabeth Julia Johnson (nee Schultz). BS in Mech. Engring., Stanford U., 1964, MS in Mech. Engring., 1965; PhD in Nuc. Engring. Scis., U. of Fla., 1971. Registered Profl. Nuclear Engr., State Bd. of Registration, Calif., 1977. Nuc. engr. Gen. Electric Nuc. Energy Divsn., San Jose, Calif., 1965; sect. leader, high temperature gas reactor, core design dept. Gen. Atomics, San Diego, 1971—75, mgr. fusion tech. devel. dept., 1975—90, dir. inertial fusion tech. divsn., 1990—2001, dir. ops. for energy group, 2001—. Mem., panel on low activation materials for fusion U.S. Dept. of Energy, Washington, 1982—83; mem., sr. com. on environment safety and econs. of fusion energy U3. .Dept. of Energy, Washington, 1985—87. Recipient Fusion Tech. award, IEEE and Nuclear Plasma Sys. Soc., 1994, Larry Foreman award, Inertial Fusion Target Fabrication Meeting, 2001. Mem.: AAAS, Am. Nuc. Soc. (bd. dirs. 2000—03, publs. steering com. 1998—2003, chair tech. jours. com. 1990—2001, fusion sci. and tech. editl. adv. com. 1986—2003). Democrat. Unitarian Universalist. Achievements include development of Gen. Atomics program to use nuclear power to produce hydrogen by thermochemical water-splitting. Avocations: swimming, old cars, big dogs. Office: General Atomics PO Box 85608 San Diego CA 92186-5608 Office Phone: 858-455-4304. E-mail: ken.schultz@gat.com.

SCHULTZ, LEANNE, violinist, performer, music educator; b. Topeka, Kans., Jan. 15, 1953; d. Ted Wilder Baehni and Lucille Elizabeth Reuter; m. Larry Wayne Schultz, June 30, 1984. BA in Music, Washburn U., 1988. Pvt. music Univ. student-tchr. of beginning pvt. music violin students Marquardt Music Store, Topeka, 1972—73; sec. Inlet Ins. Agy., Homer, Alaska, 1976—78; permanent emergency substitute music dir./educator Jr. HS, Homer, Alaska, 1978—79; permanent emergency substitute music dir./educator, band and choir Sr. HS, Homer, Alaska, 1978—79; pvt. piano and violin tchr. The Allegro Music Shop, Homer, 1978—80; permanent emergency substitute music dir./educator, 6th Grade Band Homer HS, 1978—79; escrow sec. and recorder of deeds Peninsula Title Ins. Co., Homer, 1979—80; clk. typist II, office of pers. Dept. of Adminstrn., State of Kans., Topeka, 1980—81; computer/word-processor, divsn. water resources State Bd. of Agriculture, Topeka, 1981—84; pvt. music tchr. Manning Music Store, Topeka, 1985—2000; office adminstrv. asst. III, personnel SRS Dept. Kans. State Bd. of Agrl., Topeka, 1985; music condr./tchr. Cair-Paravel/Topeka Latin Sch., Topeka, 1986—88; escrow sec. Lawyers Title of Topeka, 1988—94; pvt. prof. violin, viola and piano tchr. Topeka, 1994—; concert orch. mem., violinist

Topeka Symphony Orch., 1999—. Accompanist/pianist for all violin and viola pvt. music students' solo performances (from beginning levels to collegiate levels of piano accompaniment music repertoires) at all of the ann. CMENC-sponsored (Collegiate Music Educators Nat. Conf.) Mid. Sch. solo fest contests and at all of the ann. KSHSAA-sponsored (Kans. State HS Activities Assn.)regional and statewide solo fest contests; Accompany all of the pvt. music violin and viola students' solos, on the piano, of the Topeka Music Tchr. Assn. ann. honors recitals. Mem., sec. Latchkey bd. advisors NE Kans. Music Tchrs. Assn., 1999—2003. Recipient Scholarship winner, Sitka Music Festival Winter Session, Student-Institute Workshop, Univ. of Alaska at Juneau/Juneau, Alaska, 1980. Mem.: Washburn Univ. Alumni, Topeka HS Alumni, Kans. Music Tchrs. Assn., Nat. Piano Guild, Music Tchr. Nat. Assn., Am. Coll. of Musicians, Topeka Symphony Orch. Leaque, N.E. Kans. Music Tchr. Assn. (NEKMTA) (sec. 1998—2003), Topeka Music Tchr. Assn. (chmn. honors recitals 1999—2001), Women's Kans. Day Club, Sigma Alpha Iota. Protestant. Avocations: reading, writing, classical movies, literature, history. Home and Office: 3618 SW 33d St Topeka KS 66614-2812 Office Phone: 785-271-0402. Personal E-mail: schultzstringstorm@sbcglobal.net.

SCHULTZ, LOUIS EDWIN, management consultant; b. Foster, Nebr., Aug. 8, 1931; s. Louis Albert and Lula Pusey (Cox) S.; m. Mary Kathleen Peck, Mar. 3, 1962; children: Kurt Michael, Kristen Leigh. BSEE, U. Nebr., 1959; MBA, Pepperdine U., 1974. Mktg. mgr. Bell & Howell, Pasadena, Calif., 1962-70; dir. mktg. Cogar Corp., Utica, N.Y., 1970-71; product mgr. Pertec Corp., L.A., 1971-73; gen. mgr. Control Data Corp., Mpls., 1973-84; founder Process Mgmt. Internat., Inc., Mpls., Minn., 1984, pres., 1984-99; ptnr., mng. dir. Bluefire Ptnrs., Mpls., 1999—. Bd. dirs. CorCom Cos., Inc., Mpls., PMI Ltd, 1995-98; adv. bd. Inst. for Productivity Through Quality, U. Tenn., Knoxville, 1982-84; ptnr. CorCom Cos., Inc., 1997-99, ptnr.-mng. dir., Bulefire Ptrns. Author: Managing in the Worldwide Competitive Society, 1984, Quality Management Philosophies, 1985, Profiles in Quality, 1994; co-author: Quality Handbook for Small Business, 1994, Deming, The Way We Knew Him, 1995. Mem. Gov.'s Commn. on Productivity, St. Paul, 1986; chmn. Wirth Park Tree Restoration Com., Mpls., 1983; mem. Productivity Planning Com., St. Paul, 1985—. Staff sgt. USMC, 1952-54; advisor to Deming Forum, 1985—; judge Minn. Quality award, 1992. Recipient Profl. Partnership award U. Minn., 1987. Mem. Am. Soc. Performance Improvement (bd. dirs. 1984-89, outstanding svc. award), Minn. Coun. for Quality (bd. dirs. 1987-97), Human Sys. Mgmt. (editl. bd.), Asia-Pacific Orgn. Quality Control (life), Toastmasters Internat. Republican. Methodist. Office: Bluefire Ptnrs 150 S 5th St Ste 1300 Minneapolis MN 55402-4213 E-mail: lschultz@bluefirepartners.com.

SCHULTZ, LOUIS MICHAEL, advertising agency executive; b. Detroit, Aug. 24, 1944; s. Henry Richard and Genevieve (Jankowski) S.; children: Christian David, Kimberly Ann; m. Diane Lee; stepchildren: Vince, Andrea, Frank. BA, Mich. State U., 1967; MBA, Wayne State U., 1970. Staff Campbell-Ewald, Warren, Mich., 1967-74, v.p. group dir., 1975-77, sr. v.p., assoc. dir., 1977-82, group sr. v.p., 1982-83, exec. v.p., 1984-87, Lintas: USA, 1987-94; chmn. Lintas: WW Media Coun., 1991; mem. devel. council IPG, N.Y.C., 1984 ; pres., CEO CE Comm., 1994—; vice chmn. Campbell-Ewald, 1998-99; chmn., CEO Initiative Media N.Am., L.A., 2000—; chmn. Initiative Media WW, 2000. Advisor, Detroit Renaissance Com., 1981-84. With USAR, 1967-73. Mem. NATAS, Am. Women in Radio and TV, Am. Mktg. Assn., Detroit Advt. Assn., Promotion Mktg. Assn. (bd. dirs. 1999), Ad Club N.Y. (bd. dirs.), Adcraft Club, Old Club, Hidden Valley Club, Longboat Key Club, Detroit Athletic Club, Am. Advt. Fedn. (bd. dirs.), Forest Lake Country Club, Renaissance Club, Detroit Athletic Club. Episcopalian. Avocations: golf, tennis, travel. Home: 5011 Elmgate Dr Orchard Lake MI 48324-3014 Office: Initiative Media 5700 Wilshire Blvd Ste 400 Los Angeles CA 90036-3639

SCHULTZ, LOUIS WILLIAM, retired judge; b. Deep River, Iowa, Mar. 24, 1927; s. M. Louis and Esther Louise (Behrens) S.; m. D. Jean Stephen, Nov. 6, 1949; children: Marcia, Mark, Paul. Student, Central Coll., Pella, Iowa, 1944-45, 46-47; LLB, Drake U., Des Moines, 1949. Bar: Iowa. Claims supr. Iowa Farm Mut. Ins. Co., Des Moines, 1949-55; partner firm Harned, Schultz & McMeen, Marengo, Iowa, 1955-71; judge Iowa Dist. Ct. (6th dist.), 1971-80; justice Iowa Supreme Ct., 1980-93; county atty. Iowa County, 1960-68; ret., 1993. Served with USNR, 1945-46. Mem. Am. Bar Assn., Iowa Bar Assn. (bd. govs.), Iowa Judges Assn. (pres.)

SCHULTZ, MARVIN E. historian, educator; b. Albuquerque, N.Mex., Oct. 8, 1949; s. Marvin and Elizabeth Schultz; life ptnr. Shelia Kaye Jenkins. BA, Angelo State U., San Angelo, Tex., 1971; MA, SW Tex. State U., San Marcos, 1984; PhD, Tex. Christian U., Fort Worth, 1994. Asst. instr. history SW Tex. State U., San Marcos, 1980—84, instr. history, 1984—85; tchg. fellow Vanderbilt U., Nashville, 1985—87; adj. instr. history Vol. State CC, Gallatin, Tenn., 1987—88; tchg. asst. Tex. Christian U., Fort Worth, Tex., 1990—94; lectr. in Tex. history U. of Tex. at Dallas, Richardson, 1994; dir. Ctr. for Am. Culture and History in Edn., Malvern, Ark., 1999—; instr. history Ouachita Tech. Coll., Malvern, Ark., 1994—. Hist. cons., editor Applied Acad. Svcs., Fort Worth, Tex., 1990—92; jr. rsch. fellow Tex. State Hist. Assn., Austin, Tex., 1983—84; prodn. mgr. On With the Show, Austin, Tex., 1972—79. Editor: U. S. History Documents, 1996; contbr. articles and revs. to profl. jours., chapters to books. Commr. City Parks Commn., Malvern, Ark., 2001—; mem. Garvan Woodland Garden, Hot Springs, Ark., 2001—, Ouachita River Park Commn., 2003—; mem. adv. bd. Ark. Studies Living Curriculum Project, 2003—. Recipient Kent Trinkle Book Collecting award, Friends of the Tex. Christian U. Libr., 1991. Fellow: Grady McWhiney Rsch. Found.; mem.: Hot Spring County Hist. Assn., Ark. Hist. Assn., Friends of the Malvern/Hot Spring County Libr. (life), So. Hist. Assn., Alpha Chi. Avocations: gardening, travel, public history. Office: Ouachita Tech Coll One College Circle Malvern AR 72104 E-mail: mschultz@otcweb.edu.

SCHULTZ, NANCY REILLY, artist; b. N.Y.C., July 20, 1930; d. John Francis and Eunice Genevieve (Crowley) Reilly; m. Frederick Henry Schultz, Aug. 11, 1951; children: Catherine, Frederick, Clifford, John Reilly. BA, Smith Coll. for Women, 1951; BFA, U. North Fla., 2000. Pres. The Smash Tennis Shop, Inc., Jacksonville, Fla., 1976-86; chmn. Schultz, Barrett Interiors, Inc. Chmn. Duval County Mothers March, March of Dimes, 1958-59; mem. adv. bd. Women's Bd. Jacksonville Wolfson Children's Hosp. at Bapt. Med. Ctr.; chmn. Docents Cummer Mus. Art, 1968-70; caseworker Family Counseling Ctr., Jacksonville, 1961-62; vol. worker Cmty. Pub. TV, Am. Cancer Soc.; chmn. fund raising Symphony Show House, 1972; met. bd. dirs. YMCA of Fla.'s First Coast, 1989-91; trustee U. North Fla. Found., 1989-2002, mem. exec. com., 1992-96, hon. trustee 2002—; hon. mem. bd. dirs. U. North Fla. Found. Mem. Jr. League of Jacksonville, Phi Kappa Phi (U. N.Fla. chpt.). Democrat. Roman Catholic. Home: 505 Lancaster St Jacksonville FL 32204-4143 Office: 118 W Adams St Ste 6 Jacksonville FL 32202-3800 Office Phone: 904-354-3603.

SCHULTZ, NORBERT J. retired music educator; b. Gardner, Ill., Apr. 25, 1937; s. Lewis H. and Vera Schultz; m. Janet A. Schultz, Aug. 19, 1979; children: Sonia, Shelly Luppen 1 stepchild, John Bracamontes. BS in Music Edn., Ill. State U., 1959. Band, vocal and gen. music tchr., grade and H.S. Kempton and Cabrey (Ill.) Schs., 1959—61; vocal tchr. Piper City (Ill.) Grade and H.S., 1961—63; band and vocal dir. Taft Grade Sch., Lockport, Ill., 1963—67; band dir. Lyons (Ill.) Sch. Dist., 1967—70, Edwardsville (Ill.) elem, jr. high and H.S., 1970—85; gen. music tchr. Shenandoah and Woodward Elem. Schs., St. Louis, 1986—99; beginning and intermediate band dir. St. Paul's Luth. Sch., Troy, Ill., 1999—2001; ret., 2001. Profl. entertainer, band dir. Musical dir. chapel Charles Melvin Price Support Ctr. Army Facility, Granite City, Ill., 1995—2000; deacon Holy Cross Luth. Ch., Collinsville, Ill., 1988—96, elder, 1999, St. Paul's Luth. Ch., Troy, 2002—. Named team mem. in citizen ambassador program elementary edn. del. to Vietnam, Eisenhower award, U. Toledo, 1994; recipient numerous 1st pl. band awards at state competitions. Mem.: Music Tchrs. Nat. Assn., Ill. State Music Tchrs. Assn. Republican. Lutheran. Avocations: fishing, travel, private teaching. Home: Holiday Shores 846 Newport Bay Edwardsville IL 62025

SCHULTZ, PATRICIA BOWERS, vocal music educator, performer; b. Gomer, Ohio, Apr. 26, 1941; d. Paul Edward and Blodwen (Watkins) Bowers; m. Charles Albert Schultz; children: Todd Matthew, Vaughn Andrew, Cinnamon, Paulette. BS in Edn., French & Music, Miami U., Oxford, Ohio, 1963; MEd in Counseling, U. Ill., 1964; D of Musical Arts in Vocal Performance, U. Mo-Kansas City, 1984. Performer freelance USA and Europe, 1964—; music educator, counselor Northmont Pub. Schs., Dayton, Ohio, 1964-66; French educator Bowling Green (Ohio) H.S., 1967-68; instr. music and French Dickinson (N.D.) State U., 1972-74; instr. voice Ctrl. State U., Wilberforce, Ohio, 1975-76; dir. choral activities Savannah (Mo.) H.S., 1979-80; prof. music N.W. Mo. State U., Maryville, 1981—2002. Dir. music First United Meth. Ch., Maryville, 1977—88; tour mgr. Jenny Lind Ensemble, 1978—; musical dir. N.W. MO. State U., Maryville, 1981—2002; vis. prof. Internat. Enrichment, London, 2000, 02, 04; adjudicator Nat. Assn. Tchrs. of Singing, Mo. H.S. Activities Assn. Accomplishments in music include author, lead role in music drama Encore for Jenny Lind, 1976— (London Premiere 1992); conductor choral music Welsh Gymanfoedd Ganu, 1989— (Nat. Selection 1993); Coloratura soprano recitals and concerts throughout U.S.; soloist European tour Cin. Symphony, 1969; presentator Am. Assn. Higher Edn. Teaching Learning & Tech. Conf., 1997. Pres. Univ. Women, Maryville, 1978-79; first judge of vocal competition Nat. Glenn Miller Scholarship Competition, Clarinda, Iowa, 1992, 94, 2001; pres. Faculty Senate N.W. Mo. State U., 1993-95, Centennial Soc. 2002-; organizer, charter mem. Mo. Assn. Faculty Senates, Springfield, Mo., 1993-94. Named Faculty Fellow Mo. Coordinating Bd. for Higher Edn., 1997-98, Outstanding Alumnae Conservatory of Music, U. Mo.-Kansas City, 1990; grantee Mo. State Coun. on Arts, 1991-95. Mem. AAUW, Coll. Music Soc., Nat. Assn. Tchrs. Singing (Teacher of regional state and chpt. winners in Mo., Nebr. and eight state region 1986, 88, 90, 92, 97, 98), Am. Choral Dirs. Assn., (hon.) Mortar Bd. (Outstanding advisor, 2003), Sigma Alpha Iota (patroness and advisor 1995-2002), Delta Omicron. Avocations: gardening, reading, travel. Home: 1004 W Cooper St Maryville MO 64468-2005 Office: NW Mo State Univ Dept Music 800 University Dr Maryville MO 64468-6015

SCHULTZ, RICHARD ALLEN, lawyer, farmer; b. Emporia, Kans., Jan. 3, 1939; s. Ebur Samuel and Opal Mae (Porter) S.; m. Esther Marie Strafuss, May 8, 1971; children: William Allen, Bryan Lee. BS in Indsl. Mgmt., U. Kans., 1961; JD, Washburn U. Topeka, 1970. Bar: Kans. 1971. Sole practice law, Topeka, 1970—. Dep. dir. Kans. Govs. Com. Criminal Adminstrn., 1971-73; asst. jud. adminstr. Kans. Supreme Ct., 1973-76; ct. adminstr. 3d Jud. Dist., Kans., 1976-83; dep. sec. Dept. Corrections State of Kans., Topeka, 1983-88. Exec. bd. Topeka YMCA; dist. officer Jayhawk Area Boy Scouts Am., Nat. Eagle Scout Assn.; dir. Kans. Vets. Found., Inc. Lt. USN, 1961-67. Decorated commendation award USN. Mem. ABA, Topeka Bar Assn. (Liberty Bell award 1983), Kans. Bar Assn., Am. Legion, Vietnam Vets Am., Phi Alpha Delta, Alpha Tau Omega. Democrat. Methodist. Office: 3109 SW Stone Ave Topeka KS 66614-2821 Office Phone: 785-273-5566.

SCHULTZ, RICHARD CARLTON, plastic surgeon; b. Grosse Pointe, Mich., Nov. 19, 1927; s. Herbert H. and Carmen (Huebner) S.; m. Pauline Zimmermann, Oct. 8, 1955; children: Richard, Lisa, Alexandra, Jennifer. MD, Wayne State U., 1953. Diplomate Am. Bd. Plastic Surgery. Intern Harper Hosp., Detroit, 1953-54, resident in gen. surgery, 1954-55, U.S. Army Hosp., Ft. Carson, Colo., 1955-57; resident in plastic surgery St. Luke's Hosp., Chgo., 1957-58, U. Ill. Hosp., Chgo., 1958-59, VA Hosp., Hines, Ill., 1959-60; practice medicine specializing in plastic surgery Park Ridge, Ill., 1961-96; ret., 1996; clin. asst. prof. surgery U. Ill. Coll. Medicine, 1966-70, assoc. prof. surgery, 1970-76, prof., 1976-96, head divsn. plastic surgery, 1970-87; pres. med. staff Luth. Gen. Hosp., Park Ridge, 1977-79. Vis. prof. U. Pitts., 1972, U. Miss., 1973, U. Pisa, Italy, 1974, Jikei U. Coll. Medicine, Tokyo, 1976, Ind. U., 1977, U. Helsinki, 1977, U. N.Mex., 1978, U. Milan, 1981, So. Ill. Sch. Medicine, 1982, Tulane U. Med. Sch., 1983, Shanghai 2d Med. Coll., 1984, U. Guadalajara (Mex.), 1986, Gazi U., Turkey, 1988, U. Coll. Medicine Tsuksba, Japan, 1996, Taegu (Korea) U., 1996; sr. Fulbright lectr. U. Uppsala, Sweden, 2003; participant, guest surgeon Physicians for Peace, Turkey and Greece, 1988, Israel and Occupied Ters., 1990, Egypt, 1991, Lithuania, Estonia, 1993 (team leader); leader citizen amb. People to People Internat. Del. Plastic Surgeons to Albania & Russia, 1994, del. leader, Tibet and China, 1998. Author: Facial Injuries, 1970, 3d edit., 1988, Maxillo-Facial Injuries from Vehicle Accidents, 1975, Outpatient Surgery, 1979. Mem. sch. bd., Lake Zurich, Ill., 1966-72, pres., 1968-72; pres. Chgo. Found. for Plastic Surgery, 1966-. Served to capt. M.C., AUS, 1955-57. Recipient Auto Safety award Med. Tribune, 1967, Robert H. Ivy award 1969, Disting. Sci. Achievement award Wayne U. Coll. Medicine Alumni, 1975, Sanvenero-Rosselli award, 1981; McGregor scholar, 1946-49, scholar Fulbright Found., Sweden, 1960-61; grantee Edn!. Found. Am. Soc. Plastic and Reconstructive Surgery, 1964-65. Fellow ACS (pres. local commn. on trauma 1985-87); mem. Am. Assn. Plastic Surgeons (trustee 1990-91), Am. Soc. Plastic and Reconstructive Surgeons, Midwestern Assn. Plastic Surgeons (pres. 1978-79), Chgo. Soc. Plastic Surgeons (pres. 1970-72), Midwestern Assn. Plastic Surgeons (pres. 1978-79), Am. Soc. Maxillofacial Surgeons (pres. 1988-89, award of honor 1986), Am. Assn. Automotive Medicine (pres. 1970-71, A. Merkin award 1982), Am. Cleft Palate Assn., Am. Soc. Aesthetic Plastic Surgery, Tord Skoog Soc. Plastic Surgeons (pres. 1971-75), Can. Soc. Plastic Surgery, Chilean Soc. Plastic Surgery (corr.), Japanese Soc. Plastic Surgery (corr.), Cuban Soc. Maxillofacial Surgery (corr.), Korean Soc. Plastic Surgery (corr.). Office: PO Box 357 Northport MI 49670-0357 Office Phone: 231-386-5950.

SCHULTZ, RICHARD DALE, national athletic organization executive; b. Grinnell, Iowa, Sept. 5, 1929; s. August Henry and Marjorie Ruth (Turner) S.; m. Jacquilyn Lu Duistermars, June 26, 1949; children: Robert Dale, William Joel, Kim Marie. BS, Ctrl. Coll., Pella, Iowa, 1950; EdD (hon.), Ctrl. Coll., 1987; LLD (hon.), Wartburg Coll., 1988, Alma Coll., 1989, Luther Coll., 1991; PhD (hon.), U.S. Sports Acad., 1993; LLD (hon.), Daniel Webster Coll., 1997, Gettysburg Coll., 1998. Head basketball coach, athletic dir. Humboldt (Iowa) High Sch., 1950-60; freshman basketball coach U. Iowa, Iowa City, 1960-62, head baseball coach, assoc. basketball coach, 1962-70, head basketball coach, 1970-74, asst. v.p., 1974-76; dir. athletics and phys. edn. Cornell U., Ithaca, N.Y., 1976-81; dir. athletics U. Va., Charlottesville, 1981-87; exec. dir. NCAA, Mission, Kans., 1987-94; pres. Global Sports Enterprises, 1994-95; exec. dir. U.S. Olympic Com., Colorado Springs, Colo., 1995—; chmn. Mktg. Assocs. Internat., 2000—04; chmn., CEO, Internat. Partnerships, 2002—. Mem. honors ct. Nat. Football Found. and Hall of Fame, Nat. Basketball Hall of Fame, 1992; chmn. bd. NCAA Found., 1989; organizer Iowa Steel Mill, Inc.; bd. trustees Gettysburg Coll., 1996—. Author: A Course of Study for the Coaching of Baseball, 1964, The Theory and Techniques of Coaching Basketball, 1970; Contbr. articles to mags. Bd. dirs. Fellowship of Christian Athletes, 1986, chmn., 1990; chmn. Multiple Sclerosis, 1974-75; mem. Knight Found. Commn. on Intercollegiate Athletics, 1990—; mem. adv. com. on svc. acad. athletic programs Def. Dept. Recipient Disting. Alumni award Ctrl. Coll., Pella, 1970, 98, Lifetime Svc. award U. Iowa, 1994, Corbett award Nat. Assn. Collegiate Dirs. Athletics, 1994, medal of honor Ellis Island, 1997, Disting. Alumni award Ctrl. Coll., 1998, Casey award, 1999, Pres. and Mrs. Bush Cmty. Impact award 1999; mem. Basketball Hall of Fame Honor Ct., 1992, Sportsman of Yr. award Marine Corp., 1997; inducted into Iowa Baseball Hall of Fame, 1993, Ctrl. Coll. Hall of Honors, 2002, Des Moines Register Hall of Fame, 2003. Mem. Nat. Assn. Coll. Basketball Coaches, Ea. Coll. Athletic Assn. (mem. exec. com. 1980-81), Am. Basketball Coaches Assn. (Award of Honor 1994), Am. Football Coaches Assn. (lifetime membership award 1995). Home: 3670 Twisted Oak Cir Colorado Springs CO 80904-4720 Office Phone: 719-685-3245. E-mail: dschultz@maisponts.com.

SCHULTZ, RICHARD MICHAEL, biochemistry educator, researcher; b. Phila., Oct. 28, 1942; s. William and Beatrice (Levine) S.; m. Rima M. Lunin, Mar. 7, 1965; children: Carl M., Eli J. BA, SUNY, Binghamton, 1964; PhD, Brandeis U., 1969. Rsch. fellow Harvard U. Med. Sch., Boston, 1969-71; asst. prof. Loyola U. Stritch Sch. of Medicine, Maywood, Ill., 1971-78, assoc. prof., 1978-84, prof., 1984—, chmn. dept. molecular and cellular biochemistry, 1984-2000. Mem. adv. med. bd. Leukemia Rsch. Found., Chgo., 1987-91. Co-author: Textbook of Biochemistry; contbr. articles to profl. jours., chapters to books. Recipient Rsch. grants NIH. Achievements include in vivo evidence for the role of protease enzymes and their inhibitors in regulating tumor cell metastasis, oncogene pathways in cancer, obtaining evidence on the nature of the transition-state in enzyme catalysis. Office: Divsn Molecular & Cellular Biochemistry Loyola U Sch Medicine Maywood IL 60153 Office Phone: 708-216-9378. E-mail: rschult@lumc.edu.

SCHULTZ, RICHARD OTTO, ophthalmologist, educator; b. Racine, Wis., Mar. 19, 1930; s. Henry Arthur and Josephine (Wagoner) S.; m. Diane Haldane, Sept. 29, 1990; children: Henry Reid, Richard Paul, Karen Jo. BA, U. Wis., 1950, MS, 1954; MD, Albany Med. Coll., 1956; MSc, U. Iowa, 1960. Diplomate Am. Bd. Ophthalmology. Intern, Univ. Hosps., Iowa City, 1956-57, resident in opthalmology, 1957-60; chief ophthalmology sect. div. Indian health USPHS, Phoenix, 1960-63; practice medicine specializing in ophthalmology Phoenix, 1963; NIH spl. fellow in ophthalmic microbiology U. Calif., San Francisco, 1963-64, clin. assoc., 1963-64, research assoc., 1963-64; assoc. prof., chmn. dept. ophthalmology Marquette U. Sch. Medicine (now Med. Coll. Wis.), Milw., 1964-68, prof., chmn., 1968-97, prof. ophthalmology, 1997—2000, prof. emeritus, 2000—. Mem. nat. adv. eye coun. NIH, 1984-88; cons. VA regional ctr. Milw. Children's, Columbia, Froedert and hosps., Milw. Contbr. articles to profl. jours. Served with USPHS, 1960-63. Fellow: ACS, Am. Ophthalmol. Soc., Am. Acad. Ophthalmology; mem.: Milw. Acad. Medicine, Med. Soc. Milwaukee County, Oxford Ophthalmol. Congress (Eng.), Rsch. to Prevent Blindness, N.Y. Acad. Scis., Assn. Rsch. Vision and Ophthalmology, Milw. Ophthal. Soc., Assn. Univ. Profs. Ophthalmology. Home: 7505 S Kangaroo Lake Rd Baileys Harbor WI 54202 Office: MCW Eye Inst 925 N 87th St Milwaukee WI 53226-4812 Personal E-mail: eyeotto@aol.com.

SCHULTZ, ROGER C. career officer; b. LeMars, Iowa, Oct. 13, 1945; s. Harry Willis and Sylvia Dorothy (Aronson) S.; m. Barbara J. Kaiser, Feb. 14, 1969. BS, Upper Iowa U., 1988; MPA, Shippensburg U., 1992. Commd. USNG, advanced through grades to brig. gen., 1996; rifle platoon leader Co. A 2d Bn., 133d Inf., Ft. Carson, Colo., 1968-69; scout leader Hdqs. and Hdqs. Co. 2d Bn., 22d Inf., Vietnam, 1969; logistics, personnel, intelligence officer HHC 2d Bn., 133d Inf., Sioux City, Iowa, 1970-75, rifle co. comdr. Co. B Sheldon, Iowa, 1975-76, ops. and tng. officer HHC Sioux City, Iowa, 1976-78; brigade ops. and tng. officer 34th Brigade, 47th Inf., Boone, Iowa, 1978-81, exec. officer, 1981-82; bn. comdr. 1st Bn., 168th Inf., Council Bluffs, Iowa, 1982-84; dir. op. and tng. Iowa Army Nat. Guard, Johnston, Iowa, 1984-88, chief of staff, 1988-95, dep. adjutant gen., 1995—98; dir. Army Nat. Guard, Washington, 1998—. Lobbyist Dept. Pub. Def., Des Moines, 1996. Decorated Silver Star, 1969, Bronze Star, 1969, Purple Heart (2 awards), 1969, Legion of Merit, 1995. Presbyterian. Office: NG Bur 1411 Jefferson Davis Hwy Arlington VA 22202-3231

SCHULTZ, STANLEY GEORGE, physiologist, educator, dean; b. Bayonne, N.J., Oct. 26, 1931; s. Aaron and Sylvia (Kaplan) S.; m. Harriet Taran, Dec. 25, 1960; children: Jeffrey, Kenneth. AB summa cum laude, Columbia U., 1952; MD, NYU, 1956. Intern Bellevue Hosp., N.Y.C., 1956-57, resident, 1957-59; research assoc. in biophysics Harvard U., 1959-62, instr. biophysics, 1964-67; assoc. prof. physiology U. Pitts., 1967-70, prof. physiology, 1970-79; prof., chmn. dept. physiology U. Tex. Med. Sch., Houston, 1979-96, prof. dept. internal medicine, 1979—, prof. dept. integrative biol. pharm. physiology, 1997—, vice chmn., 1999—, dean Sch. Medicine, 2004—, Fondren chair in cell signalling, 1999—. Cons. USPHS, NIH, 1970—; mem. physiology test com. Nat. Bd. Med. Examiners, 1974-79, chmn., 1976-79 Editor Am. Jour. Physiology, Jour. Applied Physiology, 1971-75, Physiol. Revs., 1979-85, Handbook of Physiology: The Gastrointestinal Tract, 1989-91—; mem. editl. bd. Jour. Gen. Physiology, 1969-88, Ann. Revs. Physiology, 1974-81, Current Topics in Membranes and Transport, 1975-81, Jour. Membrane Biology, 1977—, Biochim. Biophys. Acta, 1987-89; assoc. editor Ann. Revs. Physiology, 1977-81; assoc. editor News in Physiol. Scis., 1989-94, editor, 1994-2003; contbr. articles to profl. jours. Served to capt. M.C. USAF, 1962-64. Recipient Rsch. Career award NIH, 1969-74, Solomon Berson award NYU, 2003; overseas fellow Churchill Coll., Cambridge U., 1975-76 Mem. AAAS, AMA (coun. on med. edn.), Am. Heart Assn. (estab. investigator 1964-68), Am. Physiol. Soc. (councillor 1989-91, pres.-elect 1991-92, pres. 1992-93, past pres. 1993-94, Guyton award 1997, Orr Reynolds award 1999, Daggs award 2003), Fed. Am. Soc. Exptl. Biology (exec. bd. 1992-95), Biophys. Soc., Soc. Gen. Physiologists, Internat. Cell Rsch. Orgn., Internat. Union Physiol. Scis. (chmn. internat. com. gastrointestinal physiology 1977-80, chmn. U.S. nat. com. 1992-98), Assn. Am. Physicians, Am. Assn. Ob-Gyn. (hon. fellow), Assn. Chmn. Depts. Physiology (pres. 1985-86), Houston Philos. Soc., Phi Beta Kappa, Sigma Xi. Home: 4955 Heatherglen Dr Houston TX 77096-4213 Office Phone: 713-500-5010.

SCHULTZ, T. PAUL, economics professor; b. Ames, Iowa, May 24, 1940; s. Theodore W. and Esther (Werth) S.; m. Judith Hoenack, Sept. 16, 1967; children: Lara, Joel, Rebecca. BA, Swarthmore Coll., 1961; PhD, MIT, 1966; MA (hon.), Yale U., 1974. Cons. Joint Econ. Com., Washington, 1964; rschr. econ. dept. Rand Corp., Santa Monica, Calif., 1965-72, dir. population rsch., 1968-72; prof. econ. U. Minn., Mpls., 1972-75, Yale U., New Haven, 1974—, dir. Econ. Growth Ctr., 1983-96; prof. econ. Malcolm K. Brachman, 1977. Cons. World Bank, Rockefeller Found., InterAm. Devel. Bank; mem. com. on population NAS, Washington, 1987-89, 90-93. Author: Structural Change in a Developing Country, 1971, Economics of Population, 1981; editor: (books) The State of Development Economics, 1988, Investment In Women's Human Capital, 1995, (periodical) Research in Population Economics, 1985, 88, 91, 96; assoc. editor Jour. Population Econs., 1991—, Econ. of Edn. Rev., 1993-2004, China Econ. Rev., 1994—. Mem. commn. on behavioral sci. and edn. Nat. Rsch. Coun., 1997-2002. Fellow: AAAS (population resources environ. com. 1985—89, nomination com. 1987—90); mem.: Econ. Rsch. Forum for Arab Countries (trustee 1993—2001), European Soc. for Population Econs. (bd. dirs., pres. 1997), Soc. for Study Social Biology (bd. dirs. 1986—89), Internat. Union for Sci. Study Population, Population Assn. Am. (bd. dirs. 1979—81), Econometrics Soc., Am. Econ. Assn. Office: Yale U Econ Growth Ctr PO Box 208269 27 Hillhouse Ave New Haven CT 06520-8269 E-mail: paul.schultz@yale.edu.

SCHULTZ, TODD R. science administrator; BA in Econs., U. Wis.; MA in Internat. Rels., Syracuse U. Trade rsch. analyst Dept. of Commerce; cons. Govt. of Madison (Wis.); Rep. technical cons. Subcom. Internat. Sci. Cooperation, Washington, 1987-89; Rep. spl. asst. Subcom. Space Sci. and Applications, House Com. Sci., Space & Tech., Washington, 1989; adminstrv. asst. Congressman F. James Sensenbrenner, Jr. U.S. House of Reps., 1989-96; chief of staff House Com. Sci., 1996—. Syracuse U. fellow. Office: House Com Sci 2320 Rayburn Office Bldg Washington DC 20515-0001

SCHULTZ, VICTOR M. physician; b. Pitts., Aug. 14, 1932; s. Irvin and Rose (Reiss) S. BS, Kent (Ohio) State U., 1955; MD, Ohio State U., Columbus, 1958. Diplomate Am. Bd. Dermatology. Pvt. practice, Santa Monica, Calif., 1965—. Fellow Am. Acad. Dermatology, Pacific Dermatologic Assn.; mem. AMA, Am. Coll. Physicians, Calif. Med. Assn., L.A. County Med. Assn. Avocations: skiing, tennis, golf, music, swimming. Office: 2461 Santa Monica Blvd Santa Monica CA 90404-2049 Office Phone: 310-828-7492.

SCHULTZ, WILLIAM JOHN, artist, educator; s. William Joseph and Lucy Alice Schultz; m. Nadya Stevens, Dec. 2, 1981. BA, Vesper George Sch. of Art, Boston, 1952. Profl. artist William J. Schultz Art Sch., Lenox, Mass., 1955—85, Vero Beach, Fla., 1985—2003; ret., 2004. Founder and dir. Am. Impressionist Soc., Ellenton, Fla., 1998—; lectr. on Impressionist art; profl. instr. watercolor, oil and pastel. Prin. works include oil portrait Center for the Arts (award), exhibitions include, N.Y.C., Boston, Santa Fe, Vero Beach, Fla. Master sgt. U. S. Army, 1942—47, ETO. Named Mastel Pastelist, Am. Pastel Soc., 1965; recipient award, Academic Artists Assn., 1968. Avocations: travel, golf, walking. Office Phone: 772-778-1760. Personal E-mail: nadyaschultz@msn.com.

SCHULZ, DIANA, film company executive; Grad. summa cum laude, Claremont McKenna Coll.; MBA, Stanford U. With Bain and Co., Microsoft Corp., McKinsey and Co. Consulting, L.A., 1991—97; mem. corp. devel. and strategic planning roup Vivendi Universal Entertainment, Universal City, Calif., 1997—99, head of group, 1999—2001, sr. v.p. corp. devel. and strategic planning, 2001—. Office: Vivendi Universal Entertainment 100 Universal City Plaza Universal City CA 91608-1002

SCHULZ, EKKEHARD, business executive; Chmn. exec. bd. Thyssen Krupp AG. Chmn. supervisory bd. Thyssen Krupp, Eisen-und Krupp Thyssen Stinless GmbH, Thyssen Krupp Materials and Svcs. AG, Thyssen Krupp; bd. dirs. Budd Co., Thyssen Inc.; mem. supervisory bds. Commerzbank AG, Hapag Lloyd AG, MAN AG, Energie AG, Strabag AG; pres. Eurofer; com. mem., bd. Wirtschaftsvereinigung Stahl, VDEh. Office: Thyssen Krupp AG August Thyssen Str 1 40211 Düsseldorf Germany

SCHULZ, HELMUT WILHELM, chemical engineer, environmental executive; b. Berlin, July 10, 1912; came to U.S., 1924; s. Herman Ludwig Wilhelm and Emilie (Specka) S.; m. Colette Marie Francoise Prieur, Mar. 6, 1954; children: Raymond A., Caroline P., Roland W., Robert B., Thomas F. BS, Columbia U., 1933, ChE, 1934, PhD, 1942. Rsch. engr. to mng. dir. Union Carbide Corp., Charleston, W.Va., 1934-69; spl. asst. to dir. def. rsch. and engring. U.S. Dept. of Def., Washington, 1964-67; spl. asst. to U.S. commr. of edn. U.S. Dept. of Edn., Washington, 1971; sr. rsch. scientist, adj. prof. chem. engring. Columbia U., N.Y.C., 1972—83; founder, dir. Urban Technology Ctr., Columbia Engring. Sch., N.Y.C., 1972—83; chmn., CEO Dynecology, Inc., Harrison, N.Y., 1974—. Contbr. articles to profl. jours. Mem. N.Y.C. Mayor's Sci. and Tech. Adv. Coun., 1973-74; bd. dirs. Charleston Symphony Orch., 1956-62, Am. Cancer Soc., W.Va., 1954-58; chmn. W.Va. Atomic Energy Commn., Charleston, 1962-64. Grantee in field; Egleston medal for disting. engring. achievement Columbia Engring. Sch. alumni assn., 2004. Fellow AIChE; mem. N.Y. Acad. Scis., Am. Chem. Soc. (emeritus), N.Y. Yacht Club, Cosmos Club. Achievements include patents for centrifugation cascade for enrichment of fissionable uranium isotope; high acceleration rocket motor; tar-free, slagging coal/waste gasifier; enhanced oil recovery process; synthesis of ethanol from ethylene and steam; waste-to-energy conservation processes; 60 U.S. and fgn. patents. Home: 611 Harrison Ave Harrison NY 10528-1406

SCHULZ, JOHN JOSEPH, communications educator; BA in Journalism, U. Mont., 1962; MPhil, Oxford U., 1979, DPhil, 1981; student, Nat. War Coll., Washington, 1985-86. Newswriter, reporter Voice of Am. News, Washington, 1971-72, corr. Hong Kong, 1972-74, bur. chief Tokyo, 1974-77; commentator BBC, London, 1977-79; coverage editor Voice of Am., 1979-82; dep. dir. Voice of Am. News Divsn., 1982—85; South Asia corr. Voice of Am. News, Islamabad, Pakistan, 1987-89; thinktank analyst Oxford Analytica, 1977-79, 84-88; prof. Nat. War Coll., Washington, 1989-91; sr. corr. Voice of Am. News, 1986—87, 1991—92; assoc. dir. publs. The Arms Control Assn., 1992-95; prof. internat. comm. Coll. Comm. Boston U., 1995—97, 2000—03, chair dept. mass. comm., advt., and pub. rels., 1997—2000, dean. Coll. Comm., 2003—; editor Arms Control Today, 1992-95. Presenter in field. Editor-in-chief Global Beat Syndicate, 2002—; contbr. articles to profl. jours. With USAF, 1963-71. Decorated 3 DFC, silver star, air medals, gallantry crosses; recipient disting. alumni award U. Mont., 1995. Office: Coll Communication 640 Commonwealth Ave Boston MA 02215-2422 Office Phone: 617-353-3488. Business E-Mail: jjschulz@bu.edu.

SCHULZ, JUERGEN, art history educator; b. Kiel, Germany, Aug. 18, 1927; came to U.S., 1938; s. Johannes Martin Askan Schulz and Ilse (Lebenbaum) Hiller; m. Justine Hume, Sept. 1951 (div. 1968); children: Christoph (dec.), Ursula, Catherine; m. Anne Markham, May 19, 1969; 1 child, Jeremy. BA, U. Calif., Berkeley, 1950; PhD in History of Art, U. London, 1958. Reporter San Francisco Chronicle, 1950-51; copy editor UPI, London, 1952-53; from instr. to prof. history of art U. Calif., 1958-68; prof. Brown, Providence, 1968-90, Andrea V. Rosenthal prof. history art and architecture, 1990-95; Samuel H. Kress prof. Nat. Gallery of Art, 2000-2001. Mem. Inst. for Advanced Study, Princeton, N.J., 1971-72. Author: Venetian Painted Ceilings of the Renaissance, 1968, Printed Plans and...Views of Venice, 1971, La cartografia tra scienza e arte, 1990, The New Palaces of Medieval Venice, 2004; also articles. Staff sgt. U.S. Army, 1945-48. Decorated grande ufficiale Ordine della Stella della Solidarieta della Repubblica Italiana; Guggenheim fellow, 1966-67. Mem. Ateneo Veneto, Centro Internaz. di Studi di Architettura A. Palladio. Office: Brown U Dept History Art and Architecture PO Box 1855 Providence RI 02912-1855

SCHULZ, KAREN ALICE, psychologist, medical psychotherapist, medical and vocational case manager; b. Detroit, Aug. 18, 1952; d. Donald E. and Ethel B. (Johnston) Wallinger. BA, Concordia U., 1974; MA, Wayne State U., 1991. Cert. cognitive behavioral sex therapist; cert. cognitive forensic therapist, cert. med. psychotherapist, disability analyst; lic. psychologist, Mich. Case mgr. Comprehensive Case Mgmt. Svcs., Dearborn, Mich., 1993—; mem. faculty Davenport U., Dearborn, 1993—. Cert. rehab. counselor, addictions counselor, Am. Bd. Disability Analysts, Am. Bd. Med. Psychotherapists; lic. profl. counselor, psychologist. Mem. CMSA, ACA, Mich. Self Insurers Orgn. Office: Comprehensive Case Mgmt Svcs PO Box 871344 Canton MI 48187-6344

SCHULZ, KEITH DONALD, corporate lawyer, writer; b. Burlington, Iowa, Dec. 20, 1938; s. Henry Carl and Laura Iral (Bowlin) S.; m. Emily Brook Roane, Apr. 19, 1985; children: Keith Jr., Sarah, Christine, Stefan. BA, U. Iowa, 1960, JD, 1963. Bar: Iowa 1963, Ill. 1966, Wis. 1990. Dep. Sec. of State, State of Iowa, Des Moines, 1965-66; atty. AT&T, Chgo., 1966-67; sec., gen. counsel Borg-Warner Acceptance Corp., Chgo., 1967-74; asst. gen. counsel Borg-Warner Corp., Chgo., 1974-84, v.p., gen. counsel, 1984-88; of counsel Bell, Boyd & Lloyd, Chgo., 1988—. Chmn., CEO Downtown Ptnrs., Inc., 1995-96. Author: (novel) Keepers of the River, 2001; contbr. articles to Harvard Bus. Rev., Jour. for Corp. Growth. Chmn. bd. dirs. Vol. Legal Svcs. Found., Chgo., 1984-91, pres.; bd. dirs. Southeast Iowa Symphony Orch., pres., 1998-2000, 2003—, Heritage Trust Found. Mem. Iowa Bar Assn., Chgo. Bar Assn. (chmn. corp. law depts. com. 1983-84), Wis. Bar Assn., Assn. of Gen. Counsel, Law Club of Chgo. Clubs: University, Economic (Chgo.). Avocations: tennis, bicycling, skiing. Office: Bell Boyd & Lloyd 70 W Madison St Ste 3300 Chicago IL 60602-4284 Office Phone: 312-372-1121. Personal E-mail: KDons@aol.com.

SCHULZ, LAWRENCE A. lawyer; b. Buffalo, Jan. 5, 1941; BA, SUNY, Buffalo, 1966, JD, 1969. Bar: N.Y. 1970, U.S. Dist. Ct. (we. dist.) N.Y. 1970, U.S. Ct. Appeals (2d cir.) 1972, U.S. Supreme Ct. 1974, U.S. Ct. Appeals (4th cir.) 1982, U.S. Dist. Ct. (no. dist.) N.Y. 1990. Pvt. practice, Orchard Park, N.Y. Confidential asst. to appellate divsn. 4th Dept., 1975-81; mem. N.Y. State Jury Selection Uniform Rules Task Force, 1977, Chief Judge's Drafting Com. Ct. Adminstrn. Stds. and Policies, 1977-78. Revision editor New York Appellate Practice, 1994, 95. With USN, 1958-62. Mem. N.Y. State Bar Assn. (com. cts. appellate jurisdiction, legis. policy com.), Erie County Bar Assn. (appellate practice com., practice and procedure in city, county and state cts. com., comml. and bankruptcy com.), Monroe County Bar Assn.

SCHULZ, MICHAEL, physicist; b. Petoskey, Mich., July 14, 1943; s. Helmuth Martin Walter and Annette Elaine Marie (Steimel) Schulz. BS in Physics, Mich. State U., 1964; PhD in Physics, MIT, 1967. Physicist Nat. Bur. Stds., Washington, 1964—65; mem. tech. staff Bell Tel. Labs., Murray Hill, NJ, 1967—69; from staff scientist to sr. scientist The Aerospace Corp., El Segundo, Calif., 1969—93; staff physicist Lockheed Martin Advanced Tech. Ctr., Palo Alto, Calif., 1993—. Co-author (with L. J. Lanzerotti): (book) Particle Diffusion in the Radiation Belts, 1974; contbr. articles to profl. jours. Recipient Outstanding Alumnus award, Coll. Natural Sci., Mich. State U., 1983; Alumni Disting. scholar, Mich. State U., 1961—64, NSF Grad. fellow, MIT, 1964—67. Fellow: Am. Geophys. Union (sec. for magnetospheric physics 1980—84), Am. Phys. Soc.; mem.: European Geophys. Soc. Home: 1037 Twin Oak Ct Redwood City CA 94061-1818 Office: Lockheed Martin Adv Technology Ctr Dept L9-42 Bldg 255 3251 Hanover St Palo Alto CA 94304-1187

SCHULZ, MICHAEL JOHN, fire and explosion analyst, consultant; b. Milw., Oct. 7, 1958; s. John F. and JoAnn E. (Carlson) S.; children: Kari L., Brian M. BS in Fire and Safety Engring. Tech., U. Cin., 1996; grad., U.S. Fire Adminstrn. Acad. Cert. fire and explosion investigator; cert. fire protection specialist; cert. fire investigation instr.; cert. fire svc. instr. II; cert. Can. fire investigator. Fire investigator Cedarburg (Wis.) Police Dept., 1979—90; capt., fire investigator Cedarburg (Wis.) Fire Dept., 1981-90; sr. staff expert John A. Kennedy & Assoc., Hoffman Estates, Ill., 1990-2000; pres. M.J. Schulz Assocs., Inc., 2000—. Cons. U.S. Fire Adminstrn.; instr. fire tech. and police sci. depts. Milw. (Wis.) Area Tech. Coll.; instr. fire sci. tech. dept. William Rainey Harper C.C.; lectr. in field. Author: Manual for the Determination of Electrical Fire Causes, 1988, Guide for Fire and Explosion Investigations, 1992, 95, 98. Recipient Common Coun. Commendation, City of Cedarburg, Wis., 1986; named Firefighter of Yr., Ozaukee County Assn. Fire Depts., 1985. Mem. ASTM, Nat. Assn. Fire Investigators (bd. dirs. 1987—, nat. cert. bd. 1987—, chmn. edn. com., editor The Nat. Fire Investigator, Man of Yr. 1991), Nat. Fire Protection Assn. (tech. com. on fire investigations 1985—, fire svc. sect., sect. rep. tech. com. on fire investigations 1985-92, sec. rep. nat. conf. on fire investigation instrn., mem. bd. dirs. fire sci. and tech. educators sect.), Fire Marshal's Assn. N.Am. (assoc.), Nat. Inst. Bldg. Scis. (reviewing mem. fire rsch. sub-com.), Bldg. Ofcls. and Code Adminstrs. Internat., Soc. Automotive Engrs., Human Factors and Ergonomics Soc., So. Bldg. Code Congress Internat., Internat. Bldg. Code Ofcls., Internat. Assn. Arson Investigators (John Charles Wilson scholarship award 1982), Ill. Chpt. Internat. Assn. Arson Investigators, Internat. Soc. Fire Svc. Instrs., Am. Soc. Safety Engrs., Nat. Conf. Fire Investigation Instrn. (bd. dirs.), Wis. Soc. Fire Svc. Instrs., Ky. Cols. Republican. Lutheran. Avocation: amateur radio. Office Phone: 630-736-0747. Personal E-mail: mjschulz@mjschulz.com.

SCHULZ, RALPH RICHARD, publishing consultant; b. N.Y.C., June 5, 1928; s. Harry and Margaret (Faecher) S.; m. Joyce S. Woolf, Sept. 9, 1951; children: Laura Stern, Barbara Tejerina, Susan. BS in Chemistry, CCNY, 1950. Asst. editor McLean-Hunter Pub. Co., Toronto, Can., 1950; assoc. editor McGraw-Hill Pub. Co., N.Y.C., 1951-60, mng. editor Chem. Week, 1960-68, editor-in-chief, 1968-73; dir. McGraw-Hill World News, N.Y.C., 1973-76; v.p. editorial dept. McGraw-Hill Pubs. Co., N.Y.C., 1976-84; sr. v.p. McGraw-Hill, Inc., N.Y.C., 1985-92; pub. cons., 1992—; mng. dir. DeSilva & Phillips Inc., N.Y.C., 1994-2001. Adj. prof. Grad. Sch. Bus. Adminstrn., Fordham U., 1990-97. Author to numerous mag. on bus. and sci. Trustee Correspondents Fund, N.Y.C., 1979—; bd. dirs. Bus. Press Ednl. Found., N.Y.C., 1986-99, McGraw-Hill Found., N.Y.C., 1987-92, Copyright Clearance Ctr., N.Y.C., 1983-92. Petty officer USN, 1946-48. Recipient Honor award for disting. svc. in journalism Ohio U., 1972, Jesse H. Neal Editorial Achievement cert. of merit Am. Bus. Press, 1972. Mem. Am. Soc. Mag. editors (exec. com. 1984-88), Overseas Press Club Am. (bd. dirs. 1969-73), Nat. Press Club, Players Club (bd. dirs. 1974-78), Silurians, Sigma Delta Chi. Personal E-mail: d5sag@aol.com.

SCHULZ, RAYMOND ALEXANDER, medical marketing professional, consultant; b. Paris, June 2, 1946; s. Helmut W. and Colette (Prieur) S.; m. Dixie Lee Suzanne Specht, Apr. 9, 1977 (div. Dec. 1990); children: Christopher, William; m. Casey Elizabeth Watson, Apr. 10, 1999; 1 child, Francis John. BA in Physics, W.Va. U., 1970; MS in Computer Sci., Columbia U., N.Y.C., 1975. Sr. programmer Meml. Sloan Kettering Cancer Ctr., N.Y.C., 1972-74; program coord. Neurol. Inst. Columbia Presbyn. Hosp., N.Y.C., 1974-76; engring. mgr. EMI Med. Systems, Northbrook, Ill., 1976-78; product mgr. Johnson & Johnson (Technicare), Solon, Ohio, 1978-80; group product mgr. Siemens Corp., Iselin, NJ, 1980-82; mktg. mgr. Toshiba Am. Med. Systems (formerly Diasonics MRI), South San Francisco, Calif., 1983-92; dir. mktg. Voxel, Laguna Hills, Calif., 1992—98; v.p. mktg. and customer support Voxel, Inc., Provo, Utah, 1999—2001; prin. RA Enterprises, San Mateo, Calif., 2001—; v.p. mktg. and sales Scanis, Inc., Foster City, Calif., 2002—03. Bd. dirs. Dynecology, Harrison, NY; presenter in field. Contbr. articles to Life mag. and profl. jours. Mem. St. Matthews Episcopal Ch., San Mateo, Calif. Recipient first prize Roentgen Centenary Congress, 1995, Best Paper prize Am. Assn. Neurosurgeon/Cong Neurosurg. Brain Tumor Meeting, San Francisco, 2000. Mem. Am. Assn. Physicists in Medicine, N.Y. Acad. Scis., Internat. Soc. Magnetic Resonance in Medicine, Med. Mktg. Assn., Larchmont Yacht Club, Commonwealth Club Calif., Eta Kappa Nu. Avocations: skiing, running, hiking, swimming, mountainbiking. E-mail: ras257@columbia.edu.

SCHULZ, RENATE ADELE, German studies and second language acquisition educator; b. Lohr am Main, Germany, Feb. 24, 1940; came to U.S., 1958; 1 child, Sigrid Diane. BS, Mankato State Coll., 1962; MA, U. Colo., 1967; PhD, Ohio State U., 1974. Edn. officer U.S. Peace Corps, Ife Ezinihitte, Nigeria, 1963-65; asst. prof. Otterbein Coll., Westerville, Ohio, 1974-76, State U. Coll. N.Y., Buffalo, 1976-77; from asst. to assoc. prof. U. Ark., Fayetteville, 1977-81; from assoc. to prof. U. Ariz., Tucson, 1981—, chair dept. German, 1984-90, chair PhD program in second lang. acquisition and teaching, 1994-97. Disting. vis. prof. USAF Acad., Colorado Springs, Colo., 1990-91. Recipient Creative Tchg. award, U. Ariz. Found., Tucson, 1984, Stephen A. Freeman award, N.W. Conf. Tchg. Fgn. Langs., 1984, Bundesverdienstkreuz, Fed. Govt. Germany, 1990, Anthony Papalia award for excellence in tchr. edn., Am. Coun. on the Tchg. of Fgn. Langs./N.Y. State Assn. Fgn. Lang. Tchrs., 2002. Mem.: MLA (del. 1989—91), Nat. Fedn. Modern Lang. Tchrs. Assns. (v.p./pres.-elect 2004—), Am. Assn. Applied Linguistics, Tchrs. of ESL, Am. Assn. Tchrs. German (v.p. 1988—90, pres. 1990—91), Am. Coun. on the Tchg. of Fgn. Langs. (exec. coun. 1979—81, Florence Steiner award 1993). Office: U Ariz Dept German Studies Tucson AZ 85721-0105 Office Phone: 520-621-7388. E-mail: schulzr@u.arizona.edu.

SCHULZ, SANDRA E. art educator; b. Dallas, July 2, 1963; d. Lionel Leigh and Ida Maria Johanna Schulz. BS in Art Edn., Tex. Woman's U., 1985, MFA in Sculpture, 1990. Cert. tchr. art all levels, Tex. Clk. and advt. Bartos Inc., Dallas, 1982—90; art tchr. 7th and 8th grades Harry Stone Mid. Sch., Dallas, 1990—91; art tchr. 9-12th grades Thomas Jefferson H.S., Dallas, 1992—. Art club sponsor, robotics team sponsor Thomas Jefferson H.S., Dallas. Chair publicity and decoration Tex. Cultural Partnership, Dallas, 1994-2001; publicity chair Am. Czech Culture Soc., Dallas, 1992-2001. Named Citizen of the Week, KRLD Radio Sta., 2002; recipient Brookhaven Coll. Pyramid award for tchg., 2001, Tex. Senate Excellence award for outstanding tchrs., Outstanding H.S. Tchr. award, Dallas Rotary Club, 2001—02. Mem. Nat. Art Educators Assn., Tex. Art Educators Assn., Dallas Art Educators Assn. (publicity chair 1996-98), Sculpture Assn. (sec. 1993-95). Lutheran. Avocations: camping, fishing, gardening, music, electric trains. Home: 9218 Clear Dr Sanger TX 76266 Office: Thomas Jefferson HS 4001 Walnut Hill Ln Dallas TX 75229-6239

SCHULZ, SUSAN, magazine editor; b. 1971; Grad., Loyola Coll. Editl. asst. Good Housekeeping; sr. articles writer YM; dep. editor CosmoGIRL, 2000—02, exec. editor, 2002—03, editor-in-chief, 2003—. Contbr. for various publ. including YM, Redbook, Shape. Office: CosmoGIRL 224 W 57th St Lobby New York NY 10019 Office Phone: 212-649-3852.

SCHULZ, WILLIAM FREDERICK, human rights association executive; b. Pitts., Nov. 14, 1949; s. William F. and Jean Smith; m. Beth Graham, 1993. AB, Oberlin Coll., 1971; MA, Meadville/Lombard Theol. Sch., 1973, DMin, 1975, DDiv, 1987; MA, U. Chgo., 1974; DHL (hon.), Nova Southeastern U., 1995, Grinnell Coll., 2004. Minister First Parish Unitarian Universalist, Bedford, Mass., 1975-78; dir. social responsibility Unitarian Universalist Assn., Boston, 1978-79, exec. v.p., 1979-85, pres., 1985-93; exec. dir. Amnesty Internat. USA, 1994—. Author: Finding Time and Other Delicacies, 1992, In Our Own Best Interest: How Defending Human Rights Benefits Us All, 2001, Making the Manifesto: The Birth of Religious Humanism, 2002, Tainted Legacy: 9/11 and the Ruin of Human Rights, 2003; editor, contbr.: Transforming Words: Six Essays on Preaching, 1984; editor, contbr.: 2d edit., 1996. Named Humanist of Yr., Am. Humanist Assn., 2000. Mem. ACLU, Unitarian Universalist Mins. Assn., Coun. Fgn. Rels. Democrat.

SCHULZE, ERIC WILLIAM, lawyer, legal publications editor, publisher; b. Libertyville, Ill., July 8, 1952; s. Robert Carl and Barbara (Mayo) S. BA, U. Tex., 1973, JD, 1977. Bar: Tex. 1977, U.S. Dist. Ct. (we. dist.) Tex. 1987, U.S. Ct. Appeals (5th cir.) 1987, U.S. Dist. Ct. (ea. and so. dists.) Tex. 1988, U.S. Dist. Ct. (no. dist.) Tex. 1989, U.S. Supreme Ct. 1989; bd. cert. civil appellate law Tex. Bd. Legal Specialization, 1990—. Rsch. asst. U. Tex., Austin, 1978; legis. aide Tex. Ho. of Reps., Austin, 1979-81; editor Tex. Sch. Law News, Austin, 1982-85; assoc. Hairston, Walsh & Anderson, Austin, 1986-87; ptnr. Walsh, Anderson, Brown, Schulze & Aldridge, Austin, 1988—, mng. ptnr., 1993-2004; editor Tex. Sch. Adminstrs. Legal Digest, Austin, 1986-92, co-pub., 1991—, mng. editor, 1992—. Editor: Texas Education Code Annotated, 1982-85; editl. adv. com. West's Edn. Law Reporter, 1996—. Del. Tex. State Democratic Conv., 1982, Travis County Dem. Conv., 1982, 84, 86. Recipient Merit award Internat. Assn. Bus. Communicators-Austin br., 1983, Merit award Coll. State Bar Tex., 1992. Mem. Fed. Bar Assn., Am. Bar Assn., Tex. Bar Assn., Travis County Bar Assn., Bar Assn. of 5th Cir., Def. Rsch. Inst., Nat. Coun. Sch. Attys., Tex. Coun. Sch. Attys., Edn. Law Assn., Toastmasters (pres. Capital City chpt. 1995). Home: 2615 Ave O 1/2 Galveston TX 77550 Office: Walsh Anderson Brown Schulze & Aldridge PO Box 2156 Austin TX 78768-2156 Office Phone: 512-454-6864.

SCHULZE, FRANZ, JR., critic, educator; b. Uniontown, Pa., Jan. 30, 1927; s. Franz and Anna E. (Krimmel) Schulze; m. Marianne Gaw, June 24, 1961 (div. 1975); children: F. C. Matthew, Lukas; m. Stephanie Mora, 1992 (div. 1996). Student, Northwestern U., 1943; PhB, U. Chgo., 1945; BFA, Sch. Art Inst. Chgo., 1949, MFA, 1950; postgrad., Acad. Fine Arts, Munich, 1956-57. Instr. art Purdue U., 1950-52; chmn. dept. art Lake Forest (Ill.) Coll., 1952-58, artist-in-residence, 1958-61, prof. art, 1961—, Hollender prof. art, 1974-91; art critic Chgo. Daily News, 1962-78, Chgo. Sun-Times, 1978-85. Chgo. corr. art Christian Sci. Monitor, 1958—62; art. and arch. critic Chicagoan, 1973—74; mem. vis. com. dept. art U. Chgo., 1974—; adj. prof. U. Ill., Chgo., 1996. Author: Art, Architecture and Civilization, 1969, Fantastic Images: Chicago Art Since 1945, 1972, 100 Years of Chicago Architecture, 1976, Stealing is My Game, 1976, Mies van der Rohe: A Critical Biography, 1985, The University Club of Chicago: A Heritage, 1987, Mariotti, 1988; co-author: Mariotti II, 2004; editor: Mies van der Rohe: Critical Essays, 1989, Mies van der Rohe Archive, 1993; editor: (with Rosemary Cowler and Arthur Miller) Thirty Miles North, 2000; editor: (with Kevin Harrington) Chicago's Famous Buildings, 1993; co-author, 2003; co-author: Philip Johnson: Life and Work, 1994; co-editor: A. James Speyer, Architect, Curator, Exhibition Designer, 1997, The Farnsworth House, 1997; contbg. editor: Art News, 1973—, Inland Arch., 1975—94, corr. editor: Art in Am., 1975—. Trustee Ragdale Found., Lake Forest, 1981—. Recipient Harbison award for tchg., Danforth Found. St. Louis, 1971, Disting. Svc. award, Chgo. Phi Beta Kappa soc., 1972, Hon. Mention Hitchcock Book award, Soc. Archtl. Historians, 1987, Excellence in Architecture award, Ill. Inst. Tech., 1999; Adenauer fellow, 1956—57, Ford Found. fellow, 1964—65, Graham Found. for Advanced Studies in the Fine Arts fellow, 1971, 1981, 1993, NEH fellow, 1982, 1988, Skidmore Owings & Merrill Found. fellow, 1983. Mem.: AAUP, Soc. Archtl. Historians (Hon. Mention Hitchcock Book award), Archives Am. Art (mem. adv. com.), Coll. Art Assn. (bd. dirs. 1983—86). Office: Lake Forest Coll Dept Art Lake Forest IL 60045 Office Phone: 847-735-5084.

SCHULZE, HORST H. hotel company executive; Pres., COO The Ritz Carlton Hotel Co., Atlanta. Office: The Ritz-Carlton Hotel Co 3414 Peachtree Rd NE Ste 300 Atlanta GA 30326-1164

SCHULZE, RICHARD HANS, engineering executive, environmental engineer; b. Buffalo, May 28, 1933; s. Hans Joachim and Lucy (Kawczynska) S.; m. Jacqueline Van Luppen, Nov. 2, 1967 (div. Aug. 1979); children: Richard Hans Jr., Linda Neale, John; m. Enika Grooters, Aug. 29, 1987. BSME, Princeton U., 1954; MBA, Northwestern U., 1958. Registered profl. engr., Tex. Rsch. analyst U.S. Steel Corp., Pitts., 1958-60; chief engr. G&H Rsch. and Devel., McKeesport, Pa., 1960-62; cons. Mgmt. and Mktg. Inst., N.Y.C., 1962-63, Ill. Inst. Tech. Rsch. Inst. mgmt. consulting divsn., N.Y.C., 1963-64; market analyst Mobil Chem. Co., N.Y.C., 1964-66; market devel. mgr., plastics divsn. Mobil Chem. Co. (now PACTIV), Jacksonville, Ill., 1966-68, dist. sales mgr. Dallas, 1967-71; pres. Ecology Audits, Inc. (Core Labs.), Dallas, 1971-74; pres., CEO, Trinity Cons., Inc., Dallas, 1974-97, chmn. bd. dirs., 1997—, CEO, 2001—. Instr. over 200 short courses on dispersion modeling of air pollutants throughout world; vis. lectr. air quality Princeton U., 1998; adv. bd. Dept. of Environ. Civil Engring, So. Meth. U., 2001—. Contbr. articles to Jour. of Air and Waste Mgmt. Assn., Atmospheric Environ., others; presented papers at sci. symposiums, seminars, confs. Mem. Dallas Symphony Assn., Mus. Art; trustee Dallas Opera, 1993—; elder Preston Hollow Presbyn. Ch., 1996-98; commr. to Grace Presbytery, 1996-98. Lt. (j.g.) USNR, 1954-56. Mem. ASME, Am. Acad. Environ. Engrs. (diplomate, trustee 2001-2003), Am. Chem. Soc., Am. Meteorol. Soc., Air and Waste Mgmt. Assn. (bd. dirs. 1986-89, 90-93, v.p. 1988-89, 1st v.p. 1990-91, pres. 1991-92, past pres. 1992-93, chmn. honors and awards com. 1996-97, vice chmn. planning com. 1999-2000), Soc. Petroleum Engrs. (chmn. environ. health and safety award com. 1994-95), Soc. for Risk Analysis, Verein Deutscher Ingenieure, Assn. Francaise des Ingénieurs et Techniciens Environ., Inst. Profl. Environ. Practice (qualified environ. profl., trustee 1993-95), European Assn. for the Sci. of Air Pollution. Home: 7619 Marquette St Dallas TX 75225-4412 Office: Trinity Cons Inc 12801 N Central Expy Ste 1200 Dallas TX 75243-1791

SCHULZE, RICHARD M. retail electronics company executive; b. 1941; With No. States Sales Co., 1962-66; founder, chmn. Besy Buy Co., Inc., Eden Prairie, Minn., 1967—, CEO, 1967—2002. Office: Best Buy 7601 Penn Ave S Minneapolis MN 55423-3645

SCHULZRINNE, HENNING G. computer science educator; b. Cologne, Germany; came to U.S., 1984; BS, Tech. U. Darmstadt, 1984; PhD, U. Mass., 1992. With AT&T Bell Labs., Murray Hill, N.J., 1992-94, GMD Fokus, Berlin, 1994-96; assoc. prof. Columbia U., N.Y.C., 1996—. Mem. IEEE. Office: Dept Computer Sci Columbia Univ New York NY 10027 E-mail: hgs@cs.columbia.edu.

SCHUMACHER, BARRET, motion picture propman, writer; b. Boulder, Colo., Sept. 16, 1965; s. Eugene Pierre and Mary Alice Schumacher; m. Beth Alice Edelstein, Mar. 24, 1996; 1 child, Tess Sara. BA screenwriting/film, San Franciso State Univ., Calif., 1990. Model maker Holt, Hinshaw, Peau Jones Arch., San Francisco, 1987—90, Clockwork Apple, Inc., N.Y., 1991—94, Cinergy Films "Judge Dredd", Lenox, Mass., 1994—95; motion picture propman I.A.T.S.E. Local 52, N.Y., 1995—. Author: (novels) Fear Itself, 2002. Avocations: guitar, hiking, skiing, drawing. Office: Universal Network TV 5801 Westside Ave North Bergen NJ 07047-5801

SCHUMACHER, CYNTHIA JO, retired elementary and secondary education educator; b. Sebring, Fla., Sept. 24, 1928; d. Floyd and Espage S. BA, Fla. State U., 1950, MA, 1951; MS, Nova U., 1978; postgrad., Fla. State U., 1968-69. English tchr. Grady County Sch. System, Cairo, Ga., 1951-53; elem. tchr. Brevard County Sch. System, Melbourne, Fla., 1953-55; elem. tchr., curriculum generalist, secondary tchr. Lake County Schs., Tavares, Fla. area, 1955-85; retired, 1985. Mem. Edn. Standards Commn., Fla., 1980-85, Quality Instrn. Incentives Coun., Fla., 1983-84. Author: (poetry) Seeds from Wild Grasses, 1988, Creekstone Crossings, 1993, Soul Candles, 1998, Wellspring Legacies, 2000; (poetry and stories) Butterfly Excursions, 1996; (children's books) Colorful Character, 1998, Searching for S, 1998. Pres. League of Women Voters of Lake County, 1989-91; mem. Lake Conservation Coun., The Nature Conservancy, Habitat for Humanity of Lake County. Named Fla. Tchr. of Yr., Fla. Fedn. Women's Clubs, 1966, Lake County Tchr. of Yr., Lake County Sch. Sys., 1985, East Cen. Fla. Tchr. of Yr. finalist, State of Fla., 1986; recipient Good Egg award, Leesburg Area C. of C., 1991, Lifetime Achieve-

ment award, Fla. Edn. Assn. United, 2000. Mem. Lake County Edn. Assn. (pres. 1971-72, cons. 1985—). Democrat. Roman Catholic. Avocations: environ. support activities, gardening, creative writing, macrobiotic cooking.

SCHUMACHER, DIANE KOSMACH, manufacturing executive, lawyer; b. Chgo., Aug. 13, 1953; BA with high honors, So. Ill. U., 1974; JD magna cum laude, DePaul U., 1977. Bar: Mo. 1977, Ill. 1978, Tex. 1983. Corp. atty. Belden Corp. (acquired by Cooper Industries Inc. 1981), 1980-81; sr. counsel Cooper Industries Inc., Houston, 1981-88, corp. sec., 1988-91, corp. v.p., 1991-93, v.p. adminstrn., corp. sec., 1993-95, sr. v.p., gen. counsel, sec., 1995—2003, sr. v.p., gen. counsel, chief compliance officer, 2003—. Bd. dirs. Gardner Denver, Inc. Mem. ABA, Am. Corp. Counsel Assn., Am. Soc. Corp. Secs. (pres. Houston chpt. 1992-93, bd. dirs. 1995-98), Am. Arbitration Assn. (bd. dirs. 1996—), State Bar Tex. Office: Copper Industries Inc Chase Tower 600 Travis St Ste 5800 Houston TX 77002-2912 E-mail: schumach@cooperindustries.com.

SCHUMACHER, H(ARRY) RALPH, internist, rheumatologist, medical educator, researcher; b. Montreal, Canada, Feb. 14, 1933; s. H. Ralph and Dorothy (Shreiner) S.; m. Elizabeth Jean Swisher, July 13, 1963; children: Heidi Ruth, Kaethe Beth. BS, Ursinus Coll., 1955; MD, U. Pa., 1959. Intern Denver Gen. Hosp., 1959-60; resident in medicine Wadsworth VA Hosp., LA, 1960-62, fellow in rheumatology, 1962-63, Robert B. Brigham Hosp. and Harvard U. Med. Sch., Boston, 1965-67; chief arthritis-immunology ctr. VA Med. Ctr., Phila., 1967—; faculty mem. U. Pa. Sch. Medicine, Phila., 1967—, prof. medicine, 1979—, acting arthritis divsn. chief, 1978-80, 91-95, prof. orthopaedics, 1998—. Vis. scholar NIH, 1994-99; lectr. in field. Author: Gout and Pseudogout, 1978, Essentials of a Differential Diagnosis of Rhematoid Arthritis, 1981, Rheumatoid Arthritis, 1988, Case Studies in Rheumatology for the House Officer, 1989, Atlas of Synovial Fluid and Crystal Identification, 1991, A Practical Guide to Synovial Fluid Analysis, 1991, The Spondylarthropathies, 1998, Classic Papersin Rheumatology, 2001; editor: Primer on Rheumatic Disease, 1981—97, Jour. Clin. Rheumatology, 1994—; mem. editl. bd. Jour. Rheumatology, 1973—, Arthritis and Rheumatism, 1981—88, Revue du Rhumatisme (now Joint, Bone, Spine), 1992—, Internat. Jour. Clin. Practice, 1992—, New European Rheumatology, 1993—, Asian Pacific League Against Rheumatism Jour. Rheumatology, 1997—, Current Rheumatology Reports, 1999—, Indian Jour. Rheumatology, 2000—, Portuguese Jour. Rheumatology, 2000—; mem. editl. bd. Resident and Staff Physician, 2001—; contbr. articles to profl. jours. Pres. Ea. Pa. chpt. Arthritis Found., 1980-82; chmn., founder Phila. Garden Tours, 1987—95; bd. dirs. Hemochromatosis Rsch. Found., 1984—, Am. Bd. Med. Advancement China, 1983-99. With M.C. USAF, 1963-65. Recipient VanBreeman award Netherland Rheumatism Soc., 1988, Philip Hench award Assn. Mil. Surgeons, 1986, Hollander award Arthritis Found., 1996; named Alumnus of Yr. Ursinus Coll, 1995; named to Sports Hall of Fame, 1997; Deposition VA grantee, 1967-95, NIH grantee, 1981, 94—. Fellow ACP; mem. AAAS, Am. Coll. Rheumatology (master; pres. Southeastern region 1981-82, Klemperer lectr. 2002), Phila. Rheumatism Soc. (pres. 1980), Phila. Electron Microscopy Soc. (chmn. 1975-76), Rheumatism Soc. Mex., Rheumatism Soc. Australia, Rheumatism Soc. Colombia, Rheumatism Soc. Chile, Rheumatism Soc. China, Rheumatism Soc. Argentina, Med. Soc. Argentina, Slovak Soc. Rheumatology, Fedn. Clin. Rsch. Office: Hosp U Pa 8 Penn Tower 3400 Spruce St Philadelphia PA 19104-4206 also: VA Med Ctr 151K Univ and Woodland Aves Philadelphia PA 19104 Business E-Mail: schumacr@mail.med.upenn.edu. *I try to teach meticulous observation and questioning of dogma both in daily care of patients and in laboratory investigation of the poorly understood rheumatic diseases.*

SCHUMACHER, HARRY RICHARD, lawyer; b. June 21, 1930; s. Henry Richard and Martha (Hagenbucher) S.; m. Katherine E. Ware, June 8, 1991; children: Richard, Garry. BA, Yale U., 1951; JD magna cum laude, Harvard U., 1958. Bar: N.Y. 1959, U.S. Supreme Ct. 1964. Assoc. firm Cahill Gordon & Reindel and predecessor firms, N.Y.C., 1958—67, ptnr., 1968—97. Chmn. Legal Svcs. for N.Y.C., Inc., 1994—2003; dir. New York Legis. Svcs., 2000—. Mem. Manhattan Borough Pres.'s Cmty. Planning Bd. 6, 1962—66; Dem. candidate N.Y. State Assembly, 1962, 1963; warden Episcopalian Ch.; bd. dirs. Incarnation Camp, Ivoryton, Conn., 1961—72. Lt. (j.g.) USNR, 1951—54. Mem.: ABA, Am. Judicature Soc., N.Y. County Lawyers Assn. (bd. dirs. 1987—93, 1996—99), Fed. Comms. Bar Assn., Assn. Bar City of N.Y., N.Y. State Bar Assn. (mem. ho. dels. 1990—94, 2001—03), Yale (N.Y.C.), Union. Home: 47 E 88th St New York NY 10128-1152 Office: Cahill Gordon & Reindel 80 Pine St Fl 16 New York NY 10005-1790

SCHUMACHER, HENRY JEROLD, museum administrator, former career officer, business executive; b. Torrance, Calif., June 17, 1934; s. Henry John and Rene (Wilcox) S.; m. Barbara Howell, Aug. 24, 1958; children: Sheri Lynn, Henry Jerold II. Student, Stanford U., 1953; BS, U.S. Mil. Acad., 1957; MS, Northeastern U., Boston, 1965; MBA, Auburn U., 1977. Commd. lt. U.S. Army, 1958, advanced through grades to maj. gen., 1982; army attaché Moscow, 1969-71; chief communications ops., 1971-72; exec. officer Office Chief of Staff, 1972-75; comdr. U.S. Army Communications Command, Panama, 1977-79; dir. network integration, Office Asst. Chief of Staff Automation and Communications, Dept. Army, 1979-81; comdr. The White House Communications Agy., Washington, 1981-82; chief U.S. Army Signal Corps, 1981-83; ret., 1983; sr. v.p. Visa Internat., 1983-86; chief oper. officer Fuel Tech., Inc., Stamford, Conn., 1986-87; pres. IMM Systems, Phila., 1987-89; exec. v.p. Cylink Corp., Sunnyvale, Calif., 1990-95; exec. dir. Hiller Mus. of No. Calif. Aviation History, Redwood City, 1995-98; mng. gen. ptnr. Distributed Syss. Ptnrs., 1999—. Decorated Def. D.S.M., D.S.M., Legion of Merit. Home: 156 Normandy Ct San Carlos CA 94070-1519 E-mail: jerry57ca@hotmail.com.

SCHUMACHER, JOEL, director, writer; b. N.Y.C., Aug. 29, 1939; s. Francis and Marian (Kantor) S. BA, Parsons U., 1965. Costume designer: (stage) The Time of the Cuckoo, 1974, (films) Play It As It Lays, 1972, The Last of Sheila, 1972, Blume In Love, 1973, Sleeper, 1973, The Prisoner of Second Avenue, 1975, Interiors, 1978; screenwriter: Car Wash, 1976, Sparkle, 1976, The Wiz, 1978; screenwriter, dir.: (films) D.C. Cab, 1983, St. Elmo's Fire, 1985, (TV movies) The Virginia Hill Story, 1974, Amateur Night at the Dixie Bar and Grill, 1979; dir.: The Incredible Shrinking Woman, 1981, The Lost Boys, 1987, Cousins, 1989, Flatliners, 1990, Dying Young, 1991, Falling Down, 1993, The Client, 1994, Batman Forever, 1995, A Time to Kill, 1996, Batman & Robin, 1997; exec. prodr.: Foxfire, 1985, Slow Burn, 1986; writer, exec. prodr.: (TV pilot) Now We're Cookin', 1983; prodn. designer: Killer Bees, 1974. also: Joel Schumacher Prodns 4000 Warner Blvd Burbank CA 91522-0001 Office: Joel Schumacher Productions 400 Warner Blvd Burbank CA 91522-0001

SCHUMACHER, JON LEE, lawyer; b. Rochester, NY, Feb. 28, 1937; s. Howard Alexander and Ruth S.; m. Katherine Truesdell, Apr. 22, 1967; children: Sara Wolff, Howard Alexander II. AB, Princeton U., 1959; JD, U. Va., 1964. Bar: N.Y. 1964. With Nixon Peabody LLP and predecessor firms, Rochester, 1964—; mem. mgmt. com. Nixon, Hargrave, Devans & Doyle, Rochester, 1986-90, mng. ptnr., 1988-90. Co-author Charitable Giving and Solicitation. Bd. dirs., officer Rochester Area Found., Inc., 1987-94, United Way, 1986—; pres. estate planning Coun. Rochester, 1986-87. Fellow Am. Coll. Trusts and Estate Counsel; mem. ABA, NY State Bar Assn. (exec. com. trusts and estates law sect. 1985-88, 94—, chmn. 1997, chmn. estate planning com. 1992-94), Monroe County Bar Assn. (found. pres. 1995-97), Country Club Rochester, Genesee Valley Club. Republican. Presbyterian. Avocation: opera. Home: 550 Allens Creek Rd Rochester NY 14618-3406 Office: Nixon Peabody LLP Clinton Sq PO Box 31051 Rochester NY 14603-1051 E-mail: jschumacher@nixonpeabody.com.

SCHUMACHER, MABEL G. director, consultant; b. Milw., Sept. 14, 1944; d. Clarence F. and Mabel Baskin Smith; m. Vernon A. Schumacher, Nov. 1, 1984. EdB, U. Wis., Whitewater, 1968, MS in Edn., 1971; PhD, U. Wis., 1978. Cert. sch. dist. adminstr. Wis., 1975, dir. instrn. Wis., 1975, dir. spl. edn. Wis., 1975, reading specialist Wis., 1971, tchr. mentally retarded Wis., 1968, tchr. learning disabled Wis., 1971, dir. pupil svcs. Wis., 1980. Tchr. mentally retarded Racine County Handicapped Children's Edn. Bd., Burlington, Wis., 1968—73, tchr. learning disabled, 1973—74, assoc. dir. spl. edn. Union Grove, Wis., 1975—84, dir. spl. edn., 1984—88; coord. spl. edn. Wauwatosa (Wis.) Sch. Dist., 1988—90, Sheboygan (Wis.) Area Sch. Dist., 1990—92; dir. instrn. Sch. Dist. Ft. Atkinson, Wis., 1992—2002; ret. Program asst. dept. edn. U. Wis., Madison, 1974—75, adj. prof., Whitewater, 1978—84; adj. prof. programs in mgmt. for adults Cardinal Stritch U., Milw., 1980—88, rev. team mem. Sch. Evaluation Consortium, Madison, 1990; staff devel. adv. com. mem. Coop. Edn. Svc. Agy. (CESA) 2, Milton, Wis., 1994—97; rev. panel Project First View-Wis. Pub. Broadcasting, Madison, 1996; ednl. cons., 2001—; presenter in field. Bd. dirs. United Way, Ft. Atkinson, 1994—2000, campaign co-chairperson, 1995, campaign chairperson, 1996; ch. organist, instr., youth leader Ft. Atkinson, 1962—84; pres. Phi Delta Kappa, Whitewater, 1977—78; sec. Wis. Sch. Pub. Rels. Assn., Madison, 1997—99, v.p., 1999—2000, pres. elect, 2000—01, pres., 2001—02, sec., 2002—. Fellow Program Assistantship, U. Wis., Madison, 1974—75; scholar, State of Wis., 1973—75, U. Wis., Whitewater, 1967—68. Mem.: Wis. Ret. Educators Assn., Walworth County Area Ret. Educators Assn., Wis. Sch. Pub. Rels. Assn. (sec. and past pres. 2002—), Kennel Club of Ft. Atkinson. Achievements include development of variety of education-related computer databases; Facilitator of Concept-Based Curriculum Project. Avocations: travel, reading, computer, cooking, pets. Home: 848 Messmer St Fort Atkinson WI 53538

SCHUMACHER, MARIA, biomedical researcher, educator; Undergradate, Portland State U.; PhD in Biochemistry, 1995. Asst. prof. biochemistry and molecular biology Oregon Health and Sci. U., 2002—. Recipient Career award in Biomedical Sciences, Burroughs Wellcome Fund Ctr., 1999—. Office: U Oregon Dept Biochemistry and Molecular Biology MRB 524A 3181 SW Sam Jackson Park Rd Portland OR 97239-3098 Office Phone: 503-494-2256. Office Fax: 503-494-8393. Business E Mail: schumacm@ohsu.edu.

SCHUMACHER, MICHAEL JOHN, allergist; b. London, 1936; MBBS, U. Melbourne, Australia, 1960. Diplomate Am. Bd. Allergy and Immunology, Am. Bd. Pediatrics. Resident in pediat. Royal Children's Hosp., Melbourne, 1963-66; resident in allergy and clin. immunology Nat. Jewish Hosp., Tucson, 1969-72; fellow in immunology Inst. Med. Rsch., Melbourne, 1977-79; mem. staff Univ. Med. Ctr., Tucson, 1979—; chief allergy/immunology, assoc. prof. U. Ariz. Coll. Medicine, Tucson, 1979—, prof., 1996—. Mem. Am. Acad. Allergy & Immunology. Office: Univ Ariz Health Sci Ctr Pediat 1501 N Campbell Ave Tucson AZ 85724-0001

SCHUMACHER, PAUL MAYNARD, lawyer; b. Columbus, Nebr., Apr. 4, 1951; s. Maynard Mathew and Rita Bell (Jarosz) S.; m. Michele Suzanne Gassé, June 26, 1976; children: Nicole Suzanne, Kristen Paulette. AA, Platte Coll., 1971; BS, Fort Hays U., 1973; JD, Georgetown U., 1976. Bar: Fla. 1976, Nebr. 1977, U.S. Dist. Ct. Nebr. 1977. Mem. staff U.S. Senate, Washington, 1974-76; sole practice Miami, Fla. and Columbus, 1976—; v.p. Community Lottery Systems, Inc., Columbus, 1990-92, pres., 1992—. V.p. Megavision Corp., Columbus, 1976—. Treas. prin. Rep. campaign com. U.S. Senate Candidate, Lincoln, Nebr., 1978-79; atty. Platte County, Columbus, 1979-87; chmn. Platte county Reps., 1988-94; mem. Nebr. Rep. State Ctrl. Com., 1994-96, 2000—; CEO Lotto Nebr., 1992—; CEO Cmty. Internet Sys., Inc., 1995-96, bd. dirs., 1995—. Mem. Nebr. Bar Assn., Fla. Bar Assn., Platte County Bar Assn. (pres. 1992-93), N.Am. Gaming Regulators Assn. (internat. gaming com.), Nat. Republican small bus. adv. council, Rotary, Elks. Roman Catholic. Avocation: physics. Home: 6255 Meyer Rd Columbus NE 68601-8044 Office: PO Box 122 Columbus NE 68602-0122 E-mail: pschumac@megavision.com.

SCHUMACHER, PHILIP GERARD, fundraising executive; b. Green Bay, Wis., Mar. 5, 1949; s. Peter John and June Elizabeth (Umberham) S.; m. Elizabeth Lucille Burke, Aug. 15, 1972 (div. Apr. 1985); children: Nicholas Philip, Eric Peter; m. Rebecca Satka, Jan. 3, 2003. BA, St. Norbert Coll., 1971; MA, St. Mary's U. Minn., 1974. Cert. fund raising exec. Tchr., coach Premontre H.S., Green Bay, 1971-73; assoc. dean students St. Mary's U. Minn., Winona, 1973-75, dir. residential life, 1975-77, v.p. student affairs, 1977-85; v.p. Maly & Co., Winona, 1985-87; dir. devel. Gundersen Med. Found., La Crosse, Wis., 1987-89; v.p. The Metanoia Group, Winona, 1989-90; dir. devel. St. Mary's U. Minn., Winona, 1989-90, v.p. instnl. advancement, 1990-93; exec. dir. devel. Gundersen Med. Found., La Crosse, 1993-96; grad. faculty St. Mary's U. Minn., 1994—; exec. dir. Gundersen Luth. Med. Found., LaCrosse, 1996—. Editor: Memoirs of Jean Pierre Schumacher, 1975. Vol. Minn. Pvt. Coll. Found., St. Paul, 1987—97; bd. dirs. Winona Cath. Schs., 1989—95; mem. nat. bd. visitors St. Mary's U. Minn., Winona, 1993—; bd. dis. Riverfront, Inc., Assn. Fundrasing Profls. Found., Canada, 2001—. Mem. Assn. Fundraising Profls. (chpt. pres. 1993-95, nat. nominating com. 1997, nat. bd. dirs., vice chair member svcs., exec. com.), Winona Country Club, La Crosse Club, Rotary (com. mem.). Roman Catholic. Avocations: tennis, travel. E-mail: pschuma@gundluth.org.

SCHUMACHER, ROBERT DENISON, banker; b. Evanston, Ill., Dec. 16, 1933; s. Frank Ade and Dorothy Ormonde (Hilton) S.; m. Mary Ann Montgomery, Aug. 25, 1956; children: Stephen Michael, Jeffrey Hilton. BA, Williams Coll., 1956; postgrad., Grad. Bus. Sch. N.Y. U., 1957-59; P.MD, Harvard Bus. Sch., 1966. With Irving Trust Co., N.Y.C., 1956-89, sr. v.p., 1977-89, mgr. adminstrv. services, 1976—89, ret., 1989. Treas. Calvary, Holy Communion and St. George's Episcopal Ch., 1976-79, warden, 1980-86, 89-93, 2001—; trustee The Church Club, 1993-2003, treas., 1994-99; mem. non-voting taxpayers Adv. com. Town of Chatham, Mass. Mem. The Church Club. Republican. Home: 431 E 20th St New York NY 10010-7502 E-mail: rschumach@aol.com.

SCHUMACHER, STEPHEN JOSEPH, lawyer, educator; b. L.A., Feb. 5, 1942; s. Joseph Charles and Theresa Isabel (Flynn) S.; m. Jeanne Keller Schumacher, Sept. 29, 1990; children by previous marriage: William Scott, Stacey Elizabeth. AB, U. So. Calif., 1963; JD, Hastings Coll. Law, U. Calif., 1967; LLM in Taxation, NYU, 1969. Bar: Calif. 1968. Assoc. Stephens, Jones, LaFever & Smith, L.A., 1967-68, Wenke, Kemble & Burge, 1970-73; ptnr. Wenke, Taylor, Schumacher & Evans, Santa Ana, Calif., 1974-79, Schumacher & Evans, Costa Mesa, Calif., 1979-87; sole practice Orange County, Calif., 1987—. Instr. real estate taxation U. Calif.-Irvine, 1980-83. Bd. dirs. Orange County Opportunities Industrialization Ctr., 1973-75. Mem. ABA, Calif. Bar Assn., Orange County Bar Assn., Balboa Bay Club. Office: 4340 Campus Dr Ste 100 Newport Beach CA 92660-1812 E-mail: sjschu42@hotmail.com.

SCHUMACHER, SUSAN LOUISE, underwriter; b. Nashville, June 30, 1943; d. Robert Lynn and Elsie (Keiter) Vetters; m. Stanley Eversole Schumacher, Sept. 9, 1967. BA, Butler U., 1967. FLMI, FALU. Actuarial clk. Indpls. Life Ins. Co., 1964-67, Midland Mut. Life Ins. Co., Columbus, Ohio, 1967-74; sr. underwriter Nationwide Life Ins. Co., Columbus, 1974-78, Puritan Life Ins. Co., Providence, R.I., 1978-80; sec. Pikeville (Ky.) Coll., 1980-81; re-ins. underwriter Lincoln Nat. Life Ins. Co., Millburn, N.J., 1981-87; underwriter Guardian Life Ins. Co., Bethlehem, Pa., 1987—. Lector Sts. Simon and Jude Roman Cath. Ch., Bethlehem, Pa., 2002—. Avocations: knitting, walking, reading, travel. Home: 4606 Cheryl Dr Bethlehem PA 18017-8705

SCHUMACHER, THOMAS, film company executive; Grad., UCLA. Past mem. staff L.A. Music Ctr. Mark Taper Forum; past sr. v.p. feature animation Walt Disney Pictures, Burbank, Calif., exec. v.p. feature animation and theatrical prodns., 1996-98; pres. Walt Disney Feature Animation and Walt Disney Theatrical Prodns., 1999—2002, Buena Vista Theatrical Group, 1999—. Line prodr. Olympic Arts Festival, 1984; asst. gen. mgr. L.A. Ballet; co-founder, assoc. dir. L.A. Festival of the Arts, 1987; mem. edn. coun. L.A. Music Ctr.; bd. dirs. Rachel Rosenthal Co. Prodr. film The Rescuers Down Under, 1990; exec. prodr. film The Lion King, 1994. Office: Walt Disney Pictures 500 S Buena Vista St Burbank CA 91521-0006*

SCHUMAN, ALLAN L. chemical company executive; b. 1937; BS, NYU, 1955. With Ecolab Inc., St. Paul, 1957—, v.p. mktg. and nat. acctg., 1972-78, v.p. mktg. devel., 1978-79, now pres., CEO. Office: Ecolab Inc Ecolab Ctr Saint Paul MN 55102

SCHUMAN, LEONARD M. medical educator, academic administrator; b. Cleve., Mar. 4, 1913; AB, Oberlin Coll., 1934; MSc, Western Reserve U., 1939, MD, 1940. Diplomate Am. Bd. Preventive Medicine. Teaching and rsch. fellow in hygiene and bacteriology Sch. Medicine Western Reserve U., 1937-39; intern U.S. Marine Hosp., Chgo., 1940-41; asst. epidemiologist Ill. Dept. Pub. Health, 1941-42, dist. health supt. dist. # 2, 1943, asst. chief divsn. local health adminstrn., 1943-45, chief divsn. venereal disease control, 1947-50, acting chief divsn. communicable disease, 1949-50, dep. dir. divsn. preventive medicine, 1950-51, 53-54; assoc. prof. Sch. of Pub. Health U. Minn., 1954-58, prof. epidemiology, 1958-83, Mayo prof. emeritus, dir. epidemiology emeritus Sch. Pub. Health, 1983—. Epidemiologist U.S. Dept. of Def., 1951-53; vis. lectr. U. Ill. Sch. of Medicine, Chgo., 1947-54; lectr. communicable diseases Springfield Meml. Hosp., Sch. of Nursing, 1947-54; cons. Communicable Disease Ctr., USPHS, 1955-83, Air Pollution Med. Program, 1958—, Nat. Cancer Inst., 1958-79, Divsn. Radiol. Health, 1961-69, Chronic Disease Divsn., 1964-72, mem. Adv. Com. Bio-Effects of Radiation, 1966-69, Grant Rev. Com. for Prevention Ctrs., Ctrs. for Disease Control, 1986-93; cons. Minn. State Health Dept., 1955-90, mem. adv. com. cancer surveillance, 1981—, tech. adv. com. non-smoking and health, 1983—; cons. Hennepin County (Minn.) Gen. Hosp., 1955—. Contbr. articles to profl. jours. With USPHS, 1941-47. Rockefeller Found. fellow, 1946; recipient Samuel Harvey award Am. Assn. Cancer Edn., 1983, Wyeth award Pacific Coast Fertility Soc., 1983, Pioneer award Minn. Dept. of Health, 1991, Recognition award Hennepin County (Minn.) Cmty. Prevention Coalition, 1994, citation from Surgeon Gen. Jocelyn Elders, 1994, Recognition award Assn. Schs. Pub. Health, 1995; named Disting. Alumnus 2000, Case Western Reserve Sch. Medicine. Fellow APHA (chmn. infectious disease monograph subcom. 1961-68, mem. com. evaluations and standards 1962-66, governing coun. 1964-70, resolutions com. 1964-65, chmn. subcom. on drugs 1964-65, vice chmn. epidemiology sect. 1966, chmn. epidemiology sect. 1967, program area com. communicable diseases 1966-70, mem. tech. devel. bd. 1966-70, v.p. 1993-94, John Snow award 1983, Sedgwick Meml. medal 1996), Am. Coll. Epidemiology (bd. dirs. 1979-89, chmn. edn. com. 1985-92, Abraham H. Lilienfeld award 1989, cert. Appreciation 1991), Am. Heart Assn. (coun. epidemiology 1965, hon.); mem AAAS, AAUP, Am. Assn. Pub. Health Physicians, Am. Coll. Preventive Medicine (sec. coun. rsch. 1956-59, chmn. 1959-64), Am. Epidemiol. Soc. (v.p. 1978), Am. Thoracic Soc. Am. Venereal Disease Assn., Am. Cancer Soc. (Minn. divsn.), Assn. Mil. Surgeons U.S., Assn. Tchrs. Preventive Medicine, Internat. Epidemiol. Soc., Internat. Soc. Cardiology, Internat. Soc. Thrombosis and Hemostasis, Mid. States Pub. Health Assn., Minn. Pub. Health Assn. (Pub. Health Achievement award 1987), N.Y. Acad. Scis., Pub. Health Cancer Assn., Soc. Epidemiol. Rsch. (exec. bd. 1980, award for Outstanding Contbns. to Field of Epidemiology 1992), Phi Beta Kappa, Alpha Omega Alpha, Phi Zeta, Sigma Xi, Phi Kappa Phi, Delta Omega (award selection com. 1985, pres. Pi chpt. 1985—, nat. pres.-elect 1990-92, pres. 1993-95). Office: U Minn Mayo Meml Bldg Box 197 420 Delaware St SE Minneapolis MN 55455-0374 Fax: 612-626-6931. E-mail: schum009@maroon.tc.umn.edu.

SCHUMAN, PATRICIA GLASS, publishing company executive, educator; b. N.Y.C., Mar. 15, 1943; d. Milton and Shirley Rhoda (Goodman) Glass; m. Alan Bruce Schuman, Aug. 30, 1964 (div. 1973); m. Stanley Robert Epstein, June 14, 1997. AB, U. Cin., 1963; MS, Columbia U., 1966. Libr. trainee Bklyn. Pub. Libr., 1963-65; tchr. libr. Brandeis High Sch., N.Y.C., 1966; asst. prof. libr. N.Y. Tech. Coll., Bklyn., 1966-71; assoc. editor Sch. Libr. Jour., N.Y.C., 1970-73; sr. editor R.R. Bowker Co., N.Y.C., 1973-76; pres. Neal-Schuman Pubs., N.Y.C., 1976—. Vis. prof. St. John's U., Queens, N.Y., 1977-79, Columbia U., N.Y.C., 1981-90, Pratt Inst., 1993-2000, Syracuse U., 1997—; cons. N.Y. State Coun. on Arts, 1987, Office Tech. Assessment, U.S. Congress, 1982, 84, Coord. Coun. Lit. Mags., N.Y.C., 1987, NEH, 1980, Temple U., 1978-80; bd. visitors Sch. Libr. and Computer Studies Pratt Inst., 1987-2001; juror Best of Libr. Lit., 1980-88; mem. adv. bd. Sch. Libr. and Info. Studies, Queens Coll., 1989-91. Author: Materials for Occupational Education, 1973, 2d edit., 1983 (Best Edn. Book award 1973), Library Users and Personnel Needs, 1980, Your Right to Know: The Call to Action, 1993; editor: Social Responsibilities and Libraries, 1976; mem. editorial bd. Urban Acad. Libr., 1987-89, Multicultural Review, 1991-95; contbr. articles to profl. jours. Bd. dirs. Women's Studies Abstracts, Albany, N.Y., 1970-74, Pratt Inst. Sch. of Libr. and Info. Studies, 1993—2000, Ctr. for Publ., NYU, 1996—, Am. Libr. in Paris, 2004—; mem. Com. To Elect Major Owens to U.S. Congress, 1983, N.Y.C. Mayor's Com. for N.Y. Pub. Ctr., 1984-85; pres. Met. Reference and Resources Coun./Met. N.Y. Libr. Coun. Recipient Fannie Simon award Spl. Librs. Assn., 1984, Disting. Alumni award Columbia U., 1992; U.S. Office Edn. fellow, 1969. Mem. ALA (councillor 1971-79, 84-88, exec. bd. 1984-88, 90-93, treas. 1984-88, chmn. legis. com. 1989-90, 94-96, chmn. internat. rels. com. 1998, 99, chmn. Libr. Advocacy NOW!, v.p., pres.-elect 1990-91, pres. 1991-92, Disting. Coun. Svc. award 1979, 88, Equality award 1993, hon. mem. Black Caucus, appreciation award 1993, Freedom to Read Found. Honor Roll 1999, Lippincott award for disting. svc. 2001), N.Y. Libr. Assn., Assn. for Libr. and Info. Sci. Edn., Spl. Librs. Assn . Office: Neal-Schuman Pubs Inc 100 William St Ste 2004 New York NY 10038 E-mail: pgs@neal-schuman.com.

SCHUMAN, STANLEY HAROLD, epidemiologist, educator; b. St. Louis, Dec. 29, 1925; married, 1952; 8 children. MD, Wash. U., St. Louis, 1948; MPH, U. Mich., 1960, DrPH, 1962; LLD (hon.), Clemson U., 1996. Diplomate Am. Bd. Pediatrics. Intern Jewish Hosp., St. Louis, 1948-49; resident Children's Hosp., St. Louis, 1950-51, Grady Hosp., 1953; clin. instr. pediatrics, sch. medicine Wash. U., 1954-59; from asst. prof. to prof. epidemiology, sch. pub. health U. Mich., Ann Arbor, 1962-73; prof. epidemiology in family practice, coll. medicine Med. U. S.C., Charleston, 1974—2002, prof. pediatrics, 1976—2002, prof. emeritus, 2002—. Med. dir. Agromedicine Program, Clemson and Med. U. S.C., 1984-2002. Author: Epidemiology, 1986, Environmental Epidemiology for the Busy Clinician, 1997, AG-MED, Rural Practitioner's Guide, 1997, User's Guide to Agromedicine, 2000; editor-in-chief Jour. Agromedicine, 1994-2002. Recipient Gov.'s Palmetto award for pub. svc., 2000, Man of Yr. award in S.C. Agr., Progressive Farmer Mag., 2000. Mem. Am. Epidemiol. Soc., Soc. Epidemiol. Rsch., Coun. Agrl. Sci. Tech., Am. Physicians' Poetry Assn. (Poetry prize 2000), Sigma Xi. Achievements include research on pesticide health effects; field trials with young drivers; epidemiology in family practice; cancer of the esophagus, health effects of heat stress, fireant anaphylaxis, agricultural and occupational medicine. Home: 1019 Scottland Dr Mount Pleasant SC 29464-3612 Office: Med U SC Agromedicine Program 171 Ashley Ave Charleston SC 29425-0001

SCHUMAN, WILLIAM PAUL, lawyer; b. Chgo., May 6, 1954; s. Alvin W. and Gloria (Kayner) S.; m. Caryn Gutmann, Dec. 20, 1980; children: Lindsey J., Lisa A., Jamie L. BBA, U. Mich., 1976; JD, Harvard U., 1979. Bar: U.S. Dist. Ct. (no. dist.) Ill. 1979. Assoc. McDermott, Will & Emery, LLP, Chgo., 1979—84, ptnr., 1985—. Mem. ABA, Ill. Bar Assn., Chgo. Bar Assn. Avocations: softball, golf, basketball. Home: 1863 Clavey Rd Highland Park IL 60035-4373 Office: McDermott Will & Emery LLP Ste 3100 227 W Monroe St Chicago IL 60606-5096 E-mail: wschuman@mwe.com.

SCHUMANN, GAIL L. plant pathologist, educator; BS in Botany, U. Mich., 1972; MS in Plant Pathology, Cornell U., 1976, PhD in Plant Pathology, 1978. From vis. lectr. to prof. U. Mass., Amherst, Mass., 1984—2001, prof. emerita, 2003—; prof. dept. biol. scis. Marquette U., Milw., 2023—. Sr. editor APS Press, 1992; chair APS Press Illustrations of Plant Pathogens and Disease Com.; editor-in-chief The Plant Health Inst., 2000—. Author: Plant Diseases: Their Biology and Social Impact, 1991; co-author: IPM Handbook for Golf Courses, 1998. Recipient APS Excellence in Tchg. award, 1993, Disting. Tchg. award U. Mass., 2994, award of merit MEDAPS, 1996. Mem.: APS (pres. N.E. divsn. 1995). Office: Marquette U Dept Biol Scis 202B Wehr Life Scis 530 N 15th St Milwaukee WI 53233 Business E-Mail: gail.schumann@marquette.edu.

SCHUMANN, J. PAUL, federal agency administrator; b. Kansas City, Mo., Dec. 10, 1937; s. Fred and Miriam E. (Penzotti) S.; m. Olva Kimmel Dorris, Dec. 23, 1960; 1 child, Robert Reynold. BA, MA, U. Miss., 1960; cert., Indsl. Coll. Armed Forces, 1966; PhD, U. Okla., 1982. Instr. polit. sci. Jacksonville (Ala.) State U., 1961-64; intelligence officer Missile and Space Intelligence Ctr., Huntsville, Ala., 1964-91, sr. intelligence officer, 1991-99, sr. intelligence analyst, 1999—. Adj. asst. prof. U. Ala., Huntsville, 1981—2001; pres. Tenn dept. Coun. on Am's Mil. Past, Huntsville, 1981—82. Contbr. articles to profl. jours. V.p. external affairs Jaycees, Jacksonville, 1963-64. Recipient achievement medal for civilian svc. U.S. Army, 1992, letter of commendation South Korean Def. Intelligence Agy., 1992; Dept. Def. scholar, 1971-72. Mem. Nat. Mil. Intelligence Assn., Am. Polit. Sci. Assn., Phi Alpha Theta, Phi Kappa Psi (treas. 1957-58), Pi Sigma Alpha. Avocations: military history, collecting books. Home: 8204 Willowbrook Cir SE Apt A Huntsville AL 35802-3335 E-mail: sch@msic.dia.mil.

SCHUMANN, LAURA ELAINE, conductor; b. Mpls., May 13, 1963; d. Aubrey Paul Schumann, Elaine Anne Topka. BMus, U. Colo., 1985; MA, U. Calif., Santa Barbara, 1988; D in Musical Arts, Tex. Tech. U., 2001. Instr. violin and string methods Wake Forest U., Winston-Salem, NC, 1990—91; instr. upper strings and music theory Winston-Salem State U., NC, 1991—92; asst. condr. orch., instr. strings Murray State U., Murray, Ky., 1992—94; asst. prof. music, dir. orchestral activities, studio strings We. State Coll., Gunnison, Colo., 1994—99; asst. prof. music, music dir., condr. SE Ohio Symphony Muskingum Coll., New Concord, Ohio, 1999—. Instr. violin and string methods Salem Coll., Winston-Salem, 1990—91; asst. condr. orch. Tex. Tech. U., Lubbock, 1997—98; music dir., condr. Ovations Youth Orch. Wheeling (W.Va.) Symphony, 2000—02; freelance violinist; competitor Jordania Internat. Conducting Competition, Kharkov, Ukraine, 2003. Recipient Women of Achievement award, YMCA/YWCA, 2001. Mem.: ASCAP (Adventurous Programming award 2001), Ohio Music Educators Assn., Coll. Music Soc., Music Educators Nat. Conf., Condr.'s Guild, Am. String Tchrs. Assn., Am. Fedn. Musicians, Am. Symphony Orch. League. Office: Music Dept Muskingum Coll New Concord OH 43762 Office Phone: 740-826-8314. E-mail: schumann@muskingum.edu.

SCHUMANN, PAULA M. L. writer; b. Phila., Pa., Oct. 23, 1938; d. Paschal Francis and Paula Marie Libonati; m. Walter Francis Schumann, June 17, 1967; 2 children. MT, PCMS, Phila. County Med. Soc., 1972. Medical Tech. Phila. Gen. Hosp. Sch. of Med. Tech., Pa., 1971. Author and pub. Renaitre Press, King of Prussia, Pa., 1998—. Author (publisher): A Chapter in the Life of a Poet (a story in verse), 1995, With His Love, Prayers and Poems, 2002; author: (poems in English) Les Saisons de la Vie, 1998. Pres. Legion of Mary, King of Prussia, Pa., 2000—02. Scholar, Franklin Sch. of Sci. and Arts, 1960 to 1961. Mem.: Phila. Writers' Conf., Poetry Soc. of Am., The Acad. of Am. Poets (Disting. mem. of the Internat. Soc. of Poets). Roman Catholic. Avocations: cooking, travel, swimming, piano, dance. Office: Renaitre Press P O Box 61163 King Of Prussia PA 19406-1163

SCHUMANN, WILLIAM HENRY, III, financial executive; b. Iowa City, Aug. 28, 1950; s. William Henry Jr. and Eunice Vere (Doak) S. BS, UCLA, 1972; MS, U. So. Calif., 1973. Program mgmt. analyst Hughes Helicopters, Culver City, Calif., 1973-75; mgr. fin. planning Sunkist Growers, Sherman Oaks, Calif., 1975-81; dir. N.Am. Ops. Agrl. Products Group, FMC Corp., Chgo., 1981—; treas. FMC Corp., 1987—, exec. dir. corp. development, 1990-93, v.p., 1995—, sr. v.p., CFO, 1999—2001, FMC Techs., 2001—. Bd. dirs. Gt. Lakes Advisors. Republican. Office: FMC Techs 200 E Randolf Dr Chicago IL 60601

SCHUMER, CHARLES ELLIS, senator; b. Brooklyn, N.Y., Nov. 23, 1950; s. Abraham and Selma (Rosen) S.; m. Iris Weinshall, 1980; children: Jessica Emily, Alison. BA magna cum laude, Harvard U., 1971, JD with honors, 1974. Bar: N.Y. 1975. Mem. staff U.S. Senator Claiborne Pell, 1973; assoc. Paul, Weiss, Rifking, Wharton and Garrison, 1974; mem. N.Y. State Assembly, 1975-80, chmn. subcom. on city mgmt. and governance, 1977, chmn. com. on oversight and investigation, 1979; mem. 97th-98th Congresses from 16th N.Y. Dist., 1981—85, 99th-105th Congresses from 10th (now 9th) N.Y. dist., Washington, 1985-98; mem. Banking & Fin. Svcs. Com.; ranking minority mem. jud. subcom. on crime; U.S. senator from NY, 1998—; senate com. on banking, housing and urban affairs 106th Congress, mem. judiciary and rules and adminstrn. Herbert Tenzer award for Pub. Service, Five Towns Jewish coun., 1995, Criminal Justice Legis. award, NY State Bar Assoc., 1999, Leadership in Govt. award, Columbia U. Bus. Sch., 1999, Travers J. Bell Mem award of Distinction, NY Dist. Econ. Edn. Found, Securities Industry, Assoc., 1999, Pub. Policy Achievement award, Amer. Cancer Society, 2000, Sound Guardian award, NY Audobon and Cons. Industry Coun. of Westchester, 2002 Mem. B'nai Brith, Phi Beta Kappa. Democrat. Jewish. Office: US Senate 313 Hart Office Bldg Washington DC 20515-0001*

SCHUMM, STEVEN A, corporate financial executive; b. 1953; B in bus. adminstrn., St. Louis U. Now mng. ptnr. Ernst & Young, St. Louis, 1974—98, nat. dir. ind. tax. services; exec. v.p. Charter Communications, 1998—2002, interim CFO, 2002—, exec. v.p., chief admin. officer, 1998—. Mem. nat. tax com. Ernst & Young; dir. of TV Gateway LLC. Mem. St. Louis Regional Commerce and Growth Assn.; Repertory Theatre of St. Louis; Boy Scouts of Am.; mem. St. Louis U. Sch. of Bus.; archdiocese of St. Louis. Office: Charter Communications 12405 Powerscourt Dr Saint Louis MO 63131

SCHUNDLER, BRET DAVIS, former mayor; b. Colonia, N.J., Jan. 14, 1959; s. Hans Otto and Gertrud (Droop) S.; m. Lynn Greenfield, Aug. 10, 1985; children: Shaylin Annedore, Hans Otto. Student, U. Haifa, Israel, 1980; BA in Sociology cum laude, Harvard U., 1981. Exec. asst. U.S. Congressman Roy Dyson, Washington, 1982-83; campaign organizer Gary Hart for Pres., Washington, 1983-84; instl. sales assoc. Salomon Bros., N.Y.C., 1984-87, C.J. Lawrence, N.Y.C., 1987-90; self-employed fin. mgr. Jersey City, 1990-92; mayor Jersey City, 1992—2001. Pres. Downtown Coalition of Neighborhood Assns., Jersey City, 1989; co-founder, co-chair Jersey City Coalition for Fair Taxation; Republican nominee for Gov. of N.J., 2001; elder Old Bergen Ch., 1989—. Republican. Presbyterian. Avocations: travel, boating, reading. Home: 299 Varick St Jersey City NJ 07302-4021 Office: 355 2nd St Jersey City NJ 07302

SCHUNICHT, SHANNON ANTHONY, retired army officer, politician; b. Miami, Nov. 17, 1961; s. Wayne Anthony Schunicht and Suzanne Chatin (Tindell) Fast. *While in the Army, Mr. Schunicht was involved in a mid-air collision rendering him unconscious for three weeks. Everything had to be relearned, as nursing actions were reported having been displayed on awakening from the extended unconsciousness (19 days). Studies while in recovery brought about some pragmatic discoveries to compensate for the residual memory deficits. The most valuable discovery was having each vowel represent a mathematical sign, i.e., "A" for multiplication implying "@"; "O" for division implying "over"; "I" for subtraction implying "minus"; "U" for addition implying "plus"; and "E" implying "Equals". Most constants and variables are consonants, e.g., C=speed of light, R=rate/time variable.* BA in Philosophy/Polit. Sci., Fla. State U., 1983; BS in Microbiology, BA in Biology, Tex. A&M U., 1994. Cert. real estate agt. Tex. With U.S. Army, 1983-90. Mem. Internat. Leprosy Assn., Am. Soc. for Microbiology. Office: 408 Eisenhower St College Station TX 77840-1715 E-mail: mandwinc@alpha1.net.

SCHUNK, MAE GASPARAC, former state official; b. Chgo., May 21, 1934; m. William Schunk; 1 child. BS in Elem. Edn., U. Wis., Eau Claire, 1958; MA in Curriculum and Instrn., Gifted Edn. in Gifted/Talented Edn., U. St. Thomas, St. Paul, 1989, lic. in adminstrv. leadership, 1992. Curriculum specialist, asst. prin., elem. tchr. various pub. schs. in Wis. and St. Paul; lt. gov. State of Minn., St. Paul, 1999—2003; instr. dept. edn. Inver Hills C.C., 2003—. Mem. Minn. Exec. Coun.; chair Capitol Area Archtl. Planning Bd.; co-chair The Minn. Alliance with Youth, the NetDay Minn. Program, Minn. Office of Citizenship and Vol. Svcs. Recipient 1st pl. state award, U. Minn. Coun. on Econ. Edn., 1984, award of commendation, Gov. Perpich, 1986, 1990, award, United Def., 1999, Hmong Am. New Yr., Inc., 1999, St. Paul Fedn. Tchrs., 1999, Mpls. Police Dept., 1999, Minn. Sch. Counselors Assn., 1999, United Vietnamese Mut. Assistance Assn., 1999, Dept. Corrections, 2000, 82d Airborne Divsn. Assn. Am.'s Guard of Honor, 2000, Forward Support Bn., 2000, Outstanding Citizen award, 2000, award, Jobs for Am. Grads., Washington, 2000, Recognition award, Gov. Jesse Ventura, 2002, Minn. State Founders award, Jobs for Minn. Grads. Bd., 2002, proclamation from Gov. Ventura, 2002. Independent. Avocations: flower and vegetable gardening, creative cooking and baking, stained glass, watercolor painting, fishing.

SCHUNK, ROBERT WALTER, space physics research administrator; b. N.Y.C. BS, NYU, 1965; PhD in Phys. Fluids, Yale U., 1970. Fellow space physics Inst. Sci. and Tech., U. Mich., 1970-71; rsch. assoc. geophysicist Yale U., 1971-73; rsch. assoc. space physics U. Calif., San Diego, 1973-76; assoc. prof. Utah State U., Logan, 1976-79, prof. physics, 1979—. Mem. Com. Solar Terrestrial Rsch., Geophys. Rsch. Bd., Nat. Acad. Sci., 1979-82, Nat. Ctr. Atmospheric Rsch. Computer Divsns. Adv. Panel, 1980-83; prin. invester Solar Terrestrial Theory Program, 1980—. Assoc. editor Jour. Geophys. Rsch., 1977-80. Recipient Gov.'s Medal Sci. & Tech., Utah, 1988. Fellow Am. Geophys. Union; mem. AAAS. Home: Utah State U Ctr Atmospheric Space Logan UT 84322-4405

SCHUPAK, DONALD, merchant banker, strategic planner, lawyer; b. N.Y.C., Apr. 2, 1943; s. Sidney and Helen (Smith) S.; m. Leslie Silverman, June 21, 1964 (div. 1981); children: Andrew, Jessica; m. Cynthia Saul, Nov. 19, 1981; children: Amanda, Philip Nicholas. BA, Syracuse U., 1964, JD, 1966; LLM in Taxation, NYU, 1970. Bar: N.Y. Assoc. various law firms, N.Y.C., 1966-70; ptnr. Schupak, Rosenfeld, Fishbein, et al, N.Y.C., 1970-82; chmn. bd., chief exec. officer Donald Schupak and Co., Inc., N.Y.C., 1982—, Safety Harbor Corp., N.Y.C., 1985-90. Vice chmn. Horn and Hardart Co., N.Y.C., 1977-88, chmn. bd., chief exec. officer, pres., 1988—. Mem. Assn. of Bar of City of N.Y., N.Y. Bar Assn., Phi Kappa Phi, Order of Coif. Clubs: Rombout Hunt (Hyde Park, N.Y.). Office: Danskin Inc 530 7th Ave New York NY 10018 also: Hardart Cons Co 730 5th Ave New York NY 10019-4105 also: Learn2 dot com Inc 1311 Mamaroneck Ave White Plains NY 10605

SCHUPBACH, ROSA LECHNER, retired economist; b. Zurich, Switzerland, June 19, 1928; arrived in U.S., 1959, naturalized, 1966; d. Florian and Marie (Ozeler) Lechner; m. Edmund W. Schupbach, Dec. 27, 1967 (dec.). BS, Columbia U., 1967, MA, 1968, MEd, 1981. Jr. economist Caltex Petroleum Corp., N.Y.C., 1967—67; economist, legal asst. Anderson Russell Kill & Olick, N.Y.C., 1971—77; rsch. asst. to prof. Fritz Machlup Dept. Econs. NYU, 1979—83; with Nat. Bur. Econ. Rsch., 1983—90; ret., 1990. Aux. police officer N.Y.C. Police Dept., 1980—; pres. East 74th St. Block Assn., N.Y.C., 1980—. Mem.: NY Acad. Scis. Home: 20 E 74th St New York NY 10021-2654

SCHUPP, PAUL EUGENE, mathematician, educator; b. Cleve., Mar. 12, 1937; s. Paul Eugene and Venna Marie Schupp; m. Elva Stewart, June 14, 1984 (div. June 14, 1984); 1 child, Jerome Oliver William. BA, Case Western Res. U., 1959; PhD, U. Mich., 1966. Asst. prof. U. Wis., Madison, 1966—67, U. Ill., Urbana, 1968—71, assoc. prof., 1971—75, prof., 1975—, assoc. mem. Ctr. for Advanced Study, 1976—77. Vis. prof. U. London, 1982, U. Paris VII, 1984—92, U. Singapore, 1982, U. Bordeaux, 1984, 96; exch. vis. USA-USSR Nat. Acads. Sci. Exch. Program, 1982. Author: (with R.C. Lyndon) Combinatorial Group Theory. Fellow, John Simon Guggenheim Found., 1977—78. Mem.: Am. Math. Soc. Greek Orthodox. Home: 310 Eliot Urbana IL 61801 Office: U Ill Dept Math Urbana IL 61801 Office Phone: 217-333-1610. E-mail: schupp@math.uiuc.edu.

SCHUPP, ROBERT WARREN, law educator; b. Miami Beach, Fla., Jan. 21, 1947; s. Frederick Anthony Schupp and Mary June (Barefoot) Schupp Goodall. B.S. in Mgmt., U. Fla., 1969, J.D., 1973. Bar: Fla. 1973, U.S. Dist. Ct. (mid. dist.) Fla. 1974. Instr. Fla. Jr. Coll., Jacksonville, 1972-73; assoc. prof. U. N. Fla., Jacksonville, 1973—; cons. Sears, Roebuck & Co., Inc., 1974. Contbr. articles to legal jours. Participant Leadership Jacksonville, 1979. Recipient Fla. Disting. Service medal Fla. N.G., 1981. Mem. Fla. Bar Assn., Beta Gamma Sigma, Delta Sigma Pi. Republican. Office: U N Fla 4567 Saint Johns Bluff Rd S Jacksonville FL 32224-2646

SCHUR, WALTER ROBERT, physician; b. Webster, Mass., June 17, 1914; s. Robert O. and Alma L. (Gatzke) S.; m. Delta Jean Newman, June 17, 1944; children: Paul, David, Jonathan, Ruth, Timothy, Peter, Stephen, Mary, Joel, Daniel, Rhoda. Student, Valparaiso U., 1931-34; MD, Middlesex U.Sch. of Med., 1940. Resident Milford (Del.) Meml. Hosp., 1940-41, Grace Hosp., Cleve., 1942-43; intern Luth. Hosp., Cleve., 1941-42; pvt. practice Oxford, Mass., 1944—. Bd. dirs., pres. Doctors Hosp., Worcester, Mass., chmn. bd., 1978-87; bd. dirs. AdCare Hosp., 1987—, chmn. bd. dirs., 1987-91, Atlantic dist. Luth. Ch.-Mo. Synod, 1978-87, mem., sec. edn. com., missions com., 1960-77, mem. stewardship com., youth com., edn. com., 1951-57, chmn. edn. com. Atlantic dist., 1954-57, mem. commn. on mission and minitry in ch., named Dist. Layman of Yr., 1966, chmn. com. on ministry Atlantic dist., 1970; bd. dirs. Luth. Assn. Works of Mercy, assn. Evang. Luth. Chs.; bd. dirs. Valparaiso U., 1969-99, sec., 1984-99; pres., scholarship chmn. N.E. dist. Luth. Laymen's League, 1957; vice chmn. Luth. Hour Oper. Com., 1958, chmn., 1959-61; New Eng. bd. dirs. Assn. Evang. Luth. Chs., 1977-87, trustee East Coast Synod, 1977-87, mem. nat. bd. dirs., 1979-88; mem. coun. New Eng. Synod Evang. Luth. Ch. Am., 1988-94; bd. dirs., vice chmn. French River Edn. Ctr., 1985—; mem. Oxford Sch. Com., 1961-86, Mass. Commn. on Christian Unity; assoc. charter mem. Park Ridge Ctr., 1986. Recipient award of merit Internat. Luth. Laymen's League, 1963, Soli Deo Gloria award New Eng. Synod, Evang. Luth. Ch. Am., 1994. Fellow Am. Acad. Gen. Practice, Am. Acad. Family Physicians (charter); mem. AMA, Mass. Med. Soc., Worcester Dist. Med. Soc., Am. Geriatrics Assn., New Eng. Ob-gyn. Soc., Valparaiso U. Alumni Assn. (past pres.), Luth. Acad. for Scholarship (bd. dirs. 1977-86), Concordia Hist. Inst., New Eng. Luth. Hist. Soc. (charter), Internat. Platform Assn., New Eng. Huguenot Soc., Rotary (past pres.). Home: 168 Charlton St Oxford MA 01540-2008 Office: 367 Main St Oxford MA 01540-1746 Office Phone: 508-987-2533.

SCHURE, ALEXANDER, university chancellor; b. Can., Aug. 4, 1920; s. Harry Joshua and Bessie (Ginsberg) S.; m. Dorothy Rubin, Dec. 8, 1943 (dec. June 1981); children: Barbara, Matthew, Louis, Jonathan; m. Gail Doris Strollo, Sept. 12, 1984. AST in Elec. Engring, Pratt Inst., 1943; BS, CCNY, 1947; MA, NYU, 1948, PhD, 1950, EdD, 1953; D in Engring. Sci. honoris causa, Nova U., 1975; DSc, N.Y. Inst. Tech., 1976; LLD, Boca Raton Coll., 1976, LI U., 1983; LHD, Columbia Coll., Calif., 1983; D of Pedagogy, N.Y. Chiropractic Coll., 1985. Asst. dir. Melville Radio Insts., N.Y.C., 1945-48; pres. Crescent Sch. Radio and TV, Bklyn., 1948-51, Crescent Electronics Corp., N.Y.C., 1951-55; founder, pres., CEO N.Y. Inst. Tech., Bklyn., 1955—82, chancellor, CEO, 1982-91, chancellor emeritus, 1991—, founder computer graphics lab., 1970-91; pres., CEO, chancellor The Univ. Fedn., Inc., 1995—; chancellor, CEO Nova U. (now NSU), 1970—85; mem. Fla. State Bd. Ind. Colls. and Univs., 1991—; pres. Vidbits, Inc., 1992, N.Y. Coll. for Wholistic Health Edn. and Rsch., Syosset, L.I., NY, 2000—. Cons. N.Y. State Dept. Edn., U.S. Office Edn., UNESCO, tech. educator sent to Venezuela to study needs, UNESCO, 1960; mem. Regents Regional Coordinating Coun. for Post-Secondary Edn. in N.Y.C., 1973—; mem., 1st inductee Nassau County Consortia on Higher Edn., L.I., 1971—, Alfred P. Sloan Found. adv. com. for expanding minority opportunities in engring., 1974; rep. to Nat. Assn. State Adv. Coun., 1975—; chmn. N.Y. Title IV Adv. Coun., 1975-77; mem. steering com. L.I. Regional Adv. Counc. 1974—; chair Regents Adv. Coun. on Learning Techs., 1986-88; mem., trustee exec. com. Commn. Ind. Colls. and Univs.; mem. adv. coun. learning techs. N.Y. State Dept. Edn., 1982—; co-founder NY. Coll. Osteo Medicine, Old Westbury, 1977; mem. Accreditation Task Force for Coun.on Postsecondary Accreditation/SHEEBO Project on Assessing Long Distance Learning Via Telecomms. (Project ALLTEL), 1982—; mem. N.Y. State Motion Picture and TV adv. bd., chair tech. com.; dir. numerous rsch. projects; expert witness Ho. of Reps. com. of Commn. on Sci. and Astronautics; mem. adv. coun. Fla. State Bd. Ind. Colls. and Univs.; vis. tech. exec. Hofstra U., L.I., N.Y., 1998, 99. Author and-or editor textbooks, film producer; prodr., dir. Tuby the Tuba; designer automatic teaching machine; built one of first computer-controlled anthropomorphic speech devices, 1959; contbr. articles to tech. publs.; patentee in field. Pres. bd. dirs., trustee L.I. Ednl. TV Coun., Channel 21, Garden City; bd. dirs. Coun. Higher Ednl. Instns., N.Y.C., 1973-83; pres. The Univ. Fedns., Fla., 1995--. Served with Signal Corps AUS, 1942-45. Recipient (2) Clio awards; 1st inductee Fine Arts Mus. of Long Island's Computer Hall of Fame, 1986. Mem. IEEE (L.I. sect. Gruenwald award 1988), N.Y. Acad. Sci., Am. Inst. Engring. Edn., N.E.A., Electronic Industries Assn. (chmn. task force curriculum devel.), Phi Delta Kappa, Delta Mu Delta, Eta Kappa Nu. Personal E-mail: schure1ufi@aol.com. *The world is an ever changing, ever challenging reality, filled with opportunities for individual fulfillment and success. A positive philosophy toward life does much to make the realization of individual potential an actuality.*

SCHURE, MATTHEW, academic administrator; b. N.Y.C., May 26, 1948; s. Alexander and Dorothy (Rubin) S.; m. Judith Z. Birchman, Aug. 12, 1973; children: Jared, Deborah. BA magna cum laude with high honors in Psychology, Queens Coll., 1969; MA, Columbia U., 1970, MPH, PhD, Columbia U., 1976. Lic. psychologist, N.Y. Mem. faculty N.Y. Inst. Tech., Old Westbury, 1969—, research assoc., instr., asst. prof., assoc. prof. behavioral scis., 1969-70, counselor, 1970-72, assoc. dir. Human Resources Devel. Ctr., 1973-77, assoc. dean acad. assessment, 1977-78, dir. Human Resources Devel. Ctr., 1978-81, pres., 1982—. Dep. provost, chmn. dept. community medicine N.Y. Coll. Osteo. Medicine, 1981-91. Author: Hannah's Trial: Our Triumph Over Infertility, 1981; contbr. articles and papers in field to profl. pubs. Trustee Commn. on Ind. Colls. and Univs., 1983-86, St. Barnabas Hosp., 1993-99, L.I. Regional Adv. Coun. on Higher Edn.; chmn. bd. trustees N.Y. State Higher Edn. Svcs. Corp., 1993-96; mem. N.Y. State Coun. on Problem Gambling, 1995; chmn. program com. Pvt. Industry Coun., Town of Oyster Bay; vice chair L.I. Works Coalition, 1999—. Mem. APA, Nassau County Psychol. Assn., Am. Assn. Colls. of Osteo. Medicine (chair, bd. govs.), Phi Beta Kappa. Office: NY Inst Tech PO Box 8000 Old Westbury NY 11568-8000

SCHURENBERG, ERIC, magazine editor; b. Cin., Aug. 23, 1953; s. Carl Joseph and Lorraine Claire (Willows) S.; m. Judith Margaret Dowd, Apr. 30, 1983; 1 child, Emilie. AB in English, Brown U., 1975. Joined Money mag., N.Y.C., 1984, sr. editor, 1990-95, asst. mng. editor, 1995—97, Fortune mag., 1997—2000; mng. editor Goldman.com, 2000—01; editor-at-large Business 2.0, 2001, deputy mng. editor, 2001—04; mng. editor Money mag., N.Y.C., 2004—. Commentator Nightly Bus. Report, PBS, 1990—; former pers. fin. reporter WCBS News. Former pers. fin. editor Marketplace Radio, Mut. Broadcasting Sys., 1988-96. Author: (books) 401K Take Charge of Your Future, 1995. Recipient Nat. Mag. award Am. Soc. Mag. Editors, 1988, Page One award Newspaper Guild of N.Y., 1989, Gerald Loeb award Anderson Sch., UCLA, 1989.*

SCHUR KAUFMAN, SUSAN, retired public affairs consultant; b. Feb. 27, 1940; d. Norman and Jeanette (Handelman) Dorfman; m. Clayton Kaufman; children from previous marriage: Diana Elisabeth Schur, Erica M. Rydzewski. BA, Goucher Coll., 1961. Adminstr. fed. housing, fgn. aid, anti-poverty programs, 1961-67; mem. Mass. Housing Appeals Com., 1977-86; mem., v.p. Bd. of Alderman, Newton, Mass., 1974-81; mem. Mass. Ho. of Reps., 1981-94; pvt. pub. affairs cons., 1995—2000. Bd. dirs. Middlesex Bank & Trust Co. Bd. dirs. Newton Cmty. Devel. Found., 1995-99; overseer New Philharmonia Orch., 1997-99; mem. Newton Dem. City Com., 1970-99.

SCHURMAN, DAVID JAY, orthopedic surgeon, educator; b. Chgo., Apr. 25, 1940; s. Shepherd P. and Dorothy (Laskey) S.; m. Martha Ellen Rocker, Mar. 8, 1967; children: Hilary Sue, Theodore Shepherd. BA, Yale U., 1961; MD, Columbia U., 1965. Intern Baylor U., Houston, 1965-67; resident in gen. surgery Mt. Sinai Hosp., N.Y.C., 1966-67; resident in orthop. surgery UCLA, 1969-72; asst. rsch. surgeon UCLA Med. Sch., 1972-73; asst. prof. orthopedic surgery Stanford Med. Sch., 1973-79, assoc. prof., 1979-87, prof., 1987—. Acting chief divsn. orthop. surgery Stanford U. Med. Ctr., 1990-93, fellowship dir. total joint replacement, 1983—, fellowship dir. sports medicine, 1992-95, dir. orthop. rsch. lab., 1973—. Capt. USAF, 1967-69. Fellow NIH, 1972-73; grantee NIH, 1976-96; recipient Top Dr. award, San Francisco Mag. Mem. Am. Orthopaedic Assn. (bd. dirs. 1994-95), Clin. Orthopaedics and Related Rsch. (bd. dirs. 1994-00), Assn. Bone and Joint Surgeons (v.p. 1996-97, pres. 1997-98). Office: Stanford U Sch Medicine R144 Divsn Orthop Surgery 300 Pasteur Dr Palo Alto CA 94304-2203

SCHURMEIER, HARRIS MCINTOSH, aeronautical engineer; b. St. Paul, July 4, 1924; m. Bettye Jo, 1949; children: Harris Jr., Sydne, Dennis, Alan. BSME, Calif. Inst. Tech., 1945, MS in Aeronautcial Engring., 1948, Profl. Engr. in Aeronautics, 1949. Sr. rsch. engr. jet propulsion lab Calif. Inst. Tech., 1949-53, chief wind tunnel sect., 1953-56, chief aerodynamics divsn., 1956-58, dep. program mgr. sgt. missile, 1958-59, mgr. systems divsn., 1959-62, project mgr. Ranger, 1962-65; project mgr. Mariner Mars 69, 1965-69, Voyager, 1970-76; asst. lab dir. energy and tech. application Calif. Inst. Tech., 1976-81, assoc. dir. def. and civil programs, 1981-85; cons., 1985—. Mem. rsch. steering com. manned space flight NASA, 1959, rsch. adv. com. missile and space vehicle aerodynamics, 1960-62, com. project. mgmt., 1980-81; chmn. W. M. Keck Obs. Project Review Bd., 1986-95, Galileo Project Standing Review Bd., 1986-95, Soaring Soc. Am. Tech. Bd., 1989-94; Von Karman lectr. Am. Inst. Aeronaut and Astronaut, 1975. Served with USN, 1942—47. Recipient Exceptional Sci. Achievement medal NASA, 1965, Exceptional Svc. medal, 1969, Dist. Svc. medal, 1981, Astronaut Engr. award Nat. Space Club, 1965, 81. Fellow AIAA; mem. AAAS, NAE, Supersonic Tunnel Assn (chmn. 1954-56), Sigma Xi.

SCHURZ, SCOTT CLARK, journalist, publisher; b. South Bend, Ind., Feb. 23, 1936; s. Franklin Dunn and Martha (Montgomery) S.; m. Kathryn Joan Foley, Aug. 5, 1967; children: Scott Clark, Alexandra Carol, John Danforth. BA, Denison U., 1957; LHD (hon.), Ind. U., 2000. Asst. instr. U. Md., 1957-58; adminstrv. asst. South Bend Tribune, 1960-66; circulation cons. Imperial Valley Press, El Centro, Calif., 1966; pres. Hoosier Times, Inc.; dir., v.p. Schurz Comms., Inc.; pub., editor-in-chief Sunday Hoosier-Times. Pres. Bloomington Boys' Club, 1970-71, Jr. Achievement Monroe County, 1971-73; bd. dirs. United Way Monroe County, 1979-81, Cmty. Found. Area Arts Coun. Served with U.S. Army, 1958-60. Mem.: Ind. U. Found. (bd. dirs. 1986—), Newspaper Advt. Bur. (bd. dirs. 1987—92), Internat. Press Inst., World Press Freedom Com. (exec. com.), Hoosier State Press Assn. (pres. 1989, 1997), Inter-Am. Press Assn. (bd. dirs. 1995—), Newspaper Assn. Am. (bd. dirs. 1992—95, 2002—, found. pres.), Inland Daily Press Assn. (pres. 1989), Internat. Newspaper Mktg. Assn. (pres. 1986, treas. 1997—), World Assn. Newspapers (bd. dirs.). Republican. Presbyterian. Office: Hoosier Times Inc 1900 S Walnut St Bloomington IN 47401-7720

SCHUSSEL, ROBERT, beverage distributing executive; CFO Nat. Distributing, Atlanta. Office: National Distributing One National Dr SW Atlanta GA 30336 Office Fax: (404) 691-6238.

SCHUSSLER, IRWIN, psychiatrist, educator; b. Bklyn., Nov. 14, 1943; s. Jack and Fannie Yetta (Blank) S.; m. Myra Yvette Paget, June 26, 1966; children: Jeffrey Mitchell, Doreen Robyn, Kimberly Beth, Howard, Brian. BS, Bklyn. Coll., 1964; DO, Chgo. Coll. Osteopathic Medicine, 1968. Diplomate Am. Bd. Psychiatry and Neurology, Am. Bd. Gen. Psychiatry and Child Psychiatry, Am. Osteopathic Bd. Neurology and Psychiatry, Am. Bd. Sexology. Intern Interboro Gen. Hosp., Bklyn., 1968-69; resident in gen. psychiatry U. Fla. Coll. Medicine, Gainesville, 1972-74, asst. prof. psychiatry and pediatrics, 1976-77, dir. in-patient psychotherapy, 1976-77, fellow in child and adolescent psychiatry, 1974-76; fellow in human sexual medicine U. Pa., Phila., 1975; practice medicine specializing in psychiatry Ft. Worth, 1977-79; clin. assoc. prof., vice chmn. dept. psychiatry North Tex. State U. Health Scis. Ctr., Tex. Coll. Osteo. Medicine, Ft. Worth, 1979—. Chmn. bd. dirs. Osteo. Med. Ctr. Tex., med. dir. psychiatry dept.; bd. dirs. Health Care Tex., Mental Health Assn.; pres. Osteo. Health Sys. of Tex. Contbr. articles to profl. jours. Bd. dirs. Mental Health Assn. Fellow Am. Coll. Neuropsychiatry, Am. Coll.

Sexology; mem. Am. Psychiat. Assn., Am. Acad. Child Psychiatrists, Am. Acad. Clin. Psychiatrists, Am. Assn. Sex Educators, Counselors and Therapists, Tex. Soc. Psychiat. Physicians (pres. Tarrant County chpt.), Am. Osteo. Assn., Tex. Osteo. Med. Assn., Fla. Osteo. Med. Assn., Masters and Johnson Found. Jewish. Home: 3712 Myrtle Springs Rd Fort Worth TX 76116-9213 Office: Psychiat Cons Ft Worth 3704 Mattison Ave Fort Worth TX 76107-2619 Office Phone: 817-732-8441.

SCHUSSLER, THEODORE, lawyer, physician, educator, consultant; b. July 27, 1934; s. Jack and Fannie (Blank) Schussler; m. Barbara Ann Gordon, June 18, 1961; children: Deborah, Jonathan, Rebecca. BA in Polit. Sci., Bklyn. Coll., 1955; LLB, Bklyn. Law Sch., 1958, JD, 1967; MD, U. Lausanne, Switzerland, 1974. Bar: N.Y. 1959, U.S. Dist. Ct. (so. and ea. dists.) N.Y. 1975, U.S. Tax Ct. 1961, U.S. Ct. Appeals (2nd cir.) 1962, U.S. Supreme Ct. 1975. Clerkship and practice, N.Y.C., 1956, 1958—59; legal editor tax divsn. Prentice-Hall, Inc., Englewood Cliffs, NJ, 1956; vol. criminal law divsn. Legal Aid Soc., N.Y.C., 1959; atty. legal dept. N.Y.C. Dept. Welfare, 1959—60; sole practice N.Y.C., 1960—. Sr. staff asst. IBM-Indsl. Medicine Program, 1969—70, 1974—76; intern in medicine St. Vincent's Med. Ctr. of Richmond, S.I., NY, 1976—77, resident emergency medicine, 1977—79; resident in gerontology, chief house physician Carmel Richmond Nursing Home, S.I., 1978—80; surg. rotation emergency dept. Met. Hosp. Ctr., 1979; house physician dept. medicine Richmond Meml. Hosp. and Health Ctr., 1979—80; gen. practice medicine, 1980—; attending physician, former chief dept. family practice, former chmn. med. care evaluation, med. records and by-laws coms., former physician Cmty. Hosp. Bklyn., 1980—94, advisor emergency dept., former mem. blood transfusion, credential's, emergency dept. coms., 1980—94, mem. med. staff, 1980—94; attending physician Meth. Hosp., Bklyn., 1984—92, supervising emergency dept. physician, dept. ambulatory care, 1980—83; attending physician Kings Hwy. Hosp., 1981—88, coord. emergency dept., 1981; clin. instr. dept. preventive medicine and cmty. health Downstate Med. Ctr. SUNY, Bklyn., 1981—88, clin. asst. prof., 1988—95, SUNY Health Sci. Ctr.; med. dir. divsn. devel. disabilities Mishkon-Jewish Bd. Family & Children's Svc., Bklyn., 1982—2000; primary care physician Jewish Home and Hosp. for Aged, N.Y.C., 1993—94; cons. in gerontology Palm Beach Home for Adults, Bklyn., 1980—92; cons. indsl. medicine IBM, 1990—92; tchr., instr., lectr., prof., 1954—95; med.-legal cons. to professions of medicine and law. Author: Torts, 1961, 1963, 1974, Jurisdiction and Practice in Federal Courts, 1967, Constitutional Law, 1973; contbr. articles to profl. jours. Recipient Pub. and Cmty. Svc. award, United Ind. Dems. 44th Assembly Dist., Bklyn. Fellow: Am. Coll. Legal Medicine; mem.: United Univ. Professions, Assn. Arbitrators of Civil Ct. of N.Y. (small claims divsn., arbitrator), Bklyn. Law Sch. Alumni Assn. (past bd. dirs.), Delta Sigma Rho. Home and Office: 760 E 10th St Apt 6H Brooklyn NY 11230-2352

SCHUSTER, CARLOTTA LIEF, psychiatrist; b. NYC, Sept. 16, 1936; d. Victor Filler and Nina Lincoln (Rayevsky) Lief; m. David Israel Schuster, Sept. 2, 1962; 1 child, Amanda. BA, Barnard Coll., 1957; MD, NYU, 1964. Cert. Am. Bd. Psychiatry and Neurology; cert. addiction psychiatry. Intern Lenox Hill Hosp., N.Y.C., 1964-65; resident St. Luke's Hosp., N.Y.C., 1965-68; fellow Inst. Sex Edn. U. Pa., Phila., 1968-69; instr. N.Y. Med. Coll., N.Y.C., 1969-72; asst. attending Met. Hosp., N.Y.C., 1969-72; assoc. attending St. Luke's-Roosevelt Hosp. Ctr., N.Y.C., 1972-95; staff psychiatrist Silver Hill Hosp., New Canaan, Conn., 1972-95; clin. assoc. instr. Columbia U., N.Y.C., 1990-95. Chief substance abuse svc. Silver Hill Hosp., New Canaan, 1976-95; dir. Recovery Clinic Bellevue Hosp., N.Y.C., 1993-2003; mem. faculty Dept. Psychiatry Sch. Medicine NYU, 1995—. Author: Alcohol and Sexuality, 1988; co-author: Chapter in Advances in Alcohol and Substance Abuse, 1987; contbr. chpts. to books. Mem. Am. Psychiat. Assn., Am. Med. Soc. on Addictions, Am. Acad. Addiction Psychiatry. Democrat. Jewish. Avocations: cooking, attending concerts, opera, films. Office: 207 E 30th St New York NY 10016-8230 Office Phone: 212-213-2513. Personal E-mail: carlotta_schuster@msn.com.

SCHUSTER, DARLEEN VICTORIA, director; b. LA, May 14, 1970; d. Ronald Edward and Marleen Virginia Schuster. BA in Polit. Sci. (magna cum laude), U. of Calif., 1992; MA in Comm. Mgmt., U. of So. Calif., 1994; MPH, Calif. State U., 1997. Cert. Health Edn. Specialist Nat. Commn. for Health Edn. Credentialing, 1997. Rsch. asst. U. So. Calif. Inst. for Prevention Rsch., LA, 1998—2001; instr. U. So. Calif. MPH Program, Alhambra, 2000—; mgr. U. of So. Calif. MPH Program, Alhambra, 2001—. Author: Jour. of Health Commn. Mem.: Nat. Notary Assn., Am. Assn. for Health Edn., Assn. of Tchrs. of Preventive Medicine, APHA, Alpha Chi Omega. Office: U So Calif Master of Pub Health Program 1000 South Fremont Ave Unit 8 Alhambra CA 91803 Personal E-mail: dvschuster@yahoo.com. E-mail: dschuste@usc.edu.

SCHUSTER, ELAINE, civil rights professional; b. Detroit, Sept. 26, 1947; d. William Alfred and Aimee Isabelle (Cote) LeBlanc; m. James William Schuster, Sept. 6, 1969; 1 child, Cambrian James. BA, Wayne State U., 1972, postgrad., 1974-75, paralegal cert., 1991. Asst. payments Mich. Dept. Social Svcs., Detroit, 1972-73; rights rep. Mich. Dept. Civil Rights, Detroit, 1973-80, 82-87, 90, asst. dir. div., 1987-90, supr., 1993-97, dir. Svc. Ctr., 1997-99, contract coord., 1999—2002, ret., 2003; ct. adminstr. Chippewa-Ottawa Conservation Ct., Bay Mills, Mich., 1980-82; quality assurance coord. State Mental Health Facility, Southgate, Mich., 1991-93; acting interim dir. Mich. Indian Commn., Detroit, 1995; proprietor Good Things to Share, 2003—; trainer HIV/AIDS health support profls., 2004. Author: Anishinaabe Language, 2003, Walking in Two Worlds, Delivering Culturally Competent Care in the American Indian Community, 2003, Critique, An Indian Tours Michilimackinac, 1981; contbr. articles and poems to mags. and profl. jours. Bd. dirs. Tri-County Native Ams., Warren, Mich., 1982-89, sec. Native Am. Sesquicentennial subcom., Mich., 1987; mem. Linking Lifetimes, mentor program for Native Am. youth, 1992-93; sec., newsletter editor various civic orgns.; also other polit. and civic activities. Native Am. fellow Mich. State U., 1989. Mem. NAACP (housing com. S. Oakland br. 2000), ACLU (bd. dirs. Union-Oakland county 1987-88). Democrat. Avocations: exploring local historical and natural places of interest, historical re-enactment, research, exercise. E-mail: ikwewe@comcast.net.

SCHUSTER, FRED, federal agency administrator; b. St. Louis; m. Donna Schuster; children: Jenny, Joshua(dec.), Sarah. BS in Indsl. Mgmt., Iowa State U., 1980. Regional dir., acting state adminstr. U.S. Sen. Charles Grassley, Iowa, 1984—2002; regional dir. Region VII U.S. Dept. HHS, Kansas City, Mo., 2002—. V.p. Cedar Falls Libr. Bd.; mem. jud. justice adv. bd. IA Gov. Mem.: Waterloo Kiwanis (pres.), Cardinal Key. Office: US Dept HHS Rm S1801 601 E 12th St Kansas City MO 64106

SCHUSTER, GARY FRANCIS, public relations executive; b. Detroit, Jan. 26, 1942; s. Dwayne Alger and Mary Elizabeth (Cullen) S.; m. Barbara Anne Leopold, Aug. 30, 1968 (dec. Sept. 1999); children— Rory Anne, Reid Patrick. BS in Journalism/Psychology, Wayne State U., 1966. Gen. assignment reporter Royal Oak (Mich.) Tribune, 1966-68; gen. assignment reporter Detroit News, 1968-70, state capital corr., 1970-74, bur. chief, 1974-75, chief asst. city editor Detroit, 1975-76, city editor, 1976-77, news editor, 1977-78, Washington Bur. chief, 1978-85, White House corr., 1978-85, CBS News, 1985—86; pvt. practice media cons., 1986-87; v.p. corp. rels. Union Pacific Corp., 1987-2000; sr. v.p. comms. Cambridge Technology Ptnrs., 2000-2001, Novell, 2001—. Mem. White House Corrs. Assn. (pres. 1985-86). E-mail: gary.schuster@novell.com.

SCHUSTER, INGEBORG IDA, chemistry professor; b. Frankfurt, W. Ger., Oct. 30, 1937; came to U.S. 1947; d. Ludwig Karl and Mariluise (Kautetzky) S. BA, U. Pa., 1960; MS, Carnegie Inst. Tech., Pitts., 1963; PhD, Carnegie Inst. Tech., 1965. Postdoctoral fellow Bryn Mawr (Pa.) Coll., 1965-67; asst. prof. chemistry Pa. State U., Abington, 1967-73, assoc. prof. chemistry, 1973-83, prof. chemistry, 1983—. Contbr. articles to profl. jours. Huff fellow, 1966; E. Gerry fellow, 1982. Mem. Am. Chem. Soc. Republican. Roman Catholic. Avocations: skiing, violin, cartooning. Office: Pa State Univ 1600 Woodland Rd Abington PA 19001-3918

SCHUSTER, JAMES EDWARD, aircraft manufacturing executive; b. Buffalo, Apr. 28, 1953; s. William Daniel and Donna Mae (Flury) S.; m. Ann Marie Evans; children: Jeremy L., Jesse D., Benjamin T., Christian D. BA, Lockhaven U., 1976; postgrad., Morehead U., 1976-77, Ill. Inst. Tech., 1978; MBA, Lake Eric Coll., 1984. Labor analyst GTE Automatic Electric, Northlake, Ill., 1977-79; mgr. corporate staff Gould Inc., Rolling Meadows, Ill., 1979-80; sr. ops. program mgr. Westinghouse Corp. (formerly Gould Inc.), Cleve., 1980-82, head metal working sect., 1982-84, mgr. electronics assembly, 1984-86, dir., mgr. mfg., 1986-88; mgr. ops. oceanic div. Westinghouse Electronics, Cleve., 1988—95; v.p. operations Aerospace Equipment Sys. Divsn. AlliedSignal Inc., Torrance, Calif., 1995—96; exec. v.p. MagneTek Inc., Nashville, sr. v.p. operations, 1996—98, pres. moters and generators divsn., 1998—99; pres. Raytheon Aircraft Integration Systems (RAIS), 1999—2001; chmn., CEO Raytheon Aircraft Co., 2001—; exec. v.p. Raytheon Co., 2001—. Mem.: Gen. Aviation Mfrs. Assn. (GAMA) (chmn. Security Issues Com. 1999—, mem. bd. dirs. 2001—, elected v.p. 2003—). Lutheran. Avocations: scuba diving, flytying, fishing. Office: Raytheon Co 9709 E Ctrl Wichita KS 67206

SCHUSTER, JULIA HORST, writer, publishing executive; b. Memphis, Tenn., June 11, 1957; d. Otto Arthur Horst and Mary Ida Gaston; m. Peter Klaus Schuster, Jan. 1, 1983; children: Tiffany Dawn Bell, Mary Katherina. Corp. sales and sys. trainer Dillard Dept. Stores, Little Rock, 1980—82, mdse. buyer Fort Worth, Tex., 1982—83, Brandise Dept. Stores, Omaha, 1984—85; preschool tchr. St. Vincent de Paul Cath. Ch., Charlotte, NC, 1998—2001; pres. and founder Emerald Coast Writers, Inc., Destin, Fla., 2002—. Mem. Sisters in Crime, 1999—, Queens Writers Group, Charlotte, 1999—, Romance Writers of Am., 1999—2002. Editor (publisher): (literary journal) SandScript - A Journal of Contemporary Writing; author: (novel) Flowers for Elvis, God Whispers. Mem. Okaloosa Arts Alliance, Fort Walton Beach, Fla., 2002, Arts Coun. of NW Fla., Pensacola, 2002, Three Arts Alliance, Santa Rosa Beach, 2002, Christ Renews His Parish, Destin; pres. Emerald Coast Writers, Inc., Destin, 2002. Roman Catholic. Achievements include short stories, essays pub. in various publications. Avocation: artist, painter. Office: Emerald Coast Writers Inc PO Box 6502 Destin FL 32550 E-mail: juliaschuster@cox.net.

SCHUSTER, MARVIN MEIER, retired physician, educator; b. Danville, Va., Aug. 30, 1929; s. Isaac and Rosel (Katzenstein) S.; m. Lois R. Bernstein, Feb. 19, 1961; children: Roberta, Nancy, Cathy. BA, BS, U. Chgo., 1951, MD, 1955. Diplomate Am. Bd. Internal Medicine. Intern Kings County Hosp., Bklyn., 1955-56; resident Balt. City Hosps., 1956-58, founder divsn. digestive disease; resident Johns Hopkins Hosp., Balt., 1958-61; Janssen emeritus, Strauss Halbreich prof. medicine and psychiatry Johns Hopkins U. Sch. Medicine, Balt., 1976-97, chief emeritus digestive disease divsn.; dir. emeritus Marvin M. Schuster Ctr. for Digestive and Motility Disorders, Balt. Author: Gastrointestinal Disorders: Behavioral and Physiological Basis for Treatment; Keeping Control: Understanding and Managing Fecal Incontinence; editor: Gastrointestinal Motility Disorders, 1981, Atlas of Gastrointestinal Motility, 1st edit. 1994, 2d edit., 2002; mem. editl. bd. Gastroenterology, 1978-81, Gastrointestinal Endoscopy, 1979-81, Psychosomatics, 1979—, Am. Jour. Gastroenterology, 1993—; contbr. chpts. to textbooks and articles to profl. jours. Bd. dirs. Beth El Congregation, 1961-76, Am. Cancer Soc., 1975—, pres., 1984-86; chmn. med. adv. bd. Balt. Ostomy Assn., 1966—; chmn. phys. divsn. Assoc. Jewish Charities, 1961-76. Recipient St. George Disting. Svc. award Am. Cancer Soc., 1979. Fellow ACP, Am. Psychiat. Assn., Am. Gastroent. Assn. (chmn. audiovisual com. 1975-78); mem. AAUP, Am. Soc. Gastrointestinal Endoscopy (governing bd. 1975-78), Am. Coll. Gastroenterology (master, pres. 1996), Am. Physiol. Soc. Democrat. Jewish. Achievements include research on gastrointestinal motility and application of biofeedback to gastrointestinal control. Home: 10 Red Cedar Ct Baltimore MD 21208-6305 E-mail: mschuster@comcast.net.

SCHUSTER, PHILIP FREDERICK, II, lawyer, writer, law educator; b. Denver, Aug. 26, 1945; s. Philip Frederick and Ruth Elizabeth (Robar) S.; m. Barbara Lynn Nordquist, June 7, 1975; children: Philip Christian, Matthew Dale. BA, U. Wash., 1967; JD, Willamette U., 1972. Bar: Oreg. 1972, Wash. 2002, U.S. Dist. Ct. Oreg. 1974, U.S. Ct. Appeals (9th cir.) 1986, U.S. Ct. Appeals (D.C. cir.) 2001, U.S. Supreme Ct. 1986. Dep. dist. atty. Multnomah County, Portland, Oreg., 1972; title examiner Pioneer Nat. Title Co., Portland, 1973-74; assoc. Buss, Leichner et al, Portland, 1975-76; from assoc. to ptnr. Kitson & Bond, Portland, 1976-77; pvt. practice Portland, 1977-95; ptnr. Dierking and Schuster, Portland, 1996—; adj. prof. law Lewis & Clark Coll., 2002. Arbitrator Multnomah County Arbitration Program, 1985—; student mentor Portland Pub. Schs., 1988—. Author: The Indian Water Slide, 1999; contbg. author OSB CLE Publ., Family Law; contbr. articles to profl. jours. Organizer Legal Aid Svcs. for Community Clinics, Salem, Oreg. and Seattle, 1969-73; Dem. committeeman, Seattle, 1965-70; judge Oreg. State Bar and Classroom Law Project, H.S. Mock Trial Competition, 1988—. Mem. ABA, ATLA, NAACP (exec. bd. Portland, Oreg. chpt. 1979-98), ACLU, Multnomah Bar Assn. (Vol. Lawyers Project), Internat. Platform Assn., Alpha Phi Alpha. Avocations: river drifting, camping, swimming, walking, writing. Office: 3565 NE Broadway St Portland OR 97232-1820 Office Phone: 503-335-7765. Business E-Mail: schuster@pcez.com. *Hard work and perseverance are the keys to accomplishing any goal. Protecting and nurturing our children and our environment are life's most noble goals. Success is the pursuit of these goals.*

SCHUSTER, ROBERT PARKS, lawyer; b. St. Louis, Oct. 25, 1945; s. William Thomas Schuster and Carolyn Cornforth (Daugherty) Hathaway; 1 child, Susan Michele. AB, Yale U., 1967; JD with honors, U. Wyo., 1970; LLM, Harvard U., 1971. Bar: Wyo. 1971, U.S. Ct. Appeals (10th cir.) 1979, U.S. Supreme Ct. 1984, Utah 1990. Dep. county atty. County of Natrona, Casper, Wyo., 1971-73; pvt. practice Casper, 1973—76; assoc. Spence & Moriarity, Casper, 1976-78; ptnr. Spence, Moriarity & Schuster, Jackson, Wyo., 1978—2002; pvt. practice Jackson, Wyo., 2002—. Trustee U. Wyo., 1985-89; Wyo. Dem. nominee for U.S. Ho. of Reps., 1994; polit. columnist Casper Star Tribune, 1987-94; pres. United Way Natrona County, 1974; bd. dirs. Dancers Workshop, 1981-83; chair Wyo. selection com. Rhodes Scholarship, 1989-98; mem. bd. visitors Coll. Arts and Scis., U. Wyo., 1991-2000; mem. Dem. Nat. Com., 1992-2000; chair Wyo. Pub. Policy Forum, 1992-98; mem. Wind River Reservation Econ. Adv. Coun., 1998-99. Ford Found. Urban Law fellow, 1970-71. Mem. ABA, ATLA, Wyo. Trial Lawyers Assn., Yale Club (pres. Wyo. chpt., 2004—). Home: PO Box 13160 Jackson WY 83002 Office: Robert P Schuster PC 250 Veronica Ln Ste 204 PO Box 13160 Jackson WY 83002 Office Phone: 307-732-7800.

SCHUTT, ALLAN JACKSON, retired medical oncologist; b. Defiance, Ohio, Mar. 7, 1932; m. Ann H. Schutt, Sept. 8, 1956 (div. Mar. 1988); 1 child, John C.; m. Marcia L. Schutt, June 2, 1990. BA, Bowling Green State U., 1954; MD, Ohio State U., 1958. Diplomate Am. Bd. Internal Medicine, Am. Bd. Gastroenterology, Am. Bd. Med. Oncology. Intern Toledo Hosp., 1958-59; fellow in internal medicine and gastroenterology Mayo Found., Rochester, Minn., 1961-65; mem. staff Fargo (N.D.) Clin., 1965-69; assoc. prof. oncology Mayo Med. Sch., Rochester, 1969-94; locum tenens, 1994-99; ret. Bd. dirs. Am. Bristlecome Home Care and Hospice, Frisco, Colo., 1997-. Mem. AMA, Am. Gastroenterol. Assn., Am. Assn. for Cancer Rsch., Optimists (pres. Breckenridge club 1996-98), Rotary Club Summit County. Republican. Presbyterian. Personal E-mail: SchuttAJ@aol.com.

SCHUTT, WALTER EUGENE, lawyer; b. Cleve., July 27, 1917; s. Erle Minchin and Elizabeth (Eastman) S.; m. Dorothy Louise Gilbert, Apr. 18, 1942 (dec. Mar. 2000); children: Gretchen Sue, Stephen David, Elizabeth Ann, Robert Barclay; m. Virginia Varley, Nov. 2, 2001. AB, Miami U., Oxford, Ohio, 1939; JD, U. Cin., 1948. Bar: Ohio 1948, U.S. Dist. Ct. (so. dist.) Ohio 1953, U.S. Supreme Ct. 1962, U.S. Tax Ct. 1983, U.S. Ct. Appeals (6th cir.) 1986. Pvt. practice, Wilmington, Ohio, 1948—; city solicitor, 1950-53. Mem. Wilmington Bd. Edn., 1958-65; chmn. Clinton County chpt. ARC, 1951-53; Wilmington chmn. Cin. Symphony Orch. Area Artists Series, 1969-71; trustee Wilmington Coll., 1962-74, sec. 1966-74; trustee Quaker Hill Found., Richmond, Ind., 1970-75, Friends Fellowship Cmty. Inc., 1986-93; rep. U.S. preparations com. 6th Internat. Assembly World Coun. of Chs., 1982. 1st lt. USAAF, 1943-46. Decorated DFC; recipient Disting. Svc. award Wilmington Jr. C. of C., 1953. Mem. Am. Bar Assn. (arms control and disarmament com. 1977-80), Ohio State Bar Assn., Clinton County Bar Assn. (past pres.), World Peace Through Law Ctr. Mem. Soc. of Friends (presiding clk. Friends United Meeting 1978-81, rep. to bd. Nat. Coun. Chs. of Christ 1985-96, presiding clk. Friends com. on nat. legis. 1984-87), Rotary. Home: 3043 W State Route 73 Wilmington OH 45177-9287

SCHUTTE, THOMAS FREDERICK, academic administrator; b. Rochester, N.Y., Dec. 19, 1935; m. Tess Lansing; children: Douglas Lindsley, David Lansing. AB, Valparaiso (Ind.) U., 1957; MBA, Ind. U., 1958; DBA, U. Colo., 1963. Dir. freshmen men's residence ctr. Valparaiso U., 1959-60, instr. econs., Sch. Bus., 1958-60; instr. U. Colo., 1960-63; project dir., rsch. assoc. Mktg. Sci. Inst., Phila., 1963-66; part-time lectr. grad. div. Wharton Sch., U. Pa., 1964-66, asst. prof. mktg., 1966-72, assoc. prof. mktg., 1972-75, asst. dean, 1973-75; pres. Phila. Coll. Art, 1975-83, RISD, 1983-88, Pratt Inst., N.Y.C., 1994—. Chmn. various task forces, lectr., cons. in field. Co-author: Brand Policy Determination, 1967; editor: A Directory for Graduate Education in Marketing, 1968, An Uneasy Coalition: Design and Corporate America, 1975; contbr. numerous articles to profl. publs. Pub. trustee Greater Phila. Cultural Alliance, 1975-83; trustee Pa. Ballet Co., 1975—; bd. dirs. Prints in Progress, 1977—, Union Ind. Colls. Art, 1975—; mem. East Coast Art Colls. Consortium, 1976—; mem. adv. bd. Design Mgmt. Inst., Cambridge, Mass., 1977—; mem. Coll. Hill Neighborhood Found., Providence, R.I., 1983—, Providence Found., 1984—, Nicholas Brown Found., 1983—, Hist. Soc. Pa., Inst. Contemporary Art, Pa. Acad. Fine Arts; mem. adv. com. The Artists Found. Inc., Boston, 1980-83; active other civic and cultural organizations. Recipient Anvil award Wharton Grad. Assn.; Most Outstanding Teaching award Wharton Eve. Div., George Norlin award U. Colo. Alumni Assn., Outstanding Alumni award Valparaiso U., Outstanding Citizen award State of R.I. Mem. Am. Mktg. Assn., Am. Coun. Edn., Art Dir.'s Club (Philadelphia), Phila. Sketch Club, East Coast Art Colls. Consortium (founding mem.), Beta Gamma Sigma (bus. hon.), Gamma Theta Epsilon, Sigma Iota Epsilon (mgmt. hon.). Avocations: Am. 18th and 19th Century architecture and art, piano, swimming, gardening, landscape design. Office: Pratt Institute 200 Willoughby Ave Brooklyn NY 11205-3899*

SCHUTZ, DONALD FRANK, geochemist, environmental corporate executive; b. Orange, Tex., Sept. 22, 1934; s. Theodore J. and Mildred Irene S.; m. Beatriz Valera, May 18, 1958; children: Delfino, Celita. BS in Geology cum laude, Yale U., 1956, PhD in Geology, 1964; MA in Geology, Rice U., 1958. Research staff geologist Yale U., New Haven, 1963-64; mgr. nuclear geochemistry dept. Teledyne Isotopes, Westwood, N.J., 1968-70, v.p., 1970-75, pres., 1975-93; engring. group exec. Teledyne, Inc., Westwood, 1989-92; chief scientist Teledyne Environ. Systems, 1992-93; gen. mgr. Teledyne Brown Engring. Environ. Svcs., 1993—99; v.p. Teledyne Environ., Inc., 1996-99; pres. Geonuclear, Inc., 1999—. Low level waste adv. com. N.J. Dept. Environ. Protection, Trenton, 1988-90; chmn. com. on radioactive materials N.J. BIA, Trenton, 1980-88. Pres. Children's Aid and Adoption Soc. N.J. Inc., Bogota, 1976-95, Am. Amateur Judo Found., River Vale, N.J., 1979-89; bd. visitors Berry Coll., 1985—; bd. dirs. Yale U. Alumni Fund, 1989-94; co-chmn. Children's Aid and Family Svcs. Inc., 1995-96, bd. dirs. emeritus, 2000—. Recipient Antarctic Service medal U.S. Congress, 1964. Mem.: Am. Assn. Engring. Soc. (engrs. forum on sustainable devel. 1995—), Am. Nuc. Soc. (chmn. no. N.J. sect. 1988—89, pub. policy com. 1991—96, coord. climate change and sustainable devel. activities UN 1994—, chair 1995—96, vice chair 2000—01, chair 2001—02), Greening Earth Soc., Am. Assn. Radon Sci. and Tech. (life; pres. 1986—89, treas. 1990—95), Yale Sci. and Engring. Alumni Assn. (bd. dirs. Bergen County and vicinity chpt. 1989—), Sigma Xi. E-mail: donald.schutz@aya.yale.edu.

SCHUTZ, JOHN ADOLPH, historian, educator, former university dean; b. L.A., Apr. 10, 1919; s. Adolph J. and Augusta K. (Gluecker) Schutz. AA, Bakersfield Coll., 1940; BA, UCLA, 1942, MA, 1943, PhD, 1945. Asst. prof. history Calif. Inst. Tech., Pasadena, 1945-53; assoc. prof. history Whittier (Calif.) Coll., 1953-56, prof., 1956-65; prof. Am. history U. So. Calif., L.A., 1965-91, chmn. dept. history, 1974-76, dean social scis. and communication, 1976-82. Author: William Shirley: King's Governor of Massachusetts, 1961, Peter Oliver's Origin and Progress of the American Rebellion, 1967, The Promise of America, 1970, The American Republic, 1978, Dawning of America, 1981, Spur of Fame: Dialogues of John Adams and Benjamin Rush, 1980, 2001, A Noble Pursuit: A Sesquicentennial History of the New England Historic Genealogical Society, 1995, Legislators of the Massachusetts General Court, 1691-1780, 1997; joint editor: Golden State Series; contbg. author: Spain's Colonial Outpost, 1985, Generations and Change: Genealogical Perspectives in Social History, 1986, Making of America: Society and Culture of the United States, 1990, rev. edit., 1992, Encyclopedia Britannica. Trustee Citizens Rsch. Found., 1985—99; mem. Neighborhoodwatch of Victor Heights, L.A., 1999—, v.p., 2004—; officer Neighborhood Coun. L.A., 2002—; mem. Hist. Cultural Neighborhood Coun., 2002—. NEH grantee, 1971; Sr. Faculty grantee, 1971-74; U. Calif. fellow, 1944-45. Mem. Am. Hist. Assn. (pres. Pacific Coast br. 1972-73, sec.-treas. 1951-88, 95-96), Am. Studies Assn. (pres. 1974-75), Mass. Hist. Soc. (corr.), New Eng. Hist. Geneal. Soc. (trustee 1988-2000, trustee emeritus 2001—, editor, author intro. book Boston Merchant Census of 1789, 1989, rec. sec. 1995-96), Colonial Soc. Mass. (corr.), St. Botolph Club (Boston). Home and Office: 1100 White Knoll Dr Los Angeles CA 90012-1353 Office Phone: 213-250-1865. Business E-Mail: jschutz@usc.edu. *The excitement of collegiate activities makes each year an adventure in learning and a renewal of one's youth.*

SCHUTZIUS, LUCY JEAN, retired librarian; b. Cin., Dec. 27, 1938; d. Gregory Girard and Harriet Elsa (Wiggers) Wright; m. Paul Robert Wilson, Aug. 25, 1962 (div. 1968); 1 child, Ellen Field; m. William Carl Schutzius, Dec. 12, 1976; stepchildren: Christopher Matthew, Catharine Alexander, John Benedict, Margaret Elizabeth. BA in French, Middlebury Coll., 1960; MLS, U. Ill., 1963. Tech. libr. Chanute AFB, Rantoul, Ill., 1963-65; libr. Coll. Prep. Sch., Cin., 1969-74; pub. svcs. libr. Raymond Walters Coll., Cin., 1974-79, dir. libr., 1979-92, sr. libr., 1988—2001, sr. libr. emerita, 2001—. Access svcs. libr. U. Cin. Coll. Engring., 1992—2001. Mem.: Friends of Univ. Librarians. Home: 3444 Stettinius Ave Cincinnati OH 45208-1204 E-mail: lucy.wilson@uc.edu.

SCHUUR, DIANE JOAN, vocalist; b. Tacoma, Dec. 10, 1953; d. David Schuur. Ed. high sch., Vancouver, Wash. Singer: (albums) Pilot of My Destiny, 1983, Deedles, Schuur Thing, 1986, Timeless (Grammy award for female jazz vocal, 1986), Diane Schuur and the Count Basie Orchestra (Grammy award for female jazz vocal, 1987), Talkin' 'Bout You, 1988, Pure Schuur, 1991 (#1 on Billboard contemporary jazz chart, 1991, nominated for Grammy award, 1991), In Tribute, 1992, Love Songs, 1993 (Grammy nomination, Best Traditional Vocal, Grammy nomination for The Christmas Song); singer: (with B.B. King) Heart to Heart, 1994 (No. 1 on Billboard contemporary jazz chart); singer: Love Walked In, 1996, Blues For Schuur, 1997, The Best of Diane Schuur, 1997, Music Is My Life, 1999, Friends for Schuur; singer: (with Maynard Ferguson) 'Swingin' for Schuur, 2001, Midnight, 2003; singer: (performances) White House, Monterey Jazz Festival, Hollywood Bowl, Carnegie Hall, Moscow Symphony, (tours) Japan, Far East, Near East, South Am., Europe, South Africa. Recipient 1st Ella Fitzgerald ann. award Montreal Jazz Festival, 1999, Helen Keller Personal Achievement award Am. Found. for Blind, 2000. Office Phone: 949-240-4400. E-mail: paulcantor@cox.net. *"There is no plateau that can't be reached, no obstacle that can't be overcome if you believe in yourself and your higher power".*

SCHUURMAN, WILLEM GERHARD, lawyer; b. June 21, 1940; s. William B. and Rina (Du Preez) S.; m. Karla Arnold, Feb. 15, 2001; children: Greg W., Bruce J., Angus D., D. Geordie. BS, U. Cape Town, South Africa, 1962, LLB, 1964; JD magna cum laude, South Tex. Coll. Law, 1981. Bar: Tex. 1981, U.S. Dist. Ct. (so. dist.) Tex. 1982, U.S. Dist. Ct. (we. dist.) Tex. 1985. Ptnr. Adams & Adams, Pretoria, South Africa, 1967—79; assoc. Arnold, White & Durkee, Houston, 1979—83, ptnr., 1983—98, Vinson & Elkins LLP, Austin, Tex., 1998—. Mem.: ABA, Internat. Assn. for the Protection of Indsl. Property, Travis County Bar Assn., Internat. Fedn. Indsl. Property Attys. U.S.,

Am. Intellectual Property Law Assn., Westwood Country Club. Office: Vinson & Elkins LLP Terrace 7 2801 Via Fortuna Ste 100 Austin TX 78746-7568 Office Phone: 512-542-8663. Business E-Mail: bschuurman@velaw.com.

SCHUYLER, ROBERT LEN, investment company executive; b. Burwell, Nebr., Mar. 4, 1936; s. Norman S. and Ilva M. (Hoppes) S.; m. Mary Carol Huston, June 13, 1958; children: Kylie Anne, Nina Leigh, Melynn Kae, Gwyer Lenn. BS, U. Nebr., 1958; MBA, Harvard U., 1960. Asst. to treas. Potlatch Forests, Inc., Lewiston, Idaho, 1962-64, dir. corp. planning San Francisco, 1964-66; mgr. fin. analysis Weyerhaeuser Co., Tacoma, 1966-68, mgr. investment evaluation dept., 1968-70, v.p. fin. and planning, 1970-72, sr. v.p. fin. and planning, 1972-85, exec. v.p., chief fin. officer, 1985-91; mng. ptnr. Nisqually Ptnrs., Tacoma, 1991-95; bd. dirs. Grande Alberta Paper, Ltd., 1992—. Past mem. nat. adv. bd. Chem. Bank, U. Wash. MBA program, coun. fin. exec. Conf. Bd., Pvt. Sector Coun., exec. com. Am. Paper Inst.; bd. dirs. Paragon Trade Brands Inc., Montrail, Inc. Past chmn. Santa Fe County Bd. Econ. Advs.; chmn. Santa Fe Bus. Incubator; past trustee Santa Fe Chamber Music Festival; commr. N.Mex. Dept. Econ. Devel. Mem. Anglers Club, Sangre de Cristo Flyfishers, Las Campanas Golf & Country Club, Don Quixote Club. Home and Office: 46 Hollyhock Cir Santa Fe NM 87506-8595 E-mail: skysantafe@msn.com.

SCHWAAB, RICHARD LEWIS, lawyer, educator; b. Oconomowoc, Wis., Nov. 15, 1945; s. Thomas L. and Phyllis N. (Lord) S.; m. Lynn Louise Howie; children: Amy, William, Andrew, Matthew. BSChemE, U. Wis., 1967; JD with honors, George Washington U., 1971, LLM in Internat. Law with highest honors, 1979. Bar: Va. 1971, U.S. Dist. Ct. (ea. dist.) Va. 1979, U.S. Supreme Ct. 1980, U.S. Ct. Appeals (fed. cir.) 1982, D.C. 1998. Ptnr. Stepno, Schwaab & Linn, Arlington, 1974-78, Schwartz, Jeffrey, Schwaab, Mack, Blumenthal & Evans, P.C., Alexandria, 1978-88; ptnr. in charge, chair dept. intellectual property Foley & Lardner, Washington, 1988-99, ptnr., 1999—. Lectr. law George Washington U., 1978-88, George Mason U., 1989—. Max Planck Inst. Fgn. and Internat. Patent, Copyright and Competition Law fellow, 1971-72. Co-author Patent Practice, 6 vols., 1976-99, International Patent Law: EPC & PCT, 3 vols., 1978; Intellectual Property Protection for Biotechnology Worldwide, 1987; contbr. articles to profl. jours. Mem. ABA, Am. Intellectual Property Law Assn., Va. State Bar (gov. 1974-78), Am. Soc. Internat. Law, Internat. Patent and Trademark Assn., Internat. Fedn. Indsl. Property Attys., Christian Legal Soc., Phi Kappa Phi, Tau Beta Pi. Home: 34205 Nashotah Rd Nashotah WI 53058-9534 Office: Foley & Lardner 3000 K St NW Ste 500 Washington DC 20007-5143 E-mail: rschwaab@foleylaw.com.

SCHWAB, CHARLES R. brokerage house executive; b. Sacramento, 1937; m. Helen O'Neill; 5 children. BA in Economics, Stanford U., 1959, MBA, 1961. Formerly mut. fund mgr., Marin County, Calif.; founder, chmn. Charles Schwab Corp., San Francisco, 1971—, CEO, chmn., 1971—2003, chmn., 2003—04, CEO, chmn., 2004—. Bd. dirs. The Gap, Inc., 1986—2004, Seibel Systems, Inc. Author: How to be Your Own Stockbroker, 1984, Guide to Financial Independence, 1998, You're Fifty - Now What?, 2001; co-author (with Carrie Schwab Pomerantz): It Pays To Talk. Chmn. All Kinds of Minds Inst.; co-founder (with Helen Schwab) and chmn. Charles and Helen Schwab Found., 2001—; bd. trustees Stanford U. Republican. Achievements include pioneer in discount brokerage business since 1974. Office: Charles Schwab & Co Inc 101 Montgomery St San Francisco CA 94104-4175*

SCHWAB, EILEEN CAULFIELD, lawyer, educator; b. N.Y.C., Feb. 11, 1944; d. James and Mary (Fay) Caulfield; m. Terrance W. Schwab, Jan. 4, 1969 (dec. Apr. 25, 2004); children: Matthew Caulfield, Catherine Grimley, Claire Gillespie. BA, Hunter Coll., 1965; JD, Columbia U., 1971; BA magna cum laude. Bar: N.Y. 1972, U.S. Dist. Ct. (so. and ea. dists.) N.Y. 1975, U.S. Ct. Appeals (2d cir.) 1975, U.S. Tax Ct. 1980, U.S. Ct. Appeals (10th cir.) 1993. Assoc. Poletti Friedin, N.Y.C., 1971-72, Hughes Hubbard & Reed, N.Y.C., 1972-75, Davis Polk & Wardwell, N.Y.C., 1975-81; dep. bur. chief Charities Bur., Atty. Gen. of N.Y., 1981-82; counsel Sidley Austin Brown & Wood LLP, N.Y.C., 1983—, ptnr., 1984. Adj. prof. N.Y. Law Sch. Trustee Cath. Communal Fund; chair planned gifts, bequests and endowment com. Archdiocese of N.Y.; mem. profl. adv. com. Mus. of Modern Art, Met. Mus. Art, Cen. Park Conservancy, Calvary Hosp., Mus. of Arts and Design, N.Y. Pub. Libr., Ascension Sch.; chmn. adv. com. Meml. Sloan-Kettering Cancer Ctr.; trustee Cooke Ctr. Learning and Devel. Fellow Am. Coll. Trust and Estate Counsel; mem. N.Y. State Bar Assn., Phi Beta Kappa. Democrat. Roman Catholic. Personal E-mail: eschwab@sidley.com.

SCHWAB, ERNEST ROE, III, physiology educator, researcher; b. Denver, Colo., July 19, 1950; s. Ernest Roe and Mary Ellen (Murray) S.; m. Patty Ann Millspaugh, May 16, 1974. Ph.D., Loma Linda U., Loma Linda, California, 1981—89; M.S., Andrews U., Berrien Springs, MI, 1975—78; B.A., Union Coll., Lincoln, NE, 1969—75. Assoc. prof. of phys. therapy, and dir. of basic sci. edn. Sch. of Allied Health Professions, Loma Linda U., Loma Linda, Calif., 1996—2003; assoc. prof. of biology La Sierra U., Riverside, Calif., 1991—96; assist. prof. of biology Loma Linda U., Riverside, Calif., 1983—91. Author (secondary author): (published and presented research) Variety of Scientific Journals and Congresses. Mem. Calif. chpt. Nat. Wilflife Fedn., 1981. Recipient Godfrey T. Anderson Award for Excellence in Tchg., Loma Linda U., 1990, Cert. of Merit, Nat. Academic Advising Assn., 1994; grantee Rsch. Opportunity Award, NSF, 1989. Mem. AAAS, Entomol. Soc. Am. (news service liaison 1986—), Union Concerned Scientists, Scientists Action Network, Internat. Bee Research Assn., Internat. Union for the Study of Social Insects, N.Y. Acad. Scis., Sigma Xi (Grad. Student Research grantee 1979), Nat. Acad. Adv. Assn. (Cert. of Merit 1994), Soc. for Neurosci., Internat. Soc. for Neuroethology, Soc. for Integrative of Comparative Biology. Democrat. Sda. Avocations: photography, travel, backpacking, piano. Home: 423 Marilyn Lane Redlands CA 92373 Office: Loma Linda University 11234 Anderson St Loma Linda CA 92350-0001 Personal E-mail: acheta1@earthlink.net. Business E-Mail: eschwab@sahp.llu.edu.

SCHWAB, FRANK, JR., management consultant; b. Brookline, Mass., Dec. 19, 1932; s. Frank Sr. and Phyllis (Robinson) F. BA, Rutgers U., 1952; MBA, Harvard Bus. Sch., 1956. Cert. mgmt. cons. Internal auditor Champion Paper, Inc., Hamilton, Ohio, 1956-57, mgmt. engr. Pasadena, Tex., 1957-58; cons., assoc. Booz Allen & Hamilton, N.Y.C., 1958-65; dir. trans. planning Planning Rsch. Corp., L.A., 1965; pres., CEO F.R. Schwab & Assocs., N.Y.C., 1965-82; pres., co-CEO Fenvessy & Schwab, N.Y.C., 1982-87; pres., CEO, Anderson & Schwab, N.Y.C., 1987—. Bd. dirs. Sugarland Oil Corp., N.Y.C., mfrs. and svcs. divsn. Nat. Mining Assn., Washington. Trustee Nat. Mining Hall of Fame and Mus., Leadville, Colo., 1992—. 1st lt. U.S. Army, 1952-54, Korea. Decorated Nat. Def. Svc. medal, Korean Svc. medal with bronze star, Commendation ribbon with medal pendant, UN Svc. medal. Mem. Inst. Mgmt. Cons. (pres. N.Y. chpt. 1975-77), Am. Arbitration Assn. (panel arbitrator), Mil. Order Fgn. Wars (vet. companion), Maidstone Club, Union Club, River Club, King Coal Club, Army and Navy Club. Republican. Avocation: tennis. Office: Anderson & Schwab Inc 444 Madison Ave New York NY 10022-6903 Fax: (212) 755-9576. E-mail: fschwab@andersonschwab.com.

SCHWAB, GEORGE DAVID, social science educator, author; b. Nov. 25, 1931; s. Arkady and Klara (Jacobson) S.; m. Eleonora Storch, Feb. 27, 1965; children: Clarence Boris, Claude Arkady, Solan Bernhard. BA, City Coll. N.Y., 1954; MA, Columbia U., 1955, PhD, 1968. Lectr. Columbia Coll., N.Y.C., 1959, CUNY, 1960-68; asst. prof. history, 1968-72; assoc. prof. history, 1973-79; prof., 1980—2000; prof. emeritus, 2001—. Mem. Columbia U. Seminar on Law and Polit. Thought and Institutions; dir. Conf. History and Politics CUNY; with Nat. Com. Am. Fgn. Policy. Author: Dayez: Beyond Abstract Art, 1967, Enemy oder Foe, 1968, Switzerland's Tactical Nuc. Weapons Policy, 1969, The Challenge of the Exception: An Introduction to the Polit. Ideas of Carl Schmitt, 1970, 2nd edit., 1989, Appeasement and Detente, 1975, 81, Carl Schmitt: Polit. Opportunist?, 1975; translator: The Concept of the Polit. with Comments by Leo Strauss (Carl Schmitt), 1976, 96, Legality and Illegality as Instruments of Revolutionaries in Their Quest for Power, Remarks Occasioned by the Outlook of Herbert Marcuse, 1978, The German State in Hist. Perspective, 1978, Ideology: Reality or Rhetoric, 1978, Ideology and Fgn. Policy, 1978, 81, The Decision: Is the Am. Sovereign at Bay?, 1978, State and Nation: Toward a Further Clarification, 1980, Am. Fgn. Politics at the Crossroads, 1980, Carl Schmitt: Through a Glass Darkly, 1980, From Quantity and Heterogeneity to Quality and Homogeneity: Toward a New Foreign Policy, 1980, Toward an Open-Society Bloc, 1980, Eurocommunism: The Ideological and Political Theoretical Foundations, 1981, Am. Fgn. Policy at the Crossroads, 1982, A Decade of the Nat. Com. on Am. Fgn. Policy, 1984, (trans.) Polit. Theology: Four Chapters on the Concept of Sovereignty (Carl Schmitt), 1985, 88, The Destruction of a Family, 1987, Elie Wiesel: Between Jerusalem and New York, 1990, The Broken Vow, The Good Obtained, 1991, Thoughts of a Collector, 1991, Carl Schmitt Hysteria in the US, 1992, Contextualizing Carl Schmitt's Concept of Grossraum, 1994; (translator) The Leviathan in the State Theory of Thomas Hobbes (Carl Schmitt), 1996, Carl Schmitt, A Note on a Qualitative Authoritarian Bourgeois Liberal, 2000, The Nat. Com. on Am. Fgn. Policy's Focus on Russia, 2000, U.S. National Security Interests Today, 2003; editor Am. Fgn. Policy Interests; series Global Perspectives in History and Politics. Trustee, pres. mem. exec. com. Nat. Com. Am. Fgn. Policy; mem. Coun. on Fgn. Rels. Decorated Order of the Three Stars (Latvia); recipient Ellis Island medal of honor. Office: Nat Com Am Fgn Policy 320 Park Ave New York NY 10022-6815 E-mail: ncafp@aol.com.

SCHWAB, HAROLD LEE, lawyer; b. NYC, Feb. 5, 1932; s. Harold Walter and Beatrice (Braverman) S.; m. Rowena Vivian Strauss, June 12, 1953; children: Andrew, Lisa, James. BA, Harvard Coll., 1953; LLB, Boston Coll., 1956. Bar: NY 1957, U.S. Ct. Mil. Appeals 1958, U.S. Dist. Cts. (so. and ea. dists.) NY 1967, U.S. Dist. Ct. (no. dist.) NY 1974, U.S. Dist. Ct. (we. dist.) NY 1988, U.S. Dist. Ct. Conn. 1995, U.S. Dist. Ct. (ea. and we. dists.) Ark. 2000, U.S. Ct. Appeals (2d cir.) 1971, U.S. Ct. Appeals (DC cir.) 1986, U.S. Ct. Appeals (11th cir.) 1988, U.S. Ct. Appeals (5th cir.) 1991, U.S. Supreme Ct. 1971. V.p. H.W. Schwab Textile Corp., NYC, 1959-60; assoc. Emile Z. Berman & A. Harold Frost, NYC, 1960-67, ptnr., 1967-74; sr. ptnr. Lester Schwab Katz & Dwyer, NYC, 1974—. Lectr. NY Jud. Seminars, 2000-02, NY State Bar Assn., NY County Lawyers Assn. Contbr. articles to legal jours.; mem. editl. bd. Jour. Products and Toxics Liability, 1976-96. Served to lt. col. USAFR. Fellow Internat. Acad. Trial Lawyers; mem. ABA, ASTM, SAE, Assn. Advancement of Automotive Medicine, Product Liability Adv. Coun., NY State Bar Assn. (chmn. trial lawyers sect. 1980-81, editor sect. newsletter 1981-84), Am. Bd. Trial Advs. (pres. NY chpt. 1982-83), Fedn. Ins. and Corp. Counsel (v.p. 1979-80), NY State Trial Lawyers Assn., Def. Assn. NY, Harvard Club NY, Downtown Assn., Ft. Hamilton Officers Club. Home: 205 Beach 142 St Neponsit NY 11694 Office: Lester Schwab Katz & Dwyer 120 Broadway Fl 38 New York NY 10271-0071 Office Phone: 212-341-4234. E-mail: hschwab@lskdnylaw.com.

SCHWAB, HERMANN CASPAR, banker; b. N.Y.C., Jan. 8, 1920; s. Hermann Caspar and Ruth (Bliss) S.; m. C. Meteer Shanks, July 5, 1955; children: Henry R., Lesley Schwab Forman, Margery Schwab Weekes, Stuart Taylor, George Bliss, Katharine Lambard Schwab Kimmick. Grad., St. Marks Sch., 1937, Yale U., 1941. With Hanover Bank, 1941-44, 46-55, asst. sec., 1949-53, asst. v.p., 1953-55; ptnr. Dick & Merle Smith, 1956; v.p. Empire Trust Co., 1957-66, sr. v.p., 1965-66; with Bank N.Y., 1966-67; sr. v.p. Schroder Trust Co., N.Y.C., 1967-73, dir., 1970-73; pres., dir. Cheapside Dollar Fund Ltd., N.Y.C., 1970-88; sr. v.p. Schroder Capital Mgmt. Inc., N.Y.C., 1973-84, cons., 1984-88. Chmn., dir. Schroder Capitol Funds Inc., 1988-98, trustee dir., 1998—. Mayor Oyster Bay Cove, N.Y., 1973-85, trustee, 1965-98; trustee St. Lukes-Roosevelt Hosp. Ctr., 1969-99. 2d lt. inf., AUS, 1943-46. Mem. Piping Rock Club (Locust Valley, N.Y.). Home: 34 Northern Blvd Oyster Bay NY 11771-4105

SCHWAB, HOWARD JOEL, judge; b. Charleston, W.Va., Feb. 13, 1943; s. Joseph Simon and Gertrude (Hadas) S.; m. Michelle Roberts, July 4, 1970; children: Joshua Raphael, Bethany Alexis. BA in History with honors, UCLA, 1964, JD, 1967. Bar: Calif. 1968, U.S. Dist. Ct. (cen. dist.) Calif. 1968, U.S. Ct. Appeals (9th cir.) 1970, U.S. Supreme Ct. 1972. Clk. legal adminstrn. Litton Industries, L.A., 1967-68; dep. city atty. L.A., 1968-69; dep. atty. gen. State of Calif., L.A., 1969-84; judge Mcpl. Ct. L.A. Jud. Dist., 1984-85; judge Superior Ct. Superior Ct. L.A. County, L.A., 1985—. Mem. faculty Berkeley (Calif.) Judicial Coll., 1987—; adj. prof. U. So. Calif. Sch Medicine. Contbr. articles to profl. jours. Recipient CDAA William E. James award Calif. Dist. Atty.'s Assn., 1981. Mem. San Fernando Valley Bar Assn. (Appreciation award as Judge of Yr. 2002_, Inn. of Ct., Phi Alpha Delta. Democrat. Jewish. Avocations: history, book collecting. Office: 9425 Penfield Ave Chatsworth CA 91311 Office Phone: 818-876-8480. E-mail: hschwab@lasuperiorcourt.org.

SCHWAB, JOHN HARRIS, microbiology and immunology educator; b. St. Cloud, Minn., Nov. 20, 1927; s. John David and Katherine (Harris) S.; m. Ruth Ann Graves, Sept. 1, 1951; children: Stewart, Thomas, Anna, Kellogg. BS, U. Minn., 1949, MS, 1950, PhD, 1953. Asst. prof. U. N.C., Chapel Hill, 1953-67, prof., 1967—; Cary C. Boshamer prof., 1982—. Scientist Lister Inst. Preventive Medicine, London, 1960, MRC Rheumatism Rsch, Unit, Taplow, England, 1968, Radiobiol. Inst., Rijswijk, The Netherlands, 1975, Pasteur Inst., Paris, 1985. Contbr. articles to profl. jours. and chpts. to books. Recipient Faculty Scholar award Josiah Macy Jr. Found., 1975; NIH Spl. fellow, 1960, 68; Fogarty Internat. fellow NIH, Paris, 1985. Mem. Am. Soc. Mibrobiology (editor Infection and Immunity jour. 1980-85), Am. Assn. Immunologists, AAAS.

SCHWAB, JOHN JOSEPH, psychiatrist, educator; b. Cumberland, Md., Feb. 10, 1923; s. Joseph L. and Eleanor (Cadden) S.; m. Ruby Baxter, Aug. 4, 1945; 1 dau., Mary Eleanor. BS, U. Ky., 1946; MD, U. Louisville, 1946; MS in Physiology (Med. fellow), U. Ill., 1949; postgrad., Duke U., 1951-52, U. Fla., 1959-61. Diplomate: Nat. Bd. Med. Examiners. Intern Phila. Gen. Hosp., 1947-48; resident medicine Louisville Gen. Hosp., 1949-50; edn. officer med. coll. U. Yokohama, 1952-54; internist, psychosomaticist Holzer Clinic, Gallipolis, Ohio, 1954-59; resident psychiatry U. Fla. Hosp., 1959-61; NIMH Career tchr. U. Fla., Gainesville, 1962-64, mem. faculty, 1961-73, prof. psychiatry and medicine, 1967-73, dir. cons. liaison program, 1964-67, resident tng. dir., 1965-71; prin. investigator Fla. Health Study, 1969-74; prof., chmn. dept. psychiatry and behavioral scis. Sch. Medicine U. Louisville, 1973-91, prof. psychiatry, 1991-93, prof. emeritus, 1993—, assoc. dir. clin. psychopharm. rsch., 1991—. Chmn. epidemiologic studies rev. com. Ctr. for Epidemiologic Studies, NIMH, 1973-75, cons. psychiatry br., 1975-92; cons. Old Order Amish Study of Depression, 1978—; vol. vis. lectr. Howard U., 1992; ann. vis. lectr. U. Würzburg, Germany, hon. faculty, 1992—; vis. prof. El-Azar U., Cairo, 1991; prin. investigator LSVL Family Health Study, 1982—; dir. U. Fla. Coll. Med. Program: History and Philosophy of Medicine, 1965-72; mem. instn;. rsch. rev. bd. U. Louisville, 2003—. Author: Handbook of Psychiatric Consultation, 1968; also articles; co-author: Sociocultural Roots of Mental Illness: An Epidemiologic Survey, 1978, Social Order and Mental Health, 1979; assoc. editor Psychosomatics, 1965-86; co-editor: Man for Humanity: On Concordance V. Discord in Human Behavior, 1972, Social Psychiatry, vol. 1, 1974, The Psychiatric Examination, 1974, first author Family Mental Health History, Epidem, Clinical Health Issues, 1993, first author Family Functioning: The General Living Systems Research Model, 2000; co-edited 9 books, 11 Monographs, and over 250 articles. Capt. USAMC, 1949-54. Recipient Disting. Mental Health award Mental Health Assn. Ky., 1992. Fellow Am. Coll. Psychiatrists (regent 1977-79), Collegium Internat. Neuro-Psychopharmacologicum, World Assn. Social Psychiatry, AAAS, Am. Psychiat. Assn. (chmn. council research and devel. 1974-75); mem. AMA, Acad. Psychosomatic Medicine (exec. 1965-72, pres. 1970-71), Group for Advancement Psychiatry (bd. dirs. 1985-87), So. Assn., Jefferson County Med. Soc., Ky. Psychiat. Assn., Am. Assn. Social Psychiatry (pres. 1971-73), Alpha Omega Alpha, (Outstanding Performance award for Affirmative Action U. Louisville 1986), World Assn. Soc. Psychiatry (internat. adv. com., Rome, 1991), Psychiatrists for Better Psychiat. (pres. 1990-99), U. of the World (co-chair health, edn. com. 1992-98). Achievements include research on applicability of psychiatric concepts to general medicine, sociocultural aspects of mental illness; establishing guidelines for identification and management of medical patients with illnesses complicated by emotional stress; epidemiology of mental illness; depression and the family; clinical psychopharmacology, historical and epidemiologic perspectives on the family. Home: 6217 Innes Trace Rd Louisville KY 40222-6008

SCHWAB, MARK, marketing executive; V.p. strategy and mktg. Hallmark Cards, Kansas City, Mo.; pres., CEO Binney & Smith subs. Hallmark Cards, Easton, Pa., 1999—. Office: Binney & Smith 1100 Church Ln Easton PA 18040-6638

SCHWAB, NELSON, JR., lawyer; b. Cin., July 19, 1918; s. Nelson Sr. and Frances Marie (Carlile) S.; m. Elizabeth Bakhaus (div.); m. Sylvia Lambert; children: Nelson III, Richard O. BA, Yale U., 1940; LLB, Harvard U., 1943. Bar: Ohio 1947. Ptnr. Graydon Head & Ritchey, Cin., 1947-95; sr. counsel, 1995—. Bd. dirs. Rotex, Inc., Ralph J. Stolle co., Security Rug Cleaning Co., Yoder Die Casting Corp. Grants Review Com. The Greater Cin. Found.; mem. Cin. Pub. Schs. Degration Task Force; former chmn. bd. Vol. Lawyers for the Poor Found.; trustee Cin. Scholarship Found., FISC; adv. bd. Cin. Playhouse in the Park;; past mem., sec. Cin. Bus. Com., 1977-88, mm. Schs. Task Force; past mem. Cin. City Mgr.'s Working Rev. Com. 2000 Plan, chmn. Reconstituted 2000 Plan Rev. Com., 1990; pres. Greater Cin. C. of C., 1973; chmn. Greater Cin. Ednl. TV, 1965-70, hon. trustee; chmn. Cincinnati and Hamilton County Am. Red Cross, 1955-57, hon. trustee; incorporator United Appeal, 1955; mem. Cin. Sch. Bd., 1959-64. Honoree Greater Cin. Region NCCJ, 1990; Great Living Cincinnatian Grater Cin. C. of C., 1991 Mem. 6th Cir. Jud. Conf., Cin. Country Club (past bd. dirs., sec.), Commonwealth Club (past pres.), Comml. Club, Recess Club (past pres.), Gyro Club (past pres.), Queen City Club, Queen City Optimists (past pres.), Cin. Yale Club (past pres.), Lincoln's Inn Soc., Delta Kappa Epsilon. Home: 2470 W Rookwood Ct Cincinnati OH 45208-3321 Office: Graydon Head & Ritchey 2471 W Rookwood Ct Cincinnati OH 45208

SCHWAB, PAUL JOSIAH, psychiatrist, educator; b. Waxahachie, Tex., Jan. 14, 1932; s. Paul Josiah and Anna Marie (Baeuerle) Schwab; m. Martha Anne Beed, June 8, 1953; children: Pual Josiah III, John Conrad, Mark Whitney. BA, North Ctrl. Coll., 1953; MD, Baylor U., 1957. Diplomate Am. Bd. Psychiatry and Neurology. Intern Phila. Gen. Hosp., 1957-58; clin. assoc. Nat. Cancer Inst., Bethesda, Md., 1958-60; resident in internal medicine U. Chgo., 1960-62, resident psychiatry, 1962-65, chief resident, instr. psychiatry, 1965, lectr. psychiatry, 1968-74, assoc. prof., 1974-79; clin. assoc., 1979-86; clin. assoc. prof., 1986—; dir. residency tng. U. Chgo., 1976-79, dir. in-patient unit and day treatment program, 1975-79; pvt. practice Naperville, Ill., 1965—; cand. Chgo. Psychoanalytic Inst., 1970-72. Clin. instr. dept. psychiatry U. Ill., Chgo., 1965—66; vis. lectr. in psychology North Ctrl. Coll., 2002—03. Contbr. articles to profl. jours. Pres. North Ctrl. Coll. Alumni Assn., 1979—80; trustee North Ctrl. Coll., chair liaison com., 1983—2004, vice-chmn. acad. and student affairs com., 1983—92, vice chair admissions fin. aid and student devel., 1992—95. Recipient Outstanding Alumnus, North Ctrl. Coll., 1983, Gael D. Swing award, 2001. Fellow: Am. Psychiat. Assn. (life Nancy C.A. Roeske award 1991); mem.: AMA, Am. Soc. Clin. Psychopharmacology, Alpha Omega Alpha. Democrat. Methodist. Home and Office: 1200 Tall Oaks Ct Naperville IL 60540-9494 Office Phone: 630-420-2090. E-mail: pauljschwab@earthlink.net.

SCHWAB, STEWART JON, dean; b. 1954; BA, Swarthmore U., 1975, MA, 1978; PhD, Mich. U., 1981. Bar: D.C. 1982. Law clk. to Hon. J. Dickson Phillips U.S. Ct. Appeals (4th cir.), 1981-82; law clk. to Hon. Sandra O'Connor U.S. Superior Ct, 1982-83; from asst. prof. to prof. law Cornell U. Law Sch., Ithaca, NY, 1983—2003, dean, 2003—; disting. visiting prof. U. Nebr. Coll. Law, Lincoln, 2003; Fulbright sr. scholar Australian Nat. Univ. Ctr. for Law & Econ., Canberra, 1998. Vis. fellow Centre Socio-Legal Studies Oxford U., 1990. Mem. Am. Econ. Assn., Am. Judicature Assn., Order of Coif; City of Ithaca bd. zoning appeals, 1985-88. Office: Cornell Law Sch Myron Taylor Hall Ithaca NY 14853 E-mail: sjs15@cornell.edu.*

SCHWAB, SUSAN CARROLL, dean; BA in Polit. Economy, Williams Coll., 1976; MA in Devel. Policy, Stanford U., 1977; PhD in Pub. Adminstrn., George Washington U., 1993. U.S. trade negotiator Office of U.S. Trade Rep., Washington, 1977-79; trade policy officer U.S. Embassy, Tokyo, 1980-81; chief economist, legis. asst. for internat. trade for Senator John C. Danforth, 1981-86, legis. dir., until 1989; asst. sec. commerce, dir. gen. U.S. and Fgn. Comml. Svc. Dept. Commerce, 1989-93; with corp. strategy office Motorola, Inc., Schaumburg, Ill., 1993-95; dean U. Md. Sch. Pub. Affairs, College Park, 1995—. Office: U Md Sch Pub Affairs College Park MD 20742-0001

SCHWAB, TERRANCE W. lawyer; b. Pitts., May 19, 1940; m. Eileen Caulfield, Jan. 4, 1969; children: Matthew Caulfield, Catherine Grimley, Claire Gillespie. BA magna cum laude, Harvard U., 1962; LLB cum laude, Columbia U., 1966. Assoc. Milbank, Tweed, Hadley & McCloy, N.Y.C., 1966-70, Kelley, Drye & Warren, N.Y.C., 1970-74, ptnr., 1975-96; sr. v.p., gen. counsel global fin. and investment banking The Sanwa Bank Ltd. (now UFJ Bank Ltd.), N.Y.C., 1996—. Lectr. various profl. orgns. Assoc. editor: Law Practice of Alexander Hamilton, 1964-1980; contbr. articles to profl. jours. Trustee, sec. Caramoor Ctr. for Music and Arts, Katonah, N.Y., 1971—; trustee Sch. of Convent of Sacred Heart, N.Y.C., 1987-93, chmn., 1990-93. Mem. ABA, N.Y. State Bar Assn., Assn. of Bar of City of N.Y., Harvard Club. Office: UFJ Bank Ltd 55 E 52nd St Fl 24 New York NY 10055

SCHWABE, JOHN BENNETT, II, lawyer; b. June 14, 1946; s. Leonard Wesley and Hazel Fern (Crouch) Schwabe. AB, U. Mo., Columbia; JD, U. Mo., Columbia, 1970. Bar: Mo. 1970, U.S. Dist. Ct. (we. dist.) Mo. 1970, U.S. Ct. Mil. Appeals 1971, U.S. Supreme Ct. 1973; ordained minister. Pvt. practice, Columbia, Mo., 1974—96, St. Louis, 1984—96. Mem. N. Am. Boxing Fedn., 1997—; minister, founder John Schwabe Ministries. Capt. JAGC USAF, 1970—74. Mem.: Lawyers Assn. St. Louis, Boone County Bar Assn. (sec. 1977—79), Am. Legion, Phi Delta Phi. Methodist. Office: John B Schwabe II Law Firm Schwabe Bldg 2 E Walnut St Columbia MO 65203-4163

SCHWALB, HARRY, artist; b. Pitts., July 2, 1924; s. Adolf and Maria (Bruder) Schwalb; m. Myrna Kline, Dec. 28, 1958 (div. May 1989); 1 child, Adam. Student, Pa. State U., 1940-42; BS summa cum laude, U. Pitts., 1947, MA, 1949. Creative dir. Fisher Sci. Co., Pitts., 1951-93; U.S. corr. ARTnews Mag., N.Y.C., 1988—. Editor The Lab. Mag., Pitts., 1960-93; art critic Pitts. Mag., 1977-95; dean Ivy Sch. Profl. Art, Pitts., 1970-72; juror, curator and cons. for arts orgns. in U.S. and Can. Illustrator: Of Long Ago, 1949, A Western Journal, 1951; one man shows include Collectors Gallery, N.Y.C., 1960, Arnot Art Gallery, Elmira, N.Y., 1962, Carnegie Mus. Art, Pitts., 1965, Westmoreland Mus. Am. Art, Greensburg, Pa., 1965, 99, Mendelson Gallery, Pitts., 1995, 98; represented in permanent collections Carnegie Mus. Art, Westmoreland Mus. Am. Art. Recipient Critical Writing Silver medal U. Kans., 1990, Golden Quill award Pitts. Press Club, 1990-95; ann. Harry Schwalb award established in 1996 Pitts. Mag. Avocations: lecturing, writing essays. Home and Office: 166 N Dithridge St Pittsburgh PA 15213-2647

SCHWALM, LAURA, school system administrator; BA, U. Calif., Riverside; MA, Calif. State U., Fullerton; PhD, U. So. Calif. Tchr. Garden Grove Unified Sch. Dist., Calif., 1973—79, prin., dir. ednl. svcs., dir. pers. svcs., supt., 1999—. Finalist Broad Prize Urban Edn., 2003. Office: Garden Grove Unified Sch Dist 10331 Stanford Ave Garden Grove CA 92840

SCHWAM, MARVIN ALBERT, graphic design company executive; b. Newark, Apr. 18, 1942; s. Meyer and Fannie (Lerman) S.; m. Jeanette Fein, June 13, 1964; children: Frederic, Matthew. BFA, Cooper Union, 1964. Staff artist Domerus & Co., 1964-66; mgr. Flowerental Corp., N.Y.C., 1966-68; pres. M. Schwam Floralart, N.Y.C., 1968-76; exec. v.p., bd. chmn. Florenco Foliate Systems Corp., N.Y.C., 1975-88; pres., chmn. bd. Am. Christmas Decorating Svc., Inc., N.Y.C., 1989—. Res. Marc Shaw Graphics, Inc., N.Y.C., Florenco Graphics Systems, Inc.; exec. v .p. Display Arts Worldwide, 1975-88; pres. Creative Animations, Inc., 1988-90; creative dir., v.p. Rennoc Animations, Inc., 1988-90; pres. Almar Comm., Ltd., 1990-94, Sayso Comm.,

Ltd., 1990-95, Gay Entertainment TV, Inc., 1992-99, Forma Studio Gallery, 1999—; chmn. bd., pres. Union Sq. Ceramic Ctr., 2002. Industry chmn. March of Dimes, 1975-78, pres. bd. dirs. Happi Found for Austic People, N.Y.C.; trustee Nat. Found. Jewish Genetic Diseases; patron Young Adult Inst. and Workshop, Inc.; co-chmn. restaurant, hotel and entertainment industry luncheon Boy Scouts Am., 1988-96; chmn. benefit com. Plan Internat. USA, 1991-92; pres. Union Square Ceramic Ctr., 2002--. Recipient award of merit for svc. to GM Corp., 1978, award for Highlight of Christmas Citibank/Citicorp Ctr., 1978, Disting. Svc. award Coler Hosp., 1982-86, Sr. Citizens of Roosevelt Island. Mem. Mcpl. Art Soc. N.Y., Am. Mus. Natural History, Alumni Assn. Cooper Union (2d Century Soc. fellow), Internat. Platform Assn. Achievements include designer largest artificial Christmas tree in U.S., Radio City Music Hall, N.Y.C., 1979; decorator Pulitzer Fountain, N.Y.C., 1979-80 Christmas season; chief designer Town Sq., New Orleans, Christmas, 1981, Albany Tricentennial, 1986; interior landscape designer La. State Pavillion World's Fair, New Orleans, 1984. Home: 7 E 17th St New York NY 10003-1913 Office: Am Christmas Decorations Inc 1135 Bronx River Ave Bronx NY 10472- Office Phone: 212-633-2026. E-mail: mschwam@nyc.rr.com.

SCHWAN, HERMAN PAUL, electrical engineering and physical science educator, research scientist; b. Aachen, Germany, Aug. 7, 1915; came to U.S., 1947, naturalized, 1952; s. Wilhelm and Meta (Pattberg) S.; m. Anne Marie DelBorello, June 18, 1949; children: Barbara, Margaret, Steven, Carol, Cathryn. Student, U. Goettingen, 1934—37; PhD, U. Frankfurt, 1941, Habilitation in Physics and Biophysics, 1946; DSc (hon.), U. Pa., 1986, U. Kuopio, Finland, 2000, U. Graz, Austria, 2001. Rsch. scientist, prof. Kaiser Wilhelm Inst. Biophysics, 1937-47, asst. dir., 1945-47, rsch. scientist USN, 1947-50, prof. elec. engring., prof. biomed. engring., prof. elec. engring. in phys. medicine, assoc. prof. phys. medicine U. Pa., Phila., 1950-83, Alfed F. Moore prof. emeritus, 1983—, dir. electromed. divsn., 1952-73, chmn. biomed. engring., 1961-73, program dir. biomed. engr. tng. program, 1960-77. Vis. prof. U. Calif., Berkeley, 1956, U. Frankfurt, Germany, 1962, U. Würzburg, Germany, 1986-87; lectr. Johns Hopkins U., 1962-67, Drexel U., Phila., 1983-90; W.W. Clyde vis. prof. U. Utah, Salt Lake City, 1980; 10th Lauristan Taylor lectr. Nat. Coun. Radiation Protection and Measurements, 1986; Fgn. sci. mem. Max Planck Inst. Biophysics, Germany, 1962—; cons. NIH, 1962-90; chmn. nat. and internat. meetings biomed. engring. and biophysics, 1959, 61, 65; mem. nat. adv. coun. environ. health HEW, 1969-71; mem. coms. NAS-NRC, 1968-87. Co-author: Advances in Medical and Biological Physics, 1957, Therapeutic Heat, 1958, Physical Techniques in Medicine and Biology, 1963; editor: Biol. Engring, 1969; co-editor: Interactions Between Electromagnetic Fields and Cells, 1985; mem. editl. bd. Environ. Biophysics, IEEE Transactions Med. Biol. Engring., Jour. Phys. Med. Biol., Nonionizing Radiation, Bioelectromagnetics; contbr. articles to profl. jours. Recipient Citizenship award Phila., 1952, 1st prize AIEE, 1953, Achievement award Phila. Inst. Radio Engring., 1963, Rajewsky prize for biophysics, 1974, U.S. Sr. Scientist award Alexander von Humboldt Found., 1980-81, Biomed. Engring. Edn. award Am. Soc. Engring. Edn., 1983, d'Arsonval award Bioelectromagnetics Soc., 1985. Fellow IEEE (chmn. and vice-chmn. nat. profl. group biomed. engring. 1955, 62-68, Phila. Achievement award 1962, Morlock award 1967, Edison medal 1983, Centennial award 1984, Phila. Sect. award 1991, Millenium medal 2000), AAAS, Am. Inst. Med. and Biol. Engring.; mem. NAE, Am. Stds. Assn. (chmn. 1961-65), Biophys. Soc. (publicity com., coun., constn. com.), German Biophys. Soc. (hon.), Nordic (Scandinavian) Bioimpedance Club (hon.), Internat. Fedn. Med. and Biol. Engring. (Otto Schmitt award 2000), Bioelectromagnetics Soc., Biomed. Engring. Soc. (founder, dir. 1968-71), Sigma Xi. Achievements include discovery of counterion relaxation; dielectric spectroscopy of cells and tissues; nonlinearity law of electrode polarization; research on nonionizing radiation biophysics; fundamentals electromagnetic bioengineering; first standard for safe exposure to electrical fields; development of biomedical engineering and education. Home: 99 Kynlyn Rd Wayne PA 19087-2849 Office: U Pa Dept Bioengring D2 Hayden Hall Philadelphia PA 19104 Business E-Mail: hschwan@seas.upenn.edu.

SCHWAN, HOWARD W. manufacturing executive; From mgr. prodn. to pres. CTI Industries Corp., Barrington, Ill., 1983—97, pres., 1997—, dir. Office: CTI Industries Inc 22160 N Pepper Rd Barrington IL 60010*

SCHWAN, LEROY BERNARD, artist, retired art educator; b. Dec. 8, 1932; s. Joseph L. and Dorothy (Papenfuss) S.; children from previous marriage: David A., Mark J., William R., Catherine L., Maria E. Student, Wis. State U., River Falls, 1951-53, Southeastern Signal Sch., Ga., 1954; BS, U. Minn., 1958, MEd, 1960, postgrad., 1961-64, No. Mich. U., 1965, Tex. Tech. U., 1970, So. Ill. U., 1978, U. Iowa, 1980, EdD (hon.), 1988. Head art dept. Unity Pub. Schs., Milltown, Wis., 1958-61; instr. art Fridley Pub. Schs., Mpls., 1961-64; asst. prof. art No. Mich. U., Marquette, 1964-66, Mankato (Minn.) State Coll., 1966-71, assoc. prof., 1971-74; tchr. off-campus grad. classes Northeast Mo. State U., John Wood Cmty. Coll.; dir. Art Workshop Educultural Ctr., 1968; dir. art edn. Quincy (Ill.) Pub. Schs., 1974-78, art tchr., 1978-88, ret., 1988. Tchr. art to mentally retarded children, Faribault, Minn., Owatonna, Minn., Mankato, Lake Owasso Children's Home, St. Paul; dir. art workshops, Mankato, 1970, St. Paul, 1972, 73, 74, 75; dir. workshops tchrs. mentally retarded Mankato, 1971, Faribault, 1972, Omaha, 1972-73, Quincy, 1974, 79, 82, 84-86, asst. adj. Ill. VA Home, 1980—. Author: Art Curriculum Guide Unity Public Schs., 1961, Portrait of Jean, 1974, Schwan's Art Activities, 1984, Poems of Life, 1995, LeRoy Remembers, 2003; co-author: Bryant-Schwan Design Test, 1971, Bryant-Schwan Art Guide, 1973; contbr. articles to profl. jours., author numerous poems; one-man shows: Estherville Jr. Coll., 1968, Mankato State Coll., 1968, 71, 73, 75, 97, Farmington, Wis., 1970-71, 91, Good Thunder, Minn., 1972, Quincy, 1975, 77, 84, Western Ill. U., 1979, St. Croix River Valley Arts Coun. Gallery, Osceola, Wis., 1993-96, The Northern Ctr. for the Arts, Amery, Wis., 1994, 2001, Borders Books Gallery, Woodbury, Wells Fargo Gallery, Woodbury, Health Ptnrs. Gallery, Woodbury, 2000, Gallery at Fortes Ins., Woodbury, 2001; exhibited in group shows at Pentagon, Washington, 1955, U. Minn., 1958, No. Mich. U., 1965, St. Cloud State Coll., 1967, Moorhead State Coll., 1967, Bemidji (Minn.) State Coll., 1967, MacNider Mus., Mason City, Iowa, 1969, 72-74, Gallery 500, Mankato, Minn., 1970, Rochester, Minn., 1972, Minn. Mus., St. Paul, 1973, Hannibal, Mo., 1976, 77-78, Quincy, Ill., 1976-77, 85, Ill. Art Educators Show, 1984-85, Tchrs. Retirement Art Show, Springfield, Ill., 1987, Phipps Ctr. Arts, Hudson, Wis., 1997-99, 2000-01, 03; prodr. edn1. TV series, 1964-65, also 2 shows Kids Komments, Sta. WGEM, Quincy; mural commd. Gem City Coll., 1977. Webelos leader Twin Valley coun. Boy Scouts Am., 1968-69; bd. dirs. Quincy Soc. Fine Arts, 1975-85, Polk County Hist. Soc., 1993—. With Signal Corps., AUS, 1954-56. Recipient cert. of accomplishment Sec. Army, 1955, Golden Poet award, 1985, 86, 88, 90, 91, Silver Poet award 1989. Mem. Nat. Art Edn. Assn., Ill. Art Edn. Assn., Cath. Order Foresters, Am. Legion, Phi Delta Kappa. Home: 849 County Road H New Richmond WI 54017-6209

SCHWANAUER, FRANCIS, philosopher, educator; b. Zsámbék, Hungary, Jan. 20, 1933; came to U.S., 1959; s. Georg and Maria (Keller) S.; m. Johanna Maria Koelln, Sept. 29, 1957; children: Stephan Michael, Miriam Frances. Maturum, Ulrich von Hutten Gymnasium, Korntal, Germany, 1954; PhD, U. Stuttgart, Germany, 1959. Asst. prof. Lebanon Valley Coll., Annville, Pa., 1960—62, U. Maine, Orono, 1962—65, U. So. Maine, Portland Gorham, 1965—67, assoc. prof., 1967—72, prof., 1972—. Author: Truth is a Neighborhood with Nothing in Between, 1977, Those Fallacies by Slight of Reason, 1978, No Many is not a One (For the Case is Comparison), 1981, The Flesh of Thought is Pleasure or Pain, 1982, To Make Sure is to Cohere, 1982, Philosophical Fact and Paradox, 1987, Fables from the Fox, 1991; contbr. articles to profl. jours. Grantee John Anson Kittredge Ednl. Fund, 1991, 93. Mem.: New Eng. Philos. Assn. Democrat. Roman Catholic. Avocation: fishing. Home: 4 Woodmont St Portland ME 04102-2709

SCHWANDA, TOM, religious studies educator; b. E. Stroudsburg, Pa., Oct. 23, 1950; s. Theodore Frank and Madlyn Betty (Backensto) S.; m. Grace Elaine Dunning, July 30, 1977; children: Rebecca Joy, Stephen Andrew. Student, Worcester Polytechnic Inst., 1968-69; BA in Econ., Moravian Coll., 1969-72; student, Gordon-Conwell Sem., 1972-74; MDiv, New Brunswick Sem., 1975; DMin, Fuller Theol. Sem., 1992. Ordained to ministry Reformed Ch. in Am., 1975. Pastor Wanaque (N.J.) Reformed Ch., 1975-87; pastor congl. care Immanuel Reformed Ch., Grand Rapids, Mich., 1987-92; interim sr. pastor Remembrance Reformed Ch., Grand Rapids, 1992-93; rsch. fellow H. Henry Meeter Ctr. for Calvin Studies Calvin Coll., Grand Rapids, 1993-95; instr. spirituality and worship Bethlehem Ctr. for Spirituality, Grand Rapids, 1993—; dir. Reformed Spirituality Network, Grand Rapids, 1992—; assoc. for spiritual formation Reformed Ch. in Am., 1995-99; prof. spiritual formation Reformed Bible Coll., Grand Rapids, Mich., 1999—. Organizer, convener Gathering Reformed Spirituality, 1993, 94, 95, 97, 99, 2001, 2004; chair spirituality com. Synod of Great Lakes, 1989-2000, mem. Christian discipleship com., 1988-94; mem. ch. life, evangelism, missions com. South Grand Rapids Classics, chair, 1992; mem. commn. on worship Reformed Ch. in Am., 1978-94; mem. care of students com. Passaic Classis, 1975, 87, chair, 1978, 83-86, pres., 1979; adj. prof. spirituality and spiritual direction and worship Fuller Theol. Sem., San Francisco Theol. Sem., No. Bapt. Theol. Sem., Western Theol. Sem., Columbia Theol. Sem., Charlotte, Orlando, Reformed Theol. Sem., Charlotte. Author: Celebrating God's Presence: The Transforming Power of Public Worship, 1995; contbr. articles to religious jours.; author poetry; manuscript reader, evaluator religious pub. co. Established, managed Wanaque Cmty. Food Pantry, 1977-87; vol. Domestic Crisis Ctr., Grand Rapids, 1988—; bd. dirs. Nat. Inst. Rehabilitation Engring., Hewitt, N.J., 1984—, pres. bd. dirs., 1986—. Recipient Barnabas award Iglesia Cristiana Ebenezer, 1987. Mem. Czechoslovak Soc. Arts and Sci., Czechoslovak Hist. Conf., Soc. for Study of Christian Spirituality. Mem. Reformed Ch. Am. Avocations: running, landscaping, genealogy/family history, amateur radio. Home: 6125 Capitan Dr SE Grand Rapids MI 49546-6721 Office: Reformed Bible Coll 3333 E Beltline Ave NE Grand Rapids MI 49525-9781 Business E-Mail: tschwanda@reformed.edu.

SCHWANTES, CARLOS ARNALDO, history educator, consultant; b. Wilmington, N.C., Mar. 7, 1945; s. Arnaldo and Frances (Casteen) Schwantes; m. Mary Alice Dassenko, Sept. 4, 1966; children: Benjamin, Matthew. BA, Andrews U., 1967; MA, U. Mich., 1968, PhD, 1976. From instr. to prof. Walla Walla Coll., College Place, Wash., 1969-85; prof. history U. Idaho, Moscow, 1984—2002; St. Louis Merc. Libr. endowed prof. transp. studies U. Mo., St. Louis, 2001, 2002—. Consult TV History Idaho, 1988. Author: (book) Coxey's Army: An Amercian Odyssey, 1985, The Pacific Northwest: An Interpretive History, 1989, Railroad Signatures Across the Pacific Northwest, 1993, Going Places: Transportation Redefines the Twentieth Century West, 2003; author or editor: 8 other books, mem. editl. bd.: Pacific NW Quart, 1982—97, Idaho Yesterdays, 1987—2002, Forest and Conservation History, 1988—95, Pacific Hist Rev, 1991—95; contbr. articles to profl. jours. Fellow NEH, 1982—83, Research, Idaho Humanities Coun, 1989—90; grantee, Idaho State Bd Educ, 1990—91. Mem.: Mo. Hist. Soc., Lexington Soc., Mining Hist. Assn. (coun 1990—94), Western Hist. Assn., Am Hist. Assn. (pres Pacific Ct br 1999—2000). Republican. Seventh Day Adventist. Avocations: photography, backpacking. Personal E-mail: CASchwantes@sbcglobal.net.

SCHWANTES, ROBERT SIDNEY, international relations executive; b. Beetown Township, Wis., July 11, 1922; s. Kurt John and Lillian Ellen (Walker) S.; m. Marion Laura Miles, July 15, 1943; children: Virginia, Janet, Ingrid. AB summa cum laude, Harvard U., 1943; MA, U. Colo., 1947; PhD, Harvard U., 1950. Instr. in history Harvard U., Cambridge, Mass., 1950-52; Carnegie resch. fellow Coun. on Foreign Rels., N.Y.C., 1952-54; various positions The Asia Found., San Francisco and Tokyo, 1954-66, dir. of programs San Francisco, 1966-69, v.p. for programs, 1969-84, exec. v.p., 1984-88; vis. rsch. scholar Hoover Inst., Stanford, 1988—. Mem. Am. adv. com. Japan Found., Tokyo, 1984-86, vis. History lectr. Harvard U., 1958. Author: Japanese and Americans, 1955, What Did You Do in the War, Daddy?, 1998; contbr. articles to profl. jours. Vestryman St. Paul's Episcopal Ch., Burlingame, Calif., 1993-95. Lt. (j.g.), USNR, 1942-46, PTO. Assn. Asian Studies, World Affairs Coun. No. Calif., Japan Soc. No. Calif. Democrat. Avocations: reading, travel. Home: 1432 Benito Ave Burlingame CA 94010-5550 E-mail: robertschwantes@msn.com.

SCHWANTNER, JOSEPH, composer, educator; b. Chgo., Mar. 22, 1943; m. Janet Elaine Rossate; 2 children. B.Mus., Chgo. Conservatory Coll.; M.Mus., Northwestern U., 1966, D.Mus., 1968. Teaching fellow Northwestern U., 1966-68; mem. faculty Chgo. Conservatory Coll., 1967-68; asst. prof. Pacific Lutheran U., 1968-69, Ball State U., 1969-70; successively asst. prof., assoc. prof., prof. Eastman Sch. Music, U. Rochester, 1970—, prof. composition, 1970—. Composer-in-residence St. Louis Symphony Orch., 1982-84 Compositions include Aftertones of Infinity (Pulitzer prize for music 1979), Diaphonia Intervallum, Chronicon, Autumn Canticle, Consortium, In Aeternum, Modis Caelestis, Canticle for the Evening Bells, Elixir, Wild Angels of the Open Hills, And the Mountains Rising Nowhere, Sparrows. Recipient Faricy award, 1965, BMI Student award, 1965, 66, 67, Bearns prize Columbia U., 1967; Nat. Inst. Arts and Letters Charles Ives scholar, 1970; N.Y. State Council on Arts Creative Arts Public Service grantee, 1973; NEA grantee; Guggenheim fellow, 1978-79 Office: Eastman Sch Music 26 Gibbs St Rochester NY 14604-2505

SCHWARCZ, STEVEN LANCE, law educator, lawyer; b. N.Y.C., Nov. 10, 1949; s. Charles and Elinor Schwarcz; m. Susan Beth Kolodny, Aug. 24, 1975; children: Daniel Benjamin, Rebekah Mara. BS summa cum laude in Aero. Engring., NYU, 1971; JD, Columbia U., 1974. Bar: N.Y. 1971, U.S. Dist. Ct. (so. dist.) N.Y. 1975. Assoc. Shearman & Sterling, N.Y.C., 1974-82, ptnr., 1983-89; ptnr., chmn. structured fin. Kaye, Scholer, Fierman, Hays & Handler, 1996—; prof. Duke U. Sch. Law, Durham, NC, 1996—, Stanley A. Star prof., 2004—; spl. counsel Kaye, Scholer, Fierman, Hays & Handler, 1996—; faculty dir. Duke Global Capital Markets Ctr. Adj. prof. law Yeshiva U., Benjamin N. Cardozo Sch. Law, N.Y.C., 1983-92; vis. lectr. Yale Law Sch., 1992-96; lectr. Columbia Law Sch., 1992-96. Contbr. articles to profl. jours. Chmn. Friends of the Eldridge St. Synagogue, N.Y.C., 1979-96, Legis. Drafting Rsch. Fund. George Granger Brown scholar, 1971; NSF grantee in Math., 1969. Fellow Am. Coll. Comml. Fin. Lawyers; mem. Am. Law Inst., Assn. of Bar of City of N.Y. (environ. law com. 1975-78, nuc. tech. com. 1979-81, sci. and law com. 1985—, chmn. 1987-90), Am. Law and Econs. Assn., Tau Beta Pi, Sigma Gamma Tau. Jewish. Office: Duke U Sch Law Box 90360 Science Dr & Towerview Rd Durham NC 27708 Office Phone: 919-613-7060. E-mail: schwarcz@law.duke.edu.

SCHWARTE, DAVID A. travel company executive; b. 1950; BA, U. Ky.; JD, Salmon P. Chase Coll. Law. Atty., legal dept. Am. Airlines, 1979—98; dir. Kelly, Hart & Hallman, Ft. Worth, 1999—2000; exec. v.p., gen. counsel Sabre Holdings, Southlake, Tex., 2000—. Mem.: ABA (past chmn., forum on air and space law), Tex. State Bar Assn. Office: Sabre Holdings 3150 Sabre Dr Southlake TX 76092*

SCHWARTZ, AARON ROBERT, lawyer, former state legislator; b. Galveston, Tex., July 17, 1926; s. Joseph and Clara (Bulbe) S.; m. Marilyn Cohn, July 14, 1951; children: Richard Austin, Robert Allen, John Reed, Thomas Lee. Pre-law student, Tex. A&M U., 1948; JD, U. Tex., 1951. Bar: Tex. 1951. Mem. Tex. Ho. of Reps., 1955-59, Tex. Senate, 1960-81, past chmn. rules, jurisprudence and natural resources coms. Chmn. Tex. Coastal & Marine Coun., U.S. Coastal States Orgn.; adj. prof., legis. and costal mgmt. law, Bates Law Sch., U. Houston, Tex. A&M U., Corpus Christi, Tex. Contbr. articles to profl. jours. Mem. emeritus exec. com. Galveston Bay Fond.; apptd. to Tex. Oil Spill Oversight Commn., 1993. Served with USN, 1944-46, 2d lt. USAFR, 1948-53. Recipient conservation and legis. awards, Outstanding Citizen award Galveston Jr. C. of C., 1981, Man of Yr., People of Vision award Galveston chpt. Soc. for Prevention of Blindness, 1986, Disting. Service award Nat. Hurricane Conf., Tex. Coastal Mgmt. Adv. Com., 1987, Lifetime Coastal Achievement award, 1997. Mem. Tex. State Bar Assn., Galveston County Bar Assn. Democrat. Jewish. Address: 1122 Colorado St Apt 2102 Austin TX 78701-2142 Personal E-mail: ars717726@aol.com.

SCHWARTZ, ALAN E. lawyer, director; b. Detroit, Dec. 21, 1925; s. Maurice H. and Sophia (Welkowitz) S.; m. Marianne Shapero, Aug. 24, 1950; children: Marc Alan, Kurt Nathan, Ruth Anne. Student, Western Mich. Coll., 1944-45; BA with distinction, U. Mich., 1947; LLB magna cum laude, Harvard U., 1950; LLD, Wayne State U., 1983, U. Detroit, 1985. Bar: N.Y. 1951, Mich. 1952. Assoc. Kelley, Drye & Warren, N.Y.C., 1950-52; mem. Honigman, Miller, Schwartz & Cohn, Detroit, 1952—, Spl. asst. counsel N.Y. State Crime Commn., 1951; bd. dirs. Pulte Corp. Editor: Harvard Law Rev., 1950. Dir. Detroit Symphony Orch.; v.p., bd. dirs. United Found.; bd. dirs. Detroit Renaissance, New Detroit, Jewish Welfare Fedn. Detroit, Wayne State Univ. Found.; trustee Cmty. Found. for Southeastern Mich., Interlochen Arts Acad.; adv. mem. Arts Commn., City of Detroit; mem. investment com. Kresge Found., Skillman Found. Served as ensign Supply Corps, USNR, 1945-46. Recipient Mich. Heritage Hall of Fame award, 1984, George W. Romney award for lifetime achievement in volunteerism, 1994, Max M. Fisher Cmty. Svc. award, 1997. Mem. Mich. Bar Assns. Clubs: Franklin Hills Country; Detroit, Economic (dir.). Office: Honigman Miller Schwartz & Cohn 2290 1st National Bldg Detroit MI 48226

SCHWARTZ, ALAN GIFFORD, sport company executive; b. N.Y.C., Nov. 7, 1931; s. Kevie Waldemar and Vera (Isaacs) S.; m. Roslyn Smulian, Sept. 6, 1958; children: Steven, Andrew, Sally, Elizabeth. BS, Yale U., 1952; MBA, Harvard U., 1954. Ptnr. Gifford Investment Co., Chgo., 1954—; CEO Tennis Corp. of Am., Chgo., 1969—, chmn. bd., 1974—. Dir. Firstar Bank Ill., Comtrex Systems, Inc., Mt. Laurel, N.J.; trustee Roosevelt U., 1994—, Inst. European & Asian Studies, 1993—; v.p. U.S. Tennis Assn., 1994—. Contbr. articles to profl. jours.; editorial cons. Club Industry mag., 1985—. Bd. dirs. Grad. Sch. of Bus., Duke U., Durham, N.C., 1977—, McCormick Boys and Girls Club, 1989—. Elected to Club Industry Hall of Fame, 1987. Mem. Standard Club of Chgo., Exec. Club. Chgo. Jewish. Avocations: travel, tennis. Office: Tennis Corp of Am 3611 N Kedzie Ave Chicago IL 60618-4513

SCHWARTZ, ALAN LEIGH, pediatrician, educator; b. N.Y.C., Apr. 25, 1948; s. Robert and Joyce (Goldner) S.; m. Judith Child, June 22, 1974; 1 child, Timothy Child. BA, PHD in Pharmacology, Case Western Res. U., 1974, MD, 1976. Diplomate Am. Bd. Pediatrics. Intern Children's Hosp., Boston, 1976-77, resident, 1976-78, fellow Dana Farber Cancer Inst., 1978-80; instr. Harvard Med. Sch., Boston, 1980-81, asst. prof., 1981-83, assoc. prof., 1983-86; prof. pediatrics, molecular biology and pharmacology Washington U. Sch. Medicine, St. Louis, 1986—, chmn. dept. pediatrics, 1995—; chmn. faculty practice plan Washington U., 1999—2001. Vis. scientist MIT, Boston, 1979-82; mem. sci. adv. bd. Nat. Inst. Child Health and Human Devel., NIH, Bethesda, Md., 1988-94; investigator Am. Heart Assn. Alumni Endowed Prof. Pediats. Wash. U. Sch. Medicine, 1987-97, Harriet B. Spoehrer Prof. Pediats., 1997—. Mem. Inst. Medicine of NAS. Office: Washington U Sch Medicine Dept Pediatrics Box 8116 One Children's Pl Saint Louis MO 63110-1093

SCHWARTZ, ALAN PAUL, corporate executive; b. N.Y.C., Nov. 5, 1949; s. William and Dorothy S.; m. Lori Jill Kleinman, Aug. 5, 1979. BS in Biology, CCNY, 1972. Investigator law and procedures N.Y. dist. FDA, 1972-77, supervisory investigator, 1977-78; cons., pres. Med. Device Inspection Co., Inc., Great Neck, N.Y., 1979-94; sr. cons. MDI Cons., Inc., Great Neck, N.Y., 1995—. Mdi Cons., Inc., Great Neck; cons., v.p. Foodworks Inc., Flushing, N.Y., 1978-85; pres. Foodworks Quality Assurance Cons., Great Neck, 1985—; v.p. Creative Sci. Tech., Inc., Great Neck, N.Y., 1987-93, CST Tech. Inc., 1993, exec. v.p., 1993; sec.-treas. Gum Tech. Inc., Flushing, 1983-85; bd. advisers Gen. Med. Corp., Cohasset, Mass.; regulatory affairs advisor MEIPEC Cons. Group, Cohasset, 1983-84; lectr. Ctr. for Profl. Advancement, 1981—; lectr. to mfrs. on govt. regulations and corp. liability; mem. adv. bd. BCR Ltd. 1986-88, Preventa-Pak USA, 1986-87, Crystal Biotech Corp., 1987-89, Med. Mfrs. Industry Coun., 1993; chmn. sci. adv. bd. Am. TV Network, 1992—; advisor Bd. Med. Manufacturer Info. Coun., 1993. Mem. editl. adv. bd. Jour. CGMP Compliance; contbr. articles to profl. jours. Mem. Regulatory Affairs Profl. Soc., Inst. Food Technologists, Environ. Mgmt. Assn., Small Mfrs. Med. Devices Assn., Assoc. Health Found., Toastmasters (sec.-treas. 1985-86), KP (Man of Yr. 1985). Office: MDI Consltants Inc 55 Northern Blvd Ste 200 Great Neck NY 11021-4058

SCHWARTZ, ALAN VICTOR, advertising agency executive; b. Detroit, July 12, 1948; s. Seymour and Adeline (Goldstein) S.; children: Stacy Ilana, Andrew Robert. BS with honors, Lehigh U., 1970; MBA with highest honors, Cornell U., 1972. CPA, N.Y. Mgr. Price Waterhouse, Huntington, N.Y., 1972-79; v.p., dir. fin. control Doyle Dane Bernbach, N.Y.C., 1979-81; v.p., CFO, Bernard Hodes Group, N.Y.C., 1981-84, sr. v.p., chief oper. and fin. officer, 1984-87, exec. v.p., COO, 1987—2001, pres., CEO, 2002—, 2002—. Bd. mgrs. Evans Tower, treas. 1991-92, pres. 1991-92. Campaign vice chmn. United Way L.I., 1978. Mem. Nat. Assn. Accts. (various directorships, treas.), N.Y. State Soc. CPAs, Lehigh Alumni Assn. (pres. L.I. chpt. 177-79, treas. 1975-77). Office: Bernard Hodes Group 220 E 42d St New York NY 10017

SCHWARTZ, ALBERT TRUMAN, chemistry professor; b. Freeman, S.D., May 8, 1934; s. Albert and Edna Kaufman Schwartz; m. Beverly Beatty, Aug. 12, 1958; children: Ronald Eric, Katherine Schwartz Herrmann. BA, U. S.D., 1956, Oxford (Eng.) U., 1958, MA, 1960; PhD, MIT, 1963; DSc (hon.), U. S.D., 1991. Rsch. chemist Procter & Gamble Co., Cin., 1963-66; asst. prof. Macalester Coll., St. Paul, 1966-72, assoc. prof., 1972-78, prof., 1978-83, DeWitt Wallace prof., 1983—, dean faculty, 1974-76, chair dept. chemistry, 1980-88, 94-95. Vis. rschr. U. Lund, Sweden, 1968, U. Mass., Amherst, 1972—73; vis. prof. U. Wis., Madison, 1979—80, U. S.D., 2000; hon. vis. prof. U. York, England, 1994; dep. dir. tchr. preparation and enhancement NSF, Washington, 1986—87. Author: Chemistry: Imagination and Implication, 1973; sr. author: Chemistry in Context: Applying Chemistry to Society, 1994, 2nd edit., 1997, And Gladly Teach: A Resource Book for Chemists Considering Academic Careers, 2003; co-editor: Motion Toward Perfection: The Achievement of Joseph Priestley, 1970; contbr. articles to profl. jours. Mem. selection com. Rhodes Scholarship Trust, 1963—, sec. Minn. and Midwest dist. coms., 1993-2001. Recipient Catalyst award in chem. edn. Chem. Mfrs. Assn., 1982, Coll. Sci. Tchr. of Yr., Minn. Sci. Tchrs. Assn., 1988; Rhodes scholar Rhodes Trust, Oxford U., 1956-58. Fellow AAAS; mem. Am. Chem. Soc. (chair divsn. chem. edn. 1989, chair mem. sect. 1992-93, mem. various coms., Conn. Sect. award 1991, Brasted award 1996, James Flack Norris award 1997). Avocations: music, photography, travel, cooking. Home: 68 Otis Ave Saint Paul MN 55104 Office: Macalester Coll 1600 Grand Ave Saint Paul MN 55105-1801 E-mail: schwartz@macalester.edu.

SCHWARTZ, ALFRED, university dean; b. Chgo., Jan. 8, 1922; s. Isadore and Lena (Ziff) S.; m. Delle Weiss, Aug. 26, 1945; children: Reid Mitchell, Karen Ruth. B.Ed., Chgo. Tchrs. Coll., 1944; MA in Polit. Sci., U. Chgo., 1946, PhD in Ednl. Adminstrn., 1949. Tchr. Chgo. pub. schs., 1944-45; contact officer VA, 1946; instr. U. Chgo. Lab. Sch., 1946-50; assoc. prof. edn. Drake U., 1950-56, U. Del.; also exec. sec. Del. Sch. Study Council, 1956-58; dean (Univ. Coll.); prof. Coll. Edn., Drake U., 1958-85, dean, 1964-79, 80-84, dean emeritus, 1985; acting v.p. acad. adminstrn. Coll. Edn., Coll. Edn., 1979-80; cons., 1985—. Adviser Iowa Dept. Pub. Instrn.; mem. coordinating bd. Nat. Council Accreditation for Tchr. Edn.; chmn. tchr. edn. and adv. com. Iowa Dept. Pub. Instrn. Author: (with Harlan L. Hagman) Administration in Profile for School Executives, 1954, (with Stuart Tiedeman) Evaluating Student Progress, 1957, (with Willard Fox) Managerial Guide for School Principals, 1965. Mem. Gov.'s Commn. State-Local Relations, pres. condo assn., 1987-97. Mem. World Council on Curriculum and Instrn., Iowa Assn. Colls. for Tchr. Edn. (pres., exec. sec.), Am. Profs. for Peace in Middle East, Am. Ednl. Research Assn., Iowa Edn. Assn., NEA, Phi Delta Kappa, Kappa Delta Pi. Home: 3450 3rd Ave Apt 511 San Diego CA 92103-4939

SCHWARTZ, ALLYSON Y. state legislator; b. N.Y.C., Oct. 3, 1948; d. Everett and Renee Perl Young; m. David Schwartz, 1970; children: Daniel, Jordan. BA, Simmons Coll., 1970; MSS, Bryn Mawr Coll., 1972. Founder, exec. dir. Elizabeth Blackwell Health Ctr. for Women, 1975-88; acting commr., 1st dep. commr. Dept. Human Svcs., 1988-90; mem. Pa. Senate, Harrisburg, 1990—, minority chmn. edn. com., 1994. Mem. Aging and Youth Com., Pub. Health and Welfare Com., Policy Commn., Banking and Ins. Commn., Judiciary Commn. Mem. Pa. State Bd. Edn., 1995—. Pa. Coun. on Higher Edn., Pa. 2000, 1990—, Pa. Hist. and Mus. Commn., Edn. Commn. States, Nat. Dem. Leadership Coun.; former vice chair Nat. Conf. State

Legislators, 1994; v.p. Women's Network; co-chair Pa. New Dem. Coalition; bd. trustees Arcadia U., Chestnut Hill Healthcare; chair Instl. Review Bd., Phila. Health Mgmt. Corp.; bd. dirs. Nat. Jewish Dem. Coun.; adv. bd. Tuition Assistance (TAP) Office: Pa Senate Senate Box 203004 182 Capitol Bldg Harrisburg PA 17120

SCHWARTZ, ANNA JACOBSON, economic historian; b. NYC, Nov. 11, 1915; married; 4 children. BA, Barnard Coll., 1934; MA, Columbia U., 1935, PhD, 1964; LittD (hon.), U. Fla., 1987, Emory U., 2000; ArtsD (hon.), Stonehill Coll., 1989; LLD (hon.), Iona Coll., 1992, Rutgers U., 1998; LHD (hon.), CUNY, 2000; LLD (hon.), Williams Coll., 2002; LHD (hon.), Loyola U., Chicago, 2003. Rschr. USDA, 1936, Columbia U. Social Sci. Rsch. Coun., 1936-41; sr. rsch. staff Nat. Bur. Econ. Rsch. Inc., N.Y.C., 1941—. Instr. Bklyn. Coll., 1952, Baruch Coll., 1959-60; adj. prof. econs. grad. CCNY, 1967-69, grad. sch. CUNY, 1986—, NYU Grad. Sch. Arts and Sci., 1969-70; hon. vis. prof. City U. Bus. Sch., London, 1984—; hon. fellow Inst. of Econ. Affairs, London, 1998. Mem. editorial bd. Am. Econ. Rev., 1972-78, Jour. Money, Credit and Banking, 1974-75, 84—, Jour. Monetary Econs., 1975—, Jour. Fin. Svcs. Rsch., 1993—; contbr. articles to profl. jours. Disting. fellow Am. Econ. Assn., 1993; hon fellow Inst. Econ. Affairs, London. Mem. Western Econ. Assn. (pres. 1987-88). Office: Nat Bur Econ Research 365 Fifth Ave 5th Fl New York NY 10016-4309 Business E-Mail: aschwartz@gc.cuny.edu.

SCHWARTZ, ANTHONY, veterinary surgeon, educator; b. Bklyn., July 30, 1940; s. Murray and Miriam Sarah (Wittes) S.; m. Claudia Rosenberg, July 21, 1963; children: Thomas Frederick, Eric Leigh. Student, Mich. State U., 1957—58; DVM, Cornell U., 1963; PhD, Ohio State U., 1972. Diplomate Am. Coll. Vet. Surgeons (bd. of regents 1989-92). Gen. practice vet. medicine, Huntington, N.Y., 1963-66; resident in surgery Animal Med. Ctr., N.Y.C., 1968-69, Ohio State U., Columbus, 1969-70, asst. prof., head sect. small animal surgery, 1973; asst. prof. then assoc. prof. comparative medicine Yale U. Sch. Medicine, New Haven, 1973-79; assoc. prof. then prof., chmn. dept. surgery, assoc. dean Tufts U. Sch. Vet. Medicine, Boston, 1979-89, assoc. dean clin. edn., 1989-93, prof., chmn. dept. surgery, assoc. dean academic affairs, 1993-97, assoc. dean for acad. and outreach programs, 1997—2002, assoc. dean for continuing edu. and outreach programs, 2003—. Cons. U.S. Surg. Corp., Norwalk, Conn., 1975—; mem. Bd. Tufts Animal Expo LLC, program dir., 1999—; mem. vet. adv. bd. PetPlace.com, Intelligent Content Corp., 2000—; exec. dir., chair bd. dirs. N.E. Vet. Conf., 2003—, chair program com., 2003-04. Author: (with others) Small Animal Surgery, 1989, Complications in Small Animal Surgery, 1996; editl. bd. Vet. Surgery, 1987-90, Jour. Investigative Surgery, 1987-98; assoc. editor: Textbook of Small Animal Surgery, 1985; contbr. articles to profl. jours. Capt. U.S. Army Vet Corps, 1966-68. Recipient 1st prize N.Y. State Vet. Med. Soc., 1963; Robert Wood Johnson Health Policy fellow, Washington, 1988-89; NIH grantee, 1975-84. Mem.: AAAS, AVMA (legis. planning com. 1989—92, coun. on govt. affairs 1992—97), Mass. Vet. Med. Assn. (chmn. 1990—91, animal welfare com. 1990—98, Merit award for leadership in pub. rels. and colleague devel. 2002), Nat. Acads. of Practice (co-chmn. acad. vet. medicine 2002—03), Assn. Am. Vet. Med. Colls. (treas. 1992—93, Washington, exec. dir.), Phi Kappa Phi, Sigma Xi. Democrat. Jewish. Office: Tufts U Sch Vet Medicine 200 Westboro Rd North Grafton MA 01536-1895 Office Phone: 508-887-4600. Business E-Mail: Anthony.Schwartz@tufts.edu.

SCHWARTZ, ARTHUR, playwright, poet; b. N.Y.C., May 20, 1931; s. Harry and Sarah Pearl Schwartz; m. Joan Klenin, June 10, 1956; children: Jessy Ann, Rachel Freyda. Student, Champlain Coll., 1950, student, 1951, student, 1952. Minor league baseball player N.Y. Yankees, 1954—55; stand-up comedian, 1968—80; playwright, poet, 1976—. Prodr.: (plays) An Apple a Day, 1977, The King of Empire Boulevard, 1978, The General and the Jew, 1979, A Choice of Weapons, 1996, If The White House Calls, I'm Out, 2000, The Intruder-The National Pastime, 2001, Naked Batting Practice, 2004, A Song for Chaim Levy, 2004;, author poetry. Named one of Best Poets of 1994, Nat. Libr. Poetry, Best Poets of 1995, Best Poets of 1996, Best Poets of 1997; recipient Writers Digest Poetry award, 1995, Outstanding Achievement award, Nat. Libr. Poetry, 1994, 1995, 1996, 1997. Home: 420 Merrick Rd Rockville Centre NY 11570 Office Phone: 717-362-6490.

SCHWARTZ, ARTHUR GERALD, microbiology educator; b. Balt., Mar. 13, 1941; s. Paul and Rose (Goldfinger) S.; m. Karen Jean Bantley, Mar. 27, 1988; 1 child, Daniel Paul. BA, Johns Hopkins U., 1961; PhD, Harvard U., 1968. Postdoctoral fellow Sir William Dunn Sch. Pathology U. Oxford, Eng., 1968-71; postdoctoral fellow dept. cell biology Albert Einstein Coll. Medicine, N.Y., 1971-72; investigator Fells Rsch. Inst. Temple U. Sch. Medicine, Phila., 1972—, asst. prof. microbiology, 1972-77, assoc. prof. microbiology, 1977-85, prof. microbiology, 1985—. Patentee method for prophylaxis of obesity and steroids useful as anti-cancer and anti-obesity agts. Jane Coffin Childs Meml. Fund for Med. Rsch. fellow, 1968. Mem. Phi Beta Kappa. Office: Temple U Sch Medicine 3307 N Broad St Philadelphia PA 19140-5104

SCHWARTZ, ARTHUR HAROLD, psychiatry educator; b. N.Y.C., Apr. 6, 1936; s. Benedict and Miriam (Patkin) S.; m. Carol Louis Caton, Dec. 19, 1964 (div. Dec. 1980); 1 child, Lisa Catherine. AB, Columbia Coll., 1957; MD, Harvard U., 1961. Diplomate Am. Bd. Psychiatry and Neurology. Acting dir. Newport (R.I.) Mental Health Clinic, 1965-67; asst. prof. Yale U. Sch. Medicine, New Haven, 1967-71, assoc. prof. clin. psychiatry, 1971-72; assoc. prof. psychiatry Mt. Sinai Sch. Medicine, N.Y.C., 1972-81; prof. psychiatry U. Medicine & Dentistry N.J., Robert Wood Johnson Med. Sch., Piscataway, N.J., 1981—, acting chmn. dept. psychiatry, 1991—. Lt. comdr. USN, 1965-67. Fellow AAAS, Am. Psychiat. Assn., Am. Psychopathol. Assn., N.Y. Acad. Medicine; mem. Am. Psychoanalytic Assn. Office: Univ Medicine and Dentistry Robert Wood Johnson Med Sch 675 Hoes Ln Piscataway NJ 08854-5627

SCHWARTZ, AUBREY EARL, artist, educator; b. N.Y.C., Jan. 13, 1928; s. Louis and Clara S. Student, Art Students League, Bklyn. Mus. Art Sch., 1969-94; prof. emeritus Harpur Coll., SUNY, Binghamton, 1994—. Prof. art Harpur Coll., SUNY, Binghamton, 1969— One-man shows Grippi Gallery, N.Y.C., 1958, Art U.S.A., N.Y. Coliseum, N.Y.C., 1959, Contemporary Graphic Art, U.S. State Dept., 1959, retrospective exhbn., MacClaren, Barrie, Ont., 2003, Odon Wagner Gallery, Toronto; group shows include Whitney Mus. Am. Art, N.Y.C., 1957, Binghamton Univ. Art Mus., 1997; represented in permanent collections Nat. Gallery Art, Washington, Bklyn. Mus. Art, Phila. Mus. Art, Library Congress, Washington, Art Inst. Chgo. Recipient 1st prize for graphic art Boston Arts Festival 1960, Europhysics prize, 2003; Guggenheim fellow, 1958-60; Tamarind fellow, 1960; N.Y. State CAPS fellow, 1973-74 Home: PO Box 6 Afton NY 13730-0006

SCHWARTZ, BARRY FREDRIC, lawyer, diversified holding company executive; b. Phila., Apr. 16, 1949; s. Albert and Evelyn (Strauss) S.; m. Sherry L. Handsman, Mar. 21, 1985; children: Fanny Rose, Abraham David. AB cum laude, Kenyon Coll., 1970; JD, Georgetown U., 1974. Bar: Pa. 1974, Ill. 1974, N.Y. 1992, U.S. Dist. Ct. (ea. dist.) Pa. 1974, U.S. Dist. Ct. (no. dist.) Ill. 1975, U.S. Dist. Ct. (so. dist.) N.Y. 1992, U.S. Ct. Appeals (7th cir.) 1977, U.S. Ct. Appeals (3d cir.) 1978, U.S. Ct. Appeals (4th cir.) 1979, U.S. Ct. Appeals (6th cir.) 1981, U.S. Supreme Ct. 1981, N.Y. 1992. Assoc. Sachnoff, Schrager, Jones & Weaver, Chgo., 1974-76; ptnr. Wolf, Block, Schorr & Solis-Cohen, Phila., 1976-89; exec. v.p. gen. counsel MacAndrews & Forbes Holdings, Inc., N.Y.C., 1989—. Trustee Kenyon Coll.; mem. adv. coun. Westchester Holocaust Commn., 2000-; mem. Adv. Com. for Justices of the Comml. divsn. Supreme Ct., New York County, 1999-. Mem.: Assn. Governing Bds. of Univs. and Colls., Revlon Consumer Products Corp., REV Holdings LLC, Sci. Games Corp. Home: 16 Brookside Park Greenwich CT 06831-5316 Office: MacAndrews & Forbes Holdings Inc 35 E 62nd St New York NY 10021-8032

SCHWARTZ, BART, diversified financial services company executive; BA, Antioch Coll., 1975; JD, U. So. Calif., 1978; MBA, Vanderbilt U., 1991. Former assoc. atty. Debevoise and Plimpton, Skadden, Arps, Slate, Meagher & Flom; former exec. v.p., gen. counsel Werthan Packaging, Inc.; former sr. v.p., gen. counsel, sec. Willis Corroon Corp., Nashville; former sr. v.p., gen. counsel The MONY Group, Inc., N.Y.C., 2000—; dep. gen. counsel, corp. sec. Marsh & McLennan Cos., Inc., N.Y.C. Mem.: ABA (com. corp. gen. counsel), Coun. Chief Legal Officers, Assn. Life Ins. Counsel, Am. Corp. Counsel Assn. (bd. dirs. N.Y. chpt.). Office: MONY Group 1740 Broadway New York NY 10019

SCHWARTZ, BERNARD See CURTIS, TONY

SCHWARTZ, BERNARD, physician; b. Toronto, Nov. 12, 1927; s. Samuel and Gertrude Schwartz; children: Lawrence Frederick, Karen Lynne, Jennifer Carla, Ariane Samara MD, U. Toronto, 1951; MS, State U. Iowa, 1953, PhD, 1959. Intern U. Hosps., State U. Iowa, 1951-52, resident ophthalmology, 1951-54; research fellow U. Iowa, 1954-58; asst. prof. to assoc. prof. Downstate Med. Center fo State U. N.Y., 1958-68; prof. ophthalmology Tufts U., 1968-93, chmn. dept., 1968-90, prof. emeritus ophthalmology, 1993—. Author: Syphilis and the Eye; editor-in-chief Survey of Ophthalmology, 1968—, Comprehensive Ophthalmology Update, 1998—; contbr. articles to profl. jours. Fellow Am. Acad. Ophthalmology, ACS; mem. Assn. Rsch. in Ophthalmology, New Eng. Ophthalmol. Soc., N.Y. Acad. Medicine, Sigma Xi. Home: 180 Beacon St Boston MA 02116-1408 Office: 7 Kent St Ste 3 Brookline MA 02445 Office Phone: 617-232-4442. Business E-Mail: glaucomares@mva.net.

SCHWARTZ, BERNARD LEON, space and communications company executive; b. Dec. 13, 1925; BBA, CCNY, 1948. Ptnr. Schnee, Hover & Schwartz, 1948—62; sr. v.p. APL Corp., Fla., 1962—68; chmn. bd., CEO Leasco Corp., Miami Beach, 1969—72; chmn., CEO Loral Corp., N.Y.C., 1972—96, pres., 1973—81; chmn., CEO, bd. dirs. Loral Space & Comm., 1996—; chmn., CEO Globalstar Telecomms. Ltd., 1996—, K&F Industries, Inc. With U.S. Army, 1943—45. Office: Loral Space & Comms 600 3rd Ave Fl 36 New York NY 10016-2001

SCHWARTZ, BRIAN S. medical educator, academic administrator; MD, Northwestern U., 1984; MS, U. Pa., 1989. Assoc. prof. Johns Hopkins U., Balt., dir. occupl. and environ. health. Office: Johns Hopkins U Dept Occupl & Environ Hlth 615 N Wolfe St Baltimore MD 21205-2103

SCHWARTZ, CARL EDWARD, artist, printmaker; b. Detroit, Sept. 20, 1935; s. Carl and Verna (Steiner) S.; m. Kay Joyce Hofmann, June 18, 1955 (div.); children: Dawn Ellen, Cari Leigh. BFA, Art Inst. Chgo. Sch.-U. Chgo., 1957. Past tchr. art, Chgo., N. Shore Art League, Suburban Fine Arts Center, Deerpath Art League; faculty art Edison C.C., Fla. Gulf Coast U. One-man shows include, South Bend (Ind.) Art Center, Feingarten Gallery, Chgo., 1960, Bernard Horwich Center, Chgo., Covenant Club, Chgo., Barat Coll., Chgo. Pub. Library, Alverno Coll., 1020 Art Center, Rosenberg Gallery, Peoria (Ill.) Art Guild, 1977, Ill. State Mus., 1977 Ill. Inst. Tech., 1978, Miller Gallery, Chgo., 1979, Union League Club, Chgo., 1982, Art Inst. Rental and Sale Gallery, Chgo., 1982, Horwich Gallery, Chgo., 1983, Lake Forest (Ill.) Coll., 1983, Campanile-Capponi Contemporary Gallery, Chgo., 1987, Nagata Gallery, Ft. Myers, Fla., 1988, Jan Cicero Gallery, Chgo., 1990, Neopolitan Gallery, Naples, Fla., 1996, 97; numerous group shows include 9th Ann. Michigana Exhbt, Detroit (Cloetingh and Deman award 1959), Hyde Park Art Center, Chgo., 1960 (5th Ann. Jury Exhbn. prize), Spectrum Exhbn. '63, Chgo. (1st prize), New Horizons Exhbt, Chgo., 1960 (Joseph Shapiro award), Nat. Design Center, Chgo., 1965 (New Horizons in Painting 1st prize), 3d Ann. Chgo. Arts Competition, 1962 (1st prize), Union League Club, Chgo., 1967 (2d prize), N. Shore Art League Ann. Drawing and Print Show, Chgo., 1965 (1st prize), Artists Guild Chgo., 1965 (prize), McCormack Pl., Chgo., 1965 (1st prize), Detroit Art Inst., 1965 (Commonwealth prize), Park Forest (Ill.) Art Exhbn, 1969 (Best of Show), 14th Ann. Virginia Beach (Va.) Show, 1969 (Best of Show), Suburban Fine Arts Center, Highland Park, Ill., 1970 (prize), 15th Ann. Virginia Beach Show, 1970 (prize), 32d Ann. Artists Guild, Chgo., 1970 (2d prize), N. Shore Art League Print and Drawing Show, 1970 (prize), 16th Ann. Virginia Beach Show, 1971 (2d prize), Ill. State Fair, 1972 (prize), Artists Guild Chgo., 1972 (1st prize), 17th Ann. Virginia Beach Exhbt, 1972 (1st prize), Artists Guild 50th Fine Art Exhbn., Chgo., 1973 (prize), Dickinson State U., 1973 (prize), N. Shore Art League Print Exhbn, 1973 (prize), Lakehurst Exhbt, 1974 (prize), Union League Art Exhbt, 1974 (1st prize), Artists Guild Fine Arts Exhbn., 1974 (best of Show), Bluegrass Painting Exhbn, Louisville, 1975 (award), Union League Art Exhbn, 1976 (prize); represented in permanent collections, Brit. Mus., London, Smithsonian Inst., Washington, Art Inst. Chgo., K. Van Ella, Chgo., Weatherburn Gallery, Naples. Home: 5825 Briarcliff Rd Fort Myers FL 33912-4204 *I am a painter of light. I'm intrigued and fascinated with form. To me, there are two worlds-the one we all live in, and the one that I create. Painting is the discipline by which I constantly rediscover both of these worlds.*

SCHWARTZ, CAROL ANN, investment company executive; m. Michael D. Schwartz, Jun., 1985; children: Matthew, Allison, Elana. B in Bus. Adminstrn., U. Cinn., 1983; M in Bus. Adminstrn., Finance, Xavier U., 1984; graduate, Grad. Real Estate Inst., 1992. Lic. real estate sales agent. Asst. v.p. Fifth Third Bank, 1984-91; exec. v.p. Morris Investment Co., 1991—. Spkr. in field. Group fundraiser United Appeal, 1986—89; group adv. Jr. Achievement, 1984—86; vol. neighborhood coord., solicitor March of Dimes, 1993—; lox box com. Orgn. Rehab. and Tng. Blue Chip chpt., 1993, 1995—96; bd. mem. Yavneh PTA, 1995—97, Sukkot decorating com., Rosh Hashanah Treats co-chair, Tu'Bishvat spkr., 1997, Tu'Bishvat Seder com., 1998; v.p. fundraising Yavneh Day Sch., 2000—, bd. dirs., 1997—, Friends of Yavneh Campaign chair, 1998—2000; young women/young leaders mission to Israel Hadassah Nat., 1997, nat. conv. chat room facilitator, 1998—99, nat. young leaders adv. coun., 1999—2000, conv. attendee, 1996—99; awards dinner com. Nat. Conf. Christians and Jews, 1993; bus. and profl. group program com. Nat. Coun. Jewish Women, 1990—91, bus. and profl. group program com., chpt. legis. com., 1991—92, bus. and profl. group program com., 1992—93, pub. affairs com., computer analysis com., 1992—93, fin. analysis com., 1993—94, life mem., 1993—; mem. United Jewish Cmtys. Nat. Young Leadership Cabinet, 2000—; bd. dirs. Hadassah Cin. chpt., 1993—, donor com. publicity, pre-donor brunch chair, 1992—93, donor com. publicity, 1996—97, chair, 1993—94, donor book, 1994—96, jewels and memorials, 1995—99, budget chair, 1995—97, com., 1997—, leading gifts divsn. co-chair, 1996—97, pres., 1997—99, cons., 1999—2000; fundraising conf. coord. Hadassah Regional, 1993, regional conf. com., 1997—98, bd. dirs., 1995—2000; Nat. Young Leaders adv. coun. rep. Hadassah Regional, 1999—; fundraising conf. attendee Hadassah Midwest Area Coop., 1993, pres. tng. attendee, 1997, young women's co-chair, 1999—2000; bd. dirs. Hillel, 1998—, alumni com., 1998—2000, auction com., 1998—2000; leadership coun. Jewish Fedn. of Cin., 1987—92, solicitor, 1991—92, lect. series com., 1989, kickoff party com., 1990, women's divsn. group, 1992—, campaign co-chair, 1996—97, bus. and profl. women co-chair, 1998—99, Israel programs cabinet, 1998—99, chair, 1999—2000, campaign cabinet program co-chair, 1999—2000, bd. dir., 1999—; hostess liquid assets luncheon Jewish Nat. Fund, 1993, bd. dirs., 1995—, v.p. edn., 1996—99, tchrs. edn. day chair, 1997—99, four star dining com., 1998—2000, trade and industry dinner com., 1997—98, Green Sunday com., 1996—, Walk for Water com., 1998—; life mem. Jewish Women's Auxilliary, 1995—; v.p. Adath Israel Synagogue, 2001—, bd. dirs., 1992—. Recipient State Member of Yr. Fin. Women Internat., 1987, Cin. chpt. Mem. of Yr., 1988, Nat. Leadership award Cin. chpt. Hadassah Ya'al Group, 1994, Clara Geller Young Leadership award Jewish Fedn. Cin.; named among Outstanding Women of Am., 1985, The Cincinnati Business Courier's Who's Who Among Women in Bus. in Cin., 1992, Top 40 Women in Bus., 1993. Mem. AAUW, Cin. Bd. of Realtors (mem. svcs. com. 1992-93), Ohio Assn. Relators (conv. attendee), Nat. Assn. Realtors (conv. attendee), Comm. Indsl. Real Estate Industry (CCIM designate), Cin. Art Mus., Cin., Historical Soc., Cin. Playhouse in the Park, Contemporary Arts Ctr., Nat. Assn. Female Execs., Nat. History Mus., U. Cin. Alumni Assn. (life mem. 1986—), Women's City Club, World Jewish Cong., Xavier U. Alumni Assn. (life).

SCHWARTZ, CAROL LEVITT, government official; b. Greenville, Miss., Jan. 20, 1944; d. Stanley and Hilda (Simmons) Levitt; m. David H. Schwartz (dec.); children: Stephanie, Hilary, Douglas. BS in Spl. and Elem. Edn., U. Tex., 1965. Mem. transiton team Office of Pres. Elect, 1980-81; con. office presdl. personnel The White House, Washington, 1981; cons. U.S. Dept. Edn., Washington, 1982; pres. sec. U.S. Ho. Reps., Washington, 1982-83; mem.-at-large Coun. of D.C., Washington, 1985-89, 97—; candidate for mayor, Washington, 1986, 1994, 1998, 2002. Vice chmn. Nat. Edn. Commn. on Time and Learning, 1992-94, Nat. Adv. Coun. on Disadvantaged Children, 1974-79; lectr. in field; radio commentator, 1990-91; chair transp., vice-chair planning bd. Coun. Govts. Regional columnist Washington Jewish Week, 1995-97. Mem. D.C. Bd. Edn., 1974-82, v.p., 1977-80; bd. dirs. Met. Police Boys and Girls Club, 1st v.p., 1989-93, pres., 1994-96, chmn. membership com., 1984-93; mem. adv. com. Am. Coun. Young Polit. Leaders, 1982-90; mem. Nat. Coun. Friends Kennedy Ctr., 1984-91; bd. dirs. Whitman-Walker Clinic, 1988—, v.p., 1995-96; bd. dirs. St. John's Child Devel. Ctr., 1989-91, Hattie M. Strong Found., 1995—; trustee Kennedy Ctr. Cmty. and Friends Bd., 1991—, chmn. ednl. task force, 1993—; trustee Jewish Coun. on Aging, 1991-93; v.p. adv. bd. Am. Automobile Assn., 1988—; bd. dirs. Washington Hebrew Congregation, 1995-98. Mem. Cosmos Club. Republican. Jewish. Office Phone: 202-724-8105.

SCHWARTZ, CAROL VIVIAN, lawyer; b. Newark, Apr. 5, 1952; d. A. Harold and Helen (Schwartz) S.; m. Robert L. Sills, June 9, 1985. BA, Tufts U., 1974; JD, Columbia U., 1977. Law clk. to presiding justice U.S. Dist. Ct. N.Y, N.Y.C., 1978-79; assoc. DeLevoise & Plimpton, N.Y.C., 1979-81; assoc. counsel Am. Express Co., N.Y.C., sr. counsel, now group counsel, 1981—. Mem. ABA. Avocation: sailing. Home: 520 E 86th St # 11A New York NY 10028-7534 Office: Am Express Co Am Express Tower 200 Vesey St New York NY 10285-1000

SCHWARTZ, CAROLYN LYNN, retail executive, musician; b. Brownwood, Tex., Apr. 14, 1957; d. Milton Frank and Ramona Villa Schwartz. BA, U. Mary Hardin, 1979; degree in nursing, Baylor U. Lic. real estate agt. Tex. Musician: (albums) Walkin Thru the Fire, 1990, Journey, 1995. Ch. musician, coord children's gospel music, Goldthwaite, Tex., 1989—. Mem.: ASCAP, Tex. Realtors. Avocations: tennis, swimming, writing music, reading.

SCHWARTZ, CHARLES, JR., federal judge; b. New Orleans, Aug. 20, 1922; s. Charles and Sophie (Hess) S.; m. Patricia May, Aug. 31, 1950 (dec.); children: Priscilla May, John Putney. BA, Tulane U., 1943, JD, 1947. Bar: La. 1947. Ptnr. Guste, Barnett & Little, 1947-70; practiced in New Orleans, until 1976; ptnr. firm Little, Schwartz & Dussom, 1970-76; dist. counsel Gulf Coast dist. U.S. Maritime Adminstrn., 1953-62; judge U.S. Dist. Ct. (ea. dist.) La., New Orleans, 1976-91, sr. judge, 1991—. Mem. Fgn. Intelligence Surveillance Ct., 1992-98; prof. Tulane U. Law Sch., 1977-99; lectr. continuing law insts., 1974-75; mem. Jud. Conf. Com. U.S. on implementation of jury system, 1981-85; mem. permanent adv. bd. Tulane Admiralty Law Inst., 1984—. Bd. editors Tulane Law Rev. Pres. New Orleans unit Am. Cancer Soc., 1956-57; v.p., chmn. budget com. United Fund Greater New Orleans Area, 1959-61, trustee, 1953-65; bd. dirs. Cancer Assn. Greater New Orleans, 1958—, pres., 1958-59, 72-73; bd. dirs. United Cancer Council, 1963-85, pres., 1971-73; mem. com. on grants to agencies Community Chest, 1965-87; men's adv. com. League Women Voters, 1966-68; chmn. com. admissions of program devel. and coordination com. United Way Greater New Orleans, 1974-77; mem. comml. panel Am. Arbitration Assn., 1974-76; bd. dirs. Willow Wood Home, 1979-85, 1989-92; bd. mgrs. Touro Infirmary, 1992—; trustee Metairie Park Country Day Sch., 1977-83; mem. La. Republican Central Com., 1961-76; mem. Orleans Parish Rep. Exec. Com., 1960-75, chmn., 1964-75; mem. Jefferson Parish Rep. Exec. Com., 1975-76; del. Rep. Nat. Conv., 1960, 64, 68; mem. nat. budget and consultation com. United Community Funds and Coun. of Am., 1961; bd. dirs. Community Svcs. Coun., 1971-73. Served to 2d lt. AUS, 1943-46; maj. U.S. Army Res.; ret. Mem. La. Bar Assn. New Orleans Bar Assn. (legis. com. 1970-75), Fed. Bar Assn., Fgn. Rels. Assn. New Orleans (bd. dirs. 1957-61), 5th Cir. Dist. Judges Assn. (pres. 1984-85), Lakewood Country Club (bd. dirs. 1967-68, pres. 1975-77). Office: 219 Northline Metairie LA 70005-4447

SCHWARTZ, CHARLES WALTER, lawyer; b. Brenham, Tex., Dec. 27, 1953; s. Walter C. and Annie (Kuehn) S.; m. Kay Anne Bryan, Sept. 24, 1996. BS, U. Tex., 1975, MA, 1980, JD, 1977; LLM, Harvard U., 1980. Bar: Tex. 1977; bd. cert. civil appellate law Tex. Bd. Legal Specialization. Law clk. U.S. Ct. Appeals (5th cir.), Austin, Tex., 1977-79; assoc. Vinson & Elkins L.L.P., Houston, 1980-86, ptnr., 1986—2003, Skadden, Arps, Seate, Meagher & Flom, 2003—. Contbr. articles to law revs. Fellow: Am. Bar Found., Tex. Bar Found. (sustaining life), Coll. State Bar Tex., Houston Bar Found. (sustaining life); mem.: ABA, Tex. Law Rev. Assn., Am. Law Inst., Bar Assn. of 5th Cir., State Bar Tex. (former chmn. grievance com. 1993—99, bd. dirs. 2000—04, exec. com. 2001—04, chmn. 2002—03, immediate past chmn. 2003—04). Home: 2154 Chilton Rd Houston TX 77019 Office: Skadden Arps Slate Meagher & Flom LLP 1600 Smith Ste 4400 Houston TX 77002 Office Phone: 713-655-5160. E-mail: Charles.Schwartz@skadden.com.

SCHWARTZ, CHERIE ANNE KARO, storyteller, writer; b. Miami, Fla., Feb. 24, 1951; d. William Howard and Dorothy (Olesh) Karo; m. Lawrence Schwartz, Aug. 12, 1979. BA in Lit., The Colo. Coll., 1973; MA in Devel. Theater, U. Colo., 1977. Tchr. English, drame, mime, creative writing, speech coach South High Sch., Pueblo, Colo., 1973-76; tchr. English and drama Rocky Mountain Hebrew Acad., Denver, 1981-83; full-time profl. storyteller throughout N.Am., 1982—. Storyteller, docent, tchr. tng., mus. outreach Denver Mus. Natural History, 1982—; trainer, cons., performer, lectr, keynote speaker various orgns., synagogues, instns., agys., confs. throughout the country, 1982—; co-founder, chairperson Omanim b'Yachad: Artists Together, Nat. Conf. Celebrating Storytelling, Drama, Music and Dance in Jewish Edn., Denver, 1993. Storyteller: (audio casette tapes) Cherie Karo Schwartz Tells Stories of Hanukkah from Kar-Ben Books, 1986, Cherie Karo Schwartz Tells Stories of Passover From Kar-Ben Books, 1986, Miriam's Trambourine, 1988, Worldwide Jewish Stories of Wishes and Wisdom, 1988; storyteller, actor: (video tape) The Wonderful World of Recycle, 1989; author: (books) My Lucky Dreidel: Hanukkah Stories, Songs, Crafts, Recipes and Fun for Kids, 1994, A Worldwide Celebration, 2000, The Kids' Catalog of Passover, 2000; co-author: (with Barbara Rush) The Kids' Catalog of Passover, Circle Spinning: Jewish Turning and Returning Tales, 2002; author numerous stories in anthologies of Jewish lit., including Chosen Tales, Because God Loves Stories, Reading Between the Lines, Gray Heroes Elder Tales from Around the World. Title III grantee State of Colo. Edn., Pueblo, 1975-76. Mem. Coalition for Advancement of Jewish Edn. (coord. Jewish Storytelling Conf. 1989-98, coord. Nat. Jewish Storytelling Network 1994-97), Nat. Assn. for Preservation and Perpetuation of Storytelling, Nat. Storytelling Assn., Rocky Mountain Storytelling Guild, Rocky Mountain Storytellers Conf. (performer, tchr.), Spellbinders (tchr., nat. bd. dirs.). Democrat. Jewish. Home: 996 S Florence St Denver CO 80247-1952 Office Phone: 303-367-8099. E-mail: schwartstory@earthlink.net.

SCHWARTZ, DANIEL BENNETT, artist; b. N.Y.C., Feb. 16, 1929; s. Bennett Henry and Lillian (Blumenthal) S.; m. Judith Nancy Kass, June 12, 1955 (div. 1980); 1 child, Claudia Bennet. Grad., High Sch. of Music and Art, N.Y.C., 1946; student, Art Students League, 1946, Y. Kuniyoshi; BFA, R.I. Sch. Design, 1949. Instr. pvt. painting class, 1965-81, 90-95, Parsons Sch. Design, 1983. One man shows include Davis Galleries, N.Y.C., 1955, 56, 58, 60, Hirschl & Adler Galleries, N.Y.C., 1963, Maxwell Galleries, San Francisco, 1964, Babcock Galleries, N.Y.C., 1967, F.A.R. Galleries, N.Y.C., 1970, Armstrong Galleries, N.Y.C., 1985, 87, Hammer Galleries, N.Y.C., 1994, Hudson River Gallery, Dobbs Ferry, N.Y., 2001; exhibited in group shows at Albany Inst. History and Art, Am. Fedn. Arts, Butler Inst. Am. Art, Libr. of Congress, Nat. Acad. Design, Pa. Acad. Fine Art, Whitney Mus. Art, Collection Nat. Portrait Gallery, Munson-Williams-Proctor Inst., Bates Coll., British Mus., Century Assn., others; subject of various articles. Louis C. Tiffany Found. grantee, 1956, 60; recipient Purchase prize Am. Acad. Arts and letters, 1964, 84, 11 Gold medals Soc. Illustrators, N.Y.C., 1960-85, Obrig prize for painting Nat. Acad. Design, 1990, winner 1st Benjamin Altman Figure prize, 1992; named to Soc. of Illustrators Hall of Fame, 2002. Mem. NAD, Century Assn. Avocation: jazz piano. Home and Office: 48 E 13th St New York NY 10003-4631 E-mail: dschwartz17@nyc.rr.com.

SCHWARTZ, DANIEL C. lawyer; b. Pa., 1943; AB, Stanford U., 1965; JD, George Washington U., 1969. Bar: D.C. 1969. Asst. to dir. Bur. Competition, FTC, Washington, 1973-75, asst. dir. evaluation, 1975-77, dep. dir., 1977-79; gen. counsel Nat. Security Agy., Washington, 1979-81; ptnr. Bryan Cave LLP, Washington. Mem. ABA. Office: Bryan Cave LLP 700 13th St NW Fl 7 Washington DC 20005-5921 Office Phone: 202-508-6025. E-mail: dcschwartz@bryancave.com.

SCHWARTZ, DEBORAH S. airport manager; b. Muncie, Ind., Oct. 4, 1954; d. Martin David and Helen Frances (Berger) Schwartz; m. Paul Hamlen Ledwell III, July 23, 1977; 1 child, Hilary R. BA cum laude, Wheaton Coll., 1975; MA, U. Houston, 1989. Accredited airport exec. Adminstrv. mgr. various cos., 1976-85; asst. airport mgr. William P. Hobby Airport, Houston, 1986-92; airport dir. Worcester (Mass.) Mcpl. Airport, 1992-94; airport mgr. Little Rock Nat. Airport, 1994—. Mem. Ark. Women's Leadership Forum, Little Rock, 1994—. Named among top 100 women in Ark. Ark. Bus., 1996. Mem. Am. Assn. Airport Execs. (vice chair diversity com. 1995—, legis. com. 1995—), Greater Little Rock C. of C. (bd. dirs. 1995—, transportation com. 1996, literacy com. 1995—, literacy com. 1995—), Phi Kappa Phi, Pi Alpha Alpha, Ark. Airport Operators Assn., Little Rock Rotary. Avocations: reading, riding, camping, hiking, parenting. Office: Little Rock Nat Airport One Airport Dr Little Rock AR 72202

SCHWARTZ, DONALD, chemistry professor; b. Scarsdale, N.Y., Dec. 27, 1927; s. Harry A. and Ethel S.; m. Lois Schwartz, Sept. 8, 1948; children: Leanne, Mark W., Scott B., Bradley F. BS, U. Mo., 1949; MS, Mont. State U., 1951; PhD, Pa. State U., 1955. Program dir. NSF, 1966-68; asso. dean Grad. Sch., Memphis State U., 1968-70; dean advanced studies Fla. Atlantic U., Boca Raton, 1970-71; v.p., acting pres. State U. N.Y., Buffalo, 1971-74; chancellor Ind. U.-Purdue U., Ft. Wayne, Ind., 1974-78; chancellor, prof. U. Colo., Colorado Springs, 1978-83, prof., 1983-93, prof. emeritus, 1993—. Cons. in field. Author papers structure of coal and organo-titanium compounds, also on higher edn. Bd. dirs., treas. Colo. Springs. Osteo. Found., 1985—. With USCG, 1945. Research fellow AEC, 1953-55; N.Y. State fellow, 1947-48 Mem. Am. Chem. Soc., AAAS, Sigma Xi, Phi Lambda Upsilon, Phi Delta Kappa. Clubs: Rotary, Shriners. Home: 21 Sanford Rd Colorado Springs CO 80906-4219 Personal E-mail: lolodo@msn.com. *Each can become all that he or she is capable of being through education, hard work and compassion for other human beings. This I believe.*

SCHWARTZ, DONALD FRANKLIN, communication scientist; b. Jamestown, ND, 1935; m. Lois Carolyn Schwartz, June 26, 1965; children: Daria, Karin, Marc. BS, ND State U., 1957, MS, 1961; PhD, Mich. State U., 1968. Asst. dir. pub. rels. ND State U., Fargo, 1959-66, chmn. social scis., 1969-71, chmn. comm., 1967-79; instr. comm. Mich. State U., East Lansing, 1966-67; vis. scientist US Dept. Agr., Washington, 1979-80; prof. comm. Cornell U., Ithaca, NY, 1980-98, chmn. dept., 1980-85, dir. undergraduate studies, 1995-98, prof. emeritus, 1998—. Vis. scholar U. N.Mex., 1994. Contbr. articles to profl. jours. Recipient Outstanding Svc. award Future Farmers Am., 1976, Svc. award USDA, 1980, A.D. White Prof. of Yr. award, 1993. Mem. AAUP, Internat. Comm. Assn. (sec., pub. rels. interest group 1992-93), Am. Acad. Mgmt., Am. Soc. Pers. Adminstrn. (chpt. pres. 1976-77), Pub. Rels. Soc. Am. (nat. faculty advisor student assn. 1989-90, vice-chair educators sect. 1992, Pres.'s Citation for Leadership 1990, nat. ednl. affairs com. 1993-96). Roman Cath. Office: Cornell U Dept Communication 331 Kennedy Hall Ithaca NY 14853-4203

SCHWARTZ, DONALD LEE, lawyer; b. Milw., Dec. 8, 1948; s. Bernard L. and Ruth M. (Marshall) S.; m. Susan J. Dunst, June 5, 1971; children: Stephanie Jane, Cheryl Ruth. BA, Macalester Coll., 1971; JD, U. Chgo., 1974. Bar: Ill. 1974. Assoc. Sidley & Austin, Chgo., 1974-80, ptnr., 1980-88, Latham & Watkins, Chgo., 1988—. Chmn. Ill. Conservative Union, 1979-81, bd. dirs. 1977-85. Served with U.S. Army, 1971-77. Mem. ABA (uniform comml. code com., comml. fin. svcs. commn.), Ill. Bar Assn. (sec. coun. banking and bankuprtcy sect. 1982-83), Chgo. Bar Assn. (chmn. comml. law com. 1980-81, fin. insts. com. 1982-83), Ivanhoe Country Club, Sea Pines Country Club, Colleton River Country Club, Met. Club. Republican. Episcopalian. Avocation: golf. Home: 191 Park Ave Glencoe IL 60022-1351 Office: Latham & Watkins Ste 5800 Sears Tower Chicago IL 60606 E-mail: Donald.schwartz@lw.com.

SCHWARTZ, EDWARD ARTHUR, lawyer; b. Boston, Sept. 27, 1937; s. Abe and Sophie (Gottheim) S.; m. Sheila Kauffman, Apr. 5, 1997; children: Eric Allen, Jeffrey Michael. AB, Oberlin Coll., 1959; LLB, Boston Coll., 1962; postgrad., Am. U., 1958-59, Northeastern U., 1970; postgrad. exec. program, Stanford U., 1979. Bar: Conn. 1962, Mass. 1965. Legal intern Office Atty. Gen. Commonwealth of Mass., 1961; assoc. Schatz & Schatz, Hartford, Conn., 1962-65, Cohn, Reimer & Pollack, Boston, 1965-67; v.p., gen. coun., sec. Digital Equipment Corp., Maynard, Mass., 1967-88; pres. New Eng. Legal Found., Boston, 1990-98. Vis. prof. law Boston Coll., 1986, adj. prof., 1987-89 bd. dirs. SatelLife Corp. Editor Boston Coll. Indsl. and Comml. Law Rev, 1960-62, Ann. Survey Mass. Law, 1960-62. Trustee Rural Land Found. Home: 62 Todd Pond Rd Lincoln MA 01773-3808

SCHWARTZ, ELEANOR BRANTLEY, academic administrator; b. Kite, Ga., Jan. 1, 1937; d. Jesse Melvin and Hazel (Hill) Brantley; children: John, Cynthia. Student, U. Va., 1955, Ga. Southern Coll., 1956-57; BBA, Ga. State U., 1962, MBA, 11963, DBA, 1969. Adminstrv. asst. Fin. Agy., 1954, Fed. Govt., Va., Pa., Ga., 1956-59; asst. dean admissions Ga. State U., Atlanta, 1961-66, asst. prof., 1966-70; assoc. prof. Cleve. State U., 1970-75, prof. and assoc. dean, 1975-80; dean, Harzfeld prof. U. Mo., Kansas City, 1980-87, vice chancellor acad. affairs, 1987-91, interim chancellor, 1991-92, chancellor, 1992-99; prof. mgmt. U. Mo. Block Sch., Kansas City, 1999—2003, prof. emeritus, 2003—. Disting. vis. prof. Berry Coll., Rome, N.Y. State U. Coll., Fredonia, Mons U., Belgium; cons. pvt. industry U.S., Europe, Can.; bd. dirs. Rsch. Med. Ctr., Waddell & Reed Funds, Inc., Toy and Miniature Mus., Menorah Med. Ctr. Found., NCAA, NCCJ, Econ. Devel. Corp. of Kansas City, Silicon Prairie Tech. Assn. Author: Sex Barriers in Business, 1971, Contemporary Readings in Marketing, 1974; (with Muczyk and Smith) Principles of Supervision, 1984. Chmn., Mayor's Task Force in Govt. Efficiency, Kansas City, Mo., 1984; mem. comm. unity planning and rsch. coun. United Way Kansas City, 1983-85; bd. dirs. Jr. Achievement, 1982-86. Named Jones Store Career Woman of Yr., Kansas City, Mo., 1989, Ctrl. Exch. Woman of Yr., 1995; named one of 60 Women of Achievement, Girl Scouts Coun. Mid Continent, 1983; recipient Disting. Faculty award, Cleve. State U., 1974, Disting. Svc. award, Kans. State U., 1992, YWCA Hearts of Gold award, 2002. Mem.: Alpha Iota Delta, Golden Key, Phi Kappa Phi.

SCHWARTZ, ELI, economics educator, writer; b. N.Y.C., Apr. 2, 1921; s. Israel and Tillie (Shapiro) S.; m. Renee S. Kartiganer, Aug. 29, 1948; children: Pamela F., Alan G. BS, Denver U., 1943; MA, U. Conn., 1948; PhD, Brown U., 1952. Instr. U. R.I., Kingston, 1947-48; asst. instr. Brown U., Providence, 1948-51; chief regional economist Office Price Stblzn., Boston, 1951-53; lectr. Mich. State U., East Lansing, 1953-54; asst. prof. econs. Lehigh U., Bethlehem, Pa., 1954-58, assoc. prof., 1958-62, prof., 1962-91, Charles Macfarlane prof. econs., 1978-91, chmn. dept. econs., 1978-84, ret., 1991; cons. econs. and fin., expert witness Schwartz-Aronson Assocs., Bethlehem, 1965—. Author: Corporate Finance, 1962, Trouble in Eden, 1980; editor: Managing Municipal Finance, 1980, 83, 87, 96, 2004, Restructuring the Thrift Industry, 1989, Theory and Application of the Interest Rate, 1993; columnist Allentown Moring Call. With U.S. Army, 1943-46, ETO. Recipient sr. teaching Lehigh U., 1972; Earhart Found. grantee, 1978 Mem. Am. Econs. Assn., Am. Fin. Assn., Nat. Assn. Forensic Econs. (founding mem.). Jewish. Home: 3185 W Cedar St Allentown PA 18104-3441 Office: Lehigh U Dept Econs Rauch Ctr 621 Taylor St Bethlehem PA 18015-3107 Office Phone: 610-758-3410. Business E-Mail: rf03@lehigh.edu. *If I have achieved any success it is because I am interested in the subject matter of my field. I am fortunate to enjoy reading, teaching, consulting and writing.*

SCHWARTZ, ELLIOTT SHELLING, composer, author, music educator; b. Bklyn, Jan. 19, 1936; s. Nathan and Rose (Shelling) S.; m. Dorothy Rose Feldman, June 26, 1960; children: Nina, Jonathan. AB, Columbia U., 1957, MA, 1958, EdD, 1962. Instr. music U. Mass., Amherst, 1960-64; from asst. prof. music to assoc. prof. Bowdoin Coll., Brunswick, Maine, 1964-75, prof. music, 1975—. Vis. prof. music Ohio State U., Columbus, 1988-92; vis. composer Trinity Coll. Music, London, 1967, U. Calif. Coll. Creative Studies, Santa Barbara, 1970, 73, 74; composer, pianist, commentator British Broadcast Corp, London, 1972, 74, 78, 83; vis. research musician Center Music Expt., La Jolla, Calif., 1978-79; disting. vis. prof. Ohio State U., 1985-86; music cons. Holt, Rinehart & Winston, Random House, Oxford Univ. Press, Schirmer Books, N.Y.C., 1977—; vis. fellow Robinson Coll., Cambridge U., U.K., 1993-94, 99. Composer: Island, 1970 (Internat. Gaudeamus prize 1970), Chamber Concertos I-IV, 1977-81, Extended Piano, 1980, Dream Music With Variations, 1983, Four Ohio Portraits, 1986, Memorial in Two Parts, 1989, Elan, 1990, Rows Garden, 1993, Equinox, 1994, Timepiece, 1994, Chiaroscuro, 1995, Reflections, 1995, Rainbow, 1996, Tapestry, 1996, Alto Prisms, 1997, Vienna Dreams, 1998, Kaleidoscope, 1999, Jack O'Lantern, 2000, Mehitabel's Serenade, 2000, Rain Forest with Birds, 2001, Voyager, 2002; author: Electronic Music: A Listener's Guide, 1973, Music: Ways of Listening, 1982, (with Daniel Godfrey) Music Since 1945: Issues, Materials and Literature, 1993; editor: (with Barney Childs) Contemporary Composers on Contemporary Music, 1967, rev. edit., 1998; contbr. articles to profl. jours. Nat. Endowment for Arts composition grantee, 1974, 76, 82; Rockefeller Found. residence fellow Bellagio, Italy, 1980, 89; MacDowell Colony resident fellow, 1965, 66; Yaddo residence fellow, 1977; recipient Maine State award Maine Commn. Arts and Humanities, 1970, McKim Commn., 1986 Mem.: Am. Composers Alliance (governing bd. 1994—2000), Am. Soc. Univ. Composers (nat. coun. 1968—72, nat. chmn 1983—88), Coll. Music Soc. (nat. coun. 1982—88, pres. 1988—90), Am. Music Ctr. (v.p. 1981—87). Home: PO Box 451 South Freeport ME 04078-0451 Office: Bowdoin Coll Dept Music Brunswick ME 04011 E-mail: eschwart@bowdoin.edu.

SCHWARTZ, ERIC, lawyer; Gen. counsel Tosco Corp., Santa Monica, Calif. Office: Tosco Corp 2300 Clayton Rd Concord CA 94520-2100

SCHWARTZ, ESTAR ALMA, lawyer; b. Bklyn., June 29, 1950; d. Henry Israel and Elaine Florence (Scheiner) Sutel; m. Lawrence Gerald Schwartz, June 28, 1976 (div. Dec. 1977); 1 child, Joshua (dec.); m. James Francis Edward Stuart, Sept. 25, 1999 (div. Aug. 2001). JD, NYU, 1980. Mgr., ptnr. Scheiner, Scheiner, DeVito & Wytte, N.Y.C., 1966-81; social security fraud specialist U.S. Govt., 1982—83; pensions Todtman, Epstein, et al, 1983—85; office mgr., sec. Sills, Beck, Cummis, 1985—86; office mgr., bookkeeper Philip, Birnbaum & Assoc., 1986—87; office mgr., sec. Stanley Posses, Esq., Queens, 1989—90; owner Estaris Paralegal Svc., Flushing, 1992—, Sutel Creative Mgmt. Agy., 1999—. Owner Estaris Paralegal Svc., Flushing, N.Y., 1992—, Sutel Creative Mgmt. Agy., Flushing, 1999—. Democrat. Jewish. Avocations: needlepoint, horseback riding, tennis, bowling, writing. Home and Office: 67-20 Parsons Blvd Apt 2A Flushing NY 11365-2960 Office Phone: 718-820-0432. E-mail: sutel@email.com., sutelmmgmt12345@msn.com., estaris@email.com.

SCHWARTZ, FRANCIS, music educator, composer; b. Altoona, Pa., Mar. 10, 1940; s. Isidore Joseph Schwartz and Simone Klughaupt; m. Martha Elena Moreno, Nov. 17, 1990; 1 child, Gabriela Raquel. BS, Juilliard Sch., 1961, MS, 1962; PhD, U. Paris, 1979. Prof. music U. of PR, San Juan, PR, 1966—99, dean Humanities Coll., 1995—99. Vis. prof. of music U. of Paris, 1977—79. Composer: (multi-sensorial sculpture-instrument) Mon Oeuf de Centre Pompidou. V.p. U. PR Press, San Juan, 1998—2000. Named Chevalier, Ordre des Arts et Lettres, French Govt., 1986. Mem.: ASCAP. Avocations: tennis, wine and food studies, travel. Home and Office: 435 South Gulfstream Ave Sarasota FL 34236 E-mail: maqroll40@yahoo.com.

SCHWARTZ, GEORGE R. physician, researcher; b. Caribou, Maine; m. Colleen Jill Schwartz; children: Ruth, Rebekah, Rachel, Moses, Abigail, John Gabriel, Aaron. BS in Chemistry with honors, Hobart Coll., 1963; MD magna cum laude, SUNY, Bklyn., 1967. Diplomate Am. Bd. Family Practice, Am. Bd. Emergency Medicine; cert. CPR instr. Intern King County Hosp., Seattle, 1967-68; instr. dept. medicine U. Wash., Seattle, 1967-68; resident in psychiatry Hillside Hosp., Glen Oaks, N.Y., 1968-69; resident in surgery Ind. U. Med. Ctr., Indpls., 1971-72; instr. emergency medicine Med. Coll. Pa., Phila., 1972-76, dir. emergency svcs., asst. dir. emergency medicine program, 1972-74; dir. emergency medicine West Jersey Hosp., 1974-76; pvt. practice, 1977; assoc. prof., dir. divsn. emergency medicine U. N.Mex., Albuquerque, 1978-83; staff mem. emergency medicine Heights Gen. Hosp., Albuquerque, 1983-85; with Los Alamos (N.Mex.) Med. Ctr., 1985-90. Vis. assoc. prof. Med. Coll. Pa., 1991—; co-founder Allied Genomics; ptnr. Brain Resuscitation Rsch. LLC; pres. Schwartz Pharm. and Med. Rsch. LLC. Author: Geriatric Emergencies, 1984; Co-author: (with Tandberg) Emergency Medicine Continuing Edn. Rev., 1981, 2d edit. 1984, (with Bosker) Geriatric Emergency Medicine, 1990; editor: Principles and Practice Emergency Medicine, 1978, 3d edit., 1992, 4th edit., 1999; co-editor Trauma Rounds, 1973-75; editorial bd. Annals Emergency Medicine, 1972-81, Resident and Staff Physician, 1978—, Emergency Med. Abstractrs, 1978-85, Med. Exam. Publ. Co., 1981-87; contbr. articles to profl. jours., chpts. to textbooks. Med. dir. The Bridge Counselling Ctrs., Los Alamos, N.Mex., 1988-91, N.Mex. Poison Ctr., 1978-83; dir. planning com. disaster exercise Phila. Internat. Airport, 1974, Camden County Poison Ctr., 1974-76. Recipient Gallup award, 1973, Giraffe award, 1990. Mem. AAAS, AMA, Am. Coll. Emergency Physicians (charter mem.; pres. N.Mex. chpt. 1980-81), N.Mex. Med. Soc., Univ. Assn. Emergency Physicians (chmn. socio-econ. com. 1976-77), Internat. Emergency Care Assn., Am. Trauma Soc. (founding mem.), Am. Acad. Clin. Toxicology, Am. Acad. Emergency Medicine (founding mem., sec. 1994, bd. dirs. 1998—), Internat. Assn. for Study of MSG and Food Additives (pres. 1988). Achievements include patent for use of a pharmaceutical agent in male impotence; research in computer applications in medicine, new medical diagnostic instruments; patentee in cerebral hypothermia field; neuropoietin research through Healing Research Institute, international patent on new neurologic drug. Address: Rsch Inst/Schwartz Pharm LLC Santa Fe NM 87504-1968

SCHWARTZ, GERALD, public relations and fundraising agency executive; b. N.Y.C., June 22, 1927; s. George and Martha F. S.; m. Felice P. Schwartz, June 25, 1950; children: Gary R., Gregg R., Wendy L. Student, N.C. State U., 1944-45; AB, U. Miami, Fla., 1949, BS, 1950, postgrad., 1966-67. Staff writer Miami Herald, 1941-44; publicity dir. U.S. Army in Europe, 1946-48; editor Miami Beach Sun, 1950-51; fund raising and pub. rels. counselor Miami, 1952-58; press sec. to Gov. Nebr., 1959—60; exec. v.p. Bar-Ilan U., Ramat Gan, Israel, 1960-61; prin. Gerald Schwartz Agy., Miami, Fla., 1962—. Editor, pub. Jewish Herald Newspaper, 1999-2000; editor, pub. emeritus Jewish Star-Times, 2000-2003. Nat. v.p. Am. Zionist Fedn., 1985—89, 1991—93; pres. Pres.'s coun. Zionist Orgn. Am., 1983—85; nat. chmn. Friends of Pioneer Women/Na'amat, 1984—98; pres. Am. Zionist Fedn. So. Fla., 1970—73, 1986—92; vice chmn. Urban League of Greater Miami, 1983—87, City of Miami Beach Planning Bd., 1953—55; bd. dirs. Greater Miami Symphony, 1982—87, Miami Beach Taxpayers Assn., 1988—89; pres. Civic League Miami Beach, 1985—87; pres. Greater Miami chpt. Assn. Welfare of Soldiers in Israel, 1983—86; chmn. City of Miami Beach Hurricane Def. Com., 1978—86, 1990—97; trustee South Shore Hosp. and Med. Ctr., Miami, 1987—2004, exec. vice-chmn. Miami Beach, 1989—2004; vice chmn. South Shore Med. Ctr. Found., 1989—2004; bd. govs. Barry U., 1985—86; chmn. Econ. Devel. Coun. City of Miami Beach, 1985—91; bd. dirs. Crimestoppers of Dade County, 1991—94; mem. exec. bd. State of Israel Bonds Orgn., 1996—; dep. chmn. Dem. Midwest Conf., 1958—60; bd. dirs. adminstrv. com. Jewish Nat. Fund of Am., 1995—, v.p. Greater Miami region, 1996—97; bd. dirs. Temple Emanu-El of Greater Miami, Papanicolaou Cancer Rsch. Inst., Miami, 1962—80. Served with U.S. Army, 1944—46. Recipient Jerusalem Peace award State of Israel Bonds, 1978, Jerusalem 3000 award State of Israel, 1996. Mem. Pub. Rels. Soc. Am. (accredited; treas. So. Fla. chpt. 1962-64), Am. Pub. Rels. Assn. (pres. chpt. 1960-61), Am. Assn. Polit. Cons., Nat. Assn. Fund Raising Execs. (pres. chpt. 1977-78), Miami Beach Taxpayers Assn. (bd. dirs. 1994-2000), Miami Internat. Press Club (bd. dirs. 1991-99), Miami Beach C. of C. (v.p. 1978-80, 81-84, 86-87, pres.-elect 1988-90, trustee 1990—), Lead and Ink, Tiger Bay Club (pres. 1986-88), Prime Minister's Club of State of Israel (Greater Miami chmn. 1997—), B'nai B'rith (pres. lodge 1964-66), Theta Omicron Pi, Omicron Delta Kappa, Alpha Delta Sigma (pres. 1965-67), Zeta Beta Tau. Office: Gerald Schwartz Agy Ste 505 600 Alton Rd Miami FL 33139-5502

SCHWARTZ, GERALD WILFRED, financial executive; b. Winnipeg, Man., Can., Nov. 24, 1941; s. Andrew O. and Lillian Arkin (Leith) S.; m. Heather Reisman, May 15, 1982; children: Carey, Jill, Anna, Anthony. B.Commerce, U. Man., 1962, LLB, 1966; MBA, Harvard U., 1970. V.p. Estabrook & Co., Inc., N.Y.C., 1970-73, Bear Stearns & Co., N.Y.C., 1973-77; pres., dir., mem. exec. com. CanWest Capital Corp., Winnipeg, 1977-83; chmn., pres., CEO ONEX Corp., Toronto, 1984—. Bd. dirs. Celestica Internat. Holdings Inc., Bank of N.S.; dir. Loews Cineplex Entertainment Corp. Bd. dirs. Can. Coun. Christians and Jews; vice chmn., bd. dirs., gov., mem. exec. com. Mt. Sinai Hosp. of Toronto; dir. bd. of assocs. Harvard Bus. Sch.; trustee Simon Wiesenthal Ctr.; mem. adv. coun. Dancer Transition Ctr.; nat. bd. dirs. Ben-Gurion U. of the Negev. With RCAF, 1958. Office: Onex Corp 161 Bay St 49th Fl PO Box 700 Toronto ON Canada M5J 2S1

SCHWARTZ, GORDON FRANCIS, surgeon, educator; b. Plainfield, NJ, Apr. 29, 1937; s. Samuel H. and Mary (Adelman) S.; m. Rochelle DeG. Krantz, Sept. 5, 1959; children— Amory Blair, Susan Leslie AB, Princeton U., 1956; MD, Harvard U., 1960; MBA, U. Pa., 1990. Intern N.Y. Hosp.-Cornell Med. Ctr., N.Y.C., 1960-61; resident in surgery Columbia-Presbyterian Med. Ctr., N.Y.C., 1963-68; instr. surgery Columbia U., N.Y.C., 1966-68; assoc. in surgery U. Pa., Phila., 1968-70; dir. clin. services Breast Diagnostic Ctr., Jefferson Med. Coll., Phila., 1973-78, asst. prof. surgery, 1970-71, assoc. prof., 1971-78, prof., 1978—, dir. breast surgery fellowship, 2003—. Practice medicine specializing in surgery and diseases of breast, Phila., 1968—; founder, chmn. acad. com, sec. of Med. bd. Breast Health Inst., 1990—; edtl. bd. The Breast Jour., 1994—. Author: (with R.H. Guthrie, Jr.) Reconstructive and Aesthetic Mammoplasty, 1989, (with Douglas Marchant) Breast Disease: Diagnosis and Treatment, 1981; mem. editl. bd. The Breast-Ofcl. Jour. of the European Soc. of Mastology, 1996—, Cancer, 1997—; co-editor Seminars Breast Disease, 1997; mem. editl. bd. ONE, Oncology Econs., 1999—; contbr. some 200 articles to profl. jours. Mem. Pa. Gov.'s Task Force on Cancer, 1976-82; mem. breast cancer task force Phila. chpt. Am. Cancer Soc.; mem. clin. investigation rev. com. Nat. Cancer Inst., 1992-95. Served to capt. AUS, 1961-63. NIH Cancer Control fellow, 1968-69 Mem. ACS, AMA, AAUP, Assn. for Acad. Surgery, Allen O. Whipple Surg. Assn., Soc. Surg. Oncology, Internat. Cardiovasc. Soc., Soc. for Surgery Alimentary Tract, John Jones Surg. Soc., Am. Soc. Clin. Oncology, Am. Soc. Breast Diseases (pres. 1981-83), Soc. Internat. Senologie (treas. 1982-90, v.p. 1990-92, sci. com. 1992—), Am. Soc. Breast Surgeons, N.Y. Acad. Scis., Am. Soc. Artificial Internal Organs, Am. Radium Soc., Philadelphia County Med. Soc. (chmn. com. on econs. 1999-2000, bd. dirs. 1999-2000), Internat. Sentinel Node Soc. (founding mem. 2003), Italian Soc. Senology (hon.), Greek Surg. Soc. (hon.), The Phila. Club, Union League, Princeton Club Phila. (pres. 1989-91), Princeton Club (N.Y.C.), Princeton Terrace Club, Nassau Club, Phi Beta Kappa, Sigma Xi, Alpha Omega Alpha, Nu Sigma Nu. Republican. Jewish. Office: 1015 Chestnut St Ste 510 Philadelphia PA 19107-4305 Office Phone: 215-627-8487. E-mail: gordonschwartz@yahoo.com.

SCHWARTZ, HERBERT FREDERICK, lawyer; b. Bklyn., Aug. 23, 1935; s. Henry and Theodora (goldberg) S.; m. Gail Lubets, Jan. 23, 1960; children: Wendy Helene, Karen Anne, Peter Andrew; m. Nan Budde Chequer, Mar. 13, 1987; stepchildren: Elizabeth Guthrie, Anne Hamilton, Laura Dunham. BSEE, MIT, 1957; MA in Applied Econs., LLB, U. Pa., 1964. Assoc. Fish & Neave, N.Y.C., 1964-70, jr. ptnr., 1970-71, ptnr., 1972—, mng. ptnr., 1985-91. Lectr. law U. Pa., Phila., 1980-89, adj. prof., 1990—, NYU, 2003-. Mem. adv. bd. PTC Jour., Washington, 1983; author: Patent Law and Practice, Federal Judicial Center, 1988, 2d edit., 1995, Bureau of National Affairs, 2d edit., 1996, 4th edit., 2003; co-author: Principles of Patent Law, 1998, 2d edit., 2001; contbr. articles to profl. jours. Vice-chmn. Jr. Yacht Racing Assn. of L.I. Sound, 1985-88. 1st lt. U.S. Army, Signal Corps, 1957-59. Mem. U.S. Trademark Assn., Assn. of Bar of City of N.Y., Am. Intellectual Property Lawyers Assn., N.Y. Intellectual Property Lawyers Assn. (pres. 1999-2000), Am. Coll. Trial Lawyers, Am. Bar Found., Am. Law Inst., Order of Coif, N.Y. Yacht Club, Riverside Yacht Club, Cruising Club of Am. Avocation: racing and cruising sailboats. Home: 24 Cherry Tree Ln Riverside CT 06878-2629 Office: Fish & Neave 1251 Avenue Of The Americas Fl 50 New York NY 10020-1105

SCHWARTZ, HERBERT S. surgical oncology educator; b. Chgo., July 22, 1955; BS, U. Ill., Chgo., 1977; MD, U. Chgo., 1981. Diplomate Am. Bd. Orthopaedic Surgery (test task force 1998—). Resident in orthopaedic surgery U. Chgo., 1981-86; fellow in orthopaedic oncology Mayo Clinic, Rochester, Minn., 1986-87; asst. prof. surg. oncology Vanderbilt U., Nashville, 1987-93, assoc. prof., 1993-97, prof., 1997—. Chief orthopaedic surgery VA Med. Ctr., Nashville, 1992—. Contbr. over 50 articles to cancer and orthopaedic jours. Fellow ACS, Am. Acad. Orthopaedic Surgeons, Am. Orthopaedic Assn. (chmn. Hatcher fellow 1999-00), Phi Beta Kappa. Achievements include patent for spinal nail. Office: Vanderbilt U T-4323 MCN Dept Orthopaedics Rehab Nashville TN 37232-2550 E-mail: herbert.s.schwartz@vanderbilt.edu.

SCHWARTZ, HOWARD WYN, business/marketing educator, consultant; b. Mpls., June 12, 1951; s. Jerry Schwartz and Geraldine (Berg) Brooks; m. Jeannie Marie Holtzmann, Aug. 2, 1975; children: Abigail Jorene, Rachel Elizabeth. BA cum laude, U. Minn., 1973, MBA, 1982, MEd, 1999. Cert. tchr. Minn. Acct. Med. Sch., U. Minn., 1973-77, bus. mgr. dept. neurology, 1977-79, adminstr. found. edn. dept., 1979-82, assoc. to chmn. dept. radiology, 1982-99; chmn. bus./mktg. edn. dept. Robbindale-Cooper H.S., New Hope, Minn., 1999—. Adj. instr. dept. radiology U. Minn., 1982—; pres. Bus. Mgmt. Svcs., Golden Valley, Minn., 1979—; lectr., author topics in bus./mktg. edn., 2000—. Editor-in-chief: RADWORKS Workload Measurement Manual, 1985-87; editor: Radiology Management, 1985-87, Purchasing the Radiology Information System, 1991, Current Concepts in Radiology Management, 1991; contbr. articles to profl. jours. Mem. Cystic Fibrosis Found., Minn., 1980—; chmn. Human Rights Commn., Robbinsdale, 1982-84; sec. Coord. Coun. Minority Concerns, 1984-85; chmn. imaging tech. adv. com. Univ. Hosp. Consortium, 1989-92; dir. Univ. Hosp. Consortium Svcs. Corp., 1990-92, Nat. Summit on Manpower, 1989-92; treas. Tech. Learning Campus Site Coun., Dist. 281, 1990-91, chmn. Bond Referendum campaign, 1995; pres. Armstrong H.S. Parent Assn., Dist. 281, 1991-92. Recipient In the Spirit of Youth Role Model award, Cmty. Ahead, 2004, Tchr. of Excellence award, Best Prep, 2004. Fellow Am. Healthcare Radiology Adminstrn. (regional pres. 1986-87, nat. pres. 1988-89, sec. edn. found. 1990-91, bd. dirs. edn. found. 1993-95, 97-98, Outstanding Author award 1990, 93, 96, Midwest Region Disting. Mem. award 1991, Gold award 1991, Cmty. award 2004); mem. Radiologists Bus. Mgrs. Assn., Delta Kappa Epsilon. Home: 7400 Winnetka Heights Dr Golden Valley MN 55427-3549 Office: PO Box 27405 Minneapolis MN 55427-0405 Personal E-mail: schwa006@ix.netcom.com.

SCHWARTZ, IRVING DONN, architect; b. Chgo., June 11, 1927; s. Simon S. and Rose P. S.; children: Charles, Linda. BS, U. Ill., 1949, BS in Architecture, 1965, MS in Architecture, 1972. Registered architect, Ill., Ind., Fla., D.C., Ohio, Ga., Ala., Calif., N.H., Va., Md., Pa, Tenn., La., N.J., Tex., Mo., N.C., S.C., Ark. Chief standard cost and indsl. engring. Lanzit Corrugated Box Co., Chgo., 1950-53; pres. Kaufman, Inc., Champaign, Ill., 1953-60; v.p. Hart Mirror Plate Co., Grand Rapids, Mich., 1953-60; assoc. Richardson, Severns, Scheeler & Assos., Inc., Champaign, 1960-71; pres. IDS, Inc., Champaign, 1971-83, ADI, Dallas, 1983-86, IDS/B, Inc., Dallas, 1986—. Prof. architecture Grad. Sch. Architecture, U. Ill., 1976-83; assoc. prof. design U. North Tex.; cons. in field. Mem. Champaign County Devel. Council; mem. Model Community Coordinating Council, Champaign; co-chmn. bldg. com. Mercy Hosp.; bd. frat. affairs U. Ill.; bd. dirs. United Fund. Served to 2d lt. U.S. Army, 1945-47. Recipient archtl. design research award, graphic design citation Progressive Architecture mag., 1974, Gold Key Design award

Hospitality Mag., 1994, John Robinson award, 2001. Fellow Am. Soc. Interior Designers (treas. 1976, nat. pres. 1978, Louis Tregre award 1992, Nat. design award 1983); mem. AIA (Design award 1983), Nat. Council Archtl. Registration Bds., Nat. Council Interior Design Qualifications (bd. dirs., pres. 1980), Tex. Assn. Interior Design (pres. 1993). Clubs: Standard (Chgo.). Home: 4928 Briarwood Pl Dallas TX 75209-2004 Office: IDS/B Inc 2777 N Stemmons Fwy Ste 1650 Dallas TX 75207-2502

SCHWARTZ, IRVING LEON, physician, scientist, educator; b. Cedarhurst, N.Y., Dec. 25, 1918; s. Abraham and Rose (Doniger) S.; m. Felice T. Nierenberg, Jan. 12, 1946; children: Cornelia Ann, Albert Anthony, James Oliver. AB, Columbia U., 1939; MD, NYU, 1943. Diplomate Am. Bd. Internal Medicine. Intern, then asst. resident Bellevue Hosp., N.Y.C., 1943-44, 46-47; NIH fellow physiology NYU Coll. Medicine, N.Y.C., 1947-50; Am. Physiol. Soc. Porter fellow, also Gibbs meml. fellow in clin. sci. Rockefeller Inst., N.Y.C., 1950-51, Am. Heart Assn. fellow, 1951-52, asst., then assoc., 1952-58; asst. physician, then assoc. physician Rockefeller Inst. Hosp., N.Y.C., 1950-58; sr. scientist Brookhaven Nat. Lab., Upton, NY, 1958-61, rsch. collaborator, 1961—97; attending physician Brookhaven Nat. Lab. Hosp., Upton, NY, 1958-97; Joseph Eichberg prof. physiology, dir. dept. U. Cin. Coll. Medicine, 1961-65; dean grad. faculties Mt. Sinai Med. and Grad. Schs., CUNY, 1965-80, prof. physiology and biophysics, chmn. dept., 1968-79, exec. officer biomed. scis. doctoral program, 1969-72, Dr. Harold and Golden Lamport disting. prof., 1979-98; dir. Ctr. Peptide and Membrane Research Mt. Sinai Med. Ctr., 1979-87; dean emeritus Mt. Sinai Grad. Sch. Biol. Scis., 1980—. Contbr. articles to sci. publs. Pres. Life Scis. Found., 1962-98, pres. emeritus, 1998--. Served from 1st lt. to capt., M.C. AUS, 1944-46. Recipient Solomon A. Berson Med. Alumni Achievement award NYU Sch. Medicine, 1973. Fellow ACP; mem. Am. Physiol. Soc., Soc. Exptl. Biology and Medicine, Am. Soc. Clin. Investigation, Am. Fedn. Clin. Rsch., Biophys. Soc., Endocrine Soc., Harvey Soc., Soc. for Neurosci., Am. Heart Assn., John Jay Assocs. Columbia Coll., AAAS, N.Y. Acad. Sci., N.Y. Acad. Medicine, Sigma Xi, Alpha Omega Alpha. Home: 1120 5th Ave # 14B New York NY 10128-0144 Office: Mt Sinai Med Ctr Grad Sch Biol Scis Box 1022 100th St & 5th Ave New York NY 10029 also: Brookhill Group 501 Madison Ave 18th Fl 10022 *The excitement and stimulation that comes from a productive collaboration with other people has been a major source of satisfaction in my life. I feel privileged to have had the opportunity to interact with a wide range of imaginative and inspiring colleagues, students and friends, including my wife of 50 years, whose extraordinary career emphasized the importance of idealism, commitment, persistence and a felicitous blending of focus and flexibility.*

SCHWARTZ, JAMES PETER, real estate broker; b. Bridgeport, Conn., Oct. 30, 1919; s. Joseph and Stephanie (Tischler) S.; m. Natalie Postol, Mar. 12, 1944; 1 child: Joseph William. Reporter Bridgeport Times-Star, 1940-41; reporter, photographer Bridgeport Post, 1942-43, 45-49; pres. Jay James Inc., Fairfield, Conn., 1949-70; owner James P. Schwartz & Assocs., Bridgeport, 1970—. Dir. Lafayette Bank & Trust Co., 1965-85, Lafayette Bancorp. 1985-88, Lafayette Am. Bank & Trust Co., 1992-93. Contbg. editor Photog. Trade News, 1960-70. Treas. Greater Bridgeport Bd. Realtors, 1974-77, sr. v.p., 1978, pres., 1979; pres. Barnum Festival Soc., 1975-76; ringmaster Barnum Festival, 1979; justice of peace, 1970-96; mem. Easton (Conn.) Zoning Bd. Appeals, 1971-76; police commr., Easton, 1976-90, chmn. bd. police commrs., 1986-88; bd. dirs. Bridgeport divsn. Am. Cancer Soc., 1977-94; bd. assocs. U. Bridgeport, 1962-94. With AUS, 1943-45. Named Man of Yr. dept. sociology U. Bridgeport, 1962, Realtor of Yr. award Greater Bridgeport Bd. Realtors, 1979. Mem. Fairfield Bd. Realtors, Nat. Assn. Realtors (bd. dirs.), Conn. Assn. Realtors (treas. 1981-82, pres. 1984-85), Masons, Corinthian Lodge. Home: Embassy Towers 2625 Park Ave Unit 10P Bridgeport CT 06604-1348

SCHWARTZ, JEFFREY BYRON, lawyer; b. Phila., Dec. 3, 1940; s. Carl Sidney and Tessie Claire (Cohen) S.; m. Joan S. Weinman, Aug. 4, 1963; children: Kevin, Jill. BS, Pa. State U., 1962; JD, U. Pa., 1965; MBA, Am. U., 1967. Bar: Pa. 1965, D.C. 1968, La. 1969. Staff acct. Price Waterhouse & Co., Washington, 1962; trial atty. SEC, Washington, 1965-68; sr. atty. New Orleans Legal Assistance, 1968-70; gen. counsel Nat. Tenants Orgn., Washington, 1970-73; litigation atty. Nat. Health and Environ. Law Project, Washington, 1971-74; chief counsel Pa. Dept. Health, Harrisburg, 1974-79; ptnr. Berriman & Schwartz, King of Prussia, Pa., 1979-85; sr. ptnr. Wolf, Block, Schorr & Solis-Cohen, Phila., 1985-92; ptnr. Cohen, Shapiro, Polisher, Shiekman & Cohen, Phila., 1992-95, Fox Rothschild, O'Brien & Frankel, LLP, Phila., 1995-99; sr. legal advisor USAID Assistance Program Bulgarian Securities and Stock Exch. Commn., 1999—; atty. J. Schwartz & Assocs., 2000—; v.p., gen. counsel Crossover Med. Tech., 2000—. Guest lectr. on welfare and health law U. Pa. Sch. Law, Tulane U. Law Sch., Wayne State U. Law Sch. and Georgetown U. Law Sch.; instr. Catholic U. Am. Law Sch., 1972-73; course planner Pa. Bar Inst., 1980—. Contbr. articles to profl. jours. Reginald Heber Smith fellow, 1968-70. Mem. Am. Soc. Hosp. Attys., Am. Health Lawyers Assn. (dir.), Pa. Soc. Hosp. Attys. (pres. 1983-85, bd. dirs. 1983-89), Hosp. Attys. Southeastern Pa., Am. Pub. Health Assn. (chmn. health law com. 1978-81), Pa. Bar Assn., D.C. Bar Assn. Democrat. Jewish. Home: 10 Radcliff Rd Bala Cynwyd PA 19004-2631

SCHWARTZ, JOHN J. association executive, consultant; b. New Rochelle, N.Y., Aug. 28, 1919; s. Edwin Benner and Marjorie Helen (James) S.; m. Katharine S. Sprackling, Jan. 6, 1942; children: Christopher Louis. Grad. high sch., New Rochelle; student, Mercersburg Acad., 1938. Campaign dir. John Price Jones Inc., N.Y.C., 1946-50; dir. pub. relations and fund raising Travelers Aid Soc., N.Y., N.Y.C., 1950-55; dir. devel. Community Service Soc., N.Y.C., 1955-57, Near East Found., N.Y.C., 1957-60; v.p. G.A. Brakeley & Co. Inc., N.Y.C., 1960-61; dir. devel. Fgn. Policy Assn., N.Y.C., 1962-64; founding pres. Greater N.Y. Nat. Soc. of Fund Raising Execs., 1964; asst. v.p. for crusade Am. Cancer Soc., N.Y.C., 1964-66; exec. dir. Am. Assn. Fund Raising Counsel, N.Y.C., 1966-68, exec. v.p., 1968-72, pres., 1972-87. Founding bd. mem. Ind. Sector, Washington, 1980-85, mem. com. to measurably increase giving; mem., former pres. Com. on Nat. Ctr. for Charitable Stats.; spl. cons. to Com. on Pvt. Philanthropy and Pub. Needs., 1973; chair pvt. adv. group Nat. Assn. Attys. Gen. Model Law Project. Author: Modern American Philanthropy; A Personal Account, 1993. Mem. adv. bd. mgmt. fund-raising cert. program NYU; mem. adv. coun. Grad. Sch. Mgmt. and Urban Professions, New Sch. Social Rsch.; active formation of 5 borough coalitions Daring Coals for Caring Soc., N.Y.C., 1987; cons. Ind. U. Ctr. on Philanthropy, 1988—91, Cmty. Counselling Serv. Co., Inc., 1988—91; pres. Nat. Philanthropy Day, 1988—90, mem. hon. com., 1981; pres. Friends of Westport Libr., 1995—98; bd. dir.-at-large USA World Fund Raising Coun., 1993; bd. dirs. Norwalk Sr. Ctr., 2001—. Capt. PTO USAF, 1941—46. Recipient Disting. Profl. Service to Philanthropy award Am. Assn. Fund-Raising Counsel, N.Y., 1976, Outstanding Agy. Profl. award United Way Am., Alexandria, 1982, Henry A. Rosso Lifetime Achievement in Ethical Fundraising award Ind. U. Ctr. on Philanthropy, 1997. Mem.: Assn. Fund Raising Profls. Fairfield County (bd. dirs. emeritus), Am. Asn. Ret. Persons (bd. dir. Andrus Found. 1983-90), Fairfield County Asn. Fundraising Profls. (bd. dir. 1992-2000, bd. dir. emeritus 2000-02), Nat. Soc. Fund Raising Execs. (bd. dirs. 1964-90, past pres.), Nat. Charities Info. Bur. (bd. dirs. 1978-94), VFW, Princeton Club (N.Y.C.), 501C-3 Soc. Democrat. Unitarian Universalist. Avocations: writing history, ship models. E-mail: jschwarz227@aol.com.

SCHWARTZ, JOHN J. biotechnology company executive; JD, Harvard Law Sch., 1958; PhD Physics, U. Rochester, 1965. Asst. prof., v.p., gen. counsel Stanford U., Calif.; pres., CEO SyStemix, Inc.; chmn. StemCells, Inc., Palo Alto, Calif. Office: StemCells Inc 3155 Porter Dr Palo Alto CA 94304

SCHWARTZ, JOHN NORMAN, human services administrator; b. Watertown, Minn., Dec. 13, 1945; s. Norman O. and Marion G. (Tesch) Schwartz. BA, Augsburg Coll., Mpls., 1967; MHA, U. Minn., 1969. Adminstrv. resident Luth. Hosp. and Med. Ctr., Wheat Ridge, Colo., 1968-69; asst. adminstr. St. Luke's Hosp., Milw., 1969-73, med. adminstr., 1973-75, v.p., 1975-84; sr. v.p., COO Good Samaritan Med. Ctr., Milw., 1984-85, pres., CEO, 1985-88; exec. v.p. Aurora Health Care Inc., Milw., 1988-89; gen. mgr. SmithKline Beecham Clin. Labs., Schaumburg, Ill., 1989-90; chief exec. adv. Trinity Hosp. Adv. Health Care, Chgo., 1991—. Bd. dirs. E. Side Bank. Gov.'s appointee Coun. Hemophilia and Related Blood Disorders, Madison, 1978; mem. Sullivan Chamber Ensemble, Milw., 1975—84; bd. dirs. Gt. Lakes Hemophilia Found., Milw., 1975—89, S.E. Chgo. Devel. Commn., 1996—; mem. S. Chgo. YMCA, 1993—. Named Exec. of the Yr., Health and Human Svcs. Ministry, 1999; recipient Bd. Mem. of the Yr. award, Gt. Lake's Hemophilia Found., 1986, Outstanding Cmty. Leadership award, Stony Island C. of C., 1996, Cir. of Distinction award, Am. Hosp. Assn., 1999. Fellow: Am. Coll. Healthcare Execs. (regent 1993—99, Regent's award for sr. exec. leadership 1999). Lutheran. Avocations: jogging, photography, music, choral singing. Office: Adv Trinity Hosp 2320 E 93rd St Chicago IL 60617 E-mail: john.schwartz@advocatehealth.com.

SCHWARTZ, JONATHAN, broadcast executive; b. LI, N.Y. Degree summa cum laude in Bus., U. Pa.; JD with hons., Stanford (Conn.) U.; MA, Cambridge (Eng.) U. Bar: D.C., N.Y. Law clk. Judge Harry T. Edwards U.S. Ct. Appeals (D.C. cir.); law clk. Justice Thurgood Marshall U.S. Supreme Ct.; fed. prosecutor Manhattan, NY; sr. positions Dept. Justice, Washington, prin. assoc. dep. atty. gen.; gen. counsel Napster, Inc.; sr. v.p., dep. gen. counsel AOL Time Warner Inc.; exec. v.p. Cablevision Sys. Corp., Bethpage, NY, gen. counsel. Named one of Top 40 Lawyers Under Age 40, Washingtonian Mag., 1998; recipient Edmund J. Randolph award, Dept. Justice, 2001; fellow, Fulbright Found., Harvard U. Inst. Politics. Office: Cablevision Systems 1111 Stewart Ave Bethpage NY 11714-3581

SCHWARTZ, JOSEPH, retired container company executive; b. N.Y.C., Apr. 22, 1911; s. Nathan and Ida (Estrich) S.; m. Hazel Shapiro, Dec. 25, 1932; children— Arlene Schwartz Bornstein, Linda Schwartz Rosenbaum Grad., high sch. Ptnr. Mut. Paper Co., Lynn, Mass., 1928-38; treas. Allied Container Corp., Hyde Park, Mass., 1938-56; pres., treas. Allied Container Corp., Dedham, Hyde Park, 1956-84. Chmn. bd. Cargal, Ltd., Lod Israel; ret. v.p. Union Camp Corp., Wayne, N.J. Fellow Brandeis U. Home: 3230 Stirling RD #1 Hollywood FL 33021-2041

SCHWARTZ, JOYCE GENSBERG, pathologist; b. San Antonio, July 24, 1950; d. Frank and Sara Gensberg; m. Alan R. Schwartz, July 17, 1977. BA, U. Tex., Austin, 1971, MA, 1972; MD, U. Tex., San Antonio, 1980. Speech pathologist N.E. Ind. Sch. Dist., San Antonio, 1971-73, vet. asst., 1973-74; resident in pathology U. Tex. Health Sci. Ctr., San Antonio, 1980-84, mem. faculty pathology, 1984-96; med. dir. southern region Quest Diagnostics, Irving, Tex., 1996—2000, chief lab. officer Teterboro, NJ, 2000—. Pres. P.I. Nixon Hist. Libr., 1991-92. Recipient Presdl. Tchg. award, 1991, Piper Prof. award, 1992; named San Antonio Women's Hall of Fame, 1995. Mem. AMA, Coll. Am. Pathologists (regional commr.), Tex. Soc. Pathologists (sec. 1994-96), Women's Faculty Assn. (pres. 1988-89), San AntonioSoc. Pathologists (pres. 1988-89), Phi Kappa Phi, Alpha Omega Alpha. Jewish. Office: Quest Diagnostics 1 Malcolm Ave Teterboro NJ 07608

SCHWARTZ, JUDY ELLEN, cardiothoracic surgeon; b. Mason City, Iowa, Oct. 5, 1946; d. Walter Carl and Alice Nevada (Moore) S. BS, U. Iowa, 1968, MD, 1971; M.P.H., Johns Hopkins U., 1996. Diplomate Am. Bd. Surgery, Am. Bd. Thoracic Surgery, Am. Bd. Med. Mgmt.; cert. physician exec. Cert. Commn. Med. Mgmt. Intern Nat. Naval Med. Ctr., Bethesda, Md., 1971-72, gen. surgery resident, 1972-76, thoracic surgery resident, 1976-78, staff cardiothoracic surgeon, 1979-82, chief cardiothoracic surgeon, 1982-83; chmn. cardiothoracic surg. dept. Naval Hosp., San Diego, 1983-85, quality assurance program dir., 1985-88. Exec. office Rapidly Deployable Med. Facility Four, 1986-88; asst. prof. surgery Uniformed Svcs. U. Health Sci., Bethesda, 1983-99; sr. policy analyst quality assurance Profl. Affairs and Quality Assurance, 1988-90, dep. dir. quality assurance, 1990; dir. clin. policy Health Svcs. Ops., Washington, 1990-94; head performance evaluation and improvement Nat. Naval Med. Ctr., 1994-99; cardiothoracic splty. cons. to naval med. command U.S. Navy, Washington, 1983-84; Dept. Def. rep. to Joint Commn. Accreditation Health Care Orgn. task force on info. mgmt., 1990-93, chmn. 1991-93, task force on IMS Tech., 1993-94; chmn. info mgmt. workshop Fed. Health Care Study Commn.'s Corrd. Fed. Health Care, 1993; corp. med. dir. Medctr. One Health Sys., 1999-2002, ND Dept. Corrections & Rehab., 1999-2002, v.p. med. affairs Medcenter One, 2002; v.p. Surg. Svc. and Electonic Med. Records Informatics, 2003—; bd. dirs. SCCI; trustee Medcenter One Health Sys., 1999-03; adv. com. Blue Cross Blue Shield Care Mgmt., 1999-2002, v.p. med. affairs, 2002. Contbr. articles to various publs. Mem. nat. physician's leadership coun. VHA, 2000—02; trustee St. Vincent's Nursing Home, 2001—. Fellow Am. Coll. Cardiology, Am. Coll. Surgeons (com. allied health pers. 1985-91, exec. com. 1987-91, accreditation review com. edn. physician asst. 1988-94, treas. accreditation review com. 1991-93, sr. mem. com. allied health pers. 1991-94); mem. AMA, Am. Thoracic Soc., Am. Med. Women's Assn., Am. Mgmt. Assn., Am. Coll. Physician Execs. Office: Medcenter One Health Systems PO Box 5525 300 N 7th St Bismarck ND 58506-5525 Office Phone: 701-323-8668. Business E-Mail: jschwartz@mohs.org.

SCHWARTZ, KENNETH ERNST, communications executive; b. Detroit, July 12, 1922; s. Bernath and Sadie (Weiss) S.; m. June Henry; m. 2d, Eileen Frances Lamb, Dec.13, 1969; children: Joshua, Sarah. Grad., U.S. Merchant Marine Acad., 1944, Am. Acad. Dramatic Arts, 1944-46. Producer/dir. Great Lakes Drama Festival, Saginaw, Mich., 1951-53; gen. mgr. Weil & Co., Detroit, 1953-55; producer/director Northland Playhouse, Southfield, Mich., 1955-69; deck officer U.S. Merchant Marine, 1969-71; freelance film producer/writer, 1971-73; pres. Cutting Edge Enterprises, Inc., Easy Edit, V & W Sound Rec., Inc., N.Y.C., 1973-89, U.S. Editing Systems and Kenedit Film Svcs., N.Y.C., 1989—. Pres. U.S. Editing Systems, N.Y.C.; dir. Midwest Alliance Summer Theatres, Detroit. Asst. producer (Broadway prodn.) Raisin in the Sun, 1959; co-producer (Broadway prodn.) Once There Was a Russian, 1961; assoc. producer (motion picture) Popcorn, 1990; co-author (film): Snapshots, 1973. Served to lt. USNR, 1944-47. Recipient Key to City of Detroit. Mem. B'nai B'rith Cinema, Radio, TV. Jewish. Office: Kenedit Film Svcs 630 9th Ave New York NY 10036-3708

SCHWARTZ, LAWRENCE, aeronautical engineer; b. N.Y.C., Nov. 30, 1935; s. Harry and Fanny (Steiner) S.; m. Cherie Anne Karo, Aug. 12, 1979; children: Ronda, Daran. SB in Aero. Engring., SM in Aero. Engring., MIT, 1958; postgrad., Ohio State U., 1960, U. Dayton, 1962-63; PhD in Engring., UCLA, 1966. Registered profl. engr., Colo., Calif. Electronics design engr. MIT Instrumentation Lab., Cambridge, 1959; aerospace engr. Wright-Patterson AFB, Wright-Patterson AFB, Ohio, 1962-63; mem. tech. staff Hughes Aircraft Co., Culver City, Calif., 1963-65, staff engr., 1965-67, sr. staff engr., 1967-72, sr. scientist, 1972-79, chief scientist lab., 1979-93, tech. mgr., 1985-87, chmn., tech. adv. bd., 1987-88, prin. scientist/engr., 1993-97, Raytheon Systems Co., Aurora, Colo., 1997-98, sr. prin. engr., 1999, engring. fellow, 1999, Raytheon Co. (formerly Raytheon Systems Co.), Aurora, 2000—. Cons., tchr. in field. Contbr. articles to profl. jours. With USAF, 1959—62. Mem. IEEE, AAAS, N.Y. Acad. Scis., Sigma Xi, Sigma Gamma Tau, Tau Beta Pi. Home: 996 S Florence St Denver CO 80247-1952 Office: 16800 E Centretech Pky Aurora CO 80011-9046 E-mail: lschwart@ieee.org.

SCHWARTZ, LEON, foreign language educator; b. Boston, Aug. 22, 1922; s. Charles and Celia (Emer) S.; m. Jeanne Gurtat, Mar. 31, 1949; children— Eric Alan, Claire Marie. Student, Providence Coll., 1939-41; BA, UCLA, 1948; certificat de phonetique, U. Paris, 1949; MA, U. So. Cal., 1950, PhD, 1962. Tchr. English, Spanish and Latin Redlands (Calif.) Jr. High Sch., 1951-54; high sch. tchr. Spanish and French, 1954-59; prof. French Calif. State U., Los Angeles, 1959-87, chmn. dept. fgn. langs. and lit., 1970-73, prof. emeritus, 1987—. Author: Diderot and the Jews, 1981; co-author: Mortier-Tresson, Dictionnaire de Diderot, 1999. Served as 2d lt. USAAF, 1942-45. Decorated Air medal with 5 oak leaf clusters; recipient Outstanding Prof. award Calif. State U. L.A., 1976. Mem. Am. Assn. Tchrs. French, Modern and Classical Lang. Assn. So. Calif., Am. Soc. 18th Century Studies, Société Diderot, Calif. State U. L.A. Emeriti Assn. (pres. 1998-2000), Phi Beta Kappa, Phi Kappa Phi, Pi Delta Phi, Sigma Delta Pi, Alpha Mu Gamma. Office: Calif State U Dept Modern Langs and Lit Los Angeles CA 90032 Personal E-mail: l_schwar@pacbell.net. Business E-Mail: lschwar@calstatela.edu.

SCHWARTZ, LEONARD JAY, lawyer; b. San Antonio, Sept. 23, 1943; s. Oscar S. and Ethel (Eastman) S.; m. Sandra E. Eichelbaum, July 4, 1965; 1 child, Michele Fay. BBA, U. Tex., 1965, JD, 1968. Bar: Tex. 1968, Ohio 1971, U.S. Supreme Ct. 1971, U.S. Dist. Ct. (no., ea., wes. and so. dists.) Tex., U.S. Dist. Cts. (no. and so. dists.) Ohio, U.S. Dist. Ct. Nebr., U.S. Ct. Appeals (5th, 6th, 7th and 11th cirs.). Assoc. Roberts & Holland, N.Y.C., 1968-70; ptnr. Rigely, Schwartz & Fagan, San Antonio, 1970-71; staff counsel ACLU of Ohio, Columbus, 1971-74; ptnr. Schwartz & Fishman, Columbus, 1974-79; elections counsel to sec. of state State of Ohio, Columbus, 1979-80; ptnr. Waterman & Schwartz and successor firms, Austin, Tex., 1981-85; mng. dir. Schwartz & Eichelbaum, PC, Austin and other cities, 1985-99, 2000—, shareholder Austin, various locations, 1985—. Gen. counsel various sch. dists., cities and counties; adj. prof. law U. Tex. Sch. Law, Austin; labor and employment law cons. and sch. law Tex. Assn. Sch. Adminstrs; condr. workshops in field; mem. com. on fed. judiciary rels. Tex. Bar. Contbr. articles to profl. jours. Mem. chancellor's coun. U. Tex. Sys.; mem. U. Tex. Pres.'s Assocs., Littlefield Soc., Sch. of Law Keeton Fellows. Recipient Outstanding Tchg. Quiz Master award U. Tex. Sch. Law, 1968. Fellow Tex. Bar Found.; mem. ABA, FBA, Tex. Bar Assn., Bar Assn. 5th Cir., Phi Delta Phi. Democrat. Jewish. Office: Schwartz & Eichelbaum PC 4201 W Parmer Ln Ste 100 Austin TX 78727 Fax: 512-472-2599. E-mail: lschwartz@edlaw.com.

SCHWARTZ, LILLIAN FELDMAN, artist, filmmaker, art analyst, writer, nurse; b. Cin., July 13, 1927; d. Jacob and Katie (Green) Feldman; m. Jack James Schwartz, Dec. 22, 1946; children: Jeffrey Hugh, Laurens Robert. BSE, U. Cin., 1947; Dr. honoris causa, Kean Coll., 1988. Nurse Cin. Gen. Hosp., 1947; head supr. premature nursery St. Louis Maternity Hosp., 1947-48; cons. AT&T Bell Labs., Murray Hill, N.J., 1968-97; pres. Computer Creations Corp., Watchung, NJ, 1989—2004; cons. Bell Communications Research, Morristown, N.J., 1984-92, Lucent Technologies/Bell Labs. Innovations, 1996—2001. Artist-in-residence Sta. WNET, N.Y.C., 1972-74; cons. T.J. Watson Rsch. Lab. IBM Corp., Yorktown, N.Y., 1975, 82-84; vis. mem. computer sci. dept. U. Md., College Park, 1974-80; adj. prof. fine arts Kean Coll., Union, N.J., 1980-82, Rutgers U., New Brunswick, N.J., 1982-83; adj. prof. dept. psychology NYU, N.Y.C., 1985-86, assoc. prof. computer sci.; guest lectr. Princeton U., Columbia U., Yale U., Rockefeller U.; mem. grad. faculty Sch. Visual Arts, N.Y.C., 1990—; dir. team from Rutgers U. to create world's first computer-generated 3-D model of Leaning Tower of Pisa to test structures, 1999; invited com. mem. info. tech. and creativity NAS, 2000-03; invited juror L'Oreal/Color/Internat., 2000-01; film retrospective Leeds, Eng. Lumen-Evolution, 2002, 2003-04. Co-author: Information Technology and Creativity, 2001, The Computer Artist's Handbook; contbd. articles to profl. jours including Scientific Am., 1995; contbr. chpts. to books, also Trans. Am. Philos. Soc., vol. 75, Part 6, 1985; one-woman shows of sculpture and paintings include Columbia U., 1967, 68, Rabin and Krueger Gallery, Newark, 1968; films shown at Met. Mus., N.Y.C., Franklin Inst., Phila., 1972, U. Toronto, 1972, am. Embassy, London, 1972, L.A. County Mus., Corcoran Gallery, Washington, 1972, Whitney Mus., N.Y.C., 1973, Grand Palais, Paris, Musee Nat. d'Art Moderne, Paris, IBM, (digital print show) Bklyn. Mus. Art, 2001, Chelsea Mus. Art, N.Y.C., 2004, others; dir.: Save the Leaning Tower. Recipient numerous art and film awards, Emmy award Mus. Modern Art, 1984, Computer Graphics World Smithsonian awards for virtual reality, art analysis, inventing computer medium for art and animation, 1993; named Outstanding Alumnus, U. Cin., 1987; grantee Nat. Endowment for Arts, 1977, 81, Corp. Pub. Broadcasting, 1979, Nat. Endowment Composers and Librettists, 1981, Arts Coun. Eng., 2003. Fellow World Acad. of Art and Sci.; mem. NATAS, Am. Film Inst., Info. Film Prodrs. Am., Soc. Motion Picture and TV Engrs., Internat. Sculptors Assn., Centro Studi Pierfrancescani (Sansepolcro, Italy, founding mem.). Achievements include pioneer in use of computers as art media; commd. to create computer poster and TV comml. for opening New Mus. Modern Art, 1984; discovered identities of the Mona Lisa, hidden and surface, 1987, and identified steps DaVinci made in transforming Isabella, Duchess of Aragon, into the Mona Lisa using his own features as the model, 1993; discovered perspective used by DaVinci in The Last Supper, 1988; identified time of day and tree of thorns in Piero della Francesca's Resurrection; discovered Elizabeth I is model for Martin Droeshout engraving of Shakespeare, 1991; performed first transmission of computer drawing between U.S. and Germany, 1990; used morphing algorithms to determine Leonardo's creative decision-making steps in transforming the Duchess of Aragon into the Mona Lisa using his own features to segue; discovered method Leonardo used to create his Grotesques, 1994; discovered new Renaissance illusion of another figure in a painting of Christ, 1996, rediscovered Renaissance illusion published in visual computer, 1997, Satan-like figure in Leonardo's Munich "Madonna", 1998; created with Professor Madara Ozot and PhD candidate Zheng Zhou, first computer-generated 3D model of the Leaning Tower of Pisa to test the structure, 1999; completed archive/collection acquired by Ohio State U., 2004; discovered why the right hand of Christ in Leonardo's "Last Supper" is in the awkward position it is in, 2004. *I have always been provoked by and concerned with the mechanical and technological world around me. I enjoy experimenting with traditional media and combining them with technology today. For example, I used computers as an art medium when computers were solely programmed for scientific purposes. By using the computer to understand the creative process I have made clear the intent of the great masters and applied their decision-making steps to my own work. The excitement in creating is to discover and to make a new world. My present success was achieved in part by being able to make new rules and not be hindered by old or obvious solutions.*

SCHWARTZ, LITA LINZEF, psychologist, educator; b. Jan. 14, 1930; d. Aaron Jerome and Dorothy Claire Linzer; m. Melvin Jay Schwartz, June 18, 1950 (div. 1983); children: Arthur Lee, Joshua David, Frederic Seth. AB, Vassar Coll., 1950; EdM, Temple U., 1956; PhD, Bryn Mawr Coll., 1964. Diplomate Am. Bd. Forensic Psychology, Am. Bd. Profl. Psychology; lic. psychologist, Pa. Part-time instr., counselor Pa. State U., Abington, 1961-66, from asst. prof. edn. psychology to assoc. prof., 1966-76, prof., 1976-93, disting. prof., prof. women's studies, 1993-95, disting. prof. emerita, 1995—. Pvt. practice, 1964—; cons. in field. Author: American Education, 1969, 74, 78, Educational Psychology, 1972, 77, The Exceptional Child: A Primer, 1975, 79, Exceptional Students in the Mainstream, 1984, (with Natalie Isser) The American School and The Melting Pot, 1985, 89, (with Natalie Isser) The History of Conversion and Contemporary Cults, 1988, Alternatives to Infertility: Is Surrogacy the Answer?, 1991, Why Give Gifts to the Gifted?: Investing in a National Resource, 1994, (with Florence W. Kaslow) The Dynamics of Divorce, 1987; editor: Mid-Life Divorce Counseling, 1994, (with Florence W. Kaslow) Painful Partings: Divorce and Its Aftermath, 1997, (with Phil Rich) The Healing Journey Through Divorce, 1999; editor: Psychology and the Media: A Second Look, 1999, (with N. Isser) Endangered Children: Neonaticide, Infanticide, Filicide, 2000; co-editor: (with F. Kaslow) Welcome Home! An International and Nontraditional Adoption Reader; contbr. numerous articles to profl. jours., chpts. to books. Recipient Humanitarian award N.Y. Philanthropic League, 1973, Christian R. and Mary F. Lindback award, 1982, Outstanding Tchr. award Pa. State U. Coll. Edn. Alumni, 1982. Fellow: APA; mem.: Ethnic Studies Assn. Delaware Valley (co-chair program com. 1986—88), Acad. for Conflict Resolution (evaluation com. child study mediation project Delaware Valley), Assn. Family and Conciliation Cts., Internat. Coun. Psychologists (bd. dirs. 1995—96), Am. Bd. Forensic Psychology, Psi Chi. Office: Pa State U Abington Coll Abington PA 19001 Business E-Mail: lls2@psu.edu.

SCHWARTZ, LLOYD, music critic, poet; b. N.Y.C., Nov. 29, 1941; s. Sam and Ida (Singer) Schwartz. BA, Queens Coll., N.Y.C., 1962; MA, Harvard U., 1963, PhD, 1976. Classical music editor Boston Phoenix, 1977—; dir. creative writing U. Mass., Boston, 1982—, 1990—2002; classical music critic Fresh Air Nat. Pub. Radio, Phila., 1987—. Prof. English U. Mass., Boston, 1986—. Author (poems): These People, 1981, Goodnight, Gracie, 1992, Cairo Traffic, 2000, Lloyd Schwartz: Greatest Hits 1973-2000, 2003; author: (plays) These People: Voices for the Stage, 1990; editor: Ploughshares, 1979, Elizabeth

Bishop and Her Art, 1983; actor: The Spider's Web, 1975—82; dir.: These People: Voices for the Stage, 1990; (Operas) L'Heure Espagnol (Ravel), 1972, Mavra (Stravinsky), 1973. Recipient Pulitzer prize for criticism, 1994; NEA creative writing fellow in poetry, 1990. Mem.: MLA, PEN, Associated Writing Programs, New Eng. Poetry Club, Poetry Soc. Am., PEN Am. Avocations: collecting old recordings, books. Home: 27 Pennsylvania Ave Somerville MA 02145-2217 Office: Boston Phoenix 126 Brookline Ave Boston MA 02215-3920 E-mail: lschwartz@phx.com.

SCHWARTZ, LYLE HOWARD, materials scientist, science administrator; b. Chgo., Aug. 2, 1936; s. Joseph K. Schwartz and Helen (Shefsky) Bernards; divorced; children: Ara, Justin; m. Celesta Sue Jurkovich, Sept. 1, 1973. BS in Sci. Engring., Northwestern U., 1959, PhD in Materials Sci., 1964. Prof. materials sci. Northwestern U., Evanston, Ill., 1964-84, dir. Materials Research Ctr., 1979-84; dir. materials sci. and engr. lab. Nat. Inst. Standards and Tech., Dept. Commerce, Gaithersburg, Md., 1984-97; pres. Associated Univs., Inc., Washington, 1997-98; interim dir. Brookhaven Nat. Lab., Washington, 1997; cons., 1998-99; dir. aerospace and material scis. Air Force Office Sci. Rsch., Arlington, Va., 1999-2001, dir., 2001—. Cons. Argonne Nat. Labs., Ill., 1965-79; vis. scientist Bell Telephone Labs., Murray Hill, N.J., 1971-73. Author: (with J.B. Cohen) Diffraction From Materials, 1977, 2d edit., 1987, also numerous articles and papers NSF fellow, 1962-63; recipient Presdl. Rank Award of Meritorious Exec. for outstanding govt. svc., 1990. Fellow Am. Soc. for Metals; mem. AAAS, AIME, Nat. Acad. Engring., Am. Phys. Soc., Am. Crystallography Assn., Materials Rsch. Soc., Sigma Xi. Office: 801 N Randolph St Ste 732 Arlington VA 22203-1977 E-mail: lyle.schwartz@afosr.af.mil.

SCHWARTZ, MARK, former retail executive; CEO Hechinger Investment, Largo, Md.; pres., COO KMart Corp., Troy, Mich., 2001—02.

SCHWARTZ, MARSHALL ZANE, pediatric surgeon; b. Mpls., Sept. 1, 1945; s. Sidney Shay and Peggy Belle (Lieberman) S.; m. Michele Carroll Walker, Oct. 16, 1971; children: Lisa, Jeffrey. BS, U. Minn., 1968, MD, 1970. Diplomate Am. Bd. Surgery, Am. Bd. Pediatric Surgery. Intern N.Y. Hosp., N.Y.C., 1970-71; resident in gen. surgery U. Minn., Mpls., 1971-73, 75-76, rsch. fellow, 1974-75; jr. resident in pediatric surgery Children's Hosp. Med. Ctr., Harvard Med. Sch., 1973-74, sr. resident in pediatric surgery, 1976-77, chief resident in pediatric surgery, 1977-78; instr. Med. Sch. Harvard U., Boston, 1978-79; asst. in surgery Children's Hosp. Med. Ctr., Boston, 1978-79; asst. prof. Med. Br. U. Tex., Galveston, 1979-81, assoc. prof., 1981-83, chief. pediatric surgery, 1980-83; assoc. prof. U. Calif., Davis, 1983-86, prof., 1986-92, chief pediatric surgery, 1983-92, vice chmn. faculty Sch. Medicine, 1990-91, chmn. faculty Sch. Medicine, 1991-92; prof. surgery and pediat. George Washington Sch. Medicine, 1992-96; surgeon-in-chief, chmn. dept. pediatric surgery Children's Nat. Med. Ctr., Washington, 1992-96; assoc. med. dir. Dupont Hosp. for Children, Wilmington, Del., 1996—2001, vice chmn. dept. surgery, 1996—2003; prof. surgery and pediat. Thomas Jefferson U., 1996—, vice chmn. dept. surgery, 1996—2003; mem. staff St. Christopher Hosp. for Children, Phila. Bd. dirs. Am. Bd. Surgery, 2003—. Mem. editl. bd. Jour. Pediat. Surgery, 1988—, Jour. ACS, 1999—. Vice chmn. Bd. of Childrens Faculty Assocs., Childrens Nat. Med. Ctr.; bd. dir. Am. Pediat. Surg. Assn., 2001—; pres. bd. dir. Sacramento Children's Hosp. Found., 1990—92; chmn. bd. dir. Delaware Valley Transplant Program, 2000—02. Recipient Basil O'Connor Rsch. award March of Dimes Found., 1981, Young Investigator award NIH, 1982, Found. for Children Rsch. award, 1982, James W. McLaughlin award U. Tex., 1983, ASPEN-Rhodes Rsch. award, 1999, Rsch. award Am. Colon and Rectal Surg. Assn., 2000. Fellow: ACS (chmn. adv. coun. for pediat. surgery); mem.: Pacific Assn. Pediat. Surgeons (pres. 1997—98), Am. Pediat. Surg. Assn. (bd. dirs.), Soc. Surgery Alimentary Tract, Am. Pediatric Surg. Assn. (bd. govs.), Soc. Univ. Surgeons, Am. Surg. Assn. Jewish. Avocations: skiing, fishing, wood working. Office: St Christopher Hosp for Children Erie Ave at Front St Philadelphia PA 19134 Personal E-mail: mzschwartz@msn.com.

SCHWARTZ, MARTIN LERNER, physician; b. Newport News, Va., 1945; PhD in Biochemistry, Duke U., 1972, MD, 1973. Resident U. N.C., Chapel Hill, 1973-77; mem. staff Bess Kaiser Hosp., Portland, Oreg., 1977-96, Providence-St. Vincent's Hosp., Portland, 1996—. Home: 7824 NW Blue Pointe Ln Portland OR 97229-9105 Office: 3550 N Interstate Ave Portland OR 97227-1196 Office Phone: 503-331-5016. E-mail: martin.l.schwartz@kp.org.

SCHWARTZ, MARVIN, lawyer; b. Phila., Nov. 3, 1922; s. Abe and Freda (Newman) S.; m. Joyce Ellen Sidner, Sept. 7, 1947; children: Daniel Bruce, Pamela Louise Pier. LL.B., U. Pa., 1949. Bar: Pa. 1950, N.Y. 1951, D.C. 1955. Law sec. to judge U.S. Ct. Appeals, 3d Circuit, Phila., 1949-50; law sec. to Justice Burton U.S. Supreme Ct., Washington, 1950-51; assoc. Sullivan & Cromwell, N.Y.C., 1951-60, ptnr., 1960-92, sr. counsel, 1993—. Mediator U.S. Dist. (so. dist.) N.Y., N.Y. Supreme Ct. Comml. Divsn.; arbitrator Am. Arbitration Assn., N.Y. Stock Exch., Nat. Assn. Securities Dealers. Spl. master appellate divsn. 1st dept. Supreme Ct. N.Y.; chmn. Zoning Bd. of Adjustment, Alpine, N.J., 1966-74; mem. Planning Bd., Alpine, 1966-67; bd. overseers emeritus U. Pa. Law Sch.; bd. dirs. Conn. Cmty. Found. With Signal Corps U.S. Army, 1943-46. Mem. ABA, N.Y. Bar Assn., D.C. Bar Assn., Am. Coll. Trial Lawyers (sec. 1986-88, bd. regents 1981-86, chmn. Downstate N.Y. com. 1976-78), Am. Law Inst. (adviser complex litigation project), Univ. Club (N.Y.C.), Litchfield (Conn.) Country Club. Democrat. Jewish. Office: Sullivan & Cromwell 125 Broad St Fl 28 New York NY 10004-2489

SCHWARTZ, MELVIN, physics educator, laboratory administrator; b. N.Y.C., Nov. 2, 1932; s. Harry and Hannah (Shulman) Schwartz; m. Marilyn Fenster, Nov. 25, 1953; children: David N., Diane R.; 1 child, Betty Lynn. AB, Columbia U., 1953, PhD, 1958, DSc (hon.), 1991, Weizmann Inst. Sci., 1995. Assoc. physicist Brookhaven Nat. Lab., 1956—58; mem. faculty Columbia U., N.Y.C., 1958—66, prof. physics, 1963—66, Stanford U., Calif., 1966—83, cons. prof., 1983—91; chmn. Digital Pathways, Inc., Mountain View, Calif., 1970—91; assoc. dir. high energy and nuclear physics Brookhaven Nat. Lab., Upton, NY, 1991—94; prof. physics Columbia U., N.Y.C., 1991—94, I.I. Rabi prof. physics, 1994—. Co-discoverer muon neutrino, 1962. Weizmann Inst. Sci. Recipient Nobel prize in Physics, 1988, John Jay award, Columbia Coll., 1989, Alexander Hamilton medal, Columbia U., 1995; fellow Guggenheim, 1968. Fellow: Am. Phys. Soc. (Hughes award 1964); mem.: NAS. Home: PO Box 5068 Ketchum ID 83340-5068 Office: Columbia U Dept Physics New York NY 10027 E-mail: melschw@cox-internet.com.

SCHWARTZ, MICHAEL, university president, sociology educator; b. Chgo., July 29, 1937; s. Norman and Lillian (Ruthenberg) S.; m. Ettabelle Slutsky, Aug. 23, 1959 (div. Jan. 1998); children: Monica, Kenneth, Rachel; m. Joanne Rand Whitmore, Nov. 10, 1998. BS in Psychology, U. Ill., 1958, MA in Indsl. Rels., 1959, PhD in Sociology, 1962; LLD (hon.), Youngstown State U., 1990. Asst. prof. sociology and psychology Wayne State U., Detroit, 1962-64; asst. prof. sociology Ind. U., Bloomington, 1964, assoc. prof. sociology, 1966-70; prof., chmn. dept. sociology Fla. Atlantic U., Boca Raton, 1970-72, dean Coll. Social Sci., 1972-76; v.p. grad. studies and rsch. Kent (Ohio) State U., 1976-78, interim pres., 1977, acting v.p. acad. affairs, 1977-78, v.p. acad. and student affairs, 1978-80, provost, v.p. acad. and student affairs, 1980-82, pres., 1982-91; pres. emeritus and trustee's prof. Kent State U., 1991; interim pres. Cleve. State U., 2001—. Trustee Ctrl. State U., 1996-97; acting dir. Inst. for Social Rsch., Ind. U., 1966-67; tng. cons. Operation Head Start in Ind., 1964-70; cons. Office of Manpower, Automation and Tng., U.S. Dept. Labor, 1964-65. Cons. editor, Sociometry, 1966-70, assoc. editor, 1970; reader Am. Sociol. Rev. papers; author: (with Elton F. Jackson) Study Guide to the Study of Sociology, 1968; contbr. articles to profl. jours., chpts. to books. Chmn. Mid-Am. Conf. Coun. Pres.; rep. Nat. Coll. Athletic Assn. Pres.'s Commn.; chmn. divsn. I, 1988; corps evaluators North Ctrl. Assn. Colls. and Schs.; mem. bd. visitors Air U., USAF; mem. Akron (Ohio) Regional Devel. Bd., N.E. Ednl. TV of Ohio, Inc., N.E. Ohio Univs. Coll. Medicine; trustee Akron Symphony Orch. Assn.; mem. State of Ohio Post-Secondary Rev. Entity, 1995; mem. Assn. of Governing Bds. Commn. on Strengthening the Presidency. Recipient Disting. Tchr. award Fla. Atlantic U., 1970-71, Meritorious Svc. award Am. Assn. State Colls. and Univs., 1990; Michael Schwartz Ctr., Kent State U., named in his honor, 1991. Mem. Ohio Tchr. Edn. and Cert. Adv. Commn., Pine Lake Trout Club. Office: Kent State U 405 White Hl Kent OH 44242-0001 E-mail: mschwartz@educ.kent.edu.

SCHWARTZ, MICHAEL ALAN, physician; b. N.Y.C., Dec. 13, 1944; s. David Henry and Ray Schwartz; m. Joan Kay Clayton, Jan. 12, 1979; children: Dana, David, Elizabeth. AB, Princeton, 1965; MD, Cornell U., 1969. Intern, medicine N.Y. Hosp., Cornell, 1969-70, resident, psychiatry Cornell, Westchester, 1970-74; clin. assoc. NIMH, Washington, 1972-74; asst. prof. psychiatry Cornell Med. Coll., N.Y.C., 1974-76; assoc. to prof. of psychiatry N.Y. Med. Coll., 1976-92; prof. dept. psychiatry Case Western Res. U., Cleve., 1992—, vice chmn. dept. psychiatry, 1992-96. Plenary spkr. symposium on advances in neurosci. Decade of the Brain, WHO, Chinese Psychiat. Assn., 1998, Internat. Congress on Psychosomatic Medicine, 2003; keynote spkr. Colegio Chileno de Neuropsicofarmacologia, Santiago de Chile, 2003; med. dir. Irwin Found., 2000-. Editor: (with Manfred Spitzer, Christoph Mundt, Friedrick Uehlein) Phenomenology, Language, and Schizophrenia, 1992, (with John Sadler and Osborn Wiggins) Psychiatric Diagnostic Classification, 1994; mem. editl. bd. Comprehensive Psychiatry, 1992—; assoc. editor Philosophy, Psychiatry, Psychology, 1993—; mem. internat. adv. bd. L'Evolution Psychiatrique, 1997-2002; mem. editorial com. Psychiatric Sciences Humaines Neurosciences; contbr. articles to numerous sci. jours. Recipient Egner-Stiftung prize Dr-Margrit Egneér-Stiftung Found., 1998, Exemplary Psychiatrist award Nat. Alliance for the Mentally Ill, 2000. Fellow Am. Psychopathol. Assn., Am. Psychiat Assn. (disting.), Am. Psychopath Assn.; mem. Ind. Psychiat. Assn. of Russia (hon.), Soc. Italiana per la Psicopatologia (hon.), Gesellschaft Philosophie und Wissenschaften der Psyche. Home: 1106 Blackacre Trail Austin TX 78746 Office: Univ Hosps Cleve Dept Psychiatry 11100 Euclid Ave Cleveland OH 44106-1736 E-mail: mas1@concentric.net.

SCHWARTZ, MICHAEL ROBINSON, insurance company executive; b. St. Louis, Mar. 18, 1940; s. Henry G. and Edith C. (Robinson) Schwartz; m. Kathleen Nowicki, Dec. 9, 1989; children from previous marriage: Christine, Richard. AB, Dartmouth Coll., 1962; MHA, U. Minn., 1964. Asst. in adminstrn. Shands Tchg. Hosp., Gainesville, Fla., 1966-67, asst. dir., 1967-68, assoc. dir., 1968-73; assoc. adminstr. St. Joseph Mercy Hosp., Pontiac, Mich., 1973-76, pres., 1976-85; exec. v.p. Mercy Health Svcs., Farmington Hills, Mich., 1985-96, COO, 1988-96; exec. v.p. Ea. Mich. region Sisters of Mercy Health Corp., 1991-92; pvt. practice Birmingham, Mich., 1996—; dir. provider rels. Blue Cross Blue Shield of Mich., 2003—. Non-resident lectr. U. Mich., 1982—93; cons. prof. Oakland U., 1980—88; asst. prof. hosp. adminstrn. U. Fla., 1967—73; pres. Eastern Mich. Regional Bd. Sisters of Mercy Health Corp., 1976—79; v.p. Lourdes Nursing Home, 1981—84, United Way-Pontiac/North Oakland, 1982—84; treas. Oakland Health Edn. Program, 1978—79; coms. Blue Cross/Blue Shield of Mich., 1978—86, chair hosp. contingent to participating hosp. agreement adv. com., 1989—96; bd. dirs. Vis. Nurse Assn., Inc., 1997—, treas., 1998—99, 2003—04, vice chair, 1999—2000, chair, 2000—02; chmn. bd. dirs., pres. Accord Ins. Co. Ltd., 1983—88; chmn. bd. dirs. Mercy Health Plans, 1986—96, Venzke Svc. Co., 1983—88, pres., 1983—84; chmn. bd. dirs., pres. Venzke Ins. Co. Ltd., 1988—96; mem. audit and fin. com. Am. Healthcare Sys., 1988—92; mem. S.E. Mich. Hosp. Coun., chmn. pub. rels. com., 1983—85; mem. Commonfund Healthcare Coun., 1999—; trustee Sisters of Mercy Health Corp., 1991—93, sec. bd. trustees, 1993; bd. dirs. Hosp. Fund, 1986—96. Mem. charitable trust Sisters of Mercy, Regional Cmty. Detroit, 1999—. With U.S. Army, 1964—66. Fellow: Am. Coll. Healthcare Execs. (mem. exec. com. higher edn. 1990—93, Mich. Regent's award 1992); mem.: Comprehensive Health Planning Coun. (com. mem. 1976—81), Am. Healthcare Sys. Risk Retention Group (bd. dirs. 1990—91), Mich. Hosp. Assn. (at-large rep. corp. bd. 1990—96, exec. com. 1992—96), Pontiac Urban League (pers. com. 1979). Office: 600 Lafayette E MCJ 744 Detroit MI 48226 Office Phone: 313-225-0705. Business E-Mail: mschwartz@bcbsm.com.

SCHWARTZ, MILDRED ANNE, retired sociologist; b. Toronto, Can., Nov. 17, 1932; d. Max and Rebecca Schwartz. BA, U. of Toronto, 1954, MA, 1956; PhD, Columbia U., N.Y., 1965. Asst. prof. U. of Alta., Calgary, Canada, 1962—64; study dir. Nat. Opinion Rsch. Ctr., Chgo., 1964—66; assoc. prof. U. of Ill., Chgo., 1966—69, prof., 1969—98, prof. emeritus, 1998—; vis. prof. Harvard U., Cambridge, 1973—73, U. of Calgary, Canada, 1999. Program dir. NSF, Arlington, Va., 1995; vis. scholar NYU, N.Y.C., 1999—. Author: (book) Public Opinion and Canadian Identity, 1967, Politics and Territory, 1974, The Party Network, 1990. Fellow Inst. for the Humanities fellowship, U. of Ill. at Chgo., 1988—89, Sr. Rsch. fellowship, Embassy of Can., 1996, Thomas O. Enders fellowship, Enders Found., 1999; grantee Rsch. Grant, Social Sci. and Humanities Rsch. coun. of Can., 1994—96, Conf. Grant, NSF, Am. Sociol. Assn., 2000. Mem.: Assn. for Can. Studies in the U.S. (exec. com. 1970—75), Can. Polit. Sci. Assn., Am. Polit. Sci. Assn. (nominating com. 1981—82), Social Sci. History Assn. (pres. 1985), Am. Sociol. Assn. (sect. chair 1998—99). Jewish. Achievements include research in parties, regionalism, nat. identity. Home: 245 Prospect Ave Apt 11C Hackensack NJ 07601 Personal E-mail: mildred@uic.edu.

SCHWARTZ, MILES JOSEPH, cardiologist; b. Richmond, Va., Aug. 7, 1925; s. Hugo and Ella ((Kramer)) Schwartz; m. Margery Baer Irish, June 7, 1956 (div. 1972); children: Elizabeth, James, Margaret; m. Katherine Rush, May 26, 1980. BS, Queens Coll., N.Y., 1947; MD, N.Y. Univ., 1951. Lic. Am. Bd. Internal Medicine, Am. Bd. Cardiovasc. Disease. Interne Mt. Sinai Hosp., N.Y.C., 1951-52; resident Bronx VA Hosp., NY, 1952-53, Mt. Sinai Hosp., N.Y.C., 1953-54; resident, fellow Bronx VA Hosp., NY, 1954-55, asst. med. sect. chief, 1956-58; resident, to chief resident St. Luke's Hosp. Ctr., N.Y.C., 1955-56, asst. attending physician to assoc. cardiologist, 1959-69, chief of hypertension clinic, 1959-81, dir. clin. cardiology tng. program, 1966—97, attending physician, 1970-98, clin. dir. pvt. med. svc., 1974-78, assoc. dir. medicine, 1978-84, assoc. dir. cardiology divsn., 1987—97; acting dir. cardiology divsn. St. Luke's Roosevelt Hosp., N.Y.C., 1995—96; pres. Williamsburg Healthcare Consortium, Va., 2001—. Cons. Sharon Hosp., Conn., 1976—91; prof. clin. med. emeritus Columbia U., Physicians and Surgeons, N.Y.C., 1998. Served in USNR, 1944—46. Fellow: ACP, Am. Heart Assn., Am. Coll. Cardiology; mem.: Phi Beta Kappa, Alpha Omega Alpha. Jewish. Avocations: travel, history, bioethics, medical edn. Home: 217 W Queens Dr Williamsburg VA 23185-4918 Personal E-mail: mjschwartz64@cox.net.

SCHWARTZ, MILTON LEWIS, federal judge; b. Oakland, Calif., Jan. 20, 1920; s. Colman and Selma (Lavenson) S.; m. Barbara Ann Moore, May 15, 1942; children: Dirk L., Tracy Ann, Damon M., Brooke. AB, U. Calif. at Berkeley, 1941, JD, 1948. Bar: Calif. bar 1949. Rsch. asst. 3d Dist. Ct. Appeal, Sacramento, 1948; dep. dist. atty., 1949-51; practice in, 1951-79; partner McDonough, Holland, Schwartz & Allen, 1953-79; U.S. dist. judge Eastern Dist. Calif., U.S. Dist. Ct., Calif., 1979-90, sr. judge, 1990—2002. Prof. law McGeorge Coll. Law, Sacramento, 1952-55; mem. Com. Bar Examiners Calif., 1971-75 Pres. Bd. Edn. Sacramento City Sch. Dist., 1961; v.p. Calif. Bd. Edn., 1967-68; trustee Sutterville Heights Sch. Dist. Served to maj. 40th Inf. Divsn. AUS, 1942-46, PTO. Named Sacramento County Judge of Yr., 1990; Milton L. Schwartz Am. Inn of Court named in his honor, Davis, Calif. Fellow Am. Coll. Trial Lawyers; mem. State Bar Calif., Am. Bar Assn., Am. Bd. Trial Advocates, Anthony M. Kennedy Am. Inn of Ct. (pres. 1988-90, pres. emeritus 1990—). Office: US Dist Ct Rm 15 200 501 I St Sacramento CA 95814

SCHWARTZ, MISCHA, electrical engineering educator; b. N.Y.C., Sept. 21, 1926; s. Isaiah and Bessie (Weinstein) S.; m. Lillian Mitchnick, June 23, 1957 (div.); 1 son, David; m. Charlotte F. Berney, July 12, 1970. B.E.E., Cooper Union, 1947; M.E.E., Poly. Inst. Bklyn., 1949; PhD in Applied Physics (Sperry Gyroscope grad. scholar), Harvard U., 1951. Project engr. Sperry Gyroscope Co., 1947-52; mem. faculty Poly. Inst. Bklyn., 1952-74, prof. elec. engring., 1959-74, head dept., 1961-65; prof. elec. engring. and computer sci. Columbia U., N.Y.C., 1974-88, Charles Batchelor prof. elec. engring., 1988-96, Charles Batchelor prof. emeritus, 1996—, dir. Ctr. for Telecommunications Research, 1985-88. Part-time tchr. Adelphi Coll., 1951-52, CCNY, 1952; cons. radiation physicist Montefiore Hosp., N.Y.C., 1954-56; vis. prof. sys. sci. dept. UCLA, 1964; vis. prof. dept. elec. engring. and computer sci. Columbia U., 1973-74; vis. prof. dept. electronic and elec. engring. U. Coll., London, 1995; vis. prof. dept. elec. and computer engring. U. Calif., San Diego, 1997; chmn. Commn. C, U.S. Nat. Com. Internat. Union Radio Sci., 1977-80; vis. scientist IBM Rsch., 1980, 94, NYNEX Sci. and Tech., 1986; vis. mem. tech. staff AT&T Bell Labs., 1995; cons. in field. Author: Information Transmission, Modulation and Noise, 4th edit., 1990, (with L. Shaw) Signal Processing, 1975, Computer Communication Network Design and Analysis, 1977, Telecommunications Networks, 1987, Broadband Integrated Networks, 1996; editor, contbr.: Communication Systems and Techniques, 1966, reissued, 1995. Trustee Gt. Neck Libr., 1997-2001, pres., 1998, 99. Served with AUS, 1944-46. NSF sci. faculty fellow, 1965-66; recipient Disting. Vis. award Australian-Am. Ednl. Found., 1975, Vis. Scientist award Nippon Tel. & Tel., 1981, Tchg. award Columbia U., 1984, Gano Dunn award Cooper Union, 1986, Mayor's award for excellence in tech., City of N.Y., 1995; finalist Mayor's Awards for Excellence in Sci. & Tech., City of N.Y., 1992, recipient Okawa award for contbns. comm., computer networks, engring. edn., 2003. Fellow AAAS, IEEE (chmn. adminstrv. com. profl. group info. theory 1964-65, bd. dirs. 1978-79, bd. govs. Comm. Soc. 1973-79, v.p. 1982-83, pres. 1984-85, Edn. medal 1983, IEEE Centennial Hall of Fame 1984, Region 1 award for leadership in mgmt. Ctr. for Telecom. Rsch. 1990, Edwin Armstrong award for contbns. to telecomm. 1994, Millennium medal 2000); mem. NAE, AAUP (chpt. pres. 1970-72), Assn. for Computing Machinery, Sigma Xi, Tau Beta Pi, Eta Kappa Nu (eminent mem. 1999). Home: 66 Maple Dr Great Neck NY 11021-1928 Office: Columbia U Schapiro CEPSR Rm 806 New York NY 10027 Office Phone: 212-854-3125. Personal E-mail: mcschw66@aol.com. Business E-Mail: schwartz@ctr.columbia.edu.

SCHWARTZ, MURRAY MERLE, federal judge; b. 1931; BS, Wharton Sch. U. Pa., 1952; LLB, U. Pa., 1955; LLM, U. Va., 1982. Part-time referee in bankruptcy Dist. of Del., 1969-74; judge U.S. Dist. Ct. Del., 1974-85, chief judge, 1985-89, sr. judge, 1989—. Author: The Exercise of Supervisory Power by the Third Circuit Court of Appeals, 1982. Mem. Del. State Bar Assn. Office: US Dist Ct Lockbox 44 844 N King St Wilmington DE 19801-3519

SCHWARTZ, NEENA BETTY, endocrinologist, educator; b. Balt., Dec. 10, 1926; d. Paul Howard and Pauline (Shulman) S. AB, Goucher Coll., 1948, DSc (hon.), 1982; MS, Northwestern U., 1950, PhD, 1953. From instr. to prof. U. Ill. Coll. Medicine, Chgo., 1953-72, asst. dean for faculty, 1968-70; prof. physiology Northwestern U. Med. Sch., Chgo., 1973-74; Deering prof. Northwestern U., Evanston, Ill., 1974—99, chmn. dept. biol. scis., 1974-78, acting dean, Coll. Arts and Scis., 1996-97, prof. emeritus, 2000—. Contbr. chpts. to books, articles to profl. jours. NIH rsch. grantee, 1955-. Fellow: AAAS (exec. bd. 1998—2002, Lifetime Mentor award 2003); mem.: Soc. for Neurosci., Am. Physiol. Soc., Soc. for Study of Reproduction (dir. 1975—77, exec. v.p. 1976—77, pres. 1977—78, Carl Hartman award 1992), Endocrine Soc. (v.p. 1970—71, mem. coun. 1979—83, pres. 1982—83, Williams award 1985, Disting. Educator award 1998), Am. Acad. Arts and Scis. Home: 1511 Lincoln St Evanston IL 60201-2338 Office Phone: 847-491-5529. Personal E-mail: n-schwartz@northwestern.edu.

SCHWARTZ, NORTON A. military officer; B in Polit. Sci. and Internat. Affairs, USAF Acad., Colorado, 1973; grad., Squadron Officer Sch., Alabama, 1977; MBA, Cen. Mich. U., 1983; grad., Armed Forces Staff Coll., Virginia, 1984, Nat. War Coll., Washington, DC, 1989; seminar fellow, Mass Inst of Tech, 1994. Commd. 2d lt. USAF, 1973, advanced through grades to lieutenant gen., 2002; action officer Directorate of Plans Hdqs. USAF, Office of Dep. Chief of Staff Plans and Ops., Washington, 1984-86; comdr. 36th Tactical Airlift Squadron, McChord AFB, Wash., 1986-88; dir. plans and policy Spl. Ops. Command Europe, Stuttgart-Vaihingen, Germany, 1989-91; dep. comdr. for ops., comdr. 1st Spl. Ops. Group, Hurlburt Field, Fla., 1991-93; dep. dir. ops., dep. dir. forces Office Dep. Chief of Staff for Plans and Ops., Hdqs. USAF, Washington, 1993-95; comdr. 16th Spl. Ops. Wing, Hurlburt Field, Fla., 1995-97, Spl. Ops. Command, Pacific, Camp H.M. Smith, Hawaii, 1997-98; dir. strategic planning Dep. Chief of Staff for Plans and Programs, Hdqs. USAF, Washington, 1998—2000; dep. comdr. and chief Spl. Ops. Command, USAF, MacDill AFB, Fla., 2000; comdr. Alaskan Command, Alaskan N. Amer. Def. Command, 2000—02; dir. of operations Joint Staff, Washington, 2002—. Decorated Def. Superior Svc. medal with oak leaf cluster, Legion of Merit with oak leaf cluster, Def. Meritorious Svc. medal, Meritorious Svc. medal with 2 oak leaf clusters; Seminar XXI fellow MIT, 1994. Office: OCJCS Public Affairs 9999 Joint Staff Rm 2D844 Washington DC 20318

SCHWARTZ, PAUL N. manufacturing executive; CFO, COO, pres. Maxxam Inc., Houston. Office: Maxxam Inc 5847 San Felipe St Ste 2600 Houston TX 77057-3268

SCHWARTZ, PAULA MAE, communications company executive; BA in English Lit., Boston U. Formerly with Newsweek; former pub. rels. profl. N.Y.C., Boston; co-founder, CEO Schwartz Comms., Inc., Waltham, Mass., 1990—. Bd. dirs. Gloucester Adventure. Avocations: hiking, theater, thriller fiction. Office: Schwartz Comms Inc Prospect Pl/230 Third Ave Waltham MA 02451 also: Schwartz Comms Inc 595 Market St Ste 2050 San Francisco CA 94105-2831

SCHWARTZ, PEPPER JUDITH, sociology educator; b. Chgo., May 11, 1945; d. Julius J. and Gertrude (Puris) S.; m. John A. Strait, June 19, 1971; m. Arthur M. Skolnik, Jan. 9, 1982; children— Cooper, Ryder. B.A., Washington U., St. Louis, 1968, M.A., 1970; M. in Philosophy, Yale U., 1972, Ph.D., 1974. Assoc. prof. sociology, adj. assoc. prof. 1972-88, prof. psychiatry and behavioral sci. U. Wash., Seattle, 1988— . Chmn. rev. com. NIMH; bd. dirs. Women's Research Ctr.; frequent guest and host local and network TV shows; apptd. to Pres. Reagan's ad hoc adv. roundtable on the family, 1984; expert appearance in NBC Sacred Sexless, 1987, Some Thoughts on Being Single, 1984, ABC After The Sexual Revolution, 1986; relationship expert Lifetime-TV.com, 1998—, PerfectMatch.com, 2003—. Bd. dirs. Nat. Abortion Rights Action League, Anti-Defamation League; guardian Ad-Litem Program; bd. dirs. Empty Space Theater, Seattle, pres., 1980; past mem. Gov.'s Commn. Venereal Disease; bd. dirs. ACLU; nat. bd. dirs. YWCA, Jewish Family Service; mem. Presdl. Adv. Roundtable on Family, 1984. Named Outstanding Young Woman of the Future, Time-Life mag., 1978; One of Most Powerful People of the 1980s, Next mag., 1981. Fellow Internat. Acad. Sex Rsch.; mem. Pacific Sociol. Assn. (pres. 2004—), Soc. for the Sci. Study of Sexuality (pres. 1998), Am. Sociol. Assn. (chair com. on coms.), Pacific Sociol. Assn. (mem. coun., pres. 2004), Nat. Conf. Family Rels., Lluminari Women's Expert Health Network, Groves Conf., Yale Club (N.Y.C.). Author: Women at Yale, 1976, Peer Marriage, 1995, The Great Sex Weekend, 1995; (with Judith Laws et al) Sexual Scripts, 1977; (with P. Blumstein) American Couples, 1983, (with V. Rutter) The Gender of Sexuality, 1995, (with D. Cappello) Ten Talks Parents Must Have with their Children About Sex and Character, 2002, Everthing You Know About Love & Sex is Wrong, 2002, Lifetime Book of Love & Sex Quizes, 2003; co-author and editor: A Student's Guide to Sex on Campus, 1971; contbr. numerous articles to mags. and jours.; profiles in Savvy, Ladies Home Jour., Playboy, Cosmopolitan, N.Y. Times, Newsweek, others; articles on work in Time, Redbook, New West, others. Office: Dept Sociology Dk 40 U Seattle WA 98195-0001 Office Phone: 206-543-4036. E-mail: pepperschwartz@hotmail.com.

SCHWARTZ, PERRY LESTER, information systems engineer, consultant; b. Bklyn., July 29, 1939; s. Max David and Sylvia (Weinberger) S.; m. Arlene Metz, Jan. 24, 1960; 3 children. BEE, CUNY, 1957-62; MS in Indsl. Engring. and Computer Sci., NYU, 1967; PhD in Engring., Thornhill U., 2001. Registered profl. engr., profl. planner, NJ; cert. mediator and arbitrator, expert witness comm. Microwave engr. Airbourne Inst. Lab., Deer Park, NY, 1962-63; engr. ITT Fed. Labs, Nutley, NJ, 1963-64; program mgr. Western Electric Co., NYC, 1964-69; dept. head RCA, Princeton, NJ, 1970-71; dir. engring. Warner Comm. Inc., NYC, 1972-74; cons. engr. Intertech Assoc., Freehold, NJ, 1974—. Adj. faculty CCNY, 1962-71, Ocean County Coll., Toms River, NJ, 1981-83, Rutgers U., New Brunswick, NJ, 1984-87; lectr. NJ Dept. Edn., 1994-95; mem. NJ State Bd. Profl. Planners, 2004—. Steering

com., trustee Intelligent Bldg. Found., 1982-89. Mem. IEEE (sr.), Am. Cons. Engr. Coun., Nat. Soc. Profl. Engr., Nat. Assn. Radio and Telecom. Engr. (sr. mem. charter mem., cert. master engr. in wire and RF, Cert. of Distinction 1994-95), Cons. Engrs. Coun. NJ, NY Acad. Sci., CCNY Engring. Sch. Alumni Assn. (v.p. 2004—), Zeta Beta Tau (chpt. founder 1958), K. P. Office: Intertech Assoc 77-55 Schanck Rd Ste A-14 Freehold NJ 07728 Office Phone: 732-431-4236. Business E-Mail: ps@intertechassociates.com.

SCHWARTZ, PETER ISAAC, poet; b. Bronx, Sept. 22, 1970; s. Earl Daniel Schwartz and Christine Ann Smith. BA in Lit., SUNY, Purchase, 2000. Musician, vocalist Insomniacs, Buffalo, 1994—98; mktg. rschr. Survey Svcs., Tonawanda, NY, 1998—2000; ptnr. Tiger Kids LLC, Augusta, Maine, 2000—. Interviewer, amateur archivist, Augusta, 2002—03. Author: (book of poetry) Unerasble Poetry, 1998, Holidays of the Moment, 2000, (poem) Truthfulness, 2003, The Soldier's Poem, 2003, The Myth of Satan, 2003, Wilderness Training Center, 2003, Ode to the Collection Agency, 2003. Mem.: Internat. Assn. Paradoxism (hon. Disting. Achievement award 2003), Acad. Am. Poets. Avocations: piano, philosophy, weightlifting. Personal E-mail: jiggyexperiences@hotmail.com.

SCHWARTZ, PHILIP, lawyer; b. June 7, 1930; s. Louis and Kate (Brodsky) S.; m. Iris M. Ballin, Nov. 28, 1953 (div. 1979); children: David, Elyse, Donna; m. Monique W. Wagner, July 26, 1982 (div. 1991); m. Carol J. Pruett, Aug. 14, 1992. BA, George Washington U., 1952, JD, 1959; LLM in Taxation, Georgetown U., 1961; postgrad., U. Paris, London Sch. Econs., Harvard U. Bar: Va. 1959, D.C. 1966, U.S. Tax Ct. 1966, U.S. Ct. Appeals (D.C. cir.) 1966, U.S. Ct. Mil. Appeals 1966, U.S. Supreme Ct. 1966, U.S. Ct. Appeals (4th cir.) 1982, U.S. Ct. Internat. Trade 1988, N.Am. Coun. London Ct. Internat. Arbitration 1988; diplomate Am. Coll. Family Law Trial Lawyers; fellow Am. Acad. Matrimonial Lawyers, Internat. Acad. Matrimonial Lawyers. Sr. intelligence analyst Nat. Security Agy., Washington, 1952-54, 56-63; assoc. Varoutsos, Koutoulakos & Arthur, Arlington, Va., 1963—68; ptnr. Schwartz & Ellis, Ltd., Arlington, 1968—2002, Schwartz & Assocs., PLLC, 2002—; of counsel Odin, Feldman & Pittleman PC, 2002—. Instr. No. Va. Life Underwriters Tng. Coun., 1974, No. Va. Paralegal Inst., Arlington, 1976; moot ct. judge George Washington U., Washington, Georgetown U., Washington, Jessup Internat. Law Competition; commr. Chancery Arlington Cir. Ct., judge Pro Tempo; spkr. in field. Contbr. articles to profl. jours. Mem. U.S. Sec. of State Adv. Com. on Pvt. Internat. Law; mem. Arlington County Bd. Zoning Appeals, 1972-85, Arlington County Coun. Human Rels., 1973; del. to Hague Conf. Pvt. Internat. Law; bd. dirs. Jewish Cmty. Ctr. Greater Washington, 1975. With M.I., U.S. Army, 1954-56. Master Barrister Am. Inns of Ct.; fellow Internat. Acad. Matrimonial Lawyers (pres. 1996-97), Am. Acad. Matrimonial Lawyers (bd. govs., v.p.); mem. ABA (chmn. family law sect. com. internat. laws 1983-86, chmn. internat. law sect. com. enforcement fgn. judgments), Internat. Bar Assn. (chmn. family law divsn. 1988-92, governing coun. gen. practice sect., liaison officer to IMF), Am. Coll. Family Trial Layers (diplomate), Va. Trial Lawyers Assn. (instr. 1984), Assn. Trial Lawyers Am. (vice chmn. internat. practice sect.), Va. State Bar (bd. govs. internat. law sect., liaison to ABA internat. law sect., spl. com. reducing litigation delay and costs, com. on bench/bar rels.), Calif. Bar Assn. (internat. law sect.), N.Y. State Bar Assn. (internat. law, family law sect.), D.C. Bar (internat. law, family law sect.), Arlington County Bar Assn. (cts. com., legis. com., jud. selection com.), Fairfax County Bar Assn. (family law and internat. law sects.), Brit. Inst. Internat. and Comparative Law, Am. Soc. Internat. Law, Union Internationale des Avocats, Inter-Am. Bar Assn., Internat. Soc. Family Law, Solicitors Family Law Assn. Eng. and Wales, Soc. English and Am. Lawyers, Am. Fgn. Law Assn., Internat. Law Assn., Asia-Pacific Lawyers Assn., Arlington Jaycees, Kiwanis, Phi Epsilon Pi, Delta Phi Epsilon, Phi Delta Phi. Office: Schwartz & Assocs PLLC 9302 Lee Hwy 11th Fl Fairfax VA 22031 Office Phone: 203-218-2121. E-mail: philip.schwartz@ofplaw.com.

SCHWARTZ, RANDY KEN, mathematician, educator; b. Washington, Aug. 30, 1956; s. Hyman Alex Schwartz and Clare Louise Carp. BA in Math., Dartmouth Coll., 1977; MA in Math., U. Mich., 1979. Computer programmer Logicon, Inc., Merrifield, Va., 1974-77; adj. instr. Washtenaw CC, Ann Arbor, Mich., 1979-84; instr. Cleary Coll., Ypsilanti, Mich., 1981-84; prof. Schoolcraft Coll., Livonia, Mich., 1984—. Author: Test Bank for Elementary Linear Algebra, 1994, 2000; editor: (newsletter) Repast, 1999—; contbr. articles to profl. jours. Mem.: Culinary Historians Ann Arbor (editor 1999—), Math. Assn. Am., Am. Math. Soc., Ann Arbor Track Club, Phi Beta Kappa. Avocations: running, poetry, blues music, cooking. Home: 1044 Greenhills Dr Ann Arbor MI 48105-2722 Office: Schoolcraft Coll 18600 Haggerty Rd Livonia MI 48152-2696 Office Phone: 734-462-4400 5290. Business E-Mail: rschwart@schoolcraft.edu.

SCHWARTZ, RENEE GERSTLER, lawyer; b. Bklyn., June 18, 1933; d. Samuel and Lillian (Neulander) Gerstler; m. Alfred L. Schwartz, July 30, 1955; children: Carolyn Susan, Deborah Jane. AB, Bklyn. Coll., 1953; LLB, Columbia U., 1955. Bar: N.Y. 1956, U.S. Dist. Ct. (so. and ea. dists.) N.Y. 1956, U.S. Ct. Appeals (2d cir.) 1956, U.S. Dist. Ct. D.C. 1983, U.S. Supreme Ct. 1986. Assoc. Botein, Hays & Sklar, N.Y.C., 1955-64, ptnr., 1965-89, Kronish, Lieb, Weiner & Hellman, N.Y.C., 1990—. Bd. dirs. New Land Found., N.Y.C., 1965—. Mem. Bar Assn. City of N.Y. Home: 115 Central Park W New York NY 10023-4153 Office: Kronish Lieb Weiner & Hellman 1114 Avenue Of The Americas New York NY 10036-7703 Office Phone: 212-479-6040. E-mail: rschwartz@kronishlieb.com.

SCHWARTZ, RICHARD BRENTON, English language educator, dean, writer; b. Cin., Oct. 5, 1941; s. Jack Jay and Marie Mildred (Schnelle) S.; m. Judith Mary Alexis Lang, Sept. 7, 1963; 1 son, Jonathan Francis. AB cum laude, U. Notre Dame, 1963; AM, U. Ill., 1964, PhD, 1967. Instr. English, U.S. Mil. Acad., 1967-69; asst. prof. U. Wis.-Madison, 1969-72, assoc. prof., 1972-78, prof., 1978-81, assoc. dean Grad. Sch., 1977, 79-81; prof. English, dean Grad. Sch., Georgetown U., Washington, 1981-98, interim exec. v.p. for main campus academic affairs, 1991-92; interim exec. v.p. for the main campus Georgetown U., Washington, 1995-96; prof. English, dean Coll. Arts and Sci. U. Mo., Columbia, 1998—. Mem. exec. bd. Ctr. Strategic and Internat. Studies, 1981-87. Author: Samuel Johnson and the New Science, 1971 (runner-up Gustave O. Arlt prize), Samuel Johnson and the Problem of Evil, 1975, Boswell's Johnson: A Preface to the Life, 1978, Daily Life in Johnson's London, 1983, Japanese edit., 1990, After the Death of Literature, 1997, Nice and Noir: Contemporary American Crime Fiction, 2002, (novels) Frozen Stare, 1989, The Last Voice You Hear, 2001, After the Fall, 2002, Into the Dark, 2002 (hon. mention genre fiction Writer's Digest); short stories, The Biggest City in America, 1999 (Choice Mag. citation); editor: The Plays of Arthur Murphy, 4 vols., 1979, Theory and Tradition in Eighteenth-Century Studies, 1990; contbr. articles to profl. jours. Served to capt. U.S. Army, 1967-69. Decorated Army Commendation medal; recipient Presdl. medal Georgetown U., 1998; Nat. Endowment Humanities grantee, 1970, 87; Inst. for Research in Humanities fellow, 1976; Am. Council Learned Socs. fellow, 1978-79; H.I. Romnes fellow, 1978-81. Mem. Mystery Writers Am., Johnson Soc. So. Calif., Johnson Soc. of London, Am. Soc. Eighteenth-Century Studies, Coun. Grad. Schs., N.E. Assn. Grad. Schs. (exec. com. 1986-88), Assn. Grad. Schs. in Cath. Univs. (exec. com. 1984-87), Assn. Literary Scholars and Critics, Nat. Assn. Scholars, N.Am. Conf. Brit. Studies, Jefferson Club, Mosaic Soc., Alpha Sigma Nu, Alpha Sigma Lambda. Roman Catholic. Home: 5800 Highlands Pkwy Columbia MO 65203-5125 Office: U Mo Coll of Arts and Sci 317 Lowry Hall Columbia MO 65211-6080 Office Phone: 573-882-4421. E-mail: schwartzrb@missouri.edu.

SCHWARTZ, RICHARD EDWARD DERECKTOR, retired sociologist, educator; b. Newark, Apr. 26, 1925; s. Selig and Tillie (Derecktor) S.; m. Emilie Zane Rosenbaum, June 30, 1946; children: David, Margaret Jane, Deborah. BA, Yale U., 1947, PhD in Sociology, 1952. Research fellow Inst. Human Relations, Yale, 1951-54, instr., asst. prof. sociology and law, 1953-61; faculty Northwestern U., Evanston, 1961-71, prof. sociology, 1964-71, prof. sociology and law, 1966-71; dir. Council Intersocietal Studies, 1965-70, co-dir. law and social sci. program, 1967-70; dean, provost Faculty of Law and Jurisprudence, State U. N.Y. at Buffalo, 1971-76; Ernest I. White rsch. prof. law Syracuse U., 1977—2004. Mem. com. law enforcement and adminstrn. of justice NAS, 1975-85; fellowship referee Russell Sage Found., 1970-77, NEH, 1972-77, NSF, 1978-81; exec. dir. NESCO, 1995-2001. Author: (with others) Society and the Legal Order, 1970, Criminal Law, 1974, Handbook of Regulation and Administrative Law, 1994, Unobtrusive Measures, 2000; founding editor: Law and Soc. Rev., 1966-69. Served with USNR, 1943-45. Ctr. for Advanced Study in Behavioral Scis. fellow, 1989—90, sr. rsch. scholar, Yale, 2002—. Fellow AAAS, Am. Acad. Polit. and Social Sci.; mem. Am. Sociol. Assn., Law and Soc. Assn. (pres. 1972-75) Jewish. Home: 40 Beach Ave Milford CT 06460-8154 Office Phone: 203-874-4586. Personal E-mail: emnred@aol.com. *I believe that we could create a better way of life if we structured society to encourage-rather than to penalize-altruism. Although I have not yet contributed much toward achieving such a society, the effort to do so has been satisfying.*

SCHWARTZ, RICHARD HARVEY, pediatrician; b. Bklyn., July 6, 1938; s. Hy and Ruth (Marshak) S.; m. Rose Lynne Hass, May 29, 1960; children: Lisa, Keith, Keira. BA, George Washington U., 1960; MD, Georgetown U., 1965. Diplomate Am. Bd. Pediat., Am. Soc. Addiction Medicine. Intern U.S. Army, 1965-66, resident in pediat., 1969-71; pvt. practice, Vienna, Va., 1972—. Contbr. articles to profl. jours. Maj. U.S. Army, 1965-69. Mem. AMA (Outstanding Contbn. in Adolescent Medicine award 1990), Am. Acad. Pediatrics (rsch. award 1989). Jewish. Avocations: walking, travel. Office: Advanced Pediatrics 115 Park St SE Vienna VA 22180-4653

SCHWARTZ, RICHARD JOHN, electrical engineering educator, researcher; b. Waukesha, Wis., Aug. 12, 1935; s. Sylvester John and LaVerne Mary (Lepien) S.; m. Mary Jo Collins, June 29, 1957; children: Richard, Stephen, Susan, Elizabeth, Barbara, Peter, Christopher, Margaret. BSEE, U. Wis., 1957; SM, MIT, 1959, ScD, 1962. Mem. tech. staff Sarnoff Rsch. Labs. RCA, Princeton, N.J., 1957-58; instr. MIT, Cambridge, 1961-62; v.p. Energy Conversions, Inc., Cambridge, 1962-64; assoc. prof. Purdue U., West Lafayette, Ind., 1964-71, prof., 1972—, head dept., 1985-95, dean engring., 1995—2001, dir. Optoelectronic Ctr., 1986-89. Co-dir. Nano Tech. Ctr. Purdue U., W. Lafayette, Ind.; cons. solar cells, 1965—. Contbr. chpts. to books, articles to profl. jours. Served to 2nd lt. U.S. Army, 1957-58. Recipient Disting. Svc. medal U. Wis., 1989, Centennial medal, 1991. Fellow: IEEE (William R. Cherry award 1998), Internat. Electronics Con.; mem.: Nat. Elec. Engring. Dept. Heads Assn. (bd. dirs.). Achievements include development of high intensity solar cells, of surface charge transfer device, and of numerical models for solar cells. Office: Purdue U 1285 ElectricalEngring West Lafayette IN 47907

SCHWARTZ, ROBERT, finance educator; b. N.Y.C., Feb. 12, 1937; s. Fred J. Schwartz and Shirley Liebowitz; m. Jody Silver Schwartz; 1 child, Emily. BA, NYU, 1959; MBA, Columbia U., 1962, PhD, 1966. Asst. prof. econs. NYU, 1965—70, assoc. prof. econs., 1970—77, prof. econs., 1977—83, prof. econs. and fin., 1983—91; prof. econs. and fin., Yamaichi Faculty fellow Stern Sch. Bus., NYU, 1991—97; Speiser prof. fin., Univ. Disting. prof. Zicklin Sch. Bus. Baruch Coll., CUNY, 1997—. Chmn. econ. adv. bd. NASDAQ, 1995—97, mem. econ. adv. bd., 1997—99. Author (with Kalman J. Cohen, Steven F. Maier and David K. Whitcomb): The Microstructure of Securities Markets, 1986; author: Equity Markets: Structure, Trading and Performance, 1988, Reshaping the Equity Markets: A Guide for the 1990s, 1991, reissue, 1993; author: (with R. Francioni) Equity Markets in Action, 2004; contbr. articles to profl. jours.; editor (with Ernest Bloch): Impending Changes for Securities Markets: What Role for the Exchanges?, 1979; editor: (with Yakov Amihud and Thomas Ho) Market Making and the Changing Structure of the Securities Industry, 1985; editor: (with Henry Lucas) The Challenge of Information Technology for the Securities Markets: Liquidity, Volatility and Global Trading, 1989; editor: Global Equity Markets: Technological, Competetive and Regulatory Challenges, 1995, The Electronic Call Auction: Market Mechanism and Trading, Building a Better Stock Market, 2001; editor: (with Antoinette Colaninno) Regulation of U.S. Equity Markets, 2001; editor: (with John A. Byrne and Antoinette Colaninno) Call Auction Trading: New Answers to Old Questions, 2003; editor: A Trading Desk's View of Market Quality, 2004, Coping with Institutional Order Flow, 2004; assoc. editor Jour. Fin., 1983—88, Rev. Quantitative Fin. and Acctg., Rev. Pacific Basin Fin. Markets and Policies, Jour. Entrepreneurial Fin. and Bus. Ventures, mem. adv. bd. Internat. Fin. Mem.: Am. Fin. Assn. Office: Baruch Coll CUNY 55 Lexington Ave Box B10-225 New York NY 10010

SCHWARTZ, ROBERT GEORGE, retired insurance company executive; b. Czechoslovakia, Mar. 27, 1928; came to U.S., 1929, naturalized, 1935; s. George and Frances (Antoni) S.; m. Caroline Bachurski, Oct. 12, 1952; children: Joanne, Tracy, Robert G. BA, Pa. State U., 1949; MBA, NYU, 1956. With Met. Life Ins. Co., N.Y.C., 1949-93, v.p. securities, 1962-70, v.p., 1970-75, sr. v.p., 1975-78, exec. v.p., 1979-80, vice chmn. bd., 1980-83, chmn. investment com., 1980-93, chmn. bd., 1983-93, chmn. bd., pres., chief exec. officer, 1989-93. Bd. dirs., mem. Horatio Alger Assn. Trustee Com. for Econ. Devel. With U.S. Army, 1950—52. Mem.: Sky Club, Alpha Chi Rho. Office: MetLife Bldg 200 Park Ave 32d Fl New York NY 10166-0005

SCHWARTZ, ROBERT M. lawyer; b. Phila., Aug. 6, 1940; s. Nathan and Miriam (Albus) S.; m. Karen Leaf, Feb. 11, 1966; children: Eric, Lauren. BS, Pa. State U., 1962; JD, Villanova U., 1965. Bar: Pa. 1965, U.S. Ct. Appeals (3rd cir.) 1965; cert. adv. bus and comml. mediator tng. Law clk. to presiding justice Common Pleas Ct. Montgomery County, Norristown, Pa., 1965; v.p., assoc. counsel Commonwealth Land Title Ins. Co., Phila., 1969—73; ptnr. in bus. dept. White and Williams, LLP, Phila., 1973—. Spkr. and expert witness in field. Mem. regional exec., civil rights com., regional bd. trustees Anti-Defamation League, vice chmn., 1997-99; bd. dirs., mem. facilities and legal coms. Police Athletic League. Named one of Pa. Superlawyers, Phila. Mag., 2004. Mem. Phila. Bar Assn. (chmn. real property com. 1981, exec. bd. real property sect. 1983-89, 91, 2002, chmn. real property sect. 1986), Am. Coll. Real Estate Lawyers (Best Lawyers in Am. award 1989-2004), Am. Coll. Mortgage Attys., Am. Land Title Assn. (lenders counsel group 1993—), Order of Coif. Republican. Jewish. Avocations: bridge, golf. Office: White and Williams 1650 Market St Fl 18 Philadelphia PA 19103-7395 Office Phone: 215-864-7188. Business E-Mail: schwartzr@whiteandwilliams.com.

SCHWARTZ, ROBERT TERRY, industrial design executive; b. Irvington, N.J., Sept. 29, 1950; s. Edward Herman and Harriet Selma (Rosenstein) S.; m. Carol Fawn Mullenix, July 27, 1975; children: Zachary Jacob, Allison Lizabeth. BFA, Kansas City Art Inst., 1973; M of Indsl. Design, R.I. Sch. Design, 1975. Red Cross project dir. R.I. Sch. Design, Providence, 1975-76; head indsl. design/architecture Red Cross Nat. Hdqrs., Washington, 1976-88; dir. sci. and tech. Health Industry Mfrs. Assn., Washington, 1988-90; exec. dir., COO Worldesign Found., Great Falls, Va., 1990-96, Indsl. Designers Soc. Am., Great Falls, 1990-99; dir. indsl. design Motorola, Inc., Ft. Lauderdale, Fla., 1999—2003; v.p. new product devel. Levolor Kirsch, High Point, NC, 2003—. Provider expert testimony before Congress, 1994, commencement address, Kansas City Art Inst., 1995; sr. tech. advisor to Peoples Republic of China, UN, 1998. Contbr. chpts. to books, articles to profl. jours.; presenter in field; holder 5 patents, 1 trademark. Recipient Project of Merit award Indsl. Design Mag., 1985, Cert. of Achievement, ARC, 1988, Louis B. Tiffany award ARC, 1987, numerous others; Nat. Endowment for the Arts grantee, 1984, 92, 94; EPA grantee, 1992. Mem. Indsl. Designers Soc. Am. (Personal Recognition award 2000). Avocations: edison antiquities collecting, sailing. Office: Levolor Kirsch 4110 Premier Dr High Point NC 27265 E-mail: designo@att.net.

SCHWARTZ, ROBERT WILLIAM, management consultant; b. N.Y.C., Oct. 23, 1944; s. Edward and Bertha R. S.; m. Gail Beth Greenbaum, Mar. 18, 1967; children: Jill, Evan. BS, Cornell U., 1967; postgrad., SUNY, Albany, 1970. Assoc. IBM, 1967-68; cons. Peat, Marwick, Mitchell & Co., Albany, 1970-71; v.p. Security Gen. Svcs., Inc., Rochester, N.Y., 1971-73; v.p. fin. and adminstrn. Gardenway Mfg. Co., Troy, N.Y., 1973-77; exec. v.p. United Telecommunications Corp., Latham, N.Y., 1977-79, pres., 1980-82, also bd. dir.; pres., chmn. Winsource, Inc., Albany, 1982-85, Schwartz Heslin Group, Inc., 1985—. Bd. dirs. Docucon, Inc., San Antonio, State Zone Capital Corp., Albany, NY, State Industries for Disabled, Donnkenny, NY; adj. prof. Rochester Inst. Tech., 1971—73, U. Albany, SUNY Albany, 1998—, Union U., 2002—. Bd. dirs. United Cerebral Palsy of Capital Dist., 1973—; trustee Newman Found., Rensselaer Poly. Inst., 1974-78, Gov. Clinton coun. Boy Scouts Am., SUNY Found. Mem. Am. Mgmt. Assn., Esarco Internat., N.Am. Tel. Assn., Assn. for Systems Mgmt., Ft. Orange Club, Econ. Club, Corenell Club (N.Y.C.). Republican. Home: 2 Myton Ln Albany NY 12204-1310 Office: 8 Airport Park Blvd Latham NY 12110-1441

SCHWARTZ, SAMUEL, retired chemical company executive, business consultant; b. Moose Jaw, Sask., Can., Nov. 12, 1927; came to U.S., 1951, naturalized, 1965; s. Benjamin and Rose (Becker) S.; m. Margaret Patterson, Feb. 20, 1956; children: Michael R., Thomas R., David C., Janet C. BA, U. Sask., 1948, B in Commerce, 1950; MBA, Harvard U., 1953. Research assoc. Harvard Bus. Sch., Boston, 1953-57; with Conoco Inc., 1957-83, sr. v.p. coordinating and planning, 1974-75, sr. v.p. corp. planning, 1975-78, sr. v.p. adminstrv., 1978-80, group sr. v.p. adminstrv., 1980-83; sr. v.p. adminstrv. E.I. duPont de Nemours & Co., Wilmington, Del., 1983-87, sr. v.p., corp. plans dept., 1987-88. Dir. Conoco Inc. Consol. Coal Co., 1981-88. Trustee Inst. for the Future, Menlo Park, Calif., 1975-92, Henry du Pont Winterthur Mus., Winterthur, Del., trustee, 1984—, chmn., 1994-97. Personal E-mail: samnmarg@aol.com.

SCHWARTZ, SANDY, publishing executive; Exec. v.p., gen. mgr. The Austin Am.-Statesman Cox Newspapers, Inc., 1996—2000; v.p. & gen. mgr. Atlanta Journal-Constitution, 2001—. Office: Atl Journ-Const PO Box 4689 Atlanta GA 30302

SCHWARTZ, SEYMOUR IRA, surgeon, educator; b. N.Y.C., Jan. 22, 1928; s. Samuel and Martha (Paul) S.; m. Ruth Elaine Wainer, June 18, 1949; children: Richard, Kenneth, David. BA, U. Wis., 1947; MD, NYU, 1950; PhD (hon.) (hon.), U. Lund, Sweden, 1989; PhD, U. Madrid, 1997. Intern Strong Meml. Hosp., Rochester, NY, 1950—51, resident, 1951—52; asst. prof. surgery U. Rochester, NY, 1959—63, assoc. prof, 1963—67, prof., 1967—, chmn. dept., 1987—98, dir. surg. rsch., 1962—82; resident Strong Meml. Hosp., Rochester, NY, 1954—57. Nat. cons. USAF, 1968—77; mem. surgery study sect. A NIH, 1974—78. Co-author: Mapping of America, 1980, Surgical Reflections, 1991; author: Mapping of the French and Indian War, 1994; co-editor: Maingot's Abdominal Operations, 2 edits.; editor-in-chief: Year Book of Surgery, 6 edits., 1969—. Lt. (j.g.) USN, 1952—54. Recipient Sesquicentennial medal, U. S.C., 1974, Acrel medal, Swedish Surg. Assn., 1974, Yandell medal, U. Louisville (Ky.), 1978, Roswell Park medal, 1989, Albert Kaiser medal, 1992; scholar John and Mary R. Markle scholar in acad. medicine, 1960. Fellow: ACS (regent 1988, chmn. bd. regents 1994—97, pres. 1997—98, programs and ethics com. 1989—), Am. Antiquarian Soc., Am. Bd. Surgery (vice chair), Am. Surg. Assn. (pres. 1993—94), Soc. Univ. Surgeons, Royal Coll. Surgeons, So. Surg. Soc., Soc. Clin. Surgery (pres. 1985), Genesee Valley Club, Cosmos Club (Washington), Grolier Club (N.Y.C.), Alpha Omega Alpha, Phi Beta Kappa; mem.: Ctrl. Surg. Soc. (pres. 1981—82). Avocation: collecting antique maps. Office: U Rochester Med Ctr 601 Elmwood Ave Rochester NY 14642-0001

SCHWARTZ, SHARON J. state representative; b. Waterville, Kans., Mar. 14, 1940; m. Leo Schwartz; children: Douglas, Cheri. Bus. mgr. Pork Chop Acres, Inc., 1983—; mem. Kans. Ho. of Reps., 1996—. Mem.: Washington Kans. C. of C., Nat. Pork Bd., Kans. Pork Prodrs. Republican. Roman Catholic. Office: 110-S State Capitol 300 SW 10th Ave Topeka KS 66612 Address: 2051 20th Rd Washington KS 66968-2419

SCHWARTZ, SHIRLEY E. chemist, researcher; b. Detroit, Aug. 26, 1935; d. Emil Victor and Jessie Grace (Galbraith) Eckwall; m. Ronald Elmer Schwartz, Aug. 25, 1957; children: Steven Dennis, Bradley Allen, George Byron. BS, U. Mich., 1957, Detroit Inst. Tech., 1978; MS, Wayne State U., 1962, PhD, 1970. Asst. prof. Detroit Inst. Tech., 1973-78, head divsn. math. sci., 1976-78; mem. rsch. staff BASF Wyandotte (Mich.) Corp., 1978-81, head sect. functional fluids, 1981; sr. staff rsch. scientist GM Rsch., Warren, Mich., 1981-99; materials engr. GM Powertrain, 1999—2003. Contbr. articles to profl. jours.; patentee in field. Recipient Gold award Engring. Soc. Detroit, 1989, Life Achievement award Soc. Women Engrs., 1999; inducted U.S. Nat. Acad. of Engring., 2000. Fellow Soc. Automotive Engrs. (Excellence in Oral Presentation award 1986, 91, 94, Arch T. Colwell Merit award 1991, Lloyd L. Withrow Disting. Spkr. award 1995), Soc. Tribologists and Lubrication Engrs. (treas. Detroit sect. 1981, vice chmn. 1982, chmn. 1982-83, chmn. wear tech. com. 1987-88, bd. dirs. 1985-91, assoc. editor 1989-90, contbg. editor 1989—2003, Wilbur Deutsch award 1987, P.M. Ku award 1994), Soc. Automotive Engrs.; mem. Soc. Tribologists and Lubrication Engrs., Am. Chem. Soc., Soc. In Vitro Biology, Mich. Women's Hall of Fame (lifetime achievement award 1996), Women of Wayne (headliners award 2000), U.S. Nat. Acad. Engring., Mensa, Classic Guitar Soc. Mich., U.S. Power Squadrons, Detroit Navigators, Sigma Xi. Lutheran. *I've spent a number of very pleasant hours trying to make water behave like oil and alcohol behave like gasoline—a quest not much different from that of the ancient alchemists, who also spent their time trying to convert one substance to another.*

SCHWARTZ, STEPHAN ANDREW, entrepreneur, writer; b. Cin., Jan. 10, 1942; s. Abraham Leon and Bertha Culbertson (Watson) S.; m. Katherine Rowland, Jan. 6, 1965 (div. 1979); 1 child, Catherine Rowland; m. Hayden Oliver Gates, July 10, 1982; 1 stepchild, Lea Daniel Meyers. Student, U. Va. Founder, chmn., rsch. dir. The Mobius Soc., L.A., 1977—; pres. S. A. Schwartz & Assocs., L.A., 1992—. Gen. ptnr. V-Partners, Inc.; chmn. Clearlight TV Prodns., L.A.; former vis. prof. John F. Kennedy U.; adv. bd. PHOENIX: New Directions in the Study of Man; sr. fellow Philos. Rsch. Soc.; cons. to oceanographer USN; spl. asst. rsch. and analysis Chief Naval Ops.; co-inventor ThighMaster; mem. bd. advisors Global Inst. Network N. Inst., Aura Comms. Sys., Inc.; cons. in field. Editor: Seapower Magazine; author: The Secret Vaults of Time, 1978, The Alexandria Project, 1980, 1983, Psychic Detectives, 1987; author: (with others) Stories From Omni, 1984; contbr. over 47 publications to profl. jours.; screenwriter spl. presentations and documentaries. Bd. dirs. World Children's Transplant Found., 1992—. Fellow Royal Geog. Soc.; mem. Internat. Soc. for Subtle Energies and Energy Medicine (bd. dirs., editor Subtle Energies Jour.,), Soc. for the Anthropology of Consciousness (past pres., founding mem.), Soc. for Hist. Archaeology, Calif.-Russia Trade Assn. (bd. dirs.), Explorer's club. N.Y. Avocations: reading, scuba diving, canoeing, sailing, hiking. Home: 9899 Santa Monica Blvd # 444 Beverly Hills CA 90212-1672 also: 4470 W Sunset Blvd Ste 339 Los Angeles CA 90027-6305

SCHWARTZ, STEPHEN BLAIR, retired information industry executive; b. Chgo., Oct. 19, 1934; s. Herbert S. and Gertrude Schwartz; m. Nancy Jean Astrof, Dec. 18, 1955; children: Debra Lee Schwartz Zaret, Susan Beth Schwartz Derene. BS in Indsl. Engring., Northwestern U., 1957. With IBM Corp., 1957-92; various mgmt. positions, dir. product programs Harrison, N.Y., to 1977; v.p. Systems Communications div., 1977-81; v.p. Armonk, N.Y., 1982-90; v.p. Am. Far East Corp. subs. IBM Corp. Tokyo, 1982-84; pres., CEO Satellite Bus. Systems, McLean, Va., 1984; v.p., asst. group exec. Telecommunications, 1985-86; v.p., pres. Systems Products Div., 1986-88; v.p., gen. mgr. Application Bus. Systems, 1988-90; sr. v.p. market driven quality, 1990-92. Bd. dirs. MFRI, Inc. Mem.: PGA Nat. Golf Club (Palm Beach Gardens, Fla.). Republican. Jewish.

SCHWARTZ, STEPHEN LAWRENCE, composer, lyricist; b. NYC, Mar. 6, 1948; s. Stanley Leonard and Sheila Lorna (Siegel) Schwartz; m. Carole Ann Piasecki, June 6, 1969; children: Scott Lawrence, Jessica Lauren. Student, Juilliard Sch. Music, 1960—64; BFA, Carnegie-Mellon U., 1968. Works include title song for Butterflies Are Free, 1969, (theatre) music and lyrics Godspell, 1971, Pippin, 1972, The Magic Show, 1974, The Baker's Wife, 1976, Children of Eden, 1991, Wicked, 2003, four songs, adaptation and direction Working, 1978, music for 3 songs Personals, 1985, (with Leonard Bernstein's) English texts for Leonard Bernstein's Mass, 1971, lyrics Rags, 1986, (films) lyrics Pocahontas, 1995 (Acad. award best original score, 1996, Acad. award best original song, 1996), The Hunchback of Notre Dame, 1996,

(music and lyrics) The Prince of Egypt, 1998 (Acad. award best original song, 1999), (TV, music and lyrics) Geppetto, 2000, (juvenile) The Perfect Peach, 1977, Captain Louie, 1983, (recording) Reluctant Pilgrim, 1997, Uncharted Territory, 2001. Recipient Drama Desk awards, 1971, 1978, 2004, Grammy awards, 1971, 1996, Golden Globe award, 1996. Mem.: ASCAP, Am. Motion Picture Arts Soc., Dramatists Guild (coun.).

SCHWARTZ, STEVE WENDELIN, physician; b. Bethesda, Md., May 16, 1955; s. Wallace John and Gwynne June (Lingenfelter) S. AB in Chemistry summa cum laude, Duke U., 1977, MD, 1981. Diplomate Am. Bd. Family Practice. Rotating intern Med. U. S.C., Charleston, 1981-82, resident in family practice, 1982-84; emergency rm. physician Coastal Emergency Svc., 1985-86; family physician Carolina Health Care, Myrtle Beach, S.C., 1984—; CEO Cactus Internat., Inc. Data processing dir. HMI, 1984—; pres. Unitrerds Software Corp., 1989—; rschr. Symbol Theory; programmer langs. Columnist SCO World Mag.; contbr. articles to profl. jours. Del. ann. meeting N.C. Med. Soc., 1980; participant Intramural Soccer, 1977-80; mem. Intramural Track, 1980, Blacknall Meml. Presbyn. Ch., 1977-80; coord. Boy Scouts Phys. Exam. Program, 1983; vol. cmty. health care project for poor East End Cmty. Health Ctr.; tchr. seminars on alcoholism for drug edn. project Holistic Medicine Group, 1980; Bible study coord. Valley of Achor. With USAF. 1973-75. First Place Durham Open Chess Tournament, 1974; recipient Grand Strand Leadership, 1986. Fellow Am. Acad. Family Physicians; mem. AMA (Physicians Recognition award 1986), So. Med. Assn., Horry County Med. Soc., Phi Beta Kappa, Upsilon Pi Epsilon. Avocations: chess, soccer. Home: 100 Lands End Blvd Apt 310 Myrtle Beach SC 29572-7005 Office: Carolina Health Care 4605 Hwy 17 Byp S Myrtle Beach SC 29577 6681

SCHWARTZ, STEVEN MARK, marketing executive; b. Phila., Feb. 26, 1948; s. Edward and Erika (Schneier) S.; m. Paula Mae Levine, May 15, 1979; 1 child, Roger. AB magna cum laude, Bowdoin Coll., 1970; MFA in Writing, Columbia U., 1973. Writer, account exec. Schneider & Rich Assocs., N.Y.C., 1973-76; sr. account exec. Richard Weiner Inc., N.Y.C., 1976-78; account supr., v.p. The Rowland Co., N.Y.C., 1978-79; project mgr. exec. comm. GE, Fairfield, Conn., 1979-83, mgr. exec. comm., 1983-84; v.p. corp. comm. Interleaf Inc., Cambridge, Mass., 1984-86, v.p. mktg. programs and comm., 1986-88, v.p. mktg., 1989 90; pres. Schwartz Comm. Inc., Waltham, Mass., 1990—, Trustee Bowdoin Coll. Mem. Appalachian Mountain Club (bd. dirs.), Am. Alpine Club (bd. dirs.), Phi Beta Kappa, Theta Delta Chi. Republican. Avocations: kayaking, climbing. Office: Schwartz Comm Inc 230 3rd Ave Waltham MA 02451-7528

SCHWARTZ, STUART R. psychiatrist; MD, SUNY Downstate Med. Ctr., Bklyn., N.Y., 1960. Diplomate Am. Bd. Psychiatry and Neurology, 1971. Intern in Psychiatry Mount Zion Hosp., San Francisco, 1960—61; resident in Psychiatry U. Calif., San Francisco, 1963—65; fellow in Psychiatry Mount Zion Hosp., San Francisco, 1965—66; pahysician dept. Psychiatry Robert Wood Johnson U. Med. Group, Piscataway, NJ, 1967—. Prof. psychiatry Robert Wood Johnson Med. U., Piscataway, NJ, 1967—. Office: Robert Wood Johnson U Med Grp 671 Hoes Ln Piscataway NJ 08854

SCHWARTZ, THEODORE A. investment company executive; Chmn., CEO Berger Holdings, Ltd., Feasterville, Pa., 1994—. Office: Berger Holdings Ltd 805 Pennsylvania Blvd Feasterville Trevose PA 19053-7813

SCHWARTZ, VICTOR ELLIOT, lawyer, educator; b. N.Y.C., July 3, 1940; AB summa cum laude, Boston U., 1962; JD magna cum laude, Columbia U., 1965. Bar: N.Y. 1965, Ohio 1974. Law clk. to judge So. Dist. N.Y., 1965-67; from asst. to assoc. prof. law U. Cin., 1967-72, prof., 1972-79, acting dean, 1973-74; vis. prof. U. Va. Law Sch., 1970-71; dist. vis. scholar U. Cin., 2002—; ptnr. firm Crowell & Moring, Washington, 1980—2001; sr. ptnr. firm Fed. Interagy. task Force on Products Liability, 1976; ptnr., chair firm's pub. policy group Shook Hardy & Bacon, Washington, 2001—. Bd. visitors U. Cin. Sch., 1998—; disting. vis. scholar U. Cin., 2003—; gen. counsel, bd. dirs. Am. Tort Reform Assn.; chmn. Civil Justice Task Force, Am. Legis. Exch. Coun.; chmn. Dept. of Commerce Task Force on Product Liability and Accident Compensation, 1977-80. Author: Comparative Negligence, 1974, 4th edit., 2002; (with Prosser and Wade) Cases and Materials on Torts, 1976, 10th edit., 2000, How to Prepare for the Multi-State Bar Examination, 1977, Products Liability: Cases and Trends, 1987, Products Liability: Asset Trends, 1988, (with Lee and Kelly) Multistate Legislation, 1985; editor: Columbia Law Rev., 1965; prin. draftsman: Model Uniform Product Liability Act. Recipient Sec. of Commerce award for disting. svc., Burton award for best law rev. writing in U.S., Tort Summit award, Am. Tort Reform Assn., 2002; named One of 100 Most Influential Attys. in U.S., Nat. Law 3, 1994, 97, Pvt. Sector Person of Yr., Am. Legis. Exch. Coun., 2003. Mem. ABA (chmn. products liability com. 1979, uniform laws com. 1981, torts and ins. practice sect.), Am. Law Inst. (life, adv. com. Restatement Third of Torts), Phi Beta Kappa. Office: Shook Hardy & Bacon LLP 600 14th St NW Ste 800 Washington DC 20005-2004 Office Phone: 202-662-4880. *The greatest joys in life are found in one's relationships, be it business, romance or friendship, with other people.*

SCHWARTZ, WALTER RICHARD, obstetrician/gynecologist, retired; b. Lancaster, Wis., Jan. 2, 1931; MD, U. Wis., 1955. Diplomate Am. Bd. Ob/gyn. Intern St. Josephs Hosp., Marshfield, 1955-56; resident in ob/gyn. Milw. County Hosp., 1958-61; staff West Allis Hosp., Wis., 1961—, Sinai Samaritan Hosp., 1961—, Elmbrook Meml. Hsop., 1971—; assoc. clin. prof. ob/gyn. Med. Coll. Wis., 1976—. Fellow Am. Coll. Obstetricians/Gynecologists, Am. Coll. Surgeons; mem. AMA, ACOG, Ctrl. Assn. Obstetricians and Gynecologists.

SCHWARTZ, WILLIAM, lawyer, educator; b. Providence, May 6, 1933; s. Morris Victor and Martha (Glassman) S.; m. Bernice Konigsberg, Jan. 13, 1957; children: Alan Gershon, Robin Libby. AA, Boston U., 1952, JD magna cum laude, 1955, MA, 1960; postgrad., Harvard Law Sch., 1955-56; LHD (hon.), Hebrew Coll., 1996, Yeshiva U., 1998. Bar: D.C. 1956, Mass. 1962, N.Y. 1989. Prof. law Boston U., 1955-91, Fletcher prof. law, 1968-70, Roscoe Pound prof. law, 1970-73, dean Sch. of Law, 1980-88, dir. Ctr. for Estate Planning, 1988-91; univ. prof. Yeshiva U., N.Y.C., 1991—; of counsel Swartz & Swartz, 1973-80; v.p. for acad. affairs, chief acad. officer Yeshiva U., N.Y.C., 1993-98; counsel Cadwalader, Wickersham and Taft, N.Y.C., Washington, Charlotte, London, 1988—; mem. faculty Frances Glessner Lee Inst., Harvard Med. Sch., Nat. Coll. Probate Judges, 1970, 77, 78, 79, 88; gen. dir. Assn. Trial Lawyers Am., 1968-73; reporter New Eng. Trial Judges Conf., 1965-67; participant Nat. Met. Cts. Conf., 1968; dir. Mass. Probate Study, 1976—; chmn. spl. com. on police procedures City of Boston, 1989, 91. Bd. dirs., chmn. UST Corp., 1993—94, chmn. bd. dirs., 1996—2000; bd. dirs. Viacom Inc., Viacom Internat., Inc., chmn., nominating com., mem. governance com., mem. compensation com.; mem. com adv. com. WCI Street, Inc.; mem. legal adv. bd. N.Y. Stock Exch. Author: Future Interests and Estate Planning, 1965, 77, 81, 86, Comparative Negligence, 1970, A Products Liability Primer, 1970, Civil Trial Practice Manual, 1972, New Vistas in Litigation, 1973, Massachusetts Pleading and Practice, 7 vols., 1974-80, Estate Planning and Living Trusts, 1990, The Convention Method: The Unused Amending Superhighway, 1995, Jewish Law and Contemporary Dilemmas and Problems, 1997, Does Time Heal All Wrongs?, 1999, Amending Irrevocable Trusts, 2003, others; note editor: Boston U. Law Rev., 1954-55; property editor: Annual Survey of Mass. Law, 1960—; contbr. articles to legal jours. Rep. Office of Pub. Info., UN, 1968—73; chmn. legal adv. panel Nat. Commn. Med. Practice, 1972—73; examiner of titles Commonwealth of Mass., 1964—; spl. counsel Mass. Bay Transp. Authority, 1979; pres. Fifth Ave. Synagogue, N.Y.C., 1997—2001, hon. pres., 2001—; trustee Hebrew Coll., 1975—, Salve Regina U., Yeshiva U. Recipient Homer Albers award Boston U., 1955, John Ordronaux prize, 1955; Disting. Service award Religious Zionists Am., 1977; William W. Treat award; William O. Douglas award. Fellow Am. Coll. Probate Counsel; mem. ABA, Am. Law Inst., Mass. Bar Assn. (chmn. task force tort liability), N.Y. State Bar Assn., Assn. Bar City N.Y., Nat. Coll. Probate Judges (hon. mem.), Phi Beta Kappa. Office: 100 Maiden Ln New York NY 10038-4818 Office Phone: 212-504-6399. *I have been guided by the maxim: "Ideals are like stars. You cannot touch them with your hands, but like the seafaring man, if you choose them as your guide and follow them, you will reach your destiny.".*

SCHWARTZ, WILLIAM BENJAMIN, internist, educator; b. Montgomery, Ala., May 16, 1922; s. William Benjamin and Molly (Vendruff) S.; children: Eric A., Kenneth B., Laurie A. MD, Duke U., 1945. Diplomate: Am. Bd. Internal Medicine (mem. test com. nephrology). Intern, then asst. resident medicine U. Chgo. Clinics, 1945-46; asst. medicine Peter Bent Brigham Hosp., Boston; also research fellow medicine Harvard Med. Sch., 1948-50; fellow medicine Children's Hosp., Boston, 1949-50; mem. faculty Tufts U. Sch. Medicine, 1950-96, prof. medicine, 1958-96, Endicott prof., 1975-76, Vannevar Bush Univ. prof., 1976-96, chmn. dept. medicine, 1971-76; mem. staff New Eng. Center Hosps., 1950-59, sr. physician, chief renal service, 1959-71, physician-in-chief, 1971-76; prof. medicine U. So. Calif., L.A., 1992—; disting. physician Dept. VA, 1994-97. Established investigator Am. Heart Assn., 1956-61; chmn. gen. medicine study sect. NIH, 1965-69; mem. sci. adv. bd. USAF, 1965-68, Nat. Kidney Found., 1968—, chmn., 1970—; mem. tng. com. Nat. Heart Inst., 1969-70; prin. adviser health scis. program, Rand Corp., 1977-88. Author numerous articles in field. Markle scholar med. scis., 1950-55 Mem. Inst. Medicine NAS, Am. Soc. Nephrology (pres. 1974-75), Acad. Arts and Scis., ACP, Am. Fedn. Clin. Research, Am. Physiol. Soc., Am. Soc. Clin. Investigation, Assn. Am. Physicians, Phi Beta Kappa, Sigma Xi, Alpha Omega Alpha. Office: 1355 San Pablo St Ste 144 Los Angeles CA 90089-0111

SCHWARTZ, WILLIAM LEWIS, retired veterinary pathologist; b. Columbus, Ohio, Dec. 11, 1931; s. Lewis Glenn and Mildred Opal (Basinger) S.; m. Barbara Ann Custer, June 21, 1953; children: Kimberly Ann Schwartz Barbour, Kay Annette Schwartz Carrabba. BSc, Ohio State U., 1953, DVM, 1957; MS, Tex. A&M U., 1970. Vet. practitioner in pvt. practice, Lancaster, Ohio, 1957-60; regulatory veterinarian Ohio Dept. Agr., Lancaster, Ohio, 1960-63, lab. diagnostician Reynoldsburg, Ohio, 1963-64; asst. prof. Ga. Coastal Plain Expt. Sta., Tifton, 1964-67; asst. prof. vet. pathology Coll. of Vet. Med., Tex. A&M U., College Station, 1967-70; vet. pathologist Tex. Vet. Med. Diagnostic Lab., College Station, 1970-99. Contbr. over 90 articles to profl. jours. Mem. AVMA, Tex. Vet. Med. Assn., Am. Assn. Vet. Lab. Diagnosticians, Ohio State Vet. Alumni Assn., Lions (pres. 1989-90), Phi Zeta, Sigma Xi. Lutheran.

SCHWARTZBERG, ALLAN ZELIG, psychiatrist, educator; b. Cleve., Dec. 5, 1930; s. Joseph and Jeanette (Eisenman) S.; m. Katherine Weiss, June 19, 1955; children: Shana, Robert. BS cum laude, Case Western Res. U., 1951; MD, Ohio State U., 1955. Diplomate Am. Bd. Psychiatry and Neurology, Am. Bd. Forensic Medicine. Intern, resident in psychiatry Johns Hopkins Hosp., Balt., 1955—59; pvt. practice Gaithersburg, Md.; assoc. clin. prof. psychiatry Georgetown U. Sch. Medicine, Washington, 1979—89, clin. prof., 1989—. Vis. prof. faculty seminar in cmty. psychiatry Harvard U. Med. Sch., Boston, 1965-67; cons. Dept. Energy, 2002-. Editor-in-chief Internat. Annals Adolescent Psychiatry, 1988—2000; co-editor Adolescent Psychiatry, Vols. 8-19; contbr. articles to med. jours. Recipient Vicennial medal Georgetown U., 1984. Fellow Am. Psychiat. Assn. (disting. life), Am. Soc. for Adolescent Psychiatry, Am. Soc. Psychoanalytic Physicians (pres. 1986-87, 2000-01), Am. Coll. Psychiatrists; mem. AMA, Am. Group Psychotherapy Assn., B'nai B'rith, Phi Beta Kappa. Republican. Jewish. Home: 6616 Kenhill Rd Bethesda MD 20817-6014 Office: Comprehensive Behavioral Svcs 9021 Shady Grove Ct Gaithersburg MD 20877-1308 Office Phone: 301-590-9000. E-mail: azsmd@aol.com.

SCHWARTZBERG, GIL N. apparel executive, lawyer; b. N.Y.C., Oct. 30, 1942; s. Julian and Juliet Schwartzberg; m. Debra Austin Sterling, May 2, 1971; children: David, Julie. BS, NYU, 1964; BSL, Glendale Coll. Law, 1974; JD, Valley U., 1976. Asst. v.p. Mfrs. Bank, L.A., 1964-69; v.p. Bri-Son Industries, L.A., 1969-72; pres. Capital Res. Devel., L.A., 1972-75; sr. v.p. Surety Nat. Bank, L.A., 1975-77; ptnr. Leeds, Schubert & Schwartzberg, Beverly Hills, Calif., 1977-89; vice chmn. L.A. Gear Inc., 1989—. Bd. dirs., chmn. of loan com. Sterling Bancorp., L.A., 1977—. Bd. Dirs. City of Hope, L.A., 1985—, Beekman Rsch. Inst., 1990—; trustee The Buckley Sch., L.A., 1990—. Office: L A Gear Inc 4221 Redwood Ave Los Angeles CA 90066-5605

SCHWARTZBERG, JOSEPH EMANUEL, b. Bklyn., Feb. 5, 1928; s. Philip and Frances (Lefkowitz) S. m. Monique Elisabeth Ribaux, Dec. 19, 1963 (div. Oct. 1998); children: Philip, Paul. BA, Bklyn. Coll., 1949; MA, U. Md., 1951; PhD, U. Wis., 1960. Geographer U.S. Army Map Svc., Brookmont, Md., 1949-51; soldier U.S. Army, Heidelberg, Germany, 1951-53; asst. prof. geography and South Asian studies U. Pa., Phila., 1960-64; assoc. prof. U. Minn., Mpls., 1964-70, prof., 1970—2001. Vis. prof. Jawaharlal Nehru U., New Delhi, India, 1979-80. Author: Occupational Structure and Level of Economic Development in India: A Regional Analysis, 1960; co-author, editor: A Historical Atlas of South Asia, 1978, 92, The History of Cartography, Vol. 2, Books 1 and 2, 1992, 94, Revitalizing the United Nations: Reform through Weighted Voting, 2004. Pres. Minn. chpt. World Federalist Assn. (now Citizens for Global Solutions), 1976-79, 96-99, 2002—, nat. bd. dirs., 1996—. Mem. Assn. Am. Geographers, Assn. Asian Studies, Am. Geographic Soc., Acad. Coun UN Sys., Amnesty Internat., Minn. Alliance of Peacemakers. Home: 5492 Bald Eagle Blvd E White Bear Lake MN 55110-1100 Office: U Minn Dept Geography Minneapolis MN 55455 E-mail: schwa004@umn.edu.

SCHWARTZEL, CHARLES BOONE, lawyer; b. Louisville, Jan. 4, 1950; s. Charles Joseph and Rosemary Jane (Redens) S.; m. Rose Marie Carlisi, June 20, 1980; children: Sally Ann, Charles Gerard. BA, Vanderbilt U., 1972; JD, U. Tex., 1975. Bar: Tex. 1975. Atty. Vinson & Elkins L.L.P., Houston, 1975-98, ptnr., 1983-98; pvt. practice Houston, 1998—. Contbr. articles to profl. jours. Councilman City of West University Place, Tex., 1985-89. Fellow Am. Coll. Trust and Estate Counsel; mem. Tex. Bar Assn. Roman Catholic. Office: Attorney at Law 1010 Lamar St Ste 1520 Houston TX 77002-6315 Office Phone: 713-654-1133.

SCHWARTZHOFF, JAMES PAUL, foundation executive; b. Waukon, Iowa, June 24, 1937; s. Harold J. and Mary (Regan) Schwartzhoff; m. Mary Lou Hess, Apr. 23, 1960; children: Tammara, Eric, Stephanie, Mark, Laurie, Michelle, Steven. B, U. Iowa, 1962. Asst. chief auditor Wis. Dept. Tax, Madison, 1962-67; mgr. treas. dept. Mead Johnson and Co., Evansville, Ind., 1967-69; v.p., treas., investment officer Kettering Found., Dayton, Ohio, 1969—. Chmn., treas. bd. Pastoral Counseling Ctr., Dayton, 1975-81; treas. Ohio River Rd. Runners, Dayton, 1986-87; spkr. nat. investment confs. Past treas. Nat. Issues Forums Inst., Coun. Pub. Policy Edn., Ctr. for Cmty. and Ednl. Devel.; mem. Donor's Forum Ohio Fin. Com., 1990-92; mem. investment com. U. Dayton; adv. com. JMB Endowment and Found. Realty Funds, 1991-94; advisor to investment com. Fetzer Inst. Cpl. U.S. Army, 1957-59. Mem. AICPA, Found. Fin. Officers Group, Southern Ohio Pension Fund Group. Avocations: bicycling, running, photography, woodworking, skiing. Office: Kettering Found 200 Commons Rd Dayton OH 45459-2799

SCHWARTZMAN, ANDREW JAY, lawyer; b. N.Y.C., Oct. 4, 1946; s. Joel Jay and Theresa (Greenhauff) S.; m. Linda Lazarus, June 8, 1986. AB, U. Pa., 1968, JD, 1971. Bar: N.Y. 1972, D.C. 1974, Temporary Emergency Ct. Appeals 1977, U.S. Dist. Ct. D.C. 1978, U.S. Ct. Appeals (D.C. cir.) 1981, U.S. Ct. Appeals (2d cir.) 1987, U.S. Ct. Appeals (3rd, 4th, 7th, 8th, 9th cirs.) 1991, U.S. Supreme Ct. 1980. Staff counsel United Ch. of Christ Office of Comm., N.Y.C., 1971-74; atty. adviser Fed. Energy Office, Washington, 1974-77; sr. atty. adviser U.S. Dept. Energy, Washington, 1977-78; bd. dirs. Safe Energy Comms. Coun., pres. bd. dirs., 1989—2003; dir. Media Access Project, Washington, 1978-96, pres., CEO, 1996—. Mem. adv. panel Study on Comms. Systems for an Info. Age; mem. adv. bd. Ctr. for Democracy and Tech., 1996—; lectr. Fairleigh Dickinson U., 1972-73; instr. Johns Hopkins U., 2003—; mem. comms. coun. forum Aspen Inst. on Comms. and Soc., 1992—; bd. dirs. Min. Media and Telecomms. Coalition, 1994—; mem. adv. bd. Nat. Inst. Entertainment and Media Law, Southwestern U. Sch. Law, 2000—, dist. lectr. in residence Southwestern U. Sch. Law Summer Entertainment and Media Law Program, Fitzwilliam Coll., Cambridge U., 2004. Contbg. author: Les Brown's Dictionary of Television, 3d edit., Ency. of the Consumer Movement, 1997; contbr. articles to legal jours. Recipient Everett Parker award United Ch. of Christ, 1994, Just Media Lifetime Achiev. award, 2004. Mem. ABA, Fed. Comms. Bar Assn., U. Pa. Alumni Assn. Office: Media Access Project # 1000 1625 K St NW Washington DC 20006-1604 Office Phone: 202-232-4300. E-mail: info@mediaaccess.org.

SCHWARTZTOL, HOLLY WECHSLER, psychologist; b. Washington, Dec. 20, 1946; d. James Arthur and Nancy (Fraenkel) Wechsler; m. Robert Ira Schwartztol, Nov. 16, 1975; children: Laurence, Andrew. BA, Finch Coll., 1968; MA, C. W. Post Coll., 1971; PhD, U. Miami, 1981. Instr. psychology C. W. Post Coll., Greenvale, N.Y., 1971; tchr. Yorktown High Sch., Yorktown Heights, N.Y., 1971-73; sch. psychologist Dade County Schs., Miami, Fla., 1973-84; pvt. practice holistic psychology Miami, 1983—; Reiki master, trainer radiant heart therapy. Adj. asst. prof. counseling psychology U. Miami, 1984-85; co-founder, co-dir. Miami Inst. Clin. Hypnosis, 1986-93; co-founder, dir. Miami Inst. Expanding Light, 1993-96. Author: (with James A. and Nancy F. Wechsler) In a Darkness, 1972, 2d edit., 1988. Reiki master, trainer and practitioner of radiant heart therapy. Mem. Dade County Psychol. Assn. (pres. 1988), Fla. Psychol. Assn., Am. Psychol. Assn., Am. Soc. Clin. Hypnosis (bd. dirs. 1998-99, pres.-elect 1999-2000, pres. 1999—), South Fla. Soc. for the Study Multiple Personality and Dissociative Disorders (bd. dirs. 1989, pres. 1991). Office: 806 S Douglas Rd Ste 560 Coral Gables FL 33134-3157

SCHWARY, RONALD LOUIS, motion picture producer; b. The Dalles, Oreg., May 23, 1944; s. Mitchell Louis and Lorraine (Ablan) S.; children: Brian L., Neil L. BS, U. So. Calif., 1967. Pres. Red Truck Prodns., Inc., L.A., 1985—. Prodr. (motion pictures) Ordinary People, 1980 (Golden Globe award 1981, Acad. award 1981), Absence of Malice, 1981, Tootsie, 1982, A Soldier's Story, 1984, Batteries Not Included, 1987, Havana, 1990, Scent of a Woman, 1992, Cops and Robbersons, 1994, Sabrina, 1995, Mirror Has Two Faces, 1996, Meet Joe Black, 1997, Random Hearts, 1999; (TV series) Tour of Duty, 1987, Now and Again, 1999, Medium, 2004. Mem. Dirs. Guild Am. Republican. Roman Catholic.

SCHWARZ, BERTHOLD ERIC, psychiatrist; b. Jersey City, Oct. 20, 1924; s. Berthold Theodore Dominick and I. Thyra W. (Ericson) Schwarz; m. Ardis Marilyn Peterson, Jan. 22, 1955; children: Lisa Thyra, Eric Rolf. AB, Dartmouth Coll., 1945; MD, NYU, 1950; MS, Mayo Grad. Sch. Medicine, 1957. Intern Mary Hitchcock Meml. Hosp., Hanover, N.H., 1950-51; psychiatrist, researcher pvt. practice, Montclair, N.J., 1955-82; Mayo Found., Rochester, Minn., 1951-55; psychiatrist, researcher pvt. practice, Vero Beach, Fla., 1982—. Cons. Essex County Hosp. Ctr., Cedar Grove, N.J., 1965-82, Med. Correctional Assn., Ossining, N.Y., 1960-72; exec. dir. Internat. Psychosomatics Inst., Mountain Lakes, N.J., 1995—. Contbr. articles to med. jours. With USNR, 1943-45. Fellow AAAS, Am. Psychiat. Assn., Am. Soc. Psychical Rsch., Am. Geriatric Soc. Republican. Avocations: ufos, paranormal aspects, swimming, walking. Home: 1070 Reef Rd Apt 305 Vero Beach FL 32963-4342 Office: 642 Azalea Ln Vero Beach FL 32963-1832 Office Phone: 772-231-5220. Personal E-mail: ardisps@aol.com.

SCHWARZ, DANIEL ROGER, English and American literature educator; b. Rockville Centre, NY, May 12, 1941; s. Joseph Alexander and Florence (Rimler) S.; m. Marcia Mitson, Sept. 1, 1963 (div. 1986); m. Marcia Jacobson, 1998; children: David K., Jeffrey C. BA, Union Coll., 1963; MA, Brown U., 1965, PhD, 1968. Asst. prof. Cornell U., Ithaca, N.Y., 1968-74, assoc. prof., 1974-80, prof., 1980—, dir. undergrad. studies in English, 1976-82, Stephen H. Weiss Presdl. fellow, 1999—. Disting. vis. Cooper prof. U. Ark., Little Rock, 1988; vis. Citizen's prof. lit. U. Hawaii, 1992-93; vis. eminent scholar U. Ala., Huntsville, 1996; U.S. Info. Svc. vis. scholar Australia, 1993, Cyprus, 1999, Italy, 2003-04; dir. Summer Seminars for Coll. Tchrs. on Modernism, NEH, 1984, 86, 88, 90, 93, Summer Seminars for Secondary Tchrs. on James Joyce, 1985, 87, 89, 91. Author: Reading The Modern British and Irish Novel, 1890-1930, 2004, Broadway Boogie Woogie: Damon Runyon and the Making of New York City Culture, 2003, Rereading Conrad, 2001, Imagining the Holocaust, 1999, Reconfiguring Modernism: Explorations in the Relationship Between Modern Art and Modern Literature, 1997, Narrative and Representation in the Poetry of Wallace Stevens, 1993, The Case for a Humanistic Poetics, 1991, The Transformation of the English Novel, 1890-1930, 1989, rev., 1995, Reading Joyce's Ulysses, 1987, rev., 1991, 2d edit., 2004, The Humanistic Heritage: Critical Theories of the English Novel from James to Hillis Miller, 1986, rev., 1989, Conrad: The Later Fiction, 1982, Conrad: Almayer's Folly to Under Western Eyes, 1980, Disraeli's Fiction, 1979; editor: The Secret Sharer (Joseph Conrad), 1997, The Dead (James Joyce), 1994; co-editor: Narrative and Culture, 1994; mem. editl. bd. The Early Novels of Benjamin Disraeli, 2004; author numerous poems. Bd. dirs. Freeville Planning Bd., 1968—74, Freeville Zoning Bd., 1968—74. Recipient Russell Disting. Tchg. award Cornell U., 1998; grantee Am. Philos. Soc., 1981, NEH, 1984-91, 93. Mem. MLA, Internat. Narrative Soc. (pres. 1990-91), James Joyce Soc., Phi Beta Kappa. Jewish. Avocations: travel, tennis, museums, theater. Home: 925 Mitchell St Apt 3 Ithaca NY 14850-4991 Office: Cornell U 242 Goldwin Smith Hall Ithaca NY 14853-3201 E-mail: drs6@cornell.edu.

SCHWARZ, EGON, humanities and German language educator, writer, literary critic; b. Vienna, Aug. 8, 1922; arrived in U.S., 1949, naturalized, 1956; s. Oscar and Erna S.; m. Dorothea K. Klockenbusch, June 8, 1950; children— Rudolf Joachim, Caroline Elisabeth, Gabriela Barbara. PhD, U. Wash., 1954, U. Vienna, 1997, U. Örebro, Sweden, 2002. Mem. faculty Harvard U., 1954-61; mem. faculty dept. Germanic langs. and lit. Washington U., St. Louis, 1961—, prof. German, 1963—, Rosa May Disting. Univ. prof. in the Humanities, 1975-93, prof. emeritus, 1993—. Vis. prof. U. Hamburg, Fed. Republic Germany, 1962-63, U. Calif., Berkeley, 1963-65, Middlebury Coll., 1969, U. Calif., Irvine, 1977, U. Tübingen, 1986; William Evans prof. U. Otago, Dunedin, N.Z., 1984; Disting. scholar Ohio State U., Columbus, 1987, U. Graz, Austria, 1989, 93, U. Siegen, 1993-94. Author: Hofmannsthal und Calderon, 1962, Joseph von Eichendorff, 1972, Das verschluckte Schluchzen- Poesie und Politik bei Rainer Maria Rilke, 1972, Keine Zeit für Eichendorff: Chronik unfreiwilliger Wanderjahre; an autobiography, 1979, rev., 1992, Dichtung, Kritik, Geschichte: Essays zur Literatur 1900-1930, 1983, Literatur aus vier Kulturen: Essays und Besprechungen, 1987, Ich bin Kein Freund allgemeiner Urteile über ganze Volker: Essays über österreichische, deutsche und jüdische Literatur, 2000, Die japanische Mauer: Ungewöhnliche Reisegeschichten, 2002, Refuge-Chronicle of a Flight from Hitler, 2002, others. Recipient Joseph von Eichendorff medal, 1986, Austrian Medal of Honor for Arts and Scis., 1991, Alexander von Humboldt prize for fgn. scholars, 1995; Guggenheim fellow, 1957-58, Fulbright fellow, 1962-63, sr. fellow NEH, 1970-71, fellow Ctr. for Interdisciplinary Studies, Bielefeld, Germany, 1980-81; grantee Am. Coun. Learned Socs., 1962-63. Mem.: MLA, German Acad. Lang. and Letters, Am. Assn. Tchrs. German, German Acad. Lang. and Lit. (hon.). Home: 1036 Oakland Ave Saint Louis MO 63122-6565 Office: Washington U German Dept Saint Louis MO 63130 E-mail: gabrielas@aol.com. *When I was young, heroic phantasies were closer to my heart than ethical ones, desires of self-fulfillment stronger than the hopes for an equitable world. Today my horizon is broader in that I wish for a society where personal satisfactions are not achieved at the expense of others, where the earth which one generation inherits is not left more depleted to the next, a society which does not coerce other societies.*

SCHWARZ, FREDERICK A.O., JR., lawyer; b. N.Y.C., Apr. 20, 1935; s. Frederick August Otto and Mary Delafield (DuBois) S.; m. Marian Ladd, June 19, 1959; children: Frederick August Otto III, Adair L., Eliza Ladd; m. Frederica Perera, May 11, 1996. BA in History magna cum laude, Harvard Coll., 1957, LLB magna cum laude, 1960; LLD (hon.), N.Y. Law Sch., 1987, CUNY, 1993. Bar: N.Y. 1961, U.S. Dist. Ct. (so. dist.) N.Y. 1963, U.S. Ct. Appeals (2nd cir.) 1978, U.S. Ct. Appeals (9th cir.) 1972, U.S. Ct. Appeals (10th cir.) 1973, U.S. Supreme Ct. 1973. Law clk. to chief judge J. Edward Lumbard U.S. Ct. of Appeals, 2d Circuit, 1960-61; asst. commr. for law revision Govt. of No. Nigeria, 1961-62; assoc. firm Cravath, Swaine & Moore, N.Y.C., 1963-68, ptnr., 1969-75, 1976-81, 87—; chmn. N.Y.C. Charter

Revision Commn., 1989; corp. counsel City of N.Y., 1982-86; chief counsel Senate Select Com. on Intelligence, 1975-76. Speaker in the field. Author: Nigeria: The Tribes, The Nation, or the Race, 1966; Editor Harvard Law Sch. Law Review. Contbr. articles to profl. jours. Chmn. Fund for the City of N.Y., 1977-81, 87-97; pres. Vera Inst. Justice, 1978-81, chmn. 1987-98; mem. bd. overseers Harvard U., 1977-83; mem. Com. to Visit Harvard Coll., N.Y.-N.J. Citizens Commn. on AIDS; trustee Experiment in Internat. Living, 1965-82; bd. dirs. NAACP Legal Def. Fund. Constl. Edn. Found., Manhattan Bowery Corp., 1970-81, Lawyers for the Public Interest, 1976-81, FAO Schwarz, 1970-85; chair leadership N.Y. Adv. Coun., 1989—; trustee Nat. Resources Def. Coun., 1987-92, chmn., 1992—, Legal Action Center, 1973-81, N.Y.C. Criminal Justice Agy., 1977-81, Town Sch., 1972-80, Am. Com. on Africa, 1965-79, Milton Acad., 1960's, NAACP Legal Def. Fund, Constitutional Edn. Found., William Nelson Cromwell Found.; trustee The A Theater Found., 1992—. Recipient Liberty award Lambda Legal Def. and Edn. Fund, 1987, The Louis Lefkowitz award Fordham Urban Law Jour. 1990, Civic Leadership award Citizens Union City of N.Y., 1990, The Whitney North Seymour Pub. Svc. award Fed. Bar Coun., 1991., Fellow N.Y. Bar Found.; mem. ABA, Assn. of Bar of City of N.Y. (mem. exec. com. 1986-90, coun. on criminal justice, chmn. juvenile justice com. 1980-81, chmn. nominating com. 1983, Cardozo lectr. 1991), Am. Law Inst., Harvard Law Sch. Assn. of N.Y.C. (pres. 1983-84), N.Y. State Bar Assn., N.Y.C. Bar Assn. Office: Ste 2003 Washington County Courthouse Washington PA 15301 also: Cravath, Swain & Moore 825 8th Ave Fl 38 New York NY 10019-7475

SCHWARZ, GERARD, conductor, musician; b. Weehawken, N.J., Aug. 19, 1947; m. Jody Greitzer, June 23, 1984; children: Alysandra, Daniel, Gabriella, Julian. BS, MA, Juilliard Sch., 1972; DFA (hon.), Fairleigh Dickinson U., Seattle U.; MusD (hon.), U. Puget Sound. Trumpet player Am. Symphony Orch., 1965—72, Am. Brass Quintet, 1965—73, N.Y. Philharm., 1973—77; trumpet player, guest condr. Aspen Music Festival, 1969—75, bd. dirs., 1973—75; music dir. Erick Hawkins Dance Co., 1967—72, SoHo Ensemble, 1969—75, Eliot Feld Ballet Co., N.Y.C., 1972—78, Music Sch. Princeton (N.J.) U., 1977—2002, N.Y. Chamber Symphony, 1977—, L.A. Chamber Orch., 1978—86, White Mountains (N.H.) Music Festival, 1978—80; music advisor Mostly Mozart Festival, Lincoln Ctr., N.Y.C., 1982—84, music dir., 1984—2001, Music Today at Merkin Concert Hall, N.Y.C., 1988—89, Liverpool Philharm. Orch., 2000—, Seattle Symphony, 2001—. Music advisor Seattle Symphony, 1983—84, prin. condr., 1984—85, music dir., 1985—, Royal Liverpool Philharm. Orch., 2001—; artistic advisor Tokyu Bunkamura's Orchard Hall, Japan, 1994—98; mem. faculty Juilliard Sch., N.Y.C., 1975—83, Mannes Coll. Music, 1973—79, Montclair (N.J.) State Coll., 1975—80; guest condr. various orchs. including Phila. Orch., L.A. Philharm., St. Louis, Buffalo, Detroit, San Francisco, Atlanta, Houston, Pitts., Minn., Jerusalem Symphonies, Israel Chamber Orch., Moscow Philharm., Moscow Radio Orch., Orch. Nat. de France, Paris, London Symphony Orch., Frankfurt Radio, Stockholm Radio, Helsinki Philharm., Ensemble InterContemporain, Monte Caarlo Philharm., Nat. Orch. Spain, English Chamber Orch., London Symphony, Scottish Chamber Orch., City of Birmingham (Eng.) Symphony, Nouvel Orchestre Philharmonique, Sydney (Australia) Symphony, Melbourne (Australia) Symphony, Orchestre Nat. de Lyon, Orchestre Philharm. de Montpellier, France, Washington Opera, Da Capo Chamber Players, 20th Century Chamber Orch., Chamber Music Soc. Lincoln Ctr., San Francisco Opera, Seattle Opera, Tokyu Bunkamura, Japan, Rseidentie Orch. of The Hague, Netherlands, St. Louis Symphony, London Mozart Players, Kirov Orch., St. Petersburg, Russia, Tokyo Philharm., Royal Liverpool Philharm., Vancouver (Can.) Symphony Orch., City of London Symphonia, Evian Festival in France; artistic adv. Tokyo Philharm., 1994—98. Rec. artist Columbia, Nonesuch, Vox, MMO, Desto, Angel, Delos Records, Season 1995. Nominee 10 Grammy awards; named Condr. of Yr., Musical Am. Internat. Directory of Performing Arts, 1994; recipient award for concert artists, Ford Found., 1973, Mumms Ovation award, Record of Yr. awards, Ditson Condrs. award, Columbia U., 1989.

SCHWARZ, GLENN VERNON, newspaper editor; b. Chgo., Nov. 24, 1947; s. Vernon Edward and LaVerne Louise (Schuster) S.; m. Cynthia Frances Meisenhoelder, June 17, 1984; 1 child, Chloe. BA, San Francisco State U., 1970. Sports writer San Francisco Examiner, 1970—87, sports editor, 1988—2000, San Francisco Chronicle, 2000—. Fundraiser San Francisco Zoological Soc., 1987—. Mem. AP Sports Editors, Baseball Writers Assn. Am. (bd. dirs. 1986-87). Avocation: nature travel. Office: San Francisco Chronicle 901 Mission St San Francisco CA 94103

SCHWARZ, H. MARSHALL, trust company executive; b. 1936; married. BA, Harvard U., 1958, MBA, 1961. With U.S. Trust Co., N.Y.C., 1967—, chmn, chief exec. officer, 1990—. Bd. dirs. Bowne & Co., Inc., Atlantic Mut. Co. Formerly chmn. ARC in Greater N.Y.C.; trustee Columbia U. Tchrs. Coll., Milton Acad., Camille and Henry Dreyfus Found. Office: US Trust Co NY 114 W 47th St New York NY 10036-1510

SCHWARZ, JOHN HENRY, theoretical physicist, educator; b. North Adams, Mass., Nov. 22, 1941; s. George and Madeleine (Haberfeld) S.; m. Patricia Margaret Moyle, July 11, 1986. AB, Harvard U., 1962; PhD, U. Calif., Berkeley, 1966. Instr. physics Princeton (N.J.) U., 1966-69, asst. prof., 1969-72; research assoc. Calif. Inst. Tech., Pasadena, 1972-85, Harold Brown prof. theoretical physics, 1985—. Co-author: Superstring Theory, 1987. Trustee Aspen (Colo.) Ctr. for Physics, 1982—. Recipient Dirac medal Internat. Ctr. for Theoretical Physics, 1989; Guggenheim fellow, 1978-79, MacArthur Found. fellow, 1987. Fellow NAS, Am. Phys. Soc., Phi Beta Kappa (vis. scholar 1990-91). Office: Calif Inst Tech # 452 48 Pasadena CA 91125-0001

SCHWARZ, JOHN J.H. state legislator, surgeon; b. Chgo., Nov. 15, 1937; s. Frank William and Helen Veronica (Brennan) S.; m. Anne Louise Ennis, Jan. 16, 1971 (dec. Feb. 1990); 1 child, Brennan Louise. BA, U. Mich., 1959; MD, Wayne State U., 1964. Physician, surgeon, Battle Creek, Mich., 1974—; mayor City of Battle Creek, 1985-87; mem. Mich. Senate from 24th dist., Lansing, 1987—; pres. pro tempore of the Senate, 1993—. Trustee Olivet Coll., 1991—, Wayland Acad., 1992-96; trustee, treas. Am. Legacy Found. Lt. USN, 1965-67. Mem. AMA, ACS, Am. Soc. for Head and Neck Surgery. Republican. Roman Catholic. Office: State Senate State Capital Lansing MI 48909

SCHWARZ, LOUISE A. band director; H.s. band dir. Bethlehem Ctrl. H.S., Delmar, N.Y. Recipient Castleman award for excellence in chamber mus. teaching, 1993. Office: Bethlehem Ctrl High Sch 700 Delaware Ave Delmar NY 12054-2436

SCHWARZ, M. ROY, physician, administrator; b. American Falls, Idaho, July 30, 1936; s. Frank and Hulda Christina (Rast) S.; m. Thelma Constance Schwarz, June 9, 1957; children: Ryan Merle, Tanna Berit. BS, Pacific Luth. U., 1959; MD, U. Wash., 1963; DS, Mont. State U., 1994, U. Idaho, 1995; LHD (hon.), Pacific Luth. U., 2002. From asst. to full prof. medicine U. Wash., Seattle, 1963-79; dean, prof. U. Colo., Denver, 1979-83; sr. v.p. Am. Med. Assn., Chgo., 1984-96; pres. China Med. Bd., N.Y.C., 1997—. Co-author (with C. Everett Koop, Clarence E. Pearson): Critical Issues in global Health, 2001; editor: Proceedings of the VI Leukocyte Culture Conf., 1971; contbr. over 150 articles to profl. jours. Office: China Med Bd 750 Third Ave 23 Fl New York NY 10017 Office Phone: 212-682-8000. E-mail: rschwarz@chinamedicalboard.org.

SCHWARZ, MICHAEL, lawyer; b. Brookline, Mass., Oct. 19, 1952; s. Jules Lewis and Estelle (Kosberg) S.; m. Rebecca Handy; 1 child, Patrick Joshua Charles. BA magna cum laude, U. No. Colo., 1975; postgrad., U. N.Mex., 1977, JD, 1980; reader in Negligence Law, Oxford U., 1978; diploma in Legal Studies, Cambridge U., 1981. Bar: N.Mex. 1980, U.S. Dist. Ct. N.Mex. 1980, U.S. Ct. Appeals (10th, D.C. and Fed. cirs.) 1982, U.S. Ct. Internat. Trade 1982, U.S. Tax Ct. 1982, N.Y. 1987, U.S. Supreme Ct. 1983. Vol. VISTA, Albuquerque, 1975-77; rsch. fellow N.Mex. Legal Support Project, Albuquerque, 1978-79; supr. law Cambridge (Eng.) U., 1980-81; law clk. to chief justice Supreme Ct. N.Mex., Santa Fe, 1981-82; pvt. practice Santa Fe, 1982—. Spl. pros. City of Santa Fe, 1985, spl. asst. atty. gen., 1986-88; mem. west editl. adv. com. Social Security Reporting Svc., 1983-95; mem. N.Mex. Supreme Ct. Com. Profl. Responsibility, 1990—, chmn., 1998—, domestiv rels. task force com., 2004—. Author: New Mexico Appellate Manual, 1990, 2d edit., 1996; contbr. articles to profl. jours. Vice-dir. Colo. Pub. Interest Rsch. Group, 1974; scoutmaster Gt. S.W. Area coun. Boy Scouts Am., 1977—79; mem. N.Mex. Acupuncture Lic. Bd., 1983; level 2 referee, master's coaching level USA Hockey; head coach Squirt Gold Santa Fe Trailrunners, 2001—03, Santa Fe Huskies, 2003—04; USA hockey adminstr. of coaching edn. for New Mex. Recipient Cert. of Appreciation Cambridge U., 1981, Nathan Burke Meml. award, 1980, N.Mex. Supreme Ct. Cert. Recognition, 1992, 93, 95, N.Mex. Supreme Ct. Cert. Appreciation Outstanding Svc. to Legal Sys., 2001. Mem.: ATLA, ABA (10th cir. editor 1998, litigation com. on profl. responsibility, mem. Ctr. Profl. Responsibility, litigation com. on pretrial practice and discovery), Am. Law Inst., N.Mex. State Bar (chmn. 1990—91, bd. dirs. employment law sect. 1990—96, family law sect. bd. 1999—2001), Bar Assn. U.S. Dist. Ct. Dist. N.Mex. (1st judical dis. bar assoc. pres. 1990—91), Santa Fe Trailrunners Hockey Assn. (bd. dirs. 2001—02). Home and Office: PO Box 1656 Santa Fe NM 87504-1656 E-mail: barristr@nm.net.

SCHWARZ, RALPH JACQUES, retired engineering educator; b. Hamburg, Germany, June 13, 1922; naturalized, 1944; s. Simon J. and Anna (Schoendorff) S.; m. Irene Lassally, Sept. 9, 1951; children: Ronald Paul, Sylvia Anne. BS, Columbia U., 1943, MS, 1944, PhD, 1949; postgrad., Poly. Inst. Bklyn., 1944-45, N.Y. U., 1946-47. Registered profl. engr., N.Y. Mem. faculty Columbia U., 1943-92, prof. elec. engring., 1958-92, chmn. dept., 1958-65, 71-72, assoc. dean acad. affairs Faculty Engring. and Applied Sci., 1972-75, acting dean, 1975-76, 80-81, vice dean, Thayer Lindsley prof., 1976-92, Thayer Lindsley prof. emeritus, 1992—; cons. systems analysis, communications and noise theory, 1945—. Vis. assoc. prof. UCLA, 1956; adviser Inst. Internat. Edn., 1952-65; vis. scientist IBM Research Center, 1969-70 Author: (with M.G. Salvadori) Differential Equations in Engineering Problems, 1954, (with B. Friedland) Linear Systems, 1965. Bd. dirs. Armstrong Meml. Research Found.; trustee Associated Univs., Inc., 1980-92. Fellow: IEEE (chmn. circuit theory group 1963—65, Centennial medal 1984). Home: 1270 North Ave # 5G New Rochelle NY 10804-2601 Business E-Mail: rjs3@columbia.edu.

SCHWARZ, RICHARD HOWARD, obstetrician, gynecologist, educator; b. Easton, Pa., Jan. 10, 1931; s. Howard Eugene and Blanche Elizabeth (Smith) S.; m. Patricia Marie Lewis, Mar. 11, 1978; children by previous marriage: Martha L., Nancy Schwarz Tedesco, Paul H., Mary Katherine Schwarz Murray. MD, Jefferson Med. Coll., 1955; MA (hon.), U. Pa., 1971. Diplomate Am. Bd. Ob-Gyn. (examiner 1977-95). Intern, then resident Phila. Gen. Hosp., 1955-59; prof. U. Pa., Phila., 1963-78; prof., chmn. Downstate Med. Ctr., Bklyn., 1978-90, dean, v.p. acad. affairs, 1983-89, provost, v.p. clin. affairs, 1988-93, interim pres., 1993-94, prof. ob.-gyn., 1990-96, disting. Svc. prof. ob.-gyn. emeritus, 1996; chmn. ob.-gyn. N.Y. Meth. Hosp., Bklyn., 1996—2002; prof. ob.-gyn. Cornell U. Med. Coll., N.Y.C., 1996—2002; vice chair for clin. svc. dept. Ob/GYN Maimonides Med. Ctr., 2002—. Obstetrical cons. March of Dimes Birth Defects Found., 1995— Author: Septic Abortion, 1968. Editor: Handbook of Obstetric Emergencies, 1984, mem. editorial bd. jour. Ob-Gyn., Milw., 1983-87; contbr. articles to profl. jours. Bd. dirs. March of Dimes, N.Y.C., 1985-95. Capt. USAF, 1959-63. Fellow Royal Coll ObGyn, 1999; mem. Am. Coll. Obstetricians and Gynecologists (chmn. dist. 2 1984-87, v.p. 1989-90, pres. elect 1990-91, pres. 1991-92). Republican. Presbyterian. Office: Maimonides Med Ctr 967 48th St Brooklyn NY 11219-3645

SCHWARZ, ROSE OBERMAN, artist; b. Jan. 24, 1910; d. William and Florence Oberman; m. Sidney Schwarz, July 31, 1929 (dec. Mar. 1984); children: Lillian, Elaine. Student, South Fla. Art Inst., 1977—99. Ins. salesperson. Exhibitions include Bacardi Gallery, Miami, Fla., 1979, Miami Beach City Hall, Fla., 1981—82, Viscaya, 1981, Met. Mus., Coral Gables, Fla., 1985, Bay Harbor Gallery, Fla., 1985—. Recipient Rex Art award, Hollywood Cultural Ctr., 1981, hon. mention, Pioneer Mus., 1982, Best in Show award, Hollywood Art Guild, 1983, hon. mention, Pioneer Mus., 1983, Best in show, Hollywood Cultural Ctr., 1984, Best in Show, 1985. Avocations: dress making, piano. Home: 6674 Via Roma Delray Beach FL 33446-3730

SCHWARZ, WOLFGANG, psychologist; b. Stuttgart, Germany, Oct. 30, 1926; came to U.S., 1934, naturalized, 1940; s. Mole and Edith (Gutstein) S.; m. Cynthia Mae Johnson, Sept. 12, 1949 (div.); children: Amy Maria, Casey Andrew, Darcy Lynn, Priscilla Anne, Lydia Beth, Emily Jane; m. Susan Decker, 1976; children: Jaime Bartholomew, Noah. AB, NYU, 1948, AM, 1949, PhD, 1956. Diplomate Am. Bd. Profl. Psychology. Intern Bellevue Med. Ctr., N.Y.C., 1949-51; chief psychology Rip Van Winkle Med. Found., Hudson, N.Y., 1951-53; dir. psychology Hillcrest Med. Ctr., Tulsa, 1953-56, Hollywood Presbyn. Hosp., L.A., 1956-58; cons. psychology Cedars Lebanon Hosp., L.A., 1956-58; spl. cons. D.C. Govt., 1959-61, NIH, Bethesda, Md., 1962-64; dir. psychol. rsch. Mass. Dept. Mental Health, Boston and Malden, 1965-68; individual practice clin. psychology Tulsa, 1953-56, Beverly Hills, Calif., 1956-59, Washington, 1959-63, Malden and Concord, Mass., 1963-73, Mt. Kisco, N.Y., 1973—. Lectr. U. Tulsa, 1953-54, L.A. State Coll., 1956-57; asst. prof. Howard U., 1961; assoc. prof. George Washington U., 1961-62; vis. rsch. asst. Harvard Psychiatry Lab., 1966-68; prof. Malden Hosp., 1968-71; cons. No. Westchester Hosp., 1974—, United Hosp., 1975—, Four Winds Hosp., 1975-80; cons. psychology Peace Corps, Mass., 1969—. Author: A Survey of the Mental Health Facilities in the Disctict of Columbia, 1961; contbr. articles to profl. jours. and chpt. to book. Mem. exec. com. Mayor's Model City Program, Malden, 1967-68. With USNR, 1945-46. Recipient Founder's Day award NYU, 1956, Individual award USPHS/NIH, 1960-64. Mem. APA, N.Y. Psychol. Assn., Mass. psychol. Assn., Washington Soc. Hist. of Medicine (exec. com. 1963-64), N.Y. Acad. Scis., Psi Chi, Beta Lambda Sigma. Home: 81 Paulding Dr Chappaqua NY 10514-2818 Office: 101 S Bedford Rd Mount Kisco NY 10549-3439 Office Phone: 914-241-3716. E-mail: drwschwarz@aol.com.

SCHWARZENEGGER, ARNOLD ALOIS, governor; b. Graz, Austria, July 30, 1947; came to U.S., 1968, naturalized, 1983; s. Karl and Aurelia (Jedrny) S.; m. Maria Owings Shriver, Apr. 26, 1986; children: Katherine Eunice, Christina Aurelia, Patrick, Christopher. BA in Bus. and Internat. Econs., U. Wis., Superior. Owner prodn. co. and real estate; gov. State of Calif., Sacramento, 2003—. Speaker Republican Nat. Convention, NYC, 2004. Actor: (films) Stay Hungry, 1976 (Golden Globe award 1976), Pumping Iron, 1977, The Villain, 1979, Conan, The Barbarian, 1982, Conan, The Destroyer, 1983, The Terminator, 1984, Commando, 1985, Red Sonja, 1985, Raw Deal, 1986, Predator, 1987, Running Man, 1987, Red Heat, 1988, Twins, 1988, Total Recall, 1990, Kindergarten Cop, 1990, Terminator 2: Judgement Day, 1991, True Lies, 1994, Junior, 1994, Terminator 2: 3-D, 1996, Jingle All the Way, 1996, Eraser, 1996, Batman & Robin, 1997, End of Days, 1999, Collateral Damage, 2002, Terminator 3: Rise of the Machines, 2003; actor, prodr. The Last Action Hero, 1993, The 6th Day, 2000; (TV spl.) Sinatra: 80 Years My Way, 1995; (TV movies) The Jayne Mansfield Story, 1980; dir. TV movie Christmas in Connecticut, 1992; host A Very Special Christmas Story; dir. The Switch, Tales from the Crypt, HBO, 1990; author: Arnold: The Education of a Bodybuilder, 1977, Arnold's Bodyshaping for Women, 1979, Arnold's Bodybuilding for Men, 1981, Arnold's Encyclopedia of Modern Bodybuilding, 1985, 2d edit. 1998; prodr. bodybuilding video tape. Nat. weight tng. coach Spl. Olympics; vol. prison rehab. programs; chmn. Pres.'s Coun. on Phys. Fitness and Sports, 1990-93. Bodybldg. champion, 1965-80; named Jr. Mr. Europe, 1965, Best Built Man of Europe, 1966, Mr. Europe, 1966; Internat. Powerlifting Championship, 1966, German Powerlifting Championship, 1968; IFFB (Internat. Fedn. Body Builders) Mr. Internat., 1968, IFFB Mr. Universe (amateur), 1969; NABBA (Nat. Assn. Body Builders) Mr. Universe (amateur), 1967, NABBA Mr. Universe (profl.), 1968, 69, 70; Mr. World, 1970; IFFB Mr. Olympia, 1970, 71, 72, 73, 74, 75, 80; recipient Golden Globe award for Best Newcomer in Films, 1976, Timmie Award The Touchdown Club, 1990; named Video Star Yr. VSDA, 1990; voted Internat. Star of 1984, ShoWest; recipient, Muhammad Ali Humanitarian award; Nat. Leadership award, Simon Wiesenthal Ctr.; Father Flanagan Svc. to Youth award, Boys and Girls Town. Republican. Office: Office of Governor State Capitol Sacramento CA 95814-4906 also: PMK 8500 Wilshire Blvd Ste 700 Beverly Hills CA 90211-3105*

SCHWARZER, WILLIAM W, federal judge; b. Berlin, Apr. 30, 1925; came to U.S., 1938, naturalized, 1944; s. John F. and Edith M. (Daniel) S.; m. Anne Halbersleben, Feb. 2, 1951; children: Jane Elizabeth, Andrew William. AB cum laude, U. So. Calif., 1948; LLB cum laude, Harvard U., 1951. Bar: Calif. 1953, U.S. Supreme Ct. 1967. Teaching fellow Harvard U. Law Sch., 1951-52; asso. firm McCutchen, Doyle, Brown & Enersen, San Francisco, 1952-60, ptnr., 1960-76; judge U.S. Dist. Ct (no. dist.) Calif., San Francisco, 1976—; dir. Fed. Jud. Ctr., Washington, 1990-95. Sr. counsel Pres.'s Commn. on CIA Activities Within the U.S., 1975; chmn. U.S. Jud. Conf. Com. Fed.-State Jurisdiction, 1987-90; mem. faculty Nat. Inst. Trial Advocacy, Fed. Jud. Ctr., All-ABA, U.S.-Can. Legal Exch., 1987, Anglo-U.S. Jud. Exch., 1994-95, Salzburg Seminar on Am. Studies; disting. prof. Hastings Coll. Law U. Calif. Author: Managing Antitrust and Other Complex Litigation, 1982, Civil Discovery and Mandatory Disclosure, 1994, Federal Civil Procedure Before Trial, 1994; contbr. articles to legal publs., aviation jours. Trustee World Affairs Coun. No. Calif., 1961-88; chmn. bd. trustees Marin Country Day Sch., 1963-66; mem. Marin County Aviation Commn., 1969-76; mem. vis. com. Harvard Law Sch., 1981-86. Served with Intelligence, U.S. Army, 1943-46. Fellow Am. Coll. Trial Lawyers (S. Gates award 1992), Am. Bar Found.; mem. ABA (Meador Rosenberg award 1995), Am. Law Inst., San Francisco Bar Assn., State Bar Calif., Coun. Fgn. Rels. Office: 450 Golden Gate Ave San Francisco CA 94102-3661

SCHWARZKOPF, H. NORMAN, retired army officer, public speaker; b. Trenton, N.J., Aug. 22, 1934; s. H. Norman and Ruth (Bowman) Schwarzkopf; m. Brenda Holsinger, July 6, 1968; children: Cynthia, Jessica, Christian. BS in engring., U.S. Mil. Acad., West Point, N.Y., 1956; MME, U. So. Calif., Los Angeles, 1964; student, U.S. Army War Coll., Carlisle Barracks, Pa., 1972-73; LHD (hon.), U. S. Fla.; D. in Leadership (hon.), U. Richmond; D. in Pub. Svc. (hon.), U. Miami, U. Fla. Commd. 2nd lt. U.S. Army, 1956, advanced through grades to gen., 1988; platoon leader, exec. officer 2nd Airborne Battle Group, 1957-59; platoon leader 6th Inf., Fed. Rep. Germany, 1959; aide-de-camp Berlin Command, Fed. Rep. Germany, 1960-61; assoc. prof. Dept. Mechanics, U.S. Army Military Acad., West Point, NY, Ga., 1965; advisor U.S. Army, Vietnam, 1965-66; commander 1st Battalion, 6th Inf., 198th Inf. brigade, 23rd Inf. Div., Vietnam, 1969-70; chief, Prof. Devel. Section, Inf. branch Office Personnel Operations, Washington, D.C., 1970-72; military asst. Office Asst. Sec. Army, Washington, D.C., 1973-74; dep. comdr. 172d inf. brigade Ft. Richardson, Alaska, 1974-76; comdr. 1st brigade 9th Inf. div., Ft. Lewis, Wash., 1976-78; dep. dir. plans U.S. Pacific Command, Camp Smith, Hawaii, 1978-80; asst. div. comdr. 8th inf. div. (mechanized) U.S. Army Europe, Fed. Republic Germany, 1980-82; dir. mil. personnel mgmt. Office Dep. Chief Staff for Personnel, Washington, 1982-83; comdg. gen. 24th inf. div. (mechanized) Ft. Stewart, Ga., 1983-85; dep. comdr. U.S. forces in Grenada operation, 1983; asst. dep. chief staff ops. Hdqrs. Dept. Army, Washington, 1985-86; comdg. gen. I corps Ft. Lewis, Wash., 1986-87; dep. chief staff for ops. and plans Hdqrs. Dept. Army, Washington, 1987-88; comdr. in chief U.S. Cen. Command, MacDill AFB, Fla., 1988-91, U.S. Forces in Ops. Desert Shield, Desert Storm, Saudi Arabia, 1990-91; ret. U.S. Army, 1992. Lecturer, 1993—; contbr. and analyst NBC News, 1995—. Author (with Peter Petre): It Doesn't Take a Hero, 1992. Chair Starbright Found., 1995—. Decorated Def. D.S.M., D.S.M. with two oak leaf clusters, D.S.M. for USN, D.S.M. for USAF, D.S.M. for USCG, Silver Star with two oak leaf clusters, Def. Superior Svc. medal, Legion of Merit, D.F.C., Bronze Star with three oak leaf clusters, Purple Heart with oak leaf cluster, Combat Infantryman badge, Master Parachutist badge, Gen. Staff Identification badge, Joint Staff Identification badge, Dept. Def. Identification badge, Presdl. Medal of Freedom; Nat. Order of Legion of Honor, hon. pfc. French Fgn. Legion (France); Order of Leopold (Belgium); knight Hon. Order of the Bath (U.K.); Decoration 1st degree (Bahrain); Sash of Independence (Qatar); Medal of Independence (United Arab Emirates); officer Order of King Abd Al Aziz 1st class (Saudi Arabia), Order of Kuwait with Sash of Most Excellent Order (Kuwait); named Father of the Yr., 1991, Toastmaster Internat. Best Spkr., 1992, Humanitarian of the Yr. United Cerebral Palsy, 1993, Living Legends M. D. Anderson Found., 1996; recipient Am. Patriot medal, 1993, Gilda Radner award Courage, 1995, N.J. Disting. Svc. medal, 1995, Vince Lombardi award Excellence, 1995, James Ewing Layman award Soc. Surg. Oncologists, 1997, Oliver R. Grace award, 1998, Ambassador Hope award, 1998, Spirit of Hope award, 1999, Leadership award Multiple Myeloma Rsch. Found., 1999, Inspirational award U. Pitts. Med. Ctr., 2000, Harry S. Truman Good Neighbor award, 2000, Pioneer in Prostate Cancer award Fla. Cancer Edn. Network, 2000, Theodore Roosevelt Am. Experience award, 2000, Award of Excellence Ronald McDonald, 2001. Avocations: hunting, fishing, skeet, trap and sporting clays. Office: Care Internat Creative Mgmt Inc 40 W 57th St New York NY 10019-4001 also: 400 N Ashley Dr Ste 3050 Tampa FL 33602-4314

SCHWARZMAN, STEPHEN ALLEN, investment banker; b. N.Y.C., Feb. 14, 1947; s. Joseph and Arline (Horelley) S.; children: Elizabeth, Edward. BA, Yale U., 1969; MBA, Harvard U., 1972. Mng. dir. Lehman Brothers, N.Y.C., 1978—84; co-founder, pres., CEO The Blackstone Group, N.Y.C., 1985—. Bd. dirs. N.Y.C. Ballet, New York Pub. Libr., N.Y.C. Partnership; chmn., bd. trustees Kennedy Ctr. Performing Arts, Wash., 2004-. Mem. Coun. on Fgn. Rels, JP Morgan Chase Nat. Advisory Bd., Harvard Bus. Sch. Vis. Com. Jewish. Office: The Blackstone Group 345 Park Ave Ste 3101 New York NY 10154-0004 E-mail: schwarzman@blackstone.com.

SCHWARZROCK, SHIRLEY PRATT, writer, educator; b. Mpls., Feb. 27, 1914; d. Theodore Ray and Myrtle Pearl (Westphal) Pratt; m. Loren H. Schwarzrock, Oct. 19, 1945 (dec. 1966); children: Kay Linda, Ted Kenneth, Lorraine V. BS, U. Minn., 1935, MA, 1942, PhD, 1974. Sec. to chmn. speech dept. U. Minn., Mpls., 1935, instr. in speech, 1946, team tchr. in creative arts workshops for tchrs., 1955—56, guest lectr. Dental Sch., 1967—72, asst. prof. (part-time) practice administrn. Sch. Dentistry, 1972—80; tchr. speech, drama and English Preston H.S., Minn., 1935—37; tchr. speech, drama and English, dir. dramatics Owatonna H.S., Minn., 1937—39; tchr. creative dramatics and English, tchr.-counselor Webster Groves Jr. H.S., Mo., 1939—40; dir. dramatics and tchr.-counselor Webster Groves Sr. H.S., 1940—43; exec. sec. bus. and profl. dept. YWCA, Mpls., 1943—45; tchr. speech and drama Convent of the Visitation, St. Paul, 1958; editor pro-tem Am. Acad. Dental Practice Adminstrn., 1966—68; editor North Country Pages, 2003—. Guest tchr. Coll. St. Catherine, St. Paul, 1969; vol. mgr. Gift Shop, Eitel Hosp., Mpls., 1981-83, Edina Cmty. Resource Pool, 1992-95; cmty. citizen mem. planning, evaluating, reporting com. Edina Pub. Sch. Sys., 1993-96; tutor for reading, writing, and speaking, 1993-96; condr. tutorials in speaking and profl. office mgmt., 1985-96; owner Shirley Schwarzrock's Exec. Support Svc., 1989-99; cons. Ergodyne Corp., St. Paul, 1991-92; freelance editor med. support bus., 1992; cons., lectr. in field. Author: Coping With Personal Identity, Coping With Human Relationships, Coping With Facts and Fantasies, Coping With Teenage Problems, 1984; individual book titles (Coping With series) include: Do I Know the "Me" Others See?, My Life-What Shall I Do With It?, Living With Loneliness, Learning to Make Better Decisions, Grades, What's So Important About Them, Anyway?, Facts and Fantasies About Alcohol, Facts and Fantasies About Smoking, Food as a Crutch, Facts and Fantasies About the Roles of Men and Women, You Always Communicate Something, Appreciating People-Their Likenesses and Differences, Fitting In, To Like and Be Liked, Can You Talk With Someone Else?, Coping With Emotional Pain, Some Common Crutches, Parents Can Be a Problem, Coping With Cliques, Crises Youth Face Today; (with L.H. Schwarzrock) Effective Dental Assisting, 1954, 1st edit., 1967, (with J.R. Jensen) 1973, 3d edit., 1982; (with J.R. Jensen, Kay Schwarzrock, Lorraine Schwarzrock) 1990, 7th edit., 1991, Workbook for Effective Dental Assisting, 1968, 5th edit., 1991; (with Donovan F. Ward) Effective Medical Assisting, 1969, 2d edit., 1976, Manual for Effective Medical Assisting, 1969, 2d edit., 1976; (with C.G. Wrenn) The Coping With Series of Books for High School Students, 1970, The Coping With Manual, 1973, Contemporary Concerns of Youth, 1980, Shirley's Supergoodies: An Old Fashioned Cookbook for the Modern Cook, 2002; cons. editor: North

Country Pages, St. Paul, 2003-04; contbr. articles to profl. jours. Pres. Univ. Elem. Sch. PTA, 1955-56; vol. judge Minn. State Hist. Day Program, 1994-98. Fellow Internat. Biog. Assn.; mem. Minn. Acad. Dental Practice Adminstrn. (hon.), Authors Guild, Minn. Hist. Soc., Minn. Geneal. Soc., Zeta Phi Eta (pres. 1948-49), Eta Sigma Upsilon. Home: 7448 W Shore Dr Edina MN 55435-4022 *Growing up as a latch key child, challenged to accomplish adult tasks accompanied by "You can do it, Kid", provided me with the ability to face challenges from scrubbing floors to delving deeply into reseach. Assured that there is a solution to every problem, I absorbed the knowledge and skills my professors taught, developed my creativity and spiritual awareness, and learned to listen sensitively and compassionately. This training enabled me to draw forth creative expression from adolescents, respond to their many needs, and to develop adults' communication skills in numerous settings.*

SCHWARZTRAUBER, SAYRE ARCHIE, former naval officer, maritime consultant; b. Zion, Ill., June 23, 1929; s. Archie Douglas and Eleanor Miriam (Sayrs) S.; m. Beryl Constance Stewart, June 27, 1953; children: Sayre Archie, Beryl Ann, Heidi, Holly. BS cum laude, Maryville Coll., 1951; MA, Am. U., 1964, PhD, 1970. Commd. ensign USN, 1952, advanced through grades to rear adm., 1976; comdr. River Squadron 5, Vietnam, 1968-69, U.S.S. Decatur guided missile destroyer, 1970-71, Navy Recruiting Area 4, 1974-76; dep. chief staff Supreme Command Atlantic (NATO), 1976-79; co-dir. U.S.-Spanish Combined Staff, Madrid, 1979-81; dir. Inter-Am. Def. Coll., Washington, 1981-83; ret., 1983; apptd. rear adm. U.S. Maritime Svc., 1984; pres. Maine Maritime Acad., 1984—86. Mem. Sec. of Navy Adv. Com., 1986-90; nat. and internat. lectr. strategic naval and maritime matters, 1973—. Author: The Three-Mile Limit of Territorial Seas, 1972, Schwarztrauber, Stewart and Related Families, 1995; editor Mass. Maritime Mag., 1987-90; contbr. articles, essays and revs. to profl. jours. Ruling elder Presbyn. Ch. U.S.A., 1965-86. Decorated Def. Disting. Svc. Medal, Legion of Merit, Cross of Gallantry (Vietnam), Gran Cruz de Merito (Spain); recipient Alfred Thayer Mahan award Navy League, 1974. Mem. SAR (pres. Cape Cod chpt. 1993-95, state reg. and genealogist 1992-2003, state pres. 1998-99, nat. trustee 1999-2000), Gamewardens of Vietnam, Nat. Geneal. Soc., U.S. Naval Inst., Am. Legion, Masons (adjutant Aleppo Temple), VFW, Mil. Order World Wars, Mensa, Travelers' Century Club, Phi Kappa Phi, Pi Gamma Mu, Pi Sigma Alpha, Theta Alpha Phi. Home and Office: PO Box 589 Osterville MA 02655-0589

SCHWEBEL, DAVID CHARLES, psychologist, educator; b. Columbus, Ohio, Apr. 25, 1972; s. Andrew I. and Carol R. Schwebel; m. Yikun Zhang, Jan. 15, 2000. BA, Yale U., 1994; PhD, U. Iowa, 2000. Lic. clin. psychologist Ala., 2000. Psychology resident U. of Wash., Seattle, 1999—2000; asst. prof. U. of Ala., Birmingham, 2000—. Contbr. articles to profl. jours. Grantee Rebecca Routh Coon Injury Prevention grant, Soc. for Pediatric Psychology, 2001. Mem.: APA, Sigma Xi. Office: University of Alabama at Birmingham 1300 University Blvd CH 415 Birmingham AL 35294 Office Phone: 205-934-8745.

SCHWEBEL, MILTON, psychologist, educator; b. Troy, NY, May 11, 1914; s. Frank and Sarah (Oxenhandler) S.; m. Bernice Lois Davison, Sept. 3, 1939; children: Andrew I., Robert S. AB, Union Coll., 1934; MA, SUNY, Albany, 1936; PhD, Columbia U., 1949; Cert. in Psychotherapy, Postgrad. Ctr. Mental Health, N.Y.C., 1958. Lic. psychologist, N.Y., N.J.; diplomate Am. Bd. Examiners Profl. Psychology. Asst. prof. psychology Mohawk Champlain Coll., 1946-49; asst. to prof. edn., dept. chmn., assoc. dean NYU, 1949-67; dean, prof. Grad. Sch. Edn., Rutgers U., New Brunswick, N.J., 1967-77; prof. Grad. Sch. Applied and Profl. Psychology, 1977-85, prof. emeritus, 1985—. Vis. prof. U. So. Calif., U. Hawaii; postdoctoral fellow Postgrad. Ctr. Mental Health, N.Y.C., 1954-58, lectr. psychology, 1958-60; cons. NIMH, U.S., state and city depts. edn., ednl. ministries in Europe, Asia, univs. and pub. schs.; pvt. cons. psychologist and psychotherapist, 1953—; disting. cons. & faculty Saybrook Grad. Sch. & Rsch. Ctr., 1999—. Author: A Guide to a Happier Family, 1989, Personal Adjustment and Growth, 1990, Student Teachers Handbook, 3d edit., 1996, Interests of Pharmacists, 1951, Health Counseling, 1953, Who Can Be Educated?, 1968, Remaking America's Three School System: Now Separate and Unequal, 2003; editor: Mental Health Implications of Life in the Nuclear Age, 1986, Facilitating Cognitive Development, 1986, Promoting Cognitive Growth Over the Life Span, 1990, Behavioral Science and Human Survival, 1965, The Impact of Ideology on the I.Q. Controversy, 1975; editor Peace & Conflict: Jour. Peace Psychology, 1993-2000; co-editor Bull. Peace Psychology, 1991-94; mem. editl. bd. Am. Jour. Orthopsychiatry, Readings in Mental Health, Jour. Contemporary Psychotherapy, Jour. Counseling Psychology, Jour. Social Issues, others. Mem. sci. adv. bd. Internat. Ctr. for Enhancement of Learning Potential, 1988—; trustee Edn. Law Ctr., 1973-81, Nat. Com. Employment Youth, Nat. Child Labor Com., 1967-75, Union Exptl. Colls. and Univs., 1976-78; pres. Nat. Orgn. for Migrant Children, 1980-85; pres. Inst. of Arts and Humanities, 1984-85. Served with AUS, 1943-46, ETO. Met. Applied Rsch. Coun. fellow, 1970-71. Fellow APA, Am. Psychol. Soc., Am. Orthopsychiatry Assn., Soc. Psychol. Study Social Issues, Jean Piaget Soc. (trustee), Am. Ednl. Rsch. Assn., N.Y. Acad. Scis., Psychologists for Social Responsibility (pres.), Inst. Arts and Humanities Edn. (pres.), Sigma Xi. Home: Apt 17L 1050 George St New Brunswick NJ 08901-1068 Office: Rutgers U Grad Sch Applied and Profl Psychology 152 Frelinghuysen Rd Piscataway NJ 08854-8085 Business E-Mail: mschwebe@rci.rutgers.edu.

SCHWEBEL, RENATA MANASSE, sculptor; b. Zwickau, Germany, Mar. 6, 1930; came to U.S., 1940, naturalized, 1946; d. George and Anne Marie (Simon) Manasse; m. Jack P. Schwebel, May 10, 1955; children: Judith, Barbara, Diane. BA, Antioch Coll., 1953; MFA, Columbia U., 1961; student, Arts Students League, 1967-69. Cartographer Ecostate Inc., Ridgewood, NJ, 1949; display artist Silvestri Inc., Chgo., 1950-51; asst. Mazzolini Art Foundry, Yellow Springs, Ohio, 1952. One-woman shows include Columbia U., 1961, Greenwich Art Barn, Conn., 1975, Sculpture Ctr., N.Y.C., 1979, Pelham Art Ctr., N.Y., 1981, New Rochelle Libr. Gallery, 1980, Outdoor Installations Katonah Gallery, 1986, 1989, Berman/Daferner Gallery, N.Y.C., 1992—93; artist (group shows) Stamford Mus., Conn., 1967, 1996, Hudson River Mus., Yonkers, N.Y., 1972, 1974, Wadsworth Atheneum, Hartford, 1974, Silvermine Art of the Northwest U.S.A. Anns., 1972, 1976, 1980, 1995, 1998, Silvermine Gallery, 1986, 1991, 2000, 2001, 2002, 2003, New Britain Mus. Am. Art, Conn., 1974, Imprimatur Gallery, St. Paul, 1985, 1986, Bergen County Mus., N.J., 1983, Sculpture Ctr., 1978—88, Katonah Gallery, N.Y., 1986—90, Cast Iron Gallery, N.Y.C., 1991, 1993, Kyoto (Japan) Gallery, 1993; exhibitions include Sculptors Guild Anns., 1974—; artist (traveling show exhibitions) in Am. cultural ctrs. in Egypt and Israel, 1981, 3 Rivers Art Festival, Pitts., 1994, FFS Gallery, N.Y.C., 1994, 1995, Russian Consulate, 1998, Long Beach Island Assn. Arts and Scis., N.J., 1999, Grounds for Sculpture, Hamilton, N.J., 1999, Chesterwood Mus., Stockbridge, Mass., 2000, Troy Arts Ctr., N.Y., 2000—01, Rockland Ctr. for Arts, 2001—02, No. Westchester Arts Coun., 2002, 2003, Westport Arts Ctr., 2003, Ednl. Alliance Gallery, N.Y.C., 2003; Represented in permanent collections S.W. Bell, Columbia U., Colt Industries, Am. Airlines, Comcraft Industries, Nairobi, Gruber Haus, Berlin, Mus. Fgn. Art, Sofia, Bulgaria, Housatonic Mus. Bd. dirs. Fine Arts Fedn., N.Y., 1985-87; trustee Sculpture Ctr., 1980-88, chmn. exhbn. com., 1986-88; adv. bd. Pehlham Art Ctr., 1982. Mem.: N.Y. Artists Equity, Silvermine Guild, Conn. N.Y. Soc. Women Artists, Conn. Acad. Fine Arts, Audubon Artists (Chaim Gross award 1980, Medal of Honor 1982, Rennick award 1986, 1990, 1992, 1995), Nat. Assn. Women Artists (Willis Meml. prize 1974, Medal of Honor 1981, Paley Meml. award 1979), Sculptors Guild (bd. dirs. 1975—94, pres. 1980—83, bd. dirs. 1995—2004), Katonah Gallery (artist mem. 1986—90), Ams. for Peace Now (bd. dirs. 1991—2001), Antioch Coll. Assn. (bd. dirs. 1971—77). Home: 10 Dogwood Hills Pound Ridge NY 10576-1508 Personal E-mail: RENATA99M@aol.com.

SCHWEBEL, STEPHEN MYRON, arbitrator, mediator, legal advisor; b. N.Y.C., Mar. 10, 1929; s. Victor and Pauline (Pfeffer) S.; m. Louise Ingrid Nancy Killander, Aug. 2, 1972; children: Jennifer, Anna. BA in Govt. magna cum laude with highest honors in govt., Harvard U., 1950; postgrad., Cambridge (Eng.) U., 1950-51; LLB, Yale U., 1954; LLD (hon.), Bhopal (India) U., 1983, Hofstra U., 1997, U. Miami, 2002. Bar: N.Y. 1955, U.S. Supreme Ct. 1965, D.C. 1976. Dir. UN hdqrs. office World Fedn. UN Assns., 1950-53; lectr. Am. fgn. policy various univs. U.S. Dept. State, India, 1952; research, drafting asst. to Trygve Lie for writing of In the Cause of Peace, 1953; assoc. White & Case, N.Y.C., 1954-59; asst. prof. law Harvard U., Cambridge, Mass., 1959-61; asst. legal advisor U.S. Dept. State, Washington, 1961-66, dep. legal advisor, 1973-81; exec. dir. Am. Soc. Internat. Law, Washington, 1967-72; Burling prof. internat. law Sch. of Advanced Internat. Studies, Johns Hopkins U., Washington, 1967-81; pres. Adminstrv. Tribunal, IMF, Washington, 1994—; judge Internat. Ct. Justice, The Hague, The Netherlands, 1981-2000, v.p., 1994-97, pres., 1997-2000; jurist-in-residence John's Hopkins Sch. Adv. Internat. Studies, 2000-01. Hon. fellow Cambridge U. Ctr. for Rsch. in Internat. Law, 1983—; mem. bd. electors Whewell Professorship in Internat. Law U. Cambridge, 1983—; hon. bencher Gray's Inn, London, 1998—; spl. rep. Micronesian claims U.S. Dept. State, 1966—71; legal adv. U.S. del. 16th-20th and 4th Spl. Gen. Assemblies UN; U.S. assoc. rep. Internat. Ct. Justice, 1962, U.S. dep. agt., 1979, U.S. counsel, 1980; U.S. rep., chmn. U.S. del. to 1st session UN Spl. Com. on Principles Internat. Law concerning friendly rels. and coop. among states, Mexico City, 1964; US rep. numerous other UN coms.; pres. So. Blue Fin Tuna Arbitration, 2000; mem. Eritrea-Yemen Arbitration Tribunal, 1998—2000, Eritrea-Ethiopia Boundary Commn., 2001—; mem. panels arbitrators and conciliators Internat. Ctr. Settlement of Investment Disputes World Bank, 2000—; chmn. or party-apptd. arbitrator 37 internat. comml. arbitrations, 1982—2004; cons. Ford Found., 1990; chmn. supr. bd. Telders Internat. Law Moot Ct. Competition, The Hague, The Netherlands, 1993—98; chmn. Hauser Scholars Selection Bd., N.Y.U. Law Sch., 1997—2000; vis. lectr. in field; pres. Barbados-Trinidad &Tobago Arbitration, 2004—. Author: The Secretary-General of the United Nations, 1952, International Arbitration: Three Salient Problems, 1987, Justice in International Law, 1994; editor: The Effectiveness of International Decisions, 1971; mem. editorial bd. Am. Jour. Internat. Law, 1967-81, hon. mem., 1996- ; chmn. editoral adv. com. Internat. Legal Materials, 1967-73. Mem. UN Internat. Law Commn., Geneva, 1977—81. Frank Knox fellow Harvard U., 1950-51, Hallows Jud. fellow Marquette U. Law Sch., 2000; recipient Gherini prize Yale Law Sch., 1954, medal of Merit, 1997, Pres. medal Johns Hopkins U., 1992, Harold Weill medal NYU, 1992, Wolfgang Friedmann award Columbia U., 1998. Mem. ABA, Am. Soc. Internat. Law (exec. v.p. 1967-73, hon. v.p. 1982-95, hon. pres. 1996-2001, Manley O. Hudson medal 2000), Internat. Law Assn., Inst. Droit Internat., Coun. Fgn. Rels., Acad. of Experts (v.p. 1995—), Harvard Club (N.Y.C.), Athenaeum (London), Cosmos Club, Met Club (Washington), Phi Beta Kappa. Avocation: music. Office: 1501 K St NW Washington DC 20005 Office Phone: 202-736-8328. Personal E-mail: judgeschwebel@aol.com.

SCHWEBLER, STEPHEN, retired chemist; b. Flemington, N.J., Dec. 5, 1928; s. Philip and Elizabeth (Pratscher) S.; m. Marian Finch, May 3, 1953; children: Bradley Stephen, Susan Elizabeth, Nancy Carol. AS, Columbia-Greene C.C., Hudson, N.Y., 1974; BS, SUNY, Saratoga, 1982. With Marshall's Chrysler-Plymouth, Ravena, N.Y., 1953-56; owner/mgr. Steve's Auto Svc., Coxsackie, N.Y., 1956-58; svc. mgr. Jackson & Boone Chrysler-Plymouth, West Coxsackie, N.Y., 1958-66; sr. lab. technician N.Y. State Dept. Health, Albany, 1966-72, N.Y. State Dept. Environ. Conservation, Albany, 1972-85; phys. chemist N.Y. State Office Gen. Svcs., Albany, 1985-88, specification writer, 1988-90, N.Y. State Thruway Authority, Albany, 1990-94; ret. Deacon New Baltimore Ref. Ch., N.Y., 1985-90; rsch. vol. Greene County Hist. Soc., West Coxsackie, 1996—. Democrat. Reformed Ch. Achievements include developing first confirmatory test for the birth defect, galactosemia, by paper chromatography; research in improved methods of sewage treatment and toxic substance monitoring of all bodies of water in N.Y. state. Home: 3931 Rt 51 Hannacroix NY 12087-9708 E-mail: SSchwebler@cs.com.

SCHWEGMANN, MELINDA, supermarket executive, former state official; b. Austin, Tex., Oct. 25, 1946; m. John F. Schwegmann; 3 children. Student, La. State U.; grad. in Edn., U. New Orleans, 1968. Former pub. sch. tchr.; past pres. La. Soc. for Prevention of Cruelty to Animals; lt. gov. La., 1991-95; now dir. Schwegmann's Giant Supermarkets; now mem. La. Ho. of Reps. Mem. bd. Schwegmann Giant Super Markets; chmn. bd. Goodwill Industries; bd. dirs. Met. Area Com. New Orleans; sec. bd. dir.s Jr. Achievement; former mem. Jefferson Beautification Com. Office: State Representative 104 Sena Srive Metairie LA 70005

SCHWEICKART, JIM, advertising executive, broadcast executive, consultant; b. Toledo, June 25, 1950; s. Norman Marvin and Anne Belle (Cress) S.; m. Deborah J., Aug. 14, 1971; children: Jennifer, Kimberly, Stephen. BA in Polit. Sci, Taylor U., Upland, Ind., 1972. News anchor, announcer Sta. WCMR, Elkhart, Ind., 1967-71; news anchor, disc jockey Sta. WWHC, Hartford City, Ind., 1971-72; gen. mgr. Sta. WTUC, Taylor U., 1971; news dir. Sta. WCMR, Elkhart, 1972-74; news anchor Sta. WOWO, Fort Wayne, Ind., 1974-78, Sta. KDKA, Pitts., 1978-79; gen. mgr. Sta. WBCL-FM, Fort Wayne, 1979-85; owner advt. agy., broadcast cons. Schweickar & Assocs. Inc., Fort Wayne, 1984—; pub Aboite Independent.com, 2004—. Mem. adv. bd. Taylor U., Fort Wayne campus. Republican. Baptist. Office: 3452 Stellhorn Rd Fort Wayne IN 46815-4630

SCHWEICKERT, RICHARD JUSTUS, psychologist, educator; b. Madison, Wis., July 19, 1946; s. Carl E. and Marie E. (Dilzer) S.; m. Carolyn M. Jagacinski, Dec. 27, 1980; children: Patrick, Kenneth. BS in Math., U. Santa Clara, 1968; MA in Math., Ind. U., 1972; PhD in Psychology, U. Mich., 1979. Statistician Bellevue Psychiatric Hosp., N.Y.C., 1969-71; asst. prof. Purdue U., West Lafayette, Ind., 1978-83, assoc. prof., 1984-91, prof., 1992—. Adv. panel on human cognition & perception NSF, 1993-96. Author: (with others) Handbook of Human Factors, 1987; editor Jour. Math. Psychology; assoc. editor Psychol. Bull. and Rev., 1993-98; mem. editl. bd. Jour. Exptl. Psychology; Learning, Memory and Cognition, 1985-89, 91-94, Jour. Math. Psychology, 1986-94; contbr. articles to profl. jours. Grantee NSF, 1981-84, 92-2000, NIMH, 1983-89. Fellow AAAS, Am. Psychol. Soc.; mem. Soc. for Math. Psychology (pres. 1990-91, bd. dirs.), Psychonomic Soc., Informs. Office: Purdue U Dept Psychol Scis Lafayette IN 47907

SCHWEIGERT, JACK, lawyer; b. July 26, 1947; s. Charles Arthur and Alma Mae S.; m. Valerie Bavero, 1981; children: Carly, Scott. BS in Econs., U. Gannon, 1969; JD, U. Akron, 1974. Bar: Hawaii 1975, U.S. Ct. Appeals (9th cir.) 1975, U.S. Supreme Ct. 1978. Pvt. practice, Honolulu, 1975—. With U.S. Army, 1969-71. Mem. Honolulu Lions Club (dist. 50 legal counsel, Melvin Jones award 1997-98). Office: The Lawyers Bldg 550 Halekauwila St Ste 309 Honolulu HI 96813-5035 Fax: 808-533-7490. Office Phone: 808-533-7491. E-mail: conlawjack@cs.com.

SCHWEIKER, RICHARD SCHULTZ, trade association executive, former senator, former cabinet secretary; b. Norristown, Pa., June 1, 1926; s. Malcolm Alderfer and Blanche (Schultz) S.; m. Claire Joan Coleman, Sept. 10, 1955; children: Malcolm C., Lani, Kyle, Richard S. Jr., Lara Kristi. BA, Pa. State U., 1950; D of Pub. Svcs. (hon.), Temple U., 1970; D.Sc. (hon.), Georgetown U., 1981. Bus. exec., 1950-60; mem. 87th-90th congresses from 13th Dist. Pa., mem. house armed services and govt. ops. coms.; U.S. senator from Pa., 1969-80; mem. appropriations com., ranking mem. Labor-HEW subcom., ranking mem. health and human resources com., ranking mem. health subcom.; sec. HHS, 1981-83; pres. Am. Council Life Ins., Washington, 1983-94. Chmn. Partnership for Prevention, 1991—97. Alt. del. Nat. Rep. Conv., 1952, 56, del., 1972, 80; designated v.p. candidate with Reagan for Pres. of U.S., 1976. Served with USNR, World War II. Recipient Disting. Alumnus award Pa. State U., 1970, Dr. Charles H. Best award Am. Diabetes Assn., 1974, Outstanding Alumnus of Yr. award Phi Kappa Sigma, 1982, Gold medal Pa. Assn. Broadcasters, 1982, Nat. Outstanding Svc. award Headstart, 1983, Pub. Svc. Gold medal Surgeon Gen. U.S., 1988, Govt. Achievement award Juvenile Diabetes Found., 1990, Disting. Achievement award Nat. Coun. on Aging, 1991, John Newton Russell award Nat. Assn. Life Underwriters, 1992; named Outstanding Young Man of Yr., Jr. C. of C., 1960. Mem. Phi Beta Kappa.

SCHWEIKERT, EDGAR OSKAR, dentist; b. Heidelberg, Germany, Aug. 30, 1938; came to U.S., 1972; s. Oskar and Priska (Zehr) S.; m. Mary Lou Como, Apr. 7, 1969; 1 child, Marisa. Degree, Hamburg Dental Sch., 1966; Dr. Med. Dentistry, U. Munich, 1969. Lic. dentist, Calif., N.Y. Dentist, U.S. Army, Frankfurt, Fed. Republic Germany, 1969-72; gen. practice dentistry, L.A., 1972-73, Bklyn., 1973—; lectr. in field. Author Multiple Cantilevers in Fixed Prosthesis, 1988, Spanish edit., 1990; contbr. articles to profl. jours. Served as capt. German Air Force, 1967-69. Mem. ADA, German Dental Assn., Second Dist. Dental Assn., Bay Ridge Dental Soc., Guild Dental Craftsmen. Home and Office: 429 77th St Brooklyn NY 11209-3205 Office Phone: 718-680-4717.

SCHWEIKERT, NORMAN CARL, retired musician; b. Los Angeles, Oct. 8, 1937; s. Carl Albert and Hilda (Meade) S.; m. Sally Hardin Haizlip, July 22, 1961; 1 son, Eric Carl. Mus.B. performer's certificate in horn, Eastman Sch. Music, 1961. Teaching assoc. Northwestern U., 1973-75, assoc. prof. (part-time), 1975-98; horn instr. Nat. Music Camp, Interlochen, 1967; curator Leland B. Greenleaf Collection Mus. Instruments, Interlochen, 1970-71 Successively 4th, 2d and 3d horn with, Rochester Philharmonic, Civic and Eastman-Rochester symphonies, 1955-62, 64-66, instr. horn, mem., Interlochen (Mich.) Arts Quintet, Interlochen Arts Acad., 1966-71, 1st horn, Rochester Chamber Orch., 1965-66, Midland (Mich.) Symphony Orch., 1969-71, 1st horn, soloist, Northwestern Mich. Symphony Orch., 1966-71, Chgo. Little Symphony, tours, 1967, 68, asst. 1st horn, soloist, Chgo. Symphony Orch., 1971-75, 2d horn, Chgo. Symphony Orch., 1975-97; appearances with, Eastman Chamber Orch., Rochester Bach Festival, Aspen Festival Orch., Moravian Music Festival, Alaska Festival, Peninsula Music Festival, Rochester Brass Quintet, Canterbury Wind Quintet, Westchester Brass Quintet, Eastman Wind Ensemble, Chgo. Symphony Winds, Quadrangle Chamber Players, Washington Island Music Festival; soloist, New Japan Philharmonic, rec. artist for, Mercury, Columbia, Everest, C.R.I., Capitol, Mark Ednl., London-Decca, DGG, RCA Victor records, Sheffield Lab, Koch, recitals, also lecture demonstrations.; Contbr. articles to profl. jours. Served with AUS, 1962-64. Recipient certificate of merit City Chgo., 1971 Mem. Internat. Horn Soc. (hon., chmn. organizing com., sec.-treas. 1970-72, adv. coun. 1972-76), Am. Mus. Instrument Soc., Phi Mu Alpha Sinfonia (life alumni mem.), Pi Kappa Lambda. Home: RR 1 Box 40-s Washington Island WI 54246-9708

SCHWEINLE, AMY, psychologist, educator; b. Kansas City, Kans., Oct. 4, 1971; d. Ernest Richard and Marilyn Sue Putthoff; m. William Edwin Schweinle III, Feb. 13, 1999. BA in Psychology, Midwestern State U., 1993; MS in Exptl. Psychology, U. Tex., Arlington, 1998, PhD in Exptl. Psychology, 2001. Adminstrv. asst. Wichita Falls (Tex.) Texans CBA, 1993—94; client devel. dir. Wichita Falls Maternity Cottage, 1993—94; case mgr. Helen Farabee Mental Health Mental Retardation Ctr., Wichita Falls, 1994—95; tchg./rsch. asst. U. Tex., Arlington, 1995—99, tchg./rsch. assoc., 1999—2001; postdoctoral rsch. assoc. U. Notre Dame, South Bend, Ind., 2001—03; vis. asst. prof. U. So. Miss., Hattiesburg, 2003; asst. prof. U. SD, Vermillion, 2003—. Statis. cons. U. Tex., Arlington, 1998—2001; ad hoc editl. cons. Ednl. Psychologist, 2002; textbook reviewer Prentice-Hall, 2003; presenter in field. Contbr. articles to profl. jours., chpt. to book. Bd. dirs. Wichita Falls Maternity Cottage, 1995. Scholar, U. Tex., Arlington, 2001; travel/rsch. grantee, Nat. Inst. Drug Abuse, 2001. Mem.: APA, Soc. for Rsch. in Child Devel., Am. Psychol. Soc. Roman Catholic. Avocations: reading, kickboxing, egg painting, gardening. Office: Univ SD Dept Counseling and Psychology Edn 414 E Clark St Vermillion SD 57069 Home: 202 S Howard St Vermillion SD 57069-2209 E-mail: aschwein@usd.edu.

SCHWEINSBURG, JANE DUBERG, librarian; b. Chgo., Oct. 24, 1946; d. John Edward and Mary Andrews Duberg; m. Richard Lyle Schweinsburg, Sept. 3, 1977. BA in Math., Goucher Coll., Towson, Md., 1967; MLS, SUNY, Albany, 1996. Reference libr. Schenectady County C.C., Schenectady, NY; reference libr. and instr. Coll. of St. Rose, Albany, NY, 1996—98; reference libr. Johnson and Wales U., Providence, 1998—99, East Providence Pub. Libr., 1999—2000; asst. dir. Coventry Pub. Libr., Coventry, RI, 2000—. Contbr. articles to encys. and publs. Co-chair Episcopal charities campaign Episcopal Diocese of R.I., Providence, 1999—2000. Recipient Profl. Achievement award, Coll. of St. Rose, 1997. Mem.: R.I. Libr. Assn. (intellectual freedom com.). Episcopalian. Home: 46 Fairway Dr Coventry RI 02816-5775 Office: Coventry Pub Libr 1672 Flat River Rd Coventry RI 02816 Office Phone: 401-822-9104. E-mail: js@coventrylibrary.org.

SCHWEITZER, CHRISTOPH EUGEN, liberal studies educator; b. Berlin, July 11, 1922; came to U.S., 1945; s. Ernst Eugen and Franziska Ida (Körte) S.; m. Catherine Ann Plescher, Sept. 3, 1949; children: Stephen Adrian, Peter Savage. MA in Spanish, U. Wis., 1949, MA in German, 1950; PhD in German, Yale U., 1954. Instr. Yale U., New Haven, 1953-57, asst. prof., 1957-59; assoc. prof., chmn. dept. German Bryn Mawr (Pa.) Coll., 1959-65, prof., 1965-70; prof., chmn. Germanic langs. U. N.C., Chapel Hill, 1970-75, prof., 1975-93. Vis. prof. U. Colo., Boulder, 1959, Yale U., 1980, U. Augsburg, Fed. Republic of Germany, 1984, Duke U., Durham, 1988. Editor: Goes Das Loffelchen, 1968, Lessing's Nathan der Weise, 1970, 84, Albertinus, Verachtung des Hoflebens, 1986, (manuscript) Deliciae Hortenses, 1982, (dictionary) Dictionary of Literary Biography, 1990, 91, Carove's Kinderleben/Sarah Austin's Story Without an End, 1995, (book) Men Viewing Women as Art Objects, 1998, Führer Wahrheit und Guter Rath, 2003; mem. editl. bd. Lessing Yearbook, 1976—, Yearbook of German-Am. Studies, 1982—, South Atlantic Rev., 1985-88. Mem. nat. adv. bd. Wayne State U. Jr. Yr. Abroad Program, 1960-93; mem. coll. bd. German Advanced Placement Test Devel. Com., 1980-87, chmn., 1983-87. Cpl. U.S. Army, 1946-47. Mem. Goethe Soc. N.Am. (pres. 1990-91). Democrat. Presbyterian. Avocation: tennis.

SCHWEITZER, GEORGE KEENE, chemistry professor; b. Poplar Bluff, Mo., Dec. 5, 1924; s. Francis John and Ruth Elizabeth (Keene) S.; m. Verna Lee Pratt, June 4, 1948; children: Ruth Anne, Deborah Keene, Eric George. BA, Central Coll., 1945, ScD in Philosophy, 1964; MS, U. Ill., 1946, PhD in Chemistry, 1948; MA, Columbia U., 1959; PhD in History, NYU, 1964. Asst. Central Coll., 1943-45; fellow U. Ill., 1946-48; asst. prof. chemistry U. Tenn., 1948-52, assoc. prof., 1952-58, prof., 1960-69, Alumni Distinguished prof., 1970—. Cons. to Monsanto Co., Proctor & Gamble, Internat. Tech., Am. Cyanamid Co., AEC, U.S. Army, Massengill, CTI-Siemens; lectr. colls. and univs.; mem. adv. bd. East Tenn. Hist. Soc. Author: Radioactive Tracer Techniques, 1950, The Doctorate, 1966, Genealogical Source Handbook, 1992, Civil War Genealogy, 1993, Tennessee Genealogical Research, 1981, Kentucky Genealogical Research, 1981, Revolutionary War Genealogy, 1982, Virginia Genealogical Research, 1982, War of 1812 Genealogy, 1983, North Carolina Genealogical Research, 1983, South Carolina Genealogical Research, 1984, Pennsylvania Genealogical Research, 1985, Georgia Genealogical Research, 1987, New York Genealogical Research, 1988, Massachusetts Genealogical Research, 1989, Maryland Genealogical Research, 1991, German Genealogical Research, 1992, Ohio Genealogical Research, 1994, Indiana Genealogical Research, 1996, Illinois Genealogical Research, 1997, Missouri Genealogical Research, 1997; also 170 articles. Faculty fellow Columbia U., 1958-60. Mem. Am. Chem. Soc., Am. Philos. Assn., History Sci. Soc., Soc. Genealogists, Phi Beta Kappa, Sigma Xi. Home: 407 Ascot Ct Knoxville TN 37923-5807

SCHWEITZER, LOREN MARCUS, computer programmer; b. Ft. Worth, Jan. 3, 1966; s. Leonard and Rose-Marie (Gustafson) S. BA in Econs., U. Tex., 1989. Analyst Nat. Asset Placement Corp., Dallas, 1995-96; programmer I Daily Data Inc., Dallas, 1996-98; programmer II Blockbuster Inc., Dallas, 1999, Bank Am., Dallas, 2000—. Mem. Delphi Developers Dallas, 1999—. Home: 14902 Preston Rd # 404-313 Dallas TX 75254-9191 E-mail: lorens@airmail.net.

SCHWEITZER, N. TINA, fiction writer, photojournalist, television producer, director, international consultant public relations, media relations, government relations; b. Hartford, Conn., Apr. 7, 1941; d. Abraham Aaron Morris and Ruth Blanche (Shifreen) S. BS, Emerson Coll., 1964. Freelance writer, Boston and Washington, 1965-67; mem. press, info. staff Embassy of Republic of Indonesia, Washington, 1967-68; researcher, writer Congl. Quar., Inc., Washington, 1969-70; owner Schweitzer Assocs., Hartford, Conn. and Washington, 1970-78, 79—. Dir. comty. rels., media rels. and govt. rels.

Advocacy Svcs. for the Deaf, West Hartford, Conn., 1978-79; del. White House Conf. Small Bus., 1986; mem. faculty Conn. Re-employment Workshop Middlesex Comty. Tech. Coll.; profl. model; ind. TV prodr. Editor, chief prodn. Focus on Indonesia, Washington, 1967-68; corr. The Farmington (Conn.) Valley Herald, 1984; first bus. columnist Hartford Woman newspaper, 1984; contbr. articles to numerous govtl. and comml. publs. including U.S.I.S.; author: Media Kit, 1978, Women's Job Hunting Guide, 1983, You Can Do It! A Practical Guide for Job Hunting and Career-Changing, 1987, Men On the Tor (Violet Hunter), 1990; writer, designer, producer first series of TV videotape pub. svc. announcements on employment deaf or hard-of-hearing in the history of Conn., 1983-84; contbr. editorials to TV Stas. WFSB, 1977, 84, 86, WVIT, 1983; writer, ind. producer, dir., talk-show host Sta. WVIT-TV, 1987; works/fiction included in permanent collection Smith Coll. Lib., Northampton, Mass. Mem. State-wide Health Coordinating Coun., a U.S. Govt./State of Conn. Health Dept. project, 1978-80; adviser Conn. Office Advocacy to Handicapped; mem. legis. task force State of Conn., 1978-79; del. first Conn. Gov.'s Conf. on Libr. and Info. Svcs., 1978; candidate Conn. Ho. of Reps., 1982; aux. police officer Hartford Police Dept., 1976-77; acting chmn. Comm. Com. Unitarian Meeting House, West Hartford; dir. pub. rels. Greater Hartford Com. UNICEF, 1984-86; affiliated Rep. Town Com., Hartford., 1989; apptd. to Nat. Pub. Rels./Advt. Adv. Coun. Am. Mensa Ltd., 1989; press liason Mensa Internat. Offices, press rep. 1st Joint Conf. Am. Coun. Edn. and Conf. European Rectors, 1989. Recipient Presdl. Sports award Pres.'s Coun. on Phys. Fitness and Sports, 1992, 93, 94, 96; hon. fellow John F. Kennedy Presdl. Libr. Mus. Found. Mem. Nat. Writers Union, Nat. Press Photographers Assn., Inter-Am. Press Assn., American Mensa, Ltd., Sherlock Holmes Soc. London, Sigma Delta Chi. Address: 576C Mountain Rd West Hartford CT 06117-1826 Home: PO Box 974 Hartford CT 06143

SCHWEITZER, PETER, advertising agency executive; b. Chgo., Aug. 31, 1939; children: Mark, Cynthia, Jenifer, Samantha; m. Elaine Elkin, 1986; children: Dana, Taylor. BA, U. of Mich., 1961; MBA, W. Mich. U., 1967. With Post div. Gen. Foods, 1961-69; v.p. Grey Advt., 1969-76; sr. v.p. J. Walter Thompson, 1976-79; sr. v.p. mktg. Burger King Corp., 1990; sr. v.p., gen. mgr., then exec. v.p., gen. mgr. J. Walter Thompson USA, Inc.-Detroit, 1995; v. chmn. of agency ops. J. Walter Thompson Co., Detroit, 1988-95, pres., 1995—, CEO, 2001—. Pres. Internat. Fedn. Multiple Sclerosis. Office: J Walter Thompson Co 500 Woodward Ave 14th Fl Detroit MI 48226-3416 also: 466 Lexington Ave New York NY 10017-3140

SCHWEITZER, SANDRA LYNN, lawyer, nurse; b. San Jose, Calif., Nov. 16, 1952; d. Raymond Oliver and Joanne McLean; children: Brian, Laura, Christopher. BSN, Cornell U., 1974; JD, Georgetown U., 1979. Bar: Md. 1980, D.C. 1980, Calif. 1994, U.S. Dist. Ct. Md. 1980, U.S. Dist. Ct. (no. dist.) Calif. 1994, U.S. Ct. Appeals (D.C., fed. and 4th cirs.) 1987, U.S. Ct. Appeals (9th cir.) 1994, U.S. Supreme Ct. 1987; RN, Calif.; cert. family law specialist, Calif. Assoc. Shulman, Rogers, Gandal et al, Silver Spring, Md., 1978-81; pvt. practice Potomac, Md., 1981-86; assoc. Miller & Chevalier, Washington, 1987; pvt. practice Bethesda, Md., 1988-89; ptnr. Johnston & Schweitzer, P.A., Washington, 1990-93; pvt. practice Bethesda, Md., 1993—94, Oakland, Calif., 1994—2000, Chico, Calif., 2000—. Adj. prof. George Washington U. Med. Sch., 1988-1994 Mem. bus. and profl. women's coun. Nat. Mus. of Women in the Arts, 1991-94. Served to capt. U.S. Army Nurse Corps, 1974-76. Fellow Am. Acad. Matrimonial Lawyers; mem. ABA, D.C. Bar Assn., State Bar Assn. Calif, Md. State Bar Assn., Calif. Women Lawyers, Butte County Bar Assn., Nat. Assn. Counsel for Children, Assn. of Family and Conciliation Cts., Assn. Cert. Family Law Specialists, Sigma Theta Tau. Office: Law Office Sandra L Schweitzer 2725 The Esplanade Chico CA 95973

SCHWEITZER, THEODORE GOTTLIEB, III, United Nations administrator; b. Hannibal, Mo., Aug. 28, 1942; s. Theodore Gottlieb Jr. and Dorothy Lois (Burnett) S. Cert. in French Lang., U. Paris, 1968; BA, U. Iowa, 1970, MA, 1974; student, Hanoi (Vietnam) Fgn. Langs. U., 1992-94. Cert. Thai Lang. Am. Univ. Alumnae Assn., Bangkok, 1976, profl. tchr., Iowa. Tchr., librarian Lewis County Schs., Ewing, Mo., 1971-73; head librarian Internat. Sch., Bangkok, 1974-76; info. officer U.S. Army, Udorn, Thailand, 1974-76; dir. media services Am. Sch., Teheran, 1976-77, dir. media svcs. Isfahan, Iran, 1977-78; refugee officer UN HCR, Geneva and Bangkok, 1979—. Founder S.E. Asia Rescue Found., Ft. Walton Beach, Fla., 1981—. Hanoi Fgn. Langs. U., 1992-94. Author: (with Malcolm McConnell) Inside Hanoi's Secret Archives-Solving the MIA Mystery, 1995. Spl. rep. to Vietnam, Office of the Sec. of Def., Washington, 1992-94. With USAF, 1959-62. Recipient Award of merit SOS Boat people Com., San Diego, 1982, replica of Nobel Peace Prize, UN High Commr. for Refugees, 1981. Mem. Mensa, BPOE. Republican. Baptist. Avocations: writing, reading, scuba diving, photography, private pilot. Office: UN High Commr for Refuges Palais Des Nations Geneva Switzerland E-mail: ted@searescue.org.

SCHWEIZER, KARL WOLFGANG, historian, educator, author; b. Mannheim, Fed. Republic Germany, June 30, 1946; came to U.S., 1988; 1 child, Paul. BA in History, Wilfrid Laurier U., Can., 1969; MA, U. Waterloo, Can., 1970; MA, PhD, Cambridge U., 1976. Prof. history Bishop's U., Lenoxville, Canada, 1976-88, chmn. dept., 1978-79, 82-84, 86; prof., chmn. humanities dept. N.J. Inst. Tech., Newark, 1988-93, prof. dept. social sci. and policy studies, 1993—, chmn. dept. humanities and social scis., 2000—03, prof. dept. humanities, 2003—; assoc. Ctr. for Study of Global Change Rutgers U., 1995—. Grad. faculty Rutgers U., 1993—; vis. lectr. U. Guelph, Can., 1978-80; rsch. assoc. Russian Rsch. Ctr., Ill., 1979-80, 99; acad. visitor London Sch. Econs., 1986, 94, vis. scholar, 1986-87, Queens U., Ont., Can., 1986-87; vis. fellow Darwin Coll., Cambridge, 1987, 94, 2003, Princeton U., 1994, Yale U., 1994; vis. prof. dept. polit. sci. Rutgers U., 1997—; sr. rsch. assoc. Peterhouse Coll., Cambridge, 2003. Author: The Art of Diplomacy, 1983, Lord Bute: Essays in Reinterpretation, 1988, England, Prussia and the Seven Years War, 1989, Frederick the Great, William Pitt and Lord Bute, 1991, Lord Chatham, 1993, François de Callières: Diplomat and Man of Letters, 1995, War, Politics and Diplomacy: The Anglo Prussian Alliance, 1756-1763, 2001, Seeds of Evil: The Gray/Snyder Murder Case, 2001, Statesmen, Diplomats and the Press, 2003; co-author: British Literary Periodicals, 1983, The Origins of War in Early Modern Europe, 1987; co-author: (with J. Osborne) Cobbett in His Times, 1990; co-author: paperback edit., 1993, The War of the Spanish Succession, 1994, British Prime Ministers, 1997, Hanoverian Britain and Empire, 1998, Oxford Dictionary of the Enlightenment, 2003, Scribners Dictionary of Modern European History, 2003, Dictionary of National Biography, 2004; editor: The Devonshire Political Diary, 1757-1762, 1982, Diplomatic Thought 1648-1815, 1982, Warfare and Tactics in the 18th Century, 1984, Herbert Butterfield: Essays on the History of Science, 1998, In Defense of Australia's Constitutional Monarchy, 2004; co-editor: Essays in European History 1648-1815 in Honour of Ragnhild Hatton, 1985, Politics and the Press in Hanoverian Britain, 1989; gen. editor: Studies in History and Politics, 1980—91, editl. cons.: Scribner's Dictionary of Modern European History, Oxford Dictionary of National Biography; contbr. articles to profl. jours. Mem. NJ Gov.'s Adv. Panel on Higher Edn. Restructuring, 1994; trustee NJ Literary Hall of Fame, 1988—92. Recipient Thesis Def. award Can. Coun., 1976, travel awards Peterhouse Coll., 1971-73, Adelle Mellen prize for outstanding contbn. to scholarship Edwin Mellen Press, 1989, Author's award N.J. Writer's Conf., 1993, Tchg. award N.J. Inst. Tech., 2000; fellow U. Waterloo, 1969-70, Province of Ont., 1969-70, Can. Coun., 1970-75; named Wilfred Laurier Proficiency scholar, 1966-69; rsch. grantee Bishop's U., 1977, 78, 80, 82, 83, postdoctoral rsch. grantee Can. Coun., 1977-78, 82-83, grantee Inter-Univ. Ctr. for European Studies, 1978, 81, conf. grantee S.S.H.R.C., 1985; travel grantee NEH, 1991, N.J. Com. for Humanities, 1988-1992; Mellon fellow Harvard U., 1978. Fellow Royal Hist. Soc.; mem. Internat. Commn. on History of Internat. Rels., Hist. Soc., Cambridge Hist. Soc., North American Conf. on Brit. Studies, Can. Assn. Scottish Studies, Can. Assn. 18th Century Studies. Avocations: music, writing, reading. Home: 49 S Passaic Ave Apt 24 Chatham NJ 07928 Office: NJ Inst Tech Dept Social Sci and Policy Newark NJ 07102

SCHWEIZER, NIKLAUS R. German educator; b. Zurich, Aug. 24, 1939; arrived in U.S., 1964; s. Rudolf Alexander Schweizer and Hedwig Louise Ulrich. BA, U. Zurich, 1964; PhD, U. Calif., Davis, 1968. Tchr. German Punahou Sch., Honolulu, 1968—70; vis. asst. prof. German Dept. European Lang. and Lit. U. Hawaii, Manoa, 1969—70, asst. prof. German, 1970—74, assoc. prof. German, 1974—83, prof. German, 1983—. Hon. consul of Switzerland, Honolulu, 1972—. Author: (novels) His Hawaiian Excellency, 1987, 1994, 2004, (book) The Ut pictura poesis Controversy in Eighteenth-Century England and Germany, 1972, A Poet Among Explorers: Chamisso in the South Seas, 1973, Hawaii und die deutschsprachigen Völker, 1982, Hawaii and the German Speaking Peoples, 1982, Seine hawaiische Exzellenz, 1990, Turning Tide: The Ebb and Flow of Hawaiian Nationality, 1999, 2002; editor: By Royal Command: Biographical Notes on Curtis Piehu Iaukea, 1988, Jour. des Malers Ludwig York Choris, 1999; contbr. articles to profl. jours., chpts. to books. Dean Consular Corps of Hawaii, 1986, historian, 1988—; pres. Friends of the Royal Hawaiian Band, 1979—99; steering com. Annexation Observance Hawai'i Loa Ku Like Kakou, 1998; bd. dirs. Friends of Iolani Palace, 1982—, chair spl. events com., 1980—; pres., mem. coun. Hui Hanai, aux. Queen Lili 'uokalani Children Trust, 1987, mem. coun., 1981—87; chmn. bd. Friends of the Royal Hawaiian Band, 1999—; bd. dirs. Ahahui Ka'iulani, 1990—, Moanalua Gardens Found., 1994—; del. Friends of Iolani Palace, 1996—. Recipient 1st Ann. Award, German-Hawaiian Friendship Club, 1998. Mem.: PEN Ctr. USA West, Pacific Translators, Royal Order of Kamehameha (hon.), German-Hawaiian Comm. and Friendship Club (hon.). Avocations: amateur radio, tennis, skiing, swimming. Office: Univ of Hawaii at Manoa Lang and Lit of Europe and the Ams 1890 East-West Rd Moore 483 Honolulu HI 96822 Office Phone: 808-956-4184. Business E-Mail: niklaus@hawaii.edu.

SCHWEIZER, PAUL DOUGLAS, museum director; b. Bklyn., Nov. 26, 1946; s. Alvin Charles and Marie Gertrude (Scholtz) S.; m. Jane Kulczycki, June 10, 1978 (div. 2004). BA, Marietta Coll., Ohio, 1968; MA, U. Del., 1975, PhD, 1979; postgrad. Mus. Mgmt. Inst., U. Calif., Berkeley, 1990. Instr. art history St Lawrence U., Canton, N.Y., 1977-78; asst. prof. St. Lawrence U., Canton, N.Y., 1978-80; curator St. Lawrence U. (Brush Gallery), Canton, N.Y., 1977-78; dir. St. Lawrence U., Canton, N.Y., 1979-80; dir. and chief curator Munson-Williams-Proctor Arts Inst. Mus. Art, Utica, 1980—; adj. prof. art history Pratt at Munson-Williams-Proctor, 2000—. Mem. vis. com. Picker Art Gallery, Colgate U., 1999—. Author exhbn. catalog; contbr. articles to profl. jours. Bd. dirs. Remington Art Mus., Ogdensburg, N.Y., 1979-80; bd. dirs. Williamstown (Mass.) Regional Art Conservation Lab., 1981-92, pres., 1988-92. Rsch. grantee Nat. Endowment for Arts, 1978. Mem. Coll. Art Assn., Assn. Art Mus. Dirs., N.Y. State Assn. Art Mus. (trustee 1993-95), Mus. Assn. N.Y. (councilor 1995-2002), Gallery Assn. of N.Y. (bd. dirs. 1996-2002, pres. 1999), Otsego Sailing Club, Alpha Sigma Phi, Omicron Delta Kappa. Office: Munson-Williams-Proctor Arts Inst Mus Art 310 Genesee St Utica NY 13502-4799 E-mail: pschweiz@mwpai.edu.

SCHWELB, FRANK ERNEST, appellate judge; b. Prague, Czechoslovakia, June 24, 1932; came to U.S., 1947; s. Egon and Caroline (Redisch) S.; m. Taffy Wurzburg, Apr. 9, 1988. BA, Yale U., 1949-53; LLB, Harvard U., 1958. Bar: N.Y. Ct. Appeals 1958, U.S. Dist. Ct. (so. and ea. dists.) N.Y. 1960, U.S. Ct. Appeals (2d cir.) 1961, U.S. Supreme Ct. 1965, U.S. Ct. Appeals (4th cir.) 1968, D.C., D.C. Ct. Appeals, U.S. Dist. Ct. D.C. 1972. Assoc. Mudge, Stern, Baldwin & Todd, N.Y.C., 1958-62; trial atty. Civil Rights Div. U.S. Dept. Justice, Washington, 1962-79, chief eastern sect., 1969, chief housing sect., 1969-79, spl. counsel for litigation, 1979; spl. counsel rev. panel on new drug regulation HEW, Washington, 1976-77; assoc. judge Superior Ct. D.C., Washington, 1979-88, D.C. Ct. Appeals, Washington, 1988—. Instr. various legal edn. activities. Contbr. articles to profl. jours. With U.S. Army, 1955-57. Recipient Younger Fed. Lawyer award, Fed. Bar Assn., 1967. Mem. Bar Assn. D.C., World Peace Through Law Ctr., World Assn. Judges, Czechoslovak-Am. Orgns., De Tocqueville Soc., Order of the Battered Boot. Achievements include proficiency in Czech, French and German. Avocations: tennis, ping pong/table tennis, sports, gilbert and sullivan operettas, shakespeare. Home: 4879 Potomac Ave NW Washington DC 20007-1539 Office: DC Ct Appeals 500 Indiana Ave NW Washington DC 20001-2138 E-mail: fschwelb@dcca.state.dc.us.

SCHWEMIN, JOSEPH, retired pharmacist; b. Blackwell, Okla., Aug. 14, 1921; s. Joseph Julian and Julia Ann (Grapes) S.; m. Bettye Mae Wright, June 12, 1943 (div. Aug. 1966); children: Sue, Mary, Joe; m. Louise Elizabeth Williams, Feb. 22, 1969; children: Julie, Joey. BS in Pharmacy, Southwestern Okla. State U., 1948. Registered pharmacist, Okla., Ark. Mgr. Madding Drug, Houston, 1950-51; owner Pharmacy, Houston, 1952-53, Vern Drug, Tulsa, 1955-75, J-Bar-J Ranch, Talihina, Okla., 1961-70; dir. Okla. State Bd. Pharmacy, Oklahoma City, 1965-89. Sgt. USMC, 1942-45, PTO. Recipient Hygeia award A.H. Robins Bowl, 1962, Disting. Alumni award Southwestern Okla. State U., 1981, Pharmacy Disting. Alumni award, 1976, Spl. Recognition award 1974, Outstanding Contbn. Pharmacy award, 1971, Gaffney Bldg. Mortgage Retirement Drive award Okla. Pharmacy Heritage Found., 1996. Mem. Nat. Assn. Bds. Pharmacy (pres. 1973, chmn.), An. Assn. Colls. Pharmacy (chmn. Dist. 6), Southwestern Okla. State U. Pharmacy Alumni Found. (pres. 1978-98), Tulsa C. of C., Lions Club (dist. gov. 3-0 1961-62), Beta Tau Beta (past pres.), Beta Tau Beta Fraternity Alumni (past pres.). Democrat. Roman Catholic. Avocations: golf, fishing. Home: 5025 NW 26th St Oklahoma City OK 73127-1750

SCHWEMM, JOHN BUTLER, printing company executive, lawyer; b. Barrington, Ill., May 18, 1934; s. Earl M. and Eunice (Butler) S.; m. Nancy Lea Prickett, Sept. 7, 1956; children: Catherine Ann, Karen Elizabeth. AB, Amherst Coll., 1956; JD, U. Mich., 1959. Bar: Ill. 1959. With Sidley & Austin, Chgo., 1959-65; with legal dept. R.R. Donnelley & Sons Co., Chgo., 1965-69, gen. counsel, 1969-75, v.p., 1971-75, pres., 1981-87, chmn., 1983-89, dir., 1980-92. Bd. dirs. William Blair Mut. Funds, Inc., Walgreen Co., USG Corp. Life trustee Northwestern U., Chgo. Mem. Law Club Chgo., Order of Coif, Phi Beta Kappa. Clubs: Chgo., Univ., Hinsdale (Ill.) Golf, Old Elm. Home (Summer): 2 Turvey Ct Downers Grove IL 60515-4530 Home and Office: 565 Sanctuary Dr Ste A401 Longboat Key FL 34228

SCHWEND, MICHAEL T. hospital administrator; m. Mary Jo Fitzpatrick. BS in Psychology, Truman State U., 1983, MA in Counseling and Guidance, 1990; MBA, William Woods U., 1997. Pres., CEO Preferred Family Healthcare, Kirksville, Mo. Mem. White House Commn. on Alcohol and Drug Abuse; sec. bd. govs. Truman State U., Kirksville, 2001—; former mem. Mo. Adv. Coun. on Alcohol and Drug Abuse; peer rev. specialist Tex. Commn. on Alcohol and Drug Abuse; active Kirksville R-III Athletic Booster Club; pres. bd. dirs. K-Life outreach program; active Immaculate Cath. Ch. Office: Preferred Family Healthcare 900 E LaHarpe Kirksville MO 63501

SCHWENDEMAN, PAUL WILLIAM, lawyer; b. Chgo., Apr. 7, 1945; s. Oscar and Edna Dorothy (Ellis) S.; m. Shirley Anne Starke; children: Paul A., John E., Thomas D. BA in Econs., Carleton Coll., 1966; MSJ, Northwestern U., 1967; JD, Duquesne U., 1978. Bar: Pa. 1978. Mgr. divsn. ops. Greater Waterbury (Conn.) C. of C., 1971-75; v.p. Greater Pitts. C. of C., 1975-78; assoc. Kirkpatrick & Lockhart, Pitts., 1978-84, ptnr., 1984—. Lt. USNR, 1971. Office: Kirkpatrick & Lockhart 1500 Oliver Bldg Pittsburgh PA 15222-2312

SCHWENDIMAN, STEPHEN GLENN, lawyer; b. Freeport, Ill., Apr. 2, 1948; s. Glenn and Helen (Snow) S.; m. Carolee Kulinsky, Sept. 3, 1971; children: Larah, Stephen, Karissa, Jeremy. BA, Brigham Young U., 1972; JD, U. Utah, 1975. Bar: Utah 1975. Asst. atty. gen. Utah, Salt Lake City, 1975—. Divsn. chief, 1983-89. Voting dist. vice chmn. Rep. Com., Salt Lake City, 1982-84, voting dist. chmn., 1988-90; scoutmaster, Boy Scouts Am., 1981-84, roundtable commr. Evergreen dist., 1980-84, asst. dist. commr., 183-85, dist. commr., 1985-89, dist. chmn., 1990-94, nat. jamboree scoutmaster, 1989, 97, dist. merit award, 1981, Silver Beaver award, 1990. Mem. Utah Bar Assn. Mem. Lds Ch. Office: Utah Atty Gen 160 E 300 S Salt Lake City UT 84111-2316

SCHWENKE, ROGER DEAN, lawyer; b. Washington, Oct. 18, 1944; s. Clarence Raymond and Virginia Ruth (Gould) S.; m. Carol Lynne Flenniken, Nov. 29, 1980; 1 child: Matthew Robert; stepchildren: Tracy L. Wolf Dickey, Mary M. Wolf. BA, Ohio State U., 1966; JD with honors, U. Fla., 1969. Bar: Fla. 1970. Instr. Coll. Law U. Fla., Gainesville, 1969-70; assoc. Carlton Fields, P.A., Tampa, Fla., 1970-74, ptnr., 1975—; adminstr., dept. head Real Estate, Environ. and Land Use Dept., 1978—99. Adj. prof. Coll. Law, Stetson U., St. Petersburg, Fla., 1979-80; mem. faculty U. Miami Coll. of Law Master of Law's in Real Estate Devel. Program, 1994-96. Author chpt. in Environmental Regulation and Litigation in Florida, 1987, chpt. in Florida Real Property Complex Transactions, 1997, 2000; contbr. articles to profl. jours., chpt. to book. Mem. diocesan coun. Episc. Diocese SW Fla., 1978-86, mem. standing com., 1989-92, chief judge Eccles. Ct., 1996—. Recipient Gertrude Brick Law Rev. prize U. Fla., 1969. Fellow Am. Coll. Real Estate Lawyers (bd. govs. 1985-88), Am. Law Inst.; mem. ABA (liaison to standong com. on environ. law 1980-87, mem. coun. real property sect. 1988-95), Fla. Bar Assn., Air and Waste Mgmt. Assn., Order of Coif, Greater Tampa C. of C. (chmn. environ. coun. 1980-81), Tampa Club. Democrat. Office: Carlton Fields PO Box 3239 Tampa FL 33601-3239 Fax: 813-229-4133. Office Phone: 813-229-4152. E-mail: rschwenke@carltonfields.com.

SCHWENN, LEE WILLIAM, retired medical center executive; b. Morrisonville, Wis., Dec. 23, 1925; s. LeRoy William and Vivian Mae (Kramer) S.; m. Glenna Edith Mehne, Jan. 16, 1947; 1 son, William Lee. BS, U. Wis., 1948; M.P.H., U. N.C., 1956. Tchr. pub. schs., Appleton, Wis., 1948-52; teaching cons. Wis. Health Dept., 1952-53; adminstrv. asst. Madison (Wis.) Health Dept., 1953-57; adminstrv. cons. U.S. Children's Bur., Atlanta Regional Office, 1957-58; adminstr. USPHS, Washington, 1958-66; assoc. dir. D.C. Dept. Health, 1966-70, D.C. Dept. Human Resources, 1970-71; exec. v.p. Maimonides Med. Center, Bklyn., 1971-88, pres., 1988-89, spl. cons. Bd. Trustees, 1989-96. Recipient Disting. Pub. Service award D.C. Govt., 1970 Mem. Delta Omega. Home: 1007 Westminster Dr Greensboro NC 27410-4551

SCHWERDTNER, FREDERICK HOWARD, lawyer, retired police commander, real estate broker; b. Chgo., Oct. 13, 1949; s. Fred and Lydia (Tatz) S.; m. Julie Anne Carramusa, Oct. 21, 1990; 1 child, Sarah Elizabeth. BS, Loyola U., Chgo., 1973, JD, 1989; MBA with distinction, DePaul U., 1983. Bar: Ill. 1989, US Dist. Ct. (no. dist.) Ill. 1989. Officer Oak Park (Ill.) Police Dept., 1973-93, commdr., 1989-93; with DuPage County Vets. Assistance Commn., 1995—, pres., 1997—99; lawyer Pvt. Practice, Ill. Contbr. articles to profl. jours. Tutor inner city high sch. students, Chgo., 1988; apptd. local bd. mem. Selective Svc. Sys., police commr. Bd. Police Commr., Village of Glendale Heights, Ill., 1999-, chmn., 2002-. Served USMC, 1965-69, Vietnam, 1967-68. Mem. ABA, Fraternal Order Police, Marine Corps League (Band of Bros. Detachment), Ill. State Bar Assn., Chgo. Bar Assn., DuPage County Bar Assn., Beta Gamma Sigma. Republican. Lutheran. Avocations: hiking, tennis, racquetball, golf. E-mail: vet-star@comcast.net.

SCHWERIN, KARL HENRY, anthropology educator, researcher; b. Bertha, Minn., Feb. 21, 1936; s. Henry William and Audrey Merle (Jahn) S.; m. Judith Drewanne Altermatt, Sept. 1, 1958 (div. May 1975); children: Karl Frederic, Marguerite DelValle; m. Partha Louise Hake Buell, Jan. 25, 1979; stepchildren: Tamara, Brent, Taryn. BA, U. Calif., Berkeley, 1958; PhD, UCLA, 1965. Instr. Los Angeles State Coll., 1963; asst. prof. anthropology U. N.Mex., Albuquerque, 1963-68, assoc. prof., 1968-72, prof., 1972-2001, asst. chmn. dept. anthropology, 1983-85, chmn. dept. anthropology, 1987-93, prof. emeritus, 2001—. Prof. invitado Inst. Venezolano de Investigaciones Cientificas, Caracas, 1979. Author: Oil and Steel Processes of Karinya Culture Change, 1966, Antropologia Social, 1969, Winds Across the Atlantic, 1970; editor: Food Energy in Tropical Ecosystems, 1985; contbr. articles to profl. jours. V.p. Parents without Ptnr., Albuquerque, 1976-77. Grantee Cordell Hull Found., Venezuela, 1961-62, N.Y. Zool. Soc., Honduras, 1981; Fulbright scholar Cañar, Ecuador, 1969-70, Paris, 1986; founded Karl H. Schwerin Fellowship in Ethnology. Fellow Am. Anthrop. Assn.; mem. Am. Ethnol. Soc., Am. Soc. Ethnohistory (pres. 1975), Southwestern Anthrop. Assn. (co-editor Southwestern Jour. Anthropology 1972-75), N.Mex. Cactus and Succulent Soc. (v.p. 1970-71), Internat. Congress of Americanists (35th-40th, 43d, 46th, 48th, 49th, 50th), Sigma Xi (chpt. pres. 1980-81). Avocations: photography, gardening, hiking, camping, bicycling. Office: U NMex Dept Anthropology Albuquerque NM 87131-0001 E-mail: schwerin@unm.edu.

SCHWERING, FELIX KARL, electronics engineer, researcher; b. Cologne, Nordrhein-Westfalen, Federal Republic of Germany, June 4, 1930; came to U.S., 1964; s. Felix Bernhard and Maria (Heinrichs) S. BS, U. Aachen, Federal Republic of Germany, 1951, Diplom-Ingenieur, 1954, PhD, 1957. Asst. prof. U. Aachen, Federal Republic of Germany, 1956-58; electronic scientist U.S. Army R & D Labs., Fort Monmouth, N.J., 1958-61; project leader AEG-Telefunken, Ulm, Federal Republic of Germany, 1961-64; rsch. scientist U.S. Army Communication Electronics Command (CECOM), Fort Monmouth, N.J., 1964-96, ret., 1996, cons., 1996—. Vis. lab. assoc. U.S. Army Rsch. Office, Rsch. Triangle, N.C., 1984-85; vis. prof. N.J. Inst. Tech., Newark, 1986—, Rutgers U., New Brunswick, N.J., 1973-87, Monmouth U., 1996—. Author: (with others) Millimeter Wave Antennas, 1988; author and editor (with others) Microwave Antennas, 1989; mem. editorial bd. Microwave and Optical Tech. Letters, 1988—; contbr. over 40 articles to profl. jours.; patentee in field. Fellow IEEE (Best Paper award Antennas and Propagation Soc. 1961, 82), Internat. Sci. Radio Union, Am. Geophys. Union, Armed Forces Comm. Electronics Assn., Sigma Xi. Roman Catholic. Office: US Army CERDEC Attn AMSRD-CER-ST-WL Fort Monmouth NJ 07703-5203 Office Phone: 732-532-0469. Business E-Mail: schwerin@mail1.monmouth.army.mil.

SCHWERT, G(EORGE) WILLIAM, III, finance educator; b. Durham, N.C., Jan. 26, 1950; s. George William Jr. and Margaret (Houlton) S.; m. Camille Matthews, Dec. 19, 1970 (div. 1983); 1 child, Lisa Margaret; m. Patricia Michel, Dec. 23, 1983; children: Michael William, Andrew Patrick. AB in Econs. with honors, Trinity Coll., 1971; MBA, U. Chgo., 1973, PhD in Fin., 1975. Asst. prof. Grad. Sch. Bus. U. Chgo., 1975-76; asst. prof. to prof. Simon Sch. Bus. U. Rochester, N.Y., 1976-86, Gleason prof. fin., 1986-98, Disting. U. prof., 1998—. Chmn. Knollwood Cons. Group, Inc., Rochester, 1987—. Co-editor Jour. Fin. Econs., 1979-86, 89-95, adv. editor, 1986-89, mng. editor 1995—; assoc. editor Jour. of Fin., 1983-2000, Jour. Monetary Econs., 1984—; contbr. articles to econs. jour. Recipient Smith-Breeden Disting. Paper prize Jour. Fin., 1990, Graham and Dodd plaque Fin. Analysts Jour., 1990. Mem. Am. Fin. Assn. (bd. dirs. 1987-89), Am. Econs. Assn., Econometrics Soc., Am. Statis. Assn. (chair bus. econs. sect. 1990-91). Avocations: tennis, boating, fishing, golf. Home: 71 Knollwood Dr Rochester NY 14618-3512 Office: U Rochester W E Simon Grad Sch Bus Adminstrn Rochester NY 14627

SCHWERTFEGER, TIMOTHY B. investment company executive; b. 1950; BA in Econs. and Fin., Northwestern U.; JD, Georgetown U.; student, Harvard Bus. Sch., Stanford U. Nat. dir. health care investment banking svcs. Nuveen Investments, Inc. (div. St. Paul Co., Inc.), 1977—86, head corp. mktg., 1987—89, exec. v.p. and bd. dirs., 1989—96, chmn. bd. dirs. Nuveen Mutual Funds and Exch.-traded Funds, 1996—, chmn. and CEO, 1996—. Pres. Hubbard St. Dance Chgo.; bd. dirs. Better Boys Found., Lyric Opera Chgo., Mus. Contemporary Art, Providence St. Mel Sch. Office: John Nuveen & Co Inc 333 W Wacker Dr Chicago IL 60606

SCHWETZ, BERNARD ANTHONY, toxicologist; b. Cadott, Wis., Nov. 27, 1940; married; 4 children. BS in Biology, U. Wis., Stevens Point, 1962; DVM, U. Minn., 1967; MS in Pharmacology, U. Iowa, 1968, PhD in Pharmacology, 1970. Diplomate Am. Bd. Toxicology. USPHS trainee dept. vet. physiology and pharmacology U. Minn., 1964-66; USPHS trainee dept. pharmacology U. Iowa, 1966-70; toxicologist Dow Chem. U.S.A., Midland, Mich., 1970-78, dir. toxicology rsch. lab., 1978-82; chief sys. toxicity br. divsn. toxicology rsch. and testing NIEHS, Research Triangle Park, N.C., 1982-92, acting dir. environ. toxicology program, 1993; dir. Nat. Ctr. for Toxicol. Rsch., Jefferson, Ark., 1993—2000; assoc. commr. for sci. FDA, Rockville, Md., 1994—, sr. advisor. Adj. prof. U. Ark. for Med. Scis., 1993—, Mich. State U., East Lansing, 1973-82, N.C. State U., Raleigh, 1985-93. Assoc. editor Fundamental and Applied Toxicology, 1983-86, editor, 1986-92; editl. adv. bd. Environ. Health Perspectives, 1984-93, Critical Revs. in Toxicology, 1984—; contbr.

numerous articles to profl. publs. Recipient Arnold J. Lehman award Soc. of Toxicology, 1991, Dir.'s award NIH, 1991, Founders award Chem. Industry Inst. of Toxicology, 1994, FDA Commr.'s Spl. citation, 1995. Mem. AVMA, Soc. Toxicology (charter mem. Mich. chpt., councilor 1984-86, pres. N.C. chpt. 1987, pres. reproductive toxicology speciality sect. 1986, pres.-elect south ctrl. chpt. 1997), Teratology Soc. (treas. 1978-82), Behavioral Teratology Soc., Phi Zeta. Avocations: fishing, photography. Office: Nat Ctr Toxicol Rsch HFT-1 3900 Nctr Rd Jefferson AR 72079-9501 Home: 4806 Waltonshire Cir Olney MD 20832-3130

SCHWIEBERT, DEBORAH JOHNSON, marketing executive; b. Moline, Ill., Apr. 26, 1952; d. Robert B. and Ruth E. Cronin; m. Mark W. Schwiebert, Oct. 10, 1987. BA in English, St. Mary's Coll., 1974. Dealer mgmt. rep. John Deere co., East Moline, Ill., 1975-77, territory mgr., 1977-85; mktg. cons. John Deere Info. Systems, East Moline, Ill., 1985-91, mgr. quality assurance, 1991-93; project mgr., product safety mktg. Deere & Co., Moline, Ill., 1993-97, divsn. mgr. retail customer, 1997-98, mgr. Deere.com, 1998—. Deere & Co. Credit Union, 1996—. Mem. St. Mary's Coll. Alumni (pres. 1998—, bd. dirs. 1994—, bd. trustees 1998—). Roman Catholic. Avocations: reading, travel. Home: 3913 14th St Rock Island IL 61201-6016 Office: Deere & Co 400 19th St Moline IL 61265-1373

SCHWIEBERT, MARK WILLIAM, lawyer, mayor; b. Moline, Ill., Aug. 2, 1950; s. Lloyd Alvin and Olive (Johnson) S.; m. Deborah L. Johnson, Oct. 10, 1987. BA, Augustana Coll., Rock Island, 1972; DHL (hon.), Augustana Coll., 2003; JD, Drake U., 1975, MA, 1976. Bar: Ill. 1975, U.S. Dist. Ct. (ctrl. dist.) Ill. 1977, Iowa 1999, U.S. Supreme Ct. 1999. With Schwiebert & Schwiebert, Moline, Ill., 1975—; mem. city coun. City of Rock Island, Ill., 1981—89, mayor, 1989—. Probate law lectr. Marycrest Coll., Davenport, Iowa, 1976-77; chmn. elected ofcls. com. Ill. Quad Cities Joint Purchasing Coun.; bd. dirs. Rock Island Econ. Growth Corp., 1982—, Quad City Arts; bd. dirs., chmn. transp. policy com. Bi-State Regional Commn., chmn., 2004—; mem. exec. com., bd. dirs. Quad-Cities Devel. Group; chmn. task force Rock Island Arsenal, 1998—, vice chmn., 2004. Mem. No. Ill. Luth. Synod Coun., 1987-90. Named One of 10 Outstanding Young Men Quad Cities, Quad City Times, 1984; recipient Outstanding Svc. award Ill. Quad Cities C.C., 1990, Rock Island Jaycees, 1991, Modern Man of Am., 2004; Paul Harris fellow 1992; inducted Hall of Fame Rock Island HS Alumni, 2004. Mem. ABA, Ill. Bar Assn. (com. on profl. competence 1980-87, cert. of Appreciation 1987), Rock Island Bar Assn., Kiwanis (bd. dirs. 1986-89, Layperson of yr. and Spiritual Aims award 1989), Rock Island Rotary (Excellence award 2001), Great River Bend Libr. Assn. (Exemplary Friend of Libr. award 2002). Avocations: writing, watercolor painting, running. Office: Schwiebert & Schwiebert 501 15th St Ste 605 Moline IL 61265-2135 Office Phone: 309-762-9369. E-mail: nws@ntexpress.net.

SCHWIER, PRISCILLA LAMB GUYTON, television broadcasting company executive; b. Toledo, Ohio, May 8, 1939; d. Edward Oliver and Prudence (Hutchinson) Lamb; m. Robert T. Guyton, June 21, 1963 (dec. Sept. 1976); children: Melissa Guyton, Margaret Guyton, Robert Guyton; m. Frederick W. Schwier, May 11, 1984. BA, Smith Coll., 1961; MA, U. Toledo, 1972. Pres. Gt. Lakes Comm., Inc., 1982—97; vice chmn. Seilon, Inc., Toledo, 1981—83, also dir. Bd. dirs. WGTE-TV, Toledo, Ohio His. Soc., Ft. Meigs. Contbr. articles to profl. jours. Trustee Wilberforce U., Ohio, 1983—, Planned Parenthood, Toledo, 1979—83, Maumee Valley Country Day Sch., Toledo; bd. dirs. N.W. Ohio Hospice, 1991—98; trustee Toledo Hosp., Maumee Country Day Sch., 1986—92; pres. Edward Lamb Found., 1987—; bd. dirs. Episcopal Ch., Maumee, Ohio, 1983—, Ft. Miegs State Meml. Democrat. Episcopalian. Home and Office: 345 E Front St Perrysburg OH 43551-2131

SCHWILLE, JOHN ROBERT, education educator, researcher; b. Delhi, NY, Aug. 27, 1941; s. Arnold Herman and Jennie Granlees Schwille; m. Sharon Louise Anderson, June 24, 1967; children: Kirsten Schwille Desai, John Arnold. BA, Harvard Coll., 1959—63; PhD, U. of Chgo., 1963—66. Ph.d candidate doing field rsch. Sorbonne & Institut d'Etudes Politiques, Paris, 1966—67; spencer fellow, rsch. officer U. of Stockholm, 1972—74; nie assoc. Nat. Inst. of Edn., Washington, 1974—75, 1975—77; assoc. prof. Coll. of Edn., Mich. State U., 1977—82, prof., 1982—84, prof./asst dean, internat. studies in edn., 1984—. Other consultancies UNDP, UNESCO, NSF, U.S. Dept of Edn., Aga Khan Found., 1988—92; vis. prof. U. of Zimbabwe, Harare, Zimbabwe, 1988, Adventist U. of Ctrl. Africa, Mudende, Rwanda, 1988; mem., bd. on internat. comparative studies in edn. NRC, Nat. Academies, Washington, 1990—96; consultancies World Bank, Washington, 1991—95; vis. prof. Chulalongkorn U., Bangkok, 1992, Tchr. Tng. Colleges, Kuala Lumpur, Malaysia, 1993, Ecole Nationale d'Administration et de Magistrature, Ouagadougou, Burkina Faso, 1996—97, U. of Que. at Montreal, Montreal, Canada, 1997, U. of Md., College Park, 1997. Editor: (book) New Paradigms and Recurring Paradoxes in Edn. for Citizenship; co-author: (jour. article) Elem. Sch. Jour., McGill Jour. of Edn., Jour. of Multilingual and Multicultural Devel., Ednl. Admin. Quar., Ednl. Policy, Teachers Coll. Record, Jour. of Curriculum Studies, Am. Jour. of Edn., Interna. Jour. of Polit. Edn., Jour. of Ednl. Measurement, Jour. of Ednl. Psychology, Peabody Jour. of Edn., Internat. Jour. of Ednl. Rsch., comparative edn. rev.; co-editor: (book) Civic Edn. Across Countries: Twenty-four Nat. Case Studies from the IEA Civic Edn. Project (Outstanding Academic Title, selected for the yr. 2000 by the jour. Choice: Current Reviews for Academic Libraries, 2000); editor: (special issue of journal) Tchr. Collegiality and Prof. Devel.: Internat. Variation in Practice and Context; co-editor: (special issue of jour.) Primary Edn. in Thailand: An Integrated Approach to Policy Rsch.; co-author: (chapter in edited book) Civic values learned in sch.: policy and practice in industrialized nations, Edn., experience and the paradox of finitude, Providing quality edn. when resources are scarce: strategies for increasing primary sch. effectiveness in Burundi. Capt. USAF, 1967—71. Recipient Jonthan L. Snyder Soc., Mich. State U. (donor recognition), 2001-2003; fellow Spencer Post-doctoral Fellowship, Univ of Stockholm &Internat. Assn. for the Evaluation of Ednl. Achievement, 1972-73. Mem.: NAFSA: Assn. of Internat. Educators, Comparative and Internat. Edn. Soc. (mem., bd. of directors 1993—96), Am. Sociol. Assn., Am. Ednl. Rsch. Assn., African Studies Assn., ACLU, Amnesty Internat. Episcopalian. Avocations: reading, exercising. Home: 1046 Lilac Ave East Lansing MI 48823 Office: Mich State U 517 Erickson Hall East Lansing MI 48824

SCHWIMMER, DAVID, actor; b. Queens, N.Y., Nov. 12, 1966; BS in Speech/Theater, Northwestern U., 1988. Co-founder The Lookingglass Theater Co., Chgo., 1988; actor Friends, 1994—. Stage appearances include West, The Odyssey, Of One Blood, In the Eye of the Beholder, The Master and Margarita; dir. The Jungle, The Serpent, Alice in Wonderland; TV appearances include Monty NYPD Blue, L.A. Law, The Wonder Years; film appearances include Flight of the Invader, 1991, Crossing the Bridge, 1993, Twenty Bucks, 1993, The Pallbearer, 1995, The Pallbearer, 1996, Apt Pupil, 1997, (TV movie) Breast Men, 1997, Kissing a Fool, 1998, (TV movie) A Celebration of Life, 1997, All the Rage, 1999, Band of Brothers, 2001, Uprising, 2001; appeared in, dir. (film) Since You've Been Gone, 1997; film prodr. Shoot the Moon, 1996, Kissing a Fool, 1998; film dir. (TV series) Friends, 1994-2004, Curb Your Enthusiasm, 2004. Office: Move/Medavoy Dirs Guild of Am Bldg 7920 W Sunset Blvd # 401 Los Angeles CA 90046-3300*

SCHWIMMER, SIGMUND, food enzymologist; b. Cleve., Sept. 20, 1917; s. Solomon and Sarah (Brown) S.; m. Sylvia Klein, Dec. 18, 1941; children: Susan, Elaine. Student Ohio State U., 1935-36; B.S., George Washington U., 1940; M.S., Georgetown U., 1941, Ph.D., 1943. From lab. asst. to research chemist USDA, Washington and Berkeley, Calif., 1936-62; adj. prof. biology Calif. Inst. Tech., Pasadena, 1963-65; chief research biochemist USDA, Berkeley, 1966-72, collaborator emeritus, 1975-; adj. prof. dept. nutritional scis. U. Calif.-Berkeley, 1985-87; sr. expert biochemistry UN Indsl. Devel. Orgn., Haifa, Israel, 1973-74; cons. food enzymology, Berkeley, 1980-; lectr. dept. biotech. food engring. Israel Inst. Tech., Haifa, 1973; vis. scientist Food Industry Rsch. and Devel. Inst., Hsinchu, Taiwan, 1992. Contbr. articles to profl. jours.; editor, Biochem. Sci. Biotech., Cambridge, Eng., 1983—, Trends in Biochemistry, Trends in Biotechnology, 1983—, Jour. Food Biochemistry, 1977-98; author: Source Book of Food Enzymology, 1982 (Jour. Assn. Coll. and Rsch. Librs. award 1983). John S. Guggenheim fellow; NSF fellow; Carlsberg Biol. Inst. fellow, Copenhagen; recipient Superior Service award USDA, 1949, 59, Lifetime Achievement award, 1993, Agrl. and Food Chemistry Divsn. award Am. Chem. Soc., 1996. Fellow Inst. Food Technologists, nominee USDA's ARS Sci. Hall of Fame, 2003; mem. Am. Soc. Biochemistry Molecular Biology, Sigma Xi. Office: Western Regional Ctr USDA 800 Buchanan St Albany CA 94710-1105 also: U Calif Dept Nutritional Sci Berkeley CA 94720-0001 Office Phone: 510-559-5870. Business E-Mail: sig@pw.usda.gov.

SCHWIND, MICHAEL ANGELO, law educator; b. Vienna, July 2, 1924; came to U.S., 1951; s. Siegfried and Sali (Salner) S. JD, U. Central, Ecuador, 1949; LL.M. in Internat. Law, NYU, 1953, LL.B., 1957. Bar: Ecuador 1949, N.Y. 1957, U.S. Supreme Ct. 1967. Pvt. practice, N.Y.C., 1957-69; Lectr. law NYU Sch. Law, 1959-63, adj. asst. prof., 1963-64, assoc. prof., 1964-67, prof., 1967-94, prof. emeritus, 1994—. Dir. Inter-Am. Law Inst., Inst. Comparative Law, NYU Sch. Law, 1967-71. Contbr. International Encyclopedia of Comparative Law, vol. 5; Bd. editors Am. Jour. Comparative Law, 1971-97. Mem.: Am. Fgn. Law Assn. (bd. dirs. 1980—83, 1984—87, 1988—91, 1993—96, 1997—2000, v.p. 1983—84, 1991—93, 1996—97, 2000—), Am. Assn. Comparative Study Law (NYU rep. on bd. dirs. 1971—2000). Office: NYU Sch Law 40 Washington Sq S Rm 423 New York NY 10012-1005 Office Phone: 212-998-6218. E-mail: schwindm@juris.law.nyu.edu.

SCHWIND, WILLIAM F., JR., lawyer, oil industry executive; b. Chgo., 1944; BS, JD, Loyola U., Chgo. Bar: Tex. 1969. With Marathon Oil Corp., Findlay, Ohio, 1974—83, gen. atty. Houston, 1984—91, gen. counsel, sec., 1992—; comml. contract mgr. Jakarta, Indonesia, 1983—84; sr. v.p. adminstrn., gen. counsel, sec. Dehli Gas Pipeline Corp., Dallas, 1991—92. Mem.: ABA, Am. Petroleum Inst. (chmn. gen. com. law), Am. Corp. Counsel Assn. Office: Marathon Oil Co PO Box 4813 5555 San Felipe Rd Houston TX 77210-4813

SCHWINGHAMER, MARY DENISE, veterinarian; b. Jasper, Ind., Aug. 25, 1953; DVM, Auburn U., 1978. Vet., Talladega, Ala., 1979—. Roman Catholic. Achievements include invention of; research in treatment for canine parvovirus enteritis; treatment for HIV-AIDS and Systemic Viremias in human population with companion animals as in vivo models. Avocations: swimming, dog breeding. Home: 78 Cromer St Talladega AL 35160 Office Phone: 256-362-1664.

SCHWINN-JORDAN, BARBARA (BARBARA SCHWINN), painter; b. Glen Ridge, NJ; d. Carl Wilhelm Ludwig and Helen Louise (Jordan) Schwinn; m. Frank Bertram Jordan, Jr.; children: Janine Jordan, Frank Bertram III. Grad., NY Sch. Fine and Applied Art, NYC and Paris; student, Grand Ctrl. Art Sch., Art Students League, NYC, Grand Chaumiere, Acad. Julien, Paris, Columbia U., NAD. Freelance painter, 1970—. Lectr., instr. illustration Parsons Sch., 1952-54; founder adv. coun. Art Instrn. Sch., 1956-70. Chmn. art com. UNICEF greeting cards, 1950-61, mem. com. Spence Chapin Sch., Philharm Soc., 1950's-60's. Author: Technique of Barbara Schwinn, 1956, World of Fashion Art, 1968; illustrator mags. including Vogue, 1930's, Ladies Home Jour., Saturday Evening Post, Colliers, Good Housekeeping, Cosmopolitan, McCall's, American, Town and Country, 1940's-60's, Women's Jour., Eng., Hors Zu, Germany, Marie Claire, France, other fgn. publs., 1950's-60's. Portrait painter, including Queen Sirikit, Princess Margaret, Princess Grace, Mrs. Alfred Lee Loomis, Conrad Hilton, Deborah Kerr; one-woman shows include Soc. of Illustrators, 1940, 50, Barry Stephens Gallery, 1950, Bodley Gallery, NYC, 1971, 80, C.C., West Mifflin, Pa., 1973, Duquesne U., 1973, Mus. Am. Illustration, NYC, 1991, Illustration House, NYC, 1991, Giraffics Gallery, East Hampton, NY, 1991-2002 (also rep.), 1999, Seventh Regiment Armory, 1991-2002; exhibited in group shows including NAD, 1955, Royal Acad., London, Guild Hall, NY, 1981, Summit, NJ Art Ctr., 1981, Meredith Long Gallery, Houston, 1983, Mus. Soc. Illustrators, NY, 1985, The Marcus Gallery, Santa Fe, 1985, 86, The Gerald Peters Gallery, Santa Fe, 1985, 86, Brandywine Mus., Pa., 1986, New Britain (Conn.) Mus. Am. Art, 1986, Armory Show, NYC, 1992-94, The Women's Ctr., Chapel Hill, NC, 1993-94, Greenville County Mus. Art, SC, 1995, The Soc. of the Four Arts, Palm Beach, Fla., 1995, The Hyde Collection, Glen Falls, NY, 1985, Ga. Mus. Art, 1995, Heckscher Mus., L.I., NY, 1995; works represented Holbrook Collection, Ga. Mus. Art, Eureka Coll., Ill., New Britain Mus. Am. Art, Mus. of Soc. Illustrators, NYC, Brandywine Mus., Pa., Sanford Low Meml. Collection, Del. Art Mus., Wilmington, Mus. Am. Illustration, NYC, Glenbow Mus., Calgary, Alta., Can.; represented in traveling show Del. Art Mus. 1994-95, The Mus. York County, Rock Hill, SC, 2002-; various pvt. and gallery collections; work featured in America's Great Women Illustrators 1850-1950, 1985. Winner prizes Art Dirs. Club, 1950, Guild Hall, 1969. Mem. Guggenheim Mus. (assoc.), Cosmopolitan Club NY. Home: 579 Fearrington Post Pittsboro NC 27312-8570

SCHWISTER, JAY EDWARD, portfolio manager; b. Milw., Apr. 16, 1962; s. Jerome Charles and Carol Christina (Keeler) Schwister; m. Sara M. Schlaudecker; 1 child, Katharine Claire. BS in Fin. cum laude, Marquette U., 1984. Chartered fin. analyst. Sr. investment officer First Wis. Trust Co., Milw., 1984-87; sr. v.p., sr. portfolio mgr. Putnam Investments, Boston, 1987—. Fin. com. mem. Hills Bd. Trustees, Wayland, Mass., 1990—; pres. coun. Marquette U., Milwaukee, Wis., 1990—. Chmn. fund raising com. Marquette U. Alumni Fund, Boston, 1989—. Mem. Assn. for Investment Mgmt. and Rsch., Boston Security Analysts Soc., Inc., Bond Analysts Soc., Inc., Beta Gamma Sigma. Avocations: golf, tennis, travel, woodworking, music. Home: 14655 Juneau Blvd Elm Grove WI 53122-1669 Office: Putnam Investments 1 Post Office Sq Fl 7 Boston MA 02109-2106

SCHWOY, LAURIE ANNETTE, professional soccer player; b. Balt., Feb. 14, 1978; Mem. U.S. Nat. Women's Soccer Team, 1997—, including U.S. Women's Cup, 1997; mem. Under-20 Women's Nat. Team, 1996—; including bronze medal team at Nordic Cup, 1996; championship team Nordic Cup, Denmark, 1997. Named Soccer Am. Freshman of Yr., 1996, ACC Rookie of Yr., 1996. Avocation: dance. Office: US Soccer Fedn 1801-1811 S Prairie Ave Chicago IL 60616

SCHWYN, CHARLES EDWARD, retired accountant; b. Muncie, Ind., Oct. 12, 1932; s. John and Lela Mae (Oliver) Schwyn; m. Mary Helen Nickey, May 25, 1952 (dec.); children: Douglas, Craig, Beth; m. Madelyn Steinmetz, June 26, 1993. BS, Ball State U., 1957. CPA Calif., DC. With Haskins & Sells, Chgo., Orlando, Fla., 1958-67; mgr. Deloitte, Haskins & Sells, Milan, 1967-70, San Francisco, 1970-80; with Deloitte, Haskins & Sells (now Deloitte & Touche), Oakland, Calif., ptnr. in charge, 1980-92; ret., 1992. Bd. dirs. Jr. Ctr. Art and Sci., 1982—89, pres., 1987—88; bd. dirs., trustee Oakland Symphony, 1982—86, 1989—91; bd. dirs. Oakland Met. YMCA, 1984—89, Oakland Police Activities League, 1981—91, Joe Morgan Youth Found., 1982—91, Summit Med. Ctr., 1989—94, 1996—99, Marcus A. Foster Ednl. Inst., 1986—95, pres., 1991—93; bd. dirs. Greater Oakland Internat. Trade Ctr., 1996—97, Ctrl. Coast Lighthouse Keepers, 2001—; mem. adv. bd. Festival of Lake, 1984—89, U. Oakland Met. Forum, 1991—99; co-chmn. Commn. for Positive Change in Oakland Pub. Schs., 1989—91; mem. campaign cabinet United Way Bay Area, 1989; bd. regents Samuel Merritt Coll., 1993—2001, chmn. bd. regents, 1996—2001; chief of protocol City of Oakland, 1996—97; mem. Calif. Coun. of the Oakland Mus. of Calif. Found., 1997—; docent Pt. Sur Hist. Lighthouse, 2000—. With USN, 1952—56. Decorated knight Order St. John of Jerusalem Knight Hospitaller; named honoree Schwyn Endowment Fund for cancer rsch., Bay Area Tumor Inst., 1998, date of job ret. in honor of his name, Oakland Mayor; recipient Cmty. Svc. award, Kiwanis Club, Orlando, cert. of Recognition, Calif. Legis. Assembly, 1988, Ctr. Ind. Living award. Mem.: AICPA (mem. coun. 1987—90), Nat. Assn. Accts. (pres. Fla. chpt. 1967), Calif. Soc. CPA (bd. dirs. 1979—81, 1983—84, pres. San Francisco chpt. 1983—84, bd. dirs. 1985—87), Oakland Met. C. of C. (pres. 1996), Oakland C. of C. (mem. exec. com. 1982—89, chmn. bd. dirs. 1987—88, Oakland Bus. Arts award for outstanding bus. leader 1992), Golf Club Quail Lodge (bd. dirs. 2000—02), Oakland 100 Club (pres. 1994), Lakeview Club (bd. govs. 1987—92), Claremont Country Club (treas., bd. dirs. 1989—97), Rotary (treas. 1984—86, bd. dirs.Oakland club 1986—88, 1991—92, pres. 1991—92), Sons in Retirement (treas. 2001—02, Little Sir 2003, Big Sir 2004). Personal E-mail: ceschwyn@aol.com.

SCIALDO, MARY ANN, music educator, musician; b. Westchester, NY, Sept. 21, 1942; d. Camille George Scialdo. MusB, Seton Hill Coll., 1963; MusM, Pius XII Inst. Fine Arts, Florence, Italy, 1964; profl. diploma, Manhattan Sch. Music, 1978; postgrad., Peabody Cons. Cert. tchr. NY, Fla. Supr. music Great Barrington (Mass.) Sch. Sys., 1967—68; music, theater prof. Simons Rock Coll., Great Barrington, 1968—70, Cath. U. PR, Ponce, 1971; performing arts instr. Briarcliff Sch. Dist., 1981, Ossining (NY) Sch. Dist., 1982, Albert Leonard Jr. H.S., 1983, Pleasantville (NY) Sch. Dist., 1984; theater and music tchr. Briarcliff Manor Schs., 1984—98; music tchr. Hillsborough County Schs., Tampa, Fla., 1999—. Dir., prodr., mus. and vocal dir., set and costume numerous student prodns. Debut concert: Merkin Hall, N.Y.C., internat. debut concert: Glinka Mus.; performer: (fund raising concert) Chopin Found. NY, (Giannini retrospective) WQXR, WNCN, (CD) Scriabin 24 Preludes, Opus 11, 1998—99. Recipient Outstanding Drama Tchr. award, Emerson Coll., 1st place award, Young Artist Nat. Competition, Nat. Fedn. Music Clubs competition, Disting. Alumna Leadership award, Seton Hill U. Mem.: Sigma Alpha Iota (life). Democrat. Roman Catholic. Office: Webb Middle Sch 6035 Hanley Rd Tampa FL 33634-4913

SCIAME, JOSEPH, university administrator; b. Bklyn., Sept. 9, 1941; s. Joseph and Sophie (Pintacuda) S. EdB, St. John's U., 1971. Fin. aid officer, asst. to dean of admissions St. John's U., Jamaica, N.Y., 1967-71, dir. fin. aid, 1971-82, dean fin. aid, 1982, v.p. fin. aid and student svcs., 1982-94, v.p. for govt. and cmty. rels., 1994—2002, v.p. for cmty. rels., 2002—. Mem. Gov. Commn. on Sch. Achievement, 1971—, chairperson, 1993—; pres. N.Y. Assn. Student Fin. Aid Adminstrn., 1980-82, Ea. Assn. Student Fin. Aid Adminstrn., 1986-87. Chmn. bd. ethics Town of North Hempstead, N.Y., 1984—; nat. chmn., bd. dirs. Garibaldi-Meucci Mus., N.Y., 1987-93, 97-99, pres., CEO, 1999-2002; mem. Providence Rest Found., 1995—; bd. dirs. St. John's Prep, 1996—; bd. mem. Queens Symphony Orch., 2000—, Boy Scouts Am., 2000—, v.p. membership, 2001—; bd. mem. Holocaust Resource Ctr., 2002—. Decorated Cavaliere Hfficiale del Merito della Repubblica Italiana, Cavaliere Ufficiale Order Merit House of Savoy; recipient Lifetime Membership award Ea. Assn., 1995, Achievement award N.Y. State Fin. Aid Adminstrs., 1982, Congl. Record award, 1979, 91, 93, 94, 95. Mem. Nat. Assn. Student Fin. Aid Adminstrs. (chmn. 1987-88, Disting. Svc. award 1988, Leadership award 1994), Assn. Equestrian Order Holy Sepulchre (knight grand cross 1991, knight invested 1980), Order Sons of Italy in Am. (lodge pres. 1974-75, state pres. 1993-97, nat. v.p. 1997—2003, nat pres. 2003—), Futures in Edn. Found. (vice chair 1991-93, chair 1994-97), Jamaica C. of C. (bd. dirs.), Queens Symphony Orch. (bd. dirs.), Boy Scouts Am.(v.p. membership com. 2001—), Holocaust Rejourne Ctr. (bd. dirs.). Roman Catholic. Avocations: walking, cooking, gardening, reading, lecturing. Home: 6 Jones St New Hyde Park NY 11040-1616 also: Trout Ln Southampton NY 11968 Office: St John's Univ Off Vp Cmty Rels 8000 Utopia Pky Jamaica NY 11439-0001 Business E-Mail: sciamej@stjohns.edu.

SCIAMMARELLA, MARIA GRACIELA, internist, cardiologist, arrived in U.S.A., 1996; d. Alfredo Maximo Sciammarella and Maria del Carmen Ciruzzi. MD with hons., U. Nac. La Plata, 1980. Cert. cardiologist Ninisterio de Salud y Argentina, 1987, diplomate Am. Bd. Internal Medicine, 2001. Intern Hosp. Jose de San martin, Buenos Aires, 1981—82; resident in cardiology Hosp. Ramos Meja, Buenos Aires, 1982—86, jr. attending CCU, 1986—87; fellow nuclear cardiology Ospedale San Raffaele, Milan, 1987—92; chief nuclear cardiology Fundacion Favaloro, Buenos Aires, 1992—95; rsch. assoc. U. Calif., San Francisco, 1996—98, resident nuclear medicine, 1998—99; resident internal medicine Calif. Pacific Med. Ctr., San Francisco, 1999—2001; attending physician nuclear cardiology Cedars Sinai Med. Ctr., LA, 2001—02; cardiology fellow U. Calif. Davis Med. Ctr., Davis, Calif., 2002—03. Co-author: Abnormalities in Cardiology, 1999; mem. editl. bd.: Revista Espanola de Cardiologia, 1999; author: Imaging in Cardiovalca, 2001; contbr. chapters to books, articles to profl. jours. Recipient Outstanding Young award, Assn. Cultural San Martiniana, 1980; scholar, Inst. Italo Latino Americano, 1987—88, Ministero di Relazioni Esteri, 1988—89. Mem.: Medline Interactivo (mem. expert com. 1997). Roman Catholic. Avocations: travel, painting, hiking, literature, art.

SCIANCE, CARROLL THOMAS, chemical engineer, educator; b. Okemah, Okla., Feb. 16, 1939; s. Carroll Elmer and Winifred (Black) Sciance; m. Anita Ruth Fischer, Jan. 30, 1960; children: Steven, Frederick, Thomas, Erica. BSChemE, U. Okla., 1960, M in Chem. Engring., 1964, PhD, 1966. With E.I. duPont de Nemours & Co., Inc., 1966-95, planning mgr. nylon intermediates divsn., petrochem. dept., 1978-80, tech. mgr., 1980-83, dir engring. rsch., engring. dept., 1983-87, prin. cons. corp. rsch. and devel. planning divsn., 1987-89; mgr. petroleum products R & D divsn. Conoco, Inc., 1989-93; dir. environ. tech. partnerships ctrl. R & D dept. DuPont, 1993-95; pres. Sci. Cons. Svcs., Inc., 1995—. Math. scis. and edn. bd. NRC, 1987—89; adv. bd. chem. sci. and tech. NIST, 1988—94; sr. lectr. U. Tex., Austin, 1996—; mem. Travis County Appraisals Rev. Bd., Tex., 1999—2004. Pres. Hudson Beach Colony Homeowners Assn., 2004—. Officer USAR, 1961—63. Fellow: AIChE (bd. dirs. material engring. and scis. divsn. 1986—92, chmn. new tech. com. 1990—92, mem. govt. rels. com. 1993—96); mem.: N.Y. Acad. Scis., Am. Chem. Soc. (mem. environ. R & D com. 1995—99), Fedn. Materials Soc. (v.p. 1988—92, pres. 1993—94), Sigma Xi. Home: 16658 Forest Way Austin TX 78734-1110

SCIARRA, JOHN J. obstetrician, gynecologist, educator; b. West Haven, Conn., Mar. 4, 1932; s. John and Mary Grace (Sanzone) S.; m. Barbara Crafts Patton, Jan. 9, 1960; chidren: Vanessa Patton, John Crafts, Leonard Chapman. BS, Yale U., 1953; MD, Columbia U., N.Y.C., 1957, PhD, 1963. Asst. prof. Columbia U., N.Y.C., 1964-68; prof., dept. head U. Minn. Med. Sch., Mpls., 1968-74; prof. Northwestern U. Med. Sch., Chgo., 1974—; chmn. ob-gyn Northwestern Meml. Hosp. and Northwestern U. Med. Sch., Chgo., 1974—2003. Editor Gyn-Ob Reference Series, 1973—, Internat. Jour. Gyn-Ob, 1985—. V.p. med. affairs Chgo. Maternity Ctr., Chgo., 1974—2003. Fellow ACS, Am. Coll. Ob-Gyn. (chmn. internal affairs com. 1985-89), Royal Coll. Ob-Gyn. (ad eundem); Internat. Fedn. Gyn-Ob. (pres. 1991-94, pres. Supporters Assn. 1994-2000); mem. Assn. Profs. Gyn-Ob. (sec. 1976-79, pres. 1980-81, Achievement award 1998, Tchg. award 2003), Am. Assn. Maternal and Neonatal Health (pres. 1980-89), Coun. Resident Edn. in Ob-Gyn., Am. Fertility Soc. (Hartman award 1965, bd. dirs. 1971-73), Assn. Profs. Gyn-Ob. Med. Edn. Found. (sec.-treas. 1987-91, pres. 1991-93), Ctrl. Assn. Ob-Gyn. (trustees 1986-90, pres. 1990-91), Chgo. Gynecol. Soc. (pres. 1990-91), Internat. Soc. Gynecol. Endoscopy (v.p. 1997-99, pres. 1999-2001), Internat. Acad. Human Reprodn., Yale Club N.Y.C., Carleton Club (Chgo.). Avocations: photography, food, wine, travel. Office: Northwestern U Med Sch Dept Ob-Gyn 680 N Lake Shore Dr Ste 1015 Chicago IL 60611-8702 E-mail: jsciarra@northwestern.edu.

SCIFRES, DONALD RAY, finance company executive; m. Carol Scifres. BS, Purdue U., 1968; MS, U. Ill., 1970, PhD, 1972; Doctorate (hon.), Purdue U., 2001. Rsch. and tchg. asst. U. Ill., Urbana, 1968-72; rsch. fellow, area mgr. Xerox Corp., Palo Alto, Calif., 1972-83; founder, pres., CEO SDL, Inc., San Jose, Calif., 1983-2001, dir., 1983-2001, chmn., 1992-2001; co-chmn., chief strategy officer JDS Uniphase Corp., 2001—03; chmn. SDL Capital, 2003—. Nat. lectr. IEEE Quantum Electronics Soc., 1979 Bd. editors Jour. Fiber and Integrated Optics, 1978; mem. editorial adv. bd. Photonics Spectra, 1992—; contbr. articles to tech. jours.; patentee in field. Recipient Disting. Engring. Alumni award, Purdue U., 1990, Outstanding Elec. Engr. award, 1992, The Gov. Nobert T. Tiernan award, Beta Sigma Pi, 2002, Engring. Alumni award, U. Ill., 1991, Alumni Honor award, 1993, Distinction in Photonics award, Laurin Pub. Co., 1999, Rank prize, Rank Found., U.K., 2001; fellow U. Ill., 1968, Gen. Telephone and Electronics, 1970—72. Fellow IEEE (Jack Morton award 1985, 3d Millenium award 2000, Robert N. Noyce medal 2003), IEEE Lasers and Electro-Optics Soc. (pres. 1992, Engring. Achievement award 1994), Optical Soc. Am. (Edward H. Land medal 1996); mem. Am. Phys. Soc.

(George E. Pake prize 1997), Lasers and Electro-Optics Mfg. Assn. (bd. dirs. 1992-, sec. 1994, pres. 1996), Nat. Acad. Engring., Tau Beta Pi, Eta Kappa Nu (Eminent Mem. award 2003), Phi Eta Sigma. Office: 2800 Sand Hill Rd Ste 120 Menlo Park CA 94025

SCIOLARO, CHARLES MICHAEL, cardiac surgeon; b. Kansas City, Kans., July 5, 1958; s. Gerald Michael and Charleen Gwen Sciolaro; m. Vicki Lynn Mizell, Sept. 29 BA in Biology and Chemistry magna cum laude, Mid Am. Nazarene Coll., 1980; MD magna cum laude, U. Kans., Kansas City, 1984. Diplomate Am. Bds. Gen. Surgery, Thoracic and Cardiac; lic. Ariz., Calif., La., Fla., Kans.; cert. advanced cardiac life support, advanced cardiac life support instr., advanced trauma life support, Calif. x-ray supr. and operator, transesophageal echocardiography. Intern gen. surgery Tucson hosps. surg. program U. Ariz., 1984-85, resident gen. surgery, 1985-86, 87-89, chief resident gen. surgery, 1989-90; biochemistry rsch. fellow U. Kans., Kansas City, 1978-79; instr. surgery Loma Linda U. Med. Ctr., Tucson, 1991-92; staff physician St. Francis Cabrini Hosp., Alexandria, La., 1993-96, Rapides Regional Med. Ctr., Alexandria, 1993-96; instr. surgery Loma Linda (Calif.) U. Med. Ctr., 1991-93; physician divsn. cardiac, thoracic and vascular surgery MacArthur Surg. Clinic, Alexandria, 1993-96, Kanza Multispecialty Clinic, Kansas City, 1996—2003; staff physician Providence Med. Ctr., Kansas City, 1996—2000, Bethany Med. Ctr., 1996—2001, Overland Park Med. Ctr., 2001—, Bapt.-Luth. Med. Ctr., 2003—, Kans. Heart and Lung Ctr., 2003—. Emergency rm. physician, cons. Nat. Emergency Corp., Tucson, 1986-87; emergency care attendent Veteran's Med. Ctr., Tucson, 1985-89, Cigna Urgent Care, 1985-89; with divsn. cardiac, thoracic and vascular surgery MacArthur Surg. Clin., Alexandria, 1993-96; pres. Kans. Heart and Lung Surgery, Chartered, 2003—; rschr., lectr., presenter in field. Author: (manuscripts) Aortic Coarctation in Infants, 1991. Mem. ACS, AMA, Am. Coll. Cardiologists, Am. Coll. Chest Physicians, La. Med. Soc., Kans. Med. Soc., Wyandotte Med. Soc., Rapides Med. Soc., Southea. Surg. Congress, Soc. Thoracic Surgery, Internat. Soc. Intraoperative Cardiovasc. Ultrasound, Internat. Coll. Surgons, Kans. Med. Soc., Wyandotte County Med. Soc., Internat. Platform Assn., Am. Heart Assn. (bd. dirs. Kansas City chpt.), Phi Delta Lambda. Republican. Avocations: photography, golf, softball. Office: 8919 Parallel Pky Ste 416 Kansas City KS 66112

SCIOLINO, ELAINE, reporter; m. Andrew Plump; children: Alessandra, Gabriela. M of History, NYU, 1971; D (hon.), Syracuse U., Canusius Coll., Dowling Coll. Vaious positions Newsweek, 1970—84, foreign corr., 1978—80, bur. chief Rome, 1980—82, internat. corr. NYC, 1983—84; metropolitan reporter UN Newspapers, 1984, bur. chief, 1985-87; diplomatic corr. The NY Times, 1987-91, covered intelligence beat, 1991-92, chief diplomatic corr., 1992-96, sr. writer, Washington bur.; sr. fellow U.S. Inst. Peace, Washington, 1998. Edward R. Murrow Press Fellow Coun. on Foreign Rels., 1982—83. Author: The Outlaw State: Saddam Hussein's Quest for Power and the Gulf Crisis, 1991, Persian Mirrors: The Elusive Face of Iran, 2000. Recipient Page One Award, 1978, Nat. Headliners Award, 1981, Overseas Press Club citation, 1983, Helen Bernstein Book Award for Excellence in Journalism, NY Public Library, 2001.

SCIORRA, ANNABELLA, actress; b. Wethersfield, Mar. 24, 1964; Appeared in films, including True Love, 1989, Internal Affairs, 1990, Cadillac Man, 1990, Reversal of Fortune, 1990, The Hard Way, 1991, Jungle Fever, 1991, The Hand That Rocks the Cradle, 1992, Whispers in the Dark, 1992, The Night We Never Met, 1993, Romeo is Bleeding, 1994, The Cure, 1995, The Addiction, 1995, The Funeral, 1996, Underworld, 1996, Copland, 1997, Mr. Jealousy, 1997, Highball, 1997, Underworld, 1997, Destination Anywhere, 1997, What Dreams May Come, 1998, New Rose Hotel, 1998, Little City, 1998, Sam the Man, 1999, King of the Jungle, 1999, American Crime, 2003, Chasing Liberty, 2004; (TV series) The Sopranos, 1999, 2001, 2002, Queens Supreme, 2003; (TV miniseries) Asteroid, 1997

SCIPIO, L(OUIS) ALBERT, II, retired aerospace science engineering educator, architect, military historian; b. Juarez, Mex., Aug. 22, 1922; s. Louis Albert and Marie Leona (Richardson) S.; m. Katherine Ruth Jones, Aug. 15, 1942; children: Louis Albert, Karen R. BS, Tuskegee Inst., 1943; B.Civil Engring., U. Minn., 1948, MS, 1950, PhD, 1958. Archtl. draftsman McKissack & McKissack, Tuskegee, Ala., 1943; instr. Tuskegee Inst., 1946; designer Long & Thorshov, Mpls., 1948-50; lectr. U. Minn., Mpls., 1950-59; research physicist Hughes Aircraft Co., Culver City, Calif., 1954; Fulbright prof. Cairo U., Giza, Egypt, 1955-56; assoc. prof. mechanics Howard U., Washington, 1959-61; Fulbright prof. Cairo U., Giza, Egypt, 1955-56; dir. grad. studies for engring. and architecture, prof. aerospace engring. Howard U., Washington, 1967-70, Univ. prof. space scis., 1970-87, Disting. Univ. prof. emeritus, 1987—; prof. phys. scis. U. P.R., Mayaguez, 1961-63; prof. aerospace engring. U. Pitts., 1963-67; pub. Roman Publs., Silver Springs, Md., 1981—; cons. in field. Author Compendium of Aircraft Stress Analysis and Design, 1956 Author: Principles on Continua with Applications, 1966, Structural Design Concepts, 1967, E.M. Collar Insignia, 1907-1926, 1981, Last of the Black Regulars, 1983, With the Red Hand Division, 1985, The 24th Infantry at Fort Benning, 1986, Pre-War Days at Tuskegee, 1987, The Collar Disk Story (1907-1999), 1999. Bd. visitors Air Force Inst. Tech., 1979-83. Served with AUS, 1943-46. Mem. N.Y. Acad. Scis., Internat. Assn. Bridge and Structural Engrs., Soc. Natural Philosophy, AIAA, AAAS; mem. Am. Phys. Soc.; mem. NSPE, Co. of Mil. Historians, Coun. on Am. Mil. Past, Phi Beta Kappa, Sigma Xi, Alpha Kappa Mu, Pi Mu Epsilon, Sigma Pi Sigma, Sigma Gamma Tau, Pi Tau Sigma. Home: 12511 Montclair Dr Silver Spring MD 20904-2053

SCIPIONE, RICHARD STEPHEN, insurance company executive, lawyer, retired; b. Newton, Mass., Aug. 27, 1937; BA, Harvard U., 1959; LLB, Boston U., 1962. Bar: Mass. 1962. Atty. John Hancock Mut. Life Ins. Co., Boston, 1965-69, asst. counsel, 1969-74, assoc. counsel, 1975-79, sr. assoc. counsel, 1980-82, 2d v.p., counsel, 1982-84, v.p. gen. solicitor, 1984-85, sr. v.p. and gen. solicitor, 1986-87, gen. counsel, 1987-2000, ret., 2000. Bd. dirs. New England Legal Found., John Hancock Advisers/Distbrs. Capt. U.S. Army, 1962-65. Mem. ABA (dir. New Eng. coun.), Assn. Life Ins. Counsel (gov. 1994-98), Chatham Yacht Club, South Shore Country Club.

SCIRICA, ANTHONY JOSEPH, federal judge; b. Norristown, Pa., Dec. 16, 1940; s. A. Benjamin and Anna (Sclafani) Scirica; m. Susan Morgan, May 6, 1966; children: Benjamin, Sarah. BA, Wesleyan U., 1962; JD, U. Mich., 1965; postgrad. Fulbright Scholar, Central U., Caracas, Venezuela, 1966. Bar: Pa. 1966, U.S. Dist. Ct. (ea. dist.) Pa. 1984, U.S. Ct. Appeals (3d cir.) 1987. Ptnr. McGrory, Scirica, Wentz & Fernandez, Norristown, Pa., 1966—80; asst. dist. atty. Montgomery County, Pa., 1967—69; mem. Pa. Ho. of Reps, Harrisburg, 1971—79; judge Montgomery County Ct. Common Pleas, Pa., 1980—84, U.S. Dist. Ct. (ea. dist.) Pa., Phila., 1984—87, U.S. Ct. Appeals (3d cir.), 1987—, chief judge, 2003—. Chmn. Pa. Sentencing Commn., 1980—85; bd. dir. William Penn Found.; trustee Temple Univ. (chmn. exec. com.); chmn. com. on rules of practice & procedure, Jud. Conf. of US; prof. Penn State U. Sch. of Law, 2004—. Scholar Fulbright scholar, Ctrl. U., Caracas, Venezuela, 1966. Mem.: ABA, Am. Law Inst., Montgomery Bar Assn., Pa. Bar Assn. Roman Catholic. Office: James A Byrne Courthouse 601 Market St Rm 2100 Philadelphia PA 19106-1715

SCISM, DANIEL REED, lawyer; b. Evansville, Ind., Aug. 27, 1936; s. Daniel William and Ardath Josephine (Gibbs) S.; m. Paula Anne Sedgwick, June 21, 1958; children: Darby Claire, Joshua Reed. BA, DePauw U., 1958; JD, Ind. U., 1965. Bar: Ind. 1965, U.S. Dist. Ct. (so. dist.) Ind. 1965, U.S. Ct. Appeals (7th cir.) 1967, U.S. Supreme Ct. 1976. Reporter Dayton (Ohio) Jour.-Herald, 1958-59; editor Mead Johnson & Co., Evansville, 1961; first assoc., then ptnr. Roberts, Ryder, Rogers & Scism and predecessor firms, Indpls., 1965—86; ptnr. Barnes & Thornburg, Indpls., 1987—2002, of counsel, 2003—. Cons. Ind. Pers. Assn., 1984-2002. Treas. Marion County chpt. Myasthenia Gravis Found., Indpls., 1970; v.p. Marion County Mental Health Assn., Indpls., 1970-71; pres. The Suemma Coleman Agy., Indpls., 1973-74; bd. dirs. Ind. Humanities Coun., 1995-2000, chmn. bd., 1997-98; trustee Indpls. Mus. Art, 2001—; bd. dirs. Westminster Village North, Inc., 2003—; pres. Persimmon Woods Homeowners Assn., 2001-03, sec. 2003-. With U.S. Army, 1959—62. Edwards fellow Ind. U., 1964. Mem. ABA, Ind. Bar Assn., Indpls. Bar Assn., Ind. State C. of C. (social legis. com. 1970-80). Clubs: Indpls. Athletic; Woodland Country (bd. dirs. 1984-88, sec. 1998-99) (Carmel, Ind.). Methodist. Home: 10909 300 Yard Dr Fishers IN 46038-9306 Office: Barnes & Thornburg 11 S Meridian St Indianapolis IN 46204-3535

SCITOVSKY, ANNE AICKELIN, economist, researcher; b. Ludwigshafen, Germany, Apr. 17, 1915; arrived in U.S., 1931, naturalized, 1938; d. Hans W. and Gertrude Margarete Aickelin; 1 child, Catherine Margaret. Student, Smith Coll., 1933—35; BA, Barnard Coll., 1937; postgrad., London Sch. Econs., 1937—39; MA in Econs., Columbia U., 1941. Mem. staff legis. reference svc. Libr. of Congress, 1941—44; mem. staff Social Security Bd., 1944—46; with Palo Alto (Calif.) Med. Found./Rsch. Inst., 1963—, chief health econs. div., 1973—94, sr. staff scientist, 1994—. Lectr. Inst. Health Policy Studies, U. Calif., San Francisco, 1975—94; mem. Inst. Medicine of NAS, Nat. Acad. Social Ins., Pres.'s Commn. for Study of Ethical Problems in Medicine and Biomed. and Behavioral Rsch., 1979—82, U.S. Nat. Com. on Vital and Health Stats., 1975—78, Health Resources and Svcs. Adminstrn., AIDS adv. com., 1990—94; cons. HHS, Inst. Medicine Coun. on Health Care Tech. Assessment, 1986—90. Home: 161 Erica Way Portola Valley CA 94028-7439 Office: Palo Alto Med Found Rsch Inst Ames Bldg 795 El Camino Real Palo Alto CA 94301-2302 Personal E-mail: ascitovsky@aol.com.

SCIVALLY, BART MURNANE, accountant, auditor; b. Oklahoma City, Mar. 13, 1944; s. Louis Frensley and Mary Helen (Boadway) S.; divorced; children: Amy D., Robyn M., Louis Francis. BS in Bus. Adminstrn., U. Ark., 1969. CPA Ark. Auditor Div. of Legis. Audit, Little Rock, 1968-73, audit supr., 1974—. Named Acct. of Yr. U. Ark., 2000. Mem.: AICPA, Assn. Govt. Accts. (cert. govt. fin. mgr. 1995). Roman Catholic. Office: Div of Legis Audit 172 State Capitol Little Rock AR 72201-1033 E-mail: bscivally@lapo.state.ar.us.

SCLAFANI, ANTHONY PAUL, plastic surgeon, educator, biomedical researcher; b. Bklyn., Oct. 3, 1963; BA, Columbia U., 1985; MD, U. Pa., 1989. Diplomate Am. Bd. Otolaryngology, Am. Bd. Facial Plastic and Reconstructive Surgery. Intern in gen. surgery Beth Israel Med. Ctr., N.Y.C., N.Y., 1989-91; resident in otolaryngology, head and neck surgery N.Y. Eye and Ear Infirmary, N.Y.C., 1991-95, assoc. prof., dir. facial plastic surgery, 1996—2004, prof., dir. facial plastic surgery, 2004—; fellow in facial plastic and reconstructive surgery St. Louis U. Sch. Medicine, 1995-96; pvt. practice, N.Y.C., N.Y., 1996—, Chappaqua, N.Y., 1998—. Assoc. editor: Facial Plastic Surgery, Facial Plastics Clins. N.Am.; contbr. articles to profl. jours. Fellow ACS, Am. Acad. Facial Plastic and Reconstructive Surgery (Sir Harold Delf Gillies award 1996, Ira Tresley Rsch. award 2002); mem. Am. Acad. Otolaryngology and Head and Neck Surgery, Am. Soc. for Laser Medicine and Surgery. Office: NY EE Infirm/Facial Pl Surg Dept Otolaryng/Head Neck 310 E 14th St 6th Fl New York NY 10003-4201 also: 59 S Greeley Ave Chappaqua NY 10514-3321 also: 1430 2d Ave Ste 110 New York NY 10021 Office Phone: 914-238-5500. E-mail: drsclafani@nyfacialsurgery.com.

SCLAFANI, SUSAN K. federal agency administrator; b. Albany, NY, Sept. 22, 1944; AB in German and Math. cum laude, Vassar Coll., 1966; MA in German Lang. and Lit., U. Chgo., 1967; ME in Ednl. Adminstrn., U. Tex., Austin, 1985, PhD, 1987. Cert. Tchr.Math. Ill., N.Y., Lifetime Tchr. Math. and German 6-12 Tex., Adminstr., Supt., Supr., Midmgr. Tex. Tchr. Ctrl. YMCA H.S., Chgo., 1971—72, Woodson Jr. H.S. Houston Ind. Sch. Dist., Tex., 1972—74, H.S. for Engring. Professions, Houston Ind. Sch. Dist., Tex., 1975—78; coord. magnet sch. Washington H.S. Houston Ind. Sch. Dist., 1978—83; ctrl. office coord. instrnl. tech. Houston Ind. Sch. Dist., Tex., 1983—84, exec. dir. curriculum devel., 1987—89, asst. supt. constrn. mgmt. and program planning, 1989—92, assoc. supt. dist. adminstrn., 1992—94, chief of staff, 1994—96, chief of staff ednl. svcs., 1996—2001; counselor to Sec. of Edn. U.S. Dept. Edn., Washington, 2001—04, acting sec., vocational & adult edn., 2003—04, asst. sec., vocational & adult edn., 2004—. V.p. and gen. mgr. Quantum Access, Inc., 1986—87; adj. prof. dept. curriculum and instrn. U. Houston, Tex., 1988—94, adj prof. dept. ednl. leadership, 1999—2001; presenter to numerous ednl. groups. Co-author (with R. Paige): (Book) Strategies for Reforming Houston's Schools; School Choice or Best Systems, What Improves Education, 2001; contbr. articles to profl. jours. Vol. Star of Hope Women and Family Shelter, Houston, 1988—90; mem. com. Tex. Alliance for Minorities in Engring., Houston, 1975—85; activity vol., conf. spkr. Coun. for Exceptional Children, Houston, 1989—91; com. mem. Tex. Task Force for the Homeless, 1990—92; mem. Hispanic Youth Leadership Forum Steering Com., Houston, 1990—, Pub. Policy, Comty. and Agy. Support, Success by Six Coms., United Way, Houston, 1987—2001; chair Children's Policy Com. United Way, Houston, 1987—2001. Office: US Dept Edn Mary E Switzer Bldg 330 C St SW Rm 4090 Washington DC 20202-7110 E-mail: susan.sclafani@ed.gov.

SCLATER, JAMES STANLEY, music educator, composer, musician; b. Mobile, Ala., Oct. 24, 1943; parents Arthur Lee and Naomi Bell Sclater; m. Ann Judy Davis; 1 child, Patricia. BMus, U. So. Miss., 1966, MMus, 1967; Dr. Mus. Arts, U. Tex., 1970. Prof. music Miss. Coll., Clinton, 1970—. Composer: (music for voice, chorus, band, orch.) Visions, 1973 (Ostwald Prize, 1974), (orchestral work) Concerto for Orchestra, 1989 (Music Award, Mississippi Institute of Arts and Letters, 1990), (choral/orchestral work) Witness to Matters Human and Divine, 1995, (piano sonata) Piano Sonata, 1975 (Bicentenniel performance at Kennedy Center, 1976), (organ and brass) Images of Southern Religion, 2000 (American Guild of Organists commission, 2001). Bd. dirs. Miss. Inst. of Arts and Letters, Jackson, 1999—2002. Named Disting. Prof. of the Yr., Miss. Coll., 1997. Mem.: ASCAP (Serious Music awards 1991—2003). Avocation: photography. Office: Mississippi College Box 4021 Clinton MS 39058 Office Fax: 601-925-3945. Personal E-mail: sclater@mc.edu. Business E-Mail: sclater@mc.edu.

SCLATER, JOHN GEORGE, geophysics educator; b. Edinburgh, Scotland, June 17, 1940; s. John George and Margaret Bennett (Glen) S.; m. Naila Gloria Sclater; children: Iain Andrew, Stuart Michael. B.Sc., Edinburgh U., 1962; PhD, Cambridge (Eng.) U., 1966. Research geophysicist Scripps Inst. Oceanography, La Jolla, Calif., 1965-72, prof., 1991—; asso. prof. MIT, 1972-77, prof., 1977-83; dir. Joint Program Oceanography Woods Hole Oceanographic Inst., 1981-83; Shell Cos. chair in geophysics U. Tex., Austin, 1983-91; prof. Scripps Instn. Oceanography, U. Calif., San Diego, 1991—, now prof. geophysics La Jolla. Sweeney lectr. Edinburgh U., 1976. Contbr. articles to profl. jours. Guggenheim Found. fellow, 1998-99; recipient Rosenstiel award oceanography, 1979, numerous award for publs. Fellow Geol. Soc. Am., Royal Soc. London, Am. Geophys. Union (Bucher medal 1985); mem. NAS (mem. ocean studies bd., 1985-92, chair 1988-91). Home: 5701 Skylark Pl La Jolla CA 92037-7742 Office: Scripps Instn Oceanography La Jolla CA 92093-0215

SCLAVOS, STRATTON, information technology executive; BS in Electrical and Computer Engring., U. Calif., Davis. Various exec. positions Megatest Corp., 1982—87; various exec. and sr. mgmt. positions MIPS Computer Systems, 1987—92; v.p. worldwide sales and bus. devel. GO Corp., 1992—93; v.p. worldwide mktg. and sales Taligent, Inc., 1994—95; chmn., CEO VeriSign, 1995—. Bd. dirs. Juniper Networks, Intuit, Keynote Systems, Marimba, Inc.; mem. Nat. Security Telecomm. Adv. Com. (NSTAC). Named Entrepreneur Yr., Silicon Valley Bus. Jour., 1998, No. Calif. Ernst & Young, 2002; named to Top 50 CEO's List, Forbes, 2001; recipient Leadership award Global Commerce, Morgan Stanley, 2001, Excellence award Online Encryption, Info. Security Mag., 2001, Editor's Choice award Managed PKI Svc., Network Computing, 2001. Achievements include the formation of the Sclavos Family Found. with wife Jody to support charitable efforts in children's edn. and med. rsch. Mailing: Investor Rels Dept 487 E Middlefield Rd Mountain View CA 94043

SCLOVE, STANLEY LOUIS, statistics educator; b. Charleston, W.Va., Nov. 25, 1940; s. Abraham Bernard Sclove and Dorothy Ruth (Gold) Broh; m. Suzan Tash, June 14, 1962 (div. Mar. 1983); children: Sarabeth, Benjamin; m. Caryl L. Wertheimer, Sept. 30, 1990; 1 child, Aaron Joseph. AB, Dartmouth Coll., 1962; PhD, Columbia U., 1967. Math. statistician USPHS, Cin., Summers 1962-64; rsch. assoc. Stanford U., Palo Alto, Calif., 1966-68, vis. asst. prof., 1971-72; asst. prof. stats. Carnegie-Mellon U., Pitts., 1968-72; assoc. prof. U. Ill., Chgo., 1972-81, prof., 1981—; vis. assoc. prof. Northwestern U., Evanston, Ill., 1980-81. Statis. cons. for various firms; expert witness in fed. ct.; contracted prin. investigator USAF Office Scientific Rsch., 1978, Office of Naval Rsch., 1980-82, Army Rsch. Office, 1982-85. Co-author: (with T.W. Anderson) Introductory Statistical Analysis, 1974, An Introduction to the Statistical Analysis of Data, 1978, 86, (with David Moore, George McCabe, William Duckworth) The Practice of Business Statistics, 2003; author of numerous articles in field. Mem. exec. bd. Friends of Libr., Highland Park, Ill., 1976-77; saxophonist, historian Highland Park Pops Jazz/Dance Band, 1976—. Mem. Am. Statis. Assn. (bd. dirs. Chgo. chpt. 1976, chmn. risk analysis sect. 1997), Classification Soc. (sec.-treas. 1997--), Inst. Math. Stats., Inst. for Ops. Rsch. and Mgmt. Scis. Avocations: play clarinet, saxophone and flute, tennis. Office: U Ill Dept Info and Decision Sci 601 S Morgan St MC 294 Chicago IL 60607-7124

SCOBEY, DAVID W., JR., telecommunications industry executive; b. Nashville; BSEE, Auburn U.; postgrad., Harvard U. With Bellsouth Advt. and Pub. - The Real Yellow Pages, Bellsouth Telecomm.; pres. long distance Bellsouth Corp., pres. small bus. svcs., 2001—. Mem. indsl. adv. bd. Auburn U. Sch. Elec. Engring.; mem. pres. coun. Harvard U.; mem. bd. elders North Atlanta Ch. Christ. Office: Bellsouth Corp 1155 Peachtree St NE Atlanta GA 30309-3610

SCOBEY, MARGARET, ambassador; b. Memphis; d. James and Delores Scobey. B in History, U. Tenn., 1971, M in History, 1973. Consular, Lima, 1981—83; polit. officer Peshawar, 1983—86; chief polit. sect. Jerusalem, 1990—91; polit. counselor U.S. Embassy, Kuwait, 1994—96; dep. chief of mission Sanaa, Yemen, 1996—99; dir. Office of Arabian Peninsula at Dept. of State, 2000—01; dep. chief of mission Am. Embassy, Riyadh, Saudi Arabia, 2001—03; amb. U.S. Embassy, Syria, 2003—. Staff asst. to asst. sec. Near East and South Asian Affairs; watch officer Operation Ctr.; polit. mil. officer Office of Israeli and Arab-Israeli Affairs, dep. dir. of sec. staff. Office: Embassy of USA Abou Roumaneh 2 Al Mansour St PO Box 29 Damascus Syria also: Embassy of USA Damascus Syria Dept State Washington DC 20521-6110

SCODEL, RUTH, humanities educator; b. Columbus, Ohio, Feb. 29, 1952; d. Alvin and Barbara (Keith) S.; 1 child, Anna Gabrielle. AB, U. Calif., Berkeley, 1973; PhD, Harvard U., 1978. Asst. prof. Harvard Coll., Cambridge, Mass., 1978-83; assoc. prof. classics of Greek and Latin U. Mich., Ann Arbor, 1983-87, prof., 1987—, dir. LSA Honors program, 1991—97. Author: Trojan Trilogy of Euripides, 1980, Sophocles, 1984, Credible Impossibilities, 1999, Listening to Homer, 2002; editor Transactions of Am. Philol. Assn., 1986-91. Office: Univ Mich Dept Classical Studies Ann Arbor MI 48109

SCOFIDIO, RICARDO, artist; Prof. arch. The Cooper Union. Co-author: Back to the Front: Tourisms of War/Visite aux armee: tourismes de guerre, FLESH; Exhibited in group shows at Richard Anderson Gallery, N.Y., 1992—93, Mus. Modern Art, N.Y.C., 1993, New Mus., N.Y., 1993, Sagacho Gallery, Tokyo, 1997, Thomas Healy Gallery, N.Y., 1998, numerous others. Recipient Chrysler award for innovation in design, 1988—89; fellow, N.Y. Found. Arts, 1998—99, Graham Found. Advancement Fine Arts, 1998—99.

SCOFIELD, DAVID WILLIAM, lawyer; b. Hartford, Conn., Oct. 17, 1957; s. Leslie Willson and Daphne Winifred (York) S. AB, Cornell U., 1979; JD, U. Utah, 1983. Bar: Utah 1983, U.S. Dist. Ct. Utah 1983, U.S. Dist. Ct. Ariz. 1993, U.S. Dist. Ct. Hawaii 1995, U.S. Ct. Appeals (10th cir.) 1990, U.S. Ct. Appeals (9th cir.) 1995, U.S. Supreme Ct. 1996, U.S. Ct. Claims, 1997. Assoc. Parsons & Crowther, Salt Lake City, 1983-87, Callister, Duncan & Nebeker, Salt Lake City, 1987-89, ptnr., 1989-92; founding ptnr. Parsons, Kinghorn, Peters, Salt Lake City, 1992—2004, pres., 1996-97; founding ptnr. Peters Scofield Price, Salt Lake City, 2004—. Mem. adv. com. on Utah rules of civil procedure Utah Supreme Ct., 2002—, mem. adv. com. on professionalism, 2003—. Author: Trial Handbook for Utah Lawyers, 1994; mem. Utah Law Rev., 1981-83; contbr. articles to legal jours. Bd. dirs. Westminster Coll. Found., 1994-96, chmn. cultivation com., 1995-96. Named to Outstanding Young Men of Am., 1986. Mem. ABA, Assn. Trial Lawyers Am., Utah Trial Lawyers Assn., Salt Lake County Bar Assn., Zeta Psi. Congregationalist. Avocations: american history, writing, sports. Home: 2331 Scenic Dr Salt Lake City UT 84109-1432 Office: Peters Scofield Price 111 East Broadway Ste 340 Salt Lake City UT 84111-5225 Office Phone: 801-322-2002 102. E-mail: dws@psplawyers.com.

SCOFIELD, GORDON LLOYD, mechanical engineer, educator; b. Huron, S.D., Sept. 29, 1925; s. Perry Lee and Zella (Reese) S.; m. Nancy Lou Cooney, Dec. 27, 1947; children: Cathy Lynn, Terrence Lee. B.M.E., Purdue U., 1946; M.M.E., U. Mo., Rolla, 1949; PhD in M.E, U. Okla., 1968. Instr. mech. engring. S.D. State Coll., Brookings, 1946-47; successively grad. asst., instr., asst. prof., asso. prof., prof. U. Mo., Rolla, 1947-69; prof., head mech. engring.-engring. mechs. dept. Mich. Technol. U., Houghton, 1969—80; disting. prof. mech. engring. S.D. Sch. Mines and Tech., Rapid City, 1981-88, asst. v.p. for acad. affairs, 1981-83, v.p., dean engring., 1984-86; pres. S.D. Sch. Mines and Tech. Found., 1982-90. Cons. U.S. Naval Ordnance Test Sta., China Lake, Calif., 1956-71; bd. dirs. Accreditation Bd. for Engring. and Tech., 1994-2000; cons. to industry. Served with USNR, 1943-46. NSF sci. faculty fellow, 1966-67; recipient alumni achievement award U. Mo., Rolla, 1975 Mem. ASME, Soc. Automotive Engrs. (pres. 1977, Excellence in Engring. Edn. award, 1999), Am. Soc. Engring. Edn., Sigma Xi, Tau Beta Pi, Pi Tau Sigma, Phi Kappa Phi. Home: PO Box 1085 Rapid City SD 57709-1085 *Satisfaction comes from sharing achievements. By acknowledging and sharing the importance of others in our success it is possible to accomplish more that is worth remembering.*

SCOFIELD, LOUIS M., JR., lawyer; b. Brownsville, Tex., Jan. 14, 1952; s. Louis M. and Betsy Lee (Aiken) S.; children: Christopher, Nicholas, Emma. BS in Geology with highest honors and high distinction, U. Mich., 1974; JD with honors, U. Tex., 1977. Bar: Tex. 1977, US Dist. Ct. (ea. and so. dists.) Tex., US Ct. Appeals (5th cir.) 1981, US Supreme Ct. 1984. Ptnr. Mehaffy & Weber, Beaumont, Tex., 1982—. Spkr. CNA Ins., Dallas, Jefferson County Ins. Adjusters, S.E. Tex. Ind. Ins. Agts., Gulf Ins. Co., Dallas, Employers Casualty Co., Beaumont, Tex. Employment Commn., Jefferson County Young Lawyers Assn., Jefferson County Bar Assn., South Tex. Coll. of Law, John Gray Inst., Lamar U., 1991, Tex. Assn. Def. Counsel, 1991; cert. arbitrator Nat. Panel of Consumer Arbitrators; arbitrator BBB; presenter Forest Park HS, Martin Elem. Sch., St. Anne's Sch. Contbr. columns in newspapers, articles to profl. jours. Patron Beaumont Heritage Soc., John J. French Mus.; bd. dir. Beaumont Heritage Soc., 1983-84, mem. endowment fund com., 1988; chmn. lawyers divsn. United Appeals Campaign, 1984; grand patron Jr. League of Beaumont, 1989, 90. Fellow: ABA (contbg. editor newsletter products, vice chmn.gen liability and consumer laws com.), State Bar of Tex. (mentors com. 1995), Tex. Bar Found. (life); mem.: Jefferson County Bar Assn. (disaster relief project 1979, outstanding young lawyer's com. 1980), Def. Rsch. Inst., Tex. Assn. Defense Counsel (dir. at large 1986—87, v.p. 1987—89, program chmn. San Diego 1989, adminstrv. v.p. 1989—90), Assn. Defense Trial Attys. (exec. coun. 1999—2002, chmn. Tex. membership com., Ctrl. US region 2000—02), Beaumont County Country Club, Phi Beta Kappa. Democrat. Episcopalian. Avocations: golf, reading, fishing. Home: 4790 Littlefield St Beaumont TX 77706-7748 Office: Mehaffy & Weber PO Box 16 Beaumont TX 77704-0016 Office Phone: 409-835-5011.

SCOFIELD, RODERICK ARTHUR, meteorologist, researcher, educator; b. Louisville, Dec. 3, 1942; s. Edward Harold and Hortense Alice (Gillespie) S.; m. Eileen Joyce Wiedmar, Aug. 22, 1964; children: Michelle Eileen, Matthew Roderick, Brett Edward. BS in Physics, U. Louisville, 1964; MS in Meteorology, U. St. Louis, 1969, PhD in Meteorology, 1973. Rschr. Nat. Weather Svc., Silver Springs, Md., 1972-74; rschr. flood prediction, precipitation forecaster Nat. Environ. Satellite Data Information Svc., Camp Springs, Md., 1974—. Cons. Project Atmosphere, Washington, 1984—; tchr. meteorol. enhancement program. Contbr. articles to profl. jours. including Monthly Weather Review, Remote Sensing Review, Bull. Am. Meteorol. Soc., Am.

Geophys. Union Newsletter. Recipient bronze medal NOAA, 1989, medal Weather Bureau of Taiwan, 1992, gold medal for outstanding rsch. and leadership in developing flash flood forecasting techniques using satellite data Dept. Commerce, 1999; named U. Louisville Arts and Scis. Alumni Fellow of Yr., 2000; fellow Univ. Louisville Arts and Sci. Alumni, 2000. Fellow: Am. Meteorol. Soc. (Reichelderfer award 1999, bronze awards for edn. and tng. flash flood forecasting techniques 1999, bronze award for edn. and tng. flash flood forecasting techniques 2001); mem.: Am. Geophys. Union, Nat. Weather Assn. (pres.-elect 1999, pres. 2000, outstanding contbns. award 1986), Sigma Xi. Episcopalian. Achievements include the development of a neural network (expert system) algorithm that uses geostationary and polar microwave date for diagnosing flash floods around the world. Home: 8850 Lowell Rd Pomfret MD 20675-3110 Office: NOAA Science Ctr 5200 Auth Rd Suitland MD 20746-4304 E-mail: roderick.scofield@noaa.gov., cbstorm@aol.com.

SCOGIN, TROY POPE, publishing company executive, accounts executive; b. Manchester, Ala., Oct. 31, 1932; s. James David and Thelma Katie (Helton) S.; m. Katie Elizabeth Bates, May 26, 1956; children: Norma Kay, Joyce Marie. BA, Howard Coll., 1955; MDiv, So. Baptist Theol. Seminary, Louisville, 1959; MA, Samford U., 1972. Ordained to ministry Baptist Ch., 1956. Pastor West Port (Ky.) Baptist Ch., 1956-58, Providence Baptist Ch., Bellevue, Ohio, 1958-61; chaplain/capt. USAF, Lincoln, Nebr., 1961-64; pastor Sycamore (Ala.) Baptist Ch., 1964-65; sales rep. Houghton Mifflin Co., Boston, 1965-74, regional mgr., 1974-89, spl. asst. to exec. v.p. coll. div., 1989-90, v.p., 1984—, nat. accounts exec., 1990-92; pastor Ross Ave. Bapt. Ch. Intercity Mission, Dallas, 1993-98; prof. Wake Tech. C.C., Raleigh, N.C., 1998—. Adv. bd. dirs. Ross Ave. Ctr.; faculty Eastfield Coll., 1992-98. Chmn. bd. deacons Ross Avenue Bapt. Ch., Dallas, 1991; trustee St. Johns Met. Cmty. Ch., Met. Cmty. Ch., Raleigh. Mem. Am. Mgmt. Assn., Am. Soc. Tng. Devel., Nat. Coun. Tchrs. English, Tex. Jr. Coll. Tchrs. Assn., N.C. C.C. Faculty Assn., Phi Kappa Phi, Omicron Delta Kappa (nat. leadership fraternity pres. 1954), Alpha Phi Omega (nat. svc. fraternity pres. 1952). Democrat. Avocations: bowling, swimming, fishing, tennis, golf. Personal E-mail: tscogin@nc.rr.com. *Accomplishment of goals requires setting priorities. Anything worth doing is worth doing well. To determine what is worthwhile decide if it is right, if it is needed, and if it is worth the cost.*

SCOGLAND, WILLIAM LEE, lawyer; b. Moline, Ill., Apr. 2, 1949; s. Maurice William and Harriet Rebecca S.; m. Victoria Lynn Whitham, Oct. 9, 1976; 1 child, Thomas. BA magna cum laude, Augustana Coll., 1971; JD cum laude, Harvard U., 1975. Bar: Ill. 1975, U.S. Dist. Ct. (no. dist.) Ill. 1975. Assoc. Wildman, Harrold, Allen & Dixon, Chgo., 1975-77, Hughes Hubbard & Reed, Milw., 1977-81; from assoc. to ptnr. Jenner & Block, Chgo., 1981—. Lectr. in law U. Chgo. Law Sch., 2000—; bd. dirs. Am. Benefits Coun., 2004—. Author: Fiduciary Duty: What Does It Mean?, 1989; co-author Employee Benefits Law, 1987; contr. Tort and Ins. Law Jour., 1989, and others. Fellow: Am. Coll. Employee Benefits Counsel; mem.: Omicron Delta Kappa, Phi Beta Kappa. Republican. Office: Jenner & Block One IBM Plz Fl 4000 Chicago IL 60611-7603 Office Phone: 312-923-2878. E-mail: wscogland@jenner.com.

SCOGNAMIGLIO, CARLO, economics and finance educator, Italian government senator; b. Varese, Italy, Nov. 27, 1944; s. Luigi and esther (Pasini) S.; m. Cecilia Pirelli, May 28, 1980; children: Filippo, Elisabetta Thea. D.Econs., U. Bocconi, Milan, Italy, 1968; spl. student, London Sch. Econs., 1970-71. Asst. prof. U. Bocconi, 1968-73, prof., 1973-79, U. Rome-Luiss, 1979—, dean and rector, 1984—. Senator Constituency of Milan, 1992—, pres. of senate, acting pres. of Republic, 1994-96, defense minister, 1998-99; pres. Corriere della Sera, 1983, Aspens Inst. Italia, 1995—. Author: The Stock Exchange, 1973, Industrial Crises, 1976, Industrial Economics, 1987, Theory of Finance, 1987, The Liberal Project, 1996. Winner prize for econs. French Acad., 1988. Avocations: golf, sailing, skiing. Office: Senato della Repubblica 00100 Rome Italy

SCOLES, CLYDE SHELDON, library director; b. Columbus, Ohio, Apr. 14, 1949; s. Edward L. and Edna M. (Ruddock) S.; m. Diane Francis, July 14, 1976; children: David, Kevin, Karen, Stephen. BS, Ohio State U., 1971; MLS, U. Mich., 1972. Librarian Columbus Pub. Library, 1972-74; library dir. Zanesville (Ohio) Pub. Library, 1974-78; asst. dir. Toledo-Lucas County Pub. Library, 1978-85, dir., 1985—. Adj. lectr., libr. bldg. cons. U. Mich.; v.p. bd. dirs. Read for Literacy. Mem. ALA, Ohio Libr. Assn., Ohio Libr. Coun., Toledo C. of C., Com. of 100, Maumee Hist. Soc. Clubs: Torch (Toledo). Lodges: Rotary.

SCOLES, EUGENE FRANCIS, law educator, lawyer; b. Shelby, Iowa, June 12, 1921; s. Sam and Nola E. (Leslie) S.; m. R. Helen Glawson, Sept. 6, 1942; children— Kathleen Elizabeth, Janene Helen. AB, U. Iowa, 1943, JD, 1945; LLM, Harvard U., 1949; JSD, Columbia U., 1955. Bar: Iowa 1945, Ill. 1946. Assoc. Seyfarth-Shaw & Fairweather, Chgo., 1945-46; asst. prof. law Northeastern U., 1946-48, assoc. prof., 1948-49, U. Fla., 1949-51, prof., 1951-56, U. Ill., Champaign, 1956-68, Max Rowe prof. law, 1982-89, prof. emeritus, 1989—; vis. prof. McGeorge Law Sch. U. Pacific, Sacramento, 1989-92; prof. U. Oreg., 1968-82, dean Sch. Law, 1968-74, disting. prof. emeritus, 1982—. Vis. prof. Khartoum U., Sudan, 1964-65. Author: (with H.F. Goodrich) Conflict of Laws, 4th edit., 1964, (with R.J. Weintraub) Cases and Materials on Conflict of Laws, 2d edit., 1972, (with E.C. Halbach, Jr., R.C. Link, P.G. Roberts) Problems and Materials on Decedents' Estates and Trusts, 6th edit., 2000, Problems and Materials on Future Interests, 1977, (with P. Hay, P.J. Borchers, S.C. Symeonides) Conflict of Laws, 3d edit., 2000; contbr. articles to profl. jours.; notes and legislation editor Iowa Law Rev., 1945; reporter Uniform Probate Code Project, 1966-70; mem. joint editorial bd. Uniform Probate Code, 1972— Mem. ABA, Soc. Pub. Tchrs. Law, Am. Law Inst., Ill. Bar Assn., Assn. Am. Law Schs. (pres. 1978), Order of Coif Office: U Oreg Sch Law 1515 Agate St Eugene OR 97403-1221 Business E-Mail: escoles@law.uoregon.edu.

SCOLESE, CHRISTOPHER, federal agency administrator; BSEE, SUNY, Buffalo; MSEE, George Washington U. EOS program mgr., dep. dir. flight programs and projects for earth sci. Goddard Space Flight Ctr., 1987; dep. assoc. adminstr. Office Space Sci. NASA, Washington; sr. analyst Gen. Rsch. Corp., McLean, Va. With USN, 1978—83. Recipient Presdl. Rank award of meritorious exec. Fellow: AIAA (assoc.; mem. astrodynamics com., chmn. nat. capitol sect. guidance navication and control tech. com., Young Engr./Scientist of Yr. award nat. capitol sect.); mem.: IEEE, Tau Beta Pi, Eta Kappa Nu. Office: NASA Hdqrs Mail Code S 300 E St SW Washington DC 20546

SCOLL, EULALIE ELIZABETH, writer, researcher; b. Vancouver, Wash., Mar. 6, 1920; d. Frederick and Elizabeth (Williamson) Laws; m. James Leslie Hildebrand; children; James, Frederick. BS, Women's U. Tex., 1941; MS, Salve Regina U., 1989, PhD, 1996. Engring. draftsman for Dr. Urey Manhattan Project, N.Y.C.; high fashion designer N.Y.C. Interior decorator. Author: The Role and Abuse of Women as Portrayed in Three Dostoevsky's Major Novels, 1989, Nietzsche Journal of Antichrist Tibetan Buddhism Versus Christianity, 1991, Dostoevsky's Sonya and Martha: Fiction and Reality, 1996. Mem. AAUW, Am. Assn. Advancement Slavic Studies, Nat. Trust for Historic Preservation, Nat. Mus. Women in the Arts, Am. Soc. Phys. Rsch., Inc., The Authors Guild, Inc., Newport Preservation Soc., Newport Hist. Soc., Asian Soc., Naval War Found., Internat. Dostoevsky Soc., Bailey's Beach Oldest Beach Club Am. Home: Cave Cliff 11 Chastellux Ave Newport RI 02840-3811

SCOLLARD, PATRICK JOHN, hospital executive; b. Chgo., Apr. 20, 1937; s. Patrick J. and Kathleen (Cooney) S.; m. Gloria Ann Carroll, July 1, 1961; children: Kevin, Maureen, Daniel, Thomas, Brian. BS in Econs., Marquette U., 1959; grad. sr. exec. program, MIT, 1976. With Equitable Life Assurance Soc. U.S., N.Y.C., 1962-79, asst. v.p., 1969-71, v.p., personnel dir., 1971-75, v.p. corp. adminstrv. svcs., 1975-79; sr. v.p. Chem. Bank, N.Y.C., 1979-80, exec. v.p., 1980-87, chief adminstrv. officer, 1987-92; pres., CEO St. Francis Hosp., Roslyn, N.Y., 1992-99; pres. Scollard Assocs. LLC, Garden City, N.Y., 1999—; pres., CEO Cath. Health Svcs. of L.I., Melville, NY, 2003—, also bd. dirs. Bd. dirs. Curaspan, Inc., Cath Health Svcs. L.I., Ebb Svcs. Office: Scollard Assocs LLP 1461 Franklin Ave Garden City NY 11530-1648 Office Phone: 516-739-5107.

SCOLLICK, BRYAN ROBERT, music educator, market research consultant; b. Harrisburg, Pa., Apr. 27, 1965; s. Gary and Diane Scollick; m. Melissa Ann Schonour, Oct. 15, 1994. BS in music edn., Lebanon Valley Coll., 1983—88. Teaching License PA, 1988. Music educator Reading Ctrl. Cath. H.S., Reading, Pa., 1989—; market rschr. Internat. Comm. Rsch., Reading, Pa., 1994—2004. Dir.: (musical theater) Godspell. Cantor St. Catharine's Roman Cath. Ch., Reading, Pa., 1998—2004. Recipient Presentor for Diocesan Edn. Conv., Dioceses of Allentown, 2003. Mem.: Music Educators Nat. Com. D-Conservative. Roman Catholic. Avocations: travel, movies, trivia/puzzles. Home: 17-5 Cranberry Ridge Reading PA 19606 Office: Reading Central Catholic HS 1400 Hill Rd Reading PA 19602 E-mail: bscollick@cchsbc.pvt.k12.pa.us.

SCOLNICK, EDWARD MARK, pharmaceutical executive; b. Boston, Aug. 9, 1940; s. Barbara (Chasen) Scolnick; m. Barbara Bachrach; children: Laura, Jason, Daniel. AB, Harvard U., 1961; MD, Harvard U. Med. Sch., 1965. Intern Mass. Gen. Hosp., 1965—66, asst. resident internal medicine, 1966—67; rsch. assoc. USPHS, 1967—69; sr. staff fellow lab. biochem. genetics NIH, 1969—70; instr. NIH Sem., 1970; sr. staff fellow viral leukemia and lymphoma br. Nat. Cancer Inst., 1970—71, spl. advisor to spl. virus cancer program, 1973—78, mem. coordinating com. for virus cancer program, 1975—78, chief. lab. tumor virus genetics, head. molecular virology sect., 1975—82; exec. dir. basic rsch. virus and cell biology rsch. Merck Sharp & Dohme Rsch. Labs., West Point, Pa., 1982—83, v.p. virus and cell biology rsch., 1983—84, sr. v.p., 1984, pres., 1985—93; sr. v.p. Merck & Co., Inc., 1991—93, exec. v.p., pres. rsch., 1993—95; pres. Merck & Co. Inc., West Point, Pa., 1995—. Adj. prof. microbiology Sch. Medicine U. Pa., 1983—86. Editor-in-chief: Jour. Virology, mem. editl. bd.: Virology; contbr. articles to profl. jours. Served with USPHS, 1965—67. Recipient Arthur S. Fleming award, 1976, Superior Svc. award, PHS, 1978, Eli Lilly award, 1980, Indsl. Rsch. Inst. medal, 1990. Mem.: NAS, Am. Soc. Microbiologists, Am. Soc. Biol. Chemists. Home: 811 Wickfield Rd Wynnewood PA 19096-1610 Office: Merck & Co Inc 7700 Sumney Townpike West Point PA 19486 also: Merck & Co Inc 1 Merck Dr Whitehouse Station NJ 08889

SCOMMEGNA, ANTONIO, obstetrician, gynecologist, educator; b. Barletta, Italy, Aug. 26, 1931; came to U.S., 1954, naturalized, 1960; s. Francesco Paola and Antonietta (Maresca) S.; m. Lillian F. Sinkiewicz, May 3, 1958; children: Paola, Frank, Roger. BA, State Lyceum A. Casardi, Barletta, 1947; MD, U. Bari (Italy), 1953. Diplomate: Am. Bd. Obstetrics and Gynecology, also sub-bd. endocrinology and reprodn. Rotating intern New Eng. Hosp., Boston, 1954-55; resident obstetrics and gynecology Michael Reese Hosp. and Med. Center, Chgo., 1956-59, fellow dept. research human reprodn., 1960-61, research asso., 1961; fellow steroid tng. program Worcester Found. Exptl. Biology, also Clark U., Shrewsbury, Mass., 1964-65; asso. prof. obstetrics and gynecology Chgo. Med. Sch., 1965-69; mem. staff Michael Reese Hosp. and Med. Center, 1961—, attending physician obstetrics and gynecology, 1961—, dir. sect. gynecologic endocrinology, 1965-81; dir. ambulatory care obstetrics and gynecology Mandel Clinic, 1968-69, chmn. dept., 1969-89; attending, chief svc. U. Ill. Chgo. Hosp. and Med. Ctr., 1989-98; trustee Mandel Clinic, 1977-80; prof. dept. ob-gyn. Pritzker Sch. Medicine, U. Chgo., 1969-89; prof., head dept. ob-gyn. Coll. Medicine, U. Ill. Chgo., 1989-98, prof. emeritus, 1999—. Author numerous articles in field. Fulbright fellow, 1954-55 Fellow Am. Coll. Obstetricians and Gynecologists, Endocrine Soc., Chgo. Inst. Medicine, Am. Gynecol. and Obstet. Soc.; mem. AMA, Ill., Chgo. med. socs., Am. Fertility Soc., Chgo. Gynecol. Soc. (sec. 1976-79, pres. 1981-82), Soc. Study Reprodn., AAAS, Soc. for Gynecologic Investigation. Home: 1023 W Vernon Park Pl Apt E Chicago IL 60607-3447 Office Phone: 312-996-0222. Business E-Mail: anmis@uic.edu.

SCORDIAS, MARGARET ANN, education educator; b. St. Louis, July 17, 1955; d. Robert Lennolan and Helen Margaret (Brannon) Lovan; m. George Joseph Scordias, Jan. 11, 1975; children: Stephen Michael, Anthony James. BA, Washington U., St. Louis, 1977; MEd, U. Mo., St. Louis, 1985; EdD, U. Mo., 2004. Cert. elem., learning disabilities, remedial reading tchr. Mo., libr. media specialist. Curriculum/ instrnl. specialist Maplewood-Richmond Heights Sch. Dist., Mo. Project dir. U. Mo., St. Louis, 2003—. Mem.: ASCD, NEA, Tchr.'s Acad. Internat. Reading Assn., Phi Delta Kappa.

SCORSESE, MARTIN, film director; b. Flushing, N.Y., Nov. 17, 1942; s. Charles and Catherine (Cappa) S.; m. Laraine Marie Brennan, May 15, 1965 (div.), 1 daughter: Catherine Terese Glinora Sophia; m. Julia Cameron, 1975 (div.), 1 daughter: Dominica Elizabeth; m. Isabella Rosellini, Sept. 29, 1979 (div. 1983); m. Barbara DeFina, Feb. 9, 1985 (div.); m. Helen Morris, 1999; 1 child, Francesca Kingsland Scorsese. BS in Film Communications, NYU, 1964, MA in Film Communications, 1966. Faculty asst., then instr. film NYU, N.Y.C., 1963-70. Films include: (dir.): The Big Shave, 1968 (also writer), Who's That Knocking at My Door?, 1968, (also writer, assoc. prodr., actor), Boxcar Bertha, 1972 (also actor), Mean Streets, 1973 (also co-writer, actor), Alice Doesn't Live Here Anymore, 1975, Taxi Driver, 1976 (Palme d'Or Cannes Internat. Film Festival), New York, New York, 1977, The Last Waltz, 1978, Raging Bull, 1980, The King of Comedy, 1983, After Hours, 1985, The Color of Money, 1986, The Last Temptation of Christ, 1988, New York Stories (Life Lessons), 1989, GoodFellas, 1990 (also co-writer), Cape Fear, 1991, The Age of Innocence, 1993 (also co-writer), Casino, 1995 (also writer), Kundun, 1997, Bringing Out the Dead, 1999, The Gangs of New York, 2002; (prodr.): The Grifters, 1990, Mad Dog and Glory, 1993; (exec. prodr.): Naked in New York, 1994, Clockers, 1995, Grace of My Heart, 1996; documentaries include: (editor): Woodstock, 1970 (also asst. dir.), Elvis on Tour, 1973; (assoc. prodr.): Medicine Ball Caravan, 1971; (dir.): Street Scenes 1970, 1970, Italianamerican, 1974, American Boy: A Profile of Steven Price, 1979, Made in Milan, 1990; co-dir. (documentary) A Personal Journey with Martin Scorsese Through American Movies, 1997, Il Mio Viaggio in Italia, 1999, The Blues, 2002; other film appearances include: Cannonball, 1976, Pavlova: A Woman for All Seasons, 1983, 'Round Midnight, 1986, Akira Kurosawa's Dreams, 1990, Guilty by Suspicion, 1991, Quiz Show, 1994, Search and Destroy, 1995 (also prodr.), The Muse, 1999, (TV films) La Memoire Retrouvee, 1996, (exec. prodr.) Kicked in the Head, 1997, The Hi-Lo Country, 1998. Recipient Edward L. Kingsley Found. award, 1963-64, 1st prize Rosenthal Found. awards Soc. Cinemetologists, 1964, 1st prize Screen Producer's Guild, 1965, 1st prize Brown U. Film Festival, 1965, Golden Lion award Venice Film Festival, 1995, Life Achievement award Am. Film Inst., 1997, Lifetime Career award Lincoln Ctr. Film Soc., 1998, Golden Globe, 2003, Evelyn F. Burkey award Writer's Guild Am. East, 2003, Lifetime Achievement award Dir.'s Guild Am., 2003, also others; named Best Dir. Cannes Film Festival, 1986. Office: Ken Starr & Co 350 Park Ave Fl 9 New York NY 10022-6022 also: Sikelia Prodns 5th Fl 110 W 57th St New York NY 10019

SCORZA, SYLVIO JOSEPH, religion educator; b. Zürich, Switzerland, Mar. 21, 1923; came to U.S., 1929; s. Joseph Peter and Helena Christina (Kopp) S.; m. Phyllis Joan VanSetters, June 6, 1952; children: Christine Marie, Philip Joseph, John Forrest. AA, Woodrow Wilson Jr. Coll., 1942; AB, Hope Coll., 1945; BD, Western Theol. Sem., Holland, Mich., 1953; ThD, Princeton Theol. Sem., 1956; PhD, U. Ill., 1972. Ordained to ministry Ref. Ch. in Am., 1955. Stated supply pastor Hickory Bottom Charge, Loysburg, Pa., 1957-58; prof. religion Northwestern Coll., Orange City, Iowa, 1959-90, prof. emeritus, 1990—. Vis. prof. Lancaster (Pa.) Theol. Sem., 1956-57, Western Theol. Sem., Holland, Mich., 1958-59; v.p. Ref. Ch. in Am., N.Y.C., 1988-89, pres., 1989-90, moderator, exec. com., 1990-91; mem. Iowa Bd. Law Examiners, 1997—2004. Co-editor: Concordance to the Greek and Hebrew Text of Ruth, The Computer Bible, Septuagint series, Vols. XXX, XXX-B, 1988-89; contbr. articles to profl. jours. County del. Iowa Dems., Ft. Dodge, 1984. Recipient Disting. Alumnus award Hope Coll., 1989, Homecoming Honors award Northwestern Coll. N Club, 1990, Handicapped Person of Siouxland award Siouxland Com. for the Handicapped, 1990, Gov.'s award Iowa Commn. of Persons with Disabilities, 1990, Victory award Nat. Rehab. Hosp., 1991, Disting. Alumnus award Western Theol. Sem., 2002. Mem. Internat. Orgn. for Septuagint and Cognate Studies, Smithsonian Instn., Nat. Geog. Soc., U.S. Chess Fedn., Iowa State Chess Assn. (v.p. 1984-85, dir. postal tournament 1987-97). Mem. Ref. Ch. In Am. Avocations: chess, bridge. Home and Office: 520 2nd St SW Orange City IA 51041-1728 E-mail: scorza@nwciowa.edu.

SCOTCHMER, SUZANNE ANDERSEN, economics professor; b. Seattle, Jan. 23, 1950; d. Toivo Matthias and Margaret (Sangder) Andersen. BA in Econ., U. Wash., 1970; MA in Stats., U. Calif., Berkeley, 1979, PhD in Econ., 1980. From asst. to assoc. prof. econ. Harvard U., Cambridge, Mass., 1981-86; prof. econ. and pub. policy U. Calif., Berkeley, 1986—. Vis. prof. Toronto Sch. Law, 1993, Tel Aviv U., 1994, U. Paris, Sonbonne, 1992, New Sch. of Econ., Moscow, 1993, U. Aukland, 2002; prin. investigator NSF, 1986-2002; lectr. in law. Mem. editl. bd. Am. Econ. Rev., 1991-95, Jour. Pub. Econ., 1986-2001, Jour. Econ. Perspectives, 1994-97, Regional Sci. and Urban Econ., 1991—, Jour. Econ. Lit., 1998—; contbr. articles to profl. jours. Hoover Nat. fellow Stanford U., 1989, Olin fellow Yale Sch. Law, 1993, Sloan fellow, 1979, Phi Beta Kappa fellow, 1978; France/Berkeley Fund grantee, 1994-95. Office: Univ Calif 2607 Hearst Ave Berkeley CA 94720-7320 Business E-Mail: scotch@socrates.berkeley.edu.

SCOTT, A. TIMOTHY, lawyer, business executive; b. Natchez, Miss., Feb. 16, 1952; s. John William and Patricia (O'Reilly) S.; m. Nancy E. Howard, June 7, 1976; children: Kevin Howard, Brian Howard. BA in Psychology, Stanford U., 1974, JD, 1977. Bar: Calif. 1977, U.S. Tax Ct. 1978. Assoc. then ptnr. Agnew, Miller & Carlson, L.A., 1977-83; assoc. Greenberg, Glusker, Fields, Claman & Machtinger, L.A., 1983; ptnr. Sachs & Phelps, L.A., 1983-91; mem. Heller, Ehrman White & McAuliffe, L.A., 1991-96, of counsel, 1996-99; sr. v.p., tax counsel Pub. Storage, Inc., Glendale, Calif., 1996—. Speaker in field. Note editor Stanford Law Rev., 1976-77; contbr. article to profl. publs., chpt. to book. Mem. ABA, L.A. County Bar Assn. (chmn. real estate taxation com. 1988-91, exec. com., taxation sect. 1989-91), Order of Coif. Democrat. Avocations: volleyball, gardening, Calif. wine, contemporary art, skiing. Office: Pub Storage Inc 701 Western Ave Glendale CA 91201-2349 E-mail: tscott@publicstorage.com.

SCOTT, ALASTAIR IAN, chemistry professor; b. Glasgow, Scotland, Apr. 10, 1928; came to U.S., 1968; s. William and Nell (Newton) S.; m. Elizabeth Wilson Walters, Mar. 4, 1950; children: William Stewart, Ann Walker. BSc, Glasgow U., 1949, PhD, 1952, DSc, 1964; MA (hon.), Yale U., 1968; DSc (hon.), U. Coimbra, Portugal, 1990, U. Pierre & Marie Curie, Paris, 1992. Lectr. organic chemistry Glasgow U., 1957-62; prof. U. B.C., Vancouver, Canada, 1962-65, Sussex (Eng.) U., 1965-68, Yale U., 1968-77; disting. prof. Tex. A&M U., 1977-80; prof. dept. chemistry U. Edinburgh, Scotland, 1980-82; Davidson prof. sci. Tex. A&M U., 1982—2001, Welch & Barton chair in chemistry, 2002—. Cons. in field. Author: Interpretations of Ultraviolet Spectra of Natural Products, 1964; contbr. articles to profl. jours. Recipient Rsch. Achievement award, Am. Soc. Pharmacognosy, 1993, Robert A. Welch award in chemistry, 2000, Disting. Tex. Scientist of Yr. award, Tex. Acad. Sci., 2002. Fellow: Royal Soc. Edinburgh (Royal medal 2001), Royal Soc. (Bakerian lectr. 1996, Davy medal 2001); mem.: Tex. Acad. Sci. (Tex. Scientist of Yr. 2002), Japan Pharm. Soc. (hon.), Chem. Soc. (Corday-Morgan medal 1964, Centenary lectr. 1994, Tetrahedron prize for creativity in organic chemistry 1995, Natural Products Rsch. award 1996), Am. Chem. Soc. (Ernest Guenther award 1976, A.C. Cope scholar 1992, Nakanishi prize 2003). Office: Tex A&M U Dept Chemistry College Station TX 77843-0001 Office Phone: 979-845-3243. Business E-Mail: scott@mail.chem.tamu.edu.

SCOTT, ALEXANDER ROBINSON, engineering association executive; b. Elizabeth, N.J., June 15, 1941; s. Marvin Chester and Jane (Robinson) Scott; m. Angela Jean Kendall, July 17, 1971; children: Alexander Robinson, Jennifer Angela, Ashley Kandall. BA in History, Va. Mil. Inst., 1963; MA in Personnel and Counseling Psychology, Rutgers U., 1965. Sales mgr. Hilton Hotels, 1967-70; meetings mgr. Am. Inst. Mining Engrs., N.Y.C., 1971-73; exec. dir. Minerals, Metals and Materials Soc., 1973—. With U.S. Army, 1965—67. Decorated Bronze Star. Mem.: Am. Soc. Assn. Execs. Republican. Baptist. Home: 107 Staghorn Dr Sewickley PA 15143-9506 Office: TMS 184 Thorn Hill Rd Warrendale PA 15086-7514 E-mail: TMSgeneral@tms.org.

SCOTT, ALICE HOLLY, retired librarian; b. Jefferson, Ga. d. Frank D. and Annie D. (Colbert) Holly; m. Alphonso Scott, Mar. 1, 1959; children— Christopher, Alison AB, Spelman Coll., Atlanta, 1957; M.L.S., Atlanta U., 1958; PhD, U. Chgo., 1983. Librarian Bklyn. Pub. Library, 1958-59; br. librarian Chgo. Pub. Library, 1959-72, dir. Woodson Regional Library, 1974-77, dir. community relations, 1977-82, dep. commr., 1982-87, asst. commr., 1987-98; ret., 1998. Doctoral fellow, 1973 Mem. ALA (councilor 1982-85), Chgo. Spelman Club, DuSable Mus., Chgo. Urban League Democrat. Baptist.

SCOTT, ANDY, Canadian government official; b. Barker's Point, N.B., Can., 1955; s. Keith and Gyda (Burns) S.; m. Denise Scott; 2 children. Degree in sociology with honors, U. N.B., 1979, grad., 1981. Mem. staff Leader of Opposition Joseph Daigle; exec. dir. Liberal Assn., 1981-89; sr. policy advisor Premier Frank McKenna, 1989-92; asst. dep. min. Dept. Intergovtl. Affairs, 1992-97; mem. House of Commons, 1997—, solicitor gen., 1997-98, former chair standing com. on justice and human rights, min. state (infrastructure), 2003—. Chair caucus com. Can. Broadcasting Corp. Co-chairperson Theatre N.B. Fundraising Campaign; bd. dirs. Can. Rehab. Coun. for the Disabled; mem. Fredericton Cmty. Literacy Com.; founding pres. Friends of Characters Inc. Office: Ho of Commons 100 Justice Ottawa ON Canada K1A 0A6 E-mail: scotta@parl.gc.ca.

SCOTT, ANNA MARIE PORTER WALL, sociology educator; b. South Fulton, Tenn. d. Thomas Madison and Jevvie Roggie (Porter) P.; m. John T. Scott Sr. (dec.); 1 child, Harvey G. BA, MEd, MSW, U. Ill. Cert. tchr. and social worker, Ill. Caseworker Dept. Pub. Aid, Champaign, Ill.; psychiat. social worker Vets. Hosp., Danville, Ill.; prof. sociology Parkland Coll., Champaign, Ill. Head Dem. 21st Congl. Dist., 1974-78; del. Nominating Conv./Mini Conv., 1975, 76; commr. Ill. Banking Bd.; mem. AME Ch., Hadassah; mem. Vet. of Armed Svcs. Named Outstanding Black Alumni, U. Ill., Urbana. Mem. LWV, NAACP, Nat. Coun. Negro Women (past pres.), Am. Legion (comdr. post 559), AMVETS, Champaign-Urbana Symphony Guild, Order Ea. Star (grand organist Eureka Grand chpt.). Avocations: pub. speaking, piano, baking, gardening, politics. Home: 309 W Michigan Ave Urbana IL 61801-4945 Office: Parkland Coll 2400 W Bradley Ave Champaign IL 61821-1806

SCOTT, ANNE BYRD FIROR, history professor; b. Montezuma, Ga., Apr. 24, 1921; d. John William and Mary Valentine (Moss) Firor; m. Andrew Mackay Scott, June 2, 1947; children: Rebecca, David MacKay, Donald MacKay. AB, U. Ga., 1941; MA, Northwestern U., 1944; PhD, Radcliffe Coll., 1958; LHD (hon.), Lindenwood Coll., 1968, Queens Coll., 1985, Northwestern U., 1989, Radcliffe Coll., 1990, U. of the South, 1990, Cornell Coll., 1991. Congressional rep., editor LWV of U.S., 1944-53; lectr. history Haverford Coll., 1957-58, U. N.C., Chapel Hill, 1959-60; asst. prof. history Duke U., Durham, N.C., 1961-67, assoc. prof., 1968-70, prof., 1971-80, W.K. Boyd prof., 1980-91, W.K. Boyd prof. emerita, 1992—, chmn. dept., 1981-85; Gastprofessor Universität, Bonn, Germany, 1992-93. Vis. prof. Johns Hopkins U., 1972-73, Stanford U., 1974, Harvard U., 1984, Cornell Coll., 1993, Williams Coll., 1994, U. Miss., 2000; Times-Mirror scholar Huntington Libr., 1995; vice chmn. Nat. Humanities Ctr., 1991-98; mem. adv. com. Schlesinger Libr.; lectr. in field. Author: The Southern Lady, 1970, 25th anniversary edit., 1995, (with Andrew MacKay Scott) One Half the People, 1974, Making the Invisible Woman Visible, 1984, Natural Allies, 1991; editor: Jane Addams, Democracy and Social Ethics, 1964, The American woman, 1970, Women in American Life, 1970, Women and Men in American Life, 1976, Unheard Voices, 1993; mem. editl. bd. Revs. in Am. History, 1976-81, Am. Quar., 1974-78, Jour. So. History, 1978-84; contbr. articles to profl. jours. Chmn. Gov.'s Commn. on Status of Women, 1963-64; mem. Citizens Adv. Council on Status of Women U.S., 1964-68; trustee Carnegie Corp., 1977-85, W.W. Ctr.

for Scholars, 1977-84; chmn. bd. dirs. Nat. Cmty. Investment Fund, 1996—2002. AAUW fellow, 1956-57; grantee NEH, 1967-68, 76-77, Nat. Humanities Ctr., 1980-81; grad. medal Radcliffe Coll., 1986, Duke U. medal, 1991, John Caldwell medal N.C. Humanities Coun., 1994; fellow Ctrl. Advanced Study in Behavioral Sci., 1986-87; Fulbright scholar, 1984, 92-93. Mem. Am. Antiquarian Soc., Orgn. Am. Historians (exec. bd. 1973-76, pres. 1983, Disting. Pub. Svc. award 2002), So. Hist. Assn. (exec. bd. 1976-79, pres. 1989), Soc. Am. Historians, Phi Beta Kappa. Democrat. Office: Duke U Dept History Durham NC 27708 E-mail: ascott2@email.unc.edu., ascott@acpub.duke.edu.

SCOTT, BERTRAM, insurance company executive; Degree, DePaul U. Former claims ops. and acct. exec. Prudential Ins. Co., Chgo., v.p. mktg. and mng. care ops., 1989; pres., CEO Horizon Mercy, 1996; pres. TIAA-CREF Life Ins., N.Y.C. Mem. Robert Wood Johnson Pediat. Hosp. Project, State of N.J. Black Infant Mortality adv. com.; chmn. United Way, Essex and West Hudson, NJ, 2000. Mem.: Nat. Assn. Urban Based HMOs, Am. Heart Assn. Office: TIAA-CREF Life Ins 730 3rd Ave New York NY 10017

SCOTT, BEVERLY JEANNE, contractor, writer; b. Mason City, Iowa, May 7, 1937; d. Dale White Dunlap and Rosetta Frances Plath; m. Dwayne Orville Scott, Feb. 14, 1958; children: Teresa Joanne Johnson(dec.), Tammy Jeanne Bartlett, Tracey Janne, Marty Lee, Eugene Dwayne. A, Grandview Coll., 1957. Ptnr., office mgr. Colonial Builders Inc, Ankeny, Iowa, 1975—. Author: (novel) Righteous Revenge, Ruth Ever, Jena's Choice. Mem.: Internat. Edsel Club (treas. 1987—2004). Presbyterian. Avocations: reading, writing, travel. Home: 6990 N W 6th Dr Ankeny IA 50021-9512 Office: Colonial Builders Inc 6990 N W 6th Dr Ankeny IA 50021-9512 E-mail: bevscott1@msn.com.

SCOTT, BLACK, investment company executive; B in Applied Math. and Econs., John Hopkins U., 1968; MBA, Harvard U. With William O'Neill Co., 1978—80; founder, pres. Delphi Mgmt., 1980—, portfolio mgr. Delphi Value Fund, 1980—. Recipient Corp. Goodwill award, Northwestern U. Ctr. for the Study Sport in Soc., 1996. Office: Delphi Mgmt Ste 540 50 Rowes Wharf Boston MA 02110*

SCOTT, BONNIE KIME, English literature and cultural educator; b. Phila., Dec. 28, 1944; d. Roy Milford and Shiela (Burton) Kime; m. Thomas Russell Scott, June 12, 1967; children: Heather Sheila, Ethan Kime, Heidi Cathryn Molly. BA, Wellesley Coll., Mass., 1967; MA, U. N.C., 1969, PhD, 1973. Asst. prof. U. Del., Newark, 1975—80, assoc. prof., 1980—86, prof., 1986—2001; prof. women's studies San Diego State U., 2001—. Author: Joyce and Feminism, 1984, James Joyce, 1988, Refiguring Modernism, 2 vols., 1995; editor: New Alliances in Joyce Studies, 1988, Selected Letters of Rebecca West, 2000; co-editor: Images of Joyce, 1998, Virginia Woolf: Turning the Centuries, 2000; gen. editor, contbr. The Gender of Modernism, 1990; contbr. articles to profl. jours. Mem. Del. Humanities Coun., 1983—87, U. Del. Ctr. for Advanced Study. Recipient Excellence in Tchg. award, Mortar Bd., 1984. Mem.: MLA, James Joyce Found. (founder women's caucus 1983—, bd. dirs. 1991—), Virginia Woolf Soc., Soc. Study Narrative Lit., Am. Conf. for Irish Studies (exec. com. 1981—83), Phi Beta Kappa (pres. Del. chpt. 1994—95). Office: San Diego State Univ Adams Humanities Dept Womens Studies San Diego CA 92182 Home: 10758 Puebla Dr La Mesa CA 91941-5711 Office Phone: 619-594-6460. E-mail: bkscott@mail.sdsn.edu.

SCOTT, BRENDA D. writer; b. Tampa-Sneads, Fla. d. Alonzie III and Felicia (Lopez) Scott. Diploma in child guidance, Lively Vocat. Tech. Ctr., Tallahassee, 1987; AA in Sci. Edn., Tallahassee C.C., 1993; BS in Reading Edn., Fla. State U., 1995; AA in Criminal Justice, Tallahassee CC, 2000. Contbr. poetry to mags., other publs including Internat. Women's Writing Guild; author: (screenplay) Surprise (Guild Membership movie), 1998, Mrs. Jellie Mae's Store, 1999, poetry book, Down-Home-News, 2000. Mem. West Fla. Literary Assn., Am. Black Book Writers Assn., Acad. Am. Poets, Internat. Soc. Poets, Women Ministering Biblically. Democrat. African Meth. Episcopalian. Avocations: reading, writing, movies, church activities, sports. Home and Office: PO Box 171 Sneads FL 32460-0171

SCOTT, BRIAN DAVID, lawyer; b. Spokane, Wash., Sept. 30, 1946; s. Dick E. and Helene L. (Johnson) S.; m. Lynita G. Muzzall, Sept. 9, 1972; children: D. Alexander, Rachel E., S. Andrew. BA, U. Wash., 1968; JD, U. Wis., 1972. Bar: Wis. 1972, Wash. 1972, U.S. Dist. Ct. (we. dist.) Wash. 1972, U.S. Dist. Ct. (we. dist.) Wis. 1972. Asst. atty. gen. Wash. State Atty. Gen.'s Office, Seattle, 1972-74; assoc. Jackson, Ulvestad, Goodwin, Grutz, Seattle, 1974-81; ptnr. Goodwin, Grutz & Scott, Seattle, 1981-96, Grutz, Scott & Kinney, Seattle, 1996-99, Grutz, Scott, Kinney & Fjelstad, Seattle, 1999—. Mem. ATLA, Wash. Trial Lawyers Assn., Wash. Athletic Club. Democrat. Avocations: boating, skiing, travel. Home: 158 Prospect St Seattle WA 98109-3750 Office: Grutz Scott Kinney & Fjelstad 600 University St Ste 1928 Seattle WA 98101-4178 E-mail: scott@gskf-law.com.

SCOTT, BRIAN WALTER, management consultant; b. Melbourne, Victoria, Australia, Apr. 23, 1935; s. Walter and Dorothy Ada (Ransom) S.; m. Dorothy Yvonne Allen, Aug. 15, 1959; children: David, Mark, Jennifer, Susan. B of Econs., Sydney (Australia) U., 1955; MBA, Stanford U., 1959; D of Bus. Adminstrn., Harvard U., 1963. Asst. prof. U. So. Calif., Los Angeles, 1961-62; cons. mgmt. W.D. Scott and Co. Pty. Ltd., Sydney, 1963-69, dir., 1969-74, mng. dir., 1974-79, chmn., 1979-85; dep. chmn. A.C.I. Internat. Ltd., Sydney, 1985-86, chmn., 1986-88; dir., mgmt. rev. Edn. Portfolio, New South Wales, 1988-90. Chmn. Mgmt. Frontiers Pty. Ltd., Sydney, Found for Devel. Cooperation Ltd., Brisbane; bd. dirs. ANZ Banking Corp. Ltd., Melbourne, Liquid Air Australia Ltd., Melbourne, James N. Kirby Found. Ltd. Chmn. Trade Devel. Coun., Canberra, 1984-90, chmn. Australian-Korean Found, 1992-2000; chmn. coun. Knox Grammar Sch., Sydney, 1981-89, Australia-Asean Bus. Coun., Canberra, 1980-82; mem. governing bd. Asian Inst. Mgmt., Manila, 1990—; co-chmn. Australia-Korea Forum, 1989-91. Named Officer, Order of Australia, 1985; recipient Australian Mfrs. Export Coun. award, 1989. Fellow Inst. Dirs. Australia (fed. pres. 1982-86), Internat. Acad. Mgmt., Australian Inst. Mgmt., Inst. Mgmt. Cons.; mem. Trade Policy Rsch. Ctr. (coun. mem. 1985-90), Sydney U. (senate 1990-95), Royal Sydney Yacht Squadron Club, Am. Club (Sydney). Avocations: reading, travel. Home: #4 2-6 Russell Ave Lindfield NSW 2070 Australia Office: Mgmt Frontiers Pty Ltd 118 Alfred St Milsons Pt North Sydney NSW 2061 Australia E-mail: mfed@mgtfrontiers.com.au.

SCOTT, BRUCE A. otolaryngologist; b. Louisville, Ky., Sept. 30, 1961; m. Christy Scott; 3 children. MD, U. Tex., 1987. Diplomate Am. Bd. Otolaryngology. Intern Sealy Hosp.-U. Galveston, 1987-88; resident in otolaryngology and head and neck surgery U. Tex. Med. Br., Galveston, 1988-92; fellow in facial plastic and reconstructive surgery U. Tex. Health Sci. Ctr., Houston, 1992-93; pvt. practice Lousiville. Tee-ball, baseball coach, basketball coach. Mem. AMA (bd. trustees, com. on membership, nominating com., AMA Found., mem. resident physician sect. governing coun., chairperson, young physician sect. governing coun., del. to ho. of dels. 1997, 98, mem. surg. caucus exec. com., reference com., mem. women in medicine adv. panel, Outreach Awards). Avocations: golf, flying radio control planes. Office: AMA 515 N State St Chicago IL 60610-4325 also: 225 Abraham Flexner Way Ste 401 Louisville KY 40202-1850

SCOTT, BRUCE K. retired military officer; b. Ft. Bliss, Tex., Apr. 22, 1950; m. Mary B. Tallman; children: Kate, Andy, Karoline, Kerney, Alec, Adam. BS, U.S. Mil. Acad., 1972; M of Internat. Rels., U. Freiburg, Germany; MPA, Harvard U., 1984. Commd. 2d lt. U.S. Army, 1972, advanced through grades to maj. gen.; dep. dir. strategy, plans and policy Office of the Dep. Chief of Staff for Ops. and Plans, to 1997; chief legis. liaison Office of Sec. of Army, Washington, 1997—2002; v.p. internat. mktg., defense ITT Industries, McLean, Va., 2002—. White House fellow, 1984—85. Decorated Army DSM, legion of Merit with oak leaf cluster, Army Commendation medal, others; Olmsted scholar. Office: ITT Industries, Defense 1650 Tysons Blvd Ste 1700 Mc Lean VA 22102*

SCOTT, BYRON ALTON, professional basketball coach, former professional basketball player; b. Ogden, Utah, Mar. 28, 1961; m. Anita Scott; children: Thomas, Londen. Student, Ariz. State U., 1979-85. With L.A. Lakers, 1983-93, 96-97; shooting guard Indiana Pacers, Indpls., 1993-95, Vancouver Grizzlies, 1995-96; asst. coach Sacramento Kings, Sacramento, 1998-00; head coach New Jersey Nets, East Rutherford, 2000—04, New Orleans Hornets, 2004—. Mem. NBA Championship Team, 1985, 87, 88. Office: c/o New Orleans Hornets 1501 Griod St New Orleans LA 70113*

SCOTT, CAMPBELL, actor; b. N.Y.C., July 19, 1962; s. George C. Scott and Colleen Dewhurst; m. Anne Scott, 1991. BA, Lawrence U., 1983. Appearences include (theatre) The Queen and the Rebels, 1982, The Real Thing, 1984, Our Town, 1984, Hay Fever, 1985, A Man For All Seasons, 1986, Dalliance, 1986, Copperhead, 1987, Ah, Wilderness!, 1987-88, Long Day's Journey Into Night, 1987-88, (TV movies) The Kennedys of Massachusetts, 1990, The Perfect Tribute, 1991, Would You Kindly Direct Me to Hell?: The Infamous Dorothy Parker, 1994, The Love Letter, 1998, The Tale of Sweeney Todd, 1998, (TV miniseries) LIBERTY! The American Revolution, 1997, (films) Five Corners, 1987, From Hollywood to Deadwood, 1988, Longtime Companion, 1989, Ain't No Way Back, 1990, The Sheltering Sky, 1990, Dying Young, 1991, Dead Again, 1991, Singles, 1992, Mrs. Parker and the Vicious Circle, 1994, The Innocent, 1994, Let It Be Me, 1995, Big Night, 1996, The Daytrippers, 1996, The Spanish Prisoner, 1996, The Imposters, 1998, Hi-Life, 1998, Top of the Food Chain, 1999, Spring Forward, 1999, Lush, 1999, Other Voices, 2000, Delivering Milo, 2000, Marie and Bruce, 2004, Loverboy, 2004; (TV movies) Follow the Stars Home, 2001, The Pilot's Wife, 2002; actor, exec. prodr. (film) Roger Dodger, 2002; actor, prodr. (film) The Secret Lives of Dentists, 2002. Address: Richard Parks Agy 138 E 16th St New York NY 10003*

SCOTT, CARL DOUGLAS, aerospace engineer; b. San Antonio, Nov. 14, 1937; s. Sparkman and Mildred Scott; m. Marcia Margaret Campbell, June 10, 1960; children: Stephen, Jacquelyn, James, Erin. BA, Rice Inst., 1960; PhD, U. Tex., 1969. Aerospace engr., physicist NASA Johnson Space Ctr., Houston, 1963—, aerothermodynamics group leader, 1985—91. Vis. prof. U. Paris Nord, Villetaneuse, France, 1991-92. Assoc. editor: Jour. Thermophysics and Heat Transfer, 1987—90; co-editor: Thermophysical Aspects of Reentry Flows, 1986; contbr. articles to profl. jours. including Jour. Thermophysics and Heat Transfer. Lt. (j.g.) USN, 1960-63. Named Tech. Person of Yr., Coun. Tech. Socs., 1987. Fellow AIAA (assoc., thermophysics tech. com. 1984-86). Methodist. Achievements include patents for an aeroassisted orbital transfer vehicle; first to determine temperature dependent catalytic recombination coefficient for oxygen and nitrogen on space shuttle tiles; development of chemical kinetics models from carbon nanotube formation. Office: ES4 Nasa Johnson Space Ctr Houston TX 77058 Office Phone: 281-483-6643.

SCOTT, CATHERINE DOROTHY, librarian, information consultant; b. June 21, 1927; d. Leroy Stearns Scott and Agnes Frances (Meade) Scott Schellenberg. AB in English, Cath. U. Am., 1950, MS in Libr. Sci., 1955. Asst. libr. Export-Import Bank USA, Washington, 1951-55, Nat. Assn. Home Builders, 1955-62, reference libr., 1956-62; founder, chief tech. libr. Bellcomm, Inc., subs. AT&T, 1962-72; chief libr. Nat. Air, Space Mus. Smithsonian Instn., 1972-82, chief libr. Mus. Reference Ctr., 1982-88, sr. reference libr., 1989-95; info. cons., 1995—. Presdl. appointee, mem. Nat. Commn. Librs., Info. Sci., 1971—76; bd. visitors Cath. U. Am. Libr. Sci. Sch., Librs., 1984—93. Editor: International Handbook of Aerospace Awards and Trophies, 1980, 81; guest editor: Aeronautics and Space Flight Collections, 1985, in Spl. Collections, 1984. Vice chmn. DC Rep. Com., Washington, 1960—68; mem. platform com. Rep. Nat. Com., 1964; del. Rep. Nat. Conv., San Francisco, 1964; sec. Rep. Nat. Com., Washington, 1968; del. Rep. Nat. Conv., Miami, Fla., 1968. Named to Hon. Order Ky. Cols., 1968; recipient Sec.'s Disting. Svc. award Smithsonian Instn., 1976, Alumni Achievement award Cath. U. Am., 1977, Century Circle, 1998—, Disting. Fed. Svc. Nat. Commn. Libr. and Info. Sci. medal, 1985. Mem.: Am. Soc. of Info. Sci, League Rep. Women DC (bd. dirs. 1995—97, nominating com. 1996—97, contbg. mem. 1999—), Nat. Fedn. Rep. Women, Cath. U. Am. Devel. Com., Friends of Cath. U. Librs. (founder, pres. 1984—88, exec. coun. 1984—96, sustaining mem. 1998—), Internat. Fedn. Libr. Assns. (del. 1976, 1983, 1985, 1988—89), Nat. Mus. Women in Arts, Am. Soc. Assn. Execs., Spl. Librs. Assn. (assn. pres., Washington chapt. pres. 1973—74, DCSLA, cons. com. 1976—91, award com. 1990—91, pres. elect 1991—92, assn. pres., Washington chapt. pres. 1973—74, pres. 1992—93, aerospace divsn., assn. pres. elect 1992—93, immediate past pres. 1993—94, chair assn. awards and honors 1994—95, chmn. cons. com. 1994—98, anniversary com. aerospace divsn. 1995, convenor ret. causus 1997—99, conf. program facilitator Indpls. 1998, conf. program facilitator Mpls. 1999, conf. program facilitator Phila. 2000, conf. program facilitator San Antonio 2001, conf. program facilitator LA 2002, conf. program facilitator NYC 2003), WW in Am. (hon.), Capital Yacht Club, Cent. Club, Legacy Club. Fax: (202) 483-9223.

SCOTT, CHARLES DAVID, chemical engineer, consultant; b. Chaffee, Mo., Oct. 24, 1929; s. Charles Perry and Alma Gertrude (Kendall) S.; m. Alice Reba Bardill, Feb. 11, 1956; children: Timothy Charles, Mary Alice, Lisa Ann. BS in Chem. Engring., U. Mo., 1951; MS in Chem. Engring., U. Tenn., 1961, PhD, 1966. Registered profl. engr., Tenn. Devel. engr. Union Carbide Corp., Oak Ridge, 1953-57; rsch. engr. Oak Ridge Nat. Lab., 1957-73, sect. chief, 1973-76, assoc. divsn. dir., 1976-83, rsch. fellow, 1983-86, sr. rsch. fellow, 1987-94; dir. bioprocessing rsch. and devel. ctr., 1991-94; engirng. R&D cons., 1994—. Adj. prof. chem. engring. U. Tenn., Knoxville. Contbr. articles to profl. jours.; patentee in field. 1st lt. AUS, 1951-53. Recipient U.S. Dept. Energy E.O. Lawrence award, 1980, U. Tenn. Nathan W. Doughtery award, 1987, U. Mo. Honor award, 1988, David Perlman award Am. Chem. Soc., 1994; Union Carbide Corp. fellow, 1983; Martin Marietta Sr. Corp. fellow, 1987. Mem. Am. Chem. Soc. (chmn. separation sci. subdivsn.), Am. Assn. Clin. Chemistry (chmn. com. advanced analytical concepts, nat. award 1980), Am. Inst. Chem. Engrs. (bd. dirs.), Nat. Acad. Engring., Sigma Xi, Alpha Chi Sigma. Lutheran. Office Phone: 865-483-5493.

SCOTT, CHARLES FRANCIS, health facility administrator; b. Phila., Mar. 21, 1950; married. BS, Princeton U., 1972; M in Bus. Adminstrn., U. Chgo., 1975. Diplomate Am. Coll. Health Care Execs. Adminstrv. intern Med. Coll. Pa. and Hosp., Phila., 1974; adminstrv. asst. Reading (Pa.) Hosp. and Med. Ctr., 1975-78; asst. adminstr. ops. Mercy Hosp., Council Bluffs, Iowa, 1979-82; assoc. exec. dir. ops. Tampa (Fla.) Gen. Hosp., 1982-84; v.p. St. Joseph's Hosp., Tampa, 1984-88, COO, adminstr., 1988-94, pres. hosp. ops., 1994-96; pres., CEO Meml. Hosp. Tampa/Town and Country Hosp., 1997-2000, Doctors' Hosp. Sarasota, Fla., 2000—. Office: Doctors Hosp Sarasota 5731 Bee Ridge Rd Sarasota FL 34233-5056

SCOTT, CHARLES LEWIS, retired photojournalist; b. Grayville, Ill., Aug. 18, 1924; s. Marvin Joseph and Prudence (Blood) S.; m. Jane Turner, Jan. 14, 1945 (dec. 1983); children— Lyntha Ann, Thomas Marvin; m. Martha McDonald, Aug. 23, 1986. BS in Journalism, U. Ill., 1948; MS, Ohio U., 1970. Photographer Champaign-Urbana (Ill.) Courier, 1946-50, chief photographer, 1953-56; photographer Ill. Natural History Survey, 1946-51, Binghamton (N.Y.) Press, 1951-53; asst. picture editor Milw. Jour., 1956-58; picture editor, 1958-66; graphics dir. Chgo. Daily News, 1966-69; instr. Sch. Journalism, Ohio U., Athens, 1969-70, asst. prof., 1971-72, asso. prof., 1972-74, 76-77, prof., 1977—; dir. Sch. Visual Communication, 1978-95, prof. emeritus visual comm., 1995; picture editor Chgo. Tribune, 1974-76; dir. photography Rocky Mountain News, Denver, 1987-88; ret., 1995. Served with U.S. Navy, 1942-45. Decorated D.F.C., Air medal (3); recipient numerous awards in regional and nat. news photo contests. Mem. Nat. Press Photographers Assn. (charter mem., Newspaper Photographer of Yr. 1952, Editor of Yr. 1966, Joseph Sprague Meml. award 1975, Robin F. Garland Educator award 1979), Soc. Profl. Journalists, Ohio News Photographers Assn. (Lifetime Achievement award 1995). Presbyterian. Home: 8559 Lavelle Rd Athens OH 45701-9190

SCOTT, CHARLOTTE H. business educator; b. Yonkers, NY, Mar. 18, 1925; d. Edgar B. and Charlotte Agnes (Palmer) Hanley; m. Nathan Alexander Scott, Jr., Dec. 21, 1946; children: Nathan Alexander Scott, Leslie Kristin Scott Ashamu. AB, Barnard Coll., 1947; postgrad., Am. U., 1949-53; MBA, U. Chgo., 1964; LL.D., Allegheny Coll., 1981. Research asso. Nat. Bur. Econ. Research, N.Y.C., 1947-48; economist R.W. Goldsmith Assos., Washington, 1948-50, 1955-56, Fed. Res. Bank, Chgo., 1956-71, asst. v.p., 1971-76; prof. bus. adminstrn. and commerce, sr. fellow Tayloe Murphy Inst., U. Va., Charlottesville, 1976-86; prof. commerce and edn. U. Va., Charlottesville, 1986-98, prof. emeritus, 1998—. Bd. dirs. Atlantic Rural Expn., Inc.; mem. adv. bd. NationsBank Charlottesville, 1991-93; mem. nat. adv. bd. coun. SBA, 1979-82; mem. consumer adv. coun. bd. govs. FRS, 1979-82, vice chmn., 1980-81, chmn., 1981-82. Mem. editorial bd. Jour. Retail Banking, 1978-85, Jour. Internat. Assn. Personnel Women, 1981-85; contbr. articles to profl. jours. Pres. women's bd. Chgo. Urban League, 1967-69; mem. Va. Commn. on Status of Women, 1982-85, Gov.'s Commn. on Va.'s Future, 1982-85, Gov.'s Commn. on Efficiency in Govt., 1985-87; treas. Va. Women's Cultural History Project, 1982-85; bd. dirs. Boys and Girls Club of Charlottesville/Albemarle; governing bd. Charlottesville Area Cmty. Found., 1993—; mem. adv. bd. Ash Lawn-Highland Mus.; treas. Episcopal Diocese, Coun. Region XV, 1999-2004. Mem. Internat. Assn. Personnel Women (v.p. mems.-at-large 1980-82), Assn. Study of Higher Edn., Va. Assn. Econs., Acad. Mgmt., Barnard Coll./Columbia U. Alumnae Assn. (bd. dirs. 1977-81, trustee 1977-81). Episcopalian. Office: U Va McIntire Sch Commerce Monroe Hall Charlottesville VA 22903 Home: 250 Pantops Mountain Rd Charlottesville VA 22911

SCOTT, D. DWIGHT, corporate financial executive; BA, U. NC, Chapel Hill; MBA, U. Tex. Mng. dir. Donaldson, Lufkin and Jenrette; sr. v.p. fin. and planning El Paso Corp., Houston, 2002, exec. v.p., CFO, 2002—. Office: El Paso Corp 1001 Louisiana St Houston TX 77002

SCOTT, DALE ALLAN, major league umpire; b. Springfield, Oreg., Aug. 14, 1959; s. Jesse Lee and Betty Ann (Potts) S. AS, Lane C.C., 1979. Radio disc jockey Sta. KBDF, Eugene, Oreg., 1976-81; minor league umpire various orgns., 1981-85; umpire Am. League, 1986-99, World Series, 1998, 2001, Major League Baseball, 2000—, All Star Game, 1993, 2001. Ofcl. Lane County Baseball Umpire Assn., 1975-81, Lane County Basketball Ofcls. Assn., 1977-85, Portland Basketball Assn., 1986-96, Lane County Football Ofcls. Assn., 1978-88, H.S. football Portland Football Ofcls. Assn., 1989-96; instr. Golden State Umpire Camp, 1991-99. Democrat. Office: Office of Commr of Baseball 245 Park Ave New York NY 10167-0002

SCOTT, DANIEL LEE, dean; b. Douglas, Ga., Aug. 24, 1952; s. Carroll Lee and Ann Trainer Scott; m. Melinda Maish, Aug. 15, 1975; children: Benjamin Lee, Gretchen Ann, Paul Landon. EdD, U. Memphis, 1984. Prof. edn. Liberia Bapt. Theol. Sem., Monrovia, 1984—90, Nigerian Bapt. Theol. Sem., Ogbomoso, 1990—2001; dean of evening and weekend studies DeVry U., Orlando, 2001—. Author: (academic textbook) A History of Educational Thought and Practice, (various monographs) Stewardship, Jesus the Teacher, Deacons.

SCOTT, DAVID ALBERT, congressman; b. Aynor, S.C., June 27, 1945; s. Albert and Mamie (Polite) S.; m. Alfredia Aaron, Oct. 26, 1969; children: Dayna Dorienda, Marcye Michelle. BA, Fla. A&M U., 1967; MBA, U. Pa., 1969. Pres., owner Dayn-Mark Advt., Atlanta; mem. Ga. Ho. of Reps., Atlanta, 1975-82, Ga. Senate, Atlanta, 1983—2002, chmn. edn. com., 1993, chmn. rules com., 1994—2002; mem. U.S. Ho. of Reps. from 13th Ga. dist., 2003—. Chmn. Atlanta Fulton Senate Del., 1992, 93, 94. Creator, prodr., dir. (film) Langston! (4 Emmy awards, best cultural affairs program award NATAS, spl. recognition Congl. Black Caucus, Bronze Jubilee award), (nat. radio program) Inside Black America (spl. cmty. svc. award Mayor of Chgo., James Weldon Johnson journalism award NAACP, spl. citation City of Highland Park, Mich., spl. broadcasting cmty. svc. award Detroit City Coun., spl. tribute Mich. Ho. of Reps.). Mem. exec. bd. dirs. U. Pa. Wharton Sch. Recipient Silver Microphone award, 1986, 92, 93, 94, Amy awards, 1993, Gov.'s award for excellence in edn., Telly award 1994. Mem. Ga. Bus. Coun., Ga. C. of C. (bd. dirs.), Nat. Assn. Black Elected Ofcls., Black Caucus, NAACP, Alpha Phi Alpha. Democrat. Baptist. Avocations: reading, writing, movies, theater. Office: 417 Cannon Ho Office Bldg Washington DC 20515-1013

SCOTT, DAVID ALLEN, mental health services professional, writer; b. Bethlehem, Pa., Sept. 26, 1945; s. Frederic Allen and Sarah Low Scott; m. Ann Elizabeth Barrier, Dec. 26, 1996; m. Sally Jane Locke, Mar. 24, 1972 (div.); children: Matthew Jacob Barrier, Eric Benson Scott. AA, Fresno City Coll., 1969; B of Psychology, Calif. State U., 1972, M of Psychology, 1974. Lic. mariage and family therapist Calif. Bd. of Behavioral Scis., Calif. C.C. counselor credential Bd. of Govs., Calif. C.C.s, Calif. C.C. instr. credential Bd. of Govs., Calif. C.C.s. Sr. lic. mental health clinician Fresno County Human Svcs. Dept. Behavioral Health, Fresno, 1996—99, clin. supr., 1999—. Author: (nonfiction) Love Answers - Based on the Bible and A Course in Miracles, 1996, A Healing Way: Psycho-Spiritual Healing Groups for Delinquent Children and their Families, 1999, (poetry) Changing Impressions - Selected Poetry of David Scott, 1999, (children's fiction) The Indian Way: A Boy Finds Peace, 2001. Treas. Sunnyside Condominiums Homeowners' Assn., Fresno, 1999—2003, v.p., 2004—. Mem.: Psi Chi, Phi Kappa Phi. Avocations: writing, photography. Office: Fresno Co Older Adult Mental Health Team Ste 230 2025 E Dakota Ave Fresno CA 93726 Office Phone: 559-453-5707. Business E-Mail: dascott@co.fresno.ca.us. E-mail: dascott@msn.com.

SCOTT, DAVID CLINTON, research scientist; b. Brighton, Colo., Sept. 5, 1960; s. Robert Glenn and Janice Elizabeth (Smith) S.; m. Dana Jungschaffer, Aug. 7, 1988; children: Clinton P., Alexander J., Eric O. BA, U. Colo., 1986; PhD, U. So. Calif., 1993. R & D chemist ICI, Hawthorn, Calif., 1987-88; rsch. asst. chemistry dept. U. So. Calif., L.A., 1988-93; rsch. scientist Jet Propulsion Lab, Pasadena, Calif., 1993-2000; sr. mem. tech. staff Atmospheric Scis., Pasadena, Calif., 2000—. Contbr. articles to profl. jours. Mem. AAAS, Am. Geophys. Union, Am. Chem. Soc., Applied Optics, Phi Beta Kappa. Avocations: mountain biking, running, swimming, skiing, hiking. Office: Jet Propulsion Lab M/S 183-401 4800 Oak Grove Dr Pasadena CA 91109

SCOTT, DAVID KNIGHT, physicist, university administrator; b. North Ronaldsay, Scotland, Mar. 2, 1940; married, 1966; 3 children. BSc, Edinburgh U., 1962; DPhil in Nuclear Physics, Oxford U., 1967. Rsch. officer nuclear physics lab. Oxford U., 1970-73; rsch. fellow nuclear physics Balliol Coll., 1967-70, sr. rsch. fellow, 1970-73; physicist Lawrence Berkeley Lab. U. Calif., 1973-75, sr. scientist nuclear sci., 1975-79; prof. physics, astronomy and chemistry Nat. Superconducting Cyclotron Lab. Mich. State U., East Lansing, 1979-93; Hannah disting. prof. physics, astronomy and chemistry Mich. State U., East Lansing, 1979-86, assoc. provost, 1983-86, provost, v.p. acad. affairs, 1986-92; Hannah Disting. prof. learning, sci. and soc. Nat. Superconducting Cyclotron Lab. Mich. State U., East Lansing, 1992-93; chancellor U. Mass., Amherst, 1993—2001. Fellow Am. Phys. Soc. Office: U Mass 418 Lederle Grad Rsrch Ctr Amherst MA 01003 E-mail: dkscott@chancellor.umass.edu.

SCOTT, DAVID RODICK, lawyer, legal educator; b. Phila., Dec. 30, 1938; s. Ernest and Lydia Wister (tunis) S.; m. Ruth Erskine Wardle, Aug. 20, 1966; children: Cintra W., D. Rodman. AB magna cum laude, Harvard U., 1960, JD, 1965; MA, Cambridge U., 1962. Bar: Pa. 1966, D.C. 1977, U.S. Dist. Ct. (ea. dist.) Pa. 1966, U.S. Ct. Appeals (3rd cir.) 1966, U.S. Ct. Appeals (D.C. cir.) 1977, U.S. Supreme Ct. 1977. Law clk. to assoc. justice Supreme Ct. Pa., Phila., 1965-66; assoc. Pepper, Hamilton & Scheetz, Phila., 1966-69, 72-76; asst. dist. atty. City of Phila., 1970-72; sr. trial atty. criminal divsn. U.S. Dept. Justice, Washington, 1976-80; chief counsel, acting dir. Office Govt. Ethics, Washington, 1980-84; univ. counsel Rutgers U., New Brunswick, NJ, 1984—2004. Acting dir. U.S. Office Govt. Ethics, 1982-83; tchr., lectr. in law Cath. U. Am., Washington, 1977-81, Inst. Paralegal Tng., Phila., 1970-74; instr. faculty of arts and scis. Rutgers U.; adj. prof. Rutgers Law Sch., Camden, 2004; lectr. in field. Contbr. chpts. to textbooks, articles to profl. jours. Trustee

United Way Greater Mercer County, 1990—, Princeton Area Cmty. Found., Inc., 1991-2002; bd. mgrs. Episc. Acad., Merion, Pa., 1970-74. Keasbey Found. fellow, 1960-62. Mem ABA, Pa. Bar Assn., Nat. Assn. Coll. and Univ. Attys. (bd. dirs. 1993-96), Am. Friends Cambridge U. (head N.J. chpt. 1987-93). Home: 255 Russell Rd Princeton NJ 08540-6733 Office: Rutgers U Office of Univ Counsel Winants Hall New Brunswick NJ 08901 E-mail: scott@oldqueens.rutgers.edu.

SCOTT, DAVID WARREN, statistics educator; b. Oak Park, Ill., July 16, 1950; s. John V. and Nancy (Mellers) S.; m. Jean Charlotte Madera, June 15, 1974; children: Hilary Kathryn, Elizabeth Alison, Warren Robert. BA, Rice U., 1972, MA, PhD, Rice U., 1976. Asst. prof. Baylor Coll. Medicine, Houston, 1976-79, Rice U., Houston, 1979-80, assoc. prof., 1980-85, chmn. stats. dept., 1990-93, Noah Harding prof. stats., 2001—; vis. prof. Stanford U., Palo Alto, Calif., 1985-86; prof. stats. Noah Harding, 2003—. Vis. prof. Dept. Def., Ft. Meade, Md., 1993-94, 99-2000. Author: Multivariate Density Estimation, 1992; mem. editl. bd. John Wiley & Sons Probability and Stats. Series, 1994—; past editor jour. Computational Stats. and Jour. Statis. Scis.; editor Jour. Computational and Graphical Stats., 2000—03, contbr. articles to profl. publs. Mem. applied and Theoretical stats. com. Nat. Rsch. Coun., 2001-05. Grantee NASA, 1982-84, Office Naval Rsch., 1985-93, NSF, 1993—. Fellow Internat. Stats. Inst., Inst. Math. Stats., Am. Statis. Assn. (assoc. editor jour. 1983-94); mem. Inst. Math. Statis. (cons.). Avocations: woodworking, hiking, family. Home: 4143 Marlowe St Houston TX 77005-1953 Office: Rice U Dept Stats 6100 Main St # Ms-138 Houston TX 77005-1827 Office Phone: 713-348-6037. Business E-Mail: scottdw@rice.edu.

SCOTT, DAVID WINFIELD, artist, museum consultant; b. Fall River, Mass., July 10, 1916; s. Benjamin David and Edith May (Romig) S.; m. Tirsa Lilia Saavedra, July 10, 1947 (dec. Jan. 1986); children: Tirsa Margaret, Edith Elizabeth; m. Doris Jean Fitch White, Aug. 19, 1988. AB, Harvard Coll., 1938; MA, Claremont Grad. Sch., 1940, MFA, 1951; PhD, U. Calif., Berkeley, 1960; DFA, Corcoran Sch. Art, 1991. Instr. art Riverside (Calif.) Jr. Coll., 1940-41; from lectr. to prof. Scripps Coll., Claremont, Calif., 1947-63; dir. Nat. Collection Fine Art, Washington, 1964-69; planning officer Nat. Gallery Art, Washington, 1969-84; acting dir. Corcoran Gallery Art, Washington, 1990; artist, cons. pvt. practice, Whitehaven, Md., 1991—. Cons. in field. Capt. USAF, 1945. Mem. Cosmos Club. Home: 2764 Whitehaven Rd Whitehaven MD 21856-2507 E-mail: scotfree@intercom.net.

SCOTT, DEBORAH ELIZABETH, school system administrator, poet; b. Middletown, Conn., July 6, 1969; d. Donald William Troxler, Sr. and Celeste Elizabeth Troxler (Jennings by later remarriage); m. Ashley Van Scott, May 13, 1967; children: Brittney Elizabeth, Ashley Celeste, Destiney Monae'. Cert. of Completion, Marine Corps Svc. Support Sch. (Adminstrn. and Typing), Camp Lejeune, NC, 1988—88; Cert. of Tng., Basic Mil. Police Sch., Ft. Jackson, SC, 1995—95. Adminstrv. clk. USMC, Camp Lejeune, NC, 1988—89; adminstrv. asst. Mayor's Office / City Hall, Baker, La., 1991—92; mil. police officer US Army N.G., Sacramento, 1994—97; adminstr. O Happy Day Christian Acad., Yuba City, Calif., 1996—97, Learning Light Acad., Lompoc, Calif., 1998—2002, Victorville, Calif., 2003—. Spl. guest poet / spkr. (holidays) Buena Vista Elem. Sch., Lompoc, Calif., 2001—02. Author: (book) Debbie ES Poetry Journals. Mem. / hostess First Assembly of God (Ch.), Victorville, Calif., 2003—04. Lance cpl. USMC, 1988—89, Camp Lejeune, North Carolina. Decorated Promotion Cert. and Insignia USMC; recipient Hon. Discharge, 1989, US Army N.G., 1997. Mem.: Spring Valley Lake Country Club. D-Conservative. Assembly Of God (Christian). Achievements include author/pub. of Debbie ES Poetry Greeting Cards; pub.author and illustrator of Personalized Children's Poetry. Avocations: poetry, sketch art, swimming, camping. Office: Learning Light Academy 8370 S V L Box Victorville CA 92392-51 Office Phone: 760-955-9641.

SCOTT, DEBORAH EMONT, curator; b. Passaic, N.J. d. Harold and Rhoda (Baumgarten) Emont; m. George Andrew Scott, June 4, 1983; children: Meredith Suzanne, Diana Faith. BA, Rutgers U., Livingston Coll., 1973; MA, Oberlin Coll., 1979. Asst. curator Allen Meml. Art Mus., Oberlin, Ohio, 1977-79; curator collections Memphis Brooks Mus. Art, 1979-83; curator The Nelson-Atkins Mus. Art, Kansas City, 1983—, chief curator, 1998—. Project dir. Kansas City Sculpture Pk., 1986-01. Author: (catalogue) Alan Shields, 1983, (essay) Jonathan Borofsky, 1988, (essay) Judith Shea, 1989, (interview) John Ahearn, 1990, (essay) Gerhard Richter, 1990, (essay) Kathy Muehlemann, 1991, (essay) Nate Fors, 1991, (essay) Julian Schnabel, 1991, (essay) Louise Bourgeois, 1994, (essay) Joel Shapiro, 1995, (essay) Lewis deSoto, 1996, (catalogue) Ursula von Rydingsvard, 1997; contbr.: Celebrating Moore: Works from the Collection of the Henry Moore Foundation, Selected by David Mitchinson, 1998, Modern Sculpture at The Nelson-Atkins Museum of Art: An Anniversary Celebration, 1999, (CD ROM) Masterworks for Learning: A College Collection Catalogue, Allen Memorial Art Museum, Oberlin College, 1998. Office: Nelson-Atkins Mus Art 4525 Oak St Kansas City MO 64111-1873

SCOTT, DEBORAH L. costume designer; Costume designer: (films) E.T. The Extra-Terrestrial, 1982, Twilight Zone-The Movie ("Kick the Can", "Nightmare at 20,000 Feet"), 1983, Back to the Future, 1985, About Last Night..., 1986, Armed and Dangerous, 1986, Who's That Girl?, 1987, Moving, 1988, Coupe de Ville, 1990, Defending Your Life, 1991, Eve of Destruction, 1991, Sliver, 1993, Jack the Bear, 1993, Legends of the Fall, 1994, Indian in the Cupboard, 1995, To Gillian on Her 37th Birthday, 1996, Titanic, 1997 (Acad. award 1998), Wild Wild West, 1999, The Patriot, 2000, Minority Report, 2001. Recipient Academy award, 1998.

SCOTT, DONAHUE, energy executive; b. Washington, Mar. 24, 1962; s. Donahue and Rachel Julia Scott; m. JoAnn Marie Burgette, Aug. 1, 1992; children: Austin Timothy, Alaya Janelle, Thais Renee, Dacia Julia, Lela JoAnn. BS in Mech. Engring., Howard U., 1987; MBA, West Chester U., 1998. Registered profl. engr., Pa., 1994, cert. energy mgr., Assn. Energy Engrs., 2000, demand-side mgmt. profl., Assn. Energy Engrs., 2000. Engr. PPL, Allentown, Pa., 1987—95; sr. energy engr. Exelon, Phila., 1995—2002; account mgr. Reliant Energy Solutions, Houston, 2002—03; dir. sales Liberty Power, 2003—. Recipient Innovator award, Electric Power Rsch. Inst., 1998. Avocation: chess.

SCOTT, DONALD LAVERN, city manager, former army officer; b. Hunnewell, Mo., Feb. 8, 1938; s. William Edward and Amanda Beatrice (Dant) S.; m. Betty Jean Forte, Mar. 3, 1962; children: Jeffrey Jerome, Merriell Edward Lavern. BA in Graphic Arts, Lincoln U., 1960; MA in Counseling and Human Devel., Troy State U., 1982. Commd. 2d lt. U.S. Army, 1960, advanced through grades to brig. gen., 1991; bn. comdr. 3d Bn., 47th Inf. Div., Ft. Lewis, Wash., 1978-80; prof. mil. sci. Tuskegee (Ala.) U., 1980-81; dep. insp. gen. U.S. Army Europe, Heidelberg, Fed. Republic Germany, 1982-83; comdr. Hohenfels (Germany) Tng. Ctr., 1983-85; insp. gen. VII U.S. Corps, Stuttgart, Fed. Republic Germany, 1985-86; asst. div. comdr. 1st Cav. Div., Ft. Hood, Tex., 1986-88; chief of staff 2d U.S. Army, Ft. Gillem, Ga., 1988-91; ret., 1991; chief of staff City of Atlanta, 1991, COO, 1991—. Bd. dirs. Atlanta Conv. and Bus. Bur., 1991—; advisor Jimmy Carter's Atlanta Project, 1992; mem. 100 Blackmen, Atlanta, 1992. Decorated D.S.M., Legion of Merit, Bronze Star (6), Meritorious Svc. medal. Mem. Assn. U.S. Army, Atlanta C. of C., Kappa Alpha Psi (reporter 1980-82). Avocations: golf, reading, jogging. Home: 2118 Tysons Executive Ct Dunn Loring VA 22027-1047 Office: City of Atlanta Office of Mayor 55 Trinity Ave SW Atlanta GA 30303-3520

SCOTT, DONALD MICHAEL, writer, educator; b. L.A., Sept. 26, 1943; s. Bernard Hendry and Marguerita (Baroni) Scott, Barbara (Lannin) Scott (Stepmother); m. Patricia Ilene Pancaost, Oct. 24, 1964 (div. June 1971); children: William Bernard, Kenneth George. BA, San Francisco State U., 1965, MA, 1986. Cert. tchr. Calif. Tchr. Mercy HS, San Francisco, 1968-71; pk. ranger Calif. State Pk. Sys., Half Moon Bay, 1968-77; tchr. adult divsn. Jefferson Union HS Dist., Daly City, Calif., 1973-87; dir. NASA-NPS Project Wider Focus, Daly City, 1983-90, also bd. dirs., dir. Geo. Sci. Spl. Projects San Francisco, 1990—; nat. pk. ranger, naturalist Grant-Kohrs Ranch Nat. Hist. Site, Deer Lodge, Mont., 1987-88; nat. pk. ranger pub. affairs fire team Yellowstone Nat. Pk., 1988. Rsch. subject NASA, Mountain View, Calif., 1986—90; guest artist Yosemite (Calif.) Nat. Pk., 1986; nat. pk. ranger Golden Gate Nat. Recreation Area Nat. Pk. Svc., San Francisco, 1986, nat. pk. svc. history cons. to Bay Dist., 1988—94; adj. asst. prof. Skyline Coll., 1989—94, Coll. San Mateo, 1992—94; aerospace edn. specialist NASA/OSU/AESP, 1994—2004; state rep. Mont. and Nev. AESP, 1999—2003; cons. Friends Eastern State Penitentiary Project, Phila., 1993. Co-author: (book) From Geos to Mars, 2004, From Montana to Mars, 2003; contbr. articles and photographs to profl. jours., mags., chapters to books; author: (book) The Geos Project, 2003. Panelist Cmty. Bds. San Francisco, 1978—87; active CONTACT Orgn., 1991—, bd. dirs., 1995—; mem. edn. working group Case for Mars VI, Boulder, 1996; pres. Youth for Kennedy, Lafayette, Calif., 1960; city chair Yes on A Com., So. San Francisco, San Mateo County, Calif., 1986. Mem.: Orange County Space Soc., Mars Soc. (founding mem., mem. ednl. task force), Planetary Soc. (charter mem.), Nat. Assn. Interpretation (founding mem.), Friends George R. Stewart, Wider Focus, Yosemite Assn. (life). Avocations: photography, hiking, camping, travel, naturism. Home and Office: PO Box 978 Oceano CA 93475

SCOTT, DORIS PETERSEN, lawyer; b. June 22, 1925; d. David Steele and Leslie Helena (Suit) Petersen; m. Charles Lurman Scott, Aug. 30, 1947; children: Charles L., David Steele. Student, Coll. of Notre Dame of Md., 1945; JD, U. Md., 1949. Bar: Md. 1949, U.S. Dist. Ct. Md. 1955, U.S. Ct. Appeals (4th cir.) 1956. Assoc. Callahan & Caldwell, Balt., 1949—51; pvt. practice Elkton, Md., 1951—82; ptnr. Scott & Scott, Elkton, 1983—. Atty., Cecil County Bd. Edn., 1954; dir. Cecil Fed. Savingss & Loan Assn.; trustee Deferred Compensation Bd., State of Md., 1975—79. Recipient Cecil County Trailblazers award, 1998, Daily Record Leadership in Law award, 2001. Mem.: ABA, Susquehana Law League, Cecil County Bar Assn. (past pres.), Md. State Bar Assn. (past mem. bd. govs.), Balt. Country Club. Democrat. Episcopalian. Office: 109 E Main St Elkton MD 21921-5906

SCOTT, DOROTHY, writer; b. Rochester, Pa., July 21, 1951; d. Mildred Boettner and James Frantz; m. Thomas C.H. Scott, June 10, 1978; children: Margaret, T.A. Malcolm. BA, U. Pitts., 1973. Asst. editor Learning Rsch. & Develop. Ctr., U. Pitts., 1973—79; manuscript editor Eye Rsch. Inst. Retina Found., Boston, 1979—81; freelance med. copy editor Pitts., 1981—86; project mgr., editor Physicians World, Secaucus, NJ, 1987—88; mng. editor Health Learning Sys., Lyndhurst, NJ, 1988—89; med. editor Discovery Internat., Deerfield, Ill., 1990—91, dir. editl. svcs., 1991—95, sr. mng. med. editor, 1995—2001; sr. med. writer CPE Comm., Chgo., 2001—03; med. writer Med. Media Comm., Rosemont, Ill., 2002—. Mem.: Am. Med. Writers Assn. Episcopalian. Avocations: bead work, singing.

SCOTT, EDWARD WILLIAM, JR., computer software company executive; b. Panama City, Panama, May 25, 1938; s. Edward William and Janice Gertrude (Grimison) S.; m. Cheryl S. Gilliland, apr. 23, 1988; children: Edward William, Heather Yolanda Deirdre, Reece Donald; 1 stepson, Erik Veit. BA, Mich. State U., 1959, MA, 1963; BA, Oxford (Eng.) U., 1962. Personnel specialist Panama Canal Co., 1962-64, staff asst. to dir. personnel, 1964-66; personnel officer IRS, Detroit, 1966-68; staff personnel mgmt specialist U.S. Dept. Justice, Washington, 1968-69, chief personnel systems and evaluation sect., 1970-72, dir. Office Mgmt. Programs, 1972-74, assoc. dep. commr. planning and evaluation U.S. Immigration and Naturalization Svc., 1974-75, dep. asst. atty. gen. adminstrn. U.S. Immigration and Naturalization Svc., 1972-75, asst. sec. for adminstrn. Trans. Dept., 1977-80; pres. Office Power, Inc., Washington, 1980-81; dir. mktg. Computer Consoles, Inc., 1981-84; v.p. mktg. Dest Systems, 1984-85; dir. govt. mktg. Sun Microsystems, Mountain View, Calif., 1985-88; exec. v.p. Pyramid Tech., Mountain View, 1988-95; founder, pres. BEA Sys., Inc., San Jose, Calif., 1995—. Founder, chmn. Ctr. for Global Devel., Washington, (with Bill Gates and George Soros) Data-Debt, AIDS, and Trade-Africa, Friends of the Global Fight, Wash.; founder, pres. escottVentures, Inc.; pres. U.S. Dept. Justice Fed. Credit Union, 1970-73. Recipient Presdl. Mgmt. Improvement certificate, 1971; Spl. Commendation award Dept. Justice, 1973; also Spl. Achievement award, 1976; William A. Jump Meml. award, 1974; presdl. sr. exec. service rank of Disting. Exec., 1980; Mich. State U. scholar, 1957-60. Mem.: Phi Kappa Phi, Phi Eta Sigma. Office: BEA Sys Inc 2315 N 1st St San Jose CA 95131-1010 E-mail: ed@escottventures.com.

SCOTT, EILEEN ROSE, retail executive; b. Jersey City, Apr. 4, 1953; d. James Anthony and Margaret Rita (D'Errico) S. BSBA, William Paterson Coll., 1976. Asst. store mgr. Supermarket's Gen. Corp. Pathmark Div., Woodbridge, NJ, 1976-79, buyer, 1979-82, buying supr., 1982-85; sales mgr. Pathmark, Carteret, NJ, dir. sales, 1989, exec. v.p. store ops., 2001—01, CEO, 2002—. Mem. Ea. Dairy Deli Assn. Democrat. Roman Catholic. Home: 506 Horizon Way Neshanic Station NJ 08853-4042 Office: Pathmark Stores Inc 200 Milik St Carteret NJ 07008-1102

SCOTT, ELOISE HALE, state legislator; b. Benton County, Miss., Jan. 24, 1932; m. Lex B. Scott; children: Kenny, Kimble. BS, Miss. U. for Women; MA, U. Miss. Mem. Miss. Ho. of Reps. Chmn. edn. com., mem. labor appropriations, banks and banking, and ethics coms. Active Lee County Ext. Svc. Mem. LWV, Dem. Women. Methodist. Democrat. Office: Miss State House State Capitol Jackson MS 39201 Home: 1275 Winwood Cv Tupelo MS 38801-6472

SCOTT, FREDERICK ISADORE, JR., editor, business executive; b. Balt., Oct. 27, 1927; s. Frederick Isadore and Rebecca Esther (Waller) S.; m. Viola Fowlkes, Feb. 4, 1949. B.E. in Chem. Engring, Johns Hopkins, 1950; MS in Mgmt. Engring, Newark Coll. Engring., 1956. Chem. process engr. in research and devel. RCA, Harrison, N.J., 1951-59; with Kearfott div. Gen. Precision Aerospace, Little Falls, N.J., 1960-62; asst. sales mgr. Isotopes, Inc., Westwood, N.J., 1964-66; mgr. capacitor sect. Wellington Electronics, Inc., Englewood, N.J., 1967-68; owner F.I. Scott & Assos. (med. equipment), Montclair, N.J., 1968-80; tech. product mktg. and editorial svcs. F.I. scott & Assocs., Check, Va., 1980-86; editor instrumentation publ. Am. Lab. and Internat. Lab., Fairfield, Conn., 1968-80, cons. editor, 1980—; pres. Group Tech., Ltd., 1979—; editor Am. Clin. Lab., 1990—. Served with AUS, 1946-47. Mem. Am. Chem. Soc. (sr.), AAAS, N.Y. Acad. Sci., IEEE (editor newsletter No. N.J. sect. 1957-58, chmn. publs. com. 1958-59), N.Y. Micros. Soc. Home and Office: 1 E Chase St Apt 410 Baltimore MD 21202-2597 Office Phone: 410-625-2065. Personal E-mail: fiscott@ziplink.net. *Perhaps the most significant aspect of my life is a long-felt realization that each person is ultimately responsible for his or her condition in life. Application of this principle continually requires that the individual assess a failure in such a way as to determine how his or her actions might have avoided it or, if unavoidable, how its recurrence can be obviated. Accepting responsibility in this manner can, I believe, lead the way toward a society based on a federation of autonomous individuals delegating authority to units of government when appropriate but clearly retaining the capability to recall that delegated authority should it be abused.*

SCOTT, G. JUDSON, JR., lawyer; b. Phila., Nov. 16, 1945; s. Gerald Judson and Jean Louise S.; m. Ildiko Kalman, Mar. 21, 1971; children: Nathan Emory, Lauren Jean. AA, Foothill Jr. Coll., Los Altos, Calif., 1965; BA, U. Calif., Santa Barbara, 1968; JD cum laude, U. Santa Clara, 1975. Bar: Calif. 1975, U.S. Dist. Ct. (no. dist.) Calif. 1975, U.S. Ct. Appeals (9th cir.) 1975, U.S. Supreme Ct. 1981. Assoc. Feldman, Waldman & Kline, San Francisco, 1975-76, Law Offices John Wynne Herron, 1976-80; of counsel Haines & Walker, Livermore, Calif., 1980; ptnr. Haines Walker & Scott, 1980-84; officer, dir., shareholder Smith, Etnire, Polson and Scott, Pleasanton, 1984-88; pvt. practice, 1988—. Judge pro tem Livermore-Pleasanton Mcpl. Ct., 1981-83; settlement commr. Alameda County Superior Ct., 1994—, judge pro tem, 2001-; lectr. Calif. Continuing Edn. of Bar. Contbg. author: Attorney's Guide to Restitution, 1976; editor: The Bottom Line, 1989-91. Pres. Walnut Creek Open Space Found., Calif., 1981-83. Rear adm. USNR, 1968-2001. Fellow: Nat. Conf. of Bar Pres., Am. Bar Found.; mem.: ATLA, ABA (ho. of dels. 2003—), Alameda-Contra Costa County Trial Lawyers Assn., Alameda County Bar Assn. (chmn. law office econs. com. 1986—87, mem. jud. nomination evaluation com. 1996—97, chair task force 1997, bd. dir. 1997—98, v.p. 1999, pres.-elect. 2000, pres. 2001), Calif. State Bar (mem. standing com. on lawyer referral svcs. 1985—88, mem. exec. com. law practice mgmt. sect. 1988—93, chair 1992—93), Ea. Alameda County Bar Assn. (v.p. 1981—82), Coll. of Master Advocates and Barristers (sr. counsel), Consumer Attys. Calif. (reviewer of pending Calif. legis.), Livermore C. of C. (past chmn. growth study 1983), Million Dollar Advs. Forum. Republican. Episcopalian. Office: 6140 Stoneridge Mall Rd Ste 125 Pleasanton CA 94588-3233 Office Phone: 925-460-0800.

SCOTT, GARY THOMAS, historian; b. Wichita Falls, Tex., Mar. 9, 1944; s. Thomas Clifford, Jr. and Lillian (Hanks) Fecher. BA, Southwestern U., Georgetown, Tex., 1966; MA, U. N.C., Chapel Hill, 1969. History instr. Tusculum Coll., Greeneville, Tenn., 1969-70, Herringswell Manor Sch., Bury St. Edmunds, UK, 1970-71; asst. to clk. of the works Washington Nat. Cathedral, 1971-75; archtl. historian Nat. Park Svc., Washington, 1976-82, regional historian, 1982-95, historian Nat. Capital area, 1995—; chief historian Nat. Capital Region, 1996—. Lectr., tour leader Smithsonian Inst., Washington, 1981—; prin. N.Am. rep. in course on archtl. conservation hist. bldgs. Property Svcs. Agy. and English Heritage of Brit. Govt., West Dean Coll., Chichester, Sussex, Eng., 1982-90. Author: The Kappa Alpha Order-1865-1897, 1994, Aquia and Seneca Stone, White House History, 1998. Rep. Nat. Park Svc., D.C. Bicentennial, Washington, 1991—; mem. Com. of One Hundred, Washington, 1993—, U.S. Capitol Cornerstone Bicentennial, Washington, 1993, Washington Monument Cornerstone Centennial, 1998; active Hist. Soc. Washington, 1977—, So. Hist. Assn., 1980—; mem. Friends Attingham Summer Sch., N.Y.C., 1981—, Preservation Roundtable, Washington, 1989—, pres. Victorian Soc., Washington, 2002—04. Recipient Disting. Pub. Svc. award, Kappa Alpha Order, 1988. Mem. Masons (33 degree), Scottish Rite, Cosmos Club Washington, Kappa Alpha Order (chief alumnus 1991-95). Episcopalian. Avocation: book and antique collecting. Office: Nat Park Svc National Capital Region 1100 Ohio Dr SW Washington DC 20242-0001

SCOTT, GENEVA LEE SMITH, nursing educator; b. Codell, Kans., Nov. 2, 1943; d. Lester Lee and Lennicejean Leota (Lynch) Smith; m. Dennis G. Scott, Feb. 20, 1965; children: J.D., Shane, Deminy. BS, Fort Hays Kans. State Coll., 1965; BS in Nursing, Fort Hays State U., 1979; MS in Nursing, West Tex. State U., 1986. Charge nurse Hadley Regional Med. Ctr., Hays, Kans.; sch. nurse Borger (Tex.) Ind. Sch. Dist.; clin. and classroom instr. North Cen. Kans. Area Vocat. Tech. Sch., Hays; nursing instr. St. Philip's Coll., San Antonio; sch. nurse Bryan Ind. Sch. Dist., 1993-97; instr. nursing edn. Blinn Coll., Bryan, Tex., 1997-98, Weatherford (Tex.) Coll., 1998, vocat. nursing instr., 1998-2000, instr. associates degree in nursing program, 2000—. Scholarship grant, 1983. Mem. Am. Nurses Assn., Phi Delta Kappa, Beta Sigma Phi (membership chairperson, Girl of Yr. 1978). Home: 405 W Spring St Weatherford TX 76086 E-mail: scott@wc.edu.

SCOTT, GEORGE ALFRED, advertising executive, writer; b. Detroit, Feb. 9, 1925; s. Frederick Harry and Irene Lottie Scott; m. Audrey Jil Scott, Dec. 16, 1950; 1 child, George A. IV; children: Mrs. Michel Princess Martin, James Sellers, Gary Sellers, Monty Sellers. BA, Mich. State Univ., Ea. Lansing, Mich., 1948. Reporter The Marion Star, Marion, Ohio, 1948—50, sports editor, 1952—53; acct. exec. Jay Maish Co., Marion, Ohio, 1953—57; adv. staff Dow Chem. Co., Midland, Mich., 1957—59; v.p. Barnes Chase Adv., San Diego, 1959—65; assoc. creative dir. MacManus, John & Adams, Bloomfield Hills, Mich., 1965—72; v.p., creative dir. D'Ary, MacManus & Masivs, Bloomfield Hills, Mich., 1972—83; sr. v.p., creative dir. D'Arcy, Masium, Benton & Bowles, Bloomfield Hills, Mich., 1979—86; pres., owner Encore South, Ft. Myers, Fla., 1986—, Encore North, Lupton, Mich., 1986—. Author: (book) Ribbons & Roses & Rice, 1984, More Ribbons, Roses & Rice, 1994, Secrets of an Ad Pro, 2001, Laughing Your Way Through Life, 2003, (books) 2 books of poetry. Worker Habitat for Humanity, Ft. Myers, Fla., 1996—2000. 1st Lt. USMC, 1943—46, 1st Lt. USMC, 1950—52. Recipient Aid to Advt., Ed. Award, Am. Advt., Ed., 1984, DMM Ad of the Yr., D'Avery, McManus & Masius, 1982. Avocations: marathons, poetry. Home and Office: 3701 Lakeside Dr Lupton MI 48635-9631

SCOTT, GEORGE COLE, III, investment advisor; b. N.Y.C., July 9, 1937; s. George Cole Scott II and Anne Blair Clark Martindell; m. Leslie Jane Daniels, Apr. 12, 1969; children: Jane Leslie, Anne Blair, John Cole. BA, U. Wash., 1969. Advt. reporter Am. Weekly, London, 1966-68; stockbroker Anderson & Strudwick, Richmond, Va., 1969-73, Scott & Stringfellow, 1973-78, Piper, Jaffray & Hopwood, Seattle, 1978-82, Wheat, First Securities, Inc., Richmond, Va., 1982-87, Anderson & Strudwick, 1988—. Pres. Closed-End Fund Advisors, Richmond, Va., 1996—; dir. Bergstrom Capital Corp., Seattle, 1976-2003. Co-author: Investing in Closed-End Funds: Finding Value and Building Wealth, 1991; pub., editor: The Scott Letter: Closed-End Fund Report, 1988--; contbr. to Closed-End Country Fund Report, Barron's and other publs. Founder Seattle-Christchurch, New Zealand Sister City Assn. With USCG, 1960-64. Recipient Disting. Citizen award State of Wash., 1981. Mem. Richmond Soc. Fin. Analysts (assoc.), Soc. Cincinnati, Country Club Va., Wash. Athletic Club (Seattle). Episcopalian. Avocations: freelance writing, travel. Home: 8659 Rio Grande Rd Richmond VA 23229-7822 Office: 707 E Main St Richmond VA 23219-2814 Office Phone: 804-344-3845. E-mail: gscott@cefadvisors.com.

SCOTT, GEORGE GALLMANN, accountant; b. Hattiesburg, Miss., July 8, 1928; s. John Havers and Rebecca Evelyn (Gallmann) S.; m. Patsy T. Womack, June 27, 1953; 1 child, George Gallmann. BS, Millsaps Coll., 1949. Accredited bus. acct., tax advisor, 1992; accredited in acctg. and taxation Nat. Accreditation Coun. for Accountancy. Clk. Spanish Trail Transport, Mobile, Ala., 1949—50, asst. auditor, 1953—55; bookkeeper Met. Engraving & Electrotype Co., Richmond, Va., 1952—53; chief clk. Mobile (Ala.) office Ctrl. Truck Lines of Tampa, Fla., 1955—56; gen. auditor M.R.&R. Trucking Co., Crestview, Fla., 1956—66, sec.-treas., 1967—77; pub. acct. enrolled to represent taxpayers before IRS, 1979—. Mem. data processing adv. com. Okaloosa-Walton Col., Niceville, Fla., 1965- 66, 72-73; mem. Okaloosa County Gen. Advisory Com. for Devel. Vocat. Edn., 1973, 79. Bd. dirs. Okaloosa Cmty. Concert Assn., 1982-87; chmn. Crestview Downtown Devel. Bd., 1988-89; bass-baritone soloist, 1953—, choir dir. Meth. Ch., 1966-83, chmn. ofcl. bd., 1971-73, chmn. fin. com., 1974-75, 79-81, audit com., 1977-86, mem. com. on lay personnel, 1979-87, chmn., 1983-87, 89-90, mem. com. on pastor-parish rels., 1980-86, coun. on ministries, 1985, trustee, 1985-87, treas., 1990-95; mem. Walton Co. C. of C. With U.S. Army, 1950-52. Mem. Nat. Assn. Accts., Nat. Assn. Enrolled Agts., Am. Trucking Assn. (nat. acctg. and fin. coun. 1956-77), Southeastern Acctg. and Fin. Coun. (bd. dirs. 1974-77), Fla. Assn. Enrolled Agts., Crestview Downtown Mchts. Assn. (bd. dirs. 1980-84, treas. 1980-84), Greater Crestview C. of C. (chmn. bus. ethics com. 1973-74, bd. dirs. 1981-83, treas. 1982-83), Fla. Accts. Assn. (bd. govs. 1979-80, pres. N.W. Fla. chpt. 1979-80), DeFuniak Springs Bus. and Profl. Assn., Kiwanis (past treas., past sec., past pres.), Pi Kappa Alpha. Home: 244 Seminole Trail Crestview FL 32536-2326

SCOTT, GLORIA RANDLE, college president; b. Apr. 14, 1938; d. Freeman and Juanita (Bell) Randle; m. Will Braxton Scott. AB, Ind. U., 1959, MA, 1960, PhD, 1965, LLD, 1977; DHL, Fairleigh Dickinson U., 1978, Westfield State Coll., 1992, Wilson Coll., 1992, Mt. Vernon Coll., Marian Coll., 1999. Rsch. assoc. in genetics Inst. Psychiat. Rsch. Ind. U. Med. Ctr., Indpls., 1961-63; instr. biology Marian Coll., Indpls., 1961-65; dean students Knoxville (Tenn.) Coll., 1965-67; asst. to pres. N.C. Agrl. and Tech. State U., 1967-68, prof., 1967-76, dir. planning Inst. Rsch., 1973-76; prof. Tex. So. U., 1976-78; v.p., prof. Clark Coll., 1978-86; prof. Grambling State U., 1987; pres. Bennett Coll., Greensboro, N.C., 1987-2001, founder Women's Leadership Inst., 1989; owner Scott's Bau Enterprises on Baffin Bay, Riviera, Tex., 1973-98. Sec. bd. dirs., founder Africa U., Mutare, Zimbabwe, 1988-97; bd. dirs. Loew Corp.; vice chair Women's Coll. Coalition, 1990-94; bd. dirs. Nat. Assn. Ind. Colls. and Univs., 1992-96, Nat. Assn. Schs. and Colls. of the United Meth. Ch., 1993-95. Del. UN Decade for Women Internat. Forum, Nairobi, Kenya, 1985; chmn. del. UN Decade for Women Conf., Beijing, 1995; chmn. bd. Nat. Scholarship Fund for Negro Students, 1984-85; 1st v.p.

Girl Scouts U.S., 1972-75, pres., 1975-78; bd. dirs. Wilson Coll., 1978-83, Nat. Urban League, 1976-85; mem bd. visitors Ind. U. Sch. Edn., Bloomington, 1988-94; bd. dirs. United Negro Coll. Fund, 1993-95, chair golden anniversary com., 1992-95; chair edn. adv. com. Delta Sigma Theta, 1989—; mem. adv. bd. James McGregor Leadership Acad., Md., 2000—; mem. divsn. III pres.'s coun. NCAA, 1998-2001; founder Nat. African Am. Women's Leadership Inst., 1999; mentor Leadership Inst., 1997-98; mem. Internat. Women's Forum; chmn. Coun. Presidents Black Coll. Fund, UMC, 1997-99. Recipient Drum Major for Justice award, 1993, N.C. Gov's. award for Outstanding N.C. Women, 1991, Achievement award Delta Sigma Theta, 1994. Mem. Rotary (organizing founder East Greensboro 2000-01). Office Phone: 361-297-5307. E-mail: randle@rivnet.com.

SCOTT, GREGORY ALAN, pharmacist, writer; b. Newport, Vt., June 10, 1954; s. S. Gerald Scott Sr. and Elizabeth A. Scott; m. Linda M. Scott, Apr. 21, 1996; children: Matthew, Ryan. BA in Chemistry, U. N.H., 1976, MS in Analytical Chemistry, 1979; PharmD, U. Pacific, 1981. Registered pharmacist. Clin./staff pharmacist Dartmouth-Hitchcock Med. Ctr., Hanover, NH, 1982—83; instr. in clin. pharmacology, dept. of medicine Dartmouth Med. Sch., Hanover, 1982—93; clin. pharmacist for drug info. Dartmouth-Hitchcock Med. Ctr., Hanover, 1982—89, asst. dir. clin. and informational pharmacy svcs., 1989—93; v.p. sci. affairs Clin. Comm. Inc., Greenwich, Conn., 1993—98; dir. continuing edn. Sci. Exch. Inc., Greenwich, 1993—2000; pres. and owner WriteHealth, LLC, Stamford, Conn., 2000—. Cons. to the therapeutic agts. and pharmacy rev. com. VA Med. and Regional Office Ctr., White River Junction, Vt., 1986—90; surveyor Accreditation Coun. for Continuing Med. Edn., Chgo., 2000—. Contbg. author: book Clinical Pharmacology Basic Principles in Therapeutics, 3rd edit., 1992; contbr. articles to profl. jours. Mem. bd. of ch. devel. First Congl. Ch. Stamford, 2002—04; bd. of trustees First Congl. Ch. of Stamford, 1996—2001. Mem.: Am. Coll. Clin. Pharmacy (reviewer Pharmaco Therapy 1989—98), Am. Soc. Health-Sys. Pharmacists (reviewer Am. Jour. Hosp. Pharmacy 1989—98), Am. Soc. Clin. Pharmacology and Therapeutics, Am. Med. Writers Assn., Alliance for Continuing Med. Edn. Avocations: carpentry, travel. Office: WriteHealth LLC 110 van Rensselaer Ave Stamford CT 06902 Office Phone: 203-325-9414. Personal E-mail: gscott@writehealth.com.

SCOTT, GREGORY KELLAM, judge trial referee, former state supreme court justice, lawyer; b. San Francisco, July 30, 1943; s. Robert and Althea Delores Scott; m. Carolyn Weatherly, Apr. 10, 1971; children: Joshua Weatherly, Elijah Kellam. BS in Environ. Sci., Rutgers U., 1970, EdM in Urban Studies, 1971; JD cum laude, Ind. U., Indpls., 1977. Asst. dean resident instrn. Cook Coll. Rutgers U., 1972-75; trial atty. U.S. SEC, Denver, 1977-79; gen. counsel Blinder, Robinson & Co., Inc., Denver, 1979-80; asst. prof. coll. law U. Denver, 1980-85, assoc. prof., 1985-93, prof. emeritus, 1993—, chair bus. planning program, 1986-89, 92-93; justice Colo. Supreme Ct., Denver, 1993-2000; gen. counselor Kaiser-Hill Co., Golden, Colo., 2000—; judge trial referee Colo. Supreme Ct., Colo., 2000. Of counsel Moore, Smith & Bryant, Indpls., 1987-90; v.p., gen. counsel Comml. Energies, Inc., 1990-91; presenter in field. Author: (with others) Structuring Mergers and Acquisitions in Colorado, 1985, Airport Law and Regulation, 1991, Racism and Underclass in America, 1991; contbr. articles to profl. jours. Mem. ABA, Nat. Bar Assn., Nat. Assn. Securities Dealers, Inc., Nat. Arbitration Panel (arbitrator), Colo. Bar Found., Sam Cary Bar Assn., Am. Inn Ct. (founding mem. Judge Alfred A. Arraj inn). Avocations: golf, reading, travel. Office: Kaiser-Hill Co LLC Rocky Flats Environ Tech Site 10808 Hwy 93 Unit B Golden CO 80403-8200

SCOTT, GREGORY W. health care company executive; B in Math. Econ., Colgate U.; MS, U. Mich. cert. CLU. Sr. v.p. Prudential Capital Corp.; gen. ptnr. RRY Ptnrs.; v.p. corp. fin. Salomon Brothers, Inc.; COO, CFO Medsite, 1999-01; exec. v.p., CFO PacifiCare Health Sys. Inc., Cypress, Calif., 2001—. Office: PacifiCare Health Sys 5995 Plaza Dr Cypress CA 90630

SCOTT, HARRY VENGHETTE, JR., choreographer, educator; b. Southampton, N.Y., Aug. 4, 1942; s. Harry Venghette and Mildred Bernice Scott. Grad., Mercy H.S., Riverhead, N.Y., 1960. Lectr., choreographer N.Y.C. Dept. Edn., N.Y.C., 1982—; dance tchr. The Dalton Sch., N.Y.C., 2001—. Vocal choreographer Motown Records, Beverly Hills, Calif., 1971—72; lectr. in field. Actor(dancer): (Broadway show) Hallelujah Baby, 1967. Vol. fundraiser Mayor John Lindsay, N.Y.C., 1965. Grantee, Bronx Coun. on the Arts, 1967. Mem.: NRA (life), Actors' Equity Assn. (life). Republican. Roman Catholic. Avocations: riding, guns, swimming, photography, travel. Office Phone: 718-515-1661. E-mail: harryvscott@verizon.net.

SCOTT, HUGH PATRICK, physician, naval officer; b. Phila., Feb. 12, 1938; s. Hugh Patrick and Martha (Papiana) S.; m. Diane Marie Lopatzie, July 1, 1961; children: Karen, Brendan, Catherine. BA, LaSalle Coll., 1960; DO, Phila. Coll. Osteo. Medicine, 1964, LLD (hon.), 1991. Diplomate Am. Osteo. Bd. Ophthalmology and Otolaryngology. Intern Detroit Osteo. Hosp., Highland Park, Mich., 1964-65, resident otorhinolatyngology, 1965-68; lt. med. corps USNR, 1967, advanced through grades to rear adm., 1991; naval med. officer U.S. Naval Dispensary N.O.B., Norfolk, Va., 1968-70, Submarine Squadron 10, Groton, Conn.; Submarine Group 2; naval med. officer Naval Submarine Med. Ctr., New London, Conn., 1975-83; dir. undersea medicine and radiation health Naval Med. Command, Washington, 1983-86; comdg. officer Naval Hosp., Groton, 1986-88, Camp Lejeune, N.C., 1988-90; fleet surgeon Comdr. in Chief, U.S. Pacific Fleet, Pearl Harbor, Hawaii, 1990-91; asst. chief for operational medicine and fleet support Bur. Medicine and Surgery, Washington, 1991-92; dir. med. resources, plans and policy Office Chief of Naval Ops., Washington, 1992-94; sr. med. advisor Northrop Grumman Info. Tech. Health Solutions, 2000—. Asst. clin. prof. medicine Mich. State U., Lansing, 1970—75; pvt. practice, Madison Heights, Mich., 1970—75; cons. Am. Coll. Undersea and Hyperbaric Medicine, Washington, 1985—86, 1994—96; sr. program mgr. Data Sys. & Svcs. divsn. Northrop Grumman Co., 1998—99; sr. med. advisor Northrop Grumman Info. Tech.; sr. v.p. Geo-Ctrs. Inc., 2000—01; mem. sr. exec. med. adv. com. for mil. medicine Johns Hopkins U. Applied Physics Lab.; mem. faculty U. So. Calf. Health Scis. Campus for Advanced Biotelecomms. and Bio Informatics. Decorated Legion of Merit, Gold Star (3). Fellow Osteo. Coll. Ophthalmology and Otolaryngology, Am. Acad. Otolaryngology and Head and Neck Surgery; mem. Am. Osteo. Coll. Otolaryngology--Head and Neck Surgery (past pres.), Assn. Mil. Osteopathic Physicians and Surgeons (2nd v.p.). Republican. Roman Catholic. Home: 3707 Merlin Way Annandale VA 22003-1326 Office: Northrop Grumman Info Tech 5201 Leesburg Pike Suite 701 Falls Church VA 22041 Office Phone: 703-575-0156. Business E-Mail: hugh.scott@ngc.com.

SCOTT, ISADORE MEYER, former energy company executive; b. Wilcoe, W.Va., Nov. 21, 1912; s. David and Libby (Roston) S.; m. Joan Rosenwald, Feb. 14, 1943; children: Betsy Scott Kleeblatt, Peggy, Jonathan D. AB, W.Va. U., 1934, MA, 1938, LLD, 1983; JD, Washington and Lee U., 1937. Bar: Va. 1937. Practiced law, Richmond, Va., 1937-38; v.p. Lee I. Robinson Hosiery Mills., Phila., 1938-42; with Winner Mfg. Co., Inc., Trenton, NJ, 1947-61, v.p., 1947-51, pres., 1951-61; chmn. bd. Tri-Instl. Facilities, Inc., Phila., 1962-78, TOSCO Corp., L.A., 1976—83, vice-chmn. bd., 1983—87, chmn. bd. Bd. dirs., chmn. Univ. City Assocs., Inc.; founder, mem. U.S. Adv. Bd. Brit.-Am. Project. Bd. dirs. S.E. Pa. chpt. ARC, Univ. City Sci. Ctr., Phila.; mem. adv. com. Urban Affair Partnership; bd. dirs. emeritus, former mem. exec. com., vice-chmn. Phila. Mus. Art; former chmn. World Affairs Coun. Phila.; mem. Phila. Com. Fgn. Rels.; trustee emeritus Washington and Lee U.; emeritus trustee George C. Marshall Found.; former chmn. Christ Ch. Preservation Fund, Phila., Jefferson House Restoration, Phila. With inf. U.S. Army, 1942-46, NATOUSA, ETO. Decorated Legion of Merit, Silver Star, Purple Heart, Bronze Star; Crown of Italy; medal of merit Czechoslovakia; Mentioned-in-dispatches, Eng.; fellow Mus. Am. Jewish History Mem. Va. State Bar, Phila. Club, Gulph Mills Golf, Anglers of Phila., Masons, Phi Beta Kappa, Omicron Delta Kappa, Order of Coif. (hon.). Democrat. Jewish.

SCOTT, IVAN CARL, historian, educator; b. Iowa City, Iowa, Sept. 9, 1928; s. Wilbur Lloyd and Gladys Georgina Scott; m. Melvia Mary Atta, 1958 (div. June 1984); children: John, Thomas, David; m. Barbara Jean Kettlewell. BA, William and Mary Coll., 1959; MA, U. Pa., 1961, PhD, 1964. Asst. prof. Memphis State U., 1964-65, W.Va. State U., Morgantown, 1965-67; prof. U. Toledo, 1967-85, prof. emeritus, 1985—. Author: The Roman Question, 1969, The Rise of the Italian State, 1980, Upton Sinclair, 1997, Bromfield, The Forgotten Author, 1998, Jew vs. Arab, 2001. With U.S. Army, 1946—49. Fulbright scholar, U. Paris, 1962—63. Mem. Delta Tau Kappa. Avocations: fiction writing, citrus growing, Tex. plantations. Home: 9143 10th St Fort Ripley MN 56449

SCOTT, JACQUELINE DELMAR PARKER, educational association administrator, business administrator, consultant, fundraiser, educator; b. L.A., May 18, 1947; d. Thomas Aubrey and Daisy Beatrice (Singleton) Parker (div.); children: Tres Mali, Olympia Ranee, Stephen Thomas. AA in Theatre Arts, L.A. City Coll., 1970; BA in Econs., Calif. State U., Dominguez Hills, Carson, 1973; MBA, Golden Gate U., 1979; EdD, Pepperdine U., 1999. Cert. parenting instr., 2000; holder various Microsoft certs. Sales clk. Newberry's Dept. Store, L.A., 1963-65; long distance operator Pacific Telephone Co., L.A., 1965-66; PBX operator Sears, Roebuck & Co., L.A., 1966-68; retail clk. Otey's Grocery Store, Nashville, 1968-69; collector N.Am. Credit, L.A., 1970-71; office mgr. Dr. S. Edward Tucker, L.A., 1972-74; staff coord. sch. edn. dept. Calif. State U., 1973-74; from bank auditor to corp. loan asst. Security Pacific Bank, L.A., 1974-77; from dist. credit analyst to asst. v.p. Crocker Nat. Bank, L.A., 1977-80; from capital planning adminstr. to project bus. mgr. TRW, Inc., Redondo Beach, Calif., 1980-87, lab. sr. bus. adminstr., 1984-86, project bus. mgr., 1986-87, div. sr. bus. adminstr., 1987-92; ptnr., co-author, co-facilitator, cons. Diversified Event Planners, Inc., L.A., 1990-93; asst. area devel. dir. United Negro Coll. Fund, L.A., 1993-96; cons. parenting edn., 1994—. Cmty. coll. instr.; cons. in field. Co-founder career growth awareness com. TRW Employees Bootstrap, Redondo Beach, Calif., 1980, pres., 1983-84; role model Inglewood High Sch., TRW Youth Motivation Task Force, Redondo Beach, 1981-83, Crozier Jr. High Sch., 1981-83, Monroe Jr. High Sch., Redondo Beach, 1981-83, Frank D. Parent Career Day, TRW Affirmative Action Com., Redondo Beach, 1987, St. Bernard's Career Day, 1991; chairperson community involvement com., 1981, chairperson disaster com., 1989-90; chairperson gen. and local welfare com. TRW Employees Charitable Orgn., 1989-90, disaster com. chair, 1988-89, bd. dirs. 1987-89; pres. Mgmt. Effectiveness Program Alumnae, L.A., 1982-83, TRW Employees Bootstrap Program Alumnae, 1983-84; group leader Jack & Jill of Am., Inc., South L.A., 1980-81, parliamentarian, 1986-87, v.p., 1981-82, chpt. pres., 1984-86, regional dir., 1987-89, nat. program dir., 1992-96, liaison to Young Black Scholars Program, 1986—; bd. dirs. Adolescent Pregnancy Child Watch, 1993—; nat. program dir., bd. dirs. Jack & Jill Am. Found., 1992-96; L.A. mem. Nat. Black Child Devel. Inst., 1994—; vol. ARC, 1994; parenting instr. Am. Red Cross, 1994-96; founder Jack & Jill of Am. Leadership Devel. Program, 1993. Recipient commendation NAACP, 1985, United Negro Coll. Fund, 1986, United Way, 1988, Austistic Children's Telephon, 1980, Inglewood Sch. Dist., 1981, Pres. award Harbor Area Chpt. Links, Inc., 1985, Women of Achievement award City of L.A., Black Pers. Assn., 1994. Mem. Black Women's Forum (sponsor), Phi Delta Kappa, Delta Sigma Theta. Avocations: reading, dance. E-mail: jscott4@earthlink.net.

SCOTT, JAMES ARTHUR, radiologist, educator; b. Cleve., Aug. 23, 1950; s. Robert James and Margaret Emma (Hinz) S.; m. Phyllis Virginia Gauthier, Oct. 3, 1981. SB, MIT, 1972; MD, Boston U., 1976. Diplomate Am. Bd. Radiology, Am. Bd. Nuc. Medicine. Resident Harvard U. Med. Sch.-Mass. Gen. Hosp., Boston, 1976-80, fellow, 1980-81, instr., 1982-83, asst. prof., 1984-93, assoc. prof., 1994—. Mem. editl. adv. bd. Jour. Nuc. Medicine, Am. Jour. Roentgen. Recipient New Investigator Rsch. award NIH, 1984-87. Mem. Soc. Sci. Exploration, Sigma Xi, Am. Coll. Radiology, AAAS, Phi Lambda Upsilon, Theta Xi. Lutheran. Avocations: writing, golf, history of religions. Office: Div Nuclear Medicine Mass Gen Hosp Boston MA 02114 E-mail: scott@helix.mgh.harvard.edu.

SCOTT, JAMES HUNTER, JR., investment executive; b. Balt., Jan. 28, 1945; s. James Hunter and Marialice (Short) S.; m. Katheen Ann Bilderback, Sep. 1, 1973; children: Andrew James, Elizabeth Ann. BA, Rice U., 1967; MS, Carnegie Mellon U., 1970, PhD, 1975. Instr. Carnegie Mellon U., Pitts., 1969-71; rsch. fellow Fed. Res. Bank of Cleve., 1971-72; asst. prof. U. Wis., Milw., 1972-75; from asst. prof. to prof./divisional rep. fin. Columbia U., N.Y.C., 1975-87; mng. dir. Prudential Ins. Co., Newark, 1987-97; chmn. PTC Svcs., Newark, 1991—; CEO Prudential Diversified Investment Strategies, Short Hills, N.J., 1994-97; sr. mng. dir. Prudential Investments, 1997—. Vis. asst. prof. Stanford (Calif.) U., 1974-75, assoc. prof., 1979; adj. prof. grad. sch. bus. Columbia U., 1988—; dir. Inst. for Quantitative Rsch. in Fin., N.Y.C., 1995—; with Goldman, Sachs, Kinsey & Co., 1981-82; trustee adminstrv. com. Eastern Air Lines Pilots Investment Plan, Miami, 1985-91; dir. Prudential Trust Co., 1996—. Bd. editors Fin. Analysts Jour., 1998—; contbr. over 25 articles to profl. jours. Pres. bd. trustees Alpine (N.J.) Cmty. Ch., 1986-89, v.p., 1998—; v.p. bd. trustees Tenafly (N.J.) Bd. Edn., 1998—; mem. Grad. Sch. Indsl. Adminstrn. Coun. on Fin., Carnegie Mellon U. Mem. Am. Econ. Assn., Am. Fin. Assn. Methodist. Office: Quantitative Mgmt Prudential Investments 2 Gateway Ctr Fl 4 Newark NJ 07102-5003

SCOTT, JANE MADELINE, language educator; b. NYC; d. Paul Henry and Elizabeth Barbara (Mitchell) Kane; m. Albert Claude Scott (dec.); children: Elizabeth, Madeline, Emmett, Meri; m. Paul E. Starnes, Feb. 1, 1944 (dec. Jan. 1987). BA in English cum laude, Calif. State Polytechnic U., 1981, MA in English, 1985. Instr. English Sawyer Coll., Pomona, Calif., 1982—85, dean acads., 1985—90; instr. English Riverside C.C., Calif., 1995—2000. Author: The Quick and the Dead, 1987, Working with Words, 1984, Soundings, 1994, Genesis II, 2000. Mem.: Sigma Tau Delta (mem. Rho Chi chpt. 1980). Avocation: dance.

SCOTT, JEAN A. university president; B in History, U. Richmond, 1968; M in History, Harvard U., 1969, PhD in History, 1974. Asst. prof. history Duke U., dir. admission; dean undergrad. admission Case We. Res. U., Ohio; assoc. provost acad. adminstrn., dean admissions Coll. William and Mary, Williamsburg, Va., 1989-94; v.p. enrollment and student svcs. SUNY, Potsdam, 1994—. Office: Potsdam Coll Pierrepont Ave Potsdam NY 13676-2294

SCOTT, JEFFREY LYLE, protective services official; b. Toledo; s. Mylous and Florastine S. Student, U. Toledo, 1977-80. Dist. mgr. DuBois Chems., Detroit, 1988-90; pres. F&S Chems., Detroit, 1991-94; police officer City of Toledo (Ohio), 1994—. Candidate Toledo City Coun., 1993, Ohio State Senate, Toledo, 1994. With Civil Air Patrol, 1995—. Recipient Lifesaving medal, Civil Air Patrol, 1994, Cert. of Appreciation, Safety Coun. NW Ohio, 2002. Mem. Smithsonian Inst.

SCOTT, JOHN ATWOOD, JR., hypnoanalyst, psychologist, marriage and family therapist; b. Darby, Pa., July 14, 1949; s. John Atwood and Mary Joyce (Forrester) S.; m. Edna Vera Newhouse, June 12, 1971; children: Abigail Rae, John Benjamin. BS, Empire State Coll., 1976; MAR, Harding Grad. Sch. Religion, 1979; postgrad., Memphis State U., 1979—. Ordained to ministry Ch. of Christ, 1969. Min., youth worker Shiloh, Inc., N.Y.C., 1969-71; youth worker, adminstr. Ctrl. Coleman Youth Devel. Project, Rochester, NY, 1971-75; counselor, hypnoanalyst John. A. Scott, PhD and Assocs., P.C., Memphis, 1975—2003; clin. psychology intern Jersey Shore Med. Ctr., Neptune, NJ, 1986-87; dir. social svcs. office Linden-Camilla Towers, Memphis, 2001—03; clin. dir. Brief Psychotherapy Inst. of the Rockies, Broomfield, Colo., 2003—. Assoc. editor Med. Hypnoanalysis, 1980-86; contbr. articles and book revs. to profl. publs. Bd. dirs. Drug and Alcohol Coun., Rochester, 1973-75; mem. 16th Ward Coalition for Neighborhood Devel., Rochester, 1973-75, chmn., 1974; mem. adv. bd. Genessee Valley Mental Health Ctr., 1974-75, chmn., 1975; neighborhood rep. to bd. dirs. Action for Better Cmty., 1974-75; founder, dir. Rochester City-Wide Basketball League, 1974-75; minister outreach to city program White Station Ch. of Christ, Memphis, 1976-91. Mem. Am. Acad. Med. Hypnoanalysts (bd. dirs. 1981—, pres. 1990-92, chmn. 1994-96, pres. 1998-2000, chmn. 2000-02), Soc. Med. Hypnoanalysts, Am. Inst. Hypnosis, Hypnosis Rsch. Found., Am. Assn. Sex Educators, Counselors and Therapists, Nat. Alliance for Family Life. Office: 1022 Depot Hill Rd Broomfield CO 80020

SCOTT, JOHN BROOKS, retired research institute executive; b. Morenci, Ariz., Aug. 8, 1931; s. Brooks and Lucile (Slagle) S.; m. Jo Ann Rohrbach, June 5, 1987; children from previous marriage: Janice, Steven, Sarah. BS, U. Ariz., 1957, MA, 1959. Asst. prof. systems engring. U. Ariz., Tucson, 1959—60; mgr. Bell Aerosystems Co., Tucson, 1961—62; sr. v.p. IIT Rsch. Inst., Annapolis, Md., 1963—90, pres. Chgo., 1990-97. Author papers on computer software, electromagnetic compatibility. Past pres. bd. dirs. Md. Hall for Creative Arts, Inc.; past chmn. Md. Hall Found.; past mem. bd. govs. IIT Rsch. Inst.; past trustee Ill. Inst. Tech. Mem. Greater Annapolis C. of C. (pres. 1987); mem. Phi Kappa Phi, Sigma Pi Sigma, Pi Mu Epsilon. Home: Apt 903 3145 S Atlantic Ave Daytona Beach FL 32118-6045 E-mail: jscott2030@cfl.rr.com.

SCOTT, JOHN D. pharmacologist; b. Edinburgh, Scotland, Apr. 13, 1958; married; 2 children. BSc in Biochemistry with honors, Herriot-Watt U., Edinburgh, 1980; PhD in Biochemistry, U. Aberdeen, 1983. NIH postdoctoral fellow dept. pharmacology U. Wash., Seattle, 1983—86, rsch. asst. prof. dept. biochemistry, 1986—88; asst. prof. dept. physiology and biophysics, dept. biol. chemistry U. Calif., Irvine, 1988—89; asst. scientist Ctr. Rsch. Occupl. & Environ. Toxicology Oreg. Health Scis. U., 1989—90, asst. scientist Vollum Inst. Advanced Biomed. Rsch., dept. biochemistry and molecular biology, 1990—92, scientist, 1993—97, sr. scientist, 1997—; investigator Howard Hughes Med. Ctr. (known as Vollum Inst.), 1997—. Spkr. in field. Mem. editl. bd. Jour. Biol. Chemistry; contbr. articles to profl. jours. Recipient John J. Abel award, Am. Soc. Pharmacology and Exptl. Therapeutics, 1996; scholar Med. Endowments Hon., U. Aberdeen, 1980—83. Mem.: Protein Soc., Biochem. Soc., Am. Soc. Biochemistry and Molecular Biology. Office: Vollum Inst Oreg Health Scis U 3181 SW Sam Jackson Park Rd Portland OR 97239-3011

SCOTT, JOHN EDWARD SMITH, lawyer; b. St. Louis, Aug. 6, 1936; s. Gordon Hatler and Luella Margarite (Smith) S.; m. Beverly Joan Phillips, Dec. 17, 1960; 1 dau., Pamela Anne. AB, Albion Coll., 1958; JD, Wayne State U., 1961. Bar: Mich. 1961, U.S. Dist. Ct. (ea. dist.) Mich. 1962, U.S. Dist. Ct. (we. dist.) Mich. 1970, U.S. Tax. Ct. 1979, U.S. Ct. Appeals (6th cir.) 1964, U.S. Supreme Ct. 1966. Law clk. Supreme Ct. Mich., Lansing, 1961-62; assoc. Dickinson, Wright, Moon, Van Dusen & Freeman, Detroit, 1962-69, ptnr., 1970—. Adj. prof. U. Detroit Law Sch., 1967-71. Supreme Ct. appointee State Bar Rep. Assembly, Detroit, 1972-77; mayor City of Pleasant Ridge, Mich., 1973-81; commr. Mich. Appellate Defender Commn., Detroit, 1979—, chmn., 1992—; hearing referee Mich. Civil Rights Commn., Detroit, 1974-80; chmn. Detroit Legal Aid & Defender Commn., 1972-77; chmn. case flow mgmt. com. Mich. Supreme Ct., 1989-90. Fellow Am. Coll. Trial Lawyers, Internat. Soc. Barristers, Internat. Acad. Trial Lawyers; mem. ABA (chmn. trial evidence com. sect. litigation 1988-91), Am. Bar Found., Mich. Bar Found., Detroit Golf Club, Order of Coif (hon.). Office: Dickinson Wright PLLC 500 Woodward Ave Ste 4000 Detroit MI 48226-3416

SCOTT, JOHN JOSEPH, lawyer; b. Chgo., Dec. 30, 1950; s. John Joseph and Alice (Pierzhala) S.; m. Maria Crawford, Aug. 17, 1974. BA, Yale U., 1972; JD, U. Chgo., 1975. Bar: Ill. 1975, U.S. Dist. Ct. (no. dist.) Ill. 1976. Assoc. Kirkland & Ellis, Chgo., 1975-82, ptnr., 1982-91; asst. gen. counsel CF Industries, Inc., Long Grove, Ill., 1991—. Mem. ABA, Chgo. Bar Assn., Am. Soc. Corp. Secs., Order of Coif. Roman Catholic. Avocations: reading, swimming, bike riding, playing tennis. Office: CF Industries Inc One Salem Lake Dr Lake Zurich IL 60047-8401

SCOTT, JOHN LENNOX, real estate company executive; Cert. residential broker. From realtor to pres. John L. Scott Real Estate, Bellevue, Wash., 1976—80, pres., 1980—, CEO, 2002—, chmn., 2002—. Founder John L. Scott Found.; bd. dir. Washington Wildlife Recreation Coalition, Bellevue (Wash.) Performing Arts Com., Ctrl. Pubet Sound Real Estate Rsch. Com., Econ. Devel. Coun. Seattle and King County. Mem.: Nat. Assn. Home Builders, Nat. Assn. Realtors (mem. exec. com., mem. large broker coun., mem. realtor safety coun., mem. budget rev. team, mem. strategic thinkers group, mem. pres. adv. group, mem. strategic investment res. adv. bd.), Realty Alliance, Wash. Assn. Realtors (mem. real estate safety coun., dir., exec. com., pres. Seattle-King county chpt., Pacesetter award, Pres.'s award 2003, Realtor of Yr. award 2002), Young Pres.'s Orgn., Rotary Internat. Office: John L Scott Real Estate 3380 146th Place SE Ste 450 Bellevue WA 98007*

SCOTT, JOHN MCGREGOR, oil and gas industry executive, real estate investor; b. Brighton, Sussex, Eng. came to U.S., Sept. 1994; s. Edward McGregor Scott and Margret Joan Goldrich; m. Candida Jane Scott, Apr. 11, 1977 (div. Sept. 1988); m. Trude Koby, June 24, 1996; 1 child, Asia Koby. BSc in civil engring., Leicester U., Eng., 1977; MBA, London Bus. Sch., 1990. Chartered engr. Assoc. dir. Global Engring., London, 1982-88; mgr. R&D Texaco, London, 1988-90, mgr. prospects, 1990-92, mgr. properties Aberdeen, Eng., 1992-94, gen. mgr. L.Am. Coral Gables, Fla., 1994-96, gen. mgr. Venezuela Houston, 1996-98, gen. mgr. Brazil, 1999—. Lectr. Inst. Project Mgrs., London, 1990-92. Dir. Jr. Achievment, Houston, 1999—, Houston Symphony, 1999—. Buddhist. Avocations: travel, motorsports, history. Office: 1111 Bagby St # 3533 Houston TX 77002-2551

SCOTT, JOHN PAUL, medical educator; b. Kamunting, Malaysia, June 26, 1956; came to U.S., 1991; s. Joseph and Agnes (Beldon) S.; m. Lesley Carol Poole, Dec. 5, 1981; children: Christopher Michael, Elizabeth Mary, David Matthew. MB ChB, Otago U., Dunedin, New Zealand, 1979, MD, 1990; MS, Cambridge U., England, 1992; MS in Econs., U. London, 1999; LLB (hon.), U. Wolverhampton, 2000; LLM, U. Glamorgan, 2003, U. Glasgow, 2002. Resident Otago U., Dunedin, New Zealand, 1979-83; assoc. prof. transplantation Mayo Clinic, Rochester, Minn., 1991-96, prof., 1996—. Contbr. articles to profl. jours. Fellow dept. pulmonary medicine Otago U., 1984-85, Cambridge U., 1985-88, sr. fellow, 1988-91. Fellow Royal Coll. Physicians (internat. advisor 2000—, assoc. dir. 2004—), Royal Australian Coll. Physicians, Am. Coll. Physicians, Royal Statis. Soc.; mem. Am. Thoracic Soc. (Minn. rep. 1993-96), Royal Soc. New Zealand, Internat. Soc. Philosophical Enquiry, Mayo Thoracic Soc. (pres. 1996-99). Avocations: philosophy, economics, chess, climbing, travel. Office: Mayo Clinic 200 1st St SW Rochester MN 55905-0002

SCOTT, JOHN ROLAND, business law educator; b. Wichita Falls, Tex, May 13, 1937; s. John and Margaret S.; m. Joan Carol Redding, Sept. 5, 1959; 1 child, John Howard. LLB, Baylor Sch. Law, Waco, Tex., 1962. Bar: Tex. 1962, Alaska 1970, Tex., 1965, U.S. Dist. Ct. (we. dist.), U.S. Dist. Ct. Alaska 1975. Assoc. litigation sect. Lynch & Chappell, Midland, Tex., 1962-65; regional atty. Atlantic Richfield Co., Midland, 1965-79; sr. atty. Anchorage, 1969-77, Dallas, 1977-80; v.p., assoc. gen. counsel Mitchell Energy & Devel. Corp., Houston, 1980-82; asst. gen. counsel Hunt Oil Co., Dallas, 1982-84, v.p., chief counsel, 1984-91, sr. v.p. gen. counsel, 1994-2001; adj. prof. bus. law Dallas Bapt. U., Dallas, 2001—. Bar examiner in Alaska, 1974-77 Mem. State Bar Tex. (lectr.), Dallas Bar Assn., ABA, Phi Alpha Delta. Republican. Office: 3801 Hanover Ave Dallas TX 75225-7117

SCOTT, JOHN WALTER, chemical engineer, research management executive; b. Berkeley, Calif., May 27, 1919; s. John Walter and Cora Viola (Wampfler) S.; m. Jane Ellen Newman, June 27, 1942; children— Nancy, Barbara, Charles, James, Richard BS in Chemistry, U. Calif., Berkeley, 1941, MSChemE, 1951. Registered profl. chem. engr., Calif. Process and catalyst research and devel. Chevron Research, Richmond, Calif., 1946-67, v.p., 1967-84, cons., 1985—. Contbr. articles to profl. jours.; patentee in field Trustee U. Calif.-Berkeley Found., 1985-91; adv. coun. Lawrence Hall of Sci., 1990-97; mem. coun. Town of Ross, Calif., 1992-96. Capt. U.S. Army, 1941-46. Fellow Am. Inst. Chem. Engrs. (awards com. 1979-84, award 1978), AAAS; mem. Nat. Acad. Engring., Am. Chem. Soc., Am. Petroleum Inst. (chmn. research data info. services 1971-73, 77-80, cert. of appreciation 1983) Avocations: history; travel. Home: 5555 Paradise Dr # 250 Corte Madera CA 94925

SCOTT, JOYCE ALAINE, university official; b. Long Beach, Calif., May 21, 1943; d. Emmett Emery Scott and Grace (Evans) Wedum. BA, U. Conn., 1964; MA, U. Va., 1966; PhD, Duke U., 1973. From instr. to assoc. prof. U. Wyo., Laramie, 1971-74, asst. dean, 1974-78, asst. v.p. acad. affairs, 1976-81, assoc. v.p. acad. affairs, 1981-84; provost, v.p. SUNY-Potsdam, 1984-86; exec. v.p. Wichita (Kans.) State U., 1986-90, v.p. on spl. assignment, 1990-91; sr. cons. Am. Assn. State Colls. and Univs., 1991-92, v.p. acad. and internat. programs, 1992-97; dep. commr. Mont. U. Sys., Helena, 1998—2003; provost, v.p. acad. and student affairs Texas A&M U., 2003—. Mem. Commn. on Ednl. Credit and Credentials of Am. Coun. on Edn., Washington, 1982-87; cons. faculty Am. Open U., Lincoln, Nebr., 1981-82. Contbr. articles to profl. jours. Trustee Jones Internat. U. Mem. MLA, AAHE, Am. Assn. Tchrs. French, Phi Beta Kappa, Phi Sigma Iota. Republican. Presbyterian. Office: Office of Provost 280 McDowell Adminstrn Bldg 2600 W Neal PO Box 3011 Commerce TX 75429-3011 Office Phone: 903-886-5018. E-mail: Joyce_Scott@tamu-commerce.edu.

SCOTT, JUSTINE FORD, counselor, educator; b. Newton, N.C., Nov. 3, 1942; d. Laddie Henry, Sr. and Vera Burton Ford; m. Jerry Scott, June 24, 1972; children: David, Alicia. BS, N.C. A&T State U., 1970; MEd, DePaul U., 1999. Cert. tchr., Ill. Customer svc., sales asst. GE, Oak Brook, Ill., 1979-92; tchr.'s aid Sch. Dist. 60, Zion, Ill., 1992-94; 6th grade tchr. Sch. Dist. 187, North Chicago, Ill., 1994-99; SEP counselor Coll. of Lake County, Grayslake, Ill., 1999—. Mentor, Sisters Taking Care, Chgo.; mem. chancel choir, 2d Bapt. Ch., Evanston, Ill. Mem. Am. Counseling Assn., Ill. Counseling Assn., Chgo. Counseling Assn. E-mail: jfordscott@msn.com.

SCOTT, KAREN BONDURANT, consumer catalog company executive; b. East Orange, N.J., June 4, 1946; d. Walter James and Wanda (French) Schmidt; m. Ian James Anderson, May 12, 1982; children: Steven, Michael. BS, U. Mass., 1968; MBA, Northwestern U., 1977. Bus. analyst Dun & Bradstreet, N.Y.C., 1968-69; asst. mgr. Shay Med. Employment, Chgo., 1970-72; mgr. recruitment Michael Reese Med. Ctr., Chgo., 1972-76; brand mgmt., new bus. devel., dir. mergers & acquisitions Kraft Foods, Inc., Glenview, Ill., 1977-95; pres. Chelsea & Scott dba One Step Ahead, Lake Bluff, Ill., 1987—. Sec.-treas. adv. bd. Lincolnshire (Ill.) Nursery Sch., 1987-89; co-leader Boy Scouts Am., Lincolnshire, 1991. Mem. Juvenile Product Mfrs. Assn. (new product judge 1992-99, speaker nat. catalog conf.), Nat. Assn. Women Bus. Owners (mem. Lake Forest cmty. task force). Office: Chelsea & Scott Ltd 75 Albrecht Dr Lake Bluff IL 60044-2226

SCOTT, KAREN ELIZABETH, information technology assistant; b. Buffalo, July 21, 1957; children: James Kenneth-Mark, Alexis Victoria Scott-Davis. BA, Empire State Coll., Buffalo, N.Y., 2002. Adminstrv. asst. WNY Libr. Resources Coun., Buffalo, 1990—97; info. asst. Rsch. Found. SUNY, Buffalo, 1997—2003. Bd. dirs. Langston Hughes Inst., Buffalo, 2000. Empire State Honors Scholarship for African Am., Latino, and Native Am. Students, Empire State Coll., 1999, 2000, 2001. Avocations: interior decorating, fashion design, current affairs.

SCOTT, KAREN LOU, systems analyst; b. Rantoul, Ill., Aug. 3, 1965; d. David Edson Bishop Jr. and Maxine Helen Bishop; m. Daniel Joseph Scott; 1 child, Margaret Helen. AS, Clinton C.C., Clinton, Iowa, 1988; BS, U. Mary Hardin-Baylor, 1992; MS, Ga. So. U., 1994; postgrad., Baylor U. Instr. Math. Ogeechee Tech. Inst., Statesboro, Ga., 1994—95, Ctr. Tex. Coll., Ft. Steward, Ga., 1995—97, Clinton C.C., Clinton, Iowa, 1997; asst. instr. U. Tex. Austin, 1998; software engr., sci. sys. analyst Comarco Inc., Ft. Hood, Tex., 1998—2000; sci. sys. analyst EWA Svcs. Inc., Ft. Hood, 2000—. Instr. Math. Ga. So. U., Statesboro, 1995, Armstrong Atlantic State U., Savannah, Ga., 1995—97; tchg. asst. Baylor U., Waco, Tex., 1998—2000; adj. prof. Math. Tarleton State U., Killeen, Tex., 2002—; guest lectr. Clinton H.S., Ellison H.S., Killeen. Contbr. articles to profl. jours. Mem.: Am. Math. Soc., Soc. Indsl. and Applied Math., Math. Assn. Am. (Presentation award), Am. Statis. Assn., Kappa Mu Epsilon. Avocations: horseback riding, sports, cooking, stained glass, animals. Office: TESCO/EWA PO Box 5400 Fort Hood TX 76544

SCOTT, KELLY, newspaper editor; Sunday Calendar editor The L.A. Times. Office: LA Times Times Mirror Sq Los Angeles CA 90053

SCOTT, KENNETH ELSNER, mechanical engineering educator; b. Webster, Mass., May 18, 1926; s. Henry Anderson and Amanda (Elsner) S.; m. Elizabeth Ann Oldham, June 21, 1952; children— Kenneth Elsner, Cynthia Lynne, Jeffrey Alan, Donald Leighton. BSMechE, Worcester Poly. Inst., 1948, MS, 1954. Faculty Worcester Poly. Inst., 1948-91, prof. mech. engring., 1966-91, prof. emeritus, 1991—, George I. Alden prof. engring., 1971-75, inst. dir. audio-visual devel., 1971-74, dir. instructional TV, 1974-90, dir. CAD Lab., 1981-93, acting head dept. mech. engring., 1988-89. Active Bd. Health, Holden, Mass., 1963-70. With AUS, 1944-46. Recipient Trustees' award for Outstanding Tchr. of Year, 1971, Tchg. Excellence and Campus Leadership award Sears-Roebuck Found., 1990-91, William R. Grogan award in recognition of support for Mission of Worcester Poly. Inst., 1998. Fellow ASME (exec. com. Worcester sect. 1952-57, sec.-treas. 1955-56, chmn. 1956-57, region I chmn. profl. divns. com. 1957-59, chmn. agenda, audit, budget and nominating com. Worcester 1957-58, chmn. symposium lubrication Worcester sect. 1957-58, chmn. Adm. Earle award com. 1958-59, chmn. devel. com. 1960-61); mem. Am. Soc. Engring. Edn. (sec.-treas. New Eng. chpt., Western Electric Fund award 1972), Sigma Xi, Pi Tau Sigma, Tau Beta Pi. Home: 9750 Cypress Lake Dr Fort Myers FL 33919-6064 Personal E-mail: easkes@aol.com.

SCOTT, KENNETH R. transportation executive; b. Iowa City; BCE, U. Iowa, 1960; MCE, U. Mo., Rolla, 1966. Commd. U.S. Army, 1961, advanced through grades, 1970; airport project engr. Norfolk (Va.) Airport Authority, 1970-72, asst. airport mgr., 1971-72, exec. dir., 1972—. Adj. prof. Embry-Riddle Aero. U. at Norfolk Naval Air Sta. and Langley AFB. Bd. dirs. Norfolk Cmty. Promotion Corp., Va. Aviation and Space Edn. Forum. Mem. Am. Assn. Airport Execs., Va. Airport Operators Coun. Office: Norfolk Airport Authority Norfolk Internat Airport 2200 Norview Ave Norfolk VA 23518-5897

SCOTT, KERRIGAN DAVIS, private investor, philanthropist; b. Magdalene, Fla., Sept. 26, 1941; s. Thurman Thomas and Jacqueline (Glenister) S.; children: Katherine, Stephanie, Jennifer. N.D. U. Va., 1964. Pvt. investor, Hilton Head Island, S.C., 1965—. Aide-de-camp to gov. of Tenn. with rank of col. Recipient Presdl. Legion Merit, Shield of Valor medal, White House Letter Commendation. Author: Aristocracy and Royalty of the World, 1983, Hereditary Baron in the Nobility of France. Mem. bd. regents Liberty U., Lynchburg, Va.; bd. dirs. Aid to Hospitalized Vets.; assoc. Library of Congress; pres. The Cittanova Found. Recognized as His Royal Highness, Prince of Cittanova by Govts. of Albania and San Marino (Italy). Episcopalian. Club: Shipyard Plantation Racquet. Home: Windmill Harbour Plantation 5 Yacht Club Dr Hilton Head Island SC 29926-1242 Office Phone: 843-681-4313.

SCOTT, LAURIE P. music educator; b. Buffalo, Oct. 6, 1955; d. Walter Francis Scott and Marion Anne Studer; m. Leslie Winters Young, Jan. 29, 1988; 1 child, Leslie Martin Young. BM in Music Edn., SUNY, Fredonia, 1977; MM in Performance, U. Nebr., 1979; PhD in Music Edn., U. Tex., 1987. Cert. tchr. N.Y., Tex. Orch. dir. St. John's Sch., Seward, Nebr., 1978—81; tchr. violin string project U. Tex., Austin, 1981—86, asst. prof., 2002—; lectr. S.W. Tex. State U., San Marcos, 1985—90; orch. dir. Austin Ind. Schs., 1986—94; asst. prof. Southwestern U., Georgetown, Tex., 1994—2002. Co-dir. Armadillo Suzuki Orgn., Austin, 1985—, Suzuki Tour Group, Austin, 1986—; dir. Austin Met. Suzuki Sch., 1985—. Contbr., articles to profl. jours. Mem. Austin Symphony Orch., 1981—2001, Austin Lyric Opera Orch., 1985—2001. Named Woman of Yr. in Arts, YWCA, 1990. Mem.: Music Educators Nat. Conf., Am. String Tchrs. Assn. (local treas.), Suzuki Assn. Ams. (chmn. pub. sch. com. 1996—98), Am. Fedn. Musicians. Avocations: hiking, furniture restoration. Office: U Tex Sch Music 1 University Station E 3100 Austin TX 78712

SCOTT, LEE (HAROLD LEE SCOTT JR.), retail executive; b. Joplin, Mo., Mar. 14, 1949; s. Harold Lee and Avis Viola (Parsons) S.; m. Linda Gale Aldridge, June 7, 1969; children: Eric Sean, Wyatt Parson. BBA, Pitts. State U., Kans., 1971. Br. mgr. Yellow Freight System, Springdale, Ark., 1972-78; mgr. Queen City Warehouse, Springfield, Mo., 1978-79; dir. transp. Wal-Mart Stores, Inc., Bentonville, Ark., 1979-83, v.p. distbn., 1983-2000, pres., CEO, 2000—. Bd. dirs. Pvt. Truck Council, Washington, 1985-86. Republican. Methodist. Avocations: reading, quail hunting. Office: Wal-Mart Stores Inc 702 SW 8th St Bentonville AR 72716-6299*

SCOTT, LEE HANSEN, retired holding company executive; b. Atlanta, Sept. 25, 1926; s. Elbert Lee and Auguste Lillian (Hansen) S.; m. Margaret Lee Smith, July 20, 1951; children: Bradley Hansen, Randall Lee. B.E.E., U. Fla., 1949. With Fla. Power Corp., St. Petersburg, 1949-94, dir. constrn., maintenance and operating, 1968-71, v.p. customer ops., 1971-77, sr. v.p. ops., 1977-83, pres., 1983-88, chmn. bd., 1988-90, also bd. dirs., Fla. Progress Corp.; ret., 1994. Bd. dirs. Sun Banks; cons. in field. Pres. St. Petersburg chpt. ARC, 1977, Pinellas Com. of 100, 1980, Community Services Council, 1970, St. Petersburg Progress, 1983, Bus. and Industry Employment Devel. Council, 1983; chmn. bd. United Way. Served with USAF, 1944-46. Named Mr. Sun of St. Petersburg, 1990. Mem. Fla. Engring. Soc., IEEE, Elec. Council Fla. (pres. 1979), St. Petersburg C. of C. (v.p. 1980), Fla. C. of C. (pres. 1987-88), Pinellas Suncoast C. of C. (past chmn., chmn. bd. trustees). Presbyterian. Home: 601 Apalachee Dr NE Saint Petersburg FL 33702-2766

SCOTT, LEIGHTON REEVES, interior designer, artist, writer; b. Columbus, Ind., Sept. 9, 1942; AB, U. Md., 1968, Knox Coll., 1964. Scientist NASA, Greenbelt, Md., 1968—73; sys. analyst NOAA, Suitland, Md., 1973—76; sr. physicist Johns Hopkins Applied Physics Lab., Laurel, Md., 1976—81; computer software cons. Westinghouse Def. Sys., Linthicum, Md., 1982—84; computer scientist Nat. Security Agy., Ft. George G. Meade, Md., 1984—94; cons., creativity trainer Mt. Airy, Md., 1995—2003. ADA program mgr. Nat. Security Agy., Ft. Meade, 1983—88. Author: (book) The Search for Manhood, 1992, Museum of the Mind, 2002, 2003. Achievements include invention of software blueprints; Vented Bennett Ion Mass Spectrometer orbiting Earth and Venus; design of National Security Agency's first electronic systems support system; U.S. government's first walk-in on-site store for disabled employees. Avocations: abstract art, interior and product design, building model railroad scenery, automobile design, group facilitation. Office: Lee Scott Design 594 Shannon Dr N Greencastle PA 17225 Home: 594 Shannon Dr N Greencastle PA 17225 Business E-Mail: leighton@leescottdesign.com.

SCOTT, LOUIS EDWARD, advertising agency executive; b. Waterbury, Conn., June 17, 1923; s. Louis Arthur and Ellen (Eckert) S.; m. Phyllis Corrine Denker, Jan. 27, 1942; children: Susan Louise, Eric Richard, Jane Lynn. BS, U. Calif., Berkeley, 1944. Sr. account exec. McCarty Co., L.A., 1946-50; from mem. staff to dir. Foote, Cone & Belding, 1950—61; dir. Foote, Cone & Belding/Honig, 1961—98. Bd. dirs. Smart and Final Corp., Casino Internat., True North Comm. Chmn. publicity com. Los Angeles Community Chest, 1960; patron mem. Los Angeles YMCA; mem. Freedoms Found.; chmn. So. Calif. advisory bd. Advt. Council; mem. exec. advisory bd. Art Center Coll. Design. Served with U.S. Maritime Service, also USNR, World War II. Named Western Advt. Man of Year, 1972 Mem. Am. Assn. Advt. Agys. (dir., past chmn. Western region), Coronado Cays Yacht Club, Rio Verde Country Club, Seattle Yacht Club, Cruising Club Am. Home: 19119 E Tonto Trail Rio Verde AZ 85263 also: PO 182247 Coronado CA 92178 E-mail: lowphyll1@cox.net.

SCOTT, MARGARET SIMON, retired mortgage broker; b. Boston, May 12, 1934; d. Frank A. and Margaret Alice (Gotham) Simon; m. Walter Neil Scott, Nov. 21, 1959 (div. June 1997); 1 child, Walter David Kimbley; m. Stephen E. Michelman, Feb. 8, 2003. BA in Physics, Wellesley Coll., 1956; MA in Polit. Sci., Boston U., 1965; MS in Human Resources Mgmt., U. Utah, 1974. Rsch. asst. Bell Tel. Labs., Whippany, N.J., 1956-58; rsch. asst. med. sch. U. Louisville, 1959-60, Harvard U., Boston, 1960-64; instr. polit. sci. Trinity U., San Antonio, 1966-67; cons. info. systems U.S. Dept. Labor, Washington, 1968; dir. manpower planning N.Y.C. Human Resources Adminstrn., 1968-71; asst. v.p. First Nat. City Bank, N.Y.C., 1972-77; v.p. Citibank, N.A., N.Y.C., 1978-86, AMEV Asset Mgmt., Inc., N.Y.C., 1986-88; pres. Mortgage Adv. Svcs., Inc., N.Y.C., 1988-99. Vol. Jr. League, Louisville, 1957; bd. mgr. N.Y. Jr. League, N.Y.C., 1970—74; sec. 1095 Park Ave Corp., N.Y.C., 1977—86; bd. mgrs. McBurney YMCA, N.Y.C., 1995—2000, chmn., 1998—2000; trustee United Adult Ministries, 1998—, mem. exec. com., 1999—, chair, fin. com., 1999—; trustee First Presbyn. Ch. in the City N.Y., 1995—98, pres., 1997—98; trustee N.Y. City Presbytery, 1996—98, treas., 1998—2002, chair coun. adminstrn. and support svcs., 2003—; ruling elder First Presbyn. Ch., 2000—03; mem. steering com. Presbyn. Welcome, 1999—2004, co-moderator, 2001—03; bd. trustees Presbyn. Synod of Northeast, 2002—; bd. dirs. YWCA, N.Y.C., 1980—85. Mem.: Wellesley Club. Democrat. Home: 441 W 24th St New York NY 10011-1253 E-mail: margaretsnyc@mac.com.

SCOTT, MARIAN ALEXIS, journalist; b. Atlanta, Feb. 4, 1949; d. William Alexander and Marian (Willis) Scott; m. Marc Anthony Lewis, Sept. 14, 1968 (div. 1973); m. David Leslie Reeves, Mar. 16, 1974 (div. 1998); children: Cinque Scott, David Leslie Jr. Student, Barnard Coll., 1966-68, Spelman Coll., 1989-90, Regional Leadership Inst., 1992; LHD, Argosy U., 2003. Reporter, asst. city editor, cable TV editor, mgr., video Atlanta Jour. & Constn., 1974-93; dir. diversity Cox Enterprises Inc., 1993-97; pub. Atlanta Daily World, 1997—. Bd. dirs. Atlanta Life Ins. Co.; vis. instr. summer program for minority journalists, Berkeley, Calif., 1980, 81, 84, 85, 87 Grady High Sch., Atlanta, 1982-83; journalist-in-residence Clark Coll., Atlanta, 1983. Rschr., writer: The history of Atlanta NAACP, 1983 (NAACP award 1984). Moderator First Congl. Ch., 1982-92. Named one of 100 Top Black Bus. and Profl. Women, 1986, 20 Women Making a Mark in Atlanta, Atlanta Mag., 1998, Top 25 Women in Bus., The Network Jour., 2004; recipient Disting. Urban Journalism award, Nat. Urban Coalition, 1980, Acad. Achievement award, YWCA, 1989, Media of Yr. award, Ga. Legisl. Black Caucus, 2001, Grimes fellow, Cox Family Enterprise Ctr., Kennesaw State U., Citizen of Yr. award, Southwest Hosp., 2001; Michele Clark fellow, Columbia U. Sch. Journalism, 1974. Mem.: Nat. Assn. Black Journalists, Atlanta Assn. Black Journalists (Commentary Print award 1983, Pioneer Black Journalist award 1998), Nat. Assn. Media Women (pres Atlanta chpt. 1985—87, Media Woman of Yr. award 1983, Media Woman of Yr. nat. award 1993), Atlanta Press Club (pres. 2000), Sigma Delta Chi (bd. dirs. 1980—84, treas. 1985—88). Office: Atlanta Daily World 145 Auburn Ave NE Atlanta GA 30303-2503

SCOTT, MARIANNE FLORENCE, retired librarian, educator; b. Toronto, Dec. 4, 1928; d. Merle Redvers and Florence Ethel (Hutton) S. BA, McGill U., Montreal, Que., Can., 1949, BLS, 1952; LLD (hon.), York U., 1985, Dalhousie U., 1989; DLitt (hon.), Laurentian U., 1990. Asst. librarian Bank of Montreal, 1952-55; law librarian McGill U., 1955-73, law area librarian, 1973-75, dir. libraries, 1975-84, lectr. legal bibliography faculty of law, 1964-75; nat. librarian Nat. Library of Can., Ottawa, Ont., 1984-99, ret., 1999. Co-founder, editor: Index to Can. Legal Periodical Lit, 1963—; contbr. articles to profl. jours. Decorated officer Order of Can., 1995; recipient Queen Elizabeth II Silver Jubilee medal, 1977, IFLA medal, 1996, Queen Elizabeth II Golden Jubilee medal, 2002. Mem. Internat. Assn. Law Libraries (dir. 1974-77), Am. Assn. Law Libraries, Can. Assn. Law Libraries (pres. 1963-69, exec. bd. 1973-75, honored mem. 1980—), Can. Library Assn. (council and dir. 1980-82, 1st v.p. 1980-81, pres. 1981-82), Corp. Profl. Librarians of Que. (v.p. 1975-76), Can. Assn. Research Libraries (pres. 1978-79, past pres. 1979-80, exec. com. 1980-81, sec.-treas. 1983-84), Ctr. for Research Libraries (dir. 1980-83), Internat. Fedn. Library Assns. (honor com. for 1982 conf. 1979-82, chair com. on copyright and other legal matters 1998-2003, hon. fellow 2003), Conf. of Dirs. of Nat. Libraries (chmn. 1988-92). Home: 119 Dorothea Dr Ottawa ON Canada K1V 7C6 E-mail: mfscott@rogers.com.

SCOTT, MARTHA G. state legislator; b. Ware Shoals, S.C., Nov. 10, 1935; d. Harold and Pearl (Wardlaw) Smith; children: Marion Jr., Deborah Ann Gilmore. Student, Highland Park Jr. Coll., 1952-54; DHH, Tenn. Sch. Religion, 1990; DHL, Urban Bible Inst., Detroit, 1994. With Mich. Bell Telephone Co., 1960-86; rep. Mich. Ho. of Reps. Mem. Mich. State Dem. Ctrl. Com., 1974-82; commr. Wayne County Bd. Commrs., 1977-80, chairwoman Human Resources Com., 1978-80; vice chairwoman Wayne County Civil Svc. Commn., 1980-82; pres. Highland Park City Coun., 1984-87; mayor City of Highland Park, 1988; Dem. precinct del. 1st Congl. Dist.; bd. dirs. Nat. Coun. Alcoholism and Other Dependencies, 1979, Detroit Osteopathic Hosp., 1990; vice chairwoman Mich. Women in Mcpl. Govt.; founding mem. Nat. Polit. Congress Black Women; adv. bd. Met. Region Bus. Alliance; vol. Residential Care Alternatives. Recipient Plaque Highland Park Sch. Bd., 1977, Nat. Polit. Congress of Black Women award, 1981, Resolution, Wayne County Bd. Commrs., 1981, Wayne County Auditors, 1981, Dollars and Sense Mag. award, 1989, Spl. Achievement award Amvets, Golden Heritage award for excellence in svc., 1988, Cmty. Svc. award Knoxville Coll. Alumni, 1988. Mem. Gamma Phi Delta. Office: Michigan House of Reps State Capitol Lansing MI 48909

SCOTT, MARY ELIZABETH, administrative educator; b. Portola, Calif., Dec. 14, 1940; d. Daniel Marchant and Gemma Rose Scott. BA, St. Mary's Coll., Notre Dame, Ind., 1963; MA, U. of the Pacific, Stockton, Calif., 1975; MEd, U. Nev., 1978; EdD, U. San Diego, 1989. Charter dir. Clark County Community Coll., Henderson, Nev., 1974-81, St. Rose de Lima Hosp. Found., Henderson, 1982-84; dir. institutional rsch. and staff devel. Community Coll. So. Nev., North Las Vegas, 1988-91; exec. dir. Ctr. for Human Empowerment Mt. Carmel Health, Columbus, Ohio, 1991-92; mem. faculty, chair dept. mgmt. C.C. So. Nev., 1922—96; instr. Clark County C.C., Las Vegas, 1992—. Adj. instr. U. Nev., 1979, St. Francis Coll., Joliet, Ill., 1983, West Hills Coll., San Joaquin, Calif., 1971-72; instr. Clark County Community Coll., Las Vegas, 1974-78, 81-87, 1992—; tchr. Dos Palos High Sch., 1971-72, Bishop Gorman High Sch., Las Vegas, 1968-71, St. Cyril's Sch., Tucson, 1963-68; cons. Mgmt. Tng. for Mgrs. and Non-Mgrs., 1981—, Master Plan Design and Execution, 1985, Cultural Mgmt./Lang. Cons., 1983, Community Demographic Study, 1982. Bd. dirs. Cath. Community Svcs. of Nev., 1988-91. Mem. Community Coll. Exchange Program, Nat. Coun. for Staff, Program and Orgn. Devel. Democrat. Roman Catholic. Avocations: music, dance, hiking, swimming, piano.

SCOTT, MCGREGOR W. lawyer; b. 1962; married; 2 children. BA History, Santa Clara Univ.; JD, Hastings Coll. of Law, Univ. of Calif. Dep. dist. atty. Contra Costa County, 1989—97; Dist. atty. Shasta County, 1997—2003; interim pending State Confirm. Dist. of Calif., 2003; US Atty. for Ea. Calif. nomination by Pres. Bush, 2003—. Office: Sacramento Fed Cthse 501 I St Ste 10-100 Sacramento CA 95814

SCOTT, MELLOUISE JACQUELINE, retired media specialist; b. Sanford, Fla., Mar. 1, 1943; d. Herbert and Mattye (Williams) Cherry; m. Robert Edward Scott, Jr., July 1, 1972; 1 child, Nolan Edward. BA, Talladega Coll., 1965; MLS, Rutgers U., 1974, EdM, 1976, EdS, 1982. Media specialist Seminole County Bd. Edn., Sanford, 1965-72, Edison (N.J.), 1972-98; ret. Edison (N.J.) Bd. Edn., 1999. Mem. ALA, N.J. Ret. Educators Assn., NEA. Baptist. Home: PO Box 1771 Sanford FL 32772-1771

SCOTT, MICHAEL COLEMAN, philosophy educator; b. Orange, Calif., Sept. 24, 1945; s. Clarence Coleman and Wilma Coetta (Neel) S.; div. Mar. 1981. BA, Calif. State U., Long Beach, 1974, MA, 1976. Cert. tchr., Calif. Instr. ESL, Coastline Coll., Fountain Valley, Calif., 1976, Santa Ana (Calif.) Coll., 1976-79; instr. philosophy Saddleback Coll. North, Irvine, Calif., 1979-80; part-time instr. philosophy Orange Coast Coll., Costa Mesa, Calif., 1980-85, instr. philosophy, 1985—. Cons. Orange County Mental Health, Santa Ana, 1975-76. Author poetry. With USN, 1962-63. Mem. People for Ethical Treatment of Animals, Rat Fan Club. Socialist. Avocations: music, ethology, science.

SCOTT, MICHAEL DENNIS, lawyer; b. Mpls., Nov. 6, 1945; s. Frank Walton and Donna Julia (Howard) S.; m. Blanca Josefina Palacios, Dec. 12, 1981; children: Michael Dennis, Cindal Marie, Derek Walton. BS, MIT, 1967; JD, UCLA, 1974. Bar: Calif. 1974, U.S. Dist. Ct. (no., so. and ctrl. dists.) Calif. 1974, U.S. Patent Office 1974, U.S. Ct. Appeals (9th cir.) 1974, U.S. Supreme Ct. 1978, U.S. Ct. Appeals (fed. cir.) 1989. Systems programmer NASA Electronics Rsch. Lab., Cambridge, Mass., 1967-69, Computer Scis. Corp., El Segundo, Calif., 1969-71, Univac, Valencia, Calif., 1971; from assoc. to ptnr. Smaltz & Neelley, LA, 1974-81; exec. dir. Ctr. for Computer/Law, LA, 1977-94; pvt. practice LA, 1981-86, 88-89; pres. Law and Tech. Press, 1981-94; ptnr. Scott & Roxborough, LA, 1986-88, Graham & James, 1989-93; v.p., gen. counsel Sanctuary Woods Multimedia, Inc., San Mateo, Calif., 1993-94; of counsel Steinhart & Falconer, San Francisco, 1995-97; ptnr. Hosie Wes Sacks & Brelsford, Menlo Park, Calif., 1997-98, Perkins Coie LLP, 1998—2003; prof. law Southwestern U., LA, 2003—. Adj. assoc. prof. law, Southwestern U., LA, 1975-80, 2001-03, Loyola U., L.A., 1997-99, 2002-, Pepperdine U., LA, 2001—; chmn. World Computer Law Congress, L.A., 1991, 93. Author: (with David S. Yen) Computer Law Bibliography, 1979, The Scott Report, 1981-86, Computer Law, 1984, Scott on Computer Law, 1991, Multimedia: Law and Practice, 1993, Scott on Multimedia Law, 1996, (with Warren S. Reid) Year 2000 Computer Crisis: Law Business Technology, 1998, Internet and Technology Law Desk Reference, 1999-, Intellectual Property and Licensing Law Desk Reference, 2001—, Telecommunications Law Desk Reference, 2003-; editor-in-chief: Computer/Law Jour., 1978-94, Software Protection, 1982-92, The Scott Report, 1985-94, Internat. Computer Law Adviser, 1986-92, Cyberspace Lawyer, 1996—, E-Commerce Law Report, 1998—. Mem. Computer Law Assn. (bd. dirs. 1994-99), Calif. State Bar Assn. Office: 675 S Westmoreland Ave Los Angeles CA 90005

SCOTT, MIMI KOBLENZ, psychotherapist, actress, publicist, journalist, playwright; b. Albany, NY, Dec. 15, 1940; d. Edmund Akiba and Tillie (Paul) Koblenz; m. Barry Stuart Scott, Aug. 13, 1961 (dec. Nov. 1991); children: Karen Scott Zantay, Jeffrey B. BA in Speech, English Edn., Russell Sage Coll., 1962; MA in Speech Edn., SUNY, Albany, 1968; M in Social Welfare, SUNY, 1985; PhD in Psychology, Pacific Western U., Encino, Calif., 1985. Cert. tchr., social worker. Tchr. English, speech Albany Pub. Schs., 1961-63; hostess, producer talkshow Sta. WAST-TV 13, Albany, 1973-75; freelance actress N.Y.C., 1975-77; producer, actress Four Seasons Dinner Theater, Albany, 1978-82; instr. of theatre Albany Jr. Coll., 1981-83; pvt. practice psychotherapy Albany, N.Y., 1985-92; exec. producer City of Albany Park Playhouse, 1989-92; actor self-employed N.Y.C., 1992—; actor Off Broadway show Grandma Sylvia's Funeral, 1996-98, Split Ends, 2004. Guest psychotherapist Sally Jessy Raphael Show, 1992, 93, Jane Whitney Show, 1994, A Current Affair, 1995, News Talk TV, 1995; founder Manhattan Playwrights Inc., 2001—, producing artistic dir., 2001—. Scriptwriter, dir., actor (TV films) To Liberty and Justice for All, 1985, featured writer Backstage, 1995—96, featured in ind. film Mr. Vincent, Sundance, 1997, book and lyricist (musical) Dressing Room, Soho Playhouse, N.Y.C., 2000; author: Mind Tricks, 2003; dir.: Mind Tricks, 2003. Event organizer AmFar, 1985; co-chmn. March of Dimes Telethon, 1985-86; fundraiser Leukemia Found., 1987, Aids Benefit, N. Miami Beach, Fla., 1988; elected to SUNY Albany U. Found., 1990. Recipient FDR Nat. Achievement award March of Dimes, 1985, Recognition Cert. Capital Dist. Psychiat. Ctr., 1983, 84, 85; named Woman of Yr. YWCA, 1986, Commr. Albany Tricentennial Celebration, 1986; Mimi Scott Day proclaimed by Mayor of Albany, 1989. Mem.: NASW, AFTRA, SAG, AEA, N.Y. League Profl. Theatre Women. Jewish. Avocations: horseback riding, boating, golf, tennis. Home and Office: 211 W 71st St Apt 6A New York NY 10023-3767 Office Phone: 917-846-2449. Personal E-mail: mscott13@aol.com.

SCOTT, NANCY ELLEN, psychologist; b. El Paso, Tex., Nov. 1, 1960; d. Robert Churchill and Annie Jo (Schmidt) S. BS, U. Tex., El Paso, 1982; MS, Springfield Coll., 1985; MA, Columbia U., 1987, EdM, 1989; PhD, Fordham U., 1996. Cert. tchr., Tex., cert. clin. hypnotherapy; lic. psychologist, N.Y. Assoc. Occupl. Health Consulting Inc., West Nyack, N.Y., 1985-88; psychiat. rehab. counselor Met. Hosp., N.Y.C., 1988-91; psychotherapist Met. Ctr. for Mental Health, N.Y.C., 1991-96; psychology intern Albert Einstein Coll. of Medicine, Bronx, N.Y., 1991-92; psychologist Albert Einstein Coll. Medicine, Bronx, N.Y., 1992-94, Bronx Psychiat. Ctr., Bronx, N.Y., 1994-95; assessor

Assessment Sys., Inc., N.Y.C., 1995; pvt. practice N.Y.C., 1995—; neuropsychologist Burke Med. Rsch. Inst., White Plains, NY, 1996-99, dir. neuropsychol. assessment program, 1999—2001. Contbr. articles to profl. jours. Mem. APA. Office: 168 Fifth Ave Ste 2N New York NY 10010 Fax: 212-304-9758. E-mail: Nscottphd5ave@cs.com.

SCOTT, NANCY L. health facility administrator, consultant; b. Berwyn, Ill., Sept. 11, 1962; d. Kenneth N. and Lolita L. Unger; m. Paul A. Scott, Dec. 29, 1990 (div. Sept. 1995). BS, Univ. of Ill., 1983; MBA with hons., U. of Chgo., 1991. Cert. CHE Am. Coll. of Healthcare Execs., Chgo., 2000. Various positions including implementation specialist to fin. product mgr. Enterprise Systems, Inc., Wheeling, Ill., 1993—96; cytogenetics technologist Univ. of Chgo., 1986—88; supr. Reproductive Genetics Inst., Chgo., 1988—90; dist. agt. The Prudential, Des Plaines, Ill., 1992; mgr., sr. cons. Cap Gemini Ernst & Young U.S., Chgo., 1996—2003; acct. exec. AHA Fin. Solutions, Inc., Chgo., 2003—. Home: 3238 Elm Ave Brookfield IL 60513 Office: AHA Financial Solutions Inc 1 N Franklin 30th Fl Chicago IL 60606-3421 E-mail: NLScott@aol.com.

SCOTT, NATHAN ALEXANDER, JR., minister, literary critic, religious educator; b. Cleve., Apr. 24, 1925; s. Nathan Alexander and Maggie (Martin) S.; m. Charlotte Hanley, Dec. 21, 1946; children: Nathan Alexander III, Leslie K. AB, U. Mich., 1944; BD, Union Theol. Sem., 1946; PhD, Columbia U., 1949; LittD, Ripon Coll., 1965, St. Mary's Coll., Notre Dame, Ind., 1969, Denison U., 1976, Brown U., 1981, Northwestern U., 1982, Elizabethtown Coll., 1989; LHD, Wittenberg U., 1965; DD, Phila. Div. Sch., 1967; STD, Gen. Theol. Sem., 1968; LHD, U. D.C., 1976; DD, The Protestant Episcopal Theological Seminary in Va., 1985; HumD, U. Mich., 1988; LHD, Wesleyan U., 1989, Bates Coll., 1990; STD, Univ of the South, 1992; DD, Kenyon Coll., 1993, Wabash Coll., 1996; Ordained priest Episcopal Ch., 1960; canon theologian Cathedral St. James, Chgo., 1967-76. dean of chapel, Va. Union U., 1946-47; instr. humanities, Howard U., 1948-51, asst. prof., 1951-53, assoc. prof., 1953-55; asst. prof. theology and literature, U. Chgo., 1955-58, assoc. prof., 1958-64, prof., 1964-72, Shailer Mathews prof. of theology and lit., 1972-76, prof. English, 1967-76; Commonwealth prof. religious studies, U. Va., 1976-81, William R. Kenan prof. religious studies, 1981-90, prof. English, 1976-90, prof. emeritus, 1990—. Author: Rehearsals of Discomposure: Alienation and Reconciliation in Modern Literature, 1952, The Tragic Vision and the Christian Faith, 1957, Modern Literature and the Religious Frontier, 1958, Albert Camus, 1962, Reinhold Niebuhr, 1963, The New Orpheus: Essays toward a Christian Poetic, 1964, The Climate of Faith in Modern Literature, 1965, The Broken Center: Studies in the Theological Horizon of Modern Literature, 1966, Ernest Hemingway, 1966, The Modern Vision of Death, 1967, Adversity and Grace: Studies in Recent American Literature, 1968, Negative Capability: Studies in the New Literature and the Religious Situation, 1969, The Unquiet Vision: Mirrors of Man in Existentialism, 1969, The Wild Prayer of Longing: Poetry and the Sacred, 1971, Nathanael West, 1971, Three American Moralists: Mailer, Bellow, Trilling, 1973, The Poetry of Civic Virtue: Eliot, Malraux, Auden, 1976, Mirrors of Man in Existentialism, 1978, The Poetics of Belief: Studies in Coleridge, Arnold, Pater, Santayana, Stevens and Heidegger, 1985, Visions of Presence in Modern American Poetry, 1993; co-editor Jour. Religion, 1963-77, (with Ronald Sharp) Reading George Steiner, 1994; adv. editor Religion and Lit., Literature and Theology, Callaloo. Fellow Am. Acad. of Arts and Scis.; mem. Soc. Arts, Religion and Contemporary Culture, Soc. for Values in Higher Edn. (Kent fellow), MLA., Am. Acad. Religion (pres. 1986), Century Assn. (N.Y.C.), Quadrangle Club, Arts Club (Chgo.), Greencroft Club (Charlottesville, Va.). Office: U Va Dept Religious Studies Charlottesville VA 22903

SCOTT, NORMAN ROY, academic administrator, agricultural engineering educator; b. Spokane, Wash., Sept. 6, 1936; s. Roy Samuel and Agnes Sarafia (Lilljegren) S.; m. Sharon R. Cogley, June 17, 1961; children: Robin, Nanette, Shirlene. BS in Agrl. Engring., Wash. State U., 1958; PhD, Cornell U., 1962. Mem. faculty agrl. engring dept. Cornell U., Ithaca, N.Y., 1962—, chmn. agrl. engring. dept., 1978-84, dir. office for rsch. agrl. experimentation sta., 1984-89, v.p. rsch. and advanced studies, 1989-98. Mem. bd. on agriculture NRC, Nat. Acad. Scis., 1993-96. Contbr. articles to profl. jours.; patentee in field. Recipient Alumni Achievement award Wash. State U., 1995. Fellow ASHRAE, Am. Inst. for Med. and Biol. Engring. (founding 1991), Am. Soc. Agrl. Engrs. (tech. v.p. 1989-92, pres. elect 1992-93, pres. 1993-94, Henry Glese award 1989, McCormick-Case Gold Medal award 2002); mem. AAAS, N.Y. Acad. Scis., Nat. Acad. Engring., Inst. Biol. Engring. (pres. 2001), Am. Soc. for Engring. Edn., Instrument Soc. Am. (sr.). Democrat. Methodist. Avocations: sailing, golf. Home: 1662 Taughannock Blvd Trumansburg NY 14886-9120 Office: Cornell U 216 Riley Robb Hall Ithaca NY 14853-5701 Office Phone: 607-255-4473. Business E-Mail: nrs5@cornell.edu.

SCOTT, OLOF HENDERSON, JR., priest; b. Phila., May 13, 1942; s. Olof Henderson and Julia Irene (Rutroff) S.; m. Eva Jakowenko, Sept. 13, 1969; children: Lisa Ann, Christopher Olof, Timothy Nicholas. BA in Physics, Franklin and Marshall Coll., 1964; MS in Nuclear Engring., Pa. State U., 1966; postgrad., St. Vladimir's Orthodox Theol. Sem., 1975-76. Ordained deacon Antiochian Orthodox Christian Ch., 1975, priest, 1976, archpriest, 1988. Ops. engr. S3G ops. Knolls Atomic Power Lab., GE Co., Schenectady, N.Y., 1966-68, project engr. S3G ops., 1968-69; lead nuclear engr. Seabrook Nuclear project Pub. Svc. Co. of N.H., Manchester, 1969-70; project engr. VEPCO projects Nuclear Energy Sys. divsn. Westinghouse Elec. Co., Monroeville, Pa., 1970-72, project mgr. VEPCO projects Nuclear Energy Sys. divsn., 1972-74, regional sales mgr. mktg., 1974-75; pastor St. George Orthodox Ch., Charleston, W.Va., 1976—; dean of clergy Appalachian-Ohio Valley Deanery, 1976—. Spiritual advisor NAC-SOYO of Archdiocese, 1977-82, vice-chmn. inter-orthodox and inter-faith rels., 1987—; exec. bd. W.Va. Coun. Chs., 1977—; bd. govs. Nat. Coun. Chs., 1977—, nominating com., 1979-81, exec. com., 1985-96, membership com., 1988-91, unity and rels., 1989-92, ch. world svc., 1997—; mem. West Va. Ecumenical Coalition on Infant Mortality, 1992-96. Contbr. articles to profl. jours. Bd. dirs. Religious Coalition for Cmty. Renewal in Charleston, 1987-95, Charleston Ch. Recreation Assn., 1998—, Kanawha Home for Children, 1986-89, pres., 1989; long-range planning com. W.Va. State Rep. Exec. Com., 1985-87; adv. bd. Nat. Ctr. for Human Rels., 1997-98; del. 8th Assembly of WCC, Harare, Zimbabwe, 1998. Named Hon. West Virginian, 2001; Olof H. Scott Day named in his honor, City of Charleston, W.Va., 2001. Mem. Acad. Parish Clergy (pres. W.Va. chpt. 1983-85), Am. Nuclear Soc., St. Vladimir's Theol. Found., Charleston Ministerial Assn., Order of St. John of Jerusalem-Knights Hospitellers (chaplain 1985—), Order of St. Ignatius of Antioch, Soc. for Preservation and Encouragement Barbershop Quartet Singing in Am. Inc. (v.p. 1984-85), Pa. State Club W.Va. (pres. 1984-88), Alden Kindred of Am., Sigma Pi Sigma, Delta Sigma Phi. Avocations: camping, barbershop quartet, motorcycling. Home: 4409 Staunton Ave SE Charleston WV 25304-1743 Office: St George Orthodox Ch PO Box 2044 Charleston WV 25327-2044 E-mail: frolof@charter.net. *My thoughts on life are but mere recitations of the Holy Scripture and my feeble attempts at making Those words and Thoughts my own.*

SCOTT, OMERIA MCDONALD, state legislator; m. Charles Scott. Mem. Miss. Ho. of Reps., 1993—. Mem. Nat. Coun. Negro Women, Federated Women Am., Assn. Excellence in Edn., Eastern Star. Democrat. Baptist. Address: 615 E 19th St Laurel MS 39440-2470 Office: Miss Ho of Reps Rm 400E-NC State Capitol Jackson MS 39205

SCOTT, PETER DALE, writer, retired English language educator; b. Montreal, Jan. 11, 1929; s. Francis Reginald and Marian Mildred (Dale) S.; m. Mary Elizabeth Marshall, June 16, 1956; children: Catherine Dale, Thomas, John Daniel; m. Ronna Kabatznick, July 14, 1993. BA, McGill U., Montreal, Que., Can., 1949, PhD, 1955; postgrad, Inst. d'Etudes Politiques, Paris, 1950, Univ. Coll., Oxford, Eng., 1950-52. Fgn. service officer Canadian Dept. External Affairs, Ottawa, Ont., 1957-61; asst. prof. speech U. Calif., Berkeley, 1961-66, from asst. prof. to assoc. prof. English, 1966-80, prof., 1980-94; ret., 1994. Author: The War Conspiracy, 1972, Crime and Cover-Up, 1977, Coming to Jakarta, 1988, Listening to the Candle, 1992, Deep Politics and the Death of JFK, 1993, Crossing Borders, 1994, Deep Politics Two, 1995, Drugs, Contras, and the CIA, 2000, Minding the Darkness, 2000, Drugs, Oil, and War, 2003; co-author: The Assassinations, 1976, The Iran-Contra Connection, 1987, Cocaine Politics, 1991. Fellow Internat. Ctr. Devel. Policy (Freedom award 1987); recipient Lannan award for Poetry, 2002. Mem. Assn. for Responsible Dissent (bd. dirs. 1988). Avocation: birdwatching. Office: U Calif Dept English Berkeley CA 94720-0001 E-mail: pdscottweb@hotmail.com.

SCOTT, PETER M. utility company executive; married; two children. BS, MBA, U. N.C. Prin., ptnr. Theodore Barry & Assocs., L.A.; pres. Scott, Madden & Assocs., Inc., 1983-2000; exec. v.p., CFO Carolina Power & Light, Raleigh, 2000—. Office: CP&L Energy Inc 411 Fayetteville St Raleigh NC 27601

SCOTT, PHYLLIS WRIGHT, coach, music educator; b. Lancaster, Pa., Nov. 9, 1925; d. George Bronson and Edythe Heckroth Wright; m. Edgar Lee Arthur Mixon, Oct. 12, 1946 (div. Nov. 1954); children: Thomas Lee, Raymond Dean, Michael George; m. Gilbert Henry Scott, June 23, 1976 (dec. May 1995). Grad., H.S., 1963; studied music, studied skating. Skating tchr. Health Ctr., Norfolk, Va., 1947, Ringing Rocks Park, Pottstown, Pa., 1945, Gt. Leopard Roller Rink, Chester, Pa., 1946—47, Ringing Rocks Park Roller Rink, Lancaster, Pa., 1948—49, Playland Roller Rink, York, Pa., 1950—51, Skateland Roller Rink, Camden, NJ, 1952—55, Exton (Pa.) Roller Rink, 1956—57; music tchr. Holiday Music, Pennsauken, NJ, 1962—64; pvt. practice Bellmawr, NJ, 1965—98; tchr. organ, piano and keyboard Keyboard Am., Lewes, Del., 1998—. Prodr.: (skating shows), 1944—62. Den mother Cub Scouts of Am., Bellmawr, NJ, 1950—54. Recipient Silver-Bronze Dance medal, Roller Skating Rinks Operator Assn., 1943, Bronze Figures award, 1944. Mem.: Order of Eastern Star. Republican. Baptist. Avocations: needlepoint, playing keyboard instruments. Home: 29261 White Pine Rd Milton DE 19968 Personal E-mail: phylliswscott@msn.com.

SCOTT, RALPH MASON, physician, radiation oncology educator; b. Leemont, Va., Nov. 23, 1921; s. Benjamin Thomas and Marion Hazel (Mason) S.; m. Alice Latine Francisco, Dec. 21, 1946; children: Susan Taylor, Ralph Mason, John Thomas. BA, U. Va., 1947; MD, Med. Coll. Va., 1950. Diplomate Am. Bd. Radiology (trustee 1965-76, treas. 1969-70, v.p. 1970-72, pres. 1972-74). Intern Robert Packer Hosp., Sayre, Pa., 1953-54, resident, 1954-57, dir. radiation therapy and nuclear medicine sect., 1957-59; with Christie Hosp. and Holt Radium Inst., Manchester, England, 1956-57; asst. prof. radiology U. Chgo. Med. Sch., 1959-60; assoc. prof. radiology, dir. radiation therapy and radioisotopes U. Louisville Med. Sch., 1960-64, prof., dir. radiation therapy, 1964-77; prof. and chmn. dept. rad. and oncology U Louisville, 1974-77; prof. radiation therapy U. Louisville Med. Sch., 1981-82; prof. emeritus U. Louisville, 1995; dir. J. Graham Brown Regional Cancer Ctr., Health Scis. Ctr. U. Louisville Med. Sch., 1981-82; dir. dept. radiation medicine Christ Hosp., Cin., 1982-93; ret. Clin. prof. radiology U. Cin. Coll. Medicine, 1982-93; prof., chmn. dept. therapeutic radiology U. Md. Sch. Med., 1977-80; dir. radiation therapy program div. cancer rsch. resources and ctrs., Nat. Cancer Inst. (on leave from U. Louisville), 1976-77. Pres. Ky. divsn. Am. Cancer Soc., 1972-73; bd. dirs. Living Arrangements for the Developmentally Disabled, 1993-95, No. Ky. Assn. for the Retarded, 1993-95, Day Spring Inc., 1993-95, United Health Care, 1994-95, Seven Counties Svcs., Inc., 1997—, J. Graham Brown Regional Cancer Ctr. Corp., 1997—. Lt. (j.g.) USNR, 1943-45. Fellow Christie Hosp. and Holt Radium Inst., Manchester, Eng., 1956-57. Mem. Am. Roentgen-Ray Soc. (exec. coun. 1968—, chmn. exec. coun. 1972-73), AMA, Am. Coll. Radiology (vice chmn. commn. on cancer 1968-69), Am. Radium Soc., Am. Soc. Therapeutic Radiologists, Assn. U. Radiologists, Radiol. Soc. N.Am., Pi Kappa Alpha, Phi Chi. Home: 5516 Tecumseh Cir Louisville KY 40207-1692

SCOTT, RAYMOND PETER WILLIAM, chemistry research educator, writer; b. Erith, Eng., June 20, 1924; came to U.S., 1969; s. Ronald and Annie (Hoadley) S.; m. Barbara Winifred Doreen Strange, Apr. 20, 1946; children: Kerry Raymond, Kevin Francis. B.Sc., U. London, 1946, D.Sc., 1958. Lab. leader Burroughs Welcome, Dartford, Eng., 1946-48; chief chemist APCM, 1948-52; research mgr. Benzole Producers, Watford, Eng., 1952-60; divisional mgr. Unilever, Sharnbrook and Bedfordshire, Eng., 1960-69; dir. phys. chemistry Hoffamn La Roche, Nutley, N.J., 1969-80; dir. applied rsch. Perkin-Elmer, Norwalk, Conn., 1980-86; sometime rsch. prof. dept. chemistry Georgetown U., Washington, 1986-2000; writer, cons., 2001—. Rsch. prof. dept. chemistry Birkbeck Coll., London. Author: Liquid Chromatography Detectors, 1977, 3d edit., 1987, Contemporary Liquid Chromatography, 1976, Liquid Chromatography Column Theory, 1991, Silica Gel and Bonded Phases, 1993, Liquid Chromatography for the Analyst, 1994, Chromatography Techniques, 1995, Chromatography Detectors, 1996, Tandem Techniques, 1996, Introduction to Analytical Gas Chromatography, 1997, Chiral Chromatography, 1998, Quantitative Chromatographer Analysis, 2000, Chromatography Theory, 2002; editor: Gas Chromatography, 1960, Small Bore Columns in Liquid Chromatography, 1983. Recipient Tswett medal Am. Internat. Symposia on Chromatography, 1978; recipient Tswett award USSR Tech. Inst. Moscow, 1978, Martin medal in chromatography Chromatography Group Gt. Britain, 1982 Fellow Royal Soc. Chemistry (chartered, Analysis and Instrumentation award 1988), Am. Inst. Chemists (cert.), Am. Chem. Soc. (Chromatography award 1977). Home: Great Sanders House Hurst Ln London TN33 0PE England

SCOTT, RICHARD ELTON, health facility administrator; b. St. Louis, Oct. 3, 0193; s. Earl Ray and Celeste (Roark) Scott; m. Carol Jenkins, Sept. 3, 1960; children: Suzanne Scott Abbe, Richard E. Jr. BA, Baylor U., 1971; MS, Trinity U., 1978. Various positions Hillcrest Bapt. Med. Ctr., Waco, Tex., 1961-78, asst. adminstr., 1973-78, v.p., 1978-90, exec. v.p., 1990-92, pres., CEO, 1992—; adminstrv. resident Scott & White Clinic, Temple, Tex., 1973—. Chmn. VHA S.W., Inc., Dallas, 1997—98; ores. Bapt. Hosp. Assn., 1999—2001; co-founder, bd. dirs. Cmty. Health Action Ptnrs.; bd. dirs. Waco Family Practice Found. Pres. exec. com., bd. Dr. Pepper Mus., Waco, 1996; chmn. Waco Bus. League, 1989; chmn. bd. United Way, Waco, 1989; chmn. Greater Waco C. of C., 1991; chmn. bd. trustees First Bapt. Ch., Waco, 2000. Named Leonard A. Duce award, Trinity U. Healthcare Alumni Assn., San Antonio, 1997, Vol. or Yr., United Way, Waco, 1991. Mem.: Vol. Hosps. Am. Southwest, Tex. Hosp. Assn., Rotary. Office: Hillcrest Health Sys 3000 Herring Ave Waco TX 76708-3239

SCOTT, RICHARD G. religious organization administrator; b. Pocatello, Idaho, Nov. 7, 1928; s. Kenneth Leroy and Mary Whittle S.; m. Jeanen Watkins, July 16, 1953; 7 children. Degree in mech. engring., George Washington U.; postgrad. in nuclear engring. Mem. staff naval and land based power plants, 1953-65; head North Mission LDS Ch., Cordoba, Argentina, 1965-69, regional rep. in Uruguay, Paraguay, N.C., S.C., Va., Washington, 1969-77, mem. 1st Quorum of Seventy, 1977-83, mem. presidency of 1st Quorum of Seventy, 1983-88, apostle, 1988—. Avocations: jazz and classical music, hiking, birding, painting. Office: LDS Ch 50 E North Temple Salt Lake City UT 84150-0002

SCOTT, RICHARD THOMAS, JR., reproductive endocrinologist; b. Selma, Ala., Nov. 28, 1958; s. Richard Thomas and Cynthia Marvin (Coleman) S.; m. Blair MacKerer, June 16, 1979; children: Whitney Blair, Katherine Leigh, Richard Thomas III. BS in Chemistry, Randolph Macon Coll., 1979; MD, U. Va., Charlottesville, 1983. Diplomate Nat. Bd. Med. Examiners, Am. Bd. Ob-Gyn., reproductive endocrinology divsn; bd. cert. high complexity lab dir. embryology, andrology, endocrinology, Am. Bd. Bioanalysts. Commd. 2nd lt. USAF, 1979, advanced through grades to lt. col., 1993; intern Wilford Hall USAF Med. Ctr., San Antonio, 1983-84, resident, 1984-87, chief reproductive endocrinology Lackland AFB, Tex., 1989-93; fellow Jones Inst. for Reproductive Medicine, Ea. Va. Med. Sch., Norfolk, 1987-89; chief reproductive endocrinology Uniformed Svcs. U. Health Scis., Bethesda, Md., 1993—, asst. prof., 1990—, assoc. prof., 1993—. Adj. scientist S.W. Found. Biomed. Rsch., 1990—, dir. Assisted Reproductive Technology, Reproductive Medicine Assocs. of N.J., Morristown, N.J. Ad hoc reviewer Fertility and Sterility, Jour. Clin. Endocrinology and Metabolism, Ob-Gyn., Am. Jour. Ob-Gyn., Contraception, Maturitas, Jour. Pediatric and Adolescent Gynecology, Internat. Jour. Infertility, Jour. In Vitro Fertilization and Embryo Transfer; contbr. articles to profl. jours. and abstracts. Lt Col USAF, 1993—95, Uniformed Services University of the Health Sciences. Grantee Surgeon Gen., Wyeth Rsch., Solvay Pharm. Rsch., Hitachi of Am., Tap Pharms. Fellow Am. Coll. Obstetricians and Gynecologists (chmns. award Armed Forces dist. meeting 1988, Searle award 1989, Prof. of Yr. 1991); mem. Am. Fertility Soc. (Best Poster award 1988), N.Am. Menopausal Soc., Soc. Air Force Clin. Surgeons, Endocrine Soc., Soc. Reproductive Endocrinologists, Phi Beta Kappa, Chi Beta Phi, Omicron Delta Kappa. Achievements include receiving several awards for research. Office: RMA of NJ 111 Madison Ave Ste 100 Morristown NJ 07960-6083 Home: 170 Post Kennel Rd Far Hills NJ 07931-2408

SCOTT, RIDLEY, film director; b. South Shields, Northumberland, Eng., Nov. 30, 1939; Ed., Royal Coll. Art, London. Dir.: (films) The Duellists, 1977, Alien, 1979, Legend, 1985, Black Rain, 1989; prodr.: The Browning Version, 1994, Clay Pigeons, 1998, Where the Money Is, 2000, Six Bullets from Now, 2002; exec. prodr.: Monkey Trouble, 1994; dir.(and prodr.): Thelma & Louise, 1991, 1492: Conquest of Paradise, 1992, G.I. Jane, 1997, Black Hawk Down, 2001, Matchstick Men, 2003; writer, dir., prodr. Boy on a Bicycle, 1965; dir.(and co-prodr.): Blade Runner, 1982, (and exec. prodr.): Someone to Watch Over Me, 1987, White Squall, 1996, Gladiator, 2000; dir., prodr., exec. music prodr. Hannibal, 2001; dir.: (TV series) Z Cars, 1962, Adam Adamant Lives, 1966, The Informer, 1966; exec. prodr.: The Hunger, 1997, AFP: American Fighter Pilot, 2002; (TV films) RKO 287, 1999, The Last Debate, 2000, The Gathering Storm, 2002. Winner Design scholarship, N.Y. Office: Creative Artists Agy 9830 Wilshire Blvd Beverly Hills CA 90212-1804

SCOTT, ROBERT, financial services company executive; CFO Morgan Stanley Dean Witter & Co., N.Y.C. Office: Morgan Stanley Dean Witter & Co 1585 Broadway New York NY 10036-8200

SCOTT, ROBERT ALLYN, academic administrator; b. Englewood, N.J., Apr. 16, 1939; s. William D. and Ann. F. (Waterman) S.; children: Ryan Keith, Kira Elizabeth. BA, Bucknell U., 1961; PhD, Cornell U., 1975; LLD, Ramapo Coll., 2000. Mgmt. trainee Procter & Gamble Co., Phila., 1961-63; asst. dir. admissions Bucknell U., Lewisburg, Pa., 1965-67; asst. dean Coll. Arts and Scis. Cornell U., Ithaca, 1967-69, assoc. dean, 1969-79, anthropology faculty, 1978-79; dir. acad. affairs Ind. Commn. for Higher Edn., Indpls., 1979-84, asst. commr., 1984-85; pres. Ramapo (N.J.) Coll., 1985-2000, Adelphi U., 2000—. Cons. Sta. WSKG Pub. TV and Radio, 1977-79, also to various colls. and univs., pubs., 1966—; mem. curriculum adv. com. Ind. Bd. Edn., 1984-87, Lilly Endowment Think Tank, 1984-86; mem. nat. adv. panel Ind. 21st Century Schooling Project, 1990-92; U.S. rep. to creation of U. Mobility Asian-Pacific, 1993—; U.S. rep. to meetings of Coun. European Rectors, 1991—; sr. advisor to U.S. State Dept. on Higher Edn. in Unesco European Region, 1997—; U.S. del. to UNESCO N.Am. and World Confs. on Higher Edn., 1998; sr. cons., chair N.J. Higher Edn. Restructuring Team, 1994; bd. dirs. iRV. Author books and monographs; editl. bd. Cornell Rev., 1976-79; book rev. editor Coll. and Univ., 1974-78; cons. editor Change mag., 1979-95; cons. editor Jour. Higher Edn., 1985—; exec. editor Saturday Evening Post book div. Curtis Pub. Co., 1982-85; contbr. articles to sociols., edn. and popular publs. Trustee Bucknell U., 1976-78, First Unitarian Ch., Ithaca, 1970-73, 78-79, chmn., 1971-73, Unitarian Universalist Ch. of Indpls., 1980-85. With USNR, 1963-65. Spencer Found. rsch. grantee, 1977; recipient Sagamore of the Wabash award, 1986, Prudential Found. Leader of Yr. award, 1987, Disting. Svc. award West Bergen Mental Health Ctr., 1991, NYU Presdl. medal, 1994, Sci. and Edn. award Boy Scouts Am., 1993, Raoul Wallenberg Humanitarian Leadership award, 2000, ACIT award for Disting. Svc., 2002, Harbor Child Care Disting. Svc. award, 2003, Huntington Chamber award for Excellence in Higher Edn., 2003, Telly award for Excellence in Cable Television Programming, 2003, Garden City Chamber Cmty. Svc. award, 2004. Fellow Am. Anthrop. Assn.; mem. Am. Sociol. Assn., Am. Assn. Higher Edn., Coun. on Liberal Arts and Scis. (chair 1990-93), Am. Coun. on Edn. Commn. On Internat. Edn. (chair 1991-93), L.I. Assn., Global Kids, Inc., Regional Plan Assn., Nat. Fgn. Lang. Ctr., Brookings Instn. Study Group, Higher Edn. Colloquium (chmn. 1982-84, 96-98), N.J. Assn. of Coll. and Univs. (chair 1991-92), Bucknell U. Alumni Assn. (bd. dirs. 1971-80, pres. 1976-78, Outstanding Achievement 1991), Indian Trail Club, Century Assn., Phi Kappa Psi, Phi Kappa Phi. Office: Adelphi U Garden City NY 11530

SCOTT, ROBERT CORTEZ, congressman, lawyer; b. Washington, Apr. 30, 1947; s. Charles Waldo and Mae (Hamlin) S. BA, Harvard U., 1969; JD, Boston U., 1973; LLD (hon.), Commonwealth Coll., Hampton, Va., 1988. Pvt. practice, Newport News, 1973—91; del. Va. Ho. Dels., Richmond, 1978—83, senator, 1983—93; mem. U.S. Congress from 3rd Va. dist., Washington, 1993—; mem. edn. and workforce com., judiciary com. Br. pres. NAACP, Newport News, 1974-80; pres. bd. Peninsula Legal Aid Ctr., Hampton, 1977-81; mem. state exec. bd. March of Dimes, Va., 1987—; chmn. 1st dist. Dem. Party Va., 1980-85; bd. dirs. Hampton Roads March of Dimes; adv. com. Peninsula Boy Scouts Am. Recipient Brotherhood Citation award Nat. Conf. Christians & Jews, 1985, Child Adv. award Va. Acad. Pediatrics, 1987, Disting. Svc. award Va. State Fraternal Order Police, 1987, Outstanding Legislator award So. Health Assn., 1989. Mem. Peninsula C. of C., Alpha Phi Alpha, Sigma Pi Phi. Democrat. Office: US House of Reps 2464 Rayburn Ho Office Bldg Washington DC 20515-4603

SCOTT, ROBERT EDWIN, dean, law educator; b. Nagpur, India, Feb. 25, 1944; came to U.S., 1955; s. Roland Waldeck and Carol (Culver) S.; m. Elizabeth (Loch) Shumaker, Aug. 14, 1965; children: Christina Elaine, Robert Adam. BA, Oberlin (Ohio) Coll., 1965; JD, Coll. of William and Mary, 1968; LLM, U. Mich., 1969, SJD, 1973. Bar: Va. 1968. From asst. to prof. Law Sch. Coll. of William and Mary, Williamsburg, Va., 1969-74; prof. law Sch. of Law U. Va., Charlottesville, 1974-82, Lewis F. Powell, Jr. prof. Sch. of Law, 1982—2003, dean and Arnold H. Leon prof., 1991—2001; Justin W. D'Atri Prof. Law, Bus. & Soc. Columbia Law Sch., 2001—02; David & Mary Harrison Dist. Prof. U. Va., Charlottesville, Va., 2003—. Author: Commercial Transactions, 1982, 91, Sales Law and the Contracting Process, 1982, 91, Contract Law and Theory, 1988, 93, Payment Systems and Credit Instruments, 1996. Fellow Am. Bar Found., Am. Acad. Arts and Scis.; mem. Va. Bar. Democrat. Methodist. Home: 1109 Hilltop Rd Charlottesville VA 22903-1220 Office: U Va Rm WB179e Sch of Law Charlottesville VA 22903 Personal E-mail: res8f@virginia.edu.

SCOTT, ROBERT HAYWOOD, JR., lawyer; b. Hazelton, Pa., Mar. 1941; s. Robert Haywood and Marjorie Jane Scott; m. Sandra Lou Carroll, June 6, 1966; children: Paige Carroll, Robert Haywood. AB magna cum laude, Kenyon Coll., 1963; JD with distinction, Duke U., 1966. Bar: Mo. 1969, Kans. 1966, Ohio 1972. Assoc. Hoskins King Springer McGannon and Hahn, Kansas City, Mo., 1970-72; operating v.p., sr. counsel Federated Dept. Stores, Cin., 1972-83; ptnr. Roberts Fleischaker & Scott, Joplin, Mo., 1983-88; chief exec. officer W&S Mfg., Inc., Joplin, 1988-92, also chmn. bd. dirs.; CEO Robert Scott Investment Banking, 1988—. Chmn. Deep Sea Archaeology Rsch. Coun., 1994—. Contbr. articles to profl. jours. Capt. USAF, 1966—70. Mem. Mo. Bar Assn., Order of the Coif, Phi Beta Kappa. Home: 1330 Valle Dr Joplin MO 64801-1074

SCOTT, ROBERT LANE, chemist, educator; b. Santa Rosa, Calif., Mar. 20, 1922; s. Horace Albert and Maurine (Lane) S.; m. Elizabeth Sewall Hunter, May 27, 1944; children: Joanna Ingersoll (dec.), Jonathan Armat, David St. Clair, Janet Hamilton. S.B., Harvard U., 1942; MA, Princeton U., 1944, PhD, 1945. Sci. staff Los Alamos Lab., 1945-46; Frank B. Jewett fellow U. Calif., Berkeley, 1946-48; faculty UCLA, 1948—, prof. chemistry, 1960-92, prof. emeritus, 1993—, chmn. dept., 1970-75. Author: (with J.H. Hildebrand) Solubility of Nonelectrolytes, 3d edit. 1950, rev., 1964, Regular Solutions, 1962, Regular and Related Solutions, 1970; Contbr. articles to profl. jours. Guggenheim fellow, 1955; NSF sr. fellow, 1961-62; Fulbright lectr., 1968-69 Fellow AAAS, Am. Phys. Soc.; mem. Am. Chem. Soc. (Joel Henry Hildebrand award 1984), Royal Soc. Chemistry (London), Sigma Xi. Home: 11128 Montana Ave Los Angeles CA 90049-3509

SCOTT, ROBERT MONTGOMERY, museum executive, lawyer; b. Bryn Mawr, Pa., May 22, 1929; s. Edgar and Helen Hope (Montgomery) S.; m. H. Gay Elliot, June 30, 1951 (div. 1997); children: Hope Tyler Scott Rogers, Janny Scott Ritter, Elliot Montgomery. AB, Harvard U., 1951; LLB, U. Pa., 1954; DHL (hon.), Thomas Jefferson U., 1996. Ptnr. Montgomery McCracken Walker & Rhoads, Phila., 1961-82, of counsel, 1982-88; spl. asst. to U.S. Amb. to Ct. of St. James, London, 1969-73; hon. Brit. consul Phila., 1979-83; pres., chief exec. officer Phila. Mus. Art, 1982-96, hon. chmn., 1997—. Pres. Acad. Music of Phila., 1973-80; mem. adv. bd. First Union Bank Atlantic. Trustee Phila. Mus. Art, 1965—, Royal Oak Found., 1978-86, Inst. Cancer Rsch., Fox Chase Cancer Ctr., 1960-86, Lankenau Hosp., 1959-86, U. Pa., 1975-80, William Penn Found., 1986-91; pres. Mary Louise Curtis Book Fedn., 1989—, Curtis Inst. of Music, 1994—; bd. dirs. Glyndebourne Assn. Am., Inc. Recipient Superior Honor award Dept. State, 1973, Gov. of Pa. award for Leadership in the Arts, 1996, Citizen of Yr. awad Penjerdel Coun., 1996, Hospitality City U.S.A. Grand award Greater Phila. Hotel Assn., 1996. Fellow Am. Bar Found.; mem. Am. Assn. Mus., Greater Phila. Cultural Alliance, Phila. Club (pres. 1997—), Knickerbocker Club, White's Club. Republican. Home: Ardrossan 807 Newtown Rd Villanova PA 19085-1031

SCOTT, RONALD, lawyer; b. Lexington, Mich., Aug. 31, 1947; BA, Baylor U., 1969; JD, U. Tex., 1975. Bar: Tex. 1975. Mem. Bracewell & Patterson, Houston. Mem. State Bar Tex., Tex. Bar Found., Houston Bar Found., Houston Bar Assn., Order of Barristers, Phi Delta Phi. Office: Bracewell & Patterson South Tower Pennzoil Pl 711 Louisiana St Ste 2900 Houston TX 77002-2781 E-mail: RScott@Bracepatt.com.

SCOTT, RONALD FRASER, civil engineering educator, engineering consultant; b. London, Apr. 9, 1929; came to U.S., 1951; s. Frederick Durham and Catherine Isobel (Fraser) S.; m. Pamela June Wilkinson, May 28, 1959; children— Grant Fraser, Craig Alistair, Roderick Jonathan B.Sc. in Civil Engring., Glasgow U., 1951; S.M. in Civil Engring., MIT, 1953, Sc.D. in Civil Engring., 1955; DEng (hon.), Glasgow U., 1995. Registered profl. engr., Calif. Soils engr. U.S. Army Corps Engrs., Boston, 1955-57; divisional soils engr Racey, McCallum & Assocs., Toronto, Ont., Can., 1957-58; prof. civil engring. Calif. Inst. Tech., Pasadena, 1958—, Dotty and Dick Hayman prof. engring., 1987—, Hayman prof. emeritus, 1998—; pvt. practice cons. engr. Pasadena, 1958—. Author: Principles of Soil Mechanics, 1963, (with Schoustra) Soil Mechanics and Engineering, 1968, (with Bolt, Horn, MacDonald) Geological Hazards, 1975, Foundation Analysis, 1981. Contbr. articles to profl. jours. Patentee in field. Overseas Fellow, Churchill Coll., Cambridge U., Fellow Guggenheim Found., 1972; Churchill Found., 1972; Rankine Lectureship, Brit. Geotech. Soc., 1987. Mem. ASCE (Huber Research prize 1968, Norman medal 1972, Middlebrooks prize 1981, Terzaghi lectureship 1983, hon. mem. 2003), Am. Geophys. Union, Nat. Acad. Engring., Earthquake Engring Inst. (hon. mem. 1999). Avocations: walking; photography. Office: Calif Inst Tech Mail Sta 104-44 1201 E California Blvd Pasadena CA 91125-0001

SCOTT, RONALD S. construction executive; b. McCook, Nebr., Apr. 29, 1942, s. Frank Maxwell and Edna Mae Scott; m. Christine S Salmon, Mar. 28, 1968; children: Ronald S Jr., Jonathan L. BS in metal tech., Bradley U., 1965. Mgr., plant maintenance Rep. Steel Corp., Chgo., 1965—87; mgr., hot mill maintenance Acme Steel Corp., Chgo., 1987—97; pres. Oak Haven Builders, Seneca, SC, 2000—. Bd. mem. Home Builders Assn., 2000—03. Pres. Homeowners Assn., 2001—03; commodore Keyowee Sailing Club, 2003—. Recipient Golden Anchor award, Keowee Sailing Club, 2002. Republican. Protestant. Home: 302 Oak Haven Ct Seneca SC 29672 Office: Oak Haven Builders Inc PO Box 41 Newry SC 29665

SCOTT, ROSA MAE, art educator, artist; b. East Hampton, N.Y., Apr. 12, 1937; d. James Alexander and Victoria (Square) Nicholson; m. Frank Albert Hanna, Apr. 1, 1957 (div. Mar. 1985); 1 child, Frank Albert Hanna III; m. Warner Bruce Scott, Aug. 3, 1985 (dec. Oct. 2002); children: Bernadine, John, Patricia, Charlene, Lawrence. AA, Dabney Lancaster, 1989; BA, Mary Baldwin, 1992. Cosmetologist Rosa's Beauty Shop, East Hampton, 1962-68; sec. Frank Hanna's Cleaning Co., East Hampton, 1962-77; cashier, clk. Brook's Pharmacy, East Hampton, 1992; lead tchr. East Hampton Day Care, 1992-94, 97-98; substitute tchr. Lexington (Va.) Schs., 1994—, East Hampton Sch. Sys., 1996-97; lead tchr. Suffolk C.C. Child Care Ctr., River Head, N.Y., 1999; substitute tchr. East Hampton Sch., 2000—03; lead tchr. after sch. program Springs Sch., 2000—02, 2004, substitute tchr., 2000—03; receptionist Montauk Artist Assn., 2003—. Receptionist, Montauk (N.Y.) Artist Assn., 2003; sec. Lylburn Downing Cmty. Ctr., Inc., Lexington, 1985-92; arts and crafts tutor, supr. East Hampton Town Youth After Sch. Program, 1996—. Acrylic painter. Pres. Rockbridge Garden Club, Lexington, 1996; co-organizer Va. Co-op. Ex. Garden Clubs, Lexington, 1995; bd. dirs. Rockbridge Area Pres. Homes, 1996, Fine Arts of Rockbridge, 1985-92, Friends of Lime Kiln, Lexington, 1985-92. Mem.: Guild Hall, East End Arts, Montauk Artists Assn. (receptionist 2003), Artist Alliance East Hampton, L.I. Black Artists (v.p. 2000—03), Rockbridge Arts Guild. Avocations: collecting emmett kelly clowns, art, reading, theater, tennis. Home: PO Box 1265 East Hampton NY 11937-0708

SCOTT, SANDRA J. not-for-profit executive; b. Kansas City, Kans., Jan. 12, 1959; d. Eartha Lee and Herman Scott; children: Sonya Lynn Allen, Jonelle Melissa Allen, Michael Lee Hunter, Jr. Exec. dir. Your Empowerment Source, Inc., Kansas City, 2003—. Author: (autobiography) Lord, Let There Be Light, Becoming Whole Before Becoming One, Baggage Handlers: My Road to Letting Go of Life's Painful Luggage. E-mail: sandra_j_scott59@yahoo.com.

SCOTT, SHIRLEY, city council; married; four children. BA, Drew U., 1965; MA Germanic Langs., U. Cin., 1968. Operator Scott Supply Svc. Inc.; city coun. Tucson City Coun., 1995—. Bd. dirs. Tucson Clean and Beautiful. Office: Tucson City Coun 8123 E Poinciana Dr Tucson AZ 85730-4641

SCOTT, SIDNEY BUFORD, financial services company executive; b. Richmond, Va., Mar. 3, 1933; s. Buford and Mary (Nixon) S.; m. Susan Elder Bailey, Sept. 19, 1959; children: Sidney Buford Jr., Elizabeth Scott Cech, George Reily Bailey. Student, Yale U., 1951-53; BA, U. Va., 1955; LLD (hon.), St. Paul's Coll., 1982. Chmn. Scott & Stringfellow Inc., Richmond, 1974—. Bd. dirs. New Market Corp.; mem. regional firms adv. com. N.Y. Stock Exch., 1982-85; chmn. bd. trustees Securities Industry Found. for Econ. Edn., 1976-86; trustee Va. Retirement Sys., 1984-94; dir. Nat. Coun. Econ. Edn. Bd. dirs. Hollywood Cemetery, Police Benevolent Assn.; trustee, chmn. Elk Hill Farm, Inc.; bd. visitors U. Va., 1987-94; former vice rector, bd. visitors Va. Commonwealth U.; past chmn. United Way Greater Richmond; vestryman, past sr. warden St. Paul's Episcopal Ch.; past pres. Sheltering Arms Hosp; past bd. dirs., v.p. Big Bros. Am.; past bd. dirs., chmn. Big Bros. Richmond, Met. Found., also others. Sgt. U.S. Army, 1956-58. Recipient Outstanding Young Man of Yr. award Richmond Jr. C. of C., 1964, outstanding svc. award Va. Coun. on Econ. Edn., 1976, 80, Brotherhood award NCCJ, 1981, George P. Baker medal Joint Coun. on Econ. Edn., 1986, Bd. Mem. of Yr. award Va. Assn. Children's Homes, 1987. Mem. Securities Industry Assn. (governing coun. 1976-78), Raven Soc., Beta Gamma Sigma. Democrat. Home: 4919 Lockgreen Cir Richmond VA 23226-1748 Office: PO Box 1575 Richmond VA 23218-1575

SCOTT, STANLEY DEFOREST, real estate executive, former lithography company executive; b. Hudson County, NJ, Nov. 2, 1926; s. Stanley DeForest and Anne Marie (Volk) S.; m. Mary Elizabeth Hazard, Dec. 30, 1953. BA, U. So. Calif., 1950. Gen. mgr. Alfred Scott Pubs., N.Y.C., 1951-56; chmn., pres. S.D. Scott Printing Co., Inc., N.Y.C., 1956-92; gen. ptnr. 145 Hudson St. Assocs.; co-chmn. mus. and art com. Fraunces Tavern Mus., 1973-87, 1998—. Assoc. J. Carter Brown Libr.; former mem. Mayor's Industry Adv. Com.; former bd. dirs., Bus. Relocation Com. With USNR, 1944-46. Recipient Frick Collection fellowship. Fellow: Am. Numismatic Soc. (trustee); mem.: Am. Assocs. Royal Acad. Arts (patron), Mt. Vernon Ladies Assn. (adv. com.), Royal Oak Found., English-Speaking Union U.S. (patron), N.Y. Hist. Soc., S.R. (bd. mgrs.), Soc. Colonial Wars, Soc. Mayflower Descs., Pilgrims U.S., Am. Mus. in Britain (coun. 1986—), Mus. Modern Art, Met. Mus. Art, Morgan Libr., Am. Friends Hermitage Mus., Am. Friends Brit. Mus. (patron), Am. Friends English Heritage, St. George's Soc., Sir John Soane's Mus. Found. (patron), The Church Club N.Y., Union Club, Knickerbocker Club, Grolier Club. Republican. Episcopalian. Home: One Sutton Pl South New York NY 10022-2471 Office: 145 Hudson St New York NY 10013-2103 Personal E-mail: ScttHUDSON@aol.com.

SCOTT, STEPHEN BRINSLEY, theater producer; b. Pitts., Aug. 27, 1950; s. Robert Crawford and Lucille (Hendrickson) S. BS in Edn., U. Kans., 1972; MA, U. Denver, 1973. Artistic dir. Creede (Colo.) Repertory Theatre, 1976-78; chair dept. theatre Baker U., Baldwin, Kans., 1978-80; dir. edn. and cmty. svcs. Goodman Theatre, Chgo., 1980-84, dir. arts in edn., 1986-88, artistic assoc., 1988-94, assoc. producer, 1994—; dir. ednl. programs Chgo. Internat. Theatre Festival, 1985-86. Spl. instr. Loyola U. Chgo., 1987-95; instr. Columbia Coll., Chgo., 1981-85, 92-97, Latin Sch. Chgo., 1984-86, Roosevelt U., 1997—; mem. arts in edn. panel Nat. Endowment for Arts, Washington, 1990-91. Mem. adv. panels Ill. Arts Coun., Chgo., 1984-87; mem. com. League Chgo. Theatres, 1990—; cmty. rep. local sch. coun. Franklin Sch., Chgo., 1990-94. pres. Chgo. Coalition for Arts in Edn., 1983-85. Named Outstanding Lectr. Chgo. Cultural Ctr., 1981, 84, Outstanding Dir. Joseph Jefferson Citation Nominations, 1987, 97, award for outstanding ensemble Joseph Jefferson Award Com., 1999, After Dark award for outstanding dir., 2001. Mem. Ill. Theatre Assn. (exec. com. 1987-97), Soc. Stage Dirs. and Choreographers Ill. Alliance for Arts in Edn., Ill. Arts Alliance, Phi Beta Kappa. Democrat. Home: 124 W Polk St Apt 207 Chicago IL 60605-1766 Office: Goodman Theatre 170 N Dearborn St Chicago IL 60601 Office Phone: 312-443-8478. Business E-Mail: stevescott@goodman-theatre.org.

SCOTT, STEPHEN CARLOS, academic administrator; b. Greenville, S.C., Sept. 20, 1949; s. Carlos O'Dell and Christina (Nikitas) S.; m. Patsy Jordan, Apr. 13, 1968; children: Stephanie Christina, Lance Stephen. BA, Clemson (S.C.) U., 1971, MEd, 1975, EdD, 1987. Owner, mgr. Scotty's Inc., restaurant, Clemson, 1967-71; tchr. math. Pickens (S.C.) Sr. High Sch., 1972-74; instr. bus. Tri-County Tech. Coll., Pendleton, S.C., 1974-76, head dept., 1976-78, dir. br. campus Easley, S.C., 1978-80; dean bus. Greenville Tech. Coll., 1980-85, assoc. v.p., 1985-88; pres. Southeastern C.C., Whiteville, N.C., 1988-99; exec. v.p. N.C. C.C. Sys., 1999—2002; pres. Lenoir C.C., Kinston, NC, 2002—. Cons. P.C.E. Fed. Credit Union, Liberty, S.C., 1975-88, Jacobs Mfg. Co., Clemson, 1979-80, Flat Rock Shelter Ctr., Easley, 1980-85; bd. mem. N.C. Rural Ctr. Contbr. articles to profl. jours. and mags. Pres. So. Shelter Ctr., Greenville, 1986—88, Good Shepherd Found., Whiteville, 1990—92; bd. dirs. Good Shepherd, 1988—91; chmn. Columbus County Sch. Bond. Dr., 1989, Am. Heart Fund Drive Columbus County, 1992; co-chmn. Columbus County Long Range Planning Com., 1989—91; vice chmn. Pvt. Industry Coun. Region O, 1992—99; funding dir. Habitat for Humanity Columbus County, 1992; pres. bd. dirs. Columbus County Rural Health Ctr., 1994; bd. dirs. N.C. Rural Ctr., 2000—02. Recipient award for patriotism U.S. Savs. Bonds Program, 1987. Mem. Am. Assn. Cmty. and Jrs. Colls. (Pres.'s Acad.), Greater Kinston C. of C. (exec. bd. 2003—), Rotary (bd. dirs. Whiteville 1990-92, pres. 1992-93). Presbyterian. Avocations: running, chess, coin collecting/numismatics, reading. Home: 104 Hibiscus Dr Clayton NC 27520-8714 E-mail: scs320@lenoircc.edu.

SCOTT, SUSAN CRAIG, plastic surgeon; b. N.Y.C., 1948; MD, Columbia U., 1974. Diplomate Am. Bd. Plastic Surgery with subspecialty in hand surgery. Intern Roosevelt Hosp., N.Y.C., NY, 1974—75, resident in gen. surgery, 1975—79; resident in plastic surgery NYU Med. Ctr., 1979—81; fellow in hand surgery Roosevelt Hosp., 1981—82; pvt. practice plastic surgery N.Y.C., 1987—. Office: 150 E 77TH St New York NY 10021-1922*

SCOTT, SUSAN SHATTUCK, retired secondary school educator; b. Cambridge, Mass., Sept. 12, 1945; d. Kenneth Elton and Phyllis Shattuck; m. Robert Allen Scott, Dec. 27, 1968 (div. 1973); 1 child, Kenneth Charles. BS in Edn., Boston State Coll., 1967; M in Math., Worcester Poly. Inst., 1990. Cert. secondary math. tchr., Mass. Tchr. South Jr. H.S., Weymouth, Mass., 1967-73; editor Houghton-Mifflin Co., Boston, 1973-74; tchr. Ctrl. Jr. H.S., Weymouth, 1974-81, South H.S., Weymouth, 1981-90, Weymouth H.S./Vocat. Tech. H.S., 1990—2002; ret., 2002. Freelance editor Houghton Mifflin, Boston, 1974-75. Treas. Singles' Group, Duxbury Bapt. Ch., 1976-78, Stone Village Condo. Assn., Wareham, Mass., 1993-. Mem. Nat. Coun. Tchrs. Math. Avocations: walking, swimming, reading, gardening, cooking. Home: 342 Rand Hill Rd Alton Bay NH 03810

SCOTT, SYLVIA JANE, small business owner; b. Charleston, Jan. 31, 1945; d. John Mitchell and Christabelle Lillian Johnson; m. Nathanial Myers, 1960 (dec. Mar. 9, 1998); children: Tia Johnson, Nathanial Myers, Norma Griffin, Tralane Mason, Sonia Melton, Troi Mack, Myer Micheal. Student, Trident Tech. Coll., 1975; cosmetology cert., 1987. Owner Shear Beauty, Charleston, SC, 1988—, Rental Units, Charleston, 1997—, Scott Supplies, Charleston, 1999—. Author: The Bookdweller, 2002. Recipient cert., Carolina Monority Supplier Council, Inc. Roman Catholic. Achievements include patents for multi-page doll bookmarks; scheduling board.

SCOTT, T. GORDON, chemistry and math educator, writer; b. Laconia, N.H., Nov. 27, 1941; s. William Stafford and Jeanne Richardson Scott; m. Elizabeth Mary Winterberg, Mar. 11, 1995. BA, U. Pa., 1963; BA with honours, Cambridge (Eng.) U., 1965, MA, 1970; PhD, U. Ill., 1969. Profl. tchg. cert., Pa.; postgrad. tchg. lic., Va. Tchg. asst. U. Ill., Champaign-Urbana, 1965-66; asst. prof. chemistry Oberlin (Ohio) Coll., 1969-70; lectr. biochemistry U. Calif., Santa Barbara, 1971; cons. Sci-Math Cons., Uniontown, Pa., 1972-75; supr. secondary studies Westminster Acad., Carmichaels, Pa., 1975-79; asst. prof. chemistry Alderson-Broaddus Coll., Philippi, W.Va., 1981-84; assoc. prof. chemistry Bryan Coll., Dayton, Tenn., 1984-86, Knoxville (Tenn.) Coll., 1987-89, Union Coll., Barbourville, Ky., 1989-91, Jarvis Christian Coll., Hawkins, Tex., 1992-98; with Chem. Edn. Cons. USA, Hawkins, Tex., 1998-2000; instr. math. Winona (Tex.) Ind. Sch. Dist., 1998-99; instr. math, chemistry and astronomy Pittsylvania County (Va.) Schs.; tchr. Dan River H.S., Ringgold, Va., 2000—02; adj. prof. chemistry and natural sci.-biochemistry Danville (Va.) C.C., 1999—2004; adj. instr. pharmacology Nat. Coll., Danville, 2001—03; assoc. prof. chemistry Winston-Salem (NC) State U., 2004—. Rsch. assoc. DuPont Chem. Co., Inc., Phila., 1963, EPA, Phila., 1988, Edgewood-Aberdeen Rsch. U.S. Army, Aberdeen Proving Ground, Md., 1993; vis. prof. La. Coll., Pineville, 1992; adj. sci. instr. Hargrove Mil. Acad., Chetham, Va., 2003; cons. with Transition State Assocs., Danville, Va. Author: (with others) Synthetic Procedures in Nucleic Acid Chemistry, 1968, Spectroscopic Model Studies of NAD, 1969; contbr. articles to Jour. Am. Chem. Soc., 1967, 1970, 1972, 2003. Musician with Danville Recorder Consort, Danville Area Choral Arts Soc. Thouron fellow to Cambridge U., 1963-65; Thouron scholar Gonville & Cains Coll., Cambridge U.; grantee NSF, 1996-97, Army Rsch. Orgn., 1993-95, Robert A. Welch Found., 1996-98, NSF, 1997-99. Mem. Am. Chem. Soc., Cambridge U. Chem. Soc., Am. Sci. Affiliation (dir. 1998), Rotary Internat. (chmn. internat. edn. com. 1977-81). Achievements include determined the fluorescent lifetime of coenzyme NADH. Avocations: baritone vocal solos, exploring ideas, renaissance music (treble and tenor blockflute), astronomy. E-mail: ps8411@adelphia.net.

SCOTT, TERRY D. military officer; b. Buffalo, Mo. Grad. (with hons.), USN Sr. Enlisted Acad., 1990; BS, So. Ill. U. With USN, 1976—, advanced through grades to master chief petty officer, 2002—. Decorated Legion of Merit, Meritorious Svc. medal, 5 Navy Commendation medals, 4 Navy Achievement medals. Office: 2 Navy Annex Rm 1046 Washington DC 20370-2000

SCOTT, TERRY LEE, communications company executive; b. Rockford, Ill., Oct. 21, 1950; s. Wilson C. and Marie G. (Bunger) S.; divorced; 1 child, Andrea; m. Jenny Scarborough, Aug. 1, 1981; children: Brady, Tiffany. BS in Acctg. magna cum laude, Bradley U., 1972. CPA Ill., Tex. Audit prin. Arthur Young and Co., Dallas, 1972-82; v.p. fin. and adminstrn., treas. Paging Network Inc., Dallas, 1982-90; sr. v.p. Paging Network, Inc., Dallas, 1990-92, pres., CEO, bd. dirs., 1993-95, Terion Inc., Melbourne, Fla., 1995-97, chmn., CEO, 1997-99, Terry Scott Enterprises, Plano, Tex., 1997—; dir. Chameleon Tech., Inc., Seattle, 2002—, Metasolv Software, Inc., Dallas, 2003—04; CFO, v.p. Fin. of Chase Med., Inc., 2003—04; pres., CEO, dir. Airimba Wireless, Inc., Plano, Tex., 2004—. Bd. dirs. XY Point Corp., Terion, Inc., Locate Networks, Inc., MobileStar Inc., Peoples Choice TV Corp. Mem. AICPA, Tex. Soc. CPAs, Phi Kappa Phi, Zeta Pi. Methodist. Office: Terry Scott Enterprises 1704 Riviera Dr Plano TX 75093-2910 Personal E-mail: tscott1704@aol.com.

SCOTT, THEODORE R. lawyer; b. Mount Vernon, Ill., Dec. 7, 1924; s. Theodore R. and Beulah (Flannigan) S.; children: Anne Laurence, Sarah Buckland, Daniel, Barbara Gomon. AB, U. Ill., 1947, JD, 1949. Bar: Ill. 1950. Law clk. to judge U.S. Ct. Appeals, 1949-51; pvt. practice Chgo., 1950—; assoc. Spaulding Glass, 1951-53, Loftus, Lucas & Hammand, 1953-58, Ooms, McDougall, Williams & Hersh, 1958-60; ptnr. McDougall, Hersh & Scott, Chgo., 1960-87; of counsel Jones, Day, Reavis & Pogue, 1987-97, Rockey, Milnamow & Katz, 1998—. 2nd lt. USAAF, 1943-45. Decorated Air medal. Fellow Am. Coll. Trial Lawyers; mem. ABA, Ill. Bar Assn., Chgo. Bar Assn., 7th Cir. Bar Assn. (past pres.), Legal Club Chgo., Law Club Chgo., Patent Law Assn. Chgo. (past pres.), Union League Club, Exmoor Country Club (Highland Park, Ill.), Phi Beta Kappa. Home: 1569 Woodvale Ave Deerfield IL 60015-2350

SCOTT, THOMAS CLIFFORD, lawyer, writer; b. Halifax, Nova Scotia, Can., Sept. 4, 1948; s. Thomas Elsworth Scott and Marion Beatrice O'Hearn; m. Patricia Lynn Adami, May 17, 1997; children: John Christopher, Maryann Elizabeth, Melissa Louise. BS, Ind. U., Indpls., 1971, JD, 1977. Mngr. mfg acctg. Schwitzer Div. Wallace-Murray, Indpls., 1969—77; owner, pres. Tom Scott & Assocs., Indpls., 1977—. Presenter in field. Author: (novels) Wicked Game, Whistle Daughter Whistle. Mem.: IBA, Nat. Assn. Chpt. Thirteen Trustees, ISBA. Office: Tom Scott & Associates 6100 N Keystone Ave Suite 454 Indianapolis IN 46220 Office Phone: 317-255-9915.

SCOTT, THOMAS EMERSON, JR., lawyer, former prosecutor; b. Pittsburg, Penn., Apr. 27, 1948; s. Thomas Emerson Sr. and Marie (Ebel) S.; m. Ginger Claud, Mar. 1978 (div. Aug. 1980); m. Joyce Newman, Aug. 6, 1983. BA in Econs. cum laude, U. Miami, 1969, JD cum laude, 1972; LLM, U. Va., 1989. Bar: Fla. 1972, U.S. Dist. Ct. (so. dist.) Fla. 1972, U.S. Ct. Appeals (5th and 11th cirs.) 1972. Law clk. to cir. judge 11th jud. cir. ct., State of Fla., Dade County, 1970-71; assoc. Bradford, Williams, McKay, Kimbrell, Hamann & Jennings, P.A., Miami, Fla., 1972-76, mem. firm, 1977-79; assoc. Huebner, Shaw & Burrell, Ft. Lauderdale, Fla., 1976-77; cir. judge 11th jud. cir. State of Fla., Miami, 1979-84; ptnr. Kimbrell, Hamann, Jennings, Womack, Carlson & Kniskern P.A., Miami, 1984-85, Steel Hector & Davis, Miami, Fla., 1990—; judge U.S. Dist. Ct. (so. dist.) Fla., Miami, 1985-90; U.S. atty U.S. So. Dist., Fla., 1997-99; ptnr. Shook Hardy & Bacon, Miami, Fla., 1999—. Chmn. security com. U.S. Dist. Ct., so. dist. Fla.; instr. litigation skills U. Miami, Coral Gables, 1984-86; instr. Nita program U. Fla.; instr. trial advocacy program Nova U.; instr. profl. responsibility and product liability St. Thomas U. Contbr. articles to profl. jours. Served to 1st lt. USAR, 1969—. Mem. ABA (co-chmn. com. on discovery litigation sect.), Fla. Bar Assn. (chmn. standing com. on professionalism, past chmn. CLE trial advocacy program), Dade County Bar Assn. (Outstanding Jurist award Young Lawyers' sect.), U.S. Dist. Judges' Assn., Product Liability Adv. Coun. Found. Republican. Roman Catholic. Avocations: running, collectibles. Office: Shook Hardy & Bacon 201 S Biscayne Blvd Ste 2400 Miami FL 33131-4313 E-mail: tscott@shb.com.

SCOTT, THOMAS JEFFERSON, JR., lawyer, electrical engineer; b. Montgomery, Ala., Dec. 30, 1943; s. Thomas Jefferson Sr. and Irene (Feagin) S.; m. Betsy Sue Mackta, Apr. 25, 1981; children: Elspeth Watts, Marghuerita Taylor, Thomas Jefferson III. BEE, Yale U., 1966, BA in Econs., 1967; JD, Vanderbilt U., 1974. Bar: Va. 1974, D.C. 1975, N.Y. 1980, U.S. Dist. Ct. D.C. 1986, U.S. Dist. Ct. (ea. dist.) Va. 1993, U.S. Tax Ct. 1981, U.S. Ct. Fed. Claims, 1982, U.S. Ct. Appeals (fed. cir.) 1982, U.S. Ct. Appeals (4th cir.) 1993, U.S. Supreme Ct. 1984. Trial atty. civil div. U.S. Dept. of Justice, Washington, 1974-78; assoc. Cooper & Dunham, N.Y.C., 1978-80, sr. trial counsel civil div., 1980-85; ptnr. Pennie & Edmonds, Washington, 1985-90, Howrey & Simon, Washington, 1990-97, Hunton & Williams, Washington, 1997—. Capt. USNR, 1966-71. Decorared D.F.C. Mem. ABA, Am. Intellectual Property Law Assn. Office: Hunton & Williams 1900 K St NW Washington DC 20006-1110 E-mail: tscott@hunton.com.

SCOTT, TIFFANY, ice skater; b. Weymouth, Mass., May 1, 1977; Student, Del. Tech. U., 1999. Pairs ice skater with Philip Dulebohn. Recipient Bronze medal, U.S. Jr. Championships, 1997. Avocations: sewing, bicycling, camping, collecting skating stamps, postcards. Office: US Figure Skating Headquarters 20 First St Colorado Springs CO 80906

SCOTT, TONY, film director; b. Newcastle, England, June 21, 1944; m. Donna Wilson. Degree in Fine Arts, Sunderland Art School; postgrad., Leeds Coll. Art, 1969; MFA, Royal Coll. Arts, 1972. Film dir. Totem Prodn., L.A., 1972—. Dir. films including One of the Mission (half-hour film, Brit. Film Inst.), Loving Memory (1-hour feature, Albert Finney), The Hunger, 1983, Top Gun, 1986, Beverly Hills Cop II, 1987, Revenge, 1990, Days of Thunder, 1990, The Last Boy Scout, 1991, True Romance, 1993, Crimson Tide, 1995, The Fan, 1996, Enemy of the State, 1998; exec. prodr., dir.: Spy Game, 2001, The Hire; Beat the Devil, 2002, exec. prodr.: Clay Piegons, 1998, Where the Money Is, 2000, Big Time, 2001, The Hire: Hostage, 2002, The Hire: Ticker, 2002, Six Bullets From Now, 2002, dir (TV episode) The Hunger, 1997; exec. prodr.: (TV movies) RKO 281, 1999, The Last Debate, 2000, The Gathering Storm, 2002, formerly dir. TV commls. Recipient numerous Clios, Gold and Silver Lions and various other awards. Office: Totem Prodns 8009 Santa Monica Blvd Los Angeles CA 90046-5008 also: Creative Artists Agy 9830 Wilshire Blvd Beverly Hills CA 90212-1804

SCOTT, VICKI SUE, school system administrator; b. Pine Bluff, Ark., Feb. 16, 1946; d. John Wesley and Ruby Gray (Whitehead) and Hannah (Lewis) S. BA, Hendrix Coll., 1968; MS in Edn., U. Cen. Ark., 1978, postgrad., 1979-84, U. Ark., 1983-85, Ark. State U., 1993-94. Cert. adminstr., secondary sch. prin., middle sch., secondary health and phys. edn. Tchr., coach Brinkley (Ark.) Pub. Schs., 1968-76, Lonoke (Ark.) Jr. and Sr. High Schs., 1976-77, S.E. Jr. High Sch., Pine Bluff, 1978-92, asst. prin., 1992-2000, dir. summer sch., 1991, 92; prin. White Hall (Ark.) Jr. H.S., White Hall, Arkansas, 2000—. AIDS educator Arkansas River Edn. Svc. Coop., Pine Bluff, 1989-92. Active Leadership Pine Bluff, 1993-94. Scholar Assn. Women Ednl. Suprs., 1985; named Outstanding Young Women of Am., 1974, Ark. Assn. of Middle Level Adminstrs. Bd., 2002-, Ark. Leadership Acad. Mem.: DAR, ASCD, NMSA, Ark. Assn. Mid. Level Adminstrs., Nat. Assn. Sch. Secondary Prins., Ark. Activities Assn., Ark. Assn. Ednl. Adminstrs., Ark. Assn. Mid. Level Educators (bd. dirs. 2002—), Order Ea. Star, Phi Delta Kappa, Delta Kappa Gamma (Epsilon chpt. pres., scholar 1994). Baptist. Avocations: tennis, reading, hiking, travel, golf. Home: 3215 S Cherry St Pine Bluff AR 71603-5983 Office: White Hall Jr HS 8106 Dollarway Rd White Hall AR 71602-6999 E-mail: scottv@whjr.arsc.k12.ar.us., vscott@seark.net.

SCOTT, W. RICHARD, retired sociologist, educator; AA, Parsons Jr. Coll., 1952; BA, U. Kans., 1954, MA, 1955; PhD, U. Chgo., 1961, Copenhagen Sch. of Bus., 2000, Helsinki Sch. Econs., Finland, 2001. Prof. sociology Stanford (Calif.) U., 1988—99, sr. scholar John W. Gardner Ctr., 2002—, sr. rschr. Stanford Collaboratory for Resume on Global Projects. Mem. health svcs. rsch. study sect. Nat. Ctr. for Health Svcs. Rsch., Washington, 1968—72; mem. epidemiol. and svcs. rsch. rev. com NIMH, Washington, 1985—88; courtesy appointee Schs. Bus., Edn. and Medicine, Stanford U., 1988—96; mem. commn. behavioral & social sci. and edn. Nat. Rsch. Coun., 1990—96; dir. Stanford U. Ctr. Orgnl. Rsch., 1988—96. Co-author (with others): Metropolis and Region, 1960; co-author: (with Peter Blau) Formal Organizations, 1961, 2d edit., 2003; co-author: (with Sanford Dornbusch) Evaluation and Exercise of Authority, 1975; co-author: (with John Meyer) Organizational Environments: Ritual and Rationality, 1983; co-author: (with Ann Barry Flood) Hospital Structure and Performance, 1987; co-author: (with others) Institutional Environments and Organizations, 1994, Institutional Change and

Healthcare Organizations, 2000; author: (Book) Organizations: Rational, Natural and Open Systems, 1981, 5th edit., 2003, Institutions and Orgnizations, 1995, 2d rev. edit., 2001; contbr. articles to profl. jours. Recipient Disting. Scholar award, Mgmt. and Orgn. Theory Divsn. Acad. Mgmt., Richard D. Irwin award, Acad. Mgmt., 1996; fellow Ctr. for Advanced Study in Behavioral Scis., 1989—90, Bellagio (Italy) Study and Conf. Ctr., 2002; Woodrow Wilson fellow, U.S. Dept. Edn., 1954—55. Mem.: Inst. of Medicine, Phi Beta Kappa. Office: Stanford Univ Dept Sociology Rm 132 450 Serra Mall Bldg 120 Stanford CA 94305-2047

SCOTT, WALTER, JR., construction company executive; b. May 21, 1931; m. Suzanne Scott. BS, Colo. State U., 1953; LittD, U. Nebr., 1983; LHD, Coll. St. Mary, 1988; D of Commerce, Bellevue U., 1996. With Peter Kiewit Sons, Inc., Omaha, 1953—, engr., project engr., dist. engr., Cleve. dist., 1959—61, asst. dist. mgr., Cleve. dist., 1961—62, dist. mgr. Cleve. dist., 1962-64, v.p., 1964, exec. v.p., 1965-79, chmn. bd., 1964, pres., 1979, chmn. bd. dirs., pres., CEO, 1979-97, dir., chmn. level 3 comm., 1997, chmn. emeritus, 1997—. Bd. trustee Open World Leadership Ctr.; dir. Berkshire Hathaway, Burlington Resources, Commonwealth Telephone Enterprises, MidAmerican Energy Holdings, RCN Corp., Valmont Industries. Served with USAF, 1954-56. Named Philanthropist of Yr., Nat. Soc. Fund-Raising Execs., 1987, Man of Yr., Mid-Am. Coun. Boy Scouts Am., 1988, King Ak-Sar-Ben XCII, Knights of Ak-Sar-Ben, 1988, Disting. Eagle Scout, Boy Scouts Am., 1991, Citizen of Yr., United Way of the Midlands, 1993, Air Force Assn., 1993, Person of Yr., Pmaha Club, 1996; named to Nebr. Bus. Hall Fame, Nebr. C. of C. and Industry, 1995, Omaha Bus. Hall Fame, Greater Omaha C. of C., 1995; recipient Nebr. Builder award, U. Nebr., 1983, Outstanding Achievement in Construction award, The Moles, 1986, Brotherhood award, Nat. Conf. Christians and Jews, 1986, Horatio Alger award, Horatio Alger Assn., 1997, Spirit Youth award, Uta Halee Girls Village, 1988, Perry W. Branch Disting. Svc. award, U. Nebr. Found., 1989, Golden Beaver for Mgmt., The Beavers, 1990, Order of Tower, U. Nebr., Omaha, 1991, Golden Plate award, Am. Acad. Achievement, 1991, Golden Apple award, Met. Cmty. Coll. Found., 1993, Headliner award, Greater Omaha C. of C., 1996, Nebraskalander award, Nebraskaland Found., 1998, Manresa award, Creighton U., 1998, Cmty. Builder award, Greater Omaha C. of C., 1999, Bus. Vol. of Yr., Nat. Alliance Bus., 1999, Midlander of Yr., Omaha World-Herald, 2000. Mem.: Chi Epsilon Soc. (hon.). Office: Peter Kiewit Sons Inc 1000 Kiewit Plz Omaha NE 68131-3302 also: Joslyn Art Mus 2200 Dodge St Omaha NE 68102-1208*

SCOTT, WALTER DILL, management educator; b. Chgo., Oct. 27, 1931; s. John Marcy and Mary Louise (Gent) S.; m. Barbara Ann Stein, Sept. 9, 1961; children: Timothy Walter, David Frederick, Gordon Charles. Student, Williams Coll., 1949-51; BS, Northwestern U., 1953; MS, Columbia U., 1958. Cons. Booz, Allen & Hamilton, NYC, 1956—58; assoc. Glore, Forgan & Co., NYC, 1958—63, ptnr. Chgo., 1963-65; pntr. Lehman Bros, Chgo., 1965-72, sr. ptnr., 1972-73, also bd. dirs.; assoc. dir. econs. and govt. Office Mgmt. and Budget, Washington, 1973-75; sr. v.p. internat. and fin. Pillsbury Co., Mpls., 1975-78, exec. v.p., 1978-80, also bd. dirs.; pres., CEO, Investors Diversified Svcs., Inc., Mpls., 1980-84; group mng. dir. Grand Met. PLC, Mpls., 1984-86, also bd. dirs.; chmn. Grand Met USA, Mpls., 1984-86; prof., sr. Austin fellow Kellogg Sch. Mgmt., Northwestern U., Evanston, Ill., 1988—. Bd. dirs., vice chmn. Intermatic, Inc. Bd. dirs. Chgo. Cmtys. in Schs., Ctr. for Exec. Women, Imagine Schs., Inc., Leadership for Quality Edn. Lt. (j.g.) USN, 1953-56. Home: 55 Meadowview Dr Northfield IL 60093-3547 Office: Northwestern U Kellogg Sch Mgmt 2001 Sheridan Rd Evanston IL 60208-0814 E-mail: wds@kellogg.northwestern.edu.

SCOTT, WILLARD HERMAN, meteorologist, newscaster; b. Alexandria, Va., Mar. 7, 1934; s. Willard Herman and Thelma Matti (Phillips) S.; m. Mary Ellen Dwyer, Aug. 7, 1959; children: Mary Phillips, Sally W. BA in Philosophy and Religion, Am. U., 1955. Page NBC, Washington, 1950; mem. Joy Boys broadcast team Sta. WOL Radio; broadcaster Sta-WRC-AM, Washington, 1953—72, Sta. WWDC, Washington, 1972—74; formerly staff announcer children's TV shows Voice of NASA radio show; weather reporter, performer Today Show and NBC Radio, N.Y.C., 1980—; host Willard Scott's Home and Garden Almanac (Cable TV). Free-lance comml. actor, narrator. Host (TV series) The New Original Amateur Hour, 1991. Active March of Dimes, Easter Seals, ARC, Am. Cancer Soc., Nat. Symphony of Washington, Nat. Park Service, Alzheimer's Found. Served with USN, 1956-58. Named Washingtonian of the Yr., Washingtonian Mag., 1979, Humanitarian in Residence, Nat. Soc. Fund Raisers, 1985, Disting. Virginian, Va. Assn. Broadcasters, 1990; recipient Pvt. Sector award, Pres. Ronald Reagan, 1985. Mem.: De Molay. Episcopalian. Office: NBC 30 Rockefeller Plz Ste 3885 New York NY 10112-0002

SCOTT, WILLIAM CLEMENT, III, private investor; b. N.Y.C., Apr. 25, 1934; s. William Clement and Susan L. (Cameron) S.; m. Cindy L. Taylor, Dec. 5, 1981; children by previous marriage: Katherine Louise, David Campbell. AB, Coll. William and Mary, Williamsburg, Va., 1956. Self-employed, 1956-64; v.p. Booz-Allen & Hamilton, N.Y.C., 1964-69; group v.p. Cordura Corp., Los Angeles, 1969-72; exec. v.p. Western Pacific Industries, N.Y.C., 1972-76, pres., chief operating officer, 1976-87; pvt. investor N.Y.C., 1987-88; chmn., CEO Panavision Inc., N.Y.C., 1988-98. Bd. dirs. Edison Control Corp., Audio Visual Svcs. Corp. Bd. dirs. Opera Orch. of N.Y., pres., 1988-97; bd. dirs. Met. Opera Club N.Y.C., pres., 2002-04. Mem. Met. Opera Club N.Y.C., Racquet and Tennis Club, Hay Harbor Club, Fishers Island Country Club, Coral Beach Club (Bermuda), Royal Bermuda Yacht Club. Republican. Episcopalian. Office: 445 Park Ave Ste 1905 New York NY 10022 E-mail: wcscott@att.net.

SCOTT, WILLIAM CORYELL, medical executive; b. Sterling, Colo., Nov. 22, 1920; s. James Franklin and Edna Ann (Schilling) S.; m. Jean Marie English, Dec. 23, 1944 (div. 1975); children: Kathryn, James, Margaret; m. Carolyn Florence Hill, June 21, 1975; children: Scott, Amy Jo, Robert. AB, Dartmouth Coll., 1942; MD, U. Colo., 1944, MS in OB/GYN, 1951. Cert. Am. Bd. Ob-Gyn., 1956, 79, Am. Bd. Med. Mgmt., 1991. Intern USN Hosp., Great Lakes, Ill., 1945-46, Denver Gen. Hosp., 1946-47; resident Ob-Gyn St. Joseph's Hosp., Colo. Gen. Hosp., Denver, 1946-51; practice medicine specializing in Ob-Gyn Tucson, 1951-71; assoc. prof. emeritus U. Ariz. Med. Sch., Tucson, 1971—; v.p. med. affairs U. Med. Ctr., Tucson, 1984-94. Contbr. articles to med. jours. and chpt. to book. Pres. United Way, Tucson, 1979-80, HSA of Southeastern Ariz., Tucson, 1985-87; chmn. Ariz. Health Facilities Authority, Phoenix, 1974-83. Served to capt. USNR, 1956-58. Named Man of Yr., Tucson, 1975. Fellow ACS, Am. Coll. Ob-Gyn, Pacific Coast Ob-Gyn Soc., Ctrl. Assn. of Ob-Gyn; mem. AMA (coun. on sci. affairs 1984-93, chmn. 1989-91), Am. Coll. Physician Execs., Ariz. Med. Assn. Republican. Roman Catholic. Avocations: golf, gardening, photography. Address: HC 1 Box 923 Sonoita AZ 85637-9705 Personal E-mail: cbarc3@hotmail.com.

SCOTT, WILLIAM FLOYD, accountant; b. Woodland, Miss., Feb. 26, 1936; s. Robert Fulton and Sarah Etta (Watson) S.; m. Carolyn Marie Pierce, Dec. 12, 1958; children: David, Ricky, Stephen, Julie. BS in Bus. Adminstrn., Delta State U., Cleveland, Miss., 1957. Staff acct. Reynolds Elec. & Engring., Las Vegas, Nev., 1957-62, sr. auditor, 1962-65, dir. internal auditing, 1965-70; sr. staff acct. Davis & Mosher, CPAs, Pasadena, Tex., 1970-72; owner Scott & Co., CPAs, Pasadena, 1972—2001; mng. dir. Scott, Forrest & Co., PLLC, Pasadena, 2002—. Chmn. fin. com. Meml. Bapt. Ch., Pasadena, 1974-80, treas., 1974—. Mem. AICPA, Tex. Soc. CPAs, Pasadena Noon Optimist Club (treas. 1973-75), Neighborhood Assn. Three Villas (treas. 2000-). Avocations: reading, gardening, sports. Office: Scott Forrest & Co PLLC CPAs 4620 Fairmont Pky Ste 200 Pasadena TX 77504-3328 Office Phone: 281-487-2501. E-mail: wmfscott@swbell.net.

SCOTT, WILLIAM PAUL, lawyer; b. Staples, Minn., Nov. 8, 1928; m. Elsie Elaine Anderson, Feb. 7, 1968; children: Jason Lee, William P., Mark D., Brian D., Scott; stepchildren: Thomas J. (dec.), Terri L. Weeding-Berg. ALA, U. Minn., 1949; BSL, St. Paul Coll. Law, 1952, JD, 1954. Bar: Minn. 1954. Atty., right of way divsn. Minn. Hwy Dept., 1945-52, civil engr., traffic and safety divsn., 1953-55; practice law Arlington, Minn., 1955-61, Gaylord, Minn., 1963-67; sr. ptnr. Scott Law Offices and predecessors, Pipestone, Minn., 1967—. Probate, juvenile judge Sibley County, Minn., 1956-61; Minn. pub. examiner, 1961-63; county atty. Sibley County, 1963-68, city atty., Pipestone, 1979-2002. Sibley County Rep. chmn., 1961. Served with USMCR, 1946-50, from 2d lt. to lt. col. USAF Res., 1950-88, ret. Recipient George Washington Honor medal Freedoms Found., 1970, 72. Mem. MOAA, VFW, DAV, Minn. Bar Assn., Mensa, Am. Legion, Mil. Officers Assn. Am. Home: PO Box 689 Pipestone MN 56164-0689 Office: Park Plz Offices Pipestone MN 56164 Office Phone: 507-825-5496. E-mail: scottlaw@rconnect.com.

SCOTT, WILLIAM PROCTOR, III, lawyer; b. Berkeley, Calif., Dec. 1, 1946; s. William Proctor Jr. and Marcia (Wood) S.; children: William Proctor IV, Jennifer Anne. BS, MIT, 1968; JD cum laude, U. Pa., 1975. Assoc. Ballard Spahr Andrews & Ingersoll LLP, Phila., 1975-82, ptnr., 1982-2000, Nixon Peabody LLP, Albany, N.Y., 2000—. Regional chmn. MIT Ednl. Coun., 1988-2000. Bd. dirs. Cathedral Village, 1998—, vice chair, 2003-; Lt. (j.g.) USNR, 1969-72. Office: Nixon Peabody LLP Omni Plz 30 S Pearl St Albany NY 12207-3425 Office Phone: 518-427-2700. E-mail: wscott@nixonpeabody.com.

SCOTT, W(ILLIAM) RICHARD, sociology educator; b. Parsons, Kans., Dec. 18, 1932; s. Charles Hogue and Hildegarde (Hewit) S.; m. Joy Lee Whitney, Aug. 14, 1955; children: Jennifer Ann, Elliot Whitney, Sydney Brooke. AA, Parsons Jr. Coll., 1952; AB, U. Kans., 1954, MA, 1955; PhD, U. Chgo., 1961; PhD in Econs. (hon.), Copenhagen Sch. Bus., 2000, Helsinki Sch. Econs., 2001. From asst. prof. to assoc. prof. sociology Stanford (Calif.) U., 1960-69, prof., 1969-99, prof. emeritus, 1999—, chair dept. sociology, 1972-75; sr. scholar John Gardner Ctr./Stanford U., 2002—; sr. rschr. Collaborating for Rsch. on Global Projects, 2003—. Courtesy prof. Sch. Medicine, Stanford U., 1972—, Sch. Edn., Grad. Sch. Bus., 1977—; fellow Ctr. for Advanced Study in Behavioral Scis., 1989-90; resident fellow Bellagio Study and Conf. Ctr., 2002; dir. Orgns. Rsch. Tng. Program, Stanford U., 1972-89, Ctr. for Orgns. Rsch., 1988-96; mem. adv. panel Sociology Program NSF, Washington, 1982-84; mem. epidemiol. and svc. rsch. rev. panel NIMH, Washington, 1984-88; mem. Commn. on Behavioral and Social Scis. and Edn., NAS, 1990-96; vis. prof. Kellogg Grad. Sch. Mgmt., Northwestern U., winter 1997, Hong Kong U. Sci. and Tech., fall 2000. Author: (with O.D. Duncan et al) Metropolis and Region, 1960; (with P.M. Blau) Formal Organizations, 1962, Social Processes and Social Structures, 1970; (with S.M. Dornbusch) Evaluation and the Exercise of Authority, 1975, Organizations: Rational, Natural and Open Systems, 1981, rev. edit., 2003; (with J.W. Meyer) Organizational Environments: Ritual and Rationality, 1983, edit., 1992; (with A.B. Flood) Hospital Structure and Performance, 1987; (with J.W. Meyer), Institutional Environments and Organizations: Structural Complexity and Individualism, 1994, Institutions and Organizations, 1995, rev. edit., 2001; (with S. Christinsen) The Institutional Construction of Organization, 1995; (with M. Ruef et al) Institutional Change and Healthcare Organizations: From Professional Dominance to Managed Care, 2000; editor Ann. Rev. of Sociology, 1986-91; (with R. Cole) The Quality Movement and Organization Theory, 1999, (with J. Davis et al) Social Movements and Organization Theory, 2004. Fellow Woodrow Wilson, 1954-55; mem. Nat. Commn. Nursing, 1980-83; chair Consortium Orgns. Rsch. Ctrs., 1989-91; elder First Presby. Ch., Palo Alto, Calif., 1977-80, 83-86. Named Edmund P. Learned Disting. Prof., Sch. Bus. Adminstrn., U. Kans., 1970—71; recipient Cardinal Citation for Disting. Svc., Labette C.C., Parsons, 1981, Disting. Scholar award, Mgmt. and Orgn. Theory divsn. Acad. Mgmt., 1988, Richard D. Irwin award for scholarly contbns. to mgmt., Acad. Mgmt., 1996; Social Sci. Rsch. Coun. fellow, U. Chgo., 0959, resident fellow, Bellagio Conf. Ctr., 2002. Mem. Inst. Medicine, Am. Sociol. Assn. (chmn. sect. on orgns. 1970-71, mem. coun. 1989-92), Acad. Mgmt., Sociol. Rsch. Assn. (exec. com. 2003—), Macro-Organizational Behavior Soc., Phi Beta Kappa. Democrat. Presbyterian. Home: 940 Lathrop Pl Stanford CA 94305-1060 Office: Stanford U Dept Sociology Bldg 120 Stanford CA 94305 Office Phone: 650-723-3959. Business E-Mail: scottwr@stanford.edu.

SCOTT-CHILDRESS, REYNOLDS JOHNSON, historian, educator; b. Charlotte, N.C., Nov. 1, 1960; s. William Newton and Osee Mac Johnson Childress; m. Katherine Grace Scott-Childress; children: Lillian Grace Childress, Elias Richard Childress. PhD, U. Md., College Park, 1993—2003. Youth counselor YMCA, N.Y.C., 1980—84; prodn. editor Guilford Publications, N.Y.C., 1983—88; mng. editor Zone Books, N.Y.C., 1988—92; conv. and publications coord. Am. Studies Assn., Washington, 1993—98; adj. prof. U. Md., Balt., 2003—04, Cath. U., Washington, 2003—04, asst. prof., 2004—; historian U. Md./U.S. Pk. Svc., College Park, 2004—. Editor: (book) Race and the Production of Modern American Nationalism. Fellow, Gilder Lehrman Inst., 2001; Keck fellow, Huntington Libr., 2000. Mem.: So. Hist. Assn., Am. Studies Assn., Orgn. Am. Historians, Am. Hist. Assn. Home: 1-D Northway Greenbelt MD 20770 Personal E-mail: rc111@umail.umd.edu.

SCOTTI, DENNIS JOSEPH, educator, researcher, consultant; b. N.Y.C., Apr. 20, 1952; s. Joseph Charles and Theresa (Giancola) S. BS, Stony Brook U., 1974; MBA, Adelphi U., 1977; MS, Temple U., 1980, PhD, 1982. Bd. cert. in healthcare mgmt.; cert. healthcare fin. profl., managed care profl.; diplomate Am. Coll. Healthcare Execs. Dep. chief adminstr. Dept. Mental Health Devel. Ctr., Suffolk, N.Y., 1975-77; asst. prof. Rutgers U., N.J., 1980-83; assoc. prof. Fairleigh Dickinson U., N.J., 1983-88, prof., 1989—; sr. prof. Ctr. Healthcare Mgmt. Studies, 2001—. Exec. v.p. Presscott Assocs., Ltd., Avon, Conn., 1989—; prof. Ctr. Healthcare Mgmt. Studies, 2001—. Author: Strategic Management in the Health Care Sector, 1988; contbr. articles to profl. jours. Mem. Regents Adv. Coun. N.J. Recipient Tchg. Excellence award Exec. Master of Bus. Adminstrn., 1997. Fellow Healthcare Fin. Mgmt. Assn. (William G. Fulmer Bronze award for meritorious svc., 1997, Robert H. Reeves Silver award for meritorious svc., 2001, co-recipient Helen M. Yerger Spl. Recognition award, 2002); mem. Am. Coll. Healthcare Execs., Med. Group Mgmt. Assn., Health Planning and Mktg. Soc., Acad. Mgmt. (co-recipient Best Theory to Practice award 2003), Peoples Med. Soc., Health Decisions Assembly, Phi Theta Kappa, Delta Mu Delta. Office: Fairleigh Dickinson U 1000 River Rd Teaneck NJ 07666-1996

SCOTTI, JAMES VERNON, astronomer; b. Bandon, Oreg., Aug. 22, 1960; s. Paul Carl and Elizabeth Louise (Garoutte) S.; m. Karriaunna K.-R. Harlan, May 15, 1983; children: Jennifer Anne, Christopher James. BS, U. Ariz., 1983. Planetarium asst. Flandrau Planetarium, Tucson, 1979-82; student rsch. asst. Lunar and Planetary Lab., Tucson, 1982-83, rsch. asst., 1983-93, sr. rsch. specialist, 1993—. Mem. Am. Astron. Soc. (assoc.), Div. for Planetary Scis., Assn. Lunar and Planetary Observers (asst. comets recorder). Achievements include being a leading observer of faint comets, being heavily involved in observing comet P/Shoemaker-Levy 9 before and during its impact on Jupiter in July 1994. Office: U Ariz Lunar And Planetary Lab Tucson AZ 85721-0001

SCOTTO, RENATA, soprano; b. Savona, Italy, Feb. 24, 1935; m. Lorenzo Anselmi. Studied under, Ghirardini, Merlino and Mercedes Llopart, Accademia Musicale Savonese, Conservatory Giuseppe Verdi, Milan. Opera singer Robert Lombardo Assocs., 1979—. Presenter master classes Juilliard Sch., N.Y.C., Curtis Inst., Phila., Yale U., Russian Opera Ctr., Moscow, Tokyo U., young artist program La Scale, Milan, N.Y. Met. Opera; opened Renata Scotto Opera Acad., Albisola Marina, Italy, 1997—, Music Conservatory of Westchester, White Plains, NY, 2003—; dir. young artist program Verdi Festival, Parma, Italy, 2000 Roles include Feldmarschallin in Der Rosenkavalier (Franco Abiati and Frankfurter Allgemeine awards), 1992, performs Les Nuits d'Ete (Berlioz), Strauss and Mahler songs, Erwartung (Schoenberg), Santa Cecilia Acad. Orch., Rome, 1994, staged Il Parata (Bellini), Festival Belliniano, Catania, Italy, 1993, staged new prodn. La Sonnambula, 1994; dir. new prodn. La Traviata, N.Y.C. Opera, 1995.Kundry in Parsifal, German Schweing Fewtival, 1995, La Voix Humaine, Maggio Musicale Fiorentino, also in Barcelona, Spain, Amsterdam, The Netherlands, Klytemnestra in Elektra, Balt., 2000; dir. Tosca, Grand Opera Miami, 2001; performs with leading orchs. of world, giving concerts and master classes Bd. dirs. Santa Cecilia Acad., Rome Recipient Emmy award for Best Live Mus. Event in TV for Live from Lincoln Ctr., 1995. Office: 5 Stone Hollow Way Armonk NY 10504 Also: care Theatre of La Scala via Filodrammatici 2 Milan Italy*

SCOTTO, ROSANNA, newscaster; b. Brooklyn; BA in Fine Arts, Catholic U. Reporter, assoc. prodr. WTBS, Atlanta; reporter WABC-TV NY, reporter Eyewitness News; corr., anchor FOX 5/WNYW News, N.Y.C., 1986—. Co-owner Fresco by Scotto, 1993—. Co-author: Fresco: Modern Tuscan Cooking for All Seasons, 1997; actor: (films) Miracle on 34th Street, 1994, Ransom, 1996, The Object of My Affection, 1998, Famous, 2000. Nominee Emmy award, 1990, 1995; recipient First Place award for indiv. reporting, NY St. Associated Press Assoc., 1995. Office: WNYW-TV/Fox Broadcasting Co 205 E 67th St New York NY 10021-6050

SCOTT-THOMAS, KRISTIN, actress; b. Redruth, Cornwall, England, United Kingdom, May 24, 1960; m. Francois Olivennes, 3 children, Hannah, Joseph, George. Student, Cen. Sch. Speech and Drama, Ecole Nat. des Arts. Stage debut in Schnitzler's La Lune Déclinante Sur 4 ou 5 Personnes Qui Danse; stage appearances include La Terre Etrangère, Naive Hirondelles, Yes Peut-Etre; appearances on French, German, Australian, U.S. and Brit. TV include L'Ami d'Enfance de Maigret, Blockhaus, Cameleon La Tricheuse, Sentimental Journey, The Tenth Man, Endless Game, Framed, Titmuss Regained, Look at it this Way, Body and Soul; film appearances include Djamel et Juliette, L'Agent Troubé, La Méridienne, Under the Cherry Moon, A Handful of Dust, Force Majeure, Bille en Tete, The Bacheloir, Bitter Moon, Four Weddings and a Funeral (B.A.F.T.A. award), Angels and Insects (Evening Standard Film award), Richard III, 1995, Angels & Insects, 1996, Somebody to Love, 1996, The Pompatus of Love, 1996, Mission: Impossible, 1996, The English Patient, 1996, Amour et confusions, 1997, Souvenir, 1998, The Revenger's Comedies, 1998, The Horse Whisperer, 1998, Up at the Villa, 1999, Random Hearts, 1999, Life as a House, 2001, Gosford Park, 2001. Office: c/o Kevin Huvane & Bryan Lourd Creative Artists Agy 9830 Wilshire Blvd Beverly Hills CA 90212*

SCOTT-WILLIAMS, WENDY LEE, information technology specialist; b. Buffalo, Jan. 22; d. Arthur Raymond and June Amelia Schutt; m. Nigel Simon Scott-Williams, Feb. 29, 1980. BA cum laude, SUNY, Buffalo, 1975; MA with honors, Cambridge U., 1979; MLIS with honors, CUNY-Queens Coll., 1987. Applications rep. Barrister, N.Y.C., 1982-83; coord. computer systems Stroock & Stroock & Lavan, N.Y.C., 1983-87; tech. svcs. mgr. Batten, Barton, Durstein & Osborn (BBDO) Worldwide, N.Y.C., 1987-92; adminstr., mgr. info. resources Fairchild Publs., N.Y.C., 1992-96; info. resource mgr. March of Dimes Birth Defects Found., White Plains, N.Y., 1996—. Active N.Y. Zool. Soc. Mem. Spl. Librs. Assn., Cambridge Union Soc., Oxford-Cambridge Soc., Nature Conservancy, Greenpeace. Presbyterian. Avocations: travel, gardening. Office: March of Dimes Birth Defects Found Nat Hdqs 1275 Mamaroneck Ave White Plains NY 10605-5298

SCOULAR, ROBERT FRANK, lawyer; b. Del Norte, Colo., July 9, 1942; s. Duane William and Marie Josephine (Moloney) Scoular; m. Donna V. Scoular, June 3, 1967; children: Bryan T., Sean D., Bradley R. BS in Aero. Engring., St. Louis U., 1964, JD, 1968. Bar: Mo. 1968, Colo. 1968, ND 1968, U.S. Supreme Ct. 1972, Calif. 1979. Law clk. to chief judge U.S. Ct. Appeals (8th cir.), 1968-69; ptnr. Bryan, Cave, McPheeters & McRoberts, St. Louis, 1969-89, mng. ptnr. LA, 1979-84, exec. com., 1984-85, sect. leader tech., computer and intellectual property law, 1985-89; ptnr. Sonnenschein, Nath, Rosenthal, Chgo., 1990—, mng. ptnr. LA, 1990—, mem. policy and planning com., 1995—. Co-leader intellectual property practice, 1990—98; dir. Mo. Lawyers Credit Union, 1978—79. Contbr. articles to profl. jours. Bd. dirs. St. Louis Bar Found., 1975—76, 1979, bd. dirs., pub. counsel, 2004—; bd. dirs., vice chmn., gen. counsel LA area coun. Boy Scouts Am.; league commr. Am. Youth Soccer Orgn.; mem. alumni coun. St. Louis U., 1979—82, dean's coun. Sch. Law, 2000—; hon. dean Dubourg Soc. Recipient Nat. Disting. Eagle Scout award. Mem.: ABA (nat. dir. young lawyers divsn. 1977—78), Fed. Bar Assn., Mo. Bar Assn. (chmn. young lawyers sect. 1976—77, Disting. Svc. award), Calif. Bar Assn., Assn. Bus. Trial Lawyers (bd. govs. 2004—), LA County Bar Assn., Bar Assn. Met. St. Louis (chmn. young lawyers sect. 1975—76, v.p. 1978—79, sec. 1979), Chancery Club. Home: 1505 Lower Paseo La Cresta Palos Verdes Peninsula CA 90274-2066 Office: Sonnenschein Nath & Rosenthal LLP 601 S Figueroa St Ste 1500 Los Angeles CA 90017-5720 Office Phone: 213-623-9300. Business E-Mail: rscoular@sonnenschein.com.

SCOVANNER, DOUGLAS, retail company executive; BS, Washington and Lee U., 1977; MBA, U. Va., 1979. With Coca-Cola Enterprises and affiliates, Atlanta, 1980-92, v.p., treas., 1989-92; sr. v.p. fin. Fleming Cos., Oklahoma City, 1992-94; CFO, sr. v.p. fin. Target Corp. (formerly Dayton Hudson Corp.), Mpls., 1994—. Office: Target Corporation 1000 Nicollett Mall Minneapolis MN 55403-2467

SCOVIL, ROGER MORRIS, international business consultant; b. Greenville, S.C., Apr. 23, 1929; s. Roger Peniston and Sophia Rose (Herbert) S.; m. Mary Earle Nock; children: Randolph, Frances, Elizabeth. Student, Davidson Coll., 1946-48; BS in Civil Engring., N.C. State U., 1951. Registered profl. engr., Ga., S.C., P.R. Project mgr. McKoy-Helgerson Co., Greenville, 1953-63; v.p., maintenance div. mgr. Daniel Constrn. Co., Greenville, 1963-66; v.p., Caribbean div. mgr. Daniel Internat. Corp., San Juan, P.R., 1966-74, v.p. Europe and Middle East Brussels and Jeddah, Saudi Arabia, 1974-79; v.p. internat. mkgt. Daniel Constrn. Co., Greenville, 1980; pres. Polysius Corp., Atlanta, 1981-88; sr. v.p., dir. Lockwood Greene Systems Corp., Atlanta, 1988-97. Pres. Lockwood Greene Internat., Atlanta, 1991-95, pres., 1995-97; mem. operating bd. Lockwood Greene Engrs., Inc., 1995-97, bd. dirs., chmn. exec. com. World Trade Ctr., Atlanta, 1995-2004; pres. World Trade Ctr. Atlanta, 2004—. Author: Get Ahead: Scovil's 7 Rules for Success in Management. Mem. Atlanta Dist. Export coun., 1996—; bus. adv. bd. So. Ctr. for Internat. Studies, 2000—; bd. dirs. N.C. State Engring. Found., 1998-2001, Ga. tech. cpt. AIESEC, 1996—. Capt. U.S. Army, 1951-53. Mem. Atlanta World trade Ctr. (bd. dirs.), Internat. Club Atlanta, Brazilian Am. C. of C. Ga. (bd. dirs. 1997—, pres. 1997-99, chmn. emeritus, 1999—), Tau Beta Pi, Chi Epsilon, Sigma Phi Epsilon. Episcopalian. Home: 6025 Riverwood Dr NW Atlanta GA 30328-3732

SCOVILLE, JAMES GRIFFIN, economics professor; b. Amarillo, Tex., Mar. 19, 1940; s. Orlin James and Carol Howe (Griffin) S.; m. Judith Ann Nelson, June 11, 1962; 1 child, Nathan James. BA, Oberlin Coll., 1961; MA, Harvard U., 1963, PhD, 1965. Economist ILO, Geneva, 1965-66; instr. econs. Harvard U., Cambridge, Mass., 1964-65, asst. prof., 1966-69; assoc. prof. econs. and labor and indsl. relations U. Ill.-Urbana, 1969-75, prof., 1975-80; prof. indsl. rels. Indsl. Rels. Ctr., U. Minn., Mpls., 1979—, dir., 1979-82, dir. grad. studies, 1990-97. Cons. ILO, World Bank, U.S. Dept. Labor, Orgn. for Econ. Cooperation and Devel., USAID; labor-mgmt. arbitrator. Author: The Job Content of the US Economy, 1940-70, 1969, Perspectives on Poverty and Income Distribution, 1971, Manpower and Occupational Analysis: Concepts and Measurements, 1972, (with A. Sturmthal) The International Labor Movement in Transition, 1973, Status Influences in 3rd World Labor Markets, 1991. Mem. Am. Econ. Assn., Indsl. Rels. Rsch. Assn. (v.p. internat. sect. 1998, pres. 1999), Internat. Indsl. Rels. Assn. Office: U Minn Ind Rels Ctr 3-289 CSOM Minneapolis MN 55455 E-mail: jscoville@csom.umn.edu.

SCOWCROFT, BRENT, retired air force officer, government official; b. Ogden, Utah, Mar. 19, 1925; s. James and Lucile (Ballantyne) S.; m. Marian Horner, Sept. 17, 1951 (dec. 1995); 1 dau., Karen. BS, U.S. Mil. Acad., 1947; MA, Columbia U., 1953, PhD, 1967; postgrad., Georgetown U., 1958. Commd. 2d lt. USAF, 1947, advanced through grades to lt. gen., 1974; asst. prof. dept. social sci. U.S. Mil. Acad., 1953-57; asst. air attache Am. Embassy, Belgrade, Yugoslavia, 1959-61; assoc. prof. dept. polit. sci. U.S. Air Force Acad., Colo., 1962-63, prof., head dept., 1963-64; mem. staff long range planning div. Office Dep. Chief Staff Plans and Ops., Washington, 1964-67; assigned Nat. War Coll., 1967-68; staff asst. Western Hemisphere region Office Asst. Sec. Def. Internat. Security Affairs, Washington, 1968-69; dep. asst. dir. plans for nat. security matters office Dep. Chief Staff Plans and Ops., 1969-70; spl. asst. to dir. Joint Staff, Joint Chiefs of Staff, 1970-71; mil. asst. to Pres., 1972-73; dep. asst. to Pres. for nat. security affairs, 1973-75; asst. to Pres. for nat. security affairs, 1975-77; mem. Pres.'s Gen. Adv. Com. on Arms Control, 1977-80; vice chmn. Kissinger Assocs., Inc., 1982-89; asst. to Pres. Nat.

Security Coun., Washington, 1989-93; pres. Forum for Internat. Policy, Washington, 1993—. Bd. dirs. Nat. Bank Washington, Qualcomm, Inc., Am. Coun. on Germany; chmn. Pres.'s Commn. on Strategic Forces; mem. Pres.'s Commn. on Def. Mgmt., Pres. Spl. Rev. Bd. on Iran/Contra Affair; pres. The Scowcroft Group, 1994—. Bd. dirs. Atlantic Council U.S.; Bd. visitors U.S. Air Force Air U., 1977-79; mem. adv. bd. Georgetown Center for Strategic and Internat. Studies. Decorated D.S.M. with two oak leaf clusters, Legion of Merit with oak leaf cluster, Air Force Commendation medal, D.S.M. Dept. Def., Nat. Security medal; recipient Medal of Freedom, 1991; named Hon. Knight Brit. Empire, 1993. Mem. Council Fgn. Relations (bd. dirs.), UN Assn. U.S. (vice chmn.), Am. Polit. Sci. Assn., Acad. Polit. Sci. Mem. Ch. Jesus Christ of Latter-day Saints. Office: # 500 900 17th St NW Ste 500 Washington DC 20006-2507

SCOZZAFAVA, DEDE, state representative; b. Buffalo, N.Y. m. Ron McDougall; children: Matt, Molly. BS, Boston U.; MBA, Clarkson Grad. Sch. of Mgmt. Trustee Village of Gouverneur, mayor, 1993—98; N.Y. state rep., 1998—. Investment advisor RBC Dain Rauscher Inc., Watertown, NY; pres. St. Lawrence County Mayors Assn., 1994—95, 1996—97. Assembly standing coms. Econ. Devel., Edn. and Social Svcs., 2001—02; apptd. ranking mem. Assembly's Local Govts. Com.; served on Task Force on Edn. Stds., Nursing Shortage Task Force. Recipient Conf. of Mayor's award, N.Y. State. Mem.: Gouverneur Arts Club (assoc.). Office: 93 E Main St Gouverneur NY 13642 Address: LOB 532 Albany NY 12248 E-mail: scozzad@assembly.state.ny.us.

SCRAGG, THOMAS WILLIAM, librarian, historical researcher, solicitor; b. Wirral, Cheshire, Eng., Sept. 19, 1940; s. Joseph and Norah Scragg, m. Isabel Mary Thomas, Apr. 3, 1972; children: Maximian Rhys Joseph, Halcyon Rosemary Louise, Sophia Isabel Hannah, Mortimer Henry Thomas. BA with honours, Sch. Slavonic and E. European Studies, U. London; B.Phil., U. Liverpool; MA, Manchester Poly., Eng.; postgrad., King's Coll., U. London, U. Wales, Aberystwyth; Dipl.Lib., F.L.A., Manchester Libr. Sch. Solicitor Supreme Ct., 1968—; music adviser, hist. rschr., program annotator Chester Festival, 1967, 1986—88, Festival in Gt. Irish Houses, 1970—81, Queen's Festival, U. Belfast, 1971, 1972, Newcastle-upon-Tyne Festival, 1972—75, Portsmouth Festival, 1977—78, Dublin Festival, Royal Dublin Soc., 1979, Alfred Beit Found., 1979—81, Leeds Castle Festival, 1987, Music Assn. Ireland, others. Phonographic cons., cataloguer Sir Compton MacKenzie's Jethou Record Collection, 1973—75; music libr. cons. Granada TV Ltd., 1973—75; libr., archivist Knowsley Libr., 1974—91. Author: festival program material, Claudio Arrau Discography, 1978, 2d edit., 1982; author: (joint) Library Association Standards for Local Studies Provision in Public Libraries, 1989; contbr. articles to profl. jours. Fellow: Libr. Assn. (Charles Nowell Meml. prize 1992), Soc. Antiquaries of Scotland, Royal Soc Arts, Royal Geog. Soc.; mem.: E.S.U., Anglo-Polish Music Circle Gt. Britain (hon. v.p. 1970), Polish Inst. Arts and Scis. Am. (assoc.), Soc. Genealogists, Royal Mus. Assn., Soc. Archivists, Law Soc., Internat. Assn. Religious Freedom. Avocations: travel, history of public concerts, historical discography. Home: The Woodcroft Barnston Wirral CH6 11BU England

SCREPETIS, DENNIS, retired nuclear engineer, consultant; b. Hoboken, N.J., Feb. 12, 1930; s. George and Athanasia (Stasinos) S.; m. Betty Pravasilis, Sept. 17, 1960. Student, Stevens Inst. Tech., Bklyn. Poly. Inst., Cooper Union, Rutgers U. Registered profl. engr., N.J., N.Y. Nuc. engr. Vitro Corp. Am., N.Y.C., 1957-60; project engr. Gen. Cable Corp., Bayonne, N.J., 1960-63; project mgr. AMF Atomics, York, Pa., 1963-65; sr. staff engr. nuc. divsn. Combustion Engring. Corp., Windsor, Conn., 1965-66; corp. engr. Std. Packaging Corp., N.Y.C., 1966-68; v.p. engring. Ea. Schokbeton, Bound Brook, N.J., 1968-74; cons. engr. Ft. Lee, N.J., 1974-99; ret., 1999. Mem. Am. Biog. Inst. Rsch. Assn. (bd. dirs.), Internat. Biog. Ctr. (bd. dirs.). Greek Orthodox. Achievements include patentee in nuclear science. Home and Office: 2200 N Central Rd Fort Lee NJ 07024-7557

SCRIBNER, CHARLES, III, publisher, art historian, writer; b. Washington, May 24, 1951; s. Charles and Joan (Sunderland) S.; m. Ritchie Harrison Markoe, Aug. 4, 1979; children: Charles IV, Christopher Markoe. AB, Princeton U., 1973, MFA, 1975, PhD, 1977. Editor Charles Scribner's Sons, NYC, 1975—, dir. subs. rights, 1978-82, pub. paperback divsn., 1982-83, exec. v.p., 1983-84; v.p. Macmillan Pub. Co., NYC, 1984-94. Instr. dept. art and archaeology Princeton U., 1976-77; mem. adv. coun. Princeton U. Libr., 1981-90, 98-2003; mem. adv. coun. dept. art and archaeology Princeton U., 1983-91, 99-2003; trustee Princeton U. Press, 1984-90, Homeland Found., 1987—; bd. advisors Wethersfield Inst., 1985—; bd. dir. Met. Opera Guild, 1990-92. Author: The Triumph of the Eucharist - Tapestries by Rubens, 1982, Rubens, 1989, Bernini, 1991. Trustee St. Paul's Sch., Concord, N.H., 1994—. Mem. Assn. Princeton U. Press, NYC Racquet and Tennis Club. Roman Catholic. Office: 155 E 72d St #5D New York NY 10021-4371 E-mail: cscribner3@yahoo.com.

SCRIBNER, MARGARET ELLEN, educational consultant, consultant; b. Pana, Ill., Oct. 20, 1948; d. William M. and Beatrice Faye (Springman) Scribner; m. John E. McNeal, Aug. 15, 1977 (div. Oct. 1981); m. Leonard P. Basak, Jr., Mar. 13, 1986; children: L. Phillip Basak III, Cassandra Basak. BS in Social Work, Spalding U., 1970. Coord. Gov.'s Inaugural Com., Springfield, Ill., 1972; sr. cons. Ill. State Bd. Edn., Chgo., 1970—, acting divsn. supr., 2001—. Bd. dirs., corp. sec. Ventura 21, Inc., Roselle, Ill., 1984—87; mem. Ill. Common Performance Mgmt. Project Team, 1996—2001. Mem. Uptown Cmty. Orgn., Chgo., 1978—80; charter mem., organizer Margate-Ainslie Block Club, Chgo., 1979—80. Mem.: Internat. Leadership Tng. Inst. (cert. 1974), Bus. and Profl. women Chgo. (historian 1978—79), Nat. Assn. State Adminstrs. and Suprs. Pvt. Schs. (sec. 1999—2002, pres.-elect 2002—04), Brookwood Country Club (Wood Dale, Ill.), Ill. Athletic Club (Chgo.). Republican. Roman Catholic. Avocations: golf, clarinet, water colors, writing. Office: Ill State Bd of Edn 100 W Randolph St Ste 14-300 Chicago IL 60601-3283

SCRIBNER, PRINCESS ROSE-MARIE, not-for-profit developer; b. Gardiner, Maine; d. Harvey Clinton and Harriet Gertrude Mason; m. Henry Elden Scribner, Jan. 18, 1958; children: Randall, Dawn, Debra, Shawn, Todd. BS, U. Ea. Conn., 1971; degree (hon.), U. Maine, 2002. Pres., founder White Cloud Indians for Devel., Norwich, Conn., 1970—86; adminstr. Indian Health Clinic, Pequot Nation, Ledyard, Conn., 1977—86. Founder, pres. Indian Women's Non-Profit Orgn., Indian Island, Maine. Active mem. Women's Polit. Caucus, Hartford, Conn., 1970, Nat. Women's Polit. Orgn., Washington, 1971. Recipient Volunteering Recognition award, Pres. Reagan. Democrat. Roman Catholic. Avocations: dance, decorating, puzzle-making, gardening, writing. Home: 65 West St II Old Town ME 04468

SCRIBNER, SHERLIE ANN, language educator; b. Mobile, Ala., Aug. 24, 1945; d. Murl and Eva Coggin Scribner; children: Michael Svestka, Lauren Svestska, Christopher Svestka. BA in English and Philosophy, Baylor U., 1966; MEd, U. Va., 1976; MA, EdD in Edn. Adminstrn., Columbia U., 1980; diploma, Nat. Def. U., 1984. Classroom tchr. Virginia Beach (Va.) Pub. Schs., 1966-69, Internat. Sch., Bangkok, 1969-70; reading resource tchr. Fairfax (Va.) County Pub. Schs., 1973-76; sr. evaluator U.S. Gen. Acctg. Office, Washington, 1980-97; CEO Children's Fund, Washington, 1997—; devel. officer Washington Episcopal Sch., Bethesda, Md., 1999-2000; program dir., tchr. profl. studies U. Va. Sch. Continuing and Profl. Studies, 2000-2001; ESL and English tchr. Fairfax (Va.) County Pub. Sch., 2001—. Contbr. articles to profl. jours., reports to U.S. Congress. Trustee Episcopal Ctr. for Children; bd. dirs. Tiny Findings Daycare Ctr., Washington; founder Children's Fund, Children's Resource Network, Ctr. for Children's Studies, Child Survival Fund, Children's Hunger Relief Network, Free the Children Fund, Children's Fund Charieies, Children's Edn. and Enrichment Fund, Children's Spl. Needs Fund, Christian Children's Relief Fund, all Washington. Mem. World Orgn. Presch. Edn. Baptist. Address: Children's Fund PO Box 7936 Mc Lean VA 22106-7936 E-mail: SherlieScribner@aol.com.

SCRICCO, FRANCIS M. electronics company executive; b. May 1949; married; 3 children. BS, Worcester Poly. Inst.; MS in Bus., Columbia U. With The Boston Cons. Group; various mgmt. positions GE Corp.; pres. Whirlpool, Can.; group pres. Fisher Sci. Internat.; exec. v.p., COO Arrow Electronics Inc., Melville, NY, 1997—99, pres., COO, 1999—2001, pres., CEO, 2000—02; also bd. dirs. Office: Arrow Electronics Inc 25 Hub Dr Melville NY 11747-3509

SCRIGGINS, LARRY PALMER, lawyer, director; b. Englewood, N.J., Nov. 27, 1936; s. Thomas Dalby and M. Patricia (Fowler) S.; m. Victoria Jackola, Feb. 17, 1979; children: Elizabeth J., Thomas P. AB, Middlebury Coll., 1958; JD, U. Chgo., 1961. Bar: Md. 1962. Law clk. to chief judge Md. Ct. Appeals, 1962; assoc. Piper & Marbury, L.L.P., Balt., 1962-69, ptnr., 1969-98, vice chmn., 1988-93, mem. exec. com., CFO, 1993-98; sr. counsel Piper Rudnick, LLP, Balt., 1999-2001, ptnr. emeritus, 2001—. Mem. legal adv. com. N.Y. Stock Exch., 1992-96; bd. dirs. USF & G Corp., 1979-98, Center Stage Assocs., 1979-89, Balt. Choral Arts Soc., 1979-96, Balt. Conv. Bur., 1982-95, YMCA of Greater Balt., 1987-94, Fund for Ednl. Excellence, 1990-98, chmn. bd. trustees, 1993-98; bd. dirs. Nat. Aquarium in Balt., bd. govs. 1987-93; bd. dirs. Balt. Symphony Orchestra, 1996-2001. Contbr. articles to profl. jours. Fellow: Am. Bar Found.; mem.: ABA (sect. on bus. law coun. 1972—76, chmn. law and acctg. com. 1985—88, vice chair and editor-in-chief The Bus. Lawyer 1989—90, chair 1991—92, chmn. com. corp. laws 1996—2000, chmn. ad hoc com. on ethics 2000 1999—2002), AICPA (planning com. 1989—92), Fin. Acctg. Stds. Bd., Task Force in Fin. Instruments, Am. Law Inst., Am. Judicature Soc., Md. Bar Assn. (coun. 1976—78, chmn. 1977—78, mem. com. on corp. laws 1981—84). Home: 13663 E Columbine Dr Scottsdale AZ 85259-3752 Office: Piper Rudnick LLP 6225 Smith Ave Baltimore MD 21209-3600 Business E-Mail: larry.scriggins@piperrudnick.com.

SCRIMGEOUR, GARY JAMES, writer, educator; b. Auckland, New Zealand, Jan. 15, 1934; came to U.S., 1957; s. Colin Graham and Caroline Lenna (Hardie) S. BA with honors, U. Sydney, Australia, 1954; MA in English, Wash. U., 1959; PhD, Princeton U., 1968. Asst. personnel officer Dexion Ltd., London, 1956-57; mem. faculty dept. English Fla. U., Gainesville, 1959-61, Rutgers U., New Brunswick, N.J., 1963-64, Ind. U., Bloomington, 1964-69; editor, writer Benjamin Blom, Inc., N.Y.C., 1969-70; chief of social systems div. and head editorial office Sch. of Pub. and Environ. Affairs, Ind. U., 1970-74; dir. Profl. Studies Assocs., Bloomington, 1973—; editor Coll. Engring. U. Nev.-Reno, 1992-94, sr. editor Coll. Bus. Adminstrn., 1994—. Cons. for research in alcoholism, ct. systems, hwy. safety and design of seminars to various govt. agys., schs. and social orgns., 1970—. Author: A Woman of Her Times, 1982, The Garden Inspector, 1993; contbr. numerous manuals on ct. systems and alcohol safety to profl. publs. and articles on lit. criticism to lit. jours. Jane E. Procter fellow Princeton U., 1968. Office: 369 Bret Harte Ave Reno NV 89509 E-mail: gscrim@unr.nevada.edu.

SCRIMSHAW, NEVIN STEWART, physician, nutrition and health educator; b. Jan. 20, 1918; m. Mary Ware Goodrich, 1941; 5 children. BA with honors, Ohio Wesleyan U., 1938; MA in Biology, Harvard U., 1939, PhD in Physiology, 1941, MPH, 1959; MD with honors, U. Rochester, 1945. Intern Gorgas Hosp., 1945-46; Rockefeller postdoctoral fellow U. Rochester, NY, 1946—47, Merck NRC fellow, 1947—49; asst. resident in ob-gyn. Strong Meml. Hosp., Genesee Hosp., NY, 1948—49; dir. Inst. Nutrition C.Am. and Panama, Guatemala, 1949—61, cons. dir., 1961—65, cons., 1965—. Cons. nutrition Pan-Am. San Bur. WHO, 1948—49, regional advisor on nutrition, 1949—53; dir. Clin. Rsch. Ctr. MIT, 1962—66, 1979—83, dir. internat. food and nutrition program, 1976—88, prof. human nutrition, 1961—76, head dept. nutrition and food sci., 1961—79, inst. prof., 1976—87, emeritus, 1988—; vis. prof. Columbia U., N.Y.C., 1976—88, vis. lectr., 1961—66, Harvard U., 1968—85; adj. prof. Tufts U.; mem. govt. adv. com. NIH; chmn. internat. com. NRC; dir. devel. studies divsn. UN U., 1985—86, food nutrition program, 1975—97, sr. advisor, 1998—; mem. adv. com. WHO, Nutrition Found., others. Editor (with others): Amino Acid Fortification of Protein Foods, 1971, Nutrition, National Development and Planning, 1973, The Economics, Marketing and Technology of Fish Protein Concentrate, 1974, Development: Significance and Potential for the Tropics, 1976, Single-Cell Protein: Safety for Animal and Human Feeding, 1979, Nutrition Policy Implementation: Issues and Experience, 1983, Diarrhea and Malnutrition: Interactions, Mechanisms and Interventions, 1983, Chronic Energy Deficiency, 1987, Acceptability of Milk and Milk Products in Populations with Lactose Intolerance, 1988, Nutrition in the Elderly, 1989, Activity, Energy Expenditure and Energy Requirements of Infants and Children, 1990, RAP: Rapid Assessment Procedures: Qualitative Methodologies for Planning and Evaluation of Health Related Programs, 1992, Protein-energy Interactions, 1992, Community-based Longitudinal Nutrition and Health Studies: Classical Examples from Guatemala, Haiti, and Mexico, 1995, The Effects of Improved Nutrition in Early Childhood: The Institute of Nutrition of Central American and Panama Follow-up Study, 1995, The Nutrition and Health Transition of Democratic Costa Rica, 1995, Energy and Protein Requirements, 1996, Causes and Consequences of Intrauterine Growth Retardation, 2000; contbr. articles to profl. jours. Trustee Rockefeller Found., 1971—83, Pan-Am. Health and Edn. Found., 1986—92; pres. Internat. Nutrition Found. for Developing Countries, 1982—. Recipient Osborne and Mendal award, 1960, Internat. award, Inst. Food Technologists, 1969, medal of honor, Fundacion F. Cuenca Villoro, Spain, 1978, Bristol-Myers prize, 1988, Alan Shawn Feinstein award, 1991, World Food prize, 1991, Kellogg award in internat. nutrition, 2002, Lifetime Achievement and Svc. award, UN, 2004. Fellow: APHA (v.p. 1978, award of excellence in promoting and protecting health of people 1974), AAAS, Am. Soc. Clin. Nutrition, Royal Soc. Health, Am. Soc. Nutritional Scis.; mem.: NAS (chair applied biol. sect. 1973—76, 1988—91), others, Internat. Epidemiol. Assn., Internat. Union Nutritional Scis. (pres. 1978—81), Am. Epidemiol. Soc., Am. Physiol. Soc., Mass. Med. Soc., New Eng. Pub. Health Assn., Mass. Pub. Health Assn., Am. Bd. Nutrition, Am. Coll. Preventive Medicine, Am. Coll. Nutrition, Am. Acad. Arts and Scis., Inst. Medicine NAS. Home and Office: Sandwich Mountain Farm 115 Sandwitch Notch Rd Box 330 Campton NH 03223-0330 Fax: 603-726-4614. E-mail: nevin@cyberportal.net.

SCRIMSHAW, SUSAN CROSBY, dean; PhD in Anthropology, Columbia U., 1974. Prof. Sch. Pub. Health UCLA, 1974—94, assoc. dean, 1988—94; dean U. Ill. Sch. Pub. Health, Chgo., 1995—. Recipient Margaret Mead award, 1985. Fellow: AAAS; mem.: Nat. Soc. Med. Anthropology (pres. 1985), Soc. Applied Anthropology, Am. Anthropology Assn., Inst. Medicine NAS. Office: Sch of Pub Health U Ill Chicago 2121 W Taylor St # Mc922 Chicago IL 60612-7260

SCRIPPS, DOUGLAS JERRY, music educator, conductor; b. Grand Rapids, Mich., Aug. 25, 1942; s. Kenneth Witvoet and Marguerite F. (Rottier) Scripps; m. Betty Ann Broersma Porter, July 24, 1963 (div. Aug. 1974); children: Elisabeth Ann Scripps Blue, Theodore Jon; m. Collins Merilee Evelyn, Apr. 5, 1975; children: Daniel Collins, Taylor Douglas, Adam Rottier. Student, Eastman Sch. Music, 1961, 62; BA, Calvin Coll., 1965; student, U. Music and Dramatic Art, Vienna, 1965—66; MM, U. Mich., 1970. Prin. trumpet player Grand Rapids Symphony Orch., 1961—65, assoc. conductor, 1976—85; dir. music Grand Rapids City Coll., 1967—78; conductor Lake St. Clair Symphony, Detroit, 1970—72, Alma (Mich.) Symphony Orch., 1985—2002; music dir. Grand Rapids Ballet, 1979—99; asst. prof. music Ctrl. Mich. U., Mt. Pleasant, 1981—84; prof. music, dept. chair Alma Coll., 1985—2002, prof. emeritus, 2003—. Guest condr. Interlochen Ctr. Arts, Joffrey Balley, Bay View Music Festival, Blue Lake Fine Arts Camp; vis. prof. Grand Valley State U., Calvin Coll., 1977—81; adjudicator various midwest comps., 1968—95; condr. Ctrl. European Youth Symphony Orch., 2004—, Am. Heritage Assn. Recipient Am. Heritage Assn. study abroad lectr., Vienna, 1999. Avocations: reading, travel, sailing. Home: PO Box 476 Northport MI 49670-0476 Office Phone: 231-386-5001. E-mail: scripps@alma.edu.

SCRIPPS, ROBERT P. publishing executive; Trustee Edward W. Scripps Trust, San Diego. Office: Edward W Scripps Trust 625 Broadway Ste 625 San Diego CA 92101-5483

SCRIVEN, JOHN G. retired lawyer, chemical company executive; Bar: Mich. 1993. Sr. staff counsel Dow Europe S.A., 1981-83; gen. counsel Dow Chem. Co., Midland, Mich., 1983-86, v.p., gen. counsel, 1986-2000, v.p., gen. counsel, sec., 1986-2000; ret., 2000. Office: Dow Chem Co 2030 Dow Ctr Midland MI 48674-0001

SCRIVER, CHARLES ROBERT, medical researcher, human geneticist; b. Montreal, Que., Can., Nov. 7, 1930; s. Walter deM. and Jessie (Boyd) S.; m. E.K. Peirce, Sept. 8, 1956; children: Dorothy, Peter, Julie, Paul. BA cum laude, McGill U., Montreal, 1951, MDCM cum laude, 1955; DSc (hon.), U. Man., 1992, U. Glasgow, 1993, U. Montreal, 1993, Utrecht U., 1999, U. B.C., 2002. Intern Royal Victoria Hosp., Montreal, 1955-56; resident Royal Victoria and Montreal Children's Hosps., 1956-57, Children's Med. Ctr., Boston, 1957-58; McLaughlin travelling fellow Univ. Coll., London, 1958-60; chief resident pediat. Montreal Children's Hosp., 1960-61; asst. prof. pediat. McGill U., 1961, prof. biology Faculty of Sci., prof. pediat. Faculty of Medicine, 1969—, Alva prof. human genetics, 1994—2002, prof. emeritus, 2002—. Mem. med. adv. bd. Howard Hughes Med. Inst., 1981-88; dir. Med. Rsch. Coun. Group in Genetics, 1972-94; assoc. dir. Can. Genetic Diseases Network, 1989-98. Co-author: Amino Acid Metabolism and Its Disorders, 1973, Garrod's Inborn Factors in Disease, 1989; sr. online editor Metabolic and Molecular Bases Inherited Disease, 1986—; contbr. more than 550 rsch. publs. in field. Decorated Order of Can. Que., Mont.; named Royal Coll. lectr., 1992, Disting. Scientist, Med. Rsch. Coun., 1995—; named to Can. Med. Hall of Fame, 2001, Can. Sci. Engring. Hall of Fame, 2001; recipient Wood Gold medal, McGill U., 1955, Gairdner Internat. award, Gairdner Found., 1979, Prix Michel-Sarrazin, Club de Rech Clin du Que., 1988, Ross award, Can. Pediatric Soc., 1990, Award of Excellence, Genet Soc. Can., 1992, Prix d'Excellence, Inst. Rsch. Clin. de Montreal, 1993, Prix du Quebec, Wilder Penfield, 1995, Medal of Merit, Can. Med. Assn., 1996, Lifetime Achievement award, March of Dimes Birth Defects Found., 1997, Querci Found. prize, Italy, 2001, Founders award, Can. Coll. Med. Geneticist, 2003; Markle scholar, 1962—67. Fellow: AAAS, Royal Soc. London (Can. Rutherford lectr. 1983), Royal Soc. Can. (McLaughlin medal 1981), Royal Coll. Physicians of Ireland (hon.), Am. Coll. Med. Genetics (hon.); mem.: Am. Acad. Pediat. (Mead Johnson award for rsch. in pediat. 1968), Soc. Francaise de Pediat., Brit. Pediat. Assn. (50th Anniversary lectr. 1978), Assn. Am. Physicians, Am. Soc. Clin. Investigation, Am. Pediat. Soc. (pres. 1994—95), Am. Soc. Human Genetics (dir. 1971—74, pres. 1986—87, William Allan award 1978, Award of Excellence in Human Genetics Edn. 2001), Soc. Pediat. Rsch. (pres. 1975—76), Can. Soc. Clin. Investigation (pres. 1974—75, G. Malcolm Brown Meml. award 1979, Henry Friesen award 2001). Office: McGill Univ-Montreal Childrens Hosp Rsch Inst 2300 Tupper St Montreal QC Canada H3H 1P3 E-mail: charles.scriver@mcgill.ca., charles.scriver@muhc.mcgill.ca.

SCRIVNER, THOMAS WILLIAM, lawyer; b. Madison, Wis., Sept. 10, 1948; s. William H. and Jane (Gehrz) S.; m. Meredith Burke, Aug. 16, 1980; children: Allison, David. AB, Duke U., 1970, MAT, 1972; JD, U. Wis., 1977. Assoc. Michael, Best & Friedrich LLP, Milw., 1978-85, ptnr., 1985—. Mem. ABA, Wis. Bar Assn., Milw. Bar Assn. (labor sect.), Corp. Practice Inst. (pres. 1989-92). Episcopalian. Home: 4626 N Cramer St Milwaukee WI 53211-1203 Office: Michael Best & Friedrich LLP 100 E Wisconsin Ave Ste 3300 Milwaukee WI 53202-4108 Office Phone: 414-225-4565. Business E-Mail: twscrivner@mbf-law.com.

SCROCCA, ANTHONY CHARLES, bank executive; b. Bristol, Pa., Aug. 28, 1966; s. Henry Richard and Marian Jeanette Scrocca; m. Lori Lee Cantell, Sept. 19, 1987; children: Austin James, Gina Lynn, Luke Anthony. AA, Bucks County CC, Newtown, Pa., 1987; student, LaSalle U. Assoc. Bucks County (Pa.) Bank, 1985—87; asst. v.p. First Union Bank, Phila., 1988—99; v.p. Citizens Bank, Horsham, Pa., 1999—2001; gen. mgr. Pa. Auto Credit, Fairless Hills, Pa., 2002—. Author: Rising Son, 1999. Republican. Roman Catholic. Avocations: boating, coin collecting/numismatics. Home: 454 Pheasant Ln Fairless Hills PA 19030 Office: Pa Auto Credit 327 Lincoln Hwy Fairless Hills PA 19030 Office Phone: 800-736-4450. Personal E-mail: ascrocca@aol.com.

SCROGGIE, WAYNE LEE, computer scientist, management consultant; b. July 19, 1949; s. James Heburn and Edith (Harrington) Scroggie. BA, Eastern Wash. State Coll., 1975; MBA, U. Wash., 1977. Indsl. engr. Boeing Comml. Airplane Co., Everett, Wash., 1978; fin. planner Boeing Marine Systems, Seattle, 1978-81; cost and schedules engr. ASW/SOW program Boeing Aerospace Co., Kent, Wash., 1981-84; cost and schedules engr. Boeing Comml. Airplane Co., Renton, Wash., 1984-87; sys. analyst Boeing Computer Svcs., 1987-94; owner N.E. Rim, Seattle, 1994-2001, 2003—; programmer Danzas AEI, Renton, 2001—02. With USAF, 1968—72. Mem.: World Affairs Coun., Assn. MBAs, Asian Mgmt. Bus. Assn., Latin Trade Com., U. Wash. MBA Alumni Assn., Assn. Internat. Students Econs. and Commerce, Asia Soc., Harbor Club, Transp. Club Seattle, China Club Seattle (pres. 1992—94, bd. dirs. 1995—), World Trade Club. Home: 2740 47th Ave SW Seattle WA 98116-2904

SCROGGINS, WESLEY ALLEN, finance educator, researcher; b. Springfield, Mo., May 30, 1965; s. Albert and Diann Scroggins; m. Susan Lynne Scroggins, Mar. 7, 1993; children: Chase Chapman, Chelsie Chapman, Kailee Nicole. BA, S.W. Bapt. U., 1987; MDiv, Midwestern Bapt. Theol. Sem., 1990; MS, S.W. Mo. State U., 1997; PhD, N.Mex State U., 2003. Instr. psychology S.W. Mo. State U., Springfield, 1997—98, asst. prof. of mgmt., 2003—. Cons. State of N.Mex. Third Jud. Dist. Ct., Las Cruces, 2000—00, Cath. Diocese Las Cruces, 2000—00, Deming Pub. Sch. Dist., 1999—99. Co-author: Employee Compensation Systems and HR Strategy: Issues adn Perspectives., In Human Resources Management: Perspectives, Context, Functions and Outcomes. Tchr. Sycamore Bapt. Ch., Springfield, 2001—02. Recipient Best Paper Track award, 2001. Mem.: S.W. Acad. Mgmt. (Outstanding Reviewer award 2001, Doctoral Student award 2002), Soc. Indsl. and Orgnl. Psychology, Acad. Mgmt., Soc. Human Resource Mgmt., Sigma Iota Epsilon. Southern Baptist. Avocation: trout fishing. Office: Southwest Missouri State University 901 S National Springfield MO 65804 Personal E-mail: was072f@smsu.edu. E-mail: was072f@smsu.edu.

SCROGGS, LARRY KENNETH, lawyer, state legislator; b. Beebe, Ark., Oct. 8, 1941; s. Kenneth Chalmers and Mildred Lorene (McDonald) S.; m. Mary Patricia Rushing, Aug. 25, 1967; children: Larry Kenneth Jr., James Kevin, Michael Kyle. BA, Harding U., 1963; JD, Vanderbilt U., 1971. Bar: Tenn. 1971, U.S. Dist. Ct. (we. dist.) Tenn. 1971, U.S. Ct. Appeals (8th cir.) 1982, U.S. Ct. Appeals (6th cir.) 1989, U.S. Supreme Ct. 1981. Assoc. Law Firm of Leo Bearman, Memphis, 1971-72, Holt, Batchelor, Spicer, Memphis, 1972-76, ptnr., 1976-80, Less & Scroggs, Memphis, 1980-92; pvt. practice, Germantown, Tenn., 1992-96; ptnr. Scroggs & Rogers, Collierville, Tenn., 1997—2003, Burch, Porter & Johnson, Memphis, 2003; mem. Tenn. Ho. of Reps., Nashville, 1996—2002. Mcpl. ct. judge City of Germantown, 1980-86; atty. for County Trustee, Shelby County, Memphis, 1990—. Mem. campaign steering com. George Bush for Pres., Memphis, 1987-92; vol. Ed Bryant for Congress campaign, Memphis, 1994, Don Sundquist for Gov. campaign, Memphis, 1994. Lt. U.S. Navy, 1964-67, Vietnam. Mem. ABA, Tenn. Bar Assn., Memphis Bar Assn. (bd. dirs. 1990-91). Republican. Mem. Ch. of Christ. Avocations: photography, boating, tennis. Office: Burch Porter & Johnson 130 N Court Ave Memphis TN 38103

SCRUGGS, CHARLES G. editor; b. McGregor, Tex., Nov. 4, 1923; s. John Fleming and Adeline (Hering) S.; m. Miriam June Wigley, July 5, 1947; children— John Mark, Miriam Jan BS, Tex. A&M U., 1947. Assoc. editor Progressive Farmer, Dallas, 1947-61, editor, 1962—, v.p., 1964—, exec. editor, 1972, editorial dir., 1973—, editor-in-chief, 1982-87; editorial chmn. So. Progress Pubs., 1987-89. Pres. Torado Land and Cattle Co., pres. Tex. Comml. Agr. Council 1953-54; chmn. bd. Sunlean Foods, Inc., 1989—. Author: The Peaceful Atom and the Deadly Fly, 1975, American Agricultural Capitalism Founding gen. chmn. Chancellors' Century Coun., Tex. A&M U. System, 1987-90; Mem. Gov.'s Com. for Agr., 1950, Tex. Animal Health Council, 1955-61; chmn. So. Brucellosis Com., 1956; pres. Tex. Rural Safety Com., 1957-59; chmn. Nat. Brucellosis Com., 1958-59, 71-72; del. World Food Congress, 1963; pub. mem. U.S. del. 17th Biennial Conf. of FAO, UN,

Rome, 1973; chmn. Joint Senate-House Interim Com. Natural Fibers, Tex. Legislature, 1971; mem. coordinating bd. Tex. Coll. and Univ. System, 1965-69; bd. regents Tex. Tech U., 1971-78; founding pres. S.W. Animal Health Research Found. 1961-63, trustee, 1961— . Served to lt. col. U.S. Army; Res., ret. Recipient Christian Svc. Mass Media award, 1995, Abilene Christian U., Southwestern Cattle Raisers award, 1962, Am. Seed Trade Assn. award, 1963, award of honor Am. Agrl. Editors Assn., 1964, Reuben Brigham award Am. Assn. Agrl. Coll. Editors, 1965, Disting. Svc. award Tex. Farm Bur., 1966, Journalistic Achievement award Nat. Plant Food Assn., 1967, Nat. award for agrl. excellence Nat. Agri-Mktg. Assn., 1983, Agrl. Vision award Nat. Forum for Agr., 1994; named Disting. Alumnus Tex. A&M U., 1982. Mem. Am. Agrl. Editors Assn. (pres. 1963), Am. Soc. Mag. Editors, Tex. Assn. Future Farmers Am. (pres. 1940-41), Dallas Agrl. Club (pres. 1951), Nat. Livestock Confedn. Mexico (hon.), The Austin Club, Headliners Club, Alpha Zeta, Sigma Delta Chi

SCRUGGS, EARL EUGENE, entertainer; b. Cleveland County, NC, Jan. 6, 1924; s. George Elam and Georgia Lula (Ruppe) Scruggs; m. Anne Louise Certain, Apr. 18, 1948; children: Gary Eugene, Randy Lynn, Steven Earl. HHD in Folk Music (hon.), Gardner-Webb Coll., 1986. Recorded album MCA Records released 2001 with guest stars Elton John, Dwight Yoakam, Billy Bob Thornton, Gary Scruggs, Travis Tritt, Melissa Etheridge, Sting, Glen Duncan, Randy Scruggs, Steve Martin, Vince Gill, Marty Stuart, Albert Lee, Paul Shaffer, Jerry Douglas, Leon russell, Rosanne Cash, John Fogerty, Don Henley and Johnny Cash. Album titled "Earl Scruggs and Friends". Banjo player, 1945—, rec. artist Columbia Records, 1950—, recorded theme song (TV series) The Beverly Hillbillies, 1962; author: Earl Scruggs and the 5-String Banjo, 1968; banjo player formed Earl Scruggs Revue, 1969—, major performances Carnegie Hall, NYC, Wembley Festival, London, Washington Moratorium for Peace, also rock festivals, coll. concerts, 1969—, appearances (TV series) NET-TV Spl. Earl Scruggs: His Family and Friends, 1971; composer (with others): (movie score) Where The Lilies Bloom, 1973; star (films) Banjo Man, 1975, appearances (TV series) Midnight Spl., NBC-Harper Valley U.S.A. Spl., NBC Country Music Awards Show, Phil Donahue Show, Mike Douglas Show, Austin City Limits, 1977, The Grand Ole Opry's 60th Anniversary Show, 1985, The Nashville Network spl. The Am. Music Shop, 1990, The Grand Ole Opry's 65th Anniversary Show, Country Music Assn. Awards Show, 1991, guest appearance (TV films) Return of the Beverly Hillbillies, 1981, appearances (TV series) Country Music Assn. Hall of Fame 25th Anniversary TV show, 1992, The Legend of The Beverly Hillbillies, CBS-TV, 1993, Folk Sound USA-Revlon Revue, The Tonight Show, Les Crane Show, Mac Davis Special, The Johnny Cash Show, The Hootenanny Show, Frank McGee's Here and Now, Ernie Ford Show, Jimmy Dean Show, The Anatomy of Pop, Kraft's Am. Profile, The Roots of Country, CBS-TV, 1994, Red Hot and Country, TNN-TV, A Night at the Ryman, TNN-TV, 1995, An Evening of Country Grt., TNN-TV, CMA 40th Anniversary Celebration, CBS-TV, 1998, albums Nashville Rock, Dueling Banjos, Kans. State, I Saw the Light, Earl Scruggs Revue, Rockin' Cross the Country, Family Portrait, Top of the World, Anniversary Spl. Vol. I and Vol. II, Live! At Austin City Limits, Earl Scruggs: His Family and Friends Soundtrack, Today and Forever, Bold and New, Am.-Made, World-Played, others, guest appearances (TV series) The Beverly Hillbillies, Earl Scruggs Revue rec. music soundtrack for (films) Where The Lilies Bloom; composer: (instrumental) Foggy Mountain Breakdown (used in movie Bonnie and Clyde) (Grammy award, 1968, Grammyy award, 2001, Broadcast Music, Inc., 1969); appearance (radio program) John Boy & Billy, 2001, BBC Radio Network, London, Eng., 2001; appearance: (TV show) The Tonight Show w. Jay Leno, 2002. Apptd. hon. mem. Lt. Gov.'s Staff State of Tenn., 1987. Nominee 13 Grammy nominations Achievements include development of Scruggs style of banjo playing; inventor Scruggs Tuning Pegs; Honored with a star in Hollywood Walk of Fame, Hollywood, Calif., 2003.

SCRUGGS, ELAINE M. mayor; m. Larry Scruggs; 1 child, Jennifer. Former mgmt. specialist; elected mem. Glendale (Ariz.) City Coun., 1990-93; mayor City of Glendale, 1994—. Past chmn. Maricopa (Ariz.) Assn. Govts., chair youth policy adv., chmn. Regional Pub. Transp. Authority, chmn. Ariz. Mcpl. Water Users Assn., chair Maricopa Assn. Govt. Regional Aviation Systems policy com.; chair Ariz. Mcpl. Tax Code Commn. Dir. Glendale Leadership Program, 1984-89; mem. Ariz. Coalition for Tomorrow, Ariz. Women in Mcpl. Govt.; mem. youth adv. commn., Mayor's Alliance Against Drugs and Gangs. Mem. Glendale C. of C. Office: Office Mayor 5850 W Glendale Ave Glendale AZ 85301-2563

SCRUGGS-LEFTWICH, YVONNE, association executive; BA in Polit. Sci. cum laude, N.C. Ctrl. U.; postgrad., Freie U., Berlin, Deutsche Hoch Schule Politics, Johns Hopkins U.; MA in Pub. Adminstrn., U. Minn.; PhD in City and Regional Planning, U. Pa. Housing rsch. technician City Phila. Evaluation Project; coord. rsch. and planning, exec. dir. The Wharton Ctr.-North Phila. Settlement House; cmty. renewal specialist Phila. Cmty. Renewal Program; assoc. dir. Phila. Coun. for Cmty. Advancement Ford Founds. Gray Areas Project, dep. dir. planning, 1962-65; fed. liaison officer U.S. Dept. HUD, 1965-69; coord. field svcs., human resources ctr. U. Pa. Wharton Sch., 1970-75; chairperson, assoc. prof. grad. dept. city/regional planning Howard U., 1974-77; prof. city and regional planning Howard U. Sch. Arch. and Planning, 1979-81; head U.S. del. to OECD and ECE U.S. Dept. HUD, 1977-79, dep. asst. sec. cmty. planning and devel., exec. dir. Pres. Carter's Urban/Regl. Policy Group, 1977-79; regional dir. DHCR, Buffalo, 1981-82; commr. N.Y. State Divsn. Housing and Cmty. Renewal, 1982-85; dep. mayor City Phila., 1985-87; bd. chair, COO Y.E.L. Corp., Bklyn. & Harlem, 1987-91; dir. Urban Pol. Inst., Nat. Pol. Inst., Exec. Leadership Seminar, Joint Ctr. for Pol. and Econ. Studies, 1991—. Lectr. grad. dept. city and regional planning U. Pa., Phila., 1970-76, vis. lectr. urban affairs program, 1978-80, vis. prof. grad. dept. city and regional planning, 1985-87, vis. prof. Fels Ctr. Govt., 1985, vis. prof. grad. program dynamics of orgn., 1987; sr. cons. Jeffalyn Johnson and Assocs., Falls Church, Va., 1980-81; adj. prof. planning SUNY, Buffalo, 1981-82; vis. prof. polit. power and urban diversity Grad. Sch. Polit. Mgmt., George Washington U., 1990-2000; vis. prof. U.S. Info. Agy., Kenya, Ethiopia, South Africa, Nigeria, Ghana; vis. expert West German Office Fgn. Rels. Bd. dirs. Crime Prevention Assn., 1964-69, Mid City YMCA, 1964-71, Gaudenzia House, 1969-72; pres. Phila. Assn. Intergroup Rels. Ofcls., 1967; trustee SUNY, Buffalo, 1982-86; pres. Geneva B. Scruggs Cmty. Health Ctr., 1982-85; bd. dirs. State N.Y. Mortgage Agy., 1983-85, Housing Fin. Agy. N.Y. State, 1983-85, N.Y. State Mortgage Loan Enforcement Corp., 1983-85, N.Y. State Project Fin. Agy.; co-chair Gov.'s Task Force on the Homeless, 1983-85; chair Gov.'s Housing Policy Task Force, 1983-85; exec. com. Women in Govt., 1984, 85; v.p., trustee Milton S. Eisenhower Found., 1991—; bd. mem. Washington Planning Workshop; v.p. Pa. Housing Fin. Agy., 1983-85, Commonwealth Pa.; commr. Mobile Home Stds. Commn., Commonwealth Pa.; bd. dirs. Phila. Coun. for Cmty. Advancement; bd. dirs., membership com. World Affairs Coun.; others. Fulbright fellow, Berlin; study scholar Johns Hopkins U.; Ford Found. grantee, 1979-81. Mem. ASPA, Am. Planning Assn., Nat. Assn. Planners (bd. mem., Diana Donald award), Nat. Coun. Negro Women, Nat. Polit. Congress Black Women, Greater Washington Urban League, Alpha Kappa Alpha (Alpha Chi chpt.), Pi Gamma Nu. Office: Black Leadership Forum Inc Po Box 34506 Washington DC 20043-4506

SCUDDAY, ROY GEORGE, lawyer; b. Odessa, Tex., Sept. 29, 1946; s. Roy Sheppard and Letitia Roselyn (Keith) S.; children— Roy Keith, John Andrew; m. Linda R. Reed, Jan. 16, 1999. BA in History, Rice U., 1968; JD, U. Tex., 1971; MA in History, S.W. Tex. U., 2001. Bar: Tex. 1971, U.S. Dist. Ct. (so. dist.) Tex. 1979, U.S. Dist. Ct. (we. dist.) Tex. 1980, U.S. Ct. Appeals (5th cir.) 1980. Hearing examiner Tex. Water Quality Bd., Austin, 1971-73; staff atty. Gulf Coast Waste Disposal Authority, Houston, 1973-79; ptnr. Fielder & Scudday, Lockhart, Tex., 1979—88; hearings atty., comptroller of pub. accounts, 1988-96; adminstrv. law judge, comptr., 1996—. Home: 502 W Prairie Lea St Lockhart TX 78644-2623

SCUDDER, CHARLES SEELYE KELLGREN, lawyer; b. London, Feb. 20, 1947; arrived in U.S., 1964; s. Evarts Seelye and Henrica Antonina (Kellgren) Scudder; m. Jannette Harris Ericson, June 20, 1970; children: John Whitney, Jocelyn Seelye, Ansley Harris. BA, Yale U., 1968; BA in Law with 2d class honors, Oxford (Eng.) U., 1973, MA (hon.), 1980; JD with honors, U. Conn., 1975. Bar: NY 76, U.S. Dist. Ct. NY 76. Assoc. Winthrop Stimson Putnam & Roberts, N.Y.C., 1975—81; sr. counsel Conoco Inc., E.I. DuPont de Nemours & Co., Wilmington, Del., 1981—87; v.p., assoc. gen. counsel Unisys Corp., Blue Bell, Pa., 1987—91; sr. v.p., gen. counsel Carnadmetalbox, Inc., Cin., 1995—96; ptnr. Obermayer Rebmann Maxwell & Hippel, LLP, Phila., 1991—94, 1996—2001; asst. gen. counsel, corp. sec. Akzo Nobel Inc., Dobbs Ferry, NY, 2001—. Editor: Conn. Law Rev., 1974. Mem. George W. Bush Campaign Com., 1997—. With U.S. Army, 1968—71. Mem.: ABA (subcom. on multinat. corps.), Am. Corp. Counsel Assn., NY State Bar Assn. Republican. Office: 7 Livinstone Ave Dobbs Ferry NY 10522

SCUDDER, RICHARD B. newspaper executive; b. Newark, May 13, 1913; s. Edward W. and Katherine (Hollifield) S.; m. Elizabeth A. Shibley, June 24, 944; children: Elizabeth H. (Mrs. Philip Difani), Charles A., Carolyn (Mrs. Peter M. Miller), Jean (Mrs. Joseph Fulmer). AB, Princeton U., 1935; LHD (hon.), Mon Coll. Reporter Newark News, 1935-37, v.p., 1941-51, pub., 1951-72; reporter Boston Herald, 1937-38; chmn. MediaNews Group, Gloucester County Times, Inc., Garden State Newspapers, Inc., Garden State Paper Co., Denver Newspapers, Inc. Trustee Riverview Hosp., N.J. Conservation Found., Monmouth County Conservation Found.; former trustee Rutgers U.; adv. com. Princeton (N.J.) Environ. Inst. Served from pvt. to maj. AUS, 1941-45. Decorated bronze star; recipient TAPPI award, 1971; Nat. Recycling award Nat. Assn. Secondary Materials Industries, 1972; Nat. Resource Recovery Man of Year award, 1978; Papermaker of Yr. award Paper Trade Jour., 1978; named to Paper Industry Hall of Fame, 1995. Mem. N.J. Audubon Soc., Rumson Country Club, Seabright Beach Club, Seabright Lawn Tennis Club, Mill Reef Club, Adirondack League Club. Office: Media News Group 1560 Broadway Ste 2100 Denver CO 80202-6000 Address: 309 S Broad St Woodbury NJ 08096-2406

SCUDDER, THAYER, anthropologist, educator; b. New Haven, Aug. 4, 1930; s. Townsend III and Virginia (Boody) S.; m. Mary Eliza Drinker, Aug. 26, 1950; children: Mary Eliza, Alice Thayer. Grad., Phillips Exeter Acad., 1948; AB, Harvard U., 1952, PhD, 1960; postgrad., Yale U., 1953-54, London Sch. Econs., 1960-61. Rsch. officer Rhodes-Livingstone Inst., No. Rhodesia, 1956-57, sr. rsch. officer, 1962-63; asst. prof. Am. U., Cairo, 1961-62; rsch. fellow Ctr. Middle East Studies, Harvard U., 1963-64; asst. prof. Calif. Inst. Tech., Pasadena, 1964-66, assoc. prof., 1966-69, prof. anthropology, 1969-2000, prof. emeritus, 2000—; dir. Inst. for Devel. Anthropology, Binghamton, NY, 1976—2002; commr. World Commn. on Dams, 1998-2000. Cons. UN Devel. Program, FAO, IBRD, WHO, Ford Found., Navajo Tribal Coun., AID, World Conservation Union, Lesotho Highlands Devel. Authority, South China Electric Power Joint Venture Corp., U.S. Nat. Rsch. Coun., Que.-Hydro, Environ. Def. Fund, Ministry of Industry and Handicrafts, Lao People's Dem. Republic. Author: The Ecology of the Gwembe Tonga, 1962; co-author: Long-Term Field Research in Social Anthropology, 1979, Secondary Education and the Formation of an Elite: The Impact of Education on Gwembe District, Zambia, 1980, No Place to Go: The Impacts of Forced Relocation on Navajos, 1982, For Prayer and Profit: The Ritual, Economic and Social Importance of Beer in Gwembe District, Zambia, 1950-1982, 1988, The IUCN Review of the So. Okavango Integrated Water Development Project, 1993. John Simon Guggenheim Meml. fellow, 1975; recipient (1st) Lucy Mair medal for applied anthropology Royal Anthropol. Inst., 1998. Mem. Am. Anthrop. Assn. (1st recipient Solon T. Kimball award for pub. and applied anthropology 1984, Edward J. Lehman award 1991), Soc. Applied Anthropology (Bronislaw Malinowski award 1999). Office: Calif Inst Tech # 228 77 Pasadena CA 91125-0001 Office Phone: 626-395-4207. Business E-Mail: tzs@hss.caltech.edu.

SCULCO, THOMAS PETER, surgeon; b. NYC, Feb. 20, 1944; s. Alfred Francis and Mary Jacqueline Sculco; m. Cynthia Davis, June 4, 1966; children: Sarah Jane, Peter. BA in Classics, Brown U., 1965; MD, Coll. of Physicians and Surgeons Columbia U., 1969. Intern in gen. surgery Roosevelt Hosp., NYC, 1969-70, resident in orthopedic surgery, 1970-71; orthop. fellowship London Hosp., 1947—75; asst. attending orthopedic surgery Meml. Hosp., NYC, 1977-83; resident in orthopedic surgery Hosp. for Spl. Surgery, 1971-74, asst. attending orthopedic surgery, 1977-83, assoc. attending orthopedic surgery, 1983-91, attending surgeon in orthopedics, 1991—, Korein-Wilson prof. orthopedic surgery; asst. attending orthopedic surgery NY Hosp., 1977-83, attending surgeon in orthopedics, 1991—; cons. orthopedic surgeon Mary Manning Walsh Nursing Home, 1978—, Meml. Hosp., 1983—, Bronx Vets. Adminstrn. Hosp., 1987—; from asst. to assoc. prof. clin. surgery Cornell U., 1977-91; dept. chmn., prof. clin. surgery in orthopedics Weill Med. Coll., Cornell U., 1991—. Chief surg. arthritis svc. Hosp. for Spl. Surgery, 1993-2003, dir. orthopedic surgery, 1993-2003, surgeon-in-chief, 2003—; sr. scientist Hosp. for Spl. Surgery, 1996—. Mem. editl. bd. Surg. Blood Mgmt. Forum, 1997. Trustee NY chpt. Arthritis Found., 1997—; mem. Carnegie Hill Assn., St. Bernard's Sch.; bd. dirs. Westerley (RI) Cmty. Chorus, 190-96; sponsor Westerley Pub. Libr., 1996; patron Met. Opera, Carnegie Hall. MC maj. USAF, 1975—77. Recipient Clint Compere award Twentieth Century Orthopedic Assn., 1997, Lifetime Achievement award Arthritis Found., 1999,; recipient numerous grants; named Best Doctors in NY, NY Mag., 2003 Mem. AMA, NY County Med. Soc., Am. Acad. Orthopedic Surgeons (com. on data svcs. chmn. 1981-85, coun. musculoskeletal specialty socs. 1986-90, coord. com. on health policy 1986-89, task force on data chmn. 1987, com. on clin. policies 1991—, patent edn. com. 1999—, liaison to bd. trustees Arthritis Found. 1999—, bd. dirs. 1999-2001), NY Acad. Medicine, NY State Orthopedic Soc., Eastern Orthopedic Soc., Am. Orthopedic Soc., Austrian Orthop. Soc. (hon.), Interurban Orthopedic Assn., Am. Rheumatism Assn., Orthopedic Rsch. and Edn. Found., Knee Soc. (founding mem. 1983, exec. com. 1983-84, program chmn. 1986, membership com. 1986-93, chmn. 1992-93, edn. com. 1990-94, chmn. 1993-94), Assn. VA Orthopedic Surgeons (founder 1986, sec.-treas. 1986-88), Assn. for Arthritis Hip and Knee Surgery, Acad. Orthopedic Soc., Physicians Sci. Soc., Med. Strollers, Internat. Soc. Tech. in Arthroplasty, Am. Austrian Found. (bd. dirs. 2000—), Hip Soc. (membership com. 2000—, Otto Aufranc Rsch. award 1991, Charnley Rsch. award 1995), Australian Orthop. Assn. (hon.). Office: The Hosp for Spl Surgery 535 E 70th St New York NY 10021 Address: Belaire Bldg 525 East 71st St 2nd Fl between York Ave and East River New York NY 10021 Office Phone: 212-606-1475. Office Fax: 212-734-9572. Business E-Mail: sculcot@hss.edu.

SCULLEY, PATRICK DAVID, retired army officer, science honor society director; b. Jamestown, N.Y., Sept. 12, 1947; s. Claude Francis and Hildegarde Ruth (Anderson) S.; m. Peggy Ann Carroll, Aug. 26, 1967; children: Patricia, Paul, Perry, Peter. BA, Washington and Jefferson Coll., 1969; DDS, SUNY, Buffalo, 1973; MA in Health Svcs. Mgmt., Webster U., 1994. Diplomate Fed. Svcs. Bd. Gen. Dentistry, Am. Bd. Oral Medicine, Am. Bd. Gen. Dentistry, Am. Coll. Health Care Execs. Commd. U.S. Army, advanced through grades to maj. gen., 1999; gen. practice resident Kimbrough Army Hosp., Ft. Meade, Md., 1973-74; gen. dentist U.S. Army MEDDAC, White Sands Missile Range, N.Mex., 1974-76; gen. dentistry resident U.S.Army DENTAC, Ft. Knox, Ky., 1977-79, clinic chief Ft. Riley, Kans., 1979-81; comdr. 576th Med. Detachment, Bad Kreuznach, West Germany, 1982-85; staff officer U.S. Army Health Svcs. Command, Ft. Sam Houston, Tex., 1985-86, asst. inspector gen., 1986-88; dental cons. Dept. Army Surgeon Gen.'s Office, Washington, 1988-90; student U.S. Army War Coll., Carlisle Barracks, Pa., 1990-91; comdr. U.S. Army Dental Activity, Ft. Bragg, N.C., 1991-92; dir. dental svcs. Health Svcs. Command U.S. Army, 1992-93, comdr. Dental Command, 1993-95, asst. surgeon gen. pers., 1996, commdg. gen. U.S. Army Ctr. Health Promotion and Preventive Medicine, 1996-99, acting dep. surgeon gen., 1998-99, dep. surg. gen./chief Army Dental Corps, chief of staff U.S. Army Med. Command, 1999—2002, ret., 2002; exec. dir. Sigma Xi, 2002—. Instr. oral medicine gen. practice residency, Ft. Riley, 1980-81; mem. bd. examiners Fed. Svcs. Bd. Gen. Dentistry, Washington, 1986-90; mem. bd. examiners Am. Bd. of Gen. Dentistry, 1991-95 Asst. high sch. football coach Bad Kreuznach Am. High Sch., 1982-83; basketball coach Vienna (Va.) Youth Inc., 1988-89, Cath. Youth Orgn., San Antonio, 1985-86; softball coach Girls Recreation Softball League, Manhattan, Kans., 1981. Fellow: Am. Coll. Dentists; mem.: ADA (alt. del. Ho. Dels. 1999—2000), Pierre Fouchard Acad., Assn. Mil. Surgeons U.S. (Fed. Healthcare Adminstr. of Yr. 2001), Am. Bd. Gen. Dentistry, Acad. Gen. Dentistry (chmn. self-assessment com. 1988—91, examination coun. 1988—92, pres. Army chpt. 1988—91, chmn. reference com. on adminstrn. comm. and constrn. bylaws 1990, ho. of dels. 1988—91, long range planning coun. 1997—98, chmn. long range planning coun. 1998—99, chmn. strategic advancement com. 1999—2002, Disting. Svc. award 1999), Am. Coll. Health Care Execs., Sigma Xi, Omicron Kappa Upsilon. Republican. Roman Catholic. Avocation: coaching athletics. Office: Sigma Xi 3106 E NC Hwy 54 Research Triangle Park NC 27709

SCULLIN, FREDERICK JAMES, JR., judge; b. Syracuse, N.Y., Nov. 5, 1939; s. Frederick James and Cleora M. (Fellows) S.; m. Veronica Terek, Aug. 31, 1984; children: Mary Margaret, Kathleen Susan, Kellie Anne, Rebecca Rose; 1 stepchild, Angel Jenette Godleski. BS in Econs., Niagara U., 1961; LLB, Syracuse U., 1964. Bar: N.Y. 1964, Fla. 1976, U.S. Dist. Ct. (no. dist.) N.Y. 1967, U.S. Supreme Ct. 1971. Assoc. Germain & Germain, Syracuse, 1967-68; asst. dist. atty. Onondaga County, Syracuse, 1968-71; asst. atty. gen. N.Y. State Organized Crime Task Force, 1971-78, dir. regional office, 1974-78; chief prosecutor, dir. Gov.'s Coun. on Organized Crime State of Fla., Tallahassee, 1978—; sole practice Syracuse, 1979-82; U.S. atty. for No. Dist. N.Y., 1982-92; judge U.S. Dist. Ct. (no. dist.) N.Y., 1992—2000, chief judge, 2000—. With U.S. Army, 1964-67, Vietnam; col. USAR. Decorated Air medal, Bronze Star; Cross of Gallantry (Vietnam); recipient Meritorious Svc. Cross, Vietnam Svc. medal, Vietnam Campaign medal, 5 stars; Nat. Def. medal, N.Y. State Dist. Svc. medal, various others. Mem. Am. Judicature Soc., Fla. Bar Assn., Fed. Bar Assn., Fed. Bar Coun., Onon City Bar Assn., Jud. Conf. U.S. Office: US Dist Ct US Courthouse 100 S Clinton St Syracuse NY 13261-6100 E-mail: fscullin@nynd.uscourts.gov.

SCULLION, ANNETTE MURPHY, lawyer, educator; b. Chgo., Apr. 6, 1926; d. Edmund Patrick and Anna (Nugent) Murphy; 1 child, Kevin. BEd, Chgo. Tchrs. Coll., 1960; JD, DePaul U., 1964, MEd, 1966, Loyola U., Chgo., 1970; EdD, No. Ill. U., 1974. Bar: Ill. 1964, U.S. Dist. Ct. (no. dist.) Ill. 1965, U.S. Ct. Appeals (D.C. cir.) 1978. Lectr. Chgo. C.C., 1964-68; pvt. practice Chgo., 1964—; from asst. prof. bus. edn. to prof. Chgo. State U., 1966-98. Founder, adviser Bus. Edn. Students Assn., Chgo. State U., 1976—; sch. law workshop coord. Ill. Divsn. Vocat. and Tech. Edn., 1981, coord. edn. workshops, 1990—. Mem. ABA, Nat. Bus. Edn. Assn., Womens Bar Assn. Ill., Am. Tchr. Edn., Beta Gamma Sigma. Home: 386 Muskegon Ave Calumet City IL 60409-2347

SCULLION, ROSEMARIE, literature educator; Co-editor: Celine and the Politics of Difference, 1995, Studies in Twentieth Century Literature, South Central Rev. Substance; contbr. articles to profl. jours. Mem.: Modern Lang. Assn. Am. (exec. coun. 2000—). Office: Univ Iowa 716 Jefferson Bldg 467 Phillips Hall Iowa City IA 52242 E-mail: rosemarie-scullion@uiowa.edu.

SCULLION, TONY, pharmaceutical executive; BSc in physiology, U. London, England; MSc in pharm., U. London. With Hoechst Roussel; sr. mktg., strategic oper. Pfizer Inc.; v.p., head global bus. devel. Glaxo Wellcome plc; dir., CEO Memory Pharm., Montvale, NJ, 2001—. Bd. dirs. Dynogen Pharm., Inc. Office: Memory Pharm 100 Philips Pkwy Montvale NJ 07645

SCULLY, BONNIE DIANE, financial planner; b. Anchorage, June 11, 1948; d. Oakley Walter and Patricia Alberta (Campbell) Baron; m. J. Robert Scully, Aug. 28, 1971; children: Amanda Rose, John Robert Jr. BA in English, Spring Hill Coll., 1970; CFP, Coll. for Fin Planning, Denver, CO, 1986. CFP. Flight attendant Delta Airlines, Atlanta, 1970; bank teller Ctrl. Nat. Bank, Richmond, Va., 1971; educator St. Elizabeth Sch., Richmond, Va., 1972-74; dept. chmn. airline and travel career program Nat. Coll. Bus., Rapid City, S.D., 1976-77; tax preparer H&R Block, Iowa City, 1978-80; bus. mgr. Dr. J. Robert Scully, Asheville, N.C., 1980-83; fin. planner Parsec Fin. Mgmt., Asheville, N.C., 1983-88; fin. counselor Cath. Social Svcs., Asheville, N.C., 1995—. Author: The Scully Files - Organizing Your Finances, 1999, The Scully Files - A Young Couple's Blueprint for Managing Money, 2000. Mem. Leadership Asheville, 1983; bd. dirs. Jr. Achievement, Asheville, 1984-86, Children's Home Soc., Asheville, 1987-89; bd. dirs., allocation com. United Way, Asheville, 1986-88; treas., bd. dirs. St. Joan of ARC Parish Coun., 1986-88; pres. PTA, Asheville Cath. Sch., 1996-97; chmn. spl. event com. St. Joseph Hosp., 1996-97; bd. dirs. Belechere Entertainment Com., bd. dirs. Jesuit House of Prayer, 1995-98; vol. ABCCM (Asheville Buncombe Community Christian Ministry), 1995-98. Mem. ADA, (regional treas. 1997-98), Buncombe County Dental Aux. (treas. 1995-98). Roman Catholic. Avocations: writing, yoga, travel, reading, sewing. Home and Office: 450 N Griffing Blvd Asheville NC 28804-2814

SCULLY, JOHN CARROLL, life insurance marketing research company executive; b. Springfield, Mass., Mar. 16, 1932; s. James and Frances (Carroll) S.; m. Barbara A. Fougere, Sept. 7, 1953; children: Kathleen, Margaret, John, James, Patricia, Mary Ellen, Susan. BA, Holy Cross Coll., 1953; C.L.U., Boston U., 1963; postgrad., Dartmouth Inst., 1977. With John Hancock Mut. Life Ins. Co., 1953-92, gen. agent, 1966-75, sr. v.p. agency dept. Boston, 1975-80, pres. retail sector, 1980-92; pres. emeritus Life. Ins. Mktg. Rsch. Assoc., Windsor, Conn., 1992-97. Bd. dirs. Greater Boston YMCA, 1975-91; chmn. Mass. campaign Holocaust Meml. Mus., 1985—; div. chmn. United Way, 1985—; bd. dirs. Cath. Charities, 1986—; trustee Springfield Coll., 1986, Suffolk U., 1986, Am. United Life Ins. Co. With U.S. Army, 1954-56. Mem. Am. Coll. Life Underwriters, Nat. Assn. Life Underwriters (v.p. Ind. 1973-75), Life Ins. Mktg. and Rsch. Assn. (past chmn.), Gen. Agts. and Mgrs. Assn. (past pres. Indpls. Nat. Mgmt. award 1973-75), Life Underwriter Tng. Coun. (past chmn.), Greater Boston C. of C. (bd. dirs. 1985—), Wellesley Club, Executives Club (past pres.), Algonquin Club (bd. dirs.), KC. Roman Catholic. Home: Unit 414 4800 N AIA Vero Beach FL 32963 Office: Limra Internat PO Box 208 Hartford CT 06141-0208 Personal E-mail: jscully@limra.com.

SCULLY, JOHN EDWARD, JR., banker; b. Chgo., Jan. 18, 1943; s. John Edward and Ann Berenice (Allenbrand) S.; m. Mary Julia Purvin, June 11, 1966; children: Melissa, Julie, John Edward III. BA, U. Notre Dame, 1964; MA, DePaul U., 1966. Supr., No. Trust Co., Chgo., 1968-69, with personnel dept., 1969-74, personnel officer, 1974-77, bond investment officer, 1977-80; asst. v.p. First Nat. Bank of Chgo., 1980-82, v.p., 1982-87; first v.p. Exch. Nat. Bank, 1987-90; sr. v.p. ABN AMRO, 1990—; mem. mgmt. com. LaSalle Bank, Chgo., 1991-2002. Bd. dirs. Chgo. Heart Assn., 1987-98; trustee Village of Riverside, 2001—; vice chair Ill. Employer Support of Guard and Res. Maj. gen., 1964-96. Mem. Soc. for Human Resource Management, Res. Officers Assn., Mil. Order World Wars, Assn. U.S. Army, Am. Legion, VFW, USO of Ill., Riverside Swim Club, Union League Chgo. (dir. 1993-96, 2d v.p., pres. 1999-2000). Roman Catholic. Home: 258 Lawton Rd Riverside IL 60546-2337 Office: LaSalle Bank Corp Chicago IL 60603

SCULLY, JOHN THOMAS, obstetrician, gynecologist, educator; b. NYC, Mar. 11, 1931; s. John Thomas and Mildred Frances (Dunstrop) S.; m. Kimberly Ann Stamberger; children: John, Helen Mary, Thomas, Nora, James, Sara, Megan, Devin. BS, Georgetown U., 1952; MD, U. Mex., 1959. Diplomate Am. Bd. Ob-Gyn. Intern, Nassau Hosp., 1959-60, resident, 1960-63; practice medicine specializing in ob-gyn, 1963—; sr. attending chmn. dept. ob-gyn St. Peter's Univ. Hosp., 1971—, chmn. dept. ob-gyn., 1971—. Fellow ACS, Am. Coll. Ob-Gyn; mem. NJ Med. Soc., Middlesex County Med. Soc., NJ Ob-Gyn Soc., NJ Right to Life (charter) Republican. Roman Catholic. Office: 23 Duke St New Brunswick NJ 08901-1738

SCULLY, MARLAN ORVIL, physics educator; b. Casper, Wyo., Aug. 3, 1939; s. Orvil O. and Thelma G. (Thoms) Scully; m. Judith Bailey, Aug. 16, 1958; children: James, Robert, Steven. AS, Casper Coll., 1959; BS, U. Wyo., 1961; MS, Yale U., 1963, PhD, 1966. Instr. Yale U., New Haven, 1967-69; asst. prof. MIT, Cambridge, 1969-71, assoc. prof., 1971-72; prof. U. Ariz., Tucson, 1972-80; disting. prof. physics U. N.Mex., Albuquerque, 1980—92; prof. physics Tex. A&M U., 1992—96; dir. Ctr. Theoretical Physics, Tex. A&M U., 1995—; Burgess disting. prof. Tex. A&M U., 1996—, prof. elec. engring., 1999—; disting. rsch. chair TEES, 2000—; dir. Inst. Quantum

Studies, Tex. A&M U., 2001—. Dir., co-founder Radtech, 1984; mem. Joint coun. on Quantum Electronics, Internat. Commn. on Optics; mem. program com. VIIth and VIIIth Internat. Conf. on Quantum Electronics (co-chmn. program com.); panel mem. Internat. Conf. on Hot Electrons in Semiconductors, North Tex. State U.; co-dir. VIIth Course of NATO Internat. Sch. Quantum Electronics; mem. program com. for OSA sponsored topical meeting on Picosecons Phenomena, Hilton Head, S.C., 1978; invited lectr. U.S.-Japan Coop. Seminar on Laser Spectroscopy, Hakone, Japan, 1977; mem. NRC panel on electron, atomic and molecular physics; advisor to ARO Nat. Acad. Panel, Los Alamos Physics Div. Author: (with others) Laser Physics, 1974; contbr. articles to profl. jours. Recipient Elliott Cresson medal The Franklin Inst., 1990; John S. Guggenheim fellow, 1970, Alfred P. Sloan fellow, 1972. Fellow AAAS, Optical Soc. Am. (dir. at large 1978-80, publs. com. 1972, Ives medal com. 1976, chmn. Wood prize com. 1978, Adolph E. Lomb medal 1970; mem. Max Planck Soc, Nat. Acad. Scis., Academia Europa. Avocations: cattle ranching, inventing.

SCULLY, MARTHA SEEBACH, speech and language pathologist; b. S.I., Nov. 1, 1951; d. Henry F. and Rose Anne (Callahan) Seebach; m. Roger Tehan Scully, Dec. 29, 1979, 1 child, Roger Tehan. BA, Trinity Coll., 1972; MS, George Washington U., 1974; postgrad., Syracuse (N.Y.) U., 1976-79. Lic. speech-lang. pathologist, Md. Clin. supr. Syracuse U., 1976-79; speech-lang. pathologist Fairfax (Va.) County Pub. Schs., 1979—. Bd. dirs. Trinity Coll., Washington, Nat. Children's Choir, 1987-91; trustee Davis Meml. Goodwill Industries, 1994-96, bd. dirs. Goodwill Guild, 1990—, chair ball; docent Folger Shakespearean Libr.; chmn. Nat. Challenge Com. of Disabled, 1985; mem. Ear Ball, 1988, 89; mem. Internat. Children's Festival, 1990, 91; co chmn. Jr. League of Washington Capital Collection, 1990; chmn. Salvation Army Garden Party, 1992, Washington Embassy Tour, 1993; mem. bd. edn. Holy Cross Sch., Garrett Park, Md., 2001-. Recipient First Order Affiliation Order of Franciscans mirror, 1985; named Outstanding Woman in Am., 1987, 88. Mem. Am. Biog. Inst., Am. Speech-Lang.-Hearing Assn., Coun. for Exceptional Children, Montgomery County Assn. for Hearing Impaired Children, Benevolent and Protective Order Elks (mem. Washinton-Rockville lodge, lecturing knight 1999, esteemed loyal knight 2000). Home: 10923 Wickshire Way Rockville MD 20852-3220

SCULLY, ROGER TEHAN, II, lawyer; b. Washington, Jan. 10, 1948; s. James Henry and Marietta (Maguire) S.; m. Martha Anne Seebach, Dec. 29, 1979. BS, U. Md., 1977; JD, Cath. U., 1980. Bar: Md. 1980, D.C. 1981, U.S. Tax Ct. 1982, U.S. Supreme Ct. 1988. V.p. Bogley Related Cos., Rockville, Md., 1971-75; law clk. to presiding justice Superior Ct. of D.C., Washington, 1979-81; assoc. Lerch, Early & Roseman, Bethesda, Md., 1981-82; gen. counsel Laszlo N. Tauber, M.D. & Assocs., Bethesda, 1982-94, Jefferson Meml. Hosp., Alexandria, Va., 1982-94; spl. counsel Venable, Baetjer, Howard & Civiletti, Washington, 1991-96. Cons. in real estate Order of Friar Minor, N.Y.C., 1977—; lectr. Mortgage Bankers Assn., Washington, 1984—; bd. dirs. Nozzoli Constrn. Co., Washington; exec. com., spl. counsel to bd. dirs., bd. dirs. Chromachron Technology Corp., Toronto; bd. dirs. MusicWorks, N.Y.C.; vice chair Sayett Tech., Inc., Rochester, N.Y.; vice chair, bd. dirs., exec. com. MediaShow, Inc., Rochester. Author: (with Quarles & Howard) Summary Adjudication Dispositive Motions and Summary Trials, 1991. Mem. pres.'s coun. St. Bonaventure U., Olean, N.Y., 1995—, chmn. pres.'s coun., 1986-96; trustee Belmont Abbey Coll., Charlotte, N.C., 1993-95; bd. trustees Edmund Burke Sch., Washington, 1984-2001, trustees emeritus, 2001-; bd. dirs. Nat. Children's Choir, Washington, 1980-94. Recipient First Order Affiliation Order of Friars Minor, 1985; named one of Outstanding Young Men in Am., 1982. Fellow D.C. Bar Assn.; mem. ABA, ATLA, FBA, Md. Bar Assn. (chmn. corp. counsel sect.), Am. Judicature Soc., Assn. Governing Bd. of Univs. and Colls., Am. Inns of Ct., Irish Legal Soc., Selden Soc., U.S. Jud. Conf. of 4th Cir. (permanent mem.), U.S. Jud. Conf. Fed. Cir. (del.), Jud. Conf. of D.C. (del.). Office: 4 Neptune Ave Madison CT 06443-3240 E-mail: rts2esq@yahoo.com.

SCULLY, STEPHEN J. plastic surgeon; b. Lawrence, Mass., Jan. 29, 1937; s. Joseph A. and Frances M. (Hart) S.; m. Diane Loretta Lizotte, Apr. 22, 1967; children: Stephen, Christopher, Caroline, Jacqueline. AB summa cum laude, Merrimack Coll., 1958; MD cum laude, Georgetown U., 1962. Surg. resident Tufts New Eng. Med. Ctr., Boston, 1962-67; plastic surg. resident NYU, N.Y.C., 1969-72. Trustee Holy Family Hosp., Methuen, Mass., 1993, Merrimack Coll., North Andover, Mass., 1993. Lt. comdr. USNR, 1967-69. Fellow ACS; mem. Am. Soc. Plastic Surgeons, Am. Soc. Aesthetic Plastic Surgery. Roman Catholic. Avocations: photography, skiing. Office: Plastic Cosmetic Reconstr Surgery Inc 451 Andover St North Andover MA 01845-5044

SCULLY, THOMAS A. lawyer, former federal agency administrator; Bachelor's Degree, U. Va.; JD, Cath. U. Staff asst. Fed. Election Commn., 1979—81, U.S. Senator Slade Gorton, 1981—85; atty. Akin, Gump, Strauss, Hauer & Feld, LLP, 1986—88; comm. staff Bush-Quayle Campaign, 1988, dep. dir. congl. affairs; assoc. dir. human resources, vets. and labor Office Mgmt. and Budget, 1989—92, counselor to the dir., 1992—93; pres., CEO Fedn. Am. Hosps., 1995—2001; ptnr. Patton Boggs, LLP, Washington; dep. asst. to the pres. White House, 2001—03; CEO, adminstr. Ctrs. for Medicare and Medicaid Svcs. Dept. Health & Human Services, Washington, 2001—03; sr. counsel Alston & Bird LLP, Washington, 2003—. Mem.: bd. dirs., SHPS, Inc., 2004-. Republican. Office: Alston & Bird LLP 601 Pennsylvania Ave NW N Bldg 10th Fl Washington DC 20004-3606*

SCURRY, BRIANA COLLETTE, professional soccer player; b. Mpls., Sept. 7, 1971; BS in Polit. Sci., U. Mass., 1995. Goalkeeper U.S. Women's Nat. Soccer Team, Chgo., 1994—99, 2002—; profl. soccer player Atlanta Beat (WUSA), 2001—03. Mem. U.S. Olympic Soccer Team, Athens, 2004. Named Goalkeeper of Yr., Mo. Athletic Club Sports Found., 1993; recipient Gold medal, Atlanta Olympics, 1996, Athens Olympic games, 2004, World Cup champion, 1999, Silver medal, Sydney Olympic Games, 2000. Office: US Soccer Fedn US Soccer House 1801 S Prairie Ave Chicago IL 60616-1319

SCUSERIA, GUSTAVO ENRIQUE, theoretical chemist; b. San Fernando, Buenos Aires, Argentina, July 30, 1956; arrived in US, 1985, naturalized; s. Eraldo L. and Alicia (Capitanelli) S.; m. Ana Inés Ilvento, Apr. 17, 1982; children: Ignacio, Tomás. BS, MS, U. Buenos Aires, 1979, PhD in Physics, 1983. Grad. asst. U. Buenos Aires, 1979-83, asst. prof., 1983-85; rsch. assoc. U. Calif., Berkeley, 1985-87; sr. rsch. assoc. U. Ga., Athens, 1987-89; asst. prof. Rice U., Houston, 1989-93, assoc. prof., 1993-95, prof., 1995-2000, Robert A. Welch prof. chemistry, 2000—. Recipient IBM Partnership award IBM Corp., 1998-99; Camille and Henry Dreyfus Teacher scholar Camille and Henry Dreyfus Found., 1992; John Simon Guggenheim Meml. Found. fellow, 2003. Fellow AAAS, Am. Phys. Soc.; mem. Am. Chem. Soc., Materials Rsch. Soc. Office: Rice U Dept Chemistry PO Box 1892 Houston TX 77251-1892 E-mail: guscus@rice.edu.

SCUTT, ROBERT CARL, lawyer; b. Newark, N.Y., Dec. 24, 1950; s. Charles E. and Lois L. (Armstrong) S. BA, Union Coll., 1973; JD, Duke U., 1976. Bar: N.Y. 1977, U.S. Dist. Ct. (we. dist.) N.Y. 1977, U.S. Tax Ct. 1978. Assoc. Harris, Beach & Wilcox, Rochester, N.Y., 1976-83, ptnr., 1984—. Mem. N.Y. State Bar Assn., Am. Health Lawyers Assn. Office: Harris Beach LLP 99 Garnsey Rd Pittsford NY 14534

SCZUDLO, WALTER JOSEPH, lawyer; b. Fairbanks, Alaska; s. Walter and Dolores J. Sczudlo; children: Lauren Hall, Elizabeth Fairbanks, Walter Christopher; m. Rebecca Grey Tucker. AB, Middlebury Coll.; JD, Golden Gate U.; LLM, Georgetown U.; post grad., U. Calif., Santa Barbara, Tulane U., Vt. Law Sch. Bar: Alaska, Calif., DC, US Ct. Appeals (9th cir.), US Ct. Appeals (DC cir.), US Dist. Ct. (no., cen., ea. and so. dists.) Calif., US Dist. Ct. Alaska, US Ct. Claims, US Tax Ct. Law clk. to presiding justice Alaska Supreme Ct.; assoc. atty. Merdes, Schaible, Staley and Delisio, Anchorage; legis. dir., gen. counsel U.S. Senator Murkowski, Washington; sr. tax assoc. Schramm and Raddue, Santa Barbara, Calif.; dir. congl. rels., counsel Natural Gas Supply Assn., Washington; Washington counsel Shell Oil Co., 1988-96; v.p., Washington counsel Intercontinental Energy Corp., 1996-99; gen. counsel, exec. v.p. pub. affairs and programs Assn. Fundraising Profls., Washington, 1999—; prin. ptnr. WEBK Broadcasting 105.3 FM, Killington, Vt., 1985—. Dir. Sun's Edge, Inc., Santa Barbara, 1987—, Natural Gas Roundtable, Washington, 1987—. Author: (with other) Washington Legal Foundation. 1988. Com. chmn. Steve Cowper for Gov., Anchorage, 1982. Recipient Am. Jurisprudence award Bancroft-Whitney Pub. Co.

SDRINGOLA-MARANGA, STEFANO, medical educator, researcher; b. Perugia, Italy, Nov. 29, 1964; arrived in U.S., 1993; s. Francesco Sdringola-Maranga and Edda Sguilla; m. Manuela Tentoni, May 22, 1993; children: Chiara, Sarah, Giulia. Diploma in medicine and surgery cum laude, U. Perugia, 1990. Diplomate Am. Bd. Internal Medicine, Am. Bd. Cardiology, Am. Bd. Interventional Cardiology. Vol. in cardiac rehab., clk. dept. internal medicine and vascular medicine U. Perugia, 1987—90, intern internal medicine dept. internal medicine and vascular medicine, 1991—93; intern dept. cardiology Silvestrini Hosp., Perugia, 1993; intern Cabrini Med. Ctr., N.Y.C., 1993; resident dept. internal medicine U. Tex., Houston, 1994—96, cardiology fellow, 1996—99, interventional cardiology fellow, 1999—2000, asst. prof. medicine, 2000—; staff mem. Meml. Hermann Hosp., 2000—. Lectr. in field. Reviewer: Circulation, 2000—, Catheterization and Cardiovascular Interventions, 2000—, Jour. Am. Coll. Cardiology, 2001—; contbr. articles to profl. jours. With Italian Mil., 1989—90. Grantee, Pfizer Pharm., 2000—01, The Weathereard P.E.T. Ctr. for Preventing and Reversing Atherosclerosis, 2000—01, 2001—02, 2002—03. Mem.: AMA, Albo dei Medici Chirurghi di Perugia, Tex. Med. Assn., Am. Coll. Cardiology. Achievements include research in techniques for optimal in vitro radiolabelling of autologous platelets with Indium-111 and subsequent clinical application in vivo; sympathetic activation in CFH; value of Hyperventilation test in patients with vasospastic or variant angina, platelets TXA2 receptor during stable and unstable coronary syndromes; stabilization and reversal of coronary artery disease; myocardial protection during coronary percutaneous revascularization; pressure wire in percutaneous coronary interventions; carotid artery stenting; percutaneous abdominal aortic aneurysm repair; sperimentation of new pharmacological approaches for the stabilization and regression of athrosclerotic coronary artery disease; noninvasive diagnosis of early coronary artery disease. Avocation: soccer. Office: Univ Tex Health Sci Ctr MSB 1245 6431 Fannin Houston TX 77030

SEABOLT, RICHARD L. lawyer; b. Chgo., Aug. 28, 1949; BGS with distinction, U. Mich., 1971; JD, U. Calif., Hastings, 1975. Bar: Calif. 1975. With Hancock, Rothert & Bunshoft, San Francisco, 1975—, ptnr., 1981—. Frequent speaker and author profl. jours.; co-author: (with Matthew Bender) California Pretrial Civil Procedure and Discovery, 2003. Mem. Am. Arbitration Assn. (mem. large complex case panel), State Bar Calif. (treas. litigation sect., mem. jury instruction adv. com.), Assn. Bus. Trial Lawyers (bd. dirs.). Office: Hancock Rothert & Bunshoft LLP Four Embarcadero Ctr San Francisco CA 94111-4106 E-mail: rlseabolt@HRBLaw.com.

SEABORG, DAVID MICHAEL, evolutionary biologist; b. Berkeley, Calif., Apr. 22, 1949; s. Glenn Theodore and Helen Lucille (Griggs) S.; m. Adele Fong Yee, June 17, 1990. BS, U. Calif., Davis, 1972; MA, U. Calif., Berkeley, 1974. Biology tchr. U. Calif., Berkeley, 1972-73; biol. rschr., photographer Trans Time Labs, Berkeley, 1978; pvt. practice, 1974—; hypnosis and self-hypnosis tchr. Open Edn. Exchange, Oakland, Calif., 1978—81; biol. tchr. Oakland Mus., Calif., 1983-87; rsch. biologist, dept. ecology and evolutionary biology U. Calif., Irvine, 1987; pres. dir. Rsch. Found. for Biol. Conservation and Rsch., Walnut Creek, Calif., 1983—; radio talk show host Sta. KPFA, Berkeley, 1996; biology and life sci tchr. Phillip and Sala Burton Acad. H.S., San Francisco, 1996-97; lab. Chem. Biodynamics U. Calif., Berkeley, 1975; comedian, 1969—. Vol. asst. to curator Smithosonian Instn. 1966-67; lectr. sci, philos., environ. issues, 1974—; Inventor game, Sum-It, 1981; originator, theory of evolution based on organisms as integrated systems; chmn. Com. for Arts and Lectures, U. Calif., Berkeley, 1974-75; chmn. Bastille Day, Lafayette (Calif.)-Langeac Soc., 1982, master of ceremonies, 1982-86, 98-2000. Contbr. articles to profl. jours. Environ. organizer, founder, pres. U Turn Soc., Glenn Seaborg Open Space Fund, World Rainforest Fund; creator, an organizer press conf. on global environ. and social issues 100th Nobel Prize Festivities, Stockholm, 2001. Recipient Meritorius Svc. award Smithsonian Inst., 1967, Animal Photograph award Soc. Photographic Scientists and Engrs., 1967, Best of Show award photo contest Klamath Basin Audubon Soc., 1991; award winning poet, 1997, 99. Mem.: Nat. Resources Def. Coun., Earth Island Inst., World Wildlife Fund, Calif. Aggie Alumni Assn., Population Connection, Save the Bay Assn., Desert Tortise Preserve Com., Greenpeace, Rainforest Action Network, Nature Conservancy, Calif. Alumni Assn., Sierra Club, Club of Rome USA (v.p. 1998—2001, bd. dirs. 1995—). Democrat. Address: 1888 Pomar Way Walnut Creek CA 94598-1424 E-mail: davidseaborg@juno.com.

SEABRA, JAMES JOSEPH, music educator, professional musician; b. Providence, Oct. 16, 1953; s. Dolores T. Case; m. Seabra (div. May 25, 1995); children: Jonathan, James, Trafford. BS applied music, Berklee Coll. of Music, Boston, Mass., 1972—76; post grad., UCLA, Los Angeles, CA, 1987—88, Calif. State Univ., Northridge, 1987—88; MATC, R.I. Coll., 1993. Educator Foster/Gloster Pub. Sch., Foster/Gloster, RI, 1989, Cranston (RI) Pub. Sch., 1989—90; band dir. Smithfield HS, Smithfield, RI, 1990—2002; assoc. prof. RI Coll., Providence, 1998—2002, Providence Coll., 2003—. Mem. Percussive Arts Soc., Cawtow, Okla., 1976—2002, Am. Feb. of Musicians, Providence, 1976—2002, Music Ed. Nat. Conf. (MENC), 1989—2002. Home: 84 Cottage Ave N Providence RI 02911-2113 Office: Smithfield HS 90 Pleasantview Ave Esmond RI 02917

SEABROOK, JOHN MARTIN, retired food products executive, chemical engineer; b. Seabrook, N.J., Apr. 16, 1917; s. Charles Franklin and Norma Dale (Ivins) S.; m. Anne Schlaudecker, Apr. 5, 1939 (div. 1951); children: Carol Ormsby (Mrs. Jacques P. Boulanger), Elizabeth Anne; m. Elizabeth Toomey, 1956; children: John Martin, Bruce Cameron. BS in Chem. Engring, Princeton, 1939; LL.D. (hon.), Gettysburg Coll., 1974. Registered profl. engr., N.J., Del. Engr. Deerfield Packing Corp., 1939-41; v.p. Seabrook Farms Co., 1941-50, exec. v.p., 1950-54, dir., 1941-59, pres., 1954-59, chief exec. officer, 1955-59; dir. Pa. Reading & Seashore Line, 1950-63, N.Y. Ctrl. R.R., 1964-69, Penn Ctrl. R.R., 1968-71; cons. IU Internat. Corp., Wilmington, Del., 1959, v.p., 1960-65, dir., 1963-87, pres., 1965-73, 74-78, chief exec., 1967-80, chmn. bd., 1969-82, chmn. exec. com., 1982-87. Pres., bd. dirs. Cumberland Automobile & Truck Co., 1954-59, Cumberland Warehouse Corp., 1954-59, Salem Farms Corp, N.J., 1948—; chmn. bd. dirs. Frick Co., Waynesboro, Pa., 1959-68; chmn., bd. dirs. S.W. Fabricating & Welding Co., Inc., Houston, 1964-68; chmn. Divcon, Inc., Houston, 1967-69; pres. bd. dirs. Internat. Utilities Overseas Capital Corp., Wilmington, 1966-82, chmn., 1970-80; v.p. Gen. Waterworks Corp., Phila., 1959-66, pres., 1966-68, chmn., 1968-71; chmn. bd. dirs. GWC Inc., Phila., 1971-73; pres. Brown Bros. Contractors, Inc., Phila., 1960, chmn. bd. dirs., 1965-67; pres. Am. Portable Irrigation Co., Eugene, Oreg., 1961, chmn. bd. dirs., 1966-68; chmn. bd. dirs. Gotaas-Larsen Shipping Corp., 1963, chmn., 1979, pres., CEO, 1982-88; chmn. bd. dirs. Amvit Corp., Cleve., 1964-68; bd. dirs. Echo Bay Mines Ltd., South Jersey Gas Co., Folsom, N.J., South Jersey Industries, Inc., Folsom, Bell Atlantic Corp.; dir. emeritus Bell Atlantic-N.J., Inc. Mem. N.J. Migrant Labor Bd., 1945-67, chmn., 1955-67; mem. N.J. Bd. Higher Edn., 1967-70, Pres.' Air Quality Adv. Bd., 1968-70; bd. dirs. Brandywine Conservancy, Inc., 1972-95, pres., 1992-93, hon. dir., 1997—; trustee Eisenhower Exch. Fellowships, 1974-85; trustee Hitchcock Found., 1991-96, chmn., 1993-96. Mem.: Coaching Club (N.Y.C. and U.K.), Wilmington (Del.) Club, Phila. Club, Knickerbocker Club (N.Y.C.), Racquet and Tennis Club (N.Y.C.), Phi Beta Kappa. Home and Office: 55 Nimrod Rd Salem NJ 08079-4323 Office Phone: 856-935-5200. E-mail: jmsdrives@snip.net.

SEABROOK, RAYMOND J. corporate financial executive; b. Toronto, Mar. 1, 1950; married; 2 children. Cert. in arch., Humber Coll., Toronto, 1972; B in Bus., McMaster U., Hamilton, Ontario, 1975. With Coopers and Lybrand, Toronto, Canada, 1976—85; v.p. fin. control Onex Packaging and Am. Can Can., 1985—91; from sr. v.p., CFO to sr. v.p. fin. Ball Packaging Products Can., Inc., Broomfield, Colo., 1991—2000, sr. v.p., CFO, 2000—. Office: Ball 10 Longs Peak Dr Broomfield CO 80021

SEACREST, RYAN, television and radio personality; b. Atlanta, Dec. 24, 1976; s. Gary and Connie Seacrest. Attended, U. Ga., 1994—95. DJ WSTR/Star 94, Atlanta, 1992—94. Host (TV series) Radical Outdoor Challenge, ESPN, 1995, American Idol, 2002—, American Juniors, 2003, host, exec. prodr. On-Air With Ryan Seacrest, 2004—, corr. Extra Weekends, 2002, host (radio) Live from the Lounge, Star 98.7, 1995—2001, Ryan Seacrest for the Ride Home, Star 98.7, L.A., 1995—2004, American Top 40, 2004—, On-Air With Ryan Seacrest, 102.7 KIIS-FM, L.A., 2004—. Office: On-Air With Ryan Seacrest Hollywood & Highland 6801 Hollywood Blvd Hollywood CA 90028*

SEADEN, GEORGE, civil engineer; b. Cracow, May 26, 1936; s. Simon and Mary (Guttman) S.; m. Linda Helen Mutch, Mar. 18, 1978; children: Amy Elisabeth, Maia Claire. BE, McGill U., Montreal, Que., Can., 1958; MS, Harvard U., 1968; postgrad., Northwestern U., 1992. Engr. Gatineau Power, Hull, Que., 1958-59, Ent. Fougerolle, Paris, 1960-62; mgr. Warnock Hersey Ltd., Montreal, 1959-60; assoc. Cartier, Coté, Piette, Montreal, 1962-67; sr. advisor Ministry Urban Affairs, Ottawa, Ont., Can., 1969-71; pres. Archer, Seaden & Assoc., Inc., Montreal, 1971-84; dir. gen. Inst. Rsch. in Constrn. Nat. Rsch. Coun., Ottawa, 1985-97, chief Constrn. Tech. Group, 1995-97; exec.-in-residence Faculty Adminstrn. U. Ottawa, 1997—2001. Vis. prof. U. Ottawa, 1968-73; mem. Can. Constrn. Rsch. Bd., 1985-91, Constrn. Industry Devel., Can., 1988-93, Civil Engring. Rsch. Found., 1993—, Rsch. Bd. Am. Pub. Works Assn., 1994-97; dir. Continental Automated Bldg. Assn., 1995-97, Can. Rsch. Mgrs. Assn., CERIU; pres. Conseil Internat. du Batiment, Rotterdam, The Netherlands, 1989-92; vice chair Constrn. for Sustainable Devel. in the Twenty First Century Conf., Washington, 1996; chair INFRA 2000, Montreal; mem. jury to select best Can. Constrn. projects and engring. design, lectr. numerous univs. and rsch. ctrs.; chmn. Internat. Symposium on Innovation, Ottawa, 2001. Contbg. author: Buildings, Culture and Environment, 2003; co-editor: Trends in Building Construction Worldwide, 1989, Innovation in Construction, 2001; mem. editl. bd. Bldg. Rsch. and Practice, Constrn. Bldg. Rev., 1991—; contbr. numerous articles to profl. pubs. Chmn. bd. dirs. St. Andrew's Sch., Westmount, Que., 1975-82. Fellow Am. Soc. Civil Engrs. E-mail: george.seaden@ragers.com.

SEADER, JUNIOR DEVERE (BOB SEADER), chemical engineering educator; b. San Francisco, Calif., Aug. 16, 1927; s. George Joseph and Eva (Burbank) S.; m. Joyce Kocher, Aug. 12, 1950 (div. 1960); m. Sylvia Bowen, Aug. 11, 1961; children: Steven Frederick, Clayton Mitchell, Gregory Randolph, Donald Jeffrey, Suzanne Marie, Robert Clark, Kathleen Michelle, Jennifer Anne. BS, U. Calif., Berkeley, 1949, MS, 1950; PhD, U. Wis., 1952. Instr. chem. engring. U. Wis., Madison, 1951-52; group supr. chem. process design Chevron Rsch. Corp., Richmond, Calif., 1952-57, group supr. engring. rsch., 1957-59; prin. scientist heat transfer and fluid dynamics rsch. Rocketdyne div. N.Am. Aviation, Canoga Park, Calif., 1959-65, sr. tech. specialist, summer 1967; prof. chem. engring. U. Idaho, 1965-66, U. Utah, Salt Lake City, 1966—2003, chmn. dept. chem. engring., 1975-78. Tech. cons.; trustee CACHE Corp., Austin, Tex., 1969—2002; lectr. AIChE, 1983, bd, dirs., 1983—85. Author 13 books; assoc. editor IEC Rsch. jour., 1986-99; co-author widely used vapor-liquid equilibrium correlation; contbr. more than 100 articles to tech. publs. Served with USNR, 1945—46. Recipient Disting. Tchg. award U. Utah, 1975, Donald L. Katz lectureship, 1990, Dean's Tchg. award U. Utah, 1998, CACHE award for excellence in computing in chem. engring. edn. Am. Soc. Engring. Edn., 2004. Fellow AIChE (Computing in Chem. Engring. award 1988, Warren K. Lewis award for chem. engr. edn. 2004); mem. Am. Chem. Soc., Sigma Xi, Phi Lambda Upsilon. Heat transfer rsch. connected with the devel. of rocket engines associated with the Apollo and Space Shuttle projects, 1960-65; rsch. on tar sands, process synthesis, catalyst effective factors, bifurcation analysis. Home: 13696 Vestry Rd Draper UT 84020-7521 Office: U Utah Dept Chem Engring Rm 3290 50 S Central Campus Dr Salt Lake City UT 84112-9203 Office Phone: 801-581-6916. E-mail: j.seader@utah.edu.

SEADLER, STEPHEN EDWARD, social scientist, philosopher, writer; s. Silas Frank and Doris Amy Seadler; m. Ingrid Linnea Adoflsson, 1954 (div. 1997); children: Einar Austin, Anna Carin. AB in Physics, postgrad., Columbia U., 1947; postgrad. studied under George Gamow, George Washington U., 1948—50. Electronic engr. Cushing & Nevell, Warner Inc., N.Y.C., 1951—54; seminar leader, leader trainer world politics Am. Found. for Continuing Edn., N.Y.C., 1955—57; exec. dir. Medimetric Inst., 1957—59; mem. long range planning com., chmn. corporate forecasting com., mktg. rsch. dir. W.A. Sheaffer Pen Co., Ft. Madison, Iowa, 1959—65; founder Internat. Dynamics Corp., Ft. Madison and N.Y.C., 1965, pres., 1965—70; originator DELTA program for prevention and treatment of violence, 1970; founder, pres. ID Ctr., Ft. Madison, Dover, N.J., 1968—. Mgmt. cons. in human resources devel. and conflict reduction, N.Y.C., 1970-73; pres. UNICONSULT computer-based mgmt. and computer scis., N.Y.C., 1973-76; speaker on decision support systems, internat. affairs and ideological arms control; author/speaker (presentation) Holocaust, History and Arms Control; originator social sci. of ideologics and ideotopology; spl. works collection accessible via On-line Computer Lib. Ctr. Instr. polit. sci. Ia. State Penitentiary, 1959-62; guest speaker on radio and television. Author: Principia Ideologica: A Treatise on Combatting Human Malignance, 1999, Ending the Bronze Age, 2001, Terror War and Peace, 2003; contbr. ideologics and ideotopology sects. to Administrative Decision Making, 1978, Management Handbook for Public Administrators, 1978, statement on ideological arms control in Part 4 of Sen. Fgn. Rels. Com. hearing on Salt II Treaty, 1979, Ideologics Extended to treat ethnic, racial, religious conflict, 1992, with first call for Abrahamic Reformation, Morristown (N.J.) Unitarian Ch., 1993; contbr. articles to profl. jours. Served with AUS, 1944—46. Recipient 20th Century Achievement Award medal Internat. Biographical Ctr., U.K., 1995; named to The Wisdom Hall of Fame by The Wisdom Soc., 1997. Mem.: IEEE, UN Assn.-USA, Forum on Physics and Soc., Fgn. Policy Assn., Am. Mgmt. Assn. (lectr. 1963—68), Am. Sociol. Assn., N.Y. Acad. Scis., Acad. Polit. Sci., Am. Statis. Assn., Am. Phys. Soc., West Point Soc. NJ, Union Concerned Scientists, Friends of West Point, Scottish Rite. Office: ID Ctr PO Box 824 Dover NJ 07802-0824 Business E-Mail: ses146@columbia.edu. *In retrospect, a single, predominant thread has woven through my entire life since childhood, sometimes as primary track, sometimes as parallel, but always as relentless destiny: to gain such learning and skills as to enable me to revolutionize mankind's thinking, slay the dragons of racism, religionism, ethnicism and other ideologies of malevolence, oppression and war, and bring true peace for the first time. To accomplish that mission requires development of a single comprehensive framework, which has become the new field of ideologics, and a single comprehensive, revolutionary work employing that framework, to appear at the foothills of the new millennium. That work is the book Principia Ideologica.*

SEAGAL, STEVEN, actor; b. Lansing, Mich., Apr. 10, 1951; m. Miyako Seagal, 1975 (div. 1986); children: Kentaro, Ayako; m. Adrienne La Russa (div.); m. Kelly LeBrock (div. 1994); children: Annaliza, Dominic San Rocco, Arissa, Savannah. Studied martial arts under masters, Japan. Founded Aikido Ten Shin Dojo, L.A. Martial arts choreographer The Challenge, 1982; actor, prodr., martial arts choreographer Above the Law, 1988, Marked for Death, 1990, My Giant, 1998; actor, martial arts choreographer Hard to Kill, 1990; actor, prodr. Out for Justice, 1991, Under Siege, 1992, Under Siege 2, 1995, Half Past Dead, 2002, The Foreigner, 2003, Out for a Kill, 2003, Belly of the Beast, 2003; actor, dir., co-prodr. On Deadly Ground, 1994; fight scene choreographer various films; appeared in films The Glimmer Man, 1996, Executive Decision, 1996, Fire Down Below, 1997, The Patriot, 1998, Get Bruce, 1999, Blood on the Moon, 2000, Exit Wounds, 2001, Ticker, 2001, Out of Reach, 2004. Achievements include first non-Asian to open martial arts acad. in Japan; black belt numerous martial arts. Office: ICM 8942 Wilshire Blvd Beverly Hills CA 90211-1934*

SEAGER, DAUNA GAYLE OLSON-STOKES, speech therapist; b. Logan, Utah, Sept. 22, 1925; d. Helmar Alexander and La Rena Barnes (Jones) Olson; m. Arch Jr. Stokes, Aug. 5, 1943 (dec. Apr. il 1970); children: Jeffrey David, John Phillip, Jeannette; m. Floyd W. Seager, July 7, 1973 (dec. Oct. 1996). AS, Weber State U., 1964; BS, MS in Audiology Speech Pathology, Utah State U.,

1969. X-ray ech., physician asst. Robins X-Ray, Ogden, Utah, 1946-52; asst. to supt. Lyman (Wyo.) Pub. Schs., 1952-60; clinic supr. Utah State U., Logan, 1965-69; speech, language, hearing therapist Weber/Davis Sch. District, Ogden, Farmington, Utah, 1969-73, various, Utah, 1970-90; co-founder, coord. Clinic at O.R.M., Ogden, Utah, 1988—. Bd. dirs. Weber County DUP Mus., Ogden. Author: Pioneer Settlers, 1990; contbr. articles to profl. jours. Co-founder Seager Indigent Clinic, Ogden Mission, Utah, 1988—; organized Stroke Club for Families of CVA Support Group, Ogden, 1972-74, Stroke Unit St. Benedict's Hosp., Ogden, 1972-74, Parent Child Tchr. Group, Ogden, 1970-73; mem. Ogden Sesquicentennial Com., OgSesqui, 2000—, Weber County Sesquicentennial, 2000; co-chair Ogden Mayor's Cemetery Enhancement Commn; mem. cmty. rels. com. McKay Dee Hosp., 2000—. Fellow Utah State U., Logan, 1967-68, 68-69; recipient Point of Light award #101 Gov. Utah, 2003. Mem.: DAR, Mus. Action Team, Fedn. Ogden Bus. Profl. Women Internat., Weber County Women's Legis. Coun. and Rep. Women, Weber Far South Ctr. Co., Utah Mus. Assn. (bd. dirs.), Ogden Mayors Project (cemetery com., sesquicentennial com.), Altrusa Internat., Daus. of Utah Pioneers, Child Culture Club, Aglaia Club. Mem. Lds Ch. Avocations: historian/lecturer, writer, golfer, bridge, swimmer, ballroom dance instr. Home and Office: 4046 South 895 East Ogden UT 84403-2416 Office Phone: 801-621-4891.

SEAGLE, EDGAR FRANKLIN, environmental engineer, consultant; b. Lincolnton, N.C., June 27, 1924; s. Franklin Craig and Lillie Mae (James) S.; m. Doris Elaine Long, Mar. 23, 1958; children: Rebecca Jane, Mary Elaine, James Craig, William Franklin. AB in Chemistry, U. N.C., 1949, MS in Pub. Health, 1954; BCE, U. Fla., 1961; DPH, U. Tex., 1974. Registered profl. engr., Ala. Sr. sanitarian Health Dept., City of Charlotte, N.C., 1950-52, chief indsl. hygiene sect., 1956-59; sanitation cons. N.C. State Bd. Health, Raleigh, 1954-56; engr. dir. USPHS, Rockville, Md., 1961-78; asst. dir. Fellowship Office Nat. Acad. Scis., Washington, 1978-83; pub. health engr. Dept. of Environ., State of Md., Balt., 1985-88; ind. engring. cons. Rockville, 1984-85, 88—. Contbr. articles to profl. publs. With USN, 1943-46, PTO. Mem. ASCE, APHA, Am. Acad. Environ. Engrs. (diplomate). Methodist. Home and Office: 14108 Heathfield Ct Rockville MD 20853-2760 Personal E-mail: efseagle@mindspring.com.

SEAGLE, J. HAROLD, lawyer; b. Marion, N.C., May 9, 1947; s. Rufus James and Alma Rhoda (McMahan) S.; m. Linda Jean Cranford, June 3, 1967; 1 child, James Mark. BA, U. N.C., 1973, JD, 1977. Bar: N.C. 1977; U.S. Dist. Ct. (ea., middle, we. dists.) N.C. 1977, 88, 92; U.S. Ct Appeals (4th cir.) 1982; U.S. Supreme Ct. 1982. Assoc. atty. Rountree & Newton, Wilmington, NC, 1977-79; ptnr. Rountree & Seagle, L.L.P., Wilmington, 1979—2001. Past pres. Fifth Jud. Dist. Bar. Bd. trustees and bd. deacons Winter Park Baptist Ch.; past moderator Wilmington Baptist Assn.; bd. dirs. Rescue Mission of Cape Fear; past adv. Bd. Coastal Bioethics Network; past chmn. annual fund drive Am. Cancer Soc.; past sect. chmn. Cape Fear United Way. Mem.: N.C. Bar Coun. of Pres. Wilmington Inns of Ct. (exec. com., master), Maritime Law Assn. of U.S. (proctor), Southeastern Admiralty Law Inst. (past chmn., chmn. adv. coun.), N.C. Coll. of Advocacy, N.C. Acad. Trial Lawyers, N.C. State Bar, N.C. Bar Assn., New Hanover County Bar Assn. Avocations: acoustic guitar, motorcycle racing. Address: 19 Treetop Dr Arden NC 28704 E-mail: haroldseagle@charter.net.

SEAGO, DIANA MARIE, college administrator; b. Kansas City, July 30, 1949; d. Gordon Eugene and Rita Marie (Ohmes) S. BA, Mt. St. Scholastica Coll., 1971. Joined Order of St. Benedict. Tchr. St. Joseph Grade Sch., Shawnee, Kans., 1971-72; asst. dir. admissions Donnelly Coll., Kansas City, Kans., 1972-73; dir. residence hall Benedictine Coll., Atchison, Kans., 1973-78; assoc. dir. campus ministry Washburn Cath. Campus Ctr., Topeka, 1978-80; dir. RCIA St. Mary Ch., Tulsa, 1980-91; comm. svc. Williams Telecom., Tulsa, 1991-92; dir. gift planning, then assoc. v.p. devel. Benedictine Coll., 1992—. Cons. in field. Author of poems. Recipient Sertoma Club Kans Citizens award, 1967. Mem. HTML Writers Guild, Scriptorium, Coun. for Advancement and Support of Edn. Democrat. Roman Catholic. Avocations: fishing, guitar, harmonica, needlecrafts, internet. Office: Benedictine Coll 1020 N 2nd St Atchison KS 66002-1402

SEAGREN, ALICE, state legislator; b. 1947; m. Fred Seagren; 2 children. BS, SE Mo. State U. Mem. Minn. Ho. of Reps., 1993—, chmn. edn. fin., 1999—. Active Bloomington (Minn.) Sch. Bd., 1989-92. Mem. Bloomington C. of C. (bd. dirs. 1990-92), Phi Gamma Nu, Alpha Chi Omega. Republican. Home: 9730 Palmer Cir Bloomington MN 55437-2017 Office: Minn Ho of Reps State Capital Building Saint Paul MN 55155-0001 E-mail: rep.alice.seagren@house.leg.state.mn.us.

SEAGREN, STEPHEN LINNER, oncologist; b. Mpls., Mar. 13, 1941; s. Morley Raymond and Carol Christine (Linner) S.; m. Jill Garrie; 1 child, Sean Garrie. AB, Harvard U., 1963; MD, Northwestern U., 1967. Diplomate Am. Bd. Internal Medicine, Am. Bd. Med. Oncology, Am. Bd. Radiology. From asst. prof. to assoc. prof. radiology and medicine U. Calif., San Diego, 1977-88, prof., 1988—, chief divsn. radiation oncology. Contbr. over 80 articles to profl. jours. Bd. dirs., chmn. profl. adv. com. Wellness Cmty., San Diego, 1988-2003; chmn. radiol. oncology com. Cancer and Acute Leukemia Group, Chgo., 1986-98; assoc. dir. U. Calif. San Diego Cancer Ctr., 1998-2000. Lt. comdr. USNR, 1971-73. Fellow ACP. Avocations: physical fitness, bridge, skiing, golf, tennis. Office: U Calif San Diego Med Ctr 200 W Arbor Dr San Diego CA 92103-9000 Office Phone: 619-543-5303. Business E-Mail: sseagren@ucsd.edu.

SEAL, JOHN S., JR., manufacturing executive, consultant; b. Phila., May 20, 1944; s. John S. Sr. and Gertrude Eva (Abbott) Seal; m. LoriAnn LaBonte; children: Kathryn, Ashley, Kristen, Heather, Stephen, Spencer, MacKenzie, Riley. BS in Econs., Drexel U., 1967; MBA, Dartmouth Coll., 1971. CPA, N.Y. Asst. to exec. v.p. fin. Gould Inc., Chgo., 1971, dir. electronics group fin. planning Newton Upper Falls, Mass., 1972-73; pres., treas., CEO Nat. Comms. Industries Co., Greenwich, Conn., 1973-76, chmn., 1973-79; exec. v.p. Boyerton (Pa.) Burial Casket Co., 1976-77; v.p., gen. mgr. comms. products divsn. FSC Corp., Pitts., 1977-79; sr. v.p. Butcher and Singer Inc. subs. Butcher and Co. Inc., Phila., 1979-85; pres. Sovereign Group Inc. subs. Butcher and Co. Inc., Phila., 1983-85, Seal Devel. Co., Phila., 1985-88; mng. dir. Essex Fin. Group, Phila., 1988-97; CFO telecoms. Spiraduct, Inc., Montgomeryville, Pa., 1997-00. Bd. dirs. RTG Svcs., Inc., 1992—, Rittenhouse Sq. Fitness Club, Phila., 1983-89. Trustee Please Touch Mus., Phila., 1987-90; bd. dirs. alumni bd. Drexel U., Phila., 1983-92. With U.S. Army, 1967-68. Mem. AICPA, N.Y. Soc. CPAs, Conn. Soc. CPAs. Republican. Mem. Ch. of Christ. Club: Union League (Phila.). Avocations: helicopter pilot, boating, travel. Home: 18210 SE Ridgeview Dr Tequesta FL 33469-8124 Office: Perfect Data Sys 18210 SE Ridgeview Dr Tequesta FL 33469 Office Phone: 561-741-7875. Fax: (561) 741-7875.

SEALE, JAMES LAWRENCE, JR., agricultural economics educator, international trade researcher; b. Memphis, Mar. 12, 1949; s. James Lawrence and Mary Helen (Keefe) S.; divorced. BA, U. Miss., 1972; postgrad., U. Chgo., 1978-79; PhD, Mich. State U., 1985. Agrl. vol. Peace Corps, Tondo, Zaire, 1973-75; agrl. advisor Harvard Inst. for Internat. Devel., Abyei, Sudan, 1978; specialist Mich. State U., Fayoum, Arab Republic of Egypt, 1980-83; asst. prof. agrl. econs. U. Fla., Gainesville, 1985-90, assoc. prof. agrl. econs., 1990-95, prof. agrl. econs., 1995—. Vis. prof. U. Leicester (Eng.), 1992, 94, hon. vis. fellow, 1995. Author: (with H. Theil and C.F. Chung) International Evidence on Consumption Patterns, 1989; editor: Journal of Agricultural and Applied Economics, 1998-2001, spl. edit., 2002-03; contbr. articles to profl. jours. Vol. Farmer to Farmer, UOCA, Namibia, 1994, Farmer to Farmer, Wenrock Internat., 1994; vol. agrl. bus. svcs. Wenrock Internat., Far Eastern Russia, 1998. NIMH scholar U. Chgo., 1978-79; traveling scholar U. Mich., 1979; rsch. fellow Cairo U., 1980-83; McKethan-Matherly rsch. fellow, 1986-88, McKethan-Matherly sr. rsch. fellow, 1991-94. Mem. Am. Econs. Assn., Am. Agrl. Econs. Assn., Internat. Assn. Agrl. Economists, Econometrics Soc., Caribbean Agro-Econ. Soc., Internat. Agrl. Trade Rsch. Consortium, Gamma Sigma Delta. Episcopalian. Avocations: scuba diving, Karate. Home: 408 W University Ave 7D Gainesville FL 32601 Office: U Fla Dept Food and Resource 2111 McCarty PO Box 110240 Gainesville FL 32611-0240 Office Phone: 352-392-1845 414.

SEALE, JAMES MILLARD, retired religious organization administrator, clergyman; b. Middlesboro, Ky., Oct. 4, 1930; s. Albert Tyler and Edith Josephine (Buchanan) S.; m. Mary Dudley Harrod; children: William Alan, Ann Lynn Seale Hazelrigg. BA, Transylvania U., 1952; BD, Lexington Theol. Sem., 1955, MDiv, 1963, D Ministry, 1981. Ordained to ministry Christian Ch. (Disciples of Christ), 1951. Student pastor various Christian Chs., Ky., 1949-54; pastor 1st Christian Ch., Pikeville, Ky., 1954-58, Erlanger (Ky.) Christian Ch., 1958-61; sr. minister 1st Christian Ch., Mt. Sterling, Ky., 1961-70, Paris, Ky., 1978-82; stewardship sec. Gen. Office Christian Ch., Indpls., 1970-74; adminstr. Christian Ch. Home of Louisville, 1974-78; dir. devel. Christian Ch. Homes Ky., Louisville, 1978; pres. Disciples of Christ Hist. Soc., Nashville, 1983-95, pres. emeritus, 1995. Author: A Century of Faith and Caring, 1983, Forward From The Past, 1991; editor jour. Discipliana, 1983-92. Pres. Kiwanis Club, Pikeville, 1957, Mt. Sterling, 1963, lt. gov., Ctrl. Ky., 1965. Mem. Christian Ch. Avocations: writing, photography, golf, fishing.

SEALE, JOHN CLEMENT, director, cinematographer; b. Warwick, Queensland, Australia, Oct. 5, 1942; s. Eric Clement and Marjorie Lyndon (Pool) S.; m. Louise Lee Mutton, Sept. 23, 1967; children: Derin Anthony, Brianna Lee. Grad. high sch., Sydney, Australia; PhD (hon.), Griffith U., 1997. Camera asst. film dept. Australian Broadcasting Com., 1962-68; freelance technician, camera operator various films, series, comms., 1968-76. Dir. feature film, Till There Was You, 1989-90. Dir. photography: Goodbye Paradise (Golden Tripod 1982), Careful, He Might Hear You (Best Cinematography 1983), Witness, 1984 (Golden Tripod 1984, Oscar nomination 1986, Brit. Acad. award nomination 1986), The Hitcher, 1985, Children of a Lesser God, 1985 (Golden Tripod 1985), The Mosquito Coast, 1986, Stakeout, 1987, Gorillas in the Mist (Brit. Acad. award nomination 1989, Premier Mag. Cinematographer of the Yr. 1989), Rainman, 1988 (Acad. award nomination 1988, Artistic Achievement award 1989), Dead Poets Society, 1989, The Doctor, 1991, Lorenzo's Oil, 1992, The Firm, 1993, The Paper, 1993, Beyond Rangoon, 1994, The American President, 1995, The English Patient, 1995-96 (Best Cinematography award L.A. Film Critics Assn., Acad. award Cinematography, 1996, Brit. Acad. award 1996, Best Cinematography award Am. Soc. Cinematographers 1996, European Best Cinematography award 1997, Chgo. Film Critics award, Fla. Film Critics award), Ghosts of Mississippi, 1996, City of Angels, 1997, At First Sight, 1998, The Talented Mr. Ripley, 1998, The Perfect Storm, 1999, Harry Potter, 2000, Dreamcatcher, 2002, Cold Mountain, 2002. Recipient Film Critics Cir. Australia 1990 Tribute; named European Cinematographer of Yr., 1997. Mem. Australian Cinematographers Soc. (named Cinematographer of Yr. 1982, 84, Inaugural mem. Hall of Fame 1997), Am. Soc. Cinematographers, Order of Australia. Avocations: building boats, sailing.

SEALE, ROBERT ARTHUR, JR., lawyer; b. Shreveport, La., July 17, 1942; s. Robert Arthur Sr. and Lucille (Frank) S.; m. Chalon Fontaine, Feb. 24, 2001; children: Robert A. III, John Meyers. BBA, La. State U., 1964, JD, 1967. Bar: La. 1967, Tex. 1969. Mem. La. Law Rev., 1965—67; rsch. asst. La. Law Inst., Baton Rouge, 1967; law clk. U.S. Dist. Ct. (we. dist.) La., Shreveport, 1967-68; atty./ptnr. Vinson & Elkins, Houston, 1968—97; sr. ptnr. Phelps Dunbar LLP, Houston, 2002—. Trustee, legal counsel The Mus. of Fine Arts, Houston, 1981-89, The Creel Found., Augusta, Ga., 1989-97; pres., trustee The Lyons Found., Houston, 1986—, M.A. and J.A. Elkins, Jr. Found. Sr. Warden St. Martin's Episcopal Ch., Houston, 1990; pres. Pine Shadows Civic Assn., Houston, 1991; trustee Episcopal High Sch., Houston, 1985-88; bd. dir. Boys' and Girls' Country, Houston, 1990-94; mem. U. Tex. Houston Health Sci. Ctr. Devel. Bd. Fellow Houston Bar Found.; mem. ABA, Tex. Bar Assn., Coronado Club (pres. 1991), Omicron Delta Kappa, Vivian Smith Found. For Neurologic Rsch. (pres., trustee). Avocations: civic and charitable activities, golf. Office: 3040 Post Oak Blvd Ste 900 Houston TX 77056 Office Phone: 713-877-5504. E-mail: sealep@phelps.com.

SEALE, ROBERT L. former state treasurer; b. Inglewood, Calif., Oct. 4, 1941; m. Judy Seale (dec.). BSA, Calif. Poly. U. Former contr. and sr. fin. officer Rockwell Internat.; sr. accountant Ernst & Ernst, L.A.; mng. ptnr. Pangborn & Co., Ltd. CPA's, 1985-88; state treas. State of Nev., 1991—99; chair. Nev. Rep. Party, 2000—03. Former treas. Nev. Rep. Com. Mem. Nat. Assn. State Treas. (past pres.). Republican.

SEALL, STEPHEN ALBERT, lawyer; b. South Bend, Ind., Oct. 24, 1940; s. Stephen Henry and Mildred Rita (MacDonald) S.; m. Barbara Ann Halloran, June 25, 1966; children: John Paul, Edward Andrew, Ann Marie. BA, Purdue U., 1963; postgrad., Cornell U. Grad. Sch. Bus. Adminstrn., 1963; LLB, U. Notre Dame, 1966. Bar: Ind. 1966, U.S. Claims Ct. 1973, U.S. Tax Ct. 1968, U.S. Ct. Appeals (6th cir.) 1980, U.S. Ct. Appeals (7th cir.) 1969, U.S. Supreme Ct. 1973. Assoc. Thornburg, McGill, Deahl, Harman, Carey & Murray, South Bend, 1966-71; ptnr. Barnes & Thornburg and predecessor firm Thornburg, McGill, Deahl, Harman, Carey & Murray, 1972—, vice chmn. and mgmt. com., mng. ptnr. South Bend office, 1985—2001. Spkr. in field. (Mem. editl. bd.) Notre Dame Law Rev., 1964—66. Mem. Mayor's Com. on Downtown Devel., South Bend, 1975-77, Mayor's Com. on Utilization of Downtown Bldgs., South Bend, 1988-96; trustee Project Future, South Bend, 1986-2002; exec. com. Meml. Hosp. South Bend, Inc., 1999-2003; dir. Meml. Health Found., 1992-98, Meml. Health Sys., 1997-2003, United Way of St. Joseph County, Inc., 1992-98, Conv. and Tourism Industry Coun., 1994-2000, CASIE Ctr., Inc., 1998—, Home Mgmt. Resources, Inc. 2003—. Fellow Am. Coll. Tax Counsel, Am. Bar Found., Ind. Bar Found.; mem. ABA (taxation sect.), Ind. State Bar Assn. (chmn. taxation sect. 1977-78), Summit Club (chmn. 1976-77), Morris Park Country Club (bd. dirs., sec. 1998-2001). Democrat. Roman Catholic. Avocations: golf, softball, weightlifting. Home: 17705 Waxwing Ln South Bend IN 46635-1328 Office: Barnes & Thornburg 600 1st Source Bank Ctr 100 N Michigan St Ste 600 South Bend IN 46601-1632 Office Phone: 574-233-1171.

SEALS, MARGARET LOUISE CRUMRINE, newspaper editor; b. Buckhannon, W.Va., Oct. 27, 1944; d. James Richard and Helen Margaret (Brown) Crumrine; m. Harry Eugene Seals, Jan. 10, 1975. BS in journalism, W. Va. U., 1966; MS in mass. comm., Va. Commonwealth U., 1983. Reporter, copy editor Democrat & Chronicle, Rochester, NY, 1966-67, Dayton (Ohio) Daily News, 1967-68; copy editor Richmond (Va.) Times-Dispatch, 1968-75, copy desk slot editor, 1975-81, exec. news editor, 1981, asst. mng. editor, 1982-92, dep. mng. editor, 1992-93, mng. editor, 1994—. Mem. Leadership Metro Richmond, 1986, mem. adv. bd. sch. mass. comm. Va. Commonwealth U., 1988-93; mem. vis. com. Sch. Journalism, W.Va. U., 1999—. Named Outstanding Woman in Comms. YWCA Met. Richmond, 1989; recipient Perley Isaac Reed award W.Va. U. Journalism Sch. Alumni Assn., 1996; inducted into Va. Comm. Hall of Fame, 2003. Mem.: Richmond Assn. Black Journalists, Nat. Assn. Black Journalists, Va. Press Assn. (dir. 2001—03, treas. 2003—), AP Mng. Editors (editor APME News 1993—94, dir. 1993—95, treas. 1996—97, dir. 1998—2001, Disting. Svc. award 2002), Va. Press Women (treas. 1986—88, 2d v.p. 1988—90, pres. 1990—92, Press Woman of Yr. 1986, Communicator of Achievement award 1997), Soc. Profl. Journalists (bd. dirs. Va. profl. chpt. 1998—2003, pres. Va. profl. chpt. 2000—02), Nat. Fedn. Press Women (bd. dirs. 1990—92, Communicator of Achievement award 1997), Phi Kappa Phi. Avocations: history, historical fiction, jazz. Office: Richmond-Times Dispatch PO Box 85333 Richmond VA 23293-5333 E-mail: lseals@timesdispatch.com.

SEALY, VERNOL ST. CLAIR, scientist; came to U.S., 1962; m. Josephine Doreen Nanton, May 8, 1965; children: Vernetta, Vernol Jr. Gen. cert. edn., U. London, 1962; LLB, La Salle Ext. U., Chgo., 1967; BS in Zoology, Howard U., 1968, Med. Tech. cert., 1969, MS in Microbiology, 1971; MPH, U. Mich., 1974; PhD in Religion summa cum laude, Trinity Theol. Sem., Newburgh, Ind., 1988; Cultural Doctorate in Sacred Philosophy, World U., Tucson, 1984. Ordained to ministry Seventh-day Adventist Ch. as elder, 1978; registered microbiologist. Elder Seventh-day Adventist Ch., mem. adminstrv. bd., 1975-81, Ypsilanti, Mich., 1981-84, dir. personal ministries, 1981-82; mem. adminstrv. bd. Oakwood Seven-day Adventist Ch., Melvindale, Mich., 1986—; med. technologist D.C. Gen. Hosp., 1970-73; clin. lab. hematologist St. Joseph Mercy Hosp., 1973—. With nursing, neuro-psychiatry unit Freedmen's Hosp., Howard U., Washington; conducted M.S. rsch. NIH, 1970-71. Past mem. Boy's Scout Assn.; commandant Brit. Red Cross Soc. Fellow Royal Soc. Health; mem. Adventist Theol. Soc., Am. Soc. Clin. Pathologists (cert. med. technologist, hematologist), N.Y. Acad. Scis., Internat. Biog. Assn. (life patron), Am. Biog. Inst. and Rsch. Assn. (rsch. bd. advisors, dep. gov. 1988—). Home: 3667 Helen St Ypsilanti MI 48197-3760 *To know the Creator-Redeemer God and to be like Him, is man's highest destiny. To reveal His presence through a constant exhibition of His love, is to know Him, and to be like Him: For God is Love.*

SEAMAN, ALFRED JARVIS, retired advertising agency executive; b. Hempstead, L.I., N.Y., Sept. 17, 1912; s. Alfred J. and Ellen (Delaney) S.; m. Mary M. Schill, Sept. 26, 1937 (dec. June 1975); children: Marilyn Hollingsworth, Susan, Barry, Deborah; m. Honor S. Mellor, July 16, 1977. BS, Columbia U., 1935; LittD, L.I. U., 1987. Account exec. Fuller & Smith & Ross, Inc., N.Y.C., 1937-41; partner Knight & Gilbert. Inc., Boston, 1941-43; with Compton Advt., Inc., N.Y.C., 1946-59, exec. v.p., creative dir., dir., 1954-59; vice chmn. bd., chmn. exec. com. SSC & B, Inc., 1959-60, pres., chief exec. officer, 1960-79, chmn., chief exec. officer, 1979-81. Dir., mem. exec. com. Interpublic Group of Cos., Inc. Hon. bd. dirs., adv. council, founding chmn. Advt. Ednl. Found.; bd. dirs., hon. dir. com. Advt. Council.; chmn. planning bd., 1962—, mayor Village Upper Brookville, 1966-98; chmn. emeritus Samuel Waxman Cancer Research Found.; dir. Jupiter Hosp., 1991-2002. Lt. USNR, 1943-46. Named to Advt. Hall of Fame, 1983 Mem.: U.S. Sr. Golf Assn., Creek (Locust Valley, L.I.) (pres.), Piping Rock (Locust Valley, L.I.), Racquet and Tennis (N.Y.C.), Jupiter Island (Fla.), Nat. Golf Links Am. (Southampton, N.Y.), Seminole (Fla.), Hobe Sound Yacht (Fla.). Home: Wolver Hollow Rd Upper Brookville Oyster Bay NY 11771 also: Jupiter Island 126 Gomez Rd Hobe Sound FL 33455-2424 Office: 220 E 42nd St New York NY 10017-5806

SEAMAN, ARLENE ANNA, retired musician, educator; b. Pontiac, Mich., Jan. 21, 1918; d. Roy Russell and Mabel Louise (Heffron) S. BS, life cert., Ea. Mich. U., 1939; MMus, Wayne State U., 1951; postgrad., Colo. Coll., 1951-52, Acad. Music, Zermatt Switzerland, 1954, 58, U. Mich. Guest conductor Shepherds and Angels, Symphonie Concertante, 1951; asst. conductor Detroit Women's Symphony, 1960-68; adjudicator Mich. State Band and Orch. Festivals, Solo and Ensemble Festivals, 1950-70, Detroit Fiddler's Band Auditions, 1948-52, Mich. Fedn. Music Clubs, 1948-55; tchr. Ea. Mich. U., 1939-42, Hartland Sch. Music, 1939-42, Pontiac (Mich.) Pub. Schs., 1942-45, Detroit Pub. Schs., 1945-73, pvt. studio, 1973-90. Performer cello South Oakland Symphony, 1958-65, Detroit Women's Symphony, 1951-68, Riviera Theatre Orch., 1959, 60, Masonic Auditorium Opera, Ballet Seasons, 1959-65, Toledo Ohio Symphony, 1963-70, others; performer trumpet Detroit Brass Quartet, 1974-78; piano accompanist various auditions, recitals, solo and ensemble festivals; composer: Let There Be Music, 1949, Fantasy for French Horn and Symphonic Band, 1951. Mem. Quota Internat., Delta Omicron. Home: 6231 N Montebella Rd #347 Tucson AZ 85704

SEAMAN, BARBARA (ANN ROSNER), author; b. NYC, Sept. 11, 1935; d. Henry Jerome and Sophie Blanche (Kimels) Rosner; m. Gideon Seaman, Jan. 13, 1957 (div.); children: Noah Samuel, Elana Felicia, Shira Jean. BA (Ford Found. scholar), Oberlin Coll., 1956, LHD (hon.), 1978; cert. in advanced sci. writing (Sloan-Rockefeller fellow), Columbia U., 1968. Columnist Brides Mag., NYC, 1964-68; columnist, contbg. editor Ladies' Home Jour., NYC, 1965-69; editor child care and edn. Family Cir., NYC, 1970-73; contbg. editor Omni mag., 1978; cons. FYI, ABC-TV, 1979-80; v.p. for devel. David Brooks Prodn., 1990-94; contbg. editor MS Mag., 1993—; columnist Hadassah Mag., 2000—03. Cons. US Senate subcom. on monopoly: Nelson pill hearings, 1970; presented testimony to Senate and Congl. coms., 1970—; lectr. in field; participant TV discussion shows; tchr. Coll. New Rochelle, 1975, Sagaris Inst., 1975, CUNY, 1993; founding mem. NY Women's Forum, 1973-99; co-founder Nat. Women's Health Network, 1975—, Comm. Consultants for Choice, 1985-86, Nat. Task Force Sexual Malpractice, 1985-86, Families Against Sexually Abusive Therapists and Other Profl., 1992—; v.p. Women's Med. Ctr., NYC, 1971-73; mem. ERA Emergency Task Force, 1979; adv. coun. Feminist Press, Old Westbury, NY, 1975; adv. bd. Feminist Ctr. for Human Growth and Devel., 1979, Women's History Libr., Berkeley, Calif., 1973-75; steering com. Women's Forum, 1974; adv. bd. NOW, NY, 1973, Women's Guide to Books, 1974, Jewish Women for Affirmative Action, Evanston, Ill., 1973—, Jour. Women and Health, 1975, Jewish Feminist Orgn., NYC, 1975; chair com. domestic violence Nat. Coun. Women's Health, 1993-98; judge for various journalism awards. Author: The Doctors' Case Against the Pill, 1969, rev. edit., 1980, 25th anniversary edit., 1995, Free and Female, 1972; (with G. Seaman) Women and the Crisis in Sex Hormones, 1977, Lovely Me: The Life of Jacqueline Susann, 1987, anniversary edit., 1996; (with Gary Null) For Women Only: Your Guide to Health Empowerment, 2000; The Greatest Experiment ever Performed on Women: exploding the Estrogen Myth, 2003; contbg. author: foreword to Lunaception, 1975; The Bisexuals, 1974, Career and Motherhood, 1979, The Menopause Industry, 1994; author (play) I Am a Woman, 1972; (movie) Scandalous Me: The Jackie Susann Story, 1998; contbr. (anthologies) Rooms with No View, 1974, Women and Men, 1975, Seizing Our Bodies, 1978, Women's Health Care: A Guide to Alternatives, 1984; Encyclopaedia of Childbirth, 1992, Lawyers Manual on Domestic Violence: Representing the Victim, 1995, The Conversation Begins, 1996, Real Majority Media Minority, 1997, The Reader's Companion to US Women's History, 1997, Jewish Women in America: An Historical Encyclopedia, 1997, Textbook of Women's Health, 1997, Women's Health, 1999, Routledge International Encyclopedia of Women,2001; George Mag., 250 ways to make Am. Better, 1999; Hands On! 33 More Things Every Girl Should Know, 2001, Sexual Revolution, 2003; cons. (film) The Pill, 1999; PBS Am. Experience the Pill, 2003; narrator (film) Taking Our Bodies Back, 1974; contbr. articles to newspapers, popular mags.; books and articles translated into Spanish, German, Dutch, Turkish, Japanese, Hebrew, French, Italian. Alumni cons. women's studies program Oberlin Coll., 1975; motivation com. Am. Cancer Soc., 1973; adv. com. Older Women's Health Project, NYU Med. Ctr., 1980; bd. dir. Safe Transp. of People, NYC, 1975, Women's Health Newsletter, 1983; adv. bd. DES Action, 1977, 7 Stories Press, 1997-; cons. Nat. Task Force on DES, 1978; contraceptive rsch. br. HEW, 1980; v.p., bd. dir. ARM (Abortion Rights Moblzn.), 1981—; hon. bd. dir. Carcinogen Info. Program, St. Louis, 1981, Am. Friends of Rabin Med. Ctr., 1998—;; trustee Nat. Coun. on Women in Medicine, 1989-1991, Nat. Coun. on Women's Health, 1992-2000; chmn. adv. bd. Coalition for Family Justice, 1991—; co-chair Domestic Violence com. NY Women's Agenda, 1992-93, del. Can.-USA Women's Health Forum, 1996; host com. Womens Health Day, Beijing, Plus-Five UN Reunion, 2000; cons. FDA Patient Labels on Oral Contraceptives, 2000-01; nat. judge Project Censored award, 1997-. Recipient citation for books as first to raise issue of sexism in health care as world-wide issue Libr. of Congress, 1973, citation as author responsible for patient package inserts on prescriptions HEW, 1970, Matrix award, 1978, Pioneer Woman award Resources Divsn. of Am. Assn. Retired Persons, 1986, Athena award Nat. Coun. Women's Health, 1992, Health Advocacy award Health Policy Adv. Ctr., APHA, 1994, Project Censored award, 1996, Postal Service Women's Rights Movement stamp, 2000; Poynter Journalism Fellow, Yale U., 2003; inviting com. Am. Writers Congress. Mem. PEN, Authors Guild, Nat. Assn. Sci. Writers. Address: 110 W End Ave Apt 5D New York NY 10023-6348

SEAMAN, DARYL KENNETH, oil company executive; b. Rouleau, Sask., Can., Apr. 28, 1922; BSME, U. Sask., 1948, LLD (hon.), 1982, U. Calgary, 1993. Cert. mech. engr. CEO Bow Valley Industries Ltd., Calgary, Alta., Can., 1962-70, 85-91, chmn., chief exec. officer, 1970-82; chmn. Box Valley Industries Ltd., Calgary, Alta., Can., 1982-85; pres. Bow Valley Industries Ltd., Calgary, Alta., Can., 1985-87, chmn., 1991-92. Bd. dir. Far West Mining Ltd., Pure Techs. Ltd., Western Lakota Energy Svcs. Inc., Bow Valley Energy Ltd.; co-owner Calgary Flames Hockey Club, bd. dir.; chmn., pres. Dox Investments, Inc.; hon. regent Athol Murray Coll. of Notre Dame, 2001—.

Mem. Royal Commn. Econ. Union and Devel. Prospects for Can., 1982-85; active numerous coms. for fundraising U. Sask.; hon. chmn. The Western Heritage Centre Soc.; chmn. nat. adv. com. Banff Sch. Mgmt. Served with RCAF, 1941-45, North Africa, Italy. There is no repetition since it is indicated as an award you received and as a membership. Mem. Assn. Profl. Engrs., Geologists and Geophysicists (hon. life, Frank Spragins award, 1985, McGill Mgmt. Achievement award, 1979), Order of Canada 1993, Western Heritage Centre Soc., Ranchmen's Club, RAF Club, Earl Grey Golf Club, Calgary Petroleum Club, Calgary Golf and Country Club, U. Calgary Chancellor's Club. Progressive Conservative. Mem. United Ch. Can. Avocations: ranching, golf, hunting, skiing. Home and Office: Dox Investments Inc 2320 300-5 Ave SW Calgary AB Canada T2P 3C4 Office Phone: 403-290-1884. E-mail: admin@doxinvestments.com.

SEAMAN, IRVING, JR., banker; b. Milw., July 14, 1923; s. Irving and Anne (Douglas) S.; m. June Carry, June 24, 1950, (dec. 2001); children: Peter Stewart, Marion Carry, Irving Osborne, Anne Douglas; m. Barbara P. Gardner, May 22, 2002. BA, Yale U., 1944. With Continental Ill. Nat. Bank & Trust Co., Chgo., 1947-61, v.p., 1959-61; pres., chief exec. officer, dir. Nat. Boulevard Bank, Chgo., 1961-65, chmn. exec. com., chief exec. officer, dir., 1966-76; vice chmn. bd., dir. Sears Bank and Trust Co., Chgo., 1976-77, pres., chief operating officer, dir., 1977-82; sr. cons. Burson-Marsteller, Chgo., 1982-94. Chmn. bd. Associated Bank Chgo., 1985—. Mem. Northwestern U. Assn.; life mem. bd. dirs. Lake Forest Hosp.; bd. dirs. United Way of Chgo., 1975-89, pres., 1979; bd. dirs. United Way/Crusade of Mercy, 1980-89, 94-95, vice chmn., 1980-81; trustee Chgo. Symphony Orch., 1987—. Lt. (j.g.) USNR, WWII. Mem. Commonwealth Club, Econ. Club, Chgo. Club, Comml Club, Racquet Club, Onwentsia Club, Winter Club, Old Elm Club (Highland Park, Ill.), Shoreacres Club (Lake Bluff, Ill.), Augusta Nat. Golf Club (Ga.), Marsh Landing Club (Fla.), Sawgrass (Fla.) Country Club. Home: 666 N Sheridan Rd Lake Forest IL 60045-1410 Office: Assoc Bank Chgo 200 E Randolph St Chicago IL 60601-6436

SEAMAN, JEFFREY, consumer products company executive; Grad., U. Pa., 1984. Pres. Rooms to Go, Feffner, Fla., 1990—. Office: Rooms to Go 11540 E Us Highway 92 Seffner FL 33584-7346

SEAMAN, JEROME FRANCIS, actuary; b. Oak Park, Ill., Nov. 4, 1942; s. William Francis and Bernice Florence (Haughey) S.; m. Jacquelyn Ann Robinson, Aug. 22, 1970; children: Carolyn, John. BA, U. Notre Dame, 1964; MA, Northwestern U., 1991. Asst. actuary Combined Ins. Co. of Am., Chgo., 1966-73; v.p., actuary United Equitable Life Ins. Co., Skokie, Ill., 1975-77; mgr. Peat Marwick Mitchell & Co., Chgo., 1973-75, 77-78; nat. dir. actuarial svcs. Arthur Young & Co., Chgo., 1978-83; pres., cons. actuary Jerome F. Seaman & Assocs., Evanston, Ill., 1983—. Dir. Polysystems, Inc., Chgo., 1987-91. Contbr. articles to profl. jours. Recipient Commendation for Svc. Pres. Ronald Reagan, 1982. Fellow Soc. of Actuaries, Conf. of Cons. Actuaries; mem. Am. Acad. Actuaries (task force on risk based capital health orgns. 1993-95). Democrat. Unitarian Universalist. Avocations: running, hiking, classical music, opera, baseball. Home and Office: Jerome F Seaman & Assocs 1864 Sherman Ave Unit 6NW Evanston IL 60201-3738 E-mail: jerryseaman@sbcglobal.net.

SEAMAN, ROBERT E., III, lawyer; b. Chgo., Apr. 2, 1947; s. Robert E. II and Rae June (Blair) S.; children: Kimberly Desiree, Charissa Alaine, Robert E. IV, Jason Robert. BA in Polit. Sci., The Citadel, 1969; JD, U. Va., 1972; postdoctoral, N.Y. Inst. Fin., 1975-77, Harvard U., 1979. Bar: N.Y. 1975, S.C. 1978, U.S. Dist. Ct. (so. dist.) N.Y. 1975, U.S. Tax Ct. 1980, U.S. Ct. Appeals (2nd cir.) 1975, U.S. Ct. Appeals (4th cir.) 1979, U.S. Supreme Ct. 1979, U.S. Ct. Mil. Appeals 1980. Assoc. Breed, Abbott & Morgan, N.Y.C., 1972-74; v.p.-legal, asst. sec. Paine, Webber, Jackson & Curtis Inc. and subs., N.Y.C., 1974-77, asst. to chmn. bd. PaineWebber Inc., 1974-77; assoc. gen. counsel Col. Life and Accident Ins. Co., Columbia, S.C., 1977-80; sole practice, 1980—. Gen. counsel Jacom Computer Services, Inc., Northvale, N.J., 1977—; chmn. The dorchester Group, 1987—; bd. dirs., gen. counsel Internat. Chem. Cons., Ltd., 1983-88; pres. Titan Trading Co., Inc., Columbia, 1984-86, Comptel Data Sys., 1984—; chief exec. officer, pub. Up2Date Market Adv. Service, Columbia, 1985-87; chmn. bd., CEO Race Mktg. Assocs. Inc.; lectr. various ednl. instns. Co-author: How to Use the Relative Strength Index to Increase Trading Profits, 1986, Legal Issues in the Leasing Process, 1991; editor in chief: The Reading Guide and Virginia Law School Outline Series, 1971-72; sr. editor Va. Law Weekly, 1970-72; contbr. articles to profl. jours. Student senator S.C. Legislature, 1968-69; mem. coll. presdl. adv. com., state dir. Collegiate Counsel of UN, 1968-69; trustee Faith United Meth. Ch.; coord. phon-a-thon campaign Midlands S.C. youth div. YMCA, 1980-82; class chmn. Citadel Devel. Found., 1980; chpt. chmn., campaign adv. com. chmn., vice chmn. exec. com. Midlands chpt. March of Dimes, 1978-81; mem. task force Greater Columbia C. of C.; vice chmn. bd. KIDS North Jersey, 1990-94; founder, chmn. The Millennium Found., 1992—. Served capt. M.I., inf. U.S. Army, 1972 -77, Res., 1977-83. Robert R. McCormick scholar McCormick Found., and Chgo. Tribune, 1965-69, DuPont scholar U. Va., 1969-72; winner Estate Planning contest 1st Nat. Bank Chgo., 1971; recipient Leadership award Citadel Devel. Found., 1979-80, named Young Man of Yr., S.C. Greater Met. Area Jaycees, 1980; recipient Recognition award Nat. March of Dimes, 1981; named Knight Comdr., Grand Cross, Min. Fin. and Advocar Gen., Order St. John Knights of Malta. Mem. Assn. of Bar of City of N.Y., ABA (state regulation of securities com., subcom. on oil and gas, subcom. on regulation of equipment leasing, securities industry assn. compliance divsn. 1974-77), Am. Assn. Equipment Lessors, Info. Tech. Resellers Assn., NYSE, AMEX, Nat. Assn. Securities Dealers (registered rep.), Commodities Futures Trading Commn. (registered prin.), N.Y. Bar Assn., S.C. Bar Assn., Citadel Brigadier Club (bd. dirs.), Ill. Citadel Club (pres.), Knights of Malta (Knighted and designated Knight Comdr., Grand Cross, Minister of Fin. and Avocar Gen. Order of St. John), Pi Sigma Alpha; Clubs: Yale Club N.Y.C., Rockland Country Club, Com. of 100 Club, Met. Bus. Club, Palmetto Soc., Toastmasters (pres. Lexington chpt., ann. impromptu speech contest champion, Toastmaster of Yr. 1979). Office: Jacom Computer Serv 2121 SW Broadway 2 Portland OR 97201-3146

SEAMAN, WILLIAM BERNARD, physician, radiology educator; b. Chgo., Jan. 5, 1917; s. Benjamin and Dorothy E. S.; m. Veryl Swick, February 26, 1944; children: Marvin Gene, Cheryl Dorothy, William David. Student, U. Mich., 1934-37; MD, Harvard U., 1941. Diplomate Am. Bd. Radiology. Intern Billings Hosp., U. Chgo., 1941-42; asst. radiology Yale U. Sch. Medicine, 1947-48, instr., 1948-49; instr. radiology Washington U. Sch. Medicine, St. Louis, 1949-51, assoc. prof., 1951-55, prof., 1955-56; prof. radiology, chmn. dept. Coll. Phys. and Surg., Columbia U., 1956-82; James Picker prof. emeritus Columbia U., 1982—. Dir. radiology service, trustee Presbyn. Hosp., N.Y.C. Served as maj. USAAF, 1942-46; flight surgeon. Recipient W.B. Cannon medal Soc. Gastro-intestinal Radiologists, 1979, Gold medal Am. Coll. Radiology, 1983 Mem. Radiol. Soc. N.A., Am. Roentgen Ray Soc. (pres. 1973-74, gold medal 1988), Am. Coll. Radiology (pres. 1980-81), Assn. U. Radiologists (pres. 1955-56, Gold medal 1979), N.Y. Roentgen Soc. (pres. 1961-62), N.Y. Gastroent. Soc. (pres. 1965-66), Soc. Chmn. Academic Radiology Depts. (pres. 1967-68), Eastern Radiol. Soc. (pres. 1985-86). Presbyterian. Home: 2108 Devonshire Way Palm Beach Gardens FL 33418-6873

SEAMANS, ROBERT CHANNING, JR., astronautical engineering educator; b. Salem, Mass., Oct. 30, 1918; s. Robert Channing and Pauline (Bosson) S.; m. Eugenia Merrill, June 13, 1942; children: Katherine (Mrs. Louis Padulo), Robert Channing III, Joseph, May (Seamans Baldwin), Daniel M. BS, Harvard U., 1939; MS, MIT, 1942, ScD, 1951; grad. exec. program bus. adminstrn., Columbia U., 1959; DSc, Rollins Coll., 1962, NYU, 1967; DEng, Norwich Acad., 1971, Notre Dame U., 1974, Rensselaer Poly. Inst., 1974, U. Wyo., 1975, George Washington U., 1975, Lehigh U., 1976, Thomas Coll., 1980, Curry Coll., 1982. Successively instr. dept. aero. engring., staff engr. instrumentation lab., asst. prof., project leader instrumentation lab., asso. prof. Mass. Inst. Tech., 1941-55; chief engr. Project Meteor, 1950-53, dir. flight control lab., 1953-55; mgr. airborne systems lab., chief systems engr. airborne systems dept. RCA, 1955-58, chief engr. missile electronics and controls div., 1958-60; asso. adminstr. NASA, 1960-68, dep. adminstr., 1965-68, cons., 1968-69; vis. prof. MIT, 1968, Hunsaker prof., 1968-69; sec. air force, 1969-73; pres. Nat. Acad. Engring., 1973-74; adminstr. ERDA, Washington, 1974-77; Henry R. Luce prof. environment and pub. policy MIT, 1977-84, sr. lectr. dept. aeros. and astronautics, 1984-96, dean Sch. Engring., 1978-81. Mem. sci. adv. bd. USAF, 1957-62, assoc. adviser, 1963-67. Bd. overseers Harvard U., 1968—74; trustee emeritus Mus. Sci., Boston, Sea Edn. Assn., Nat. Geog. Soc., Carnegie Inst., Washington, Woods Hole Oceanographic Inst. Recipient naval ordnance devel. award 1945, Godfrey L. Cabot award Aero Club New Eng., 1965, disting. svc. medal NASA, 1965, 69, Robert H. Goddard meml. trophy, 1968, disting. pub. svc. medal Dept. Def., 1973, exceptional civilian svc. award Dept. Air Force, 1973, Gen. Thomas D. White U.S. Air Force Space Trophy, 1973, Ralph Coats Roe medal ASME, 1977; achievement award Nat. Soc. Profl. Engrs., Thomas D. White Nat. Def. award, 1980, exceptional svc. award Dept. Air Force, 1985. Fellow Am. Acad. Arts and Scis., Am. Astron. Soc., IEEE, AIAA (hon., Lawrence Sperry award 1951); mem. Internat. Acad. Astronautics, Am. Soc. Pub. Adminstrn., Nat. Acad. Engring. (Arthur M. Bueche Award, 1994, Daniel Guggenheim award 1996), AAAS, Air Force Acad. Found., Fgn. Policy Assn., Coun. on Fgn. Rels., Sigma Xi. Clubs: Harvard (Boston); Manchester Yacht (Mass.); Essex County (Mass.); Chevy Chase, Metropolitan (Washington); Cruising of Am. (Boston Sta.).

SEAMANS, WILLIAM, writer, commentator, former television and radio journalist; b. Providence, July 8, 1925; s. William and Mary Seamans; m. Jane Kingsbury, Sept. 15, 1951; children: Laurie, Jonathan, Adam. AB, Brown U., 1949; MS, Columbia U., 1952. Freelance journalist, 1952-53; journalist CBS News, 1953-63; producer evening news ABC News, 1963-65, European producer, 1965-70, field producer N.Y.C., 1970-72, corr., bur. chief Tel Aviv, 1972-92; commentator Vt. Pub. Radio, lectr., freelance writer, 1992—. Producer Nightline in Israel Week (including Palestinian-Israeli town meeting) (Emmy award, Dupont award). Served with inf. AUS, 1942-45. Decorated Bronze Star medal; CBS Murrow News fellow Columbia U., 1961-62. Mem. Writers Guild Am., Nat. Acad. TV Arts and Scis. (Emmy award 1961, 89), Overseas Press Club Am. (award for best radio reporting invasion of Cyprus 1974, award for best fgn. affairs documentary Yitzhak Rabin biography 1975), Nat. Press Club (Washington), Fgn. Corrs. Assn. in Israel. E-mail: bseamans@worldpath.net.

SEAPKER, JANET KAY, museum and architectural history consultant; b. Pitts., Nov. 2, 1947; d. Charles Henry and Kathryn Elizabeth (Dany) S.; m. Edward F. Turberg, May 24, 1975. BA, U. Pitts., 1969; MA, SUNY, Cooperstown, 1975. Park ranger Nat. Park Svc., summers 1967-69; archtl. historian N.C. Archives and History, Raleigh, 1971—76, hist. preservation adminstr., 1976—77, grant-in-aid adminstr., 1977—78; dir. Cape Fear Mus. (formerly New Hanover County Mus.), Wilmington, NC, 1978—2000, ret.; archtl. historian-preservation/mus. cons.; curator U. N.C. Wilmington's Kenan House, 2003—04; bd. dirs. Wrightsville Beach Mus., 2004—. Bd. dirs. Bellamy Mansion Found., Wilmington, 1986-89, 91-97, Lower Cape Fear Hist. Soc., Wilmington, 1985-88; N.C. rep. S.E. Mus. Conf., 1986-90; bd. dirs. Cape Fear Coast Conv. and Vis. Bur., 1997-2001, sec., 2001, Wrightsville Beach Mus., 2004-; field reviewer Inst. Mus. Svcs., 1982-2001 Contbr. articles to profl. jours. Bd. dirs. Downtown Area Revitalization Effort, Wilmington, 1979-81, Thalian Hall Ctr. for Performing Arts, 1996-98; bd. dirs. Hist. Wilmington Found., 1979-84, pres., 1980-81; mem. Cmty. Appearance Commn., Wilmington, 1984-88, 250th Anniversary Commn., Wilmington, 1986-90. Grad. program fellow SUNY, Cooperstown, 1969-70; recipient Profl. Svc. award N.C. Mus. Coun., 1982, Woman of Achievement award YWCA, 1994, William T. Alderson awardN.C. Mus. Coun., 2004. Mem. Am. Assn. Mus. (accreditation vis. com. 1983-2001, reviewer mus. assessment program 1982-2002), Nat. Trust Hist. Preservation, Southeastern Mus. Conf. (N.C. state rep. 1986-90), N.C. Mus. Coun. (sec.-treas. 1978-84, pres. 1984-86; recepient William T. Anderson award, 2004), Hist. Preservation Found N.C. (sec. 1976-78). Presbyterian. Home and Office: 307 N 15th St Wilmington NC 28401-3813 Office Phone: 910-762-6301. Personal E-mail: jseapker@ec.rr.com.

SEAR, MOREY LEONARD, federal judge, educator; b. New Orleans, Feb. 26, 1929; s. William and Yetty (Streiffer) S.; m. Lee Edrehi, May 26, 1951; children: William Sear II, Jane Lee. JD, Tulane U., 1950, LLD (hon.), 1999. Bar: La. 1950. Asst. dist. atty., Parish Orleans, 1952-55; individual practice law Stahl & Sear, New Orleans, 1955-71; spl. counsel New Orleans Aviation Bd., 1956-60; magistrate U.S. Dist. Ct. (ea. dist.) La., 1971-76, judge, 1976—, chief judge, 1992-99; judge Temp. Emergency Ct. of Appeals, 1982-87. Adj. prof. Tulane U. Coll. Law; former chmn. com. on adminstrn. of bankruptcy sys., former chmn. adv. com. on bankruptcy rules, former mem. com. on adminstrn. of fed. magistrate sys. Jud. Conf. U.S., mem. jud. panel on multidist. litigation; former mem. Jud. Conf. of U.S. and Its Exec. Com.; former mem. cir. coun. 5th Cir. of U.S.; founding dir. River Oaks Pvt. Psychiat. Hosp., 1968. Pres. Congregation Temple Sinai, 1977-79; bd. govs. Tulane Med. Ctr., 1977—; former chmn. Tulane Med. Ctr. Hosp. and Clinic, 1980-85. Decorated Order of Vasco Nunez de Balboa (Panama) with grade of grand ofcl. Mem. ABA, La. Bar Assn., New Orleans Bar Assn., Order of Barristers, Order of the Coif (hon.). Office: US Dist Ct C-256 US Courthouse 500 Camp St New Orleans LA 70130-3313

SEARBY, RICHARD HENRY, academic administrator, lawyer; b. July 23, 1931; s. Henry and Mary Searby; m. Caroline McAdam, 1962; 3 sons. MA (hons.), U. Oxford. Bar: London 1956, Victoria, Australia 1957. Assoc. to Chief Justice of Australia Rt. Hon. Sir Owen Dixon, 1956-59; ind. lectr. law relating to executors and trustees U. Melbourne, Australia, 1961-72; bd. dirs. News Corp. Ltd., Australia, 1977-92, chmn., 1981-91; bd. dirs. News Internat. plc, U.K., 1981-92, dep. chmn., 1987-92; bd. dirs., chmn. Equity Trustees Executors and Agy. Co. Ltd., 1975—2000, S. China Morning Post, 1987—92; chancellor Deakin U., 1997—. Bd. dirs. Shell Australia Ltd., 1977-98, Rio Tinto Ltd., 1977-97, Rio Tinto plc, 1995-997 Times Newspapers Holdings Ltd., dep. chmn., 1981-91; bd. dirs. Woodside Petroleum Ltd. Chmn. Geelong Grammar Sch., 1983-89; mem. coun. Nat. Libr. Australia, 1992-95, Mus. of Victoria, 1993-97. Decorated QC (Australia) 1971. Mem.: Melbourne Club. Avocations: reading, music, tennis, fishing. Office: 25 Flinders Ln Melbourne 3000 Australia also: 23A Hampden Rd Armadale 3143 Victoria Australia

SEARCY, ASHBURN PIDCOCK, SR., anesthesiologist; b. Thomasville, Ga., Oct. 23, 1937; s. Floyd Hartsfield and Anna Ashburn (Pidcock) S.; m. Nancy Rieves Ford, July 6, 1963; children: Ann Maxwell, Ashburn Pidcock Jr. BA in Humanities, Emory U., 1959; MD, Med. Coll. Ga., 1965. Fellow pathology Med. Coll. Ga., Augusta, 1962-63, resident in anesthesiology, 1966—68; rotating intern U. Hosp., Augusta, 1965-66; staff St. Joseph's Hosp., Augusta, 1968-76, Univ. Hosp., Augusta, 1968-76, Ga. Bapt. Med. Ctr., Atlanta, 1976-77, Northside Hosp., Atlanta, 1977-78, Kennestone Hosp., Marietta, Ga., 1978—2000, emeritus staff, 2000—; staff Columbia Marietta Surg. Ctr., 1989—2001, Emory-Adventist Hosp., Smyrna, Ga., 1991-2001, Wellstar Paulding Hosp., Dallas, Ga., 1998—, Mountainside Med. Ctr., Jasper, Ga., 1999—2001, 2004—; chief anesthesiology Mid. Ga. Hosp., Macon, 2001—02; staff Macon Outpatient Surgery, Inc., 2000—. Staff Coffee Reg. Med. Ctr., Douglas, Ga., 1999-2000, Archbold Meml. Hosp., Thomasville, Ga., 2000, Colquitt Reg. Med. Ctr., Moultrie, Ga., So. Surgery Ctr., La Grange, Ga., 2000, Appling County Health Sys., Baxley, Ga., 2000, Chestatee Reg. Med. Ctr., Dahlonega, Ga., 2000-2002, Tanner Med. Ctr., Villa Rica, Ga., 2000-01, 04—, So. Crescent Anesthesiology, Inc., Newnan Hosp., Newnan, Ga., 2000—, Chestatee Regional Hosp., Dahlonega, 2000-02, 04—, Ga. Bone and Joint Outpatient Surgery, Newman, W. Ga. Regional Health Sys., LaGrange, Ga., 2003—, West Ga. Regional Health Sys., LaGrange, 2003—, Washington County Regional Med. ctr., Sandersville, Ga., 2003—, Med. Ctr. Ctrl. Ga., Macon, 2004—, Henry Regional Med. Ctr., Stockbridge, Ga., 2004—, Sumter Regional Med. Ctr., Americus, Ga., 2004—; adv. dir. Citizens Bank, Cairo, Ga., 1995—. Mem. AMA, Am. Soc. Anesthesiologists, Ga. Soc. Anesthesiologists, Med. Assn. Ga. Bahá'I.

SEARCY, DOROTHY JAMES, missionary; b. Yalaha, Fla., Oct. 8, 1924; d. Roland and Irma Kathryn (Bayan) James; married, Mar. 29, 1942 (widowed 1999); children: Gloria Rolanda Searcy Baird, Paul Raphael, Martha Loraine Searcy Bullard. Student, Lee Coll. (now Lee U.), Cleveland, Tenn., 1959-60. Missionary, Ch. of God, Nigeria, 1956-59, Panama and Canal Zone, 1960-66; editor-in-chief Ch. of God newsletters, various chs., various cities and countries, 1966—. Republican. Avocations: writing, songwriting, crafts, Scrabble, nature walks. Home: 27440 Lime Ave Yalaha FL 34797-3204

SEARCY, LEON, JR., professional football player; b. Washington, Dec. 21, 1969; m. Sonya; children: Malika-Maya, Kenya Imani; stepchild, Willie. Degree in Sociology, Miami. Offensive tackle Pittsburgh Steelers, 1992-95; football player Super Bowl, 1995; offensive tackle Jacksonville Jaguars, 1996—2001; guard Miami Dolphins, 2002—. Active Searcy Found., Jacksonville, Orlando, Fla., Jacksonville's Lee Boys and Girls Club; supporter numerous holiday efforts to feed homeless and assist elderly; supporter coll. scholarships to deserving H.S. students; spokesperson Kidney Found., 1999, Jacksonville Bone Marrow Donor Registry. Named All-Pro team Sports Illustrated, 1995, second-team All-Pro, AP, Pro Football Newsweekly, 1999, Best Right Tackle in NFL, The Sporting News, 1999; named to Pro Bowl, 1999. Office: Miami Dolph 7500 SW 30th St Fort Lauderdale FL 33314

SEARCY, WILLIAM NELSON, lawyer, director; b. Moultire, Ga., June 26, 1942; s. Floyd Hartsfield and Anna (Pidcock) Searcy; m. Camille Heery, June 17, 1967; 1 child, Amelia Ashburn. AB, U. Ga., 1964, JD, 1967; LLM in Taxation, Washington U., St. Louis, 1968. Bar: Ga. 1967, U.S. Dist. Ct. (so. dist.) Ga. 1970, U.S. Ct. Appeals (5th and 11th cirs.) 1976, U.S. Tax Ct. Assoc. Bouhan, Williams & Levy, Savannah, Ga., 1970-73; ptnr. Brannen, Searcy & Smith LLP, Savannah, 1973—. Chmn. bd. dirs. Citizens Bank; sec. Am. Fed. Savs. and Loan Assn., 1978—81; mem. adv. bd. Liberty Savs. Bank, 1984—88. Pres. Chatham-Savannah Voluntary Action Ctr., Inc., 1978—80. Served to maj. gen. Ga. N.G. U.S. Army, 1967—2004, comdr. Ga. N.G. U.S. Army, 2000—04. Mem.: ABA (sec. spl. liaison tax com. S.E. region 1983—85, chmn. 1984—85), Inst. Continuing Legal Edn., Savannah Estate Planning Coun., Am. Judicature Soc., Savannah Bar Assn. (pres. Younger Lawyers sect. 1975—76), State Bar Ga. (mem.-at-large exec. coun. Young Lawyers sect. 1975—78, chmn. conf. with Ga. Soc. CPAs 1979—81, chmn. sect. taxation 1983—84, Ga. commn. continuing lawyer competency 1989—95, vice chmn. 1995), N.G. Assn. U.S. (chmn. air resolution com. 2001—03, bd. dirs. 2002—04, chmn. resolutions com. 2003—), Georgian Club, Savannah Golf Club, Oglehtorpe Club, Rotary (pres. Savannah West 2004—). Office: PO Box 8002 Savannah GA 31412-8002

SEARFOSS, DAVID W. insurance company executive; B in Acctg., Bentley Coll.; MBA, U. Conn. CPA, CFA, CLU. With Price Waterhouse, Orion Capital Corp.; sr. v.p., CFO Phoenix Home Life Mutual Ins. Co., 1987-94; exec. v.p., CFO Phoenix Co. (formerly Phoenix Home Life Mutual Ins. Co.), 1994—. Bd. dirs. PXRE. Mem. AICPA, Assn. for Investment Mgmt. Rsch., Conn. Soc. CPA, Hartford Soc. Fin. Analysts. Office: Phoenix Home Life Mutual Ins Co One American Row Hartford CT 06102

SEARING, MARJORY ELLEN, government official, economist; b. N.Y.C., Mar. 29, 1945; d. William Edgar Searing and Jean Frances (Smith) Searing Fusaro; 1 child, Stephanie Anne Lane. BA in Econs., SUNY-Binghamton, 1966; MA in Econs., Georgetown U., 1969, PhD in Econs., 1972. Economist Bur. Econs. Analysis U.S. Dept. Commerce, Washington, 1967-73, internat. economist Bur. East-West Trade, 1973-74, dir. Office Internat. Sector Policy, 1980-84, dir. Office Industry Assessment, 1984-86, acting dep. asst. sec. sci. and electronics, 1984-85, dir. Office Multilateral Affairs, 1986-90, dep. asst. sec. for Japan, 1991-97, asst. sec., acting dir. Gen. U.S. and Fgn. Comml. Svc., 1997-98; dep. asst. sec. for Asia and the Pacific, 1998—; sr. internat. economist Office Trade Policy U.S. Dept. Treasury, Washington, 1974-76, dir. Office East-West Econ. Policy, 1976-79. Contbr. numerous articles to profl. publs. N.Y. State Regents scholar, 1962-65; Georgetown U. fellow, 1966-71 Office: US Dept Commerce Constitution Ave NW Washington DC 20230-0001

SEARLE, ANDREW BARTON, fund raising consultant; b. Washington, Aug. 30, 1962; s. Harvey Russell and Louise Morgan (Cowles) S.; m. Samuel C. Pang, July 5, 2003. BA, Haverford Coll., 1984. Asst. to exec. dir. Springfield (Mass.) Ctr. Bus. Dist., Inc., 1984-86; asst. dir., regional capital campaign Smith Coll., Northampton, Mass., 1986-88; assoc. dir. devel. Watkinson Sch., Hartford, Conn., 1988-91; dir. devel. Wilmington (Del.) Friends Sch., 1991-93, Lawrence Acad., Groton, Mass., 1993-96; prin. Andrew Searle Fund Raising Counsel, Groton, Mass., 1996—. Trustee Alumni Program Coun., 1992-2000, v.p., 1999-2000, spkr./panelist various confs., 1989-00; spkr./panelist various confs. Coun. for Advancement and Support of Edn., 1991-98; spkr. Nat. Assn. of Ind. Schs., 2000. Contbr. articles to profl. publs.; columnist Funding Private Schools, Boston, 1996-2002. Trustee Summer Theatre at Mount Holyoke Coll., South Hadley, Mass., 1994—2001, pres., 1997—98; trustee Svc. Providers, Inc., Springrield, 1988—91, Groton (Mass.) Pub. Libr., 1998—2003; corporator StageWest, Springfield, 1988—91; bd. dirs. Gay & Lesbian Advs. and Defenders, Boston, 2001—. Avocation: genealogical research. Office: PO Box 6074 Lincoln MA 01773 Mailing: 4 Brooks Hill Rd Groton MA 01450 E-mail: absearle@comcast.net.

SEARLE, BERNARD G. pharmacologist, dental educator; b. N.Y.C., June 9, 1919; s. Harry Shapiro and Anna Banner; m. Norma D. Searle, Feb. 7, 1949. PhD, NYU, 1959. Rsch. scientist N.Y.C. Dept. of Health, N.Y.C. Cpl. U.S. Army, 1943—46. Decorated Good Conduct Medal. Jewish. Achievements include development of method for determining lead in blood using atomic absorption spectrophotometer; procedure for detecting phenylketonuria. Avocation: reading. Home: 3769 W McNab Rd #10A Pompano Beach FL 33069

SEARLE, PHILIP FORD, banker; b. Kansas City, Mo., July 23, 1924; s. Albert Addison and Edith (Thompson) S.; m. Jean Adair Hanneman, Nov. 22, 1950 (dec. Nov. 1990); 1 child, Charles Randolph; m. Jean Walker, Oct. 4, 1992 (dec. oct. 1993); m. Elizabeth Gordon, Nov. 4, 1994. AB, Cornell U., 1949; grad. in banking, Rutgers U., 1957, 64. With Geneva (Ohio) Savs. & Trust Co., 1949-60, pres., 1959-60; pres., sr. trust officer Northeastern Ohio Nat. Bank, Ashtabula, 1960-69; pres., CEO BancOhio Corp., Columbus, 1969-75; chmn., CEO Flagship Banks, Inc., Miami, 1975-84; chmn. bd. Sun Banks, Inc., Orlando, 1984-85, cons., 1986-94. Mem. faculty Sch. Banking, Ohio U., 1959-70, Nat. Trust Sch., Northwestern U., Evanston, Ill., 1965-68; corp. adv. com. Nat. Assn. Securities Dealers, 1981-83; v.p., fed. adv. coun. to bd. govs. FRS, 1983-85; chmn. Nat. Adv. Bd. to Oversight Bd. for Resolution Trust Corp., 1991-92. Co-author: The Management of a Trust Department, 1967. Past chmn. bd. regents Stonier Grad. Sch. Banking, Rutgers U., 1974-76, past mem. faculty; trustee Fin. Acctg. Found., Norwalk, Conn., 1989-93. Capt. AUS, 1943-46, 51-52, ETO. Decorated Bronze Star; named outstanding citizen in Ashtabula County, 1967. Mem. Am. Bankers Assn. (bd. dirs. 1972-74, governing coun.), Bank Adminstrn. Inst. (nat. chmn. 1987-88, bd. dirs. Chgo. 1985-89), Fla. Bankers Assn. (bd. dirs. 1979-81, coun. 1981), Ohio Bankers Assn. (pres. 1970-71), Assn. Bank Holding Cos. (pres. 1979-81), Fla. C. of C. (bd. dirs. 1978-82), Royal Poinciana Golf Club (Naples, Fla.), Naples Yacht Club, Catawba Island Club (Port Clinton, Ohio), Phi Kappa Tau.

SEARLE, ROBERT FERGUSON, minister; b. Auburn, NY, July 13, 1951; s. Loren Rawson and Esther Lucille (Ferguson) S.; m. Elizabeth Jane Anderson. BS, Cornell U., 1973; MDiv, Princeton Theol. Sem., 1977; DMin, Asbury Theol. Sem., 1997. Ordained deacon United Meth. Ch., 1978, ordained elder United Meth. Ch., 1980, cert. in pastoral care, bd. cert. chaplain Nat. Assn. Vet. Affairs Chaplains, 2004. Pastor of Blodgett Mills Freetown and McGraw (NY) United Meth. Ch., 1978-84; pastor Pennsylvania Ave. United Meth. Ch., Pine City, NY, 1984-98; chaplain resident Duke U. Med. Ctr., 1998-99; chaplain U.S. Army Res., 1991—; pastor Clyde United Meth. Ch., 1999—2003; adj. prof. spiritual formation Northeastern Sem., Rochester, NY, 2000—; contract chaplain Canandaigua and Syracuse VA Hosp., 2000—; mobilized as chaplain Operation Enduring Freedom, 2003; pastor Red Creek

Westbury Sterling United Meth. Chs., 2004—. Mem. dist. bd. Ordained Ministry, Syracuse, NY, 1980-84, mem. conf. bd., 1980-85, dist. youth dir., Syracuse, 1981-84; mem. Cortland County Youth Bur., 1980-81; mem. hosp. com. Cortland County Coun. of Chs., 1980-84. Mem. McGraw Bd. Edn., 1981-84; bd. dirs. Meals on Wheels, Elmira, 1985-88, CPC, Elmira, 1985-93; mem. edn. and rsch. instl. rev. bd. Arnot Ogden Hosp., Elmira, 1995-98; mem. cmty. bd. Southport Correctional Facility, 1987-98; spiritual dir. Spiritual Exercises, High Acres, Geneva, NY, 1986-98, 99-2003, spiritual dir. Walk to Emmaus, Rome, NY, 1993; mem. design team Ctrl. Lakes Dist. Acad. Spiritual Devel., 1999—. Mem.: Charles Wesley Soc., Am. Assn. Christian Counselors, Masons, KT. Republican. Avocations: reading, exercise, travel, music. Home: 5905 Draper St Wolcott NY 14590-1148 Office Phone: 315-754-8853. E-mail: r0027@aol.com.

SEARLE, RODNEY NEWELL, state legislator, farmer, insurance agent; b. Camden, N.J., July 17, 1920; s. William Albert and Ruby Marie (Barrus) S.; m. Janette Elizabeth Christie, May 17, 1941 (dec.); children: R. Newell Jr., Linda Jennison Grant, Alan John; m. Ruth Anne Bartlett, May 6, 2001. BA, Mankato State U., 1960; DHL, Winona State U., 2001. Prodn. coordinator Johnson & Johnson, New Brunswick, N.J., 1940-47; farmer Waseca, Minn., 1947—; spl. agt. John Hancock Mut. Ins. Co., Waseca, Minn., 1961-84; mem. Minn. Ho. of Reps., St. Paul, 1957-80, speaker, 1979—. Author: Minnesota Standoff—The Politics of Deadlock, 1990. Lay reader St. John's Episcopal Ch., 1952—; chmn. Upper Mississippi River Basin Commn., 1981-82; pres. Minn. State U. Bd., 1981-92; chmn. Minn. Higher Edn. Bd., 1991-92; bd. dirs. Minn. Wellsprings, 1984-90; emeritus mem. adv. bd. Hubert H. Humphrey Inst.; emeritus mem. coun. Minn. Hist. Soc.; bd. dirs. Minn. Agrl. Interpretive Ctr., 1983-2002; mem. Waseca County Hist. Bd., 1995—; capt. Minn. Wing of the Civil Air Patrol. Named Minn. State Tree Farmer of Yr., 1978 Mem. Am. Tree Farm System, Nat. Conf. State Legislators, Minn. Forestry Assn. (bd. dirs. 1991-2001), Masons, Rotary (pres. club 1968). Republican.

SEARLES, EDNA LOWE, artist, illustrator, composer; b. Minden, La., Sept. 10, 1936; m. Thomas D. Searles. AA, Mont. Coll., 1975; BA in Edn., La. Poly., 1958. Tchr. pub. sch., 1958—65. Guest curator Delaplaine Visual Arts Ctr., Frederick, Md., 1995, East Meets West. Illustrator Soy for the 21st Century, 1984, ABC Coloring Book, 1994, Mind Children, 1995, Mind Travel, 1998, About You, 1998, Choose Life, 2002, (coloring book) Animal Alphabet Book, 2003; one-woman shows include Arnot Art Mus., Elmira, N.Y., 1988, Va. Tech State U., 1989, Gwinnett Coun. of the Arts Gallery, Ga., 1990, VA Honorarium, 1990, Other: Affiliation and Exhibits, Janice Aldridge Gallery, Georgetown, Washington, 1996, Sculpture on the Ground, Md., 1994, 1999, The Artist's Gallery, Frederick, Md., 1997—2002, The Garden Gallery, Carlisle, Pa., 1999—, Nancy Stamm's Galleria, 1999—, Gallery of New Masters, Sandy Spring, Md., 2000—01, Millinneum Exhibit Music for the Eyes, 1999—2000, Musicians and All that Jazz, Frederick, Md., 2000, Gallery of New Masters, Olney, Md., 2000—01, Boarman Art Ctr., Martinsburg, W.Va., 2001, exhibited in group shows at Nat. League Am. Pen Women, 2003, Summer Sch. Mus., Washington, 2004, Sandy Spring Mus., Md., 2004, Friendship Gallery, Chevy Chase, 2004. Past pres. Clarksburg (Md.) Cmty. Assn. Recipient Juror's award for painting Montgomery County Art, 1993, Internat. Gold medal for painting Accademia Italia, 1973; named Wilson Wims Citizen of Yr. Clarksburg Comm. Assn., 1974. Mem.: DAR (vice regent Pleasant Plains of Damascus chpt. 2001—02), Nat. League Am. Pen Women (pres. Chevy Chase br. 1980—82, 2002—04, Md. state pres. 2004—, 3d v.p. Chevy Chase br. 2004—, Poetry award). Methodist. Achievements include invention of music system for the deaf to "see" music as art. Avocations: hammered dulcimer, composing music, folk singer, harp, piano.

SEARS, DAVID ALAN, medical educator; b. Portland, Oreg., Oct. 20, 1931; s. Harry J. and Huldah M. (Meyer) S.; m. Yvonne D. Bowles, June 22, 1958; children: Geoffrey B., Cameron J., Andrea Y. Sears Andrews. BS, Yale U., 1953; MS, U. Oreg., 1958, MD, 1959. Cert. in internal medicine and hematology. Intern, resident in internal medicine U. Rochester (N.Y.) Sch. Medicine and Dentistry, 1959-62, fellow in hematology, 1962-63; rsch. hematologist Walter Reed Army Inst. Rsch., Washington, 1963-66; asst. prof. hematology U. Rochester Sch. Medicine and Dentistry, 1966-69; from assoc. prof. to prof. medicine U. Tex. Health Scis. Ctr., San Antonio, 1969-80; prof. medicine Baylor Coll. Medicine, Houston, 1980—2002, prof. emeritus, 2002—. Local, state and nat. bd. dirs., various other offices Am. Cancer Soc., 1971—. Contbr. chpts. to books, articles to profl. jours. Elder Presbyn. Ch. Capt. U.S. Army, 1963-66. Recipient St. George medal Am. Cancer Soc., Anne Norris Humanitarian award Sickle Cell Assn. Mem. ACP, Am. Soc. Hematology (Disting. emeritus mem.), Am. Fedn. Med. Rsch., Internat. Soc. Hematology, Alpha Omega Alpha. Office: Baylor Coll Medicine 1 Baylor Plz Houston TX 77030-3411

SEARS, DAVID O'KEEFE, psychology educator; b. Urbana, Ill., June 24, 1935; s. Robert R. and Pauline (Snedden) S.; divorced; children: Juliet, Olivia, Meredith. BA in History, Stanford U., 1957; PhD in Psychology, Yale U., 1962. Asst. prof. to prof. psychology and polit. sci. UCLA, 1961—, dean social scis., 1983-92. Dir. Inst. for Social Sci. Rsch., 1993—. Author: Public Opinion, 1964, Politics of Violence, 1973, Tax Revolt, 1985, Political Cognition, 1986, Social Psychology, 11th edit., 2003, Racialized Politics, 2000, Oxford Handbook of Political Psychology, 2003. Fellow Am. Acad. Arts and Scis.; mem. Soc. for Advancement Socio-Econs. (pres. 1991-92), Internat. Soc. Polit. Psychology (pres. 1994-95). Office: UCLA Psychology Dept Los Angeles CA 90095-0001 Office Phone: 310-825-2160. Business E-Mail: sears@psych.ucla.edu.

SEARS, EDWARD L. English language educator, real estate investor; b. Pratt, Kans., Jan. 27, 1954; s. Melvin Leroy and Deloris Fay (Owens) S.; m. Janeth (Bontia). BA in English, West Tex. State U., 1990; MA in English, Tex. Tech. U., 1993. Firefighter Dodge City (Kans.) Fire Dept., 1981-83, Amarillo (Tex.) Fire Dept., 1983-86; tutor Writing Ctr. West Tex. State U., Canyon, 1987-90, Tex. Tech. U., Lubbock, 1990-92, tchg. asst., 1990-92; writing lab. super. South Plains Coll., Levelland, Tex., 1992—2001, asst. prof. English, 1993—. Ssgt. USAF, 1977-81. Democrat. Roman Catholic. Office: South Plains Coll Reese Ctr 528 Gilbert Dr Lubbock TX 79416

SEARS, EDWARD MILNER, JR., newspaper editor; b. Bluefield, W.Va., Dec. 28, 1944; s. Edward Milner and Helene (Stras) S.; m. Jo Ann Langworthy, May 15, 1971; 1 child, Helene Mateer. BS in Journalism, U. Fla., 1967. Makeup editor Atlanta Constn., 1970, news editor, 1971-73, feature editor, 1974, city editor, 1975-76, asst. mng. editor, 1977, mng. editor, 1978-80, Atlanta Jour., 1980-82, Atlanta Jour. and Atlanta Constn., 1982-85; editor Palm Beach Post, 1985—. Served with U.S. Army, 1968-69. Named Editor of the Yr., Editor & Pub., 2003 Mem. Fla. Soc. Newspaper Editors, Am. Soc. Newspaper Editors, Sigma Delta Chi. Home: 230 Dyer Rd West Palm Beach FL 33405-1218 Office: Palm Beach Post 2751 S Dixie Hwy West Palm Beach FL 33405-1233 E-mail: esears@pbpost.com.

SEARS, JOHN PATRICK, lawyer; b. Syracuse, N.Y., July 3, 1940; s. James Louis and Helen Mary (Fitzgerald) S.; m. Carol Jean Osborne, Aug. 25, 1962; children: James Louis, Ellen Margaret, Amy Elizabeth. BS, Notre Dame U., 1960; LLB, JD, Georgetown U., 1963. Bar: N.Y. 1963. Clk. N.Y. Ct. Appeals, 1963-65; assoc. firm Nixon, Mudge, Rose, Guthrie, Alexander & Mitchell, 1965-66; mem. staff Richard M. Nixon, 1966-69; dep. counsel to Pres. Nixon, 1969-70; ptnr. Gadsby & Hannah, Washington, 1970-75, Baskin & Sears, Washington, 1977-84; pvt. practice Washington, 1984—. Mgr. Ronald Regan's Presdl. Campaign, 1975-76, 79-80; polit. analyst NBC Today Show, 1984-89; mem. Wall Street Jour. bd. of polit. experts, 1984—; columnist LA Times, Newsday, 1992—. Sr. advisor Jack Kemp for v.p. Campaign, 1996. Fellow Kennedy Inst. Politics, Harvard U., 1970. Home: 2801 New Mexico Ave NW Washington DC 20007-3921 Office: 2021 K St NW Washington DC 20006-1003

SEARS, JOHN WINTHROP, lawyer; b. Boston, Dec. 18, 1930; s. Richard Dudley and Frederica Fulton (Leser) S.; m. Catherine Coolidge, 1965 (div. 1970). AB magna cum laude, Harvard U., 1952, JD, 1959; MLitt, Oxford U., 1957. Bar: Mass. 1959, U.S. Dist. Ct. Mass. 1982. Rep. Brown Bros. Harriman, N.Y.C., 1959-63, Boston, 1963-66; mem. Mass. Ho. Reps., 1965-68; sheriff Suffolk County, Mass., 1968-69; chmn. Boston Fin. Commn., 1969-70, Met. Dist. Commn., 1970-75; councilor-at-large Boston City Coun., 1980-82; trustee Sears Office, Boston, 1975—. Contbr. articles to profl. jours. Apptd. bd. dirs. Fulbright Scholarship, 1991-93; trustee Christ's Ch., Longwood, Brookline, Mass., 1965—, Sears Trusts, Boston, 1975—; hon. trustee J. F. Kennedy Libr., 1991—; bd. dirs. Am. Mus. Textile Heritage, 1987-97, Shirley-Eustis Assoc., Environ. League, Mass., 1994-97; Rep. candidate Sec. State, Mass., 1978, Gov. of Mass., 1982; vice chmn. Ward 5 Rep. Com., 1965-69, 75-85; chmn. Rep. State Com., 1975-76, mem., 1980-85; del. Rep. Nat. Conv., 1968, 76, State Conv., 1966-92; mem. U.S. Electoral Coll., 1984; bd. dirs. United South End Settlements, 1966—, chmn., 1977-78. Lt. comdr. USNR, 1952-54, 61-62. Recipient Outstanding Pub. Servant award Mass. Legis. Assn., 1975; Rhodes scholar, 1955 Mem. Mass. Bar Assn., New Eng. Hist. and Geneal. Soc. (bd. dirs., councillor 1977-82), Mass. Hist. Soc., Handel and Haydn Soc. (gov. 1982-87), Signet Soc., Boston Atheneum, Tennis and Racquet Club, Somerset Club, The Country Club (Brookline), St. Botolph Club, Club of Odd Vols., Wednesday Evening Club of 1777, Thursday Evening Club of 1846 (pres. 1999), Spee Club (Cambridge chpt., pres., trustee), Phi Beta Kappa. Republican. Home: 7 Acorn St Boston MA 02108-3501 *As the working years come to an end, some of us look for ways to teach, to help neighbors, especially those in need, to build up the beauty and excellence we may have encountered in our own lives, and do our best to pass them on to others.*

SEARS, KENT T. automotive executive; BS in Bus. Plant mgr. Flint Engine Plant, GM, 1987—91, Doraville Assembly Plant, Atlanta, 1991—93; dir. mfg. transmissions Powertrain Group, 1993—96; mfg. mgr. GM Truck Group, Pontiac, 1996—99; exec. in charge quality N. Am. GM, 1999—2001; v.p. quality GM N. Am., 2001—. Office: GM Corp PO Box 300 300 Renaissance Ctr Detroit MI 48265-3000

SEARS, LEAH J. state supreme court justice; b. June 13, 1955; d. Thomas E. and Onnye J. Sears; married; children: Addison, Brennan. BA, Cornell U., 1976; JD, Emory U., 1980; M in Apellate Jud. Process, U. Va.; JD (hon.), Morehouse Coll., 1993. Judge City Ct. Atlanta; atty. Alston & Bird, Atlanta; trial judge Superior Ct. Fulton County; justice Supreme Ct. Ga., Atlanta, 1992—. Contbr. articles to profl. jours. Bd. dirs. Sadie G. Mays Nursing Home, Ga. chpt. Nat. Coun. Christians & Jews; mem. adv. bd. United Way Drug Abuse Action Ctr., Outdoor Activity Nature Ctr.; mem. Cornell U. Women's Coun.; mem. steering com. Ga. Women's History Month, Children's Def. Fund Black Cmty. Crusade Children; founder Battered Women's Project, Columbus, Ga. Recipient Outstanding Young Alumna award Emory U., One of 100 Most Influential Georgians Ga. Trend mag., Excellence in Pub. Svc. award Ga. Coalition Black Women, 1992, Outstanding Woman of Achievement YWCA Greater Atlanta, One of Under Forty & On the Fast Track, 1993. Mem. ABA (chair bd. elections), Nat. Assn. Women Judges, Ga. Bar Assn., Women's Forum Ga., Gate City Bar Assn., Atlanta Bar Assn. (past chair jud. sect.), Ga. Assn. Black Women Attys. (founder, pres.), Fourth Tuesday Group, Jack & Jill Am. (Atlanta chpt.), Links Inc. (Atlanta chpt.), Alpha Kappa Alpha. Office: Ga Supreme Ct 244 Washington Street Atlanta GA 30334-9007

SEARS, MARY HELEN, lawyer; b. Syracuse, N.Y. d. James Louis and Helen Mary (Fitzgerald) Sears. AB, Cornell U., 1950; JD with honors, George Washington U., 1960. Bar: Va. 1960, D.C. 1961, U.S. Supreme Ct. 1963. Chemist Allied Chem. and Dye Corp., Syracuse, 1950-52, Hercules Powder Co., Wilmington, Del., 1952-55; patent examiner U.S. Patent Office, Washington, 1955-60; pvt. practice Washington, 1960-61; assoc. Irons, Birch, Swindler & McKie, Washington, 1961-69; mem. firm Irons and Sears, Washington, 1969-84; chmn. trade regulation practice dept. Memel, Jacobs, Pierno, Gersh & Ellsworth, Washington, 1984-87; ptnr., chmn. intellectual property and unfair competition practice dept. Ginsburg, Feldman & Bress, Washington, 1987-91; ptnr., chmn. intellectual property and telecomm. practice group Reid & Priest, Washington, 1991-94; founder, chmn. M. H. Sears Law Firm, 1994—. Mem. adv. bd. Boardroom Reports, Inc., N.Y.C., 1980-85; mem. Cornell U. Coun., 1981-87, 89-93, life mem., 1995—, mem. adminstrv. bd., 1984-86. Contbr. articles to various publs. Recipient Outstanding Performance award U.S. Dept. Commerce, 1957; named to Guide to the World's Leading Patent Law Experts Euromoney Publs., PLC, 1995, 97. Mem.: ABA (co-chmn. appellate practice com., litigation sect. 1989—92), D.C. Bar Assn., Va. State Bar Assn., Internat. Trademark Assn., Am. Soc. Internat. Law, Am. Intellectual Property Law Assn., George Washington U. Law Alumnae Assn. (bd. dirs. 1995—2001), Order of Coif, Phi Alpha Delta. Republican. Office: MH Sears Law Firm Chartered NW Ste 800 910 17th St Washington DC 20006-2601 Office Phone: 202-463-3892. E-mail: mhsears@mhsears.com.

SEARS, MICHAEL M. former aerospace transportation executive; b. St. Louis, July 16, 1947; s. Murlin Mitchell, Mary Rassieur (Parsons); m. Debra Sue Tompkins, Aug. 23, 1969; children: Matthew Mitchell, Mark Michael. BS in elec. engring., MS in elec. engring., Purdue U.; MS in engring. mgmt., U. Mo. Rolla; Ph. D science (hon.), U. Mo.-St.Louis, 2001; Ph. D in engring. (hon.), Purdue U., 2002. Avionics engr., F-15 and ATF McDonnell Aircraft Co., St. Louis, 1969—84; radar mgr. McDonnel Aircraft Co., St. Louis, 1984—87, chief program engr. for advanced F/A18 strike fighter studies, 1987—88; program mgr. new bus. devel. McDonnell Douglas, 1988—90, v.p., gen. mgr. new aircraft products divsn., 1990-97; pres. McDonnell Douglas Aerospace, 1997; pres., McDonnell military aircraft and missile systems div. The Boeing Co., St. Louis, 1997—98, pres., military aircraft and missile systems, 1998—2000, sr. v.p., 1998—2000, exec. v.p., CFO, 2000—03. Major Mo. Army Nat. Guard, 1970-78; V.p. Naval Aviation Mus. Found.; dir. March of Dimes; bd. trustees St. Louis Sci. Ctr., Washington U. Recipient Alumni Achievement award, U. Mo.-Rolla, Outstanding Elec. Engr. award, Purdue U., Disting. Alumni award, 1988, Laurel award, Aviation Week, 1995, Hap Arnold award for excellence in aeronautical program mgmt.,(AIAA), 1998, Robert J. Collier award, Nat. Aeronautic Assn., 1999, Fleet Admiral Chester A. Nimitz award, Navy League, 2000. Fellow Am. Insts Aeronautics and Astronautics. Avocations: antique furniture, bowling, coaching children.

SEARS, ROBERT STEPHEN, finance educator, university dean; b. Odessa, Tex., May 27, 1950; s. William Bethel and Leola Vernon (Little) S.; Reva Dana Flournoy, Aug. 17, 1973; children: Matthew Stephen, Elizabeth Rea. AAS, Odessa Jr. Coll., 1970; BA summa cum laude, Tex. Tech. U., 1973, MS, 1976; PhD, U. N.C., 1980. Supr. Bethel Enterprises, Odessa, Tex., 1973-74; tchg. asst. Tex. Tech U., Lubbock, 1974-76, dir. Inst. Banking and Fin. Studies, 1988-98; tchg. asst. U. N.C., Chapel Hill, 1976-79; asst. prof. U. Ill., Champaign, 1979-85, assoc. prof., 1985-88; rsch. prof. Bur. Econ. and Bus., Champaign, 1984; tchg. asst. Lubbock Bankers Assn., 1990—; chmn. dept. fin. Tex. Tech U., 1997-2001; interim dean Tex. Tech U. Coll. Bus., 2000, sr. exec. assoc. dean, Coll. Bus, 2001—03. Cons. Cameron Brown Mortgage Co., Raleigh, N.C., 1978-80, Howard Savs. Bank, Livingston, N.J., 1980; asset mgr., trustee, pvt. investors, 1984—. Author: Investment Management, 1993, (chpt), Modern Real Estate, 1980, 84; assoc. editor Rev. of Bus. Studies, 1989-95, Jour. Fin. Rsch., 1990-96, Internat. Chmn. fin. com. Temple Bapt. Ch., Champaign, Ill., 1982, bd. deacons, 1982-88, chmn. deacons, lay leader, 1983; Sunday sch. tchr. Carrboro (NC) Bapt. Ch., 1977-79; bd. deacons Ind. Ave. Bapt. Ch., Lubbock, 1989-96, Sunday sch. tchr., 1991-92, master design com., 1993-96; trustee All Saints Episcopal Sch., 1995-2003, treas., 2000-03; bd. deacons Southcrest Bapt. Ch., Lubbock, 1998—. Rsch. grantee Cameron Brown Mortgage Co., Raleigh, N.C., 1978-80, U. Ill, Champaign, 1980-84, 86-87, Investors in Bus. Edn., Champaign, 1980-81, 84; recipient Excellence in Undergrad. Tchg. award U. Ill. Champaign, 1984-85, Award for Outstanding Coll. Educator Champaign-Urbana, Ill. Jaycees, 1983-84, Coll. of Commerce Alumni Assn. Undergrad. Excellence in Tchg. award U. Ill., 1981-82; Mortar Bd., Omicron Delta Kappa Leadership scholarship and Svc. award Tex. Tech U., 1997-98, Pres.'s Excellence in Tchg. award Tex. Tech U., 1993-94, Acad. Achievement award Tex. Tech U., 1994-95. Mem. Am. Fin. Assn., Southwestern Fin. Assn. (pres. 1989-90, v.p., program chmn. 1988-89, sec., treas. 1986-88, bd. dirs. 1984-86, mem. program com. 1985-86, 89—), Fin. Mgmt. Assn. (mem. program com. 1986, 89-94, 97, 99-2004), So. Fin. Assn. (mem. program com. 1986), Western Fin. Assn. (mem. program com. 1986), Ea. Fin. Assn., Lake Ridge Country Club. Republican. Baptist. Avocations: golf, walking, participating in sports with my children. Office: Tex Tech U COBA Lubbock TX 79409-2101 Home: 4203 88th Pl Lubbock TX 79423-2909 Office Phone: 806-742-3377.

SEARS, SANDRA LEE, computer consultant; b. Rochester, N.Y., Apr. 25, 1952; AB with distinction, Cornell U., 1974; MA, U. Conn., 1976, postgrad., 1976-81. Cert. in data processing. Tng. cons. Ins. Crime Prevention Inst., Westport, Conn., 1977-78; systems analyst Data Directions, Bloomfield, Conn., 1978-79; prin. S. S. Prindle Consulting, Manchester, Conn., 1979-81; dir. info. svcs. Conn. Attys. Title Ins., Rocky Hill, Conn., 1981-85; mgr., systems, programming Community Health Care Plan, Inc., Wallingford, Conn., 1985-87; assoc. dir. Mass. Mutual Life Ins., Springfield, Mass., 1987-91; cons. mgr. Coopers & Lybrand Cons., East Hartford, Conn., 1991-96; dir. info. architecture and data warehousing CIGNA Healthcare, Bloomfield, Conn., 1996-97; divsn. dir. advanced devel. solutions divsn. Advanced Computing Techniques, Glastonbury, Conn., 1997-98; practice dir. data warehousing and knowledge mgmt. PRT Group, Inc., Windsor, Conn., 1998-99; sr. mgr. KPMG Cons., Hartford, 1999-2001; prin. The Preceptor Group, Manchester, Conn., 2001—. Adj. faculty U. New Haven, West Haven, Conn., 1976-77, Eastern Conn. State U., Willimantic, 1986-2001, Manchester C.C., 1989—; participant Tex. Instruments' Case Satellite Seminar, 1989. Mentor Career Beginnings, Hartford, 1991-95. Presdl. scholar Nat. Merit Program, 1970, William Stout scholar Cornell U., 1973, AAUW fellow U. Conn., 1981. Mem. Cornell Club of Greater Hartford (mem. admissons vol. programs alumni adv. com., exec. bd., book award chair 1987—), Cornell Alumni Admissions Amb. Network (chair 1983-86), Mortar Board, Phi Kappa Phi, Pi Mu Epsilon. Office: The Preceptor Group 10 Gardner St Manchester CT 06040-5625 E-mail: slsears@preceptorgroup.com.

SEARS, WINSOME EARLE, congressman; b. Kingston, Jamaica, Mar. 11, 1964; m. Terence Owen Sears; children: DeJon L. Williams, Katia E., Janel C. AA cum laude, Tidewater C.C., 1992; BA in English, Old Dominion U., 1992; MA in Orgnl. Leadership, Regent U., 2003—. Mem. Va. Ho. of Dels., 2002—04; candidate 3d Congl. Dist., Va., 2004—. With USMC, 1983—86. Republican. Address: PO Box 12912 Norfolk VA 23541 Office Phone: 757-687-8211. Personal E-mail: winsea@msn.com.

SEARSON, DEE, retail products executive; CFO MTS, Inc., West Sacramento. Office: MTS Inc PO Box 919001 West Sacramento CA 95691-9001

SEARY, LAWRENCE ANTHONY, cinematographer, news assignment editor, field operations administrator; b. NYC, June 13, 1951; m. Phyllis Cole, Oct. 2, 1976; children: Tara Ann, Paul Anthony. BFA, NYU, 1973. News cameraman, assignment desk supr., prodr. NBC, N.Y.C., 1974—. Recipient N.Y. State Broadcast award UPI, 1987. Mem. Nat. TV Acad. (bd. govs. 1996-2000, 2003—, nat. bd. trustees 2003—, awards com., Emmy award nominations 1978, 82, 94-95, 2003, Emmy awards 1978, 2 Emmy awards 2003), Mensa, N.Y. Press Club (2d v.p., 2002—, Feature Video award 1994). Democrat. Roman Catholic. Office: NBC 30 Rockefeller Plz Rm 728E New York NY 10112-0002 E-mail: larry.seary@nbc.com.

SEASE, GENE ELWOOD, public relations company executive; b. Portage, Pa., June 28, 1931; s. Grover Chauncey and Clara Mae (Over) S.; m. Joanne D. Cherry, July 20, 1952; children: David Gene, Daniel Elwood, Cheryl Joanne. AB, Juniata Coll., 1952; B.D., Pitts. Theol. Sem., 1956, Th.M., 1959; PhD, U. Pitts., 1965, M.Ed., 1958; LL.D., U. Evansville, 1972, Butler U., 1972; Litt.D., Ind. State U., 1974; DD, U. Indpls., 1989. Ordained to ministry United Methodist Ch., 1956; pastor Grace United Meth. Ch., Wilkinsburg, Pitts., 1952-63; conf. dir., supt. Western Pa. Conf. United Meth. Ch., Pitts., 1963-68; lectr. grad. faculty U. Pitts., 1965-68; mem. staff U. Indpls., 1968-89, asst. to pres., 1968-69, pres., 1970-88, chancellor, 1988-89, pres. emeritus, 1989—; chmn. Sease, Gerig & Assocs., Indpls., 1989—. Bd. dirs. Bankers Life Ins. Co. of N.Y. Author: Christian Word Book, 1968; also numerous articles. Pres. Greater Indpls. Progress Com., 1972-75, Marion County Sheriff's Merit Bd.; mem. Ind. Scholarship Commn.; cons. Time Warner; bd. dirs. Indpls. Conv. Bur., Ind. Law Enforcement Tng. Acad., 500 Festival, Crossroads coun. Boy Scouts Am., Community Hosp. Indpls., St. Francis Hosp.; chmn. Ind. State Fair Commn. Mem. Internat. Platform Assn., English Speaking Union, Japan-Am. Soc. Ind., Ind. C. of C. (bd. dirs.), Indpls. C. of C. (bd. dirs.), Ind. Schoolmen's Club, Ind. State Fair Commn. (chmn.), Econ. Club of Indpls. (bd. dirs.), Skyline Club (bd. dirs.), Phi Delta Kappa, Alpha Phi Omega, Alpha Psi Omega. Clubs: Mason (Indpls.) (33 deg., Shriner), Kiwanian. (Indpls.), Columbia (Indpls.). Office Phone: 317-634-1171.

SEASHORE, MARGRETTA REED, physician, educator; b. Red Bank, N.J., June 20, 1939; d. Robert Clark and Lillie Ann (Heaviland) Reed; m. John Seashore, Dec. 26, 1964; children: Robert H., Carl J., Carolyn L. BA, Swarthmore Coll., 1961; MD, Yale U., 1965. Diplomate Am. Bd. Pediatrics, Am. Bd. Med. Genetics, Nat. Bd. Med. Examiners. Intern in pediat. Yale U. Sch. Medicine, New Haven, 1965-66, asst. resident in pediat., 1966-68, postdoctoral fellow in genetics and metabolism, depts. pediat. and medicine, 1968-70, asst. clin. prof. human genetics and pediat., 1974-78, from asst. prof. to assoc. prof., 1978-90, prof. genetics and pediatrics, 1990—; clin. asst. prof. pediat. U. Fla. Coll. Medicine, Gainesville, 1970-71, asst. prof., 1971-73; attending physician Duvall Med. Ctr., U. Hosp. Jacksonville, 1970-73, asst. prof., 1970-71; attending physician Hope Haven Children's Hosp., Jacksonville, Fla., 1970-73, Shands Tchg. Hosp., Gainesville, 1971-73, Danbury (Conn.) Hosp., 1977—, Yale-New Haven Hosp., 1974—, dir. Genetic Consultation Svc., 1977-86, 1989—; cons. physician Bridgeport (Conn.) Hosp., 1974—, Lawrence and Meml. Hosp., New London, Conn., 1979—, Norwalk (Conn.) Hosp., 1981—. Contbr. chapters to books. Fellow: Am. Coll. Med. Genetics (founding fellow), Am. Acad. Pediat. (mem. screening com. Conn. chpt. 1977—, mem. genetics com. 1989—94, chair com. genetics 1990—94); mem.: AAAS, AMA, New Eng. Genetics Group (chmn. outreach com. 1979—89, mem. steering com. 1979—98, chmn. screening com. 1989—93, co-dir. 1992—95), Soc. Study Inborn Errors of Metabolism, Am. Bd. Med. Genetics (bd. dirs. 2004—), Soc. Inherited Metabolic Disorders (bd. dirs. 1989—, sec. 1991—96, pres. 1997), Am. Soc. Human Genetics (mem. genetic svcs. com. 1986—91). Avocations: music, gardening, sewing, computers. Office: Yale U Sch Med Dept Genetics 333 Cedar St New Haven CT 06510-3289 Office Phone: 203-785-4938. Business E-Mail: margretta.seashore@yale.edu.

SEATON, CAROLLE CARTER, educator, writer; b. Oklahoma City, Okla., Sept. 18, 1939; d. Robert Henry and Claire (Haggard) Carter; m. James Cagney Seaton, Oct. 24, 1959 (dec.); children: Jene, James II, Ernest. B degree, U. West Fla., 1975, M degree, 1980, cert. edn. specialist, 1990. Kindergarten tchr. Santa Rosa Schs., Gulf Breeze, Fla., 1975-83, head gifted programs, 1983-85, staffing specialist Milton, Fla., 1985-95, program facilitator, 1995—. Editor: One Kid at a Time; author poetry. Chairperson Interagy. Coun., Milton, 1995-96; comdr. Gulf Breeze Sail and Power Squadron, 2002--. Mem. Fla. Assn. for the Gifted (regional rep. 1985-95), NEA. Avocations: diving, photography, charter boat captain, biking. Home: 907 Aquamarine Dr Gulf Breeze FL 32563-3001 Office: Santa Rosa Sch Dist 6751 Berryhill St Milton FL 32570-4824

SEATON, EDWARD LEE, editor, publishing executive; b. Manhattan, Kans., Feb. 5, 1943; s. Richard Melvin and Mary (Holton) Seaton; m. Karen Mathisen, Sept. 4, 1965; children: Edward Merrill, John David. AB cum laude, Harvard U., 1965; postgrad., U. Ctr., Quito, Ecuador, 1965-66, U. Mo., 1966—67. Staff writer Courier-Jour., Louisville, 1968—69; editor-in-chief, pub. Manhattan Mercury, 1969—. Bd. dirs., officer 8 newspaper and broadcasting affiliates; mem. adv. com. Knight Internat. Press Fellowship Program; mem. Pulitzer Prize Bd., 1992—2001, chmn., 2001; mem. Cabot Awards bd. Columbia U., 1995—2003. Contbr. articles to profl. jours. Chmn. Alfred M. Landon lecture patrons Kans. State U.; chmn. Latin Am. Scholarship Program Am. Univs., Cambridge, Mass., 1986—87. Decorated comendador Order Christopher Columbus (Dominican Republic); recipient Cabot prize, Columbia U., 1993; Fulbright scholar, 1965. Mem.: Internat. Press Inst., Internat. Ctr.

Journalists (bd. dirs. 1990—2001), Inter-Am. Press Assn. (pres. 1989—90), Am. Soc. Newspaper Editors (pres. 1998—99, Found. pres. 1994—), Kans. C. of C. and Industry (pres. 1987), Fly Club (Harvard U.). Avocations: tennis, cooking. Office: 318 N 5th St Manhattan KS 66505-0787

SEATON, ROBERT FINLAYSON, retired finance company executive; b. Hancock, Mich., Nov. 28, 1930; s. Donald W. and Mary Lucille (Finlayson) S.; m. Helen Jean Robarts, Apr. 18, 1954; children: Scott, Sandy. BS, Mich. Technol. U., 1952; MBA, Stanford, 1956; postgrad., Ind. U., 1966, U. So. Calif., 1973. Asst. sec. Palo Alto (Calif.) Mut. Savs. and Loan Assn., 1956-60; asst. v.p. Am. Savs. and Loan Assn. No. Calif., 1960-63; v.p. 1st Western Savs. and Loan Assn., Las Vegas, 1963-67; v.p., sec. Fed. Home Loan Bank, Cin., 1967-72; pres., chief exec. officer 2d Fed. Savs. and Loan Assn., Cleve., 1973, Cardinal Fed. Savs. Bank, Cleve., 1973-87, chmn., 1987-88; sr. v.p. Planned Giving Systems, Inc., Cleve., 1989-90, pres., 1990-94. V.p. Luth. Housing Corp.; trustee, treas. N.E. Ohio Coun. Higher Edn.; hon. trustee ParkWorks. Lt. USNR, 1952—54. Republican. Methodist. Home: 16 Pepper Creek Dr Cleveland OH 44124-5248

SEATON, SHIRLEY SMITH, academic administrator, consultant; b. Cleve. d. Kibble Smith and Cecil Wright; m. J. Lawrence Seaton, Oct. 2, 1965; 1 child, Eric Dean. *Son Eric Dean Seaton, BA 1991, Ohio State University, is a member of the Director's Guild of America and is currently a director of Disney Channel's #1 hit show, "That's So Raven."* BA, MA in History, Howard U., 1949; MEd, Case Western Res., 1956; EdD, U. Akron, 1981; cert. in Chinese history and culture, Beijing Normal U. Tchr. Cleve. Dist., 1950-59, dir. social studies, 1976-87; prin. Lafayette, Dike, Cleve., 1959-63, 65-76; with Stas. WEWS-TV, WVIZ-TV, Cleve., 1963-67; adj. prof. Cleve. State U., 1988-90; adminstr. John Carroll U., University Heights, Ohio, 1990—. Program dir. Office Econ. Opportunities, Cleve., 1965; peer rev. Ohio Profiency Test, 1986—; cons. Basics and Beyond, Cleve., 1990—. *John Carroll University recognized Shirley Smith Seaton for her outstanding service, scholarship and loyalty by inducting her as an honorary member of Alpha Sigma Nu, the Jesuit Honor Society.* Coord. Ctr. Civic Edn., 11th Congress Dist., 1987—; peer interview chair Fulbright tchr. exch. U.S. Dept. State, 1994-99, 2001-04; trustee Western Res. Hist. Soc., Cleve., 1996—, Ret. Vol. Program, Cleve., 1997-2003; commr. City of Cleveland Heights, Ohio, 1997—. Recipient Ohio Humanitarian award Govt. of Ohio, 1992; Fulbright grantee USIA, 1959, 82. Mem. Fulbright Assn., Nat. Alliance Black Edn., Coalition 100 Black Women, Am. Assn. Univ. Women, Phi Delta Kappa, Alpha Kappa Alpha, Phi Beta Delta, Alpha Sigma Nu, Am. Assn. U. Women. Episcopalian. Avocation: bridge. Home: 3680 Bendemeer Rd Cleveland Heights OH 44118 Office: John Carroll U 20700 North Pk Blvd University Heights OH 44118 E-mail: sseaton@jcu.edu.

SEATON, VAUGHN ALLEN, retired veterinary pathology educator; b. Abilene, Kans., Oct. 11, 1928; m. Clara I. Bertelrud; children: Gregory S., Jeffrey T. BS, DVM, Kans. State U., 1954; MS, Iowa State U., 1957. Pvt. practice, Janesville, Wis., 1954; instr. pathology Vet. Diagnostic Lab. Iowa State U., Ames, 1954-57, from asst. to assoc. prof. pathology Vet. Disgnostic Lab., 1957-64, prof., head Vet. Diagnostic Lab., 1964-94. Lab. coord. regional emergency animal disease eradication orgn. Animal and Plant Health Inspection Svc. USDA, 1974—; mem. rsch. com. Iowa Beef Industry Coun., 1972-85; mem. adv. bd. Iowa State Water Resources Rsch. Inst., 1973-80; cons. several orgns. Co-author: (monographs) Feasibility Study of College of Veterinary Medicine, 1972, Veterinary Diagnostic Laboratory Facilities-State of New York, 1970; bd. dirs. Iowa State U. Press, 1985-88, mem. manuscript com., 1982-85; contbr. articles to profl. jours. Trustee Ames Pub. Libr., 1979-85; mem. Iowa State Bd. Health, 1971-77, v.p., 1976-77; bd. dirs. Masonic Edn. Found., 1985-88. Mem. AVMA, Am. Assn. Vet. Lab. Diagnosticians (bd. govs. 1973-88, pres. 1968, E.P. Pope award 1980), Am. Coll. Vet. Toxicologists, U.S. Animal Health Assn., Iowa Vet. Med. Assn. (pres. 1971), North Ctrl. Assn. Vet. Lab. Diagnosticians, Western Vet. Conf. (exec. bd. 1986-90, v.p. 1994, pres.-elect 1995, pres. 1996), World Assn. Vet. Lab. Diagnosticians (pres. 1980-86), Ames C. of C. (bd. dirs. 1970-73), Phi Kappa Phi, Phi Zeta (pres. 1964), Alpha Zeta, Gamma Sigma Delta. Office: Iowa State U Coll Vet Medicine Vet Diagnostic Lab Ames IA 50011-0001

SEATS, PEGGY CHISOLM, marketing executive; b. Lisman, Ala., Oct. 12, 1951; d. William H. and Bernice (Berry) Chisolm; m. Melvin Seats (div.). BA in Communications cum laude, Lewis U., 1974; grad. cert. in event mgmt., George Washington U., 1995; MA in Pub. Comm., Am. U., 1997; grad. cert. in intercultural comm., Vaxjo (Sweden) U., 1997. Account exec. Globe Broadcasting, Chgo., 1976-78, Merrill Lynch, Chgo., 1978-79, Transp. Displays, Inc., Chgo., 1979-81; with Reverie, Inc., 1981—; nat. accounts mgr. Soft Sheen Products Co., Chgo., 1981-83; mktg. cons. Reverie, Inc., Chgo., 1983-85; pub. rels., mktg. mgr. Proctor & Gardner Advt., Chgo., 1985-86; dir. pub. rels., mktg. Morris Brown Coll., Atlanta, 1986-87; mgr. mktg. Howard U. Press, Washington, 1989-90; cons. White House Initiative on Historically Black Colls., Univs., 1990-92. State advisor U.S. Congl. Adv. Bd., Ill., 1982. Contbr. numerous articles to newspapers and mags. Founder Benjamin Banneker Meml. Found., Washington, 1996; organizer S.W. Waterfront Initiative, 2000—; mem. L'Enfant Plaza Revitalization Project, 1997—; bd. dir. Congl. Award Found. Recipient Kizzie award Black Women Hall of Fame, Chgo., 1981, Svc. award Nat. Assn. Women in Media, Chgo., 1982. Mem. Internat. Platform Assn., Internat. Assn. Bus. Communicators, Internat. Spl. Events Soc., Pub. Rels. Soc. Am., Black Pub. Rels. Soc. (founder Atlanta chpt.), Nat. Assn. Market Developers, World Affairs Coun., Comittee of 100, Lewis U. Alumni Assn. (bd. dirs. Ill. 1979), Washington Interdependence Coun. (founder, exec. dir. 1996), Benjamin Banneker Inst. Math. and Sci. (founder). Unitarian Universalist. Avocations: music, art collecting, reading. Home: 2020 Pennsylvania Ave NW Washington DC 20006-1811 Office Phone: 202-387-3380. E-mail: seatspc@aol.com.

SEAU, JUNIOR (TIANA SEAU JR.), professional football player; b. Samoa, Jan. 19, 1969; Student, U. So. Calif. Linebacker San Diego Chargers, 1990—2003, Miami Dolphins, 2003—. Player Super Bowl XXVIV, 1994. Named to Sporting News Coll. All-Am. Team, 1989, to Pro Bowl Team, 1991-2000, 2002, to Sporting News NFL All Pro Team, 1992, 93. Office: Miami Dolphins 7500 SW 30th St Davie FL 33324

SEAVER, JEFFREY MARK, SR., lawyer; b. Hartford, Conn., Feb. 4, 1960; s. Herbert Lawrence and Mary Muriel S.; m. Brenda Colette Seaver, June 23, 1983; children: Arielle, Lunden, Jared. B in Gen. Studies, La. Tech. U., 1988; JD, So. Univ. Law Ctr., Baton Rouge, 1997. Bar: La. 1997. With USAF, 1977-89, advanced through grades to tech. sgt., 1987, inflight refueling technician, 1977-89; dir. bank resolutions FDIC, Washington, 1990-94; mng. ptnr. Seaver Law Firm, Baton Rouge, 1997—2002; atty. at law The Simmons Law Firm, LLC, 2002—. Bd. dirs. Krewe of Orion, Baton Rouge. Author: Career Transition and Placement Training Manual, 1994. Recipient pro-bono award Baton Rouge Bar Assn., 1998. Mem. ABA, Assn. Trial Lawyers Am., La. Trial Lawyers Assn., La. State Bar Assn., Baton Rouge Bar Assn. Republican. Roman Catholic. Avocations: hunting, fishing. Home: 11070 Mead Rd Apt 205 Baton Rouge LA 70816-2279

SEAVER, ROBERT LESLIE, retired law educator; b. Brockton, Mass., June 13, 1937; s. Russell Bradford and Lois (Marchant) S.; m. Marjorie V. Rote, Aug. 21, 1960 (div. 1974); children: Kimberly, Eric, Kristen; m. Elizabeth A. Horwitz, May 22, 1984. AB cum laude, Tufts U., Medford, Mass., 1958; JD, U. Chgo., 1964. Bar: Ohio 1964, U.S. Ct. Appeals (6th cir.) 1964, U.S. Dist. Ct. (so. dist.) Ohio 1965. Assoc. Taft, Stettinius and Hollister, Cin., 1964-66; v.p., sec., gen. counsel IDI Mgmt. Inc., Cin., 1966-74; pvt. practice Cin., 1974-75; prof. law emeritus No. Ky. U. Salmon P. Chase Coll. Law, Highland Heights, 1975—; of counsel Cors & Bassett, Cin., 1993-99; ret., 1999. Cons. in field, 1975-00. Author/editor: Ohio Corporation Law, 1988; contbr. chpts. to books. Advisor subcom. on pvt. corps of Ky. Commn. on Constl. Rev., 1987. With USMC, 1958-61. Recipient Justice Robert O. Lukowsky award of Excellence Chase Law Sch. Student Bar Assn., 1986. Republican. Unitarian Universalist. Avocations: duplicate bridge (life master), history. E-mail: rseaver@cinci.rr.com.

SEAVEY, CHRISTOPHER GORDON, psychotherapist, addiction counselor; b. Syracuse, N.Y., Dec. 4, 1942; s. Gordon Crowell and Shirley Edith Seavey; m. Eudene Sawyer, Aug. 8, 1965 (div. Mar. 1983); children: Sandra, Sherry, Gordon; m. Nancy Bowen, 1983. BA in Human Svcs., U. Mass., Boston, 1986; MA in Rehab. Counseling, U. South Fla., Ft. Myers, 1991; PhD in Psychotherapy, Internat. U. Grad. Studies, 2001. Sr. counselor Project Turnabout, Hingham, Mass., 1982-86; counselor Coastal Cmty. Counseling, Braintree, Mass., 1986-87, South Shore Coun. on Alcoholism, Quincy, Mass., 1987; chem. dependency counselor II David Lawrence Ctr., Naples, Fla., 1989-90; vocat. rehab cons. Intracorp, Naples, 1990-96; acting dir. Addiction Recovery Ctr., Ft. Myers, Fla., 1993-98; clin. dir. Assisted Addiction Recovery, Naples, 1995—. Bd. dirs. AAR Counseling, Naples, Human Svc. Inc., Ft. Myers, 1995-97; mem. adv. bd. Naples Rehab. Inc., 1994-97. Mem. adj. bd. Project Help, Naples, 1996—; chmn. Collier County Depression Coalition, Naples, 1997. Recipient Book award U. Mass., Boston, 1986; U. Calif. San Francisco fellow, 1986; Tobacco Coalition grantee, 1998. Mem. NADAAC, ACA, Internat. Assn. Rehab. Profls., Internat. Coun. on Alcohol and Addictions, Fla. Rehab. Assn. (pres. S.W. Fla. chpt. 1994—, Svc. award 1999), S.W. Fla. Marriage and Family Counseling Assn., Fla. Mental Health Counselors, Gulf Coast Mental Health Counselors Assn. (past pres.), Phi Kappa Phi. Office: AAR Counseling 1061 Collier Centerway Ste 6 Naples FL 34110-1603 Office Phone: 239-436-7939. E-mail: chriseavey@earthlink.net.

SEAVEY, WILLIAM ARTHUR, lawyer, vintner; b. Los Angeles, Aug. 28, 1930; s. Arthur Jones and Dorothy (Keyes) S.; m. Mary van Beuren, June 25, 1955; children: Dorothy K., Arthur V.B., William G., Frederic A., Charles K. AB, Princeton U., 1952; LLB, Harvard U., 1955; grad. Inst. Internat. Studies, U. Geneva, Switzerland, 1956, D in Polit. Sci., 1970. Bar: Calif. 1957, U.S. Dist. Ct. (so. and no. dist.) Calif. 1957, U.S. Ct. Appeals (9th cir.) 1957. Assoc. Luce, Forward, Kunzel & Scripps, San Diego, 1956-57; asst. U.S. atty. U.S. Dist. Ct. (so. dist.) Calif., 1957-59; with Noon & Seavey, San Diego, 1959-65; lectr. in internat. law and econ., asst. to pres. Mills Coll., Oakland, Calif., 1968-74; ptnr. Richards & Seavey, San Francisco, 1974-76, Davis, Stafford, Kellman & Fenwick, San Francisco, 1976-78; of counsel Friedman, Olive, McCubbin, Spalding, Bilter, Roosevelt etal, San Francisco, 1987—2003. Proprietor Seavey Vineyard, Napa County, 1981—. Author: Dumping Since the War: The Gatt and National Laws, 1970. Councilman City of Coronado, Calif., 1960-62, mayor 1962-64; trustee French-Am. Internat. Sch., San Francisco, 1968-96; pres. English Speaking Union, San Francisco, 1982-85, Alliance Francaise, San Francisco, 1979-81; chair Javits Fellowship Bd., Washington, 1989-92; mem. Columbus Fellowship Found. Bd., Washington, 1993-99; bd. dirs. San Francisco Com. on Fgn. Rels., 1995-98, 2001—, chmn., 1998-2001. Mem. ABA, Calif. Bar Assn., Am. Soc. Internat. Law. Clubs: Pacific Union, Cercle de l'Union, World Trade (San Francisco), The Met. (Washington). Republican. Avocations: skiing, jazz piano. Home: 90 Hazel Ln Piedmont CA 94611-4033 Office: 425 California St Fl 21 San Francisco CA 94104-2102 also: 1310 Conn Valley Rd Saint Helena CA 94574-9624 E-mail: waseavey@pacbell.net., was@seaveyvineyard.com.

SEAWELL, DONALD RAY, lawyer, publisher, arts center executive, producer; b. Jonesboro, NC, Aug. 1, 1912; s. A.A.F. and Bertha (Smith) S.; m. Eugenia Rawls, Apr. 5, 1941; children: Brook Ashley, Donald Brockman. AB, U. N.C., 1933, JD, 1936, DLitt, 1980; LHD, U. No. Colo., 1978. Bar: N.C. 1936, N.Y. 1947. With SEC, 1939-41, 45-47, Dept. Justice, 1942-43; chmn. bd., dir., pub., pres. Denver Post, 1966-81; chmn. bd., dir. Gravure West, L.A., 1966-81; dir. Swan Prodns., London; of counsel firm Bernstein, Seawell, Kove & Maltin, N.Y.C., 1979—; chmn. bd., chief exec. officer Denver Ctr. for Performing Arts, 1972—. Ptnr. Bonfils-Seawell Enterprises, N.Y.C.; bd. vis. U. N.C. Chmn. bd. ANTA, 1965—; theatre panel Nat. Coun. Arts, 1970-74; bd. govs. Royal Shakespeare Theatre, Eng.; trustee Am. Acad. Dramatic Arts, 1967—, Hofstra U., 1968-69, Cen. City Opera Assn., Denver Symphony; bd. dirs., Air Force Acad. Found., Nat. Ints. Outdoor Drama, Walter Hampden Meml. Library, Hammond Mus.; pres. Helen G. Bonfils Found., 1972-97, pres. emeritus, 1997—, chmn. fin. com., 1997—, Denver Opera Found.; Population Crisis Com., 1982-91; bd. dirs. Family Health Internat., Found. for Internat. Family Health; bd. visitors N.C. Sch. Arts, 1992-98; pres. Frederick G. Bonfils Found., 1972-92; chmn. Civilian Mil. Inst. Named Officer, Most Excellent Order of the Brit. Empire, 2002; recipient Am. Acad. Achievement award, 1980, Tony award for producing, On Your Toes, 1983, Vocie Rsch. and Awareness award, Voice Found., 1983, Arts and Entertainement Cable Network award, 1987, Third Millennium Leadership award, Am. Diabetes Assn., 1996, Colo. Tourism Hall of Fame award, 1999, Thomas Degaetani award, U.S. Inst. for Theatre Tech., 2000, Benjamin F. Stapleton, Jr. award, 2000, Disting. Svc. award, U. Colo., 2000, Downtown Denver award for Tantalus, 2001, AWARD Honoree award, 2001. Mem. Bucks Club (London), Dutch Treat Club (N.Y.C.), Denver Country Club, Denver Club, Cherry Hills Country Club, Mile High Club (Denver), Garden of Gods Club (Colorado Springs, Colo.), Order of Brit. Empire (officer). Office: Denver Ctr for Performing Arts 1050 13th St Denver CO 80204-2157 E-mail: geary@dcpa.org.

SEAWELL, WILLIAM THOMAS, former airline executive; b. Pine Bluff, Ark., Jan. 27, 1918; s. George Marion and Harriet (Aldridge) S.; m. Judith Alexander, June 12, 1941; children: Alexander Brooke, Anne Seawell Robinson. BS, U.S. Mil. Acad., 1941; JD, Harvard U., 1949. Commd. 2d lt. U.S. Army, 1941; advanced through grades to brig. gen. USAF, 1959; comdr. 401st Bombardment Group, ETO, World War II, 11th Bomb Wing SAC, 1953-54; dep. comdr. 7th Air Div., 1954-55; mil. asst. to sec. USAF, 1958-59, to dep. sec. def., 1959-61; comdt. cadets U.S. Air Force Acad., 1961-63; ret., 1963; v.p. operations and engring. Air Transport Assn. Am., Washington, 1963-65; sr. v.p. ops. Am. Airlines, N.Y.C., 1965-68; pres. Rolls Royce Aero Engines Inc. U.S. subsidiary Rolls Royce, Ltd., 1968-71; pres., chief operating officer Pan Am. World Airways Inc., N.Y.C., 1971-72, chmn. bd., CEO, 1972-81. Decorated Silver Star, D.F.C. with three oak leaf clusters, Air medal with three oak leaf clusters; Croix de Guerre with palm France). Mem. Pine Bluff Country Club, Wings (N.Y.C.). Home: 21 Westridge Dr Pine Bluff AR 71603-7149

SEAWRIGHT, JAMES L., JR., sculptor, educator; b. Jackson, Miss., May 22, 1936; s. James L. and Josephine (Power) S.; m. Mabelle M. Garrard, June 22, 1960; 1 child, James Andrew. Student, U. of South, 1953-54, Delta State Coll., 1954-55; BA in English, U. Miss., 1957; postgrad., Art Students League of N.Y., 1961-62. Tech. supr. Columbia-Princeton Electronic Music Center, N.Y.C., 1963-69; tchr. Sch. Visual Arts, 1967-69; dir. visual arts program Princeton U., 1972-2001, prof. coun. of humanities and visual arts, 1992—. Asst. to choreographer, Henry St. Playhouse, N.Y.C., 1962-63, spl. effects, tech. cons., Mimi Garrard Dance Co., N.Y.C., 1964—; sculptor represented in permanent collections, Mus. Modern Art, N.Y.C., Whitney Mus., N.Y.C., N.J. State Mus., Trenton, Guggenheim Mus., N.Y.C., Wadsworth Atheneum, Hartford, Conn., others; pub. commns. for SEA-TAC Internat. Airport, Seattle, Logan Internat. Airport, Boston; also pvt. collections. Served with USN, 1957-61. Recipient Theodoron award Guggenheim Mus., 1969, Am. Acad. Arts and Letters Art award, 1997, Lifetime Achievement award, Miss. Inst. Arts and Letters, 2003; Graham Found. Advanced Study in Arts fellow, 1970. Mem. Am. Abstract Artists, Phi Delta Theta. Democrat. Episcopalian. Office: 185 Nassau St Princeton NJ 08544-2003 Office Phone: 609-258-5098. E-mail: jims@princeton.edu., james@seawright.net.

SEBASTIAN, PETER, international affairs consultant, former ambassador; b. June 19, 1926; m. Harvel Huddleston, Dec. 11, 1951; 1 child, Christopher. BA, U. Chgo., 1950; postgrad., U. d'Aix-Marseille, Nice, France, 1949, New Sch. for Social Research, N.Y.C., 1950, Nat. War Coll., 1969-70. Dir., owner cons. co., N.Y.C., 1950-57; U.S. Fgn. Service officer Dept. State, Washington, 1957-76, dep. exec. sec., 1976-77, sr. seminar, 1977-78; U.S. consul gen. Casablanca, Morocco, 1978-80; minister, counselor Am. embassy, Rabat, Morocco, 1980-82; dir. for North Africa Dept. State, Washington, 1982-84; ambassador to Tunisia Tunis, 1984-87; ambassador-in-residence Ctr. for Strategic Internat. Studies, Georgetown U., Washington, 1987-88; cons in fgn. affairs to the public and pvt. sector, lectr., 1988—. Mem. V.P. Bush's task force on border control, 1988—89. Contbr. poems to Osmose, 1949; author studies for the pvt. sector U.S. Dept. State and other U.S agys. Served to sgt. AUS, 1944-46 Decorated Ouissam Alaouite (Morocco), numerous U.S. mil. decorations; recipient Presdl. Meritorious Service award, 1985. Mem. Am. Fgn. Svc. Assn., Nat. Geog. Soc., Mid. East Inst. Episcopalian. Avocations: painting, drawing, photography. Office Phone: 505-983-6364. E-mail: Batuta@aol.com.

SEBASTIAN, PHYLIS SUE (INGRAM), real estate broker, antique appraiser; b. Childersburg, Ala., Jan. 24, 1945; d. Albert Freeman and Era Mae (McGowin) Ingram; m. Robert Emmett Martin, March 31, 1965 (div. Sept. 1976); children: Connie, Michael, Toni, Steve; m. Thomas Haskell Sebastian III, June 26, 1985; stepchildren: Shellie, Tabatha, Cherie, Thomas IV. Ordained minister Progressive Universal Life Ch., 2002; lic. real estate broker Mo., real estate appraiser Tenn., Mo., PREA, CIMA. Owner, broker Phylis Sebastian Real Estate, Farmington, Mo., 1989—, U.S. Auto Sales, Park Hills, Mo., 1993—96; owner Bus. Legal Svs., Park Hills, Mo., 1993—; ptnr. La Femme Fine Antique Auction Svc., Ironton, Mo., 1997—. Owner Astrology Cons., 1970—; numerous appearances St. Louis TV; hostess radio show, St. Louis. Contbr. articles to newspapers; author: Marriages in Madison County Missouri for 1848-1868, 1998, 1910 Census for Madison County Missouri, 1998, numerous poems. Co-founder Astrological Assn., St. Louis, 1976-77, Mo. Mental Health Consumer Network, 1989-93, Mineral Area chpt. 1989-93. Mem. Nat. Gardening Club, Libr. Congress, Smithsonian, Nat. Hist. soc., Geneal. Assn. Madison County, Mo. (founder, sec., treas., genealogist). Mem. Lds Ch. Avocations: studying genealogy, astrology, natuapathy, herbal medicine, metaphysics, quatum physics, & parapsychology., reading, walking, gardening, pianist and guitarist. Home: 5231 West 72 Highway Fredericktown MO 63645 Office: Arcadia Valley Auction Company Inc and Real Estate 315A W Russell St Ironton MO 63650-1316 Office Phone: 573-546-3900. E-mail: phylis@phylissebastian.com.

SEBASTIAN, SUZIE, producer; b. Redding, Calif., Aug. 2, 1962; d. Richard Werner and Hildegard (Goettel) Guenther; m. Ted Sebastian, June 6, 1984 (div. July 1990). AA, Shasta Coll., 1985. Freelance tv prodr., prodn. mgr. commls., 1985-91; freelance underwater model, stunt woman; expedition leader, hostess Adventures on Scuba Dive Travel, Santa Barbara, Calif., 1991—; documentary TV prodr. Discovery Channel, 1998-2000. Asst. instr. Filming Sharks in the Wild, Nassau, Bahamas, 1996—. Prodr.: documentaries, ednl. videos; picture editor, underwater model: Tom Campbell's Film and Video Prodns., 1991—; prodr.: Navy Seals: In Harms Way, How to Survive Hellweek, FBI: Critical Incident Class 234. Mem.: Internat. Documentary Assn., Divers Alert Network, Aquatic Bodyworks. Avocations: skiing, triathlon. Home: 919 Veronica Springs Rd Santa Barbara CA 93105-4500 Office: Adventures on Scuba 238 Las Alturas Rd Santa Barbara CA 93103-2170 E-mail: suzies@silcom.com.

SEBASTIANELLI, CARL THOMAS, clinical psychologist; b. Jessup, Pa. s. Carlo and Antonia (Antonelli) S. BS in Psychology magna cum laude, U. Scranton, 1965; MA in Psychology, Temple U., 1967; postgrad. in clin. psychology, L.I. U., 1968-70; PhD in Psychopathology/Psychotherapy, Clayton U., 1983. Lic. psychologist, Pa. Psychologist Farview State Hosp., Waymart, Pa., 1967-68; clin. psychology doctoral intern N. Dauphin Mental Health/Mental Retardation Ctr., 1970-71; clin. psychology doctoral intern family therapy ctr. Harrisburg (Pa.) State Hosp., 1970-71, clin. psychologist, 1971-77, chmn. psychology forum, 1974-76, clin. psychologist Psychiat. Treatment Ctr., 1977-79; pvt. practice clin. psychology Comprehensive Health Svcs. Ctr., Dunmore, Pa., 1979-90, ind. pvt. practice clin. psychology, 1990—. Mem. adj. faculty U. Scranton, 1979-86, Pa. State U., 1973-86; mem. state bd. Pa. Social Services Union, 1974-75; media commentator psychopathology topics, 1979—. Contbr. articles to profl. jours., UPI; interviewed for articles in newspapers and nat. mags.; featured in Pa. Dept. Welfare publ. on subject of family therapy tng. Pa. Profl. Edn. Program scholar L.I. U.; recipient award N.E. Pa. chpt. Am. Diabetes Assn., 1980. Mem. APA, Internat. Acad. Behavioral Medicine Counselling and Psychotherapy, Anxiety Disorders Assn. Am., Nat. Register Health Svc. Providers in Psychology. Home: 1224 Monroe Ave Scranton PA 18509-2808

SEBASTIANELLI, MARIO JOSEPH, internist, nephrologist, health services administrator; b. Jessup, Pa., Sept. 14, 1935; s. Carlo and Antonia (Antonelli) S.; m. Alena Marie Drazdauskas, June 26, 1993 (div. 7/7/2004); children: Mario, Alexa, Marco. BS in Biology, U. Scranton, 1958; MD, Jefferson Med. Coll., 1962. Diplomate Am. Bd. Internal Medicine. From sr. instr. to assoc. prof. medicine Hahnemann U., Phila., 1969-87; pvt. practice Scranton, Pa., 1971—; chief nephrology, founding dir. hemodialysis Moses Taylor Hosp., Scranton, 1972-76; founding med. dir. Pa. Regional Tissue Bank, Scranton, 1983-91; dir. inpatient hemodialysis svcs. Comty. Med. Ctr., Scranton, 1996—; founding med. dir. Fresenius Med. Care Dialysis Svcs. Dunmore, Scranton, 2001—. Mem. senateconfirmed gov. apptd. Govs. Renal Disease Adv. Com., Harrisburg, Pa., 1973-76; creator, owner Comprehensive Health Svcs. Ctr., Dunmore, Pa., 1979—; founding med. dir. Diagnostic Lab., Dunmore, 1981-95. Contbr. articles to profl. jours. Bd. dirs. Scranton Lackawanna Human Devel. Agy., Scranton, 1977-82. Lt. USNR, 1963-65. Fellow: ACP; mem.: KC (4th degree), AMA, Renal Physicians Assn., Internat. Soc. Nephrology, Am. Soc. Nephrology, Alpha Omega Alpha. Republican. Roman Catholic. Avocations: fishing, swimming, travel, sports cars, reading. Office: Comprehensive Health Svcs Ctr 1416 Monroe Ave Ste 206 Dunmore PA 18509-2477 Office Phone: 570-347-5212.

SEBASTIEN, ANYA CELITA, academic administrator, consultant; d. Errol Olliver Sebastien and Grace Elma Audain Sebastien. BS in Elem. and Spl. Edn., Lesley Coll., 1975; MS in Exceptional Citizen Edn. and Learning Disabilities, U. Miami, Fla., 1979; EdD in Higher Edn. Adminstrn., George Washington U., 1989. Spl. edn. tchr. Govt. of V.I., Dept. Edn., St. Thomas, 1975—78, resource specialist, 1983—84; dean's grant coord. Coll. of V.I., St. Thomas, 1979—81; info. and referral specialist Info. Ctr. for Handicapped Individuals, Inc., Washington, 1981—82; asst. prof. edn. U. V.I., St. Thomas, 1990—91, exec. asst. to v.p. acad. affairs, 1992—95; sec. to bd. trustees, exec. asst. to pres. Chgo. State U., 1995—97; assoc. provost St. Petersburg (Fla.) Coll., Seminole Campus, 1998—. Mem. selection com. Leadership Pinellas, Clearwater, Fla., 2002—. Grantee, U.S. Dept. Edn., 1991; participant Nat. Identification Program for Advancement of Women in Higher Edn., Am. Coun. Edn., 1996. Mem.: AAUW (assoc.), Coun. for Exceptional Children (assoc.; pres. St Thomas, V.I. chpt. 1977—78), Am. Assn. Higher Edn. (assoc.), Caribbean Studies Assn. (assoc.). Office: St Petersburg Coll PO Box 13489 Saint Petersburg FL 33733 Personal E-mail: acseb@aol.com. E-mail: sebastiena@spcollege.edu.

SEBBA, ROSANGELA YAZBEC, pianist, music educator, theorist; b. Goiania, Goias, Brazil, Jan. 1, 1971; d. Taufic Jose and Leila (Yazbec) Sebba. BMus, U. Fed. de Goias, Goiania, 1991; MuxM, U. Wyo., 1996; DMA, U.So. Miss., 2000. Pianist MMTA, 2001. Prof. Conservatorio Estadual Gustav Ritter, Goiania, Brazil, 1989—94; adj. prof. U. of So. Miss., Hattiesburg, 2000; adj. porfessor Pearl River C.C., Poplarville, Miss., 2000—01; asst. prof. Miss. State U., Starkville, Miss., 2001—. Pianist, accompanist etc. Freelance, 1996—; lectr./recital Coll. Music Soc. Internat. Conf., Costa Rica, 2003; founder, coord. Brazilian Music Festival. Concert tour Teatro Goiania, Teatro Pirinopolis, Teatro Sao Joaquim, Orche. Camara Goyazes, Brazil, 2003; concert tour Mexico. Performer. Recipient First prizes in Brazilian Nat. Competitions, 1986-1994; grantee, Humanities and Arts Rsch. Program, 2002, Schillig, H.A.R.P., Office Rsch. Mem.: Music Tchrs. Nat. Assn., Miss. Music Tchrs. Assn., Coll. Music Soc. Office Phone: 662-325-2854. E-mail: rys3@colled.msstate.edu.

SEBEJAIS, MELANIE, federal agency administrator; m. Bob Sabelhaus; 2 children. With IBM; founder Exclusive Interim Properties Ltd. (now Bridgestreet Accomodations), Balt., 1986—97; v.p. global sales Bridgestreet Accomodations (formerly Exvlusive Interim Properties Ltd.), 1997—98; deputy adminstr. Small Bus. Adminstrn., Washington, 2002—. Bd. dirs. United Way, Alzheimer's Assn. Ctrl. Md.; co-chair Nat. Summit Women in Philanthropy. Recipient Outstanding Vol. Fundraiser of Yr. award, Assn. Fundraising Profls., Md., 2002. Office: Small Bus Adminstrn 409 3d St SW Washington DC 20416

SEBELIUS, KATHLEEN GILLIGAN, governor; b. Cin., May 15, 1948; d. John J. and Mary K. (Dixon) Gilligan; m. Keith Gary Sebelius, 1974; children: Edward Keith, John McCall. BA, Trinity Coll., 1970; MA in Pub. Adminstrn., U. Kans., 1977. Exec. dir. Kans. Trial Lawyers Assn., 1978—86; mem. Kans. Ho. of Reps., 1987-95; ins. commr. State of Kans., 1995—2002, gov., 2003—. Founder Women's Polit. Caucus; precinct committeewoman, 1980-86; mayor, Potwin, 1985-87; appointed Presdl. adv. commn. consumer protection and quality in Health Care, 1997. Mem. Common Cause (state bd., nat. gov. bd. 1975-81), Nat. Assn. Ins. Commrs. (chair). Democrat. Roman Catholic. Office: Office of the Gov State Capitol 2nd Fl Topeka KS 66612-1590 Home: 1 SW Cedar Crest Rd Topeka KS 66606-2275

SEBOLD, ALICE, writer; b. Madison, Wis., 1963; d. Jane and Russell Sebold; m. Glen David Gold, 2001. B.A., Syracuse U., 1984; studied poetry, U. Houston, 1984—85; M.F.A. in fiction, U. Calif., Irvine, 1998. Author: (memoir) Lucky, 1999, The Lovely Bones, 2002. Office: c/o Steven Barclay Agy 12 Western Ave Petaluma CA 94952

SEBOLD, RUSSELL PERRY, III, Romance languages educator, writer; b. Dayton, Ohio, Aug. 20, 1928; s. Russell Perry and Mary (Kiger) Sebold; m. Jane Norvell Hale, Nov. 24, 1955; children: Mary Norvell, Alice Hale. Student, U. Chgo., 1945-47; BA, Ind. U., 1949; MA (Woodrow Wilson fellow), Princeton U., 1951, PhD, 1953; D.Phil. and Letters (hon.), U. Alicante, Spain, 1984. Instr. Spanish, Duke U., 1955-56; instr. Spanish, U. Wis., 1956-58, asst. prof., 1958-62, assoc. prof., 1962-66; prof. Spanish, chmn. dept. fgn. langs. and lits. U. Md., 1966-68; prof. Spanish, U. Pa., 1968-88, chmn. dept. Romance langs., 1968-78, Edwin B. and Leonore R. Williams prof. Romance langs., 1988—. Mem. adv. com. Soc. Ibero-Am. Enlightenment, 1968—, treas., 1969—; mem. steering com. Am. Soc. Eighteenth Century Studies, 1970—; corr. academician Royal Spanish Acad., 1993—, Royal Acad. Humane Letters of Barcelona, 1993—. Author: Tomás de Iriarte: poeta de rapto racional, 1961, El rapto de la mente, 1970, 1989, Colonel Don José Cadalso, 1970, Cadalso: el primer romántico europeo de España, 1974, Novela y autobiografía en la Vida de Torres Villarroel, 1975, Trayectoria del romanticismo español, 1983, Descubrimiento y fronteras del neoclasicismo español, 1985, Bécquer en sus narraciones fantásticas, 1989, De llustrados y románticos, 1992, La novela romantica en España, 2000, La perduración de la modalidad clásica, 2001, Lírica y poética en España, 1536-1870, 2003, Ensayos de meditacion y critica literaria, 2004; contbr. articles to profl. jours. Recipient Elio Antonio de Nebrija Internat. prize, U. Salamanca, 2001; grantee, Am. Philos. Soc., 1971, 1976, 1982; Guggenheim fellow, 1962—63, Am. Coun. Learned Socs. fellow, 1979—80. Mem.: Hispanic Soc. Am., Sociedad de Literatura Española del Siglo XIX, Ctr. 18th Century Studies (Oviedo, Spain), Am. Assn. Tchrs. French, Am. Assn. Tchrs. Spanish and Portuguese, Sigma Delta Pi, Phi Gamma Delta, Phi Beta Kappa. Episcopalian. Home: 16 Flintshire Rd Malvern PA 19355-1108 Office: U Pa Dept Romance Langs Philadelphia PA 19104-6305 E-mail: rpsebold@earthlink.net.

SEBOROVSKI, CAROLE, artist; b. San Diego, June 16, 1960; d. Stanley and Eleanor Ononsko S. BFA, Calif. Coll. Arts and Crafts, 1982; MFA, Hunter Coll., 1987. Artist: solo exhibitions include: Damon Brandt Gallery, N.Y.C., 1986, Hunter Coll. Art Gallery, N.Y.C., 1986, Lorence-Monk Gallery, N.Y.C., 1988, 89, Galerie Karsten Greve, Paris, 1991, 94, 2003, Cologne, 1992, 2004, Milan, 1995, 2001, Angles Gallery, Santa Monica, Calif., 1991, 92, 93, 96, Betsy Senior Contemporary Prints, N.Y.C., 1993, John Weber Gallery, N.Y.C., 1993, 95, John Berggruen Gallery, San Francisco, 1994, Locks Gallery, Phila., 1997, Karsten Greve, Koln, 1997, Galerie Karsten Greve, Milan, Italy, 1997, 2001, John Weber Gallery, N.Y.C., 1998, Cheryl Haines Gallery, San Francisco, 2000, 2002, Mitchell-Innes and Nash Gallery, N.Y.C., Miller Block Gallery, Boston, 2001; group exhbns. at: Willard Gallery, N.Y.C., 1984, Nora Haime Gallery, N.Y.C., 1985, 86, 93, 95, 2002, Manhattan Arts Ctr., N.Y.C., 1985, Hillwood Art Gallery L.I. Univ., Brookville, N.Y., 1985, Damon Brandt Gallery, 1985, 86 (2), 87, Mus. de Arte, La Tertuila, Columbia, 1986, Weatherspoon Gallery, Greensboro, N.C., 1986, Barbara Krakow Gallery, Boston, 1986, 88, 90 (travels to John C. Stoller & Co., Mpls.), Anne Plumb Gallery, N.Y.C., 1987, Am. Acad. and Inst. Arts and Letters, 1987, Bklyn. Mus., 1987, Lorence-Monk Gallery, 1987, 89 (3), 90, 91 (2), Carnegie Mellon U. Art Gallery, Pitts., 1988, Reynolds/ Minor Gallery, Richmond, Va., 1988, John Good Gallery, N.Y.C., 1988, 92, Pamela Auchincloss Gallery, N.Y.C., 1988, Dart Gallery, Chgo., 1988, Angles Gallery, 1989, Persons & Lindell Gallery, Helsinki, Finland, 1989, Anderson Gallery Va. Commonwealth U., Richmond, 1989, Baxter Gallery, Richmond, 1989, Hillwood Art Gallery, Brookville (travels through 1991 to Blum Helman Gallery, N.Y.C., Richard F. Brush Gallery, Canton, N.Y., Contemporary Mus. Art, Caracas, Venezuela), Cheryl Haines Gallery, San Francisco, 1989, 94, 96, 2003, Security Pacific Corp. Gallery, Santa Monica, 1990, Meml. Art Gallery U. Rochester, N.Y., 1990, Hood Mus. Art Dartmouth Coll., Hannover, N.H., 1990, San Francisco Mus. of Art, 1991, Pfizer, Inc. (Mus. Modern Art, N.Y. Collection), 1991, John Berggruen Gallery, 1991, travelling exhbn. to Anthony Ralph Gallery at Earl McGrath, L.A., Mars Gallery, Tokyo, Katonah Mus. Art, N.Y., Ind. U. Fine Arts Gallery, Kerr Gallery, Alberta Coll. of Art, Can., Huntsville Mus. Art, Ala., Worcester Art Mus., Mass., Lamont Gallery N.H., San Diego State U. Gallery, 1992, Barbara Mathes Gallery, N.Y.C., 1993, Transamerica Pyramid Lobby, San Francisco, 1993, travelling exhbn. to The Drawing Ctr., N.Y., Corcoran Gallery Art, Washington, Santa Monica Mus., L.A., The Forum, St. Louis, Am. Ctr., Paris, 1993, Addison Gallery, Andover, Mass., 1994, John Weber Gallery, 1994, 96, Huntington Gallery Mass. Coll. Art, Boston, 1995, Rice U. Art Gallery, Houston, 1995, The Altered Stages, N.Y., 1995, Brooke Alexander Gallery, N.Y.C., 1995, Thread Waxing Space, N.Y., 1996, Duchess County C.C., N.Y., 1996, Gallery 7, Hong Kong, 1996, Century Club, N.Y.C., 1996, Dutchess Coll., N.Y., 1997, Vassar Coll., Poughkeepsie, N.Y., 1997, Mus. Cantonale d'Arte, Lugano, Switzerland, 1997, Kunst-Mus., Ahlen, Germany, 1998, Kunstmus., Winterhur, Switzerland, 1998, Acad. der Kunste, Berlin, 1999, Mitchell-Innes and Nash, N.Y.C., Nohra Haime Gallery, N.Y.C., 2002, Maragaret Thatcher Projects, N.Y.C., 1999, 2002, San Francisco Mus. Modern Art, Calif., 2000, Block Mus., Chgo., 2000, Contemporary Mus., Honolulu, 2000, Fogg Art Mus., 2000, Neuberger Mus. Art, Purchase, NY, 2000, Lyman Allyn Mus, Conn., 2000, Yale Art Galley, 2002, Bertha and Karl Leubsdorf Art Gallery, N.Y.C., 2002, Charles Cowles Gallery, N.Y.C., 2002, Krannert Art Gallery, Ill., 2002, Anthony Grant, Inc., 2003, Cin. Art Mus., 2003, The Workspace, N.Y.C., 2003, others; represented in permanent collections including Whitney Mus. Art, N.Y., Paine Webber, N.Y., Weatherspoon Art Gallery, Greensboro, N.C., J. Walter Thompson, N.Y., Refco Collection, Chgo., Panza Collection, Italy, San Francisco Mus. Modern Art, Mus. Modern Art, N.Y., Mus. Cantonale d'Arte, Lugano, Switzerland, Met. Mus. Art, N.Y., Merril Lynch Inc., N.Y., MIT Visual Ctr., Hood Mus. Art, Hanover, N.H., Fogg Art Mus., Harvard U., Cambridge, Mass., Cleve. Ctr. Contemporary Art, Chase Manhattan Bank, N.Y., Carnegie Mus. Art, Pitts., Bklyn. Mus., Balt. Mus., Anderson Collection, Calif., Addison Gallery, Phillips Acad., Andover, Mass., Bklyn. Mus., Yale U. Art Gallery, Wadsworth Atheneum, Conn., Tel Aviv Mus., Nat. Gallery Art, Washington. Grantee Pollock-Krasner Found., 1986, NEA, 1991, Art Devel. Com., 1997; named Artist in Residence, Villa Monalvo, Saratoga, Calif., 1989, Djerassi Found., Calif., 1990; Agnes Bourne fellow in visual arts, 1990. Home: 171 E 81st St Apt #3A New York NY 10028

SEBREN, LUCILLE GRIGGS, retired private school educator, public school educator; b. Chesterfield, S.C., May 21, 1922; d. Manley Oscar and Clara Blanche (Rivers) Griggs; m. Herbert Lee Sebren, Dec. 19, 1943; children: Herbert Lee Jr., George Hall, Samuel Robert Franklin. BA, Flora Macdonald Coll., Red Springs, N.C., 1942; MEd, Coll. of William and Mary, 1966. Cert. tchr., Va., N.C., S.C. Tchr. Cheraw (S.C.) Elem. Sch., 1942-44; tchr. kindergarten Larchmont Meth. Ch., Norfolk, Va., 1951-53; tchr. Norfolk Acad., 1953-89, supr., cons., adminstr. primary dept., 1970-89, master tchr., cons. elem. grades, 1970-89, asst. to dir. of admissions, 1987—. Contbr. articles to profl. jours. Mem. Va. Symphony and Symphony Aux., Norfolk, 1946—, Norfolk Soc. Arts, 1970—, Chrysler Mus., Norfolk, 1965—, Va. Opera Assn., Norfolk, 1974—, Norfolk Forum, 1980—, U.S. Capitol Hist. Assn., 1983—, ODU Roundtable, 1990-, Little Theater Norfolk, 1992-, Smithsonian Instn., Met. Opera Guild, Va. Hist. Assn., World Affairs Coun., 2001—, Heritage Found., Nat. Trust Historic Preservation, Hermitage Mus. Found. Aux.; pres. Philanthropic Ednl. Orgn., 1993-96, v.p., 2001—; bicentennial mem. Libr. Congress. Recipient Disting. Svc. award Norfolk Acad., 1991. Mem. AAUW (sec. exec. bd. 1974-76), Joie de Vivre (treas. 1994—), Old Dominion U. Faculty Wives Club (pres. 1958-60), Town-N-Gown (bd. dirs. 1992—, chaplain 1993-96, v.p. 1995-96, pres.-elect 1996-97, pres. 1997-98), Old Dominion U. Town-N-Gown (pres.-elect 1998-99, pres. 1999-2001), bd. dirs. Old Dominion U. Town-N-Gown, 1992—, parliamentarian, 2001-03, Nat. Cathedral Assn., Nat. Trust for Historic Preservation, Nat. M.I. Hummel Club, Hon. Order Ky. Cols., Internat. Assn. Torch Clubs, Inc., Alpha Delta Kappa Internat. (pres., past state, provincial, nat. pres. 1993—, pres. Va. 1978-80, S.E. region 1981-83, internat. grand chaplain 1983-85, internat. grand pres.-elect 1985-87, internat. grand pres. 1987-89, internat. exec. bd. 1985-91, pres.-elect internat. past state pres. 1993-95, pres. 1995—), Kappa Delta Pi. Republican. Baptist. Avocations: reading, travel, collecting antique glassware and Hummels, music. Office: Norfolk Acad 1585 Wesleyan Dr Norfolk VA 23502-5591

SEBRING, MARJORIE MARIE ALLISON, former home furnishings company executive; b. Burnsville, N.C., 1926; d. James William and Mary Will (Ramsey) Allison Shockey; 1 child, Patricia Louise Banner Krohn. Student, Mars Hill Coll., 1943, Home Decorators Sch. Design, N.Y.C., 1948, Wayne State U., 1953; cert. home furnishings rep., U. Va., 1982. Dir. decorating divsn. Robinson Furniture, Detroit, 1949-57; head buyer Tyner Hi-Way House, Ypsilanti, Mich., 1957-63, Town and Country, Dearborn, Mich., 1963-66; instr. Nat. Carpet Inst., 1963-71; owner Adams House, Inc., Plymouth, Mich., 1966-72; exec. v.p. mktg. and sales, regional sales and mktg. mgr. Triangle Industries, L.A., 1972-89; co-owner Markham-Sebring, Inc., St. Petersburg, Fla., 1983-89. Dir. contract divsn. Kane Furniture, 1984-85; co-owner Accessories, Etc., 1985-89; chmn. bd. Heritage Lakes, U.S. Home; co-owner, dir. Talamanca Pipeline Ltd., Costa Rica. Vol. coord. Pasco County Clk. Ct., Suncoast Theatre; adv. bd. Webster Coll.; charter mem. Presdl. Task Force; pres. Presbyn. Ch. Seven Springs; bd. dirs. Fla. Health and Human Svc., Fla. Presbyn. Homes, Gills Trinity YMCA, 2001—; chmn. bd. dirs. Two Westminster Condominium Assn.; mem. Tampa Bay Presbytery Rev. and Evaluation; bd. dirs. James P. Gills Suncoast YMCA, 2001—; citizens adv. com. Pasco County, 2001-. Recipient recognition for work with youth and aged; named to Fla. Finest List, Gov. of Fla., 1994. Mem. Internat. Home Furnishings Assn., Fla. Home Furnishings Rep. Assn. (officer), Am. Security Coun. (coun.), Williamsburg Found., USCG Aux., Nat. Audubon Soc., Internat. Platform Assn., Pasco County Planning Com., Heritage Lake Assn. (bd. dir. 2002-04, chmn.), II Westminster Assn.(pres. 2004), Pasco Rep. Club. Republican. Achievements include contbr. creative display to Better Homes & Gardens, 1957-64. Home: 4902 Cathedral Ct New Port Richey FL 34655-1486 Fax: 727 375-7702.

SEBRIS, ROBERT, JR., lawyer; b. N.Y.C., May 20, 1950; s. Robert and Ruth (Kagis) Sebris; m. S. Lawson Hollweg, Sept. 8, 1973; children: Jared Matthew, Bryan Taylor. BS in Indsl. Labor Rels., Cornell U., 1972; JD, George Washington U., 1978. Bar: DC 1978, Wash. 1980. Labor rels. specialist Onondaya County Office labor rels., Syracuse, NY, 1973-74, U.S. Dept. Labor, Washington, 1972-75; labor rels. mgr. U.S. Treasury Dept., Washington, 1975-78, employee rels. mgr., 1978-80; assoc. Davis, Wright, Todd, Riese & Jones, Seattle, 1980-84; ptnr. Davis, Wright, Tremain, Bellevue, Wash., 1985-92, Sebris Busto James, Bellevue, 1992—. Expert witness T.E.A.M. Act Amendments NLRA U.S. Senate hearing, 1997. Co-author: (book) Employer's Guide to Strike Planning, 1985; contbr. articles to profl. jours. Mem. Bellevue CC Found., 1988—95, pres., 1995—96; chair employment law cert. program U. Wash. Law Sch., 1996—97. Mem.: ABA (health law forum, labo and employment law sect., mem. com. employee rights), Soc. Human Resource Mgmt., Am. Health Lawyers Assn., Pacific Coast Labor Law Conf. (planning com. 1980—93, chmn. 1991—92), Seattle/King County Bar Assn. (chmn. labor law sect. 1991—92), DC Bar Assn., Wash. Bar Assn. Avocation: golf. Home: 16301 Mink Rd NE Woodinville WA 98072-9463 Office: Sebris Busto James Ste 325 14205 SE 36th St Bellevue WA 98006 Office Phone: 425-450-0300. E-mail: rsebris@sebrisbusto.com.

SECCOMBE, STEPHEN DANA, computer engineer; s. Stanley Gordon Seccombe and Eleanor Joan Dreher. BSEE, MIT, Cambridge, Ma, 1971; MSEE, MIT, Cambridge, Mass., 1971; EE, MIT, Cambridge, 1972. Exec. vice president R & D Applied Sci. Fiction, Austin, Tex., 1999—2002; vice pres. and gen. mgr. inkjet supplies Hewlett Packard Co., Palo Alto, Calif., 1972—99; pres. Tactyx, 2002—. Chmn. digital subcommittee solid state circuits conf. IEEE, Piscataway, NJ, 1983—87. Editor: (special issue on microprocessors) IEEE Transactions (Cledo Brunetti Award, 1993). Fellow, NSF, 1971. Mem.: IEEE. Achievements include patents for inkjet technology; invention of NMOS-III; 32b processor system and associated IC's; development of 32b RISC processor system (Spectrum); dry photo processing system. E-mail: seccombe@tactyx.com.

SECHREST, LARRY J. economist, educator; b. Detroit, Oct. 12, 1946; s. Howard J. and Frances C. Sechrest; children: J. Kyle, R. Tara. BA in History, U. Tex., Arlington, 1968, MA in Econs., 1985, PhD in Econs., 1990. Instr. U. Tex., Arlington, 1985-90; prof. econs. Sul Ross State U., Alpine, Tex., 1990—. Adj. scholar Ludwig von Mises Inst., Auburn, Ala., 1996—; rsch. fellow Ind. Inst., Oakland, Calif.; found. scholar Found. Advancement of Monetary Edn., 1996—; bd. advisors Def. of Freedom Found., Newport Beach, Calif. Author: Free Banking, 1993; contbr. chapters to books, articles to profl. jours.; co-editor (with Jorg Guido Hulsmann): Capital and Production, 2000; mem. editl. bd. Quar. Jour. Austrian Econs., 1996—, bd. advisors Jour. Ayn Rand Studies, 1999—. Fellow Inst. Humane Studies, Fairfax, Va., 1987-88; listed Guide to Pub. Policy Experts, Heritage Found., Washington, 2000. Mem. Nat. Assn. Scholars, U.S. Naval Inst., Assn. Pvt. Enterprise Edn., The Hist. Soc., Soc. Devel. Austrian Econs., Internat. Maritime Econ. History Assn., So. Econ. Assn., N.Y. Acad. Scis. Libertarian. Avocations: maritime history, yacht design, firearms, marine art, golf. Office: Sul Ross State U 400 N Harrison St Alpine TX 79832-8300 Office Phone: 432-837-8069. Business E-Mail: larrys@sulross.edu.

SECHRIST, CHALMERS FRANKLIN, JR., electrical engineering educator; b. Glen Rock, Pa., Aug. 23, 1930; s. Chalmers F. and Lottie V. (Smith) S.; m. Lillian Beatrice Myers, June 29, 1957; children: Jonathan A., Jennifer N. BE in Elec. Engring., Johns Hopkins U., 1952; MS, Pa. State U., 1954, PhD in Elect. Engring., 1959. Sr. engr. Bendix Corp., summers 1952, 53, 54; instr. elec. engring. Pa. State U., 1954-55; staff engr. HRB-Singer, Inc., State College, Pa., 1959-65; from asst. prof. to prof. elec. engring. U. Ill., Urbana, 1965-96, assoc. head instructional programs dept. elec. and computer engring., 1984-86, asst. dean engring., 1986-96, prof. Emeritus, 1996—; program dir. divsn. undergrad. edn. NSF, Washington, 1992-96; adj. prof. engring. Fla. Gulf Coast U., 1998—. Acting sci. sec. Sci. Com. on Solar-Terrestrial Physics, 1981; chmn. publs. com. Middle Atmosphere Program, 1980-86, editor handbook, 1981-86; mem. adv. com. on tech. edn. Fla. Dept Edn., 2001-. Editor: Proc. Aeronomy Confs, 1965, 69, 72; contbr. articles to profl. jours. Grantee NSF. Fellow: IEEE (edn. activities bd. 1990, tech. activities bd. 1991—92, edn. activities bd. 1992—93, chmn. com. on pre-coll. edn. ednl. activities bd. 1997—99, edn. activities bd. 1997—99, awards and recognition com. edn. activities bd. 2000—01, oversight subcom. Virtual Mus. 2000—02, precoll. edn. coord. com. edn. activities bd. 2000—03, Millennium medal 2000); mem.: Internat. Tech. Edn. Assn., Am. Soc. Engring. Edn., Am. Meteorol. Soc., Am. Geophys. Union, Edn. Soc. of IEEE (v.p. 1989—90, pres. 1991—92, achievement award 1993). Office Phone: 239-454-0640. Personal E-mail: csechrist@comcast.net.

SECK, MAMADOU MANSOUR, ambassador, military officer; b. Dakar, Senegal, July 3, 1935; children: Ndeye, Safi, Makura, Astou Dior, Sonia Penda. Attended, St. Cyr Milit. Acad., France, Salon Air Force Acad., French Air War Coll., Institut des Hautes Etudes de la Def. Nat. Commanding officer 1st Senegalese Air Force Squad, 1966; comdr. 1st Senegalese Air Force, 1972; dep. chief gen. staff, 1980-84; spl. chief of staff to Pres. of Republic of Senegal, chief of staff of Sene-Gambia Confedn., 1984; gen. chief of staff, gen. chief Confedn., 1988; chmn. Joint Chiefs of Staff of Senegal, 1988-93; amb. to U.S. Govt. of Republic of Senegal, 1993—; amb. to Mex., Argentina, Jamaica, Haiti, Trinidad and Tobago, Barbados, 1993—. Decorated Senegal, France, Gabon, Hollan, Luxembourg. Office: Embassy of Republic of Senegal 2112 Wyoming Ave NW Washington DC 20008-3926

SECOLA, JOSEPH PAUL, lawyer; b. Hartford, Conn., May 18, 1959; s. Pasquale Anthony and Anna Maria; m. Mary Alice Ipavich, June 20, 1982; children: Peter, Sharon, Mary Joy, Timothy, Paul, Andrew. BA in History, Fairfield U., 1981; JD, Oral Robert U., 1984. Bar: Conn. 1984, N.Y. 1985, U.S. Dist. Ct. Conn. 1985, Va. 1986, U.S. Dist. Ct. (so. dist.) N.Y. 1988, U.S. Ct. Appeals (2d cir.) 1989, U.S. Supreme Ct. 1990, U.S. Dist. Ct. (we. dist.) N.Y. 1996. Pvt. practice, Brookfield, Conn., 1984—; judge of probate Dist. of Brookfield, 2001—. Mem. bd. edn. City of Milford, Conn., 1989-90, Greater Danbury (Conn.) Cath. Elem. Schs., 1992-96. Mem. ABA, Nat. Employment Lawyers Assn., Am. Trial Lawyers Assn., Conn. Trial Lawyers Assn., Conn. Bar Assn., Conn. Employment Lawyers Assn., Litchfield County Bar Assn., Greater Danbury Bar Assn. Republican. Roman Catholic. Avocations: sports, N.Y. Yankees. Office: Ste 500 67 Federal Rd Bldg A Brookfield CT 06804-2538 Fax: (203) 740-2355. E-mail: jpsecolalaw@aol.com.

SECOR, DONALD TERRY, JR., geologist, educator; b. Oil City, Pa., Nov. 22, 1934; s. Donald Terry and Mary Elizabeth (LaRue) S.; m. Dorothy Eisenhart, June 15, 1959; children: Beth Ann, Jane Marie, Carol Lynn. BS, Cornell U., 1957, MS, 1959; PhD, Stanford U., 1963. Asst. prof. geology U. S.C., Columbia, 1962-66, assoc. prof., 1966-79, prof., 1979-99, chmn. dept., 1966-68, 77-81, disting. prof. emeritus, 1999—. Am. Assn. Petroleum Geologists Disting. lectr., 1978-79; recipient U. S.C. Ednl. Found. award, 1991; NSF grantee, 1966-70, 76-94, U.S. Geol. Survey grantee, 1979-82. Fellow Geol. Soc. Am.; mem. Am. Geophys. Union, AAAS Office: U SC Dept Geol Scis Columbia SC 29208-0001 Personal E-mail: donsecor@bellsouth.net.

SECOR, HAROLD EDWIN, retired obstetrician/gynecologist; b. Towanda, Pa., Mar. 21, 1925; Student, The Citadel, 1943-44, U. Mo., 1945; MD, Baylor U., 1949. Diplomate Am. Bd. Ob-Gyn. Intern Robert Packer Hosp., Sayre, Tex., 1949-50; resident Meth. Hosp., Houston, 1952-54; pvt. practice Bellaire, Tex., 1954-61; fellow Precept-Gulf Coast Med. Ctr., Wharton, Tex., 1961-63; obstetrician, gynecologist Rugley and Blasiogome Clin., 1963-89, ret., 1989. Mem. hon. staff Gulf Coast Med. Ctr., Wharton, 1994. Capt. Med. Svc. Corps. U.S. Army, 1950-52, Korea. Mem. ACOG, Tex. Assn. Ob-Gyns.

SECORD, LLOYD DOUGLAS, healthcare administrator; b. Lachine, Que., Can., Nov. 22, 1946; s. George William and Gladys Mable (Wilson) S.; m. Louise Margaret Morrison, Dec. 21, 1966; children: Steven Lloyd, Gordon Arthur, Mary Elizabeth. BS in Chemistry, U. New Brunswick, 1968; M of Adminstrn., U. Toronto, Ont., Can., 1970. Cert. accreditation surveyor Can. Coun. on Health Facilities, 1990-92. Adminstrv. resident Toronto East Gen. and Orthopaedic Hosp., 1969-70; adminstrv. asst. Moncton Hosp., summer 1968, asst. adminstr., 1970-75; exec. dir. Kiwanis Nursing Home Inc., 1975—; facility adminstr. Region 2 Hosp. Corp., Sussex, N.B., Can., 1992-98; sec. Sussex Health Ctr. Svcs. Inc., Bryant Dr. Holdings Inc., 1975—, CEO, adminstr. Sussex Hosp., 1975-98; region dir. capital projects Atlantic Health Scis. Corp., 1998—2003. Chmn. adv. com. Min. Health; mem. Fundy Linen Svcs. Inc., 1976-92; mem. regional hosp. planning com. Health Region II, 1974-76; commr. of oaths, 1975—. Bd. dirs. Atlantic Bapt. Sr. Citizen's Home Inc., 1973-79, original bldg. com., 1971-74, rec. sec., 1971-74, chmn. bldg. com.; founding chmn. Comty. Based Svcs. Coord. Com. for Sussex, 1981; founding pres. Sussex Sr. Housing Inc., 1981, 82; established Sussex Health Ctr. Svcs. Inc., 1991, Bryant Dr. Holdings Inc., 1992-93; founding sec. Kings County Wellness Ctr., 1997; bd. trustees, bd. deacons Sussex United Bapt. Ch.; dir. Sussex br. Order of St. John, 1976-78, 90-92; trombonist Sussex Comty. Adult Band, 1989—; sec. Kings County Wellness Ctr., 1997—. Lord Beaverbrook scholar, Leonard Found. scholar. Fellow Can. Coll. Health Svc. Execs., Soc. Mgmt. Accountants Can., Am. Coll. Health Care Execs. (affiliate, regent for Atlantic provinces and Quebec 1992-2001, membership oral examiner 1984, 85, 86, 88, 93, 95, 96, mem. ethics com. 1985-88), Can. Coll. Health Svc. Execs. (various provincial coms., nat. bd. dirs. 1997-2000), Soc. Mgmt. Accts. Can. (cert., mem. provincial coun. 1977-88, provincial sec.-treas. 1982, provincial chmn. 1987, nat. edn. svcs. com. 1985, 86, nat. bd. dirs. 1986, 87, nat. strategic planning com. 1986); mem. New Brunswick Hosp. Assn. (numerous provincial coms.), New Brunswick Assn. Nursing Homes (numerous provincial coms.), Northeastern Can./Am. Health Coun. (Can. co-chmn. 1991-94, co-chair internat. mini conf. on rural health care New London, N.H. 1988, chair bi-ann. conf. Montreal 1991), Provincial Ambulance Operators Assn. (exec. com. 1990-96), Sussex and Dist. C. of C. (pres. 1985), Kiwanis Club Sussex Inc. (pres. 1985, 99). Avocations: band, golf, gardening, painting, education. Office: Kiwanis Nursing Home 11 Bryant Dr Sussex NB Canada E4E 2P3 Office Phone: 506-432-3207.

SECREST, JAMES SEATON, SR., lawyer; b. Middletown, Ky., Dec. 9, 1930; s. Elmer S. and Linney (Witherbee)S.; m. Mary Sue Corum, Sept. 2, 1950; children: James Seaton, Lynne Suzanne. JD, U. Louisville, 1954. Bar: Ky. 1954. Ptnr. Goad & Secrest, Scottsville, Ky., 1955-62; solo practice Scottsville, Ky., 1962-77; ptnr. Secrest & Secrest, Scottsville, 1977—. City judge pro tem Scottsville, 1955-58; judge Allen County, 1958-61; city atty. Scottsville, 1962-66; atty. Allen County, 1966-89, dep. judge-exec., 1990-99; bd. dirs. Barren River Area Devel. Dist., 1970, mem. regional bd. ethics; mem. adv. bd. dirs. Starbank, Scottsville, 1998; bd. dirs. Commonwealth Health Corp. Mem. Scottsville C. of C. (pres. 1962), Ky. County Attorneys Assn. (pres. 1973), Ky. Assn. Counties (bd. dirs. 1985-86), ABA, Ky. Bar Assn. Clubs: Rotary (pres. 1960). Republican. Methodist. Home: 714 Secrest Ln Scottsville KY 42164 Office: Secrest & Secrest PO Box 35 210 W Main St Scottsville KY 42164-1123 E-mail: jsecrest@nctc.com.

SECREST, MERYLE, writer; arrived in U.S., 1953; d. Albert Edward Doman and Olive Edith May Love; m. Thomas Gattrell Beveridge, Nov. 25, 1975; m. David Waight Secrest, Sept. 12, 1953 (div. Feb. 1965); children: Cary Doman, Martin Adams, Gillian Anne Clark. Women's editor Hamilton News, Canada, 1949—50, 1951—53; reporter Bristol Evening News, England, 1950—51; editor Columbus Citizen, Ohio, 1955—57; feature writer/editor/art critic Washington Post, 1964—76. Author: (biography) Between Me and Life: A Biography of Romaine Brooks (ALA Thirty Best Books of 1974), Being Bernard Berenson, 1979, Kenneth Clark, 1984, Salvador Dalí, 1986, Frank Lloyd Wright, 1992 (Book of the Month Club/Quality Paperback choice; Ken Burns documentary.), Leonard Bernstein, 1994, Stephen Sondheim: A Life, 1999 (NY Times 100 Most Notable Books of 1998, George Freedley Meml. award Theatre Libr. Assn.), Somewhere for Me: A Biography of Richard Rodgers, 2001 (One of the five best books of 2001, Sunday Times of London), Joseph Duveen: A Life in Art, 2004. Guggenheim fellow, 1981—82. Mem.: Cosmos Club of Washington (art, libr. and award coms. 1993—). Democrat. Mem. Ch. Of Eng. Avocations: travel, painting, interior decor, French language and literature. Mailing: c/o Janklow & Neabit Assoc Lit Agency 445 Park Ave New York NY 10022-2606

SECULAR, SIDNEY, writer, weather forecaster, actor, model, fundraiser, consultant; b. N.Y.C., Dec. 20, 1940; s. Benjamin and Mollie (Stern) Secular; m. Mildred Vance, Oct. 31, 1969. BA, SUNY, Stony Brook, 1962. Cert. HS tchr. Contract asst. U.S. Army, Bklyn., 1962-66; contract specialist USN, Washington, 1966-67, FDA, Washington, 1967-68; contracting officer Dept. Justice, Washington, 1968-81; conf./expo organizer, counselor to small bus. SBA, Washington, 1986-97; govt. mktg. cons. to small bus. Silver Spring, Md., 1997—. Mem. consumer bd. Giant Food corp., WSSC Water Utility; freelance writer, Silver Spring, Md., 1985—; weather broadcaster Washington Weatherline, Bethesda, Md., 1982—91, Comprehensive Weather Svcs., 1982—85, Verizon Comm., 1991—; total quality mgmt. cons., 1995—. Activist East Sliver Spring Citizens Assn., 1981—; chief election judge Montgomery County, Md., 1998—. With U.S. Army, 1963—69. Recipient Performance and Suggestion awards, U.S. DEA and SBA. Mem.: ASPA, Area Small and Disadvantaged Bus. Coun., Am. Meteorol. Soc., Nat. Contract Mgmt. Assn., Ctr. Hiking Club (trails dir. 1975), Masons. Avocations:

investments, immigration reform, entrepreneurial activities, American history, environmental improvement. Home: 740 Silver Spring Ave Silver Spring MD 20910-4661 Office Phone: 301-588-7668. Personal E-mail: SidSecular1@aol.com.

SECUNDA, EUGENE, marketing professional, educator; b. Bklyn., June 15, 1934; s. Sholom and Betty (Almer) Secunda; m. Shirley Carol Frummer, Sept. 23, 1961; children: Ruthanne, Andrew. Comml. degree, N.Y. Inst. Photography, 1955; BS, NYU Sch. Bus., 1956; MS, Boston U., 1962; PhD, NYU, 1988. News editor Sta.-WBMS, Boston, 1956-57; reporter New London (Conn.) Daily Day, 1958-59; publicist various Broadway shows, 1959-62; sr. publicist 20th Century Fox Film Corp., N.Y.C., 1962-65; with J. Walter Thompson Co., N.Y.C., 1965-73, dir. corp. and pub. affairs, 1974-78, sr. v.p., dir. entertainment group, 1974-80, dir. entertainment divsn., 1978-80; sr. v.p., dir. comm. svcs. N.W. Ayer Internat., N.Y.C., 1980-82; pres. Barnum/Secunda Assocs., N.Y.C., 1982-85, Secunda Mktg. Comm., N.Y.C., 1985—. Adj. prof. media studies NYU, N.Y.C., 1972—2003, prof. mktg. and advt. Grad. Sch. Bus., 1985—88, prof. mktg., 1993—96, adj. prof. mktg. and media studies, 1996—; prof. mktg. and advt. Baruch Coll. CUNY, 1988—93; prof. mktg. Adelphi U., Garden City, NY, 1993—96; guest lectr. FBI Acad., Columbia U., UCLA. Contbr. articles to profl. jours. Mem. Greenwich Village Trust. With USAR, 1957—63. Mem.: NATAS, Am. Mktg. Assn., Mcpl. Arts Soc., Am. Acad. Advt., Internat. Advt. Assn., Internat. Comm. Assn., Greenwich Village Preservation Soc., Mooring Mates. Address: 30 5th Ave New York NY 10011-8859

SEDACCA, ANGELO ANTHONY, police investigator, educator, notary public; b. Bronx, N.Y., Mar. 14, 1971; s. Marie Ann and Joseph Sedacca; m. Diane F. Bockino, Mar. 15, 1997 (div.); children: Christopher M., Nicholas A. B.A. - French Studies, B.A. - Italian Studies, Fordham U., Bronx, NY, 1989—93; M.A. - French Lang. and Civilization, NY U., New York, NY, 1993—95; M.A. - Religious Studies, St. Joseph's Sem., Yonkers, NY, 1996—2003. Adj. prof. theology Fordham U., Bronx, 2000—; highway safety officer NYC Police Dept., 40th precinct, 1999—; IAB investigator NYC Police Dept., 2002—04; sgt. NYC Police Dept., 42nd precinct, 2004—. Adj. prof. French Fordham U., 2001—. Active mem. Cath. League, New York, NY, 1993; eucharistic min., lectr. St. Clare of Assisi Ch., Bronx, NY, 1993, lector, 1993; professed mem. Secular Franciscan Order, Yonkers, NY, 1995; 4th-degree mem. KC, Bronx, NY, 1991. Recipient Heydt French Gold Medal, Fordham U., 1993, Founder Diplomatic Counsellor, London Diplomatic Acad., 2000, Dean's List, Fordham U., 1992-1993, Summa Cum Laude, St. Joseph's Sem., 2003, Cavalier (rank and decoration), World Order of Sci., Edn., Culture, 2002, Knight Chevalier (rank and decoration), Order of St. Michael the Archangel, 2002, Amb. of Grand Eminence, Am. Biog. Inst., 2002, Internat. Cultural Diploma of Honor, Internat. Sash of Academia, Internat. Who's Who of Intellectuals, Internat. Biog. Assn., 1999. Mem.: Am. Soc. Notaries, Nat. Notary Assn. (corr.; notary pub. 1996), Internat. Police Assn. (corr.; mem. 1998), Fraternal Order of Police (corr.; mem. 1998), Alpha Mu Gamma (life; pres. 1992—93, Michael Marinaro award 1993), Gamma Kappa Alpha (life; pres. 1992—93). Roman Catholic. Avocations: oenology, philosophy, martial arts. Office: Fordham U E Fordham Rd Duane Libr Bronx NY

SEDARIS, AMY, writer, actress; b. NYC, Mar. 19, 1961; d. Lou Sedaris. Performer: (TV series) Exit 57, 1995—96; co-writer (TV series) Exit 57, 1995—96, co-creator, 1995—96; performer: (TV series) Strangers With Candy, 1999—2000; co-writer (TV series) Strangers With Candy, 1999—2000, co-creator, 1999—2000; actor(guest appearances): (TV series) Just Shoot Me, Monk, Sex and the City, Ed, Cracking Up,: (films) Commandments, 1997, Bad Bosses Go to Hell, 1997, Six Days Seven Nights, 1998, Jump Tomorrow, 2001, Maid in Manhattan, 2002, The School of Rock, 2003, Elf, 2003, My Baby's Daddy, 2004; (TV films) Untitled New York Pilot, 2003; (plays) Jamboree, 1993; co-author (with brother David Sedaris): (plays) Jamboree, 1993; actor: (plays) Stump the Host, 1993; co-author (with brother David Sedaris): (plays) Stump the Host, 1993; actor: (plays) One Woman Shoes, 1995; co-author (with brother David Sedaris): (plays) One Woman Shoes, 1995 (Obie award, 1995); actor: (plays) Froggy, The Country Club, 1998—99 (nominated Drama Desk award, 1999), The Most Fabulous Story Ever Told, 1998—99, The Little Freida Mysteries, 1999; co-author (with brother David Sedaris): (plays) The Little Freida Mysteries, 1997; actor: (plays) The Book of Liz; co-author (with brother David Sedaris): (plays) The Book of Liz, 2001; co-author: (book), 2002; actor: (plays) Drama Department, 2001, Wonder of the World, 2001—02 (Lucille Lortel award for outstanding featured actress League of Off-Broadway Theatres and Prodrs., 2002), (short film) Wheels of Fury, 1998; co-writer (short film) Wheels of Fury, 1998; co-author (with brother David Sedaris): (plays) Stitches, Incident at Cobbler's Knob; co-author: (book) Wigfield: The Can-Do Town That Just May Not, 2003. Office: c/o Jonathan Bluman Paradigm 10100 Santa Monica Blvd 25th Fl Los Angeles CA 90067

SEDARIS, DAVID RAYMOND, writer; b. Johnson City, N.Y., Dec. 26, 1956; s. Lou Sedaris. Student, Kent State U.; BFA, Art Inst. Chgo., 1987. Tchr. writing Art Inst. Chgo., 1987—90. Worker moving co.; elf SantaLand Macy's Dept. Store; cleaner various apts. Author: (books) Stories and Essays, 1994, Holidays on Ice, 1997, Naked, 1997, Me Talk Pretty One Day, 2000, Dress Your Family in Corduroy and Denim, 2004; author with sister Amy under the name The Talent Family: plays Stump the Host, Stitches, One Woman Shoe (Obie award, 1995), Incident at Cobbler's Knob, The Little Freida Mysteries, 1997, The Book of Liz, 2001; writer: (TV series) Exit 57, 1995; author: (commentaries) Nat. Pub. Radio, 1992—; frequent appearances: NPR program This Am. Life; contbg. author: Esquire, The New Yorker. Named Humorist of Yr., Time mag., 2001; recipient Thurber prize for Am. humor, 2001, Lambda award, Adv., 2001. Office: care of Don Congdon Assocs 156 5th Ave Ste 625 New York NY 10010-7002*

SEDDON, JOHANNA MARGARET, ophthalmologist, epidemiologist; b. Pitts. BS, U. Pitts., 1970, MD, 1974; MS in Epidemiology, Harvard U., 1976. Intern Framingham (Mass.) Union Hosp., 1974-75; resident Tufts New Eng. Med. Ctr., Boston, 1976-80; fellow ophthalmic pathology Mass. Eye and Ear Infirmary, Boston, 1980-81, clin. fellow vitreoretinal Retina Svc., 1981-82; instr. clin. ophthalmology Harvard Med. Sch., Boston, 1982-84, asst. prof., asst. surgeon ophthalmolgy, 1984, assoc. prof., 1989—; assoc. surgeon, dir. ultrasound svc. Mass. Eye and Ear Infirmary, Boston, 1989—, orgn. epidemiology rsch. unit, 1984-85, dir. epidemiology unit, 1985—, surgeon in ophthalmology, 1992—; assoc. prof. faculty dept. epidemiology Harvard Sch. Pub. Health, Boston, 1992—. Mem. com. vision Commn. Behavioral and Social Scis. and Edn., NRC, NAS, Washington, 1984; mem. divsn. rsch. grants NIH, 1987-89, 94—; mem. sci. adv. bd. Found for Fighting Blindness, 1994—, Macular Degeneration Internat., 1994—, adv. panel, Age-Related Macular Degeneration Alliance Internat.; spkr. in field; lectr. in field. Author books and articles in field, especially in field of ocular tumors and macular degeneration; mem. editl. staff ophthalmic jours. Recipient NIH Nat. Svc. Rsch. awards, 1975, 80-81, Lewis R. Wasserman merit award Rsch. to Prevent Blindness for contbns. to ophthalmic rsch., 1996; grantee, prin. investigator Nat. Eye Inst., 1984—, Nat. Cancer Inst., 1986; med. sch. scholar, 1970-74, Henry H. Clark Med. Edn. Found. scholar, 1973, voted one of Am.'s top ophthalmologists, Consumer Rsch. Coun. Am., 2004. Mem. AMA (Sr. Honor award 2003), APHA, Am. Acad. Ophthalmology (Honor award 1990, Sr. Honor award 2003), Am. Med. Women's Assn., Assn. Rsch. in Vision and Ophthalmology (elected, chair epidemiology sect. 1990, trustee clin. vision epidemiology sect. 1992-97. v.p. 1996-97), Soc. Epidemiologic Rsch., New Eng. Ophthal. Soc., Am. Coll. Epidemiology, Retina Soc., Macula Soc., Mass. Soc. Eye Physicians and Surgeons (v.p. 2000-2002, Spl. Recognition award 1997), Am. Epidemiol. Soc., Am. Ophthal. Soc. Achievements include first to field of nutrition and age-related eye diseases. Home: 4 Louisburg Sq Boston MA 02108-1203 E-mail: jseddon@earthlink.net.

SEDDON, PRISCILLA TINGEY, painter; b. Boston, Apr. 1, 1938; d. Richard Hume and Mildred Gurina (Lundgren) Tingey; m. James Alexander Seddon, Jr., Nov. 28, 1959; children: Amy, Sarah, Carroll, Alice. BFA, Tufts U., 1989; Cert., Sch. of the Mus. of Fine Arts, Boston, 1990, Postgrad. 5th Yr., 1991. Associated with Imagining Angels: World AIDS Day Show, Howard Yezersky Gallery, Boston, 1995, others. Exhbns. include: U. Bridgeport, Conn., 1997, Gallery 84, N.Y.C., 1996, Erector Square Gallery, New Haven, Conn., 1996, Harvard U., Cambridge, Mass., 1996, ArtsWorcester Gallery, Worcester, Mass., 1995, Wellesley Coll., Mass., 1994, Grove Street Gallery, Worcester, 1993, Carvajal Sculpture Gallery, Boston, 1992; works include metal work, paintings and sculptures. Grantee MIT Coun. for Arts, Cambridge, 1988, Firstnight, Inc., Boston, 1991, Hingham Edn. Found., Mass., 1993. Mem. Womens Caucus for Art, Visual AIDS. Avocation: watercolour.

SEDELL, JAMES, parks director; PhB, Willamette U., 1966; D in Biology and Ecology, U. Pitts., 1971. Rschr. Weyerhauser Co.; rsch. assoc., asst. prof. Oreg. State U.; rsch. ecologist Pacific N.W. Rsch. Sta.'s Lab., Corvallis, Oreg., 1980, program mgr. for aquatic/land interaction rsch.; inter-dep. water coord. Forest Svc., 1980—; nat. dir. wildlife, fish, watershed and air rsch. USDA Forest Svc., Arlington, Va., 2003—.

SEDELMAIER, J. J. filmmaker; b. Chgo., Mar. 11, 1956; s. John Josef and Marie S.; m. Patrice Estella Masters, Nov. 4, 1981. Student, Millikin U., 1974-75; BS in Art, U. Wis., 1979. Asst. animator Perpetual Motion Pictures, N.Y.C., 1981-82; asst. animator, animator Buzzco Prodns., N.Y.C., 1982-84, The Ink Tank Corp., N.Y.C., 1984-85, producer, 1985-86, exec. producer, 1986-88, assoc. dir., dir., exec. producer, rep., 1989-91; pres., producer, dir. J. J. Sedelmaier Prodns., White Plains, N.Y., 1991—. Launched Beavis and Butthead for MTV-(Art Dirs. Club gold medal, BDA awards, Comm. awards, Hatch awards; subject of retrospectives: Ottawa Animation Festival, 1997, Cinematique Quebecoise, 1997; acclaimed series of cartoons for "Saturday Night Live", animated peacocks for NBC, Captain Linger series for Cartoon Network; co-creator Ambiguously Gay Duo, X-Presidents, Fun with Real Audio; prodr. (3 episodes) Schoolhouse Rock; prodr., dir. Harvey Birdman Attorney@Law; vis. artist Sch. Visual Arts, assisted in saving and restoration of Dempster St. terminal, Skokie, Ill., adv. bd., Mercy Coll. Prodr., dir. Saturday TV Funhouse, Captain Linger, Harvey Birdman-Attorney at Law. Recipient Annecy Film Festival, France, N.Y. Festivals, Annie award, Mobius award, medal Multiple N.Y. Festivals, Multiple Worldfest. Mem. Am. Inst. Graphic Artists, Assn. Internat. Film Animation, Art Dirs. Club (2 Gold medals), Shore Line Interurban Hist. Soc., Chgo. Transit Posters Archtl. Restoration. Avocations: collecting illustrations, animation art, animation film cons, architectural historic restoration. Office: 199 Main St White Plains NY 10601-3200 E-mail: sedelmaier@aol.com.

SEDELMAIER, JOHN JOSEF, filmmaker; b. Orrville, Ohio, May 31, 1933; s. Josef Heinrich and Anne Isabel (Baughman) S.; m. Barbara Jean Frank, June 6, 1965; children: John Josef, Nancy Rachel, Adam Frederich. BFA, Art Inst. Chgo. at U. Chgo., 1955. Dir. art Young and Rubicam, Chgo., 1955-61; dir. art, assoc. creative dir. Clinton E. Frank, Chgo., 1961-64; dir. art, producer J. Walter Thompson, Chgo., 1964-67; pres. Sedelmaier Film Prodns., Chgo., 1967—. Spkr. Brit. design and art direction Pres. Lectr. Series, London, 1998; spkr. Harvard Bus. Sch., 2003. Retrospective exhibit, Mus. Broadcast Comms., Chgo., 1988, Mus. Broadcasting, L.A., 1991, Mus. TV and Radio, N.Y.C., 1992; dir.: (films) OpenMinds, 2003 (Sundance Film Festival Official Selection, 2003). Recipient Golden Ducat award for short film MROFNOC Mannheim Film Festival, 1968, Golden Gate award for short film Because That's Why, San Francisco Film Festival, 1969, 82 Clio awards, 1968-92, numerous Gold, Silver and Bronze Lion awards Cannes Film Festival, 1972-90, Gold Hugo award Chgo. Film Festival, 1976, 91, 2d Ann. IDC Creative award, Chgo., 1980, Internat. Broadcasting award for world's best TV comml., 1980, 86, Clio award for dir. of yr., 1981, London Internat. Advt. awards, 1986-88, numerous awards Internat. Festival of N.Y., 1984-93, Ann. Achievement award Assn. Ind. Comml. Producers, 1988; named Advt. Person of Yr., Chgo. Advt. Club, 1984, Jewish Communicator of Yr., 1985; named one of 50 Pioneers & Visionaries Who Made TV America's Medium, Advt. Age Mag., 1995; profiled in Communication Arts mag., Mar. 1976, Print mag., Jan. 1982, Fortune mag., June 1983, Newsweek mag., Nov. 1986, numerous others; featured on 60 Minutes, 48 Hours; subject of cover story Esquire mag., Aug. 1983; included in Arts & Entertainment's Top 10 Greatest Commls. of All Time, 1999; inducted The Art Dirs. Hall Fame, 2000. Office: Sedelmaier Film Prodns Inc 858 W Armitage Ave # 267 Chicago IL 60614-4329 Office Phone: 312-822-0110.

SEDEÑO, EUGENE RAYMOND, electronics engineer, consultant; b. Honolulu, Aug. 31, 1952; s. Josephine Marie Sedeño Rosa; m. Theresa Ann Contreras, Dec. 28, 1980; children: Roxanne Guadelupe, Raymond Contreras, Darrell Kealoha Albright. ASET, Heald Engring. Coll., 1974; BSEE, Coll. Allied Sci., 1980; MBA, Calif. Coast U., 2002. Field svc. engr. Bausch & Lomb, San Leandro, Calif., 1974—81; project mgr. Tylan Corp., Carson, Calif., 1981—85; field svc. supr. Sci. Atlanta, Santa Fe Springs, Calif., 1985—86; facilities and systems engr. Refractory Composities, Inc., Whittier, Calif., 1986—90, cons., 1985—91; supr. test and integration Thermco Systems, Orange, Calif., 1989—90; field engring. So. Calif. Edison, 1990—. With U.S. Army, 1970—76. Mem. Am. Mgmt. Assn., Mensa. Democrat. Roman Catholic. Avocations: kenpo karate, kobudo, kajukenbo, photography, collecting antique books. Home: 16137 Minnetonka St Victorville CA 92392-9146 Office: So Calif Edison 12353 Hesperia Rd Victorville CA 92392-4797 Office Fax: 760-951-3115. Business E-Mail: Eugene.Sedeno@sce.com.

SEDER, JEFFREY A. entrepreneur; b. Phila., Sept. 1, 1948; m. Nina L.S. Burnaford, Aug. 29, 1998; 1 child, Meriwether Jessica. AB magna cum laude, Harvard U., 1970, JD, MBA, 1976. Bar: Pa. 1976. CEO EOB, Inc., Chester County, Pa., 1977—99, Craftex Mills, Inc., Blue Bell, Pa., 1984-99, Boston Stores, L.A., 1991-93; exec. dir. non-profit youth svc. Big Picture Alliance, Phila., 1994—. Contbr. articles to profl. jours. Bd. dirs. Buck and Doe Trust, Unionville, Pa., 1984—. John Harvard scholar Harvard U., 1968, 69, 72. Mem. Phila. Bar Assn., Phi Beta Kappa. Avocations: dance, motorcycle roadracing, horseback riding. Home: Houyhnhnm Farm 1055 Doe Run Rd Coatesville PA 19320 Office: EQB Inc 501 Hicks Rd West Grove PA 19390

SEDERBAUM, ARTHUR DAVID, lawyer; b. N.Y.C., Sept. 14, 1944; s. William and Harriet (Warschauer) Sederbaum; m. Francine Haba, Dec. 30, 1967 (div. Aug. 1982); children: Rebecca, David; m. Phyllis Padow, Jan. 18, 1988 (div. Aug. 2002); 1 child, Elizabeth. AB cum laude, Columbia U., 1965, JD, 1968; LLM, NYU, 1972. BAr: N.Y. 1968, Fla. 1980, U.S. Dist. Ct. (so. and ea. dists.) N.Y. 1972. Assoc. Zissu Nelper & Martin, N.Y.C., 1968-70, Berlack, Israels & Liberman, N.Y.C., 1970-72, Rubin Baum Levin Constant & Friedman, N.Y.C., 1972-76; ptnr. Certilman, Haft, Balin, Buckley, Kremer & Hyman, N.Y.C., 1976-88, Olshan, Grundman, Frome, Rosenzweig & Orens, N.Y.C., 1988-92, Patterson, Belknap, Webb & Tyler, L.L.P., N.Y.C., 1992—. Mem. adv. bd. Bur. Nat. Affairs Estates, Gifts and Trusts Jour.; mem. adv. bd. NYU Inst. Fed. Taxation, CCH Fin. and Estate Planning. Author: Setting Up and Executing Trusts, 1988; contbr. articles to Tax Mgmt. Estates, Gifts and Trusts Jour. Recipient J.K. Lasser Tax prize NYU Inst. Fed. Taxation, 1968. Fellow Am. Coll. Trusts and Estates Coun.; mem. ABA, N.Y. State Bar Assn. (vice chmn. com. on estate planning trusts and estates law sect.), Assn. Bar City N.Y. (com. surrogates cts.), Practicing Law Inst. (chmn. income taxatin of estates and trusts program). Office: Patterson Belknap Webb & Tyler LLP Ste 1405 1133 Avenue Of The Americas New York NY 10036-6710 Home: 91 High St Armonk NY 10504-1226 Office Phone: 212-336-2550. E-mail: adsederbaum@pbwt.com.

SEDERBAUM, WILLIAM, b. N.Y.C., Dec. 22, 1914; s. Harry and Sarah (Steingart) S.; m. Harriet Warschauer, Aug. 29, 1940 (dec. Mar. 1980); children: Arthur David, Caroline Joan; m. Pearl Leibowitz, Jan. 11, 2003. BS, NYU, 1936, MA, 1943, PhD. Assoc. Sigmund Pines Co., Pub. Accts., 1935-38; tchr. N.Y.C. pub. schs., 1935-39; restaurant propr., 1939-41; v.p. Schenley Distillers Co., N.Y.C., 1941-61; pres. Distbrs. New Eng., 1956-61, Melrose Distillers Co., 1959-60, Park & Tilford Distillers Co., 1959-61; exec. v.p. Meade & Co., 1961-62; v.p., mktg. dir. J. T. S. Brown Distillers Co., 1962-65; mktg. cons., 1965-67; exec. v.p., gen. mgr. Fulton Distbg. Co., 1967-77; asst. gen. mgr., dir. spl. projects Am. Distbrs. Fla., 1977—. Instr. acctg. Fla. Jr. Coll., 1984-89 Mem. Eleanor Roosevelt Cancer Com.; mem. U.S. Olympic Games Com.; exec. com. Fedn. Jewish Charities, March of Dimes; bd. dirs. Jacksonville Urban League, 1975-87; mem. Com. of 100; bus. cons. Jr. Achievement Project, Jacksonville; chmn. bd. trustees, pres. men's club Reform Cong. of Merrick, L.I. Recipient Arch award NYU; named Chevalier, Confrerie de la Chaine des Rotisseurs, Bailliage de Jacksonville, Fla. Mem. Jacksonville Wholesale Liquor Assn. (pres. 1970-76), Jacksonville Symphony Assn., Jacksonville Civic Music Assn., Jacksonville C. of C. (econ. edn. com., airline svc. com., hon. adm. of flag ship Am. Airlines), Kappa Phi Kappa. Clubs: River, Carriage (N.Y.C.); NYU, Playboy, Key. Office: Am Distbrs Fla 6867 Stuart Ln S Jacksonville FL 32254-3438 Home: 3820 La Vista Cir Unit 108 Jacksonville FL 32217 *Live life the way it should be-not the way it is.*

SEDGWICK, ALEXANDER, historian, educator; b. Boston, June 8, 1930; s. William Ellery and Sarah (Cabot) S.; m. Charlene Mary Maute, June 24, 1961; children— Catherine Maria, Alexander Cameron BA, Harvard U., 1952, PhD in History, 1963. Asst. prof. history Dartmouth Coll., 1962-63; assoc. prof. U. Va., Charlottesville, 1963-66, 1966-74, prof., 1974—, chmn. history dept., 1979-85, dean Coll. Arts and Scis., 1985-90, dean grad. studies, 1990-95, univ. prof., 1995-97, univ. prof. emeritus, 1997—. Mem. adv. com. in history Sr. Fulbright Awards Council for Internat. Exchange of Scholars. Author: The Ralliment in French Politics 1890-98, 1965, The Third French Republic, 1870-1914, 1968, Jansenism in Seventeenth Century France, Voices in the Wilderness, 1977, The Travails of Conscience. The Arnauld Family and the Ancien Regime, 1998; co-author: Church, State and Society Under the Bourbon Kings of France, 1982, For Want of a Horse, 1985, That Gentle Strength, 1980, Les Discour sur les Révolutions, 1991, History Today, 1991, Chroniques de Port-Royal, 1993, 95. Served with U.S. Army, 1952-54. Fulbright fellow, 1960-62; recipient Am. Coun. Learned Socs. grant-in-aid, 1967-68, Am. Philos. Soc. grant-in-aid, 1971. Mem. AAUP (nat. council 1976-79), Soc. French Hist. Studies (sec. 1979-83, pres. 1983-84), Am. Hist. Assn., Century Assn. Home: 1409 Rugby Rd Charlottesville VA 22903-1240 E-mail: as6d@virginia.edu.

SEDGWICK, KYRA, actress; b. N.Y.C., Aug. 19, 1965; m. Kevin Bacon, 1988; children: Travis, Sosie. Appeared in off-Broadway prodns. Time Was, 1981, Dakota's Belly Wyoming, 1989; stage appearances in Ah Wilderness!, 1988 (Theatre World award), Maids of Honor, 1990, Oleanna, 1994; TV appearances include (miniseries) Family Pictures, 1983, (spls.) ABC Afternoon Spls., 1985, Am. Playhouse, 1987, 88, (TV movies) The Man Who Broke 1,000 Chains, 1987, Women & Men II, 1991, Hallmark Hall of Fame, 1992 (Golden Globe award nomination 1993), The Wide Net, 1997, Door to Door, 2002, Talk to Me, 2000, (series) Another World, 1982-83, Ally McBeal, 2002; film appearances include War and Love, 1985, Tai-Pan, 1986, Kansas, 1988, Born on the Fourth of July, 1989, Mr. and Mrs. Bridge, 1990, Pyrates, 1991, Singles, 1992, Heart and Souls, 1993, Murder in the First, 1995, Something to Talk About, 1995, Losing Chase (also exec. prodr.), 1996, Phenomenon, 1996, Montana (also assoc. prodr.), 1997, Critical Care, 1997, Twelfth Night, 1998, The Red Door, 1999, Labor Pains, 1999, What's Cooking, 2000, Just a Kiss, 2002, Behind the Red Door, 2002, Secondhand Lions, 2003, The Woodsman, 2004, Cavedweller, 2004, Loverboy, 2004. Address: WMA 151 S El Camino Dr Beverly Hills CA 90212-2704*

SEDGWICK, SALLY BELLE, publishing company executive; b. Chgo., July 6, 1947; d. William Morton and Dorothy Hyde (Dunlap) Price; m. Roger Stephen Sedgwick, Sept. 7, 1968 (div.); children: Peter, Andrew. BA, Lawrence U., 1968; MFA, U. Alaska, 1974; MA, Gen. Theol. Sem., N.Y.C., 1986; DMin, Grad. Theol. Found., Donaldson, Ind., 1996. Instr. Lake Region Jr. Coll., Devils Lake, N.D., 1974-77; dir. Carousel Creative Arts Program, Oakes, N.D., 1978-80; pricing analyst Orgn. Resources Counselors, N.Y.C., 1981-85; exec. dir. Ch. Periodical Club, N.Y.C., 1985-90; assoc. dir. Forward Movement Publs., Cin., 1990—. Bd. mem. Fountain Sq. Fools, Cin., 1992-95; cons. Episcopal Diocese N.D., 1974-80. Mem. Episcopal Communicators, Nat. Network Lay Profls. Episcopalian. Office: Forward Movement Publs 412 Sycamore St Ste 3 Cincinnati OH 45202-4195

SEDIA, JOHN MICHAEL, lawyer; b. Buffalo, Aug. 29, 1954; s. Pasquale Joseph and Anne Marie (Delollis) S.; m. Rosemary Piccirilli, Sept. 24, 1983. AB in Journalism and Spanish, Ind. U., 1976; J.D., 1979. Bar: Ind. 1979, U.S. Dist. Ct. (no. dist.) Ind. 1979. Assoc. Saul I. Ruman & Assocs., Hammond, Ind., 1979-80, Bainbridge & Tweedle, Highland, Ind., 1980-83; ptnr. Tweedle & Sedia, Highland, 1983—99; pvt. practice, Highland, 1999-; referee juvenile divsn. Lake Superior Ct., 1994—; adj. prof. In. U. N.W., 2002—. Ind. U. Alumni Assn. scholar U. Ind., Bloomington, 1976. Mem. Justinian Soc. Lawyers (treas. N.W. Ind. chpt. 1983—), Ind. U. Alumni Assn., Ind. State Bar Assn., Blue Key, Pi Kappa Alpha. Roman Catholic. Home: 120 Pine St Schererville IN 46375-1016 Office: Highland Office Ctr 2646 Highway Ave Ste 106 Highland IN 46322 Office Phone: 219-838-1952.

SEDLACEK, RICHARD LEO, retired surgeon; b. Iowa City, Apr. 13, 1924; MD, U. Iowa Coll. Medicine, 1948. Cert. surgery. Intern Letterman Gen. Hosp., San Francisco, 1948-49, resident in surgery, 1949-52; with St. Luke's Hosp. and Mercy Hosp., Cedar Rapids, Iowa, 1956-89; retired, 1989. Mem. AMA, Iowa State Med. Assn., LoCMS.

SEDLACEK, WILLIAM, education educator; b. Chgo., Jan. 4, 1939; s. Edward Joseph and Walborg Selma Sedlacek; m. Alexandra Dominguez, May 13, 1979; 1 child, Joseph Sung. BS, Iowa State U., 1960, MS, 1961; PhD, Kans. State U., 1966. Rsch. psychologist Assn. of Am. Med. Colls., Evanston, Ill., 1964—67; asst. dir. Counseling Ctr. U. of Md., College Park, prof. of edn. Adj. prof. of pharmacy U. of Md., Balt. Author: (book) Racism in American Education: A Model for Change, Beyond the Big Test: Noncognitive Assessment in Higher Education, (journal article) Measurement & Evaluation in Counseling & Development; contbr. articles to profl. jours. (Rsch. award, 1997). Recipient Rsch. fellowship, Greater Kans. City Mental Health Found., 1962—63, Outstanding Contbn. to Med. Edn. award, Assn. of Med. Minority Educators, 1983, John B. Muir Writing award, Nat. Assn. for Coll. Admission Counseling, 1993. Mem.: APA (sr. scholar 2002), Nat. Coun. on Measurement in Edn., Am. Ednl. Rsch. Assn., Am. Coll. Pers. Assn. (sr. scholar 1998—2003, sr. scholar, diplomate 2003, Contbn. to Knowledge award 2004, Diamond honoree 2002), Am. Counseling Assn. (Ralph F. Berdie Meml. Rsch. award 1992). Office: U Md 1101B Shoemaker Bldg College Park MD 20742-8111

SEDLAK, JAMES WILLIAM, organization administrator; b. Tarrytown, N.Y., Nov. 17, 1943; s. Jacob Frank and Catherine Eva (Sedlak) S.; m. G. Michaeleen Bizub, June 17, 1967; children: Frank George, Jeanette Michele Sedlak Veltri, Terri Lynn Rose Sedlak Ferrara. BS in Physics, Manhattan Coll., 1967; MS in Indsl. Adminstrn., Union Coll., Schenectady, 1975. Customer engr. IBM, N.Y.C., 1963-67, semicondr. engr. East Fishkill, N.Y., 1967-80, sr. engr. Harrison, N.Y., 1980-92; co-founder, nat. dir. Stop Planned Parenthood, La Grangeville, N.Y., 1986-93; pres., writer, editor The Ryan Report, STOPP (Stop Planned Parenthood) Internat., La Grangeville, 1994-98; v.p. pub. policy and edn. Am. Life League, Inc., Stafford, Va., 1998—. Former guest lectr. med. ethics Mt. St. Mary's Coll., Newburgh, N.Y.; guest lectr. ethics Vassar Coll., Poughkeepsie, N.Y., 1986-92. Author: Quarterly Dividends, 1975, Parent Power!!, 1990, Deadly Deception, 1996; co-author: Title X: The Six Billion Dollar Scam, 1997; contbr. to pro-life publs. Past pres. PTO; mem. bd. advisors Am. Life League, Inc.; former mem. faculty Apostles of Life Leadership Acad., Human Life Internat.; cons. to nat. and internat. pro-life groups; speaker numerous state-wide pro-life convs. and events, U.S., Can., Mex., Italy, Australia, No. Ireland, Eng. and New Zealand; workshop presenter nat. convs. Concerned Women for Am., Human Life Internat., Am. Life League; numerous appearances on radio and TV. Recipient Dutchess County Right to Life Pro-Lifer of Yr. award, 1984, Expectant Mother Care N.Y. Pro-Life Champion award, 1987, family life award Parent's Roundtable, 1987, Unsung Hero award Am. Life League, 1988, Disting. Svc. to Life award Grand Haven (Mich.) Pro-Lifers, 1993, Svc. to Life award N.W. and Putnam Life Ctr., NY, 2003, also others. Mem. KC (3d degree). Roman Catholic. Office: Am Life League Inc PO Box 1350 Stafford VA 22555-1350 E-mail: jwsedlak@aol.com.

SEDLAK, VALERIE FRANCES, retired English language educator, retired academic administrator; b. Balt., Mar. 11, 1934; d. Julian Joseph and Eleanor Eva (Pilot) Sedlak; 1 child, Barry. AB in English, Coll. Notre Dame of Md., 1955; MA, U. Hawaii, 1962; PhD, U. Pa., 1992. Grad. tchg. fellow East-West Cultural Ctr. U. Hawaii, 1959-60; adminstrv. asst. Korean Consul Gen., 1959-60; tchr. Boyertown (Pa.) Sr. H.S., 1961-63; asst. prof. English U. Balt., 1963-69; assoc. prof. Morgan State U., Balt., 1970-2000, assoc. prof. English emerita, 2001—, asst. dean Coll. Liberal Arts, 1995-2000, sec. to faculty, 1981-83, faculty rsch. scholar, 1982-83, 92-93, comm. officer, 1989-90, dir. writing for TV program, 1990-97; exec. dir. Renaissance Inst. Coll. of Notre Dame of Md., 2000—03, ret., 2003—. Cons. scholar Md. Humanities Coun., 1992—; adj. prof. York (Pa.) Coll., 2004-. Author numerous poems and lit. criticism; editor Liberal Arts Rev., 1996-2000; mem. editl. bd., assoc. editor Md. English Jour., 1994-2000, Morgan Jour. Undergrad. Rsch., 1995-2000, CEA MAGazine, 2002—; assoc. editor, CEA Critic, 2003—; contbr. articles to lit. jours. Coord. Young Reps., Berks County, Pa., 1962-63; chmn. Md. Young Reps., 1964; election judge Baltimore County, Md., 1964-66; regional capt. Am. Cancer Soc., 1978-79; mem. adv. bd. Md. Our Md. Anniversary, 1984, The Living Constitution: Bicentennial of the Fed. Constitution, 1987. Morgan-Penn Faculty fellow, 1977-79, NEH fellow, 1984; named Outstanding Tchg. prof., U. Balt. Coll. Liberal Arts, 1965. Mem. MLA, South Atlantic MLA, Coll. Lang. Assn., Coll. English Assn. (Mid-Atlantic Group v.p. 1987-90, pres. 1990-92, exec. bd. 1992—, nat. bd. dirs. 2001-04, nat. liaison officer 1993-2004), Women's Caucus for Modern Langs., Md. Coun. Tchrs. English, Md. Poetry and Lit. Soc., Md. Assn. Depts. English (bd. dirs. 1992—), Mid. Atlantic Writers' Assn. (founding 1981, exec. assoc. editor Mid. Atlantic Writers' Assn. Rev. 1989-2000), Delta Epsilon Sigma (v.p. 1992-94, pres. 1994-96), Pi Kappa Delta. Roman Catholic. Home: 17049 Keeney Mill Rd New Freedom PA 17349 Personal E-mail: vfsedlak@aol.com.

SEDLER, ROBERT ALLEN, law educator; b. Pitts., Sept. 11, 1935; s. Jerome and Esther (Rosenberg) S.; m. Rozanne Friedlander, Jan. 24, 1960; children: Eric, Beth. BA, U. Pitts., 1956, JD, 1959. Bar: D.C. 1959, Ky. 1968, Mich. 1979; U.S. Supreme Ct. 1969. Asst. prof., assoc. prof. law St. Louis U., 1961-65; assoc. prof. law, asst. dean Addis Ababa U., Ethiopia, 1963-66; assoc. prof. to prof. law U. Ky., Lexington, 1966-77; prof. law Wayne State U., Detroit, 1977—, disting. prof. law, Gibbs chair civil rights & civil liberty, 2000—. Author: American Constitutional Law, 2000, Across State Lines, 1989: Applying the Conflict of Law to Your Practice, 1989 (with R. Cramton) The Sum and Substance of Conflict of Laws, 1987, Ethiopian Civil Procedure, 1968; contbr. articles to profl. jours. Gen. counsel ACLU Ky., 1971-76. Gershenson Disting. Faculty fellow, Wayne State Univ., 1985-87. Mem. ABA, AAUP, Phi Beta Kappa, Order of the Coif. Democrat. Jewish. Home: 18851 Capitol Dr Southfield MI 48075-2680 Office: Wayne State U 468 Ferry Mall Detroit MI 48202-3620 Office Phone: 313-577-3968. Personal E-mail: rsedler@aol.com. Business E-Mail: rsedler@wayne.edu.

SEDLER, ROZANNE FRIEDLANDER, social worker, educator; b. Greensburg, Pa., June 16, 1938; d. Ernest and Belle (Marchel) Friedlander; m. Robert Allen Sedler, Jan. 24, 1960; children: Eric Mark, Beth Ellen. BA, U. Pitts., 1960; MSW, St. Louis U., 1962. Social worker Family & Children's Svc., St. Louis, 1962-63; lectr. Sch. of Social Work Haile Selassie U., Addis Ababa, Ethiopia, 1963-66; social worker U. Ky. Med. Ctr., Lexington, 1966-68, Renaissance Home Health Care, Detroit, 1984-86; geriatric social worker Jewish Family Svc., Southfield, Mich., 1986—. Chair Jewish Family Svc.-Am. Fedn. of State, County, Mcpl. Employees Local 1640; mem. exec. bd. AFSCME Local 1640; chair Oakland County bd. dirs. ACLU. Mem. ACLU (pres. chpt.), Am. Fedn. State, County and Mcpl. Employees (exec. bd. Local 1640, chair Jewish Famil Svc. Bargaining Unit, bd. dirs.). Democrat. Jewish. Home: 18851 Capitol Dr Southfield MI 48075-2680 Office: Jewish Family Svc 24123 Greenfield Rd Southfield MI 48075-3116 Office Phone: 248-559-1500. Personal E-mail: rozsedler@aol.com.

SEDLIN, ELIAS DAVID, physician, orthopedic researcher, educator; b. N.Y.C., Jan. 21, 1932; s. Arnold Boris and Sonia Lipschitz Sedlin; m. Barbara Sue Zidell, July 9, 1960; children: Faith Avril, Adrian. BS in Biology, U. Ala., 1951; MD, Tulane U., 1955; D.Med. Sci., U. Gothenburg, Sweden, 1966. Diplomate: Am. Bd. Orthopedic Surgery. Intern Mobile (Ala.) Gen. Hosp., 1955-56; resident Charity Hosp., New Orleans, 1956-57; chief resident Bronx (N.Y.). Mcpl. Hosp., 1959-60; sr. resident Henry Ford Hosp., Detroit, 1960-61, rsch. assoc., emergency room lectr., 1961-63, NIH fellow, 1963-64; jr. attending physician Detroit Receiving Hosp., 1962-63; spl. NIH fellow dept. orthopedic surgery Sahlgrenska Sjukhuset, Gothenburg, 1964-66; asst. prof. dept. orthopaedic surgery Albert Einstein Coll. Medicine, 1966-69, assoc. prof., 1969-75, prof., 1975—, dir. orthopaedic surgery, 1969-79; prof. orthopaedic surgery Mt. Sinai Sch. Medicine, 1980—. Contbr. to multiple symposia, profl. meetings, also articles to profl. jours. Served to capt. AUS, 1957-59. Fulbright scholar, 1962; NSF postdoctoral fellow, 1964; recipient P.D. McGehee award Mobile Gen. Hosp., 1956; Ludvic Hektoen gold medal AMA, 1963; Nicholas Andry award Assn. Bone and Joint Surgeons, 1964 Fellow ACS, AAAS, Am. Acad. Orthopaedic Surgeons; mem. Orthopaedic Rsch. Soc., Phi Beta Kappa. Office: 133 E 73d St New York NY 10021 Office Phone: 212-861-9000.

SEDMAK, DANIEL D. academic administrator; b. Columbus, Ohio, Apr. 18, 1952; m. Peggy Sedmak; 5 children. BS in biology, U. Cin.; MD, Ohio State U., 1980. Resident in pathology Cleveland Clinic Found., 1980—84, fellow in immunopathology, 1984—85; joined faculty Ohio State U., 1985; dir. nephropathology and transplant pathology programs Ohio State U. Hosp.; prof. and chair pathology Coll. Medicine and Pub. Health, Ohio State U., 1997, interim dean, sr. assoc. v.p. health sci. and exec. vice dean; exec. dean Georgetown U. Sch. Medicine, 2003—; exec. v.p. health sci. Georgetown U., 2003—. Office: Georgetown U Med Ctr 4000 Reservoir Rd NW Washington DC 20057 Office Phone: 202-687-4600. Business E-Mail: sedmak@georgetown.edu.

SEDOR, FRANK A. chemist; b. E. Chgo., Ind., Nov. 21, 1944; s. Stephen and Julia S.; m. Judith Anne Sedor; 1 child, Julia Christine. BA, Wabash Coll., 1966; PhD, U. Fla., 1971. Diplomate Am. Bd. Clin. Chemistry. Asst. dir. clin. chemistry Duke U. Med. Ctr., Durham, NC, 1978-82, dir. outpatient labs., 1982-92, dir. clin. chemistry, 1992—. Contbr. articles to profl. jours. Mem. Am. Assn. Clin. Chemistry (pres. 2000—); fellow Nat. Acad. Clin. Biochemistry (bd. dirs. 1993-98). Avocations: gardening, books. Office Phone: 919-304-6878. E-mail: fas7273@mebtel.net.

SEDRA, ADEL SHAFEEK, electrical engineering educator, academic administrator; b. Assuout, Egypt, Nov. 2, 1943; arrived in Can., 1966; s. Chafik and Hélène (Monsour) S.; m. Doris M. Barker, May 5, 1973; children: Paul Douglas, Mark Andrew. BSEE, Cairo U., 1964; MASc in Elec. Engring., U. Toronto, Ont., Can., 1968, PhD in Elec. Engring., 1969; DSc (hon.), Queen's U., 2003. Registered profl. engr., Ont. Instr. Cairo U., 1964-66; asst. prof. elec. engring. U. Toronto, 1969-72, assoc. prof., 1972-78, prof., 1978—2003, chmn. dept., 1986-93, v.p., provost, chief acad. officer, 1993—2002; prof. elec. engring., dean faculty of engring. U. Waterloo, Canada, 2003—. Pres. Elec. Engring. Consociates Ltd., Toronto, 1979-81; bd. dirs. Info. Tech. Rsch. Ctr., Toronto, 1988-93; mem. rsch. coun. Can. Inst. for Advanced Rsch., 1994—; del. Oxford U. Press, 1995—. Co-author: Filter Theory and Design, 1978, Microelectronic Circuits, 1982, 5th edit., 2004 (also Spanish, Korean, Greek, Italian, Portuguese, Chinese, Persian, and Hebrew transls.), SPICE, 1997; contbr. over 120 articles to sci. jours. Operating grantee Nat. Scis. and Engring. Rsch. Coun. Can., 1970—; Ryerson Poly. Inst. fellow, 1988. Fellow IEEE (Darlington best paper award 1984, Edn. medal 1996, Cir. and Sys. Soc. Edn. award 1994, Guillemin Cauer Best Paper award 1987, Golden Jubilee medal 2000, 3d Millennium medal 2000), Can. Acad. Engrs., Royal Soc. Can., Am. Soc. Engring. Edn. (Terman award 1988); mem. Info. Tech. Assn. Can. (Tech. Achievement award 1993), Assn. Profl. Engrs. Ont. (Excellence award 2002). Home: 18 High Park Blvd Toronto ON Canada M6R 1M4 Office: U Waterloo Dean of Faculty of Engring 200 University Ave W Waterloo ON Canada N2L 3G1

SEDWAY, LYNN MASSEL, real estate economist; b. Washington, Nov. 26, 1941; d. Mark S. and Jean M. (Magnus) Massel; m. Paul H. Sedway, June 12, 1966; children: Mark, Carolyn, Jan. BA in Econs., U. Mich., 1963; MBA, U. Calif., Berkeley, 1976. Economist San Rafael (Calif.) Redevel. Agy., 1976-78; prin. Sedway Group, San Francisco, 1978—99; exec. mng. dir. CB Richard Ellis, San Francisco, 1999—. Instr. Appraisal Bus. Sch. U. Calif., Berkeley; bd. dirs. San Francisco Devel. Fund; corporate bd. mem. Hunting Gate Capital, Sertg Co. AMB Alliance Fund III. Mem. Berkeley Bus. Sch. Fund Council, 1984-86, Internat. Coun. of Shopping Ctrs.; chmn San Rafael Downtown Retail Com., 1985; mem. Fisher Center Policy Advisory Bd. of the Haas School; trustee Urban Land Inst., former chmn. retail comml. coun., San Francisco District Council, former chmn., Housing Devel. Fin. Corp., bd. dirs. Marin, Calif. chpt. 1984—. Fellow, Homer Hoyt. Mem. Counselors of Real Estate, San Francisco Chamber of Commerce (former bd. of dirs.), City Club Intl. House, Marin C. of C. (bd. dirs. 1984-87), San Rafael C. of C., Lambda Alpha (past pres., bd. dirs.), Internat. Land Econs. Soc., San Francisco Municipal Fiscal Advisory Com. Avocation: tennis. Home: 765 Market St Apt 26G San Francisco CA 94103-2038 Office Phone: 415-733-5321. Personal E-mail: lynn.sedway@cbre.com.

SEDWICK, DEBORAH, state agency administrator; BS, Boston U.; M, U. Alaska. V.p. Jack White Real Estate, Anchorage; commr. Alaska State Dept. Cmty. & Econ. Devel., 1997—. Office: AIDEA 813 W Northern Lights Blvd Anchorage AK 99503

SEE, CAROLYN, English language educator, novelist, book critic; b. Pasadena, Calif., Jan. 13, 1934; d. George Newton Laws and Kate Louise (Sullivan) Daly; m. Richard Edward See, Feb. 18, 1955 (div. June 1959); 1 child, Lisa Lenine; m. Tom Sturak, June 11, 1959; 1 child, Clara Elizabeth Marya. BA, Calif. State U., L.A., 1958; PhD, UCLA, 1963. Prof. English Loyola Marymount Coll., L.A., 1970-85, UCLA, 1985—; book critic L.A. Times, 1981-93, Washington Post, 1993—. Author: Rhine Maidens, 1980, Golden Days, 1986, Making History, 1991, Dreaming: Hard Luck and Good Times In America, 1995, The Handyman, 1999, Making a Literary Life, 2002. Bd. dirs. Calif. Arts Coun., L.A., 1987-91, Day Break, for homeless, Santa Monica, Calif., 1989—, Friends of English, UCLA, 1990—; buddy for life AIDS Project L.A., AIDS relief, L.A., 1990—. Recipient award Sidney Hillman Found., 1972, Robert Kirsch award L.A. Times, 1994; PEN Ctr. USA West Lifetime Achievement award 1998; grantee Nat. Endowment for Arts, 1980, Guggenheim fellow, 1990-91. Mem. Writers Guild Am., Libr. Found. Calif., PEN Ctr. USA West (pres. 1990-91), Nat. Book Critics Cir. (bd. dirs. 1986-90). Democrat. Avocations: gardening, sailing, dance, brush clearing. Home: 17339 Tramonto Dr Pacific Palisades CA 90272-3124 Office: UCLA Dept English 405 Hilgard Ave Los Angeles CA 90095-9000 Office Phone: 310-454-7724.

SEE, EDMUND M. lawyer; b. Marietta, Ohio, Oct. 9, 1943; s. Edgar Thorpe and Katherine M. (Merriam) S.; m. Ellen Engler, June 5, 1976; children: Kevin, Gregory, Tyler. BA, Wesleyan U., Middletown, Conn., 1965; JD, Harvard U., 1971. Bar: Conn. 1971. Assoc. Day, Berry & Howard LLP, Hartford, Conn., 1971-77, ptnr., 1978—. Chmn. Mcpl. Fin. Practice Group. Vol. Peace Corps, Gabon, 1965-67, Vista, 1968-69; pres. bd. dirs. Legal Aid Soc., 1977-85, Hartford Arch. Conservancy, 1983-86; trustee St. Joseph Coll., 1991-2003; dir. Conn. Bar Found., 1994-; corporator Hartford Sem., 1994-. Mem. ABA, Conn. Bar Assn., Hartford County Bar Assn., Nat. Assn. Bond Lawyers, Conn. Govtl. Fin. Officers Assn., U.S. Govtl. Fin. Officers Assn., Phi Beta Kappa. Office: Day Berry & Howard LLP Cityplace 25th Fl Hartford CT 06103-3499 E-mail: emsee@dbh.com.

SEE, HAROLD FREND, judge, law educator; b. Chgo., Ill., Nov. 7, 1943; s. Harold Frend and Corinne Louise (Rachau) S.; m. Brenda Jane Childs, Dec. 2, 1978; children: Callie Suzanne, Garrett Brittain; children by previous marriage: Mary Elisabeth, Eric Palmer. Student, U. Chgo., 1962-63; BA, Emporia State U., 1966; MS, Iowa State U., 1969; JD, U. Iowa, 1973. Bar: Ill. 1973, U.S. Dist. Ct. (no. dist.) Ill. 1973, Ala. 1981, U.S. Ct. Appeals (fed. cir.) 1991; U.S. Supreme Ct. Instr. econs. Iowa State U., Ames, 1967-69; asst. prof. econs. Ill. State U., Normal, 1969-70; assoc. Sidley & Austin, Chgo., 1973-76; assoc. prof. law U. Ala., Tuscaloosa, 1976-78, prof., 1978-97; justice Supreme Ct. Ala., 1997—. Contbr. to books, also articles and book reviews. Mem. ABA, Ala. Bar Assn., Am. Econ. Assn., Am. Law and Econs. Assn., Soc. Profls. in Dispute Resolution, Am. Law Inst., Ala. Law Inst. Baptist. Office: Supreme Ct Ala 300 Dexter Ave Montgomery AL 36104-3741

SEE, ROBERT FLEMING, JR., lawyer; b. Kansas City, Mo., Apr. 23, 1942; s. Robert Fleming and Betty (Conard) S.; m. Leslie, Apr. 26, 1985 (dec.). BA with honors, U. Tex., 1964, JD with honors, 1966. Bar: Tex. 1966. Assoc. Locke, Purnell, Rain, Harrell and predecessor, Dallas, 1966-72, ptnr., 1972-89, pres., 1989-96; ptnr. Locke, Liddell & Sapp LLP and predecessor, Dallas, 1996—2001; pres., owner Robert F. See, Jr. & Assocs., P.C., Dallas, 2001—. Spkr. in field. Contbg. author: Loan Documentation Guide, 1990. Chmn. bd. commrs. Dallas Housing Authority; bd. dirs. The Real Estate Coun., Dallas Citizens Coun. Mem. Tex. Bar Assn., Dallas Bar Assn., Greater Dallas C. of C., North Dallas C. of C., Salesmanship Club Dallas. Office: Robert F See Jr & Assocs PC 901 Main St Ste 3601 Dallas TX 75202 Office Phone: 214-761-3001. E-mail: rsee@rseelaw.com.

SEE, SAW-TEEN, structural engineer; b. Georgetown, Penang, Malaysia, Mar. 23, 1954; came to US, 1974; d. Hock-Eng and Ewe-See (Lim) S.; m. Leslie Earl Robertson, Aug. 11, 1982; 1 child, Karla Mei. BSCE, Cornell U., 1977, MCE, 1978. Registered profl. engr., NY, Calif., Conn., Fla., Mass., Md., NJ, Ohio, Pa., Wash., Ark., Ill., Tex. Design engr. Leslie E. Robertson Assocs., R.L.L.P., NYC, 1978-81, assoc., 1981-85, ptnr., 1986—, mng. ptnr., 1990—. Cons. M of Engring. class Cornell U., 1994-95, mem. adv. coun. Sch. Civil and Environ. Engring., 1999—; project dir., project mgr. Miho Mus., Kyoto, Japan, West Side HS, NYC, Jr. HS 234, Bklyn., Jewelry Trade Ctr., Bangkok, Bilboa (Spain) Emblematic bldgs., Internat. Trade Ctr., Barcelona, Spain, Seattle Art Mus., San Jose (Calif.) Convention Ctr., San Jose Arena; project dir. Hong Kong Sta. South West & North East Tower Structural Audit, Balt. Conv. Ctr., Rock 'N Roll Hall of Fame and Mus., Cleve., Pontiac Marina Hotel and Retail, Singapore, acad. bldgs. and greenhouse, SUNY, Binghamton, NY; project mgr. Coll. of Law bldg. U. Iowa, Iowa City, Neiman-Marcus store, San Francisco, AT&T Exhbn. bldg., NYC, Bank of China Tower, Hong Kong, AIG Tower, Hong Kong, Bellevue Hosp., NYC, W.J. Clinton Presdl. Ctr., Little Rock, Ark., Shanghai World Fin. Ctr., PPG Hdqs., Pitts., AT&T Corp. Hdqs., NYC; ptnr.-in-charge Nat. Constn. Ctr., Phila. Contbr. articles to profl. jours. Named to Those Who Made Marks in the Constrn. Industry in 1988, Engring. News Record, NYC, 1989, Spl. Recognition award Profl. Women in Constrn., 2002. Mem. ASCE (performance study team World Trade Ctr. with FEMA-)(hon.), Archtl. League, Coun. on Tall Bldgs. and Urban Habitat (past chairperson com. on gravity loads and temperature effects 1982-85), Architects, Designers, Planners for Social Responsiblity, NY Assn. Cons. Engrs. (dir. 1989-93, structural codes com. 1991—). Avocations: sailing, skiing, reading, photography. Home: 45 E 89th St Apt 25C New York NY 10128-1230 Office: Leslie E Robertson Assocs RLLP 30 Broad St Fl 47 New York NY 10004-2304 Office Phone: 212-750-9000. E-mail: sts@lera.com.

SEE, SCOTT WILLIAM, history professor; b. Washington, Oct. 12, 1950; s. John W. and Nathalie L. See; m. Mylese J. Johnson, Aug. 26, 1978; children: Hadley E., Hilary P. BA, Muskingum Coll., New Concord, Ohio, 1972; MA, U. Maine, Orono, 1980, PhD, 1984. Prof. history U. Vt., Burlington, 1985—97; Libra prof., chair history U. Maine, Orono, 1997—. History tchr. Canterbury Sch., New Milford, Conn., 1983—85; mem. Gorsebrook Rsch. Inst., Halifax, N.S., Canada, 2002—. Author: (textbook) The History of Canada, 2001, (scholarly book) Riots in New Brunswick: Orange Nativism and Social Violence in the 1840s, 1993; contbr. articles to profl. jours.; mem. editl. bd.: Acadiensis, Am. Rev. of Can. Studies. Recipient Kroepsch-Maurice award for tchg., U. Vt., 1989; Fulbright rsch. fellow, 1995—96, sr. fellow, Canadian Embassy, 2001. Mem.: Assn. for Can. Studies in the U.S. (exec. coun. 1995—99), Can. Hist. Assn., Am. Hist. Assn. (joint com. with Can. Hist. Assn. 1994—96), Phi Alpha Theta. Avocations: photography, golf, hiking. Home: 1 Frost Ln Orono ME 04473 Office: U Maine History Dept Stevens Hall Orono ME 04469 Office Phone: 207-581-1923. E-mail: scottsee@maine.edu.

SEEBACH, LYDIA MARIE, physician; b. Red Wing, Minn., Nov. 9, 1920; d. John Henry and Marie (Gleusen) S.; m. Keith Edward Wentz, Oct. 16, 1959; children: Brooke Marie, Scott. BS, U. Minn., 1942, MB, 1943, MD, 1944, MS in Medicine, 1951. Diplomate Am. Bd. Internal Medicine. Intern Kings County Hosp., Bklyn., 1944; fellow Mayo Found., Rochester, Minn., 1945-51; pvt. practice Oakland, Calif., 1952-60, San Francisco, 1961—. Asst. clin. prof. U. Calif., San Francisco, 1981—; mem., vice chmn. Arthritis Clinic, Presbyn. Hosp., San Francisco, 1961-88, pharmacy com., 1963-78; chief St. Mary's Hosp. Arthritis Clinic, San Francisco, 1968-72; exec. bd. Pacific Med. Ctr., San Francisco, 1974-76. Contbr. articles to med. jours. Fellow ACP; mem. AMA, Am. Med. Womens Assn. (pres. Calif. chpt. 1968-70), Am. Rheumatism Assn., Am. Soc. Internal Medicine, Pan Am. Med. Womens Assn. (treas.), Calif. Acad. Medicine, Calif. Soc. Internal Medicine, Calif. Med. Assn., San Francisco Med. Soc., San Francisco Med. Assn., San Francisco Soc. Internal Medicine, No. Calif. Rheumatism Assn., Internat. Med. Women's Assn., Mayo Alumni (bd. dirs. 1983-89), Iota Sigma Pi. Republican. Lutheran. Avocations: music, cooking, gardening, needlepoint. Office: 490 Post St Ste 939 San Francisco CA 94102-1414 Office Phone: 415-397-9571.

SEED, BRIAN BRUCE, music educator; b. Anchorage, Alaska, Jan. 4, 1966; s. Gerald Bruce and Marilyn Marie Seed; m. Stephanie Louise Brown, June 24, 1995; children: James, Mark. Grad., Armed Forces Sch. of Music, Norfolk, Va., 1984—85; BMus Edn., Willamette U., 1990, MA Tchg., 1991. Cert. tchr. Oreg., 1991. Announcer KSJJ - KPRB Radio, Redmond, Oreg., 1987—88; announcer/news reporter KBND-KLRR Radio, Bend, Oreg., 1989—91; youth program dir. Holland Am. Cruise Line, Seattle, 1992—95; advt./tech. cons. The Mattress Factory, Inc., Bend, 1997—2002; band dir. Molalla H.S./Molalla River Sch. Dist., Oreg., 1991—2001, Summit H.S./Bend-LaPine Sch. Dist., Bend, 2001—; v.p. The Mattress Factory, Inc., 2002—. Dir. band exch. program with Matsudo Mcpl. HS, Japan, 1996—. Chair North Lancaster Neighborhood Assn., Salem, Oreg., 1994—98; founder, pres. Molalla River Cmty. Concert Assn., 1998—2001. Specialist 4 U.S. Army, 1984—87, Ft. Hood, Tex. Recipient Army Commendation Medal, U.S. Army, 1987, Army Achievement Medal, 1986—87, Good Conduct Medal, 1987. Mem.: Oreg. Edn. Assn., Oreg. Music Educators Assn., Music Educators Nat. Conf., Arthritis Found., Am. Legion. Conservative. Mem. Christian Ch. (Disciples Of Christ). Avocation: music, computers, movies, history, travel. Home: 2446 NE 6th St Bend OR 97701 Office: Summit HS 2855 NW Clearwater Dr Bend OR 97701 Personal E-mail: seedb@bendnet.com.

SEEDS, SHARON LYNN, bank processor; d. Don A. and Marguerite Morairty Seeds. BA in Edn. with high distinction, Ariz. State U., 1972. Tchr. gen. and vocal music edn. Paradise Valley Unified Sch. Dist. # 69, Phoenix, 1973—76; advt. coord. Greater Phoenix Jewish News, 1976—83; disbursements/loan rev. processor Merabank, Phoenix, 1984—88; loan processor II Citibank, Scottsdale and Mesa, Ariz., 1989—91; acctg. specialist, ops. processor I and II, store acctg. support, mortgage lending home equity Internet divsn. Wells Fargo & Co., Phoenix, 1992—. Festival adjudicator Ariz. Solo and Ensemble Festival, Phoenix, 1973—99; jr. choir dir. Christ Ch. of the Ascension, Paradise Valley, 1983—87; soloist, sect. leader Congregation Ch., Tempe, Ariz., Presbyn. Ch., Phoenix, Ch. of Divine Sci.; soloist, sect. leader Trinity Episcopal Cathedral Trinity Cathedral St. Barnabas-on-the Desert, 1976—2002. Contr.ghost editor: textbook Arizona Construction Lending and the Law, 1988; actor: (theatrical prodns.) various locations. Vol. libr. catalog area Lillian Vallely Sch., Blackfoot, Idaho, 2002; neighborhood activist on hist. preservation com. Sunview Estates II, Phoenix, 2002—; vol. press release area Episcopal Ch. Gen. Conv., Phoenix, 1991. Mem.: Am. Choral Dirs. Assn., Music Educators Nat. Conf., Phi Kappa Phi, Kappa Delta Pi, Pi Lambda Theta, Sigma Alpha Iota (local chair/co-chair for nat. bazaar at triennial conv. 1987—, nat. elections chair triennial conv. 2003, Sword of Honor 1972, Rose of Honor 1995, Rose of Dedication 2003). Episcopalian. Avocations: music theater/liturgical drama, needlecrafts, reading.

SEEGER, GUENTER OTTO, chef; b. Loffenau, Baden, Germany, Mar. 23, 1949; s. Otto Emil and Margarete (Temme) S.; m. Marion Boehmlander (div. Aug. 1991); children: Diana, Denise. Student, Cook and Hotel Sch., Lucerne, Switzerland. Apprentice Hotel Funk, Dobel, Germany, 1963-66; cook various locations, Switzerland, 1966-77; owner, operator restaurant Pforz Heim, Germany, 1977-84; exec. chef maifar Regent Hotel, Washington, 1984-85; exec. chef dining rm. Ritz-Carlton Hotel, Atlanta, 1985—. Pres., cons., produce developer Smi, Inc., Atlanta, 1993. Editor calendars, 1982, 83 (award 1982). Named Best Chef of Atlanta, Atlanta Mag., 1993. Mem. Chefs Collaborative 2000 (bd. overseers 1994). Avocation: Kung Fu. Office: The Ritz-Carlton Buckhead 3434 Peachtree Rd NE Atlanta GA 30326-1172

SEEGER, LEINAALA ROBINSON, law librarian, educator; b. Wailuku, Hawaii, July 2, 1944; d. John Adam and Anna Hiilani (Leong) Robinson; 1 child, Maile Lea. BA, U. Wash., 1966; JD, U. Puget Sound, 1977; M in Law Librarianship, U. Wash., 1979. Bar: Wash. 1977. Reference librarian U. Puget Sound Sch. Law., Tacoma, 1977-79, assoc. law librarian, 1981-86; asst. librarian McGeorge Sch. Law, U. of Pacific, Sacramento, 1979-81; assoc. librarian pub. svc. Harvard Law Sch., Cambridge, Mass., 1986-89; dir. law library, assoc. prof. law U. Idaho Coll. Law, Moscow, 1989-97, U. Hawaii Sch. of Law, Honolulu, 1997—. Mem. Assn. Am. Law Schs. (librs. and technol. com. 1997-99, chmn. 1998-99), Wash. state Bar Assn., Am. Assn. Law Librs. (chmn. minority com. 1990-91, v.p., pres.-elect Western Pacific chpt. 1985-86, 90-91, pres. 1991-92, vice chmn. edn. com. 1991-92, chmn. 1992-93). Avocations: scuba, snorkeling, wine education, flying, aerobics.

SEEGER, MELINDA WAYNE, realtor; m. Robert Charles Seeger; 1 child, Jeffrey Wayne. Chief occupl. therapy Rehab. Inst. Oreg., Portland, 1964-66; supr. phys. disabilities and gen. medicine and surgery occupl. therapy Mpls. VA Hosp., 1966-68; supr. phys. disabilities occupl. therapy Nat. Naval Med. Ctr., Bethesda, Md., 1968-71; assoc. chief rehab. svcs., dir. occupl. therapy UCLA Med. Ctr., 1974-85, cons., prin. investigator rheumatology divsn. dept. medicine, 1985-86; realtor Merrill Lynch Realty, L.A., 1987-95, Re/Max Estate Properties, Beverly Hills, Calif., 1995-96, Nelson Shelton & Assocs., Beverly Hills, 1996—. Author, editor articles in field. Mem. utilization rev. com. Vis. Nurse Assn. L.A., 1975-85, mem. profl. adv. com., 1979-80; mem. exec. com. Allied Health Professions sect. Arthritis Found., 1980-85, chmn. edn. com., 1982-85, mem. profl. edn. com.; bd. dirs. Calif. Occupl. Therapy Found., 1984-85, Westwood-Holmby Hills Homeowners Assn.; mem. adv. bd. Save Westwood Village L.A. Recipient Spl. Achievement award Nat. Naval Med. Ctr., 1971, Outstanding Performance award, 1971, Spl. Performance award UCLA, 1980, 84, Addie Thomas Svc. award for outstanding svc. to rheumatology cmty. Arthritis Found., 1986, Cert. of Appreciation award, 1989; mem. Million Dollar Club. Mem. Am. Occupl. Therapy Assn., Occupl. Therapy Assn. Calif., Allied Health Professions Assn. (chmn. edn. com. 1982—), L.A. Bd. Realtors, San Fernando Valley Bd. Realtors, West L.A. C. of C., Million Dollar Club, Blue Diamond Club. Office: 355 N Canon Dr Beverly Hills CA 90210-4704

SEEGERS, LORI C. lawyer; b. Miami Beach, Fla., June 17, 1955; BA cum laude, U. Pa., 1977; JD, Fordham U., 1982. Bar: N.Y. 1983, Ill. 2002, U.S. Dist. Ct. (so. dist.) N.Y. 1983. Ptnr. Anderson, Kill & Olick, P.C., N.Y.C.; gen. counsel PPM Am., Inc. Contbr. articles to profl. jours. Mem. ABA, N.Y. State Bar Assn. (sect. banking, corp. and bus. law), Assn. of Bar of City of N.Y. Office: PPM Am Inc Ste 1200 225 W Wacker Dr Chicago IL 60606-1276 E-mail: lori.seegers@ppmamerica.com.

SEEGMILLER, RAY REUBEN, manufacturing executive; b. Dysart, Iowa, May 15, 1935; s. Reuben Jacob and Lola Fern (Gnagy) S.; m. Nancy Louise Schilz, July 27, 1958; children: Jane Rae, Ann Carla; m. Connie Callam, May 30, 1981 BS in bus. adminstrn., Drake U., 1957. Acct. Arthur Andersen & Co., Chgo., 1957-61; div. controller S.W. Forest Industries, Phoenix, 1961-63; asst.

controller Allison Steel Mfg. Co., Phoenix, 1963-68; with Marathon Mfg. Co., Houston, 1969—, pres., CEO, 1986—; pres. & CEO Cabot Oil & Gas Corp., Houston. Mem. Am. Inst. C.P.A.s, Fin. Execs. Inst. Office: Cabot Oil & Gas Corp PO Box 4544 Houston TX 77210-4544

SEEHAUSEN, RICHARD FERDINAND, architect; b. Indpls., Mar. 17, 1925; s. Paul Ferdinand and Melusina Dorothea (Nordmeyer) S.; m. Phyllis Jean Gates, Dec. 22, 1948; children: Lyn, Dirk. Student, DePauw U., 1943-44, Wabash Coll., 1944, State U. Iowa, USN Pre Flight, 1944; BArch, U. Ill., 1949. Registered profl. arch. Ptnr. Johnson, Kile, Seehausen & Assocs., Inc. archs., engrs., Rockford, Ill., 1955-82, pres., 1974-82, Richard F. Seehausen-Arch., Inc., Rockford, Ill., 1983—. Mem. com. jail planning and constrn. stds. Bur. Detention Facilities, Ill. Dept. Corrections, 1970-73; analyst Dept. Def., 1962-66; analyst Fed. Fall-Out Shelter, 1962—. Prin. works include No. Ill. U. Ctr., Harrison Hall, Lorado Taft, Oreg., Health Svc. Bldg., No. Ill. U., (Renovation) Old Winnebago County Pub. Safety Bldg., Rockford, Ill., St. Mark Luth. Ch., Christ Meth. Ch., Forest Hills Free Ch., Page Park Spl. Edn. Sch., Winnebago County Courthouse, Court Street Meth. Ch., Willows Personal Care Ctr., 1st Presbyn. Ch., Rochelle, Ill., Messiah Luth. Ch., Rock Falls, Ill., Rockford Mut. Ins. Home Office Bldg., Ch. of the Nazarene, Freeport, Ill., Stephenson County Courthouse, LDS Temple, McHenry County Ct. House, Woodstock, Ill., Ogle County Pub. Safety Bldg., Oreg., DeKalb H.S., Social Security bldgs., Racine, Sheboygan, Oshkosh and Janesville, Wis., Freeport YWCA Bldgs., renovation Carroll County Ct. House, DeKalb Area Retirement Ctr., Oak Crest Retirement Ctr., Sycamore/DeKalb, Ill., St. Paul Ch. of Christ, Davis, Ill., Savanna Meth. Ch., Savanna, Ill., others. Bd. dirs. Rockford Boys Club, Lincoln Pk. Boys Club, past dir.; trustee Emmanuel Luth. Ch., Rockford, 1989-92; mem. Nat. Trust Hist. Preservation, 2000—. Served with USN, 1943-45, USNR, 1945 47, lt. USAF, 1949-55. Mem. AIA (dir. No. Ill. chpg. 1966-68, 75-77, pres. chpt. 1978-79), Ill. Coun. of Am. Inst. Archs., U. Ill. Alumni Assn., Mason (Shriner), Kiwanian, Forest Hills Country Club (gov. 1970-72), Saddle Brooke Country Club, Saddle Brooke Arc. Com., Lamdba Chi Alpha. Lutheran. Office: Richard F Seehausen Arch Inc 65297 E Emerald Ridge Dr Tucson AZ 85739-1434 E-mail: dicknjean@worldnet.att.net.

SEEHRA, MOHINDAR SINGH, physics educator, researcher; b. Panjab, Pakistan, Feb. 14, 1940; came to U.S., 1963; s. Bakhshish Singh and Rattan (Kaur) S.; m. Harbhajan Kaur, May 12, 1963; children: Jasmeet, Parveen. BS, Panjab U., 1959; MS, Aligarh (India) U., 1962; PhD, U. Rochester, 1969. Instr. chemistry Arya Coll., Nawanshahr, India, 1959-60; lectr. physics Jain Coll., Ambala City, India, 1962-63; asst. prof. physics W.Va. U., Morgantown, 1969-73, assoc. prof., 1973-77, prof., 1977-91, Eberly disting. prof. physics, 1992—. Contbr. more than 200 articles to profl. jours. Rsch. fellow A.P. Sloan Found., 1973-75, ORAU Summer fellow, 1976, 77, 84, 85; recipient Outstanding Rsch. award Coll. Arts and Scis., U. W.Va., 1985. Fellow Am. Phys. Soc., Inst. Physics (Eng.). Office: WVa State U Dept Physics PO Box 6315 Morgantown WV 26506-6315 Office Phone: 304-293-3422 x 1473. E-mail: mseehra@wvu.edu.

SEELAND, ARTHUR DAVID, bishop; b. Jersey City, Oct. 31, 1931; s. Theodore Arthur and Dorothea Augusta (Thomas) Seeland; m. Mary Ann Hove, Apr. 10, 1954; children: John Robert, Eric David, Tellef Martin, Karen Victoria. *Father's family emigrated from Norway to New Jersey about 1900. Mother's family emigrated from England to West Jersey, now Salem County, New Jersey, about 1680. Son John, Financial Operations Manager, Martin Memorial Health System, Stuart, Florida; married Diane Benfield. Son Eric, Captain, USNR, Commanding Officer, Defense Intelligence Agency Headquarters 0797; married Donna Durham. Son Tellef, independent contractor, one son, Christopher. Daughter Karen, homemaker; married Nacif Colton Zacca, Director of Operations, Professional Payroll Solutions, Conshohocken, Pennsylvania; one daughter, Hannah, two sons Asher and Matthias* BA, Houghton Coll., 1953; MDiv, Temple U., 1958; D Ministry, McCormick Theol. Sem., 1978; grad. with highest distinction, U.S. Naval War Coll., 1981; ThM, Princeton Theol. Sem., 1973. Diplomate Am. Bd. Med. Psychotherapists. Pastor NJ United Meth. Conf., 1953—64; commd. lt. (j.g.) USN, 1963, advanced through grades to comdr., 1975, chaplain, 1964—87; clin. dir. Family and Psychol. Svcs., Cherry Hill, NJ, 1987—90; rector Holy Sacraments Anglican Cath. Ch., King of Prussia, Pa., 1988—93; archdeacon Diocese of the Resurrection, Quakertown, Pa., 1990—93; bishop Diocese of the Pacific and SW of the Anglican Rite Cath. Ch., L.A., 1993—. Lectr. med. ethics Med. Sch. Uniformed Services U., Bethesda, Md., 1980—84; lectr. ethics U.S. Nat. War Coll., Washington, 1980—84; asst. prof. Pa. State U., Hershey. *Chaplain, Groveville, New Jersey Fire Company #9. Founding member, Yardville, New Jersey, First Aid Squad. Member, 1960 White House Conference on Children and Youth. Liaison Officer between U.S. Navy Middle East Force and the ruler of Bahrain, 1967-1970. Drafted first Federal Government "Do Not Resuscitate Order Guidelines" in 1982. First Chairman, National Naval Medical Center Medical Ethics Committee, 1982. Organized first joint National Institutes of Health-National Naval Medical Center Medical Ethics Seminar 1982. Advisor to Secretary of Defense Staff on Just War aspects of nuclear weapons, 1981-1983. Guest Lecturer on "Just War" to Joint Chiefs of Staff nuclear weapons targeting staff, 1981-1983.* Contbr. articles to profl. jours. Editl. bd. Jour. of Christian Bioethics, Waco, Tex., 1994—99; pres. Houghton (NY) Coll. Alumni, 1981—83. Master: Masons (life; grand chaplain NJ 1963—, grand chaplain France 1977—); mem.: Assn. of Mil. Surgeons of the U.S. (life), NY Acad. of Scis. (life). Holy Catholic Church (Anglican Rite). Avocations: sailing, travel, hiking, hunting. Home: 764 West Bay Ave Barnegat NJ 08005 Office: Diocese of the Pacific and Southwest 6752 East Ramsey Rd Hereford AZ 85615

SEELENFREUND, ALAN, retired pharmaceutical company executive; b. N.Y.C., Oct. 22, 1936; s. Max and Gertrude (Roth) S.; m. Ellyn Bolt; 1 child, Eric. BME, Cornell U., 1959, M. in Indsl. Engring., 1960; PhD in Mgmt. Sci., Stanford U., 1967. Asst. prof. bus. adminstrn. Grad. Sch. Bus. Stanford U., Palo Alto, Calif., 1966-71; mgmt. cons. Strong, Wishart and Assocs., San Francisco, 1971-75; various mgmt. positions McKesson Corp., San Francisco, 1975-84, v.p., chief fin. officer, 1984-86, exec. v.p., chief fin. officer, 1986-89, chmn., CEO, 1989-97, chmn., 1997-99, also bd. dirs., chmn., 1997—2002; ret., 2002. Mem. Nature Conservancy, World Wildlife Fund, St. Francis Yacht Club, Villa Taverna Club, Pacific Union Club. Avocations: sailing, skiing, hiking. Office: McKesson Corp 1 Post St Ste 3275 San Francisco CA 94104-5296

SEELER, RUTH ANDREA, pediatrician, educator; b. N.Y.C., June 13, 1936; d. Thomas and Olivia (Patten) S. BA cum laude, U. Vt., 1959, MD, 1962. Diplomate Am. Bd. Pediatrics, Am. Bd. Pediatric Hematology/Oncology. Intern Bronx (N.Y.) Mcpl. Hosp., 1962—65; pediats. hematology/oncology fellow U. Ill., 1965—67; dir. pediatric hematology/oncology Cook County Hosp., 1967—84; prof. pediatrics and pediatric edn. Coll. Medicine U. Ill., Chgo., 1984—; assoc. chief pediatrics Michael Reese Hosp., Chgo., 1990—97, acting chief pediatrics, 1997—99; pediatrician St. Anthony's Hosp./U. Ill. Coll. Medicine, 1999—2001. Course coord. pediatrics Nat. Coll. Advanced Med. Edn., Chgo., 1987-96; mem. subboard Pediatric Hematology/Oncology, Chapel Hill, 1990-95. Mem. editl. bd. Am. Jour. Pediat. Hematology/Oncology, 1985-95. Founder camp for hemophiliacs Hemophilia Found., Ill., 1973—2000, med. dir., pres., 1981—85; jr. and sr. warden, treas. Ch. Our Saviour, Chgo., 1970—92. Mem.: U. Vt. Med. Sch. Alumna Assn. (sec.), Phi Beta Kappa, Gamma Phi Beta Found. (trustee 1994—2000, 2002—). Avocations: triathalons, biking, swimming. Office: U Ill Coll Medicine Pediats M/C 856 840 S Wood St Chicago IL 60612-7317 Office Phone: 312-355-1021.

SEELEY, JOHN GEORGE, horticulture educator; b. North Bergen, N.J., Dec. 21, 1915; s. Howard Wilson and Lillian (Fiedler) S.; m. Catherine L. Cook, May 28, 1938 (dec. Feb. 1999); children: Catherine Ann, David John (dec. 1995), Daniel Henry, George Bingham, Thomas Dyer. BS, Rutgers U., 1937, MS, 1940; PhD, Cornell U., 1948. Research asst. N.J. Agrl. Exptl. Sta., 1937-40, foreman ornamental gardens, 1940-41; instr. floricultural sci. Cornell U., Ithaca, N.Y., 1941-43, 45-48, asst. prof., 1948-49, prof. floricultural sci., 1956-83, prof. emeritus, 1983—, head dept. floriculture, 1956-70; prof. floriculture Pa. State U., 1949-56; D.C. Kiplinger chair floriculture, prof. horticulture Ohio State U., 1984-85. Asst. agronomist Bur. Plant Industry Dept. Agr., 1943-44; chemist Wright Aero. Corp., Paterson, N.J., 1944-45. Trustee Kenneth Post Found., 1956-84, Fred. C. Gloeckner Found., 1970—, pres., 1993—2004. Recipient Best Sr. award in Agriculture, Rutgers U., 1937, S.A.F. Found. for Floriculture Rsch. & Edn. award, 1965, Cornell Edgerton Career Teaching award, 1983. Fellow: AAAS, Am. Soc. Hort. Sci. (pres. 1982—83, chmn. bd. 1983—84, Leonard H. Vaughan rsch. award 1950, Bittner Extension award 1982); mem.: Pa. Flower Growers Assn., N.Y. Flower Growers Assn., Am. Carnation Soc., Ohio Florists' Assn. (hon.), Internat. Soc. Hort. Sci. (hon.), Am. Acad. Floriculture (hon.), Mass. Hort. Soc. (Silver medal 1980), Soc. Am. Florists (Hall of Fame 1979), Am. Hort. Soc. (Liberty Hyde Bailey award 1998), Rotary (dist. gov. 1973—74), Pi Alpha Xi (pres. 1951—53), Phi Kappa Phi, Sigma Xi, Phi Epsilon Phi, Epsilon Sigma Phi, Alpha Zeta (chancellor 1936—37). Presbyterian. Home: 403 Savage Farm Dr Ithaca NY 14850-6506

SEELEY, MARK, agronomist; b. Gary, Ind., May 3, 1942; s. Clayton Barron and Margaret Louise (Cook) Seeley. BS, Purdue U., 1967; MA in Edn., Austin Peay State U., 1971. Staff asst. Purdue U., 1962; tchr. sci. Lake Ctrl. Sch. Corp., St. John, Ind., 1967-68, Gary, 1972-73; mgr. agronomic crops R.L. Schultz Farms, Hobart, Ind., 1973-94, dir. Lupin introduction and devel., 1980-94. Bd. dirs. On Line Electric Inc., mem. exec. steering com. Mem. Lake Area United Way Vol. Svc., Lake County Health Fair, 1974; sci. and engring. judge 26th and 27th Calumet Regional Sci. Fairs. Mem.: NSPE, AAAS, Am. Soc. Quality, U.S. Hang Gliding Assn., Soil Sci. Soc. Am., Internat. Soc. Hort. Sci., Fedn. Am. Scientists, Crop Sci. Soc. Am., Coun. Agrl. Sci. and Tech. (mem. Century Club 1983), Am. Soc. Plant Physiologists, Am. Soc. Agronomy, Ind. Soc. Profl. Engrs. (mem. scholarship com. Calumet chpt. 1982—83, co-chmn. 1984—85), Am. Soc. Agrl. Engrs. (pres.'s club 1980—94), Am. Soc. Hort. Sci. (food quality and nutrition working group), Am. Inst. Biol. Scis., Lake Michigan Flyers Assn. Address: 6126 Colorado Street Hobart IN 46342

SEELIG, GERARD LEO, management consultant; b. Schluchtern, Germany, June 15, 1926; came to U.S., 1934, naturalized, 1943; s. Herman and Bella (Bach) S.; m. Lorraine Peters, June 28, 1953; children: Tina Lynn, Robert Mark and Carol Ann (twins). BEE, Ohio State U., 1948; MS in Indsl. Mgmt, N.Y. U., 1954. Registered profl. engr., Ohio. Electronics engr. Martin Corp., Balt., 1948-50; sr. engr. Fairchild Aircraft Co., Farmingdale, N.Y., 1950-54; program mgr. RCA, Moorestown, N.J., 1954-59, Van Nuys, Calif., 1959-61; div. mgr. Missile & Space Co. div. Lockheed Aircraft Corp., Van Nuys, 1961-63; v.p., gen. mgr. Lockheed Aircraft Corp. (Lockheed Electronics div.), Los Angeles, 1963-68; exec. v.p. Lockheed Electronics Co., Inc., Plainfield, N.J., 1968-69, pres., 1969-71; group exec., exec. asst. to office of pres. ITT, N.Y.C., 1971-72, corp. v.p., 1972-79, sr. v.p., 1979-81, exec. v.p., 1981-83; pres. indsl. and tech. sector Allied Corp., exec. v.p., 1983-87. Disting. exec. lectr. Rutgers Grad. Sch. Mgmt.; exec.-in-residence, vis. prof. Columbia U. Grad. Sch. Bus.; bd. dirs. 5 corps.; cons. various investment firms. Served with AUS, 1944-46. Recipient Disting. Alumnus award Ohio State U., 1987. Fellow AIAA (assoc.); mem. IEEE (sr.).

SEELIG, JILL, publishing executive; MBA, Fordham U., NY. With fin. svcs. ind., 1984—89; sales rep. NY Mag.; beauty dir. Self Mag., 1994—95; advt. sales rep. Self Mag., 1996—99; advt. dir. Vanity Fair, 1998—99, O, The Oprah Mag., 1999—2000, pub., 2000—. Office: O, The Oprah Magazine 1700 Broadway New York NY 10019

SEELMAN, KATHERINE DOLORES, institute administrator; b. Boston, May 26, 1938; d. Frederick George and Loretta (Tetu) S. BA, Hunter Coll., 1964; MA, NYU, 1970, PhD, 1982. Tchr. N.Y.C. Schs., 1966-73; instr., rschr. N.Y. Inst. Tech., NSF, N.Y.C., 1973-75; project mgr. Nat. Coun. Chs., N.Y.C., 1976-82; cons. Am. Assn. Retired Persons, Washington, 1982-83; rsch. scholar Gallaudet U., Washington, 1984-86; dir. pub. edn. Mass. Comm. for Deaf and Hard of Hearing, Boston, 1986-89; rsch. specialist Nat. Coun. on Disability, Washington, 1989-93; dir. program devel. Adminstrn. on Devel. Disability, Washington, 1993-94; dir. Nat. Inst. on Disability and Rehab. Rsch., Washington, 1994—. Switzer scholar Nat. Rehab. Assn., 1991, Disting. Switzer fellow Dept. Edn. Nat. Inst. Disability and Rehab. Rsch., 1985-86; recipient Scholarships NYU, 1973, Am. Law Inst./ABA, 1977, Fellowships NSF, 1974, Resources for the Future, 1976; named to Hall of Fame Alumni Assn. Hunter Coll., 1995; recipient pub. svc. award Assn. Acad. Physiatrists, 2000. Mem. RESNA, AAAS, Am. Pub. Health Assn. (Disability Achievement award 1999), Assn. for Advancement of Sci., Soc. for Disability Studies, Self-Help for Hard of Hearing. Office: Nat Inst Disability and Rehab Rsch 600 Independence Ave SW Washington DC 20202-0004

SEELY, JAMES MICHAEL, defense consultant, retired naval officer, small business owner; b. Los Angeles, Oct. 15, 1932; s. Louis K. and Mary Edith (Gleason) S.; m. Gail Margaret Deverman, July 13, 1957; children: Ted Andrew, Nina Marie. BS, UCLA, 1955; MS, George Washington U., 1976. Commd. ensign USN, 1955, advanced through grades to rear adm.; student pilot, 1955-56; attack pilot, 1957-75; comdg. officer Attack Squadron 165, Naval Air Sta. Whidbey Island, Wash., 1972-73; comdr. Carrier Air Wing 9, Naval Air Sta. Lemoore, Calif., 1974-75; comdg. officer U.S. Naval Air Sta., Whidbey Island, 1977-79; dep. dir. DCNO (Air Warfare, OP-50), Pentagon, Washington, 1979-82; dir. Joint Analysis Directorate, Office Joint Chiefs Staff, Washington, 1982-84; comdr. Medium Attack Tactical Electronic Warfare Wing, Pacific Fleet, Naval Air Sta. Whidbey Island, 1984-86; dir. DCNO (Air Warfare, OP-50), Pentagon, 1986-88; dep. comptr. of Navy, Pentagon, 1988-89; ret., 1989; with RRP Def. Cons. Assocs., Arlington, Va., 1989—2002; owner, pres. JMS Cons., 2002—. Vietnam combat duty with Attack Squadrons 93, 152, 165 flying from aircraft carriers USS Enterprise, Hancock, Bon Homme Richard, Shangri-La and Constellation; 447 combat missions. Decorated Defense Superior Service, Legion of Merit (3), D.F.C. (4), Bronze Star, Air Medal (43), Navy Commendation medal with combat v (7). Mem. Naval Inst., Tailhook Assn., Assn. Naval Aviation, Marine Corps Aviation Assn., Red River Valley Fighter Pilots Assn., Navy League, Assn. Old Crows, Golden Eagles, Sigma Pi. Republican. Roman Catholic. Avocations: sports, automobiles. Home: 5730 Shropshire Ct Alexandria VA 22315-4027 Office Phone: 703-971-3695. E-mail: jim.seely@cox.net.

SEELY, ROBERT DANIEL, physician, medical educator; b. Woodmere, N.Y., Nov. 4, 1923; s. Harry and Ethel (Weil) S.; m. Marcia Ann Wells, June 19, 1953; children: Ellen Wells, Anne Wells. BS, NYU, 1943; MD, Columbia U., 1946. Intern Mt. Sinai Hosp., N.Y.C., 1946-47, asst. resident in medicine, 1950-51, resident in pathology, 1951-52, chief resident in medicine, 1952-53; Sara Welt fellow in cardiovascular research Presbyn. Hosp., N.Y.C., 1953-54; instr. dept. physiology, cardiovascular research Western Res. U., Cleve., 1947-48; chief rheumatic heart disease clinic Mt. Sinai Hosp., N.Y.C., 1961-70, attending physician medicine and cardiology, 1978—, chief of service dept. medicine, 1979—, clin. prof. medicine, cardiology Sch. Medicine, 1970—; practice medicine specializing in cardiovascular disease N.Y.C., 1953—. Contbr. articles to profl. jours. Served to capt. M.C. AUS, 1948-50. Recipient Solomon Berson Meml. award Mt. Sinai Hosp., 1977 Fellow Am. Coll. Cardiology, ACP; mem. N.Y. Heart Assn., AMA, N.Y. County Med. Soc., Soc. Cert. Internists N.Y., Phi Beta Kappa, Alpha Omega Alpha, Beta Lambda Sigma Office: 49 E 96th St # 11D New York NY 10128-0782 Personal E-mail: billybobseedy@cs.com.

SEEMAN, NADRIAN CHARLES, chemistry professor; b. Chgo., Dec. 16, 1945; s. Herman and Emma (Klaman) S. BS, U. Chgo., 1966; PhD, U. Pitts., 1970. Rsch. assoc. biology Columbia U., N.Y.C., 1970-72; postdoctoral fellow biology MIT, Cambridge, 1972-77; asst. prof. biology SUNY, Albany, 1977-83, assoc. prof. biology, 1983-88; prof. chemistry NYU, N.Y.C., 1988—, Margaret and Herman Sokol chair in chemistry, 2001—. Sr. cons. Molecular Biophysics Tech., Inc., Phila., 1983-87; cons. Lifecodes Corp., Inc., Elmsford, N.Y., 1983-87, Datascope, Malvern, Pa., 1989-93, Chiron Corp., 1993-98. Contbr. articles to profl. jours. Recipient Sidhu award Pitts. Diffraction Soc., 1974, Rsch. Career Devel. award NIH, 1982-87, Feynman prize in nanotechnology, 1995, Emerging Tech. prize, 1997; Basil O'Connor fellow March of Dimes, 1978-81, DNA-based Computation award, 2004; Rsch. grantee NIH, 1979—, ONR, 1989—. Mem. Internat. Soc. for Nanoscale Sci., Computation and Engring. (founding pres. 2004-2005), Am. Crystallographic Assn., Biophys. Soc., Am. Chem. Soc., Am. Soc. Biochemistry and Molecular Biology. Achievements include founding DNA nanotechnology; construction of 1st DNA truncated octahedron, theory of DNA knot design, construction of DNA double crossover molecules; discovery of antijunctions and mesojunctions, first synthetic DNA KNOT, development of 3D, 3-connected DNA object, of first geometrical DNA object, of first specific proposal for a biochip, DNA nanomechanical device of testable theory of macromolecular design and crystal formation, of theory and demonstration of immobile nucleic acid junctions, of theory of sequence-specific recognition of nucleic acids, of first crystal structure of RNA double helices, and of first crystal structure of a dinucleoside phosphate. Office: NYU Dept Chemistry New York NY 10003 Business E-Mail: ned.seeman@nyu.edu.

SEEMANN, ROSALIE MARY, international business and foreign policy association executive; b. St. Louis, July 30, 1942; d. Ulysses Sylvester and Helen Maire (Hootselle) Simon; m. Richard Vaughn, Jan. 20, 1968 (dec.); 1 child, Heather Elizabeth. Student, Lindenwood Colls., St. Charles, Mo., 1973-76, Harris Tchrs. Coll., St. Louis, 1961, U. Fla., Gainesville, 1964. Vol. U.S. Peace Corps, Brazil, 1964-66; tech. analyst, group leader Conductron-Mo., St. Charles, 1966-71, bus. mgr., 1971-77; maintenance engr. McDonnell Douglas Astronautics, St. Louis, 1977-78; mgr. supply support Northrop Def. Systems Divsn., Rolling Meadows, Ill., 1978-80; logistics mgmt. cons. Logistic Support Svcs., Spring Grove, Ill., 1980-85; mgr. reliability, maintanability, integrated logistic Recon/Optical, Inc., Barrington, Ill., 1985-90; v.p., exec. dir. Mid Am. Com. Internat. Bus. & Govt. Coop., Chgo., 1991-97; exec. dir. World Affairs Coun., St. Louis, 1997-99; founder, pres. Mid-West Inst. Internat. Exch., 1999—; v.p. global initiatives World Trade Ctr., St. Louis, 1999—2001. Bd. dirs. Libr. Internat. Rels., Chgo.-Kent Coll. Law, Prime Med. Products. Bd. dirs. U. Mo.-St. Louis Chancellor's Coun., internat. affairs com.; bd. dirs. World Affairs Coun. Am.; mem. women's bd. Goodman Theatre, Chgo.; active Girl Scouts U.S.A. Recipient commendation Conductron-Mo., 1967, pres. award Recon-Optical, 1989. Mem. Am. Soc. Assn. Execs. (internat. sect. coun. 1996—), Nat. Coun. Internat. Visitors, Am. Women Internat. Understanding, Soc. Logistics Engrs. (Mem. of Yr. award, sr. mem.), English Speaking Union, Japan Am. Soc., Chgo. Coun. Fgn. Rels. (Chgo. com.), Assn. Old Crows, Coun. Women Leaders, Execs. Club Chgo., Arts & Edn. Coun. Greater St. Louis, Internat. Trade Assn., Senate Constantine Prophyrogenetus Internat. Assn. (Greece, hon. pres.), Inst. Mid. East Studies Al-Mamun. Fax: 636-745-2352. Office Phone: 636-745-2352. E-mail: rseemann@earthlink.net.

SEENITH, SIVASUNDARAM, mathematician, educator; s. Sam Seenith and Tham Kanaga; m. Irene M Siva, May 21, 1973; 1 child, Diantha A Siva. PhD, U. Tex., 1987. Prof. Embry-Riddle Aero. U., Daytona Beach, Fla., 1989—. Organizer Conf. Nonlinear Problems in Aviation and Aerospace, Conf. Math. Problems in Engring. and Aerospace Scis. Author: Vector Lyapunov Functions and Stability Analysis of Nonlinear Systems, 1991, College Mathematics for Aviation I, 1992, College Mathematics for Aviation II, 1993, Dynamics Systems on Measure Chain, 1996, Advances in Nonlinear Dynamics, 1997, Nonlinear Problems in Aviation and Aerospace, 2000, Advances in Dynamics and Control, 2004; editor-in-chief Jour. Nonlinear Studies. Mem.: AAUP, Soc. Indsl. and Applied Math., Internat. Fedn. Nonlinear Analysts (charter), Math. Assn. Am. (charter mem. math. for bus., industry and govt. 1999), Acad. Nonlinear Scis., Am. Math. Soc. Avocations: travel, cricket. Office: Embry-Riddle Aero U 600 S Clyde Morris Blvd Daytona Beach FL 32114 Business E-Mail: siva@erau.edu.

SEETHALER, WILLIAM CHARLES, international business executive, consultant; b. N.Y.C., Dec. 4, 1937; s. William Charles and Catherine Frances (Flaherty) Seethaler. Student, Quinnipiac Coll., Conn., 1955-56, Ohio State U., 1956-58; BSBA, U. San Francisco, 1977; MBA, Pepperdine U., 1982; grad. global enterprise mgmt. program, Oxford U., Eng., 2000. Lic. real estate salesperson Calif. Asst. to v.p. sales T. Sendzimir, Inc., Waterbury, Conn. and Paris, 1960-66; mgr. internat. ops. Dempsey Indsl. Furnace Co., East Longmeadow, Mass., 1966-67; mgr. internat. sales Yoder Co., Cleve., 1967-74; mng. dir., owner Seethaler & Assocs., Palo Alto, Calif., 1974—; owner, chief exec. officer Seethaler Internat. Ltd., Palo Alto, Calif., 1982-92; ptnr. DFS Computer Assocs., San Jose, Calif., 1976-87; v.p. mktg. and sales Telewave Inc., Mountain View, Calif., 1996—2001; rep. IMSM, Malmesbury, England, 2002—, Spacesonic, San Carlos, Calif., 2004—. Bd. dirs. Palo Alto Fund, 1979—93, chmn., 1986—88; cmty. rels. advisor Stanford U., 1986—2003; mem. Friends of Rewley House, Oxford U., 2001—. Mem.: Joint Venture: Silicon Valley (bd. dirs. 1992—95), Assn. MBA Execs., Assn. Iron and Steel Engrs. (life), Inst. Indsl. Engrs. (sr.; v.p. profl. rels. Peninsula chpt. 1988—90, bd. dirs. 1988—, del. to Silicon Valley Engring. Coun. 1991—97), Ohio State U. Alumni Assn., Stanford U. Alumni Assn. (life), Palo Alto C. of C. (bd. dirs. 1975—79, v.p. orgn. affairs 1976—77, pres. 1977—78), Pepperdine U. Alumni Assn., U. San Francisco Alumni Assn., Stanford Diamond Club. Office: 345 Stanford Shopping Ctr #144 Palo Alto CA 94304-1412

SEFF, RICHARD, actor, writer; b. N.Y.C., Sept. 23, 1927; s. Chester and Henrietta (Levy) Siff. BA, NYU, 1947. Agt. MCA, Inc., N.Y.C., 1954-62; sec., treas. Hesseltine, Bookman & Seff, N.Y.C., 1962-69; v.p. Creative Mgmt. Assn., N.Y.C., 1969-74. Staff writer Theater Week Magazine, N.Y.C, 1988—. Author: (musical book) Shine!, 2001; (plays) Paris Is Out, 1969-70, The Whole Ninth Floor starring Alan Alda, 1966; appeared on Broadway in Darkness At Noon, 1950-52, Herzl, 1976, The Seagull, 1982, End of the World, 1984, Musical Comedy Murders of 1940, 1987; off-Broadway in Modigliani, 1979-80, Childe Byron, 1981, Richard II, 1982, Angels Fall, 1984, Only You, 1987, Summer and Smoke, 1988, Established Price, 1990, Countess Mitzi, 1991, Lend Me a Tenor, 1991, The Cocktail Hour, 1992, The Truth Teller, 1995, The Countess, 1999-2000; appeared in films The Onion Field, 1979, Being There, 1979, Where The Buffalo Roam, 1980, A Stranger is Watching, 1982, Quiz Show, 1994, The Hours, 2002. Recipient Carbonell award for best featured actor in play Angels Fall, Carbonell (Fla.) Com., 1984. Avocations: financial planning, theatrical investment, travel.

SEFFRIN, JOHN REESE, health science association administrator, educator; b. Hagerstown, Ind., May 19, 1944; s. Theodore H. and Mary Ellen (Reese) Seffrin; m. Carole Sue Washburn, Apr. 16, 1966; 1 child, Mary. BS in Edn., Ball State U., 1966, DSc (hon.), 1994; MS, U. Ill., 1967; PhD in Health Edn., Purdue U., 1970. Asst. prof. health edn. Purdue U., West Lafayette, Ind., 1970—76, assoc. prof., 1976—79; prof., chmn. dept. applied health sci. Ind. U., Bloomington, 1979—92; CEO Am. Cancer Soc., Atlanta, 1992—. Trustee Am. Cancer Soc. Found., 1992—; guest lectr. various pub. health orgns. and schs., 1970—; bd. dirs. Healthcare Inc.; mem. subcom. on cessation Dept. HHS, Washington, 2002—; charter mem., mem. steering com. Nat. Dialog on Cancer, 1999. Nat. bd. dirs. Am. Lung Assn., 1980—90; treas. Partnership for Prevention of Premature Death, Disease and Disability, 1991—; mem. Pres.'s Commn. on Improving Econ. Opportunity in Cmtys. Dependent on Tobacco Prodn. While Protecting Pub. Health, 2000—01; pres. State Welfare Bd. Ind. Dept. Pub. Welfare, 1979—80, 1982—84; treas. Midwest Nuc. Bd., 1973—75; chmn. cmty. edn. com. Am. Lung Assn., 1981—83, v.p., 1980, pres., 1982; chmn. bd. dirs. Nat. Health Coun., 1998—2000; bd. dirs. Nat. Ctr. for Tobacco-Free Kids, 1996—; bd. trustees The Scripps Rsch. Inst., 1999—; bd. advisors Discovery Health Media, 2000—; bd. dirs. Wabash Ctr. for the Mentally Retarded, 1970—73. Named commr.-at-large, Nat. Commn. Health Edn. Credentialing, 1995—2000, Sagamore of Wabash, State of Ind., 1980, 1988; recipient cert. appreciation, Surgeon Gen. of Pub. Health Svc., 1992, Outstanding Alumn us award, Ball State U., 1982. Fellow: Am. Sch. Health Assn. (mem. governing coun. 1979—81, 1982—89, pres. 1987—88, Howe award 1991); mem.: NAS (Nat. Cancer Policy Bd. 1997—), AMA, Am. Acad. Family Physicians (pub. adv. bd. 1999—), Rsch. Am. (bd. dirs. 1996—), Independent Sector (bd. dirs. 1997—, 1997—), Nat. Interagy. Coun. on Smoking and Health (bd. dirs. 1979—), Internat. Union Against Cancer (ex-officio mem. U.S. nat. com. 2000—, pres. 2002—), Ind. Assn. for Health, Phys. Edn. and Recreation (pres. 1976, Cert. of Appreciation 1977, Honor award 1982), Am. Cancer Soc. (dir. Ind. Divsn. 1977—90, chmn. Ind. Divsn.

1982—85, dir.-at-large to nat. bd. dirs., chmn. nat. pub. edn. com. 1984—87, nat. v.p. 1986—87, chmn. nat. bd. dirs. 1989—91), Ind. Thoracic Soc. (mem. governing coun. 1977—84), Ind. Family Health Coun. (dir. 1979—81, v.p. 1980—81, pres. 1981), Ind. Assn. Health Educators (pres. 1975—76, chair 1997—2000), Assn. for Advancement Health Edn. (bd. dirs. 1989—92), Nat. Assn. State Bds. of Edn. (commn. on sch. cmty. role in improving adolescent health 1989—90), Eta Sigma Gamma, Phi Delta Kappa. Roman Catholic. Office: Am Cancer Soc 1599 Clifton Rd NE Atlanta GA 30329-4250*

SEGAL, BARRY, company executive; CEO Bradco Supply, Avenell, N.J. Office: Bradco Supply 13 Production Way Avenel NJ 07001-1628

SEGAL, BERNARD LOUIS, physician, educator; b. Montreal, Quebec, Canada, Feb. 13, 1929; came to U.S., 1961, naturalized, 1966; s. Irving and Fay (Schecter) S.; m. Idajane Fischman, Feb. 17, 1963; 1 dau., Jody Segal Reinbold. BSc cum laude, McGill U., 1950, postgrad., 1950-51, MD, C.M. high standing, 1955. Diplomate Am. Bd. Internal Medicine. Intern Jewish Gen Hosp., Montreal, 1955-56; resident Balt. City Hosp., 1956-57, Beth Israel Hosp., Boston, 1957-58, Georgetown Med. Ctr., Washington, 1958-59, St. George's Hosp., London, 1959-61; pvt. practice internal medicine and cardiology Phila., 1961—; prof. medicine Med. Coll. Pa., Hahnemann U., 1996—; prof. medicine, sr. attending physician Jefferson Med. Coll./Thomas Jefferson U., 1998—. Dir. cardiology Thomas Jefferson U., 1998. Author: Auscultation of the Heart, 1965; Editor: Theory and Practice of Auscultation, 1964, Engineering in the Practice of Medicine, 1966, Your Heart, 1972, Arteriosclerosis and Coronary Heart Disease, 1972; mem. editl. bd. Am. Jour. Cardiology, 1970—, Clin. Echocardiography, 1978; contbr. articles to profl. jour. Fellow ACP, Am. Coll. Cardiology (chmn. scholar-trainee com., trustee 1969-71), Am. Coll. Chest Physicians; mem. NY Acad. Sci., Alpha Omega Alpha. Home: 1156 Red Rose Ln Villanova PA 19085-2121 Office: Jefferson Heart Inst 925 Chestnut St Mezzanine Philadelphia PA 19107-4824 also: 401 E City Line Ave Ste 525 Bala Cynwyd PA 19004-1125 Office Phone: 610-666-5555., 215-955-8145.

SEGAL, DAVID ROBERT, sociology educator; b. N.Y.C., June 22, 1941; s. Harry and Daisy Rose Segal; m. Mady Wechsler, Dec. 25, 1976; 1 child, Eden Heather. BA, Harpur Coll., 1962; MA, U. Chgo., 1963, PhD, 1967; DHL (hon.), Towson U., 1991. From asst. prof. to assoc. prof. U. Mich., Ann Arbor, 1966-75; tech. area chief U.S. Army Rsch. Inst., Arlington, Va., 1973-75; prof. U. Md., Coll. Pk., 1975—; dir. Ctr. Rsch. Mil. Orgn., Coll. Pk., 1995—. Vis. rsch. fellow U. Bonn, Germany, 1971; guest scholar Brookings Inst., Washington, 1981-84; disting. vis. prof. U.S. Mil. Acad., W. Point, N.Y., 1988-89; mem. bd. visitors U.S. Army War Coll., Carlisle, Pa., 1997-01. Co-author: The All-Volunteer Force, 1977, Recruiting for Uncle Sam, 1989, Peace Keepers and Their Wives, 1993, The Postmodern Military, 2000. Spl. asst. peace ops. Chief Staff U.S. Army, Washington, 1993-95; mem. task force Def. Sci. Bd., Washington, 1998-00. Fellow Inter-Univ. Sem. Armed Forces and Soc. (pres. 1995—); mem. Am. Sociol. Assn. (chair sect. peace and war 1991-92), D.C. Sociol. Soc. (pres. 1994-95, Morris Rosenberg award 1997). Avocations: tennis, astronomy. Office: U Md Dept Sociology College Park MD 20742-1315 Office Phone: 301-405-6439. E-mail: dsegal@socy.umd.edu.

SEGAL, HELENE ROSE, periodical editor; b. L.A., Jan. 31, 1955; d. Alan and Lila E. Segal. Student, Calif. State U., Fullerton, 1973-75; BA in English, U. Calif., Santa Barbara, 1978. Library asst. ABC-CLIO, Santa Barbara, 1979-80, editorial asst., 1980-81, asst. editor, 1981-83; mng. editor ABC POL SCI, ABC-CLIO, Santa Barbara, 1983-2001; project mgr. ABC-CLIO, Santa Barbara, 2001—. Mem. Am. Polit. Sci. Assn., Current World Leaders (adv. bd. 1989—). Avocations: reading, collecting, swimming. Home: 142 La Vista Grande Santa Barbara CA 93103-2817 Office: ABC CLIO 130 Cremona Dr Ste C Santa Barbara CA 93117-5505 E-mail: hsegal@abc-clio.com.

SEGAL, HOWARD PAUL, history educator; b. Phila., July 15, 1948; s. Alexander David and Irene Sylvia (Goldsmith) S.; m. Deborah D. Rogers, Nov. 26, 1988; children: Richard William Rogers, Raechel Maya Rogers. AB, Franklin and Marshall Coll., Lancaster, Pa., 1970; MA, Princeton U., 1972, PhD, 1975. Lectr. and Taft postdoctoral fellow in history U. Cin., 1975-76; lectr. and Killam postdoctoral fellow in history Dalhousie U., Halifax, N.S., Can., 1976-78; asst. prof. history U. Mich., Ann Arbor, 1978-83; lectr. in history of sci. Harvard U., Cambridge, Mass., 1984-86; asst. prof. history U. Maine, Orono, 1986-88, assoc. prof. history, 1988-92, prof. of history, 1992-96, Bird and Bird prof. history, 1996—. Author: Technological Utopianism in American Culture, 1985, (with A. Marcus) Technology in America: A Brief History, 1989, 2d edit. 1999, Future Imperfect, 1994; co-editor: Technology, Pessimism and Post-Modernism, 1994. Am. Philos. Soc. rsch. grantee, 1979; Andrew Mellon faculty fellow, 1984-85. Mem. Am. Hist. Assn., Orgn. Am. Historians, Am. Studies Assn., Soc. for History of Tech., Am. Soc. Engring. Edn., Phi Beta Kappa, Phi Alpha Theta. Democrat. Jewish. Office: Univ of Maine Dept of History 5774 Stevens Hall Orono ME 04469-5774

SEGAL, ILYA R. finance educator; PhD, Harvard U., Cambridge, Mass., 1991—95. Assoc. prof. econs. Stanford U., Calif., 1999—2002, prof. humanities, scis., 2002—. Vis. asst. prof. econs. MIT, Cambridge, Mass., 1995—95; asst. prof. econs. U. Calif., Berkeley, 1995—99; nat. fellow Hoover Instn. War, Revolution, and Peace, Stanford, Calif., 1998—99; mem. Inst. Advanced Study, Princeton, NJ, 2002—03. Fellow Rsch. Fellowship, Alfred P. Sloan Found., 1999-2001, John Simon Guggenheim Meml. Found., 2002-2003; grantee Rsch. grants, NSF, 1998-2004. Fellow: Econometric Soc. Office: Dept Econs Stanford Un Stanford CA 94305

SEGAL, JACK, mathematics professor; b. Phila., May 9, 1934; s. Morris and Rose (Novin) S.; m. Arlene Stern, Dec. 18, 1955; children: Gregory, Sharon. BS, U. Miami, 1955, MS, 1957; PhD, U. Ga., 1960. Instr. math. U. Wash., Seattle, 1960-61, asst. prof., 1961-65, assoc. prof., 1965-70, prof., 1970-1999, prof. emeritus, 2000—, chmn. dept., 1975-78. Author: Lecture Notes in Mathematics, 1978, Shape Theory, 1982. NSF postdoctoral fellow Inst. Advanced Study, Princeton, N.J., 1963-64; Fulbright fellow U. Zagreb, Croatia, 1969-70, U. Coll. London hon. rsch. fellow, 1988; NAS exch. prof. U. Zagreb, 1979-80. Mem. Am. Math. Soc. Home: 8711 25th Pl NE Seattle WA 98115-3416 Office: U Washington Dept Mathematics Seattle WA 98195-0001 Office Phone: 206-543-1914. E-mail: segal@math.washington.edu.

SEGAL, JANE, newscaster; b. N.Y. BS in Edn., Bernard M. Baruch Coll. Gen. assignment reporter, weekend anchor WLBT, Jackson, Miss.; reporter, anchor WMC-TV, Memphis, 1983; anchor WLBT, Jackson. Avocations: old movies, foreign films. Office: WLBT 715 S Jefferson St Jackson MS 39201

SEGAL, JONATHAN BRUCE, editor; b. NYC, May 12, 1946; s. Clement and Florence Lillian (Miller) S.; m. Haidi Kuhn, June 30, 1974. BA, Washington Coll., 1966. Writer, editor NY Times, NYC, 1966-73; editor Quadrangle/NY Times Book Co., NYC, 1974-76; sr. editor Simon & Schuster, NYC, 1976-81; exec. editor, editor-in-chief, editl. dir., v.p. Times Books, NYC, 1981-89; editor-at-large Random House, NYC, 1985-89; v.p., sr. editor Alfred A. Knopf, NYC, 1989—. Contbr. articles to popular jour. Democrat. Jewish. Home: 115 E 9th St Apt 12E New York NY 10003-5420 Office: Alfred A Knopf 1745 Broadway New York NY 10019 E-mail: jsegal@randomhouse.com.

SEGAL, LORE, writer; b. Vienna, Mar. 8, 1928; came to U.S., 1951, naturalized, 1956; d. Ignatz and Franzi (Stern) Groszmann; m. David I. Segal, Nov. 3, 1960 (dec.); children: Beatrice Ann, Jacob Paul. BA in English, Bedford Coll., U. London, Eng., 1948. Prof. writing div. Sch. Arts, Columbia U., also Princeton U., Sarah Lawrence Coll., Bennington Coll.; prof. English U. Ill., Chgo., 1978-92, Ohio State U., 1992-97. Author: Other People's Houses, 1964; Lucinella, 1976, Her First American, 1985; (children's book) Tell Me A Mitzi, 1970, All the Way Home, 1973, Tell Me a Trudy, 1977; The Story of Mrs. Brubeck and How She Looked for Trouble and Where She Found Him, 1981, The Story of Mrs. Lovewright and Purrless Her Cat, 1985, Morris the Artist, 2003, Why Mole Shouted and Other Stories, 2004; translator: (with W.D. Snodgrass) Gallows Songs, 1968, The Juniper Tree and Other Tales from Grimm, 1973, The Book of Adam to Moses, 1987, The Story of King Saul and King David, 1991; contbr. short stories, articles to N.Y. Times Book Rev., Partisan Rev., New Republic, The New Yorker, others. Guggenheim fellow, 1965-66; Council Arts and Humanities grantee, 1968-69; Artists Public Service grantee, 1970-71; CAPS grantee, 1975; Nat. Endowment Arts grantee, spring 1982, 1987; NEH grantee, 1983; Acad. Arts and Letters award, 1986. Address: 280 Riverside Dr New York NY 10025-9010 E-mail: Lore@usa.net.

SEGAL, MARTIN ELI, retired actuarial and consulting company executive; b. Vitebsk, Russia, Aug. 15, 1916; came to U.S., 1921, naturalized, 1928; s. Isidor and Anna (Title) S.; m. Edith Levy, June 17, 1937; children: Susan Segal Rai, Paul. LHD (hon.), Pratt Inst., 1976; MusD (hon.), Mannes Coll. Music, 1976; LHD (hon.), Grad. Ctr. CUNY, 1979, L.I. U., 1986, NYU, 1988; D in Music (hon.), Manhattan Sch. Music, 1999. Various positions ins. industry, 1935-39; founder The Segal Co., consultants and actuaries, N.Y.C., 1939, pres., CEO, 1939-67, chmn. bd., 1967-91, chmn. emeritus, 1991—. Pres. Wertheim Asset Mgmt. Svcs., Inc., N.Y.C., 1972-75, chmn., bd., 1975-82; ptnr. Wertheim & Co., investment bankers, N.Y.C., 1967-82. Founding chmn. The N.Y. Internat. Festival of the Arts, Inc., 1985-2002; chmn. bd. Lincoln Ctr. Performing Arts, Inc., 1981-86, chmn. emeritus, 1986—; organizing co-chmn. Internat. Conf. on Future of Arts Edn., 1999; bd. dirs. Pub. Radio Internat., 1981-94, dir. emeritus, 1994-98; counselor at large, 1998—; co-chmn. Conf. on Intellectual Property The Arts and Tech., 1994; chmn. arts and culture com., N.Y. 92, N.Y. 93, N.Y. 94, N.Y. 95; mem., bd. dirs. Nat. Bldg. Mus., 1983-91; founding mem., bd. advisers Libr. of Am., 1984—; trustee Am.-Scandinavian Found., 1986-91, adv. trustee, 1991—; bd. visitors Grad. Sch. and Univ. Ctr., CUNY, 1983-96; bd. dirs. The Grad. Ctr. Found., Inc., 1996—, vice chmn. bd. trustees, 2003—; bd. dirs. ASCAP Found., 1997-2003; mem. adv. com. arts Harvard and Radcliffe, 1993-99, mem. office for the arts coun., 1999—; bd. trustees, chmn. exhibitions com. Mus. Modern Art, 1978-81; trustee Inst. for Advanced Study, Princeton, N.J., 1972-91, trustee emeritus, 1991—; trustee City Ctr. Music and Drama, 1971—, pres. Cultural Assistance Ctr., Inc., 1977-82, chmn., 1982-84; founding pres. Film Soc. of Lincoln Ctr., 1968-78, pres. emeritus, 1978—; mem. adv. com. Tony voter Am. Theater Wing, 2000—; mem. adv. coun. Theatre Devel. Fund, 1992—; mem. nat. bd. Young Audiences, Inc., 1979—; mem. adv. bd. Concert Artists Guild, 1983-2000; founding mem. publs. com. The Pub. Interest, 1965-2002; mem. vis. com. Harvard U. Sch. Pub. Health, 1979-92, dean's coun. Sch. Pub. Health, 1990—; mem. adv. bd. Studio in a Sch. Assn., 1988—; bd. dirs. Helena Rubinstein Foundn., 1972-95; chmn. mayor's Com. on Cultural Policy, 1974; founding chmn. Commn. for Cultural Affairs City of N.Y., 1975; chmn. pub. svc. awards com. Fund for City of N.Y., 1978, 79, bd. dirs., 1978-87; co-chair China cultural exchange mission, Ctr. US-China Arts Exchange, 1979; founder Film Guild N.Y., 1940-41. Decorated Royal Swedish Order of Polar Star, 1984; officer of Arts and Letters, Ministry of Culture of French Govt., 1984; recipient cert. of merit Mcpl. Art Soc., 1974; spl. award Internat. Film Importers and Distbrs. Am., 1973; N.Y.C. Mayor's award of honor for arts and culture, 1982; Ann. award of distinction Mus. City of N.Y., 1982; Concert Artists Guild award, 1983; Disting. Am. of Fgn. Birth award Internat. Ctr. N.Y.C., 1985; John H. Finley medal Alumni Assn. CCNY, 1985; Town Hall Friend of the Arts award, 1987; Dirs. Emeriti award Lincoln Ctr. for Performing Arts, Inc., 1987; N.Y. State Gov's. Arts award, 1989; Pres.'s award Grad. Sch. and Univ. Ctr. of City Univ. of N.Y., 1990; City of N.Y. Edn. Fund award LWV, 1984; award for svc. to music Third Street Music Sch. Settlement, 1981; Annual Arts Leadership award Alumni and Friends of LaGuardia H.S., 1985; Songwriters' Hall of Fame Patron of the Arts award, 1988; Nat. Fedn. Music Clubs Presdl. Citation award, 1989; Creative Arts Rehab. Ctr. Pub. Spirit award, 1989; Honor medal The Nat. Arts Club, 1992; Lincoln Ctr. Laureate, 1997; Our Town Treasure award Mus. City of N.Y., 1998; Civic Leadership award Citizens Union, 1998; Arts Roundtable award of honor, 1998; Martin E. Segal Theatre Ctr., CUNY Graduate Ctr, 2000; Acting Co. Joan Warburg Humanitarian award, 2001; S.L.E. Found. (lupus) award, 2001. Breukelein Inst. Gaudlum award, 2002. Fellow: Royal Soc. (London); mem.: Players Club, The Pilgrims of the U.S., Century Assn. Democrat. Jewish. Office: 375 Park Ave Ste 2602 New York NY 10152-2699

SEGAL, MINDY, chef; Grad., Kendall Coll. Pastry asst. Ambria, Chgo.; pastry chef Charlie Trotter's, Chgo., Gordon, Chgo., Marche, Chgo., Spago, Chgo., MK the Restaurant, Chgo. Developed dessert menus Mia Francesca, Harvest on Huron, Thyme. Office: 868 N Franklin Chicago IL 60610

SEGAL, PHYLLIS NICHAMOFF, mediator; b. Apr. 18, 1945; d. Sidney and Theresa Helen (Uroff) Nichamoff; m. Eli J. Segal, June 13, 1965; children: Jonathan, Mora. Student, Brandeis U., 1962-65; BA, U. Mich., 1966; JD, Georgetown U., 1973. Bar: N.Y. 1974, U.S. Dist. Ct. (so. and ea. dists.) N.Y. 1975, Mass. 1983, U.S. Supreme Ct. 1979. Deputy atty. gen. Commonwealth Mass., 1986—88; assoc. Weil, Gotshal and Manges, N.Y.C., 1973-77; legal dir. NOW Legal Def. and Edn. Fund., N.Y.C., 1977-82, gen. counsel, 1986—94; mediator ADR Assoc., L.L.C., Boston, 2001—. Chmn. Fed. Labor Rels. Auth., Washington, 1994-2000; gen. counsel Exec. office Transp. and Constrn., Commonwealth of Mass., 1984-86; adj. asst. prof. law NYU, 1980-82; fellow Bunting Inst. Radcliffe Coll., 1982-83; cons. U.S. Commn. Civil Rights. Contbr. articles to profl. jours. Mem. Commn. on Party Reform Nat. Dem. Party, 1972-73, mem. Compliance Rev. Commn., 1974-76; mem. adv. bd. Mass. Commn. Against Discrimination, 1983—; bd. chmn. Handgun Control Inc./Ctr. to Prevent Handgun Violence; former chairwoman Nat. Labor Rels. Authority. Mem. ABA, Fedn. Women Lawyers Jud. Screening Panel, Mass. Bar Assn. Office: ADR Assoc LLC 85 Newbury Street Ste 3 Boston MA 02116

SEGAL, ROBERT MARTIN, lawyer; b. Atlantic City, N.J., Apr. 7, 1935; s. Nathan Albert and Edna (Dutkin) S.; m. Rhoda Sue Luber, June 8, 1958; children— Deborah Ann, William Nathan, Elizabeth Ann Student, Cornell U., 1953-54; BS in Econs., U. Pa., 1957; LLB cum laude, Harvard Law Sch., 1960. Bar: Pa. 1961. Assoc. Wolf, Block, Schorr & Solis-Cohen LLP, Phila., 1960-69, ptnr., 1969—, chmn., exec. com., 1978-79, 82-83, 86-87, 89-98. Hon. pres. Jewish Employment and Vocat. Svc.; bd. dirs. Orleans Homebuilders, Inc. Contbr. articles to profl. jours. and mags. Constable of elections Lower Merion Twp., Pa., 1970-72; bd. dirs. Jewish Family and Children's Agy., Am. Jewish Com., Feinstein Ctr. for Am. Jewish History at Temple U., Greater Phila. Urban Affairs Coalition; bd. govs. Rep. Jewish Coalition; past trustee Hahnemann U., Fedn. Jewish Agys., Phila. Rehab. Plan, Inc., Rosenbach Mus. and Libr. Mem. ABA, Pa. Bar Assn., Phila. Bar Assn., Internat. Coun. Shopping Ctrs., Urban Land Inst. (assoc.), Am. Coll. Real Estate Lawyers, Phila. Bar Found. (trustee 1981-87), Am. Law Inst., Harvard Law Sch. Assn. Phila., Federalist Soc., Wharton Club, Chaine des Rotisseurs, L'Ordre Mondial, Sunday Breakfast Club, La Coquille Club, Harvard Club, Beta Gamma Sigma. Avocations: golf, swimming. Office: Wolf Block Schorr & Solis-Cohen LLP 1650 Arch St Fl 22 Philadelphia PA 19103-2097 Office Phone: 215-977-2230. E-mail: rsegal@wolfblock.com.

SEGAL, ROBERT S. retail executive; b. New Haven, Conn., Nov. 4, 1954; s. Leonard and Barbara Segal; m. Mariquita A.K. Segal, Aug. 7, 1977; 1 child, James Q. AB, Ripon Coll., 1975; MA, NYU, 1977; postgrad., U. Ill., 1981. Buyer Hecht Co., Arlington, Va., 1981-87; mktg. mgr. Lechmere, Woburn, Mass., 1987-89; v.p. merchandising Rickel Home Ctr., Plainfield, N.J., 1989-90; dir. merchandising Best Products, Richmond, Va., 1990-93; sr. v.p. merchandising Fresh Fields, Rockville, Md., 1993-94; v.p. merchandising Shopko, Green Bay, Wis., 1995—. Mem. adv. bd. Internat. Housewares Show, Chgo., 1998—. Contbr. articles to profl. jours. Bd. dirs. Autism Soc. of Am. Found., 2000-2001, Orgn.for Autism Rsch., 2002—. Mem. Phi Beta Kappa. Office Phone: 920-429-4120.

SEGAL, SHELDON JEROME, biologist, educator, foundation administrator; b. N.Y.C., Mar. 15, 1926; s. Morris M. and Florence (Bogan) S.; m. Harriet Ellen Feinberg, May 22, 1961; children: Amy Robin, Jennifer Ann, Laura Jane. BA, Dartmouth Coll., 1947; postgrad., U. Geneva, 1947-48; MS, U. Iowa, 1951, PhD, 1952; MD (hon.), U. Tampere, Finland, 1984, U. Upssala, Sweden, 1985. Rsch. scientist William S. Merrill Co., Cin., 1952-53; rsch. assoc., asst. prof. U. Iowa, 1953-56; asst. med. dir. Population Coun., N.Y.C., 1956-63, med. dir., 1963-78, v.p., 1969-76, sr. v.p., 1976-78; affiliate Rockefeller U., N.Y.C., 1956-76, adj. prof., 1977-87; dir. population scis. Rockefeller Found., 1978-91; disting. scientist Population Coun., N.Y.C., 1991—. Lectr. Columbia U., 1959-61; vis. prof. All-India Inst. Med. Scis., New Delhi, 1962-63, Amir Chand lectr., 1975; mem. Marine Biol. Lab, Woods Hole, Mass.; cons. World Bank, WHO, NIH, Ford Found., Indian Govt., UN Office Sci. and Tech., UN Fund Population Activities; mem. com. on contraceptive tech. NAS, 1977-80, com. on health effects of marijuana Inst. Medicine, 1981-82, NAS com. on demographic impact of contraceptive tech., 1988-89, nat. rsch. con., overview com. for Indo-U.S. sci. initiative, 1985—; adv. com. on human reproduction FDA; cons. to dir. Nat. Inst. Child Health and Human Devel., 1978-80; plenary lectr. 3d World Congress Endocrinology, 1968, Upjohn lectr. Am. Fertility Soc., 1971, plenary lectr. World Fertility Congress, 1975, Sigma Xi lectr. U. Idaho, 1976, plenary lectr. World Congress on Ob-Gyn., 1976, lectr. Chinese Acad. Scis., 1977, Carl Gemzell lectr. U. Upssala, 1982, Pierre Soupart lectr. Axel Munthe Found., 1988, Alpha Omega Alpha lectr. U. Pa. Coll. Medicine, 1989, plenary lectr. World Congress on Human Reproduction, 1990; hon. prof. Peking Union Med. Coll., Beijing, 1987, Chinese Acad. Scis., 1988; trustee Marine Biol. Lab., 1985—, chmn. bd. trustees, 1991—; pres. 10th World Congress on Human Reproduction, 1999. Co-editor 8 books; contbr. numerous articles to profl. jours. Trustee Rye Country Day Sch., 1979—, pres. bd. trustees, 1981-85; trustee Ctr. for Reproductive Law and Policy, 1992—. Lt. (j.g.) USNR, 1943-45. Decorated Order Comdr. of Lion (Finland); recipient Honor award Innsbruck U., Austria, hon. citation Pres. of India, 1978, Clarence J. Gamble award World Acad. Arts and Scis., 1980, Joseph C. Wilson award Rochester Assn. for UN, 1981, UN Population award, 1984, Axel Munthe award in medicine Axel Munthe Found., Italy, 1985, Sci. award Planned Parenthood Fedn. Am., 1990, Dmitirus N. Chorafas award in medicine Swiss Acad. Scis., 1995. Fellow AAAS; mem. Royal Coll. Obstetricians and Gynecologists (hon.), Am. Fertility Soc. (hon. v.p. 1975-76, trustee found. 1975-77), Endocrine Soc., Am. Assn Anatomists, Internat. Soc. for Study Reprodn. (pres. 1968-72), Internat. Inst. Embryology, Am. Soc. Zoologists, Coun. Fgn. Rels., Mexican Acad. Medicine (hon.), Inst. Medicine, Dartmouth Club N.Y., Woods Hole Yacht Club. Home: 9 Topland Rd Hartsdale NY 10530-3001 Office: Population Coun One Dag Hammarskjold Plz New York NY 10017

SEGAL, SIMON, real estate executive, finance company executive; b. Havana, Cuba, Apr. 16, 1941; arrived in U.S., 1955, naturalized, 1970; s. Govsey and Julia (Getzug) Segal. BCE, Cornell U., 1965; MS in Mgmt., Fla. Internat. U., 1982, MS in Fin., 1987, MBA, 1999. Registered profl. engr., Fla.; real estate and mortgage broker Fla. Owner Simon Segal Constrn. Co., Miami Beach, Fla., 1971—75; pres. Investex Realty Corp., Miami, Fla., 1973—75, S.S. Investments, Inc., Miami, 1975—85, Siber, Inc., Miami, 1985—2001; adj. prof. Jerome Bain Real Estate Inst., Fla. Internat. U., 2000—; pres. Fla. Real Estate of Miami Corp., 2001—. Nominee White House Fellows, Wash., D.C., 1972; recipient Key to City of Miami, 1974, Key to City of South Miami, 1975. Mem.: ASCE (sec. 1970), NSPE, Soc. Am. Mil. Engrs., Jaycees, Internat. C. of C. (senator), Cuban Am. C. of C. (founder, pres. 1971), Greater Miami C. of C., Cornell Soc. Engrs., Fla. Engring. Soc., Fla. Internat. U. Alumni Assn., Cornell U. Alumni Assn., Peekskill Mil. Acad. Alumni Assn., Beta Gamma Sigma. Home: 8777 Collins Ave Unit1203 Surfside FL 33154-3406 Office: Fla Real Estate of Miami Corp 2740 NW 112 Ave Miami FL 33172

SEGAL, URIEL, music director; b. Jerusalem, 1944; Asst. condr. N.Y. Philharm.; condr. laureate Century Orch., Osaka, Japan; music dir. Chautauqua Symphony, N.Y., Louisville Orch. Rec. for London-Decca, EMI; condr. European tour Stuttgart Radio Symphony, 1972, now prin. guest condr. Condr. English Chamber Orch., Israel Philharm., Berlin Philharm., royal Concertgebouw, London Symphony, Orch. Paris; condr. orchs. in Houston, Chgo., Dallas, St. Paul, Colo., Milw., Cin. Recipient 1st prize Internat. Mitropolous Conducting Competition, 1969. Office: Louisville Orch 300 W Main St Ste 100 Louisville KY 40202-2930

SEGALAS, HERCULES ANTHONY, investment banker; b. N.Y.C., Mar. 21, 1935; s. Anthony Spiros and Katherine A. (Michas) S.; m. Margaret Wharton, Sept. 18, 1956; children: Donnell Anthony, Stephen Wharton, Katherine Lacy Devlin. BS, Yale U., 1956. Various engring. and mfg. positions Procter & Gamble Co., Cin., 1956-65; pres. for Latin Am., mgr. Internat. Flavors and Fragrances, N.Y.C., 1965-68; exec. v.p. William D. Witter Inc., N.Y.C., 1969-76; sr. v.p. Drexel Burnham Lambert Inc., N.Y.C., 1976-87, mng. dir., 1987-88, also bd. dirs., 1976-88; mng. dir. head consumer products investment banking group PaineWebber Inc. Investment Banking Group, N.Y.C., 1988-99, also bd. dirs.; mng. dir., chmn. global consumer products Investment Banking Group, Schroder & Co., Inc., N.Y.C., 1999-2000; mng. dir., chmn. consumer products investment group Solomon Smith Barney, N.Y.C., 2000—01; ptnr. Sawaya, Segalas & Co., N.Y.C., 2001—. Bd. dirs. Nantucket Land Coun., Mass., 1982-85; mem. corp. Nantucket Cottage Hosp., 1984-85. Mem. Morristown Field Club, Nantucket Yacht Club (bd. govs. 1987-93, mem. exec. com. 1988-93), The Windsor Club. Republican. Avocations: tennis, sailing, languages, woodworking, golf. Home: 10625 Wittington Ave Vero Beach FL 32963-4734 Office: Sawaya Segalas & Co 888 7th Ave 8th Fl New York NY 10019 Office Phone: 212-331-0150. E-mail: hsegalas@aol.com.

SEGALL, DANIEL OWEN, psychologist, researcher; b. Los Angeles, Calif., June 2, 1957; married. Ph.D., U. of Ill., Urbana-Champaign, 1979—83. Mgr., psychometric rsch. Dept. of Def., Seaside, Calif., 1996—, Def. Manpower Data Ctr., Seaside, Calif., 1996—. Achievements include research in the areas of psychometrics and computerized adaptive testing. Office: Def Manpower Data Ctr 400 Gigling Rd Seaside CA 93955 Office Phone: 831-583-2400. Personal E-mail: dan@danielsegall.com. E-mail: dan.segall@osd.pentagon.mil.

SEGALLA, THOMAS FRANCIS, lawyer; b. Lee, Mass., Apr. 7, 1943; s. Stanley John and Ann (Finnegan) S.; m. Mary Louise, Aug. 5, 1967. BBA cum laude, U. Miami, Coral Gables, Fla., 1965; JD cum laude, SUNY-Buffalo, 1972. Bar: N.Y. 1973, U.S. Dist. Ct. (we.dist.) N.Y. 1973, U.S. Supreme Ct. 1983. Prodn. mgr. UniRoyal Inc., Naugatuck, Conn., 1966-69; law asst. N.Y. Atty. Gen., Buffalo, 1971; ptnr. Saperston & Day, PC, Buffalo, 1972-2001, Goldberg Segalla, Buffalo, 2001—. Lectr. Erie C.C., Buffalo, 1970-73, Bryant & Stratton Inst., Buffalo, 1975; assoc. prof. SUNY, 1985-90. Editor SUNY Buffalo Law Rev., 1971-72. Mem. ABA, Def. Rsch. Inst., Erie County Bar Assn., Fed. Def. and Corp. Counsel, Internat. Assn. Def. Counsel, Kappa Sigma (pres. Miami 1964-65). Roman Catholic. Home: 25 Westfield Rd Buffalo NY 14226-3492 Office: Goldberg Segalla 665 Main St Ste 400 Buffalo NY 14203

SEGEL, J. NORMAN, garment manufacturing company executive; b. Toledo, Aug. 1, 1939; BBA, Western Res. U., 1961; MBA, Adelphi U., 1980. Accountant Bobbie Brooks, Cleve., 1961-62; contr. Stacy Ames, Long Island City, N.Y., 1962-65, dir. finance, 1965-66, sec.-treas., 1966-70, exec. asst. to pres., 1968-70; v.p. Fairfield-Noble, Inc., N.Y., 1970-77; treas. Levin & Hecht Inc., N.Y.C., 1977-79; v.p. fin. Parsons Place Apparel Co. Ltd., N.Y.C., 1979-89, dir., 1982-86; v.p. fin. DLH Apparel Co. dba Diana Hartman, 1989-91; contr. Hiram Cohen & Son, Inc., 1991—. Treas. Stephanie Queller Ltd., 1982-86; pres. Jupiter Internat. Inc., 1994-96; sec., treas. JZNS Assoc., 1985-2000, pres., 2000—. Home: 3447 5th St Oceanside NY 11572-5133 Office: 486 Willis Ave Williston Park NY 11596-1737 Office Phone: 516-742-7180.

SEGEL, KAREN LYNN JOSEPH, lawyer, taxation specialist; b. Youngstown, Ohio, Jan. 15, 1947; d. Samuel Dennis and Helen Anita Joseph; m. Alvin Gerald Segel, June 9, 1968 (div. Sept. 1976); 1 child, Adam James. BA in Soviet and East European Studies, Boston U., 1968; JD, Southwestern U., 1975. Bar: Calif., 1996, U.S. Tax Ct., 1996, U.S. Dist. Ct. (cen. dist.) Calif., 1996, U.S. Ct. Appeals (9th cir.), 1997. Adminstrv. asst. Olds Brunel & Co., N.Y.C., 1968-69, U.S. Banknote Corp., N.Y.C., 1969-70; tax acct. S.N. Chilkov & Co. CPA's, Beverly Hills, Calif., 1971-74; intern Calif. Corps. Commr., 1975; tax. sr. Oppenheim Appel & Dixon CPA's, L.A., 1978, Fox,

Westheimer & Co. CPA's, L.A., 1978, Zebrak, Levine & Mepos CPA's, L.A., 1979; ind. cons. acctg., taxation specialist Beverly Hills, 1980—. Settlement officer L.A. County Superior Ct., 2000; law student mentor Southwestern U., 1996-2002, tax moot ct. judge, 1997. High sch. amb. to Europe People-to-People Orgn., 1963. Mem. Calif. State Bar, Women's Inner Circle of Achievement, So. Calif. Bus. Litig. Inns of Ct., L.A. County Bar Assn, Beverly Hills Tinseltown Rose Soc. Avocations: collecting seashells, lhasa apso dog breeding, art, travel, music. E-mail: kjslaw@earthlink.net.

SEGELHORST, CINDY MARIE, pre-school educator; b. St. Louis, Oct. 2, 1957; d. Bernard Anthony and Marjorie Ann Engler; children: April Christine Brooks, Kenneth Andrew. BS in Edn., U. Mo., St. Louis, 1994; MA, Lindenwood U., 1998. Cert. early childhood edn. Dept. Elem. and Secondary Edn., Mo., 1994, elem. edn. Dept. Elem. and Secondary Edn., Mo., 1994, middle sch. social studies Dept. Elem. and Secondary Edn., Mo., 1994, early childhood spl. edn. Dept. Elem. and Secondary Edn., Mo., 1998, trainer work sampling sys. assessment. Early childhood educator Francis Howell Sch. Dist., St. Charles, Mo., 1995—; adj. instr. St. Charles C.C., St. Peters, Mo., 2001—. Cooperating tchr. for student teachers Lindenwood U. and U. of Mo. at St. Louis, St. Charles, 1997—; chairperson for cmty. wellness fair Francis Howell Pub. Sch. Dist., St. Charles, 1998—; mentor for new educators Francis Howell Sch. Dist., St. Charles, 1998—; contbg. mem. Pub. Sch. Kindergarten Transition Team, St. Charles, 2000—; adv. bd. mem. St. Charles C.C. Child Care and Early Childhood, St. Peters, 2001—; contbg writer for fine arts and math curriculum Francis Howell Sch. Dist., St. Charles, 2001—; adv. bd. mem. for pre-kindergarten math stds. Dept. Elem. and Secondary Edn., Jefferson City, Mo., 2001—; mentor for new educators Francis Howell Sch. Dist., St. Charles, 2001—02; dist. rep. Francis Howell Sch. Dist. Profl. Devel Com., St. Charles, 2002—. Mem. Citizens for a Healthy Environment, St. Charles, 2001—03. Named Tchr. of the Yr., Walmart Stores, 1997—98, Tchr. of the Week, St. Charles Jour., 2002; recipient Golden Apple for Early Childhood, St. Peters C. of C., 1996—97. Mem.: Mo. CC Assn., Nat. Assn. Edn. Young Children. Avocations: remodeling, reading, travel, tennis, gardening. Home: 1312 Presidents Landing Dr O Fallon MO 63366-8480 Office: Francis Howell Sch Dist 2555 Hackmann Rd Saint Charles MO 63303

SEGELMAN, ALVIN BURTON, pharmaceutical executive, researcher, scientist, health science consultant, educator; b. Boston, Sept. 27, 1931; s. Joseph Theodore and Anna (Klein) Segelman; m. Florence Hannah Pettler, Apr. 27, 1972 (dec. Jan. 7, 1994); children: Lauren Beth, Sheera Toba. BS, Mass. Coll. Pharmacy, 1954, MS, 1967; PhD, U. Pitts., 1971. Registered pharmacist Mass., cert. nutritional specialist Am. Coll. Nutrition. Chief pharmacist Kenmore Pharmacy, Boston, 1954—61; pres. Bell Pharmacy, Somerville, Mass., 1961—67; instr. pharmacognosy and microbiology pharmacognosy dept. U. Pitts., 1967—71; asst. prof. pharmacognosy dept. Rutgers U., Piscataway, NJ, 1971—74, assoc. prof., chmn. pharmacognosy dept., 1974—90; v.p. R&D health scis. Nature's Sunshine Products, INc., Provo, Utah, 1990—2000; CEO Pharmacognosy Rsch. Inst., Orem, Utah, 2001—. Prin. investigator rsch. Rutgers Biomed. Rsch. Grants, New Brunswick, 1972—85, U.S. Pub. Health Svc. Grant, Washington, 1973; co-prin. investigator rsch. Am. Cancer Soc., Washington, 1987—88; expert med. cons. U.S. Congress Select Com. on Aging, Washington, 1981—83; vis. prof. Jagellonian U., Cracow, Poland, 1989, Patrice Lamumbe U., Moscow, 1999; cons. in field. Co-author: Antibiotics in Historical Perspective, 1981; contbr. articles to profl. jours.; sci. reviewer: various profl. and sci. jours. Mem. various coms. Acad. Pharm. Scis., Washington, 1976—89; mem. med. adv. com. Planned Parenthood Middlesex County, New Brunswick, NJ, 1979—90. 2nd lt. U.S. Army, 1957—59. Fellow: Linnean Soc. Avocations: small arms pistol competition, ethnopharmacognosy research and writing, mountain climbing. Home and Office: Pharmacognosy Rsch Inst 54 West 680 South Orem UT 84058

SEGELNICK, STUART LAWRENCE, periodontist; b. Bklyn., Aug. 11, 1967; s. Saul Irving and Harriet S.; m. Tina Hope Segelnick, Nov. 16, 1997. DDS, SUNY, Buffalo, 1992; Cert. in Periodontology, Temple U., Phila., 1994. Periodontist JHB Periodontal Services, PC, Bklyn., 1994—2000; divsn. chief Brookdale Hosp., Bklyn., 1996—; pres. Advanced Periodontal Svcs., PC, Bklyn., 2000—; sect. chief Wyckoff Heights Med. Ctr., Brooklyn, NY, 2000—; attending NY Hosp. Queens, Queens, NY, 2003—; clin. asst. prof. NYU Coll. of Dentistry, 1999, Columbia U. Sch. Dental and Oral Surgery, New York, 2004—. Disaster mortuary operational rescue team HHS and the Office of Emergency Preparedness. Mem.: ADA, Second Dist. Dental Soc., Am. Bd. Forensic Dentistry, Am. Soc. Forensic Odontology, Acad. Osseointegration, Am. Acad. Implant Dentistry, Northeastern Soc. Periodontology, Am. Acad. Periodontology, Acad. Gen. Dentistry. Avocations: song writing, piano, collecting autographs. Office: Advanced Periodontal Svcs PC 1603 Voorhies Ave 2nd Fl Brooklyn NY 11235 E-mail: eperiodr@aol.com.

SEGERBLOM, SHARON B. social services administrator; b. Miami, Okla., Dec. 19, 1948; d. Charles L. and Doris E. (Randall) Butler; m. Richard Segerblom; children: Eva, Carl. Student, Okla. State U.; degree in nursing, U. Tulsa, 1971; BA in Polit. Sci., U. Nev. Past mgr. Neighborhood Response divsn. City of Las Vegas, past intergovtl. cmty. rels. cood., past chief asst. to the mayor, dir. Neighborhood Svcs., 1997—. Rschr. Focus on Nev.'s Children, 1987, Focus on Nev.'s Women, co-editor, video writer, prodr. Issues chairperson Gov.'s Conf. on Women, 1989-90; 1st v.p. Clark County Area Coun. PTA, 1989-90, Girl Scouts USA Frontier Coun., 1991-93; bd. dirs. WE Can, 1989-90, Martin Luther King Jr. Com., Weed and Seed Steering Com.; bd. dirs., past pres. Clark County Atty.'s Wives, 1988-89; past pres. Women's Dem. Club Clark County; mem. Clark County Dem. Ctrl. Com., 1989-90; past bd. dirs. Jr. League of Las Vegas, 1990; mem. adv. bd. REACH-OUT; fundraiser Boy Scouts Am., Boulder Dam Coun. Recipient Cmty. Svcs. award for excellence Gov.'s Conf. on Women, 1990, Heart of Gold award Focus on Nev.'s Women, Jr. League of Las Vegas, 1989-90. Mem. Assn. for Children for Enforcement of Support (bd. dirs. 1989-90). Office: Dept Neighborhood Svcs City Las Vegas City Hall 400 Stewart Ave Las Vegas NV 89101-2927

SEGERHAMMAR, SHARON K. special education administrator; b. Marysville, Kans., June 25, 1947; d. Wayne P. and Laura O. Baker; m. Carl R. Segerhammar; children: Todd R., Kyle W. (dec.). BS in Elem. Edn., Emporia State U., 1969, MS in Curriculum and Instrn., 1974; EdS in Edn. Leadership, U. Ala., 1996, EdD in Edn. Leadership, 2000. Tchr. elem. edn. USD 244, Burlington, Kans., Saudi Arabia Internat. Sch., Riyadh; tchr. spl. edn. Learning Coop. N. Ctrl. Kans., Concordia, Calhoun County Schs., Anniston, Ala., Rome (Ga.) City Schs.; spl. edn. adminstr. Cobb County Schs., Marietta, Ga. Mem. ASCD, Profl. Orgn. Ga. Educators, Coun. Exceptional Children. Avocations: reading, counted cross stitch, knitting, bridge. Office: Cobb County Schs 514 Glover St Marietta GA 30060 E-mail: ssederhammar@aol.com.

SEGERLIND, LARRY J. agricultural engineering educator; Prof. emeritus dept. agrl. engring. Mich. State U. Mem. Am. Soc. Agrl. Engrs. (A.W. Farrall Young Educator award 1976, Paper award, Massey-Ferguson medal 1996) Office: Mich State U Rm 205 AW Farrall Hall East Lansing MI 48824-1323 E-mail: segerlin@egr.msu.edu.

SEGERSTEN, ROBERT HAGY, lawyer, investment banker; b. Boston, June 24, 1941; s. Wendell C. and Claire H. Sergersten; m. Marie E. Mankinen, Feb. 13, 1965; children: Amanda Beth Sergersten, Vanessa Bryce Sergersten. AB, Bates Coll., 1963; JD, Boston U., 1970. Bar: Mass. 1970. Assoc. Nessen & Csaplar, Boston, 1970-75; v.p. March Co., Boston, 1975-77; pres. March-Eton Corp., Concord, Mass., 1977-82; ptnr. Nessen, Goodwin & Segersten, Concord, 1977-82, Kane & Segersten, Dedham, Mass., 1983-85; pres. Woodbine Optical Corp., Boston, 1990—. Adj. prof. real estate law Bentley Coll. Officer, bd. dirs. Friends of Jimmy Fund, Boston. Served to lt. USN, 1963—67. Mem.: ACLU, Mass. Bar Assn. Democrat. Episcopalian. Home: 64 Folsom Ave Hyannis MA 02601-4823

SEGESVARY, VICTOR GYÖZÖ, retired diplomat; b. Miskolc, Hungary, Feb. 20, 1929; came to U.S., 1984; s. Viktor and Margit (Kovács) S.; m. Andrea Bárczay, Jan. 20, 1955 (div. Nov. 1957); 1 child, Gábor; m. Monika Schwarz, Dec. 28, 1968. PhD in Polit. Sci., Grad. Inst. Internat. Studies, Switzerland, 1968; DD, U. Geneva, 1973. Asst., libr. Reformed Theol. Acad., Budapest, Hungary, 1953-56; sec. gen. African Inst., Geneva, 1961-63; asst. editor, market rsch. officer Bus. Internat. S.A., Geneva, 1963-66; market rsch. officer SESAF S.A., Geneva, 1967-68; chief rsch. dept. Henry Dunant Inst. Internat. Red Cross, Geneva, 1968-71; cons. Internat. Trade Ctr., UNCTAD/GATT, Geneva, 1969-71; tech. advisor market rsch.-market study Internat. Trade Ctr., Algiers, Algeria, 1971-72; sr. trade promotion advisor, project mgr. UNCTAD/GATT/ITC, Algiers, 1973-74, chief advisor in internat. econ. rels., project mgr. Kabul, Afghanistan, 1975-79, Bamako, Mali, 1979-83; sr. advisor, cons. UN Devel. Programme, African countries, 1984-93. Sr. advisor, cons. dept. for tech. cooperation for devel. UN, N.Y.C., 1985-88. Author: Le réalisme khrouchtchévien: Politique soviètique au Proche-Orient, 1968, La Rèforme et l'Islam, 1500-1550, 1973, reprinted with English preface and summary, 1998, A Ràday Könyvtár 18. századi törtènete, 1992, Inter-Civilizational Relations and the Destiny of the West: Dialogue or Confrontation?, 1998, 2d edit., 2000, From Illusion to Delusion: Globalization and the Contradictions of Late Modernity, 1999, 2d edit., 2001, Existence and Transcendence: An Anti-Faustian Essay in Philosophical Anthropology, 1999, 2d edit., 2002, Dialogue of Civilizations: An Introduction to Civilizational Analysis, 2000, A Nyugati Civilizacis Ezredvegi Va/lsnga, 2001. Sec.-gen. Internat. Fedn. Students in Polit. Sci., Geneva, 1958-59.

SEGGER, MARTIN JOSEPH, museum director, art history educator; b. Felixtowe, Eng., Nov. 22, 1946; s. Gerald Joseph and Lillian Joan (Barker-Emery) S.; m. Angele Cordonier, Oct. 4, 1968; children: Cara Michelle, Marie-Claire, Margaret Ellen. BA, U. Victoria, B.C. Can., 1969, diploma in edn., 1970; MPhil, U. London, 1973. Prof. art history U. Victoria, 1970-74; museologist Royal B.C. Mus., Victoria, 1974-77; dir. Maltwood Art Mus., prof. art history U. Victoria, 1977—, dir. cmty. rels., 2001—. Cons. Nat. Mus. Corp., Ottawa, 1977, UNESCO, O.E.A., Cairo, 1983; bd. dirs. Canadian Cultural Rsch. Network, 2002—, Victoria Coll. Art, 2001—, Can. Rsch. Alliance; bd. advisors Greater Victoria Economic Devel. Commn.; v.p. Commonwealth Museums Assn. Author: exhbn. catalogue House Beautiful, 1975, Arts of the Forgotten Pioneers, 1971, Victoria: An Architectural History, 1979, (commendation Am. Assn. State and Local History 1980), This Old House, 1975, This Old Town, 1979, British Columbia Parliament Buildings, 1979, The Heritage of Canada, 1981, Samuel Maclure: In Search of Appropriate Form, 1986 (Hallmark award 1987, 98), (a guide) St. Andrew's Cathedral, 1990, The Development of Gordon Head Campus, 1988, An Introduction to Museum Studies, 1989, An Introduction to Heritage Conservation, 1990, Botswana Live, 1994, Exploring Victoria's Architecture, 1996; contbr., cons. British Columbia Encyclopedia, 2000. Mem. heritage policy rev. com. Govt. Can., 2001—; Canadian Decorative Arts Soc., 2001—; mem. cultural diversity experts com. Govt. Can., 2002—; v.p. Commonwealth Museums Assn., 2003—; bd. govs. Heritage Can. Found., 1979—83; chmn. City of Victoria Heritage Adv. Com., 1975—79; bd. dirs. Downtown Victoria Cmty. Alliance, Heritage Trust, 1977—86, B.C. Touring Coun., Sta. CFUV Radio, B.C. Govt. Ho. Found., Royal B.C. Mus., 1996—99; co-chair B.C. Arts Festival; mem. B.C. Heritage Adv. Bd., 1973—83; councillor City of Victoria, 1987—93; vice-chair Provincial Capital Commn., 1991—2001; pres. Assn. Vancouver Island Municipalities, 1993—94; chmn. B.C. Festival of the Arts, 1999; bd. dirs. Internat. Coun. Mus.-Can., 1999, Victoria Coll. Art, 2001—, Victoria Harbour Authority, 2002—, dir. Decorated knight Equestrian Order of Holy Sepulchre of Jerusalem; named Hon. Citizen, City of Victoria, 2000, Arts Citizen of Yr., 2001; recipient award, Heritage Can. Comm., 1976, Heritage Conservation award, Lt. Gov. B.C., 1989, Harley J. McKee award, Assn. Preservation Tech., 1994, Queen's Golden Jubilee medal. Fellow Royal Soc. Arts, Can. Mus. Assn. (counsellor 1975-77); mem. Internat. Coun. Mus. (chair internat. com. for tng. of pers. 1995-98), Internat. Coun. Monuments and Sites (bd. dirs. 1980-82), Soc. Study Architecture Can. (bd. dirs. 1979-81), Can Mus. Dirs. Orgn., Union Club (Victoria). Roman Catholic. Avocations: travel, motor mechanics, water color painting. Home: 1035 Sutlej St Victoria BC Canada V8V 3P2 E-mail: msegger@uvic.ca.

SEGGERMAN, ANNE CRELLIN, foundation executive; b. Los Angeles, May 13, 1931; d. Curtis Vergil and Yvonne (LaGrave) Crellin; m. Harry G.A. Seggerman, Apr. 14, 1951; children: Patricia, Henry, Marianne, Yvonne, Suzanne, John. Studies with Albert Levesque, Paris, 1948-50; Student, Sch. Decorative Arts, Paris, 1950, Sch. of the Louvre, 1950, Albertus Magnus Coll., 1951; D.H.L. (hon.), Sacred Heart U., 1980. French tchr., Beverly Hills, Calif., 1958-60; translator World Affairs Council, Los Angeles, 1958-60; staff mem. West Side Sch. Gifted Children, Beverly Hills, 1958-60; pres. Huxley Inst. for Bio-Social Research, Fairfield, Conn., 1972—, 4th World Found. Interfaith Media Action, Fairfield, 1977—, Steiner Prodns., Fairfield, 1981—; founder The Com. for Guadalupe Research, Fairfield, 1982—. Bd. dirs. Anuk, Inc. Co-founder Christian/Jewish Ctr. Understanding Sacred Heart U., Fairfield, Conn.; active Pres. Reagan's Health Task Force Resources Com. on Health Adv. Couns. of U.S. Dept. Health and Human Svcs.; mem. Pres.'s Com. Mental Retardation, 1981-86, Com. Housing Handicapped Families, 1989; mem. Nat. Coun. on Disability, 1992-95; bd. dirs. Easter Seal Rehab. Ctr., Fairfield, Internat. Coll. Applied Nutrition, World Health Med. Group, Cath. League for Religion and Civil Rights. Recipient Am. Assn. Sovereign Mil. Order of Malta, 1991, Cmdr. of Equestrian Order of Holy Sepulchre of Jerusalem, 1991. Mem. Nat. Health Fedn., The Inst. for Study of Human Knowledge, Am. Holistic Med. Inst., Internat. Acad. Preventive Medicine, Calif. Orthomolecular Soc., Am. Phys. Rsch., Fairfield County Organic Gardeners.

SEGGEV, MEIR, radiologist, educator; b. Burgas, Bulgaria, Jan. 23, 1939; came to U.S., 1969, naturalized, 1976; s. Bouco and Helen (Bejerano) S.; m. Ruth Lerner, Dec. 30, 1964 (div. Apr. 1978); 1 child, Yael.; m. Sandra Lee Slarsky, Apr. 7, 1979. MD, Hebrew U. Hadassah, Jerusalem, 1969. Diplomate Am. Bd. Radiology. Resident in radiology Beth Israel Hosp. Harvard Med. Sch., Boston, 1970-73; radiologist Peter Bent Brigham Hosp., 1973-74, Hale Hosp., Haverhill, 1974—. Clin. instr. radiology Harvard Med. Sch., Boston, 1973—; assoc. radiologist Beth Israel Hosp., 1974—. Mem. AMA, Am. Inst. Ultrasound in Medicine, Am. Roentgen Ray Soc., Radiol. Soc. N.Am., Am. Coll. Radiology, Mass. Med. Soc., Harvard Club. Home and Office: 236 Fairview Rd Palm Beach FL 33480-3320 E-mail: meirseggev@aol.com.

SEGIL, LARRAINE DIANE, materials company executive; b. Johannesburg, South Africa, July 15, 1948; came to U.S., 1974; d. Jack and Norma Estelle (Cohen) Wolfowitz; m. Clive Melwyn Segil, Mar. 9, 1969; 1 child, James Harris. BA, U. Witwatersrand, South Africa, 1967, BA with honours, 1969; JD, Southwestern U., L.A., 1979; MBA, Pepperdine U., 1985. Bar: Calif. 1979, U.S. Supreme Ct. 1982. Cons. in internat. transactions, L.A., 1976-79; atty. Long & Levit, L.A., 1979-81; chmn., pres. Marina Credit Corp., L.A., 1981-85; pres., chief exec. officer Electronic Space Products Internat., L.A., 1985-87; mng. ptnr. The Lared Group, L.A., 1987—; pres. Lared Presentations Inc.; keynote spkr. and expert on alliances, globalization, and leadership. Author: (novel) Belonging, 1994, Intelligent Business Alliances, 1996. Bd. govs. Cedars Sinai Med. Ctr., L.A., 1984—; bd. dirs. So. Calif. Tech. Execs. Network, 1984-86, DARE. Mem. ABA (chmn. internat. law com. young lawyers div. 1980-84), Internat. Assn. Young Lawyers (exec. coun. 1979-81, coun. internat. law and practice 1983-84), World Tech. Execs. Network (chmn.). Avocations: piano, horseback riding. Office: The Lared Group 1901 Ave of Stars Los Angeles CA 90067-6001

SEHILI, MAHMOUD, artist; b. Tunis, July 27, 1931; m. Gabriele Buth, Apr. 11, 1959; children: Thouraya, Lilia, Raouf. Student, Fine Arts Sch., Tunis; diploma supérieur des arts plastiques, Ecole des Beaux-Arts, Paris. Tchr. Inst. Technol. d'Art, d'Arch. et d'Urbanisme, Tunis; dir. Irtissem Art Gallery, Tunis, 1977—. Recipient Golden medal Cagnes sur Mer, 1st prize Town of Tunis, 1963, others. Avocations: music, playing the luth, composition of arabic music, fishing. Home: 4 Rue Victor Hugo Carthage Tunisia

SEHLAOUI, ABDELILAH SALIM, science educator, researcher; s. Mohamed Sehlaoui and Fatima Ezzakri; m. Khadija Sebbar, July 19, 1965; children: Ayoub, Morad, Wiam. BA, Med Ben Abellah U., Fes, Morocco, 1984; M Ed, Faculty of Scis. Edn., Rabat, Morocco, 1985; MA, Ind. U. of Pa., 1995, EdD, 1999. Assoc. prof. Emporia State U., Emporia, Kans., 1999—, dir. tchr. edn. programs, 1999—. Grantee 3.8 Million Dollars, US Dept. of Edn., for 5 years since 2001. Mem.: ASCD, KATESOL (assoc.), TESOL, Inc (assoc.), Assn. of Tchr. Educators (life), MATE (life). Achievements include Major Federal Grant Awards for designing an Online TESOL Teacher Certification Model. Avocations: reading, travel. Office Phone: 620-341-5237.

SEHORN, JASON, professional football player; b. Sacramento, Calif., Apr. 15, 1971; m. Angie Harmon. Student in Comm., U. S.C. Football player minor leagues Chgo. Clubs Orgn.; profl. football player N.Y. Giants, 1994—2003, St. Louis Rams, 2003—. Established Sehorn's Ctr. to assist single-parent families; supporter Homes for the Holidays programs, other programs, Newark. Recipient MVP honors. Office: St Louis Rams One Rams Way Saint Louis MO 63045

SEI, IBRAHIM, process engineer; b. Freetown, Sierra Leone, Mar. 23, 1969; s. Juma Mohamed and Ayeshat S.; m. Aminata Bailoh-Jalloh, July 10, 1999; children: Juma, Kenya. BS, U. Md., 1995, PhD, 2000. Process engr. IBM, Endicott, N.Y., 1996-99; sr. process engr. Intel Corp., Rio Rancho, N.Mex., 2000—. Mem. AIChE, Am. Electroplaters and Surface Finishers Soc., Inc., Am. Chem. Soc., Nat. Soc. Black Engrs. Office: Intel Corp 4100 Sara Rd Rio Rancho NM 87124 Home: 8300 Wyoming Blvd NE Apt 3222 Albuquerque NM 87113-2175 E-mail: ibrahim.sei@intel.com.

SEIB, BILLIE MCGHEE RUSHING, nursing administrator, consultant; b. Brookport, Ill., Mar. 04; d. Frank and ILA (Paris) McGhee; m. Alfred Rushing, Jan. 2, 1958 (dec.); children: Lisa, Libbi; m. Bob Seib, Mar. 21, 1986. Diploma, DePaul Sch. Nursing, St. Louis, 1947; postgrad. in oper. rm. nursing, Washington U., St. Louis, 1950; BS, U. St. Francis, Joliet, 2002. Cert. geriat. nurse, ANCC. Dir. oper. rm. Jennie Stuart Med. Ctr., Hopkinsville, Ky.; clin mgr. oper. rm. Meml. Med. Ctr., Savannah, Ga.; mgr. oper. rm. Meth. Med. Ctr., Oak Ridge, Tenn.; coord. oper. rm. Parkwest Hosp., Knoxville, Tenn.; mem. oper. rm. pool Ft. Sanders Park West Hosp., Knoxville, 1992-93; geriat. supr. Briarcliff Health Care Ctr., Oak Ridge, Tenn., 1993-96, Windwood Health Care Ctr. (now Beverly Health & Rehab. Ctr.), Clinton, Tenn., 1996—, asst. DON, 1997—2001. Cons. Washington, Fla., Ky., Nev.; mgr., owner N.Y. Fashio Her Way, Oak Ridge, Tenn., 1997—. Mem. Assn. Oper. Rm. Nurses (cert., bd. dirs., past pres. East Tenn. chpt.), Am. Gerontol. Nursing Assn. Home: 133 Lakeview Hills Ln Clinton TN 37716-5957 E-mail: B23P@comcast.net.

SEIBEL, KLAUSPETER, conductor; b. Offenbach, Germany; Assoc. music dir. Freiburg, Lubeck, Kassel, Frankfurt operas, 1963-75; music dir. Freiburg Opera and Philharmonic; assoc. music dir. Hamburg Opera; prof. conducting Hamburg Conservatory; music dir. Nuremberg Symphony, 1980, Kiel Opera and Philharmonic, 1987, La. Philharmonic Orch., 1995—. Permanent guest condr. Hamburg and Dresden operas; guest condr. symphony orchs. Berlin, Hamburg, Frankfurt, Bratislava, Copenhagen, Reykjavik; guest condr. Am. Opera of Julliard Sch. in N.Y., San Diego Symphony, New Orleans Opera, Spokane Symphony. Recipient Prize Nicolai Malko and Dimitri Mitropoulos competitions. Office: La Philharmonic Orch 305 Baronne St Ste 600 New Orleans LA 70112-1619 E-mail: KPSeibel@aol.com.

SEIBER, RICHARD ALLAN, retired minister; b. L.A., Nov. 15, 1932; s. Edward Maurice and Dorothy Mildred (Ball) S.; m. Wilma Ellen Shook, Sept. 24, 1955; children: Bruce Wayne, Roger Kent, Dale Eugene, Michael Allan. BA in History, U. Puget Sound, 1958; MDiv, Garrett Biblical Inst., 1960; grad., Air Command & Staff Coll., Maxwell AFB, 1962, Air War Coll., 1970. Ordained elder United Meth. Ch., 1960. Enlisted USAF, 1950, advanced through grades to lt. col., ret., 1976, chaplain, 1960-76; student pastor Meth. Ch., Algona-Pacific, Wash., 1955-57, Sciota-Friendship, Ill., 1957-60; pastor United Meth. Ch., Spanaway, Wash., 1976-83, Epworth-LeSourd United Meth. Ch., Tacoma, 1983-97; ret. United Meth. Ch., Tacoma, 1997. Mem. editl. bd. Meth. History United Meth. Ch., Madison, NJ, 1982—86, mem. gen. conf. archives and history, 1980—88, mem. jurisdictional conf. archives and history, 1980—, pres. jurisdictional conf. archives and history, 1980—84; chmn. com. on chaplains Pacific N.W. Conf., 1977—88. Editor: Memoirs of Puget Sound: David Blaine, 1978, Methodist History Index: Oct. 1962-July 1982, 1984, Jour. Henry Bridgeman Brewer, 1839-48, 1986; contbr. Sprague, Lamont, Edwall, WA, 1881-1981, 1982; contbr. Religious Heritage of Washington State, 1988, Illustrated History of Methodism, 1999. Mem. Tacoma Mayor's Task Force on Vets. Affairs, 1986-91; chmn. Ministry with Service People—Co-NeXion, Tillicum, Wash., 1976-79, 87-90; mem. Wesley Homes Corp., Des Moines, Wash., 1984—; v.p. exploring, exec. com. Mount Rainier Coun., Boy Scouts Am., 1976-81, v.p. rels., 1981-92, mem. nat. coun., rep. Pacific Harbors coun., 1999—. Recipient Silver Beaver award Boy Scouts Am., 1977, God and Svc. recognition award Boy Scouts Am., 1988, James E. West fellow, 1997. Fellow Internat. Biog. Assn. (life); mem. SAR (chpt. pres. 1989-91), Air Force Assn. (state pres. 1994-98, Sigma Chi raternity, 1955, Exceptional Svc. award 1999), Mil. Chaplain's Assn. (Puget Sound chpt. pres. 1985-93, 2002), Nat. Eagle Scout Assn., Scouting Heritage Assn. (life, charter), Air Force Hist. Found., Mil. Officers' Assn. (life), Air War Coll. Alumni Assn. (life), Sigma Chi. Avocations: stained glass, genealogy, clocks, early northwest church history, collecting royal doulton. Home: 5514 89th Avenue Ct W University Place WA 98467-1532

SEIBERG, NATHAN, physics educator; b. Israel, Sept. 22, 1956; married; two children. BSc with high distinction, Tel-Aviv U., 1977; PhD, Weizmann Inst. Sci., Israel, 1982. Sr. scientist Weizmann Inst., 1985-86, assoc. prof., 1986-89, prof., 1989-91, Rutgers U., 1989-90, prof. II, 1990-97; prof. Inst. Advanced Study, Princeton, N.J., 1997—. Vis. mem. Inst. for Advanced Study, 1994-95. With Israeli Def. Force, 1977-82. Recipient Israel Phys. Soc. prize, 1976, Mifal Hapais prize, 1979, Michael Landau prize, 1981, J.F. Kennedy prize, 1982, N.J. Pride award N.J. Monthly Mag., 1996, Bd. Trustees award Rutgers U. for Excellence in Rsch., 1996, Dannie Heineman prize Am. Inst. of Physics, 1998; named Racah lectr. Weizmann Inst. Sci., 1985, Oskar Klein lectr. and Oskar Klein medal, 1995, Disting. IFT lectr. U. Fla., 1996; Amos de-Shalit Found. scholar, 1976; John D. and Catherine T. MacArthur Found. fellow, 1996. Fellow: Am. Acad. Arts and Scis. Office: Inst for Advanced Study Sch Natural Sci Einstein Dr Princeton NJ 08540 E-mail: seiberg@ias.edu.

SEIBERLICH, CARL JOSEPH, retired naval officer; b. Jenkintown, Pa., July 4, 1921; s. Charles A. and Helen (Dolan) S.; m. Trudy Germi, May 29, 1952; children: Eric P., Heidi M., Curt A. BS, U.S. Mcht. Marine Acad., 1943; grad., Armed Forces Staff Coll., 1959. Commd. ensign U.S. Navy, 1943, advanced through grades to rear adm., 1971; designated naval aviator, 1947; comdg. officer Airship ZPM-1, 1949—51, Air Anti-Submarine Squadron 26, 1961—62, U.S.S. Salamonie, 1967—68, U.S.S. Hornet, 1969—70; dir. recovery astronauts Apollo 11 and 12 lunar missions, 1969; comdr. anti-submarine warfare group 3 Flagship U.S.S. Ticonderoga, 1971—73; dir. aviation programs, 1973—75; comdr. task force 74 Viet Nam Ops., 1972; asst. dep. chief naval ops. for air warfare Navy Dept., 1975-77; dep. chief naval personnel, 1977-78; comdr. Naval Mil. Personnel Command, 1978-80; with VSE Corp., 1980-82; pres. U.S. Maritime Resource Ctr.; dir. mil. program Am. Pres. Lines, 1983-95, TranSystems Corp., Reston, Va., 1996—; chmn. bd., CEO Dellaware River Maritime Enterprise Coun., 2000—01; U.S. rep. intermodal and short sea shipping subcom. Internat. Orgn. for Standardization; ISO del. Internat. Maritime Orgn., maritime safety com. and maritime security working group, 2001—. Co-chmn. intermodal task force Nat. Rsch. Coun., Transp. Bd.; mem. NAFTA Info. Exch. & Automation working group. Vice pres. Naval Aviation Mus. Found.; active Boy Scouts Am. Decorated Legion of Merit (6), Air medal; recipient Harmon Internat. trophy for devel. 1st variable depth towed sonar, 1951; Vincent T. Hirsch Maritime award Navy League, 1995, Its Am. award for Intermodal Transp. Achievement, 2002. Mem. VFW, AIAA, Am. Soc. Naval Engrs., Soc. Naval Architects and Marine Engrs., Intelligent Transp. Sys. Am., Am. Helicopter Soc., U.S. Naval Inst., U.S. Naval Sailing Assn. (commodore 1979), Am. Angus Assn., Tailhook Assn., Navy Helicopter Assn., Naval Airship Assn., Early and Pioneer Naval Aviators Assn., Nat. Def. Transp. Assn., Navy League U.S. (maritime affairs com.), Propeller Club, Order of Daedalians, U.S. Mcht. Marine Acad. Alumni Assn., Assn. Naval Aviation, Am. Legion, Nat. Space Club, Delta Sigma Pi.

Home: Seagate Farm 1510 Loudoun Dr Haymarket VA 20169-1120 Office: TranSystems Corp 2100 Reston Pkwy Ste 202 Reston VA 20191-1200 *Maintain a clear set of moral values, prepare yourself professionally, maintain physical fitness, persevere as you move toward your goal. Value personal relationships. Never give less than your best; never accept less than the best. Don't trade on the accomplishments of yesterday. Have fun and at times pause and admire the flowers.*

SEIBERLING, JOHN FREDERICK, former congressman, law educator, lawyer; b. Akron, Ohio, Sept. 8, 1918; s. J. Frederick and Henrietta (Buckler) S.; m. Elizabeth Pope Behr, June 4, 1949; children— John B., David P., Stephen M. AB, Harvard U., 1941; LLB, Columbia U., 1949. Bar: N.Y. 1950, Ohio 1955. Assoc. mem. firm Donovan, Leisure, Newton, Lumbard & Irvine, N.Y.C., 1949-53; atty. Goodyear Tire & Rubber Co., Akron, 1954-71; mem. 92d-99th Congresses from 14th Ohio Dist.; mem. com. on judiciary, com. on interior and insular affairs, chmn. subcom. on public lands; vis. prof. law U. Akron, 1987, 90, dir. Ctr. for Peace Studies, 1991-96; ptnr. Goldman, Seiberling, Davis & Tsarnas, Akron, 1988-89. Served to maj. AUS, 1942-46. Mem. United Ch. of Christ. Home: 154 Tecumseh Ln Akron OH 44321-2753

SEIBERT, ANN, state legislator, physical therapist; b. Jamestown, N.Y., Jan. 22, 1934; m. Dean J. Seibert; 4 children. BA, Russell Sage Coll., Troy, N.Y., 1956; grad. in phys. therapy, Albany Med. Ctr. Phys. therapist; mem. Vt. Ho. of Reps., Montpelier, 1988—. Bd. dirs. The Family Place, White River Junction, Vt. Bd. dirs. The Family Place, White River Junction, Vt. Mem. LWV, Vt. Lung Assn., Women's Network Upper Valley, Norwich Women's Club. Home: 386 Main St Norwich VT 05055-9453 Office: Vt Ho of Reps Office Of House Mems Montpelier VT 05602

SEIBERT, RUSSELL JACOB, botanist, research associate; b. Shiloh Valley, Ill., Aug. 14, 1914; s. Erwin W. and Helen A. (Renner) S.; m. Isabelle L. Pring, Dec. 26, 1942; children: Michael, Donna, Lisa. AB, Washington U., St. Louis, 1937, MS, 1938, PhD, 1947. With U.S. Dept. Agr., 1940-50, botanist-geneticist rubber plant investigations, 1941-42, botanist-geneticist, 1943-46, 1947-49; dir. Los Angeles State and County Arboretum, Arcadia, Calif., 1950-55, Longwood Gardens, Kennett Square, Pa., 1955-79; adj. curator tropical horticulture Marie Selby Bot. Garden, Sarasota, Fla., 1979-96. Adj. prof. dept. hort. U. Del., 1960-79; head dept. arboreta and bot. gardens, Los Angeles County, 1952-55; Am. del. Internat. Soc. Hort. Sci., 1960-70; chmn. Am. Hort. Council-U.S.A. (hort. exhbn.), 1960; (floriade), Rotterdam, Holland; v.p. XVII Internat. Hort. Congress, 1966; chmn. Am. Hort. Film Festival, 1964-69 Recipient Frank N. Meyer Meml. medal Am. Genetic Soc., 1966, Arthur Hoyt Scott Garden and Horticulture medal Swarthmore Coll., 1975, Disting. Svc. awrd Hort. Soc. N.Y., 1969, award of merit Am. Assn. Bot. Gardens and Arboreta, 1982. Mem. AAAS, Am. Hort. Soc. (pres. 1964-65, Liberty Hyde Bailey medal 1975), Am. Inst. Biol. Scis., Rotary, Sigma Xi, Phi Sigma, Gamma Sigma Delta. Home: 7333 Scotland Way #1218 Sarasota FL 34238

SEIBOLD, JAMES RICHARD, physician, educator; b. Washington, Apr. 5, 1950; s. Herman Rudolph and Clara Bond (Taylor) S.; m. Margaret Frances Bennett, Jan. 20, 1968; children: Jon Drew, Zachary Bennett. BS, La. State U., 1972; MD, SUNY, Stony Brook, 1975. Diplomate Am. Bd. Internal Medicine, Am. Bd. Rheumatology. Intern in medicine L.I. Jewish Hosp., New Hyde Park, N.Y., 1975-76, resident in medicine, 1976-78; fellow in rheumatology U. Pitts., 1978-80; asst. prof. medicine Robert Wood Johnson Med. Sch. U. Medicine and Dentistry N.J., New Brunswick, 1980-86, assoc. prof., 1986-92, prof., 1992—, chief rheumatology, 1986-91, dir. clin. rsch. ctr., 1989-95; prof., dir. scleroderma program U. Mich., Ann Arbor, 2004—. Mem. adv. bd. Ctr. for Advanced Biotech. and Medicine, Piscataway, N.J., 1989-95, dir. Scleroderma program 1995—; W.H. Conzen chair clin. pharmacology Schering-Plough Found., 1989; prof. internal medicine Scleroderma Program U. Mich., dir. Author: (chpt.) Rheumatology, 1988, 91, 94, 95, 99, 2001, 03; contbr. over 300 articles to profl. jours. Bd. dirs. Arthritis Found. Fellow ACP, Am. Coll. Rheumatology (regional coun. 1985), Scleroderma Clin. Trials Consortium (founder 1994). Mem. Soc. Of Friends. Home: 1622 Kriss Crossing Brighton MI 48114 Office: U Mich Health Sys 3918 Taubman Ctr 1500 E Medical Center Dr Ann Arbor MI 48109-0358 Office Phone: 734-936-5561. Business E-Mail: jseibold@med.umich.edu.

SEIDE, PAUL, civil engineering educator; b. N.Y.C., July 22, 1926; s. Julius David and Sylvia (Eiler) S.; m. Joan Cecilia Matalka, Jan. 7, 1951; children: Richard Laurence, Wendy Jane Seide Kielsmeier. B.C.E., CCNY, 1946; M. Aero. Engring, U. Va., 1952; PhD, Stanford U., 1954. Aero. research scientist Nat. Adv. Commn. for Aeros., Langley AFB, Va., 1946-52; research asst. Stanford Calif. U., 1952-53; research engr. Northrop Aircraft Co., Hawthorne, Calif., 1953-55; head methods and theory sect. TRW Inc., Los Angeles, 1955-60; head methods and research sect. Aerospace Corp., El Segundo, Calif., 1960-65; prof. civil engring. U. So. Calif., L.A., 1965-91, prof. emeritus, 1991—, assoc. chmn. dept. civil engring., 1971-73, 81-83; Albert Alberman vis. prof. Technion-Israel Inst. Tech., Haifa, 1975; vis. prof. U. Sydney, Australia, 1986, U. Canterbury, N.Z., 1986. Cons. Northrop Inc., 1972-77, Aerospace Corp., 1966-68, Rockwell Inc., El Segundo, 1982-85 Author: Small Elastic Deformations of Thin Shells, 1975; contbr. numerous articles to profl. jours. NSF fellow, 1964-65 Fellow (life) ASME, Am. Acad. Mechanics; mem. ASCE (life), Tau Beta Pi, Sigma Xi. Democrat. Jewish. Home: 300 Via Alcance Palos Verdes Peninsula CA 90274-1105

SEIDEL, ARTHUR HARRIS, lawyer; b. N.Y.C., May 25, 1923; s. Philip and Pearl (Geller) S.; m. Raquel Eliovich, Aug. 21, 1949; children: Stephen A., Paul B., Mary Beth Sharp. BS, CCNY, 1942; A.M., U. Mich., 1943; JD with honors, George Washington U., 1949. Bar: D.C. 1949, Pa. 1956, N.Y. 1957. Atty. patent dept. Gulf Oil Corp., Washington and Pitts., 1947-52; individual practice law, 1952-64; sr. ptnr. firm Seidel & Gonda, 1964-68, Seidel, Gonda & Goldhammer (P.C.), Phila., 1968-72, pres., 1972-84, Seidel, Gonda, Goldhammer & Abbott, P.C., Phila., 1984-88, Seidel, Gonda, Lavorgna & Monaco, Phila., 1988-2001; of counsel Drinker, Biddle & Reath, Phila., 2001—. Lectr. in Intellectual Property Temple U. Law Sch., 1973-86, Am. Law Inst. Editor: George Washington Law Rev, 1949; author: (with others) Trademark Practice, 2 vols, 1963, Monographs on Patent Law and Practice, 5th edit, 1993, Trademarks and Copyrights, 6th edit., 1992, Trade Secrets and Employment Agreements 3d edit, 1995; also articles. Mem. Adv. Com. for Restatement of Law of Unfair Competition. Mem. ABA, Am. Law Inst., Pa. Bar Assn., Phila. Bar Assn., Am. Intellectual Property Law Assn., Phila. Intellectual Property Law Assn., Order of Coif. Home: 904 Centennial Rd Narberth PA 19072-1408 Office: Drinker Biddle & Reath LLP One Logan Sq Philadelphia PA 19103 Office Phone: 215-988-3317. E-mail: seidelah@dbr.com. *My entire professional career has been devoted to the question of innovation, patents for inventions, trademarks for new businesses and copyrights for new writings. I have seen the United States become the world's leader in technology and business.*

SEIDEL, CARL WILLIAM, business executive, consultant; b. Hempstead, NY, Aug. 18, 1938; s. Charles Francis and Wilma Marie Seidel; m. Suzanne Winslow Dana; children: Lisa Marie, Michael Dana, Rebecca Suzanne, Elaine Marie. BS in Chemistry, U. Wis., 1959; MS in Chemistry, U. Notre Dame, 1962. Chemist, mktg. mgr. Nuclear Sci. and Engring., Pitts., 1962-69; product mgr. New England Nuclear, Billerica, Mass., 1969-73, asst. divsn. mgr., 1973-79, gen. mgr. new products, 1979-81; various positions, mfg. mgr. pharm. divsn. DuPont, Billerica, 1981-91; assoc. dir. DuPont Merck, Billerica, 1991-97; pres., CEO Internat. Isotopes, Denton, Tex., 1997-99; pres. Carl W. Seidel & Assocs., Cons., 1999—. Cons. Dept. of Energy, Washington, 1990-2001; tech. advisor U.S. Pharmocpiea, Bethesda, 1995-2000; com. mem. Am. Nat. Stds. Inst., Gaithersburg, 1975. Co-editor Mössbauer Effect Methodology, Vol. 8, 1973, Vol. 9, 1974, Vol. 10, 1976; editor: The Mössbauer Effect and Its Application in Chemistry, 1967. Town rep., Chelmsford, Mass., 1980-97. Mem. Internat. Isotope Soc., Am. Coll. Nuclear Physicians, Legatus, Soc. of Nuclear Medicine (sec.-treas. therapy coun.), Am. Chem. Soc., European Soc. of Nuclear Medicine, Russell Mill Swim and Tennis (pres. 1972-75), C. of C. Republican. Roman Catholic. Avocations: tennis, travel. Home and Office: 4 Thresher Rd Nashua NH 03063 E-mail: carl.w.seidel@mindspring.com.

SEIDEL, FREDERICK LEWIS, poet; b. St. Louis, Feb. 19, 1936; s. Jerome Jay and Thelma (Cartun) S.; children: Felicity, Samuel. AB, Harvard U., 1957. Occasional lectr., Rutgers U., New Brunswick, 1964—; Paris editor, Paris Review, 1961, advisory editor, 1962. Author: (poetry) Final Solutions, 1963, Sunrise, 1979 (Lamont Poetry prize Acad. Am. Poets 1980, Am. Poetry Rev. prize 1980, Nat. Book Critics Circle award for poetry 1981), Men and Woman: New and Selected Poems, 1984, Poems 1959-1979, 1989, These Days, 1989, My Tokyo, 1993, Going Fast, 1998, The Cosmos Poems, 2000, Life on Earth, 2001, Area Code 212, 2002, The Cosmos Triology, 2003, Barbados, 2004. Guggenheim Fellow, 1993, Pen/Voelcker award for poetry, 2002.

SEIDEL, GEORGE ELIAS, JR., animal scientist, educator; b. Reading, Pa., July 13, 1943; s. George E. Sr. and Grace Esther (Heinly) S.; m. Sarah Beth Moore, May 28, 1970; 1 child, Andrew. BS, Pa. State U., 1965; MS, Cornell U., 1968, PhD, 1970; postgrad., Harvard U. Med. Sch., Boston, 1970-71. Asst. prof. physiology Colo. State U., Ft. Collins, 1971-75, assoc. prof., 1975-83, prof., 1983-93, univ. disting. prof., 1993—. Vis. scientist Yale U., 1978-79, MIT, 1986-87; mem. bd. on agr. NRC. Co-editor: New Technologies in Animal Breeding, 1981; contbr. articles to profl. jours. Recipient Alexander Von Humboldt award, N.Y.C., 1983, Animal Breeding Research award Nat. Assn. Animal Breeders, Columbia, Mo., 1983, Clark award Colo. State U., 1982, Upjohn Physiology award, 1986; Gov's. award for Sci. and Tech., Colo., 1986. Mem. AAAS, NAS, Am. Dairy Sci. Assn., Am. Soc. Animal Sci. (Young Animal Scientist award 1983), Soc. for Study of Reprodn., Internat. Embryo Transfer Soc. (pres. 1979, disting. svc. award 2001). Home: 3101 Arrowhead Rd Laporte CO 80535-9374 Office: Colo State U Animal Repro Biotech Lab Fort Collins CO 80523-1683 Office Phone: 970-491-5287.

SEIDEL, JOAN BROUDE, securities trader, investment advisor; b. Chgo., Aug. 16, 1933; d. Ned and Betty (Treiger) Broude; m. Arnold Seidel, Aug. 18, 1957; children: David, Craig. BA, UCLA, 1954; postgrad., N.Y. Inst. Fin. Registered prin., investment advisor Morton Seidel & Co. Inc., L.A., 1970-74, v.p., 1974-93; pres., 1993—; also bd. dirs. Morton Seidel & Co. Inc., L.A. Instr. UCLA Extension, 1979-84. Treas. City of Beverly Hills, Calif., 1990-2001, chmn. rent adjustment bd., 1989-90, mem., 1983-89; mem. investment com. YWCA of greater L.A., 1987-2002, treas. 1992-95; bd. dirs. Discovery Fund for Eye Rsch., L.A., 1987—, treas., 1999—; corp. dir. Queen's Care; bd. dirs. L.A. Opera, 2002—; CFO The Maple Couns. Ctr., 2002—04. Named Citizen of Yr. Beverly Hills C. of C., 1993. Fellow Assn. for Investment Mgmt. and Rsch.; mem. Am. Technion Soc. (v.p. 1998-2002, pres. So. Calif. chpt. 2001—, nat. bd. dir. 2002—, internat. bd. 2003—), Nat. Assn. Security Dealers (dist. bus. conduct com. 2S 1993-95, 98-2000, small firm adv. bd. 1998-2000, chair dist. 2 1999-2000), L.A. Soc. Fin. Analysts, Orgn. Women Execs., Rotary, Phi Sigma Alpha. Avocations: reading, travel. Office: Morton Seidel & Co Inc 8730 Wilshire Blvd Ste 530 Beverly Hills CA 90211-2792 E-mail: seidel350@aol.com.

SEIDEL, ROBERT WAYNE, science historian, educator; b. Kansas City, Mo., June 9, 1945; s. Wayne Herman and Harriet Anita (Day) S.; m. Alison Publicover, Aug. 26, 1972 (div. 1989); 1 child, Mary Ruth; m. Christine Ruth Stack, July 1, 1993. BA, Westmar Coll., 1967; MA, U. Calif., Berkeley, 1968, PhD, 1978. Exhibit designer Lawrence Hall Sci., Berkeley, 1970-72; specialist Poland 4-city tour USIA, Warsaw, 1971-72; grad. rsch. and teaching asst. U. Calif., 1972-78; asst. prof. Tex. Tech U., Lubbock, 1978-83, dir. rsch. history of engring. program, 1979-83; rsch. historian U. Calif., Berkeley, 1980-82, Laser History Project, Albany, Calif., 1983-85; adminstr. Bradbury Sci. Mus., Los Alamos, N.Mex., 1985-90, overview project leader, 1990-92; sr. staff mem. Ctr. Nat. Security Studies, Los Alamos, N.Mex., 1992-94; dir. Charles Babbage Inst., U. Minn., Mpls., 1994-99; ERA Land Grant prof. History of Tech. U. Minn., Mpls., 1994-99, prof. chem. engring., 1999—. Author: Lawrence and His Laboratory: A History of the Lawrence Berkeley Laboratory, 1989, Los Alamos and the Making of the Atomic Bomb, 1995. Mem. N.Mex. Sci. Ctr. Commn., 1989-92; bd. dirs. The Bakken Mus., 1994—. Woodrow Wilson fellow, 1967, U. Calif. Regent's fellow, 1968, German Marshall Fund fellow, Grenoble, France, 1975, Sr. fellow Dibner Inst., MIT, 2001; recipient Bicentennial Essay prize Nat. Sci. Tchrs. Assn., 1976. Mem. AAUP, History Sci. Soc., Soc. for History Tech. Democrat. Avocation: computer simulations. Home: 5625 Woodlawn Blvd Minneapolis MN 55417-2667 Office: 151 Amundson Hall/U Minn Minneapolis MN 55455 E-mail: rws@tc.umn.edu.

SEIDEL, SELVYN, lawyer, educator; b. Long Branch, N.J., Nov. 6, 1942; s. Abraham and Anita (Stoller) S.; m. Deborah Lew, June 21, 1970; 1 child, Emily. BA, U. Chgo., 1964; JD, U. Calif., Berkeley, 1967; diploma in law, Oxford U., 1968. Bar: N.Y. 1970, D.C. Ct. Appeals 1982. Ptnr. Latham & Watkins, N.Y.C., 1985—. Adj. prof. Sch. Law, NYU, 1974-84; instr. Practicing Law Inst., 1980-81, 84. Contbr. articles to profl. jours. Bd. dirs. Citizen Scholarship Fund Am., 1995-2000. Mem. ABA, N.Y. County Bar Assn., N.Y.C. Bar Assn. (mem. fed. cts. com. 1982-85, internat. law com. 1989-92, 95-96, art law com. 1997-2000), Boalt Hall Alumni Assn. (bd. dirs. 1980-82). Office: Latham & Watkins 885 3rd Ave New York NY 10022-4802 Office Phone: 212-906-1312. Business E-Mail: selvyn.seidel@lw.com.

SEIDELMAN, SUSAN, film director; b. Pa., Dec. 11, 1952; Student, Drexel U., NYU. Dir. films, including: Smithereens, 1982, Desperately Seeking Susan, 1985, Making Mr. Right, 1987, Cookie, 1989, She-Devil, 1990, The Dutch Master (nominee Acad. award in dramatic short category), 1994, The Barefoot Executive, 1995; directorial debut with short film: You Act Like One, Too (Student Film award AMPAS), 1997, HBO Sex and The City, 1999, A Cooler Climate, 1999. Office: care Michael Shedler 350 5th Ave New York NY 10118-0110 also: Gary Pearl Pictures 10956 Weyburn Ave Ste 200 Los Angeles CA 90024-2834

SEIDEN, DAVID, anatomist, academic administrator; b. New York, NY, Apr. 14, 1946; PhD, Temple U., 1967—71. Assoc. dean UMDNJ-Robert Wood Johnson Med. Sch., Piscataway, NJ, 1990—, prof. of neuroscience, 1996—. Sch. bd. East Brunswick Bd. of Edn., 1977—95. Office: UMDNJ-Robert Wood Johnson Medical School 675 Hoes Lane Piscataway NJ 08854

SEIDEN, HENRY (HANK SEIDEN), advertising executive; b. Bklyn., Sept. 6, 1928; s. Jack S. and Shirley (Berkowitz) S.; m. Helena Ruth Zaldin, Sept. 10, 1949; children: Laurie Ann, Matthew Ian. BA, Bklyn. Coll., 1949; MBA, CCNY, 1954. Trainee Ben Sackheim Advt. Agy., 1949-51; nat. promotion mgr. N.Y. Post Corp., 1951-53; promotion mgr. Crowell-Collier Pub. Co., Inc., 1953-54; copy group head Batten, Barton, Durstine & Osborn, Inc., 1954-60; v.p., creative dir. Keyes, Madden & Jones, 1960-61; sr. v.p., assoc. creative dir. McCann-Marschalk, Inc., 1961-65, chmn. plans bd., 1964-65; creative dir., dir., prin. Hicks & Greist, Inc., N.Y.C., 1965—, sr. v.p., 1965-74, exec. v.p., 1974-83, COO, 1983—, pres., 1986—; CEO Ketchum/Hicks & Greist Inc., 1987-89; chmn., CEO Ketchum Advt., 1989-91; exec. v.p. Ketchum Comm. Inc., also bd. dirs.; vice chmn. Jordan, McGrath, Case & Taylor, Inc., 1992—97; chmn., CEO The Seiden Group, Inc. Bd. dirs. Ketchum Internat. Inc.; guest lectr. Bernard M. Baruch Sch. Bus. and Pub. Adminstrn., CCNY, 1962—, Baruch Coll., 1969—, New Sch. Social Scis., 1968, 72,73, Sch. Visual Arts, 1979, 80—, Lehman Coll., CCNY, 1980—, Ohio U., 1981, Newhouse Grad. Sch., Syracuse U., 1981, NYU, 1983; cons. pub. rels. and comm. to mayor City of New Rochelle, N.Y., 1959—; cons. mktg. dept. Ohio State U.; cons. to pres. N.Y.C. City Coun., 1972-73; cons. Postmaster Gen. U.S., 1972-74; comm. advisor to commr. N.Y.C. Police Dept., 1973—, hon. dept. commr., 1991—, spl. cons. to commr., 1992—; mem. bd. advisors Stillman Sch. Bus., Seton Hall U., 2002; adv. circle, Columbia U., Health Sci. Divsn., 2003. Author: Advertising Pure and Simple, 1976, Advertising Pure and Simple: The New Edition, 1990; contbg. editor: Madison Ave. mag, 1966-, Advt. Age, Mag. Age; guest columnist: N.Y. Times, 1972. Vice commr. Little League of New Rochelle; bd. dirs. Police Res. Assn. N.Y.C., 1973—, pres. exec. com.; bd. dirs. Cancer Rsch. and Treatment Fund, Inc., pres., 1992—; bd. dirs. Am. Heart Assn., 2002, Transmedia Network, Inc.; bd. dirs., chmn. New York's Finest Found., 1975—, pres., 1996, chmn., 2002; bd. dirs., chmn., sr. v.p. Drug Enforcement Agy. Found., 1995—; advisors cir. Columbia Presbyn. Hosp., 2002; assoc. Marine Corps Univ. Found., 2004. Recipient award Four Freedoms Found., 1959, award Printers Ink, 1960, promotion award Editor and Pub., 1955, Am. TV Commls. Festival award, 1963-69, Effie award Am. Mktg. Assn., 1969, 70, award Art Dirs. Club N.Y., 1963-70, award Am. Inst. Graphic Arts, 1963, Starch award, 1969, spl. award graphic art lodge B'nai B'rith Greater N.Y., 1971, 87, award of highest honor FBI Nat. Acad., 1994, Commendation, 1995. Mem. NATAS, Am. Inst. Mgmt. (assoc.), Drug Enforcement Agts. Found. (sr. v.p. 1995), Advt. Club N.Y. (exec. judge Andy awards, award 1963-65), Advt. Writers Assn. N.Y. (Gold Key award for best newspaper and mag. advts. 1962-640, Copy Club (co-chmn. awards com., Gold Key award for best TV comml. 1969), Alpha Phi Omega. Home: 1056 5th Ave New York NY 10028-0112 Office: The Seiden Group 708 3rd Ave New York NY 10017-4201 Office Phone: 212-655-1051. E-mail: hankruthseiden@aol.com., handseiden@theseidengroupadv.com. *Be yourself but don't take yourself too seriously.*

SEIDEN, PAUL, insurance agent, consultant; b. Rzeszow, Poland, Nov. 16, 1920; came to U.S., 1939, naturalized, 1943; s. Simon and Amalia Grauer S.; m. Ida Perlin, Nov. 27, 1943 (div. 1961); children: Mark D., Henry A.; m. Judith Ellen Barkalow, Jan. 19, 1962; children: Lewis J., Eve M. Student, CUNY, 1939-41; MS in Mgmt., MS in Fin. Svcs., Am. Coll., 1985. Real estate broker Simon J. Boss Realty Co., Bklyn., 1948-51; life ins. agt. Phoenix Mutual Life Ins. Co., N.Y.C., 1952-56; asst. gen. agr. Aetna Life Ins. Co., Miami, 1956-61; gen. agt. Nat. Life Vt., Beverly Hills, Calif., 1962-90, agt. Encino, Calif., 1991—. Cons. mktg., pres. Income Devel. Corp., Encino, 1968—. 1st Lt. U.S. Army, WWII ETO, 1942-46. Mem. Nat. Assn. Life Underwriters, U.S. Army Ret. Officers Assn., West Dade Masonic Lodge # 388, Am. Legion, Kosciuszko Found., Simon Wiesnthal Ctr. Jewish. Avocations: trap and skeet shooting, dance, swimming, history studies, teaching. Home: 24671 Cordillera Dr Calabasas CA 91302-2512 Office: Income Devel Corp 5729 Ostrom Ave Encino CA 91316-1407

SEIDEN, STEVEN ARNOLD, executive search consultant; b. N.Y.C., Feb. 18, 1936; s. Leon and Eleanor (Troy) S.; m. Katherine Cohen, June 8, 1965; children: Lisa Brooke, Hilary Anne. AB, Yale U., 1958. Pres. Seiden Krieger Assocs., 1984—. Mem. N.Y. Stock Exch. Regulatory Adv. Com., 1981-83, policy com. Am. Coun. for Capital Formation, 1982-87. *Steven Seiden is known for his expertise in recruiting top executives for corporations in transition. Among his clients are many of America's most publicized acquisitive entrepreneurs who seek out under managed companies needing new chief executives as well as operational, financial, and marketing talent. These include conglomerates, international holding companies, merchant banks, LBO organizations, and venture capitalists. Additionally, he finds new management and directors for companies emerging from bankruptcy or involved in proxy contests.* Mem. adv. bd. Registered Rep. Mag., 1982-84. Served with U.S. Army, 1961—62. Mem.: U.S. C. of C. (small bus. coun. 1985—89), Internat. Assn. Corp. and Profl. Recruiters (editl. bd. 1993—95), N.Y. Biotech. Assn., Turnaround Mgmt. Assn. (program co-chair N.Y. chpt. 1991—92), N.Y. Soc. Security Analysts, Securities Industry Assn. (bd. dirs. 1981—83), Assn. Corp. Growth (asst. v.p. 1987—88, bd. dirs.), Wall St. Tax Assn. (bd. dirs. 1981—83), Bond Club, Century Country Club. Republican. Office: Seiden Krieger Assocs 375 Park Ave New York NY 10152-0002 Office Phone: 212-688-8383. Business E-Mail: steven@seidenkrieger.com.

SEIDENBERG, IVAN G. telecommunications company executive; b. N.Y.C., Dec. 10, 1946; s. Howard and Kitty (Zaretsky) S.; m. Phyllis A. Maisel, Dec. 13, 1969; children: Douglas, Lisa. BS in Math., CUNY, 1972; MBA in Mktg. Mgmt., Pace U., 1980. Various engring. positions N.Y. Tel., 1966-74; dist. mgr. transmission design AT&T, Basking Ridge, NJ, 1974-76, dist. mgr. tech. planning, 1976-78, div. mgr. fed. regulatory N.Y.C., 1978-81, asst. v.p. mktg., 1981-83; v.p. fed. relations Nynex Corp., Washington, 1983-86, former v.p. external affairs, former pres. and vice chmn., chmn., CEO, 1995-98, Bell Atlantic Corp, N.Y.C., 1999-2000; CEO Verizon Comm. (formerly Bell Atlantic Corp.), N.Y.C. Bd. dirs. Boston Properties Inc., CVS Corp., Honeywell, Wyeth. Bd. dirs. N.Y. Hall Sci., Nat. Urban League., Pace U., Mus. TV and Radio, Verison Found. Sgt. U.S. Army, 1966—68, Vietnam. Mem. U.S. Telephone Assn. (bd. dirs. 1985—), Rockland Bus. Council (trustee 1987). Office: Verizon Communications Ste 200b 1095 Avenue Of The Americas New York NY 10036-6704*

SEIDENSTICKER, EDWARD GEORGE, Japanese language and literature educator; b. Castle Rock, Colo., Feb. 11, 1921; s. Edward George and Mary Elizabeth (Dillon) S. BA, U. Colo., 1942; MA, Columbia U., 1947; postgrad., Harvard U., 1947-48; LittD (hon.), U. Md., 1991. With U.S. Fgn. Service, Dept. State, Japan, 1947-50; mem. faculty Stanford U., 1962-66, prof., 1964-66; prof. dept. Far Eastern langs. and lit. U. Mich., Ann Arbor, 1966-77; prof. Japanese Columbia U., 1977-85, prof. emeritus, 1986—. Author: Kafu the Scribbler, 1965, Japan, 1961, Low City, High City, 1983, Tokyo Rising, 1990, Very Few People Come This Way, 1994; transl.: (by Murasaki Shikibu) The Tale of Genji, 1976. Served with USMCR, 1942-46. Decorated Order of Rising Sun Japan; recipient Nat. Book award, 1970; citation Japanese Ministry Edn., 1971; Kikuchi Kan prize, 1977; Goto Miyoko prize, 1982; Japan Found. prize, 1984; Tokyo Cultural award, 1985; Yamagata Banto prize, 1992. Home: 1350 Ala Moana Blvd Apt 3103 Honolulu HI 96814-4229 *"Make yourself a routine and stick to it," said my childhood piano teacher when I went off to college. I have never had, as some people seem to have, great plans for my future; but if a person has a serious routine and sticks resolutely with it, something is bound to get accomplished.*

SEIDENWURM, RICHARD LEWIS, lawyer; b. N.Y.C., Feb. 1, 1941; s. Jesse and Lillian (Epstein) S.; m. Carol Ann Wender, Aug. 14, 1965; children: Amy, Robert. BA, Williams Coll., 1962; JD, Columbia U., 1965. Bar: N.Y. 1966, Calif. 1973, U.S. Dist. Ct. (so. and ea. dists.) N.Y. 1966, U.S. Dist. Ct. (so. dist.) Calif. 1973. Assoc. counsel OEO, Washington, 1965-66; assoc. Davis Polk & Wardwell, N.Y.C., 1966-72; ptnr. Solomon, Ward, Seidenwurm & Smith and predecessor firms, San Diego, 1973—. Mem. State Bar Calif. (lectr. continuing edn. divsn. 1980, 83, 85). Home: 4597 Vista De La Patria Del Mar CA 92014-4151 Office: Solomon Ward Seidenwurm & Smith 401 B St Ste 1200 San Diego CA 92101-4295 E-mail: rseidenwurm@swsslaw.com.

SEIDER, WARREN D. engineering educator; b. N.Y.C., Oct. 20, 1941; s. Harry Aaron and Ida Posner Seider; m. Diane Harwith, Aug. 24, 1944; children: Deborah Anne Shapiro, Benjamin Herschel. B in Chem. Engring., Poly. Inst. Bklyn., 1962; PhD, U. Mich., 1966. Prof. chem. engring. U. Pa., Phila., 1967—. Author: FLOWTRAN Simulation - An Introduction, Introduction to Chem. Engring. and Computer Calculations, Product and Process Design Principles: Synthesis, Analysis, and Evaluation; contbr. scientific papers to profl. journals. Mem.: AIChE (dir. 1984—86, Computing in Chem. Engring. award 1992, Warren K. Lewis award 2004), Am. Soc. Engring. Edn., Am. Chem. Soc. Jewish. Avocations: hiking, tennis, choir member. Home: 6 Rose Valley Rd Rose Valley PA 19063-4218 Office: University of Pennsylvania Dept of Chem Eng 220 S 33rd St Philadelphia PA 19104-6393 Office Phone: 215-898-7953. Business E-Mail: seider@seas.upenn.edu.

SEIDLER, B(ERNARD) ALAN, lawyer; b. NYC, Nov. 26, 1946; s. Aaron H. and Ethel T. (Berkowitz) S.; m. Lynne Aubrey, Jan. 21, 1978; children: Jacob A., Morgan H., Lily R. BA, Colgate U., 1968; JD, Seton Hall U., 1972. Bar: N.Y. 1973, U.S. Dist. Ct. (ea., no. and so. dists.) N.Y. 1975, U.S. Ct. Appeals (2d cir.) 1976, U.S. Ct Appeals (3d cir.) 1984,U.S. Ct Appeals (4th cir.) 2004, U.S. Supreme Ct. 1977. Staff atty. N.Y. Legal Aid Soc., N.Y.C., 1972-75; sole practitioner N.Y.C., 1975—. Mem. Snedens Landing Tennis Assn. (Palisades, N.Y.), Palisades Swim Club. Office: 580 Broadway New York NY 10012 Office Phone: 212-334-3131.

SEIDLER, DORIS, artist; b. London, Nov. 26, 1912; m. Bernard Seidler, Sept. 5, 1935; 1 son, David. Group exhbns. include Bklyn. Mus. Bi-Ann., Vancouver Internat., Honolulu Acad. Arts, Pa. Acad. Fine Arts, Phila., Soc. Am. Graphic Artists, Assoc. Am. Artists Gallery, Jewish Mus., N.Y.C., Albright-Knox, 1994, Brit. Mus. Recent Acquisitions, 1997, Whitworth Gallery, Manchester, Eng., 2003; represented in permanent collections Libr. of Congress, Smithsonian Instn., Washington, Phila. Mus. Art, Bklyn. Mus., Seattle Mus. Art, Whitney Mus., Nat. Gallery Art, Nassau County (N.Y.) Mus. Fine Arts, Brit. Mus., London, Victoria and Albert Mus. London, Pallant House Coll., Eng., Portland Mus. Art, Oreg., Birmingham Mus., Eng., 1999. Address: 14 Stoner Ave Great Neck NY 11021-2101

SEIDMAN, CHRISTINE E. medical educator; BA, Harvard U.; MD, George Washington U., 1978. Resident in internal medicine Johns Hopkins U., Balt.; resident in cardiology Mass. Gen. Hosp., Boston; staff Brigham and Women's Hosp. Harvard U., Boston, 1987, dir. cardiovasc. genetics svc., prof.; assoc. investigator Howard Hughes Med. Inst. Mem.: Inst. Medicine. Office: Harvard U Med Sch Genetics NRB 256 77 Avenue Louis Pasteur Boston MA 02115

SEIDMAN, DAVID N(ATHANIEL), materials science and engineering educator; b. N.Y.C., July 5, 1938; s. Charles and Jeanette (Cohen) S.; m. Shoshanah Cohen-Sabban, Oct. 21, 1973; children: Elie, Ariel, Eytan. BS, NYU, 1960, MS, 1962; PhD, U. Ill., Urbana, 1965. Postdoc. assoc. Cornell U., Ithaca, N.Y., 1964-66, asst. prof. materials sci. and engring., 1966-70, assoc. prof. materials sci. and engring., 1970-76, prof. materials sci. and engring., 1976-85, Northwestern U., Evanston, Ill., 1985-96, Walter P. Murphy prof. materials sci. and engring., 1996—. Vis. prof. Technion, Haifa, 1969-70, Tel-Aviv U., Ramat-Aviv, 1972; Lady Davis vis. prof. Hebrew U., Jerusalem, 1978, 80-81, prof. materials sci., 1983-85; vis. scientist C.E. de Grenoble, 1981, C.N.E.T.-Meylan, 1981, C.E. de Scalay, 1989, U. Goettingen, 1989, 92; sci. cons. Argonne (Ill.) Nat. labs., 1985-94. Mem. editl. bd., editor spl. issues (jour.) Interface Sci., 1993—2001, editor-in-chief, 2002—, mem. editl. bd. Materials Sci. Forum, 1996—; contbr. numerous articles to profl. jours. Recipient Max Planck Rsch. prize Max-Planck-Gesellschaft and the A. von Humboldt-Stiftung, 1993; Guggenheim fellow, 1972-73, 80-81, Humboldt fellow, 1989, 92; named chair for phys. metallurgy Gordon Conf., 1982. Fellow Am. Phys. Soc., The Minerals Metals Materials Soc. (mem. fellows award com. 2002--, Hardy Gold medal 1967); mem. AAAS, Am. Soc. Metals Internat., Am. Ceramic Soc., Am. Chem. Soc., Materials Rsch. Soc., Microscopy Soc. Am., A. von Humboldt Soc. Am., Internat. Field-Emission Soc. (mem. steering com. 1997—2002, pres. 2000—02), Böhmische Phys. Soc. Democrat. Jewish. Achievements include research in nanostructural temporal evolution, internal interfaces, atomic-scale imperfections in metals and semiconductors, three-dimensional atom-probe microscopy and electron microscopy. Avocations: reading, history, travel. Home: 9056 Tamaroa Ter Skokie IL 60076-1928 Office: Northwestern U MS&E Dept Cook Hall Evanston IL 60208-3108 Business E-Mail: d-seidman@northwestern.edu.

SEIDMAN, ELLEN SHAPIRO, lawyer, government official; b. N.Y.C., Mar. 12, 1948; d. Benjamin Harry Shapiro and Edna (Eysen) Stern; m. Walter Becker Slocombe, June 14, 1981; 1 child, Benjamin William. AB, Radcliffe Coll., 1969; JD, Georgetown U., 1974; MBA, George Washington U., 1988. Bar: D.C., 1975. Law clk. U.S. Ct. of Claims, Washington, 1974-75; assoc. Caplin & Drysdale, Washington, 1975-78; atty., advisor U.S. Dept. of Transportation, Washington, 1978-79, dep. asst. gen. counsel, 1979-81; assoc. gen. counsel Chrysler Corp Loan Guaranty Bd., Washington, 1981-84; atty., advisor U.S. Dept. of Treasury, Washington, 1981-86, spl. asst. to the Under Sec. Fin., 1986-87; dir. strategic planning Fed. Nat. Mortgage Assn., Washington, 1987-88, v.p., asst. to chmn., 1988-91, sr. v.p. regulation rsch. and econs., 1991-93; spl. asst. to the pres. for econ. policy The White House, Washington, 1993-97; dir. Office Thrift Supervision U.S. Dept. Treasury, Washington, 1997—2001; sr. counsel, Minority Staff, fin. svcs. com. U.S. Ho. of Reps., Washington, 2002; sr. mng. dir. nat. practice Shorebank Adv. Svcs., 2002—. Office Phone: 202-822-9146. Business E-Mail: eseidman@sasbk.com.

SEIDMAN, GLENN ELLIOTT, sales executive, marketing professional; b. June 18, 1953; m. Charlene Goldberg, 1988; children: Brooke, Michelle. BA, CUNY, 1975; MA, NYU, 1977. Asst. dir. student activities Columbia U., N.Y.C., 1978-83; assoc. dean students Poly. U., Bklyn., 1983-88; territory mgr. Quality Products & Svcs., Reading, Pa., 1988—. Mem. Queens Coll. Alumni Assn. (pres. 1987-89). Home: 19 Beach Pl Huntington NY 11743 E-mail: oxfordbcg@aol.com.

SEIDMAN, JONATHAN G. genetics educator; BA in Biochemistry, Harvard U.; PhD, U. Wis. Prof. Harvard Med. Sch., Boston; investigator Howard Hughes Med. Inst. Office: Havard Med Sch, Seidman Lab Warren Alpert Bldg Rm 533B 200 Longwood Ave Boston MA 02115-5701

SEIDMAN, L(EWIS) WILLIAM, television commentator, publisher; b. Grand Rapids, Mich., Apr. 29, 1921; s. Frank E. and Esther (Lubetsky) S.; m. Sarah Berry, Mar. 3, 1944; children: Thomas, Tracy, Sarah, Carrie, Meg, Robin. AB, Dartmouth Coll., 1943; LL.B., Harvard U., 1948; MBA, U. Mich., 1949. Bar: Mich. 1949, D.C. 1977. Spl. asst. fin. affairs to gov. of Mich., 1963-66; nat. mng. partner Seidman & Seidman C.P.A.s, N.Y.C., 1969-74; asst. for econ. affairs to Pres. Gerald R. Ford, 1974-77; dir., chief fin. officer Phelps Dodge Corp., N.Y.C., 1977-82, vice chmn., 1980-82; dean Coll. Bus. Adminstrn. Ariz. State U., Tempe, 1982-85; chmn. RTC FDIC, Washington, 1989-91; chief commentator Sta. CNBC-TV, 1991; pub.-bd. Bank Dir. Mag., 1992. Chmn. Detroit Fed. Res. Bank Chgo., 1970, RTC, 1989-91; co-chair White House Conf. on Productivity, 1983-84. Lt. USNR, 1942-46. Decorated Bronze Star. Mem. D.C. Bar Assn., Chevy Chase Club (Md.), Univ. Club (N.Y.C.), Crystal Downs Club (Mich.), Nantucket Yacht Club (MA). Home: 825 Audubon Dr Bradenton FL 34209-7304 Office: CNBC 8th Flr 1025 Connecticut Ave NW Washington DC 20036-5405 Office Phone: 202-530-0910. Personal E-mail: lws1025@aol.com.

SEIDMAN, STEPHEN BENJAMIN, dean, computer science educator; b. N.Y.C., Apr. 13, 1944; s. Sylvan and Anne (Levine) S.; m. Barbara Heidemarie Koppe, Aug. 24, 1969; children: Miriam, Naomi. BS, CCNY, 1964; AM, U. Mich., 1965, PhD, 1969. Asst. prof. math. NYU, 1969-72, George Mason U., Fairfax, Va., 1972-76, assoc. prof. math., 1976-84, prof. computer sci., 1984-90; prof., dept. head computer sci., engring. Auburn (Ala.) U., 1990-96; prof., chair dept. computer sci. Colo. State U., Ft. Collins, 1996—2001; dean Coll. Computing Sci. NJ Inst. Tech., Newark, 2001—. Author: Assembly Language programming in Compass, 1987. Mem. IEEE Computer Soc. (bd. govs. 2003—), Assn. for Computing Machinery.

SEIDMAN, THOMAS ISRAEL, mathematics professor; b. NYC, Jan. 7, 1935; s. Sol H. and Sadie (Rattner) S.; m. Marjorie Shiro, Nov. 28, 1969; 1 child, Gregory. AB, U. Chgo., 1952; MA, Columbia Teachers Coll., 1953; MS, NYU, 1954, PhD, 1959. Lectr. UCRL, Livermore, Calif., 1958-60, UCLA, 1960—61, Math. Rsch. Ctr., U. Wis., Madison, 1961-62, Boeing Sci. Rsch. Lab., Seattle, 1962-64; assoc. prof. Wayne State U., Detroit, 1964-67, Carnegie-Mellon U., Pitts., 1967-72; assoc. prof., prof. U. Md. Balt. County, 1972—; vis. prof. U. Nice, France, 1980—81. Cons. Westinghouse, Pitts., Northrop Grumman, others. Contbr. articles to profl. jours. Rsch. grant USAF Office Sci. Rsch., NSF. Mem. Am. Math. Soc., Soc. Indsl. and Applied Maths. Home: 10355 Buglenote Way Columbia MD 21044-3816 Office: U Md Dept Math and Stats U Md Baltimore County Baltimore MD 21228 Office Phone: 410-455-2438. Business E-Mail: seidman@math.umbc.edu.

SEIERSEN, NICHOLAS STEEN, management consultant; b. Geneva, June 23, 1955; s. Ove Steen and Kamini Shoshiela (Bhandari) S.; m. Sylvie Jacqueline Fenouillet, Nov. 7, 1981. BSc with honors, U. Sussex, 1976; MBA, Pacific State U., L.A., 1987. Project chief Metra Proudfoot Internat. Mgmt. Cons., Brussels, 1977-81; unit mgr. Auchan Hypermarkets, Paris, 1981-83; internat. controller Pain Jacquet Group, Paris, 1983-85; sr. cons. A.T. Kearney Mgmt. Cons., Paris, 1985-88; European mktg. mgr. Digital Equip. Corp., Paris, 1988-95; dir. sales, mktg., logistics and distbn. European Mfg. Expertise Ctr., Digital Equipment Corp., Paris, 1995-96; prin. KPMG Mgmt. Consulting (now BearingPoint, LP), Toronto, Canada, 1996—99, sr. mgr., 1999—. Sci. bd. Logistique & Mgmt. Jour. (in French); adv. bd. Petrah Knowledge Solutions; editl. com. Global Supply Chain Forum mgmt. jour., Logistics Quarterly. Editl. adv. bd.: Logistics Quar. Jour., 2001—03. Can. exec. editor:, 2003—; contbr. articles to profl. jours. Mem. U.S. Bus. Logistics Assn. (coun. logistics mgmt., v.p. 1998-2000, pres. Toronto Roundtable) 2000-2002, Can. Assn. for Logistics Mgmt., French Assn. Logistics Mgmt. (bd. dirs. 1994-96, v.p. internat. affairs 1994-96). Office: BearingPoint Inc 20 Bay St Ste 940 Toronto ON Canada M5J 2X9 E-mail: nicholas.seiersen@bearingpoint.com.

SEIFER, ARNOLD DAVID, systems engineer; b. Newark, Apr. 22, 1940; s. Abe W. and Bessie R. (Coopersmith) Seifer. BS in Math., Rensselaer Poly. Ins., 1962, MS, 1964, PhD, 1968. Rsch. specialist Gen. Dynamics Corp., Groton, Conn., 1967—73; sr. staff mathematician Applied Physics Lab., Laurel, Md., 1973—76; sr. staff engr. Emerson Elec. Co., St. Louis, 1976—80; prin. engr. Raytheon Co., Wayland, Mass., 1980—92; sr. prin. systems engr. BAE Systems, Nashua, NH, 1992—. Contbr. articles to profl. jours. Mem.: IEEE (sr.), Soc. Indsl. and Applied Math., Sigma Xi. Home: 16 Ledgewood Hills Dr Apt 303 Nashua NH 03062-4452 Office: BAE Systems PO Box 868 Nashua NH 03061-0868

SEIFER, RONALD LESLIE, psychologist; b. Liberty, N.Y., Oct. 23, 1942; s. Leon and Pearl (Treibitz) S.; m. Gail Sandra Eagerman, May 29, 1967; children: David Marc, Robert Eric. BA, Queens Coll., 1964; MA, Northeastern U., 1967; PhD, U. Maine, 1971. Lic. psychologist, Fla., N.Y. Intern psychologist Albert Einstein Coll. Medicine, Bronx, N.Y., 1968-69; psychologist St. Vincent's Hosp., Harrison, N.y., 1969-71; supervising psychologist Saratoga County Mental Health Ctr., Saratoga Springs, N.Y., 1971-76; psychologist Brevard County Mental Health Ctr., Melbourne, Fla., 1976-79; pvt. practice clin. psychology Melbourne and Palm Bay, Fla., 1978—; med. staff Holmes Regional Med. Ctr., Melbourne, 1979—. Coord. TOP Soccer, Fla. Youth Soccer Assn., 1990-95; chair, psychology dept., psychiatry dept., Holmes Regional Med. Ctr., Melbourne, 2000—. Rsch. fellow Northeastern U., 1964-66. Mem.: APA, Brevard County Psychol. Assn. (founding pres. 1979—80), Fla. Psychol. Assn. (founding pres. Child/Adolescent/Family divsn. 1997—98). Avocations: gardening, fishing, parenting. Office: 2123 Franklin Dr NE Palm Bay FL 32905 Office Phone: 321-724-1614.

SEIFERT, DUSTIN DAVID, conductor, music educator; b. Lancaster, Ohio, Oct. 25, 1972; s. John Franklin and Stephanie Lynn Seifert; m. Stephanie M. Cortez, May 9, 1977. MusB Summa Cum Laude, U. Akron, OH, 1991—96; MusM in edn., U. Ill., Champaign, 1996—98. Grad. tchg. asst. U. of Ill., Champaign, 1996—98; asst. dir. bands Iowa State U., Ames, 1998—2000; dir. bands Ea. N.Mex U., Portales, 2000—. Dir. enmu concert band clinic, enmu summer music edn. seminar. Ch. musician, Portales, N.Mex., Clovis, N.Mex. Recipient Presser Scholar, Theodore Presser Co., 1994, Guy M. Duker award, U. Ill. Bands, 1998, Outstanding Undergraduate Brass Performer, U. Akron, 1996. Mem.: N.Mex Music Educators Assn. (exec. sec., SE dist. 2002—03), Nat. Band Assn. (N.Mex state chair 2002—03), Music Educators Nat. Conf., Golden Key Nat. Honor Soc., Pi Kappa Lambda (hon.), Kappa Delta Pi (hon.), Tau Beta Sigma (hon.), Kappa Kappa Psi (hon.; SW dist. gov. 2000—01). R-Liberal. Avocations: travel, conventioneering, reading. Home: 1920 S Ave O Portales NM 88130 Office: Eastern New Mexico U 1500 S Ave K Station 16 Portales NM 88130 Office Phone: 505-562-2671. Business E-Mail: dustin.seifert@enmu.edu.

SEIFERT, GEORGE, retired professional football coach; b. San Francisco, Jan. 22, 1940; m. Linda Seifert; children: Eve, Jason. Grad., U. Utah, 1963. Asst. football coach U. Utah, 1964; head coach Westminster Coll., 1965; asst. coach U. Iowa, 1966, U. Oreg., 1966-71; secondary coach Stanford U., 1972-74; head coach Cornell U., 1975-76; from secondary coach to defensive coord. San Francisco 49ers, 1980-89, head coach, 1989-96, Carolina Panthers, Charlotte, 1999—2001. With AUS, 1963. Named NFL Coach of Yr. The Sporting News, 1990, 94.

SEIFERT, KATHI P. manufacturing executive; b. Appleton, Wis., 1949; m. Steve Seifert; children: Erin, Andrew. BA Valparaiso U., 1971. Various mgmt. positions P&G, Beatruce Foods, Fort Howard Paper Co., 1972—78; from product mgr. to mktg. dir. feminine care products Kimberly-Clark, Inc., Neenah, Wis., 1978—92, pres. feminine care sectory, 1992—94, group pres. N. Am. consumer products, 1994—95, group pres. N. Am. personal care products, 1995—98, group pres. personal care products, 1998—99, exec. v.p., group pres. global personal care products, 1999—. Bd. dirs. Eli Lilly and Co. Bd. dirs. U.S. Fund for UNICEF; bd., dirs. Fox Cities Performing Art Ctr., 1999—, chmn. of bd., 2003—; bd. dirs. Theda Health Care Group, Wis. Commn. in Arts Edn. Office: Kimberly Clark Corp 355 Phelps Dr Irving TX 75038

SEIFERT, PATRICIA CLARK, cardiac surgery nurse, educator, consultant; b. Springfield, Mass., Apr. 4, 1945; d. Thomas W. and Kathleen E. (O'Malley) Clark; m. Gary F. Seifert, Sept. 10, 1966; children: Kristina S. Glenn, Philip A. BA in History, Trinity Coll., 1967; ADN, No. Va. Community Coll., 1976; MS in Nursing, Cath. U. Am., 1988. RN, Va., D.C.; cert. oper. rm. nurse, first asst. nurse. Head nurse cardiac surgery Fairfax Hosp., Falls Church, Va., 1976-88; adminstrv. dir. Washington Hosp. Ctr., 1988-89; oper. room coord. cardiac surgery Arlington (Va.) Hosp., 1989-97, Alexandria (Va.) Hosp., 1995—97; mgr. open heart surgery Halifax Med. Ctr., Daytona Beach, Fla., 1997—98; coord. cardiovasc. svcs. Arlington (Va.) Hosp., 2000—02; innovations liaison Sandel Med. Industries, Chatsworth, Calif., 2002—02; perioperative cardiac care coord. Inova Fairfax Hosp., Falls Church, Va., 2002. Mem. adv. bd. Surg. Info. Sys., Ethicon Endo-surgery Nursing; lead coord. Nursing Orgns. Alliance, 2001—; lectr., cons. in field. Author: (books) Clinical Assessment Tools for Use with Nursing Diagnosis, 1989, Cardiac Surgery, 1994, 2002; contbr. chpts. in Alexander's Care of the Patient in Surgery, 12th rev. edit., 2002, Cardiovascular Nursing, 7th rev. edit., 1991, Perioperative Care Planning, 2d rev. edit., 1996, The RN First Assistant: An Expanded Perioperative Role, 3d rev. edit., 1999, Core Curriculum for the RN First Assistant, 3d rev. edit., 1999, CNOR Study Guide, rev. edit., 1999; contbr. numerous articles to profl. jours. Fellow: Am. Acad. Nursing; mem.: Va. Nurses's Assn. (dist. 8 bd. dirs. 1987—91, Nurse of Year award 1984), Assn. Perioperative RN's (nat. nominating com. 1991—93, pres. No. Va. chpt. 1994—95, nat. bd. dir. 1994—98, nat. pres.-elect 1999—99, nat. pres. 1999—2000, RN 1st asst.), Am. Heart Assn. (coun. on cardiovasc. nursing), Assn. Perioperative RN's Found. (sec. 1999—2001), Am. Assn. for History of Nursing, Sigma Theta Tau (pres. Eta Alpha chpt. 1990—92, Virginia Henderson fellow). Home: 6502 Overbrook St Falls Church VA 22043-1942 Fax: 703-237-1259. E-mail: seifertpc@aol.com.

SEIFERT, SHELLEY JANE, bank executive, human resources specialist; b. Aug. 12, 1954; BS in Consumer Econs. and Journalism, U. Mo., 1976; MBA in Fin. with honors, U. Louisville, 1980. Fin. analyst Nat. City Bank, Ky., 1979-81, compensation analyst, 1981-85, mgr. compensation, 1985-86, mgr. compensation, recruiting and tng., 1986-91; mgr. compensation and devel. Nat. City Corp., Cleve., 1988-91, human resource dir., 1991-94, sr. v.p., corp. human resource dir., 1994—2000, exec. v.p., dir. corp. human resources, 2000—. Spkr. in field. Grad. Leadership Cleve.; vice chair bd. dirs. Bus. Vols. Unlimited, Vis. Nurse Assn. Greater Cleve.; bd. dirs. Arthritis Found.; mem. Cleve. Commn. on Econ. Partnership and Inclusion. Recipient Woman of Distinction award YMCA. Mem. Urban League (bd. dirs., chair employment com., Ohio labor adv. com.). Office: Nat City Corp Nat City Ctr 1900 E 9th St Cleveland OH 44114-3401

SEIFERT, THOMAS LLOYD, lawyer; b. Boston, June 6, 1940; s. Ralph Frederick and Hazel Bell (Harrington) S.; m. Ann Cecelia Berg, June 19, 1965. BS cum laude, Ind. U., 1962, JD cum laude, 1965. Bar: Ill. 1965, Ind. 1965, N.Y. 1979. Assoc. law firm Keck, Mahin & Cate, Chgo., 1965-67; atty. Essex Group, Inc., Ft. Wayne, Ind., 1967-70, Amoco Corp., Chgo., 1970-73; assoc. gen. counsel, asst. sec. Canteen Corp., Chgo., 1973-75; sec., gen. counsel The Marmon Group, Inc. (and predecessor cos.), Chgo., 1975-78; v.p., gen. counsel, sec. Hanson Industries, Inc., N.Y.C., 1978-82; sr. v.p. law, chief fin. officer Petrie Stores Corp., N.Y.C., 1982-83; mem. Finley, Kumble, Wagner, Heine, Underberg, Manley, Myerson & Casey, N.Y.C., 1983-87, Paul, Weiss, Rifkind, Wharton & Garrison, N.Y.C., 1987-91; gen. counsel, chief legal officer Sterling Grace Capital Mgmt., L.P. and affiliated cos., N.Y.C., 1991—. Note editor Ind. Law Jour., 1964-65. Named to Ind. Track and Cross Country Hall of Fame, 1993. Mem. ABA, N.Y. State Bar Assn., Order of Coif, The Creek, Beta Gamma Sigma. Home: Museum Tower 15 W 53d St Apt 31 E New York NY 10019-5401 Office: Sterling Grace Capital Mgmt 405 Park Ave Ste 1203 New York NY 10022 E-mail: tlseifert@msn.com.

SEIFF, E. KENNETH, Internet company executive; b. N.Y.C. m. Nicole Seiff; 2 children. BS in Econs., U. Pa., 1986. With Lorne Weil, Inc., N.Y.C.; founder, pres. Pivot Rules, Inc., 1991—94, founder, chmn., CEO, 1994—98; CEO Bluefly, Inc., N.Y.C., 1998—. Named to, Crain's N.Y. Bus. "40 under 40", 2004. Office: Bluefly Inc 42 W 39th St New York NY 10018*

SEIFF, ERIC A. lawyer; b. Mt. Vernon, N.Y., Apr. 25, 1933; s. Arthur N. and Mathilde (Cohen) S.; m. Sari Ginsburg, June 26, 1960 (div. Oct. 1983); children: Judith C., E. Kenneth, Dean A.; m. Meredith Feinman, Jan. 15, 1984; children: Abigail, Sarah. BA, Yale U., 1955; LLB, Columbia U., 1958. Bar: N.Y. 1958, U.S. Dist. Ct. (so. dist.) N.Y. 1960, U.S. Dist. Ct. (ea. dist.) N.Y. 1981, U.S. Ct. Appeals (2d cir.) 1965, U.S. Supreme Ct. 1967. Assoc. Bower and O'Connor, N.Y.C., 1959-60, Yellin, Kramer & Levy, N.Y.C., 1961; asst. dist. atty. N.Y. County Dist. Atty.'s Office, 1962-67; asst. counsel Agy. for Internat. Devel., Washington, 1967-70, counsel Rio de Janeiro, 1970-72; gen. counsel N.Y. State Divsn. Criminal Justice Svcs., 1972-74; dep. chief atty. Legal Aid Soc. Criminal Def., N.Y.C., 1974-75; first dep. commr. N.Y. State Investigation Commn., 1975-77, chmn., 1977-79; ptnr. Seiff, Kretz & Abercrombie (formerly Scoppetta & Seiff), N.Y.C., 1981—; spl. dist. atty. Bronx County, 1986-89. Spl. asst. atty. gen. State of N.Y., Gov.'s Task Force Investigating Conduct of Attica Prosecutions, 1975. Bd. dirs. Legal Aid Soc., N.Y.C., 1994-2000; Prisoners' Legal Svcs., N.Y.C., 1989—, Lawyers Fund for Client Protection, N.Y., 1980—. Recipient Frank S. Hogan Meml. award Frank S. Hogan Assn., 1994. Mem.: N.Y. State Assn. Criminal Def. Lawyers (bd. dirs. 2001—), Bar Assn. City N.Y. (chmn. project on the homeless 1999—2003), N.Y. Criminal Bar Assn. (bd. dirs. 1980—, past pres.). Office: Seiff Kretz & Abercrombie 645 Madison Ave New York NY 10022-1010 Office Phone: 212 371 4500.

SEIFF, STEPHEN S. ophthalmologist; b. L.A., Sept. 30, 1925; s. Max and Minnie F. (Feldman) S.; m. Gloria Louise Holtzman, Apr. 16, 1950; children: Stuart R., Sherri Seiff Sloane, Karen Seiff Sacks. AA, UCLA, 1945; AB, U. Calif., Berkeley, 1946; MD, U. Calif., San Francisco, 1949. Diplomate Am. Bd. Ophthalmology. Intern County Gen. Hosp., L.A., 1949-50; fellow in anesthesiology Lahey Clinic, Boston, 1950-51; resident in ophthalmology U. Calif., San Francisco, 1952-55; clin. prof. dept. ophthalmology UCLA, 1956—2002, emeritus clin. prof., 2002—; pvt. practice Beverly Hills, Calif., 1955—; clin. chief divsn. ophthalmology Cedars/Sinai Med. Ctr., L.A., 1957—; attending ophthalmologist Children's Hosp., L.A., 1956-94. Lectr. in field; assoc. examiner Am. Bd. Ophthalmology. Collaborating author: Clinical Anticoagulant Therapy, 1965; contbr. articles to profl. jours. Bd. dirs. That Man May See Inc., San Francisco; former exec. com. mem. UCLA Hosp. Lt. M.C. USNR, 1950-52. Recipient Sr. Honor award UCLA Dept. Ophthalmology, 1994. Fellow ACS, Am. Acad. Ophthalmology; mem. L.A. Soc. Ophthalmology (past pres.), Frederick Cordes Eye Soc. (past nat. pres.), Am. Soc. Cataract and Refractive Surgery (founding mem.). Avocation: sailing. Office: 435 N Roxbury Dr Ste 107 Beverly Hills CA 90210-5003 Personal E-mail: sseiff@aol.com.

SEIFOULLAEV, ROUSTAM KAFAR, mathematician, programmer; b. Baku, Azerbaijan, Mar. 30, 1953; s. Kafar Suleiman and Alexandra Konstantin (Sen) S.; m. Alia Anatoly Guseinova, Nov. 28, 1981 (div. Oct. 1994); 1 child, Anar; m. Zemfira Djafar Ismail-zade, Nov. 24, 1997; chldren: Zaour, Anar. MS, Baku State U., 1975, PhD, 1979; DSc, Inst. Math. and Mechs., Baku, 1994. Prof. Baku State U., 1979-97, Western U., Baku, 1995-97, head dept. fgn. rels., 1995-97; sr. rsch. fellow Inst. Math. and Mechanics, Baku, 1992-97; prof. Univ. extension U. Tex., Austin, 1998—, prof., rsch. fellow Inst. for Geophysics, 1998—. Sys. cons. DHV Cons. BV, Amersfort, Netherlands; expert Higher Attestation Commn., Baku, 1996-97. Mem. editl. bd. Singular Integral Operators, 1983-97. Internat. Sci. Found. grantee, 1993; Brit. Coun. scholar, 1983-84. Mem. N.Y. Acad. Sci., Azerbaijan Math. Soc. (treas. 1981-90, editor Procs. 1994-97), Soc. Exploration Geophysicists, U. Tex. Club. Avocations: music, chess, swimming. Office: U Tex Inst for Geophysics Bldg 600 Rm 135 4412 Spicewood Springs Rd Austin TX 78759-8500 E-mail: roustam@utig.ig.utexas.edu.

SEIGEL, JAN KEARNEY, lawyer; b. Bayonne, N.J., Feb. 7, 1947; s. Max and Margaret (Kearney) S.; m. Judy L. Mascuch, Aug. 29, 1971; children: Margaret, Emily, Jonas, Luke. BSBA, Georgetown U., 1968, JD, 1971; LLM in Taxation, NYU, 1974. Bar: N.J. 1971, D.C. 1972, Ga. 1972, U.S. Ct. Appeals (3d cir.) 1979, U.S. Supreme Ct. 1979. Law sec. to Hon. Theodore Rosenberg Superior Ct. of N.J., Paterson, NJ, 1971—72; asst. prosecutor Passaic County Pros.'s Office, Paterson, NJ, 1972—76; prin. Seigel & Assocs., Ridgewood, NJ, 1976—. Mem. faculty William Paterson Coll., 1974-79; lectr. N.J. Inst. for Continuing Edn., 1981—, N.J. State Bar and various county bar assns. Recipient Police Hon. Legion award Police Chiefs Assn. of N.J., 1980. Mem. ABA (rep. of N.J. young lawyers divsn. 1980-82), N.J. State Bar Assn. (Young Lawyer of Yr. award 1983, bd. trustees 1978-79), Passaic County Bar Assn. (bd. trustees 1973-81), Bergen County Bar Assn. Office: Seigel & Assoc 505 Goffle Rd Ridgewood NJ 07450-4027 Office Phone: 201-444-4000.

SEIGEL, JERROLD EDWARD, historian, writer; b. St. Louis, June 9, 1936; s. William and Katherine (Ginsberg) S.; m. Jayn Rosenfeld, Aug. 28, 1966; children: Micol, Jessica. AB, Harvard U., 1958; PhD, Princeton U., 1963. Instr. Princeton (N.J.) U., 1962-65, asst. prof., 1965-68, assoc. prof., 1968-78, prof. history, 1978-88, NYU, N.Y.C., 1988—; Kenan prof., 1994—. Vis. prof. history Maitre d'Etudes, Ecoles des hautes études, Paris, 1988-94; finalist Nat. Book Critics Cir., 1987. Author: Rhetoric and Philosophy, 1968, Marx's Fate, 1978, Bohemian Paris, 1986, Private Worlds of Marcel Duchamp, 1995, The Idea of the Self, 2004. Fulbright fellow Inst. Internat. Edn., 1961-62; NEH fellow, 1979-80, 87-88; resident Am. Acad. Rome, 2000; Guggenheim fellow, 2004—. Mem. N.Y. Inst. for Humanities, Phi Beta Kappa. Home: 48 Horatio St New York NY 10014-1614 Office: NYU History Dept 53 Washington Sq S New York NY 10012-1098 E-mail: jes3@nyu.edu.

SEIGEL, RICHARD M. consumer products company executive; Chmn., CEO SYSCO Food Svcs., L.A., 1990-97; dir. Indsl. Distbn. Group, Atlanta, 1997—, chmn., acting CEO, 1998—. Office: Indsl Distbn Group 950 E Paces Ferry Rd NE Atlanta GA 30326-1180

SEIGEL, STUART EVAN, retired lawyer; b. N.Y.C., Mar. 25, 1933; s. Philip Herman and Betty Sarah (Leventhal) S.; m. Joyce Roberta Meyers (div.); children: Charles Meyers, Lee Bennett, Suzanne Marcie; m. Sherry Diane Jackson,Sept. 24, 1989. BS, N.Y. U., 1953, LLB, 1957; LLM in Taxation, Georgetown U., 1960. Bar: N.Y. 1958, D.C. 1958. Atty. Office Chief Counsel, IRS, Washington, 1957-65, Office Tax Legis. Counsel, Dept. Treasury, Washington, 1965-69, assoc. tax legis. counsel, 1968-69; ptnr. firm Cohen and Uretz, Washington, 1969-77; chief counsel IRS, Washington, 1977-79; ptnr. firm Williams and Connolly, Washington, 1979-89, Arnold and Porter, N.Y.C., 1989—2002. Lectr. George Washington U. Sch. Law, 1970-73; adj. prof. law Antioch Sch. Law, 1973-76, Georgetown U. Sch. Law, 1981. Mem. ABA, Am. Law Inst., Am. Coll. Tax Counsel, N.Y. State Bar Assn. Clubs: Metropolitan (Washington).

SEIGENTHALER, JOHN LAWRENCE, retired newspaper executive; b. Nashville, July 27, 1927; s. John and Mary (Brew) Seigenthaler; m. Dolores Watson, Jan. 3, 1955; 1 child, John Jr. Staff corr. Nashville Tennessean, 1949-60, editor, 1962-72, pub., 1973-82, pres., 1979-82, chmn., 1982-92; editorial dir. USA Today, 1982-92, ret., 1992. Chmn. freedom forum First

Amendment Ctr., Vanderbilt U., Nashville, 1992—; adminstrv. asst. to atty. gen. U.S., 1961; dir. Tennessean Newspapers, Inc., 1963—79, 1978—83. Mem. U.S. Adv. Commn. Info., 1962—64, Pres.'s Jud. Nominating Commn., 1978—79, Nat. Commn. Electoral Reform, 2001—02. Nieman fellow, Harvard U. Mem.: Am. Soc. Newspaper Editors (dir., pres.), Sigma Delta Chi. Office Phone: 615-385-5006. Business E-Mail: johns@fac.org.

SEIGLER, DAVID STANLEY, botanist, educator, chemist; b. Wichita Falls, Tex., Sept. 11, 1940; s. Kenneth R. and Floy M. (Wilkinson) S.; m. Janice Kay Cline, Jan. 20, 1961; children: Dava, Rebecca. BS in Chemistry, Southwestern (Okla.) State Coll., 1961; PhD in Organic Chemistry, U. Okla., 1967. Postdoctoral assoc. USDA No. Regional Lab., Peoria, Ill., 1967-68; postdoctoral fellow dept. botany U. Tex., Austin, 1968-70; asst. prof. botany U. Ill., Urbana, 1970-76, assoc. prof., 1976-79, prof. botany, 1979—, head dept. plant biology, 1988-93. Curator U. Ill. Herbarium, 1993—. Author: Plant Secondary Metabolism, 1999; editor: Crop Resources, 1977, Phytochemistry and Angiosperm Phylogeny, 1981; contbr. numerous articles to profl. jours. Recipient Fulbright Hays Lecturer award Fulbright Commn., Argentina, 1976, (alternate) Germany, 1995-96, study award Deutsche Akademischer Austauschdienst, Germany, 1995, Rupert Barneby award N.Y. Bot. Garden, 1997. Mem. Phytochem. Soc. N.Am. (pres. 1988-89), Bot. Soc. Am., Am. Chem. Soc., Am. Soc. Plant Taxonomists, Internat. Soc. Chem. Ecology (pres. 1990-91). Mem. Assembly of God Ch. Avocation: genealogy. Home: 510 W Vermont Ave Urbana IL 61801-4931 Office: U Ill Dept Plant Biology 265 Morrill Hall 505 S Goodwin Ave Urbana IL 61801-3707 Office Phone: 217-333-7577. Business E-Mail: seigler@life.uiuc.edu.

SEIGLER, MICHAEL EDWARD, lawyer, librarian; b. Tallahassee, Oct. 14, 1948; s. Claude Milo and Roberta Bradford (Whitfield) S.; m. Janet Cummings, Feb. 19, 1971; children: Kelly Elizabeth, Megan Whitfield. AA, Lake Sumter C.C., 1968; BS, Fla. State Univ., 1970; MS, 1974; JD, Atlanta Law Sch., 1980. Bar: Ga. 1980, U.S. Ct. Appelas (5th cir.) 1980, U.S. Ct. Appeals (11th cir.) 1980, U.S. tax Ct. 1985, U.S. Supreme Ct. 1985, Cert. tchr. Libr. tchr. Sumter Correctional Inst., Bushnell, Fla., 1970-73; asst. libr. dir. Leesburg Pub. Libr. (Fla.), 1974-75, libr. dir., 1975-77, Atlanta Law Sch., 1979-81; atty. Brooks & Brock, Marietta, Ga., 1981-83; libr. Port Charlotte Pub. Libr., 1983-84; assoc. Brooks & Brock, Marietta, Ga., 1985, Brock & Barr, Marietta, 1985-86, Brock & Clay, 1987; judge pro hoc vice State Ct. of Cobb County, 1986; pvt. practice, 1986—. Asst. dir. Pine Mountain Regional Libr., 1988-95; libr. dir. Smyrna Pub. Libr., 1995—; design judge Ben Franklin Awards, 2001, 03. Columnist Smyrna Vinings Living, 2000-02; contbr. articles to jours. Vol. worker ACLU, Atlanta, 1979; mem. Fla. State U. Libr. Com., Tallahassee, 1974, Children's Program Com., Port Charlotte, 1983, Port Charlotte Cultural Ctr. Adv. Com., 1984, Pine Mountain Arts Coun., past bd. dirs.; mem. Cobb County Dem. Exec. Com., 1986-87; exec. com. Cobb Christmas, 1986-87; com. mem. Smyrna Cmty. Culture, 2000-2002, bd. dirs. 2003—; sec. program com. WRFG Cmty. Radio, 2002, bd. dirs., 2003--, chair fin. com., 2003--. Named Tchr. of Yr., Sumter Correctional Inst., 1973. Mem. Nat. Libr. Assn. (com. chmn. 1975-76), Fla. Libr. Assn. (caucus chmn. 1976-77), Ga. Libr. Assn. (mem. com. chmn. 1992—, sec. 1993-94, parliamentarian 1997, 1st v.p. 1999, pres. 2000), Metro Atlanta Libr. Assn. (v.p. 1997, pres. 1998), Southeastern Libr. Assn. (mem. com. 1988—, convention chair 2000, com. chair 2001—), ALA (con. spkr.), Atlanta Law Sch. Alumni Assn. (treas. 1986-90), Fla. State U. Alumni Assn. (life), Ga. Libr. Video Assn. (pres. 1991-92), Mensa (sec. 1987, 89, pres. Ga. chpt. 1988, mediator Ga. chpt. 2000-02, rgional vice chmn. 2003—, trustee Mensa Edn. and Rsch. Found. (v.p. 1993), Ga. Coun. Media Orgn. (chair steering com. 2000), Leadership Meriwether (pres. 1993). Home: 3023 Bay Berry Dr SW Marietta GA 30008-5674 Office: 100 Village Green Cir SE Smyrna GA 30080-3478 Office Phone: 770-431-2860. E-mail: m.seigler@comcast.net., mjseigler@msn.com.

SEIGLER, RUTH QUEEN, college nursing administrator, educator, consultant, nurse; b. Conway, S.C., July 31, 1942; d. Charles Isaac and Berneta Mae (Weaks) Queen; m. Rallie Marshall Seigler, Sept. 1, 1963; children: Rallie Marshall Jr., Scot Monroe. ADN, Lander Coll., 1962; BSN, U. S.C., 1964, MSN, 1980. Pub. health nurse Richland County Health Dept., Columbia, S.C., 1964-66; dir. nurses Columbia Area Mental Health Ctr., 1966-69; program nurse specialist Midlands Health Dist., 1969-72; discharge planner Richland Meml. Hosp., 1972-73, clin. dir., 1973-75; exec. dir. S.C. State Bd. Nursing, 1976-83; v.p. nursing dept. Self Meml. Hosp., Greenwood, S.C., 1983-86; exec. dir. S.C. Commn. on Aging, Columbia, 1986-95; asst. dean Coll. Nursing U. S.C., Columbia, 1995-96, assoc. clin. prof., 1996—; dir. Cockcroft Leadership Program for Nurse Execs., 2002—. Cons. intergenerational family studies, 1999—; bd. dirs. Queen Gas Co., Barnwell, S.C.; nurse cons. Creative Nursing Mgmt., Mpls., 1984—; dir. Ctr. for Nursing Leadership. Advisor: The Role of County Mental Health Nurse, 1971. Moderator Trinity Presbyn. Ch., 2003—. Recipient Disting. Alumni award Lander Coll., 1978, career Woman recognition award Columbia YWCA, 1980, William S. Hall award S.C. Assn. Residential Care Homes, 1988, U. S.C. Coll. Nursing Disting. Alumni award, 1993, award for excellence S.C. League for Nursing, 1995, Svc. Recognition award S.C. AARP, 1995; named one of Ten Women of Achievement, S.C. March of Dimes, 1987. Mem. ANA, APHA, S.C. Nurses Assn. (sec. 1965-68, bd. dirs. 1986-88, Excellence award 1984, Recognition award 1984), S.C. Hosp. Assn., S.C. Gerontol. Soc., S.C. Nurses Found., S.C. Healthy People 2000 (vice chair), Partnership for Older South Carolinians (founder, chair bd. dirs.), Columbia Luncheon Club (pres. 1997-98), S.C. Fedn. Older Ams., Evening Mission Action Group, Bd. Nursing Home Examiners, Pilot Club, Inc. (pres. 1988-89, 97-98), Vols. of Am.-Carolinas (bd. dirs., chair, 1998-00, elder, 1999-01), Rotary Internat., Sigma Theta Tau, Beta Sigma Phi (pres. chpt. 1997-98). Presbyterian. Avocations: gardening, travel. Home: 6 Beaver Dam Ct Columbia SC 29223-3100 Office: U SC Coll Nursing Deans Office Columbia SC 29208-0001

SEIL, FREDRICK JOHN, retired neuroscientist; b. Nove Sove, Yugoslavia, Nov. 9, 1933; s. Joseph and Theresa (Krieger) S.; m. Daryle Faith Wolfers, July 2, 1955; children: Jonathan Fredrick, Joel Philip Timothy. BA, Oberlin Coll., 1956; MD, Stanford U., 1960. Intern Kaiser Found. Hosp., San Francisco, 1960-61; resident in neurology Stanford (Calif.) U., 1961-64, fellow in neurology, 1964-66; staff neurologist VA Med. Ctr., Palo Alto, Calif., 1969-76, clin. investigator Portland, Oreg., 1976-79, staff neurologist, 1979-81, dir. VA office regeneration research programs, 1981—2001, ret., 2001. Asst. prof. neurology Stanford U., 1969-75, assoc. prof. neurology Oreg. Health and Sci. U., Portland, 1976-78, prof. neurology, 1978-2001, prof. cell and devel. biology, 1990-2001, prof. emeritus neurology, 2001—. Editor: Nerve, Organ and Tissue Regeneration: Research Perspectives, 1983, Neural Regeneration, 1987, 94, Current Issues in Neural Regeneration Rsch., 1988, Current Issues in Neural Regeneration and Transplantation, 1989, Advances in Neural Regeneration Research, 1990, Neural Injury and Regeneration, 1993, Multiple Sclerosis: Current Status of Research and Treatment, 1994, Neural Regeneration, Reorganization, and Repair, 1997, Neural Plasticity and Regeneration, 2000; contbr. articles to profl. jours. Served to capt. U.S. Army, 1966-68. Grantee VA, 1970-2001, NIH, 1986-95. Mem. Internat. Brain Rsch. Orgn., Internat. Soc. Develop. Neurosci., Am. Neurol. Assn., Am. Assn. Neuropathologists, Soc. Neurosci., Soc. Exptl. Neuropathology. Democrat. Home: 10306 SW Radcliffe Rd Portland OR 97219-7956 Personal E-mail: seilf@comcast.net.

SEILACHER, ADOLF, special education educator; b. Stuttgart, Germany, Feb. 24, 1925; came to U.S., 1987; s. Adolf and Frida (Pfitzer) S.; m. Edith Drexler, July 20, 1957; children: Ulrike, Peter. PhD, U. Tübingen (Germany), 1951. Asst. prof. Tübingen U., 1951-57; docent Frankfurt (Germany) U., 1957-59; lectr. Baghdad (Iraq) U., 1959-61; prof. Göttingen (Germany) U., 1961-64, Tübingen U., 1964-90; adj. prof. geology & geophysics Yale U., New Haven, 1987—. Mem. adv. bd. Sendenberg Mus., Frankfurt, Naturkunde Mus., Berlin. Editor Neues Jahr Geol. Paleontol., Stuttgart, 1965—. With German Navy, 1943-45. Recipient Crafoord prize Swedish Acad. Sci., Stockholm, 1992. Fellow AAAS; mem. Acad. Scis. Heidelberg, Geol. Soc. London (hon.), Royal Phys. Soc. Lund (hon.), Paleontology Assn. (hon.). Avocation: ballroom dancing. Home: 25 Engelfriedschalde D-72076 Tübingen Germany Office: Dept Geology Yale U 210 Whitney Ave New Haven CT 06511-8902

SEILER, CHARLOTTE WOODY, retired educator; b. Thorntown, Ind., Jan. 20, 1915; d. Clark and Lois Merle (Long) Woody; m. Wallace Urban Seiler, Oct. 10, 1942 (dec. Aug. 2002); children: Patricia Anne Seiler Bootzin, Janet Alice Seiler Sawyer. AA, Ind. State U., 1933; AB, U. Mich., 1941; MA, Ctrl. Mich. U., 1968. Tchr. elem. schs., Whitestown, Ind., 1933-34, Thorntown, 1934-37, Kokomo, Ind., 1937-40, Ann Arbor, Mich., 1941-44, Willow Run, Mich., 1944-46; instr. English divsn. Delta Coll., University Center, Mich., 1964-69, asst. prof., 1969-77; ret., 1977. Organizer, dir. Delta Coll. Puppeteers, Midland, Mich., 1972—77. Mem. Friends of Grace A. Dow Meml. Libr., 1974-2000, treas., 1974-75, 77-79, corr. sec., 1975-77; leader Sr. Ctr. Humanities program Midland Sr. Ctr., 1977-94; vol. Quality Health Care, North Port, Fla., 2001—; leader bridge refresher Harbor Cove, North Port, 2002—. Mem. AAUW (fellow 1979), Mich. Libr. Assn., Harbor Cove Civic Assn., Pi Lambda Theta, Chi Omega. Presbyterian. Home: 652 Blackburn Blvd North Port FL 34287

SEILER, FRITZ ARNOLD, physicist; b. Basel, Switzerland, Dec. 20, 1931; came to U.S., 1980; s. Friedrich and Marie (Maibach) S.; m. Mary Catherine Coster, Dec. 22, 1964; children: Monica, Simone, Daniel. BA in Econs., Basel Sch. of Econs., 1951; PhD in Physics, U. Basel, 1962. Rsch. assoc. U. Wis., Madison, 1962-63; scientific assoc. U. Basel, 1963-69, privat dozent, 1969-75, dozent, 1975-80; sr. scientist Lovelace Inhalation Toxicology Inst., Albuquerque, 1980-90; sr. tech. assoc. IT Corp., Albuquerque, 1990-92, disting. tech. assoc., 1992-96; v.p. Inst. Regulatory Sci., Albuquerque, 1996-97; prin. Sigma Five Cons., Los Lunas, N.Mex., 1997—. Cons. Swiss Dept. Def., 1968-74; vis. scientist Lawrence Berkeley Labs., 1974-75. Contbr. numerous articles to profl. jours. With Swiss Army staff, 1964-75. Fellow Am. Phys. Soc., Health Physics Soc., Soc. for Risk Analysis, Fachverband fuer Strahlenschutz, Am. Nat. Stds. Inst. (mgmt. coun. 1987-2002, com. N14 1986-2002). Office: Sigma Five Consulting PO Box 1709 Los Lunas NM 87031-1709 Office Fax: 505-866-5197. Business E-Mail: faseiler@nmia.com.

SEILER, JAMES ELMER, judge; b. LaCrosse, Wis., Sept. 2, 1946; s. Elmer Bernard and Margaret Theresa (Mader) Seiler; m. Sonia Gonzales, Feb. 9, 1968; children: Rebecca, Cristina. BA, U. Wis., LaCrosse, 1968; JD, U. Wis., 1973. Bar: Wis. 1973, Minn. 1981, U.S. Supreme Ct. 1985, Mo. 1986. Pvt. practice, Balsam Lake, Wis., 1973-81; in-house counsel Farm Credit Banks, St. Paul, 1981-85; corp. counsel Hussmann Corp., St. Louis, 1985-94; adminstrv. law judge Social Security, Evansville, Ind., 1994-95, Office Hearings and Appeals, Creve Coeur, Mo., 1995—, chief adminstrv. law judge, 1997—. Candidate dist. atty. Polk County, Wis., 1980. With U.S. Army, 1969—71. Avocations: soccer coach, swimming, water-skiing, Senior Olympics. Home: 18 Harbor Point Ct Lake Saint Louis MO 63367-1336 Office: 11475 Olde Cabin Rd Saint Louis MO 63141-7130

SEILER, KAREN PEAKE, organizational psychologist; b. Seattle, Jan. 31, 1952; d. Louis Joseph and Donna Mae (Waters) Tomaso; m. Arthur J. Seiler; children from previous marriage: Jeremy S. Peake, Anthony K. Peake. BA/BSW magna cum laude, Carroll Coll., 1987; postgrad., MIT, 1994. Cert. strategic planning Pacific Inst.; cert. orgnl. cons. Covey Learning Ctr., 1993. Admissions counselor Shodair Children's Hosp., Helena, Mont., 1984-86; asst. dir., counselor Career Tng. Inst., Helena, 1986-90; pres. Corp. Cons., Helena, 1990—. Apptd, amb. Mont. Ambs., 1990—; active Gov.'s Task Force on Econ. Devel., 1991-94; chairperson Mont. Dist. Export Coun./U.S. Dept. Commerce, 1992-96; exec. com. mem. Mont. World Trade Ctr., Missoula, 1995—, chmn. 1996—; pres. Coun. Carroll Coll., 1997—. Mem. YWCA, 1986-90, pres., 1989; mem. Bus. and Profl. Women's Orgn., 1987-93, sec., 1990; pres. Helena Area Econ. Devel. Coun., 1989-92; exec. com. Leadership Helena, 1990-91; monitoring chair Concentrated Employment Program Pvt. Industry Coun., Mont., 1990—; bd. dirs., exec. com. Mont. Women's Capital Fund, 1990-95; exec. com. Mont. Race for the Cure, 1994—. Mem. NAFE, Partnership for Employment and Tng., Delta Epsilon Sigma (Outstanding Citizen award). Roman Catholic. Avocations: sailing, world travel. Home and Office: 6970 Viscaya Ln Helena MT 59602-6445

SEILER, STEVEN LAWRENCE, health facility administrator; b. Chgo., Dec. 30, 1941; married. B, U. Ariz., 1963; M, U. Iowa, 1965. Adminstrv. resident Rush-Presbyn.-St. Luke's Med. Ctr., Chgo., 1965, adminstrv. asst., 1965-68; asst. adminstr. Lake Forest (Ill.) Hosp., 1968-71, adminstr., 1971-73, pres., 1973-86; exec. v.p Voluntary Hosps. Am., Park Ridge, Ill., 1987-89, sr. v.p., 1986-92; CEO Good Samaritan Regional Med. Ctr., Phoenix, 1992—. Adj. prof. Contbr. articles to profl. jours. Mem. AHA (svc. com.), Ill. Hosp. Assn. (chair 1980-81). Home: 3930 E Rancho Dr Paradise Valley AZ 85253-5025 Office: Good Samaritan Regional Med Ctr 1111 E Mcdowell Rd Phoenix AZ 85006-2612

SEILS, WILLIAM GEORGE, lawyer; b. Chgo., Aug. 9, 1935; s. Harry H. and Hazel C. (Sullivan) S.; m. Evelyn E. Oliver, Sept. 8, 1956; children: Elizabeth Ann, Ellen Carol, Eileen Alison. AB, JD, U. Mich., 1959. Bar: Ill. bar 1959. Since practiced in, Chgo.; ptnr. Arvey, Hodes & Costello & Burman, 1968-87; gen. counsel, sec., sr. v.p. Richardson Electronics, Ltd., LaFox, Ill., 1986—. Contbr. articles to profl. jours.; asst. editor: Mich. Law Rev, 1958-59. Mem. Ill. Bar Assn., Order of Coif. Office: Richardson Electronics Ltd PO Box 393 40w267 Keslinger Rd Lafox IL 60147-0393 E-mail: wgs@rell.com.

SEINFELD, JERRY, comedian, actor, television producer, scriptwriter; b. Bklyn., Apr. 29, 1954; s. Kalman and Betty S.; m. Jessica Sklar, Dec. 25, 1999; children: Sascha, Julian. Grad. with degree in theatre communications, Queens (N.Y.) Coll., 1976. Former salesman. Stand-up comedian, 1976—; joke-writer (TV series) Benson, ABC, 1980; actor, co-writer, prod. (TV series) Seinfeld, NBC-TV, 1990-97 (Emmy award Outstanding Comedy Series, 1993, Emmy nomination, Lead Actor - Comedy Series, 1994, Golden Globe winner, 1994, best actor comedy series), (TV movie) The Ratings Game, 1984, I'm Telling You for the Last Time, 1999; (TV specials) The Tommy Chong Roast, 1986, The Seinfeld Chronicles, 1989; (film) Comedian (also exec. prodr.), 2002; writer Jerry Seinfeld-Stand-Up Confidential, 1987; author: Sein Language, 1993; guest appearances The Larry Sanders Show, 1992, News Radio, 1995. Recipient Am. Comedy award funniest male comedy stand-up, 1988, funniest actor in a TV series, 1992, 93; Screen Actors Guild award, Outstanding Performance by an Ensemble in a Comedy Series, 1994, 96, 97; People's Choice award, Favorite TV Comedy Series, 1998. Jewish. Avocations: zen, yoga.

SEINFELD, JOHN HERSH, chemical engineering educator; b. Elmira, N.Y., Aug. 3, 1942; s. Ben B. and Minna (Johnson) S. BS, U. Rochester, 1964; PhD, Princeton U., 1967; DSc honoris causa, U. Patras, Greece, 2002, Carnegie Mellon U., 2002. Asst. prof. chem. engring. Calif. Inst. Tech., Pasadena, 1967-70, assoc. prof., 1970-74, prof., 1974—, Louis E. Nohl prof., 1980—, exec. officer for chem. engring., 1973-90, chmn. engring. and applied sci. div., 1990-2000. Allan P. Colburn meml. lectr. U. Del., 1976; Camille and Henry Dreyfus Found. lectr. MIT, 1979; mem. coun. Gordon Rsch. Confs., 1980-83; Donald L. Katz lectr. U. Mich., 1981; Reilly lectr. U. Notre Dame, 1983; Dean's Disting. lectr. U. Rochester, 1985; Katz lectr. CUNY, 1985; McCabe lectr. N.C. State U., 1986; Lewis lectr. MIT, 1986; Union Carbide lectr. SUNY, Buffalo; Van Winkle lectr. U. Tex., 1988; Bicentennial lectr. La. State U., 1988; Ida Beam lectr. U. Iowa, 1989, David Mason lectr. Stanford U., 1989; Julian Smith lectr. Cornell U., 1990; Merck lectr. Rutgers U., 1991; Henske Disting. lectr. Yale U., 1991; lectr. AIChE, 1980; Centennial lectr. U. Pa., 1993; Miles Disting. lectr. U. Pitts., 1994; Kelly lectr. Purdue U., 1996; Disting. rsch. lectr. Carnegie Mellon U., 1998; Berkeley lectr. U. Calif., Berkeley, 1998; Sigma Xi lectr., 1998—, Merck Sharp & Dohme lectr. U. P.R., 1998; Hess lectr. U. Va., 1998; inaugural disting. lectr. U. Toledo, 1999; Priestley lectr. Commonwealth Scientific and Indsl. Rsch. Orgn., 2000; Amundson lectr. U. Houston, 2002, Hottel lectr. MIT, 2002, Lowrie lectr. Ohio State U. Author: Numerical Solution of Ordinary Differential Equations, 1971, Mathematical Methods in Chemical Engineering, Vol. III, Process Modeling, Estimation and Identification, 1974, Air Pollution: Physical and Chemical Fundamentals, 1975, Lectures in Atmospheric Chemistry, 1980, Atmospheric Chemistry and Physics of Air Pollution, 1986, Fundamentals of Air Pollution Engineering, 1988, Distributed Parameter Systems--Theory and Applications, 1989, Atmospheric Chemistry and Physics, 1998; assoc. editor Environ. Sci., Tech., 1981-97; mem. editorial bd. Computers, Chem. Engring, 1974-96, Jour. Colloid and Interface Sci, 1978-95, Advances in Chem. Engring, 1980-03, Revs. in Chem. Engring, 1980—, Aerosol Sci. and Tech., 1981-93; assoc. editor: Atmospheric Environment, 1976—. Recipient Donald P. Eckman award Am. Automatic Control Coun., 1970, Pub. Svc. medal NASA, 1980, Disting. Alumnus award U. Rochester, 1989, Nev. medal Desert Rsch. Inst., 2001, Haagen-Smit Clean Air award Calif. Air Resources Bd., 2003; Camille and Henry Dreyfus Found. Tchr. Scholar grantee, 1972. Fellow AIChE (bd. dirs. 1988-91, mem. editl. bd. jours. 1985—, Allan P. Colburn award 1976, William H. Walker award 1986, Warren K. Lewis award 2000), NAE, AAAS, Japan Soc. Promotion Sci., Am. Geophysical Union; mem. Am. Soc. Engring. Edn. (Curtis W. McGraw Rsch. award 1976, George Westinghouse award 1987), Assn. Aerosol Rsch. (bd. dirs. 1983—, v.p. 1988-90, pres. 1990-92), Am. Acad. Arts and Scis., Am. Chem. Soc. (Svc. through Chemistry award 1988, Creative Advances in Environ. Sci. and Tech. award 1993), Internat. Aerosol Rsch. Assembly (Fuchs award 1998), Sigma Xi, Tau Beta Pi. Home: 4409 Beulah Dr La Canada CA 91011 Office: Calif Inst Tech Divsn Engring Applied Sci 210-41 Pasadena CA 91125-0001 E-mail: seinfeld@caltech.edu.

SEIP, TERRY LEE, history professor; b. Pawnee City, Nebr., Oct. 26, 1944; s. Leslie Grant and Mildred Marie Seip; m. Patricia Sejkora, June 18, 1966; children: Jeremy Grant, Brandon Ray, Ginger Suzanne Seip-Nuno. BA, Kans. State U., 1967; MA, La. State U., 1970, PhD, 1974. Assoc. prof. history U. of So. Calif., LA, 1974—. Author: (scholarly history) The South Returns to Congress: Men, Economic Measures, and Intersectional Relationships, 1868-1879, 1983, (booklet on pedagogy) We Shall Gladly Teach: Preparing History Graduate Students for the Classroom, 1999. Recipient Grant-in-Aid for Basic Rsch., Am. Philos. Soc., 1983. Mem.: So. Hist. Assn., Orgn. of Am. Historians, Am. Hist. Assn. (Nancy Lyman Roelker Mentorship award for undergraduate tchg. 1997). Home: 1538 N Harding Ave Pasadena CA 91104 Office: Univ So Calif Univ Park Los Angeles CA 90089-0034 E-mail: tseip@usc.edu.

SEIPLE, JOHN W., JR., corporate financial executive; b. July 20, 1958; married; 3 children. BA in Econs., Davidson Coll.; MBA, Tex. Christian U. With Interfirst Bank Dallas, N.A.; ptnr., sr. v.p. Trammell Crow Co.; v.p., market officer Prologis, Houston, 1993—94, sr. v.p., regional dir., 1994—97, mng. dir. S.E. region, 1997—99, COO, 1999, pres., chief investment officer N.Am., 2004—, chair N.Am. mgmt. com., chair N.Am. investment com., mem. Office of the Chmn. Office: Prologis 14100 E 35th Pl Denver CO 80011*

SEITELMAN, MARK ELIAS, lawyer; b. N.Y.C., Apr. 14, 1955; s. Leo Henry and Pearl (Elias) S. BA, Bklyn. Coll., 1976; JD, Bklyn. Law Sch., 1979. Bar: N.Y. 1980, U.S. Dist. Ct. (ea., so., and we. dists.) N.Y. 1980, U.S. Supreme Ct. 1995, U.S. Ct. Mil. Appeals, 1995. Law asst. Criminal Ct., Bklyn., 1979; law clk. to Hon. Justice Aaron D. Bernstein N.Y. Supreme Ct., Bklyn., 1980; assoc. Lester, Schwab, Katz & Dwyer, N.Y.C., 1981-87, Weg and Myers, 1987-88, Kroll & Tract, 1988-90; pvt. practice N.Y.C., 1990—. Appeared on WABC TV Eyewitness News; interviewed by N.Y. Daily News, N.Y. Newsday, N.Y. Law Jour., Crain's NY Bus. Mem. ABA, ATLA (sustaining mem. motor vehicle and small practice sect.), N.Y. State Bar Assn., N.Y. County Bar Assn. (ins. and supreme ct. coms.), N.Y. State Trial Lawyers Assn. (sustaining mem., bd. dirs., mem. spkrs. bur., conv. com., legis. com., contbg. editor Trial Lawyers Quar.), N.Y. State Trial Lawyers Inst. (CLE program chmn., lectr.), Bklyn. Bar Assn. (legis. com., employment law com.), Millon Dollar Advocats Forum. Office: 111 Broadway 9th Fl New York NY 10006 Office Phone: 212-962-2626. Personal E-mail: mail@seitelman.com.

SEITMAN, JOHN MICHAEL, arbitrator, mediator, lawyer; b. Bloomington, Ill., Feb. 9, 1942; BS, U. Ill., 1964, JD, 1966. Bar: Calif., U.S. Dist. Ct. (so., ctrl., no. and ea. dists.) Calif., U.S. Ct. Appeals (9th cir.). Prin. Lindley, Lazar & Scales, San Diego, 1966-97; full-time neutral affiliated with JAMS, 1997—. Lectr. in continuing legal edn. Bd. dirs. San Diego County Bar Found., 1983-89, treas., 1983-84, pres., 1988-89; del. to 9th Cir. Jud. Conf., 1986, 88. Fellow Am. Bar Found.; mem. ABA, State Bar Calif. (pres. 1991-92), San Diego County Bar Assn. (pres. 1986). Office: PO Box 2156 Del Mar CA 92014-1456 Office Phone: 858-793-4555. Personal E-mail: jseitman@pacbell.net.

SEITZ, CHARLES LEWIS, computer scientist and engineer; b. Phila., Jan. 1, 1943; s. Philip Franz Durham and Elaine Marie (Good) S.; m. Jean Marie Austin, July 5, 1963 (div. 1981); children: Elizabeth, Russell. BSE, MIT, 1965, MS, 1967, PhD, 1971. Asst. prof. computer sci. U. Utah, Salt Lake City, 1970-72; cons. Burroughs Corp., LaJolla, Calif., 1971-78; prof. computer sci. Calif. Inst. Tech., Pasadena, Calif., 1977-94; pres. Myricom, Inc., Arcadia, Calif., 1994—. Cons. Strategic Def. Initiative Orgn., Washington, 1985-87; panelist U.S. Congress Office Tech. Assessment, Washington, 1986-87; mem. Computer Sci. and Telecomms. Bd., NRC, 1992—. Contbr. articles to profl. jours; patentee in field. Recipient Goodwin medal MIT, 1968, Leonard G. Abraham award IEEE, 1971, Cert. Appreciation, City Oceanside, Calif., 1984. Mem. NAE, Assn. Computing Machinery, Sigma Xi. Avocation: hiking. Office: Myricom Inc 325 N Santa Anita Ave Arcadia CA 91006-2870

SEITZ, FREDERICK, former university administrator; b. San Francisco, July 4, 1911; s. Frederick and Emily Charlotte (Hofman) S.; m. Elizabeth K. Marshall, May 18, 1935. AB, Leland Stanford Jr. U., 1932; PhD, Princeton U., 1934; Doctorate Hon. Causa, U. Ghent, 1957; DSc (hon.), U. Reading, 1960, Rensselaer Poly. Inst., 1961, Marquette U., 1963, Carnegie Inst. Tech., 1963, Case Inst. Tech., 1964, Princeton U., 1964, Northwestern U., 1965, U. Del., 1966, Poly. Inst. Bklyn., 1967, U. Mich., 1967, U. Utah, 1968, Brown U., 1968, Duquesne U., 1968, St. Louis U., 1969, Nebr. Wesleyan U., 1970, U. Ill., 1972, Rockefeller U., 1981; LLD (hon.), Lehigh U., 1966, U. Notre Dame, 1962, Mich. State U., 1965, Ill. Inst. Tech., 1968, N.Y. U., 1969; LHD (hon.), Davis and Elkins Coll., 1970, Rockefeller U., 1981, U. Pa., 1985, U. Miami, 1989. Instr. physics U. Rochester, 1935-36, asst. prof., 1936-37; physicist research labs. Gen. Electric Co., 1937-39; asst. prof. Randal Morgan Lab. Physics, U. Pa., 1939-41, assoc. prof., 1941-42; prof. physics, head dept. Carnegie Inst. Tech., Pitts., 1942-49; prof. physics U. Ill., 1949-57, head dept., 1957-64, dir. control systems lab., 1951-52, dean Grad. Coll., v.p. research, 1964-65; exec. pres. Nat. Acad. Scis., 1962-69; pres. Rockefeller U., N.Y.C., 1968-78; dir. Richard Lounsbery Found., N.Y.C., 1980—, pres., 1995—2002, U. Miami (Fla.), 1989. Trustee Ogden Corp., 1977—; dir. tng. program Clinton Labs., Oak Ridge, 1946-47; chmn. Naval Rsch. Adv. Com., 1960-62; vice chmn. Def. Sci. Bd., 1961-62, chmn., 1964-68; sci. adviser NATO, 1959-60; mem. nat. adv. com. Marine Biomed. Inst. U. Tex., Galveston, 1975-77; mem. adv. group White House Conf. Anticipated Advances in Sci. and Tech., 1975-76; mem. adv. bd. Desert Rsch. Inst., 1975-79, Ctr. Strategic and Internat. Studies, 1975-81; mem. Nat. Cancer Adv. Bd., 1976-82; dir. Akzona Inc. Author: Modern Theory of Solids, 1940, The Physics of Metals, 1943, Solid State Physics, 1955, The Science Matrix, 1992, On the Frontier: My Life in Science, 1994, Stalin's Captive: Nikolaus Riehl and the Soviet Race for the Bomb, 1995, Electronic Genie: The Tangled History of Silicon. Trustee Rockefeller Found., 1964-77, Princeton U., 1968-72, Lehigh U., 1970-81, Rsch. Corp., 1966-82, Inst. Internat. Edn., 1971-78, Woodrow Wilson Nat. Fellowship Found., 1972-82, Univ. Corp. Atmospheric Rsch., Am. Mus. Natural History, 1975—; trustee John Simon Guggenheim Meml. Found., 1973-83, chmn. bd., 1976-83; mem. Belgian Am. Edn. Found. Decorated Order of the Brilliant Star (Republic of China); recipient Franklin medal Franklin Inst. Phila., 1965, Hoover medal Stanford U., 1968, Nat. Medal Sci., 1973, James Madison award Princeton U., 1978, Edward R. Loveland Meml. award ACP, 1983, Vannevar Bush award Nat. Sci. Bd., 1983, J. Herbert Holloman award Acta Metallurgica, 1993, Von Hippel award Materials Rsch. Soc., 1993, Joseph Henry medal Smithsonian Instn., 1997. Fellow Am. Phys. Soc. (pres. 1961); mem. NAS, Am. Acad. Arts and Scis., AIME, Am. Philos. Soc., Am. Inst. Physics (chmn. governing bd. 1954-59),

Inst. for Def. Analysis, Finnish Acad. Sci. and Letters (fgn. mem.), Phi Beta Kappa Assos.; mem. GM Adv. Council, Cancer Rsch. Found. Address: Rockefeller U 1230 York Ave New York NY 10021-6307

SEITZ, JAMES EUGENE, retired college president, freelance writer; b. Columbia, Pa., July 27, 1927; s. Joseph Stoner and Minnie (Frey) S.; m. Florence Arlene Dutcher, Apr. 6, 1950; children: Diane Louise, Ellen Kay, Linda Marie, Karl Steven. BS, Millersville State Coll., 1950; MEd, Pa. State U., 1952; PhD, So. Ill. U., 1971. Tchr. pub. schs., Pa., 1950-56; lectr. Temple U., Phila., 1956-62; asst. prof. engr. tech. Kans. State U., Pitts., 1962-65; dean Mineral Area Coll., Flat River, Mo., 1965-69, Coll. of Lake County, Grayslake, Ill., 1969-73; founding pres. Edison State Community Coll., Piqua, Ohio, 1973-85; freelance writer Sidney, Ohio, 1985—. Founding sec.-treas. Ohio Tech. and C.C. Assn., Columbus, 1976; speaker in field. Author: Woodcarving: A Designer's Notebook, 1989, Country Creations, 1991, Selling What You Make, 1992, Effective Board Participation, 1993, Substance for the Soul, 1999, Practical Woodcarving Design and Application, 2003; contbr. articles to profl. jours. Founding pres. Exch. Club Grayslake, 1970; pres. Epicurian Soc., Sidney, Ohio, 1978-79; mediator Mcpl. Ct., Sidney, 1992-2003; sr. citizens' steering com. Arbor Day Found.; founding pres. Sr. Ctr. of Sidney-Shelby Co., 1996—, choir, 2001—; trustee Sidney Meml. Bldg., 2003-; named Outstanding Sr. Citizen, 2001. Recipient Leadership and Svc. award, Pa. State U. Alumni Soc., 1990. Mem. Am. Assn. Ret. Persons (founding chpt. pres. 1990-91), Assn. for Career & Tech. Edn., VFW (charter Post 8757), Am. Legion (scholarship com. and judge Post 217 1996-97, exec. com. 1997—, publicity dir. 1998-2000), Sidney Singing Soldiers, 1996— (pres., 1998), Shelby Woodcarvers Guild (founding pres. 1999), Iota Lambda Sigma. Avocations: woodworking, lecturing. Home: 55 Brown Rd Sidney OH 45365-8949 E-mail: jseitz@voyager.net.

SEITZ, KARL RAYMOND, editor; b. Corpus Christi, Tex., Sept. 26, 1943; s. Kerlin McCullough and Martha Elisabeth (Tillman) S.; m. Patricia Jean Floyd, June 13, 1970; 1 child, Lee Kerlin. BA, Birmingham So. Coll., 1970. Copy editor Birmingham (Ala.) Post-Herald, 1967-70, asst. news editor, 1970-73, chief editorial writer, 1973-78, editor editorial page, 1978—. Dir. Birmingham Post-Birmingham Typographical Union Pension Plan, 1983-90, chmn., 1986-90; dir. Goodfellow Fund, Inc., Birmingham, 1983—, v.p., 1986—. Active exec. in residence Birmingham So. Coll., 1987. Leadership Birmingham, 1986—, mem. mem.'s coun., 1998—2001. With USN, 1961—64. Mem. Am. Acad. Polit. and Social Sci., Nat. Conf. Editorial Writers, Acad. Polit. Sci. Home: 1212 30th Street S Birmingham AL 35205-1910 Office: Birmingham Post Herald PO Box 2553 Birmingham AL 35202-2553 Office Phone: 205-325-2488. E-mail: kseitz@postherald.com.

SEITZ, MARY LEE, mathematics professor; BS in Edn. summa cum laude, SUNY, Buffalo, 1977, MS in Edn., 1982. Cert. secondary tchr., N.Y. Prof. math. Erie C.C.-City Campus, Buffalo, 1982—. Reviewer profl. jours. and coll. textbooks. Mem. NY Maths. Assn. Two Yr. Colls., Assn. Maths. Tchrs. NY, NY Assn. Two Yr. Colls., Inc., Pi Mu Epsilon. Avocations: gardening, photography, bird watching. Office: Erie C C-City Campus 121 Ellicott St Buffalo NY 14203-2601 E-mail: seitzm@ecc.edu. *Consider the words of Peter Marshall, U.S. Senate chaplain, who said, "Give to us clear vision that we may know where to stand and what to stand for— because unless we stand for something, we shall fall for anything.".*

SEITZ, NICHOLAS JOSEPH, magazine editor, journalist; b. Topeka, Kans., Jan. 30, 1939; s. Frank Joseph and Lydia Natalie (Clerico) S.; m. Velma Jean Pfannenstiel, Sept. 12, 1959; children: Bradley Joseph, Gregory Joseph. BA, U. Okla., 1966. Sports editor Manhattan (Kans.) Mercury, 1960-62, Norman (Okla.) Transcript, 1962-64, Okla. Jour., Oklahoma City, 1964-67; staff Golf Digest mag., Norwalk, Conn., 1967—, editor, 1973-82; editorial dir. Golf Digest and Tennis, 1982-90; editorial dir. Sports/Leisure divsn. N.Y. Times Co. Mag. Group, 1991-92, sr. v.p., editor in chief, 1992-98, editor at large, 1999—. Syndicated golf instrn. and commentary CBS Radio Network; commentary ESPN TV Network. Author: Superstars of Golf, 1978; (with Dave Hill) Teed Off, 1977; (with Tom Watson) Getting Up and Down, 1983, Getting Back to Basics, 1991, Tom Watson's Strategic Golf, 1993; contbr. articles to profl. jours.; anthologized in: Best Sports Stories. Named Okla. Sports Writer of Year Nat. Sportswriters and Sportscasters Assn., 1965; winner contests Nat. Basketball Writers Assn.; winner contests Golf Writers Assn.; recipient Lincoln A. Werden award for outstanding contbn. to golf journalism, 1993, Meml. Tournament Golf Journalism award, 2000, PGA Lifetime Achievement in Journalism award, 2002. Home: 36 Hunt St Norwalk CT 06853-1015 Office: 20 Westport Rd Wilton CT 06897-0850 Office Phone: 203-761-5239. Personal E-mail: nseitz@optonline.net.

SEITZ, PATRICIA ANN, federal judge; b. Washington, Sept. 2, 1946; d. Richard J. and Bettie Seitz; m. Alan Graham Greer, Aug. 14, 1981. BA in History cum laude, Kans. State U., 1968; JD, Georgetown U., 1973. Bar: Fla. 1973, D.C. 1975, U.S. Dist. Ct. (no., mid., so. dists., trial bar) Fla., U.S. Ct. Appeals (5th and 11th cirs.), U.S. Supreme Ct. Reporter Dallas Times Herald, Washington, 1970-73; law clk. to Hon. Charles R. Richey U.S. Dist. Ct., Washington, 1973-74; assoc. Steel, Hector & Davis, Miami, Fla., 1974-79, ptnr., 1980-96; dir. office legal counsel Office of Nat. Drug Control Policy, Exec. Office of Pres., Washington, 1996-97; judge U.S. Dist. Ct. (so. dist.) Fla., 1998—. Adj. faculty U. Miami Law Sch., Coral Gables, Fla., 1984-88; faculty Nat. Inst. Trial Advocacy, Boulder, Colo., 1982, 83, 95, Chapel Hill, N.C., 1984, 87, Fla. region, 1989; lectr. in field. Contbr. numerous articles to law jours. Mem. Dade Munroe Mental Health Bd., Miami, 1982-84, United Way of Greater Miami comty. devel. com., 1984-87; chmn. family abuse task force United Way of Greater Miami, 1986; chmn. devel. com. Miami City Ballet, 1986-87, bd. dirs., 1986-90. Fellow Am. Bar Found., Am. Bd. Trial Advocacy, Internat. Soc. Barristers; mem. ABA (chmn. various coms. 1979-85, Ho. Dels. 1992-96), Am. Arbitration Assn. (nat. bd. dirs. 1995-97, complex case panel arbitrator), The Fla. Bar (bd. govs. young lawyer divsn. 1981-82, bd. govs. 1986-92, pres. 1993-94, bd. cert. civil trial), Fla. Assn. Women Lawyers, Dade County Bar Assn. (pub. interest law bank). Roman Catholic. Avocations: travel, art. Office: Fed Courthouse Square 301 N Miami Ave Fl 5 Miami FL 33128-7702

SEITZ, VICTORIA ANN, marketing educator; b. Rio de Janeiro, Aug. 7, 1956; (parents Am. citizens); d. Richard Joseph and Betty Jean (Merrill) S.; m. James Milton Smallwood, Jan. 5, 1985 (div. Aug. 1987); m. Stephen P. Wilson, Aug. 29, 1992 (div. Nov. 2000). BS in Apparel Design, Kans. State U., 1978; MS in Apparel Merchandising, Okla. State U., 1984, PhD in Apparel Merchandising, 1987. Fashion coord. Burdines Dept. Stores, Miami, Fla., 1978-80; asst. dept. mgr. Saks Fifth Avenue, Ariz., 1980-81, dept. mgr., 1981-82; grad. teaching asst. clothing, textiles and mdse. dept. Okla. State U., Stillwater, 1983-85, grad. teaching and rsch. assoc., 1986-87; asst. prof. U. North Tex. Sch. Human Resource Mgmt., Denton, 1988-91; prof. dept. mktg. Calif. State U., San Bernardino, 1991—. Asst. fashion designer, cons. Fred Baggs Inc., Miami, 1978-85; panel moderator, participant, presenter numerous confs. and convs.; cons. on image direct mktg., advt., pub. rels. and merchandising, various cos. Author: Power Dressing, 1991, Your Executive Image, 1992, 2000; syndicated fashion columnist, 1985-89; columnist Beauty-Walk.com, 2001--; contbr. articles to profl. jours. Recipient numerous grants and awards; fellow Eleanor Radell Sole Acad.; scholar Fulbright, Romania, 2002—03. Mem.: Direct Selling Ednl. Found. (bd. dirs. 1999—2002), Inland Empire Ad Club (pres., bd. dirs.), Direct Mktg. Assn. North Tex. (bd. dirs. 1988—91). Republican. Roman Catholic. Avocations: travel, exercise. Office: Calif State U Dept Mktg 5500 University Pkwy San Bernardino CA 92407-2318

SEITZ, VIRGINIA A. lawyer; BA summa cum laude, Duke U., 1978; MA, Oxford (Eng.) U., 1980; JD, SUNY. Bar: Pa. 1985, D.C. 1986. Jud. law clk. to Hon. Harry T. Edwards, U.S. Ct. Appeals for D.C. Circuit, Washington, 1985-86; jud. law clk. to Hon. William J. Brennan, Jr. U.S. Supreme Ct., Washington, 1986-87; ptnr. Sidley & Austin, Washington. Bd. dirs. Congl. Office Complaince, Washington. Rhodes scholar, 1979-80. Mem. Phi Beta Kappa. Office: Sidley & Austin 1722 E St NW Washington DC 20006 Fax: 202-736-8711. E-mail: vseitz@sidley.com.

SEITZ, WALTER STANLEY, cardiovascular research consultant; b. L.A., May 10, 1937; s. Walter and Frances Janette (Schleef) S. BS in Physics and Math., U. Calif., Berkeley, 1959; PhD in Biophysics, U. Vienna, 1981, MD, 1982. Health physicist U. Calif. Radiation Lab., 1959-61; rsch. assoc. NIH at Pacific Union Coll., 1961-63; physicist Lockheed Rsch. Labs., Palo Alto, Calif., 1961-63; staff scientist Xerox Corp., Pasadena, Calif., 1963-66; sr. scientist Applied Physics Cons., Palo Alto, 1966-75; instr. clin. sci. U. Ill Coll. Medicine, Urbana, 1983-84; cons. cardiology Cardiovascular Rsch. Inst. U. Calif. Sch. Medicine, San Francisco, 1987—; sr. scientist Inst. Med. Analysis and Rsch., Berkeley, 1987—. Contbr. articles to profl. jours. Postdoctoral Rsch. fellow, U. Calif. San Francisco, 1984. Fellow Am. Coll. Angiography; mem. AAAS, Royal Soc. Medicine London, N.Y. Acad. Scis., Physicians for Social Responsibility. Avocations: reading, music, hiking. Office: IMAR Cons Inc 38 Panoramic Way Berkeley CA 94704-1828 Office Phone: 510-843-7192. Business E-Mail: imar@transbay.net.

SEIVERS, LANA C. commissioner of education; b. Clinton, Tenn, 1951; BEd, Middle Tenn. State U.; MA in Ednl. Adminstrn., D in Ednl. Leadership, U. Tenn. Speech pathologist Spl Edn. Oak Ridge Sch. System, Tenn.; adminstr. early childhood and edn programs Oak Ridge Sch. System, prin. Linden Elem. Sch.; supt. Clinton City Schs., Tenn., 1989—2003; commr. Tenn. Dept. Edn., Nashville, 2003—. Design cons. Inst. Sch. Leaders; mem. adv. coun. Edn of Childen with Disabilities. Mem.: Assn. Ind. and Mcpl. Schs. (bd. dirs.), Tenn. Orgn. Sch. Supts. (treas.), E. Tenn. Supts. Stidy Coun. (chair), So. Assn. Colls. and Schs. (chair). Office: Tenn Dept Edn 6th Fl Andrew Johnson Twr 710 James Robertson Pkwy Nashville TN 37243

SEIWALD, ROBERT J. retired inventor; b. Ft. Morgan, Colo., Mar. 26, 1925; BS in Chemistry, U. San Francisco; PhD in Organic Chemistry, St. Louis U., 1954. Prof. organic chemistry U. San Francisco, 1957-89; ret., 1989. Served in WWII. Inducted Nat. Inventors Hall of Fame, 1995. Achievements include invention of first patented antibody labeling agent. Office: Nat Inventors Hall of Fame 221 S Broadway St Akron OH 44308-1505*

SEJNOWSKI, TERRENCE JOSEPH, science educator; b. Cleve., Aug. 13, 1947; s. Joseph Francis and Theresa (Cudnik) S.; m. Beatrice Alexandra Golomb, Mar. 24, 1990. BS, Case Western Res. U., 1968; PhD, Princeton U., 1978. Rsch. fellow Harvard Med. Sch., Boston, 1979-82; prof. biophysics Johns Hopkins U., Balt., 1982-90; prof. Salk Inst. U. Calif. San Diego, La Jolla, 1988—, dir. computational neurobiology tng. program, 2004—. Investigator Howard Hughes Med. Inst., 1991—; bd. dirs. San Diego McDonnell-Pew Ctr. for Cognitive Neurosci., 1990-98, Inst. for Neural Computation, U. Calif. San Diego., 1990—. Editor-in-chief Neural Computation, 1989—; co-inventor: (with others) the Boltzmann machine and NET talk; mem. editl. bd. Sci. Mag., 1990—. Pres. Neural Info. Processing Sys. Found. Recipient Presdl. Young Investigator award NSF, 1984, Wright prize Harvey Mudd Coll., 1996; Sherman Fairchild Disting. scholar Calif. Inst. Tech., 1993. Fellow IEEE (Neural Network Pioneer award 2002; mem. Soc. for Neurosci., Am. Phys. Soc., Internat. Neural Network Soc. (governing bd. 1988-92, Hebb prize 1999), Am. Math. Soc., Assn. Rsch. in Vision and Ophthalmology, Am. Assn. Artificial Intelligence, Biophys. Soc., Optical Soc. Am., Am. Psychol. Soc., Am. Psychol. Assn., N.Y. Acad. Scis., Fedn. Am. Soc. Exptl. Biophysics, Soc. Neuroscience, Internat. Soc. Neuroethology, Soc. Math. Biology, Johns Hopkins U. Soc. of Scholars. Achievements include co-invention of the Boltzmann machine, of NETtalk, a neural network for text-to-speech. Office: Salk Inst PO Box 85800 San Diego CA 92186-5800 Office Phone: 858-453-4100. E-mail: sejnowski@salk.edu.

SEKANINA, ZDENEK, astronomer; b. Mlada Boleslav, Czechoslovakia, June 12, 1936; came to U.S., 1969; s. Frantisek Sekanina and Hedvika Sekaninova; m. Jana Soukupova, Apr. 1, 1966; 1 child, Jason. Diploma, Charles U., Prague, Czechoslovakia, 1959, PhD in Astronomy, 1963. Astronomer Stefanik Obs., Prague, 1959-66, Ctr. for Numerical Math., Charles U., Prague, 1967-68; vis. scientist Inst. d'Astrophysique, Univ. de Liege, Cointe-Ougree, Belgium, 1968-69; physicist Smithsonian Astrophys. Obs., Cambridge, Mass., 1969-80; mem. tech. staff Jet Propulsion Lab., Pasadena, Calif., 1980-81, rsch. scientist, 1981-84, sr. rsch. scientist, 1984—. Assoc. Harvard Coll. Obs., Cambridge, 1969-80; mem. NASA Comet Sci. Working Group, 1977-80; cons. Jet Propulsion Lab., 1977-80; prin. U.S. co-investigator Particulate Impact Analyzer Experiment, Dust Impact Detector Sys. Experiment, European Space Agy.'s Giotto Mission to Comet Halley, 1980-89; mem. NASA-European Spacy Agy. Comet Halley Environ. Working Group, 1980-89; discipline specialist Near Nucleus Studies Network, Internat. Halley Watch, 1982-90; mem. imaging sci. subsys. team Comet Rendezvous Asteroid Flyby Mission, 1986-92; mem. sci. definition team ESA/NASA Comet Nucleus Sample Return Mission, 1988—; co-investigator STARDUST Discovery Mission, 1994—. Editor Comet Halley Archive, 1982-91; mem. editorial bd. Kosmicke Rozhledy, 1963-69. Recipient Exceptional Sci. Achievement medal NASA, 1985; minor planet named Sekanina, 1976. Mem. Internat. Astron. Union (mem. commns. 15, 20, 22, mem. organizing commn. 22 1976-82, organizing commn. 15 1979-85, mem. working group on comets 1988—, assoc. dir. Ctrl. Bur. for Astron. Telegrams 1970-80), COSPAR (working group 3, panel C, exec. mem. 1980-82), Learned Soc of Czech Republic (hon. 1996—), Czech Astron. Soc. (hon. 2001-). Roman Catholic. Office: Jet Propulsion Lab 4800 Oak Grove Dr Pasadena CA 91109-8001 E-mail: zs@sek.jpl.nasa.gov.

SEKERKA, ROBERT FLOYD, physics educator, scientist; b. Wilkinsburg, Pa., Nov. 27, 1937; s. John Jacob and Vivian Mae (Smith) S.; m. Dianne Thompson, Apr. 30, 1960 (div. Apr. 1981); children: Lee Ann, Robert Thompson; m. 2d Carolyn Lee Confer, May 24, 1981. BS in Physics, U. Pitts., 1960; AM, Harvard U., 1961, PhD, 1965; PhD (hon.), U. Timisora, Romania, 1996. Engr. Westinghouse Rsch. Labs., Pitts., 1965-68, mgr. materials growth and properties dept., 1968-69; lectr. Carnegie-Mellon U., Pitts., 1967-69, assoc. prof., 1969-72, prof. metallurgy and materials sci., 1972-82, dept. head, 1976-82, prof. physics and math., dean Mellon Coll. Sci., 1982-91, Univ. Prof., 1991—. Mem. space studies bd. NRC, 1989-91. Assoc. editor Jour. Crystal Growth, 1971-94; Metallurgical Trans., 1970-76; editorial bd. Applied Microgravity Tech., 1987-90. Past bd. dirs. Forbes Health Sys., Pitts., Pitts. Regional Ctr. for Sci. Tchrs.; past vice chmn. bd. dirs. NMR Inst.; past mem. rsch. com. Allegheny Singer Rsch. Inst., Pitts. Recipient A.G. Worthing award U. Pitts., 1959, Philip M. McKenna Meml. award, 1980, Bruce Chalmers award TMS, 1998; Woodrow Wilson fellow, 1960, NSF fellow, 1962-65. Fellow: Am. Phys. Soc., Am. Soc. Metals, Japanese Soc. for Promotion of Sci.; mem.: Internat. Orgn. Crystal Growth (pres. 2001, Frank prize 1992), Am. Assn. Crystal Growth (mem. exec. com.), Minerals Metals Materials Soc., Edgewood Country Club, Sigma Xi, Phi Beta Kappa, Omicron Delta Kappa. Home: 307 S Dithridge St Atrium 911 Pittsburgh PA 15213-3519 Office: Carnegie Mellon U Dept Physics 6416 Wean Hall Pittsburgh PA 15213-3890 Office Phone: 412-268-2362. Business E-Mail: sekerka@cmu.edu.

SEKHAR, JAINAGESH AKKARAJA, entrepreneur, educator; B in Tech., U. Ill., 1977, PhD, 1981. Prof. and dir. icm U. Cin., Cin., 1988—. Contbr. articles to profl. jours.;, author books in field. Pres. bd. dirs. Acad. Greater Cin. Recipient Entrepreneur of Yr. award, 2003, R&D 100 award, 2000, 2001, 2004; fellow, U. Cin., 2001. Fellow: ASM Internat. Achievements include patents for Over 60; patents in field. Office: U Cin 412 B Rhodes Cincinnati OH 45221-0012 Office Phone: 513-556-3105. E-mail: jainagesh.sekhar@uc.edu.

SEKIGUCHI, EUGENE, dentist, dental association executive; DDS in elec. engring., MS in elec. engring., U. So. Calif. Pvt. practice dentist, Monterey Park, Calif.; clinical prof., assoc. dean internat. profl. and legis. affairs U. So. Calif. Sch. Dentistry. Pres. ADA, 2003—04, former trustee; past. pres., interim exec. dir. Calif. Dental Assn.; past pres. San Gabriel Valley Dental Soc. Office: 823 S Atlantic Blvd Ste 1 Monterey Park CA 91754 Office Phone: 323-283-3662.

SEKLER-KATZ, RUDOLFINE, internist, psychiatrist; b. Cernowitz, Romania, Aug. 11, 1924; came to U.S., 1967; d. Aron and Anna Sekler; widowed. MD, U. West Timisoara, Romania, 1950. Resident St. John's Hosp., Queens, N.Y., Mt. Sinai Hosp./Elmhurst Divsn.; attending physician in internal medicine, psychiat. cons. N.Y.C., 1971—. Office: 96-08 70th Ave Forest Hills NY 11375-5823

SEKOWSKI, CYNTHIA JEAN, corporate executive, contact lens specialist; b. Chgo., Feb. 14, 1953; d. John L. and Celia L. (Matusiak) S. PhD in Health Svcs. Adminstrn., PhD in Health Scis., Columbia Pacific U., 1984; grad., Realtor Inst., 1998. Chief contact lens dept. Lieberman & Kraff, Chgo., 1974-87; pres., CEO Seko Eye Care, Inc., Chgo., 1988—; realtor Country Club Realty Group, Naples, Fla., 1995—2002, John R. Wood, Inc. Realtors, 2002—. Rschr., technologist U. Ill., Chgo., 1976-78. Mem. Chgo. Zool. Soc., 1984—. Little City Inner Circle, 1991—; sponsor Save the Children Orgn., 1983—; asst. to campaign mgr. Rep. state senatorial candidate, Chgo., 1972; pres. Compass Point Condo Assn., Naples, Fla., 1996-99; budget com. Windstar Country Club Master Homeowner's Assn., Naples, 1996-99. Fellow: Contact Lens Soc. Am.; mem.: Women's Coun. Realtors, Naples Area Bd. Realtors, Nat. Assn. Realtors, Fla. Assn. Realtors, Nat. Contact Lens Examiners, Better Vision Inst., Opticians Assn. Am., Ill. Soc. Opticianry, Soc. of the Little Flower, The Phoenix Soc. (med. profl.), Nat. Wildlife Fedn., S.W. Fla. Conservancy, Nat. Geog. Soc., U.S. Golf Assn., Columbia Pacific U. Alumnae Assn., Bear's Paw Country Club (mktg. com. 2002—), Vanderbilt Country Club (residents adv. bd. 1999—2001, vice-chmn. adminstrn. com. 2001—03). Roman Catholic. Avocations: gardening, reading, photography, poetry, golf. Office: John R Wood Inc Realtors 3255 Tamiami Trl N Naples FL 34103 Office Phone: 239-269-5000. E-mail: luvfla@mindspring.com.

SEKULER, ROBERT WILLIAM, psychologist, educator; b. Elizabeth, N.J., May 7, 1939; s. Sidney and Mary (Siegel) Sekuler; m. Susan Pamela Nemser, June 25, 1961; children: Stacia, Allison, Erica. AB, Brandeis U., 1960; MSc, Brown U., 1963, PhD, 1964; postgrad. (NIH postdoctoral fellow), MIT, 1964-65. Prof. psychology Northwestern U., Evanston, Ill., 1973-89, prof. ophthalmology Med. Sch., 1978-89, prof. neurobiology and physiology, 1982-89, John Evans prof. neuroscience, 1986-89, chmn. dept., 1975-79, assoc. dean Coll. Arts and Scis., 1985-89; v.p. Optronix, Inc., 1980-82; Louis and Frances Salvage prof. psychology Brandeis U., Waltham, Mass., 1989—, provost, dean faculty, 1989-91, dir. program cognitive scis., 1998—, chair program on neurosci., 2003—; mem. Ctr. Complex Sys., 1990—. Rsch. prof. biomed. engring. Boston U., 1992—, adj. prof. cognitive and neural sys., 1994—2001; vis. prof. psychology U. Toronto, 2000; cons. NWSF, NIH, AAAS, USAF, U. Calif., APA; chmn. vision com. NRC-NAS; chmn. working group on visual function and aging NRC, chmn. working group on aging workers and visual impairment; scientist Rotman Inst. Baycrest Geriatric Ctr., 2000. Author (with D. Kline and K. Dismukes): (book) Aging and Human Visual Function, 1981; author: Star Trek on the Brain, 1998, Star Trek on the Brain, paperback edit., 1999, Star Trek on the Brain, Japanese edit., 2000; author: (with R. Blake) Perception, 1985, Perception, Hungarian edit., 2000, Perception, 4th edit., 2001; editor: Perception & Psychophysics, 1971—86, Jour. Exptl. Psychology, 1973—74, Vision Rsch. Jour., 1974—79, 1980—92, Optics Letters, 1977—79, Am. Jour. Psychology, Ophthalmic and Physiol. Optics, 1986—99, Intelligent Sys., 1986—92, Psychology and Aging, 1987—92; co-author: Oxford Textbook of Geriatric Medicine, 1992, 1999, Ency. Psychology, 1999; contbr. articles to profl. jours. Grantee, Nat. inst. Neurol. Diseases and Stroke, USAF, NSF, Nat. Eye Inst., Nat. Inst. Aging, USN, James McDonnell Found., Alzheimer's Found. Fellow: AAAS, Am. Psychol. Soc., Optical Soc. Am.; mem.: Knowles Inst. for Hearing Rsch. (bd. dirs. 1988—90), Psychonomic Soc., Neurosci. Soc., Assn. Rsch. in Vision and Ophthalmology, Sigma Xi. Home: 64 Strawberry Hill Rd Concord MA 01742-5502 Office: Brandeis U Ctr for Complex Systems Waltham MA 02454

SEKULIC, DUSAN P. science educator, researcher; b. Novi Sad, Vojvodina, Former Yugoslav Federation, June 21, 1949; s. Petar and Djurdjinka Sekulic; m. Gorana Jesic, Dec. 17, 1949; children: Visnja, Aleksandar. B in Engring., U. Novi Sad, 1972, BS in Physics, 1976; MME, U. Belgrade, 1976, DSc, 1981. Cert. Profl. Mech. Engr., Yugoslavia, 1973. Prof. U. of Novi Sad, Yugoslavia, 1976—95; vis. rschr. Tech. U. Munich, 1977; vis. scholar Duke U., 1988—89; vis. scientist MIT, 1989; vis. prof. Marquette U., 1994—96; sr. rsch. scientist UK Ctr. for Mfg., Lexington, Ky., 1997—; adj. prof. U. Ky., 2002—. Contbr. articles to profl. jours. Grantee Materials Sci. and Advanced Mfg., NSF, 1999—2003, Heat Exch. and Boundary Layer Phenomena, KFA-Julich, Germany, 1989—91, Ky. Sci. and Engring. Found., 2003—04; Cryogenics Rsch. grant, Dept. of Energy, 1988—91, Sr. Fulbright scholar, 1988—89. Mem.: Yugoslav Soc. of Physicist, Mathematicians and Astronomers, Yugoslav Assn. of Engineers, Am. Welding Soc., Am. Soc. of Mech. Engring. Home: 1064 Albert Ln Lexington KY 40514 Office: University of Kentucky 210 CRMS Bldg Lexington KY 40506 Office Phone: 859-257-2972. Business E-Mail: sekulicd@engr.uky.edu.

SEKULOVICH, MALDEN See MALDEN, KARL

SELANNE, TEEMU, professional hockey player; b. Helsinki, Finland, July 3, 1970; Hockey player Winnipeg Jets, 1992—95, Phoenix Coyotes, 1995—97, Anaheim Mighty Ducks, 1997—2001, San Jose Sharks, 2001—. Player All-Star Game, 1993, 94, 96. Named Rookie of Yr., Sporting News, 1992—93; named to All rookie Team, 1992—93; recipient Calder Meml. Trophy, 1992—93. Office: San Jose Sharks HP Pavilion 525 West Santa Clara Street San Jose CA 95113

SELBERG, ATLE, retired mathematician; b. Langesund, Norway, June 14, 1917; came to U.S., 1947; D, U. Oslo, 1943; postgrad. Inst. Advanced Study, Princeton U., 1947-48, 49. Rsch. fellow U. Oslo, 1942-47; assoc. prof. math. Syracuse U., 1948-49; prof. Inst. Advanced Study, Princeton U., 1949-87, prof. emeritus, 1987—. Editor: (with others) Axel Thue's Selected Mathematical Papers, 1977; author: Reflections Around the Ramanujan Centenary, 1989, Number Theory, Trace Formulas & Discrete Groups, 1989, Collected Papers, 1991. Recipient Fields medal Internat. Congress Math., Harvard U., 1950, Wolf Prize, 1986. Mem. Norwegian Acad. Sci., Royal Danish Acad. Scis. and Letters, Am. Acad. Arts and Scis. Achievements include elementary proof of the prime number theorem, with a generalisation to primes in an arbitrary arithmetic progression. Office: Inst Advanced Studies Sch Math 1 Einstein Dr Princeton NJ 08540

SELBY, CECILY CANNAN, dean, educator, scientist; b. London, Feb. 4, 1927; d. Keith and Catherine Anne Cannan; m. Henry M. Selby, Aug. 11, 1951 (div. 1978); children: Norman, William, Russell; m. James Stacy Coles, Feb. 21, 1981. AB cum laude, Radcliffe Coll., 1946; PhD in Phys. Biology, MIT, 1950. Teaching asst. in biology MIT, 1948-49; adminstrv. head virus study sect. Sloan-Kettering Inst., N.Y.C., 1949-50, asst. mem. instr., 1950-55; instr. microscopic anatomy Cornell U. Med. Coll., 1955-57; tchr. sci. Lenox Sch., N.Y.C., 1957-58, headmistress, 1959-72; nat. exec. dir. Girl Scouts U.S.A., N.Y.C., 1972-75; adv. com. Simmons Coll. Grad. Mgmt. Program, 1977-78; mem. Com. Corp. Support of Pvt. Univs., 1977-83; spl. asst. acad. planning N.C. Sch. Sci. and Math., 1979-80, dean acad. affairs, 1980-81, chmn. bd. advisors, 1981-84. Cons. U.S. Dept. Commerce, 1976-77; dir. Avon Products Inc., RCA, NBC, Loehmanns Inc., Nat. Edn. Corp. pres. Am. Energy Ind., 1976; co-chmn. commn. pre-coll. math. and sci. Nat. Sci. Bd., 1982-83; adj. prof. NYU, 1984-86, prof. sci. edn., 1986-94; mem. policy steering com. Gov. Cuomo's Conf. on Sci. and Engring., 1989-90; affil. scholar Radcliffe Pub. Policy Ctr. of Harvard U., 2000-2001. Contbr. articles to profl. jours., chpt. to book. Founder, chmn. N.Y. Ind. Schs. Opportunity Project, 1968-72; mem. invitational workshops Aspen Inst., 1973, 75, 77, 79; trustee MIT, Bklyn. Law Sch., Radcliffe Coll., Woods Hole Oceanographic Instn., Women's Forum N.Y., N.Y. Hall of Sci., 1982—, vice chmn., 1989—, trustee Girls Inc., 1992—, Nat. Coun. Women in Medicine, 1990-94; mem. Yale U. Peabody Mus. Adv. Coun., 1981-89; co-chair program in sci., soc. and gender Radcliffe Inst. of Harvard U., 1999-2001. Named affiliated scholar, Harvard U., 2001; recipient Woman Scientist of Yr. award, N.Y. chpt. Am. Women in Sci., 1992, Alumnae Achievement award, Radcliffe Coll., 2001. Fellow Am. Women Sci., N.Y. Acad Scis.; mem. Century Assn. Club, Woods Hole Golf Club, Cosmo-

politan Club, The Explorers Club, Sigma Xi, Phi Delta Kappa. Home and Office: 1 E 66th St New York NY 10021-5854 also: 100 Ransom Rd Falmouth MA 02540-1652 E-mail: selbyc@aol.com.

SELBY, DIANE RAY MILLER, fraternal organization administrator; b. Lorain, Ohio, Oct. 11, 1940; d. Dale Edward and Mildred (Ray) Miller; m. David Baxter Selby, Apr. 14, 1962; children: Elizabeth, Susan, Sarah. BS in Edn., Ohio State U., 1962. Sec. Kappa Kappa Gamma Frat., Columbus, Ohio, 1962-63, editor, 1972-86; tchr. Hilliard (Ohio) High Sch., 1963-65; exec. dir. Mortar Bd., Inc. Nat. Office, Columbus, Ohio, 1986—. Editor The Key of Kappa Kappa Gamma Frat, 1972-86 (Student Life award, 1983, 84, 85). Founding officer Community Coordinating Bd., Worthington, Ohio, 1983; pres. PTA Coun., Worthington, 1984, Worthington Band Boosters, 1985; sec., treas. Sports and Recreation Facilities Bd., Worthington, 1986—; mem. sustaining com. Jr. League Columbus, 1991-93, docent Kelton House, 1979—. Mem. Mortar Bd., Inc., Twig 53 Children's Hosp. (assoc.), Assn. Coll. Honor Soc. (mem. exec. com. 1999-2001, 2003-04, 04—. chmn. bylaws com., trustee 2004—), Ladybugs and Buckeyes, Kappa Kappa Gamma (House Bd. v.p. 1997-2000). Republican. Lutheran. Home: 6750 Merwin Pl Columbus OH 43235-2838 Office: Mortar Bd Inc 1200 Chambers Rd Ste 201 Columbus OH 43212-1754 Office Phone: 614-488-4094. Business E-Mail: selby.1@osu.edu.

SELBY, FREDERICK PETER, investment banker; b. Mannheim, Germany, Mar. 31, 1938; s. Ernest and Margaret (Lassman) S.; m. Lillian E. Howard, Sept. 18, 1960; children: Christopher, Andrea, Stephanie. BS in Econ., U. Pa., 1960. Various positions Weyerhaeuser Timber Co., 1960—62; football coach William Penn Charter Sch., Phila., 1960—62; mktg. cons. Barrington Assocs., NYC, 1962—64; adviser Nepal Indsl. Devel. Corp. (U.S. Dept. State and AID), Kathmandu, 1962—. Mgmt. cons., 1963-65; v.p., dir. Reeves Broadcasting Corp., N.Y.C. 1965-67; dir., CEO Previews, Inc., 1966-67; mng. ptnr. Graham Loving & Co., mems. N.Y. Stock Exchange, N.Y.C., 1968-69; v.p. corp. fin. Burnham & Co., N.Y.C., 1969-70; dir. corp. fin. Wood, Walker & Co., N.Y.C., 1971-74; cons. corp. devel. Penn-Dixie Industries, N.Y.C.; cons. corp. fin. Bankers Trust Co. cons. to chmn. G & W Natural Resources Co., N.Y.C., 1974-79; pres., CEO H.C. Sleigh N.A., Inc. subs. H.C. Sleigh Ltd., Australia, 1980-84; sr. v.p., dir. corp. fin. Banque Arabe Internationale D'Investissement, N.Y.C., 1984-85; chmn., CEO Randy Internat. Air Freight, N.Y.C., 1986-87; chmn., mng. dir. Selby Capital Ptnrs., N.Y.C., 1987-99; bd. dirs. Gristede's Foods, Inc. (formerly Designcraft Corp.), 1987—, fin. advisor to chmn.; ltd. ptnr., mng. dir., Chart Group, N.Y.C., 2000-01. Co-author: Why, When and How to Go Public, Corporate Earnings, Cash or Cosmetics, Foreign Investment in the USA; contbr. articles to travel publs. Fellow Royal Geographical Soc., Explorers' Club (lectr., fin. com., specialist on Nepal and Himalayas); mem. N.Y. Soc. Security Analysts, Am. Alpine Club, Kappa Sigma. Home: 301 E 79th St Apt 29A New York NY 10021-0947

SELBY, JEROME M. mayor; b. Wheatland, Wyo., Sept. 4, 1948; s. John Franklin and Claudia Meredith (Hudson) S.; m. Gloria Jean Nelson, June 14, 1969; children: Tyan, Cameronn, Kalen. BS in Math., Coll. Idaho, 1969, MA in Edn. Adminstrn., 1974; MPA, Boise State U., 1978. Assoc. engr. Boeing Co., Seattle, 1969-71; dir. evaluation WICHE Mountain States Regional Med. Program, Boise, 1971-74; dir. rsch., evaluation Mountain States Health Corp., Boise, 1974-76, with health policy analysis and accountability, 1976-78; dir. health Kodiak (Alaska) Area Native Assn., 1978-83; mgr. Kodiak Island Borough, 1984-85, mayor, 1985-98, bus., mcpl. and fisheries cons., 1998—; regional dir. planning and devel. Providence Health System, 1998—2003. Propr. Kodiak Tax Svc., 1978—, Registered Guide, Kodiak, 1987—; cons. Nat. Cancer Inst., Washington, 1973-78, others. Contbr. articles to profl. jours. Treas. ARC, Kodiak, 1978-93, bd. dirs., 1978-95, chmn., 1989-90, mem. western ops. hdqrs. adv. bd., 1986-92, mem. group IV and V nat. adv. coj., 1986-89, nat. bd. govs., 1989-95, chmn. chpt. rels. com., 1994-95, mem. Alaska statewide chpt. bd. dirs., 2002—; pres. S.W. Alaska Mcpl. Conf., Anchorage, 1988-89, v.p., 1986-87, treas., 1996-98, bd. dirs., 1986-98; pres. Alaska Mcpl. League Investment Pool, Inc., 1992-98; v.p. Alaska Mcpl. League, 1988-90, pres., 1990-91, bd. dirs., 1988-98; bd. dirs. Alaska Mcpl. League Jt. Ins. Assn. Bd., 1995—, v.p., 1996-98, pres., 1998-2000; mem. Alaska Resource Devel. Coun., 1987-2001, exec. com., 1989-2000; bd. dirs. Alaska State C. of C., 2000—, exec. com., 2002-; mem. policy com. of outer continental shelf adv. bd. U.S. Dept. Interior, 1990—, vice chair, 1996-98, chair, 1998-2000; chmn. Natural Gas Subcom., 2000-01; co-chair Alaska Task Force, 1995—; mem. Com. on Oil Pollution Act, 1995; mem. Nat. Assn. Counties, Cmty. and Econ. Devel. Steering Com., 1990-98, Alaska govtl. roles task force, 1991-92; mem. Alaska state/local govt. task force, 1996-98; chmn. Kodiak Island Exxon Valdez Restoration Com., 1991-95; bd. dirs. Kodiak Health Care Found., 1992—, v.p. 1992—; co-chmn. Arctic Power, 1993—; bd. dirs. Western Interstate Region Nat. Assn. of Counties, 1993-98; bd. dirs. Alaska Oceans, Seas, Fisheries Rsch. Found., 1998—, pres., 1998—; mem. environment, energy and land use steering com. Nat. Assn. Counties., 1997-98; mem. grad. med. edn. com. Alaska Family Practice Residency, 2000-01; mem. Koniag Edn. Found., 2002-03; mem. Oiled Regions of Alaska, 2001—, pres., 2002—. Paul Harris fellow, 1987, 88, 91, 92, 96; recipient Outstanding Contbn. award Alaska Mcpl. League, 1994, Disting. Alumni award Albertson Coll. of Idaho, 1997, Lifetime Achievement award Alaska Mcpl. League, 1998. Mem. Alaska Conf. Mayors, Nat. Soc. Tax Profls., Acad. Polit. Sci., Alaska Mcpl. Mgrs. Assn., Kodiak C. of C. (dir. 1983-99), Rotary (bd. dirs. 1989-97, treas. 1989-93, v.p. 1993-94, pres.-elect 1994-95, pres. 1995-96). Office: Kodiak Tax Svc 1120 Baranof St Kodiak AK 99615 Office Phone: 907-486-4833. E-mail: jselby@ptialaska.net.

SELBY, LELAND CLAY, lawyer; b. Granite City, Ill., July 4, 1944; s. William Edward and Agnes (Newell) S.; m. Diane Schryver, Aug. 20, 1966; children: Leland Clay, Timothy Schryver, Amanda Elizabeth. BA, U. Richmond, 1966; LLB, U. Va., 1969. Bar: Conn. 1969, N.Y. 1989. Assoc. Hirschberg, Pettengill & Strong, Greenwich, Conn., 1969-74; ptnr. Hirschberg, Pettengill, Strong & Nagle, Greenwich, 1974-78, Whitman & Ransom, Greenwich, 1978-93, Whitman Breed Abbott & Morgan, Greenwich, 1993-95; mem. Fogarty Cohen Selby & Nemiroff LLC, Greenwich, 1995—. Bd. dirs., v.p. Stamford (Conn.) Ctr. for Arts, 1989—2003; chmn. adv. coun. Stanford Ctr. for Arts, 2003—; chmn. bd. govs. Greenwich Found. for Cmty. Gifts, 1980-90; pres. United Way of Greenwich, 1978-80; bd. dirs. Retirement Sys., Town of Greenwich, 1993-2001, Greenwich Symphony Orch., 1986-95; co-pres. Greenwich chpt. English-Speaking Union; bd. dirs. exec. com. English-Speaking Union U.S. Named Greenwich Young Man of Yr., Greenwich Jaycees, 1974. Fellow Am. Coll. Trust and Estate Counsel; mem. ABA, Conn. Bar Assn., N.Y. State Bar Assn., Greenwich Bar Assn., Preston Mountain Club (sec. 1999—), Riverside Yacht Club, Va. Club of N.Y.C., Harpoon Club of Greenwich. Episcopalian. Avocations: fly fishing, sporting clays, hiking, reading, travel. Home: 155 Field Point Rd Greenwich CT 06830 Office: Fogarty Cohen Selby & Nemiroff 88 Field Point Rd Greenwich CT 06836-2508

SELCER, DAVID MARK, lawyer; b. Cleve., Feb. 12, 1943; s. Lester and Sylvia (Esral) S.; m. Belinda Weine, Aug. 8, 1968 (div. 1986); children: Daniel, Anne, Emily; m. Susan Merwin, Mar. 22, 1993. BA, Northwestern U., 1965; JD, Ohio State U., 1968. Bar: Ohio, 1968, Ill. 1969, U.S. Dist. Ct. (so. dist.) Ohio 1971, U.S. Dist. Ct. (no. dist.) Ohio 1973. Ptnr. Porter, Wright, Morris & Arthur, Columbus, Ohio, 1973-78, Krupman, Fromson & Selcer, Columbus, 1979-81, Baker & Hostetler, Columbus, 1981—. Adj. prof. Capitol U. Law Sch., Columbus, 1973-74; bd. dirs. Consolidated Stores Corp., 1990-91. Trustee Temple Israel, Columbus, 1987-94; v.p. Jewish Family Svc., 1987-94. Recipient Disting. Service award Columbus Symphony Orch., 1986-87. Mem. ABA (equal employment opportunity subcom. of labor com 1978—), Nat. Labor Relations Bd (asst. bd. mem. 1967-68), Ohio Bar Assn., Columbus Bar Assn. Office: Baker & Hostetler 65 E State St Ste 2100 Columbus OH 43215-4260

SELDEN, ANNIE, mathematics professor; b. Torrington, Conn., Feb. 1, 1938; d. Adolf Laurer and Annie (Wopperer) Anderson; m. Herbert Lloyd Alexander Jr., Oct. 7, 1961 (div. July 1970); children: Neil Brooks, Kim Anne; m. John Selden, May 24, 1974. BA, Oberlin Coll., 1959; MA, Yale U., 1962; PhD, Clarkson U., 1974. Instr. SUNY, Potsdam, 1969-71; sr. lectr. Bayero U., Kano, Nigeria, 1978-85; asst. prof. Hampden Sydney (Va.) Coll., 1973-74, Bosphorus U., Istanbul, Turkey, 1974-78, Tenn. Technol. U., Cookeville, 1985-90, assoc. prof., 1990—95, prof., 1995—2003, emerita, 2003—. Vis. scholar ctr. for sci. edn. in math., sci. and tech. U. Calif., Berkeley, 1993; sec.-treas. Math. Edn. Resources Co., 1994—; external examiner Fed. Advanced Tchrs. Coll., Katsina, Nigeria, 1979-82, Gumel, Nigeria, 1981-82; reader advanced placement calculus exams., 1990-92; vis. scholar Ctr. for Rsch. in Math. and Sci. Edn., San Diego State U., 1995-96; vis. prof. Ariz. State U., 1999-2000; adj. prof. N.Mex. State U., 2003—. Dept. editor: UME Trends: News and Reports on Undergrad. Math. Edn., 1989—96, MAA Online's Tchg. and Learning Sect., 1996—; mem. editl. bd. Jour. Computers in Math. and Sci. Teaching, 1992—96, Jour. for Rsch. in Math. Edn., 1997-2000; assoc. editor for tchg. and learning MAA Online, 1997—; assoc. editor Media Highlights sect. Coll. Math. Jour., 1994—contbr. articles to profl. jours. Named Fulbright scholar, 1959-60, Woodrow Wilson fellow, 1960-61, NSF grad. trainee Clarkson U., 1972-73, NSF grantee, 1971, 94-96. Fellow AAAS; mem. AAUP (Tenn. Tech. chpt. sec. 1991-92, v.p. 1992-93, pres. 1994—95), Am. Math. Soc., Math. Assn. Am. (dept. rep. 1986—2000, coord.-elect spl. interest group on rsch. in undergrad. math. edn. 1999-2000, coord. 2000-02, past coord. 2002-03), Assn. Women in Math. (Louise Hay award for contbns. to math. edn. 2002), Nat. Assn. Math., Am. Math. Assn. Two-Yr. Colls., Benjamin Banneker Assn., Nigerian Math. Soc. (organizer 5th ann. conf. 1984), Internat. Group for Psychology Math. Edn., Am. Ednl. Rsch. Assn., Nat. Coun. Tchrs. Math., Rsch. Coun. for Math. Learning, Tenn. Acad. Sci., Women in Higher Edn. Tenn. (Tenn. Tech. chpt. pres. 1990-92, state 1st v.p. 1991-92, state pres. 1992-93), Women Organizing Women (treas. 1992-93), Am. Coun. Edn. (nat. indentification program for women com. 1992-93), Assn. for Sci. Study of Consciousness, Phi Beta Kappa, Sigma Xi, Pi Mu Epsilon, Kappa Mu Epsilon. Office: NMex State U Dept Mathematical Scis PO Box 30001 Las Cruces NM 88003-0001 E-mail: aselden@nmsu.edu.

SELDEN, ROBERT WENTWORTH, physicist, science advisor; b. Phoenix, Aug. 11, 1936; s. Edward English and Mary Priscilla (Calder) S.; m. Mary Tania Hudd, June 1958 (div. 1976); 1 child, Ian Scott; m. Marjorie Anne Harmon, Feb. 20, 1977; children: Brock, Thane, Shawna, Kirsten. BA in Physics cum laude, Pomona Coll., 1958; MS in Physics, U. Wis., 1960, PhD in Physics, 1964. Rsch. assoc. Lawrence Livermore (Calif.) Nat. Lab., 1965-67, staff mem., 1967-73, group leader, 1973-78, asst. assoc. dir., 1978-80; div. leader applied theoretical physics Los Alamos (N.Mex.) Nat. Lab., 1980-83, dep. assoc. dir. strategic def. rsch., 1983-84, assoc. dir. theoretical and computational physics, 1984-86, dir. Ctr. for Nat. Securities Studies, 1986-88, assoc. dir. for lab. devel., 1991-94; chief scientist USAF, Washington, 1988-91, panel chmn. sci. adv. bd., 1984-88, 91-96, 1991—96, 2002—, chmn. sci. adv. bd., 1999—2002, mem., 2002—; cons. Los Alamos, 1994—. Chmn. study group on reactor materials and nuclear explosives U.S. Dept. Energy, 1976-78; mem. ballistic missile def. techs. adv. panel U.S. Congress Office Tech. Assessment, 1984-85, The Pres.'s Defensive Tech. Study Team, Washington, 1983; strat. adv. group U.S. Strat. Command, 1996—, panel chair, 2003-; strat. adv. group jt. adv. com. Sec. Def., Sec. Energy, 1996—. Editor Rsch. Jour. Lawrence Livermore Nat. Lab., 1976-77; contbr. sci. and tech. papers to profl. jours. Pres. Livermore Cultural Arts Coun., 1969-72; chmn. Livermore Sister City Orgn., 1973, Planning Commn. City of Livermore, 1971-76; bd. dirs. Orch. of Santa Fe, 1986-88. Capt. U.S. Army, 1964-67. Grad. fellow Edward John Noble Found., 1958-62; recipient Theodore von Karman award for outstanding contbn. to def. sci., 1989, medal for outstanding pub. svc. U.S. Sec. Def., 1996; decorated for exceptional civilian svc. USAF, 1988, 91, 96. Mem. AAAS, Am. Phys. Soc., N.Y. Acad. Sci., Air Force Assn. Avocations: tennis, hiking, music. Office: 624 La Bajada Los Alamos NM 87544-3805 E-mail: selden@cybermesa.com.

SELDES, MARIAN, actress; b. N.Y.C. d. Gilbert and Alice (Hall) S.; m. Julian Claman, Nov. 3, 1953 (div.); 1 child, Katharine; m. Garson Kanin, June 19, 1990 (dec. Mar. 1999). Grad., The Dalton Sch., N.Y.C., 1945, Neighborhood Playhouse, 1947; DHL, Emerson Coll., 1979; DFA (hon.), Julliard Sch., 2003. Faculty drama and dance divsn. Juilliard Sch. Lincoln Center, N.Y.C., 1969-91; faculty drama dept. Fordham U., 2003. Appeared with Cambridge (Mass.) Summer Theatre, 1945, Boston Summer Theatre, 1946, St. Michael's Playhouse, Winooski, Vt., 1947-48, Bermudiana Theatre, Hamilton, Bermuda, 1951, Elitch Gardens Theatre, Denver, 1953, The Cretan Woman, Lysistrata, 1955 (actress/artist-in residence Stanford U.); Broadway appearances include Medea, 1947, Crime and Punishment, 1948, That Lady, 1949, Tower Beyond Tragedy, 1950, The High Ground, 1951, Come of Age, 1952, Ondine, 1954, The Chalk Garden, 1955, The Wall, 1960, A Gift of Time, 1962, The Milk Train Doesn't Stop Here Any More, 1964, Tiny Alice, 1965, A Delicate Balance, 1967 (Tony award for best supporting actress), Before You Go, 1968, Father's Day, 1971 (Drama Desk award, Tony nomination), Mendicants of Evening (Martha Graham Co.), 1973, Equus, 1974-77, The Merchant, 1977, Deathtrap, 1978 (tony nomination), Ivanov (Drama Desk nomination), 1997, Ring Round the Moon, 1999 (Tony nomination), 45 Seconds from Broadway, 2001 Dinner At Eight, 2003 (Tony nomination); off-Broadway appearances include Diff'rent, 1961, The Ginger Man, 1963 (Obie award), All Women Are One, 1964, Juana LaLoca, 1965, Three Sisters, 1969, Am. Shakespeare Festival, Stratford, Conn., Mercy Street at Am. Place Theater, N.Y.C., 1969, Isadora Duncan, 1976 (Obie award), Painting Churches, 1983, 84 (Outer Critics Circle award 1984), Other People, Berkshire Theatre Festival, 1969, The Celebration, Hedgerow Theater, Pa., 1971, Richard III, N.Y. Shakespeare Festival, 1983, Remember Me, Lakewood Theatre, Skowhegan, Maine, Gertrude Stein and a Companion, White Barn Theatre, Westport, Conn., 1985, Lucile Lortel Theatre, N.Y.C., 1986, Richard II, N.Y. Shakespeare Festival, 1987, The Milk Train Doesn't Stop Here Anymore, WPA Theatre, N.Y.C., 1987, Happy Ending, Bristol (Pa.) Riverside Theatre, 1988, Annie 2 John F. Kennedy Ctr., Washington, 1989-90, Goodspeed Opera House, Chester, Conn., 1990, A Bright Room Called Day, N.Y. Shakespeare Festival, 1991, Three Tall Women, River Arts, Woodstock, N.Y., 1994, Another Time, Am. Jewish Theatre, 1993, Breaking the Code, Berkshire Theatre Festival, 1993, Three Tall Women, Vineyard Theatre, N.Y.C., 1994, Promenade Theatre, 1994-95, nat. tour, 1995-96, Boys From Syracuse, City Ctr., N.Y.C., 1997, Dead End: Williamstown, 1997, Dear Liar, Irish Repertory Theater, 1999, The Matchmaker: Williamstown, 1998, Tongue of a Bird, Mark Taper Forum, 1998, Sail Away, Carnegie Hall, 1999, Mad About The Boy, Carnegie Hall, 1999, The Torch-Bearers, 2000, Ancestral Voices, 2000, The Skin of our Teeth, 2000, Williamstown, The Play About the Baby, Alley Theatre, Houston, 2000, The Butterfly Collection, Playwrights Horizon, NY, 2000, The Play About the Baby, Helen, N.Y., 2001, Play Yourself, N.Y. Theater Workshop, 2002, Beckett/Albee, Century Ctr. Theatre, N.Y.C., 2003, The Royal Family Ahmanson Theatre, L.A., 2004; nat. tour Three Tall Women, 1995-96; film appearances include The Greatest Story Ever Told, Gertrude Stein and a Companion, 1988, In a Pig's Eye, 1988, The Gun in Betty Lou's Handbag, 1992, Tom and Huck, 1995, Digging to China, 1997, Home Alone 3, 1997, Affliction, 1997, Celebrity, 1998, One Life to Live, 1998, Remember WENN, 1999, The Haunting, 1999, Town and Country, 1999, Duets, 1999, Hollywood Ending, 2002, Mona Lisa Smile, 2003; (TV series) Good and Evil, 1991, Murphy Brown, 1992, Truman, 1995, Cosby, 1996, 98, Trinity, 1998, The Others, 2000, If These Walls Could Talk 2, 2000, Nero Wolfe, 2001 (A&E), The Education of Max Bickford, 2002, American Masters PBS "Juillard Documentary, 2003", Hallmark Hall of Fame, 2004, Frasier, 2004; also appeared on radio CBS Mystery Theater, 1976-81, Theatre Guild on The Air; author: The Bright Lights, 1978, Time Together, 1981. Bd. dirs. Neighborhood Playhouse, The Acting Co., Nat. Repertory Theatre, Theatre Hall of Fame, 1996; bd. trustees Broadway Cares/Equity Fights Aids. Winner Ovation award Theater L.A. for Three Tall Women, 1996, Conn. Critics award for Three Tall Women, 1996; recipient Madge Kennedy/Sidney Kingsley award Dramatists Guild Fund, 2000, Obie award for sustained achievement, Lucille Lortel award for Sustained Achievement, 2003, Edwin Booth award, Players Club, 2003, Lifetime Mem. award Theatre Libr. Assn., 2003, Breukelein Inst. Gaudium award, 2003. Mem. Players Club, Century Assn. Home: 210 Central Park S Apt 19D New York NY 10019-1426

SELDIN, DONALD WAYNE, physician, educator; b. N.Y.C., Oct. 24, 1920; s. Abraham L. and Laura (Ueberal) S.; m. Muriel Goldberg, Apr. 1, 1943; children: Leslie Lynn, Donald Craig, Donna Leigh. BA, NYU, 1940; MD, Yale U., 1943; DHL (hon.), So. Meth. U., 1977; DSc (hon.), Med. Coll. Wis., 1980, Yale U., 1988; D honoris causa, Univ. de Paris VI, Pierre et Marie Curie, 1983. Diplomate Am. Bd. Internal Medicine (test com. on nephrology 1970-73). Intern New Haven Hosp., Yale U., 1943-44, resident, 1944-46, instr. medicine, 1948-50, asst. prof. internal medicine, 1950-51; mem. faculty U. Tex. Southwestern Med. Sch., Dallas, 1951—, William Buchanan prof. internal medicine, 1969—, Univ. Tex. System prof., 1988-98, chmn. dept. internal medicine, 1952-88; chief med. service Parkland Meml. Hosp., Dallas, 1952-98; chmn. dept. medicine Lisbon VA Hosp., Dallas, ret. 1987; pres. emeritus Southwestern Med. Found., 1988-97; prof. internal medicine Southwestern Med. Sch. U. Tex., Dallas. Cons. Baylor Hosp., St. Paul's Hosp., Presbyn. Hosp., Dallas, Brooke Army Hosp., Ft. Sam Houston, Walter Reed Army Hosp., Washington, also to Surgeon Gen. U.S., Surgeon Gen. USAF, and Eli Lilly Co., 1972—; mem. Bur. Budget, Exec. Office of Pres., 1966-67; chmn. dialysis and transplantation com. of sci. adv. bd. Nat. Kidney Found.; mem. bd. sci. councillors Nat. Inst. Arthritis and Metabolic Diseases, NIH, 1968-71; trustee Rand Corp., 1975-93, adv. trustee, 1993—. Editorial bd.: Jour. Lab. and Clin. Medicine, 1958-60, Nephron, The Clinician, Medicine, Mineral and Electrolyte Metabolism, 1977-79; cons. editor: Am. Jour. Medicine; assoc. editor: Kidney Internat., 1973-79; contbr. articles to profl. jours. Served as capt. U.S. Army, 1946-48. Recipient Disting. Achievement award Modern Medicine, 1977, John P. Peters award Am. Soc. Nephrology, 1983, Disting. U.S. Scientist award Alexander von Humboldt Found., 1989, John K. Lattimer award Am. Urol. Assn., 1989; Friedrich Von Muller hon. lectr. U. Munich, 1968. Master ACP (Disting. Teaching award 1980); Fellow Royal Soc. Medicine, Am. Acad. Arts and Sci.; mem. AMA, Dallas County Med. Soc., Tex. Med. Assn., Dallas Diabetes Assn., So. Soc. Clin. Investigation (pres. 1964, Founders medal 1975), Central Soc. Clin. Research (pres. 1963), Am. Fedn. Clin. Research, Am. Soc. Clin. Investigation (pres. 1966), Assn. Profs. Medicine (pres. 1971, Robert H. Williams Disting. Chmn. Medicine award 1977), Assn. Am. Physicians (pres. 1980, Kober medal 1985), Am. Physiol. Soc., Am. Soc. Nephrology (pres. 1968), Nat. Kidney Found. (David Hume award 1981), Am. Heart Assn., Am. Clin. and Climatol. Assn., Soc. Med. Cons. to Armed Forces, Internat. Soc. Nephrology (councillor 1973-78, pres. 1984-87), Southwestern Med. Found. (pres. 1988-93, vice chmn. 1993—), Australian Soc. Nephrology (hon.), Gesellschaft für Nephrologie, (Volhard medal 1986), Alpha Omega Alpha. Office: U Tex Southwestern Med Sch 5323 Harry Hines Blvd Dallas TX 75390-7208

SELDIN, GLORIA, state legislator; b. Bklyn., Apr. 7, 1924; Mem. N.H. Ho. of Reps. (dist. 17), Concord, 1996—; mem. labor, indsl. and rehab. svcs. N.H. Ho. of Reps., Concord, 1996—. Mem. Svc. Coun. Commn., 1983-87, N.H. Women's Lobby, 1989-92, Older Womans League, N.H. Hospice Program; founder Concord Share Program. Jewish. Home: 54 Church St Concord NH 03301-4550

SELDMAN, NEIL NORMAN, cultural organization administrator; b. Bklyn., Aug. 2, 1945; s. Fred Herman and Sylvia (Flaster) S.; m. Laura Jane Klugherz, Feb. 22, 1968; children: Oliver, Chloe. BS in Indsl. and Labor Rels., Cornell U., 1966; MS in Internat. Communism, George Washington U., 1968, PhD in Internat. Rels., 1974. Asst. to pres. B.H. Krueger Co., Bklyn., 1969-72; assoc. prof., lectr. George Washington U., Washington, 1974-76, asst. dir. exptl. program, 1976-77; founder Inst. for Local Self-Reliance (ILSR), Washington, 1974—, pres., 1980—. Cons. World Bank/UN Environ. Program, Washington, 1980-81, City Coun., Phila., 1984-90. Author: Common Sense Radicalism, 1976, Waste to Wealth: A Guide for Community Enterprise, 1985; co-author: Integrated Resource Recovery-Recycling from Municipal Refuse: A State-of-the-Art Review and Annotated Bibliography, 1985, Proven Profits from Pollution Prevention, 1986, Garbage in Europe: Economics, Technologies, Trends, 1987; contbr. article to Ency. of Energy Tech. and the Environment, 1995. Fabrangen Cheder Jewish Community Orgn.; elected chair Neighborhood Planning Coun., Washington, 1976-82; co-founder D.C. Interracial Coalition for Environ. Equity, Washington, 1989, Nat. Recycling Coalition, 1980, Grass Roots Recycling Network, 1996. With NG, 1968-74. Grantee Moriah Fund, 1990-95, Pew Charitable Trusts, 1991, NSF, 1979-80, H. Heinz Endowment, 1995-96, EPA, 1993-98, Turner Found., 1995-98. Jewish. Avocations: fast pitch softball, nineteenth-century literature, French and Russian revolutions.

SELES, MONICA, professional tennis player; b. Novi Sad, Yugoslavia, Dec. 2, 1973; came to U.S., 1986; d. Karolj and Esther Seles. Profl. tennis player, 1989—. Mem. U.S. Fed Cup Team, 1996, 99, 2000, WTA Tour Players' Coun., 1998—99. Author: (novels) From Fear to Victory, 1996. Active Spl. Olympics. Winner WTA Singles Championship, 1990-92, Roland Garros, 1990, 91, 92, French Open, 1990, 91, 92, U.S. Open, 1991, 92, Australian Open, 1991, 92, 93, 96, 53 Career Singles Titles and 6 Career Doubles Titles, WTA Tour; named Yugoslavia's sportswoman of yr., 1985, Tennis Mag./Rolex Watch Female Rookie of Yr., 1989, WTA Tour Player of Yr., 1991, Comeback Player of Yr. Tennis mag., 1995, Profl. Female Athlete by Yr., 1995, Most Exciting Player as voted by fans, 1995, 97, Female Pro Athlete of the Yr., Fla. Times-Union, 1998; recipient 1990 Rado Topspin award, Ted Tinling Diamond award Va. Slims, 1990, Inaugural Sanex Hero of the Yr. award, 2002. Achievements include 3rd player in the Open-era to capture the Australian and Roland Garros in same calendar year; World #1 ranked player, 1991, 92, 95; named youngest #1 ranked player in tennis history for women and men at 17 years, 3 months, 9 days. Office: c/o Internat Mgmt Group 1 Erieview Plz Cleveland OH 44114-1715

SELESKY, DONALD BRYANT, software developer; b. Englewood, N.J., Jan. 7, 1948; s. Harold Francis and Bernice Evelyn (Deacon) S.; m. Janet Borna (div.); m. Sandy Lynn Berke, Sept. 11, 1983. BA in Econ., Cornell U., 1970; MBA in Mktg., Columbia U., 1977; MS in Computer Sci., Boston U., 1990. Sr. Arthur Andersen & Co., N.Y.C., 1971-75; bus. sys. analyst Nabisco Inc., East Hanover, N.J., 1975-77; cons., 1977-81, 82-83; mgr. data processing Kings Dept. Stores, Watertown, Mass., 1981-82; sys. analyst The Analytical Scis. Corp., Reading, Mass., 1983-84; prin. software engr. Lotus Devel. Corp., Cambridge, Mass., 1984-86; prin. Ksoft, Westford, Mass., 1986—. Sr. software engr. Kurzweil Applied Intelligence, Waltham, Mass., 1995-98, product mgr., 1997-98; patentee in field. Author (software) @BASE, 1987; co-author (software) Look and Link, 1988, Monarch, 1991, Monarch for Windows, 1994; patentee in field. Mem. Nashoba Valley Photo Club, Appalachian Mountain Club. Avocations: backpacking, photography, kayaking, shooting, biking. Home and Office: Ksoft 15 Bradley Ln Westford MA 01886-2544

SELETZ, JULES MORTIMER, surgeon; b. Chgo., 1930; BA in Biology, Va. Mil. Inst., 1953; MD, U. Health Scis., Chgo., 1958. Diplomate Am. Bd. Surgery, FACS. Intern, then resident in gen. surgery Boston City Hosp., 1958-63, mem. staff, 1963-74; mem. faculty Sch. Medicine Tufts U., 1963-82; mem. staff Newton Weslesley Hosp., 1963-82; mil. surgeon U.S. Army, 1982-94; mem. staff Keller Army Cmty. Hosp., West Point, N.Y., 1990-94; physician surveyor Joint Com. Accreditation Healthcare Orgn., 1994-01. Author mystery/med. thriller novels and hist. fiction. Home: PO Box 1087 Lincoln NH 03251-1087 E-mail: jseletz@earthlink.net.

SELF, JIMMIE EVERETTE, music educator, musician; b. Kingsport, Tenn., Feb. 28, 1952; s. Clarence Edward and Wilma Orenta (Harris) Self; m. Nancy Bernice Arnold, Feb. 24, 1973; children: Christopher, Candace, Doris. AAS, CC of Air Force, 1979; BA, U. NH, 1980. Musician trombone and euphonium USAF Band, 1972—94, program mgr., 1994—98; instr. low brass East Tenn. State U., Johnson City, 1999—. Prin. trombonist Montgomery (Ala.) Symphony Orch., 1974—76; co-prin. trombonist Kingsport Symphony Orch., 2001—. Arranger (music) Shortnin' Bread, 2002. Dir. Cmty. Chest, Church Hill, Tenn., 1999—; mem. Rep. Nat. Com., 2002—. Chief master sgt. USAF, 1972—98. Recipient Commendation medal, USAF, 1978, Achievement medal, 1991, Meritorious Svc. medal, 1998. Mem.: Internat. Tube/Euphonium Assn., Non-Commd. Officers Assn. (life), Air Force Sgts. Assn. (life). Baptist. Achievements include performing for 4 U.S. presidents and many foreign heads of state. Avocations: gentleman farming, model railroading, motorcycles. Office: E Tenn State U Dept Music PO Box 70661 Johnson City TN 37614-1701 E-mail: selfj@mail.etsu.edu.

SELF, MADISON ALLEN, finance company executive; b. Ozawkie, Kans., June 30, 1921; s. Benjamin B. and Margaret E. (Allen) S.; m. Lila M. Reetz, Sept. 1, 1943; 1 son, Murray A. BS in Chem. Engring, U. Kans., 1943. Engr. York Corp., 1943-44; salesman and researcher Sharples Chems., Inc., 1944-47; with Bee Chem. Co., Lansing, Ill., 1947-84, chmn. bd., chief exec. officer, 1986; pres. Allen Fin., Inc., 1984—; chmn. bd. dirs. Tioga Internat., Inc., 1989-99. Life trustee Ill. Inst. Tech. Mem. Chief Exec. Orgn., World Pres.'s Orgn., Hinsdale Golf Club. Office: Allen Fin Inc 907 N Elm St Ste 302 Hinsdale IL 60521-3645 Office Phone: 630-371-4848.

SELF, MARK EDWARD, communications consultant; b. Tyler, Tex., Dec. 6, 1955; s. Edward and Ruby (Rogers) S.; m. Dianne Logan; children: Patricia Bartlett, Marcile Christine. Student, Tenn. Tech. Sch., 1973-76. Gen. mgr. Gulf Telephone Inc., Beaumont, Tex., 1980-82; gen. sales mgr. CSC Telephone Inc., Tyler, Tex., 1982-83; v.p. sales Teleci Inc., Irving, Tex., 1983-85; cons. Self & Assocs., Inc., Grapevine, Tex., 1985—; pres. S&A Equipment Co., Grapevine, 1990—; v.p. mktg. Hicom, Inc., Euless, Tex., 1994—. Fundraiser Freedom Ride Found., Dallas, 1987. Named Outstanding Young Men of Am., 1985. Mem. Am. Hotel and Motel Assn., Nat. Office Machine Dealer Assn., Nat. Fedn. Ind. Bus., Dallas C. of C., Masons. Avocations: fishing, hunting, woodworking. Home: 3442 Spring Willow Dr Grapevine TX 76051-6516 Office: Self & Assocs PO Box 1258 Colleyville TX 76034 Office Phone: 817-571-7900. E-mail: sna7900@aol.com., markself@snaequipment.com.

SELF, W. M. textile company executive; Pres., bd. dirs. Greenwood (S.C.) Mills. Inc., until 1996, chmn., CEO, 1996—. Office: Greenwood Mills Inc PO Box 1017 Greenwood SC 29648-1017

SELFE, EDWARD MILTON, lawyer; b. St. Paul, Sept. 26, 1921; s. Edward Milton and Eleanor (Moen) S.; m. Rena Hill McMurry, July 10, 1950 (div. Oct. 1979); children: Murry, Edward, James; m. Jane Comer Bowron, Dec. 31, 1979. BA, Presbyn. Coll., Clinton, S.C., 1943; LLB, U. Va., 1950. Bar: N.Y., Va., Ala. Asst. prof. law Law Sch., U. Va., Charlottesville, 1950-51; assoc. Shearman & Sterling, N.Y.C., 1951-52, Bradley Arant Rose White, Birmingham, Ala., 1952-57, ptnr., 1957-2000, of counsel, 2000—; vice chmn. Secor Bank, Birmingham, 1988-91, gen. counsel, 1991-93. Lectr. Law Sch., U. Ala., Tuscaloosa, 1968—90. Chmn. Birmingham-Jefferson County Transit Authority, 1972-82. Served to capt., inf. U.S. Army, 1943-47, ETO. Decorated Silver Star, Bronze Star (V), Purple Heart. Fellow Am. Coll. Tax Counsel; mem. ABA, Ala. Bar Assn., Birmingham Bar Assn. Democrat. Avocation: tennis (ranked 5th nationally USTA in men's singles-age 80, 2003). Home: 84 Arlington Crest 2600 Arlington Ave S Birmingham AL 35205-4167 Office: Bradley Arant Rose & White One Federal Pl 1819 Fifth Ave N Birmingham AL 35203-2104 Office Phone: 205-521-8280. Business E-Mail: eselfe@bradleyarant.com.

SELFRIDGE, GEORGE DEVER, retired dentist, retired naval officer; b. Pitman, N.J., Sept. 24, 1924; s. William John and Edith (Gorman) S.; m. Ruth Motisher, 1948; children: Pamela Ruth, Kimberly Dawn, Cheryl Beth. Student, Gettysburg Coll., 1942-43, Muhlenburg Coll., 1943-45; DDS, U. Buffalo, 1947; MA, George Washington U., 1974. Commd. lt. (j.g.) USN, 1948, advanced through grades to rear adm., 1973; intern Naval Dental Sch., Bethesda, Md., 1948-49, Naval Hosp., St. Albans, N.Y., 1949-50; asst. dental officer U.S.S. Midway, 1949-51; with USN, 1951-64; sr. dental officer U.S.S. Randolph, 1958-60, U.S.S. Cadmus, 1964-65, U.S.S. Vulcan, 1965-66, Svc. Force, 1964-66, Submarine Force, Atlantic Fleet, 1967-69; from asst. dir. grad. edn. to comdg. officer Navy Grad. Dental Sch., Bethesda, 1969-76; exec. officer Norfolk (Va.) Navy Dental Clinic, 1972-73; ret. USN, 1976; dean Dental Sch., Washington U., St. Louis, 1976-86; dir. dental services Barnes Hosp., St. Louis, 1976-87, Children's Hosp., St. Louis, 1976-87; exec. dir. Am. Bd. Orthodontics, 1986-97; ret., 1998. Adv. bd. VA Hosp., St. Louis, 1977-79; mem. exec. coun. Cen. Region Testing Svc., 1976-86; adv. com. St. Louis Jr. Coll. Dist., 1976-86. Contbr. articles to med. jours. Decorated Legion of Merit; recipient commendation medals, Greater St. Louis Gold Medallion award, 1995, Spl. Recognition award Am. Bd. Orthopedics, 1996. Mem. ADA, Am. Coll. Dentists (past pres.), Internat. Coll. Coll. Dentists (dep. registrar, sec. U.S. sect.), Assn. Mil. Surgeons U.S., Omicron Kappa Upsilon. Republican. Home: 14545 Foxham Ct Chesterfield MO 63017-5620

SELICK, HOWARD E. (BARRY SELICK), biotechnology executive; BA in Biophysics, PhD in Molecular Biology, U. Pa. Am. Cancer Soc. fellow U. Calif. San Francisco Sch. Medicine; Damon Runyon-Walter Winchell Cancer Fund fellow Protein Design Labs.; former v.p. rsch. Affymax Rsch. Inst.; pres., CEO Camitro Corp., Menlo Park, Calif. Office: 1300 Seaport Blvd #5 Redwood City CA 94063-5538

SELIG, ALLAN H. (BUD SELIG), Major League Baseball Commissioner; b. Milw., July 30, 1934; s. Ben and Marie Selig; m. Suzanne Lappin Steinman, Jan. 18, 1977; children: Sari, Wendy. Grad., U. Wis., Madison, 1956; LHD (hon.), Lakeland Coll., 1989. With Selig Ford (became Selig Chevrolet 1982), West Allis, Wis., 1959-90, pres., owner, 1966-90; with Selig Exec. Leasing Co., West Allis, 1959—, pres., owner, 1977—; part owner Milw. Braves (became Atlanta Braves 1965), 1963-65; co-founder Teams, Inc., 1964; co-owner, pres., chief exec. officer Milw. Brewers Baseball Club, Inc., 1970-98; interim commr. Maj. League Baseball, 1991-98, commr., 1998—. Bd. dirs. Green Bay Packers Profl. Football Team., Marcus Corp., Oil-Dri Corp. Am. Co-founder Child Abuse Prevention Fund, 1988. With U.S. Army, 1956-58. Recipient Major League Exec. of Yr. award UPI, 1978, Internat. B'nai B'rith Sportsman of Yr. award 1981, Sportsman of Yr. award U.S. Olympic Com., 1988, August A. Busch, Jr. award for long and meritorious svc. to baseball, 1989, Ellis Island Congl. medal of honor, 1993, Anti-Defamation League's "A World of Difference Award" 1994, Herbert Hoover Humanitarian award Boys and Girls Clubs for Outstanding Svc. to Benefit Am.'s Youth, 1998. Office: Office of the Commr Major League Baseball 245 Park Ave New York NY 10167-0002*

SELIG, JOEL LOUIS, lawyer, educator; b. Boston, Apr. 12, 1944; s. William Max and Ruth Horton (Berger) S.; m. Ruth Mildred Osterweis, Oct. 6, 1968; children— William Osterweis, Deborah Osterweis. A.B., Harvard U., 1965, J.D., 1968. Bar: Mass. 1968, U.S. Dist. Ct. Mass. 1969, U.S. Supreme Ct. 1973, U.S. Ct. Appeals (9th cir.) 1974, U.S. Ct. Appeals (D.C. cir.) 1974, U.S. Ct. Appeals (5th cir.) 1975, D.C. 1976, U.S. Ct. Appeals (6th cir.) 1976, U.S. Dist. Ct. D.C. 1976, U.S. Ct. Appeals (10th cir.) 1977, U.S. Ct. Appeals (11th cir.) 1981. Atty. Mass. Law Reform Inst., Boston, 1969; atty., employment sect., civil rights div. Dept. Justice, Washington, 1969-73, atty., appellate sect., 1977-78, dep. chief, housing and credit sect., 1978-79, dep. chief, gen. litigation sect., 1979-82, sr. trial atty., fed. enforcement sect., 1982-83; dir. govt. employment discrimination project Lawyers' Com. for Civil Rights Under Law, Washington, 1973-77; vis. prof. law U. Wyo. Coll. Law, Laramie, 1983-84, prof. law, 1984—, centennial disting. prof. of law, 1992-95; temporary recorder Supreme Ct. Wyo. Permanent Rules Adv. Com., 1983-84, reporter, 1984— . Office: Univ Wyo Coll Law Dept 3035 1000 E Univ Ave Laramie WY 82071-3035

SELIG, KARL-LUDWIG, language and literature educator; b. Wiesbaden, Germany, Aug. 14, 1926; naturalized, 1948; s. Lucian and Erna (Reiss) S. BA, Ohio State U., 1946, MA, 1947; postgrad., U. Rome, Italy, 1949-50; PhD, U. Tex., 1955. Asst. prof. Romance langs. and lit. Johns Hopkins U., Balt., 1954-58; assoc. prof. U. N.C., Chapel Hill, 1958-61, U. Minn., Mpls., 1961-63; vis. prof. U. Tex., Austin, 1963-64, prof. Romance langs. and lit., 1964-65; Hinchliff prof. Spanish lit. Cornell U., Ithaca, N.Y., 1965-69, dir. grad. studies in Romance lit., 1966-69; prof. Spanish lit. Columbia U., N.Y.C., 1969—. Brown Found. fellow, vis. prof. Spanish and comparative lit. U. of the South, Sewanee, Tenn., 1990; vis. prof. U. Munich, 1963-64, U. Berlin, 1967; vis. prof. U. Greifswald, Germany, 1991-96, hon. prof., 1996—; cons. prof. Ohio State U., Columbus, 1967-69; vis. lectr. U. Zulia, Maracaibo, Venezuela, 1968; dir. summer seminar NEH, 1975, cons., 1975-77; vis. scholar Ga. U. Sys., 1977; vis. rsch. scholar Fondation Hardt, Vandoeuvres, Switzerland, 1959, Herzog August Bibliothek Wolfenbüttel, Fed. Repubic Germany, 1979—; mem. com. grants-in-aid Am. Coun. Learned Soc., 1969-73; chmn. Comparative Lit. Program and Colloquia, Columbia Coll., 1976-88. Author: (books) The Libr. of Vincencio Juan de Lastanosa, Patron of Gracián, Geneva, 1960, Studies on Alciato in Spain, 1990, Studies on Cervantes, 1993, also numerous articles, revs.; editor: (books) (Thomas Blundeville) of Councils and Counselors, 1963; editor: (with A.G. Hatcher) Studia Philologica et Litteraria in Honorem L. Spitzer, 1958; editor: (with J.E. Keller) Essays in Honor of N.B. Adams, 1966; editor: (with R. Brinkmann) Theatrum Europaeum. Festschrift E.M. Szarota, 1982; editor: (with S. Neumeister) Theatrum Mundi Hispanicum, 1986; editor: (with R. Somerville) Florilegium Columbianum: Essays in Honor of Paul Oskar Kristeller, 1987; editor: (with E. Sears) The Verbal and the Visual: Essays in Honor of William Sebastian Heckscher, 1990; editor: Polyanthea Essays on Art and Lit. in Honor of William Sebastian Heckscher, 1993, Mira de Amescua, La hija de Carlos Quinto, 2002; assoc. editor: Modern Lang. Notes, 1955—58, mng. editor: Romance Notes, editor U. N.C. Studies in Comparative Lit., Bull. Comediantes; assoc. editor: Bull. Comediantes, mem. editl. bd.: Bull. Comediantes, co-editor Yearbook of Comparative Lit., Vol. IX; editl. bd.: Colección Támesis, London, editl. bd.: Romania Rev., editl. bd.: Tchg. Lang. Through Lit., assoc. editor: Hispania, assoc. editor: Ky. Romance Quar., gen. editor: Revista Hispánica Moderna, mem. nat. adv. bd.: MLA Internat. Bibliography, mem. editl. bd.: Edición Reichenberger, Kassel, Germany, editl. bd.: Yale Italian Studies. Recipient Mark Van Doren award Columbia, 1974, spl. citation Columbia Coll. Alumni Assn., 1991, Festschrift, Über Texte, 1997; fellow Fulbright Found., Rome, 1949-50, Newberry Libr., 1958, Folger Shakespeare Libr., 1959, 63, Belgian Am. Ednl. Found., 1961, 62; sr. fellow Mediaeval and Renaissance Inst. Duke U., 1978; Fulbright rsch. scholar Utrecht, The Netherlands, 1958-59; DAAD rsch. grantee, 1979; Karl-Ludwig Selig scholarship named in his honor, Columbia Coll., 2001. Mem. MLA (sec., then chmn. Romance sect. 1965-66, chmn. comparative lit. 1973, James Russell Lowell prize com. 1989-90, chmn. 1990), Internat. Assn. Hispanists, Acad. Lit. Studies, Am. Friends Herzog August Bibliothek (bd. dirs. 1996—), Phi Beta Kappa (hon.). Home: 333 W 86th St Apt 406 New York NY 10024

SELIG, WILLIAM GEORGE, university official; b. Prince Rupert, B.C., Can., Sept. 25, 1938; s. George Oliver Selig and Minerva Junuetta (Brand) Goodale; m. Judith Margaret Sprague, June 20, 1964; children: Cheryl, Cynthia. BA, Cen. Washington State Coll., 1961, MA, 1968; CAGS, U. Mass., 1972, EdD, 1973. Tchr. Sharon (Mass.) High Sch., 1963-64, Hydaburg (Alaska) Grade Sch., 1964-65, W. Puyallup (Wash.) Jr. High Sch., 1966-69; dir. spl. edn. Northampton (Mass.) Schs., 1969-73, 1974-76, asst. prof. Westfield (Mass.) State Coll., 1973; dir. pupil svcs. Longmeadow (Mass.) Pub. Schs., 1976-80; prof. Regent U., Virginia Beach, Va., 1980-83, dean, prof., 1984-89, provost, 1989-2000; Disting. prof. ednl. leadership, 2000—. Bd. dirs. Set Net, Virginia Beach; pres. Motivational Teaching Systems, Inc.; spl. edn. adv. bd. dirs. Virginia Beach Pub. Schs.; bd. trustees Klingberg Family Ctrs., New Britain, Conn., 1991—2000. Author: Training for Triumph, 1984, Loving Our Differences, 1989, Handbook of Individualized Strategies for Classroom Discipline, 1995; editor Or Gavett Meanliffe, 2001; contbr. chpt. to book. Episcopalian. Avocations: skiing, tennis. Office: Regent University 1000 Regent University Dr Virginia Beach VA 23464-9800 E-mail: georsel@regent.edu.

SELIGA, CHARLES G. airport administrator; BS, MBA, Seton Hall U. Mgmt. analyst Port Authority of N.Y. and N.J., N.Y.C., 1966, exec. asst. to dep. dir. World Trade Ctr., sr. exec. asst. to dir. World Trade Dept., project dir. World Trade Ctr.; asst. gen. mgr. aviation mktg. econs. N.Y.-N.J. Regional Airport Sys., N.Y.C., gen. mgr. ctrl. bus. adminstrn.; mgr. bus. adminstr. JFK Internat. Airport, Jamaica, N.Y., 1987-94, mgr. security and landside ops., 1994-96, gen. mgr., 1996—2000; mng. dir., pres., CEO Nat. Express Corp., Stewart Internat. Airport, Newburgh, NY, 2000—. Office: Stewart Internat Airport Newburgh NY 12550*

SELIGER, MARK ALAN, photographer; b. Amarillo, Tex., May 23, 1959; s. Maurice and Carol Lee (Singer) S. BS, East Tex. State U., 1981. Chief photographer Rolling Stone Mag., N.Y.C., 1989-93, GQ mag., N.Y.C., 2001—; contbg. photographer Vanity Fair. Recipient Excellence in Journalism award Page One, 1988, Excellence awards Comm. Arts, 1988, 89, 90, 91, 92, 93, Creativity certs. Distinction Art Direction Mag., 1989, 93, Merit award Art Dirs. Club, 1991, Distinctive Merit award 1991, 92, Excellence certs. Am. Photography, 1991, 92, Distinctive Merit awards Soc. Pub. Designers, 1992, Distinguished Alumni award East Tex. State U., 1993; Mark Seliger Photography Scholarship named in his honor East Tex. State U., 1994, Alfred Eisenstuedt Photography award Single Image, 1999. Mem. Am. Soc. Mag. Photographers.

SELIGMAN, DANIEL, editor; b. N.Y.C., Sept. 25, 1924; s. Irving and Clare (O'Brien) S.; m. Mary Gale Sherburn, May 23, 1953; children: Nora, William Paul. Student, Rutgers U., 1941-42; AB, NYU, 1946. Editl. asst. New Leader, 1946; asst. editor Am. Mercury, 1946-50; assoc. editor Fortune, 1950-59, editl. bd., 1959-66, asst. mng. editor, 1966-69, exec. editor, 1970-77, assoc. mng. editor, 1977-87, contbg. editor, 1988-97, Forbes, 1997—. Sr. staff editor all Time, Inc. (publs.), 1969-70. Author: A Question of Intelligence: The IQ Debate in America, 1992. Home: 190 E 72nd St New York NY 10021-4370 E-mail: ad453@aol.com.

SELIGMAN, FREDERICK, lawyer; b. Bklyn. s. Martin and Florence (Alperin) S.; m. Delice Felice. AB, Clark U., 1957; JD, N.Y. Law Sch., 1972. Bar: N.Y. 1973, U.S. Dist. Ct. (so. and ea. dists.) N.Y. 1974, U.S. Tax Ct. 1974, U.S. Ct. Appeals (2d cir.) 1975, U.S. Supreme Ct. 1979. Atty. N.Y.C. (N.Y.) Police Dept., 1972-73; asst. dist. atty. N.Y. County, N.Y.C., 1973-79; pvt. practice N.Y.C., 1980-85; ptnr. Seligman & Seligman, N.Y.C., 1986—. Mem. N.Y. Criminal Bar Assn., N.Y. State Defenders Assn. Home: Runge Rd Shokan NY 12481 Office: Seligman & Seligman 26 Broadway New York NY 10004-1703 Office Phone: 212-785-1800. E-mail: frederli@aol.com.

SELIGMAN, JOEL, dean; b. N.Y.C., Jan. 11, 1950; s. Selig Jacob and Muriel (Bienstock) S.; m. Friederike Felber, July 30, 1981; children: Andrea, Peter. AB magna cum laude, UCLA, 1971; JD, Harvard U., 1974. Bar: Calif. 1975. Atty., writer Corp. Accountability Rsch. Group, Washington, 1974-77; prof. law Northeastern U. Law Sch., 1977-83, George Washington U., 1983-86, U. Mich., Ann Arbor, 1986-95; dean law U. Ariz., Tucson, 1995-99; dean sch. law Washington U., St. Louis, 1999—. Cons. Fed. Trade Commn., 1979-82, Dept. Transp., 1983, Office Tech. Assessment, 1988-89; chair adv. com. on mkt. info. SEC, 2000-2001; reporter Nat. Conf. of Commrs. on Uniform State Laws, Uniform Securities Act, 2002. Author (with others) Constitutionalizing the Corporation: The Case for the Federal Chartering of Giant Corporations, 1976, The High Citadel: The Influence of Harvard Law School, 1978, The Transformation of Wall Street: A History of the Securities and Exchange Commission and Modern Corporate Finance, 1982, 3d edit., 2003, The SEC and the Future of Finance, 1985, (multi-volume) Securities Regulation, The New Uniform Securities Act, 2002; contbr. articles to profl. jours. Mem. AICPA (profl. ethics exec. com. 2000-02), NASD (bd. govs.), State Bar Calif., Am. Law Inst. (adv. com., advisor corp. governance project). Office: Washington U Sch Law CB 1120 1 Brookings Dr Saint Louis MO 63130-4862

SELIGMAN, MARTIN E.P. psychologist, educator; b. Albany, N.Y., Aug. 12, 1942; s. Adrian and Irene Seligman; m. Mandy M. Seligman; children: Amanda, David, Lara, Nicole, Darryl, Carly, Jenny. AB, Princeton U., 1964; PhD in Psychology, U. Pa., 1967; PhD (hon.), Uppsala (Sweden) U., 1989, Mass. Coll. Profl. Psychology, 1997. Cert. psychologist Pa. Asst. prof. Cornell U., 1967-70; assoc. prof. psychology U. Pa., 1972-76, prof., 1976—, Fox Leadership prof., 1999—, dir. clin. program, 1980-94. Vis. fellow Maudsley Hosp. Inst. Psychiatry, U. London, 1975; hon. prof. psychology U. Wales, Cardiff. Author: Helplessness, 1975, Learned Optimism, 1991, What You Can Change & What You Can't, 1993, The Optimistic Child, 1995, Authentic Happiness, 2002 (Best Psychology Book 2003), (with Christopher Peterson) Character Strengths and Virtues, 2004; co-author: Character Strengths and Virtues, 2004; contbr. numerous articles to profl. jours. Recipient MERIT award, 1991, William James fellow award Am. Psychol. Soc., 1992, James McKeen Cattell Fellow award, 1995; NIMH grantee, 1969—; NSF fellow, 1963-64, Woodrow Wilson fellow, 1964-65, Guggenheim fellow, 1974-75, Ctr. Advanced Study in Behavioral Scis. fellow, 1978-79, Theodore Roosevelt fellow, 2002, Am. Acad. Polit. and Social Sci. Fellow AAAS, APA (pres. divsn. clin. psychology 1993-95, pres. 1997-99); mem. Ea. Psychol. Assn. (bd. dirs.), Psychonomic Soc., Assn. Advancement Behavior Therapy, Am. Psychopathol. Assn., Am. Psychosomatic Soc., Phi Beta Kappa, Sigma Xi. Office: 3720 Walnut St Philadelphia PA 19104-6196

SELIGMAN, NICOLE K. broadcast executive, lawyer; BA, Harvard Coll. (Radcliffe), 1978; JD, Harvard Law Sch., 1983. Assoc. editl. page editor The Asian Wall St. Jour., Hong Kong, 1978—80; law clk. to Judge Harry T. Edwards U.S. Ct. of Appeals, Wash., DC, 1983—84; law clk. to Justice Thurgood Marshall U.S. Supreme Ct., 1984—85; ptnr. Williams & Connolly LLP, Wash., DC; exec. v.p., gen. counsel Sony Corp. of Am., 2001—. Office: Sony Corp of Am 550 Madison Ave New York NY 10022

SELIG-PRIEB, WENDY, sports team executive; JD, Marquette U., 1988. With broadcasting dept. Milw. Brewers, from 1982; exec. trainee Office of Baseball Commr.; corp. atty. Foley & Lardner, to 1990; gen. counsel Milw. Brewers, 1990-95, v.p., gen. counsel, 1995-98, now pres., CEO, 1998—. Office: Milw Brewers Baseball % Miller Park 1 Brewers Way Milwaukee WI 53214-3651

SELIGSON, CARL H. business executive; b. N.Y.C., Feb. 25, 1935; s. Harold P. and Lilian (Yohalem) Seligson; m. Bonnie Laskin, Mar. 6, 1983; children: Susan S. Pattenaude, Barbara S. Zweig, Nina Priven, Eric M. Drath. AB, Brown U., 1956; postgrad., NYU Grad. Sch. Bus. Adminstrn., 1961—63. Textile salesman Cohn, Hall, Marx Co., Montreal, Canada, 1958—61; security analyst Burnham & Co., N.Y.C., 1961—67, Kuhn, Loeb & Co, N.Y.C., 1967—71; mng. dir. Merrill Lynch, N.Y.C., 1971—87, Kidder, Peabody & Co., N.Y.C., 1987—90; sr. exec. cons. regulated industries Deloitte & Touche, N.Y.C., 1990—92; mng. dir. Prudential Securities, N.Y.C., 1992—95; sr. advisor Andersen Consulting, N.Y.C., 1996—2000; sr. v.p. energyLeader.com, N.Y.C., 2000; sr. advisor Prospect Street Ventures, N.Y.C., K Road Mgmt., 2002—. Contbr. articles to profl. jours. including Pub. Utilities Fortnightly, Telephony, Fin. Exec., The Southern Banker, Coal Monthly and Energy News. Mem. strategic issues com. and adv. coun. Elec. Power Rsch. Inst., Palo Alto, Calif., 1998—; bd. dirs. Nuc. Energy Inst., Washington, 1988—95. With Counter Intelligence Corps U.S. Army. Fellow Fin. Analysts Fedn.; mem. Univ. Club. Avocations: water sports, travel, theater. Office: K Road Mgmt LLC 330 Madison Ave 25th fl New York NY 10017 Office Phone: 212-351-0538. Business E-Mail: carls@kroadpower.com.

SELIGSON, GARY MARC, musician; b. West Orange, N.J., Sept. 14, 1960; s. Kurt and Lore Seligson; m. Lucy Gentry Vance, July 1, 2000. MusB cum laude, U. Hartford, 1983; studied with Alexander Lepak; studied with Gary Chester, N.Y.C., 1984-85. Endorser, clinician, tchr. various instruments. Drummer, percussionist: (Broadway shows) The King and I, Disney Radio City Music Hall, Christmas, N.Y.C., 1983-84, On Your Toes, Dreamgirls, N.Y.C. and nat. andinternat. tours, 1985-87, Cats, Les Miserables, Miss Saigon, nat. and internat. tours, 1988-97; Broadway and studio drummer Lion King, Chicago, Rent, N.Y.C., 1999; drummer, house contractor, arranger: (Broadway show) Aida, N.Y.C., 1999-2003 (Tony award 2000, Grammy award 2000); drummer, arranger: (Broadway show) Gershwin's Fascinating Rhythm, 1999, Original Band Ejectrode, 1998—; drummer: (Broadway show) Wicked, 2003; co-composer: The Alchemist; TV appearances include NBC Today Show, 1999, ABC Good Morning America, 2000, ABC The View, 2000; percussionist: (rec.) Compassion, 1999; featured in Modern Drummer Mag. Mem. Am. Fedn. Musicians. Home: 371 Ft Washington Ave Apt 2I New York NY 10033

SELIGSON, JUDITH, artist; b. Phila., July 8, 1950; d. David and Harriet Tutelman Seligson; m. Allan M. Greenberg, Sept. 7, 1938; 1 child, Hannah Leah. BA cum laude, Harvard U., 1973. One-woman shows include Jane Haslem Gallery, Washington, 1992, Anita Friedman Fine Art, N.Y.C., 1997, Schlesinger Libr., Radcliffe Coll., Cambridge, Mass., 1997, exhibited in group shows at Gary Snyder Fine Art, N.Y.C., 1998, 2002, Signal 66, Washington, 2001, Exit Art, N.Y.C., 2002, Amram Sunday Scholars Series, Washington, 2000; contbr. articles to profl. jours. and pubs.

SELIGSON, MITCHELL A. Latin American studies educator; b. Hempstead, N.Y., Nov. 12, 1945; m. Susan Berk, June 18, 1967; 1 child, Amber Lara. BA cum laude, Bklyn. Coll., 1967; MA, U. Fla., 1968; PhD, U. Pitts., 1974. Vol. U.S. Peace Corps, Costa Rica, 1968-70; asst. prof./assoc. prof. U. Ariz., Tucson, 1974-85; prof. U. Pitts., 1986-93, Daniel H. Wallace prof. polit. sci., 1994—, dir. Latin Am. studies, 1986-92, rsch. prof., 1992—; Centennial prof. Vanderbilt U., Nashville, 2004—. Cons. to U.S. AID, Guatemala, Honduras, Nicaragua, Costa Rica, Ecuador, Jamaica, Panama, El Salvador, Peru, Bolivia, Paraguay, 1980—. Author, editor: Peasants of Costa Rica and the Development of Agrarian Capitalism, 1980, The Gap Between Rich and Poor, 1984, Authoritarians and Democrats, 1987, Elections and Democracy in Central America, 1989, rev. edit. 1995, Development and Underdevelopment, 1993, The Political Economy of Global Inequality, 2003. Fulbright fellow, Costa Rica, 1986, Rockefeller Found. fellow, 1985-86; grantee Social Sci. Rsch. Coun., Ford Found., NSF, Mellon Found., Heinz Endowment. Mem. Am. Polit. Sci. Assn., Latin Am. Studies Assn. (chmn. fin. com. 1991). Office: Vanderbilt U Dept Polit Sci Nashville TN 37235 E-mail: m.seligson@vanderbilt.edu.

SELIGSON, THEODORE H. architect, art appraiser, interior designer; b. Kansas City, Mo., Nov. 10, 1930; s. Harry and Rose (Haith) S.; m. Jacqueline Rose, Dec. 27, 1964 (div. 1976). BArch, Washington U., St. Louis, 1953. Registered architect, Mo., Kans. Intern Marshall & Brown, Kansas City, Mo., 1949-54; designer, head design Kivett & Myers, Kansas City, Mo., 1954-62; prin. Design Assocs., 1955—, Atelier Seligson, Kansas City, Mo., 1962-64; pres. Seligson, Eggen, Inc., Kansas City, 1964-73, Seligson Assocs., Inc., Architects Planners, Kansas City, 1973-97; prin. Foss, Seligson, Lafferty, 1997—. Vis. lectr. adult edn. U. Mo.-Kansas City, 1958-61, vis. prof. arch., 1989—, vis. prof. urban design, 2002--; tchr., critic Kansas City Art Inst., Mo., 1961-64, 71-72, adj. prof., 1986, 89, 91, 92; adj. prof. Kans. State U., 1991-92, 97; vis. prof. Washington U., St. Louis, 1975, 77, 78, 81, 86, 91, U. Kans., Lawrence, 1978, 79, 80, 91, 92; art cons. Design Assocs., Kansas City, Mo., 1955—. Projects pub. in archtl. jours. V.p. Friends of Art Nelson-Atkins Mus. Art, Kansas City, bd. dirs. 1963-67, chmn. selections com., 1981, vis. curator, 1972, 87; chmn. Capitol Fine Arts Commn. Mo., 1983-90, Kansas City Worlds Fair goals and themes subcom., 1985-90; bd. dirs. Westport Tomorrow, Kansas City, 1980-87, Hist. Kansas City Found., 1984-90; pres. Native Sons of Kansas City, 1989, bd. dirs. 1978-94, Westport Cmty. Coun., 1973-75; bd. govs. Truman Med. Ctr., Kansas City, 1998-2002, mem. bd. advisors, 2002--; mem. Kansas City Key to City Commn., 2001-02; bd. dirs. Sacred Structures, 2003—. Recipient Urban Design award Kansas City Mcpl. Art Commn., 1968, 74, 78; Nat. Archtl. award Am. Inst. Steel Constrn., 1970; Nat. award ASID/DuPont Corian, 1989. Fellow AIA (Kansas City chpt. pres. 1983, bd. dirs. 1979-84, Design Excellence award 1966, 68, 70, 74, Ctrl. States Regional award 1974, 78, Honor award for outstanding svc. to chpt. and profession 1982-83); mem. Mo. Coun. Archs., Am. Soc. Interior Designers, Nat. Coun. Archtl. Registration Bds. (task analysis adv. com. 1988-90), Soc. Archtl. Historians (pres. 1973-75, bd. dirs. 1994-97). Jewish. Office: Foss Seligson Lafferty 106 W 14th St Kansas City MO 64105-1914

SELIN, IVAN, entrepreneur; b. N.Y.C., Mar. 11, 1937; s. Saul and Freda (Kuhlman) Selin; m. Nina Kallet, June 8, 1957; children: Douglas, Jessica. BE, Yale U., 1957, ME, 1958, PhD, 1960; DSc, U. Paris, 1962. Rsch. engr. Rand Corp., Santa Monica, Calif., 1960-65; sys. analyst Dept. Def., Washington, 1965-67, dep. asst. sec. def., 1967-69, acting asst. sec. for systems analysis, 1969-70; founder, chmn. bd. Am. Mgmt. Systems, Inc., Arlington, Va., 1970-89; undersec. state Dept. State, Washington, 1989-91; chmn. NRC, Washington, 1991-95; chmn., CEO Phoenix Internat., Washington, 1995—; chmn. BZL Biologics, Inc., 1998—, Enumerale Solutions, Inc., 1998—. Lectr. UCLA, 1961-63; chmn. mil. econ. adv. panel to CIA, 1978-89; chmn. e-Numerate Solutions, Inc., BZL Biologics. Author: Detection Theory, 1964;

contbr. articles to profl. jours. Pres. Corp. Against Drug Abuse, 1988-95; bd. dirs., gov. UN Assn. U.S., 1979-89; exec. com. Greater Washington Research Ctr., Fed. City Council; trustee Asia Soc., 1996-98; chmn., bd. dirs. Smithsonian Nat. Mus. of Am. History, 1996—. Yale U. Coun., 2000—. Recipient Disting. Civilian Svc. medal, 1970, Disting. Svc. medal Sec. of State, 1991; Fulbright scholar, 1959-61; Ford Found. grantee, 1952-54. Mem. IEEE (editor Trans. on Info. Theory 1960-65), Coun. Fgn. Rels., Yale Club, Sigma Xi, Tau Beta Pi. Office: Phoenix Internat Inc PO Box 58277 Washington DC 20037-5503 Home: PO Box 58277 Washington DC 20037-8277

SELIN, LISA K. physician; b. Helsinki, Finland, Apr. 8, 1952; d. Lauri Oscar and Hilma K Selin. BSc, Dalhousie Univ, 1970—74; MD, Dalhousie U., 1974—79, FRCP, 1980—84; PhD, Univ. Man., 1986—93. Med. intern Dalhousie U., Halifax, Canada, 1979—80, resident in internal medicine, 1980—84; fellow in infectious diseases Univ of Man., Winnipeg, Canada, 1984—86; doctoral student Univ of Man., 1986—91; postdoctoral fellow Univ. Mass. Med. Sch., 1992—95, instr., 1995—96; asst. prof. Univ. Mass. Med Sch., 1996—2001; assoc. prof. Univ. Mass. Med. Sch., 2001—. Contbr. articles to profl. jours. Med. Coun. of Can. Student fellowship, Med. Coun. of Can., 1986—91, Dalhousie Entrance schoarship, Dalhousie Univ, 1970, Izaak Walton Killam scholarship, Izaak Walton Killam Found., 1984—86, Clin. Investigator award, Nat. Inst. of Health, 1996—99, Rsch. grant, NIH- NIAID, 2000—, NIH-NIAID, 2001—, 1999—2003. Mem.: Can. Infectious Disease Soc., Am. Assn. of Immunologists. Achievements include research in T cell-mediated heterologous immunity in viral infections. Avocations: painting, cross country skiing, swimming, gardening, travel. Office: Univ Mass Med Sch 55 Lake Ave North Worcester MA 01655 E-mail: liisa.selin@umassmed.edu.

SELIN, NINA EVVIE, philanthropist; b. N.Y.C., Dec. 16, 1935; d. Louis Harry and Ida Cantor; m. Ivan Selin, June 8, 1957; children: Douglas Scott, Jessica Beth. BS, Boston U., 1957. Cert. elem. tchr., Conn. Tchr. West Haven (Conn.) Sch. Dist., 1957-60; dir. Nat. Consumers League, Washington, 1968-75; propr. Relax-Relocation Cons., Washington, 1975-80; vice chmn. Phoenix Internat. Power Plant Co., Washington, 1995-98; chmn. Nat. Aquarium, Washington, 1986—. Bd. dirs. Am. Cancer Soc., 1972-87, Nat. Geog. Soc., 1995—, Mt. Sinai Hosp. Found., Miami Beach, Fla., 1998—, Rep. Nat. Com., 1991—; chmn. Selin Family Found., Del., 1995; judge Nathan Davis award AMA, Washington, 2001. Recipient Disting. Svc. award Am. Cancer Soc., 1987, Mt. Sinai Found., 1999. Mem. Internat. Club III, Welcome to Washington Internat. Club. Avocations: exotic travel, scuba diving, reading, public service. Home: 1455 Ocean Dr Apt 1602 Miami FL 33139 Office: Phoenix Internat 1050 17th St NW Washington DC 20036 E-mail: nselin@phnx-intl.com.

SELINGER, JERRY ROBIN, lawyer; b. Peekskill, N.Y., Nov. 3, 1947; s. Philip R. and Helen D. (Klein) S.; m. Barbara D. Wax, Aug. 2, 1969; children: Elise, Scott. BS in Engring. Sci., SUNY, Buffalo, 1969; MS, Columbia U., 1971; JD, George Washington U., 1975. Bar: Md. 1975, D.C. 1976, U.S. Ct. Appeals (fed. cir.) 1977, U.S. Supreme Ct. 1978, Tex. 1980, U.S. Ct. Appeals (5th and 11th cirs.) 1981, U.S. Ct. Appeals (3d cir.) 1982. Atty. Arent, Fox, Kintner, Plotkin & Kahn, Washington, 1975-79, Richards, Harris & Medlock, Dallas, 1979-82; mem., dir. Baker, Mills & Glast, Dallas, 1982-90; ptnr. Vinson & Elkins LLP, Dallas, 1990-97; shareholder Jenkens & Gilchrist, Dallas, 1997—. Contbr. articles to profl. jours. Bd. trustees Dallas Bar Found., 2001—. Mem. ABA, Tex. Bar Assn. (chair intellectual property law sect. 1996-97, bd. dirs. 1998-2001), Dallas Bar Assn. (bd. dirs. 1995-96), Tex. Young Lawyers Assn. (bd. dirs. 1984-86, Pres. award 1986), Am. Intellectual Property Law Assn. (bd. dirs. 2002—), Dallas (Tex.) Bar Found. (bd. trustees, 2001—), Dallas Assn. Young Lawyers (sec. 1983, treas. 1984), Order of Coif, Phi Delta Phi. Home: 10414 Woodford Dr Dallas TX 75229-6317 Office: Jenkens & Gilchrist 1445 Ross Ave Ste 3200 Dallas TX 75202-2785 Office Phone: 214-855-4776. E-mail: jselinger@jenkens.com.

SELIS, STUART L. financial consultant, underwriter; b. Washington, Feb. 1, 1951; s. Sidney M. Selis and Betty (Pollock) Kuhne; m. Pamela Naftolin, Oct. 27, 1977 (div. Mar. 1989); children: Michael J., Lisa K.; m. Cherie Sternberg, June 20, 1990. BA, Mich. State U., 1973. CLU, chartered fin. con. Account mgr. Sagemark Consulting of Lincoln Nat. Corp., Southfield, Mich., 1980—. Pres. Farmington Green West Homeowners Assn., Farmington Hills, Mich., 1984-85; mem. Farmington Hills Parks and Recreation Commn., 1987-97; mem. Mich. regional adv. bd. Anti-Defamation League of B'nai B'rith, 1991-96; bd. dirs. Young Israel West Bloomfield, 1995—1999, bd. dirs. Bais Chabad of W. Bloomfield, 2003-. Mem. Nat. Assn. Life Underwriters, Am. Soc. CLU's. Republican. Jewish. Home: 6436 Summer Ct West Bloomfield MI 48322-2234 Office: Sagemark Consulting Inc 26555 Evergreen Rd Ste 1600 Southfield MI 48076-4206

SELKIRK, JAMES KIRKWOOD, biochemist, researcher; b. N.Y.C., Dec. 3, 1938; s. James Kirkwood and Doris (Schuler) S.; m. Carole Ann Bozzone, Sept. 16, 1961; children: James Kirkwood, David Edward. BS, Coll. Environ. Sci. and Forestry, Syracuse (N.Y.) U., 1964; PhD, Syracue U. Upstate Med. Ctr., Syracuse, 1969. Postdoctoral fellow McArdle Lab. Cancer Rsch., U. Wis., Madison, 1969-72; staff fellow Nat. Cancer Inst., NIH, Bethesda, Md., 1972-74, sr. staff fellow, 1974-75; sr. staff scientist unit leader chem. carcinogenesis biology divsn. Oak Ridge (Tenn.) Nat. Lab., 1975-85; chief carcinogenesis and toxicology evaluation br. nat. toxicology program Nat. Inst. Environ. Health Scis., 1985-89, assoc. dir. divsn. toxicology rsch. and testing, 1989-92, chief carcinogen mechanism group Lab. Molecular Carcinogenesis, 1992—97; spl. asst. to sci. dir. for technology devel. Nat. Inst. Evniron. Health Scis., 1997-2000; deputy dir. Nat. Ctr. Toxicogenomics, 2000—; adj. prof. Oak Ridge Biomed. Grad. Sch., U. Tenn., 1975-85; mem. breast cancer task force NIH, 1979-82; mem. com. on pyrenes and analogs NAS, 1981-83; chmn. Interagy. Testing Commn., 1986-90. Author rsch. articles, chpts. in books; mem. editl. bd. Carcinogenesis Jour., 1984-87, 91-93, Cancer Rsch., 1981-86, Environ. Health Perspectives, 1993-98, contbg. editor, 2003—. Mem. Orange County Planning Bd., 1997—; chmn. Weaver Dairy Precinct, Dem. Party Orange County, 1996-99. With AUS, 1959-61. Recipient U.S. Interagy. Testing Com. Exemplary Svc. award, 1992. Mem. Am. Cancer Soc. (carcinogenesis study sect. 1975-78, 92-96). Home: 30119 Settle Dr Chapel Hill NC 27517 Office: Nat Inst Environ Health Scis PO Box 12233 Research Triangle Park NC 27709 Office Phone: 919-541-2548. E-mail: selkirk@niehs.nih.gov.

SELKOE, DENNIS JESSE, neurologist, researcher, educator; b. N.Y.C., Sept. 25, 1943; s. Herbert E. and Mary P. (Lille) S.; m. Polly Ann Strasser, June 24, 1967; children: Gregory, Kimberly. BA, Columbia U., 1965; MD, U. Va., 1969. Diplomate Am. Bd. Psychiatry and Neurology, Nat. Bd. Med. Examiners. Intern in medicine Hosp. U. Pa., Phila., 1969-70; rsch. assoc. NIH, Bethesda, Md., 1970-72; resident in neurology Peter Bent Brigham/Children's Hosp., Boston, 1972-74, chief resident in neurology, 1974-75; rsch. assoc. Harvard Med. Sch., Boston, 1975-78, asst. prof. neurology, 1978-82, assoc. prof., 1982-85, assoc. prof. neurology and neurosci., 1985-90, faculty mem. divsn. on aging, 1980—, prof. neurology and neurosci., 1990—. Vincent and Stella Coates prof. neurol. diseases, 2001—; co-dir. Ctr. Neurologic Diseases Brigham and Women's Hosp., Boston, 1985—. Mem. sci. adv. bd. Alzheimer's Disease Assn., Chgo., 1983-89; mem. Gov.'s Commn. on Alzheimer's Disease, Mass., 1985-87; neurosci. adv. com. Howard Hughes Med. Inst., 1996—. Author over 200 articles, book chpts. on biochemistry and molecular biology of Alzheimer's Disease. Asst. surgeon USPHS, 1970-72. Recipient Wood-Kalb Found. prize Alzheimers Disease Assn., 1984, Med. Rsch. award Met. Life Found., 1986, LEAD award Nat. Inst. on Aging, 1988, NIH Merit award, 1991—, Arthur Cherkin award UCLA, 1995, Mathilde Solowey award in neurosci. Found. for Advanced Edn. in Scis., NIH, 1998, Rita Hayworth award Alzheimer's Assn., 1995, Boerhaave medal U. Leiden, 1998, Pioneer award Alzheimer's Assn., 1999; grantee Bristol-Myers Squibb Neurosci., 1990. Fellow AAAS, Am. Acad. Neurology (Potamkin prize 1989, Dr. A.H. Heineken prize for Medicine 2002); mem. Am. Neurol. Assn., Soc. for Neurosci., Am. Assn. Neuropathologists, World Fedn. Neurologists. Office: Harvard Med Sch Brigham & Womens Hosp 77 Avenue Louis Pasteur Boston MA 02115-5727

SELKOWITZ, ARTHUR, retired advertising agency executive; b. N.Y.C., May 26, 1943; s. Harry and Anne (Lichten) S.; m. Betsey Wattenberg, Apr. 15, 1967; children: Adam, Jed. AB, Syracuse (N.Y.) U., 1965. Account exec. Dancer Fitzgerald Sample, 1969-71; with Benton & Bowles, Inc., N.Y.C., 1971-82, v.p., account supr., 1972-75, sr. v.p., mgmt. supr., 1975-81, sr. v.p., account dir., 1981-82; founder, pres. Penchina, Selkowitz Inc., N.Y.C., 1982-90; exec. v.p. internat. D'Arcy, Masius, Benton & Bowles, N.Y.C., 1990-94, pres. Asia and Pacific, 1995-96, pres. N.Am., 1996-97, chmn., CEO, 1997-2000; vice chmn., chief client officer BCom3 Group, Inc., N.Y.C., 2001—02, Publicis Groupe, 2002. Dancer Fitzgerald Sample, N.Y.C., 1966-71. E-mail: arthur@sunrockholdings.com.

SELL, NOEL BRUCE, music educator; b. Allentown, Pa., Nov. 7, 1955; s. Frederick Franklin and Irene Lillian Sell; m. Valerie Grace Schultz, July 28, 1979; children: Warren Frederick, Sarah Katherine. MusB in Music Edn .(hon.), Westminster Choir Coll., Rider U., 1978. Music Comprehensive K-12 NJ State Bd. of Examiners - Deparment of Edn., 1978. Tchr., choral dir. Sampson G. Smith Intermediate Sch., Somerset, NJ, 1978—; dir. music Hillsborough Ref. Ch., Millstone, 1979—82; dir. music, organist Packanack Cmty. Ch., Wayne, 1982—84, Pluckemin Presbyn. Ch., 1984—. Mentoring student tchrs. and new tchrs. Sampson G. Smith Intermediate Sch., Somerset, 1985—. Musician (choral dir.): (gifted and talented choir) Performance of Choral Music (N.J. State Teen Arts Festival, 2001, 2002, 2003, 2004), gifted and talent choir, gifted and talented choir. Mem. Calvary Moravian Ch., Allentown, Pa., 1968—2003; union assn. rep. Franklin Twp. Edn. Assn., Somerset, 2003—04. Mem.: NEA, N.J. Music Educators Nat. Conf., Music Educators Nat. Conf., N.J. Edn. Assn., Am. Guild of Organists, Amercian Guild English Handbell Ringers, Am. Choral Directors Assn., Round Valley Trout Assn. (trustee 1980—82), Knee Deep Club. Moravian. Achievements include Member/Soloist Westminster Choir (1975-1978); Member, Choir in Residence, Festival of Two Worlds, Charleston, South Carolina and Spoleto Italy (1975-1978); Gifted and Talented Choir of SGS Int. Sch. received outstanding ratings in the 27th-30th and 32nd-38th Annual Jr. High Mid. Sch. Choral Festival sponsored by NJMENC. Avocations: fishing, collecting and running o gauge toy trains, gardening. Home: 108 Van Dyke Court Hillsborough NJ 08844-3417 Office: Sampson G Smith Intermediate School 1649 Amwell Road Somerset NJ 08873 Office Phone: 732-873-2800 769. E-mail: nsell@franklinboe.org.

SELL, ROBERT EMERSON, electrical engineer; b. Apr. 23, 1929; s. Cecil Leroy and Ona Arletta (Stevens) S.; m. Ora Lucile Colton, Nov. 7, 1970. BS, U. Nebr., 1962. Registered profl. engr., Nebr., Mo., Ill., Ind., Ohio, W.Va., Ky., Ark., Tex., Oreg., Wash., Calif. Chief draftsman Dempster Mill Mfg. Co., Beatrice, Nebr., 1949-53; designer-engr. U. Nebr., Lincoln, 1955-65; elec. design engr. Kirkham, Michael & Assocs., Omaha, 1965-67, Leo A. Daly Co., Omaha and St. Louis, 1967-69; mech. design engr. Hellmuth, Obata, Kassabaum, St. Louis, 1969-70; chief elec. engr. Biagi-Hannan & Assocs., Inc., Evansville, Ind., 1971-74; elec. project engr. H.L. Yoh Co. under contract to Monsanto Co., Creve Coeur, Mo., 1974-77, Dhillon Engrs., Inc., Portland, Oreg., 1978-85; project coord. Brown-Zammit-Enyeart Engring., Inc., San Diego, 1985-88; elec. engr. Morgen Design, Inc., San Diego, 1988; lead elec. engr. Popov Engrs., Inc., San Diego, 1988-89; mech. and elec. specialist Am. Engring. Labs., Inc. divsn. Profl. Svc. Industries, Inc., San Diego, 1990—. Instr. Basic Inst. Tech., St. Louis, 1971. Mem. ASHRAE, IEEE. Home and Office: PO Box 261578 San Diego CA 92196-1578

SELLECCA, CONNIE, actress; b. Bronx, N.Y., May 25, 1955; m. Gil Gerard (div.); m. John Tesh, 1992; children: Gilbert Gerard, Prima Tesh. Appeared in The Bermuda Depths, TV films include Somebody's Killing the World's Greatest Models, Captain America, The Last Fling, Flying High, 1978, Captain America II, 1979, Circus of the Stars #5, 1980, Hotel, 1982, International Airport, 1985, Downpayment on Murder, 1987, Breotherhood of the Rose, 1989, Turn Back the Clock, 1989, Miracle Landing, 1990, People Like Us, 1990, P.S.I. Luv U, 1991, House of Secrets and Lies, 1992, Passport to Murder, 1993, She Led Two Lives, 1994, The Surrogate, 1995, Holiday to Remember, 1995, A Dangerous Affair, 1995, While My Pretty One Sleeps, 1997, Something Borrowed, Something Blue, 1997, Domesday Rock, 1997, Dangerous Waters, 1999, Anna's Dream, 2002; TV series include Beyond Westworld, Flying High, The Greatest American Hero, Arthur Hailey's Hotel, PS I Luv U; films I Saw Mommy Kissing Santa Claus, 2002. Address: William Morris Agy 151 El Camino Dr Beverly Hills CA 90212 also: Richard Grant and Assocs 8489 W Third St Los Angeles CA 90048*

SELLECK, TOM, actor; b. Detroit, Jan. 29, 1945; s. Robert D. and Martha S.; m. Jacquelyn Ray, 1970 (div. 1982); 1 stepson, Kevin; m. Jillie Joan Mack, Aug. 7, 1987; 1 child, Hannah Margaret. Student, U. So. Calif. TV appearances include The Rockford Files, Friends, 1996, 2000; star TV series Magnum P.I. 1980-88, The Closer, CBS series, 1998—;; co-producer and star TV Film Monte Walsh; films include Midway, 1976, Coma, 1982, High Road to China, 1983, Lassiter, 1984, Runaway, 1985, Three Men and a Baby, 1987, Her Alibi, 1989, An Innocent Man, 1989, Quigley Down Under, 1990, Three Men and a Little Lady, 1990, Folks!, 1992, Mr. Baseball, 1992, In and Out, 1997, The Love Letter, 1999; TV films include The Sacketts, 1979, Divorce Wars, 1982, Louis L'Amour's "The Shadow Riders", 1982, Broken Trust, 1995, Ruby Jean and Joe, 1996, Last Stand at Saber River, 1998, Louis l'Amour's Crossfire Trail, 2000, Monte Walsh, Reversible Errors, Thunder in June. Office: care Esme Chandlee 2967 Hollyridge Dr Los Angeles CA 90068-1949

SELLER, GREGORY EROL, marketing executive, writer, consultant; b. Denver, Oct. 4, 1953; s. Otto Gustave and Dolores Louise (Crawford) S. BBA, U. Colo., 1975. Account exec. Gt.-West Life, L.A., 1975-79, asst. v.p. group devel. Denver, 1980-84; v.p. govt. mkts. and nat. accts. Great-West Life, L.A., 1988—; pres., chief exec. officer Benefits Communication Corp., Denver, 1985-87, sr. v.p. govt. mkts., 1991—. Bd. dirs. Benefits Communication Co. Editor newsletter Focus on 457, 1988—. Mem. vestry, treas. St. Thomas Episc. Ch., Hollywood, Calif., 1989-93. Mem. Delta Upsilon. Democrat. Office: Great West Life Ste 560 18111 Von Karman Ave Irvine CA 92612-7131 Home: 22822 Via Orvieto Monarch Beach CA 92629-3452

SELLER, ROBERT HERMAN, cardiologist, physician; b. Phila., Mar. 21, 1931; s. David and Elsie (Straussman) S.; m. Maxine Schwartz, June 3, 1956; children: Michael, Douglas, Stuart. AB, U. Pa., 1952, MD, 1956. Intern. Grad. Hosp. of U. Pa., Phila., 1956-57; research asst. dept. pharmacology U. Pa., 1953-55; resident in cardiology, research fellow Am. Heart Assn., Phila. Gen. Hosp., 1957-58; resident in internal medicine Albert Einstein Med. Ctr., Phila., 1958-59, chief resident, 1959-60; instr. medicine Hahnemann Med. Coll. and Hosp., Phila., 1960-64, asst. prof., 1964-69, assoc. prof., 1969-72, dir. Service F, 1962-67, asst. coordinator mil. edn. for nat. def., 1961-64, dir. div. family medicine, 1967-72, acting chmn. dept. family medicine and community health, 1972-74, prof. medicine, family medicine and community health, 1973-74; practice medicine, specializing in cardiology Buffalo, 1974—; prof., chmn. dept. family medicine, prof. medicine SUNY-Buffalo, Deaconess Hosp., 1974-82, chmn. dept. family practice and dir. family practice residency program, 1974-82; prof. medicine and family medicine SUNY-Buffalo, 1974-2000; emeritus prof. medicine and family medicine, 2000—. Author: Differential Diagnosis of Common Complaints, 1986, 4th edit., 2000, Diagnosis of Common Complaints, 2004; contbr. articles to profl. jours. NIH grantee, 1972-75; Deaconess Hosp. family practice resident tng. grantee, 1975-; health professions spl. projects grantee, 1975- Fellow ACP, Am. Coll. Cardiology, Am. Acad. Family Physicians, Phila. Coll. Physicians; mem. AMA, N.Y. Med. Soc., Erie County Med. Soc., Am. Fedn. Clin. Research, Am. Heart Assn., Soc. of Tchrs. of Family Medicine, N.Y. Acad. Sci., N.Y. Acad. Family Physicians. Home: 125 Crestwood Ln Buffalo NY 14221-1462 Office: 1542 Maple Rd Buffalo NY 14221-3625 Office Phone: 716-568-3402.

SELLERS, BARBARA JACKSON, federal judge; b. Richmond, Va., Oct. 3, 1940; m. Richard F. Sellers; children: Elizabeth M., Anne W., Catherine A. Attended, Baldwin-Wallace Coll., 1958-60; BA cum laude, Ohio State U., 1962; JD magna cum laude, Capital U. Law Sch., Columbus, Ohio, 1979. Bar: Ohio 1979, U.S. Dist. Ct. (so. dist.) Ohio 1981, U.S. Ct. Appeals (6th cir.), 1986. Jud. law clk. Hon. Robert J. Sidman, U.S. Bankruptcy Judge, Columbus, Ohio, 1979-81; assoc. Lasky & Semons, Columbus, 1981-82; jud. law clk. to Hon. Thomas M. Herbert, U.S. Bankruptcy Ct., Columbus, 1982-84; assoc. Baker & Hostetler, Columbus, 1984-86; U.S. bankruptcy judge So. Dist. Ohio, Columbus, 1986—. Lectr. on bankruptcy univs., insts., assns. Recipient Am. Jurisprudence prize contracts and criminal law, 1975-76, evidence and property, 1976-77, Corpus Juris Secundum awards, 1975-76, 76-77. Mem. Columbus Bar Assn., Am. Bankruptcy Inst., Nat. Conf. Bankruptcy Judges, Order of Curia, Phi Beta Kappa. Office: US Bankruptcy Ct 170 N High St Columbus OH 43215-2403 E-mail: barbara_sellers@ohsb.uscourts.gov.

SELLERS, DONALD R. biotechnology company executive; AB, Lafayette Coll.; M.Internat. Mgmt., Am. Grad. Sch. Internat. Mgmt. Counter-intelligence spl. agt. Spl. Forces U.S. Mil. Intelligence; country mgr. Vietnam and Hong Kong Pfizer Pharm., 1973; dir. worldwide exports Revlon Health-care Group, Pacific area dir.; v.p. mktg. and ops. Asia Sterling Drug Internat., 1983—90, pres. L.Am. Andina Group; corp. v.p. Getz Bros., 1990—93, pres. Japanese ops.; mng. dir. SciClone Pharms. Internat., Ltd., 1993—; CEO, pres., dir. SciClone Pharms., Inc., San Mateo, Calif., 1996—. Office: Sci Clone Pharmaceuticals Inc 901 Mariners Island Blvd #205 San Mateo CA 94404

SELLERS, FRED EVANS, accounting educator; b. Lexington, Mo., Feb. 28, 1941; s. James MacBrayer and Rebekah Hall (Evans) S.; m. Katherine Ann Griggs, May 3, 1969; children: Mark Griggs, Rebekah Field. BA in History, Yale U., 1965; MBA, U. Kans., 1976, PhD in Bus., 1984. CPA Tex. Reporter Kansas City (Mo.) Star, 1965-66, copy editor, 1966-70, Washington Star, 1970-72, asst. nat. editor, 1972-73; asst. prof. U. Tulsa, 1979-87; assoc. prof. Southwestern U., Georgetown, Tex., 1987—, chmn. dept. econs. and bus., 1994—2004. Sec., treas. planning com. U. Tulsa Conf. Accts., 1980-87. Contbr. articles to profl. jours. Trustee Wentworth Mil. Acad., Lexington, Mo., 1986—, pres., 1990-92; trustee Williamson County (Tex.) Literacy Coun., 1989-91; treas., bd. dirs. St. John's Presch., Tulsa, 1984-87; conv. del. Episc. Diocese Okla., 1984, 85; audit com. St. John's Episc. Ch., Tulsa, 1983-87; bishop's com. Grace Episc. Ch., 1989, jr. warden, 1989, bishop's warden, 1990, chmn., audit com., 2004, mem. rector search com., 2004; alt. Tex. State Rep. Conv., 1988; treas. Georgetown Area United Way, 1993-99; mem. Georgetown Ethics Commn., 2004—. Mem. Inst. Mgmt. Accts. (dir. manuscripts Austin chpt. 1988-96), Am. Acctg. Assn. (membership com. 1980-81), AICPA, Tex. Soc. CPAs (ednl. instns. com. Austin chpt.), Rotary. Avocations: bridge, piano, singing, jogging. Home: 1610 E 15th St Georgetown TX 78626-7206 Office: Southwestern U Dept Econs and Bus Adminstrn Georgetown TX 78627-0770 Office Phone: 512-863-1574.

SELLERS, FRED WILSON, accountant; b. Alexander City, Ala., Apr. 29, 1942; s. Fred Wilson and Helen (Hagan) Sellers; m. Nancy Wilbanks, July 11, 1964; children: Fredrick Hagan, Robert Wilbanks. BS, U. Ala., 1964; MBA, L.I. U., 1966; postgrad., U. Wis., Madison, 1974. CPA, N.C., Ala.; cert. fraud examiner. Staff acct. Ernst & Young, Winston-Salem, N.C., 1966-69; comptr. Citibanc Group, Inc., Andalusia, Ala., 1969-73; various positions, then sr. v.p., gen. auditor AmSouth Bank, Birmingham, Ala., 1973-98. Bd. dirs. Better Bus. Bur., Mobile, Ala., 1984-86. Mem. budget com. United Way, Birmingham, 1982-83. Mem. AICPA, N.C. Assn. CPAs, Ala. Assn. CPAs, Ala. United States Air Force Acad. Parents Club (pres. 1993-94, 94-95), Vestavia Country Club, The Club, Univ. Club (Tuscaloosa). Avocations: travel, photography. Home and Office: 2112 Viking Cir Birmingham AL 35216-3325

SELLERS, GREGORY JUDE, physicist; b. Far Rockaway, N.Y., June 20, 1947; s. Douglas L. and Rita R. (Dieringer) S.; m. Lucia S. Kim, Nov. 26, 1983; 1 child, Kristin Kim. AB in Physics, Cornell U., 1968; MS, U. Ill., 1970, PhD, 1975. Sr. scientist B-K Dynamics, Inc., Rockville, Md., 1974-76; with Allied-Signal Corp., Morristown, N.J., 1976-88, applications physicist, 1977-88; product supr. Amphenol Fiber Optic Products, Naperville, Ill., 1985-88; mgr. Cinch Connectors, Elk Grove, Ill., 1988-91; pres. Forss, Inc., Naperville, 1991-96, Fotron, Inc., Naperville, 1995—. Bd. dirs. Thermo-Tek, Inc., N.J., Fotron. Mem. AAAS, IEEE, Am. Phys. Soc. Achievements include development and commercialization of electronic connectors and fiber optic products; development of applications for polymeric materials and glassy metals in the electrical and electronics arena. Co-inventor adhesive bonding metallic glass, electromagnetic shielding, testing of thermal insulation, amorphous antipilferage marker, amorphous spring-shield, multiple fiber positioner for optical fiber connection, raised rib waveguide ribbon for precision optical interconnects. Home and Office: Fotron Inc 7S 515 Oak Trails Dr Naperville IL 60540

SELLERS, JIMMIE, construction executive; b. Florence, S.C., Aug. 4, 1951; s. Kisar and Evell Sellers; m. Lorrainne Conley Sellers, Aug. 25, 1996; children: Jimmy, Nikita Renee 1 stepchild, Teran Correia. Advanced welding cert., Coosa Valley Vocat.-Tech. Sch., 1971; small bus. mgmt. course, Floyd Jr. Coll., 1974. Cardiac care provider Am. Heart Assn., Rome, Ga., 1997; medic 1st aid EMP Am., Catersville, Ga., 2002. Author: (poetry) America at the Millennium, 2000. Min. Pentecostal Assembly of the World. Sgt. 1st class U.S. Army, 1988. Mem.: Handyman Club Am., VA Assn. Pentecostal. Avocations: drawing, wood carving, playing guitar, writing, building. Home: 109 Battey Dr Rome GA 30165

SELLERS, KATE M. art museum director; From dir. devel. and comm. to acting dir. Walters Art Gallery, Balt., 1987-94; dir. devel. and external affairs Cleve. Mus., 1995-97, dep. dir., 1997-2000; dir. Wadsworth Atheneum, Hartford, Conn., 2000—. Office: Wadsworth Atheneum Mus Art 600 Main St Hartford CT 06103-2990

SELLERS, MARK S. retail executive; BBA, U. Kans.-Mo., Kansas City. CEO, CFO S.W. Supermarkets, LLC, Schwegmann Giant Super Markets, LLC, Bay Area Foods Holding Co., Bay Area Foods, Inc., Homeland Holding Co., Homeland Stores, Inc.; vice chmn., CFO Pameco Corp., Norcross, Ga., 1999—. Office: Pameco Corp Ste D2 1865 Beaver Ridge Cir Norcross GA 30071-3845

SELLERS, PETER HOADLEY, mathematician, educator; b. Phila., Sept. 12, 1930; s. Lester Hoadley and Therese (Tyler) S.; m. Lucy Bell Newlin, June 21, 1958; children: Mortimer, Therese, Mary, Lucy Bell BA, U. Pa., 1953, MA, 1958, PhD, 1965. Math. tchr. Kangaru Sch., Embu, Kenya, 1961-63; programmer U. Pa., Phila., 1958-61; mem. faculty Rockefeller U., N.Y.C., 1966—. Johnson Found. postdoctoral fellow, 1963-65 Mem. editl. bd. Genomics, 1986-97; author: Combinatorial Complexes, 1979; contbr. articles to profl. jours. Trustee Coll. of the Atlantic, Bar Harbor, Maine, 1985-96; curator Rockefeller Hist. Instrument Collection, 1997—. Lt (j.g.) USNR, 1953-55 Mem. Am. Math. Soc., Math. Assn. Am., Soc. Indsl. and Applied Math. Democrat. Episcopalian. Avocations: boat building, sailing. Home: 413 W Stafford St Philadelphia PA 19144-4407 Office: Rockefeller Univ 1230 York Ave New York NY 10021-6399 Business E-Mail: sellers@rockefeller.edu.

SELLERS, WAYNE CHADICK, retired newspaper publisher, editor; b. Brady, Tex., Mar. 10, 1916; s. Marcellus Stephenson Sellers and Martha Jane Chadick; m. Camilla Ann Browning, June 29, 1946 (dec. June 1996). BA, Tex. Tech U., 1938; postgrad., U. Tex., 1940-41. Statistician Ft. Worth Star-Telegram, 1943-50; prodn. mgr. San Francisco News, 1951-52; bus. mgr. Sherman (Tex.) Democrat, 1953-59; pub. Rock Hill (S.C.) Herald, 1959-66; editor, pub. Palestine (Tex.) Herald-Press, 1966-80. Mem. bd. mgrs. Tex. State R.R., 1969-73; mem. adv. coun. U. Tex. Coll. communication, Austin, 1979—. Chmn. Palestine United Way, 1968, Northeast Tex. Lib. Sys. Adv. Coun., Garland, 1986—, Palestine Pub. Libr. Bd., 1979—; vol. lobbyist Tex. Libr. Assn., 1983; chmn. Reporter Bd., United Meth. Ch., Dallas, 1980-82. Named to Hall of Fame Tex. Tech U. Sch. Mass Comm., Lubbock, 1979; named Trustee of Yr. Tex. Libr. Assn., Houston, 1981, Nat. Advocacy Honor Roll Mem., Am. Libr. Assn., chgo., 2000, Builder of Palestine, Palestine C. of c., 1982, Mr. Books, Tex. State Libr. and Archives Commn., Austin, 1983. Democrat. Methodist. Avocations: amateur radio, travel, collecting books. Home: 215 Stephanie Dr Palestine TX 75803-8505 E-mail: wcsellers@earthlink.net.

SELLES, ROBERT HENDRIKUS, retired actuary; b. Amsterdam, Nov. 8, 1938; arrived in U.S., 1969; s. Albertus Henrikus and Jansje Suzanna (Cordes) Selles; m. Manuela Ioana Comnene, Aug. 26, 1966 (div. Mar. 1978); 1 child, Melina Joanna. B of Commerce with honors, U. Manitoba, 1961. Actuarial asst. Can. Premier Life Ins. Co., Winnipeg, Canada, 1961-62; asst. actuary Sun Life Assurance Co. Can., Montreal, 1962-69; sr. v.p. Hay/Huggins Co., Inc., Phila., 1969—91, ret., 2004. Fellow: Soc. Actuaries; mem.: Gavel Soc., Western Pension and Benefits Conf., Am. Acad. Actuaries, Conf. Cons. Actuaries, Netherlands Am. Assn. Delaware Valley (bd. dirs. 1993—96), Rainbor River Inc. (pres. 1995—), Netherlands Soc. Phila. (bd. dirs. 1991—, pres. 1993—96, 1999—2000), Internat. Benefits Found., Actuaries Club San Francisco. Home: 1420 Locust St Apt 34-A Philadelphia PA 19102-4220 Personal E-mail: robert@selles.us.

SELLEY, MICHAEL L. pharmaceutical company executive; b. Woking, Surrey, U.K., Jan. 20, 1948; s. Stanley John and Rosina Lillian Selley; m. Angela Grace Charlton, July 30, 1966 (div. Sept. 1976); 1 child, Michelle Louise; m. Pamela Kay Foulser, Oct. 29, 1977; 1 child, Timothy Michael. BSc, U. London, 1968; MSc, U. Alta., Edmonton, 1971; PhD, U. Sydney, 1975. Sr. rsch. scientist Sandoz Pharma Ltd., Basle, Switzerland, 1975-84; sr. rsch. fellow John Curtin Sch. Med. Rsch. Inst. Advanced Studies, Australian Nat. U., Canberra, 1985-95; chief of staff Office of the Min. for Sci. Tech., Canberra, 1996-97; chmn. and mng. dir. Pan Australia Labs Pty. Ltd., Symondstown, 1997-98; pres., CEO Angiogen Pharms. Pty. Ltd., Weston Creek, 1999—. Cons. Asia/Pacific region Panlabs Inc., Seattle, 1988-95. Contbr. articles to profl. jours. Anutech Canberra Tech. Partnership grantee, 1991-93. Fellow Royal Australian Chem. Inst. Achievements include research on the role of free radicals in neurodegenerative disease; the development of new anti-angiogenesis drugs. Home: 19 Holmes St Turramurra NSW 2074 Australia Office: Level 31 ABN AMRO Tower 88 Phillip Street Sydney NSW 2000 Australia Home Fax: 61 2 9144 3175. E-mail: mllselley@angiogen.com.au.

SELLICK, KATHLEEN A. hospital administrator; b. Phoenix, Ariz. m. Phil Sellick; 1 child, Grace. BS, Ariz. State U.; MBA, U. Chgo. Grad. Sch. Bus., 1984. With Am. Med. Internat., Beverly Hills, Calif., Westgate Med. Ctr., Denton, Tex.; adminstrv. resident Mayo Clinic, Rochester, Minn.; v.p. adminstrn. and dir. outreach devel. Hoag Meml. Hosp. Presbyn., Newport Beach, Calif.; exec. v.p. and COO St. Joseph Hosp., Orange, Calif.; assoc. exec. dir. and COO U. Wash. Med. Ctr., Seattle, 1999—2001, acting exec. dir., 2000—01, exec. dir., 2001—. Clin. asst. prof., dept. health services U. Wash. Sch. of Public Health and Community Medicine. Office: U Wash Med Ctr 1959 NE Pacific St Box 356151 Seattle WA 98195-6151 Office Fax: 206-598-6292.*

SELLIN, THEODORE, foreign service officer, consultant; b. Phila., June 17, 1928; s. Thorsten and Amy (Anderson) S.; m. Taru Jarvi, July 10, 1965; 1 child, Derek. Student, U. Uppsala, Sweden, 1946-48; BA, U. Pa., 1951, MA, 1952. Joined Fgn. Svc., Dept. State, 1952; vice consul Copenhagen, 1952-56; rsch. analyst Dept. State, Washington, 1956-58; program officer Office Internat. Confs., 1965-67; acad. tng. staff U. Ind., 1958-59; 2d sec. Am. Embassy, Helsinki, Finland, 1959-64, 1st sec., polit. officer, 1971-73, 1st sec., labor-polit. officer Oslo, 1967-71; polar affairs officer Dept. State, 1975; consul gen. Goteborg, Sweden, 1978-80; fgn. rels. cons. Dept. State, Washington, 1980—. Office: Dept State A/RPS/IPS/CR/IR Washington DC 20520

SELLINGSLOH, JOHN S. lawyer; b. Houston, Sept. 6, 1922. B.A., Rice U., 1947; LL.B., U. Tex., 1950. Bar: Tex. 1950. Practice, Houston; mem. Baker & Botts. Mem. Houston Bar Assn., ABA, State Bar Tex., Phi Beta Kappa, Order of Coif, Phi Delta Phi. Club: Chancellors. Editor-in-chief Tex. Law Rev. Office: Baker & Botts 1 Shell Plz Houston TX 77002

SELLKE, FRANK WILLIAM, cardiothoracic surgeon, researcher; b. Ft. Wayne, Ind., Feb. 5, 1956; s. Erwin A. and Anna Luise (Schumacher) S.; m. Amy Marie Brill, Jan. 31, 1987; children: Michelle, Eric, Nicholas, Amanda. AB summa cum laude, Wabash Coll., 1978; MD, Ind. U., Indpls., 1981. Diplomate Am. Bd. Thoracic Surgery, Am. Bd. Surgery. Intern Ind. U. Hosp., Indpls., 1981-82; emergency physician Culver Union Hosp., Crawfordsville, Ind., 1982-83; resident in surgery Akron (Ohio) City Hosp., 1983-87; postdoctoral fellow cardiac surgery U. Iowa, Iowa City, 1987-90; from instr. to asst. prof. surgery Harvard Med. Sch., Boston, 1990-95, assoc. prof. surgery, 1995—2000, prof. surgery, 2000—; cardiothoracic surgeon Beth Israel Hosp., Boston, 1990—; chief cardiothoracic surgery Beth Israel Deaconess Med. Ctr., Boston, 1999—. Editorial board journal of thoracic and cardiovascular surgery, —, journal of surgical research. Contbr. rsch. articles to profl. jours. Fellow Am. Coll. Cardiology, Am. Coll. Surgeons; mem. AMA, Am. Surg. Assn., Am. Heart Assn., Am. Physiol. Soc., Am. Coll. Chest Physicians, Soc. Univ. Surgeons, Assn. Acad. Surgeons, Am. Assn. for Thoracic Surgery, Soc. Thoracic Surgeons, Phi Beta Kappa. Lutheran. Home: 121 Monadnock Rd Chestnut Hill MA 02467-1136 Office: Beth Israel Deaconess Med Ctr 110 Francis St Boston MA 02215 Office Phone: 617-632-8383. Business E-Mail: fsellke@bidmc.harvard.edu.

SELLS, BOAKE ANTHONY, private investor; b. Ft. Dodge, Iowa, June 24, 1937; s. Lyle M. and Louise (Gadd) S.; m. Marian S. Stephenson, June 20, 1959; children: Damian, Brian, Jean Ann. BSC, U. Iowa, 1959; MBA, Harvard U., 1969. Bus. office mgr. Northwestern Bell Tel., Des Moines, 1959-63; salesman Hydraulic Cos., Ft. Dodge, 1964-67; pres. Cole Nat. Corp., Cleve., 1969-83; vice chmn. Dayton Hudson Corp., Mpls., 1983-84, pres., 1984-87; chmn., pres., chief exec. officer Revco D.S., Inc., Twinsburg, Ohio, 1987-92. Bd. dirs. Promus Cos. (name changed to Harrah's Entertainment, Inc. Trustee Mus. Contemporary Art, Cleve., Cleve. Play House.

SELLS, BRUCE HOWARD, biomedical sciences educator; b. Ottawa, Ont., Can., Aug. 15, 1930; s. Charles Henry and Nell (Worth) S.; m. Bernice May Romain, Sept. 19, 1953; children: Jennifer, Monica, David, Lisa. BS, Carleton U., 1952; MA, Queen's U., 1954; PhD, McGill U., 1957. Demonstrator McGill U., Montreal, Ont., Can., 1954-57; rsch. assoc. Columbia U., N.Y.C., 1961-62; asst. prof. St. Jude Children's Hosp.-U. Tenn., Memphis, 1962-68; assoc. prof. St. Jude Children's Hosp., Memphis, 1964-72, mem., 1968-72; prof., dir. molecular biology Meml. U. Nfld., St. John's, Can., 1972-83, assoc. dean, 1979-83; prof. molecular biology U. Guelph, Ont., Can., 1983-96, dean biol. sci., 1983-95, univ. prof. emeritus, 1997—; exec. dir. Can. Fed. Biol. Socs., 1999—; interim dir. Nat. Inst. Nutrition, 2003—04. Adv. com. Ont. Health Rsch. Coun., 1992. Contbr. articles to profl. jours. Rsch. fellow Damon Runyon Meml. Fund, Brussels, 1957-59, Copenhagen, 1959-60; Killam Sr. Rsch. fellow U. Paris, 1978-79; grantee NIH, 1963-72, NSF, 1965-69, Med. Rsch. Coun. Can., 1972-93, Damon Runyon Meml. Fund for Cancer Rsch., 1962-76, Nat. Found.-March of Dimes, 1974-78, Muscular Dystrophy Assn. Can., 1974-78, Nat. Cancer Inst. Can., 1979-83, Nat. Scis. and Engring. Rsch. Coun., 1990-2001, Vis. Prof. award Institut Pasteur, Paris, 1989; Exch. fellow Natural Scis. and Engring. Rsch. Coun. of Can., 1994. Fellow Royal Soc. Can. (rapporteur microbiology and biochemistry divsn. 1985-87, convenor 1987-89); mem. Acad. Sci. of Royal Soc. Can. (life scis. divsn. fellowship rev. com. 1990-92), Am. Soc. Microbiologists, Can. Biochemistry Soc. (pres. 1981-82, Ayerst award selection com. 1990), Med. Rsch. Coun. (Centennial fellowships com., chmn. com. on biotech. devel. grants 1983-85, standing com. for Can. Genetic Disease Network 1991-92, chmn., 1992-97), Nat. Rsch. Coun. Can. (biol. phenomena subcom. 1983-86, chmn. steering group, sci. criteria for environ. quality com. 1986, E.W.R. Steacie Prize com. 1986-88), Assn. Can. Deans of Sci. (co-founder 1989). Home: 277 Coutts Bay Rd RR # 5 Perth ON Canada K7H 3C7 Office: Can Fedn Biol Socs 305-1750 Courtwood Crescent Ottawa ON Canada K2C 2B5 Office Phone: 613-225-8889. E-mail: bsells@CFBS.org., Bruce.Sells@sympatico.ca.

SELLS, CLIFFORD WAYNE, pediatrician; m. Beth Riley; children: Jasmine children: Quincy. MD, Med. Coll. of Wis., Milw. WI, 1984—88. Medicine, Board Certified in Pediatrics 1992, MPH 1994, Board Certified Adolescent Medicine 1997. Dir., divsn. of adolescent health OHSU, Portland, Oreg., 1996—. Med. dir. Outside In Homeless Ctr., Portland, Oreg., 1997—. Fellow: AAP (life); mem.: Oreg. Pediatric Soc. (exec. bd. 1998—2003), Soc. for Adolescent Medicine. Office: OHSU 707 SW Gaines Rd CDRC-P Portland OR 97239

SELLS, COLIN DAVID, meteorologist; b. Nuremberg, Germany; s. Jack David Sells and Ursula Daltrop; m. Mary Alice Loedding, July 18, 1981; 1 child, James Walter Sells. BA in Polit. Sci., U. South Fla., 1974; AS in Meteorology, C.C. USAF, Washington, 1985. Agrl. technician, climatologist Fla. Inst. Food and Agrl. Scis., Ruskin, Fla., 1988—90; meteorol. technician Nat. Weather Svc., St. Paul Island, Alaska, 1990—91; meteorologist, Nat. Weather Svc. Anchorage, 1991—. Guest lectr. U. dept. geography U. Alaska, Anchorage, 1994-01; mem. Baseline Proficiency Standards team Nat. Weather Svc., 1999-2001. Contbr. articles to profl. jours. Judge Alaska State Sci. Fair, Anchorage, 1993, 97, 99, 2003; union steward Nat. Weather Svc. Employees Orgn., Anchorage, 1994-2002; spokesman local TV Christmas children's spl., Anchorage, 1996-99. Served with USAF, 1977-87. Mem. Am. Meteorol. Soc., Am. Geophys. Union. Avocations: chess, martial arts. Home: 1600 Turpin St Anchorage AK 99504-2559 Office: Nat Weather Svc Ctr Weather Svc Unit 700 N Boniface Ave Anchorage AK 99506-1612 E-mail: Colin.Sells@NOAA.GOV.

SELLS, KEVIN DWAYNE, marine engineer; b. Conn., 1958; m. Ketruthai Houngsatjakul; children: Corey, David III, Vidhya. BSc in Quality Assurance, Ft. Steilacoom C.C., Tacoma, 1984; BS in Marine Engring., Pierce Coll., 1987. Nuc. shipfitter elec. boat divsn. Gen. Dynamics, Groton, Conn., 1976-79; quality assurance surveyor Tacoma Boatbuilding Co., 1979-81, marine constrn. planner, 1981-84, sr. logistics engr. F.E. Basil, Washington, 1984-86; ship repair engr. C. Long Assocs., Bangkok, Thailand, 1987-89, sr. logistics analyst Tucson, 1989—. Mem. Soc. Naval Architects, Am. Archeology Soc., Smithsonian Inst., Libr. Congress. Achievements include research and implementation of modular shipbuilding techniques; revamped Saudi Arabian naval supply system.

SELLS, LARRY JOE, writer; b. Waterloo, Iowa, Mar. 1, 1960; s. Larry Lyle and Joyce Sells. BA in English, U. of No. Iowa, 1994—96. Author: (novels) The Headless Ghostman, Chattanooga Factory, (short stories) Spiritual Realm and Other Stories, 303 East Street and Other Stories, (poetry book) Images of Nature, Visions of Light and Darkness, Drunken Verses, Visions of an Outsider, A Voice Out of the Darkness; editor: (short story anthology) Freaky Frights. Mem.: Iowa Poetry Assn., HWA. Home: 320 Pearl St Cedar Falls IA 50613 Personal E-mail: deathwalk@earthlink.net.

SELM, ROBERT PRICKETT, engineer, consultant; b. Cin., Aug. 9, 1923; s. Frederick Oscar and Margery Marie (Prickett) S.; m. Rowena Imogene Brown, Nov. 25, 1945 (div. Jan. 1975); children: Rosalie C. Selm Pace, Linda R. Selm Partridge, Robert F., Michael E.; m. Janis Claire Broman, June 24, 1977. BSChemE, U. Cin., 1949. Registered profl. engr. Enlisted U.S. Army, 1943, advanced through grades to sgt., 1943-46, commd. capt., 1949, resigned, 1954; design engr. Wilson & Co., Salina, Kans., 1954-67, gen. ptnr., 1967-81, sr. ptnr., 1981-89; ptnr. in charge Wilson Labs., Salina, Kans., 1956-88, chmn. bd. dirs.; dir. Upper Eagle Valley Water Authority, Avon, Colo., 1994—; ind. investor Salina, Kans., 1989—. Contbr. articles to profl. jours.; patentee in field. Mem. Gov.'s Adv. Commn. on Health and Environ. Named Engr. of Yr. Kans. Engring. Soc., Topeka, 1986. Fellow AIChE; mem. NSPE (state chmn. environ. resource com., nat. legis. and govt. affairs com. 1988-91), Am. Chem. Soc., Am. Water Works Assn., Water Pollution Control Fedn., Am. Acad. Environ. Engrs. (diplomate), Petroleum Club, Salina Country Club (pres. 1986), Elks, Shriners. Republican. Episcopalian. Avocations: golf, lapidary arts. Office: Wilson & Co 1700 E Iron Ave Salina KS 67401-3403 Home: 2160 Sherwood Ln Salina KS 67401-6979

SELMIC, RASTKO R. engineering educator; b. Belgrade, Yugoslavia, Nov. 4, 1970; m. Sandra Selmic, Dec. 2, 2000; 1 child, Mila. PhD, U. Tex., Arlington, 2000. Digital signal processing sys. engr. Signalogic, Dallas, 2000—02; asst. prof. La. Tech U., Ruston, 2002—. Achievements include patents for intelligent control of actuator nonlinearities. Office: La Tech U Arizona Ave Nethken Hall 229 Ruston LA 71270 Office Phone: 318-257-4641. E-mail: rselmic@latech.edu.

SELOVER, WILLIAM CHARLTON, corporate communications and governmental affairs executive; b. Long Beach, Calif., Dec. 12, 1938; s. John Jesse and Myrtis Charlton (Holmes) S.; m. Mary-Louise Hutchins, Jan. 5, 1963 (div. 1985); children: Victoria, Edward. BA, Principia Coll., 1960; MA, U. Va., 1962. Editl. staff Christian Sci. Monitor, from congl. corr. to diplomatic corr., 1964-71; spl. asst. to sec. of the navy USN, 1971; mem. White House Coun. on Internat. Econ. Policy, Washington, 1971-72; history and archives divsn. chief Cost of Living Coun., Exec. Office of the Pres., Washington, 1973-74; asst. to adminstr. U.S. EPA, Washington, 1974-75, 77-78; from staff mem. White House Domestic Coun. to asst. to V.P. Nelson Rockefeller White House, Washington, 1975-76; speechwriter Pres. Gerald R. Ford, Washington, 1976; pub. affairs exec. Ford Motor Co., Detroit, 1978-88, pub. affairs mgr. diversified products ops., regional pub. affairs mgr., 1988-91; v.p. corp. comms. and govtl. affairs USL Capital Corp. (subs. Ford Fin. Svcs. Group), 1991-96; prin. The Chaparral Working Group, San Francisco, 1997—. Speechwriter for chmn. and CEO of Ford Motor Co., Henry Ford II; editor autobiography former Pres. Richard M. Nixon, 1977. Helen Dwight Reid Found. fellow, Carnegie Found./Maxwell Grad. Overseas fellow, 1962. Mem. Conference Bd. (coun. corp. comm. execs.), Nat. Press Club, Press Club Detroit, Press Club L.A., Motor Press Guild, Internat. Motor Press Assn., Leadership Detroit Alumni Assn., Am. Polit. Sci. Assn. Address: 1257 Union St San Francisco CA 94109-1922

SELTEN, REINHARD, retired economist, educator; b. Breslau, Germany, Oct. 5, 1930; s. Adolf and Käthe (Luther) S.; m. Elisabeth Amalie Laugreiner, Feb., 1959. Diploma in math., Frankfurt U., 1957, PhD, 1961, habilitation in econs., 1968; PhD in Econs. (hon.), U. Bielefeld, Germany, 1989, Johann-Wolfgang-Goethe U., Frankfurt, Germany, 1996, U. Graz, Austria, 1996, U. Breslav, Poland, 1996, U. Norwich, Eng., 1997, ENS Cachan, 1998, U. Innsbruck, Austria, 2000. Asst. Frankfurt (Germany) U., 1957-67, private docent, 1968-69; vis. prof. U. Calif., Berkeley, 1967-68; prof. Free U. Berlin, 1969-72, U. Bielefeld, Germany, 1972-84, U. Bonn, Germany, 1984-96, prof. emeritus, 1996—; hon. prof. Jiaotong U., Shanghai, 1996. Author: Models of Strategic Rationality, 1988, (with J. Harsanyi) A General Theory of Equilibrium Selection in Games, 1988. Recipient Nobel Prize in econs., 1994, Prize of State North-Rhine Westfalia. Fellow Econometric Soc.; mem. NAS (fgn. assoc.), North-Rhine Westfalian Acad. Scis., Am. Acad. Arts and Scis. (fgn. hon.), Berlin-Brandenburgian Acad. Scis., European Econ. Assn. (pres.), Am. Econ. Assn. (hon.). Home: Hardtweg 23 Königswinter D-53639 Germany Office: Lab Wirtschaftsforschung U Bonn Adenauerallee 24-42 53113 Bonn Germany*

SELTSER, RAYMOND, epidemiologist, educator; b. Boston, Dec. 17, 1923; s. Israel and Hannah (Littman) S.; m. Charlotte Frances Gale, Nov. 16, 1946; children: Barry Jay, Andrew David. MD, Boston U., 1947; MPH, Johns Hopkins U., 1957. Diplomate Am. Bd. Preventive Medicine (trustee, sec.-treas. 1974-77), Am. Bd. Med. Specialties (mem. exec. com. 1976-77). Asst. chief med. info. and intelligence br. U.S. Dept. Army, 1953-56; epidemiologist divsn. internal health USPHS, 1956-57; from asst. prof. to prof. epidemiology Johns Hopkins U. Sch. Hygiene and Pub. Health, Balt., 1957-81, assoc. dean, 1967-77, dep. dir. Oncology Ctr., 1977-81; dean U. Pitts. Grad. Sch. Pub. Health, 1981-87, prof. epidemiology, 1981-88, emeritus dean, emeritus prof. epidemiology, 1988—; assoc. dir. USPHS Ctrs. for Disease Control, Rockville, Md., 1988-90; assoc. dir. Ctr. for Gen. Health Svcs. Extramural Rsch. Agy. for Health Care Policy and Rsch., Rockville, 1990-95, sr. advisor spl. population rsch. Ctr. Primary Care Rsch., 1995-98; med. and healthcare advisor Dept. Va Office Inspector Gen. Office Health Care Inspections, Chevy Chase, Md., 1997—2000. Cons. NIMH, 1958-70, also various govtl. health agys., 1958-79; expert cons. Pres.'s Commn. on Three Mile Island, 1979-80; mem. Three Mile Island Adv. Panel Health, Nat. Cancer Inst. Cancer Control Grant Rev. Com., Pa. Dept. Health Preventive Health Service Block Grant Adv. Task Force, Gov.'s VietNam Herbicide Info. Commn. Pa.; chmn. Toxic/Health Effects Adv. Com., 1985-87. Trustee, mem. exec. com., chmn. profl. adv. com. Harmarville Rehab. Ctr., Pitts., 1982-87; bd. dirs. Health Edn. Ctr., Media Info. Svc.; chmn. USPHS Task on Improving Med. Criteria for SSA Disability Determination, 1988-92. Served to capt. AUS, 1951-53, Korea. Decorated Bronze Star; recipient Centennial Alumni citation Boston U. Sch. Medicine, 1973; elected to Johns Hopkins Soc. of Scholars, 1986. Fellow AAAS, APHA (mem. governing coun. 1975-77, chmn. EPI sect. coun. 1979-80), Pa. Pub. Health Assn. (bd. dirs. 1985-88, pres.-elect 1986-88), Am. Coll. Preventive Medicine, Am. Heart Assn.; mem. Am. Epidemiol. Assn., Internat. Epidemiol. Assn., Am. Soc. Preventive Oncology, Am. Cancer Soc. (bd. dirs. Pa. divsn. 1985-87, mem. exec. com. 1986-87), Assn. Schs. Pub. Health (sec. 1969-71, mem. exec. com., chmn. edn. com. 1983-87), Soc. Med. Cons. Armed Forces, Soc. Epidemiologic Rsch., Nat. Coun. Radiation Protection and Measurements (consociate), Johns Hopkins Alumni Coun. (mem. exec. com. 1994-97), Sigma Xi, Delta Omega.

SELTZER, BARRY S. federal judge; b. 1954; BA magna cum laude, Hamilton Coll., 1976; MBA, JD, NYU, 1980, LLM in Taxation, 1984. Atty Trenam, Simmons, Kemker, Scharf, Barkin, Frye & O'Neill, Tampa, Fla., 1980-82; asst. U.S. atty. So. Dist. Fla., 1984-88; judge Broward County Ct., 1988-91; magistrate judge U.S. Dist. Ct. (so. dist.) Fla., Ft. Lauderdale, 1991—. Comment editor NYU Law Rev. of Law and Social Change. Recipient Spl. Achievement award Dept. Justice, commendations Drug Enforcement Agy., U.S. Secret Svc., Bur. of Alcohol, Tobacco and Firearms, Postal Inspection Svc., U.S. Customs Svc., USDA. Mem. ABA, Fed. Bar Assn., Fla. Bar, Broward County Bar Assn., Fed. Magistrate Judges Assn., Stephen Booner Inn of Ct. (past pres.), B'nai B'rith Justice Unit, Beta Gamma Sigma. Office: 109 US Courthouse 299 E Broward Blvd Fort Lauderdale FL 33301-1944

SELTZER, BOB, public relations executive; Grad., Syracuse U. Journalist Gannett Pubs.; mem. corp. pub. rels. dept. GAF Corp.; gen. mgr., pres. Porter Novelli, N.Y.C.; chmn., CEO Ogilvy Pub. Rels. Worldwide, N.Y.C. Office: Ogilvy Public Relations Worldwide 909 3rd Ave New York NY 10022-4731

SELTZER, JEFFREY LLOYD, diversified financial services company executive; b. Bklyn., July 27, 1956; s. Bernard and Sue (Harris) S.; m. Ana Isabel Sifre, Sept. 2, 1985; children: Ian Alexander, Pamela Allison. BS in Econ. cum laude, U. Pa., 1978; JD, Georgetown U., 1981. Bar: N.Y. 1982. Assoc. Austrian, Lance & Stewart, N.Y.C., 1981-85; assoc. gen. counsel, asst. v.p. Shearson Lehman Bros., N.Y.C., 1986; mng. dir. Lehman Bros., N.Y.C., 1986-94; dep. chmn., mng. dir. CIBC Oppenheimer Corp., N.Y.C., 1994-99; exec. v.p., COO Adirondack Trading Ptnrs., N.Y.C., 1999—; faculty assoc. Merrill Lynch Ctr. for Study of Internat. Fin. Mkts. and Svcs., Zarb Sch. Bus., Hofstra U., 2001—. Spl. prof. law Hofstra U., 1999. Author: The U.S. Greeting Card Market, 1977, Starting and Organizing a Business, 1984, Swap Risk Management: A Primer, 1988, A View for the Top: The Role of the Board of Directors and Senior Management in the Derivatives Business, 1995, Financial Strategy Roundtable: Derivatives, 1995. Mem. Nat. Policy Forum, 1994—97; mem. U.S. Trade Adv. Com. on Svc. Industries, Washington, 1990—94; mem. local adv. bd. County of Nassau, 1997—99; mem. adv. bd. Huntsman Program in Internat. Studies and Bus. U. Pa., Phila., 1997—; mem. securities industry coalition Bush-Quayle campaign, 1992; mem. small bus. adv. coun. Rep. Nat. Com., Washington, 1984—90; mem. nat. adv. coun. U.S. SBA; policy analyst Reagan-Bush Com., Arlington, Va., 1980; advisor Friends of Giuliani, N.Y.C., 1989, New Yorkers for Lew Lehrman, N.Y.C., 1981—82; dir. Nassau County Sports Commn., 1997—, mem. exec. com.; vice chmn., trustee Inst. Internat. Bankers, 1998—99; chmn. Class of 1978 reunion com. U. Pa., 1997—. Recipient Disting. Alumnus award W. C. Mepham H.S., 1994. Mem. ABA, Re. Nat. Lawyers Assn., Federalist Soc., Ctr. for Study of Presidency, Securities Industry Assn. (chmn. swap and derivative products com. 1990-94). Office: 120 W 45th St New York NY 10036

SELTZER, LEO, documentary filmmaker, educator, lecturer; b. Montreal, Que., Can., Mar. 13, 1910; came to U.S., 1916; s. Boris and Atalia (Gerowitz) S.; m. Elaine Basil, Apr. 15, 1941 (div. 1950); children: Janzie, John; m. Dicky Ransohoff, 1951 (div. 1963). BA, U. Mass., 1979. Faculty CCNY, 1949-54, New Sch. Social Rsch., 1949-51; pres. Leo Seltzer Assocs., Inc., N.Y.C., 1950-90; faculty Columbia U., 1954-60, Phila. Coll. Art, 1955-56, NYU, N.Y.C., 1966-67; dir. audio-visual therapy program pediatrics ward Univ. Hosp., N.Y.C., 1970-76; instr. film prodn. workshop Sch. Visual Arts, N.Y.C., 1969-84; adj. prof. performing and creative arts Coll. S.I., N.Y., 1977-78; prof. film Bklyn. Coll., 1978-83, prof. emeritus film, 1983—. Lectr. in U.S. and abroad, including Mus. Modern Art, N.Y.C., Marymount Coll., Ghent U., Belgium, Libr. Congress, others. Prodr., dir. over 60 social documentaries and TV films in 35 countries, including First Steps, UN Divsn. Social Affairs, 1946 (Acad. award for best documentary 1947), Fate of a Child, UN Divsn. Tech. Assistance, 1949, For the Living, City of N.Y., 1952, (with Walter Cronkite) Conquest of Aging, 1958, All the Years, 1959, Jacqueline Kennedy's Asian Journey, 1962, Progress Through Freedom (pres. Kennedy's visit to Mex.), 1962, (with Edward R. Murrow) The American Commitment, USIA, 1963, Report on Acupuncture, 1977, (with John Huston) Let There Be Light; prodr., dir.: Nat. Film Bd. Can., 1941, films include Air-Sea Rescue Techniques; chief cons. visual aids City of N.Y., 1941-42; prodr.: N.Y.C. Mcpl. Film and TV Unit Sta. WNYC, 1949-50; film biographer to White House for Pres. Kennedy, 1962; exec. prodr. Quadrant Comms., Inc., 1973-75 (7 citations Cannes and Edinburgh Film Festivals 1948-63); films are in U.S. Nat. Archives, Libr. of Congress, in collection and distributed by Mus. Modern Art; photographs are in Houston Mus. Fine Arts collection, Nat. Gallery Can., Visual Studies Workshop, Rochester, N.Y., N.Y.C. 5th Ave. Libr.; reconstructed 6 Am. social documentaries of 1930's in 1978 for Mus. Modern Art Film Archives, 1976-77,; edited and filmed much of original footage; subject of TV program by Bill Moyers, A Walk Through the Twentieth Century, Blackside Prodns., CBC, BBC TV; contbr. film footage to Nat. Geographic, History Channel, others. 1st lt. Signal Corps. U.S. Army; directed tng. and information films for U.S. Army and public; officer in charge of Film and Equipment Depot, ETO, 1947. Recipient Acad. award for best documentary, 1948, Silver medals Venice Film Festival, 1949, Freedom's Found. award, 1953, Golden Reel award Scholastic Mag., 1955, Robert Flaherty award CCNY, 1956, Silver medal Atlanta Internat. Film Festival, 1977; honored in tribute Mus. Modern Art, 1990; oral history N.Y. Fifth Ave. Libr. Archives. Mem. Dirs. Guild Am. (charter). Achievements include research on American social documentary films. Home and Office: 368 E 69th St New York NY 10021-5706 Office Phone: 212-879-0990.

SELTZER, MITCHELL SHERMAN, hotel executive; b. Abington, Pa., June 10, 1948; s. Larry and Mary Ellen (Gallagher) S.; m. Laura Ann Hayhurst Seltzer; 1 child, M. Babe. BA, Pa. State U., 1971. Chef Valley Forge Hilton Hotel, King of Prussia, Pa., 1974-77, Cutillo's Restaurant, Pottstown, Pa., 1977-79; gen. mgr. Unisys Edn. Ctr., Malvern, Pa., 1984-88; gen. mgr. Dave Thomas Ctr. Duke U., Durham, N.C., 1988-90; gen. mgr. Am. Coll. Marriott Corp., Bryn Mawr, Pa., 1990-92; gen. mgr. Certain-teed Corp. World Hdqr. Marriott Corp., 1992-94; gen. mgr., operating ptnr. First Noah's Corp., 1994-97, Hospitality Staff Phila., 1997-98; gen. mgr. Profl. Edn. and Conf. Ctr., Kent State U., 1999—2004; gen. mgr. Regional Learning Alliance, 2004—. Avocations: skiing, golf. Home: 572 Evergreen Ct Mars PA 16046

SELTZER, RICHARD C. lawyer; b. N.Y.C., Sept. 3, 1943; s. Edward and Beatrice (Fishman) S.; m. Carol Reische, Aug. 31, 1969; children: Wendy, Mark. BA, Harvard U., 1965; JD, Columbia U., 1968. Bar: N.Y. 1969, U.S. Dist. Ct. (so. and ea. dists.) N.Y. 1969, U.S. Ct. Appeals (5th cir.) 1978, U.S. Ct. Appeals (2nd cir.) 1987, U.S. Supreme Ct. 1995. Ptnr. Kaye Scholer LLP, N.Y.C., 1969—. Mem. ABA, Assn. of Bar of City of N.Y. Office: Kaye Scholer 425 Park Ave New York NY 10022-3506

SELTZER, RICHARD WARREN, JR., writer, editor, consultant; b. Clarksville, Tenn., Feb. 23, 1946; s. Richard Warren and Helen Isabella (Estes) S.; m. Barbara Ann Hartley, July 28, 1973; children: Robert, Heather, Michael, Timothy. BA, Yale U., 1969; MA in Comparative Lit., U. Mass., 1972. Editor

Benwill Pub., Boston, 1973-79; sr. communications cons., Internet cons. Digital Equip. Corp., Maynard, Mass., 1979-98; ind. internet cons. and writer, 1998—. Pub. B&R Samizdat Express, Boston, 1974—. Author: Name of Hero, 1981, Lizard of Oz, 1974, Now and Then, 1976, The Alta Vista Search Revolution, 1997, Shop Online the Lazy Way, 1999, Ethiopia Through Russian Eyes, 2000, Take Charge of Your Website, 2001, Web Business Boot Camp, 2001, My Internet: A Personal View of Internet Business Opportunities; editor: Internet-on-a-Disk, 1994—, Please Copy This Disk, 1993—; author short stories. With USAR, 1969-75. Mem. Internat. Assn. Bus. Communicators, U.S. Chess Fedn. Avocations: chess, internet, russian translation. Home: PO Box 161 West Roxbury MA 02132-0002 E-mail: seltzer@samizdat.com.

SELTZER, VICKI LYNN, obstetrician, gynecologist; b. June 2, 1949; d. Herbert Melvin and Marian Elaine (Willinger) Seltzer; m. Richard Stephen Brach, Sept. 2, 1973; children: Jessica Lillian Brach, Eric Robert Brach. BS, Rensselaer Poly. Inst., 1969; MD, NYU, 1973. Diplomate Am. Bd. Ob-Gyn. (examiner 1988-2001). Intern Bellevue Hosp., N.Y.C., 1973-74, resident in ob-gyn., 1974-77; fellow gynecol. cancer Am. Cancer Soc., N.Y.C., 1977-78, Meml. Sloan Kettering Cancer Ctr., N.Y.C., 1978-79; assoc. dir. gynecol. cancer Albert Einstein Coll. Medicine, N.Y.C., 1979-83, prof. ob-gyn., 1989—, Edie and Marvin H. Shur prof. ob-gyn. and women's health, 2003—; assoc. prof. ob-gyn. SUNY, Stony Brook, 1983-89. Dir. ob-gyn. Queens Hosp. Ctr., Jamaica, NY, 1983—93, pres. med. bd., 1986—89; chair ob-gyn. L.I. Jewish Med. Ctr., 1993—; v.p. women's health svcs. North Shore-L.I. Jewish Health Sys., 1999—; chair ob-gyn. North Shore U. Hosp., 1999—, chair med. bd., 2001—; mem. N.Y. State Coun. Grad. Med. Edn., 2003—. Author: Every Woman's Guide to Breast Cancer, 1987; editor-in-chief: Primary Care Update for the Ob-Gyn, 1993—; editor: Women's Primary Health Care, 1995, 2d edit., 2000; mem. editl. bd. Women's Life mag., 1980—82, Jour. Jacobs Inst. Women's Health, 1990—95, mem. internat. editl. bd. Jour. Soc. Obstreticians and Gynecologists Can., 2000—; contbr. articles to profl. jours.; host (TV series) Weekly Ob-Gyn. program, Lifetime Med. TV. Mem. Mayor Beame's Task Force on Rape, N.Y.C., 1974—76; chair health com. Nat. Coun. Women, N.Y.C., 1979—84; bd. govs. Nat. Coun. Women's Health, 1985—94; chair Coun. Resident Edn. Ob-Gyn., 1987—93. Recipient citation, Nat. Safety Coun., 1978, Achiever award, L.I. Ctr. Bus. and Profl. Women, 1987; Galloway Fund fellow, 1975. Fellow: ACOG (mem. gynecol. practice com. 1981, v.p. 1993—94, pres.-elect 1996—97, pres. 1997—98), N.Y. Obstet. Soc. (pres. 1999—2000); mem.: Am. Hosp. Assn. (mem. governing coun. maternal and child health 2004—), N.Y. Cancer Soc., Am. Med. Women's Assn. (com. chair 1975—79, mem. editl. bd. jour. 1986—2002, citation 1973), Internat. Fedn. Gynecology and Obstetrics (mem. internat. steering com. to reduce maternal mortality 2000—02), Women's Med. Assn. (v.p. N.Y. 1974—79, mem. resident rev. com. ob-gyn. 1993—98, Lila Wallis Lifetime Achievement award 2002), NYU Sch. Med. Alumni Assn. (bd. govs. 1979—, v.p. 1987—91, pres. 1992—93), Alpha Omega Alpha. Office: LI Jewish Med Ctr New Hyde Park NY 11040 Office Phone: 718-470-7660. Business E-Mail: vseltzer@lij.edu.

SELTZER, WILLIAM, statistician, social researcher, former international organization director; b. N.Y.C., Sept. 22, 1934; s. William B. Seltzer and Edith S. (Goldman) Alt.; m. Jane E. Berger, Nov. 20, 1970; children: Benjamin, Ezra. BA, U. Chgo., 1956. Rsch. asst. Health Info. Found., N.Y.C., 1957-60; statistician U.S. Bur. Census, Suitland, Md., 1960-64; advisor Pakistan Inst. Devel., Econs. and Cen. Statis. Office, Karachi, 1964-68; staff assoc. Population Coun., N.Y.C., 1968-74; br. chief UN Statis. Office, N.Y.C., 1974-86, dir., 1986-94; sr. advisor to under-sec.-gen. Dept. Econ. and Social Info. and Policy Analysis, N.Y.C., 1993-94; sr. rsch. schlar Fordham U., N.Y.C., 1995—. Mem. com. on population and demography, chair panel on data collection NAS, Washington, 1977-82, mem. Roundtable on the Demography of Forced Migration, 2001--; cons. UN Population Fund, 1995, Internat. Criminal Tribunal for Rwanda, 1996, UN Stats. Divsn., 1996-98, Internat. Labor Office, 1997, World Bank, 1997-98. Author: Poems, 1960, Politics and Statistics, 1994; co-author: Population Growth Estimation, 1973; also various UN documents, jour. articles, reports. Fellow Am. Statis. Assn. (chair social stats. sect. 1983-84, chair com. on internat. rels. 1986-87, chair com. on profl. ethics 2000—), Royal Statis. Soc. (hon.;); mem. Population Assn. Am., Internat. Statis. Inst., Internat. Assn. Ofcl. Statisticians. Mem. Soc. Of Friends. Office: Fordham U Dept Sociology and Anthropology 441 E Fordham Rd Bronx NY 10458-5149 Office Phone: 718-817-3868. E-mail: seltzer@fordham.edu.

SELVADURAI, ANTONY PATRICK SINNAPPA, civil engineering educator, applied mathematician, consultant; b. Matara, Sri-Lanka, Sept. 23, 1942; arrived in Can., 1975; s. Kanapathiyar Sinnappa and W. Mary Adeline (Fernando) S.; m. Sally Joyce; children: Emily, Paul, Mark, Elizabeth. Diploma in Engring., Brighton Poly., U.K., 1964; Diploma, Imperial Coll./London U., 1965; MS, Stanford U., 1967; PhD in Theoretical Mechanics, U. Nottingham, 1971; DSc, U. Nottingham, Eng., 1986. Registered profl. engr., Can.; chartered mathematician, UK. Staff rsch. engr. Woodward Clyde Assoc., Oakland, Calif., 1966-67; rsch. assoc. dept. theoretical mechanics U. Nottingham, 1969-70; lectr. dept. civil engring. U. Aston, Birmingham, England, 1971-75; asst. prof. civil engring. Carleton U., Ottawa, Canada, 1975-76, assoc. prof., 1976-81, prof., 1982-93, chmn. dept., 1982-90, Davidson Dunton Rsch. lectr., 1987; prof., chmn. dept. civil engring./applied mechanics McGill U., Montreal, Canada, 1993-96. Vis. rsch. sci. Bechtel Group, Inc., San Francisco, 1981-82; vis. prof. U. Nottingham, 1986, Inst. de Mécanique de Grenoble, France, 1990; cons. Atomic Energy of Can. Ltd., Pinawa, Man., 1983-96—, Ministry of Transp. Ont., Toronto, 1984-97, Fleet Tech., Ottawa, 1988—, Atomic Energy Control Bd., 1987—. Author: Elastic Analysis of Soil Foundation Interaction, 1979, (with R.O. Davis) Elasticity and Geomechanics, 1996, (with R.O. Davis) Plasticity and Geomechanics, 2002; editor: Mechanics of Structured Media, 1981, (with G.Z. Voyiadjis) Mechanics of Material Interfaces, 1986, Developments of Mechanics, 1987, (with M.M. Zaman and C.S. Desai) Recent Accomplishments and Future Trends in Geomechanics in the 21st Century, (with M.J. Boulon) Mechanics of Geomaterial Interfaces, 1995, Mechanics of Poroelastic Media, 1996, Partial Differential Equations in Mechanics, Vol. 1, Fundamentals, Laplace's Equation, Diffusion Equation, Wave Equation, 2000, Vol. 2, The Biharmonic Equation, Poisson's Equation, 2000. Recipient Rsch. award Alexander von Humboldt Found., 1997; King George VI Meml. fellow English Speaking Union of Commonwealth, 1965, rsch. fellow SRC, UK, 1969, Erskine fellow U. Canterbury, New Zealand, 1992, 98, Killam rsch. fellow Can. Coun. for Arts, 2000-02. Fellow Am. Acad. Mechanics, Can. Soc. Civil Engring. (Leipholz medal 1991), Assoc. Prof. Engrs. of Ont. (Engring. medal for rsch. 1993), Engring. Inst. Can., Inst. Math. and Its Applications; mem. Internat. Assn. for Computer Methods and Advances in Geomechanics (award for significant paper in the category theory computational analytical 1994, paper prize computational and analytical theory category 1997, John Booker medal 2001), Max Planck Soc. (Max Planck Rsch. prize 2003). Roman Catholic. Office: McGill U Dept Civil Engring Montreal PQ Canada H3A 2K6 E-mail: patrick.selvadurai@mcgill.ca.

SELVAGGI, SUZANNE MARIE, pathologist, educator; b. Amityville, N.Y., Apr. 6, 1952; d. Gerald Anthony and Gilda Mary Selvaggi; m. Robert Bruce Washabaugh, June 10, 1978; 1 child, Sarah Jane Washabaugh. BA in Biology, Case Western Res. U., 1974; MD, Albert Einstein Med. Coll., 1978; pathologist, NYU Med. Ctr., 1983. Asst. prof. pathology Cornell Med. Ctr., N.Y.C., 1983-85, Wayne State U., Detroit, 1987-90; assoc. prof. pathology U. Mich., Ann Arbor, 1990-97, Loyola U. Med. Ctr., Maywood, Ill., 1997—2001; prof. U. Wis., Madison, 2001—. Author: (book) Fine Needle Aspiration of Pelvic Organs, 1997; mem. editl. rev. bd. Diagnostic Cytopathology, 1995—, Cancer Pathology, 1997—; sect. editor Diagnostic Cytopathology, 1999—; contbr. articles to med. jours. Mem. Am. Soc. Clin. Pathologists, Am. Soc. Cytopathology, Am. Soc. Gynecologic Pathologists, Papanicolaou Soc. Cytopathology. Home: 2940 Ivanhoe Glen Fitchburg WI 53711 Office: U Wis Hosp and Clinics 600 Highland Ave Madison WI 63792 E-mail: sselvaggi@facstaff.wisc.edu.

SELVAGGIO, PIERO, restauranteur; b. Modica, Sicily, Italy; married; 3 children. Owner Valentino, Santa Monica, Calif., 1972—, Primi, Santa Monica, Calif., 1986—2000, Posto, San Fernando Valley, Calif., 1992—, Valentino Las Vegas, 1999—. Author (with Karen Stabiner): The Valentino Cookbook, 2001; co-author: Five Brothers: A Year of Tuscan Cooking, 1997; host (radio shows) KNX 1070 AM, L.A., Good Food, KCRW. Active Meals on Wheels, Am. Cancer Soc., Five Star Sensation, Planned Parenthood, Santa Monica Rape Crisis Ctr., Pediat. AIDS Found., Share Our Strength, The Arthritis Found.; Calif. Restaurant Assn. Ednl., L.A. Children's Mus. Named Man of Yr., Italian Wine and Spirit Awards, 1985; named an Outstanding Friend of Brunello in the World of Wine; named to Who's Who in Am. Hall of Fame, Cook's Mag.; recipient Leccio d'Oro award, 1995, award, Gayot's L.A. Restaurant, 1995, Outstanding Svc. award, James Beard Found., 1996, Cavaliere award, Pres. of Sicilian Region, 1997, Outstanding Native Son award, Ivy award of distinction, Restaurants and Instns., 2000, Comune di Roma award. Office: Valentino 3115 Pico Blvd Santa Monica CA 90405

SELVAKUMAR, ARIAMALAR, environmental engineer; b. Jaffna, Sri Lanka, June 16, 1957; d. Arumugam and Thavamany Veluppillai; m. Kumar Selvakumar, Aug. 20, 1982; 1 child, Anuja. BSc in Environ. Engring., U. Peradeniya, Sri Lanka, 1976—80; Master's Engring. (Environ. Engring.), Asian Inst. Tech., Bangkok, Thailand, 1982—84; PhD in Engring., N.J. Inst.Tech., Newark, 1984—88. Cert. profl. engr., N.J. State Bd. of Engrs. and Land Surveyors, 1992. Environ. engr. Foster Wheeler Corp., Livingston, NJ, 1990—99, U.S. Environ. Protection Agy., Edison, NJ, 1999—. Home: 9 Kady Ln Kendall Park NJ 08824 Office: US Environ Protection Agy 2890 Woodbridge Ave Edison NJ 08837 Office Phone: 732-906-6990. Business E-Mail: selvakumar.ariamalar@epa.gov.

SELVIG, JETTIE PIERCE, lawyer; b. Bee Branch, Ark., Dec. 16, 1932; d. Jefferson Davis Pierce and Ruba Ann Bivens; m. Rolf S. Selvig Sr., Jan. 27, 1962; children: Rolf S. Jr., Erik K., John L. LLB, U. Ark., 1954. Bar: Ark. 1953, Calif. 1961, U.S. Supreme Ct. 1969. Pvt. practice, 1961—. Bd. dirs. San Francisco Neighborhood Legal Assistance Found., 1975. Recipient Cert. of Honor, Bd. Suprs. of City and County of San Francisco, 1969, Countess of Pulaski Proclamation, Quorum Ct. of Pulaski County, 1969, Silver Bowl of Appreciation, Girl Scouts Am.; named Hidden Heroine, San Francisco Bay Girl Scout Coun., 1976. Mem. Nat. Assn. Women Lawyers (state del., assembly del., bus. mgr., treas., v.p., pres.-elect, pres. 1969-70, chairperson, mem. women in pub. svc. com. 1971-75), Calif. State Bar (disciplinary com. 1972-74), Calif. Applicants' Attys. Assn. (dir. No. Calif. chpt. 1974, v.p. 1975, pres. 1976, 77, sec. and pres.-elect statewide assn., pres. statewide assn. 1981-82, life mem.), Queen's Bench (life, asst. sec.-treas., dir. 1972, treas. 1973, mem. Law Day com., chmn. publicity com., v.p. 1974, pres. 1975, Lifetime Achievement award 1995, pres. Queen's Bench Found., 1974-76), Women's Equity Action League (treas. Calif. divsn. 1970-72, pres. Calif. divsn. 1973), Legal Aid Soc. San Francisco (bd. dirs. 1976), Lawyer's Club San Francisco (life), del. to state bar conv.) Democrat. Home and Office: 469 Molino Ave Mill Valley CA 94941-3380 Fax: 415-383-9105. Office Phone: 415-383-9105. E-mail: jettiecoleen@msn.com.

SELVY, BARBARA, dance instructor; b. Little Rock, Jan. 20, 1938; d. James Oliver and Irene Balmat Banks; m. Franklin Delano Selvy, Apr. 15, 1959; children: Lisa Selvy Yeargin, Valerie Selvy Miros, Lauren Kroll, Franklin Michael, Madison Banks Selvy. Student, U. Ctrl. Ark., 1955—57. Founder, dir. Carolina Ballet Theater, Greenville, SC, 1973—; pres. Dance Arts Inc. and Incentives, Inc. Mem. adv. bd. dirs. Met. Arts Coun., and S.C. Govs. Sch., St. Marys Cath. Sch. Appeared in numerous TV commls., on Goodson-Toddman game show Play Your Hunch, 1958-59; toured Far East with TV show Hit Parade, 1958; named Miss Ark., 1956, Mrs. S.C., 1981; dir. and staged Mrs. Va., Mrs. N.C., Mrs. S.C. pageants; choreographed Little Theater prodns., Furman U. Opera. Mem. Nat. Rep. Congl. Com., 2003, Pres. Bush Small Bus. Adv. Coun., 2003. Mem. So. Assn. Dance Masters (ballet adviser, regional dir.), Dance Educators Am., Dance Masters of Am., Profl. Dance Tchrs. Home: 206 Honey Horn Dr Simpsonville SC 29681-5814

SELWAY, PHILLIP JAMES, musician; b. Huntingdon, England, May 23, 1967; married. Student in English and History, Liverpool (Eng.) Poly. Drummer touring musicals; sub-editor; tchr. English; drummer Radiohead, 1992—. Musician: (albums) Pablo Honey, 1993, The Bends, 1995, OK Computer, 1997 (Grammy award, 97), Kid A, 2000 (Grammy award, 2000), Amnesiac, 2001, I Might Be Wrong: Live Reocrdings, 2001, Hail to the Thief, 2003. Office: Capital Records 1750 North Vine St 10th Fl Hollywood CA 90028

SELWYN, DONALD, engineering administrator, researcher, inventor, educator; b. N.Y.C., Jan. 31, 1936; s. Gerald Selwyn and Ethel (Waxman) Selwyn) Moss; m. Delia Nemec, Mar. 11, 1956 (div. Mar. 1983); children: Laurie, Gerald, Marcia; m. Myra Rowman Markoff, Mar. 17, 1986 BA, Thomas A. Edison Coll. N.J., 1977. Svc. engr. Bendix Aviation, Teterboro, N.J., 1956-59; svc. mgr. Bogue Electric Mfg. Co., Paterson, N.J., 1959; proposal engr. advanced design group Curtiss-Wright Corp., East Paterson, N.J., 1960-64; ind. bioengr., rehab. engring. cons. N.Y.C., 1964-67; pres. bd. trustees, exec. tech. and tng. dir. Nat. Inst. for Rehab. Engring., Hewitt, N.J., 1967—. Cons. N.Y. State Office Vocat. Rehab., 1964—, Pres.'s Com. on Employment of Handicapped, 1966—, bus. and industry and for Am. with Disabilities Act compliance, also numerous state rehab. agys., health depts., vol. groups, agys. for handicapped in fgn. countries; cons., trainer computer applications. Contbr. articles on amateur radio, rehab. of severely and totally disabled to profl., gen. mags. Trustee Nat. Inst. for Rehab. Engring., Rehab. Research Center Trust. Decorated Knight of Malta; recipient Humanitarian award U.S. Ho. of Reps., 1972, Bicentennial Pub. Service award, 1975. Mem. Am. Acad. Consultants, I.E.E.E. (sr.), Soc. Tech. Writers and Pubs. (sr.), Nat. Rehab. Assn., N.Y. Acad. Scis., Mensa. Achievements include being the developer or co-developer field-expander glasses for hemianopsia, tunnel and monocular vision, electronic speech clarifiers, electronically guided wheelchairs, off-road vehicles and cars for quadriplegics, others; patentee indsl., mil. and handicapped rehab. inventions; expert, cons. on handicapped employment, handicapped product safety including design, manufacture, labelling and user instrnl. material, 1990—. Office: Nat Inst Rehab Engring PO Box T Hewitt NJ 07421-1020 Office Phone: 973-853-6585., 800-736-2216. E-mail: dons@theoffice.net. *As I travel the road of life, it becomes more and more evident to me that people matter most, and technology is useful and good only so long as it serves man, and man is not made to serve technology. From technician I have evolved to humanist, using technology only as a tool. Always think positive. Don't waste your time or emotional energy on people who do not appreciate your good will. Think only about those who do, and you'll achieve more and enjoy life.*

SELYA, BRUCE MARSHALL, federal judge; b. Providence, May 27, 1934; s. Herman C. and Betty (Brier) S.; children: Dawn Meredith Selya Sherman, Lori Ann BA magna cum laude, Harvard U., 1955, JD magna cum laude, 1958. Bar: D.C. 1958, R.I. 1960. Law clk. U.S. Dist. Ct. R.I., Providence, 1958-60; assoc. Gunning & LaFazia, Providence, 1960-62; ptnr. Gunning, LaFazia, Gnys & Selya, Providence, 1963-74, Selya & Iannuccillo, Providence, 1974-82; judge U.S. Dist. Ct. R.I., Providence, 1982-86, U.S. Ct. Appeals (1st cir.), Providence, 1986—. Judge Lincoln Probate Ct., R.I., 1965-72; mem. R.I. Jud. Council, 1964-72, sec., 1965-70, chmn., 1971-72; mem. Gov.'s Commn. on Crime and Adminstrn. Justice, 1967-69; del. Nat. Conf. on Revisions to Fed. Appellate Practice, 1968-82; mem. various spl. govtl. commns. and adv. groups Chmn. bd. trustees Bryant Coll., Smithfield, R.I., 1986-92; bd. dirs. Lifespan Health Sys., chmn. bd. dirs., 1994—, mem. bd. trustees R.I. Hosp. subs. Recipient Louis Dembitz Brandeis medal for disting. legal svc. Brandeis U., 1988, Neil Houston award Justice Assistance of Am., 1992. Mem. ABA, FBA, Fed. Judges Assn., R.I. Bar Assn. (chmn. various coms.), R.I. Bar Found., U.S. Jud. Conf. (mem. com. on jud. br.), Am. Arbitration Assn., Am. Judicature Soc. (bd. dirs.). Jewish. Home: 224 George St Providence RI 02906-3115 Office: US Ct Appeals US Courthouse 1 Exchange Terr Rm 316 Providence RI 02903

SELZ, PETER HOWARD, art historian, educator; b. Munich, Mar. 27, 1919; came to U.S., 1936, naturalized, 1942; s. Eugene and Edith S.; m. Thalia Cheronis, June 10, 1948 (div. 1965); children: Tanya Nicole Eugenia, Diana Gabrielle Hamlin; m. Carole Schemmerling, Dec. 18, 1983 Student, Columbia U., U. Paris; MA, U. Chgo., 1949, PhD, 1954; DFA, Calif. Coll. Arts and Crafts, 1967. Instr. U. Chgo., 1951-56; asst. prof. art history, head art edn. dept. Inst. Design, Ill. Inst. Tech., Chgo., 1949-55; chmn. art dept., dir. art gallery Pomona Coll., 1955-58; curator dept. painting and sculpture exhbns. Mus. Modern Art, 1958-65; dir. univ. art mus. U. Calif., Berkeley, 1965-73, prof. history of art, 1965—; Zaks prof. Hebrew U., Jerusalem, 1976. Vis. prof. CUNY, 1987; mem. pres.'s council on art and architecture Yale U., 1971-76. Author: German Expressionist Painting, 1957, New Images of Man, 1959, Art Nouveau, 1960, Mark Rothko, 1961, Fifteen Polish Painters, 1961, The Art of Jean Dubuffet, 1962, Emil Nolde, 1963, Max Beckmann, 1964, Alberto Giacometti, 1965, Directions in Kinetic Sculpture, 1966, Funk, 1967, Harold Paris, 1972, Ferdinand Holder, 1972, Sam Francis, 1975, The American Presidency in Political Cartoons, 1976, Art in Our Times, 1981, Art in a Turbulent Era, 1985, Chillida, 1986, Twelve Artists from the GDR, 1989, Max Beckmann: The Self Portraits, 1992, William Congdon, 1992, Beckmann, 1996, Gottfried Helnwein, 1997, Beyond the Mainstream, 1997; co-author: Theories and Documents of Contemporary Art, 1996, Beyond the Mainstream, 1998, Barbara Chase-Riboud, 1999, Nathan Oliviera, 2001; editor: Art in Am., 1967—, Art Quar., 1969-75, Arts, 1981-92, Cross-Currents in Modern Art, 2000; contbr. articles to art publs. Trustee Am. Crafts Coun., 1985—89; mem.adv. coun. archives Am. Art, 1971—; mem. acquisitions com. Fine Arts Mus., San Francisco, 1993; pres. Berkeley Art Project, 1988—93; project dir. Christo's Running Fence, 1973—76; commr. Alameda County Art Commn., 1990—95; bd. dirs. Richmond Art Ctr., 1998—2004; chair Berkeley Arts Festival, 1997—2000; trustee Neue Galerie, New York, 2001—, Amster Kala Inst., 2004. Decorated Order of Merit Fed. Republic Germany; Fulbright grantee Paris, 1949-50; fellow Belgian-Am. Ednl. Found.; sr. fellow NEH, 1972; resident Rockefeller Found. Study Ctr., Bellagio, 1994. Mem. Coll. Art Assn. Am. (dir. 1959-64, 67-71), AAUP, Internat. Art Critics Assn. Office: U Calif Dept Art History Berkeley CA 94720-0001 Office Phone: 510-524-5402.

SEMAK, MICHAEL WILLIAM, photographer, educator; b. Welland, Ont., Can., Jan. 9, 1934; s. John and Lena (Roketsky) S.; m. Annette Antoniuk, Jan. 30, 1960; children: James, Arlene. Student archtl. tech., Ryerson Poly. Inst., 1956-58. Freelance photographer Toronto-Pickering, 1961—; mem. faculty York U., Toronto, 1971—, assoc. prof. photography, 1977—. Exhibitor one-man shows, Image Gallery, N.Y.C., 1972, Il Diaframma Canon Gallery, Milan, Italy, 1976, Enjay Gallery, Boston, 1977, Ukraina Soc., Kiev, U.S.S.R., 1980, 81, group shows, Ont. Art Gallery, 1967, Expo '67 Internat. Exhbn., Montreal, 1967, Neikrug Gallery, N.Y.C., 1971; represented in permanent collections, Nat. Film Bd. Can., Ottawa, Nat. Gallery Can., Ottawa, Mus. Modern Art, N.Y.C., UN, Geneva. Recipient Photo Excellence Gold medal Nat. Film Bd., 1969; recipient Excellence award Pravda newspaper, Moscow, 1970, 71, Excellence diploma Fedn. Intenationale de l'art Photographique, Switzerland, 1972 Home: 1796 Spruce Hill Rd Pickering ON Canada L1V 1S4 Office: Dept Photography York U 4700 Keeles St Toronto ON Canada M3J 1P3 *I see many contradictions around us, social realities which I believe rob us of our self-esteem and individuality. Must we continually accept and succumb to the never-ending hot baths for the mind society offers us? I wish my photography and words to disturb the complacent and the sleeper. I offer you cold showers for the mind.*

SEMANS, MARY DUKE BIDDLE TRENT, foundation administrator; b. N.Y., Feb. 21, 1920; d. Anthony Joseph Drexel and Mary (Duke) B.; m. Josiah Trent; m. James H. Semans. Attended, Hewitt Sch., N.Y.; AB in History, Duke U.; LLD (hon.), N.C. Cen. U., 1963; HHD (hon.), Elon Coll., 1965; degree (hon.), Davidson Coll., N.C. Wesleyan Coll., 1982, U.N.C. at Chapel Hill, Duke U., 1983; LLD (hon.), Furman U., 1993. Trustee emeritus Duke U., 1961-81; chmn. The Duke Endowment, 1960—; various positions N.C. Sch. Arts, 1981—; former trustee Davidson Coll., N.C. Mus. Art, 1961-83, Shaw U., Converse U., Lincoln Hosp.; vice chmn. The Mary Duke Biddle Found., 1960—; chmn. Angier B. Duke Meml., Exec. Mansion Fine Arts Com., 1965—, Friends of Duke U. Library; pres. Durham Homes, Inc., 1968; mem. bd. dirs. Goodwill Industries of the Rsch. Triangle Area, 1964—, First Union Corp., 1980-82, N.C. State Library, 1958-61, Durham Pub. Library; numerous other positions. Mem. Durham City Coun., 1951-55; mayor pro-tem City of Durham, 1953-55; commencement speaker Duke U., 1983. Recipient Merit award Duke U. Health and Hosp. Adminstrn. Alumni Assn., 1989, Giannini medal for meritorious svc. to N.C. Sch. of the Arts, 1990, Alan Keith-Lucas Friend of Children award N.C. Childcare Assn., 1991, Elna Spaulding award Women-in-Action, 1993, Outstanding Philanthropist award Triangle Chpt. Nat. Soc. Fund Raising Execs., 1993, Sam Ragan award St. Andrews Coll., 1993. Mem. LWV, Bus. and Profl. Women's Club, Altrusa Club, Half Century Club, Rotary Club. Democrat. Methodist. Home: 1415 Bivins St Durham NC 27707-1519 Office: The Mary Duke Biddle Found 1044 W Forest Hills Blvd Durham NC 27707-1678

SEMAS, PHILIP WAYNE, editor; b. Gilroy, Calif., Feb. 23, 1946; s. Louis Alexander and Marian (Crapper) S.; m. Robin Lucille Tuttle, Sept. 7, 1967; children: Katherine Lucille, Anna Marian, Ellis Jeremy. Student, U. Oreg., 1963-67. Editor Coll. Press Service, Washington, 1967-68; free-lance writer Berkeley, Calif., 1968-69; asst. editor Chronicle of Higher Edn. Inc., Balt. and Washington, 1969-76, 1976-78, mng. editor, 1978-88, editor, new media, 1995—2002, editor in chief, 2002—; editor Chronicle of Philanthropy, Washington, 1988—95. Recipient Higher Edn. Writers award, AAUP, 1974 Mem. Am. Soc. Mag. Editors Office: Chronicle of Higher Edn 1255 23rd St NW Ste 700 Washington DC 20037-1125 Office Phone: 202-466-1000.

SEMBLER, MELVIN F. ambassador, real estate developer; b. St. Joseph, Mo, 1930; m. Betty Schlesinger; children: Steve, Brent, Greg. BS, Northwestern U., 1952. Developer shopping ctrs.; chmn. bd. The Sembler Co., St. Petersburg, Fla., 1962—; US amb. to Australia & Nauru US Dept. State, Canberra, 1989-93; US amb. to Italy U.S. Dept. State, Rome, 2001—. Committeeman Rep. Nat. Com., Fla., S.E. regional chmn., nat. adv. coun. Team 100; bd. trustees George Bush Presdl. Libr. Found., Eckerd Coll., Internat. Coun. Shopping Ctrs.; bd. dirs. Pratt Industries, First Union Nat. Bank Fla., Pro Hispanic Polit. Action Com., Bush/Quayle Alumni Assn., Nat. Jewish Coalition, Holocaust Meml. Mus. Madiera Beach; resident mem. Fla. Coun. of 100. Mem. Internat. Coun. Shopping Ctrs. (pres. 1986-87). Office: 9500 Rome Pl Washington DC 20521 also: Am Embassy Via Vittorio Veneto 119A 00187 Rome Italy

SEMEL, GEORGE HERBERT, plastic surgeon; b. N.Y.C., Apr. 20, 1938; s. Louis Bennett and Sara Sonja (Eutis) S. AB, Columbia U., 1959; MD, Boston U., 1963. Diplomate Am. Bd. Plastic Surgery. Intern L.A. County Gen. Hosp., 1963-64; resident gen. surgery Long Beach (Calif.) VA Hosp., 1964-67; residency in plastic surgery Mayo Clinic, Rochester, Minn., 1967-69; chief resident plastic surgery Med. U. S.C., Charleston, 1969-70; pvt. practice L.A., 1970—; staff Midway Hosp. Founder L.A. Music Ctr., 1978, Mus. Contemporary Art, 1980. With Calif. NG, 1964-69, USNG, 1969-73. Mem. AMA, Am. Soc. Plastic Surgery, Am. Lipoplasty Soc., L.A. Soc. Plastic Surgeons, Phi Gamma Delta. Office: 450 S Beverly Dr Beverly Hills CA 90212-4402 Office Phone: 310-274-7547. E-mail: drsemel@drsemel.com.

SEMEL, TERRY S. Internet company executive; b. NYC, Feb. 24, 1943; s. Ben and Mildred S.; m. Jane Bovingdon, Aug. 24, 1977; children: Eric Scott, Courtenay Jane, Lily Bovingdon Semel, Kate Bovingdon Semel. BS in Acctg., L.I.U., 1964; postgrad. in market research, CCNY, 1966-67. Domestic sales mgr. CBS Cinema Center Films, Studio City, Calif., 1970-72; v.p., gen. mgr. Walt Disney's Buena Vista, Burbank, Calif., 1972-75; pres. W.B. Distbn. Corp., Burbank, 1975-78; exec. v.p., chief operating officer Warner Bros., Inc., Burbank, 1979-80, pres., chief operating officer, 1980-94, chmn., co-CEO, 1994-99, Warner Music Group Inc, 1995-99; chmn., CEO Yahoo! Inc., 2001—. Bd. dirs. Revlon., Polo Ralph Lauren Corporation Vice chmn. Pres.'s Com. for the Arts and Humanities; vice chair San Diego Host Com. for 1996

Rep. Nat. Conv.; bd. dirs. Solomon R. Guggenheim Mus., Edn. First, Cedars Sinai Med. Ctr., Environ. Media Assn. Pioneer of the Year, 1990, Found. of Motion Pictures Pioneers. Office: Yahoo! Inc 701 First Ave Sunnyvale CA 94089*

SEMMEL, BERNARD, historian, educator; b. NYC, July 23, 1928; s. Samuel and Tillie (Beer) S.; m. Maxine Loraine Guse, Mar. 19, 1955; 1 child, Stuart Mill. BA, CCNY, 1947; MA, Columbia U., 1951, PhD, 1955; postgrad., London Sch. Econs., 1959-60. With Nat. Citizens Commn. for Pub. Schs. and Coun. for Fin. Aid to Edn., N.Y.C., 1951-55; asst. prof. history Park Coll., Parkville, Mo., 1956-60; mem. faculty SUNY, Stony Brook, 1960-91, prof. history, 1964-91, chmn. dept., 1966-69; Disting. prof. Grad. Sch. CUNY, 1991-96. Vis. prof. Columbia U., 1966-67. Author: Imperialism and Social Reform, 1960, Jamaican Blood and Victorian Conscience, 1963, The Rise of Free Trade Imperialism, 1970, The Methodist Revolution, 1973, John Stuart Mill and the Pursuit of Virtue, 1984, Liberalism and Naval Strategy, 1986, The Liberal Ideal and The Demons of Empire, 1993, George Eliot and the Politics of National Inheritance, 1994; editor: Occasional Papers of T.R. Malthus, 1963; editor, translator: Halévy's The Birth of Methodism in England, 1971; editor Jour. Brit. Studies, 1969-74, Marxism and the Science of War, 1981. Rockefeller Found. grantee, 1959-60; Am. Council Learned Socs. fellow, 1964-65; Guggenheim fellow, 1967-68, 74-75; Nat. Humanities Ctr. fellow, 1986-87 Fellow Royal Hist. Soc.; mem. Am. Hist. Assn. (profl. divsn. 1984-86), Conf. Brit. Studies, Cosmos Club, Phi Beta Kappa. Home: PO Box 1162 Stony Brook NY 11790-0749

SEMMES, SALLY PETERSON, choreographer, educator, performer; b. Rockford, Ill., Nov. 17; d. Edwin Carl and Eva Victoria Peterson; m. David Hamilton Semmes, Jan. 8, 1955; children: Melissa Kay Semmes-Thorne, Laurie Ruth. BS in Edn., U. Wis., 1953, postgrad., 1957-58, 61-62, San Diego State U., London campus, 1976, Northwestern U., 1977. Cert. English, speech/theater tchr., Wis. Tchr. English and speech Oshkosh (Wis.) H.S., 1953-54, Madison (Wis.) East H.S., 1955; instr. Patricia Stevens Finishing Sch., 1956; pvt. tchr. dance Phillips, Wis., 1957-60; project asst. Wis. Idea Theatre U. Wis, Madison, 1963-66; test adminstr. Manitowoc (Wis.) Counseling Ctr., 1967; tchr. English and speech Valders (Wis.) H.S., 1978-81; pub. info. U. Wis., Manitowoc, 1970-72, instr. dance, 1972-78, instr. pub. speaking, 1983—, instr. remedial Coll. English, 1992, freelance instr. dance, 1982-95, tchr. Hatrack Kids classes reading motivation, 1982—; owner Sally Semmes Ednl. Workshops, 1983—; staff Next Act Theatre, 2000. Narrator Green Bay (Wis.) Symphony Childrens Concerts, 1977-81, Manitowoc Symphony Orch., 1992; founder, pres., treas. The Hatrack Storytellers, Inc., 1967—; mem. Readers Theatre Reading Incentive Program for Children, 1967—. Choreographer (musicals) Anything Goes, Mame, Guys and Dolls, The Fantasticks, Broadway Bound, Joseph and the Amazing Technicolor Dreamcoat, (mus. revues including) 7 Showtime Shows, Manitowoc; dir.: (plays) Anything Goes, The Male Animal, The Boor, The Ugly Duckling, Our Town, The Sandbox, The Staring Match, The Imaginary Invalid; performer: (numerous productions) Daytrips, Trip to Bountiful, Tuck Everlasting, Love Letters, Dancing at Lughnasa, Lovers, Rules of the Game, The Resounding Tinkle, Baby with the Bathwater, The Man Who Came to Dinner, Blithe Spirit, The Glass Managerie, The White House, The Royal Family, See How They Run, Talking With, Marvin's Room, Eleemosynary, (groups) Milw. Repertory Theater, First Stage Milw., Kohler Arts Ctr., Next Act Theatre, Renaissance Theatreworks. Pub. svc. videos City of West Allis, Am. Cancer Soc., assisted living, 1998; lay reader St. James Episcopal Ch., Manitowoc, 1984—97; dir. Miss Manitowoc pageant, 1972—75, Miss Calumet County pageant, New Holstein, Wis., 1974; guest artist Creative Arts Week Minn. Episcopal Cathedral, Mpls., 1997; editor's asst. Wis. Mag. of History of Wis. State Hist. Soc., 1958. Recipient Cultural Achievement award Manitowoc and Two Rivers C. of C., 1984, Cert. of Appreciation Manitowoc Pub. Libr., 1987; named Sec. of Yr. Manitowoc Manpower, 1983; elected to Natl. Museum of Women in the Arts, 2002. Mem.: AAUW, AARP, LWV, Nature Conservancy, Environ. Defense, Arthritis Found., Wis. Alumni Assn., World Wildlife Fedn., PEO Sisterhood, Sierra Club, Phi Beta. Avocations: baking, travel, reading, film. Home and Office: 8501 Old Sauk Rd 305 Middleton WI 53562

SEMON, MARK DAVID, physicist, researcher; b. Milw., Mar. 27, 1950; s. Milton K. and Joyce Gloria (Kupper) S. Student, Imperial Coll., London, 1973-74; AB magna cum laude, Colgate U., 1971; PhD, U. Colo., 1976. Rsch. asst. Kitt Peak Nat. Obs., Tucson, Ariz., 1970, Los Alamos (N.Mex.) Sci. Lab., 1974; asst. prof. physics Bates Coll., Lewiston, Maine, 1976-83, assoc. prof., 1983-88, prof. physics, 1990—. Vis. prof. physics Amherst (Mass.) Coll., 1988-90; accident reconstructionist Med. and Tech. Cons., Portland, Maine, 1986—; referee Am. Jour. Physics, 1988—, Founds. of Physics, 1989—. Asst. editor Am. Jour. Physics, 1988-90; contbr. articles to Phys. Rev., Il Nuovo Cimento, other profl. jours. Woodrow Wilson fellow, 1971; grantee NSF, 1980, Nat. Rsch. Corp., 1978. Mem. Am. Phys. Soc., Am. Acad. Forensic Scientists, Am. Assn. Physics Tchrs., Am. Coll. Forensic Examiners, Coun. Undergrad. Rsch., Soc. Woodrow Wilson Fellows. Achievements include evaluation of expectation values in Aharonov-Bohm Effect; co-authoring new equation of state for liquid/gas systems near critical point, alternative formulation of quantum electrodynamics; new interpretation of the electromagnetic vector potential, new geometric model of velocity addition in special relativity. Office: Bates Coll Dept Physics 44 Campus Ave Lewiston ME 04240-6018 Office Phone: 207-786-6324. E-mail: msemon@bates.edu.

SEMON, WARREN LLOYD, retired computer sciences educator; b. Boise, Ida., Jan. 17, 1921; s. August and Viola Lorreta (Eastman) S.; m. Ruth Valerie Swift, Dec. 1, 1945; children— Warren Lloyd, Nolan David, Jonathan Richard, Sue Anne. Student, Hobart Coll., 1940-43; S.B., U. Chgo., 1944; MA, Harvard, 1949, PhD, 1954. Instr. math. Hobart Coll., 1946-47; lectr. applied math. Harvard U., Cambridge, Mass., 1956-61, asst. dir. computation lab., 1954-61; head applied math. dept. Sperry Rand Research Ctr., Sudbury, Mass., 1961-64; mgr. computation and analysis lab. Burroughs Research Ctr., Paoli, Pa., 1964-67; prof. computer sci. Syracuse (N.Y.) U., 1967-84, prof. emeritus, 1984—, dir. system and information sci., 1968-76, dean Sch. Computer and Info. Sci., 1976-84. Cons. USAF, 1957, NSA, 1957, Lockheed Electronics Corp., 1967, Monsanto Co., 1972. Contbr. profl. jours. Served to 1st lt. USAAF, 1943-46, MTO. Fellow IEEE; mem. Assn. Computing Machinery, Math. Assn. Am., IEEE Computer Soc. (chmn. publs. com. 1972-74, bd. govs. 1973-74, editor-in-chief 1975-76), Sigma Xi. Address: PMB F54807 3590 Round Bottom Rd Cincinnati OH 45244-3026

SEMONES, CHARLES W. retired elementary school educator, writer; b. Harrodsburg, Ky., Aug. 25, 1937; s. Charles Fred and Della Tyler Semones. BS, Eastern Ky. Univ., Richmond, 1964. Cert. tchg. dept. edn. Tchr. Mercer County Pub. Sch., Harrodsburg, Ky., 1956—58, 1962—88; ret.; asst. editor Christian Voice, Harrodsburg, Ky., 2000—01. Author 3 vols. of poetry, 1 vol. essays. Mem.: Ky. Ret. Tchrs. Assn., Acad. of Am. Poets. Democrat. Protestant. Avocations: music, gardening, genealogy, antiques. Home: 327 N Greenville St Apt 10 Harrodsburg KY 40330

SEMONIN, RICHARD GERARD, retired state official; b. Akron, Ohio, June 25, 1930; s. Charles Julius and Catherine Cecelia (Schooley) S.; m. Lennie Stuker, Feb. 3, 1951; children: Cecelia C., Richard G. Jr. (dec.), James R., Patricia R. BS, U. Wash., 1955. With Ill. State Water Survey, Champaign, 1955-91, chief, 1986-91, chief emeritus, 1991—; co-chmn. Ill. Water Rsch. & Land Use Planning Task Force, 1992-94. Adj. prof. U. Ill., 1975-91; chmn. Ill. Low-Level Radioactive Waste Task Group, 1994-96. Contbr. chpts. to books and articles to profl. jours.; co-editor: Atmospheric Deposition, 1983. Staff sgt. USAF, 1948-52. Grantee NSF, 1957-76, U.S. Dept. Energy, 1965-90. Fellow AAAS, Am. Meteorol. Soc. (councilor 1983-86); mem. Nat. Weather Assn. (councilor 1978-81), Weather Modification Assn., Ill. Acad. Scis., Sigma Xi. Roman Catholic. Avocations: civil war, golf, fishing, genealogy. Home: 1002 Devonshire Dr Champaign IL 61821-6620 Office: Ill State Water Survey 2204 Griffith Dr Champaign IL 61820-7495 E-mail: semonin@uiuc.edu.

SEMPLE, CECIL SNOWDON, retired manufacturing company executive; b. Assam, India, Aug. 12, 1917; came to U.S., 1927, naturalized, 1948; s. Fordyce B. and Anne (Munro) S. BA, Colgate U., 1939. Buyer R.H. Macy & Co., 1939-42, 46-48; buyer, div. supt. Montgomery Ward, 1948-50; v.p. Nachman Corp., Chgo., 1950-55; sales mgr. radio receiver dept. Gen. Elec. Co., Bridgeport, Conn., 1955-60, mktg. cons. merchandising N.Y.C., 1966-67, gen. mgr. audio products dept., 1967-68, dep. div. gen. mgr. housewares div., 1968-69, gen. mgr. housewares div., 1969, v.p., 1969-71, v.p. corp. customer relations, 1971-85; v.p. Rich's Inc., Atlanta, 1960-62, sr. v.p., dir., 1962-66. Trustee Peoples Bank., Bridgeport, 1975-89, trustee emeritus. Bd. dirs. Nat. Jr. Achievement Inc., 1974-86, Bridgeport Area Found., 1970-91, dir. emeritus, 1991—; bd. dirs. Bridgeport Hosp., 1970-93, chmn., 1983-89, dir. emeritus, 1993—; bd. trustees Colgate U., 1970-84, vice chmn. 1978-84; trustee emeritus, past pres., bd. dirs. Alumni Corp.; chmn. So. Conn. Health Svc. Inc., 1990-93. Served to maj. USAAF, 1942-46. Mem. St. Andrews Soc. State N.Y. (chmn. bd. mgrs. 1968-70), Delta Kappa Epsilon Clubs: Brooklawn Country (Fairfield, Conn.), Fairfield Country. Home: 25 Cartright St Bridgeport CT 06604-2047

SEMPLE, JAMES WILLIAM, lawyer; b. Phila., Nov. 18, 1943; s. Calvin James and Marie (Robinson) S.; m. Ellen Burns, Nov. 26, 1966; children: Megan Semple Greenberg, Luke Robinson. AB, St. Josephs U., Phila., 1965; JD, Villanova U., 1974. Bar: Del. 1974, U.S. Dist. Ct. Del. 1974, D.C. 1975, U.S. Ct. Appeals (3d cir.) 1982, U.S. Tax Ct. 1996. Ptnr. Morris, James, Hitchens & Williams, Wilmington, 1983—. Lectr. numerous seminars; mediator Superior Ct. Voluntary Mediation Program. Mem.: ABA, Fedn. Defense and Corp. Counsel, Am. Bd. Trial Advs. Office: Morris James Hitchens & Williams, LLP PO Box 2306 Wilmington DE 19899-2306 E-mail: jsemple@morrisjames.com.

SEMPLE, LLOYD ASHBY, lawyer; b. St. Louis, June 7, 1939; s. Robert B. and Isabelle A. S.; m. Cynthia T. Semple, Aug. 26, 1961; children: Whitney, Sarah, Lloyd Jr., Terrell. BA, Yale U., 1961; JD, U. Mich, 1964. Bar: Mich. 1964. Assoc. Dykema Gossett, Detroit, 1964-70, ptnr., 1971—, chmn., 1994—2002. Bd. dirs. SenSystech, Inc., 2003—. Councilman, mayor pro tem City of Grosse Pointe Farms, Mich., 1975—83; chmn. exec. com. Detroit Zool. Soc.; dir., trustee Karmanos Cancer Inst.; chmn. bd. trustees Detroit Med. Ctr. Corp., 1996—2001. Mem. ABA, Mich. Bar Assn., Detroit Bar Assn., Country Club Detroit, Yondotega Club, Detroit Athletic Club, Yale Club (N.Y.C.), Bohemian Club (San Francisco). Episcopalian. Home: 57 Cambridge Rd Grosse Pointe Farms MI 48236-3004 Office: Dykema Gossett 400 Renaissance Ctr Ste 3500 Detroit MI 48243-1602 E-mail: lsemple@dykema.com.

SEMPLE, ROBERT BAYLOR, JR., newspaper editor, journalist; b. St. Louis, Aug. 12, 1936; s. Robert B. and Isabelle Ashby (Neer) S.; m. Susan Riker Kirk, Aug. 19, 1961 (div. Feb. 1980); children: Robert Baylor III, Elizabeth, William, Mary; m. Lisa Pulling, Jan. 10, 1981. Grad., Phillips Acad., 1954; BA, Yale U., 1959; MA, U. Calif., Berkeley, 1961. Reporter Nat. Observer, 1961-63; corr. N.Y. Times, 1963-68, White House corr., 1968-72, dep. nat. editor, 1973-75, London bur. chief, 1975-77, fgn. editor, 1977-82, op-ed page editor, 1982-88, assoc. editor editorial page, 1988—. Recipient Pulitzer prize for editorial writing, 1996; Carnegie fellow, 1959-60; Woodrow Wilson fellow, 1960-61. Mem. Century Assn. (N.Y.C.), Yale Club (N.Y.C.). Episcopalian. Office: 229 W 43rd St New York NY 10036-3913 E-mail: semple@nytimes.com.

SEMROD, T. JOSEPH, banker; b. Oklahoma City, Dec. 13, 1936; s. L.J. and Theda Jo (Hummel) S.; m. Janice Lee Wood, June 1, 1968 (div. 1988); children: Ronald, Catherine, Christopher, Elizabeth; m. Jaye Patricia Hewitt, May 27, 1989; 1 child, Kelsey. BA in Polit. Sci., U. Okla., 1958, LLB, 1963. Bar: Okla. 1963. With Liberty Nat. Bank, Oklahoma City, 1963-81, v.p., 1967-69, sr. v.p., 1969-71, exec. v.p., 1971-73, pres., 1973-81, Liberty Nat. Corp., Oklahoma City, 1976-81; chmn. bd., pres., CEO United Jersey Banks (now UJB Fin. Corp.), Princeton, N.J., 1981-96; chmn., CEO Summit Bancorp. (merged with UJB Fin. Corp.), Princeton, 1996—; chmn., bd. dirs., CEO Summit Bank, Princeton, N.J., 1981—; vice chmn. Fleet Boston Fin., 2001—; chmn. Fleet Bank, N.J., 2001—. Bd. dirs. Fed. Res. Bank N.Y., Internat. Fin. Conf., chmn., 1994. Trustee, mem. exec. com. Nat. Urban League, 1963-95; mem. bd. advisors Outward Bound, Inc., 1984-2000, Ind. Coll. Fund N.J., 1986-90; commr. Citizens Commn. on Aids, 1988-90; chmn. bd. regents Stonier Grad. Sch. Banking, Rutgers U., 1983; mem. N.J. Transp. Trust Fund Authority, 1985-87; chmn. The Partnership for N.J., 1989-2001, trustee; mem. N.J. Com.-U.S. Savings Bonds com.; chmn. banking industry U.S. Savs. Bonds campaign, 1992-93. 1st lt. U.S. Army, 1958-60. Mem. Am. Bankers Assn., N.J. Bankers Assn., N.J. Bar Assn., Okla. Bar Assn., Bankers Roundtable (bd. dirs. 1995-97), Regional Plan Assn. (bd. dirs. 1989-91), Youn Pres. Orgn., Am. Running and Fitness Assn. (bd. dirs. 1983-86), N.J. C. of C. (bd. dirs., vice chmn. 1998-99, co-chair prosperity N.J. 1998-2000, chmn. 1999-2000), Drumthwacket Found. (chmn. 1990-94), Bedens Brook Club (Skillman, N.J.), River Club (N.Y.C.), Jasna Polana TPC (Princeton), Coral Beach Club (Bermuda), Nassau Club, Tournament Players Club, Adirondack League Club (Old Forge, N.Y.), The Port Royal Club (Naples, Fla.). Democrat. Roman Catholic. Office: FleetBoston Fin 301 Carnegie Ctr Princeton NJ 08540

SEMSEKWA, AMIR A.M.T. JUMA, management consultant; b. Dar-Es-Salaam, Tanzania, 1942; s. Juma J.M.S. Semsekima and Aisha Ibrahim; m. Said Kivugo; 4 children. Grad., U. Calif. Sch. Internat. Law, 1989; cert., Columbia Pacific U., San Rafael, Calif., 1989. Investor Avington Internat., The Netherlands, 1991-96; agt. Elsevier Sci. Tech., London, 1996-97, BDI Germany Supplies, Mindelheim, 1996—, Thomas Register, N.Y.C., 1997, MRI Catalogue Scis., Oxford, Eng., 1997, Lab. Safety Supply, Wis., 1996-97, Agent Export Directory, U.S., 1988, Internat. Tech., U.S., 1990—, NRI, U.K., 1990—; asst. mgr. Pharm/Chem., Tanzania, 1990—. Author: Statistical Analysis, 1987, Analyzing Statistical Science, 1992, Statistical Methods, 1992, 2d edit., 1997, Practical Methods for Design, 1995; contbr. articles to profl. jours. Mem. CCM, Tanzania, 1972—, Tafori, Tanzania, 1992, CRDB 1996; limited membership of bd. dirs. AS Membership Share, Tanzania. Mem. N.Y. Acad. Scis. Muslim. Avocation: sports.

SEMYONOV, OLEG G. research scientist; b. Abakan, Siberia, Russia, Jan. 3, 1944; arrived in U.S., 1997; s. Gabriel P. and Anna G. Semyonov; m. Eugenia V. Khorochilova, Oct. 15, 1971; children: Xenia, Nick. MS, Moscow State U., 1967; PhD, Lebedev Inst. Physics, Moscow, 1981. Rsch. scientist VNIIEF, Arzamas, Russia, 1967—70, Inst. Atomic Energy, Moscow, 1970—71; sr. scientist Lebedev Inst. Physics, Moscow, 1971—97; sr. rsch. engr. Applied Laser and Fusion Tech., Hull, Canada, 1999—2001; sr. rsch. scientist SUNY, Stony Brook, 2001—. Cons. ALFT, Inc., Hull, 2001; tech. transl. KAHOT, Inc., Bklyn., 1998. Contbr. articles to profl. publs. Russian Orthodox. Achievements include patents for 4 patents in field of x-ray sources and their application; discovery of effect of polarization of x-ray lines of highly ionized atoms in a high-current discharge and suggested a theoretical model to explain it; microrelief and internal structure modification of solid films irradiated by pulsed x-rays; fluorescent biomedical imaging of tumors in vivo; optical powering of sensors and actuators. Avocations: tennis, guitar. Office: SUNY Stony Brook 212 Old Chemistry Bldg Stony Brook NY 11794 Office Phone: 631-632-1402. E-mail: osemyonov@ecesunysb.edu.

SEN, AMARTYA KUMAR, economist, educator; b. Santiniketan, India, Nov. 3, 1933; s. Ashutosh and Amita Sen. BA, Calcutta U., 1953, Cambridge (Eng.) U., 1955; PhD, 1959; DLitt (hon.), U. Sask., 1979, Visva-Bharati U., 1983, U. Essex, 1984, Georgetown U., 1989, Jødavpur U., 1990, Kalyani U., 1990, Athens U. Econs. and Bus., 1991, Williams Coll., 1991, London Guildhall U., 1991, New Sch. Social Rsch., 1992, Calcutta U., 1992, Oberlin Coll., 1993, Syracuse U., 1994, Wesleyan U., 1995, Oxford, 1996; DSc (hon.), U. Bath, 1984, U. Edinburgh, 1995; D (hon.), U. Caden, 1987, Louvain, 1989, U. Valencia, 1994, U. Zurich, 1994, U. Antwerp, 1995, U. Stockholm, 1996; dottore ad honorem, U. Bologna, 1988; LLD (hon.), U. Tulane, 1990, Queen's U., 1993. Prof. econs. Jadavpur U., Calcutta, 1956-58; fellow Trinity Coll., Cambridge U., 1957-63; prof. econs. Delhi U., 1963-71, London Sch. Econs., 1971-77, Oxford (Eng.) U., 1977-80, Drummond prof. polit. economy, 1980-88; prof. econs. and philosophy Harvard U., Cambridge, Mass., 1987-98, Lamont univ. prof., 1988-98, vis. prof., 1968-69; master Trinity Coll. Cambridge U., 1998—. Vis. prof. U. Calif., Berkeley, 1964-65; Andrew D. White prof.-at-large Cornell U., Ithaca, N.Y., 1978-84; chmn. expert group role advanced skill and tech. UN, 1967; hon. fellow Trintiy Coll., Cambridge Inst. Social Studies, The Hague, Inst. Devel. Studies, U. Sussex, London Sch. Econs., U. London. Author: Choice of Techniques, 11960, Collective Choice and Social Welfare, 1970, Growth Economics, 1970, On Economic Inequality, 1973, Employment, Technology and Development, 1975, Poverty and Famines: An Essay on Entitlement and Deprivation, 1981, Utilitarianism and Beyond, 1982, Choice, Welfare and Measurement, 1982, Resources, Values and Development, 1984, Commodities and Capabilities, 1985, On Ethics and Economics, 9187, The Standard of Living, 1987, Hunger and Public Action, 1989, Inequality Reexamined, 1992, Quality of Life, 1993, India: Economic Development and Social Opportunity, 1995; contbr. articles to profl. jours. Recipient Mahalanobis award, 1976, Rank E. Seidman Disting. award in Polit. Economy, 1986, Agnelli Internat. prize, 1990, Alan Shawn Feinstein World Hunger award, 1990, Jean Mayer Global Citizenship award, 1993, Indira Gandhi Gold Medal award, Asiatic Soc., 1994, Edinburgh Medal, 1997, 9th Catalonia Internat. prize, 1997, Nobel prize in econ. scis., 1998; co-recipient Wassily Leontief prize for advancing frontiers econ. thought Tufts Global Inst. for Environ. and Devel., 2000. Fellow Brit. Acad., Econometric Soc. (past pres.); mem. AAAS (fgn. hon.), Am. Econ. Assn. (past pres.), Indian Econ. Assn. (past pres.), Royal Econ. Soc. (v.p.), Indian Econometric Conf., Devel. Studies Assn. (past pres.), Internat. Econ. Assn. (pres. 1986-89, hon. pres.). Office: Lamont U Prof Dept Econs Harvard U Cambridge MA 02138

SEN, ASHISH KUMAR, government administrator, urban planner, educator, statistician; b. Delhi, India, June 8, 1942; came to U.S., 1967, naturalized, 1985; s. Ashoka Kumar and Arati Sen; m. Colleen Taylor. BS with honors, Calcutta U., 1962, MA, U. Toronto, Ont., Can., 1964, PhD, 1971. Research assoc., lectr. dept. geography Transp. Center, Northwestern U., 1967-69; mem. faculty Center Urban Studies, U. Ill., Chgo., 1969—, prof., 1978—, dir. Sch. Urban Planning, 1991; dean Center Urban Studies, U. Ill. (Sch. Urban Scis.), 1977-78, acting dir., 1992; pres. Ashish Sen. and Assocs., Chgo., 1977-98; dir. Urban Transp. Ctr., 1997-98; dir. Bur. Transp. Stats. U.S. Dept. Transp., 1998—2002; mng. dir. TransInfo LLC, Chgo., 2003—. Author: Regression Analysis: Theory, Methods and Applications, 1990, Gravity Models of Spatial Interaction Behavior, 1995; also articles. Mem. Chgo. Bd. Edn., 1990-95; chmn. budget com. 1992-94; bd. trustees Asian Inst., 1993-95. Fellow Royal Statis. Soc., Am. Statis. Assn.; mem. Regional Sci. Assn., Transp. Rsch. Bd., Cliffdwellers. Hindu. Home: 2557 W Farwell Ave Chicago IL 60645-4617

SEN, LAURA J. wholesale distribution executive; Exec. v.p. merchandising BJ's Wholesale Club, Inc., Natick, Mass., 1996—. Office: BJs Wholesale Club Inc 1 Mercer Rd Natick MA 01760-2400 Fax: 508-651-6114.

SENA, JAMES ANTHONY, finance educator, department chairman; b. Cin., Ohio, Aug. 23, 1938; s. Janet Sena; m. Nancy Lynn Wilson, July 18, 1981; children: Joseph, James, Jennifer, Mark, Julie Davis. BS in Math., Xavier U., Cin., 1961, MBA in Quantitative Methods, 1964; MS in Info. Sci., U. Dayton, Ohio, 1967; PhD, U. Ky., Lexington, 1971. CCNA Cisco learning Inst., 2001. Computer programmer NCR, Dayton, Ohio, 1962—68; sr. sys. scientist Spindletop Rsch., Lexington, Ky., 1968—73; prof. U. Louisville, 1973—78; sr. rsch. scientist Battelle Inst., Houston, 1978—81; prof. U. Houston, Clear Lake City, 1981—84, Tex. A&M, Coll. Sta., 1984—87, Calif. Polytechnic State U., San Luis Obispo. Vis. rschr. Norwegian Inst. of Tech., Trondheim, Norway, 1993—94. Sgt. USAR, 1957—63. Home: 1183 Vista Del lago San Luis Obispo CA 93405 Office: Calif Polytech State Univ Coll of Business San Luis Obispo CA 93407 E-mail: jsena@calpoly.edu.

SENA, KATHLEEN F. academic administrator; d. Arthur Antonio and Margaret Mae Sena; 1 child, Christopher Kyle. BS, U. N.Mex., 1980. Exec. dir. N.Mex. FHA-HERO Assn., Albuquerque, 1981—85; program coord. N.Mex. Engring. Rsch. Inst., Albuquerque, 1985—86; admissions supr. U. N.Mex., Albuquerque, 1986—88, from asst. registrar to registrar, 1988—. Mem.: Rocky Mountain Assn. Collegiate Registrars and Admissions Officers (treas. 1999—2001, pres. 2001—), Am. Assn. Collegiate Registrars and Admissions Officers (com. mem. 1999—2003). Avocations: horses, reading. Office: Univ NMex Office of the Registrar SSC 261D Central/Stanford Ave Albuquerque NM

SENCHUK, DENNIS M. philosopher, educator; b. Chgo., Oct. 14, 1945; s. Michael and Loretta Senchuk; m. Karen Hanson, Aug. 22, 1970; children: Chloë Miranda, Tia Elizabeth. BA in Philosophy, U. Ill., Chgo., 1967; PhD in Philosophy, U. Minn., 1973; postgrad., Harvard U., 1975—76. Provisional elem. tchr. Chgo. Bd. Edn., 1966—67; psychiat. social worker Chgo. State Hosp., 1967; lectr. Northeastern U., Boston, 1971—75; asst. prof. continuing edn. Boston State U., 1975; tchg. asst. Harvard Grad. Sch. Edn., Cambridge, Mass., 1975; rsch. asst. Harvard Project Zero, Cambridge, 1975—76; assoc. prof. philosophy Ind. U., Bloomington, 1976—, adj. prof. edn. and Am. studies, 1976—. Mem. sci. com. Cognitio: Revista De Filosofia, Sao Paulo, Brazil, 2001—03. Editor: (other) Philosophical Studies in Education, 1981—83; author: Against Instinct: From Biology to Philosophical Psychology, 1991; contbr. articles to profl. jours. Grantee, NSF, 1979. Mem.: Ohio Valley Philosophy Edn. Soc. (pres. 1985), Ind. Philos. Assn. (pres. 1999—2000), Radical Philosophy Assn. (ctrl. divsn. pres. 1988—89, chair program com. ctrl. divsn. 1988—2003). Home: 3678 Sterling Ave Bloomington IN 47401 Office: Ind Univ Philosophy Dept 1033 E 3rd St Bloomington IN 47405 Office Phone: 812-855-3106.

SENDAK, MAURICE BERNARD, writer, illustrator; b. Bklyn., June 10, 1928; s. Philip and Sadie (Schindler) S. Student, Art Students League, N.Y.C., 1949-51; LHD, Boston U., 1977; hon. degree, U. So. Miss., 1981, Keene State Coll., 1986. Window display artist Timely Svc., N.Y.C., 1946; display artist FAO Schwartz, N.Y.C., 1948-51; co-founder, artistic dir. The Night Kitchen, 1990—. One-man shows include Gallery Sch. Visual Arts, N.Y.C., 1964, Rosenbach Found., Phila., 1970, 75, Trinity Coll., 1972, Galerie Daniel Keel, Zurich, 1974, Ashmolean Mus., Oxford, 1975, Am. Cultural Center, Paris, 1978, Pierpont Morgan Library, N.Y.C., 1981; author, illustrator: Kenny's Window, 1956 (Spring Book Fesitval honor book 1956), Very Far Away, 1957, The Acrobat, 1959, The Sign on Rosie's Door, 1960, The Nutshell Library (contains Chicken Soup with Rice, One Was Johnny, Alligators All Around, Pierre: A Cautionary Tale), 1962, Where The Wild Things Are, 1963 (N.Y. Times Best Illustrated Book award 1963, Caldecott medal 1964, Lewis Carroll Shelf award 1964, Internat. Bd. on Books for Young People award 1966, Art Books for Children award 1973, 74, 75, Best Young Picture Books Paperback award Redbook Mag. 1984, Children's Choice award 1985), Hector Protector and As I Went Over the Water: Two Nursery Rhymes, 1965, Higglety, Pigglety, Pop!; or, There Must Be More to Life, 1967 (Am. Book award nomination 1980), In the Night Kitchen, 1970 (N.Y. Times Best Illustrated Book award 1970, Caldecott medal nomination 1971, Art Books for Children award 1973, 74, 75, Redbook Mag. award 1985), Ten Little Rabbits: A Counting Book with Mino the Magician, 1970, Pictures by Maurice Sendak, 1971, Maurice Sendak's Really Rosie, 1975, Some Swell Pup; or, Are You Sure You Want A Dog, 1976, Seven Little Monsters, 1977, Outside Over There, 1981 (N.Y. Times Best Illustrated Book award 1981, Boston Globe/Horn Book award 1981, Caldecott medal nomination 1982, Am. Book award 1982), We Are All in the Dumps with Jack and Guy, 1993, Tsippi, 1994, Moishe, 1994, Max, 1994; illustrator: Atomics for the Millions, 1947, Good Shabbos, Everybody!, 1951, The Wonderful Farm, 1951, A Hole is to Dig, 1952 (N.Y. Times Best Illustrated Book award 1952), Maggie Rose: Her Birthday Christmas, 1952, The Giant Story, 1953, Hurry Home Candy, 1953, Shadrach, 1953, A Very Special House, 1953 (Caldecott medal nomination 1954), I'll Be You and You Be Me, 1954 (N.Y. Times Best Illustrated Book award 1954), Happy Hanukkah, Everybody, 1954, The Tin Fiddle, 1954, Magic Pictures, 1954, Mrs. Piggle-Wiggle's Farm, 1954, The Wheel on the School, 1954, Charlotte and the White Horse, 1955, The Little Cow and the Turtle, 1955, Singing Family of the Cumberlands, 1955, What Can You Do With a Shoe?, 1955, Happy Rain, 1956, The House of Sixty Fathers, 1956, I Want to Paint My Bathroom Blue, 1956 (N.Y. Times Best Illustrated Book award 1956), Birthday Party, 1957 (N.Y. Times Best Illustrated Book award 1957), Circus Girl, 1957, You Can't Get There From Here, 1957, Little Bear,

1957, Along Came a Dog, 1958, No Fighting, No Biting!, 1958, Somebody Else's Nut Tree, 1958, What Do You Say, Dear?, 1958 (N.Y. Times Best Illustrated Book award 1958, Caldecott medal nomination 1959), The Moon Jumpers, 1959 (Caldecott medal nomination 1960), Father Bear Comes Home, 1959 (N.Y. Times Best Illustrated Book award 1959), Seven Tales, 1959, Dwarf Long-Nose, 1960, Little Bear's Friend, 1960, Open House for Butterflies, 1960 (N.Y. Times Best Illustrated Book award 1960), Let's Be Enemies, 1961, The Tale of Gockel, Hinkel and Gackeliah, 1961, What Do You Do, Dear?, 1961, Little Bear's Visit, 1961 (Caldecott medal nomination 1962), Schoolmaster Whackwell's Wonderful Sons, 1962, Mr. Rabbit and the Lovely Present, 1962 (Caldecott medal nomination 1963), The Singing Hill, 1962 (N.Y. Times Best Illustrated Book award 1962), Nikolenka's Childhood, 1963, She Loves Me, She Loves Me Not, 1963, The Bat-Poet, 1964 (N.Y. Times Best Illustrated Book award 1964), How Little Lori Visited Times Square, 1964, Pleasant Fieldmouse, 1964, Lullabies and Night Songs, 1965, The Animal Family, 1965 (N.Y. Times Best Illustrated Book award 1965), Zlateh the Goat, 1966 (N.Y. Times Best Illustrated Book award 1966), The Golden Key, 1967, Poems from William Blake's Songs of Innocence, 1967, The Big Green Book, 1968, Griffin and the Minor Canon, 1968, A Kiss for Little Bear, 1968 (N.Y. Times Best Illustrated Book award 1968), The Light Princess, 1969 (N.Y. Times Best Illustrated Book award 1969), The Bee-Man of Orn, 1971, Sarah's Room, 1971, The Juniper Tree and Other Tales from Grimm, 1973 (N.Y. Times Best Illustrated Book award 1973), Fortunia: A Tale by Mme. D'Aulnoy, 1974, Fly by Night, 1976 (N.Y. Times Best Illustrated Book award 1976), King Grisly-Beard: A Tale from the Brothers Grimm, 1978, The Nutcracker, 1984 (N.Y. Times Best Illustrated Book award 1984), In Grandpa's House, 1985, The Children's Books of Randall Jarrell, 1988, Dear Mili: An Old Tale by Wilhelm Grimm, 1988, I Saw Esau, 1992, The Ubiquitous Pig, 1992; author: Fantasy Sketches, 1970, Collection of Books, Posters, and Original Drawings, 1984, The Love for Three Oranges: The Glyndebourne Version, 1984, Posters, 1986, Caldecott & Co.: Notes on Books and Pictures, 1988, Maurice Sendak Book and Poster Package: Wild Things, 1991; editor: Maxfield Parrish Poster Book, 1974, The Disney Poster Book, 1977; contbr.: The Publishing Archive of Lothar Meggendorfer, 1975, Babar's Anniversary Album, 1981, Masterworks of Children's Literature, Vol. 7, 1984, Victorian Color Picture Books, 1985, Winsor McCay: His Life and Art, 1987, Mickey Mouse Movie Stories, 1988; dir., lyricist: Really Rosie, 1975; lyricist, set designer: Really Rosie, 1978; lyricist, set designer, costume designer: Where the Wild Things Are, 1980, Higglety, Pigglety, Pop!, 1984; set designer, costume designer: The Magic Flute, 1980, The Cunning Little Vixen, 1981, Love for Three Oranges, 1982, The Goose of Cairo, 1984, Idomeneo, 1988, L'Enfant et les Sortileges, 1989, L'Heure Espagnol, 1989, It's Alive!, 1994, So, Sue Me, 1994; photographer: The Cunning Little Vixen, 1985; set designer: The Nutcracker, 1983, Hansel and Gretel, 1998, Brundibar, 2004; designer: (film) The Nutcracker, 1986. Recipient Chandler Book Talk Reward of Merit, 1967, Hans Christian Andersen Internat. medal, 1970, Laura Ingalls Wilder award Assn. Libr. Svc. to Children, 1983, Nat. Medal Arts, 1997, Lindgren award, 2003, Pell Lifetime Achievement award, 2003, Lifetime Achievement award Child mag., 2004. Office: Harper Collins Childrens Divsn 1350 Ave of the Americas New York NY 10019*

SENDAX, VICTOR IRVEN, dentist, educator, dental implant researcher; b. N.Y.C., Sept. 14, 1930; s. Maurice and Molly R. S.; m. Deborah deLand Cobb, Dec. 17, 1969 (div. June 1976); 1 child, Jennifer Reiland; m. Marcia Ayer Pearson, Dec. 13, 1986; children: Anneliese Chase, Cordelia Ayer. Grad., Tanglewood Music Ctr., 1953; BA, NYU, 1951, DDS, 1955; postgrad., Harvard U. Sch. Dental Medicine, 1969-72. Diplomate Am. Bd. Oral Implantology/Implant Dentistry (pres. 1996, dir.). Commr. N.Y. State Dental Svc. Corp., 1969-73; pres., dir. BioDental Rsch. Found., Inc., N.Y.C., 1975—; pres. Victor I. Sendax, D.D.S., P.C., N.Y.C., 1972—, Sendax Mini Dental Implant Ctrs. Mgmt., Inc., 1985—; assoc. attending implantologist St. Lukes-Roosevelt Hosp. Dental Implant Ctr., N.Y.C., 1979—; vol. attending implantologist Beth Israel Hosp., N.Y.C., 1991—, Beth Israel North Hosp., N.Y.C., 1991—. Adj. assoc. prof. implant prosthodontics Columbia U. Sch. Dental and Oral Surgery, N.Y.C., 1974-92; vis. lectr. dept. implant dentistry NYU Coll. Dentistry; faculty 1st Dist. Dental Soc. Sch. for Continuing Dental Edn.; mem. dental implant rsch. programs adv. com. Nat. Inst. Dental Rsch., HHS; cons. Julliard Sch. Voice and Drama, N.Y.C., 1972—, Vocal Dynamics Lab. Dept. Otolaryngology, Lenox Hill Hosp., N.Y.C., 1970-90; founder Sendax Seminars; 1st dir. implant prosthodontics resident program Columbia U. Sch. Dental and Oral Surgery and Columbia Presbyn. Hosp. Editor: Dental Clinics of North America: HA-Coated Dental Implants, 1992; mem. editl. bd. Oral Implantology, 1979—; patentee in mini-implants, oral implant magnetics, implant abutments and sinus graft implant stabilizers. Bd. dirs. City Ctr. Music and Drama, Inc. divsn. Lincoln Ctr. Performing Arts, N.Y.C., 1966-75; mem. adv. bd. Amagansett (N.Y.) Hist. Assn., 1969-89; trustee Leukemia Soc. Am., N.Y.C., 1967; bd. dirs. Schola Cantorum, 1980-90, Soc. Asian Music, 1965-76. Capt. Dental Corps USAF, 1955-57. Recipient Cert. of Honor, Brit. Dental Implant Assn., 1988., Aaron Gershkoff Meml. award for Outstanding Contbns. and Dedication to Oral Implantology Am. Acad. of Implant Dentistry, 1996. Fellow: Royal Soc. Medicine Gt. Britain, Am. Acad. Implant Dentistry (nat. pres. 1981), Internat. Coll. Dentists, Am. Coll. Dentists; mem.: ADA (ho. of dels. 1969), Japan Soc., N.Y. Acad. Scis., Internat. Assn. Dental Rsch., Am. Assn. Dental Rsch. (implant group), Fedn. Dentaire Internat., Am. Analgesia Soc., Acad. of Osseointegration, Am. Assn. Dental Schs. (chmn. spl. interest group on dental implant edn.), Century Assn., Sigma Epsilon Delta. Home: 70 E 77th St Apt 6A New York NY 10021-1811 Office: Mini Dental Implant Ctr 30 Central Park S Rm 14B New York NY 10019-1628 E-mail: vis@sendax-minidentimpl.com. *I stand in awe of mankinds' eternal need to innovate and push back the frontiers of knowledge, while tempering the harsher realities of existence with a perspective born of our cultural heritage.*

SENDERLING, JON TOWNSEND, journalist, public affairs specialist; b. Phila. s. John Chester and Elizabeth (Nogle) S.; m. Elizabeth Marie Broadbent, Mar. 27, 1965; children: Jon, Tracy. Student, Ursinus Coll., 1960, Temple U., 1961-64; student (fellow), Stanford U., 1970. Reporter Bucks County Courier Times, Levittown, Pa., 1966-68, Wilmington (Del.) News-Jour., 1968-70; reporter, mag. writer, columnist, spl. projects editor Trenton (N.J.) Times, 1970-76; gen. assignments editor, state editor, nat.-fgn. editor Dallas Times Herald, 1976-80, editorial page dir., 1981-86; dep. fgn. editor Newsday, Melville, L.I., N.Y., 1987-89; pub. affairs mgr. EDS Corp., Dallas, 1989-97, mgr. corp. message strategy, 1997-99; pub. affairs mgr. LandSafe, Plano, Tex., 2000-01; exec. dir. news and info. U. Tex. at Dallas, Richardson, 2001—. Author: play The Trashman, 1970. Recipient disting. service award for editorial writing Sigma Delta Chi, 1982, also 16 awards state press assns. Office: U Tex Dallas PO Box 830688 MS: AD38 Richardson TX 75093-0688 Office Phone: 972-883-2565. Business E-Mail: jsender@utdallas.edu.

SENDO, TAKESHI, mechanical engineering educator, researcher, author; b. Ena City, Japan, Aug. 5, 1917; s. Shigeyoshi and Michie (Yamamoto) S.; m. Hide Okamoto, Apr. 16, 1945; children: Mitsuyoshi, Sachiko, Kazuyasu. B of Engring., Tokyo U., 1941. Prof. mech. engring. Meijo U., Nagoya City, Japan, 1959-90, hon. prof., 1990—. Curator libr. Meijo U., Nagoya City, 1975-80. Author: Treatise of High Speed Deformation of Metal, 1993, 2nd edit., 1994, Experiment: Behavior of Al Column by Drop Hammer Test, 1959-90; contbr. over 60 articles to profl. jours. Mem. cmty. activity com. Local Self-Governing Orgn., Moriyama City, Japan, 1990, 91. Served to lt. comdr. Japanese Navy, 1941-45. Fellow Japan Soc. Mech. Engring., Japan Soc. Precision Engring. Avocations: composing haiku and tanka, trying essay, jogging. Home: 21-8 Choei Moriyama-ku Nagoya 463 Japan

SENDROW, JERROLD B. financial services executive; b. NYC, Oct. 1, 1944; s. Harry and Sylvia (Greenberg) S.; m. Silvia Escalante, Sept. 30, 1989 (div. Sept. 1995); children: Eric, Lisa. BBA, Baruch Coll., 1970. CFP. Treas. Thomas Cook Travel, Inc., N.Y.C., 1974-84, Don Travel, Inc., N.Y.C., 1984-86; contr. Pisa Bros., Inc., N.Y.C., 1987-93; v.p. fin. MSW Columbia Travel Group, N.Y.C., 1993-94; v.p., CFO, bd. dirs. 800 Travel Sys., Inc., Tampa, Fla., 1994-99; prin., owner e*Travelmart.com, Tampa, Fla., 1999—2001; prin. J.B. Sendrow & Assocs., N.Y.C., 1987—. Bd. dirs. 321 Apts. Corp., N.Y.C. Bd. dirs. Carrollwood Key Homeowners Assn., Tampa. With U.S. Army, 1965-67. Republican. Avocations: sailing, travel, chess, computers. Home: 5546 Carrollwood Key Dr Tampa FL 33624-5732 E-mail: cfp.jbs@verizon.net.

SENECA, MICHAEL JOSEPH, historian; b. Phila., Sept. 16, 1973; s. Michael and Joan Ann Seneca. BA in history, Rutgers U., 1995, MA in history, 1997. Asst. archivist Campbell Soup Co., Camden, NJ, 1999; rsch. coord. The Athenaeum of Phila., 2000—. Co-curator N.Y. Shipbuilding in WWII exhibit Camden County Hist. Soc., 1999—2001. Contbr. Naval Warfare: An International Encyclopedia, 2002; author: The Fairmount Park Motor Races, 1908-1911, 2003. Mem.: Orgn. of Am. Historians, Nat. Coun. on Pub. History. Republican. Office: The Athenaeum of Phila 219 So Sixth St Philadelphia PA 19106

SENECHAL, ALICE R. federal judge, lawyer; b. Rugby, N.D., June 25, 1955; d. Marvin William and Dora Emma (Erdman) S. BS, N.D. State U., 1977; JD, U. Minn., 1984. Bar: Minn. 1984, U.S. Dist. Ct. Minn. 1984, N.D. 1986, U.S. Ct. Appeals (8th cir.) 1987. Law clk. U.S. Dist. Judge Bruce M. Van Sickle, Bismarck, N.D., 1984-86; with Robert Vogel Law Office, Grand Forks, N.D., 1986—. U.S. magistrate judge, 1990—.

SENER, JOSEPH WARD, JR., securities company executive; b. Balt., June 30, 1926; s. Joseph Ward and Clara (Hodshon) S.; m. Ann Clark TenEyck, May 3, 1952 (dec. Oct. 1967); children: J. TenEyck, Beverley T., Joseph Ward III; m. Jean Eisenbrandt-Johnston, Feb. 6, 1971. AB, Haverford (Pa.) Coll., 1950; diploma, Inst. Investment Banking, U. Pa., 1954. With John C. Legg & Co., Balt., 1950-70, gen. partner, 1961-70; exec. v.p., dir. Legg, Mason & Co., Inc., Balt., 1970-72; vice chmn. bd. dirs., chief adminstrv. officer Legg Mason Wood Walker, Inc., Balt., 1976-80; dir. Legg Mason, Inc., 1982-96. Bd. dirs. Chesapeake Bank and Trust, Chestertown, Md., 1986-96, chmn., 1992-96. Trustee emeritus Boys' Latin Sch., Balt., pres. bd. trustees, 1980-82; chmn. emeritus bd. govs. Chesapeake Bay Maritime Mus. Served with USAAF, 1944-46. Mem. Nat. Assn. Securities Dealers (past dist. chmn.), Balt. Security Analysts Soc. (past pres.), Md. Club (Balt.). Republican. Episcopalian.

SENESE, DONALD JOSEPH, former government official, research administrator; b. Chgo., Apr. 6, 1942; s. Leo Carl and Joan (Schaffer) S.; m. Linda Faye Wall, Dec. 29, 1973; 1 dau., Denise Nicole. BS in History, Loyola U., 1964, MA, 1966; PhD, U. S.C., 1970; postgrad., Sophia U., Tokyo, 1970, Nat. Chengchi U., Taipei, Taiwan, 1971; cert. in adminstrv. procedures, U.S. Dept. Agr. Grad. Sch., 1976. Assoc. prof. history Radford (Va.) U., 1969-72; legis. asst. Senator from Va., 1973; legis. dir. to Rep. from Tex., 1973-76; sr. research assoc. House Republican Study Com., U.S. Ho. of Reps., Washington, 1976-81; asst. sec. for ednl. research and improvement U.S. Dept. Edn., Washington, 1981-85; pres. Senese Edn. Enterprises, Inc., 1985-96; dep. asst. sec. to asst. sec. Office Territorial and Internat. Affairs, Dept. Interior, Washington, 1989-93; writer, cons. SEE, Inc., Alexandria, Va.; instr. US Dept. of Agrl. Grad. Sch., 1995—2003. Mem. child care liability task force study Dept. Labor, 1989; v.p. dir. rsch. The 60 Plus Assn., Rosslyn, Va., 1997—2002. Author: Indexing the Inflationary Impact of Taxes, 1978, Modernizing the Chinese Dragon, 1980, Asianomics: Challenge and Change in Northeast Asia, 1981; editor: Ideas Confront Reality, 1981, Sweet and Sour Capitalism, 1985, Democracy in Mainland China, 1986; co-author: Can The Two Chinas Become One?, 1989; editor: George Mason and The Legacy of Constitutional Liberty, 1989. Vice chmn. Alexandria (Va.) Rep. Com., 1976-78, staff Rep. Nat. Com., 1987-89; mem. Alexandria Hist. Records Commn., 1979-84; mem. Fairfax County History Commn., 1985—, chmn., 1990-91; Fairfax County Bicentennial of U.S. Constn. Com., 1986-91; dir. Nat. Ctr. for Presdl. Rsch., 1987—; dir. opposition rsch. Rep. Nat. Com., 1995-96; dir. of rsch Co-Chairman Rep. Nat. Com., 1996. Recipient William P. Lyons Master Essay award, 1967; Freedoms Found. award, 1981, 85, 90; named Outstanding Man of Yr. Jaycees, 1976, 78, Sec. Labor Exceptional Achievement award, 1990; inducted St. Rita H.S. (Chgo.) Hall of Fame, 1984. Mem. Univ. Profs. for Acad. Order, No. Va. Assn. History, Order Sons of Italy, Pi Gamma Mu, Phi Alpha Theta, Delta Sigma Rho-Tau Kappa Alpha. Republican. Roman Catholic. Office: PO Box 6886 Alexandria VA 22306-0886 Office Phone: 703-768-6198. E-mail: doctor_don42@yahoo.com. *It has been important to have a philosophy of government which emphasizes honesty, integrity, a Ciceronian concept of duty, cost-effective public service, and a committment to the American heritage and traditions. These views have been reinforced by the support of family, friends, and a spiritual faith.*

SENFT, MASON GEORGE, musician; b. Bklyn., Nov. 1, 1942; s. Arthur and Ann (Nagel) S. BA cum laude, Adelphi U., 1964. Pvt. practice accompanist/vocal coach, Roslyn Heights, N.Y., 1964—. Tchr. Adelphi U., Garden City, N.Y., 1964-73; dir. Nat. Scholastic Aptitude Tng. Inst., Garden City, 1966-69; musical dir. Tibbits Opera House, Coldwater, Mich., 1972-73, Canal Fulton (Ohio) Playhouse, 1974-84, Island Lyric Opera, Garden City, 1980—, A Small Co. in America, Glen Cove, N.Y., 1984—; cons. Island Chamber Symphony Orch., Glen Head, N.Y., 1985—, Nat. Grand Opera, Tilles Ctr., Greenvale, N.Y., 1988—, PBS TV spl. Christmas with Flicka, 1988, Dark Summer debut by Christine Berl, Lincoln Ctr. Chamber Soc., Alice Tully Hall, N.Y., 1989, Glimmerglass Opera, 1992—; accompanist to Frederica von Stade 350th Convocation Celebration, Harvard U., Cambridge, Mass., 1986; accompanist ARC benefit concert In Concert, Carnegie Hall, 1989, Met. Opera Gala, N.Y.C., 1994; music coach The Aspern Papers, Dallas Opera, debut 1988; cons. N.Y. Virtuoso Chamber Symphony, 1989—; music coach DiCapo Opera Co., 1975—; accompanist concert in honor of Queen Margrethe II of Sweden, The White House, 1991, hist. gala concert at Steinway Hall, N.Y., 1991, gala concert for Met. Opera Four Seasons Hotel, 1993. Author: Chimera, 1997, Elusive Thought, 1998, Windows, 1998; orchestrator: (films) Liberty Heights, 1998; prodr.: (CD) A Memorial Tribute-To the Fallen Heroes of September 11, 2001; musician (with violinist Jeremy Cushman): (TV broadcast) Madison Sq. Garden, N.Y.C., 2003. Apptd. to the Rep. Presdl. Task Force, 2001. Recipient citation for lifetime achievement N.Y. State Assembly, 1994. Mem. Musicians Union Local 802, L.I. Singers Soc. (accompanist 1985-96), Mensa. Avocations: travel, writing, metaphysics. Home: 18 Osborne Ln Greenvale NY 11548 E-mail: msenft@optonline.net.

SENG, COLEEN JOY, mayor; b. Council Bluffs, Iowa, Feb. 8, 1936; d. Otis A. and Helen V. (Anderson) McElwain; m. Darrel E. Seng, Oct. 22, 1960 (dec. 1993); children: Marcee Lee, Christopher Charles, Phillip Scott. BA, Nebr. Wesleyan U., 1958. Dist. dir. Girl Scouts U.S.A., Saginaw, Mich., 1958-60, Lincoln, Nebr., 1960-62; cmty. ministry 1st United Meth. Ch., Lincoln, 1977-97; mem. Lincoln City Coun., 1987—2003; mayor City of Lincoln, 2003—. Mem. Mayor's first multi-cultural task force, co-chair of Gov. Nelson's urban adv. team, chmn. railroad transp. safety dist. Lincoln/Lancaster county joint budget com., mem. Lincoln/Lancaster county homeless coalition; active U. Place Cmty. Orgn. N.E. Family Resource Ctr.; past chair Lincoln/Lancaster county family resource ctr. bd.; past pres. Lincoln Fellowship of Chs.; mem. Lincoln Interfaith Coun.; mem Lincoln Urban Ministries com.; past pres. Homestead Girl Scouts Coun. Democrat. United Methodist. Avocations: reading, movies, gardening. Home: 6101 Walker Ave Lincoln NE 68507-2467 Office: County City Bldg 555 S 10th St Lincoln NE 68508-2810

SENGERS, JOHANNA M. H. LEVELT, thermophysicist; b. Amsterdam, The Netherlands, Mar. 4, 1929; married, 1963; 4 children. Drs, U. Amsterdam, 1954, PhD in Physics, 1958; PhD (hon.), Delft U. Tech., 1992. Rsch. assoc. U. Amsterdam, Van der Waals Lab, 1954-58, 59-63, U. Wis., Inst. Theoretical Chemistry, Madison, 1958-59; physicist heat divsn. Inst. Basic Stds., Nat. Bur. Stds., Gaithersburg, Md., 1963-78; group leader thermophysics divsn. Nat. Engring. Lab., 1978-87; sr. fellow thermophysics divsn. Nat. Inst. Standards and Tech., 1983-95, fellow emeritus, 1995—. Lectr Cath. U., Louvain, Belgium, 1971; rsch. assoc. Inst. Theoretical Physics, U. Amsterdam, 1974-75; regent's prof. chemistry U. Calif., L.A., 1982. Chair working group A Internat. Assn. Properties Steam, 1985-90; pres. Internat. Assn. Properties Water and Steam, 1991-92. Recipient Silver medal U.S. Dept. Commerce, 1972, Gold medal, 1978, Wise award Interagy. Com. Women in Sci. and Engring., 1985, Alexander von Humboldt Rsch. award Alexander von Humboldt-Stiftung, Bonn, Germany, 1991, L'Oreal-UNESCO Women in Sci. award, 2003. Fellow: AAAS, Am. Phys. Soc., Internat. Assn. Properties Water and Steam (hon.); mem.: ASME, AIChE, Physical Soc., Assn. Women in Sci., Royal Holland Soc. of Scis. and Humanities, Dutch Phys. Soc., Netherlands Royal Acad. Arts and Sci. (corr.), European Phys. Soc., Nat. Acad. Engring., Nat. Acad. Sci., Cosmos Club. Office: Phys & Chem Properties Div Nat Inst Stds & Tech 100 Bureau Dr Stop 8380 Gaithersburg MD 20899-8380 Office Phone: 301-975-2463. Business E-Mail: johanna.sengers@nist.gov.

SENGPIEHL, PAUL MARVIN, lawyer, former state official; b. Stuart, Nebr., Oct. 10, 1937; s. Arthur Paul and Anne Marie (Andersen) S.; B.A., Wheaton (Ill.) Coll., 1959; M.A. in Pub. Adminstrn., Mich. State U., 1961; J.D., Ill. Inst. Tech.-Chgo. Kent Coll. Law, 1970; m. June S. Cline, June 29, 1963; children— Jeffrey D., Chrystal M. Bar: Ill. 1971, U.S. Supreme Ct. 1982. Adminstrv. asst. Chgo. Dept. Urban Renewal, 1962-65; supr. Ill. Municipal Retirement Fund, Chgo., 1966-71; mgmt. officer Ill. Dept. Local Govt. Affairs, Springfield, 1971-72, legal counsel, Chgo., 1972-73; spl. asst. atty. gen. Ill. Dept. Labor, Chgo., 1973-76; asst. atty. gen. Ct. of Claims div. Atty. Gen. of Ill., 1976-83; hearing referee Bd. Rev., Ill. Dept. Labor, 1983-84; local govt. law columnist Chgo. Daily Law Bull., 1975-84; instr. polit. sci. Judson Coll., Elgin, Ill., 1963. Republican candidate for Cook County Recorder of Deeds, 1984; dep. committeeman Oak Park Twp Rep. Orgn.; elected alt. del., served del. Rep. Nat. Conv., 1992; People's Choice candidate pres. Oak Park Village, 1993; elected Rep. committeeman Oak Park Twp., 1994-98; elected del. Rep. Nat. Convention, 1996; co-chmn. Cook County Jail Ministry Bd., chmn. 2003. Mem. Ill. Bar Assn. (local govt. law sect. council 1973-79, vice chmn. 1976-77, co-editor local govt. newsletter 1976-77, chmn. 1977-78, editor newsletter 1977-78, state tax sect. council 1979-82, 84-85), Chgo. Bar Assn. (local govt. com., chmn. legis. subcom. 1978-79, sec. 1979-80, vice chmn. 1980-81, chmn. 1981-82, state and mcpl. tax com.), John Ericsson Rep. League Ill. (state sec. 1983-85, 95—, sec. Cook County 1982-97, pres. 1997—), Oak Park-River Forest C. of C. (sm. bus. coun., 1991—). Baptist (vice chmn. deacons 1973-76, 79-80, moderator 1983-86, supt. Sunday sch. 1986-93). Home: 727 N Ridgeland Ave Oak Park IL 60302-1735

SEN GUPTA, BARUN KUMAR, geology educator, researcher; b. Jamshedpur, Bihar, India, July 31, 1931; s. Tarapada and Sulata (Das Gupta) Sen Gupta; m. Mandira Gupta, May 12, 1956; children: Sagaree, Upal. BS with honors, Calcutta U., 1951, MS, 1954, Cornell U., 1961; PhD, Indian Inst. Technology, Kharagpur, India, 1963. Apprentice geologist Dalmia Cement Ltd., Calcutta, India, 1955; from asst. lectr. to lectr. Indian Inst. Tech., Kharagpur, 1955-66; postdoct. fellow, rsch. scientist Bedford Inst. Oceanography, Dartmouth, Canada, 1966-68; from asst. prof. to prof. U. Ga., Athens, 1969-79; prof. geology La. State U., Baton Rouge, 1979—2001, H.V. Howe prof. geology, 2001—03, H.V. Howe prof. emeritus, 2003—. Vis.prof. U. Rio Grande do Sul, Porto Alegre, Brazil, 1974, U. Bordeaux, France, 1985—86; vis. scientist Petrobras, Rio de Janeiro, 1999; vis. prof. U. São Paulo, Brazil, 2004. Editor: (Book) Modern Foraminifera, 1999; contbr. numerous articles to profl. jours. and chpts. to books. Fellow, pres. Cushman Found. Foraminiferal Rsch., 1987-88. Fulbright sr. fellow U. Utrecht (The Netherlands), 1992-93; rsch. grantee NSF, 1969-72, 75-79, 82-90, NATO, 1986-92, Minerals Mgmt. Svc., 1995—. Fellow Geol. Soc. Am. (W.S. Cole award 1995); mem. AAAS, AAUP, Paleontol. Soc. Office: La State U Dept Geology & Geophysics Baton Rouge LA 70803-4101 E-mail: barun@geol.lsu.edu.

SENGUPTA, MRITUNJOY, mining engineer, educator; b. Cuttack, Orissa, India, Oct. 24, 1941; came to U.S., 1968; s. Chandi P. and Bani S.; m. Nupur Bagchi, Jan. 15, 1981; children: Shyam S. ME, Columbia U., 1971, MS, 1972; PhD, Colo. Sch. of Mines, 1983. Mining engr. Continental Oil Co., Denver, 1977-78, United Nuclear Corp., Albuquerque, 1978-80, Morrison-Knudson Co., Boise, Idaho, 1975-77, 80-82; assoc. prof. U. Alaska, Fairbanks, 1983-88, prof., 1989-95. Cons. UN Devel. Program, 1987. Author: Mine Environmental Engineering, vols. I and II, 1989, Environmental Impacts of Mining, 1992, Bioremediation Engineering for Mining and Mineral Processing Wastes, 1997, Mineral Industry of India: Planning, Development and Foreign Investment Opportunities, 2001; contbr. articles to profl. publs. Recipient Gold medal Mining Metall. Inst. of India, 1976, Among Most Outstanding Intellectuals of Twenty First Century, Cambridge, Eng., 2004; Nat. Merit scholarship Govt. of India, 1959-63. Mem. NSPE, AAAS, So. Mining Engrs. Achievements include development of new concepts for mine design in oilshale in Colo. Home: PO Box 13713 Mill Creek WA 98082-1713 E-mail: msengupta@msn.com.

SENGUPTA, SOMINI, reporter; b. Calcutta, India; BA in English and Devel. Studies, U. Calif., Berkeley, 1988. With Newsday, N.Y.C.; West African bur. chief N.Y. Times, N.Y.C., 2003—. Recipient Feature Writing award, Newswomen's Club N.Y., 1997, SAJA Journalism award, 1999, George K. Polk award for fgn. reporting, 2004. Office: NY Times 229 W 43rd St New York NY 10036-3959*

SENGUPTA-GOPALAN, CHAMPA, research scientist, educator; b. Chittagong, Bangladesh, Sept. 22, 1949; d. Ananda Gopal and Renuka Sengupta; m. Aravamudan Srinivasan Gopalan, Aug. 5, 1980; children: Anjali Gopalan, Vivek Gopalan. BSc, U. Jodhpur, India, 1969; MSc, Kalyani U., India, 1972; PhD, Ohio State U., Columbus, 1978. Postdoctoral assoc. McGill U., Montreal, Canada, 1978—80, Stanford U., Palo Alto, Calif., 1980—81; rsch. scientist Agrigenetics, Madison, Wis., 1982—85; assoc. prof. N.Mex. State U., Las Cruces, 1985—92, prof., 1992—. Scientific advisor S.W. Consortium for Plant Genetics, 1995—; panel mem. USDA Nat. Rsch. Inst. grants, 1995. Contbr. articles to profl. jours.; monitoring editor Plant Physiology, Rockville, Md., 1998—2001. Mem.: Internat. Soc. of Plant Molecular Biology, Am. Soc. Plant Biology. Avocations: reading, cooking, gardening. Office: Dept Agronomy & Horticulture N Mex State Univ N127 Skeen Hall Las Cruces NM 88003

SENHAUSER, DONALD A(LBERT), pathologist, educator; b. Dover, Ohio, Jan. 30, 1927; s. Albert Carl and Maude Anne (Snyder) S.; m. Helen Brown, July 22, 1961; children: William, Norman. Student, U. Chgo., 1944-45; BS, Columbia U., 1948, MD, 1951; grad. with honors, U.S. Naval Sch. Aviation Medicine, 1953. Diplomate Am. Bd. Pathology. Intern Roosevelt Hosp., N.Y.C., 1951-52; resident Columbia-Presbyn. Hosp., N.Y.C., 1955-56, Cleve. Clinic, 1956-60; instr. in pathology Columbia U., 1955-56; fellow in immunopathology Middlesex Hosp. Med. Sch., London, 1960-61; mem. dept. pathology Cleve. Clinic Found., 1961-63; assoc. prof. pathology U. Mo., 1963-65; prof., asst. dean Sch. Medicine U. Mo., 1969-70, dir. teaching labs., 1968-70, prof., vice-chmn. dept. pathology, 1965-75; prof., chmn. dept. pathology Coll. Medicine Ohio State U., 1975-92, chair emeritus, 1992, prof. Sch. Allied Med. Professions, 1975-95, prof. emeritus, 1995—, endowed named prof., 2003. Dir. labs. Ohio State U. Hosps., 1975-92; pres. Univ. Reference Lab., Inc., 1984-86, CEO, 1986-92; bd. dirs. Columbus area chpt. ARC, 1978-82; cons. in field; WHO-AMA Vietnam med. edn. project mem. U. Saigon Med. Sch., 1967-72; vis. scientist HEW, 1972-73; acting dir. Ctrl. Ohio Regional Blood Ctr., 1976-79. Mem. editorial bd. Am. Jour. Clin. Pathology, 1965-76. With USN, 1945-46; lt. M.C. USNR, Korea, China; now capt. USNR ret. Served with USN, 1945-46; served as lt. M.C. USNR, Korea, China; now capt. USNR, Ret. Recipient Lower award, Bunts Ednl. Found., 1960—61; professorship endowed in his name, Ohio State U. Med. Sch., 2003. Mem. AAAS, Coll. Am. Pathologists (bd. govs. 1980-86, v.p. 1989-90, pres.-elect 1990-91, pres. 1991-93, immediate past pres. 1993—, Pathologist of Yr. 1994, Hartman award 1998), Am. Soc. Clin. Pathologists, Assn. Pathology Chmn., Am. Assn. Pathology, Internat. Acad. Pathology, Assn. Am. Med. Colls., Am. Assn. Blood Banks, Ohio Soc. Pathologists (gov. 1979, pres. 1987-89), Ohio Hist. Soc., Masons, Sigma Xi. Lutheran. Home: 1256 Clubview Blvd N Columbus OH 43235-1226 E-mail: donaldsenhauser@cs.com.

SENHAUSER, JOHN CRATER, architect; b. New Philadelphia, Ohio, Apr. 7, 1947; s. Edwin Crater and Margaret Jean (Huffman) S.; m. Teri A. Schleyer, June 25, 1988. BS in Architecture, U. Cin., 1971. Registered architect, Ohio, Ky. Designer Jones, Peacock, Garn & Ptnrs., Cin., 1971-72; project architect Smith Stevens Architects, Cin., 1972-76; project mgr. Herrlinger Enterprises, Cin., 1976-79; prin., owner John C. Senhauser, Architect, Cin., 1979—. Adj.

assoc. prof. Sch. Architecture and Interior Design, U. Cin., 1992-98 Exhibited in group shows at Toni Birckhead Gallery, 1990, Contemporary Arts Ctr., Cin., 1993, 98, Canton (Ohio) Art Inst., 1993; prin. works include residences. Mem. historic conservation bd. City of Cin., 1986-98, chmn. 1998—; mem. urban design rev. bd., 1998—; mem. dean's adv. coun. Coll. Design Architecture Art and Planning U. Cin., 1990; mem. design rev. com. U. Cin., 1997—. Recipient Merit award Builder mag., 1985, 88, 94, 96, 99, Grand award, 1990, Grand Best in Region award Profl. Builder, 1988, 90, Grand award for Best Overall Design, Custom Home Mag., 1996, 97, Merit award, 1990, 94, other awards. Fellow AIA (pres. 1991, Honor award Cin. chpt. 1983, 85, 90, 91, 92, 93, 94, 95, 96, 2000, Merit award 1990, 93, 94); mem. AIA Ohio (bd. dirs., sec. 1997-98, v.p. 1999, pres. 2000, regional dir. nat. bd. dirs. 2001—, Honor award 1985, 90, 91, 93, 94, 99). Office: John C Senhauser Architect 1118 Saint Gregory St Cincinnati OH 45202-1724

SENIOR, BRENT ANTHONY, otolaryngologist, educator; b. Detroit, June 7, 1964; s. Gerald William and Juanita Ann (Brondell) S.; m. Dana Lynn Dystant, Sept. 8, 1990; children: Rebecca, Benjamin, Grace, Anna. BS summa cum laude, Wheaton Coll., 1986; MD, U. Mich., 1990. Diplomate Am. Bd. Otolaryngology. Intern Boston U., 1990-91; resident Boston U.-Tufts U., 1991-95; fellow U. Pa., Phila., 1995-96; sr. staff Henry Ford Hosp., Detroit, 1996-99; assoc. prof. otolaryngology, head and neck surgery U. N.C., 1999—. Contbr. articles to profl. jours. Fellow ACS; mem. Am. Acad. Otolaryngology (mem. continuing edn. faculty 1997—), Am. Acad. Otolaryngology Head and Neck Surgery, Am. Rhinology Soc. (cons. to bd. dirs.), Soc. Univ. Otolaryngologist Head & Neck Surgeons, Am. Acad. Sleep Medicine, Christian Med. and Dental Soc., Newton Fisher Soc., Walter Work Soc. Office: UNC Otolaryngology Head & Neck Surgery 610 Burnett Womack Clb # 7070 Chapel Hill NC 27599-0001 Address: 106 Brannon Ct Chapel Hill NC 27516-8099 E-mail: Brent_senior@med.unc.edu.

SENIOR, ENRIQUE FRANCISCO, investment banker; b. Havana, Cuba, Aug. 3, 1943; came to U.S., 1960; s. Frank and Dolores (Hernandez) Senior; m. Robin Suffern Gimbel, Sept. 7, 1977; children: Tailer, Heather, Fern, Seanna. BA in Architecture, Yale U., 1964, BS in Elec. Engring., 1967; MBA, Harvard U., 1969. Corp. fin. exec. White, Weld & Co., NYC, 1969-73; v.p. Allen & Co., Inc., NYC, 1973-80, exec. v.p., mng. dir., 1980—. Bd. dirs. Allen & Co., Inc., Dick Clark Prodns., Inc., Burbank, Calif. Mem. The Brook Club, Piping Rock Club, Farmington Country Club, Phi Beta Kappa, Tau Beta Pi. Avocations: flying, fishing, hunting, skiing, woodworking. Office: Allen & Co Inc 711 5th Ave Fl 8 New York NY 10022-3111*

SENIOR, RICHARD JOHN LANE, textile rental service executive; b. Datchet, Eng., July 6, 1940; arrived in U.S., 1972, naturalized, 1977; s. Harold Dennis Senior and Jane Lane Dorothy (Chadwick) Senior Rigg; m. Diana Morgan, Dec. 19, 1966; children: Alden, Alicia, Amanda. MA, Oxford U., 1962; MIA, Yale U., 1964. Jr. mgr. Tate & Lyle, 1964—66; mgmt. cons. McKinsey & Co., Inc., London, Chgo., 1967-74; pres., CEO Morgan Svcs., Inc., Chgo., 1974—. Bd. dirs. Ball Hort. Co.; Chgo. Crime Commn., 1994-99, Northwestern Meml. Healthcare, 1992-2001, Northwestern Meml. Found., 2001—, Near South Planning Bd., 2001-2003; regional adv. bd. Kemper Ins. Cos., 1994-96. Pres. bd. trustees Latin Sch., Chgo., 1979-83. Hon. scholar Oxford U., 1960-1962. Mem. Uniform and Textile Svc. Assn. (bd. dirs. 1996-99, exec. com. 2001—, chmn. 2002-04), Textile Rental Svcs. Assn. Am. (pres. 1983-85, dir., exec. com. 1978-86), Northwestern U. Assocs., Racquet Club (bd. govs. 1983-91), Chgo. Club, Glen View Club, Casino (bd. govs. 1991-96, treas. 1993-94), Econ. Club, Yale Club Chgo. (bd. dirs. 1991-95, AYA del. 1992-95). Home: 1500 N Lake Shore Dr Chicago IL 60610-6657 Office: Morgan Svcs Inc 323 N Michigan Ave Chicago IL 60601-3798 E-mail: senior@morganservices.com.

SENIOR, THOMAS BRYAN A. electrical engineering educator, researcher, consultant; b. Menston, Yorkshire, Eng., June 26, 1928; came to U.S., 1957; s. Thomas Harold and Emily Dorothy (Matthews) S.; m. Heather Margaret Golby, May 4, 1957; children— Margaret, David, Hazel, Peter. B.Sc., Manchester U., 1949, M.Sc., 1950; PhD, Cambridge U., 1954. Sr. sci. officer Royal Radar Establishment, Malvern, Eng., 1952-57; rsch. scientist U. Mich., Ann Arbor, 1957-69, prof. elec. engring., 1969-84, prof. elec. and computer sci., 1984-98, Arthur F. Thurnau prof., 1990-98, prof. emeritus, 1998—, dir. radiation lab., 1975-87, assoc. chmn. elect. engring. & computer sci. dept., 1984-90, acting chmn., 1987-88, assoc. chmn. acad. affairs, 1991-98. Cons. in field. Author: (with Bowman and Uslenghi) Electromagnetic and Acoustical Scattering by Simple Shapes, 1969; Mathematical Methods in Electrical Engineering, 1986; (with Volakis) Approximate Boundary Conditions in Electromagnetics, 1995; contbr. articles to profl. jours. Fellow IEEE (3d Millennium medal, AP-S Disting. Achievement award 2000); mem. Internat. Sci. Radio Union (chmn. U.S. nat. com. 1982-84, vice chmn. Com. B. 1985-87, chmn. 1988-90, pres. 1996-99, Van der Pol Gold medal 1993). Home: 1919 Ivywood Dr Ann Arbor MI 48103-4527 Office: U Mich Dept Elec Engring Comp S Ann Arbor MI 48109 E-mail: senior@eecs.umich.edu.

SENKIW-RUDOWSKY, PATRICIA JOAN, artist, writer, educator; b. Newark, Jan. 20, 1961; d. James Zenon Senkiw and Joan Marie Kleinschmidt; m. Jay Mark Rudowsky, Oct. 15, 1983; 1 child, Luke Zenon. BA, Kean Coll., 1983, postgrad., 1996, St. Peter's Coll., 1989—90. Cert. prevention specialists S.A.C., 1997. With Child Assault Prevention Program, Union and Essex Counties, NJ, 1985—89; educator Irvington (N.J.) Bd. Edn., 1989—90; actress Bloomfield (N.J.) Culture Soc., 1992—93; asst. dir. Livingston (N.J.) Youth & Cmty. Svcs., 1995—2000, program dir., 2000—01; freelance writer, artist NJ, 2001—. Author: Believe, 2001, (screen) Down the Shore, 2002, The Good Life, 2003. Mem. St. Helen's Ch., Westfield, NJ. Recipient Extraordinary Svc. to Children award, Livingston Mall Alliance, 2001, 1st pl. Essay Contest, My Hero Contest, Livingstone, 2001, Best in Show hon. mention, Westfield Art Assn., 2003. Roman Catholic. Avocations: swimming, art, golf, reading, music. Office: 1201 Ocean Ave Unit 1A Bradley Beach NJ 07020 Office Phone: 732-221-3488.

SENKLER, ROBERT L. insurance company executive; BA in Math. and Stats., Minn. Duluth Coll., 1974. Began Minn. Life Ins. Co., 1974—, v.p. Individual Ins. Divsn., 1987-94, pres., 1994—, CEO, 1994—, chrmn, 1995—. Past chrmn Ins. Fed. Minn.; pres. Minn. Bus. Prtnrshp., 2003; chrmn Cap. City Prtnrshp. Recipient Univ. Minn.-Duluth Acad. Sci. Engring., 2003. Fellow Soc. Actuaries. Office: 400 Robert St N Saint Paul MN 55101-2015*

SENN, DEBORAH, insurance commissioner; m. Rudi Bertschi. BA, MA, U. Ill.; JD, Loyola U. Rep. cmty. groups, consumers, women & family groups, labor and small bus.; elected Wash. state ins. commr., 1992-96. Avocations: hiking, outdoors. Office: Insurance Bldg PO Box 40255 Olympia WA 98504-0255

SENNEMA, DAVID CARL, museum and arts administration consultant; b. Grand Rapids, Mich., July 6, 1934; s. Carl Edward and Alice Bertha (Bieri) S.; m. Martha Amanda Dixon, Feb. 22, 1958; children: Daniel Ross, Julia Kathryn, Alice Dixon. BA, Albion Coll., 1956. Mgr. Columbia Music Festival Assn., 1964-67; exec. dir. S.C. Arts Commn., Columbia, 1967-70; assoc. dir. Fed.-State Partnership and Spl. Projects program Nat. Endowment for the Arts, Washington, 1971-73; prof. arts adminstrn., dir. cmty. arts mgmt. program Sangamon State U., Springfield, Ill., 1973-76; dir. S.C. Mus. Commn., Columbia, 1976-85; bus. mgr. Palmetto Mastersingers, 1986-96. Cons. in field. Co-author: Columbia, S.C. A Postcard History, 1997. Mem. adv. panel Nat. Endowment for the Arts Music, 1968-70; chmn. Springfield Arts Commn., 1975-76. Served with U.S. Army, 1957-58. Mem. Rotary. E-mail: dsennema@sc.rr.com.

SENNETT, DAVID, theater educator, actor; b. Champaign, Ill., July 7, 1954; m. Eileen S. Cowel, Aug. 15, 1993; 1 child, Tate Matthew. M.F.A., Va. Commonwealth U., Richmond, Va., 1997—99; B.A., S.U.N.Y. Empire State Coll., NY, 1994—96. Producing artistic dir. Richmond Ensemble Theatre, 2002—; faculty Sch. of the Performing Arts in the Richmond Cmty., 1997—, Governor's Sch. for the Visual and Performing Arts, 2002—; assoc. artist - actor, dir., educator TheatreVirginia, 1997—2002; free-lance theatre artist NY, 1982—. Mem. Alliance for the Performing Arts, 2002—03; dir. Richmond Ensemble Theatre, 2002—03. Fellow Directing Fellow, U. of Iowa, 1996-97, Va. Commonwealth U., 1997 - 1999. Mem.: Lincoln Ctr. Directors Lab, SAG, Actors Equity Assn. Avocations: travel, fishing, film. Office: Richmond Ensemble Theatre 4630 Patterson Avenue Richmond VA 23226 Personal E-mail: ecowel@erols.com. E-mail: richmondensembletheatre@erols.com.

SENSABAUGH, MARY ELIZABETH, financial consultant; b. Eastland, Tex., Aug. 15, 1939; d. Johnnie and L.G. (Tucker) Roberts; m. Dwight Lee Sensabaugh, Dec. 22, 1956; children: Robert Lee, Mark Jay. Student, Odessa Jr. Coll., 1959-63, U. North Tex., 1963-67. Sr. acct. Braniff Internat. Airlines, Dallas, 1967-68; acct. Computer Bus. Services, Dallas, 1968-72; sec.-treas. Robert D. Carpenter, Inc., Dallas, 1972-76; controller Broadway Warehouses, Dallas, 1976-78; asst. controller S.W. Offset, Dallas, 1978-79; sec.-treas., cons. Carpenter, Carruth & Hover, Inc., Dallas, 1979-92; sec.-treas. Roberts, Taylor and Sensabaugh, Inc., Hurst, Tex., 1992-95; pvt. practice Irving, Tex., 1995—. Mem. Nat. Assn. Women in Constrn. (bd. dirs. Dallas chpt. 1983-84), Internat. Platform Assn., Beta Sigma (pres. Irving, Tex. chpt. 1973-74), NAFE. Avocations: playing organ and piano, reading, handcrafts. Home and Office: 702 Hughes Dr Irving TX 75062-5601

SENSENBRENNER, F(RANK) JAMES, JR., congressman; b. Chgo., June 14, 1943; s. F. James and Margaret Sensenbrenner; m. Cheryl Warren, Mar. 26, 1977; children: F. James III, Robert Alan. AB, Stanford U., 1965; JD, U. Wis., 1968. Bar: Wis. 1968, U.S. Supreme Ct. 1972. State rep. Wis. Assembly, Madison, 1969-75; state sen. Wis. Senate, Madison, 1975-79; asst. minority leader, 1976-79; mem. U.S Ho. of Reps. from 5th Wis. district, Washington, 1979—; chmn. jud. com. U.S Ho. of Reps., Washington, 2001—, chmn. sci. com., 1997-2001. Mem. Friends of Milw. Mus., Riveredge Nature Ctr. Mem. Am. Philatelic Soc., Chenequa Country Club, Capitol Hill Club. Republican. Episcopalian. Office: 2449 Rayburn House Office Bldg Washington DC 20515-4905 Office Phone: 202-225-5101.

SENSENICH, ILA JEANNE, judge; b. Pitts., Mar. 6, 1939; d. Louis E. and Evelyn Margaret S. BA, Westminster Coll., 1961; JD, Dickinson Sch. Law, 1964, JD (hon.), 1994. Bar: Pa. 1964. Assoc. Stewart, Belden, Sensenich and Harrington, Greensburg, Pa., 1964-70; asst. pub. defender Westmoreland (Pa.) County, 1970-71; U.S. magistrate judge We. Dist. Pa., Pitts., 1971—. Adj. prof. law Duquesne U., 1982-87. Author: Compendium of the Law of Prisinor's Rights, 1979; contbr. articles to profl. jour. Trustee emeritus Dickinson Sch. Law. Vis. fellow Daniel & Florence Guggenheim program in criminal justice Yale Law Sch., 1976-77. Mem. ABA, Fed. Magistrate Judges Assn. (sec. 1979-81, 88-89, treas. 1989-90, 2d v.p. 1990-91, pres.-elect 1992-93, pres. 1993-94), Pa. Bar Assn. (comn. on women in the profession 1998—), Nat. Assn. Women Judges, Westmoreland County Bar Assn., Allegheny County Bar Assn. (fed. ct. sect., com. women in law), Womens Bar Assn. We. Pa., Am. Judicature Soc. Democrat. Presbyterian. Avocations: skiing, sailing, bicycling, classical music, cooking. Office: US PO a nd Courthouse 3d Fl Pittsburgh PA 15219

SENSIPER, SAMUEL, electrical engineer; b. Elmira, NY, Apr. 26, 1919; s. Louis and Molly (Pedolsky) S.; m. Elaine Marie Zwick, Sept. 10, 1950; children: Martin, Sylvia, David. BSEE, MIT, 1939, ScD, 1951; MSEE, Stanford U., 1941. Asst. project engr. to sr. project engr., cons. Sperry Gyroscope, Garden City, Great Neck, NY, 1941-51; sect. head and sr. staff cons. Hughes Aircraft, Culver City, Malibu, Calif., 1951-60; lab. divsn. mgr. Space Gen. Corp., Glendale, Azuza, L.A., 1960—67; lab. mgr. TRW, Redondo Beach, Calif., 1967—70; cons. elec. engr. L.A., 1970—73; dir. engring. Transco Products, Venice, Calif., 1973—75; cons. elec. engr. in pvt. practice L.A., 1975—95; cons., 1995—. Faculty U. So. Calif., L.A., 1955-56, 79-80. Contbr. articles to profl. jours.; patentee in field. Recipient Cert. of Commendation U.S. Navy, 1946; indsl. electronics fellow MIT, 1947-48. Fellow IEEE, AAAS; mem. Calif. Soc. Profl. Engrs., MIT Alumni Assn., Stanford Alumni Assn., Electromagnetics Acad., Sigma Xi, Eta Kappa Nu. Home and Office: 3775 Modoc Rd #109 Santa Barbara CA 93105-4465 Office Phone: 805-879-7756. Personal E-mail: sensiper1@ieee.org.

SENSOR, MARY DELORES, hospital official, consultant; b. Erie, Pa., July 20, 1930; d. Sergie Pavl Malinowski and Leocadia Mary Francis (Machalinski) Harner; m. Robert Louis Charles Sensor, Apr. 21, 1945; children: Robert Louis Paul, Stephen Maxmillian Augustus, Therese Blaze, Kathryn Anne. MS in Health Care Adminstrn., Gannon U., 1986, MS in Health Svc. Adminstrn., 1988; BS in Hosp. Adminstrn., Daemon Coll., 1972. Intern in hosp. adminstrn. Harvard U., Boston, 1972; dir. med. records St. Mary Hosp., Langhorne, Pa., 1972-74, Moses Taylor Hosp., Scranton, Pa., 1975-77, Erie County Geriatric Ctr., Fairview, Pa., 1988-92; dir. utilization rev. Millcreek Cmty. Hosp., Erie, Pa., 1983—. Cons. prof. in hosp. adminstrn. and med. records U. Pitts., 1972-74, Temple U., 1972-74; contbr. paper 6th World Congress Automated Med. Data, Washington; presenter paper Computer Adaptation of SNOMed to DRG Assignment, to 12th Ann. Symposium on Coomputer Application in Med. Care, Washington. Bd. dirs. St. John Kanty Prep. Sch., Erie, 1970-71, pres. Ladies Aux., 1970-71; mem. Siebenburger Singing Soc. Mem. Am. Med. Record Assn., Pa. Med. Record Assn., N.W. Pa. Med. Record Assn. (2d treas. 1982-84), Nat. Assn. Quality Assurance Profls., Pa. Assn. Quality Assurance Profls. Roman Catholic. Avocations: professional classical dancing, researcher early man's migration patterns, gourmet cooking, collecting jazz. Home: 2023 Harrison St Erie PA 16510-1403

SENTELL, SUSAN B. telecommunications company executive; married; 2 children. BS in Bus. Adminstrn., Miami U., Oxford, Ohio. In comm. industry, 17 yrs.; market mgr., regional sales dir., various mgmt. positions Sprint, Chgo., from 1987, asst. v.p. mktg. comm., v.p. mktg. and product mgmt.; now pres. mtkg. and ops. Spring Bus. Svcs. Group, Dallas. Office: Sprint Bus Svcs Group 5420 LBJ Fwy Dallas TX 75240-6222

SENTELLE, DAVID BRYAN, federal judge; b. Canton, N.C., Feb. 12, 1943; s. Horace Richard Jr. and Maude (Ray) Sentelle; m. Jane LaRue Oldham, June 19, 1965; children: Sharon Lewis, Regan Herman, Rebecca Acheson. BA, U. N.C., 1965, JD with honors, 1968. Bar: N.C. 1968, N.C. (U.S. Dist. Ct. (we. dist.)) 1969, (U.S. Ct. Appeals (4th cir.)) 1970. Assoc. Uzzell & Dumont, Asheville, NC, 1968—70; asst. U.S. atty. City of Charlotte, NC, 1970—74, dist. judge, 1974—77; ptnr. Tucker, Hicks, Sentelle, Moon & Hodge, P.A., Charlotte, 1977—85; judge U.S. Dist. Ct. (we. dist.) N.C., Charlotte, 1985—87, U.S. Ct. Appeals D.C., 1987—. Adj. prof UNC, 1991—92; adj. prof. Fla. State U. Coll. Law, 1993; presiding judge Spl. Divsn. for Appointment of Ind. Counsels, 1992—; Disting. adj. prof. George Mason U. Sch. Law. Contbr. articles to profl. jours. Chmn. Mecklenburg County Rep. Com., 1978—80, N.C. State Rep. Conv., 1979—80. Fellow, Dameron Found., 1967. Mem.: Mecklenburg County Bar Assn., Shriners, Masons (Scottish Rite), Am. Inn of Ct. Found. (bd. dir.), Edward Bennett Williams Inn of Ct. (pres.). Baptist. Office: US Court of Appeals 333 Constitution Ave NW Washington DC 20001-2866

SENTER, LYONEL THOMAS, JR., federal judge; b. Fulton, Miss., July 30, 1933; s. L. T. and Eva Lee (Jetton) S. BS, U. So. Miss., 1956; LL.B., U. Miss., 1959. Bar: Miss. 1959. County pros. atty., 1960-64; U.S. commr., 1966-68; judge Miss. Circuit Ct., Circuit 1, 1968-80, U.S. Dist. Ct. (no. dist.) Miss., 1980-82, chief judge, 1982-98, sr. judge, 1998—. Mem. Miss. State Bar Office: Clerk US Dist Ct 2012 15th St Ste 403 Gulfport MS 39501

SENTHIL NATHAN, SELVARAJ, internist, geriatrician; b. Madras, India, July 11, 1957; s. Selvaraj and Duraichi Chellappa. MBBS, Madras U., 1981, MD, 1984, DM, 1989. Diplomate Am. Bd. Internal Medicine, Am. Bd. Geriatrics., Am. Bd. Hospice and Palliative Medicine; cert. med. rev. officer; bd. cert. in hospice and palliative medicine. Resident in internal medicine Stanley Med. Coll., Madras, 1981-84; fellow in pathology Madras Med. Coll., 1985-87; fellow in oncology Cancer Inst., Madras, 1987-89; resident in internal medicine Eng., Ireland, 1990-93; resident in inteneral medicine U. Medicine and Dentistry of N.J., 1993-95; fellow in internal medicine/geriatrics U. Tex. Med. Br., Galveston, 1995-96; physician internal medicine and geriatrics Cmty. Action Orgn. of Lawrence County, 1996-97; med. dir. Holzer Sr. Care Ctr., Bidwell, Ohio, 1997—. Cons. internal medicine and geriat. Holzer Med. Ctr., Gallipolis, Ohio; clin. asst. prof. dept. family and cmty. health Marshall U. Sch. Medicine, Huntington, W.V. Fellow Acad. Medicine of N.J.; mem. ACP. Avocations: internet, surfing, computers, alternative medicine research. Home: 25 E South St Jackson OH 45640-1638 Office: 90 Jackson Pike Gallipolis OH 45631-1560

SENTURIA, YVONNE DREYFUS, pediatrician, epidemiologist; b. Houston, Jan. 16, 1951; BA in Biology and Sociology, Rice U., 1973; MD, U. Tex., San Antonio, 1977; MSc in Epidemiology, London Sch. Hygiene and Tropical Medicine, 1985. Diplomate Am. Bd. Pedias. Pediat. resident Shands Tchg. Hosp., Gainesville, Fla., 1977-79, Tex. Children's Hosp., Houston, 1979-80; instr., asst. prof. Coll. Medicine, Baylor U., Houston, 1980-82; sr. clin. med. officer Hammersmith and Fulham Health Authority, London, 1982-83; cons. pediatrician Kingston (Eng.) Hosp., 1983, Northwick Park Hosp., London, 1983; rsch. pediatrician Charing Cross Hosp. Med. Sch., London, 1984-85; clin. lectr. Inst. Child Health, London, 1985-88; attending pediatrician and epidemiologist Children's Meml. Hosp., Chgo., 1989-96; attending pediatrician Jacobi Hosp., Bronx, N.Y., 1996—. Fellow Am. Acad. Pediat.; mem. Ambulatory Pediat. Assn. Office: Albert Einstein Coll Medicine Nurses Residence 7 S 12 1300 Morris Park Ave Bronx NY 10461-1926

SENTURK, UFUK, ceramics engineer, researcher; s. Nail Senturk. BS, Mid. East Tech. U., Ankara, Turkey, 1990; MS, Mid. East Tech. U., 1993; PhD, N.Y. State Coll. of Ceramics, Alfred, 1997. Rsch. scientist SUN Y-Stony Brook, 1997—99; rsch mgr PQ Corp, Conshohoken, Pa., 1999—. Home: 46 East 4th St Bridgeport PA 19405 Office: PQ Corp 280 Cedar Grove Rd Conshohocken PA 19428

SENZEL, ALAN JOSEPH, analytical chemistry consultant, music critic; b. L.A., May 26, 1945; s. Bernard and Esther Mildred (Shykin) S.; m. Phyllis Sharon Abt, June 22, 1969; children: Richard Steven, Lisa Beth. BS in Chemistry, Calif. State U., Long Beach, 1967; MS, UCLA, 1969, PhD, 1970. Assoc. editor Am. Chem. Soc., Washington, 1970-74; methods editor Assn. Ofcl. Analytical Chemists, Washington, 1974-78; info. dir. Chemistry Industry Inst. Toxicology, Research Triangle Park, NC, 1978-79; pvt. cons. Raleigh, NC, 1978—. Sr. tech. writer Cardinal Health, Morrisville, N.C., 2002—; music critic Raleigh News and Observer, 1982-90, Spectator Mag., 1990-94; dep. mgr. Environ. Sys. Group, Environ. Resources Mgmt. Inc., Exton, Pa., 1988; project scientist Agrl. divsn. Residu Chem. dept. CIBA-GEIGY Corp., Greensboro, N.C., 1989-93; analytical contract lab. mgr. Entropy, Inc., 1995-96. Editor: Instrumentation in Analytical Chemistry, 1973, Newburger's Manual of Cosmetic Analysis, 1977 (FDA award 1978), Safety in the Laboratory, 1984 (STC award 1985); assoc. editor: Official Methods of Analysis, 1975; editor Inclusions Quar., 1993-94; publs. mgr. Internat. Union Pure and Applied Chemistry, 1999-2002. Pres. Congregation Sha'arei Israel, 1981-83, Raleigh Chamber Music Guild, 1997-99. Mem. Soc. Tech. Comm. (treas. 1983-85, v.p. 1985-87, achievement award 1985, excellence award 2002), Am. Chem. Soc., Assn. Ofcl. Analytical Chemists, Bridge Club (Raleigh), Capitol Club, Vanderbilt Club, B'nai B'rith. Republican. Jewish. Avocations: music, tennis, basketball, bridge. Home and Office: 7704 Audubon Dr Raleigh NC 27615-3403 Office Phone: 919-465-8632. E-mail: asenzel@yahoo.com.

SENZEL, MARTIN LEE, lawyer; b. Rochester, N.Y., June 21, 1944; s. Albert Benjamin and Besse (Lipson) S.; m. Dagni Maren Belgum, Feb. 17, 1979; 1 child, Whitney. BA, Yale U., 1966, LLB, 1969. Bar: N.Y. 1971, U.S. Dist. Ct. (so. dist.) N.Y., U.S. Ct. Appeals (2nd cir.) 1973. Assoc. Cravath, Swaine & Moore LLP, N.Y.C., 1969—77, ptnr., 1977—2000. Bd. dir. Medinol Ltd. Mem. ABA, N.Y. State Bar Assn., Assn. Bar City N.Y. Home: 101 Central Park W New York NY 10023-4204 Office: Cravath Swaine & Moore LLP Worldwide Plz 825 8th Ave Fl 38 New York NY 10019-7475 Office Phone: 212-474-1520. E-mail: msenzel@cravath.com.

SEPNAFSKI, BILL G. secondary school educator, consultant; b. Manitowoc, Wisc., May 27, 1950; s. William Peter and Marian Sepnafski; m. Ellen Jean Hanley, Aug. 10, 1974; children: Megan, Rob. BS, Univ. Wisc., Eau Claire, Wisc., 1972. Head resident housing dept. Univ. Wis., Eau Claire, Wis., 1972—73; social studies educator Eau Claire N H.S., Eau Claire, Wis., 1973—74; social studies educator, social studies dept. chair, K-12 social studies coord. Menasha H.S., Menasha, Wis., 1974—. Youth adv. bd. Fox Cities/Kurgan Russia-Sister Cities Program, Appleton, Wis., 2003—; trainer, cons. evaluator svc. learning Nat. Svc. Learning Exch., Wis., 1994—. Bd. dirs. Boys Girls Brigade, Neenah, 2004—, Habitat for Humanity, Fox Cities, Wis., 2002, Heckrodt Wetlands Res., Menasha, 2002—. Recipient Tchr. of the Yr., Menasha Joint Sch. Dist., 2002. Global Educator, Wis. Dept of Pub. Instrn., 2004; Kohl Fellowship, Kohl Found., 2002—03. Master: Assn. for Supervision and Curriculum and Devel.; mem.: Wisc. Basketball Coaches Assn., Orgn. of Am. Historians, Nat. Coun. for Social Studies, Wis. Coun. for Social Studies. Avocations: sports, travel, reading, service learning, environmentalism. Home: 1150 Meadow Ln Menasha WI 54952 Office: Menasha H S 420 Seventh St 54952

SEPULDADL, LYNN, utility company executive; CFO NGTS, Dallas. Office: NGTS 8150 N Central Expy Ste 525 Dallas TX 75206-1867

SEPULVADO, JOSEPH MICHAEL, computer information scientist; b. Cheyenne, Wyo., Aug. 16, 1952; s. Joseph Martin and Ann Mildred (Shipp) S.; m. Cynthia Marie Howell, July 31, 1982 (div. Aug. 1987); m. Shirley Rae Benham; children: Julie Ann, Angela Dyan. BS, U. Okla., 1972. Cert. data processor, data educator, computer programmer. Sr. systems analyst Pub. Svc. Co. of Okla., Tulsa, 1978-80; application supr. Cotton Petroleum Corp., Tulsa, 1980-81; cons. Forte Info. Svcs., Tulsa, 1981-82; instr. Tulsa Jr. Coll., 1982-84; sr. systems analyst Citgo Petroleum Corp., Tulsa, 1984; cons. Computer Horizons, inc., Jacksonville, Fla., 1984-85, Computer Assistance, Inc., Dallas, 1985-87, IMI Systems, Inc., Dallas, 1987-97; ind. contractor, 1997—. With USAF, 1981. Roman Catholic. Avocations: reading, fishing. Home: 1701 Windmire Dr Mesquite TX 75181-1555

SEPULVEDA, EDUARDO SOLIDEO, chemical engineer; b. Loay, Philippines, Jan. 5, 1945; came to U.S., 1981; m. Consuelo S. Araneta, May 18, 1977; children: Edward, Josephus, Blaise. BSChE, De La Salle U., 1966; M of Chem. Engring., U. Philippines, 1972. Lic. profl. engr., Calif. Instr. U. Philippines, Quezon City, 1968-70; sr. instr. De La Salle U., Manila, Philippines, 1970-71, asst. prof., 1971-73; process engr. Philippines Petroleum Corp., Makati, 1973-74, sr. process engr., 1974-75, mgr. tech. svc., 1975-81; sr. engr. C F Braun & Co., Alhambra, Calif., 1981; prin. engr. Brown & Root Braun, Alhambra, Calif., 1987-94, L.G. Engineering Co., Ltd., Seoul, Korea, 1994-96; supervising process engr. Parsons, Martinez, Calif., 1997—. Reviewer chem. bd. De La Salle U., 1970-79. Mem. St. John Corregidor Lodge, Manila, 1979. Mem. AIChE, Project Mgmt. Inst., Phi Kappa Phi. Achievements include designed and engineered a fluid catalyst transport system to hydrocracker reactor. Home: 3700 Oaklawn Ln Pico Rivera CA 90660-5941 Office: Parsons E & C 2000 Marina Vista Ave Martinez CA 94553-1301 Office Phone: 925-313-5187. E-mail: ed.sepulveda@parsonsec.com., essep@aol.com.

SEPULVEDA, NICASIO, hydrologist, researcher; b. Adjuntas, PR, Sept. 24, 1960; s. Agustin A. Sepulveda and Matilde C. Alancastro; m. Marta J. Gonzalez, Feb. 3, 1965; children: Nicholas Brian, Jonathan Paul. PhD, Brown U., 1986. Mem. tech. staff AT&T Bell Labs., Whippany, NJ, 1986—; rsch. hydrologist U.S. Geol. Survey, Altamonte Springs, Fla., 1988—2003. Mem.: Am. Geophys. Union (corr.). Independent. Roman Catholic. Achievements include development of algorithm to estimate water-table altitude from digital elevation model and minimum water table based on lake elevations and stream stages; ground-water flow model for the Floridan Aquifer System in peninsular

Florida; solved nonlinear problems in surface water and ground-water. Avocation: tennis. Office: U S Geological Survey 224 W Central Parkway Suite 1006 Altamonte Springs FL 32712 E-mail: nsepul@usgs.gov.

SEPÚLVEDA, SANDRA, communications educator; b. N.Y.C., N.Y., Sept. 14, 1948; d. Samuel Sepúlveda and Maria Trinidad. PhD, U. P.R., Rio Piedras, 2000. Cert. life cert. Tchr. Dept. Edn., P.R. Prof. U. P.R., Rio Piedras, PR, 1986—. V.p. acad. affairs Nat. Coll., Bayamon and Arecibo, PR, 1994—95; dean acad. affairs Sch. Fine Arts, San Juan, PR, 1997—99; cons. in field, PR, 1996—; mem. consultative bd. Coun. Higher Edn., PR, 1996—. Pres. editl. bd.: Nat. Coll. Bull., 1989—95. Mem. P.R. chpt. ARC, 1990, Preservation Trust of P.R., 1995—. Mem.: AAUW, MLA, Phi Delta Kappa. Avocations: travel, photography, reading, decoration, cooking. Home: PO Box 195081 San Juan PR 00919-5081 Office: U PR Rio Piedras Campus Coll Bus Adminstrn PO Box 23332 San Juan PR 00931

SEQUEIRA, MANUEL ALEXANDRE, JR., lawyer; b. Oct. 31, 1931; came to U.S., 1946, naturalized, 1954; s. Manuel Alexandre and Cecilia Maria (Xavier) S.; m. Angela Maria Lopes, Feb. 15, 1958; children: Joseph, Michael, Peter, Robert. BA, U. Notre Dame, 1955, JD, 1956. Bar: N.Y. 1957, U.S. Dist. Ct. (so. and ea. dists.) N.Y. 1958, U.S. Ct. Appeals (2d cir.) 1967, U.S. Supreme Ct. 1971. Assoc. atty. Hill Rivkins & Hayden LLP, N.Y.C., 1956-67; litigation house counsel Am. Internat. Group (Sequeira, Rienzo & Gillies), N.Y.C., 1967-82; pvt. practice Mahopac, N.Y., 1983—. Mem. Christian Legal Soc. Roman Catholic. Office: PO Box 563 Mahopac NY 10541-0563 Office Phone: 845-628-1818. E-mail: sequeira.law.office@rcn.com.

SÉQUIN, CARLO H. computer science educator; b. Winterthur, Switzerland, Oct. 30, 1941; came to U.S., 1970; s. Carl R. and Margrit (Schaeppi) S.; m. Margareta Frey, Oct. 5, 1968; children: Eveline, Andre. BS, U. Basel, Switzerland, 1965, PhD, 1969. Mem. tech. staff Bell Labs., Murray Hill, N.J., 1970-76; vis. Mackay lectr. U. Calif.-Berkeley, 1976-77, prof. elec. engring. computer scis., 1977—, assoc. chmn. computer sci., 1980-83, assoc. dean capital projects, 2001—. Author: First Book on Charge-Coupled Devices, Charge Transfer Devices, 1975; contbr. over 230 articles to profl. jours. Fellow IEEE (Tech. Achievement award 2003), Assn. Computing Machinery, Swiss Acad. Engring. Scis. Achievements include patents for integrated circuits. Office: U Calif Dept EECS Computer Scis Divsn Soda Hall Berkeley CA 94720-1776 Business E-Mail: sequin@csberkeley.edu.

SERAFIN, DONALD, plastic surgeon, educator; b. NYC, Jan. 18, 1938; s. Stephen Michael and Julia (Sopko) S.; m. Patricia Serafin; children: Allison Elizabeth, Christina Julia, Donald Stephen, Lara Leigh. AB, Duke U., 1960, MD, 1964. Diplomate Am. Bd. Surgery, Am. Bd. Plastic Surgery. Surg. intern Grady Meml. Hosp., Atlanta, 1964-65; resident in surgery Emory U. Hosp., Atlanta, 1965-69; asst. resident in plastic and reconstructive surgery Duke U. Med. Ctr., Durham, N.C., 1971-73, chief resident, 1973-74; Christine Kleinert fellow in hand surgery U. Louisville Hosp., 1972-73; practice medicine specializing in plastic surgery, Durham. Mem. staff N.C. Splty. Hosp., Durham Regional Hosp., Maria Parham Hosp.; attending faculty Durham VA Med. Ctr.; asst. prof. plastic, reconstructive and maxillofacial surgery Duke U., 1974-77, assoc. prof., 1977-81, prof., 1981-2000, prof. emeritus, 2000—, chief divsn. plastic reconstructive and maxillofacial and oral surgery, 1985-95, chmn. Plastic Surgery Rsch. Coun., 1983. Assoc. editor Jour. Reconstructive Microsurgery; contbr. articles to profl. jours. Served to maj. M.C., USAF, 1969-71, to col. M.C., USAR. Decorated Air Force Commendation medal, Army Commendation medal, Army Achievement medal. Fellow ACS; mem. AMA, Internat. Soc. Reconstructive Microsurgery, Am. Soc. Plastic Surgeons, Am. Assn. Plastic Surgeons, Am. Soc. Aesthetic Plastic Surgery, Am. Soc. Surgery Hand, Am. Assn. Hand Surgery, Am. Burn Assn., Plastic Surgery Rshc. Coun., N.C. Soc. Plastic, Maxillofacial and Reconstructive Surgeons, Southeastern Soc. Plastic and Reconstructive Surgeons. Office: NC Specialties Hosp 1110 N Main St Durham NC 27701 also: 511 Rain Creek Rd Ste 104B Lakeview NC 28350 Office Phone: 919-220-7711., 252-438-8152. Personal E-mail: seradonald@aol.com.

SERAFIN, JOHN ALFRED, art educator; b. Washington, Nov. 3, 1942; Student, Syracuse U., 1967-69, MS, 1974; BFA, U. Utah, 1971. Cert. tchr., N.Y. Graphic artist Sears, Roebuck and Co., Syracuse, 1967-68; dir. advt. Around the Town mag., Syracuse, 1969; tchr. art Blodgett Jr. High Sch., Syracuse, 1971-76, Roberts Elem. Sch., Syracuse, 1986-87, Fowler High Sch., Syracuse, 1976—; full-time artists. Yearbook adviser Blodgett Jr. High Sch., 1971-75, coach track, 1971-74, coach cross-country, 1972-74; jr. class adviser Fowler High Sch., 1977-78. Artist mag. cover design U. Utah Pharmacy Mag., 1970, Fine Art Index Internat., 1995 edit., Chgo.; group exhbns. include Syracuse Stage, 1989-92, N.Y. State Fair, 1977, 89, 90, Everson Mus., Syracuse, 1985, Cooperstown (N.Y.) Nat. Show, 1991, Westmoreland Nat. Art Show, Latrobe, Pa., 1995, Nat. Design Congress of Art & Design Exhbn. Art Reach '95, Salt Lake City, Tex. Nat. Show, Stephen Austin State U., 1996, Stad Diksmuide World Show, Brussels, 1996; represented by Montserrat Art Gallery, N.Y.C., Limner Gallery, N.Y.C., Agora Gallery, N.Y.C.; painting included in Mut. of N.Y. M.O.N.Y. Art Collection, N.Y.C., Hudson Gallery, Toledo, Delevan Art Gallery, Syracuse. Recipient award of Excellence, Manhattan Arts Mag., N.Y.C. Mem. N.Y. State United Tchrs., Syracuse Tchrs. Assn. (rep. 1972-75), Associated Artists Galleries, Allied Artists of N.Y., Nat. Art Educators Assn., Cooperstown Art Assn. Democrat. Home: 113 Euclid Dr Fayetteville NY 13066-1919 *The artist can turn the not yet into reality.*

SERAFIN, ROBERT JOSEPH, science center administrator, electrical engineer; b. Chgo., Apr. 22, 1936; s. Joseph Albert and Antoinette (Gazda) S.; m. Betsy Furgerson, Mar. 4, 1961; children: Katherine, Jenifer, Robert Joseph Jr., Elizabeth. BSEE, U. Notre Dame, 1958; MSEE, Northwestern U., 1961; PhDEE, Ill. Inst. Tech., 1972. Engr. Hazeltine Rsch. Corp. Ill. Inst. Tech. Rsch. Inst., 1960-62; assoc. engr., rsch. engr., sr. rsch. engr. Nat. Ctr. for Atmospheric Rsch., Boulder, Colo., 1962-73, mgr. field observing facility, 1973-80, dir. atmospheric tech. div. Bouulder, Colo., 1981-89, dir. ctr., 1989-2000. Chair Nat. Weather Svc. Modernization Com. Author: Revised Radar Handbook, 1989; contbr. numerous articles to profl. jours.; editl. bd./com. Acta Meteorologica Sinica; editl. founder Jour. Atmospheric and Oceanic Tech.; patentee in field. Speaker various civic groups in U.S. and internationally. Fellow IEEE, Am. Meteorol. Soc. (pres.); mem. NAE, NAS (human rights com.), Boulder C. of C., Sigma Xi. Avocations: golf, fishing, skiing. Office: Nat Ctr Atmospheric Rsch 1850 Table Mesa Dr PO Box 3000 Boulder CO 80307-3000

SERAFIN, THOMAS JOSEPH, photographer, writer; b. Buffalo, July 28, 1952; s. Joseph Thomas and Mary Helen Serafin; 1 child, Christine. Photographer Modernage, L.A., 1984—. Author: (book) Relics-The Forgotten Sacramental, 1999, The Simony Report, 1999. Founder Internat. Crusade Holy Relics, L.A., 1996—2002; dep. mem. assembly Internat. Parliament Safety & Peace, Palermo, Italy, 2001—. With USAR, 1970—76. Decorated knight Order Immaculate Conception Vila Vicosa, Duke Braganca, 36th Titular King of Portugal, comdr. St. Michael of the Wing; named Officer, Imperial Order of Dragon of Annam-Liaison to His Royal Highness Prince Nhiep Chinh Nguyen-Phuc Buu Chanh, Vietnam. Mem.: Apostolate Holy Relics (pres., CEO 2002). Roman Catholic. Office: Ichrusa/Apostolate Holy Relics PO Box 21301 Los Angeles CA 90021 Office Phone: 818-416-9279. Business E-Mail: tom@ICHRusa.com.

SERAJI-BOZORGZAD, NASRINE, architecture educator; b. Tehran, Iran, 1957; Bachelor's, Yale U., 1978; diploma, Archtl. Assn. Sch., London, 1983; MArch, Harvard U., 1985. Instr. study abroad program U. Toronto; founder Atelier Seraji; prof. and dir. Meisterschulen fur Architektur Akademie der Bildenden Kunste, Vienna; instr. Archtl. Assn. Sch., London; chair Coll. Arch., Art and Planning Cornell U., 2001—. Prin. works include Temporary Am. Cultural Ctr., Paris, 1991, Pavilion of Caverne du Dragon in Chemin des Dames, Aisne, France, 1996—98. Home: 11 Rue Des Arquebusiers 75003 Paris France Office: Coll Arch Art and Planning Cornell U 129 Sibley Dome Ithaca NY 14853

SERATT, RODGER CALVIN, manufacturing executive; b. Poplar Bluff, Mo., Feb. 5, 1950; s. Calvin Eulas Seratt and Evelyn Berneice Mitchell. BS, U. Ark., 1971. Lic. Real Estate Broker Ark. V.p. rsch., editor newsletter Energy Independence Techs. Corp., Fayetteville, Ark., 1976-80; pres., CEO Ozark River Farms, Inc., Fairdealing, Mo., 1980—, Colombian Leather Co., Inc., Fairdealing, Mo., 1999—; owner, mfr. Cole Manufactured Housing, 2001—. Instr. Escuelas Aeronauticas, Naylor, Mo., 1998—. Author: Future Trends in Personnel Management, 1970, The Alcohol Fuel Book, 1981, Fly Safe and Easy, 1998, Vuelo Facil Y Seguro, 2000; editor: The Alcohol Fuel Rev., 1978. Deacon Order of Grand Masons, Fayetteville, 1971-74; active Jaycees, chmn. Lake Wilson project, Fayetteville, 1974-76; mem. pub. rels. com. C. of C., Fayetteville, 1976-78; mem. broker adv. com. Ark. Bd. Realtors, Fayetteville, 1974-76; elected Constable 5th Dist., Fayetteville, 1979-81. 1st lt. inf. U.S. Army, 1971-74. Recipient Athletic scholarship U. Ark., 1970, 71, scholarship award Men's Interhouse Congress U. Ark., 1969. Mem. Aircraft Owners and Pilots Assn., Experimental Aircraft Assn., Nat. Arbor Day Found., Nat. Audubon Soc. Avocations: swimming, flying, playing guitar, building cars. Home: RR 1 Box 2000 Naylor MO 63953 Office: Ozark River Farms Inc RR 1 Box 2001 Naylor MO 63953 Fax: 573-857-2034. E-mail: rodger@semo.net., sales@coleleather.com.

SERATTI, LORRAINE M. state legislator; b. Oct. 30, 1949; V.p. Wis. Fedn. Taxpayers Orgn.; pres. Florence County Taxpayers Alliance; Wis. state assemblywoman dist. 36, 1992—. Small bus. owner. Mem. Florence Hist. Soc. Mem. NRA. Republican. Address: HC 2 Box 588 Florence WI 54121-9620 Office: Wis Assembly PO Box 8952 Madison WI 53708-8952

SERBAROLI, FRANCIS J. lawyer, educator, writer; b. N.Y.C., Feb. 8, 1952; AB, Fordham U., 1973, JD, 1977. Bar: N.Y. 1978, U.S. Dist. Ct. (ea. and so. dists.) N.Y. 1978, U.S. Ct. Appeals (2d and D.C. cirs.) 1979, U.S. Supreme Ct. 1983. Asst. atty. gen. N.Y. State Dept. Law, 1978-80; ptnr. Cadwalader Wickersham & Taft, N.Y.C., 1995—. Vice chmn. N.Y. State Pub. Health Coun., 1995—; health law columnist The N.Y. Law Jour. Author: The Corporate Practice of Medicine Prohibition in the Modern Era of Health Care, 1999. Chmn. bd. trustees Loyola Sch., N.Y.C. Fellow N.Y. Acad. Medicine; mem. Am. Health Lawyers' Assn., N.Y. State Bar Assn., Assn. Bar City N.Y. Office: Cadwalader Wickersham Taft LLP 100 Maiden Ln New York NY 10038-4818

SERBER, WILLIAM, radiation oncologist, educator; b. Phila., Oct. 26, 1912; s. David and Rose Jean (Frankel) S.; m. Jane Greenberg, June 16, 1938; children: John, Ellen. BA, Yale U., 1934; MD, U. Pa., 1938. Bd. cert. in radiology and nuclear medicine; lic. physician, Pa. Intern. Phila. Gen. Hosp., 1938-40, resident in radiology, 1940-42; assoc. in radiology Hahnemann Med. Coll., 1951-52, asst. prof., 1952-60; instr. in radiology U. Pa., 1947-52, vis. lectr., 1952-61, clin. asst. prof., 1961-66, asst. prof. clin. radiology, 1966-77; from assoc. prof. to prof. clin. radiation oncology Hahnemann U., Phila., 1977-91, prof. therapeutic radiology, 1991-95; prof. radiation oncology and nuclear medicine Med. Coll. Pa. and Hahnemann U., Phila., 1995-97; staff Hahnemann U. Hosp., Phila., 1977-97. Assoc. dir. dept. radiology Albert Einstein Med. Ctr., Phila., 1950-60; staff radiation oncology Sacred Heart Hosp., Norristown, Pa., 1978-94, mem. cancer com., 1978-94; staff radiation oncology Montgomery Hosp., Norristown, 1978-97, Suburban Gen. Hosp., Norristown, 1988-97; contbr. articles to profl. jours. Maj. U.S. Army, 1942-46. Recipient award for outstanding leadership Brady Cancer Rsch. Inst., 1994. Fellow Am. Coll. Radiology; mem. Am. Radium Soc., Am. Soc. for Therapeutic Radiology and Oncology, Phila. County Med. Soc. Home: Apt 231 5555 Paradise Dr # 231 Corte Madera CA 94925-1851 E-mail: serberw@comcast.net.

SERCHUK, IVAN, lawyer; b. N.Y.C., Oct. 13, 1935; s. Israel and Freda (Davis) S.; children: Camille, Bruce Mead, Vance Foster. BA, Columbia U., 1957, LLB, 1960. Bar: N.Y. 1961, U.S. Dist. Ct. (so. dist.) N.Y. 1963, U.S. Ct. Appeals (2d cir.) 1964, U.S. Tax Ct. 1966. Law clk. to judge U.S. Dist. Ct. (so. dist.) N.Y., N.Y., 1961-63; assoc. Kaye, Scholer, Fierman, Hays & Handler, 1963-68; dep. supt., counsel N.Y. State Banking Dept., N.Y.C., Albany, 1968-71; mem. Berle & Berle, 1972-73; spl. counsel N.Y. State Senate Banks Com., 1972; mem. Serchuk & Zelermyer LLP, White Plains, NY, 1976—2003, Todtman, Nachamie, Spizz & Johns, PC, 2003—. Lectr. Practising Law Inst., 1968-71. Mem. N.Y. State Bar Assn., Assn. of Bar of City of N.Y. Home: Mead St Waccabuc NY 10597 Office: Todtman Nachamie Spizz & Johns 425 Park Ave New York NY 10022 E-mail: iserchuk@tnsj-law.com.

SERCK-HANSSEN, EILIF, air transportation executive; BS in Civil Engring., U. Bergen; BA in Mgmt. Sci., U. Kent, Canterbury; MBA, U. Chgo. Former mgr. PricewaterhouseCoopers, London, PepsiCo; former mng. dir. fin., asst. treas. N.W. Airlines; sr. v.p.-fin., treas. US Airways Group, Inc., US Airways, Inc., Arlington, Va., 2003—. Mem.: Inst. Chartered Accts. Eng. and Wales. Office: US Airways 2345 Crystal Dr Arlington VA 22227*

SERCOMBE, WILLIAM JOHN, geologist; b. Strathroy, Ont., Mar. 26, 1955; came to U.S., 1981; s. Raymond S.; 1 child, Daniel. BASc in Applied Sci., U. Toronto, 1978. Profl. engr. Geologist Amoco, various locations, 1978—. Contbr. numerous articles to sci. jours. Active Boy Scouts Am. Achievements include first to interpret Himalayas and Carpathians correctly. Home: PO Box 4381 Houston TX 77210-4381

SERDARI, THOMAÏ, historian, librarian; b. Athens, Greece, May 5, 1970; d. Vasilis Serdaris and Despina Serdari. MA in Architecture, Nat. Tech. U. of Athens, 1994; MA in Media Studies, New Sch. for Social Rsch., N.Y.C., 1997; MA in Art History, postgrad., NYU, 2001—. Cert. archtl. engr., Hellenic Republic Tech. Chamber of Greece. Arch., Lamia, Greece, 1994—95; art and architecture libr. Dept. Fine Arts NYU, 1999—. Founder, editor-in-chief (jour.) POLIS. Scholar, Pratt Inst., Bklyn., 1999—2000; Bogardus scholar, 1999—2000. Mem.: Art Librs. Soc. N.Am., Soc. Archtl. Historians, Ind. Press Assn., Documentation and Conservation of Bldgs., Sites and Neighborhoods of the Modern Movement.

SEREBRIER, JOSÉ, musician, conductor, composer; b. Montevideo, Uruguay, Dec. 3, 1938; came to U.S., 1956; s. David and Frida (Wasser) S.; m. Carole Farley, Mar. 29, 1969; 1 child, Lara Adriana Francesca. Diploma, Nat. Conservatory, Montevideo, 1956, Curtis Inst. Music, 1958; BA, U. Minn., 1960; studied with Aaron Copland, Anatal Dorati, Pierre Monteux. Ind. composer, condr., 1955—. Apprentice condr. Minn. Orch., 1958-60; assoc. condr. Am. Symphony Orch., N.Y.C., 1962-66; music dir. Am. Shakespeare Festival, 1966; composer-in-residence Cleve. Orch., 1968-71; artistic dir. Internat. Festival of Arts., Miami, 1984—, Festival Miami, 1985—; guest condr. numerous orchs. including London Symphony, London Philharm., Paris Radio, Cleve. Symphony Orch., Phila. Symphony Orch., Pitts. Symphony Orch.; founder, artistic dir. Festival Miami (internat. arts festival), 1984. Composer: (for orch.) Variations on a Theme from Childhood, (for chamber) Symphony for Percussion, Concerto for Violin and Orch. (recorded by Royal Phila. Orch. on ASV), (concerto for harp and orch.) Colores Magicos, 1970, also works for chorus, voice, keyboard; recs. for RCA, CRI, ASV, KEM, Disc, Trax Classique, EMI, Tioch, Chandos, Varese-Sarabande Decca, IMG, Pickwick, BMG, BIS Records, Vox, Dinemec, Conifer Classics, Decca, Warner Classics, Naxos, with various orchs.; condr. for many recs. including Sibelius Symphony No. 1, Holst's The Planets, Carmen, Poulenc's opera La Voix Humaine, Shostakovich Film Suites vol. 1, 2 and 3(Deutsche Schallplatten award 1988), Carole Farley Sings French Songs (Deutsche Schallplaten award 1988), (home video) Kultur, Prokoviev's Alexander Nevsky, Beethoven's Eroica and Tchaikovsky Symphony No. 1 with Sydney and Melbourne Symphony Orch., Mendelssohn Symphonies, Beethoven Symphonies, Bloch's Violin Concerto and Serebrier's Poema Elegiaco CD, 1992, Le Orchestral Music of Tchaikovsky (several vols.), Laserdisc of Operas The Telephone by Menotti and La Voix Humaine by Poulenc with Scottish Chamber Orch., 1992, Royal Philharm. Orch., 1992, Dvörak Symphonies with Czech State Philharm. for Conifer/BMG, Music of Janacek and Chadwick (4 CDs) for R.R., Hindemith CD with Philharmonia Orch. for ASV; (first complete recording) Partita, Ned Rorem For Naxos; (world-premiere recordings) Winterreise, Fantasia; solo-violin sonata with London Philharm. Orch.; Gershwin CD with Royal Scottish Nat. Orch. for Dinemic; Delius songs and orch. works, Grieg songs, London Philharmonic Orch. recording for Dinemic; conductor Grammy Awards, 2003; recordings: music by William Schuman (2 Grammy nominations), Ives Symphony No. 4 (Grammy nomination). Recipient Ford Found. Condr.'s award, Alice M. Ditson award, 1976, commn. award Nat. Endowment Arts, 1978, Deutsche Schall Platten Critics award, Music Retailers Assn. award for Best Symphony Rec., 1991, 2002; Guggenheim fellow, 1958-60; Rockefeller Found. grantee, 1968-70. Mem. Am. Symphony Orch. League, Am. Music Ctr., Am. Fedn. Musicians. Home: 270 Riverside Dr New York NY 10025-5209 E-mail: caspi123@aol.com. *A composer has the duty to communicate with his audience. The academic-intellectual composer of the 50's has become obsolete. Writing just for one's colleagues has fortunately been proven a dead-end.*

SERENBETZ, ROBERT, financial planner, retired manufacturing executive; b. Rockville Centre, N.Y., Apr. 18, 1944; s. Raymond Robert Serenbetz and Mildred (Egner) Clapp; m. Karen Jeanne Jackson, Dec. 30, 1967; children: Todd, Gregg, Kathryn. AB, Dartmouth Coll., 1966; MBA, Harvard U., 1968. Cert. fin. planner. Mktg. staff asst. to group product mgr. Colgate-Palmolive Co., N.Y.C., 1968-75; dir. mktg. Colgate-Palmolive Colombia, Cali, Colombia, 1975-77; v.p. mktg. Colgate-Palmolive Canada, Toronto, Ont., Can., 1977-81; v.p. mktg. western hemisphere Warner-Lambert Co., Morris Plains, N.J., 1981; pres. Warner-Lambert Can., Toronto, 1981-85; pres. Latin Am., Asia, Australia Warner-Lambert Co., Morris Plains, 1986-89; pres. Am. Chicle, Morris Plains, 1989-91; pres., COO DNA Plant Tech. Corp., Cinnaminson, N.J., 1991-92, pres., CEO Oakland, Calif., 1992-94, chmn., CEO, 1994-96; COO DNAP Holding Corp., Oakland, Calif., 1996-98; pvt. practice CFP, 2003—. Mem. adv. bd. Coun. Ams., N.Y.C., 1987-89; mem. steering com. Pharm. Mfrs. Assn., Washington, 1987-89; bd. dirs. Caribbean/Cen. Am. Com., Washington, 1989; mem. adv. bd. Coun. for Internat. Unity, N.Y.C., 1987-89. Bd. dirs. Notch Brook Resort Gen. Ptnrs. Condominium Assn., Stowe, Vt., 1988-94; pres. bd. dirs. Seaside Homeowners Assn., Isle of Palms, S.C., 1997—; mem. U.S. Postal Svc. Mktg. Adv. Bd., 1990-2004, vice chmn., 1998-2004. Mem. Nat. Candy Wholesalers Assn. (bd. dirs. 1989-91), Morris County C. of C. (bd. dirs. 1989-91), Leadership Inc. (bd. dirs. Phila. br. 1993-94), Fin. Planning Assn., Wild Dunes Club (Isle of Palms, S.C.), Lookaway Golf Club (Buckingham, Pa.), Trillium Links and Lake Club (Cashiers, N.C.). Republican. Episcopalian. Avocations: golf, stamp collecting/philately, photography, tennis. E-mail: bobserenbetz@prodigy.net.

SERENE, HARRY E. surgeon; b. Pitts., June 4, 1943; s. Michael Francis and Clara Louise (Huff) S.; m. Linda Jean Hootman, Feb. 28, 1970; children: Amy, Scott. BA, California U. Pa, 1965; MD, Creighton U., 1969. Diplomate Am. Bd. Surgery. Intern Harrisburg (Pa.) Hosp., 1969-70; resident Western Pa. Hosp., Pitts., 1970-74; pvt. practice Pitts. Mem. staff St. Clair Meml. Hosp., Pitts. Mem. ACS, AMA, Pa. Med. Soc., Masons. Republican. Presbyterian. Office: Serene Surgery Assocs Ltd 1050 Bower Hill Rd Ste 205 Pittsburgh PA 15243-1868

SERENO, KEALA, musician; b. Honolulu, Jan. 8, 1959; s. Kenneth Sereno and Vera Egge; m. Yolanda Morrobel de los Santos, June 6, 1987; children: Natalie Noelani, Joel Kawika, Joshua Liko. MusB in Composition, U. of So. Calif., L.A., 1982. Piano player Saskatchewan Six, Fountain Valley, Calif., 1975—77; tuba player L.A. Lakers Pep Band, 1980—81; vol. stage mgr. Arnold Shoenberg Inst., L.A., 1980—82; vocal accompanist Vocal Studio of Betty Zukov, Fountain Valley, Calif., 1977; singer/keyboard player in a musical duo Seafood Galley, Redondo Beach, Calif., 1981; musician (tuba) with the Blazin' Brass Band Disneyland, Anaheim, Calif., 1981—82; musician (tuba); arranger; choreographer Future World Band Walt Disney World, 1982—93; rehearsal pianist So. Ballet Theatre, Orlando, Fla., 1995; musician (tuba and keyboard) with the Main St. Philharm. and the Tomorrowland Countdown bands Walt Disney World, Lake Buena Vista, Fla., 2000—. Co-worship leader (pianist/singer/arranger/composer/translator) Ch. for the Nations/Iglesia Para Las Naciones, Kissimmee, Fla., 2003—; music arranger, piano tchr., trumpet coach Iglesia Casa de Alabanza, Kissimmee, 1997—98; musician for jail ministry 33rd St. Prison, Orlando, Fla., 2000—00; studio musician (keyboard) Kids Colors Ministry (Christian radio ministry), Orlando, 2000—00; keyboard player First Bapt. Ch., St. Cloud, 1997; wedding pianist and singer, Orlando, 1982—2003; worship singer Iglesia Discipulos De Cristo, Kissimmee, 1998—2001; co-dir. of coro mayor (spanish ch. choir) Iglesia Discipulos de Cristo, Kissimmee, 1997—2001, ch. pianist, 1995—2001; choir dir. for Las Voces de Betania (spanish ch. choir) Iglesia Betania, Orlando, Fla., 1988—92, ch. pianist, 1988—94; interim worship dir. (pianist/singer) Alliance Ch., Kissimmee, 1998—99; ch. pianist Internat. Filipino Christian Ch., Kissimmee, 1994; musical arranger Northland Cmty. Ch. - Spanish Ministries, Longwood, Fla., 1999. Vocalist Nace Una Estrella (Top-Ten Finalist christian vocal competition, 2003); author: (self-study book with audio cd's) Listening by the Numbers (work in progress); arranger (music) Thriller Medley; composer: (art song) Un Barco Triste (Aired on Spanish radio sta. Easter Sunday, 1991); translator (with Alvin Robles): (cantata) Call His Name Jesus; translator: (arranger for Las Voces de Betania) arranged over 60 two-part songs for choir; arranger/transcriber over 70 coritos for Northland Cmty. Ch. Spanish Ministries, 1999; arranger Grand opening of Captain EO exhibit in Epcot. Recipient Meritorious Performance award for Mendelssohn's Concerto in G minor, 7th Ann. Young Artist Concerto Competition, Orange County Calif., 1977, Bank of Am. Achievement award in music, Bank of Am., 1977; scholar First Ann. David Buffington Meml. scholar for music, Fountain Valley H.S., 1977; Band grantee, U. of So. Calif. Trojan Marching Band, 1980. Mem.: Nat. Music Tchrs. Assn., Musicians Assn. of Ctrl. Fla., US Chess Fedn. Evangelical Christian. Avocation: chess. Home: 2409 Franklin Dr Kissimmee FL 34744 Office: Walt Disney World Co Lake Buena Vista FL Office Phone: 407-934-2678. Personal E-mail: keala1959@juno.com.

SERETEAN, MARTIN B. (BUD SERETEAN), carpet manufacturing company executive; b. N.Y.C., 1924; married. BS, Okla. A&M Coll., 1949; MS, NYU, 1950. With Abraham & Straus Inc., 1950-51, Allied Stores Corp., 1951-53; sales mgr. Katherine Rug Mills, Inc., 1953-56; with Coronet Industries, Inc., Dalton, Ga., 1956—, pres., chief exec. officer, 1962-72, chmn. bd., chief exec. officer, 1972-80, chmn. bd., from 1980, also bd. dirs.; bd. dirs. Atlanta Hawks, 1975—. Office: Atlanta Hawks One CNN Ctr South Tower Ste 405 Atlanta GA 30303

SEREYAN, ANDY, publishing executive; m. Nancy Marshall; children: Alex, Eliza. B in Econs. summa cum liade, Middlebury Coll.; MBA, Stanford U. Various consumer mktg. positions Time, Inc., 1987—91; consumer mktg. dir. Entertainment Weekly, 1991—93, v.p. comsumer mktg. & devel., 1993—97; v.p., assoc. pub. InStyle Mag., 1997—99; founding pub. Real Simple, 2000; with The Parenting Group, 2001; pres. Entertainment Weekly, 2002—. Office: Entertainment Weekly 111 8th Ave New York NY 10011

SERGEL, ALFRED E., III, (AL SERGEL), music educator; b. Bronx, N.Y., May 14, 1946; s. Alfred E. Sergel, Jr. and Gertrude Lina (Koenig) Sergel; m. Deanna Carol Greear; children: Alfred E. IV, Audra DeAnn. BMusEd, Fla. State U., 1969; MMusEd, U. Fla., Gainesville, 1974; EdS in Music Adminstrn., N.W. Mo. State, Maryville, 1989; post grad. in higher edn. adminstrn., U. Mo., Kan. City, 1988—93. Asst. band dir. Thomasville Pub. Sch., Ga., 1969; dir. of bands Auburndale Pub. Sch., Fla., 1969—73; grad. asst. dir. of bands U. Fla., Gainesville, 1973—74; dir. of bands and fine arts White Settlement Ind. Sch. Dist., Tex., 1974—81; dir. of bands N.W. Mo. State, Maryville, Mo., 1981—, dir. of freshman seminar, 1999—. Dir. N.W. Mo. State Summer Music Camps, Maryville, Mo., 1981—; creator and organizer N.W. Mo. State Four State Honor Music Festival, Maryville, 1983—; sponsor Kappa Delta chpt. Kappa Kappa Psi, Maryville, 1995—; pres. faculty senate N.W. Mo. State, Maryville, 1999—2000; mem. organizing com. Mo. Fine Arts Acad., 1995—96; mem. nominating com. John Phillip Sousa Legion of Honor, Terra Haute, Ind., 1998—. Author: Warming Up Your Concert Band, 2004; composer: (percussion solos) Emma's Snare Drum Sundae, 2001, Abbie's Waltz, 2001, Audra's Rudimental Ragtime, 2001, Alfred's Challenge, 2002, Kevin's March, 2002. Named to Fla. State U. Band Alumni Wall of Fame,

2002; recipient Phi Mu Alpha Orpheus award. Mem.: Mo. Music Educators Assn. (dist. pres. 1984—90, v.p. coll. affairs 1989—91), Coll. Band Dir. Nat. Assn. (Mo. state chair 1988—96), Phi Mu Alpha, Kappa Kappa Psi (midwest dist. gov. 1995—99, nat. coun. v.p. profl. rels. 1997—2001, nat. bd. trustees 2003—, midwest dist. gov. 2001—03, Outstanding Chpt. Sponsor 1997, Disting. Svc. to Music medal 2003). Avocations: fishing, travel. Home: 1207 Parkdale Rd Maryville MO 64468 Office: NW Mo State Univ 800 Univ Dr Maryville MO 64468

SERGENT, JOHN S. hospital administrator, medical educator; m. Carole Sergent; children: Ellen, Katie. MD, Vanderbilt U., 1966. Pvt. practice; chair dept. medicine St. Thomas Hosp., Nashville, 1988—95; mem. faculty Vanderbilt U., Nashville, 1975—88, prof. medicine, 1988—; chief med. officer Vanderbilt U. Hosp. and Clinic, Nashville, 1995—2003; vice chmn. for edn. Vanderbilt U. Sch. of Medicine, Nashville, 2003—, prog. dir. resident tng., dept. medicine, 2003—. Mem.: Am. Coll. Rheumatology (pres. 1992—). Office: Vanderbilt U 111 21st Ave S D-3300 MCN Nashville TN 37232-2104*

SERGEY, JOHN MICHAEL, JR., investment company executive; b. Chgo., Nov. 17, 1942; s. John Michael and Helen Ann (Bruchan) S.; m. Sharon Lee Ourada (div. 1982); children: John Michael III, Elisabeth Ann, Mark William, Tanya Ruth; m. Pamela Lynne Murphy, Aug. 8, 1987; children: Brian M., Sarah L. BA in Bus., Northwestern U., 1968; MBA, U. Chgo., 1976. Mgr. rolled products A. M. Castle, Chgo.; v.p. Dietzgen Corp., Chgo.; dir. sales and mktg. Avery Label, Azusa, Calif., 1978-80; v.p., gen. mgr. Fasson Roll div. Avery, Painesville, Ohio, 1980-84; group v.p. Soabar Products Group div. Avery, Phila., 1984-87, Materials Group div. Avery, Painesville, 1987 89; pres., CEO GAF Materials Corp., Wayne, N.J., 1989 96; CEO Strategic Distbn., Inc., Bensalem, Pa., 1997—2001; chmn. Jay 3 Corp., 2002—. Office: Jay 3 Corp 517 Falcon Point Dr New Hope PA 18938

SERGI, ARTURO, tenor, music educator, academic administrator; b. N.Y.C., Nov. 8, 1925; s. Maxwell and Sophie Kagan; m. Leonore Glickman, Apr. 29, 1959; children: Arturo, David. Student, Manhattan Sch. of Music, 1947—48, Conservatorio Giuseppe Verdi, Milan, Italy, 1948—51, Conservatorio Santa Cecelia, Rome, 1951—54; pvt. study, Maestro Sergi Nazor, Italy and Germany, 1954—69. Leading tenor Städtische Bühnen, Wuppertal, Germany, 1954—57, Frankfurt, Germany, 1957—60, Staatsoper, Hamburg, Germany, 1958—62, Met. Opera Assn., N.Y.C., 1962—67, 1979—84; assoc. prof. voice U. Tex., Austin, Tex., 1971—77; cantor Congregation Beth Israel, Houston, 1972—85; leading tenor, concert artist various opera cos. and symphony orchs., 1980—90; founding pres. East-West Internat. Music Acad., Altenburg, Germany, 1990—. With U.S. Army, 1946—47, U.S. and Japan. Recipient Kulturpreis der Stadt Altenburg, City of Altenburg, Germany, 1998, Fed. Republic of Germany Friendship award, German Amb. to U.S., 2003; grantee, U.S. State Dept., 1992—2002. Mem.: Coll. Music Soc. (life), Rotary (hon.). Democrat. Jewish. Avocations: swimming, exercise. Home: 600 Leah Ave Apt 1404 San Marcos TX 98666 Office: Ost-West Internationale Musik-Akademie Rudolf-Harbig-Str 30A 42377 Radevormwald Germany Office Phone: 49-2195-689102. Office Fax: 49-2195-689102. Personal E-mail: sergiassociates@centurytel.net. E-mail: owima10@aol.com.

SERIG, DANIEL, art educator, researcher; b. Santa Clara, Calif., Nov. 1, 1969; s. Joe Allen and Beverly Joan Serig; m. Angela Suarez, July 30, 1994; 1 child, Sofia Isabelle. BFA, Wash. U., St. Louis, 1992. Art educator Concordia Internat. Sch., Shanghai, 1998—2001; rsch. assoc. The Ctr. for Arts Edn. Rsch., N.Y.C., 2002—. Profl. devel. coord. Mo. Dept. of Elem. and Secondary Edn., St. Louis, 1997—98. Recipient scholarship for doctoral studies, Art and Art Edn. Dept. - Teachers Coll., Columbia U., 2002 - Present. Mem.: Nat. Art Edn. Assn. Democrat-Npl. Roman Catholic. Achievements include reseach to assist in evaluating and assessing arts education programming. Avocation: travel.

SERIO, JOHN N. language educator; b. Buffalo, Oct. 8, 1943; s. Nicola and Amelia (Zona) S.; m. Faye Ann Walters, Aug. 19, 1972; children: Alisa, Alexis, Andrew. BS, SUNY, Buffalo, 1965; MA, Northwestern U., 1966; PhD, U. Notre Dame, 1974. Instr. English Valparaiso (Ind.) U., 1966-70; tchg. asst. U. Notre Dame, Ind., 1971-73; asst. prof., assoc. prof. Clarkson U., Potsdam, N.Y., 1974-89, prof., 1989—. Pres. Wallace Stevens Soc., Potsdam, 1983—, jour. editor, 1983—; sec.-treas. Coun. Editors of Learned Jours., Gainesville, Fla., 1990-95. Author: Annotated Bib of W. Stevens, 1994, Teaching W. Stevens, 1994; contbr. articles to profl. jours. Recipient Fulbright award to Greece Coun. Internat. Exch. Scholars, 1993, Belgium, 1998; grantee NEH, 1976, 84, 91, Phoenix award for significant editl. achievement, Coun. Editors Learned Jours., 1990, Outstanding Tech. Article award Tech. Comm., 1989. Office: Clarkson Univ 8 Clarkson Ave Potsdam NY 13676-1403 E-mail: serio@clarkson.edu.

SERKES, JEFFREY D. energy executive; BBA in Acctg., George Washington U.; MBA in Fin., Rutgers U. With RJR Nabisco; from v.p. fin, sales and distbn. to v.p., treas. IBM, 1995—2002; pres. JDS Opportunities, LLC, 2002—03; sr. v.p., CFO Allegheny Energy, Hagerstown, Md., 2003—. Bd. adv. Rutgers U.; dir., chmn., audit com., compensation com. REFAC. Office: Allegheny Energy 10435 Downsville Pike Hagerstown MD 21740-1766

SERLE, JANET BARBRA, ophthalmologist, educator; b. N.Y.C., Jan. 30, 1956; d. Seymour and Anita Serle; m. Ira Malin; children: Allison, Beth. MD, Harvard U., 1980. Diplomate Am. Bd. Ophthalmology, Nat. Bd. Med. Examiners. Asst. prof. Mt. Sinai Hosp., N.Y.C., 1986—91, assoc. prof., 1991—, asst. attending ophthalmology, 1986—91, assoc. attending ophthalmology, 1991—. Residency program dir. dept. ophthalmology Mt. Sinai Sch. Medicine, N.Y.C., 1986—98, glaucoma fellowship dir. dept. ophthalmology, 1999—; clin. asst. Elmhurst Gen. Hosp., Queens, NY, 1986—87, clin. assoc., 1991—93, asst. attending, 2000—; part-time staff physician Bronx (N.Y.) Vets. Adminstrn. Hosp., 1987—91; dir. glaucoma svcs. St. Joseph's Hosp., Flushing, NY, 2002—; assoc. examiner Am. Bd. Ophthalmology, Boston, 1993, Boston, 97; mem. adv. com. FDA, 1995—98; mem. adv. coun. Faculty Practice Assocs., 2002—. Mem. editl. bd.: Jour. Glaucoma, 1995—, Glaucoma editor: Focal Points, 1996—99, asst. editor: Mt. Sinai Jour. Medicine, 2000—; contbr. articles to profl. jours. Recipient William Warner Hoppin award, N.Y. Acad. Medicine, 1984; grantee, Allergan Pharm. Co., 1999—; Regents scholar, 1972—76, Assn. Rsch. Vision Ophthalmology Travel fellow, Nat. Eye Inst., 1983. Fellow: Am. Acad. Ophthalmology (Honor award 1995), Soc. HEED Fellows; mem.: N.Y. State Ophthalmol. Soc., N.Y. Soc. for Clin. Ophthalmology (pres. 1998—99, mem. exec. com. 1993—98), Manhattan Ophthalmol. Soc., N.Y. Glaucoma Soc. (program chmn. 1991—), Rsch. to Prevent Blindness, N.Y. County Med. Soc., Am. Glaucoma Soc. (exec. com. member-at-large 1995—98), Mt. Sinai Med. Ctr. Alumni Assn., Harvard Med. Alumni Assn., Assn. for Rsch. in Vision and Ophthalmology. Achievements include patents for method for reducing intraocular pressure and treating glaucoma. Home: 49 Shelter Ln Roslyn Heights NY 11577 Office: Mt Sinai Hosp One Gustave L Levy Pl New York NY 10029 Office Phone: 212-241-0939.

SERLETIC, MATTHEW, recording industry executive; s. Matt and Deanie Serletic; m. Ramona Bajnauth, Mar. 1999; 2 children. B in Music Performance, U. Miami, 1992, M in Music Performance, 1994. Founder, prodr. Melisma Records, 1998—2002; chmn., CEO Virgin Records Am., 2002—. Prodr.: Matchbox Twenty, Santana, Aerosmith, Collective Soul, Angie Aparo, Edwin McCain, Celine Dion. Named to, Crain's N.Y. Bus. "40 under 40", 2004; recipient Grammy award Prodr. for Album of Yr., 2000, Grammy award Prodr. Record of Yr., 2000. Office: Virgin Records 338 N Foothill Rd Beverly Hills CA 90210*

SERNA, PATRICIO, state supreme court justice; b. Reserve, N.Mex., Aug. 26, 1939; m. Eloise Serna; children: Elena Patricia, Anna Alicia 1 stepchild, John Herrera. BSBA with honors, U. Albuquerque, 1962; JD, U. Denver, 1970; LLM, Harvard U., 1971; postgrad., Nat. Jud. Coll., 1985, postgrad., 1990, postgrad., 1992, postgrad., 1994; LLD (hon.), U. Denver, 2002. Bar: N.Mex. 1970, Colo. 1971, U.S. Dist. Ct. N.Mex. 1970. Probation and parole officer State of N.Mex., Santa Fe, Las Cruces, 1966—67; spl. asst. to commn. mem. Equal Opportunity Commn., Washington, 1971—75; asst. atty. gen. State of N.Mex., Santa Fe, 1975—79; pvt. practice Santa Fe, 1979—85; dist. judge First Jud. Dist., Santa Fe, 1985—96; supreme ct. justice N.Mex. Supreme Ct., Santa Fe, 1996—2001, chief justice, 2001—02. Adj. prof. law Georgetown U., Washington, 1973, Cath. U., Washington, 1974—75; faculty advisor Nat. Jud. Coll., Reno, 1987. Bd. dirs. Santa Fe Group Homes Inc. With U.S. Army, 1963—65. Mem.: Santa Fe Bar Assn., No. N.Mex. Am. Inns of Ct., Nat. Hispanic Bar Assn. (HNBA Judge of Yr. award 2002, Judge of Yr. 2002), N.Mex. Hispanic Bar Assn., N.Mex. Bar Assn., Elks, Phi Alpha Delta. Avocations: hiking, fishing, Ping Pong, chess, painting. Office: NMex Supreme Ct PO Box 848 Santa Fe NM 87504-0848

SERNETT, RICHARD PATRICK, lawyer; b. Mason City, Iowa, Sept. 8, 1938; s. Edward Frank and Loretta M. (Cavanaugh) S.; m. Janet Ellen Ward, Apr. 20, 1963; children: Susan Ellen, Thomas Ward, Stephen Edward, Katherine Anne. BBA, U. Iowa, 1960, JD, 1963. Bar: Iowa 1963, Ill. 1965, U.S. Dist. Ct. (no. dist.) Ill. 1965, U.S. Supreme Ct. 1971. House counsel, asst. sec. Scott, Foresman & Co., Glenview, Ill., 1963-70, sec., legal officer, 1970-80; v.p., law sec. SFN Cos., Inc., Glenview, 1980-83, sr. v.p., sec., gen. counsel, 1983-85, exec. v.p., gen. counsel, 1985-87; pvt. practice Northbrook, Ill., 1988-90; v.p., sec., gen. counsel Macmillan/McGraw-Hill Sch. Pub. Co., 1990-92; v.p. Bert Early Assoc., Chgo., 1992-93; ptnr. Sernett & Blake, Northfield, Ill., 1993-95; ret., 1995. Mem. U.S. Dept. State Adv. Panel on Internat. Copyright, 1972-75. Chmn. bd. dirs. Iowa State U., Broadcasting Co., 1987-94. Mem. ABA (chmn. copyright divsn. 1972-73, com. on copyright legis. 1967-70, com. on copyright office affairs 1966 67, 79 81, com. on program for revision copyright law 1971 72), Am. Intellectual Property Law Assn., Am. Soc. Corp. Secs., Ill. Bar Assn. (chmn. copyright com. 1971-72), Chgo. Bar Assn., Patent Law Assn. Chgo. (bd. mgrs. 1979-82, chmn. copyright law com. 1972-73, 77-78), Copyright Soc. U.S.A. (trustee 1972-75, 77-80), Wyndemere Country Club (Naples, Fla.). Home: 2579 Fairford Ln Northbrook IL 60062-8101

SEROKA, JAMES HENRY, social sciences educator, university administrator; b. Detroit, Mar. 5, 1950; s. Henry S. and Mary (Wyoral) S.; m. Carolyn Marie White, June 27, 1970; children: Mihail, Maritsa. BA, U. Mich., 1970; MA, Mich. State U., 1972, PhD, 1976. Labor mkt. analyst U.S. Dept. of Labor, Washington, 1970-71; asst. prof. U. N.C., Greensboro, 1976-77, Appalachian State U., Boone, N.C., 1977-79, So. Ill. U., Carbondale, 1979-81, assoc. prof., 1981-87, prof., dir., 1987-88; prof., head div. humanities and social scis. Pa. State U., Erie, 1988-90; prof. U. North Fla., Jacksonville, 1990-98; dir. Ctr. for Pub. Leadership, Jacksonville, 1991-98; vis. prof. internat. security studies U.S. Air War Coll., Maxwell AFB, Ala., 1997-98; prof. Auburn (Ala.) U., 1998—; dir. Ctr. for Govtl. Svcs., Auburn. Dir. Master of Pub. Affairs Program Soc. Ill. U., 1987-88, Rural and Small Town Adminstrn. Project, 1980-85; asst. dir. Appalachian Regional Bur. Govts., Boone, N.C., 1977-79; manpower planning analyst U.S. Dept. Labor, Washington, 1970-71; exchange prof. Fakultet Politickih Nauka, Univerzitet u Beogradu, Yugoslavia, 1986; vis. prof. Air War Coll., Montgomery, Ala.; sr. researcher Coun. for the Internat. Exchange Scholars Yugoslavia, 1980; mem. state adv. com. Gov.'s Rural Affairs Coun. for State of Ill., 1988; dir. Ctr. Govt. Svcs., Auburn, 1998—. Co-author: Political Organizations in Social Yugoslavia, 1986 (Choice award 1987); editor Rural Public Adminstration, 1986; co-editor: Developed Socialism, 1982, Comparative Political Systems, 1990, Yugoslavia: The Failure of Democratic Transformation, 1992; contbr. numerous articles to profl. jours. Recipient Akademischer Austausch Dienst Lang. scholar Fed. Republic of Germany, 1988 and numerous other grants, traveling fellows. Mem. Am. Soc. Pub. Adminstrn. (so Ill. chpt. 1982-83), Nat. Civic League, Am. Polit. Sci. Assn., Internat. Polit. Sci. Assn., Midwest Polit. Sci. Assn., So. Polit. Sci. Assn., Southwestern Polit. Sci. Assn., Western Polit. Sci. Assn., Policy Studies Orgn., Acad. Polit. Sci., Rural Sociol. Assn., Internat. Studies Assn., Am. Assn. Advancement of Slavic Studies, Western Social Sci. Assn., Cmty. Devel. Soc., Rotary Internat. (Paul Harris fellow). Office: Auburn U Ctr Govtl Svcs 2236 Hayden Ctr Auburn AL 36849

SEROTA, JAMES IAN, lawyer; b. Chgo., Oct. 20, 1946; s. Louis Henry and Phyllis Estelle (Horner) S.; m. Susan Perlstadt, May 7, 1972; children: Daniel Louis, Jonathan Mark. AB, Washington U., St. Louis, 1968; JD cum laude, Northwestern U., 1971. Bar: Ill. 1971, US Dist. Ct. (no. dist.) Ill. 1972, DC 1978, US Supreme Ct. 1978, US Ct. Appeals (DC cir.) 1978, U.S. Dist. Ct. (DC dist.), US Ct. Claims 1980, NY 1981, US Dist. Ct. (so. and ea. dists.) NY, 1981, US Dist. Ct. (no dist.) NY, 2003, US Ct. Appeals (2d cir.) 1983. Trial atty. Antitrust div. US Dept. Justice, Washington, 1971—77; assoc. Bell, Boyd & Lloyd, Washington, 1977—81; ptnr. Werner, Kennedy & French, NYC, 1982—85, Levitsky & Serota, 1985-86, Huber, Lawrence & Abell, NYC, 1987—98, Vinson & Elkins, NYC, 1998—2002; shareholder Greenberg Traurig, NYC, 2003—. Contbr. articles to profl. jours.; editor Law Rev., Law bd., Northwestern U.; ed bd., antitrust columnist CCH Power and Telecom Law jour. Recipient Spl. Achievement award U.S. Dept. Justice, 1976. Mem. ABA (chmn. ins. industry com. 1987-90, vice chair program com. 1990-91, chair annual mtg. program 1991-94, chair fuel & energy com. 1994-97, coun. 1997-2000), N.Y. State Bar Assn., Assn. of Bar of City of N.Y. (antitrust and trade regulation com. 1988-91), Fed. Bar Council. Office: Greenberg Traurig LLP 885 Third Ave New York NY 10022-4834 Office Phone: 212-801-2277. Business E-Mail: serotaj@gtlaw.com.

SEROTA, SCOTT, medical association administrator; BA, Purdue U.; MA in Health Admin. and Planning, Wash. U. Sch. of Med., St. Louis. Creator, leader Physicians Preferred Health Inc., Mo.; v.p. health care mgmt. PruCare, St. Louis, 1980; v.p. group ops., v.p. health care mgmt. Prudential Ins. Co., Chgo.; pres., CEO Rush Prudential Health Plans, Chgo., 1993—96; exec. v.p. system devel. Blue Cross and Blue Shield Assn., COO, 1994—96, exec. v.p. sys. devel., 1996—2000, pres., CEO, 2000—. Founding mem. Inst. on Healthcare Costs and Solutions Wash. Bus. Group on Health; bd. mem. Council for Affordable Quality Healthcare, Nat. Ctr. for Healthcare Leadership, Partnership for Prevention, Nat. Alliance for Health Info. Tech., Accrediting Commn. on Edn. for Health Services Admin.; mem. Am. Coll. of Healthcare Executives. Office: Blue Cross Blue Shield Assn 225 N Michigan Ave Chicago IL 60601

SERPICK, ARTHUR ALLEN, health facility administrator, physician; b. Balt., Md., Feb. 21, 1935; s. Jacob and Dorothy (Tapper) S.; married, Sept. 13, 1979. BS, Univ. Md., 1957, MD, 1959. Staff assoc. Nat. Cancer Inst., Bethesda, Md., 1963-65; head med. svc. Balt. Cancer Soc., Balt., 1965-70; head oncology Md. Gen. Hosp., Balt., 1970-87; head dept. medicine St. Joseph Med. Ctr., Towson, Md., 1983—2002, v.p. med. affairs, 2002—. Medicare Carrier adv. com. for Md. Active Am. Cancer Soc., 1968-76. Fellow Am. Coll. Physicians, Internal Soc. Hemtology; mem. Am. Coll. Physicians Execs., Am. Soc. Clinical Oncology, Am. Soc. Hematology. Office: St Joseph Med Ctr 7601 Osler Dr Towson MD 21204-7508 E-mail: arthurserpick@chi-east.org.

SERRA, JOE, investment company executive; Pres. Team Mgmt., Dearborn, Mich.; pres., CEO Al Serra Chevrolet, Grand Blanc; pres., COO Saturn Enterprises, Inc., Charlotte, N.C., 1998-99; CEO, chmn. Serra Investments, Grand Blanc, Mich., 1999—. Office: Serra Investments 3118 E Hill Rd Grand Blanc MI 48439-8106

SERRA, MATTHEW D. consumer products company executive; b. 1945; With R.H. Macy & Co., 1962—69, Bloomingdale's, 1969—76; divisional merchandising mgr. men's wear Lord & Taylor, 1976; v.p. & divisional merchandise mgr. Saks Fifth Ave, NYC, 1976—78, assoc. gen. merchandise mgr. men's and boys' wear, 1978—79, sr. v.p. & gen. merchandise mgr. men's and boys' wear, 1979—83; pres. Gimbels NY divsn., 1983, Gimbels East, 1983—86, CEO, 1985—86; pres. Sibleys, Rochester, NY, 1986—90, CEO, 1987—90; pres. CEO Seaman's Furniture Co., NY, 1991—92; chmn., CEO Sterns divsn. of Federated Dept. Stores Inc., 1993-98; pres., CEO Foot Locker Worldwide, 1998—2000; COO Foot Locker Inc. (formerly Venator Group Inc.), 2000—01, pres., 2000—, CEO, 2001—, chmn., 2004—. Office: Foot Locker Inc 112 W 34th St New York NY 10120*

SERRA, MATTHEW D. retail executive; With Macy's NY, 1966, Bloomingdale's, Saks Fifth Ave.; pres. Gimbels, 1983—86, COO, 1984—86, CEO, 1984—86; pres., CEO Sibleys, 1986—90, G. Fox, 1986—90, Seamans, 1991—92; chmn., CEO Sterns, 1993—98; pres., CEO worldwide divsn. Foot Locker, Inc., 1998—2000, COO, 2000—01, pres., 2000—, CEO, pres., 2001—. Office: 112 W 34th St New York NY 10120

SERRA, PATRICIA JANET, social services administrator; b. St. Louis, Mo., Aug. 9, 1933; d. Lewis John and Constance Loyola (Egan) Protheroe; m. Mauricio Tadeo, Sept. 3, 1960; children: Mauricio Antonio, Patricia Suzanne, Mark Lewis. BS, St. Louis U., 1955; MSW, San Jose (Calif.) State U., 1974. Social worker Associated Catholic Charities, New Orleans, 1956-61; med. social worker Charity Hosp., New Orleans, 1961-63; counselor City of New Orleans, 1963-64; child welfare worker City of San Francisco, 1964-66; social worker Cath. Social Svc., San Francisco, 1970-74; counselor Golden Gate Regional Ctr., 1974-76; case mgr. San Andreas Regional Ctr., San Jose, 1976-84; program mgr. United Cerebral Palsy Assn. Santa Clara, Mountain View, Calif., 1984—. Faculty field instr., San Jose State U., San Jose, 1985—. Recipient awards of recognition United Cerebral Palsy Assn. Santa Clara, San Mateo Counties, 1989, Bd. Suprs. County San Mateo, Calif., 1989, Spl. Tech. Ctr., Mountain View, Calif., 1991. Mem. Nat. Assn. Social Workers, Acad. Cert. Social Workers; lic. clin. Soc. Worker (LCSW). Republican. Roman Catholic. Avocations: travel, skiing, theater, reading. Home: 4556 Bald Eagle Way San Jose CA 95118-2019 Office: 480 San Antonio Rd Ste 215 Mountain View CA 94040-1218 E-mail: patlito@ix.netcom.com., pat@ucpscsm.org.

SERRAGLIO, MARIO, architect; b. Bassano, Veneto, Italy, Apr. 13, 1965; arrived in U.S., 1972; s. Luciano G. and Maria P. (Bellon) Serraglio. BS in Architecture, Ohio State U., 1988. Real estate agent Four Star Realty, Columbus, Ohio, 1984—; treas. Columbus Masonry, Inc., 1985-86; v.p. Serraglio Masonry, Inc., Columbus, 1986-87; pres. Serraglio Constrn., Columbus, 1987—; residential designer Gary A. Bruck, SGR, Inc., Columbus, 1988-89, Sullivan Gray Ptnrs., Columbus, 1989-92; project mgr. John Regan Archs., Columbus, 1992-93; prin. Architettura Serraglio, Inc., Reynoldsburg, Ohio, 1995—. Mem.: AIA, Nat. Assn. Realtors. Office: Architettura Serraglio 7404 E Main St 2d Fl Reynoldsburg OH 43068-2166 Fax: (614) 759-6986. E-mail: mario@iwaynet.net.

SERRANO, JORGE LUIS, education educator, writer; b. Bronx, N.Y. s. Valentin and Carmen Iris Serrano. BA, Columbia U., 1990; MA, Yale U., 1994. Tchr. educator Nat. Puerto Rican Forum, Inc., N.Y.C.; adj. prof. Coll. New Rochelle; Latin tchr. Frederick Douglass Acad., Philippa Schuyler Sch. Cpl. USMC. Fellow: Am. Classical League.

SERRANO, JOSE E. congressman; b. Mayaguez, P.R., Oct. 24, 1943; s. Jose E. and Hipolita (Soto) S.; m. Mary Serrano; children: Lisa Marie, Jose Marco, Justine, Jonathan, Benjamin. With Mfrs. Hanover Trust Co., 1961-69; mem. Bd. Edn. N.Y., 1969-74; former N.Y. State Assemblyman Albany, from 1975; mem. 102nd-108th Congress from 18th (now 16th) N. Y. dist.N.Y., Washington, 1991—; chmn. Congl. Hispanic Caucus, 1993-94; mem. 107th Congress appropriations com., 1996—. Ranking Dem. transp. com. Ranking mem. subcom., legis. br., mem. 4 subcom. agrl. Rural Devel., Food & Drug Adminstrn. and related agys. Democrat. Roman Catholic. Office: 2227 Rayburn Hob Washington DC 20515-0001 also: 890 Grand Concourse Bronx NY 10451-2828

SERRE, JEAN-PIERRE, mathematician, scholar; b. Bages, France, Sept. 15, 1926; s. Jean and Adèle (Diet) S.; m. Josiane Heulot, Aug. 10, 1948; 1 child, Claudine. Baccalauréat, Lycée de Nîmes, France, 1944; agrégation, Ecole Normale Supérieure, France, 1948; Phd, U. Paris, 1951; PhD (hon.), Cambridge (Eng.) U., 1978, U. Stockholm, 1980, U. Glasgow, Scotland, 1983, U. Athens, 1996, Harvard U., 1998, Durham U., 2000, London U., 2001, U. Oslo, 2002, U. Oxford, 2003, Acad. Bucharest, 2004. Prof. Coll. de France, Paris, 1956—, prof. emeritus. Author: Groupes algébriques et corps de classes, 1959, Corps Locaux, 1962, Lie Algebras and Lie Groups, 1965, Représentations linéaires des groupes finis, 1968, Cours d'arithmétique, 1970, Trees, 1980, Local Algebra, 2000, Collected Papers, 1986, 2000. Recipient Fields Medal, 1954, Prix Balzan, 1985, Leroy P. Steele prize Am. Math. Soc., 1995, Wolf prize, Israel, 2000, Abel prize, 2003. Mem. Acad. Sci. Paris, Royal Soc. London (hon. fellow), London Math. Soc. (hon.), Nat. Acad. Sci. U.S. (fgn.), Nederland Acad. Sci. (fgn.), Acad. Sci. Stockholm (fgn.), Russian Acad. Sci. (fgn.). Home: 6 Ave de Montespan 75116 Paris France Office: Coll de France 75005 Paris France Business E-Mail: serre@dma.ens.fr.

SERRES, GREGORY A. prosecutor; BBA, Texas A&M U.; JD, Baylor U., 1986. Prosecutor Harris Co. Dist. Atty. Office, Tex., 1987—92; asst. US atty. US Dept. Justice, Southern Dist., Tex., 1992—95, chief, Special Prosecutions Div., 1995—98, first asst. US atty., 1998—, interim US atty., 2001. Grantee Nat. Merit Scholar, Lechner Fellowship. Office: US Attorney Southern Dist of Tex PO Box 61129 Houston TX 77208

SERRIE, HENDRICK, retired anthropology and international business educator; b. Jersey City, July 2, 1937; s. Hendrick and Elois (Edge) S.; m. Gretchen Tipler Ihde, Sept. 3, 1959; children: Karim Jonathan, Keir Ethan. BA with honors, U. Wis., 1960; MA, Cornell U., 1964; PhD with distinction, Northwestern U., 1976. Dir. Solar Energy Field Project, Oaxaca, Mex., 1961-62; instr. U. Aleppo, Syria, 1963-64; asst. prof. Beloit (Wis.) Coll., 1964-69, Calif. State U., Northridge, 1969-70, Purdue U., West Lafayette, Ind., 1970-72, New Coll./U. South Fla., Sarasota, 1972-77; tchr. Pine View Sch., Sarasota, 1978; prof. anthropology, internat. bus. Eckerd Coll., St. Petersburg, Fla., 1978—2002, dir. internat. bus. overseas programs, 1981—2002; ret., 2002. Sr. rsch. assoc., Human Resources Inst., St. Petersburg, 1988—. Author, editor: Family, Kinship, and Ethnic Identity Among the Overseas Chinese, 1985, Anthropology and International Business, 1986, What Can Multinationals Do for Peasants, 1994, The Overseas Chinese: Ethnicity in National Context, 1998; writer, dir. films: Technological Innovation, 1962, Something New Under the Sun, 1963; contbr. articles to Wall Street Jour. and Wall Street Jour. Europe. Tchr. Sunday sch., North United Methodist Ch., Sarasota, 1977—. Exxon scholar, So. Ctr. for Internat. Issues, Atlanta, 1980-81; Presdl. fellow Am. Grad. Sch. Internat. Mgmt., 1991; recipient Leavy award, Freedoms Found., Valley Forge, Pa., 1989. Fellow Am. Anthropol. Assn., Soc. Applied Anthropology; mem. So. Ctr. Internat. Issues, Acad. Internat. Bus., Tampa Bay Internat. Trade Coun., Internat. Soc. Intercultural Edn., Tng. and Rsch. Republican. Avocations: singing, drawing, beach walking, bicycling, sailing. Home: 636 Mecca Dr Sarasota FL 34234-2713 Office Phone: 941-355-2560. Business E-Mail: serrieh@eckerd.edu.

SERRIN, JAMES BURTON, mathematics professor; b. Chgo., Nov. 1, 1926; s. James B. and Helen Elizabeth (Wingate) S.; m. Barbara West, Sept. 6, 1952; children: Martha Helen Stack, Elizabeth Ruth, Janet Louise Sucha. Student, Northwestern U., 1944-46; BA, Western Mich. U., 1947; MA, Ind. U., PhD, 1951; DSc, U. Sussex, 1972; DSc in Engring., U. Ferrara, Italy, 1992; DSc in Math., U. Padova, Italy, 1992. With MIT, Cambridge, 1952-54; mem. faculty U. Minn., Mpls., 1955—, prof. math., 1959-95, Regents prof., 1968—, head Sch. Math., 1964-65; emeritus, 1995. Vis. prof. U. Chgo., 1964, 75, Johns Hopkins U., 1966, U. Sussex, 1967-68, 72, 76, U. Naples, 1979, U. Modena, 1988, Ga. Inst. Tech., 1990. Author: Mathematical Principles of Classical Fluid Mechanics, 1957. Mem. Met. Airport Sound Abatement Council, Mpls., 1969— . Recipient Disting. Alumni award Ind. U., 1979 Fellow AAAS; mem. NAS, Am. Math. Soc. (G.D. Birkhoff prize 1973), Math. Assn. Am., Soc. for Natural Philosophy (pres. 1969-70), Finnish Acad. Sci. and Letters. Home: 4422 Dupont Ave S Minneapolis MN 55409-1739 Office Phone: 612-624-9530.

SERRITELLA, JAMES ANTHONY, lawyer; b. Chgo., July 8, 1942; s. Anthony and Angela (Deleonardis) S.; m. Ruby Ann Amoroso, Oct. 3, 1981. LLD, North Park U., 1996; BA, SUNY-S.I., 1965, Pontifical Gregorian U., Rome, 1966; postgrad., DePaul U., 1966-67; MA, U. Chgo., 1968, JD, 1971. Bar: Ill. 1971, U.S. Dist. Ct. (no. and ea. dist.) Ill. 1971, U.S. Supreme Ct. 1976, U.S. Tax Ct. 1985, U.S. Ct. Appeals (fifth cir.) 1995, U.S. Ct. Appeals

(sixth cir.) 1992, U.S. Ct. Appeals (seventh cir.) 1993, U.S. Ct. Appeals (ninth cir.) 1996. Ptnr. Kirkland & Ellis, Chgo., 1978; ptnr. Reuben & Proctor, Chgo., 1978-86, Mayer, Brown & Platt, Chgo., 1986-97, Burke, Warren, MacKay & Serritella, PC, Chgo., 1997—. Lectr. in field. Contbr. articles to profl. jours. Exec. bd. govt. rels. com. United Way of Chgo., 1979-84; bd. dirs. Child Care Assn. Ill., 1975-79, Lyric Opera Guild, 1979-84; v.p. Comprehensive Community Svcs. of Met. Chgo., 1976-81; chmn. adv. bd. DePaul U. Coll. Law Ctr. Ch./State Studies, 1982—, dean's vis. com., 1982—; trustee Mundelein Coll., 1982-86, St. Xavier Coll., St. Mary of the Lake Sem., 1982-83, Sta. WTTW Chgo. Pub. TV, 1978-81, Loretto Hosp., 1989-91; mem. geriatrics/gerontology steering com. McGaw Med. Ctr. Northwestern U., 1981-82; adv. bd. N.Am. Coll., 1990-92; mem. Bus. Execs. for Econ. Justice, 1988-94, State wide citizens com. on Child Abuse and Neglect, 1988-94; bd. advisors Alzheimer's Ctr. Rush-Presbyn.-St. Luke's Med. Ctr., 1990—; cons. Union of Bulgarian Founds., 1992, Internat. Acad. for Freedom of Religion and Belief, Budapest, Hungary, 1992. Recipient St. Joseph Sem. Rerum Novarum award, 1999. Fellow Am. Bar Found.; mem. ABA, FBA, NCCJ (adv. com. on ch., state and taxation), Am. Assn. homes for Aging, Nat. Health Lawyers Assn., Ill. State Bar Assn. (bd. govs., spl. com. on jud. redistricting), Ill. Bar Found. (charter), Chgo. Bar Assn. (com. on evaluation of jud. candidates), Cath. Lawyers Guild (bd. govs.), Canon Law Soc. Am. (active mem.), Diocesan Attys. Assn. (exec. com.), Nat. Cath. Cemetery Conf., Cath. Health Assn., The Chgo. Club, Econ. Club, Tavern Club. Office: Burke Warren MacKay & Serritella PC IBM Plaza 22nd Fl 330 N Wabash Ave Chicago IL 60611-3603 E-mail: jserritella@burkelaw.com.

SERRITELLA, WILLIAM DAVID, lawyer; b. Chgo., May 16, 1946; s. William V. and Josephine Dolores (Scalise) S. JD, U. Ill., Champaign, 1971. Bar: Ill. 1971, U.S. Dist. Ct. (no. and cen. dists.) Ill. 1972, U.S. Dist. Ct. (ea. and we. dists.) Wis. 1995, U.S. Ct. Appeals (7th cir.) 1974, U.S. Supreme Ct. 1979, U.S. Dist. Ct. (so. dist.) Ind. 1997. Law clk. U.S. Dist. Ct., Danville, Ill., 1971-72; ptnr. Ross & Hardies, Chgo., 1972—2003, McGuire Woods, Chgo., 2003—. Arbitrator Am. Arbitration Assn. Mem. ABA, Ill. Bar Assn., Chgo. Bar Assn., Nat. Assn. R.R. Trial Counsel (Ill.), Soc. Trial Lawyers, Defense Rsch. Inst., Trial Lawyers Club (Chgo.), Lawyers Club Chgo. Office: McGuire Woods 150 N Michigan Ave Ste 2500 Chicago IL 60601-7567 Office Phone: 312-750-8643. Business E-Mail: wserritella@mcguirewoods.com.

SERSEN, HOWARD HARRY, retired interior designer, cabinetry consultant; b. Chgo., Apr. 20, 1929; s. Harry S. and Bertha A. Sersen; m. Judith Ann Nelson, Sept. 22, 1956; children: Mark Howard, Diane Lynn Krause, Karen Judith Skadow, Amy Louise Gibbons. BFA, Sch. Art Inst. Chgo., 1956. Cert. kitchen designer. Engaged in store planning, mdse. display, furniture design Paul MacAlister and Assocs., Lake Bluff, Ill., 1952-55, Silvestry Art, Chgo., 1955-56, Montgomery Ward & Co., Chgo., 1956-60, Riebold Co., Chgo., 1960-61, Sears, Roebuck & Co., Chgo., 1961-68; custom cabinet and kitchen design Reynolds Enterprises, Inc., River Grove, Ill., 1967-76; prin. Howard Sersen design, Park Ridge, Ill., 1976—2002; ret., 2002. Design and planning cons. for kitchens and related storage cabinetry for homes and offices; mfr., distbr. to showrooms; visual merchandising display cons. to small retail stores. Editor Qualified Remodeler mag.; contbr. articles to display, home improvement and kitchen mags.; feature in several books and in Chgo. Tribune. Art dir. park Ridge Party, 1964; mem. Park Ridge Heritage com., 1992—; v.p. Park Ridge Hist. Soc., 1996-97, bd. dirs., 1995, v.p., 1996-97, pres., 1998-99. Served with U.S. Army, 1952-54. Recipient 1st Place award Bicentennial Kitchen Design Contest, Wood-Mode Cabinets, 1974, Design award Wood Office Furniture Inst. Design Competition, 1952, award Design in Hardwoods Competition, 1958, Showroom Design award Nat. Kitchen and Bath Assn., 1st Place award for kitchen design/21st Century Elkay Mfg. Co., 1996, others. Mem. Soc. Cert. Kitchen Designers (sec. Chgo.-Midwest chpt. 1974-75, bd. councillors 1977-81, gov. 1978-82, designer emeritus 1998, Kitchen Design award 1972), Park Ridge Jaycees, Park Ridge C. of C., Park Ridge Univ. Club, Rotary (bd. dirs., bull. editor, historian), Masons, Order de Molay (chevalier). Home: 1608 Courtland Ave Park Ridge IL 60068-5335

SERSTOCK, DORIS SHAY, retired microbiologist, educator, civic worker; b. Mitchell, SD, June 13, 1926; d. Elmer Howard and Hattie (Christopher) Shay; m. Ellsworth I. Serstock, Aug. 30, 1952; children: Barbara Anne, Robert Ellsworth, Mark Douglas. BA, Augustana Coll., 1947; postgrad., U. Minn., 1966-67, Duke U., summer 1969, Communicable Disease Ctr., Atlanta, 1972. Bacteriologist Civil Svc., S.D., Colo., Mo., 1947-52; rsch. bacteriologist U. Minn., 1952-53; clin. bacteriologist Dr. Lufkin's Lab., 1954-55; chief technologist St. Paul Blood Bank of ARC, 1959-65; microbiologist in charge mycology lab. VA Hosp., Mpls., 1968-93; ret. Instr. Coll. Med. Scis., U. Minn., 1970-79, asst. prof. Coll. Lab. Medicine and Pathology, 1979-93. Contbr. articles to profl. jours. Mem. Richfield Planning Commn., 1965-71, sec., 1968-71; extended ministries commn. Wood Lake Luth. Ch., Richfield, 1993-94; rep. religious coun. Mall Am., Bloomington, Minn., 1993-94; chief nursery caregiver Christ the King Luth. Ch., Bloomington, 1994-99, Hope Presbyn. Ch., Richfield, Minn., 1994-2003; mem. Rep. Presdl. Task Force, Nat. Rep. Senatorial Com., 1997. Fellow Augusta Coll.; named to Exec. and Profl. Hall of Fame; recipient Alumni Achievement award Augustana Coll., 1977, Superior Performance award VA Hosp., 1978, 82, Cert. of Recognition, 1988, Golden Spore awards Mycology Observer, 1985, 87, Congl. Order of Merit Nat. Rep. Congl. Com., 2003; name engraved on founders' wall Ronald Reagan Rep. Ctr., 2000; named Minn. Rep. of Yr. Nat. Rep. Congl. Com., 2003. Mem. Richfield Women's Garden Club (pres. 1959), Wild Flower Garden (chmn. 1961). Republican. Home: 7201 Portland Ave Minneapolis MN 55423-3218 E-mail: dsv9@juno.com.

SERTICH, KELLI ANN, land use planner; b. Riverside, Calif., Nov. 9, 1959; d. Robert Sr. and Lillian Patricia (Hale) S. AAS in Constrn. Drafting, Glendale C.C., 1981; BS in Design Urban Planning, Ariz. State U., 1983; MPA, Western Internat. U., 2002. Draftsman, facilities planner Washington Elem. Sch. Dist., Phoenix, 1980-83; planner various pvt. sector planning & archtl. firms, Phoenix, 1983-88; dir. planning & econ. devel. Town of Buckeye (Ariz.), 1988-93; dir. tourism & econ. devel. City of Williams (Ariz.), 1993-95; dir. cmty. devel., interim city mgr. City of Bisbee (Ariz.), 1995-98; sr. planner Cmty. Scis. Corp., Phoenix, 1998; sr. planner policy analyst Maricopa County Dept. Transp., Phoenix, 1998-2000; regional area planning mgr. Flood Control Dist. Maricopa County, Phoenix, 2000—. Pres. Bisbee Christmas in April, 1997; chmn. Ariz. Cmty. Found. Cochise Project Team, Bisbee, 1997; chmn. Buckeye Clean and Beautiful, 1989-93. Mem. Am. Planning Assn., Ariz. Planning Assn. (dir.-at-large 1993-2001, sec. 1994-99, pres. 2003—). Roman Catholic. Avocations: sewing, horseback riding, travel, gardening. Office: Maricopa County Flood Control 2801 W Durango St Phoenix AZ 85009-6357

SERVAAS, BEURT RICHARD, manufacturing executive; b. Indpls., May 7, 1919; s. Beurt Hans and Lela Etta (Neff) S.; m. Cory Jane Synhorst, Jan. 7, 1950; children: Eric, Kristin, Joan, Paul, Amy. Student, U. Mex., Mexico City, 1938-39; AB, Ind. U., 1940, MD, 1970; postgrad., Purdue U., 1941; D Bus. Mgmt., Ind. Inst. Tech.; LHD (hon.), Butler U. Agt. CIA, China, 1946; v.p. constrn. Vestar Corp., N.Y.C., 1948; founder, chief exec. officer, chmn. bd. No. Vernon Forge, Inc. Rev. Pub. Co., SerVaas Labs., Indpls., 1949—. Chmn. bd. SerVaas, Inc., Indpls. and affiliated cos. Curtis Pub. Co., Forge Mexicana, Edgerton Tool, Dependable Engring., SerVaas Mgmt., SerVaas Rubber, Premier, Indpls. Rubber Co., Bridgeport Brass Co.; bd. dirs. Bank One Ind. Pres. City-County Coun., Indpls.; chmn. Ind. State Commn. Higher Edn., Kirksville Coll. Osteo. Medicine; bd. dirs. Coll. Univ. Corp., Ind. Pub. Health Found., Robert Schuller Ministries; past chmn. bd. dirs. Ind. State Bd. Health, Nat. Fgn. Rels. Commn. With USNR, 1941—45. Decorated Bronze Star, Army Commendation medal; recipient Horatio Alger award, 1980. Mem. NAM, Am. Acad. Achievement (Golden Plate award 1973), Assn. Am. Med. Colls., Ind. C. of C., Indpls. C. of C., Marion County Hist. Soc., Ind. Hist. Soc., Newcomen Soc. N.Am., U.S. Naval Res. Assn., World Future Soc., Am. Legion, Columbia Club, Econ. Club, Indpls. Athletic Club, Indpls. Press Club, Meridian Hills Country Club, Phi Delta Kappa. Presbyterian. Home: 2525 W 44th St Indianapolis IN 46228-3249 Office: Office of the City County Coun 241 City-County Bldg 200 E Washington St Indianapolis IN 46204-3307 also: SerVaas Inc 1000 Waterway Blvd Indianapolis IN 46202-2155

SERVAAS, CORY, health sciences association administrator; Pres., CEO Saturday Evening Post, Indpls. Office: Saturday Evening Post 1100 Waterway Blvd Indianapolis IN 46202-2174

SERVEDIO, DOMINICK MICHAEL, engineering executive; b. NYC, Aug. 7, 1940; s. Daniel and Margaret (Ingenito) S.; m. Patricia L. Filatro, July 26, 1969; children: Dominique, Daniel. BEE, NYU, 1962; MBA, St. John's U., 1972. Registered profl. engr., NH, Mass. Engr. in tng. NY Cen. R.R., NYC, 1962-63, engr., 1965-67; elec. engr. Citizen Utility Co., NYC, 1967-68; project engr. L.I. R.R., NYC, 1968-73; asst. dir., supervising engr. Met. Transp. Authority, NYC, 1973-77; from v.p. transportation STV Group, Inc., NYC, 1977—87, pres. and COO Pottstown, 1987, exec. v.p., 1987, pres. and COO NYC, 1993—, CEO and chmn., 1999—, bd. dir., 1992. Bd. dirs. NY Bldg. Congress, NY Assn. Consulting Engrs., Coun. on Transportation, NY State Transportation Engring. Alliance, Moles. Mem. Columbus Citizens Found., Inc., NYC., 1990, NJ Alliance for Action, Edison, 1991; active Greater NY March of Dimes, 1991, Greater NY Couns. Boy Scouts Am., 1991. 1st lt. US Army, 1963-65. Mem. NSPE, Soc. Am. Mil. Engrs.(past pres.), NY R.R. Club Inc., Soc. for Mktg. Profl. Svcs. Avocations: golf, skiing, reading. Office: 225 Park Ave S New York NY 10003-1604 Office Phone: 212-777-4400. Office Fax: 212-529-5237.*

SERVICE, JOHN GREGORY, law educator; b. Batesville, Ind., May 30, 1949; s. Henry David and Martha Geneva (Ennis) S.; m. Rosemarie Pinkocze, June 16, 1974; children: Patrick David, Kimberly Marie. AA, Broward Jr. Coll., 1969; BBA, Fla. Atlantic U., 1971; JD, U. Miami, 1974. Bar: Fla. 1974, U.S. Dist. Ct. (so. dist.) Fla. 1976. Claims adjuster Allstate Ins. Co., Coconut Creek, Fla., 1975; atty. Legal Aid Svc. Broward County, Inc., Ft. Lauderdale, Fla., 1975-77; house counsel Liberty Mut. Ins. Co., Ft. Lauderdale, Fla., 1977-78; prof. law and econs. Broward C.C., Coconut Creek, 1978—. Adj. prof. Palm Beach Jr. Coll., Boca Raton, Fla., 1982—, Coll. of Boca Raton, 1983—; cons. on hotel and motel liability problems, Delray Beach, Fla.; mediator Fla. Dept. of Ins. Program; cons. premise liability. Co-author: The Police Use of Force, 1981, Security Litigations and Related Matters, 1982; author: Hotel-Motel Law: A Primer on Innkeeper Liability, 1983, Security for Hotels and Motels: A Perspective on Liabilities, 1986; contbr. articles on hotel-motel law and liability problems to legal jours. Mem. Fla. Bar Assn., Nat. Assn. Securities Dealers (arbitrator, mediator). Republican. Methodist. Home: 7020 NW 5th Ave Boca Raton FL 33487-2381 Office: Broward Community College 1000 Coconut Creek Blvd Pompano Beach FL 33066-1697 Office Phone: 954-201-2215. E-mail: GService@Broward.edu., JGService@aol.com.

SERVICE, WILLIAM W. restaurant company executive; CEO Jaspers Food Mgmt., Inc., 1993—, CBW Inc., 1995—99, Oreg. Food Mgmt., Inc., 1996—; CEO, CFO Elmer's Restaurants, Inc., Portland, Oreg., 1998—. Office: Elmer's Restaurants Inc 11802 SE Stark St Portland OR 97292

SERVODIDIO, PAT ANTHONY, broadcast executive; b. Yonkers, N.Y., Nov. 9, 1937; s. Pasquale and Catherine (Verdisco) S.; children: Christian, Alexa. BS, Fordham U., 1959; postgrad., St. John's U., N.Y.C., 1960-63. Asst. to bus. mgr. Sta. WCBS-TV, N.Y.C., 1960-64; account exec. Sta. WTNH-TV, New Haven, 1964-66; account exec., N.Y. sales mgr. RKO TV Reps., N.Y.C., 1967-74; v.p., N.Y. sales mgr. Sta. WOR-TV, N.Y.C., 1974-79, v.p., gen. sales mgr., 1979-81; v.p., gen. mgr. Sta. WNAC-TV, Boston, 1981-82; pres. RKO TV, N.Y.C., 1982-87, RKO Gen., Inc., N.Y.C., 1987—91, also bd. dirs.; v.p., gen. mgr. Sta. WKYC-TV, Cleve., 1991-92; pres. Multimedia Broadcasting Co., Cin., 1992-94; broadcast cons., 1995—. Bd. regents St. Peter's Coll., 1983-99; mem. com. future financing Rutgers U., New Brunswick, N.J., 1983-85; dir. TV bur. Advt. Bd., 1993-94; bd. dirs. Internat. Radio and TV Found., 1983-93, Assn. for Maximum Svc. TV, Inc., 1993-95. With U.S. Army, 1959-62. Office: 380 Lexington Ave Ste 1700 New York NY 10168-0002

SERWATKA, WALTER DENNIS, publishing executive; b. Irvington, NJ, July 19, 1937; s. Walter F. and Grace R. (Sheehan) S.; m. Beverly M. Farrell, Aug. 10, 1963 (div. Feb. 1988); children: David, Nora, Nancy; m. Constance L. Holcomb, May 10, 1991. BBA in Acctg., Upsala U., 1959; MBA in Fin., Fairleigh Dickinson U., 1966; postgrad., Harvard U., 1978, Columbia U., 1979, Stanford U., 1985. With treas.'s dept. WESTVACO, NYC, 1964-68; dir. fin. analysis Random House Co., NYC, 1968-72; with McGraw-Hill Info. Systems Co., 1972-83; from contr. Sweet's divsn. to asst. contr. McGraw-Hill, Inc., NYC, 1972-76, sr. v.p., contr., 1976-79, group v.p. real estate info. svcs., 1979-83, sr. v.p. group mfg. and circulation svcs., 1985, exec. v.p., CFO, 1985-88, exec. v.p. ops., 1989—92; exec. v.p. fin. and svc. McGraw-Hill Publ. Co., NYC, Nebr., 1983-84; pres. McGraw-Hill Info. Svc., NYC, 1988-89; sr. advisor Whitestone Comm., Inc., 1993—. Trustee Upsala Coll., East Orange, NJ; bd. dirs. Am. Cancer Soc. Served with U.S. Army, 1959—62. Mem. Fin. Exec. Inst., Mag. Pubs. Assn., Am. Inst. Accts., Planning Execs. Inst., Pvt. Sector Council.

SERWER, ALAN MICHAEL, lawyer; b. Detroit, Aug. 31, 1944; s. Bernard Jacob and Marian (Borin) S.; m. Laurel Kathryn Robbert, June 6, 1968; children: David Matthew, Karen Anne. BA in Econs., U. Mich., 1966; JD, Northwestern U., 1969. Bar: Ill. 1969, D.C. 1980, U.S. Dist. Ct. (no. dist.) Ill. 1970, U.S. Ct. Appeals (7th cir.) 1979, U.S. Supreme Ct. 1979, U.S. Ct. Appeals (6th cir.) 1982, U.S. Ct. Appeals (5th cir.) 1983, U.S. Ct. Appeals (11th cir.) 1984, U.S. Ct. Appeals (9th cir.) 1986. Trial atty. U.S. Dept. Labor, Chgo., 1969-78, counsel safety and health, 1978-79; assoc. Haley, Bader & Potts, Chgo., 1979-82, ptnr., 1983-87; mem. Bell, Boyd & Lloyd, Chgo., 1987—. Ill. Bar Assn., Chgo. Bar Assn. Home: 233 Woodland Rd Highland Park IL 60035-5052 Office: Bell Boyd & Lloyd 70 W Madison St Ste 3200 Chicago IL 60602-4244

SESHADRI, ARATHI H. research scientist, educator; d. Seshadri Holur and Usha Seshadri; 1 child, Pratheeksha Mallikarjun. BSc in Horticulture, U. Agrl. Scis., Bangalore, 1988, MS in Genetics and Plant Breeding, 1991; D in Life Scis., Indian Inst. Sci., Bangalore, 1997. Rsch. assoc. U. Minn., St. Paul, 1998—2000, U. Kans., Lawrence, 2001—02; asst. prof. in ecology Adelphi U., Garden City, NY, 2002—. Contbr. articles to profl. jours. Mem.: NA-SIUSSI, Entomol. Soc. Am.

SESHAIYER, PADMANABHAN, mathematician, educator; b. Chennai, Tamil Nadu, India; B. with honors in engring., Birla Inst. Tech. and Sci., India, 1994; MSc with honors, Birla Inst. Tech. and Sci., 1994; PhD, U. Md., 1998. Rsch. assoc. Tex. A&M U., Coll. Sta., Tex., 1998—2000; asst. prof. Tex. Tech U., Lubbock, Tex., 2000—. Recipient Grad. Prof. of Yr., SIAM Chpt., Tex. Tech U., 2002; Tex. Project NExT fellow, Math. Assn. of Am., Tex. Chpt., 2001-2002, Std. Rsch. grant, NSF, 2002-2005, Std. Conf. grant, 2003-2004, Whitaker Found., 2003-2004. Mem.: Tchg. Academy, Tex. Tech. U. Office: Tex Tech U Box 41042 Math Stats Lubbock TX 79409-1042 E-mail: padhu@math.ttu.edu.

SESONSKE, ALEXANDER, nuclear and chemical engineer; b. Gloversville, N.Y., June 20, 1921; s. Abraham and Esther (Kreitzer) S.; m. Marjorie Ann Mach, Apr. 17, 1952 (dec. Jan. 1995); children: Michael Jan, Jana Louise. B.Chem. Engring., Rensselaer Poly. Inst., 1942; MS, U. Rochester, 1947; PhD, U. Del., 1950. Engr. Chem. Constrn. Corp., N.Y.C., 1942; chem. engr. Manhattan Project, 1943-45, Columbia-So. Chem. Corp., 1945-46; staff Los Alamos Sci. Lab., 1950-54, 60-61, cons., 1961-63; faculty Purdue U., Lafayette, Ind., 1954, prof. nuclear and chem. engring., 1959-86, prof. emeritus, 1986—, asst. chmn. dept. nuclear engring., 1966-73. Cons. Oak Ridge Nat. Lab., 1963-67, Electric Power Research Inst., 1974; mem. rev. com. Argonne (Ill.) Nat. Lab., 1965-67, 75-81; ind. cons. 1986—. Author: (with Samuel Glasstone) Nuclear Reactor Engineering, 1963, 4th edit., 1994, Nuclear Power Plant Design Analysis, 1973; mem. editorial bd. Advances in Nuclear Sci. and Tech., 1972—; contbr. numerous articles to profl. jours. Recipient Wall of Fame award U. Del., 1988. Fellow Am. Nuclear Soc. (Arthur H. Compton award 1987); mem. Am. Inst. Chem. Engrs., Am. Soc. Engring. Edn., Sigma Xi, Omega Chi Epsilon. Achievements include research on nuclear fuel mgmt., liquid metal heat transfer and nuclear reactor engring. Home and Office: 700 Black Lake Blvd SW Apt 109 Olympia WA 98502 Office Phone: 360-943-5467. Personal E-mail: alses1@cs.com.

SESSIONS, BETTYE JEAN, humanities educator; b. Jacksonville, FL, Jan. 29, 1934; d. John Henry and Willene Porter Hayes; m. Malcolm G.A. Sessions, July 7, 1956; children: Sabrina F., Malcolm G.A. II, Byron Craig. BA, Fla. A&M U., 1956; MAT, Jacksonville U., 1967. Tchr. English, humanities Duval County Pub. Schs., Jacksonville, Fla., 1957—72; prof. humanities Fla. C.C., Jacksonville, Fla., 1972—90; news corr. Fla. Times - Jacksonville Jour., 1981—86; profl. writer, author and poet Jean-Aubrey Ideas, Inc., Jacksonville, 1985—2001.

SESSIONS, CICERO COLUMBUS, lawyer; b. Empire, C.Z., Oct. 5, 1908; s. Varner Vaughn and Laura Caroline (Browning) S.; m. Phyllis Dilworth, Apr. 12, 1941; 1 dau., Mary Susan Sessions Hadley. Student La. State U., 1926-29; J.D., Tulane U., 1932. Sole practice, New Orleans, 1932-40; gen. counsel La. Dept. Revenue, asst. atty. gen. State of La., 1940-42; asst. city atty., New Orleans, 1946; ptnr. Montgomery, Barnett, Brown, Sessions & Read, New Orleans, 1946-53; sr. ptnr. Sessions, Fishman, Rosenson, Boisfontaine, Nathan & Winn, New Orleans, 1953-81, ret., 1981, now of counsel. Served to 1st lt. JAGC, AUS, 1942-45; ret. lt. col. AUS, 1968. to lt. col. JAGC, USAR, 1946-68. Fellow Am. Coll. Trial Lawyers (state chmn. 1963, com. to preserve oral argument in appellate cts. 1976—, chmn. 1977-78, mem. com. to preserve oral argument in trial cts. 1978-81), Internat. Soc. Barristers; mem. ABA (spl. com. to cooperate with Internat. Commn. of Jurists 1957-64), La. Bar Assn. (chmn. sect. internat. comparative and mil. law 1949-51, chmn. ins. sect. 1958-59, ho. of dels. 1957-60), New Orleans Bar Assn. (chmn. com. on jud. reform 1952-54, chmn. com. on dist. ct. rules 1963-64, 1966-67, exec. v.p. 1965), Assn. Bar City N.Y., Bar Assn. of U.S. 5th Cir. Ct. Appeals, Am. Judicature Soc., Am. Soc. Internat. Law, Judge Advs. Assn., Fedn. Ins. Counsel, Internat. Assn. Ins. Counsel (chmn. marine ins. com. 1957-58), Maritime Law Assn., U.S. Assn. Def. Counsel, La. Assn. Def. Counsel, New Orleans Assn. Def. Counsel, New Orleans Assn. Commerce (chmn. aviation com. 1950-52), U.S. Fifth Cir. Ct. Appeals Jud. Conf. (hon. life), Supreme Ct. Hist. Soc. (founding), Levere Meml. Found., Sigma Alpha Epsilon, Pi Sigma Alpha, Tau Kappa Alpha. Republican. Presbyterian. Clubs: Masons, Petroleum of New Orleans, Carnival. Co-author: Statement of the Rule of Law in the United States, 1965. Office: 601 Poydras St Fl 25 New Orleans LA 70130-6029

SESSIONS, JEFFERSON BEAUREGARD, III, senator; b. Hybart, Ala., Dec. 24, 1946; s. Jefferson Beauregard and Abbie (Powe) S.; m. Mary Montgomery Blackshear, Aug. 9, 1969; children: Mary Abigail, Ruth Blackshear, Samuel Turner BA, Huntingdon Coll., Montgomery, Ala., 1969; JD, U. Ala., 1973. Bar: Ala. 1973. Assoc. Guin, Bouldin & Porch, Russellville, Ala., 1973-75; asst. U.S. atty. U.S. Dept. Justice, Mobile, Ala., 1975-77, U.S. atty., 1981-93; assoc., ptnr. Stockman & Bedsole Attys., Mobile, Ala., 1977-81; ptnr. Stockman, Bedsole & Sessions, Mobile, 1993-94; atty. gen. State of Ala., 1995—97; U.S. senator from Ala., 1997—. Mem. U.S. atty. gen.'s. adv. com., 1987-89, vice-chmn. 1989; mem. judiciary, health, edn., labor & pensions armed svcs. coms. Presdl. elector State of Ala., 1972; trustee, mem. exec. com. Mobile Bay Area Partnership for Youth, 1981-95; chmn. adminstrv. bd. Ashland Pl. United Meth. Ch., Mobile, 1982; 1st v.p. Mobile Lions Club, 1993-94. Capt. USAR, 1975-85 Recipient U.S. Atty. Gen's. award for significant achievements in the war against drug trafficking U.S. Atty. Gen. William P. Barr, 1992. Mem. ABA, Ala. Bar Assn., Mobile Bar Assn. Republican. Home: 1119 Hillcrest Xing E Mobile AL 36695-4505 Office: 335 Senate Russell Office Bldg Washington DC 20510-0001 E-mail: senator@sessions.senate.gov.

SESSIONS, KATHRYN L. state legislator, educator; b. Jackson, Wyo., Feb. 13, 1942; widowed; 3 children. BS, Utah State U., 1970; MS, Leslie Coll., 1990. Educator, Wyo., 1970—; mem. Wyo. Ho. Reps., Cheyenne, 1992-98, Wyo. Senate, Dist. 7, Cheyenne, 1998—; mem. appropriations com. Wyo. Senate, Cheyenne, mem. rules and procedures. com. Mem. NEA, LWV, Wyo. Edn. Assn., Alpha Delta Kappa (edn. com.). Democrat. Mem. Lds Ch. Home: 930 Centennial Dr Cheyenne WY 82001-7407 Office: Wyo Senate State Capitol Cheyenne WY 82002-0001

SESSIONS, PETE, congressman; b. Mar. 22, 1955; m. Juanita; children: Bill, Alex. Grad., Southwestern U., 1978. With Southwestern Bell Telephone Co., Southwestern Com. Rsch.; v.p. pub. policy Nat. Ctr. Policy Analysis; mem. U.S. Congress from 32nd Tex. dist. (formerly 5th), 1997—; mem. rules com., homeland sec. com. Bd. mem. YMCA; active United Meth. Ch. Mem. Rotary Club. Republican. Avocations: hiking, mountain climbing, running.

SESSIONS, ROY BRUMBY, otolaryngologist, educator; b. Houston, July 28, 1937; s. Roy Brumby and Elizabeth (Compton) S.; m. Mary Cousart, Aug. 28, 1976; children: Kate, Elizabeth, Abigail, Matthew. BS, La. State U., Baton Rouge, 1958; MD, La. State U., New Orleans, 1962. Resident gen. surgery and otolaryngology Washington U. Sch. Medicine, St. Louis, 1965-69; asst. prof. Baylor Coll. Medicine, Houston, 1969-73, assoc. prof., 1973-83; prof. head and neck surgery Meml. Sloan Kettering Cancer Ctr., N.Y.C., 1983-89; prof., chmn. dept. otolaryngology, head and neck surgery Med. Sch. Georgetown U., Washington, 1989-97; chmn. dept. otolaryngology, head and neck surgery Beth Israel Med. Ctr., N.Y.C., 1998—, assoc. dir. Cancer Ctr., co-dir. Inst. Head and Neck Surgery, 1998—. Contbr. articles to profl. jours., chpts. to books; author one textbook. Lt. comdr. USN, 1962-65. Roman Catholic. Home: 411 Forest St Rye NY 10580 Office: Beth Israel Med Ctr 10 Union Sq E Ste 4J New York NY 10003-3314

SESSIONS, WILLIAM STEELE, former government official, lawyer; b. Ft. Smith, Ark., May 27, 1930; s. Will Anderson and Edith A. (Steele) S.; m. Alice Lewis, Oct. 5, 1952; children: William Lewis, Mark Gregory, Peter Anderson, Sara Anne. BA, Baylor U., 1956, LLB, 1958; hon. degree, John C. Marshall Law Sch., St. Mary's U., 1989; LLD (hon.), Dickinson Coll., 1988, Flager Coll., 1990, Davis & Elkins Coll., 1992, McMurry U., 1997. Bar: Tex. 1959; U.S. Dist Ct. (Western Dist.) Tex.; Ct. Appeals (5th Cir.). Ptnr. McGregor & Sessions, Waco, Tex., 1959-61; assoc. Tirey, McLaughlin, Gorin & Tirey, Waco, 1961-63; ptnr. Haley, Fulbright, Winniford, Sessions & Bice, Waco, 1963-69; sect. chief, govt. ops sect. criminal divsn. U.S. Dept. Justice, Washington, 1969-71; U.S. atty. U.S. Dept Justice, U.S. Dist. Ct., (we. dist), San Antonio, 1971-74; dist. judge U.S. Dist. Ct. (we. dist.) Tex., San Antonio, 1974-87, chief judge, 1980-87; dir. FBI, Washington, 1987-93; ptnr. Sessions & Sessions, San Antonio and Washington, 1995-2000, Holland & Knight, LLP, San Antonio and Washington, 2000—. Bd. dirs., chmn. book com. Fed. Jud. Ctr., Washington, 1981—; mem. Tex. Commn. on Judicial Efficiency, 1995, Tex. Commn. on a Representative Student Body, 1998, Gov.'s Task Force on Homeland Security, Gov.'s Anti-Crime Commn., Tex., 2002, ABA Standing Com. on the 21st Century Judiciary, ABA Standing Com. on the Libr. of Congress; mem. steering com. of coastal Tex. Contbr. articles to profl. jours. Active Dr. Martin Luther King Jr. Fed. Holiday Commn., 1991-96, hon. bd. dirs., 1993-94; bd. trustees Nat. Environ. Edn. & Tng. Found., Inc., 2001—. Lt. USAF, 1951-55; capt. USAFR, Recipient Rosewood Gavel award St. Mary's U. Sch. Law, San Antonio, 1982, Disting. Alumni award Baylor U., Golden Plate award Am. Acad. Achievement, 1988, Law Enforcement Leadership award Assn. Fed. Investigators, 1989, medal of honor DAR, 1989, Disting. Eagle Scout award Boy Scouts Am., 1990, Person of Yr. award Am. Soc. for Indsl. Security, 1990, Magna Charta award Baronial Order of Magna Charta, 1990, Price Daniel Disting. Pub. Svc. award Baylor U., 2002; named Lawyer of Yr., Baylor Law Sch., 1988, Father of Yr., Nat. Fathers Day Com., 1988, Ellis Island Congl. Medal of Honor, 1992; inducted into Eagle Scout Hall of Fame, 1998. Fellow ABA (chmn. spl. com. on judicial independence 1997—, Nat. Law Day chmn. 2000-02, hon. co chmn., pres. commn. on the 21st Century Judiciary, 2002-,); mem. Jud. Conf. U.S. (com. on ct. adminstrn., chmn. jud. improvements subcom. 1983-85, ad hoc com. on automation to subcom. 1984-87, mem. ad hoc ct. reporter com. 1984-87), San Antonio Bar Assn. (bd. dirs. 1973-74), Fed. Bar Assn. (pres. San Antonio sect. 1974), Am. Judicature Soc. (exec. com. 1982-84), Dist. Judges Assn. of 5th Cir. (pres. 1982-83), State Bar of Tex. (chmn. com. to develop procedures for cert. state

law questions to Supreme Ct. by Fed. Cts. 1983-85), Waco McLennan County Bar Assn. (pres. 1968), San Antonio Inns of Ct. (pres. 1986), William S. Sessions Inns of Ct. Republican. Methodist. Avocations: hiking, climbing, canoeing. Office: Holland & Knight LLP Ste 100 2099 Pennsylvania Ave NW Washington DC 20006 Fax: (202) 955-5564. E-mail: wscssions@hklaw.com.

SESSLE, BARRY JOHN, adult education educator, researcher; b. Sydney, NSW, Australia, May 28, 1941; arrived in Can., 1971; s. Frederick George and Sadie Isobel (Lawson) S.; m. Mary Baldwin; children from previous marriage: Erica Jane, Claire Marie. BDS, Sydney U., New South Wales, 1963, MDS, MSc, Sydney U., New South Wales, 1965; PhD, U. New South Wales, 1969, DSc (hon.), 2000. Scholar Dental Found. Sydney U., 1963-64; tchg. fellow U. New South Wales, 1965-68; vis. assoc. U.S. Nat. Inst. Dental Rsch., Bethesda, Md., 1968-70; assoc. prof. U. Toronto Dental Sch., Canada, 1971-76, prof., 1976-85, chmn. divsn. biol. scis., 1978-84, assoc. dean rsch., 1985-90, dean, 1990-2001. Mem. com. on dental scis. Can. Med. Rsch. Coun., Ottawa, 1979-82; mem. com. grants rev. U.S. NIH, Bethesda, 1976-. Author: The Neural Basis of Oral and Facial Function, 1978; editor: Mastication and Swallowing, 1976, Oro-facial Pain and Neuromuscular Dysfunction, 1985, Effects of Injury of Trigeminal and Spinal Somatosensory Systems, 1987, Trigeminal Neuralgia: Current Concepts Regarding Pathogenesis and Treatment, 1991, Temporomandibular Joint and Masticatory Muscle Disorders, 1994, Temporomandibular Disorders and Related Pain Conditions, 1995, Neurobiology of Mastication, 1999, Orofacial Pain, 2001; mem. editl. bd. Arch. Oral Biol. Jour., 1988—, Pain Jour., 1986-90, Jour. Dental Rsch., 2003—, Dysphagia Jour., 1990—, Pain Rsch. and Mgmt. Jour., 1995—, Oral Biosci. and Medicine, 2003—, Jour. of Oral Rehab., 2003—, editor-in-chief Jour. Orofacial Pain, 1997—. Can. rsch. chair, 2001—. Recipient Tchr. award Can. Fund for Dental Edn., 1977, Disting. Career award Can. Pain Soc., 1999, Nat. Recognition award Am. Assn. Orofacial Pain, 2004; grantee Med. Rsch. Coun., 1971—, NIH, 1974—. Fellow Royal Soc. Can., Can. Acad. Sci., Internat. Coll. Dentists; mem. Internat. Assn. Study Pain (sec. Can. chpt. 1982-87, mem. coun. 1993-96, pres.-elect 1997-99, pres. 1999-2002), Soc. Neurosci. (pres. South Ont. chpt. 1982-83), Internat. Assn. Dental Rsch. (pres. Can. divsn. 1977-78, sec.-treas. 1976-79, pres. neurosci. group 1985-86, pres. 1994-95, Oral Sci. award 1976, Pindborg Oral Biol. prize 1994), Internat. Union Physiol. Sci. (sec. oral physiology commn. 1983-90). Office: Faculty Dentistry U Toronto 124 Edward St Toronto ON Canada M5G 1G6

SESSLER, ANDREW MARIENHOFF, physicist; b. Bklyn., Dec. 11, 1928; s. David and Mary (Baron) S.; m. Gladys Lerner, Sept. 23, 1951 (div. Dec. 1994); children: Daniel Ira, Jonathan Lawrence, Ruth. BA in Math. cum laude, Harvard U., 1949; MA in Theoretical Physics, Columbia U., 1951, PhD in Theoretical Physics, 1953. NSF fellow Cornell U., Ithaca, NY, 1953—54; asst. prof. Ohio State U., Columbus, 1954, assoc. prof., 1960; on leave Midwestern Univs. Rsch., 1955—56; vis. physicist Lawrence Radiation Lab., 1959—60; vis. physicist, summer Niels Bohr Inst., Copenhagen, 1961; rschr. theoretical physics Lawrence Berkeley Lab. U. Calif., Berkeley, 1961—73, rschr. energy and environment Lawrence Berkeley Lab., 1971—73, dir. Lawrence Berkeley Lab., 1973—80, sr. scientist plasma physics Lawrence Berkeley Lab., 1980—94, disting. sr. staff scientist Lawrence Berkeley Lab., 1994—2001, disting. vis. scientist Lawrence Berkeley Lab., 2001—02, disting. scientist Lawrence Berkeley Lab., 2002—, dir. emeritus, 2003—. U.S. advisor Panjab U. Physics Inst., Chandigarh, India; mem. U.S.-India Coop. Program for Improvement Sci. Edn. in India, 1966, high energy physics adv. panel to U.S. AEC, 1969-72, adv. com. Lawrence Hall Sci., 1974-78; chmn. Stanford Synchrotron Radiation Project Sci. Policy Bd., 1974-77, EPRI Advanced Fuels Adv. Com., 1978-81, BNL External Adv. Com. on Isabelle, 1980-82; mem. sci. pol. bd. Stanford Synchrotron Radiation Lab., 1991-92; L.J. Haworth dist. scientist Brookhaven Nat. Lab., 1991-92. Mem. editl. bd. Nuclear Instruments and Methods, 1969—; correspondent Comments on Modern Physics, 1969-71; contbr. articles in field to profl. jours. Mem. hon. adv. bd. Inst. Advanced Physics Studies, LaJolla Internat. Sch. Physics, 1991—; mem. Superconducting Super Collider Sci. Policy Com., 1991—93. Recipient E.O. Lawrence award U.S. Atomic Energy Commn., 1970, U.S. Particle Accelerator Sch. prize, 1988; fellow Japan Soc. for Promotion Sci. at KEK, 1985. Fellow AAAS (nominating com. 1984-87), Am. Phys. Soc. (chmn. com. internat. freedom scientist 1982, study of directed energy weapons panel 1985-87, chmn. panel pub. affairs 1988, chmn. divsn. physics of beams 1990, chmn. com. applications of physics 1993, councilor for divsn. physics of beams 1994-97, pres.-elect 1997, pres. 1998, past pres. 1999, Nicholson medal 1994, Robert R. Wilson prize 1997); mem. NAS, IEEE, Fedn. Am. Scientists Coun. (vice chmn. 1987-88, chmn. 1988-92), N.Y. Acad. Sci., Assoc. Univ. Inc. (bd. dirs. 1991-94). Office: Lawrence Berkeley Lab Univ Calif MS 71R0259 1 Cyclotron Rd Bldg Berkeley CA 94720-8211 Office Phone: 510-486-4992. Business E-Mail: AMSessler@lbl.gov.

SESSOMS, ALLEN LEE, academic administrator, former diplomat, physicist; b. NYC, Nov. 17, 1946; s. Albert Earl and Lottie Beatrice (Leff) Sessoms; children from previous marriage: Manon Elizabeth, Stephanie Csilla. BS, Union Coll., Schenectady, N.Y., 1968; PhD, Yale U., 1972; DSc (hon.), Union Coll., 1998; PhD (hon.), Soka U., Japan, 2000. Sci. assoc. CERN, Geneva, 1973-78; asst. prof. physics Harvard U., Cambridge, Mass., 1974-81; sr. tech. advisor OES, State Dept., Washington, 1980-82; dir. Office Nuclear Tech. & Safeguards, State Dept., Washington, 1982-87; counselor for sci. and tech. U.S. Embassy, Paris, 1987-89, polit. minister, counselor Mexico City, 1989-91, dep. chief of mission, 1991-93; exec. v.p., v.p. for acad. affairs U. Mass. Sys., Boston, 1993-95; pres. CUNY Queens Coll., Flushing, N.Y., 1995-2000; lectr., fellow Belfer Ctr. for Sci. and Internat. Affairs, JFK Sch. Govt., Harvard U., Cambridge, Mass., 2000—03; pres. Del. State U., 2003—. Mem. adv. com. U.S. Sec. Energy, 1995-2002; mem. NCAA Pres. Coun., 1996-2000; mem. nuc. energy rsch. adv. com. U.S. Dept. Energy. Contbr. articles to profl. jours. Bd. dirs. Milestone Fund, Drawing Ctr., Big Apple Circus; mem. adv. coun. Toda Internat. Ford Found. travel/study grantee, 1973-74; Alfred P. Sloan Found. fellow, 1977-81; recipient Wilbur Cross medal Yale Grad. Sch. Alumni, 1999, Medal of Highest Honor, Soka U., 1999; officer dans l'Order des Palmes Académiques, 1999. Mem. AAAS, Am. Phys. Soc., N.Y. Acad. Sci., Cosmos Club. Office: Office of the Pres Del State Univ 1200 N Dupont Hwy Dover DE 19901 Office Phone: 302-857-6001. Personal E-mail: vonsessoms@aol.com. Business E-Mail: asessoms@desu.edu.

SESSUMS, T. TERRELL, lawyer; b. Daytona Bch., Fla., June 11, 1930; m. Neva Ann Steeves, Aug. 16, 1958; children: Thomas T. Jr., Richard H., Sandra Sessums Moneyham. BA in polit. sci., U. Fla., 1952; JD, U. Fla. Coll. Law, 1958; grad., Fla. Exec. Mgmt. Program, 1993; LLD (hon.), Fla. So. Coll., 1973; D of pub. adminstrn. (hon.), Rollins Coll., 1974; LLD (hon.), Flagler Coll., 1988; LHD (hon.), U. So. Fla., 1995. Assoc. atty. Hardee & Ott, Tampa, 1958—60; legis. aide/legal asst. to State Senator Sam Gibbons, Fla. Senate, 1959—61; ptnr. Albritton, Sessums Jordan & Ryder, Tampa, 1961—84; shareholder, mng. ptnr. Macfairlane Ferguson & McMullen, 1984—97; ptnr. Salem Saxon, P.A., 1998—2003; of counsel Salem Law Group, P.A., Tampa, 2003—. Spkr. Fla. Ho. Rep., 1972—74; adj. prof. U. S. Fla., Tampa, 1974—75; gen. coun. Tampa Port Authority, 1974—89; colloquium bd., lectr., ednl. policy issues Harvard U. Grad. Sch. Edn., 1977; chmn. Fla. Bar Legis. Com., 1977—78; coun. Fla. Conf. Cir. Judges, 1978; spl. coun. Fla. Bar/Workers' Compensation Section, 1978—79, chmn., 1979—80; served on Fla. Bd. Regents, 1979—88, chmn., 1986—88; spl. coun. to US Senator Bob Graham, 1995; dir. GTE Fla., 1986—93; dir. region II, cons. bd. Southeast Bank, N.A., Tampa Bay, 1973—91; dir. Blue Cross Fla., 1977—78; trustee, exec. com., gen. coun. Time Warner Trust, Tamps, 1983—98; dir. Family TV Co. (WFTV, Channel 28), 1978—84; pres. Ashley St. Properties, Inc., 1986—89, Golden Pond Groves, Inc., Tampa, 1986—89, Halifax Mgmt. Co., 1994—97; v.p. Trouble Creek Properties, Inc., 1988—2001; mem. Tampa Bay Area Com. on Fgn. Rels., 1982—; state dir., sr. mem. Orange Bowl. Com., 1991—; dir. Mus. Sci. and Industry (MOSI), Tampa, 1990—94, adv. coun., 1994—; founding pres. Georgia Seagle Alumni Assn., Inc., 1982—84, dir., 1984—94, adv. coun., 1994—2004. Contbr. articles to jour. Bd. trustees exec. com. U. S. Fla. Found., 1979—89; bd. dir. Moffitt Cancer Ctr., Inc., 1984—91; ednl. mission to coll. and U. in China and Japan U. S. Fla., 1986, life mem. pres. coun.; trustee Found. Eye Rsch., Inc., 1987—91; dir. Fla. State Fair Authority, 1995—96; pres. Greater Tampa C. of C., 1983—84, gen. coun., 1979—87, exec. com., 1988—91, chmn. com. of 100, 1986; dir. Fla. C. of C., 1987—96, v.p. pub. affairs, 1988—89, mem. project cornerstone adv. com., 1988—89, vice chmn. programs, 1989—90, chmn. rsch. and info. coun., 1990—91, chmn., 1992—93, exec. com., 1988—94, bd. gov., 1996—; pres. alumni coun. U. Fla. Coll. Law, 1984 85, mem. major gifts com./Hillsborough County chmn., 1989—91; trustee U. Tampa, 1978—91, chmn. strategic planning com., 1987—88, vice chmn. bd. trustees, 1987—88, chmn. bd. trustees, 1988—90, bd. overseers; trustee Fla. So. Coll., 1989—, chmn. long range planning com., 1990—, pres. coun., 1983—, chmn. bd. trustees, 1993—2003, emeritus chmn. bd.; parents' coun. Wofford Coll., 1981—85, pres. coun., 1982—85; trustee Inter Am. Scholarship Found., Inc.; asst. scoutmaster Boy Scouts Am., Tampa, 1976—79; organizing com. mem. Tampa Bay Performing Arts Ctr., 1980, trustee, 1980—88; mem. Found. Excellence in Edn., 1987—90; dir. Fla. Independent College Fund, 1988—90; fed. judicial nom. com. Fla. (Middle Dist. Panel), 1997—2001; chmn. adv. coun. Tampa United Meth. Ctr., 1989—94; trustee United Meth. Found. Higher Edn., 1998—; dir. Nat. Conf. Christians and Jews, Tampa Bay Chpt., 1990—94. Named diplomat, Fla. Demolay Hall Fame, 1995; recipient Disting. Alumnus award, U. Fla., 1973, CHIEF award (Champion Higher Independent Edn. in Fla.), Pres. Independent Coll. and U. in Fla., 1974—75, Pres. Disting. Citizen award, U. So. Fla., 1975, Don L. and Ruth E. Smith Founders award, 1980, Nat. Football Found. award, Contbn. to Cmty. and Football Tampa Chpt., 1982, Person of Vision award, Nat. Soc. Prevent Blindness, 1986, "Class of 56" award, U. So. Fla. Alumni Assn., 1988, Silver Medallion award, Nat. Conf. Christians and Jews, 1990, Disting. Svc. award, Fla. Assn. Coll. and U., 1993, Francis Asbury award, Fla. Annual Conf., United Meth. Ch., 1998. Mem.: Fla. Bar Assn., Hillsborough Bar Assn., Tampa Bar Assn., Hall Fame Bowl Assn. (founding dir. 1986—88), Kiwanis Club Tmap, Tampa Yacht and Country Club, U. Club Tampa, Omicron Delta Kappa. Achievements include named in honor, Terrell Sessums Mall at U. So. Fla., 2001; named in honor, Terrell Sessums Elem. Sch., 2004. Office Phone: 813-224-9000.

SESTINI, VIRGIL ANDREW, retired biology educator; b. Las Vegas, Nov. 24, 1936; s. Santi and Merceda Francesca (Borla) S. BS in Edn., U. Nev., 1959; postgrad., Oreg. State U., 1963-64; MNS, U. Idaho, 1995; postgrad., Ariz. State U., 1967, No. Ariz. U., 1969. Cert. tchr., Nev. Tchr. biology Rancho H.S., 1960-76; sci. chmn., tchr. biology Bonanza H.S., Las Vegas, 1976-90, ret., 1990. Co-founder, curator exhibits Meadows Mus. Nat. History, 1993-94; part-time tchr., sci. chmn. Meadows Sch., 1987-94; ret., 1994; edn. specialist, cell biologist SAGE Rsch., Las Vegas, 1993, ret., 1998; founder Da Vinci Enterprises, Las Vegas, 1995. Author: Lab Investigations for High School Honors Biology, 1992, Laboratory Investigations in Microbiology, 1992, Genetics Problems for High School Biology, 1995, Science Laboratory Report Data Book, 1995, Field and Museum Techniques for the Classroom Teacher, 1995, Selected Lab Investigations and Projects for Honors and AP Biology, Vol. I Microbiology, 1995, Telecommunications: A Simulation for Biology Using the Internet, 1995; co-author: A Biology Lab Manual for Cooperative Learning, 1989, Metrics and Science Methods: A Manual of Lab Experiments for Home Schoolers, 1990, Experimental Designs in Biology I: Botany and Zoology, 1993, Designs in Biology: A Lab Manual, 1993, Integrated Science Lab Manual, 1994, Supplemental Experiments and Field Studies for AP Biology, 1998; contbr. articles to profl. jours. including The Sci. Tchr., Am. Biology Tchr., Fine Scale Models, Ships in Scale, IPMS Jour. With USAR, 1959-65. Reciepient Rotary Internat. Honor Tchr. award, 1965, Region VIII Outstanding Biology Tchr. award, 1970, Nev. Outstanding Biology Tchr. award Nat. Assn. Biology Tchrs., 1970, Nat. Assn. Sci. Tchrs., Am. Gas Assn. Sci. Tchg. Achievement Recognition award, 1976, 80, Gustov Ohaus award, 1980, Presdl. Honor Sci. Tchr. award, 1983; Presdl. award excellence in math. and sci. tchg., 1984, Celebration of Excellence award Nev. Com. on Excellence in Edn., 1986, Hall of Fame award Clark County Sch. Dist., 1988, Excellence in Edn. award, 1987, 88, Spl. Edn. award 1988, NSEA Mini-grants, 1988, 89, 92, World Decoration of Excellence medallion World Inst. Achievement, 1989, Cert. Spl. Congrl. Recognition, 1989, Senatorial Recognition, 1989, mini-grant Jr. League Las Vegas, 1989, Excellence in Edn. award Clark Country Sch. Dist., 1989; named Nev. Educator of Yr., Milken Family Found./Nev. State Dept. Edn., 1989; grantee Nev. State Bd. Edn., 1988, 89, Nev. State Edn. Assn., 1988-89. Mem. AAAS, NEA, Nat. Assn. Taxidermists, Nat. Sci. Tchrs. Assn. (life, Nev. state membership chmn. 1968-70), Nat. Assn. Biology Tchrs. (life, OBTA dir. Nev. state 1991-93), Am. Soc. Microbiology, Coun. for Exceptional Children, Am. Biographic Inst. (rsch. bd. advisors 1988), Nat. Audubon Assn., Nat. Sci. Suprs. Assn., Am. Inst. Biol. Scis., Nautical Rsch. Guild, Internat. Plastic Modelers Soc., So. Nev. Scale Modelers (Las Vegas coord., Modeloberfest, 1995), Silver State Scale Modelers Guild. Avocations: scale models, military figures, scale models circus, photography. E-mail: v.sestini@lvcm.com.

SESTRIC, ANTHONY JAMES, lawyer; b. St. Louis, June 27, 1940; s. Anton and Marie (Gasparovic) S.; m. Carol F. Bowman, Nov. 24, 1966; children: Laura Antonette, Holly Nicole, Michael Anthony. Student, Georgetown U., 1958-62; JD, Mo. U., 1965. Bar: Mo. 1965, Minn. 1996, U.S. Ct. Appeals (8th cir.) 1965, U.S. Ct. Appeals (7th cir.) 1984, U.S. Dist. Ct. Mo. 1966, U.S. Dist. Ct. (no dist.) Tex. 1985, U.S. Dist. Ct. Ill. 1994, U.S. Tax Ct. 1969, U.S. Supreme Ct. 1970, U.S. Claims Ct. 1986. Law clk. U.S. Dist. Ct., St. Louis, 1965-66; ptnr. Sestric, McGhee & Miller, St. Louis, 1966-77, Fordyce and Mayne, 1977-78, Sestric & Garvey, 1978-96, Sestric Law Firm, St. Louis, 1996—. Spl. asst. to Mo. atty. gen., St. Louis, 1968, spl. asst. circuit atty., 2001—; mem. Fed. Jud. Selection Commn., 1993, U.S. Jud. Selection Commn., 1993-94; gen. chmn. 22nd jud. cir. bar com., 1995, mem. Region XI disciplinary com., 2001—. Contbr. articles to profl. jours. Hearing officer St. Louis Met. Police Dept.; active St. Louis Air Pollution Bd. Appeals and Varience Rev., 1966-73, chmn., 1968-73; active St. Louis Airport Commn., 1975-76; dist. vice-chmn. Boy Scouts Am., 1970-76; bd. dirs. Full Achievement, Inc., 1970-77, Legal Aid Soc. St. Louis, 1976-77, Law Libr. Assn. St. Louis, 1976-78, Thomas Dunn Memls., 1995-98, Marquette Learning Ctr., 1995-98; v.p. bd. St. Elizabeth Acad., 1985-86 Mem. ABA (state chmn. judiciary com. 1973-75, cir. chmn. com. condemnation, zoning and property use 1975-77, standing com. bar activities 1982-88), Nat. Conf. Bar Pres.'s (exec. coun. 1987-90), Mo. Bar Assn. (vice-chmn. young lawyers sect. 1973-76, bd. govs. 1974-77, chmn. law practice mgmt. com. 1997-99), Bar Assn. Met. St. Louis (chmn. young lawyers sect. 1974-75, exec. com. 1974-83, 94-95, pres. 1981-82, bd. govs. 1995-98, chmn. survey com. 1999). Home: 3967 Holly Hills Blvd Saint Louis MO 63116-3135 Office Phone: 314-351-2512. E-mail: ajsestric@juno.com.

SETCHELL, CHARLES MARSHALL, retired music educator; b. Mendota, Ill., Feb. 15, 1948; s. Floyd D. and Elaine M. Setchell. MusB in Edn., Ill. Wesleyan U., 1970; MusM in Edn., Ill.State U., 1987. Vocal music tchr. Unit 4 Schs., Heyworth, Ill., 1971—80; gen. music specialist Bloomington (Ill.) Pub. Schools, 1980—2004; ret., 2004. Asst. dir. Turnabout Songs, NYC, 1976—. Pvt. U.S. Army, 1970—70, Fort Lewis. Scholar, State of Ill., 1966—70. Mem.: NEA, Ill. Music Educators Assn., Music Educators Nat. Conf., Bloomington Edn. Assn. (bldg. del. 1998—2003), Ill. Edn. Assn., Elks, Mendota Masonic Lodge (life), Bloomington Consistory (life), Pi Kappa Lambda, Phi Mu Alpha (warden 1969—70, advisor 1971—91, advisor emeritus 2002—, Orpheus Award 1984). Republican. Methodist. Avocations: reading, writing, travel, gardening, piano. Home: 210 S Gridley St #2 Bloomington IL 61701 Personal E-mail: csetchel@mindspring.com.

SETHER, DIANE M. research scientist; d. Merle Raymond and Virginia LaVelle Sether; m. Mark Andrew Houston, Dec. 0, 1994. BS, Oreg. State U., Corvallis, OR, 1989; MS, Oreg. State U., 1991; PhD, U. of Hawaii, 2002. Prodn. mgr. Janet Starnes Nursery, Molalla, Oreg., 1979—91; grad. rsch. asst. Oreg. State U., Corvallis, 1989—91; rschr. U. of Hawaii, Honolulu, 1991—. Contbr. articles to profl. jours. Recipient Best Paper in Plant Pathology, U. of Hawa, CTAHR Student Competition, 1998, Oreg. scholar, State of Oreg., 1982, Pa'ani Polo 'O Hawai'i Mahalo Ho'omaika'i, Honolulu Polo Club, 2003; fellow Outstanding Student in Entomology fellow, Jackman Found., Oreg. State U., 1990—91; grantee Rsch. grantee, USDA-CSREES, 1998—2001, Pest Mgmt. Alternatives Rsch. grantee, 2003—. Mem.: Am. Phytopathological Soc., Entomol. Soc. of Am., Hawaiian Entomol. Soc., Hawaii Humane Soc., Humane Soc. of the US, Lyon Arboretum (assoc.), Honolulu Polo Club, Gamma Sigma Delta, Alpha Omicron Pi (various 1983—85). Achievements include patents for Development of monoclonal antibodies for pineapple closteroviruses; research in Etiology of mealybug wilt of pineapple. Avocations: collector of bromeliads, golf. Office: University of Hawaii 3190 Maile Way St John 310 Honolulu HI 96822 Office Phone: 808-956-2830. Personal E-mail: sether@hawaii.edu. E-mail: sether@hawaii.edu.

SETHI, SANDEEP, environmental engineer; b. New Delhi, Jan. 27, 1969; came to U.S., 1991; s. Satish Kumar and Champa (Bhasin) S. BS in Civil Engrng. with honors, Birla Inst. Tech. & Sci., Pilani, India, 1991; MS in Environ. Engrng., Rice U., 1994, PhD in Environ. Engrng., 1997. Registered profl. engr., Calif. Engr. Nat. Informatics Ctr., New Delhi, 1991; rsch. asst. Rice U., Houston, 1991-97; sr. engr. Metcalf & Eddy, Inc., Atlanta, 1997-99; project and rsch. engr. Carollo Engrs., Santa Ana, Calif., 1999—. Chair, invited spkr. membrane technology sessions ASCE 1999 Conf.; lectr. Calif. State U., Long Beach, 2000. Contbr. articles to internat. and profl. jours.; reviewer: Jour. Environ. Engrng., Jour. Am. Water Works Assn. Mem. Water Environment Fedn., Am. Water Works Assn. (invited spkr. 1999 conf.), N.Am. Membrane Soc., Santa Ana River Basin Sect. Calif. Water Environment Assn. (rsch. achievement award com. 1999). Achievements include first to simulate comparison of constant pressure and constant flux modes of operation in ultrafiltration and microfiltration based on detailed mathematical modeling; development of a unified model for performance of membrane filtration processes, incorporating multiple transport mechanisms, which can predict the observed minimum in permeate flux with particle size; a cost model for membrane processes incorporating separate correlations for major system components and a changing economy of scale with the design mix; a computer software package for membrane systems for the U.S. EPA; the optimization of hollow-fiber membrane design, membrane system operation, & single and integrated nanofiltration systems; research in numerical simulation, sensitivity analysis, and optimization of non-linearly constrained systems and application of advanced computational techniques to solve complex research engineering problems. Avocations: music, computer programming, literature, photography, travel.

SETHI, SHYAM SUNDER, management consultant; b. Rawalpindi, Pakistan, July 11, 1942; s. Balraj and Shakuntala (Sawhney) S.; m. Kiran Nair, Oct. 17, 1972; children: Seema, Shana. B.E. in Mech. Engrng., Birla Inst. Tech., Ranchi, India, 1964; MSI.E., U. Wis., 1970. Cert. mgmt. cons. V.p. Drake Sheahan/Stewart Dougall, N.Y.C., 1970-80; pres., ptnr. Distbn. Mgmt. Assocs., Inc., Princeton, N.J., 1980-96; exec. dir. Dechert-Hampe & Co./DMA, Princeton, 1996-2000; pres. Distbn. Mgmt. Assocs., Inc., Princeton, 2001—. Cons. in supply chain, logistics, inventory mgmt., ops. for maj. consumer goods, indsl. and retail cos., Europe, S.Am. and U.S.; spkr. internat. logistics conf. Contbr. articles to profl. jours. Pres. N.J. chpt. Coun. Logistics Mgmt., 1987-88, N.J. chpt. Inst. Mgmt. Consultants, 1987-88. Mem. Yacht Assn. India. Hindu. Avocations: tennis, sailing. Home: 4 Haelig Ct Bridgewater NJ 08807-2377 Office: DMA Inc PO Box 6843 Bridgewater NJ 08807-0843 E-mail: sethinj@optonline.net.

SETHI, VIKRAM, finance educator; PhD, U. Pitts., 1992. Cert. engr., India, 1984. Assoc. prof. S.W. Mo. State U., Springfield, 1992—2000; assoc. prof., doctoral coord. U. Tex., Arlington, 2000—03; prof., chair Wright State U., Dayton, Ohio, 2003—. Author: Organizational Transformation Through Business Process Reengineering, 1998; contbr. articles to prof. jours., confs., chapters to books. Office: Wright State U 3640 Colonel Glenn Hwy Dayton OH 45435 E-mail: vsethi@world.std.com.

SETHNA, BEHERUZ NARIMAN, university president, marketing, management educator; b. Bombay, July 31, 1948; came to U.S., 1973; s. Nariman Dhanjishaw and Mithu Nariman (Mistry) S.; m. Madhavi Kaji, May 25, 1974; children: Anita B., Shaun B. B in Tech. with honors, Indian Inst. Tech., Bombay, 1971; MBA, Indian Inst. Mgmt., Ahmedabad, 1973; MPhil, Columbia U., 1975, PhD in Bus., 1976; student, Ind. U., 1986, Harvard U., 1991. Cert. computing profl. Inst. for Cert. Computing Profls. Engring. and mgmt. trainee various corps., Bombay, 1968-69, 70-72; case writer, trainee Clarion Advt., Bombay, 1973; project mgr., cons. Lever Bros. Co., N.Y.C., 1974-76; prof., chair mktg. and mgmt. info. systems Clarkson U., Potsdam, N.Y., 1976-89, dir. grad. programs, 1978-80; mktg., rsch. and strategic planning mgr. Procter & Gamble (India)/Richardson Hindustan (Vicks), Bombay and Westport, Conn., 1980-81; interim exec. v.p. acad. and student affairs; dean Coll. of Bus., chief acad. officer Lamar (Tex.) U., 1989-94, Gulf States Utilities prof. bus., 1991-94; pres. State U. W. Ga., Carrollton, 1994—; interim sr. vice chancellor Univ. Sys. Ga., 1999—; pres. Ga. Assn. Colls., 2000-2001. Mem. adv. coun. SUNY-Canton (N.Y.) Coll., 1975-89; cons. in field. Author: Research Methods in Marketing, 1984; contbr. articles to profl. jours. Scoutmaster Boy Scouts Am., Potsdam, 1987-89, pack com. chair, den leader, 1987-89, mem. dist. bd., 1991-94, mem. exec. bd. Atlanta Area coun., 1997—, Pres.'s Scout Gold Cord, 1966; leader Girl Scouts U.S., Beaumont, 1989-94. Recipient Instrl. Innovation award Decision Scis. Inst., 1984, 85, 86, 87, 88, 89, Minority Achiever's award Role Model award, 1991, Dean's Leadership award Acad. Bus. Adminstrn., 1993, Nat. Svc. award, 1996, Alumnus award (hon.), 1999, Disting. Alumnus award Indian Inst. Tech., Bombay, 2000, Carroll County Citizen of Yr., 1999, rated first among Carroll County's Movers, Shakers and Newsmakers, 2002; named one of 100 Most Influential Georgians, Ga. Trend, 2003, Resolution of Commendation, State Senate, 2003; Fulbright scholar U.S. Info. Agy., 1986-87; U.S. Dept. Energy grantee, 1980, IBM Corp. grantee, 1984, AT&T grantee, 1985; Paul Harris fellow Rotary Internat., 1997. Mem. Rotary (polio plus edn. chair). Avocations: family, scouting. Home: 107 Windsong Ct Carrollton GA 30117-8978 Office: State U W Ga Office Pres Carrollton GA 30118-0001 E-mail: bsethna@westga.edu.

SETLIFFE, CHARLES DAVID, hospital administrator; b. Aug. 11, 1931; s. David Bert and Willie Mae (Fussell) S.; m. Eva Gertrude Holladay, Nov. 17, 1951; children: Charles Vaden, David Scott, Susan Lynn. BS, U. Chattanooga, 1956; MHA, Washington U., St. Louis, 1965. Sales rep. Chemetron Corp., Chattanooga, 1956—59; hosp. purchasing dir. Meml. Hosp., Chattanooga, 1960-63; asst. adminstr. Ft. Sanders Presbyn. Hosp., Knoxville, Tenn., 1964-67, Sts. Mary and Elizabeth Hosp., Louisville, 1968-81, adminstr., 1975-81; pres., CEO Wilson Meml. Hosp., N.C., 1981-91, pres. emeritus, 1992—; bd. dir. Centura Bank, Wilson, NC. Health care cons., 1992—; cons. United Emergency Svcs., Inc., 1999—; mem. found. bd. dirs. Meml. Healthcare Sys., Inc., Chattanooga, 1996—; chmn. Meml. Healthcare Sys., Chattanooga, 1999—2001; adminstr. Univ. Surg. Assocs., Inc., Chattanooga, 1995; dir. Statewide Health Coord. Coun., Ky., 1982—83, Ky. Health Sys. Agy.-West, Louisville, 1978—81. Bd. dirs. Wilson Concerts, Inc., 1982—85, Wilson ARC, United Way Wilson County, 1982—86, 1988—91; mem. adv. com. Wilson County Tech. Coll.; bd. dirs. Health Edn. Found. Ea. N.C., 1981—91, treas., 1982—91, exec. com., 1985—91, chmn. bldg. study com., 1984—85, N.C. Constituent of Nat. League Nursing, 1986—91, chmn. fin. com., 1987; bd. dirs. Hospice of Wilson, Inc., 1983—91; sec., treas. Hosp. Adminstrs. Ea. N.C., 1983, vice chmn., 1984; bd. dirs. Centura Bank, Wilson, NC, 1989—91; mem. adv. com. Blue Cross-Blue Shield N.C. Sgt. USAF, 1951—55. Recipient Cross Mil. Svc., John W. Dunham chpt. United Daus. Confederacy, 1989; named Ky. Col., 1977. Mem. Ky. Hosp. Assn. (life, bd. dirs. 1976-81), N.C. Hosp. Assn. (life, mem. coun. fin.), Tenn. Hosp. Assn., Westfield Condominiums Assn., Inc. (treas. Signal Mountain, Tenn. 2000-2003), Wilson County C. of C. (bd. dirs. 1984-86, chmn. accreditations com. 1986, health care cost containment com. 1983-91), Am. Legion. Republican. Presbyterian. Avocations: tennis, travel. Home: 35 Oliver Ct Signal Mountain TN 37377-2456 Office: Wilson Medical Ctr Inc 1705 Tarboro St SW Wilson NC 27893-3437

SETLOW, JANE KELLOCK, biophysicist; b. N.Y.C., Dec. 17, 1919; d. Harold A. and Alberta (Thompson) Kellock; m. Richard Setlow, June 6, 1941; children— Peter, Michael, Katherine, Charles. BA, Swarthmore Coll., 1940; PhD in Biophysics, Yale U., 1959. With dept. radiology Yale U., 1959-60; with biology div. Oak Ridge Nat. Lab., 1960-74; biophysicist Brookhaven Nat. Lab., Upton, N.Y., 1974—. Mem. recombinant DNA molecule program adv.

com. NIH, chmn., 1978-80 Author articles; mem. editorial bd. jours. Predoctoral fellow USPHS, 1957-59; postdoctoral fellow, 1960-62 Mem. Biophys. Soc. (pres. 1977-78), Am. Soc. Microbiology. Democrat. Home: 57 Valentine Rd Shoreham NY 11786-1243 Office: Biology Dept Brookhaven Nat Lab Upton NY 11973

SETLOW, NEVA DELIHAS, artist, research biologist; b. New Haven, Dec. 29, 1940; d. Nevins Donald and Eve Mary (Kokojan) Cummings; m. Nicholas Delihas, Aug. 21, 1961 (div. 1986); m. Richard Burton Setlow, Mar. 3, 1989; children: Nicholas Delihas, Marcia Hermus, Cynthia DiGiacomo. BA, Empire State Coll., 1975. Rschr. Brookhaven Nat. Lab., Upton, N.Y., 1976-96. Exhibited in group shows at Guild Hall, East Hampton, 1985—98, 2004, Ward Nasse Gallery, N.Y.C., 1993, Islip Art Mus., 1993, 1996, Planetary Art Soc., Pasadena, Calif., 1997, Salon des Femmes, Southampton, 1997, The Islip (N.Y.) Mus., 1997, Faber Biren Color Award Show, Stamford, Conn., 1997, 2001, Smithtown Arts Coun., 1998, Elaine Benson Gallery, Bridgehampton, N.Y., 1999, Broome St. Gallery, N.Y.C., 1999—2003, Islip Art Mus., 2000, Shelter Rock Art Gallery, Manhasset, N.Y., 2000, Gallery at Edison, Piqua, Ohio, 2001, Huntington Arts Coun., Melville, N.Y., 2001, Grounds for Sculpture, N.J., 2001, Binney and Smith Gallery, Bethlehem, Pa., 2002, East End Arts Coun. (Contact!), Riverhead, N.Y., 2003, Tex. A&M Coll., Station, Tex., 2004, J. Wayne Stark Galleries, Tex., 2004. Recipient Purchase prize, Berkshire Art Assn., Pittsfield, Mass., 1972, 25th Anniversary award, Silvermine Art Guild, New Canaan, Conn., 1972, Sculpture award, Huntington Twp. Art League, 1974, 1976, Painting award, North Shore Art Guild, 1996, Am. Icon - Outer Space award, Nat. Assoc. of Women Artists, 2001, Cleo Hartwig award, 2002, The Gretchen Richardson Meml. award. Mem.: Am. Soc. of Contemporary Artists, Nat. Assoc. of Women Artists, Internat. Scupture Coun. Home and Office: 4 Beachland Ave East Quogue NY 11942-4941 Personal E-mail: setlow@optonline.net.

SETLOW, RICHARD BURTON, biophysicist, researcher; b. N.Y.C., Jan. 19, 1921; s. Charles Meyer and Elsie Setlow; children: Peter, Michael, Katherine, Charles; m. Neva Delihas, Mar. 3, 1989. AB, Swarthmore Coll., 1941; PhD, Yale U., 1947; DSc, U. Toronto, 1985; MD, U. Essen, 1993. Assoc. prof. Yale U., 1956-61; biophysicist Oak Ridge (Tenn.) Nat. Lab., 1961-74, sci. dir. biophysics and cell physiology, 1969-74; dir. U. Tenn.-Oak Ridge Grad. Sch. Biomed. Scis., 1972-74; sr. biophysicist Brookhaven Nat. Lab., Upton, N.Y., 1974—, chmn. biology dept., 1979-87, assoc. dir. life scis., 1985-98, assoc. lab. dir., 1998. Prof. biomed. scis. U. Tenn., 1967-74; adj. prof. biochemistry SUNY, Stony Brook, 1975—. Author: (with E.C. Pollard) Molecular Biophysics, 1962; editor: (with P.C. Hanawalt) Molecular Mechanisms for Repair of DNA, 1975. Recipient Finsen medal Internat. Assn. Photobiology, 1980, Enrico Fermi award U.S. Dept. Energy, 1988, Environ. Mutagen Soc. award, 2002. Mem. NAS, Am. Acad. Arts and Scis., Biophys. Soc. (pres. 1969-70), Internat. Com. Photobiology (pres. 1972-76), Radiation Rsch. Soc., Am. Soc. Photobiology, Am. Soc. Biochemistry and Molecular Biology, Am. Soc. Cancer Rsch., Environ. Mutagen Soc., 11th Internat. Congress on Photobiology (hon. pres. 1992), Phi Beta Kappa. Home: 4 Beachland Ave East Quogue NY 11942-4941 Office: Brookhaven Nat Lab Dept Biology Upton NY 11973 Office Phone: 631-344-3391. Personal E-mail: setlow@optonline.net. Business E-Mail: setlow@bnl.gov.

SETLOW, VALERIE PETIT, health science association director; b. New Orleans, Jan. 24, 1950; d. Alvin Joseph and Lorraine Catherine (Kelly) Petit; m. Loren William Setlow, June 26, 1976; children: Daniel Lawrence, Craig Anthony. BS, Xavier U. La., 1970; PhD, Johns Hopkins U., 1976. Dir. policy USPHS, Washington, 1990-92, dept. dir., 1992, asst. dir. nat. aids policy office, 1992-93; dir. health scis. policy Inst. Medicine Nat. Acad. Scis., Washington, 1993-98; dep. dir. Tulane/Xavier Ctr. Bio-Environ. Rsch., New Orleans, 1998—. Cons. NIH, Fairfax County Schs. Contbr. articles to profl. jours. Mem. AAAS, Am. Soc. Biochemists and Molecular Biologists. Avocations: quilting, gardening. Office: Tulane/Xavier Ctr Bio-Environ Rsch 1430 Tulane Ave # Sl3 New Orleans LA 70112-2699

SETO, WILLIAM RODERICK, public accounting company executive; b. N.Y.C., July 2, 1954; s. James and Dorothy (Tsang) S. BS, U. Pa., 1976; JD, Cornell Law Sch., 1979. Bar: N.Y. 1980; CPA. Ptnr. Ernst & Young, Atlanta; S.E. area dir. internat. tax, 1986—. Mem. bd. advisors Fgn. Sales Corp./Domestic Internat. Sales Corp. Tax Assn., 1994-95; lectr. in field. Mem. editl. bd. Atlanta Internat. Mag., 1992-94. Mem. Leadership Atlanta. Named one of Top Tax Advisors in U.S., Internat. Tax Rev. mag., 1995. Mem. ABA, AICPA, N.Y. Bar Assn., Internat. Fiscal Assn. Office: Ernst & Young 2800 Nations Bank Plz 600 Peachtree St NE Ste 2800 Atlanta GA 30308-2215

SETRAKIAN, BERGE, lawyer; b. Beirut, Apr. 14, 1949; came to U.S. 1976; s. Hemayak and Armine S.; m. Vera L. Nazarian, Nov. 22, 1975; children: Ani, Lara. Diplome d'Etudes de Doctorat, U. Lyons, France, 1973; Diplome d'Etudes de Doctorat Droit Compare, F.I.E.D.C., Strasbourg, France, 1974; Licence en Droit Francais, Licence en Droit Libanais, U. St. Joseph, Beirut, 1972. Bar: Beirut 1972, N.Y. 1983. Assoc. Tyan & Setrakian, Beirut, 1972-76; ptnr. Whitman & Ransom, N.Y.C., 1976-93, Whitman, Breed, Abbott & Morgan, N.Y.C., 1993-2000, Winston & Strawn, N.Y.C., 2000—. Bd. dirs. Cedars Bank, Calif., 1987—, Bank Audi, U.S.A., 1991; fgn. law cons., N.Y., 1978. Pres. Armenian Gen. Benevolent Union, N.Y.C., 2002-; bd. dirs. Armenian Assn. of Am., Washington, 1978-87; bd. dirs. Am. Task Force for Lebanon, 1988—; bd. dirs. Am. U. Armenia, 1992—. Mem. ABA, N.Y. Bar Assn., Beirut Bar Assn., Am. Fgn. Law Assn., Englewood Field Club. Office: Winston & Strawn 200 Park Ave New York NY 10166-0005 E-mail: bsetrakian@winston.com.

SETRIGHT, MILDRED ALBERTA, educator; b. Milw., Apr. 10, 1919; d. Edward Peter and Adelheid M. (Schultz) S. BS, Milw. State Tchrs. Coll., 1941. Tchr. Bd. of Edn., Elcho, Wis., 1941-43, Waukesha, Wis., 1943-44, Appleton, Wis., 1944-45, Milw., 1944-46, 60-87, Downers Grove, Ill., 1947-48, Cath. Bd. of Edn., Milw., 1958-60, Bd. Edn., Milw., 1960-87. Mem. Emily's List, Washington, 1995—; treas. Shorewood Sr. Ctr., Milw., 1988-91, sec. 1992-94, vice chmn. 1995, chmn. 1995-97, governing bd. 1995-97; pres. Christian Women's Assn., 1995-2000; mem. SS Peter and Paul Ch., Milw. Mem. AAUW, Milw. Retired Tchrs. Assn., Wis. Retired Tchrs. Assn., U. Wis.-Milw. Guild for Learning in Ret., Florentine Opera Club, Whitefish Bay Woman's Club, Riverside H.S. Alumni Assn, Milw. (bd. dirs.) Avocations: music, painting, travel, reading, needlecrafts. Home: 2631 N Murray Ave Milwaukee WI 53211-3624

SETSER, CAROLE SUE, retired food science educator; b. Warrenton, Mo., Aug. 26, 1940; d. Wesley August and Mary Elizabeth (Meine) Schulze; m. Donald Wayne Setser, June 2, 1969; children: Bradley Wayne, Kirk Wesley, Brett Donald. BS, U. Mo., 1962; MS, Cornell U., 1964; PhD, Kans. State U., 1971. Grad. asst. Cornell U., Ithaca, N.Y., 1962-64; instr. Kans. State U., Manhattan, 1964-72, asst. prof., 1974-81, assoc. prof., 1981-86, prof., 1986-2001, prof. emeritus, 2001—. Vis. prof. Bogazici U., Istanbul, Turkey, 2000—01. Recipient Rsch. Excellence award Coll. of Human Ecology, Manhattan, 1990. Mem.: Inst. Food Techs. (chmn. sensory evaluation divsn. edn. com. 1989—92, continuing edn. com. 1992—95, sec. product devel. divsn. 1997—99, also other offices), Am. Assn. Cereal Chemists (assoc. editor 1989—93), Kappa Omicron Nu (Excellence for Rsch. award 1987), Sigma Xi, Phi Tau Sigma (Outstanding Food Scientist 1998), Gamma Sigma Delta, Phi Upsilon Omicron, Phi Kappa Phi (Scholar award 1998). Business E-Mail: setser@ksu.edu.

SETTERHOLM, JEFFREY MILES, systems engineer; b. Rochester, N.Y., May 8, 1946; s. Vernon Miles and Grace Lorraine (Bogema) S.; m. Donna Jean Stollenwerk, July 6, 1974; children: Gregory Todd, Vincent Michael. BS in Engring., Applied Sci. cum laude, Yale U., 1968; MS in Sys. Sci. and Math., Washington U., 1976. Electronic engr. McDonnell Douglas Aircraft Divsn., St. Louis, 1974, sr. engr. flight simulation, 1976-78; prin. devel. engr. mil. avionics divsn. Honeywell Inc., Mpls., 1978-84; prin. engr. aerospace divsn. Rosemount, Inc., Burnsville, Minn., 1984-92; ind. software tech. cons. Lakeville, Minn., 1992-94; geodetic scientist Geospan Corp., Mpls., 1994—2003. Author: The Philosophy Works Manual, 1993, The Philosophy Works Manual, 2004. Capt. USAF, 1969-73. Decorated DFC. Mem. AIAA, Soc. Automotive Engrs. Lutheran. Achievements include patents in field; origination of the computer configurable six-axis hand controller concept; invention of surveying from non-coplanar images; research in virtual cockpit concepts. Home: 8095 230th St E Lakeville MN 55044-8287 E-mail: jeff@setterholm.com.

SETTIS, SALVATORE, archaeologist, art historian; b. Rosarno, Italy, June 11, 1941; s. Rocco and Carmela (Megna) Settis; m. Chiara Frugoni, Dec. 9, 1965 (div. 1982); children: Silvano, Andrea, Marta; m. Maria Michela Sassi, Jan. 4, 1984; children: Bruno, Nicola. Degree, U. Pisa, Italy, 1963; PhD, Scuola Normale Superiore, Pisa, 1965. Asst. prof. U. Pisa, 1965—69, lectr., 1969—75, prof., 1976—84, dean Faculty Letters and Philosophy, 1978—81; prof. Scuola Normale Superiore, Pisa, 1984—, dean Faculty Letters and Philosophy, 1986—91, dir., 1999—. Getty Rsch. Inst. for History Art and Humanities, Santa Monica, Calif., 1994—99. Author: La Tempesta Interpretata, 1978, La Colonna Traiana, 1988, I Greci, 5 vols., 1996—2001, Laocoonte Fama e Stile, 1999, Italia SpA L'assalto al patrimonio culturale, 2002, Futuro del "Classico", 2004. Office: Scuola Normale Superiore Piazza dei Cavalieri 7 56125 Pisa Italy Office Phone: +39050509215. E-mail: direttore@sns.it.

SETTLE, MARK, information technology executive; CIO Occidental Petroleum, 1997—99; exec. v.p., systems and processing Visa Internat., 1999—2001; v.p., CIO Arrow Electronics, Inc., Melville, NY, 2001—. Office: Arrow Electronics 3514-B Bush St Melville NY 11747

SETTLER, EUGENE BRIAN, recording industry executive; b. Balt., Apr. 24, 1936; s. Myer Martin and Esther (Levinson) Settler; m. Phyllis Goldfinger, June 10, 1956 (div. Oct. 1975); m. Sharon O'Brasky, May 27, 1976 (div. July 1988); children: Richard Dean, Michael Scott, Robert Marc; m. Margery Shulman, June 1, 1991; children: Gabrielle Shulman, Whitney Shulman. BS in Bus., Loyola Coll., Balt., 1957. V.p. Edge Ltd., Washington, 1954-65; dir. mktg. Epic Records, N.Y.C., 1965-71; exec. v.p. Music West/Music 2, N.Y.C., 1971-73; exec. v.p. mktg. RCA Records, N.Y.C., 1971-73; pres. Rimiro Corp., N.Y.C., 1971-73; exec. v.p. Transcontinental Music Corp., Los Angeles, 1973-76; pres. Request Records, Hollywood, Fla., 1976-82; exec. v.p. Kid Stuff div. IJE, Inc., Plantation, Fla., 1982-87; pres. Internat. Mgmt. and Mktg. Sales Co., 1987-88; pres., COO The Singing Machine Co., Inc., Boca Raton, 1988-96; COO, dir. Golden Entertainment Corp., 1996—. Cons. in field; bd. dirs. LCS Entertainment, Inc., Music W./Music 2, Singing Machine Co., Inc., Parker Highland E. Corp., Monad Records, Inc.; pres. Setco, Inc., Oldies But Goodies, Inc., USA Oldies.com, Music Oldies.com. Music arranger: (films) Raiders of the Lost Ark, 1981; music arranger: albums Hooked on Exercise, 1983. Dir., treas. Ft. Lauderdale Film Festival, 1986—88. Mem.: NARAS, Friars Club, B'nai B'rith, Masons. Home and Office: 4605 S Ocean Blvd Apt 4C Highland Beach FL 33487-5339 Office Phone: 561-272-1985. Personal E-mail: esett@aol.com.

SETTLES, F. STAN, JR., engineering educator, manufacturing executive; b. Denver, Oct. 3, 1938; s. Frank S. and Dorothy Marie (Johnson) S.; m. Evelyn Brown, June 10, 1961; children: Frank S. III, Richard, Charles, Michael. BS in Prodn. Tech., Indsl. Engring., LeTourneau Coll., Longview, Tex., 1962; MS in Indsl. Engring., Ariz. State U., 1967, PhD in Indsl. Engring., 1969. Sr. systems analyst AiResearch Mfg. Co., Phoenix, 1968-70, project mgr., 1970-74, mgr. operational planning, 1974-80; mgr. indsl. engrs. Garrett Pneumatic Systems, Phoenix, 1980-83; mgr. indsl. mfg. engring. Garrett Turbine Engring. Co., Phoenix, 1983-85; v.p. mfg. ops. AiResearch Mfg. Co., Torrance, Calif., 1985-87; dir. indsl. mfg. engring. The Garrett Corp., Phoenix, 1987-88; dir. planning Garrett Engine Div., Phoenix, 1988-92; asst. dir. White House Office of Sci. and Tech. Policy, 1992-93; program dir. NSF, 1992-94; prof., chmn. indsl. and systems engring. dept. U. So. Calif., L.A., 1994—2001, IBM prof. engring. mgmt., 2001—. Faculty assoc. Ariz. State U., Tempe, 1974-85, 90-92, rsch. prof., 1992-94. Mem. sch. bd. Tempe Elem. Sch. Dist., 1976-80; mem. YMCA Indian Guides, nat. chief, 1978-79. Fellow Inst. Indsl. Engrs. (pres. 1987-88, Ops. Rsch. award 1980), Inst. Ops. Rsch. and Mgmt. Sci., Nat. Acad. Engrs., Soc. Mfg. Engrs. (sr.), IEEE Engring. Mgmt. Soc., Am. Soc. Quality Control, Am. Soc. Engring. Edn. Republican. Presbyterian. Home: 1310 E Ocean Blvd Unit 1602 Long Beach CA 90802-6917 Office: U So Calif Dept Indsl Sys Engring Los Angeles CA 90089-0001 Office Phone: 213-740-0263. E-mail: settles@usc.edu.

SETTLES, JEANNE DOBSON, librarian; b. Covington, Tenn., Nov. 21, 1928; d. Garrett Edward and Lula Mai (Birmingham) Dobson; m. Andrew Settles, Dec. 26, 1948; children: Thomas E., Anthony Dobson. BS, Memphis State U., 1966, MEd, 1977. Cert. tchr., Tenn. Libr. Memphis City Schs., 1966-72, 77-91. Mem. Delta Kappa Gamma (treas.). Avocations: painting, writing, sewing, travel.

SETZER, ARLENE J. state representative, retired secondary school educator; b. Dayton, Ohio, Mar. 2, 1944; BS in Bus. Adminstrn., U. Dayton, 1966; MEd, Wright State U., 1973. Tchr. Vandalia-Butler HS, 1967—2000; rep. Ohio State Ho. Reps., Columbus, 2000—. Mem. agr. and natural resources com. Ohio State Ho. Reps., chmn. edn. com., mem. energy and environ. com., mem. ins. com., vice chmn. mcpl. and govt. and urban revitilization com. Mem. ins. rev. com. City of Vandalia, 1998—2000; chair Vandalia-Butler Food Pantry Bldg. Fund; pres. Pres.'s Club of Vandalia, 1997—99; precinct capt. Montgomery County Rep. Party, mem. ctrl. com., exec. com.; mem. Vandalia City Coun., vice-mayor, 1986—88, 1995—2000. Named Rep. Woman of Yr., 1997, 2001, 2003; recipient Clara Weisenborn award, 1999, Horace M. Huffman Jr. Svc. to Bicyclists award, Ohio Bicycle Fedn., Appreciation award, S.W. Ohio Hemophilia Found. and W. Ctrl. Ohio Hemophilia Ctr.; scholar Martha Holden Jennings scholar, 1983—84. Mem.: Sister Cities of Vadalia, Montgomery County Farm Bur., Inc., Montgomery County Cattlemen's Assn., Montgomery Agrl. Soc., Miami Valley Mil. Affairs Assn., Vandalia-Butler (Ohio) Hist. Soc. (v.p. 2000), Rotary (hon.; Dist. 6670 dir. 1992—96, pres. 1994—95, Dist. 6670 scholarship com. 1997, Dist. 6670 bd. dirs., asst. dist. gov. 1998—2000, named to Hall of Fame). Republican. Office: Ohio State Ho of Reps 77 S High St 13th Fl Columbus OH 43215-6111

SETZLER, EDWARD ALLAN, lawyer; b. Kansas City, Mo., Nov. 3, 1933; s. Edward A. and Margaret (Parshall) S.; m. Helga E. Friedemann, May 20, 1972; children: Christina, Ingrid, Kirstin. BA, U. Kans., 1955; JD, U. Wis., 1962. Bar: Mo. 1962, U.S. Tax Ct. 1962. Assoc. Spencer, Fane, Britt & Browne, Kansas City, 1962-67, ptnr., 1968-2000, mng. ptnr., 1974-77, 78-82, chmn. trust and estate sect., 1974-2000; ptnr. Husch & Eppenberger, LLC, 2000—. Co-author: Missouri Estate Administration, 1984, supplements, 1987—2004; contbg. editor: Understanding Living Trusts, 1990—2004; co-author: Missouri Estate Planning, 1986; co-author Missouri Estate Planning, supplements, 1988—2004; contbg. editor: A Will is Not the Way--The Living Trust Alternative, 1988; bd. editors: Wis. Law Rev., 1961—62. Amb., bd. govs., bd. dirs., chmn. found. com. Am. Royal, 1982—; mem. planning giving com. Nelson Atkins Mus. Art, 1984—95; mem. deferred giving com. Children's Mercy Hosp., 1991—; mem. Kansas City Estate Planning Symposium Com., 1984—92, chmn., 1991; mem. adv. com. Greater Kansas City Cmty. Found., 2000—; trustee Zoo Learning Fund, 2002—; mem. adv. bd. Children's Svc. League, 2003—. Fellow: Am. Coll. Trust and Estate Counsel (state chmn. 1992—97, mem. state membership com. 1986—2001); mem.: Assn. Conflict Resolutions, Estate Planning Soc. Kansas City (co-founder 1965, pres. 1983—84, dir. 1984—85, mem. social com. 1968—), Kansas City Met. Bar Assn. (lectr., chmn. probate and trust 1979, 1992, vice chmn. 1983—85, 1991, legis. rev. com. 1991—95), Mo. Bar Assn. (lectr., vice chmn. probate and estate planning com. 1994—97), Sigma Xi, Order of the Coif, Phi Delta Phi. Office: 1200 Main St Ste 1700 Kansas City MO 64105-2100 Fax: 816-421-0596. Office Phone: 816-283-4684. E-mail: edward.setzler@husch.com.

SETZLER, WILLIAM EDWARD, chemical company executive; b. Bklyn., Dec. 20, 1926; s. William Edward and Gertrude A. (Seyer) S.; m. Dorothy C. Kress, Dec. 2, 1950 (dec. Mar. 1987); children: William John, Heather A.; m. Lenore Kelly, July 13, 1991. B of Chem. Engring., Cooper Union, 1950; MS in Liberal Studies, Columbia U., 1993. V.p. ops. Argus Chem. Corp., N.Y.C., 1950-66; v.p. engring., then group v.p. Witco Chem. Corp. (now Crompton Corp.), N.Y.C., 1966-75, exec. v.p., 1975-90, ret., 1990, also bd. dirs.; chmn. and CEO Faimount Chem. Inc., 1993-97. Author and patentee in field. Served with USAAF, 1945-46. Mem. Am. Inst. Chem. Engrs., Soap and Detergent Assn. (bd. dirs.), The Dorothy Setzler Fund (pres. 1991—). Home: 3921 Lincoln St Seaford NY 11783-2115 E-mail: billchair@att.net.

SEUNG, THOMAS KAEHAO, philosophy educator; b. Jungju, Korea, Sept. 20, 1930; m. Kwihwan Hahn, May 29, 1965; children: Hyunjune Sebastian, Kwonjune Justin, Haesue Florence. BA, Yale U., 1958, MA, 1961, PhD, 1965. Instr. Yale U., 1963-65; asst. prof. Fordham U., 1965-66; mem. faculty dept. philosophy U. Tex., Austin, 1966—, prof. in philosophy, 1972—, prof. in govt., 1985—, prof. in law, 1993—, Jesse H. Jones prof. liberal arts, 1987—. Author: The Fragile Leaves of the Sybil, 1962, Kant's Transcendental Logic, 1969, Cultural Thematics, 1976, Structuralism and Hermeneutics, 1982, Semiotics and Thematics, 1982, Intuition and Construction, 1993, Kant's Platonic Revolution, 1994, Plato Rediscovered, 1996. Served as officer Korean Army, 1950-53. Recipient Wilbur Lucius Cross medal Yale Grad. Sch. Alumni Assn., 1988; Soc. Religion in Higher Edn. fellow, 1969-70; Am. Council Learned Soc. fellow, 1970-71; NEH fellow, 1977-78 Office: U Tex Dept Philosophy Austin TX 78712 Mailing: PO Box 28055 Austin TX 78755 Office Phone: 512-471-6808. E-mail: t.k.seung@mail.utexas.edu.

SEURKAMP, MARY PAT, college president; b. Pitts., Sept. 6, 1946; d. Frank H. and Loretta (Husic) Reuwer; m. Robert W. Seurkamp, Aug. 6, 1983; children: Kris, Robert, Brooke. BA, Webster U., 1968; MA, Washington U., 1969; PhD, SUNY, Buffalo. Counselor to dir. student living Gannon U., Erie, Pa., 1969-76; assoc. v.p. St. John Fisher Coll., Rochester, N.Y., 1976-92, adj. asst. prof. dept. psychology, 1992—, acting v.p. academic affairs, dean, 1992-98; pres. Coll. of Notre Dame of Md., Balt., 1998—. Mem. planning team Monroe County Ednl. Outcomes Conf.; bd. dirs. Bishop Kennedy High Sch.; cons. Women's Career Ctr., Rochester, N.Y., 1987—. Com. mem. various parish coms., Pittsford, N.Y., 1983—, Diocesan Com. Devel. of Mins. and Employees, Rochester, 1986-89, Internat. Alliance Leadership Conf., 1991; mentor Career Beginnings Program; vol. Career Connections Mentoring Program, 1988-90. Mem. AAUP, Am. Assn. High Edn., Nat. U. Continuing Edn. Assn., Rochester Women's Network. Republican. Roman Catholic. Home: 5502 Lombardy Pl Baltimore MD 21210-1420 Office: Coll Notre Dame Md 4701 N Charles St Baltimore MD 21210-2404

SEVART, DANIEL JOSEPH, lawyer; b. Oswego, Kans., June 25, 1944; s. Vernon Joseph and Alma Bridget (Carland) S.; m. Shoko Kato, Apr. 17, 1968; 1 child, Eric J. AA, Parsons Jr. Coll., 1964; BA, Washburn U., 1973, JD with honors, 1975. Bar: Kans. 1976, U.S. Dist. Ct. Kans. 1976, U.S. Ct. Appeals (10th cir.) 1976. Assoc. Render & Kamas, Wichita, Kans., 1976-78, ptnr., 1978-82, Schartz & Sevart, Wichita, 1982-83, Sevart & Sevart, Wichita, 1983—. Bd. dirs. Wichita Symphony Soc., Inc., 1989—. Served to staff sgt. USAF, 1965-72. Mem. Assn. Trial Lawyers Am., Kans. Bar Assn. (bd. govs. 1995-98, 2000-01, sec.-treas. 1998-99, v.p. 2001-02, pres.-elect 2002-03, Kans. Trial Lawyers Assn. (bd. govs. 1989—), Wichita Bar Assn. (bd. govs. 1988-90, sec.-treas. 1990-91, v.p. 1991-92, pres.-elect 1992-93, pres. 1993-94), Wichita C. of C. Democrat. Roman Catholic. Avocations: classical music, gardening, fishing, camping, travel. Office: Sevart & Sevart 100 S Main St Ste 400 Wichita KS 67202-3208 also: 1900 L St NW Ste 500 Washington DC 20036-5031

SEVCENKO, IHOR, history and literature educator; b. Radosc, Poland, Feb. 10, 1922; came to U.S., 1949, naturalized, 1957; s. Ivan and Maria (Cherniatynska) S.; m. Oksana Draj-Xmara, Apr., 1945 (div. 1953); m. Margaret M. Bentley, July 16, 1953 (div. 1966); m. Nancy Patterson, June 18, 1966 (div. 1995); children: Catherine, Elisabeth. Dr.Phil., Charles U., Prague, Czechoslovakia, 1945; Doct. en Phil. et Lettres, U. Louvain, Belgium, 1949; PhD (hon.), U. Cologne, Germany, 1994; D in Hist. Scis. (hon.), U. Warsaw, Poland, 2001. Fellow in Byzantinology Dumbarton Oaks, 1949-50, dir. studies, 1966, prof. Byzantine history and lit., 1965-75, sr. research assoc., 1975—; lectr. Byzantine and ancient history U. Calif., Berkeley, 1950-51; fellow Byzantinology and Slavic lit., research program USSR, 1951-52; instr., then asst. prof. Slavic langs. and lit. U. Mich., 1953-57; mem. faculty Columbia U., 1957-72, prof., 1962-65, adj. prof., 1965-72; vis. prof. Harvard U., 1973-74, prof., 1974-92, emeritus, 1992. Vis. fellow All Souls Coll., Oxford U., 1979—80, Wolfson Coll., Oxford U., 1987, 93, Onasis Found., Athens, 2002; vis. mem. Princeton Inst. for Advanced Study, 1956; vis. prof. Munich U., 1969, Coll. de France, 1985, Cologne U., 1992, 96, Ctrl. European U., Budapest, 1995, Budapest, 97; treas., acting treas., bd. dirs. Am. Rsch. Inst. in Turkey, 1964—66, 1967, 1975—; assoc. dir. Harvard Ukrainian Rsch. Inst., 1973—89, acting dir., 1977, 1985—86; chmn. Nat. Com. Byzantine Studies, 1966—77; mem. Internat. Com. for Greek Paleography, 1983—; guest of the rector Collegium Budapest, 1998. Author: Etudes sur la polémique entre Théodore Métochite et Nicéphore Choumnos, 1962, Society and Intellectual Life in Late Byzantium, 1981, Ideology, Letters and Culture in the Byzantine World, 1982, Byzantium and the Slavs in Letters and Culture, 1991, Ukraine Between East and West, 1996; co-author: Der Serbische Psalter, 1978, Life of St. Nicholas of Sion, 1984; contbr. articles to profl. jours. Recipient Hrusevs'kyj medal, Sci. Ševcenko Soc., 1996, Antonovych Lit. prize, Kiev, 2000; Guggenheim fellow, 1963, Humboldt-Forschungspreistraeger, 1985. Fellow Medieval Acad. Am., Brit. Acad. (corr.); mem. Am. Philos. Soc., Am. Acad. Arts and Scis., Ukrainian Acad. Arts and Scis. (hon. pres. 2003-), Sci. Sevcenko Soc., Société des Bollandistes Belgium (adj.), Accademia di Palermo (fgn.), Accademia Nazionale dei Lincei (fgn.), Internat. Assn. Byzantine Studies (v.p. 1976-86, pres. 1986-96, hon. pres. 1996—), Christian Archeological Soc. of Athens (hon.), Austrian Acad. Sci. (corr.), Accademia Pontaniana of Naples (fgn.), Nat. Acad. of Sci. Ukraine (fgn.), Acad. Humanities Rsch. (Moscow), Accademia Nazionale Dei Lincei, Cosmos Club (Washington), Harvard Club (N.Y.C.), Phi Beta Kappa (hon.). Office: Harvard Univ 204 Boylston Hall Cambridge MA 02138 Office Phone: 617-495-4027.

SEVER, JOHN LOUIS, medical researcher, educator; b. Chgo., Apr. 11, 1932; s. John Louis and Harriet (Link) Sever; m. Gerane Werle, Mar. 3, 1956; children: Kimberly, Beverly, Valerie. BA, U. Chgo., 1952; BS, MD, MS, PhD, Northwestern U., 1957. Head sect. infectious diseases NINDS, NIH, Bethesda, Md., 1960—71, chief infectious diseases, 1971—88; chmn. pediat. Children's Nat. Med. Ctr., Washington, 1988—90, prof. pediat., ob-gyn., immunology, microbiology and tropical medicine, 1988—. Cons. Rotary Internat., Evanston, Ill., 1964—, NIH, Bethesda, 1988—, WHO, Geneva, 1991—. Editor: 11 med. books; contbr. more than 600 articles to profl. jours. Capt. USPHS, 1960—88. Recipient Kimbel award, Am. Soc. for Microbiology, 1979, Wellcome Diagnostics award, Pan Am. Med. Virology, 1989, Meritorious Alumni award, Northwestern U., 1989, Pasteur award, Microbiology Soc., 1987, Abbott award, 1996, Soc. for Biomolecular Screening award, 2001. Mem.: Pan Am. Soc. Rapid Viral Diagnosis (pres. 1995—96), Assn. Med. Lab. Immunologists (pres. 1994—95, Erwin Niter award 1997), Teratology Soc. (pres. 1976—77), Assn. Med. Clin. and Lab. Immunologists (pres. 1992—94), Infectious Disease Soc. of Ob-gyn. (pres. 1994—96, Ortho-McNeill award 1998), Country Glen Club, Potomac Rotary Club. Avocation: gardening.

SEVERDIA, ANTHONY GEORGE, chemistry researcher; b. Sharon, Pa., Sept. 20, 1946; s. George Anthony and Angela Mary (Tomich) S. BS, Pa. State U., 1968; MS, Case Western Reserve U., 1971, PhD, 1974. Rsch., teaching assoc. Rensselaer Poly. Inst., Troy, N.Y., 1975-77; chemist N.Y. U., 1977-79, 82-83, Columbia U., N.Y.C., 1979-82; analytical chemist Mallinckrodt Group, Terre Haute, Ind., 1983-92; sr. chemist analytical sci. Sanofi-Synthelabo Rsch., Gt. Valley, Pa., 1992—. Presenter in field. Contbr. articles to profl. jours. Summer fellow NSF, Cleve., 1971. Mem. Am. Chem. Soc. (exec. com., treas. Terre Haute sect. 1991-92), Soc. Applied Spectroscopy, The Internat. Soc. for Optical Engring. Home: 301 Pritchard Ln Wallingford PA 19086-6104 Office Phone: 610-889-6103. Personal E-mail: aseverdia@comcast.net.

SEVERIN, BLAINE FRANK, environmental engineer; b. Bay City, Mich., Oct. 24, 1952; BS in Biology with honors, U. Ill., 1974, MS in Environ. Engring., 1975, PhD in Environ. Engring., 1982. Registered profl. engr., Mich., Tenn. Rsch. asst. U. Ill., 1974-75, 75-76, 1979-82; rsch. engr. environ. equipment divsn., project leader FMC Corp., Itasca, Ill., 1976 79; sr. environ. engr. water and waste treatment devel. Tenn. Eastman Co., Kingsport, 1982-86, oper. divsn. rep., sr. process engr., 1986-88, sr. environ. engr., process mgr., 1988-90; sr. engr. Mich. Biotech. Inst., Lansing, 1990-94, dir. environ. techs., 1994—. Vis. assoc. prof. dept. civil and environ. engring. Mich. State U., 1991; presenter in field. Contbr. articles to profl. jours.; patentee in field. Recipient Acad. Excellence award Ctrl. States Water Pollution Control Assn., 1982, Water Environ. Fedn. Willem Rudolfs medal, 1986. Mem. Water Envrion. Fedn., Sigma Xi. Office: Mich Biotech Inst 3900 Collins Rd Lansing MI 48910-8543

SEVERIN-HANSEN, JEANNE ANNE, poet; b. Delhi, NY, Aug. 29, 1948; d. Frank Rivers and Rosellen MacGowan; married; 1 child, Margaret Eun Sil. AA, Suffolk C.C., Selden, N.Y., 1975; BA, SUNY Empire State, Old Westbury, 1994. Adminstrv. asst. to pres. Go-Lo Resources, 1995—99; customer svc. asst. State Farm Ins., Melville, NY, 2000—02; freelance writer. Editor (monthly column): Threshold, Open Door Soc., 1985—87; author: numerous poems. Mem.: Hunting Sch. Ballet Guild. E-mail: nseverinhansen@netscape.net.

SEVERINI, THOMAS ALAN, statistician and educator; b. Butler, Pa., Aug. 15, 1959; s. Carl Thomas and Rose (Morozowich) Severini; m. Karla Jean Engel, Aug. 11, 1988; children: Katherine, Anthony, Joseph, Elisabeth. BS, Pa. State U., 1981; MS, U. Mich., 1982; PhD, U. Chgo., 1987. Reliability engr. IBM, Rochester, Minn., 1982—83; asst. prof. statistics U. Wis., Madison, 1987—89; cons. Arthur D. Little, Washington, 1989—90; asst. prof. statistics Northwestern U., Evanston, Ill., 1990—94, assoc. prof., 1994—2000, prof., 2000—. Dept. chair Northwestern U., Evanston, 2001—; cons. in field. Author: (book) Likelihood Methods in Statistics, 2000; contbr. articles to profl. jours. Mem.: Inst. Math. Statistics, Am. Statis. Assn., Phi Beta Kappa. Office: Northwestern Univ 2006 Sheridan Rd Evanston IL 60208-0852 Office Phone: 847-467-1254. Business E-Mail: severini@northwestern.edu.

SEVERINO, ROBERTO, foreign language educator, academic administration executive; b. Catania, Italy, July 19, 1940; s. Giuseppe and Alba (Scroppo) S. Student, State U. Catania, Italy, 1960-62; BA, Columbia Union Coll., 1967; MA, U. Ill., 1969, PhD, 1973. Head acct., pers. dir. Industria Nazionale Apparecchiature Scientifiche, Milan, 1961-63; teaching asst., lang. lab. supv. Columbia Union Coll., Takoma Park, Md., 1965-67; grad. teaching asst. U. Ill., Urbana, 1967-70, coord. Corr. Sch., 1970-71; instr. dept. French and Italian U. Mass., Amherst, 1971-73; prof. dept. Italian Georgetown U., Washington, 1973—, acting chmn., 1987, chmn. dept., 1988—; pres., co-founder Nat. Inst. Contemporary Italian Studies, 1986—; co-founder Associazione Internazionale del Diritto e dell'Arte, 1994—; pres. emeritus Am. U. of Rome, 1990-93, chair. Lit. dir. Georgetown U. Elec. Text Repository, Italian Archive, 1988-91, Ultramarina, 1992-96; mem. adv. bd. Nat. Italian Am. Found. Nat. Christopher Columbus 1992 Celebration; mem. U.S. delegation to 1st Conf. on Italian lang. and culture in U.S., 1987; lectr., speaker in field; founder Georgetown Poetry Series; pres. Coun. Promotion of Italian Lang. in Am. Schs., 1999—; hon. pres. U.S. Assn. Internat. Antonietta Labisi, 2000—. Author: Le soluzioni immaginarie, 1985, The Signs and Sounds of Italian, 1985, A carte scoperte, 1990, Presente imperfetto ed altri tempi, 1992, The Battle for Humanism, 1994, A Dumas: Mariano Stabile Sindaco di Palermo, 1994; co-author: Periscopio, 1986, International Nuclear Agreements Multilingual Glossary, 1988, United Nations Organization Multilingual Glossary, 1988, Regularizing the Irregular Italian Verb, 1990, Preserving and Promoting Italian language and Culture in North America, 1997, Napoleon: One Image, Ten Mirrors, 2002; translator: The Next 6000 Days by Saverio Avveduto, 1987; editor: (serials) Segni, 1985-88, Hispano-Italic Studies, 1976, 79; mem. editorial bd. Educazione Comparata, 1993—; contbr. articles to profl. jours.; translator: Angelo Scandurra: The Hot-Tempered Musician and Other Poems, 1996, M. Rotelli's E. Sanguineti, If, For Me, You Write a Poem, 1999, Francesco Battiato: Amnesia of the Blue, 2000; editor: Giuseppe Severino: Ricordi di Castelnuovo primi '900. Scene di vita paesana, 1992; co-founder, U.S. editor: Colophon, An Internat. Jour. Arts and Letters, 1997—. Trustee Joel Nafuma Refugee Ctr., Rome, 1993—; chmn. Strega Lit. Prize, Washington D.C. Jury, 1997-2001; mem. jury Prima Parete in Concerto, Lion's Internat. Art Prize, Catania, 1998—, Spoleto Poetry Prize, 1999—. Rsch. grantee Interuniversity Ctr. European Studies, 1977; recipient Accademia Internazionale di Lettere, Scienze, Arti medal, 1983, Internat. Poetry prize, 1986, Gold Cross Cavaliere dell'Ordine al Merito della Repubblica Italiana, 1983, Gold medal Italian Ministries of Univs. and Sci. Rsch., 1988, Marranzano d'Argento prize, 1989, Gold Commander class Cross al Merito della Repubblica Italiana, 1990, Georgetown U. Vicennial Disting. Svc. medal, 1994, Telamone prize, 1995, Top Sprint: Siciliani nel Mondo award, 2000. Mem. MLA, So. Atlantic Modern Lang. Assn., Nat. Assn. Secondary Sch. Prins. (mem. sch. partnerships internat. Italian adv. coun. 1988—), Italian Am. Cultural Found., Italian Cultural Soc. (pres. 1979-81, 83-85, Outstanding Svc. award 1983, chmn. acad. policy com. 1981—), Assn. Internationale Critiques Literaires and Associazione Italiana Critici Letterari, Greater Washington Assn. Tchrs. Fgn. Langs. (mem. award selection com. 1983-85), Manuscript Soc., Renaissance Soc. Am., Circolo Culturale Italiano (hon.), Am. Club (Rome), Touring Club Italiano (hon.), Gamma Kappa Alpha (v.p. 1990—, sec.-treas. and chpt. advisor 1985-90), World Jurist Assn. Ctr. Assocs. (U.S. pres. 1993—, chmn. program devel. and fin. com. 2000—), Associazione Internazionale del Diritto e dell'Arte (v.p. 1994—), Nat. Italian Am. Found. Coun. of 1,000, Napoleonic Soc. Am., Soc. di Studi Valdesi, Istituto Internazionale di Epistemologia la Magna Grecia, Unione Nazionale per la lotta contro l'Analfabetismo, Sons of Italy. Home: 4949 Quebec St NW Washington DC 20016-3230 Office: Georgetown U Dept Italian 37th And O Sts NW ICC 307 Washington DC 20057-0001 E-mail: Severiro@gunet.georgetown.edu.

SEVERINSEN, DOC (CARL H. SEVERINSEN), conductor, musician; b. Arlington, Oreg., July 7, 1927; m. Emily Marshall; children: Nancy, Judy, Cindy, Robin, Allen. Ptnr. Severinsen-Akwright Co.; pops condr. The Phoenix (Ariz.) Symphony Orchestra; prin. pops condr. Minn. Orch., 1993. Address: Minn Orch 1111 Nicollet Mall Minneapolis MN 55403-2406 also: c/o William Morris Agency 151 S El Camino Dr Beverly Hills CA 90212-2704 also: c/o The Phoenix Symphony Orch 455 N 3rd St Ste 390 Phoenix AZ 85004-3942

SEVERO, RICHARD, writer; b. Newburgh, N.Y., Nov. 22, 1932; s. Thomas and Mary Theresa (Farina) S.; m. Emöke Edith de Papp, Apr. 7, 1961. BA, Colgate U., 1954; postgrad., NYU Inst. Fine Arts, 1955-56, Columbia U. Sch. Architecture and Urban Planning, 1964-65. News asst. CBS, N.Y.C., 1954-55; reporter Poughkeepsie (N.Y.) New Yorker, 1956-57, A.P., Newark, 1957-61, N.Y. Herald Tribune, 1961-63; writer TV news CBS, N.Y.C., 1963-66; reporter Washington Post, 1966—68; reporter, fgn. correspondent, feature writer, feature obituarist, sci. and environ. reporter N.Y. Times, N.Y.C., 1968—. Assoc. Seminar on the City, Columbia U., 1966-69; vis. lectr. Am. culture Vassar Coll., 1985-99; bd. dirs. Hudson Valley Philharm., 1998-99, Colgate U. Alumni Corp., 1988-92. Author: Lisa H., 1985; (with Lewis Milford) The Wages of War, 1989 (Am. Legion Nat. Comdr.'s award 1990); contbr. articles to mags. Established Thomas and Mary Severo Scholarship funds for majors in music and Italian Vassar Coll., 2002. Poynter fellow-in-residence Vassar Coll., 1974-75; CBS News fellow, 1964-65; Recipient Front Page award Washington-Balt. Newspaper Guild, 1967; Journalistic award H.A.V.E.N., 1969; Schaeffer Gold Typewriter award N.Y. Newspaper Reporters Assn., 1969; Page One award Newspaper Guild of N.Y., 1970; hon. mention Mike Berger award Columbia U., 1970; Leone di San Marco award Italian Heritage and Culture Com., 1982; George Polk Meml. award L.I. U. Sch. Journalism, 1975; Hudson River Fisherman's Assn. award, 1976; Mike Berger award Columbia U., 1976; James Wright Brown award Deadline Club, Sigma Delta Chi, N.Y.C., 1976; Feature award N.Y. Press Club, 1977; Page One award Newspaper Guild N.Y., 1977, 82; Media award Am. Cancer Soc., 1977; hon. mention Heywood Broun Meml. award Am. Newspaper Guild, 1977; Penney-Mo. Newspaper award U. Mo. Sch. Journalism, 1978; Media award Agt. Orange Victims Internat., 1982; Page One award N.Y. Newspaper Guild, 1982; Gift of Life award N.Y. Blood Ctr., 1991, Spl. Writing award Soc. of the Silurians, 1992. Home: 83 Balmville Rd Newburgh NY 12550-1917 Office Phone: 212-556-1659. E-mail: severo@nytimes.com.

SEVERS, CHARLES A., III, lawyer; b. N.Y.C., Sept. 16, 1942; s. Charles A. and Gertrude (O'Neill) S.; m. Regina Ferrone, Sept. 4, 1965; children: Charles A. IV, Cornelius Forsythe, Rudyard Pierrepont, Olivia Consuelo Poor. BA, Georgetown U., 1964, JD, 1967. Bar: N.Y. 1968, D.C. 1985. Ptnr. Dewey Ballantine, N.Y.C., 1967-96; gen. counsel, exec. v.p. Nat. Madison Group, N.Y.C., 1996-97. Lectr. various continuing legal edn. programs. Contbr. articles to profl. jours. Dir., trustee various orgns. Fellow Am. Coll. Trust and Estate Counsel; mem. ABA, N.Y. State Bar Assn., Assn. of Bar of City of N.Y., D.C. Bar Assn., Union Club. Address: High Meadow Old Chatham NY 12136

SEVERS, WALTER BRUCE, pharmacology educator, researcher; b. Pitts., June 10, 1938; s. Walter Bruce and Pauline Marie (Sever) S.; m. Anne Elizabeth Daniels, Apr. 25, 1970; children: Mary, Jane, Steven, William, Katherine. BS, U. Pitts., 1960, MS, 1963, PhD, 1965. Postdoctoral fellow NIH, Bethesda, Md., 1966-68; asst. prof. pharmacology Coll. Medicine, Pa. State U., Hershey, 1968-71, assoc. prof., 1971-77, prof., 1977-99, prof. emeritus, 1999—. Cons. pharmacology/toxicology, 1999—; v.p. for sci. affairs Ednl. Horizons, Inc., Lemoyne, Pa., 1998—; ad hoc grant cons. NIH, U.S. Army, NSF. Mem. editl. Bd. Am. Jour. Physiology, 1978-98; assoc. editor Pharmacology, 1998-2000; contbr. numerous articles, chpts., revs. to profl. publs. Recipient Disting. Alumnus award U. Pitts., 1978, I.M. Setchenov medal Acad. Med. Sci. USSR, 1983, Blue medal for sci. Acad. Med. Sci., Bulgaria, medal for sci. U. Belgrade; NASA grantee, 1976-98. Fellow Am. Coll. Clin. Pharmacology; mem. Am. Physiol. Soc., Am. Soc. Pharmacology and Exptl. Therapeutics, Soc. for Neurosci., Soc. for Exptl. Biology and Medicine, Sigma Xi (pres. Pa. State U. chpt. 1981-82), Kiwanis (pres. Hershey area 1980, bd. dirs.). Republican. Roman Catholic. Avocations: reading, camping, hiking. Home: 1011 Grubb Rd Palmyra PA 17078-3510 Office: Pa State U Coll Medicine Dept Pharm Mail Code H78 500 University Dr Hershey PA 17033-2360 Business E-Mail: wbs2@psu.edu.

SEVERS, WILLIAM FLOYD, actor; b. Britton, Okla., Jan. 8, 1932; s. Harry Lysander Fletcher and Katherine Lucinda (McAuliffe) S.; m. Mary Anne Proctor, Jan. 18, 1964 (div. 1971); 1 child, Pilar; m. Barbara Alice Schonger, Sept. 9, 1978; children: Katherine Meghan, Erin Christine. AA, Pasadena Playhouse Coll., 1956. Appeared on Broadway in Cut of the Axe, 1959-60, The Moon Is Blue, 1962, On Borrowed Time, 1991-92, nat. tour Look Homeward, Angel, 1960; co-star nat. tour Spoon River, 1964; actor Secret Storm, All My Children, One Life to Live, Guiding Light, Texas, Search for Tomorrow, Another World, Loving, 1963-93; other TV appearances include Armstrong Circle Theatre, 1963, The Defenders, 1964, World War II, A GI Diary, 1978, Nurse, 1980, Muggable Mary, 1986, Law and Order, recurring role as Hon. Henry Fillmore, 1990-99, Hallmark Hall of Fame, Grace and Glorie, 1998, Law and Order: Criminal Intent, 2000; appeared in films including Funny Farm, 1988, Regarding Henry, 1991, Meet the Parents, 2000, Revolution #9, 2000, 13 Conversations About 1 Thing, 2001; actor European tour West Side Story, 1990-91, 94, Asian tour West Side Story, 1999; actor, voice artist numerous commls., 1964—. Staff sgt. USAF, 1946-53. Mem. SAG, AFTRA, Actors Equity Assn., Pasadena Playhouse Alumni Assn. Democrat. Avocations: reading, golf. Home: 10 Waterside Plz Apt 6F New York NY 10010-2610 Office: Michael Hartig Agency Ltd 156 5th Ave New York NY 10010-7002 E-mail: wfsevers@rcn.com.

SEVERSON, ROGER ALLAN, bank executive; b. Thief River Falls, Minn., Sept. 2, 1932; s. Alfred Gerhard and Esther Olga (Landro) S.; m. Beverly Diane Hays, Aug. 30, 1953; children: Eric Hays, Holle Diane. BS, U. Minn., 1954. Group v.p. First Nat. Bank, Mpls., 1952-73; pres. FBS Fin., Inc., Mpls., 1974-77; exec. v.p. F&M Savs. Bank, Mpls., 1977-82; sr. v.p. First Nat. Bank, St. Paul, 1983-85; exec. v.p. Shelard Nat. Bank, Mpls., 1985-86, TCF Bank Savs., Mpls., 1986-92; ret., 1992. Mem. Robert Morris Assocs., 1980-92; trustee Heitman Mortgage Investors, Chgo., 1970-71, Mass. Mut. Mortgage Realty Investors, Springfield, 1972-85. Vice chmn. bd. of trustees The Am. Luth. Ch. Synod, Mpls., 1976-81; trustee Children's Health Ctr., Mpls., 1971-72; bd. dirs. Goodwill Industries, Mpls., 1967-70. Fellow Versterheim Mus.; mem. Ethics in Pub. Policy Ctr., Ctr. for Am. Experiment. Home: 8321 Essex Rd Chanhassen MN 55317-8705

SEVERSON, SALLY, meteorologist; married; 2 children. Student, No. Ill. U., U. Wis., Milw.; BS in Meteorology, Miss. State U. Meteorologist WISN, Milw., 1986—. Vol. Children's Hosp. of Wis. Avocations: hiking, bicycling, astronomy, boating. Office: WISN PO Box 402 Milwaukee WI 53201

SEVIK, MAURICE, acoustical engineer, researcher; b. Istanbul, Turkey, Mar. 19, 1923; s. Benjamin and Esther (Barzilai) S.; m. Jacqueline Delannoy, June 2, 1953; children: Michele, Martine. DIC, Imperial Coll. Sci. Tech., London, 1946; PhD, Pa. State U., 1963. Registered profl. engr., Ont. With Bristol Aircraft Corp., U.K., 1946-51; sr. structures engr. Avro Aircraft Ltd., Can., 1952-59; prof. aerospace engring., dir. Garfield Thomas Water Tunnel, Pa. State U., University Park, 1959-72; mem. assoc. tech. dir. ship signatures directorate David Taylor Rsch. Ctr., Bethesda, Md., 1972-96, sr. rsch. scientist, 1996-99; ret., 1999. Vis. prof. Cambridge (Eng.) U., 1970; cons. USAF Office Sci. Rsch. 1965; cons. applied physics lab. U. Wash., Seattle, 1999—. Contbr. articles to profl. jours. Overseas fellow Churchill Coll., Cambridge U., 1970; recipient Gold Medal award The Am. Soc. of Naval Engrs., 1990, Disting. Alumni award Central Pa. chpt. Acoustical Soc. of Am., Charles B. Martell Tech. Excellence award Nat. Security Indsl. Assn., 1992, Robert Dexter Conrad award Office Naval Rsch., 1996, French decoration Ordre Nat du Mérite, 1997; Dr. M. M. Sevik Acoustic Data Analysis Ctr. Bldg. named in his honor. Fellow ASME (Rayleigh lectr. 1995, Per Bruel Gold medal for noise control and acoustics 1996), Acoustical Soc. Am., Sigma Xi; mem. Nat. Acad. Engring. Home: 2 Spruce Ct Hilton Head Island SC 29928 Office: David Taylor Model Basin 9500 Macarthur Blvd West Bethesda MD 20817-5700 Personal E-mail: msevik@aol.com.

SEVILLA, STANLEY, lawyer; b. Cin., Apr. 3, 1920; s. Isadore and Dienna (Levy) S.; m. Lois A. Howell, July 25, 1948; children: Stanley, Susan, Donald, Carol, Elizabeth. BA in Econs. with high honors, U. Cin., 1942; JD, Harvard U., 1948. Bar: Calif. 1949. Since practiced in, Los Angeles; assoc. Williamson, Hoge & Curry, 1948-50; mem. firm Axelrod, Sevilla and Ross, 1950-75, Stanley Sevilla (P.C.), 1975—. Gen. counsel La.-Pacific Resources, Inc., 1970-90. Bd. dirs. Caesars World, Inc., 1989-95. With USAAF, 1942-46. Mem. Beverly Hills Bar Assn., Phi Beta Kappa, Tau Kappa Alpha. Home: 16606 Merrivale Ln Pacific Palisades CA 90272-2236 Office: PO Box 308 Pacific Palisades CA 90272-0308

SEVILLA-SACASA, FRANCES ALDRICH, bank executive; BA in Langs., U. Miami, 1977; MA in Internat. Mgmt., Am. Grad. Sch. Internat. Mgmt., 1978. Joined Bankers Trust, 1983; mng. dir. L.Am. pvt. banking Bankers Trust Internat. Pvt. Banking Group, Miami, Fla.; sr. v.p. pvt. client svcs. Lehman Bros., Miami, 1997—98; mng. dir. L.Am. pvt. bank divsn. Deutsche Bank; pres. Bankers Trust Internat. Pvt. Banking Corp., 1998—2000; mng. dir., S.E. region head Citibank Pvt. Bank, 2000—01; mng. dir., head L.Am. Citigroup, N.Y.C., 2001—, head Europe Citigroup Pvt. Bank, 2003—. Office: Citigroup Pvt Bank 153 E 53rd St New York NY 10043

SEVIN, DIETER HERMANN, language and literature professional, educator; b. Mühlanger, Germany, Nov. 5, 1938; came to U.S. 1958; s. Wolf-Dieterich and Erna (Brockmann) S.; m. Ingrid Antje Dirks, June 15, 1963; children: Sonja, Karen. BA, San Jose State U., 1963; MA, U. Wash., 1964, PhD, 1967. Asst. prof. Pacific Lutheran U., Tacoma, 1967-68, Vanderbilt U., Nashville, 1968-73, assoc. prof., 1973-82, prof., 1982—, chair dept., 2002—. Author: Individuum und Staat, 1972, Zur Diskussion: A Modern Approach to German Conversation, 3d edit., 1987, Teststrategien in DDR-Prosawerken zwischen Bau und Durchbruch der Berliner Mauer, 1994, Christa Wolf (interpretation), 4d edit., 2000, Wie Geht's? An Introductory German Course, 7th edit., 2003; editor: Die Resonanz des Exils, 1992; contbr. numerous articles on German lit. and culture to profl. jours. Fellow Am. Philos. Soc. (grant 1991), Am. Council of Learned Socs. (grant 1981-82), German Academic Exchange Svc. (grant 1980). Avocations: travel, reading, music. Office: Vanderbilt U Dept Germanic And Slav Nashville TN 37235 Office Phone: 615-322-2611.

SEVY, ROGER WARREN, retired pharmacology educator; b. Richfield, Utah, Nov. 6, 1923; s. Carl Spencer and Maude (Malmquist) S.; m. Barbara Florence Snetsinger, Aug. 16, 1948; children— Pamela Jane, Jonathan Carl. Student, Utah State U., 1941-43, Harvard, 1943-45; MS, U. Vt., 1948; PhD, U. Ill., 1951, MD, 1954. Asst. physiology U. Ill., 1948-51, instr., 1951-54; asst. prof. pharmacology Temple U., Phila., 1954-56, prof., 1956-89, chmn. dept., 1957-73, dean Sch. Medicine, 1973-79, prof. emeritus, 1989—. Served with AUS, 1943-45. Mem. Am. Soc. Pharmacology and Exptl. Therapeutics, Am. Physiol. Soc., Endocrine Soc., AAAS, Sigma Xi., Alpha Omega Alpha. Achievements include research on hypertension and cardiovascular pharmacology. Home: 100 West Ave Apt D17 Jenkintown PA 19046-2652 Office: Temple U 3420 N Broad St Philadelphia PA 19140-5104

SEWALD, CARL MARTIN, music educator; s. Carl Frederick and Eileen Catherine Sewald; m. Rita Ann Mathis, Aug. 20, 1966; 1 child, Jill Marie. M of Ch. Music, Southwestern Bapt. Theol. Sem., Ft. Worth, 1969. Min. of music, youth, edn. Red Star Bapt. Ch., Cape Girardeau, Mo., 1970—71; dir. of vocal and choral music So. Bapt. Coll., Walnut Ridge, Ark., 1971—77; choral and orch. dir. Pine Bluff (Ark.) H.S., 1977—. Specialist 4th class U.S. Army N.G. Named S.E. Ark. Choral Dir. of the Yr., S.E. Ark. Choral Dir.'s Assn., 1989 90; recipient, 1993—94, 2000—01, 2003—04. Mem.: Am. Choral Dirs. Assn. Office: Pine Bluff H S 711 W 11th St Pine Bluff AR 71601 Office Phone: 870-543-4313.

SEWALL, SARAH LEE, foundation administrator; BA, Harvard Coll.; MA, Oxford U. Assoc. dir. Am. Acad. Arts/Scis.; dep. asst. sec. defense Peacekeeping and Humanitarian Assistance, 1993-96; sr. foreign policy advisor Sen. George J. Mitchell, 1987-93. Vis. scholar Harvard Program on Negotiation, lectr. internat. affairs, Stanford U., Washington, D.C.; exec. bd. Women in Internat. Security. Recipient Rhoades scholar, Harvard Coll. and Oxford U. Office: Coun Livable World 322 4th St NE Washington DC 20002-5824

SEWARD, GEORGE CHESTER, lawyer; b. Omaha, Aug. 4, 1910; s. George Francis and Ada Leona (Rugh) S.; m. Carroll Frances McKay, Dec. 12, 1936 (dec. 1991); children: Gordon Day, Patricia McKay (Mrs. Dryden G. Liddle), James Pickett, Deborah Carroll (Mrs. R. Thomas Coleman). BA, U. Va., 1933, LLB, 1936. Bar: Va. 1935, N.Y., Ky., D.C., U.S. Supreme Ct. With Shearman & Sterling, N.Y.C., 1936-53, Seward & Kissel LLP, N.Y.C., 1953—. Dir. Witherbee Sherman Corp., 1952-66, pres. 1964-66, Howmet Corp., 1955-75, Chas. P. Young Co., 1965-72, Howmedica Inc., 1970-72, Benson Mines, Inc., 1980-85; trustee Benson Iron Ore Trust, 1969-80. Author: Basic Corporate Practice, 1977, Seward and Related Families, 1994; co-author: Model Business Corporation Act Annotated, 1960, We Remember Carroll, 1992. Trustee Arts and Scis. Coun. U. Va., 1983-93, pres., 1991-93; trustee Edwin Gould Found. for Children, 1955-96, Nature Conservancy of Ea. L.I., 1969-80, N.Y. Geneal. and Biog. Soc. Named to Louisville Male H.S. Alumni Assn. Hall of Fame, 1991; commd. Ky. Col., 1993. Fellow: N.Y. State Bar Found., Am. Bar Found.; mem.: ABA (chmn. sect. com. corp. laws 1952—58, chmn. bus. law sect. 1958—59, ho. of dels. 1959—60, chmn. sect. banking com. 1960—61, ho. of dels. 1963—74, joint com. with Am. Law Inst. on continuing legal edn. 1965—74), Internat. Bar Assn. (hon. life pres., lectr. series by heads of state named in his honor, New Delhi 1988, Lisbon 1992, Budapest 1993, Geneva 1994), Downtown Assn. (N.Y.C.), Athenaeum Lit. Assn. (Louisville), Greencroft Club (Charlottesville, Va.), Univ. Club (Chgo.), Met. Club (Washington), Bohemian Club (San Francisco), Gardiner's Bay Country Club (Shelter Island, N.Y.), N.Y. Yacht Club, Knickerbocker Club, Delta Sigma Rho, Theta Chi, Phi Beta Kappa, Phi Beta Kappa Fellows (pres. 1969—75), Order of Coif, Raven Soc., Cum Laude Soc. Home: 48 Greenacres Ave Scarsdale NY 10583-1436 Office: Seward & Kissel LLP One Battery Park Plz New York NY 10004 also: Internat Bar Assn 271 Regent St London W1R 7PA England

SEWARD, JAMES PICKETT, internist, educator; b. N.Y.C., Oct. 14, 1949; s. George C. and Carroll Frances (McKay) S. AB, Harvard U., 1971; M of Pub. Policy, U. Calif., Berkeley, 1977; MD, U. Calif., San Francisco, 1977; M of Med. Mgmt., Tulane U., 2003. Diplomate Am. Bd. Internal Medicine, Am. Bd. Occupational Medicine, Am. Bd. Med. Mgmt. Resident U. Calif. Hosps., San Francisco, 1977-80; Robert Woods Johnson postdoctoral fellow U. Calif., San Francisco, 1980-82; med. dir. health svcs. Lawrence Livermore Nat. Lab., 1994—; dir. preventive medicine residency U. Calif., Berkeley, 1991-95, assoc. clin. prof. San Francisco, 1983—, assoc. clin. prof. Sch. Pub. Health Berkeley, 1986—2004, clin. prof. Sch. Pub. Health, 2004—. Fulbright scholar, 1972-73. Fellow Am. Coll. Preventive Medicine, Am. Coll. Occupl. and Environ. Medicine, Am. Coll. Physicians Execs., Calif. Acad. Preventive Medicine (past pres.), We. Occupl. and Environ. Med. Assn. (v.p.), Calif. Med. Assn. Office: HSD L723 LLNL PO Box 808 Livermore CA 94551-0808

SEWARD, NANCY H. retired band director, composer; b. Henryetta, Okla., Aug. 9, 1930; d. Albert Louis and Grace Wood Heitmann; m. Raymond Kenneth Seward, Aug. 21, 1952 (dec. Dec. 1980); children: Steven Kenneth, Lynn Annette Seward Fryer. B Music Edn. cum laude, Ctrl. Meth. Coll., 1952; postgrad., U. Mich., 1952, U. Mo., Columbia, 1964, U. Mo., Kansas City, 1973-74. Band dir. Leavenworth (Kans.) pub. schs., 1952-54, Excelsior Springs (Mo.) pub. schs., 1954-58, Ruskin H.S., Hickman Mills, Mo., 1958-64, Ctrl. Meth. Coll., Fayette, Mo., 1964-66, Richmond (Mo.) pub. schs., 1967-81, Stet Pub. Schs., 1967-73, Polo (Mo.) pub. schs., 1982-90; ret., 1990. Dir. band in Tournament of Roses Parade, Pasadena, Calif., 1960, several televised half-time shows for Kansas City Chiefs football games, also Kansas City Royals and St. Louis Cardinals; adjudicator, clinician at festivals and contests in Midwest and Can., 1964—. Composer, arranger numerous works for concert bands. Recipient 2d pl. award Richmond Band, Internat. Youth and Music Festival, Vienna, Austria, 1981, disting. alumni award Ctrl. Meth. Coll., 1978; named to Mo. Bandmasters Hall of Fame, 1993. Mem. World Assn. for Symphonic Bands and Ensembles, Nat. Band Assn., Women Band Dirs. Internat., Mo. Bandmasters' Assn., Tex. Bandmasters' Assn., Music Educators Nat. Conf., Mo. Music Educators Assn., Phi Beta Mu, Avocations: reading, genealogy. Home and Office: 1204 N Ridge Ave Liberty MO 64068-1359

SEWARD, RICHARD BEVIN, lawyer; b. Bartlesville, Okla., May 27, 1932; s. Fredrick W. and Kittie Lea (Hudson) S.; m. Loydell E. Nash, Aug. 1, 1954; children: Ann M., Elizabeth, Amy M. BS, Okla. State U., 1954; postgrad., Tulsa U., 1959-62; JD, So. Methodist U., 1971. Bar: Tex. 1968. Personnel mgr. Unit Rig and Equipment Co., Tulsa, 1958-62, Gifford-Hill Cos., Dallas, 1962-66; labor cons. Dallas, 1966-68; partner firm Stanfield & Seward, Dallas, 1978-83; sole practice law Farmersville, Tex., 1983—. Served with AUS, 1955-57. Mem. Order of Coif. Home and Office: 14340 County Road 550 Farmersville TX 75442-7034 Office Phone: 972-784-6266. E-mail: sewfolly@aol.com.

SEWARD, WILLIAM W(ARD), JR., writer, retired educator; b. Surry, Va., Feb. 2, 1913; s. William Ward and Elizabeth (Gwaltney) S.; m. Virginia Leigh Widgeon, Dec. 27, 1941; children: Virginia S. Godwin, Leigh S. Huston. AB, U. Richmond, 1934, MA, 1935; grad. fellow, Duke U., 1938-39, 40-41. English tchr. pub. schs., 1935-38; instr. U. Richmond, 1939-40, summer 1944; head English dept. Greenbrier Mil. Sch., 1941-42; prof., head English dept. Tift Coll., 1942-45; faculty Old Dominion U., Norfolk, Va., 1945, 47—, prof., 1957-77, prof. emeritus, 1977—, head dept. English, 1947-61. Lectr. U. Va. extension div., 1952-54 Author: The Quarrels of Alexander Pope, 1935; editor: The Longer Thou Livest the More Fool Thou Art (W. Wager), 1939, Literature and War, 1943, Skirts of The Dead Night, 1950, Foreword to Descent of the White Bird (Barbara Whitney), 1955, Contrasts in Modern Writers, 1963, My Friend Ernest Hemingway: An Affectionate Reminiscence, 1969, 2003; contbr. to book: The True Gen: An Intimate Portrait of Hemingway by those Who

Knew Him (Denis Brian), 1988, Remembering Ernest Hemingway (interviews by James Plath and Frank Simons), 1999; mem. editl. bd.: Lyric Virginia Today, 1956; contbr. articles to profl. jours. Recipient Charles T. Norman medal for best grad. in English U. Richmond, 1934 Mem. Poetry Soc. Va. (pres. 1952-55), Hemingway Soc., Internat. Mark Twain Soc. (hon.), Va. Writers Club (emeritus), Virginia Beach Sports Club, Phi Beta Kappa, Kappa Alpha, Pi Delta Epsilon. Methodist. Home: 701 Cavalier Dr Virginia Beach VA 23451-3837

SEWELL, ANDREW, music director; m. Mary Anne Sewell; children: Anna, Lydia, Alistair. MMus, U. Mich.; studied with Gustav Meier. Past asst. condr. Memphis Symphony; past resident condr. Toledo Symphony Orch.; music dir. Mansfield (Ohio) Symphony, Wis. Chamber Orch., Madison; music dir., condr. Wichita (Kans.) Symphony Orch., 2000—. Guest condr. orchs. Detroit, Japan, Mex., Can., New Zealand. Recipient Young Achiever's award Australian Guarantee Corp., Star award New Zealand Aotea Performing Arts Trust, 1997. Office: Wichita Symphony Orch 225 W Douglas Ave Ste 207 Wichita KS 67202-3181

SEWELL, BETH PERRY, gas industry executive; Pres., CEO Perry Gas Cos., Inc., Houston, 1993—. Office: Perry Gas Cos Inc 952 Echo Ln Ste 450 Houston TX 77024-2781 E-mail: energy@perrygas.com.

SEWELL, CECIL W., JR., bank executive; BS in Econ., U. N.C., Chapel Hill; MBA, Rollins Coll. Exec. v.p. Peoples Bank of Mid-South Bank, Sanford, 1973-87; pres. Peoples Bancorporation, 1987-93; pres., COO Centura, 1993—. Office: Centura Bank PO Box 1220 Rocky Mount NC 27802-1220

SEWELL, GLORIANA, piano teacher; b. Huntington, N.Y., June 6, 1948; d. Reavis Staggs and Evelyn (Vilches) Kurlowich; m. C. Eugene Sewell, Aug. 8, 1969; children: Keren Ligowski, Daniel Sewell. BA in Piano, Bob Jones U., 1970. Piano tchr. in pvt. practice, Santa Barbara, Calif., 1970-71, Sodus, N.Y., 1971-78; Suzuki piano tchr. in pvt. practice Quakertown, Pa., 1979-86, Milford Square, Pa., 1986—; Kindermusik tchr. Milford Square Music Studio, 1996—. Piano accompanist ch. choir Assembly of the Word, Milford Square, 1993—. Recipient Tchr. award for 1st Pl. Winner, Baldwin Jr. Keyboard Competition, 1985, 1992, 2000, Tchr. of Yr. award, 1989, award, Music Tchrs. Nat. Assn. Student Composition Competition, 1993, 1994, 2001, Tchr. award 1st Pl., Yamaha H.S. Keyboard Competition, 2002. Mem.: Dalcroze Soc. Am., Nat. Guild Piano Tchrs., Am. Orff-Schulwerk Assn., Kindermusik Educations Assn., Suzuki Assn. of Ams., Pa. Music Tchrs. Assn. (pres. Lehigh Valley chpt. 1991—92, co-dir. spring music festival 1997, v.p. 1999—2001, pres. 2001—03, immediate past pres. 2003—), Music Tchrs. Nat. Assn. (Disting. Svc. award 2003). Avocation: gardening. Home and Office: Milford Square Music Studio PO Box 199 2244 Milford Square Pike Milford Square PA 18935

SEWELL, JOAN MARSHALL, retired elementary school educator; b. Nashville, Nov. 5, 1936; d. Willie Eston Marshall and Omer Lee Denny; m. Shirley Starr Sewell, Dec. 8, 1956 (dec.); children: Gina Marie, Donna Lee, Lisa Gaye, Sheila Kaye. BA, Ga. State U., 1961, EdS, 1980; MEd, U. Ga., 1971. Classroom tchr. Dekalb County Pub. Schs., Decatur, Ga., 1961—64, Gwinnett County Pub. Schs., Lawrenceville, Ga., 1966—76, 1985—94, instrnl. lead, asst. prin., 1976—85; ret., 1994. Item writer Ednl. Testing Svc., 1992—94; del. to nat. conf. NEA, Mpls. and Miami, Fla., 1976—77. Author: (play) Murder on the Menu, 1999, (column) Kaleidoscope for Walton Tribune, 1998—. Blood dr. worker ARC; investigator Faith Is Serving Humanity, Monroe, Ga.; chmn. Jud. Foster Care Rev. Panel, Lawrenceville, 1994—96, Juvenile Ct. Youth Divsn. Panel, Lawrenceville, 1995—97; bd. dirs. Eastside Sr. Friends, 1994—2004, pres., 2003—04, former rec. sec., v.p.; Bible class tchr. Ch. of Christ. Named Sr. of Yr., Gwinnett Coun. for Srs., 2002; recipient Cmty. Svc. award, 1997. Mem.: Ga. Ret. Educators Assn., Gwinnett County Ret. Educators Assn. (mem. legis. com. 2004), U. Ga. Alumni Assn. (licentiate), Alpha Delta Kappa (past pres. Beta Sigma chpt.). Republican. Mem. Ch. Of Christ. Avocations: gardening, travel, reading, volunteer work. Home: 1386 Tipperary Ct Monroe GA 30656-4580

SEWELL, JOHN WILLIAMSON, research association executive; b. Cleve., Dec. 19, 1935; s. William and Hilda F. (Gaunt) S.; m. Maryann Strauss, July 19, 1958; children: Gregory J., Michael P. BA, U. Rochester, 1957; MA, NYU, 1967. Fgn. service officer Dept. State, 1961-68; asst. to dir. Bur. Intelligence Research, Dept. State, Washington, 1968-70; asst. to pres. Brookings Inst., Washington, 1970-71; v.p. Overseas Devel. Council, Washington, 1971-77, exec. v.p., 1977-79, pres., 1980-2000; sr. scholar Woodrow Wilson Internat. Ctr., 2001—. Mem. Bretton Woods Com., North-South Roundtable; former vice chair Internat. Ctr. for Rsch. on Women; mem. Internat. Adv. Group for 1995 World Summit for Social Devel.; spl. advisor to the adminstrn. UNDP, 1988-99; chair Working Group on Devel. of Role of Internat. Monetary Fund; global advisor World Resources Inst.; advisor UN ASsn. USA. Author: U.S. Foreign Policy and the Third World Agenda, 1985-86; Growth, Exports, & Jobs in a Changing World Economy: Agenda 1988, The Real Politik of Poverty; co-editor: United States Budget for a New World Order, FY, 1992, Challenges and Priorities in the 1990s: An Alternative U.S. International Affairs Budget, FY, 1993; contbr. articles to jours. Pres. Nat. Choral Found., 1969-75. With U.S. Army, 1958-60. Mem. Coun. on Fgn. Rels. Home: 7614 Morningside Dr NW Washington DC 20012-1557

SEWELL, RICHARD HERBERT, historian, educator; b. Ann Arbor, Mich., Apr. 11, 1931; s. Herbert Mathieu and Anna Louise (Broene) Sewell; m. Natalie Paperno, Jan. 13, 1971; 1 child, Rebecca Elizabeth. AB, U. Mich., 1953; MA, Harvard U., 1954, PhD, 1962. Asst. prof. No. Ill. U., DeKalb, 1962-64, U. Wis., Madison, 1965-67, assoc. prof., 1967-74, prof, 1974-95, prof. emeritus, 1995—. Vis. lectr. U. Mich., Ann Arbor, 1964—65; adv. bd. Lincoln and Soldiers Inst. Gettysburg Coll., Pa., 1990—. Author: (book) John P. Hale and the Politics of Abolition, 1965, Ballots for Freedom, 1976, A House Divided, 1988; contbr. articles to profl. jours. Lt. (j.g.) USNR, 1954—57. Fellow: Wis. Hist. Soc. (hon.); mem.: Orgn. of Am. Historians, So. Hist. Assn., Soc. Civil War Historians, Phi Beta Kappa, Phi Kappa Phi. Avocation: white-water rafting. Home: 2206 Van Hise Ave Madison WI 53726 E-mail: rhsewell@wisc.edu.

SEWELL, ROBERT DALTON, pediatrician; b. Newman, Calif., Apr. 28, 1950; s. James Dalton and Mary Louise (Hartwell) S.; m. Laura Slinkard-Ekberg, May 21, 1998; children: Kevin, David; stepchildren: Nicole, Samantha. BA magna cum laude, Pacific Union Coll., 1972; MD, Loma Linda U., 1975. Diplomate Am. Bd. Pediatrics. Pediat. intern and resident White Meml. Med. Ctr., L.A., 1975-77; pediat. resident, chief resident Milton S. Hershey Med. Ctr., Pa. State U., Hershey, 1977-80; pediatrician Children's Med. Ctr. Asheville, N.C., 1980-81, Lincoln City (Oreg.) Med. Ctr. P.C., 1982-95; examining physician C.A.R.E.S. Ctr. Emanuel Hosp. & Health Ctr., Portland, Oreg., 1988-90; asst. prof. Loma Linda (Calif.) U. Sch. Medicine, 1995-97; with Good Shepherd Med. Group, Hemiston, Oreg., 1998-2001; physician examiner Guardian Care Ctr., Pendleton, Oreg., 1999-2001. Chmn. child protection team North Lincoln Hosp., Lincoln City, 1983-89, sec. med. staff, 1990-92, pres. med. staff, 1992-94; mem. Citizens' Rev. Bd. Lincoln County, Newport, Oreg., 1986-92, Early Intervention adv. com., Newport, 1986-90. Mem. North Lincoln Local Sch. Com., Lincoln City, 1983-94, chmn., 1986-90; bd. dirs. Lincoln Shelter and Svcs., Inc., Lincoln City, 1983-89, chmn., 1987-89; mem. North Lincoln divsn. Am. Heart Assn., Lincoln City, 1986-89, v.p., 1987-89; mem. Drug and Alcohol Task Force, Lincoln City, 1988; mem., 2d vice-chmn. Yr. 2000 Plan housing com. Lincoln City Planning Commn., 1987-88; mem. AIDS task force Lincoln County Sch. Dist., 1987-89; mem. Lincoln County Children's Agenda Taskforce, 1988; mem. med. rev. com. Oreg. Med. Assn., 1990-95, mem.-at-large med. staff sect. gov. bd., 1993-95. Named Citizen of Yr. child protection com. Lincoln County, 1984, Man of Yr. Lincoln City C. of C., 1988. Mem. Am. Acad. Pediatrics (sect. on child abuse), Am. Profl. Soc. of Abuse of Children (charter mem.), Nat. Assn. Counsel for Children, Internat. Soc. for Prevention Child Abuse and Neglect, Oreg. Profl. Soc. on Abuse of Children (founding pres. 1992-94), Oreg. Med. Assn. (mem. health care fin. com. 1999-2001). Democrat. Seventh-day Adventist. Avocations: music, sports, boating, auto racing. E-mail: kidsdr@eoni.com.

SEWELL, RODNEY MILTON, biologist; b. Frederick, Md., July 5, 1946; BS in Psychobiology, Hood Coll., 1974. Operating room tech. USN, 1967-70; biologist NIMH/LBEB, 1974-79; systems integrator LAMDA, 1983—. Mem. IEEE Computer Soc., N.Y. Acad. Scis., AAAS, Am. Chem. Soc., Am. Psychol. Soc. Achievements include research in developmental and comparative aspects of neurobiology and behavior, computer-assisted learning devices. Office: Lab Med Devices PO Box 30634 Bethesda MD 20824-0634

SEWELL, WILLIAM GEORGE, III, electronics engineer, writer; b. Roanoke, Va., Dec. 14, 1950; s. William George Jr. and Elizabeth Marie (Morrison) S.; m. Verna Landry, Aug. 25, 1970 (div. 1974); children: Ronald Allen, Bryan Joseph; m. Colleen Rose Gaynor, May 15, 1981. BS in Engring., U. Ill., Chgo., 1980; PhD, Calif. U., Modesto, 1983. Electronic technician 928 Airlift Group, Chgo., 1972-74; with FAA, Chgo., 1974-85, staff engr. Wheeling, Ill., 1980-82, regional nav. and landing systems engr. Chgo., 1982-85, nat. program mgr., 1985—87; with Jerry Thompson & Assocs., Kensington, Md., 1987-88; v.p. Navcom Systems, Inc., 1988-89, B2 Software, Inc., 1988-89; v.p., CEO The Thinkk Corp., 1988-89; founder, CEO Software Coalition, 1989—; sr. v.p., gen. mgr. DMJM Tech., 2004—. Dir. comm. and info. systems group SEMA, Inc., 1990—93; dir. comm. solutions Jacobs Facilities, Inc., 1993—2000; Sverdrup fellow, 1998; v.p. Holmes & Narver, Inc., 2000—01, DMJM Holmes & Narver, Inc., 2001—03; sr. v.p. AECOM Tech. Corp., 2004—; pres. GEOLINC, 2002—; cons. engr. W.G. Sewell & Assocs., Internat., Niles, Ill., 1981—88; chair TIA Indsl. Telecoms Standards Body, 1999—2001; sr. v.p. DMJM Tech., 2003—; mem. JV bd. Lawa Assoc. Contbr. articles to profl. jours.; author: Building Security: Handbook for Architectural Planning and Design, 2004. Mem. Chgo. Coun. Fgn. Rels., 1976-80. Served with USAF, 1970-72, Vietnam. Recipient 1st prize, Am. Soc. Electro-Surgery, 1982. Mem. IEEE (chair telecomm. industry assoc. indsl. stds. group), Soc. Automotive Engrs., Aircraft Owners and Pilots Assn. Achievements include invention of high speed turn control for land vehicles, 1980; co-inventor child's hidden identification and location device, 1990. Office: 1300 Wilson Blvd Ste 1100 Arlington VA 22209-2307 E-mail: bill.sewell@dmjm.com.

SEXSON, RICHMOND LOCKWOOD, professional baseball player; b. Portland, Oreg., Dec. 29, 1974; m. Kerry Sexson. Player Milw. Brewers, 2000—03, Ariz. Diamondbacks, Phoenix, 2003—. Achievements include third in Brewers franchise history to hit 40 home runs in a season; named to All-Star game, 2002-03. Office: c/o Ariz Diamondbacks 401 E Jefferson Phoenix AZ 85004*

SEXSON, STEPHEN BRUCE, education writer, educator; b. Silver City, N.Mex., May 29, 1948; s. Ralph Dale and Wanda Claudean (McMahan) S.; m. Barbara Jane Davis, May 24, 1968; children: David Paul, Linda Carol. BA in Rhetoric and Pub. Address, Pepperdine U., 1969, MA in Pub. Comm., 1975; PhD in Higher Edn., Okla. State U., 1990. Asst. to supt. Morongo Unified Sch. Dist., Twentynine Palms, Calif., 1973-77; corp. trainer Merrill Lynch Realty, Dallas, 1979-81; sch. psychologist Texhoma (Tex.) Sch. Dist., 1982-83; assoc. prof., dir. Christian Student Ctr. Okla. Panhandle State U., Goodwell, 1982-84; rsch. resident Okla. State U., Stillwater, 1984-87; spl. programs staff LA Unified Sch. Dist., 1987—93; dir. Edwest Edn. Rsch., Burbank, Calif., 1991—; prof. Copper Mountain Coll., 2003—. Lectr. Chapman U., 1998—. Verbal Comm. Inst., Palm Desert, Calif., 2001—; guest lectr. edn. Okla. State U., Stillwater, 1993-94, U. Tulsa, 1993-94; spkr. Merrill Lynch Realty-Relo, Atlanta, 1979; prof. Chapman U., 1998—. Author: The Magic Classroom, 1995, The Values Rich Teacher, 1996, Dad's Role in the New Age, 2003; contbr. articles to profl. jours. Mem. ASCD, Am. Assn. Sch. Adminstrs., Nat. Assn. of Sch. Psychologists, Lions Club, Phi Delta Kappa. Avocations: computing, travel, theater. Home: PO Box 845 Twentynine Palms CA 92277-0845 Office: Chapman U Coachella Valley Campus 42-600 Cook St Ste 134 Palm Desert CA 92211 E-mail: SteveSexson@aol.com.

SEXSON, WILLIAM ROBERT, pediatrician, educator; b. Washington, Dec. 3, 1945; children: Sara Kristen, Ryan William. BS, USAF Acad., 1967; MD, U. Miss., 1971. Diplomate Am. Bd. Pediatrics, Am. Bd. Neonatal-Perinatal Medicine. Pediat. resident Wilford Hall USAF Med. Ctr., 1994; fellow in neonatology Vanderbilt U., Nashville, 1976; staff neurologist Crawford Long Hosp., Atlanta, 1984—, Egleston's Children's Hosp., Atlanta, 1984—; dir. nurseries Grady Meml. Hosp., Atlanta, 1987-94; vice-chair dept. pediatrics, assoc. prof. Emory U. Sch. Medicine, Atlanta, 1994—, interim assoc. dean clin. affairs, 1998-2000, assoc. dean clin. affairs, 2000—; chief pediatrics Grady Health Sys., Atlanta, 1994—. Active Ga. Policy Coun. for Children and Families, 1995-2000; co-chair Children's Health Com., Ga. Dept. Med. Assts.; child health adv com., physicians adv. coun. Ga. Medicaid, 2001—; chmn. health and safety com. Boy Scouts Am. Atlanta Area Coun., 1998—. Col. USAFR. Named Outstanding Citizen of Ga., 1990. Mem. Am. Acad. Pediatrics (v.p. Ga. chpt. 1990-92, pres. 1993-96, exec. com. 1996—, chair com. on bioethics for Ga., chair hosp. ethics com. 1987—), Coun. on Maternal and Infant Health (chair 1993-95), Ga. Perinatal Assn. Home: 804 Springdale Rd NE Atlanta GA 30306-4618 Office: Grady Health Sys 68 Armstrong St SE Atlanta GA 30303-3040 E-mail: swexson@emory.edu.

SEXTON, BRENDA, film agency director; b. N.Y.C., Aug. 1, 1954; d. Daniel Francis and Eve (Lucas) Sexton; m. James Daniel Ryndak, July 7, 1984 (div. Sept. 1990); 1 child, Christine Ryndak; m. M. Blair Hull, Nov. 30, 1995 (div.). BA, U. Denver, 1977; M of Internat. Mgmt., Am. Grad. Sch. Internat. Mgmt., Phoenix, 1980. Account exec. Ogilvy & Mather, N.Y.C., 1980-81, J. Walter Thompson, Chgo., 1981-82; sr. v.p. Irvine Assocs., Chgo., 1982-86; sr. mng. dir. Julien J. Studley, Chgo., 1987-93; pres. corp. svcs. The Galbreath Co., Chgo., 1993-97; sr. mng. dir. The Williams Co., Chgo., 1997—2003; mng. dir. Ill. Film Office, Chgo., 2003—. Editl. bd.: Bldg. and Owners Management Organization, Chgo., 1995-96. Chmn. State Street Revitalization Task Force, Chgo., 1996-97, The Latin Sch./Silent Auction Restaurant Com., Chgo., 1996-97, Major Fundraising Com./Old Saint Patrick's Sch., Chgo., 1993-94; officer Chgo. Film Critics' Assn.; mem. women's bd. Goodman Theatre; v.p. exec. bd. PAWS (Pets Are Worth Saving), Chgo. Named to Top 40 Under 40 Crain's Chgo. Bus., 1994, Top Comml. Broker in Chgo., Sun Times, 1991, 95, Top Broker in U.S., Julien J. Studley, 1995, Hot Broker, Comml. Property News, 1994, one of Chgos. 100 Most Influential Women, Crain's Chgo. Bus., 2004. Mem. Econ. Club of Chgo., The Exec. Club, The Glen View Club. Office: Ill Film Office Ste 3-400 100 W Randolph Chicago IL 60601*

SEXTON, CAROL BURKE, consultant; b. Chgo., Apr. 20, 1939; d. William Patrick and Katharine Marie (Nolan) Burke; m. Thomas W. Sexton Jr., June 30, 1962 (div. June 1976); children: Thomas W., J. Patrick, M. Elizabeth. BA, Barat Coll., 1961; cert. legal, Mallinckrodt Coll., 1974. Tchr. Roosevelt High Sch., Chgo., 1961-63, St. Joseph's Sch., Wilmette, Ill., 1975-80; dir. Jane Byrne Polit. Com., Chgo., 1980-81; mgr. Chgo. Merc. Exch., 1981-84, sr. dir. govt. and civic affairs, 1984-87, v.p. pub. affairs, 1987-94, exec. v.p. corp. rels., 1995-2001. Mem. internat. trade an investment subcom. Chgo. Econ. Devel. Commn., 1989, 90. Bd. dirs. Chgo. Sister Cities, 1992—2000, Ill. Ambs., 1991—98, pres., 1994—98; bd. dirs., sec. Internat. Press Ctr., 1992—97, chmn. bd., 1994. Mem. Execs. Club of Chgo. (bd. dirs. 1992-2001), Chgo. Conv. and Tourism Bur. (sec. 1989-90, exec. com. 1987-2000, chmn.-elect 1990, chmn. 1991-92), Econ. Club of Chgo. Roman Catholic. Avocations: books, gardening, travel.

SEXTON, DAVID FARRINGTON, lawyer, investment banking executive; b. Montclair, N.J., Aug. 20, 1943; s. Dorrance and Marjorie (McComb) S.; m. Ann Hemelright, Feb. 27, 1971; children: James, Ashley, Christopher. AB cum laude, Princeton U., 1966; JD cum laude, U. Pa., 1972. Bar: N.Y. 1972. Assoc. Sullivan & Cromwell, N.Y.C., 1972-77; with First Boston Corp., N.Y.C., 1977-90, v.p., gen. counsel, 1980-83, mng. dir., gen. counsel, 1983-86; mng. dir., pres. First Boston Internat. Ltd., 1986-90; sr. exec. v.p., dir. Yamaichi Internat. (America), Inc., N.Y.C., 1990-95, vice-chmn., 1995-98; pres., CEO The Farrington Group, LLC, Greenwich, Conn., 1998—2002. Adj. prof. law Fordham U., 1985—86; mem. U.S.-Japan Friendship Commn., Washington, 1990—94; adv. bd. mem. Manifold Products, LLC. Lt. USNR, 1966-69. Mem. Assn. Bar City N.Y., Racquet and Tennis Club, N.Y. Yacht Club, Ivy Club, Bucks Harbor Yacht Club (bd. govs. 1991-, commodore 2003-), The Nat. Assn. of Japan Am. Socs. (bd. dirs. 1998-, dir. exec. com. 1997-). Republican. Presbyterian. Office: The Farrington Group 186 Field Point Rd Ste 1B Greenwich CT 06830

SEXTON, DONALD LEE, retired business administration educator; b. New Boston, Ohio, June 14, 1932; s. Benjamin Franklin and Virgie Marie (Jordan) S.; m. Levonne Bradley, June, 1954 (div. June 1964); 1 child, Rhonda Jane; m. Carol Ann Schwaller, Dec. 18, 1965; children: David Lee, Douglas Edward. BS in Math. and Physics, Wilmington Coll., 1959; MBA, Ohio State U., 1966, PhD in Mgmt., 1972. Indsl. engr. Detroit Steel Corp., Portsmouth, Ohio, 1959-61; sr. rsch. engr. Rockwell Internat., Columbus, Ohio, 1961-68; v.p. merchandising R.G. Barry Corp., Columbus, 1968-74; v.p., gen. mgr. Henri Fayette, Inc., Chgo., 1976; gen. mgr. M.H. Mfg. Co., Jackson, Miss., 1976-77; assoc. prof. Sangamon State U., Springfield, Ill., 1977-79; Caruth prof. entrepreneurship Baylor U., Waco, Tex., 1979-86; Davis prof. entrepreneurship Ohio State U., Columbus, 1986-94, prof. emeritus, 1994—; dir. Nat. Ctr. for Entrepreneurial Rsch. Kauffman Found., Kansas City, Mo., 1994-97, scholar-in-residence, 1997-2000. Adj. faculty Nova Southeastern U., Ft. Lauderdale, Fla., 1997-99; mem. adv. bd. SBA, Columbus, 1986-94; rsch. adv. bd. U. So. Calif., L.A., 1986-90. Co-author: Entrepreneurship Education, 1981, Experiences in Small Business, 1982, Starting A Business in Texas, 1983; co-editor: Encyclopedia of Entrepreneurship, 1981, Art and Science of Entrepreneurship, 1986, Women Owned Business, 1989, Entrepreneurship: Creativity and Growth, 1990, The State of the Art of Entrepreneurship, 1991, Leadership and Entrepreneurship, 1996, Entrepreneurship: 2000, 1996, The Handbook of Entrepreneurship, 1999, Strategic Entrepreneurship, 2002. Served to staff sgt. USAF, 1951-55. Recipient Leavy Free Enterprise award Freedoms Found. Valley Forge, 1985, Cert. Appreciation SBA, Washington, 1984, 85, Outstanding Contbn. to Entrepreneurship Edn. award Assn. Coll. Entrepreneurs, 1991, Disting. Alumni award Wilmington Coll., 1993, Entrepreneurship Adv. of the Yr., 1997; named Adv. of Yr.-Innovation SBA, Dallas, 1982, 83, 84. Mem. Internat. Coun. for Small Bus. (sr. v.p. 1986), U.S. Assn. for Small Bus. (v.p. pub. rels. 1987), Acad. Mgmt. (chmn. entrepreneurship com. 1981, mem. adv. bd. 1984-85)), Masons, Shriners, Eagles, Am. Legion, Alpha Tau Omega. Republican. Baptist. Avocation: golf. Home: 196 Bellerive Ln Summerville SC 29483-5032 E-mail: dlsexton@aol.com.

SEXTON, JOHN EDWARD, academic administrator, law educator; b. Bklyn., Sept. 29, 1942; s. John Edward and Catherine (Humann) S.; m. Lisa Ellen Goldberg; children: Jed, Katherine. BA, Fordham U., 1963, PhD, 1978; JD, Harvard U., 1979. Bar: NY 1981, US Supreme Ct. 1984. Prof. religion St. Francis Coll., Bklyn., 1965-75; law clk. U.S. Ct. Appeals, Wash., 1979, 80, U.S. Supreme Ct., Wash., DC, 1980-81; prof. law NYU, NYC, 1981—, dean law sch., 1988—2002, pres., 2002—. Dir. Washington Sq. Legal Services, NYC, 1983-2002, Pub. Interest Law Found., N.Y.C., 1983-85. Author: A Managerial Model of the Supreme Court, 1985, Federal Jury Instructions-Civil, 1985, How Free Are We? A Study of the Constitution, 1985, Cases and Materials in Civil Procedure, 1988. Dir. Root-Tilden Scholarship Program, 1984-88. Mem. Assn. of Am. Law Schs. (pres. 1997-98). Home: 29 Washington Sq W New York NY 10011-9180 Office: NYU Sch Law 70 Wash Sq S Rm 1216 New York NY 10012-1385

SEXTON, JOHN JOSEPH, oral and maxillofacial surgeon, educator; b. Boston, Dec. 4, 1947; s. Bernard Thomas and Margaret Theresa (Carrigg) S.; m. Judith Whelden, Aug. 21, 1971; 1 child, Benjamin. BS, Boston Coll., 19770; DMD, Tufts U., 1975; MScD, Boston U., 1978, CAGS, 1979. Diplomate Am. Bd. Oral and Maxillofacial Surgery. Orthognathic fellow Boston U. Inst. for Correction of Facial Deformities, 1976-77; intern, jr. resident, chief resident Boston U./Tufts U., 1975-79; asst. prof. Goldman Sch. Dental Medicine, Boston U., 1979-81; chief oral and maxillofacial surgery Beth Israel Hosp., Boston, 1981—2001, dir. maxillofacial trauma svc., 1990—2001, dir. mucosal disorders unit, 1990—2001; chief oral and maxillofacial surgery Lahey Clinic Med. Ctr., Burlington, Mass., 2001—. Cons. dermatology Beth Israel Hosp.; asst. prof. oral and maxillofacial surgery Harvard Med. Sch., Boston. Contbr. numerous articles to profl. jours. Avocations: philosophy, physics, history, travel. Office: 372 Washington St Ste 2500 Wellesley MA 02481-6202 Office Phone: 781-235-4554. E-mail: john_sexton@lahey.org.

SEXTON, ROBERT FENIMORE, educational organization executive; b. Cin., Jan. 13, 1942; s. Claude Fenimore and Jane (Wisenall) S.; m. Pam Peyton Papka, Sept. 15, 1985; children: Rebecca, Robert B., Ouita Papka, Paige Papka, Perry Papka. BA, Yale U., 1964; MA in History, U. Wash., Seattle, 1968, PhD in History, 1970; DHL (hon.), Berea Coll., 1990, Georgetown Coll., Ky., 1993, Eastern Ky. U., 2000. Asst. prof. history Murray (Ky.) State U., 1968-70; dir. Office Acad. Programs, Commonwealth of Ky., Frankfort, 1970-73; assoc. dean, exec. dir. Office Exptl. Edn. U. Ky., Lexington, 1973-80; dep. exec. dir. Ky. Coun. Higher Edn., Frankfort, 1980-83; exec. dir. Prichard Com. for Acad. Excellence, Lexington, 1983—; founder, pres. Ky. Ctr. Pub. Issues, Lexington, 1988—94. Vis. scholar Harvard U., Cambridge, Mass., 1992, 94; chair Nat. Ctr. for Internships, Washington, 1973-80, Coalition for Alternatives in Post-Secondary Edn., Washington, 1977-80; bd. dirs. Editl. Projects in Edn., Consortium Policy Rsch. in Edn., Ky. Long Term Policy Rsch. Ctr., Edn. Trust, Trust for Early Edn., 1992-94. Pub. The Ky. Jour., 1988-2001; editor book series: Public Papers of Governors of Kentucky, 1973-86, Mobilizing Citizens for Better Schools, 5 books, 2004; contbr. articles to profl. jours. Co-chmn. Carnegie Ctr. for Literacy, Lexington, 1990-93; mem. Gov.'s Task Force on Health Care, Frankfort, 1992-99; bd. dirs. Ky. Inst. Edn. Rsch. Fund for Improvement in Postsecondary Edn., 1993-2000; chair Bluegrass Edn. Work Coun., Lexington, 1978-80; founder, steering com. Gov.'s Scholars Program, Frankfort, 1983-85. Recipient Charles A. Dana award for pioneering achievement, 1994. Mem. Am. Assn. Higher Edn. (bd. dirs. 1979-83). Democrat. Avocations: fishing, travel. Office: Prichard Com Acad Excell 167 W Main St Ste 310 Lexington KY 40507-1702

SEYBERT, JOANNA, federal judge; b. Bklyn., Sept. 18, 1946; BA, U. Cin., 1967; JD, St. John's U., 1971. Bar: N.Y. 1972, U.S. Dist. Ct. (ea. and so. dists.) N.Y. 1973. Trial staff atty. Legal Aid Soc., N.Y.C., 1971-73, sr. staff atty. Mineola, N.Y., 1976-80; sr. trial atty. Fed. Defender Svc., Bklyn., 1973-75; bur. chief Nassau County Atty's Office, Mineola, 1980-87; judge Nassau County Dist. Ct., Hempstead, N.Y., 1987-92, Nassau County Ct., Mineola, 1992-94, U.S. Dist. Ct. (ea. dist.) N.Y., Uniondale, 1994—. Mem.: Nassau Lawyers Assn. (past pres.), Fed. Judges Assn. (v.p.), Theodore Roosevelt A. Inns of Ct. (past pres.), Suffolk County Bar Assn., Internat. Assn. Judges (del.). Office: 1034 Federal Plz Central Islip NY 11722-4443

SEYDOUX, GERALDINE, molecular biologist; BS, U. Maine, 1986; PhD in Molecular Genetics, Princeton U., 1991. Postdoctoral trainee Carnegie Instn. Washington, Balt., 1991—95; asst. prof. molecular biology and genetics Sch. Medicine Johns Hopkins U., Balt., 1995—. Recipient Jr. Faculty Rsch. award, Am. Cancer Soc., 1996, Searle Scholars award, 1997, Presdl. Early Career award for scientists and engrs., NIH, 1999; fellow, Packard Found., 1996, MacArthur Found., 2001; scholar Basil O'Connor Starter scholar, March of Dimes, 1996. Office: Johns Hopkins U Sch Medicine 725 N Wolfe St 1515 PCTB Baltimore MD 21205

SEYEDI, NAHID, physiologist, researcher; b. Shiraz, Fars, Iran, Nov. 22, 1949; arrived in U.S., 1987; d. Abbas and Legha Seyedi. MS, Pahlavi Med. Coll., Shiraz, Iran, 1978, N.Y. Med. Coll., Valhalla, N.Y., 1993, PhD, 1994. Lectr. physiology Urima Univ., Urmia, Iran, 1973—78; tchg. asst. N.Y. Med. Coll., Valhalla, NY, 1988—94; rsch. assoc. Weill Med. Coll., Cornell Univ., 1998—. Mem.: APA, Am. Soc. for Pharmacology, Am. Heart Assn. Achievements include discovery of local Bradikimin prodn. from isolated symaptosomes of guine-pig heart; local nitric oxide prodn. from coronary micro vessels of heart. Office: Weill Md Coll 1300 York Ave New York NY 10021

SEYED-YAGOOBI, JAMAL, mechanical engineering educator; b. Tabriz, Azarbaijan, Iran, Dec. 28, 1954; came to U.S., 1978; s. Ali-Asghar and Maryam Seyed-Yagoobi. BSME, Shariff U. Tech., Tehran, 1978; MSME, U. Ill., 1981, PhD in Mech. Engring., 1984. Registered profl. engr., Tex. Rsch. asst. U. Ill., Urbana, 1979-84, teaching asst., 1979-84; rsch. engr. Westvaco Corp., Covington, Va., 1984-87; asst. prof. Tex. A&M U., College Station, 1987-92, assoc. prof., 1992-98, prof., 1998—2001; prof. and chair dept. mechanical, materials and aerospace engring. Ill. Inst. Tech., Chicago, 2002—. Cons. Westvaco Corp., Covington, 1987-88, Bommer Engr. Co., San Antonio, 1990, WEB Systems, Inc., Boulder, Colo., 1990, Frito Lay, Inc., Irving, Tex., 1990-92, ABB Flakt Ross, Inc., Appleton, Wis., 1991-95, Pizza Hut, Inc., Wichita, Kans., 1991-92, Johnson & Johnson Med., Inc., Sherman, Tex., 1994-95, Tex. Instruments, Inc., Plano, 1994, Kimberly-Clark Corp., Neenah, Wis., 1996-97, Gas Rsch. Inst., Chgo., 1998—. Author: Advances in Drying, 1992, (anthology) Energy Engineering and Management, 1991, Advances in Heat Transfer, 1999; contbr. articles to profl. jours.; patentee electrohydrodynamic induction pumping thermal energy transfer system and method, slot jet reattachment nozzle, method of using jet reattachment combustion nozzles for flame heating of surfaces, viscometric thermometer. Recipient numerous grants and awards. Fellow ASME; mem. ASHRAE (assoc.), IEEE, Am. Soc. Engr. Edn., Tech. Assn. Pulp and Paper Industries, Sigma Xi, Phi Kappa Phi, Tau Beta Pi, Pi Tau Sigma. Avocations: travel, running. Office: Tex A&M Univ Dept Mech Engring College Station TX 77843-0001 E-mail: jyagoobi@mengr.tamu.edu.

SEYFERT, WAYNE GEORGE, secondary education educator, anatomy educator; b. Roslyn Park, N.Y., Nov. 23, 1947; s. George William Seyfert and Helen Francis (Weiss) Marks; m. Kathleen A. Kearns, May 23, 1970 (div. 1980); children: Sean Francis, Kerry Noelle, Adam Wayne. BS in Biology, SUNY, Cortland, 1969; MS in Biology, L.I. U. at C.W. Post, 1973; profl. diploma in sch. adminstrn., CUNY at Queen's Coll., N.Y.C., 1988. Cert. biology and secondary sci. tchr., N.Y.; cert. sch. adminstr. and supr., N.Y.; cert. sch. dist. adminstr., N.Y. Jr. h.s. sci. tchr. Port Washington (N.Y.) Schs., 1969-70; sci. tchr. Lawrence (N.Y.) Pub. Schs., 1970—2003; instr. North Shore Sci. Mus., Plandome, NY, 1973—75; adj. prof. human anatomy and physiology Nassau C.C., Garden City, NY, 1975—, N.Y. Inst. Tech., 1994—. Summer program dir. Sci. Mus. L.I., Plandome, 1976-85; environ. cons. Town of Brookhaven, L.I., 1978-80. Contbr. articles to profl. publs. Membership chmn. Boy Scouts Am., Sunrise dist., N.Y., 1978-79; mem. conservation adv. coun. Town of Brookhaven, 1977-79; mem. L.I. Sci. Congress exec. bd., 1985-98. Recipient Ednl. Leadership award Lawrence Ednl. Found., 1998, named L.I. Educator of Month, Hofstra U./TV Channel 12, L.I., 1995, Person of the Yr., Nassau Herald, 1998, STANYS Nassau County H.S. Sci. Tchr. of Yr., 1998. Mem. AAAS, Am. Fedn. Tchrs., Adj. Faculty Assn., Nat. Sci. Tchrs. Assn., Nat. Biology Tchr. Assn., Am. Philatelic Soc., Am. 1st Day Cover Soc., Am. Revenue Assn., Am. Perfin Soc., Am. Precanceled Stamp Soc., United Postal Stationary Soc., Meter Stamp Soc., State Revenue Assn., Am. Airmail Soc., Aerogramme Soc., Christmas Seal and Charity Seal Soc., N.Y. Acad. Scis., N.Y. State United Tchrs., Sci. Tchrs. Assn. N.Y. State, Lawrence Tchrs. Assn. (1st v.p. 1984-2001), MACUB Soc. for Neutobiology. Achievements include writing first history of America's first prairie and performance of first environmental study to trace an area's environmental change since first European encroachment. Home: PO Box 116 Woodmere NY 11598-0116

SEYFERTH, DIETMAR, chemist, educator; b. Chemnitz, Germany, Jan. 11, 1929; arrived in U.S., 1933; s. Herbert C. and Elisabeth (Schuchardt) S.; m. Helena A. McCoy, Aug. 25, 1956; children— Eric Steven, Karl Dietmar, Elisabeth Mary. BA summa cum laude, U. Buffalo, 1951, MA, 1953; PhD, Harvard, 1955; Dr. honoris causa, U. Aix-Marseille, 1979, Paul Sabatier Univ., Toulouse, France, 1992. Fulbright scholar Tech. Hochschule, Munich, Germany, 1954-55; postdoctoral fellow Harvard U., 1956-57; faculty MIT, 1957—, prof. chemistry, 1965-2000, prof. emeritus, 2000—, Robert T. Haslam and Bradley Dewey prof., 1983-99. Cons. to industry, 1957—; prof. emeritus, 2000—. Author: Annual Surveys of Organometallic Chemistry, 3 vols, 1965, 66, 67; regional editor: Jour. Organometallic Chemistry, 1963-81; coordinating editor revs. and survey sects., 1964-81; editor: Organometallics, 1981—; contbr. research papers to profl. lit. Recipient Disting. Alumnus award U. Buffalo, 1964, Alexander von Humboldt Found. sr. award, 1984, Clifford C. Furnas Meml. award SUNY-Buffalo, 1987; Guggenheim fellow, 1968. Fellow AAAS, Am. Inst. Chemists, Inst. Materials, Am. Acad. Arts and Scis.; mem. NAS, Am. Chem. Soc. (Frederic Stanley Kipping award in organosilicon chemistry 1972, disting. svc. award advancement inorganic chemistry 1981, award in organometallic chemistry, 1996, Arthur C. Cope Sr. Scholar award 2003), Materials Rsch. Soc., Am. Ceramic Soc., Royal Soc. Chemistry, Gesellschaft Deutscher Chemiker, German Acad. Scientists-Leopoldina, Phi Beta Kappa, Sigma Xi. Office: MIT 77 Massachusetts Ave Rm 4-382 Cambridge MA 02139-4307 Office Phone: 617-253-1861. Business E-Mail: seyferth@mit.edu.

SEYFERTH, VIRGINIA M. public relations executive; b. Detroit; BA, Grand Valley State U., Allendale, Mich. With pub. rels. dept. St. Jude Children's Rsch. Hosp., 1977-79, AMOCO Oil Co., 1979-81, Amway Corp., 1981-84; pres. Seyferth & Assocs., Inc., Grand Rapids, Mich., 1984—. Office: Seyferth & Assocs Inc Ste 202 40 Monroe Ctr NW Grand Rapids MI 49503

SEYFFARTH, LINDA JEAN WILCOX, corporate executive; b. Montour Falls, N.Y., May 10, 1948; d. Maurice Roscoe and Theodora (Van Tassell) Wilcox; m. P. Tomlin Agnew, June 29, 1991; 1 child by previous marriage, Kristin. BA magna cum laude, Syracuse (N.Y.) U., 1970; MBA with honors, NYU, 1977. Programmer Prudential Ins. Co., Newark, 1970-73; with Hoffmann-La Roche Inc., Nutley, N.J., 1973—, corp. controller, 1985-88, v.p., contr., 1989-95, v.p. fin., 1995-99, v.p., treas. U.S., 1999—. Bd. dirs. St. Barnabas Burn Found., West Orange, N.J.; vice chmn. Ind. Coll. Fund, Summit, N.J.; bd. dirs., treas. Glen Ridge (N.J.) Ednl. Found. Mem. Nat. Assn. Accts., Fin. Execs. Inst., Leadership N.J., Phi Beta Kappa, Beta Gamma Sigma. Office: Hoffmann-LaRoche Inc 340 Kingsland St Nutley NJ 07110-1199

SEYFRIED, VINCENT F. historian; b. N.Y.C., Apr. 18, 1918; s. Christian F. and Ottilie J. Seyfried; m. Constance J. Goldsmith, July 1, 1955. AB, Fordham U., 1939, MA, 1941. Tchr. N.Y.C. Bd. Edn., 1945—79; ret., 1979; historian City of Garden City, NY, 1979—. Historian L.I. R.R., Jamaica, NY, 1984—; cons. Trustees of Garden City, Jamaica Bd. Dirs. 1st lt. USAF, 1942—45. Roman Catholic. Avocations: history, books, languages. Home: 163 Pine St Garden City NY 11530

SEYMORE, JAMES W., JR., magazine editor; Exec. editor People Magazine, 1988—90; mng. editor Entertainment Weekly, N.Y.C., 1990—2002; editor at-large Time Inc., 2002—03.

SEYMOUR, CHARLENA, academic administrator; m. Harry Seymour. BA, Howard U., 1965; MA, Ohio State U., 1967, PhD in Speech and Hearing Sci., 1981. Asst. prof. U. Mass., Amherst, 1971—78, assoc. prof., 1978—89, chair dept. comm. disorders, 1984—92, dean Grad. Sch., 1994—2001, provost, 2001—. Chair Coun. Grad. Schs. Adv. Com. on Minorities in Grad. Edn. Creative editor: Communication Disorders Textbook Series. Recipient Disting. Alumni award, Sch. Intercultural and Race Rels., Harvard Found., Harvard U., 1997. Fellow: Am. Speech-Lang. Hearing Assn.; mem.: N.E. Assn. Grad. Schs. (pres.-elect). Office: U Mass Office of the Provost 362 Whitmore Bldg 181 Presidents Dr Amherst MA 01003*

SEYMOUR, EVERETT HEDDEN, JR., lawyer; b. Tuxedo Park, N.Y., Apr. 16, 1958; s. Everett Hedden and Deborah (Robinson) S. BA, Yale U., 1980; JD, U. Va., 1986. Bar: N.Y. 1988, U.S. Dist. Ct. (so. and ea. dists.) N.Y. 1988, Conn. 1988, U.S. Dist. Ct. Conn. 1988. Law clk. to justice U.S. Dist. Ct., New Haven, 1986-87; assoc. Davis Polk & Wardwell, N.Y.C., 1987-97; v.p., asst. gen. counsel J.P. Morgan Chase & Co., N.Y.C., 1997—. Articles rev. editor U. Va. Law Rev., 1984-86. Office: JP Morgan Chase & Co 270 Park Ave 39th Fl New York NY 10017-2014

SEYMOUR, FREDERICK PRESCOTT, JR., industrial engineer, consultant; b. Oak Park, Ill., June 19, 1924; s. Frederick Prescott and Ivy Louise (Horder) S.; m. Janet Mary Stocking, Oct. 15, 1960; children: Robert Prescott, Bruce Stocking, Mary Janet. BS, Cornell U., 1948; MS in Commerce, U. Ill., 1951, MBA, U. Chgo., 1957. Indsl. engr., dir. planning, exec. salesman R R Donnelley and Sons Co./Lakeside Press, Chgo., 1951-72; regional dir. U.S. Postal Svc., Chgo., 1972-76; dir. advt. Spiegel, Inc., Chgo., 1976-80; pres. Frederick P. Seymour and Assocs., Inc., Winnetka, Ill., 1980—. Pres. Cornell Univ. Club. Chgo., 1960-61, Exec. Program Club, Chgo., 1972-73; mem. Postmaster Gen.'s tech. adv. com., Washington, 1973—. Contbg. editor: Gravure mag., 1982—; contbr. articles to profl. jours. Precinct capt. New Trier Rep. Orgn., Winnetka, 1970-72. With USN, 1944-46, PTO. Mem. ASME (life), Cornell Soc. Engrs., Graphic Comms. Assn. (Innovator award 1988), Gravure Assn. Am., Graphic Arts Industry Rsch. and Engring. Coun. (Non Pareil Soc. award 1990), Assn. Postal Commerce (bd. dirs. 2003), Econ. Club Chgo. (life).

SEYMOUR, JANE, actress; b. Hillingdon, Middlesex, Eng., Feb. 15, 1951; came to U.S., 1976; d. John Benjamin and Mieke Frankenberg; m. David Flynn, July 18, 1981 (div. 1991); 2 children; m. James Keach, May 15, 1993; 2 children (twins). Student, Arts Ednl. Sch., London. Appeared in films Oh What A Lovely War, 1968, The Only Way, 1968, Young Winston, 1969, Live and Let Die, 1971, Sinbad and the Eye of the Tiger, 1973, Somewhere in Time, 1979, Oh Heavenly Dog, 1979, Lassiter, 1984, Head Office, Scarlet Pimpernel, Haunting Passion, Dark Mirror, Obsessed with a Married Woman, Killer on Board, The Tunnel, 1988, The French Revolution, Tochiny Wild Horses, 2002; TV films include Frankenstein, The True Story, 1972, Captains and The Kings, 1976 (Emmy nomination), 7th Avenue, 1976, The Awakening Land, 1977, The Four Feathers, 1977, Battlestar Galactica, Dallas Cowboy Cheerleaders, 1979, Our Mutual Friend, PBS, Eng., 1975, Jamaica Inn, 1982, Sun Also Rises, 1984, Crossings, 1986, Keys to Freedom, Angel of Death, 1990, Praying Mantis, 1993; A Passion for Justice: The Hazel Brannon Smith Story, 1994; Broadway appearances include Amadeus, 1980-81, I Remember You, 1992, Matters of the Heart, 1991, Sunstroke, 1992, Praying Mantis, 1993, Heidi, 1993; TV mini-series include East of Eden, 1980, The Richest Man in the World, 1988 (Emmy award), The Woman He Loved, 1988, Jack the Ripper, 1988, War and Remembrance, 1988, 89; host PBS documentary, Japan, 1988; TV series: Dr. Quinn: Medicine Woman, 1993-98 (Emmy nomination, Lead Actress Drama, 1994, 98, Golden Globe award 1996), A Marriage of Convenience, CBS, 1998, A Memory in My Heart, CBS, 1999, Murder in the Mirror, CBS, 2000, Enslavement: The True Life Story of Fanny Kemble, Showtime, 2000, Blackout, CBS, 2000, Yesterday's Children, CBS, Dr. Quinn Winters Heart, 2001, Heart of a Stranger, 2002; author: Jane Seymour's Guide to Romantic Living, 1986, Two at a Time, 2001; co-author: Yum, Splat, 1998, Boing, 1999. Decorated Order Brit. Empire; recipient OBE award, 2000; named Hon. Citizen of Ill., Gov. Thompson, 1977. Mem. Screen Actors Guild, AFTRA, Actors Equity, Brit. Equity. Office: Guttman Assocs 118 S Beverly Dr Ste 201 Beverly Hills CA 90212-3016*

SEYMOUR, JEFFREY ALAN, governmental relations consultant; b. L.A., Aug. 31, 1950; s. Daniel and Evelyn (Schwartz) S.; m. Valerie Joan Parker, Dec. 2, 1973; 1 child, Jessica Lynn. AA in Social Sci., Santa Monica Coll., 1971; BA in Polit. Sci., UCLA, 1973; MPA, 1977. Councilman aide L.A. City Coun., 1972-74; county supr.'s sr. dep. L.A. Bd. Suprs., 1974-82; v.p. Bank of L.A., 1982-83; prin. Jeffrey Seymour & Assocs., L.A., 1983-84; ptnr. Morey/Seymour & Assocs., L.A., 1984—2002, Seymour Consulting Group, 2002—. Mem. comml. panel Am. Arbitration Assn., 1984—90. Chmn. West Hollywood Parking Adv. Com., L.A., 1983-84; chmn. social action com. Temple Emanuel of Beverly Hills, 1986-89, bd. dirs. 1988-93, v.p. 1990-93; v.p. Congregation N'Vay Shalom, 1994-95; mem. Pan Pacific Park Citizens Adv. Com., L.A., 1982-85; bd. dirs. William O'Douglas Outdoor Classroom, L.A., 1981-88; mem. bd. regents U. Calif., 2001-02; pres. Alumni Assns. U. Calif., 2000-02; chair UCLA Fund, 2002—. Recipient plaques for svcs. rendered Beverlywood Cheviot Hills Dem. Club, L.A., 1981, Jewish Fedn. Coun. Greater L.A., 1983, certs. of appreciation, L.A. Olympic Organizing Com., 1984, County of L.A., 1984, City of L.A., 1987, Santa Monica Mountains Conservancy, 1999, UCLA Alumni Assn., 2002, others; commendatory resolutions, rules com. Calif. State Senate, 1987, Calif. State Assembly, 1987, 96, County of L.A., 1987, City of L.A., 1987; mem. bd. Regents of U. Calif., 2000-2002. Mem. ASPA, UCLA Alumni Assn. (mem. govtl. steering com. 1983-97, bd. dirs. 1995—, chair govtl. rels. steering com. 1995-97, pres. 1998-2000); exec. sect. Calif. Fedn. Young Dems., 1971; mem. Calif. Dem. Cen. Com., 1979-82; pres. Beverlywood-Cheviot Hills Dem. Club, L.A., 1978-81; co-chmn. Westside Chancellor's Assocs. UCLA, 1986-88; mem. L.A. Olympic Citizens Adv. Com.; mem. liaison adv. commn. with city and county govt. for 1984 Olympics, 1984; v.p. comty. rels. metro region, Jewish Fedn. Coun. of L.A., 1985-87, co-chmn. urban affairs commn., 1987-89, vice chmn., 1989-90, subcom. chmn. local govt. law and legislation commn., 1990, chmn. campus outreach task force, 1994; mem. adv. bd. Nat. Jewish Ctr. for Immunology & Respiratory Medicine, 1991-93; bd. dirs. Hillel Coun. of L.A., 1991; mem. platform on world peace and internat. rels. Calif. Dems., 1983; pres. 43d Assembly Dist. Dem. Coun., 1975-79; arbitrator BBB, 1984; trustee UCLA Found., 1989-97; pres. UCLA Jewish Alumni, 1992-95; mem. Santa Monica Mountains Conservancy adv. com., 1996-99; mem. cabinet Jewish Cmty. Rels. Com. Greater L.A., 1994, chair campus outreach task force, 1994-95, govtl. rels. commn., 1995-96, v. chair Jewish Cmty. Rels. com. Jewish Fedn. Coun. Greater L.A., 1998; mem. bd. dirs., Century City C of C, 1998-2000, adv. bd. L.A. Peace Now, UCLA Fund (chair 2002—), Alumni Assn. of U. Calif. (pres. 2001-2002, chmn. 2002-2004, bd. govs. 2004—, mem. adv. com. 2004—). Office: Seymour Consulting Group 15233 Ventura Blvd Ste 1002 Van Nuys CA 91403 Office Phone: 818-905-0283. Business E-Mail: jeff@jseymourgroup.com

SEYMOUR, JOSEPH JOHN, air transportation executive; b. Herkimer, N.Y., July 11, 1947; s. John Edward and Julia (Crough) S.; m. Susan Elizabeth LathburySept. 19, 1970; children: Abigail, Christopher. BBA, Northeastern U., 1970; M in City Planning, U. R.I., 1976. Dir. urban renewal City of East Rochester, N.Y., 1967-76; spl. asst. for downtown devel. City of Rochester, N.Y., 1977-78; dir. planning and devel. City of Peekskill, N.Y., 1978-82; commr. planning and devel. City of Yonkers, 1983-84; city mgr. City of Peekskill, 1984—89; commsr. of general services NY, 1990—95; exec. dep. commsr. NY Dept. of Motor Vehicles, 1995—2001; exec. dir. NY Port Authority, 2001—. Ind. cons. Village of Hilton, Village of East Rochester, Village of Fairport, Town of Webster, City of Naughatuck, Conn.; corp. dir. Unique Homes of N.Y. Inc. Mem. Internat. City Mgrs. Assn., Am. Planning Assn., Nat. Assn. Housing and Renewal Ofcls. Avocations: skiing, sailing, biking.

SEYMOUR, LESLEY JANE, magazine editor-in-chief; b. San Juan, P.R. BA, Duke U., 1978. Reporter Women's Wear Daily, 1978, N.Y. Daily News Tonight, 1981—82; writer, sr. editor Vogue Mag., 1982—91; beauty dir. Glamour Mag., 1994—97; editor-in-chief YM/Young & Modern, N.Y.C., 1997—98, Redbook, 1998—2001, Marie Claire mag., N.Y.C., 2001—. Office: Marie Claire 1790 Broadway New York NY 10019

SEYMOUR, LISA, museum director; b. Oct. 30, 1962; m. E. David Seymour. BA in Mass Comms., U. Denver, 1984; MA in Mass Comms., 1985. Grad. teaching asst. U. Denver, 1985; records clk. typist Kingman (Ariz.) Police Dept., 1985-86; sec. First Presbyn. Ch., Elko, Nev., 1986-87; exec. dir. Elko (Nev.) County Against Domestic Violence, 1987; exec. dir. of found. Elko (Nev.) Gen. Hosp. Found., 1989-90; mgr. cmty. rels. Elko (Nev.) Gen. Hosp., 1987-90; adtg. mgr. Elko (Nev.) Ind., 1990-91, newspaper editor, reporter, photographer, 1991-94; archivist and oral historian Northeastern Nev. Mus., Elko, 1994-95; interim mus. adminstr., 1995; mus. dir., 1996-99. Grantee Newmont Gold Co., E.L. Cord Found., E.L. Wiegard Found., 1996. Office: c/o Northeastern Nev Mus 1515 Idaho St Elko NV 89801-4021

SEYMOUR, MCNEIL VERNAM, lawyer; b. St. Paul, Dec. 21, 1934; s. McNeil Vernam and Katherine Grace (Klein) S.; children: Margaret, McNeil Vernam, James, Benjamin; m. Mary Katherine Velner, May 15, 1993. AB, Princeton U., 1957; JD, U. Chgo., 1960. Bar: Minn. 1960, U.S. Dist. Ct. Minn. 1960. Mem. Seymour & Seymour, St. Paul, 1960-71; mem. firm Briggs & Morgan, St. Paul, 1971—, ptnr., 1976—. Chmn., bd. trustees Thomas Irvine Dodge Nature Ctr.; sec., bd. dirs. Ramsey County Law Libr., 1972—76; pres., treas. White Bear Unitarian Ch., 1964—65; trustee Oakland Cemetery Assn. With U.S. Army, 1960—62. Mem. Minn. Bar Assn., Ramsey County Bar Assn., Somerset Country Club. Republican. Unitarian Universalist. Home: 886 S Highview Cir Mendota Heights MN 55118-3686 Office: Briggs & Morgan W-2200 1st Nat Bank Bldg Saint Paul MN 55101 Office Phone: 651-808-6601. E-mail: MSeymour@Briggs.com.

SEYMOUR, PAUL DOUGLAS, mathematician, educator; b. Plymouth, Devon, England, July 26, 1950; s. Percival Douglas and Daisy Amelia (Williams) Seymour; m. Shelley Jane MacDonald, Aug. 25, 1979; children: Amy Elizabeth, Emily Miriam. BA, Oxford (England) U., 1971, MSc, 1972, D Phil, MA, Oxford (England) U., 1974. Rsch. fellow U. Swansea, Wales, 1974—76; jr. rsch fellow Merton Coll., Oxford, 1976—80; vis. rsch. assoc. U. Waterloo, Canada, 1978—79; assoc. and full prof. Ohio State U., Columbus, 1980—83; mem. of tech. staff, sr. scientist Bellcore, Morristown, NJ, 1983—96; prof. dept. math. Princeton (N.J.) U., 1996—. Cons. Telcordia Technologies, Morristown, 1996—. Contbr. more than 140 articles to profl. jours.; editor-in-chief: Jour. Graph Theory, 1994—. Co-recipient D.R. Fulkerson prize, 1994; recipient, Am. Math Soc., 1979, G. Polya prize, Soc. Indsl. and Applied Math., 1983; fellow, Sloan Found., 1983. Atheist. Achievements include patents for comm. network ring router (with W. Cook). Home: 100 Cold Soil Rd Lawrenceville NJ 08648 Office: Princeton U Math Dept Fine Hall Washington Rd Princeton NJ 08544

SEYMOUR, RACHEAL, human services administrator; M in Pub. Policy, Harvard U., 1997; BA in Internat. Studies, U. of Wash., 1994. Commr. Beverly Hills (Calif.) Human Rels. Commn., 2000—. Actor: Strong Medicine, Surplus Male. Recipient Truman scholarship, H.S. Truman Found., 1993, Key to the City of Cambrige, Mass. Mem.: SAG (bd. dirs. 2002), Harvard Club of So. Calif. Avocations: horseback riding, golf, Japanese literature, football, martial arts. Office: Beverly Hills Human Rels Commn 455 N Rexford Dr Beverly Hills CA 90210-4817 E-mail: raseymour@aol.com.

SEYMOUR, RICHARD DEMING, technology educator; b. Shelby, Ohio, Oct. 3, 1955; s. G. Deming and Elizabeth (Peterson) S.; m. Vicki Stebleton; 1 child, Ryan. BS in Edn., Ohio State U., 1978; MA, Ball State U., 1982; EdD, W.Va. U., 1990. Tchr. Crestview Sr. High Sch., Ashland, Ohio, 1978-81; from instr. to assoc. prof. Ball State U., Muncie, Ind., 1982—. Vis. instr. W.Va. U., Morgantown, 1985, Oreg. State U., 1990-91. Co-author: Exploring Communications, 1987, rev. edit., 2000; co-editor: Manufacturing in Technology Education, 1993. Advisor 4-H Clubs, Richland County, Ohio, 1978-81; dir. tech. in-svc. workshops Ind. Dept. Edn., Indpls., 1988-2000. Named technology tchr. educator of yr. Coun. on Technology Tchr. Edn., 1998. Mem.: Tech. Edn. Collegiate Assn. (internat. advisor 1990—92, nat. contest coord. 1992—), Am. Soc. Engring. Edn., Tech. Educators Ind. (pres. 1995—96), Ind. Math., Sci., Tech. Alliance (bd. dirs. 1994—), Coun. on Tech. Tchr. Edn. (v.p. 2003—), Soc. Mfg. Engrs., Internat. Tech. Edn. Assn. (bd. dirs. 1992—94, chmn. internat. conf. 1999, award of distinction 1999), Phi Delta Kappa, Epsilon Pi Tau. Methodist. Avocations: model railroads, sports, travel. Office: Ball State U Dept Industry Tech Muncie IN 47306-0255 E-mail: rseymour@bsu.edu.

SEYMOUR, SCOTT, science administrator; BEE, Poly. U., Bklyn.; JD, Western State U. From engr. to v.p., B-2 program mgr. Northrop Grumman Corp., 1983—97, v.p. air combat sys., 1998—2001, corp. v.p., pres. integrated sys., 2001—. With USMC. Office: Northrop Grumman Corp Air Combat Sys Integrated Sys One Northrop Grumman Ave El Segundo CA 90245-2804

SEYMOUR, SLOAN, publishing executive; V.p. Publisher PC Week, Medford, MA.

SEYMOUR, STEPHANIE, model; b. San Diego, July 23, 1968; children: Dylan, Peter Jr., Harry. Appeared on the covers of Vogue, Elle, Cosmopolitan, Allure, Marie Claire; featured in comml. Diet Coke, Victoria's Secret, L'Oreal; worked with Helmut Newton, Herb Ritts, Francesco Scavullo, Irving Penn, Albert Watson, Arthur Elgort, Richard Avedon. Office: IMG Models 304 Park Ave S Ph N New York NY 10010-5339

SEYMOUR, STEPHANIE KULP, federal judge; b. Battle Creek, Mich., Oct. 16, 1940; d. Francis Bruce and Frances Cecelia (Bria) Kulp; m. R. Thomas Seymour, June 10, 1972; children: Bart, Bria, Sara, Anna. BA magna cum laude, Smith Coll., 1962; JD, Harvard U., 1965. Bar: Okla. 1965. Practice, Boston, 1965—66, Tulsa, 1966—67, Houston, 1968—69; assoc. Doerner, Stuart, Saunders, Daniel & Anderson, Tulsa, 1971—75, ptnr., 1975—79; judge U.S. Ct. Appeals (10th cir.) Okla., Tulsa, 1979—94, 2000—, chief judge, 1994—2000. Mem. U.S. Jud. Conf., 1994—, com. defender svcs., 1985—90, chmn., 1987—90, com. to review cir. council conduct and disability, 1996—; joint fed. tribal rels. com. 9th and 10th cirs., 1993—; mem. Okla. State Fed. Tribal Judicial Coun., 1993—94. Task force Tulsa Human Rights Commn., 1972—76; legal adv. panel Tulsa Task Force Battered Women, 1971—77; trustee Tulsa County Law Libr., 1977—78. Mem.: ABA, Am. Inns of Ct. (Council Oak chpt.), Nat. Assn. Women Judges, Fed. Judges Assn., Tulsa County Bar Assn., Okla. Bar Assn. (assoc. bar examiner 1973—79), Phi Beta Kappa. Office: US Courthouse 333 W 4th St Ste 4-562 Tulsa OK 74103-3819

SEYMOUR, THADDEUS, English educator; b. N.Y.C., June 29, 1928; s. Whitney North and Lola Virginia (Vickers) S.; m. Polly Gnagy, Nov. 20, 1948; children— Elizabeth Halsey, Thaddeus, Samuel Whitney, Mary Duffie, Abigail Comfort AB, U. Calif., 1950; MA, U. N.C., 1951, PhD, 1955; D.H.L. (hon.), Wilkes Coll., 1968; LL.D. (hon.), Butler U., 1971, Ind. State U., 1976; LLD (hon.), Wabash Coll., 1984, U. Cen. Fla., 1990, Stetson U., 1990; DHL (hon.), Rollins Coll., 1990. Mem. faculty Dartmouth Coll., 1954-69, prof. English, dean coll., 1959-69; pres. Wabash Coll., Crawfordsville, Ind., 1969-78, Rollins Coll., Winter Park, Fla., 1978-90, prof. English, 1978—. Pres. Ind. Conf. Higher Edn., 1977; v.p. Assoc. Colls. Ind., 1978; vice-chmn. Fla. Ind. Colls. Fund Past mem. Ind. Bicentennial Commn.; trustee Park-Tudor Sch., 1970-78, Bach Festival Soc., Winter Park Pub. Libr., 1998—; chmn. Fla. selection com. Rhodes Scholarship Trust, 1983-88; chmn. Habitat for Humanity of Winter Park, 1994—; sec.-treas. Winter Park Health Found., 1998—. Mem. Cmty. Found. Ctrl. Fla. (bd. dirs.), Ring 219 (charter), Internat. Brotherhood Magicians, Century Assn., Rotary, Omicron Delta Kappa. Home: 1350 College Pt Winter Park FL 32789-5700 E-mail: tseymour@rollins.edu.

SFEKAS, STEPHEN JAMES, lawyer, educator; b. Balt., Feb. 12, 1947; s. James Stephen and Lee (Mesologites) S.; m. Joanne Lorraine Murphy, May 27, 1973; children: James Stephen, Andrew Edward Stephen, Christina Marie; m. Elizabeth Ruff, Nov. 1, 1997. BS in Fgn. Svc., Georgetown U., 1968, JD, 1973; MA, Yale U., 1972. Bar: Md. 1973, U.S. Dist. Ct. Md. 1974, U.S. Ct. Appeals (4th cir.) 1974. Law clk. U.S. Dist. Ct., Balt., 1973-74; assoc. firm Frank, Bernstein, Conaway & Goldman, Balt., 1974-75; asst. atty. gen. State of Md., Balt., 1975-81; assoc. firm Tydings & Rosenberg, Balt., 1981-82, ptnr., 1983-86; with firm Miles & Stockbridge, Balt., 1986-90; ptnr. Weinberg & Green, Balt., 1991-98, Saul, Ewing, LLP, Balt., 1998—2001; counsel Cook & Di Franco, LLC, 2001—. Instr. legal writing C.C. Balt., 1976-79; instr. legal ethics Goucher Coll., Balt., 1979; adj. prof. adminstrv. law U. Md., Balt., 1981-93, health, 1993—, law sch. U. Balt., 1993—. Editor Georgetown Law Jour., 1972-73; contbr. articles to legal publs. Bd. dirs. Md. region NCCJ, 1981-89, co-chmn. Md. region, 1986-89, Orthodox Christian Laity, 1990—98, Ctrl. Md. Ecumenical Coun., 1991—93, ARC of Balt. Vol. for Med. Engring., 2001-; mem. Piraeus Sister City Com., City of Balt., 1983-89; mem. parish coun. Greek Orthodox Cathedral of Annunciation, Balt., 1981-84; mem. internat. com. Balt. region ARC, 1984-85; mem. adv. com. on bread for the world Dept. Ch. and Soc., Greek Orthodox Archdiocese North and S.Am., 1984—; pres. Greek Orthodox Counseling and Social Svcs. of Balt., 1984-88; mem. bylaw com. Girl Scouts Ctrl. Md., 1989-91, Md. Leadership Program, 1997; mem. pres.'s adv. coun. U. Md., Baltimore County; mem. human rights

com. ARC of the U.S., 2002—. Danforth fellow, Woodrow Wilson fellow, WHO fellow, London, 1979. Fellow: Md. Bar Found., Soc. for Values in Higher Edn. (bd. dir. 2002—); mem.: ABA (forum com. on health law, Grant Morris fellow 1979), Am. Health Lawyers Assn., Bar Assn. Balt. City, Md. Bar Assn. Democrat. Office: Cook & Di Franco LLC Ste 1810 120 E Baltimore St Baltimore MD 21202 Office Phone: 410-223-1590 225. E-mail: ssfekas@cookanddifranco.com.

SFERRAZZA, ANTHONY CARL, historian, writer; b. N.Y.C., June 13, 1959; s. Carl Richard and Marie Jane (Martirano) Sferrazza. BA in History, George Washington U., 1983. Writer Presdl. Inaugural Book Com., Washington, 1980—81, 1984—85, 1988—89, Exec. Office of Pres., Washington, 1981—82, White House Preservation Fund, Washington, 1983—84; speechwriter Office of First Lady Nancy Reagan, Washington, 1985—86; instr. George Washington U., Washington, 1994; contbg. editor George Mag., N.Y.C., 1997—99; bibliographer, bd. dirs. Nat. First Ladies Libr, Canton, Ohio, 1996—. Freelance hist. writer Style sect. Washington Post, Washington, 1985—98; hist. cons. Nat. Mus. Am. History, Smithsonian Instn., Washington, 1990—92; hist. source Office of First Lady Hillary Clinton, Washington, 1993—2001. Author: First Ladies: The Saga of the Presidents' Wives and Their Power, 1789,1990, 2 vols., 1990—91, As We Remember Her: Jacqueline Kennedy Onassis in the Words of Her Friends and Family, 1997, Florence Harding: The First Lady, The Jazz Age and the Death of America's Most Scandalous President, 1998, The Kennedy White House: Family Life and Pictures, 1961-1963, 2001, America's First Families, 2000. Named Bicentennial Honoree, U. Louisville, 1997; recipient Spl. Book Collections, Brandeis U. Libr., 2001. Episcopalian. Avocations: hiking, boxing, tennis.

SFIKAS, PETER MICHAEL, lawyer, educator; b. Gary, Ind., Aug. 9, 1937; s. Michael E. and Helen (Thureanos) S.; m. Freida Platon, Apr. 24, 1966; children: Ellen M., Pamela C., Sandra N. BS, Ind. U., 1959; JD, Northwestern U., 1962. Bar: Ill. 1962, U.S. Dist. Ct. (no. dist.) Ill. 1963, U.S. Ct. Appeals (7th cir.) 1963, U.S. Supreme Ct. 1970, U.S. Ct. Appeals (9th cir.) 1976, U.S. Ct. Appeals (3d cir.) 1981, U.S. Ct. Appeals (D.C. cir.) 1984, U.S. Ct. Appeals (8th cir.) 1995, U.S. Dist. Ct. (cen. dist.) Ill. 1988. Atty. Legal Aid Bur., United Charities Chgo., 1962-63; sr. ptnr. Peterson & Ross, Chgo., 1970-95; chief counsel, assoc. exec. dir. divsn. legal affairs ADA, Chgo., 1995—; ptnr. Bell, Boyd & Lloyd, Chgo., 1996—. Prosecutor Village of LaGrange Park, Ill., 1969-74; mem. rules com. Ill. Supreme Ct., 1975-95, mem. spl. joint com. on discovery rules, 1995; arbitrator Nat. Panel Arbitrators, 1972—; adj. prof. Loyola U. Sch. Law, 1978—; guest lectr. U. Ill. Coll. Dentistry, 1988-95; lectr. corp. counsel inst. Northwestern U. Sch. Law, 1984, lectr. Ray Garret Jr. Corp. and Securities Law Inst., 1996. Co-author: Antitrust and Unfair Competition Practice Handbook, 1996; contbr. articles to profl. jours. Mem. Ill. steering com. Ct. Watching Project, LWV, 1975-77; pres. Holy Apostles Greek Orthodox Ch. Parish Coun., 1987-89; co-pres. Oak Sch. PTO, 1989-90; mem. com. to select sch. supr., dist. 86, DuPage County, Ill., 1993-94. Recipient Maurice Weigle award, Chgo. Bar Found., 1973, Fones award and hon. membership, Conn. Dental Assn., 1998. Fellow Am. Bar Found., Am. Coll. Trial Lawyers, Chgo. Bar Found. (life); mem. ABA (editor in chief Forum Law Jour. sect. ins., negligence and compensation law 1972-76), Ill. Bar Found. (bd. dirs. 1975-77), Northwestern U. Law Alumni Assn. (1st v.p. 1985-86, pres. 1986-87, Svc. award 1990), Ill. State Bar Assn. (bd. govs. 1970-76, chmn. antitrust law sect. coun. 1986-87), Chgo. Bar Assn. (editl. bd. Chgo. Bar Record 1973-84), Bar Assn. 7th Fed. Cir. (chmn. com. on meetings 1973-75), Ill. Inst. Continuing Legal Edn. (chmn. profl. antitrust problems program 1976, author program on counseling corps., antitrust and trade regulation), Legal Club Chgo. (sec.-treas, 1984-86, v.p. 1989-90, pres. 1990-91). Office: Bell Boyd & Lloyd 70 W Madison St Ste 3300 Chicago IL 60602-4284 Office Phone: 312-807-4348. E-mail: psfikas@bellboyd.com.

SFORZA, ALFRED VINCENT, dentist, educator, writer; b. Huntington, N.Y., Aug. 26, 1939; s. Alfred Anthony and Lena Sforza; m. Barbara Joan Albin, June 10, 1961; children: Anthony V., Debra Ann Smith, Sharon Lee Buehrig. BA, N.Y. U., U. Heights N.Y., 1961; DDS, NYU, 1965. Cert. D.D.S. N.Y. Officer Suffolk County Police, L.I., NY, 1963—65; dentist pvt. practice, Huntington, NY, 1965—; assoc. clin. prof. NYU Coll. of Dentistry, N.Y.C., 1965—. Author: Portrait of a Small Town Huntington Station, 1996, Portrait of a Small Town II Huntington 'In the Beginning', 2001. Bd. of trustees Huntington Historical Soc., 1996—; Anniversary Com. Huntington 350th Anniversary, 2002—. Mem.: Dentist For A Better Huntington, Suffolk County Dental, Am. Dental Assn. (assoc.). Avocations: skiing, hiking, history. Office: Alfred V Sforza DDS PC 44 West Neck Road Huntington NY 11743

SFORZINI, RICHARD HENRY, aerospace engineer, educator; b. Rochester, N.Y., July 25, 1924; m. Corinne Lorenz, 1947; children: Richard Jr., Suzanne Simonelli, Deborah Pugh, Michael, Stephen, Andrew, Mark. Degree of Mech. Engr., MIT, 1954; BS, U.S. Mil. Acad., 1947. Instr. ordnance U.S. Mil. Acad., 1954-56, asst. prof., 1956-57; project dir. anti-tank missile sys. R&D Army Rocket and Guided Missile Agy., Redstone Arsenal, Ala., 1958-59; engr. Huntsville divsn. Thiokol Chem. Corp., Ala., 1959-62, mgr. engring. dept., 1962-64, dir. engring. space booster divsn., 1964-66; vis. prof. Auburn (Ala.) U., 1966-67, prof., 1967-85, prof. emeritus aerospace engring., 1985—. Home and Office: 912 Cherokee Rd Auburn AL 36830-2723

SGANGA, JOHN B. furniture holding company executive; b. Bronx, N.Y., Nov. 21, 1931; s. Charles and Marie (Crusco) S.; m. Evelyn Joan Battilana, Jan. 19, 1957; children: Mark, John B. Jr., Matthew. BS in Acctg. cum laude, Bklyn. Coll., 1961; postgrad., Bernard Baruch Coll. Systems analyst DIVCO, Wayne, N.Y., 1965-67; mgr. mgmt. cons. svcs. Coopers & Lybrand, CPAs, N.Y.C., 1967-74; sr. v.p. fin. and adminstrn. Aurora Products Co. subs. RJR Nabisco, West Hempstead, N.Y., 1974-79; contr. Gt. Lakes Carbon Corp., N.Y.C., 1979-80, v.p., 1980-81, sr. v.p. fin., CFO, 1981-86; v.p. Cunard Line, Ltd., N.Y.C., 1988; exec. v.p. CFO Consolitated Furniture Corp. (formerly Mohasco Corp.), N.Y.C., 1989—, also bd. dirs. Contbr. articles to profl. jours.; editl. adv. to Financial Management mag. Served with USNR, 1950-54. Mem. Inst. Cert. Mgmt. Cons. (a founder), Inst. Mgmt. Accts., Fin. Execs. Internat. (past chmn. com. M.I.S.), Treas.'s Club. Home: 21312 Tarraco Mission Viejo CA 92692-5921 Office: Consolidated Furniture Corp 445 Park Ave at 57th St Ste 905 New York NY 10022-2606

SGARRO, DOUGLAS A. pharmaceutical executive, lawyer; b. NY, 1959; m. Breda Sgarro; 3 children. Grad, Hamilton Coll., 1981; law degree, Univ. of Va. Sch. of Law, 1984. Assoc. Brown & Wood LLP, New York, NY, 1984—93, ptnr., 1993—97; sr. v.p. and chief legal officer CVS Pharmacy, Woonsocket, RI, 1997—2004; pres. CVS Realty Co., Woonsocket, RI, 1999—; sr. v.p. and chief legal officer CVS Corp., Woonsocket, RI, 2000—04; dir. Econ. Devel. Corp., Woonsocket, RI, 2000—; exec. v.p. Strategy, Chief Legal Officer CVS Corp., CVS Pharmacy, 2004—. Dir. Providence Children's Mus., United Way, Rye, NY. Mem.: Am. Bar Assoc. Bus. Law Sect., Internat. Assoc. of Atty. Exec. in Corp. Real Estate. Avocations: reading, watch CNN on TV, exercise. Office: Office Chief Legal Officer CVS Corp One CVS Dr Woonsocket RI 02895

SGRO, BEVERLY HUSTON, day school administrator, educator, state official; b. Ft. Worth, Jan. 12, 1941; d. James Carl and Dorothy Louise (Foster) Huston; m. Joseph Anthony Sgro, Feb. 1, 1964; children: Anthony, Jennifer. BS, Tex. Woman's U., 1963; MS, Va. Poly. Inst. and State U., 1974, PhD, 1990. Cert. tennis teaching profl. Instr. of deaf Midland (Tex.) Ind. Sch. System, 1963-64; speech pathologist Arlington (Tex.) Pub. Sch. System, 1964; rsch. asst. Tex. Christian U., 1964-65; tennis profl. Blacksburg (Va.) Country Club, 1977-81; from coord. for Greek affairs to exec. asst. to v.p. student affairs Va. Poly. Inst. and State U., Blacksburg, 1981-89, dean of students, 1989-93; sec. of edn. Commonwealth of Va., Richmond, 1994-98; interim head Collegiate Sch., Richmond, 1998-99; head Carolina Day Sch., Asheville, N.C., 1999—. Adj. faculty Coll. Edn., Va. Poly. Inst. and State U.; lectr., presented papers at numerous symposia and convs., 1983—. Trustee Foxcroft Sch., Middleburg, Va., 1989-98, pres. bd. trustees, 1993-96; bd. dirs. Habitat Humanity. Mem. AACD, Nat. Assn. Student Pers. Adminstrs., Am. Coll. Pers. Assn. (sec., com. mem. 1986-88), Omicron Delta Kappa, Phi Kappa Phi, Phi Upsilon Omicron, Pi Lambda Theta, Sigma Alpha Eta, Zeta Phi Eta. Avocations: reading, travel, theater. Home: 22 Hilltop Rd Asheville NC 28803-3030 Office: Carolina Day Sch 1345 Hendersonville Rd Asheville NC 28803-1923 Office Phone: 828-274-0757.

SGRO, JOSEPH ANTHONY, retired psychologist, educator; b. New Haven, Nov. 22, 1937; s. Fred and Tullia (Francesconi) S.; m. Beverly Ann Huston, Feb. 1, 1964; children: Anthony, Jennifer. BA, Trinity Coll., 1959; MS, Lehigh U., 1961; PhD, Tex. Christian U., 1966. Asst. prof. Old Dominion U., Norfolk, Va., 1965-67, Va. Poly. Inst. & State U., Blacksburg, 1967-71, assoc. prof., 1971-79, prof., 1979-99; prof. emeritus, 1999—; dept. head psychology Va. Poly. Inst. & State U., Blacksburg, 1982-96, mem. exec. bd., sec.-treas. coun. grad. dept. psychology, 1990-92, chmn., 1992-93; adj. prof. Warren Wilson Coll., 2000, U. NC Asheville, 2004. Vice-chmn. Va. Bd. Psychologists Examiners, Richmond, 1970-75. Editor: Virginia Tech Symposium on Applied Behavioral Science, 1980. Mem. Am. Psychol. Assn., Southeastern Psychol. Assn. (chmn. assn. heads depts. psychology 1987-89), Ea. Psychol. Assn., Va. Psychol. Assn. (pres. 1974-76), Omicron Delta Kappa, Psi Chi, Sigma Xi. Avocations: golf, cooking, yoga. Home: 22 Hilltop Rd Biltmore Forest NC 28803 E-mail: jsgro@charter.net.

SGRO, JUDY, Canadian government official; b. New Brunswick, Can., Dec. 16, 1944; Mem. Can. Parliament, 1999—; parliamentary sec. to the min. pub. works and govt. svcs. Govt. Can., 2003, min. citizenship and immigration, 2003—. Vice chair Toronto Police Svcs. Bd., 1998; mem. North York City Coun., 1987—93; regional councillor Met. Toronto Coun., 1994. Office: House of Commons Ottawa ON Canada K1A 0A6 also: Jean Edmonds Bldg Tower South 21st Fl 365 Laurier St West Ottawa ON Canada K1A 1L1*

SHAAR, H. ERIK, academic administrator; V.p. acad. affairs Shippensburg U. of Pa., until 1986; pres. Lake Superior State U., Sault Sainte Marie, Mich., 1986-92, Minot (N.D.) State U., 1992—. Office: Minot State U Office of Pres 500 University Ave W Minot ND 58707-0002

SHABAIK, AHMED, pathologist, educator; s. Abdelkader Emara Shabaik and Aziza. MB, BChir, Cairo U., 1977. Anatomic and Clin. Pathology Am. Bd. of Pathology, 1990, Cytopathology Am. Bd. of Pathology, 1992. Assoc. prof. pathology U. Calif. San Diego, 1992—. Contbr. numerous med. pubs. Fellow: Coll. Am. Pathologists, Am. Soc. Clin. Pathologists; mem.: Islamic Med. Assn. N.Am., Am. Soc. Cytopathology (assoc.), U.S. and Can. Acad. Pathology. Muslim. Office: Univ of California San Diego 9500 Gilman Dr La Jolla CA 92093-0612 E-mail: ashabaik@ucsd.edu.

SHABAZ, JOHN C. judge; b. West Allis, Wis., June 25, 1931; s. Cyrus D. and Harriet T. Shabaz; children: Scott J., Jeffrey J., Emily D., John D. LLB, Marquette U., 1957; BS in Polit. Sci., U. Wis., 1999. Comd. 2d. lt. U.S. Army, 1954, assigned to inactive reserves as capt., 1964; pvt. practice law West Allis, Wis., 1957—82; mem. Wis. Assembly, 1965—81; judge U.S. Dist. Ct. (we. dist.) Wis., 1982—96, chief judge, 1996—2001. Office: US Dist Ct PO Box 591 Madison WI 53701-0591

SHABAZZ, AMILCAR, historian, humanities educator; s. Edward Al and Winona St. Julian Frank; m. Demetria Rougeaux Shabazz; children: Mandela, Amilcar II. BA in Econs., U. Tex., 1982; MA in History, Lamar U., 1990; PhD in History, U. Houston, 1996. Fellow in history and provost office adminstrv. intern U. Houston, 1996—97; asst prof. Am. studies U. Ala., Tuscaloosa, 1997—2004, assoc. prof., 2004—. Dir. African Am. studies program U. Ala., Tuscaloosa, 1997—. Panel mem. nat. register hist. places rev. Ala. Hist. Commn., 2001—; dist. 7 rep. Ala. Hist. Commn. Black Heritage Coun., Ala., 2001—; rep. Houston Archaeological and Hist. Commn., 1995—97; bd. chair Coalition Alabamians Reforming Edn., Ala., 1999—2003; founding bd. mem. Rutherford B. H. Yates Mus. Printing History, Houston, 1995—97. Fellow Summer Seminar at U. Calif. Irvine, Nat. Endowment for the Humanities, 1991, Wye Faculty Seminar, The Aspen Inst., 2001; Fellow-in-residence at the Harry Ransom Humanities Rsch. Ctr., Andrew W. Mellon Found., 1998. Mem.: Orgn. Am. Historians, Assn. for the Study African Am. Life and History (life). Avocations: art, music, travel. Office: Univ Ala AMS Box 870214 Tuscaloosa AL 35487-0214 Office Phone: 205-348-2532. Business E-Mail: amilcar@bama.ua.edu.

SHABAZZ, DAVID LORENZO, vocational school educator; b. Clinton, SC, Oct. 26, 1969; s. Moses Jackson Dillard and Mary Leola Byrd. BA in Journalism, Benedict Coll., 1991; MA in Mass. Comms., U. SC, 1994; MEd, Wake Forest U., 1998. Reporter SC Black Media Group, Columbia, 1989—93, Clinton (SC) Chronicle, 1991, Winston-Salem (NC) Chronicle, 1993—95; news dir. WKWQ Radio FM, Batesburg, SC, 1990—91; author, lectr. Awesome Records, Clinton, 1995—; instr. Forsyth Tech. C.C., Winston-Salem, 2001—, Ky. State U. Author: Dolemite: The Story of Rudy Ray Moore, 1996, Public Enemy Number One, 1999, Discover Your Mind, 2001. Recipient Editor's Choice award, Internat. Soc. Poets, 1999. Home: 720 Ridgeview Dr Apt 909 Frankfort KY 40601 E-mail: info@DavidShabazz.com.

SHABEL, NORMAN, lawyer; b. New York, NY, Jan. 28, 1937; s.: Samuel and Jeanette Shabel; m. Arleen Jones, June 10, 1962; children: Daniel Adam, Alexandria. JD, Rutgers U., 1969. Bar: NJ 1969, Supreme Ct. 1978, 5th Cir. Ct. of Appeals 1975. Attorney Shabel and Shabel, Mt. Laurel, NJ, 1989—96, Shabel and DeNittis, Mt. Laurel, NJ, 1996—. Author: God Knows No Heroes, 2001, The Corporation, 2004, The Badger Game, 2004. Office: 5 Greentree Ctr Ste 302 Marlton NJ 08053-3422

SHABICA, CHARLES WRIGHT, geologist, earth science educator; b. Elizabeth, N.J., Jan. 2, 1943; s. Anthony Charles and Eleanor (Wright) S.; m. Susan Ewing, Dec. 30, 1967; children: Jonathan, Andrew, Dana. BA in Geology, Brown U., 1965; PhD, U. Chgo., 1971. Prof. earth sci. Northeastern Ill. U., Chgo., 1971—; disting. prof., 1991; pres. Shabica & Assocs. Coastal Cons., Inc., Northfield, Ill., 1985—. Chmn. bd. dirs. Aesti Corp., 1991-96; rsch. collaborator Nat. Park Svc., 1978-82, 89—; adj. prof. Coll. V.I., St. Thomas, 1980, adj. prof. environ. sci. Northwestern U., Evanston, 1999—; Kellogg fellow Northeastern Ill. U., 1979—; chmn. Task Force on Lake Michigan, Chgo., 1986-89; mem. Chgo. Shoreline Protection Commn., 1987-88; cons. Shedd Aquarium, Chgo., 1991; mem. Ft. Sheridan Commn., 1989-90; bd. dirs. Winnetka (Ill.) Hist. Soc. Editor: (with Andrew A. Hay) Richardson's Guide to the Fossil Fauna of Mazon Creek, 1997. Commr., packmaster Boy Scouts Am., Winnetka, Ill., 1984-88. Coop. Inst. for Limnology and Ecosystems Rsch. Lab. fellow. Mem. ASCE, Internat. Assn. for Great Lakes Rsch., Am. Shore and Beach Preservation Assn. (bd. dirs., pres. Great Lakes chpt.), Sigma Xi. Home: 326 Ridge Ave Winnetka IL 60093-3842 Office: 550 W Frontage Rd Ste 3735 Northfield IL 60093-1246 Office Phone: 847-446-1436. Personal E-mail: charles@shabica.com.

SHABOT, MYRON MICHAEL, surgeon, critical care educator, informaticist; b. Houston, Aug. 5, 1945; s. Sam and Mona Doris (Stalarow) S.; 1 child, Samuel Laib. Student, Tulane U., 1963-64; BA, U. Tex., Austin, 1966; MD, U. Tex., Dallas, 1970. Intern Parkland Meml. Hosp., Dallas, 1970—71; resident Harbor Gen. Hosp., Torrance, Calif., 1973—78; lectr. surgery UCLA Sch. Medicine, 1977-78, asst. prof., 1978-82, clin. assoc. prof. surgery and anesthesiology, 1983-97, prof. surgery, 1997—; dir. surg. ICU, LA County Harbor Med. Ctr.-UCLA Sch. Medicine, 1980-82; med. dir. Enterprise Info. Svcs. Cedars-Sinai Med. Ctr., LA, dir. surg. ICU, 1982—, chief of staff, 2002—03. Sec. Cedars-Sinai Med. Ctr. Attending Staff, 1999—. Contbr. articles to profl. jours. Served to lt. comdr. USPHS, 1971-73. Fellow ACS (So. Calif. chpt. bd. dirs. 1988—, pres. 1992-93, gov., 1992—), Am. Coll. Critical Care Medicine, Am. Coll. Med. Informatics; mem. Western Surg. Assn., Pacific Coast Surg. Assn., Soc. Critical Care Medicine, Am. Assn. Surgery of Trauma, Soc. Computers in Critical Care and Pulmonary Medicine (bd. dirs. 1988—, treas. 1989—, pres., 1993-94), Soc. Clin. Data Mgmt. Systems (pres. 1985-86), L.A. Surg. Soc. (pres. 1997-98), Phi Eta Sigma. Jewish. E-mail: michael.shabot@cshs.org.

SHACK, R. BRUCE, plastic surgeon; b. Vernon, Tex., Oct. 7, 1947; s. Nathan Lee and Patsy Lee (Holliday) S.; m. Sharon Summers Frazier, Aug. 16, 1969 (div. 1982); children: Robert David, Nathan Andrew; m. Wanda Kaye, Nov. 11, 1984; children: Jerion Elizabeth, Austin Ryan. BS, Midwestern U., 1969; MD, U. Tex., 1973. Diplomate Am. Bd. Plastic Surgery. Resident in gen. surgery Vanderbilt U. Med. Ctr., Nashville, 1973-78, resident in plastic surgery, 1978-80; asst. prof. surgery Johns Hopkins Med. Sch., Balt., 1980-82; from asst. prof. to prof., chmn. plastic surgery Vanderbilt U. Med. Ctr., 1982—. Fellow Am. Coll. Surgeons, So. Surg. Assn.; mem. AMA, Am. Assn. Plastic Surgeons, Am. Soc. Maxillofacial Surgeons, Am. Soc. Plastic Surgeons, Am. Soc. Reconstructive Microsurgery, Am. Soc. Aesthetic Plastic Surgery, H. William Scott, Jr. Soc., John B. Lynch Soc., John Staige Davis Soc. Plastic Surgeons Md., Nashville Acad. Medicine, Nashville Surg. Soc., Southeastern Soc. Plastic and Reconstructive Surgeons, So. Med. Assn., Tenn. Soc. Plastic Surgeons. Republican. Methodist. Avocations: golf, travel, shooting. Office: Vanderbilt U Med Ctr 2100 Pierce Ave Ste 230 Nashville TN 37236-3156 Office Phone: 615-936-0169. Business E-Mail: bruce.shack@vanderbilt.edu.

SHACKELFORD, JAMES FLOYD, materials science educator, researcher; b. Springfield, Mo., Sept. 1, 1944; s. Amos Franklin and Opal Leona Shackelford; m. Penelope Lea Openshaw, Dec. 11, 1971; 1 child, Scott. BS, U. Wash., Seattle, 1966, MS, 1967; PhD, U. Calif., Berkeley, 1971. Postdoctoral fellow U. Calif., Berkeley, 1971, McMaster U., Hamilton, Canada, 1972—73; asst. prof. U. Calif., Davis, 1973—79, assoc. prof., 1979—84, prof., 1984—, assoc. dean, 1984—2001, dir. integrated studies honor program, 2001—. Author: Introduction to Materials Science for Engineers, 1984, 5th edit., 2000, (book) Bioceramics, 1999; editor: CRC Handbook of Materials Science and Engineering, 1992, CRC Practical Handbook of Materials Selection, 1995, CRC Materials Science and Engineering Handbook, 2nd Edition, 1994, Bioceramics - Applications of Ceramic and Glass Materials in Medicine, 1999, CRC Handbook of Materials Science and Engineering, 3rd Edition, 2001. Fellow: Am. Ceramic Soc. (Outstanding Educator 1996); mem.: ASM Internat. Office: U Calif Dept Chem Engring and Materials Sci Davis CA 95616 Business E-Mail: jfshackelford@ucdavis.edu.

SHACKLEFORD, WILLIAM ALTON, SR., minister; b. Red Springs, N.C., Aug. 5, 1947; s. Purcell and Pearl (Walton) S.; m. Rebecca Belsches, Dec. 2, 1972; children: Kristal Lynn, William Alton Jr. Student, Hampton U., 1965-67, U. Richmond, 1969, 70; DD (hon.), Va. Sem. and Coll., 1990. Ordained to ministry Unity Bapt. Mins.' Conf., 1977. Pastor Cedar Grove Bapt. Ch., Charles City, Va., 1979-82, St. Paul High Street Bapt. Ch., Martinsville, Va., 1986—. Past pres. Bapt. Sunday sch. and Bapt. Tng. Union Congress of Va., chmn. exec. bd., 1997—; past pres. Sunday sch. Union of Hampton and Adjoining Cities, Unity Bapt. Min.'s Conf., Newport News, Va.; corr. sec. Va. Bapt. State Conv., 1986-96; sr. technician tech. svc. Badishe Corp., Williamsburg, Va., 1967-81, asst. supr. corp. office svcs., 1981-86. Author: Replacing the Fallen Angels, 2000; contbr. articles to Martinsville Bull. Apptd. supt. Schs. Adv. Coun.; mem. Child Abuse and Neglect Multidiscipline Team; exec. bd. Martinsville Voter's League, 1987—; mem. overall econ. devel. com., ad hoc drug and alcohol abuse com., past mem. adminstrv. bd. Martinsville Dept. Social Svcs.; adv. coun. Good News Jail and Prison Ministries; past chmn. bd. dirs., adv. com., mem. editl. bd. Patrick Henry Drug and Alcohol Coun.; mem. Martinsville City Sch. Bd., 1991-2000, chmn. 1998-2000; past chmn. bd. trustees Va. Sem. and Coll., Lynchburg, Va., 1992-96; v.p. Va. One Ch. One Child, 1992—; mem. edn. com. Va. Mcpl. League, 1993-95. Named Outstanding Min. Nat. Hairston Clan, 1988; recipient Dedicated Svc. award Va.'s One Ch. One Child Program, 1989, others. Mem. NAACP, Smith River Bapt. Assn. (moderator 2000—), Martinsville and Henry County Ministerial Alliance (com.). Home: 145 Yeatts Rd Martinsville VA 24115-5223 Office: St Paul High St Bapt Ch PO Box 1003 401 Fayette St Martinsville VA 24112-2514 E-mail: pastorwmshackleford@peoplepc.com. *I live with the assurance that the invisible hand of God works to bless and exalt those who commit the totality of their existence to serve God and benefit humanity.*

SHACKLETON, RICHARD JAMES, lawyer, director; b. Orange, N.J., May 24, 1933; s. S. Paul and Mildred W. (Welsh) S.; m. Katharine L. Richards, June 16, 1956; children: Katharine Margaret, Julia Anne, Forrest Maxwell. Student, Kalamazoo Coll., 1957; JD, Rutgers U., 1961. Bar: N.J. 1961, U.S. Dist. Ct. N.J. 1967, U.S. Dist. Ct. (ea. dist.) N.Y. 1987, U.S. Dist. Ct. (so. dist.) N.Y. 1986, U.S. Dist. Ct. (we. and no. dists.) N.Y. 1997, U.S. Ct. Appeals (3rd cir.) 1983, U.S. Ct. Appeals (4th cir.) 1986, U.S. Supreme Ct. 1969, Fed. Bar Coun. N.J. 1988. Ltd. atty. Berry Whitson & Berry, 1961; practice Ship Bottom, NJ, 1961—; sr. ptnr. Shackleton, Hazeltine & Dasti, Ship Bottom, NJ, 1965—, Shackleton, Hazeltine & Bishop, 1984—2003, Shackleton & Hazeltine, 2003—. Pres. Beach Haven Inlet Taxpayers Assn., 1958—68, Ocean County Vis. Homemakers Assn., 1966—72, Brodhead Watershed Assn., 1997—98; mem. U.S. Dist. Ct. N.J. Hist. Soc.; mem. exec. com., bd. dirs. Mount Pocono Water Quality Com.; bd. dirs., v.p. Brodhead Protective Assn. Mem. ABA (litigation sect., product liability com.), Am. Judicature Soc., Fed. Bar Coun. N.Y., N.J. Bar Assn., N.Y. Bar Assn., Ocean County Bar Assn., Def. Rsch. Inst. (mem. med. device and products sect.), Ocean County Lawyers Club, Henryville Conservation Club (chmn. bd.), Henryville Flyfishers Club (pres., bd. dirs., chmn.), The Anglers' Club Phila., Phila. Gun Club (bd. dirs., sec.), Sandy Island Gun Club (life, bd. dirs., pres.), NRA (life), Gun Owners Am. (life), U.S. Sportsman's Alliance, Brodhead Protective Assn. (bd. dirs.), Brodhead Watershed Assn. (bd. dirs., pres. 1997-98, 2001-02), Ancient Inc. Order of the Beefeater. Home: 5614 West Ave Beach Haven NJ 08008-1059 Office: 22d St at Long Beach Blvd Ship Bottom NJ 08008 E-mail: shblaw@aol.com.

SHACKLEY, DOUGLAS JOHN, fire alarm company executive; b. Oakland, Calif., Sept. 21, 1938; s. Floyd H. and Margqret I. Shackley; m. Chloe Jeanne Olson, Sept. 11, 1965; children: Derek Todd, Darren James, Daniel John, Christina Louise. Student, San Jose State U., 1957, Chabot Coll., 1962-63; diploma in bus. mgmt., LaSalle Extension U., 1972. Officer mgr. service dept. Am. Dist. Telegraph Co. (ADT), Oakland, 1961-67; office mgr. Pacific Aux. Fire Alarm Co., San Francisco, 1967-69, mgr., 1969-73, pres., gen. mgr., 1973—, also dir. Mem. task force for improved fire protection Gov. of Calif., 1989. Contbg. mem. Alarm Industry Telecommunications Com. Pres., Chabot Sch. Dad's Club, 1969-70, Chabot Sch. Parent's Club, 1971-72; moderator Eden United Ch. of christ, 1980-81, vice moderator, 1987-88; mem. Eden Area YMCA, San Francisco YMCA, Boy Scouts Am.; sustaining mem. Calif. Republican Com.; mem. Rep. Presdl. Task Force, 1994-95. Served with USMC, 1957-61. Recipient Art Kane Meml. award, CAFAA, 2000. Mem. Nat. Fire Preventnion Assn., Nat. Automatic Fire Alarm Assn. (bd. dirs. 2003—), Calif. Automatic Fire Alarm Assn. (bd. dirs. 1986-87, 94-95, pres. 1988-89, 2003—, v.p. for No. Calif. 1987-88, 96-2000, pres. 2003, Art Kane Meml. award 2000), Lake Mont Pine Home Owner Assn. (bd. dirs. 1988-89), San Francisco C. of C. (code com.), Rotary. Home: 1380 Carlton Pl Livermore CA 94550-6400 Office: Pacific Aux Fire Alarm Co 95 Boutwell St San Francisco CA 94124-1903 Office Phone: 415-467-9393. E-mail: doug@shackley.com., doug@pafa.com.

SHACKMAN, DANIEL ROBERT, psychiatrist; b. N.Y.C., Nov. 15, 1941; s. Nathan H. and Dorothy K. Shackman. BA, Columbia U., 1962, MD, 1966. Diplomate Am. Bd. Psychiatry and Neurology. Intern Mount Sinai Hosp., N.Y.C., 1966-67, resident, chief resident, fellow, 1967-70; psychiatrist USAF, Spokane, Wash., 1970-72; clin. and adminstrv. staff Brentwood VA Hosp., L.A., 1972-79; pvt. practice psychiatry L.A., 1975-87, Santa Barbara, Calif., 1984—. Asst. clin. prof. UCLA Sch. Medicine, L.A., 1975—87; psychiat. cons. CAlif. Dept. Rehab., L.A., 1975—87; cons. psychiatrist Sanctuary Psychiat. Ctrs., Santa Barbara, 1984—2001; chmn. dept. psychiatry Santa Barbara Cottage Hosp., 1990—92. Bd. dirs. Family Counseling Svc., Spokane, 1971-72. Maj. USAF, 1970-72. Mem. Am. Psychiat. Assn., Am. Acad. Child/Adolescent Psychiatry, So. Calif. Psychiat. Soc. (dist. councillor 1989-92), Am. Soc. Clin. Psychopharmacology. Avocations: photography, travel, music, computer science. Office: 924 Anacapa St Santa Barbara CA 93101-2115

SHACKOULS, BOBBY S. oil and gas industry executive; BSChemE, Miss. State U. Various mgmt. positions in oil and gas industry; sr. mgmt. positions Torch Energy Advisors affil. Torchmark Corp., Plains Resources, Houston Oil & Minerals; exec. v.p., COO Burlington Resources, 1993-95; pres., CEO, 1995—; also chmn.; exec. v.p. Meridian Oil Inc. subs. Burlington Resources, Houston; pres., CEO, 1994. Office: Burlington Resources 5051 Westheimer Houston TX 77056

SHACTER, DAVID MERVYN, lawyer; b. Toronto, Ont., Can., Jan. 17, 1941; s. Nathan and Tillie Anne (Schwartz) S. BA, U. Toronto, 1963; JD, Southwestern U., 1967. Bar: Calif. 1968, U.S. Ct. Appeals (9th cir.) 1969, U.S. Supreme Ct. 1982. Law clk., staff atty. Legal Aid Found., Long Beach, Calif., 1967-70; asst. city atty. City of Beverly Hills, Calif., 1970; ptnr. Shacter & Berg, Beverly Hills, 1971-83, Selwyn, Capalbo, Lowenthal & Shacter Profl. Law Corp., 1984-99; pvt. practice, 1999—. Del. State Bar Conf. Dels., 1976—; lectr. Calif. Continuing Edn. of Bar, 1977, 82, 83, 86; judge pro tem L.A. and Beverly Hills mcpl. cts.; arbitrator L.A. Superior Ct., 1983—, also judge pro tem; disciplinary examiner Calif. State Bar, 1986. Bd. dirs. and pres. Los Angeles Soc. Prevention Cruelty to Animals, 1979-89. Mem.: City of Hope Med. Ctr. Aux., Am. Arbitration Assn. (nat. panel arbitrators, neutral arbitrator, panel chmn.), Beverly Hills Bar Found. (pres. 1995—97, bd. govs. 1998—2001), Beverly Hills Bar Assn. (bd. govs. 1985—, sec. 1987—88, treas. 1988—89, v.p. 1989—90, pres.-elect 1990—91, pres. 1991—92, editor-in-chief jour.), Nat. Assn. Securities Dealers (arbitrator 1998—), West Los Angeles C. of C. Office: 10801 National Blvd Ste 608 Los Angeles CA 90064 Office Phone: 310-474-4115. E-mail: david@shacter.org.

SHACTER, JAMES DETMERS, editor, writer; b. Chgo., Apr. 14, 1926; s. Joseph Andrew and Helen Seidman Shacter; m. Nancy Louise Blankenberg, Dec. 30, 1997; m. Ruth Evelyn Bjorn, Aug. 1, 1958 (dec. Sept. 5, 1994); 1 child, Joseph Edwin. BS, U. Ill., 1948. Copy editor UP, Milw., Chgo., Detroit, Washington, N.Y.C., 1947—55; chief copy editor World Book Ency., Chgo., 1955—81; freelance editor, writer Chgo., 1981—. Author: Piano Man, 1975, Loose Shoes, 1994, Jazz Party, 2000. Yeoman 3d class USN, 1944—46. Avocation: traditional jazz.

SHADDIX, JAMES W. retired lawyer; b. 1946; BBA, U. Tex., 1968, JD, 1971. Bar: Tex. 1971. With U.S. Treasury-IRS, 1972-77; atty. Pennzoil Co., 1977-79, asst. gen. counsel, 1977-90, gen. counsel, 1990-98; gen. cousnel Pennzoil-Quaker State Co., 1998—2001. Office: Pennzoil-Quaker State Co PO Box 2967 Houston TX 77252-2967

SHADDOCK, CARROLL SIDNEY, lawyer; b. Beaumont, Tex., July 7, 1940; s. Carroll Bitting Jr. and Hulda Martha (Gaertner) S.; m. Dorothea Schulze, Nov. 30, 1963; children: Carroll Christian, Peter Eric, Matthew Nolan. BA, Rice U., 1962; JD, Yale U., 1965. Ptnr. Locke Liddell & Sapp LLP, Houston, 1967—. Chmn. Scenic Am., Washington, 1985-92, Scenic Tex., 1992—, Trees for Houston, 1982—, Billboards Limited, Houston, 1982-92. Republican. Lutheran. Avocations: music, golf, travel. Home: 1715 South Blvd Houston TX 77098-5419 Office: Locke Liddell & Sapp LLP JP Morgan Chase Tower 600 Travis St Ste 3400 Houston TX 77002-3095 E-mail: cshaddock@lockeliddell.com.

SHADE, LINDA BUNNELL, university chancellor; d. Byron and Bobbye Bunnell. BA in English and Comm., Baylor U., 1964; MA in English Lang. and Lit., U. Colo., 1967, PhD in English Lit., 1970. Asst. prof. English U. Calif., Riverside, 1970-77, asst. dean coll. humanities, 1972—77; from asst. dean to dean academics Calif. State U. Sys., 1977-87; vice chancellor acad. affairs Minn. State U. Sys., St. Paul, 1987-93; chancellor U. Colo., Colorado Springs, 1993—2001; sr. v.p. higher edn. Coll. Bd., 2001—02; CEO Bunnell Assocs., Colo. Springs, Colo., 2002—04; chancellor U. Wis., Stevens Point, 2004—. Active Minn. Women's Econ. Round Table, 1989-93; mem. exec. com. Nat. Coun. for Accreditation Tchr. Edn., 1996-99. Mem. St. Paul chpt. ARC; mem. cmty. bd. Norwest Bank, Colorado Springs, 1997—, mem. El Pomar awards for Excellence com., 1997—; mem. leadership commn. Am. Coun. Edn., 1997—; mem. subcom. ROTC; mem. edn. com. U.S. Army. Recipient Disting. Alumni award Baylor U., 1995; named leader of yr., Colo. Springs Econ. Devel. Coun., 2001; Woodrow Wilson dissertation fellow, Univ. Colo. Avocations: gardening, baseball, cooking, sable burmese cats. Office: U Wis Stevens Point 2100 Main St Stevens Point WI 54481-3897 Business E-Mail: lbunnell@uwsp.edu.

SHADEGG, JOHN B. congressman; b. Phoenix, Oct. 22, 1949; s. Stephen and Eugenia Shadegg; m. Shirley Shadegg; children: Courtney, Stephen. BA, U. Ariz., 1972, JD, 1975. Advisor U.S. Sentencing Commn.; spl. asst. atty. gen. State of Ariz., 1983-90; spl. counsel Ariz. State Ho. Rep. Caucus, 1991-92; pvt. practice; mem. U.S. Congress from 4th Ariz. dist., 1995—; mem. commerce com., fin. svcs. com., homeland sec. com.; asst. whip U.S. Ho. Reps. Mem. Victims Bill of Rights Task Force, 1989-90; mem. Fiscal Accountability and Reform Efforts Com., 1991-92; counsel Arizonian's for Wildlife Conservation, 1992; chmn. Proposition 108-Two-Thirds Tax Limitation Initiative, 1992. Rep. Party Ballot Security chmn., 1982; active Corbin for Atty. Gen., 1982-86; Rep. Precinct committeeman; chmn. Ariz. Rep. Caucus, 1985-87; chmn. Ariz. Lawyers for Bush-Quayle, 1988; mem. steering com., surrogate spkr. Jon Kyl for Congress, 1988-92; former pres. Crime Victim Found.; founding dir. Goldwater Inst. Pub. Policy; chmn. Ariz. Juvenile Justice Adv. Coun.; mem. adv. bd. Salvation Army; mem. vestry Christ Ch. of Ascension, 1989-91; mem. class II Valley Leadership; bd. dirs. Ariz. State U. Law Soc. Republican. Episcopalian. Office: US House Reps 306 Cannon Ho Office Bldg Washington DC 20515-0001

SHADER, BRYAN LYNN, mathematics professor; b. Laramie, Wyo., Dec. 17, 1961; s. Leslie Elwin and Patricia Ann (Tigges) S. BS, U. Wyo., 1984; MA, U. Wis., 1987, PhD, 1990. Postdoctoral fellow Inst. of Math. and its Applications, Mpls., 1991-92; asst. prof. U. Wyo., Laramie, 1990—, prof. math. Contbr. articles to profl. publs. U. Wyo. grantee, 1991. Mem. Am. Math. Soc., Math. Assn. Am. Office: U Wyo Ross Hall Laramie WY 82071

SHADER, RICHARD IRWIN, psychiatrist, pharmacologist, educator; b. Mt. Vernon, NY, May 27, 1935; s. Myer and Beatrice (Epstein) Shader; m. Aline Brown, Sept. 21, 1958 (dec. Aug. 10, 2002); children: Laurel Beth, Jennifer Robin, Robert Andrew; m. Cynthia H. Livingston, Dec. 6, 2003. Student, Harvard U., 1952-56; MD, NYU, 1960; grad., Boston Psychoanalytic Inst., 1970. Diplomate Am. Bd. Psychiatry and Neurology (dir. 1977-84, treas. 1982-83, pres. 1984). Intern Greenwich Hosp., Conn., 1960-61; resident in psychiatry Mass. Mental Health Ctr., Boston, 1961-62, 64-65, NIMH, Bethesda, Md., 1962-64; assoc. prof. psychiatry Harvard Med. Sch., 1970-79; psychiatrist in chief New Eng. Med. Ctr. Hosp., Boston, 1979-91; prof. dept. psychiatry Tufts U. Med. Sch., Boston, 1979—, chmn. dept., 1979-91, prof. pharmacology, 1989—, chmn. dept. pharmacology and exptl. therapeutics, 1991-93, dir. grad. program pharmacology and exptl. therapeutics, 1999—. Author (with A. DiMascio): Psychotropic Drug Sides Effects, 1970; author: (with D. J. Greenblatt) Benzodiazepines in Clinical Practice, 1974; author: Manual of Psychiatric Therapeutics, 1975, 3d edit., 2003; editor: Psychiatric Complications of Medical Drugs, 1972; editor: (with A. DiMascio) Clinical Handbook of Psychopharmacology, 1970, Butyrophenones in Psychiatry, 1972; editor: (with D. J. Greenblatt) Pharmacokinetics in Clinical Practice, 1985, MAOI Therapy, 1988; editor: (with J. P. Tupin and D. S. Harnett) Handbook of Clinical Psychopharmacology, 1988; editor: (with D.A. Ciraulo) Pharmacotherapy of Depression, 2004; editor: (with others) Drug Interactions in Psychiatry, 1989, 2d edit., 1995; editor: Clinical Manual of Chemical Dependence, 1991; editor-in-chief Jour. Clin. Psychopharmacology, 1980—. Bd. dirs. Med. Found., Inc., 1980—87. With USPHS, 1962—64. Recipient Seymor Vestermark award, Am. Psychiat. Assn., 1988, 1990; fellow, Ctr. Advanced Study Behavioral Scis., Stanford, Calif., 1990—91; Joseph J. Michaels Merit scholar, 1968—69. Mem.: AMA, Am. Soc. Pharmacology and Exptl. Therapeutics, Am. Soc. Clin. Pharmacology & Therapeutics, Am. Coll. Neuropsychopharmacology (v.p. 1984, pres. 1990), Mass. Med. Soc. Democrat. Jewish. Office: Tufts U Sch Medicine 136 Harrison Ave Boston MA 02111-1817

SHADID, ANTHONY, journalist; married; 1 child. Student, U. Okla.; B in journalism, U. Wis., Madison, 1990; postgrad., Columbia U., 1993—94. With AP, Milw., 1990—93; editor AP Internat. Desk, NYC, 1993—95; reporter, editor AP, Cairo, 1995—99, news editor LA, 1999—2000; reporter Boston Globe, 2000—03, Wash. Post, 2003—. Author: (book) Legacy of the Prophet: Despots, Democrats, and the New Politics of Islam, 2002. Named Joe Alex Morris Jr. Meml. Lectr., Nieman Found. Journalism, Harvard U., 2004; recipient Bob Considine award, Overseas Press Club, 1997, Ralph O. Nafziger award for disting. achievement, U. Wis., Madison, 2002, George Polk award for foreign reporting, 2003, Pulitzer Prize for internat. reporting, 2004, Michael Kelly Award, Atlantic Media Co., 2004; fellow in Arabic language, Am. U. Cairo, 1991—92. Office: Washington Post 1150 15th st NW Washington DC 20071*

SHADLEY, ROBERT D. retired army officer; b. Circleville, Ohio, Aug. 5, 1942; BS in Indsl. Engring., MS in Indsl. Engring., Purdue U.; M of Mil. Arts and Scis., Army Command/Gen. Staff Coll. Commd. 2d lt. U.S. Army, 1965, advanced through grades to maj. gen., 1997; served in Vietnam and Desert Shield/Desert Storm; exec.officer to the comdg. gen. U.S. Army Materiel Command, 1992-94; dir. for logistics U.S. Atlantic Command, 1994-95; chief of ordnance, comdg. gen. U.S. Army Ordnance Ctrs. and Schs., 1995-97; dep. comdg. gen. for ordnance U.S. Army Combined Arms Support Command, Aberdeen Proving Ground, Md.; dep. chief of staff for logistics Hdqrs. U.S. Army Forces Command, Ft. McPherson, Ga., 1997-2000. Decorated Disting. Svc. medal, Legion of Merit with 2 oak leaf clusters, Bronze Star medal with oak leaf cluster, others. Address: Alliant Techsystems MN07-ME10 4700 Nathan Ln North Plymouth MN 55442-2512

SHADOAN, WILLIAM LEWIS, judge; b. Galesburg, Ill., July 12, 1931; s. William Parker and Hortense (Lewis) S.; m. Katherine E. Thomson, 1961; children: Ann-Wayne Harlan, Kate, Tom. BS, U. Ky., 1955; JD, U. Louisville, 1961. Bar: Ky. 1961, U.S. Dist. Ct. (we. dist.) Ky. 1961. City atty., Wickliffe, Ky., 1963; county atty. Ballard County, Ky., 1963-76; chief regional judge 1st cir. Wickliffe, Ky., 1983—. Chmn. Ballard County Dem. Party, 1963; trustee Meth. Ch., Wickliffe, 1961-84; advisor Selective Svc., Peducah, Ky., 1968; chmn. Wickliffe C. of C., 1967-71; mem. exec. com. Ky. Hist. Soc., Frankfort; vice chmn. Ky. Cert. of Need and Lic. Bd., 1973-84; named assoc. justice Ky. Surpeme Ct., 1984. Capt. U.S. Army, 1955-59. Mem. ABA, Ky. Health Systems Assn. (vice chmn. 1976-82), Ky. Bar Assn. (Outstanding Judge 1997), Assn. Trial Lawyers Am., Ky. County Ofcls. Bd. (chmn. 1976-80), Miss. River Commn. (chmn. 1976-83), Ky. County Attys. Assn. (pres. 1966-77), First Dist. Bar Assn. (pres.), Masons (Wickliffe, 32 degree), Shriners (Madisonville, Ky.), Orer Ea Star, Elks. Home: RR 2 Wickliffe KY 42087-9804 Office: Ballard Courthouse 4th St Wickliffe KY 42087

SHADUR, MILTON IRVING, judge; b. St. Paul, June 25, 1924; s. Harris and Mary Shadur; m. Eleanor Pilka, Mar. 30, 1946; children: Robert, Karen, Beth. BS, U. Chgo., 1943, JD cum laude, 1949. Bar: Ill. 1949, U.S. Supreme Ct. 1957. Pvt. practice, Chgo., 1949-80; assoc. Goldberg, Devoe & Brussell, 1949-51; ptnr. Shadur, Krupp & Miller and predecessor firms, 1951-80; judge U.S. Dist. Ct. (no. dist.) Ill., Chgo., 1980-92, sr. judge, 1992—. Commr. Ill. Supreme Ct. Character and Fitness, 1961-72, chmn., 1971; gen. counsel Ill. Jud. Inquiry Bd., 1975-80; chmn. adv. com. on evidence rules to Jud. Conf. of U.S., 1999-2002, mem. adv. com., 1992-99. Editor-in-chief: U. Chgo. Law Rev., 1948-49. Chmn. visiting com. U. Chgo. Law Sch., 1971-76, mem. vis. com., 1989-92, 99-2002; bd. dirs. Legal Assistance Found. Chgo., 1972-78; trustee Village of Glencoe, 1969-74, Ravinia Festival Assn., 1976-93, exec. com. 1983-93, vice chmn. 1989-93, life trustee, 1994—. Lt. (j.g.) USNR, 1943-46. Fellow Am. Bar Found.; mem. ABA (spl. com. on youth edn. for citizenship 1975-79), Ill. State Bar Assn. (joint com. on rules of jud. conduct 1974), Chgo. Bar Assn. (chmn. legis. com. 1963-65, jud. com. 1970-71, profl. ethics com. 1975-76, sec. 1967-69), Chgo. Council Lawyers, Order of Coif Office: US Dist Ct 219 S Dearborn St Ste 2388 Chicago IL 60604-1800 Office Phone: 312-435-5766.

SHADYAC, THOMAS, film director, producer; b. Falls Church, Va., 1960; Grad., U. Va.; MA in Film, UCLA, 1989. Stand-up comedian Improv, L.A. Motion pictures include: (dir.) Ace Ventura: Pet Detective, 1994, The Nutty Professor, 1996, Liar, Liar, 1997; (dir., prodr.) Patch Adams, 1998, Dragonfly, 2002, Bruce Almighty, 2003; (prodr.) Nutty Professor II: the Klumps, 2000. TV movies: (dir.) Frankenstein: The College Years, 1991. TV series: (exec. prodr.) 8 Simple Rules for Dating My Teenage Daughter, 2002-. Office: United Talent Agy care Dan Aloni 9560 Wilshire Blvd Fl 5 Beverly Hills CA 90212-2400 Studio: 8 Simple Rules 500 S Buena Vista St, Stage 6 Burbank CA 91521-2901

SHAEFFER, CHARLES WAYNE, investment counselor; b. Bridgeton, Pa., Dec. 12, 1910; s. Bartram Augustus and Carolyn I. (Morton) S.; m. Ruth S. Smyser, Oct. 2, 1937; children— Charles Wayne, Ann B. (Mrs. Clark F. MacKenzie), Julia P. BA, Pa. State U., 1933; MBA, Harvard, 1935; LL.D., Loyola Coll., 1974. Investment counselor Mackubin Legg & Co., Balt., 1935-37; with T. Rowe Price Assos., Inc. (formerly T. Rowe Price & Assos., Inc.), Balt., 1938—, chmn. bd., 1966-76, pres., 1963-74, cons., 1976—; pres. T. Rowe Price Growth Stock Fund, Inc., 1968-74, chmn. bd., 1974-76, Rowe Price New Income Fund, 1973—. Dir. Rowe Price New Horizons Fund, Inc., 1966—, Rowe Price New Era Fund, Inc., Rowe Price Prime Res. Fund; trustee Monumental Properties Trust; lectr. investment mgmt. Balt. Coll. Commerce, 1938-70, Johns Hopkins, 1960-72 Trustee Pa. State U., Franklin Sq. Hosp.; bd. mgrs. Bryn Mawr Sch., U. Balt.; bd. dirs. Md. chpt. Nature Conservancy; chmn. bd. dirs. Md. Shock-Trauma Found. Recipient Distinguished Alumni award Pa. State U. Coll. Bus. Adminstrn., 1971-72 Mem. Investment Counsel Assn. Am. (pres. 1970-73, gov. 1965—), No-Load Mut. Fund Assn. (pres. 1972-75), Investment Co. Inst. (gov. 1968—, chmn. 1975-76), Alpha Sigma Phi, Pi Gamma Mu, Delta Sigma Pi. Clubs: Maryland (Balt.), L'Hirondelle (Balt.), Merchants (Balt.), Center (Balt.), Elkridge (Balt.); Green Spring Valley Hunt (Garrison, Md.); Laurel Fish and Game Assn. (York, Pa.), Lafayette (York, Pa.); Seaview Country (Absecon, N.J.); Farmington Country (Charlottesville, Va.). Episcopalian. Home: 603 Brightwood Club Dr Lutherville Timonium MD 21093-3632 Office: 100 E Pratt St Baltimore MD 21202-1009

SHAEFFER, JOHN NEES, historian, educator; b. Wapato, Wash., Dec. 7, 1929; s. John Nees Shaeffer and Helen May Kerns. BA, Wash. State U., 1953; AM, Harvard U., 1957; PhD, U. Wis., 1968. Instr. history Columbia Basin Coll., Pasco, Wash., 1957—63; prof. history Calif. State U., Northridge, 1968—92, prof. emeritus, 1992—. Contbr. articles to profl. jours. 1st lt. USAF, 1953—57, Korea. Mem.: Orgn. Am. Historians (life), Am. Hist. Assn. (life), Phi Kappa Phi (life).

SHAEVSKY, MARK, lawyer; b. Harbin, Manchuria, China, Dec. 2, 1935; came to U.S., 1938, naturalized, 1944; s. Tolio and Rae (Weinstein) S.; m. Lois Ann Levi, Aug. 2, 1964; children: Thomas Lyle, Lawrence Keith. Student, Wayne State U., 1952-53; BA with highest distinction, U. Mich., 1956, JD with highest distinction, 1959. Bar: Mich. 1959. Law clerk to presiding judge U.S. Dist. Ct., Detroit, 1960-61; assoc. Honigman Miller Schwartz & Cohn, Detroit, 1961-64; ptnr. Honigman, Miller, Schwartz & Cohn, Detroit, 1965-69, sr. ptnr., 1969—2001, of counsel, 2001—. Instr. law Wayne State U. Law Sch., Detroit, 1961-64; comml. arbitrator Am. Arbitration Assn., Detroit; bd. dir. Charter One Fin. Inc., Charter One Bank, H.W. Kaufman Fin. Group, Inc., USF Ins. Co. Contbr. Wayne State U. Law Rev., U. Mich. Law Rev., 1957-59, asst. editor, 1958-59. Dir. Detroit Mens Orgn. of Rehab. through Tng., 1969—79; trustee William Beaumont Hosp., 1997—, Beaumont Found., 1997—, Jewish Vocat. Svcs., 1973—76; mem. exec. bd. Am. Jewish Com., 1965—74; sec., dir. Am. Friends Hebrew U., 1976—84; mem. capital needs com. Jewish Welfare Fedn., 1986—97; bd. dir. William Beaumont Hosp., 2002—, Shaevsky Family Found., 2000—. With U.S. Army, 1959—60. Burton Abstract fellow, 1959. Mem. ABA, Mich. Bar Assn., Franklin Hills Country Club, Detroit Athletic Club, Order of the Coif, Phi Beta Kappa. Home: The Hills of Lone Pine 4750 N Chipping Gln Bloomfield Hills MI 48302-2390 Office: Honigman Miller Schwartz & Cohn 32270 Telegraph ste 225 Bingham Farms MI 48025 Office Phone: 248-566-8498. E-mail: mshaevsky@honigman.com.

SHAFER, CAROL LARSEN, retired book reviewer; b. Spencer, Iowa, Sept. 20, 1907; d. John Adolph and Emma Louise (Cook) Larsen; m. Boyd Carlisle Shafer, June 6, 1932 (dec. Feb. 1992); children: Kirstin A. Moritz, Anders C. Shafer. BA, Morningside Coll., 1930; MA, U. Iowa, 1931. Social worker United Charities, Chgo., 1931-32; supr. social work Dunn County, Menomonie, Wis., 1933-35; book reviewer Mpls. Tribune and Mpls. Star, 1964-73, Tucson, 1975-86. Author: Filter of Time, 1996; co-author: Life, Liberty and the Pursuit of Bread, 1940; contbr. articles to profl. jours. Mem. AAUW. Home: 1923 E Joyce Blvd # HC Fayetteville AR 72703-5398

SHAFER, ERIC CHRISTOPHER, minister; b. Hanover, Pa., Apr. 10, 1950; s. B. Henry and Doris M. (Von Bergen) S.; m. Kristi L. Owens, Nov. 24, 1973. BA, Muhlenberg Coll., 1972; MDiv, Hamma Sch. Theology, 1976. Ordained to ministry Luth. Ch. Am., 1976. Pastor Holy Trinity Meml. Luth. Ch., Catasauqua, Pa., 1976-83; asst. to Bishop Northeastern Pa. Synod, Wescosville, Pa., 1983-92; staff commn. for fin. support Evang. Luth. Ch. in Am., Chgo., 1988-92, asst. dir. dept. for comm., 1992-93, dir. dept. for comm., 1993—. Contbg. editor The Lutheran mag., 1989-92. Trustee Muhlenberg Coll., Allentown, Pa., 1972-83; bd. dirs. Luth. Film Assn., 1993—; chmn. comm. commn. Nat. Coun. Chs. in USA, 1996—2003, mem. exec. bd., 1996—2003. Democrat. Lutheran. Avocations: running, computers, photography, travel. Office: Evang Luth Ch in Am 8765 W Higgins Rd Chicago IL 60631-4178 Office Phone: 773-380-2960. Business E-Mail: eshafer@elca.org.

SHAFER, JOHN MILTON, hydrologist, consultant, software developer; b. Findlay, Ohio, Mar. 18, 1951; s. Paul Eugene and Mary Ethel (Schwyn) S.; m. Elise Ann Dunne, Apr. 11, 1980; children: Paul Emery, Jessica Elise, Elise Ann. BS in Earth Sci., Pa. State U., 1973; MS in Resource Devel., Mich. State U., 1975; PhD in Civil Engring., Colo. State U., 1979. Cert. hydrologist #218. Asst. rsch. prof. Colo. State U., Fort Collins, 1979-80; rsch. engr. Battelle Meml. Inst., Richland, Wash., 1980-83, sr. rsch. engr., 1983-84; hydrologist Ill. State Water Survey, Champaign, 1984-85, asst. head ground water sect., 1985-90, prin. hydrologist, 1988-91, head hydrology div., 1990-92; assoc. dir., rsch. prof. Earth Scis. and Resources Inst., U. S.C., Columbia, 1992-95, dir., 1995—. Cons. pvt. cos., 1984—; owner GWPATH, Columbia, S.C., 1992; v.p. Environ. and Archtl. Signage, Findlay, Ohio; prin. hydrologist, co-owner Applied Hydrogeologic Rsch., Inc., Seattle, 1995-00. Developer software, 1987; contbr. articles to profl. jours. Recipient John C. Frye Meml. award in geology, 1991, Ill. Groundwater Sci. Achievement award, 1993. Mem. Intergovt. Coord. Com. Groundwater, Am. Geophys. Union, Am. Inst. Hydrology (pres. Ill. sect. 1985-92), Nat. Ground Water Assn., Ill. Groundwater Assn., Sigma Xi. Presbyterian. Avocations: tennis, handball, woodworking, model building. Home: 321 Lake Front Dr Columbia SC 29212-2426 Office: Earth Scis Resouces Inst U SC 901 Sumter St Columbia SC 29201-3961 E-mail: jshafer@sc.rr.com.

SHAFER, ROBERT TINSLEY, JR., judge; b. Cin., Sept. 11, 1929; s. Robert Tinsley and Grace Elizabeth (Welsh) S.; m. Barbara Jean Hough, Dec. 27, 1950; children: Richard Hough, Janet Lee Shafer Davis, Charles Welsh. BA, Coll. of Wooster, 1951; JD, U. Cin., 1956. Bar: Fla. 1956, U.S. Ct. Appeals (5th cir.) 1963, U.S. Dist. Ct. (so. dist.) Fla. 1961, U.S. Supreme Ct. 1965. Asst. trust officer 1st Nat. Bank, Ft. Myers, Fla., 1956-57; ptnr. Henderson, Franklin, Starnes & Holt, P.A., Ft. Myers, 1957-77; cir. judge 20th Jud. Cir. State of Fla., Ft. Myers, 1977-92, chief cir. judge, 1985-89, sr. judge, 1992—. Former mem. com. for ret. and sr. judges Nat. Conf. State Trial Judges. Contbr. article to Corp. Law, 1955-56 (Goldsmith Corp. Law prize, 1956). Elder Covenant Presbyn. Ch., 1982-85; mem. jud. commn. Fla. Presbyn. Synod, 1960-63; chmn. Lee County chpt. Red Cross, Ft. Myers, 1963; chair Permanent Judicial Commn., Peace River Presbytery, Presbyn. Ch. U.S.A. 2nd lt. USMCR, 1951-53, PTO, Korea. Mem. ABA, Fla. Conf. Cir. Judges (exec. com. 1986-88), Fla. Bar Assn. (bd. govs. Jr. Bar sect. 1961-64), Lee County Bar Assn. (pres. 1968), Am. Judges Assn., Am. Judicature Soc., Nat. Conf. Met. Cts. Calusa Inn of Ct. Republican. Avocations: bicycling, travel, reading, walking. Home: 2704 Shriver Dr Fort Myers FL 33901-5931

SHAFER-KENNEY, JOLIE E. writer, columnist; b. Roswell, N.Mex., Oct. 26, 1953; d. Jack Ernest and Betty Marie (Halstead) Shafer; m. David A. Kenney (div.); children: Matthew Alan, Jack Andrew. Grad., Parks Sch. Bus., 1972; student, Colo. State U., 1971, 74, U. Pitts., 1995-96. Dept. mgr. Joslins Dept. Store, Aurora, Colo., 1972-73; flight attendant United Airlines, 1974-84, publicity rep. com., 1980-84; v.p. Surg. Assocs., Inc., Latrobe, Pa., 1991-98; asst. Women and Talent Gifted Women Forum, Am. Online, 1997-98; ind. contractor AOL, Inc., 1997-99; staff Online Psychol. Svcs., Inc. AOL, 1995-97, seminar host, 1995-97; with prodn. staff AOL's Comty. Matters, 1997-98, AOL's Alt. Health and Healing, 1997-98. Editl. dir. CelebrityStores.com., 1999—; editor-in-chief Winetree Pub. and The Wine Mag., 1999-2000. Feature/content writer Entertainment Asylum, 1997-99, Electra, 1997-98; editl. dir. Celebritystores.com, 1999—; editor-in-chief Winetree Pub., 1999-2000, www.thewineadvisor.com, www.thewinemagazine.com, www.winetreepublishing.com, 1999-2000; featured columnist ShoutingOut.com; contracted feature writer Gaiam, Inc., 2000—; nat. content writer digitalcity.com, 2000—; author: ASK JES, 1999 (pub. in Chicken Soup for the Soul 1999); contbr. 6th Bowl of Chicken Soup for the Soul, 1999; journalist: AOL's Internat. News, 1997-98, AOL TW's Digital City, Inc. (www.digitalcity.com, cbsswitchboard.com, AOL KW: Pitts.), 1999—; lic. syndicated columnist, ASK JES tm and TEENS ASK JESTm; content provider: iSyndicate.com, 1999—; mng. editor: Feedbackforthought.com, 2001—; contbr. articles to online jours. and newspapers; patent pending in field. Mem. AAUW, Nat. Mus. of Women in Arts, Inst. Noetic Scis., Sea Shepherd Conservation Soc., Ctr. for Marine Conservation, Sierra Club, MADD. Avocations: french language and culture, philosophy, gun control, patient's rights, spirituality. Office: 988 E Pittsburgh Street Ste 13 Greensburg PA 15601 E-mail: jolie@askjes.com.

SHAFF, KAREN E. lawyer, insurance company executive; BA, Northwestern U., Evanston, Ill.; JD, Drake U., Des Moines. Atty. Austin and Gaudineer, Des Moines, 1979—82, Principal Fin. Group, 1982—83, asst. counsel, 1983—86, assoc. counsel, 1986—90, sr. v.p., gen. counsel, 1999—2004, exec. v.p., 2004—, gen. counsel, 2004—. Bd. mem. Hospice of Ctrl. Iowa Found., Sci. Ctr. of Iowa. Mem.: ABA, Am. Life Ins. Coun., Am. Corp. Counsel Assn., Polk County Bar Assn., Iowa Bar Assn., Am. Coun. Life Ins. Office: Principal Fin Group 711 High St Des Moines IA 50392

SHAFFER, ALFRED GARFIELD (TERRY SHAFFER), retired service organization executive; b. Sunbury, Pa., Jan. 5, 1939; s. Alfred G. and Betty Marjorie (Vogel) Shaffer; m. Nancy Jane Dawson, Aug. 29, 1976. BS, Susquehanna U., 1961. Cert. tchr., Pa. Tchr. Danville (Pa.) Sch. Dist., 1962-69; mgr. club svc. Kiwanis Internat., Chgo., 1969-74, dir. program devel., 1974-81, dir. program svcs. Indpls., 1982-85, dir. spl. svcs., 1985-87, asst. sec. spl. svcs., 1987-88, asst. to internat. sec., 1988-94, exec. dir., 1994—2003, archivist/historian, 2003—04; corp. affairs cons. Nat. Easter Seal Soc., Chgo., 1981-82; adminstr. Cir. K Internat., Chgo., 1982; mem. Pres.'s Com. on Employment of Handicapped, 1983-86. Chmn. adv. coun. 70001 Ltd., Indpls., 1984-86; mem. adv. bd. Salvation Army, Indpls., 1996—; bd. govs. Children's Miracle Network, 2001-04. Recipient Gold Key of Svc., Pa. Dist. Key Clubs, 1964, Tablet of Honor Kiwanis Internat. Found., award of gold Ind. Kiwanis. Mem. Indps. Athletic Club, 500 Festival Assocs., USAC Winners' Cir., Travelers Protective Assn., Kiwanis (pres. Selinsgrove, Pa. 1964, lt. gov. Pa. 1966-67, pres. Chgo. 1970-72, pres. Northwest Indpls. 1991-92, lt. gov. Ind., 2004-, found. exec. com., Outstanding Svc. award 1981, Kiwanian of Yr. 1966, 85). Lutheran. Home: 5688 N Broadway St Indianapolis IN 46220-3073

SHAFFER, ANITA MOHRLAND, counselor, educator; b. Racine, Wis., Apr. 5, 1939; d. Milton Arthur and Gudrun Amanda Stoffel. BS magna cum laude, U. Wis., 1961; MEd, U. Wash., 1966; postgrad., Ariz. State U., 1971-76. Cert. in elem. edn., social sci. secondary edn., spl. edn., Tex., Ariz.; lic. profl. counselor, Tex.; diplomate Internat. Acad. Behavioral Medicine, Counseling and Psychotherapy. Tchr. Racine Unified Dist. 1, 1961-63, Edmonds Sch. Dist. 15, Lynnwood, Wash., 1963-70, Ariz. Dept. Corrections, Phoenix, 1971-77; tchr. spl. edn. Pasadena (Tex.) Ind. Sch. Dist., 1977-78, spl. edn. counselor, 1978-90, elem. counselor, 1990-98; univ. supr. U. Houston, 1998—. Ednl.

cons., 1998—. Mem. Tex. Counseling Assn., Houston Counseling Assn., Mus. Fine Arts Houston (patron), Houston Lic. Profl. Counselors Assn., Pi Lambda Theta. Home: 5905 Woodway Place Ct Houston TX 77057-2005

SHAFFER, AUDREY JEANNE, health information administrator, educator; b. Hutchinson, Minn., Nov. 24, 1929; d. Floyd R. and Edna C. (Seppman) Kleiman; m. Frank L. Shaffer, July 15, 1948; 1 child, Cynthia Lou Shaffer Wilkinson. BS, Loma Linda U., 1973; MA, Ctrl. Mich. U., 1982. Registered health info. adminstr. Med. records clk. San Bernardino County Hosp., Calif., 1948-50; radiology receptionist White Meml. Med. Ctr., L.A., 1950-52; med. records clk. Portland (Oreg.) Adventist Hosp., 1952-53; mgr. med. records Tempe (Ariz.) Cmty. Hosp., 1953-54; mem. faculty Loma Linda (Calif.) U., 1975-96, 99—. Dir. med. info svcs. Corona Cmty. Hosp., Corona, Calif., 1973—89; cons. med. info. and quality improvement Calif., Utah, Fla., and Philippines, 1981—93; cons. Health Info. and Quality Improvement, Hang-Zhou, China, 1993—; cons. med. records, Mexico; pilot and med. asst. Liga Internat., Mexico, 1964—68; chmn. Corona Blood Bank, 1957—68. Chmn. vols. Corona Cmty. Hosp. Aux., 1965—68; supr. archaeology Caesarea Expdn. Am. Sch. Oriental Rsch., Israel, 1974—. Recipient Vol. Svc. award, Corona Cmty. Hosp., 1968, Congeniality award, Caesarea Archeol. Exhbn., 1975, Alumna of Yr. award Sch. Allied Health Professions, Loma Linda U., 1992. Mem.: Inland Quality Assurance Network (pres. 1988), Nat. Assn. Healthcare Quality, Inland Area Health Info Assn. (pres. 1992—93), Calif. Health Info. Assn. (quality assurance com. 1980—81, pub. rels. com. 1988—91), Am. Health Info. Mgmt. Assn., Loma Linda U. Med. Rec. Alumni (pres. 1979—81), Archeol. Inst. Am., Corona Flying Club (sec. 1960—68), Women's Improvement Club (program chmn. 1960—61). Home and Office: 880 Encanto St Corona CA 92881-3501

SHAFFER, BERNARD WILLIAM, mechanical and aerospace engineering educator; b. N.Y.C., Aug. 7, 1924; s. Abraham and Eva (Ellinsky) S.; m. Florence Solow, Feb. 23, 1947 (dec. Oct. 29, 1986); children: Janet Ilene, Roberta Franceen. BME, CCNY, 1944; MSME, Case Inst. Tech., 1947; PhD, Brown U., 1951. Registered profl. engr., N.Y., R.I. Aero. rsch. scientist flight propulsion rsch. lab. NACA (now NASA), Cleve., 1944-47; spl. lectr. applied mechanics Case Inst. Tech. (now Case Western Reserve Univ.), Cleve., 1946-47; rsch. assoc., grad. div. applied math. and engring. instr. Brown U., Providence, 1947-50; asst. prof. mech. engring. NYU, N.Y.C., 1950-53, assoc. prof., 1953-58, prof., project dir. rsch. divsn., 1958-73; prof. dept. mech. and aerospace engring. Poly. U., Bklyn. and Farmingdale, N.Y., 1973-93, prof. emeritus, 1993—. Cons. in field; mem. adv. coun. Coll. Aeros., N.Y.C., 1982—; vis. rsch. prof. mech. engring. Fla. Atlantic U., Boca Raton, 1992, Disting. vis. rsch. prof., 1993-95, 97—. Contbr. articles to profl. jours. Bd. dirs. Harbor Hills Civic Assn., Great Neck, N.Y., 1968-71. With USAAF, 1944-47. Recipient various govt. grants. Fellow ASME (Richards Meml. award 1968); mem. AIAA (assoc. fellow), Sigma Xi, Tau Beta Pi, Pi Tau Sigma. Avocations: golf, swimming.

SHAFFER, CHARLES ALAN, lawyer; b. Wilkes-Barre, Pa., July 22, 1938; s. Joseph and Irene G. (Murzin) S.; m. Barbara A. Kurlancheek, July 30, 1961; children— Jonathan David, Susan Deborah. BS in Econs., U. Pa., 1960, JD, 1963. Bar: Pa. 1963, U.S. Dist. Ct. (mid. dist.) Pa. 1968, U.S. Ct. Appeals (3d cir.) 1975, U.S. Supreme Ct. 1976; diplomate Nat. Bd. Trial Advocacy; cert. civil trial adv. Sole practice, 1963-68; asst. pub. defender Luzerne County, Pa., 1965-67; law clk. Ct. Common Pleas of Luzerne County, 1967-69; 1st clk. of Orphans' Ct., dep. register of wills, 1972-83; ptnr. Flanigan, Doran, Biscontini & Shaffer, Wilkes-Barre, 1968-86, Mahler, Shaffer & Pugliese, 1986—; mem. faculty Wilkes Coll., 1964-70; lectr. Pa. Bar Inst., 1988; nat. panel arbitrators Am. Arbitration Assn.; Pa. coun. mediators; cert. mediator U.S. Dist. Ct. spl. trial master Ct. of Common Pleas, Pa. Contbr. articles to profl. jours. Bd. dirs. Jewish Community Ctr., Wilkes-Barre, 1970-76, Fine Arts Fiesta, Sordoni Gallery Wilkes U., pres., 1986-90; pres. United Rehab. Services, Inc., 1970-72; treas., bd. dirs. Temple B'nai B'rith, Kingston, Pa., 1980; incorporator, bd. dirs. Health Services Agy. Northeastern Pa. Mem. Luzerne County Bar Assn. (pres. 1998-2000), Pa. Bar Assn. (judicial adminstrn. com. and dispute resolution com.), ABA (litig. sect. com. on trial practice), Pa. Trial Lawyers Assn., ATLA, Pa. Def. Rsch. Inst., Westmoreland (Wilkes-Barre) Club. Avocations: skiing, photography, science fiction. Home e-mail: cas866@aol.com; office e-mail: cshaffer@usnetway.com. Home: 866 Nandy Dr Kingston PA 18704-5608 Office: Mahler Shaffer & Pugliese 575 Pierce St Ste 500 Kingston PA 18704-5754

SHAFFER, CLARENCE F. retired electronics executive; b. Williamsport, Pa., Sept. 19, 1910; s. Howard Edward and Zita Agnes (Gonsman) S.; m. Gertrude Alice Gray, Dec. 16, 1933; 1 child, Nancy Shaffer Ivanski. Student, Pa. State Coll., 1929-30, Harvard U., 1961. Pres., owner Shaffer Constrn. Co., Williamsport, 1930-39; dist. sales mgr., v.p. Pitney Bowes, Stamford, Conn., 1939-55; v.p., gen. sales mgr. Harris Intertype Co., Cleve., 1960-61; gen. mgr. bus. machines divsn. Fairchild Camera & Ins. Co., 1961-63, v.p., 1963-65; pres., owner Distbrs. Leasing and Sales, Cleve., 1966-75. Contbr. over 500 articles to computer mags. or books; holder 18 patents on bldg. industry products, including centerline sawing sys. Mem., pres. task force, mem. steering com. Rep. Nat. Com.; mem. Nat. Rep. Senatorial Com. Recipient silver medal Olympics; heavyweight champion Golden Gloves (oldest living champion). Mem. N.Am. Yacht Racing Union, Interlake Yachting Assn., Cleve. Yachting Club, Boater Luncheon Club (pres. 1949-97), Masons (32d degree), Shriners. Methodist. Avocations: painting, photography, yacht racing, computers, writing. Home: 19757 Roslyn Dr Rocky River OH 44116-1643

SHAFFER, DAVID JAMES, lawyer; b. Springfield, Ohio, July 30, 1958; s. Frank James Shaffer and Martha Isabelle (Hardman) Matthews; children: Brynn Danielle, Jedediah Clay. BA, Wittenberg U., 1980; JD, Stanford U., 1983. Bar: Calif. 1984, U.S. Dist. Ct. (no. and ea. dists.) Calif. 1984, U.S. Ct. Appeals (9th cir.) 1984, U.S. Dist. Ct. (so. dist.) Calif. 1985, U.S. Dist. Ct. (we. dist.) Wash. 1986, D.C. 1988, U.S. Dist. Ct. D.C. 1988, U.S. Ct. Appeals (D.C. cir.) 1988, U.S. Dist. Ct. (no. dist.) Tex. 1991, U.S. Supreme Ct. 1993, Md. 1994, U.S. Dist. Ct. Md. 1997. Supr. field ops. U.S. Census Bur., Columbus, Ohio, 1980; legal intern Natural Resources Def. Coun., Inc., San Francisco, 1982-83; assoc. Gibson, Dunn & Crutcher, San Jose, Calif., 1983; law clk. to Judge Betty B. Fletcher, U.S. Ct. Appeals for 9th Cir., Seattle, 1983-84; assoc. Gibson, Dunn & Crutcher, San Jose, 1984-87, Arnold & Porter, Washington, 1987-92; ptnr. Semmes, Bowen & Semmes, Washington, 1992-94, Arter & Hadden, Washington, 1995-99, Thelen Reid & Priest LLP, Washington, 1999—. Contbr. articles to profl. and legal jours. Campaign mgr. Clark County Dem. Party, Springfield, 1978-80; organizer Citizens for Sensible County Planning, Fairfax, Va., 1989-94. Alumni scholar Wittenberg U., 1976. Mem. ABA, FBA (chmn. EEO com. 1992-94, individual rights and responsibilities 1994-95, co-chmn. alt. dispute resolution 1995-96, mem. governing bd. labor law and labor rels. sect., editor newsletter Labouring Oar, Outstanding Svc. award 1992), D.C. Bar Assn., Calif. Bar Assn., Order of Coif. Avocations: music, hiking, nature study. Office: Thelen Reid & Priest LLP 701 Pennsylvania Ave NW Washington DC 20004-2608 E-mail: dshaffer@thelenreid.com.

SHAFFER, DENNY RICHARD, small business owner; b. Altoona, Pa., Feb. 13, 1931; s. Melvin Anson and Mildred Catherine Shaffer; m. Kim Martin, May 6, 1984; 1 child, Francesca Martin; m. Betty Blair (dec. Dec. 1972); children: Robert Daniel, David Richard. BBA, U. Pitts., 1952; student, Inst. for Advanced Pastorial Studies, Bloomsfield Hill, Mich., 1968. Mgr. One Hour Koretizing / One Hour Martinizing, Fayetteville, NC, 1954—66, Burlington, 1954—66, Durham, 1954—66, Rocky Mount, 1954—66, Charleston, SC, 1954—66; v.p. One Hour Koretizing, Lynchburg, NC, 1962—66; field mgr. One Hour Valet, Miami, Fla., 1963—65; pres. Kore-O-Mat of Fayetteville, 1965—2003, One Hour Koretizing, Fayetteville, 1966—99, Shaffer Mgmt. Co., Fayetteville, 1966—99; ptnr. Scots Hills Floral Nursery, Cameron, NC, 1968—75. Author: (oral history forward) Ted Synder, 1984, Brock Evans, 1987, (book forward) Images of Wilderness, 1993. Mem. Fayetteville City Coun., 1967—71; del. Sierra Club Coun., San Francisco, 1972—77; lobbyist Easter Wilderness Bill, Washington, 1974, chmn. nat. membership com., 1976—79; nat. bd. dirs. Sierra Club, Washington, 1977—84, bd. dirs., 1985—91, 1994—97; pres. Nat. Sierra Club, 1982—84, treas., CFO, 1978—82, 1985—86, 1994—95, sec., 1997, v.p. for planning, v.p. for electoral politics, 1982—85, 1987—94; mem. bd. trustees The Sierra Club Found., 1979—86, 1991—94; founding mem. Sierra Club of Fayetteville, NC Group, 1970; chmn. NC Conservation, 1972—74; exec. com. mem Sierra Club Coun., 1974—77; founding dir. Hillsboro St. Sch., 1958, Spainhour Sch., 1967—84, The People's Clinic, 1968—72. Recipient Gov.'s award, 1983, Realtor's Cup, Fayetteville C. of C., 1967, William Colby award, Sierra Club, 1996, Disting. Environ. Series, Bancroft Libr., 2003, U. Calif., Berkley, 2003, Order of the Long Leaf Pine, State of N.C., 2003. Democrat. Presbyterian. Avocations: golf, hiking. Home: 2910 Skye Dr Fayetteville NC 28303-5925

SHAFFER, DONALD S. retail executive; b. Philippi, W.Va., Mar. 22, 1943; m. Leslie Stalker; 1 child. AA, Potomac State Coll.; BS in Acctg., W.Va. U. Mgmt. trainee Sears, Roebuck and Co., USA, 1968-70, pers. mgr., 1970-72, Landover, Md., 1972-73, asst. store mgr. Washington, 1973-75, soft lines mdse. mgr., 1975-78, store mgr. Watertown, N.Y., 1978-81, zone oper. mgr. Albany, N.Y., 1981-82, store mgr. New Brunswick, N.J., 1982-83, with planning dept. nat. hdqs. Chgo., 1983-86, regional mgr., 1986-87; v.p. field sales ops. Sears Can. Inc., Toronto, 1987, v.p. field sales ops. and real estate, 1988; regional gen. mgr. Sears, Roebuck and Co., USA, Detroit, 1989, nat. bus. mgr. womens apparel, accessories nat. hdqs. Chgo., 1989-90, nat. mdse. mgr. furniture, 1990-93; exec. v.p., COO Sears Can. Inc., Toronto, 1993—94, pres., CEO, 1994—97; chmn., CEO Western Auto, Kansas City, Mo., 1997—99; pres., CEO Heilig-Myers, 1999—2001, Dollar General, Goodlettsville, Tenn., 2001—. Bd. dirs. Sears Acceptance Co.; bd. mem. Retail Coun. Can. Bd. govs. Jr. Achievement Can. 1st lt. U.S. Army, 1965-67. Office: Dollar General 100 Mission Ridge Goodlettsville TN 37072-1284

SHAFFER, DOROTHY BROWNE, retired mathematician, educator; b. Feb. 12, 1923; arrived U.S., 1940; d. Hermann and Steffy (Hermann) Browne; m. Lloyd Hamilton Shaffer, July 25, 1943 (dec. 1978); children: Deborah Lee, Diana Louise, Dorothy Leslie. AB, Bryn Mawr Coll., 1943; MA, Harvard U., 1945, PhD, 1962. Mathematician MIT, Cambridge, 1947-48; assoc. mathematician Cornell Aero. Lab., Buffalo, 1952-56; mathematician Dunlap & Assocs., Stamford, Conn., 1958-60; lectr. grad. engring. U. Conn., Stamford, 1962; prof. math. Fairfield (Conn.) U., 1963-92, prof. emeritus, 1992—. Vis. prof. Imperial Coll. Sci. and Tech., London, fall 1978, U. Md., College Park, spring 1981; vis. prof. U. Calif.-San Diego, summer 1981; vis. scholar, 1986; NSF faculty fellow IBM-T.J. Watson Research Center, Yorktown Heights, N.Y., 1979. Contbr. numerous papers in math. analysis. Mem. Am. Math. Soc., Math. Assn. Am., Assn. Women in Math., London Math. Soc. Achievements include patent in Viscosity Stabilized Solar Pond. Home: Apt 3119 122 Palmers Hill Rd Stamford CT 06902 Office: Fairfield U Dept Math & Computer Sci Fairfield CT 06430 E-mail: dbshaffer@fair1.fairfield.edu.

SHAFFER, GAIL DOROTHY, secondary school educator; b. Summit, N.J., May 7, 1936; d. Franklin Clifford Jr. and Mildred Edna (Burgmiller) S. AB, Hood Coll., 1958. Tchr. Sherman Sch., Cranford, N.J., 1959-60, Gov. Livingston High Sch., Berkeley Heights, N.J., 1960—. Vol. intake worker Covenant House, N.Y.C., 1982-92, spkrs. bur., 1986—, bd. dirs., Newark, 1993—; mem. juvenile conf. Family Ct. Union County, Elizabeth, N.J., 1968—; project dir. Berkeley Heights (N.J.) Alliance Against Drugs and Alcohol, 1990-95; active Berkeley Heights Youth Com., 1960-65. Named Berkeley Heights Citizen of Yr. by Jr. C. of C., Speaker of Yr. by Covenant House Corp., Vol. of Yr. by Covenent House, Union County Tchr. of Yr., 1992-93, N.J. State Tchr. of Yr., 1992-93. Mem. DAR (Beacon Fire chpt.), ASCID, NEA, N.J. Edn. Assn., N.J. State Tchrs. of the Yr. (pres.), Union County Edn. Assn. Republican. Methodist. Avocations: reading, travel, U.S. history, needlework, Victoriana. Home: 522 Plainfield Ave Berkeley Heights NJ 07922-1919 also: 7 Embury Ave Ocean Grove NJ 07756-1354 Office: Gov Livingston High Sch 175 Watchung Blvd Berkeley Heights NJ 07922-2799

SHAFFER, HAL J. bank executive, lawyer; b. Phila., June 13, 1958; BA, Pa. State U., 1980; JD, Temple U., 1983. Bar: N.J. 1983, Pa. 1983, U.S. Dist. Ct. (ea. dist.) Pa., U.S. Dist. Ct. N.J., U.S. Ct. Appeals (3d cir.), U.S. Supreme Ct. Ptnr. Dilworth, Paxson, Kalish & Kauffman; mng. ptnr. Shaffer, Bonfiglio, Scerni & D'Elia, LLC, Mt. Laurel, N.J.; chmn. First Bank of Phila. Bond counsel N.J. Econ. Devel. Authority; spl. condemnation counsel Casino Reinvestment Devel. Authority; lectr. in field. Mem. bd. trustees N.J. Alliance for Action, 1992—, Rowan Coll., N.J., 1995—, Pa. State U., 1979-80; mem. N.J. Sports Law Com.; bd. dirs. Corp. for Bus. Assistance N.J.; bd. dirs. Cherry Hill Econ. Devel. Corp.; mem. March of Dimes Banquet Com. Mem. ABA, N.J. State Bar Assn. (fin. transactions com.), Coml. Law League Am., Nat. Assn. Bond Lawyers, Pa. Bar Assn., Camden County Bar Assn., Phila. Bar Assn. Office: First Bank Phila 1632 Walnut St Philadelphia PA 19103-5403 Fax: 215-790-1038. E-mail: shafferlaw@wld.com.

SHAFFER, HARRY GEORGE, economics professor; b. Vienna, Aug. 28, 1919; arrived in U.S., 1940; s. Max Schaffer and Teofilia (Infeld) Schaffer Weissman; m. Betty Rosenzweig, June 7, 1987; children by previous marriages: Bernard Charles, Ronald Eric, Len Joseph, Tanya Elaine; stepchildren: Rene Carlis, Jamie Paul. BS, NYU, 1947, MA, 1948, Ph.D, 1958. Instr. Concord Coll., Athens, W.Va., 1948-50, U. Ala., Tuscaloosa, 1950-56; from asst. prof. to prof. U. Kans., Lawrence, 1956-69, prof. econs. and Soviet and East European studies, 1969—90, prof. emeritus, 1990—. Vis. prof. Portland State Coll., Oreg., summer 1963, U. Calif.-Davis, 1973-74. Author: English-Language Periodic Publications on Communism, 1971, Periodicals on the Socialist Countries and on Marxism, 1977, Women in the Two Germanies, 1981, American Capitalism and the Changing Role of Government, 1999; author booklet: The U.S. Conquers the West, 1974; editor: The Soviet Economy, 1963, rev. edit., 1969, The Soviet System in Theory and Practice, 1965, 2d edit., 1984, The Communist World: Marxist and Non-Marxist Views, 1967; (with Jan Prybyla) From Under-Development to Affluence: Western, Soviet and Chinese Views, 1968; editor, contbg. author: The Soviet Treatment of Jews, 1974, Soviet Agriculture, 1977, American Capitalism and the Changing Role of Government, 1999; contbr. articles to profl. jours. Served with M.I., U.S. Army, 1943-44 Mem. Am. Econ. Assn., Assn. Comparative Econ. Studies, AAUP, Ams. for Dem. Action, Common Cause, NAACP, Unity Ch., Beta Gamma Sigma Democrat. Jewish. Home: 2510 Jasu Dr Lawrence KS 66046-4537 Office: U Kans Dept Econs 2260 Summerfield Hall Lawrence KS 66045-7522

SHAFFER, JACK, real estate company executive; Co-founder Hiffman Shaffer Assocs., Inc., Chgo.; CEO HSA Comml., Chgo., 2000—04, chmn., 2000—. Office: HSA Comml Ste 500 180 N Wacker Dr Chicago IL 60606*

SHAFFER, JUDY ANN, educator, data processing professional; b. Dec. 24, 1942; d. Vernon Sherwood and Josephine (Bean) Peterson; m. James Nelson Shaffer Jr., Feb. 28, 1970. BS, Morningside Coll., 1965; MS, Iowa State U., 1969; postgrad., NC State U. Tchr. math. Plaza Jr. H.S., Virginia Beach, Va., 1971; instr. Ivy Ind. Vocat. Tech. Coll., Ft. Wayne, Ind., 1973—74, Ind. Purdue U., Ft. Wayne, 1974—76; programmer Bowmar, Ft. Wayne, 1976—77; programmer analyst GTE Data Svc., Ft. Wayne, 1977—79, Experior Corp., Ft. Wayne, Ind., 1979—87, 1990; instr. dept. math. scis. Ind. Purdue U., Ft. Wayne, 1987—89; edn. specialist Misys Health Care Sys., 1993—2002; ret., 2002. Instr. Star II Purdue U., Lafayette, Ind.; mem. assoc. faculty Ind. Purdue U., Ft. Wayne, 1984—85. Charter mem. Ft. Wayne Area Cmty. Band, 1979—90; mem. Raleigh Concert Band, 1990—2002, Kingdom of the Sun Cmty. Band, 2002—. Mem.: PEO, Kappa Mu Epsilon. Avocations: music, model railroading, golf. E-mail: jnshaffer@earthlink.net.

SHAFFER, MARGARET MINOR, retired library director; b. New Orleans, Sept. 20, 1940; d. Milhado Lee and Margaret Minor (Krumbhaar) S. BS, Nicholls State U., Thibodaux, La., 1962; MLS, La. State U., 1965. Asst. dir. Terrebonne Parish Pub. Libr., Houma, La., 1965-72, dir., 1973-95; ret., 1995. Named Woman of Yr., Houma Bus. and Profl. Women's Club, 1981. Mem. ALA, La. Libr. Assn. (chmn. pub. libr. com. 1986-87), Southeastern Libr. Assn. Democrat. Episcopalian. Avocations: crafts, travel. Home: 2678 Highway 311 Schriever LA 70395-3240

SHAFFER, MARY LOUISE, art educator; b. Blufton, Ind., Nov. 23, 1927; d. Gail H. and Mary J. (Graves) S. AB, Northwest Nazerene U., 1950; MA, Ball State U., 1955; EdD, MS, Ind. U., 1964. Art and music tchr. Kuna (Idaho) H.S., 1950-55; asst. prof. art Northwest Nazarene U., Nampa, Idaho, 1955-56, head art dept., 1971-98, dir. Friesen Art Galleries, 1997-2000, faculty emeritus, 1998; asst. prof. art Pasadena (Calif.) U., 1956-61; prof. art Olivet Nazarene U., Kankakee, Ill., 1964-71. Dir. music Kankakee Congl. Ch., 1964-71, Nampa Christian Ch., 1971-76, Nampa Meth. Ch., 1976-81; juror Nampa Art Guild Painting Show, 1994, 2003; head art policy coun. Northwest Nazarene U.; spkr. in field. One-woman show Friesen Art Galleries, 1999; participant European Images Art Show, 1989; cover artist Nazarene Internat. Mag., 1989; painting retrospective, 1999; juror Nampa Art Guild Painting Show, 2003. Dir. music Van Nuys (Calif.) Nazarene Ch., 1957-60. E.I. Lilly grantee, 1961-62; women's singles tennis champion Kankakee, Ill., 1966, 67, 68, Boise (Idaho) Racquet and Swim Club, 1973, Idaho Sr. Tennis champion Sun Valley, 1984; watercolor Sun Valley Mountain selected to go to moon on Endeavour Space Shuttle, 1992. Mem. NAFE, Nat. Art Edn. Assn., Idaho Arts Edn. Assn., Nat. Assn. Univ. Women, Nat. Mus. Women in the Arts, Boise Racquet Swim Club, Boise Art Mus. Avocations: travel, music, renovating buildings, watercolor painting, tennis. Home: Shaffer Studios 4755 E Victory Rd Meridian ID 83642-7011

SHAFFER, MICHAEL L. transportation company executive; b. Eldorado, Ill., Dec. 28, 1945; s. L.E. Jim Shaffer and Berniece (Belva) Andrews; m. Mary Elaine Charboneau, Jan. 30, 1970; children: Michelle, James. Dispatcher Atlas Van Lines, Inc., Long Beach, Calif., 1969-73, ops. mgr. Hyattsville, Md., 1973-75, Evansville, Ind., 1975-80, asst. sec., 1980-84; v.p., gen mgr. Atlas Van Lines Texas, Austin, 1983-84; v.p. ops. Atlas Van Lines, Inc., Evansville, 1984-88, sr. v.p., 1988-90; pres. U.S. Transp. Group, 1991-98; chmn., CEO Atlas Van Lines, Inc., 1998—. With U.S. Army, 1963-65, Vietnam. Roman Catholic. Home: 3599 Crossgate Ct Newburgh IN 47630-9661 Office: Atlas Van Lines Inc 1212 Saint George Rd Evansville IN 47711-2364

SHAFFER, OREN GEORGE, former manufacturing company executive; b. Sharpsville, Pa., Aug. 13, 1942; s. Oren G. and Alice Marie (Miller) S.; m. Evelyne Soussan, Oct. 2, 1965; children: Kathleen R., Oren O. BSBA, U. Calif., Berkeley, 1968; MS, MIT, 1985. Mem. internal tng. squad Goodyear Tire and Rubber Co., Akron, Ohio, 1968-69, asst. comptr., 1983-84, v.p., treas., 1985-87, exec. v.p., CFO, 1987-90; mem. fin. staff Goodyear SA, Diegem, Belgium, 1969-70, fin. mgr. Benelux, 1970-75; CFO, Goodyear France, Paris, 1975-80, pres., 1981-83; CFO, Goodyear Tyre and Rubber Co., Wolverhampton, Eng., 1980-81; exec. v.p., CFO Ameritech Corp., Chgo., 1994-2000; pres., COO Sorrento Networks Corp., San Diego, 2000—02, advisor, 2000—02; vice chmn., CFO Quest Communications Internat., Denver, 2002—. Bd. dirs. Akron Priority Corp., pres. 1987. Mem. Nat. Assn. Accts., Fin. Execs. Inst., Officer's Conf. Group. Clubs: Firestone Country, Portage Country (Akron). Office: Quest Communications 1801 California St Denver CO 80202

SHAFFER, PAUL, musician, bandleader; b. Thunder Bay, Ont., Can., Nov. 28, 1949; m. Cathy Vasapoli; 1 child, Victoria Lily. Mem. band Fabulous Fugitives, Thunder Bay, 1964-68; keyboardist NBC's Saturday Night Live, 1975-80; musical dir. Blues Bros. Band, 1978-79; leader, keyboardist The World's Most Dangerous Band NBC's Late Night with David Letterman, 1982-1993; music director The Late Show with David Letterman (CBS), 1993—. Mus. dir. (Toronto, Ont. prodn.) Godspell, 1972; musician: (N.Y.C. prodn.) The Magic Show, 1974, (Gilda Radner's mus. revue, also co-composer) Live in New York, 1979, (off-Broadway prodn.) Leader of the Pack, 1984; rec. artist, keyboardist: (with Barry Manilow) This One's For You, 1976, (with National Lampoon) Good-Bye Pop, 1976, (with the Jeff Healey Band) Feel This, 1977, (Blues Bros.) Briefcase Full of Blues, 1978, Made in America, 1980, (with Jaon Armatrading) Me Myself, 1980, (with Nina Hagen) Nunsexmonkrock, 1980, (with Diana Ross) Silk Electric, 1981, (with Yoko Ono) It's Alright, 1982, (Honey Drippers) The Honey Drippers, 1985, (film soundtrack) The Karate Kid II, 1986, (with Dion, Ben. E. King, Bobby Womack and Wilson Pickett) Coast to Coast, 1991, (with Blues Traveler) Save His Soul, 1993, (with the Party Boys of Rock 'n' Roll) The World's Most Dangerous Party, 1993; regular mem. cast (TV series) A Year at the Top, 1977; film appearances include This Is Spinal Tap, 1984; solo album Coast to Coast, 1989 (2 Grammy nominations). Office: Late Show w/ David Letterman CBS 530 W 57th St New York NY 10019-2902

SHAFFER, PAUL E. retired banker; b. Rockford, Ohio, Aug. 3, 1926; s. Randall J. and Zelah V. (Alspaugh) S.; m. Dorothy L. Schumm, June 26, 1951; children: Paula Kay, Patti Lee. Grad., U. Wis. Sch. Banking, 1954; cert., Am. Inst. Banking; DHL (hon.), Purdue U., 1985. With Rockford Nat. Bank, 1945-48; asst. nat. bank examiner Treasury Dept., 1948-52; with Ft. Wayne (Ind.) Nat. Bank, 1952-65, from exec. v.p. to chmn., CEO, 1965-70, chmn., CEO, 1970-92, chmn. emeritus, 1993-95, ret., 1995, 1996. Bd. dirs. Old First Nat. Bank, Bluffton, Ind. Pres. Downtown Fort Wayne Assn., 1965, Credit Bur., Fort Wayne, 1962, Jr. Achievement, 1967-69; treas. Fort Wayne Better Bus. Bur., 1968, Ind.-Purdue Devel. Fund; mem. regional adv. com. Comptroller Currency, 1968-70; commr. Ft. Wayne Conv. and Tourism Authority.; past bd. dirs. Fort Wayne Conv. Bur., Fort Wayne Philharmonic Orch., Parkview Meml. Hosp.; bd. dirs. Caylor-Nickel Hosp., Ft. Wayne campus Ind. U., Ind.-Purdue Found., Taxpayers Research Assn.; past bd. dirs. United Community Services, chmn. drive, 1970-71; past bd. dirs. Fort Wayne YMCA, v.p., 1964-67; bd. adviser Ind. U.-Purdue U., Ft. Wayne; mem. fin. adv. bd. Luth. Social Services; bd. govs. Assn. Colls. Ind.; chmn. vol. com. U.S. Savs. Bonds, Allen County, Ind., numerous other civic activities. Served with USAAF, 1945. Mem. Am. Inst. Banking (past pres. Ft. Wayne chpt.), Am. Bankers Assn. (governing coun. 1978-79), Ind. Bankers Assn. (past pres., bd. dirs.), Ft. Wayne C. of C. (past v.p., bd. dirs.), Ind. C. of C. (state dir.), Execs. Club (past pres.), Ft. Wayne Country Club, Summit Club, Quest Club, Ft. Wayne Press Club, Mad Anthonys Club, Sycamore Hills Country Club, Masons (33rd degree), Shriners, Bonita Bay (Fla.) Golf Club. Home: 11132 Carnoustie Ln Fort Wayne IN 46814-9014

SHAFFER, PETER (SIR PETER SHAFFER), playwright; b. Liverpool, Eng., May 15, 1926; s. Jack and Reka (Fredman) S. BA, Cambridge U., Eng., 1950. Conscript coal mines, Eng., 1944-47; with N.Y. Pub. Libr., N.Y.C., 1951-54, Boosey & Hawkes, London, 1954-55; lit. critic Truth, 1956-57; music critic Time and Tide, 1961-62; freelance playwrite, 1957—. Vis. prof. contemporary drama Oxford (Eng.) U., 1994-95. Author: (plays) Five Finger Exercise, 1958 (Evening Standard Drama award 1958, N.Y. Drama Critics Cir. award 1960), The Private Ear, 1962, The Public Eye, 1962, It's About Cinderella, 1963, The Royal Hunt of the Sun, 1964, Black Comedy, 1965, The White Liars, 1967, The Battle of Shrivings, 1970, Equus, 1973 (Best Play Tony award 1975, Outer Critics Cir. Best Play award 1975), Amadeus, 1979 (Evening Standard Drama award 1979, London Drama Critics award 1979, Best Play Tony award 1980, Plays and Players Best Play award 1980), Yonadab, 1985, Lettice and Lovage, 1987 (Evening Standard Drama award 1988), The Gift of the Gorgon, 1992, Whom Do I Have the Honor of Addressing?, Chichester Festival Theatre, 1996, (screenplays) Follow Me!, 1971, Equus, 1977 (Acad. award nomination for best screenplay adaptation 1977), Amadeus, 1984 (Acad. award for best screenplay adaptation 1984), (TV plays) The Salt Land, 1955, Balance of Terror, 1957, (radio plays) The Prodigal Father, 1955, Whom Do I Have the Honor of Addressing?, 1989, (novels) The Woman in the Wardrobe, 1951, (novels, with Anthony Shaffer), How Doth the Little Crocodile?, 1952, Withered Murder, 1955. Created knight, 2001; decorated comdr. Order Brit. Empire; recipient Hamburg Shakespeare prize, 1987, William Inge award for disting. achievement in Am. theatre, 1992. Fellow Royal Soc. Lt. (London chpt.). Address: 173 Riverside Dr New York NY 10024

SHAFFER, RICHARD, communications executive; BA in Philosophy, U. Okla. Prin., founder, pub. Technologic Ptnrs., 1984—. Past sci. and tech. editor Wall Street Jour.; past columnist Forbes; columnist Fortune; editl. dir. Fortune Tech. Guides, Wall St. Jour. Tech. Summits, Wall St. Jour. Healthcare Summits. Mem. vestry St. Bartholomew's Episcopal Ch., N.Y.C. Office: Technologic Pntrs 120 Wooster St New York NY 10012-5200

SHAFFER, RICHARD JAMES, lawyer, former manufacturing company executive; b. Pe Ell, Wash., Jan. 26, 1931; s. Richard Humphrys and Laura Rose (Faas) S.; m. Donna M. Smith, May 13, 1956; children: Leslie Lauren Shaffer Litsinger, Stephanie Jane Athenton. BA, U. Wash.; LL.B., Southwestern U. Bar: Calif. Vice pres., gen. counsel, sec. NI, Inc., Long Beach, Calif., 1974—89; gen. counsel Masco Bldg. Products Corp., Long Beach, 1985—89; pvt. practice Huntington Beach, Calif., 1989—98; internat. ops. officer Newport Fin. Group; CFO Dream Quest Entertainment, Ltd., 2003—. Mem. ltd. liability co. drafting com. and task force Calif. State Bar, 1992-94; lectr. in field. Trustee Ocean View Sch. Dist., 1965-73, pres., 1966, 73; mem. fin. adv. com. Orange Coast Coll., 1966; mem. Long Beach Local Devel. Corp., 1978-89, Calif. Senate Commn. on Corp. Governance, Shareholders' Rights and Securities Transactions, 1986-97, chmn. drafting com. ltd. liability co. act for senate com., 1991-93; mem. Pers. Commn. City of Huntington Beach, 1996-98; mem. Huntington Beach clean water subcom. Huntington Harbour; bd. dirs. Huntington Beach Libr. Patrons, 1996-98. Mem. ABA, Nat. Assn. Securities Dealers (bd. arbitrators), Calif. Bar Assn. (exec. com. corp. law dept. com. bus. sect. 1981-88), Orange County Bar Assn., Huntington Harbour Yacht Club, Catalina Island Yacht Club, Wanderlust Skiers of Huntington Harbour (pres.).

SHAFFER, SHEILA WEEKES, mathematics educator; b. Syracuse, N.Y., Oct. 20, 1957; d. Carroll Watson and Reina Lou (Yonker) Judd; m. Jason Craig Shaffer, June 4, 1983 (div. Sept. 1994). BA, SUNY, Albany, 1979, MS, 1982. Cert. tchr. English/Math., N.Y. English tchr. Cortland (N.Y.) HS, 1979-81, Prince George's County, Upper Marlboro, Md., 1984-86, math. tchr., 1986-87, math. tchr./coord., 1990-95, 96-99; math./English tchr. Camden HS, St. Mary's, Ga., 1988-90; math tchr. Frederick County, Va., 1995-96, Kingston City (N.Y.) Schs., 1999—. Mem. SAT com. The Coll. Bd., N.Y.C., 1993-96. Mem.: Nat. Coun. Tchrs. Math. Avocations: reading, hiking, gardening. Office: Kingston City Schools 61 Crown St Kingston NY 12401-3833

SHAFFER, SHERRILL LYNN, economist; b. Tyler, Tex., Aug. 1, 1952; s. Douglas Marsene and Ethel Elizabeth (Green) S.; m. Margaret Jane Ahrens, Jun. 20, 1987; 1 child, David Carsten. BA, Rice U., 1974; MA, Stanford U., 1978, PhD, 1981. Rsch. asst. Stanford U., Calif., 1976—79, instr., 1979—80; from economist to chief Fed. Res. Bank N.Y., N.Y.C., 1980—88; from rsch. officer, economist to asst. v.p./discount officer Fed. Res. Bank Phila., 1988—97; John A. Guthrie disting. prof. banking and fin. svcs. U. Wyo., Laramie, 1997—. Vis. scholar Stanford U., 2004; chmn. tenure and promotion com., grad. coun., 2000-02, MBA adv. com., grad. admissions com., 1999-2000, grad. program rev. com., 2000-02; violinist solo and with orchs., Calif., NY, 1976-88; cons. asst. Rosse & Olszewski, Palo Alto, Calif., 1978-80; cons. in field. Assoc. editor to editor Jour. Econs. and Bus., 1993—; mem. editl. bd. Jour. Regulatory Econs., 2002—; contbr. articles to profl. jours. Sec. bd. dirs. N.Y. Arts Group, N.Y.C., 1982—83; mem. program com. So. Fin. Assn., 1996; exec. adv. coun. mem. dept. fin. Temple U., 1996—97; bd. advisors cultural programs series U. Wyo., 1999—; mem. fin. com. St. Matthew's Cathedral, Laramie, Wyo., 1998—2004, mem. vestry, 1999—2002; bd. dirs. artist selection com. Tri-County Concerts Assn., 1996—. Recipient Messier cert. Astronomical League, 1993; vis. scholar, Stanford Univ., 2004. Mem. AAAS, Am. Econ. Assn., Am. Math. Soc., Math. Assn. Am., N.Am. Econs. and Fin. Assn., Indsl. Orgn. Soc., N.Y. Acad. Scis., Fin. Mgmt. Assn. (program com. 1991, 01, 03, 04, nat. awards com. 2000, 01), So. Fin. Assn. (program com. 1996), Delaware Valley Amateur Astronomers (observing chmn. 1993, publicity chmn. 1994-96), Chamber Music Am. Episcopalian. Avocations: hiking, astronomy, computer programming, theology, number theory, cycling (medalist). Home: 30 Silver Spur Rd Laramie WY 82072-9563 Office: U Wyo Dept Econs and Fin PO Box 3985 Laramie WY 82071-3985 Business E-Mail: shaffer@uwyo.edu.

SHAFFER, SUSAN E. nutrition specialist; b. Nashville, Apr. 14, 1947; d. James G. and Esther W. Shaffer. B.A. in English, Elmhurst (Ill.) Coll., 1969; MS in Nutrition, Rutgers U., 1992. Mem. claim dept. Allstate Ins. Co., 1971-76, unit mgr., Springfield, Pa., 1976-77, regional life claim mgr., Basking Ridge, N.J., 1977-79, dist. claim mgr., Latham, N.Y., 1979-87; rsch. asst. food sensory lab. Rutgers U., New Brunswick, N.J., 1991-94, asst. to dir. mkgt. Rescar Inc., Downers Grove, Ill, 1994-99; adminstrv. mgr. Millennium Rail, Inc., 1999—. Mem. Ins. Inst. Am. (assoc. in mgmt.). Office: Millennium Rail Inc 3 Westbrook Corporate Ctr Westchester IL 60154

SHAFFER, TERRY GEORGE, pastor; b. Meadville, Pa., Oct. 22, 1953; s. George William and Arlene (Robinson) S.; m. Sondra Lee Knight, July 21, 1973 (div. Mar. 1994); m. Beverly LoElen Buckner, July 1, 1994. BA in Sociology, Edinboro (Pa.) U., 1975; MDiv, Wesley Theol., Washington, 1978. Assoc. pastor Sharpsville (Pa.) United Meth. Ch., 1978-79; pastor Tenth St. United Meth. Ch., Erie, Pa., 1979-85, Marchand (Pa.) Charge Ch., 1985-90, Laketon Heights United Meth. Ch., Pitts., 1990-94, Albright United Meth. Ch., Pitts., 1994—. Assoc. dean We. Pa. Sch. of Mission, Pitts., 1995-96, dean, 1996-98; pres. Zoarhome, Pitts., 1995-98; vice chair chaplains, U. Pitts., 1997-98; mission amb. for African Ch. in We. Pa., 1994-95. V.p. Zoar Home, 1998—2001; chmn. mission support We. Pa. Conf. United Meth. Ch., 2002. Recipient Cmty. Spirit award Jewish Assn. of Aging for Alleghany County, 1999. Mem. Kiwanis (lt. gov. Pitts. divsn. 1998-2000, chair human spiritual values Pa. dist. 2000-02, We. Pa. Conf. Mission Support 2002, co-chmn. mid-winter convention 2003), Pa. Kiwanis Found.(bd. dirs.). Avocations: model railroading, travel, camping. Home and Office: Albright United Meth 486 S Graham St Pittsburgh PA 15232-1267 E-mail: TGshaffer@aol.com.

SHAFFER, THOMAS LINDSAY, lawyer, educator; b. Billings, Mont., Apr. 4, 1934; s. Cecil Burdette and Margaret Jeanne (Parker) S.; m. Nancy Jane Lehr, Mar. 19, 1954; children: Thomas, Francis, Joseph, Daniel, Brian, Mary, Andrew, Edward. BA, U. Albuquerque, 1958; JD, U. Notre Dame, 1961; LL.D., St. Mary's U., 1983. Bar: Ind. 1961. Assoc. Barnes, Hickam, Pantzer, & Boyd, Indpls., 1961-63; prof. law U. Notre Dame, Ind., 1963-80, assoc. dean, 1969-71, dean, 1971-75, Robert and Marion Short prof., 1988-97; Robert and Marion Short prof. emeritus, 1997—; supervising atty. Notre Dame Legal Aid Clinic, 1991—; prof. law Washington and Lee U., 1980-87, Robert E.R. Huntley prof. law, 1987-88. Vis. prof. UCLA, 1970-71, U. Va., 1975-76, U. Maine, 1982, 87, 98, Boston Coll., 1992; mem. Ind. Constl. Revision Commn., 1969-70, Ind. Trust Code Study Commn., 1968-71; reporter Ind. Jud. Conf., 1963, 67. Author: Death, Property, and Lawyers, 1970, The Planning and Drafting of Wills and Trusts, 1972, 4th edit., 2001, Legal Interviewing and Counseling, 1976, 3rd edit., 1998, On Being a Christian and a Lawyer, 1981, American Legal Ethics, 1985, Faith and the Professions, 1987, Moral Memoranda From John Howard Yoder, 2002; co-author: Lawyers, Law Students, and People, 1977, Cases in Legal Interviewing and Counseling, 1980, American Lawyers and Their Communities, 1991, Property Cases, Materials and Problems, 1992, 2nd edit., 1998, Lawyers, Clients, and Moral Responsibility, 1994; co-editor: The Mentally Retarded Citizen and the Law, 1976; contbr. articles to legal jours. Served with USAF, 1953-57. Frances Lewis scholar Washington and Lee U., 1979; recipient Emil Brown Found. Preventive Law prize, 1966, Presdl. citation U. Notre Dame, 1975, St. Thomas More award St. Mary's U., 1983, Law medal Gonzaga U., 1991, Jour. Law and Religion award, 1993. Mem. Ind. State Bar Assn., Jewish Law Assn., Nat. Lawyers Assn. Roman Catholic. Home: 1865 Champlain Dr Niles MI 49120-8935 Office: Notre Dame Legal Aid Clinic 725 Howard St South Bend IN 46617-1529

SHAFFERT, KURT, retired lawyer, chemical engineer; b. Vienna, July 20, 1929; s. Rudolph nee Schafranik and Irma (Altar) S.; m. Judith Pytel, June 12, 1955; children: Elona Ruth, Robin Laurette. BChemE, CCNY, 1951; LLB cum laude, NYU, 1963. Bar: N.Y. 1963, D.C. 1965, U.S. Supreme Ct. 1967, U.S. Patent and Trademark Office 1964. Chem. engr. Diamond Alkali Co., Newark, 1951-54; process devel. engr. Am. Cyanamid Co., Stamford, Conn., 1957-59; patent liaison engr. Uniroyal Inc., 1959-63; assoc. Arthur, Dry & Kalish, N.Y.C., 1963-66, Office of Robert F. Conrad, Washington, 1966-69; sr. ptnr. Shaffert, Miller & Browne, Washington, 1970-74; sr. trial atty. intellectual property sect. Antitrust divsn. Dept. of Justice, Washington, 1974-85, professions and intellectual property sect., 1985-94, intellectual property guidelines task force, 1994, civil task force, 1994-2000; ret., 2000. Mem. Bethesda-Chevy Chase Jewish Comm. Group, 1965, pres., 1973-74, v.p. 1972-73, treas. 1971-72; mem. Jewish Comm. Ctr. of Greater Wash., 1970-78, bd. dirs., 1973-78; provided tape recorded Holocaust recollections for Stephen Spielberg Holocaust Archive Survivors of the Shoa Visual History Found., 1998. With U.S. Army, 1955-56. Mem. ABA (antitrust sect., patent, trademark and copyright sect.), Profl. Assn. Antitrust Divsn. Dept. of Justice (pres. 1978-79), Bar Assn. D.C. (council del. 1972-74), D.C. Bar Assn.

SHAFFLER, RHONDA, news correspondent; B in broadcast journalism and polit. sci., Penn. State U. Various positions in broadcast and bus. news fields, 1987—95; anchor WPEN-AM, Phila., WMGK-FM, Phila.; broadcast editor AP; news editor, editor Dow Jones Voice Info. Network; freelance reporter News 12, Long Island, NY; reporter, writer bus. and gen. news WPHL-TV Inquirer News Tonight, Phila.; field prodr. CNN Bus. News, 1995—96, corr., 1996; anchor Moneyline Weekend Edit., CNN Bus. News; sr. corr. NY Stock Exchange CNNfn and CNN Bus. News; anchor CNNfn Market Call. Office: CNN 5 Penn Plz Fl 20 New York NY 10001-1810 Office Phone: 212-714-7800.

SHAFFNER, PATRICK NOEL, retired architectural engineering executive; b. Burlington, N.C., Nov. 1, 1939; s. Samuel Hubert and Martha Jane (Noel) Shaffner; m. Patricia Anne Anders, June 12, 1961; children: Scott Anders, Kimberly Page, Melissa Hope. BS, Va. Poly. and State U., 1961. Registered profl. engr., Va. Structural engr. Hayes, Seay, Mattern & Mattern, Roanoke, Va., 1963-68; sr. structural engr. Sherertz & Franklin, Roanoke, 1968-72; ptnr. Sherertz, Franklin, Crawford, Shaffner, Roanoke, 1972-87; chmn., CEO Sherertz, Franklin, Crawford, Shaffner, Inc., Roanoke, 1988-98. Bd. dirs. Mill Mountain Theatre, Va. Tech. Coll. Engring. Com. 100; CHIP, v.p. Roanoke Found. for Downtown, Inc.; bd. trustees Va. Bapt. Children's Home and Family Svcs. Capt. Corps. Engrs., U.S. Arm, 1961-63. Paul Harris fellow. Fellow ASCE; mem. AIA (assoc.), Roanoke Regional C. of C. (Small Bus. Person of Yr. 1991), Rotary (pres. Roanoke club 1986). Lodges: Rotary (Roanoke) (pres. 1986). Republican. Baptist. Home: 2635 Turnberry Rd Salem VA 24153-7483 E-mail: shaffner@adelphia.net.

SHAFFNER, RANDOLPH PRESTON, shop owner, educator, writer, publisher; b. Winston-Salem, N.C., Jan. 17, 1940; s. Emil Nathaniel and Anna Jackson (Preston) S.; m. Margaret Farmer Rhodes; children: Eric Randolph, Edward David, Joseph Andrew, Thomas Matthew, Jackson Rhodes. Student, Davidson Coll., 1958-60; BA in English with honors in writing, U. N.C., 1962, MA in Comparative Lit., 1969, PhD, 1973. Surveyor's lineman Joyce Mapping Co., Winston-Salem, 1955-58, 62; counselor, scoutmaster Camp Sequoyah, Weaverville, N.C., 1959; track repairman Alaska R.R., Anchorage, 1960; case handler Emard Packing Co., Anchorage, 1960, AYR Canneries, Seldovia, Alaska, 1961; tchr. U.S. Peace Corps., Chiengrai, Thailand, 1963-65, St. Christopher's Sch., Richmond, Va., 1969-71; instr. U. N.C., 1968-69, 71-73; asst. prof. Fairfield U., Conn., 1973-78, Western Carolina U., 1984, 87, Continuing Edn. program World Masterpieces, Highlands, NC, 1987—89; moderator Highlands lecture series Western Carolina U., 1989-92. Instr. carolina environ. program U. NC, Chapel Hill, 2003; editor John F. Blair Pub., Winston-Salem, 1966-68; bookseller, owner Cyrano's Bookshop, Highlands, NC, 1978—; founder, pub. Faraway Pub., 2001; asst. to dean Sch. Libr. Scis. U. NC, Chapel Hill, 1973-74; literary mag. adv., various subcoms. Dept. Eng. Fairfield U., 1973-78. Author: Apprenticeship Novel, 1984, Tree Ordinance for Town of Highlands, 1987, Good Reading Material, Mostly Bound and New: The Hudson Library 1884-1994, 1994, Heart of the Blue Ridge: Highlands, North Carolina, 2001; (with others) Nineteenth Century Literature Criticism, Vol. 21, 1989; contbr. poetry to N.C. Poetry Soc. anthology Here's to the Land, 1992; contbr. short stories to mags; contbr. Heritage of Macon Co., N.C., Vol. 2, 1999. Lectr. with Alexander, String Quartet, Words & Music, 1989, 92, 94, for Western Carolina U., Highlands lectr. series, 1991-93, 2000; instr. Ctr. for Life Enrichment, 2000; chmn. ARC Disaster Svcs., Fairfield, 1974-78, Zoning Bd. of Adjustment, Highlands, 1981-83, 85-90; pres., bd. trustees Hudson Libr., Inc., Highlands, 1987-90, 99-2001, chmn. libr. com., 1995-99; trustee Hudson Libr. Bascom-Louise Art Gallery, 1987-90, 95-99, Highlands Land Trust, Inc., 1995-96; bd. dirs. ARC, Fairfield, 1974-78, Highlands Cultural Art Ctr., 1987; fundraisingcom. Highlands Permanent Endowment Scholarships, 1987-89; Town of Highlands Millennium Com., 1999; historian Highlands Hist. Soc., Inc., 1999—, adv. com., 2001-; vice-chmn. bd. missions Greenfield Hill Congl. Ch., Fairfield, Conn., 1977, chmn. scholarship co., 1975-77; chaperon Am. Inst. for Fgn. Study, Grenoble, France, 1970. Recipient God and Country award, 1955, Outstanding Pres. and Trustee award Hudson Libr. and Bascom-Louise Gallery, 1990, Daniel Boone Coun. Boy Scouts Am. Disting. Citizen award, 2002, Gertrude and Dolly Harbison award, Hudson Libr., 2004; Goethe Inst. scholar German Embassy, Munich, Fed. Rep. Germany, 1965, Univ. Besançon, France, 1965. Mem.: Highlands Biol. Found. (bd. trustees 1981—, fund raising com. 1986, environ. protection com. 1986—88, exec. com. 1986—, treas. 1990—2004, adv. com. on Nature Ctr. 1992), Highlands Mchts. Assn. (chmn. fin. com., treas. 1984—87, chmn. tree com. and beautification com. 1984—89), Southeastern Booksellers Assn., Am. Booksellers Assn., Am. Acad. Poets, N.C. Poetry Soc., Writers' Workshop, Am. Comparative Lit. Assn., Internat. Comparative Lit. Assn., N.C. Soc. Historians (History Book award 2002), Nat. Peace Corps Assn., Clan Morrison Soc., Highlands C. of C., Highlands Hist. Soc., Trail Hikers Am., Rotary (Outstanding Vol. award 1989), Lambda Iota Tau (faculty moderator Delta Omicon Ch. 1975—80, founder). Democrat. Moravian. Avocations: construction, reading, travel, hiking, camping. Home: 608 Hickory St Highlands NC 28741-0765 Office: Cyrano's Bookshop 390 Main St Highlands NC 28741-0765 E-mail: cyranos@nctv.com.

SHAFFRON, J. JANET, legislative administrator; b. Welch, W.Va., Mar. 27, 1947; BS, W.Va. U., 1969. Legis. dir. to Rep. Frank R. Wolf U.S. Ho. of Reps., Washington, 1984—. Office: US Ho of Reps 241 Chob Washington DC 20515-0001 E-mail: janet.shaffron@mail.house.gov.

SHAFII, BAHMAN, statistician, educator, researcher; b. Tehran, Iran, Dec. 12, 1954; s. Mahmood and Akhtar Shafii; m. Sima Safaei; children: Omid, Farid children: Sara Azar. BS with hon., Rezaeyeh U., Rezaeyeh, Iran, 1977; MS, U. Idaho, 1980, MS, 1982, PhD, 1988. Lectr. Wash. State U., Pullman, Wash., 1984—88; dir. statis. programs U. of Idaho, Moscow, Idaho, 1988—. Contbr. articles over 70 to profl. jours. Recipient Paul Howe Shepard award, Am. Pomological Soc., 1998, award of Excellence, Weed Sci. Soc. Am., 2002. Mem.: AAAS, NCR-170 Coord. Rsch. Advances Agrl. Statistics (sec. 1995—2001), Am. Statis. Assn. (pres. 1995—96, Snake River chpt.), Internat. Biometric Soc., Sigma Xi. Avocations: travel, music, poetry. Office: Statistical Programs University of Idaho PO Box 442337 Moscow ID 83844-2337 Business E-Mail: bshafii@uidaho.edu.

SHAFIR, ROBERT S. finance company executive; BA, Lafayette Coll.; MBA, Columbia U. With Morgan Stanley & Co., 1985—90; sr. mgmt. positions Lehman Brothers Holdings Inc., 1990—2000, co-head, global equities, 2000—. Mem. exec. com. Lehman Brothers Holdings Inc. Office: Lehman Brothers Holdings Inc 745 Seventh Ave New York NY 10019

SHAFRITZ, DAVID ANDREW, physician, research scientist; b. Phila., Oct. 5, 1940; s. Saul and Ethel (Kohn) S.; m. Sharon C. Klemow, Aug. 16, 1964; children: Gregory S., Adam B., Keith M. AB in Chemistry with honors, U. Pa., 1962, MD, 1966. Diplomate Nat. Bd. Med. Examiners, Am. Bd. Internal Medicine. Intern, then asst. resident U. Md. Hosp., Balt., 1966-68; rsch. assoc. NIH, Bethesda, Md., 1968-71; clin. and rsch. fellow Mass. Gen. Hosp., Boston, 1971-73; instr. Harvard Med. Sch., Boston, 1971-73, asst. prof. medicine, 1973; asst. prof. medicine and cell biology Albert Einstein Coll. Medicine, Yeshiva U., Bronx, N.Y., 1973-76, assoc. prof., 1976-81, prof. medicine and cell biology, 1981—, dir. Marion Bessin Liver Rsch. Ctr., 1985—, Herman Lapota prof. liver disease rsch. (endowed chair), 1992—. Cons. integrated Genetics, Inc., Framingham, Mass., 1981-86, Immuno, Vienna, Austria, 1986-91, Innovir, Inc., N.Y.C., 1991-98, Eugenetech Internat., Inc., Ramsey, N.J., 1991-93, Ctrs. for Med. Innovation, 1997-2001; temp. advisor WHO, Geneva, 1983; mem. Nat. Com. for Clin. Lab. Stds., Villanova Pa., 1983—, Renaissance Techs., 1996—, Affymetrix, Inc., 1997—; sci. adv. bd. com. liver cancer program Inst. for Cancer Rsch., Fox Chase and Phila., 1987—, mem. rev. panel C. study sect. Nat. Inst. Diabetes and Digestive and Kidney Diseases, 1988-92, chmn., 1991-92; mem. cen. coord. com. Liver Tissue Procurement and Distbn. Sys., 1986-95, Nat. Inst. Health Metabolic Pathology Study sect., 1995-99; mem. Nat. Bd. Med. Examiners and U.S. Med. Exam. Com., 1996-98. Co-author: The Liver: Biology and Pathobiology, 1982, 4th edit., 2001, Hepatobiliary Diseases, 1991; assoc. editor Hepatology, 1981-86; mem. editl. bd. Jour. Med. Virology, 1982-93, Hepatology, 1990-96, Jour. Virology, 1992-98; contbr. numerous rsch. articles and revs. to profl. publs.; contbr. chpts. to books; patentee in field. Trustee Westchester Jewish Ctr., Mamaroneck, N.Y., 1980-86. Lt. comdr. USPHS, 1968-71. Recipient Merck award U. Pa., 1962, Morton McCutcheon Meml. Rsch. prize Sch. Medicine, 1966, Career Scientist award Irma T. Hirschl Trust, N.Y.C., 1974-79, NIH Merit award, 1994, Disting. Rsch. Achievement award Am. Liver Found., 2000; European Molecular Biology Orgn. fellow, 1978; recipient Rsch. Career Devel. award NIH, 1975-80, spl. rsch. fellow, 1971-73, rsch. grantee, 1974—. Mem. Am. Assn. for Study of Liver Diseases, Internat. Assn. for Study of Liver, Am. Gastroenterol. Assn., Am. Soc. Biochemistry and Molecular Biology, Am. Soc. Investigative Pathology, Am. Soc. Clin. Investigation, Assn. Am. Physicians, N.Y. Acad. Scis., Harvey Soc., Interurban Clin. Club (sec./treas. 1996-99, pres. 1999-2000). Democrat. Jewish. Avocations: jogging, tennis. Home: 4 Pheasant Run Larchmont NY 10538-3423 Office: Yeshiva U Albert Einstein Coll Med Marion Bessin Liver Rsch Ctr 1300 Morris Park Ave Bronx NY 10461-1926 E-mail: shafritz@aecom.yu.edu.

SHAFTMAN, FREDRICK KRISCH, telephone communications executive, lawyer; b. Roanoke, Va., Apr. 9, 1948; s. Sydney and Rosalie (Krisch) S.; m. Diane Hasson, Dec. 27, 1970; children: Stephanie, Emily. BSBA, U. Ala., 1970, JD, 1973. Bar: Va. 1973. Gen. counsel Bell South Comm. Sys. (formerly Universal Comm. Sys., Inc.), Roanoke, 1973-74, v.p., gen. counsel, 1974-79, pres., 1979-84, CEO, 1984-99, also bd. dirs.; pres. Bus. BellSouth Corp, Atlanta, 2000—. V.p. Am. Motor Inns, Inc. Bd. dirs. United Way Roanoke Valley, Roanoke Mill Mountain Zoo; trustee North Cross Country Day Sch., Roanoke, Roanoke Valley Sci. Mus., Roanoke Valley ARC. Recipient President's Disting. Svc. award N.Am. Telecom. Assn., 1985, achievement award United Jewish Assn., 1989. Mem. ABA, N.Am. Tel. Assn. (bd. dirs.), Western Va. BBB (bd. dirs.), Va. Bar Assn., Rotary. Office: Bellsouth Bus Sys 1100 Peachtree St NE Ste 1000 Atlanta GA 30309-4501

SHAFTO, ROBERT AUSTIN, retired insurance company executive; b. Council Bluffs, Iowa, Sept. 15, 1935; s. Glen Granville and Blanche (Radigan) S.; m. Jeanette DeFino, Dec. 17, 1954; children: Robert, Dennis, Teri, Shari, Michael. BS in Actuarial Sci., Drake U., Des Moines, 1959. Mgr. computer svcs. Guarantee Mut. Life Ins. Co., Omaha, 1959-65; v.p. Beta div. Electronic Data Systems, Dallas, 1965-71; from 2d v.p. to v.p. for computer systems devel. and info. svcs. New England Mutual Life Ins. Co., Boston, 1972-75, sr. v.p. policy holder and computer svcs., 1975-81, adminstrv. v.p., 1981-82, exec. v.p. individual ins. ops., 1982-86, exec. v.p. ins. and employee benefits ops., 1986-88, pres. ins. and personal fin. svcs., 1988-90, pres., chief oper. officer, 1990-92, pres., CEO, 1992-93, pres., CEO, chmn., 1993-98, also bd. dirs.; ret., 1998. Bd. dirs., pres. New Eng. Variable Life, Fleet Bank of Mass., Am. Coun. Life Ins. Bd. overseers Children's Hosp., Boston, 1989—; mem. corp. Dana Farber Cancer Inst., Northwestern U.; bd. dirs. United Way of Mass; trustee Am. Coll. Mem. Greater Boston C. of C. (bd. dirs.). Roman Catholic. Avocations: tennis, golf, scuba diving, jogging. Office: New Eng Mut Life Ins Co 501 Boylston St Boston MA 02116-3769

SHAGAM, MARVIN HÜCKEL-BERRI, private school educator; b. Monongalia, W.Va.; s. Lewis and Clara (Shagam) S. AB magna cum laude, Washington and Jefferson Coll., 1947; postgrad., Harvard Law Sch., 1947-48, Oxford (Eng.) U., 1948-51. Tchr. Mount House Sch., Tavistock, Eng., 1951-53, Williston Jr. Sch., Easthampton, Mass., 1953-55, Westtown (Pa.) Sch., 1955-58, The Thacher Sch., Ojai, Calif., 1958—; English dept. head Kurasini Internat. Edn. Centre, Dar-es-Salaam, Tanzania, 1966-67; dept. head Nkumbi Internat. Coll., Kabwe, Zambia, 1967-68. Vol. visitor Prisons in Calif., 1980-95, Calif. Youth Authority, 1983-93; sr. youth crisis counsellor InterFace, 1984-94. With U.S. Army, 1942-46, 1st lt. M.I. res.,1946-57. Danforth Found. fellow, 1942; Coun. for the Humanities fellow, Tufts U., 1983. Mem. Western Assn. Schs. and Colls. (accreditation com.), Great Teaching (Cooke chair 1977—), Phi Beta Kappa, Delta Sigma Rho, Cum Laude Soc. Republican. Avocations: hiking, camping, travel. Home: 5025 Thacher Rd Ojai CA 93023-8304 Office: The Thacher Sch 5025 Thacher Rd Ojai CA 93023-9001 Fax: 808-646-9490. E-mail: mshagam@thacher.org.

SHAGAN, BERNARD PELLMAN, endocrinologist, educator; b. Bklyn., Sept. 29, 1935; s. Samuel David and Pearl (Pellman) S.; m. Maureen Helen Oshever Amster, June 24, 1957 (div. 1970); children: Ellen Ruth Basch, Brian Ross; m. Phoebe Orange, Aug. 24, 1972; 1 child, Adam Irwin. AB, Harvard U., 1956; MD, NYU, 1960. Diplomate Am. Bd. Internal Medicine; bd. cert. endocrinology and metabolism. Chief sect. endocrinology Coney Island Hosp., Bklyn., 1968-79; chief sect. endocrinology, assoc. prof. medicine East Tenn. State U. Quillen Dishner Coll. Medicine, Johnson City, 1979-84; assoc. chmn., then acting chmn. dept. medicine Nassau County Med. Ctr., East Meadow, NY, 1984-87; assoc. prof. clin. medicine SUNY, Stony Brook, 1985-87; chmn., program dir. dept. medicine Monmouth Med. Ctr., Long Branch, NJ, 1987-96, dir. Diabetes Edn. Ctr., 2002—; pvt. practice in endocrinology and metabolism Shrewsbury, NY, 1997-98, West Long Branch, NJ, 1998—2002; pvt. practice of endocrinology Long Branch, NJ, 2002—; clin. prof. medicine Drexel U. Med. Ctr. Clin. prof. medicine Med. Coll. Pa. Hahnemann U., Phila., 1988—2002; clin. prof. medicine Coll. Medicine Drexel U., Phila., 2004—. Contbr. articles to med. jours. Capt. M.C., U.S. Army, 1966-68. Fellow ACP (gov. N.J. 1996-2000), Am. Coll. Endocrinologists; mem. Am. Assn. Clin. Endocrinologists, Am. Diabetes Assn., Endocrine Soc. Jewish. Avocations: music, singing, piano. Office: Diabetes Edn Ctr Alexander Pavilion 300 2d Ave Long Branch NJ 07740 Office Phone: 732-923-5026. E-mail: bshagan@monmouth.com.

SHAGAN, STEVE, screenwriter, novelist, film producer; b. N.Y.C., Oct. 25, 1927; m. Elizabeth Florance, Nov. 1956. Film technician Consol. Film, Inc., N.Y.C., 1952-56, RCA, Cape Canaveral, Fla., 1956-59; asst. to publicity dir. Paramount Pictures, Hollywood, Calif., 1962-63. Prodr.: (TV series) Tarzan, 1966; prodr., writer movies for TV, Universal and CBS, Hollywood, Calif., 1968-70; writer original screenplay: Save the Tiger, 1972 (Writers Guild award, Acad. award nominee 1973); prodr. film, author screenplay: City of Angels (produced as movie Hustle), 1975, novel, screenplay The Formula, 1979, screenplay Voyage of the Damned, 1976 (Acad. award nominee); writer, prodr. film The Formula, 1980; author: (novels) Save the Tiger, 1972, City of Angels, 1975, The Formula, 1979, The Circle, 1982, The Discovery, 1985, Vendetta, 1986, Pillars of Fire, 1989, A Cast of Thousands, 1993, (screenplays) Primal Fear, 1996, Gotti, 1996 (Emmy nominee Best Screenplay). Served with USCG, 1944-46. Mem. Writers Guild Am. (bd. dirs. West chpt. 1978-82).

SHAH, AASHIT K. neurologist; b. Baroda, India, Feb. 19, 1964; m. Jigna Shah; children: Aashka, Ananya. MBBS, N.H.L. Mcpl. Med. Coll., Gujarat, India, 1987. Diplomate Am. Bd. Neurology. Intern Interfaith Med. Ctr., Bklyn., 1988-89; res. Wayne State U. Detroit Med. Ctr., 1989-92, fellowship, 1992-93; staff neurologist Hutzel Hosp., Detroit, 1993, Harper Hosp., Detroit, 1993, Detroit Rec. Hosp., 1993. Assoc. prof. Wayne State U., 1993. Office: 8A-UHC/Dept Neur 4201 Saint Antoine St Detroit MI 48201-2153 Office Phone: 313-745-4275. Business E-Mail: ashah@med.wayne.edu.

SHAH, AJAY, electronics company executive; Chmn., pres., CEO Smart Modular Tech., Fremont, Calif. Office: Smart Modular Tech PO Box 1757 Fremont CA 94538-0175

SHAH, ARVIND, trade consultant, industrial designer; s. Shantilal and Aban Shah; m. Aban Wadia; 1 child, Sapna. BS in Indsl. Design, U. Mich., 1967. Internat. trade cons. Scaindia/Arvind Group, Santa Barbara, Calif., 1973—, product design cons., 1973—. Scholar Nat. Def. Award. Achievements include design of form and function stainless steel barware. Personal E-mail: arvingroup@cs.com.

SHAH, HARESH CHANDULAL, civil engineering educator; b. Godhra, Gujarat, India, Aug. 7, 1937; s. Chandulal M. and Rama Shah; m. Mary-Joan Dersjant, Dec. 27, 1965; children: Hemant, Mihir. BEngring., U. Poona, 1959; MSCE, Stanford U., 1960, PhD, 1963. From instr. to assoc. prof. U. Pa., Phila., 1962-68; assoc. prof. civil engring. Stanford (Calif.) U., 1968-73, prof., 1973—, chmn. dept. civil engring., 1985-94, John A. Blume prof. engring., 1988-91, Obayashi prof. engring., 1991-97, dir. Stanford Ctr. for Risk Analysis, 1987-94, Obayashi prof. engring. emeritus, 1998—. Trustee Geohazards Internat.; bd. dir. OYO-RMS, Inc., Japan, ERS, R.M. Software Ltd., India, Risk Mgmt. Solutions, Inc., World Seismic Safety Initiative, Buildfolio, Inc.; cons. in field; pres. World Seismic Safety Initiative, 1994—. Author 1 book; contbr. over 250 articles to profl. jours. Mem. ASCE, Am. Concrete Inst., Earthquake Engring. Rsch. Inst., Seismol. Soc. Am., Sigma Xi, Tau Beta Pi. Avocations: hiking, climbing, travel. Office: Risk Mgmt Solutions Inc 7015 Gateway Bldg Newark CA 94560 E-mail: hshah@stanford.edu., haresh.shah@rms.com.

SHAH, JAMES M. actuary; b. Amadhara, India, Feb. 4, 1943; came to U.S., 1980; s. Manekchand Keshrichand and Kamuben Manekchand Shah; m. Urmila Jashwantlal Shah, May 16, 1966; children: Meeta, Keena, Jatin. BS, Gujarat U., India, 1965; MS, Gujarat U., 1969; MA, Georgetown U., 1983; MS, U. Nebr., 1986. Sr. rsch. asst. Nat. Inst. Rural Devel., Hyderabad, India, 1972-74; rsch. officer Population Ctr. World Bank Population Project, Bangalore, India, 1974-77; actuarial analyst Shelby Ins. Co., Ohio, 1987-90; actuary ins. dept. State of ND, Bismarck, ND, 1990-91; pres. A S D Consulting Svc., Mansfield, Ohio, 1991-2000; asst. actuary Blue Cross Blue Shield Utica, Utica, NY, 2000. Contbr. articles to profl. jours. UN fellow Ministry of Fgn. Affairs, 1978; recipient Outstanding Young Person award Garden City Jaycees, 1977, 7th Summer Seminar award U. Hawaii, 1976. Mem. Internat. Actuarial Assn. (cert. 1996), Internat. Union for Sci. Study of Population, Soc. Actuaries (cert. 1994), Am. Acad. Actuaries (cert. 1994). Avocations: travel, reading, ping pong/table tennis. Home: 91 S Ireland Blvd Mansfield OH 44906-2220 Office: ASD Cons Svc 91 S Ireland Blvd Mansfield OH 44906 E-mail: shahjames@hotmail.com.

SHAH, JAMI J. mechanical engineering educator, researcher; s. Maqsood A. and Nasim K. Shah. BSME, NED Engring. Coll., Karachi, 1973; MSMetE, U. Pitts., 1976; PhDME, Ohio State U., 1984. Engr. Pakistan Steel, Karachi, 1973-75; prodn. engr. Pakistan Oxygen, Karachi, 1976-80; assoc. prof. Ariz. State U., Tempe, 1984—2003, prof., 1995—. Cons. rsch. area in application of artificial intelligence techniques to engring. design and mfg. automation; tchr. creativity techniques in engring. & bus. Author: 2 books; contbr. more than 150 rsch. papers to profl. jours.; founding editor: ASME Transactions,: Jour. Computing and Info. Sci. Fellow: ASME. Avocations: hiking, climbing, desert plants. Office: Ariz State U Dept Mech Engring Tempe AZ 85287

SHAH, NANDLAL CHIMANLAL, retired physiatrist; b. Sadra, Gujarat, India, July 3, 1933; came to U.S., 1969; s. Chimanial D. and Dahiben C. (Shah) Shah; m. Indira N. Shah, May 15, 1960; children: Sandip N., Tushar N. Student, M.G. Sci. Inst., Ahmedabad, India, 1952; MB, BS, B.J. Med. Coll., Ahmedabad, India, 1957. Diplomate Am. Bd. Phys. Medicine and Rehab., Am. Bd. Quality Assurance and Utilization Review Physicians. Intern Yonkers (N.Y.) Gen. Hosp., 1970; resident in internal medicine St. Barnabas Hosp., Bronx, N.Y., 1971; resident in phys. medicine and rehab. Albert Einstein Coll. Medicine, Bronx, 1971-74; staff physiatrist, dir. med. svcs. Inst. Phys. Medicine and Rehab., Peoria, Ill., 1974-79; med. dir. Thomas Rehab. Hosp., Asheville, N.C., 1979-81; staff physiatrist phys. medicine and rehab. Charlotte (N.C.) Inst. Rehab. (formerly Charlotte Rehab. Hosp.), 1981; pvt. practice Carolina Rehab. Clinic, Charlotte, 1981-99, ret., 2001. Mem. Greater Charlotte (N.C.) Assn. Physicians Indian Origin (chartered), N.C. Assn. Physicians Indian Origin (past pres.), Masons. Hindu. Avocations: Indian classical music, social, cultural and religious programs.

SHAH, NAYAN, internist; b. Botad, India, July 21, 1956; came to U.S., 1978; s. Rasiklal Shah; m. Jayu Shah; children: Suketu, Shalin. MD, Bombay U., 1979. Diplomate Am. Bd. Internal Medicine, Am. Bd. Gastroenterology. Pvt. practice, Hollywood, Md., 1984—. Dir. Tri-County Endoscopy Ctr., Hollywood, 1989. Fellow Am. Coll. Gastroenterology; mem. Am. Soc. Gastrointestinal Endoscopy. Office: 24035 Three Notch Rd Hollywood MD 20636

SHAH, RAMESH KESHAVLAL, researcher, engineering educator; b. Bombay, Sept. 23, 1941; came to U.S., 1963; s. Keshavlal M. and Hiraben K. (Kothari) S.; m. Rekha R. Maniar, Jan. 22, 1968; children: Nilay R., Nirav R. BME, Gujarat U., Ahmedabad, Gujarat, 1963; MS, Stanford U., 1964, ME, 1970, PhD in Mech. Engring., 1972. Project engr. Air Preheater Co., Wellsville, N.Y., 1964-66, Avco-Lycoming, Charleston, S.C., 1966-69; rsch. engr. Harrison Radiator Divsn. GM, Lockport, N.Y., 1971-75, tech. dir. rsch. Harrison Radiator Divsn., 1976-88, sr. staff rsch. scientist Delphi Harrison Thermal Systems, 1989-95; chmn. dept. mech. engring. U. Ky., Lexington, 1995-97; sr. staff rsch. scientist Delphi Harrison Thermal Systems, Lockport, 1997—2001; rsch. prof. Rochester (N.Y.) Inst. Tech., 2001—. Tchr. short courses, presenter keynote lectrs., seminars on heat exchanger design nd fuel cell tech. at various univs. and rsch. insts. in U.S., India, Can., U.K., Turkey, Yugoslavia, Germany, China, Japan, Australia, Argentina, Brazil, Portugal, Czechoslovakia, Hungary, Taiwan, South Korea, Israel, Belgium, Sweden, Lithuania, Russia, Greece, Italy, Malta, Singapore, Ukraine, France, Poland, South Africa, Bangladesh. Author: (with A.L. London) Laminar Flow Forced Convection in Ducts, Suppl. 1 to Advances in Heat Transfer, 1978; editor: (with S. Kakac and A.E. Bergles) Low Reynolds Number Flow Heat Exchangers, 1983, (with S. Kakac and W. Aung) Handbook of Single-Phase Convective Heat Transfer, 1987, (with E.C. Subbarao and R.A. Mashelkar) Heat Transfer Equipment Design, 1988, (with E.N. Ganic and K.T. Yang) Experimental Heat Transfer, Fluid Mechanics and Thermodynamics, 1988, (with A.D. Kraus and D.E. Metzger) Compact Heat Exchangers: A Festschrift for Professor A.L. London, 1990, (with H. Md. Roshan, V.M.K. Sastri and K.A. Padmanabhan) Thermomechanical Aspects of Manufacturing and Materials Processing, 1991, (with J.F. Keffer and E.N. Ganic) Experimental Heat Transfer, Fluid Mechanics and Thermodynamics, 1991, (with A. Hashemi) Aerospace Heat Exchanger Technology, 1993, (with M.D. Kelleher, K.R. Sreenivasan and Y. Joshi) Experimental Heat Transfer, Fluid Mechanics and Thermodynamics, 1993, (with S.P. Sukhatme, V. Venkat Raj and V.M.K. Sastri) Heat and Mass Transfer, 1994, (with G.P. Celata) Two-Phase Flow Modelling and Experimentation, 1995, Compact Heat Exchangers for the Process Industries, 1997, (with G.P. Celata and P. Di Marco) Two-Phase Flow Modeling and Experimentation, 1999, Compact Heat Exchangers and Enhancement Technology for the Process Industries, 1999, Compact Heat Exchangers and Enhancement Technology for the Process Industries, 2001, Fundamentals of Heat Exchanger Design, 2003, Compace Heat Exchangers and Enhancement Technology for the Process Industries, 2003; editor 12 symposium vols.; founding co-editor, editor-in-chief Exptl. Thermal and Fluid Sci., 1987-95; tech. papers reviewer ASME Jour. Heat Transfer, Internat. Jour. Heat and Mass Transfer, Internat. Jour. Heat Fluid Flow, Jour. Enhanced Heat Transfer, Jour. Numerical Heat Transfer, AIChE Jour., ASME Jour. Fluids Engring., Heat Transfer Engring. Jour., numerous fgn. jours. NSF grantee (10), 1981-95, NATO grantee (4), 1980-87, 96-97, UN grantee, 1985-86, 88-89. Fellow ASME (Region III Tech. Achievement award 1979, Valued Svc. award 1986, 87, 92, 50th Anniversary award of Heat Transfer Divsn. 1988, Charles Russ Richards Meml. award 1989, Heat Transfer Meml. award 2000), Soc. Automotive Engrs.; mem. AIChE, Indian Soc. Heat and Mass Transfer (life), Am. Soc. Engring. Edn., Niagara Frontier Assn. R&D Dirs. Jain. Avocations: travel, reading, bridge. Office: Rochester Inst Tech Dept Mech Engring Rochester NY 14623-5604 E-mail: rkshah@attglobal.net.

SHAH, SHIRISH KALYANBHAI, computer science, chemistry and environmental science educator; b. Ahmedabad, India, May 24, 1942; came to U.S., 1962, naturalized, 1974; s. Kayyanbhai T. and Sushilaben K. S.; m. Kathleen Long, June 28, 1973; 1 son, Lawrence. BS in Chemistry and Physics, St. Xavier's Coll. Gujarat U., 1962; PhD in Phys. Chemistry, U. Del., 1968; cert. in bus. mgmt., U. Va., 1986; PhD in Cultural Edn. (hon.), World U. West, 1986. Asst. prof. Washington Coll., Chestertown, Md., 1967-68; dir. quality control Vita Foods, Chestertown, Md., 1968-72; asst. prof., assoc. prof. sci., adminstr. food, marine sci. and vocat. programs Chesapeake Coll., Wye Mills, Md., 1968-76; assoc. prof., prof. sci., chmn. dept. tech. studies C.C. of Balt., 1976-91; assoc. prof. chemistry Coll. Notre Dame of Md., 1991—2002. Chmn. computer sys. and engring. techs., 1982-89, project facilitator telecom. curriculum and lab., 1985-89, coord. tech. studies, 1989-91; adj. prof. Phys. Sci. Coppin State Coll., 1996-98; mem. Balt. City Adult Edn. Adv. Com., 1982-89, Distance Learning Task Force, 1996-97; chmn. Coll. wide computer user com., 1985-91; coun. mem. Faculty R&D, 1994-97; adj. prof. chemistry Towson U., 1998—, Morgan State U., 1999—; lectr./prof. chemistry Villa Julie Coll., 2002—; cons. joint apprentice com. Baltimore City Govt., 1980-91. Contbr. articles to profl. jours. Permanent mem. Rep. Senatorial Com.; charter mem. Rep. Presdl. Task Force; mem. Congl. Adv. Com., 1983—; adviser Young Reps., 1992-2002. Recipient Phoenix award Am. Chem. Soc., 1996, 97, Pub. Rels. award, 1996, Sci. Policy award, 2000. Fellow Am. Inst. Chemists (co-chair internat. com. 2002); mem. IEEE, APHA, NSTA, Am. Lung Assn. (chair environ. affairs com., 1976-80), Am. Lung Assn. Md. (bd. dirs. 1971-80), Am. Chem. Soc. (chmn.-elect Md. Sect. 1995-96, chmn. 1996-98, chair kids and chemistry program of Md. sect. 1996-99, sec. Mid-Atlantic regional conf., 2002-, chmn. com. govt. rels. Md. sect. 1998-, chair pub. rels. com. 2000-, pres.-elect Chesapeake sect. 2002-03, sec. Mid Atlantic sect. 2003—), Indsl. Hygiene Assn. (pres. Chesapeake sect. 2003-04), Nat. Environ. Tng. Assn., Nat. Assn. Indsl. Tech. (dir. local region, bd. accreditors 1989-95), Am. Vocat. Assn., Am. Tech. Edn. Assn., Am. Fedn. Tchrs., Md. State Tchrs. Assn., Md. Assn. Cmty. and Jr. Colls. (v.p. 1977-78, pres. 1978-97), Sigma Xi, Epsilon Pi Tau, Iota Lambda Sigma Nu. Roman Catholic. Home: 5605 Purlington Way Baltimore MD 21212-2950 Office: Chemistry Dept Towson University Towson MD 21252- Office Phone: 410-704-2720. Personal E-mail: dr.shah@juno.com. Business E-Mail: sshah@towson.edu.

SHAH, SURENDRA POONAMCHAND, engineering educator; b. Bombay, Aug. 30, 1936; s. Poonamchand C. and Maniben (Modi) S.; m. Dorothie Crispell, June 9, 1962; children: Daniel S., Byron C. BE, B.V.M. Coll. Engring., India, 1959; MS, Lehigh U., 1960; PhD, Cornell U., 1965. Asst. prof. U. Ill., Chgo., 1966-69, assoc. prof., 1969-73, prof., 1973-81; prof. civil engring Northwestern U., Evanston, Ill., 1981—, dir. Ctr. for Concrete and Geomaterials, 1987—, prof. civil engring., 1989—, Walter P. Murphy prof. of engring., 1992—. Cons. govt. agys. and industry, U.S.A., UN, France, Switzerland, People's Republic China, Denmark, The Netherlands; vis. prof. MIT, 1969, Delft U., The Netherlands, 1976, Denmark Tech. U., 1984, LCPC, Paris, 1986, U. Sidney, Australia, 1987; NATO vis. sci. Turkey, 1992; disting. vis. prof. Nat. Singapore U., 1999, vis. chair prof. Denmark Tech. U., 2002; hon. prof. Hongkong Poly. U, 2003. Co-author: Fiber Reinforced Cement Composites, 1992, High Performance Concrete and Applications, 1994, Fracture Mechanics of Concrete, 1995; contbr. more than 400 articles to profl. jours.; editor 12 books; mem. editorial bds. 2 internat. jours.; editor-in-chief Jour. Materials and Structures. Recipient Thompson award ASTM, Phila., 1983, Disting. U.S. Vis. Scientist awrd Alexander von Humboldt Found., 1989, Swedish Concrete award, Stockholm, 1993, Engring. News Record award of Newsmaker, 1995, Charles Perkow award, 1997. Fellow Am. Concrete Inst. (chmn. tech. com., Anderson award 1989, 99, Henry Crown award 2000, Symposium in his honor 2002), Internat. Union Testing and Rsch. Labs. Materials and Structures (chmn. tech. com. 1989—, mgmt. adv. bd. 1996—, Gold medal 1980); mem. ASCE (past chmn. tech. com., mem. exec. com., mem. adv. bd., Richard J. Caroll Meml. Lectr. 2001). Home: 921 Isabella St Evanston IL 60201-1773 Office: Northwestern U Tech Inst Rm A130 2145 Sheridan Rd Evanston IL 60208-0834

SHAH, Y. T. academic administrator; BSChemE, U. Mich.; MS, ChE, DSc, MIT. Prof. chem. engring. U. Pitts., 1969—87; dean engring. and sci. U. Tulsa, 1987—91; disting. prof., dean Coll. Engring. Drexel U., Phila., 1991—97; sr. vice provost for rsch. and grad. studies, chief rsch. scientist Clemon U., 1997; provost U. Mo., Rolla, 2002—. Mem.: AIChE, Am. Chem. Soc., Am. Soc. Elec. Engring. Office: Office of the Provost 204 Parker Hall 1870 Miner Cir Rolla MO 65409*

SHAHAN, SHERRY JEAN, writer, educator; b. Long Beach, Calif., Aug. 14, 1949; d. Frank Rowe Webb and Sylvia Jean (Brunner) Benedict; m. Edgar Harold Shahan, Oct. 23, 1982; children: Kristina Michelle Beal, Kyle Shannon Beal. BS in Social Scis., Calif. Poly. State U., San Luis Obispo, 1978. Lectr. Saddleback Coll. Writers Conf., Orange County, Calif., 1992, Cuesta Community Coll., San Luis Obispo, 1988—, Calif. Reading Assn., 1998—, Nat. Coun. Tchrs. English, 1999—. Author: Dashing Through the Snow: The Story of the Jr. Iditarod (a photo essay, 1997), (mid. grade novel) Frozen Stiff, 1998, (photoessay) The Little Butterfly, 1998, (photoessays) The Sunflower Family, 1996, Feeding Time at the Zoo, 2000, (picture book) A Jazzy Alphabet, 2002, Working Dogs, 1999, Willie Covan Loved to Dance!, 2004; contbr. articles, photographs numerous regional and nat. newspapers and mags. Mem.: Children's Bookwriters and Illustrators, So. Calif. Children's Book Sellers, Am. Travel Writers, Authors Guild, Pi Gamma Mu. Home and Office: 2603 Richard Ave Cayucos CA 93430 E-mail: Kidbooks@thegrid.net.

SHAHANI, SAPNA, broadcast executive; b. Bombay, Aug. 6, 1978; d. Surinder and Rosabelle Shahani. BS, Gustavus Adolphus Coll., St. Peter, Minn., 2000. Pub.'s asst. India-West newspaper, San Leandro, Calif., 2000—01; facility mgr. Berkeley Cmty. Media, Calif., 2001—. Co-founder South Asian Sisters, San Francisco, 2000—04. Prodr.: (video) Berkeley Speaks. Office: Berkeley Community Media 2239 Martin Luther King Jr Way Berkeley CA 94704 E-mail: sapna@betv.org.

SHAHEEN, C. JEANNE, political organization administrator, former governor; b. St. Charles, Mo., Jan. 28, 1947; m. William H. Shaheen; 3 children. BA, Shippensburg U., 1969; M of Social Sci. in Polit. Sci., U. Miss., 1973. Campaign mgr. Pres. Jimmy Carter, 1980, Gary Hart, 1984, Gov. Paul McEachon, 1986, 1988; mem. N.H. Senate, 1991-96; gov N.H., 1997—2003; vice chair Democratic Nat. Convention Com., 2004—; nat. chair John Kerry Presidl. Campaign, 2004—. Democrat. Protestant. Office: Democratic Nat Convention Com 53 State St Fourth Fl Boston MA 02109*

SHAHEEN, GEORGE T. management consultant; b. 1944; Mng. ptnr.-cons. for N.Am., Andersen Worldwide Orgn., until 1989; mng. ptnr., CEO Andersen Cons., Chgo., 1989-99; chmn., CEO Webvan Group, Inc., Foster City, Calif., 1999—. Office: Webvan Group Inc # F 1155 Triton Dr Foster City CA 94404-1251

SHAHEEN, GERALD L. manufacturing executive; With Caterpillar Inc., Peoria, Ill., 1967—, mng. dir. Geneva, Switzerland, 1995, v.p. engring. products divsn. Peoria, 1995, group pres., 1998—. Bd. dir. U.S. Chamber of Commerce, UtiliCorp United, National City Corp. Office: Caterpillar Inc 100 NE Adams St Peoria IL 61629-0002

SHAHEEN, JACK GEORGE, communications educator; b. Pitts., Sept. 21, 1935; s. Jack and Nazara (Jacob) S.; m. Bernice Marie Rafeedie, Jan. 22, 1966; children: Michael A., Michele L. BFA, Carnegie Inst. of Tech., 1957; MA, Pa. State U., 1964; PhD, U. Mo., 1969. Entertainment dir. U.S. Spl. Svcs., Berlin, Germany, 1960-63; spl. programs dir. UCLA, 1965-67; asst. instr. mass communications U. Mo., Columbia, 1967-69; prof. mass communications So. Ill. U., Edwardsville, 1969-94. Cons. Inst. for Internat. Rsch. Inc., Washington, 1986—; cons. mid. east affairs CBS News, 1994—. Author: The TV Arab, 1984 (Outstanding Book of Yr., Choice Mag. 1984), Reel Bad Arabs: How Hollywood Vilifies A People, 2001, editor: Nuclear War Films, 1978; contbr. more than 300 articles, essays to newspapers and mags. Scholar-diplomat Dept. State, 1980; Fulbright scholar, 1975, 82. Democrat. Mem. Eastern Orthodox Ch. Avocations: tennis, swimming. Home: 1 Dahlgren Ln Hilton Head Island SC 29928-3939

SHAHEEN, SHAHEEN AZEEZ, textile executive; b. Chgo., Jan. 23, 1928; s. Azeez and Saleemeh (Balluteen) S.; m. Pierina Barbaglia, June 30, 1951; children: John A., David M. BS, Ill. Inst. Tech., 1949. Regional sales Katherine Rug, Dalton, Ga., 1949-53; chmn., pres., founder World Carpets, Inc., Dalton, Ga., 1954-92. Author: World Carpets-The First Thirty Years, 1984; mineral exhbn. Dalton State Coll., Ga., 2000-. Min. Jehovah's Witnesses, 1942--; helped establish Fed. Housing Authority carpet standards, Washington, 1970-75; mem. stay-in-sch. task force Dalwhichcom Found., Dalton, 1984-90; participant, bd. dirs. Harvest Outreach Rehab. Ctrs. for the Homeless, Dalton, 1990-2000; pres., treas. Dalton Land Co., 1982—. Named Permanent Carpet Industry Elected Mem. of World Floor Covering Hall of Fame, World Floor Covering Assn., Anaheim, Calif. Established modern carpet production and technology, by pioneering methods and techniques for carpet production in areas of manufacturing, equipment development and innovation, quality assurance, continuous dyeing, product flow, distribution, marketing, merchandising, personell incentives and programs, profit sharing, direct private trucking, and related areas that resulted in common, everyday usage of wall to wall carpet worldwide. Office: Dalton Land Co PO Box 187 Dalton GA 30722-0187

SHAHIDEHPOUR, MOHAMMAD, dean, academic administrator, engineering educator; b. Tehran, Iran, July 27, 1955; came to U.S., 1977; m. Jamie Winkler, Sept. 8, 1989; children: Dustin, Ryan, Andrew. BS, Sharif U., Tehran, 1977; MS, U. Mo., 1978, PhD, 1981. Prof. Ill. Inst. Tech., Chgo., 1983—, dean, 1994—, assoc. v.p. rsch., 1999—. Author: Power Systems, 1999; contbr. articles to profl. jours. Named Oustanding Rschr. Edison Electric Inst. Mem. IEEE (editor 1999—), HKN (pres. 2000—), Sigma Xi, Tau Beta Pi. Achievements include 2 patents. Office: Ill Inst Tech 3300 S Federal St Chicago IL 60616-3793

SHAHID-GARCIA, MARIA DE LOURDES, foreign language educator; b. Lagos de Mareno, Jalisco, Mex., May 10, 1960; d. Jose Isabel García and Marcelina García-Diaz; m. Shahid Iqbal, Oct. 9, 1990; children: Mussarat Iqbal, Maira Iqbal. M in Internat. Pub. Comm., Calif. State U., Chico, 1988, M in Internat. Pub: Comm., 1994. Spanish prof. Butte Coll., Oroville, Pa., 1989—, Calif. State U., Chico, 1989—. Author: Tips for Successful Spanish, 1994, Say it in Spanish, 1998; editor, prodr. (T.V. program) Sabias Que?, 1992—. Chmn. Sch. Evangelization, Chico, 2001. Recipient First prize San Francisco Poetry Contest, 1986. Mem. Calif. Tchrs. Assn., Hispanic C. of C. (pres. 1999—). Roman Catholic. Home: 4 Roberto Ct Chico CA 95928

SHAHIED, ISHAK I. science educator; BA, Eastern Nazarene Coll., 1959; MS, U. Tenn., 1964; PhD, Colo. State U., 1973. Sr. rsch. chemist Aerospace Med. Rsch. Lab. USAF, Dayton, 1973—74; prof., dept. chmn. St. George's Med. Coll., Grenada, 1977—86; prof. Cleveland Coll., Kansas City, Mo., 1986—89; prof., head biochemist Life U., Marietta, Ga., 1989—94; prof. St. Matthew's Med. Coll., Belize, 1997—98, Ctrl. Bapt. Coll., Conway, Ark., 2001—02; prof., exec. dean St. James Sch. Medicine, Bonaire, Netherlands Antilles, 2002—. Taught at Cleve. Chiropractic Coll., Kansas City, Mo., 1976-77, 86-89. Author: Biochemistry of Foods and the Biocatalysts, 1977, (textbook) Physiology, 1980. Named Hon. fellow Truman Libr. Inst.; recipient Best Instr. award, 1984. Mem. N.Y. Acad. Sci. Avocations: writing, swimming.

SHAHINFAR, SHAHNAZ, pharmaceutical executive, nephrologist; b. Mashad, Iran, Mar. 12, 1950; arrived in U.S., 1975; d. Mohammad Shahinfar and Meymanat Rajabiun; m. Ali Ahmadinejad, June 1975; children: Laila, Tina, Tara. MD, Ferdowsi U., Mashad, 1975. Diplomate Am. Bd. Pediat., Am. Bd. Pediat. Nephrology. Resident Georgetown U. Hosp., Washington, 1976—79, fellow, 1979—81; assoc. dir. Merck & Co., Inc., West Point, Pa., 1981—86, dir. drug experiments and epidemiology Blue Bell, Pa., 1986—88, dir. CV clin. rsch., 1988—97, sr. dir. CV clin. rsch., 1997—. Adj. assoc. prof. pediat. U. Pa., 1991—; presenter in field. Contbr. articles to profl. jours.; author: numerous abstracts and publs. in area of hypertension and kidney disease. Recipient Pahlavi award, Iranian Min. Edn., 1973, Medal award, 1975, award, Nat. Kidney Found., 1998. Mem.: AHA - Kidney Coun., Am. Soc. Nephrology, Internat. Soc. Nephrology. Achievements include patents for method of treating renal disease using an ACE inhibitor and an AII anatagonist; research in alpha and beta receptors in platelets and white blood cells in labile hypertension; efficacy of enalapril in mild to moderate hypertension; many others; clin. trials in diabetes (RENAAL); design of clinical trails in pediatric hypertension for ACIEs and ARB; implementation of Phase II-V clinical trials. Avocations: cooking, poetry. Office: Merck & Co Inc PO Box 4 BLX-21 West Point PA 19486

SHAHON, SUSAN VALERIE, marketing director; b. Waukegan, Illinois, Aug. 13, 1948; d. Raymond James and Dorothy Evelyn (Chisholm) Proctor; m. David N. Shahon; children: Michael Darin, Laura Evelyn. Student, Lake County Coll., Grayslake, Ill., 1973—81; grad. media tng., Jack Franchetti Comm., Inc., Manhasset, N.Y., Internat. Assn. Fin. Planners, Telesis, N.Y. profl. model cert. John Robert Powers, Chgo. Svc. mgr., bookkeeper Nat. Co., Chgo., 1965—76; svc. mgr. A and P, Chgo., 1978—82; futures researcher MBH Commodities, Winnetka, Ill., 1980—93; dir. mktg. Jean D'Estrees Cosmetics, 1985—87; nat. account mgr., product mgr. J.C. Penny Co., N.Y., Dallas, 1987—92; v.p. mktg. Annuity Fin. Svc., Dallas, 1993; nat. corp. sales, mktg. mgr. Fine Jewelers Guild Zale Corp., Irving, Tex., 1993—96; v.p. mktg. Annuity Fin. Svc., Dallas, 1992—93; nat. corp. sales, mktg. mgr. Zale Corp., Fine Jewelers Guild, Irving, 1994—96; v.p. mktg. Perussina Ambrose and Assoc., San Francisco, 1996—97; co-founder, exec. v.p. Life Map Comm., Inc., Walnut Creek, Calif., 1997—2003; dir. mktg. Hotch Kiss Ins. Agy., Carrollton, Tex., 2003—. Dir. mktg., cons., and spl. events coord. Extract, Inc., Miami, Fla., 1984; nat. mgr. Fernand Aubry Cosmetics J.C. Penney Corp., Dallas, 1987—; vis. tchr.; dir. numerous cosmetic and skincare seminars; profl. model, 1983—; cons. Futures Symposium, Tucson, 1983—; aerobic instr. Karcher Retirement Home, Waukegan, Ill. Recipient tennis award Libertyville Park Dist., Ill., 1973; various Blue Ribbon and 1st Pl. Awards Libertyville Men's Garden Club, 1982, various rose growers awards, 1983. Mem. DAR, Am. Rose Soc. (Best Climber nat. trophy 1985), Dallas Rose Soc. (sec., recipient trophies for rose growing), Northeastern Ill. Rose Growers (treas.), No. Ill. Rose Growers Assn., Am. Running and Fitness Assn., Fashion Group Dallas. Republican. Office Phone: 972-931-3750 x260. Business E-Mail: sshahon@hotchkissins.com.

SHAHSHAHANI, AHMAD, economics professor; b. Tehran, Iran, Sept. 14, 1947; came to U.S., 1971; s. Housein Shahshahani and Zahra (Heshmat) Zommorodian; m. Shahla Mohtasham; 1 child, Ramina. Cert. in English, U. Cambridge, 1968; BS, U. Tehran, 1969; MA, U. Colo., 1973, PhD, 1976. Asst. prof. econs. Tehran U., 1976-80; research fellow Hoover Instn., Stanford, Calif., 1980-82; fin. analyst Unity in Diversity Council, L.A., 1983-84; asst. prof. Calif. State U., L.A., 1984-91, Northridge, 1985-87; economist U.S. Dept. Treasury, Glendale, Calif., 1991-93; economist, mgr. U.S. Dept. Treasury, IRS, L.A., 1993—. Mem. corp. fin. team Baraban Securities, Culver City, Calif., 1983-87; fellow Internat. Rsch. Ctr. Energy and Econ. Devel., Boulder, 1976-87; fin. advisor Tissurama-Knitex Industries, L.A., 1987-91. Author: Economics for Students, 1972, 2d edit., 1977, An Introduction to the Theory of Employment, 1974, 2d edit., 1977, An Econometric Model of Iran, And Its Application, 1978, Economist Report Writing Guide for Transfer Pricing, 2001, Economist Report Writing Guide for Intangible Assets, 2003, Economist Program website, 1999—; editor Econ. Issues, 1995-2000; also articles to profl. jours. Fellow Tehran U., 1974-76, scholar U. Colo., Boulder, 1973-74. Mem. Nat. Assn. Securities Dealers (series 7 lic.), Omicron Delta Epsilon. Avocations: tennis, jogging, travel. Home: 11939 Gorham Ave Apt 101 Los Angeles CA 90049-5362 Office: US Dept of Treasury IRS 225 W Broadway Glendale CA 91204-1331 Office Phone: 818-265-2323.

SHAIKH, MUZAFFAR ABID, management science educator; b. Bombay, Jan. 5, 1946; came to U.S., 1966; s. Shaikh A. Razzaque and Khudaija R. Shaikh; m. Farhat Anjum, Dec. 29, 1968; children: Mahjabeen, Shahbaaz, Shoaib. BS, U. Bombay, 1966; MS, Kans. State U., 1968; PhD, U. Ill., 1983. Mgmt. sci. rsch. analyst Caterpillar Inc., Peoria, Ill., 1968-85; sr. staff engr. Harris Corp., Melbourne, Fla., 1985-87; assoc. prof. Fla. Inst. Tech., Melbourne, 1987-92, prof. mgmt. sci., 1992—, assoc. dean Sch. Bus., 1992—97, head engring. sys. Coll. Engring., 1999—. Cons. Harris Corp., Melbourne, 1987-92, Grumman Corp., Melbourne, 1987-92. Assoc. editor Trans. of Simulation, 1989-96, INCOSE Sys. Engring. Jour., 1998-; N.Am. editor Bus. Process Mgmt. Jour., 2002-; contbr. over 1000 articles to profl. jours. Fellow

Sigma Xi; sr. mem. Ops. Rsch. Soc. Am., Inst. Mgmt. Sci., Inst. Indsl. Engrs. Home: 409 Crystal Lake Dr Melbourne FL 32940-1934 Office: Fla Inst Tech 150 W University Blvd Melbourne FL 32901-6975

SHAIKH, NAZRUL ISLAM, industrial engineer, researcher; s. Nisar Ahmed and Deeba Shaikh. B in Chem. Engring., India Inst. Tech., Bombay, 2000; MSEE, MS in Indsl. Engring., postgrad., Pa. State U., 2002—. Intern Nat. Chem. Labs, Pune, India, 1997—99; grad. lectr. Pa. State U., State College, 2001, tchg. asst., 2001, rsch. asst. indsl. engring., 2000—. Contbr. articles to profl. jours. Scholar Nat. Merit scholar, Govt. of India, Jit Paul scholar, Apeejay Edn. Soc. Mem.: IIE, INFORMS, Interact Club (dir.), Tau Beta Pi. Office: Dept Indsl Engring 310 Leonhard Bldg State College PA 16802 also: 333 Logan Ave Apt 107 State College PA 16801-4646 E-mail: nis109@psu.edu.

SHAIN, IRVING, retired chemical company executive and university chancellor; b. Seattle, Jan. 2, 1926; s. Samuel and Selma (Blockoff) S.; m. Mildred Ruth Udell, Aug. 31, 1947; children: Kathryn A., Steven T., John R., Paul S. BS in Chemistry, U. Wash., 1949, PhD in Chemistry, 1952. From instr. to prof. U. Wis., Madison, 1952-75, vice chancellor, 1970-75, chancellor, 1977-86; provost, v.p. acad. affairs U. Wash., Seattle, 1975-77; v.p. Olin Corp., Stamford, Conn., 1987-92, ret., 1992, also bd. dirs. Mem. tech. adv. bd. Johnson Controls, Inc., Milw., 1980-2003; trustee Univ. Rsch. Park, Inc., Madison, pres., 1984-86, v.p., 1987—; mem. Nat. Commn. on Superconductivity, 1989-90. Contbr. articles on electroanalytical chemistry to profl. jours. Bd. dirs. Madison Gen. Hosp., 1972-75; v.p. Madison Cmty. Found., 1984-86; mem. CEO adv. bd. Kamehameha Schs./Bishop Estates, 2002-04. With U.S. Army, 1943-46, PTO. Fellow AAAS, Wis. Acad. Scis., Arts and Letters; mem. Am. Chem. Soc., Electrochem. Soc., Conn. Acad. Sci. and Engring., Phi Beta Kappa, Sigma Xi, Phi Kappa Phi. Home: 2820 Marshall Ct # 8 Madison WI 53705-2270 E-mail: i.shain@att.net.

SHAINE, FREDERICK MORDECAI, newspaper executive, consultant; b. Cambridge, Mass., Feb. 5, 1916; s. Joseph and Mollie (Prescott) S.; m. Sylvia Pollack, Mar. 21, 1944; 1 child, Frederick Mordecai Jr. (Rick). Student, U. Vt., 1934-35; BA in Gen. Studies, Columbia U., 1970. From copy boy to advt. sales rep. Boston Herald, 1933, 36-41; advt. rep. O'Mara & Ormsbee, N.Y.C., 1946-58; advt. dir. Book Rev. N.Y. Herald Tribune, 1958-63; bus. mgr. Book Week Nat. Sun newspaper supplement, 1963-66; bus. mgr. Book World, Sun. book rev. Washington Post/Chgo. Tribune, N.Y.C., 1966-72; dir. N.Y. ops. European Stars and Stripes, N.Y.C., 1972-95. Cons. to Armed Forces Info Svcs., Dept. Def., 1996-97; transl. from Italian: And No Quarter, 1972; reviewer and translator various publs. Mem. adv. coun. Casa Italiana, Columbia U., 1967-70. With USCG, 1941-45. Grantee Ford Found. New Career Scholarship, 1970. Mem. Soc. for Italian Hist. Studies, Columbia Club. Avocations: reading, travel, translating, bridge. Home: 930 5th Ave Apt 12F New York NY 10021-2651

SHAINMAN, IRWIN, music educator, musician; b. N.Y.C., June 27, 1921; s. Samuel and Gussie (Pollack) S.; m. Bernice Cohen, Aug. 29, 1948; children—Joan, Jack. BA, Pomona Coll., 1943; MA, Columbia, 1948; Premier Prix, Conservatoire Nat. de Musique de Paris, France, 1950. Prof. music, curator Paul Whiteman collection Williams Coll., Williamstown, Mass., 1948-91, prof. emeritus, 1991—; chmn. music dept., 1971-77; dean faculty, 1972-73; coordinator performing arts, 1973-76; Class of 1955 prof. music, 1980-91. Tchr. ext. U. Mass., 1952-55, Mass. State Coll., North Adams, 1957, also Bennington Coll. Composer's Conf. and Chamber Music Ctr.; cons. advanced placement program Coll. Entrance Exam. Bd., 1969-75; mem. edn. com. Saratoga Performing Arts Ctr., 1967-68; pres. Williamstown Theatre Found., 1972-77, South Mountain Concert Assn., 1980-96; lectr. J.F. Kennedy Ctr. for Performing Arts, Washington, 1994—. Condr., Berkshire Symphony, 1950-65, also Williams Coll. band, brass ensemble and woodwind ensemble, 1st trumpet, Albany (N.Y.) Symphony Orch., 1960-65, Vt. Symphony Orch., 1954-58; contbr. articles to profl. jours.; columnist: Berkshire Eagle; author: Avoiding Cultural Default and Other Essays, 1991. Mem. merit aid panel Mass. Arts Council, 1984. Served with AUS, 1942-45. Decorated Bronze Star, Purple Heart, Combat Inf. badge.; N.Y. Philharmonic scholar, 1934-35; Recipient Danforth Found. Tchrs. award, 1957-58 Mem. Am. Musicological Soc., Coll. Music Assn., Music Critics Assn. Home: 88 Baxter Rd Williamstown MA 01267-2111

SHAINWALD, SYBIL, lawyer; b. N.Y.C., Apr. 27, 1928; d. Samuel and Anne; m. Sidney Shainwald; children: Robert, Louise, Laurie, Marsha. BA, Coll. William and Mary, 1948; MA, Columbia U., 1972; JD, N.Y. Law Sch., 1976, LLD (hon.), 2000. Bar: N.Y. 1976. Legal advisor Am. Found. for Maternal Child and Health; adj. prof. dept. law Baruch Coll., 1981—82. Co-editor: Jour. Women and Health; contbr. articles to profl. jours. Active Abortion Rights Action; co-founder, bd. mem. Trial Lawyers for Pub. Justice, 1982—88; bd. mem. Hysterectomy Edn. Resources and Svcs., 1985—, Dalkon Shield INfo. Network, Nat. Network to Prevent Birth Defects, No. Ariz. Sch. Midwifery, 1989—; bd. advisors Med. Legal Aspects of Breast Implants; bd. dirs. Consumer Interest Rsch. Inst.; fellow Roscoe Pound Inst., Morgan Libr.; trustee Civil Justice Found., 1998—99; bd. dirs. Am. Friends of Tel Aviv Mus., 2000, Friends of Tel Aviv Mus., 2000-; trustee N.Y. Law Sch., 2000—; adv. bd. Southampton The Hamptons Shakespeare Festival, 2000—; co-chair Take Home a Nude N.Y. Acad. Art, 2001; active Sybil Shainwald Charitable Found., N.Y.C. Comptrs. Health Task Force. Recipient Susan B. Anthony award, NOW; grantee, Nat. Endowment for the Humanities, Rockefeller Found., Gov. W. Averell Harriman; scholar Pres. Bryan scholar, Coll. of William and Mary, Edward Coles scholar. Mem.: ATLA (chair environ. and toxic tort sect. 1988—89, co-chair breast implant litigation group 1992—2000, mem. Dalkon shield litigation group 1995, mem. contraceptive implant litigation group 1995, co-chair DES litigation group, environ. law adv. com.), N.Y. State Trial Lawyers (bd. govs.), Assn. of the Bar of the City of N.Y. (judge nat. moot ct. competition 1988—2003), Soc. Med. Jurisprudence, Health Action Internat.-U.S. (co-founder, mem. steering com.), Lawyers Com. for Human Rights, Am. Soc. Law, Medicine and Ethics, Nat. Women's Health Alliance (pres.), Nat. Women's Health Network (bd. mem. 1980—86, chair litigation svc. 1980—86, chair health law and regulation 1981—88, chmn. bd. dirs. 1982—86, chair N.Y. state affiliate), Phi Beta Kappa. Avocations: art, music. Home: 25 Sutton Pl New York NY 10022-2445 Office: 950 Third Ave 10th Fl New York NY 10022

SHAKEEL, ARIF, retail executive; BSME, Memphis (Tenn.) State U.; MBA, Pepperdine U. From product mgr. to COO Western Digital Corp., Lake Forest, Calif., 1985—2001, COO, 2001—, pres., 2002—. Bd. dir. Share Our Selves, Calif. Office: Western Digital Corp 20511 Lake Forest Dr Lake Forest CA 92630-7741*

SHAKELY, JOHN BOWER (JACK SHAKELY), foundation executive; b. Hays, Kans., Jan. 9, 1940; s. John B. and Martha Jean (Gaston) S.; 1 child, Benton. BA, U. Okla., 1962. Vol. Peace Corps., Costa Rica, 1963-64; editor publs. Dept. Def., 1967-68; dir. devel. U. Okla., 1968-70, Resthaven Mental Health Ctr., L.A., 1970-74; pres. Jack Shakely Assocs., L.A., 1974-75; sr. adv. Grantsmanship Ctr., L.A., 1975-79, Coun. on Founds., Washington, 1979; pres. Calif. Community Found., L.A., 1980—. Lectr. in field. Bd. dirs. Emergency Loan and Assistance Fund, 1985—, chair bd. dirs., 1988-93; mem., vice chair L.A. Am. Indian Commn.; bd. dirs. So. Calif. Assn. Philanthropy, 1980—, Comic Relief, 1987—; chmn. bd. dirs. Nonprofit Channel. Served to 1st lt. U.S. Army, 1965-68. Decorated Army Commendation medal; named Nat. Philanthropy Day Outstanding Exec., L.A. Com. Nat. Philanthropy Day, 1989. Office: 445 S Figueroa St Ste 3400 Los Angeles CA 90071-1638

SHAKER, WILLIAM HAYGOOD, marketing professional, public policy reformer; b. Downey, Calif., Apr. 22, 1938; s. Elmer S. and Marylee Shaker; m. Joanna Drummond, Jan. 28, 1966; children: Catherine Patricia, Marylee, Marcus, Matthew. BS in Engring., U. So. Calif., 1964; MS in Engring., U. Mich., 1969. Registered profl. engr., Calif. Exec. Dow Chem. Co., Midland, Mich., 1966-78; v.p. Nat. Legal Ctr. for the Pub. Interest, Washington, 1979; exec. v.p. Nat. Tax Limitation Com., Washington, 1980-86; pres. Am. Coun. for Health Care Reform, Arlington, Va., 1982—, Heart to Heart Found., Arlington, 1982—; CEO Washington Mktg. Group, Arlington, 1987—; pres. Health PAC, Arlington, 1994—. Pres. RepublicanPac.com, 2000—, Rule of Law Com., 2001—. Author: Health Care Reform, 1994, also legis. and govt. publs.; editor: Electric Power Reform, 1979; editor, pub. millennium edit. The Man of Galilee, 2001; contbr. articles to profl. jours. Founder, chmn. Taxpayers United, Mich., 1972-84. Mem. Govtl. Rsch. Assn. (most effective presentation of govtl. rsch. award 1973), Direct Mktg. Assn. (Echo award 1982-97, Maxi award 1987-2001), Pub. Rels. Soc. (Silver Anvil 1979), Am. Conservative Union (Health Care Reform award 1995). Republican. Lutheran. Office: Washington Mktg Group 2507 N Harrison St Arlington VA 22207 Office Phone: 703-534-8180. E-mail: william.shaker@twmg.com.

SHAKESPEARE, FRANK, ambassador; b. N.Y.C., Apr. 9, 1925; s. Francis Joseph and Frances (Hughes) S.; m. Deborah Anne Spaeth, Oct. 9, 1954; children: Mark, Andrea, Fredricka. BS, Holy Cross Coll., 1945; D.Eng. (hon.), Colo. Sch. Mines, 1975; DCS (hon.), Pace U., 1979; LLD (hon.), Del. Law Sch., 1980, Sacred Heart U., 1985, U. Dallas, 1987, Pepperdine U., 1990, Nichols Coll., 1991, Marquette U., 1993; D of Pub. Svc. (hon.), Hillsdale Coll., 1996. Formerly pres. CBS-TV Services; exec. v.p. CBS-TV Stas.; dir. USIA, 1969-73; exec. v.p. Westinghouse Electric Corp., 1973-75; pres. RKO Gen. Inc., N.Y.C., 1975-85, vice chmn., 1983-85; U.S. ambassador to Portugal Lisbon, 1985-87; U.S. ambassador to The Holy See Vatican City, 1987-89. Chmn. Heritage Found., 1975-85, dir., 1989—; chmn. Radio Free Europe/Radio Liberty, Inc., 1976-85; dir. Bradley Foundtn., 1989—. Served to lt. (j.g.) USNR, 1945-46. Mem.: Union League. Home: 1517 Hommen Rd Deerfield WI 53531-9678

SHAKHMUNDES, LEV, mathematician; b. Leningrad, USSR, 1933; came to Can., 1975; s. Yudel and Alexandra (Voitsekhovskaya) S.; children: Nadia, Daniel. MS, Leningrad U., 1957; PhD, Leningrad Poly. Inst., 1965. Engr., rsch. assoc., cons. various instns., Leningrad, 1957-74; rsch. asst. U. Toronto, 1976-78; sr. cons. analyst Union Gas Ltd., Chatham, Canada, 1978—98, cons., 1998—. Author: We Are Different, So What, 1999, A Better Organization: Facing Challenges to Mankind and Civility, 2001; co-author: Economic Efficiency of Capital Expenditures (in Russian), 1969; contbr. articles to Soviet and U.S. acad. periodicals; patentee Ministry Sci. and Tech. USSR. Mem. Assn. Profl. Engrs. Ont., Can. Econs. Assn. Avocation: sports. Home: PO Box 383 Chatham ON Canada N7M 5K5 Business E-Mail: lev@WeAreDif.net.

SHAKNO, ROBERT JULIAN, hospital and social services administrator; b. Amsterdam, Holland, Aug. 15, 1937; came to U.S., 1939, naturalized, 1944; s. Rudy C. and Gertrude S.; m. Linda, June 10, 1962; children: Steven Lee, Deborah Sue. BBA (scholar 1955), So. Methodist U., 1959; M.H.A., Washington U., St. Louis, 1961. Adminstrv. asst. Mt. Sinai Hosp., Chgo., 1961—63; asso. adminstr. Tex. Inst. Rehab. and Research, Houston, 1963—65; asst. adminstr. Michael Reese Hosp., Chgo., 1965—70, v.p., hosp. dir., 1970—73; asso. exec. dir. Cook County Hosp., Chgo., 1973—75; pres. Hackensack Med. Center, NJ, 1975—85, Mt. Sinai Med. Ctr., Cleve., 1985—96; dir. nat. strategy practice KPMG Peat Marwick, 1996-98; v.p. med. affairs, vice dean sch. of medicine Case Western Res. U., 1998—2002; pres., CEO, Jewish Family Svc., Cleve., 2002—. Bd. dirs. Ohio Hosp. Inc. Co. Mem. editorial bd. Mgmt. Series, Am. Coll. Healthcare Execs. Mem. Leadership Cleve.; bd. dirs. Premier Hosp. Alliance, chmn., 1994-96; bd. dirs. The New Cleve. Inc., Univ. Circle Inc., Cleve., Cleve. Sight Ctr.; trustee Hope Lodge, Cleve. chpt. Am. Cancer Soc.; chmn. elect, bd. dirs. Jewish Family Svcs.; chmn. social svcs. divsn. United Jewish Appeal, Cleve., 1987-88, chmn. health cabinet, 1990, gen. co-chmn., 1990—; chmn. Hosp. Pacesetter campaign United Way, chmn. health svcs. portfolio, 1988-89, oversight commn., 1992-93. Served to 1st lt. USAR, 1960-66. Named Young Adminstr. of Yr., Washington U., 1968 Fellow Am. Coll. Hosp. Adminstrs.; mem. Am. Hosp. Assn. (coun. urban hosps., del. coun. on met. hosps., rep. regional policy bd.), Washington U. Alumni Assn. (past pres.), Greater Cleve. Hosp. Assn. (bd. dirs.), Ohio Hosp. Assn. (bd. dirs.), Cleve. Sight Ctr. (trustee, bd. dirs.), Sigma Alpha Mu (past pres.). Home: 32050 Meadow Lark Way Pepper Pike OH 44124-5508 Office: Jewish Family Svcs Assn 3659 S Green Ste 321 Cleveland OH 44122

SHAKOW, ALEXANDER, economist, government official; b. Apr. 12, 1937; s. David and Sophie (Harap) S.; m. Patricia Connell, Dec. 26, 1967; children: John, Peter, Thomas. BA with honors, Swarthmore Coll., 1958; PhD in Internat. Rels./Econ. Devel., London Sch. Econs., 1962. Assoc., dep., then dir. Indonesia program U.S. Peace Corps, Washington and Jakarta, Indonesia, 1963-65, asst., dep. then dir. Office Vol. Tng. Washington, 1965-67; dir. Office Indonesia Affairs-Office Asia Devel. Planning, US AID, Washington, 1968-74, dep. asst. adminstr., then asst. adminstr. program-policy, 1974-81; spl. policy advisor, chief policy unit, sr. advisor internat. econ. affairs World Bank, Washington, 1981-85, chief internat. econ. affairs, 1985-87, dir. strategic planning and rev., dir. external affairs, 1987-94, exec. sec. World Bank/IMF devel. com., 1995—2002; dep. sec. World Bank group World Bank/IMF, 1997—2002, acting v.p., sec., 2001—02. Chmn. bd. sci. and tech. for internat. devel. NAS, Washington, 1989-95; bd. trustees Enterprise Works Worldwide, 2003—. Bd. govs. Inst. Devel. Studies, Sussex, Eng., 1991-2002, hon. gov., 2002—. Recipient William A. Jump Meritorious award for outstanding pub. svc. William A. Jump Meml. Found., 1967. Mem. Am. Friends London Sch. Econs. (founding). Avocations: grandchildren, carpentry, gardening, reading. Fax: 301-933-3218. E-mail: ashakow@worldbank.net.

SHALALA, DONNA E. university administrator, former federal official, political scientist, educator; b. Cleve., Feb. 14, 1941; d. James Abraham and Edna (Smith) S. AB, Western Coll., 1962; MSSC, Syracuse U., 1968, PhD, 1970; 39 hon. degrees, 1981-91. Vol. Peace Corps, Iran, 1962-64; asst. prof. polit. sci. CUNY, 1970-72; assoc. prof. politics and edn. Tchrs. Coll. Columbia U., 1972-79; asst. sec. for policy devel. and research HUD, Washington, 1977-80; prof. polit. sci., pres. Hunter Coll., CUNY, 1980-87; prof. polit. sci., chancellor U. Wis., Madison, 1987-93; sec. Dept. HHS, Washington, 1993-2001; pres. U. Miami, 2001—. Dir., treas. Mcpl. Assistance Corp. for the City of N.Y., 1975—77. Author: Neighborhood Governance, 1971, The City and the Constitution, 1972, The Property Tax and the Voters, 1973, The Decentralization Approach, 1974. Mem. Trilateral Commn., 1988—92, Knight Commn. on Intercollegiate Sports, 1989—91; bd. govs. Am. Stock Exch., 1981—87; trustee TIAA, 1985—89, Com. Econ. Devel., 1982—92, Brookings Inst., 1989—92; bd. dirs. Children's Def. Fund, 1980—93, Am. Ditchley Found., 1981—93, Spencer Found., 1988—92, M&I Bank of Madison, 1991—92, NCAA Found., 1991, Inst. Internat. Econs., 1981—, Gannett Co., Inc., McLean, Va., United Health Group, Mpls., Lennar Corp., Miami; trustee emeritus Kennedy Ctr. Bd. of Trustees, Washington. Ohio Newspaper Women's scholar, 1958, Western Coll. Trustee scholar, 1958-62; Carnegie fellow, 1966-68; Guggenheim fellow, 1975-76; recipient Disting. Svc. medal Columbia U. Tchrs. Coll., 1989. Mem. ASPA, Am. Polit. Sci. Assn., Nat. Acad. Arts and Scis., Nat. Acad. Pub. Adminstrn., Coun. Fgn. Rels., Nat. Acad. Edn. (Spencer fellow 1972-73). Office: U Miami Office Pres 230 Ashe Bldg Coral Gables FL 33146

SHALES, THOMAS WILLIAM, television and film critic, writer, journalist; b. Elgin, Ill., Nov. 3, 1953; s. Clyde LeRoy and Hulda Louise (Reko) S. BA, Am. U., 1973. Entertainment editor Washington Examiner, 1968-71; writer style sect. Washington Post, 1972—77, chief TV critic, 1977—, TV editor, 1979—; film critic, modular arts service Nat. Public Radio, 1970-79, film critic, Morning Edit., 1979—. Adj. prof. Am. U., 1978; syndicated columnist On the Air, Washington Post Writers Group, 1979— Author: The American Film Heritage, 1972, On the Air!, 1982, Legends, 1989; Co author: Live from New York: An Uncensored History of Saturday Night Live, 2002. Recipient Disting. Alumnus award Am. U., 1978. Recipient Pulitzer Prize for criticism, 1988, Disting. Writing Award, Am. Soc. Newspaper Editors, 1988. Office: Washington Post Co 1150 15th St NW Washington DC 20071-0002*

SHALHOUB, MICHAEL See SHARIF, OMAR

SHALHOUB, TONY, actor, television producer; b. Green Bay, Wis., Oct. 9, 1953; Student, coll., Portland, Maine; grad. student Sch. of Drama, Yale U. Actor: (films) Longtime Companion, 1990, Quick Change, 1990, Barton Fink, 1991, Honeymoon in Vegas, 1992, Searching for Bobby Fischer, 1993, Addams Family Values, 1993, I.Q., 1994, Big Night, 1996 (Nat. Soc. Film Critics award best supporting actor, 1996), Men in Black, 1997, Gattaca, 1997, A Life Less Ordinary, 1997, Primary Colors, 1998, Paulie, 1998, The Siege, 1998, The Impostors, 1998, A Civil Action, 1998, The Tic Code, 1998, The Man Who Wasn't There, 2001, Spy Kids, 2001, Thir13en Ghosts, 2001, Men in Black II, 2002, Life or Something Like It, 2002, Impostor, 2002, Something More, 2003, Against the Ropes, 2003, Spy Kids 3-D: Game Over, 2003, T for Terrorist, 2003; actor, dir.: (films) Made-Up, 2002; actor: (TV films) Alone in the Neon Jungle, 1988, Money, Power, Murder, 1989, Day One, 1989, Gypsy, 1993, Radiant City, 1996, That Championship Season, 1999, The Heart Department, 2001, (video game) Fallout: A Post-Nuclear Role-Playing Game, 1997; (TV series) Wings, 1991—97, Stark Raving Mad, 1999—2000; prodr., actor: (TV series) Monk, 2002 (Golden Globe award, 2002, Emmy award best actor in a comedy, 2003, Screen Actors Guild Award for best actor in a comedy series, 2004), (TV guest appearances) Late Late Show with Craig Kilborne, Ally McBeal, Frasier, Almost Perfect, The X Files, many others. Office: UTA 9560 Wilshire Blvd # 500 Beverly Hills CA 90921

SHALHOUP, JUDY LYNN, marketing communications executive; b. Charleston, W.Va., Oct. 25, 1940; d. George Ferris and Mary Margaret (Moses) Shalhoup; m. William Mainella. BA, Morris Harvey Coll., Charleston, 1967; MS, W.Va. U., 1970. With Union Carbide Corp., 1960-92, publicity mgr. plastics, 1971-73, coatings materials divsn. advt. mgr., 1973-82, mgr. mktg. comm. splty. chems. div., 1982-85, mgr. mktg. comm., solvents and coatings materials div., 1982-92; chmn. GMJC Assocs., 1992—. V.p., gen. mgr. Fruit Bowl, Charleston, 1975-78. Recipient Best Teller award Bus. Profl. Advt. Assn., 1978-84, 86-87, Pro-Com award, 1991, Excellence in Bus.-to-Bus. Advt. award, 1989, Objectives and Results Advt. award Am. Bus. Press, 1978, Clio Advt. Recognition award, 1978-86, Clio award, 1984, Andy award, 1983, 84, Nutmegger award, 1985. Mem. Telefood Assn., Internat. Platform Assn., Assn. Nat. Advt., Inc., SSPC, AAAS, Nat. Paint and Coatings Assn. (comm. com.), Fedn. Socs. Coatings Tech., Bus. Profl. Advt. Assn. (Star awards for excellence 1989-90, Procom award 1990). Office Phone: 304-346-5553.

SHALIKASHVILI, JOHN MALCHASE, retired military career officer; b. Warsaw, June 27, 1936; s. Dimitri and Maria (Ruediger) S.; m. Joan E. Zimpelman, Dec. 27, 1966; 1 child, Brant. BSME, Bradley U., 1958; attended, Naval War Coll., 1969—70, U.S. Army War Coll., 1977—78; MA in Internat. Affairs, George Washington U., 1970; LLD (hon.), U. Md., 1993, Bradley U., 1994. Joined U.S. Army, 1958, advanced through grades to gen., 1992—, various troop and staff assignments Alaska, U.S., Fed. Republic of Germany, Vietnam, Korea, Italy, Belgium, 1959-75, commdr. 1st bn. 84th field arty., 1975-77; dep. chief of staff ops. So. European Task Froce U.S. Army, Vicenza, Italy, 1978-79; comdr. div. arty., 1st Armored Div. U.S. Army, Nuernberg, Fed. Republic of Germany, 1979-81, chief., politico-mil div., later dep. dir. ODCSOPS Washington, 1981-84, asst. div. comdr. 1st. Armored div. Nuernberg, Fed. Republic of Germany, 1984-86, dir. strategy, plans, policy ODCSOPS Washington, 1986-87; comdg. gen. 9th inf. div. Ft. Lewis, Wash., 1987-89; dep. comdr.-in-chief Hdqrs. USAREUR and 7th Army, Heidelberg, Fed. Republic of Germany, 1989-91; asst. to chmn. Joint Chiefs of Staff, Washington, 1991-92; Supreme Allied Comdr. Europe, Comdr.-in-Chief U.S. Forces Europe, 1992-93; chmn. Joint Chiefs of Staff, 1993-97. Bd. trustees Bradley U.; mem. Buffalo Soldier Meml. Hon. Com. Decorated Def. D.S.M. with 3 oak leaf clusters, D.S.M. (Army) with oak leaf cluster), D.S.M. (Navy), D.S.M. (Air Force), D.S.M. (Dept. Trans.), Legion of Merit with 2 oak leaf clusters, Bronze Star medal with V device, Meritorious Svc. medal with 3 oak leaf clusters, Air medal, Joint Svc. Commendation medal, Army Commendation medal, Nat. Def. Svc. medal with bronze svc. star, Armed Forced Expeditionary medal, Republic of Vietnam Svc. medal with silver service star, S.W. Asia Svc. medal with bronze svc. star, Humanitarian Svc. medal, Army Svc. Ribbon, Overseas Svc. Ribbon with bronze Arabic numeral 5, Inter-Am. Def. Bd. medal, Kuwait Liberation medal, Order of Combat Infantryman badge, Parachutist badge, Joint Chiefs of Staff Identification badge, Army Staff Identification badge, Brazilian Order of Mil. Merit with 1st and 2d award, French Grand Officer of Nat. Merit, Belgian Grand Cordon of Order of Leopold, German Order of Merit with star and sash, Japanese Order of Rising Sun, Argentine Order of May in Grade of Gt. Cross for Mil. Merit, Korean Order of Nat. Security Merit, Tong-IL medal, Bintang Yudha Dharama Utama Hon. Decoration (Indonesia), Kuwait Def. medal, Grand Cross of Royal Norwegian Order of Merit, Grand Cross of Mil. Merit medal of Portuguese Republic, Republic of Vietnam Gallantry Cross with 2 silver and 1 bronze star, Republic of Vietnam Armed Forces Honor medal 1st class, Republic of Vietnam Armed Forces Honor medal 1st class, Republic of Vietnam Campaign medal, Republic of Vietnam Chung My medal 2d class, Tng. Svc. medal 1st class, Netherlands Comdr. Order Orange Nassau with swords, Mexican U.S. Mil. Merit 1st class, Great Cross Repub. Poland; recipient Chilean Bernardo Higgins award, Dwight D. Eisenhower Dist. Svc. award Vets. Fgn. Wars, Dist. Alumni Achievement award George Washington U.

SHALITA, ALAN REMI, dermatologist; b. Bklyn., Mar. 22, 1936; s. Harry and Celia; m. Simone Lea Baum, Sept. 4, 1960; children: Deborah (dec.) and Judith (twins). AB, Brown U., 1957; BS, U. Brussels, 1960; MD, Bowman Gray Sch. Medicine, 1964; DSc (hon.), L.I. U., 1990. Intern Beth Israel Hosp., N.Y.C., 1964-65; resident dept. dermatology NYU Med. Ctr., 1967-68, NIH tng. grant fellow dept. dermatology, 1968-70, instr. dermatology, 1970-71; asst. prof. NYU, 1971-73, Columbia U., 1973-75; assoc. prof. medicine, head divsn. dermatology SUNY Downstate Med. Ctr., Bklyn., 1975-79, prof., 1979—, head divsn. dermatology, 1979-80, chmn. dept. dermatology, 1980—, asst. dean, 1977-83, acting dean Queens campus, 1983-84; assoc. dean clin. affairs SUNY Health Sci. Ctr., Bklyn., 1989-92, assoc. provost for clin. affairs, 1992-93, assoc. v.p. clin. affairs, 1993—, assoc. dean grad. med. edn., 1999—. Disting. tchg. prof. SUNY Health Sci. Ctr., Bklyn., 1996—; asst. attending in dermatology Univ. Hosp., N.Y.C., 1970-73, Bellevue Hosp. Ctr., 1970-73, Manhattan VA Hosp., 1971-73, Presbyn. Hosp., 1973-75; med. bd. Kings County Hosp. Ctr.; cons. dermatology Bklyn. VA Hosp., 1975—; chief dermatology Brookdale Med. Ctr., 1977-90; chief dermatology Univ. Hosp. of Bklyn., 1975—; chief dermatology Kings County Hosp. Ctr., Bklyn., 1975—, acting med. dir., 1989-92; med. dir. Univ. Hosp. Bklyn., 1992-96. Pres. Temple Shaaray Tefila, N.Y.C., 1982-86, chmn. bd. trustees, 1987-95. Lt. M.C. USNR, 1965-67. Recipient Torch of Liberty award Anti-Defamation League, 1987, Surg. and Pediat. awards Beth Israel Hosp., NYC, 1965, Leah Dickstein Man of Good Conscience award Women's Med. Assn. NY, 1999, Leadership in Urban Med. Edn. award Arthur Ashe Inst. for Urban Health, 1999; Spl. fellow NIH, 1970-73. Mem.: AMA, Venezuelan Dermatology Soc., Argentina Dermatology Soc., Brit. Assn. Dermatologists, N.Y. Dermatol. Soc. (pres. 1989—90), Dermatol. Soc. Greater N.Y. (pres. 1980—81), N.Y. State Dermatol. Soc., N.Y. Acad. Medicine, N.Y. State Med. Soc., N.Y. Acad. Scis., Internat. Soc. Dermatology, Assn. Profs. Dermatology (sec.-treas. 1988—94, pres. 1996—98), Am. Soc. Dermatol. Surgery (past bd. dirs.), Am. Dermatol. Assn. (sec.-treas. 1996—2001, pres. 2001—02), Dermatology Found. (past trustee), Soc. Investigative Dermatology, Am. Acad. Dermatology (bd. dirs. 1983—87, v.p. 1995—96), Polish Dermatology Soc. (hon.), Soc. Francaise de Dermatology (hon.), Alpha Omega Alpha. Republican. Home: 70 E 77th St New York NY 10021-1811 Office: 450 Clarkson Ave Brooklyn NY 11203-2056 Office Phone: 718-270-1229. Business E-Mail: ashalita@downstate.edu. *Treat others with compassion, dignity and respect, add a little humor to everyone's life. Speak up for what you truly believe, be charitable.*

SHALKOP, ROBERT LEROY, retired museum director; b. Milford, Conn., July 30, 1922; s. Bertram Leroy and Dorothy Jane (Boardman) S.; m. Antoinette Joan Benkowsky, Dec. 7, 1963; 1 son, Andrew Goforth. Student, Maryville (Tenn.) Coll., 1940-42; MA, U. Chgo., 1949; postgrad., Sorbonne, 1951-52. Dir. Rahr Civic Center, Manitowoc, Wis., 1953-56, Everhart Mus., Scranton, Pa., 1956-62, Brooks Meml. Art Gallery, Memphis, 1962-64; assoc. dir. Colorado Springs (Colo.) Fine Arts Center, also curator Taylor Mus., 1964-71; dir. Anchorage Mus. History and Art, 1972-87; pvt. practice mus.

cons. Salisbury, N.C., 1987-94; archaeologist Smithsonian Instn., 1948, 50. Am. Found. Study Man, 1951, U. Wash., 1953, State U. Idaho, 1960. Author: Wooden Saints, the Santos of New Mexico, 1967, A Comparative View of Spanish Colonial Sculpture, 1968, Arroyo Hondo, the Folk Art of a New Mexican Village, 1969, A Comparative View of Spanish Colonial Painting, 1970, A Show of Color: 100 Years of Painting in the Pike's Peak Region, 1971, Russian Orthodox Art in Alaska, 1973, Sydney Laurence, an Alaskan Impressionist, 1975, Eustace Ziegler, 1977, Contemporary Native Art of Alaska, 1979, Henry Wood Elliott, 1982; Editor: An Introduction to the Native Art of Alaska, 1972; assoc. editor: Exploration in Alaska, 1980. Served with USAAF, 1942-45. Home and Office: 309 W Marsh St Salisbury NC 28144-5345

SHALLCROSS, DEANNE J. finance company executive; Mktg. exec. TIAA-CREF, N.Y.C., 1996—. Office: TIAA-CREF 730 3d Ave New York NY 10017 E-mail: dshallcross@tiaa-cref.org.

SHALLCROSS, DORIS JANE, creative behavioral educator; b. Cranford, N.J., Feb. 28, 1933; d. John William and Ethel Belle (Ruth) S. BA, Montclair State Coll., 1955; MA, Wesleyan U., Middletown, Conn., 1962; EdD, U. Mass., 1973. Tchr. Hunterdon Cen. High Sch., Flemington, N.J., 1955-61, Roosevelt Jr. High Sch., Cleveland Heights, Ohio, 1961-65, Cleveland Heights H.S., 1965-67; adminstr. Cleveland Heights Pub. Schs., 1967-69; dir. humanistic edn. Montague (Mass.) Pub. Schs., 1972-75; program devel. specialist Tchr. Corps., SUNY, Oneonta, N.Y., 1976-78; asst. prof. edn. divsn. home econs. U. Mass., Amherst, 1978-82, prof., dir. grad. studies in creativity, 1982-95; pres. Shallcross Creativity Inst., Haydenville, Mass., 1995—. Pres. bd. trustees Creative Edn. Found., Buffalo, 1989-94; co-dir. Global Odyssey, 1992—; bd. dirs. Ctr. for Critical and Creative Thinking, Hartford, Conn., 1989-92, 95—; prof. internat. grad. program in creativity U. Santiago, Santiage de Compostela, Spain, 1999. Author: Teaching Creative Behavior, 1981; co-author: The Growing Person, 1985, Leadership: Making Things Happen, 1987, Intuition: An Inner Way of Knowing, 1989; cons. editor Jour. Creative Behavior, 1967—; contbr. articles to profl. jours. Mem. Planning Bd., Town of Williamsburg, 1981-89; v.p. bd. dirs. Pioneer Valley Performing Arts H.S., 1995-98, pres., 1998—; chair edn. com. Arts in Edn. Ctr., 1997—, pres. 2002-; bd. dirs. Mass. Charter Schs. Assn., 2001—; mem. Creative Problem Solving Inst. Coun. Recipient Disting. Leader award, Creative Edn. Found., 1986; inductee Creative Problem Solving Inst. Hall of Fame, 2004; grantee, NSF, 1987-89, U. Mass., 1987-89. Mem. NEA, Mass. Soc. of Profs., Inst. for Noetic Scis., Am. Creativity Assn. (bd. dirs. 1990-93). Avocations: music, golf, reading, gardening. Home and Office: 26 S Main St Haydenville MA 01039-9735

SHALLCROSS, RICHARD, corporate financial executive; BS in Acctg., U. Denver. CPA. Audit mgr. Arthur Andersen & Co.; v.p. fin., chief fin. officer Rose Health Care System, Denver; pres. fin. and managed care HCA, Inc., Colo., 1995—96, chief fin. officer, 1996—97, 1997—2001, Nashville, 2001—. Mem.: Colo. Soc. CPA's, Health Care Fin. Mgmt. Assn. Office: HCA Inc 1 Park Plz Nashville TN 37203

SHALOM, LILIANE WINN, investment company executive, consultant; b. Casablanca, Morocco, May 28, 1940; d. Joseph and Madeleine Levy; 1 child, Dominique Winn. Brevet Etudes Premier Cycle, Alliance Israelite, Casablanca, 1956; cert. proficiency in English, U. Mich., 1960. English tchr. U.S. Info. Agy., Casablanca, 1959-61; multilingual guide, interpreter for VIPs, heads of state UN, N.Y.C., 1962-65; designer-ptnr., v.p. I.Q. Originals, Inc., N.Y.C., 1977-82; pres. EON Holdings, Inc., N.Y.C., 1981—, L.S. Cons., 1991—; cons. Applied Energy Svcs., Alexandria, Va., 1992—95, Airbus Industrie, Toulouse, France, 1999—2000. Editor, pub., contbr. The Sephardi World quar. mag., 1975-82. Fin. com. Carter for Pres., N.Y.C., 1975-76, Moynihan for Senate, N.Y.C., 1976, Dukakis for Pres., N.Y.C., 1987-88; chmn. fundraising Congl. Fgn. Rels. Com., N.Y.C., 1986. Recipient Louise Waterman Wise award Am. Jewish Congress, 1984, Stanley Isaacs Human Rels. award Am. Jewish Com., N.Y., 1986; named Comdr. of Ouissam Alaouite, King of Morocco, 1987. Mem. Am. Sephardi Fedn. (pres. 1975-82), World Zionist Congress (presidium 1971—), Moroccan Jewish Orgn. (founder, chmn. 1978), United Jewish Appeal (bd. dirs.), Hebrew Immigration Aid Soc. (v.p. 1990—), World Jewish Congress (econ. and social commn.). Democrat. Office: 645 5th Ave Ste 710 New York NY 10022-5910

SHALOWITZ, ERWIN EMMANUEL, civil engineer; b. Washington, Feb. 13, 1924; s. Aaron Louis and Pearl (Myer) S.; m. Elaine Mildred Langerman, June 29, 1952; children: Ann Janet, Aliza Beth, Jonathan Avram. Student, U. Pa., U. Notre Dame, 1944-45; BCE, George Washington U., 1947, postgrad., 1948-49; grad. soil mechanics, Cath. U., 1951; MA in Pub. Adminstrn. (fellow U.S. Civil Service Commn.), Am. U., 1954. Registered profl. engr., Washington. Engr. Klemitt Engring. Co., N.Y.C., 1947; with cons. firm Whitman, Requardt & Assos., Balt., 1947-48; chief structural rsch. engr., head def. rsch. sect., project officer and tech. adviser for atomic tests Bur. Yards and Docks, Dept. Navy, Washington, 1948-59; supervisory gen. engr. spl. asst. for protective constrn. programs, project mgr. for bldg. systems, chief rsch. br., chief mgmt. info, chief contracting procedures and support, chief contract evaluation and analysis, team leader/project mgr. acquisition sys., acquisition/procurement exec., Pub. Bldg. Svc., Gen. Svcs. Adminstrn., Washington, 1959—98; mgr. ednl. svc. for individual improvement Silver Spring, Md., 1998—. Chmn. fed. exec. tng. program U.S. Civil Service Commn., 1950; fallout shelter analyst Dept. Def.; chmn. GSA Fire Safety Com., GSA Fallout Protection Com., GSA Bldg. Evaluation Com.; mem. Interagy Com. on Housing Rsch. and Bldg. Tech.; mem. Nat. Evaluation Bd. Architect-Engr. Selections; mem. standing com. on procurement policy Nat. Acad. Sci. Bldg. Research Adv. Bd. and Interagency Com. on Procurement Curriculum Rev.; coordinator pub. bldgs. design and constrn. Small Bus. Program and Minority Enterprise and Minority Subcontracting Programs. Contbr. articles profl. jours. Served to engring. officer USNR, 1944-46. Recipient Commendable Svc. award GSA, 1968, Outstanding Performance recognition, 1976, 77, 79, 83, 87, 93-96, Superior Accomplishment award, 1995, others; Engr. Alumni Achievement award George Washington U., 1985. Fellow ASCE, Am. Biog. Inst.; mem. Soc. Advancement Mgmt., Am. Biog. Inst. (nat. bd. advisors), Soc. Am. Mil. Engrs., Sigma Tau, Pi Sigma Alpha. Jewish. Home: 3122 Gracefield Rd Apt 108 Silver Spring MD 20904-5801 E-mail: eshalowitz@aol.com. *PRINCIPLES: Look beyond the material for lasting values and meaning, optimize managerial effectiveness by creating an objective and challenging climate in an organization, delve into the underlying causes of problem areas for meaningful solutions, and persevere in spite of obstacles. IDEAS: Cultural pluralism; the intrinsic potential of each individual; and love, appreciation, and support of one's family as indispensable for real accomplishment. GOALS: To attain the highest level of professional accomplishment within my capabilities and to continue to have a rich, happy, and fulfilling family life. STANDARDS OF CONDUCT: To be fair, consistent, and straightforward; and to avoid over-reacting.*

SHAM, LU JEU, physics educator; b. Hong Kong, Apr. 28, 1938; s. T.S. and Cecilia Maria (Siu) Shen; m. Georgina Bien, Apr. 25, 1965; children: Kevin Shen, Alisa Shen. GCE, Portsmouth Coll., Eng., 1957; BS, Imperial Coll., London U., Eng., 1960; PhD in Physics, Cambridge U., Eng., 1963. Asst. rsch. physicist U. Calif. at San Diego, La Jolla, 1963-66, assoc. prof., 1968-75, prof., 1975—, chair dept. physics, 1995-98, dean div. natural scis., 1985-89; asst. prof. physics U. Calif. at Irvine, 1966-67; rsch. physicist IBM Corp., Yorktown Heights, N.Y., 1974-75. Reader Queen Mary Coll., U. London, 1967-68. Assoc. editor Physics Letters A., 1992—; contbr. sci. papers to profl. jours. Recipient Churchill Coll. studentship, Eng., 1960-63, Sr. U.S. Scientist award Humboldt Found., Stuttgart, Germany, 1978, Faculty Rsch. lectr. award, 2000; fellow Guggenheim Found., 1984, Chancellor Assocs. award for Excellence in Rsch., 1995. Fellow Am. Phys. Soc.; mem. AAAS, NAS, Acad. Sinica Republic of China, Optical Soc. Am. Democrat. Avocations: tennis, folk dancing. Office: U Calif San Diego Dept Physics 0319 La Jolla CA 92093-0319 Office Phone: 619-534-3269. E-mail: lsham@ucsd.edu.

SHAMASH, YACOV, dean, electrical engineering educator; b. Iraq, Jan. 12, 1950; BSEE, Imperial Coll., London, 1970; PhD in Control Systems, Imperial Coll., 1973. Postdoctoral fellowin elec. engring. Tel-Aviv U., 1973-75, from lectr. elec. engring. to sr. lectr. elec. engring., 1975-78; prof. elec. engring. Fla. Atlantic U., Boca Raton, 1977-85; prof., chair dept. elec. engring. dept. Wash. State U., Pullman, 1985-92; dean engring. SUNY, Stony Brook, 1992—. Bd. dirs. KeyTronics, Spokane, Wash., 1990—; vis. asst. prof. U. Pa., Phila., 1976-77. Contbr. over 100 articles to profl. jours., book chpts. Fellow IEEE (sr.). Office: SUNY Coll Engring & Applied Sci Stony Brook NY 11794-2200

SHAMBAN, AVA T. dermatologist; BS, Harvard U., 1977; MD, Case Western Res. U. Pvt. practice dermatology, Santa Monica, Calif.; asst. clin. prof. dermatology UCLA. Cons. ABC's Extreme Makeover; investigator Nat. Acne Rsch. Project; featured regarding cosmetic dermatology Discovery Channel. Bd. dirs. Santa Monica Coll. Found. Fellow: Am. Acad. Dermatology. Office: Laser Inst for Dermatology 2021 Santa Monica Blvd #600E Santa Monica CA 90404

SHAMBAUGH, DAVID LEIGH, political scientist, educator, writer; b. Chgo., Jan. 18, 1953; s. George E. Shambaugh, Jr. and Genevieve (Krum) Shambaugh; m. Ingrid Cecile Larsen, Aug. 7, 1982; children: Christopher Leigh, Alexander George. BA in East Asian Studies, George Washington U., 1977; MA in Internat. Affairs, Johns Hopkins U., 1980; PhD in Polit. Sci., U. Mich., 1989. Prof. U. London, 1988—96, George Washington U., Washington, 1996—; sr. fellow Brookings Instn., 1998—. Cons. U.S. Dept. State, Dept. Def., other govt. agys., Ford Found., 1983—87, Am. Express, 1994—2000, Rand Corp., 1998—2000, Rockefeller Found., 1998, Microsoft Corp., 1999—2000, others. Editor China Quar., 1991—96, mem. editl. bd., 1989—, Studies on Contemporary China, 1991—, Internat. Security, 2003—, China Perspectives, 1998—, Current History, 1999—; author: The Making of a Premier: Zhao Ziyang's Provincial Career, 1984, Beautiful Imperialist: China Perceives America, 1972-1990, 1991, China and Europe, 1949-1995, 1996, Modernizing China's Military Progress, Problems, and Prospects, 2002; editor, contbr. American Studies of Contemporary China, 1993, Greater China: The Next Superpower?, 1995, Deng Xiaoping: Portrait of a Chinese Statesman, 1995, China's Military in Transition, 1997, Contemporary Taiwan, 1998, The Modern Chinese State, 2000, Is China Unstable?, 2000, co-editor Chinese Foreign Policy: Theory and Practice, 1994, co-editor, contbr. China's Military Faces the Future, 1999, The China Reader: The Reform Era, 1999, Making China Policy: Lessons from the Bush and Clinton Administrations, 2001. Grantee, Brit. Acad./Econ. & Social Rsch. Coun. China Exch. Program, 1990, 1994, Chiang Ching-kuo Found., 1998—2000; Rsch. fellow, Pacific Cultural Found., 1998—2000, Woodrow Wilson fellow, 2002—03, others. Mem.: Pacific Coun. on Internat. Policy, Coun. on Fgn. Rels., Asia Soc., Internat. Studies Assn., Assn. for Asian Studies, Coun. on Security Coop. in the Asia Pacific, Nat. Com. U.S.-China Rels., Internat. Inst. Strategic Studies, World Econ. Forum. Democrat. Avocations: travel, basketball, tennis, canoeing, bluegrass music. Home: 1600 N Highland St Arlington VA 22201 Office: George Washington Univ Elliott Sch Internat Affairs 1957 East St NW Ste 503 Washington DC 20052 Business E-Mail: shambaug@gwu.edu.

SHAMBAUGH, IRVIN CALVIN, JR., aptitude test firm executive; b. Harrisburg, Pa., June 7, 1943; s. Irvin Calvin and Viola Mary (Deibler) S.; m. Amy Willcox, Jan. 3, 1975. BS in Geol. Sci., Pa. State U., 1964; postgrad. MIT, 1964-65, Tex. Christian U., Ft. Worth, 1974-76, East. Tex. State U., 1976-77. Rsch. coord. Johnson O'Connor Rsch. Found., Ft. Worth, 1965-76; pres., chief scientist Aptitude Inventory Measurement Svc., Dallas, 1976—; centennial fellow Coll. Earth and Min. Scis. Pa. State U., 1996. Author: The Test-Taker's Guide to Career Literature, 1982, Test Manual for Selected AIMS Worksamples, 1986, Books About Careers, 1986, Career Facts: Where to Find Them and How to Use Them, 1992, The AIMS Guide to Career Facts, 1997; co-author: AIMS Information About Aptitudes, 1979, The Aptitude Handbook: A Guide to the AIMS Program, 1996, 3d edit., 2004, Career Facts: In Print and on the World Wide Web, 2003; co-author, editor: You and Your Aptitudes, 1983; developer Activity Preference Questionnaire, 1994, psychometric instrument III Interest Inventory, 1996; contbr. articles to profl. jours.; developer AIMS test battery, 1976—. With USMC, 1966-68. Mem. ACA, APA, AAAS, Assn. Assessment in Counseling and Edn., Am. Psychol. Soc., Nat. Coun. Measurement in Edn., Am. Statis Assn., Nat. Assn. Coll. Admissions Counselors, Nat. Assn. Test Dirs. Home: 934 Westbrook Dr Garland TX 75043-5243 Office: Aptitude Inventory Measurement Svc 12160 Abrams Rd Ste 314 Dallas TX 75243-4525

SHAMBAUGH, STEPHEN WARD, lawyer; b. South Bend, Ind., Aug. 4, 1920; s. Marion Clyde and Anna Violet (Stephens) S.; m. Marilyn Louise Pyle (dec. 1993); children: Susan Wynne Shambaugh Hinkle (dec. 1998), Kathleen Louise Shambaugh Thompson. Student, San Jose State Tchrs. Coll., 1938-40, U. Ark., 1951; LLB, U. Tulsa, 1954. Bar: Okla. 1954, Colo. 1964. Mem. staff Reading & Bates, Inc., Tulsa, 1951-54; v.p., gen. mgr., legal counsel Reading & Bates Drilling Co. Ltd., Calgary, Alta., Can., 1954-61; sr. ptnr. Bowman, Shambaugh, Geissinger & Wright, Denver, 1964-81; sole practice Denver, 1981-97; now ret. Dir., fin. counsel various corps. Col. USAF ret. Mem. Colo. Bar Assn., Okla. Bar Assn., P-51 Mustang Pilots Assn., Masons, Elks, Phi Alpha Delta.

SHAMBO, JAMES ALAN, accountant; b. Chicago Heights, Ill., July 16, 1950; s. Gerald G. and Bernice R. (Sharp) S.; m. Elaine Kern, Oct. 19, 1975. BS in Acctg., No. Ill. U., 1972. CPA, Colo., Ariz. Staff acct. First Am. Realty, Chgo., 1972-73; office mgr. Robert Worley & Co., CPA's, Phoenix, 1973-79; tax mgr. Gustafson, Crandall, Sanden & Duncan, Inc., CPAs, Colorado Springs, Colo., 1980-84; mng. ptnr., v.p. Sanden, Shambo and Anderson, P.C., Colorado Springs, 1984—; pres. Lifetime Planning Concepts P.C., Colorado Springs, 1995—. Mem. com. Specialization Oversight Bd., Denver, 1984-86; chmn. Accreditation of Fin. Planning Specialists Com., N.Y.C., 1986-91; v.p. Nat. Accreditation Bd. for CPA Specialists, N.Y.C., 1987. Cons. Hispanic & Native Am. Srs., Colorado Springs, 1989-91. Mem. AICPA (chmn. accreditation pers. fin. specialist subcom. 1987-91, exec. com. pers. fin. planning divsn. 1990-96, vice chair pers. fin. planning exec. com. 1992-93, chmn. pers. fin. planning exec. com. 1993-95, mem. pers. fin. specialist subcom. 1996—), Ariz. Soc. CPAs, Colo. Soc. CPAs (bd. dirs. 1988-89, pub. issues assessment com. 1990-91, v.p. 1991-92), Colorado Springs Estate Planning Coun. (treas. 1990—). Avocations: lyric writing, reading and writing books, camping. Office: Lifetime Planning Concepts PC 3355 American Dr Ste 200 Colorado Springs CO 80917-5706*

SHAMBROOM, PAUL, artist, photographer; b. Teaneck, N.J., 1956; BFA, Mpls. Coll. Art Design, 1978. One-man shows include Film in the Cities, St. Paul, 1979, Minn. Hist. Soc., 1984, Bockley Gallery, Mpls., 1990, CEOA Gallery and Medaillel Coll., Buffalo, 1995, Walker Art Ctr., Mpls., 1995, Tanya Bonakdar Gallery, N.Y.C., 1997—98, exhibited in group shows at Camerawork Gallery, San Francisco, 1979, Northlight Gallery, Tempe, Ariz., 1981, Forecast Pub. Artspace Prodns., Mpls., 1981, Univ. Gallery, U. Minn., 1986, Minn. Coll. Art Design, 1988, Film in the Cities, St. Paul, 1990, Mpls. Inst. Arts, 1990, 1996, Bockley Gallery, Mpls., 1991, Mus. Modern Art, N.Y.C., 1996, Whitney Mus. Am. Art, 1997, Represented in permanent collections, San Francisco Mus. Modern Art, L.A. County Mus. Art, Mus. Modern Art, N.Y.C., Walker Art Ctr., Mpls., Mpls. Inst. Arts, Mus. Fine Arts, Houston. Fellow Photography fellow, McKnight Found., Mpls., 1985, 1989, 1995, Visual Arts fellow, Jerome Found., St. Paul, 1987, Artist Assistance fellow, Minn. State Arts Bd., 1988, 1993, Artist fellow, Bush Found., St. Paul, 1992; Dayton Hudson Found. grantee, Mpls., 1979, Jerome Found. grantee, St. Paul, 1996. Office: c/o Bonakdar Jancou Gallery 521 W 21st St New York NY 10011-2811

SHAMBUREK, ROLAND HOWARD, physician; b. Adell, Wis., June 7, 1928; s. William and Catherine (Illig) Shamburek; m. Gladys Irene Gibbons, June 21, 1952; children: Steven J., Robert D., Daniel J. BS, U. Wis., 1950, MD, 1953; MPH, Harvard U., 1960; grad., U.S. Army War Coll., Carlisle Barracks, Pa., 1972. Diplomate Am. Bd. Preventive Medicine. Commd. 1st lt. M.C., U.S. Army, 1953, advanced through grades to col., 1968; intern St. Joseph's Hosp., Marshfield, Wis., 1953-54; grad. U.S. Naval Sch. of Aviation Medicine, Pensacola, Fla., 1957; resident in preventive (aerospace) medicine USAF Sch. Aerospace Medicine, Brooks AFB, 1960-63; service in 216th Field Artillery (Atomic) Battalion, 1954—56, 1966, Office of Army Surgeon Gen., Washington, 1966—70, 1972—75; comdr. 67th EVAC Hosp., Vietnam, 1970-71, U.S. Army Med. Pers. Support Agy., 1975-77; ret. U.S. Army, 1977; exec. v.p. Aerospace Med. Assn., 1977-79; clin. practice Pentagon Health Clinic, Washington, 1981-85; med. researcher Office of Army Surgeon Gen., 1985-87. Med. monitor Canary Island Tracking Sta. for Gemini missions NASA, 1965—66. Contbr. scientific papers in field. Decorated Legion of Merit with oak leaf cluster, Army Commendation medal, Meritorious Svc. medal. Mem.: AMA (del. 1978), Internat. Acad. Aviation and Space Medicine, Soc. NASA Flight Surgeons, U.S. Army Flight Surgeons, Soc. Med. Cons. Armed Forces, Aerospace Med. Assn. (v.p. 1968—69), Am. Coll. Preventive Medicine (v.p. 1968—69), Assn. Mil. Surgeons (John Shaw Billings award 1968). Address: 3700 Moss Dr Annandale VA 22003-1915

SHAMIM, MAH TALAT, chemist; b. Karachi, Pakistan, Sept. 7, 1952; came to U.S., 1976; d. Syed Hasan and Askaribi (Nuzhat) Akhtar; m. A. Najm Shamim, Dec. 20, 1975. BS in Chemistry, Karachi U., 1972, MS in Chemistry, 1973, Howard U., 1981, PhD in Chemistry, 1983. Postdoctoral fellow NIH, Bethesda, Md., 1983-89, sr. staff fellow, 1989-91; chemist EPA, Washington, 1991-93, sect. chief environ. fate and effects divsn., 1993-97, chief environ. risk br. environ fate and effects divsn., 1997—. Panelist U.S. Merit Sys. Protection Adv. Bd., Washington, 1996—; mem. internat. environ. fate workgroups. Co-author: Rejection Rate Analysis: Environmental Fate Guidelines, 1995; contbr. articles to profl. jours. Mem. Am. Chem. Soc., Assn. Asian-Pacific Ams. Avocations: gardening, sewing, painting, writing. Office: Environ Protection Agy 401 M St SW Washington DC 20024-2610 E-mail: shamim.mah@epa.gov.

SHAMMAS, NAZIH KHEIRALLAH, environmental engineer, consultant, engineering educator; b. Homs, Syria, Feb. 18, 1939; arrived in U.S., 1991; s. Kheirallah Hanna and Nazha Murad (Hamwi) Shammas; m. Norma Massouh, July 28, 1968; children: Samerl Erick, Samer Sam. Degree in engirng. with distinction, Am. U., Beirut, 1962; MS in Sanitary Engring., U. N.C., 1965; PhD in Civil Engring., U. Mich., 1971. Instr. civil engring. Am. U., Beirut, 1965-68, asst. prof. civil engring., 1972-76; tchg. fellow U. Mich., Ann Arbor, 1968-71; asst. prof. civil engring. King Saud U., Riyadh, Saudi Arabia, 1976-78, assoc. prof., 1978-91; prof. environ. engring. Lenox (Mass.) Inst. Water Tech., 1991-2001, dean edn., 1992-93. Cons., ptnr. Cons. and Rsch. Engrs., Beirut, 1973—76; advisor, cons. Ar-Riyadh Devel. Authority, 1977—93, Riyadh Water and Sanitary Drainage Authority, 1979—83, Assoc. Cons. Engring. Team, 1994—99; adj. prof. environ. sci. Berkshire CC, 1995—; planning assoc. Berkshire Regional Planning Commn., 1999—. Co-author: Environmental Sanitation, 1988, Wastewater Engineering, 1988, Physicochemical Treatment Processes, 2004; contbr. articles to profl. jours. and confs. Recipient Excellence in Tchg. award, King Saud U., 1981, 1984; Block grantee, U. Mich., 1968—70. Mem.: ASCE, Assn. Environ. Engring. and Sci. Profs., Internat. Water Assn., New Eng. Water Works Assn., New Eng. Water Environ. Assn., Am. Water Works Assn., Water Environ. Fedn. Achievements include research in biological and physiochemcial remediation processes; mathematical modeling of nitrification process; water and wastewater management in developing countries; water conservation; wastewater treatment and reuse; appropriate technology for developing countries; multidisciplinary studies in environmental management and planning. Home: 35 Flintstone Dr Pittsfield MA 01201 Personal E-mail: shammas@earthlink.net.

SHAMMAS, NICOLAS WAHIB, internist, cardiologist; b. Amyoun, El-Koura, Lebanon, Jan. 31, 1963; arrived in U.S., 1988; s. Wahib Nicolas and Vera Yousuf (El-Helou) Shammas; m. Gail Ann Hanson, Feb. 22, 1991; children: Waheeb John, Andrew Nicolas, Anna Elizabeth. BSc with distinction, Am. U. Beirut, 1983, MD, MSc in Physiology, Am. U. Beirut, 1987, Diploma in Computer Programming, 1985. Diplomate Am. Bd. Internal Medicine, Am. Bd. Cardiology and Interventional Cardiology. Postdoctoral rsch. fellow Am. U. Beirut, 1987-88; resident in internal medicine U. Iowa Hosps., Iowa City, 1988-91; instr. medicine, clin. fellow cardiology U. Rochester (N.Y.) Med. Ctr., 1991-94; fellow assoc. in cardiology U. Iowa Hosps., Iowa City, 1994—95; mem. staff Genesis Med. Ctr., Davenport, Iowa, 1995—; clin. asst. prof. U. Iowa. Founder Mastermind Pub., 1995, Phenix Realty Co., 1997; founder, pres. Midwest Cardiovasc. Rsch. Found., 2002. Author (with others): Flavors of Lebanon, 1995; contbr. articles to profl. jours. Am. U. Beirut Univ. Rsch. Bd. awardee, 1986-87, John C. Sable Meml. Heart award J.C. Sable Fund, 1993, Trainee Investigator award for clin. rsch. meeting, Balt., 1994. Fellow: ACP, Am. Coll. Chest Physicians, Internat. Coll. Angiology, Am. Coll. Cardiology, Soc. Cardiac Angiography and Interventions; mem.: AMA, Am. Soc. Nuclear Cardiology, Iowa Med. Soc., Am. Soc. Internal Medicine, Am. Fedn. Clin. Rsch. Achievements include research in basic cardiology: prostacyclin and transmembrane calcium movements; adrenergic binding sites in hypertrophied rat hearts induced by renovascular hypertension; myocardial viability in hybernating myocardium; coronary flow reserve; principal investigator at Genesis Medical Center for several large multicenter national and international clinical trials, including SYMPHONY, BEST, LIMIT-AMI, ATLAS; SPORT, ASSENT.2, SLIDE, SUPORT, NOET, XaNADU, INFLAME, MiniCrown Registry, JUMBO, LUNAR, CHARISMA, others. Office: Cardiovasc Medicine PC 1236 E Rusholme St Ste 300 Davenport IA 52803-2400

SHAMOO, ADIL ELIAS, biochemist, biophysicist, educator; b. Baghdad, Iraq, Aug. 1, 1941; came to U.S., 1964, naturalized, 1973; s. Elias M. and Mariam T. (Mansour) S.; m. Joan Hutchison, Dec. 16, 1967 (div. Dec. 1997); children: Abraheem, Zachary, Jessica. B.Sc. in Physics, U. Baghdad, 1962; MS in Physics (grad. fellow), U. Louisville, 1966; PhD in Biophysics, CUNY, 1970. Instr. engring. physics Speed Sch., U. Louisville, 1965-68; asst. prof. physiology City U. N.Y., 1971-73; guest worker Lab. Biophysics and Neurochemistry, NIH, Bethesda, Md., 1972-73; asst. prof. radiation biology and biophysics U. Rochester, 1973-75; guest prof. Max-Planck Inst. Biophysics, Frankfurt, West Germany, 1977-78; assoc. prof. radiation biology and biophysics U. Rochester, 1975-79; prof., chmn. dept. biol. chemistry U. Md., Balt., 1979-82, prof. biochemistry and molecular biology, 1982—, prof. epidemiology and preventive medicine, 2003—, head membrane biochemistry research lab., 1982-90. Cons. div. biol. scis. Kodak Co., Rochester, 1976-77; NIH tng. fellow U. Louisville, 1967; investigator Am. Heart Assn., 1976-79; Neurosci. Rsch. Program fellow, Boulder, Colo., summer 1977; chmn. symposia, various coms. in field; mem. organizing coms. workshops in field; adj. profl. dept. physics East Carolina U., Greenville, N.C., 1996-2000; bd. dirs. Friends Rsch. Inst., 1994-2001; ethics cons. Armed Forces Epidemiol. Bd.; chair ethics adv. group GlaxoSmithKline Co., 2003. Editor (with M.W. Miller) Membrane Toxicity, 1977, Carriers and Channels in Biological Systems, 1975, Carriers and Channels in Biological Systems-Transport Proteins, 1980, Regulation of Calcium Transport Across Muscle Membranes, 1985, Principles of Research Data Audit, (with R. Verna) Biotechnology Today, 1995, Ethics in Neurobiological Research with Human Subjects, 1997; editor in chief Membrane Biochemistry, 1977-93, Accountability in Research: Policies and Quality Assurance, 1988—; mem. editl. bd. Molecular and Cellular Biochemistry, 1987-94, Quality Assurance: Good Practice Regulation and Law, 1991—; contbr. articles and abstracts to profl. jours., chpts. to books. Bd. dirs. Alliance for Mentally Ill of Md., 1990-93, Friends Rsch. Inst. Inc., 1994-2002; mem. rsch. monitoring com. Nat. Alliance for Mentally Ill, bd. dirs. 1994-97; pres. faculty senate U. Md., Balt., 1993-94; mem. coun. univ. systems U. Md., 1994-97; mem. adv. com. Vantage Pl., 1995-97; bd. dirs. Howard County Mental Health Authority, 1997-00, pres., 1997-2000; bd. dirs. Citizens for Responsible Care and Rsch., 1998—, v.p., 1998—; mem. Nat. Human Rsch. Protections Adv. Com., 2000-02. Recipient Advocacy award Mental Health Assn. Md., 1994, Disting. Svc. award Alliance for Mentally Ill of Md., 1994, Howard County Mental Health Auth., 1999. Mem. AAAS, AAUP (chpt. sec. 1971-72), Basic Sci. Council of Am. Heart Assn., Am. Soc. Biol. Chemists and Mol. Biol., Am. Coll. Sports Medicine, Am. Assn. Physics Tchrs., Am. Soc. Bioethics and Human Values, Am. Physiol. Soc., Biophys. Soc. (Cole Membrane Award Com. 1983-84, chmn. biophysics subgroup 1982-83, council 1986-89), Membrane Biophys. Group (chmn. 1982-83, sec.-treas. 1983-85, co-chmn. U.S. bioenergetics group 1979-80), Md. Acad.

Scis. (chmn. com. programs and exhbns. 1986-87, sci. council 1985-89), N.Y. Acad. Scis., Coun. of Biology (editor 1989—), Soc. Quality Assurance. Achievements include patents for liquid scintillators. Office: 108 N Greene St Baltimore MD 21201-1503 E-mail: ashamoo@umaryland.edu.

SHAMOON, MONTAHA JIRGES, educator, researcher; d. Jirges Shamoon Kakose and Gorgia Yaldo. BSc, U. Basrah, Iraq, 1976—2001; MSc, U. Manchester, Eng., 1981, PhD, 1984. Lectr. U. Basrah, Iraq, 1984—93; asst. prof. Saddam U., Baghdad, Iraq, 1993—96; assoc. prof. Alzaytoonah U., Amman, Jordan, 1996—99; adj. prof. U. Detroit, 1999—2002, Lawrence Technol. U., Southfield, Mich., 2000—03, U. Mich., Dearborn, 2002—. Translator: Introduction to Numerical Analysis. Office: Univ Mich 4901 Evergreen Rd Dearborn MI 48128 E-mail: shamoon@umd.umich.edu.

SHAMOUN, JOHN MILAM, plastic surgeon; b. Greenville, Miss., Apr. 1, 1960; s. Joseph David Shamoun and Phyllis Ann Joseph. BS, U. Miss., 1982, MD, 1986. Bd. cert. Am. Bd. Surgery, Am. Bd. Plastic and Reconstructive Surgery, Am. Bd. Facial Plastic and Reconstructive Surgery, Am. Bd. Forensic Examiners. Gen. surgeon U. South Ala., Mobile, 1986-91; plastic surgeon U. Tex., Dallas, 1991-93, Mt. Sinai Hosp., Miami Beach, Fla., 1993-94, Plastic Surgery Ctr. of the Pacific, Honolulu, 1994-95, Atlanta Plastic Surgery, 1994-95, Newport Inst. Plastic Surgery, Newport Beach, Calif., 1995—. Legal cons. Law Firm of Charles G. Shamoun, Dallas, 1995—. Author: (books) Aesthetic Surgery, 1996, Microvascular Atlas, 1997; contbr. articles to profl. jours. Fellow ACS; mem. Am. Soc. Plastic and Reconstructive Surgery, Calif. Soc. Plastic Surgery, Anti Aging Soc., Alpha Omega Alpha. Roman Catholic. Avocations: skiing, hunting, fishing, horseback riding. Office: 360 San Miguel Dr Ste 406 Newport Beach CA 92660-7822

SHAMPO, MARC ANTHONY, retired medical editor, writer; b. Green Bay, Wis., Oct. 20, 1924; s. Norman Joseph Shampo and Antoinette Rondou; m. Norma Eileen Beyea, Oct. 23, 1945 (div. Oct. 1965); 1 child, Teresa; m. Lila Irene Mayhew, July 29, 1967; children: Barbara, Charles, Nancy, Scott. BS, U. Wis., 1948, MS, 1949, PhD, 1960. H.S. tchr., Pewaukee, Wis., 1949—51, Racine, Wis., 1951—58; prof. Duquesne U., Pitts., 1958—62; med. editor Mayo Clinic, Rochester, Minn., 1962—89; ret., 1989. Contbr. articles to profl. jours., chpts. to books. With U.S. Army, 1943—46, ETO. Mem.: Phi Delta Kappa, Phi Eta Sigma. Home: 2828 Wellington Ln SW Rochester MN 55902

SHAMSHAM, FADI MICHEL, cardiologist; b. Beirut, Nov. 28, 1968; arrived in U.S., 1994; s. Michel Salim Shamsham and Marie Assi Gemayel. BS, Am. U. of Beirut, 1989, MD, 1993. Diplomate Am. Bd. Internal Medicine, Am. Bd. Internal Medicine with subspecialities in cardiovascular diseases and interventional cardiology. Resident in internal medicine S.I. U. Hosp., S.I., NY, 1994—97; fellow in cardiovascular diseases SUNY, Bklyn., 1997—2000; fellow in interventional cardiology Kaiser Permanente Found. Hosp., L.A., 2000—01; fellow in vascular medicine Charleston Area Med. Ctr., W.Va., 2001—02; cardiologist Med. Group of North Fla., Tallahassee, 2002—; med. staff Tallahassee Meml. Hosp., Fla., 2002—, Capital Regional Med. Ctr., 2002—. Clin. inst. SUNY, Bklyn., 1997—2000. Contbr. articles to profl. jours. Fellow: Soc. Cardiac Angiography and Interventions, Am. Coll. Cardiology; mem.: AMA, ACP. Office: Med Group of North Florida 2626 Care Dr Ste 100 Tallahassee FL 32308 Office Phone: 850-656-2656.

SHAN, KESAVAN, cardiologist, researcher; b. Jaffna, Sri Lanka, Dec. 6, 1965; s. Krishnambal and Shanmuganathan; m. Girija Shan, Nov. 28, 1992; children: Tamara, Devan. BSc with honors, U. London, 1987, MBBS MD with honors, 1990. Diplomate Am. Bd. Internal Medicine, 1996, Nat. Bd. Echocardiography, 1999, cardiovas. diseases Am. Bd. Internal Medicine, 2000, cert. nuc. cardiology Am. Bd. Nuc. Medicine, 2001. Clin. instr. medicine Baylor Coll. Of Medicine, Houston, 1998—2000; cardiologist Tex. Heart Inst., Houston, 1999—2001, Cardiology Of Houston, 2001; clin. asst. prof. medicine U. Tex., Houston, 2001—. Med. edn. com. S.W. Meml. Hosp., Affiliate U. Tex., Houston. Contbr. articles to profl. jours. Fellow: Am. Coll. Cardiology (fellow, Merck award and Young Clin. Investigator award finalist 1999); mem.: Royal Coll. Physcians. Achievements include research in cardiovascular MRI echocardiography; discovery of tissue doppler changes and diastolic dysfunction in hibernating myocardium; cardiovascular MRI and nuclear cardiology. Office: Cardiology Of Houston 7737 SW Freeway Ste 780 Houston TX 77074 E-mail: shankg@att.net.

SHANAHAN, BRENDAN FREDERICK, professional hockey player; b. Mimico, Ont., Canada, Jan. 23, 1969; With N.J. Devils, 1987—91; with St. Louis Blues, 1991—95, Hartford Whalers, 1995—97, Detroit Red Wings, 1997—. Player NHL All-Star Game, 1994, 96, 97, 98, 99, 2000, All-Star Game, 2002; mem. Stanley Cup Champions, Detroit Red Wings, 1997, 98, 2002, Can. Olympic Hockey Team, 2002. Named to NHL All-Star 1st Team, 1993—94; recipient Gold medal, Olympic Games, 2002. Office: care Detroit Red Wings 600 Civic Center Dr Detroit MI 48226-4408

SHANAHAN, EUGENE MILES, flow measurement instrumentation company executive; b. Great Falls, Mont., Sept. 18, 1946; s. Raymond Eugene and Helen Marjorie (Graham) S.; m. Beverly Ann Braaten, Sept. 8, 1967; children— Bret Allen, Shaun Eugene, Shae Erin BS in Mech. Engring., Mont. State U., 1968; MS, Mont. State U., 1969; MBA, Portland State U., 1976. Registered profl. engr., Oreg. Mech. engr. Tektronix, Beaverton, Oreg., 1968-71; mech. engr. Shell Oil Co., Martinez, Calif., 1967; chief mech. project engr. Mears Controls, Beaverton, 1971-76, mktg. mgr., 1976-79; v.p., gen. mgr. Eaton Corp., Beaverton, 1979-87; v.p. Asia Pacific Dieterich Standard (a Fisher-Rosemount Co.), Boulder, Colo., 1987-98; with Rosemount Inc., Chanhassen, Minn. Served with N.G., 1969-75 NSF trainee, 1969 Mem. ASME, Instrumentation Soc. Am., Tau Beta Pi, Phi Kappa Phi, Pi Tau Sigma. Office: Rosemount Inc 8200 Market Blvd Chanhassen MN 55317-9687 Home: 7460 Windmill Dr Chanhassen MN 55317-9362

SHANAHAN, MICHAEL FRANCIS, retired manufacturing executive, former hockey team executive; b. St. Louis, Oct. 29, 1939; m. Mary Ann Barrett; children: Megan Elizabeth, Michael Francis Jr., Maureen Patricia. BS in Commerce, St. Louis U.; postgrad., Washington U., St. Louis; LHD (hon.), St. Louis Rabbinical Coll., 1987; PHD LLB (hon.), St. Louis U., 2002. With McDonnell Douglas Automation Co., St. Louis, 1962-73, sales mgr., 1969-71, br. mgr., 1971-72, mktg. dir. cen. region, 1972-73; mktg. v.p. Numerical Control Inc., St. Louis, 1973-74, pres., 1974-79; v.p. Cleve. Pneumatic Co. (formerly Numerical Control Inc.), St. Louis, 1979-82; chmn., chief exec. officer Engineered Air Systems Inc., St. Louis, 1982—; former chmn., ceo St. Louis Blues Hockey Team. Bd. dirs. Engineered Air Systems Inc. (chmn.), St. Louis Blues Hockey Inc. (chmn.); adv. com. Nat. Hockey League; mem. U.S. Senatorial Bus. Adv. Bd.; bd. dirs. Capital Bank and Trust of Clayton, The Graphic Arts Ctr. Inc., Kilo Rsch. Found. (vice chmn.). Bd. dirs. Am. Heart Assn., St. Louis Ambassadors, Catholic Charities of St. Louis, Galway Sister City Com., The Backstoppers, Christmas in St. Louis Found.; nat. bd. dirs. Boys Hope; bd. trustees, pres. coun. St. Louis U.; adv. bd. Safe Kids; hon. bd. Paraquad; hon. chmn. Small Bus. Week in St. Louis, 1989; hon. co-chmn. Veteran's Day Observance and Parade, 1989; co-chairperson AMC Cancer Rsch. Ctr. Community Svc. award. Named St. Louis Ambassador of Yr., 1986, Olivette Businessman of Yr., 1987, St. Louis Bus. Leader of Yr. Coll. Bus. Adminstrn., So. Ill. U. at Carbondale, 1987,Outstanding Philanthropist St. Louis chpt., Nat. Soc. Fund Raising Execs., 1987; recipient Spirit of Life award City of Hope Labor Mgmt., 1987, St. Louis U. Alumni Merit award, 1987, Meritorious Svc. to Sports award MS Soc., 1987, Presdl. Sports award Maryville Coll., 1987, Sales Exec. of Yr. award Sales and Mktg. Execs. of Met. St. Louis, 1988, St. Louis Port Coun.'s Mgmt. Man of the Yr. award Greater St. Louis Area and Vicinity Port Council, Maritime Trades Dept., AFL-CIO,, 1989. Mem. Alzeimer's Disease and Related Disorders Assn. (hon.), St. Louis Counts, Hawthorn Found., St. Louis Club, Mo. Athletic Club, Old Warson Country Club, Boone Valley Country Club. Office: Engineered Support Systems Inc 1270 N Price Rd Saint Louis MO 63132-2316 Home: 10 Trent Dr Saint Louis MO 63124-1033

SHANAHAN, MICHAEL GEORGE, police officer; b. Seattle, Oct. 14, 1940; s. Raymond Roderick and Carletta (Anderson) S.; m. Jo-Anne Genevieve David, Sept. 16, 1961; children: Patrick, Matthew, Raymond. BA in Psychology, Stanford U., 1962. Asst. police chief U. Wash., Seattle, 1971-75, vol. police cons. and mgmt. pvt. sector issues, 1995—. Mem. law enforcement task force interim mcpl. com. Wash. State Legis., 1970-71, campus law enforcement task force-higher edn. com., 1970-71; co-chmn. Wash. Law Enforcement Standards Task Force; founding chmn. Washington Law Enforcement Exec. Forum, 1981, Operation Bootstrap, 1985, others. Author: Private Enterprise and the Public Police: The Professionalizing Effects of a New Partnership, 1985; contbr. articles to profl. jours. Mem. nat. exploring com. Boy Scouts Am., 1977, exec. bd., chief Seattle council, 1984-88; mem. Blanchet High Sch. Bd., Seattle, 1978-79, Gov.'s Coun. on Criminal Justice, 1980-81, Gov.'s Coun. Food Assistance, 1983-86. Major U.S. Army, 1963-70, Vietnam. Decorated Bronze Star; recipient award for pub. svc. U.S. Dept. Transp., 1984, Humanitarian award Seattle chpt. NCCJ, 1985, Silver Beaver award Boy Scouts Am., 1986, St. Matthew award Northwest Harvest, 1987, Paul J. Breslin award Internat. Security Mgrs. Assn., 1990, Criminal Justice award of excellence Wash. State U., 1989, Service Above Self awd. Rotary Intl., 1998. Mem. FBI Nat. Acad. Assocs., Nat. Inst. Justice (peer rev. program), Internat. Assn. Chiefs of Police (life, bd. officers 1983-84, gen. chmn. divsn. state assns. 1983-84, co-chmn. pvt. sector liaison com.), Police Exec. Rsch. Forum, Wash. Assn. Sheriffs and Police Chiefs, Rotary Internat. (Svc. Above Self award 1998, pres. Univ. Rotary Club Seattle 1985-86, Svc. Above Self award 1988, founding chmn. Rotary Op. First Harvest), Univ. Dist. Club (local award). Roman Catholic. Avocations: fishing, gardening.

SHANAHAN, MIKE, professional football coach; b. Oak Park, Ill., Aug. 24, 1952; m. Peggy, children: Kyle, Krystal. BS Phys. Edn., Eastern Illinois U., Charleston, Ill., 1974; MS Phys. Edn., 1975. Student coach Eastern Illinois U.; asst. coach U. Oklahoma, 1975-76; offensive coord., No. Ariz. U., 1976-77, Ea. Ill. U., 1977-78, U. Minn., 1979-80; offensive coord., U. Fla., 1980-84, asst. head coach, 1983-84; receivers coach Denver Broncos, 1984-87; head coach Los Angeles Raiders, 1988-89; asst. coach Denver Broncos, NFL, 1989-91; offensive coordinator San Francisco 49ers, 1992-94; head coach Denver Broncos, 1995—. Avocations: golf, travel. Office: Denver Broncos 13655 Broncos Pkwy Englewood CO 80112-4150

SHANAHAN, SHEILA ANN, pediatrician, educator; m. Justin Laurence Cashman Jr., Sept. 14, 1968; children: Justin III, Gillis. BA, Trinity Coll., 1963; MD cum laude, Med. Coll. Pa., 1969. Diplomate Nat. Bd. Med. Examiners, Am. Bd. Pediats. Intern Presbyn. Hosp., N.Y.C., 1969-70, resident in pediats., 1970-72, asst. in clin. pediats., 1972-75, assoc. clin. pediats., 1975-78; pvt. practice specializing in pediats. Greenwich, Conn., 1972-78; asst. attending Greenwich Hosp., 1972-73, assoc. attending, 1973-78; from instr. to assoc. Columbia Coll. Physicians and Surgeons, N.Y.C., 1972-78; asst. prof. pediats. George Washington U. Sch. Medicine, Washington, 1980—, Georgetown U. Sch. Medicine, Washington, 1984—; pvt. practice specializing in pediats. Washington, 1984—. Attending dept. ambulatory medicine Children's Hosp. Nat. Med. Ctr., Washington, 1980-84; courtesy staff Georgetown U. Hosp., Washington, 1984—, George Washington U. Hosp., 1984—, Sibley Meml. Hosp., Washington, 1984—, Columbia Hosp. for Women, 1984-2002, Children's Hosp. Nat. Med. Ctr., 1984—. Fellow Am. Acad. Pediats.; mem. Am. Women's Med. Assn. Office: 4900 Massachusetts Ave NW Washington DC 20016-4358

SHANAHAN, THOMAS M. judge; b. Omaha, May 5, 1934; m. Jane Estelle Lodge, Aug. 4, 1956; children: Catherine, Thomas M. II, Mary Elizabeth, Timothy F. AB magna cum laude, U. Notre Dame, 1956; JD, Georgetown U., 1959. Bar: Nebr., Wyo. Mem. McGinley, Lane, Mueller, Shanahan, O'Donnell & Merritt, Ogallala, Nebr.; assoc. justice Nebr. Supreme Ct., Lincoln, 1983-93; judge U.S. Dist. Ct. Nebr., Omaha, 1993—. Office: US Dist Ct 111 S 18th Plz Ste 3141 Omaha NE 68102

SHANAHAN, WILLIAM STEPHEN, consumer products company executive; b. Cin., Apr. 15, 1940; s. William Stephen and Dorothea (Murken) S.; children: Kimberly, Michael Erika, Alejandra. BA, Dartmouth Coll., 1962; postgrad., U. Calif.-Berkeley, 1962-63, Internat. Christian U., Tokyo, 1963-64, U. Philippines-Manila, 1964-65. Joined Colgate-Palmolive Co., 1965, pres., gen. mgr., 1972-76, v.p. mktg. services div. Colgate U.S.A. N.Y.C., 1976-78; pres., CEO Helena Rubinstein, N.Y.C., 1978-80; v.p. western hemisphere, group v.p. Colgate-Palmolive Co., N.Y.C., sr. exec. v.p. ops., until 1989, chief oper. officer, 1989-2000, pres., 2000—. Office: Colgate-Palmolive Co 300 Park Ave New York NY 10022-7402

SHANAS, ETHEL, sociology educator; b. Chgo., Sept. 6, 1914; d. Alex and Rebecca (Rich) S.; m. Lester J. Perlman, May 17, 1940; 1 child, Michael Stephen AB, U. Chgo., 1935, AM, 1937, PhD, 1949; LHD (hon.), Hunter Coll., N.Y.C., 1985. Instr. human devel. U. Chgo., 1947-52, rsch. assoc. prof., 1961-65; sr. rsch. analyst City of Chgo., 1952-53; sr. study dir. Nat. Opinion Rsch. Ctr., Chgo., 1956-61; prof. sociology U. Ill., Chgo., 1965-82, prof. emerita, 1982—. Vice chmn. expert com. on aging UN, 1974; mem. com. on aging NRC, Washington, 1978-82, panel on statistics for an aging population, 1984-86; mem. U.S. Com. on Vital and Health Stats., Washington, 1976-79. Author: The Health of Older People, 1962; (with others) Old People in Three Industrial Societies, 1968; editor: (with others) Handbook of Aging and the Social Sciences, 1976, 2d edit., 1985 Bd. govs. Chgo. Heart Assn., 1972-80; mem. adv. council on aging City of Chgo., 1972-78 Keston lectr. U. So. Calif., 1975; recipient Burgess award Nat. Council on Family Relations, 1978; Disting. Chgo. Gerontologist award Assn. for Gerontology in Higher Edn., 1988. Fellow: Am. Sociol. Assn. (chmn. sect. on aging 1985—86, Disting. Scholar award 1987), Gerontol. Soc. Am. (pres. 1974—75, Kleemeier award 1977, Brookdale award 1981); mem.: Inst. Medicine of NAS, Midwest Sociol. Soc. (pres. 1980—81). Home: 222 Main St Evanston IL 60202-2488

SHANDLER, GEOFF, publishing executive; b. N.Mex. Student, Yale U., Harvard U. Editl. asst. Random Ho., 1993—97; sr. editor Pub. Affairs, 1997—2000; exec. editor Little Brown & Co., Time Warner, N.Y.C., 2000—04, editor-in-chief, 2004—. Office: Little Brown & Co 1271 Ave of Ams New York NY 10020*

SHANDLING, GARRY, comedian, scriptwriter, actor; b. Chgo., Nov. 29, 1949; s. Irving and Muriel S. BA in Marketing, U. Ariz. TV screenwriter: Sanford and Son, Welcome Back Kotter, Three's Company; guest host The Tonight Show, 1986-88; host Emmy Awards 1987, 88, Grammy Awards 1990, 91, 92; writer, prodr. (comedy specials) Garry Shandling: Alone in Las Vegas, 1984; exec. prodr., writer (comedy specials) It's Garry Shandling's Show 25th Anniversay Special, 1986, (TV Series) It's Garry Shandling's Show, 1986-90 (CableACE award best comedy series 1989, 90, CableACE award best actor in a comedy series, 1990), Garry Shandling: Stand-Up, 1991; writer, exec. prodr., dir. (TV Series) The Larry Sanders Show, 1992-98 (Emmy award for outstanding writing, 1998, CableACE award writing in a comedy series, 1993, 94, 95, 96, CableACE award best actor in a comedy series, 1995, 96); actor (films) Love Affair, 1994, Mixed Nuts, 1994, Doctor Doolittle (voice), 1998, Hurlyburly, 1998, What Planet Are You From? 2000 (also writer, prodr.), Town & Country, 2001, Run Ronnie Run!, 2002, Comedian, 2002. Office: Endeavor Talent Agy 9701 Wilshire Blvd Fl 10 Beverly Hills CA 90212*

SHANDS, GAIL MAXINE, environmental scientist; b. Bklyn., Apr. 10, 1952; d. Leon and Mitzi (Edelman) Shands; m. Miles B. Kessler, Dec. 30, 1973; children: Marc Philip, Jeff Eric. BS, Cornell U., 1973; MS, Purdue U., 1975; MPA, NYU, 1985. Soil scientist USDA-NRCS, Colo., 1976, soil conservationist, 1977; project mgr. U.S. AID, Washington, 1978-82; owner/mgr. Coll. Scholarship Network, Colo., 1988-90; dir. urban edn. project Denver Audubon Soc., 1993-97; owner Gail Shands Assocs., Inc., 1998—. Cons. natural resources, environ. scis., NEPA compliance; reservist Fed. Emergency Mgmt. Agy. Reviewer state environ. edn. master plan Colo. Alliance for Environ. Edn.; vol. denver Russian REsettlement Program, 1992-94, Women's Am. Orgn. for Rehab. and Tng., Denver, 1993—. NYU Acad. scholar, 1982-85. Mem. Am. Soc. Pub. Adminstrn., Am. Soc. Agronomy, Am. Planning Assn. (task force on pub. lands policy 1985). Achievements include participation in initial evaluation of the Senegal River basin development.

SHANDS, WILLIAM RIDLEY, JR., lawyer; b. Richmond, Va., Nov. 23, 1929; s. William Ridley and Josephine (Winston) S.; m. Lynneth Williams, May 31, 1958; children: William Tyler, Laura Sawyer. BA, Hampden-Sydney Coll., 1952; LLB, U. Va., 1958. Bar: Va. 1958. Atty., assoc. Christian, Barton, Epps, Brent & Chappell, Richmond, 1958-61; counsel The Life Ins. Co. of Va., Richmond, 1961-66, asst. gen. counsel, 1966-68, assoc. gen. counsel, 1968-71, gen. counsel, 1971-73, v.p., gen. counsel, 1973-78, sr. v.p., gen. counsel, 1978-79; sr. v.p. law and public affairs Continental Fin. Services Co., Richmond, 1980-85; sr. v.p., sec. Life Ins. Co. Va., Richmond, 1985-88; sr. counsel Sands, Anderson, Marks & Miller, Richmond, 1988-98; ret., 1998. Chmn. Eastern Appeal Bd. Selective Svc. System, 1969; pres., chmn. bd. dirs. Trinity Episcopal High Sch., 1971-72; bd. dirs. Richmond Area Heart Assn., 1965-71, Southampton Cotillion, 1970-72; vestryman St. Michael's Episc. Ch., 1965-68, sr. warden, 1968. Served with AUS, 1952-55, Philippines. Mem. Va. Bar Assn., Richmond Bar Assn., Assn. Life Ins. Counsel (pres. 1987-88), Am. Coun. Life Ins. (chmn. legal sect. 1982 83), Commonwealth Club, Country Club Va. Home: 3811 Darby Dr Midlothian VA 23113-1318

SHANE, DONEA LYNNE, retired nursing educator; b. Jefferson, Iowa, Mar. 5, 1939; m. William D. Shane, Jr., Dec. 30, 1962; children: Craig Lloyd, Lynnea Lee. Diploma, Iowa Meth. Sch. Nursing, 1960; BSN, Calif. State U., Long Beach, 1984; MS in Health Edn., U. N.Mex., 1973, PhD in Ednl. Adminstrn., 1986. RN, N.Mex. Insvc. instr., supr. Bernalillo County Med. Ctr., Albuquerque, 1969-71; dir. health edn. group N.Mex. Regional Med. Program, Albuquerque, 1972-75; coord. RN-BSN nursing students U. N.Mex., Albuquerque, 1975-82, assoc. dean baccalaureate program Coll. Nursing, 1987-96, dean, 1996-97; ret., 1997; exec. dir. N.Mex. Consortium for Nursing Workforce Devel., 1999—. Author: Returning to School: A Guide for Nurses; contbr. articles to profl. publs. Mem. ANA, N.Mex. Nurses Assn. (state pres. 1978-80), Nat. League for Nursing (state pres. 1998-00), Sigma Theta Tau.

SHANE, JEFFREY NEIL, government official, lawyer; b. NYC, Mar. 27, 1941; s. Albert and Ann (Semanoff) S.; m. D. Jean Wu, June 27, 1992. AB, Princeton U., 1962; LLB, Columbia U., N.Y.C., 1965. Bar: D.C. 1966. Trial atty. FPC, Washington, 1966-68, Dept. Transp., Washington, 1968-70, spl. asst. to gen. counsel, 1970-72; traveled in Africa, Europe, 1972-73; researcher Environ. Law Inst., Washington, 1974-75; mem. UN Task Force on Human Environ., Bangkok, 1975-77; atty., cons. environ. law in developing countries, Washington, 1978-79; asst. gen. counsel internat. law Dept. Transp., Washington, 1979-83, dep. asst. sec. policy and internat. affairs, 1983-85, asst. sec. policy and internat. affairs, 1989—93, assoc. dep. sec., 2002—03, under sec. for policy, 2003—; dep. asst. sec. transp. affairs Dept. of State, Washington, 1985-89; counsel Wilmer, Cutler & Pickering, Washington, 1993-96, ptnr., 1997-2000, Hogan & Hartson, Washington, 2000—02. Adj. prof. law Georgetown U., Washington, 1985-89; cons. and lectr. transp. law and policy; mem. Archl. and Transp. Barriers Compliance Bd., 1989-93, vice-chmn., 1992-93; vice chmn. Adv. Com. on Confs. in Ocean Shipping, 1990-91; chmn. commn. on air transport Internat. C. of C., Paris, 1994-2001. Co-author: Developing Economies and the Environment, 1978; co-author-editor: NEPA in Action: The Impact of the National Environmental Policy Act on Federal Decision-Making, 1975, Environmental and Natural Resource Management in Developing Countries, 1979. Recipient Presdl. Meritorious Rank award, 1988. Mem.: ABA (chmn. forum on air and space law 2001), Nat. Defense Transp. Assn. (chmn. mil. airlift com. 1994—2001, air transp. stabilization bd. 2004—), Columbia Country Club (Chevy Chase, Md.), Wings Club (N.Y.C. bd. govs. 1995—98), Internat. Aviation Club (Washington pres. 1999—2000), Aero Club (Washington bd. govs. 1984—86), Cosmos Club (Washington). Home: 5015 Rockwood Pkwy NW Washington DC 20016-1913 Office: Dept Transp 400 7th St NW Washington DC 20590 Office Phone: 202-366-1815. Business E-Mail: joeff.shane@ost.dot.gov.

SHANE, JOHN MARDER, endocrinologist; b. Kansas City, Mo., Oct. 5, 1942; s. Henry Kamsler and Ruth (Marder) S.; m. Eileen Goodart, June 18, 1967; children: Robert M., Edward G. BS, U. Okla., 1964, MD, 1967. Diplomate Am. Bd. Ob-Gyn., Am. Bd. Reproductive Endocrinology; cert. master gardener. Resident Harvard Med. Sch., Boston, 1970-73, fellowship, 1973-75, instr., 1970-75, asst. prof., 1975-78; pvt. practice Tulsa, 1978-99. Lectr., cons. Tutorial Svcs. Internat., England, 1984—; bd. dirs. St. Francies G.I.F.T. Lab., Tulsa; cons. to preimplantation genetics project Chapman Genetics Inst., Children's Med. Ctr., Tulsa. Author: CIBA Symposium Infertility: Diagnosis and Treatment; contbr. articles to profl. jours. and publs.; exhibitions include Okla. Woodturners, The Philbrook Mus. Active Tulsa Garden Ctr., 1988—; bd. dirs. Temple Israel, Tulsa, 1985-86, Up With Trees Found., 2000—, Tulsa, master gardener. Capt. USAF, 1967-69. Recipient Annual award Boston Obstet. Soc., 1977; named one of Best Doctor's in Am., Tulsa's Best Doctors, Tulsa People Mag. Mem. ACS, Tulsa Gynecol. Soc. (past pres. 1986-87), Soc. Reproductive Endocrinologists, Tulsa bonsai Soc. (bd. dirs. 1988—), Am. Coll. Ob-Gyn. (v.p. 1971-92, pres. New England Jr. divsn. 1972-73), Am. Bonsai Soc. (nat. bd. dirs.), Chanie des Rotisseurs (l'Ordre Mondial, Tulsa v.p., Bronze Star 2001), Southside Rotary of Tulsa (bd. dirs., pres. 1997—98, Nat. Arboretum Bonsai Pavillion (nat. bd. dirs.), Rotary Club. Republican. Jewish. Avocations: gardening, bonsai, collector oriental arts, woodturning.

SHANE, LAWRENCE EDWARD, music educator; m. Randi Clein, June 18, 1969; children: Zachary Miles, Dylan Jacob. BM, U. of Miami, 1986—91. Band dir. Coral Shores HS, Key Largo, Fla., 1992—96, Miami Southridge Sr. HS, Miami, Fla., 1996—99, John I. Leonard HS, Lake Worth, Fla., 1999—. Music instr. / cons. Dutch Boy Drum & Bugle Corps, Kitchener, Ontario, Canada, 1992—93, Blue Knights Drum & Bugle Corps, Denver, 1994—2003, Magic of Orlando Drum & Bugle Corps, Orlando, Fla., 2004—. Tee-ball coach West Boynton Little League, Boynton Beach, Fla., 2003. Mem.: Music Educators Nat. Conf., Phi Mu Alpha Sinfonia, Pi Kappa Lambda. Personal E-mail: bbtrpt1@earthlink.net.

SHANE, RITA, opera singer, educator; b. N.Y.C. d. Julius J. and Rebekah (Milner) S.; m. Daniel F. Tritter, June 22, 1958; 1 child, Michael Shane. BA, Barnard Coll., 1958; postgrad., Santa Fe Opera Apprentice Program, 1962-63, Hunter Opera Assn., 1962-64; pvt. study with, Beverly Peck Johnson, Elizabeth Schwartzkopf, Bliss Hebert. Adj. prof. voice Manhattan Sch. of Music, 1993-95. Prof. voice Eastman Sch. Music Rochester U., 1989—, Aspen Music Sch., 1999, Hamamatsu, Japan, 2000—02; pvt. tchr., N.Y.C., 1978—; judge Richard Tucker Music Found., Met. Opera Regional Auditions, Licia Albanese Puccini Found. Performer with numerous opera cos., including profl. debut, Chattanooga Opera, 1964, Met. Opera, San Francisco Opera, N.Y.C. Opera, Chgo. Lyric Opera, San Diego Opera, Santa Fe Opera, Teatro alla Scala, Milan, Italy, Bavarian State Opera, Netherlands Nat. Opera, Geneva Opera, Vienna State Opera, Phila., New Orleans, Balt. Opera, Opera du Rhin, Strasbourg, Scottish Opera, Teatro Reggio, Turin, Opera Metropolitana, Caracas, Portland Opera, Minn. Opera, also others; world premiere Miss Havisham's Fire, Argento; Am. premieres include Reimann-Lear, Schat-Houdini, Henze-Elegy for Young Lovers; participant festivals, including Mozart Festival, Lincoln Center, N.Y.C., Munich Festival, Aspen Festival, Handel Soc., Vienna Festival, Salzburg Festival, Munich Festival, Perugia Festival, Festival Canada, Glyndebourne Festival, performed with orchs. including Santa Cecilia, Rome, Austrian Radio, London Philharm., Louisville, Cin., Cleve., Phila., RAI, Naples, Denver, Milw., Israel Philharm., rec. artist, RCA, Columbia, Louisville, Turnabout, Myto labels, also radio and TV. Recipient Martha Baird Rockefeller award, William Matheus Sullivan award. Mem. Am. Guild Mus. Artists, Screen Actors Guild, Nat. Assn. Tchrs. Singing. Office: care Daniel F Tritter 330 W 42nd St New York NY 10036-6902 E-mail: rtritter@earthlink.net.

SHANE, WILLIAM WHITNEY, astronomer; b. Berkeley, Calif., June 3, 1928; s. Charles Donald and Mary Lea (Heger) S.; BA, U. Calif., Berkeley, 1951, postgrad., 1953-58; ScD, Leiden (The Netherlands) U., 1971; m.

Clasina van der Molen, Apr. 22, 1964; children: Johan Jacob, Charles Donald. rsch. assoc. Leiden U., 1961-71, sr. scientist, 1971-79; prof. astronomy, dir. Astron. Inst., Cath. U. Nijmegen, The Netherlands, 1979-88; guest prof. astronomy Leiden U., 1988-93; C.H. Adams fellow Monterey (Calif.) Inst. Rsch. Astronomy, 1994—. With USN, 1951-53. Fellow AAAS; mem. Internat. Astron. Union (commns. 33, 34), Am. Astron. Soc., Astron. Soc. Netherlands, Astron. Soc. of the Pacific, Phi Beta Kappa. Achievements include research on structure and dynamics of galaxies, observational astronomy. Home: 9095 Coker Rd Prunedale CA 93907-1401 Office: Monterey Inst Rsch Astronomy 200 8th St Marina CA 93933-6002 Office Phone: 831-883-1000.

SHANEFIELD, DANIEL JAY, ceramics engineering educator; b. Orange, NJ, Apr. 29, 1930; s. Benjamin and Nan (Leichter) S.; m. Elizabeth Davis, June 28, 1964; children: Alison, Douglas. BS in Chemistry, Yale U., 1952; PhD in Chemistry, Rutgers U., 1962. Sr. project engr. ITT Group, Nutley, NJ, 1962-67; sr. mem. tech. staff AT&T Bell Labs., Princeton, NJ, 1967-86; disting. prof. Rutgers U., New Brunswick, NJ, 1986—. Adv. panel NSF, 1990—; course dir. Ctr. for Profl. Advancement, U.S. and The Netherlands, 1993—; cons., presenter in field. *Dr. Shanefield developed a new ceramic insulator via the "tape casting" process. Over 200 million of these have been made, and there is one in almost every telephone line in the United States. He also invented a method for electroplating less gold than usual on contacts, which resulted in cost reductions for AT&T of eleven million dollars per year. Bell Labs advertised this resource-saving advancement in The New Yorker, the Scientific American, etc. Dr. Shanefield also developed the double-blind audio test for hi-fi components and wrote four cover stories for Stereo Review, etc.* Author: Organic Additives and Ceramic Processing, 1996; co-author: Defects in Gold Plating, 1981, Industrial Electronics for Engineers, Chemists and Technicians, 2000; contbr. 4 chpts. to books, articles to profl. jours.; co-inventor 17 patents; mem. editl. bd. Jour. Am. Ceramic Soc., 1987-99. With U.S. Army, 1952-54, Korea. Fellow Am. Inst. Chemists, Am. Ceramic Soc. (Best Paper award); mem. IEEE (life; chmn. stds. com. 1984-99), Am. Chem. Soc., Ceramic Assn. of N.J. (Man of Yr. award 1996). Republican. Avocations: modifying sports cars, writing audio, stereo articles. Office: Rutgers U Ceramics Engring Dept 607 Taylor Rd Piscataway NJ 08854-8065

SHANK, CHARLES VERNON, science administrator, educator; b. Mt. Holly, N.J., July 12, 1943; s. Augustus Jacob and Lillian (Peterson) S.; m. Brenda Buckhold, June 16, 1969. BS, U. Calif., Berkeley, 1965, MS, PhD, 1969. Mem. tech. staff AT&T Bell Labs., Holmdel, N.J., 1969-76, head quantum physics and electronics dept., 1976-83, dir. Electronics Rsch. Lab., 1983-89; dir. Lawrence Berkeley Lab., faculty mem. chemistry, physics, elec. engring. and computer scis. U. Calif., Berkeley, 1989—. Numerous patents in field. Recipient E. Longstreth medal Franklin Inst., Phila., 1982, Morris E. Leeds award IEEE, 1982, David Sarnoff award IEEE, 1989. R.W. Wood prize. Fellow AAAS, Am. Phys. Soc. (George E. Pake prize 1996, Arthur L. Schawlow prize 1997), Optical Soc. Am. (R. W. Wood prize 1981); mem. NAS, NAE, Am. Acad. Arts and Scis. Home: 9 Ajax Pl Berkeley CA 94708-2119 Office: Lawrence Berkeley Nat Lab Ms 50A 4119 Berkeley CA 94720-0001

SHANK, MAURICE EDWIN, aerospace engineering executive, consultant; b. N.Y.C., Apr. 22, 1921; s. Edwin A. and Viola (Lewis) S.; m. Virginia Lee King, Sept. 25, 1948; children: Christopher K., Hilary L. Shank-Kuhl, Diana L. Shank. BS in Mech. Engring., Carnegie-Mellon U., 1942; D.Sc., MIT, 1949. Registered profl. engr., Mass. Assoc. prof. mech. engring. MIT, Cambridge, 1949-60; dir. advanced materials R&D Pratt & Whitney, East Hartford, Conn., 1960-70; mgr. materials engring. and rsch., 1971-72; dir. engring. tech., 1972-80; dir. engine design and structures engring. Pratt & Whitney, East Hartford, Conn., 1980-81, dir. engring. tech., 1981-85, dir. engring. tech. assessment, 1985-86; v.p. Pratt Whitney of China, Inc., East Hartford, 1986-87; pvt. exec. cons. to industry and govt., 1987—. Cons. editor McGraw-Hill Book Co., N.Y.C., 1960-80; adv. com. to mechanics div. Nat. Bur. Standards, Washington, 1964-69; vis. com. dept. mech. engring. Carnegie-Mellon U., Pitts., 1968-78; corp. vis. coms. depts. materials sci. and engring., dept. aeros. and astronautics MIT, 1968-74, 79-92; mem. rsch. and tech. adv. coun. com. on aero. propulsion NASA, Washington, 1973-77, mem. aero. adv. com., 1978-86; mem. aero. and space engring. bd. NRC, 1989-92; lectr. in field. Contbr. articles to profl. jours. Served to maj. U.S. Army Corps. of Engrs., Ordnance Corps, 1942-46, Middle East/North Africa. Fellow AIAA, ASME, AIME, Am. Soc. Metals; mem. Nat. Acad. Engring., Conn. Acad. Sci. and Engring. Clubs: Cosmos. Episcopalian. Avocations: boating; fishing.

SHANK, RUSSELL, librarian, educator; b. Spokane, Wash., Sept. 2, 1925; s. Harry and Sadie S.; m. Doris Louise Hempfer, Nov. 9, 1951 (div.); children: Susan Marie, Peter Michael, Judith Louise. BS, U. Wash., 1946, BA, 1949; MBA, U. Wis., 1952; DrLS, Columbia U., 1966. Reference libr. U. Wash., Seattle, 1949; asst. engring. libr. U. Wis.-Madison, 1949-52; chief pers. Milw. Pub. Libr., 1952; engring.-phys. scis. libr. Columbia U., N.Y.C., 1953-59, sr. lectr., 1964-66, assoc. prof., 1966-67; asst. univ. libr. U. Calif.-Berkeley, 1959-64; dir. sci. libr. N.Y. Met. Reference and Rsch., 1966-68; dir. librs. Smithsonian Instn., Washington, 1967-77; univ. libr. prof. UCLA, 1977-89, asst. vice chancellor for libr. and info. svcs. planning, 1989-91, univ. libr., prof. emeritus, 1991—. Cons. Indonesian Inst. Sci., 1970; bd. cons. Pahlavi Nat. Library, Iran, 1975-76; pres. U.S. Book Exchange, 1975; bd. trustees Freedom to Read Found., 1989—. Trustee OCLC, Inc., 1978-84, 87, chmn., 1984; mem. library del. People's Republic of China, 1979; bd. dirs. Am. Council on Edn., 1980-81. Served with USNR, 1943-46. Recipient Disting. Alumnus award U. Wash. Sch. Librarianship, 1968, Role of Honor award Freedom to Read Found., 1990, Disting. Alumnus award Columbia U. Sch. Libr. Sci., 1992; fellow Coun. on Libr. Resources, 1973-74. Fellow AAAS; mem. ALA (pres. 1978-79, coun. 1961-65, 74-82, exec. bd. 1975-80, chmn. internat. rels. com. 1980-83, pres. info. sci. and automation div. 1968-69), Assn. Coll. and Rsch. Librs. (pres. 1972-73, Hugh Atkinson award 1990), Assn. Rsch. Librs. (bd. dirs. 1974-77), Beta Phi Mu. Home: 12919 Montana Ave Apt 101 Los Angeles CA 90049-4843 E-mail: RShank@ucla.edu. *Intellectual freedom is the paramount human right. It is the American's premier heritage. Without it the claim to democracy is a sham. Should the principles of our society fade or perish, the survival of this freedom alone would justify the nation's experience. The freedom to think, to read, and to speak will be our enduring monument. Their diffusion throughout the world must be our unending crusade.*

SHANK, SUZANNE ADAMS, lawyer; b. Kansas City, Mo., Nov. 13, 1946; d. Howard Howe and Bettie Ann (Winkler) Hettick; m. Martin Smoler, May 18, 1991. BJ, U. Mo., 1972; MPA in Health Adminstrn., JD, U. Mo., Kansas City, 1982. Bar: Mo. 1982, U.S. Dist. Ct. (we. dist.) Mo. 1982. Journalist U. Kans. Med. Ctr., Kansas City, 1972-73; asst. editor Am. Family Physician, Kansas City, Mo., 1973-75; exec. dir. Lambert Med. Clinic, Kansas City, Mo., 1975-80; assoc. Shughart, Thomson & Kilroy, Kansas City, 1982-85; v.p. GE/Employers Reins. Corp., Overland Park, Kans., 1985-2000; sr. v.p. Attys. Liability Assurance Soc., Chgo., 2000—. Mem. Friends of Zoo, Kansas City, Mo., 1981—, Menorah Med. Ctr. Aux., Kansas City, 1982—, Women's Vision Internat., Kansas City, Mo., 1999—; mem. Internat. Rels. Coun., 1999—; bd. dirs. Friends Conservatory Music, Kansas City, 2002—, Found. on Aging, Kansas City, 2003—. Mem. ABA, Mo. Bar Assn., Kansas City Bar Assn. (chmn. ins. law com.), Soc. Profl. Journalists, Soc. CPCU (rsch. com.), Com. to Protect Journalists, Kappa Tau alpha. Home: 2703 W 66th Ter Shawnee Mission KS 66208-1810 Office: Attorneys Liability Assurance Soc 311 S Wacker 5700 Chicago IL 60606

SHANK, WILLIAM O. lawyer; b. Hamilton, Ohio, Jan. 11, 1924; s. Horace Cooper and Bonnie (Winn) S.; m. Shirleen Allison, June 25, 1949; children—Allison Kay, Kristin Elizabeth. BA, Miami U., Oxford, Ohio, 1947; JD, Yale, 1950. Bar: Ohio, Ill., U.S. Supreme Ct. Pvt. practice, Hamilton, Ohio, 1951-55, Chgo., 1955—; mem. firm Shank, Briede & Spoerl, Hamilton, Ohio, 1951-55; assoc. Lord, Bissell & Brook, Chgo., 1955-58; atty. Chemetron Corp., 1958-60, sr. atty., 1960-61, gen. atty., asst. sec., 1961-71, sec., gen. counsel, 1971-78; v.p., gen. counsel, sec. Walgreen Co., Deerfield, Ill., 1978-89; ptnr. Burditt & Radzius, Chartered, Chgo., 1989-98; exec. v.p. Internat. Bus. Resources, Inc., Chgo., 1993—2000; ptnr. Williams Montgomery & John Ltd., Chgo., 1998—2003; of counsel Hinshaw & Culbertson, Crystal Lake, Ill., 2003—. Mem. bus. adv. coun. Miami U., Oxford, Ohio, 1975—; arbitrator 19th Jud. Cir., Ill., 1995—; adv. bd. eLawForum, Washington, 1999—. Bd. dirs. Coun. for Cmty. Svcs. Met. Chgo., 1973-77; trustee Libr. Internat. Rels., 1971-78; bd. dirs. Chgo. Civic Fedn., 1984-89, Walgreen Drug Stores Hist. Found., 1990—; mem. Chgo. Crime Commn., 1985-89. 1st lt., pilot 8th Air Force, USAAF, World War II, ETO. Fellow Am. Bar Found. (life); mem. ABA (com. corp. gen. counsel), Ill. State Bar Assn., Chgo. Bar Assn. (chmn. com. on corp. law depts. 1971-72, 89-90), Am. Soc. Corp. Secs. (pres. Chgo. regional group 1983-84, nat. bd. dirs. 1984-87), Yale U. Law Sch. Assn. (past pres. Ill. Alumni, exec. com. New Haven), Walgreen Alumni Assn. (pres. 1992-94), Legal Club (pres. 1979-80), Law Club, Lawyers Club (Chgo.), Univ. Club, Econ. Club, Yale Club of Chgo., Omicron Delta Kappa, Phi Delta Phi, Sigma Chi. Home: 755 S Shore Dr Crystal Lake IL 60014-5530 Office: Hinshaw & Culbertson 453 Coventry Ln Crystal Lake IL 60014 E-mail: wshank@hinshawlaw.com.

SHANKAR, GAUTHAM, associate, financial services & sales trader; b. Mumbai, Maharashtra, India, Sept. 6, 1974; s. A.G. Shankar, Lalitha Shankar. Bachelor of Pharmacy (Honors), Birla Institute of Technology & Science, Pilani, Pilani, Rajasthan, India 333031, 1992—96; Master of Business Administration, Pennsylvania State University, Smeal College of Business, State College, PA, 1996—98. Consultant i2 Technologies Inc., Dallas, 1998—2000; Associate Goldman, Sachs & Co., New York, NY, 2000—02; v.p. Soundview Tech. Group, Conn., 2003—. Author: (Publication) Impact of GATT on Indian Pharmaceutical Markets, 1996. Mem.: Penn State Alumni Association (Member 1998—2002).

SHANKAR, RAVI, musician, sitar player, composer; b. Apr. 7, 1920; m. Sukanya Rajan; children: Shubho, Geetali, Anoushka. Studied under, Ustad Allauddin Khan of Maihar; trained in Guru-Shishya tradition, pupil of Ustad Allauddin Khan, 1938. Solo sitar player; former dir. music All India Radio, also founder Nat. Orch.; founder, dir. Kinnara Sch. Music, Bombay, 1962, Kinnara Sch. Music, L.A., 1967; many recordings of traditional and exptl. variety in India, U.K., U.S., including Tana Mana, 1987; concert tours in Europe, U.S., The East; vis. lectr. U. Calif., 1965; appeared in film Raga, 1974; fellow Sangeet Natak Akademi, 1976; responsible for music and choreography for ASIAD, 1982; film scores: Pather Panchali, The Flute and the Arrow, Nava Rasa Ranga, Charly, Gandhi, and many musical compositions including Concerto for Sitar No. 1, 1971, No. 2, 1981, Ghanashyam, 1989, and numerous ragas and talas; author: My Music, My Life, 1969, Rag Anurag (Bengali), (autobiography) Raga Mala, 1997. Recipient Deshikottam award, 1982; Silver Bear of Berlin; award of Indian Nat. Acad. Music, Dance and Drama, 1962; award of Padma Bhushan, 1967, Padma Vibushan, 1981, Internat. Music Coun. UNESCO award, 1975; elected to the Rajya Sabha, India, 1986; recipient 16 hon. doctorates around the world; recipient Grand prize Fukuoka Asian Cultural Prizes, Japan, 1991, Ramon Magsaysay award, The Philippines, 1992, Bharatiya Vidya Bhavan Mahatma Gandhi award, 1992, U.K. Ho. of Commons Shield, 1995, Crystal award, Switzerland, 1995, Premium Imperial Arts award, Japan, 1997, Light of Asia award, U.S., 1997, Juliet Hollister award, U.S., 1998, The Polar Music prize, Sweden, 1998, Bharat Ratna, India, 1999, Hon. KBE, 2000; named Commdr. of Legion of Honour, France, 2000. Address: care Sulivan Sweetland 28 Albion St London W2 2AX England

SHANKAR, VENKY N. transportation engineer, educator; arrived in U.S., 1988; s. Subramaniam and Shyamala Venkataraman; life ptnr. Angela R. Linse. PhD, U. Wash., Seattle, 1997. Profl. engr., Bd. of Engrs. and Land Surveyors, 1994. Pvt. practice cons., Seattle and Bellevue, 1989—96; rsch. engr. Wash. State Dept. of Transp., Olympia, 1996—99; asst. prof. U. Wash., Seattle, 1999—2004; assoc. prof. Penn State U., 2004—. Expert witness, Seattle, 2003—03; cons. to law firms, Seattle; vis. prof. Nagoya Found. Mem.: Inst. of Transp. Engrs. Achievements include research in Nagoya Found. Promotion of Sci. Office: U WA 133C Box 352700 More Hall Seattle WA 98195 Personal E-mail: vns_puli@yahoo.com. E-mail: vns@u.washington.edu.

SHANKEL, DELBERT MERRILL, microbiologist, biologist, educator; b. Plainview, Nebr., Aug. 4, 1927; s. Cecil Wilfred and Gladys Dalton (Dodd) Shankel; m. Carol Jo Mulford, Sept. 10, 1962; children: Merrill, Jill, Kelley. BA, Walla Walla Coll., 1950; PhD, U. Tex., 1959. Tchr. Walla Walla Coll. Acad., College Place, Wash., 1950-51; instr. San Antonio Coll., 1954-55; asst. prof., assoc. prof. microbiology and biology U. Kans., Lawrence, 1959-68, prof., 1968—, asst. dean, assoc. dean arts and sci., 1966-72, acting dean, 1973, exec. vice chancellor, 1974-80, 86, 90-92, acting chancellor, 1980-81, chancellor, 1994-95, chancellor emeritus, 1996. Cons., evaluator N. Ctrl. Assn. Colls. and Schs., Chgo., 1969—96, commr., 1991—95. Editor: Atimutagenesis and Anticarcinogenesis: Mechanisms, Vols. I-III, 1986, 1993; assoc. editor: Mutation Rsch., 1992—95. Active numerous civic orgns. With U.S. Army, 1952—54. Named Disting. Alumnus of the Yr., Walla Walla Coll., 1989; recipient Outstanding Educator award, Mortar Bd., U. Kans., 1982, 1985, 1990; numerous rsch. grantee. Fellow: Am. Acad. Microbiology; mem.: Radiation Rsch. Soc., Soc. Gen. Microbiology (Eng.), Genetics Soc. Am., Environ. Mutagen Soc. (chmn. pub. policy com. 1991—93, mem. nat. coun. 1994—97), Am. Soc. Microbiology (past chmn. edn. com., chmn. numerous coms.), Kans. Alumni Assn. (interim pres.and CEO 2004—), U. Kans. Alumni Assn. (interim pres., CEO 2004), Sigma Xi (pres. U. Kans. chpt. 1967). Republican. Unitarian Universalist. Avocations: sports, music, theater, reading. Office: U Kans 1002 Haworth Hl Lawrence KS 66045-0001 Office Phone: 785-864-3150. Business E-Mail: shankel@ku.edu.

SHANKLIN, CAROL W. dietician; BS in Home Econs. Edn., U. Tenn., Martin, 1973; MS in Food Sys. Adminstrn., U. Tenn., Knoxville, 1974, PhD in Food Sys. Adminstrn., 1976. Asst. prof. foods and nutrition Tex. Tech. U., 1977—78; asst. food svc. dir. Highland Hosp., Lubbock, Tex., 1978; asst. prof. food sys. mgmt. Tex. Women's U., 1978—82, assoc. prof. food sys. mgmt., 1982—88, assoc. prof., chair Dept. Nutrition and Food Scis., 1985—87, prof., chair Dept. Nutrition and Food Scis., 1987—90; tech. advisor, cons. Miss. Inst. Higher Learning, 1988—89; grad. program dir., prof. dept. hotel, restaurant, instn. mgmt. and dietetics Kans. State U., Manhattan, 1990—2001, asst. dean. grad. sch., prof. dept. hotel, restaurant, instn. mgmt. and dietetics, 2001—. Contbr. articles to profl. jours. Recipient Michael Olsen Rsch. Achievement award, U. Del. Mem.: Am. Dietetic Assn. (Medallion award 2001). Achievements include research in on environmental issues in the foodservice and hospitality industry; dietetics and hospitality education; quality service in foodservice operations; and foodservice management, food safety and nutrition in foodservice operations. Office: Kansas State U Graduate Sch 103 Fairchild Manhattan KS 66502-1404 Office Phone: 785-532-7927. Business E-Mail: shanklin@ksu.edu.

SHANKLIN, CAROL WILLIAMS, academic administrator, researcher; b. Dyersburg, Tenn., Jan. 13, 1952; d. Marion Fisher and Martha Doris Williams; m. Larry Duane Williams, Mar. 19, 1970; 1 child, William Christopher. PhD, U. of Tenn., 1976, MS, 1974, BS, 1973. Registered Dietitian Commn. on Dietetic Registration, 1976. Prof., hrimd & asst. dean of grad. sch. Kans. State U., Manhattan, Kans., 1990—2003; dept chair and prof. Tex. Woman's U., Denton, Tex., 1985—90. Asst./assoc./prof. Tex. Woman's U., Denton, Tex., 1978—85; asst. prof. Tex. Tech U., Lubbock, Tex., 1977—78. Recipient Medallion award, Am. Dietetic Assn., U. Del. Michael D. Olsen Rsch. Achievement award, 2004. Mem.: Am. Dietetic Assn. (profl. interest del. and chair of rsch. com. 2003—, Mediallion Award 2001). Office: Dept HRIMD Kansas State University 103 Justin Hall Manhattan KS 66506-1404 Office Phone: 785-532-7927. Office Fax: 785-532-5522. E-mail: shanklin@ksu.edu.

SHANKS, ANN ZANE, filmmaker, producer/director, photographer, writer; b. N.Y.C. d. Louis and Sadye (Rosenthal) Kushner; m. Ira Zane (dec.); children— Jennifer, Anthony; m. Robert Horton Shanks, Sept. 25, 1959; 1 child, John. Student, Carnegie-Mellon U., Columbia U., 1949. Tchr., moderator spl. symposiums Mus. Modern Art, N.Y.C.; tchr. New Sch. U. Photographer, writer: for numerous mags. and newspapers; prodr., dir. (movie shorts) Ctrl. Pk., 1969 (U.S. entry Edinburgh Film Festival, Cine Golden Eagle award, Cambodia Film Festival award), Denmark...A Loving Embrace (Cine Golden Eagle award, 1973), Tivoli, 1972—79 (San Francisco Film Festival award, Am. Film Festival award), (TV series) Am. Life Style (Silver award, 5 Gold medal awards Internat. TV and Film Festival N.Y., 2 Cine Golden Eagle awards), He's Fired, She's Hired; prodr.: (CBS TV Drop-Out Mother); prodr., dir., writer (TV short) Mousie Baby; dir.: (TV movie) Drop-Out Father, CBS; prodr.: (plays, video spl.) The Avante-Garde in Russia 1910-1930, Arts and Entertainment channel, ABC Morning Show, Good Afternoon Detroit (Emmy award nomination); prodr., dir. (TV spl.) A Day in the Country, PBS, (Off Broadway play) S.J. Perelman in Person; prodr.: (Broadway plays) Lillian; exhibited (photographs) Mus. Modern Art, Mus. City N.Y., Transit Mus., Bklyn. Heights, N.Y., Met. Mus. Art, Jewish Mus., Howard Greenberg Gallery, N.Y.C., 1999, photographer (one-woman shows) Ann Shanks one-person exhibition, N.Y. Hist. Soc., N.Y.C., 2003—04, (accompanying catalogue (64 pages) "Ann Zane Shanks Behind the Lens", 2003; prodr.: Discovery channel, U.S.; author: (photographs and text) The Name's the Game, New Jewish ency.; author: (photographer, writer) (book) Old is What You Get, Busted Lives..Dialogues with Kids in Jail, 1983; writer, photographer: book Garbage and Stuff; photography (in collections of) Merv Griffin, N.Y. Pub. Libr., Mus. of City of N.Y., Met. Mus., N.Y., others, represented (permanent collections) N.Y. Pub. Libr. Recipient awards from internat. photography competitions. Mem. Am. Soc. Mag. Photographers (bd. govs.), Women in Film (v.p.), Dirs. Guild Am.; trustee Overseas Press Club. *I guess I have "adolescent enthusiasm" for most of my work. It gives me infinite pleasure to be alive and have the chance to take an idea and see it through to its final form on the screen, or on the television set or the theater...savoring all the headaches, joys and the working together— step-by-step. I seek responsibility for my work, my family, and those I love.*

SHANKS, DAVID, publishing executive; Grad, Holy Cross Coll., 1968. V.p., dir. of sales Berkley Pub. Co. (now known as Penguin Putnam Pub. Co.), 1979—82, sr. v.p., dir. of planning ops., 1982—85, sr. v.p., 1985—91, pres., 1991—97, COO, 1997—2001; CEO Penguin Putnam Pub. Co., 2001—. Office: Penguin Group USA Inc 375 Hudson St New York NY 10014

SHANKS, EARL, marketing professional; married; 2 children. BSc, MA in Acctg., U. Ill. CPA AICPA. Mgr. Peat Marwick Mitchell & Co., Chgo.; from dir. tax to v.p., treas. Farley Industries Inc., 1983—96; v.p. The Convergys Corp., Cin., 1996—, treas., 1996—, CFO, 2003—. Office: Convergys Corp 201 E 4th St Cincinnati OH 45202*

SHANKS, EUGENE BAYLIS, JR., banker; BA, Vanderbilt U., 1969; MA, PhD, Stanford U., 1974. With Bankers Trust Co., N.Y.C., 1973—78, 1980—95, pres., dir., 1992-95; pres. NetRisk, Inc., Greenwich, Conn., 1997—2002. Treas. Tenn. Valley Bancorp, 1978—80, Commerce Union Bank, 1978—80. Trustee Vanderbilt U.; bd. dir. Posse Found, IFL, Ltd., Catamount Inv. Gr., AMA, New Power, Inc. Office: NetRisk Inc 500 W putnam Ave Ste 410 Greenwich CT 06830

SHANKS, HERSHEL, editor, writer; b. Sharon, Pa., Mar. 8, 1930; s. Martin and Mildred (Freedman) S.; m. Judith Alexander Weil, Feb. 20, 1966; children: Elizabeth Jean, Julia Emily. BA, Haverford (Pa.) Coll., 1952; MA, Columbia, 1953; LLB, Harvard, 1956. Bar: D.C. 1956. Trial atty. Dept. Justice, 1956-59; pvt. practice Washington, 1959-88; ptnr. Glassie, Pewett, Beebe & Shanks, 1964-88; editor Bibl. Archaeology Rev., Washington, 1975—. Pres. Bibl. Archaeology Soc., 1974—, Jewish Ednl. Ventures Inc., 1987—. Author: The Art and Craft of Judging, 1968, The City of David, 1973, Judaism in Stone, 1979, Jerusalem--An Archaeological Biography, 1995, The Mystery and Meaning of the Dead Sea Scolls, 1998, also articles; co-author: (with Ben Witherington III) The Brother of Jesus, 2003; co-editor: Recent Archaeology in the Land of Israel, 1984; editor: Ancient Israel, A Short History, 1988, revised edit., 1999, Christianity and Rabbinic Judaism, 1992, Understanding the Dead Sea Scrolls, 1992; editor Bible Rev., 1985—, Moment mag., 1987—2004, Archaeology Odyssey, 1998—; contbr. articles to profl. jours. Fellow Royal Asiatic Soc.; mem. ABA, D.C. Bar Assn., Am. Schs. Oriental Rsch., Soc. Bibl. Lit., Cosmos Club, Phi Beta Kappa. Home: 5208 38th St NW Washington DC 20015-1812 Office: Bibl Archaeology Soc 4710 41st St NW Washington DC 20016-1706 E-mail: hshanks@bib-arch.org. *I try to take time to identify what is important in my life, to focus on that and ignore the rest when it conflicts. It takes conscious effort not to dissipate energy on activities and attitudes that don't matter in the big picture of my priorities. Free to concentrate on what I value most, I try to accomplish something each day in a regular, habitual way.*

SHANKS, JUDITH WEIL, editor; b. Montgomery, Ala., Nov. 2, 1941; d. Roman Lee and Charlotte (Alexander) Weil; m. Hershel Shanks, Feb. 20, 1966; children: Elizabeth Shanks Alexander, Julia Emily. BA in Econs., Wellesley Coll., 1963; MBA, Trinity Coll., 1980. Econs. asst. Export-Import Bank, Washington, 1963-68; cons. econs. and social sci., 1968-76; rschr. Time-Life Books, Alexandria, Va., 1976-80, prin. rschr., 1980-83, illustrations editor, 1983, adminstrv. editor, 1984-95, dir. editl. adminstrn., 1996; assoc. curator SC Jewish Heritage Exhibit, Coll. Charleston, 1998—2003. Vol. Mentors, Inc. Recipient Sr. Rsch. award Hadassah Brandeis Inst. Democrat. Jewish. Avocations: dance, scuba diving, hiking, gardening, research on women. Home: Box 42456 Washington DC 20015

SHANKS, KATHRYN MARY, health care administrator; b. Glens Falls, NY, Aug. 4, 1950; d. John Anthony and Lenita (Combs) S. BS summa cum laude, Spring Hill Coll., 1972; MPA, Auburn U., 1976. Program evaluator Mobile (Ala.) Mental Health, 1972-73; dir. spl. projects Ala. Dept. Mental Health, Montgomery, 1973-76; dir. adminstrn. S.W. Ala. Mental Health/Mental Retardation, Andalusia, 1976-78; adminstr. Mobile County Health Dept., 1978-82; exec. dir. Coastal Family Health Ctr., Biloxi, Miss., 1982-95; cons. med. group practice, 1995—; ptnr. Shanks & Allen, Mobile, 1979—; health-care consulting pvt. practice, 1995—; practice dir. USA Health Svcs. Found., 1999—2001; practice mgr. Humana Mil. Healthcare Svcs., 2002—. Cons. S.W. Health Agy., Tylertown, Miss., 1984-86; instr., mgr. dept. pediats. U. South Ala., 1997-99; preceptor Sch. Nursing, U. So. Miss., Hattiesburg, 1983, 84; advisor Headstart Program, Gulfport, Miss., 1984-95; LPN Program, Gulf Coast C.C., 1984-95; lectr. Auburn U., Montgomery, 1977-78. Bd. dirs. Mobile Cmty. Action Agy., 1979-81, Moore Cmty. House; mem. S.W. Ala. Regional Goals Forum, Mobile, 1971-72, Cardiac Rehab. Study Com., Biloxi, Miss., 1983-84, Mothers and Babies Coalition, Jackson, Miss., 1983-95, Gulf Coast Coalition Human Svcs., Biloxi, 1983-95; exec. dir. Year for Miss., 1993-94. Pres.'s scholar, Spring Hill Coll., 1972. Mem. ACLU, Miss. Primary Health Care Assn. (pres.), Med. Group Mgmt. Assn., Soc. for Advancement of Ambulatory Care, Spring Hills Alumni Assn. Avocations: tennis, home restoration, golf.

SHANKS, PATRICIA L. lawyer; b. Salt Lake City, Apr. 3, 1940; BA in Microbiology with honors, Stanford U., 1962; JD, U. Colo., 1978. Bar: Calif. 1978. Mng. ptnr. McCutchen, Doyle, Brown & Enersen, L.A., 1990-94, ptnr., 1985—. Trustee L.A. County Bar Found. Recipient West Publishing award; Stork scholar. Mem. Order of the Coif, Practice in Environ. Law. Office: McCutchen Doyle Brown & Enersen 355 S Grand Ave Ste 4400 Los Angeles CA 90071-3106

SHANKS, SANFORD H. sales executive, writer; b. Brainard, Minn., Sept. 23, 1943; s. Sanford Hugh and Ardyce (Mathison) Shanks; m. Florence Kathryn Colby, Oct. 1, 1965; children: Collin, Adam. BA in Comprehensive Social Studies History emphasis, St. Cloud State Coll., 1965. Tchr. Belview Jr. and Sr. H.S., Minn., 1965—67, Redwood Falls H.S., Minn., 1967; sales mgr. Field Enterprixes, Chgo., 1970—71; sales rep. Gallo Wine Co., Commerce, Calif., 1974—85; store mgr. Clyde Blanchard & Assocs., San Dimas, Calif., 1985—97; sales assoc. Levitz Furniture, San Dimas, 1997—. Author (pen name Sandy Shanks): (novels) The Bode Testament, 2001, Impeachment; contbr. articles also; columnist: newspaper column Hibbing Daily Tribune, 2001—. 1st lt. USMC, 1971—74. Home: 2116 Mardina St West Covina CA 91791 E-mail: fs.shanks@verizon.net.

SHANKS, WILLIAM ENNIS, JR., lawyer; b. Jackson, Miss., Sept. 5, 1950; s. William Ennis and Alice Josephine (Crisler) S.; m. Jean F. Steinschneider, Sept. 7, 1974; children: William E. III, Amanda Catherine. B.A., Harvard U., 1972; J.D. cum laude, Emory U., 1976; LL.M. with highest honors in Taxation, Ala. U., 1979. Bar: Ga. 1976, Ala. 1976. Ptnr. Balch & Bingham, LLP, Birmingham, Ala., 1976—. Bd. dirs. Birmingham Festival Theatre, 1980-88, treas., 1980-84; trustee Creative Montessori Sch., 1995—; bd. dirs. Greystone Outreach Legacy Found., Ala. Leukemia and Lymphoma Soc. Named One of Best Lawyers in Am., 1992—. Mem. Birmingham Estate Planning Coun., Birmingham Employee Benefit Forum, Birmingham Profit Sharing Group, ABA, Summit Club, Exch. Club (bd. dirs. 1984-85, sec. 1985-86, v.p. 1985-86, pres. 1986-87, sec. 2002-04), Harvard Club Birmingham (v.p. 1996-98, 2001—, pres. 1998-2001), Order of Coif. Presbyterian. Home: 4516 Old Leeds Rd Birmingham AL 35213-3304 Office: Balch & Bingham LLP 1901 Sixth Ave S Ste 2600 Birmingham AL 35203-2206 Business E-Mail: wshanks@balch.com.

SHANMAN, JAMES ALAN, lawyer; b. Cin., Aug. 1, 1942; s. Jerome D. and Mildred Louise (Bloch) S.; m. Marilyn Louise Glassman, June 11, 1972; 1 child, Ellen Joan. BS, U. Pa., 1963; JD, Yale U., 1966. Bar: N.Y. 1967, U.S. Ct. Mil. Appeals 1971, U.S. Supreme Ct. 1971, U.S. Ct. Appeals (2d cir.) 1972, U.S. Dist. Ct. (so. and ea. dists.) N.Y. 1972, U.S. Ct. Internat. Trade 1976, U.S. Ct. Appeals (fed. cir.) 1987, U.S. Dist. Ct. (ea. dist.) Mich. 1989, U.S. Ct. Appeals (7th cir.) 1999. Assoc. Cahill Gordon & Reindel, N.Y.C., 1971-74, Freeman, Meade, Wasserman, Sharfman & Schneider, N.Y.C., 1974-76; mem. firm Sharfman, Shanman, Poret & Siviglia, P.C., N.Y.C., 1976-95; ptnr. Camhy Karlinsky & Stein LLP, N.Y.C., 1995-96; mem. firm Sharfman, Siviglia, Poret, Kook, Ross & Shanman, P.C., N.Y.C., 1996-98; ptnr. Edwards & Angell, LLP, N.Y.C., 1998—. Speaker on reins. law topics. Contbr. articles to profl. jours. Capt. USAF, 1966-71. Mem.: ABA, ARIAS.US (cert. arbitrator), Bailliage de Conn., Confrérie de la Chaine des Rôtisseurs, Am. Arbitration Assn. (comml. panel arbitrators 1980—), Assn. of Bar of City of N.Y. (com. ins. law 1985—88, 1990—92, 1998—2001, com. profl. liability ins. 1988—92, com. on assn. ins. plans 1989—), N.Y. State Bar Assn. Office: Edwards & Angell LLP Three Stamford Plz 301 Tresser Blvd Stamford CT 06901 Business E-Mail: jshanman@edwardsangell.com.

SHANMUGAM, GANAPATHY, geologist, researcher; b. Sirkali, Tamilnadu, India, Apr. 23, 1944; came to U.S., 1970; s. Ganapathy Mudaliar and Sambooranam; m. Jean Marie Barham, Aug. 21, 1976. BSc in Geology and Chemistry, Annamalai U., South India, 1965; MSc in Applied Geology, Indian Inst. Tech., Bombay, 1968; MS in geology, Ohio U., 1972; PhD in Geology, U. Tenn., 1978. Rsch. geologist Mobil Exploration & Product Tech. Ctr., Dallas, 1978-82, sr. rsch. geologist, 1982-84, assoc., 1984-85, rsch. assoc., 1985-89, sr. rsch. assoc., 1989-93, assoc. geol. rsch. advisor, 1993-96, geol. scientist, 1996-2000; adj. prof. geology U. Tex., Arlington, 2000—. Conf. chmn. Geol. Soc. London, 1996; debate panelist Am. Assn. Petroleum Geologists, Dallas, 1997. Author: Dimensions and Geometries of Deep-Water Systems, 1998; contbr. over 100 articles to profl. jours. Geology adv. bd. U. Tenn., Knoxville, 1985-89. Recipient Silver medal Indian Inst. Tech., 1968; Penrose grantee Geol. Soc. Am., 1976-78; recipient best Paper award Nigerian Assn. Petroleum Explorationists, 1995. Mem. Soc. Sedimentary Geology (nominating com. 1993), Nat. Geog. Soc., Sigma Gamma Epsilon (v.p. 1976-77). Achievements include questioning of the deep-water turbidite paradigm and advocation of sandy debris flows in forming deep-water petroleum reservoirs. Avocation: photography. Office: U Tex Arlington Dept Geology PO Box 19049 Arlington TX 76019-0001 E-mail: shanshanmugam@aol.com.

SHANNON, ANGELA LYNN, minister; BA, Valparaiso U., 1984; MDiv, Luth. Sch. of Theology at Chgo., 1996. Pastor Augustana Evang. Luth. Ch., Houston, 1997—2000; Shalom Zone Inst. coord. Tex. Ann. Conf. of United Meth. Ch., 2001; adminstrv. support Rothko Chapel, Houston, 2002; summer pastor in residence Friends Congl. Ch., College Station, Tex., 2002; assoc. pastor for mission and outreach Trinity English Luth. Ch., Ft. Wayne, Ind., 2002—. Spkr., presenter in field. Vol. docent Ft. Wayne Children's Zoo; adv. bd. mem. Rotating Cir. of Briget's Pl., Christ Ch. Cathedral, Houston, 2000—02; mem. Ft. Wayne Urban Ministries, 2003, Samaritan Ctr. for Counseling, Ft. Wayne. Democrat. Avocations: travel, reading, handicrafts, activism. Office: Trinity English Luth Ch 405 W Wayne St Fort Wayne IN 46802 Personal E-mail: revangelas@netzero.net. E-mail: pshannon@trinityenglish.org.

SHANNON, BARBARA, dean, nutrition educator; PhD in Nutrition, Purdue U., 1971. Prof. nutrition, dean Coll. Health and Human Devel. Pa. State U., University Park. Achievements include research on application of nutrition principles, behavior change theory and educational methods to the improvement of human dietary habits. Office: Office of Dean Coll Health Pa State Univ 201 Henderson Bldg University Park PA 16802-6501

SHANNON, CAROLYN JEAN, real estate company executive; b. Vincennes, Ind., Nov. 22, 1943; d. Melvin Eugene and Melita Harriet (Bair) Powell; m. Thomas E. Battle III; children: Timothy Carl, Heather Caroline. BA in Telecomms. and Interior Design, Ind. U., 1985. Interior designer Buchanan & Sons Furniture, also Kitchen and Bath Ctr., Bloomington, Ind., 1975-81; also freelance Bloomington, 1975-81; sales mgr. Kittle's Ethan Allen, Bloomington and Indpls., 1981-82; owner, cons. The Profl. Woman, career enhancement seminars, Bloomington, 1982-84; interior designer Interiors, Bloomington, 1984-87; owner Carolyn Shannon Interiors, Bloomington and Chgo., 1987—. Dir. Atlas Galleries, Chgo., 1991—94; exec. dir. Inner Cir. Edn./Realty U., 2000—; v.p. membership Realty U., 2002—. Rep. Local Coun. of Women, owners Bloomington Hosp., 1985—. Mem.: Am. Soc. Interior Designers, NAFE, Real Estate Educators Consortium, Phi Beta Kappa, Golden Key, Phi Delta Kappa (scholarship 1984), Psi Iota Xi. Methodist. Avocations: bridge, travel, tennis, antique collecting and dealing. Home: 10471 W Grandview Dr Columbus IN 47201-8699 E-mail: cjshannon@insightbb.com.

SHANNON, CHRIS, economics professor; BS, U. Kans., 1984—88; PhD, Stanford U., 1988—92. Prof. economics UC Berkeley, 1992—, prof. math., 2002—. Office: UC Berkeley Dept Economics 549 Evans Hall Berkeley CA 94720 Office Phone: 510-643-7283. Home Fax: 510-642-6615; Office Fax: 510-642-6615.

SHANNON, DAVID M. lawyer; b. Gardena, Calif., July 22, 1955; s. William R. Shannon and Delores Ann (Nettleton) DeBenedictis; m. Maureen Michelle Green, Feb. 18, 1978; 1 child, Ryan Edward. BA, Pepperdine U., 1976, JD cum laude, 1985. Law clk. Office of Dist. Atty. County of Ventura, Calif., 1984-85; assoc. Gibson, Dunn & Crutcher, L.A., 1985-87, San Francisco & San Jose, Calif., 1987—. Mem. ABA, Calif. Bar Assn., L.A. County Bar Assn. Avocations: swimming, basketball. Office: Gibson Dunn & Crutcher 50 W San Fernando St San Jose CA 95113-2429

SHANNON, DONALD HAWKINS, retired editor; b. Auburn, Wash., Feb. 1, 1923; s. Ernest Victor and Fern (McConville) S.; m. Sally van Deurs, June 13, 1952; children— John McConville, Susanna Shepard. BA, Stanford, 1944; postgrad., Law Sch., 1946-47. Reporter Brazil Herald, Rio de Janeiro, 1947-48; Reporter UPI, London, 1949-51, Western Reporters, Washington, 1951-53; mem. staff L.A. Times, 1954-92, bur. chief Paris, 1962-65, bur. chief Africa, 1965-66, bur. chief Tokyo, 1966-71; bur. chief UN, NYC, 1971—75, Washington, 1975—92; sr. editor Georgetown and Country, Washington, 1996-99; ret., 1999. Served with AUS, 1944-46, PTO. Mem. Nat. Press Club, Fed. City Club, City Tavern Club, Overseas Press Club (N.Y.C.), Phi Gamma Delta. Address: 1068 30th St NW Washington DC 20007-3822

SHANNON, GLENN A. real estate company executive; BA, Williams Coll.; JD, U. Mich. With Shearman & Sterling LLP, N.Y.C., 1982—94, ptnr., 1990—94; mng. dir. Shorenstein Co., N.Y.C., 1994—2000; pres. Shorenstein Realty Svcs. LP, San Francisco, 2000—. Mem.: Lincoln Ctr. Real Estate and Constrn. Coun. (bd. mem.), Urban Land Inst., Lambda Alpha Internat. Office: Shorenstein Co LLC 49th Fl 555 California St San Francisco CA 94104*

SHANNON, IRIS REED, health consultant; b. Chgo. d. Ira Paul and Iola Sophia Reed. BS in Nursing, Fisk U.-Meharry Med. Coll., 1948; MA, U. Chgo., 1954; PhD, U. Ill., Chgo., 1987; D in Pub. Svc. (hon.), Elmhurst Coll., 1993. Staff nurse Chgo. Bd. Health, 1948-50; instr. pub. health nursing Meharry Med. Coll., Nashville, 1951-56; tchr.-nurse, health coordinator child devel. Head Start, Chgo. Bd. Edn., 1957-66; dir. community nursing Mile Sq. Neighborhood Health Center, Presbyn.-St. Luke's Hosp., Chgo., 1966-69; co-dir. nurse assoc. programs Rush Presbyn.-St. Luke's Hosp., 1971-76; chairperson community nursing Rush U., Chgo., 1972-77, acting chairperson, 1988-90; asst. prof. pub. health nursing U. Ill., 1971-74; assoc. prof. cmty. nursing Rush U., 1974-97, health sys. mgr., 1988—, health cons., 1974—. Adj. faculty Sch. Pub. Health, U. N.C., 1977—85; mem. profl. adv. bd. Vis. Nurse Assn. Chgo., 1973—75; cons. Video Nursing, Inc., 1977—; mem. profl. adv. com. Mile Sq. Home Health Unit, Chgo., 1975—77; mem. nat. adv. coun. on nurse tng. HEW, 1978—81; mem. Nat. Task Force on Credentialing in Nursing, 1979—82; mem. Chgo. regional com. Ill. White House Conf. on Children, 1979—80; v.p. Chgo. Bd. Health, 1989—99. Named Prin. for a Day, Brownell Elem. Sch., Mayor's Office, City of Chgo., 1998—99, Englewood Tech. Prep. Acad., 2000—01; recipient award of merit, Ill. Pub. Health Assn., 1979, 1989—2000, Outstanding Achievement award, YWCA of Met. Chgo., 1988, Disting. Svc. award, Chgo. chpt. Meharry Alumni, 1989, Lowenberg Chair of Excellence in Nursing, Memphis State U., 1993, Bd. Trustees' Svc. medal, Rush-Presby. St. Luke's Med. Ctr., 1996, Lifeline award, Cmty. Mental Health Coun., 2002. Fellow: APHA (chmn. pub. health nursing sect. 1977—79, governing coun. 1980—82, exec. bd. 1985—87, pres. 1988—89, governing coun. 1989—99), Am. Acad. Nursing, Royal Soc. Health (hon. 1989); mem.: ANA (Pearl McIver Pub. Health Nurse award 1998), Inst. of Medicine of NAS, Delta Sigma Theta, Sigma Theta Tau. Home: 3100 S King Dr Chicago IL 60616-3634 Office Phone: 312-842-6164. E-mail: irisshannon@aol.com.

SHANNON, JACQUELINE, association executive; married; 2 children. MA in Edn., Angelo State U.; postgrad., Villanova U. Formerly tchr. English and reading; pres. nat. bd. dirs. Nat. Alliance for the Mentally Ill, 1998—. A founder Concho Valley (Tex.) affil. chpt. Nat. Alliance for the Mentally Ill, 1980s, pres. Tex. bd. dirs. Recipient Helen Farabee Wings award Tex. Dept. Mental Health/Mental Retardation, 1995, Friend of Counseling award Three River Counseling Assn., 1995, others. Office: Nat Alliance Mentally Ill 2107 Wilson Blvd Ste 300 Arlington VA 22201-3042

SHANNON, JOE, JR., lawyer; b. Nov. 9, 1940; s. Joe and Juanita Elizabeth (Milliorn) S.; children: Kelley Jane, Joseph Patrick, Shelley Carol. BA, U. Tex., 1962, LLB, 1963. Bar: Tex. 1963, U.S. Supreme Ct. 1977, U.S. Dist. Ct. (no. dist.) Tex. 1970, U.S. Ct. Appeals (5th cir.) 1977, U.S. Dist. Ct. (we. dist.) 1998; cert. family law Tex. Bd. Legal Specialization, matrimonial arbitrator. Ptnr. Shannon & Shannon, Ft. Worth, 1963-72; adminstrv. asst. to spkr. Tex. Ho. of Reps., Austin, 1970; chief criminal div. Tarrant County Dist. Atty., Ft. Worth, 1972-78; pvt. practice Ft. Worth, 1978-99; ptnr. Snakard & Gambill, Ft. Worth, 1986-90; chief econ. crimes Tarrant County Dist. Atty., 1999—. Adj. prof. Tex. Weslyan Sch. Law. Mem. Tex. Ho. of Reps., 1964-70. Fellow Tex. Bar Found., Am. Acad. Matrimonial Lawyers (cert.); mem. ABA, State Bar of Tex. (adv. com. family law, state bd. legal specialization 1985-99, dist. grievance com. 1973-76, chmn. 1975-76, 95—, sec. 2d ct. appeals adv. com. 1995—), Tarrant County Family Law Bar Assn. (pres. 1998), Tarrant County Bar Assn. (dir. 1999-2001, sec. treas. 2002, 2d v.p. 2003, pres.-elect, 2003, pres. 2004), Phi Alpha Delta, Masons, Shriners. Office: 401 W Belknap Fort Worth TX 76196 Office Phone: 817-884-1661. E-mail: joelaw@atsweb.net. *Notable cases include: State vs. Cullen Davis, 1977, richest man to be tried for murder; State vs. Mutscher, bribery conspiracy trial of Tex. House Speaker and assocs.*

SHANNON, JOHN SANFORD, lawyer, retired railway executive; b. Tampa, Fla., Feb. 8, 1931; s. George Thomas and Ruth Evangeline (Garrett) S.; m. Elizabeth Howe, Sept. 22, 1962; children: Scott Howe, Elizabeth Garrett, Sandra Denison. AB, Roanoke Coll., 1952; JD, U. Va., 1955. Bar: Va. 1955. Assoc. Hunton Williams Gay Powell & Gibson, Richmond, Va., 1955-56; solicitor Norfolk & Western Ry., Roanoke, Va., 1956-60, asst. gen. solicitor, 1960-64, gen. atty., 1964-65, gen. solicitor, 1965-68, gen. counsel, 1968-69, v.p. law, 1969-80, sr. v.p. law, 1980-82; exec. v.p. law Norfolk (Va.) So. Corp., 1982-96, ret., 1996. Bd. dirs. Norfolk So. Ry. Co., Pocahontas Land Corp., Va. Holding Corp., Norfolk and Western Ry. Co. Editor-in-chief: Va. Law Rev, 1954-55. Chancellor Episcopal Diocese Southwestern Va., 1974-82; pres. bd. trustees North Cross Sch., Roanoke, 1973-82; trustee, past chmn. exec. com. Roanoke Coll., Salem, Va.; bd. dirs. Legal Aid Soc., Roanoke Valley, 1969-80, pres., 1970-79; trustee Chrysler Mus., Norfolk, 1982-94, Norfolk Acad., 1987-99. Mem. Va. Bar Assn., Norfolk and Portsmouth Bar Assn., Shenandoah Club, Roanoke Country Club, Norfolk Yacht and Country Club, Order of Coif, Sigma Xi, Omicron Delta Kappa, Phi Delta Phi. Home: 7633 Argyle Ave Norfolk VA 23505-1701

SHANNON, KYLE, Internet company executive; Founder Urban Desires, World Wide Web Artists Consortium; co-founder Agency.com, 1995, chief creative officer, 1995-2000, chief people officer. Office: Agency dot com 20 Exchange Pl New York NY 10005-3201

SHANNON, LARRY REDDING, public relations executive; b. St. Joseph, Mo., Apr. 5, 1949; s. Charles R. Jr. and Dorothy May (Dunham) Redding. Student, U. Tex., Arlington, 1967-69. Announcer Sta. KVIL, Dallas, 1968, Sta. KFJZ, Ft. Worth and Dallas, 1968-78; pvt. practice pub. rels. and advt., Ft. Worth, 1978-85; pvt. practice pub. rels., advt. and mgmt., N.Y.C., 1985-86; adminstrv. asst. to former spkr. Jim Wright, U.S. Ho. of Reps., Ft. Worth, 1986-97; dir. investor comm. Arch Petroleum Inc., Ft. Worth, 1998—. Pres. First Strategy Corp.; bd. dirs., founder Tex. Radio Hall of Fame. Democrat. Avocations: reading, travel. Office: PO Box 123694 Fort Worth TX 76121-3694

SHANNON, LYLE WILLIAM, sociology educator; b. Storm Lake, Iowa, Sept. 19, 1920; s. Bert Book and Amy Irene (Sivits) S.; m. Magdaline W. Shannon, Feb. 27, 1943 (dec. Sept. 2001); children: Mary Shannon Will, Robert William, John Thomas, Susan Michelle. BA, Cornell Coll., Mount Vernon, Iowa, 1942; MA, U. Wash., 1947, PhD, 1951. Acting instr. U. Wash., 1950-52; mem. faculty dept. sociology U. Wis., Madison, 1952-62, assoc. prof., 1958-62; prof. sociology U. Iowa, Iowa City, 1962—, chmn. dept. sociology and anthropology, 1962-70, dir. Iowa Urban Cmty. Rsch. Ctr., 1970-91, dir. emeritus, 1991—, prof. emeritus, 1991—. Vis. prof. Portland State U., Wayne State U., U. Wyo., U. Colo. Author: Underdeveloped Areas, 1957, Minority Migrants in the Urban Community, 1973, Criminal Career Continuity: Its Social Context, 1988, Changing Patterns of Delinquency and Crime: A Longitudinal Study in Racine, 1991, Developing Areas, 1995, Socks and Cretin: Two Democats Helping Bill with the Presidency, 1995, Alcohol and Drugs, Delinquency and Crime, 1998; editor: Social Ecology of the Community series, 1974-76. With USNR, 1942-46. Mem. AAAS, Am. Sociol. Assn., Midwest Sociol. Soc., Population Assn. Am., Soc. Applied Anthropology, Am. Soc. Criminology, Kiwanis, Phi Beta Kappa. Democrat. Home: River Heights Iowa City IA 52240-9147 Office: Univ Iowa Dept Sociology W140 Seashore Hall Iowa City IA 52242-1407 Office Phone: 319-335-2525.

SHANNON, MALCOLM LLOYD, JR., lawyer; b. Phila., 1946; m. Jeanne Marie Halle, 1974; children: Travis Alan, Kate Meredith. BBA, U. N.Mex., 1968, JD, 1971. Bar: N.Mex. 1971, U.S. Supreme Ct. 1976, Tex. 1981, Colo. 1984, Calif. 1986. Counsel Gen. Atomics, 1991—. Lectr. mining and pub. land law U. N.Mex. Adv. com. solar energy application Tech. Vocat. Inst. of Albuquerque Pub. Schs., 1976; judge N.Mex. State Sci. Fair 1978-80; mem. ednl. accountability com. Cherry Creek Sch. Dist., 1984-86; bd. dirs. Denver U./Pioneer Jr. Hockey Assn., 1991-94. Author publs. in field. Mem. ABA, Am. Corp. Counsel Assn. Republican. Roman Catholic. Office: 7800 E Dorado Pl Ste 200 Englewood CO 80111

SHANNON, MARGARET ANNE, lawyer; b. Detroit, July 6, 1945; d. Johannes Jacob and Vera Marie (Spade) Van De Graaf; m. Robert Selby Shannon, Feb. 4, 1967. Student, Brown U., 1963-65; BA in History, Wayne State U., 1966, JD, 1973. Bar: Mich. 1973. Housing aide City of Detroit, 1967-68; employment supr. Sinai Hosp., Detroit, 1968-69; assoc. gen. counsel regulatory affairs Blue Cross Blue Shield Mich., Detroit, 1969-80; ptnr. Honigman Miller Schwartz and Cohn, Detroit, 1980-95, of counsel, 1996—. Nat. Merit scholar, 1963-66. Mem. Mich. State Bar (chmn. health care com. 1991, 92, co-chmn. payor subcom. health law sect.). Home: 1111 Orinoco Way Palm Beach Gardens FL 33410 Office: Honigman Miller Schwartz and Cohn 2290 First National Bldg Detroit MI 48226-3583 Office Phone: 313-465-7552. E-mail: mshannon@honigman.com.

SHANNON, MARGARET T. nursing administrator, educator; b. New Haven, June 23, 1939; d. Michael Joseph and Ellen (McNamara) S. MS in Chemistry, St. Louis U., 1967; BSN, Northwestern State U. of La., Natchitoches, 1978; MN, La. State U., New Orleans, 1981; PhD., U. New Orleans, 1987. Staff nurse Touro Infirmary, New Orleans, 1978-80; instr. nursing Touro Infirmary Sch. Nursing, New Orleans, 1980-85; asst. prof. nursing La. State U. Health Sci. Ctr., New Orleans, 1985-88; prof., dean divsn. nursing Our Lady of Holy Cross Coll., New Orleans, 1988—. Author: Giovani & Hayes Drugs and Nursing Implications, 8th edit., 1995, (with B.A. Wilson and C. Stang) Nurses' Drug Guide (Annual), 1993, 94, 95, 96, 97, 98, 99, 00. Mem. ANA, NLN, La. League for Nursing, La. State Nurses Assn., Sigma Theta Tau, Phi Kappa Phi, Phi Delta Kappa.

SHANNON, MARY LOU, adult health nursing educator; b. Memphis, Apr. 4, 1938; d. Sidney Richmond Shannon and Lucille (Gwaltney) Cloud. BSN, U. Tenn., 1959; MA, Columbia U., 1963, MEd, 1964, EdD, 1972. Staff nurse City of Memphis Hosps., 1959—60, instr. Sch. Nursing, 1960—62; asst. prof. U. Tenn., Memphis, 1964—70, assoc. prof., 1970—73, prof., 1973—89; prof., chair adult health dept. Sch. Nursing U. Tex., Galveston, 1989—98, prof., 1989—2000, prof. emeritus, 2000—. Bd. dirs. Nat. Pressure Ulcer Adv. Panel, Buffalo, 1987-96; vis. prof. U. Alta., Edmonton, Can., 1982, Union U., Memphis, 2001, Bapt. Coll. Health Scis., 2003; mem. project adv. bd. RAND, Santa Monica, Calif., 1994. Contbr. chpts. to books in field and to periodicals; mem. editl. bd. Advances in Wound Care, 1987-2000. Trustee Nurses Edn. Funds, N.Y.C., 1972-86. Mem. AAAS, ANA, Nat. League Nursing (bd. of rev. 1983-86), Orthopedic Nurses Assn., So. Nursing Rsch. Soc., Am. Assn. for History of Nursing, Sigma Xi, Sigma Theta Tau, Phi Kappa Phi. Avocations: travel, reading.

SHANNON, MARYLIN LINFOOT, state legislator, educator; b. LaGrande, Oreg., Sept. 7, 1941; BA in Edn., Ctrl. Wash. U. Mem. Oreg. Legislature, Salem, 1994—, mem. edn. com., mem. gen. govt. com., mem. health and human svcs. com., chair transp. com., mem. water and land use com. Republican. Home: 7955 Portland Rd NE Brooks OR 97305-9401 Office: S 218 State Capitol Salem OR 97310

SHANNON, PATRICK S. retail executive; Sr. acct. Arthur Andersen LLP; asst. controller AGCO Corp., Duluth, Ga., v.p., controller, v.p., dir. fin., v.p., CFO, 1998-2000; sr. v.p., CFO US Gifts Corp., Atlanta, 2000—. Office: Onecoast Network 2925 Monroe Dr NE Atlanta GA 30324-4830

SHANNON, PETER MICHAEL, JR., lawyer; b. Chgo., Oct. 13, 1928; s. Peter Michael Sr. and Marian (Burke) S.; m. Anne M. Mueller, April 3, 1969; children: Peter III, Stephen, Heather, Eamon. BA, St. Mary of the Lake, Mundelein, Ill., 1949, MA, 1952, STL, 1953; JCL, Gregorian U., Rome, 1958; JD, U. Calif., Berkeley, 1971. Bar: Calif. 1972, D.C. 1972, Ill. 1988, U.S. Dist. Ct. Md. 1972, U.S. Dist. Ct. D.C. 1972, U.S. Dist. Ct. (no. dist.) Ill. 1988, U.S. Ct. Appeals (1st, 2d, 3d, 4th, 5th, 6th, 7th, 8th, 9th, 10th and D.C. cirs.) 1972-75, U.S. Supreme Ct. 1975. Supervisory atty. litigation U.S. Dept. of Justice, Washington, 1971-75; sr. appellate atty. ICC, Washington, 1975-77, dir. enforcement, 1977-80; ptnr. Shannon, et al, Washington, 1980-82, Keck, Mahin & Cate, Chgo., 1982-96, Arnstein & Lehr, Chgo., 1996—2001; pvt. practice Western Springs, Ill., 2001—. Author: Energy and Transportation Implications of Ratemaking Policy Concerning Sources of Energy, 1980, Disposition of Real Estate by Religious Institutions, 1987, The Dual Approach of Civil Law Courts to Ecclesiastical Related Disputes, 1988. Mem. ABA (chmn. transp. com., adminstrv. law and regulatory practice sect. 1984-87, coun. mem. 1988-91), Ill. Bar Assn., Chgo. Bar Assn., Am. Acad. Hosp. Attys., Assn. Transp. Law, Logistics and Policy, Canon Law Soc. (pres. 1965-66), Ctr. for Disability and Elder Law (pres. 1997-99). Office: 4546 Wolf Road Western Springs IL 60558-1562 Office Phone: 708-784-0171.

SHANNON, ROBERT RENNIE, optical sciences center administrator, educator; b. Mt. Vernon, NY, Oct. 3, 1932; s. Howard A. and Harriebell Shannon; m. Helen Lang, Feb. 13, 1954; children: Elizabeth, Barbara, Jennifer, Amy, John, Robert. BS, U. Rochester, 1954, MA, 1957. Dir. Optics Lab. ITEK Corp., Lexington, Mass., 1959-69; prof. Optical Scis. Ctr., U. Ariz., Tucson, 1969—, dir., 1983-92; prof. emeritus Optica Scis. Ctr., U. Ariz., Tucson, 1992—. Cons. Lawrence Livermore Lab., 1980-90; trustee Aerospace Corp., 1985-94, 96—; mem. Air force Sci. Adv. Bd., 1986-90; mem. NRC Commn. on Next Generation currency, 1992-94, NRC Commn. on Optical Sci. and Engring., 1996-97; mem. com. on def. space tech. Air Force Studies Bd., 1989-93, Hubble Telescope Recovery Panel, 1990; mem. tech. adv. bd. Nat. Reconnaissance Office, 1999-2001; bd. dirs. Precision Optics Corp. Editor: Applied Optics and Optical Engineering, Vol. 7, 1980, Vol. 8, 1981, Vol. 9, 1983, Vol. 10, 1987, Vol. 11, 1992, Art and Science of Optical Design, 1997; editor Engring. and Lab. Notes, 1995-98. Recipient Lifetime Achievement award, Internat. Optical Design Conf., 2002. Fellow Optical Soc. Am. (pres. 1985, engring. coun. 1989-91), Soc. Photo-Optical Instrumentation Engrs. (pres. 1979-80, SPIE/OSA jt. task force 1998, Goddard award 1982, Gold medal 1996, treas. internat. commn. for optics, 1993-99); mem. NAE, Tucson Soaring Club (past pres.), Sigma Xi. Home: 7040 E Taos Pl Tucson AZ 85715-3344 Office: U Ariz Optical Scis Ctr Tucson AZ 85721-0001 E-mail: rshannon@u.arizona.edu.

SHANNON, STEPHEN CURTIS, dean, occupational health physician; b. Frederick, Md., Dec. 9, 1948; s. James Lee and Mary Catherine (Fry) S.; m. Barbara Jean Winterson, Jul. 31, 1971; children: Joyce Megan Shannon-Winterson, Sally Catherine Shannon-Winterson. BA in hist., U. Md., 1971, MA in Am. hist., 1975; DO, U. New Eng. Coll. Osteopathic Medicine, 1986; MPH, Harvard U., 1990. Diplomate Am. Bd. Preventive Medicine and Family Practice. Program mgr. WESM-FM Radio, Prince Frederick, Md., 1971-73; instr. Am. hist. U. Md., College Park, 1973-79; congl. rels. analyst U.S. Dept. Energy, Washington, 1979-80; family practice resident Brighton Medical Ctr., Portland, Maine, 1986-88; preventive medicine resident U. Mass. Medical Ctr., Worcester, Mass., 1988-90; medical epidemiologist Mass. Dept. Pub. Health, Boston, 1990-92; asst. prof. U. New Eng. Coll. Osteopathic Medicine, Biddeford, Maine, 1990-95; medical dir. Ctr. Health Promotion Brighton Medical Ctr., 1991-95; dir. occupational health Maine Bureau of Health, Augusta, 1990-95; acting dean U. New Eng. Coll. Osteo. Medicine, 1995—. Med. epidemiologist cons. Maine Bur. Health, 1990-91; chair occupational health sect. Brighton Med. Ctr., 1994—. Editor: The Maryland Historian, 1976-78; contbr. articles to profl. jours. Exec. com. York County Health Svcs. Bd., Saco, Maine; bd. dirs. Maine Inst. Occupational Health Edn., Waterville, Maine, 1993—, Brighton Consotrium, 1991—. Recipient New Eng. Found. Osteopathic Medicine award, 1986, U.S. Sec. Health & Human Svcs. award for Health Promotion, 1984, Ciby-Geigy award for Outstanding Comm. Svc., 1984, fellow William Randolph Hearst, U. Md., 1979. Mem. Am. Pub. Health Assn., Maine Pub. Health Assn. (bd. dirs. 1993—), Am. Osteopathic Assn., Maine Osteopathic, Physicians for Nat. Health Program, Am. Coll. Occupational & Environ. Medicine. Democrat. Avocations: canoeing, hiking, camping, writing, reading. Office: U New Eng 11 Hills Beach Rd Biddeford ME 04005-9599

SHANNON, THOMAS A. religious studies educator; b. Indpls., Sept. 28, 1940; s. John E. and Clara J. Shannon; m. Catherine Haenn Shannon, Aug. 12, 1972; children: Ashley E., Courtney M. BA, Quincy U., 1964; STB, St.

Josephs Sem., 1968; STM, Boston U., 1970, PhD, 1973; DHL (hon.), Quincy U., 1994. Instr. theology Quinty U., Ill., 1968—69; prof. religion and ethics Worcester Polytech Inst., Mass., 1973—. Co-author: The New Genetic Medicine, 2003. Democrat. Home: 123 Winifred Ave Worcester MA 01602 Office: Dept Humanities 100 Inst Rd Worcester MA 01609

SHANNON, THOMAS ALFRED, retired educational association administrator emeritus; b. Milw., Jan. 2, 1932; s. John Elwood and Eleanor Ann (Mitchell) S.; m. Barbara Ann Weidner, June 26, 1954; children: Thomas Alfred, Paul J., Suzanne L., Terrence D. BS, U. Wis, 1954; JD, U. Minn., 1961. Bar: Minn. 1961, Calif. 1963, U.S. Supreme Ct. 1965, D.C. 1977, Va. 1984; Life cert. as sch. adminstr., Calif.; cert. assoc. exec. Am. Soc. Assn. Execs. Pvt. practice law, Mpls., 1961-62; schs. atty. San Diego City Schs., 1962-73; dept. supt., gen. counsel, 1973-77; exec. dir. Nat. Sch. Bds. Assn., Washington, 1977-97, ret., 1997. Adj. prof. law and edn. U. San Diego; vis. prof. edn. U. Va.; adv. mem. Edn. Commn. of States; prof. Nat. Acad. Sch. Execs., 1971-77; legal counsel Am. Assn. Sch. Adminstrs., 1973-77; adj. prof. ednl. adminstrn. George Washington U., 1996-97. Exec. pub. The Am. Sch. Bd. Jour., 1977-96, Exec. Educator, 1978-96, Sch. Bd. News, 1981-96. Chmn. San Diego County Juvenile Justice Commn., 1973-74; mem. nat. coun. Boy Scouts Am., 1979-97; bd. dirs. Found. for Teaching Econ., San Francisco, 1993-2003. With USN, 1954-59. Mem. VFW (life), Am. Bar Assn. (chmn. com. public edn. 1978-82), Nat. Orgn. on Legal Problems of Edn. (pres. 1973), Nat. Sch. Bds. Assn. (chmn. council sch. attys. 1967-69) Home: 3811 26th St N Arlington VA 22207-5241 Personal E-mail: tombar2@juno.com.

SHANNON, THOMAS FREDERIC, German language educator; b. Cambridge, Mass., Mar. 16, 1948; m. Christine D. Höner. BA in German summa cum laude, Boston Coll., 1969; MA in German Lit., SUNY, Albany, 1973; MA in Theoretical Linguistics, Ind. U., 1975, PhD in Germanic Linguistics, 1982. Instr. in German Boston Coll., 1969-70; tchg. fellow in German SUNY, Albany, 1971-73; univ. fellow Ind. U., Bloomington, 1973-74, assoc. instr., 1974-76, 79-80; acting asst. prof. in Germanic linguistics U. Calif., Berkeley, 1980-82, asst. prof., 1982-87, assoc. prof., 1987-94, prof., 1994—, dir. lang. lab., 1989-92, assoc. dir. Berkeley Lang. Ctr., 1994-95, dir. edn. abroad study ctr., 2000—02. Co-organizer Berkeley Confs. on Dutch Lang. and Lit., 1987, 89, 91, 93, 95, 97, 10th Interdisciplinary Conf. Netherlandic Studies, 2000; econs. presenter and spkr. in field. Contbr. articles to profl. jours.; mem. editl. adv. bd. Am. Jour. Germanic Linguistics, 1998—. With USAR, 1970-76. Grantee Fulbright Found., 1976-78, U. Calif. Berkeley, 1983-84, 94-95, ACLS, 1987, Internat. Assn. Netherlandic Studies, 1988, 91, 94, 97, German Acad. Exch. Svc., summer 1996; NDEA fellow, 1969; Fulbright rsch./lectr. grantee Rijksuniversiteit Groningen, Netherlands, 1992-93; Inst. fuer deutsche Sprache summer rsch. grantee, Mannheim, Germany, 1997. Mem. MLA (exec. com. discussion group in Germanic philology 1989-94, discussion group for Netherlandic Studies 1995-99, divsn. on lang. change 1995-99), Am. Assn. Netherlandic Studies (exec. com. 1988—, editor newsletter 1989-95, series editor publs. 1994—), Am. Assn. Tchrs. German, Internat. Assn. Netherlandic Studies, Linguistic Soc. Am., Pacific Ancient and Modern Lang. Assn., European Linguistic Soc., Soc. Germanic Philology (v.p. 1991-92, 95-99), Internat. Cognitive Linguistics Soc., Alpha Sigma Nu. Home: 770 Rose Dr Benicia CA 94510-3709 Office: U Calif Dept German 5319 Dwinelle Hall Berkeley CA 94720-3243 Office Phone: 510-642-2004. E-mail: tshannon@socs.berkeley.edu.

SHANNON, W. PATRICK, telecommunications industry executive; BSBA, U. Ga. CPA. With Arthur Andersen, Atlanta, 1983—91; dir. fin. planning, analysis, dir. investor rels., dir. tech. acctg. U.S. West, Inc., 1991—94, v.p. corp. devel., 1994; v.p., chief fin. officer MediaOne, Inc., 1994—97; v.p. fin., chief fin. officer domestic ops., controller Bellsouth Corp., Atlanta, 1997—. Office: Bellsouth Corp 1155 Peachtree St NE Atlanta GA 30309-3610

SHANNON, WILLIAM NORMAN, III, marketing and international business educator, food service executive; b. Chgo., Nov. 20, 1937; s. William Norman Jr. and Lee (Lewis) S.; m. Bernice Urbanowicz, July 14, 1962; children: Kathleen Kelly, Colleen Patricia, Kerrie Ann. BS in Indsl. Mgmt., Carnegie Inst. Tech., 1959; MBA in Mktg. Mgmt., U. Toledo, 1963. Sales engr. Westinghouse Electric Co., Detroit, 1959-64; regional mgr. Toledo Scale, Chgo., 1964-70; v.p. J. Lloyd Johnson Assoc., Northbrook, Ill., 1970-72; mgr. spl. projects Hobart Mfg., Troy, Ohio, 1972-74; corp. v.p. mktg. Berkel, Inc., La Porte, Ind., 1974-79; gen. mgr. Berkel Products, Ltd., Toronto, Can., 1975-78; chmn. Avant Industries, Inc., Wheeling, Ill., 1979-81; chmn., pres. Hacienda Mexican Restaurants, South Bend, Ind., 1978—; chmn. Ziker Shannon Corp., South Bend, 1982-88, Hacienda Franchising Group, Inc., South Bend, Ind., 1987—. Assoc. prof. mktg. and internat. bus. St. Mary's Coll., Notre Dame, Ind., 1982—; chmn. Hacienda Franchise Group, Inc., 1987-96, Hacienda Mex. Restaurants Mgmt., Inc., 1994-96; sr. chmn. Hacienda Mex. Restaurants, 1996—; mem. London program faculty, 1986, 89, 92, 94, coord. internat. bus. curriculum, 1989—, mktg. curriculum, 1983, 88, 95—; advisor Coun. Internat. Bus. Devel., Notre Dame, 1991—; mng. dir. Alden & Torch Lake Railway, 1995—. Co-author: Laboratory Computers, 1971; columnist Bus. Digest mag., 1988—; mem. editl. bd. Jour. Bus. and Indsl. Mktg., 1986—, South Bend Tribune Business Weekly, 1990—; contbr. articles to profl. jours. V.p. mktg. Jr. Achievement, South Bend, Ind., 1987-90; pres. Small Bus. Devel. Coun., South Bend., 1987-90; bd. dirs. Ind. Small Bus. Coun., Indpls., 1986—, Mental Health Assn., South Bend, 1987-90, Michiana World Trade Orgn., Internat. Bus. Edn., 1989-91; Entrepreneurs Alliance Ind., 1988-92, Nat. Small Bus. United, Washington, 1989-92, Women's Bus. Initiative, 1986-90, dir. ednl. confs., 1986-90; chmn. bd. trustees, Holy Cross Coll., Notre Dame, Ind., 1987—, chmn. edn. com., 1993—; chmn. St. Joseph County Higher Edn. Coun., 1988-91, Nat. Coun. Small Bus., Washington, 1988—; Midwest region adv. coun. U.S. SBA, 1988-91; at-large mem. U.S. Govt. Adv. Coun. on Small Bus., Washington, 1988-90, 1994—, chmn. Bus. and Econ. Devel. Com., 1988-90, 1994—; vice chmn. Internat. Trade Com., 1994—; nat. adv. coun. Women's Network for Entrepreneur Tng., 1991—; vice chmn. State of Ind. Enterprise Zone Bd., 1991—; elected del. White House Conf. Small Bus., Washington, 1986; bd. dirs. Ind. Small Bus. Devel. Ctrs. Adv. Bd.; co-pres. Helena Twp. Downtown Devel. Authority, 2002—. Named Small Bus. Person of the Yr., City of South Bend, 1987, Small Bus. Advocate of the Yr., State of Ind., 1987, Ind. Entrepreneur Advocate of the Yr., 1988. Mem. Am. Mktg. Assn. (chmn. Mich./Ind. chpt., pres. 1985-86), U.S. Assn. Small Bus. and Entrepreneurship (nat. v.p. for entrepreneurship edn. 1991-92, nat. v.p. entrepreneurship devel. 1992—), Ind. Inst. New Bus. Ventures (mktg. faculty 1987-91), Michiana Investment Network (vice chmn. 1988-91), SBA (adminstrn. adv. coun. 1988—, contbg. editor Our Town Michiana mag. 1988-91), U.S. C. of C., Nat. Coun. Small Bus. (Washington), South Bend C. of C. (bd. dirs. 1987—, vice chmn. membership 1993—), Assn. for Bus. Communications (co-chmn. Internat. Conf. 1986), Univ. Club Notre Dame (vice chmn.), Shamrock Club Notre Dame (exec. dir., trustee 1993—), Rotary. Roman Catholic. Home: 2920 S Twyckenham Dr South Bend IN 46614-2116 Office: Saint Mary's Coll Dept Bus Adminstrn Eco Notre Dame IN 46556 *Enjoy good fortune resulting from LUCK, an acronym for (L) Learning how to (U)Use your talents with genuine (C) Concern on how your (K) Knowlege can benefit others.*

SHANNY, RAMY, physicist; b. Jerusalem, Nov. 6, 1935; s. Meir and Batia Shanny, Batia Shanny; m. Laura Eileen Hamilton; children: Emily, 0000 0000; m. Shula Dafny (div. Dec. 0, 1976); children: Ronnit, Micky. PhD, Princeton U. Rsch. physicist GE, Valley Forge, Pa., 1968—69, Naval Rsch. Lab., Washington, 1969—70, br. head, 1971—75; plasma physics dir., supt. NRL, 1971—75; pres. INESCO, Inc., Washington, 1977—84, LaJolla, Calif., 1977—84; pres., CEO Advanced Power Techs., Inc., 1986—2003; v.p., gen. mgr. AT, BAE Systems, 1986—2003. Recipient Exec. Svc. award, Naval Rsch. Lab., 1974. Fellow: Am.Phys. Soc.; mem.: IEEE, N.Y. Acad. Sci. Office: Advanced Power Technologies, Inc 1250 24th St NW 8th Fl Washington DC 20037 Business E-Mail: shanny@yahoo.com.

SHANSBY, JOHN GARY, investor; b. Seattle, Aug. 25, 1937; s. John Jay and Jule E. (Boyer) S.; m. Joyce Ann Dunsmore, June 21, 1959 (div.); children: Sheri Lee, Kimberly Ann, Jay Thomas; m. Barbara Anderson De Meo, Jan. 1, 1983 (div.); m. Jane Robinson Dettner, May 1, 1990. BA, U. Wash., 1959. Mktg. exec. Colgate-Palmolive Co., N.Y.C., 1959-67; subs. pres. Am. Home Products Corp., N.Y.C., 1968-71; v.p. Clorox Co., Oakland, Calif., 1972-73; ptnr. Booz, Allen & Hamilton, San Francisco, 1974-75; chmn. bd., chief exec. officer, dir. Shaklee Corp., San Francisco, 1975-86; mng. gen. ptnr. The Shansby Group, San Francisco, 1986—. Former chmn. Calif. State Commn. for Rev. of Master Plan Higher Edn.; founder J. Gary Shansby chair mktg. strtegy U. Calif., Berkeley; trustee Calif. State U. Mem. San Francisco C. of C. (past pres.), Villa Traverna Club, Pennask Lake Fishing Club (B.C.), Sky Club of N.Y.C., Sigma Nu. Republican. Office: The Shansby Group 600 Montgomery St Ste 2900 San Francisco CA 94111 Office Phone: 415-217-2330.

SHAO, JOHN JIANPING, finance educator; b. Xinyu, China, Apr. 26, 1963; came to U.S., 1985; s. Zhikui and Juying (Li) S.; m. Diana Wang, Mar. 10, 1990; children: Matthew Stephen, Sarah Gladys. MA in Internat. Bus., U Tex., 1987; MS in Statistics, Va. Tech. Inst., 1990, PhD in Fin., 1991. CFA. Prof. fin. Oklahoma City U., 1991—; pres. Pinnacle Fin. Mgmt., Oklahoma City, 1991—. Mem. Assn. Investment Mgmt. & Rsch. Office: Oklahoma City U 2501 N Blackwelder Ave Oklahoma City OK 73106-1493 Home: 12716 Whitefield Cir Oklahoma City OK 73142-3129

SHAO COLLINS, JEANNINE, magazine publisher; married; 1 child. BA in Econs., U. Rochester. Various advt. sales mgmt. positions Woman's Day, N.Y.C., Prevention mag.; N.Y. advt. mgr. Ladies' Home Jour., Meredith Corp., N.Y.C., 1993-95, advt. dir. Better Homes and Gardens, Des Moines, 1995-98, assoc. pub., 1998-99, pub., 1999—2002, v.p., 2000—02, v.p., group pub. N.Y.C., 2002—.

SHAPARD, ROBERT, gas industry executive; BA in Acctg., Texas Tech., 1977. cert. CPA. CEO TXU Co., Australia; exec. v.p., CFO Ultramar Diamond Shamrock Corp, 2000—. Office: Ultramar Diamond Shamrock 6000 N Loop 1604 W San Antonio TX 78249

SHAPEERO, LORRAINE G. physician, researcher, educator; d. Ezra and Goldine Shapeero. BA, U. Calif., Berkeley, 1964; MD, U. Calif., San Francisco, 1968. Diplomate Am. Bd. of Radiology, 1974. Resident to faculty U. Pa., Phila., 1970—74; fellowship Inst. of Orthop. Royal Nat. Orthop. Hosp., London, 1975—76; faculty U. Calif., San Francisco, 1977—82, 1984—95, Columbia U., NY, 1982—84, Institut Gustave Roussy, France, 1990—; chief Uniformed Svcs. U., Musculoskeletal Radiology Sect., Bethesda, Md., 1995—; attending radiologist Walter Reed Army Med. Ctr., Wash., DC, 1995—; dir. US Mil. Cancer Inst., Bone and Soft Tissue Sarcoma Program, Wash., DC, 2000—. Contbr. articles various profl. jours. and rsch. publs. Mem.: Internat. Skeletal Soc. (chair, grants com.), Radiology (mem. editl. bd.), Acad. Radiology (mem. editl. bd.), Assn. U. Radiologists (bd. dirs.), Alliance Med. Student Educators in Radiology (mem. exec. com.), Am. Roentgen Ray Soc., Am. Coll. Radiology, Radiol. Soc. North Am., Internat. Soc. Magnetic Resonance in Medicine (sec., Musculoskeletal Study Group), Connective Tissue Oncology Soc., Radiology Rsch. Alliance (pres.-elect), Phi Beta Kappa. Office: Uniformed Svcs U 4301 Jones Bridge Rd Bethesda MD 20814

SHAPELL, NATHAN, financial and real estate executive; b. Poland, Mar. 6, 1922; s. Benjamin and Hela S. Shapell; m. Lilly Szenes, July 17, 1948; children: Vera Shapell Guerin, Benjamin(dec.). Co-founder Shapell Industries, Inc., Beverly Hills, Calif., 1955, now chmn. bd., CEO, 1989—. Mem. adv. bd. Union Bank, Beverly Hills, Calif.; mem. residential bldgs. adv. com. Calif. Energy Resources Conservation and Devel. Commn.; speaker in field. Author: (novels) Witness to the Truth, 1974. Mem. adv. coun. Pres.'s Commn. on the Holocaust, 1979; pres. Am. Acad. Achievement, 1975—; prisoner in Auschwitz, 1943—45; Mem. Calif. Commn. Govt. Reform, 1978; Atty. Gen. Calif. Adv. Coun.; Dist. Atty. Los Angeles County Adv. Coun.; chmn. Calif. Govt. Commn. Orgn. and Economy, 1975—; mem. Gov.'s Task Force on Affordable Housing, 1980—; mem. dean's coun. UCLA Sch. Architecture and urban Planning, 1976—; trustee U. Santa Clara, Calif., 1976—; bd. councillors U. So. Calif. Med. Sch., 1973—. Recipient Golden Plate award, Am. Acad. Achievement, 1974, Fin. World award, 1977. Mem.: Hillcrest Country Club (Los Angeles). Jewish. Address: Shapell Industries Inc 8383 Wilshire Blvd Beverly Hills CA 90211-2410

SHAPERE, DUDLEY, philosophy educator; b. Harlingen, Tex., May 27, 1928; s. Dudley and Corinne (Pupkin) S.; m. Hannah Hardgrave; children: Hannah Elizabeth, Christine Ann; children by previous marriage: Alfred Dudley, Catherine Lucretia. BA, Harvard U., 1949, MA, 1955, PhD, 1957. Instr. philosophy Ohio State U., 1957-60; asst. prof. U. Chgo., 1960-65, assoc. prof., 1965-67, prof., 1967-72, mem. com. on evolutionary biology, 1969-72, chmn. undergrad. program in history and philosophy of sci., 1966-72, chmn. com. on conceptual founds. sci., 1970-72; prof. U. Ill., Urbana, 1972-75, chmn. program in history and philosophy of sci., 1972-75; prof. U. Md., College Park, 1975-84; Z. Smith Reynolds prof. philosophy and history of sci. Wake Forest U., 1984—2002; ret., 2002. Mem. com. on history and philosophy of sci. U. Md., 1975-84, chmn. program in history and philosophy of sci., 1983-84.; vis. prof. Rockefeller U., 1965-66, Harvard U., 1968; mem. Inst. Advanced Study, Princeton, N.J., 1978-79, 81, 89, Otto Neugebauer fellow, 2001; spl. cons. (program dir.) program in history and philosophy of sci. NSF, 1966-75; Sigma Xi nat. bicentennial lectr., 1974-77. Author: Philosophical Problems of Natural Science, 1965, Galileo: A Philosophical Study, 1974, Reason and the Search for Knowledge, 1984; editorial bd.: Philosophy of Sci., Studies in History and Philosophy of Sci.; rev. bd.: Philosophy Research Archives; contbr. articles to profl. jours. Served with AUS, 1950-52. Recipient Quantrell award for excellence in undergrad. tchg. U. Chgo., 1968; Disting. Scholar-Tchr. award U. Md., 1979-80. Fellow AAAS (sec. sec. 1972); mem. APA, Philosophy of Sci. Assn., History of Sci. Soc., Am. Philos. Assn., Acad. Internat. de Philosophie des Scis. Home: 3125 Turkey Hill Ct Winston Salem NC 27106-4951 E-mail: shapere@wfu.edu.

SHAPERO, HARRIS JOEL, pediatrician; b. Winona, Minn., Nov. 22, 1930; s. Charles and Minnie Sara Shapero; m. Byong Soon Yu, Nov. 6, 1983; children by previous marriage: Laura, Bradley, James, Charles. AA, UCLA, 1953; BS, Northwestern U., 1954, MD, 1957. Diplomate in occup. medicine Am. Bd. Preventive Medicine; qualified med. evaluator Indsl. Med. Coun.; ind. med. examiner, Calif.; cert. aviation medicine FAA. Intern Los Angeles County-Harbor Gen. Hosp., 1957-58, resident in pediatrics, 1958-60, staff physician, 1960-64; attending physician Perceptually Handicapped Children's Clinic, 1960-63; disease control officer for Tb Los Angeles County Health Dept., 1962-64; pvt. practice medicine specializing in pediatrics and occup. medicine, Cypress, Calif., 1965-86; pediatric cons. L.A. Health Dept., 1983-85, disease controll officer sexually transmitted diseases, 1968-78; emergency rm. dir. AMI, Anaheim, Calif., 1968-85; mem. med. staff Anaheim Gen. Hosp., Beach Cmty. Hosp., Norwalk Cmty. Hosp.; courtesy staff Palm Harbor Gen. Hosp., Bellflower City Hosp.; pediatric staff Hosp. de General, Ensenada, Mex., 1978—; primary care clinician Sacramento County Health, 1987-88; practice medico-legal evaluation, 1986-92. Founder Calif. Legal Evaluation Med. Group; apptd. med. examiner in preventive and occup. medicine State of Calif. Dept. Indsl. Rels., 1989; health care provider, advisor City of Anaheim, City of Buena Park, City of Cypress, City of Garden Grove, Cypress Sch. Dist., Magnolia Sch. Dist., Savanna Sch. Dist., Anaheim Unified Shc. Dist., Orange County Dept. Edn.; pediatric and Tv cons. numerous other orgns.; FAA med. examiner; founder Pan Am. Childrens Mission. Author: The Silent Epidemic, 1979. Named Headliner in Medicine, Orange County Press Club, 1978. Fellow Am. Coll. Preventive Medicine; mem. Los. Angeles County Med. Assn., Los angeles County Indsl. Med. Assn., Am. Pub. Health Assn., Mex.-Am. Border Health Assn. Republican. Jewish. Avocations: antique books and manuscripts, photography, graphics, beekeeping. Home: PO Box 1488 34995 Cameron Ln Wildomar CA 92595 Office: 5411 Madison Ave Ste 1 Sacramento CA 95841-3151 Personal E-mail: hjswilton2000@yahoo.com.

SHAPINSKY, DAVID FRAZIER, journalist, historian; b. N.Y.C., Mar. 13, 1960; s. Harold Shapinsky and Kathryn Sophronia Peters; m. Helen J. Wechsler, Mar. 23, 1997; children: Tobias Joseph, Theodore Aaron. BA, Pitzer Coll., Claremont, Calif., 1978—82; MA, U. Chgo., 1982—83, PhD, 1983—90. Vis. asst. prof. Coll. Wooster, Ohio, 1990—92; dir. of govtl. & strategic studies Citizens Against Govt. Waste, Washington, 1992—93; prodr. ABC News, Washington, 1993—2000; exec. prodr. Kaisernetwork.org, Kaiser Family Found., Washington, 2000—03; sr. prodr. Howard U. TV PBS, Washington, 2002—. Author: (weekly column for abcnews.com) News This Week; prodr.: (documentary series) The Brown Decision: Howard Law & the Struggle for Justice; sr. prodr. (documentary) The Long Walk (Telly Award, 2003), (TV series) On Health with George Strait, Evening Exchange with Kojo Nnamdi, @Howard, reportorial prodr. (magazine show investigation) Rush to Read (Peabody, Emmy, 1995); exec. prodr.: (live webcast coverage) Internat. AIDS Conf., Barcelona, 2002. Mem.: NATAS, Assn. Health Care Journalists, Investigative Reporters and Editors, Orgn. Am. Historians. Achievements include overseeing creation of international webcasting service, which served as the official webcaster for the UNAIDS conference; working to establish Board of Ethics for the city of Chicago. Office: Howard Univ Television 2222 4th St NW Washington DC 20059 E-mail: dshapinsky@howard.edu.

SHAPIRA, DAVID S. food products/retail grocery executive; b. 1942; married. BA, Oberlin Coll., 1964; MA, Stanford U., 1966. V.p. Giant Eagle, Inc. (formerly Giant Eagle Markets, Inc.), Pitts., 1974—81, pres., 1981—94, CEO, also bd. dirs.; chmn. & CEO Giant Eagle, Youngstown; chmn. bd. Phar-Mor Inc., Youngstown.

SHAPIRO, ANGELA, broadcast executive; BA, St. Peter's Coll. Co-owner Brookville Mktg/Greybark Advt.; owner, oper. several businesses; co-founder, pub. Soap Opera Digest, 1975, Soap Opera Update, 1988; co-prodr. Soap Opera Awards; sr. v.p. mkg. and promotion ABC Daytime, 1995, pres., 1998, Buena Vista Prodns., 2000; pres. ABC Family Channel Walt Disney Co., Burbank, Calif., 2002—03; pres. Fox TV Studios, 2004—. Office: 500 S Buena Vista St Burbank CA 91521-9722

SHAPIRO, ASCHER HERMAN, mechanical engineer, educator, consultant; b. Bklyn., May 20, 1916; s. Bernard and Jennie (Kaplan) S.; m. Sylvia Charm, Dec. 24, 1939 (div. 1959); children: Peter Mark, Martha Ann, Bernett Mary; m. Regina Julia Lee, June 4, 1961 (div. 1972); m. Kathleen Larke Crawford, Sept. 6, 1985. Student, CCNY, 1932-35; SB, MIT, 1938, ScD, 1946; DSc (hon.), Salford U., Eng., 1978, Technion-Israel Inst. Tech., 1985. Asst. mech. engring. MIT, 1938-40, faculty, 1940—, prof. mech. engring., 1952—, prof. charge fluid mechanics divsn., mech. engring. dept., 1954-65, Ford prof. engring., 1962-75, chmn. faculty, 1964-65, head dept. mech. engring., 1965-74, inst. prof., 1975-86, inst. prof. emeritus, sr. lectr., 1986—; vis. prof. applied thermodynamics U. Cambridge, Eng., 1955-56; Akroyd Stuart Meml. lectr. Nottingham (Eng.) U., 1956; editor Acad. Press, Inc., 1962-65. Cons. United Aircraft Corp., M.W. Kellogg Co., Arthur D. Little, Inc., Hardie-Tynes Mfg. Co., Carbon & Carbide Chems. Corp., Oak Ridge, Rohm & Haas Co., Ultrasonic Corp., Jackson & Moreland (Engrs.), Stone & Webster, Bendix Aviation, Oak Ridge Nat. Lab., Acushnet Processing Co., Kennecott Copper Co., Welch Sci., Sargent-Welch, Bird Machine Co., Organogenesis, Inc., CARR Separations, Inc., others; served on sub-coms. on turbines, internal flow, compressors and turbines NACA; mem. Lexington Project to study and report on nuclear powered flight to AEC, summer 1948; dir. Project Dynamo to study and report to AEC on technol. and econs. nuclear power for civilian use, 1953, Lamp Wick study Office Naval Research, 1955; mem. tech. adv. panel aeronautics Dept. Def.; cons. ops. evaluation group Navy Dept.; sci. adv. bd. USAF, 1964-66; founder, mem. Nat. Com. for Fluid Mechanics Films, 1962—, chmn., 1962-65, 71—; chmn. com. on ednl. films Commn. on Engring. Edn., 1962-65; dir. lab. for devel. power plants for use in torpedoes Navy Dept., 1943-45; mem. ad hoc med. devices com. FDA, HEW, 1970-72; mem. com. Nat. Council for Research and Devel., Israel, 1971—; mem. com. sci. and pub. policy Nat. Acad. Scis., 1970-74 Author: The Dynamics and Thermodynamics of Compressible Fluid Flow, vol. 1, 1953, vol. 2, 1954 (with Chinese translation), Shape and Flow, 1961 (Japanese, Italian, German and Spanish translations); also 3 ednl. films, 39 videotape lecture series: Fluid Dynamics, 1984; contbr. over 130 articles to sci. jours.; mem. editl. bd. Applied Mechanics, 1955-56; mem. editl. com. Ann. Rev. Fluid Mechanics, 1967-71; mem. editl. bd. MIT Press, 1977-87, chmn., 1982-87; patentee fluid metering equipment, combustion chamber, propulsion apparatus, gas turbine aux., magnetic disc, magnetic disc storage device, vacuum pump (2), low-density wind tunnel, recipe calculator, decanter. Mem. Town Meeting Arlington, Mass.; chmn. 1st Mass. chpt. Atlantic Union Com., 1951-52, mem. council, 1954—; bd. govs. Technion, Israel Inst. Tech., 1968-89. Recipient Naval Ordnance Devel. award, 1945; joint certificate outstanding contbn. War and Navy depts., 1947; Richards Meml. award ASME, 1960; Worcester Reed Warner medal, 1965; Fluids Engring. award, 1981; Townsend Harris medal Coll. City N.Y., 1978 Fellow AIAA, ASME (hon., Richards Meml. award 1960, Worcester Reed Warner medal 1965, Fluids Engring. award 1981, Daniel C. Drucker medal 1999), Am. Acad. Arts and Scis. (councillor 1967-71); mem. AAAS, NAS (sci. and pub. policy com. 1973-77), Am. Sci. Films Assn., Nat. Acad. Engring. (adv. com. on edn. 1985-89), Am. Inst. Med. and Biol. Engring. (founding fellow), Biomed. Engring. Soc. (charter mem. 1968), Am. Soc. Engring. Edn. (Lamme medal 1977), MIT Faculty Club, Cavendish Club (Brookline, Mass.), Sigma Xi, Tau Beta Pi, Pi Tau Sigma. Home: 111 Perkins St Apt 86 Jamaica Plain MA 02130-4320

SHAPIRO, BRAHM, nuclear medicine physician, endocrinologist; b. Johannesburg, Feb. 2, 1949; came to U.S., 1979; s. Norman and Claudia (Botha) S.; m. Lorraine Marilyn Fig, January 26, 1975; children: Jonathan Daniel, Bernard Joel. MB BChir, U. Cape Town, South Africa, 1973, PhD, 1978; student, Hammersmith Hosp., London, 1975; MSc in Nuc. Medicine, U. London, 1979. Diplomate Am. Bd. Nuc. Medicine. Intern Groote Schuur Hosp., Cape Town, 1974, resident, 1974-76-78; fellow in endocrinology U. Cape Town, 1976-78; registrar in nuc. medicine St. Bartholomew's Hosp., London, 1978-79; fellow in endocrinology U. Mich., Ann Arbor, 1979-81, from asst. prof. to prof. internal medicine, 1981—, prof. radiology, 2000—; mem. staff VA Med. Ctr., Ann Arbor, 1992—. Editor Internal Medicine; Clin. Exptl., 1992—, Thyroidology; Clin. Lab., 1993—; mem. editl. bd. Nuc. Medicine Comm. 1996—, Jour. Nuc. Medicine, 1999; contbr. over 90 chpts. to books, over 225 articles to profl. jours. Fellow Am. Coll. Endocrinology; mem. NRA, Am. Thyroid Assn., Soc. Nuc. Medicine, Endocrine Soc., European Assn. Nuc. Medicine, Jews Preservation Firearms Ownership, Alpha Omega Alpha (hon.). Avocations: medical history, marksmanship, metal working. Home: 1484 Green Rd Ann Arbor MI 48105-2808 Office: U Mich Med Ctr 1500 East Med Ctr Dr Ann Arbor MI 48109 Business E-Mail: brshapir@umich.edu.

SHAPIRO, BURTON LEONARD, oral pathologist, geneticist, educator; b. N.Y.C., Mar. 29, 1934; s. Nat Lazarus and Fay Rebecca (Gartenhouse) S.; m. Eileen Roman, Aug. 11, 1958; children— Norah Leah, Anne Rachael, Carla Faye. Student, Tufts U., 1951-54; D.D.S., NYU, 1958; MS, U. Minn., 1962, PhD, 1966. Faculty U. Minn. Sch. Dentistry, Mpls., 1962—, assoc. prof. div. oral pathology, 1966-70, prof., chmn. div. oral biology, 1970-79, prof., chmn. dept. oral biology, 1979-88, prof. dept. oral pathology and genetics, 1979-88, dir. grad. studies, mem. grad. faculty genetics, 1966—, prof. dept. oral sci., 1988—, mem. grad. faculty pathobiology, 1979; prof. dept. lab. medicine and pathology U. Minn. Med. Sch., 1985—, mem. Human Genetics Inst., 1988—, univ. senator, 1968-72, 88-93; also mem. med. staff U. Minn. Health Scis. Center; exec. com. Grad. Sch. U. Minn., chmn. health scis. policy rev. council, chmn. univ. faculty consultative com., 1988-92; chmn. univ. fin. and planning com. Grad. Sch. U. Minn., 1988. Hon. research fellow Galton Lab. dept. human genetics Univ. Coll., London, 1974; spl. vis. prof. Japanese Ministry Edn., Sci. and Culture, 1983 Mem. adv. editorial bd.: Jour. Dental Research, 1971—; Contbr. articles to profl. jours. Served to lt. USNR, 1958-60. Am. Cancer Soc. postdoctoral fellow, 1960-62; advanced fellow, 1965-68; named Century Club Prof. of Yr., 1988. Fellow Am. Acad. Oral Pathology, AAAS; mem. Internat. Assn. Dental Research (councilor 1969), Am. Soc. Human Genetics, Craniofacial Biology Soc. (pres. 1972), Sigma Xi,

Omicron Kappa Upsilon. Home: 148 Nina St # 2 Saint Paul MN 55102-2160 Office: U Minn Sch Dentistry Dept Oral Sci Minneapolis MN 55455 Office Phone: 612-624-3991. Business E-Mail: burt@umn.edu.

SHAPIRO, DAVID, artist, art historian; b. NYC, Aug. 28, 1916; s. Jacob and Ida (Katz) S.; m. Cecile Peyser, June 18, 1944; children: Deborah Jane, Anna Roberta. Student, Ednl. Alliance Art Sch., 1933-35, Am. Artists Sch., 1936-39. Instr. Smith Coll., 1946-47, Bklyn. Coll., summer, 1947; asst. prof. art U. B.C., 1947-49; mem. faculty dept. art New Coll., Hofstra U., 1961—63; prof. fine art New Coll., Hofstra U., 1972—81, prof. emeritus, 1981—; prof. fine art, artist in residence U. Belgrade, 1981. Vis. critic Vt. Studio Ctr., Johnson, Vt., 1990. Author: Social Realism: Art as a Weapon, 1973, Abstract Expressionism: A Critical Record, 1989; one-man shows include Ganso Gallery, NYC, 1955, Milch Gallery, NYC, 1958, 61, 63, Galleria Dell'Orso, Milan, 1971, U. Belgrade Gallery, 1981; 50 yr. retrospective T.W. Wood Art Gallery, Vt. Coll. Arts Ctr., 1987; represented in permanent collections Bklyn. Mus., Met. Mus., Libr. Congress, Nat. Mus., Smithsonian Instn., Phila. Mus. Art. Fulbright grantee, 1951-52, 52-53; MacDowell fellow, 1976; Tamarind fellow, 1976; Nat. Endowment Arts, grantee, 1978; Fulbright grantee, 1980-81. Mem. Soc. Am. Graphic Artists (pres. 1968-70), LA Printmakers, Coll. Art Assn. Home: 453 Atkinson Rd Cavendish VT 05142-9602 Home (Winter): 926 Ave Majorca Apt K Laguna Woods CA 92653 *My work and my family are the main interests in my life. Both make it very worthwhile.*

SHAPIRO, DAVID, newspaper editor; b. Culver City, Calif., Sept. 1, 1948; m. Maggie Shapiro; children: Treena, Jared. BA in Am. History, U. Hawaii. Editorial asst. Star-Bulletin, Hilo, Hawaii, 1968-87, mng. editor Honolulu, 1987—. Office: Star Bulletin 605 Kapiolani Blvd Honolulu HI 96813 5129

SHAPIRO, DAVID BENJAMIN, researcher; b. Chgo., Apr. 7, 1954; s. Leopold Julius and Virginia Lucille Shapiro. BA, Reed Coll., 1982; MA, Northwestern U., Evanston, Ill., 1986, U. Chgo., 1988; PhD, U. Ill., 1993. Computer operator Joslyn Mfg., Chgo., 1974—75; rschr. Survey Ctr., Chgo., 1982—83; rsch. analyst AMA, Chgo., 1988—89, United Way, Chgo., 1990—92; rschr. Inst. on Disability and Human Devel., U. Ill., Chgo., 1993—95. Mem.: Am. Polit. Sci. Assn. Avocations: reading, parrots.

SHAPIRO, DAVID L. lawyer; b. Corsicana, Tex., May 19, 1936; s. Harry and Alice (Laibovitz) S. BA, U. Tex., 1967; JD, St. Mary's U., 1970. Bar: Tex. 1970, U.S. Dist. Ct. (we. dist.) Tex. 1972, U.S. Supreme Ct. 1975, U.S. Ct. Appeals (5th cir.) 1981. Assoc. Law Office Jim S. Phelps, Houston, 1971; pvt. practice, Austin, 1972—. Spl. counsel com. human resources Tex. Ho. Reps., Austin, 1973-74; counsel subcom. health svcs. Tex. Senate, Austin, 1983-87. With U.S. Army, 1959-61. Mem.: Travis County Bar Assn., Austin Criminal Def. Lawyers Assn., Coll. of State Bar of Tex., Travis County Bar Assn. (sec.-treas. 1977—78, dir. 1979, pres. family law sect. 1980—81), State Bar Tex. (chmn. lawyer referral svc. com. 1980—82, adminstrn. of justice com. 1990—93, jury svc. com. 1998—2001, contbr. Media Law Handbook supplement 1986). Democrat. Avocations: automobiles, reading. Office: 1200 San Antonio St Austin TX 78701-1834 Office Phone: 512-474-2900. Personal E-mail: daveinaustintexas@yahoo.com.

SHAPIRO, DAVID W. prosecutor; Graduate, State U. NY, Binghamton; JD, State U. NY, Buffalo. Fed. Prosecutor Eastern Dist., NY, 1986—92, chief organized crime unit; Fed. Prosecutor Dist. of Ariz., 1992—94; chief Appellate Div. Northern Dist., Calif., 1994—2001, chief Criminal Div., 1994—2001, U.S. Atty., 2001—02; partner Boies, Schiller & Flexner, 2002—. Office: Boies, Schiller & Flexner 1999 Harrison Street Ste 900 Oakland CA 94612

SHAPIRO, EDWARD MURAY, dermatologist; b. Denver, Oct. 6, 1924; s. Isador Benjamin and Sara (Berezin) Shapiro; m. Ruth Young, Oct. 14, 1944; children: Adrian Michael, Stefanie Ann; m. Dorothy Rosmarin, July 22, 1990. Studied, U. Colo., 1941—43; AB with honors, U. Tex., 1948, MD, 1952. Diplomate Am. Bd. Dermatology. Intern Jefferson Coll. Medicine Hosp., Phila., 1952—53; resident in dermatology U. Tex. Med. Br., Galveston, 1953—55, Henry Ford Hosp., Detroit, 1955—56, assoc. in dermatology divsn., 1956—57; clin. instr., dermatology Baylor U. Coll. Medicine, Houston, 1957—68, assoc. clin. prof., 1968—; staff mem. Ben Taub Gen. Hosp., Houston, 1958—; active staff mem. Columbia Bayshore Hosp., 1962—, Hosp. S.E., Houston, 2000. Contbr. articles to profl. jours. With USAAF, 1943—46. Grantee, Henry J.N. Taub, 1958—60. Fellow: Am. Acad. Dermatology; mem.: AAPS (pres. 2003—), AMA, Am. Physicians Art Assn. (v.p. 1993, pres. 2003), Gulf Coast Art Soc., Houston Art League, Houston Dermatology Assn., Harris County Med. Assn. (pres., S.E. br. 1968—69), South Ctrl. Dermatol. Assn. (bd. dirs. 1987—88), Tex. Dermatol. Soc. (pres.-elect 1988, pres. 1989—90), Tex. Med. Assn., Rotary Internat. (Paul Harris fellow 1995, 1997), B'nai B'rith. Office: 1020 Pasadena Blvd Pasadena TX 77506-4700 Office Phone: 713-477-8183.

SHAPIRO, EDWARD ROBERT, psychiatrist, administrator educator psychoanalyst; b. Boston, Sept. 13, 1941; s. Jacob and Ruth (Yankelovich) S.; m. Donna Elmendorf; 1 child, Joshua Jackson; 1 child from previous marriage, Jacob Matthew; 1 stepchild, Zachary Andrew Robbins. BA magna cum laude, Yale U., 1962; MA in Anthropology, Stanford U., 1966; MD, Harvard U., 1968. Diplomate Am. Bd. Psychiatry and Neurology. Intern in medicine Beth Israel Hosp., Boston, 1968-69; resident in psychiatry Mass. Mental Health Ctr., Boston, 1969-72, chief resident in psychiatry, 1971-72; clin. assoc. NIMH, Bethesda, Md., 1972-74; dir. Adolescent and Family Treatment and Study Ctr. McLean Hosp., Belmont, Mass., 1974-89, dir. Psychosocial Tng. and Consultation, 1989-91; bd. dirs. Ctr. for Study of Groups and Social Systems, Boston, 1983-90, A.K. Rice Inst., Washington, 1983-90, dir. Nat. Group Rels. Conf., 1989-91; faculty mem. Boston Psychoanalytic Inst., 1978—; assoc. clin. prof. psychiatry Harvard Med. Sch., Boston, 1982—; med. dir., CEO The Austen Riggs Ctr., Stockbridge, Mass., 1991—; tng. and supr. analyst Psychoanalytical Inst. of the Berkshires, 2003—. Dir. The Erik H. Erikson Inst. for Edn. and Rsch., 1994-2000. Co-author: (with A.W. Carr) Lost in Familiar Places: Creating New Connections Between the Individual and Society, 1991; editor: The Inner World in the Outer World: Psychoanalytic Perspectives, 1997; mem. editorial bd. Jour. Adolescence, 1977-82, Psychiatry, 1988—; assoc. editor Jour. Adolescence, 1982-84; contbr. articles to profl. jours. Mem. Yale Russian Chorus. With USPHS, 1972-74. Recipient Isenberg teaching award McLean Hosp., 1980, Rsch. prize Soc. for Family Therapy and Rsch., 1984, Felix and Helen Deutsch Sci. prize Boston Psychoanalytic Inst., 1980. Fellow Am. Psychiat. Assn. (disting.), Am. Coll. Psychoanalysis, A.K. Rice Inst.; mem. Am. Psychoanalytic Assn. Achievements include helping develop the Erik H. Erikson Inst. for Edn. and Rsch. as a vehicle for applying the clinical insights developed at Riggs to larger social issues. Avocation: music. Office: The Austen Riggs Ctr PO Box 962 25 Main St Stockbridge MA 01262-0962

SHAPIRO, EDWIN STANLEY, lawyer, judge; b. Bklyn., Jan. 14, 1931; s. Harry I. and Ann (Safanie) S.; m. Sandra I. Bernstein, Sept. 15, 1957; children: James A., Sarah E. BA, Trinity Coll., Hartford, Conn., 1952; LLB, JD, Harvard Law Sch., 1955. Bar: N.Y. 1956, U.S. Dist. Ct. (so. and ea. dist.) N.Y. 1956, U.S. Ct. Appeals 1957. Atty. Levin & Weintraub, N.Y.C., 1956-57; pvt. practice N.Y.C., 1957-59; ptnr. Smith, Shapiro & Scheier, N.Y.C., 1959-62, Basch, Seits & Shapiro, N.Y.C., 1970-74, Seits & Shapiro, N.Y.C., 1974-81; town justice Ossining, N.Y., 1980—; pvt. practice N.Y.C., 1981-95, Briarcliff Manor, N.Y., 1996—. Lawyer Staten Island Open Lands Found., 1965-67. Mem. Assn. of Bar of City of N.Y. (environ. law com. 1970-73, com. on state cts. 1982-83, corrections com. 1996-98), Ossining Area Bar Assn. (pres. 2003). Business E-Mail: shaplaw@bestweb.net.

SHAPIRO, ELI, business consultant, educator, economist; b. Bklyn., June 13, 1916; s. Samuel and Pauline (Kushel) S.; m. Beatrice Ferbend, Jan. 18, 1946 (dec. July 1999); 1 child, Laura J. AB, Bklyn. Coll., 1936; A.M., Columbia U., 1937, PhD, 1939. Instr. Bklyn. Coll., 1936-41; rsch. assoc. Nat. Bur. Econ. Rsch., 1938-39, cons., 1939-42, mem. rsch. staff, 1955-62; asst. prof. fin. U. Chgo., 1946-47, asso. prof., 1948-52, prof., 1952; prof. fin. Mass. Inst. Tech., 1952-61; assoc. dean Mass. Inst. Tech. (Sch. Indsl. Mgmt.), 1954-58, Alfred P. Sloan prof. mgmt., 1976-84, Alfred P. Sloan prof. emeritus, 1984—; prof. fin. Harvard Bus. Sch., 1962-72, Sylvan C. Coleman prof. fin. mgmt., 1968-72; chmn. fin. com., dir. Travelers Ins. Cos., Hartford, Conn., 1971-78, vice chmn. bd., dir., 1976-78; chmn. bd. Mass. Co., 1971-72; pres. Nat. Bur. Econ. Research, 1982-84. Chmn. bd. Fed. Home Loan Bank Boston, 1970-89; econ. analyst div. monetary rsch. US Dept. Treasury, 1941-42; economist rsch. div. OPA, 1941-42; staff cons. Com. Econ. Devel., 1950-51, mem. rsch. adv. com., 1961-64, 69—, project dir., 1966-69; cons. sec. treasury; mem. enforcement commn. WSB, 1952-53; cons. Inst. Def. Analyses; dep. dir. Rsch. Com. Money Credit, 1959-61. Author: (with others) Personal Finance Industry and Its Credit Standards, 1939, (with Steiner) Money and Banking, 1941, Development of Wisconsin Credit Union Movement, 1947, Money and Banking, 1953, (with others), 1958, (with D. Meiselman) Measurement of Corporate Sources and Uses of Funds, 1964, (with others) Money and Banking, 1969, (with Wolf) The Role of Private Placement in Corporate Finance, 1972; Editor: (with W.L. White) Capital for Productivity and Growth, 1977. Served from ensign to lt. USNR, 1942-46. Recipient Econ. Dept. award Bklyn. Coll., 1936, Honors Day award distinguished alumni, 1949 Fellow Am. Acad. Arts and Scis.; mem. Nat. Bur. Econ. Research (pres.), Am. Econ. Assn., Council Fgn. Relations, Am. Fin. Assn. Home and Office: 180 Beacon St Boston MA 02116-1408 Office Phone: 617-266-5512.

SHAPIRO, FANIA, computer company executive; CEO Setka Computer Cons., San Ramon, Calif. Office: Setka Computer Cons 3223 Crow Canyon Rd Ste 250 San Ramon CA 94583-1332 Fax: 925-824-0222.

SHAPIRO, FLORENCE, state legislator, advertising, public relations executive; b. N.Y.C., May 2, 1948; d. Martin Nmi and Ann (Spiesman) D.; m. Howard Nmi Shapiro, Dec. 28, 1969; children: Lisa, Todd, Staci. BS, U. Tex., 1970. Tchr. Richardson High Sch., Tex., 1970-72; advt., pub. rels. Shapiro & Co., Plano, Tex., 1982—; formerly mayor and mem. city coun. City of Plano, Tex.; now mem. Tex. Senate, 1992—, chmn. edn. com., mem. fin. com., natural resources com., and infrastructure, devel. and security com. Bd. dirs. Plano C. of C., Presbyn. and Children's Healthcare Ctr., Plano Econ. Devel. Bd., U. Tex. at Dallas Adv. Coun., The North Tex. Commn., The Dallas Regional Mobility Coalition; mem. nat. bd. dirs. Susan B. Komen Breast Cancer Found.; mem. adv. bd. Children's Edn. Fund Dallas, Dallas County Domestic Violence Task Force, Family Violence Prevention Coun. Injury Prevention Ctr. Greater Dallas. Recipient Plano Vol. of Yr. award, 1983, Plano Citizen of Yr. award, 1985, Athena award Plano C. of C. for Businesswoman of Yr., 1990, Child Advocate award Dallas Children's Advocacy Ctr., 1995, Legislator of Yr. award Tex. Mcpl. League, 1995, 97, Nat. Rep. Legislators Assn., 1997, Tex. Ct. Apptd . Spl. Advs., 1997; Outstanding Legislator of Yr. award Tex. Police Chiefs Assn., 1995, Legislator of Yr. award, 1997, Friend of the Taxpayer award Citizens for a Sound Economy, 1999, Centennial Hero award Plano Ind. Sch. Dist., 1999, Voice of Children award, Ct. Apptd. Spl. Advs. of Collin County, 2001, others; Outstanding Legislator award Tex. Assn. Dist. and County Attys., 1997, Leader of Excellence award Free Market Com., 1997, Senate Statesman award Lonestar Found., 1997, Polit. Courage award John Ben Sheppard Pub. Leadership Forum, 1997; named One of 10 Best Legislators family law session State Bar Tex., 1997, One of 3 State Senators on YCT Honor Roll, 1997, Legis. Star, Tex. Classroom Tchrs. Assn., 1997, Guardian of Free Enterprise, Nat. Fedn. Ind. Bus., 1999, Woman of Yr., Les Femmes du Monde, 2002, Woman of Yr., Women's Transp. Seminar Dallas-Ft. Worth, 2002, others; honored by Texans for Lawsuit Reform, 1997, Assn. Ob-Gyn. and Southwestern Med. Sch., 1997. Mem. Rotary (Paul Harris fellow 1990), Alpha Epsilon Phi (Nat. Outstanding Young Alumnae award). Republican. Jewish. Office: Tex Senate PO Box 12068 Austin TX 78711-2068 Home: 1500 Eastwick Ln Plano TX 75093-2443

SHAPIRO, FRED DAVID, lawyer; b. Cleve., Nov. 10, 1926; s. Isadore R. and Lottie (Turetsky) S.; m. Helen Solomon, Sept. 5, 1948; children— Gary N., Ira R., Diane S. BA cum laude, Ohio State U., 1949; LL.B., Harvard U., 1954. Bar: Ohio 1954. Since practiced in, Cleve.; sr. ptnr. Shapiro and Lodwick, Co., L.P.A, 1994—. Served with USNR, 1945-46. Mem. Ohio Bar Assn., Greater Cleve. Bar Assn., Cuyahoga County Bar Assn., The Rowfant Club, Phi Beta Kappa. Jewish. Home: 29226 S Woodland Rd Cleveland OH 44124-5737 Office Phone: 216-378-9730. E-mail: fshapo@aol.com.

SHAPIRO, GAIL GREENBERG, pediatric allergy educator; b. N.Y.C., Jan. 11, 1947; d. Jay and Roberta (Falk) Greenberg; m. Peter Shapiro, July 13, 1967; children: Jessica, Evan. BA, Brown U., 1967; MD, Johns Hopkins U., 1970. Diplomate Am. Bd. Pediatrics, Am. Bd. Allergy and Immunology (editorial bd. 1987—), Nat. Bd. Med. Examiners. Intern Johns Hopkins Hosp., Balt., 1970-71; resident in pediatrics U. Wash. and Children's Orthopedic Hosp. and Med. Ctr., Seattle, 1971-72, fellow in allergy and clin. immunology, 1972-74; clin. instr. pediatrics U. Wash., Seattle, 1974-75, clin. asst. prof., 1975-77, clin. assoc. prof., 1977-83, clin. prof., 1983—; clin. prof. allergy div. Children's Hosp. and Med. Ctr., Seattle, 1988-89. Vis. prof. Mayo Clinic, August, 1983, Nat. Jewish Hosp., Feb., 1984, Oakland Children's Hosp., June, 1988, Children's Meml. Hosp., Sept., 1989; mem. pulmonary and allergy adv. panel FDA, 1988—. Author: (with others) Current Therapy, 1975, Muscular Exercise and the Lung, 1977, The Critically Ill Child, 1977, Allergic Diseases of Infancy, Childhood and Adolescence, 1980, Practice of Pediatrics, 1980, A Differential Diagnosis of Pediatric Allergy, 1981, The Allergy Encyclopedia;, 1981, Allergy and Immunology, 1984, Recent Advances in Otitis Media with Effusion, 1984, The Critically Ill Child, 1985, Childhood Asthma Pathophysiology and Treatment, 1987, Current Therapy, 1988, Conn's Current Therapy, 1988; contbr. numerous articles to profl. jours. Fellow Am. Acad. Pediatrics (chmn. 1982-84, chmn. sect. allergy and program 1981-82, mem. exec. com. 1980-86), Am. Acad. Allergy and Immunology (chmn. seminars com. 1985-86, chmn. continuing med. edn. com. 1988—, chmn. pub. edn. and info. on accepted med. practices subcom. 1989—); mem. AMA, Am. Bd. Allergy and Immunology (bd. dirs. 1984-89, chmn. bd. dirs. 1987-88, chmn. exam. com. 1986-87), Wash. State Soc. Allergy and Immunology (past pres.), Wash. State Pediatric Soc., Wash. Lung Assn., Wash. State Thoracic Soc., Puget Sound Allergy Soc. (past pres.), King County Med. Soc., Wash. State Med. Soc., King County Med. Svc. Bur., Western Soc. Allergy and Immunology. Office: NW Asthma & Allergy Ctr PS 4540 Sand Point Way NE # 200 Seattle WA 98105-3941

SHAPIRO, GARY EVAN, newspaper journalist; b. Lewiston, Maine, Feb. 5, 1964; s. Sherman George and Charlotte (Cominsky) S. AB, Harvard U., 1986; JD, Columbia U., 1993. Assoc. Skadden Arps Slate Meagher & Flom, N.Y.C., 1993-94; writer, event prodr. N.Y.C., 1994-99; journalist Forward newspaper, N.Y.C., 1999—. Contbg. editor Am. Scholar, 2000—; note editor Columbia Jour. Environ. Law, 1993; contbr. numerous articles to profl. jours.; prodr. numerous programs on diplomacy, history, arch., bus., arts and lit., politics and econs., sci., edn., philosophy. Recipient Charles William Eliot medal for Citizenship, 1986, Cox Medal, Phillips Exeter, 1982; John Finley Traveling fellow, 1986. Mem. Overseas Press Club, Nat. Arts Club (lit. com. 1997—), Harvard Club (program com. 1995-2000). Avocation: book collecting. Home: 27 W 44th St # 50 New York NY 10036-6613 Office: Forward Newspaper 45 E 33rd St New York NY 10016-5336

SHAPIRO, GARY JOHN, retired lawyer; b. San Francisco, Oct. 4, 1941; s. Herbert H. and Raye (Wall) S.; m. Dana Bloom, July 5, 1964; children: Karen Hillary, Anne S. Mulvaney. BS, U. Calif.-Berkeley, 1963, JD, 1966. Bar: Calif. 1966, Fed. Dist. Ct. 1967, U.S. Ct. Appeals 1967. Law clk. Oliver D. Hamlin, U.S. Ct. Appeals, 9th Cir., 1966-67; assoc. Dinkelspiel & Dinkelspiel, San Francisco, 1967-69; ptnr. firm Buchman, Kass & Shapiro, Profl. Corp., Oakland, Calif., 1970-75; of counsel Steefel, Levitt & Weiss, 1985—2002. Judge pro tem Alameda County Mcpl. Ct., San Leandro-Hayward Jud. Dist., 1972; ptnr. Shapiro Assocs., Mill Valley; mem. faculty San Francisco Law Sch., 1968-71; mem. faculty John F. Kennedy U. Sch. Law, Sch. Bus. Adminstrn., 1977-79, Am. Coll., Bryn Mawr, Pa., 1977-79, Golden Gate U. Grad. Sch. Banking, Fin. and Real Estate, 1979-81; lectr. various tax and real estate seminars. Contbr. articles to legal jours. Pres. Estate Planning Coun. of East Bay, San Francisco, 1980; trustee, sec. Jacques and Esther Reutlinger Found.; trustee Helzel Family Found.; trustee, chair, chair fin. com. Pacific Grad. Sch. Psychology; trustee, chair investment com. St. Francis Hosp. Found.; trustee, pres., chair fin. com. Judah L. Magnes Mus.; bd. dirs. Temple Emanu El, San Francisco, 1989—95, Am. Friends Ben Gurion U.; Bd. dirs., pres. Endowment Found. of Jewish Welfare Fedn., 1985—87; Jewish Nat. Fund; bd. dirs., treas. Jewish Family Svc. Agy, Alameda County, Am. Friends Shaare Zedak Hosp.; Jewish Fedn. Greater East Bay. Mem.: Hebrew Free Loan Assn. (bd. dirs.), Am. Israel Pub. Affairs Com. of No. Calif. (bd. dirs., vice chmn., nat. exec. com.), Troon Club, Lake Merced Club, Concordia Argonaut Club, Order of Coif. Republican. Jewish. Office: 44 Montgomery St 41st Fl San Francisco CA 94104 E-mail: shapirog@alumni.haas.org.

SHAPIRO, GEORGE HOWARD, retired lawyer; b. St. Louis, Nov. 10, 1936; s. Isadore T. and Alice (Schucart) S.; m. Mary Kenney Leonard, 1977 (div. 1994); m. Ray Ann Kremer, 1999; 1 child, Ellen. BA, Harvard U., 1958, LLB, 1961; postgrad., London Sch. Econs., 1961-62. Bar: Ga. 1960, D.C. 1963. Atty. U.S. Dept. Labor, Washington, 1962-63; assoc. Arent Fox Kintner Plotkin & Kahn, Washington, 1963-69, ptnr., 1970-99; ret., 2000. Co-author: 'Cable Speech' The Case for First Amendment Protection, 1983; editor: New Program Opportunities in the Electronic Media, 1983, Current Developments in CATV, 1981. With USAR, 1962-68. Frank Knox Meml. fellow Harvard U., 1961-62. Mem. D.C. Bar Assn., Fed. Communications Bar Assn. Democrat. Jewish. Avocation: skiing. Home: Apt 906 3180 Mathieson Dr NE Atlanta GA 30305-1871 E-mail: GHSinATL@aol.com.

SHAPIRO, HAROLD DAVID, lawyer, educator; b. Chgo., Apr. 15, 1927; s. Charles B. and Celia (Nierenberg) S.; m. Beatrice Cahn, June 6, 1950; children: Matthew D., Michal Ann, Nicholas J. BS, Northwestern U., Chgo., 1949, JD, 1952. Adminstrv. asst. State of Ill. Dept. Fin., Springfield, 1952; assoc. Sonnenschein Nath & Rosenthal, Chgo., 1953-59, ptnr., 1959—; Edward A. Harriman adj. prof. law Northwestern U., Chgo., 1970—. Sec., bd. dirs. West Side Affordable Housing, Inc., West Side Village, Inc. Trustee, mem. exec. com., sec. Jr. Achievement of Chgo.; bd. dirs. Schwab Rehab. Ctr., Chgo.; pres. Homan & Arthington Found., 1995—96; trustee The Ringer Found., 2000—, The Guthman Found., 2003—; pres. Northwestern U. Law Sch. Alumni Assn., Chgo., 1984—85, chmn. dean's adv. coun., 1997—99; trustee The Guthman Foundation, 2003—. Served with Seabees USNR, 1945—50, PTO. Recipient Merit award Northwestern U., 1988. Mem. Ill. Bar Assn., ABA, Chgo. Bar Assn., Chgo. Council Lawyers, Legal Club of Chgo. (pres.), Law Club of Chgo., Order of Coif, Wigmore Key, Standard Club, Met. Club, Cliff Dwellers, Chicago Club, Lake Shore Country Club. Democrat. Jewish. Home: 34 Linden Ave Wilmette IL 60091-2837 Office: Sonnenschein Nath & Rosenthal 8000 Sears Tower 233 S Wacker Dr Ste 8000 Chicago IL 60606-6491

SHAPIRO, HAROLD TAFLER, former academic administrator, economist; b. Montreal, Que., Can., June 8, 1935; s. Maxwell and Mary (Tafler) Shapiro; m. Vivian Bernice Rapoport, May 19, 1957; children: Anne, Marilyn, Janet, Karen. BComm, McGill U., Montreal, 1956; PhD in Econs. (Harold Helm fellow, Harold Dodds sr. fellow), Princeton U., 1964. From asst. prof. to assoc. prof. econs. U. Mich., 1964—70, prof., 1970-76, prof. econs. and pub. affairs, 1977, chmn. dept. econs., 1974-77, v.p. acad. affairs, 1977-79, pres., 1980 87; rsch. adv. Bank Can., 1965-72; pres. Princeton (N.J.) U., 1988-2001, pres. emeritus, prof. econ. and pub. affairs Woodrow Wilson Sch., 2001—. Mem. exec. com. Assn. of Am. Universities, 1985—89; trustee N.J. Commn. Sci. and Tech., 1988—91; mem. Pres.'s Coun. Advisors Sci. and Tech., 1990—92; chmn. com. employer-based health benefits Inst. Medicine, 1991; bd. overseers Robert Wood Johnson Med. Sch., 2000—; bd. dirs. Dow Chem., DeVry Inst., Hastings Ctr., HCA. Editor (with William G. Bowen): (book) Universities and Their Leadership, 1998. Chair Nat. Bioethics Adv. Commn., 1996—2001; trustee Alfred P. Sloan Found., 1980—, Interlochen Ctr. Arts, 1988—95, U. Pa. Med. Ctr., 1992—; chmn. spl. Presdl. com. Rsch. Librs. Group, 1980—91; mem. Gov.'s High Tech. Task Force, Mich., 1980—87, Gov.'s Commn. Jobs and Econ. Devel., Mich., 1983—87, Carnegie Commn. Coll. Retirement, 1984—86, Pres. Bush Coun. Advisors Sci. and Tech., 1990—92; dir. Am. Coun. Edn., 1989—92; trustee Univ. Corp. Advanced Internet Devel., 2000—, Ednl. Testing Svc., 1994—2000. Recipient Lt. Gov.'s medal in commerce, McGill U., 1956. Fellow: Am. Acad. Arts and Scis., Mich. Soc. Fellows (sr.); mem.: Am. Philos. Soc., Inst. Medicine of NAS, Univs. Rsch. Assn. (trustee 1988—). Office: Princeton U Woodrow Wilson School 355 Wallace Hall Princeton NJ 08544-1013 Office Phone: 609-258-6184. Business E-Mail: hts@princeton.edu.

SHAPIRO, HARRY DEAN, lawyer; b. Louisville, June 21, 1940; s. Herman Shapiro and Toby (Spector) Levy; m. Linda Siegel, Dec. 19, 1970; 1 child, Deborah Anne. BS, U. Louisville, 1962, JD, 1964. Bar: Ky. 1964, D.C. 1968, Md. 1970. Trial and appellate atty. U.S. Dept. Justice, Washington, 1964-70; assoc. Venable, Baetjer & Howard, Balt., 1970-74, ptnr., 1975-87; sr. ptnr., head of tax practice Weinberg & Green, Balt., 1987—98, chmn. corp. dept., 1993-95; transaction group coord., 1995-98; head tax practice Saul Ewing LLP (formerly Saul, Ewing, Remick & Saul LLP), 1998-99; chmn. tax dept. Saul Ewing LLP (formerly Saul, Ewing, Remick & Saul LLP), 1999—. Author: Federal Tax Liens, 1981; contbr. articles to profl. jours. Mem. Md. State Bd. Edn., 1990-97; v.p. Assoc. Jewish Charities of Balt., Inc. 1991-94; vice chmn. The Assoc. Jewish Cmty. Fedn. Balt. 1987-89, asst. treas., 1989-91, mem. exec. com., 1993-97; trustee Sinai Hosp., Balt., 1987-90; counsel Balt. Mus. Art, 1984-97, trustee, 1984-96, sec., 1985-92, v.p., sec., 1992-94, v.p., 1994-96; dir., 1989-96; chmn. Joint Budgeting Coun., 1993-96, Coun. Jewish Fedns.; trustee Acad. Art Mus., Easton, 1998—. Capt. USAR, 1967-70. Recipient Disting. Alumni award Brandeis Sch. of Law, 1996, Chmn.'s award Balt. Mus. Art, 1996. Mem. ABA (tax sect.), Md. State Bar Assn., Ky. Bar Assn., D.C. Bar Assn., Md. Club, Center Club. Home: 7903 7 Mile Ln Baltimore MD 21208-4306 Office: Saul Ewing LLP 100 S Charles St Ste 1500 Baltimore MD 21201-2771 Office Phone: 410-332-8658. E-mail: hshapiro@saul.com. *Our country is at a crossroads in its history, and it is becoming clear that a sea change is necessary. Basic reforms must occur in our governmental and educational structures. The question is whether we have the intelligence to reject the cries for bigger government and more taxes to solve these problems when fundamental action is required.*

SHAPIRO, HARVEY, poet; b. Chgo., Jan. 27, 1924; s. Jacob J. and Dorothy (Cohen) S.; m. Edna Lewis Kaufman, July 23, 1953 (div.); children— Saul, Dan. BA, Yale U., 1947; MA, Columbia U., 1948. Instr. English Cornell U., 1949-50, 51-52; creative writing fellow Bard Coll., 1950-51; mem. editl. staff Commentary, New Yorker, 1955-57, N.Y. Times Mag., N.Y.C., 1957, asst. editor, 1964-75; editor N.Y. Times Book Rev., 1975-83; dep. editor N.Y. Times Mag., 1983-96, consulting editor, 1996—2002. Author: The Eye, 1953, The Book and Other Poems, 1955, Mountain, Fire Thornbush, 1961, Battle Report, 1966, This World, 1971, Lauds, 1975, Nightsounds, 1978, The Light Holds, 1984, National Cold Storage Company, 1988, A Day's Portion, 1994, Selected Poems, 1997, How Charlie Shaver Died and Other Poems, 2001; editor: Poets of World War II, 2003. Served with USAAF, World War II. Decorated D.F.C., Air medal with 3 oak leaf clusters.; Rockefeller Found. grantee in poetry, 1967 Club: Elizabethan (New Haven), Century (N.Y.).

SHAPIRO, HARVEY, journalist, writer, lyricist; b. Bklyn., Mar. 18, 1937; s. Louis and Pauline (Watson) S.; m. Judith Shapiro, June 16, 1962 (div. Dec. 1982); children: Eric, Elyse; m. Eileen Strachman, Apr. 20, 1985. BA in Journalism, L.I. Univ., 1958. Enlisted USAR, 1954; honorably discharged U.S. Army, 1962; reporter, editor various publs., 1958-1982; sports writer, sports slotman Dayton (Ohio) Daily News, 1974-79; founder, editor, pub. World of Speed, Dayton, 1979-81; copy editor Lake County Telegraph, Painesville, Ohio, 1982; gen. sales mgr. Del Rey Plastics Corp., N.Y.C., 1982-95. Author: Faster Than Sound, 1975 (named 1st in book divsn. 1976), Sports Stars Cookbook, 1978, Where Eagles Fly, 1996, Man Against the Salt, 1997 (named 1st in book divsn. 1997), Class of '68, 1998; composer: (with Hanan Harchol) A Simple Silver Band, 1989, We Love You, Welcome Home, 1991, Where Are You America?, 1992; contbr. articles to profl. jours. Recipient numerous writing awards AP, 1972-82; mag. named Top Nat. Motorsports Mag., Dayton Auto Racing Fan Club, 1980. Mem. ASCAP, Am.

Automobile Racing Writers and Broadcasters Assn. (writing awards 1974-98), Vietnam Vets. Am. (assoc. chpt. 151), Nat. Forget-Me-Nots. Avocations: photography, golf, concerts, whale watching. Home: 370 Buckskin Path Centerville MA 02632-2206

SHAPIRO, HOWARD, newspaper editor; Travel editor The Phila. Inquirer. Office: The Philadelphia Inquirer 400 N Broad St Philadelphia PA 19130-4015 E-mail: hshapiro@phillynews.com.

SHAPIRO, IRWIN IRA, physicist, researcher; b. N.Y.C., N.Y., Oct. 10, 1929; s. Samuel and Esther (Feinberg) S.; m. Marian Helen Kaplun, Dec. 20, 1959; children: Steven, Nancy. AB, Cornell U., 1950; A.M., Harvard U., 1951, PhD, 1955. Mem. staff Lincoln Lab. MIT, Lexington, 1954-70; Sherman Fairchild Distinguished scholar Calif. Inst. Tech., 1974; Morris Loeb lectr. physics Harvard, 1975; prof. geophysics and physics MIT, 1967-80, Schlumberger prof., 1980-84; Paine prof. practical astronomy, prof. physics Harvard U., 1982-97; sr. scientist Smithsonian Astrophys. Obs., 1982—; dir. Harvard-Smithsonian Ctr. for Astrophysics, 1983—; prof. Harvard U./Timken, 1997—. Cons. NSF, NASA. Contbr. articles to profl. jours. Recipient Albert A. Michelson medal Franklin Inst., 1975, award in phys. and math. scis. N.Y. Acad. Scis., 1982, Einstein medal Einstein Soc. Bern, 1994; Guggenheim fellow, 1982. Fellow AAAS, Am. Geophys. Union (Charles A. Whitten medal 1991, William Bowie medal 1993), Am. Phys. Soc.; mem. AAAS, NAS (Benjamin Apthorp Gould prize 1979), Am. Astron. Soc. (Dannie Heineman award 1983, Dirk Brouwer award 1987, Gerard Kuiper award 1997), Am. Philos. Soc., Internat. Astron. Union, Phi Beta Kappa, Sigma Xi, Phi Kappa Phi. Home: 17 Lantern Ln Lexington MA 02421-6029 Office: Harvard-Smithsonian Ctr Astrophysics 60 Garden St Cambridge MA 02138-1516 E-mail: ishapiro@cfa.harvard.edu.

SHAPIRO, ISAAC, lawyer; b. Tokyo, Jan. 5, 1931; s. Constantine and Lydia (Chernetzky) S.; m. Jacqueline M. Weiss, Sept. 16, 1956; children: Tobias, Alexandra, Natasha. AB, Columbia U., 1954, LLB, 1956; postgrad., U. Paris, 1956—57. Bar: N.Y. 1957, U.S. Supreme Ct. 1971, Paris 1991. Assoc. Milbank, Tweed, Hadley & McCloy, N.Y.C., 1956-65, ptnr., 1966-86, resident ptnr. Tokyo, 1977-79; ptnr. Skadden Arps Slate Meagher & Flom LLP, N.Y.C., 1986—2001; resident ptnr. Skadden Arps Slate Meagher & Flom, Hong Kong, 1989-90, Paris, 1990—2001; of counsel Skadden Arps Slate Meagher & Flom LLP, N.Y.C., 2001—; tchg. fellow comparative law NYU, 1959-61. Lectr. Soviet law, 1961-67; adj. asst. prof. NYU, 1967-69, adj. assoc. prof., 1969-71, 74-75; adj. prof., dir. Russian legal studies Columbia Law Sch., 1999-2000; bd. dirs. Bank of Tokyo Mitsubishi Trust Co., N.Y.C., 1975-77, 80-2001, Enherent, Inc., Windsor, Conn., 1981-2003. Author: (with Hazard and Maggs) The Soviet Legal System, 1969; author: Japan: The Risen Sun (in Japanese), 1982; editor: The Middle East Crisis-Prospects for Peace, 1969; contbr. articles to profl. jours. Mem. Joint Com. U.S.-Japan Cultural and Ednl. Cooperation, Washington, 1972-78; mem. Japan-U.S. Friendship Commn., 1975-78; mem. svcs. policy adv. com. to U.S. Trade Rep., 1981-91; trustee Nat. Humanities Ctr., Triangle Park, N.C., 1976-89, Bank of Tokyo Mitsubishi Found., 1996—; trustee, v.p. Chamber Music Soc. Lincoln Ctr., 1980-86, Isamu Noguchi Zaidan, Japan, 1999—; trustee, pres. Isamu Noguchi Found., N.Y., 1985—; trustee, chmn. Ise Cultural Found., 1984-90; bd. dirs. Bus. Coun. for Internat. Understanding, 1989-95, Nat. Com. for U.S.-China Rels., 1989-95, Asian Cultural Coun., 1980—; bd. adv. Trust for Mutual Understanding, N.Y.C., N.Y., 1985-. With U.S. Army, 1950-52. Fulbright scholar, 1956-57. Mem.: ABA, Barristers Chambers London, N.Y. State Bar Assn., Coun. Fgn. Rels., Japan Soc., Century Assn. (N.Y.C.), Cercle de l'Union Interalliee (Paris), Royal Automobile Club (London). Office: Skadden Arps Slate Meagher & Flom LLP 4 Times Sq New York NY 10036-6522 Office Phone: 212-735-3480. Business E-Mail: ishapiro@skadden.com.

SHAPIRO, ISADORE, materials scientist, consultant; b. Mpls., Apr. 25, 1916; s. Jacob and Bessie (Goldman) Shapiro; m. Mae Hirsch, Sept. 24, 1938; children: Stanley Harris, Jerald Steven. BChemE summa cum laude, U. Minn., 1938, PhD, 1944. Registered profl. engr., Calif. Asst. instr. chemistry U. Minn., 1938—41, rsch. fellow, 1944—45; rsch. chemist E.I. duPont de Nemours and Co., Phila., 1946; head chem. lab. U.S. Naval Ordnance Test Sta., Pasadena, Calif., 1947—52; dir. rsch. lab. Olin-Mathieson Chem. Corp., 1952—59; head chemistry Hughes Tool Co., Aircraft divsn., Culver City, Calif., 1959—62; pres. Universal Chem. Sys. Inc., 1962—, Aerospace Chem. Sys., Inc., 1964—66; dir. contract rsch. HITCO, Gardena, Calif., 1966—67; prin. scientist Douglas Aircraft Co. of McDonnell Douglas Corp., Santa Monica, Calif., 1967, McDonnell Douglas Astronautics Co., 1967—70; head materials and processes AiResearch Mfg. Co., Torrance, Calif., 1971—82, cons., 1982—. Inaugurated dep. gov. Am. Biog. Inst. Rsch. Assn., 1988; dep. dir. gen. Internat. Biog. Ctr., 1989, vice consul, 2002—; eng. rater U.S. Civil Svc. Bd. Exam, 1948—52. Contbr. articles to tech. publs. 1st lt. AUS, 1941—44. Fellow: AIAA (assoc.), Am. Inst. Chemists; mem.: AIM, AAAS, Internat. Plansee Soc. for Powder Metallurgy, Am. Powder Metallurgy Inst., Nat. Inst. Ceramic Engrs., Am. Ceramic Soc., Am. Assn. Contamination Control, NY Acad. Scis., Am. Phys. Soc., Am. Inst. Physics, Soc. Advancement Materials and Process Engring., Soc. Rheology, Am. Chem. Soc., Am. Ordnance Assn., Phi Lambda Upsilon, Tau Beta Pi, Sigma Xi. Achievements include patentee, discoverer series of carborane compounds; created term "carborane"; formulator of universal compaction equation for powders (metals, ceramics, polymers, chemicals). Home: 5624 W 62nd St Los Angeles CA 90056-2009

SHAPIRO, JAMES EDWARD, judge; b. Chgo., May 28, 1930; BS, U. Wis., 1951; JD, Harvard U., 1954. Bar: Wis. 1956, U.S. Dist. Ct. (ea. dist.) Wis. 1956, U.S. Ct. Appeals (7th cir.) 1962, U.S. Supreme Ct. 1971. Sole practice, Milw., 1956-57; resident house counsel Nat. Presto Industries, Eau Claire, Wis., 1957-60; ptnr. Bratt & Shapiro, Milw., 1960-64; sole practice Milw., 1964-74; ptnr. Frank, Hiller & Shapiro, Milw., 1974-82; judge U.S. Bankruptcy Ct., Milw., 1982—, chief judge, 1996-2000. Mem. Bayside Bd. Appeals, Wis., 1969-77; Milwaukee County Ct. commr., 1969-78; dir. Milw. Legal Aid Soc., 1969-77. Served to 1st lt. U.S. Army, 1954-56. Jewish. Office: US Courthouse 140 Fed Bldg 517 E Wisconsin Ave Milwaukee WI 53202-4500 E-mail: james_e_shapiro@wieb.uscourts.gov.

SHAPIRO, JOAN ISABELLE, lab administrator, medical/surgical nurse; b. Aug. 26, 1943; d. Macy James and Frieda Lockhart; m. Ivan Lee Shapiro, Dec. 28, 1968; children: Audrey, Michael. Diploma, Peoria Meth. Sch. Nursing, 1964. RN. RN Nurse Grant Hosp., Columbus, Ohio, 1975-76, Cardiac Thoracic and Vascular Surgeons Ltd., Geneva, Ill., 1977—, mgr. non-ivasive lab., 1979—. Owner operator Shapiro's Mastiff's 1976-82; sec.-treas. Sounds Svcs., 1976—, Mainstream Sounds Inc., 1980-84; co-founder Cardio-Phone Inc., 1982-99, Edgewater Vascular Inst., 1987-89, Associated Profls., 1989-92; v.p. Computer Specialists Inc., 1986-89; founder, pres. Vein Ctr., Edema Ctr. Ltd. Mem. DAR (sec. Katahdin Valley-Lydia Putman chpt. 2004—), Soc. Non-invasive Technologists, Soc. Peripheral Vascular Nursing (cmty. awareness com. 1984-2004), Oncology Nursing Soc., Internat. Soc. Lymphology, Kane County Med. Soc. Aux. (pres. 1983-84, adviser, 1984-85). Lutheran. Home: Cardiac Thoracic/Vas Surg PO Box 325 Fort Fairfield ME 04742-0325 E-mail: joan@ivanshapiro.com.

SHAPIRO, JOEL ELIAS, artist; b. N.Y.C., Sept. 27, 1941; s. Joseph and Anna (Lewis) S.; m. Ellen Phelan; 1 dau., Ivy Bess. BA, NYU, 1964, MA, 1969. One-person shows include Paula Cooper Gallery, N.Y.C., 14 shows 1970-90, The Clocktower Gall., Inst. Art and Urban Resources, NYC, 1973, Mus. Contemporary Art, Chgo., 1976, Albright-Knox Art Gallery, Buffalo, 1977, Gallery M. Bochum, W. Ger., 1978, Galerie Mukai, Tokyo, 1980, 81, 88, 91, Asher/Faure, L.A., 1980, 89, 91, Whitechapel Gallery, London, 1980, Haus Lange, Krefeld, W.Ger., 1980, Moderna Museet, Stockholm, 1980, Brown U., 1980, Ackland Art Mus., Chapel Hill, N.C., 1981, Contemporary Arts Ctr., Cin., 1981, Israel Mus., Jerusalem, 1981, Portland Ctr. Visual Arts, Oreg., 1982, Whitney Mus. Am. Art, N.Y.C., 1982, Galerie Aronowitsch, Stockholm, 1984, Delahunty Gallery, Dallas, 1980, Donald Young Gallery, Chgo., 1987, Stedelijk Mus., Amsterdam, 1985, Kunstmuseum, Dusseldorf, 1985, Staatliche Kunsthalle, Baden-Baden, 1986, Seattle Art Mus., 1986, Galerie Daniel Templon, Paris, 1986, 88, The John and Mable Ringling Mus., Sarasota, 1986, John Berggruen Gallery, San Francisco, 1987, Hirshhorn Mus. and Sculpture Garden, Washington, 1987, Hans Strelow, Dusseldorf, Germany, 1988, Toledo Mus. Art, 1989, Waddington Gallery, London, 1989, Museet I Varberg, Sweden, 1990, Balt. Art Mus., 1990, Des Moines Art Ctr., 1990, Ctr. for Fine Arts, Miami, 1991, IVAM Centre Julio Gonazlez, Valencia, Spain, 1990, John Berggruen Gallery, San Francisco, 1991, Pace Gallery, 1993, Galerie Karsten Greve, Cologne, Germany, 1993, Gallery Seomi, Seoul, 1994, 96, Galerie Aronowitsch, Stockholm, 1995, Karsten Greve, Paris, 1995, Walker Art Ctr./Mpls. Sculpture Garden, 1995, Nelson-Atkins Mus. Art/Kansas City Sculpture Park, 1996, Pace Wildenstein Gallery, N.Y., 1995, 96, 98, 2001, 02, 03, Galerie Biedermann, Munich, Germany, 1997, Addison Gallery, Andover, Mass., 1997, Haus der Kunst, Munich, 1997, Barlach Halle K, Hamburg, 1998, Galerie Jamileh Weber, Zurich, Switzerland, 1997, Pace Wildenstein, L.A., 1999, Am. Acad. in Rome, 1999, Boston Mus. Fine Arts, 1999, New Art Ctr., Salisbury, Eng., 1999, Yorkshire Sculpture Park, Wakefield, Eng., 1999-2000, Nat. Gallery Can., 1999-2000, John Berggruen Gallery, San Francisco, 2000, Timothy Taylor Gallery, London, 2000, Spoleto Festival USA, Charleston, S.C., 2000, McNay Art Mus., San Antonio, 2000-01, Denver Art Mus., 2001, Galerie Daniel Templon, Paris, 2001, 04, The Met. Mus. Art, N.Y., 2001, Gerald B. Cantor Rooftop Galleries, N.Y., 2001, L.A. Louver Gallery, 2004; numerous group exhibits; permanent collections and commns. include Mus. Modern Art, N.Y.C., Whitney Mus. Art, N.Y.C., Walker Art Center, Mpls., Met. Mus. Art, N.Y.C., Albright Knox Art Gallery, Buffalo, Detroit Inst. Art, Stedelijk Mus., Amsterdam, Moderna Museet, Stockholm, Dallas Mus. Art, Centre Pompidou, Paris, Nat. Gallery Art, Washington, Brit. Mus., London, Bklyn. Mus., Cocoran Gallery, Washington, Fogg Art Mus. at Harvard U., Cambridge, Mass., High Mus. Art, Atlanta, Hirshhorn Mus. and Sculpture Garden at Smithsonian Instn., Washington, Israel Mus., Jerusalem, Kunsthaus Zürich, Switzerland, Mus. Contemporary Art, L.A., Mus. Fine Arts, Boston, Mus. Modern Art, Friuli, Italy, Parrish Art Mus., Southampton, N.Y., Phila. Mus. Art, Tate Gallery, London, Cleve. Mus. Art, N.C. Mus. Art, Raleigh, Des Moines Art Ctr.; commns. include Cigna Corp., Phila., 1983-84, Fukuoka (Japan) Sogo Bank, 1988, Creative Artists Agy., L.A., 1988-89, Kawamura Meml. Mus. Art, Chiba, Japan, 1988-89, Govt. Svc. Adminstrn., L.A., 1988-90, Hood Mus. Art at Dartmouth Coll., Hanover, N.H., 1989-90, U.S. Holocaust Meml. Mus., Washington, 1993, Sony Music Entertainment, N.Y.C., 1994-95, Friedrichstadt Passagen, Berlin, 1994-95, Kansas City (Mo.) Internat. Airport, 1995-96, Embassy of U.S.A., Ottawa, 1999, Koln Skulpture Park, 1999. Recipient Nat. Endowment for Arts award, 1975, Brandeis award, 1984, Skowhegan medal, 1986. Mem. Am. Acad. and Inst. Arts and Letters (Merit award 1990), Am. Acad. Arts and Letters, Swedish Royal Acad. Art. Office: care Pace Idenstein 32 E 57th St New York NY 10022-2513

SHAPIRO, JUDITH R. academic administrator, anthropology educator; b. N.Y.C., Jan. 24, 1942; Student, Ecole des Haute Etudes Inst. d'Etudes Politiques, Paris, 1961—62; BA, Brandeis U., 1963; PhD, Columbia U., 1972. Asst. prof. U. Chgo., 1970—75; fellow U. Calif., Berkeley, 1974—75; Rosalyn R. Schwartz lectr., asst. prof. anthropology Bryn Mawr Coll., Pa., 1975—78, assoc. prof., 1978—85, prof., 1985—94; pres. Barnard Coll., 1994—. Chmn. dept. Bryn Mawr Coll., 1982—85, acting dean undergrad coll., 1985—86, provost, 1986—94. Contbr. articles to profl. jours. Nat. adv. com. Woodrow Wilson Nat. Fellowship Found.; chair bd. dirs. Consortium on Financing Higher Edn.; bd. dirs. Fund for the City of N.Y.; chair bd. dirs. Women's Coll. Coalition. Fellow, Woodrow Wilson Found., 1963—64, Columbia U., 1964—65, Younger Humanist fellow, NEH, 1974—75, Am. Coun. Learned Socs., 1981—82, Ctr. for Advanced Study in the Behavioral Scis., 1989; grantee Summer Field Tng. grant, NSF, 1965, Ford Found., 1966, NIMH, 1974—75, Social Sci. Rsch. Coun., 1974—75. Mem.: Social Sci. Rsch. Coun. (com. social sci personnel 1977—80), Am. Anthrop. Assn. (ethics com. 1976—79, bd. dirs. 1984—86, exec. com. 1985—86), Am. Ethnol. Soc. (nominations com. 1983—84, pres. elect 1984—85, pres. 1985—86), Phila. Anthrop. Soc. (pres. 1983), Women's Forum, Sigma Xi, Phi Beta Kappa. Office: Barnard Coll Office of the Pres 3009 Broadway New York NY 10027-6501

SHAPIRO, KENNETH N. neurosurgeon; b. Bklyn., Aug. 7, 1943; Degree in politics, Princeton U., 1965; MD, U. Pitts., 1970. Diplomate Am. Bd. Neurol. Surgery, Am. Bd. Pediat. Neurol. Surgery. Intern Montefiore Hosp. Med. Ctr., Bronx, NY, 1970—71, resident in neurol. surgery, 1971—72, Albert Einstein U. Hosp., NY, 1972—74, 1977—78, fellow in neurol. surgery, 1974—76; registrar Hosp. for Sick Children, Gt. Ormond St., London; dir. pediat. neurosurgery Albert Einstein Coll. Medicine, 1978—86; founder Neurosurgeons for Children, Dallas, 1985—; attending neurosurgeon Children's Med. Ctr., Dallas, 1987—, med. dir. pediat. neurooncology program, 1991—; attending neurosurgeon Med. City Dallas Hosp., 1987—, Parkland Meml. Hosp., 1987—. Consulting neurosurgeon Tex. Scottish Rite Hosp. for Children, 1987—; asst. prof. pediat. Albert Einstein Coll. Medicine, 1978—83, assoc. prof. neurol. surgery, 1983—87, assoc. prof. pediat., 1984—87; clin. assoc. prof. U. Tex. Southwestern Med. Sch., Dallas, 1987—; presenter in field. Editor: (books) Pediatric Head Trauma, 1983, Hydrocephalus, 1984; editor Pediat. Neurosurgery jour. Office: Children's Med Ctr - Neurosurgery 1935 Motor St Dallas TX 75235

SHAPIRO, LARRY, lawyer, Internet company executive; B, U. Pa.; JD, U. Mich. Assoc. Weil, Gotshal & Manges, L.A., O'Melveny & Myers, L.A.; v.p., counsel corp. legal dept. Walt Disney Co.; exec. v.p. bus. devel. and ops. Buena Vista Internat Group subs. Walt Disney Co., sr. v.p. bus. and legal affairs; exec. v.p. bus. devel. and ops., gen. counsel Walt Disney Internet Group, North Hollywood, Calif., 1999—. Office: Walt Disney Internet Group 5161 Lankershim Blvd North Hollywood CA 91601

SHAPIRO, LARRY J. pediatrician, scientist, educator; b. July 6, 1946; s. Philip and Phyllis Shapiro; m. Carol-Ann Uetake; children: Jennifer, Jessica, Brian. AB, Washington U., St. Louis, 1968, MD, 1971. Diplomate Am. Bd. Pediat., Am. Bd. Med. Examiners, Am. Bd. Med. Genetics. Intern St. Louis Children's Hosp., 1971—72, resident, 1971—73; rsch. assoc. NIH, Bethesda, Md., 1973—75; asst. prof. Sch. Medicine UCLA, 1975—79, assoc. prof., 1979—83, prof. pediat. and biol. chemistry, 1983—91; investigator Howard Hughes Med. Inst., 1987—91, investigator, W.H. and Marie Wattis Disting. prof.; prof., chmn. dept. pediat. U. Calif.-San Francisco Sch. Medicine, 1991—2003; chief pediat. svcs. U. Calif.-San Francisco Med. Ctr., 1991—2003; Spencer T. and Ann W. Olin Disting. prof., exec. vice chancellor for med. affairs, dean Washington U. Sch. Medicine, St. Louis, 2003—. Contbr. numerous articles to profl. publs. Served to lt. comdr. USPHS, 1973—75. Fellow: AAAS, Am. Acad. Pediat. (E. Mead Johnson award in rsch. 1982); mem.: Am. Acad. Arts and Scis., Am. Pediatric Soc. (coun. mem. 1999—2001, pres. 2003—04), Am. Soc. Clin. Investigation, Am. Soc. Human Genetics (coun. 1985—88, pres.-elect 1995, pres. 1997), Assn. Am. Physicians, Soc. for Inherited Metabolic Disease (coun. 1983—88, pres. 1986—87), Western Soc. for Pediatric Rsch. (coun. 1983—87, pres. 1989—90, Ross award in rsch. 1981), Soc. Pediatric Rsch. (coun. 1984—87, pres. 1991—92), Inst. Medicine of NAS. Office: Wash U 660 S Euclid campus box 8106 Saint Louis MO 63110

SHAPIRO, LEO J. social researcher; b. N.Y.C., July 8, 1921; m. Virginia L. Johnson, Feb. 9, 1952; children: David, Erik, Owen, Amy. BA, U. Chgo., 1942, PhD, 1952. Survey specialist Fed. Govt. Agy., Washington, 1941-45, Sci. Rsch. Assn., Chgo., 1948-52; prin., founder Leo J. Shapiro and Assocs., Chgo., 1952-91; pres. Greenhouse, Inc., 1991—2001, SAGE LLC Survival & Growth Enterprise, Chgo., 2002—. Bd. dirs. Field of Flowers. Fellow U. Chgo., 1949. Fellow Social Sci. Rsch. Coun.; mem. Am. Sociol. Assn., Phi Beta Kappa.

SHAPIRO, LUCY, molecular biology educator; b. N.Y.C., July 16, 1940; d. Philip and Yetta (Stein) Cohen; m. Roy Shapiro, Jan. 23, 1960 (div. 1977); 1 child, Peter; m. Harley H. McAdams, July 28, 1978; stepchildren: Paul, Heather. BA, Bklyn. Coll., 1962; PhD, Albert Einstein Coll. Medicine, 1966. Asst. prof. Albert Einstein Coll. Medicine, N.Y.C., 1967-72, assoc. prof., 1972-77, Kramer prof., chmn. dept. molecular biology, 1977-86, dir. biol. scis. divsn., 1981-86; Eugene Higgins prof., chmn. dept. microbiology, Coll. Physicians and Surgeons Columbia U., N.Y.C., 1986-89; Joseph D. Grant prof. devel. biology Stanford (Calif.) U. Sch. Medicine, 1989-97, chmn. dept. devel. biology, 1989-97, Virginia and D.K. Ludwig prof. of cancer rsch. dept. devel. biology, 1998—; dir. Beckman Ctr. Molecular & Genetic Medicine Stanford U., 2001—. Mem. bd. sci. counselors NIH, Washington, 1980—84; mem. bd. sci. advisors G.D. Searle Co., Skokie, Ill., 1984—86; mem. sci. adv. bd. SmithKline Beecham, 1993—2000; bd. dirs. SmithKlineBeecham, 1994—2000; bd. dirs., mem. sci. adv. bd. GlaxoSmithKline, 2001—; mem. sci. adv. bd. Anacor Pharms., 2001—, PathoGenesis, 1995—2000, Ludwig Found., 2000—; trustee Scientists Inst. for Pub. Info., 1990—94; lectr. Harvey Soc., 1993; DeWitt Stetten disting. lectr., 89, 2002; John M. Lewis lectr. Rockefeller U., 1998; Marker lectr. Pa. State U., 1999; Lundberg lectr. Gothenburg U., Sweden, 1999; honors lectr. NYU, 1998; disting. scientist lectr. NAS, 1999; Crawford lectr. U. Iowa, 1999; Oshman lectr. Baylor U., 2000; Adam Neville lectr. U. Dundee, Scotland, 2001; Genome lectr. Harvard U., 2001; Jesup lectr. Columbia U., 2002; Hopwood lectr. John Ennes Inst., Norwich, England, 2003; mem. grants adv. coun. Bechman Found., 1999—; Stanier lectr. U. Calif., Berkeley, 2003. Editor: Microbiol. Devel., 1984; mem. editl. bd. Jour. Bacteriology, 1978-86, Trends in Genetics, 1987—, Genes and Development, 1987-91, Cell Regulation, 1990-92, Molecular Biology of the Cell, 1992-98, Molecular Microbiology, 1991-96, Current Opinion on Genetics and Devel., 1991—; contbr. articles to profl. jours. Mem. sci. bd. Helen Hay Witney Found., N.Y.C., 1986-94, Biozentrum, Basel, 1999-2001, Hutchinson Cancer Ctr., Seattle, 1999; mem. grants adv. bd. Beckman Found., 1999—; co-chmn. adv. bd. NSF Biology Directorate, 1988-89; vis. com., bd. overseers Harvard U., Cambridge, Mass., 1987-90, 2003—; mem. sci. bd. Whitehead Inst., MIT, Boston, 1988-93; mem. sci. rev. bd. Howard Hughes Med. Inst., 1990-94, Cancer Ctr. of Mass. Gen. Hosp., Boston, 1994; mem. Presidio Coun. City of San Francisco, 1991-94; mem. pres. coun. U. Calif., 1991-97. Recipient Hirschl Career Scientist award, 1976, Spirit of Achievement award, 1978, Alumna award of honor Bklyn. Coll., 1983, Excellence in Sci. award Fedn. Am. Soc. Exptl. Biology, 1994; Jane Coffin Child fellow, 1966; resident scholar Rockefeller Found., Bellagio, Italy, 1996. Fellow AAAS, Am. Acad. Arts and Scis., Am. Acad. Microbiology, Calif. Coun. on Sci. and Tech.; mem. NAS, Inst. Medicine of NAS, Am. Philos. Soc., Am. Soc. Biochemistry and Molecular Biology (nominating com. 1982, 87, coun. 1990-93), Am. Heart Assn. (sci. adv. bd. 1984-87). Avocation: watercolor painting. Office: Stanford U Sch Medicine Beckman Ctr Dept Devel Biology Stanford CA 94305 Office Phone: 650-725-7678.

SHAPIRO, MARC J. bank executive; b. Houston, 1947; Grad., Harvard U., 1969; MBA, Stanford U., 1972. With Tex. Commerce Bancshares, Inc., Houston, 1972—, exec. v.p., 1976-82, vice chmn., 1982-89, CFO, until 1989, CEO, pres., 1989—, now chmn.; v. chmn. fin. Chase Manhattan Corp., N.Y.C. Chmn., CEO Tex. Commerce Bank N.A., Houston, vice chmn. fin., head risk mgmt. Chase Manhattan Corp., 1997—. Bd. dirs. Cornell U. Med. Coll., United Way N.Y.C., Local Initiatives Support Corp., Baylor Coll. Medicine; bd. visitors M.D. Anderson Cancer Ctr.; co-chmn. Houston Music Hall Found.; past chmn. Greater Houston Partnership. Office: JP Morgan Chase & Co 270 Park Ave Fl 8 New York NY 10017-2014

SHAPIRO, MARK, advertising executive; b. St. Louis, June 7, 1951; s. Harvey and Florley (Schimmel) S.; m. Patricia Suzanne Moore, Nov. 26, 1975; children: Andrew Phillip, Max Manlin. BA in English, Wash. U., 1973; MA in Journalism, U. Mo., 1975. Writer Maritz Inc., St. Louis, 1975-77, assoc. creative dir., 1977-78; creative dir. The Hanley Partnership, St. Louis, 1979-81, sr. v.p., 1981-84; mng. ptnr. The Hermann Group, St. Louis, 1984-86, pres., 1986—, Louis London (formerly The Hermann Group), St. Louis, 1988-90; CEO Louis London, St. Louis, 1990-99; chmn. & CEO Momentum N. Am., St. Louis MO, 1999—. Recipient N.Y. Art Dirs. award, 1982, Print ICA award, 1981-82. Mem. St. Louis Advt. Club, St. Louis Advt. Fed. (Flair award 1982-86, Addys award 1987), NIJADC-St. Louis, Phi Beta Kappa.

SHAPIRO, MARK HOWARD, physicist, educator, academic dean, consultant; b. Boston, Apr. 18, 1940; s. Louis and Sara Ann (Diamond) S.; m. Anita Rae Lavine, June 8, 1961; children: David Gregory, Diane Elaine, Lisa Michelle. AB with honors, U. Calif., Berkeley, 1962; MS (NSF coop. fellow), U. Pa., 1963, PhD, 1966. Research fellow Kellogg Radiation Lab., Calif. Inst. Tech., Pasadena, 1966-68; vis. assoc. divsn. math., physics and astronomy Calif. Inst. Tech., 1976—; research assoc. Nuclear Structure Research Lab. U. Rochester (N.Y.), 1968-70; mem. faculty Calif. State U., Fullerton, 1970—2002, prof. physics, 1978—2002, acting assoc. dean Sch. Math., Sci. and Engring., 1985-86, acting dir. Office Faculty Research and Devel., 1986-87, chmn. physics dept., 1989-96, 98-01, prof. physics emeritus, 2002—; dir. tchr. enhancement program NSF, Washington, 1987-88. Tour speaker Am. Chem. Soc., 1983-85 Editor, publisher: The Irascible Professor, 1999; contbr. over 125 articles to profl. jours. Pres. Pasadena Young Democrats, 1967-68; mem. pub. info. and edn. com. Calif. Task Force on Earthquake Preparedness, 1981-85; bd. dirs. Calif. State U. Fullerton Found., 1982-85. Grantee Research Corp., 1971-74, Calif. Inst. Tech., 1977-78, U.S. Geol. Survey, 1978-85, Digital Equipment Corp., 1982, NSF, 1985-87, 90—. Mem. AAAS, Am. Phys. Soc., Am. Assn. Physics Tchrs. (profl. concerns com. 1990-93, chmn. 1991-93), Am. Geophys. Union, N.Y. Acad. Scis., Materials Rsch. Soc., Coun. on Undergrad. Rsch. (physics/astronomy councillor 1993—). Achievements include research in experimental nuclear physics, experimental nuclear astrophysics, geophysics and atomic collisions in solids. Office: Calif State Univ Physics Dept Fullerton CA 92834-6866 Business E-Mail: mshapiro@fullerton.edu.

SHAPIRO, MARVIN LINCOLN, communications company executive; b. Erie, Pa., Feb. 12, 1923; s. Hyman and Flora (Burstein) S.; m. B. Gertrude Berkman, Oct. 25, 1946; children: Susan Jo, Barbara Ann, Jonathan David. BS, Syracuse U., 1948; postgrad., Williams Coll., 1966, Columbia U., 1975. Account exec. WSYR, Syracuse, 1948-50; account exec. sta. WCAU-TV, Phila., 1950-55, nat. sales mgr., 1956-58; account exec. CBS TV Spot Sales, Chgo., 1955-56, N.Y.C., 1958-60; with TV Advt. Reps., Inc., N.Y.C., 1961-66, exec. v.p., 1965-66, pres., 1968-69, dir., vice chmn., 1969-77, chmn., 1978; pres. Radio Advt. Reps., Inc., N.Y.C., 1966-68, dir., vice chmn., 1969-77; exec. v.p., COO, pres. sta. group Westinghouse Broadcasting Co., Inc., N.Y.C., 1969-77, sr. v.p., 1978-83, also dir., 1969-83; pres., dir. Foxwood Comm. Inc., N.Y.C., 1983—; mng. dir. Veronis Suhler Stevenson, N.Y.C., 1983—; pres., dir. Farragut Comm., Inc., N.Y.C., 1992-99, Columbia Empire Broadcasting Corp., Yakima, Wash., 1992-96. Bd. dirs. Broadcasting Ptnrs. Holdings, L.P., 1996-2000, VS&A Spectrum, Inc., 1997-2000; chmn. bd. Micro-Relay, Inc., 1974-83; chmn. bd. dirs., pres. CATV Enterprises, Inc., 1970-83. Boxing official Pa. Athletic Commn., 1952-55; Bd. dirs. TV Bur. Advt., 1974-81, chmn., 1977-79; bd. dirs. Radio Advt. Bur., 1970-77; With USAAF, 1942-45. Decorated Air medal with 9 oak leaf clusters.; recipient Communications Alumni award Syracuse U., 1960 Mem. Internat. Radio and TV Soc., DAV, Alpha Epsilon Rho (hon.). Clubs: Long Ridge (Stamford). Home: 26 Foxwood Rd Stamford CT 06903-2207 Office: Veronis Suhler Stevenson 350 Park Ave New York NY 10022-6022

SHAPIRO, MARVIN SEYMOUR, lawyer; b. N.Y.C., Oct. 26, 1936; s. Benjamin and Sally (Book) S.; m. Natalie Kover, July 12, 1959; children: Donna, Meryl. AB, Columbia U., 1957, LLB, 1959. Bar: D.C. 1959, Calif. 1962. Atty. appellate sect. Civil Div. U.S. Dept. Justice, Washington, 1959-61; ptnr. Irell & Manella, L.A., 1962-99, mng. ptnr., 1992-97. Lectr. U. So. Calif. Tax Inst., Calif. Continuing Edn. of the Bar, Practising Law Inst. Articles editor Columbia Law Rev., 1958-59. V.p., bd. dirs. Jewish Fedn. Coun., L.A., 1985-95; treas. Alan Cranston Campaign, 1974, 80, 86; chmn. credentials com. Dem. Nat. Com., 1972-76; bd. dirs. L.A. Opera Co., 1997—. Mem. Beverly Hills Barristers (pres. 1970). Avocations: travel, golf. Home: 432 N Cliffwood Ave Los Angeles CA 90049-2620

SHAPIRO, MATTHEW DAVID, economist, educator; b. Mpls., Apr. 11, 1958; s. Irving and Janet (Reinstein) S.; m. Susan L. Garetz, Oct. 21, 1989; children: Benjamin Avigdor, Molly Kendall. BA summa cum laude, MA, Yale U., 1979; PhD, MIT, 1984. Jr. staff economist Coun. Econ. Advisers, Washington, 1979-80, sr. economist, 1993-94; asst. prof. Yale U., New Haven, 1984-89; assoc. prof. U. Mich., Ann Arbor, 1989-95, prof., 1995—, sr. rsch. scientist, 2000—. Rschr. Nat. Bur. Econ. Rsch., Cambridge, Mass., 1986—;

mem. acad. adv. coun. Fed. Res. Bank Chgo., 1995-; mem. com. on nat. stats. NAS, 1999-2002; mem. Fed. Econ. Stats. Adv. Com., 2000-. Bd. editors Am. Econ. Rev., 1993-96, 00—, co-editor, 1997-00; contbr. articles to profl. jours. Recipient Paul A. Samuelson Cert. of Excellence, TIAA-CREF, 1997; Olin fellow Nat. Bur. Econ. Rsch., Cambridge, 1986-87, Alfred P. Sloan fellow Sloan Found., 1991-93. Mem. Am. Econ. Assn., Econometric Soc., Phi Beta Kappa. Office: U Mich Dept Econs 611 Tappan Ave Ann Arbor MI 48109-1220

SHAPIRO, MAURICE MANDEL, nuclear astrophysicist; b. Jerusalem, Nov. 13, 1915; came to U.S., 1921; s. Asher and Miriam R. (Grunbaum) S.; m. Inez Weinfield, Feb. 8, 1942 (dec. Oct. 1964); children: Joel Nevin, Elana Shapiro Ashley Naktin, Raquel Tamar Shapiro Kislinger; m. Ruth Auslander, Nov. 30, 2002. BS, U. Chgo., 1936, MS, 1940, PhD, 1942. Instr. physics and math. Chgo. City Colls., 1937-41; chmn. dept. phys. and biol. scis. Austin Coll., 1938-41; instr. math. Gary Coll., 1942; physicist Dept. Navy, 1942-44; lectr. physics and math. George Washington U., 1943-44; group leader, mem. coordinating council of lab. Los Alamos Sci. Lab., U. Calif., 1944-46; sr. physicist, lectr. nucleonics tng. sch. Oak Ridge Nat. Lab., Union Carbon and Carbide Corp., 1946-49. Cons. div. nuc. energy for propulsion aircraft Fairchild Engine & Aircraft Corp., 1948-49; head cosmic ray br. nucleonics div. U.S. Naval Research Lab., Washington, 1949-65, supt. nucleonics div., 1953-65, founder, chief scientist Lab for Cosmic Physics, 1949-82, apptd. to chair of cosmic ray physics, 1966-82, chief scientist emeritus, 1982—; lectr. U. Md., 1949-50, 1952—, assoc. prof., 1950-51, vis. prof. physics and astronomy, 1986—; vis. prof. physics and astronomy U. Iowa, 1981-84; vis. prof. astrophysics U. Bonn, 1982-84; vis. scientist Max Planck Inst. für Astrophysik, W. Ger., 1984-85; cons. Argonne Nat. Lab., 1949; cons. panel on cosmic rays U.S. nat. com. IGY; lectr. physics and engring. Nuclear Products-Erco div. ACF Industries, Inc., 1956-58; lectr. E. Fermi Internat. Sch. Physics, Varenna, Italy, 1962; vis. prof. Weizmann Inst. Sci., Rehovoth, Israel, 1962-63, Inst. Math. Scis., Madras, India, 1971; Inst. Astronomy and Geophysics Nat. U. Mex., 1976; vis. prof. physics and astronomy Northwestern U., Evanston, Ill., 1978, exec. dir. Astrophysics Assocs.(non profit corp.) 1995—; cons. space rsch. in astronomy Space Sci. Bd., Nat. Acad. Scis., 1965; cons. Office Space Scis., NASA, 1965-66, 89; prin. investigator Gemini S-9 Cosmic Ray Expts., NASA, 1964-69, Skylab, 1967-76, Long Duration Exposure Facility, 1977—; mem. Groupe de Travail de Biologie Spatiale, Council of Europe, 1970—; mem. steering com. DUMAND Consortium, 1976—, mem. exec. com., 1979-82, mem. sci. adv. com., 1982—; lectr. Summer Space Inst., Deutsche Physikalische Gesellschaft, 1972; founder, dir. Internat. Sch. Cosmic-Ray Astrophysics, Ettore Majorana Centre Sci. Culture, Erice, Italy, 1977—; chmn. U.S. IGY com. on interdisciplinary research, mem. nuclear emulsion panel space sci. bd.; Nat. Acad. Scis., 1959—; chief U.S. rep., steering com. Internat. Coop. Emulsion Flights for Cosmic Ray Research; cons. CREI Atomics, 1959—; vis. com. Bartol Research Found., Franklin Inst., 1967-74; mem. U.S. organizing com. 13th and 19th Internat. Confs. on Cosmic Rays; mem. sci. adv. com. Internat. Confs. on Nuclear Photography and Solid State Detectors, 1966—; mem. Com. of Honor for Einstein Centennial, Acad. Naz. Lincei, 1977; mem. Internat. Organizing com. Tex. Symposia on Relativistic Astrophysics, 1976—; Regents lectr. U. Calif. Riverside, 1985; Edison lectr. Naval Rsch. Lab award, 1990; plenary lectr. Oppenheimer Centennial, Gamow Centennial, 2004. Mem. editorial bd. Astrophysics and Space Sci., 1968-75; assoc. editor: Phys. Rev. Letters, 1977-84; editor (NATO) ASI Series on Cosmic-Ray Astrophysics; contbr. to Am. Inst. Handbook of Physics, various encys. Mem. exec. bd. Cong. Beth Chai, Washington, 1987—; trustee Nat. Capital Astronomers, Washington, 1989—; mem. internat. panel Chernobyl World Lab., 1988. Recipient Disting. Civilian Svc. award Dept. Navy, 1967, medal of honor Soc. for Encouragement au Progrés, 1978, Sr. U.S. Scientist award Alexander von Humboldt Found., 1982, Profl. Achievement citation U. Chgo., 1992; Guggenheim fellow, 1962-63. Fellow Am. Phys. Soc. (chmn. organizing com. div. cosmic physics, chmn. 1971-72, com. on publs. 1977-79), AAAS, Washington Acad. Scis. (past com. chmn., Disting. Career in Scis. award, 1993); mem. Am. Astron. Soc. (exec. com. div. high-energy astrophysics 1978—, chmn., 1982), Philos. Soc. Washington (past pres.), Am. Technion Soc. (Washington bd.), Alexander von Humboldt Assn. of Am. (pres. Washington area chpt. 2000—), Assn. Los Alamos Scientists (past chmn.), Assn. Oak Ridge Engrs. and Scientists (past chmn.), Fedn. Am. Scientists (past mem. exec. com., nat. council), Internat. Astron. Union (organizing com. commn. on high-energy astrophysics), Internat. Conf. on Cosmic Rays (Victor Hess Meml. lectr., Rome, 1995), Phi Beta Kappa, Sigma Xi (Edison lectr. 1990). Clubs: Cosmos (Washington). Achievements include patents in field; discovery of first definitive evidence for production of cosmic ray secondaries in the interstellar medium; first determination of the source composition of cosmic rays; prediction of isotopic composition of "arriving" cosmic rays, co-discovery of the sigma hyperon; research in cosmic radiation, composition, origin, propagation, and nuclear transformations; in high-energy astrophysics; in particles and fields; in nuclear physics, neutron physics and fission reactors; in hydrodynamics and piezoelectricity, in gamma-ray and neutrino astronomy; design of a low-enrichment nuclear reactor for submarines used at Shippingport and in various naval ships; identification of the fissile fuel in the first Soviet atomic explosion as plutonium. Address: 5809 Nicholson Ln # 801 North Bethesda MD 20852 Office Phone: 301-984-5992. *In scientific achievement, good judgement (e.g., in choice of research problems)is sometimes more important than brilliance.*

SHAPIRO, MEL, playwright, director, drama educator; b. Bklyn., Dec. 16, 1935; s. Benjamin Shapiro and Lillian (Lazarus) Bestul; m. Jeanne Elizabeth Shapiro, Feb. 23, 1963; children: Joshua, Benjamin. BFA, MFA, Carnegie-Mellon U., 1961. Resident dir. Arena Stage, Washington, 1963-65; producing dir. Tyrone Guthrie Theater, Mpls., 1968-70; master tchr. drama NYU, N.Y.C., 1970-80; guest dir. Lincoln Ctr. Repertory, N.Y.C., 1970; dir. N.Y. Shakespeare Festival, N.Y.C., 1971-77; prof. Carnegie Mellon U., Pitts., 1980-90, head. dept., 1980-87. Head acting UCLA Sch. Theater, Film and TV, 1990—. Dir. N.Y.C. prodns. The House of Blue Leaves, 1970, Bosoms and Neglect, 1978, Marco Polo Sings a Solo, 1998, Taming of the Shrew, 1999, Big Love (L.A.), 2002; co-adaptor mus. Two Gentlemen of Verona, 1971 (Tony award); author: (plays) The Price of Admissions, 1984 (Drama-Logue mag. award), The Lay of the Land (Joseph Kesselring award 1990), A Life of Crime, 1993; (books) An Actor Performs, 1996, The Director's Companion, 1998. With U.S. Army, 1955-57. Recipient N.Y. Drama Critics award, 1971, 72, Obie award Village Voice, 1972, Drama Desk award, 1973, Drama-logue award, 1993. Mem. Soc. Stage Dirs. and Choreographers (founder, editor The Jour. 1978). Office: UCLA Sch Theatre Film & TV 405 Hilgard Ave Los Angeles CA 90095-9000 E-mail: mshapiro@ucla.edu.

SHAPIRO, MICHAEL, supermarket corporate officer; b. N.Y.C., Mar. 3, 1942; s. Jack and Celia (Schwartzbaum) S.; m. Sara Louise Ress, Mar. 22, 1964; children: Jeffrey, Lisa, Kenneth. BS, CCNY, 1962. CPA, N.Y., N.J. Acct. Sidney Kaminsky & Co., N.Y.C., 1964-68; supr. Hurdman Cranston, Penney & Co. (C.P.A.s), N.Y.C., 1968-71; with Mayfair Super Markets Inc., Elizabeth, N.J., 1971-87, v.p. fin. and adminstrn., 1978-80, sr. v.p. fin. and adminstrn., 1980-86, exec. v.p. fin. and corp. devel., 1986-87, also dir.; self employed ins. cons., 1988-89; v.p. Fin. Fidelity Land Devel. Corp., Chatham, N.J., 1989-92; v.p. fin. and ops. Apex One Inc., Piscataway, N.J., 1992-94; sr. v.p., CFO, treas. Foodarama Supermarkets, Inc., Freehold, N.J., 1994—. Mem. AICPA, N.Y. State Soc. CPAs. Office: Foodarama Supermarkets Inc 922 Highway 33 Ste 6 Freehold NJ 07728-8453 E-mail: michael.shapiro@wakefern.com.

SHAPIRO, MICHAEL BRUCE, lawyer; b. Akron, Ohio, 1947; BBA summa cum laude, Kent State U., 1969; JD magna cum laude, U. Mich., 1972. Bar: Mich. 1972. Ptnr. Honigman Miller Schwartz & Cohn, LLP, Detroit. Mem. Nat. Assn. of Real Estate Investment Trusts subcom. on state and local taxes, citizens property tax commn. Mich. Senate, 1986-87. Mem. ABA, Am. Property Tax Counsel, State Bar of Mich., Inst. Property Taxation, Order of the Coif, Beta Alpha Psi, Pi Sigma Alpha, Beta Gamma Sigma. Office: Honigman Miller Schwartz & Cohn 2290 1st Nat Bldg Detroit MI 48226 E-mail: mbs@honigman.com.

SHAPIRO, NEAL, broadcast executive, television producer; s. Sumner and Mildred Shapiro; m. JuJu Chang, Dec. 2, 1995; 1 child. BA in History and Polit. Sci., Tufts U., 1980. With ABC News, 1980—93; spl. segment prodr. World News Tonight, 1986—89; broadcast prodr. PrimeTime Live, 1989—93; exec. prodr. NBC News, Dateline, N.Y.C., 1993—2001; pres. NBC News, 2001—. Recipient George Polk award, 1992, 2000, 2 Emmy awards, Investigate Reporter and Editor award. Office: NBC News 30 Rockefeller Plz New York NY 10112-0036*

SHAPIRO, NELLA IRENE, surgeon; b. NYC, Nov. 13, 1947; d. Eugene and Ethel (Pearl) S.; m. Jack Schwartz, Oct. 16, 1977; children: Max, Molly. BA, Barnard Coll., 1968; MD, Albert Einstein Coll., 1972. Resident in gen. surgery Montefiore Hosp., N.Y.C., 1972-76; mem. staff North Ctrl. Hosp., Bronx, NY, 1976-77, Bronx Mcpl. Hosp., 1977-87; chief gen. surgery Bronx Mcpl. Hosp. Ctr., 1983-87; mem. staff in gen. surgery Albert Einstein Coll. Hosp., Bronx, 1977-93, chief gen. surgery, 1991-93; atty. Lear Surg. Assocs., 1993-94; pvt. solo practice Bronx, 1994—. Asst. prof. surgery Albert Einstein Coll., Bronx, 1980—; assoc. dir. gen. surgery Weller Hosp., Bronx, 1991-93; co-founder Whaecom Breast Ctr., Bronx, 1991—. Fellow: ACS. Avocations: travel, skiing, opera. Office: 2425 Eastchester Rd Bronx NY 10469 Office Phone: 718-405-0400.

SHAPIRO, NELSON HIRSH, lawyer; b. Feb. 3, 1928; s. Arthur and Anna (Zenitz) S.; m. Helen Lenora Sykes, June 27, 1948; children: Ronald Evan, Mitchell Wayne, Jeffrey Mark, Julie Beth. BEE, Johns Hopkins U., 1948; JD, George Washington U., 1952. Bar: D.C. 1952, Va. 1981. Patent examiner U.S. Patent Office, 1948-50; patent advisor U.S. Signal Corps, 1950-52; mem. Shapiro & Shapiro, Arlington, Va., 1952 98, Vorys, Sater, Seymour and Pease LLP, Washington, 1998-2001, Miles & Stockbridge, McLean, Va., 2001—. Patentee; contbr. articles to legal publs. and Ency. of Patent Practice and Invention Mgmt., 1964. Mem. ABA, Am. Patent Law Assn., Bar Assn. D.C., Order of Coif, Tau Beta Pi. Home: 7001 Old Cabin Ln Rockville MD 20852-4531 Office: 1751 Pinnacle Dr Ste 500 Mc Lean VA 22102-3833 E-mail: nshapiro@milesstockbridge.com.

SHAPIRO, NORMA SONDRA LEVY, federal judge; b. Phila., July 27, 1928; d. Bert and Jane (Kotkin) Levy; m. Bernard Shapiro, Aug. 21, 1949; children: Finley, Neil, Aaron. BA in Polit. Theory with honors, U. Mich., 1948; JD magna cum laude, U. Pa., 1951. Bar: Pa. 1952, U.S. Supreme Ct. 1978. Law clk. to presiding justice Pa. Supreme Ct., 1951-52; instr. U. Pa. Law Sch., 1951-52, 55-56; assoc. Dechert Price & Rhoads, Phila., 1956-58, 67-73, ptnr., 1973-78; judge U.S. Dist. Ct. (ea. dist.) Pa., 1978—. Assoc. trustee U. Pa. Law Sch., 1978-93; former trustee Women's Law Project, Albert Einstein Med. Ctr.; v.p. Jewish Pub. Soc.; trustee Fedn. Jewish Agys., 1980-83; mem. lawyers adv. panel Pa. Gov.'s Commn. on Status of Women, 1974; legal adv. regional Coun. Child Psychiatry, bd. dirs. Women Judges' Fund for Justice. Guest editor: Shingle, 1972. Mem. Lower Merion County (Pa.) Bd. Sch. Dirs., 1968-77, pres., 1977, v.p., 1976; v.p. Jewish Community Relations Council of Greater Phila., 1975-77; chmn. legal affairs com., 1978; pres. Belmont Hills Home and Sch. Assn., Lower Merion Twp.; legis. chmn. Lower Merion Sch. Dist. Intersch. Council; mem. Task Force on Mental Health of Children and Youth of Pa.; treas., chmn. edn. com. Human Relations Council, Lower Merion; v.p., parliamentarian Nes Ami Penn Valley Congregation, Lower Merion Twp. Named Woman of Yr., Oxford Circle Jewish Community Center, 1979, Woman of Distinction, Golden Slipper Club, 1979; Gowen fellow, 1954-55; recipient Hannah G. Solomon award Nat. Coun. Jewish Women, 1992. Mem. Am. Law Inst., Am. Bar Found., ABA (ho. dels. 1990-96, coun./chmn. conf. fed. judges 1986-87, chmn. jud. divsn. 1996-97), Pa. Bar Assn. (ho. of dels. 1979-81), Phila. Bar Assn. (chmn. com. women's rights 1972, 74-75, chmn. bd. govs. 1977-78, chmn. pub. rels. com. 1978), Fed. Bar Assn. (Bill of Rights award 1991), Nat. Assn. Women Lawyers, Phila. Trial Lawyers Assn., Am. Judicature Soc., Phila., Nat. Assn. Women Judges, Fellowship Commn., Order of Coif (chpt. pres. 1973-75), Tau Epsilon Rho. Office: US Dist Courthouse Independence Mall West 601 Market St Rm 10614 Philadelphia PA 19106-1714

SHAPIRO, NORMAN RICHARD, Romance languages and literatures educator; b. Boston, Nov. 1, 1930; s. Harry Alexander and Eva (Goldberg) S. BA, Harvard U., 1951, MA, 1952, PhD, 1958; diplôme de Langue et Lettres Françaises, Université d'Aix-Marseille, 1956; MA (hon.), Wesleyan U., 1972. Instr. French Amherst Coll., 1958-60; asst. prof. romance langs. and lits. Wesleyan U., 1960-65, assoc. prof., 1965-71, prof., 1971—. Writer-in-residence Adams House Harvard U. Editor: Echos, 1965, Palabres, 1973; translator, editor: Négritude, 1971; translator: Four Farces by Georges Feydeau, 1970, Comedy of Eros, 1971, Kamouraska by Anne Hébert, 1973, Virginie, or the Dawning of the World by Joseph Majault, 1974, The Camp of The Saints by Jean Raspail, 1975, Feydeau, First to Last, 1982, Fables from Old French: Aesop's Beasts and Bumpkins, 1983, A Fitting Confusion by Georges Feydeau, 1985, The Pregnant Pause, or Love's Labor Lost, by Georges Feydeau, 1987, The Brazilian by Henry Meilhac and Ludovic Halévy, 1987, A Slap in the Farce by Eugène Labiche, 1988, A Matter of Wife and Death by Eugène Labiche, 1988, Fifty Fables of La Fontaine, 1988, The Fabulists French: Verse Fables of Nine Centuries, 1992, La Fontaine's Bawdy: Of Libertines, Louts and Lechers, 1992, A Flea in Her Rear, or Ants in Her Pants, and Other Vintage French Farces, 1994, Fifty More Fables of La Fontaine, 1998, Selected Poems from Les Fleurs du Mal, 1998, One Hundred and One Poems of Paul Verlaine, 1999 (MLA Scaglione award 2000), All Gall: Malicious Monologues and Ruthless Recitations, 1999, Once Again, La Fontaine, 2001, Take Her, She's Yours, or Till Divorce Do Them Part, by Georges Feydeau, 2001, The Jew of Seville, by Victor Séjour, 2002, The Fortune Teller, by Victor Séjour, 2002, Lyrics of the French Renaissance: Marot, Du Bellay and Ronsard, 2002, Creole Echoes: Francophone Poetry of 19th Century Louisiana, 2003; composer: Three Songs, 1961; mem. editl. bd. Tex. Rev.; contbr. articles, transls. and revs. to profl. jours. Mem. African Studies Assn., Am. Assn. Tchrs. French, Universala Esperanto-Asocio, Esperanto League N.Am., Judezmo Soc., Am. Lit. Transl. Assn. (Disting. Translation award 1992), Am. Translators Assn., Dramatists Guild, Beast Fable Soc. (editorial bd. Bestia), Poetry Soc. of Am., Acad. of Am. Poets, Signet Soc. of Harvard, Delta Kappa Epsilon. Jewish. Office: Wesleyan U Dept Romance Langs & Lit 300 High St Middletown CT 06459-3233 Office Phone: 860-685-3089. E-mail: nshapiro@wesleyan.edu.

SHAPIRO, PAUL SAUVEUR, chemical engineer, researcher; b. Pitts., Dec. 4, 1942; s. Carl Lynwood and Lillian Ruth (Simon) S.; m. Melissa Friedland, Jan. 19, 1986 (div. 1997); 1 child, Felix Benjamin. SB in Chem. Engring., MIT, 1963, SM in Chem. Engring., 1965, postgrad., 1967-71; EdM in Ednl. Planning, Harvard U., 1966. Expert cons. HEW and Action, Washington, 1972-76; sr. staff officer NRC, Washington, 1976-77; cons. Office Sci. and Tech. Adviser World Bank, Washington, 1977-80; cons. on nat. and internat. sci. and tech. AID, NSF and other agys., Washington, 1980-81; cons. Office Toxic Substances EPA, Washington, 1981-82, environ. engr. Office of Solid Waste, 1983-84, program mgr. Office R&D, 1985-94, CSI coord. Office R&D, 1994—. Vis. sr. rschr. Tel Aviv (Israel) U., 1979. Contbr. over 20 articles to profl. publs. Vol., advisor Vols. in Tech. Assistance, Arlington, Va., 1978-81; chmn. career edn. adv. coun. Washington Pub. Schs.; vice chmn. Early Environs., Inc. Fellow NDEA, NDFL, 1967, 70. Mem. AIChE (program coord.), Fed. Water Quality Assn. (sec.), Air and Waste Mgmt. Assn. (work group leader), MIT Club of Washington (pres.), MIT Luncheon Club (pres.), Sigma Xi, Phi Delta Kappa. Democrat. Jewish. Achievements include development of mitigation research programs for radon, indoor air pollution, stratospheric ozone protection, global climate change, and mixed hazardous and radioactive wastes; development of pollution prevention research programs with metal finishing and electronics industries; development with SBA and DOC of cooperative technical assistance programs for small business; co-development and implementation of EPA's highest priority program, The Common Sense Initiative including development of the first national sectoral environmental R&D plan; project officer environmental research grants. Home: 1312 4th St SW Washington DC 20024-2202 Office: EPA Office R&D (8722F) 1200 Pennsylvania Ave NW Washington DC 20024-2610

SHAPIRO, PHILIP ALAN, lawyer; b. Chgo., May 14, 1940; s. Joe and Nettie (Costin) Shapiro; m. Joyce Barbara Chapnick, May 29, 1966; children: David Ian, Russell Scott, Mindi Jennifer. AA, Wilson Coll., 1960; BS in Fin., So. Ill. U., 1965; MBA, Nat. Univ., San Diego, Calif., 1975; MBA in Mktg. with distinction, San Diego State U., San Diego, 1977; JD, Western State U., 1985. Bar: Calif. 1988. Spl. agt. U.S. Secret Svc., Washington, 1965-67, Chgo., 1967-77; mgr. divsn. sales Roche Labs. divsn. Hoffman-La Roche, Inc., Chgo.; account exec. Cellular Comm., Inc., San Diego, 1985; with Complete Comm., San Diego, 1983—; assoc. Law Office Jeffrey S. Schwartz, 1988-91; pvt. practice, 1991—. Chair gen. and solo practice sect. State Bar of Calif. Editor (law rev.): We. State U. Coll. Law. Mem. adv. bd. Spreckes Elem. Sch., San Diego, 1976—77; mem. Univ. City Town Coun., San Diego, 1977; pres. Congregation Beth El, La Jolla, Calif., 1976—79. With USMC, 1958—60. Recipient Merit award, U.S. Treasury Dept., 1965, Israel Solidarity award, 1977, U. Of Judaism award, 1978. Mem.: ABA (vice chmn. gen. practice sect.), Assn. Former Agts. of U.S. Secret Svc., San Diego Bus. Referrals (pres. 1998—99), San Diego County Bar Assn., State Bar Calif. (exec. com. gen. practice sect., Wiley W. Manuel award 1990—91), Calif. Trial Lawyers Assn., Thomas Jefferson Sch. of Law Alumni Assn. (pres. 2004—, bd. dirs.). Office: PO Box 178475 San Diego CA 92177-8475 Fax: 858-483-4639. Office Phone: 858-581-2477. E-mail: pshaplaw@san.rr.com.

SHAPIRO, RAYMOND L. lawyer; b. N.Y.C., Aug. 1, 1934; s. Alexander and Sadye (Morrison) S.; m. Judith Manis, Dec. 23, 1956; children: Joel, Todd, Lisa. BS, Temple U., 1956, LLB, 1959. Bar: N.Y., Pa. Ptnr. Wexler, Weisman, Forman & Shapiro, Phila., 1959-84, Blank, Rome LLP, Phila., 1984—. Author: Dunlap-Hanna Pa. Forms, 1963-83, Pa. Civil Practice Handbook, 1973-83; contbg.-author: Business Workouts Manual. Trustee Phila. Fedn. Jewish Agys., 1979—, treas., 1984-87, v.p., 1987-90; pres. Jewish Pub. Group, 1992-95. Fellow Am. Coll. Bankruptcy (v.p., chmn. bd. dirs. 1997-2001, chmn. found. 2002—); mem. ABA, Nat. Bankruptcy Conf., Pa. Bar Assn., Phila. Bar Assn., Am Coll. Bar Suply Found. (chmn 2002-). Office: Blank Rome LLP One Logan Sq Philadelphia PA 19103-6998 also: Blank Rome LLP 405 Lexington Ave New York NY 10174

SHAPIRO, RICHARD ALAN, surgeon; b. Chgo., 1927; MD, Loyola U., Maywood, Ill., 1949. Diplomate Am. Bd. Surgery, Am. Bd. Hospice and Palliative Medicine. Intern Michael Reese Hosp., Chgo., 1949—50, resident in surgery, 1950—51, 1953—56, sr. attending surgeon; clin. prof. U. Ill.; physician Chgo. ctrl. program Vitas Hospice, Ill.; pvt. practice, 1956—95. Fellow: ACS; mem.: Acad. Hospice Physicians. Office: 700 N Sacramento Blvd Ste 201 Chicago IL 60612 E-mail: RichardShapiro@vitas.com.

SHAPIRO, RICHARD CHARLES, publishing executive, sales executive, marketing professional; b. Bklyn., May 28, 1936; s. Isidore and Sylvia (Rappaport) Shapiro; m. Marilyn Joyce Baily, Feb. 17, 1957 (div. 1974); children: Joseph, Scott; m. Francine L. Shaw, Sept. 19, 1975. BS in Edn., Golden State U., 1978, MBA, 1981; PhD in Bus. Adminstrn. and Mktg., Honolulu U., 1987. Lic. real estate broker Ill. Sales mgr. Coca Cola Bottling Co. of N.Y., 1955-62; affiliate Effective Motivation Assocs./Success Motivation inst., Bethpage, N.Y., 1965-68; v.p. sales, dir. Field Enterprises, Chgo., 1962-78; pres., CEO Snack-In, Inc., Detroit, 1978-82; sr. ptnr. Directions Growth and Strategy Cons., Chgo., 1982-95; v.p. domestic & internat. mktg. & sales, oper. officer Ency. Brit.-Compton's Learning Co., 1991-93, specialist network mktg. & relationship mktg., CEO, pres., bd. dirs.; CEO Am.'s Home Detailing Corp., 1995—, CEO, chmn. bd., 2001—; pres., COO Am.'s Deep Clean Divsn., Deerfield, Ill., 1995—2000; CEO, chmn. emeritus Am.'s Home Detailing Corp., Deerfield, Ill.; instr. grad. studies mktg. mgmt., instr. human resources mgmt. Robert Morris Coll., Chgo., 2001—. Instr. planning Life Underwriter Tng. Coun., L.I., 1965—66; assoc. editor Media Technics Pub. Assn., Lake Forest, 1988; bd. dirs. Master Deep Clean Co., Nat. Video Libr.; spkr. on mktg., sales and leadership; cons. in field; liaison Chgo. Daily News, Chgo. Sun Times, Sta. WFLD-TV; founder Discovery Toy Divsn.; tennis pro, instr. Frank Sacks Tennis Camps, Chgo., 2001—; profl. tennis registry tennis instr., 2002—. Pub.: Real Estate Property Marketing News; author: self-improvement cassettes; contbr. articles to profl. jours. Active Explorers, high schs., youth clubs, 1965—74; founder, pres. Abundance and Goodwill Soc., 1968—. With USAF, 1957—60. Named Sales/Mktg. Execs. Leadership Recruiter/Trainder of Decade award; recipient Leadership award, Am. Sales Masters, 1968, 1999—2000, POPAI-OMA Best Industry Point of Purchase Display and Mktg. award, 1992. Mem.: Chgo. Computer Soc., Effective Motivation Assocs., Salesman with a Purpose, Deercreek Tennis Club (tchr., mem. rels. 2000—). Avocations: white-water rafting, white-water canoeing, camping, tennis, writing. Office Phone: 847-459-3435. E-mail: ahd10@yahoo.com., tennistowin@yahoo.com.

SHAPIRO, RICHARD GERALD, retired department store executive, consultant; b. N.Y.C., Apr. 24, 1924; s. David and Sophie (Hayflich) S.; m. Lila Eig, July 27, 1951; children— Judith, Amy, Donald. BA, U. Mich., 1946; MBA, Harvard, 1948. With Lord & Taylor, N.Y.C., 1948-64, v.p., 1959-63, sr. v.p., 1963-64; also mem. adv. bd.; pres. Wm. Filene's Sons Co., Boston, 1965-68, chief exec. officer, chmn. bd., 1968-73; pres. Gimbel Bros. Corp., N.Y.C., 1973-76; v.p W.R. Grace & Co., pres. sporting goods div., 1977-79, pres. splty. store div., 1979-84; pres. Richard Shapiro Assocs., 1979—; sr. v.p. Montgomery Ward, Inc., 1986-88. Bd. dirs. Assoc. Merchandising Corp., Nitrotec Corp., Capital Market Fund; retail chmn. Greater N.Y. Fund, 1963; chmn. merc. div. Mass. Bay United Fund, 1967 Mem. corp. Simmons Coll., Boston Mus. Fine Arts (permanent); bd. dirs. Mass. Mchts.; bd. dirs Family Counseling and Guidance Centers, 1969-72, v.p., 1970; trustee Brandeis U. Served with AUS, 1942-46. Mem. Harvard Bus. Sch. Assn. (gov.) Home: 10019 Gable Manor Ct Potomac MD 20854-5000 E-mail: rgsle@webtv.net.

SHAPIRO, RICHARD STANLEY, physician; b. Moline, Ill., June 11, 1925; s. Herbert and Esther Dian (Grant) S.; m. Arlene Blum, June 12, 1949; children: Michele Pamela, Bruce Grant, Gary Lawrence; m. Mary Lou Coook, Oct. 11, 1971. BS in Pharmacy, MS in Preventive Medicine & Environ., U. Iowa, 1951, MD, 1957. Diplomate Am. Bd. Allergy and Immunology. Pharmacist, Rock Island, Ill., 1951-53; rsch. asst. U. Iowa Coll. Medicine, Iowa City, 1950-51, 53-57; practice medicine specializing in allergy Beverly Hills, Calif., 1958-62, Lynwood, Calif., 1962—. Attending physician Good Hope Found. Allergy Clinic, Los Angeles, 1958-62, Cedars of Lebanon Hosp., Hollywood, Calif., 1959-68, U. So. Calif.-Los Angeles County Med. Center, 1962—; physician St. Francis Hosp., Lynwood, 1962—; assoc. clin. prof. medicine U. So. Calif., 1978-84, emeritus, 1984—. Contbr. articles to profl. jours. Bd. dirs. Westside Jewish Cmty. Ctr., 1961—65, Camp JCA, 1964—65. With USNR, 1943—46. Fellow Am. Geriatric Soc., Am. Coll. Allergy, Am. Assn. Clin. Immunology & Allergy; mem. AMA, AAAS, Am. Soc. Tropical Medicine and Hygiene, Am. Acad. Allergy, Am. Soc. Internal Medicine, Am. Heart Assn., West Coast Allergy Soc., Calif. Med. Assn., Calif. Soc. Internal Medicine, Calif. Soc. Allergy, L.A. County Med. Assn., L.A. Allergy Soc., Sierra Club, B'nai B'rith, Masons, Sigma Xi. Jewish. Office: 8301 Florence Ave Ste 104 Downey CA 90240-3946 Office Phone: 562-862-1991.

SHAPIRO, ROBERT, lawyer; b. Plainfield, N.J., Sept. 2, 1942; BS in Fin., UCLA, 1965; JD, Loyola U., L.A., 1968. Bar: Calif. 1969, U.S. Ct. Appeals (9th cir.) 1972, U.S. Dist. Ct. (ctrl., no. and so. dists.) Calif. 1982. Dep. dist. atty. Office of Dist. Atty., L.A., 1969-72; sole practice L.A., 1972—87; of counsel Bushkin, Gaims, Gaines, Jonas, L.A., 1987-88, Christensen, Miller, Fink & Jacobs, L.A., 1988-95; ptnr. Christensen, Miller, Fink, Jacobs, Glaser, Weil & Shapiro, L.A., 1995—. Author: Search for Justice, 1996, Misconception, 2001. Recipient Am. Jurisprudence award Bancroft Whitney, 1969. Mem. Nat. Assn. Criminal Def. Lawyers, Calif. Attys. for Criminal Justice, Trial Lawyers for Pub. Justice (founder 1982), Century City Bar Assn. (Best Criminal Def. Atty. 1993). Office: 10250 Constellation Ave 19th Fl Los Angeles CA 90067

SHAPIRO, ROBERT B. former food products manufacturing executive; b. N.Y.C., Aug. 4, 1938; s. Moses and Lilly (Langsam) Shapiro; m. Berta Gordon, Mar. 27, 1964; children: James Gordon, Nina Rachel. AB, Harvard U., 1959; LLB, Columbia U., 1962. Bar: N.Y. 1963. Assoc. in law Columbia U., 1962—63; atty. firm Poletti Freidin Prashker Feldman & Gartner, N.Y.C.,

1963—67; spl. asst. to gen. counsel and undersec. U.S. Dept. Transp., Washington, 1967—69; assoc. prof. law Northeastern U., Boston, 1969—71; asst. prof. law U. Wis., Madison, 1971—72; v.p., gen. counsel Gen. Instrument Corp., N.Y.C., 1972—79, G.D. Searle & Co., Skokie, Ill., 1979—82; pres. NutraSweet Group divsn. G.D. Searle & Co., Skokie, Ill., 1982—85; chmn., pres., CEO Nutra Sweet Co. subs. Monsanto, Skokie, Ill., 1985—95, also bd. dirs, 1992—; chmn., CEO Monsanto Co., St. Louis, 1995—2000; chmn. Pharmacia Corp., St. Louis, 2000—01. Bd. dirs. NY Stock Exchange, 2003—. Mem. bus. adv. com. White House Domestic Policy Rev. on Indsl. Innovation, 1978—79; nat. bd. trustees Boys Clubs of Am.; mem. Mass. Gov.'s Transp. Task Force, 1970—71; mem. com. on procedure CAB, 1975—76. Recipient John R. Miller award as outstanding corp. mktg. exec., 1984, Outstanding Achievement award, Sales and Mktg. Mgmt. Mag., 1984. Mem.: ABA (vice chmn. com. on corp. counsel 1981—82), N.Y. State Bar Assn., U.S. C. of C. (coun. on antitrust policy 1981—82). Office: Pharmacia Corp 800 N Lindbergh Blvd Saint Louis MO 63167-0001*

SHAPIRO, ROBERT FRANK, investment banking company executive; b. St. Louis, Dec. 19, 1934; s. Eugene J. and Clara (Katz) S.; m. Anna Marie Susman, Dec. 21, 1960; children: Albert Andrew, Robert Jr., Jeanne Savitt. Grad., St. Louis Country Day Sch., 1952; BA, Yale U., 1956. Assoc. Lehman Bros., N.Y.C., 1956-67, ptnr., 1967-73, dir., sr. mng. dir., 1970-73; ptnr. Wertheim & Co., 1974; exec. v.p. Wertheim & Co., Inc., N.Y.C., 1974-75, pres., 1975-86; co-chmn. Wertheim Schroder & Co., Inc., 1986-87; chmn. RFS and Assocs., Inc., N.Y.C., 1988—, New Street Capital Corp., 1992-94; vice-chmn. Klingenstein, Fields & Co., L.P., N.Y.C., 1997—. Bd. dirs. TJX Cos., Inc., Genaera Corp., The Burnham Fund, chmn. nominating com. N.Y. Stock Exch., 1980, mem. regulatory adv. com., 1988—, surveillance com., 1989—; bd. govs. Am. Stock Exch., 1970-76. Trustee Lenox Hill Hosp., Skowhegan; mem. gov. bd. Yale U. Art Gallery, New Haven, 1993—; trustee Louis Comfort Tiffany Found. Mem. Securities Industry Assn. (chmn. 1985, Bond Club N.Y. (pres. 1987-88, Yale Club, Century Country Club, Knickerbocker Club. Office: Klingenstein Fields & Co LLC 787 7th Ave New York NY 10019-6018

SHAPIRO, ROBERT JACOB, economic affairs executive; b. Balt., Oct. 4, 1948; AB, U. Chgo., 1970; MS, London Sch. Econs. and Polit. Sci., 1972; MA, Harvard U., 1980, PhD. Dir. econ. studies, co-founder Progressive Found., Washington; sr. advisor to Sec. of Commerce, Washington; under sec. of commerce for econ. affairs Dept. of Commerce, Washington, 1998—; v.p., co-founder Progressive Policy Inst., Washington, 1998—; dep. nat. issues dir./chief econ. policy Dukakis-Bentsen Presdl. Campaign, 1988; prin. econ. adv. Gov. Bill Clinton presdl. campaign, 1991-92. Legis. dir., tax coun., legis. asst. for budget policy to Sen. Daniel Patrick Moynihan of N.Y.; pres. Com. on Free Trade and Econ. Growth; advisor to members of Congress; cons. to maj. U.S. corps. and fin. instns. Assoc. editor U.S. News and World Report; contbg. editor The New Rep., Internat. Economy, IntellectualCapital.com.; contbr. articles to profl. jours. Office: Dept Commerce Econ and Stats Adminstrn 14th And Constitution NW Washington DC 20230-0001

SHAPIRO, ROBYN SUE, lawyer, educator; b. Mpls., July 19, 1952; d. Walter David and Judith Rae (Sweet) S.; m. Charles Howard Barr, June 27, 1976; children: Tania Shapiro-Barr, Jeremy Shapiro-Barr, Michael Shapiro-Barr. BA summa cum laude, U. Mich., 1974; JD, Harvard U., 1977. Bar: D.C., 1977, Wis., 1979, U.S. Supreme Ct., 1990. Assoc. Foley & Lardner, Washington, 1977-79; ptnr. Barr & Shapiro, Menomonee Falls, Wis., 1980-87; assoc. Quarles & Brady, Milw., 1987-92; ptnr. Michael Best & Friedrich, Milw., 1992—, chair, Health Law Practice, 2003—. Adj. asst. prof. law Marquette U., Milw., 1979-83; assoc. dir. bioethics ctr. Med. Coll. Wis., Milw., 1982-85, dir., 1985—; asst. prof. bioethics Med. Coll. Wis., 1984-89, assoc. prof. bioethics, 1989-97, prof. bioethics, 1997—, Ursula Von der Ruhr prof. bioethics, 2000—; dir. Wis. Ethics Com. Network, 1987-98, Midwest Ethics Com. Network, 1998—; bd. dirs. Wis. Health Decisions, 1990-93; drug safety and risk mgmt. adv. com. FDA, 2003—; mem. data & safety monitoring bd. Med. Coll. Wis., 2003—. Mem. editl. bd. Cambridge Quar., 1991—, HEC Forum, 1988-91, Human Rights, 1998—; contbr. articles to profl. jours. Mem. ethics com. St. Luke's Med. Ctr., Milw., 1983—, Elmbrook Meml. Hosp., Milw., 1983-86, Cmty. Meml. Hosp., Menomonee Falls, 1984—, Aurora Sinai Med.Ctr., Milw., 1986—, Milw. County Mental Health Complex, 1984—, Froedtert Meml. Luth. Hosp., 1985—; mem. subcom. organ transplantation Wis. Health Policy Coun., Madison, 1984, bioethics com., 1986-89; mem. com. study on bioethics Wis. Legis. Coun., Madison, 1984-85; bd. dirs. Jewish Home and Care Ctr., 1994—, chair ethics com., 1994—; chair Bayside Ethics Bd., 1994—; bd. dirs. Milw. area chpt. Girl Scouts U.S., Am. Bioethics Assn., 1995-97, Wis. Perinatal Found., 1996-99, Am. Soc. Bioethics and Humanities, 1997-2000, Manor Park Found., 2002—; mem. sec.'s adv. com. on xenotransplantation U.S. Dept. Health and Human Svcs., 2001—; mem. sci. adv. com. Alzheimer's Assn. Southeastern Wis., 1997—; mem. data and safety monitoring bd. GlaxoWellcome, 1995—2003; mem. med. aid cmty. adv. bd. After Breast Cancer Diagnosis, 1999—; mem. drug safety and risk mgmt. adv. com. USDA, 2003—. James B. Angell scholar, 1971-72. Mem. ABA (health law sec., vice chair clin. ethics group 1998-2001, individual rights and responsibilities sect., health rights com. chair 1994-99, coun. 1999—, coordinating com. on bioethics and law 1993—, chair 1995-99, adv. nat. conf. of commrs. on uniform state laws, misuse of genetic info. study group 2002—, mem. working group on health info. privacy 2000-02, AIDS coordinating com. 2003-), Am. Health Lawyers Assn., Am. Hosp. Assn. (bioethics tech. panel 1991-94, spl. com. HIV practitioners 1991-93), Wis. Bar Assn. (chair Wis. health law sect. 1988-89, individual rights sect. coun. 1987-90), Assn. Women Lawyers, ACLU, Wis. Found. (Atty. of Yr. 1988), Assn. Post-Doctoral Programs in Clin. Neurophysiology (bd. dirs.), Am. Soc. Law, Medicine, and Ethics, Milw. Acad. Medicine (coun. 1992-98, chair bioethics com. 1992-98), Milw. AIDS Coalition (steering com. 1988-91), Am. Soc. Transplant Surgeons (ethics com. 1999—), Internat. Bioethics Assn. (chair task force on ethics coms.), Profl. Dimensions (Golden Compass award 1994), Phi Beta Kappa (Wis. chpt. scholarship com. chair 1990-93), Susan G. Komen Breast Cancer Found., others. Home: 9474 N Broadmoor Rd Milwaukee WI 53217-1309 Office: Med Coll Wis Bioethics Ctr 8701 Watertown Plank Rd Milwaukee WI 53226-3548 Business E-Mail: rshapiro@mcw.edu.

SHAPIRO, RONALD GARY, psychologist; b. Providence, Oct. 10, 1953; s. Nathan and Raquel (Rebe) S. BA, U. Rochester, 1975; MA, Ohio State U., 1977, PhD, 1981. Cert. human factors profl. Teaching, rsch. assoc. Ohio State U., Columbus, 1975-81; asst. prof. Denison U., Granville, Ohio, 1981-82; prin. assoc. Dunlap and Assocs. Inc., Norwalk, Conn., 1982-85; sr. engring. mgr. IBM, Poughkeepsie, N.Y., 1985-96, cons. human resources profl., 1996—, program mgr. enterprise-wide tech. and strategic learning curricula, US external edn. univ. programs, 2002—. Evening faculty U. Conn., Stamford, 1983-85, Dutchess C.C., Poughkeepsie, 1986-94; bd. cert. Profl. Ergonomics Recert. Com. Contbr. articles to Psychol. Rev., Jour. Exptl. Psychology and other profl. jours. Recipient Grad. Sch. Leadership award Ohio State U., 1979; recipient Sr. Engring. Mgr. promotion IBM, 1993. Fellow Human Factors and Ergonomics Soc. (nat. program com. 1994-97, tech. program com. 1997-2000, chair computer sys. tech. group 1999-2000, chair coun. tech. groups 2001-02, vol. chair 2003—, chair nat. ergonomics mth. 2003—); mem. APA, Soc. Indsl. Orgnl. Psychologists, SHARE, Inc. (IBM rep. 1987-91), Sigma Xi, Phi Kappa Phi. Achievements include design of computer products for easy use by people. Home and Office: 17 Brookway Rd Providence RI 02906 E-mail: rshapiro@us.ibm.com.

SHAPIRO, SANDRA, lawyer; b. Providence, Oct. 17, 1944; d. Emil and Sarah (Cohen) S. AB magna cum laude, Bryn Mawr Coll., Pa., 1966; LLB magna cum laude, U. Pa., 1969. Bar: Mass. 1970, U.S. Dist. Ct. Mass. 1971, U.S. Ct. Appeals (1st cir.) 1972, U.S. Supreme Ct. 1980. Law clk. U.S. Ct. Appeals (1st cir.), Boston, 1969-70; assoc. Foley, Hoag & Eliot LLP, Boston, 1970-75, ptnr., 1976—. Mem. bd. bar overseers Mass. Supreme Judicial Ct., 1988-92, mem. gender bias study com., 1986-89; dir. Mass. Govt. Land Bank, 1994-96. Contbr. articles to profl. jours. Bd. dirs. Patriots' Trail coun. Girl Scouts U.S., 1994—97; mem. bd. overseers Boston Lyric Opera, 1993—99, New Eng. Conservatory of Music, 1995—2001, Celebrity Series of Boston, 1997—, chair, 2003—. Woodrow Wilson fellow, 1966. Mem.: ABA (ethics, profl. and pub. edn. com. 1994—), U. Pa. Law Sch. Alumni Assn. (bd. mgrs. 1990—94), Boston Bar Assn. (mem. coun.), Mass. Bar Assn. (chmn. real property sect. coun., com. on profl. ethics), Nat. Women's Law Ctr. Network, New Eng. Women in Real Estate, Women's Bar Assn. Mass. (pres. 1985—86), Boston Club, Order of Coif. Office: Foley Hoag LLP 155 Seaport Blvd Boston MA 02210-2600 Business E-Mail: sshapiro@foleyhoag.com.

SHAPIRO, STEPHEN MICHAEL, lawyer; b. Chgo., May 3, 1946; s. Samuel H. and Dorothy A. (D'Andrea) S.; m. Joan H. Gately, Oct. 30, 1982; children: Dorothy Henderson, Michael Clifford. BA magna cum laude, Yale U., 1968, JD, 1971. Bar: Ill. 1971, Calif. 1972, D.C. 1991, U.S. Dist. Ct. (no. dist. trial bar) Ill. 1992, U.S. Ct. Appeals (all cirs.), U.S. Supreme Ct. 1975. Law clk. U.S. Ct. Appeals (9th cir.), San Francisco, 1971-72; ptnr., sr. mem. appellate practice Mayer, Brown & Platt, Chgo., 1972-78, 83—; asst. to solicitor gen. U.S. Dept. Justice, Washington, 1978-80, dep. solicitor gen., 1981-82. Trustee Product Liability Adv. Found. Co-author: Supreme Court Practice, 2002; contbr. articles to profl. jours. Mem. ABA, Am. Law Inst., Am. Acad. Appellate Lawyers, Supreme Ct. Hist. Soc., Phi Beta Kappa. Republican. Jewish. Office: Mayer Brown Rowe & Maw 190 S La Salle St Ste 3100 Chicago IL 60603-3441

SHAPIRO, STEPHEN RICHARD, retired air force officer, physician; b. Bklyn., Dec. 30, 1934; s. George Daniel and Bertha Brinna (Bazerman) S.; m. Myrna Farber, May 28, 1960; children: David C., Robert S., Marc E. BA, Bklyn. Coll., 1956; MD, SUNY Downstate Med. Ctr., 1960. Diplomate Am. Bd. Internal Medicine, Am. Bd. Allergy and Immunology, Am. Bd. Med. Mgmt. Commd. 2nd lt. USAF, 1960, advanced through grades to brig. gen., 1987; intern, then resident and fellow Walter Reed Gen. Hosp., Washington, 1960-65; asst. chief allergy Wilford Hall USAF Med. Ctr., San Antonio, 1965-73; chief clin. svc. Ramstein (Germany) Clinic, 1973-74; chief divsn. clin. medicine Hdqrs. USAFE/SG, Ramstein, 1974-76; comdr. USAF Hosp. RAF, Upper Heyford, Eng., 1976-80; dep. surgeon Hdqrs. AFSC/SG, Andrews AFB, Md., 1980-82; surgeon Hdqrs. AFRES/SG, Robins AFB, Ga., 1982-84; command surgeon Hdqrs. AFSC/SG, Andrews AFB, Md., 1984-87; comdr. Malcolm Grow USAF Med. Ctr., Andrews AFB, 1987-89; command surgeon Hdqrs. AFLC/SG, Wright-Patterson AFB, Ohio, 1989-92, Hdqrs. AFMC, 1991-92; chief of staff VA Health Care Ctr., El Paso, Tex., 1992—. Fellow Aerospace Med. Assn. (assoc.); mem. Am. Coll. Physician Execs., Am. Acad. Allergy and Immunology, Air Force Soc. Flight Surgeons, Air Force Soc. Physicians, Alpha Omega Alpha. Jewish. Avocations: gardening, reading, travel. Office: 5001 N Piedras St El Paso TX 79930-4210

SHAPIRO, STEVEN DAVID, dermatologist; b. Oakhurst, N.J., Oct. 15, 1961; s. Alfred J. and Marilyn G. S.; m. Lynn A. Shapiro Feb. 6, 1993. BA cum laude, Vanderbilt U., 1984; MD, N.J. Med. Sch., 1988. Diplomate Nat. Bd. Med. Examiners, Am. Bd. Dermatology; lic. MD N.J., Fla. Intern internal medicine Hahnemann Univ. Hosp., Phila., 1988-89; resident in dermatology Mt. Sinai Med. Ctr. Greater Miami, Miami Beach, Fla., 1989-90; chief resident in dermatology U. Miami Sch. of Medicine, VA Med. Ctr., Mt. Sinai Med. Ctr., Miami, Fla., 1991-92; dermatologist pvt. practice Long Branch, N.J., 1992-95; dermatologist Dermatology Specialists of Palm Beach County P.A., Boca Raton, Fla., 1995-97, Steven B. Rosenberg MD P.A., W. Palm Beach, Fla., 1995-98; pvt. practice Gardens Dermatology and Cosmetic Surgery Ctr., Palm Beach Gardens, Fla., 1997—. Affiliate Palm Beach Gardens Med. Ctr., Palm Beach Gardens, St. Mary's Hosp, Good Samaritan Hosp., W. Palm Beach, Jackson Meml. Hosp., VA Med. Ctr., Miami; assoc. prof. dept. dermatology and cutaneous surgery, U. Miami Sch. of Medicine; cons. Innovative Clin. Solutions, 1998—. Contbr. articles to profl. jours. including Internat. Jour. Dermatology, Cutaneous Pathology and others. Chmn. profl. edn. com. Monmouth County chpt. Am. Cancer Soc., 1992-94, vol. coord. skin cancer screenings, 1992-95, chmn. task force on skin cancer, 1994-95, v.p. 1995; presenter workshops to Am. Acad. Dermatology, San Francisco, 1989, Dermatology Nurses Assn., Atlanta, 1990, Skin Signs of Internal Disease Conf., Neptune, N.J., 1991. Finalist Marion Merrel Dow Pharm. Clin. Cases in Dermatology, 1991; named Physician of Yr. Monmouth County Chpt. Am. Cancer Soc., 1994. Fellow Am. Acad. Dermatology; mem. AMA (Physician's Recognition award 1991), Am. Soc. Dermatologic Surgery, Am. Soc. Dermatology, Am. Soc. Moh's Surgery, Phi Eta Sigma, Alpha Lambda Delta. Avocations: golf, water sports, weight tng. Home: 8246 Man O War Rd Palm Beach Gardens FL 33418-7719 also: 3401 Pga Blvd Ste 450 Palm Beach Gardens FL 33410-2841

SHAPIRO, STEVEN J. energy executive; BS, Union Coll.; MBA, Harvard U. Formerly with treasury and bus. devel. depts. ARCO, former v.p. corp. planning, former pres. ARCO Coal Australia; sr. v.p., CFO, bd. dirs. Vastar Resources, Inc., 1993—2000; sr. v.p., CFO Burlington Resources, Inc., Houston, 2000—02, exec. v.p., CFO, 2002—. Office: Burlington Resources Inc 5051 Westheimer Ste 1400 Houston TX 77210-4239

SHAPIRO, STEVEN R. legal association administrator; JD, Harvard U., 1975. Law clk. to Hon. J. Edward Lumbard U.S. Ct. Appeals, 2nd cir., 1975—76; with ACLU, 1976—, assoc. legal dir., 1987—93, legal dir., 1993—. Adj. prof. Columbia U. Mem.: bd. dirs., Advisory Com. of Asia Watch, Policy Com. of Human Rights Watch, Lawyers Com. for Human Rights. Office: ACLU 125 Broadway New York NY 10006-1605*

SHAPIRO, STUART CHARLES, computer scientist, educator; b. N.Y.C., Dec. 30, 1944; s. Louis M. and Bertha (Rubinstein) S.; m. Caren Dee Knight, July 16, 1972. BS, MIT, 1966; MS, U. Wis., 1968, PhD, 1971. Lectr. computer scis. dept. U. Wis., Madison, 1971; vis. asst. prof. Ind. U., Bloomington, 1971-72, asst. prof., 1972-77, assoc. prof., 1977-78; asst. prof. SUNY, Buffalo, 1977-78, assoc. prof., 1978-83, prof., 1983—, chmn., 1984-90, 96-99. Pres. Principles of Knowledge Representation and Reasoning, Inc., 1998-2000; rsch. scientist Nat. Ctr. for Geographic Info. and Analysis, 1989—. Author: Techniques of Artificial Intelligence, 1979, LISP: An Interactive Approach, 1986, Common Lisp: An Interactive Approach, 1992; editor: Encyclopedia of Artificial Intelligence, 1987, paperback edit., 1990, 2d edit., 1992, (with Lucja Iwanska) Natural Language Processing and Knowledge Representation: Language for Knowledge and Knowledge for Language, 2000; contbr. articles to profl. jours. Grantee NSF, 1971—; recipient numerous grants for computer sci. research, 1971—. Fellow Am. Assn. Artificial Intelligence; mem. IEEE (sr.), Assn. Computing Machinery (chmn. spl. interest group on artificial intelligence 1991-95), Assn. Computational Linguistics, Cognitive Sci. Soc., Sigma Xi. Home: 142 Viscount Dr Buffalo NY 14221-1770 Office: Univ at Buffalo Dept of Comp Sci & Engring 201 Bell Hall Buffalo NY 14260-2000 Office Phone: 716-645-3180 125. Personal E-mail: shapiro@adelphia.net. Business E-Mail: shapiro@cse.buffalo.edu.

SHAPIRO, SUMNER, retired naval officer; b. Nashua, N.H., Jan. 13, 1926; s. Maurice David and Hannah (Goodman) S.; m. Eleanor S. Hymen, June 14, 1949; children: Martha, Steven, Susan. BS, U.S. Naval Acad., 1949; MS, George Washington U., 1966; postgrad., Naval War Coll., 1966, U.S. Army Inst. Advanced Soviet and Eastern European Studies, 1961. Commd. ensign U.S. Navy, 1949; advanced through grades to rear adm.; asst. naval attache U.S. Navy (Am. embassy), Moscow, 1963-65; dep. asst. chief of staff for intelligence U.S. Naval Forces Europe, London, 1967-69; comdg. officer Naval Intelligence Processing System Support Activity, Washington, 1969-72; asst. chief staff for intelligence U.S. Atlantic Command and U.S. Atlantic Fleet, Norfolk, Va., 1972-76; dep. dir. naval intelligence, 1976-77; comdr. Naval Intelligence Command, Washington, 1977-78; dir. naval intelligence Washington, 1978-82; ret., 1982; v.p. for advanced planning BDM Internat., 1983-89; pres. The Sumner Group Inc., 1989—. Pres. Naval Intelligence Found. Decorated D.S.M., Legion of Merit and others., Nat. Intelligence D.S.M., Netherlands Order Orange-Nassau, Brazil Order Naval Merit, French Nat. Order Merit, others Mem. Naval Intelligence Found. (pres.), Naval Intelligence Profls. (bd. dirs.), U.S. Naval Inst., Assn. Former Intelligence Officers, Nat. Mil. Intelligence Assn., Nat. Security Industries Assn., U.S. Naval Acad. Alumni Assn., Naval Submarine League.

SHAPIRO, THEODORE, psychiatrist, educator; b. N.Y.C., Feb. 26, 1932; s. Herman Alexander and Nettie (Rosenblatt) S.; m. Joan May Itkin, June 26, 1955; children: Susan, Alexander Herman. BA, Wesleyan U., 1953; MD, Cornell U., 1957. Diplomate Am. Bd. Psychiatry and Neurology, Am. Bd. Child Psychiatry, Am. Psychoanalytic Assn. Intern Montefiore Hosp., N.Y.C., 1957—58; resident in psychiatry NYU-Bellevue Hosp., 1958—61; instr. to prof. NYU Sch. Medicine, 1960—76; rsch. assoc. child psychiatry NYU-Bellevue Hosp., 1961—65; asst. lectr. N.Y. Psychoanalytic Inst., N.Y.C., 1970—86; prof. psychiatry and pediatrics Cornell U. Med. Coll., N.Y.C., 1976—2002; tng. and supervising analyst N.Y. Psychoanalytic Inst., N.Y.C., 1986—; vice chair for child and adolescent psychiatry, 1995—2002; emeritus prof. Cornell U. Med. Coll., N.Y.C, 2002—. Cons. alcohol, drug abuse and mental health adminstrn. WHO, Washington, Geneva and Copenhagen, 1980—82, Am. Acad. Child and Adolescent Psychiatry, Washington; chair com. on stewardship Task Force Future, 1980—82, acad. sec., 1981—83, chair work group on sci. issues, 1988—89, chair com. editorship and stewardship of jour., 1984—86, 1990—92; participant APA bilateral exch. in Ea. Europe, 1992; mem. reviewer child psychopathology and treatment rev. com. NIMH, 1994—98; lectr. in field. Author: Clinical Psycholinguistics, 1979; co-editor: Infant Psychiatry, 1976; editor: Psychoanalysis and Contemporary Science, 1976, Structure in Psychoanalysis, 1991, Affect: Psychoanalytic Perspectives, 1992; co-author: Manual of Panic-Focused Psychodynamic Psychotherapy, 1996; editor Jour. Am. Psychoanalytic Assn., 1984-93; book rev. editor Internat. Jour. Psychoanalysis, 1993-2002; co-editor Research in Psychoanalysis, 1995; contbr. articles to profl. jours. Keynote lectr. Am. Psychoanalytic Assn., Boston, 2003, H. Harmann Meml. NY Psychoanalytic Inst., 2004. Recipient recipient Wilfred C. Hulse award N.Y. Coun. Child Psychiatry, 1982, Harry Bakwin Meml. award NYU, 1982, Heinz Hartmann award N.Y. Psychoanalitic Inst., 2004; grantee NIMH, 1976-86 Fellow Am. Acad. Child Psychiatry (sec. 1981-83), Am. Psychiat. Assn.; mem. Soc. Profs. Child Psychiatry (chmn. com. on edn. 1982-90, keynote spkr. 1999), Group for Advancement of Psychiatry (chmn. com. on child psychiatry 1985-90), Am. Bd. Psychiatry & Neurology (com. on child and adolescent psychiatry 1987-93, chmn. 1992-93), N.Y. Psychoanalytic Soc. Jewish. Office: Weill Med Coll Cornell U Payne Whitney Clinic PO Box 140 New York NY 10021-0012 Office Phone: 212-746-5713. Business E-Mail: tshapiro@med.cornell.edu.

SHAPIRO, WALTER ELLIOT, political columnist; b. N.Y.C., Feb. 16, 1947; s. Salem Seeley and Edith Geraldine (Herwitz) S.; m. Meryl Gordon, Aug. 24, 1980. BA, U. Mich., 1970, postgrad., 1970-71. Reporter Congl. Quarterly, Washington, 1969-70; editor Washington Monthly, 1972-76; spl. asst. U.S. Sec. Labor, Washington, 1977-78; Presdl. speechwriter The White House, Washington, 1979; reporter Washington Post, 1979-83; gen. editor Newsweek, N.Y.C., 1983-87; sr. writer Time Mag., N.Y.C., 1987-93; White House corr. Esquire mag., 1993-97; polit. columnist USA Today, 1995—. Contbg. editor Washington Monthly, 1976—. Author: (book) One-Car Caravan: On the Road with the 2004 Democrats Before America Tunes In", 2003. Leadership fellow Japan Soc., U.S.-Japan, 1991. Mem.: White House Correspondents Assn., Judson Welliver Soc., Author's Guild. Jewish. Avocations: standup comedy, rotisserie baseball. Home: 201 W 86th St Apt 1105 New York NY 10024-3351 Office: 3133 Connecticut Ave NW Apt 315 Washington DC 20008-5105 Office Phone: 202-462-2957.

SHAPIRO, ZALMAN MORDECAI, chemist, consultant; b. Canton, Ohio, May 12, 1920; s. Abraham and Minnie (Pinck) S.; m. Evelyn Greenberg, June 24, 1945; children: Joshua, Ezra David, Deborah Esther. BA, Johns Hopkins U., 1942, MA, 1945, PhD, 1948. Rsch. assoc. Johns Hopkins for Nat. Rsch. Coun., Balt., 1942—45; instr. chemistry Johns Hopkins U., 1946—48; sr. engr. Westinghouse Electric Corp., Pitts., 1948; mgr. phys. chemistry, mgr. chem. metallurgy AEC Bettis Naval Nuc. Power Lab., Westinghouse, West Mifflin, Pa., 1949—56, asst. divsn. mgr. pressurized water reactor divsn., 1956—57; pres., chmn. bd. Nuc. Materials and Equipment Corp., Apollo, Pa., 1957—70, Numec Instruments and Controls Corp., Apollo, 1960—70, Numec Decontamination Corp., Apollo, 1961—70, Isotope & Radiation Enterprises, Israel, 1964—70; pres. Assoc. Tech. and Bus. Consultants, Pitts., 1970—. V.p. Arco Chem. Co., Phila., 1967-70. Contbr. 2 chpts. to books; patentee in field. Mem. Govs. Sci. and Tech. Coun., Harrisburg, 1963-64; cons. Pa. Subcom. on Atomic Energy, Harrisburg, 1970-71; founder, vice-chmn., Ams. for Energy Independence, Washington, 1975—; organizer Project Pacesetter, Allegheny County, 1976. Named hon. fellow Technion Israel Inst. Tech., Haifa, 1988, Disting. Alumnus, Johns Hopkins U., 2002. Fellow Am. Nuc. Soc. (citation of merit); mem. AAAS, Am. Soc. Metals, Am. Chem. Soc., Phi Beta Kappa, Sigma Xi. Avocations: sailing, wood working. Home and Office: ASTECH 1045 Lyndhurst Dr Pittsburgh PA 15206 E-mail: zalmanms@aol.com.

SHAPO, MARSHALL SCHAMBELAN, lawyer, educator; b. Phila., Oct. 1, 1936; s. Mitchell and Norma (Schambelan) S.; m. Helene Shirley Seidner, June 21, 1959; children: Benjamin, Nathaniel. AB summa cum laude, U. Miami, 1958, JD magna cum laude, 1964; AM, Harvard U., 1961, SJD, 1974. Bar: Fla. 1964, Va. 1977, Ill. 1993. Copy editor, writer Miami (Fla.) News, 1958-59; instr. history U. Miami, 1960-61; asst. prof. law U. Tex., 1965-67, asso. prof., 1967-69, prof., 1969-70; prof. law U. Va., 1970-78, Joseph M. Hartfield prof., 1976-78; Frederic P. Vose prof. Northwestern U. Sch. Law, Chgo., 1978—; of counsel Sonnenschein, Nath & Rosenthal, Chgo., 1991-2001. Vis. prof. Juristisches Seminar U. Gottingen (Fed. Republic Germany), 1976; cons. on med. malpractice and tort law reform U.S. Dept. Justice, 1978-79; mem. panel on food safety Inst. Medicine, NAS, 1978-79; vis. fellow Centre for Socio-legal Studies, Wolfson Coll., Oxford, vis. fellow of Coll., 1975, Wolfson Coll., Cambridge, 1992, 2001; mem. Ctr. for Advanced Studies, U. Va., 1976-77; cons. Pres.'s Commn. for Study of Ethical Problems in Medicine and Biomed. and Behavioral Rsch., 1980-81; reporter Spl. Com. on Tort Liability System Am. Bar Assn., 1980-84; del. leader People to People Citizen Amb. program delegation to East Asia Tort and Ins. Law, 1986; lectr. appellate judges' seminars ABA, 1977, 83, 90; reporter symposium on legal and sci. perspectives on causation, 1990; advisor Restatement of the Law, Third, Torts: Products Liability, 1992-97. Author: Tort Law and Culture, 2003, Towards a Jurisprudence of Injury, 1984, Tort and Compensation Law, 1976, The Duty to Act: Tort Law, Power and Public Policy, 1978, A Nation of Guinea Pigs, 1979, Products Liability, 1980, Public Regulation of Dangerous Products, 1980, The Law of Products Liability, 1987, Tort and Injury Law, 1990, 2d edit., 2000, The Law of Products Liability, 2 vols., 2d edit., 1990, 4th edit., 2001, supplements, 1991, 92, 93, 95, 96, 97, 98, 99, 2002, 03, Products Liability and the Search for Justice, 1993, (with Helene Shapo) Law School Without Fear, 1996, 2d edit., 2002, Basic Principles of Tort Law, 1999, 2d edit., 2003; (with Page Keeton) Products and the Consumer: Deceptive Practices, 1972, Products and the Consumer: Defective and Dangerous Products, 1970, (with D. Jacobson & A.N. Weber) International e-Commerce: Business & Legal Issues, 2001, (with G. Hernandez & others) eBusiness & Insurance, 2001, Concise Hornbook on Tort Law, 2003; mem. editl. bd. Jour. Consumer Policy, 1980-88, Products Liability Law Jour.; author: A Representational Theory of Consumer Protection: Doctrine, Function and Legal Liability for Product Disappointment, 1975; mem. adv. bd. Loyola Consumer Law Reporter; contbr. articles to legal and med. jours. Recipient Andrew J. Hecker award Fedn. Ins. and Corp. Counsel, 2001; NEH sr. fellow, 1974-75 Mem. Am. Law Inst., Am. Assn. Law Schs. (chmn. torts compensation systems sect. 1983-84, torts round table coun. 1970). Home: 1910 Orrington Ave Evanston IL 60201-2910 Office: Northwestern U Sch Law 357 E Chicago Ave Chicago IL 60611-3059

SHAPOFF, STEPHEN H. financial executive; b. N.Y.C., Nov. 1, 1944; s. Barney and Freda Shapoff; m. Andrea Dorin, May 30, 1967; 1 child, Matthew F. BBA, Pace U., 1967. CPA, N.Y. With audit dept. Ernst & Young, N.Y.C., 1967-72; asst. controller Seeburg Industries, Inc., 1972-74, 1967-72; with Estee Lauder, Inc., N.Y.C., 1974-78; controller Coleco Industries, Inc., Hartford, Conn., 1978-79; sr. v.p. fin. Ivy Hill Corp. subs. of Time Warner Inc., N.Y.C., Conn., 1979-85; exec. v.p. Ivy Hill Corp., N.Y.C., 1985—. Adj. asst. prof. Pace U., N.Y.C., 1971-83. Editl. bd. Fin. Exec. mag., 1996—. Mem. AICPA, Fin. Exec. Inst. (pres. L.I. chpt. 1988, 92-94, chair nat. membership com., nat. dir. 1996—), N.Y. Soc. CPAs, Nat. Assn. Accts. Office: Ivy Hill Corp 375 Hudson St Fl 7 New York NY 10014-3658

SHAPPIRIO, DAVID GORDON, biologist, educator; b. Washington, June 18, 1930; s. Sol and Rebecca (Porton) S.; m. Elvera M. Bamber, July 8, 1953; children: Susan, Mark. BS with distinction in Chemistry, U. Mich., 1951; A.M., Harvard U., 1953, PhD in Biology, 1955. NSF postdoctoral fellow in biochemistry Cambridge U., Eng., 1955-56; rsch. fellow in physiology Am. Cancer Soc.-NRC, U. Louvain, Belgium, 1956-57; mem. faculty U. Mich., Ann Arbor, 1957—, prof. zool. and biology, 1967-99, Arthur F. Thurnau prof., 1989-94, prof. emeritus, 1999—, assoc. chair div. biol. scis., 1976-83, acting chair, 1978, 79, 80, 82, coord. NSF undergrad. sci. edn. program, 1962-67, dir. honors program Coll. Lit. Sci. and Arts, 1983-91. Vis. lectr. Am. Inst. Biol. Scis., 1966-68; reviewer, cons. to pubs. on textbook devel.; reviewer rsch. and ednl. tng. grant proposals NSF, NIH, mem. program site visit teams. Author rsch. on biochemistry and physiology growth, devel., dormancy; invited spkr., rsch. symposia of nat. and internat. orgns. in field. Recipient Disting. Teaching award U. Mich., 1967, Excellence in Edn. award, 1991, Bausch & Lomb Sci. award, 1974; Lalor Found fellow, 1953-55; Danforth Found. assoc. Fellow AAAS; mem. Am. Inst. Biol. Scis. (vis. lectr. 1966-68), Am. Soc. Cell Biology, Biochem. Soc., Soc. Exptl. Biology, Assn. Biol. Lab. Edn., Xerces Soc., Phi Beta Kappa (v.p. U. Mich. chpt. 1995-97, pres. 1997—). Office: U Mich Dept Biology 1123 Natural Sci Bldg Ann Arbor MI 48109-1048

SHARAN, ASHWINI D. neurosurgeon, researcher; b. Patna, India, Sept. 18, 1970; arrived in U.S., 1971; s. Guru and Kumud Sharan; m. Kanu Priya Sharan; 1 child, Isha Priya. BA magna cum laude, Boston U., 1992; MD, UMDNJ, 1995. Surg. intern U. Conn. Health Care, 1995—96, neurosurg. trainee, 1996—98, Thomas Jefferson U., 1998—2001, resident, 2001; fellow functional neurosurgery Cleve. Clinic Found., 2001—02, fellow spine surgery, 2001—02; neurosurgeon Thomas Jefferson U. Hosp., Phila., 2002— Asst prof. neurosurgery Thomas Jefferson U., 2002, asst. prof. neurology, 03; presenter in field. Contbr. articles to profl. jours. Grantee, NIH, 2002, 2003, 2003. Mem.: AMA, Internat. Stds. Orgn., Movement Disorders Soc., Congress Neurol. Surgeons, Am. Assn. Neurol. Surgeons (William Sweet Young Investigator's award 2002), Phi Beta Delta. Hindu. Achievements include research in MRI safety and deep brain stimulation systems; HIV infection of cultured neural cells; genetic influences on human epilepsy. Avocations: music, travel, exercise. Office: Thomas Jefferson Univ Hosp Dept Neurosurgery 909 Walnut St 2rd Fl Philadelphia PA 19107

SHARAPOVA, MARIA, professional tennis player; b. Nyagan, Russia, Apr. 19, 1987; d. Yuri and Yelena Sharapova. Trained, Bollettieri's Acad., 1996. Prof. tennis player WTA Tour, 2001—; model IMG Modeling Agy., 2003—; winner Wimbledon, 2004. Nominee Laureus World Newcomer Yr., 2004. Achievements include 4 career singles championships; 3 career doubles championships; first Russian woman to win at Wimbledon, 2004. Avocations: singing, reading, stamp collecting/philately, fashion, Russian music. Office: One Progress Plz Ste 1500 Saint Petersburg FL 33701*

SHARBEL, JEAN M. editor; b. Lansford, Pa. d. Joseph and Star S. BA in Journalism, Hunter Coll. Editl. dir., v.p. Dauntless Books, N.Y.C., 1962-75; editor romance mags., True Confessions mag. Macfadden Holdings, Inc., N.Y.C., 1976-92; freelance editor fiction and non-fiction books, N.Y.C., 1989—. Home: 165 E 66th St New York NY 10021-6132

SHARBONEAU, LORNA ROSINA, artist, educator, author, poet, illustrator; b. Spokane, Wash., Apr. 5, 1935; d. Stephen Charles Martin and Midgie Montana (Hartzel) Barton; m. Thomas Edward Sharboneau, Jan. 22, 1970; children: Curtis, Carmen, Chet, Cra, Joseph. AA in Arts, Delta Coll., 1986; studies with Steve Lesnick, Las Vegas, Nev.; studies with Bette Myers/Zimmerman, Phoenix and Bonners Ferry, Idaho. Prin. Sharboneau's Art Gallery, Spokane, 1977-80; tchr. art Michell's Art Gallery, Spokane, 1978-79; art therapist Vellencino Sch. Dist., Calif., 1981-83; ind. artist Lind, Wash., 1948—. Dir., producer, stage designer Ch. of Jesus Christ of LDS, San Jose, Sonora, Modesto, Calif., 1978 (1st. place road show San Jose); dir. Sharboneau's Art Show, Spokane, 1979, Hands On-Yr. of the Child; platform spkr., poet, fundraiser, libr., 1984-87; asst., apprentice to Prof. Rowland Cheney, Delta Coll., Stockton, Calif., 1985, 86, 87; demonstrated drip oil technique, Bonners Ferry, Idaho, Spokane, Wash., Stockton, Calif., Delta Coll. Author, illustrator: Through the Eyes of the Turtle Tree, The One-Armed Christmas Tree, The Price of Freedom, 1994, William Will, Bill Can, Song of the Turtle Tree, Chet's Ottle-Bottle: The Unbreakable Bottle, One Drop of Water and a Grain of Sand, The Price of Freedom; poet; prolific artist completed over 4000 paintings and drawings, displayed works in galleries through western states; featured in Magnolia News, Seattle, Delta Coll. Impact, Stockton, Calif., Stockton Record, Union Democrat, Sonora, Calif., Lincoln Center Chronicle, Stockton, Calif., Spokesman Rev., Spokane, Wash., Modesto (Calif) Bee, Angels Camp, Calif., Union Democrat, Sonora, Calif., New-Letter, Ch. of Jesus Christ of L.D.S 1st ward, Sonora; artist mixed media, oil, drip oil works, sculptures, pastel, watercolor; illustrations pen and ink, acrylic; sculptor bronze, lost wax method, ceramic art, soap stone, egg-tempra, original techniques, collage, variation on a theme. Dir., programmer, fundraiser Shelter Their Sorrows, Sonora, Calif., 1989-92, vol. Cmty. Action Agy. and Homeless Shelter; fundraiser for Homeless Flood Victims of No. Calif., 1997. Recipient Golden Rule award J.C. penny, 1991, Recognition award Pres. George Bush, cert. Spl. Congl. Recognition Congressman Richard H. Lehman, 3rd Pl. Best Show East Valley ARtists/Pala Show, 1973, 74, 75, 3d Pl. Artist of Yr., 1974, Valley Fair, Santa Clara, Calif., 1974, 1st and 2d Pl. Spokane County Fair, 1978, 3 honorable mentions, 4 premiums, 1979, 3 1st Pl., 3 2d Pl., 2 3rd Pl., honorable mention Calaveras County Fair/Angels Camp, Calif., 1983, 1st and 3rd Pl. Unitarian Art Festival, Stockton, Calif., 1984, 2d Pl., 1985, 3d Pl., 1986, 1st Pl. Lodi Art Ann., 1985, 3rd Pl., 1986, 1st Pl. 1987, 1st Pl., 1988, honorable mental SJCAC Junque Art Show, Stockton, 1985, 1st Pl Ctrl. Calif. Art League, Modesto, 1986, 88, 2d Pl. 1995; 3d Pl. Camilla Art Show, San Jose, Calif., 1974, and numerous others; 1st, 2d, and 3d Pl., Spokane County Fair, 1978; 4 honorable mentions, Sonora, Calif., 1993, 2nd Pl. Ctrl. Calif. Art Show, 1996. Mem. Ctrl. Sierra Arts Coun., Mother Lode Artists Assn., Sacramento Fine Arts Ctr., Inc., Internat. Platform Assn. (Judges Choice conv. arts competition 1993), The Planetary Soc., The Nat. Mus. of Women of Arts. Mem. Ch. of Jesus Christ of LDS. Achievements include: homeless shelter kitchen named in her honor, Sonora. Office: PO Box 5015 Sonora CA 95370-2015

SHARER, JOHN DANIEL, lawyer; b. Bklyn., Sept. 19, 1950; s. Albert Robert and Alda Loretta (Tapiro) S.; m. Kathleen Gail Donaldson, Feb. 14, 1981; 1 child, Stephanie Erin. AB, Dartmouth Coll., Hanover, N.H., 1972; JD, U. Pa., 1975. Bar: Pa. 1975, N.J. 1975, D.C. 1976, N.Y. 1989, Va. 1994. Law clk. Superior Ct. Pa., Hon. Edmund B. Spaeth, Jr., Phila., 1975-76; assoc. Sutherland, Asbill & Brennan, Washington, 1976-82, ptnr., 1982-94; counsel Christian & Barton, L.L.P., Richmond, Va., 1994-95, ptnr., 1996-99; sr. counsel Dominion Resources Svcs. Inc., 1999-2001; mng. counsel electric delivery and telecom., 2001—. Mem. faculty Va. State Bar Professionalism Course, 2001—; mem. Third Dist. Disciplinary Comm. Sect. III, 2003—. Bd. dirs. Wakefield Sch., Marshall, Va., 1990-94; pres. Dartmouth Club of Cen. Va., 1997-2003 Mem. Va. State Bar, Phi Beta Kappa. Republican. Avocations: classical music, judicial biographies, computers, Norfolk Terriers. Home: 12317 Northlake Ct Richmond VA 23233-6635 Office: 120 Tredegar St PO Box 26532 Richmond VA 23261-6532 Office Phone: 804-819-2271. E-mail: john_d_sharer@dom.com.

SHARER, KEVIN W. healthcare products company executive; b. Clinton, Iowa, Mar. 2, 1948; m. Faye M. Sharer; children: Heather, Keith. BS in Aero. Engring, U.S. Naval Acad., 1970; MS in Aero. Engring., U.S. Naval Postgrad. Sch., 1971; MBA, U. Pitts., 1982. Commd. lt. USN, 1970, advanced through grades to lt. comdr., resigned, 1978; with AT&T, 1978-82; cons. McKinsey & Co., 1982-84; pres., chief exec. officer GE Am. Communications, Princeton, NJ, 1984-89; exec. v.p., bus. markets div. MCI Telecommunications Corp., Washington, 1989—92; pres., COO Amgen Inc., Thousand Oaks, Calif., 1992-2000, pres., CEO, 2000—, chmn., bd. dirs., 2000—. Dir. Unocal Corp., 3M, Northrup Grumman Corp. Office: Amgen Inc 1 Amgen Ctr Dr Thousand Oaks CA 91320-1799*

SHARER, WILLIAM E. state senator; Owner small bus.; Rep. senator dist. 1 N.Mex. State Senate. Mem. edn., Indian and cultural affairs coms. N.Mex. State Senate. Home: Box 203 Farmington NM 87499 Office: NMex State Senate State Capitol Mail Rm Dept Santa Fe NM 87503 E-mail: senate@state.nm.us.

SHARETT, ALAN RICHARD, lawyer, environmental and disability litigator, mediator and arbitrator, law educator; b. Hammond, Ind., Apr. 15, 1943; children: Lauren Ruth, Charles Daniel; m. Cherie Ann Vick, Oct. 15, 1993. Student, Ind. U., 1962-65; JD, DePaul U., 1968; advanced postgrad. legal edn., U. Mich. and U. Chgo., 1970-71; postgrad. in human resource law, Fla. Internat. U., 1999-2000; cert. mediator, Am. Arbitration Assn., 1994; cert. tng. and human resource devel., Fla. Internat. U., 2000. Bar: Ind. 1969, N.Y. 1975, U. S. Ct. Appeals (2d cir.) 1975, U.S. Ct. Appeals (7th cir.) 1974, U.S. Supreme Ct. 1973. Assoc. World Peace Through Law Ctr., Washington, 1967-68, Call, Call, Borns and Theodoros, Gary, Ind., 1969-71; judge protem Gary City Ct., 1970-71; environ. dist. atty. 31st Jud. Cir., Lake County, Ind., 1971-75; counsel Dunes Nat. Lakeshore Group, Ind., 1971-75; mem. Cohan, Cohan and Smulevitz, 1971-75; town atty. Independence Hill, Ind., 1974-75; judge pro tem Superior Ct. (31st cir.), Lake County, Ind., 1971-75; pvt. practice Flushing, N.Y., 1980-82, Miami Beach, Fla., 1988—; lead trial counsel, chmn. lawyers panel No. Ind. ACLU, 1969-71; liaison trial counsel Lake County and Ind. State Health Depts., and Atty. Gen., 1971-75. Professorial dir. NYU Pub. Liability Inst., N.Y.C., 1975-76; adj. faculty prof. constl. law Union Inst., Miami, Cin., 1990-92; adj. prof. environ. litigation and alternative dispute resolution Ward Stone Coll., Miami, 1994; guest prof. internat. environ. law Dept. Internat. and Comparative Law, U. Miami, 1992—; mem. adv. panel internat. environ. law Hemispheric Interam. Dialogue on Water Mgmt.(U.N. Agenda 21), 1993; mem. Nat Dist Attys Assn., 1972-75, mem. environ. protection com.; pres. ESI Group, Nat. Environ. Responsibility Cons. Inc.; spkr. in field. Editor-in-chief DePaul U. The Summons, 1967-68; mem. staff DePaul Law Rev., 1968; contbr. articles to profl. jours. Gen. counsel Marjory Stoneman Douglas Friends of Everglades, 1992-93; asst. atty. gen., chair fed. and constnl. practice litigation group N.Y. State, N.Y.C., 1976-78; mem. Coalition Fla. Save Our Everglades Program; diplomate, vice chancellor Law-Sci. Acad. Am., 1967; dir. edn., dir. grants and funding The US Space Walk of Fame Found. Recipient Honors award in forensic litigation Law-Sci. Acad. Am., 1967; Presidential Medal Coalition Recipient, Washington D.C., 1992-93; Internat. fellow, Eco-Ethics Internat. Union, 2003-. Mem. ABA (nat. article editor law student divsn. 1967-68, nat. com. environ. litigation, com. fed. procedures, com. toxic torts, hazardous substances and environ. law, com. energy resources law, com. internat. environ. law, com. internat. litigation, environ. interest group, sect. natural resources, energy and environ. law, judge negotiation competition championship round, law student divsn., midyr. meeting 1995, sect. sci. and tech., biotech. com., environ. law and pub. health com., standing com. sci. evidence, spl. com. legal edn., nat. toxic and hazardous substances and environ. law com., sect. tort and ins. practice, corp. gen. counsel com., non-profit orgns. com., media law and defamation torts com., tort and hazardous substances and environ. law com., govt. and pub. sector lawyers divsn.), Judicature Soc., Soc. Am. Arbitration Assn. (cert. program in mediation 1993), N.Y. County Lawyers Assn. (com. on fed. cts., environ. law, insurance and health law, arbitration and alternative dispute resolution, labor relations and employment law, tech. and automation), ATLA (nat. coms. toxic, environ. and pharm. torts, environ. litigation), Ill. State Bar Assn. (staff editor 1967-68), N.Y. State Bar Assn. (environ. law sect., family law sect.), Ind. State Bar Assn. (environ. law sect., internat. law sect., trial practice sect.), Greater Miami C. of C. (trustee 1993-94, com. environ. awareness, environ. econs., biomed. exch., planning and growth mgmt., internat. econ. devel., bus. and industry econs. devel., govtl. affairs, ins., internat. banking, Europe/Pacific), The Planetary Soc., Natural Assn. Sci. Wrriters, New Eng. Sci. Writers, Assn. Fundraising Profls., Space Coast Grant Profls. Network, Grant Profls. Network Ctrl. Fla. Office: ESI Grp Nat Environ Resp Cons 492 Banyon Tree Cir Ste L04 Maitland FL 32751-5995 E-mail: arsharett@mindspring.com.

SHARF, STEPHAN, automotive company executive; b. Berlin, Dec. 30, 1920; came to U.S., 1947; s. Wilhelm and Martha (Schwartz) S.; m. Rita Schantzer, June 17, 1951. Degree in Mech. Engring., Tech. U., Berlin, Fed. Republic Germany, 1947. Tool and die maker Buerk Tool & Die Co., Buffalo, 1947-50; foreman Ford Motor Co., 1950-53, gen. foreman, 1953-58; with Chrysler Corp., Detroit, 1958-86, master mechanic Twinsburg stamping plant, 1958-63, mfg. engring. mgr., 1963-66, mrg. prodn. Twinsburg stamping plant, 1966-68, plant mgr. Warren stamping plant, 1968-70, plant mgr. Sterling stamping plant, 1970-72, gen. plants mgr. stamping, 1972-78, v.p. Engine and Casting div., 1978-80, v.p. Power Train div., 1980-81, exec. v.p., mfg., dir., 1981-85, exec. v.p. internat., 1985-86, also bd. dirs.; pres. SICA Corp., Bloomfield Hills, Mich., 1986—. Columnist Ward's Auto World Common Sense mag., 1987—. Bd. dirs. Jr. Achievement, Detroit council Boy Scouts Am.; trustee, v.p. Oakland U. Mem. Soc. Auto Engrs., Detroit Engring. Soc. Clubs: Wabeek Country. Home: 966 Adams Castle Dr Bloomfield Hills MI 48304-3713 Office: SICA Corp PO Box 623 Troy MI 48099-0623 Office Phone: 248-433-3688. E-mail: SICA@concentric.net.

SHARFMAN, STEPHEN L. lawyer; b. 1944; AB, George Washington U., 1966; JD, Georgetown U., 1969. Bar: D.C. 1970. Asst. gen. coun. Met. Area Transit Comn., Washington; gen. counsel Postal Rate Comnn., Washington. Bd dir. Danbury Forest Civic Assn.; Lakeside Village Cmty. Assn; Oak Marr Homeowners Assn. Office: Office Gen Counsel 1333 H St NW Washington DC 20268-0001 E-mail: sharfman@prc.gov.

SHARGEL, GERALD L. lawyer; b. New Brunswick, N.J., Oct. 5, 1944; BA, Rutgers U., 1966; JD, Bklyn. Law Sch., 1969. Bar: N.Y. 1969, U.S. Dist. Ct. (ea. and so. dists.) N.Y. 1969, U.S. Ct. Appeals (2nd, 3rd, 5th and 9th cirs.) 1969. Pvt. practice, N.Y.C., 1970—. Faculty mem. Practising Law Inst., 1976—77; adj. assoc. prof. law NYU, 1977—82; adj. prof. law Bklyn. Law Sch.; mem. adv. bd. NYU Sch. Law, Ctr. for Rsch. in Crime and Justice, 1984—88. Mem.: ABA, Fed. Bar Coun., N.Y. State Trial Lawyers Assn., N.Y. County Lawyers Assn., Assn. Bar City N.Y., N.Y. State Bar Assn., Criminal Bar Assn. Office: 16th Fl 570 Lexington Ave New York NY 10022

SHARICK, MERLE DAYTON, JR., sales executive; b. Bloomington, Ill., May 5, 1946; s. Merle Dayton and Joyce Madeline (Reed) Sharick; m. Cheryl Jean Easterday, Dec. 28, 1966; children: Amber Dawn, Cami Nicole. BA, Southwestern Coll., Winfield, Kans., 1968; MS in Edn., U. Kans., 1970. Tchr., coach Kans. High Schs., Lawrence, Hutchinson, 1968-73, asst. prin., prin. Buhler, Inman, Leoti, 1973-77; auctioneer, real estate salesman R.E.I.B., Inc., Hutchinson, 1977-78; acct. exec. Mortgage Guaranty Ins. Co., Hutchinson, 1978-81, regional sales mgr. Shawnee Mission, Kans., 1981-83, Houston, 1983-86, divsn. risk mgr. Atlanta, 1986-90, regional dir. Charlotte, NC, 1990-93; v.p., mgr. risk mgmt. Republic Mortgage Ins. Co., Winston-Salem, NC, 1993-99; mgr. S.E. divsn. Sheldon Good & Co. Auctions, Charlotte, 1999-2001; sr. v.p. Infinity Info. Solutions and Gen. Info. Svcs., Chapin, SC, 2001—03; dir. sales Mortgage Asset Rsch. Inst., Prosperity, SC, 2003—. Sports editor Winfield (Kans.) Daily Couier, 1966—68; owner, operator Riverside Home Style Laundry, South Hutchison, 1975—79; founder, owner Sport Shack, Hutchison, 1977—79; mem. UNBOG adv. group Freddie Mac, 1995—; spkr. in field. Active Rep. support groups, Houston, Atlanta, 1983—. Fellow: Inst. Devel. Ednl. Adminstrs.; mem.: Charlotte Region Comml. Bd. Realtors, Nat. Auctioneers Assn., Nat. Assn. Realtors, Housing Roundtable, Charlotte Mortgage Bankers, Tex. Mortgage Bankers, Fla. Mortgage Bankers, S.C. League Savs. Instns., N.C. Alliance Cmty. Fin. Instns., N.C. Bankers Assn., Mortgage Bankers Carolinas, Ga. Mortgage Bankers, Mortgage Bankers Am., Nat. Assn. Rev. Appraisers and Mortgage Underwriters, Charlotte Touchdown Club, Town Club (Charlotte). Baptist. Personal E-mail: msharick@mari-inc.com.

SHARIF, M. ALAN, interventional cardiologist; b. Damascus, June 24, 1967; Aleppo Med. Sch., 1990. Diplomate Am. Bd. Internat. Medicine, Am. Bd. Cardiology, Am. Bd. Nuclear Cardiology, Am. Bd. Interventional Cardiology. Intern, then resident Sinai Hosp., Wayne State U., Detroit, 1992-95; chief resident Sinai Hosp., Detroit, 1995-96; fellow in cardiology Brown U., Providence, 1996-99; interventional cardiology fellow Brown U., Miriam Hosp., Providence, 1999-2000; chmn. divsn. cardiology Ingham Regional Med. Ctr., Lansing, Mich., 2002—03; asst. prof. Mich. State U., 2000—03; clin. asst. prof. Tex. Tech. U., Lubbock, 2004—. Fellow: ACP, Am. Soc. Internal Medicine., Am. Coll. Cardiology. Office: Cardiologist Lubbock 3506 21st St Lubbock TX 79424 Home: 9702 York Ave Lubbock TX 79424 Office Phone: 806-788-0050. Personal E-mail: asharif@coltexas.com.

SHARIF, OMAR (MICHAEL SHALHOUB), actor; b. Alexandria, Egypt, Apr. 10, 1932; s. Joseph and Claire (Saada) Shalhoub; m. Faten Hamama, Feb. 5, 1955 (div. 1966); 1 child, Tarek. Attended, Victoria Coll., Cairo. Appeared in numerous Egyptian, French and Am. films including (debut) Ciel d' enfer, 1953, The Mamluks, The Blazing Sun, Goha, Lawrence of Arabia, 1962 (Golden Globe award for best supporting actor, Most Promising Newcomer-Male), Behold a Pale Horse, 1964, The Fall of the Roman Empire, 1964, Genghis Khan, 1965, The Yellow Rolls Royce, 1965, Doctor Zhivago, 1966 (Golden Globe award best actor), Night of the Generals, 1967, More Than a Miracle, 1967, Funny Girl, 1968, Mayerling, 1969, Che!, 1969, MacKenna's Gold, 1969, The Appointment, 1969, The Horsemen, 1970, The Last Valley, 1971, The Burglars, 1972, The Tamarind Seed, 1974, The Mysterious Island of Captain Nemo, 1974, Juggernaut, 1974, Funny Lady, 1975, Crime and Passion, 1975, Ace Up The Sleeve, The Pink Panther Stikes Again, The Right To Love, Ashanti, 1979, Bloodline, 1979, Oh Heavenly Dog, 1980, The Baltimore Bullet, 1980, Green Ice, Chanel Solitaire, Top Secret, 1984, The Rainbow, 1989, Mountains of the Moon, 1990, Journey of Love, 1990, (voice) Umm Kulthum, 1996, Heaven Before I Die, 1997, The 13th Warrior, 1998, Mysteries of Egypt, 1998, The 13th Warrior, 1999, The Parole Officer, 2001, Hidalgo, 2004; TV appearances include S*H*E*, Pleasure Palace, The Far Pavillion, Mrs. 'arris Goes to Paris, 1992, Shaka Zulu: The Citadel, 2001; (TV movie) Lie Down with Lions, 1994; (TV miniseries) Peter the Great, 1986, Anastasia: The Mystery of Anna, 1986, Grand Larceny, Gulliver's Travels, 1996, Katharina die Grote, 1995, also Omar Sharif Returns to Egypt, The Mysteries of the Pyramids (host). Author: The Eternal Male, 1977; author syndicated columns on bridge. Office: William Morris Agy care Ames Cushing 151 S El Camino Dr Beverly Hills CA 90212-2775*

SHARIFY, NASSER, educator, author, librarian; b. Tehran, Iran, Sept. 23, 1925; came to U.S., 1953, naturalized, 1972; s. Ebrahim and Eshrat (Saghafy) S.; m. Homayoun Taslimy, June 14, 1950 (div. 1978); children: Sharareh, Shahab. Licencie es Lettres, U. Tehran, 1947; MS, Columbia U., 1954, Dr. L.S., 1958. Editorial staff Teheran jours. Rah-e Now, Jahan-e Now, Saba, Jonb va Jush, 1943-51; translator, announcer All India Radio, 1948-49; librarian, dep. dir. Library of Parliament Iran, Tehran, 1949-53; cataloger Library of Congress, 1954-55; program asst. libraries devel. sect. UNESCO, Paris, 1959-61; acting chief servicing sect. Dept. Edn., 1962-63; dir. gen. Ministry Edn., Tehran, 1961-62; asst. prof. library and info. scis. and internat. edn. U. Pitts., 1963-66; founder, dir. Internat. Library Info. Center, 1964-66; vis. lectr. SUNY Albany Sch. Library Sci., summer, 1966; dir. internat. librarianship and documentation, internat studies and world affairs SUNY, Oyster Bay, 1966-68; dean, prof. grad. sch. library and info sci. Pratt Inst., Bklyn., 1968-87, chmn. inst. research council, 1971-89, disting. prof., dean emeritus sch. computer, info. and library scis., 1987—; pres. B.E.L.T., Inc., internat. planning cons., 1981—. Dir. Grad. Library Tng. Program, UNESCO Mission, Nat. Tchrs. Coll., Tehran, 1960; Iran's Ofcl. del. to UNESCO Conf. Ednl. Pubs., Geneva, 1961, SE Asia Edn. Secs. Conf., Murree, Pakistan, 1961, Internation Conf., on Cataloging Prins., Paris, 1961, CENTO Libr. Devel. Conf., Ankara, Turkey, 1962; chmn. standing com. for preparation reading materials for new literates UNESCO, Tehran, 1961-62; mem. U.S. AID Mission, Turkey, Iran, Pakistan, 1966; dir. Conf. on Internat. Responsibility Coll. and Univ. Librarians, Oyster Bay, 1967; U.S. del. 33d Conf. and Internat. Congress on Documentation, Tokyo, 1967; ALA del. UN Conf. on Non-Govtl. Orgn., 1969; cons. U.S. AID, Conf. on Book Devel., 1967; mem. adv. bd. Ency. Libr. and Info. Scis., 1969—; chmn. Pre-Am. Library Assn. Conf. Inst. on Internat. Libr. Manpower, Edn. and Placement in N.Am., Detroit, 1970; mem. Am. del. Internat. Fedn. Libr. Assn. Conf., Liverpool, Eng., 1971, Budapest, 1972, Grenoble, France, 1973, Washington, 1974, Brussels, 1977, Montreal, 1982, Chgo., 1985, Barcelona, 1992; organzier USAID sponsored Global Info. Village Conf., Rabat, Morocco, Bklyn., N.Y., 1997, spkr., 1997; bldg. cons. Learning Resources Center, Nat. Tchrs. Coll., Iran, 1972-73, cons. campus planning, 1972-73; UNESCO cons. missions to plan and evaluate Nat. Sch. Info. Sci., Morocco, 1973-74, 79-81, 89; cons. U.S. Info. Agy., Morocco, 1991, 92, 95; chmn. Conf. on Orgn. and Control of Info for Islamic Research, 1982; chmn. bd. cons. to Nat. U. Iran, 1974-75, Pahlavi Nat. Library of Iran, 1975-77; speaker Symposium Internat. sur l' information Economique, Casablanca, Morocco, 1990; inaugural speaker Ctr. Documentation et D'Information Multimedia, Rabat, Morocco, 1995. Author: cataloging of Persian works Including Rules for Transliteration Entry and Description, 1959, Book Production, Importation and Distribution in Iran, Pakistan and Turkey, 1966; Beyond the National Frontiers: The International Dimension of Changing Library Education for a Changing World, 1973; The Pahlavi National Library of the Future, 17 vols., 1976, other books; contbr. to Ency. of Library and Info. Sci., 1969, ALA World Ency. Library and Info. Services, 1980, 86, library jours., 1973—, Bookmark, 1972, Library Education in the Middle East, 1991, Remembering Rangathan: A Sentimental Reflection, 1992; contbr. poetry to various jours. and anthologies, 1947-51, 67, 91-93 lyrics to Iranian motion pictures and recs., 1948-52; works on display at Archieves of Hoover Inst. on War Revolution and Peace, Stanford U.; Contbr. to: film script for motion picture Morad, 1951-52. Trustee Bklyn. Public Library, 1970-82; pres. Maurice F. Tauber Found., 1981— . Recipient Taj (crown) medal and citation for disting. svc. Mohammad Reza Shah Pahlavi, Shah of Iran, 1978, Kaula Gold medal and citation for disting. svc. to internat. librarianship, 1985; named for Annual Nasser Sharify Lecture Series, Sch. of Computer Info. and Libr. Scis., Pratt Inst., 1988—; writings by and about Nasser Sharify are preserved at Archives of Hoover Instn. on wars, revolutions and peace., Stanford U., Stanford, Calif. Mem. ALA (chmn. com. equivalencies and reciprocity 1966-71, mem. UNESCO panel, mem. nominating com. 1970-71, chmn. Pakistan, Iran, Turkey, Morocco, and Middle East Resource panels, internat. library edn. com. 1973—, mem. com. internat. library schs. div. library edn. 1968-72, coordinator country resources panels, internat. library edn. com. library edn. div. 1973-78), N.Y. Library Assn. (dir. library edn. sect. 1969-72), Pub. Library Assn. (task force on internat. relations 1981-86), Am. Assn. Library Schs. (chmn. govtl. relations com., 1984-88), Am. Soc. Info. for Sci., Spl. Librarian Assn., Internat. Fedn. Library Assns. (adv. group library edn. 1971-73, v.p. library schs. sect. 1973-77). Home: 252 Jericho Tpke Westbury NY 11590-1213 Office: Pratt Inst Sch Info and Libr Sci 200 Willoughby Ave # 4 Brooklyn NY 11205-3899 Office Phone: 212-647-7691. E-mail: nsharify@aol.com. *If I am asked to wash a car, I try to make it spotless. If I am to write a book, I try to make it faultless. But it seems that I always find spots on the shining surface of the car, and faults in many well-written pages of the book. This gives me another reason to live for another day.*

SHARKEY, LEONARD ARTHUR, automobile company executive; b. Detroit, May 21, 1946; s. Percy and Lillian (Peros) S.; m. Irene Johnson, Aug. 9, 1969 (div. Nov. 1991); children: Michelle, Wesley Tucker (step-son). Cert. pvt. pilot. Tool and diemaker Ford Motor Co., Dearborn, Mich., 1965-85; indsl. hazardous substance educator Ford Motor co., Dearborn, Mich., 1985-86, indsl. health, safety and energy control educator, 1987-88, tool and diemaker leader, 1989—; non-fiction author Individual Initiative, Brighton, Mich., 1989—. Author: Journey Into Fear (reprinted title Split Decision, 1997), 1995, Hidden Shadows - An Opening to the Windows of the Mind, 1996. Mem. Nat. Geog. Soc., Nat. Rifle Assn., Boat U.S., Drummond Island Sportsman's Club, Mich. United Conservation Clubs. Avocations: boating, shooting sports, political awareness studies, biblical prophetic studies, theater.

SHARKEY, MICHAEL JOSEPH, education educator, researcher; b. Kitchener, Can., Nov. 2, 1953; arrived in US, 1996; s. Patrick Joseph and Anne (Gelineau) Sharkey; m. Susana Monica Roibas, Aug. 19, 1979; children: Alixa, Stephania, Philip. BSc, U. Guelph, Ontario, Can., 1977; MSc, McGill U., Montreal, Quebec, Can., 1981, PhD, 1984. Biologist Agrl. Can., Ottawa, Canada, 1982—84, rsch. scientist, 1994—96; prof. U. Ky., Lexington,

1996—. Rsch. assoc. LA County Mus., LA, 1999—; adj. prof. Oreg. State U., Corvallis, 2001—; adv. bd. Discover Life in Am., Gatlinberg, Tenn., 1999—2003; curator U. Ky. Arthropod Mus., 1996—. Editor: Manual of New World Genera of Braconidae, 1997, Can. Entomologist, 1996—. Grantee, NSF, 1998, 2003, USDA, 2002. Mem.: Soc. Systematic Biologists, Willi Hennig Soc. Achievements include research in hymenoptera phylogeny and evolutionary methods of theory. Avocation: running. Home: 1118 Slashes Rd Lexington KY 40502 Office: Univ Ky Dept Entomology Lexington KY 40546-0091 Business E-Mail: msharkey@uky.edu.

SHARKEY, THOMAS DAVID, botanist, educator; b. Detroit, Jan. 28, 1953; s. Robert Hugh and Patricia June (Elliott) S.; m. Paulette Marie Bochnig June 21, 1974; 1 child, Jessa Sung. BS in Biology, Mich. State U., 1974, PhD in Botany and Plant Pathology, 1980. Postdoctoral fellow Australian Nat. U., Canberra, 1980-82; assoc. rsch. prof. Desert Rsch. Inst., Reno, Nev., 1982-87; asst. prof. U. Wis., Madison, 1987-88, assoc. prof., 1988-91, prof., 1991—. Assoc. dir. Biolog. Scis. Ctr., Reno, Nev., 1983-87; chmn. dept. botany U. Wis., Madison, 1992-94; dir. Inst. Cross-Coll. Biology Edn. Editor: Trace Gas Emissions from Plants, 1991, Photosynthesis: Physiology and Metabolism, 2000; contbr. more than 120 articles to profl. peer-reviewed jours. Mem.: AAAS, Am. Geophysics Union, Internat. Soc. Photosynthesis Rsch., Am. Soc. Plant Biologists. Home: 5901 S Highlands Ave Madison WI 53705-1108 Office: Univ Wis Dept Botany 430 Lincoln Dr Madison WI 53706-1313 Office Phone: 608-262-6802. Business E-Mail: tsharkey@wisc.edu.

SHARLACH, JEFFREY, public relations executive; b. Conn., June 11, 1953; BA, Northwestern U., 1974; JD, NYU, 1977. V.p., client svc. mgr. Burson-Marsteller, N.Y.C., 1982-85; v.p., dir. creative svcs. Carl Byoir & Assocs., N.Y.C., 1986-88; exec. v.p. internat. ops. Rowland Worldwide, N.Y.C., 1988-93; pres., CEO Jeffrey Group, Miami Beach, Fla., 1993—. Mem. Pub. Rels. Soc. Am. Office: Jeffrey Group 1111 Lincoln Rd Ste 800 Miami Beach FL 33139-2451

SHARLET, ROBERT, political science educator, researcher; b. Boston, Mass., Aug. 11, 1935; s. Irving Arnold and Evelyn Lillian Sharlet; children: Jocelyn Cordelia, Jeffrey Charles. BA in Am. Civilization, Brandeis U., 1960; cert. in Russian and East European studies, Ind. U., 1961, PhD in Polit. Sci., 1968; cert. in fgn. and comparative law, Columbia U., 1975. Rsch. assoc. U.S. ACDA, Washington, 1965—67; prof. of polit. sci. Union Coll., Schenectady, NY, 1967—96; sr. coord. Rule of Law Consortium, Washington, 1994—96; Chauncey Winters rsch. prof. of polit. sci. Union Coll., NY, 1996—. Profl. adv. bd. Harriman Inst., Columbia U., N.Y.C., 1996—; bd. of advisors Jour. of East European Law, Columbia U. Law Sch., N.Y.C., 1994—; editl. bd. Demokratizatsiya: The Jour. of Post-Soviet Democratization, Washington, 1997—; vis. prof. polit. sci. Columbia U., N.Y.C., 1980—81; vis. lectr. polit. sci. Yale U., New Haven, 1976—77; vis. asst. prof. law U. Wis. Law Sch., Madison. Author: (scholarly book) Soviet Constitutional Crisis, 1992; co-editor, transl.: scholarly book Stuchka: Selected Writings on Soviet Law and Marxism, 1988, co-editor, contbr.: scholarly book The Soviet Union Since Stalin, 1980 (Main Selection, Polit. and Internat. Affairs Book Club, 1980); co-editor: Pashukanis: Selected Writings on Marxism and Law, 1980; author: The New Soviet Constitution of 1977, 1978; co-author: The Soviet Legal System and Arms Inspection, 1972; contbr. articles to profl. jours. Cons. Ctrl. and East European Legal Inititiative, ABA, Washington, 1992—98; East European coord. Amnesty Internat. USA, N.Y.C., 1977—84. With U.S. Army Security Agy., 1956—58. Co-recipient grant for team study of Russia, Carnegie Corp. of N.Y., 1997—99, grant, NEH, 1980—81, Nat. Coun. for Soviet and East European Rsch., 1979—80, grant for team study, Ford Found., 1975—77; recipient award, Am. Coun. of Learned Socs., 1973—74, fellowship to study in Moscow under U.S.-USSR Cultural Exch., Inter-Univ. Exch. Com., 1963—64; fellow, Ford Found., 1963—65, Nat. Def. Ednl. Act, 1960—63. Mem.: Am. Assn. for the Advancement of Slavic Studies. Independent. Jewish. Avocations: downhill skiing, visiting art museums, collecting graphic art, reading memoirs. Office: Union Coll Dept Polit Sci Schenectady NY 12308

SHARMA, ARJUN DUTTA, cardiologist; b. Bombay, June 2, 1953; came to U.S., 1981; s. Hari D. and Gudrun (Axelsson) S.; m. Carolyn D. Burleigh, May 9, 1981; chldren: Allira, Eric, Harrison. BSc, U. Waterloo, Ont., Can., 1972; MD, U. Toronto, Ont., 1976. Intern Toronto Gen. Hosp., 1976-77, resident in medicine, 1978-80, St. Michael's Hosp., Toronto, 1980-81; residency medicine Toronto Gen. Hosp., 1977-78; Rsch. assoc. Washington U., St. Louis, 1981-83; asst. prof. pharmacy and toxicology U. Western Ont., London, 1985-89, asst. prof. medicine, 1983-89, assoc. prof. medicine, 1989-90; dir. interventional electrophysiology Sutter Meml. Hosp., Sacramento, 1990-95. Abstract reviewer, faculty of ann. sci. sessions N.Am. Soc. for Pacing and Electrophysiology, 1993-97; assoc. clin. prof. U. Calif., Davis, 1990-96, clin. prof. medicine, 1997-2002; cons. Medtronic Inc., Mpls., 1985-2000, Telectronics Pacing Sys., Inc., 1990-94, Ela Med., 2000-03, Guidant, 2000—, Cardiometrics, 1995, Cardema, 2003—; mem. rsch. com. Sutter Inst. Med. Rsch., 1991-97; mem. exec. com. Sutter Heart Inst., 1992; program dir. Update in Tachyarhythmia Mgmt., Palm Springs, 1996, Pacing Defibrillation and Electrophysiology, Squaw Valley, 1997; mem. atrial fibrillation adv. bd. Guidant Inc.; cons. St. Jude Med., 2003—. Reviewer profl. jours., including Circulation, Am. Jour. Cardiology; contbr. articles to profl. publs. Mem. coun. for basic sci. Am. Heart Assn., chmn. ann. sci. session, 1989, resychronization co-chair, 2003. Recipient John Melady award, 1972, Dr. C.S. Wainwright award, 1973-75, Rsch. prize Toronto Gen. Hosp., 1979, 80, Ont. Career Scientist award Ont. Ministry of Health, 1983-89; Med. Rsch. Coun. Can. fellow, 1981-83. Fellow ACP, Am. Coll. Cardiology; mem. Am. Fedn. Clin. Rsch., Canadian Cardiovasc. Soc., N.Y. Acad. Scis., Sacramento Eldorado Med. Soc. Avocations: skiing, tennis, stamp collecting/philately. Office: 3941 J St Ste 260 Sacramento CA 95819-3633 E-mail: skeedud1@aol.com.

SHARMA, MARTHA BRIDGES, geography educator; b. Balt., Feb. 2, 1945; d. Gail and S. Evelyn Bridges; m. Narendra P. Sharma, Aug. 16, 1968; 1 child, Stephanie. BA in Geography, Internat. Studies, U. N.C., 1967; postgrad., U. Hawaii, 1967-68, George Washington U., 1986. Geography tchr. Washington Internat. Sch., 1976-80; dir. records/accounts Washington Internat. Sch., 1981-82, adminstrv. dean, 1983-84; geography tchr. Nat. Cathedral Sch., Washington, 1984—. Geography cons.; lectr. in field. Contbr. articles to profl. jours.; joint author: 7-12 Geography: Themes, Key Ideas, and Learning Opportunities, 1989; co-author: The National Council for Geographic Education: The First Seventy-Five Years and Beyond, 1990; contbg. author: Revisiting the Americas: Teaching and Learning the Geography of the Western Hemisphere, 1992. Mem. Nat. Coun. Geographic Edn. (v.p. pubs. and products 1992—, gender/ethnicity project task force 1991—, dir. spl. pub.s 1989-92, Region VIII awards com. 1988-90), Assn. Am. Geographers, Soc. Woman Geographers. Avocations: reading, music, needlecrafts, travel. Office: Nat Cathedral Sch 3609 Woodley Rd NW Washington DC 20016-5096

SHARMA, RAJESH, research scientist; b. Agra, U.P., India; arrived in U.S., 1997; s. G. C. and S. Sharma; m. Alka Sharma, July 9, 2000. PhD, U. Ark., Little Rock, AR, 2004. Grad. rsch. asst. U. Fla., Gainesville, 1997—99; rschr. U. Ark., Little Rock, 1999—. Contbr. articles to profl. jours. Recipient M.K. Testerman Excellence in Rsch. award, U. Ark. at Little Rock, 2002. Mem.: IEEE (Industrial Applications Soc.), Electrochem. Soc., Electrostatic Soc. of Am., Am. Chem. Soc. Home: # A106 3401 Fairpark Blvd Little Rock AR 72204 Office: Univ Ark ETAS 575 2801 South Univ Ave Little Rock AR 72204 Office Phone: 501-569-8055. E-mail: rxsharma@ualr.edu.

SHARMAN, RICHARD LEE, telecommunications executive, consultant; b. Warren, Pa., Oct. 23, 1932; s. Scott Albert Sr. and Viola Lena Marie (Kittner) S.; m. Diane Lee Van Patten, Nov. 3, 1973; children: Daria Lee, Deedra Lee; children by previous marriage: Suzanne Annette, Cynthia Lee. BS in Engring. Physics, U. Toledo, 1959; MSEE, Cornell U., 1961. Project engr. advanced electronics ctr. GE, Syracuse, N.Y., 1965-68, mgr. infrared and optics, electronics lab., 1965-68, mgr. info. networks, info. sys. divsn. Bethesda, Md., 1968-73; mgr. comml. analysis Xerox Corp., Rochester, N.Y., 1973-78, mgr. mktg. sys., 1978-80; v.p. bus. sector GTE Corp., Stamford Conn., 1980-84; v.p. mktg. GTE Mobilnet Inc., Houston, 1984-87, gen. mgr. Tex. region, 1987-90; v.p. ops. GTE Mobilnet Inc. Hdqrs., Houston, 1990-92; pres., owner Mgmt. Consulting Svcs. Co., The Woodlands, Tex., 1993—. Adj. faculty Montgomery Coll., Conroe, Tex., 1997—; bd. dirs. Cellular Comms. Corp., Irvine, Calif., 1985-87; mem. Svc. Corps of Ret. Execs., 1998—. Contbr. articles to profl. jours. With USCG, 1951-54. Mem. Am. Mktg. Assn. (exec.), Cornell Alumni Assn. (admissions amb.), Tau Beta Pi. Republican. Episcopalian. Avocation: photography. Home and Office: 26 Fernglen Dr The Woodlands TX 77380-3955 Office Phone: 281-364-0164. Business E-Mail: RLS36@cornell.edu.

SHARMAN, WILLIAM, professional basketball team executive; b. Abilene, Tex., May 25, 1926; m. Joyce Sharman; children from previous marriage: Jerry, Nancy, Janice, Tom. Student, U. So. Calif. Basketball player Washington Capitols, 1950-51, Boston Celtics, 1951-61; coach LA/Utah Stars, 1968-71, LA Lakers, 1971-76, gen. mgr., 1976-82, pres., 1982-88, spl. cons., 1991—. Author: Sharman on Basketball Shooting, 1965. Named to All Star 1st Team, NBA, 1956-59, 2nd Team, 1953, 55 (game MVP), 60, All League Team, 7 times, named Coach of Yr., 1972, One of Top Players in NBA History, league 50th anniversary, 1997, league leader free-throw percentage, 7 times; named to Basketball Hall of Fame, 1975, Naismith Basketball Hall of Fame (as player), 1976, as coach (3d man ever as both player and coach), 2004; named All-Am., twice; inductee U. So. Calif. Hall of Fame, 1994; Porterville H.S. gymnasium renamed in his honor, 1997; recipient John Wooden All-Time All-Am. award, 2003.

SHARON, NATHAN, biochemist; b. Brisk, Poland, Nov. 4, 1925; arrived in Israel, 1934; m. Rachel Itzikson, 1948; children: Esther, Osnat. MS, Hebrew U., Jerusalem, 1950, PhD, 1953; Dr. (hon.), U. Rene Descartes, Paris, 1990. Rsch. asst. Agrl. Rsch. Sta., Rehovot, Israel, 1949-53; rsch. asst. dept. biophysics Weizmann Inst. Sci., Rehovot, Israel, 1954-57, rsch. assoc. dept. biophysics, 1957-60, sr. scientist dept. biophysics, 1960-65, assoc. prof. dept. biophysics, 1965-68, prof. dept. biophysics, 1968-90, prof. emeritus, 1991—. Vis. scientist numerous univs. and colls. Author: Complex Carbohydrates: Their Chemistry, Biosynthesis and Functions, 1975; co-editor: Biotechnological Applications of Proteins and Enzymes, 1977, The Lectins: Properties, Functions and Applications in Biology and Medicine, 1986; co-author: Lectins, 1989; contbr. over 400 articles to profl. jours. Recipient Laundau prize Mifal Hapyis, Israel, 1973, Weizmann prize in exact scis. City of Tel Aviv, 1977, Olitzki prize Israel Soc. Microbiology, 1989, Datta lectureship award Fedn. European Biochem. Socs., 1987, Bijvoet medal Utrecht U., 1989, Israel prize in Biomed. and Med. Rsch., 1994. Mem. Am. Chem. Soc., Biochem. Soc. Eng., Am. Soc. Biol. Chemists (hon.), European Molecular Biology Orgn., Israel Acad. Scis. and Humanities, Academia Europaea, Polish Acad. Sci. (fgn. mem.), Am. Soc. Microbiology (hon.),, Internat. Sci. Writers Assn., Israel Biochem. Soc. (pres. 1969-70), Soc. for Complex Carbohydrates, Fedn. European Biochem. Socs. (chmn. 1980-81), Internat. Glycoconjugate Orgn. (pres. 1989-91), Am. Soc. Microbiology (hon.). Avocation: swimming. Home: 77 Mishmeret Afeka Tel Aviv 69012 Israel Office: Weizmann Inst Sci Biol Chemistry Rehovot 76100 Israel E-mail: nathan.sharon@weizmann.ac.il.

SHARON, THOMAS E. science company executive; CEO Electromagnetic Scis., Inc., Norcross, Ga. Office: EMS Tech Inc Technology Park 660 Engineering Dr Norcross GA 30092

SHARON, TIMOTHY MICHAEL, physicist; b. Portsmouth, Va., Aug. 21, 1948; s. Lester Clark and Ruth May (Banister) Sharon; m. Carla Deon Colley, Dec. 17, 1977. Student, Santa Ana Coll., 1966—68; BA, U. Calif., Irvine, 1970, MA, 1972, PhD, 1976. Jr. specialist solid state theory U. Calif., Irvine, 1976; rsch. asst. radiation physics Med. Ctr. and Sch. Medicine, 1976—77; cons. to attending staff Rsch. and Edn. Found., 1976—77; mktg. physicist Varian Assoc., Irvine, 1977—78; prin. engr., program mgr. Spectra Rsch. Sys., Newport Beach, Calif., 1977—82; v.p. Brewer-Sharon Corp., Newport Beach, Calif., 1981—86, Micor Instruments, Inc., Irvine, Calif., 1983—86; pres., CEO Medelec Instruments Co., Inc., Newport Beach, Calif., 1986—88; pres. Pacific Crest Enterprises, El Toro, Calif., 1988—91; pres., CEO Novus Group NA, El Toro, Calif., 1991—96; pres. Instafil, Lake Forest, Calif., 1995—. Adj. faculty physics and engring. Columbia Pacific U., San Rafael, Calif., 1981—87; dean Sch. Engring., Newport U., Newport Beach, Calif., 1983—87; mem. adv. panel on pub. Am. Inst. Physics, 1974—75. Editor (assoc.): (jour.) Future Oncology, 2000—01; contbr. articles to profl. jours. Fellow: Brit. Interplanetary Soc. (assoc.); mem.: Nat. Hist. Soc., Am. Film Inst., Assn. Advancement Med. Instrumentation, IEEE, Am. Assn. Physicists in Medicine, Am. Phys. Soc., AAAS, Club 33, Smithsonian Instn., Nat. Geographic Soc., Intertel, Mensa, Acad. Magical Arts, Festival of Arts Laguna Beach, Alpha Gamma Sigma, Phi Theta Kappa, Sigma Pi Sigma.

SHARON, YITZHAK YAAKOV, physicist, researcher; b. Tel Aviv, Feb. 29, 1936; came to U.S., 1948; s. Abraham Sharon-Schwadron and Dina Freidenberg; m. Sandra Brook, Jan. 13, 1991; 1 child, Dina Avrahama. AB with highest honors, Columbia U., 1958; MA in Physics, Princeton U., 1960, PhD in Physics, 1966. Asst. Inst. for Advanced Study, Princeton, N.J., 1965-66; asst. prof. Northeastern U., Boston, 1966-72; assoc. prof. Richard Stockton Coll., Pomona, N.J., 1972-75, prof. physics, 1975—, trustee fellow in scis., 2000-01. Cons. Ednl. Svcs., Inc. Phys. Sci. Study Commn., 1962-63; vis. prof. Temple U., Phila., 1970-71, U. Montreal, 1970; vis. fellow Princeton U., 1980-82, 91-92; summer physicist Nat. Bur. Standards, Washington, 1971, Oak Ridge (Tenn.) Nat. Lab., 1969, Lawrence Radiation Lab., Berkeley, Calif., 1968; vis., cons. Rutgers U., 1995—. Contbr. articles to profl. jours. Grantee NSF, N.J. Dept. Higher Edn., Ctr. for Theology and Natural Scis. Mem. Am. Phys. Soc., Am. Assn. Physics Tchrs., Sigma Xi, Phi Beta Kappa. Jewish. Home: 19 James Ave Kendall Park NJ 08824-1620 Office: Richard Stockton Coll NJ Dept Physics Pomona NJ 08240 Office Phone: 609-652-4500.

SHARP, ALLEN, federal judge; b. Washington, D.C., Feb. 11, 1932; s. Robert Lee and Frances Louise (Williams) S.; children: Crystal Catholyn Sharp Bauer, Scarlet Frances Thomas. Student, Ind. State U., 1950-53; AB, George Washington U., 1954; JD, Ind. U., 1957; MA, Butler U., 1986. Bar: Ind. 1957. Practiced in, Williamsport, 1957-68; judge Ct. of Appeals Ind., 1969-73, U.S. Dist. Ct. (no. dist.) Ind., South Bend, 1973—. Served to JAG USAF, Res. Mem. Ind. Judges Assn., Blue Key, Phi Delta Kappa, Pi Gamma Mu, Tau Kappa Alpha. Republican. Mem. Christian Ch. Club: Mason. Office: US Dist Ct 124 Fed Bldg 204 S Main St South Bend IN 46601-2122

SHARP, ANNE CATHERINE, artist, educator; b. Red Bank, N.J., Nov. 1, 1943; d. Elmer Eugene and Ethel Violet (Hunter) S. BFA, Pratt Inst., 1965; MFA, Bklyn. Coll., CUNY, 1973. Tchr. art Sch. Visual Arts, 1978-89, NYU, 1978, SUNY, Purchase, 1983, Pratt Manhattan Ctr., N.Y.C., 1982-84, Parsons Sch. Design, N.Y.C., 1984-90, Visual Arts Ctr. of Alaska, Anchorage, 1991, Anchorage Mus. Hist. and Art, 1991, 93, 94, 95, U. Alaska, Anchorage, 1994-96, Fashion Inst. Tech., SUNY, 1997-98; lectr. AAAS, The 46th Arctic Divsn. Sci. Conf., U. Alaska, Fairbanks, 1995. One-person shows Pace Editions, N.Y.C., Ten/Downtown, N.Y.C., Katonah (N.Y.) Gallery, 1974, Contemporary Gallery, Dallas, 1975, Art in a Public Space, N.Y.C., 1979, Eatontown Hist. Mus., N.J., 1980, N.Y. Pub. Library Epiphany Br., 1988, Books and Co., N.Y., 1989, The Kendall Gallery, N.Y.C., 1990, Alaska Pacific U., Carr-Gottstein Gallery, Anchorage, 1993, Internat. Gallery Contemporary Art, Anchorage, 1993, Art Think Tank Gallery, N.Y.C., 1994, U.S. Geol. Survey, Reston, Va., 1994, Stonington Gallery, Anchorage, 1994, on TV Ltd. Benefit, N.Y.C., 1998-2000; group shows include Arnot Art Mus., Elmira, N.Y., 1975, Bronx Mus., 1975, Mus. Modern Art, N.Y.C., 1975-76, Nat. Arts Club, N.Y.C., 1979, Calif. Mus. Photography, Riverside, 1983-92, Jack Tilton Gallery, N.Y.C., 1983, Lincoln Ctr., N.Y.C., 1983, Cabo Frio Print Biennale, Brazil, 1983, Pratt Graphic Ctr., N.Y.C., 1984, State Mus. N.Y., Albany, 1984, Kenkeleba Gallery, N.Y.C., 1985, Hempstead Harbor Art Assn., Glen Cove, N.Y., 1985, Mus. Mod. Art, Weddel, Fed. Republic of Germany, 1985, Kenkeleba Gallery, N.Y.C., 1985, Paper Art Exhbn. Internat. Mus. Contemporary Art, Bahia, Brazil, 1986, Mus. Salon-de-Provence, France, 1987, Mus. Contemporary Art, Sao Paulo, Brazil, 1985-86, Salon de Provence, France, 1987, Adirondack Lakes Ctr. for Arts, Blue Mountain Lake, N.Y., 1987, Kendall Gallery, N.Y.C., 1988, Exhibition Ctr. Parsons Sch. Design, N.Y.C., 1989, F.M.K. Gallery, Budapest, Hungary, 1989, Galerie des Kulturbundes Schwarzenberg, German Dem. Republic, Q Sen Do Gallery, Kobe, Japan, 1989, Anchorage Mus. History and Art, 1990-91, 94, U. Alaska, Anchorage, 1990, 91, Coos Art Mus., Coos Bay, Oreg., 1990, Spaceship Earth, Mus. Internat. de Neu Art, Vancouver, Can., 1990, Councourse Gallery, Emily Carr Coll. Art and Design, 1990, Nat. Mus. Women in the Arts, Washington, 1991, Visual Arts Ctr. Alaska, 1991, 92, Nomad Mus., Lisbon, Portugal, 1991, Mus. Ostdeutsche Gallery, Regensberg, Germany, 1991, Mcpl. Mus. Cesley Krumlov (So. Bohemia) CSFK, Czechoslovakia, 1991, Böltmiche Dörter Exhbn. Hochstrass 8, Munich, 1992, BBC-TV, Great Britain, U.K., Sta. WXXI-TV, Rochester, N.Y., 1992-93, Site 250 Gallery Contemporary Art., Fairbanks, 1993, Santa Barbara (Calif.) Mus. Art, 1993, The Rochester (N.Y.) Mus. and Sci. Ctr., 1990-94, Space Arc: The Archives of Mankind, Time Capsule in Earth Orbit, Hughes Comm., Divec TV Satellite Launch, 1994, Stonington Gallery, Anchorage, 1994, 95, UAA Art Galley U. Alaska, 1995, Arctic Trading Post, Nome, Alaska, 1995, Allan P. Kikbuarts Ctr. Gallery at the Lawrenceville (N.J.) Sch., 1996, Blue Mountain Gallery, N.Y., 1998, The Book Room, Jersey City, 2000, 01, A.I.R. Gallery, 2002, 03, 04, others; represented in permanent collections Smithsonian Instn., Nat. Air and Space Mus., Washington, Albright Knox Gallery, Buffalo, St. Vincent's Hosp, N.Y.C., N.Y. Pub. Libr., N.Y.C., U.S. Geol. Survey, Reston, Va., White House (Reagan, Bush adminstrns.), Site 250 Gallery Contemporary Art, Fairbanks, Alaska, Anchorage Mus. History and Art, others; Moon Shot series to commemorate moon landing, 1970-76, Cloud Structures of the Universe Painting series, 1980-86, Am. Landscape series, 1987-89, Thoughtlines, fall 1986, Swimming in the Mainstream with Her, U. Va., Charlottesville; author: Artist's Book - Travel Dreams U.S.A., 1989, Artworld-Welt Der Kunst, Synchronicity, 1989—, Art Think Tank: Projects in Art and Ecology, 1990—, The Alaska Series, 1990—, Potraits in the Wilderness, 1990—; columnist: Anchorage Press, 1995. Sponsor Iditorod Trail Com., Libby Riddles. Tchg. fellow Bklyn. Coll., 1972; Artist-in-residence grantee Va. Ctr. for Creative Arts, 1974, Artpark, Lewiston, N.Y., 1980, Vt. Studio Colony, 1989; recipient Pippin award Our Town, N.Y.C., 1984, certificate of Appreciation Art in Embassy program U.S. Dept. State, 1996. Mem. Mus. Women in Arts, Pratt Inst. Alumni Assn., Internat. Assn. Near-Death Studies. Address: Murray Hill Station PO Box 1776 New York NY 10156-1776 also: Decker Morris Gallery 621 W 6th Ave Anchorage AK 99501-2200 also: On Television Ltd 388 Broadway New York NY 10013-3542 *As an active painter I explore the mysteries of the 21th century space adventure in my American landscapes, painted directly from nature and in planetary landscapes, fantastic pictures of the cosmos. I believe it is in the reconciliation between inner and outer experience, through a personal sense of humor and use of universal symbols that a mystical or cosmic harmony can be expressed in art.*

SHARP, BARRY J. utilities executive; CPA. Dir. fin. and adminstrn. The AES Corp., Arlington, Va., 1986—87, v.p., CFO, 1987, sr. v.p., 1998, exec. v.p., 2001—, COO, 2002—. Office: The AES Corp 1001 N 19th St Arlington VA 22209

SHARP, DANIEL ASHER, foundation executive; b. San Francisco, Mar. 29, 1932; s. Joseph C. and Miriam (Asher) S.; m. Jacqueline Borda, 1967 (div. 1975); 1 son, Benjamin Daniel; m. Revelle Pergament Allen, 1989. BA, U. Calif.-Berkeley, 1954; JD, Harvard U., 1959. Bar: Calif. 1959. Dep. atty. gen. State of Calif., San Francisco, 1959-61; asst. dir. internat. programs U.S. Peace Corps, Washington, 1961-62, assoc. dir. Cuzco, Peru, 1962-64; acting dir. Peace Corps, La Paz, Bolivia, 1964; creator, dir. Staff Tng. Ctr. Peace Corps, Washington, 1965-68; dir. div. edn. resources U.S. Peace Corps, 1966, 1988—; dir. edn. and Latin Am. programs, asst. dir. Adlai Stevenson Inst. Internat. Affairs, U. Chgo., 1968-70; dir. tng. ITT, Latin Am., 1970-72; mgr. meml. devel. ITT World Hdqrs., N.Y.C., 1973; from dir. human resources devel. to dir. inter-Am. affairs Xerox Corp. (Xerox LatinAm. group), 1973—79; from dir. internat. affairs to internat. cons. Xerox Corp. Hdqrs., 1979—97, sr. internat. advisor InterMatrix Group, 1990—; cons. on global strategy Various corps. including Gen. Goods, IBM, Tex. Instruments, Xerox, 1987—; pres., CEO Columbia U. Am. Assembly, 1987—2002, Royal Instn. World Sci. Assembly, 2002—. Adj. prof. internat. and pub. affairs Columbia U., 1991—; sr. moderator, faculty Aspen Inst., 1995—; chmn.'s coun. Eisenhower Exch. Fellowships, 2000—; U.S. del. UN Econ. and Social Coun., Geneva, 1961, OAS, San Juan, 1986; negotiated 6 treaties U.S. Govt.; U.S. rep. Internat. Conf. on Vol. Programs, The Hague, Netherlands, 1961; outside bd. adv. coun. Macmillan Ltd. (U.K.), 1982; rep. U.S. bus. cmty. nat. task force on Europe Bus. and Industry Adv. Com., regional trade blocs, Paris, 1989; cons. in field. Editor: United States Foreign Policy and Peru, 1972, Los Estados Unidos y La Revolucion Peruaña, 1972; US editor European Business Jour., 1988-95; contbr. articles to profl. jours., chpts. to books. Chmn. adv. bd. Coun. of Ams., 1978-85; bd. dirs. Overseas Devel. Coun., 1980-96, Internat. Ctr. of N.Y., 1980-88, Fund for Multinat. Mgmt. Edn., 1979-85, Accion, 1980-88, World Press Inst., 1986-89, Forum for World Affairs, 1987-95, Stamford Symphony, 1987-91; bd. advs. Landegger Program in Internat. Bus. Diplomacy, Sch. Fgn. Svc., Georgetown U., 1981-92, Econ. Growth Ctr., Yale U., 1987, Consortium on Competitiveness and Coop., U. Calif., 1987-90, Fletcher Sch. Law and Diplomacy, 1984-89; bd. vis. Duke U. Inst. of Policy Scis. and Pub. Affairs, 1988-91; active U.S./Mex. Bus. Coun., 1981-87. With U.S. Army, 1954-55; capt. Res. Recipient Medalla de Oro y Diploma de Honor del Consejo Provincial del Cuzco, 1963, Manchester Leadership award, 1992; Woodrow Wilson fellow Princeton, N.J., 1981-85. Mem. State Bar Calif., Coun. on Fgn. Rels., Century Assn., Mid-Atlantic Club (bd. dirs.), Nat. Com. on US-China Rels., Club of Madrid (gen. coord. founding conf. 2001, adv. sec. gen. 2002—). Home and Office: 94 Campbell Dr Stamford CT 06903-4032 *Changing careers frequently keeps life exciting, as one must constantly learn new roles and ideas and organizations. Public service and the not-for-profit sector are ultimately more satisfying, but the management skills learned in the private sector are practically indispensable.*

SHARP, DAVID HOWLAND, physicist; b. Buffalo, Oct. 14, 1938; s. Russel Howland and Margaret (Dorries) E.; m. Gloria Evanitsky, Jan. 9, 1982; children: Lisa E., Michelle L.; stepchildren: Brian P. Riepe, Michael A. Riepe. AB, Princeton U., 1960; PhD, Calif. Inst. Tech., 1964. Mem. staff Los Alamos Nat. Lab., N.Mex., 1974—84, fellow, 1984—, group leader complex systems group, theoretical divsn., 2002—, sci. advisor applied physics divsn., 2002—. Mem. indsl. adv. bd. Inst. Math. and Its Applications, 2002—. Mem. editl. bd.: Jour. Math. Physics, 1985—87. Recipient def. programs award of excellence, U.S. Dept. Energy, 2001. Fellow AAAS, Am. Phys. Soc.; mem. Am. Math Soc., Internat. Assn. Math. Physicists, NY Acad. Scis., Soc. Indsl. and Applied Math., Soc. Petroleum Engrs., N.Mex. Acad. Scis. Home: 174 Laguna St Los Alamos NM 87544-2603 Office Phone: 505-667-5266. E-mail: dhs@lanl.gov., dglsharp@earthlink.net.

SHARP, ELAINE CECILE, obstetrician, gynecologist; b. Hoven, SD, Feb. 19, 1952; d. Lewis Ralph and Bernadette Teresa (Bastien) Arbach; m. Walton H. Sharp, Oct. 26, 1979 (div.); m. Shane Daigle, Nov. 1991; 1 child, Sean Patrick Daigle. BA, No. State U., 1974, BS, 1976; MD, U. Tex., Houston, 1985. Diplomate Am. Bd. Ob-Gyn. Pvt. practice, Pensacola, Fla., 1989—. Speaker, chmn. Body Talk, Milton, Fla., 1989—. Mem. Am. Med. Women's Assn., Am. Diabetes Assn., Am. Bus. Women's Assn., Am. Coll. Ob-Gyn, Soc. Laparoendoscopic Surgeons, Fla. Ob-Gyn Soc., Exec. Club (asst. chmn. cancer com.), Flying Physicians Assn., Am. Yankee Assn. Republic. Roman Catholic. Avocations: biking, running, swimming, boating, racquetball. Office: PO Box 449 Centralia IL 62801

SHARP, ISADORE, hotel facility executive; b. Toronto, Ont., Can., Oct. 8, 1931; m. Rosalie Wise; children: Jordan, Gregory, Anthony, Christopher (dec.). Degree in architecture, Ryerson Inst. Tech., 1952; LLD (hon.), U. Guelph, 1992, U. Toronto, 1994. Founder Four Seasons Hotels and Resorts, Toronto, 1960—, chmn., CEO, 1961—. Dir. Bank Nova Scotia, Clairvest Group, Inc.; mem. adv. bd. Fin. Post; mem. Premier's adv. com. on exec. resources Province Ont. Active Can. Cancer Soc.; dir. Terry Fox Humanitarian Award Program, Nat. Terry Fox Run, Coun. Can. Unity; founder Terry Fox Run Program; co-chmn. United Jewish Appeal, 1985; mem. bd. govs. Mt. Sinai Hosp., Toronto; mem. govs. coun. N. York Gen. Hosp. Recipient Ruth Hartman Frankel Humanitarian award Can. Cancer Soc., Disting. Svc. award

N.Y.-based World Rehab. Fund, 1989, Ryerson Alumni Award of Distinction, 1998; named Corp. Hotelier of World, Hotels and Restaurants Internat. Mag., 1988, Officer de Confrerie des Amis de L'hotellerier Internat., Internat. Hotel Assn., 1988, NEGEV Dinner Honoree, Jewish Nat. Fund. Can., 1989, Man of Yr., Foodsvc. and Hospitality mag., 1989, CEO of Yr., Fin. Post Mag., 1992, Officer of Order of Can., Gov. Gen. Can., 1993; named to Can. Bus. Hall of Fame, 1998; Ryerson U. fellow, 1983. Office: Four Seasons Hotels 1165 Leslie St Toronto ON Canada M3C 2K8 E-mail: nicola.blazier@fourseasons.com.

SHARP, J(AMES) FRANKLIN, finance educator, portfolio manager; b. Johnson County, Ill., Sept. 29, 1938; s. James Albert and Edna Mae (Slack) S. BS in Indsl. Engring., U. Ill., 1960; MS, Purdue U., 1962, PhD, 1966, cert. mgmt. acctg., 1979. Chartered fin. analyst, 1980; cert. in fin. mgmt., 1997. Asst. prof. engring., econs. Rutgers U., New Brunswick, N.J., 1966-70; assoc. prof. NYU Grad. Sch. Bus., N.Y.C., 1970-74; supr. bus. research AT&T, N.Y.C., 1974-77, dist. mgr. corp. planning, 1977-81, dist. mgr. fin. mgmt. and planning, 1981-85; prof. fin. Grad. Sch. Bus. Pace U., N.Y.C., 1975-91; chmn. Sharp CFA Rev. & Inst. for Investment Edn., 1987-96, Sharp Seminars, 1996—. Speaker, moderator meetings, 1965—; cons. Sharp Investment Mgmt., 1967—. Contbr. numerous articles to profl. publs.; corr.: Interfaces, 1975-78; fin. editor: Planning Rev., 1975-78. Mem. N.Am. Soc. Corp. Planning (treas. 1976-77, bd. dirs. at large 1977-78), Inst. Mgmt. Sci. (chpt. v.p. acad. 1972-74, chpt. v.p. program 1974-75, chpt. v.p. membership 1975-76, chpt. pres. 1976-77), Internat. Affiliation Planning Socs. (coun. 1978-84), N.Y. Soc. Security Analysts (CFA Rev. 1985-87), Ops. Rsch. Soc. Am. (pres. corp. planning group 1976-82), AAUP (v.p. Pace U. chpt. 1988-90), Theta Xi. Republican. Office: 315 E 86th St Apt 7H New York NY 10028-4740

SHARP, JANE SHRIVER, artist; b. Dechard, Tenn., Oct. 14, 1931; d. Paul and Jane (Brown) Shriver; m. Benjamin Thomas Sharp, Sept. 26, 1953; children: Jane Ashton Sharp, Anne Dudley, Julia Shriver. Student, Art Acad., Cin., 1948, Wesleyan Women's Coll., Macon, Ga., 1949-52, U. Chattanooga, 1953, Ecole Beaux Arts, Geneva, 1968-70. Transp. line designer TVA, Chattnooga, 1952-55. Founder Artist's Studio Gallery, Palos Verdes Art Ctr., Palos Verdes Estates, Calif., 1987, bd. dirs., 1985-88; coord. art displays Hall of Adminstrn., L.A., 1987—. One-woman show includes Security Pacific Bank, Palos Verdes Estates, 1988; juried shows include Palos Verdes Art Ctr., 1988, 89; group exhbns. include The Artist's Studio Gallery, Rancho Palos Verdes, 1991; permanent collections include Wesleyan Coll., Macon, Ga., City Hall Palos Verdes Estates; pvt. collections in Geneva, Switzerland and Wilmington, Del.; executed mural Children at Play, Nemours Inst., 1961. Artistic cons. Peninsula Beautification Com., Palos Verdes Estates, Calif., 1987—. Recipient Profl. Artist award Los Angeles County Suprs., 1989; tchr.'s scholar Art Acad., 1948. Mem. Los Angeles County Mus. Art, Mus. Contemporary Art (charter), Armand Hammer Mus. (charter), Beverly Hills Art League, 242 Art Gallery Palos Verdes, Jr. League L.A. (sustaining), Pacific Arts Group (pres. 1976-78), Peninsula Six Artists Groups (pres. 1985-88). Republican. Episcopalian. Avocations: tennis, swimming, skiing. Home: 2405 Via La Selva Palos Verdes Estates CA 90274-1017

SHARP, LEWIS I. museum director; Dir. Denver Art Mus. Office: Denver Art Mus 100 W 14th Avenue Pkwy Denver CO 80204-2749

SHARP, LINDA, professional basketball coach; Profl. basketball coach U. S.C., 1977—89, L.A. Sparks of WBNA, 1997; head coach Concordia U., 2000; profl. basketball coach Phoenix Mercury, 2002—. Color commentator Fox TV. Named WCAA Coach of Yr., Sporting News Coach of Yr.; named to Women's Hall of Fame, 2001. Office: 201 E Jefferson St Phoenix AZ 85004

SHARP, MARSHA, basketball coach; b. Wash. Bachelor's, Wayland Bapt. U., 1974; Master's, West Tex. State U., 1976. Grad. asst. basketball coach The Flying Queens Wayland Bapt. U., 1974-75; asst. basketball coach Lockney U., 1976-82; head coach Lady Raiders basketball Tex. Tech. U., Lubbock, 1982—. Led Lady Raiders to NCAA Championship, 1993, 5 S.W. Conf. titles, 3 post-season crowns; named Nat. Coach of Yr. Women's Basketball News Svc., Ohio Touchdown Club, 1993, Nat. Coach of Yr. Women's Basketball Coaches Assn., 1994. Office: Tex Tech/United Spirit Arena Jones Stadium North 18th & Indiana Ave Lubbock TX 79409

SHARP, PAUL DAVID, institute administrator; b. Youngstown, Ohio, Nov. 3, 1940; s. Robert Henderson and Kathryn (Tadsen)S.; m. Carole G. Graff, Sept. 16, 1967; children: David Allen, Kathryn Sharp Snyder. BA cum laude, Kenyon Coll., Gambier, Ohio, 1962; MPA, Auburn U., 1974. Commd. 2d lt. USAF, 1962, advanced through grades to col., 1983, comdr. Detachment 1, 7450th Intelligence Squadron, 1980-83, comdr. 480th Reconnaissance Tech. Group Langley AFB, Va., 1983-85, dir. intelligence systems HQ Tactical Air Command, 1985-86, dep. chief intelligence Tactical Air Command, 1986-88; mgr. operational intelligence group Battelle Meml. Inst., Columbus, Ohio, 1988-89, mgr. fgn. tech. assessment group, 1989-91, mgr. intelligence projects/programs, 1991-92, v.p. bus. devel. fgn. sci. and tech., 1992-95, dir. fgn. sci. and tech. programs, 1995-98; dir. Air Force spl. programs Battelle Meml. Inst., Columbus, Ohio, 1998-99, mgr. spl. programs office, 1999-2000; mgr. Internat. Tech. Assessments Product Line, 2000—. Student career coun. Kenyon Coll., Columbus, 1992—. Trustee Brandywine Assn., Yorktown, Va., 1987, Chase Assn., Powell, Ohio, 1991. Decorated Legion of Merit. Mem. Nat. Mil. Intelligence Assn., Armed Forces Communications and Electronics Assn., Air Force Assn., Retired Officers Assn., Sigma Pi (pres. Lambda chpt. 1961-62). Republican. Episcopalian. Avocations: golf, woodworking, photography, music. Office: Battelle Meml Inst 505 King Ave Columbus OH 43201-2681

SHARP, PAUL FREDERICK, former university president, education consultant; b. Kirksville, Mo., Jan. 19, 1918; s. Frederick J. and L. Blanche (Phares) S.; m. Rosella Ann Anderson, June 19, 1939; children: William, Kathryn, Paul Trevor. AB, Phillips U., 1939; PhD, U. Minn., 1947; LLD (hon.), Tex. Christian U., 1961, Austin Coll., 1978, Drake U., 1980; LHD (hon.), Buena Vista Coll., 1967, U. Nev., Towson State U., 1980, Oklahoma City U., 1996, U. Okla., 1997; LittD (hon.), Limestone Coll., 1971; HHD, Okla. Christian U. Sci. & Arts, 1992. Instr. U. Minn., 1942, 46-47, vis. lectr., 1948; asso. prof. Am. history Iowa State U., 1947-54; prof. Am. history, chmn. Am. Instns. program U. Wis., 1954-57, vis. lectr., 1953, San Francisco State Coll., 1950, U. Oreg., 1955; Fulbright lectr. Am. Instns., univs. Melbourne, Sydney, 1952; pres. Hiram Coll., 1957-64; chancellor U. N.C., Chapel Hill, 1964-66; pres. Drake U., Des Moines, 1966-71, U. Okla., Norman, 1971-78, pres. emeritus, Regents' prof., 1978-88, pres. emeritus, Regents' prof. emeritus, 1988—; disting. prof. history U. Sci. and Arts, Okla., 1990—96. Dir. Am. Coun. on Edn. Insts. for Coll. and Univ. Presidents, 1977-79; vis. lectr. Harvard U. Bus. Sch. summer session, 1970-72. Author: Agrarian Revolt in Western Canada, 1948, Old Orchard Farm, Story of an Iowa Boyhood, 1952, Whoop-Up Country, Canadian American West, 1955; cons. author: Heritage of Midwest, 1958; editor: Documents of Freedom, 1957; contbr. articles to profl. jours. Pres. Norman Cmty. Found., 1995-97, Okla. State Coun. Aging, 1997-99. USN liaison officer His Majesty's Australian Ship, Hobart, 1943-46. With USNR, 1943-47. Recipient Iowa State U. Alumni Fund award, 1952, award of merit Am. Assn. State and Local History, 1955, Silver Spur award Western Writers Am., 1955, Fulbright award to Australia, 1952; named to Okla. Higher Edn. Hall of Fame, 1995; Minn. Hist. Soc. grantee, 1947, 48, Social Sci. Rsch. Coun. grantee, 1949, 51; Ford Faculty fellow, 1954, Guggenheim fellow, 1957. Mem. Phi Beta Kappa, Phi Kappa Phi, Phi Delta Kappa, Pi Gamma Mu, Phi Alpha Theta. Mem. Christian Ch. (Disciples Of Christ). Home: 701 Mockingbird Ln Norman OK 73071-4829

SHARP, RICHARD L. retail company executive; b. Washington, Apr. 12, 1947; Student, U. Va., 1965-66, Coll. of William and Mary, 1968-70. Programmer Group Health Inc., Washington, 1970-75; founder, pres. Applied Systems Corp., Washington, 1975-81; with Circuit City Stores, Inc., Richmond, Va., 1982—, exec. v.p., 1982-84, pres., 1984-86, pres., CEO, 1986-94, chmn., pres., CEO, 1994-97, chmn., CEO, 1997-2000, chmn., 1997—. Bd. dirs. Flextronics Internat. With USAF, 1967-70.

SHARP, ROB, investment company executive; BA summa cum laude, Union Coll.; MBA, Columbia Bus. Sch. Assoc. mergers and acquisitions group Drexel Burnham Lambert; exec. v.p. Remsen Ptnrs. Ltd.; v.p. BT Securities; prin. Investcorp Internat. Inc.; mng. dir. DB Capital Ptnrs.; ptnr. MidOcean Ptnrs. Bd. dirs. Jenny Craig, Inc., Jostens, Inc., Prestige Brands Internat., Inc., Stratus Tech., Global Sight, Illumin. Mem.: Phi Beta Kappa. Office: MidOcean Ptnrs 320 Park Ave Ste 1700 New York NY 10022

SHARP, ROBERT R. publishing executive; Publisher Going Places mag. AAA, Tampa, Fla. Office: AAA PO Box 31087 Tampa FL 33633-0001

SHARP, RONALD ALAN, English literature educator, dean, author; b. Cleve., Oct. 19, 1945; s. Jack Trier and Florence (Tenenbaum) S.; m. Inese Brutans, June 22, 1968; children: Andrew Janis, James Michael. BA, Kalamazoo Coll., 1967; MA, U. Mich., 1968; PhD, U. Va., 1974. Instr. in English Western Mich. U., Kalamazoo, 1968-70; from instr. to prof. English Kenyon Coll., Gambier, Ohio, 1970—2002, assoc. provost, provost, acting pres., 2002—03; prof. English, dean of faculty Vassar Coll., Poughkeepsie, NY, 2003—. Dir. Keats Bicentennial Conf., Harvard U., 1995. Author: Keats, Skepticism and the Religion of Beauty, 1979, Friendship and Literature: Spirit and Form, 1986; translator: Teatro Breve (Garcia Lorca), 1979, editor (with Eudora Welty) The Norton Book of Friendship, 1991, (with Nathan Scott) Reading George Steiner, 1994, (with Robert Ryan) The Persistence of Poetry: Bicentennial Essays on John Keats, 1998, Selected Poems of Michael Harper, 2002; co-editor Kenyon Rev., 78-82; contbr. articles to profl. jours. Recipient award for editl. excellence Ohioana Assn., 1980; fellow Nat. Humanities Ctr., 1981, 86, NEH, 1981, 84-87, 93, 94, 96, 98, Ford Found., 1971, Mellon Found., 1980, Danforth Found., 1971, English Speaking Union, 1973, Am. Coun. Learned Socs., 1986. Mem. MLA, NEH (chmn's. adv. group humanities edn. 1987), Wordsworth-Coleridge Assn., Keats-Shelley Assn. Jewish. Office: Dean of Faculty Vassar Coll Box 4 Poughkeepsie NY 12604 Office Phone: 845-471-7435. Business E-Mail: sharp@vassar.edu.

SHARP, RONALD ARVELL, sociology educator; b. Vivian, La., Sept. 29, 1941; s. Walter Arvell and Virginia (Refield-King) S.; m. Imelda Idalia Pena, Sept. 16, 1967; children: Ronald Arvell II, Donald Allen. BS in Edn., Cameron U., 1976; BA in Sociology, SUNY, Albany, 1977; MEd in Counseling Psychology, U. Okla., 1978; PhD in Sociology, Clayton U., 1985. Ret. radiologic technologist and instr. U.S. Army, 1960-82; radiologic technologist VA Hosp., Temple, Tex., 1983-84; vets. counselor Vets. Outreach Program, San Antonio, 1982-83; dir. personnel & mktg. Heran Pharms., San Antonio, 1988-91; prof. sociology Ctrl. Tech. Coll., Killeen, 1991-95; instr. sociology Tex. State Tech. Coll., Waco, 1995-96, Academia Assocs., 1996—. Part-time instr. Ctrl. Tex. Coll., 1980-82, City Coll. Chgo., 1981, Big Bend C.C., Mannheim, Germany, 1981-82; instr. Acad. Health Scis., 1977-79. Contbr. articles to profl. jours. Coach Youth Soccer Orgns., San Antonio and Mannheim, 1976-82. Nat. Coll. Radiology Technologists fellow, 1968. Mem. AAUP, DAV (past comdr.), VFW (past comdr.), Uniformed Svcs. Disabled Retirees (nat. vice-commdr., treas.), Am. Sociol. Assn., Soc. Applied Sociology, Nat. Assn. Medics and Corpsmen (PNC), Am. Mil. Ret. Assn. (PNVP), Combat Medics Assn. (nat. dir.), La. Archeol. Soc., Choctaw Nation of Okla., Okla. Anthrop. Soc., La. Archeol. Conservancy, Caddoan Hist. Soc., Okla. Anthropol. Survey, Order of Alhambra, KC, Masons, Soc. for the Study of Social Problems, Four Winds Intertribal Soc., Hokshichankiya Soc., Psi Beta (chpt. sponsor), Alpha Kappa Delta, Psi Chi, Sigma Eta Sigma (nat. dir.). Roman Catholic. Avocations: soccer, golf, paleo-historic anthropology. Home: 9310 Oak Hills Dr Temple TX 76502-5272 Office: Academia Assocs Waco TX 76705

SHARP, STEVEN, information technology executive; Chmn., pres., CEO TriQuint Semiconductor, Hillsboro, Oreg. Recipient Oreg. Entrepreneur of Yr. award, 2000, Technology Exec. of Yr. award, 2001. Office: TriQuint Semiconductor 2300 NE Brookwood Pkwy Hillsboro OR 97124

SHARP, TIMOTHY ALLEN, editor; b. Winfield, Kans., Jan. 23, 1960; s. Roland Eugene and Shirley Anne Sharp; life ptnr. Gage Robert Church, May 7, 1964. BS in Journalism, U. Kans., 1982. Online editor Des Moines Register, 1998—; copy editor The Coloradoan, Fort Collins, 1983—84, Austin Am.-Statesman, 1984—87, St. Petersburg Times, Fla., 1987—97; asst. tech. editor NY Times Digital, 1997—98. Finalist Feature Journalism, Online News Assn., 2002; named Best Website, Iowa Newspaper Assn., 2000, Best Local News Site, Gannett Co., 2000; recipient Merit award, Des Moines Register, 2004. Mem.: Nat. Lesbian and Gay Journalists Assn. (pres. Tampa Bay chpt. 1996—97). Avocations: genealogy, comic books, travel. Office Phone: 515-286-2591.

SHARP, WILLIAM J. manufacturing executive; b. Huntington, W.Va., Nov. 2, 1941; BA in Indsl. Rels., U. Akron, 1964. Prodn. scheduler Goodyear Tire & Rubber Co., Akron, Ohio, 1964, various positions, to supt. prodn. various cities, 1964-79, mgr. prodn. Lawton, Okla., 1979-81, plant mgr., tire prodn. facilities various cities, Luxembourg, France, 1981-83, dir. domestic tire prodn. Akron, 1983-84, dir. European tire prodn. Brussels, 1984-87, v.p. tire mfg. Akron, 1987-91, exec. v.p. product supply, 1991-92, pres., gen. mgr. European region Brussels, 1992-96, pres. global support ops., 1996-99, pres. N.Am. Tire, 1999—.

SHARP, WILLIAM WHEELER, geologist; b. Shreveport, La., Oct. 9, 1923; s. William Wheeler and Jennie V. (Benson) S.; m. Rubylin Slaughter, 1958; children: Staci Lynn, Kimberly Cecile; 1 child from previous marriage, John E. BS in Geology, U. Tex., Austin, 1950, MA, 1951. Lic. pvt. pilot. Geol. Socony-Vacuum, Caracas, Venezuela, 1951-53, surface geol. chief Creole, 1953-57; dist. devel. geologist, supr. exploration, devel. unitization of 132 multi-pay oil and gas fields, expert geol. witness, coll. recruiter, rsch. adviso ARCO, 1957—85. Discovered oil and gas at Bayou Boullion, Bayou Sale, Jeanerette, La., Chandeleur Sound and Beauregaurd Parish, La.; petroleum exploration in Alaska, Aus., Can., U.S. and S.A. Contbr. articles to profl. jours.; author numerous corp. rsch. and ops. reports; included in From Acorn to Oakbourne—History of Oakbourne Country Club, 1998.; contbr. artifacts/photos to Nimitz Mus., Fredricksburg, Tex., Nat. Mus. Pacific War, Nat. WWII Meml., Washington, Tex. Meml. Mus., Benson Latin Am. Libr., U. Tex., Austin. Past dir. and chmn. U.S. Tennis Assn. Tournaments; pres. Lafayette Tennis Adv. Com., 1972; pres. Oakbourne Tennis Assn.; past dir. Jr. Achievement and United Fund Programs; contbr. to various mus. With USAF, 1943-46, PTO. Winner and finalist more than 75 amateur tennis tournaments including Confederate Oil Invitational, Gulf Coast Oilmen's Tournament, So. Oilmen's Tournament, Tex.-Ark.-La. Oilmen's Tournament, top La. State Ranking; named Hon. Citizen of New Orleans, 1971, recipient Key to New Orleans; named in Registry of Remembrances Nat. WWII Meml., Washington. Mem. Dallas Geol. Soc., Lafayette Geol. Soc. (bd. dirs. 1973-74), Am. Assn. Petroleum Geologists (emeritus, co-author Best of SEG conv. 1982), Tex. Astron. Soc., VFW, Am. Legion, Lafayette Petroleum Club, Appaloosa Horse Club, Collin County Hist. Soc., Brookhaven Country Club (Dallas), Oakbourne Country Club Tennis Assn. (pres. 1976, organizer USTA nat. boys tennis tournament 1976). Republican. Methodist. Achievements include drilling of more than 30 successful wells at Bayou Boullion Field; report/recommendations that resulted in Atlantic Refining Co. office at Anchorage, 1962. Avocations: sports, music, history. Home: 7312 Mimosa Ln Dallas TX 75230-5446

SHARPE, CALVIN WILLIAM, law educator, arbitrator; b. Greensboro, N.C., Feb. 22, 1945; s. Ralph David and Mildred (Johnson) S.; m. Maya Annette Hall, Jan. 25, 1970 (div. Oct. 1975); 1 child, Kabral; m. Janice M. Jones, Apr. 13, 1978; children: Melanie, Stevie. BA, Clark Coll., 1967; postgrad., Oberlin Coll., 1968; MA, Chgo. Theol. Sem., 1996; JD, Northwestern U., Chgo., 1974. Bar: Ill. 1974. Tchr. elem. sch. N.Y. Sch. System, Bklyn., 1968-69; dir. homework study ctr. Ocean Hill Brownsville, Bklyn., 1969; investigator Ill. Gov.'s Task Force on Cook County Property Tax, Chgo., 1972-73; law clk. to judge Hubert L. Will U.S. Dist. Ct. (no. dist.) Ill., Chgo., 1974-76; assoc. Cotton, Watt, Jones, King & Bowlus, Chgo., 1976-77; trial atty. NLRB, Winston-Salem, N.C., 1977-81; asst. prof. U. Va., 1981-84; assoc. prof. Case Western Res. U., Cleve., 1984-88, prof., 1988—, John Deaver Drinko-Baker & Hostetler prof. law, 1999—, acad. dean, 1991-92. Exec. bd. Pub. Sector Labor Rels. Assn., Ohio, 1986—; chmn. evidence sect. Assn. Am. Law Schs., 1987-88; mem. Am. Labor Law Project to Soviet Union and Western Europe-People to People, 1988; mem. Youth Svcs. Adv. Bd. of the Cuyahoga County Juvenile Ct., 1989-91; cons. So. African Commn. on Concilation, Mediation and Arbitration, 1998—. Co-author: Understanding Labor Law, 1999. Bd. trustees Cleve. Hearing and Speech Ctr., 1985-88; bd. dirs. Garrett-Evang. Theol. Sem., 1999—, Cleve. Pub. Radio, 1993-94. Mem. Soc. Profls. in Dispute Resolution, Internat. Soc. Labor Law and Social Security, Indsl. Rels. Rsch. Assn. (convener and first chair labor and employment law sect. 1995-97), Labor Law Group Trust, Nat. Acad. Arbitrators (bd. govs. 2001—), Soc. of Benchers. Office: Case Western Res U Law Sch 11075 East Blvd Cleveland OH 44106-5409

SHARPE, DONALD CHARLES, service manager; b. Durham, N.C., July 28, 1956; s. Lawrence Albright and Virginia Ann (Pacofsky) S. Electrician, ICS Corr. Schs., Scranton, Pa., 1983. Cert. chlorofluorocarbons, motor vehicle air conditioning, pool and spa operator, notary pub., N.C., 1997; lic. real estate agt., N.C. Electrician USN, 1974-88; maintenance engr. Holiday Inn Exec. Ctr., Virginia Beach, Va., 1988-94; ind. contractor Virginia Beach, 1994-95; maintenance asst. Sterling Forest Apts. Grubb Mgmt., Raleigh, N.C., 1995, svc. supr. Sterling Brook Apts. Carrboro, N.C., 1995-98; svc. mgr. Four Seasons Apartments, Raleigh, N.C., 1998-2000, Summit Properties, Durham, N.C., 2000—. Republican. Christian. Avocations: rare collectibles and books, archaeology, biblical research, history.

SHARPE, HENRY DEXTER, JR., retired manufacturing company executive; b. Providence, May 5, 1923; s. Henry Dexter and Mary Elizabeth (Evans) S.; m. Peggy Plumer Boyd, Aug. 1, 1953; children: Henry Dexter, Douglas, Sarah. Grad., Brown U., 1945. With Brown & Sharpe Mfg. Co., Providence, 1946-96, v.p., 1950-51, pres., 1951-76, chmn., CEO, 1976-80, chmn., 1980-96, ret., 1996. Vice chancellor Brown U., 1986-87. Bd. dirs. R.I. Pub. Expenditure Coun.; trustee, fellow Brown U., 1954-99; trustee Coll. of the Atlantic, 1992-2003. Lt. (j.g.) USNR, 1943-46. Mem. Nat. Machine Tool Builders Assn. (pres. 1969-70), Machinery and Allied Products Inst. (ret. mem. exec. com.) Office: 30 Pojac Point Rd North Kingstown RI 02852-1031

SHARPE, JAMES SHELBY, lawyer; b. Ft. Worth, Sept. 11, 1940; s. James Henry and Wanzel (Vanderbilt) S.; m. Martha Moudy Holland, June 9, 1962; children: Marthanne Freeman, Caren Sharp, Stephen. BA, U. Tex., 1962, JD, 1965. Bar: Tex. 1965, U.S. Dist. Ct. (no. dist.) Tex. 1966, U.S. Dist. Ct. (ea. dist.) Tex. 1993, U.S. Dist. Ct. (ea. and we. dists.) Ark. 1997, U.S. Ct. Appeals (5th and 6th cirs.) 1982, U.S. Ct. Appeals (fed. cir.) 1983, U.S. Ct. Appeals (10th cir.) 1992, U.S. Supreme Ct. 1972. Briefing atty. for chief justice Supreme Ct. of Tex., Austin, 1965-66; ptnr. Brown, Herman, Scott, Dean & Miles, Ft. Worth, 1966-84, Gandy Michener Swindle Whitaker & Pratt, Ft. Worth, 1984-87; shareholder Sharpe & Tillman, Ft. Worth, 1988—. Adj. prof. polit. sci. Tex. Christian U., Ft. Worth, 1969-79, Dallas Bapt. U., 1987, 1992-94; gen. counsel U.S.A. Radio Network, Internat. Christian Media, Denton Pub. Co. Pres. Ft. Worth-Tarrant County Jr. Bar, 1969-70, bd. dirs., sec., 1968, v.p., 1968-69; head marshal USA-USSR Track and Field Championships, Ft. Worth, USA-USSR Jr. Track and Field Championships, Austin, Tex., Relays, Austin, 1963—, NCAA Nat. Track and Field Championships, 1976, 80, 85, 92, 95, S.W. Conf. Indoor Track and Field Championships, 1987-96, Olympic Festival, San Antonio, 1993, Colorado Springs, 1995; 12 time head marshal S.W. Conf. Track and Field Championships, Big 12 Outdoor Conf. Track and Field Championship, 1997-99, 2001-03, head marshall Olympic Trials in Track and Field, 2000, 04. USA/Mobil Track Championship, 1994, 95; USA Nat. Jr. Track Championship, 1994, 95, 98, 99, USA Track and Field Track Championship, 1997, 2001-03, Master's Nat. Track and Field Nat. Championship, 1996, 98, 2002. Mem. ABA, State Bar of Tex. (dist. 7-A grievance com. 1983-85, com. adminstrn. of justice 1985-92, com. on ct. rules 1992-2003, chmn. 1992-93, 93-94). Baptist. Office: Sharpe & Tillman 6100 Western Pl Ste 1000 Fort Worth TX 76107-4679 Office Phone: 817-338-4900. E-mail: utlawman@aol.com.

SHARPE, KATHRYN MOYE, psychologist; b. Barnesville, Ga., Nov. 27, 1922; d. Herbert Johnston and Henri Lucile (Winter) Moye; m. William Herschel Sharpe, Mar. 2, 1946; children: William Herschel Jr., Mark Stephens. AB, Piedmont Coll., Demorest, Ga., 1942; MA, U. N.C., 1947; PhD, U. S.C., 1975. Tchr., guidance counselor Charleston (S.C.) Pub. Schs., 1947-66; prof. sociology, chmn. dept. Bapt. Coll. at Charleston, 1966-88, prof. emeritus, 1988—; pvt. practice psychology, Charleston, 1975—. Named One of Twelve Outstanding Women in Greater Charleston by The Ctr. for Women; Kathryn Moye Sharpe scholarship given in her honor Bapt. Coll. at Charleston, 1988. Fellow Am. Assn. for Marriage and Family Therapy (approved supr., pres. S.C. div. 1975-77, disting. svc. award S.C. chpt. 1999). Congregationalist. Home and Office: 6 Cavalier Ave Charleston SC 29407-7702

SHARPE, KEITH YOUNT, retired lawyer; b. Hiddenite, NC, July 11, 1930; s. Ruel Yount and Eileen Lois (Lackey) S.; m. Margaret Joyce Land, Aug. 27, 1955 (div.); children: Jonathan, Matthew, Leonora, Felicia. AB, Duke U., 1952; JD, Wake Forest U., 1957, MBA, 1982; MLA, U. NC, Asheville, 2001. Bar: NC 1957. Pvt. practice law, Winston-Salem, NC, 1957-62, 82-94; asst. solicitor Mcpl. Ct. of Winston-Salem, 1958-60; with Pilot Freight Carriers Inc., Winston-Salem, 1962-82, sr. v.p., 1967-76, v.p., 1976-82, also dir.; v.p., dir. Comml. Automotive Co., 1967-76, Terminal Warehouse Corp., 1967-82. Bd. govs. So. Motor Carriers Rate Conf., 1977-81. Served with inf. U.S. Army, 1952-54. Mem. Assn. Transp. Practitioners, Phi Alpha Delta, Theta Chi. Democrat. Episcopalian. Home: Apt 118 M 4755 Country Club Rd Winston Salem NC 27104-3551

SHARPE, MYRON EMANUEL, publisher, editor, writer; b. Chester, Pa., Sept. 10, 1928; s. Abraham Maxwell and Emma (Friedman) S.; m. Jacqueline Steiner, 1959 (div.); children: Susanna, Matthew; m. Carole S. Brafman, 1983; children: Elizabeth, Hannah. BA, Swarthmore Coll., 1950; MA, U. Mich., 1951; PhD, Madison U., 2000. Pres. Modern Factors Corp., Phila., 1957; founder, chmn. bd., pres. M.E. Sharpe, Inc. (Pub.), Armonk, N.Y., 1958—, writer, editor, 1955—. Founder, exec. dir. Com. to Save the Life of Henry Spetter, 1974; co-founder, coord. Initiative Com. for Nat. Econ. Planning, 1974-76; participant in drafting Full Employment and Balanced Growth Act of 1978; co-founder, pres. M.E. Sharpe, Ltd. (Arts and Antiques), New Canaan, Conn., 1981-83. Author: John Kenneth Galbraith and the Lower Economics, 1973. Chmn. Pro Arte Chamber Singers of Conn., 1982-83; pres. Waveny Chamber Music Soc., 1987-98; econ. advisor to Senator Birch Bayh for presdl. campaign, 1975. Office: M E Sharpe Inc 80 Business Park Dr Armonk NY 10504-1715 E-mail: wordsloo@aol.com.

SHARPE, ROBERT FRANCIS, equipment manufacturing company executive; b. Buffalo, Mar. 29, 1921; s. Bertram Francis and Agnes (Coppinger) S.; m. Audrey Rembe, July 10, 1943; 1 son, Robert Francis. BS in Chem. Engring, Rensselaer Poly. Inst., 1942. With Duriron Co., 1946—, mgr. pump sales, 1955-58, dir. research, devel., 1958-63, v.p. plastics ops., 1963-65, exec. v.p., 1967-68, pres., chief operating officer, 1968-69, pres., 1969-76, chief exec. officer, 1969-79, chmn. bd., 1978-83. Served with USAAF, 1943-46. Mem. Am. Inst. Chem. Engrs., Hydraulic Inst. Home: 15520 Whitney Ln Naples FL 34110-7611

SHARPE, ROBERT FRANCIS, JR., lawyer; b. Long Branch, N.J., Mar. 9, 1952; s. Robert Francis and Audrey Carolyn (Rembe) S.; 1 child, Robert Francis III; m. Maria S. Renna, Sept. 9, 2000. BA, DePauw U., 1975; BSE, Purdue U., 1975; JD, Wake Forest U., 1978. Bar: NC 1978. Atty. Capital Synergistics Corp., Winston-Salem, N.C., 1977-80; asst. counsel R.J. Reynolds Industries, Winston-Salem, 1980-82, assoc. counsel, 1983-85, counsel, 1985-86; corp. and comml. counsel R.J. Reynolds Tobacco Co., Winston-

Salem, 1986-87; sr. counsel, asst. sec. R.J. Reynolds Nabisco, Inc., Atlanta, 1987-88, asst. gen. counsel, asst sec., 1989-93, v.p., sec., gen. counsel, 1996-97; v.p. mergers and acquisitions Tyco Internat., 1994-95; sr. v.p. pub. affairs & gen. coun. PepsiCo, Inc., Purchase, NY, 1998—2002; ptnr., Brunswick Grp., Inc., 2002—. Bd. dirs. Whitman Corp., Pepsi Bottling Group. Active Jr. Achievement, U.S. C. of C. Bd. dirs. Whitman Corp., Pepsi Bottling Group. Mem. ABA, N.C. Bar Assn., Am. Corp. Counsel Assn. Republican. Episcopalian. Avocations: golf, fishing. Office: Brunswick Group 135 E 57th St New York NY 10022

SHARPE, ROBERT KENT, writer, director, producer, photographer; b. Chgo., Nov. 17, 1930; s. Byron C. and Helen Lee Sharpe; m. Mary Kahn, 1955 (div. 1971); m. T. Tina Ditta, Apr. 26, 1980; children: Steven W., Sharon E., Jonathan K., Julia A. BA in English, Brown U., 1953. Writer, dir. Ford Found., NYC, 1956-57, CBS, NYC, 1957-58, NBC Spl. Projects Dept., NYC, 1959-61, freelance dir., 1962-63; pres. RKS Devel. Corp., Ardsley, 1963-75, Robert K. Sharpe Prodns., Inc., Ardsley, NY, 1965—, Hastings on Hudson, NY, 1965—. Prodr., writer, dir.: (documentary) Before the Mountain Was Moved, 1969 (awards 1969-70); writer, dir.: (shorts) Night in a Pet Ship, 1959 (awards 1959-60), prodr., writer, dir. (shorts) Pancho, 1966-67 (awards 1966-67), Joe, 1965 (awards 1965), Face of Excellence, 1962, The Forgotten, 1958 (awards 1958-59); screenwriter: (films) WFAT, 1982, The Long Night, 1962, Barbero, 1983, A Dead Issue, 1963, Computer, 1965, A Letter Home, 1965, Squaw Gap Speaking, 1976; dir.: (TV) The Twentieth Century Series, 1962-63, Keep It Cool, Rhodes Scholar, The Jazz of Dave Brubeck, The Songs of Harold Arlen, Fire Brand on Ice - Stan Mikita, Here is New York, Buildings for Business and Government, Call it Courage, Equestrianism, others; staff writer, dir.: (TV) Wisdom Series, 1959-61, The Ordeal of Woodrow Wilson as Told by President Herbert Hoover, The Seven Lively Arts Series, Omibus Series, 1956-57; prodr., dir. (films) The Great Debate, 1963; writer, dir. (films) Light as You Like It, 1958; photographic series Assisi, 1953, Spanish Patterns, 1990, Interplay, 1998, The Unseen, 1999, Changes, 2003, Portugal, 2003. Mem. Am. Soc. Media Photographers, Dirs. Guild Am., Photographic Adminstrs., Inc., Phi Beta Kappa. Democrat. Jewish. Avocations: amateur radio, hi-fi & electronics, wood working. Home and Office: 765 N Broadway Apt 15E Hastings On Hudson NY 10706 Office Phone: 914-478-3434. E-mail: rsharpe@earthlink.net.

SHARPE, ROLAND LEONARD, structural engineer, consultant; b. Shakopee, Minn., Dec. 18, 1923; s. Alfred Leonard and Ruth Helen Sharpe; m. Jane Esther Steele, Dec. 28, 1946; children: Douglas Rolfe, Deborah Lynn, Sheryl Anne. BSCE, U. Mich., 1947, MSE, 1949. Registered civil engr., structural engr. Designer Cummins & Barnard, Inc., Ann Arbor, Mich., 1947-48; instr. engring. U. Mich., 1948-50; exec. v.p. John A. Blume & Assocs., engrs., San Francisco, 1950-73; chmn., founder Engring. Decision Analysis Co., Inc., Cupertino, Calif., 1974-87; cons. earthquake engr. Sharpe Structural Engrs., Los Altos, Calif., 1987—. Mng. dir. EDAC, GmbH, Frankfurt, Germany, 1974—82; pres. Calif. Devel. & Engring. Co., Inc., Las Vegas, Nev., 1973—81; mem. nat. earthquake hazard reduction program adv. com. overviewing Fed. Emergency Mgmt. Agy., U.S. Geol. Survey, NSF and Nat. Inst. Stds. and Tech., 1990—93. Author (with J. Blume, E. G. Kost): (book) Earthquake Engineering for Nuclear Facilities, 1971; co-author: DOE Seismic Safety Manual, 1996; contbr. articles to profl. jours. Mem. Planning Commn., Palo Alto, 1955—60; mng. dir. Applied Tech. Coun., Palo Alto, 1973—83; dir. Earthquake Engring. Rsch. Inst., 1972—75, mem.; project dir., editor Tentative Provision Devel. Seismic Regulations Bldgs., 1978; tech. mgr., contbr., editor Data Processing Facilities: Guidelines Earthquake Hazard Mitigation, 1987. With USMC, 1942—46. Recipient citation for contbn. to constrn. industry, Engring. News Record, 1978—79, 1986—87, chmn. U.S. Joint Com. Earthquake Engring., 1982—88. Fellow: ASCE (hon.; chmn. dynamic effects com. 1978—80, exec. com. structural divsn. 1980—84, chmn. 1983, exec. com. structural divsn. 1989—93, mgmt. group B 1989—93, Earnest E. Howard award 1994); mem.: Structural Engrs. World Congress (pres. 1995—, chair 1998), Structural Engrs. Assn. Calif. (dir. 1971—73, chmn. seismology com. 1972—74), Structural Engrs. No. Calif. (hon.; dir. 1969—71), Japan Structural Cons. Assn. (hon.), Am. Concrete Inst. (life). Home: 10320 Rolly Rd Los Altos CA 94024-6568 Office: Sharpe Struct Engrs 10320 Rolly Rd Ste 1 Los Altos CA 94024-6568 Office Phone: 650-948-9095. E-mail: rsharpe3@mindspring.com. *Personal philosophy: One's conduct should be beyond reproach both morally and ethically and I should serve each of my clients to the best of my ability.*

SHARPE, SHANNON, commentator, retired professional football player; b. Chgo., June 26, 1968; Student, Savannah State U. Tight end Denver Broncos, 1990—99, Balt. Ravens, 2000—02, Denver Broncos, 2002—04; commentator NFL Today, CBS, 2004—. Named to Pro Bowl Team, 1992—98, 2001. Achievements include ranks no. 1 in NFL history in recieving yards, receptions, and touchdowns for a tight end; mem. of Superbowl Championship Team, Denver Bronco's, 1997, 1998, Baltimore Ravens, 2000. Office: NFL Today 51 W 52nd St New York NY 10019

SHARPE, STERLING, former professional football player, sports commentator; b. Chgo., Apr. 6, 1965; BA, U. S.C., 1987. With Green Bay Packers, 1988-95; analyst, broadcaster ESPN, Bristol, Conn., 1995—. Named to Sporting News Coll. All-Am., 1987; named receiving leader NFL, 1989, 92, wide receiver All-Pro Team NFL, 1989. Achievements include playing in Pro Bowl, 1989, 90, 92; named to Pro Bowl, 1993.

SHARPE, WILLIAM FORSYTH, economics professor; b. Cambridge, Mass., June 16, 1934; s. Russell Thornley Sharpe and Evelyn Forsyth (Jillson) Maloy; m. Roberta Ruth Branton, July 2, 1954 (div. Feb. 1986); children: Deborah Ann, Jonathan Forsyth; m. Kathryn Dorothy Peck, Apr. 5, 1986. AB, UCLA, 1955, MA, 1956, PhD, 1961; DHL (hon.), DePaul U., 1997; D (hon.), U Alicante, Spain, 2003, U. Vienna, Austria, 2004. Economist Rand Corp., 1957—61; asst. prof. econs. U. Wash., 1961—63, assoc. prof., 1963—67, prof., 1967—68, U. Calif., Irvine, 1968—70; Timken prof. fin. Stanford (Calif.) U., 1970—89, Timken prof. emeritus, 1989—92, prof. fin., 1993—95, STANCO 25 prof. fin., 1995—99, prof. emeritus, 1999—; prin. William F. Sharpe Assocs., 1986—92; chmn. Fin. Engines, Inc., 1996—2003. Author: The Economics of Computers, 1969, Portfolio Theory and Capital Markets, 1970; co-author: Fundamentals of Investments, 1989, 3d edit., 2000, Investments, 6th edit., 1999. With U.S. Army, 1956—57. Recipient Graham and Dodd award, Fin. Analysts' Fedn., 1972, 1973, 1986—88, Nicholas Molodovsky award, 1989, Nobel prize in econ. scis., 1990, UCLA medal, 1998. Mem.: Am. Econ. Assn., Ea. Fin. Assn. (Disting. Scholar award 1991), Western Fin. Assn. (Enduring Contbn. award 1989), Am. Fin. Assn. (v.p. 1979, pres. 1980), Phi Beta Kappa.

SHARPE, WILLIAM NORMAN, JR., mechanical engineer, educator; b. Chatham County, N.C., Apr. 15, 1938; s. William Norman and Margaret Horne (Womble) S.; m. Margaret Ellen Strowd, Aug. 21, 1959; children: William N., J. Ashley. BS, N.C. State U., 1960, MS, 1961; PhD, Johns Hopkins U., 1966. Registered profl. engr., Mich., La., Md. Assoc. prof. Mich. State U., East Lansing, 1970-75, prof., 1975-78; prof., chmn. dept. mech. engring. La. State U., Baton Rouge, 1978-83; prof., dept. mech. engring. Johns Hopkins U., Balt., 1983—, Decker prof. mech. engring., 1985—. Recipient Alexander von Humboldt award, Fed. Republic Germany, 1989 Fellow ASME (Nadai award 1993), Soc. Exptl. Mechanics (Tatnall award, exec. bd. 1979-81, pres. 1984-85); mem. ASTM, Am. Soc. Engring. Edn. Home: 220 Ridgewood Rd Baltimore MD 21210-2539 Office: Johns Hopkins U Dept Mech Engring 200 Latrobe Hall Rm 122 Baltimore MD 21218

SHARPE, WILLIAM R. state legislator, electrical contractor; m. Pauline Lester. Student, Bliss Engring. Sch., Salem Coll., W.Va. U. Registered profl. engr., W.Va. Mem. W.Va. Senate, Charleston, 1980-80, 84—, majority whip, 1972-80, pres. pro tem., 1990-94. Mem. banking and ins. com., energy com., industry and mining com., fin. com., health and human resources com., rules com., small bus. com. Mem. W.Va. Dem. Exec. Com. Mem. Internat. Brotherhood Elec. Workers, Fraternal Order Eagles, Masons, Shriners, Elks, Moose. Methodist. Office: WVa Senate 1900 Kanawha Blvd E Rm 206W Charleston WV 25305-0009 also: 607 Center Ave Weston WV 26452-2122

SHARPE-ARRANT, KATHLEEN DIANE, accountant, small business owner; b. Suffern, N.Y., Sept. 29, 1955; d. Robert C. and Shirley A. (Oakley) Conklin; m. Leland J. Sharpe Jr., Sept. 26, 1986 (div. Apr. 1993); children: Angela D. Causey, Leland J. III; m. Laurence P. Arrant, Sept. 23, 2000. Asst. to project dir. S.C. Gov.'s Office, Columbia, 1982-83; asst. to exec. dir. S.C. Sentencing Guidelines Com., Columbia, 1983-86; probation/parole officer S.C. Probation, Parole and Pardon Svcs., Columbia, 1986-88; staff acct. Levitan & Yegidis, CPA's, Middletown, N.Y., 1988-91; mng. dir. Periwinkle Nat. Theatre, Monticello, N.Y., 1991-94; owner, operator AAA Books & Tax, Bloomingburg, N.Y., 1990—, Country Steppin' Prodns., Inc., Bloomingburg, 1993—. Owner, operator New To You Consignment Boutique, Montgomery, N.Y., 1999—. Founding dir. non-profit 501(C)(3) Gowns to Girls Program, 2000—. With Signal Corps U.S. Army, 1975—77, USACC, Ft. Jackson, S.C. Mem. Nat. Tchrs. Assn., Nat. Soc. Accts. Republican. Lutheran. Avocations: singing, country dance instruction and choreography. Home: 7 Ivy Ln Bloomingburg NY 12721-4506 Office: 110 Clinton St Montgomery NY 12549 Office Phone: 845-457-3747. E-mail: Karrant@hvc.rr.com.

SHARPLES, D. KENT, college administrator; b. Swanton, Ohio, May 26, 1943; s. Morrill and Doris Elizabeth (Saeger) S.; m. Linda Mancini Sharples; children: Dawn, Steven. BS, Bowling Green State U., 1965, MEd, 1966; PhD in Ednl. Adminstrn., Ohio U., 1973. Tchr. Maumee (Ohio) Jr. H.S., 1966-67; instr. dept. engring. graphics Coll. Engring. and Tech., Athens, Ohio, 1967-73; project dir. S.C. State Bd. for Tech. and Comprehensive Edn., West Columbia, 1973-76; v.p. for edn., dean of instrn. Tri-County Tech. Coll., Pendleton, S.C., 1976-80; pres. Horry-Georgetown Tech. Coll., Conway, S.C., 1980-99, Daytona Beach (Fla.) C.C., 1999—. Mem. Am. Assn. Community and Jr. Colls. (chair small/rural coll. commn. 1983-87, bd. dirs. 1987), Assn. Community Colls Trustees, So. Assn. of Colls. and Schs., Council for Occupational Edn., Am. Tech. Edn. Assn., Rotary. Episcopalian. Office: Daytona Beach CC PO Box 2811 Daytona Beach FL 32120-2811

SHARPLES, RUTH LISSAK, communications executive; b. N.Y.C., Feb. 3, 1952; d. Saul and Nettie (Field) Lissak; m. Winston Sharples, June 26, 1981; stepchildren: Hadley, John, Gillian. BA, CUNY, 1973; MFA, Columbia U., 1975. Rschr. Am. Film Inst./Motion Picture Divsn. of Libr. of Congress, Washington, 1977-79; mgr. audio-visual programs Am. Soc. Microbiology, Washington, 1979-82; mgr. video tech. Am. Gas Assn., Arlington, Va., 1982-96; dir. comm. Am. Gas Cooling Ctr., Arlington, 1996—. V.p., corp. sec. Cantab Motors, Ltd., Purcellville, Va., 1988—; corp. sec. Am. Gas Cooling Ctr., Arlington, 1996—. Editor Cool Times Newsletter, 1996-98. Mem. Nat. Trust Historic Preservation, Nature Conservancy, Mass. Audubon Soc., English Heritage, Nat. Trust, Internat. TV Assn. Avocations: hiking, archaeology. Office: Am Gas Cooling Ctr 420 N Capitol St NW Washington DC 20001-1504

SHARPLES, WINSTON SINGLETON, automobile importer and distributor; b. Springfield, Mass., Oct. 24, 1932; s. Winston Singleton and Carmela (Parrino) S.; m. Jeanette Williams, July 1961 (div. Apr. 1981); children: John, Hadley, Gillian; m. Ruth Emily Lissak, June 26, 1981. BA, Harvard Coll., 1953; postgrad. drama, Yale U., 1956-57; MFA, Carnegie Mellon U., 1959; postgrad., Univ. Md., 1978-80. Freelance writer, 1959—; producer, dir. Mon. Valley Playhouse, Charleroi, Pa., 1959, Robin Hood Theater, Arden, Del., 1960-61; pres., film and music editor Synchro-Sound Inc., N.Y.C., 1961-71; prof. CUNY, N.Y.C., 1969-74, Temple Univ., Phila., 1974-76, U. Md., College Park, 1978-79; adminstr. film preservation and documentation Am. Film Inst., Washington, 1976-78; prof. Howard Univ., Washington, 1978-80; pres. Cantab Motors, Ltd., Puncellville, Va., 1984—. Author: (with others) A Primer for Film-Making, 1971—; supr. Am. Film Inst. Catalog of Feature Films, 1960-69, 77; editor, music editor films and cartoons; contbr. articles to profl. jours. and mags. With U.S. Army, 1953-56. Nat. Endowment for the Humanities grantee, 1977. Mem. ASCAP, Archeol. Soc. Va., Am. Studies Assn., Univ. Film Assn. (v.p. 1975-76), Soc. for Cinema Studies, Soc. Automotive Engrs., Washington Automotive Press Assn., Morgan Car Club, Land Rover Owners Assn. Va., British Automobile Mfrs. Assn., Harvard Club (N.Y.C.). Democrat. Avocations: forestry, archeology. Home: 16657 Tree Crops Ln Round Hill VA 20141-2236 Office: Cantab Motors Ltd Valley Indsl Park 37251 E Richardson Ln Purcellville VA 20132-3505

SHARPLESS, JOSEPH BENJAMIN, retired county official; b. Takoma Park, Md., Feb. 4, 1933; s. William Raiford and Julia Maude (Rouse) Sharpless; m. Nancy Kathleen Steffen, July 28, 1962 (dec. Feb. 1988); 1 child, Carole Marie. BA, Earlham Coll., 1955; MS, Pa. State U., 1960. Instr. recreation Montgomery County Recreation Dept., Rockville, Md., 1957—58; from program supr. to dir. Recreation and Parks Dept., Livingston, NJ, 1959—70; chief recreation svc. Md.-Nat. Capital Park and Planning Commn. Prince George's County, Riverdale, Md., 1970—77, parks and recreation div. chief, 1977—95; ret., 1995. Mem. bd. regents, instr. Sch. Sports Mgmt. N.C. State U., 1989—92. Contbr. articles to profl. jours. Dir. volleyball Spl. Olympics Inc., 1994—; tech. del. Spl. Olympics World Summer Games, 1995, 1999, 2003; trustee U.S. Volleyball Edn. Found., 1976—, sec., 1996—; nat. volleyball chmn. AAU, 1966—69, 1972; nat. commr. U.S. Volleyball, 1976—81; mem. volleyball games staff 1996 Olympic Games, Atlanta; staff World Volleyball Congress, Atlanta, 1996; v.p. Montpelier Cmty. Assn., South Laurel, Md., 1983—84, pres., 1985; mem. Md. Sports Adv. Com., 1988—92, Md. State Games Commr., 1986—91; volleyball chmn. N.J. assn., 1961—70, Potomac Valley Assn., 1971—73; pres. NJAAU, 1968—70. Recipient Pioneer award, AAU, 1998. Fellow: Nat. Recreation Pks. Assn. (Berman Profl. Citation award Mid-Atlantic Regional Coun. 1995, Disting. Svc. award 1995); mem.: N.J. Soccer Ofcls. Assn. (sec., treas. 1966—70), Nat. Capitol Area Bd. Volleyball Ofcls. (sec. 1985—89), Sch. and Coll. Soccer Ofcls. Assn. (sec., treas. 1965—70, del. Mid-Atlantic NRPA regional coun. 1969—79), Md. Recreation and Pk. Assn. (v.p. 1975—77, pres. 1977—78, Mem. of the Yr. 1975, citation 1985), N.J. Recreation and Pks. Assn. (sec. 1965, v.p. 1966, pres. 1967), Am. Pk. and Recreation Soc. (bd. dirs. 1977—80, nat. coun., coun. affiliate pres.), Nat. Intercollegiate Soccer Ofcls. Assn. (sec. 1966—68, treas. 1968—70), U.S. Volleyball Assn. (regional commr. 1965—78, nat. ofcl. 1967—96, v.p. 1973—90, bd. dirs. 1973—, mem. exec. com. 1976—80, 1985—89, exec. cons. 1989—91, mem. exec. com. 1992—96, corp. sec. 1992—96, mng. editor pubs. 1994—98, v.p. 1996—2004, regional commr., referee, scorekeeper emeritus 2000, numerous awards), Ret. Life Profl. (Disting. Fellow award 1996). Republican. Mem. Soc. Of Friends. Home: 26205 S Cedarcrest Dr Sun Lakes AZ 85248-7206 Personal E-mail: chessycrab@aol.com.

SHARPLESS, K. BARRY, chemist, educator; b. Phila., Apr. 28, 1941; m. Jan Dueser, Apr. 28, 1965; children: Hannah, William, Isaac. BA, Dartmouth Coll., 1963, hon. doctorate, 1995; PhD, Stanford U., 1968; hon. doctorate, Swedish Royal Inst. Tech., 1995, Tech. U. Munich, 1995, Cath. U. Louvain, Belgium, 1996. Postdoctoral assoc. Harvard U., Stanford U., to 1970, faculty dept. chemistry, 1977-80; faculty MIT, Cambridge, 1970-77, 1980-90; W. M. Keck prof. chemistry Scripps Rsch. Inst. and Skaggs Inst. of Chem. Biology, La Jolla, Calif., 1990—. Recipient Pual Janssen prize for Creativity in Organic Synthesis, Chem. Pioneer award, Am. Inst. Chemists, 1988, Prelog medal, Swiss Fed. Inst. Tech., Zurich, 1988, Scheele medal and prize, Swedish Acad. Pharm. Scis., Tetrahedron prize for Creativity in Organic Chemistry, 1993, King Faisal Internat. prize for sci., 1995, Microbial medal, Kitasato Inst., Tokyo, 1997, Harvey medal, Technion-Israel Inst. Tech., 1998, Benjamin Franklin medal in chemistry, 2001, Wolf prize in chemistry, 2001, Nobel prize in Chemistry, 2001; fellow A. P. Sloan, 1987—88, Guggenheim, 1987—88; scholar Camille and Henry Dreyfus Tchr. . Fellow: AAAS, Am. Acad. Arts and Scis., Royal Soc. Chemistry (hon.); mem.: NAS (Award in Chemical Sciences 2000), Am. Chem. Soc. (Creative Work in Synthetic Organic Chemistry award 1983, Harrison Howe award Rochester chpt. 1987, Remsen award Md. sect. 1989, Arthur C. Cope award 1992, Roger Adams award 1997, Richards medal Northeastern sect. 1998, Top 75 Contbrs. to Chem. Enterprise 1998). Office: Scripps Rsch Inst BCC 315 10550 N Torrey Pines Rd La Jolla CA 92037-1000

SHARPLESS, MATTIE R. ambassador; b. Hampstead, N.C., July 1943; BA in Bus. Edn., N.C. Coll.; MBA, N.C. Cen. Univ. Former acting adminstr. USDA/Fgn. Agr. Svc.; various positions with Fgn. Agr. Svc., 1965—2001; spl. envoy to emerging economies USDA, 1999—2001; U.S. Amb. to Cen. African Rep., 2001—. Named to USDA's Yearbook of Outstanding Employees, 1990; recipient Presdl. Meritorious Svc. award. Office: DOS Amb 2060 Bangui Pl Washington DC 20521

SHARPNACK, RAYONA, management consultant; b. 1952; 1 child, Chelsea. Grad., U. Nev., Reno. Founder, pres. Inst. Women's Leadership, Redwood City, Calif., 1992—. Faculty Mills Coll., Women in Mgmt. program, 1994; bd. dirs. Profl. Bus. Women Calif. Conf., 1994—99; co-chair State of World Forum, Investing in Women Initiative, 1998—99; pres. Prof. Bus. Women in Calif., 1999; adv. coun. mem. Internat. Mus. Women, 1999—2001; player, mgr. Internat. Women's Profl. Softball League, 1979; shortstop Calif. Express. Office: Inst Women's Leadership PO Box 58 Redwood City CA 94064-0058

SHARPTON, ALFRED CHARLES, JR., minister, political activist; b. Bklyn., Oct. 3, 1954; m. Kathy Jordan, 1983; children: Dominique, Ashley. Student, Bklyn.Coll., 1973—75. Cert. ordained a Rev. 1964. Youth dir. Operation BreadBasket, 1969; founder Nat. Youth Movement, 1971—; road mgr. James Brown concert tours, 1973—80; founder, pres., CEO Nat. Action Network, Inc., Bklyn., 1991—. Candidate NY State Senate, 1978, US Senate, 1992, 94, NYC mayor, 1997, Pres., 2004. Co-author (with Anthony Walton): Go Tell the Pharaoh: The Autobiography of Reverend Al Sharpton, 1996; co-author: (with Karen Hunter) Al on America, 2002. Pentecostal. Office: Al Sharpton for Pres 1001 6th Ave Ste 1211 New York NY 10018 E-mail: info@sharpton2004.org.*

SHARPTON, THOMAS, physician; b. Augusta, Ga., July 15, 1949; s. Thomas and Elizabeth (Dozier) S. BA, Northwestern U., 1971; MS, Stanford U., 1973, MD, 1977. Intern Martinez (Calif.) VAMC, 1977-78, resident, 1978-80; mem. staff Kaiser Permanente Med. Group, Oakland, Calif., 1980—; asst. clin. prof. medicine U. Calif., San Francisco, 1994—. Cons. Berkeley (Calif.) Free Clinic, 1977—; chmn. peer review Kaiser Permanente Med. Group, Oakland, 1985-86; clin. mem. faculty U. Calif., San Francisco, 1992, asst. clin. prof., 1994; chair AIDS therapeutics com. No. Calif. Kaiser Hosps., 1996-2000. Mem. Alameda County Profl. Adv. Com., Oakland, 1984-88, Alameda County AIDS Task Force, Oakland, 1985-88. Fellow ACP; mem. Calif. Med. Assn., Alameda-Contra Costa Med. Assn., Am. Soc. Microbiology, Mensa, Sigma Pi Sigma, Phi Beta Kappa. Clubs: Phi Beta Kappa of No. Calif. Republican. Avocation: classical piano. Office: Kaiser PMG 280 W Macarthur Blvd Oakland CA 94611-5642 Business E-Mail: Thomas.Sharpton@kp.org.

SHARROW, MARILYN JANE, library administrator; b. Oakland, Calif. d. Charles L. and H.Evelyn Sharrow; m. Larry J. Davis. BS in Design, U. Mich., 1967, MALS, 1969. Libr. Detroit Pub. Libr., 1968-70; head fine arts dept. Syracuse (N.Y.) U. Librs., 1970-73; dir. libr. Roseville (Mich.) Pub. Libr., 1973-75; asst. dir. librs. U. Wash., Seattle, 1975-77, assoc. dir. librs., 1978-79; dir. librs. U. Man., Winnipeg, Can., 1979-82; chief libr. U. Toronto, Can., 1982-85; libr. U. Calif., Davis, 1985—. Chair bd. North Regional Libr. Facility, 1999—2001. Recipient Woman of Yr. in Mgmt. award Winnipeg YWCA, 1982; named Woman of Distinction, U. Calif. Faculty Women's Rsch. Group, 1985. Mem. ALA, Assn. Rsch. Librs. (bd. dirs., v.p., pres.-elect 1989-90, pres. 1990-91, chair sci. tech. work group 1994-98, rsch. collections com. 1993-95, 2000-2002, preservation com. 1997-99, 2003—), OCLC-Rsch. Librs. Adv. Com. (vice-chair 1992-93, chair 1993-94), Calif. State Network Resources Libr. Com., Can. Assn. Rsch. Libr. (pres. 1984-85). Office: U Calif Shields Libr 100 NW Quad Davis CA 95616-5292 E-mail: mjsharrow@ucdavis.edu.

SHARTLE, STANLEY MUSGRAVE, engineering executive, consultant, surveyor; b. Brazil, Ind., Sept. 27, 1922; s. Arthur Tinder and Mildred C. (Musgrave) Shartle; m. Anna Lee Mantle, Apr. 7, 1948; 1 child, Randy. Student, Purdue U., 1947—50. Registered profl. engr., land surveyor. Ind. chief dep. surveyor Hendricks County, Danville, Ind., 1941-42, dep. county surveyor, 1944-50, county engr., surveyor, 1950-54, county hwy. engr., 1975-77; asst. hydrographer Fourteenth Naval Dist., Pearl Harbor, Hawaii, 1942-44; staff engr. Ind. Toll Rd. Commn., Indpls., 1954-61; chief right of way engring. Ind. State Hwy. Commn., Indpls., 1961-75; owner, civil engr. Shartle Engring., Indpls., 1977-89; prin. Parsons Cunningham & Shartle Engrs., Inc., Indpls., 1990—. Right of way engring. cons. Gannett Fleming Transp. Engrs., Inc., Indpls., 1983—88; part-time lectr. Purdue U. Ind. State Hwy. Commn., 1965—67. Author: Shartle Genealogy, 1955, Musgrave Family History, 1961, 1995, Right of Way Engineering Manual, 1975, (novels) Her Word of Honor, 2001; contbr. articles to tech. and sci. jours. Ex-officio mem., charter mem. exec. sec. Hendricks County Planning Commn., 1951—54; mem. citizen adv. com. Hendricks County Subdivision Control Ordinance, 1988—. Named Stanley Shartle Day, Hendricks County, 1997; recipient Outstanding Contbn. award, Henricks County Soil and Water Conservation Dist., 1976. Mem.: Geog. and Land Info. Soc., Internat. Right of Way Assn. (founder chpt. 10), Ind. Toll Rd. Employees Assn. (pres. 1959—60), Nat. Geneal. Soc., Nat. Soc. Profl. Surveyors (Quarter Century Club), Ind. Soc. Profl. Land Surveyors (life; bd. dirs. 1979), Am. Congress Surveying and Mapping (life). Avocations: astronomy, genealogy, geodesy.

SHASHA, DENNIS ELLIOTT, computer scientist, author; b. White Plains, NY, Aug. 15, 1955; s. Alfred and Hanina (Zilkha) S.; m. Karen Shashoua, June 5, 1983; children: Cloe, Liane, Tyler, Eli. BS, Yale U., 1977; MA, Syracuse U., 1980; PhD, Harvard U., 1984. Engr. IBM, Poughkeepsie, N.Y., 1977-80; from asst. to assoc. prof. NYU, N.Y.C., 1984-95, prof., 1995—. Cons. AT&T Bell Labs., Summit, N.J., 1985-94, Union Bank Switzerland, 1994-98, Bellcore, 1994, Morgan Stanley Dean Witter, 1999—. Author: The Puzzling Adventures of Dr. Ecco, 1988, Codes, Puzzles and Conspiracy, 1992, Out of their minds: the lives and discoveries of 15 great computer scientists, 1995, Pattern Discovery in Biomolecular Data, 1999, Database Tuning: Principles, Experiments, and Trouble Shooting Techniques, 2002, Red Blues, 2002, Dr. Eclo's Cyber Puzzles, 2002, High Performance Discovery in Time Series Data, 2004; columnist Sci. Am. Dr. Dobb's Jour. Office: NYU 251 Mercer St New York NY 10012-1110 Business E-Mail: shasha@cs.nyu.edu.

SHASHIDHARAN, KALATHIL KUNGATTY, emergency physician, internist; b. Cannanore, Kerala, India, Dec. 10, 1945; came to U.S., 1971; Student, St. Joseph's Coll., Calicut, India, 1963-64; MD, Jawaharlal Inst. PG Medicine, Pondicherry, 1970. Diplomate Am. Bd. Internal Medicine, Am. Bd. Emergency Medicine. Intern Providence Hosp., Washington, 1972; resident internal medicine Howard U., Washington, 1973-75; ER attending physician Church Hosp., Balt., 1975-88, St. Agnes Hosp., Balt., 1988-92, Sinai Hosp., Balt., 1992-93, Good Samaritan Hosp., Balt., 1993—. Mem. AMA, Am. Coll. Emergency Physicians.

SHASTEEN, DONALD EUGENE, government official; b. Englewood, Colo., Dec. 3, 1928; s. George Donald and Frances True (Meyers) S.; m. Shirley Mae Johnson, Aug. 8, 1954; children: Jon Randolph, Ron Winston, Sherilyn Sue Kosman. *Donald's mother Frances Meyers Shasteen received her BA in 1951 from Colorado State Teacher's College and her MA in 1961 at Adams State Teacher's College. She retired in 1971 after 37 years as an elementary and junior high math teacher. She was named Outstanding Community Service Volunteer by Arkansas Valley Retired School Employees Association and she received the Sunshine Award for Beautifying the Community of La Junta, CO with her flower garden.* BA in Journalism, U. Colo., 1950. Reporter Omaha World-Herald, Des Moines, 1954-58, Lincoln, Nebr., 1958-66; exec. asst. to Senator Carl T. Curtis of Nebr., Washington, 1966-73, adminstrv. asst., 1973-78, to Sen. Gordon J. Humphrey, 1979-80; with transition group Senate Republican Conf., 1980; dep. under sec. for legislation and intergovtl. affairs Dept. Labor, 1981-83, dep. asst. sec. for vets. employment, 1983-85, asst. sec. for vets. employment and tng., 1985-89. Pres. Shasteen Assocs. Rep. nominee for U.S. Senate Nebr., 1978. Served with U.S. Army, 1951-52. Mem. Am. Legion, VFW, Am. Vets., Disabled Am. Vets., Phi Delta Theta. Republican. Lutheran. E-mail: shasteens@juno.com., shasteen@msn.com.

SHASTID, JON BARTON, wine company executive; b. Hannibal, Mo., Nov. 21, 1914; s. Jon Shepherd and Mary (Barton) S.; m. Natalie Kiliani, Dec. 16, 1944; children— Lucinda, Jon G.H., Victoria A., Thomas Bartwyn. Bar: Calif. bar 1959; C.P.A., Calif., Kans. Pub. accountant, Dodge City, Kans., 1938-42; v.p. finance Johnson Bronze Co., New Castle, Pa., 1946-54; exec. v.p., treas. E. & J. Gallo Winery, Modesto, Calif., 1954-88; pres. Gallo Wine Co. of La. at New Orleans, 1960-89. City councilman, Modesto, 1961-69. Served to capt. USAAF, 1942-46. Mem. State Bar of Calif., Am. Bar Assn., Calif. Soc. C.P.A.'s. Home and Office: 1700 Tice Blvd #209 Walnut Creek CA 94595

SHATIN, JUDITH, music composing educator; b. Boston, Nov. 11, 1949; d. Leo and Harriet Evelyn (Sommer) S.; m. Michael Kubovy, June 28, 1992. AB, Douglass, Coll., 1971; MM, Julliard Sch., 1974; PhD, Princeton U., 1979. Asst. prof. U. Va., Charlottesville, 1979-85, assoc. prof., 1985-92, prof., 1992—, chmn. McIntire dept. music, 1995—, William R. Kenan, Jr. prof., 1999—. Dir. Va. Ctr. Computer Music, 1988—. Composer: (orch.) Aura, 1981, (piano concerto) Passion of St. Cecilia, 1985, (flute concerto) Ruah, 1985, (piano trio) View from Mt. Nebo (commd. by Garth Newel Chamber Players), 1985, (piano trio) Ignoto Numine (commd. Monticello Trio), 1986, (flute, clarinet, violin, cello) Secret Ground (commd. by Roxbury Chamber Players), 1990, (soprano and tape) Three Summers Heat, 1989 (Barlow Found. Commn.), (orch.) Piping the Earth (commd. by Women's Philharm.), 1990, (flute and piano) Gabriel's Wing (commd. by Julia Bogorad and the Upper Midwest Flute Assn.), 1990, (flute and electronics) Kairos (Commd. Va. Commn. for the Arts), 1991, (chorus, brass quintet, tympani) We Hold These Truths (commd. U. Va., for Thomas Jefferson's 250th birthday), 1992, (string orch.) Stringing the Bow (commd. Va. Chamber Orch.), 1992, COAL (commd. as part of 2-yr. retrospective of work, sponsored by Lila Wallace- Readers Digest Arts Ptnrs. Program), 1994, (piano and percussion) 1492 (commd. Arioso Ensemble), 1992, (piano) Chai Variations on Eliahu HaNavi, 1995, (flute and guitar) Dreamtigers (commd. Ekko!), 1996, (chorus) Adonai Roi, 1995, (string quartet) Janus Quartet (commd. for the Arcata Quartet), 1994, (string quartet and electronic playback) Elijah's Chariot (commd. Kronos Quartet), 1995, (amplified clarinet with PVC extensions effects processor, foot pedals and playback sys.) Sea of Reeds (commd. F. Gerard Errante), 1997, (chorus and piano) Songs of War and Peace, 1998, (brass quintet) Fantasia sobre el Flamenco, 1998, (piano, cello, percussion) Houdini: Memories of a Conjurer, 1999 (commd. Core Ensemble), (wind quintet and piano) Ockeghem Variations (commd. Hexagon Ensemble), 2000, Run (piano quartet) (commd. Currents) 2001, Singing the Blue Ridge (commd. Wintergreen Performing Arts through Ams. for the Arts), 2002, Tree Music (coomd. U. Va. Art Mus., interactive electronics), 2003, Penelope's Song (viola and electronics), 2003, Amulet (commd. N.Y. Treble Singers, SSA Chorus), 2003. Nat. Endowment for Arts Composer fellow, 1980, 85, 89, 92; recipient award Va. Commn. for the Arts, 1989, 2002. Mem. Am. Music Ctr., Am. Women Composers (pres. 1989-93), Am. Composers Alliance (bd. dirs. 1993-98), Internat. Alliance for Women in Music (chair nominating com. 1996-98, adv. bd. 1999—). E-mail: shatin@virginia.edu.

SHATNER, WILLIAM, actor; b. Montreal, Que., Can., Mar. 22, 1931; s. Joseph and Anne S.; m. Gloria Rand, Aug. 12, 1956 (div. Mar. 1969); three children; m. Marcy Lafferty, Oct. 20, 1973 (div. 1996); m. Nerine Kidd, Nov. 15, 1997 (dec. Aug. 1999); m. Elizabeth Martin, Feb. 2001. BA, McGill U., 1952. Stage debut, 1952; appeared Montreal Playhouse, summers 1952, 53; played juvenile roles Canadian Repertory Theatre, Ottawa, 1952-53, 53-54; appeared Stratford Shakespeare Festival, Ont., 1954-56; Broadway appearances include Tamburlaine the Great, 1956, The World of Suzie Wong, 1958, A Shot in the Dark, 1961; films include The Brothers Karamazov, 1958, The Explosive Generation, 1961, Judgement at Nuremburg, 1961, The Intruder, 1962, The Outrage, 1964, Dead of Night, 1974, The Devil's Rain, 1975, Star Trek, 1979, The Kidnapping of the President, 1979, Star Trek: The Wrath of Khan, 1982, Star Trek III: The Search for Spock, 1984, Star Trek IV: The Voyage Home, 1986, (dir.) Star Trek V: The Final Frontier, 1989, Star Trek VI: The Undiscovered Country, 1991, National Lampoon's Loaded Weapon, 1992, Star Trek: Generations, 1994, Trekkies, 1997, Free Enterprise, 1998, Shoot or be Shot, 2000, Groom Lake, 2000, Miss Congeniality, 2000, American Psycho II, 2001, Osmosis Jones, 2001, Dodgeball: A True Underdog Story, 2004; also TV movies and appearances on The Andersonville Trial, The Bastard, 1978, Disaster on the Coastliner, 1979, Secrets of a Married Man, 1984, North Beach and Rawhide, 1985, Columbo, 1993; star of TV show Star Trek, 1966-69, animated series, 1973-75; TV series Barbary Coast, 1975-76, The Babysitter, 1979, T.J. Hooker; host (TV series) Rescue 911, CBS, 1989—, Third Rock From the Sun, 1996, The Practice, 2004, Boston Legal, 2004—; dir. TV movie TekWar; author: (novels) TekWar, 1989, TekLords, 1991, TekLab, 1991, Tek Vengeance, 1992, Tek Secret, 1993, (memoirs) Star Trek Memories, 1993, Star Trek Movie Memories, 1994, Tek Power, 1994, Tek Money, 1995, The Ashes of Eden, 1995, Man O' War, 1996, Tek Kill, 1996, The Return, 1996, Avenger, 1997, Delta Search: Quest for Tomorrow, 1997, Delta Search: In Alien Hands, 1998, Delta Search: Step Into Chaos, 1999, I'm Working on That, 2002. Recipient Tyrone Guthrie award, 1956, Theatre World award, 1958. Mem. Actors Equity Assn., AFTRA, SAG, Dirs. Guild. Address: care of Melis Prodns 760 N La Cienega Blvd Los Angeles CA 90069-5204

SHATNEY, CLAYTON HENRY, surgeon; b. Bangor, Maine, Nov. 4, 1943; s. Clayton Lewis and Regina (Cossette) S.; m. Consuelo Perez Santibañez; children: Tony, Andy, Joel. BA, Bowdoin Coll., 1965; MD, Tufts U., 1969. Asst. prof. surgery U. Md. Hosp., Balt., 1979-82; assoc. prof. U. Fla. Sch. Medicine, 1982-87; clin. assoc. prof. Stanford (Calif.) U. Sch. Medicine, 1987—. Dir. traumatology Md. Inst. Emergency Med. Svcs., Balt., 1979-82; dir. trauma U. Hosp., Jacksonville, 1982-85; assoc. dir. trauma Santa Clara Valley Med. Ctr., 1992—; cons. VA Coop. Studies Program, Washington, 1980-90. Mem. editl. bd. Circulatory Shock, 1989-94, Panam Jour. Trauma, 1995-2000, Jour. Investigative Surgery, 2001--. Maj. U.S. Army, 1977-79. State of Maine scholar Bowdoin Coll., 1961-65. Fellow ACS, Southeastern Surg. Congress, Southwestern Surg. Congress, Soc. Surg. Alimentary Tract, Am. Assn. Surg. Trauma, Soc. Internat. de Chirurgie, Western Surg. Assn., Pacific Coast Surg. Assn., Phi Kappa Phi. Home: 900 Larsen Rd Aptos CA 95003-2640 Office: Valley Med Ctr Dept Surgery 751 S Bascom Ave San Jose CA 95128-2604 Office Phone: 408-885-6060. E-mail: cshatney@yahoo.com.

SHATTUCK, CATHIE ANN, lawyer, former government official; b. Salt Lake City, July 18, 1945; d. Robert Ashley S. and Lillian Culp (Shattuck). BA, U. Nebr., 1967, JD, 1970. Bar: Nebr. 1970, U.S. Dist. Ct. Nebr. 1970, Colo. 1971, U.S. Dist. Ct. Colo. 1971, U.S. Supreme Ct. 1974, U.S. Ct. Appeals (10th cir.) 1977, U.S. Dist. Ct. D.C. 1984, U.S. Ct. Appeals (D.C. cir.) 1984. V.p., gen. mgr. Shattuck Farms, Hastings, Nebr., 1967-70; asst. project dir. atty. Colo. Civil Rights Commn., Denver, 1970-72; trial atty. EEOC, Denver, 1973-77, vice chmn. Washington, 1982-84; pvt. practice law Denver, 1977-81; mem. Fgn. Svc. Bd., Washington, 1982-84, Presdl. Pers. Task Force, Washington, 1982-84; ptnr. Epstein, Becker & Green, L.A. and Washington, 1984—. Lectr. Colo. Continuing Legal Edn. Author: Employer's Guide to Controlling Sexual Harrassment, 1992; co-editor Nat. Employment Law Insider, 2004-; mem. editl. bd. The Practical Litigator, 1988-2003. Bd. dirs. KGNU Pub. Radio, Boulder, Colo., 1979, Denver Exch., 1980-81, YWCA Met. Denver, 1979-81. Recipient Nebr. Young Career Woman Bus. and Profl. Women, 1967; recipient Outstanding Nebraskan Daily Nebraskan, Lincoln, 1967. Fellow Am. Coll. of Labor and Employment Lawyers; mem. ABA (mgmt. chair labor and employment law sect. com. on immigration law 1988-90, mgmt. chair com. on legis. devels. 1990-93), Nebr. Bar Assn., Colo. Bar Assn., Colo. Women's Bar Assn., D.C. Bar Assn., Nat. Women's Coalition, Delta Sigma Rho, Tau Kappa Alpha, Pi Sigma Alpha, Alpha Xi Delta, Denver Club. Office Phone: 202-861-1863.

SHATTUCK, GEORGE CLEMENT, retired lawyer; b. Syracuse, N.Y., Sept. 2, 1927; s. Frank M. and Geneveive Mary (Hannon) S.; m. Sheila Eagan, Sept. 21, 1957 (div. 1985); children: Edward, George, Frank, Mark, Patrick; m. Carla A. Amussen, June 16, 1987; 1 child, Morgan. BS in Mgmt., Syracuse U., 1950, JD, 1953. Bar: N.Y. 1954, U.S. Supreme Ct. 1973. Retired ptnr., estate planning splty. practice group Bond, Schoeneck & King Law Firm, Syracuse, 1954—94. Author: Letters to Room Five, 2002, Mahatawee, 2002, Molly Byron, 2002, Ugly Woman's Son, 2002, Oneida Land Claims, 1991, Estate Planning for the Small Business Owner, 1993. Mem. Syracuse Bd. Edn., 1968-75. Roman Catholic. Avocations: writing, reading history and philosophy, fishing. Home: 5158 W Lake Rd Cazenovia NY 13035-9616

SHATTUCK, JOHN, diplomat, civil rights lawyer, educator, academic administrator; b. Pasedena, Calif., Sept. 22, 1943; s. H. Francis Jr. and Ruth (Murphy) S.; m. Petra Tölle, May 17, 1970 (dec. Mar. 1988); m. Ellen Hume, Feb. 14, 1991; children: Jessica, Rebecca, Peter, Susannah. BA magna cum laude, Yale U., 1965, JD, 1970; MA with 1st class hon. in internat. law, Cambridge U., Eng., 1967; doctorate (hon.), CUNY, 1995, Kenyon Coll., 2001; doctorate (hon.), U. R.I., 2002. Law clk. to Hon. Edward Weinfeld U.S. Dist. Ct. (so. dist.) N.Y., 1970-71; nat. counsel ACLU, 1971-77, dir. Washington office, 1977-84; v.p. govt., community and pub. affairs Harvard U., 1984-93, sr. assoc. sci. tech. and pub. policy program John F. Kennedy sch. govt., 1984-93; asst. sec. of state bur. democracy, human rights and labor Dept. of State, Washington, 1993-98; U.S. amb. Czech Republic, 1998-2000; CEO John F. Kennedy Presdl. Libr. Found., 2001—. Lectr. Harvard Law Sch., 1986—93. Author: Freedom on Fire: Human Rights, Wars & American's Response, 2003; contbr. articles to profl. jours. Bd. dir. The Petra Fedn., Am. Friends of Czech Republic, ABA Ctrl. & E. Law Inst., Common Cause. Recipient UN Assn. Human Rights award 1998, Am. Bar Assn. Ambassador award 2000, H.L. Mencken award Free Press Assn. 1985, Pub. Svc. award Yale U. Law Sch. 1988, Roger Baldwin medal 1984. Office: John F Kennedy Presdl Libr and Found/Columbia Point Boston MA 02125 Office Phone: 617-514-1671. E-mail: jhshattuck@aol.com.

SHATTUCK, MAYO ADAMS, III, integrated utility executive, b. Boston, Oct. 7, 1954; s. Mayo Adams Jr. and Jane (Bergwall) S., m. Molly Anne George, Sept. 29, 1997; children: Mayo Adams IV, Kathleen Elizabeth, Spencer George, Wyatt Augustus, Lillian Jessie. BA, Williams Coll., 1976; MBA, Stanford U., 1980. Analyst Morgan Guaranty Trust Co., N.Y.C., 1976-78; mgr. Bain & Co., Menlo Park, Calif., 1980-83; v.p. to mng. dir. and head of corp. fin. Alex Brown & Sons, San Francisco, 1985-91, pres. and COO Balt., 1991-97; co-chmn., CEO BT Alex Brown Inc., from 1997; vice chmn. Bankers Trust N.Y., from 1997; co-chmn., co-CEO, Deutsche Banc Alex Brown Inc., Balt., 1999—2001; pres., CEO, chmn. bd. Constellation Energy Group, Balt., 2001—02, chmn., pres., CEO, 2002—. Bd. dirs. Constellation Energy, Gap Inc., Nuc. Energy Inst., Edison Electric Inst., Capital One Fin. Trustee Noble & Greenough Sch.; adv. dir. U. Md. Balt. County, Johns Hopkins Medicine. Avocations: tennis, golf. E-mail: Mayo.Shattuck@constellation.com.

SHATTUCK, ROGER WHITNEY, author, educator; b. N.Y.C., Aug. 20, 1923; s. Howard Francis and Elizabeth (Colt) S.; m. Nora Ewing White, Aug. 20, 1949; children— Tari Elizabeth, Marc Ewing, Patricia Colt, Eileen Shepard. Grad., St. Paul's Sch., Concord, N.H., 1941; BA, Yale U., 1947; DHC (hon.), U. Orléans, France, 1990, Univ. of the South (Sewanee), 2003, St. Michael's Coll., Burlington, Vt., 2003. Information officer UNESCO, Paris, France, 1947-48; asst. editor Harcourt, Brace & Co., 1949-50; mem. Soc. Fellows, Harvard, 1950-53, instr. French, 1953-56; faculty U. Tex., Austin, 1956-71, prof. English, French, 1968-71, chmn. dept. French and Italian, 1968-71; Commonwealth prof. French U. Va., Charlottesville, 1974-88; univ. prof., prof. modern fgn. langs. Boston U., 1988-97. Mem. adv. bd. Nat. Translation Center, 1964-69, chmn., 1966-69; provediteur gen. Coll. de Pataphysique, Paris, 1961—; Fulbright prof. U. Dakar, Senegal, 1984-85, elected bd. mem. Mt. Abraham Union H.S., 2000—. Author: The Banquet Years, 1958; poems Half Tame, 1964, Proust's Binoculars, 1963, Marcel Proust, 1974 (Nat. Book award 1975), The Forbidden Experiment, 1980, The Innocent Eye, 1984, Forbidden Knowledge, 1996, Candor and Perversion, 1999, Proust's Way, 2000; editor or co-editor: Selected Writings of Guillaume Apollinaire, 1950, Mount Analogue, (René Daumal), 1959, The Craft and Context of Translation (with William Arrowsmith), 1961, Selected works of Alfred Jarry, 1965, Occasions by Paul Valéry, 1970, The Story of My Life (by Helen Keller), 2003; mem. editl. bd. PMLA, 1977-78. Capt. USAAF, 1942-45. Decorated Ordre Palmes Academiques (France).; Guggenheim fellow, 1958-59; Fulbright rsch. fellow, 1958-59; ACLS rsch. fellow, 1969-70. Fellow AAAS; mem. Assn. Literary Scholars and Critics (pres. 1995-96).

SHATZ, CARLA J. biology professor; b. N.Y.C. BA in Chemistry, Radcliffe Coll., 1969; MPhil, Univ. Coll., London. 1971; PhD, Harvard U., 1976, postdoc., 1976—78. Assoc. prof. neurobiology Sch. Medicine Stanford U., Palo Alto, Calif., 1985—89, prof. neurobiology, 1989—92; investigator Howard Hughes Med. Inst., 1994—2000; Class of 1943 prof. neurobiology U. Calif., Berkeley, 1992—2000; prof., chair dept. neurobiology Harvard Med. Sch., Boston, 2000—. Mem. commn. on life scis. NRC, 1990—96; nat. adv. NIH, 1996—99; mem. coun. NAS, 1998—2001. Fellow: Inst. Medicine, Am. Philos. Soc., NAS, AAAS. Office: Harvard Med Sch Dept Neurobiology 220 Longwood Ave Boston MA 02115-5701

SHATZ, MARK ALLEN, psychologist, educator; b. Chgo., Apr. 7, 1955; s. Michael and Serna S.; m. Amanda L., June 26, 1999. BS, Ea. Ill. U., 1976, MA, 1977; PhD, U. Fla., 1983. Instr. Ea. Ill. U., Charleston, 1978-80; prof. psychology Ohio U., Zanesville, 1983—. Trainer, cons. Hospice Sout Ea. Ohio, Zanesville, 1988—; ethics com. Genesis Hosp., Zanesville, 1996—; crisis team Zanesville City Schs., 1996—. Author: Kissing Golf: The Keep it Simple (Stupid) Instructional Method, 1997; contbr. articles to profl. jours. Mem. Assn. Death Edn. Counseling (cert.), Am. Psychol. Soc. Avocations: bicycling, golf, hiking. Office: Ohio U Zanesville 1425 Newark Rd Zanesville OH 43701 E-mail: shatz@ohiou.edu.

SHATZ, PHILLIP, lawyer; b. White Plains, N.Y., Sept. 1, 1926; s. Hyman and Ruth (Futoran) S.; m. Bettie Dorsey, Oct. 18, 1957 (dec.); children: Phillip Dorsey, Sallie Dean; m. Natalie Marshall, May 27, 1988. BS, Syracuse U., 1948; LLB, Columbia U., 1954. Bar: N.Y. 1954, U.S. Dist. Ct. (so. dist.) N.Y. 1955, U.S. Supreme Ct. 1960. Pres., chmn. bd. Rich, Shatz and Duncan, Inc., Mahopac, N.Y., 1948-75; v.p. Putnam County Fed. Savs. and Loan Assn., 1953-63, pres., chmn. bd., 1933-78; sole practice Mahopac, 1954-70; ptnr. Shatz & Braatz, Mahopac, 1970-74, Shatz & Thomsen, Mahopac, 1974-77, Shatz, Thomsen & Mace, Mahopac, 1977-80; sr. ptnr. McCabe & Mack, Poughkeepsie, NY, 1980—2000, of counsel, 2000—. Spl. prosecutor Putnam County; dir. Mid-Hudson Legal Svcs. Chmn. Putnam County Young Republicans. With USNR, 1943-46. Mem. ABA, N.Y. State Bar Assn., Dutchess County Bar Assn., Assn. Bar City of N.Y., Univ. Club (N.Y.C.). Home: 157 Skidmore Rd Pleasant Valley NY 12569-5001 Office: McCabe & Mack LLP 63 Washington St Poughkeepsie NY 12601-2313 Office Phone: 845-486-6880. E-mail: pshatz@mccm.com.

SHATZ, STEPHEN SIDNEY, mathematician, educator; b. Bklyn., Apr. 27, 1937; s. Nathan and Agusta S.; children: Geoffrey, Adria. AB, Harvard U., 1957, MA, 1958, PhD, 1962; MA (hon.), U. of Pa., 1971. Instr. Stanford U., 1962-63, acting asst. prof., 1963-64; asst. prof. U. Pa., Phila., 1964-67, assoc. prof., 1967-69, prof. math., 1969—, chmn. dept. math., 1983-86. Vis. prof. U. Pisa, 1966-67; mem. Math. Scis. Rsch. Inst., 1986-87, Inst. Advanced Study, 1997. Author: Profinite Groups, Arithmetic and Geometry, 1972; contbr. articles to profl. jours. Mem. Am. Math. Soc. (editor Trans. 1975-78, coun. 1975-80, exec. com. coun. 1979-80). Office: U Pa Dept Math Philadelphia PA 19104-6395

SHAUGHNESSY, EDWARD LOUIS, Chinese language educator; b. Sewickley, Pa., July 29, 1952; s. James Francis and Marie Rosalie (Kraus) S.; m. Gina Lynn Look, May 15, 1976 (div. Sept. 1992); m. Elena Valussi, Sept. 6, 1997. BA, U. Notre Dame, 1974; MA, Stanford U., 1980, PhD, 1983. Asst. prof. U. Chgo., 1985-90, assoc. prof., 1990-96, prof., 1996—, Lorraine J. and Herrlee G. Creel prof. of early China. Assoc. editor: Early China, 1985-88, editor, 1988-96; editor: New Sources of Early Chinese History: An Introduction to the Reading of Inscriptions and Manuscripts, 1997, (with Michael Loewe) The Cambridge History of Ancient China: From the Origins of Civilization to 221 B.C., 1999, China Empire and Civilization, 2000; author: Sources of Western Zhou History: Inscribed Bronze Vessels, 1991, I Ching, The Classic of Changes: The First English Translation of the Newly Discovered Second-Century B.C. Mawangdui Manuscripts, 1996, Before Confucius: Studies in the Creation of the Chinese Classics, 1997, (with Robert Poor and Harrie A. Vanderstappen) Ritual and Reverence: Chinese Art at the University of Chicago, 1989, (with Cai Fangpei and James F. Shaughnessy) A Concordance of the Xiaotun Nandi Oracle-Bone Inscriptions, 1988; contbr. essays to books. Andrew W. Mellon fellow for Chinese studies, 1984-85; Divsn. of Humanities jr. faculty fellow U. Chgo., 1986; J. William Fulbright fellow in China, 2003-04. Home: 711 S Dearborn St Apt 506 Chicago IL 60605-3819 Office: U Chgo East Asian Langs/Civilizat 1050 E 59th St Chicago IL 60637-1559 E-mail: e-shaughnessy@uchicago.edu.

SHAUGHNESSY, MARIE KANEKO, artist; b. Detroit, Sept. 14, 1924; d. Eishiro and Kiyo (Yoshida) Kaneko; m. John Thomas Shaughnessy, Sept. 23, 1959. Assocs. in Liberal Arts, Keisen U., Tokyo, 1944. Ops. mgr. Webco Alaska, Inc., Anchorage, 1970-88; ptnr. Webco Partnership, Anchorage, 1983-98, also bd. dirs. Faculty Art League Sch., Alexandria, Va. Paintings, Lilacs, 1984, Blooms, 1985, The Fence, 1986 (Purchase award, 1986). Bd. dirs. Alaska Artists Guild, 1971—87; commr. Mcpl. Anchorage Fine Arts Commn., 1983—87; organizing com. Japanese Soc. Alaska, 1987. Recipient Art Affiliate award, Anchorage C. of C., 1975, 1978, 1984, Univ. Artists award, Alaska Pacific U., 1986, Am. Juror's Choice award, Sumi-E Soc. Am., 1994, Ikebana Internat. award, 1994, Dorothy Klein Meml. award, 1995, Yasutomo Calligraphy award, 1997, 1998, Oriental Calligraphy award, 1997, 1998, Sarasota Chpt Painting award, 1999, Paul Schwartz Meml. award, 2001, Sm. Works Exhibit 1st Pl. award, Wash. Watercolor Assn., 2001, Wang Chi Yuan award, 2000. Mem.: Nat. League Am. Penwomen (Grumbacher Gold medal award excellence 1993), Vienna Art Soc. (bd. dirs. 1995—96), Sumi-E Soc. Am. (past pres. 1992—94, bd. dirs., Nat. Capital Area chpt. past pres. awards 1990, Nat. Capital Area chpt. award 1990—92, 1994, Purchase award 1993), Va. Watercolor Soc. (pres. 1993, co-chmn. 2004 All State Juried Show), Potomac Valley Watercolorists (exhibits chair 1989—93, bd. dirs. 1989—99, newsletter editor 1993—96, v.p., workshop chair 1996—2001, historian 2003, awards 1989, 1991, Spl. award 1995), Alaska Watercolor Soc. (life; charter, Grumbacher Silver medal 1989), McLean Arts Club (1st pl. award 1991). Republican. Roman Catholic. Office Phone: 703-893-8116. Personal E-mail: markaneko@aol.com.

SHAUGHNESSY, MEGHANN, professional tennis player; b. Richmond, Apr. 13, 1979; d. Bill and Joy. Profl. tennis player, 1996—. Recipient WTA Tour Doubles Title, Quebec City, 2000, German Open, 2001, Gold Coast, 2002, Moscow, 2003, WTA Tour Singles Title, Shanghai, 2000, Quebec City, 2001, Canberra, 2003, Ranked #17, WTA, Ranked #6 Among U.S. Players, Highest Season Ending Single's Ranking #12, 2001, Resident Pro, Scottsdale Hyatt Gainey Ranch Resort, 6 Internat. Women's Circuit Singles Titles. Mem.: U.S. Fedn. Cup Team. Office: WTA Tour Corporate Headquarters One Progress Plz Ste 1500 Saint Petersburg FL 33701

SHAUGHNESSY, THOMAS WILLIAM, retired librarian; b. Pitts., May 3, 1938; s. Martin T. and LaVerne (O'Brien) Shaughnessy; m. Marlene D. Reuben, Aug. 11, 1968; 1 child, Mark Andrew. AB, St. Vincent Coll., 1961; MLS, U. Pitts., 1964; PhD, Rutgers U., 1970. Asst. dean Rutgers U., New Brunswick, NJ, 1969-71, libr. dir. Newark, 1971-74; assoc. dean U. So. Calif., L.A., 1974-78; asst. libr. dir. U. Houston, 1978-82; libr. dir. U. Mo., Columbia, 1982-89; univ. libr., dir. U. Minn., Mpls.-St. Paul, 1989—2002; ret., 2002. Rsch. dir. Chgo. Pub. Libr. Survey, 1968—69; cons. U. Tulsa Libr., 1982—83; mem. faculty exch. USIA, Poland, 1998; trustee OCLC, Inc., 1997—2004. Author (with Lowell A. Martin): (book) Library Response to Urban Change, 1969, Developing Leadership Skills: A Source Book for Librarians, 1990. Recipient Hugh C. Atkinson Meml. award, 1996; fellow, Coun. Libr. Resources, 1973; U.S. Office Edn. grantee, Rutgers U., 1971, Sr. fellow, Coun. Libr. Resources, 1985. Mem.: ALA, Minn. Libr. Assn. (Disting. Achievement award 2002), Assn. Rsch. Librs. (cons. tng. fellow 1981, bd. dirs. 1989—92), Assn. Coll. and Rsch. Librs. Home: 5705 Wycliffe Rd Minneapolis MN 55436-2264 E-mail: tws@umn.edu.

SHAVELSON, MELVILLE, writer, theatrical producer and director; b. N.Y.C., Apr. 1, 1917; s. Joseph and Hilda (Shalson) S.; m. Lucille T. Myers, Nov. 2, 1938; children: Richard, Carol-Lynne. AB, Cornell U., 1937. Mem. faculty sch. profl. writing U. So. Calif., 1998—2002. Author: How to Make a Jewish Movie, 1970, Lualda, 1975, The Great Houdinis, 1976, The Eleventh Commandment, 1977, Ike, 1979, Don't Shoot, It's Only Me, 1990; writer Bob Hope Pepsodent Show, NBC radio, 1938-43; screenwriter The Princess and the Pirate, 1944, Wonder Man, 1944, Room for One More, 1951, I'll See You in My Dreams, 1952; screenwriter, dir. The Seven Little Foys, 1954, Beau James, 1956, Houseboat, 1957, The Five Pennies, 1958, It Started in Naples, 1959, On the Double, 1960, Yours, Mine and Ours, 1968, The War Between Men and Women, 1972, The Legend of Valentino, 1975, Deceptions, 1985; screenwriter, dir., producer The Pigeon That Took Rome, 1962, A New Kind of Love, 1963, Cast a Giant Shadow, 1966, Mixed Company, 1974, The Great Houdinis, 1976, Ike, 1979; dir. The Other Woman, 1983; creator TV shows including Danny Thomas Show, ABC-TV, 1953, My World— and Welcome To It, NBC-TV, 1969; author Broadway mus. Jimmy, 1969. Recipient Screen Writers Guild award, 1959, Christopher award; 1959, Sylvania TV award, 1953, Acad. Award nominations (screenplay), 1955, 58, Screen Writers Ann. award nominations (screenplay), 1952 (2), 58, 59, 62, 68, 72, 75, Screen Writers award (best written Am. mus.), 1959, Award of Merit United Jewish Appeal, 1966. Mem. Dirs. Guild Am., Writers Guild Am. (exec. bd. dirs 1960-75, 78, pres. screen writers br. 1967, pres. found. 1975-96, pres. emeritus 1997—, v.p. 1996—), Acad. Motion Picture Arts and Scis. (mem. bd. govs.), Writer Guild Am. West (pres. 1969-70, 79-81, 85-87, Valentine Davies award 1979, Laurel award 1984, Morgan Cox award 1998), Sigma Delta Chi. Home and Office: 11947 Sunshine Ter Studio City CA 91604-3708 Office Phone: 818-762-6314.

SHAVENDER, MARILYN FAYE, elementary school educator; b. Washington, Feb. 22, 1938; d. Redden Hudnell and Alice Gray Shavender; 1 child, Annette Byrd. BS in Elem. Edn., East Carolina U., 1959. 2d grade tchr. Virginia Beach Sch. Sys., Va., 1959—, lang. arts com., 1988—2003; ret., 2003. Author: (book) Poetry by Grammy, 2000. Mem.: DAR, Virginia Beach Edn. Assn. Republican. Mem. Church Of Christ. Avocations: piano, writing, antiques, gardening.

SHAVER, JAMES PORTER, education educator, university dean; b. Wadena, Minn., Oct. 19, 1933; BA magna cum laude, U. Wash., Seattle, 1955; MA in Teaching, Harvard U., 1957, EdD, 1961. Instr. Grad. Sch. Edn., Harvard U., 1961-62; assoc. prof., dir. Social Studies Curriculum Ctr., Ohio State U., Columbus, 1964-65; mem. faculty Utah State U. Coll. Edn., Logan, 1962-64, prof., 1965—, chmn. Bur. Rsch. Svcs., 1965-93, assoc. dean rsch., 1978-93, acting dean Sch. Grad. Studies, 1990-91, 92-93, dean, 1993-99, prof. emeritus secondary edn., 1999—. Mem. Commn. Youth Edn. for Citizenship, ABA, 1975-81; mem. edn. task force Am. Hist. Assn.-Am. Polit. Sci. Assn. Project '87, 1981-84; tech. advisor Nat. Ctr. on Effective Secondary Schs., 1988-91; mem. adv. bd. program in civic and moral edn. Inst. for Philosophy and Pub. Policy, U. Md., 1992—; mem. steering com. Nat. Assessment Ednl. Progress Civics Consensus Project, 1995-96. Co-author: Teaching Public Issues in the High School, 1966, 2d edit., 1974, Facing Value Decisions: Rationale-building For Teachers, 1976, 2d edit., 1982; editor: Building Rationales for Citizenship Education, 1977, Handbook of Research on Social Studies Teaching and Learning, 1991; co-editor: Democracy, Pluralism, and the Social Studies, 1968; also others. Recipient Outstanding Svc. and Tchg. award Utah Coun. for the Social Studies, 1975, 78, Lifetime Achievement award, 1998. Mem. AAAS, AAUP, Nat. Coun. Social Studies (pres. 1976, Exemplary Rsch. award 1977, Exemplary Rsch. Editor award 1991), Am. Ednl. Rsch. Assn., Phi Beta Kappa, Phi Kappa Phi. Home: PO Box 176 Hyrum UT 84319-0176 Office: Utah State U 2815 Old Main Hill Logan UT 84322-2815 Office Phone: 435-797-1471. Business E-Mail: shaver@cc.usu.edu.

SHAVER, JOAN LOUISE FOWLER, dean; BS in Nursing, U. Alberta, Can., 1966; M in Nursing, U. Wash., 1968-70, PhD in Physiology and Biophysics, 1976. Nursing instr. chair med. surgical prog. Holy Cross Hosp.

Sch. Nursing, Calgary, Can., 1966-68; staff nurse Virginia Mason Hosp., Seattle, 1970-71; asst. prof. Sch. Nursing U. Ariz., Tucson, 1976-77; assoc. prof. U. Calgary, Can., 1977-80; asst. prof. Dept. Physiological Nursing U. Wash., Seattle, 1980-85, rsch. affil. Regl. Primate Rsch. Ctr., 1983-86, assoc. prof., 1985-89, chair Dept. Physiological Nursing, 1988-95, prof., 1989-95, prof., chair Dept. Biobehavioral Nursing & Health Systems, 1995-96, co-dir. Ctr. Women's Health Rsch., 1989-96; prof., dean Coll. Nursing U. Ill., Chgo., 1996—, co-dir. Rsch. Core Nat. Ctr. Excellence in Women's Health, 1997—. Mem. editl. bd. Health Care for Women Internat., 1984—, Heart and Lung: The Jour. of Critical Care, 1988-90, Jour. of Applied Nursing Rsch., 1988-91, IMAGE: Jour. Nursing Scholarship, editl. adv. bd. Nursing Rsch., 1997—, Biol. Rsch. for Nursing, 1999—, Jour. Nursing Scholarship, 2000—; contbr. artilces to profl. jours. Abe Miller Meml. scholar Alberta Assn. Registered Nurses, 1968-69; Kathryn McLaggen Meml. fellow Can. Nurses Found., fellow Am. Acad. Nursing Am. Nurses Assn., 1988—. Office: U Ill Coll Nursing 845 S Damen Ave # Mc802 Chicago IL 60612-7350*

SHAVER, KATHRYN, retired performing company executive, design educator; b. LaFayette, Ala., July 5, 1945; d. Edwin Wood and Kathryn (Simmons) Shaver; m. Edwin Hampton Perry, May 26, 1976. BFA in visual desing, Auburn U., 1967; postgrad., U. Louisville, 1977—82, U. Louisville, 1986. Creative dir. Fred Worrill Advt., Atlanta, 1968—71, Pruitt Printing, Atlanta, 1971—73; art. dir. David Advt., Louisville, 1973—75; pvt. practice in adv., 1975—90, 1984—90; ptnr., vice chmn., CFO Sheehy, Knopf, and Shaver, 1990; interim CEO Louisville Ballet, 2001—03. Tchr. effective bus. practices to fgn. countries; pvt. con. Romania, Bucharest; guest lectr. mktg., adv., bus. Ky. colls.; tchr. sr. level graphic design classes U. Louisville; designer costumes several small theatres, Atlanta; graphic artist, creative dir. adv. industry. Contbr. articles to profl. jours. 1st woman chmn. bd. trustees Spalding U.; vice chmn. Louisville Area C. of C.; chmn. Louie Creative Competition; mem. bd. dirs. Louisville Orch. Bd. Dirs.; mem. bd. dirs. Leadership Louisville, Jr. Achievement, Mary Anderson Ctr. for Arts, U. Louisville Bus. Sch. Adv. Coun., Friends U. Louisville Music Sch., Louisville Collegiate Sch. Mem.: C. of C. (v. chmn. 1984—86), Adv. Club Louisville (dir. 1977—, pres. 1984—85, chmn. 1985—86, 5-Star award 1983, Rosenthal Achievement award 1984). Office: 315 E Main St Louisville KY 40202-1215

SHAVER, PHILIP ALCOTT, lawyer; b. Oberlin, Ohio, Mar. 17, 1938; s. Chester Linn and Alice Louise (Crafts) S.; m. Viola Golod, July 29, 1961 (div. 1980); children: Peter Vaughan, Emily Anne, Andrew Alcott; stepchild, Michele Lynn Cooke Andresen; m. Barbara King, Mar. 14, 1981. Student, Harvard Coll., Cambridge, 1954-55; AB, Oberlin Coll., 1959; LLB, Yale U., 1962. Bar: Ohio 1963, Mass. 1965, N.J. 1977, U.S. Ct. Appeals (3d cir.) 1995. Assoc. Allen Hull, Cleve., 1962-65; atty., sec. Fed. Res. Bank Boston, 1965-69; assoc. coun. 1st Nat. Bank, Boston, 1969-77; sec., legal coun. City Fed. Savs. & Loan, Somerville, N.J., 1977-80; assoc. coun. United Jersey Banks, Princeton, N.J., 1980-81; pvt. practice, Princeton, 1981—. Editor: Federal Banking Laws, 1969, ann. supplements, 1967-72. Trustee Princeton Cemetery, 1988—; leader walking tours Princeton and Princeton Cemetery; allocations com. United Way, Princeton, 1986-96; deacon Nassau Presbyn. Ch., 1996-99, elder, 1985-88; trustee Rockingham Assn., 1997—. Mem. Am. Honky Tonk Bar Assn., Princeton Bar Assn. (trustee 1993-97, pres. 1996-97), Hist. Soc. Princeton (trustee 1987-94, Outstanding Vol. Svc. 1995). Home: 25A Chestnut Ct Princeton NJ 08540-1716 Office: 33 Witherspoon St Princeton NJ 08542-3207 Office Phone: 609-924-6581.

SHAVERS, CHERYL L. technology and business consultant; married; 3 children. BS in Chemistry, PhD in Solid State Chemistry, Ariz. State U.; hon. grad. degree in engring. mgmt., Calif. Poly. State U., 1996. Practicing registered patent agent Patent and Trademark Office of Dept. of Commerce. Prod. engr. Motorola; process devel. engr. Hewlett-Packard, patent agent, tech. legal dept.; microelectronics sect. mgr. Wiltron Co.; engring. mgr., thin films devel. lab. Varian Associates; sector mgr. microprocessor div., corp. bus. devel. div. Intel Corp.; under sec. commerce for tech. U.S. Dept Commerce, 1999—2001; chmn., CEO Global Smarts, Inc., Santa Clara, Calif., 2001—. Spkr., workshop leader in field; non-exec. chmn. BitArts Ltd., 2001—03; bd. dirs. Rockwell Collins, Inc., 2002—. Weekly columnist San Jose Mercury News Bus. Sect.; contbr. articles to profl. publs.; featured in articles, books and Web sites; TV appearances include documentary Wizards and Alchemists, 1995, Real Science Program, Sta. KTEH-TV, NBC New Media News, Women in Technology, 1997 Active numerous outreach programs, including Real Sci., Wizards and Alchemists, KTEH Silicon Valley Report, KRON New Media News programs; bd. dirs. San Jose Tech Mus. of Innovation, 1996—; former bd. dirs. Internat. Network Women in Tech., 1995-96, ARC, 1995-96. Recipient Janet Gray Hayes award, award Phi Lambda Upsilon, Outstanding Presenter of Yr., San Francisco Bay Area chpt. Nat. Assn. of Black MBAs, 1998; Henry Crown fellow Aspen Inst.'s Crown Fellowship Program; inductee Internat. Women in Tech. Hall of Fame, Coll. Liberal Arts and Scis. Hall of Fame, Ariz. State U., 1997, Internat. Network of Women in Tech. Hall of Fame, 1996. Mem. Libr. of Congress (assoc.). Office: Global Smarts Inc 3333 Bowers Ave Ste 130 Santa Clara CA 95050*

SHAVIN, HELENE B. venture capital company executive; b. 1954; BA, Queens Coll.; MBA, Baruch Coll. Sr. acct. KPMG Peat Marwick, Hawaii; CPA Citicorp Venture Capital Ltd., NY, 1986—2000, v.p., 1999—2000; v.p., controller Harris & Harris Group, Inc., NY, 2001—. Office: Harris & Harris Group Inc 111 W 57th St Ste 1100 New York NY 10019 also: Harris & Harris Group Inc 11150 Santa Monica Blvd Ste 1200 Los Angeles CA 90025 Office Phone: 212-582-0900., 310-479-2595. Office Fax: 212-582-9563., 310-312-1868. Business E-Mail: admin@tinytechvc.com.

SHAW, ALAN, lawyer, corporate executive; b. Long Branch, N.J., July 23, 1930; m. Margaret Knight, Oct. 15, 1959; children: Andrew Macbeth, Adriane Macbeth. AB, U. Mich., 1952; LLB, Harvard U., 1955. Bar: Mass. 1955, N.Y. 1958. Atty. Skadden, Arps, Slate, Meagher & Flom, N.Y.C., 1958-65; v.p., gen. counsel, sec. Athlone Industries Inc., Parsippany, N.J., 1966-93, also bd. dirs. Adj. prof. of Law, Fordham U., 1996—; arbitrator Am. Arbitration Assn., Nat. Assn. of Securities Dealers Dispute Resolution, N.Y. Stock Exch. Mem. membership com. Jefferson Soc. Morristown Meml. Hosp.; panelist Contract Dispute Resolution Bd., City of N.Y. With U.S. Army, 1955-57. Mem. ABA (sect. on corps., alt. dispute resolution sect.), N.J. Gen. Counsel Group, Assn. Bar City N.Y., Soc. Profls. in Dispute Resolution, Morristown (N.J.) Club, Washington Assn. Morristown (bd. trustees), Morris County Golf Club (Convent Station, N.J.), Harvard Club (N.Y.C.). Home: 490 S Maple Ave Basking Ridge NJ 07920-1327 Office: 1812 Front St Scotch Plains NJ 07076 Office Phone: 908-322-3610.

SHAW, ALAN BOSWORTH, geologist, paleontologist; b. Englewood, N.J., Mar. 28, 1922; s. Carroll Harper and Natalie Frederique (Howe) S.; m. Helen Louise Wilson, Nov. 2, 1945 (div. Apr. 1952); m. Marian Tavenner Stoll, Mar. 11, 1954 (dec. Apr. 1981); children: Nancy Jeanne, Sally Ann; m. Mary Elizabeth Merrem, Sept. 3, 1982. AB magna cum laude, Harvard Coll., 1946; AM, PhD, Harvard U., 1949. Asst. prof. geology U. Wyo., Laramie, 1949-55; paleontologist Shell Oil Co., Denver, 1955-60; owner Nat. Elec. Svc., N.Y.C., 1960-61; consulting geologist Denver, 1961; supr. Pan Am. Rsch. currently BPAmoco, Tulsa, Okla., 1961-68; various positions Pan Am. Petroleum, Denver, 1968-76; chief paleontologist Amoco Prodn., Chgo., 1976-77, chief geologist, 1977-81; geol. rsch. cons. Amoco Rsch., Tulsa, 1981-85; ret., 1985. Oil industry rep. NRC Com. on Paleontology, Washington, 1963-69; mem. Com. on Paleontology and Stratigraphy Deep Sea Drilling Program, 1973-75. Author: Time in Stratigraphy, 1964; contbr. numerous articles to profl. jours. Served to 1st lt., USAAF, 1943-45. Recipient Moore Paleontology medal Soc. Sedimentary Geology, 1996. Achievements include invention of graphic correlation system for use of fossils in making time correlations of sedimentary rocks. Home: 210 Kamira Kerrville TX 78028-8867 Personal E-mail: shaw99@ktc.com.

SHAW, ALAN ROGER, financial executive, educator; b. Bklyn., July 7, 1938; s. Sewall S. and Vera (Dimmick) S.; children: Stephen S., Todd J., Bradley C.; m. Mary Elizabeth Hogg, May 30, 1987. Student, Susquehanna U., 1957, Adelphi U., 1963-66; LLD (hon.), Susquehanna U., 1999. Analyst Harris Upham & Co., N.Y.C., 1958-71, asst. v.p., 1971-73, v.p., 1973-75; 1st v.p. Smith, Barney, Harris, Upham & Co., N.Y.C., 1975-80; sr. v.p. Smith Barney, N.Y.C., 1980—. Tchr. N.Y. Inst. Fin., 1966— Mem. Market Technicians Assn. (pres. 1974), N.Y. Soc. Security Analysts, Securities Industry Assn. Inst. (trustee 1986-92), Southward Ho Country Club, Unqua Corinthian Yacht Club (commodore 1988-90). Home: 87 Wagstaff Ln West Islip NY 11795-5206 Office: Citigroup Smith Barney 388 Greenwich St 30th fl New York NY 10013-2339

SHAW, ANTHONY, pediatric surgeon, retired educator; b. Shanghai, Oct. 31, 1929; s. Bruno and Regina (Hyman) S.; m. Iris Violet Azian, Mar. 12, 1955; children: Brian Anthony, Diana Shaw Clark, Daniel Aram. BA cum laude, Harvard Coll., 1950; MD, NYU, 1954. Diplomate Am. Bd. Surgery; cert. spl. competence pediat. surgery. Intern and resident in surgery Columbia-Presbyn. Med. Ctr., N.Y.C., 1954-56, 58-62; resident in pediat. surgery Babies Hosp., N.Y.C., 1962; asst. prof. surgery Columbia U. Coll. Physicians and Surgeons, N.Y.C., 1965-70; chief pediat. surgery St. Vincent's Hosp., N.Y.C., 1963-70, Harlem Hosp. Ctr., N.Y.C., 1965-70; prof. surgery U. Va., Charlottesville, 1970-81, chief pediat. surgery Med. Ctr., 1970-81; prof. surgery UCLA, 1981-2001, emeritus prof. surgery, 2001—; chief pediat. surgery Olive View-UCLA Med. Ctr., Sylmar, 1986-2001, cons. surgeon, 2003—. Expert witness on child abuse L.A. Superior Ct., 1986—; chmn. gov.'s adv. com. child abuse and neglect Commonwealth of Va., 1975-80; vis. prof. pediat. surgery People's Republic of China, 1985. Contbr. more than 220 articles to profl. jours. Mem. Gov.'s Task Force on Child Abuse Va., 1973-74. Capt. U.S. Army, 1956-58. Recipient Commrs. award Va. Dept. Social Svcs., 1980, award Gov.'s Adv. Bd., Cert. of Recognition HEW, 1978. Fellow Am. Pediat. Surg. Assn. (sec. 1982-85), ACS (v.p. 1987-89); mem. AMA, Pacific Coast Surg. Assn. (v.p. 1989-90), Am. Soc. Law, Medicine, and Ethics, Am. Profl. Soc. on Abuse of Children, Alpha Omega Alpha. Avocations: writing humor, grandchildren. Home and Office: One S Orange Grove Blvd # 9 Pasadena CA 91105 Office Phone: 626-796-8588. Personal E-mail: shawpas@pacbell.net.

SHAW, ARTIE, musician, writer, lecturer; b. N.Y.C., May 23, 1910; s. Harry and Sarah Shaw; m. Margaret Allen; m. Lana Turner; m. Elizabeth Kern Kern; 1 child, Steven Kern; m. Ava Gardner (div. Oct. 1946); m. Kathleen Winsor, Oct. 1946; m. Doris Dowling (div.); 1 child, Jonathan; m. Evelyn Keyes, 1957 (div. June 1985). Extension work in lit., Columbia U.; MusD (hon.), U. Nebr., 1938, LittD (hon.); LHD (hon.), Calif. Luth. U., 1987; DFA (hon.), U. Ariz., 1995. Former owner firm Shooters Svc. and Dewey (gun mfrs.); pres. Artixo Prodns., Ltd. (film distbn. co.); lectr. colls. and univs. U. Calif., Santa Barbara, Oxnard Coll., Camarillo, Calif., Yale U., U. Pa., Memphis U. Orch. leader, 1936—54, appeared (films) Dancing Coed, Second Chorus; engaged in film, theatrical prodn.; prodr.: (Broadway plays, mus.) The Great Gatsby; rec. Stardust (Nat. Acad. Rec. Arts and Scis., 1977); composer (condr. numerous songs and orchestral works): including Concerto for Clarinet; author: author: A Clarinet Method; The Trouble with Cinderella; I Love You, I Hate You, Drop Dead! Three Variations on a Theme; The Best of Intentions, and Other Stories, 1989. Former mem. exec. council, bd. Hollywood Ind. Citizens Com. Arts, Scis. and Professions. Served with USNR, 1942—44. Recipient Presdl. award, Am. Soc. Mus. Arrangers, 1990, Downbeat award best Am. swing band, Esquire Mag. Poll award as favorite band of armed services, Hall of Fame award for rec. Begin the Beguin, Jazz Wall of Fame award, ASCAP, 2000. Achievements include Achievements include being subject of film: Artie Shaw: Time is All You've Got (Academy Award for best feature-length documentary 1986).

SHAW, BILLY, retired professional football player; b. Natchez, Miss., Dec. 15, 1938; Student, Ga. Inst. Tech. Guard Buffalo Bills, 1961—69. Named All-Am. lineman, Ga. Inst. Tech., 1961; named to 1st team All-AFL, 1962—66, 2d team All-AFL, 1968, 1969, 8 AFL All-Star Games, All-Time AFL Team, All-Decade Team of '60's, Pro Football Hall of Fame, 1999. Home: Pro Football Hall of Fame 2121 Geore Halas Dr NW Canton OH 44708-2630

SHAW, CAROLE, editor, publisher; b. Bklyn., Jan. 22, 1936; d. Sam and Betty (Neckin) Bergenthal; m. Ray Shaw, Dec. 27, 1957; children: Lori Eve Cohen, Victoria Shaw Locknar. BA, Hunter Coll., 1962. Singer Capitol Records, Hilton Records, Rama Records, Verve Records, 1952-65; TV appearances Ed Sullivan, Steve Allen, Jack Paar, George Gobel Show, 1957; owner The People's Choice, L.A., 1975-79; founder, editor-in-chief Big Beautiful Woman mag., Beverly Hills, Calif., 1979—. Creator Carole Shaw and BBW label clothing line for large-size women. Author: Come Out, Come Out Wherever You Are, 1982. Avocations: piano, painting, swimming, travel. Office: BBW Mag 6666 Brookmont Ter Apt 412 Nashville TN 37205-4622

SHAW, CHARLES ALDEN, engineering executive; b. Detroit, June 8, 1925; s. Fred Alden and Amy (Ellis) S.; m. Barbara Loveland, Mar. 9, 1963 (div. 1979); children: Amy Elizabeth, Polly Nicole; m. Jeanne Steves Partridge, Apr. 22, 1989. BS, Harvard U., 1945; MSEE, Syracuse U., 1958. Test and design engr. G.E., Syracuse-Schenectady, N.Y., 1947-51; chief engr. electronics divsn. Onondaga Pottery Co., Syracuse, 1951-60; mgr. semiconductor div. G.E., Syracuse-Schenectady, 1960-66; cons. to gen. dir. Bull-G.E., Paris, 1966-69; mgr. CAD sect. integrated cir. product dept. G.E., Syracuse, 1969-71, mgr. CAD ctr. solid state applied ops., 1971-78, mgr. computer support solid state applied ops., 1978-81; dir. CAD G.E. Intersil, Cupertino, Calif., 1981-88; cons. in field Cupertino, 1988-89; mgr. tech. program Cadence Design Systems, Santa Clara, Calif., 1989—. Trustee Hidden Villa, Los Altos Hills, Calif., 1986—92; bd. dirs. Unitarian Universalist Ch., Livermore, 1999—2002. With USN, 1942—45, PTO. Mem. IEEE, Assn. Computing Machinery (chmn. spl. interest group SIGDA 1986-91), Design Automation Conf. (exec. bd. 1985-95), Harvard Club of Silicon Valley. Democrat. Unitarian Universalist. Home: 4925 Monaco Dr Pleasanton CA 94566-7671 Office: 555 River Oaks Pkwy San Jose CA 95134-1917 Office Phone: 408-428-4459. Personal E-mail: shawcha@comcast.net. Business E-Mail: shaw@cadence.com.

SHAW, CHARLES ALEXANDER, judge; b. Jackson, Tenn., Dec. 31, 1944; s. Alvis and Sarah S.; m. Kathleen Ingram, Aug. 17, 1969; 1 child, Bryan Ingram. BA, Harris Stowe State Coll., 1966; MBA, U. Mo., 1971; JD, Cath. U. Am., 1974. Bar: D.C. 1975, Mo. 1975, U.S. Ct. Appeals (8th and D.C. cirs.) 1975, U.S. Dist. Ct. (ea. dist.) Mo. 1976, U.S. Ct. Appeals (6th and 7th cirs.) 1976. Tchr. St. Louis Pub. Schs., 1966-69, D.C. Pub. Schs., Washington, 1969-71; law clk. U.S. Dept. Justice, Washington, 1972-73, NLRB, Washington, 1973-74, atty., 1974-76; assoc. Lashly, Caruthers, Theis, Rava & Hamel, St. Louis, 1976-80, asst. U.S. atty., 1980-87; judge Mo. Cir. Ct., St. Louis, 1987-94, asst. presiding judge, 1993-94; judge U.S. Dist. Ct., St. Louis, 1994—. Hearing officer Office of the Mayor, Washington, 1973-74; instr. U. Mo., St. Louis, 1980-81. State bd. dirs. United Negro Coll. Fund, St. Louis, 1979-83; trustee St. Louis Art Mus., 1979-82, 89-96; bd. dirs. Arts and Edn. Coun., 1992-96, Metro Golf Assn., 1993-2000, Landmarks Assn., St. Louis, 1980-82. Named Disting. Alumnus, Cath. U., 2001; Danforth Found. fellow, 1978-79; Cath. U. Am. scholar, 1971-74. Mem. D.C. Bar Assn., Mo. Bar Assn., Mound City Bar Assn., Bar Assn. Met. St. Louis, Harris-Stowe State Coll. Alumni Assn. (Disting. Alumni 1988), Nat. Assn. Guardsmen (sec. St. Louis chpt. 1999-2001), Phi Alpha Delta (svc. award 1973-74), Sigma Pi Phi (pres. St. Louis chpt. 1999-2001). Avocation: golf. Office: 111 S 10th St Saint Louis MO 63102 Office Phone: 314-244-7480.

SHAW, CHARLES RAYMOND, journalist; b. Phila., Feb. 2, 1951; s. Charles Raymond Sr. and Dorothy Blanche (Buckman) S.; m. Francine Ruth Pennock, Jan. 14, 1983. BS in Journalism, Temple U., 1972; MS in Journalism, Columbia U., 1973. Staff writer Intelligencer Jour., Lancaster, Pa., 1973-83, asst. news editor, 1983-88, news editor, 1989-97, editor, 1997—. Mem. Pa. Soc. of Newspaper Editors, Am. Soc. Newspaper Editors, Pa. Assoc. Press (bd. dirs.). Office: Lancaster Newspapers Inc Intelligencer Jour 8 W King St Lancaster PA 17603-3824 E-mail: rshaw@lnpnews.com.

SHAW, CHARLES RUSANDA, retired government investigator; b. Detroit, Aug. 17, 1914; s. Leonard George and Harriet (Kratzer) S.; m. Sally Madeline Jock, May 3, 1947 (dec. June 1996); children: Patrick R., Sandra L. Keding (dec.), Janice L., Lisa Keding. Cert., Wicker Sch. of Fine Arts, 1936, Mich. Acad. Advt. Art, 1937; student, Intelligence Corps Sch., 1947. Freelance artist, Detroit, 1936-39; spl. agt. U.S. Army Counter Intelligence Corps, Washington, 1947-48, Office Spl. Investigations, USAF, Washington, 1948-66; pvt. investigator Charles Shaw Assocs., Mt. Clemens, Mich., 1966-84; contract investigator USAF & U.S. Customs Svc., Washington, 1984-94; entrepreneur-inventor neoteric products, patents pending C.R. Shaw Assocs., 1994—. Author: Immaculate Misconception, 1999. Master sgt. U.S. Army, 1939-45, PTO, ETO. Mem. Assn. Former OSI Spl. Agts. (chartered), VFW, Pearl Harbor Survivors Assn. Democrat. Roman Catholic. Avocations: fine arts, photography, gardening, home improvements. Home and Office: 59295 Bates Rd New Haven MI 48048-1728 Office Phone: 586-749-9223.

SHAW, CURT, lawyer, communications executive; B with honors, Trinity Coll.; JD, Columbia U. Assoc. gen. counsel Occidental Chem. Corp., 1983—88, v.p., gen. counsel, 1986—88; counsel NYNEX, 1988—97; sr., v.p., gen. counsel Charter Comm., St. Louis, 1997—, also sec. bd. dirs. Office: Charter Comm Legal Dept 12405 Powerscourt Saint Louis MO 63131

SHAW, CURTIS S, lawyer; b. 1948; B in econ. with honors, Trinity Coll., 1970; JD, Columbia U. Sch. of Law, 1973. Assoc. gen. counsel Occidental Chemical Corp.; v.p., gen. counsel divsn. of Occidental Chemical Corp.; corp. counsel NYNEX; sr. v.p., gen. counsel and sec. Charter Commn., 1997—. Mailing: Charter Communications Inc 12405 Powerscourt Dr Saint Louis MO 63131

SHAW, DANNY WAYNE, educational consultant, musician; b. Detroit, Jan. 18, 1947; s. George L. and Nina Margarete (Smith) Shaw; m. Nancy Rivard, Feb. 29, 1980; 1 child, Christina Marie. BS, Wayne State U., 1973, MusM, 1975, EdS, 1979, PhD, 1982. Tchr. Dearborn (Mich.) Pub. Schs., 1973-74, Lincoln Park (Mich.) Schs., 1974-98, Beaufort County (SC) Schs., 1998—. Rsch. asst. Wayne State U., 1980—81, adj. faculty, 1981—85; pres. Sys. Support Svcs., Lincoln Park, Trenton, Mich., 1982—98; adj. faculty Marygrove Coll., Detroit, 1984. Mem. music adv. panel Mich. Coun. Arts, 1976—84; mem. cultural commn. City of Trenton, 1997—98; mem. Leadership Beaufort (S.C.) Class 2000; pres. Beaufort Orch., 2001—02, bd. dirs. With USMC, 1965—68, Vietnam. Decorated Presdl. Unit citation, Campaign medal Republic of Vietnam; recipient cert. for outstanding acad. achievement, Mich. Ho. Reps., 1975. Mem.: VFW, Shriners, Masons, Phi Delta Kappa. Home: 9319 SE 137th St Rd Summerfield FL 34491

SHAW, DAVID LYLE, journalist, columnist; b. Dayton, Ohio, Jan. 4, 1943; s. Harry and Lillian (Walton) Shaw; m. Alice Louise Eck, Apr. 11, 1965 (div. Sept. 1974); m. Ellen Torgerson, July 17, 1979 (dec.); stepchildren: Christopher Torgerson, Jordan Torgerson; m. Lucy Stille, Apr. 14, 1988; 1 child, Lucas. BA in English, UCLA, 1965. Reporter Huntington Park Signal (Calif.), 1963—66, Long Beach Independent (Calif.), 1966—69, L.A. Times, 1968—74, media critic, 1974—2002, columnist, 2003—. Chair Nat. Restaurant awards com. James Beard Found. Author: (book) WILT: Just Like Any Other 7-Foot, Black Millionaire Who Lives Next Door, 1973, The Levy Caper, 1974, Journalism Today, 1977, Press Watch, 1984, The Pleasure Police, 1996; contbr. articles to Esquire, Food & Wine, Cigar Afficionado, others. Recipient Nat. award, Mellet Fund, 1983, PEN West award, 1990, Gold Medallion, Calif. Bar Assn., 1990, Pulitzer Prize for disting. criticism, 1991, Non-Deadline Reporting award, Soc. Profl. Journalists, 1999. Office: LA Times Times Mirror Sq Los Angeles CA 90012 E-mail: david.shaw@latimes.com.

SHAW, DAVID TAI-KO, electrical and computer engineering educator, university administrator; b. China, Mar. 13, 1938; came to U.S., 1960, naturalized, 1972; m. Katharine Lin-Yee Yang; children: Albert, Stanley. BSM.E., Nat. Taiwan U., Taipei, 1959; MS in Nuclear Engring., Purdue U., 1961, PhD, 1964. Asst. prof. div. interdisciplinary studies and research Sch. Engring., SUNY-Buffalo, 1964-67, assoc. prof. faculty engring. and applied scis., 1967-74, prof. elec. engring. and nuclear engring., aerospace and engring. sci., 1974-77, prof. elec. engring., 1974—, dir. lab. for power and environ. studies, 1978—90. Exec. dir. State Inst. on Superconductivity, 1987-97; vis. prof. U. Paris, 1976-77; vis. scientist Centre d'Etudes Nucleairs de Fontenay-aux-Roses (France) Commissariat a L'Energie Atomique, 1976-77; vis. assoc. dept. environ. health engring. Calif. Inst. Tech., 1970-71; mem. U.S. del. French Commissariat a L'energie ATomique, 1974, U.S. del. Joint Nuclear Energy Agy. IAEA Internat. Liaison Group on Thermionic Elec. Power Generation, Paris, 1974; mem. U.S. vis. team USSR Acad. Scis. Editor: Fundamentals of Aerosol Science, 1978, Recent Developments in Aerosol Science, 1978, Assessment of Airborne Radioactivity, 1978; editor-in-chief: Jour. Aerosol Sci. and Tech., 1982-93; contbr. numerous articles to profl. publs. Mem. IEEE, ASME, AAAS, Am. Assn. Aerosol Rsch. (pres. 1982-85, Assn. award 1984, Internat. Aerosol Fellow award 1994), Sigma Xi, Sigma Pi Sigma. Office: SUNY-Buffalo Materials Rsch Lab/Ctr for Innovation Engring 330 Bonner Hall Buffalo NY 14260-1900 E-mail: dshaw@eng.buffalo.edu.

SHAW, DIANNE ELIZABETH, school administrator; b. Greenville, Tex., Feb. 9, 1950; d. Charles V. Marshall and Margaret Virginia (Cowen) Johnson; m. Gary Allen Shaw, June 8, 1968; children: Daniel Phillip, Andrew Joseph. BA, East Tex. State U., 1978; MEd, Stephen F. Austin U., 1996. Cert. tchr., Tex.; cert. elem. edn. grades 1-8 and English; mid-mgmt. cert. Asst. ctr. supr. recreation dept. City of Arlington, Tex., 1968-73; substitute tchr. Quitman (Tex.) Ind. Sch. Dist., 1974-78; youth dir. 1st United Meth. Ch., Quitman, 1976-78; tchr. 1st grade Pine Tree Ind. Sch. Dist., Longview, Tex., 1978-81; kindergarten tchr. 1st Christian Ch., Longview, 1981-88; lead tchr., math. coord., environ. coord. K-12 Trinity Sch. of Tex., Longview, 1988-96; head of sch. St. Cyprian's Episcopal Sch., Lufkin, Tex., 1996-2001, Trinity Episcopal Sch., Marshall, Tex., 2001—. Elected to Diocese of Tex. Schs. Commn., 2000—; pres. East Tex. Heads of Sch., 1999-2001. Grad. Leadership Lufkin, 1999; organizer comty. recycling project Trinity Sch. of Tex., Longview, 1994; mem. Angelina Beautiful Clean, C. of C., Lufkin, 1996-2001, mem. drug task force, 1996-2001; mem. Chamber Coalition for Better Cmty., 1999-2001; adv. com. Tex. State Tech. Coll., Marshall, 2002-; mem. adv. bd. The Assn. Retarded Citizens, 2003-2004; bd. dirs. Marshall Regional Arts Coun., 2001-. Presdl. scholar East Tex. State U., 1978; tech. grantee T.L.L. Temple Found., 1998, 99, 2000; recipient Dr. John M. Davis Disting. Ednl. Achievement award, 2003. Mem. ASCD, DAR, Nat. Assn. Episc. Schs., Southwestern Assn. Episc. Schs. (accrediting team 1995—, chair accrediting team 1998-99), Tex. Assn. Non-Pub. Schs. (regional dir. 1998—, v.p. 2003—), So. Assn. Colls. and Schs. (Tex. state chair elem. and mid. schs. com. 2000—. exec. com. commn. on elem. and mid. schs. 2000—, commn. on elem. and mid. schs., chair non-pub. and spl. purpose schs. commn. com. 2002—), Marshall C. of C. (edn. com. 2001—), Marshall Rotary Club (bd. dirs. 2002—), Phi Delta Kappa. Episcopalian. Avocations: reading, hiking, cross country skiing. Office: Trinity Episcopal Sch 2905 Rosborough Springs Marshall TX 75672 E-mail: dianne.shaw@att.net.

SHAW, DONALD LESLIE, Spanish language educator; b. Feb. 11, 1930; s. Stephen Leslie and Lily (Hughes) S.; m. Maria Concetta Cristini, June 30, 1958; children: Andrew Leslie, Sylvia Maria Pierina. BA, U. Manchester, Eng., 1952, MA, 1953; PhD, U. Dublin, Ireland, 1960. Asst. lectr. U. Dublin, 1955-57, U. Glasgow, Scotland, 1957-64, U. Edinburgh, Scotland, 1964-69, sr. lectr., 1969-72, reader, prof. spanish, 1972-86; prof. spanish U. Va., Charlottesville, 1986—. Vis. prof. Brown U., Providence, 1967, U. Va., Charlottesville, 1983. Author: Historia de la Literatura Española, Siglo XIX, 1973, La Generación del 98, 1977, Nueva Narrativa Hispanoamericana, 1981, Alejo Carpentier, 1985, Borges' Narrative Strategies, 1992, Antonio Skármeta and the Post-Boom, 1994, The Post-Boom in Spanish American Fiction, 1998, A Companion to Spanish American Fiction, 2001. Served with RAF, 1953-55. Avocation: cycling. E-mail: dls6h@vriginia.edu. Home: 1800 Jefferson Park Ave Charlottesville VA 22903-3554 Office: U Va 115 Wilson Hall Charlottesville VA 22903-3238 Office Phone: 804-924-4658. Business E-Mail: dls61@virginia.edu.

SHAW, DORIS BEAUMAR, film and video producer, executive recruiter, management consultant; b. Pitts., July 13, 1934; d. Emerson C. and Doris Llorene (Rees) Beaumar; m. Robert Newton Shaw, July 6, 1957. BA summa cum laude, Lindenwood Coll., St. Charles, Mo., 1955. Writer, asst. to pres. Baker Prodns., Benton Harbor, Mich., 1955; asst. prodn. mgr. Condor Films, Inc., St. Louis, 1955-57; chief editor, asst. to v.p. Frederick F. Watson Inc., N.Y.C., 1957-58; v.p. Gen. Pictures Corp., Cleve., 1958-71; dir., editor, unit mgr. Cinecraft Inc., Cleve., 1971-72; mgr. audio-visual dept. Am. Greetings Corp., Cleve., 1972-73; proprietor Script to Screen Svcs., Chagrin Falls, Ohio, 1973-76; pres. D & B Shaw, Inc., Chardon, Ohio, 1976-87, Hudson, Ohio, 1987—, Execusearch, Inc., Hudson, 1987—, Infosearch Inc., Hudson, 1994—, Cybersearch, Inc., Hudson, 1995—, Wellness Unltd. N.A., Inc., Pennisula, 2003—. Film festival judge, tchr. Martha Holden Jennings Found./Hawken Sch., Gates Mills, Ohio, 1970-85; advisor teenage film contests, seminars Cleve. Bd. Edn., 1970-88; contest judge/film and video WVIZ-TV, Channel 25, Parma, Ohio, 1971—; guest lectr. Lindenwood Coll., 1973-80; adj. prof. U. Akron, 1990—; cons. to bus. and industry regarding sales, mktg., bus. mgmt., info. and rsch. svcs., computer multimedia prodn., web page design and devel. Writer, dir., editor, prodr. hundreds of film, video, multi-image, multi-media, audio/visual prodn., radio, TV commls. and programs; contbr. articles to profl. jours. Bd. trustees Ohio Boys Town, Cleve., 1957-68; mem. alumnae coun. Lindenwood Coll., 1973-77; publicity chmn. Geauga County Preservation Soc., 1984-91; active various charitable orgns. Named Outstanding Young Woman of Am., Fedn. of Women's Clubs, 1965, Alumna of Yr. Merit award Lindenwood Coll., 1971; recipient numerous awards and grants for film, video projects including Gold Camera Best Documentary award, 1979. Mem. Soc. Motion Picture and TV Engrs., Info. Film Prodrs. Am., Assn. for Multi Image (charter), Detroit Prodrs. Assn., Internat. TV and Video Assn. (charter), Internat. Comm. Industries Assn., Alpha Epsilon Rho. Republican. Avocations: science, travel, physical fitness, environmental issues, organic horticulture. Office: D & B Shaw Inc PO Box 335 Peninsula OH 44264-0335

SHAW, E. CLAY, JR., (CLAY SHAW), congressman; b. Miami, FL, Apr. 19, 1939; s. E. Clay and Rita (Walker) S.; m. Emilie Costar, Aug. 22, 1960; children: Emilie, Jennifer, E. Clay, John C. BS, Stetson U., 1961, JD, 1966; MBA, U. Ala., 1963. Bar: Fla. 1967; CPA, Fla. Asst. city atty. City of Ft. Lauderdale, 1968, chief city pros., 1968-69, assoc. mcpl. judge, 1969-71, city commr., 1971-73, vice mayor, 1973—75, mayor, 1975 80; mem. U.S. Congress from 22nd (formerly 15th) Fla. dist., 1981—; mem. ways and means com.; chmn. subcom. on human resources, 1995-98; chmn. social security subcom., 1999—. U.S. spl. ambassador to Papua New Guinea Independence; pres. U.S. Conf. Republican Mayors; mem. adv. and exec. bd. U.S. Conf. Mayors.; former chmn. mcpl. div. Ft. Lauderdale United Fund Campaign, 1971; former Young Rep. Club Broward County, Ft. Lauderdale Rep. Exec. Com.; past mem. exec. com. Rep. Nat. Com.; former mem. house select com. narcotics abuse and control; past bd. dirs. Broward County Traffic Assn.; mem judiciary com. Pub. Works and Transp. Bd. overseers Stetson Coll. Law. Republican. Home: 700 Coral Way Fort Lauderdale FL 33301-2532 Office: US Ho of Reps 2408 Rayburn Ho Office Bldg Washington DC 20515-0922

SHAW, EARL D. academic administrator, physics educator; b. Clarksdale, Miss., 1937; BS in Physics, U. Ill., 1960; MA, Dartmouth Coll., 1964; PhD in Physics, U. Calif., Berkeley, 1969. Rsch. scientist Bell Labs., Murray Hill, NJ; prof. physics and astronomy Rutgers U., Newark, 1991—; chmn. physics dept. Rutgers-Newark U., Newark, 1996—. Contbr. articles to profl. jours. Mem.: Nat. Soc. Black Physicists. Achievements include invention of spin-flip tunable laser. Office: Rutgers the State U of NJ Smith Hall # 211 101 Warren St Newark NJ 07102

SHAW, ELEANOR JANE, newspaper editor; b. Columbus, Ohio, Mar. 23, 1949; d. Joseph Cannon and Wanda Jane (Campbell) S. BA, U. Del., 1971. With News-Jour. newspapers, Wilmington, Del., 1970-82, editor HEW desk, asst. met. editor, 1977-80, bus. editor, 1980-82; topics editor USA Today, 1982-83; asst. city editor The Miami Herald, 1983-85; projects editor The Sacramento Bee, 1985-87, news editor, 1987-91, exec. bus. editor, 1991-93, editor capitol bur. news, 1993-95, state editor, 1995-99; mgr. employee comm. The McClatchy Co., Sacramento, 1999—2004. Bd. dirs. Del. 4-H Found., 1978-83, Safety Ctr., Inc., Sacramento. Mem. Calif. Soc. Newspaper Editors (bd. dirs. 1990-96), No. Calif. Wine Soc. (v.p. 1987-93, pres. 1993-2002).

SHAW, ELIZABETH ORR, retired lawyer; b. Monona, Iowa, Oct. 2, 1923; d. Harold Topliff and Hazel (Kean) Orr; m. Donald Hardy Shaw, Aug. 16, 1946; children: Elizabeth Ann, Andrew Hardy, Anthony Orr. AB, Drake U., 1945; postgrad., U. Minn., 1945—46; JD, U. Iowa, 1948. Bar: Ill. 1949, Iowa 1956. Assoc. Lord Bissell & Brook, Chgo., 1949-52; pvt. practice Arlington Heights, Ill., 1952-56; ptnr. Wood & Shaw, Davenport, Iowa, 1968-72; mem. Iowa Ho. of Reps., Des Moines, 1967-72, Iowa Senate, Des Moines, 1972-77; county atty. Scott County, Davenport, 1977-78; corp. atty. Deere & Co., Moline, Ill., 1979-89; pvt. practice Davenport, 1990-98; ret., 1999. Mem. Scott County Bar Assn. (com. chmn. 1970-72), Iowa State Bar Assn. (chmn. family law com. 1970-76), Order of Coif, Phi Beta Kappa, Kappa Kappa Gamma, PEO. Republican. Mem. United Ch. of Christ.

SHAW, GAYLORD, newspaper executive; b. El Reno, Okla., July 22, 1942; m. Judith Howard, 1960; children: Randall, Kristine, Kelly. Attended, Cameron Coll., 1960-62, U. Okla., 1962-64. Night police reporter Lawton (Okla.) Constitution Press, 1960-62; Okla. City bur. night editor, statehouse correspondent AP, 1962-66, Washington bur. night editor, investigative reporter, spl. assignment team editor, White House correspondent, 1966-75; asst. mng. editor to mng. editor/news Dallas Times Herald, 1981-83; editor-in-chief Shaw Comms. Inc., Charlotte, N.C., 1983-85; correspondent Washington, Denver L.A. Times, 1975-81, correspondent, projects coord. Washington bur., 1985-88; Washington bur. chief Newsday, 1988-95, sr. corr., 1995—. Recipient Pulitzer Prize Nat. Reporting, 1978, Disting. Svc. award for Washington correspondence Sigma Delta Chi/Soc. Profl. Journalists, 1978, Loeb award Disting. Bus. Reporting, 1978, Disting. Reporting award Merriman Smith/White House Correspondents Assn., 1974, Worth Bingham Disting. Reporting award, 1968, Washington Correspondence award Nat. Press Club, 1991. Home: 2815 Otsego Dr Herndon VA 20171-2444 Office: Washington Bur Newsday 1730 Pennsylvania Ave NW Washington DC 20006-4706

SHAW, GEORGE M. hematologist, educator; b. 1953; Undergrad., Dartmouth Coll., 1975; MD, PhD, Ohio State U., 1980. Resident in internal medicine U. Mich., 1983; postdoctoral fellow NIH, U. Ala., Birmingham; mem. faculty U. Ala., Birmingham, 1985, dep. dir. AIDS Ctr., dir. dept. medicine divsn. hematology/oncology, prof. hematology and oncology dept. medicine, 1985. Investigator Howard Hughes Med. Inst., 1997. Recipient Pew scholarship, 1986. Office: U Ala-Birmingham Rm 558 1824 6th Ave S Birmingham AL 35294-

SHAW, GRACE GOODFRIEND (MRS. HERBERT FRANKLIN SHAW), publisher, editor; b. N.Y.C. d. Henry Bernheim and Jane Elizabeth (Stone) Goodfriend; m. Herbert Franklin Shaw (dec. 1992); 1 son, Brandon Hibbs. Student, Bennington Coll.; BA magna cum laude, Fordham U., 1976, MSE, 1991. Reporter Port Chester (N.Y.) Daily Item; editorial coordinator World Scope Ency., N.Y.C.; assoc. editor Clarence L. Barnhart, Inc., Bronxville, N.Y.; freelance-writer for reference books; editing supr. World Pub. Co., mng. editor, sr. editor; mng. editor Peter H. Wyden Co., N.Y.C., 1969-70; assoc. editor Dial Press, N.Y.C., 1971-72, sr. editor, 1972, David McKay Co., N.Y.C., 1972-75, Grosset & Dunlap, 1975-79; chief editor Today Press (Grosset), 1977-79; sr. editor, coll. dept. Bobbs-Merrill, N.Y.C., mng. editor, exec. editor trade div., 1979-80, pub., 1980-84; mng. editor Rawson Assocs. div. Macmillan Pub., 1985-91; pres. Grace Shaw Assocs., Scarsdale, N.Y., 1991-97; profl. respite provider Westchester Jewish Cmty. Svcs., N.Y., 1997—. Home: 85 Lee Rd Scarsdale NY 10583-5212

SHAW, HAROLD (FRANCIS HAROLD SHAW), retired performing arts administrator; b. Hebron, N.Y., June 11, 1923; Student, Ithaca Coll., 1942, Columbia, 1944, N.Y. U. Extension, 1948. Former assoc. Hurok Concerts, Inc., N.Y.C.; chmn., owner Shaw Concerts, Inc., N.Y.C., 1969-99; ret., 1999; performing arts dir. Seattle World's Fair, 1961-62. Former concert mgr. Nathan Milstein, Vladimir Horowitz, Dame Janet Baker, Jessye Norman, Helen Donath, Jacqueline duPre, Wolfgang Holzmair, Jard van Nes, Mitsuko Uchida, Garrick Ohlsson, Shura Cherkassky, Horacio Gutiérrez, Julian Bream, John Williams, Elmar Oliveira, Kyoko Takezawa, Robert Shaw, Andrew Davis, and over 100 artists and attractions; exec. dir. President's Shakespeare Ann. Com., 1964. Dir. exec. staff, mem. performing arts com. Cultural Commn., N.Y.C., 1966; nat. chmn. Performing Arts Energy Commn., 1974; chmn. bd. trustees Am. Shakespeare Theatre, Strafford, Conn., 1974. With USAAF, 1942-43. Mem.: Am. Summer Stock Mgrs. Assn. (co-founder), Actors Equity Assn., Assn. Coll., Univ. and Cmty. Arts Adminstrs., Am. Symphony Orch. League, Internat. Performing Arts Adminstrs., Athletic Club, Phi Mu Alpha Sinfonia. E-mail: hshaw611@msn.com.

SHAW, HELEN LESTER ANDERSON, retired dean, nutrition educator, researcher; b. Lexington, Ky., Oct. 18, 1936; d. Walter Southall and Elizabeth (Guyn) Anderson; m. Charles Van Shaw, Mar. 14, 1988. BS, U. Ky., 1958; MS, U. Wis., 1965, PhD, 1969. Registered dietitian. Dietitian Roanoke (Va.) Meml. Hosp., 1959-60, Santa Barbara (Calif.) Cottage Hosp., 1960-61; dietitian, unit mgr. U. Calif., Santa Barbara, 1961-63; rsch. asst., NIH fellow U. Wis., Madison, 1963-68; from asst. prof. to prof. U. Mo., Columbia, 1969-88, assoc. dean, prof., 1977-84; prof., chair dept. food and nutrition U. N.C., Greensboro, 1989-94, dean Sch. Human Environ. Scis., 1994-2000; ret., 2000. Cluster leader Food for 21st Century rsch. program U. Mo., 1985-88. Contbr. articles to rsch. publs. Elder 1st Presbyn. Ch., Columbia, 1974-89, Greensboro, 1992—. Recipient Teaching award Home Econ. Alumni Assn., 1981, Gamma Sigma Delta, 1984; rsch. grantee Nutrition Found., 1971-73, NIH, 1972-75, NSF, 1980 83. Mem. Am. Soc. for Nutrition Scis., Am. Bd. Nutrition, Am. Soc. for Clin. Nutrition, Am. Dietetic Assn., Sigma Xi, Phi Upsilon Omicron, Kappa Omicron Nu. Democrat. Avocations: tennis, choral singing, art, volunteering.

SHAW, JACK ALLEN, communications company executive; b. Auburn, Ind., Jan. 1, 1939; s. Marvin Dale and Vera Lucille (Harter) S.; m. Martha Sue Collins, Aug. 24, 1963; 1 child, Mark Allen. BSEE, Purdue U., 1962; DSc (hon.), Capitol Coll., 1994, DSc (hon.), 1995; D in Engring. (hon.), Purdue U., 1998. Project engr. Hughes Aircraft Co., El Segundo, Calif., 1962-69; dir. program mgmt. ITT Space Comms., Ramsey, N.J., 1969-74; v.p., corp. devel. Digital Comms. Corp., Gathersburg, Md., 1974-78, exec. v.p., COO Germantown, Md., 1978-81, pres., CEO, 1981-84, M/A-com Telecom divsn., Germantown, Md., 1984-87; chmn., CEO Hughes Network Sys., Inc., 1988—, chmn., also bd. dirs., 1978—, 1987-2000, corp. sr. exec. v.p. enterprise sector, 2000—; pres., CEO Hughes Elecs., 2001. Bd. dirs. XM Satellite Radio, Guidant Corp.; exec. v.p. Hughes Electronics, 1999. Mem.: IEEE (sr.), Radio Club Am. (hon.). Republican.

SHAW, JEANNE OSBORNE, editor, poet; b. Stone Mountain, Ga., June 1, 1920; d. Virgil Waite and Daisy Hampton (Scruggs) Osborne; m. Harry B. Shaw, Dec. 10, 1982; children: Robert Allan Gibbs, Marilyn Osborne Gibbs Barry. BA, Agnes Scott Coll., 1942. Editl. staff Atlanta Constitution, 1942; feature writer New London (Conn.) Day, 1943; book reviewer Atlanta Constitution, 1940—42, Atlanta Jour., 1945—48; poetry editor Banner Press, Emory U., 1957—59; book editor Georgia Mag., Decatur, 1957—73. Author: The Other Side of the Water, 1970 (author of yr. in poetry award Dixie Coun. Authors and Journalists), Unravelling Yarn, 1979, (chapbook) From Cowslip to Cobalt, 1971, Third Millennium Christmas, 2001, The First Easter Parade, 2003; co-author: Noel: Poems of Christmas, 1979, They Continued Steadfastly, History of Druid Hills Baptist Church, 1987; author: Faithbuilders, 1982—84; contbr. poems, pen and ink sketches mags. Mem. nat. arts and humanities com. Learning for Life Boy Scouts Am., 2000—; Pres. Newton class Druid Hills Bapt. Ch., 1973—74, dir. ch. tng., 1978—79, ch. clk., 1995—2001. Recipient internat. narrative poem award Poets and Patrons, Inc., Chgo., 1992, Robert Martin, Burke, Otto, In Praise of Poetry awards N.Y. Poetry Forum, 1973, 79, 81, Westbrook award Ky. Poetry Soc., 1976, Ariz. award, 1981, Ind. State Fedn. of Poetry Clubs award, Ala. State Poetry Soc. award, 1990, Rev. Earl M. Smith meml. award, 1997, Joseph V. Hickey meml. award, 1998, Nat. Fedn. State Poetry Socs. Mem.: Ga. Poetry Soc. (artistic dir. 2000, judge Nat. River of Words Contest 2002—04, Traditional award 1984, Cole and Ledford award 1986, Goreau award 1987, Melissa Henry award 1989, Charles and Virginia Dickson award 1990, Jo Ann Yeager Adkins award 1991, Poem About Atlanta award 1992, Goreau award 1993, Free Verse award 1993, My Very Best Poem award 1995, Traditional award 1997, Jabberwocky award 1997, Annette Peery award 1998, 1999, Charles Bruehler award 2000, Annette Peery award 2001, 22d Anniversary award 2002, Mikki Morris award 2002), Atlanta Writers Club (pres. 1949—50, Aurelia Austin Writer of Yr. in poetry 1971, Wyatt award 1986, Light Verse award 1989, 1990, Daniel Whitehead Hicky award 1991, F. Levering Neely award 1991, Poet Laureate's award 1993, Wyatt award 1995, Gerry Crocker award 1995, Daniel Whitehead Hicky award 1995, Villanelle award 1997, 1998, Virginia Cole Veal award 1999, Light Verse award 2001, Ben Willingham award), Poetry Soc. Ga. (John Clare prize 1955, Katharine H. Strong prize 1975, Eunice Thomson prize 1976, Jimmy Williamson prize 1977, Capt. Frank Spencer prize 1985, Conrad Aiken prize 1987, Capt. Frank Spencer prize 1988, Conrad Aiken prize 1988, Sarah Cunningham prize 1989, Soc. prize 1989, Lucy McEntire prize 1990, Grace Schley Knight prize 1991, Gerald Chan Sieg prize 1991, Eunice Thomson prize 1992, Grace Schley Knight prize 1993, Sarah Cunningham prize 1994, Lucy McEntire prize 1994, Harriet Ross Colquitt prize 1994, Gerald Chan Sieg prize 1995, Harriet Ross Colquitt prize 1995, Eva Tennyson Forbes Meml. prize 1996, Sarah Cunningham prize 1997, About Holes prize 1998, Soc. prize 2001, Formal prize 2001, Monday prize 2001, Lucy McEntire prize 2004, Formal prize 2004, 2004), Ga. Writers Assn. (Lit. Achievement award 1971), Phi Beta Kappa. Achievements include reading poetry at Atlanta Centennial Olympic Pk., 2002; poems in Ga. Coun. Teachers of English Anthology, 2003; judge, sch. contest of Ga. Poetry Soc., 2003. Home: 809 Pinetree Dr Decatur GA 30030-2332

SHAW, JIM, JR., broadcast executive; b. Ontario, Can., July 29, 1957; m. Wanda Shaw; children: Haley Morgan, Parker James. Various mgmt. positions Shaw Comm., Inc., Calgary, Canada, 1982, past pres. cable TV, past sr. v.p. ops., pres., CEO, 1995—. Chmn. bd. dirs. Vision.com, Canada; bd. dirs. Microcell Telecomm., Montreal, CableLabs, Montreal; mem. adv. coun. faculty bus. U. Alta.; owner Shaw FiberLink, Shaw DBS Ventures, YTV, SEGA Channel, Digital Music Express, Microcell; operator 9 radio stas. Gov. Shawnigan Lake Sch., B.C.; active Young Pres. Orgn.; past bd. dirs. Cable TV Stds. Found. Office: Shaw Comm 630 3d Ave SW Calgary AB Canada T2P 4L4

SHAW, JOHN FREDERICK, retired naval officer; b. Dallas, Oct. 14, 1938; s. John Frederick and Sarah E. (Crouch) S.; m. Janice Muren, July 14, 1962; children: Elizabeth Lee, Suzanne Michele. BS, U.S. Naval Acad., 1960; MS in Mgmt. with distinction, Naval Postgrad. Sch., Monterey, Calif., 1970; grad., Armed Forces Staff Coll., 1971. Commd. ensign USN, 1960, advanced through grades to rear adm., 1983; exec. officer USS Long Beach (CGN 9), 1978-79; comdg. officer USS Bainbridge (CGN 25), 1980-83; dir. guided missile destroyer 51, Arleigh Burke program Comdr. Naval Sea Systems Command, Washington, 1983-85, mgr. AEGIS shipbldg. program, 1985-87; comdr. Cruiser-Destroyer Group One, San Diego, 1987-88; dep. chief staff plans and policy Supreme Allied Comdr., Atlantic, Norfolk, Va., 1988-89, chief staff, 1989-91; ret., 1991; prof. joint mil. ops. Coll. Continuing Edn., Naval War Coll., San Diego, 1992-94. Bd. advisors United Svc. Benefit Assn., Kansas City, Kans., 1987-93; mem. cmty. bd. advisors Sam and Rose Stein Inst. for Rsch. on Aging, 1998-2004; membership chmn., 1999-2000, sec.-treas., 2000-2004; tax. cons. for elderly, AARP, 2000—. Trustee Coronado Libr., 1998—, exec. sec., 2001—02, pres., 2002—, trustee, 2004—. Decorated Def. D.S.M., Legion of Merit with two gold stars, Meritorious Svc. medal with gold star, Navy Commendation medal with gold star, Meritorious Unit Commendation (civilian) USN . Mem. AARP, U.S. Naval Inst. (life), U.S. Naval Acad. Alumni Assn. (life, pres. Washington chpt. 1986, bd. govs. San Diego/Coronado chpt. 1996-99), Surface Navy Assn. (life), San Diego Navy League (dir. 1997-2002). Avocations: golf, reading, economics, travel. E-mail: jshaw14@aol.com.

SHAW, JOHN W. lawyer; b. Mo., 1951; BA, MA, U. Mo., 1973, JD, 1977. Bar: Mo. 1977. Ptnr. Bryan Cave, Kansas City, 1977-92, Lathrop & Norquist, 1983-92, Bryan Cave LLP, 1992-98, Berkowitz Stanton Brandt Williams and Shaw LLP, Kansas City, 1998—. Mem. ABA, Securities Industry Assn. (legal and compliance group), Mo. Bar, Def. Rsch. Inst. (chmn. firearms litigation subcom.), Order of Coif. Office: Berkowitz Stanton Brandt Williams and Shaw LLP Two Emmanuel Cleaver Blvd Ste 500 Kansas City MO 64112

SHAW, JOSEPH THOMAS, Slavic languages educator; b. Ashland City, Tenn., May 13, 1919; s. George Washington and Ruby Mae (Pace) S.; m. Betty Lee Ray, Oct. 30, 1942 (dec. Sept. 2002); children: David Matthew, Joseph Thomas, James William (dec. Jan. 1999). AB, U. Tenn., 1940, AM, 1941, Harvard, 1947, PhD, 1950. Asst. prof. Slavic langs. Ind. U., 1949-55, assoc. prof., 1955-61; prof. Slavic langs. U. Wis., 1961-89, prof. emeritus, 1989—, chmn. dept. Slavic langs., 1962-68, 77-86, chmn. div. humanities, 1964-65, 72-73, assoc. dean Grad. Sch., 1965-68. Author: The Letters of Alexander Pushkin, 1963, Pushkin's Rhymes: A Dictionary, 1974, Baratynskii: A Dictionary of the Rhymes and a Concordance to the Poetry, 1975, Batiushkov: A Dictionary of the Rhymes and a Concordance to the Poetry, 1975, Pushkin: A Concordance to the Poetry, 1985, American Association Teachers Slavic and East European Languages: The First Fifty Years 1941-91, 1991, Pushkin's Poetry of the Unexpected: The Nonrhymed Lines in the Rhymed Poetry and the Rhymed Lines in the Nonrhymed Poetry, 1994, Pushkin, Poet and Man of Letters, and His Prose (collected works, vol. 1), 1995, Pushkin Poems and Other Studies (collected works vol. 2), 1996, The Letters of Alexander Pushkin (collected works vols. 3-5), 3d edit., 1997, Konkordans k stikham Pushkina, 2000, Pushkin's Rhymes: A Dictionary (collected works, vol. 6-7), 2d edit., 2001, Batiushkov: A Dictionary of the Rhymes & A Concordance to the Poetry (collected works, vol. 8), 2d edit., 2001, Baratynskii: A Dictionary of the Rhymes & A Concordance to the Poetry (collected works, vol. 9), 2d edit., 2001, Poeziia neozhidannogo u Pushkina, 2002, Studies in Pushkin's Rhyming: Theory from Practice (collected works, vol. 10), 2002, The Letters of Alexander Pushkin(vol. 10-12 in The Complete Works of Alexander Pushkin 15 vols.1999-2003) 4th edit.; editor: The Slavic and East European Jour., 1957-70; contbr. articles to profl. jours. Served to capt. USNR, 1942-46, 51-53. Mem. Am. Assn. Tchrs. Slavic and East European Langs. (mem. exec. council 1953-70, 73-80, pres. 1973-74) Home: 4505 Mineral Point Rd Madison WI 53705-5071

SHAW, KENDALL (GEORGE SHAW), artist, educator; b. New Orleans, Mar. 30, 1924; s. George Kendall and Florence Gladys (Worner) S.; m. Frances (Glenn) Fort, Oct. 31, 1955. Student, Ga. Inst. Tech., 1944-46; BS in Chemistry, Tulane U., 1949, MFA, 1959; postgrad., La. State U., 1950. Instr. Columbia U., 1961-66, Hunter Coll., 1966-68, Parsons Sch. Design, N.Y.C., 1966-86, Lehman Coll., 1968-70, Bklyn. Mus. Art Sch., 1970-76; US del. to UNESCO Conf., London, 1965. One-man shows include Orleans Gallery, New Orleans, 1960, 61, 63, Columbia U., 1962, 65, Bienville Gallery, New Orleans, 1968, Tibor de Nagy Gallery, N.Y.C., 1964, 65, 67, 68, Southampton Coll., 1969, John Bernard Myers Gallery, 1972, Alessandra Gallery, 1976, Lerner Heller Gallery, N.Y.C., 1979, 81, 82, Nature Morte, N.Y.C., 1983, Bernice Steinbaum Gallery, N.Y.C., 1991, Artists Space, N.Y.C., 1992, The Gallery of South Orange, NJ, 1997, U. Richmond, Va., 1999, Tulane U., 2001; group shows include Downtown Gallery, New Orleans, 1959, Mus. Contemporary Art, Nagaoka, Japan, 1965, Alessandra GAllery, N.Y.C., 1976, P.S.I., N.Y.C., 1977, Gladstone Villani Gallery, N.Y.C., 1978, Galerie Habermann, Cologne, 1979, Modern Art Gallery, Vienna, 1980, Jacksonville Art Mus.,Fla., 1983, The Ogden Mus. So. Art, New Orleans, 2001-04, others; represented in permanent collections Sammlung Ludwig, Aachen, Bklyn. Mus., Albright Knox Gallery, Buffalo, Mus. Contemporary Art, Nagaoka, Japan, Everson Mus., Syracuse, Chase Bank, N.Y.C., N.Y. Univ., Polk Mus. Art, Lakeland, Fla., Orlando Mus. Art, Weatherspoon Art Gallery, Greensboro, NC, Marsh Art Gallery, Richmond, Va., Tulane U., New Orleans, New Orleans Mus. Art, Miss. Mus. Art, The Ogden Mus. So. Art, New Orleans. Served in USN, 1943-46. Named Disting. Alumnus, Tulane Coll., 2001. Mem. Coll. Art Assn., N.Y., Artists Equity Assn. Address: 916 President St Brooklyn NY 11215-1604 Office Phone: 718-398-5595. Personal E-mail: kendallshaw@aol.com.

SHAW, KENDRICK MATTHEW, software engineer; b. Portland, Oreg. s. Donald and Kathey Irene S. BS in Computer Sci., MS in Computer Sci., Case Western Res. U., 1997; postgrad., U. Wash. Software design engr. Microsoft Corp., Redmond, Wash., 1997—2003. Home: 9611 163rd Pl NE Redmond WA 98052-3134

SHAW, KENNETH ALAN, university president; b. Granite City, Ill., Jan. 31, 1939; s. Kenneth W. and Clara H. (Lange) Shaw; m. Mary Ann Byrne, Aug. 18, 1962; children: Kenneth William, Susan Lynn, Sara Ann. BS, Ill. State U., 1961, DHL, 1987; EdM, U. Ill., 1963; PhD, Purdue U., 1966, EdD (hon.), 1990; DHL, Towson State, 1979, Ill. Coll., 1986. Tchr. history, counselor Rich Twp. High Sch., Park Forest, Ill., 1961-63; residence hall dir., instr. edn. Ill. State U., 1963-64; counselor Office Dean of Men, Purdue U., 1964-65, Office Dean of Men, Purdue U. (Office Student Loans), 1965-66; asst. to pres., lectr. sociology Ill. State U., 1966-69; v.p. acad. affair, dean Towson State U., Balt., 1969-76; pres. So. Ill. U., Edwardsville, 1977-79; chancellor So. Ill. U. System, Edwardsville, 1979-86; pres. U. Wis. System, Madison, 1986-91; chancellor, pres. Syracuse U., 1991—. Bd. dirs. Unity Mutual Life Ins. Co., Key Bank of Ctrl. N.Y. Trustee CICU, Albany, NY, 1993—, Am. Coll. Testing, 1990—; bd. dirs. NCAA Pres. Commn., 1993—. Named Citizen of Yr., So. Ill. Inc., 1985; named to Ill. Basketball Hall of Fame, 1983; recipient Young Leader in Edn. award, 1980, Silver Anniversary award, NCAA, 1986, Coaches Silver Anniversary award, Nat. Assn. Basketball, 1986. Mem.: State Higher Edn. Exec. Officers Assn., Am. Higher Edn. Assn., Am. Social. Assn., Am. Coun. Edn. (com. on minorities in higher edn. 1987—91), Am. Assn. State Colls. and Univs. (external rels. com. 1986—88), Met. Devel. Assn. (bd. dirs. 1991—), Syracuse C. of C. (bd. dirs. 1991—), Pi Gamma Mu, Phi Delta Kappa. Office: Syracuse Univ Office of Chancellor 300 Tolley Admin Building Syracuse NY 13244-0001

SHAW, L. EDWARD, JR., retired lawyer; b. Elmira, N.Y., July 30, 1944; s. L. Edward and Virginia Anne (O'Leary) S.; m. Irene Ryan; children: Christopher, Hope, Hillary, Julia, Rory BA in Econs., Georgetown U., Washington, 1966; JD, Yale U., New Haven, 1969. Bar: N.Y. 1969. Assoc. Milbank, Tweed, Hadley & McCloy, N.Y.C., 1969-77, ptnr., 1977-83; sr. v.p., gen. counsel Chase Manhattan Corp., N.Y.C., 1983-85, exec. v.p., gen. counsel, 1985-96; vice chmn., gen. counsel Natwest Markets, N.Y.C., 1996-97, pres., 1997-99; gen. counsel Aetna Inc., 1999—2004; ret., 2004. Mem. Assn. Bar City N.Y., Winged Foot Golf Club, Phi Beta Kappa. Roman Catholic. Avocations: youth athletics, golf.

SHAW, LARRY, state legislator; b. June 15, 1949; m. Evelyn Shaw. BS, Ala. State U., 1972, MS, 1974. Mem. N.C. Ho. of Reps., Raleigh, 1995-96, N.C. Senate, Raleigh, 1997—. Mem. appropriations/base budget com., appropriations on natural resources com., commerce com., fin. com., ranking minority mem. pensions and retirement and ins. com., chmn. transp. com. Office: NC Senate 625 Legis Office Bldg 303 N Salisbury St Raleigh NC 27603-1359 also: PO Box 1195 1528 Nicklaus Dr Fayetteville NC 28303-3066

SHAW, LEANDER JERRY, JR., retired state supreme court justice; b. Salem, Va., Sept. 6, 1930; s. Leander J. and Margaret S. BA, W.Va. State Coll., 1952, LLD (hon.), 1986; JD, Howard U., 1957; PhD (hon.) in Pub. Affairs, Fla. Internat. U., 1990; LLD (hon.), Nova Law Sch., 1991, Washington & Lee Law Sch., 1991. Asst. prof. law Fla. A&M U., 1957-60; sole practice Jacksonville, Fla., 1960-69, 72-74; asst. pub. defender, 1965-69; asst. state's atty., 1969-72; judge Fla. Indsl. Relations Commn., 1974-79, Fla. Ct. Appeals (1st dist.), 1979-83; justice Fla. Supreme Ct., Tallahassee, 1983—2003, chief justice, 1990-92. Personal E-mail: slawjustice@earthlink.net. Business E-Mail: SupremeCourt@flcourts.org.

SHAW, LEONARD GLAZER, retired electrical engineering educator, consultant; b. Toledo, Aug. 15, 1934; s. A. Daniel and Mary (Glazer) S.; m. Susan Gail Weil, Dec. 24, 1961; children: Howard Benjamin, Mitchell Bruce, Jenny

Louise. BSEE, U. Pa., 1956; MSEE, Stanford U., 1957, PhD, 1961. From asst. to assoc. prof. Polytech. U. N.Y., Bklyn., 1960-75, prof., 1975—98, prof. emeritus, 1998—, head dept. elec. engring. and computer sci., 1982-90, dean Sch. Elec. Engring. and Computer Sci., 1990-94, vice provost for undergrad. studies, 1995-96. Vis. prof. Tech. U., Eindhoven, Netherlands, 1970, Ecole Nationale Superieure de Mecanique, Nantes, France, 1977, U. Sussex, Brighton, Eng., 1998; cons. Sperry Systems Mgmt. Div., Great Neck, N.Y.; mem. grant rev. panels NSF, 1986-98. Co-author: Signal Processing, 1975; contbr. articles to profl. jours. Rsch. grantee NSF, 1973, 81. Fellow: IEEE (mem. pub. bd. 1961—92, mem. various coms., editor-in-chief IEEE Press 1988—91, gen. chmn. Conf. of Decision and Control 1989, chmn. Tech. Field Award Coun. 1995—97), Control Sys. Soc. of IEEE (fin. v.p. 1992—93, 2000, pres.-elect 2001, pres. 2002). Office: Polytech U 6 Metrotech Ctr Brooklyn NY 11201-3840 Business E-Mail: lshaw@poly.edu.

SHAW, M. THOMAS, III, bishop; b. Battle Creek, Mich., Aug. 28, 1945; s. M.T. and Wilma Janes Shaw. BA, Alma (Mich.) Coll.; master's, Cath. U.; MDiv, Gen. Theol. Sem.; DD (hon.), Seabury We. Ordained priest Episcopal Ch., 1971. Mem. Co. of Mission Priests, Eng., 1970-72, 1972-74, Soc. St. John the Evangelist, Cambridge, Mass., 1974—; bishop Episcopal Diocese of Mass., 1994—. Episcopalian. Office: 138 Tremont St Boston MA 02111-1318

SHAW, MICHAEL, biologist, educator; b. Barbados, W.I., Feb. 11, 1924; s. Anthony and Myra (Perkins) S.; m. Jean Norah Berkinshaw, Oct. 16, 1948; children: Christopher A., Rosemary E., Nicholas R., Andrew L. BSc, McGill U., 1946, MSc, 1947, PhD, 1949, DSc (hon.), 1975, U. B.C., 2003. NRC Can. postdoctoral fellow Botany Sch., Cambridge U., 1949-50; assoc. prof. biology U. Sask., Canada, 1950-54, prof., 1954-67, prof., head dept. biology, 1961-67; dean faculty agrl. scis. U. B.C., Canada, 1967-75, v.p. acad. devel., 1975-81, acad. v.p., provost, 1981-83, univ. prof., 1983-89, univ. prof. emeritus, 1989—. Mem. Sci. Coun. Can., 1976-82, Natural Scis. and Engring. Rsch. Coun. Can., 1978-80. Contbr. articles to profl. jours. Recipient Queen's Silver Jubilee medal, 1977, Gold medal Biol. Coun. Can., 1983. Fellow Royal Soc. Can. (Flavelle medal 1976), Can. Phytopath. Soc., Am. Phytopath. Soc.; mem. AAAS, Can. Bot. Assn., Can. Soc. Plant Physiologists (Gold medal 1971), Am. Soc. Plant Biologists. Home: 1792 Western Pky Vancouver BC Canada V6T 1V3

SHAW, MICHAEL EVAN, librarian; b. N.Y.C., June 20, 1960; s. Lawrence Taylor and Noreen Mary Shaw. BA, Antioch Coll., Yellow Springs, Ohio, 1986; MLS, U. Pitts., 1993. Dir. libr. Ctr. Econ. Rsch. & Grad. Edn., Prague, Czech Republic, 1993; law libr. Affiliates, L.A., 1992—98; libr. L.A. Pub. Libr., 1994-98; br. mgr. Norfolk (Va.) Pub. Libr., 1998—. Internet trainer L.A. Pub. Libr., 1995, mem. collection devel. policy com., 2002—. Mem. election com. Am. Fed. State, County and Mcpl. Employees, L.A., 1998. Mem. ALA, Va. Libr. Assn., Colonial Pl./Riverview Civic League. Avocations: literacy, exercise, bicycling, environment. Home: 4409 Newport Ave Norfolk VA 23508 Office: Norfolk Pub Libr 6525 Hampton Blvd Norfolk VA 23508 E-mail: mshaw@norfolk.gov.

SHAW, MILTON CLAYTON, mechanical engineering educator; b. Phila., May 27, 1915; s. Milton Fredic and Nellie Edith (Clayton) S.; m. Mary Jane Greeninger, Sept. 6, 1939; children: Barbara Jane, Milton Stanley. BSME, Drexel Inst. Tech., 1938; M of Engring. Sci., U. Cin., 1940, ScD, 1942; PhD (hon.), U. Louvain, Belgium, 1970; DEng (hon.), Drexel U., 1996. Rsch. engr. Cin. Milling Machine Co., 1938-42; chief materials br. NACA, 1942-46; with MIT, 1946-61, prof. mech. engring., 1953-61, head materials processing divsn., 1952-61; prof., head dept. mech. engring. Carnegie Inst. Tech., Pitts., 1961-75; univ. prof. (hon.) Carnegie-Mellon U., 1974-77; prof. engring. Ariz. State U., Tempe, 1977-86, emeritus prof. engring., 1986—. Cons., lectr. in field; pres. Shaw Smith & Assos., Inc., Mass., 1951-61; Lucas prof. Birmingham (Eng.) U., 1961; Springer prof. U. Calif., Berkeley, 1972; Distinguished guest prof. Ariz. State U., 1977; mem. Nat. Materials Adv. Bd., 1971-74; v.p. conf. com. Engring. Found., 1976-78. Recipient Outstanding Research award Ariz. State U., 1981, Am. Machinist award, 1972, Schlesinger award German Govt., 1997; P. McKenna award, 1975; Guggenheim fellow, 1956; Fulbright lectr. Aachen T.H., Germany, 1957; OECD fellow to Europe, 1964—. Fellow Am. Acad. Arts and Scis., ASME (Hersey award 1967, Thurston lectr. 1971, Outstanding Engring. award 1975, ann. meeting theme organizer 1977, Gold medal 1985, hon. 1980), Am. Soc. Lubrication Engrs. (hon., nat. award 1964), Am. Soc. Metals (Wilson award 1971, fellow 1981); mem. Internat. Soc. Prodn. Engring. Research (pres. 1960-61, hon. mem. 1975), Am. Soc. for Engring. Edn. (G. Westinghouse award 1956), Soc. Mfg. Engrs. (hon. mem. 1970, Gold medal 1958, Internat. Edn. award 1980, M.C. Shaw award 1999), Nat. Acad. Engring., Polish Acad. Sci., Am. Soc. Precision Engrs. (hon.), Japan Soc. Precision Engrs. (Internat. award 1999), Drexel 100. Home: Unit C119 2625 E Southern Ave Tempe AZ 85282-7633 Office: Ariz State U Engring Dept Tempe AZ 85287-6106 Fax: 480-965-1384.

SHAW, MILTON HERBERT, conglomerate executive; b. Phila., June 16, 1918; s. Milton Herbert and Ethel (Shane) S.; m. Rita P. Revins, Nov. 24, 1971. BS, U. Pa., 1949. cons. indsl. safety and workmen's compensation. Accountant Franklin Sugar Refinery, Phila., 1945-52; with Kaiser Metal Products, Inc., Bristol, Pa., 1952-61, mgr. ins. and taxes, 1955-61; with Kidde Consumer Durables Corp., Bala Cynwyd, Pa., 1961-88, asst. v.p., 1968-88, dir. corp. svcs. and risk mgmt., 1977-88; cons. Indsl. Safety-Workmans Compensation, 1988; cons. risk mgmt. Hanson Ind., 1989-98. Risk mgmt. and indsl. safety cons., 1988-99; owner Golden Grain Goldens; co-owner Potpourri Doll Promotions, Rita P. Shaw Porcelain Studio. Served with USNR, 1936-45. Mem. NRA, VFW (life), Escort Carriers Assn., Nat. Wildlife Fedn., Sigma Kappa Phi. Home and Office: 2209 Blackhorse Dr Warrington PA 18976-2118

SHAW, MONTGOMERY THROOP, chemical engineering educator; b. Ithaca, N.Y., Sept. 11, 1943; s. Robert William and Charlotte (Throop) S.; m. Stephanie Habel, Sept. 5, 1966 (dec. 1989); 1 child, Steven Robert; m. Maripaz Nespral, June 25, 1994. BChemE, MS, Cornell U., 1966, Princeton (N.J.) U., 1968, PhD, 1970. Engr., project scientist Union Carbide Corp., Bound Brook, N.J., 1970-76; assoc. prof. Dept. Chem. Engring., U. Conn., Storrs, 1977-83, prof., 1983—; sabbatical prof. Sandia Nat. Labs., Albuquerque, 1983-84. Vis. scientist E.I. Dupont de Nemours and Co., Experimental Station, Wilmington, Del., 1991-92; adv. bd. Jour. of Applied Polymer Sci., 1984-89. Co-author: Polymer-Polymer Miscibility, 1977, Computer Programs for Rheologists, 1994. Grantee Alcoa Found., 1985, Exxon Edn. Found., 1986. Mem. IEEE (sr. mem., assoc. editor transactions on dielectrics and elec. insulation), Soc. Rheology (sec. 1977-81, treas. 1997—), Am. Chem. Soc., Am. Phys. Soc. Achievements include patents on rheological measurement method and apparatus and low density microcellular foams. Office: U Conn IMS 97 N Eagleville Rd Storrs Mansfield CT 06269-3136 E-mail: shawmt@uconnum.uconn.edu.

SHAW, RAYMOND ARTHUR, retail manager; b. Clarion, Iowa, Aug. 28, 1960; s. James Gilbert and June Arlene Shaw; m. Catherine Marie Fritz, Apr. 7, 1990; children: Nicholas Arthur, Alex Michael, Ryan Patrick, John David, Scott Taylor. Cert., Loyalist Coll., 2002. Mgr. svc. desk Structure, Omaha, 1997—2002, incident mgr., 2002—03. Sgt. USAF, 1980—83. Decorated The Air Force Achievement medal USAF. Republican. Lutheran. Avocations: fishing, writing, family, genealogy, reading. Home: 14220 Birchwood Circle Omaha NE 68137

SHAW, RICHARD DAVID, marketing and management educator; b. Pittsburg, Kans., Aug. 25, 1938; s. Richard Malburn and Jessie Ruth (Murray) S.; m. Adolphine Catherine Brungardt, Aug. 21, 1965; children: Richard David Jr., John Michael, Shannon Kathleen. BSBA, Rockhurst Coll., 1960; MS in Commerce, St. Louis U., 1964. Claims adjuster Kemper Ins. Group, Kansas City, Mo., 1961; tchr. acctg. Corpus Christi High Sch., Jennings, Mo., 1961—63; assoc. prof. econs. Fontbonne Coll., St. Louis, 1963—70, chmn. social behavioral sci. dept., 1968—70; mem. faculty, chmn. bus. div. Longview Community Coll., Lee's Summit, Mo., 1970—81, coord. mktg., 1979—81; workshop leader Rockhurst U., Kansas City, 1975—2003, prof. mktg., 1981—2003, chmn. mgmt. and mktg., 1983—85, co-chair MBA program, 1996—2003, co-chair Sch. of Mgmt. Undergrad. Programs, 1998—2003; ret., 2003. Faculty moderator Jr. Execs. Assn., The Rock yearbook, Rockhurst U. Reps., Rockettes, co-chair undergrad. Sch. of Mgmt. programs, 1998—; pvt. cons., 1981—, chmn. freshman seminar com., 1994; instr. principles of mktg. on The Learning Channel on Cable TV for the PACE Program, 1994; chmn. sch. mgmt. curriculum com., 1993—; co-chair Task Force on Diversity, 1997. Author: Personal Finance, 1983, Principles of Marketing Study Guide, 1993, Contemporary Marketing Study Guide, 1994, Consumer Behavior Study Guide, 1997, Instructor's Manual for Michael Solomon's Consumer Behavior; co-author: Instructor's Resource Manual and Video Guide for Philip Kotler's Marketing Management, 9th edit.; cooperating author: Philip Kotler's Marketing Management. Mem. alumni bd. assessment task force Rockhurst U., 1971-73, 78-80, chmn. 30 yr. reunion com., 1990, 35 yr. reunion com., 1995, chmn. curriculum com., curriculum task force; chmn. Eastwood Hills Coun., Kansas City, 1974-76, bd. dirs., 1988-91, co-chmn. of Solid Rocks Faculty-Staff Fund Raising Campaign, 1994; lead couple Marriage Preparation Classes, Kansas City St. Joseph Dioceses, 1983--; co-chmn. Kansas City Vols. Against Hunger, 1975-80; campaign mgr. Larry Ferns for City Coun., Kansas City, 1975; bd. govs. Citizens Assn., 1976—. With USAR, 1960-64. Recipient Gov.'s Excellence in Teaching award, Mo., 1993, Harry B. Kies award Rockhurst U.; Hallmark fellow Rockhurst U., 1981-86; faculty devel. grantee Sch. Mgmt., Rockhurst U., 1984, 93, 95, 99. Mem. Am. Mktg. Assn., Soc. for Advancement of Mgmt., Mid-Am. Mktg. Assn., Alpha Sigma Nu, Kappa Delta Pi. Roman Catholic. Avocations: gardening, genealogy, photography. Home: 11014 Washington St Kansas City MO 64114-5177 Office: Rockhurst U 1100 Rockhurst Rd Kansas City MO 64110-2508

SHAW, RICHARD EUGENE, cardiovascular researcher; b. Springfield, Ohio, Jan. 20, 1950; s. Eugene Russell and Marjorie Caroline Shaw; m. Nov. 26, 1976; 2 children. BA, Duquesne U., 1972; MA, U.S. Internat. U., San Diego, 1977; PhD, U. Calif., San Francisco, 1984. Cert. nuc. med. technologist. Nuclear Medicine Tech. Cert. Bd. Staff nuc. med. technologist Scripps Meml. Hosp., La Jolla, Calif., 1975-79; rsch. asst. U. Calif. San Francisco Sch. Medicine, 1980-85; mgr. rsch. programs San Francisco Heart Inst., Daly City, Calif., 1985-87, dir. rsch., 1988-90, dir. rsch. and ops., 1991—2003; dir. rsch., quality and edn. Sutter Pacific Heart Ctrs., 2003—. Sr. advisor steering com. for databases Daus. of Charity Nat. Health Sys., St. Louis, 1993-96. Editor-in-chief Jour. Invasive Cardiology, 1989—; contbr. more than 200 articles and book chpts. to med. lit. Coach Am. Youth Soccer Orgn. and Youth Baseball Assn., bd. dirs., Burlingame, Calif., 1990-94; pres. Burlingame H.S. Athletic Boosters, 2000—. Fellow Am. Coll. Cardiology (nat. cardiac database com., outcomes assessment subcom. 1998—, NCDR task force 2001—, publs. subcom. 2001—), Am. Coll. Angiology; mem. Am. Heart Assn., Soc. for Clin. Trials, N.Y. Acad. Scis., Am. Statis. Assn., Am. Med. Informatics Assn., Soc. Behavioral Medicine. Avocation: music. Office: Sutter Pacific Heart Ctr CPMC 2340 Clay St #120 San Francisco CA 94115 Office Phone: 415-600-5897. E-mail: shawr@sutterhealth.org.

SHAW, RICHARD GLENN, financial analyst; b. Queens, N.Y., Oct. 11, 1956; s. Martin and Patricia Ann Shaw; m. Karla K. Shaw; 1 child, Michael Stone. BA, Jacksonville U., 1978. CFP, Registry of Certified Financial Planning Practitioners. Mgr. real estate devel. firm, 1980-84; owner mktg. corp., 1985-88; fin. advisor Lincoln Fin. Group, Overland Park, Kans., 1988—. Bd. dirs., trustee U. Mo.-Kansas City Conservatory Music. Mem. Internat. Assn. Fin. Planning, Estate Planning Soc. Kansas City, Internat. Baseball Fedn. Office: Lincoln Fin Group 5343 N 16th St Ste 400 Phoenix AZ 85016

SHAW, RICHARD LESLIE, engineering company executive; b. Beaver, Pa., May 8, 1927; s. George L. and Marguerite (Clements) S.; m. Margaret Powell, Nov. 30, 1951; children: Leslie P., Sidney. BS, U. Pitts., 1950. Ordering corr. Westinghouse Elec. Corp., Beaver, 1950-52; with Michael Baker Jr. Inc., Beaver, 1952-73; pres. and chief exec. officer Michael Baker Corp., Beaver, 1984—, now chmn. bd. dirs. Mem. legis. com. Am. Pub. Transit Assn., Washington. Co-chmn. Beaver County Alliance of Southwestern Pa. Growth Alliance; bd. dirs. Profls. Coalition; pres., bd. dirs. United Way Beaver County, 1985-87. Served to sgt. U.S. Army, 1940-44. Mem. Pa. Cons. Engrs. Council (bd. dirs. 1987—), Engrs. Soc. Western Pa., Pa. SW Assn. (bd. dirs. 1978—), Beaver County Corp. Econ. Devel. (bd. dirs. 1985—), Corp. Owner/Operator Projects. (bd. dirs. 1984—). Republican. Presbyterian. Avocations: golf, reading. Home: 360 Lincoln Ave Beaver PA 15009-2316 also: Michael Baker Jr Inc PO Box 280 4301 Dutch Ridge Rd Beaver PA 15009-9600 Office: Michael Baker Jr Inc 100 Airside Dr Coraopolis PA 15108-4740

SHAW, ROBERT, newspaper editor; Bur. chief AP, Little Rock, 1980—. Office: Ste 100 10802 Executive Center Dr Little Rock AR 72211-4377

SHAW, ROBERT BURNS, poet, educator; b. Phila., July 16, 1947; s. Gordon Walter and Elizabeth Anne Shaw; m. Nancy Anne Olenchuk, June 21, 1969; children: Catherine Frances, Anthony Peter Gordon. BA, Harvard Coll., 1969; MPhil, Yale U., 1973, PhD, 1974. Briggs-Copeland lectr. English Harvard U., Cambridge, Mass., 1974-76; from asst. prof. to assoc. prof. English Yale U., New Haven, Conn., 1976-83; assoc. prof. English Mt. Holyoke Coll., South Hadley, Mass., 1983-91, prof. English, 1991—. Vis. prof. U. Fla., Gainesville, spring 1996. Author: (poetry collections) Comforting the Wilderness, 1977, The Wonder of Seeing Double, 1988, The Post Office Murals Restored, 1994, Below the Surface, 1999, Solving for X, 2002. Recipient James Boatwright prize for poetry, 1992, Hollis Summers prize, 2002; Creative Writing fellow NEA, 1987, fellow Ingram Merrill Found., 1990. Mem. Assn. Literary Scholars and Critics, Authors Guild, Poetry Soc. Am., Acad. Am. Poets. Democrat. Episcopalian. Avocations: walking, swimming, gardening. Office: Mt Holyoke Coll English Dept 50 College St South Hadley MA 01075 E-mail: rshaw@mtholyoke.edu.

SHAW, ROBERT E. carpeting company executive; b. Cartersville, GA, 1931; Pres., CEO, Star Finishing Co. Inc. (merged into Shaw Industries Inc.), Dalton, Ga., until 1969; now pres., CEO Shaw Industries Inc., Dalton, Ga., 1969-96, chmn., CEO, 1996—, also bd. dirs. Office: Shaw Industries Inc 616 E Walnut Ave Dalton GA 30721-4409

SHAW, ROBERT EUGENE, retired minister, administrator; b. Havre, Mont., Apr. 8, 1933; s. Harold Alvin and Lillian Martha (Kruse) S.; m. Marilyn Grace Smit, June 14, 1957; children: Rebecca Jean, Ann Elizabeth, Mark David, Peter Robert. BA, Sioux Falls Coll., 1955; MDiv, Am. Bapt. Sem. of West, 1958; DD (hon.), Ottawa u., 1976, Judson Coll., 1984. Ordained to ministry Am. Bapt. Chs. U.S.A., 1958. Pastor First Bapt. Ch., Webster City, Iowa, 1958-63, Cmty. Bapt. Ch., Topeka, Kans., 1963-68; sr. pastor Prairie Bapt. Ch., Prairie Village, Kans., 1968-78; pres., prof. religion Ottawa U., Kans., 1978-83; exec. minister Am. Bapt. Chs. Mich, East Lansing, 1983-98; ret., 1998; exec. min. emeritus Am. Bapt. Chs. Mich., 2000—. Mem. gen. bd. Am. Bapt. Chs. U.S.A., Valley Forge, Pa., 1972-80, nat. v.p., 1978-80; nat. v.p. Am. Bapt. Minister Coun., Valley Forge, 1969-72, nat. pres., 1972-75; nat. chair Am. Bapt. Evang. Team, 1988-93; mem. Internat. Commn. on Edn. and Evangelism, Bapt. World Alliance, 1990—; mem. nat. exec. com. Am. Bapt. Adminstrs. Colls. and Univs., 1980-82; vis. prof. Evangelism Ctrl. Bapt. Theol. Sem., Kansas City, 1999-2000. Bd. dirs. Kans. Ind. Coll.s Assn., 1980-82; trustee No. Bapt. Theol. Sem., Lombard, Ill., 1983-98, Kalamazoo Coll., Mich., 1983-92, Judson Coll., Elgin, Ill., 1983-96; dir. Webster City C. of C., 1961-62, Ottawa C. of C., 1980-82. Recipient Firman Early award Disting. ministry to ch. and comty. U. Sioux Falls, 1996.

SHAW, ROBERT GILBERT, state senator, restaurant executive; b. Erwin, N.C., Nov. 22, 1924; s. Robert Gilbert B. and Annie Elizabeth (Byrd) S.; m. Grace Lee Wilson, Jan. 29, 1951 (div. 1976); children: Ann Karlen, Barbara Jean; m. Linda Owens, May 27, 1982. AA, Campbell U., 1948; postgrad., U. N.C., 1948-50. Restaurateur, 1951—. County commr. County of Guilford, Greensboro, N.C., 1968-76; chair N.C. Rep. Party, Raleigh, 1975-77; minority leader N.C. Senate, Raleigh, 1984—; chair Guilford County Rep. Party, 1973-75; mem. Rep. Nat. Com., Washington, 1975-77. With USAAC, 1943-46. Named Legislator of Yr. Nat. Fedn. Wildlife, 1990. Mem. Elks (life, bd. govs. 1953—). Presbyterian. Avocations: fishing, hunting, politics. Home: 5105 Bennington Dr Greensboro NC 27410 Office: NC Senate 1129 Legislative Bldg Raleigh NC 27611 E-mail: RGB112224@aol.com.

SHAW, ROBERT WILLIAM, JR., management consultant, venture capitalist; b. Ithaca, N.Y., Aug. 10, 1941; s. Robert William and Charlotte G. (Throop) Shaw; m. Anne P. Meads, Aug. 29, 1964; children: Mark Andrew, Christopher Matthew. B of Engring. Physics, MSEE, Cornell U., 1964; PhD, Stanford U., 1968; MPA, Am. U., 1981. Postdoctoral fellow Cavendish Lab., Cambridge, Eng., 1968-69; mem. tech. staff Bell Tel. Labs., Murray Hill, NJ, 1969-72; with Booz Allen Hamilton, Bethesda, Md., 1972-83, sr. v.p. energy and environ. divsn., 1979-83, mem. oper. coun., 1981-83, also bd. dirs.; pres. Arete Ventures, Inc., 1983-97, Utech Venture Capital Corp., 1985—2003, Utech, LLC, 2003—; gen. ptnr. Utech Venture Capital Corp. Fund I, 1985—2000, Utech Venture Capital Corp. Fund II, 1988—2003, Utech Venture Capital Corp. I Parallel Fund L.P., 1988—2001, Utech Venture Capital Corp. II Parallel Fund, L.P., 1991—2003, Utech Climate Challenge Fund, L.L.C., Bethesda, 1995—; v.p. Can. Energy and Environment Ventures, Inc., 1993-95; pres. Arete Corp., Center Harbor, NH, 1997—. Spl. ltd. ptnr. Nth Power Techs. Fund II; mem. investment com. Sustainable Asset Mgmt. Pvt. Equity Fund, Commons Capital LLC; mng. ptnr. Micro-Generation Tech. Fund, LLC, 1997—; mem. bd. energy and environ. sys. Nat. Rsch. Coun.; mem. energy com. Aspen Inst. Humanistic Studies, Investor's Cir., Solar Cir.; bd. councillors China-U.S. Ctr. Sustainable Devel.; chmn. bd. dirs. CellTech Power, Inc., Distributed Energy Sys. Corp.; bd. dirs. Evergreen Solar, Inc., H2Gen Innovations, Inc. Contbr. articles to profl. jours. Named NASA trainee; Office Sci. Rsch. fellow, USAF, 1968—69. Mem.: AAAS, Social Venture Network, Inst. Noetic Scis., Assn. Humanistic Psychology, Orgnl. Devel. Network, Nat. Venture Capital Assn., Am. Phys. Soc., Tau Beta Pi, Sigma Xi, Kappa Delta Rho, Pi Alpha Alpha, Phi Kappa Phi. Home: PO Box 1664 Center Harbor NH 03226-1664 Office: PO Box 1299 Center Harbor NH 03226-1299 Office Phone: 603-253-9797. E-mail: aretecorp@cyberportal.net.

SHAW, RODERICK KIRKPATRICK, III, dentist; b. Tallahassee, Fla., Dec. 15, 1956; s. Roderick Kirkpatrick, Jr. and Floride Wilkinson Shaw; m. Kathleen Bentley, Jan. 11, 1991; 1 child, Roderick Kirkpatrick VIII. BS in Biochemistry, Auburn U., 1981; DMD, U. Fla. Coll. Dentistry, 1986, cert. comprehensive dental program #22, 2003. Pvt. practice, Madison, Fla., 1997—. Contbr. articles to profl. jours. Elder Madison Presbyn. Ch., Fla., 1996—2000; fin. chmn. First United Meth. Ch. of Madison, Fla., 2003; treas. Madison Presbyn. Ch., Fla., 1998—2000. Fellow: Acad. Gen. Dentistry; mem.: ADA, Comprehensive Dental Program 22, NE Dist. Dental Assn., Fla. Dental Assn., Fla. Acad. Cosmetic Dentistry. Conservative. Methodist. Avocations: boating, running. Home: 529 W Base St Madison FL 32340 Office: 317 N Duval St Madison FL 32340

SHAW, RONALD AHREND, physician, educator; b. Toledo, July 20, 1946; s. Harold Michael and Eve Helen (Ganch) S.; m. Carol Ann Rapp, June 13, 1970; children: Robert, Benjamin, Daniel. BS, U. Toledo, 1968; MD, Washington U., 1972. Diplomate Am. Bd. Emergency Medicine. Intern, then resident in surgery St. Luke's Hosp., St. Louis, 1972-73, resident in surgery, 1973; mem. staff Bapt. Med. Ctr.-Montclair, Birmingham, Ala., 1976-81, chief emergency svc., 1979-81; assoc. dir. lifesaver flight ops. Caraway Meth. Med. Ctr., Birmingham, 1981-85; dir. emergency svc. sch. medicine U. Ala., 1985-89; asst. dir. emergency svc. R.I. Hosp., Providence, 1989-95; attending physician emergency dept. Bapt. Med. Ctr., Montgomery, Ala., 1996—; med. dir. emergency dept. Jackson Hosp., 2000—01; sec.-treas., med. staff Bapt. Med. Ctr., 2001—03. Cons. U. Tex., Houston, 1986, Bell Helicopter, Ft. Worth, 1986, Mut. Assurance, Birmingham, 1986-89, NYU, 1988-89, R.I. State Med. Examiners Office, 1991-96, Fla. Dept. Health, EMS Office, 1991—, Joint Underwriters Assocs. of R.I., 1991-96; chmn. adv. bd. emergency svc. Ala. Dept. Pub. Health, 1986-89; med. dir. Emergency Med. Svcs. div. R.I. Dept. Health, 1990-95; med. dir. Health Care Rev., Inc., 1995-96. Bd. dirs. MADD, Ala., 1986, Univ. Emergency Medicine Found., 1995-96; mem. planning com. Youth Baseball, Vestavia Hills, ala., 1986, 87; mem. disaster com. City of Birmingham, 1984-89; mem. 911 Commn., State of R.I., 1991-96. Recipient Disting. Achievement award Birmingham Emergency Med. Svc., 1988. Fellow Am. Coll. Emergency Physicians (bd. dirs. Ala. chpt. 1984-89, steering com. EMS sect. 1991-94, sec.-treas. R.I. chpt. 1995-96); mem. AAAS, ACS (state com. on trauma R.I. chpt. 1990-96), N.Y. Acad. Sci., Med. Assn. Ala. (mem. coun. med. svc. 1985-86). Republican. Avocations: hunting, stamp collecting and computer programming.

SHAW, RUSSELL BURNHAM, author, journalist; b. Washington, May 19, 1935; s. Charles Burnham and Mary (Russell) S.; m. Carmen Hilda Carbon, July 19, 1958; children: Mary Hilda, Emily Anne, Janet, Charles, Elizabeth. BA, Georgetown U., 1956, MA, 1960. Staff writer Cath. Standard, Washington, 1956-57; reporter Nat. Cath. News Svc., 1957-66; dir. publs., pub. info. Nat. Cath. Ednl. Assn., 1966-69; dir. Nat. Cath. Office for Info., 1969-73; assoc. sec. for communication U.S. Cath. Conf., 1973-74, sec. for pub. affairs Nat. Conf. Cath. Bishops, 1975-87; dir. pub. info. KC, 1987-97; Washington corr. Our Sunday Visitor, 1997—; assoc. prof. Pontifical Univ. of the Holy Cross, 1996—; editor The Pope Speaks, 1998—. Consultor Pontifical Coun. for Social Comms., 1984—89, 2001—. Author: The Dark Disciple, 1961, Abortion on Trial, 1968, Church and State, 1979, Choosing Well, 1982, Why We Need Confession, 1986, Renewal, 1986, Signs of the Times, 1986, Does Suffering Make Sense?, 1987, To Hunt, To Shoot, To Entertain, 1993, Understanding Your Rights, 1994, Papal Primacy in the Third Millennium, 2000, Ministry or Apostolate—What Should the Catholic Laity Be Doing?, 2002; co-author: S.O.S. for Catholic Schools, 1970, Beyond the New Morality, 3d edit., 1988, Fulfillment in Christ, 1991,Personal Vocation, 2003, others; editor Ency. of Cath. Doctrine, 1997; columnist monthly mag. Washington Report, 1966—; columnist weekly newspaper Cath. Herald, 1999—. Mem. Equestrian Order of Holy Sepulchre of Jerusalem, Phi Beta Kappa. Roman Catholic. Home and Office: 2928 44th Pl NW Washington DC 20016-3555 Office Phone: 202-363-9566. Personal E-mail: rshaw10290@aol.com.

SHAW, RUTH G. energy company executive; m. Colin Stuart Shaw; 2 children. BA in English magna cum laude, East Carolina U.; PhD, U. Tex. Pres. Central Piedmont Cmty. Coll., 1986—92; v.p. corp. comms. Duke Energy Corp., Charlotte, NC, 1992-94, sr. v.p. corp. resources, 1994-97, exec. v.p., chief adminstrv. officer, 1997—2002, pres., 2003—, El Centro Coll., Dallas. Dir. Wachovia Corp., MedCath Corp.; mem. bd. dirs. Edison Electric Inst., Nuclear Energy Inst., S. E. Electric Exchange; chair Charlotte Rsch. Inst.; mem. Palmetto Bus. Forum. Mem. Order of the Long Leaf Pine; trustee U. N.C., Charlotte; bd. dirs. Rsch. Triangle Found. of N.C.; mem. Conf. Bd. Chief Adminstrv. Officer's Coun.; chmn. Found. for the Carolinas; elder 1st Presbyn. Ch., Charlotte; active United Way, Arts and Scis. Coun., YMCA, Boy Scouts Am. Named Outstanding Alumni, East Carolina U., disting. grad. U. Tex., Charlotte Woman of Yr., 1992, Businesswoman of Yr., 1995; recipient award for comms. excellence, 1997. Office: Duke Energy Corp 526 S Church St Charlotte NC 28202-1802

SHAW, SANDRA, newscaster; Student, U. Miss. Anchor WRKG-TV, Mobile, Ala.; weather anchor, reporter WRBL-TV, Columbus, Ga.; anchor NBC 17, Raleigh, NC. Vol. Duke Children's Hosp. Avocations: running, kickboxing, weightlifting, fishing, reading. Office: NBC 17 Studios 1205 Front St Raleigh NC 27609

SHAW, STANLEY MINER, nuclear pharmacy scientist; b. Parkston, S.D., July 4, 1935; s. George Henry and Jensina (Thompson) S.; m. Excellda J. Watke, Aug. 13, 1961; children: Kimberly Kay, Renee Denise, Elena Aimee. BS, S.D. State U., 1957, MS, 1959; PhD, Purdue U., 1962. Instr. S.D. State U., 1960-62; asst. prof. bionucleonics Purdue U., West Lafayette, Ind., 1962-66, assoc. prof., 1966-71, prof. nuclear pharmacy, 1971—, head. divsn. nuclear pharmacy, 1990—; acting head Purdue U. Sch. Health Scis., 1990-93. Bd. pharm. spltys. Splty. Council Nuclear Pharmacy, 1978-82. Contbr. articles to profl. jours. Recipient Lederle Pharmacy faculty awards, 1962, 65, Parenteral Drug Assn. Rsch. award, 1970, Henry Heine Outstanding Tchr. award Sch. Pharmacy Purdue U., 1989, 93, 99, Disting. Alumnus award S.D. State U.,

1991, Disting. Pharmacy Educator award AACP, 1994. Fellow Acad. Pharmacy Practice (chmn. sect. nuclear pharmacy 1979-80, historian 1981-85, mem.-at-large 1993-95, chmn.-elect 1995-96, chmn. 1996-97, Disting. Achievement award 1998), Am. Soc. Hosp. Pharmacy, Am. Pharm. Assn.; mem. Health Physics Soc., Am. Pharm. Assn. (ho. of dels. 1977, 79, 86, 92, Founder's award, Daniel B. Smith Practice Excellence award 2000), Sigma Xi, Phi Lambda Upsilon, Phi Lambda Sigma, Rho Chi. Home: 7208 W Greenview Dr Battle Ground IN 47920-9732 Office: Purdue U Sch Pharmacy West Lafayette IN 47907-1336 Office Phone: 765-494-1443.

SHAW, TALBERT O. university president; BD, Andrews U., 1963; MA, U. Chgo., 1968, PhD, 1973. Dean of students Oakwood Coll., Huntsville, Ala., 1965-71; dean Howard U., Washington, 1971-76; dean Coll. Arts and Scis. Morgan State U., Balt., 1976-87; pres. Shaw U., Raleigh, NC, 1987—2003.

SHAW, THEODORE M. legal association administrator; b. N.Y., Nov. 24, 1954; BA with honors, Wesleyan U., 1976; JD, Columbia U., 1979. Bar: Calif. Trial atty. Civil Rights Divsn. U.S. Dept. Justice, 1979—82; dir. ednl. docket NAACP Legal Def. and Ednl. Fund, 1982—87; assoc. dir.-counsel NAACP Legal Def. Edn. Fund, Inc., N.Y.C., 1993—2004, pres., dir.-counsel, 2004—; founder, counsel Legal Def. and Edn. Fund's Western Regional Office, 1987—90; faculty U. Mich. Law Sch., 1990—93. Recipient Lawrence A. Wein prize for social justice, Columbia U., Baldwin medal, Wesleyan U. Mem.: ABA, Langston Bar Assn., L.A. County Bar Assn., Nat. Bar Assn. (A. Leon Higginbotham Jr. Meml. award Young Lawyers Divsn.). Office: NAACP Legal Def and Ednl Fund Inc Ste 1600 99 Hudson St New York NY 10013*

SHAW, THERESA (TERRI) S. federal official; married; 2 children. BS, George Mason U., 1960; Grad. Exec. Devel. Program, George Washington U., 1991. From staff to sr. v.p. and chief info. officer SLM Corp., Reston, Va., 1988—99; exec. v.p., COO eNumerate Solutions, Inc, McLean, Va., 2000—02; COO Fed. Student Aid U. S. Dept. Edn., Washington, 2002—. Office: US Dept Edn 400 Maryland Ave SW Washington DC 20202

SHAW, TIANNA, biomedical engineer; married; 1 child. BS in Biomedical Engring., BSEE, U. So. Calif.; postgrad., Calif. State U., Sacramento. Exptl. facilities engr. NASA Ames Rsch. Ctr. Mem. multicultural leadership coun. NASA Ames Rsch. Ctr., chairperson Native Am. adv. com. Mem.: Am. Indian Sci. and Engring. Soc. (v.p. Calif. profl. chpt.). Office: NASA Ames Rsch Ctr Bldg 239 Rm 213 Moffett Field CA 94035 Business E-Mail: tshaw@mail.arc.nasa.gov.

SHAW, TIMOTHY MILTON, political science educator; b. Frimley, Surrey, Eng., Jan. 27, 1945; came to Can., 1971; s. Arnold J. and Margaret E. (Milton) S.; m. Jane L. Parpart, Sept. 2, 1983; children: Laura, Lee Parpart; m. Susan M. Sturt, July 8, 1967 (div. 1980); children: Benjamin, Amanda. BA, Sussex U., Brighton, Eng., 1967; MA, E. Africa U., Kampala, Uganda, 1969, Princeton U., 1971, PhD, 1975. Prof. polit. sci. Dalhousie U., Halifax, Canada, 1971—2002; dir. Ctr. African Studies, Halifax, 1983-89, Ctr. for Fgn. Policy Studies, Halifax, 1993-2000, Internat. Devel. Studies Program, 1986-89; dir. BA and MA program, 1998-2000; dir. Pearson Inst., Halifax, 1985-87, Canadian Internat. Devel. Agy., 1994-95. Vis. faculty Makerere U., Kampala, 1968-70, U. Zambia, Lusaka, 1973-74, Carleton U., Ottawa, Ont., Can., 1978-79, U. Ife, Nigeria, 1979-80, U. Zimbabwe, 1989, Rhodes U., South Africa, 1993, 2002-03, Warwick U., U.K., 1997, U. Western Cape & Stellenbosch U., South Africa, 1998—, Mbarara U. Sci. and Tech., 1998—, Aalborg U., 2000-01; cons. UN Econ. Commn. for Africa, Addis Ababa, Ethiopia, 1983-88 Editor: Palgrave Macmillan Internat. Polit. Economy Series, London, 1984—, Ashgate Publishing Series on the International Political Economy of New Regionalisms; author: Reformism and Revisionism in Africa's Political Economy in the 1990s, 1993, (with Julius Ihonvbere) Illusions of Power: Nigeria in Transition, 1998; co-editor: (with Julius Nyangoro) Beyond Structural Adjustment in Africa, 1992, Corporatism in Africa, 1988, (with Kevin Dunn) Africa's Challenge to International Relations Theory, 2001, (with Sandra Maclean & John Harker) Advancing Human Security & Development in Africa, 2002, (with Fredrik Soderbaum) Theories of New Regionalism: A Palgrave Reader, 2003, others. Mem. New Dem. Party, Halifax, 1984—. Grantee, Social Sci. & Humanities Rsch. Coun. Can., Africa, 1981—, Ford Found., 1999—2001. Mem. Internat. Polit. Soc. Assn. (chair rsch. com. #40 on New World Orders, 1997-2003), Can. Assn. Devel. Studies (pres. 1993-94), European Assn. Devel. Inst. (co-chmn. working group on new regionalisms), Can. Assn. African Studies (pres. 1984-85), Internat. Studies Assn. (pres. global devel. sect. 1995-96), Waegwoltic Club (Halifax). Avocations: jogging, cooking, building, travel. Home: 5556 Atlantic St Halifax NS Canada B3H 1G4 Office: Inst Commonwealth Studies U London 28 Russell Sq London WC1B 5DS England Fax: (44)20-7862 8813. Office Phone: (44)20-7862 8826. E-mail: tim.shaw@sas.ac.uk.

SHAW, WILLIAM FREDERICK, statistician; b. Bklyn., Feb. 24, 1920; s. Charles Peter and Josephine Veronica (Seusing) S.; m. Josephine Cannington Kerbey, Jan. 18, 1947; children— William Frederick, Teresa Anne. BBA, U. Miami, 1949; MA, George Washington U., 1953; postgrad. studies in econometrics, math. and computer scis., U.S. Dept. Agr. Grad. Sch., 1964-74; PhD (fellow), Walden U., 1977. Rsch. asst. U. Miami, 1948—49; with Rsch. and Stats. divsn. FHA, Washington, 1950—73, chief statistician Rsch. and Stats. divsn., 1969—; chief statistician, dir. Advanced Statis. Analysis and Computer Applications Staff HUD, 1974—82, chief statistician, dir. housing stats. divsn., 1982—89, chief statistician, dir. info. sys. divsn., 1990—91, chief statistician, dir. Office of Evaluation, 1991—. Pres. Kerbey-Shaw Assos. Served with F.A. AUS, 1943-45. Decorated Bronze Star medal valor in ground combat; recipient Superior Performance award HUD, 1977; named by Info. Resources Adminstrn. Coun. as Fed. Office Sys. Profl. of Yr., 1983. Mem. AAAS, Am. Statis. Assn., Am. Risk and Ins. Assn., Am. Real Estate and Urban Econ. Assn., Am. Econ. Assn., Am. Fin. Assn., N.Y. Acad. Scis., Nat. Assn. Rev. Appraisers and Mortgage Underwriters, Soc. Cost Estimating and Analysis, Res. Officers Assn. U.S., 101st Airborne Divsn. Assn., Air Force Assn., Alpha Kappa Psi. Roman Catholic. Home: 6527 Byrnes Dr Mc Lean VA 22101-5227 Office: HUD 7th And D Sts SW Washington DC 20411-0001

SHAW, WILLIAM J. hotel facility executive; b. Arlington, Va., Oct. 3, 1945; married; 3 children. BBA, U. Notre Dame, 1967; MBA, Washington U., 1972. With Arthur Andersen & Co., 1972-74, Marriott, 1974-79, corp. controller, 1979-82, corp. v.p., 1982-85, sr. v.p. fin., head dept. tax and risk mgmt., 1985-88, treas., 1986, CFO, exec. v.p., 1988-92; pres. Marriott's Svc. Group, 1992-97; pres., COO Marriott Internat., Inc., Washington, 1997—; chmn. bd. Host Marriott Svcs. Corp., Bethesda, Md., 1995-99, Sodexho Marriott Svcs., Gaithersburg, Md., 1998. Bd. trustees Suburban Hosp. Found.; Bd. trustees U. Notre Dame, South Bend, Ind. Office: Marriot Internat Marriot Dr Washington DC 20058-0001*

SHAW-COHEN, LORI EVE, magazine editor; b. Manhattan, N.Y., Apr. 22, 1959; d. Ray and Carole (Bergenthal) Shaw; m. Robert Mark Cohen, Sept. 20, 1981; children: Joshua Samuel, Drew Taylor, Logan Shaw. BA in Journalism, U. So. Calif., 1981. Editl. asst., writer BBW: Big Beautiful Woman Mag., L.A., 1979-80, Intro Mag., L.A., 1980-81; mng. editor 'Teen Mag., L.A., 1981-86. Writer, interviewer Stan Rosenfeld & Assocs. Pub. Rels., L.A., 1980-81; cons. BBW: Big Beautiful Woman Mag., 1981—, Media Rsch. Group, L.A., 1984; condr. seminars Women in Communication, L.A., 1983, Pacific N.W. Writers Conf., Seattle, 1984 Patentee children's toy, 1971; lyricist for songs, 1977—; contbr. articles and poems to profl. jours. and mags. Avocations: travel, reading, photography, horseback riding. Office: BBW: Big Beautiful Woman Mag 6666 Brookmont Ter Apt 412 Nashville TN 37205-4622

SHAWVER, LAURA K. biotechnology company executive; PhD Pharmacology, U. Iowa, 1983. With Triton Bioscis., 1989—92; from dir. preclin. devel. to sr. v.p. preclin. & pharm. devel. Sugen, Inc., San Francisco, 1992—2002. Office: 5871 Oberlin DR #200 San Diego CA 92121-3702

SHAY, ANTHONY VICTOR, choreographer, dance historian; b. L.A., Oct. 31, 1936; s. Jack Wendell Shay and Margaret Martha Read. MLS, UCLA, L.A., 1963; MA anthropology, Calif. State Univ., L.A., 1970; MA, UCLA, 1971; PhD dance hist. and theory, Univ. Calif. Riverside, Riverside, Calif., 1997. Artistic dir. Aman Folk Ens., L.A., 1960—77, Avaz Internat. Dance Theatre, L.A., 1977—. Author: Choreographic Politics, 2002 (Outstanding dance svc., 2002), Chorephobia, 1999; choreographer over 250 works (Calif. Arts Coun. Lifetime Acheivement award, 2001). James Irvine Choreographic fellow, 1998, Soc. Sci. Rsch. Coun. fellow, 2000, NEH fellow, 2003. Home: 3756 Aloha St Los Angeles CA 90027

SHAY, ROSHANI CARI, political science educator; b. Milw., Oct. 5, 1942; d. Walter John and Dorothee May (Dahnke) O'Donnell; 1 child, Mark Sather. Student, Willamette U., 1960—63; BA, U. Oreg., 1968, MA, 1971, PhD, 1974. Adminstrv. asst. Dept. of Youth Svcs., Lubbock, Tex., 1963; tchg. asst., instr. U. Oreg., Eugene, 1969-72; vis. asst. prof. Oreg. State U., Corvallis, 1973-74, Willamette U., Salem, Oreg., 1973-79, Lewis and Clark Coll., Portland, Oreg., 1976, 78; from asst. prof. to prof. Western Oreg. U., Monmouth, 1979—2003, chair history, polit. sci., pub. adminstrn. dept., 1991-94, chair social sci. divsn., 1994-2000; exec. dir. Hawaii Wellness Inst., Honolulu, 2003—. Author: (with others) The People of Rajneeshpuram, 1990, Annual Yearbook in the Sociology of Religion, 1995, (simulation) European Unity Project, 1982. Co-founder, v.p., sec.-treas Ind. Opportunities Unltd., Salem, 1986—; co-founder, sec. Inst. for Justice and Human Rights, San Francisco, 1988-94; bd. dirs. Oreg. UN Assn., Portland, 1982-2000, Salem UN Assn., 1982-91; v.p., pres., bd. dirs. Garten Svcs. Inc. for Disabled, Salem, 1989-2003; pres. Assn. Oreg. Faculties, 1989-91; adv. bd. Connections Program for Disabled Deaf, Salem, 1989-2003, pres., bd. dirs. Model UN of the Far West, San Francisco, 1981-84, 86-88, 95-2000, 2002-03; Oreg. Women's Polit. Caucus. Danforth Found. fellow, 1968-74; named Woman of Achievement YWCA Tribute, Salem, 1990, Mem. of Yr., Oreg. Rehab. Assn., 1995. Mem. AAUW, Am. Fedn. Tchrs. (v.p., legis. officer local 2278 1982-88), Western Polit. Sci. Assn., Communal Studies Assn., Mental Health Assn. Oreg., Oreg. Acad. Sci., Soc. for Utopian Studies, Oreg. Hosp. Found., Oreg. Internat. Coun., Oreg. Mediation Assn., Phi Kappa Phi (pres., sec., treas.), Phi Alpha Delta (Outstanding Faculty Advisor in USA, 2000). Democrat. Avocations: volunteer work with multiply disabled deaf, reading, meditation. Home: 3355 Paty Dr Honolulu HI 96822 Office: Hawaii Wellness Inst 3670 Kalihi St Honolulu HI 96819 Office Phone: 808-848-5544. Business E-Mail: shayr@wou.edu. E-mail: hwi@earthlink.net.

SHAYE, ROBERT KENNETH, cinema company executive; s. Max and Dorothy S.; m. Eva G., 1970; children: Katja, Juno. BBA, U. Mich., 1960; postgrad., Sorbonne U., 1961; JD, Columbia U., 1964. Bar: N.Y. 1967. Chmn. of the bd., CEO New Line Cinema Corp., N.Y.C., 1967—. Trustee Columbia Coll., Chgo. Bd. dirs. Legal Aid Soc., N.Y.C. Recipient 1st prize Rosenthal competition Soc. Cinematologists, 1964; recipient cert. of merit Inst. Copyrights and Patents, U. Stockholm, 1966; Recipient award ASCAP/Nathan Burkan Meml. competition, 1964; Fulbright scholar, 1964-66. Mem. Motion Picture Pioneers (bd. dirs.), Friar's Club (N.Y.C.). Office: New Line Cinema 116 N Robertson Blvd West Hollywood CA 90048-3103 also: New Line Cinema Corp 888 7th Ave Fl 19 New York NY 10106-2599 Office Phone: 310-854-5811., 212-649-4900. *Life is a lot tougher than television watching in the '50's led me to believe.*

SHAYMAN, JAMES ALAN, nephrologist, educator; b. Chgo., June 14, 1954; s. Benjamin and Chernie (Abrams) S.; children: Rebecca Lynn, David Aaron. AB, Cornell U., 1976; MD, Washington U., St. Louis, 1980. Intern and resident Barnes Hosp., St. Louis, 1980-83; instr. Washington U., St. Louis, 1985-86; asst. prof. U. Mich., Ann Arbor, 1986-92, assoc. prof., 1992-97; prof. internal medicine and pharmacology, 1997—; assoc. chair rsch. programs dept. internal medicine U. Mich., Ann Arbor, 1997—. Mem. Am. Soc. Nephrology, Internat. Soc. Nephrology, Am. Diabetes Assn., Am. Soc. Clin. Investigation, Am. Physiol. Soc., Phi Beta Kappa, Phi Kappa Phi, Alpha Omega Alpha. Achievements include research in renal inositol phosphate metabolism and renal glycolipid metabolism.

SHAYS, CHRISTOPHER, congressman; b. Darien, Conn., Oct. 18, 1945; m. Betsi deRaismes, 1968; 1 child. BA, Principia Coll., 1968; MBA, NYU, 1974, MPA, 1978. Vol. U.S. Peace Corps, 1968-70; state rep. State of Conn. (Dist. 147), Stamford, 1974—87; mem. U.S. Congress from 4th Conn. Dist., Washington, 1987—, mem. fin. svcs. com., vice chmn. govt. reform com., vice chmn. budget com., mem. select com. on homeland securitychmn. subcom. on nat. security. Republican. Office: House of Reps 1126 Longworth Ho Office Bldg Washington DC 20515-0704 also: 10 Middle St 11th Fl Bridgeport CT 06604 also: Government Center 888 Washington Blvd Stamford CT 06901

SHAYWITZ, BENNETT ARTHUR, medical educator; MD, Yale U., 1963. Prof. pediats. and neurology Sch. Medicine Yale U., 1972—; co-founder, co-director National Inst. Child Health & Human Development-Yale Ctr. for the Study of Learning and Attention. Mem.: Inst. Medicine. Office: Yale New Haven Hosp LMP 3089 20 York St New Haven CT 06504-8900

SHAYWITZ, SALLY E. pediatrics educator; Grad., CUNY; MD, Albert Einstein Coll. Medicine. Resident pediat. Albert Einstein Coll. Medicine, postdoctoral fellow in developmental/behavioral pediat.; faculty mem. Yale U., 1979—, founder, dir. learning disabilities unit dept. pediat., co-dir. Ctr. for the Study of Learning and Attention, prof. pediat. Participant Nat. Summit on Learning Disabilities; spl. advisor U.S. Congress, U.S. Dept. Edn.; cons. Nat. Inst. Child Health and Human Devel., Nat. Inst. Deafness and Other Comm. Disorders; spkr. in field. Active Nat. Reading Panel; mem. com. to prevent reading difficulties in young children Nat. Rsch. Coun. Recipient Disting. Alumnus award Albert Einstein Coll. Medicine, 1995, Clin. Svc. award Soc. for the Advancement of Women's Health Rsch., 1998. Mem. NAS-Inst. Medicine, Dana Alliance for Brain Initiatives, Phi Beta Kappa. Achievements include research on differences between dyslexic and nonimpaired readers in the neural circuitry of the brain for reading; principal investigator of the Connecticut Longitudinal Study a prospective study of reading development based on a representative sample of school children followed since kindergarten. Office: Yale-New Haven Hosp Childrens Hosp 20 York St LMP 3089 New Haven CT 06504 E-mail: sally.shaywitz@yale.edu.

SHCHERBAKOVA, ESTELLA, chemist, mathematician, educator; b. Dnepropetrovsk, Ukraine, Oct. 15, 1938; arrived in Russia, 1951,arrived in U.S., 1994; d. Stepan and Fira (Poltorak) Masko; m. Stanislav Shcherbakov; 1 child, Yuriy Shcherbakov. MA math and drawing, State Pedagogical Inst., Moscow, Russia, 1956—61; PhD chem. sci., Post grad. Sch. of L. Karpov Rsch. Physical Chem. Inst., Moscow, Russia, 1968—74. Math tchr. HS #79, Moscow, 1961—62; engr. State Inst. of Caouchouc, Moscow, 1962—64; sci. worker from jr. to maj. L. Karpov Rsch. Phys. Chem. Inst., Moscow, 1964—94. Cons. and joint rsch. Inst. of Thin Chem. Tech., Moscow, 1971—89, State External Polytech. Inst., Moscow, 1978—90. Co-author: (articles) 113 articles, SU Jour. Miscellaneous reports, 1961—91, (book, monograph) Math Matters of Investigation of Chem. Equilib., 1978, (3 inventions) SU Bull. of Inventions, 1985, 1992—93. Recipient Semicentennial, L. Karpov Inst./ Moscow, Russia, 1988. Finding common math tech. for investigation of the multiple equilibriums in solutions and applying it to various chem. sys., including solutions of bromine and iodine that brought to inventions of Indsl. modus of their deriving from a leach. Finding the method for nonlinear optimizations; as to apply non-equilibrium thermodynamics to processes of polymerizations. Home: 2820 W 32nd St Apt 3E Brooklyn NY 11224 E-mail: shchest@aol.com. *She evacuated in Kuybishev (Samara) Russia, 1941-1945; resided in Mosco from 1951 because of father's job in aerospace engineering.*

SHE, QING-BAI, biologist, researcher; s. Changan She and Xiuyun Huang; m. Qing Ye; children: Yixia, Brian Minghan. BS, Fuzhou U., China, 1980—84; MS, Gifu U., Japan, 1990—92, PhD, 1992—95. Scientist Akitaya-Hoten Co., Gifu, Japan, 1995—97; postdoctoral fellow Chinese U. Hong Kong, 1997—98, U. Minn., Austin, 1998—2001, Mt. Sinai Sch. of Medicine, New York, NY, 2001—02; sr. rsch. scientist Meml. Sloan-Kettering Cancer Ctr., N.Y.C., 2002—. Contbr. articles to profl. jours.; manuscript reviewer Jour. Chromatography B Biomed. Scis. and Applications, 2000—01. Mem.: Am. Assn. Cancer Rsch. (assoc.). Achievements include patents pending for Placental alkaline phosphatase promotes mitogenesis in cells derived from human fetus: placental alkaline phosphatase is a potential growth factor for the fetus. Avocations: travel, ping pong/table tennis, volleyball. Office: Meml Sloan-Kettering Cancer Ctr 1275 York Ave Box 271 New York NY 10021

SHEA, BERNARD CHARLES, retired pharmaceutical company executive; b. Bradford, Pa., Aug. 7, 1929; s. Bernard and Edna Catherine (Green) S.; m. Marilyn Rishell, Apr. 12, 1952; children— David Charles, Melissa Leone. BS in Biology, Holy Cross Coll., Worcester, Mass. Dir. mktg. Upjohn Co., Kalamazoo, Mich., 1954-80; pres. pharm. div. Pennwalt Corp., Rochester, N.Y., 1980-86, v.p. health div. Phila., 1986, sr. v.p. health div., 1987-88, sr. v.p. chemicals, 1988-89; group pres. Atochem N.Am., Inc., Phila., 1989-90, pharm. cons., 1990-93. Served to lt. (j.g.) USN, 1951-54, Korea

SHEA, BRENT MACK, social sciences educator; b. Oneida, NY, June 3, 1946; s. Mack Evered and Alice May (Meeker) Shea. BA, SUNY, Binghamton, 1968, MA, 1972, PhD, 1977. Vis. instr. Harpur Coll. SUNY, Binghamton, 1975-76, resident dir. Coll.-in-the-Woods, 1976-78, rsch. assoc., 1977-78; from asst. prof. to prof. Sweet Briar Coll., Va., 1978—92, chmn. dept. anthropology and sociology, 1986—90, prof., 1992—, chmn. dept. anthropology and sociology, 1996—99. Vis. fellow Yale U., New Haven, 1984—85, postdoctoral fellow, 1985—86; sci. collaborator Centro studi per l'Evoluzione Umana, Rome, 1990—; vis. scholar Summer Inst. Survey Rsch. U. Mich., 1991; presenter, rschr. in field. Co-editor, contbg. author: Social Psychiatry across Cultures, 1995, editor: conf. procs. Work and Mental Health, 1996; mem. editl. bd. Internat. Scope Rev., 1999—; co-editor: Internat. Scope Rev., 2000—01; contbr. articles to profl. jour., chapters to books. Regents scholar, Harpur Coll. SUNY, 1964—68, Faculty Rsch. fellow, Sweet Briar Coll., 1984—85, 1992—93, NIMH Postdoctoral Rsch. fellow, Instn. Social and Policy Studies, Yale U., 1985—86. Mem.: AAUP (chpt. pres. 1996—99, chair state com. on coll. and univ. governance 1998—2001, state exec. com. 1998—2001), Va. Sociol. Assn. (mem. exec. com. 1980—81, pres.), Ea. Eddl. Rsch. Assn. (dir. rsch. ethics 1979—83, bd. dirs. 1979—85, gen. sec. 1983—85), Ius Primi Viri Internat. Assn. Rome (v.p. bd. govs. 1994—), Internat. Sociol. Assn. (v.p. exec. bd. 1994—98, mental health and illness rsch. com.), Am. Sociol. Assn. (task force on internat. focus of Am. sociology 1999—2002), Soc. Automotive Historians. Avocations: classical piano, classic cars. Home: PO Box 1 Sweet Briar VA 24595-0001 Office: Sweet Briar Coll Dept Anthropology & Sociology Sweet Briar VA 24595

SHEA, CHRISTINA, former mayor; Mayor City of Irvine, Calif., 1996—2000; pres. Christina Shea Consulting. E-mail: christina@christinashea.com.

SHEA, DANIEL BARTHOLOMEW, JR., English language educator, actor; b. Mpls., Oct. 29, 1936; s. Daniel Bartholomew and Dorothea (Lonergan) S.; m. Kathleen Anne Williams, June 3, 1978; children: Timothy, Matthew, Catherine, Daniel, Emily. BA summa cum laude, Coll. St. Thomas, 1958; MA, Stanford U., 1962, PhD, 1966. Teaching asst. Stanford U., 1959-61; instr. to prof. English Washington U., St. Louis, 1962—, chmn. dept., 1978-84, 95-98; acting chair performing arts, prof. drama, 1995. Fulbright-Hays lectr. Univs. of Caen and Nice, France, 1968-69; vis. fellow Clare Hall, U. Cambridge, Eng., 1984-85 Author: Spiritual Autobiography in Early America, 1968, 2d edit., 1988; editorial bd.: Early Am. Lit, 1972-74; sect. editor: Columbia Literary History of the United States; contbr. chpts. to books. Woodrow Wilson fellow, 1958; NEH summer grantee, 1971 Mem. MLA (del. gen. assembly 1977-78), AFTRA, Equity, Phi Beta Kappa. Home: 6138 Kingsbury Ave Saint Louis MO 63112-1102 Office: Washington Univ Dept of English Saint Louis MO 63130 E-mail: dbshea@artsci.wustl.edu.

SHEA, DAVID MICHAEL, state supreme court justice; b. Hartford, July 1, 1922; s. Michael Peter and Margaret (Agnes) S.; m. Rosemary Anne Sasseen, Apr. 28, 1956; children: Susan, Kathleen, Margaret, Rosemary, Christina, Michael, Maura, Julie BA, Wesleyan U., 1944; LLB, Yale U., 1948. Bar: Conn. 1948. Assoc. Tunick & Ferris, Greenwich, Conn., 1948-49; assoc. Bailey & Wechsler, Hartford, 1949-57; ptnr. Bailey, Wechsler & Shea, Hartford, 1957-65; judge Conn. Superior Ct., Hartford, 1966-81; justice Conn. Supreme Ct., Hartford, 1981-92, state judge referee, 1992—. Served with U.S. Army, 1943-46 Democrat. Roman Catholic. Office: Conn Superior Ct 95 Washington St Hartford CT 06106-4431

SHEA, DEBBIE BOWMAN, state legislator; b. Butte, Mont., June 26, 1951; divorced. BS in Elem. Edn., Eastern Mont. Coll., 1974; MA in Edn., U. Mont., 1989. Formerly tchr. 8th grade pub. schs.; mem. Mont. Ho. of Reps., 1994-96, Mont. Senate, Dist. 18, Helena, 1997—; mem. joint appropriations subcom. on corrections/pub. safety Mont. Senate; mem. edn. and cultural resources com. Mont. State Senate, mem. hwys. and transp. com., mem. fin. and claims com. Democrat. Home: 100 Moon Ln Butte MT 59701-3975

SHEA, DERMOT P. consumer advocate, lawyer; b. Springfield, Mass., Sept. 3, 1916; s. Michael Ignatius and Madeleine Helena (Mahoney) S. Student, U. Ottawa, 1934-36; JD, Boston Coll., 1939. Bar: D.C. 1950, U.S. Ct. Appeals (D.C. cir.) 1951, U.S. Supreme Ct. 1963. Law clk. Law Office of John D. O'Connor, Chicopee Falls, Mass., 1939-40; asst. to chief of press Fed. Pub. Housing Authority, Washington, 1941; pub. info. officer USIA, Washington, 1941; asst. to office of the chief Office of War Info., Washington, 1941-42; regional pub. rels. officer War Shipping Adminstrn., New London, Conn., 1942-46; claims atty. Aetna Casualty Ins. Co., Springfield, Mass., 1946-64; consumer advisor Spkr. of Mass. Ho. of Reps., Boston, 1972-85; pres. Mass. Consumers Assn., Boston, 1976-80; consumer advisor Mass. Consumers' Coalition, Boston, 1980—. Aide de camp Gov. Endicott Peabody, Boston, 1963-64. Exec. sec. Mass. Consumers Coun., Boston, 1964-72; bd. dirs. Consumer Fedn. of Am., Washington, 1989-98, Boston Concert Opera, 1979-84; town moderator Town Meeting, Granby, Mass., 1963-69; mem. Ward 5 Dem. Com., Boston, 1986—. Lt. U.S. Maritime Svc., 1942-46. Recipient Esther Peterson Consumer Svc. award, Consumer Fedn. Am., 2001. Democrat. Roman Catholic. Home: 1109 Boylston St Apt 1 Boston MA 02215

SHEA, DION WARREN JOSEPH, university official, fund raiser; b. New London, Conn, June 10, 1937; s. Frank Steven and Violette Marie (Dion) S.; m. Elizabeth M. Siaba, Dec. 31, 1986; children from previous marriage: Dion Warren Joseph, Nancy Wallace. AB, ScB in Physics, Brown U., 1959; MA in Physics, Boston U., 1962; PhD in Physics, U. Colo., 1968. Mem. tech. staff RCA, 1959-62; asst. prof. physics Creighton U., 1967-68; NRC/Environ. Sci. Svc. Adminstrn. fellow, rsch. assoc. Environ. Sci. Svc. Adminstrn., Boulder, Colo., 1968-70; exec. dir. Soc. Physics Students, Am. Inst. Physics, 1970-87, mgr. edn. div., 1972-87; cons. ednl. and computer sytems, 1988—; dir. alumni affairs US Mcht. Marine Acad., Kings Point, NY, 1989-93; asst. dir. devel. CUNY Grad. Sch., 1993-99. Author sci. articles. Fellow AAAS; mem. Am. Phys. Soc., Am. Assn. Physics Tchr., Assn. Coll. Honor Soc. (exec. com. 1984-86), Am. Soc. Assn. Exec., Assn. Fundraising Profl., Planned Giving Group Greater NY, Coun. Advancement and Support Edn., Sigma Xi, Sigma Pi Sigma, Sigma Chi, Huntington Bicycle Club (treas. 2000-01), Colo. Mountain Club, Port Dive Club (treas. 1980-83). Home: 11821 Lionel Ln Golden CO 80403 Office: 11821 Lionel Ln Golden CO 80403 Office Phone: 303-642-0699. E-mail: Dion_Shea@yahoo.com.

SHEA, DONALD WILLIAM, priest, retired military officer; b. Butte, Mont., Apr. 15, 1936; s. Edward Joseph and Agnes C. (Stanton) S. BA, Carroll Coll., 1958; BTh, St. Paul (Minn.) Sem., 1962; MA in Human Rels., U. Okla., 1984; MEd, L.I. U., 1975; MA in Pers. Mgmt., Cen. Mich. U., 1981. Ordained priest Roman Cath. Ch., 1962. Commd. 1st lt. U.S. Army, 1966, advanced through grades to maj. gen.; student Basic Chaplain Officer Sch., Ft. Hamilton, N.Y., 1966, Airborne Sch., Ft. Bragg, N.C., 1966; with 3d Brigade, 5th Inf. Div. Dept. of the Army, Ft. Carson, Colo., 1966; student spl. forces officer course Ft. Bragg, N.C., 1967; chaplain 10th Spl. Forces Group Dept. of the Army,

Bad Toelz, Germany, 1967, chaplain 5th Spl. Forces Group Vietnam, 1968, chaplain 1st Brigade, 7th Inf. Div., 1969, chaplain 15th Field Arty. Group, 1970, chaplain 4th Bn., 10th Inf., 1972, chaplain 2d Brigade, 9th Inf. Div., 1975, chaplain 1st Brigade, 1st Armored Div., 1977; student Command and Gen. Staff Coll., Ft. Leavenworth, Kans., 1978; div. chaplain 1st Armored Div. Dept. of the Army, Germany, 1978, with office Chief of Chaplains, 1979; student U.S. Army War Coll., Carlisle Barracks, Pa., 1984; chaplain VII Corps U.S. Army, Germany, 1984; staff chaplain U.S. Army Europe, 7th Army U.S. Army War Coll., Germany, 1986; exec. officer, chief of chaplains U.S. Army, Washington, 1989; dep. chief of chaplains U.S. Army War Coll., Washington, 1990-94; chief of chaplains U.S. Army, 1994-99; pastor St. Patrick Parish and St. Joseph Parish, Butte, Mont., St. Catherine Cath. Parish, Bigfork, Mont., 2003—, St. Ann's Parish, Somers, Mont. Civilian aide Sec. of the Army for Mont., 2003—. Trustee Carroll Coll., Helena, Mont. Apptd. Domestic Prelate Pope John Paul II, 1992. Office: St Catherine Parish PO Box 277 105 Oliver Ln Bigfork MT 59911*

SHEA, EDWARD EMMETT, lawyer, educator, author; b. Detroit, May 29, 1932; s. Edward Francis and Margaret Kathleen (Downey) S.; m. Ann Marie Conley, Aug. 28, 1957; children: Michael, Maura, Ellen. AB, U. Detroit, 1954; JD, U. Mich., 1957. Bar: Mich. 1957, Fla. 1959, N.Y. 1961. Assoc. Simpson Thacher & Bartlett, N.Y.C., 1960-63, Dykema, Wheat, Spencer, Detroit, 1963-69, Cadwalader Wickersham & Taft, N.Y.C., 1969-71; v.p., gen. counsel, chmn. Reichhold Chems., White Plains, N.Y., 1971-81; adj. prof. Pace U. Grad. Sch. Bus., N.Y.C., 1982—; counsel, ptnr. Windels, Marx, Davies & Ives, N.Y.C., 1982-84; ptnr. Windels, Marx, Lane & Mittendorf, N.Y.C., 1986—; sr. v.p., gen. counsel GAF Corp., 1984-86. Sec. Peridot Chems., 1988-97; lectr. N.Y. Inst. Fin., 1995—. Author: An Introduction to the U.S. Environmental Laws, 1995, The Lead Regulation Handbook, 1996, The McGraw-Hill Guidebook to Acquiring and Divesting Businesses, 1998, Environmental Law and Compliance Methods, 2002; editor: The Acquisitions Yearbook, 1991-93; contbr. articles to profl. jours. Mem. adv. bd. N.Y. State Small Bus. Ctr. Program, 1988-93. 1st lt. JAGC, USAF, 1957-60. Mem. N.Y. Athletic Club. Office: Windels Marx Lane & Mittendorf 156 W 56th St Fl 23 New York NY 10019-3867 Office Phone: 212-237-1140. E-mail: eshea@windelsmarx.com.

SHEA, GWYN, former secretary of state; 2 children. Student, U. North Tex.; student, Dallas Baptist U.; grad., Dallas Baptist U. Police Acad. Served Tex. Ho. Reps., 1982—92, Ho. Ways and Means Com., Ho. Ins. Com.; pres. Nat. Coun. Ins. Legislators; apptd. Tex. Worker's Compensation Ins. Facility, 1995; Sec. of State State of Tex., 2002—03. Constable Dallas County Precint 2 Irving, Coppell, North Dallas, 1994, 96, 2000. Pres. Tex. Healthy Kids Corp., 1997; former dir. Irving C. of C.; past pres. Women's Divsn. of C.; mem. adv. bd. Irving CARES, Profl. Secs. Internat.; mem. 1st Baptist Ch., Irving; mem. adv. bds. Irving Infant Intervention Ctr. Named to legis. commitment to people of Tex., Tex. Mun. League, Tex. Assn. Bus., Tex. Civil Justice League, Tex. Assn. Concerned Tax Payers; recipient Legislative Leadership award, Tex. C. of C. Republican.

SHEA, JAMES BRYAN, writer; b. Newark, N.J., Sept. 19, 1954; s. Francis V. and Jeanne R. Shea. BA in History, Mt. St. Mary's Coll., 1976. Author: SERIAL, 2000, Diary of the Unspoken, 2002. Bd. dirs. Cmty. YMCA, Red Bank, NJ, 1990—. Mem.: Affiliated Rep. Club Monmouth County. Republican. Roman Cath. Home: PO Box 183 Hazlet NJ 07730

SHEA, JAMES F. manufacturing executive; CEO Fairmont Homes, Nappanee, Ind. Office: Fairmont Homes 502 S Oakland Ave Nappanee IN 46550-2332

SHEA, JAMES WILLIAM, lawyer; b. N.Y.C., July 10, 1936; s. William P. and Mildred E. (McCaffrey) S.; m. Ann Marie Byrne, June 6, 1964; children: James T., Kathleen A., Tracy A. BS, St. Peters Coll., 1957; JD, Fordham U., 1962; LLM in Taxation, NYU, 1965. Bar: N.Y. 1962, U.S. Dist. Ct. (so. and ea. dists.) N.Y. 1966, U.S. Supreme Ct. 1967. Revenue agt. U.S. Treasury Dept., N.Y.C., 1961-63; tax atty. Kennecott Copper Corp., N.Y.C., 1963-67; tax counsel CBS Inc., N.Y.C., 1968-71; ptnr. Hunton & Williams and predecessor firm Conboy, Hewitt, O'Brien & Boardman, N.Y.C., 1971—2001, sr. counsel, 2001—. Rep. committeeman, S.I., N.Y., 1980; mem. adv. com. tax and fin. N.Y. State Charter Commn. City of S.I. Served to 1st lt. U.S. Army, 1957-61, to capt. USAR, 1962-72. Mem. N.Y. State Bar Assn., Richmond County Country Club S.I. (sec. 1993-96, v.p. 1996-98, pres. 1998-2000, bd. dirs. 1993-2004). Republican. Roman Catholic. Home: 399 Tysens Ln Staten Island NY 10306-2844 Office: Hunton & Williams 200 Park Ave Rm 4300 New York NY 10166-0091 Office Phone: 718-987-9798. E-mail: jws@si.rr.com.

SHEA, JIM, Olympic athlete; b. Hartford, Conn., June 10, 1968; Mem. U.S. Skeleton Team. Vol. fireman, Lake Placid, NY. Named Athlete of Month, USA Today, 1995, Rookie of Yr., 1995; recipient Gold medal, Nat. Championships, Lake Placid, 1996, 1st pl., Push Championships, 1995, 1997, 1998, Gold medal, Skeleton World Cup, 1998, Stubai Cup, 1999, 1st pl., Skeleton World Championship, Winterberg, Germany, 1999, Gold medal, Winter Goodwill Games, Lake Placid, 2000; mem., US Nat. Team and World Cup Team, 9502, 1st American to win World Cup, 10 World Cup medals worldwide. Address: PO Box 681367 Park City UT 84068 Office Phone: 435-602-6786. E-mail: dkeletonwc@aol.com.

SHEA, JOHN F. construction executive, contractor; Pres., prin., owner J.F. Shea Co., Inc., Redding, Calif., 1968—. Office: JF Shea Co Inc 655 Brea Canyon Rd Walnut CA 91789 Fax: 530-246-9940.

SHEA, JOHN JOSEPH, electrical engineer; b. Buffalo, Aug. 18, 1962; s. John Anthony and Julia Anne (Browne) S.; m. Lisa Anne Hahne, Nov. 4, 1989. PhD in Elec. Engring., SUNY, Buffalo, 1989. Sr. engr. Westinghouse Sci. and Tech. Ctr., Pitts., 1988—94; consulting engr. Eaton Elec., Pitts., 1994—. Contbr. over 27 articles to profl. jours. Recipient Erle Shobert Prize paper, 2002; Hughes Aircraft fellow, 1985. Mem. IEEE (sr. mem.), Tau Beta Pi, Eta Kappa Nu. Achievements include 12 patents in arc interruption and conductive current limiting polymers; created plasma physics lab. at Eaton Electrical. Office: Eaton Elec RIDC Park W 170 Industry Dr Pittsburgh PA 15275-1014

SHEA, MARTIN M. communications executive; BS, U. Harford. Various positions, investor relations Paramount Comm. Inc. (formerly Gulf & Western), 1977—94; v.p. investor relations Viacom, Inc. (formerly Triarc Companies, Inc.), 1994; sr. v.p., corp. comm. Viacom, Inc., sr. v.p., investor relations, 1998—. Office: Viacom Inc 1515 Bdwy New York NY 10036

SHEA, MEGAN CARROLL, lawyer, law educator; b. Lake Forest, Ill., Sept. 7, 1967; d. Barry Joseph and Barbara (Pehrson) C.; m. Timothy J. Shea II. Student, Middlebury Coll., Paris, 1987-88; BA in Philosophy, French Lit., Boston Coll., 1989, JD, 1992. Bar: Mass., 1993, Ill. 1994, D.C. 1995. Law clk. Middlesex County Probate & Family Ct., Cambridge, Mass., 1990-91; assoc. Powers & Hall, Boston, 1991; asst. dist. atty. Norfolk County, Mass., 1992; prin., owner Carroll Assocs., Counsel for the Arts, Boston, 1994—. Bd. dirs. Carroll Internat. Corp., Des Plaines, Ill.; adj. prof. law New Eng. Sch. Law, 1998—. Arts review writer various publs. Mem. Am. Ireland Fund, Boston, Chgo., 1985—, Phillips Acad. Alumni Coun., Andover, Mass., 1991-95; trustee Regency Pk. Condominiums, Brookline, Mass., 1989-91; sec. Phillips Acad. Alumni Class of 1985, Andover, 1989-95; bd. overseers Boston Ballet, 2000—, French Libr., Boston, 2000—; bd. dirs. Alliance Française, Boston, 1998-2000; mem. exec. com. capital campaign Boston Coll., 1998—. Recipient Golden Key Nat. Honor Soc., Boston Coll., 1989, Order of the Cross and Crown, Scholar of the Coll., 1989. Mem. ABA, Arts and Media Law Assn. of Boston Coll. (pres., founder), Social Register, Woman's Athletic Club Chgo., Order of Malta Aux., DAR (vice regent Wellesley, Mass. 1999—), Jr. Internat. Club Lauterbach (Germany), East Chop Beach Club, East Chop Yacht Club, East Chop Tennis Club, Boston Coll. Club (bd. dirs. 1998—), Phi Delta Phi. Republican. Roman Catholic. Avocations: classical ballet, choreography, scuba diving, flying (lic. pilot). Home: 24 Columbia St Wellesley Hills MA 02481-1603 Office: Carroll Assocs 200 Linden St # 322 Wellesley MA 02482-7964

SHEA, PATRICK A. lawyer, educator; b. Salt Lake City, Feb. 28, 1948; s. Edward J. and Ramona (Kilpack) S.; m. Deborah Fae Kern, Sept. 1, 1980; children: Michael, Paul. BA, Stanford U., 1970; MA, Oxford (Eng.) U., 1972; JD, Harvard U., 1975. Bar: Utah 1976, DC 1979. Mem. profl. staff majority leader's office U.S. Senate, 1971, asst. staff dir. intelligence com., 1975—76; assoc. VanCott, Bagley, Salt Lake City, 1976—79, ptnr., 1980—85; counsel fgn. rels. com. U.S. Senate, 1979—80; gen. counsel KUTV, Comm. Investment Corp., Std. Comm., 1985—91; dir. Bur. of Land Mgmt. Dept. of Interior, 1997-98; dep., asst. sec. interior Land & Minerals Mgmt., 1998-2000; of counsel Ballard, Spahr, Andrews & Ingersoll LLP, Salt Lake City, 2000—. Cons. judiciary com. U.S. Ho. of Reps., 1972-73; adj. prof. polit. sci. U. Utah, Salt Lake City, 1981-97, Kans. State U., 2002—. Chmn. Utah Dem. Party, Salt Lake City, 1983-85; v.p. Tomorrow-Today Found., Salt Lake City, 1982-84. Mem. Am. Rhodes Scholar Assn., Utah Bar Assn., D.C. Bar Assn., Stanford Alumni Assn. (pres.-elect 1983-84), Alta. Club. Roman Catholic. Office: Ballard Spahr Andrews & Ingersoll LLP One Utah Ctr Ste 600 201 S Main St Salt Lake City UT 84111-2221 E-mail: sheap@ballardspahr.com.

SHEA, WILLIAM J. insurance company executive; With Coopers & Lybrand, 1974—93; vice chmn., CFO BankBoston Corp., Boston, 1993—98; chmn. Demoulas Supermarkets, Tewksbury, Mass., 1998—99; CEO View Tech, Camarillo, Calif., 1999—2000; pres., CEO Conseco, 2001—. Office: 11825 N Pennsylvania St Carmel IN 46032

SHEA, WILLIAM RENE, historian, science philosopher, educator; b. Gracefield, Que., Can., May 16, 1937; s. Herbert Clement and Jeanne (Lafreniere) S.; m. Evelyn Fischer, May 2, 1970; children: Herbert, Joan-Emma, Louisa, Cecilia, Michael. BA, U. Ottawa, 1958; LPh, Gregorian U., Rome, 1959; LTh, Gregorian U., 1963; PhD, Cambridge U., Eng., 1968. Assoc. prof. U. Ottawa, Ont., Can., 1968-73; fellow Harvard U., Cambridge, Mass., 1973-74; prof. history and philosophy of sci. McGill U., Montreal, 1974—; dir. d'etudes Ecole des Hautes Etudes, Paris, 1981-82. Sec.-gen. Internat. Union of History and Philosophy of Sci., 1981-89, pres., 1990-93; mem. gen. com. Internat. Coun. of Sci. Union, Paris, 1983-89; cons. Killam Found., Ottawa, Ont., 1983-85; mem. McGill Centre for Medicine, Ethics and Law, 1990-95; Hydro Que. prof. environ. ethics, 1992—; vis. prof. U. Rome, 1992; dir. Inst. History of Sci., U. Louis Pasteur, Strasbourg, 1995-2003; Galileo chair history of sci. U. Padua, 2003—. Author: Galileo Intellectual Revolution, 1972, The Magic of Numbers and Motion, 1991, Copernico, 2001, Designing Experiments and Games of Chance, 2003; co-author: Galileo Florentine Residences, 1979, Galileo in Rome, 2003; editor: Nature Mathematized, 1983, Otto Hahn and the Rise of Nuclear Physics, 1983, Revolutions in Science, 1988, Creativity in the Arts and Science, 1990, Persuading Science: The Art of Scientific Rhetoric, 1991, Interpreting the World, Science and Society, 1991, Energy Needs in the Year 2000: Ethical and Environmental Perspectives, 1994, Science and the Visual Image in the Enlightenment, 2000. Can. Coun. fellow, 1965-68, Can. Cultural Inst. fellow, Rome, 1973, Social Scis. and Humanities Rsch. Coun. Can., 1980-81, Inst. of Advanced Studies in Berlin fellow, 1988-89; recipient The Alexandre Koyre medal Internat. Acad. of History of Sci., 1993, Knight of the Order of Malta, 1993. Fellow Royal Soc. Can.; mem. Royal Swedish Acad. Scis. (fgn.), Acadmie D'Alsace, Academia Europaea (mem. coun., 2003-), History of Sci. Soc. (coun. 1973-76), European Sci. Found. (standing com. for humanities 1989-95, chmn. 1999-2003), Can. Nat. Com. of History and Philosophy of Sci. (coun. 1982-93), Can. Philos. Assn., Internat. Acad. History of Sci. (pres. 1997-2001), Rotary. Office: Univ Padua Galileo Chair History of Sci via G Jappelli I-35121 Padova Italy Home: 35 Via Guglielmo Marconi 35122 Padova Italy Fax: +39-049-827-5068. Office Phone: +39-049-827-5073.

SHEAD, WILLIAM C. lawyer; b. Sulphur Branch, Tex., Mar. 23, 1927; m. Thalia Smith, Dec. 19, 1950; children— Suzie, Sheri, Ginny, Libby, Katie. B.S., U. Houston, 1952, LL.M., 1954; J.D., South Tex. Coll. Law, 1959. Bar: Tex. 1960. Chief scout Mid-Continent div. Tidewater Oil Co.; lectr. Downtown Sch., U. Houston; asst. city atty. City of Houston; sole practice, Houston, 1960-86; assoc. judge, State of Tex., 1986—. Candidate Tex. Ho. Reps., 1962. Mem. ABA, Am. Judicature Soc., Assn. Trial Lawyers Am., Harris County Criminal Def. Lawyers Assn., Houston Bar Assn. (prison pre-release com., jud. qualifications com.), Nat. Assn. Criminal Def. Lawyers, Pasadena Bar Assn., Tex. Criminal Def. Lawyers Assn., Tex. Trial Lawyers Assn. Lodges: Masons, Lions. Office: 2927 Broadway St Houston TX 77017-1705

SHEAFFER, RICHARD ALLEN, electrical engineer; b. Bronxville, NY, May 30, 1950; s. Harold Aumond and Carol Lois (Henry) Sweet; children: Alan Michael Sheaffer, Russell Logan Sheaffer, Neil Andrew Sheaffer. BSEE, Pa. State U., 1972; MSEE, U. So. Calif., 1975; MBA, Pepperdine U., 1996. Registered profl. engr., Calif., Fla. Elec. engr. So. Calif. Edison Co., Rosemead, 1973-79, 80-90, Harris Controls divsn., Melbourne, Fla., 1979-80; cons. to elec. utility industry, 1990-91; sr. transmission planner San Diego Gas & Electric, 1991-2000; San Diego Gas & Electric rep. for decommissioning San Onofre Nuc. Generating Sta. Unit 1, 2000—. Project leader nomogram study for Pacific and S.W. transfer subcom. Western Systems Coordinating Coun., 1988, 91; project leader Ariz.-Calif. 7550 NW Path Rating, 1994-97. Author: 1984 West-of-the-River Operating Study, 1985, December 22, 1982 Disturbance Study, 1983. Mem. IEEE (Power Engring. Soc., Engring. Mgmt. Soc.), Am. Nuc. Soc., Phi Eta Sigma.

SHEAFFER, STEVEN L. medical association administrator, medical educator; Prof., vice chair exptl. learning U. Scis. Phila.; pres. Am. Soc. Health Sys. Pharmacists, Md. Office: U Scis Phila 600 S 43d St Philadelphia PA 19104

SHEAFFER, WILLIAM JAY, lawyer; b. Carlisle, Pa., Jan. 18, 1948; s. Raymond Jay and Barbara Jean (Bell) S.; m. Carol Ann Madison, Jan. 5, 1974. BA cum laude, U. Cen. Fla., 1975; JD, Nova U., 1978. Bar: Fla. 1978, U.S. Dist. Ct. (mid. dist.) Fla. 1979, U.S. Dist. Ct. (so. and no. dists.) Fla. 1981, U.S. Ct. Appeals (5th and 11th cirs.) 1981, U.S. Supreme Ct. 1983. Atty. State of Fla., Orlando, Fla., 1978-79; pvt. practice, 1979—. Apptd. to merit selection panel to consider U.S. Magistrate Judge Applicants, 1995, 97, 99. Pres. City Coun. Edgewood, Fla., 2000—02, coun. mem., 2003—. Served to ensign class 4 USN, 1967—71. Named The Best Lawyers in America, 2003. Mem.: ACLU, NACDL, ABA, Assn. Federal Defense Attys., Ctrl. Fla. Assn. Criminal Def. Attys., Nat. Bd. Trial Advocacy (bd. cert. criminal trial specialist), Am. Inns of Ct. (ctrl. Fla. master), Fed. Trial Lawyers Assn., Fla. Assn. Criminal Def. Lawyers Inc., Fed. Bar Assn., Orange County Bar Assn. (Guardian Ad Litem of Yr. 1994, award of excellence 1995), Fla. Bar Assn. (cert. criminal trial specialist, vice chmn. 9th jud. cir. grievance com. 1997, 1998). Democrat. Avocations: boating, running, skiing. Office: 609 E Central Blvd Orlando FL 32801-2916 Fax: 407-648-0683. Business E-Mail: mail@defenselaw.net.

SHEAGREN, JOHN NEWCOMB, physician, educator; b. Aurora, Ill. s. John Wesley Sheagren and Mary Elizabeth Newcomb; m. Victoria Anne Kneevers, July 5, 1958; children: John Frederick, Martha Anne Beals, Erik Peter. BA, Carleton Coll., 1957; MD, Columbia Coll. of Physicians and Surgeons, 1962. American Board of Internal Medicine Phila, PA, 1969, Infectious Disease ABIM, 1972. Resident in medicine Mass. Gen. Hosp., Boston, 1962—64; clin. assoc. U.S. Pub. Health Svc., NIH, Bethesda, Md., 1964—71; assoc. prof. of medicine Howard U. Coll. of Medicine, Washington, 1971—72; chief, Howard U. Med. svc. D.C. Gen. Hosp., Washington, 1972—75; prof. of medicine Howard U. Coll. of Medicine, Washington, 1972—75, George Wash. U. Sch. of Medicine, Washington, 1975—77; prof. of internal medicine U. of Mich. Med. Sch., 1977—89; chief, med. svc. Ann Arbor Veterans Adminstrn. Hosp., 1977—83; assoc. chmn. Dept. of Internal Medicine, Ann Arbor, Mich., 1983—87; assoc. dean U. of Mich. Med. Sch., 1983—87; chief of staff Ann Arbor Veterans Adminstrn. Med. Ctr., Mich., 1987—88; chmn., dept. of internal medicine Ill. Masonic Med. Ctr., 1989—2001; prof. of medicine U. of Ill. Coll. of Medicine, 1989—94, Rush Med. Coll., 1994—2000, U. of Ill. Coll. of Medicine, 2000—; chmn., dept. of internal medicine Adv. Ill. Masonic Med. Ctr., 2001—. Acting chmn., dept. of medicine and dir., divsn. of infectious diseases George Wash. U. Sch. of Medicine, 1975—77. Clin. investigator U.S. Pub. Health Svc., 1964—67, Bethesda, MD. Fellow: ACP (life); mem.: Am. Soc. for Clin. Investigation. Achievements include research in identifying soluble substances produced by activated lymphocytes (now know as lymphokines); rediscovered that nasal carriers of Staphylococcus aureus were at risk of infections; presently designing how a risk factor oriented approach to organizing clinical data enhances patient diagnosis and treatment decision-making. Avocations: golf, orchid culture, crossword puzzles, fly fishing. Office: Advocate Illinois Masonic Medical Center 836 West Wellington Ave Chicago IL 60657-5193 Office Phone: 773-296-7084. E-mail: john.sheagren@advocatehealth.com.

SHEAHAN, JOHN BERNARD, economist, educator; b. Toledo, Sept. 11, 1923; s. Bernard William and Florence (Sheahan) S.; m. Denise Eugénie Morlino, Nov. 29, 1946; children: Yvette Marie, Bernard Eugene. BA, Stanford U., 1948; PhD, Harvard U., 1954. Econ. analyst Office Spl. Rep. in Europe, ECA, Paris, France, 1951-54; mem. faculty Williams Coll., 1954-94, prof. econs., 1966-94, prof. emeritus. Mem. devel. adv. service Colombia adv. group Harvard, 1963-65; nat. research prof. Brookings Instn., 1959-60; vis. prof. El Colegio de México, Mexico City, 1970-71; Fulbright research scholar Institut de recherche économique et de planification, Université de Grenoble, France, 1974-75; vis. scholar Inst. Devel. Studies, U. Sussex, 1981-82; vis. fellow Ctr. for U.S.-Mexican Studies, U. Calif. at San Diego, 1991. Author: Promotion and Control of Industry in Postwar France, 1963, The Wage-Price Guideposts, 1967, An Introduction to the French Economy, 1969, Patterns of Development in Latin America, 1987, Conflict and Change in Mexican Economic Strategy, 1992, Searching for a Better Society: The Peruvian Economy from 1950, 1999. Mem. Presdl. Price Adv. Com., 1979-80. Mem. Latin Am. Studies Assn., New England Coun. Latin Am. Studies (pres. 1989-90), Phi Beta Kappa. Home: Syndicate Rd Williamstown MA 01267 Office: Williams Coll Dept Econs Williamstown MA 01267

SHEAHAN, MICHAEL JOHN, lawyer; b. St. Paul, Minn., Jan. 27, 1934; s. Louis Patrick and Evelyn Sylvia (Frediani) S.; m. Charlene Ruth Schermerhorn, Nov. 5, 1960; children: John M., Mark W., Stephen P. BS, U. Minn.-Mpls., 1960, LL.B., 1961. Bar: Minn. 1961, U.S. Dist. Ct. Minn. 1964. Assoc. T. O. Kachelmacher, Mpls., 1961; ptnr. Cummins, Gislason, & Sheahan, Ltd., St. Paul, 1973-76, Peterson, Gray & Sheahan, Ltd., St. Paul, 1976-85; prin. Michael J. Sheahan, P.A., St. Paul, 1985—. Chmn. Ramsey County Bar Fund, St. Paul, 1983-84. Mem., sec. St. Paul City Charter Commn., 1976-80; dean Acad. Cert. Trial Lawyers Minn., 1995-96. Trustee, St. Thomas Acad., St. Paul, 1983-95. Served with U.S. Army, 1955-57. Named Minn. Super Lawyer, Minn. Law and Politics mag., 1998. Mem. Minn. Trial Lawyers Assn. (dir.), Ramsey County Bar Assn., Minn. State Bar Assn., Nat. Bd. Trial Advocacy, St. Paul Athletic Club (past sec., dir.), Optimists Club (past pres.), Phi Delta Phi. Roman Catholic. Home: 8160 Emerald Ln Saint Paul MN 55125-3325

SHEAHAN, ROBERT EMMETT, lawyer, consultant; b. Chgo., May 20, 1942; s. Robert Emmett and Lola Jean (Moore) S.; m. Pati Smith, Mar. 20, 1991. BA, Ill. Wesleyan U., 1964; JD, Duke U., 1967; MBA, U. Chgo., 1970. Bar: Ill. 1967, La. 1975, N.C. 1978. Vol. VISTA, N.Y.C., 1967-68; trial atty. NLRB, Milw., New Orleans, 1970-75; ptnr. Jones, Walker, Waechter, Poitevent, Carrere & Denegre, New Orleans, 1975-78; pvt. practice High Point, N.C., 1978—. Bd. dirs. Inst. for Effective Mgmt., Bus. Publs. Inst. Author: Employees and Drug Abuse: An Employer's Handbook, 1994, The Encyclopedia of Drugs in the Workplace, Labor and Employment Law in North Carolina, 1991, Personnel and Employment Law in North Carolina, 1992, Desk Book of Labor and Employment Law for Healthcare Employers' Desk Manual, 1995, North Carolina Lawyers' Desk Book; contbg. author: The Developing Labor Law, 1975—; editor: The World of Personnel; contbg. editor: Employee Testing and the Law; contbr. periodic supplements N.C. Gen. Practice Deskbook, 1992—. Bd. dirs. High Point United Way, 1979-83; mem. congl. action com. High Point C. of C., chmn., 1991—, bd. dirs., 1996—. Mem. ABA, N.C. Bar Assn., High Point Bar Assn., Ill. Bar Assn., La. Bar Assn., Sedgefield (N.C.) Country Club, String and Splinter Club, Bald Head Island Club. Republican. Roman Catholic. Home: 101 Bellwood Ct Jamestown NC 27282 Office: Robert E Sheahan & Assocs 603 Eastchester Dr Ste B High Point NC 27262-7647

SHEALY, COURTNEY, Olympic athlete; b. Columbia, S.C., Dec. 12, 1977; Student, U. Ga. Team capt. Ga. Bulldogs, 1999—2000. Recipient Gold medal 4 x 100-meter freestyle Sydney Olympics, 2000; named co-NCAA Swimmer of Yr., 2000, 2-time world record holder, 1 olympic record, 2-time NCAA team champion, 3-time NCAA individual champion, 5-time Am. record holder, 26 1st team all-am. awards (most by any Ga. athlete), Ramsey scholar, 1997-2000, NCAA Acad. All-Am., 1997, 1998, 2000, SEC swimmer of the yr., 2000 Office: USA Swimming 1 Olympic Plz Colorado Springs CO 80909-5746

SHEAN, TIMOTHY JOSEPH, manufacturing executive; b. Norfolk, Va., Sept. 19, 1945; s. Hobart Philip S.; m. Adriana Bergo, July 12, 1970; children: Jonathan Michael, Arianne Marie. BSME, U. Notre Dame, 1967; postgrad., U. Va., 1991. Sales engr. Shean Equipment Co., Syracuse, N.Y., 1967-69; application engr. Gen. Electric Co., Schenectady, 1970-71, prodn. control supr., 1972-75, process devel. engr., 1975-78, project mgr., 1978-80, mgr. facilities and engring., 1980-83; plant mgr. Hughes Tool Co., Bristol, Va., 1983-85; mgr. mfg. Sandvik Rock Tools, Inc., Bristol, 1985-89, gen. mgr., 1989-92, v.p., 1992-2000; pres. Sandvik Mineral Tools USA, Bristol, 2000—02, Sandvik CPD-MTD Prodn. Co., Bristol; pres., CEO R.P. Abrasives and Machine, Inc., Rochester, NH, 2002—. Sr. patrolman Nat. Ski Patrol Sys., Wilmington, Vt., 1970-80; instr., trainer first aid ARC, Schenectady, 1975-78, vice-chmn. disaster svcs., 1976-77; mem. sch. bd. Schalmont Ctrl. Sch. Dist., Schenectady, 1979-82; cmty. involvement com. Bristol Sch. Dist., 1990; chmn. Literacy Acad. Bristol, 1991-92; chmn. fin. coun. St. Anne's Cath. Ch., 1992-96; mem. Va. Atty. Gens. Commn., 1995-96, Commn. on Future S.W. Va., 1995-97; bd. fellows Va. Intermont Coll., 1996-99; mem. pres.'s adv. bd. King Coll., 1997-2002; bd. dirs. Mfg. Tech. Ctr. S.W. Va., 1998-2002, Va. Mfg. Assn., 1999-2000, mem. The Conf. Bd., 1999-2002. Named one of Outstanding Young Men of Am., U.S. Jaycees, 1979. Mem. Soc. Mfg. Engrs., Nat. Mining Assn. (chmn. resins group 1989-95, tech. com. 1990-96), Va. Coal Coun. (bd. dirs. 1993-2002), Bristol C. of C. (bd. dirs. 1994-2000, chmn. 1999-2000). Roman Catholic. Avocation: skiing. Office: R P Abrasives & Machine Inc 194 Milton Rd Rochester NH 03868 Office Phone: 603-335-2132. Business E-Mail: joe@abrasives.com.

SHEAR, IONE MYLONAS, archaeologist; b. St. Louis, Feb. 19, 1936; d. George Emmanuel and Lella (Papazouglou) Mylonas; m. Theodore Leslie Shear, June 24, 1959; children: Julia Louise, Alexandra. BA, Wellesley Coll., 1958; MA, Bryn Mawr Coll., 1960, PhD, 1968. Rsch. asst. Inst. for Advanced Study, Princeton, N.J., 1963-65; mem. Agora Excavation, Athens, 1967, 72-94; lectr. art and archaeology Princeton U., 1983-84; lectr. Am. Sch. Classical Studies, Athens, summers 1989-98. Also excavator various other sites in Greece and Italy. Author: The Panagia Houses at Mycenae, 1987, Tales of Heroes: The Origins of the Homeric Texts, 2000; contbr. articles to profl. jours. Mem. Archaeol. Inst. Am., Greek Archaeol. Soc. (hon.). Address: 87 Library Pl Princeton NJ 08540-3015 also: Deinokratous 30 Athens 106-76 Greece

SHEAR, NATALIE PICKUS, conference and event management executive; b. N.Y.C., Oct. 18, 1940; d. Sam and Mildred (Shulman) Pickus; m. Daniel H. Shear, Dec. 14, 1968 (dec. Apr. 1989); children: Adam Brian, Tamara Beth; m. Henry D. Lewis, Jan. 10, 1999. BA in Journalism, Fairleigh Dickinson U., 1962. Editorial asst. Show Bus. Newspaper, N.Y.C., 1962-64, The Jewish News, Newark, 1964-66; dir. Manhattan women's div., program asst. Am. Jewish Congress, N.Y.C., 1966-68; mng. editor The Jewish Week, Washington, 1968-71; dir. pub. rels. United Jewish Appeal, Washington, 1973-74; pub. affairs dir. Leadership Conf. on Civil Rights, Washington, 1977-83; pres.

Natalie P. Shear Assocs., Inc., Washington, 1983—. Editor (newspaper) Books Alive, 1973-74; editor, pub. (newsletter) Trends, Inc., 1989-94. Vol. nat. bd. Ams. Dem. Action, 2001—; vol., bd. dirs. Nat. Jewish Dem. Coun., Washington, 1996—; bd. dirs. Urban Philharm. Soc., 1998-99; chairperson women's task force Am. Jewish Congress, Washington, 1984-86; v.p. Nat. Child Rsch. Ctr., Washington, 1974-76; pres. Ohr Kodesh Sisterhood, Chevy Chase, Md., 1980-82. Mem. Nat. Press Club. Avocations: needlecrafts, crafts. Home: 4701 Willard Ave Chevy Chase MD 20815-4643 Office: 1730 M St NW Ste 801 Washington DC 20036 Business E-Mail: natalie@nataliepshear.com.

SHEAR, RICHARD GARY, education administrator; b. Yonkers, N.Y., June 5, 1953; s. Ralph Leon and Florence Shear; m. Benay Ava Shear, July 15, 1983; 1 child, David. BA, SUNY, Oneonta, 1975; MA, SUNY, Stony Brook, 1982; EdD, Fordham U., 1996. Tchr. Sachem H.S., Lake Ronkonkona, N.Y., 1975-87; adminstr., tchr. G.W. Hewlett H.S., Hewlett, N.Y., 1987-94; prin. Westhampton Beach H.S., Westhampton, N.Y., 1994-95; adminstr. supr. Hewlett-Woodmere Schs., 1995-97; prin. Long Beach (N.Y.) H.S., 1997—. Mem. dean's adv. coun. to Sch. Edn., C.W. Post Coll., L.I. U., Brookville, N.Y., 1992-95. Zone leader Nassau County Dem. Com., North Bellmore, N.Y., 1984-85, mgr. polit. campaign, Nassau, 1986. Named Nassau County Tchr. of Yr., L.I. U., 1991. Mem. Nat. Assn. Secondary Sch. Prins., Nassau County Prins. Assn. Avocations: tennis, reading, sports. Office: Long Beach HS 322 Lagoon Dr W Lido Beach NY 11561-4908

SHEAR, THEODORE LESLIE, JR., archaeologist, educator; b. Athens, Greece, May 1, 1938; s. Theodore Leslie and Josephine (Platner) S.; m. Ione Doris Mylonas, June 24, 1959; children: Julia Louise, Alexandra. AB summa cum laude, Princeton (NJ) U., 1959, MA, 1963, PhD, 1966. Instr. Greek and Latin Bryn Mawr (Pa.) Coll., 1964-66, asst. prof., 1966-67; asst. prof. art and archaeology Princeton U., 1967-70, assoc. prof., 1970-79, chmn. program in classical archaeology, 1970-85, assoc. chmn. dept. art and archaeology, 1976-78, 82-83, prof. classical archaeology, 1979—; prof. archaeology Am. Sch. Classical Studies, Athens, 1988-94. Mem. mng. com. Am. Sch. Classical Studies, Athens, 1972—; mem. archaeol. expdns. to Greece and Italy, including Mycenae, 1953-54, 58, 62-63, 65-66, Eleusis, 1956, Perati, 1956, Corinth, 1960, Morgantina, Sicily, 1962; mem. Ancient Agora of Athens, 1955, 67, field dir., 1968-94; trustee William Alexander Procter Found., 1982-89, Princeton Jr. Sch., 1983—, pres., 1994—. Author: Kallias of Sphettos and the Revolt of Athens in 286 B.C., 1978; contbr. articles to profl. jours. White fellow Am. Sch. Classical Studies, 1959-60. Mem. Archaeol. Inst. Am., Am. Philol. Assn., Coll. Art Assn., Archaeol. Soc. Athens (hon.), Century Assn. Club (NYC); Nassau Club (Princeton), Princeton Club (NYC), Hellenic Yacht Club (Piraeus, Greece), Phi Beta Kappa. Republican. Episcopalian. Home: 87 Library Pl Princeton NJ 08540-3015 also: 30 Deinokratous St Athens Greece

SHEARD, CHARLES, III, dermatologist; b. Toronto, Ontario, Can., Nov. 22, 1914; came to U.S., 1945; s. Charles Jr. and Alice Elizabeth (Ramsay) S.; m. Katherine Patricia Murphy, Nov. 19, 1937; children: Joan Virginia Sheard Cumming (dec.), Pamela Carol Sheard McGuiness, Wendy Alice Sheard Geyer. Sr. matriculation, Upper Can. Coll., Toronto, 1933; MD, U. Toronto, 1939. Diplomate Am. Bd. Dermatology. Intern Toronto Gen. Hosp., 1939-40; instr. physiology, anatomy U. Toronto Med. Faculty, 1940-41; surgical asst. resident Hosp. for Sick Children, Toronto, 1945; from resident to chief resident dermatologist Columbia Presbyn. Hosp., N.Y.C., 1945-49; assoc. prof. medicine Cornell U. Med. Coll., N.Y.C., 1950-94, assoc. prof. emeritus, 1994—. Author: (textbook) Treatment in Dermatology, 1978; contbr. articles to profl. jours. Flight lt. RCAF, 1941-45. Fellow ACP, Royal Coll. Physicians (Can.); mem. Metro-Manhattan Dermatol. Soc. N.Y.C. (sec. 1970-80), Royal Can. Yacht Club, Muskoka Lakes Golf and Country Club. Republican. Episcopalian. Avocations: sailing, fishing, golf.

SHEARER, ALAN, newspaper editor; b. Arlington, Va., Mar. 19, 1948; Editl. dir., gen. mgr. Washington Post Writers Group, Washington, 1991—. Office: Washington Post Writers Group 1150 15th St NW Washington DC 20071-0002

SHEARER, CHARLES LIVINGSTON, academic administrator; b. Louisville, Ky., Nov. 23, 1942; s. Guy Cooper and Kathryn (Aufenkamp) S.; m. Susan Pulling Shearer, Nov. 30, 1968; children: Todd A., Mark G., Scott B. BS, U. Ky., 1964, MA, 1967, Mich. State U., 1973, PhD, 1981. Instr. Henderson (Ky.) Community Coll., 1967-69; asst. prof. Ferris State Coll., Big Rapids, Mich., 1969-71; grad. asst. Mich. State U., East Lansing, 1971-73; dir. mgmt. program Albion (Mich.) Coll., 1973-75, dir. ops., 1975-79; v.p. fin. Transylvania U., Lexington, Ky., 1979-83, pres., 1983—. Bd. dirs. Lexington Philharm. Soc., 1983-89; mem. adv. bd. Salvation Army, Lexington, 1983-87; mem. Henry Clay Meml. Found., Lexington, 1983-89. Capt. U.S. Army Nat. Guard, 1966-76. Named One of Outstanding Young Men in Am., 1978. Mem. Am. Econs. Assn., Lexington C. of C. (bd. dirs. 1985—), Rotary. Mem. Disciples Of Christ Ch.

SHEARER, DEREK NORCROSS, international studies educator, diplomat, administrator; b. L.A., Dec. 5, 1946; s. Lloyd and Marva (Peterson) S.; 1 child, Casey (dec.); stepchildren: Anthony, Julie. BA, Yale U., 1968; PhD, Union Grad. Sch., Yellow Springs, Ohio, 1977. Lectr. U. Calif., L.A., 1979-81; dir. internat. and pub. affairs ctr., prof. of pub. policy Occidental Coll., L.A., 1981-94, 98—; dep. undersec. U.S. Dept. Commerce, Washington, 1993; U.S. amb. to Finland U.S. Dept. State, Washington, 1994-97; prof. internat. affairs Occidental Coll., L.A., 1997—; internat. advisor Ziff Bros. Investments, 1998—. Fellow Econ. Strategy Inst., Washington, 1993; policy adv. to Presidential Candidate Bill Clinton, 1990-92; adv. on NATO peace keeping USN, 1997—; pub. policy fellow Woodrow Wilson Internat. Scholars Ctr., 1999-2000; dir. global affairs Occidental Coll., 2001—, Chevalier prof. diplomacy and world affairs, 2002—; founder Pacific Coun. Internat. Policy, 1994—. Contbr. articles to profl. publs. Planning commr. City of Santa Monica (Calif.), 1984; bd. mem. Nat. Consumer Bank, Washington, 1991. Fellow Guggenheim Found., 1984, U.S.-Japan Leadership fellow Japan Soc., 1991. Democrat. Avocations: basketball, tennis, travel, mysteries. Office: Global Affairs Occidental Coll Los Angeles CA 90041 Office Phone: 323-259-1459. Business E-Mail: dshearer@oxy.edu.

SHEARER, ELLEN MARIE, music educator; b. Cleburne, Tex., Aug. 2, 1948; d. Palmer Gaines and Martha June (Henderson) O'Barr; m. Robert Lynn Shearer, Nov. 20, 1976; children: Dane Robert, Darren Paul. MusB Ed., Samford Univ., Birmingham, Al, 1966—71; MusM Ch. music, So. Baptist Theological Seminary, Louisville, Ky, 1974—76. Organist, child. choir dir. First Bapt. Ch., Shelbyville, Ky., 1975—77; organist Ninth St. Bapt. Ch., Cincinnati, Ohio, 1977—78; piano instr. Pvt. Piano Studio, Cincinnati, Ohio, 1978—85; elem. sch. music tchr. Harbison West Elem. Sch., Columbia, SC, 1985—96; pianist Harbison Bapt. Ch., Columbia, SC, 1985—90; piano instr. Ben Lippen Sch., Columbia, SC, 1990—98; pianist Harbison Bapt. Ch., Columbia, SC, 1995—2000. Piano instr. Columbia Internat. Univ., Columbia, SC, 1994—98, Accompanist, 1994—96; piano instr. Piano Praise Studio, Columbia, SC, 1996—; pianist Pk. St. Bapt., Columbia, SC, 2000—01. Recipient Horace Mann Award for Tchr. Excellence, Harbison West Elem./Columbia, SC, 1995. Mem.: Dutch Fork Music Tchr. Assoc. (v.p. 1996—), Columbia Music Tchr. Assoc. (v.p. 1996—). Achievements include my elem. sch. chorus was chosen to sing for the 1994 Gov. Inauguration for David Beasley. Avocations: aerobics, walking, music, accompanying concerts. Home: 141 Shadow Pine Rd Columbia SC 29212

SHEARER, HARRY JULIUS, screenwriter, director, actor; b. LA, Dec. 23, 1943; s. Mack Shearer and Dora (Kohn) Warren; m. Penelope Joyce Nichols, Oct. 1974 (div. 1977); m. Judith Owen, March 28, 1993. BA in polit. sci., UCLA, 1964; postgrad. in urban govt., Harvard U., 1964-65. Cert. secondary tchr., Calif. Reporter Newsweek mag., LA, Boston, 1964-65; legis. intern Calif. State Assembly, Sacramento, 1965-66; tchr. Compton (Calif.) Unified Sch. Dist., 1966-68; writer, actor, producer The Credibility Gap, LA, 1968-76; creator nat. pub. radio show Sta. KCRW, Santa Monica, Calif., 1983—. Author: (weekly column) Man Bites Town, 1990—; actor: (films) Cracking Up, 1977, American Raspberry, 1977, Fish That Saved Pittsburgh, 1979, Loose Shoes, 1980, The Right Stuff, 1983, Plain Clothes, 1988, Oscar, 1991, Pure Luck, 1991, Blood and Concrete, 1991, The Fisher King, 1991, A League of Their Own, 1992, Wayne's World 2, 1993, I'll Do Anything, 1994, Little Giants, 1994, Speechless, 1994, My Best Friend's Wedding, 1997, Godzilla, 1998, Almost Heroes, 1998, The Truman Show, 1998, Edtv, 1999, Dick, 1999, Haiku Tunnel, 2001, Out There, 2002, (voice) Animalympics, 1980, Flicks, 1987, My Stepmother is an Alien, 1988, Small Soldiers, 1988, Encounter in the Third Dimension, 1999, Ghost Dog: The Way of the Samurai, 1999, Edward Fudwupper Fibbed Big, 2000, Haunted Castle, 2001; actor, writer, composer: This is Spinal Tap, 1984; actor, dir. Portrait of a White Marriage, 1988; actor, writer, dir., exec. prodr. Teddy Bears' Picnic, 2002; actor, composer A Mighty Wind, 2003; actor: (TV films) Serpico: The Deadly Game, 1976, Million Dollar Infield, 1982, Hometown By Makes Good, 1990, (voice) Spitting Image: Down and Out in the White House, 1986, Spitting Image: The Ronnie and Nancy Show, 1987; actor, writer, composer, prodr. (TV films) The T.V. Show, 1979; actor, dir.: (TV films) The History of White People in America, 1985; The History of White People in America: Volume II, 1996; actor: (TV series) The Simpsons, 1989—, Sunday Best, 1991, The News Hole, 1995, State of the Union Undressed, 1996; actor, writer (TV series) Saturday Night Live, 1979—80 (Emmy award nomination for Outstanding Writing Variety or Music Program, 1980), 1984—85, Likely Stories, Vol. 1, 1981; actor(voice): (TV specials) The Simpsons Christmas Special, 1989; actor, writer, composer: videos Spinal Tap: Break Like the Wind - The Videos, 1992; actor: (numerous TV guest appearances); writer, composer, prodr.: (TV films) A Spinal Tap Reunion: The 25th Anniversary London Sell-Out, 1992; composer: (films) Waiting for Guffman, 1996; writer (TV films) Disco Beaver from Outer Space, 1978, Real Life, 1979, (TV series) America 2-Night, 1978 (Emmy award nomination for Outstanding Writing Comedy-Variety or Music Series, 1978). Recipient Cable ACE award for Best Game Show Series or Special, 1995.*

SHEARER, PAUL SCOTT, government relations professional; b. Clinton, Ill., Feb. 27, 1948; s. Lloyd Jr. and Pauline Lucille (Glosser) S.; m. Barbara Boston, July 3, 1981; children: Jason J. Brunk, Carrie K. Premo. BS, U. Ill., 1970, MS, 1975. Asst. dir. cash mgmt. State Treas. Ill., Springfield, 1973-74, asst. CFO, 1974-77, chief fiscal officer, 1977-78; dir. vehicle svc. State of Ill., Springfield, 1978-81; legis. asst. Senator Dixon U.S. Senate, Washington, 1981-84; exec. dir. Nat. Corn Growers Assn., St. Louis, 1984-90; dir. govt. rels. Halfpenny, Hahn, Roche & Marchese, 1990-93; dep. asst. sec. congl. rels. USDA, 1993-96; dir. nat. rels. Farmland Industries, Inc., Washington, 1996—2003; v.p. Bergner, Bockorny and Hawkins, 2003—. Mem. adv. com. Ill. Atty.'s Gen. Agr. Law, State of Ill., 1985-91; dean Coll. Agriculture, U. Ill., 1989-90, U. Ill. Dept. Agrl. Econs., 1986-89; mem. agrl. tech. com. for trade in animals and animal products USDA/U.S. Trade Rep., 1998-2002; U.S. del. to WTO Ministerial Conf., 1999; food security adv. com. USAID, 1998-2002. Del. Dem. Nat. Conv., 1978, Mo. Dem. State conv., 1988, Va. Dem. State Conv., 1992, 93, 94, 96, 97, 2000; mem. Police Bd. Commrs., Chesterfield, Mo., 1988-90; pres. Mo. River Dem. Club, 1987-89. Named to Hon. Order of Ky. Cols., 1990, Alpha Gamma Sigma nat. merit award, 1991; named to Villa Grove (Ill.) HS Alumni Hall of Fame. Mem. St. Louis Agr.-Bus. Club (sec.-treas. 1987-88, 2d v.p. 1988-89, v.p. 1989-90, pres. 1990), U. Ill. Alumni Assn., U. Ill. Coll. Agr. Alumni Assn. (dir. at large 1990), Ill. Group (chmn. 1993), Ill. State Soc. (bd. dirs. 1996—, pres. 2002-2003), Mo.-Kans. Forum (chmn. 1998-2000), Alpha Zeta (Honor Roll), Nat. Democrat Club. Methodist. Home: 2744 Clarkes Landing Dr Oakton VA 22124-1120 Office: Bergner Bockorny and Hawkins 1101 16th St NW Ste 500 Washington DC 20036 E-mail: sshearer@bbchb.com.

SHEARER, ROBERT K. apparel executive; CFO, v.p. VF Corp., Greensboro, N.C. Office: VF Corp PO Box 21488 628 Green Valley Rd Ste 500 Greensboro NC 27408-7791

SHEARER, RONALD ALEXANDER, economics professor; b. Trail, B.C., Can., June 15, 1932; s. James Boyd and Mary Ann (Smith) S.; m. Renate Elizabeth Selig, Dec. 20, 1956 (dec.); children: Carl, Bruce. BA, U. B.C., 1954; MA, Ohio State U., 1955, PhD, 1959. Asst. prof. econs. U. Mich., 1958-62; economist Royal Commn. Banking and Fin., Toronto, Canada, 1962-63; mem. faculty U. B.C., Vancouver, 1963—, prof. econs., 1970-98, emeritus prof., 1998—, head dept., 1972-76. Co-author: Money and Banking, 1975, The Economics of the Canadian Financial System, 1994; editor: Trade Liberalization and a Regional Economy, 1971. Mem. Can. Econs. Assn. Office: U BC Dept Econs Vancouver BC Canada E-mail: rshearer@interchange.ubc.ca.

SHEARER, WILLIAM KENNEDY, lawyer, publisher; b. Marysville, Calif., Jan. 21, 1931; s. William and Eva (Kennedy) S.; m. Eileen Mary Knowland; Nov. 25, 1956; 1 child, Nancy Lorena; stepchildren: David, Douglas, Dianne. BA, San Diego State U., 1955; JD, Western State U., 1975. Bar: Calif. 1975, U.S. Dist. Ct. (so. dist.) Calif. 1975, U.S. Ct. Claims 1976, U.S. Supreme Ct. 1982, U.S. Ct. Appeals (fed. cir.) 1982, U.S. Ct. Appeals (9th cir.) 1983. Legis. asst. to Congressman James Utt, 1953, 55-56; exec. dir. San Diego County Rep. Cen. Com., 1956-58; pub. Oceanside-Carlsbad Banner, Oceanside, Calif., 1958-63; adminstv. asst. Assemblyman E.R. Barnes, Sacramento, Calif., 1963-65; polit. campaign cons. Banner Advt., San Diego, Los Angeles, 1964-75; atty. Duke, Gerstel, Shearer LLP, San Diego, 1975—. Pub. newsletters Calif. Statesman, 1962—, Legis. Survey, 1963—, Fgn. Policy Rev., 1972—, Am. Ind., 1974—. Rep. nominee for State Assembly, San Diego County, 1956, 58; state chmn. Am. Ind. Party, Calif., 1967-70, nat. chmn. 1968-71, 73-77; nat. vice chmn. U.S. Taxpayers Party, 1992-96, chmn. 1996-99; Am. Ind. nominee for Gov., 1970; adv. com. Elections Com., Calif. Legislature, Sacramento, 1971-76; mem. Blue Ribbon Task Force on Calif.'s Home Constrn. Industry, 1996-97; bd. dirs. San Diego Gilbert & Sullivan Co., 1984-90, pres. 1986-88, v.p., 1985-86, 88-90. With U.S. Army, 1953-55. Mem. Calif. Bar Assn., San Diego County Bar Assn. Avocations: ancient near eastern history, gardening, music. Home: 8160 Palm St Lemon Grove CA 91945-3028 Office: Duke Gerstel Shearer LLP WKS 101 W Broadway Ste 1120 San Diego CA 92101-8296 Office Phone: 619-460-4484.

SHEARER, WILLIAM THOMAS, pediatrician, educator; b. Detroit, Aug. 23, 1937; BS, U. Detroit, 1960; PhD, Wayne State U., 1966; MD, Washington U., St. Louis, 1970. Diplomate Am. Bd. Pediat., Am. Bd. Allergy and Immunology (chmn. 1994-95, dir. 1990-95, chair nominations com., clin. immunology soc.), Nat. Bd. Med. Examiners, cert. in diagnostic lab. immunology. Post-doctoral fellow in biochemistry dept. chem. Indiana U., Bloomington, 1966—67; intern in pediat. St. Louis Children's Hosp., 1970—71, resident in immunology in pediat., 1971—72, dir. divsn. allergy and immunology, 1974—78; fellow in immunology in pediat. Barnes Hosp., Washington U., St. Louis, 1972—74; spl. USPHA sci. rsch. fellow in medicine dept. medicine Washington U., 1972—74, assoc. prof., 1978, prof., 1978; prof. pediat., microbiology, immunology Baylor Coll. Medicine, Houston, 1989—, dir. AIDS rsch. ctr., 1991—; head sect. allergy & immunology Tex. Children's Hosp., Houston, 1978—. Mem. ACTU Cmty. Adv. Bd. Tex. Children's Hosp., Houston, 1991—; chmn. pediat. core com. pediat. AIDS clin. trial group Nat. Inst. Allergy and Infectious Diseases, NIH, Bethesda, Md., 1989—, ad hoc reviewer, 1991, mem. therapeutics subcom. AIDS rsch. adv. com., 1993—, chmn. pediat. AIDS clin. trial group immunology com., 1994—, mem. pediat. AIDS clin. trials group exec. Com., 1991—95, mem. spl. rev. com. persons affected by chronic granulomatous disease, 1992; site visitor Gen. Clin. Rsch. Ctr. NIH, Bethesda, Md., 1993, vice chmn. pediat. AIDS clin. trials group exec. com., 1996—; chmn. study populatoin/patient mgmt. com. Clin. Ctrs. for the Study of Pediat. Lung and Heart Complications of HIV Infection, Nat. Heart, Lung and Blood Inst., NIH, Bethesda, Md., 1989—, mem. AIDS ad hoc work group, 1991; dir. Pediat. HIV/AIDS Clin. Rsch. Ctr., Houston, 1988—; chmn. exec. com. clin. trial intravenous gammaglobulin in HIV infected children Nat. Inst. Child Health and Human Devel., Bethesda, 1989—; dir. Am. Bd. Allergy and Immunology, 1990—95, chair, 1994—95; vice-chair exec. com. Pediat. AIDS Clin. Trials Group, 1996—2001. Editor: Pediatric Asthma, Allergy, and Immunology, 1989; editl. bd. Jour. Allergy and Clin. Immunology, 1993—, Clin. and Diagnostic Lab. Immunology, 1994—, editor Pediatric Allergy and Immunology, 1995—, Allergy and Immunology Tng. Program Dir.; assoc. editor: Jour. Allergy and Clin. Immunology, 2003—; guest editor Seminar Pediatric Infectious Disease, 1990, contbr. intro. Allergy: Princples and Practice, 1992, contbr. articles to profl. jours. including New Eng. Jour. Medicine. AIDS cons. Houston Ind. Sch. Dist., 1986—; med. adv. Spring Br. Ind. Sch. Dist., Houston, 1987—, chmn. cmty. HIV/AIDS adv. group Tex. Med. Ctr., 1991—. Recipient faculty rsch. award, Am. Cancer Soc., 1977—79, Myrtle Wreath award, Hadassah, 1985, spl. recognition award, Am. Acad. Allergy and Immunology, 1994; grantee NIH, 1988—; scholar rsch., Cystic Fibrosis Found., 1974—77. Mem.: Clin. Immunology Soc. (chair Am. Bd. Allergy and Immunology nominations com. 1994—96, pres. 2001—02), Am. Acad. Allergy, Asthma and Immunology (assoc. chmn. for planning of 1997-98 internat. meetings, profl. ednl. coun.), Am. Acad. Allergy and Immunology (chmn. clin. and lab. immunology com. 1994—96, chmn. tng. program dirs. nat. issues subcom. 1994—96), Tex. Allergy and Immunology Soc. (chmn. nat. issues com. 1992—96, pres. 1994—96), Tex. Allergy Soc. (exec. com. 1990—), Am. Acad. Pediat. (exec. com. sect. allergy and immunology 1991—), Am. Soc. Clin. Investigation. Achievements include research in half-matched T-cell-depleted bone marrow transplants; membrane signal pathway of human B lymphcytes. Office: Baylor Coll Med Allergy/Immun Clinic 6621 Fannin MC FC 330 01 Houston TX 77030-2600

SHEARES, BRADLEY T. pharmaceutical executive; BA in Chemistry, Fisk U., 1978; PhD in Biochemistry, Purdue U., 1982. Rsch. fellow dept. biochem. regulation Merck Inst. for Therapeutic Rsch., MRL, Rahway, NJ, 1987—90; hosp. specialist internat. mktg. mgmt. MSD Internat., West Point, Pa., 1990; product mgr. AIDS/Devel. products Hosp. Products Mktg. Group, MSD, 1991; product mgr./sr. product mgr. U.S. Human Health, 1991—92, dir. external bus. devel., 1992—93, sr. dir. hosp. bus. group, 1993—94, exec. dir. anti-infectives bus. group, 1995—96, v.p. anti-infectives bus. group, 1996—98, v.p. hosp. mktg. and sales, 1998—2001; pres. human health Merck & Co., Inc., Whitehouse Station, NJ, 2001—. Fellow NIH Postdoctoral, Ctr. for Cancer Rsch., MIT, 1983—85; scholar Lucille P. Markey, 1985—87. Mem.: AAAS, Am. Soc. for Microbiology, Am. Soc. Biol. Chemists (assoc.). Office: Merck and Co Inc 351 N Sumneytown Pike North Wales PA 19454

SHEARIER, STEPHEN JAMES, language educator; b. Milw., June 30, 1952; s. Donald Arthur and Marie Frances Shearier; m. Margret Tierney, Aug. 27, 1993; 1 child, Phillip Walzak. MA in Comparative Lit., U. Wis., Milw., 1977; MA in German, U. Wis., Madison, 1980, PhD in German (cum laude), 1986. Prof. German NYU, NYC, 1987—89, Barnard Coll., NYC, 1993—95; tchr. English NYC Pub. Schs., NYC, 1996—; prof. German New Sch. U., NYC, 1993—, Rutgers U., Newark, 2002—. Lang. cons. Robert Bosch Found., Stuttgart, Germany, 1995—2001; selection com. Congress-Bundestag, Pa. Contbr. Dictionary of Literary Biography: German and Austrian Dramatists; translator: Auschwitz Chronicle: 1939-1945; author: Das junge Deutschland (1917-1920): Expressionist Theater in Berlin; contbr. articles to profl. publs. Fellow, Mellon Found., 1986—87; grantee Rsch. award, Robert Bosch Found., 2001; scholar, U. Bonn, Germany, 1983—84, Deutsche Akademische Austauschdienst, 1984—85. Avocations: nature, poetry, art. Home: 77 Park Terr East D87 New York NY 10034

SHEARIN, MORRIS LEE, minister; b. Garysburg, N.C., Dec. 11, 1940; s. Simon and Bernice (Porch) S.; m. Bertha Cotton, Mar. 29, 1964; children: Felicia S., Morris Lee Jr. BA, MDiv, Shaw U., 1976; DMin, Howard U., 1981. Ordained to ministry Bapt. Ch., 1971. Pastor Cedar Grove Bapt. Ch., Lawrenceville, Va., 1970-74, Pleasant Grove Bapt. Ch., Adams Grove, Va., 1972-74, Mt. Olive Bapt. Ch., Lewiston, N.C., 1974-88, Israel Bapt. Ch., Washington, 1988—. Commr. Northampton County, Jackson, N.C., 1982-86; organizer Nation Share Cropper Assn., Wadesboro, N.C., 1982-83; bd. dirs. Montana Terrace Boys/Girls Club, 1990—, Stoddard Bapt. Home, 1990—. Mem. NAACP (chaplain D.C. br., pres. Seaboard, N.C. chpt. 1980-88, 2d v.p. Charlotte, N.C. chpt. 1984-88, 1st v.p. 1986-88, Outstanding Performance award 1987), Shaw Theol. Alumni Assn. (pres. of approval 1977), Howard U. Theol. Alumni Assn. (pres. 1990—), Omega Psi Phi (scroll of honor 1979), Century Club. Democrat. Office: Israel Bapt Ch 1251 Saratoga Ave NE Washington DC 20018-1025

SHEARING, GEORGE ALBERT, pianist, composer; b. London, Aug. 13, 1919; arrived in U.S., 1947, naturalized, 1956; s. James Philip and Ellen Amelia (Brightman) Shearing; m. Beatrice Bayes, May 1, 1941 (div.); 1 child, Wendy Ann; m. Eleanor Geffert, July 28, 1984. Student, Linden Lodge Sch. for Blind, London; D Music (hon.), Westminster Coll., Salt Lake City, 1975, Hamilton Coll., 1994. Composer: (songs) Lullaby of Birdland, numerous other popular songs; recs. English Decca and Parlophone, Am. Savoy, London, MGM Capitol, Sheba Records, Concord Jazz, Telarc, albums An Evening with George Shearing and Mel Torme, 1982 (Grammy, 1982), Top Drawer, 1983 (Grammy, 1983), An Evening at Charlie's, 1984, Grand Piano, 1985, An Elegant Evening, 1986, George Shearing and Barry Tuckwell Play the Music of Cole Porter, 1986, More Grand Piano, 1987, (with Marian McPartland) Alone Together, 1981, George Shearing and Dakota Staton: In the Night, A Vintage Year, 1987, George Shearing In Dixieland, 1989, I Hear a Rhapsody: Live at the Blue Note, 1994, On a Clear Day, 1980, How Beautiful is Night, Best of George Shearing, 1993, That Shearing Sound, 1994, Walkin' - Live at the Blue Note, The George Shearing Quintet: By Request, Jazz Moments, 1995, Paper Moon: Music of Nat King Cole, George Shearing and Friends, 1996, appearance London Symphony Pops Concerts, 1986, 1987, London Paladium, Concord Jazz Festival, Japan, 1987, Hong Kong Cultural Ctr., 1992, European Jazz Festivals, 1995, Birmingham (Eng.) Symphony with Sir Simon Rattle, 1995, Can. Tour, 1995, Japan Tour, New Eng. Jazz Festival, Tanglewood, Mass., US Tour, 1996, others, 1996. Bd. dirs. Guide Dogs for Blind San Rafael, Hadley Sch. for Blind, Winnetka, Ill. Named top English pianist, 1941—47; recipient all Am. jazz polls, also many pvt. awards, Golden Plate award, Am. Acad. of Achievement, 1968, Helen Keller Achievement award, 1995. Mem.: Broadcast Music Inc., Bohemian Club (San Francisco), Lotos Club (N.Y.), Friars Club. Avocations: walking, listening to tennis and cricket matches, bridge, quiet dinners. Office: care Joan Shulman 103 Avenue Rd Ste 301 Toronto ON Canada M5R 2G9

SHEARING, MIRIAM, state supreme court justice; b. Waverly, NY, Feb. 24, 1935; BA, Cornell U., 1956; JD, Boston Coll., 1964. Bar: Calif. 1965, Nev. 1969. Justice of peace Las Vegas Justice Ct., 1977-81; judge Nev. Dist. Ct., 1983-92, chief judge, 1986; justice Nevada Supreme Ct., Carson City, 1993-97, chief justice, 1997—. Mem. ABA, Am. Judicature Soc. (chair 2001-), Nev. Judges Assn. (sec. 1978), Nev. Dist. Ct. Judges Assn. (sec. 1984-85, pres. 1986-87), State Bar Nev., State Bar Calif., Clark County Bar Assn. Democrat. E-mail: shearing@nvcourts.state.nv.us.

SHEARN, MICHAEL JOSEPH, lawyer, arbitrator, mediator; BA with honors, U. Tex., 1973, JD, 1976; Cert. Internat. Law, London Sch. Econs., 1974. Bar: D.C. 1976, Tex. 1976, U.S. Supreme Ct. 1980. Assoc. Surrey & Morse, Washington, 1976-80; shareholder Law, Snakard, Gambill, Ft. Worth, 1981-84, Cox & Smith, San Antonio, 1984-90; gen. counsel Tex. Nat. Rsch. Lab. Commn., De Soto and Waxahachie, Tex., 1991; counsel Don McManus Law Offices, San Antonio, 1992-94; pvt. practice San Antonio, 1994—2000; assoc. gen. counsel Ilex Oncology Inc., San Antonio, 2000—. Troop com. mem. Boy Scouts Am., San Antonio, 1993—97; trustee Univ. Meth. Ch., San Antonio, 1995—97. Fellow: Tex. Bus. Law Found.; mem.: Phi Delta Phi, Phi Beta Kappa. Office: PO Box 781466 San Antonio TX 78278

SHEA-STONUM, MARILYN, federal bankruptcy judge; b. 1947; AB, U. Santa Cruz, 1969; JD, Case Western Res. U., 1975. Law clk. to Hon. Frank J. Battisti, Cleve., 1975-76; ptnr. Jones, Day, Reavis & Pogue, Cleve., 1984—94; bankruptcy judge U.S. Dist. Ct. (no. dist.) Ohio, Akron, 1994—. Editor-in-chief Am. Bankruptcy Law Jour., Nat. Conf. Bankruptcy Judges. Mem. Order of Coif. Office: US Bankruptcy Ct No Dist Ohio 240 Fed Bldg 2 S Main St Akron OH 44308-1813 Office Phone: 330-375-5780.

SHEATH, ROBERT GORDON, botanist, educator; b. Toronto, Dec. 26, 1950; arrived in U.S., 1978; s. Harry Gordon and Shirley Irene (Rose) Sheath. BSc, U. Toronto, 1973, PhD, 1977. Nat. Rsch. Coun. Can. postdoctoral fellow

U. B.C., 1977-78; asst. prof. aquatic biology U. RI, Kingston, 1978-82, assoc. prof., 1982-86, chmn. dept. botany, 1986-90, prof., 1987-91; head dept. biology Meml. U., St. Johns, Canada, 1991-95; dean coll. biol. sci. U. Guelph, Ont., 1995-2001; provost Calif. State U., San Marcos, 2001—. Mem. evolution and ecology grant selection com. NSERC, 1994—97, chair, 1996—97, selection com. life scis., 1996, chair maj. facilities access life scis. subcom., 2001; mem. Can. Rsch. Chairs Coll. of Reviewers, 2000—01. Editor (with M. M. Harlin): Freshwater and Marine Plants of RI, 1988; editor: (with K. M. Cole) Biology of the Red Algae, 1990; editor: (with J.D. Wehr) Classification and Ecology of Freshwater Algae of North America, 2003; contbr. more than 120 articles to profl. jours. Recipient G. A. Cox Gold medal, U. Toronto, 1973, Darbaker prize, Bot. Soc. Am., 1997, T. Christensen prize panel, 2000; grantee, NSF, 1980—91, 2001—, NSERC, 1991—2002. Mem.: Japanese Phycological Soc. (editl. bd. 2000—03), Brit. Phycological Soc. (freshwater flora com. 1993—2002, overseas v.p. 1997—99, assoc. editor 1999—2001), Arctic Inst. N.Am., Phycological Soc. Am. (editl. bd. 1983—86, assoc. editor 1984—89, pres. 1991—92, editl. bd. 1996—2000, publs. com. chair 2001—, bd. trustees 2001—, Bold award 1976), Internat. Phycological Soc. (editl. bd. 1993—95, T. Christensen prize panel 2000, nominating com. 2000—01). Office: U Calif San Marcos Office of Provost San Marcos CA 92096-0001 Office Phone: 760-750-4050. E-mail: rsheath@csusm.edu.

SHEATS, JOHN EUGENE, chemistry professor; b. Atlanta, Dec. 20, 1939; s. Eugene Harold and Mildred Virginia (Pendergrass) S.; m. Margaret Joann Lee, May 27, 1972; 1 child, David S. BS in Chemistry, Duke U., 1961; PhD in Chemistry, MIT, 1966. Asst. prof. Bowdoin Coll., Brunswick, Maine, 1965-70; assoc. prof. chemistry Rider Coll. (name changed to Rider U. 1995), Lawrenceville, N.J., 1970-78, prof., 1978—. Presbyterian. Avocation: scuba diving. Office: Rider U 2083 Lawrenceville Rd Lawrenceville NJ 08648-3099 Office Phone: 609-895-5413. E-mail: sheats@rider.edu.

SHEBLE, WALTER FRANKLIN, retired lawyer; b. Chestnut Hill, Pa., Sept. 14, 1926; s. Franklin and Harriett Elizabeth (Smith) S.; m. Nancy Altemus, July 7, 1956; 3 children. AB, Princeton U., 1948; JD, George Washington U., 1952, LLM, 1953. Bar: U.S. Dist. Ct. D.C. 1952, U.S. Ct. Appeals D.C. 1952, U.S. Supreme Ct. 1953, U.S. Ct. Appeals Md. 1960. Assoc. Hudson & Creyke, Washington, 1953-56, H. William Tanaka, Washington, 1956-61, 63-66; cons. Office of Pres., Washington, 1961-63; spl. asst. to postmaster gen., U.S. rep. Univ. Postal Union, Bern, Switzerland, 1966-70; spl. asst. to gen. counsel Interam. Devel. Bank, Washington, 1970-88. Trustee New Engl. Coll. Mem. bd. mgrs. Chevy Chase Village, 1985-89; pres. Parents Assn. Nat. Cathedral Sch., 1969-70, mem. governing bd. 1970. Mem. ABA (exec. coun. gen. practice sect. 1982-87), Bar Assn. D.C., Colonial Club, Barristers Club, Met. Club, Chevy Chase Club. Avocations: gardening, surf fishing.

SHECHTMAN, RONALD H. lawyer; b. Hartford, Conn., Sept. 26, 1946; s. Allen A. and Jean (Bernstein) S.; m. Carolyn Meadow, Dec. 11, 1982; 1 child, Jonathan. BA, Amherst Coll., 1968; JD, NYU, 1972. Bar: U.S. Dist. Ct. (so. dist.) N.Y. 1973, N.Y. 1973, U.S. Ct. Appeals (2d cir.), U.S. Supreme Ct. Ptnr. Gordon & Shechtman PC, N.Y.C., 1972-85, Pryor, Cashman, Sherman & Flynn, N.Y.C., 1985—. Free speech com. ACLU, 1972, labor & employment com. N.Y.C. Bar Assn., 1988-91. Bd. advisors NYU Law Sch. Ctr. for Labor and Employment Law, 1997—; bd. dirs. The Creative Coalition, 1996-99. Office: Pryor Cashman Sherman & Flynn 410 Park Ave Fl 10 New York NY 10022-4407

SHECKLER, ROSS DAVID, engineering executive; b. Cato, NY, Mar. 24, 1966; m. Cynthia Rose Delaney, June 1, 1996. MS in Aerospace Engring., Iowa State U., 1991. Sr. engr. Boeing Comml. Aircraft, Seattle, 1991—95; mem. tech. staff 5 Dynacs Engring., Seattle, 1995—97; mgr. Dynacs, Inc., Cato, 1997—2002; pres. Calmar Rsch. Corp., Cato, 2002—. Adj. prof. Syracuse (NY) U., 2001; pres. indsl. adv. com. Iowa State U., Dept. Aerospace Engring., Ames, 2001—. Mem. bd. trustees Lang Meml. Libr., Cato, 2000. Mem.: AIAA, Soc. Automotive Engrs., Exptl. Aircraft Assn. Conservative. Achievements include patents pending for Ltd. injection cycle safety syringe. Office: Calmar Rsch Corp PO Box 247 Cato NY 13033

SHEDAKER, KATHLEEN EDITH, publishing executive; b. Boston, May 2, 1953; d. Richard Flave Shedaker and Jessica Mae Gould; m. Jon Patterson Speller Sr.; 1 child, Jon Patterson Speller Jr. AAS in Bus. Adminstrn., Monroe Coll., 2001, BBA in Bus. Mgmt., 2003. Rschr. Press Office Saudi Arabia, N.Y.C., 1986-96, Bosniac Nat. Coun. of Sanjak, N.Y.C., 1996, Backster Rsch. Found., San Diego, 1985; pub. Morning Star Chapel & Press, N.Y.C., 1986—. Dir. microgenepools.com, N.Y.C., 2000—. Author: The American Dynasty, 1998, The Classic Seed Money in Action, 2003, Awaken the Sleeping Angel Within You, 2004. Exec. dir. Anti-Communist Internat., N.Y.C., 1985—. Recipient Cold War Victory medal Anti-Communist Internat., 2000. Mem.: N.Y. Geneal. and Biog. Soc., Morning Star Chapel (co-founder, Interfaith award 1996). Avocations: genealogy, music, art, poetry. Office: Anti-Communist Internat PO Box 1095 New York NY 10163-1095 E-mail: kshedaker5154@monroecollege.edu.

SHEDD, DENNIS W. federal judge; b. 1953; BA, Wofford Coll., 1975; JD, U. S.C., 1978; LLM, Georgetown U., 1980. Bar: S.C. Law clerk Harry Dent & Assoc., 1977—78; admin. asst. US Senator Strom Thurmond, 1982—84; chief counsel US Senate Jud. Com., Washington, 1985-86; of counsel Bethea, Jordan & Griffin, Columbia, S.C., 1988-90; pvt. practice, 1989-90; judge U.S. Dist. Ct. S.C., Greenville, 1990—2002, US Ct. of Appeals (4th cir.), 2002—. Adj. prof. U. SC, 1989-92. Mem. SC Bar Assn., Richland County Bar Assn., Phi Beta Kappa. Office: US Courthouse 100 Laurel St Columbia SC 29201-2431

SHEDD, DONALD POMROY, surgeon; b. New Haven, Aug. 4, 1922; s. Gale and Marion (Young) S.; m. Charlotte Newsom, Mar. 17, 1946; children: Carolyn, David, Ann, Laura BS, Yale U., 1944, MD, 1946. Diplomate Am. Bd. Surgery. Intern Yale New Haven Hosp., 1946-47, asst. resident, resident, 1949-53; instr. surgery Yale U. Med Sch., New Haven, 1953-54, asst. prof., 1954-56, assoc. prof., 1956-67; chief dept. head and neck surgery Roswell Park Cancer Inst., Buffalo, 1967-96, prof. emeritus, 1996—; rsch. prof. emeritus SUNY at Buffalo, 1996—. Co-editor: Surgical and Prosthetic Speech Rehabilitation, 1980, Head and Neck Cancer, 1985, The Early History of Hospice Buffalo, 2003; author: Historical Landmarks in Head and Neck Cancer Surgery, 2000; contbr. numerous articles to profl. jours. Founding bd. dirs. Hospice Buffalo, Inc., 1973-83. Served to capt. U.S. Army, 1947—49. Mem. Am. Head and Neck Soc., Soc. Univ. Surgeons, Soc. Surg. Oncology, New Eng. Surg. Soc., Soc. Head and Neck Surgeons (pres. 1976-77). Avocations: sailing, windsurfing, tennis, history of medicine. Home: 671 Lafayette Ave Buffalo NY 14222-1435 Office: Roswell Park Cancer Inst Elm & Carlton Sts Buffalo NY 14263-0001 Office Phone: 716-845-3281. E-mail: donshedd@adelphia.net.

SHEDLARZ, DAVID L. pharmaceutical company executive; b. New York; m. Patricia Shedlarz; 1 child, Danielle. BS in Econs. and Math., Mich. State U., 1970; MBA in Fin. and Acctg., NYU, 1975. Various positions Pfizer Inc., N.Y.C., 1976-79, prodn. contr. U.S. Pharms. divsn., 1979-81, asst. group contr. U.S. Pharms. divsn., 1981-84, group contr., 1984-89, v.p. fin. U.S. pharms. group, 1989-92, corp. officer, v.p. fin. parent co., 1992-95, CFO, 1995—, sr. v.p., 1997-2000, exec. v.p., 2000—, also mem. corp. mgmt. com.; dir. Pitney Bowes Inc., 2001—. Office: Pfizer Inc 235 E 42d St New York NY 10017-5755

SHEDLOCK, JAMES, library director, consultant; b. Detroit, Nov. 25, 1950; BA in English, U. Notre Dame, 1974; AM in LS, U. Mich., 1977. Reference and serials libr. St. Joseph Mercy Hosp., Pontiac, Mich., 1977-79; document delivery libr. Wayne State U. Med. Libr., Detroit, 1979-81; coord. online search svc. U. N.C. Health Scis. Libr., Chapel Hill, 1982-84; head pub. svcs. Med. Libr., Northwestern U., Chgo., 1985-88, assoc. dir., 1988-91, dir. Galter Health Scis. Libr., 1991—. Cons. U.N. High Commr. for Refugees, Cyprus, 1993-94, Med. Coll. Wis. Libr., 1996-97, La Porte (Ind.) Hosp., 1998. Mem. ALA, Med. Libr. Assn. (bd. dirs. 1997-99), Am. Med. Informatics Assn., Assn. Acad. Health Scis. Libr. Dirs. (rep.), Acad. Health Info. Profls. (disting.). Office: Northwestern U Galter Health Scis Libr 303 E Chicago Ave Chicago IL 60611-3093 Office Phone: 312-503-8133. E-mail: j-shedlock@northwestern.edu.

SHEDRINSKY, ALEXANDER MIKCHAIL, chemistry professor, conservator, consultant; b. Leningrad, USSR, Mar. 27, 1943; arrived in USA, 1980. s. Mikchail Alexander Shedrinsky and Mussa A. (Gordon) Tsipkina; m. Raissa A. (Bekker), Oct. 16, 1965 (div. Apr. 1975); one child, Mikchail Alexander; m. Maria G. (Kurbatova), June 30, 1982; one child, Maria Antonia. MS in Chemistry, Leningrad U., 1965; MS in Organic Chemistry, N.Y. Univ., 1983, PhD in Organic Chemistry, 1986. Rsch. asst. State Sci. Rsch. Inst. Pulp and Paper, Leningrad, 1971—72; asst. prof. chemistry Leningrad N.W. Poly. Tech., 1972—75, LI Univ., Bklyn., 1988—92; lectr. in organic chemistry Leningrad Pharm. Sch., 1976—79; tchg. fellow NY Univ., NYC, 1981—83, postdoctoral fellow Conservation Ctr. Inst. Fine Arts, 1986—88; assoc. prof. chemistry LI Univ., Bklyn., 1992—97; adj. assoc. prof. Conservation Ctr. Inst. Fine Arts NY Univ., NYC, 1993—97; cons. Met. Mus. Art, NYC, 1994—; prof. chemistry LI Univ., Bklyn., 1997—; adj. prof. Conservation Ctr. Inst. Fine Arts NY Univ., NYC, 1998—99; cons. internat. coun. Mus. Modern Art, 2001—. Vis. scientist Am. Mus. Natural History, NYC, 1995—; vis. prof. Forchheimer, 1997, Hebrew U. Jerusalem; Fulbright prof. USIA, St. Petersburg (Russia) Acad. Art, 1995, 2001-02. Contbr. chpt. to book, articles to internat. scientific journals; reviewer, Jour. Analytical and Applied Pyrolysis, Curator, Archeometry, 1989—. Andrew W. Mellon Fellow Met. Mus. Art, Dept. Object Conservation, 1988-90, Charles and Francis Atkins Fellow Met. Mus. Art, Dept. Paintings Conservation, 1984-86. Mem. Am. Chem. Soc. (tour spkr.) Washington,1992-, Internat. Inst. Conservation, NY Acad. Sci. Achievements include synthesis of new synthetic varnish for the purpose of painting conservation; introducing analytical pyrolysis in the field of art conservation (first rev. on the subject in 1989); devel. of new analytical approach (Py-GC and Py-GC-MS) to analysis of different ambers. Office: LIU 1 Univ Plz Brooklyn NY 11201-5301 Office Phone: 718-488-1208.

SHEDROFF, SHARON D. psychologist, researcher, anthropologist, consultant; b. Middletown, Conn., Feb. 7, 1952; d. Leon and Sylvia Shedroff. BA summa cum laude, Syracuse U., N.Y., 1974; MA, Calif. Sch. Profl. Psychology, San Diego, 1979. Lic. marriage, family and child counselor Calif., 1981. Psychology intern T.R.I. Cmty. Svcs., San Diego, 1978—81, marriage, family & child counselor, 1981—82; rsch. psychologist Grid Rsch., San Diego, 1983—85; founder, ptnr. Edwards Assocs., San Diego, 1985—, Strategic Vision Inc., San Diego, 1989—, Inst. for Value-Centered Life, San Diego, 1999—. Author: (novels) Dakota Dreams, 2003; contbr. articles to profl. jours. Sustaining mem. Rep. Nat. Com., 2000—03. Mem.: Am. Morgan Horse Assn., U.S.A. Equestrian. Avocations: skiing, competitive horseback riding. Home: PO Box 420036 San Diego CA 92142 Office: The Edwards Assocs PO Box 420429 San Diego CA 92142 Office Phone: 858-576-7141.

SHEEDY, ALLY (ALEXANDRA ELIZABETH SHEEDY), actress; b. N.Y.C., June 13, 1962; d. John and Charlotte (Baum) S.; m. David Lansbury; 1 child, Rebecca. Student, U. So. Calif. Past ballet dancer. Film debut in Bad Boys, 1983; other films include Wargames, 1983, Oxford Blues, 1984, The Breakfast Club, 1985, St. Elmo's Fire, 1985, Twice in a Lifetime, 1985, Short Circuit, 1986, Blue City, 1986, Maid to Order, 1987, Heart of Dixie, 1989, Betsy's Wedding, 1990, Only the Lonely, 1991, Home Alone II: Lost in New York, 1992, The Pickle, 1992, Man's Best Friend, 1993, Tattle Tale, 1993, One Night Stand, 1995, Groupies, 1997, Highball, 1997, Crossroads of Destiny, 1997, Country Justice, 1997, Amnesia, 1997, High Art, 1998 (Best Actress award Nat. Soc. Film Critics 1998, Ind. Spirit award for best female lead 1999), Autumn Heart, 1998, I'll Take You There, 1999, Advice From a Caterpillar, 1999, Just a Dream, 2002, Happy Here and Now, 2002, A Good Night to Die, 2003, Shelter Island, 2003, Noise, 2004; TV films include The Best Little Girl in the World, 1981, The Day the Loving Stopped, 1981, The Violation of Sarah McDavid, 1981, Splendor in the Grass, 1981, Dead Lessons, 1983, We Are the Children, 1987, Fear, 1990, The Lost Capone, 1990, Lethal Exposure, 1993, Chantilly Lace, 1993, The Hauting of Sea Cliff Inn, 1994, Ultimate Betrayal, 1994, Parallel Lives, 1994, Tin Soldier, 1995, Hijacked: Flight 285, 1996, Sleeping With the Devil, 1997, Buried Alive 2, 1997, Amnesia, 1997, Myth America, 1998, High Art, 1998, (TV) The Fury Within, 1998, Sugar Town, 1999, Autumn Hart, 1999, (TV) Our Guys, 1999, The Warden, 2001, The Interrogation of Michael Crowe, 2002, Life On the Line, 2003, (TV guest appearances) The Dead Zone, 2002; author (children's book) She Was Nice to Mice, 1975, (poetry) Yesterday I Saw the Sun, 1991. Address: Don Buchwald & Assocs Ste 2200 6500 Wilshire Blvd Los Angeles CA 90048 also: PO Box 523 Topanga CA 90290-0523 also: 11766 Wilshire Blvd #1610 Los Angeles CA 90025-6555*

SHEEDY, KATHLEEN ANN, lawyer; b. June 18, 1956; d. Patrick Thomas Sheedy and Margaret Pelkey Mulvaney; m. Mark Louis Pedriani, Sept. 25, 1982; children: Gabrielle, Katherine, Jennifer. BS in Bus. Adminstrn., Georgetown U., 1978; JD, Marquette U., 1981. Bar: Wis. 1981, Ill. 1981, U.S. Dist. Ct. (no. dist.) Ill. 1981, U.S. Dist. Ct. (ea. dist.) Wis. 1981. Assoc. Chapman & Cutler, Chgo., 1981-83; mgr. Peat Marwick, Paris, 1983-84; assoc. Quarles & Brady, Milw., 1984-86; sr. mgr. KPMG Peat Marwick, Paris, 1986-90; sr. atty. Kohler (Wis.) Co., 1991—. Office: Kohler Co Legal Dept 444 Highland Dr Kohler WI 53044-1500

SHEEDY, PATRICK THOMAS, judge; b. Green Bay, Wis., Oct. 31, 1921; s. Earl P. and Elsie L. (Brauel) S.; m. Margaret P. Mulvaney, Sept. 6, 1952; children: Michael, Mary, Kathleen, Patrick Thomas, Ann, Maureen. BS in Bus. Adminstrn., Marquette U., 1943, JD, 1948; LLM in Taxation, John Marshall Law Sch., 1972. Bar: Wis. 1948. Pvt. practice, Milw., 1948-80; judge Wis. Cir. Ct., Milw., 1980-90; chief judge 1st Jud. Dist., Milw., 1990-98. Past vice chmn. Archdiocesan Sch. Bd., Milw., chairperson, 1986—. Served to col. USAR, 1942-73. Decorated Legion of Merit. Mem.: ABA (state del. 1983—85, 1989—92, bd. govs. 1985—88), Wis. Bar Assn. (pres. 1974—75, bd. govs., exec. com.), Exchange (pres.). Roman Catholic.

SHEEHAN, CAROL SAMA, magazine editor; Editor-in-chief Country Home Mag., Des Moines, 1997—. Office: Country Home Magazine 1716 Locust St Des Moines IA 50309-3038

SHEEHAN, EDWARD JAMES, technical consultant, former government official; b. Johnstown, Pa., Dec. 31, 1935; s. Louis A. and Ethel F. (Schaefer) S.; m. Florence Ann Hartnett, June 17, 1958; children— Edward, James, John, William, Mary. BS in Physics, St. Francis Coll., 1959; MS (Sloan fellow), Mass. Inst. Tech., 1972. Project engr. Electronics Command, Dept. Army, 1959-61, project team leader electro-optic equipment for tanks, 1961-63, project team leader electro-optic equipment for infantry, 1963-65, tech. area dir. electro-optic night vision equipment, 1965-73, asso. lab. dir. for devel. engring., 1973-76; lab. dir. Night Vision Lab., Fort Belvoir, Va., 1976-79; founder, pres. Sheehan Assos. Inc., Alexandria, Va., 1979-92; founder, CEO, chmn. Stardyne, Inc., Johnstown, 1990-96. Chmn. Nat. and Internat. Symposia for Electro-Optical Tech. and Applications. Recipient numerous awards including Meritorious Civilian Svc. award Dept. Army, Disting. Alumnus award in sci. St. Francis Coll., 1989; named Man of Yr., Combined Svc. Clubs, Johnstown, Pa., 1993. Home: 809 Luzerne St Johnstown PA 15905-2301

SHEEHAN, JAMES JOHN, historian, educator; b. San Francisco, May 31, 1937; s. James B. and Sally W. (Walsh) S.; m. 1960; 1 child, Michael L.; m. Margaret L. Anderson, Sept. 2, 1989. BA, Stanford U., 1958; MA, U. Calif., Berkeley, 1959, PhD, 1964. From asst. to assoc. prof. Northwestern U., Evanston, Ill., 1964-79; prof. Stanford (Calif.) U., 1979-86, chmn. dept., 1982-89, Dickason prof. in humanities, 1986—. Author: Lujo Brentano, 1966, German Liberalism, 1978, German History 1770-1866, 1989, Der Ausklang des alten Reiches, 1994, Museums in German Artworld, 2000; editor: The Boundaries of Humanity, 1991; contbr. articles to profl. jours. Decorated officer's cross Order of Merit; fellow Am. Council Learned Socs., 1981-82, NEH, 1985-86, Wissenschaftskolleg Berlin; Guggenheim fellow, 2000—. Fellow AAAS (Humboldt Rsch. prize 1995), Am. Acad. Berlin; mem. Royal Hist. Soc. (corr.), Am. Hist. Assn. (nominating com. 1979-81, chmn. conf. group on Ctrl. European history 1985-86, pres.elect 2004), Am. Philos. Soc. Office: Stanford U Dept History Stanford CA 94305 Business E-Mail: sheehan@stanford.edu.

SHEEHAN, JAMES PATRICK, printing company executive, former media company executive; b. Jersey City, June 6, 1942; s. John Patrick and Helen Teresa (Woods) S.; m. Mary Ellen Finnell, July 1, 1967; children: James, Christopher. BS, Seton Hall U., 1965; MBA, Wayne State U., 1973. Contr. Otis Elevator Co. N.Am., Farmington, Conn., 1976-78, dir. mfg. Yonkers, N.Y., 1978-80; v.p., contr., Pratt & Whitney Aircraft, East Hartford, Conn., 1980-82; sr. v.p. A. H. Belo Corp., Dallas, 1982-84; CFO, A.H. Belo Corp., Dallas, 1984-86, pres., COO, 1987-93, CEO, 1993-99; pres., CEO, chmn. Goss Graphic Systems, Westmont, Ill., 1999—. Mem. devel. bd. U. Tex.-Dallas, 1985—; bd. dirs. United Way, The Dallas Partnership, The Dallas Morning News Charities; trustee St. Paul Med. Ctr. Found. Served to Lt. (j.g.) USN, 1967-69, Vietnam. Mem. Am. Newspaper Pubs. Assn., So. Newspaper Pubs. Assn. Roman Catholic. Avocations: tennis; racquetball; golf; jogging. Office: Goss International 3 Territorial Ct Bolingbrook IL 60440-3557

SHEEHAN, JEREMIAH J. former metal company executive; b. N.Y.C., Oct. 21, 1938; m. Mary Rita Sheehan; 3 children. BA in Econs., Hunter Coll.; postgrad., U. Chgo. With Continental Can Co., pres., gen. mgr. beverage packaging; v.p. can divsn. Reynolds Metals Co., Richmond, Va., 1988—90, exec. v.p. consumer and packaging products, 1990—93, exec. v.p. fabricated products, 1993—94, pres., COO, bd. dirs., 1994—96, chmn. bd., CEO, 1996—99. Bd. dirs. Union Camp Corp.; fed. resident Bank of Richmond. Mem. Bus. Roundtable, Va. Bus. Coun., Richmond Mgmt. Roundtable; adv. coun. on Rev. Estimates State of Va.; bd. trustees Va. Found. Ind. Colls.; mem. adv. coun. E. Clairborne Robins Sch. Bus., U. Richmond; bd. dirs. Va. Commonwealth U. Sch. Engring. Found., Richmond Met. Coalition Against Drugs; former chmn. bd. Keep Am. Beautiful, Inc. Office: Reynolds Metals Co 6601 W Broad St Richmond VA 23230-1723

SHEEHAN, JOHN D. automotive executive; b. Trumbull, Conn. BBA in Acctg., St. Bonaventure U., NY. CPA. Chief acctg. officer, contr. Delphi Corp., Troy, Mich., 2002—. Mem.: Am. Inst. Cert. Pub. Accts. Office: Delphi Corp World Headquarters 5725 Delphi Dr Troy MI 48098-2815

SHEEHAN, JOHN R. food products executive; Degree, So. Meth. U. With Albertson's Supermarkets, Calif., 1978—96; sr. v.p. ops. Pathmark, 1996—97, exec. v.p. store ops., 1997—2000; sr. v.p. Winn-Dixie Stores, Inc., Jacksonville, Fla., 2000—01, dir. sales and procurement, 2000—01, sr. v.p. ops., 2001—. Office: Winn Dixie Stores Inc 5050 Edgewood Ct Jacksonville FL 32254-3699

SHEEHAN, LAWRENCE JAMES, lawyer; b. San Francisco, July 23, 1932; AB, Stanford U., 1957, LLB, 1959. Bar: Calif. 1960. Law clk. to chief judge U.S. Ct. Appeals 2d Cir., N.Y.C., 1959-60; assoc. O'Melveny & Myers, L.A., 1960-68, ptnr., 1969-94, of counsel, 1995—. D. dirs. FPA Mut. Funds, Source Capital, Inc. Mem. ABA, Los Angeles County Bar Assn., Calif. Bar Assn., Order of Coif. Office: O Melveny & Myers 1999 Avenue Of The Stars Los Angeles CA 90067-6035 also: 400 S Hope St Los Angeles CA 90071-2801 Office Phone: 310-246-6895. Business E-Mail: lsheehan@omm.com.

SHEEHAN, LINDA SUZANNE, education administrator; b. Dayton, Ohio, Aug. 1, 1950; d. Paul J. and Betty L. (Fowler) King; 1 child, Amy Elizabeth. BS in Edn. with honors, Ohio State U., 1971; MEd, U. Tex., 1974; adminstrn. cert., Houston Bapt. U., 1983. Tchr. Upper Arlington Schs., Columbus, Ohio, 1971-72, Brown Sch., San Marcos, Tex., 1972-73, Comal Ind. Schs. Dist., New Braunfels, Tex., 1973-75, Allief Ind. Sch. Dist., Houston, 1975-79; asst. prin. Killough Mid. Sch., Houston, 1979-84; prin. Olle Mid. Sch., Houston, 1984-92, Blue Ribbon Sch., 1991-92, Holub Mid. Sch., 1992—. Named Tchr. of Yr. Olle Mid. Sch., Houston, 1978; recipient Mary Knotts Perkins Exemplary Leadership award, 1998, Blue Ribbon Sch. award 1991-92. Mem. Nat. Mid. Sch. Assn., Nat. Assn. Secondary Sch. Prins., Tex. Assn. Secondary Sch. Prins., Tex. Mid. Sch. Assn. (dir. 1979-91, pres. 1991-92, state convention chair 1993-94, 97-98), Houston Coun. Social Studies, Kappa Delta Pi (pres. 1984-85), Phi Delta Kappa. Roman Catholic. Home: 526 Nottingham Oaks Trail Houston TX 77079-6332 Office: Holub Mid Sch 9515 S Dairy Ashford St Houston TX 77099-4909

SHEEHAN, MICHAEL ANDREW, diplomat; b. Red Bank, N.J., Feb. 10, 1955; s. John M. and Janet M. (Purcell) S.; m. Sita Sheehan; children: Alexandra, Michael BS, US Mil. Acad., 1977; MS in Fgn. Svc., Georgetown U., 1988. Commd. 2d lt. U.S. Army, 1977-97, advanced through grades to lt. col., ret., 1997; intelligence analyst White House Staff, Washington, 1989-91; dir. internat. programs Nat. Security Coun., Washington, 1992-93, dir. global issues, 1995-97; dir. POLMIL affairs U.S. Mission to UN, N.Y.C., 1993-95; dept. asst. sec. for internat. org. affairs U.S. Dept. State, Washington, 1997-98; coord. for counter terrorism Dept of State, Washington, 1998-2000; asst. sec. gen. Dept. Peacekeeping Ops., UN, N.Y.C., 2001—03; dep. commr. counter-terrorism N.Y. Police Dept., N.Y.C., 2003—. Mem.: Coun. on Fgn. Rels., Spl. Forces Assn. Roman Catholic.

SHEEHAN, MICHAEL GERARD, allergist; b. Syracuse, N.Y., Oct. 15, 1958; MD, SUNY, Syracuse, 1984. Diplomate Am. Bd. Allergy & Immunology. Resident in internal medicine Allegheny Genl. Hosp., Pitts., 1984-87; fellow in infectious diseases Presbyn. U. Hosp., Pitts., 1987-88; with Group Practice Settings in Internal Medicine, 1988-91, Group Practice in Allergy and Clin. Immunology, 1994—; fellow in allergy & rheumatology Strong Meml. Hosp., Rochester, NY, 1991—94. Home: 5110 Reis Cir Fayetteville NY 13066 Office: 1200 E Genesee St Ste 103 Syracuse NY 13210-1936 Business E-Mail: mgsheehan@twcny.rr.com.

SHEEHAN, MIKE, advertising executive; m. Maureen Sheehan. Student, U.S. Naval Acad.; BA in English, St. Anselm Coll. With Leo Burnett, Chgo., Clarke Goward and Ingalls Quinn & Johnson, Boston; exec. creative dir. Hill Holliday, Connors, Cosmopulos Interpub. Group, Boston, DDB, Chgo., Hill Holliday, Connors, Cosmopulos Interpub. Group, N.Y.C., 2000—02, pres., 2002—, CEO, 2003—. Vice chmn., bd. trustees St. Anselm Coll. Named Nat. Creative Dir. of Yr., Adweek, 1998; recipient Grand Clio award, One Show Gold award, Cannes Lions award, Best of Show award, Hatch, Communication Arts award. Office: Hill Holliday Franfurt Balkind 622 3RD Ave #15 New York NY 10017-6710

SHEEHAN, NEIL, reporter, scholarly writer; b. Holyoke, Mass., Oct. 27, 1936; s. Cornelius Joseph and Mary (O'Shea) Sheehan; m. Susan Margulies, Mar. 30, 1965; children: Maria Gregory, Catherine Fair. AB cum laude, Harvard, 1958; LittD (hon.), Columbia Coll., Chgo., 1972; LHD (hon.), Am. Internat. Coll., 1990, U. Lowell, 1991. Vietnam bur. chief UPI, Saigon, 1962—64; reporter N.Y. Times, N.Y.C., Djakarta, Saigon, Washington, 1964—72. Author: The Arnheiter Affair, 1972, A Bright Shining Lie: John Paul Vann and America in Vietnam, 1988 (Nat. Book award, 1988, Pulitzer Prize for gen. non-fiction, 1989, Robert F. Kennedy Book award, 1989, Vetty award Vietnam Vets. Ensemble Theatre Co., 1989, Spl. Achievement award Vietnam Vets. Am., 1989, Outstanding Investigative Reporting award Investigative Reporters and Editors Inc. of U. Mo. Sch. Journalism, 1989, Amb. award English Speaking Union, 1989, John F. Kennedy award Holyoke, Mass., 1989, selected by Modern Libr. as one of the 100 best works of non-fiction of the 20th century 1999), After the War Was Over: Hanoi and Saigon, 1992; contbr. articles and book revs. for popular mags., The Pentagon Papers, 1971. With U.S. Army, 1959—62. Recipient Louis M. Lyons award for conscience and integrity in journalism, 1964, Silver medal, Poor Richard Club, Phila., 1964, Cert. of Appreciation for best article on Asia, Overseas Press Club Am., 1967, 1st Ann. Drew Pearson prize for excellence in investigative reporting, 1971, Columbia Journalism award, 1972, 1989, Sidney Hillman Found. awards, 1972, 1988, Page One award, Newspaper Guild N.Y., 1972, Disting. Svc. award and Bronze medallion, Sigma Delta Chi, 1972, Citation of Excellence, Overseas Press Club, 1972, Lit. Lion award,

N.Y. Pub. Libr., 1992; Guggenheim fellow, 1973—74, Adlai Stevenson fellow, 1973—75, Lehrman Inst. fellow, 1975—76, Rockefeller Found. fellow in humanities, 1976—77, Woodrow Wilson Internat. Ctr. for Scholars fellow, 1979—80. Mem.: Am. Acad. Achievement, Soc. Am. Historians, Lansdowne Club (London). Achievements include obtaining Pentagon Papers, 1971. Home: 4505 Klingle St NW Washington DC 20016-3580

SHEEHAN, PATTY, professional golfer; b. Middlebury, Vt., Oct. 27, 1956; 4th ranked woman LPGA Tour, 1992; winner U.S. Women's Open, 1992, 94, McDonald's LPGA Championship, 1983-84, 93. Inductee LPGA Hall of Fame, 1993, Sports Illustrated Sportsman of the Yr., 1987. Achievements include being the winner for 31 LPGA Tournaments including Mazda Japan Classic, 1981, 88, Inamori Classic, 1982-83, 86, Orlando Lady Classic, 1982, Safeco Classic, 1982, 90, 95, LPGA Corning Classic, 1983, LPGA Championship, 1983-84, 93, Henredon Classic, 1983-84, Elizabeth Arden Classic, 1984, McDonald's Kids Classic, 1984, 90, Sarasota Classic, 1985-86, 88, J&B Scotch Pro AM, 1985, Konica San Jose Classic, 1986, Rochester Internat., 1989-90, 92, 95, Jamaica Classic, 1990, Ping-Cellular One Championship, 1990, Orix Hawaiian Ladies Open, 1991, Jamie Farr Toledo Classic, 1992, Weetabix Women's Brit. Open, 1992, U.S. Women's Open, 1992, 94, Mazda LPGA Championship, 1993, The Nabisco Championship, 1996; in 17 tournaments earning $179,453, 1997, 16 tounaments earning $342,391, 1996, 35th victory, Nabisco Dinah Shore earning 6th major champ. title, crossed $5 million mark in career earnings, 1996, winner Michelob Light Front Runner Awd. for leading most rounds in season, 1996. Office: LPGA 100 International Golf Dr Daytona Beach FL 32124-1092

SHEEHAN, ROBERT C. lawyer; b. N.Y.C., Oct. 12, 1944; s. John Edward and Mary Elizabeth (Trede) Sheehan; m. Elizabeth Mary Mammen, Aug. 17, 1968; children: Elizabeth, Robert, William. BA, Boston Coll., 1966; LLB, Univ. Pa., Phila., 1969. Bar: NY 1970. Ptnr. Skadden, Arps, Slate, Meagher & Flom LLP, N.Y.C., 1978—, exec. ptnr., 1994—. Office: Skadden Arps Slate Meagher Flom LLP 4 Times Sq New York NY 10036-6595

SHEEHAN, ROBERT JAMES, II, management and market research consultant; b. Pitts., May 13, 1937; s. Regis James and Helen Lillian (O'Leary) S.; m. Marie Elizabeth Yoskovich, Apr. 24, 1964; children: Stephanie Ann, Robert James III. AB in Econs., U. Pitts., 1967, MA, 1970; postgrad., Am. U. Cert. mgmt. cons. Rsch. analyst Action Housing Inc., Pitts., 1960-63; from project rep. to dir. rehab. Urban Redevel. Authority Pitts., 1963-73; assoc. chief economist, dir. econ. rsch. Nat. Assn. Homebuilders, Washington, 1973-82, v.p econ. policy analysis, 1982-83; v.p. Regis J. Sheehan & Assocs., McLean, Va., 1983-96, pres., 1997—. Founding dir. Georgetown Cons., Inc., 1993—; vice-chmn. Fairfax County Housing and Redevel. Authority, 1988-92, chmn. 1993-95. cons. in field. Author: The Basics of Land Acquisition, 1985; co-pub., prin. contbr. Mgmt./Econs. & Constrn. Real Estate newsletters; contbr. articles to profl. jours. Pres. bd. dirs. Touchstone Theatre Co., 1984-2003; pres. Caths. for Housing, 1998-2003; founding mem. Superior Bus. Roundtable. Mem. ASTD, Nat. Economists Club, Inst. Mgmt. Cons. (pres. Washington chpt. 1989-96), Nat. Assn. Bus. Econs., KC, Soc. for Human Resource Mgmt. Roman Catholic. Avocations: walking, jogging, reading.

SHEEHAN, SAMANTHA, gymnast; b. Cincinnati, OH, May 20, 1986; d. Kevin and Cindy Sheehan. Gymnast Cincinnati Gymnastics/U.S. Natl. Team, 2002—. Achievements include Level 10 National Bar Champion; Level 10 State Champion; Qualified to 2001, 02 U.S. Gymnastics Championships, World Championships, 2002; Bronze Medal Floor Exercise, World Championships, 2002; 1st place All Around, USA-Belgium dual competition, 2003. Office: 3635 Woodbridge Blvd Fairfield OH 45014

SHEEHAN, SUSAN, writer; b. Vienna, Aug. 24, 1937; arrived in U.S., 1941, naturalized, 1946; d. Charles and Kitty C. (Herrmann) Sachsel; m. Neil Sheehan, Mar. 30, 1965; children: Maria Gregory, Catherine Fair. BA, Wellesley Coll., 1958; DHL (hon.), U. Lowell, 1991. Editl. rschr. Esquire-Coronet, N.Y.C., 1959-60; freelance writer N.Y.C., 1960-61; staff writer New Yorker mag., N.Y.C., 1961—; contbg. writer Archtl. Digest, 1997—. Writer-in-residence, lectr. Georgetown U., 1999. Author: Ten Vietnamese, 1967, A Welfare Mother, 1976, A Prison and a Prisoner, 1978, Is There No Place on Earth for Me?, 1982, Kate Quinton's Days, 1984, A Missing Plane, 1986, Life For Me Ain't Been No Crystal Stair, 1993, The Banana Sculptor, the Purple Lady, and the All-Night Swimmer, 2002; contbr. articles to various mags., including N.Y. Times Sunday Mag., Washington Post Sunday Mag., Harper's, Atlantic, New Republic, McCall's, Holiday, Boston Globe Sunday Mag., Life. Judge Robert F. Kennedy Journalism awards, 1980, 84; mem. lit. panel D.C. Commn. on Arts and Humanities, 1979-84; mem. pub. info. and edn. com. Nat. Mental Health Assn., 1982-83; mem. adv. com. on employment and crime Vera Inst. Justice, 1978-86; chair Pulitzer Prize nominating jury in gen. non-fiction for 1988, 1994, mem., 1991. Recipient Sidney Hillman Found. award, 1976, Gavel award ABA, 1978, Individual Reporting award Nat. Mental Health Assn., 1981, Pulitzer prize for gen. non-fiction, 1983, Feature Writing award N.Y. Press Club, 1984, Alumnae Assn. Achievement award Wellesley Coll., 1984, Carroll Kowal Journalism award NASW, 1993, Disting. Grad. award Hunter Coll. H.S., 1995, Pub. Awareness award Nat. Alliance for Mentally Ill, 1995, Casey medal for meritorious journalism, 1997; Durant scholar Wellesley Coll., 1958; fellow Guggenheim Found., 1975-76, Woodrow Wilson Internat. Ctr. for Scholars, 1981, Open Soc. Inst., 1998-99. Mem. Soc. Am. Historians, Phi Beta Kappa, Authors Guild, Lansdowne Club (London). Home: 4505 Klingle St NW Washington DC 20016-3580 Office: New Yorker Mag 4 Times Sq New York NY 10036-7441

SHEEHY, BARRY MAURICE, management consultant; b. Nov. 17, 1951; came to the U.S., 1991; BA in History, Econs. cum laude, Loyola Coll., 1975; MA in History, McGill U., 1977; Comms. & Electronics and Engring., Can. Forces Sch. Comm. Electronic Engring. Officer Canadian Armed Forces, Savannah, Ga., 1975-80; quality mgr. City of Calgary, 1980-85; mgr. orgnl. efectiveness No. Telecom, 1985-87; pres. Achieve Internat., 1987-91, CPC Econometrics, Inc., 1991-94, CPC Econometrics Inc., Savannah, Ga., 1997—; ptnr. The Atlanta Cons. Group, 1994-96, Sentry Technology Group, 1996-97; pres. CPC Econometrics Inc., Savannah, Ga., 1998—. Mem. faculty Estes Pk.(Healthcare) Inst., Healthcare Governance Inst., Healthcare Forum; guest spkr. U.S. C. of C., Quality Coun. Can., Quality Coun. Mex., Microsoft Healthcare Forum, INC 500, Am. Express Bank Global Forum, others. Author: In Search of Quality: 4 Unique Perspectives, 43 Different Voices (Exec. Excellence 1995); (with others) Firing on All Cylinders, 1992, Economic Divide: Winners and Losers in an Age of Abundance, 1996, Winning the RAce, 1996; contbr. articles to profl. jours. Guest spkr. SCLC, Savannah Found. Officer Can. Armed Forces. Co-recipient Am. Soc. Indsl. Engrs. award, 1985. Office: CPC Econometrics Inc 38 Mulberry Bluff Dr Savannah GA 31406-3269

SHEEHY, FRANCES DIANE, lawyer; b. Mason City, Iowa, Jan. 1, 1947; d. M. ARthur and Adeline K. (Huizel) McCoid; m. Michael J. Sheehy, DEc. 17, 1967 (div. June 1989); children: D. Michael, Peter J. BS in Acctg., Bus. adminstrn., U. Ariz., 1984, JD, 1987. Bar: Ariz. 1987, Fla. 1988, U.S. Tax Ct. 1987, U.S. Dist. Ct. (so. dist.) Fla. 1992. Spl. asst. U.S. atty. Chief Counsel IRS, Miami, 1987-92; assoc. Patricia A. Redmond, Miami, 1992; pvt. practice Ft. Lauderdale, Fla., 1992-94; ptnr. Gutter, Josepher, Ruffin & Sheehy, P.A., Ft. Lauderdale, 1994-96; pvt. practice Coconut Creek, Fla., 1996—. Adv. group IRS Commrs., 1996-98. Mem. Fla. Bar Assn. (govt. lawyers sect., exec. coun. 1990—), Fla. Assn. Women Lawyers, Dade County Bar Assn. Roman Catholic. Avocations: golf, reading, dance. Office: 1367 Lyons Rd Coconut Creek FL 33063-3908 Office Phone: 954-977-4878.

SHEEHY, GAIL HENION, author; b. Mamaroneck, NY, Nov. 27, 1937; d. Harold Merritt and Lillian Rainey (Paquin) Henion; m. Albert F. Sheehy, Aug. 20, 1960 (div. 1967); 1 adopted child, Mohm 1 child, Maura; m. Clay Felker, Dec. 16, 1984. BS, U. Vt., 1958; fellow, Journalism Sch., Columbia U., 1970. Traveling home economist J.C. Penney & Co., 1958-60; fashion editor Rochester Democrat & Chronicle, 1961-63; feature writer N.Y. Herald Tribune, N.Y.C., 1963-66; contbg. editor New York mag., 1968-77. Contbr. to NY Times Mag., Parade, New Republic, Washington Post; polit. contbg. editor Vanity Fair mag., 1988—; author: Lovesounds, 1970, Panthermania: The Clash of Black Against Black in One American City, 1971, Speed Is of the Essence, 1971, Hustling: Prostitution in Our Wide-Open Society, 1973, Passages: Predictable Crises of Adult Life, 1976, Pathfinders, 1981, Spirit of Survival, 1986, Character: America's Search for Leadership, 1988, Gorbachev: The Man Who Changed the World, 1990, The Silent Passage: Menopause, 1992, New Passages: Mapping Your Life Across Time, 1995, Hillary's Choice, 1999, Middletown, America: One Town's Passage From Trauma to Hope, 2003; (plays) Maggie and Misha, 1991; co-author: Discovering the Power of Self-Hypnosis, 1999. Adv. bd. Women's Health Initiative, NIH; bd. dirs. Girls, Inc., Poets and Writers; eminent citizen's com. UN Internat. Conf. on Population and Devel., 1994. Recipient 5 Front Page awards Newswomen's Club NY, Nat. Mag. award Columbia U., 1973, Penney-Mo. Journalism award U. Mo., 1975, Anisfield-Wolf Book award, 1986, Best Mag. Writer award Wash. Journalism Rev., 1991, NY Pub. Libr. Literary Lion, 1992; Columbia U. fellow, 1970; Alicia Patterson Found. grantee, 1974. Mem. PEN, NOW, Authors Guild. Address: c/o Doug Stumpf Vanity Fair 4 Times Sq New York NY 10036-6522*

SHEEHY, JANICE ANN, education technology coordinator; b. Jersey City, Mar. 18, 1955; d. Thomas Patrick and Norma Grace (Hultman) Sheehy; m. L. Hillen, June 19, 1976 (div. 1982); 1 child, Adrienne Grace; m. I. Richard Feingold, May 17, 1987. BA, Jersey City State Coll., 1977; student, Fairleigh Dickinson U., 1978-80; EdM, Rutgers U., 1992; EdD, Nova Southeastern U., 1997. Cert. elem. tchr., supr. K-12, adminstr. K-12. Tchr. 2d grade Roosevelt Sch., Union City, N.J., 1977-88, tchr. math., 1988 98, chair sch. improvement team, 1994-98; tech. coord. Christopher Columbus Sch., Union City, N.J., 1999—. Mem. N.J. Math. Coalition, 1994—, N.J. Math. Curriculum Frameworks Dist. Leadership Team, Framework, 1994—. Com. woman Dem. Com., Hudson County, N.J., 1985-86. Mem. ASCD, AAUW, Nat. Coun. Tchrs. Math., Assn. Math. Tchrs. N.J., Kappa Delta Pi, Phi Delta Kappa. Avocations: travel, reading, computers. Home: 360 Roosevelt St Fairview NJ 07022-1716 Office: Christopher Columbus Mid Sch 1500 New York Ave Union City NJ 07087-4324

SHEEHY, JEROME JOSEPH, electrical engineer; b. Hartford, Conn., Dec. 3, 1935; s. Jeremiah and Anna (Foley) S.; m. Jean Ann Baldassari, Oct. 13, 1962; children: Caroline, Jerome, Daniel, Carlene. BSEE, U. Conn., 1962, MSEE, 1967. Electronic engr. USN Underwater Sound Lab., New London, Conn., 1962-69; mem. tech. staff Rockwell Internat., Anaheim, Calif., 1969-74; staff engr. Hughes Aircraft Co., Fullerton, Calif., 1974-83; systems engr. Norden Systems, Santa Ana, Calif., 1983-89; advanced engring. specialist Lockheed Martin Aircraft Svc., Ontario, Calif., 1990-97. Contbr. articles to Jour. Acoustical Soc. Am. With USAF, 1954-57. Mem. Acoustical Soc. Am., Tau Beta Pi, Eta Kappa Nu. Achievements include research in detection and estimation theory for non-gaussian noise, non-normal statistics. Home: 8 Sagitta Way Coto De Caza CA 92679-5102 Personal E-mail: jandjsheehy@cox.net.

SHEEHY, JOHN PAUL, pediatrician; b. Jan. 19, 1949; AB, Bowdoin Coll., 1970; MD, N.Y. Med. Coll., 1975. Diplomate Am. Bd. Pediat., Am. Bd. Quality Assurance and Utilization Review Physicians. Intern N.Y. Med. Coll. Met. Hosp. Ctr., resident; chmn. quality assurance North Shore U. Hosp., Glen Cove, N.Y., 1988—, dir. dept. pediats., 1990—, chmn. med. bd., 2000—. Contbr. articles to profl. jours. Office: 10 Medical Plz Glen Cove NY 11542-2193

SHEEHY, ROBERT J. health facility administrator; With UnitedHealthcare, Unitedhealth Group, Inc., Minnetonka, Minn., 1992—, CEO, UnitedHealthcare Ohio, 1994—98, pres. UnitedHealthcare, 1998—2000, CEO, 2000—. Office: Unitedhealth Group Ctr 9900 Bren Rd E Minnetonka MN 55343

SHEEKEY, KATHLEEN D. advocate, director; Legislative dir. Common Cause, 1981-91; dir. congressional relations Fed. Trade Commn.; legislative dir. Consumer Federation of Am.; co-dir. Advocacy Inst., 1992. Office: Advocacy Inst 1707 L St NW Ste 400 Washington DC 20036-4213 Fax: 202-659-8484. E-mail: info@advocacy.org.

SHEELEY, STEVEN M. academic administrator, minister, education educator; b. Springfield, Mo., Dec. 2, 1956; s. Charles B. and V. Ruth Sheeley; m. Elizabeth A. Lowry; children: Kristen R., Mary E. BS in edn., SW Mo. State U., 1979; MDiv, Southwestern Bapt. Theol. Sem., 1983; PhD, The So. Bapt. Theol. Sem., 1987. Asst. prof. of religion Shorter Coll., Rome, Ga., 1988—93, assoc. prof. of religion, 1993—2001, assoc. dean of the coll., 1997—2000, asst. v.p. for academic affairs, 2000—, prof. of religion, 2001—. Spl. studies editor Nat. Assn. of Bapt. Professors of Religion, 1997—; pres. Nat. Assn. of Bapt. Professors of Religion - Southeastern Region, 2001—02. Author: (book) Narrative Asides in Luke-Acts, The Bible in English Translation: An Essential Guide, Choosing a Bible; editor: A Community of Scholars; contbr. articles to jours. Co-pres. Rome H.S. PTSO, Ga., 2002—; min. of music North Broad Bapt. Ch., Rome, Ga., 2004—. Summer Seminar for Coll. Teachers grant, Nat. Endowment for the Humanities, 1991. Mem.: Soc. of Bibl. Lit., Nat. Assn. of Bapt. Professors of Religion (spl. studies editor 1997—2003), Seven Hills Rotary Club (bd. mem. 2001—02, cmty. svc. dir. 2001—02, v.p. 2003—04, pres. elect 2004—05), Phi Kappa Phi, Sigma Tau Delta, Theta Alpha Kappa (treas. 2002—). Baptist. Avocations: golf, reading. Office: Shorter College 315 Shorter Ave Rome GA 30165 E-mail: ssheeley@shorter.edu.

SHEEN, CHARLIE (CARLOS IRWIN ESTEVEZ), actor; b. N.Y.C., Sept. 3, 1965; s. Ramon (Martin Sheen) and Janet Estevez; m. Donna Peele, Sept. 3, 1995 (div. 1996); 1 child: Cassandra; m. Denise Richards, June 15, 2002; 1 child: Sam. Appearances include (film) Grizzly II: The Predator, 1984, Red Dawn, 1984, The Boys Next Door, 1985, Ferris Bueller's Day Off, 1986, Lucas, 1986, Platoon, 1986, Wisdom, 1986, The Wraith, 1986, A Life in the Day, 1986, Wall Street, 1987, No Man's Land, 1987, Three for the Road, 1987, Eight Men Out, 1988, Young Guns, 1988, Major League, 1989, Never on Tuesday, 1989, (also prodr.) Comicitis, 1989, Courage Mountain, 1990, Navy SEALS, 1990, Backtrack, 1990, Hot Shots!, 1990, Men At Work, 1990, The Rookie, 1990, Cadence, 1991, Beyond the Law (aka Fixing the Shadow), 1992, Hot Shots, Part Deux, 1993, The Three Musketeers, 1993, Loaded Weapon I, 1993, Deadfall, 1993, (also exec. prodr.) The Chase, 1994, Major League 2, 1994, Terminal Velocity, 1994, The Shadow Conspiracy, 1995, Shockwave, 1995, Loose Women, 1996, (voice) All Dogs Go to Heaven 2, 1996, The Arrival, 1996, Postmortem, 1997, Bad Day On the Block, 1997, Money Talks, 1997, (also writer, narrator) Mission to Mars, 1997, (also exec. prodr., writer) No Code of Conduct, 1998, Free Money, 1998, Letter From Death Row, 1998, Five Acres, 1999, Being John Malkovich, 1999, Rated X, 2000, Famous, 2000, Good Advice, 2001, Scary Movie 3, 2003, Deeper Than Deep, 2003, The Big Bounce, 2004; (TV movies) Execution of Private Slovik, 1974, Silence of the Heart, 1984, The Fourth Wise Man, 1985, Out of the Darkness, 1985; (tv series) Sugar Hill, 1999, Spin City, 2000-02 (Golden Globe award bext actor, 2001), Two and a Half Men, 2003-. Office: ICM 8942 Wilshire Blvd Beverly Hills CA 90211-1934*

SHEEN, MARTIN (RAMON ESTEVEZ), actor; b. Dayton, Ohio, Aug. 3, 1940; s. Francisco and Mary Ann (Phelan) Estevez; m. Janet Sheen, Dec. 23, 1961; children: Emilio, Ramon, Carlos, Renee. Grad. high sch. Made NY stage debut as mem. Living Theatre in The Connection, 1959; Broadway debut in Never Live Over a Pretzel Factory, 1964; other stage appearances include The Subject Was Roses, 1964-66, The Wicked Crooks, 1967, Hamlet, 1967, Romeo and Juliet, 1968, Hello and Goodbye, 1969, The Happiness Cage, 1970, Death of a Salesman, 1975, Julius Caesar, 1988; film appearances include The Incident, 1967, The Subject Was Roses, 1968, Catch-22, 1970, No Drums, No Bugles, 1971, Rage, 1972, Badlands, 1973, The Legend of Earl Durand, 1974, The Cassandra Crossing, 1976, The Little Girl Who Lives Down the Lane, 1977, Apocalypse Now, 1979, The Final Countdown, 1980, Gandhi, 1982, That Championship Season, 1982, The King of Prussia, 1982, No Place to Hide, 1983, The Dead Zone, 1983, Man, Woman, and Child, 1983, Enigma, 1983, Eagle's Wing, 1983, Firestarter, 1984, The Believers, 1987, Wall Street, 1987, Siesta, 1987, Judgement in Berlin, 1988, Walking After Midnight, 1988, Da, 1988 (exec. producer, dir.), Beverly Hills Brats, 1989, Cadence, 1991 (dir.), JFK, 1991 (narrator), Hot Shots, Part Deux!, 1993 (cameo), Hear No Evil, 1993, Gettysburg, 1993, The Break, 1995, The American President, 1995, The War At Home, 1996, Truth or Consequences, 1997, Spawn, 1997, Letter From Death Row, 1998, Stranger in the Kingdom, 1998, Storm, 1998, Monument Avenue, 1998, Free Money, 1998, Catch Me If You Can, 2002; TV series include As the World Turns, The Edge of Night, The West Wing, 1999— (Golden Globe award, 2001, SAG award, 2001, 2002); TV movies and miniseries include Then Came Bronson, 1969, The Subject Was Roses, 1969, Mongo's Back in Town, 1971, Welcome Home, Johnny Bristol, 1972, That Certain Summer, 1972, Catholics, 1973, The Execution of Private Slovik, 1974, The California Kid, 1974, The Story of Pretty Boy Floyd, 1974, The Missiles of October, 1974, Sweet Hostage, 1975, The Last Survivors, 1975, Blind Ambition, 1979, Taxi!!, 1978, The Long Road Home, 1980, Fly Away Home, 1981, Kennedy, 1982, Choices of the Heart, 1983, The Atlanta Child Murders, 1985, Consenting Adult, 1985, Out of Darkness, 1985, Shattered Spirits, 1986, Samaritan, 1986, News at Eleven, 1986, Babies Having Babies (dir.), 1986, Conspiracy: The Trial of the Chicago 8, 1987, No Means No (exec. producer), Night Breaker, 1989, Project Alf, 1996, Marlon Brandon: The Wild One, 1996, D.R.E.A.M. Team, 1999; other TV appearances include Mannix, 1967, The Streets of San Francisco, 1972, Murphy Brown, 1988 (Emmy award, Guest Actor - Comedy Series, 1994), The Simpsons (voice), 1989, The Great War, 1996, The Elevator, 1996, Entertaining Angels, 1996, Spin City, 1996, Medussa's Child, 1997, 187 Documented, 1997, Titanic: Anatomy of a Disaster (narrator), 1997, Tudjman (narrator), 1997 Babylon 5. The River of Souls, 1998, Letter From Death Row, 1998, Ambrose Chapel, 1998, Gunfighter, 1998, No Code of Conduct, 1998, Shadrach (voice), 1998, Stranger in the Kingdom, 1998, Talk of the Town, 1998, Voyage of Terror, 1998, Celebrity Poker Showdown, 2003. Named Favorite Actor in a New Series, TV Guide Awards; recipient Lifetime Achievement award, Imagen Found., 1998. Roman Catholic.

SHEEN, PORTIA YUNN-LING, retired physician; b. Republic of China, Jan. 13, 1919; came to U.S., 1988; d. Y. C. and A. Y. (Chow) Sheen; m. Kuo, 1944 (dec. 1970); children: William, Ida, Alexander, David, Mimi. MD, Nat. Med. Coll. Shanghai, 1943. Intern, then resident Cen. Hosp., Chungking, Szechuan, China, 1943; with Hong Kong Govt. Med. and Health Dept., 1948-76; med. supt. Kowloon (Hong Kong) Hosp., 1948-63, Queen Elizabeth Hosp., Kowloon, 1963-73, Med. and Health Hdqrs. and Health Ctr., Kowloon, 1973-76, Yan Chai Hosp., New Territories, Hong Kong, 1976-87; ret., 1987. Fellow Hong Kong Coll. Family Physicians; mem. AAAS, British Med. Assn., Hong Kong Med. Assn., Hong Kong Pediatric Soc., N.Y. Acad. Sci. Methodist. Avocations: reading, music. Home: 1408 Golden Rain Rd Apt 7 Entry 1 Roosmoor Walnut Creek CA 94595-2442

SHEERAN, MICHAEL JOHN LEO, priest, college administrator; b. N.Y.C., Jan. 24, 1940; s. Leo John and Glenna Marie (Wright) S. AB, St. Louis U., 1963, PhL, 1964, AM in Polit. Sci., 1967, AM in Theology, STL, St. Louis U., 1971; PhD, Princeton U., 1977. Joined Soc. of Jesus, 1957; ordained priest Roman Catholic Ch., 1970. Exec. editor Catholic Mind, N.Y.C., 1971-72; assoc. editor Am. Mag., N.Y.C., 1971-72; assoc. chaplain Aquinas Inst., Princeton, N.J., 1972-75; asst. dean Regis Coll., Denver, 1975-77, dean of Coll., 1977-82, v.p. acad. affairs, 1982-92, acting pres., 1987-88, pres., 1993—. Retreat dir., cons. on governance for religious communities, 1970—. Author: Beyond Majority Rule, 1984; contbr. articles and editls. to publs. Trustee Rockhurst Coll., Kansas City, Mo., 1982—91, Creighton U., Omaha, 1985—95, U. San Francisco, 1985—94, 2001—, Loyola U., New Orleans, 1994—96, Rocky Mountain Coll. Art and Design, Denver, 1994—99, Regis Jesuit H.S., 1999—; chmn. Mile High United Way, Denver, 1999—2000; mem. adv. bd. Cmty. Coll. Aurora, Colo., 2001—; nat. bd. dirs. Campus Compact, 2002—; bd. dirs. Colo. Inst. Tech., 2001—. Ford Found. scholar, 1963. Democrat. Roman Catholic. Home: 3333 Regis Blvd Denver CO 80221-1099 Office: Regis U 3333 Regis Blvd Denver CO 80221-1099 Office Phone: 303-458-4190. Business E-Mail: president@regis.edu.

SHEERAN, ROBERT, academic administrator; b. Troy, N.Y. B in Classical Langs., Seton Hall U., 1967; postgrad., U.S. Sem., N.Am. Coll., Rome; theology licentiate degree, Gregorian U., Rome, 1971; MA in Theology, Princeton U.; D in Theology, Angelicum U., 1979; mgmt. devel. program, Harvard U., 1989. Ordained priest, 1970. Rector St. Andrew's Coll. Sem. Seton Hall U., 1980, asst. provost, 1987, assoc. provost, 1991, exec. vice chancellor, 1993-95, pres., 1995—. Participant Priests-in-Residence program Seton Hall U.; dir. advising program N.Am. Coll., Rome, 1974-79. Fellow Am. Coun. on Edn. (mem. Commn. on Women in Higher Edn.). Office: Seton Hall U 400 S Orange Ave South Orange NJ 07079-2697

SHEERR, DEIRDRE MCCRYSTAL, architectural firm executive; m. Clinton Jay Sheerr (dec. 1997); m. Martin L. Gross, 2000. BA, Monmouth Coll., 1969; MArch, U. Colo., 1978; MA in Counseling Psychology, Antioch U., 1995. Registered architect, N.H., Colo. Computer systems and program analyst, 1970-75; pres. McCrystal Design & Devel., Inc., Denver, 1976-83; ptnr., head housing divsn. Sheerr & McCrystal, Inc., New London, N.H., 1983-97, pres., 1997-98; owner, pres. Sheerr & White Residential Architecture, 1998—. Instr. passive solar design Denver Free U.; cons. solar and low income housing design Capitol Hill Architects and Planners; solar cons. Bros. Redevelopment, Inc.; bd. dirs. Ledyard Nat. Bank. Prin. works include Lawrence Berkeley (Calif.) Lab., Solar Homestead, Boulder, Colo. (Nat. Passive Solar Design award HUD), 1515 South Pearl St., Curtis Pk. Face Block Renovation Project, Denver (Nat. Honor award AIA), St. Paul's Episcopal Ch. (Archtl. award Gov.'s Commn. Handicapped 1987). Mem. Leadership, N.H., 1998-99; mem. pres.'s adv. coun. Colby Sawyer Coll., 1987-91; mem. fundraising com., chmn. bd., Ausbon Sargent Land Preservation Trust, 1989—, 1998—; chmn. Lands Com., 1993-96, trustee, 1991—; bd. dirs. 1992—, vice-chmn. 1996-98; New London Town Zoning Bd., 1998—, mem. affordable housing task force charrette for City of Laconia, N.H. Housing Authority, 1989; mem. bus. adv. coun. Town of New London, 1990-94; active Nature Conservancy, Wilderness Soc., Sierra Club, Nat. Audubon Soc. Recipient Main St. Comml. Beautification award New London Garden Club, Best Restoration of Yr. award Denver Mag., 1983, Heritage Concord Grand award 1994; Nat. Hist. Preservation grantee Sec. of Interior, 1980. Mem. AIA (bd. dirs. N.H. chpt. 1984-89, sec. 1985, pres.-elect 1986, pres. 1987, immediate past pres. 1988, mem. exec. bd. New Eng. regional coun., 1986-87, spkr. N.W. regional conf., Denver Housing Authority Low Income Housing Design co-winner 1976, Western Regional Merit award 1981, 15 awards for Excellence in Architecture N.H. chpt. 1983, 85, 86, 88, 90, 91, 92, 93, 94, 95, 96, 99, Nat. Honor award 1983), Nat. Trust Hist. Preservation, Homebuilder's Assn. N.H. (SAM Gold award 1999, Silver award 1998, Bronze award 1999), N.H. Hist. Soc., New London Hist. Soc., Appalachian Mountain Club (adv. bd. 2002—). Office: Sheerr & White Architecture PO Box 2445 177 Main St New London NH 03257-2445

SHEETS, CYNTHIA ANN, elementary school educator, gifted and talented educator; b. Kans. City, Kans., Oct. 16, 1950; d. Dee Farris and Mary Lou White; m. Fred T. Sheets, Aug. 7, 1971; children: Jason Daniel, Jonathan Edward. BS in Edn., U. Mo., 1972; MA in Tchg., Webster U., ', 1981. Cert. tchr. Kans., 1991. Elem. tchr. Consol. Sch. Dist., Kans. City, Mo., 1973—89; elem. gifted edn. tchr. Shawnee Mission (Kans.) Sch. Dist., 1989—. Math coord. Hickman Mills Sch. Dist., Kans. City, 1985—89, profl. devel. cadre, Kansas City, Mo., 1987—89; site coun. Highlands Elem. Shawnee Mission (Kans.) Sch. Dist., 2001—; profl. devel. coun. Shawnee Mission Sch. Dist., Shawnee Mission, Kans., 2002—; effective instrn. cadre The Learning Exch., Kans. City, 1983—85; instr. Johnson County C.C., Overland Pk., Kans., 1990—; presenter in field. Web page creator KGTC (Academic Excellence award Lightspan, 2002). Vol. food preparer Kans. City (Mo.) Cmty. Kitchen, Kans. City, 1994—2001; bd. dir. Mother's Day Out Program Ruskin Presbyn. Ch., Kans. City, 1982—84; vol. Ea. Jackson County Parenting/Life Skills Program Episcopal Social Svcs., Lee's Summit, Mo., 1999—2001. Recipient Teaching award, Best Buy, 2004; grantee, Shawnee Mission (Mo.) Edn. Found., 1998, 2003. Mem.: NEA, Nat. Assn. Gifted Children, Kans. Assn.

Gfited, Talented and Creative (v.p. 1994—2004, pres., rep., Gifted Adv. award 2001), Jacomo Chorale (sec. 1998—2004), Sigma Alpha Iota (edn. officer 2000—01). Episc. Avocations: music, computing. Home: 1526 NE Yorkshire Dr Lee's Summit MO 64086 Office: Highlands Elementary School 6200 Roe Ave Mission KS 66205 Office Phone: 913-993-3346. Personal E-mail: cindys2449@aol.com. Business E-Mail: cindysheets@smsd.org.

SHEETS, DOROTHY JANE, school librarian, retired elementary school educator; b. Grant, Ala., Jan. 17, 1933; d. Walker Samuel and Floria Mae (Parks) Campbell; m. Paul Beauford Sheets, Jan. 1, 1958 (div. July 1972); children: Wanda Kay, Jeffrey Lee, Sue Ann Sheets Cagle. AS, Snead Jr. Coll., 1953; BS, U. Ala., Tuscaloosa, 1956; MEd, Auburn U., 1968; grad., Writer's Digest Sch., Cin., 1996, Inst. Children's Lit., 1992; student, Nat. Radio Inst., Washington, 1997. Cert. tchr. and sch. libr., Ala. Children's libr. Cleve. Pub. Libr., 1956-58; tchr. reading Marshall County Bd. Edn., Guntersville, Ala., 1962-76, elem. libr., 1976-91. Pvt. tutor, Albertville, Ala., 1968—. Vol. tax preparer RSVP, Guntersville, 1992—. DAR scholar, 1955. Mem. NEA (life), Ala. Edn. Assn., Ala. Ret. Tchrs. Assn., Marshall County Ret. Tchrs. Assn., Am. Assn. Ret. Persons. Avocations: reading, storytelling, volunteering, gardening. Home: 407 Pecan Ave Albertville AL 35950-2733 E-mail: djsheets3@juno.com.

SHEETS, FREDRICK SIDNEY, retired military officer, auditor; b. Greenville, S.C., Aug. 16, 1946; s. Sidney Wesley Sheets and Mabel Eve (Whitfield) Becht; m. Mary Cahterine White, July 14, 1973; children: Brenda Justine, Valerie Claire, Brian Arthur. BA, Ohio U., 1969; BBA, U. Tex., El Paso, 1986, M in Accountancy, 1988. CPA, Fla.; cert. acquisition profl. Dept. Def. Commd. 2d lt. U.S. Army, 1969, advanced through grades to lt. col., 1991, served in Korea, Germany, Vietnam, Md., Tex., Wash., to 1997; sr. auditor Def. Contract Audit Agy., Palm Bay, Fla., 1988—. Counselor, Vol. Income Tax Assistance, Melbourne, Fla., 1993—. Decorated Bronze Star. Mem. Inst. Mgmt. Accts., Am. Inst. CPA, Assn. Govt. Accts. (cert. govt. fin. mgr., pres-elect, sec.-treas., chpt. pres. 1989—, Mem. of Yr. 1994, 98, Superior Performance award 1995), Assn. Cert. Fraud Examiners, Brevard Fla. Inst. CPA (pvt. practice chair 1994—), Am. Volkssport Assn. (dir. S.E. region 1996—, Disting. Achievement award 1995), Fla. Volkssport Assn. (treas., pres. 1991—). Republican. Avocation: walking. Home: 378 Godfrey Rd SE Palm Bay FL 32909-8841 Office: PO Box 61419 Palm Bay FL 32906-1419

SHEETS, HERMAN ERNEST, marine engineer; b. Dresden, Germany, Dec. 24, 1908; s. Arthur Chitz and Gertrude (Stern) S.; m. Norma Sams, Oct. 17, 1942 (dec. Dec. 1970); m. Paulann Hosler, May 29, 1982; children: Lawrence S., Michael R., Arne H., Diana E., Elizabeth J., Karn N. M.E., U. Dresden, 1934; Dr. Tech. Scis. in Applied Mechanics, U. Prague, Czechoslovakia, 1936. Engr. Prvni Brněnska Strojima, Brno, 1936-39; Chief engr. Chamberlin Research Corp., East Moline, Ill., 1939-42; mgr. research St. Paul Engring. & Mfg. Co., 1942- 44; project engr. Elliott Co., Jeannette, Pa., 1944-46; engring. mgr. Goodyear Aircraft Corp., Akron, Ohio, 1946-53; v.p. Electric Boat div. Gen. Dynamics Corp., Groton, Conn., 1953-69; v.p. engring, and research; prof. dept. ocean engring. U. R.I., Kingston, 1969-80, dept. chmn., 1971-79; dir. engring. Analysis and Tech., North Stonington, Conn., 1979-84; cons. engr. Groton, 1980—. Author numerous articles in field. Recipient citation sec. war. Fellow AIAA (assoc.), ASME, AAAS; mem. N.Y. Acad. Scis., Nat. Acad. Engring., Soc. Naval Architects and Marine Engrs., Am. Soc. Naval Engrs., Marine Tech. Soc., Pi Tau Sigma. Home and Office: Mumford Cove 87 Neptune Dr Groton CT 06340-5421 Fax: 860-572-8266. E-mail: phsheets@mindspring.com.

SHEETS, NELDA, artist; b. Roger Mills County, Okla., Oct. 31, 1931; d. Merril Ezra and Alice (Tucker) Johnson; m. Willis Davis Sheets, Nov. 12, 1949; children; Steve, Dana. Intr. Silva Method of Mind Devel., Laredo, Tex., 1967—; lectr., author Creativity Workshop, Tex., 1968—; artist Webb Gallery, Amarillo, Tex., 1980—. Trainer of instrs. Silva Method, 1971-85, conv. dir., 1973-80. Author: (book) Creative Study Skills, 1990, The Creativity Workshop, 1968; author, presenter workshop Creative Parenting. Pres. Area Arts Found., Amarillo, 1986; adv. com. Amarillo Coll. Adult Program, 1991. Democrat. Methodist. Personal E-mail: nelsheets@aol.com.

SHEETZ, JOSEPH S. retail grocery executive; BS, Bentley Coll.; MBA, Pace U. CFO Sheetz, Altoona, Pa. Office: Sheetz 5700 6th Ave Altoona PA 16602

SHEETZ, MICHAEL PATRICK, cell biology educator; b. Hershey, Pa., Dec. 11, 1946; s. David Patrick and Mary Patricia (Blumer) S.; m. Katherine Elliott, Jan. 25, 1968; children: Jonathan Patrick, Jennifer Mikaere, Courtney Elizabeth. BA, Albion Coll., 1968; PhD in Chemistry, Calif. Inst. Tech., 1972. Postdoctoral rsch. fellow U. Calif., San Diego, 1972-74; asst. prof. cell biology dept. physiology U. Conn. Health Ctr., Farmington, 1974-79, assoc. prof., 1980-85; prof. dept. cell biology and physiology Sch. Medicine, Washington U., St. Louis, 1985-90; prof., chmn. dept. cell biology Med. Sch., Duke U., Durham, N.C., 1990-00; prof. dept. biol. sci. Columbia U., N.Y.C., 2000—. Presenter profl. confs. Established investigator Am. Heart Assn., 1981-86. Javits Neurosci. grantee, 1986-93. Office: Columbia U Dept Biol Sci 1212 Amsterdam Ave New York NY 10027-7003 E-mail: ms2001@columbia.edu.*

SHEETZ, STANTON R. grocery retail executive; b. May 26, 1955; BS, Bentley Coll.; MBA, Pace U. N.Y. With Colt Industries, 1977-81, Sheetz Inc., Altoona, Pa., 1981—95, CEO, 1995—. Mem.: Nat. Assn. Convenience Stores (vice chmn. 2000—). Office: Sheetz Inc 5700 6th Ave Altoona PA 16602-1111

SHEFELMAN, JANICE JORDAN, writer; d. Gilbert John and Vera Tiller Jordan; m. Thomas Whitehead Shefelman, Sept. 18, 1954; children: Karl Jordan, Daniel Whitehead. BA, So. Meth. U., Dallas, 1951, MEd, 1953. Cert. libr. cert. U. Tex., 1980. Elem. tchr. Dallas I Sch. Dist., 1953—54, St. Andrews Episcopal Sch., Austin, 1955—57; libr. Lake Travis I. Sch. Dist., Austin, 1980—84; children's book writer, 1984—. Author: A Paradise Called Texas, 1983, Willow Creek Home, 1985, Spirit of Iron, 1987, Victoria House, 1988, A Peddler's Dream, 1992 (Am. Bookseller award, 1992, Reading Rainbow Book award, 1996), A Mare for Young Wolf, 1993, Young Wolf's First Hunt, 1995, Young Wolf and Spirit Horse, 1997, Comanche Song, 2000 (Best Book for Teen Age, 2001), Son of Spirit Horse, 2004. Mem.: Tex. Writers League, Soc. Children's Book Writer's & Illustrators, The Authors Guild. Home and Office: 1405 W 32d St Austin TX 78703 Home Fax: 512-477-9562. E-mail: tjshef@aol.com.

SHEFFEL, IRVING EUGENE, psychiatric institution executive; b. Chgo., July 5, 1916; s. Joseph and Jennie (Leibson) S.; m. Beth Silver, Aug. 2, 1942 (dec.); 1 child, Anita (dec.); m. Peggy Shelton, Apr. 6, 1996. AB, U. Chgo., 1939; M.P.A., Harvard U., 1946; LHD (hon.), Washburn U., 1987. Insp., wage and hour div. Dept. Labor, Chgo., 1940-41; mgmt. and budget analyst VA, Washington, 1946-48; budget analyst U.S. Bur. of Budget, Washington, 1948-49; controller, treas. Menninger Found., Topeka, 1949-73, v.p., 1973-93, v.p. emeritus, 1993—. Instr. Menninger Sch. Psychiatry. Bd. dirs. Washburn U. Art Center, 1969—, pres., 1971-73; treas. Karl Menninger lect. series, 1983—. Served to maj. U.S. Army, 1942-45. Fellow Assn. Mental Health Adminstrs. (charter); mem. Am. Soc. Public Adminstrn. (charter), Topeka Opera Soc. (treas. 1985—). Jewish. Home: 1215 SW 29th Ter Topeka KS 66611-2192

SHEFFER, BRENT ALAN, lawyer; b. Canton, Ohio, Nov. 7, 1957; s. Dwight W. and JoAnne Sheffer; m. Hillary Ann Taylor, Sept. 2, 1995. BS in Fin. and Acctg., Ohio State U., 1979; JD, Capital U. Law Sch., 1990. Bar: Ohio 1990, U.S. Tax Ct. 1991, U.S. Dist. Ct. (so. dist.) Ohio 1992, U.S. Supreme Ct., 1995; CPA, Ohio. Contract specialist Ohio State U., Columbus, 1978-79; supr. auditing Coopers & Lybrand, CPA's, Columbus, 1979-85; internal auditor Ctrl. Ohio Transit Authority, Columbus, 1985-86, mgr. fin. planning and budget, 1986-89, mgr. fin., 1989-90; tax supr. Norman, Jones, Enlow & Co., Dublin, Ohio, 1990-92; pvt. practice Columbus, 1992-97; assoc. Havens Willis, LLC, 1998—2001; sr. assoc. Saltz Shamis and Goldfarb, 2001—02; pvt. practice, 2002—. Advisor Jr. Achievement, 1980-85, Hugh O'Brien Youth Leadership Seminars, 1985-91; ent. com. German Village Oktoberfest, 1986-96; dir. of race ops, Columbus 500 Rd. Race, 1987-1988; Timing & Scoring Volunteer, Mid-Ohio Sports Car Course, 1984-1995; bd. dir. Ohio 4-H Found., 1975-77, mem. adv. com., 1988-90; bd. dir. Columbus Jaycee Youth Found., 1985-91, 93-98; legal counsel Columbus Flight Watch, 1993-97, dir., 1997-99, pres. 1999-2001, dir. 2001—; mem. Ctrl. Ohio Amateur Radio Emergency Svc., 2000—, dir. Columbus 500 Rd. Race ops. 1987-88 Named one of Outstanding Young Men of Am., 1986; recipient Jr. Chamber Internat. Senatorship, 1997. Mem. ABA (tax com. 1990—), Ohio State Bar Assn., Columbus Bar Assn. (tax com. 1990—), AICPA, Inst. Mgmt. Acctd. (dir. 1985-88, 91-97, v.p. adminstrn. 1992-93, pres. 1993-94, editor program book 1995-97, bd. dir. 1996-98), Ohio Soc. CPA (Ohio Accountancy Bd. liaison 1991-93), Am. Assn. Atty.-CPA, Columbus Jaycees (dir. 1985-88, 90-91, 93-99, Presdl. Achievement award 1986, Membership award 1987, newsletter editor 1993-94, pres. 1996-97, state pres. quarter award 1997, region Pres. of Yr. award 1997, bd. chmn. 1997-98), Sports Car Club Am. (chmn. membership 1982-83, regional exec. 1984-85, Regional Exec. Worker award 1983, Regional Exec. award 1984, Regional Race Worker of Yr. award 1988, Jim Trueman Meml. Trophy 1988), Am. Radio Relay League, Ctrl. Ohio Amateur Radio Emergency Svc., Ohio State U. Sports Car Club (pres. 1978-80), Stuart Cameron McLeod Soc., 1996, Phi Delta Phi (charter com. 1988, treas. 1989-90, alumni chmn. 1990—. Avocations: sports car racing, rallying, bicycling, reading, skiing, amateur radio. Home and Office: Sheffer Law Office 8050 Abbeyshire Ct Dublin OH 43016-8622 E-mail: bsheffer@columbus.rr.com.

SHEFFERY, MICHAEL B. investment company executive; BA in biology, PhD in molecular biology, Princeton U. Head of lab, gene structure and expression Meml. Sloan-Kettering Cancer Ctr.; sr. analyst, biotechnology Mehta, 1996, Isaly, 1997; dir. NeoGenesis Pharm., Biosynexus Inc., Memory Pharm. Corp.; mng. gen. ptnr. Orbimed Advisors, LLC, N.Y.C., 1996—. Office: Orbimed Advisors LLC 767 Third Ave 30th Fl New York NY 10017

SHEFFEY, RUTHE GARNET, English and humanities educator, speaker; m. Vernon R. Sheffey, Dec. 29, 1950; children: Illona Sheffey Rawlings, Renata Sheffey Strong. BA, Morgan State U., Balt., 1947; MA, Howard U., 1949; PhD, U. Pa., 1959. Prof. English Morgan State U., Balt., 1949—, chair dept. English, 1970-76. Author: Impressions in Asphalt, 1969, Trajectory (My Collected Essays), 1989; editor Zora Neale Hurston Forum, 1986—. Named Md. Outstanding Faculty Mem. of Yr., 1994, Disting. Scholar in African-Am. Studies for Yr., Towson State U., 2002, Sheroe as Honor, Women for Responsive Govt., Inc., 2003; named to Morgan State U. Hall of Fame, 2000. Mem. Nat. Coun. Tchrs. English (past mem. coll. bd.), Coll. English Assn. (past pres. Mid. Atlantic Group), Zora Neale Hurston Soc. (founder, 1984, pres.), Langston Hughes Soc. (past pres.), other lit. socs. Mem. United Ch. of Christ. Avocations: reading, theatre-going, dance.

SHEFFIELD, ALDEN DANIEL, JR., lawyer; b. St. Paul, Sept. 10, 1947; s. Alden Daniel Sheffield and Martha Terrell Yaeger; m. Pamela Roesner, Oct. 8, 1983; children: Charles Alden Sheffield, Elliot Alden Sheffield. BA, Colo. Coll., 1969; JD, U. Minn., 1974. Bar: Min. 1974, Ariz. 1975, Colo. 1991. Atty. Ryley Carlock & Applewhite, Phoenix, 1975-92; sole practice Colorado Springs, 1992—. With U.S. Army, 1970-72. Home: 1624 Culebra Pl Colorado Springs CO 80907-7333 Office: 24 South Weber St Ste 300 Colorado Springs CO 80903-1914 Office Phone: 719-635-6003. E-mail: s91287@hotmail.com.

SHEFFIELD, CAROLE JEAN, political science educator; b. Norwich, Conn., Dec. 25, 1947; d. John Moore and Doris Edna Sheffield; m. David A. Orthmann, Aug. 10, 1985. BS, Eastern Conn. State coll., 1969; MA, Miami Ohio U., 1970, PhD, 1973. Prof. polit. sci. and women's studies William Paterson U., Wayne, N.J., 1973—. Author: Sexual Terrorism, 1994; contbr. articles to profl. jours. Named N.J. Prof. of Yr. The Carnegie Found., 1997, Outstanding Tchr. in Polit. Sci. Am. Polit Sci. Assn., Pi Sigma Alpha, 1998. Mem. Nat. Women's Studies Assn. Home: 56 Allison Ave Newfoundland NJ 07435 Office: William Paterson U 300 Pompton Rd Wayne NJ 07470-2152 E-mail: sheffieldc@wpunj.edu.

SHEFFIELD, DEBORAH LAGRETA, poet, writer; b. Ft. Lauderdale, Fla., Sept. 8, 1966; d. Mary Alice Ward-Sheffield-Davis and Douglas McArthur Sheffield Sr. Grad. in psychology, U. Mo., St. Louis, 2002; grad. in arts and sci. (hon.), Forest Pk. Coll., St. Louis, 1999. Med. records coord. Metro Heart Group, St. Louis, 1998—2000; office mgr. Law Office of Inez J. Ross, St. Louis, 2001—03. Author numerous poems. Behavioral medicine vol. St. Mary's Hosp., St. Louis, 1998—2000; singing Antinoch Dist. Choir, St. Louis, 2003. With USN, 1984—86. Mem.: Am. Bus. Assn. Am. (life). Democrat. Baptist. Avocations: poetry, singing, travel. Office: Poetry On The Mind 1211 Gregan Pl Saint Louis MO 63133 Personal E-mail: dbaby987@earthlink.net.

SHEFFIELD, ELIZABETH BAKER, special education educator, lecturer, consultant; b. Cin., Oct. 28, 1926; d. Charles Wentworth Jr. and Beatrice (Carmichael) B.; m. Samuel Sanford Jr., Dec. 27, 1949; children: Samuel III, Anne Vanoy, William C., Charles T. BA magna cum laude, Smith Coll., 1948; MA in Spl. Edn., U. Cinn., 1972. Cert. learning disabilities and behavioral disorders tchr., Ohio. Reading specialist Lotspeich Schs., Cin., 1968-72, head spl. reading dept., 1972-78; dir. summer reading program 7 Hills Schs., Cin., 1973-76; tchr. aux. svcs. Cin. Pub. Schs., 1974-75; coop. tchr. U. Cin., 1975-76; adj. instr. Spl. Edn. Regional Resource Ctr., Cin., 1977—; pvt. practice learning disabilities Cin., 1978—; master tchr. Butler U., 1987-88. Lectr. in learning disabilities, 1972—, tchr. grad. course, Miami U. Ohio, 1992—; fellow Orlon-Gillingham Acad., 1995—. Recipient Outstanding Svc. award Southwestern Ohio Speech, Lang. and Hearing Assn., 1992, Lifetime Achievement award, Internat. Dyslexia Assn., 2001, Cin. Jr. League Outstanding Sustainer award, 2004. Mem. Orton Dyslexia Soc. (founder Ohio Valley br. 1979, nat. v.p. 1986-92), Cin. Tennis Club, Jr. League, Phi Beta Kappa, Sigma Xi. Home: 3054 Griest Ave Cincinnati OH 45208-2430

SHEFFIELD, GARY ANTONIAN, professional baseball player; b. Tampa, Fla., Nov. 18, 1968; Baseball player Milw. Brewers, 1986-92, San Diego Padres, 1992-93, Florida Marlins, 1993-98, L.A. Dodgers, 1999—2001, Atlanta Braves, 2002—03, N.Y. Yankees, 2004—. Mem. Nat. League All-Star Team, 1992-93, 96, 98, 99, 2000, 2003, Am. League All-Star Team, 2004; Sporting News Player of the Year, 1992; Comeback Player of Yr., Sporting News, 1992. Nat. Batting League Champion, 1992. Office: c/o NY Yankees Yankee Stadium E 161 St and River Ave Bronx NY 10451*

SHEFFIELD, JOVONNA MICHELE, music educator; b. Okla. City, May 6, 1971; d. Ron J. and Elvonda L. Williams; m. Michael Edward, Jr. Sheffield, June 15, 1991; children: Ryan Matthew, Erin Elizabeth. MusB in Performance, West Tex. A&M U., 1993, MA in Music, 2001. Pvt. piano instr., Canyon, Tex., 1991—; culty Odessa Coll., Tex., 1994. Author: (masters thesis) Tchg. Ear Tng. Skills to the Young Student: A Curriculum; musician: (piano ensemble) WTAMU Showcase of Music, (piano duo) Amarillo Internat. Soc. Music of Australia Concert, sr. solo piano recital; dancer (exhbn. performance) Rededication of the Tex. Capitol Bldg. Mem.: Music Tchrs. Nat. Assn., Tex. Music Tchrs. Assn., Amarillo Music Tchrs. Assn. (treas. 2002—04). Conservative. Avocations: travel, reading, dance. Home: 2613 11th Ave Canyon TX 79015

SHEFFIELD, LEWIS GLOSSON, physiologist; b. Adel, Ga., Oct. 30, 1957; s. Eugene Davis and Martha Sue (Sinclair) S.; m. Mary Frances Tanner, July 18, 1980. MS, Clemson U., 1980; PhD, U. Mo., 1983. Rsch. asst. Clemson (S.C.) U., 1978-80, U. Mo., Columbia, 1980-83; postdoctoral assoc. Mich. State U., East Lansing, 1983-86; asst. prof. dairy sci. dept. U. Wis., Madison, 1986-91, assoc. prof. dairy sci., 1991—, dir. endocrinology-reproductive physiology program, 1990—. Contbr. articles to profl. jours. Recipient First award NIH, 1988. Mem. Am. Dairy Sci. Assn. (milk synthesis chair 1991-92), Com. on Mammary Gland Biology, Endocrine Soc., Sigma Xi. Achievements include demonstration that epidermal growth factor interacts with estrogen and progesterone to regulate mammary devel. and are working to understand the cellular and molecular basis of that interaction; that prolactin causes a decrease in epidermal growth factor-induced growth responses, which appears to be related to mammary gland differentiation. The molecular regulation of this response is under investigation. Office: U Wis 864 Animal Scis Bldg 1675 Observatory Dr Madison WI 53706-1205

SHEFFIELD, NANCY, city agency administrator; b. Mpls. BA in Sociology and Psychology, U. Minn., 1969; postgrad., U. Wis., 1992. Participant City of Aurora (Colo.) Supervisory Cert. Series Program, 1988-90. Social worker LeSueur County Human Svcs., Le Centre, Minn., 1969-71; quality control reviewer Minn. Dept. Human Svcs., St. Paul, 1971-74, quality control supr., 1974-75; neighborhood planner City of Aurora, 1987, neighborhood support supr., 1987-94, acting mgr. Original Aurora Renewal, 1994-95, acting mgr. neighborhood support divsn., 1995, dir. neighborhood svcs., 1996—. Mem. PTO, vol. elem. sch. media ctr., 1980-86. Office: City Aurora Dept Neighborhood Svcs 15151 E Alameda Pkwy Aurora CO 80012 Office Phone: 303-739-7280. E-mail: nsheffie@auroragov.org.

SHEFFIELD, SCOTT D. oil industry executive; BS in Petroleum Engring., U. Tex. Prodn. and reservoir engr. Amoco Prodn. Co.; petroleum engr. Parker & Parsley Devel. Co., 1979—85, v.p. engring., 1981—85, pres., bd. dirs., 1985—89, chmn., CEO, 1989; pres., bd. dirs. Parker & Parsley Petroleum Co., 1990—97, chmn., CEO, 1990—97; pres., CEO Pioneer Natural Resources, 1997—, chmn. bd. dirs., 1999—. Office: 1400 Williams Sq W Irving TX 75039

SHEFTALL, BEVERLY GUY, women's studies educator; B in English, Spelman Coll.; postgraduate study, Wellesley Coll.; M in English, Atlanta U.; PhD. English instr. Ala. State U., Montgomery; Anna Julia Cooper prof. women's studies Spelman Coll., 1971—; founding dir. Women's Rsch. and Resource Ctr., 1981—. Adj. prof. Emory U. Inst. Women Studies. Founding editor Sage: A Scholarly Journal on Black Women, 1983; co-editor (with Roseann P. Bell and Bettye Parker Smith): Sturdy Black Bridges: Visions of Black Women in Literature, 1979; co-editor: (with Rudolph P. Byrd) Traps: African American Men on Gender and Sexuality, 2001; author: Daughters of Sorrow: Attitudes Toward Black Women, 1880-1920, 1991, Words of Fire: An Anthology of African American Feminist Thought, 1995; co-author (with Johnetta B. Cole): Gender Talk, 2003. Bd. mem. Nat. Coalition 100 Black Women, Nat. Black Women's Health Project, Nat. Coun. Rsch. on Women; bd. trustees Dillard U., New Orleans. Nat. Kellogg Fellowship, Woodrow Wilson Fellowship. Office: Spelman Coll 350 Spelman Ln SW Atlanta GA 30314 Office Phone: 404-681-3643.

SHEFTEL, ROGER TERRY, merchant banker; b. Denver, Sept. 10, 1941; s. Edward and Dorothy (Barnett) S.; m. Phoebe A. Sherman, Sept. 7, 1968; children: Tisha B., Ryan B. BS in Econs., U. Pa., 1963. Comml. lending officer Provident Nat. Bank, Phila., 1963-65; asst. to pres. Continental Fin. Corp., Denver, 1965-68; v.p. Eastern Indsl. Leasing Corp., Phila., 1968-71, exec. v.p., dir., 1971-73, HBE Leasing Corp., Phila., 1971-73; dir. Kooly Kupp, Inc., Boyertown, Pa., 1974-77, pres., dir., 1977; prin. Trivest, Phila., 1973-77, pres., 1977-78, 1670 Corp., 1978-82, Am. Cons. Group, Inc., 1982-83; exec. v.p., dir. Argus Rsch. Labs., Inc., 1982-83; pres. Leasing Concepts, Inc., 1983-87, Brice Capital Corp., 1987-92, Rhodes Fin., Inc., 1992—. Dir. strategic planning Wharton Sch., U. Pa., 1999; pres. AttendByWeb, Inc., 1999—, AssignByWeb, Inc., 1999—; CEO, chmn. FlyOff, Inc., 1998—. Mem.: Friars Club. Home: 414 Barclay Rd Bryn Mawr PA 19010-1218 Office: Rhodes Fin Inc PO Box 7338 Saint Davids PA 19087-7338

SHEHATA, SAID AHMED, surgeon, researcher; b. Alexandria, Egypt, Jan. 15, 1938; came to U.S., 1972; s. Ahmed Hassan and Nagia Aly (Abdeen) S.; m. Soraya Zakareya, Aug. 17, 1966; children: Samer, Deena, Sherene. MBChB cum laude, Alexandria U., 1962, M of Surgery, 1969. Diplomate Am. Bd. Surgery. Rotating intern Alexandria U. Hosp., 1962-63, surg. resident, 1963-66; surgeon Univ. Student Hosp.-Alexandria U. Sch. Medicine, 1966-70, lectr. surgery, 1969-70; sr. surg. registrar Whipps Cross Hosp., London, 1970-72; sr. chief surg. resident med. edn. program U. Ariz. Tucson Hosp., 1973-75; clin. assoc. prof. surgery Med. Coll. Ohio, Toledo, 1976—; pvt. practice Bowling Green, Ohio, 1975—. Dir. Vascular Lab. NW Ohio, Bowling Green, 1985—; cons. Ministry of Health, Saudi Arabia, 1981; vis. prof. State of Qatar, 1984, Alexandria U., 1986. Author: Cancer of Esophagus, 1969; contbr. articles to profl. jours. Maj. Egyptian Army, 1967-68. Fellow ACS, Royal Coll. Surgeons Edinburgh, Am. Coll. Abdominal Surgery; mem. Wood County Med. Soc. (pres. 1986-88). Republican. Moslem. Avocations: travel, tennis, fishing. Home: 284 Gould Ln Montecito CA 93108-2650

SHEI, H. RAY, food products executive; b. Ind. Sr. mgr. transp. and logistics Keebler Co., 1991—97, v.p. info. sys., 1997—2001; v.p., chief info. officer Kellogg Co., 2001—. Office: Kellogg PO Box 3599 1 Kellogg Sq Battle Creek MI 49016-3599

SHEIK, DUNCAN, singer, songwriter; b. Montclair, N.J., Nov. 18, 1969; Degree in semiotics, Brown U., New Providence, RI, 1992. Performed with bands His Boy Elroy, 1993, Liz and Lisa. Singer, musician: (albums) Duncan Sheik, 1996; singer, musician, co-prodr.: albums Humming, 1998, Phantom Moon, 2001, Daylight, 2002, songs "Wishful Thinking", 1998; TV Appearances: Boston Public, 2003, American Dreams, 2003; composer: (plays) (musical score) Spring Awakening. Office: c/o Atlantic Records Inc 1290 6th Ave Flr 28 New York NY 10104

SHEIKH, JAVED, physician, educator; BA, Johns Hopkins U., Balt., 1990; MD, W. Va. U., 1994. Cert. Am. Bd. of Pediat., 1997, Am. Bd. of Allergy & Immunology, 1999, lic. Calif., 1995, Mass., 2001. Clin. allergy and immunology Cedars Sinai Med. Ctr., LA, 1999—2001; clin. allergy & immunology Beth Israel Deaconess Med. Ctr., Boston, 2001—03; instr. medicine Harvard Med. Sch., Boston, 2001—. Author: (med. and sci. articles) Annals of Allergy, Asthma and Immunology. Office: Beth Israel Deaconess Med Ctr 330 Brookline Ave DA-617 Boston MA 02215

SHEILS, DENIS FRANCIS, lawyer; b. Ridgewood, NJ, Apr. 7, 1961; s. Denis Francis and Anna Marie (Clifford) Sheils; m. Harriet A. Bonawitz, Sept. 17, 1988; children: Denis F., Dylan I., Matthew D. BA, La Salle Coll., 1983; JD, Fordham U., 1986. Bar: NY 1987, Pa. 1987, U.S. Dist. Ct. (ea. dist.) Pa. 1987, U.S. Ct. Appeals (3d cir.) 1987, U.S. Dist. Ct. (so. and ea. dists.) NY 1992, U.S. Supreme Ct. 1994, U.S. Dist. Ct. (no. dist.) NY 1997, U.S. Ct. Appeals (2d cir.) 1999, Nev. 2003, U.S. Dist. Ct. Nev. 2003. Assoc. Kohn, Swift & Graf, PC, Phila., 1987—97, shareholder, 1997—. Active Lower Makefield Twp. Cable TV Adv. Bd. Mem.: ABA, Phila. Bar Assn. Roman Catholic. Office: Kohn Swift & Graf PC 21st Fl One South Broad St Philadelphia PA 19107 Home: The Dorchester 226 W Rittenhouse Sq unit 1613 Philadelphia PA 19103 Office Phone: 215-238-1700. E-mail: dsheils@kohnswift.com.

SHEIMAN, RONALD LEE, lawyer; b. Bridgeport, Conn., Apr. 26, 1948; s. Samuel Charles and Rita Doris Sheiman; m. Deborah Joy Lovitky, Oct. 16, 1971; children: Jill, Laura. BA, U. Mich., 1970; JD, U. Conn., 1973; LLM in Taxation, NYU, 1974. Bar: Conn. 1973, US Ct. Appeals (2d cir.) 1975, US Supreme Ct. 1977, DC 1978, NY 1981. Tax atty. Office Regional Counsel IRS, Phila., 1974-78; pvt. practice Westport, Conn., 1978—. Mem.: ABA, Conn. Bar Assn., Fed. Bar Assn. Home: 128 Random Rd Fairfield CT 06432-1408 Office: 1804 Post Rd E Westport CT 06880-5607

SHEIN, JAY LESING, financial planner; b. Chgo., Jan. 27, 1951; s. Garrett Melchior and Evelyn (Blitt) Hamm; m. Val Margaret Rich, Dec. 14, 1984; children: Melissa Loree, Blair Charles, Christina Anne, Allison Marie, Lindsay Gayle. Student, Broward C.C., Davie, Fla., 1969-72, Cleve. Inst. Electronics, 1973-74; CFP, Coll. for Fin. Planning, Denver, 1990; MS in Taxation and Fin., PhD, LaSalle U., 1994; postgrad., U. Pa., 1998, NYU, 2002. Cert. investment mgr. analyst, investment strategist. Tech. technician Broward County Sch. Bd., Ft. Lauderdale, Fla., 1973-76; owner, mgr. Bus. and Tax Consulting Firm, Ft. Lauderdale, 1976-83; dist. mgr. United Group and Group One, Ft. Lauderdale, 1983-84; from account exec. to v.p. Compass Fin. Group, Inc., Lighthouse Point, Fla., 1984-90, pres., CEO, 1990—. Mem. adv. bd. devel. coun.

Highlands Christian Acad., Pompano Beach, Fla., 1992—; mem. adj. faculty Rollins Coll., 1996; adj. prof. La Salle U., 1994-2001, Nova Southeastern U. Sch. Bus., 1995-2000, Fla. State U., 2000, Fla. Gulf Coast U., 2001—, IMCA Cert. Investment Mgmt. Analyst Program, U. Pa. Wharton Sch., 1998—; apptd. bd. dirs. Cert. Fin. Planner Bd. Examiners. Author: Asset Allocation and Portfolio Structure, 1999; contbr. articles to newspapers and pubs. in field. Mem. Estate Planning Coun. of Broward County. Named One of Best 250 Fin. Advisers in Country, Worth mag., 2000-02; named one of Top 100 Fin. Planners, Mut. Fund mag., 2001, 02. Mem. Investment Mgmt. Cons. Assn. (mem. editl. bd. Jour. Investment Consulting), Inst. CFP, Fin. Planning Assn., South Fla. Soc. of Inst. of CFPs (dir. ethics 1993-94, edn. chmn. 1994, pres. 1997, chmn. 1998), Fin. Planning Assn. South Fla. (chmn. edn. programs 1999—), Broward County Assn. Life Underwriters (v.p. 1992-94), Greater Ft. Lauderdale Tax Coun., Marine Industries of South Fla. Republican. Baptist. Avocations: volleyball, racquetball, travel. Office: Compass Fin Group Inc 3050 N Federal Hwy Ste 208 Lighthouse Point FL 33064-6866 E-mail: compassfinancial@hotmail.com.

SHEINBAUM, GILBERT HAROLD, international management consultant; b. N.Y.C., Apr. 20, 1929; s. Herman and Selma (Klimberg) S.; m. Inger Fredebo Thomsen, Aug. 28, 1971; children: Neil, Britt. AB in History, NYU, 1950; postgrad., CUNY, 1954-55, New Sch. for Social Rsch., 1955-56. Various fgn. svc. posts, Washington, Laos, France, Vietnam, Denmark, 1957-72; polit. officer U.S. Dept. of State, Washington, 1972-75; chargé d'affaires Am. Embassy, Antananarivo, Madagascar, 1975-77, dep. chief of mission Lilongwe, Malawi, 1977-79; Am. consul Cebu, Philippines, 1979-83; polit. counselor U.S. Mission to the UN, Geneva, 1983-86, dir. Colombo Plan (internat. orgn.), Colombo, Sri Lanka, 1986-91; cons. Nat. Security Edn. Program, Washington, 1992-95, Internat. Found. for Election Sys., Washington, 1995-96; sr. cons., advisor U.S. Dept. State, 1997—. Internat. observor Sri Lankan elections, 1993, 94; convenor Shepherd's Ctr. World Affairs Program, Vienna, Va. Author and editor articles on econ. devel. in Asia. Co-founder, trustee George Keyt Cultural Found., Colombo, 1987-91; bd. chmn. Overseas Children's Sch., Colombo, 1987-90; commr. Boy Scouts Am., Geneva, 1984-86; stage mgr., bd. dirs. Am. Light Opera Co., Washington, 1962-64. 1st lt. U.S. Army, 1951-53. Recipient Award of Recognition, Mindanao State U., Marawi, Philippines, 1983. Mem.: Assn. Diplomatic Studies, UN Assn. of U.S., Diplomatic and Consular Officers Ret., Asia Soc., World Affairs Coun. of Washington DC, Am. Fgn. Svc. Assn., Soc. Internat. du Mekong (founder, pres.). Avocations: tennis, running, touring, reading, public speaking. Home: 407 East St NE Vienna VA 22180-3577 E-mail: gsheinbaum@aol.com.

SHEINDLIN, JUDITH, television personality, judge; b. Bklyn., Oct. 21, 1942; d. Murray and Ethel Blum; m. Ronald Levy, 1964 (div. 1976); children: Jamie, Adam; m. Gerald Sheindlin, 1977; stepchildren: Greg, Jonathan, Nicole. BA, Am. U., Wash., DC, 1963; law degree, NY Law Sch., 1965; LLD (hon.), Elizabethtown Coll. Supervising judge, Manhattan, NYC, 1986—96; judge Family Ct., Bronx, 1982—86, pros. atty. NYC, 1978—82. Appeared as herself (TV films) ChiPs '99, 1998, (TV series) Judge Judy, 1996— (nominee Daytime Emmy for outstanding special class series, 1999, 2000, 2001, 2002, 2003); author: Don't Pee on My Leg and Tell Me It's Raining: America's Toughest Family Court Judge Speaks Out, 1996, Beauty Fades, Dumb is Forever: The Making of a Happy Woman, 1999, Keep It Simple, Stupid: You're Smarter Than You Look: Uncomplicating Families in Complicated Times, 2000, Judge Judy Sheindlin's Win or Lose by How You Choose, 2000, You're Smarter Than You Look: Uncomplicating Relationships in Complicated Times, 2001, Judge Judy Sheindlin's You Can't Judge a Book By Its Cover: Cool Rules for School, 2001. Office: Judge Judy PO Box 949 Los Angeles CA 90078

SHEINER, LEWIS B. pharmacist, educator; b. N.Y.C., N.Y., May 27, 1940; PhD honoris causa(hon.), U. Uppsala, Sweden, 1995. Cert. Am. Bd. Internal Medicine. Intern in medicine Columbia Presbyn. Med. Ctr., 1965, resident in medicine, 1966; rsch. assoc. NIMH, NIH, 1968; rsch. physician divsn. computer rsch. and tech. NIH, 1969; resident in medicine Stanford U. Sch. Medicine, 1970; rsch. fellow divsn. clin. pharmacology U. Calif., San Francisco, 1972, instr. depts. lab. medicine and medicine, Sch. Medicine, 1972—73, asst. prof. lab. medicine and medicine and Sch. Pharmacy, dept. biopharm. scis., 1973—78, assoc. prof. lab. medicine and medicine and Sch. Pharmacy, dept. biopharm. scis., 1978—82, prof. lab. medicine and medicine and Sch. Pharmacy, dept. biopharm. scis., 1982—. Mem. anti-virals adv. com. Ctr. for Drug Evaluation and Rsch., FDA, 1991—94; chair Gordon Conf. on Stats. in Chemistry and Chem. Engring., 1989; John G. Wagner lectr. pharmaceutics U. Mich. Coll. Pharmacy, 1994; Leon Goldberg lectr. clin. pharmacology U. Chgo., 1995; Sidney Riegelman lectr. U. Calif., San Francisco, 2000. Mem. editl. bd.: European Jour. Pharm. Scis., Clin. Pharmacology and Therapeutics, 1985—; editor: (pharmacokinetics sect.) Jour. Pharmacokinetics and Biopharmaceutics, 1981—. Recipient MERIT award, NIH, 1996, rsch. grants in field. Fellow: Am. Coll. Clin. Pharmacology (hon.; Therapeutics Frontiers lectr. award 1987); mem.: Am. Soc. for Clin. Investigation (emeritus mem.), Am. Soc. for Clin. Pharmacology and Therapeutics (Rawls-Palmer lectr. on progress in medicine 1989, pres. 1990). Office: U Calif Dept Lab Medicine Box 0626 C255 San Francisco CA 94143-

SHEINFELD, MYRON M. lawyer, educator; b. Mass., Mar. 18, 1930; s. Robert and Sadye (Rosenberg) S.; m. Christina Trzcinski, Mar. 30, 1985; children: Scott, Tom. BA, Tulane U., 1951; JD, U. Mich., 1954. Bar: Mich. 1954, Tex. 1956. Rschr. Legis. Rsch. Inst., U. Mich., 1954; asst. U. S. atty. So. Dist. Tex., 1958-60; law clk. U.S. Dist. Judge, 1960-61; ptnr. Strickland, Gordon & Sheinfeld, Houston, 1961-68; shareholder, of counsel Sheinfeld, Maley & Kay, P.C., Houston, 1968-96, counsel to firm, 1996—2001; sr. counsel Akin, Gump, Strauss, Hauer & Feld LLP, 2001—. Past adj. prof. law U. Tex.; mem. Nat. Bankruptcy Conf.; former chmn. Tex. Bankruptcy Adv. Commn., Tex., Bus. Law Section; bd. dirs. Nabors Industries, Ltd.; mem. Tex. Bd. Legal Specialization; chmn. ABA Standing Com. on Specialization. Bd. editors Collier On Bankruptcy (15th edit.); contbr. articles to profl. jours. With JAG U.S. Army, 1955-58. Fellow Am. Coll. Bankrupcty; mem. State Bar Mich., Tex. (former chmn. bus. law section), Nat. Assn. Corp. Dirs. (bd. dirs. Houston chpt.), Houston Ctr. Club (bd. dirs.), Phi Beta Kappa, Phi Sigma Alpha. Office: Akin Gump Strauss Hauer & Feld LLP Pennzoil Pl-South Tower 44th Fl 1111 Louisiana St Houston TX 77002-5200 Office Phone: 713-220-5801. Personal E-mail: msheinfeld@akingump.com.

SHEINGOLD, DANIEL H. electrical engineer; b. Boston, Sept. 26, 1928; s. Louis S. and Elsie (Frank) S.; m. Ann Silverman, Aug. 2, 1953 (dec. Feb. 1995); children: Mark J., Laura S. Duffy. BSEE with distinction, Worcester Poly. Inst., 1948; MSEE, Columbia U., 1949. Engr. George A. Philbrick Rschs. Inc., Boston, 1949-55, application engring. mgr., 1957-63; v.p. George A. Philbrick Researches, Inc., Dedham, Mass., 1964-67; staff cons. Teledyne Philbrick, Dedham, 1967-68; tech. mktg. mgr. Analog Devices, Inc., Norwood, Mass., 1969—. Editor: Analog-Digital Conversion Handbook, 1972, 3d edit., 1986, Nonlinear Circuits Handbook, 1974, Transducer Interfacing Handbook, 1980; editor Analog Dialogue jour., 1969—, others. With AUS, 1955-57. Fellow IEEE; mem. IEEE Instrumentation and Measurement Soc. (sec.-treas. 1976, v.p. 1977, pres. 1978), AAAS. Jewish. Avocations: music, walking, crosscountry skiing, reading. Office: Analog Devices Inc PO Box 9106 3 Technology Way Norwood MA 02062-9106 E-mail: dan.sheingold@analog.com.

SHEININ, ROSE, biochemist, educator; b. Toronto, Ont., May 18, 1930; d. Harry and Anne (Szyber) Shuber; m. Joseph Sheinin, July 15, 1951; children: David Matthew Khazanov, Lisa Basya Judith, Rachel Sarah Rebecca. BA, U. Toronto, 1951, MA (scholar), 1953, PhD in Biochemistry, 1956, LHD, 1985; DHL (hon.), Mt. St. Vincent U., 1985; DSc (hon.), Acadia U., 1987, U. Guelph, 1991. Demonstrator in biochemistry U. Toronto, Ont., Can., 1951-53, asst. prof. microbiology, 1964-75, asst. prof. med. biophysics, 1967-75, prof. microbiology, 1975-90, assoc. prof. med. biophysics, 1975-78, prof. med. biophysics, 1978-90, chmn. microbiology and parasitology, 1975-82, vice dean Sch. Grad. Studies, 1984-89; vice-rector acad. Concordia U., Montreal, Que., Can., 1989-94, prof. dept. biology, 1989-2000. Mem. Health Scis. Com.; vis. rsch. assoc. chem. microbiology Cambridge U., 1956-57, Nat. Inst. Med. Rsch., London, 1975-58; rsch. assoc. fellow divsn. biol. rsch. Ont. Caner Inst., 1958-67; sci. officer cancer grants panel Med. Rsch. Coun. Can.; mem. Can. Sci. Del. to People's Republic of China, 1973; mem. adv. com. Provincial Lottery Health Rsch. Awards; mem. adv. com. on biotech. NRC Can., 1984-87; mem. Sci. Coun. Can., 1984-87; adv. com. on sci. and tech. CBC, 1980-85; mem. bd. dirs. Can. Bacterial Disease Network, 1989-94; vis. prof. biochemistry U. Alta., 1971. Assoc. editor Can. Jour. Biochemistry, 1968-71, Virology, 1969-72, Intervirology, 1974-85; editl. bd. Microbiol. Revs., 1977-80; author, co-author various publs. Nat. Cancer Inst. Can. fellow, 1953-56, 58-61; Brit. Empire Cancer Campaign fellow, 1956-58; recipient Queen's Silver Jubilee medal, 1978, Woman of Distinction award Health and Edn., YWCA, 1988, Josiah Macy Jr. faculty scholar, 1981-82; fellow Ligue Contre le Cancer, France, 1981-82, Massey Coll., U. Toronto, 1981—, continuing sr. fellow, 1994—; hon. fellow Ryerson Polytech. U., 1993. Fellow Am. Acad. Microbiology, Royal Soc. Can. (chair women in scholarship com. 1990-93); mem. Can. Biochem. Soc. (pres. 1974-75), Can. Soc. Cell Biology (pres. 1975-76), Am. Soc. Virology, Am. Soc. Microbiologists, Can. Assn. Women in Sci., Internat. Assn. Women Bioscientists, Sigma Xi Rsch. Soc., Scitech. Soc. Complex Carbohydrates, Toronto Biochem. and Biophys. Soc. (pres. 1960-70, coun. 1970-74) E-mail: rosesheinin@sympatico.ca.

SHEINMAN, MORT, editor, consultant, writer, photographer; b. N.Y.C., Oct. 7, 1933; s. Irving and Molly (Feigenblatt) S.; m. Claire Rosenfeld, Aug. 27, 1967 (div.). BA in English, CCNY, 1954. Sports tabulator New York Daily News, 1956-58; reporter Women's Wear Daily, N.Y.C., 1960-69, news editor, 1970-71, mng. editor, 1971-2000, W Mag., N.Y.C., 1972-82, assoc. editor, 1982-2000; editl. dir. Publicis Dialog N.Y., N.Y.C., 2000-01; journalism instr. Fashion Inst. Tech., 2001—. Cons., writer ATT Summer Olympics Exhibit, L.A., 1984, Pru Ctr. Obs., Boston, 1995. Contbr. articles and photographs to various publs. including Diverson mag., 1979—. With U.S. Army, 1954-56. Mem.: CCNY Comm. Alumni (Hall of Fame 2003), Soc. of the Silurians, Nat. Arts Club. Home: 60 Gramercy Park N New York NY 10010-5423 E-mail: mortone@aol.com.

SHEK, ALLEN, pharmacist, educator; m. Erika Shek. BS in Pharmacy, SUNY, Buffalo, N.Y., 1991; PharmD, U. Ill., 1998. Registered pharmacist Calif., Ill. Pharmacist Sutter Merced (Calif.) Med.Ctr., 1991—97; computer cons. Rush Presbyn. - St. Luke's Med. Ctr., Chgo., 1997—99; resident in primary care U. Ill., Chgo., 1998—99, clin. assoc., 1998—99; ambulatory care clin. pharmacist San Joaquin Gen. Hosp., 1999—, interim dir. pharmacy, 2001—02. Asst. prof. pharmacy U. of The Pacific, Stockton, Calif., 1999—; pharmacy clin. coord. Health Plan San Joaquin, Stockton, 2002—; mem. pharmacy and therapeutic com. Health Plan of San Joaquin, Stockton, 2001—02; treas. Ctrl. Valley Soc. Hosp. Pharmacist, 2000—02. Contbr. articles to profl. jours. Fellow, Thomas J. Long Found., 2002—03. Mem.: Am. Assn. Colls. Pharmacy (Rufus A. Lyman award 2002), Am. Coll. Clin. Pharmacy, Am. Soc. Health-Sys. Pharmacists. Office: University of the Pacific 3601 Pacific Ave Stockton CA 95211

SHEKAR, SAM, health facility administrator; MD, MPH, U. Mich. Asst. surgeon gen., rear admiral USPHS Commd. Corps.; assoc. adminstr., field ops. Bur. Health Profls., 1998—2000; assoc. adminstr., health professions HRSA, 2000—02; assoc. adminstr., primary healthcare & svcs. adminstrn. Bur. Primary Healthcare, HHS, 2002—; dir. Bur. Primary Health Care. Leader Cmty. Health Ctr. Progra. Fellow: Am. Coll. Preventtive Medicine (bd. cert.). Office: US Dept Health and Human Svcs Health Resources and Svcs Adminstrn 4350 East-West Hwy Bethesda MD 20814

SHEKHAR, STEPHEN S. obstetrician, gynecologist; b. New Delhi, Jan. 13, 1944; arrived in U.S., 1972; s. S.P. Jain and Shakuntala Mithal; m. Claudette Dorita, Jan. 6, 1978; children: Sasha, Stephen. MBBS, Punjabi U., Patiala, India, 1966. Surgeon Nat. Health Svc. U.K., 1966-72; intern Roosevelt Hosp.-Columbia Coll. Physicians and Surgeons, N.Y.C., 1972-73; resident in ob-gyn. St. Clare's Hosp., N.Y. Med. Coll., N.Y.C., 1973-76, Harlem Hosp.-Columbia U., N.Y.C., 1976-77; pvt. practice Studio City, Calif., 1977—. Mem. staff L.A. County-U. So. Calif. Med. Sch.; clin. prof. ob-gyn. and family medicine U. So. Calif. Sch. Medicine, Oreg. Health Scis. U. Sch. Medicine. Fellow ACS, Am. Coll. Ob-Gyn., L.A. Soc. Ob-Gyn.; mem. AMA, Calif. Med. Assn., L.A. County Med. Assn., Oreg. Med. Assn., Jackson County Med. Assn. Home and Office: PO Box 1742 Medford OR 97501-0136 Office Phone: 541-292-0920.

SHELANSKI, MICHAEL L. cell biologist, educator; b. Phila., Oct. 5, 1941; s. Herman Alder and Bessie B.; m. Vivien Brodkin, June 9, 1963; children: Howard, Samuel, Noah. Student, Oberlin Coll., 1959-61; MD (Life Ins. Med. Research Fund fellow), U. Chgo., 1966, PhD, 1967. Intern in pathology Albert Einstein Coll. Medicine, N.Y.C., 1967-68, fellow in neuropathology, 1968-70, asst. prof. pathology, 1969-74; staff scientist NIH, Bethesda, Md., 1971-73; vis. scientist Inst. Pasteur, Paris, 1973-74; assoc. prof. neuropathology Harvard U., Cambridge, Mass., 1974-78; sr. research assoc., asst. neuropathologist Children's Hosp. Med. Center, Boston, 1974-78; prof., chmn. dept. pharmacology N.Y. U. Med. Center, N.Y.C., 1978-86; Delafield Prof., chmn. dept. pathology Coll. Physicians and Surgeons, Columbia U., N.Y.C., 1987—; dir. pathology services Presbyn. Hosp., N.Y.C., 1987—; co-dir. Taub Inst. for Rsch. on Alzheimer's Disease and the Aging Brain, N.Y.C., 1998—. Mem. Neurology A study sect. NIH, 1974-78; Pharmacological Scis. study sect., 1986-90; mem. sci. and med. adv. bd. Alzheimer's Disease and Related Disorders Assn., 1985-92, sec., 1987-92, mem. Zenith award panel, 1993-95; chmn. overhead powerline adv. panel State of N.Y., 1981-87; dir. Alzheimer's disease rsch. ctr. Columbia U., 1989—; mem. Am. Cancer Soc. IRG Panel, 1989-93, sci. adv. bd. Dystonia Assn., Amyotrophic Lateral Sclerosis Assn; elected mem., Inst. of Medicine, 1999. Mem. editl. bd. Jour. Neurochemistry, 1982-90, Jour. Neuropathology and Exptl. Neurology, 1983-85, Neuroscis., 1985—, Neurobiology of Aging, 1988-95, Lab. Investigation, 1989—, Brain Pathology, 1990-93. Served as sr. asst. surgeon USPHS, 1971-73. Guggenheim fellow, 1973-74 Mem. Am. Soc. Cell Biology, Inst. Medicine NAS, Am. Assn. Neuropathologists, Assn. Med. Coll. Pharmacologists, Am. Soc. Neurochemistry, Am. Assn. Physicians. Achievements include research on fibrous proteins of brain, aging of human brain, devel. neurobiology. Office: Columbia U Coll Physicians and Surgeons Dept Pathology 630 W 168th St New York NY 10032-3702

SHELBURNE, JOHN DANIEL, pathologist; b. Washington, Aug. 27, 1943; s. Clarence Daniel and Edith (McDanel) S.; m. Katherine Howard Parrish, June 17, 1966; children: Mark, Kerri. BA, U. N.C., 1966; PhD, Duke U., 1971, MD, 1972. Intern, then resident Duke U. Med. Ctr., Durham, N.C., 1972-76; asst. prof. Duke U., Durham, 1973-78, assoc. prof., 1978-85, prof. pathology, 1985—; dir. electron microscopy lab. VA Med. Ctr., Durham, 1976-92, chief lab. svc., 1983-99, chief of staff, 1999—. Adv. WHO, Manila, 1990; panel mem. VA Program, Washington, 1987—; participant Nordrhein/Westfalen Exchange, Germany, 1988. Editor: Basic Methods in Biological X-Ray Microprobe, 1983; author, editor: Microprobe Analysis in Medicine, 1989, Biomedical Applications of Microprobe Analysis, 1999. Mem. Appalachian Trail Conf., Harpers Ferry, West, Va., 1970—; bd. dirs. Cen. Carolina Youth Soccer, Durham, 1987-90; founding mem. N.C. Soc. for Electron Microscopy and Microprobe, Research Triangle Park, N.C., 1980—. Recipient Morehead scholarship, 1961-66, AOA Med. Honorary Duke Med. Sch., 1970; named Med. Scientist Tng. Program participant NIH, 1966-72, Shelley Meml. lectr., 1985, Florey Meml. lectr., 1988. Fellow Coll. Am. Pathologists; mem. Am. Assn. Pathologists, Microscopy Soc. Am., Microbeam Analysis Soc. Democrat. Episcopalian. Home: 4302 Malvern Rd Durham NC 27707-5451 Office: Duke U Dept Pathology PO Box 3712 Durham NC 27710-3712 Business E-Mail: john.shelburne@med.va.gov.

SHELBY, BRYAN ROHRER, information systems management consultant; b. Bryn Mawr, Pa., June 26, 1952; s. Albert Rohrer and Elizabeth Ellen (Griffinger) S.; m. Linda Yale Pole, Sept. 9, 1972; children: Caroline Belle, Christina Marie, Heather Lynn. AB in Math. cum laude, Harvard U., 1974. Programmer Litton Industries, Morris Plains, N.J., 1974-75; mgr. info. svcs. The Becker Co., East Orange, N.J., 1975-81; mgr. design and devel. Key Fin. Sys., Pine Brook, N.J., 1982-85; v.p., group project mgr. Bankers Trust Co., Jersey City, N.J., 1985-93; pres. Contek Sys., Inc., Madison, N.J., 1993—; prin. ITR Group LLC, Madison, 2002—, Total Rights Mgmt., Inc., Madison, 2003—. Process reengring., project mgmt. and strategic tech. planning cons.; program mgmt. and life cycle methodology specialist; corp. expert in enterprise project mgmt. setup and adminstrn.; designer, project mgr., sys. integrator fin., portfolio mgmt., trust acctg., telecom., pub. Designer/project mgr./sys. integrator fin./portfolio mgmt./trust acctg./telecom./pub. Mem. IEEE, Am. Soc. Pension Actuaries. Democrat. Avocations: reading, building sandcastles. Office: ITR Group LLC 235 Main St # 307 Madison NJ 07940-0292 Office Phone: 973-966-1845. Business E-Mail: brian.shelby@itrgroupllc.com.

SHELBY, JAMES STANFORD, cardiovascular surgeon; b. Ringgold, La., June 15, 1934; s. Jesse Audrey and Mable (Martin) S.; m. Susan Rainey, July 15, 1967; children: Bryan Christian, Christopher Linden. BS in Liberal Arts, La. Tech. U., 1956; MD, La. State U., 1958. Diplomate Am. Bd. Surgery, Am. Bd. Thoracic Surgery. Intern Charity Hosp. La., New Orleans, 1958-59, resident in surgery and thoracic surgery, 1959-65; fellow in cardiovasc. surgery Baylor U. Coll. Medicine, Houston, 1965-66; practice medicine specializing in cardiovasc. surgery Shreveport, La., 1967—2004; ret., 2004. Mem. staff Schumpert Med. Ctr., Highland Hosp., Willis-Knighton Med. Ctr.; assoc. prof. surgery La. State U. Sch. Medicine, Shreveport, 1967—. With M.C., AUS, 1961-62. Recipient Woer of Medallion award La. Tech. U., 1982. Mem. AMA, Am. Coll. Cardiology, Soc. Thoracic Surgeons, Am. Heart Assn., Southeastern Surg. Congress, So. Thoracic Surgery Assn. Home: 6003 E Ridge Dr Shreveport LA 71106-2425 Office: 2751 Albert Bicknell Dr Ste 2G Shreveport LA 71103-3970 Office Phone: 318-632-9434 E-mail: jshelby@worldnet.att.net.

SHELBY, MICHAEL T. lawyer; b. Nov. 1958; BS, Tex. A&M U., 1981; JD, U. Tex., 1984. Asst. U.S. atty. So. Dist. Tex., 1989—91, 1992—97, Dist. Ariz., 1997—2001; U.S. atty. So. Dist. Tex., 2002—. Office: PO Box 61129 910 Travis St Houston TX 77208

SHELBY, NINA CLAIRE, special education educator; b. Weatherford, Tex., Oct. 23, 1949; d. Bill Hudson and Roselle (Price) S.; m. Richard Dean Powell, May 29, 1971 (div. 1973); 1 child, Stoney Hudson. BA in English, Sul Ross State U., 1974, MEd, 1984; MA in English, U. Tex., 1995. Jr. high lang. arts educator Liberty Hill, Tex., 1974-75; H.S. resource educator Georgetown (Tex.) I. S. D., 1976-77; intermediate resource educator Raymondille (Tex.) I. S. D., 1977-81; educator of severe profound Napper Elem. Pharr (Tex.) San Juan Alamo Ind. Sch. Dist., 1981-90; H. S. life skills educator Pharr (Tex.) San Juan Alamo ISD North H.S., 1990-93; intermediate inclusion educator Carman Elem. Pharr (Tex.) San Juan Alamo Ind. Sch. Dist., 1993—2000, chair dept. spl. edn. Carman Elem., 1998—2000; primary resource/inclusion educator Elgin (Tex.) Elem. Sch., 2000—, chair dept. spl. edn., 2002—. Coach asst. Tex. Spl. Olympics, Pharr, 1981—, sponsor vocat. adj. club, 1990-93, adaptive asst. device team, Edinburg, Tex., 1993-95; spl. edn. rep. to Elgin Primary Campus Performance Adv. Coun., 2000--. Asst. cub scout leader Boy Scouts Am., 1994-95, sec. parental com. bd. rev., 1997—; parent vol. boy's and girl's Club McAllen, 1992-96. Mem. DAR, Assn. of Tex. Profl. Educators, Alpha Delta Kappa. Democrat. Mem. Ch. Of Christ. Avocations: reading, horticulture, piano, opera. Home: PO Box 426 Elgin TX 78621-0426 Office: Elgin Elem Sch Elgin ISD 1001 W 2d St Elgin TX 78621 Office Phone: 512-281-3457.

SHELBY, RICHARD CRAIG, senator, former congressman; b. Birmingham, Ala., May 6, 1934; s. O.H. and Alice L. (Skinner) S.; m. Annette Nevin, June 11, 1960; children: Richard Craig, Claude Nevin. AB, U. Ala., 1957, LLB, 1963. Bar: Ala. 1961, D.C. 1979. Law clk. Supreme Ct. of Ala., 1961-62; practice law Tuscaloosa, Ala., 1963—78; prosecutor City of Tuscaloosa, 1963—71; spl. asst. atty. gen. State of Ala., 1968—71; U.S. magistrate No. Dist. of Ala., 1966—70; mem. Ala. State Senate, 1971—78, 96th-99th Congresses from 7th Ala. dist., 1979-87; mem. energy and commerce com.; mem. vets. affairs com.; U.S. senator from Ala., 1987—; mem. com. on appropriations, com. on banking, housing, and urban affairs, chmn. com. on govtl. affairs, spl. com. on aging; chmn. senate banking com. Active Boy Scouts Am.; pres. Tuscaloosa County Mental Health Assn., 1969-70; bd. govs. Nat. Legis. Conf., 1975-78. Mem. ABA, Ala. Bar Assn., Tuscaloosa County Bar Assn., D.C. Bar Assn., Exch. Club. Republican. Presbyterian. Home: 1414 High Forest Dr N Tuscaloosa AL 35406-2152 Office: US Senate 110 Hart Senate Bldg Washington DC 20510-0001

SHELBY, RONALD VAN DORN, information technology executive; b. Covington, Ind., Jan. 14, 1948; s. Richard Van Dorn and Edna Belle Shelby; m. Susan Gail Bamford, Dec. 28, 1984; 1 child, Richard James Harold. BA, Wabash Coll., 1970; MAT, Ind. U., 1973; MBA, U. Toronto, 1984. Project leader Travelers Ins. Co., Toronto, Ont., 1976-79, mgr. data adminstrn., 1979—84; data adminstr. U.S. Dept. Interior, Washington, 1984—86; prin. Am. Mgmt. Sys., Arlington, Va., 1986—89; v.p. info. and tech. svcs. Conn. Mut. Life, Hartford, 1989—96; v.p. tech. leader Am. Express Co., Phoenix, 1996—98; chief tech. officer General Motors corp., Detroit, 1998—2000; CEO XML Solutions corp., McLean, Va., 2000—01, e Fusion Solutions, LLC, Vienna, Va., 2001—. Author: Selecting a DBMS, 1984, Project Manager's Guide to System Development, 1985, also chpts. to books; reviewing editor Data Resource Mgmt., 1989—. Mem. Data Adminstrn. Mgmt. Assn. (adv., bd. dirs., founder Washington chpt. 1988—, internat. pres. 1990). Episcopalian. Avocations: photography, baseball, jogging. Home: PO Box 2409 Vienna VA 22183 E-mail: ron@theshelbys.com.

SHELBY, TIM OTTO, secondary school educator; b. Longview, Wash., Mar. 23, 1965; s. William Richard and Ruth (Masser) S. BA in Edn., Eastern Wash. U., 1989; MA in Counseling, U. LaVerne, 2003. Cert. grades 4-12 English tchr., Wash., Calif. English tchr., head basketball and football coach Kahlotus (Wash.) H.S., 1989-90; tchr. various dists., 1990-92; English tchr., asst. basketball coach Kalama (Wash.) H.S., 1992-95; tchr. English, head basketball coach Frazier Mountain H.S., Lebec, Calif., 1995-97; English tchr., asst. basketball coach Shafter (Calif.) H.S., 1997-98; English tchr., asst. basketball coach, English dept. chmn. Mojave (Calif.) H.S., 1998—. Mem. ASCD, Nat. Coun. Tchrs. Eng., Calif. Edn. Assn. Roman Catholic. Avocations: travel, reading, coaching sports, theater, movies. Home: 21330 Santa Barbara Dr Tehachapi CA 93561-8715 Office: Mojave Unified Sch Dist Mojave CA 93501

SHELDON, BETTI L. state legislator; b. Aberdeen, Wash. 5 children. Student, Gonzaga U. Mem. Wash. Senate, Dist. 23, Olympia, 1992—; majority flood leader Wash. Senate, Olympia, 1999—; mem. Dem. flood leader Wash. Legislature, Olympia, 1997-98, majority caucus vice chair, 1995, majority whip, 1995-96, majority asst. floor leader, 1993-95, mem. higher edn. com., mem. rules com., mem. ways and means com. Bd. dirs. Small Bus. Improvement Coun., Commn. on Student Learning's K-123 Accountability Task Force, Nat. Assn. Adminstrv. Rules Rev., YMCA Youth and Govt., Gov.'s Regulatory Reform Task Force, Big Bros. and Big Sisters Kitsap County, Kitsap County Econ. Devel. Coun., Puget Sound Naval Bases Assn., West Sound Arts Coun., Bremerton Olympic Peninsula Coun. Navy League; mem. Wash. Devel. Fin. Authority; mem. adv. bd. for corp. rels. Martha & Mary Luth. Svcs.; mem. delivery plan adv. group Dept. Health Am. Indian Health Care; trustee Keyport Naval Underseas Mus. Found. Recipient Woman of Yr. Bremerton Kitsap YWCA, 1993, Strong Kids, Strong Families, Strong Cmtys. award YMCA, 1999, Dem. Woman of Yr. Wash. State Fedn. Women's Clubs, 1997. Mem. Bremerton Area C. of C. (past exec. dir.), Wash. C. of C. Execs. (v.p.). Democrat. Office: 410A Legislative Bldg Olympia WA 98504-0482

SHELDON, DEENA LYNN, television camera operator; b. Groveland, Mass., Mar. 10, 1962; d. Frederic J. and Penny Margolis. BS, Boston U., 1984. Co. mem. Body Lang. Dancers, 1986; mem. Michael Macchio's Jazz Co., 1980-85, Danny Sloan's Repertory, 1980-82, Celtic's Green Gang, 1980-82, Dean Brittenham's Shiley Elite Athletic Program. Camera operator Redsox and Bruins, Sta. WSBK-TV, Boston, 1985, Am.'s Cup, Maj. League Baseball and postseason play, Homerun Derby, Boston Marathon, Extreme Games,

ESPN, 1986—; NY Mets and NY Islanders, Sportschannel, 1987-92; NY Mets, Sta. WWOR-TV, 1987-92; Monday Night Football, Superbowl XXXIV, Superbowl XXXVII, Acad. Awards, NBA Championship, Ky. Derby, Triple Crown, Indy 500, Rose Bowl, Pro Bowl, NFL Hall of Fame game, Superbowl XXIX halftime show, Dem. and Rep. convs., Presdl. inaugurations, 1993, 97, ABC, 1992—, Late Night with David Letterman, NFL, Triple Crown, Olympics, Phil Donahue Show, Macy's Day Parade, NBC, 1986—; Superbowl XXXVIII, NFL and championship games, Daytona 500, Joan Rivers Show, Major League Baseball and postseason play, CBS, 1987—; Superbowl XXXI, World Series, NFL, NHL, Fox Sports, 1994—; robotic camera operator Met. Life and Fuji blimps, NFL championship and playoff games, Daytona 500, Indy 500, 1989—. Youth counselor and instr. athleticism. Recipient Emmy awards for CBS's Postseason Major League Baseball, 1990, CBS's Daytona 500, 1993, ESPN's Extreme Games, 1995-98, NY Emmy for NY Mets, 1992-93, 93-94, Fox's Postseason Maj. League Baseball, 1999; Emmy nominee for ESPN's Am.'s Cup, 1995. Mem. NABET, Internat. Brotherhood Elec. Workers, Internat. Alliance Theatrical Stage Employees. Avocations: trail running, dance, sunshine, instructing in athleticism. Home: 70445 Mottle Cir Rancho Mirage CA 92270 Office Phone: 760-522-1020. E-mail: deena.sheldon@verizon.net.

SHELDON, ELEANOR HARRIET BERNERT, sociologist, writer; b. Hartford, Conn., Mar. 19, 1920; d. M.G. and Fannie (Myers) Bernert; m. James Sheldon, Mar. 19, 1950 (div. 1960); children: James, John Anthony. AA, Colby Jr. Coll., 1940; AB, U. N.C., 1942; PhD, U. Chgo., 1949. Asst. demographer Office Population Rsch., Washington, 1942-43; social scientist USDA, Washington, 1943-45; assoc. dir. Chgo. Community Inventory, U. Chgo., 1947-50; social scientist Social Sci. Rsch. Coun., N.Y.C., 1950-51, rsch. grantee, 1953-55, pres., 1972-79; rsch. assoc. Bur. Applied Social Rsch. Columbia U., 1950-51, lectr. sociology, 1951-52, vis. prof., 1969-71; social scientist UN, N.Y.C., 1951-52; rsch. assoc., lectr. sociology UCLA, 1955-61; assoc. rsch. sociologist, lectr. Sch. Nursing U. Calif., 1957-61; sociologist, exec. assoc. Russell Sage Found., N.Y.C., 1971—72; vis. prof. U. Calif., Santa Barbara, 1971. Author: (with L. Wirth) Chicago Community Fact Book, 1949, America's Children, 1958, (with R.A. Glazier) Pupils and Schools in N.Y.C, 1965; editor: (with W.E. Moore) Indicators of Social Change, Concepts and Measurements, 1968, Family Economic Behavior, 1973; contbr. articles to profl. jours. Bd. dirs. Colby-Sawyer Coll., 1979-85, UN Rsch. Inst. for Social Devel., 1973-79; trustee Rockefeller Found., 1978-85, Nat. Opinion Rsch. Ctr., 1980-87, Inst. East-West Security Studies, 1984-88, Am. assembly, 1976-95. William Rainey Harper fellow U. Chgo., 1945-47 Fellow AAAS, Am. Acad. Arts and Scis., Am. Sociol. Assn., Am. Statis. Assn.; mem. U. Chgo. Alumni Assn. (Profl. Achievement award), Sociol. Rsch. Assn. (pres. 1971-72), Coun. on Fgn. Rels., Am. Assn. Pub. Opinion Rsch., Ea. Sociol. Soc., Internat. Sociol. Assn., Internat. Union Sci. Study of Population, Population Assn. Am. (2d v.p. 1970-71), Inst. of Medicine (chmn. program com. 1976-77), Cosmopolitan Club. Home and Office: 630 Park Ave New York NY 10021-6544

SHELDON, GEORGE FRANK, medical educator; b. Dec. 20, 1934; s. Richard Robert and Helen Irene (Zerzan) S.; m. Ruth Guy, Aug. 28, 1959; children: Anne Anderson, Elizabeth, Julia. BA, U. Kans., 1957, MD, 1961; postgrad., Mayo Clinic Grad. Sch., 1965. Intern Kans. U. Med. Ctr.; resident in surgery U. Calif., San Francisco, 1965-69; fellow in surg. biology Harvard Med. Sch. of Peter Bent Brigham Hosp., 1969-71; from asst. to prof. U. Calif., 1971-82; Dr. Zack D. Owens Disting. prof. surgery, dept. chmn. U. N.C., Chapel Hill, 1984—2001. Chmn. residency rev. com. accreditation Coun. for Grad. Med. Edn.; mem. Coun. Grad. Med. Edn. of Health and Human Svcs., 1986, chmn. 1998; mem. adminstrv. bd. Coun. Acad. Socs., chair, 1998-99; chmn. Merit Rev. Bd. for Surgery Va., AAMC, 2000, 01; pres. vis. bd. UN Formed Svcs. U. Health Scis., 2002-03. Author: (with J.B. Runnell) Pictorial History of Kansas Medicine, 1961; (with Jill Ridky) Managing in Academics, 1993; editor: (with J.B. Davis) Clinical Surgery, 1995. With USPHS, 1962-64. Recipient Surgeon's award for Svc. to Safety, Nat. Safety Coun., 1993, Douglass Stubbs award Nat. Med. Assn., 1991, Disting. Faculty award Med. Alumni Assn. U. N.C., 2001; named Disting. Med. Alumnus, Kans. U., 2000. Hon. fellow Royal Coll. Surgeons of Edinburgh, Royal Coll. Surgeons Eng., European Surg. Assn., Assn. of Surgeons of Gt. Britain and Ireland, Phila. Acad. Surgeons (Hunterian Orator 2001); mem. ACS (sec. bd. govs., regent 1984-93, pres. 1998, Surgeon of Yr. 2001, Fitts Orator, 1987), Am. Bd. Surgery (chmn. 1989-90), Nat. Bd. Med. Examiners (test com. 1981-84), Am. Assn. Surgery of Trauma (pres. 1984, Fitts medal), Am. Surg. Assn. (sec. 1989-94, pres. 1994-95), Assn. Am. Med. Colls. (exec. com., chair elect 1999, chair 2000-01), Soc. Surg. Chmn. (pres.), Coun. Acad. Socs. (chmn. 1998—, com. on gender equity and com. on health workforce), Inst. Medicine (sec. com. on employer based health ins. and tech. assessment edn. bds., Fluid Resuscitation com. on Nation's Physician Workforce 1996). Office: U NC at Chapel Hill Dept Surgery Campus Bx 7050 136 Burnett-Womack Bldg Chapel Hill NC 27599-7228 Office Phone: 919-966-4052. E-mail: gsheldon@med.unc.edu.

SHELDON, GILBERT IGNATIUS, clergyman; b. Cleve., Sept. 20, 1926; s. Ignatius Peter and Stephanie Josephine (Olszewski) S. Student, John Carroll U.; M.Div., St. Theol. Sem., 1970; D.Min., St. Mary Sem. and Ohio Consortium of Sems., 1974; HHD, Jesuit U. of Wheeling, 1993; STD, Franciscan U., Steubenville, 1994. Ordained priest Roman Cath. Ch., 1953, bishop, 1976. Assoc. pastor Cleve. Diocese, 1953-64, diocesan dir. propagation of faith, 1964-74; pastor, Episcopal vicar Lorain County, Ohio, 1974-76; aux. bishop Cleve., 1976—; vicar for Summit County, 1979-80, So. Region, 1980-92; bishop Steubenville, 1992—. Bd. dirs. Soc. Propagation of Faith, 1968-74, Diocesan Presbyteral Coun.; instr. theology St. John Coll.; clergy adv. bd. econ. edn. Akron U.; mem. Bishop's Com. Latin Am.; bd. trustees St. Mary Seminary, Diocesan Health Ins. Adv. Bd., Cath. Charities Corp.; former mem. bd. trustees Borromeo Coll.; mem. acad. bd. St. Mary Seminary; bd. dirs. Bishops' Com. Latin Am., adminstrv. com. Nat. Conf. Cath. Bishops/USCC, Nat. Adv. Coun., Bishops' Com. for Missions, Nat. Bd. Soc. for Propagation of Faith; bd. trustees Pontifical Coll. Josephinum, Bishop Emeritus of Steubenville, 2002, Adj. Faculty, Franciscan U. of Steubenville, 2003. Goals for Greater Akron. Served with USAF, 1944—45. Mem. Nat. Conf. Cath. Bishops (adminstrv. bd. 1985—), Am. Legion, Cath. War Vets., Knights of Columbus, Order of Alhambra., Rotary Club Akron and Steubenville. Clubs: K.C. Lodges: Rotary (Akron). Roman Catholic. Avocations: golf, astronomy, photography, history, travel. Office: Diocese of Steubenville PO Box 969 Steubenville OH 43952-5969 E-mail: lnichols@diosteub.org.

SHELDON, INGRID KRISTINA, former mayor, bookkeeper; b. Ann Arbor, Mich., Jan. 30, 1945; d. Henry Ragnvald and Virginia Schmidt (Clark) Blom; m. Clifford George Sheldon, June 18, 1966; children: Amy Elizabeth, William David. BS, Eastern Mich. U., 1966; MA, U. Mich., 1970; doctorate (hon.), Cleary U., 2001. Cert. tchr., Mich. Tchr. Livonia (Mich.) Pub. Schs., 1966-67, Ann Arbor Pub. Schs., 1967-68; bookkeeper Huron Valley Tennis Club, Ann Arbor, 1978—; acct. F.A. Black Co., Ann Arbor, 1984-88; coun. mem. Ward II City of Ann Arbor, 1988-92, mayor, 1993-2000. Commr. Housing Bd. Appeals, Ann Arbor, 1988—91; vice chmn. fin. and budget com. S.W. Mich. Coun.Govts.; treas. Huron Valley Child Guidance Clinic, Ann Arbor, 1984—, Ann Arbor Hist. Found., 1985—, Parks Adv. Commn., 1987—92, Ann Arbor Planning Commn., 1988—89; excellence com. Ann Arbor Pub. Schs. reorgn., 1985; treas. SOS Cmty. Crisis Ctr., Ypsilanti, Mich., 1987—93; chair United Meth. Retirement Cmty., Ann Arbor, 2003; trustee Cmty. Found., 2001—; pres. Ann Arbor Summer Festival, 2003; precinct ward city vice chmn. Ann Arbor Rep. City Com., 1978—. Recipient Cmty. Svc. award Ann Arbor Jaycees, 1980, DAR Cmty. Svc. award, 1997; AAUW fellow, 1982. Mem.: Mich. Mcpl. League (del. 1989—97, trustee 1997—, pres. 1999—2000), Rotary (former dir. Ann Arbor chpt.), Ann Arbor Women's City Club (chair endowment com. 1989—90, fin. com. 1987—90, treas. 2003), Alpha Omicron Pi, Kappa Delta Pi. Republican. Methodist. Avocation: musical theatre. Home: 1416 Folkstone Ct Ann Arbor MI 48105-2848 E-mail: aasheldon@aol.com.

SHELDON, J. MICHAEL, lawyer, educator; b. Mt. Carmel, Pa., Sept. 1, 1951; s. Lloyd Loomis and Helen Roberta (Sosnoski) S. AA, Harrisburg (Pa.) Community Coll., 1978; BS, Pa. State U., 1980; M in Journalism, Temple U., 1991; JD, Widener U. Sch. Law, 1996. News announcer Sta. WNUE-AM, Ft. Walton Beach, Fla., 1974-76, Sta. WFEC-AM, Harrisburg, 1977-78; announcer Sta. WCMB-AM, Wormleysburg, Pa., 1979-80; writer newspaper Pa. Beacon, Harrisburg, 1982-85; media specialist Commonwealth Media Svcs., Harrisburg, 1982-86; dir. communications Pa. Poultry Fedn., Harrisburg, 1986-89; news anchor Sta. WGAL-TV, Lancaster, Pa., 1989-90; dir. pub. rels. Profl. Ins. Agts. - Pa., Md., Del., Mechanicsburg, Pa., 1990-92; v.p. comm. and mktg. United Way of the Capital Region, Harrisburg, Pa., 1992-93, Widener U. Sch. of Law, 1994-96; pres. Open Mike Comm., Harrisburg, 1994—. Mem. adj. faculty dept. journalism Temple U., 1992; mem. faculty dept. humanities Pa. State U., 1995-97, 99—. Contbg. author: Pa. 12th Annual Civil Litigation Update, Spoliation of Evidence: Why You Can't Have Your Cake and Eat it Too, 1999; contbg. editor: A Practical Guidebook to Massachusetts Aviation Law, 1999; Contbr. articles to profl. jours. Pub. rels. advisor Cen. Pa. Leukemia Soc., Harrisburg, 1989-90; media advisor Polit. Campaign, Hershey, Pa., 1990. With USAF, 1969-73. Mem. U.S. Fed. Mid. Dist. Bar, Pa. Bar, Dauphin County Bar, VFW (life), Am. Legion, Knights of Columbus (4th degree Knight), Chi Gamma Iota, Delta Tau Kappa. Republican. Roman Catholic. Avocations: motorcycles, music, electronics, martial arts. Office: 6059 Allentown Blvd Harrisburg PA 17112-2672

SHELDON, Mrs. JOHN See GIBBONS, CELIA

SHELDON, KATHLEEN EDDY, historian; b. Hartford, Conn., June 9, 1952; d. Austin Mather and Sylvia Desmond Sheldon; m. Stephen Tarzynski, Dec. 28, 1974; children: Mercie Sheldon-Tarzynski, Benjamin Sheldon-Tarzynski. PhD, U. of California, Los Angeles, 1977—88; MA, African Area Studies, U. of Calif., Los Angeles, 1975—77; BA, History, Northwestern U., Evanston, Ill., 1970—74. Vis. rsch. scholar UCLA Ctr. for the Study of Women, 1988—. Author: (history book) Pounders of Grain: A History of Women, Work, and Politics in Mozambique; editor: (book of essays) Courtyards, Markets, City Streets: Urban Women in Africa. Commr. Commn. on the Status of Women, Santa Monica, Calif., 1992—2002. Recipient Catherine Prelinger Prize, Coordinating Coun. for Women in History, 1999. Mem.: Lusophone African Studies Orgn. (founding chair 1999—2004, editor h-luso-africa listserve 2002—), African Studies Assn. (women's caucus treas. 1997—2003).

SHELDON, LOIS ELIZABETH, social services administrator; b. Marion, Va., Oct. 20, 1942; d. Godfrey Hudson Coombs, Margaret Lillian Coombs; m. Jack Maurice Sheldon, Nov. 24, 1985. BS, San Diego State U., 1968; MPH, Loma Linda U., 1982; MDiv, Fuller Sem. Cert. med. technologist Calif. Med. technologist Sharp Hosp., San Diego, 1979—82; staff mem. Cmty. Health Agy., Romona, Calif., 1982—84, Health Sys. Agy., San Diego, 1984—86; dir. Christian Social Concerns, San Diego, 1986—99; cons. Ministries Enterprises, San Diego, 1999—. Author: The Rape of Ariel House, 1998; contbr. articles to profl. jours. Recipient Leadership award, Channel 10, 1996, Brad Truax award, San Diego AIDS Assn., 1994. Mem.: APHA, Jr. League (Award 1992). Home: 6662 Del Cerro Blvd San Diego CA 92120

SHELDON, RICHARD NEIL, retired historian; b. Mpls., June 12, 1934; s. Raymond Sedgwick and Rebecca Brokken Sheldon; m. Martha Marie Mortensen, Oct. 10, 1964. BS, Ariz. State U., 1958, MA, 1964; PhD, U. Ariz., 1970. Asst. prof. Rollins Coll., Winter Park, Fla., 1969—71; lectr. U. Md., College Park, 1972, Montgomery Coll., Rockville, Md., 1972—81, George Mason U., Fairfax, Va., 1985—87; program dir. U.S. Nat. Archives, Washington, 1974—95; ret., 1995. Rsch. cons. U. Va., Charlottesville, 1971—74. Author: Hammarskjold, 1987; contbr. articles to profl. jours. Sgt. USMC, 1952—55. Grantee, Rollins Coll., 1970. Mem.: Assn. Documentary Editing (disting. svc. award 1995), Orgn. Am. Historians. Home: 10898 N Sand Canyon Pl Tucson AZ 85737

SHELDON, RICHARD ROBERT, Russian language and literature educator; b. July 12, 1932; s. Richard Robert and Helen Irene (Zerzan) S.; m. Karen Ryden Sears, Feb. 8, 1964; children: Katherine Palmer, John Ryden, Robert Charles, Rebecca Ann. BA, U. Kans., 1954; JD, U. Mich., 1960, MA, 1962; PhD, Mich. U., 1966. Chmn. Russian dept. Grinnell (Iowa) Coll., 1965-66; asst. prof. Dartmouth Coll., Hanover, N.H., 1966-70, assoc. prof., 1970-75, prof. Russian lang. and lit., 1975—, chmn. dept., 1970-81, 90-00, formerly dir. fgn. studies programs, chmn. com. on orgn. and policy, com. on admissions, com. on diversity, com. on off-campus study, dean of humanities, 1984-89, acad. dir. alumni coll., 1990. Vis. prof. U. Calif. Berkeley, 1968, Stanford (Calif.) U., 1974; cons. Coun. Internat. Ednl. Exchange, N.Y.C., 1967-83, Dept. Edn., Washington, 1979—, Cornell U. Press, Ithaca, N.Y., 1970—; sr. assoc. mem. St. Antony's Coll., Oxford, Eng., 1983-84. Translator, editor: (books by V. Shklovsky) A Sentimental Journey, 1970, Zoo or Letters Not About Love, 1971, Third Factory, 1977; compiler: Viktor Shklovsky: An International Bibliography of Works by and about Him, 1977; co-editor: Soviet Society and Culture, 1988; author articles, book revs., other transls. Chmn. bd. Norwich (Vt.) Day Care Ctr., 1980-81. Pfc. U.S. Army, 1955-57. Summerfield scholar, 1952-54; Nat. Def. Act fellow Dept. Edn., Washington, 1961-64, Alfred P. Lloyd fellow U. Mich., Ann Arbor, 1964-65, Ctr. Advanced Study fellow U. Ill., Urbana, 1969-70, Am. Coun. Learned Socs. fellow, 1970; Internat. Rsch. and Exchanges Bd. study grantee, USSR, 1964-65. Mem. Am. Assn. Advancement of Slavic Studies, Am. Assn. Tchrs. Slavic and East European Langs., Coun. of Mem. Instns. (exec. com., adv. com. to pres., vice chair 1995-97, subcom. priorities), Phi Beta Kappa, Phi Alpha Theta, Phi Delta Theta (pres. 1953), Delta Sigma Rho. Democrat. Episcopalian. Home: 86 S Main St Hanover NH 03755-2029 Office: Dartmouth Coll Russian Dept 44 N College St Hanover NH 03755-1801

SHELDON, SIDNEY, author, producer, director; b. Chgo., Feb. 11, 1917; s. Otto and Natalie (Marcus) S.; m. Jorja Curtright, Mar. 28, 1951 (dec. 1985); 1 dau., Mary; m. Alexandra Kostoff, 1989. Ed., Northwestern U. Started as reader, Universal and 20th Century Fox Studios; author: (novels) The Naked Face, 1970, The Other Side of Midnight, 1975, A Stranger in the Mirror, 1976, Bloodline, 1977, Rage of Angels, 1980, Master of the Game, 1982, If Tomorrow Comes, 1985, Windmills of the Gods, 1987, The Sands of Time, 1988, Memories of Midnight, 1990, The Doomsday Conspiracy, 1991, The Stars Shine Down, 1992, Nothing Lasts Forever, 1994, Morning, Noon and Night, 1995, The Best Laid Plans, 1997, Tell Me Your Dreams, 1998, The Sky is Falling, 2000, Are You Afraid of the Dark?, 2004; creator, writer, producer: Nancy, The Patty Duke Show, I Dream of Jeannie; created TV show Hart to Hart; author: plays including Roman Candle, Jackpot, Dream With Music, Alice in Arms, Redhead; writer: screenplays including Billy Rose's Jumbo, The Bachelor and the Bobby-Soxer, 1947, Easter Parade (Box Office Blue Ribbon award), Annie Get Your Gun; writer, dir.: screenplays including Dream Wife, Buster Keaton Story; writer: screenplays including Anything Goes, Never Too Young; recipient Acad. award for screenplay The Bachelor and the Bobby-Soxer 1947, Tony award for Redhead 1959, Writers Guild Am. Screen awards for Easter Parade 1948, Annie Get Your Gun 1950, Edgar Allan Poe award Mystery Writers Am. for Naked Face, 1970. Served with USAAF, World War II. Inducted into the Guinness Book of Records as the Most Translated Author for 1997; recipient Will Rogers Meml. award, 2002. Address: care Warren Cowan Warren Cowan & Assocs 8899 Beverly Blvd # 919 Los Angeles CA 90048

SHELDON, TED PRESTON, library dean; b. Oak Park, Ill., July 5, 1942; s. Preston and Marjorie Sheldon; m. Beverly Stebel; children: Kathy, Mark. BA, Elmhurst (Ill.) Coll., 1964; MA, Ind. U., 1965, PhD, 1976; MLS, U. Ill., 1977. Asst. archivist U. Ill., Urbana, 1976-77; reference librarian U. Kans., Lawrence, 1977-79, head collection devel., 1979-81; assoc. dir. libraries SUNY, Binghamton, 1981-83, U. Mo., Kansas City, 1983-85, dean libraries, 1985—. Pres. Mo. Libr. Network Corp., 1991-95. Author: Population Trends, 1976, Kans. Coll. Devel. Policy, 1978, History, Sources Social Science, 1985; co-author: ANSI/ISO/AES audio/video data preservation stds., 1997—. Mem. ALA, Am. Nat. Stds. Inst./Audio Engring. Soc. (joint tech. commn. 1994—), Internat. Assn. Sound Archives, Assn. Recorded Sound Collection (mng. editor jour 1988-95, pub. jour. 1995—, pres. 1996-98, pub. 1996—). Office: U Mo Libraries 5100 Rockhill Rd Kansas City MO 64110-2499 Office Phone: 816-235-1531. Business E-Mail: sheldont@umkc.edu.

SHELDON, TERRY EDWIN, lawyer, business consultant, advisor; b. Sacramento, June 22, 1945; s. Earl M. and Christine M. S.; m. Jan L. Winters, Aug. 26, 1966; children: Jeffrey, Tiffini, Melissa. BS magna cum laude, Abilene Christian U., 1967; JD, So. Meth. U., 1970. Bar: Calif. 1970. Assoc. Bronson, Bronson & McKinnon, San Francisco, 1970-74; gen. counsel, also dir. Consol. Capital Cos., Emeryville, Calif., 1974-83, exec. v.p., chief oper. officer, 1984-85, cons., advisor, 1986-87; pres., trustee Consol. Capital Spl. Trust, 1980-85; exec. v.p., trustee Consol. Capital Realty Investors, 1975-85, Consol. Capital Income Trust, 1978-85, Consol. Capital Income Opportunity Trust, 1983-85, Consol. Capital Income Opportunity Trust 2, 1985; chmn. Nat. Syndication Forum (a div. of RESSI), 1981-82; real estate securities specialist RESSI. V.p., prin. Alpha Venture Corp., Walnut Creek, Calif., 1987; bus. cons., 1988—. Chmn. bd. visitors adv. com. Coll. of Bus. Adminstrn. Abilene Christian U., 1990. Mem. ABA, Calif. Bar Assn., Nat. Assn. Securities Dealers (direct participation programs com., real estate com., standing adv. com. to bd. govs. 1980-83), Nat. Syndication Forum. Republican. Mem. Ch. of Christ.

SHELDON, THOMAS DONALD, academic administrator; b. Canastota, NY, July 15, 1920; s. Harry Ellsworth and Sadie Joyce (McNulty) S.; m. Helen Elizabeth Kyser, Aug. 29, 1941; children: Thomas, Paul, Edward, Patricia, Curtis, Roberta, Kevin, Kelly. BS, Syracuse U., 1942, MS, 1949, Ed.D., 1958; grad., Air Command and Staff Coll., 1972. Tchr. sci., coach Split Rock (N.Y.) High Sch., 1942-43; tchr. sci., coach, vice prin., prin. Minoa (N.Y.) High Sch., 1946-59; prin., asso. supt. Hempstead (N.Y.) High Sch., 1959-63; supt. Hempstead Pub. Schs., 1963-68, Balt. City Schs., 1968-71; dep. commr. N.Y. State Edn. Dept., Albany, 1971-77; pres. Utica Coll. of Syracuse U., 1977-82; interim pres. Mohawk Valley Community Coll., 1983; then interim pres. Onondaga Community Coll., 1984, now hon. pres. emeritus; prof. ednl. adminstrn. Syracuse U., N.Y., 1984-85; supt. Sewanhaka Central High Sch. Dist., 1985-86; interim pres. Munson-Williams-Proctor Inst., 1990-91; exec. dir. Syracuse U. Relations, N.Y.C., 1987-93; chmn. Edn. Profls. Internat., 1977-9. Co-author and editor various N.Y. State Regents publs., 1971-76. Served with U.S. Army, 1943-46; served to col. USAF, 1972-77, Berlin; to brig. gen. Air N.G. 1955-77. First recipient Outstanding Grad. award Syracuse U. Sch. Edn., 1977; recipient Outstanding Md. Educator award Md. State Council PTA's, 1969; Disting. Am. Educator award Freedoms Found., 1966; Conspicuous Service medal N.Y. State Gov., 1976; N.Y.C. PSAL medal, 1978; named to Balt. Afro-Am. Honor Roll, 1970 Mem. VFW (life), N.Y. State PTA (hon. life), N.Y. State Coaches Assn. (pres. 1957), Am. Legion, Phi Delta Kappa. Clubs: Lions (hon. life). Home: 437A Fox Rd Bridgeport NY 13030 Office: Edn Profls Internat 437 Fox Rd Bridgeport NY 13030

SHELDRICK, GEORGE MICHAEL, chemistry educator, crystallographer; b. Huddersfield, Great Britain, Nov. 17, 1942; s. George and Elizabeth S.; m. Katherine E. Herford, 1968; 4 children. Student, Huddersfield New Coll., Jesus Coll., Cambridge. Lectr. Cambridge U., Eng., 1966-78; prof. structural chemistry U. Göttingen, Germany, 1978—; with Inst. Anorg Chemie, Göttingen, Germany. Contbr. numerous articles to profl. jours. Recipient Meldola and Corday-Morgan medals, Royal Soc. Chemistry, Leibniz prize, Deutsche Forschungsgemeinschaft, A.L. Patterson award, Am. Crystallographic Assn., 1993, Carl-Hermann medal, Deutsche Gesellschaft fur Kristallographie, 1999, Dorothy Hodgkin prize, Brit. Crystallographic Assn., 2004, Max Perutz prize, European Crystallographic Assn., 2004. Fellow: Royal Soc. (London). Achievements include authorship of widely used computer programs for crystal structure determination; mineral sheldrickite named in his honor. Office: Lehrstuhl Strukturchemie Tammannstrasse 4 D-37077 Göttingen Germany E-mail: gsheldr@shelx.uni-ac.gwdg.de.

SHELINE, RAYMOND K. nuclear chemistry educator; b. Port Clinton, Ohio, Mar. 31, 1922; s. Raymond Kaiser and Rozena (Huard) S.; m. Yvonne Faith Engwall, June 9, 1951; children: Yvette Ingrid, Raymond Kenneth, Jonathan Lee, Hans Eric, Rebecca Ruth, Martin Engwall, Christian Thomas. BS summa cum laude, Bethany Coll., 1943; PhD, U. Calif. at Berkeley, 1949. Research asst. Manhattan Project War Research, Columbia, 1943-45; jr. sci. U. Calif. at Los Alamos Lab., 1945-46, cons., 1961; instr. Inst. Nuclear Studies and chemistry dept. U. Chgo., 1949-51; assoc. prof. chemistry Fla. State U., 1951-55, prof., 1955-58, prof. chemistry and physics, 1958-99, Robert O. Lawton disting. prof. chemistry and physics, 1966-99, chmn. nuclear sci. program, 1959-70; research prof. Niels Bohr Inst., Copenhagen, 1964, Nordita prof., 1972. Fulbright lectr., Denmark, Holland, Germany, Norway, Sweden, 1955-58; Egyptian nat. lectr. Ein Shams U., Cairo, Egypt, 1956; cons. chem. div. Oak Ridge Nat. Lab., 1959-64; Nordita prof. U. Lund, Sweden; mem. Woodrow Wilson Fellowship Com., 1958-61; mem. com. on postdoctoral fellowships in chemistry Nat. Acad. Scis., 1958-63; mem. Gov.'s Com. on Quality Edn., 1961-63; cons. phys. facilities program NSF, 1963-66; cons. Los Alamos Sci. Lab., 1961-95; co-chmn. Gordon Research Conf. on Nuclear Chemistry, 1967; cons. Lawrence Livermore Lab., 1975-97; Chmn. rev. com. Nuclear Chemistry div. Lawrence Livermore Lab., 1979-80; mem. sci. and adv. com. on adminstrn. of Lawrence Livermore Nat. Lab. and Los Alamos Nat. Sci. Lab. U. Calif., 1981-89; lectr. Nuclear Physics Summer Sch., Mikolaki, Poland, 1974; Gillon lectr. Nat. U. Zaire, Kinshasa, 1976; vis. research prof. Inst. für Kernphysik, Kernforschungsanlage, Julich, Fed. Republic Germany, 1976; vis. fellow nuclear physics Australian Nat. U., 1982-83; appointee Ford Found. research project Internat. Coop. Atomic Energy, 1957-58 Contbr. articles numerous sci. jours., profl. publs. Served with AUS, 1943-46. Fulbright fellow Copenhagen, 1955-56, 57-58; Guggenheim fellow, 1955-56, 57-58, 64-65; recipient Niels Bohr award for coop. in devel. nuclear chemistry lab. Inst. Theoretical Physics, Copenhagen, 1958; alumni outstanding achievement award Bethany Coll., 1965; Nat. fellow, 1966; Distinguished Prof. of Year Fla. State U., 1966; Alexander von Humboldt Sr. Scientist award, 1976; Fulbright prof. U. Kinshasa, 1984. Fellow Am. Phys. Soc.; mem. Am. Chem. Soc. (Fla. award 1980, Nuc. award 1998), Danish Royal Acad. Scis. (fgn. 1974), Sigma Xi. Home: 3913 Lucina Ct Fort Myers FL 33908-1609

SHELL, KARL, economist; b. Paterson, N.J., May 10, 1938; s. Joseph J. and Grace (De Young) S.; m. Susan Witherow Schulze, Jan. 27, 1962; children: Stephanie Shell Read, Jason. AB in Math. with honors, Princeton U., 1960; PhD in Econs., Stanford U., 1965; MA (hon.), U. Pa., 1971. Asst. and assoc. prof. econ. MIT, Cambridge, 1964-68; assoc. prof. U. Pa., Phila., 1968-70, prof., 1970-87; prof. econs. Cornell U., Ithaca, NY, 1986—. Vis. prof. Stanford U., Calif., 1972-73, Autonomous U. Barcelona, 1989, Bocconi Inst. Mgmt., Milan, Italy, 1990, U. Calif., San Diego, 1992, Doshisha U., Kyoto, Japan, 1995, NYU, 2000; adj. prof. U. Paris, 1979-81, 91; rschr. CEPREMAP, Paris, 1977-78; dir. Ctr. for Analytic Rsch. in Econs. and the Social Scis., Phila., 1975-86; Ctr. for Analytic Econs., Ithaca, 1986-92. Co-author: Economic Theory of Price Indices, 1972, Economic Analysis of Production Price Indexes, 1998; editor: Optimal Economic Growth, 1967, Jour. Econ. Theory, 1968—; co-editor: Investment and Finance, 1972, Hamiltonians, 1976, Economic Complexity, 1989. Woodrow Wilson Found. fellow, 1960-61, 63-64; Ford Found. faculty rsch. fellow, 1967-68; Guggenheim fellow, 1977, Ctr. for Advanced Study in Behavioral Sci. fellow, 1984; Fulbright scholar, Barcelona, Spain, 1989, fellow Churchill Coll., Cambridge, England, 1996. Fellow Econometric Soc.; mem. Am. Econ. Assn., Econ. Study Soc., Soc. for Promotion of Econ. Theory, Princeton Club (N.Y.C.), Sigma Xi. Republican. Episcopalian. Home: 3409 Beacon St Pompano Beach FL 33062-2922 Office: Cornell U Dept Econs 402 Uris Hall Ithaca NY 14853-7601 Office Phone: 607-255-5277.

SHELL, LOUIS CALVIN, lawyer; b. Dinwiddie County, Va., Dec. 8, 1925; s. Roger LaFayette and Susie Ann (Hill) S.; m. Barbara Marie Pamplin, Aug. 5, 1950; children: Pamela Shell Baskervill, Patricia Shell Caulkins. BA, U. Va., 1946, LLB, 1947. Bar: Va. 1947. Sr. trial atty. Shell, Johnson, Andrews Baskervill & Petersburg. Va. chmn. Petersburg Electoral Bd., 1952, vice mayor city coun., 1957-60; trustee Petersburg Dist. United Meth. Ch. Named Outstanding Young Man, Petersburg Jr. C. of C., 1956. Fellow Am. Coll. Trial Lawyers; mem. Petersburg Bar Assn., Va. State Bar Assn. (coun. 1972-75), Kiwanis. Home: 10813 Lakeview Dr Petersburg VA 23805-7152 Office: Shell Johnson Andrews & Baskervill PO Box 3090 Petersburg VA 23805-3090

SHELL, OWEN G., JR., retired bank executive; b. Greenville, S.C., June 19, 1936; s. Owen and Katherine S.; m. Mary Ruth Trammell, Aug. 9, 1980; children: Katherine Sloan, Mary Carroll, Robert Owen, James Walker. BS, U. S.C., 1960; postgrad., Stonier Grad. Sch. Banking, 1971; grad., Advanced Mgmt. Program, Harvard U., 1979. Tech. supt. Deering-Milliken, Inc., 1962-63; v.p. Citizens & So. Nat. Bank S.C., Columbia, 1968-71, sr. v.p., 1971-74, exec. v.p., 1974-79; pres., dir., chief exec. officer First Am. Nat. Bank, Nashville, 1979-86; vice chmn. bd., dir. First Am. Corp., 1979-86; chmn., pres., chief exec. officer Sovran Bank/Tenn., Nashville, 1986-91; pres. Nations Bank of Tenn. (formerly Sovran Bank), Nashville, 1992-96; pres. asset mgmt. group NationsBank Corp., St. Louis, 1997-99; pres. Asset Mgmt. Bank of Am., St. Louis, 1997—2002; ret., 2002. Bd. dirs. Nashville br. Fed. Res. Bank, Atlanta; corp. dir. Lifepoint Hosp. Inc., Ctrl. Parkins, inc. Chmn. Leadership Nashville, Tenn. Performing Arts Found., Mid. Tenn. coun. Boy Scouts Am., Vanderbilt U. Owen Grad. Sch. Mgmt.; trustee Met. Nashville Pub. Edn. Found.; chmn. bd. INROADS/Nashville; bd. dirs. Tenn. Bus. Roundtable, Tenn. Tomorrow. Mem.: Assn. Res. City Bankers, Old Warson Country Club (St. Louis), Harvard Club N.Y.C., Belle Meade Country Club (Nashville), Kappa Alpha. Presbyterian. Home: 4412 Chickering Ln Nashville TN 37215-4915 also: 114 Tern Dr Anna Maria FL 34216

SHELL, ROBERT J. construction executive; b. Honolulu, Oct. 16, 1930; s. Roscoe and Gladys Rose (Callahan) S.; m. Virginia Louise Brooks, Apr. 7, 1973; children: Linda Shell Squires, Vickie Doss, Scott, Cathy, Allison Nelson. Grad. high sch., Little Rock, 1947. Project mgmt. acct. The Baldwin Co., Little Rock, 1950-61, sec., treas., 1961-76, exec. v.p., 1976-83, pres., 1983—, also bd. dirs.; pres. Baldwin & Shell Constrn., Little Rock, 1980 . Treas., bd. dirs. River City Investment Co. Chmn. Little Rock Censor Bd., 1969, Little Rock Bd. Adjustment, 1979; pres. Pulaski Acad., Little Rock, 1984-85, Ark. Arthritis Assn., 1991—; treas. Metro YMCA; bd. dirs., pres. Bapt. Med. System Found.; pres. 50 For The Future, 2000; charter mem. Ark. Constrn. Hall of Fame, 20000; chmn. found. bd. U. Ark., Little Rock, 2004; bd. mem. Twin City Bank. Mem. Am. Arbitration Assn., Am. Inst. Constructors, Associated Gen. Contractors Am. (nat. bd. dirs. 1982—, Disting. Svc. award 1984, Ark. Bus. Exec. of the Yr. 1991, vice chmn.), Ark. C. of C. (bd. dirs. 1986). Clubs: Pleasant Valley Country (Little Rock) (sec. 1985-86). Baptist. Home: 4 Bretagne Cir Little Rock AR 72223-9136 Office: Baldwin & Shell Constrn 523 Ringo PO Box 1750 Little Rock AR 72203-1750

SHELLEDY, JAMES EDWIN, III, newspaper editor; b. Spencer, Iowa, Nov. 11, 1942; s. James E. Jr. and Patricia L. (Cornwall) S.; m. Susan Emily Thomas, Mar. 7, 1986; 1 child, Ian Whittaker. BA, Gonzaga U., 1966. Reporter Spkesman-Rev., Spokane, Wash., 1963-66; tchr., coach Kootenai High Sch., Harrison, Idaho, 1967-71; reporter AP, Boise, Idaho, 1971-72; reporter, editor Lewiston (Idaho) Morning Tribune, 1973-80; editor, pub. Moscow, Idaho, 1981-91; editor The Salt Lake Tribune, Salt Lake City, 1991—; editor, pub. Daily News, Pullman, Wash., 1981—91. Juror Pulitzer Prize Com., Columbia U., 1987-88; dir. Investigative Reporters and Editors, 1978-82; bd. dirs. New Directions for News, 1989-96, Newspaper Agy. Corp., 1994-99; mem. AP audit com., N.Y.C., 1982-91. Dir. Idaho Parks Found., Boise, 1976-78, Idaho-Washington Symphony, Pullman, Wash., 1986-89; commr. Idaho Lottery Commn., Boise, 1989-91; adv. bd. Utah YWCA, 1992-97; bd. visitors La. State U. Sch. Comms., 1995—, mem. Utah Alliance for Unity, 2001--, adv. bd, comm. dept. Utah State U., 2002--. Roman Catholic. Avocations: golf, sailing. Office: The Salt Lake Tribune 143 S Main St Ste 400 Salt Lake City UT 84111-1945

SHELLER, G. A. artist, educator; d. Fred Russell Johnson and Gertrude Josephine Burke-Johnson; m. Francis Xavier Sheller, July 2, 1960; children: Patrick, Francis, Nancy. BA, Coll. New Rochelle, 1958; postgrad., Pa. State U., 1959, Yale U., 1983. Cert. tchr. Pa., N.Y. Art supr. Logan Area Sch. Sys., Altoona, Pa., 1958—61; art instr. Meml. Art Gallery, U. Rochester, 1983—. Guest lectr. U. Rochester, 1999, U. Galway, Ireland; artist-in-residence Irondequtt Schs., Rochester, 2002; instr. various painting workshops; art cons., juror in field. Represented in permanent collections Meml. Art Gallery, U. Rochester. Finalist Artisans award, N.Y. State, 1985; recipient Painting Exhbn. award, Eagles Mere Art, 1997. Mem.: Atlanta Artists Ctr. (Juried Mem. of Merit award), Pittsford Art Group (bd. dirs. 1981—, libr. liason 1982—, Merit award 1993), Rochester Art Club (bd. dirs. 1978—2003, program dir. 2003—04, Jurors award 1996), Selection for Arts. Avocations: golf, tennis, paddle tennis, photography. Home: 106 Overbrook Rd Rochester NY 14618 Office Phone: 585-381-0758.

SHELLEY, CAROLE, actress; b. London, Aug. 16, 1939; arrived in U.S., 1964; d. Curtis and Deborah (Bloomstein) Shelley; m. Albert G. Woods, July 26, 1967 (dec.). Student, Arts Ednl. Sch., 1943-56, Prepatory Acad. Royal Acad. Dramatic Art, 1956-57; studied with Iris Warren and Eileen Thorndike. Trustee Am. Shakespeare Theatre, 1974—82. Actor: (plays) The Odd Couple, 1965, Absurd Person Singular, 1973, The Norman Conquests (L.A. Drama Critics Cir. award, 1975), As You Like It, King Lear, She Stoops to Conquer, 1972, The Country Wife, 1973, A Doll's House, Man and Superman, 1977, Misalliance, 1980, Grand Hunt, 1980, The Play's the Thing, 1978, Lion in Winter, 1987, The Elephant Man (Outer Critics Cir. award, 1979, Tony award for Best Actress, 1979), What the Butler Saw, 1989, Broadway Bound, 1987—88, Lettice and Lovage, 1989—90, The Miser, 1990, Cabaret Verboten, 1991, The Destiny of Me, 1992—93, Later Life, 1993 (Outer Critics nominee), Richard II, 1994, London Suite, 1995, Show Boat, 1995—96, 1998, The Film Society, 1997, The Last Night of Ballyhoo, 1997—98, Cabaret, 1999—2002, Wicked, 2002—04; (films) The Boston Strangler, The Odd Couple, The Super, 1990, Devlin, 1991, Quiz Show, 1993, The Road to Wellville, 1993, others; (TV series) The Odd Couple, Robin Phillips Grand Theatre Co., 1983—84, Nat. Co. The Royal Family (L.A. Drama Critics Cir. award, 1977); (Broadway plays) Noises Off, 1985, Stepping Out, 1986 (Tony nominee, 1986), Waltz of the Toreadors, 1986, Oh Coward, 1986—87, Broadway Bound, 1987—88; voice actor: (films) Robin Hood; The Aristocats; Hercules. Recipient Obie award for Twelve Dreams, N.Y. Shakespeare Festival, 1982. Jewish. Office: Robert Duva 277 W 10th St New York NY 10014

SHELLEY, CLYDE BURTON, artist; b. Murphy, Tex., Mar. 21, 1922; s. Jesse Dewey and Florrie Elizabeth (Eldridge) S.; m. Freddie Lavern Mitchell, Aug. 31, 1946 (dec. Aug. 1978); m. Grace Rosamond Muder, Dec. 24, 1979. Student, Ohio Weslayan U., 1944-45, Art Ctr. Sch., L.A., 1957-58. Artist Interstate Theatres, Inc., Dallas, 1941-42, Oakite Products, N.Y.C., 1946-47; cartoonist Reddy Kilowatt, Inc., N.Y.C., 1947-50; freelance cartoonist, comml. artist N.Y.C., 1950-52, Dallas, 1952-55, L.A., 1955-56, Las Vegas, 1970-75; comml. artist Northrop Corp., Hawthorne, Calif., 1956-59; indsl. illustrator Douglas Aircraft Corp., Long Beac, El Segondo, Calif., 1959-62; comml. artist Nortronics, Palos Verdes, Calif., 1962-64; sr. illustrator Holmes & Narver, Inc., Honolulu, 1964-70, Las Vegas, 1964-70; sr. artist Houston Post Newspaper, 1975-87. One man shows at First City Nat. Bank, 1985, 87; exhibited in group shows at Clampitt Paper Co., Houston, 1985, Sportsman's Gallery, Galleria, Houston, 1986, Marriott Hotel, Houston, 1990, Lone Star Restaurant, Houston, 1991-92, CMR Gallery, Corpus Christi, Tex., 1994, 96; contbr. cartoons Am. Mag., Bluebook Mag., King Features Syndicate, AT&T, Las Vegas Sun, Las Vegas Rev./Jour., others; caricaturist Mem. Houston World Affairs Coun., 1996—. With U.S. Navy, 1942-46. Mem. Houston Mus. Fine Arts, Braeburn Valley West Civic Club, Am. Legion. Avocations: running, physical fitness, reading, politics, world affairs. Home and Office: 9443 Portal Dr Houston TX 77031-2212

SHELLEY, HERBERT CARL, lawyer; b. Stamford, Tex., Jan. 28, 1947; s. Carl B. and Lourena A. (Whitley) S.; m. Jerilyn S. Ray, Aug. 9, 1969; children: Megan, Caitlyn, Daniel. BA, Columbia Coll., 1969; JD, Vanderbilt U., 1972; LLM in Internat. and Comparative Law magna cum laude, Vrije U. Brussels, 1973. Bar: D.C. 1973, Md. 1985, U.S. Ct. Appeals (fed. cir.) 1981, U.S. Ct. Internat. Trade 1982, U.S. Supreme Ct. 1987. Atty./adv. U.S. Tariff Commn., Washington, 1973-74; Internat. trade specialist, asst. Office dir. Office Tariff Affairs U.S. Dept. Treasury, Washington, 1974-76; internat. trade negotiator Office Spl. Trade Reps., Geneva, Switzerland, 1976-79; ptnr. Plaia & Schaumberg, Washington, 1979-86, Howrey & Simon, Washington, 1986-99, Steptoe & Johnson LLP, Washington, 1999—. Mem. ABA, D.C. Bar Assn., Md. Bar Assn. Avocations: skiing, golf, cooking, travel. Office: 1330 Connecticut Ave NW Washington DC 20036-1704 Office Phone: 202-429-8146. E-mail: hshelley@steptoe.com.

SHELLEY, KEVIN, state official; b. Nov. 1955; s. Jack and Thelma Shelley; m. Dominique Shelley; 1 child, Jack. BA in Polit. Sci., U. Calif., Davis; JD, Hastings Coll. Law. With U.S. Congressman Phil Burton; mem. bd. suprs., pres. bd. San Francisco Bd. Suprs., 1990; mem., majority leader Calif. State Assembly, 1996—2002; sec. state State of Calif., 2003—. Mem.: Calif. State Bar. Office: 1500 11th St Sacramento CA 95814

SHELLEY, LORE, writer, small business owner, realtor; b. Lubbecke, Nordrhein Westfalen, Germany, Feb. 19, 1924; d. Siegfied and Meta Weinberg; m. Sucher Szaldajewski, Aug. 19, 1951; 1 child, Gabriela. Student, U. Bonn, 1955; Certificat Propedeutique, U. Geneva, 1956; MA in Exptl. Psychology, New Sch. Social Rsch., 1958; MSW, San Francisco State U., 1978; PhD in Philos., The Fielding Inst., 1984. Author: Secretaries of Death, Criminal Experiments on Human Beings in Auschwitz and War Research Laboratories, Auschwitz - the Nazi Civilization, The Union Kommando in Auschwitz, Post Auschwitz Fragments, The Fatherland's Gratitude is Guaranteed. Vol. tutor adults and children The Jewish Agy., Jerusalem, 1974—75, Maalot, 1974—75; mem. San Francisco Commn. Aging, 1977—83; vol., active mem. Bay Area Coun. on Soviet Jewry, 1971—80; co-founder The Shelley Charitable Trust Hasidim Gur, Jerusalem, 1976—2004; cofounder, bd. mem. Tikva (a support orgn. for aging Holocaust survivors), San Francisco, 1997—2002. Democrat. Jewish. Avocations: travel, yoga, bicycling, dog training.

SHELLEY, WALTER BROWN, physician, educator; b. St. Paul, Feb. 6, 1917; s. Patrick K. and Alfaretta (Brown) S.; m. Marguerite H. Weber, 1942 (dec.); children: Peter B., Anne E. Kiselewich, Barbara A. (dec.); m. E. Dorinda Loeffel, 1980; children: Thomas R., Katharine D., William L. BS, U. Minn., 1940, PhD, 1941, MD, 1943; MA honoris causa, U. Pa., 1971; MD honoris causa, U. Uppsala, Sweden, 1977. Diplomate: Am. Bd. Dermatology (pres. 1968-69, dir. 1960-69). Instr. physiology U. Pa., Phila., 1946-47, asst. instr. dermatology and syphilology, 1947-49, asst. prof. dermatology, 1950-53, assoc. prof., 1953-57, prof., 1957-80, chmn. dept., 1965-80; prof. dermatology U. Ill. Peoria Sch. Medicine, 1980-83; prof. medicine (dermatology) Med. Coll. Ohio, 1983-97, emeritus prof. medicine, 1997—. Instr. dermatology Dartmouth Coll., 1949-50; Regional cons. dermatology VA, 1955-59; mem. com. on cutaneous system NRC, 1955-59, Commn. Cutaneous Diseases, Armed Forces Epidemiological Bd., 1958-61, dep. dir., 1959-61; cons. dermatology Surgeon Gen. USAF, 1958-61, U.S. Army, 1958-61; mem. NRC, 1961-64 Author (with Crissey): Classics in Clinical Dermatology, 1953, 2003; author: (with Pillsbury, Kligman) Dermatology, 1956; author: Cutaneous Medicine, 1961; author: (with Hurley) The Human Apocrine Sweat Gland in Health and Disease, 1960; author: (with Botelho and Brooks) The Endocrine Glands, 1969; author: Consultations in Dermatology with Walter B. Shelley, 1972, Consultations II, 1974; author: (with Shelley) Advanced Dermatologic Therapy, 1987; author: Advanced Dermatologic Diagnosis, 1992, A Century of International Dermatological Congresses, 1992, Advanced Dermatologic Therapy II, 2001, Shelley's 77 Skins, 2001; mem. editl. bd. Jour. Investigative Dermatology, 1961—64, Archives of Dermatology, 1961—62, Skin and Allergy News, 1970—93, Excerpta Medica Dermatologica, 1960—, Cutis, 1972—, Jour. Geriatric Dermatol, 1993; assoc. editor: Jour. Cutaneous Pathology, 1972—81; editl. cons. Medcom, 1972—. Served as capt. M.C. AUS, 1944-46. Recipient Spl. award Soc. Cosmetic Chemists, 1955, Hellerstrom medal, 1971, Am. Med. Writers Assn. Best Med. Book award, 1973, Dohi medal, 1981, Rothman medal Soc. for Investigative Dermatology, 1987, Rose Hirschler award, 1990. Master ACP; fellow Assn. Am. Physicians, St. John's Dermatol. Soc. London (hon.); mem. AMA (chmn. residency rev. com. for dermatology 1963-67, chmn. sect. dermatology 1969-71), Assn. Profs. Dermatology (pres. 1972-73), Pacific Dermatol. Assn. (hon.), Am. Dermatol. Assn. (hon., dir., pres. 1975-76), Soc. Investigative Dermatology (hon. pres. 1961-62), Am. Physiol. Soc., Phila. Physiol. Soc., Brit. Dermatol. Soc. (hon.), Phila. Dermatol. Soc. (pres. 1960-61), Mich. Dermatol. Soc., Ohio Dermatol. Soc. (hon.), Am. Acad. Dermatology (Gold medal 1992, hon. pres. 1971-72), Pa. Acad. Dermatology (pres. 1972-73), Am. Soc. Dermatologic Surgery, N.Am. Clin. Dermatol. Soc. (hon.), Noah Worcester Dermatol. Soc., Royal Soc. Medicine; corr. mem. Nederlandse Vereniging Van Dermatologen, Israeli Dermatol. Assn., Finnish Soc. Dermatology, Swedish Dermatol. Soc., French Dermatologic Soc.; fgn. hon. mem. Danish Dermatol. Assn., Japanese Dermatol. Assn., Dermatol. Soc. S.Africa, Austrian Dermatol. Soc. Home: 21171 W River Rd Grand Rapids OH 43522-9703 Office: Med Coll Ohio 3120 Glendale Ave Toledo OH 43614-2595 Office Phone: 419-383-3720. Business E-Mail: ancampbell@mco.edu.

SHELLHORN, RUTH PATRICIA, landscape architect; b. L.A., Sept. 21, 1909; d. Arthur Lemon and Lodema (Gould) S.; m. Harry Alexander Kueser, Nov. 21, 1940. Student dept. landscape architecture, Oreg. State Coll., 1927—30; landscape architecture program, Cornell U. Coll. Architecture, 1930—33. Pvt. practice landscape architecture, various cities, Calif., 1933—; exec. cons. landscape arch. Bullocks Stores, Calif., 1945-78, Fashion Sqs. Shopping Ctrs., Calif., 1958-78, Marlborough Sch., L.A., 1968-93, El Camino Coll., Torrance, Calif., 1970-78, Harvard Sch., North Hollywood, Calif., 1974-90. Cons. landscape arch., site planner Disneyland, Anaheim, Calif., 1955, U. Calif., Riverside Campus, 1956-64, numerous others, also numerous gardens and estates; landscape arch. Torrance (Calif.) City Goals Com., 1969-70; cons. landscape arch. City of Rolling Hills (Calif.) Cmty. Assn., 1973-93. Contbr. articles to garden and profl. publs.; subject of Oct. 1967 issue Landscape Design & Constrn. mag. Named Woman of Year, L.A. Times, 1955, Woman of Year, South Pasadena-San Marino (Calif.) Bus. Profl. Women, 1955; recipient Charles Goodwin Sands medal, 1930-33, Landscape Architecture award of merit Calif. State Garden Clubs, 1984, 86, Horticulturist of the Yr. award So. Calif. Hort. Inst., numerous nat., state, local awards for excellence. Fellow Am. Soc. Landscape Archs. (past pres. So. Calif. chpt.), Phi Kappa Phi, Kappa Kappa Gamma (Alumni Achievement award 1960). Achievements include oral history and biography published by Pasadena Heritage, 2002. Home and Office: 362 Camino De Las Colinas Redondo Beach CA 90277-6435 *Integrity, honesty, dependability, sincerity, dedication, and a willingness to give more than is expected in service, are the basic principles which have guided my career. Never losing sight of the importance of the individual, I have tried to create total environments of harmony and beauty to which each individual can relate in a very personal and pleasureable way, and for a little while, can find a calm oasis in a busy and demanding world.*

SHELLMAN-LUCAS, ELIZABETH C. special education educator, researcher; b. Thomas County, Ga., Feb. 5, 1937; d. Herbert and Juanita (Coleman) Smith; m. John Lee Lucas, Jr. (div.); 1 child, Sandie Juanita Lucas Boyce; m. Eddie Joseph Shellman; 1 child, Eddie Joseph Shellman, Jr. MS in Edn., CUNY, 1990. Cert. tchr., N.Y. Pvt. practice cosmetologist, N.Y.C., 1959—; tchr. N.Y.C. Bd. of Edn. High Sch. Dist., 1984—. Vol. various community orgns.; citizen amb. del. People to People Internat., 1994. Mem. Coun. for Exceptional Children. Avocations: reading, music, dance, jogging, languages.

SHELLOW, ROBERT, management service company executive, consultant; b. Milw., Sept. 22, 1929; s. Henry G. and Sadie (Myers) S.; m. Dorothea Laadt, Aug. 30, 1963; children: Sarah Katherine, Leslie Suzzane. BA, Reed Coll., 1951; MA, U. Mich., 1952, PhD, 1956. Commd. USPHS, Bethesda, Md., 1955; advanced through grades to commdr. Psychol. U.S. Bureau Prisons, 1955-58; asst. dep. dir. Nat. Adv. Commn. on Civil Disorders, 1967-68; dir. pilot programs D.C. Dept. Pub. Safety, 1968-70; prof. Carnegie-Mellon U., Pitts., 1970-76; pres. IMAR Corp., Washington, 1978—. Cons. in field; expert witness psychol. deterence, security negligence cases, state and fed. cts., 1978—; mng. dir., PSC-I, LLC. Author: Issues in Law Enforcement, 1976; contbr. numerous articles to profl. jours. USPHS fellow U. Mich., 1953. Fellow Am. Psychol. Assn.; mem. Nat. Bus. Aircraft Assn., Internat. Assn. Profl. Security Cons. (v.p. 1987-89, pres. 1989-91), Sigma Xi. Avocations: sailing, automobile and boat restoration. Office: IMAR Corp PO Box 34528 Bethesda MD 20827-0528 Office Phone: 301-530-8000. Personal E-mail: imarcorp@mindspring.com. E-mail: robshellow@mindspring.com.

SHELLY, ANN CONVERSE, education educator, administrator; b. Lansing, Mich., July 5, 1943; d. Marshall Hough and Adelaide Louise (Crowell) Converse; m. Robert Keith Shelly, Sept. 12, 1964; children: Marshall Keith, Elizabeth Louise. BA, Mich. State U., 1965, MA, 1970, PhD, 1973. Asst. prof. SUNY, Geneseo, 1974-77; coord. tchr. prep. W.Va. State Dept. Edn., Charleston, 1977—78; prof., dir. tchr. prep. Bethany (W.Va.) Coll., 1978—90; prof. chair curriculum and instrn. U. Ala., Birmingham, 1990—94; prof., dean Coll. Edn. Ga. So. U., Statesboro, 1994—96; chair, tchr. edn. Ashland (Ohio) U., 1996—2000; prof. Ashland (Ohio) U., Ohio, 1996—, assoc. dean, 2003—. Cons. in field. Contbg. author: Mainstreaming Preparation, 1989; contbr. articles to profl. jours. Sec., bd. dirs. Interfaith Hospitality House, Birmingham, 1991—; bd. dirs. A.G. Gaston Boys and Girls Club, Birmingham, 1992—. NSF grantee, 1992. Mem. ASCD (bd. dirs. 1987-91), Am. Assn. Colls. of Tchr. Edn. (inst. rep., bd. dirs. 1987-90), Assn. Tchr. Educators, Kappa Delta Epsilon, Kappa Delta Pi, Phi Delta Kappa, Phi Kappa Phi. Democrat. Episcopalian. Avocations: sewing, quilting. Office: Ashland U Coll Edn 319 Bixler Ashland OH 44805 Office Phone: 419-289-5388. Business E-Mail: ahshelly@ashland.edu.

SHELLY, CHRISTINE DEBORAH, foreign service officer; b. Pontiac, Mich., May 1, 1951; d. Chester Price and Margaret Alice (Neafie) S. BA cum laude, Vanderbilt U., 1973; MA, Tufts U., 1974, MA in Diplomacy, 1975. Fgn. affairs analyst Intelligence and Rsch. Bur. Dept. State, Washington, 1975-77, desk officer Near Eastern Affairs, 1977-79; fin. attaché Am. Embassy, Cairo, 1979-81; asst. v.p. BankAmerica Internat., N.Y.C., 1981-82; spl. asst. Near Eastern Affairs Dept. State, Washington, 1982-83; econ. and polit. officer Am. Embassy, Lisbon, Portugal, 1983-87; dep. econ. advisor U.S. Mission to NATO, Brussels, 1987-90, dep. cabinet dir. Sec. Gen., 1990-93; dep. spokesman, dep. asst. sec. pub. affairs Dept. State, Washington, 1993-95, mem. Sr. Exec. Seminar, 1995-96; min. counselor polit. affairs Am. Embassy, Ottawa, Ont., Can., 1996-99; polit. adviser to chief of staff Dept. Army, Washington, 1999—. Avocations: equestrian, triathlete. Office: Dept Army DACS-ZK 200 Army Pentagon Rm 3c568 Washington DC 20310-0200

SHELLY, THADDEUS RUBEZ, III, trust company executive; b. Memphis, Aug. 29, 1953; s. Thaddeus R. and Beverly Claire Agnew S.; m. Helen Totty Edwards, June 26, 1982; children: Charles Edwards, James Thaddeus, Robert Willis, Beverly Lee. BA in Econs., Hampden-Sydney Coll., 1975; MBA, Coll. William & Mary, 1984. Tchr. Amezia (Va.) Acad., 1975-77; coach Hampden-Sidney (Va.) Coll., 1977-78; coach, athletic dir. Carlyle Sch., Martinsville, Va., 1978-80; tchr., coach Norfolk (Va.) Acad., 1980-82; v.p. Goldman, Sachs & Co., Phila., 1984-92; v.p., dir. pvt. client svcs. Legg Mason, Inc., Balt., 1992-98; mng. dir., resident mgr. Bessemer Trust Co., Washington, 1998—. Youth league coach Severna Park (Mass.) Green Hornets, 1995—; past vice chmn. Md. chpt. U.S. Olympic Com., Balt., 1994-96. Recipient Alumni Svc. award, Coll. William & Mary, 1994. Republican. Presbyterian. Avocations: youth sports, boating, skiing. Office: Bessemer Trust Co 1050 Connecticut Ave NW Washington DC 20036

SHELOV, STEVEN PATRICK, pediatrician, educator; b. Honolulu, Nov. 19, 1944; s. Sidney M. and Faith R. S.; m. Marsha Liberman, Aug. 30, 1968; children: Joshua, Danielle, Eric. BS, Yale, 1966; MD, Med. Coll. Wisc., 1971; MS in Med. Admin., U. Wisc., 1995. Diplomate Am. Bd. Pediatrics. Intern, then resident Montefiore Med. Ctr., Bronx, 1971-74, chief resident, 1974-75; asst. dir. amb. pediat. Albert Einstein Coll. Med., Bronx, N.Y., 1977-79; dir. pediat. edn. Montefiore Med. Ctr., Bronx, 1980—, prof. and vice chmn. pediat., 1989-97; chmn. pediat. Infants and Children's Hosp. of Bklyn., Maimonides Med. Ctr., Bklyn., 1997—; prof. Mt. Sinai Sch. Medicine. Editor: Caring for Your Baby and Young Child: Birth to 5, 1991, 1996, 2004, Pediatrics for Medical Students, 2003, Guide to Your Child's Symptoms, 1997, The First Year of Life, 2004. Recipient Geo. Armstrong award Ambulatory Pediat. Assn., 1996, Lifetime Achievement in Edn. award Am. Acad. Pediat., 2002. Office: Maimonides Med Ctr 4802 10th Ave Brooklyn NY 11219-2844 Office Phone: 718-283-6150. Business E-Mail: sshelov@maimonidesmed.org.

SHELP, RONALD KENT, non-profit, business and trade association executive, author, lecturer, consultant; b. Cartersville, Ga., Sept. 29, 1941; s. Clarence Harrison Mulkey and Willie Marion (Puckett) Shelp; m. Anna June Mueller, Feb. 14, 1982. AB cum laude, U. Ga., 1964; MA, Johns Hopkins SAIS, Washington, 1966; postgrad., London Sch. Econs., 1981—. Asst. to U.S. Senator Richard Russell, Washington, 1964—66; exec. sec. Internat. Ins. Adv. Coun., Washington, 1966—73; co-founder, exec. v.p. Art Enterprise Internat., Washington, 1970—72; asst. mgr. internat. divsn. U.S. C. of C., Washington, 1970—73; exec. sec. Assn. Am. C. of C. in Latin Am., Washington, 1969—73; v.p. Am. Internat. Group, N.Y.C., 1973—85; v.p., mem. pres.' operating com. Celanese Corp., N.Y.C., 1985—87; v.p. Hoechst Celanese Corp., 1987; pres., CEO N.Y.C. Partnership, 1987—93, N.Y. C. of C. and Industry, 1987—93; exec. com. Burson-Marsteller, N.Y.C., 1994—96, vice-chmn., 1995—96; chmn., CEO Kent Global Strategies, N.Y.C., 1996—; exec. com. Dieferbach, Elkins, NY, 1996—97; chmn., CEO Curatorial Art. Adv. Svc., N.Y.C., 1998—; pres., CEO B2Bstreet.com, 1999—2001; chmn. Anne McBride Co., 2001—02; mng. dir. FPA Search, N.Y.C., 2003—. Bd. dirs. Advantage Internat., Inc., MIMS Corp.; cons. OECD, Paris, 1982, mem. U.S. Del., 1978-85; chmn. U.S. Govt.-Svcs. Ind. Adv. Com., Washington, 1980-85; adj. prof. internat. bus. and econs. NYU, 1982-84. Co-author: Reference Manual on Doing Business in Latin America, 1979, A New International Commodity Regime, 1979, Service Industries and Economic Development, 1984, Industrial Policy: Business and Politics in The United States and France, 1985, The U.S. Trade Deficit: Impact and Implications, 1985, Revitalizing the U.S. Economy, 1986, Services in Transition: The Impact of Information Technology on the Service Sector, 1986, The Insurance Industry in Economic Development, 1986, Entrepreneurship: The Key to Economic Growth, 1986, Managing Services: Marketing Operations and Human Resources, 1988; author: Beyond Industrialization, 1981, (3d edit. in Japanese); contbr. articles to Foreign Policy, Wall Street Jour., N.Y. Times, L.A. Times, Boston Globe, Forbes, Christian Science Monitor, Jour. Social Econ. Studies, Across the Board, Financier, Georgetown Law Jour., Policy Options, contbr. and coord. artwork (book) Wrestling With History, 1996; cons.: book Testimony: Vernacular Art of the African-American South, 2001. Dir. Pan Am. Devel. Found., Washington, 1981-87, Johns Hopkins SAIS, Washington, 1982-89, 90-95, Internat. Peace Acad., N.Y.C., 1983-89; trade and econ. advisor Presdl. Campaign of Sen. Gary Hart, Washington, 1983-84, 86-87; adv. bd. Overseas Devel. Council, Washington, 1983-91, N.Y.C. Coun. on Econ. Edn., 1988-95; bd. dirs. Citizens Budget Commn., N.Y.C., 1985-87, Fund for Modern Ctrs., N.Y.C. Indsl. Tech. Assistance Corp., 1987-89, Mus. American Folk Art, 1987-90, Corp. Fund for Dance, 1987-91, Econ. Devel. Corp., N.Y.C., 1988-93, Manhattan Theatre Club, 1992-2001, N.Y.C. Housing Partnership Devel. Co., vice chmn., 1992-94; chmn. World Environ. Ctr., 1987-88; mem. Mayor's Mgmt. Adv. Task Force, 1990-93, Mayor's Adv. Com. to Productivity, 1990-93, Mayor's Task Force on Telecommunications Network Reliability, 1990-93, N.Y. State Indsl. Cooperation Coun., 1989-93, N.Y. State Job Trng. Partnership Coun., 1989-94, N.Y. State Telecomm. Exchange, 1992-93, Mayor's Coun. of Econ. Advisors, 1992-93; bd. dirs. Exhbns. Internat., N.Y.C., 2002—. With USAR, 1966-72. Crown Zellerbach fellow Johns Hopkins SAIS, 1964, Francis P. Bolton fellow, 1965. Mem. Coun. Fgn. Rels., Econ. Club N.Y., Phi Beta Kappa. Democrat. Avocations: collecting African Am. vernacular art of the South, tennis, skiing, exploration, fly fishing. Home: 5 E 16th St New York NY 10003-3112 Office: FPA Search 5 E 16th St New York NY 10003 E-mail: rkshelp@fpaus.com.

SHELTON, CRAIG, food service executive; b. Rye, N.H., naturalized, U.S., naturalized, France; trained with Joel Rubochon, trained with Ferran Adriá, trained with Paul Haeberlin. Chef Ma Maison, L.A., Rainbow Rm., Le Chantilly, Le Bernardin, Bouley; chef, owner Ryland Inn, Whitehouse, NJ, 1991—. Named Relais Gourmand, Relais & Chateaux, 1999; recipient Best

award Excellence, Wine Spectator's, 1994—, James Bears award, 2000. Mem.: N.J. Restaurant Assn. (bd. dirs.), Internat. Assn. Culinary Profls. Office: Ryland Inn Rt 22 W Whitehouse NJ 08888

SHELTON, DAVID E. retail executive; BS in Math., Berea Coll., Ky.; M, PhD, U. N.C., Greensboro. With Lowe's Cos., Inc., 1970—, various pos., including store mgr., corp. store ops. analyst, v.p. pricing and tng., v.p. store ops., sr. v.p. real estate, engring. and constrn., 1997—. Office: Lowes Cos Inc 1605 Curtis Bridge Rd Wilkesboro NC 28697

SHELTON, DAVID HOWARD, economics professor; b. Winona, Miss., Nov. 30, 1928; s. Tuttle M. and Kate (Moss) S.; m. Margaret Murff, Feb. 4, 1951; children: David Keith, Sarah Katherine, Susan Esther. BA, Millsaps Coll., 1951; MA, Ohio State U., 1952, PhD, 1958. Instr. Ohio State U., 1958; asst. prof. U. Del., 1958-63, assoc. prof., 1963-65; prof. U. N.C., Greensboro, 1965—93, head dept. econs., bus. adminstrn., 1967-70, dean Sch. Bus. and Econs., 1970-83, head dept. econs., 1988-93, prof. emeritus, 1993—. Cons. Joint Coun. on Econ. Edn., 1969-72, N.C. Dept. Pub. Instrn., 1970-73. Trustee N.C. Coun. on Econ. Edn., 1971-96, chmn., 1971-75, pres., 1975-85. Served with USN, 1946-48. M.D. Lincoln fellow, 1956-57; H.L. and Grace Doherty fellow, 1957. Mem. Beta Gamma Sigma, Omicron Delta Kappa, Kappa Sigma. Episcopalian. Home: 3609 Dogwood Dr Greensboro NC 27403-1010 Office: UNC 462 Bryan Bldg Greensboro NC 27412-0001

SHELTON, GAIL, writer; b. Fairborn, Ohio, Sept. 8, 1954; d. Robert Carl Young and Celia Clare Stripling; m. W. Myles Shelton III, Apr. 24, 1976; children: April Shelton Galyardt, W. Rhys, Robert C. BA in Journalism, Baylor U., 1975, MA in History, 1981. Instr., history/govt. Hill Coll., Hillsboro, Tex., 1982—87; mng. editor Whitney (Tex.) Messenger, 1988; editor/writer Cleburne (Tex.) Eagle, 1991; instr. Cedar Valley Coll.-Dallas County C.C., Dallas, 1991; legal asst., chief clk. Hill County Attys. Office, Hillsboro, Tex., 1992—99; columnist Clarendon (Tex.) Enterprise, Tex., 1999—; freelance writer Tex., 1995—. Author: Hide-and-Sheikh, 2001 (Rita finalist, 2002), Her Convenient Millionaire, 2003. Bd. dirs. Whitney City Libr., 1988; dist. chair Bluebonnet Girl Scout Coun., Whitney, 1983—84; pres. Friends of Libr., Clarendon. Mem.: Panhandle Profl. Writers (contest chair 2000—), Romance Writers of Am. Baptist. Avocations: singing, needlecrafts, travel, gardening. E-mail: gail@gaildayton.com.

SHELTON, GREGORY S. electronics executive; b. Calif. m. Trish Shelton. BS, Calif. Poly. U.; MS, UCLA. Former v.p., product line mgr. air missiles and advanced programs and tech. Hughes Missile Systems, Raytheon Co.; v.p. engring. Hughes Weapons Systems, Raytheon Co.; v.p. engring., missiles divsn. Raytheon Co., 1998—2001, v.p. engring. tech., mfg. and quality, 2001—. Bd. dirs. HRL Rsch. Labs. Mem. indsl. adv. coun. U. Ariz.; mem. Joint Ariz. Ctr. for Mfr., Edn. and Tng.; vice chmn. Pres.'s Coun. for Olin Coll. Engring.; mem. engring. adv. bd. U. Ariz., Tuskegee U.; mem. exec. operating com. and engring. in mass collaborative exec. com. MIT. Office: Raytheon Co 141 Spring St Lexington MA 02421

SHELTON, HENRY H. former chairman of joint chiefs; b. Tarboro, N.C., Jan. 2, 1942; m. Carolyn L. Johnson; children: Jon, Jeff, Mark. BS, N.C. State U.; MS, Auburn U.; grad., Air Command and Staff Coll., Nat. War Coll. Commd. 2d lt. U.S. Army, 1963, advanced through grades to gen., 1996; with 5th Spl. Forces Group, Vietnam, 173d Airborn Brigade, Vietnam; comdr. 3d Bn., 60th Infantry, 9th Infantry Divsn., Ft. Lewis, asst. chief of staff for ops.; comdr. 1st Brigade, 82d Airborne Divsn., Ft. Bragg, N.C.; chief of staff 10th Mountain Divsn., Ft. Drum, N.Y.; with ops. directorate Joint Chiefs of Staff, Washington, 1987, asst. divsn. comdr. for ops. 101st Airborne Divsn., 1989-91; comdr. 82d Airborne Divsn., Ft. Bragg, N.C., XVIIIth Airborne Corps., 1993, Chief of U.S. Spl. Ops. Comman, 1996; chmn. Joint Chiefs of Staff, Washington, 1997—2001. Decorated Def. D.S.M. with two oak clusters, D.S.M., Bronze Star with V device with three oak clusters, Purple Heart, Legion of Merit with oak leaf cluster. Fax: 908-771-8618.

SHELTON, JAMES D. (DENNY SHELTON), hospital management company executive; BA in polit. sci. and history, La. State U.; MS in pub. adminstrn., U. Mo. Hosp. adminstr. La., Iowa, NC, Ga., Ill., Mo.; exec. dir. Westbank Hosp. Ops. Nat. Med. Enterprises (now Tenet Healthcare Corp.), New Orleans, 1984—86, v.p. ops., 1986—90, sr. v.p. ops., 1990—93, exec. v.p. ctrl. divsn., 1993—94; pres Ctrl. Group Columbia/HCA, 1994—98, pres. Pacific Group, 1998—99; chmn., CEO Triad Hospitals Inc., 1999—. Chmn. Fedn. of Am. Hospitals, 1999, mem. bd. govs., 1999—2002; bd. dirs. Am. Hosp. Assn. Office: Triad Hospital Inc 5800 Tennyson Pkwy Plano TX 75024-3548*

SHELTON, JAMES DOUGLAS, banker; b. Boynton Beach, Fla., Feb. 28, 1939; s. Clarence Wilton and Lou Anna (Ward) S.; m. Claudia Ellen Marshall, Oct. 20, 1973; children: Christopher John, Ryan Marshall. BA, Duke U., 1961; MDiv, Union Sem., 1965; STM, Boston U., 1966; SEP, Stanford U., 1975. Adj. prof. NY Sem., NYC, 1966-68; asst. treas. Bankers Trust Co., NYC, 1968-71; v.p. Chase Manhattan Bank, NYC, 1971-84; sr. v.p. Conn. Bank & Trust, Hartford, Conn., 1984-88; chmn., pres., chief exec. officer First Fed. Savs., East Hartford, Conn., 1988-2001. Bd. dir. Conn. On-Line Computer Ctr., Avon, chmn., 1989-2001; bd. dir. Community Bank League of New Eng., Boston, chmn., 1989-96; mem. Conn. Legislature Interstate Banking Task Force, Hartford, 1989-90. Bd. dir. Jr. Achievement North Ctrl. Conn., Windsor, 1986-90, Sci. Ctr. Conn., West Hartford, 1988-94, Riverfront Recapture, Inc., Hartford, 1994-98, Charter Oak State Coll. Found., New Britain, Conn., 2004—; corporator Am. Sch. for the Deaf, West Hartford, 1986-2001. Mem. Am. Cmty. Bankers Assn. (bd. dir. 1995-2001), New Eng. Automated Clearing House Assn. (bd. dir. 1983-98), mem. Rotary Internat., 1989-2002; mem., The Country Club of Farmington, 2002-present.

SHELTON, JAMES KEITH, journalism educator; b. Altus, Okla., Oct. 28, 1932; s. Willis Oscar and Theodosia Agnes (Rupert) S.; m. Deborah Kennedy Evans, Dec. 26, 1953; children: Leslie Lynn, Lawrence Evans. BA, Midwestern State U., 1954; MA, U. North Tex., 1972. Reporter Lawton (Okla.) Constn., 1954; wire editor Wichita Falls (Tex.) Record-News, 1956-59; city hall reporter, polit. writer Dallas Times Herald, 1959-65; mng. editor, exec. editor Denton (Tex.) Record-Chronicle, 1965-69, 79-88; faculty mem., dir. pub. info. U. North Tex., Denton, 1969-79, journalist-in-residence, 1988—2002; ret. Author: What Journalists Should Know About Business, 1993. Mem. Supreme Ct. Task Force on Jud. Ethics, Austin, 1992-94. with U.S. Army, 1954-56. Mem. Soc. Profl. Journalists, Freedom on Info. Found. of Tex., Inc. (sec., bd. dirs.). Democrat. Methodist. Home: 621 Grove St Denton TX 76209-7323 E-mail: shelton@unt.edu.

SHELTON, MICHAEL PATRICK, principal; b. Seymour, Ind., July 16, 1972; s. John Michael Shelton and Paula Michelle Kemp, William Newt Kemp (Stepfather); m. Stacy Leigh Conway, Aug. 12, 1995; children: Katelyn Grace children: Brendan Patrick, Kelsey Rae. MusB, Culver-Stockton Coll., 1994—94; MS in Edn., So. Ill. U., Edwardsville, 2002. Dir. of vocal music Staunton (Ill.) Cmty. Unit Sch. Dist., 1994—2002; prin. Wood River (Ill.) -Hartford Elem. Sch. Dist., 2002—. Pres. St. Paul United Ch. of Christ, Staunton, 2001—02. Mem.: ASCD, Nat. Assn. Elem. Sch. Prins., Nat. Assn. Elem. Sch. Prins., Nat. Assn. Elem. Sch. Prins., Ill. Music Educators Assn., Ill. Music Educators Assn., Ill. Principals Assn., Staunton Optimist Club (pres. 2000—02), Delta Upsilon (vice-president 1993—94). Avocations: golf, music, travel. Home: 610 Stone Creek Dr Staunton IL 62088 Office: Hartford Elem Sch 110 W Second St Hartford IL 62088 E-mail: pshelton@madison.k12.il.us.

SHELTON, NICOLINA SYLVESTER, journalist, public relations executive; b. New Rochelle, N.Y., Nov. 29; d. Angelo and Filomena (Loungo) Sylvester. Attended, Columbia U., 1947; degree, Westchester Bus. Sch., 1948; student, Iona Coll., 1999—2002; cert., Monroe Coll., 1998. Dir. women's market Seagram Distillers Co., 1952—61; account exec. Fletcher Richards Calkins and Holden Advt. / Pub. Rels., 1962—64; dep. pub. rels. dir. U.S. Pavilion, Dept. of Commerce, N.Y. World's Fair, 1964—65; account exec. Harry W. Graff Advt. / Pub. Rels., 1967—69; news & info. asst. GAF Corp., N.Y.C., 1971—73; press relations officer Paul Andrews Pub. Rels., 1973—82; asst. pub. rels., mktg. dept. Omni Berkshire Hotel, 1988—91. Mem.: Sports Rites Scuba Club (service award 2000), Caribbean Tourism Assn. (service award 2003). Avocations: swimming, scuba diving, singing, piano. Home: 21 Rhodes St New Rochelle NY 10801

SHELTON, PATRICIA A. gas company executive; BBA, MBA, U. Tex., El Paso. CPA; cert. mgmt. acct. With El Paso Natural Gas El Paso Energy Corp., v.p. rates and regulation, 1994-96, v.p. fin., 1996, pres. El Paso Natural Gas Co., 2000—. Mem. AICPA, Tex. Soc. CPAs, Inst. Mgmt. Accts. Office: El Paso Natural Gas 8645 Railroad Dr El Paso TX 79904-2218

SHELTON, RALPH K. fuel company executive; m. Christine Shelton. Degree in sociology; MBA, Wake Forest U. Dir. corp. warehousing, mgr. svcs. purchasing Burlington Industries; CEO, S.E. Fuels Inc., Greensboro, N.C. Office: SE Fuels Inc PO Box 4061 Greensboro NC 27404-4061

SHELTON, ROBERT NEAL, physics educator, researcher; b. Phoenix, Oct. 5, 1948; s. Clark B. and Grace M. (McLaughlin) S.; m. Adrian Ann Millar, Aug. 30, 1969; children: Christian, Cameron, Stephanie. BS, Stanford U., 1970; MS, U. Calif., San Diego, 1973, PhD, 1975. Postdoctoral researcher U. Calif.-San Diego, La Jolla, 1975-76, asst. rsch. physicist, 1976-78; asst. prof. Iowa State U., Ames, 1978-81, assoc. prof., 1981-84, prof. physics, 1984-87; prof. physics, chmn. dept. U. Calif.-Davis, 1987-90, vice chancellor for rsch., 1990-96, vice provost for rsch., 1996-2001; exec. vice chancellor, provost U. North Carolina, Chapel Hill, 2001—. Contbr. over 200 articles to profl. jours. Fellow Am. Phys. Soc., Calif. Coun. on Sci. and Tech.; mem. AAAS, Materials Rsch. Soc., Sigma Xi, Phi Beta Kappa. Office: U North Carolina 104 South Bldg CB#3000 Chapel Hill NC 27599-3000 E-mail: robert_shelton@unc.edu.

SHELTON, STEPHANI, broadcast journalist, consultant; b. Boston; d. Phil and Babette (Belloff) Saltman; m. Frank Herold. BS, Boston U. Corr. CBS News, N.Y.C., 1973-84; news corr. WWOR-TV, N.Y.C., 1984-88; corr., anchor Fin. News Network, N.Y.C., 1989-91. Freelance reporter Sta. WPIX-TV, 1991-95, Sta. WNBC-TV, 1993-96, WWOR-TV, 2003; prodr. CNBC, 2003-; cons. trainer Ctrl. and Eastern Europe broadcast journalists, 1998—; med. health prodr.-reporter PBS, The Learning Channel, 1997—99; co-owner The Fred Group Ltd., video prodn. co., 1998—; freelance radio documentary writer Westinghouse Group W Broadcasting, N.Y.C., 1970-73. Recipient Peabody award, 1972, N.J. Best Spot News award AP, 1987, 88, N.J. Working Press award, 1992-94; Emmy nominee, 1994-95, 98-99. Mem. Soc. Profl. Journalists (award 1999), Radio and TV News Dirs. Assn., N.Y.C. Press Club, Investigative Reporters and Editors, Com. to Protect Journalists. E-mail: backbay38@aol.com., fred@fredgroupltd.com. *Guiding principles: a questioning mind, a refusal to take no for an answer and the memory of 28 marathons. If you don't ask "why", you are not a journalist.*

SHELTON, VIRGINIA KAYE, director; b. Dallas, June 21, 1963; d. James Milton and Gloria Louise Clark; m. Ricky O'Dale Shelton, Dec. 1, 1983; children: Timothy James, Matthew Tyler, Nathan Chase. B in Arts and Scis., Dallas Bapt. U., 1999; MS in Edn., Calif. State U., Hayward, 2001. Cert. online instr. Dir. online edn. Dallas Bapt. U., 1998—; instrnl. program mgr. distance learning Fla. C.C. at Jacksonville, 2003. Cons. Edn. Pathfinders, Arlington, Tex., 1999—2003. Office: Dallas Bapt U 3000 Mountain Creek Pky Dallas TX 75211 Office Phone: 214-333-5283. E-mail: kaye@dbu.edu.

SHELTRA, NANCY J. state legislator, legal assistant, auditor; b. Newport, Vt., July 30, 1948; m. Dennis Sheltra; two children. Student, C.C. Vt., Newport. Auditor, Derby, Vt.; legal asst.; mem. Vt. Ho. of Reps., Burlington, 1989—. Mem. fish and wildlife com., 1991-92, mem. transp. com., 1993—. Treas. Derby Rep. Party; v.p. New Eng. Regional Vt. Rep. Assembly. Home: 388 Palin Farm Rd Derby VT 05829-9530 Office: Vt House of Reps Office of House Mems Montpelier VT 05602

SHEMCHUK, MARY ELIZABETH, occupational therapist; b. Meriden, Conn., Dec. 17, 1954; d. Paul John and Rose Virginia (Piccolo) S. AS, Middlesex C.C., Middletown, Conn., 1977; BS, Eastern Mich. U., 1983. Registered occupl. therapist Minn., Conn. Staff occupl. therapist Gaylord Rehab. Hosp., Wallingford, Conn., 1985-89, sr. staff occupl. therapist, 1989-95; clin. supr. occupl. therapy Sundance Rehab. Corp., East Berlin, Conn., 1995; lead therapist in occupl. therapy Symphony Rehab. Svcs., Minnetonka, Minn., 1995—. Guest spkr. Bridgeport (Conn.) Arthritis Support Group, 1992; cons. for hearing impaired Gaylord Hosp., Wallingford, 1992-94. Former church organist Our Lady of Mt. Carmel Ch., Meriden, Conn.; guest spkr. Quota Club of Hamden (Conn.), 1986; vol. St. Vincent DePaul Soc. of Meriden Shelter, Inc., 1988. Mem. Am. Occupl. Therapy Assn. (cons. on hearing impaired 1992—), Minn. Occupl. Therapy Assn., Conn. Occupl. Therapy Assn., Self Help for Hard of Hearing, Inc., Minn. Arthritis Found. Avocations: horseback riding, nature walks, playing piano and organ, handicrafts. Home: 42 Antonio Ave # 3 Meriden CT 06451-2806

SHEMIN, BARRY L. insurance company executive; b. Bklyn., Dec. 17, 1942; AB magna cum laude, Brown U., 1963; MA, U. Mich., 1964. With John Hancock Life Ins. Co., Boston, 1968—2003, sr. v.p., corp. actuary; cons actuary. Chmn. bd. dirs. ARC of Mass. Bay; bd. dirs. Harvard Pilgrim Health Care Fellow: Soc. Actuaries (bd. govs.); mem.: Am. Acad. Actuaries, Sigma Xi, Phi Beta Kappa. Office: John Hancock Life Ins Co PO Box 111 Boston MA 02117-0111

SHEMWELL, MARY ANNE, adapted physical education specialist; b. Shreveport, La., Mar. 16, 1942; d. James Dee Jr. and Frances (Oden) Youngblood; children from previous marriage: Dee Wade, Charles James. BS, Centenary Coll., 1965; postgrad., La. Poly. Inst. Phys. edn. tchr. Midway Jr. H.S., Shreveport, 1965-69; adapted phys. edn. specialist Caddo Parish Pub. Schs., 1982—. Phys. edn. tchr. for track and field events for physically handicapped State of La.; v.p., fundraising chmn. Games Uniting Mind and Body. Coach United Cerebral Palsy of La.; mem. Rep. Women's Orgn., 1989—; treas. Rep. Profl. Women's Club, 1993—94. Named G.U.M.B.O. coach of the Yr., State of La., 1994. Mem.: La. Fedn. Tchrs., La. Assn. Health Phys. Edn. and Recreation, Coun. Exceptional Children, Jr. League Shreveport, Plantation Club, Cotillion Club. Republican. Methodist. Avocations: reading, tennis, walking, swimming, coaching handicapped students. Home: 4431 Fern Ave Shreveport LA 71105-3103

SHEN, BA-ZHONG, mathematician, computer scientist; s. Min-De Shen and Jia-Hua Wu; m. Qi Zhang; 1 child, Siyu Shen. MS, Xidian U., Xi'an, China, 1988; PhD, Eindhoven U. Tech., The Netherlands, 1992. Asst. lectr. Xidian U., Xi'an, 1988; adj. asst. prof. and rsch. scientist Lehigh U., Bethlehem, Pa., 1993—96; prin. engr. Quantum Corp., Shrewsbury, Mass., 1996—99; sr. staff scientist Broadcom Corp., Irvine, Calif., 1999—. Mem.: IEEE. Achievements include patents for parallel concatenated code with soft-in soft-out interactive turbo decoder; modified Reed-Solomon error correction system using (W+i+1)-bit representations of symbols of GF(2.sup.w+i); two-level error correction encoder; error correction encoder/decoder; modified Reed-Solomon code selection and encoding system; patents pending for variable code rate and signal constellation turbo trellis coded mudulation code; close two constituent trellis of a turbo encoder within the interleave block; metric calculation design variable code rate decoding of broadband trellis, TCM, or TTCM; turbo coding for upstream and downstream transmission in cable system; low density parity check(LDPC) decoder using min*, min*-, min*, abd/or min*-; the inverse of Min*: Min*-(The inverse of Max&: Max*-); patents for stopping criteria for iterative decoding; patents pending for 8-PSK rotationally invariant turbo trellis coded modulation without parallel transitions; true bit-level decoding of turbo trellis coded modulation; method and apparatus for parallel decoding of turbo encoded data; patents for parallel input output combined system for producing error correction code redundancy symbols and error syndromes; error correction system for five or more errors; combined system for producing error correction code symbols and error syndromes; system for finding roots of degree three and degree four error locator polynomials over GF(2M); galois field multiplier; Five-error correction system; pub. numerous sci. papers on the subjects of algebraic-geometric codes, turbo codesx, decoding error-correcting codes and etc. on the jour: IEEE transaction on Info. Theory. Office: Broadcom Corp 16215 Alton Pky Irvine CA 92619 Office Phone: 949-926-6019. E-mail: bzshen@broadcom.com.

SHEN, BENJAMIN SHIH-PING, scientist, engineer, educator; b. Hangzhou, China, Sept. 14, 1931; s. Nai-cheng and Chen-chiu (Sun) S.; m. Lucia Elisabeth Simpson, 1971; children: William, Juliet. AB, Assumption Coll., Mass., 1954, ScD (hon.), 1972; AM in Physics, Clark U., 1956; DSc d'Etat in Physics, U. Paris, 1964; MA (hon.), U. Pa., 1971. Tchr. Assumption Prep Sch., Mass., 1954-56; asst. prof. physics SUNY, Albany, 1956-59; assoc. prof. space sci., dept. aeros. and astronautics Engring. Sch., NYU, 1964-66; assoc. prof. astronomy and astrophysics U. Pa., Phila., 1966-68, prof., 1968-72, Reese W. Flower prof. astronomy and astrophysics, 1972-96, Reese Flower prof. emeritus, 1996—, chmn. coun. grad. deans, 1979-81, assoc. provost, 1979-80, provost, 1980-81, chmn. dept. astronomy and astrophysics, 1973-79, dir. Flower and Cook Obs., 1973-79, mem. Ctr. for Energy and Environment, 1976-93, chmn. roundtable on sci., industry and policy, 1976-96, prof. Sch. Engring. and Applied Sci., 1980-85. Mem. U.S. Nat. Sci. Bd., 1990-94, chmn. U.S. sci. and engring. indicators, 1990-92, chmn. Task Force on Sci. Literacy, 1992-94; mem. Nat. Coun. on Sci. and Tech. Edn., 1996—; cons. GE, 1961-68, Office Tech. Assessment, U.S. Congress, 1977-78; sci. and tech. adviser U.S. Senate Budget Com., 1976-77; guest staff Brookhaven Nat. Lab., 1963-64, 65-70; chmn. Commn. on Pub. Understanding of Sci., N.Y. Acad. Scis., 1972-75; mem. adv. com. Mt. John Obs., New Zealand, 1978-84. Author: Nuclear Problems in Radiation Shielding in Space, 1963, Passage des Protons dans des Milieux Condenses, 1964; co-editor, co-author: High-Energy Nuclear Reactions in Astrophysics, 1967; Spallation Nuclear Reactions and Their Applications, 1976, Research in the Age of the Steady-state University, 1982; mem. editorial bd. Earth and Extraterrestrial Scis., 1974-78, assoc. editor, 1978-79; assoc. editor: Comments on Astrophysics, 1979-85; contbr. articles to profl. jours. Mem. Hayden Planetarium com. of bd. trustees Am. Mus. Natural History, 1978—; mem. sci. adv. bd. Children's TV Workshop, N.Y.C., 1977, 79-00; mem. ABA-AAAS Nat. Conf. Bd. Lawyers and Scientists, 1986-92; former trustee or bd. dirs. NSF, N.Y. Acad. Scis., Pa. Ballet Co., Assumption Coll., University City Sci. Ctr., Phila., U. Pa. Rsch. Found., Morris Arboretum, Phila., Univ. Mus., Phila. Decorated Ordre des Palmes Academiques (France); recipient Vermeil medal for sci. Soc. d'Encouragement au Progres, France, 1978. Fellow AAAS (emeritus), Am. Phys. Soc., Royal Astron. Soc. (U.K.); mem. Internat. Astron. Union. Office: U Pa Dept Physics & Astronomy Philadelphia PA 19104-6396 E-mail: bshen@sas.upenn.edu.

SHEN, CHIA THENG, former steamship company executive, religious institute official; b. Chekiang, China, Dec. 15, 1913; came to U.S., 1952, naturalized, 1964; s. Foo Sheng and Wen Ching (Hsai) S.; m. Woo Ju Chu, Apr. 21, 1940; children: Maria May Shen Jackson, Wilma Way Shen George, David Chuen-Tsing, Freda Foh. BEE, Chiao Tung U., 1937; LittD (hon.), St. John's U., 1973. With Central Elec. Mfg. Works, China, 1937-44, factory mgr., 1942-44; dep. coordinating dept. Nat. Resources Commn., Govt. of China, 1945-47; pres. China Trading and Indsl. Devel. Corp., Shanghai, 1947-49; mng. dir. China Trading & Indsl. Devel. Co. Ltd., Hong Kong, 1949-53; with TransAtlantic Financing Corp., 1954-62, pres., 1958-62, Pan-Atlantic Devel. Corp., N.Y.C., 1955-70; with Marine Transport Lines Inc., N.Y.C., 1958-70, sr. v.p., 1964-70; with Am. Steamship Co., Buffalo, 1967-80, chmn. bd., chief exec. officer, 1971-80. Trustee Inst. Advanced Studies World Religions, N.Y., 1970—, chmn. bd., chief exec. officer, 1970-92, pres., 1970-84, 90—; trustee China Inst. in Am., N.Y.C., 1963-90, vice chmn., 1970-79, chmn., 1979-80, mem. exec. com., 1963-84; trustee, v.p. Buddhist Assn. U.S., N.Y.C., 1964—. Mem. Chinese Inst. Engring. Home and Office: 2020 Route 301 Carmel NY 10512-3426 Fax: (845) 225-0447. E-mail: chiatshen@yahoo.com. *To benefit all human beings and to work toward freeing them from fear is my goal. The collective wisdom of all world religions furnishes us the direction and means to achieve that goal. To introduce such wisdom into the daily life of mankind in general and America in particular, is therefore what I devote my energy to.*

SHEN, E-CHIN, dentist, periodontist; b. Keelung, Taiwan, June 19, 1955; s., Yuei-Hwa and Huei-Lien (Wang) S.; m. Chi Yang, Jan. 23, 1982; 1 child, John T. B of Dental Surgery, Nat. Def. Med. Ctr., Taipei, Taiwan, 1981; MS, cert. periodontist, Northwestern U., 1995. Resident, chief resident Tri-Svc. Gen. Hosp., Taipei, Taiwan, 1987-90, physician, 1991—; lectr. NAt. Defense Med. Ctr., Taipei, Taiwan, 1991—; physician Air Force Gen. Hosp., Taipei, Taiwan, 1991-93; sect. head dental dept. Hsin Chu Mil. Hosp., Taiwan, 1995-96; dir. dental dept. Tao Yuan Mil. Gen. Hosp., Taiwan, 1996—. Contbr. articles to profl. jours. Col. Taiwan Mil., 1996—. Mem. Am. Acad. Periodontology, Dental Assn. China (sec. 1991-93, 97-99), Acad. Periodontology (bd. dirs. 1989-91, 95—). Avocations: travel, tennis, golf. Office: Tao Yuan Mil Gen Hosp #168 Chung Shing Rd Lung-tan 325 Taiwan

SHEN, HUNG TAO, hydraulic engineering educator; b. Shanghai, May 4, 1944; s. Chin Mei and Ai-Yuan (Chen) S.; m. Hayley Hsi, May 26, 1973; children: Scott P., June P. BSCE, Chung Yuan U., Chungli, Taiwan, 1965; ME, Asian Inst. Tech., Bangkok, 1969; PhD in Mechanics and Hydraulics, U. Iowa, 1974. Engring. analyst Sargent & Lundy, Chgo., 1974-76; asst. prof. Clarkson U., Potsdam, N.Y., 1976-81, assoc. prof., 1981-83, prof. civil and environ. engring., 1983—, chair fluid mechanics and thermal sci. program, 1980-88, interim chair, dept. of civil and environ eng., 2004. Monbusyo spl. vis. prof. Min. Edn. Iwate U., Hokkaido River Disaster Prevention Rsch. Ctr., Japan, 1998-99; expert, cons. U.S. Army Cold Regions Rsch. and Engring., Hanover, N.H., 1984-95; vis. prof. Lulea (Sweden) U., 1990-91; advisor China Inst. Water Resources and Hydropower Rsch., Beijing, 1994—; chmn. 14th Internat. Ice Symposium. Editor: Frontiers in Hydraulic Engineering, 1983, Ice in Surface Waters, 1998; assoc. editor Jour. Cold Regions Engring. ASCE, 1994-97, 2002— editor, 1997-2002; mm. editorial bd. Jour. Hydraulic Rsch., 1993—; contbr. articles to Jour. Hydraulic Engring., Geophys. Rsch., Cold Reions Sci. and Tech., Hydraulic Rsch., Fluid Mechanics. Bd. dirs. Asian Inst. Tech. Found., N.Y., 1984-90. U.S. Nat. Acad. Sci. vis. scholar, 1991; grantee NSF, U.S. Army Rsch. Office, NOAA, Dept. Transp., World Bank. Mem. ASCE (tech. coms. 1980—, Can.-Am. Civil Engring. Amity award 2000, Harold R. Peyton award 2000), Am. Geophys. Union, Can. Geophys. Union (R.L. Gerard medal 2001), Internat. Assn. Hydraulic Rsch. (mem. ice rsch. and engring. com. 1986-94, 98—, chmn. 2000-2004, chair 14th Internat. Symposium on Ice), Internat. Assn. Great Lakes Rsch. Achievements include development of first comprehensive computer model on river ice, and theories on frazil jam evolution, and dynamic transport and jamming of surface ice in rivers; computer models on oil/chemical spills in rivers. Office: Clarkson U Dept Civil-Environ Engring PO Box 5710 Potsdam NY 13699-5710 E-mail: htshen@clarkson.edu.

SHEN, LIANG CHI, electrical engineer, educator, researcher; b. China, Mar. 17, 1939; came to U.S., 1962; s. Kuang Huai and Ting Chin (Yu) S.; m. Grace Liu, June 26, 1965; children: Michael, Eugene. BSEE, Nat. Taiwan U., Taipei, 1961; PhD, Harvard U., 1967. Registered profl. engr., Tex. Prof., chmn. electrical engring. dept. U. Houston, 1977-81, prof., dir. well logging lab., 1978—. Author: Applied Electromagnetism, 1987, 3d edit., 1995. Fellow IEEE. Office: U Houston Dept Elec Engring Houston TX 77204-0001

SHEN, MASON MING-SUN, medical center administrator; b. Shanghai, Jiang Su, China, Mar. 30, 1945; came to U.S., 1969; s. John Kaung-Hao and Mai-Chu (Sun) S.; m. Nancy Hsia-Hsien Shieh, Aug. 7, 1976; children: Teresa Tao-Yee, Darren Tao-Ru. BS in Chemistry, Taiwan Normal U., 1963-67; MS in Chemistry, S.D. State U., 1971; PhD in Biochemistry, Cornell U., 1977; postgrad., U. Calif., Berkeley, 1977-79, Lawrence Livermore Nat. Lab., 1979-80; MS in Chinese Medicine, China Acad., Taipei, Taiwan, 1982; OMD, San Francisco Coll Acupuncture, 1984; D Acupuncture Medicine (hon.), Asian Am. Acupuncture Coll., San Diego, 1985; MD (Medicina Alternativa), Internat. U., Colombo, Sri Lanka, 1988. Diplomate Nat. Commn. for Cert. of Acupuncturists; lic. acupuncturist, clin. chemist technologist, Calif. Rsch. assoc. Lawrence Livermore (Calif.) Lab., 1979-80; assoc. prof. Nat. Def. Med.

Coll., Taipei, 1980-82; prof. Inst. of Chinese Medicine China Acad., Taipei, 1981-82, San Francisco Coll. Acupuncture, 1983-85, Acad. Chinese Culture and Health Scis., Oakland, Calif., 1985-86, U. No. Calif., 2001—. Pres. Florescent Inst. Traditional Chinese Medicine, Oakland, Calif., 1995—2001; adminstr. Am. Ea. Med. Inst., Pleasanton, Calif., 1993—; acupuncture com. State of Calif., 1988—92; chief acupuncturist Acupuncture Ctr. Pleasanton, 1993—2000, Acupuncture Ctr. Tracy, 1995—98, Ea. Med. Ctr. Danville, Calif., 1996—99; v.p. Modern Medicine, Hayward, Calif., 1997—98, U. Health Sci., Honolulu, 1997—99; adminstrv. officer Rsch. Inst. Chinese Medicine, San Francisco, 1998—; chief acupuncturist Ea. Med. Ctr. Pleasanton, Calif., 2000—; bd. dirs. Am. Inst. Acupuncture Orthopedics and Traumatology, San Francisco, 1998—. Contbr. over 50 articles to profl. jours. Mem. Danville Rep. Com., 1988-93; bd. dirs. Asian Rep. Assembly, 1989-98; mem. presdnl. adv. com. Republican Presdl. Task Force, 1992-99; mem. chmn's. adv. bd. Republican Nat. Com., 1993—; pres. Internat. Congress Chinese Medicine, Calif., 1987—. Recipient Nat. Rsch. Svc. award NIH, 1977, Presdl. Order of Merit, Pres. of the U.S., 1991. Mem.: Ea. Med. Assn. (pres. 2002—), United Calif. Practioners Chinese Medicine (bd. dir. 1995—98, dep. supr. 1998—2001, hon. cons. 2001—), Presdl. Round Table (presdl. adv. com.), Am. Assn. Traditional Chinese Medicine (exec. dir. 1997—2001), Nat. Acupuncture Detoxification Assn. (cons. 1987—), Am. Assn. Acupuncture & Oriental Medicine (bd. dir. 1987—92, pres. 1989—90, Acupuncturist of Yr. 1998), Am. Acupuncture Assn. (bd. dir. 1986—90, v.p. 1987—89), Calif. Cert. Acupuncturists Assn. (pres. 1985—86, mem. polit. action com. 1995—, supr. 1999—), NY Acad. Sci. (bd. dir. 1984—93), Hong Kong & Kowloon Chinese Med. Assn. (hon.; life pres. 1985). Republican. Avocations: travel, horse back riding. Home: 3240 Touriga Dr Pleasanton CA 94566-6966 Office: Eastern Med Ctr 3510 Old Santa Rita Rd Ste D Pleasanton CA 94588-3466 Fax: 925-847-4180. E-mail: masonmshen@yahoo.com.

SHEN, MICHAEL, lawyer; b. Nanking, Jiangsu, Peoples Republic of China, Aug. 15, 1948; came to U.S. 1951; s. James Cheng Yee and Grace (Pai) S.; m. Marina Manese (div.); m. Pamela Nan Bradford, Aug. 12, 1983; 1 child, Jessica Li. BA, U. Chgo., 1969; MA, U. Pa., 1970; JD, Rutgers U., 1979. Bar: U.S. Dist. Ct. N.J. 1979, N.Y. 1980, U.S. Dist. Ct. (so., no. and ea. dists.) N.Y. 1980, N.J. 1981, U.S. Ct. Appeals (2d cir.) 1987, U.S. Supreme Ct. 1988, U.S. Ct. Appeals (3rd cir.) 1996. Staff atty. Bedford Stuyvesant Legal Svcs., Bklyn., 1979-80, Com. for Interns and Residents, N.Y.C., 1980-81; ptnr. Shneyer & Shen, P.C., N.Y.C. 1981—. Pres. bd. dirs. Asian Am. Legal Def. and Edn. Fund, N.Y.c.; of counsel 318 Restaurant Workers Union, N.Y.C., 1984—. Bd. dirs. Nat. Asian Pacific Am. Legal Consortium, N.Y.C., Nat. Employment Law Project; past bd. dirs. N.Y. Civil Liberties Union, N.Y.C., 1987-98. Mem. Internat. Platform Assn., Nat. Employees Lawyers Assn., N.Y. State Bar Assn., N.Y. County Bar Assn., Nat. Lawyers Guild. Avocations: arts, reading. also: 1085 Cambridge Rd Teaneck NJ 07666-1901 E-mail: shenlaw@compuserve.com.

SHEN, QING, urban planning educator, researcher; b. Jinyun, Zhejiang, China, Apr. 5, 1962; s. Xianxing and Aili (Cheng) S.; m. Yongmei Zhu, Aug. 25, 1989; 1 child, Sophie. BS, Zhejiang U., 1982; MA in Urban Planning, U. of B.C., Canada, 1986; PhD in Urban Planning, U. Calif., Berkeley, 1993. Asst. prof. Urban Studies & Planning MIT, Cambridge, 1993-99, assoc. prof. Urban Studies & Planning, 1999—2001; assoc. prof. urban studies and planning U. Md., Coll. Pk., Md., 2001—. Affiliate faculty Ctr. Trans. Studies MIT, 1996—; affiliate faculty Nat. Ctr. Smart Growth Rsch. and Edn. U. Md., 2001—; mem. jour. adv. bds. Contbr. articles to profl. jours. Emerging Scholar Paper award Assn. Am. Geographers, 1999; Horwood Critique prize Urban and Regional Info. Sys. Assn, 1998. Mem. Assn. Collegiate Schs. Planning, Assn. Am. Geographers, Transp. Rsch. Bd., Urban and Regional Info. Sys. Assn. Avocations: poetry, tennis. Office: Univ Maryland 1215 Sch Architecture College Park MD 20742-1411 Business E-Mail: qshen@umd.edu.

SHEN, QUANG, science educator; s. Chang-ling Shen and Tak-Wah Sze; m. Mary-ellen Mitchell, Nov. 11, 1976; children: Alan Michael, Stephen Thomas. BS, Furman U., 1970; PhD, Oreg. State U., 1973. Post doctoral fellow U. Windsor, Canada, 1973—76, U. Trondheim, Norway, 1976—78; post doctroal fellow ND State U., Fargo, 1978—80; asst. prof. Colgate U., Hamilton, NY, 1980—87, assoc. prof., 1988—94, prof. chemistry, 1994—. Contbr. articles various profl. jours. Rsch. grant, Norwegian Marshall Fund, 1985, NATO, 1990, NSF (REU), 1990—2000, Rsch. grants, PRF Am. Chem. Soc., 2002—05. Office: Colgate U 13 Oak Dr Hamilton NY 13346 Business E-Mail: mshen@mail.colgate.edu.

SHEN, SIN-YAN, physicist, conductor, acoustics specialist, music director; b. Singapore, Nov. 12, 1949; came to the U.S., 1969, naturalized, 1984; s. Shao-Quan and Tien-Siu (Chen) S.; m. Yuan-Yuan Lee, Aug. 4, 1973; children: Jia, Jian. BSc, U. Singapore, 1969; MS, Ohio State U., 1970, PhD, 1973. Concert recitalist on Erhu Chinese fiddle, 1963—; instr. math. U. Singapore, 1969; asst. prof. physics Northwestern U., Evanston, Ill., 1974-77, assoc. prof., 1977-81; faculty assoc. Argonne (Ill.) Nat. Lab., 1974-77, scientist, 1977-83, sr. rsch. leader, 1983—. Dir. rsch. divsn. natural resource mgmt. SUPCON Internat., 1988—; prof. Harvard U., 1989—; meeting series reviewer NSF, Washington, 1981—; coord. Tech. Rev., Argonne, Atlanta, Phoenix, Portland, Oreg., 1983—; dir. Global Warming Internat. Ctr., 1991—, chmn. Internat. Conf. Chgo., 1990-93, San Francisco, 1994-95, Vienna, 1996, Columbia U., N.Y.C., 1997, Hong Kong U. Sci. and Tech., 1998, Yamanashi Inst. Environ. Scis., 1999, Harvard U., 2000, Cambridge U., 2001, Max Planck Inst., 2002, Mass. Inst. Tech., 2003; Chinese Music Internat. Conf., 1991, 94, 2002; advisor Internat. Energy Agy., 1986—, Gas Rsch. Inst., 1984—, SUPCON Internat., 1986—, Nat. Geog., 1986—, Internat. Boreal Forest Rsch. Assn., 1991—, Electric Power Rsch. Inst., 1992—, World Climate Rsch. Programme WMO, 1993—, UN Devel. Program, 1993—, World Bank, 1994—, US Dept. Energy and US EPA, 1995—; prof. Chinese Acad. Forestry, 1986—; panel on biol. diversity Nat. Acad. Scis., Smithsonian Instn., 1986; chmn. internat. program com. Austrian Acad. Scis., 1995-96, Columbia U., 1996-97, Japan Environ. Agy., 1998-99, Intergovt. Panel on Climate Change, 1999—; music dir. Orch. Chinese Music Soc. N.Am., 1976—, Silk & Bamboo Ensemble, 1981—; adv. Ctrl. Traditional Orch., 1984—; del. leader, UN Conf. Environ. and Devel., Rio, 1992; del. chmn. Third All China Arts Festival, Kunmin, 1992; panelist Nat. Endowment for Arts, 1981—, New Eng. Found. for Arts, 1987—, Arts Midwest, 1985—, Ill. Arts Coun., 1982—, Chgo. City Arts, 1990—, Ill. Art's Alliance Found., adv. coun., 1992—, adv. coun. Mid-Am. Arts Alliance, 1992—, bd. dirs.; tech. adv. Shanghai Nat. Musical Instrument Co., 1985—; adv. West Lake Qin Soc., Hangzhou, China, 1991—. Author: Superfluidity, 1982, Acoustics of Ancient Chinese Bells, 1987, Chinese Music and Orchestration: A Primer om Principles and Practice, 1991, Global Warming Science and Policy, 1992, The Boreal Forests and Global Change, 1993, Global Warming Eludidated, 1994, Chinese Musical Instruments, 1999, Global Warming and Public Health, 1999, China: A Journey through Its Musical Art, 1999, Chinese Music in the 20th Century, 2001; editor-in-chief Chinese Music Internat. Jour., 1978—; mem. internat. editl. bd. World Resource Rev., 1989—, Internat. Boreal Forest Rsch., 1992—, Ency. of Life Support Sys., 1994—; advisor Ency. Brit., 1983—; contbr. over 300 articles to profl. jours.; patentee molten liquids, 1974, 80. Recipient Mich. Heritage award, 1992; Fulbright scholar U.S. State Dept., 1969; merit scholar Govt. Singapore, 1967; named Artistic Treasure Gov. Jim Edgar of Ill., 1998. Mem. AAAS, Am. Phys. Soc., Ops. Rsch. Soc. Am., Acoustical Soc. Am., Chinese Music Soc. N.Am. Achievements include rsch. in renewable energy and materials techs.; global change and global warming; extreme event index; indsl. sonic techs.; energy policy, planning and economics; acoustics; cultural acoustics. Office: Chinese Music Soc N Am 2329 Charmingfare Dr Downers Grove IL 60517-2910 also: SUPCON Internat PO Box 5275 Woodridge IL 60517-0275

SHEN, THOMAS TO, environmental engineer; b. Chia-Shing, Chekiang, China, Aug. 14, 1926; m. Cynthia Shen; children: Grace, Joyce. BS in Civil Engring., St. John's U., Shanghai, China, 1948; MS in Sanitary Engring., Northwestern U., 1960; PhD in Environ. Engring., Rensselaer Poly. Inst., 1971. Registered profl. engr., Wash., N.Y. Assoc. engr. Boeing Co., Renton, Wash., 1961-63; sanitary engr. Wash. State Health Dept., Seattle, 1963-66; sr. sanitary engr. N.Y. State Health Dept., Albany, 1966-70; sr. rsch. scientist N.Y. State Dept. Environ. Conservation, Albany, 1970-93. Adj. prof. Columbia U., N.Y.C., 1981-93; mem. U.S. EPA Sci. Adv. Bd., 1987-90; cons. UN's Environ. Protection Program, various Asian cities, 1983—; lectr. various U.S. and fgn. univs., 1978—; cons. World Bank, 1990; tech. reviewer Annual Pres. Bush's Environ. and Conservation Challenge awards, 1991, 92. Author: Air Pollution and Its Control, 1985, Hazardous Waste Incineration, 1982, Assessment and Control of VOC Emissions from Waste Treatment and Disposal Facilities, 1993, Industrial Pollution Prevention, 1995, 2d edit., 1999; author: (with others) Electrostatic Precipitator, 1979, Air Quality Assessment, 1989; contbr. articles to profl. jours. Bd. dirs. Internat. Ctr. of the Capital Region, Albany, 1984-88, Am. Bur. Med. Advancement of China, N.Y.C., 1985—. Recipient Svc. award Phi Tau Phi, 1986, Nat. award Indsl. Wast. Minimization Taiwan Environ. Protection Adminstrn., Ministry Econ. Affairs, 1993, Man of Yr. award N.Y. State Capital Region Chinese Am. Alliance, 1995; Named for Outstanding Editorial Contbn. on Pollution Engring., Chgo., 1978, 81. Fellow ASCE (chmn. N.Y. State Coun. 1979-80); mem. Am. Acad. Environ. Engrs. (diplomate 1973), Air and Waste Mgmt. Assn. (com. chmn. 1985—, Frank Chamber award for Outstanding Achievement in Sci. of Air 1993), Delmar Club (pres. 1979-80), Rotary. Avocations: travel, music appreciation. Home: 146 Fernbank Ave Delmar NY 12054-4215 Personal E-mail: cs.tt.shen@att.net.

SHEN, TSUNG YING, medicinal chemistry educator; b. Beijing, Sept. 28, 1924; came to U.S., 1950; s. Tsu-Wei and Sien-Wha (Nieu) S.; m. Amy T.C. Lin, June 20, 1953; children: Bernard, Hubert, Theodore, Leonard, Evelyn, Andrea. B.Sc., Nat. Ctrl. U., Chongqing, China, 1946; diploma, Imperial Coll. Sci. and Tech., London, 1948; PhD, U. Manchester, Eng., 1950, D.Sc., 1978. Research assoc. Ohio State U., Columbus, 1950-52, MIT, Cambridge, 1952-56; sr. research chemist Merck, Sharp & Dohme Research Labs., Rahway, N.J., 1956-65, dir. synthetic chem. research, 1966-76, v.p. membrane chem. research, 1976-77, v.p. membrane and arthritis research, 1977-86; A. Burger prof. medicinal chemistry U. Va., Charlottesville, 1986-96, emeritus and rsch. prof., 1996—. Vis. prof. U. Calif., Riverside, 1973, U. Calif., San Francisco, 1985, Harvard Med. Sch., 1986; adj. prof. Stevens Inst. Tech., Hoboken, N.J., 1982-85; hon. prof. Beijing Med. U., Chinese Acad. Med. Sci., Inst. Material Medica, China Pharm. U.; mem. sci. bd. CytoMed, 1989-96, T Cell Sci, 1988-93, Gene Labs., 1989-94, Osteo Arthritis Sci, 1993-95, Argonex, 1994-98. Mem. editl. bd. Clinica Europa Jour., 1977, Prostaglandins and Medicine, 1978, Medicinal Rsch. Revs., 1979-94, Jour. Medicinal Chemistry, 1980-83, Medicinal Chem. Rsch., 1991; patentee in field. Recipient Outstanding Patent award N.J. Research and Devel. Council, 1975, Rene Descartes medal U. Paris, 1977, medal of Merit Giornate Mediche Internazionali del Collegium Biologicum Europea, 1977, cert. of merit Spanish Soc. Therapeutic Chemistry, 1983, achievement award Chinese Inst. Engrs.-U.S.A., 1984. Mem. AAAS, Am. Chem. Soc. (1st Alfred Burger award in medicinal chemistry 1980), N.Y. Acad. Scis., Acad. Pharm. Assn. (hon.), Chinese Am. Chem. Soc. (bd. dirs. 1995-97). Office: U Va Dept Chem Charlottesville VA 22901 Home: 238 Eliot St Chestnut Hill MA 02467-1447

SHEN, VIRGINIA SHIANG-LAN, Spanish and Chinese language educator; b. Kaohsiung, Taiwan, July 30, 1955; d. Mu-hsing and Ah-hsin (Huang) Li; m. Eric Yao-chu Shen, May 15, 1983; children: Andrew David, Alan Michael. BA in Spanish, Fu-Jen Cath. U., 1977; MA in Latin Am. Lit., Inst. Caro y Cuervo, 1983; PhD in Spanish, Ariz. State U., 1988. Instr. Wen Tzao Jr. Coll., Kaohsiung, 1982-83; tchg. assoc. Ariz. State U., Tempe, Ariz., 1983-87; asst. prof. N.Mex. State U., Las Cruces, N.Mex., 1987-88, La. State U., Shreveport, La., 1988-91, Chgo. State U., Ill., 1991-94, assoc. prof., 1994-99, prof., 1999—. Author: Encyclopedia of World Literature in the Twentieth Century, 3rd. edit., 1999, El Teatro Español del siglo XX y su contexto, 1994, Critical Perspectives of the Works of Enrique Jaramillo-Levi, 1996, Literatura y Cultura, 2000, Literatura y cultura Narrativa Colombiana del siglo XX, 2000; contbr. articles to profl. jours. Mem. Am. Assn. Tchrs. Spanish and Portuguese, Am. Coun. on Tchg. of Fgn. Langs., Ill. Coun. Tchg. of Fgn. Langs. Office: Chgo State U 9501 S King Dr Chicago IL 60628-1598 E-mail: vshen@csu.edu.

SHEN, XIAOHUI, application developer, researcher; s. Decheng Shen and Youfen Liang; married. MS, Tsinghua U., Beijing, 1994; PhD, Northwestern U., 2001. Rsch. asst. Northwestern U., Evanston, Ill., 1997—2001; sr. software engr. Motorola Inc., Libertyville, Ill., 2001—. Program com. mem., session chair numerous internat. confs. Contbr. articles to profl. jours., 2001. Recipient Guanghua prize, Guanghua Edn. Found., 1990. Mem.: IEEE (sr.). Home: 15 S Bristol Ct Mundelein IL 60060 Office: Motorola Inc 1000 Technology Way Libertyville IL Personal E-mail: shen_xh@yahoo.com. Business E-Mail: axs095@email.mot.com.

SHEN, YUEN-RON, physics educator; b. Shanghai, Mar. 25, 1935; came to U.S. BS, Nat. Taiwan U., 1956; MS, Stanford U., 1959; PhD, Harvard U., 1963; DSc (hon.), Hong Kong U. Sci. and Tech., 1997, Nat. Chiao-Tung U., Taiwan, 1998. Rsch. asst. Hewlett-Packard Co., Palo Alto, Calif., 1959; rsch. fellow Harvard U., Cambridge, Mass., 1963-64; asst. prof. U. Calif., Berkeley, 1964-67, assoc. prof., 1967-70, prof., 1970—, chancellor's prof., 1997-2000. Prin. investigator Lawrence Berkeley Nat. Lab., 1967—. Author: The Principles of Nonlinear Optics, 1984. Recipient Charles Hard Townes award Am. Phys. Soc., 1986, Arthur L. Schawlow prize Am. Phys. Soc., 1992, DOE Alexander von Humboldt award, 1984, DOE Outstanding Rsch. award DOE-MRS Rsch., 1983, DOE Sustained Outstanding Rsch. award, 1987, Max Planck Rsch. award, 1996, Materials Sci. award Solid State Physics, 1997; Sloan fellow, 1966-68, Guggenheim Found. fellow, 1972-73. Fellow Am. Phys. Soc. (disting. traveling lectr. Laser Sci. Topical Group 1994-96, Frank Isakson prize 1998), Photonics Soc. Chinese-Ams., Optical Soc. Am.; mem. AAAS, NAS, Acad. Sinica, Chinese Acad. Scis. (fgn.). Achievements include research in nonlinear optics and condensed matter physics. Office: U Calif Berkeley Dept Physics Berkeley CA 94720-0001

SHENAI, DEODATTA VINAYAK, chemical engineer; b. Bombay, Jan. 5, 1959; s. Vinayak Ramkrishna Shenai and Rekha Vinayak Shenai; m. Usha Nilkanth Nimbalkar, Apr. 14, 1990; 1 child, Anisha. BS in Chemistry and Physics, Bombay U., 1976, BS in Chem. Engring., 1979; MS in Polymer and Fiber Sci., Manchester (Eng.) U., 1980, PhD in Polymer Sci., 1983; MBA, Suffolk U., 2001. Postdoctoral rschr. Liverpool (Eng.) U., 1984-85; acad. staff U. St. Andrews, Scotland, 1985-88; tech. mgr. Rohm and Haas Co., North Andover, Mass., 1988—. Contbr. articles to profl. jours., including Jour. Crystal Growth, Chemtronics, others; patentee in field. Home: 5 Surrey Ln Danvers MA 01923 E-mail: dshenai@aol.com.

SHENAI-KHATKHATE, DEODATTA VINAYAK, chemical researcher; b. Kankavli, India, Jan. 5, 1959; s. Vinayak Ramkrishna and Rekha Vinayak Shenai-K.; m. Usha Nilkanth Nimbalkar, Apr. 14, 1990; 1 child, Anisha Shenai-K. BSc with honors in chemistry and physics, Mumbai U., 1976, BSc in Polymer and Paint Tech., 1979; MSc in Polymer Tech., U. Manchester, U.K., 1980, PhD in Polymer Tech., 1983; MBA, Suffolk U., 2001. Tech. sales and mktg. mgr. Asian Paints (India) Ltd., Mumbai, India; rsch. fellow, acad. staff U. Liverpool, U.K., 1984-85, U. St. Andrews, U.K., 1985-88; tech. mgr. R&D and quality control Rohm and Haas Metalorganics, North Andover, Mass., 1988—. Dir. Shishubharati Sch. of Culture and Langs., Burlington, Mass., 1998-2002. Dalton chem. rsch. fellowship U. Manchester; Joseph Greenhall Harrison Rsch. scholarship U. Manchester, 1980-83. Achievements include patents on synthesis of trimethylindium trialkylarsenics, trialkylantimonides,dialkyltellurides and dialkylselenides; invention of synthesis of ultrapure MOVPE Precursors, purification of MOVPE Precursors, adduct purification MOVPE precursors, compound semiconductors. Office: Rohm and Haas Metalorganics 60 Willow St North Andover MA 01845 E-mail: dshenai@aol.com.

SHENDE, RAJESH V. chemical engineer, materials scientist, researcher; b. Nagpur, Maharashtra State, India, Mar. 13, 1965; arrived in U.S., 1999; s. Vitthalrao Ganpatrao and Kamaltai Kashikae Shende; m. Anuradha Rajesh Deshmukh, Mar. 31, 1996; 1 child, Shaunak Rajesh Shende. BS in Physics, Chemistry, Math.h.), U. of Nagpur, 1986; PhD in Chem. Engring., MS in Chem. Tech., U. of Bombay, Matunga, 1995. Dep. mgr. Khatau Dyes Ltd., Ankleshwar, India, 1995—96; asst. mgr., process tech. cell devel. incharge Indian Dyestuff Industries Ltd., Kalyan, 1996—98; rsch. scientist Inst. of Chemistry, Ljubljana, Slovenia, U. of Mo., Columbia. Contbr. rsch. publs. to sci. jours. Recipient postdoctoral fellowship, U. of Mo., 1999—, Inst. of Chemistry, Lab. for Catalysis and Chem. Reaction Engring., 1998—99, sr. rsch. fellowship for PhD, Univ. Grants Commn., 1991—95, His-Holiness the Pope Merit scholarship for MS, U. of Bombay, 1989. Mem.: Am. Chem. Soc. (reviewer Jour. Indsl. and Engring. Chemistry Rsch., reviewer Jour. Environ. Sci. and Tech.), Sigma Xi. Home: 2601 Hillshire Dr Columbia MO 65203 Office: U Mo Dept Chem Engring Columbia MO 65211 Personal E-mail: shender@missouri.edu. E-mail: rajeshshende@hotmail.com.

SHENEFELT, ARTHUR B. transportation executive, consultant; b. Boston, May 5, 1920; s. Arthur Merle and Martha Marion (Baird) S.; m. Gloria Mae Willis, Apr. 28, 1948; 1 child, Michael Baird. BA, Miami U., Oxford, Ohio, 1942; student, Garrett Theol. Sem., Evanston, Ill., 1942-44, Columbia U., 1946-47. Dir. pub. rels. Brotherhood of Locomotive Engrs., Cleve., 1951-56; dir. press rels. N.Y. Ctrl. R.R., N.Y.C., 1956-57; transp. editor Jour. of Commerce, N.Y.C., 1957-59; asst. tp pres. for pub. affairs Freight Forwrders Inst., Washington, 1959-71; dir. comms. N.Y. State Trucking Assn., N.Y.C., 1960-61, Trucking Employers Inc., Washington, 1970-71; press sec. to chmn. U.S. Senate Transp. Com., Washington, 1971-73; personal transp. adviser to Gov. of Pa., Harrisburg, 1973-77. Cons. Fed. Appalachian Regional Commn., Harrisburg and Washington, 1977-79, Japanese Nat. Ry., N.Y.C. and Tokyo, 1980-85; chmn. Bucks HUB Conf., Bristol, Pa., 1985—; chmn. Super Mag. Coalition, Washington, 1988—; chmn. Amtrak for Profit Coalition, Washington, 1995-97; pres. Interstate Maglev Inc., Bristol, 1992—; dir., chmn. Office of Transp. Tech., Strategy and Planning, 1998—. Contbr. articles, stories and features to most maj. Am. newspapers and trade jours. Lt. (j.g.), pub. info. officer USN, 1944-46, PTO. Avocation: music. Office: Bucks HUB Conf 1200 New Rodgers Rd Bristol PA 19007-2525 E-mail: shenefelt@surface.transportation.com.

SHENEFELT, PHILIP DAVID, dermatologist; b. Colfax, Wash., July 31, 1943; s. Roy David and Florence Vanita (Cagle) S.; m. Debrah A. Levenson; children: Elizabeth, Sara, Shaina. BS with honors, U. Wis. Madison, 1966, MD, 1970, MS in Adminstrv. Medicine, 1984. Intern U.S. Naval Hosp., Bethesda, Md., 1970-71; gen. practice Oreg. (Wis.) Clinic, 1975; resident in dermatology U. Wis. Hosp., Madison, 1975-78, mem. staff, 1978-87; asst. prof. dermatology sect. Dept. Internal Medicine U. South Fla., Tampa, 1987-97, assoc. prof., 1997—. Chief dermatology sect. VA Hosp., Bay Pines, Fla., 1987—89, asst. chief, Tampa, 1988—2002, chief, 2002—; dermatologist Univ. Health Svc. U. Wis., Madison, 1978—87, VA Hosp., Madison, 1982—85. Served to lt. comdr. USN, 1969-74; capt. USNR (ret.). Kellogg fellow, 1980-82. Mem.: AMA, Soc. Clin. Exptl. Hypnosis, Noah Worcester Dermatol. Soc., Fla. West Coast Dermatol. Soc., Fla. Dermatol. Soc., Am. Soc. Clin. Hypnosis, Am. Coll. Physician Execs., Am. Acad. Dermatology. Home: 15919 Notting Hill Dr Lutz FL 33548-6147 Office: U South Fla Internal Medicine/Dermatol 12901 Bruce Downs Blvd #79 Tampa FL 33612-4742 Office Phone: 813-974-2188. Business E-Mail: pshenefe@hsc.usf.edu.

SHENG, MICHAEL M. historian, educator; b. Shanghai, Dec. 29, 1950; arrived in U.S., 1992; s. Shouren Sheng and Xingde Xiang; children from previous marriage: Julie, Michael. BA, Shanghai Normal U., 1983; MA, U. N.B., Fredericton, Can., 1988; PhD, York U., Toronto, Can., 1992. Lectr. history dept. Shanghai Normal U., 1983—86; prof. S.W. Mo. State U., Springfield, 1992—, head history dept., 2003—. Author: Battling Western Imperialism: Mao, Stalin and the United States, 1997. Office: SW Mo State U History Dept 901 S National Ave Springfield MO 65804 Office Phone: 417-836-6730. Business E-Mail: mms493f@smsu.edu.

SHENG, QUAN, chemist; b. Changzhou, China, Nov. 7, 1947; arrived in U.S., 1997; s. Benyu Sheng and Yuru Lu; m. Chimin Jiang, Oct. 28, 1982; 1 child, Yiqing. BSc, Nanjing U., China, 1982, MSc in Polymer Chemistry, 1985; MSc, Laurentian U., Sudbury, Ont., Canada, 1992; PhD in Polymer Chemistry, McMaster U., Hamilton, Ont., Canada, 1997. Technician Jiangsu Jintan Pharm. Factory, Jintan, China, 1973-78; lectr., vice dir. Polymer Chemistry Inst. Dept. Chemistry Nanjing (China) U., 1985-91; rsch. chemist postdoctoral fellow Nat. Ctr. for Agrl. Utilization Rsch. USDA, Peoria, Ill., 1997-98; chemist OMG Ams., Research Triangle Park, NC, 1998—2003; global mgr. rsch. & devel. Microbond EPM, UMICORE, Raleigh, 2003—. Vice dir. Polymer Chemistry Inst. Nanjing U., China, 1985-91. Contbr. articles to profl. jours.; solder paste trade secrets and patents. Coord. Canada-China Friendship Assn., Hamilton, Ont., Canada, 1995-97. Mem.: Am. Chem. Soc. Achievements include research in polyurethanes, ionomers, polysulfone and selective functionalization of polymers; development of anti-corrosive coatings, no-clean solder paste, water-soluble solder paste, RMA solder paste and lead free solder paste for SMT and die attach applications. Avocations: Chinese finger calligraphy, ping pong/table tennis, travel, reading. Office: Microbond EPM, Umicore 3420 Tarheel Dr Ste 100 Raleigh NC 27609 Home: 807 Bristol Blue St Apex NC 27502 E-mail: quan.sheng@am.umicore.com.

SHENK, GEORGE H. lawyer; b. N.Y.C., Sept. 10, 1943; BA, Princeton U., 1965; M in Internat. Affairs, Columbia U., 1967; JD, Yale U., 1970. Bar: N.Y. 1971, Calif. 1985. Assoc. Coudert Bros., Paris, 1970, N.Y.C., 1970-73, Hong Kong, 1973-75, Tokyo, 1975-78, ptnr. N.Y.C., 1978-91, San Francisco, 1991-94, Heller Ehrman, White & McAuliffe, 1994—. Exec. dir. San Francisco Com. on Fgn. Rels. Contbr. articles to publs. Mem. Bar Assn. City of N.Y., Calif. State Bar Assn., Coun. Fgn. Rels., Pacific Coun. on Internat. Policy. Office: Heller Ehrman White & McAuliffe 333 Bush St San Francisco CA 94104-2806

SHENK, LOIS ELAINE LANDIS, writer; b. Ephrata, Pa., May 30, 1944; d. Raymond Earle and Esther May (Forry) Landis; m. John Barge Shenk, June 12, 1965; children: Philip Jon, Matthew Alan. BA in English, Eastern Mennonite Coll., 1966; MS in Edn., Temple U., 1984. English mistress Githumu Secondary Sch., Thika, Kenya, 1966-68; English tchr. Kraybill's Jr. High, Mount Joy, Pa., 1976-77; freelance writer, 1978—; religious news corr. Gospel Herald, Scottdale, Pa., 1978-82. Observer, corr. The U.S. Senate, Washington, 1987—99. Author: Out of Mighty Waters, 1982 (R.I.M. excellence award 1983), The Story of Ephrata Mennonite School, 1996; (one act play) A House for David in (anthology) Swords into Plowshares, 1983; (study guide for Christian edn.) Hebrews, 1988; contbr. poems, stories & features to jours.; editl. work Mennonite Ctrl. Com., Akron, Pa., 1977. Cmty. living advisor Friendship Cmty., Lititz, Pa., 1997-99; Sunday sch. tchr. Ephrata Mennonite Ch., 1997-99. Recipient Rep. Senatorial Medal of Honor, many other honors and awards. Avocations: reading, cooking, music, gardening. Home and Office: 157 E New St Lancaster PA 17602

SHENK, THOMAS EUGENE, molecular biology educator, academic administrator; b. Bklyn., Jan. 1, 1947; s. Eugene Richard and Helen Marie (Deffenbaugh) S.; m. Susan Mary Hillman, July 4, 1979; children— Christopher Thomas, Gregory Thomas BS, U. Detroit, 1969; PhD, Rutgers U., 1973. Asst. prof. molecular biology U. Conn., Farmington, 1975-80; prof. molecular biology SUNY, Stony Brook, 1980-84, Princeton U., 1984—, Am. Cancer Soc. prof., 1986—, now chmn. dept. molecular biology, 1996—. Co-editor: Enhancers and Eukaryotic Gene Expression, 1983. Mem. Am. Soc. Microbiology (Eli Lilly award 1982) Office: Princeton U Dept Molecular Biology Princeton NJ 08544-0001

SHENK, WILLIS WEIDMAN, newspaper executive; b. Manheim, Pa., Nov. 2, 1915; s. John Horst and Amanda (Weidman) S.; m. Elsie Sherer, Aug. 31, 1940; 1 son, J. David. Acct. Raymond D. Shearer, Lancaster, Pa., 1937-39; sr. acct. Lancaster Newspapers, Inc., 1940-50, sec.-controller, 1950-61, v.p., sec., 1961-76, pres., 1977-83, chmn. bd., 1984—. Pres. United Way of Lancaster County, 1961; pres., bd. trustees Lancaster Country Day Sch., 1971-72; trustee Franklin and Marshall Coll., Lancaster, 1977-85; sec. Pequea Twp. Planning Commn., 1965-77. Mem. Nat. Assn. Accts., Pa. Inst. CPAs, Lancaster Country Club. Clubs: Hamilton, Masons. Lutheran. Office: Lancaster Newspapers Inc PO Box 1328 8 W King St Lancaster PA 17603-3824

SHENKER, IRA RONALD, physician; b. July 8, 1934; s. Morris and Rose (Wilner) Shenker; m. Caroline Cabin, June 27, 1958; children: Diane Amy, Mitchell Steven. BS, U. Wis., 1955, MD, 1958. Diplomate Am. Bd. Pediatrics. Intern L.I. Jewish Med. Ctr., New Hyde Park, NY, 1958—59, resident pediats., 1959—61; resident pub. health Hassau County Health Dept., NY, 1961—62; coll. health physician Mt. Holyoke Coll., 1962—64; chief adolescent medicine L.I. Jewish Med. Ctr., 1965—; assoc. prof. pediat. SUNY-Stony Brook, 1979—; prof. pediat. Albert Einstein Coll. Medicine, 1989—. Author: Human Figure Drawings in Adolescance, 1972; editor: Adolescent Medicine, 1981, Clinical Monographs in Pediatrics: Adolescent Medicine, 1994; contbr. articles to profl. jours. Bd. dirs. Roslyn Sr. Citizens, NY, 1975—78. Recipient Adele Hoffman award, 2001; grantee USPHS, 1965—82. Fellow: Am. Acad. Pediats.; mem.: Soc. Adolescent Medicine (pres. 1986), N.Y. Pediat. Soc., Nassau Pediat. Soc., N.Y. Pediat. Soc. (pres. 1986—87), Queens Pediat. Soc. (pres. 1981—82). Home: 5 Fairway Rd Roslyn NY 11576-1099 Address: 270-05 76th Ave New Hyde Park NY 11040-1433 Office: Schneider Children's Hosp of LI Jewish Med Ctr New Hyde Park NY 11042 E-mail: rshenker@lij.edu.

SHENKER, JOSEPH, academic administrator; b. N.Y.C., Oct. 7, 1939; s. George and Isabelle (Schwartz) S.; m. Adrienne Green (div. 1979); children: Deborah, Karen; m. Susan Armiger, Jan. 2, 1988; children: Sarah Gabrielle, Jordan. BA in Psychology, Hunter Coll., 1962, MA in Econ., 1963; EdD in High Edn., Tchrs. Coll., 1969. Dean, community coll. affairs CUNY, 1967-69; acting pres. Kingsborough Community Coll., N.Y.C., 1969-70; chief negotiator for mgmt. CUNY, 1977; acting pres. Hunter Coll., N.Y.C., 1979-80; founding pres. LaGuardia Community Coll., N.Y.C., 1970-88; pres. Bank St. Coll. Edn., N.Y.C., 1988-95; provost C.W. Post Campus, L.I. U., 1995—. Bd. dirs. Sch. & Bus. Alliance, N.Y.C.; ptnr. N.Y.C Partnership, 1990—; advisor Consortium for Worker Edn., 2001--; bd. dirs. DeWitt Wallace Reader's Digest Fund, 2001--. Chmn. Liberty Scholarship Adv. Com., Albany, N.Y., 1989—; co-chmn. Task Force on Early Childhood Edn., N.Y.C., 1989—, Agenda for Children Tomorrow, 1989—; chmn. Chancellor's Com. on U./Sch. Collaboratives, N.Y.C., 1988. Recipient Distinguished Alumni award Tchrs. Coll. Columbia, N.Y.C., 1990. Office: C W Post Campus Long Island U 720 Northern Blvd Greenvale NY 11548-1319

SHENKER, JOSEPH C. lawyer; b. N.Y.C., Nov. 6, 1956; BS in Acctg., CUNY, 1977; JD, Columbia U., 1980. Bar: N.Y. 1981, U.S. Dist. Ct. (ea. and so. dists.) N.Y 1981, U.S. Claims Ct. 1982, U.S. Tax Ct. 1982, U.S. Supreme Ct. 1988. Assoc. Sullivan & Cromwell, N.Y.C., 1980-86, ptnr., 1986—. Contbr. articles to profl. jours. Pres. Met. Coun. on Jewish Poverty. Fellow Am. Bar Found.; mem. ABA, N.Y. State Bar Assn., Assn. Bar City N.Y. Office: Sullivan & Cromwell 125 Broad St Fl 33 New York NY 10004-2400 E-mail: shenkerj@sullcrom.com.

SHENKIR, WILLIAM GARY, business educator; b. Three Rivers, Tex., June 27, 1938; s. William and Lydia (Jancik) S.; m. Missy Smith, Jan 1, 1973. BBA, Tex. A & M U., 1960; postgrad. (Rockefeller Bros. Theol. fellow), Drew U. Sem., 1960-61; MBA, U. Tex., 1962, PhD, 1964. Asst. prof. McIntire Sch. Commerce, U. Va., Charlottesville, 1967-69, assoc. prof., 1969-72, prof., 1972—75, dean, 1977-92, Paul Goodloe McIntire prof., 1977—82; William Stamps Farish prof. McIntire Sch. Commerce U. Va., 1982—. Project dir. Fin. Acctg. Stds. Bd., Stamford, Conn., 1973—76; vis. prof. NYU Grad. Sch. Bus., N.Y.C., 1976—77; bd. dirs. ComSonics Corp., Harrisburg, Va. Editor: Carman Blough: His Professional Career and Accounting Thought, 1978; co-author: The University of Virginia's McIntire School of Commerce: The First 75 Years, 1921-96, 1996, Open-Book Management: Creating an Ownership Culture, 1998, Making Enterprise Risk Management Pay Off, 2001, Making Enterprise Risk Management Pay Off: How Leading Companies Implement Risk Management, 2002, Enterprise Risk Management: Pulling It All Together, 2002; contbr. articles to profl. jours. Served to lt. USAF, 1964-67. Mem. AICPA, Am. Acctg. Assn. (former v.p.), Acctg. Edn. Change Commn. (former vice chmn.), Am. Assembly Collegiate Schs. of Bus. (former bd. dirs., pres. 1990-91), Fin. Execs. Inst., Va. Soc. CPAs, Raven Soc., Landfall Club, Farmington Country Club, Phi Delta Kappa, Beta Gamma Sigma, Phi Kappa Phi. Presbyterian. Home: 420 Rookwood Dr Charlottesville VA 22903-4732 Office Phone: 434-924-4146. E-mail: wgs2Z@virginia.edu.

SHENKMAN, MARK RONALD, investment and finance executive; b. Providence, Aug. 17, 1943; s. George and Florence (Littman) S.; children: Andrew Harris, Gregory Alexander; m. Rosalind Schmidt, Aug. 10, 1997; 1 stepson, Justin Warren Slatky. BA, U. Conn., 1965; MBA, George Washington U., 1967. Security analyst New Eng. Mchts. Bank, Boston, 1969-71; fin. analyst Stone & Webster Securities Corp., Boston, 1971-73; rsch. analyst, portfolio mgr. Fidelity Mgmt. & Research Co., Boston, 1973-79; v.p. Lehman Bros. Kuhn Loeb, N.Y.C., 1979-83; pres. First Investors Asset Mgmt. Co., N.Y.C., 1983-85; pres., chief exec. officer Shenkman Capital Mgmt. Inc., N.Y.C., 1985—. Vice chmn. bd. trustees Wilbraham (Mass.) and Monson Acad.; bd. dirs. U. Conn. Found.; bd. visitors George Washington U. Sch. Bus., bd. trustees; mem. bd. advisors Coll. William and Mary Sch. Bus. 1st lt. U.S. Army, 1967-69. Mem. Am. Bankruptcy Inst., N.Y. Soc. Security Analysts, Boston Security Analysts Soc., Am. Statis. Assn., Assn. Investment Mgmt. and Rsch. Home: Gaston Farm Rd Greenwich CT 06831 Office: 461 Fifth Ave New York NY 10017-6234 Office Phone: 212-867-9090.

SHENKMAN, RICHARD BENNETT, journalist, historian; b. N.Y.C., Dec. 23, 1954; s. Sidney and Phyllis Ann Shenkman; m. John Walter Stucky, Oct. 20, 1965. BA in History, Vassar Coll., 1976. Editor History News Network, Seattle, 2001—. Author: (history book) Presidential Ambition: Gaining Power at any Cost, 2000. Recipient Rocky Mountain Emmy award, Rocky Mountain Emmy, 1991. Home: Apt 103 2120 8th Ave N Seattle WA 98109 Office: History News Network Ste 220 119 S Main St Seattle WA 98104 Office Phone: 206-228-4386. Personal E-mail: editor@historynewsnetwork.org.

SHENON, PHILIP, journalist; b. San Francisco, June 26, 1959; s. Peter and Philippa (Richards) Shenon. BA in English Lit., Brown U., 1981. Reporter N.Y. Times, N.Y.C., 1983—85, corr. Washington, 1985—90, S.E. Asia corr. Bangkok, 1991—95, def. corr. Washington, 1996—97, diplomatic corr., 1997—99, investigative corr., 2000—. Office: NY Times Washington Bur 1627 I St NW Washington DC 20006-4007

SHEON, AARON, art historian, educator; b. Toledo, Oct. 7, 1937; s. Benjamin William and Katherine (Rappoport) S.; m. Martine Bruel, Jan. 26, 1963 (div. 1986); children: Sandrine, Nicolas; m. Jill Belasco, Nov. 11, 2000. BA, U. Mich., 1959, MA, 1960; M.F.A. (Wilson fellow), Princeton U., 1962, PhD, 1966; postgrad., U. Paris, 1962-63. Staff officer, dir. gen.'s cabinet UNESCO, Paris, 1963-66; asst. prof. U. Pitts., 1966-69, asso. prof., 1969-78, acting chmn. dept. fine arts, 1969, 79-80, dir. univ. program, 1974-75, prof. art history, 1979—2003, prof. emeritus, 2004; vis. prof. Carnegie-Mellon U., 1981, 2002—03. Vis. exhbn. curator Mus. Art, Carnegie Inst., Pitts., 1977-81; program cons. Nat. Endowment Arts and Humanities, 1978-85; visual arts cons. Pa. Arts Council, 1981; vis. mem. Inst. for Advanced Study, Princeton, 1984-85 Author: The Gosman Collection, 1969, Monticelli, His Contemporaries, His Influence, 1978, Organic Vision, The Architecture of Peter Berndtson, 1980, Monticelli, 1986, Paul Guigou, 1987. Recipient Charles E. Merrill faculty award, 1968; Chancellor Bowman award, 1976; Honor award Pa. Soc. Architects, 1982, Innovation award in tchg. Art History Course for Blind Students U. Pitts., 2001; grantee Ford Found., 1967, NEH, 1979; Gould Arts Found. fellow, 1986; Bellet Teaching award, 2002, Innovation in Tchg. award, 2003. Mem. Coll. Art Assn., Société de l'histoire de l'art français, Am. Assn. of Mus. Office: U Pitts Dept History Arts & Arch Pittsburgh PA 15260

SHEP, ROBERT LEE, editor, publisher, textile book researcher; b. L.A., Feb. 27, 1933; s. Milton and Ruth (Miller) Polen S. BA, U. Calif., Berkeley, 1955; student, Royal Acad. Dramatic Art, London, 1956; B Fgn. Trade, Am. inst. Fgn. Trade, 1960. Asst. area mgr. fgn. dept. Max Factor, Hollywood, Calif., 1960-65; editor, pub. The Textile Booklist, Lopez Island, Wash., 1980-84; freelance writer/book reviewer/libr. appraiser/book repairer. Sponsor Triannual R.L. Shep Symposium, L.A. County Mus. Art, R.L. Shep Book award Textile Soc. Am., R.L. Shep Endowment, UCLA Fowner Mus.; curator of art Vashon Cmty. Care Ctr. Author: Cleaning and Repairing Books, 1980, Cleaning and Care for Books, 1983, Bhutan - Fibre Forum, 1984, Civil War Gentleman, 1994, Late Victorian Women's Tailoring, 1997, Regency Etiquette, 1997, Early Victorian Men, 2001; co-author: (annotated editl) The Costume or Annals of Fashion, 1986, Dress and Cloak Cutter: Women's Costume 1877-1882, 1987; Federalist and Regency Costume: 1790-1819, 1998, Shirts and Men's Haberdashery 1840's to 1920's; editor: The Handbook of Practical Cutting, 2d rev. edit., 1986, RAGS: Quarterly Revs. Costume, Clothing & Ethnic Textile Books; pub. Ladies' Guide to Needle Work, 1986, Edwardian Ladies' Tailoring, 1990, Art of Cutting and History of English Costume, 1987; editor, pub. Tailoring of the Belle Epoque, 1991, Late Georgian Costume, 1991, Civil War Cooking, 1992, Art in Dress, 1993, Minister's Complete Guide to Practical Cutting, 1993, Freaks of Fashion, 1993, 1999, The Great War Fashions of the 1910s Women's costume 1877-1885, 2002.; pub. Civil War Era Etiquette, 1988, Ladies Self Instr., 1988; mem. editl. bd. The Cutter's Rsch. Jor. Bd. dirs. AIDS Care and Edn. Svcs., Pacific Textiles. Mem. Costume Soc. London, Costume Soc. Am. (bd. dirs. 1985-87, bd. dirs. region V 2000—), Costume Soc. Ont., Mendocino County HIV Consortium (mem. steering com.), Australian Costume and Textile Soc., U.S. Inst. Theatre Tech., Textile Soc. Am., Seattle Textile and Rug Soc. E-mail: rlshep@cablespeed.com.

SHEPARD, BEATRICE L. retired microbiologist, historian; b. Hillsdale, Mich., May 15, 1919; d. James Wesley Shepard and Ona Ola Kinney. AB in Zoolog., U. Calif., Berkeley, 1940. Regional lab. dir. L.A. County Health Dept., L.A., 1945-46; sr. biologist, sr. chemist S.E. Regional Lab., Juneau, Alaska, 1946-67; acting chief of labs. Alaska Dept. Health & Social Svcs., Juneau, 1967-70; microbiologist in charge S.E. Regional Lab., Alaska Dept. Health and Social Svcs., 1967—77; ret., 1977. Chemist L.A. County Health Dept., 1944-45, L.A. County Gen. Hosp., 1943-44; dir. pub. health lab. Health Dept. Riverside (Calif.) County, 1942-43. Author: Praise the Lord and Pass the Penicillin, 1979; co-author: Have Gospel Tent, Will Travel, History of 100 Years of Alaskan Methodism, 1986; editor: (newsletter) Western Cir. Rider, 1998—, Eagle River United Meth. Camp, 1998—; contbr. articles to profl. jours., chapters to books. Docent Alaska State Mus., 1992—; mem. Juneau Borough Commn. on Aging, 1997—; curator Alaska State Mus., 2003; mem. gen. commn. archives and history United Meth. Ch. Archives Ctr., Madison, NJ, 1988—96; historian Alaska Meth. Ch., Alaska Missionary Conf., Anchorage, 1980—; bd. dirs., advocacy chair Mus. Alaska, 1992—; sec. bd. dirs. Eagle River Meth. Camp, 1955—; bd. dirs. Western Jurisdictional Commn. on Archives and History, 1984—; chair Alaska Missionary Conf. Commn. on Archives and History, 1980—. Named Outstanding Lay Person of Yr. award Alaska Missionary Conf. of United Meth. Ch., 1986; recipient Meritorious Health Svc. award Alaska Pub. Health Assn., 1990. Mem.: Friends of Alaska State Mus. (hon.; life), Museums Alaska (hon.; life). Avocation: photography. Home: 12585 Glacier Hwy Juneau AK 99801 E-mail: BShep98308@aol.com.

SHEPARD, DAVID HASPEL, film restoration specialist; b. N.Y.C., Oct. 22, 1940; s. Bertram David Shepard and Marjorie (Haspel) Markley; m. Kimberly Fetter, Mar. 26, 1977 (div.); 1 child, Benjamin Baker. AB, Hamilton Coll., 1962; MA, U. Pa., 1963. Asst. prof. theatre Pa. State U., State College, 1965-68; film acquisitions mgr., programmer Am. Film Inst., Washington, 1968-73; v.p. Blackhawk Films, Inc., Davenport, Iowa, 1973-76; spl. projects officer Dirs. Guild Am., Hollywood, Calif., 1976-87; adj. prof. cinema-TV U. So. Calif., L.A., 1982—2002; owner Film Preservation Assocs., Hat Creek, Calif., 1989-2000; managing dir. Film Preservation Assocs., Inc., 2000—. Trustee Internat. Film Seminars, N.Y.C., 1972-82; mem. adv. bd. Hollywood (Calif.) Entertainment Mus., 1984—, San Francisco Silent Film Festival, 1998—. Prodr. (video restoration series) Chaplin: A Legacy of Laughter, 1992-93, Masterworks of D.W. Griffith, 1992/2002, Landmarks of Early Soviet Cinema, 1992—, Great British Documentary Movement, 1993-2003, Golden Age of German Cinema, 1994—, Art of Buster Keaton, 1995, Douglas Fairbanks: King of Hollywood, 1996, Cecil B. De Mille: The Visionary Years, 1997— Slapstick encyclopedia, 1998, Les Vampires (1915 serial), 1998, Lon Chaney: Behind the Masks, 1997-2003, Valentino Lives!, 2002. Recipient Preservation award Soc. Cinephiles, 1970, 95, 2 Emmy awards Acad. TV Arts & Scis., 1973, Scholarship and Preservation award Internat. Documentary Assn., 1989, Prix Jean Mitry, Giornate des Cinema Muto, Pordenone, Italy, 1993, Saturn award Acad. Sci. Fiction, Horror and Fantasy Films, 1999, Mel Novikoff award San Francisco Internat. Film Festival, 2000. Mem.: Soc. Cinema and Media Studies (hon. life), Acad. Motion Picture Arts and Scis. Home: PO Box 71 Hat Creek CA 96040-0071 Office Phone: 530-335-7420. E-mail: DShepFilm@aol.com.

SHEPARD, DONALD J. insurance company executive; MBA, U. Chgo. Various mgmt. positions Life Investors, Inc., 1970-85; exec. v.p., COO Life Investors, Inc. (consolidated with AEGON), 1985-89; chmn., pres., CEO AEGON USA, Balt., 1989—2002; mem. exec. bd. AEGON N.V., 1992—, chmn., 2002—. Bd. dirs. AEGON USA, Mercantile Bankshares Corp., CSX Corp., U.S. C. of C. Bd. dirs. Balt. Symphony Orch.; trustee Johns Hopkins Health Sys. Corp., Johns Hopkins Hosp., Johns Hopkins U., Walters Art Gallery. Office: AEGON NV AEGON plein 50 PO Box 202 2501 CE The Hague Netherlands*

SHEPARD, DONALD SLOANE, public policy research educator; b. N.Y.C., Sept. 15, 1947; s. Bertram David Shepard and Marjorie (Haspel) Markley; m. Emily A. Maitin, Aug. 17, 1980; children: Melissa R. Maitin-Shepard, Jeremy B. Maitin-Shepard. BA, Harvard U., 1969, M in Pub. Policy, 1973, PhD, 1976. Lectr. U. Nairobi, Kenya, 1970-71; sr. economist Mass. Dept. Pub. Health, Boston, 1977-79; dir. econ. rsch. Vets. Adminstrn., West Roxbury, Mass., 1979-85; lectr. Harvard U., Cambridge, Mass., 1977-80, assoc. prof., 1980-91; prof. Brandeis U., Waltham, Mass., 1991—. Mem. pub. policy adv. com. Am. Found. for AIDS Rsch., Washington, 1991-95; vis. lectr. Harvard U., 1992-99; adj. faculty Boston U., 1995—; affiliated faculty Brown U., Providence, 1995—. Author: Assessing Costs for Cost-Effectiveness Analysis, 1988, Analysis of Hospital Costs: A Manual for Managers, 2000; mem. editl. bd. Evaluation and Program Planning, 1977-92. Bd. advisors Sabin Vaccine Found., New Canaan, Conn., 1994—; bd. councilors Pediat. Dengue Vaccine Initiative, 1992—; den leader Cub Scouts Am., Wellesley, Mass., 1995-97. Grad. fellow NSF, 1971; rsch. grantee Nat. Inst. on Drug Abuse and Nat. Inst. on Alcohol Abuse and Alcoholism, 1993—. Mem. APHA, Mass. Pub. Health Assn., Phi Beta Kappa. Jewish. Avocations: cross country skiing, swimming. Home: 16 Cranmore Rd Wellesley MA 02481-1329 Office: Brandeis U Heller Sch 415 South St Waltham MA 02454-9110 Office Phone: 781-736-3975. E-mail: shepard@brandeis.edu.

SHEPARD, GEOFFREY CARROLL, insurance executive; b. Santa Barbara, Calif., Nov. 7, 1944; s. James J. and Barbara (Hoose) S.; m. Saundra Gayle Carlton, Jan. 10, 1973; children: Jonathan Pettus, William Dabney. BA, Whittier Coll., 1966; JD, Harvard U., 1969. Bar: Wash. 1970, D.C. 1972, Pa. 1977, U.S. Supreme Ct. 1973. White House fellow, 1969-70; staff asst. to Pres. White House, 1970-72, assoc. dir. domestic coun., 1972-75; sr. assoc. Steptoe & Johnson, Washington, 1975-77; sr. v.p., assoc. gen. counsel CIGNA Corp., Phila., 1977-91; sr. v.p., gen. counsel, corp. sec. Reliance Ins. Group, Phila., 1991-94; pres. corp. divsn. Karr Barth Assocs., Phila., 1994—. Mem. pvt. security adv. coun. Dept. Justice, 1975-77. Adv. coun. on gen. govt. Rep. Nat. Com., 1977-78; Phila. Cmty. Leadership Seminar, 1978-79, exec. com. Boy Scouts Am., Phila, 1981-83, exec. bd. Valley Forge Coun., 1994-96; mem. exec. bd. Cradle of Liberty Coun., 1996-2001; bd. dirs. Sacred Heart Med. Ctr., 1983-85, Swarthmore Presbyn. Ch., 1984-86, 97-2000, Wallingford Hills Civic Assn., 1983-85, Com. of 70, 1985-87, Acad. Natural Scis., Phila., 1987-93, Pub. Affairs Coun., Washington, 1986-89, Episc. Acad., 1987-90; mem. exec. com. White House Fellows Regional Selection Panel, 1987-93; prin. counsel Excellence in Govt., 1994-96; bd. dirs. White House Fellows Found., 1997-2000; trustee Whittier Coll., 2002—. Mem. ABA, Assn. for Advancement Life Underwriting, Pa. Bar Assn., Phila. Assn. of Life Underwriters, D.C. Bar Assn., White House Fellows Alumni Assn., Met. Club (Washington), Union League Club (Phila.), Harvard Club (N.Y.C.). Office: Karr Barth Assocs Inc Corp Divsn 40 Monument Rd Bala Cynwyd PA 19004-1797

SHEPARD, JEAN HECK, retired publishing consultant; b. N.Y.C., Feb. 2, 1930; d. Chester Reed and Anna S. (Charig) Heck; m. Lawrence Vaeth Hastings, Mar. 29, 1950 (div. 1953); 1 child, Lance Clifford Hastings; m. Daniel A. Shepard, July 26, 1954 (div. 1981); 1 child, Bradley Reed. BA, Barnard Coll., 1950; postgrad., Columbia U., 1952. Mem. sch. and libr. svc. Viking Press, N.Y.C., 1956-57; asst. dir. sch. and libr. promotion E.P. Dutton, N.Y.C., 1957-58; dir. advt. publicity and promotion Thomas Y. Crowell Co., N.Y.C., 1958-62; dir. advt. and promotion Charles Scribner's Sons, N.Y.C., 1962-67; cons. Stephen Greene Press, Brattleboro, Vt., 1970-73; mktg. mgr. A&W Publishers, N.Y.C., 1979-80, Franklin Watts Publ., N.Y.C., 1980-82; pub. 2 mags., divsn. advt. & promotion mgr. McGraw Hill Book Co., N.Y.C., 1983-85; cons. Monitor Publ. Co., N.Y.C., 1988-2000. Author: Simple Family Favorites, 1971, Herb and Spice Sampler, 1972, Cook With Wine!, 1973, Earth Watch: Notes on a Restless Planet, 1973, Harvest Home Steak Cookbook, 1974, Fresh Fruits and Vegetables, 1974, Yankee Magazine, 1972, Let Them be Sea Captains. Mem. Authors Guild, Pub. Ad Club, Am. Libr. Assn., Women's Nat. Book Assn. Methodist. Avocations: the dance, reading, writing, travel, music. Home: 73 Kingswood Dr Bethel CT 06801-1834 Office Fax: 203-798-2924. E-mail: shepardagcy@mindspring.com.

SHEPARD, JUDITH BETHEA, librarian; b. Tuscaloosa, Ala., Apr. 12, 1947; d. Odis Hamner Reynolds and Audrea Earle Thomas; m. James Crenshaw Shepard, Feb. 19, 1978; children: Angela Elaine Ashcraft, Penelope Lea Perry. BA, Ala. Coll., 1969; MLS, U. Ala., 1974. Tchr., libr. Decatur City Schs., Ala., 1969—71; libr. Gadsden Pub. Libr., Ala., 1974—76; libr., head of info. svcs. Ala. Pub. Libr. Svc., Montgomery, 1976—. Contbr. articles to profl. jours. Mem. Montgomery Mus. Fine Arts, Ala., 1999—2004, Montgomery Zool. Soc., Ala., 2002—04. Mem.: Ala. Libr. Assn. (moderator ref. and adult svcs. roundtable 2000—03). Republican. Roman Catholic. Achievements include development of State of Ala. Resource Sharing Sys. Avocations: painting, travel, reading. Home: 30 Tecumseh Dr Montgomery AL 36117 Office: Ala Pub Libr Svc 6030 Monticello Dr Montgomery AL 36130

SHEPARD, KATHRYN IRENE, public relations executive; b. Tooele, Utah, Jan. 6, 1956; d. James Lewis and Glenda Verleen (Slaughter) Clark; m. Mark L. Shepard, June 5, 1976. BA in History, Boise State U., 1980. On-air writer Sta. KTTV, Channel 11, L.A., 1982-85; publicity dir. Hollywood C. of C., Calif., 1985-87; pres. Kathy Shepard Pub. Rels., Burbank and Portland, 1987-93; dir. pub. rels. Las Vegas Hilton, 1993-94; dir. comms. Hilton Gaming, 1994-96; dir. corp. comms. Hilton Hotels Corp., 1996—97, v.p. corp. comms., 1997—. Instr. pub. rels. ext. program UCLA, 1991-92. Contbr. articles to profl. publs. Mem.: Pub. Rels. Assn. Am., Pub. Communicators L.A. (pres. 1991—92, bd. dirs. 1987—91). Avocations: genealogy, film, travel. Office: Hilton Hotels Corp PR Dept 9336 Civic Center Dr Beverly Hills CA 90210-3604 E-mail: kathy_shepard@hilton.com.

SHEPARD, RANDALL TERRY, state supreme court chief justice; b. Lafayette, Ind., Dec. 24, 1946; s. Richard Schilling and Dorothy Ione (Donlen) S.; m. Amy Wynne MacDonell, May 7, 1988; one child, Martha MacDonell. AB cum laude, Princeton U., 1969; JD, Yale U., 1972; LLM, U. Va., 1995; LLD (hon.), U. So. Ind., 1995. Bar: Ind. 1972, U.S. Dist. Ct. (so. dist.) Ind. 1972. Spl. asst. to under sec. U.S. Dept. Transp., Washington, 1972-74; exec. asst. to mayor City of Evansville, Ind., 1974-79; judge Vanderburgh Superior Ct., Evansville, 1980-85; assoc. justice Ind. Supreme Ct., Indpls., 1985-87, chief justice, 1987—. Instr. U. Evansville, 1975-78, Indiana U., 1995, 99 Author: Preservation Rules and Regulations, 1980; contbr. articles to profl. publs. Bd. advisors Nat. Trust for Hist. Preservation, 1980-87, chmn. bd. advisors, 1983-85, trustee, 1987-96; dir. Hist. Landmarks Found. Ind., 1983—, chmn., 1989-92, hon. chmn., 1992—; chmn. State Student Assistance Commn. on Ind., 1981-85; chmn. Ind. Commn. on Bicentennial of U.S. Constn., 1986-91; vice chmn. Vanderburgh County Rep. Ctrl. Com., 1977-80. Recipient Friend of Media award Cardinal States chpt. Sigma Delta Chi, 1979, Disting. Svc. award Evansville Jaycees, 1982, Herbert Harley award Am. Judicature Soc., 1992. Mem. ABA (coun. mem. sect. on legal edn. 1991—, chair sect. on legal edn. 1997—, immediate past chair appellate judges conf. 1997-98), Ind. Bar Assn., Ind. Judges Assn., Princeton Club (N.Y.), Capitol Hill Club (Washington), Columbia Club (Indpls.). Republican. Methodist. Home: 3644 Totem Ln Indianapolis IN 46208-4171 Office: Ind Supreme Ct 304 State House Indianapolis IN 46204-2213

SHEPARD, ROBERT M. lawyer, investment banker, engineer; b. Amityville, N.Y., Feb. 15, 1932; s. Sidney M. and Undine L. (Lehmann) Shapiro; m. Barbara S. Stannard, June 25, 1955 (div. 1980); children: Karen Michele Shepard Sweer, Daniel Robert; m. Joanne E. Devlin, May 16, 1981 (div. 1993); m. Martha Kothe, Nov. 24, 1999. B.C.E., Cornell U., 1954; MBA, Hofstra Coll., 1960; LL.B., Yale U., 1963; LLM, NYU, 1988. Bar: N.Y. 1964; registered profl. engr., N.Y., Conn. Project engr. Lockwood Kessler & Bartlett, Syosset, N.Y., 1956-60; assoc. atty. Cravath, Swaine & Moore, N.Y.C. and Paris, 1963-70; gen. ptnr. Kuhn, Loeb & Co., N.Y.C., 1970-77; sr. v.p. Donaldson, Lufkin & Jenrette, N.Y.C., 1977-83; gen. ptnr. Donovan Leisure Newton & Irvine, N.Y.C., 1983-89, Adler & Shepard, N.Y.C., 1989-91, Shepard & van Essche, N.Y.C., 1991, Ballon Stoll Bader & Nadler, P.C., N.Y.C., 1992—. Note and comment editor: Yale Law Jour., 1962-63. Bd. dirs. N.Y. Grand Opera, Regency Whist Club. Recipient Fuertes Medal Cornell U., 1953 Mem. ABA, Am. N.Y. State Bar Assn., Pub. Power Assn., Nat. Assn. Bond Lawyers, Order of Coif, Union League Club, Regency Whist Club, Inc., Tau Beta Pi, Chi Epsilon. Home: 750 Park Ave Apt 2C New York NY 10021-4252 Office: Ballon Stoll Bader & Nadler 1450 Broadway New York NY 10018-2201

SHEPARD, ROGER NEWLAND, psychologist, educator; b. Palo Alto, Calif., Jan. 30, 1929; s. Orson Cutler and Grace (Newland) S.; m. Barbaranne Bradley, Aug. 18, 1952; children: Newland Chenoweth, Todd David, Shenna Esther. BA, Stanford U., 1951; PhD, Yale U., 1955; AM (hon.), Harvard U., 1966; ScD (hon.), Rutgers U., 1992. Rsch. assoc. Naval Research Lab., 1955-56; rsch. fellow Harvard, 1956-58; mem. tech. staff Bell Telephone Labs., 1958-66, dept. head, 1963-66; prof. psychology Harvard U., 1966-68, dir. psychol. labs., 1967-68; prof. psychology Stanford U., 1968-98, Ray Lyman Wilbur prof. social sci., 1989-96, Ray Lyman Wilbur prof. emeritus social sci., 1996—. Guggenheim fellow Center for Advanced Study in Behavioral Scis., 1971-72; recipient, N.Y. Acad. Scis. award, 1987, Nat. Medal of Sci., 1995, Gold medal Am. Psychol. Found., 2000. Fellow AAAS, APA (pres. exptl. div. 1980-81, Disting. Sci. Contbn. award 1976); mem. Am. Acad. Arts and Scis., Nat. Acad. Scis., Psychometric Soc. (pres. 1973-74), Psychonomic Soc., Soc. Exptl. Psychologists (Howard Crosby Warren medal 1981), Am. Philos. Soc., Yale Grad. Sch. Alumni Assn. (Wilbur Cross medal 2001).

SHEPARD, SAM (SAMUEL SHEPARD ROGERS), playwright, actor; b. Ft. Sheridan, Ill., Nov. 5, 1943; s. Samuel Shepard and Jane Elaine (Schook) Rogers; m. O-Lan Johnson Dark, Nov. 9, 1969 (div.); 1 child, Jesse Mojo; life ptnr. Jessica Lange; children: Hannah Jane, Samuel Walker. Student, Mt. San Antonio Jr. Coll., Walnut, Calif., 1961-62. Playwright-in-residence Magic Theatre, San Francisco. Author: (plays) Cowboys, The Rock Garden, 1964, 4-H Club, Up to Thursday, Dog, Rocking Chair, 1965, Chicago, 1965 (Obie award, 1966), Icarus's Mother, 1965 (Obie award, 1966), Fourteen Hundred Thousand, 1966, Red Cross, 1966 (Obie award, 1966), Melodrama Play, 1966 (Obie award, 1968), La Turista, 1967 (Obie award, 1967), Cowboys #2, 1967, Forensic and the Navigators, 1967 (Obie award, 1968), The Holy Ghostly, The Unseen Hand, 1969, Operation Sidewinder, Shaved Splits, 1970, Mad Dog Blues, Terminal, (with Patti Smith) Cowboy Mouth, Black Bog Beast Bait, 1971, The Tooth of Crime, 1972 (Obie award, 1973), Blue Bitch, (with Megan Terry and Jean-Claude van Itallie) Nightwalk, 1973, Geography of a Horse Dreamer, Little Ocean, Killer's Head, 1974, Action, 1974 (Obie award, 1975), Starving Class, 1977, Buried Child, 1978 (Obie award, 1977, Pulitzer Prize in drama, 1979, Obie award, 1979), Tongues, Savage/Love, Seduced, 1979, True West, 1981, Fool for Love, 1983 (Obie award, 1984), Superstitions, The Sad Lament of Pecos Bill on the Eve of Killing his Wife, 1983, A Lie of the Mind, 1985 (New York Drama Critics' Circle award, 1986), States of Shock, 1991, Simpatico, 1993, (collections of plays) Five Plays by Sam Shepard, 1967, The Unseen Hand and Other Plays, 1971, 1986, Mad Dog Blues and Other Plays,

1972, The Tooth of Crime and Geography of a Horse Dreamer, 1974, Angel City, Curse of the Starving Class and Other Plays, 1976, Buried Child, Seduced, Suicide in B-Flat, 1979, (collection of plays) Four Two-Act Plays by Sam Shepard, 1980, Chicago and Other Plays, Seven Plays, 1981, Fool for Love and The Sad Lament of Pecos Bill on the Eve of Killing His Wife, 1983, Fool For Love and Other Plays, 1984, 1986, contbr. to Oh! Calcutta, 1976, (with Bob Dylan) Renaldo and Clara, 1978, (collection of plays) Paris, Texas, 1984, (other writings) Rolling Thunder Logbook, 1977, Hawk Moon: A Book of Short Stories, Poems and Monologues, 1981, Motel Chronicles, 1982; dir.(writer): (plays) Fool for Love, 1983, A Lie of the Mind, 1985; (screenplays) Far North, 1988, Silent Tongue, 1993; actor: (films) Renaldo and Clara, Days of Heaven, 1978, Resurrection, 1980, Raggedy Man, 1981, Frances, 1982, The Right Stuff, 1983 (Academy award nomination best supporting actor, 1984), Country, 1984, Fool for Love, 1985, Crimes of the Heart, 1986, Baby Boom, 1987, Steel Magnolias, 1989, Hot Spot, 1990, Bright Angel, Defenseless, 1991, Thunderheart, 1992, The Pelican Brief, 1993, Safe Passage, 1994, The Good Old Boys, 1995, Curtain Call, The Only Thrill, 1997, All the Pretty Horses, 2000, The Pledge, 2001, Swordfish, 2001, Black Hawk Down, 2001, Leo, 2002; (TV films, performance) Streets of Laredo, 1995, Lily Dale, 1996, Purgatory, Dash & Lilly, 1999, Hamlet, 2000 (nominated for Golden Globe, Best Actor). Named to Theater Hall of Fame, 1994; recipient Nat. Inst. and Am. Acad. Arts and Letters award for lit., 1974, Creative Arts award Brandeis U., 1975; grantee Rockefeller Found., 1967, Guggenheim Found., 1968, 1971; Fellow, U. Minn., 1966, Yale U., 1967. Mem.: Am. Acad. and Inst. of Arts and Letters. Office: Internat Creative Mgmt 8942 Wilshire Blvd Beverly Hills CA 90211-1934

SHEPARD, STEPHEN BENJAMIN, journalist, magazine editor; b. N.Y.C., July 20, 1939; s. William and Ruth Shepard; m. Lynn Povich, Sept. 16, 1979; children: Sarah, Ned. BS, CCNY, 1961; MS, Columbia U., 1964. Reporter, editor, writer Bus. Week, N.Y.C., 1966—75; asst. prof., dir. Walter Bagehot fellowship program econs. and bus. journalism Columbia U., N.Y.C., 1975—76; sr. editor Newsweek, N.Y.C., 1976—81; editor Saturday Rev., N.Y.C., 1981—82; exec. editor Bus. Week mag., N.Y.C., 1982—84, editor in chief, 1984—. Adj. prof. Columbia Grad Sch. Journalism, 1971—75. Bd. visitors Columbia Grad. Sch. Journalism. Recipient Lifetime Achievement award, Gerald Loeb Found., 1999, Henry Johnson Fisher award, Mag. Publs. Am., 2000, President's award, Overseas Press Club, 2003. Mem.: Coun. Fgn. Rls., Am. Soc. Mag. Editors (v.p. 1990—92, pres. 1992—94, Hall of Fame 1999), Century Assn. Office: Business Week McGraw Hill Inc 43rd Fl 1221 Ave Of The Americas New York NY 10020-1001

SHEPARD, STEVEN LOUIS, graphic artist, painter; b. Port Arthur, Texas, Mar. 23, 1955; Attended, Workshops Contemporary Art, Santa Fe, 1976; BFA (hon.), U. South Ala., 1977. Author: Chgo. Pub. Libr., 1987; one-man shows include Wake Forest U., Winston - Salem, 1988, Southeastern Ctr. for Contemporary Art, 1997, U. West Fla., 1998, Miss. Mus. Art, Jackson, 1999; artist (permanent collections) Mobile Mus. Art, Ala.; murals commd. by J.L. Scott Marine Edn. Ctr., Biloxi, Miss., murals commd. by George Ohr Mus., works pub. in various publ.; illustrator Elvis Hornbill: Internat. Bus. Bird, 1991, artist (group shows) U. South Ala., 1988, 2002, Mont. Mus. Art, 2003. Mem.: Nat. Assn. Ind. Artists. Address: America Oh Yes Gallery Joe Adams PO Box 3078 Hilton Head Island SC 29928-0078 E-mail: shepart@datasync.com.

SHEPARD, THOMAS HILL, physician, educator; b. Milw., May 22, 1923; s. Francis Parker and Elizabeth Rhodes (Buchner) S.; m. Alice B. Kelly, June 24, 1946; children: Donna, Elizabeth, Ann. AB, Amherst Coll., 1945; MD, U. Rochester, 1948. Intern Strong Meml. Hosp., Rochester, NY, 1948-49, resident, 1950-52, Albany (N.Y.) Med. Ctr., 1949-50; pediatric endocrine fellow Johns Hopkins Hosp., 1954-55; pediatrician U. Wash., Seattle, 1955-61, teratologist, 1961—, prof. pediat., head ctrl. lab. for human embryology, 1961-93, prof. emeritus, 1993—; embryologist dept. anatomy U. Fla., 1961-62; rsch. assoc. dept. embryology Carnegie Inst., 1962, U. Copenhagen, 1963. Cons. NIH, FDA, EPA, 1971-; vis. prof. pediat. U. Geneva, 1972, 73-74. Author: A Catalog of Teratogenic Agents, 1973, 11th edit., 2004; contbr. articles to profl. jours. Served with U.S. Army, 1946—48, served with USAF, 1952—54. Mem.: Am. Pediatric Soc., Western Soc. Pediatric Rsch. (pres. 1970), Orgn. for Teratogen Answering Svcs. (hon. Thomas Shepard Ann. lectr.), Japanese Teratology Soc. (hon.), Teratology Soc. (hon.; pres. 1968). Home: 3015 98th Ave NE Bellevue WA 98004-1818 Office: U Wash Sch Medicine Dept Pediatrics Seattle WA 98195-0001

SHEPARD, THOMAS ROCKWELL, III, advertising executive; b. Greenwich, Conn., Apr. 21, 1951; s. Thomas Rockwell Jr. and Nancy (Kruidenier) S.; m. Margaret O'Neal, Sept. 1, 1972; children: Amanda Marie, Thomas Rockwell IV, Brian Dickinson. BA, Amherst Coll., 1973. Salesman Union Carbide Battery Products, N.Y.C., 1974-78; advt. dir. Good Housekeeping mag., 1984—90; pub. Country Living mag., 1990—93, Redbook mag., 1993—97; v.p. network advt. sales Manursing Club, N.Y. Athletic Club; sr. v.p. network advt. sales Hearst HomeArts, 1997—99; pres. King Features Syndicate, N.Y.C., 1999—. Office: King Features Ltd 2nd Fl 888 7th Ave New York NY 10106-0003 E-mail: trshepano@hearst.com.

SHEPARD, W. BRUCE, academic administrator; m. Cyndie Shepard. BA in Polit. Sci., U. Calif., Riverside, 1969, MS in Polit. Sci., 1970, PhD in Polit. Sci., 1972. Prof. polit. sci., provost, v.p. acad. affairs Ea. Oreg. U., LaGrande, 1995—2002; mem. faculty dept. polit. sci. Oreg. State U., Oreg.; chancellor U. Wis., Green Bay, Wis., 2002—. Vis. scientist Population Study Ctr., Seattle; vis. fellow Sch. Comm. and Liberal Studies MItchell Coll. Advanced Edn., Bathurst, Australia. Office: U Wis Office Chancellor 2420 Nicolet Dr Green Bay WI 54311-7001

SHEPARD, WILLIAM SETH, government official, diplomat, writer; b. Boston, June 7, 1935; s. Robinson and Myra Ellen (Foster) S.; m. Lois Rosalie Burke, June 25, 1960; children— Stephanie Lee, Cynthia Robin, Warren Burke (dec.) AB cum laude, Wesleyan U., Middletown, Conn., 1957; JD, Harvard U., Cambridge, Mass., 1961. Bar: N.H. 1961, U.S. Ct. Mil. Appeals 1962 U.S. Supreme Ct., 1970. Aide to ambs. Henry Cabot Lodge and Ellsworth Bunker, Am. embassy, Saigon, Vietnam, 1966-67; staff officer Exec. Secretariat Dept. of State, Washington, 1967-69; consul, polit. officer Am. Embassy, Budapest, Hungary, 1970-73; desk officer Hungarian affairs Dept. State, Washington, 1973-75; desk officer Singapore and Malaysian affairs Dept. of State, Washington, 1975-77; dep. polit. counselor Am. embassy, Athens, Greece, 1978-80; consul gen. Am. Consulate Gen., Bordeaux, France, 1983-85; dir. Office Congl. Affairs, ACDA, Washington, 1987-89; cons. to gen. counsel USDA, Washington, 1991-92. Lectr. internat. law U. Singapore, 1965-66; CEO The Shepard Internat. Group, Inc., 1994—. Author: Consular Tales, 2001, Murder on the Danube, 2001, Vintage Murder, 2002, Foreign Service Tales, 2002, Shepard's Guide to Mastering French Wines, 2003; wine editor: Bonjour Paris, 2002—. Candidate for Rep. nomination 8th Md. Congl. Dist., 1985-86, Rep. nominee for Gov. of Md., 1990, candidate, 1994; del. Rep. Nat. Conv., 1992; Md. co-chmn. Dole Presdl. Campaign, 1996. Recipient Pro Libertate Hungariae Commemorative medallion, 1981, Pub. Svc. Leadership award U.S.-Baltic Found., 1996, George L. Plimpton Pub. Svc. award Tilton Sch., 2003; French Govt. teaching asst. and Fulbright travel grantee, 1957-58; Congl. fellow Am. Polit. Sci. Assn. and fgn. policy legis. asst. to Senator Robert Dole, 1982-83. Mem. Soc. Mayflower Desc., Gov. Bradford Compact, Soc. Desc. Colonial Govs. (chancellor gen. 1993-95), Soc. Desc. Colonial Wars, Montesquieu Acad. France (corr.), City Tavern Club (Washington), Miles River Yacht Club, Flagon and Trencher (Trencher award 2003), Les Chevaliers de Bretvin, Ordre des Compagnons de Bordeaux, Connetablie de Guyenne, La Jurade de St. Emilion, Bontemps Medoc et des Graves, Tred Avon Players. Republican. Unitarian Universalist. Avocations: reading, vintage Bordeaux wines, travel, gastronomy. Home: 4540 Boone Creek Dr Oxford MD 21654 *I remember Himalayan peaks, Asian sunsets, Greek islands and Bordeaux vineyards. Along the way, hard work in a principled cause is its own reward. In the end, family life and friends, a foyer, pets, a book worth reading, and a glass of wine matter most.*

SHEPHARD, BRUCE DENNIS, obstetrician, educator, medical writer; b. San Francisco, Apr. 21, 1944; s. Richard G. and Madelyn (Rogers) S.; children: Christopher, Carleton, Elizabeth. BA in History, U. Calif., Berkeley, 1966; MD, U. Calif., San Francisco, 1970. Diplomate Am. Bd. Obstetrics and Gynecology. Intern Jackson Meml. Hosp.-U. Miami (Fla.), 1970-71, resident in ob-gyn., 1971-74; pvt. practice Tampa, 1976—; clin. assoc. prof. obstetrics U. So. Fla. Sch. Medicine, Tampa, 1976—. Bd. dirs. Ctr. of Excellence, 1983-90, Humana Women's Hosp., Tampa, Fla., 1983-90, Gulf Coast Health Systems Agy., 1980-83, Sta. WEDU, Tampa, 2000-; mem. midwifery adv. com. Fla. Dept. Health and Human Resources, Tallahassee, 1982-86. Author: (with Carroll Shephard) The Complete Guide to Women's Health, 1982, 3d rev. edit., 1997; prin., writer, spokesperson (series of TV commls.) The Healthy Woman (Gold Link award 1987); mem. med. adv. bd. Baby Talk mag., 1995—; contbr. articles to profl. jours. and women's mags. Lectr. Continuing Edn., Inc., 2002—; mem. Agy. Health Care Adminstrn., Dept. Health and Rehab. Svcs., Fla., cert. med. expert, 2001—; v.p. Hillsborough County Med. Assn., 2003—04; med. adv. bd. Welcare HMO, 1996—2004; pres. coun. AVMED HMO, 1999—2002. Served as maj. USAF, 1974—76. Mem. AMA, Am. Coll. Obstetricians and Gynecologists (patient edn. com. 1984-86, John McCain fellow 1981), Hillsborough County Med. Assn. (v.p. 2003-04), Phi Beta Kappa. Democrat. Lutheran. Avocations: tennis, photography, golf, antique collecting, running. Home: 8649 N Himes # 1123 Tampa FL 33614 Office: 4302 N Habana Ave Ste 300 Tampa FL 33607-6316

SHEPHARD, MARK SCOTT, civil and mechanical engineering educator; b. Buffalo, Oct. 27, 1951; s. William N. and Beatrice (Hass) S.; m. Sharon L. Nirschel, Nov. 25, 1972; children: Steven W., Kari L. BS, Clarkson U., 1974; PhD, Cornell U., 1979. Asst. prof. civil engring. and mech. engring. Rensselaer Poly. Inst., Troy, N.Y., 1979-84, assoc. prof., 1984-87, prof., 1988—, dir. Sci. Computation Rsch. Ctr., 1990—, Samuel A. and Elisabeth C. Johnson Jr. prof. engring., 1993—; assoc. dir. Rensselaer Design Rsch. Ctr., Troy, N.Y., 1980-90. Vis. rsch. fellow GE Corp., R & D Schenectady, 1985, cons., 1984-87; cons. GM Rsch. Lab., Detroit, 1980—, also other orgns.; mem. tech. adv. bd. Aries Tech., Lowell, Mass., 1987-89. Editor: Engring. with Computers; mem. editl. bd. Internat. Jour. Numerical Methods Engring., Computer Methods in Applied Mechanics and Engring., Engring. Applications of Artificial Intelligence, Internat. Jour. Engring. Analysis and Design, Computational Mechanics; contbr. articles to profl. jours., chpts. to books. Fellow ASME, AIAA (assoc.), U.S. Assn. for Computational Mechanics (past pres.), Internat. Assn. for Computational Mechanics (exec. bd.); mem. Am. Soc. Engring. Edn., Am. Acad. Mechanics, Sigma Xi, Tau Beta Pi, Phi Kappa Phi. Home: 305 Algonquin Beach Rd Averill Park NY 12018-6007 Office: Rensselaer Poly Inst 110 8th St Troy NY 12180-3522

SHEPHARD, ROBERT PARRISH, historian, educator; b. Washington, Dec. 6, 1952; s. Charles Perry and Dorothy Parrish Shephard; m. Sandra Leslie Keith, July 7, 1987; 1 child, Alex. BA, Evergreen State Coll., Olympia, Wash., 1975; MA, Claremont Grad. Sch., Calif., 1981; PhD, Claremont Grad. Sch., 1985. Asst. prof. history Elmira Coll., NY, 1987—95, assoc. prof. history, 1995—. Contbr. articles to profl. jours. Fellow Danforth Grad. fellow, Danforth Found., 1977—81, Regional Vis. fellow, Inst. for European Studies, Cornell U., 1999—2002. Mem.: N.Am. Conf. on Brit. Studies, Sixteenth Century Studies Conf., Am. Hist. Assn., Phi Beta Kappa (pres. Elmira Coll. chpt. 2002—). Office: Elmira College One Park Pl Elmira NY 14901

SHEPHARD, WILLIAM DANKS, physicist, educator; b. Gary, Ind., July 8, 1933; m. Barbara Ann Parker, July 25, 1959 (dec. Apr. 26, 1996); m. Nancy S. Kavadas, May 24, 2003. BA, Wesleyan U., 1954; MS, U. Wis., 1955, PhD, 1962. Asst. prof. U. Ky., Lexington, 1960—63; Fulbright sr. rsch. fellow Max Planck Inst. fur Physik und Astrophysik, Munich, 1962—63; asst. then assoc. prof. U. Notre Dame, Ind., 1963—73, prof., 1973—2004; guest prof. U. Nijmegen, Netherlands, 1975—76; prof. emeritus, 2004. Vis. scientist Fermilab, Batavia, Ill., 1971—; guest scientist Stanford Linear Accelerator Ctr., Palo Alto, Calif., 1980—; vis. scientist Brookhaven Nat. Lab., Upton, NY, 1960—; guest physicist and cons. Argonne Nat. Lab., Ill., 1963—80; organizer XII Internat. Symposium on Multiparticle Dynamics, Notre Dame, 1981. Editor: Multiparticle Dynamics 1981, 1982; contbr. over 240 articles to profl. jours. Deacon 1st Presbyn. Ch., South Bend, Ind., 1997—99, v.p., 1999—2000, 2003—04, elder, 2000—02, pres., 2001—02, elder, 2004—. Fellow Predoctoral fellow, NSF, 1954—55, 1956—57; grantee Rsch. grantee, 1963—; scholar Fulbright Sr. Rsch. scholar, U.S. Govt., 1962—63. Mem.: AAUP, Am. Phys. Soc., Sigma Xi (pres., Notre Dame chpt. 1977—78), Phi Beta Kappa (pres. Epsilon chpt. Ind. 1991—93), Chi Psi. Office: Univ Notre Dame Dept Physics 225 Nieuwland Notre Dame IN 46556-5670 E-mail: shephard.1@nd.edu.

SHEPHERD, ALAN J. construction executive, management consultant; b. Bklyn., Jan. 15, 1942; s. Morris Elijah and Jean (Birnbaum) Shapiro; children: Robin Elyse, Kevin Peter BS in Mech. Engring., Mich. State U.; MS in Indsl. Engring., Wayne State U., 1966. Mgmt. trainee Chrysler Corp., Detroit, 1964-65, product engr., 1965-66; exec. v.p. Bruce Erts & Assocs., Southfield, Mich., 1966-70; pres. Creative Mgmt. Group, Inc., Southfield, Mich., 1970-76, chmn. bd., 1976, pvt. cons., 1976-79. Dir. planning and coordination Mgmt. Support Assocs., Tel Aviv, Israel, 1979-81, gen. mgr., 1981-82; mgmt. cons. MSA Consortium, Washington, 1982-83; regional mktg. dir. Hill Internat., Washington, 1983-84; mng. v.p. spl. projects CRS Sirrine, Inc., Washington, 1984-85; dir. advanced mgmt. program BDM Corp., McLean, Va., 1986-89; v.p. Hill Internat., Inc., Willingboro, N.J., 1989-90; v.p. mktg. and bus. devel. AWD Techs., Inc., Rockville, Md., 1990-94; dir. bus. devel. and cons. Brown & Root, Inc., Washington, 1994-98; v.p. Montgomery Watson, Washington, 1998—. Mem. Am. Inst. Indsl. Engrs., Project Mgmt. Inst., Soc. Am. Mil. Engrs. Office: Montgomery Watson 819 7th St NW Ste 200 Washington DC 20001-3771

SHEPHERD, CYBILL LYNNE, actress, singer; b. Memphis, Feb. 18, 1950; d. William Jennings and Patty Shobe (Micci) S.; m. David Ford, Nov. 19, 1978 (div., 1982); 1 child, Clementine; m. Bruce Oppenheim, March 1, 1987 (div., 1990); children: Molly Ariel and Cyrus Zachariah (twins) Student, Hunter Coll., 1969, Coll. of New Rochelle, 1970, Washington Sq. Coll., NYU, 1971, U. So. Calif., 1972, NYU, 1973. Appeared in motion pictures Last Picture Show, 1971, The Heartbreak Kid, 1973, Daisy Miller, 1974, At Long Last Love, 1975, Taxi Driver, 1976, Special Delivery, 1976, Silver Bears, 1977, The Lady Vanishes, 1978, Earthright, 1980, The Return, 1986, Chances Are, 1988, Texasville, 1990, Alice, 1990, Once Upon a Crime, 1992, Married to It, 1993; star TV series The Yellow Rose, 1983-84, Moonlighting, 1985-89, Cybill, 1994-98 (also prodr.); TV films include A Guide for the Married Woman, 1978, Secrets of a Married Man, 1984, Seduced, 1985, The Long Hot Summer, 1985, Which Way Home, 1991, Memphis, 1992 (also co-writer, co-exec. prodr.), Stormy Weathers, 1992, Telling Secrets, 1993, There Was a Little Boy, 1993, Journey of the Heart, 1997, Due East, 2002, Martha, Inc.: The Story of Martha Stewart, 2003; record albums include Cybill Does It To Cole Porter, 1974, Cybill and Stan Getz, 1977, Vanilla with Phineas Newborn, Jr, 1978; appeared in stage plays A Shot in the Dark, 1977, Picnic, 1980, Vanities, 1981, The Muse, 1999, Marine Life, 2000; co-author Cybill Disobedience, 2000.

SHEPHERD, DONNA LOU, interior designer; b. Uvalde, Tex., Sept. 25, 1948; d. Herbert Quarrels Jr. and Wanna Lou (Ray) Haile; m. Richard Ray Shepherd, June 2003; children from previous marriage: Laura Anne Howell, Christopher J. Huffman. BS, U. Houston, 1969, MEd, 1973. Owner Rainbow Design LLC, Littleton, Colo., 1975—. Spkr. in field. Designer Parade of Homes, 1989, Jr. Symphony Guild Showhome, 1996, designs featured in Colo. Homes and Lifestyles, Denver Post. Founder, pres. Prime Time Today, Littleton. Republican. Baptist. Avocations: water fitness, fly fishing, whitewater rafting. Office: PO Box 3285 Littleton CO 80161-3285

SHEPHERD, DOUGLAS, hospital administrator; b. Aug. 1, 1944; married; three children. BA in Zoology, Miami U., 1966, postgrad., 1966-68; MHA, U. Mich., 1970. Grad. rsch. asst. in zoology Miami U., Oxford, Ohio, 1967-68; resident Ohio State U. Hosp., Columbus, 1969; asst. to adminstrv. officer Nat. Naval Med. Ctr., Bethesda, Md., 1970-73, hosp. project officer, 1973-79; assoc. adminstr. for clin. affairs Washington Hosp. Ctr., Washington, 1979-84; COO, sr. v.p. Nat. Rehab. Hosp., Washington, 1984—. Bd. trustees Commn. on Accreditation of Rehab. Facilities; faculty George Washington U., Washington, Ithaca Coll., N.Y. Cons. editor: Hospital Topics mag.; editl. adv. bd. Aspen Publishers, Inc., Jour. of Rehab. Adminstrn. Lt. comdr USN, 1970. Fellow Am. Coll. of Healthcare Execs. (bd. govs., regent-at large dist. 2, 1993-2002); mem. Am. Hosp. Assn. (governing coun. sect. of rehab. hosps. and programs 1986, chmn. 1991, former house of dels.), D.C. Hosp. Assn. (past chmn.), Md. Hosp. Assn. (past pres.), Va. Hosp. Assn. (past pres.), Am. Congress Rehab. Medicine, Assn. Health Care Adminstrs. of Nat. Capital Area (pres. 1978-79), others. E-mail: douglas.shepherd@medstar.net.

SHEPHERD, ELSBETH WEICHSEL, supply chain consultant; b. Youngstown, Ohio, Dec. 5, 1952; d. Richard Henry and Lesley Frances (Lynn) Weichsel; m. Gordon Ray Shepherd, Aug. 28, 1976. BS in Math, Carnegie-Mellon U., 1974; MBA, U. Cin., 1979. Asst. indsl. engr. Armco, Inc., Middletown, Ohio, 1974-76, assoc. indsl. engr., 1976-78, indsl. engr., 1978-82, sr. ops. engr., 1982-86, supr. process planning, 1986-88; project mgr. Integrated Mfg., Middletown, 1988-91, supt. primary ops. scheduling, 1991-92; sr. assoc. Coopers & Lybrand, Cin., 1992-93, mng. assoc., 1993-94; sr. cons. CSC Consulting, Cin., 1995—2002, prin., 1998, ptnr., 2003. Vol. Miami Purchase Assn. Am. Iron and Steel Inst. Fellow, 1978-81; mem. news mag. staff Jr. League Cin., 1980-81. Mem. Soc. Women Engrs. (pres. sect. 1981-82, provisional regional dir. 1983-84), Assn. Computing Machinery, Am. Inst. Indsl. Engrs. (v.p. services, pres. 1985-86), Tech. Socs. Coun. Cin. (pres. 1986-87, 1st v.p. 1985-86, 2d v.p. 1984-85, treas. 1983-84), Engrs. and Scientists of Cin. (sec. 1986-87, pres. elect 1987-88, pres. 1988-89, treas. 1990-95). Home: 7382 Ridgepoint Dr Cincinnati OH 45230-4398 Office: 27th Flr 255 E 5th St Ste 27 Cincinnati OH 45202-4700 Office Phone: 513-763-2961. E-mail: eshepherd@cinci.rr.com., eshepher@csc.com.

SHEPHERD, GAAL, artist; b. Gainesville, Fla., Jan. 25, 1951; d. Charles Claypoole and Ruby Frances (Grogan) S.; m. John Allen Crowl. Student, Stella Adler Theater Studio, 1968-73, U. Tampa, 1974-75, Corcoran Sch. Art, 1985-88. Artist, Atlanta, Tampa, Ga., Fla., 1973-76; graphic designer Art Prodn., Inc., Washington, 1976-79; art dir., illustrations editor Chronicle Higher Edn., Washington, 1979-88; painter, sculptor South Woodstock, Vt., 1988—. Exhbn. agt. The Carving Studio, West Rutland, Vt., 1996—. One-woman shows include Pierre Antoine Gallery, Washington, 1987, 1989, Beside Myself Gallery, Arlington, Vt., 1993, Bromfield Gallery, Boston, 1993, Colby-Sawyer Coll., New London, NH, 1993, Lyndon State Coll., Lyndonville, Ct., 1993, Chaffee Art Ctr., Rutland, Vt., 1994, 1997, 1998, 2002, Vt. Coun. on Arts, Montpelier, 1995, Clarke Galleries, Stowe, Vt., 1995, Between the Muse Gallery, Rockland, Maine, 1996, No B.I.A.S. Gallery, Bennington, Vt., 1997, Steinway Gallery, Chapel Hill,NC, 1998, Red Mill Gallery, Johnson, Vt., AVA Gallery, Lebanon, N.H., 2003, Vt. Supreme Ct., Montpelier, 2003, exhibited in group shows at Middletown (NY) Arts Ctr., 1994, Vt. State Craft Ctr. at Frog Hollow, Middlebury, 1994, Attleboro (Mass.) Mus., 1996, Helen Day Art Ctr., Stowe, 1996, Vt. Coun. on Arts, West Rutland, 1996, AVA Gallery, Lebanon, NH, 1996, Harvard U., Cambridge, Mass., 1996, Ashuah-Irving Gallery, Boston, 1996, Ctr. for Contemporary Arts, Santa Fe, N.Mex., 1997, Guadalupe Fine Arts, Santa Fe, 1997, State Capitol Rotunda, 1997, Vt. Inst. Natural Sci., Woodstock, 1997, Beside Myself Gallery, Arlington, Vt., 1998, Maine Coast Artists, Rockport, 1999, Shelburne Farms, Vt., 2001, N.Mex. State Capitol, Santa Fe, 2002, two-person shows, Colby-Sawyer Coll., New London, NH, 1997, Milton Acad., Mass., 1998, The Munson Gallery, Chatham, Mass., 2001, exhibited in group shows at N.Mex. State Capital, Santa Fe, 2002, Rosewood Gallery, Sunapee, N.H., 2002, Munson Gallery, Chatham, Mass., 2002, Woodstock (Vt.) Folk Art, 2002, Elements Gallery, Rockland, Maine, 2002, Alliance for Visual Arts, Lebanon, N.H., 2003; author: Tranquil Vermont, 2000. Democrat. Avocations: mycology, gardening. Home: Thistle Hill Rd PO Box 307 North Pomfret VT 05053-0307

SHEPHERD, GILLIAN MARY, physician; b. Mar. 12, 1948; d. John Thompson and Helen (Johnston) S.; m. Eduardo Goar Mestre, Aug. 4, 1973; children: Laura Elena, Cristina Alicia, Eduardo Goar. BA, Wheaton Coll., Norton, Mass., 1970; postgrad., Tufts U., 1970-73; MD, N.Y. Med. Coll., 1976. Diplomate Am. Bd. Internal Medicine, Am. Bd. Allergy and Immunology. Intern, resident Lenox Hill Hosp., N.Y.C., 1976-79; fellow in allergy and immunology N.Y. Hosp./Cornell Med. Sch., N.Y.C., 1979-81; assoc. prof. medicine Cornell U. Med. Coll., N.Y.C., 1988—, clin. assoc. prof. medicine, 1995—. Assoc. attending physician N.Y. Hosp., N.Y.C.; cons. allergy and immunology dept. medicine Meml. Sloan-Kettering Cancer Ctr., N.Y.C., 1982—. Contbr. articles in field to profl. jours. Fellow ACP, Am. Acad. Asthma, Allergy and Immunology (chair Edn. and Rsch. Trust 1999-2001, bd. dirs. 2000-2003); mem. AAAS, Am. Fedn. for Clin. Rsch., Joint Coun. Allergy and Immunology, N.Y. Allergy Soc. (exec. com. 1982-94, pres. 1991-92), N.Y. County Med. Soc. Office: 235 E 67th St Rm 203 New York NY 10021-6040 Office Phone: 212-288-9300.

SHEPHERD, GORDON GREELEY, space physics educator, researcher; b. Senate, Sask., Can., June 19, 1931; s. George Fredrick and Irene Eleanor (Thompson) S.; m. Marian Margaret Morgenroth, Aug. 15, 1953; children: Theodore Gordon, David Michael, Paul Ronald; m. Marianna Genova Gerdjikova, Dec. 19. 1987. B.Sc. in Engring. Physics, U. Sask., Saskatoon, Can., 1952; M.Sc. in Physics, U. Sask., 1953; PhD in Physics, U. Toronto, Ont., Can., 1956. Asst. prof. physics U. Sask., 1957-64, assoc. prof., 1964-69; prof. York U., Toronto, 1969—, dir. Ctr. for Rsch. in Earth and Space Sci., 1994—. Author: Spectral Imaging of the Atmosphere, 2002. Recipient John H. Chapman award of excellence, Canadian Space Agy., 2003. Fellow Royal Soc. Can., Can. Aeronautics and Space Inst. (Alouette award 2004), Am. Geophys. Union; mem. Optical Soc. Am., Can. Assn. Physicists Mem. United Ch. of Can. Avocations: swimming; diving; skiing. Home: 14 E Humber Dr King City ON Canada L7B 1B6 Office: York Univ/Ctr Rsch E/S Sci 4700 Keele St Toronto ON Canada M3J 1P3

SHEPHERD, JOHN FREDERIC, lawyer; b. Oak Park, Ill., May 22, 1954; s. James Frederic Shepherd and Margaret Joanne (Crotchett) Woollen; m. Jane Lowell Montgomery; children: Eliza Marion, Justine Catherine, Austin Frederic, Jack Lowell. AB magna cum laude, Dartmouth Coll., Hanover, N.H., 1976; JD, U. Denver, 1979. Bar: Colo. 1979, U.S. Dist. Ct. Colo. 1979, D.C. 1981, U.S. Dist. Ct. D.C. 1981, U.S. Ct. Appeals (10th cir.) 1981, U.S. Ct. Appeals (D.C. cir.) 1982, U.S. Ct. Appeals (9th cir.) 1990, U.S. Supreme Ct. 1984. Assoc. Holland & Hart, Denver, 1979-81, Washington, 1981-85, ptnr., 1985-87, Denver, 1987—; natural resources disting. practitioner in residence U. Denver Coll. Law, 1998. Reporter Mineral Law Newsletter, 1985-92. Mem. 50 for Colo., Denver, 1989. Mem. ABA (chmn. pub. lands and land use com. 1991-93, mem. coun. for sect. of natural resources energy and environ. law 1993-96), Rocky Mountain Mineral Law Found. (mem. long-range planning com. 1988-2001, trustee 1993-95), Dartmouth Alumni Club (pres. Washington chpt. 1985-86, trustee Rocky Mt. chpt., 1998-2001), Denver Athletic Club. Avocations: flyfishing, basketball, running. Home: 320 Clermont St Pky Denver CO 80220-5642 Office: Holland & Hart 555 17th St Ste 3200 Denver CO 80202-3950 Office Phone: 303-295-8309. E-mail: jshepherd@hollandhart.com.

SHEPHERD, JOHN MICHAEL, lawyer; b. St. Louis, Aug. 1, 1955; s. John Calvin and Bernice Florence (Hines) S.; m. Deborah Tremaine Fenton, Oct. 10, 1981; children: Elizabeth White, Katherine Tremaine. BA, Stanford U., 1977; JD, U. Mich., 1980. Bar: Calif. 1981, D.C. 1991, U.S. Dist. Ct. (no. dist.) Calif. 1981. Assoc. McCutchen, Doyle, Brown & Enersen, San Francisco, 1980-82; spl. asst. to asst. atty. gen. U.S. Dept. Justice, Washington, 1982-84, dep. asst. atty gen., 1984-86; assoc. counsel to The President The White House, Washington, 1986-87; sr. dep. comptroller of the currency Dept. Treasury, Washington, 1987-91; spl. counsel Sullivan & Cromwell, N.Y.C., 1991-93, Washington, 1993; exec. v.p., gen. counsel Shawmut Nat. Corp., Boston, 1993-95; ptnr. Brobeck, Phleger & Harrison LLP, San Francisco, 1995-2000; exec. v.p., gen. counsel and sec. Bank of New York Co., Inc., N.Y.C., 2001—. Contbr. articles to profl. jours. Asst. dir. policy Reagan-Bush Presdl. Transition Team, Washington, 1980-81; bd. dirs. Reagan Dep. Asst. Secs., Washington, 1985-90, Episc. Charities N.Y., Mus. Law, Common Good;

trustee New Eng. Aquarium, 1994-96. Named one of Outstanding Young Men Am., U.S. Jaycees, 1984; Wardack Research fellow Washington U., 1976. Mem. ABA (chmn. fin. markets and ins. com., antitrust law sect. 1992-95, banking law com. 1983—, vice chair 1998-2002, chmn. bank holding co. acquisitions subcom. 1995-98, bus. law sect., standing com. on law and nat. security 1984-96), D.C. Bar Assn., New Eng. Legal Found. (bd. dirs. 1994-96), Pacific Coun. Internat. Policy, Coun. Fgn. Rels., River Club, Chevy Chase Club, Univ. Club, Met. Club, Olympic Club, Wilson Coun. Woodrow Wilson Internat. Ctr. for Scholars, 2000—. Office: Bank of NY Co Inc One Wall St New York NY 10286 E-mail: mshepherd@bankofny.com.

SHEPHERD, JOHN THOMPSON, physiologist; b. No. Ireland, May 21, 1919; s. William Frederick and Matilda (Thompson) S.; m. Helen Mary Johnston, July 28, 1945; children: Gillian Mary, Roger Frederick John; m. Marion G. Etzwiler, Apr. 22, 1989. Student, Campbell Coll., Belfast, No. Ireland, 1932-37; MB, BCh, Queen's U., Belfast, 1945, MChir, 1948, MD, 1951, DSc, 1956, DSc (hon.), 1979; MD (hon.), U. Bologna, 1984, U. Gent, 1985. Lectr. physiology Queen's U., 1948-53, reader physiology, 1954-57; assoc. prof. physiology Mayo Found., 1957-62, prof. physiology, 1962—, chmn. dept. physiology and biophysics, 1966-74; bd. govs. Mayo Clinic, 1966-80; trustee Mayo Found., 1969-81, dir. rsch., 1969-77, dir. for edn., 1977-83, chmn. bd. devel., 1983-88; dean Mayo Med. Sch., 1977-83; assoc. dir. Gen. Rsch. Ctr. Mayo Clinic, Rochester, 1992-94. Chmn. U.S. Nat. Com. for the Internat. Union of Physiol. Scis., 1991-95; vis. prof. U. Auckland, New Zealand, 1997; vis. prof. cardiovasc. divsn. U. Minn., 1995; Soma Weiss meml. lectr. Third Internat. Congress WHMA, Pecs, Hungary, 1996. Author, editor: Physiology of the Circulation in Human Limbs in Health and Disease, 1963, Cardiac Function in Health and Disease, 1968, Veins and Their Control, 1975, Human Cardiovascular System, 1979, Handbook of Physiology, The Cardiovascular System Peripheral Circulation and Organ Blood Flow, 1983, Vascular Diseases in the Limbs, 1993, Nervous Control of the Heart, 1996; co-editor: Exercise: Regulation and Integration of Multiple Systems. Handbook of Physiology, 1996; mem. editl. bd. Hypertension, 1973—, Am. Jour. Physiology, Am. Heart Jour., Microvascular Rsch.; cons. editor Circulation Rsch., 1981—; editor-in-chief News in Physiol. Sci., 1988-94; mem. editl. adv. bd. Clin. Autonomic Rsch., 1990—, Jour. Autonomic Nervous Sys., 1994—, Exptl. Physiology, 1994—, Vascular Medicine, 1995—, Internat. Angiology Adv. Com., 1994—, Cardiovasc. Rsch., 1997—; contbr. more than 590 sci. articles to profl. jours. Recipient NASA Skylab Achievement award, 1974, A. Ross McIntyre medal for achievement, 1991; Brit. Med. Assn. scholar, 1949-50, Fulbright scholar, 1953-54; Anglo-French Med. exch. bursar, 1957; Internat. Francqui chair, 1978; Einthoven lectr. 1981, Volhard lectr., 1990. Fellow Am. Coll. Cardiology (hon.), Royal Coll. Physicians (London, hon.), Royal Coll. Physicians Ireland (hon.), Royal Acad. Medicine (Belgium); mem. NAS (space sci. bd. 1973-74, chmn. com. space biology and medicine 1973), Am. Physiol. Soc. (Disting. Svc. award 1990, Ray G. Daggs award 1997), Louis Rapkine Assn., Am. Heart Assn. (dir. 1968—, pres. 1975-76, chmn. vascular medicine and biology task force 1990, hon. fellow coun. clin. cardiology), Physiol. Soc. Gt. Brit., Med. Rsch. Soc. London, Assn. Am. Physicians, Internat. Union of Angiology (hon.), Worldwide Hungarian Med. Acad. (hon.), Rappaport Inst. Israel (sci. adv. bd.), Sigma Xi. Office: Mayo Clinic Plummer Bldg N-10 Rochester MN 55905 Office Phone: 507-284-0497.

SHEPHERD, KAREN, retired congresswoman; b. Silver City, N.Mex., July 5, 1940; m. Vincent P. Shepherd. BA, U. Utah, 1962; MA, Brigham Young U., 1963. Former instr. Brigham Young U., Am. U., Cairo; former pres. Webster Pub. Co.; former adminstr. David Eccles Sch. Bus., U. Utah; former dir. Salt Lake County Social Svcs., Utah; former dir. continuing edn. Westminster Coll.; former mem. Utah Senate; mem. 103d Congress from 2d Utah dist., Washington, 1993—94; exec. dir., U.S. rep. European Bank for Reconstruction Devel., London, 1996—2002; mem. exec. com., chair East West Trade and Investment Forum Am. C. of C., England, 1998—2002; dir. EMILY's List, 2002. Mem. Nat. Common Cause Governing Bd., Washington, 1995-96, Internat. Delegation to Monitor Elections in West Bank and Gaza, Israel, Nat. Planned Parenthood Action Fund, 2004—; founder Karen Shepherd Fund; founding mem. Utah Women's Polit. Caucus, Project 2000; mem. trustee KeyBank Victory Funds; dir. UBS Bank, USA. Former mem. United Way, Pvt. Industry Coun.; former mem. adv. bd. U.S. West Grad. Sch. Social Work; trustee Westminster Coll.; bd. dirs. ARC, 2002—; bd. dir. Utah Red Cross, 2003—; chair Grad. Sch. Social Work, U. Utah. Recipient Women in Bus. award U.S. Small Bus. Assn., Woman of Achievement award, Pathfinder award, YWCA Leadership award, 1st place award Nat. Assn. Journalists, Disting. Alumni award U. Utah Coll. Humanities, Eleanor Roosevelt award Utah Dem. Party, 2002, Merit of Honor award U. Utah, 2004. Fellow Inst. Politics Kennedy Sch. Govt., Internat. Women's Forum, Salt Lake Area C. of C. (pub. rels. com.)., Coun. on Fgn. Rels. Home: PO Box 1049 Salt Lake City UT 84110-1049 Office: 21 G St Salt Lake City UT 84103-2949

SHEPHERD, KATHLEEN SHEARER MAYNARD, television executive; b. N.Y.C., June 14, 1950; d. Theodore E. and Phyllis (Wildman) Shearer; m. Charles Dix Shepherd; m. Joseph Ashton Maynard (div. June 1977); 1 child, Natasha Candice. Student, Duke U., Durham, N.C., 1972-73, Westchester Community Coll., White Plains, N.Y, 1974-75, NYU, 1975-77. Atty. Tufts U., Medford, Mass., 1968-69; from administrv. asst. to assoc. producer WCBS-TV, N.Y.C., 1973-74, producer, 1975-76; from program devel. supr., exec. producer to dir. pub. affai WPIX TV, N.Y.C., 1977-84, v.p. pub. affairs, prodn., exec. producer, v.p. local prodn. and cmty. affairs. Trustee Coll. Mt. St. Vincent, Nat. Coalitin of 100 Black Women, lower Fairfield chpt., Conn., 1987; bd. dirs. Childrens Village, Dobbs Ferry, N.Y., 1988, Partnership for a Drug Free Am., mem. advt. coun. adv. com. Mem. NATAS. Democrat. Episcopalian. Avocations: jogging, exercise. Office: WPIX Inc 220 E 42nd St New York NY 10017-5806

SHEPHERD, MARK, JR., retired electronics company executive; b. Dallas, Jan. 18, 1923; s. Mark and Louisa Florence (Daniell) S.; m. Mary Alice Murchland, Dec. 21, 1945; children: Debra Aline Shepherd Robinson, MaryKay Theresa, Marc Blaine. BSEE, So. Meth. U., 1942; MSEE, U. Ill., at Urbana, 1947. Registered profl. engr., Tex. With GE, 1942-43, Farnsworth TV and Radio Corp., 1947-48, Tex. Instruments, Dallas, 1948-88, v.p., gen. mgr. semicondr.-components div., 1955-61, exec. v.p., chief operating officer, 1961-66, pres., chief operating officer, 1967-69, pres., chief exec. officer, 1969-76, chmn. bd. dirs., chief exec. officer, 1976-84, chmn. bd. dirs., chief corp. officer, 1984-85, chmn., 1985-88; ret. Hon. trustee Com. for Econ. Devel.; councillor conf. Bd.; mem. Bus. Coun. Lt. (j.g.) USNR, 1943-46. Fellow IEEE; mem. NAE, Sigma Xi, Eta Kappa Nu.

SHEPHERD, MARY LOU, state representative; b. Spokane, Wash., Apr. 18, 1933; m. James Shepherd; children: Mona, Jerry, Randy, David, Kevin, Glenn, Gaill. Attended, Alan Hancock Coll., 1965—70, North Idaho Coll., 1985—87. State rep. dist. 2A Idaho Ho. of Reps., Boise, 1999—, mem. state afairs and transp. and def. coms. Sec.-treas. Pritchard-Murray Fire Dept.; bd. dirs. Annexation Ad Hoc com., 2000—, Idaho Rural Partnership, 2000—; mem.e-commerce interim com.; bd. dirs. State Hosp. North, 2000—. Democrat. Office: State Capitol Bldg PO Box 83720 Boise ID 83720

SHEPHERD, PAUL H. school system administrator; b. Salt Lake City, Sept. 6, 1955; s. Richard Lawrence and Janis (Hoskings) S.; m. Marlene Wade, Aug. 31, 1978; children: Janice, Faith, Matthew, Andrew, Luke, Christian. BS in Elem. Edn., U. Utah, 1981, MEd, 1985. Cert. elem. tchr. Utah, adminstrv. certification Utah. Printer Transamerica Film Svc., Salt Lake City, 1978-81; tchr. Granite Sch. Dist., Salt Lake City, 1981—. Pres. Granite Fedn. Tchrs., 1985-87, treas., 1990-92. Active mem. State House of Reps., 1992-94; Bishop LDS Ch., West Jordan, Utah, 1988; mem. Oquivrh Shadows Community Coun., West Jordan, 1987; chmn. rels. com. Boy Scouts Am., 1972—. Recipient Outstanding Tchr. award Excel Found., 1985, Elem. Tchr. of Yr. award Utah Fedn. Tchrs., 1991. Mem. ASCD, Utah Assn Gifted Children. Democrat. Avocations: fishing, guitar. Home and Office: 6644 W 5095 S West Jordan UT 84084-7728 E-mail: shepfam@concentric.net., paul.shepherd@granite.k12.ut.us.

SHEPHERD, STEVEN STEWART, auditor, consultant; b. Pauls Valley, Okla., Aug. 7, 1956; s. Lloyd Thomas and Barbara Lou Shepherd; m. Dawn Rachelle Godwin, Aug. 22, 1981 (div. Dec. 2001); children: Shane, Lauren. BBA, U. Tex., 1981, MBA, 1990. Internal auditor Ark-La. Gas Co., Shreveport, La., 1982-84; sr. constrn. auditor Cen. & S.W. Svcs., Inc., Dallas, 1984-87; constrn. audit supr. City of Ft. Worth, 1987-96; city auditor City of Garland, Tex., 1996—. Cons. Constrn. Mgmt. Svcs., Arlington, Tex., 1990—, Eagle Tax Svcs., Arlington, 1990—; mem. adv. com. for acctg. program Tarrant County Jr. Coll., 1995-97; mem. internal audit adv. bd. U. North Tex., 1993-96. Contbr. articles to profl. jours. Mem. allocation com. Tarrant County United Way, Ft. Worth, 1991; bd. dirs. Charlotte Anderson Elem. Sch. PTA, Mansfield, Tex., 1990-91. Mem. Inst. Internal Auditors (bd. govs. Ft. Worth chpt. 1990-96, sec. 1990-91, treas. 1991-92, v.p. 1992-93, pres. 1993-94), Mansfield Youth Baseball Assn. (bd. dirs. 1993-95), Nat. Assn. Local Govt. Auditors (bd. dirs. 2002), Delta Upsilon (bd. dirs. 1991-96, sec. 1994-95). Republican. Mem. Ch. of Christ. Avocations: little league coach, horseback riding, water-skiing, skiing, scuba diving.

SHEPHERD, TERRY L. health facility administrator; BS, Purdue U.; MBA, Ind. U. V.p., CFO Cardiac Pacemakers, Inc.; dir. bus. devel. med. devices and diagnostics divsn., CFO Lilly Industries, Ltd., U.K.; pres. Hybritech Eli Lilly and Co.; pres. heart valve divsn. St. Jude Med. Inc., St. Paul, 1994, mgr. internat. ops., 1996, pres., CEO, 1999—, chmn., 2002—. Office: St Jude Med Inc 1 Lillehei Plz Saint Paul MN 55117-9983

SHEPHERD, WILLIAM MICHAEL, music educator, musician; b. Ft. Knox, Ky., Mar. 26, 1949; s. Elisha and Zella Shepherd; m. Shelley Alice Jaffe, Feb. 10, 1985; children: Kevin, Marc. Student, Vallejo (Calif.) Jr. Coll., 1968—70; B in Music Edn., Ea. Ky. U., 1975; postgrad., U. Calif., Davis, 1986; MusM, U. Oreg., 1987. Music tchr. Dayton (Ohio) City Schs., 1975—77; profl. musician Stan Kenton, Les Brown, 1977—80; music tchr. Vallejo Unified Schs., 1980—83, Ukiah (Calif.) Unified Schs., 1983—94, Brookings (Oreg.)-Harbor Schs., 1994—. Dir. Curry Big Band, Brookings; leader Banana Belt Brass Quintet, Brookings. Mem.: Internat. Assn. Jazz Educators, Internat. Trumpet Guild, Phi Mu Alpha. Avocations: shooting, sports, fishing, model aviation. Home: 337 Mill Beach Rd Brookings OR 97415 Office: Brookings Harbor Sch Dist 564 Fern Ave Brookings OR 97415 Office Phone: 541-469-2108. Business E-Mail: shepherd@harborside.com.

SHEPHERDSON, JAMES A. (JAMIE), diversified financial services company executive; Past COO McGuinness; mng. dir. Equitable Distbrs., Inc., 1994—2000, sr. v.p., 1996—2000; co-CEO, Security First Group Met. Life Ins. Co., 2000—02; sr. v.p. and pres., retirement svcs. John Hancock Fin. Svcs., Inc., Boston, 2003—04, exec. v.p. mutual funds, 2004—. Office: John Hancock Fin Svcs Inc John Hancock Pl PO Box 111 Boston MA 02117

SHEPLER, JOHN EDWARD, engineering executive; b. Freeport, Ill., June 23, 1950; s. Edward Charles and Joyce Margaret (Wagner) S.; m. Barbara Jeanne Heinrich, Sept. 11, 1976. BSEE, Milw. Sch. Engring., 1972. Lic. FCC gen. class radiotelephone operator. Disc jockey, chief engr. Sta. WACI, Freeport, 1972-73, owner, ops. mgr., 1974-75; asst. chief engr. Sta. WROK, Rockford, Ill., 1973-74, chief engr., 1975-79; project engr. Martin Automatic, Rockford, 1979-80; engring. mgr. Pacific Scientific, Rockford, 1984-86; design engr. Sundstrand Corp., Rockford, 1980-84, engring. mgr., 1986-99; Internet entrepreneur, 1998—; owner LongDistanceRateFinder.com, 2001—, John Shepler.com, 2002—, T1RexX.com, 2003—, CallBird.com, 2003—. Tech. instr. Rock Valley Coll., Rockford, 1981-84; tech. cons. various broadcasters, 1979-94; columnist Electronic Servicing and Tech. Mag., 1990-94. Author: Sensational Sound Handbook, 1981, Shepler's Weekly News and Views, Celebrating Great People Doing Great Things, 1993-98, John Shepler's Writing in a Positive Light, 1998—; columnist Radio World mag., 1982-94; tech. illustrator, cartoonist, 1989-94; contbg. reviewer Epinions, 2000—; mem. poetry rev. bd. Rockford Rev., 1997-99; contbr. articles to profl. jours.; patentee in field. Named Outstanding Alumnus Milw. Sch. Engring., 1987. Mem.: Broadcast (v.p. 1971-72). Avocations: photography, poetry, writing. Home and Office: 5653 Weymouth Dr Rockford IL 61114-5544

SHEPLEY, HUGH, architect; b. Boston, Mar. 17, 1928; s. Henry Richardson and Anna Lowell (Gardiner) S.; m. Mary Waters Niles, Dec. 27, 1950; children: Hamilton Niles, Philip Foster. BA, Harvard U., 1951; BArch., Boston Archtl. Ctr., 1958; postgrad., Mass. Inst. Tech., 1958-59. Mem. archtl. firm Shepley, Bulfinch, Richardson & Abbott, Boston, 1955-63, ptnr., 1963-91. Bd. dirs. Greater Boston Red Cross, 1967-73, mem. exec. com., 1968-69; bd. dirs. Cmty. Music Ctr., Boston, 1968-72, Boston Ctr. for Blind Children, 1979-87; trustee New Eng. Conservatory Music, 1978-83, overseer, 1983—; trustee Univ. Hosp., 1980-96, mem. exec. com., 1981-92, vice chmn. bd. dirs., 1985-89, chmn. bd. dirs., 1989-92; trustee Am. Coll. of Greece, 1983-92, treas., 1986-88; trustee, sec. Rotch Travelling Scholarship, 1987-93, v.p., 1993—; mem. adv. coun. Boston U. Med. Ctr., 1990-96, Corp. Old South Assn., 1993-2002; bd. dirs. Manchester (Mass.) Hist. Soc., 1994-2002; overseer Spaulding Rehab. Hosp., 2003—. Fellow AIA; mem. Mass. Assn. Architects (pres. 1972), Boston Soc. Architects (pres. 1974), Boston Archtl. Ctr. (pres. 1969-71). Clubs: Tavern (Boston); Manchester Yacht (commodore 1985-87). Republican. Episcopalian. Home: 8 Andover Ct Bedford MA 01730

SHEPLEY, MARDELLE MCCUSKEY, architect, educator; b. Bethesda, Md., June 28, 1949; d. E. Scott McCuskey (father) & James R. and Yvonne Hudson S.; m. Laurence Berger, 1974 (div. 1978); m. Michael Curtis Blair, Sept. 5, 1981; children: Colin, Ian, Teal. BA, Columbia U., 1971, MArch, 1974; MA, U. Mich., 1979, DArch, 1981. Registered architect Calif. Urban designer N.Y.C. Dept. City Planning, 1972—74; planner Min. Planning & Econ. policy, Panama, Panama, 1975—77; lectr., teaching asst. U. Mich., Ann Arbor, 1977—81; assoc. Tai Assocs. Architects, San Francisco, 1981—85, The Design Partnership, San Francisco, 1985—93; asst. prof. Tex. A&M U., College Station, 1993—97, assoc. prof., 1997—2003, prof., 2003—, coord. PhD program, 1999-2001, assoc. dean for students, 2001—. Rsch. com. Ctr. Health Design, Martinez, Calif., 1993—; assoc. dir. Ctr. Health Sys. and Design, 1995—2004, interim dir., 2004—. Co-author: Healthcare Environments for Children and Their Families, 1998. Bd. dirs. Assn. for Care of Children's Health, Mt. Royal, N.J., 1998-2000; mem. parent bd. Oakland (Calif.) Montessori Sch., 1991-93. Recipient Health Facilities Rsch. award AIA, 1992; Tex. A&M U. scholar, 1998; Tex. A&M U. faculty fellow, 2001-, William Pena Endowed Prof., 2003-. Office: Tex A&M U Dept Architecture College Station TX 77843-3137

SHEPP, BRYAN EUGENE, psychologist, educator; b. Cumberland, Md, Sept. 13, 1932; s. Bryan Evert and Dorothy Lorene (Stell) S.; m. June Lee Langeluttig, Jan. 31, 1953; children— Karen Suzanne, David Bryan. BS, U. Md., 1954, MS, 1956, PhD, 1960; MS with honors, Brown U., 1966. Rsch. prof. U. Conn., 1961-63; asst. prof. psychology George Peabody Coll., Nashville, 1963-64, Brown U., Providence, 1964-66, assoc. prof., 1966-69, prof., 1969-98, prof. emeritus, 1998—, chmn. dept., 1983-88, assoc. dean faculty, 1988-91, dean faculty, 1991-96. Cons. in field; vis. scientist Oxford (Eng.) U., 1970 Contbr. numerous articles to profl. publ.; ad hoc editor for several psychol. jour. Served with USN, 1955-59. Decorated letter of commendation Sec. of Navy; USPHS postdoctoral fellow, 1959-61; Nat. Inst. Child Health and Human Devel. grantee, 1965—82. Fellow APA, Am. Psychol. Soc. (founding fellow); mem. AAAS, AAUP, Psychonomic Soc., Univ. Club. Personal E-mail: bjshepp@gwi.net.

SHEPPARD, BEN H., JR., lawyer; b. Amarillo, Tex., Jan. 18, 1943; BA, U. North Tex., 1965; LLB, U. Tex., 1968. Bar: Tex. 1968. Mem. Vinson & Elkins L.L.P., Houston. Adj. prof. U. Houston Law Ctr. Editor-in-chief: Internat. Arbitration News. Adv. bd. Inst. Transnat. Arbitration. Mem. Chancellors, Order of Coif, Phi Delta Phi. Office: Vinson & Elkins 3300 First City Tower 1001 Fannin St Ste 3300 Houston TX 77002-6706

SHEPPARD, C. JAMES, composer, educator; s. Charles J. and Margaret Carol Sheppard; m. Linda Lee Moore (dec.); children: Susanna Lee, Zachary James. BFA, U. Omaha, 1967; MusM in Theory and Composition, U. Mass., 1968; PhD, U. Iowa, 1975; postgrad., W.Va. U., 1976—78, Miami U., Oxford, Ohio, 1978—. CPA Ohio. Asst. prof. composition W.Va. U., Morgantown; prof. composition Miami U., Oxford, Ohio. Music performance Electric Wind Performance, Oxford, 1983—; coord. Internat. Music at the Millennium Project, Oxford, 1998—2002. Composer (performer): (electronic composition) Starjammer (Individual Artist fellow Ohio Arts Coun., 2001), Meditation on B, Study in Contrasts. Staff sgt. USAF, 1968—72. Recipient Std. Panel awards, Am. Soc. Composers, Authors, Pubs., 1981—; Summer Rsch. Appointments in Composition, Miami U., 1979, 1982, 1985, 1990, 1997, Individual Artist fellow, Ohio Arts Coun., 1984, 1989, 2001, Rsch. Challenge grantee, State Ohio, 1986, Composing Residency, MacDowell Colony, 2001, Va. Ctr. for the Creative Arts, 2001. Mem.: Soc. Composers, Inc., Soc. Electro-Acoustic Music, USA, Am. Music Ctr., Am. Soc. Composers, Authors, Publishers. Achievements include recording: composition Snowfall, Michele Gingras, SNE CD 631; composition recording: Luminaria, Ariel, Opus One LP 126; recording: composition Cat Dreams of Flying, Sandra Seefeld, Opus One 85; recording: composition Echo in Amber, James Sheppard, Opus One 126.

SHEPPARD, JOHN WILBUR, computer research scientist; b. Pitts., Aug. 21, 1961; s. Harry Reid and Mary Jane (Amon) S.; m. Justina Anne Pape, Oct. 29, 1988; children: Jesse Carl, Jeannette Alida. BS, So. Meth. U., 1983; MS, Johns Hopkins U., 1989, PhD ., 1996. Systems analyst Sheppard Internat., Inc., Hermitage, Pa., 1979-86; fellow ARINC Engring. Svcs., LLC, Annapolis, Md., 1986—; lectr. Johns Hopkins U., 1994—. Co-author: System Test and Diagnosis, 1994; author, editor: Research Perspectives and Case Studies in System Test and Diagnosis; contbr. articles to profl. jours. Mem. YMCA, Hermitage, 1979-85, Md. Hall for the Creative Arts, Annapolis, 1988-90; pres. Univ. Chapel Campus Ministry, Dallas, 1982-83. Mem. IEEE (sr.), Mensa, Kappa Mu Epsilon. Republican. Lutheran. Achievements include patents for methods and apparatus for diagnostic testing; patents pending for aircraft condition analysis and monitoring system; development of explanation-based learning approach for fault diagnosis; multi-agent learning approaches for solving Markov games. Home: 1203 Willobrook Dr Pasadena MD 21122-2133 Office: ARINC Inc 2551 Riva Rd Annapolis MD 21401-7461 E-mail: jsquad@cablespeed.com., jsheppar@arinc.com.

SHEPPARD, SCOTT, magazine publisher; With So. Progressive Corp., 1975—; midwest sales mgr. So. Living, So Progress Corp.19, 1982—86; nat. sales mgr. So. Living, So. Progress Corp., 1986—87, v.p., advt. dir., 1987—89; v.p., pub. Southpoint Mag. (formerly Southern Mag.), So. Progressive Corp., 1989—91; dir. corp. advt. sales So. Living Progress Corp., 1990—91; v.p., assoc. pub. So. Living, So. Progress Corp., 1990—92; pub. Southern Living, So. Progress Corp., Birmingham, Ala., 1992—95, exec. v.p. Southern Living, Group pub., 1995—. Office: Southern Progress Corp 2100 Lakeshore Dr Birmingham AL 35209-6721

SHEPPARD, WILLIAM STEVENS, investment banker; b. Grand Rapids, Mich, Apr. 29, 1930; s. James Herbert and Emily Gilmore (Stevens) S.; m. Jane Steketee, 1956 (dec. 1975); children: Stevens C., Elizabeth W., Emily R.; m. Patricia Gillis Bloom, Dec. 2, 1978. BA in Econs, U. Va., 1953. Trainee J.P. Morgan & Co., Inc., NYC, 1955-58; investment adv. Delafield & Delafield, NYC, 1958-71; from salesman to sr. v.p and dir. F.S. Smithers & Co., NYC, 1971-76; sr. v.p., dir. successor Paine, Webber, Jackson & Curtis, Inc., 1976-81; pres., chief exec. officer, dir. Paine Webber Real Estate Securities Inc., 1980-85; mng. dir. Paine Webber Capital Markets, NYC, 1985-88, Berkshire Capital Corp., NYC, 1988-95, adv. dir., 1995—2003; adminstr. Pequot Investment Advisors, Inc., Southport, Conn., 1995—; ret.; adv. dir. MGR Asset Mgmt., Inc., Southport, Conn., 2001—03. Chmn. bd. dirs. Ea. Bancorp; adv. dir. Putnam Trust Co., Greenwich, Conn. An editor: Ginny Mae Manual, 1979; contbr. to handbooks. Trustee, treas. Riot Relief Fund City NY, 1970—. Served to lt. USNR, 1953-55. Mem. NY Yacht Club, Country Club of Fairfield (Conn.), Pequot Yacht Club, Mashomack Fish and Game Club, North Haven Casino Club, Cruising Club of Am., Mountain Lake Club. Republican. Home: 167 Salt Meadow Rd Fairfield CT 06430-6370 Office: HGK Asset Mgmt Inc PO Box 139 Southport CT 06490-0139 E-mail: pequotshep@aol.com.

SHEPPE, JOSEPH ANDREW, surgeon; b. Huntington, W.Va., Sept. 24, 1953; m. Kathy Chapman; children: Sheree Nicole, Natalee Marie, Brittany Lee. BS summa cum laude in Chemistry and Zoology, Marshall U., 1975; MD, W.Va. U., 1979. Diplomate Am. Bd. Surgery, Am. Bd. Colon and Rectal Surgery. Intern in gen. surgery Charleston (W.Va.) Area Med. Ctr., 1979-84; fellow in colon and rectal surgery William Beaumont Army Med. Ctr., Royal Oak, Mich., 1984-85; pvt. practice Columbia, S.C., 1985—. Physician Bapt. Med. Ctr., Columbia, Providence Hosp., Columbia, Richland Meml. Hosp., Columbia, Lexington Med. Ctr., West Columbia, S.C.; clin. instr. in gen./colorectal surgery U. S.C. Med. Sch. Fellow ACS, Am. Soc. Colon and Rectal Surgery; mem. S.C. Med. Soc., Columbia Med. Soc. Home: 204 Leaning Tree Rd Columbia SC 29223-3009 Office: 1333 Taylor St Ste 4-a Columbia SC 29201-2949

SHEPPERD, THOMAS EUGENE, accountant; b. Pekin, Ill., Aug. 19, 1941; s. William Thomas and Marguerite Louise (Meisinger) S.; m. Susan Abbott Belville, Oct. 7, 1960; children: Scott Thomas, Allison Marie Shepperd-Henry, Michele Lea. BS in Acctg., U. Ill., 1964. CPA, Ill., Mo., Iowa, Ind. From jr. acct. to mgr. Haskins & Sells, St. Louis, 1964-74, mgr. Washington, 1974-75, ptnr., 1975-77, Deloitte Haskins & Sells (formerly Haskins & Sells), St. Louis, 1977-89, Deloitte & Touche (merger Deloitte Haskins & Sells and Touche Ross & Co.), St. Louis, 1989—. Treas. Shepley concert com. Christ Ch. Cathedral, St. Louis, 1989; bd. dirs., treas. Care & Counseling, Inc., Howard Park Early Childhood Ctr.; trustee, chmn. bd. Diocesian of Mo. Investment Trust. Mem. AICPA (various coms., mem. exec. coun. 2003--), Mo. Soc. CPAs (adminstrv. v.p., bd. dirs. 1988-92, treas. 1992-95, v.p. 1996-97, pres.-elect 1997-98, pres., 1998-99, chair long range fin. planning com. and the office location com., terms on the tech. standards peer review exec., profl. ethics coms., legislation com., acctg. and auditing procedures com., bd. dirs. 2003--), U. Ill. Press. Coun., David Kinley Assn., Noonday Club (treas., bd. dirs. 1977-81), Glen Echo Country Club. Republican. Episcopalian. Avocations: golf, travel, sports. Home: 15977 Chamfers Farm Rd Chesterfield MO 63005-4717 Office: Deloitte & Touche LLP 1 City Ctr Ste 2200 Saint Louis MO 63101-1819

SHER, ALAN, health science association administrator, immunologist; b. Nutley, N.J., Apr. 12, 1945; AB, Oberlin (Ohio) Coll., 1966; PhD in Biology, U. Calif., San Diego, 1972. Postdoctoral rschr. Divsn. Parasitology Nat. Inst. Med. Rsch., London, 1972—74; prin. assoc. in pathology Harvard Med. Sch., Cambridge, Mass., 1974—76, asst. prof. pathology, 1976—80, Peter Bent Brigham Hosp., Boston, 1976—80; head Immunobiology Sect. NIH, Bethesda, Md., 1980—. Lectr. in field; mem. adv. panel Fogarty Internat. Ctr. NIH, 1989—95; mem. adv. panel Burroughs Wellcome Molecular Parasitology Award Program, 1989—95; mem. adv. bd. Heska Corp., 1989—99, Genzyme Corp., 1995—98; mem. numerous coms. Mem. editl. bd.: Exptl. Parasitology, 1979—83, Infection and Immunity, 1981—87, Molecular and Biochemical Parasitology, 1984—91, Parasite Immunology, 1987—, Infection and Immunity, second term, 1992—, Parasitology, 1993—, The Jour. Exptl. Medicine, 1995—, forum editor: Microbes and Infection, 1997—; co-editor: Current Opinion in Immunology, 1993—; dep. editor: The Jour. of Immunology, 1987—92. Recipient Issac Roitman prize, 1988, Bailey K. Ashford medal, The Am. Soc. Tropical Medicine and Hygiene, 1990, Superior Svc. award, USPHS, 1994; grantee four rsch. grants, Edna McConnell Clark Found., 1977—92, Nat. Inst. Allergy and Infectious Diseases, 1978—80, The Rockefeller Found., 1979—81, nine rsch. grants, WHO, 1980—, U.S. Agy. Internat. Devel., 1986. Mem.: Brit. Soc. Parasitology, Am. Soc. Tropical Medicine and Hygiene, Am. Assn. Immunologists. Office: Lab Parasitic Diseases NIH 4 Center Dr Bldg 4 Rm B1 01 Bethesda MD 20892-0425

SHER, ELLEN, allergist; b. Red Bank, N.J., July 5, 1960; MD, Georgetown U., 1986. Diplomate Am. Bd. Allergy and Immunology, Am. Bd. Internal Medicine. Intern, resident internal medicine Thomas Jefferson U. Hosp., Phila., 1986-89, fellow pulmonary medicine, 1989-90; fellow allergy and

immunology Nat. Jewish Ctr. Respiratory Disorders, Denver, 1990-92; allergist Atlantic Allergy and Asthma Ctr., West Long Branch, N.J., 1992—. Allergist Monmouth Med. Ctr., Long Branch, N.J., Riverview Med. Ctr., Red Bank, U. Hosp., Newark; clin. asst. prof. U. Medicine & Dentistry N.J.-U. Hosp. Newark. Fellow Am. Coll. Allergy, Asthma & Immunology; mem. ACP, Am. Coll. Chest Physicians, Am. Acad. Allergy and Immunology. Office: Atlantic Allergy & Asthma Ctr 802 W Park Ave Ste 213 Ocean NJ 07712-8523 Also: 8 Tindall Rd Middletown NJ 07748-2740

SHER, GEORGE ALLEN, philosophy educator; b. N.Y.C., Nov. 10, 1942; s. Daniel and Clara (Landesberg) S.; m. Emily Fox Gordon, July 10, 1972; 1 child, Sarah Landesberg. BA, Brandeis U., 1964; PhD, Columbia U., 1972. Instr. philosophy Fairleigh Dickinson U., Teaneck, N.J., 1966-72, asst. prof. philosopy, 1972-74; assoc. prof. philosophy U. Vt., Burlington, 1974-80, prof., 1980-91; Herbert S. Autrey prof. philosophy Rice U., Houston, 1991—, chmn. dept. philosophy, 1993-2000. Mem. Inst. for Advanced Study, Princeton, N.J., 1987-88. Author: Desert, 1987, Beyond Neutrality: Perfectionism and Politics, 1997, Approximate Justice: Studies in Non-Ideal Theory, 1997; editor: Moral Philosophy: Selected Readings, 1989, 2d edit., 1996; contbr. articles to profl. jours. Named fellow Nat. Humanitics Ctr., Rsch. Triangle Park, N.C., 1980 81. Mem. Am. Philos. Assn. Home: 2425 Dryden Rd Houston TX 77030-1001 Office: Rice U Dept Philosophy MS 14 6100 Main St Houston TX 77251-1892 Office Phone: 713-348-2723. Business E-Mail: gsher@rice.edu.

SHER, LEO, psychiatrist; b. Kiev, Ukraine, June 13, 1961; s. Alexander and Ivetta (Iokhved) Sher. MD summa cum laude(hon.), Ukrainian Nat. Med. U., Kiev, 1985. Sr. staff fellow NIMH, Bethesda, Md., 1997 2000; asst. clin. prof. psychiatry and behavioral scis. The George Washington U., Washington, 2000—02; rsch. psychiatrist N.Y. State Psychiat. Inst., Columbia U. Med. Ctr., N.Y.C., 2000—; asst. clin. prof. psychiatry Columbia U. Coll. Physicians and Surgeons, 2001—; asst. attending physician The N.Y. Presbyn. Hosp., Columbia U. Med. Ctr., 2001—. Contbr. over 150 articles to profl. jours., chpts. to books. Recipient Charlotte Marker Zitrin, M.D. award, Albert Einstein Coll. of Medicine Psychiatry Residency Program at L.I. Jewish Med. Ctr., 1997. Jewish. Achievements include patents for in field. Personal E-mail: drleosher@aol.com.

SHERBELL, RHODA, artist, sculptor; b. Bklyn. d. Alexander and Syd (Steinberg) S.; m. Mervin Honig, Apr. 28, 1956; 1 child, Susan. Student, Art Students League, 1950—53, Bklyn. Mus. Art Sch., 1959—61; pvt. study art, Italy, France, Eng., 1956. Cons., coun. mem. Emily Lowe Gallery, Hofstra U., Hempstead, N.Y., 1978, pres., 1989-81, instr., 1991—, life mem. bd. friends, pres. bd. trustees; tchr. instr. Mus. Modern Art, N.Y.C., 1959, NAD Art Sch., N.Y.C., 1985—, Art Students League, N.Y.C., 1980—; Nat. Portrait Gallery Mus. rep. to 150th anniversary Smithsonian Instn., Washington, 1996lectr. Nat. Arts Club, N.Y.C. One-woman shows include Haulington Township Art League,, Embassy of U.S., Prague, 2002-03, Country Art Gallery, Locust Valley, N.Y., Bklyn. Mus. Art Sch., 1961, Adelphi Coll., A.C.A. Galleries, N.Y.C., 1967, Capricorn Galleries, Rehn Gallery, Washington, 1968, Huntington Hartford Mus., N.Y.C., 1969, N.Y. Cultural Ctr., 1970, Nat. Arts Collection, Washington, 1970, Montclair Mus. of Art, 1976, Nat. Art Mus. Sport, 1977, Jewish Mus. N.Y.C., 1980, Morris (N.J.) Mus. Arts and Scis., 1980, Black History Mus., 1981, Queens Mus., 1981-82, Nat. Portrait Gallery, Smithsonian Inst., Washington, 1981-82, Bergen Mus. Arts and Scis., N.J., 1984, William Benton Mus., Conn., 1985, Palace Theatre of the Arts, Stamford, Conn., Bronx Mus. Arts, 1986, Hofstra Mus. Art, L.I., N.Y., 1989-90, 97-98, County Art Gallery, N.Y.C., 1990, Hecksher Mus., 2000, Bronx Mus., N.Y., Bklyn. Mus., Mus. Modern Art, N.Y.C., Country Art Gallery, 1990, Port Washington Libr., Nat. Mus. Am. Art, Smithsonian Instn., 1982, NAD, N.Y.C., 1984, 89, Castle Gallery Mus., N.Y.C., 1987, Emily Lowe Mus., N.Y.C., 1987, Heckshire Mus., N.Y.C., 1989, Islip Art Mus., N.Y.C., 1989, Gallery Emanuel, N.Y.C., 1993, Sundance Gallery, Bridgehampton, N.Y., 1995, Castiron Gallery SoHo Show, 1995, NAD Exhbn., 1995, Main St. Petile Gallery, 2003, Huntington Arts Coun., 2003, 04, Huntington Twp. Art League, 2002-03, The Art Students League Instructors Exhbn., Salandes O'Reilly Gallery, N.Y.C., 2003; 2 person exhbn. Works on Paper, Hofstra Mus., 1997-98; exhibited in group shows at Heckscher Mus., 1989, Islip Mus., 1989, Nassau Dept. Recreation and Parks, 1989, Downtown Gallery, N.Y.C., Maynard Walker Gallery, N.Y.C., F.A.R. Gallery, N.Y.C., Provincetown Art Assn., Detroit Inst. Art, Pa. Acad. Fine Arts, Old Westbury Gardens, Audubon Artists, NAD, Allied Artists, Heckscher Mus., Nat. Art Mus. Sports, Mus. Arts and Scis., L.A., Am. Mus. Natural History, Post of History Mus., 1987-88, Caslte Gallery Mus., N.Y.C., 1987, Emily Lowe Gallery Mus., N.Y., 1987, Bronx Mus. Arts, 1987, Chgo. Hist. Soc., Mus. Modern Art, N.Y.C., 1988, Sands Point Mus., L.I., Hofstra Mus., 1990, Nat. Mus. Sports Art, 1991, Indpls. Art Mus., Phoenix Mus. Art, Corcoran Mus. Art, Washington, IBM, N.Y.C., Fire House Gallery Mus. Nassau Cmty. Coll., L.I., 1992, Nat. Arts Club, 1992, IBM, N.Y.C., 1992, Nat. Sculpture Soc. and The Regina A Quick Ctr. for The Arts Fairfield U. Centennial Anniversary Exbn., 1993, Mus. Modern Art, N.Y.C., Nat. Sculpture Soc. 100 Anniversary Exhbn., 1993, 97, Italy, 1994, 98, Provincetown Assn. and Art Mus., 1993, Kyoto (Japan) Mus. Sculpture Guild, 1993, Nat. Sculpture Soc. Exhbn. in Italy, Lucca, 1994, Sculptures Guild, N.Y.C., 1994-95, Cline Gallery, Santa Fe, 1995, Smithtown Township Art Coun., N.Y.C., 1997, Hofstra Mus. Art, Hempstead, 1997, Hofstra Mus., 1997—, Smithsonian Inst. Nat. Portrait Gallery, 1997, Nat. Sculpture Soc., 1997-99, 2001, Nature Arts Club, 1999, Molloy Coll. Art Gallery, 1999, Nat. Acad. Art, 1999, Nat. Acad. Group Show, 1999, Portrait in bronze of Senator Norman J. Levy for Merrick Train Station, 2000, Aaron Copland's America, Heckscher Mus. Art, 2000, Nat. Art Mus., 2002-, Huntington Arts Coun. Inc., 2003, Petite Gallery, Baseball Hall of Fame & Mus., Cooperstown, N.Y., 2004, Queens Mus., N.Y., 2004, Allied Arts of Am., 2003-04 (New Foundry award, 2004); represented permanent collections, Stony Brook Hall of Fame, William Benton Mus. Art, Colby Coll. Mus., Oklahoma City Mus., Montclair (N.J.) Mus., Schonberg Libr. Black Studies, N.Y.C., Albany State Mus., Hofstra U., Bklyn. Mus., Colby Coll. Mus., Nat. Arts Collection, Nat. Portrait Gallery, Smithsonian Instn., Baseball Hall of Fame Cooperstown, N.Y., Nassau C.C., Hofstra U. Emily Lowe Gallery, Art Students League, Jewish Mus., "The Subway Series: The New York Mets Our National Pastime," Queens Mus., Black History Mus., Nassau County Mus., Stamford Mus. Art and Nature Ctr., Jericho Pub. Libr., N.Y., African-Am. Mus., Hempstead, N.Y., 1988, Stamford (Conn.) Mus. Art and Scis., Silvermine Artists North East exhbn., 1989, Nassau C.C. Fire House Gallery, 1992, Nat. Portrait Gallery Smithsonian Instn., 1996, Monument Work, Base Ball Club, The Family Grp., TheSea Dogs, 1999, MTA, Pub. Monument for Senator Norman J. Levy Merrik R.R. Sta., N.Y., 1999, Yogi Berra Portrait, Nat. Gallery Smithsonian Inst., 2001, Raphare Soyer Portrait, 2001, others; also pvt. collections, TV shows, ABC, 1968, 81; edml. TV spl. Rhoda Sherbell-Woman in Bronze, 1977; works include Seated Ballerina, portraits of Aaron Copland (Bruce Stevenson Meml. Best Portrait award Nat. Arts Club 1989), Eleanor Roosevelt, Variations on a Theme (36 works of collaged sculpture), 1982-86; appeared several TV shows; guest various radio programs; contbr. articles to newspapers, popular mags. and art jours.; mem. Conservation Art Group Coun. City of N.Y., 1994-97; group exhbn., The Nat. Acad. Mus., 2003-04. Coun. mem. Nassau County Mus., 1978, trustee, 1st v.p. coun.; assoc. trustee Nat. Art Mus. of Sports, Inc., 1975—; cons., cmty. liaison WNET Channel 13, cultural coord., 1975-83; host radio show Not for Artists Only, 1978-79; trustee Women's Boxing Fedn., 1978; mem. The Art Commn. of The City of New York, 1993. Recipient Gold medal Allied Artists Am., 1989, Alfred G. B. Steel Meml. award Pa. Acad. Fine Arts, 1963-64; Jersey City Mus. prize for sculpture, 1961, 1st prize sculpture Locust Valley Art Show, 1966, 67, Ann. Sculpture prize Jersey City Mus., Bank for Savs. 1st prize in sculpture, 1950, Ford Found. purchase award, 1964, 2 top sculpture awards Mainstreams 77, Cert. of Merit Salmagundi Club, 1978, prize for sculpture, 1980, 81, award for sculpture Knickerbocker Artists, 1980, 81, top prize for sculpture Hudson Valley Art Assn., 1981, Sawyer award NAD, 1985, Gold medal of honor Audubon Artists, 1985, Silvermine Exhbn. award, Gold medal Allied Artists Am., 1990, Pres.' award Nat Arts Club N.Y.C.; MacDowell Colony fellow, 1976, AAAL and Nat. Arts and Letters grantee, 1960, Louis Comfort Tiffany Found. grantee, 1962, Ford Found. grantee, 1964, 67, also award, New Foundry award, Allied Artists Am., 2004; named one of top 5 finalist to do Monument of Queen Catherine of England, 1991; named to represent Nat. Portrait Gallery at Smithsonian Mus., 1996, sculpture selected to represent Nat. Portrait Gallery Mus., 1997; guest at Dept. of State Embassy Program, Prague, Czech Republic, 2003-04. Fellow Nat. Sculpture Soc.; mem. Sculpture Guild (dir.), Nat. Assn. Women Artists (Jeffery Childs Willis Meml. prize 1978), Allied Artists Soc. (dir., Gold medal 1990, The Pietro and Alfrieda Montana Meml. award 2000, award 2001), Audubon Artists (dir., Greta Kempton Walker prize 1965, Chaim Gross award, award for disting. contbr. to orgn. 1979, 80, Louis Weskeem award), Woman's Caucus for Art, Coll. Art Assn., Am. Inst. Conservation Hist. and Artistic Works, N.Y. Soc. Women Artists, Artists Equity Assn. N.Y., Nat. Sculpture Soc. (E.N. Richard Meml. prize 1989), Internat. Platform Assn., Profl. Artists Guild L.I., Painters and Sculptors Soc. N.J. (Bertrum R. Hulmes Meml. award), Am. Watercolor Soc. (award for disting. contbn. to orgn.), Catharine Lorillard Wolfe Club (hon. mention 1968), Nat. Arts Club (N.Y.C., Stevenson Meml. award 1989, Pres. award 1992, Robert Sayford award 2000, Bruce Stevenson Meml. award for Portrait 2000, Siegfort award 2000, ward for sculpture 2004), NAD (Helen F. Barnett prize 1965, Leila Gordon Sawyer prize 1989, The Dessle Green prize 1993, Charlotte Deenevidde award 2003). Home: 64 Jane Ct Westbury NY 11590-1410

SHERBERT, SHARON DEBRA, financial services executive; b. Bklyn., Aug. 18, 1953; d. Joseph George and Leah (Katzman) Goldstein; m. Robert Fisher, Oct. 20, 1973 (div. Nov. 1981); 1 child, Meredith Audra Fisher; m. Michael Sherbert, Apr. 4, 1982; 1 child, Jared Alan. Grad. high sch., Bklyn. Cert. fin. planner; registered fin. cons. Real estate agent Century 21 R.E., Sepulveda, Calif., 1976-80; life ins. agt. Prudential Life Ins., North Hollywood, Calif., 1980-82; sr. v.p. Profl. Planning, Encino, Calif., 1982-90; exec. v.p. Comprehensive Fin. Svcs., Burbank, Calif., 1992—. Columnist on Internet Web site Women in Tech., Inc., Van Nuys, Calif., 1996—. Co-host: (TV show) You and Your Money, 1993—. Mem. NAFE, Nat. Assn. Women Bus. Owners, Internat. Assn. for Fin. Planners, Inst. Cert. Fin. Planners, Zonta Club of Santa Clarita Valley (sunshine sec. 1992-93). Office: Comprehensive Fin Svcs 3811 W Burbank Blvd Burbank CA 91505-2116

SHERBORNE, ROBERT, editor; b. Fairborn, Ohio, Mar. 26, 1950; s. Henry Hall and Lauramay (Rider) S.; m. Pamela Saunders, Apr. 16, 1988; children: Laura, Sophie. BS in Comms., U. Tenn., 1976. Reporter Clarksville (Tenn.) Leaf Chronicle, 1976, Tullahoma (Tenn.) News, 1976-77, The Tennessean, Nashville, 1977-92, regional editor, 1993-94, spl. project editor, 1995—. Recipient Nat. Gold Mass Media award Nat. Conf. Christians & Jews, 1983; spl. citation Nat. Headliners award Press Club of Atlantic City, N.J., 1983. Office: The Tennessean 1100 Broadway Nashville TN 37203-3134 E-mail: sherborne@comcast.net.

SHERBURN, ERIC W. neurosurgeon; s. James Ross and Shirley Minton Sherburn; m. Leigh Ann Moss, Oct. 5, 1991; children: Madeleine Moss, Claire Minton. BS in Zoology, BA in Philosophy, U. Okla., Norman, 1989; MD, U. Okla., Tulsa, 1993. Diplomate Nat. Bd. Med. Examiners, cert. State of Mo., 1996, State of Okla., 2000. Intern in gen. surgery Washington U., Barnes Hosp., St. Louis, 1993—94, resident of neurol. surgery, 1994—2000, resident in pediat. neurosurgery, 1996; attending neurosurgeon Okla. Spine & Brain Inst., Tulsa, 2000—. Clin. instr. of neurosurgery U. Okla. Coll. Medicine, Tulsa, 2001—. Contbr. articles to profl. jours. Grantee, NIH, 1997—99. Mem.: Okla. State Med. Assn., Tulsa County Med. Soc., Mo. State Neurosurgical Soc., Congress of Neurol. Surgeons, Am. Assn. Neurol. Surgeons. Avocations: running, golf, skiing. Office: Okla Spine & Brain Inst 1919 S Wheeling Ste 600 Tulsa OK 74104

SHERBY, KATHLEEN REILLY, lawyer; b. St. Louis, Apr. 5, 1947; d. John Victor and Florian Sylvia (Frederick) Reilly; m. James Wilson Sherby, May 17, 1975; children: Michael R.R., William J.R., David J.R. AB magna cum laude, St. Louis U., 1969, JD magna cum laude, 1976. Bar: Mo. 1976. Assoc. Bryan Cave, St. Louis, 1976-85; ptnr. Bryan Cave LLP, St. Louis, 1985—. Contbr. articles to profl. jours. Bd. dirs Jr. League, St. Louis, 1989-90, St. Louis Forum, 1992-99, pres., 1995-97; chmn. Bequest and Gift Coun. of St. Louis U., 1997-99; jr. warden Ch. of St. Michael and St. George, 1998-2000; bd. dirs. Bistate chpt. ARC, 2000—; bd. trustees St. Louis Sci. Ctr., 2000—. Fellow Am. Coll. Trust and Estate Coun. (regent 1997—), Estate Planning Coun. of St. Louis (pres. 1986-87), Bar Assn. Met. St. Louis (chmn. probate sect. 1986-87), Mo. Bar Assn. (chmn. probate and trust com. 1996-98, chmn. probate law revision subcom. 1988-96). Episcopalian. Home: 47 Crestwood Dr Saint Louis MO 63105-3032 Office: Bryan Cave LLP 1 Metropolitan Sq Ste 3600 Saint Louis MO 63102-2733 Office Phone: 314-259-2000.

SHERE, DENNIS, lawyer, retired publishing executive; b. Cleve., Nov. 29, 1940; s. William and Susan (Luskay) S.; m. Maureen Jones, Sept. 4, 1965; children: Rebecca Lynn, David Matthew, Stephen Andrew. BS in Journalism, Ohio U., 1963, MS in Journalism, 1964; JD, DePaul U., 2003. Staff writer Dayton (Ohio) Daily News, 1966-69; asst. prof. Sch. Journalism Bowling Green (Ohio) State U., 1969-70; fin. editor Detroit News, 1970-72, city editor, 1973-75; editor Dayton Jour. Herald, 1975-80; pub. Springfield (Ohio) Newspapers Inc., 1980-83, Dayton Newspapers, Inc., 1983-88; gen. mgr. Media Group Moody Bible Inst., 1989—2001; with death penalty trial assistance divsn. Il. State Appellate Defender's Office, 2004—. Served with AUS, 1964-66. Mem. Sigma Alpha Epsilon, Omicron Delta Kappa. Office Phone: 312-793-6959. Business E-Mail: Dennis.Shere@moody.edu.

SHERER, SAMUEL AYERS, lawyer, urban planning consultant; b. Warwick, NY, June 17, 1944; s. Ernest Thompson and Helen (Ayers) S.; m. Dewi Sudewinahidah, June 28, 1980 (dec. Dec. 2000). AB magna cum laude, Oberlin Coll., 1966; JD, Harvard U., 1970; M in City Planning, MIT, 1970. Bar: DC 1972, U.S. Supreme Ct. 1979. Atty., advisor HUD, Boston, 1970; sr. cons. McClaughry Assocs., Washington, 1970-71, 74-76; cons. Urban Inst., Washington, 1971-72; atty., urban planner IBRD Jakarta (Indonesia) Urban Devel. Study, 1972-74; atty., advisor Office Minority Bus. U.S. Dept. Commerce, Washington, 1976-77; ptnr. Topping & Sherer, Washington, 1977-90; pres. Sherer-Axelrod-Monacelli, Inc., Cambridge, Mass., 1978-99; prin. The Washington Team, Inc., 1992—2002, Richardson & Sherer, LLC, 2000—. Bd. dirs. EnviroClean Solutions, Inc., The Urban Agr. Network; rep. Internat. Devel. Law Inst., Washington, 1983-90; sr. fellow Climate Inst., 1988—; cons. in field. Co-author: Urban Land Use in Egypt, 1977; editor: Important Laws and Regulations Regarding Land, Housing and Urban Development in the Arab Republic of Egypt, 1977, Important Laws and Regulations Regarding Land, Housing and Urban Development in the Hashemite Kingdom of Jordan, 1981. Bd. dirs. MIT Enterprise Forum of Washington-Balt., 1980-82; mem. DC Rep. Ctrl. Com., 1984-88; mem. nat. governing bd. Ripon Soc., Washington, 1977-83. Urban Studies fellow HUD, 1969-70. Mem. ABA, DC Bar Assn., Am. Planning Assn., Am. Soc. Internat. Law, Asia Soc., Phi Beta Kappa. Avocations: tennis, reading. Home: 4600 Connecticut Ave NW Apt 205 Washington DC 20008-5702 Office: 7 Brookes Ave Gaithersburg MD 20877-2754 Office Phone: 301-527-2766. E-mail: washteam@aol.com.

SHERIDAN, FREDERICK, architectural firm executive; Ceo Sheridan, Behm, Eustice & Assocs., Arlington, Va. Office: Sheridan Behm Eustice & Assocs 3440 Fairfax Dr Arlington VA 22201-4431

SHERIDAN, JAMES EDWARD, history professor; b. Wilmington, Del., July 15, 1922; s. Phillip Lambert and Ida Alverna (Green) S.; m. Sonia Landy, Sept. 27, 1947; 1 son, Jamy. BS, U. Ill., 1949, MA, 1950; PhD, U. Calif. at Berkeley, 1961. Lectr. Chinese history Stanford U., 1960; mem. faculty Northwestern U., 1961—, prof. history, 1968—, chmn. dept., 1969-74, assoc. dean Coll. Arts and Scis., 1985-89, prof. emeritus, 1992—. Author: Chinese Warlord: The Career of Feng Yu-hsiang, 1966, China: A Culture Area in Perspective, 1970, China in Disintegration: The Republican Era in Chinese History, 1912-1949, 1975, A Community of Caring: An Introduction to Kendal at Hanover, 1998; editor: The Transformation of Modern China series, 1975— . Served to ensign USN, 1941-46. Fulbright fellow, France, 1950-51; Ford Found. fellow, 1958-60; grantee Am. Coun. Learned Socs.-Social Sci. Rsch. Coun., 1966-67, 71-72 Home: 80 Lyme Rd Apt 438 Hanover NH 03755-1236 Office: Northwestern Univ Dept History Evanston IL 60201 E-mail: james.e.sheridan@valley.net.

SHERIDAN, JIM, director, screenwriter; b. Dublin, 1949; Student, Univ. Coll., Dublin. Artistic dir. Project Arts Theatre, 1976—80, N.Y. Irish Arts Ctr., 1982—87; founder Children's Theatre Co., Dublin. Screenwriter: Into the West, 1993; dir.: My Left Foot, 1989, The Field, 1990, In the Name of the Father, 1993, The Boxer, 1997, In America, 2001; prodr., exec. prodr. Some Mother's Son, 1996, Agnes Browne, 1999, On the Edge, 2000, Borstal Boy, 2000, Bloody Sunday, 2001. Office: Hells Kitchen Ltd 21 Mespil Rd Dublin 4 Ireland also: Creative Artists Agy 9830 Wilshire Blvd Beverly Hills CA 90212-1804 E-mail: hellskit@iol.ie.

SHERIDAN, JOHN J. musician, music educator; s. John J. and Martha S. Sheridan; m. Colleen M. Smith, May 5, 1989; children: Erin Colleen, Kelly Ann. AA, Bucks County C.C., 1985; MusB, Temple U., 1989; MA, NYU, 2000. Freelance performer, Bristol, Pa., 1985—; adj. faculty jazz studies Bucks County C.C., Newtown, 1994—. Arts tech. com. Bucks County C.C., Newtown, Pa., 2002—, music tech. coord., 1996—. Composer, studio musician: songs Another View Point, studio musician: rec. Purity, Is You Is. Mem. Dem. Com., Bristol, 2002—; exec. com. mem. Bucks County Dem. Party, Doylestown, Pa., 2002—. Democrat. Roman Catholic. Office: Bucks County C C 275 Swamp Rd Newtown PA 18940-4106 E-mail: sheridaj@bucks.edu.

SHERIDAN, JOHN ROBERT, lawyer; b. Upland, Pa., Oct. 8, 1944; s. John Paul and Theresa Valerie (Dawson) Sheridan; m. Barbara Ann Bigelow, Aug. 18, 1973; children: Daniel, Timothy. BA, U. Del., 1966; JD, U. Balt., 1972. Bar: Pa. 1973, Del. 1975, U.S. Dist. Ct. Del. 1976. Law clk. Herlihy & Herlihy, Wilmington, Del., 1971—72; asst. city solicitor City of Wilmington, 1973—98, first asst., 1998—2000, city solicitor, 2001—. Mem. City Dem. Com., Wilmington, 1977—94; alt. del. State Dem. Com., Del., 1984, regular del., 1988; mem. Frawley for Wilmington, 1984, 1988, Citizens for Biden, 1970—, Maloney for Senate, 1976. With USAR, 1966—72. Mem.: ABA, Del. Bar Assn., Pa. Bar Assn., Kiwanis Club of Wilmington (pres. 1998—99), Sierra Club. Democrat. Roman Catholic. Home: 1611 Mt Salem Ln Wilmington DE 19806-1134 Office: Office of City Solicitor 800 N French St Wilmington DE 19801-3590

SHERIDAN, MARK WILLIAM, mechanical engineer, strategic planner; b. Bryn Mawr, Pa., July 9, 1959; s. Phillip Frederick and Shirley (Frazer) S. BSME, Lafayette Coll., 1981; MBA, Cornell U., 1987, M. Engring. (Mech.), 1988. Registered profl. engr., Ohio. Project engr. Internat. Paper Co., Mobile, Ala., 1981-83, sr. process engr., 1983-85; assoc. Booz-Allen & Hamilton, Cleve., 1988-90; coord. long range planning appliance motor divsn. Emerson Electric Co., St. Louis, 1990-93, resident engr. Paragould Plant, 1993-96; dir. mfg. Thermodisc, Mansfield, Ohio, 1996—2002, dir. ops. devel., 2002—. Summer intern Saturn Corp., Troy, Mich., 1986, 87. Patentee in field. Bd. dirs. ABC Condominium Assn., St. Louis, 1992-94; chmn. JGSM Student Faculty Com./Quality of Life Com., Ithaca, N.Y., 1985-87; pres. Mobile Soap Box Derby, 1983-85; v.p. ways and means, bd. dirs. Mobile Jaycees, 1984-85; mem. Leadership Unltd., 2003-04; active YMCA; treas. First Presbyn. Ch. of Mansfield, 1998-03. Lester B. Knight scholar Cornell U., 1986-88, J. Stanford Smith scholar Cornell U., 1985-87; named Outstanding Young Man of Am., 1984, 85, 87. Mem. ASME, Inst. Indsl. Engrs., The Planning Forum, Soc. Indsl. Archaeology, World Future Soc., St. Louis Jaycees (bd. dirs. 1992-94), Am. Mensa. Republican. Avocations: golf, reading, computing, weightlifting. Home: 2403 Ranchwood Dr Mansfield OH 44903-9044 Office: Thermodisc 1320 S Main St Mansfield OH 44907-5500 Office Phone: 419-525-8295.

SHERIDAN, PATRICK MICHAEL, finance company executive, retired; b. Grosse Pointe, Mich., Apr. 13, 1940; s. Paul Phillip and Frances Mary (Rohan) S.; m. Diane Lorraine Tressler, Nov. 14, 1966; children: Mary, Patrick, Kelly, Kevin, James. BBA, U. Notre Dame, 1962; MBA, U. Detroit, 1975. Acct. Peat, Marwick, Mitchell & Co., Detroit, 1962-72, audit mgr., 1969-72; exec. v.p. fin. Alexander Hamilton Life Ins. Co., Farmington, Mich., 1973-76; sr. v.p. ops. Sun Life Ins. Co. Am., Balt., 1976-78, exec. v.p., 1978-79; pres. Sun Ins. Services, Inc., 1979-81; pres., chief exec. officer Am. Health & Life Ins. Co., Balt., 1981-85; chief exec. officer Gulf Ins. Co., 1985-86; sr. v.p., chief fin. officer Comml. Credit Co., 1985-86, sr. v.p. audit, 1987; exec. v.p., chief fin. officer Anthem, Inc., Indpls., 1987-99, ret., 1999. Rep. candidate for U.S. Congress, 1972; past pres. Charlesbrooke Cmty. Assn.; past. v.p. Jr. Achievement of Met. Balt., 1984-85; bd. dirs. Goodwill Industries of Balt., 1986, bd. govs. 1994; bd. dirs. Family Svcs. Assn., 1994, Goodwill Industries of Indpls., 1994; mem. adv. coun. Clowes Meml. Hall. Capt. AUS, 1963-65. Recipient various Jaycee awards. Fellow Life Mgmt. Inst.; mem. Am. Mgmt. Assn. (pres.'s assn.), AICPAs, Mich. Assn. CPAs, Md. Assn. CPAs, Am. Soc. CLUs, U.S. Jaycees (treas. 1973-74), Mich. Jaycees (pres. 1971-72), Detroit Jaycees (pres. 1968-69), Balt. C. of C. (bd. dirs.), Mensa, Notre Dame Club, Skyline Club.

SHERIDAN, RICK D. educator; b. Lawrence, Kans., Aug. 26, 1957; s. Richard Bert and Audrey Marion Sheridan. MA, U. Kans., 1988. Journalist United Press Internat., Madison, Wis., 1990—95; adj. prof. Calif. State U., Chico, Calif., 1997—2003, Butte Coll., Chico, Calif., 1996—. Dir. Accelerated Learning Rsch., 2001. Home: 1745 Louisiana St Lawrence KS 66044 Personal E-mail: ricksheridan57@yahoo.com.

SHERIDAN, SONIA LANDY, artist, retired art educator; b. Newark, Ohio, Apr. 10, 1925; d. Avrom Mendel and Goldie Cornelia (Hanon) Landy; m. James Edward Sheridan, Sept. 27, 1947; 1 son, Jamy. AB, Hunter Coll., 1945; postgrad., Columbia U., 1946-48; MFA with high honors, Calif. Coll. Arts and Crafts, 1961. Tchr. art public high schs., Calif., 1951-57; chmn. dept. art Taipei (Taiwan) Am. Sch., 1957-59; instr. Calif. Coll. Arts and Crafts, 1960-61; asst. prof. art Sch. Art Inst. Chgo., 1961-67, assoc. prof., 1968-75, prof., 1976-80, prof. emeritus, 1980—, founder, head generative sys. program, 1970-80. Artist-in-residence 3M Corp., 1970, 76; cons. French Ministry of Culture, 1986; artist-in-residence Xerox Corp., 1981; lectr., univs., museums, art schs., workshops; lectr. Hungarian Acad. Scis. Symposium Collected Essays & Exhbn., Budapest, 1989, Internat. Soc. of Electronic Arts, Liverpool, UK. One-woman shows include Rosenberg Gallery, Chgo., 1966, Visual Studies Workshop, Rochester, N.Y., 1973, Iowa Mus. Art, Iowa City, 1976, Mus. Sci. Industry, Chgo., 1978; two-person show Mus. Modern Art, N.Y.C., 1974; exhibited in group shows at Print Ann, Boston Mus., 1963, Software, Jewish Mus., N.Y.C., 1969-70, Photography into Art, London, 1972-73, Photokino, Cologne, Germany, 1974, San Francisco Mus. Art, 1975, U. Mich. Mus. Art, 1978, Toledo Mus. Art, 1982-83, Mus. Modern Art, Paris, 1983, Siggraph, U.S., Japan, France, 1982, 83, Reina Sofia Mus., Madrid, Spain, 1986, Smithsonian Instn., 1990, Tokyo Met. Mus. Photography, 1991, Madrid City Cultural Ctr., 1992, Karl Ernst Osthaus Mus., Hagen, Germany, 1992, Circulo des Belles Artes, Madrid, 1992, Yale U. Art Gallery, 1995, Tokyo Intercom. Ctr., 1995, U. Montreal, 1995, Internat. Soc. Electronic Arts, Liverpool, Eng., 1998, Hungarian Art Mus., 1995 Scripton Mus., Netherlands, 1997, Video Gallery, Hungary, 2000-02, Mus. for Kommunikation, Frankfort, Germany, 2001, 2nd biennial, Museo Nacional de Belles Artes, Buenos Aires, 2002; major permanent collection at Hood Mus. Art, Dartmouth; represented in permanent collections Art Inst. Chgo., San Francisco Mus. Art, Mus. Sci. and Industry, Chgo., U. Iowa Mus. Art, Nat. Gallery Art, Ottawa, Can., Visual Studies Workshop, Rochester, Tokyo Met. Mus. Photography, Fundacion Arte y Technologia, Madrid, Tweed Mus., Univ. Minn., 1997, Scryption Mus., Tilburg, Netherlands, 1998; author: Energized Artscience: Sonia Landy Sheridan, 1978; co-editor Leonardo jour., hon. editor, 2000; contbr. articles, essay to profl. jours. Guggenheim fellow, 1973; Nat. Endowment for Arts workshop grantee 1974, pub. media grantee, 1976, artist grantee 1981; Union Ind. Colls. Art grantee 1975. Mem. Coll. Art Assn., Internat. Soc. for Interdisciplinary Study of Symmetry, Internat. Soc. of Electronic Arts. E-mail: sonia.sheridan@valley.net.

SHERIDAN, THOMAS BROWN, mechanical engineering and applied psychology educator, researcher, consultant; b. Cin., Dec. 23, 1929; s. Mahlon Brinsley and Esther Anna (Brown) S.; m Rachel Briggs Rice, Aug. 1, 1953; children: Paul Rice, Richard Rice, David Rice, Margaret Lenore. BS, Purdue U., 1951; MS, UCLA, 1954; ScD, MIT, 1959; Dr. (hon.), Delft U. Tech., The Netherlands, 1991. Registered profl. engr., Mass. Asst. prof. mech. engring. MIT, Cambridge, 1959-65, assoc. prof., 1965-70, prof., 1970-78, prof. engring. and applied psychology, 1978-94, prof. aeronautics and astronautics, 1994—, Ford prof., 1995—. Lectr. U. Calif., Berkeley, Stanford U., 1968; vis. prof. U. Delft, The Netherlands, 1972, Stanford U., 1989, Ben Gurion U., Israel, 1995; chmn. com. human factors, mem. com. aircrew-vehicle interaction, com. on commercially developed space facility, com. on human factors in air traffic control, NRC, mem. com. on nat. automated hwy. sys., com. on setting and enforceing speed limits, com. on intelligent vehicle initiative; mem. adv. com. on applied phys., math. and biol. scis. NSF; mem. life scis. adv. com., study group on robotics, oversight com. flight telerobotic servicer NASA; mem. task force on appropriate tech. U.S. Congress Office Tech. Assessment; mem. study sect. accident prevention and injury control NIH; mem. Def. Sci. Bd. Task Force on Computers, Tng. and Gaming, Nuclear Regulatory Commn. on Nuclear Safety Rsch. Rev. Com. Author: Telerobotics, Automation and Human Supervisory Control, 1992, Humans and Automation; co-author: Man Machine Systems, 1974; editor: (with others) Monitoring Behavior and Supervisory Control, 1976, Perspectives on the Human Controller, 1997; assoc. editor Automatica, 1982-94; co-editor: Perspectives on the Human Controller, 1997; mem. edtl. adv. bd. Tech. Forecasting and Social Change, Computer Aided Design, Advanced Robotics, Robotics and Computer Integrated Mfg.; sr. editor Presence: Telerobots and Virtual Environments, 1991—. Served to 1st lt. USAF, 1951-53. Recipient Nat. Engring. award Am. Assn. Engring. Socs., 1997, Rufus Oldenburger medal ASME, 1997. Fellow IEEE (pres. Systems, Man and Cybernetics Soc. 1974-76, Centennial medal 1984, Norbert Wiener award 1993, Joseph G. Wohl award 1995, Millenium medal 2000), Human Factors Soc. (Paul M. Fitts award 1977, Arnold Small award 2000, pres. 1990-91, Pres. Disting. Svc. award 2000), Nat. Acad. Engring. Democrat. Mem. United Ch. of Christ. Home: 32 Sewall St Newton MA 02465

SHERIDAN LABARGE, JOAN RUTH, publishing executive; b. Forest Hills, N.Y., July 3, 1956; d. Thomas Patrick and Ruth B. (Stalzer) S.; 1 daughter. BS magna cum laude in Communication Arts, St. John's U., Jamaica, N.Y., 1978. Media planner BBDO, N.Y.C., 1978-81; media supr. Ted Bates & Co., N.Y.C., 1982-84; v.p., assoc. media dir. FCB Leber Katz Ptnrs., N.Y.C., 1985-87; v.p., assoc. pub., Woman's Day Hachette Filipacchi Mags., N.Y.C., 1987—95, v.p., pub. Family Life Mag., 1995—99; exec. v.p., group pub. dir. Weider Pub., 1999—2000; corp. pub., new bus. devel. G + J USA Publishing, 2001—, pub. Rosie, 2001—02, pub. YM Mag., 2003—. Named Top Media Sales Rep, Mediaweek, 1992. Office: G + J USA Publishing 375 Lexington Ave New York NY 10017*

SHERIF, S. A. engineering educator; b. Alexandria, Egypt, June 25, 1952; came to U.S., 1978; s. Ahmed and Ietedal H. (Monib) S.; m. Azza A. Shamseldin, Feb. 6, 1977 (div.); children: Ahmed S., Mohammad S.; m. Vitrell Lynn McNair, May 30, 2003. BSME (hon.), Alexandria U., 1975, MSME, 1978; PhD in Mech. Engring., Iowa State U., 1985. Tchg. asst. mech. engring. Alexandria U., 1975-78; tchg. assoc. mech. and environtl. engring. U. Calif., Santa Barbara, 1978-79; rsch. asst. mech. engring. Iowa State U., Ames, 1979-84; asst. prof. No. Ill. U., Dekalb, 1984-87, U. Miami, Coral Gables, Fla., 1987—91; assoc. prof. mech. engring. U. Fla., Gainesville, 1991-2001, prof. mech. engring., 2001—, mem. doctoral rsch. faculty, 1992—, founding dir. Wayne K. and Lyla L. Masur HVAC Lab., 1995—, asst. dir. Indsl. Assessment Ctr., 2001—. ABET coord. for mech. engring., 1997—; coord. for mech. engring. So. Assn. Colls. and Schs., 2001—; affiliate Inst. for Sci. and Health Policy U. Fla., 2001—; cons. Solar Reactor Techs., Inc., Miami, 1988-91, Dade Power Corp., Miami, 1988-91, Ind. Energy Sys., Miami, 1988-91, Carey Dwyer Eckhart Mason Spring & Beckham, P.A. Law Offices, Miami, 1988-89, Michael G. Widoff, P.A., Attys. at Law, Ft. Lauderdale, Fla., 1989-93, Law Offices Pomeroy and Betts, Ft. Lauderdale, 1991-92, Ctr. for Indoor Air Rsch., 1994-2000; cons. Fla. Power and Light Co., 1996-98; external examiner U. Roorkee, 1994-95, 98—. Indian Inst. Tech., Delhi, 2002-, Alexandria U., Egypt, 2000-; adj. faculty cons. Kennedy Western U., Thousand Oaks, Calif., 1994-97; resident assoc. Argonne (Ill.) Nat. Lab., Tech. Transfer Ctr., summer 1992; faculty fellow NASA Kennedy Space Ctr., Cape Canaveral, Fla., summer 1993; rsch. assoc. summer faculty rsch. program USAF Office Sci. Rsch., Arnold Engring. Devel. Ctr., Arnold AFB, Tenn., 1994; faculty fellow NASA Marshall Space Flight Ctr., Huntsville, Ala., 1996, 97; ABET coord. for aerospace engring., 2002-; coord. for aerospace engring., So. Assn. Colls. and Schs., 2002-. Co-editor: Industrial and Agricultural Applications of Fluid Mechanics, 1989, The Heuristics of Thermal Anemometry, 1990, Heat and Mass Transfer in Frost and Ice, Packed Beds, and Environmental Discharges, 1990, Industrial Applications of Fluid Mechanics, 1990, rev. edit., 1991, Mixed Convection and Environmental Flows, 1990, Measurement and Modeling of Environmental Flows, 1992, Industrial and Environment Applications of Fluid Mechanics, 1992, rev. edit., 1998, Thermal Anemometry-1993, 1993, Developments in Electrorheological Flows and Measurement Uncertainty-1994, 1994, Heat, Mass and Momentum Transfer in Environmental Flows, 1995, Thermal Anemometry, 1996, Fluid Measurement Uncertainty Applications, 1996, Devices for Flow Measurement and Analysis, 1997, Heat and Mass Transfer in Environmental Flows, 1998, Industrial and Environmental Applications of Fluid Mechanics, 1999, rev. edit., 2001, Measurement and Modeling of Environmental Flows, 2002, Industrial and Environmental Applications of Fluid Mechanics, 2003, Fluid Measurement Uncertainty Applications, 2003; reviewer more than 40 internat. jours., more than 200 conf. procs.; mem. editl. com. SECTAM XXI, 2001-2002; book rev. editor ASME Applied Mech. Revs., 2001-; assoc. tech. editor Solar Energy jour., 2002—; guest editor Solar Energy Jour. Spl. Issue on Hydrogen Prodn., 2003—; contbr. numerous articles to profl. jours. NASA ambassador, 1996-98, lab. host student sci. tng. program Ctr. for Precollegiate Edn. and Tng., 1997—; mem. environ. awareness adv. com., Dade County Pub. Schs., 1989-91, lab. dir. cmty. lab. rsch. program, 1989-91, also faculty liaison design svcs. dept.; active Com. for Nat. Inst. for Environ., 1992—; mem. senate U. Fla., 1994-95, mem. OUTREACH Spkrs. program, 1996-98. Recipient Kuwait prize for applied scis., 2002, cert. recognition for rsch. contributions, NASA, 1993, 1996, 1997. Fellow ASME (mem. energy resources bd. 2001-03, chmn steering com. internat. energy conversion engring. conf., 2002-03, coord. group fluid measurements, fluids engring. divsn. 1987—, vice chmn. 1990-92, chmn. 1992-94, fluids engring. divsn. adv. bd. 1994—, fed. honors and awards com. 1995-2001, mem. fluid mechs. tech. com. 1990—, fluid mech. com. 1987-90, K-19 com. on environ. heat transfer 1987—, chmn. 2003—, mem. K-6 com. on heat transfer in energy systems, 2001—, mem. fluid applications and systems tech. com. 1990—, systems analysis tech. com. advanced energy sys. divsn. 1989—, newsletter editor advanced energy sys. divsn. 1995-98, exec. com., 1999—, mem.-at-large honors awards 1999-2000, sec., treas. 2000-2001, vice chmn., 2001-02, chmn., 2002-03, sr. mem. and past chmn., 2003-04, fundamentals and theory tech. com. solar energy divsn. 1990-97, chmn. CGFM nominating com. 1992-94, mem. 1994-98, chmn. profl. devel. com. Rock River Valley sect. 1987, tech. activities operating com. Gator sect. 1994-96, MFFCC subcom. 1 on uncertainties in flow measurements 1995-2000), ASHRAE (mem. heat transfer fluid flow com. 1988-92, 93-97, corr. mem. 1992-93, 97—, mem. thermodynamics and psychrometrics com. 1988-92, 96-2002, corr. mem. 1992-96, vice chmn. 1990-92, mem. liquid to refrigerant heat exchs. com. 1989-93, 96-97, sec. 1990-92, corr. mem. 1993-96, 97-2001, corr. mem. air-to-refrigerant heat transfer com., 2000—, chmn. stds. project com. on measurement of moist air properties 1989-95, corr. mem. refrigeration load calculations com., 1999—, mem. tech. activities com. 2004—, E.K. Campbell award of merit 1997, Disting. Svc. award 2003), AIAA (assoc., mem. terrestrial energy systems tech. com. 2001—); mem. AIChE, Internat. Assn. Hydrogen Energy, Internat. Solar Energy Soc., Am. Soc. for Engring. Edn., Internat. Energy Soc. (mem. sci. coun.), European Assn. Laser Anemometry (ASME/FED rep., mem. steering com.), Internat. Inst. Refrigeration (U.S. nat. com.), Sigma Xi. Moslem. Avocations: reading, soccer, basketball, history, astronomy. Office: U Fla Dept Mech and Aerospace Engrng 232 MAE Bldg B PO Box 116300 Gainesville FL 32611-6300 Home: 3440 NE 41st Pl Ocala FL 34479 Office Phone: 352-392-7821. E-mail: sasherif@ufl.edu.

SHERIFF, SEYMOUR, retired lawyer; b. Rye, N.Y., Aug. 22, 1917; s. Michael and Anna (Rosenfeld) S.; m. Selene Gloria Wolf, Oct. 15, 1950; children: Steven, Susan, Ellen, Carol. BSS cum laude, CCNY, 1935; JD cum laude, Yale U., 1938. Bar: D.C. 1938, N.Y. 1938, Md. 1957. Pvt. practice, Washington, 1938-58; sr. ptnr. Gardner, Morrison, Sheriff & Beddow, Washington, 1958-2000; ret., 2000. With AUS, 1942-45. Decorated Legion of Merit. Mem. Order of Coif, Phi Beta Kappa.

SHERIN, EDWIN, theatrical and film director, actor; b. Danville, Pa., Jan. 15, 1930; s. Joseph and Ruth (Berger) S.; m. Jane Alexander, Mar. 29, 1975; children: Anthony J., Geoffrey B. (dec.), Jonathan E.; 1 stepchild, Jason E. AB in History and Polit. Sci., Brown U., 1952. Acting tchr. Am. Theatre Wing, N.Y.C., 1962-64; acting tchr. Am. Theatre Tng. Inst. Southeastern Mass. U., South Dartmouth, 1974; Lucille Lortel Disting. guest artist U. Bridgeport (Conn.), 1980; dir. Sch. Theatre Arts Boston U., 1981; acting tchr. Okla. Summer Arts Inst., 1985-86, One on One, L.A., 1989, 90; exec. v.p. Altion Prodns., L.A., 1985-93; pres. Pumpkin House Prodns., 1993—. Mem. nat. adv. for Mus. Am. Theatre; instr. Okla. Summer Arts Inst., guest dir. Calif. Inst. Arts; prof. dept. drama Fla. State U. Actor with Houseman's troupe Phoenix Theatre, N.Y.C., 1957-58, actor N.Y. Shakespeare Festival, 1956-60; appeared as: Octavius Caesar in, Anthony and Cleopatra, 1958; appeared in Broadway plays Come Blow Your Horn, 1960, Desert Incident, 1961, Romulus, 1962, Face of a Hero, 1963; TV films Playhouse 90, 1956-58, Studio One, 1956-58, Omnibus, 1957-60, East Side/West Side, 1960; dir. Broadway plays including The Great White Hope, 1968, Glory Hallelujah, 1969, 6 RMS RIV VU, 1973, Find Your Way Home, Of Mice and Men, 1974, Red Devil Battery Sign, 1975, Sweet Bird of Youth, 1976, Eccentricities of a Nightingale, 1976, The First Monday in October, 1978, Goodbye Fidel, 1980, The Visit, 1992; assoc. producing dir. Washington's Arena Stage, 1964-68; dir. Cosi Fan Tutte, N.Y. City Opera Co., 1972, A Streetcar Named Desire, Piccadilly Theatre, London, 1973, Semmelweiss, Studio Arena Theatre, Buffalo, N.Y., 1978, Outrage, Kennedy Ctr., Washington, 1982; films including Valdez is Coming, 1970, My Old Man's Place, 1971; producing artistic dir. Showdown at Adobe Hotel, Semmelweiss, Hedda Gabler, Night Must Fall, A Streetcar Named Desire, Hartman Theatre, Stamford, Conn., 1980-85; dir. Chelsea Walls, Naked Angels, N.Y.C., 1990, Karla, Long Wharf Theater, 2002, Ghosts, Shakespeare Theater, Washington, 2002, TV programs Hill Street Blues, Moonlighting, WIOU, L.A. Law, Tour of Duty, MEN; co-exec. prodr. Law and Order, 1993-94, exec. prodr., 1994-2000, (TV films) The Father Clements Story, Lena, My 100 Children, Daughter of the Streets, Getting Even, A Marriage: Georgia O'Keeffe and Alfred Stieglitz, 1991. With USN, 1952-56, Korea. Recipient Outer Circle award, 1969; New Eng. Theatre award, 1969, N.Y. Drama Critics award, 1969, Drama Desk award, 1969, L.A. Drama Cir. award, 1971, Recipient Tony nomination, 1974, London Evening Std. citation, 1973, Joseph Jefferson award, 1976, Buffalo drama award, 1978, Emmy award, 1997; New Eng. Theatre Conf. award; Ford Found. grantee, 1965-66; Am. Theatre fellow Coll. of Am. Theatre. Mem. AFTRA, SAG, Actors Equity Assn., Dirs. Guild Am. (nat. v.p. 1997—), Dramatists Guild, Soc. Stage Dirs. and Choreographers (v.p. 1970-80), Lincoln Soc., Phi Gamma Delta.

SHERIN, KEITH S. electrical manufacturing company executive; BA, U. Notre Dame, 1981; MBA, Columbia U., 1991. With fin. mgmt. prgram GE, 1981-84, mem. corp. audit staff, 1984, exec. audit mgr., mgr. programs and planning; mgr. fin. comml. engine ops. GE Aircraft Engines, 1992-93; dir. fin. GE Plastics Europe, 1993-95; mgr. global fin. and fin. svcs. GE Med. Sys., 1995-96, v.p. fin. and fin. svcs. ops., 1996-98, sr. v.p. fin., CFO, 1998—; CFO General Electric Co., Fairfield, CT. Office: GE 3135 Easton Tpke Fairfield CT 06431-0002

SHERK, KENNETH JOHN, lawyer; b. Ida Grove, Iowa, Feb. 27, 1933; s. John and Dorothy (Myers) Sherk; children: Karin Fulton, Katrina, Keith, Kyle. BSC, U. Iowa, 1955; JD, George Washington U., 1961. Bar: Ariz. 1962, U.S. Dist. Ct. Ariz. 1962, U.S. Ct. Appeals (9th cir.) 1966, U.S. Supreme Ct. 1974. Assoc. Moore & Romley, Phoenix, 1962-67, ptnr., 1967-79, Romley & Sherk, Phoenix, 1979-85; dir. Fennemore Craig, Phoenix, 1985—. 1st lt. U.S. Army, 1955-58, Korea. Recipient Profl. Achievement Svcs. award George Washington Law Assn., 1986, Ariz. Judges Assn., 1989, Disting. Svc. award Phoenix Assn. Def. Counsel, 1990; named Mem. of Yr. State Bar of Ariz., 1994. Fellow Am. Coll. Trial Lawyers, Am. Acad. Appellate Lawyers, Am. Bar Found., Ariz. Bar Found. (Walter E. Craig award 1999); mem. ABA (ho. of dels. 1990-93), Ariz. Bar Assn. (pres. 1985-86), Maricopa County Bar Assn. (pres. 1978-79). Republican. Congregationalist. Avocations: fishing, hiking, bicycling. Home: 1554 W Las Palmaritas Dr Phoenix AZ 85021-5429 Office: Fennemore Craig 3003 N Central Ave Ste 2600 Phoenix AZ 85012-2913

SHERLAND, BARBARA C. lawyer; married; 3 children. BA magna cum laude, Hood Coll., 1974; JD, U. Wash., 1984. Bar: Wash., U.S. Dist. Ct. (we. dist.) Wash. Law clk. to Hon. Eugene Wright U.S. Ct. Appeals (9th cir.), 1984; with Stoel River LLP, Seattle. Mem. adv. bd. Stat. KCTS-TV. Vice chmn. bd. dirs. Puget Sound Blood Ctr.; mem. adv. bd. Fred Hutchinson Cancer Rsch. Ctr., Am. Lung Assn.; mem. endowment bd. United Way King County. Named one of Wash.'s Super Lawyers, Wash. Law & Politics, 1999, 2000, 2002, Seattle's Top 100 Lawyers, Seattle Mag., 2001. Fellow: Am. Coll. Trust and Estate Counsel; mem.: Wash. Plannned Giving Coun. (mem. exec. com.), Wash. State Bar Assn. (chair real property, probate and trust sect.). Office: 600 University St Ste 3600 Seattle WA 98101 Business E-Mail: bcsherland@stoel.com.

SHERLING, FRED W. lawyer; b. Dec. 22, 1933; s. Weaver V. and Ruth M. (Bowen) S.; m. Camille Margaret Brochetto, Nov. 29, 1969; children: Charlotte, Sharon, Cheryl. BS in Chem. Engring., U. Tenn., 1957; LLB, George Washington U., 1961. Bar: U.S. Ct. Appeals (D.C. cir.) 1963, U.S. Ct. Customs and Patent Appeals 1963, U.S. Ct. Appeals (fed. cir.), 1982, U.S. Supreme Ct. 1982. Patent examiner U.S. Patent Office, Washington, 1957—63; assoc. solicitor, 1963—86; sole practice, 1986—. Mem. Patent Office Soc. Baptist. Personal E-mail: charlotte2002c@aol.com., fredweaver@excite.com.

SHERMAN, ALAN ROBERT, psychologist, educator; b. N.Y.C., Nov. 18, 1942; s. David R. and Goldie (Wax) S.; m. Llana Helene Tobias, Aug. 14, 1966 (div. 1989); children: Jonathan Colbert, Relissa Anne; m. Ann Marie Redington, Aug. 22, 2002. BA, Columbia U., 1964; MS, Yale U., 1966, PhD, 1969. Lic. psychologist, Calif. Faculty psychology U. Calif., Santa Barbara, 1969—; clin. psychologist in pvt. practice Santa Barbara, 1981—. Cons. in field. Author: Behavior Modification, 1973; contbr. articles to profl. jours. and chpts. in books. Pres. Santa Barbara Mental Health Assn., 1978, 84-85, 91, Mountain View Sch. Site Coun., Santa Barbara, 1978-84. Recipient Vol. of Yr. award Santa Barbara Mental Health Assn., 1979, Tchg. Excellence awards Delta Delta Delta, Alpha Chi Omega, Gamma Phi Beta, Santa Barbara; NIMH predoctoral rsch. fellow, 1964-69; grantee in field. Fellow Behavior Therapy and Rsch. Soc.; mem. APA, AAUP (chpt. pres. 1978-79), Calif. Psychol. Assn., Assn. for Advancement of Behavior Therapy, Santa Barbara County Psychol. Assn. (pres. 1985), Phi Beta Kappa (chpt. pres. 1977-78), Sigma Xi, Psi Chi (chpt. faculty advisor, 1979—). Office: Univ Calif Dept Psychology Santa Barbara CA 93106-9660 Office Phone: 805-893-3534. E-mail: sherman@psych.ucsb.edu. *Pursuing a creative profession which allows one to help improve the condition of others, provides intrinsic rewards that make the work process satisfying in itself. I am fortunate to be involved in two such professions, college teaching and psychotherapy. When you genuinely enjoy what you are doing, you are likely to be successful at it.*

SHERMAN, ARTHUR, theater educator, writer, actor, composer, sculptor; b. Dec. 5, 1920; s. Herman and Fay (Epstein) S.; m. Margery Frost Sherman, Apr. 15, 1974 (div. Sept. 1989); children: Claudia, Andrew Jay. MusB, Juilliard Sch. Music, 1955; M in Music Edn., Manhattan Sch. Music, 1957; Doctoral Equivalency, CUNY, 1969. Dir. performing arts N.Y.C. (N.Y.) Tech. Coll., 1964-72; prof. speech and theatre John Jay Coll., N.Y.C., 1990—, Borough Man C.C., N.Y.C., 1990—. Judge Film Award Com., Australia, 1972-89, Acad. Awards, 1990; cons. Min. for Edn., Tasmania, Australia, 1977; presenter in field. Author: (screenplays) Thistle and Thorn, 1982, Same Difference, 1983, (book and lyrics) Lenore and the Wonder House, 1964, Prisms in the Looking Glass, 1993, Once Upon a Crime, We the Common Earth; (book) Paradise Lagoon, 1989, Picture Book for Young Adults Paintings, Music and Lyrics, 1998, An Adventure in the New Mythology, 1999, Songwriting Is Easy and Fun, 1996, Red Herr, 2003; (comedy theater) But Its Not Chekhov, 1999; (comic screenplay) Weaning, 1999; (7-book novel) The Pleiades, Burning in Heaven, Freezing in Hell, Bloody Mooring, Scoring in Limbo, Chasing the Phoenix, The Pleiades and Beyond Adventure Etc., Betrayal of Self; (with Edward Mapp) The Road to Mainstream, 1999; (play) To Hell with Buffalo Wings-Anyone for Eagle Wings?, 1999, Warsaw Ghetto Uprising, 2001; actor, dir. films, TV, theater in U.S. and Australia; actor: (films) The Punisher, 1979, Death of a Soldier, 1985, Les Patterson Saves the World, 1988, The Last Bastion, 1987; sculptures displayed YWCA, Hamilton, Ont., Can., 1967, Lincoln Ctr., N.Y.C., 1969, State Bank, Sydney, Australia, 1974; bust of Louis Armstron Meml. Mus. and House, Dame Judith Anderson Australian Consulate N.Y.; contbr. design WTC 9/11 Meml., 2003. Pres. United Fedn. Coll. Tchrs., N.Y.C., 1971. With USN, 1943-46. With U.S. Army, 1943—45. Grantee Australian Film Commn., 1981. Mem. ASCAP, Australasian Performing Rights Assn., Actors' Equity U.S. and Australia. Home: 315 W 57th St New York NY 10019-3158 Office: John Jay Coll 58th St 10th Ave New York NY 10019 Business E-Mail: asherman@jjaycuny.edu.

SHERMAN, BEATRICE ETTINGER, business executive; b. N.Y.C., May 29, 1919; d. Max and Stella (Schrager) Ettinger; m. Herbert Jacob Howard, Feb. 15, 1942 (dec. 1971); children: Robert David Howard, Carolyn Howard Smith; m. Ernest John Sherman, Dec. 29, 1974 (dec. Oct. 2000). Student, Gulf Park Jr. Coll., Gulfport, Miss., 1934-35, Shimer Jr. Coll., Mt. Carroll, Ill., 1936-38; BA, U. Miami, 1940; postgrad., Harvard U., 1940, Paris-Am. Acad., Paris, 1972, Alliance Française, 1973. Corp. sec., dir. Save Electric Corp., Toledo, 1940—67, Verd-A-Ray Corp., Toledo, 1944—67, Penetray Corp., Toledo, 1962—67; ptnr. Stella Assocs., Newark, 1960—80, BHS Ptnrs., Miami, 1983—; pres. Besman Inc., Miami, 1976—, All Am. Mobile Tel. Co., Coral Gables, 1986—2000, Besman Hospitality, Gainesville, Fla., 1997—. Vol. worker Jewish Welfare Fedn., Toledo, 1942-69; vol. nurse's aid ARC, 1942-45; nat. spkr. United Jewish Appeal; mem. womens divsn. Greater Miami Jewish Fedn., 1969—, trustee, 1986-95; adv. bd. Miami Bell South; active Miami advertiser adv. bd. Bell South Advt. and Pub. Co.; vol. Nat. Coun. Jewish Women, Toledo, 1946-67, v.p., 1964-67, v.p., Miami, 1970-73; active Toledo chpt. Hadassah, 1943-67. Recipient Lion of Judah award Greater Miami Jewish Fedn., 1986. Mem. Assn. Telemessaging Svcs. Internat., Pioneers of Miami Beach. Home: 5108 SW 72d Ave Miami FL 33155-5530 Office: PO Box 558446 Miami FL 33255

SHERMAN, BRADLEY JAMES, congressman; b. LA, Oct. 24, 1954; s. Maurice H. and Lane (Moss) S. BA summa cum laude, UCLA, 1974; JD magna cum laude, Harvard U., 1979. Bar: Calif. 1979; CPA, Calif. Pvt. practice, L.A., 1980-91; chmn. Calif. Bd. Equalization, Sacramento, 1991-95; mem. US Congress from 27th Calif. dist., 1997—; mem. banking and fin. svcs. com., internat. rels. com. Lectr. on tax law and policy; mem. Calif. Franchise Tax Bd., 1991-95. Contbr. articles to legal jours. Bd. dirs., rep. on tax issues Calif. Common Cause, 1984-89; mem. exec. com. Calif. Dem. Com., 1991—. Mem. Calif. State Bar. Democrat. Jewish. Office: US Ho Reps 1030 Longworth HOB Washington DC 20515-0527 E-mail: brad.sherman@mail.house.gov.

SHERMAN, CINDY, artist; b. Glen Ridge, N.J., 1954; Student, State Univ. Coll. Buffalo, 1972-76. One-woman exhbns. include Hallwalls Gallery, Buffalo, 1976, 77, Contemporary Arts Mus., Houston, 1980, The Kitchen, N.Y., 1980, Metro Pictures, N.Y., 1980, 83, Saman Gallery, Genoa, 1981, Young/Hoffman Gallery, Chgo., 1981, Chantal Crousel Gallery, Paris, 1982, Stedelijk Mus., Amsterdam, 1982, St. Louis Art Mus., 1983, Fine Arts Ctr. Gallery, SUNY-Stony Brook, 1983, Rhona Hoffman Gallery, Chgo., 1983, Douglas Drake Gallery, Kansas City, 1983, 84, Seibu Gallery Contemporary Art, Tokyo, 1984, Akron Art Mus., 1984, Linda Cathcart Gallery, Santa Monica, Calif., 1992, Museo de Monterrey, Mex., 1992; group exhbns. include Albright-Knox Art Gallery, Buffalo, 1975, Artists Space, N.Y., 1978, Max Protetch Gallery, N.Y., 1979, Castelli Graphics, N.Y., 1980, Lisson Gallery, London, 1980, Centre Pompidou, Paris, 1981; NIT, 1981, Renaissance Soc. U. Chgo., 1982, Metro Pictures, N.Y., 1982, La Ciennale de Venezia, Venice, Italy, 1982, Documenta 7, Kassel, West Germany, 1982, Chantall Crousel Gallery, Paris, 1982, San Francisco Mus. Modern Art, 1982, Inst. Contemporary Art, London, 1982, Grey Art Gallery, N.Y., 1982, Inst. Contemporary Art, Phila., 1982, Young Hoffman Gallery, Chgo., 1983, Hirshhorn Gallery, Washington, 1983, 1983, Whitney Mus. Am. Art, N.Y., 1983, 85, 91; represented in permanent collections Mus. Fine Arts, Houston, Albright/Knox Art Gallery, Buffalo, Dallas Mus. Fine Arts, Mus. Boymans-van Beuningen, Rotterdam, Akron Art Mus., Ohio, Mus. Modern Art, N.Y.C., Walker Art Ctr., Mpls., Tate Gallery, London, Rose Art Mus., Brandeis U., Centre Pompidou, Paris, Stedelijk Mus., Amsterdam, Met. Mus. Art, N.Y., St. Louis Art Mus., San Francisco Mus. Modern Art. Address: METRO PICTURES 519 W 24th St New York NY 10011-1104*

SHERMAN, DEANE MURRAY, culture organization administrator; b. Beulah, N.D. m. John F. Sherman, Feb. 8, 1944; children: Betsy Deane, Mary Ann. Student, N.D. State U., George Washington U. Emeritus Arts Coun. Montgomery County, Md., 2000—. Bd. trustees Internat. Conservatory of Music, 1981—, sponsor Phia Berghout Harp Series, 1996-97. Decorated chevalier Ordre des Palm Academiques;recipient Hornbook award Montgomery County Tchrs. Assn., 1967, Leadership award Am. Biog. Inst., 1995, Strathmore Hall Found. award, 1998; honored guest Fukui Harp Festival, 1982, Internat. Harp Contest, Israel, 1988-94, U.S., 1991-95, Perugia Classico IV, 1998, Russian Internat. Festival and Harp Competition, 2000. Mem.: Friends of Franklin (founding mem., bd. dirs. 2003—), Help and Resource Porject (chmn. 1989—), World Harp Congress (founder, v.p. 1990—), Women's Com. for Nat. Symphony, Md. Congress PTA (life), Nat. Congress PTA (life), Western Club Glasgow, Elstophos Sci. Club Washington. Home: 11016 Ardwick Dr North Bethesda MD 20852-3204

SHERMAN, DEMING ELIOT, lawyer; b. Providence, July 22, 1943; s. Edwin Fisk and Martha Amy (Parkhurst) S.; m. Jane Catherine Bauer, Dec. 20, 1966; children: Melissa Jane, Nicholas Deming. BA, Amherst (Mass.) Coll., 1965; JD, U. Chgo., 1968. Bar: R.I. 1968, U.S. Dist. Ct. R.I. 1970, U.S. Supreme Ct. 1974, Mass. 1985, U.S. Dist. Ct. Mass. 1985. Ptnr. Edwards & Angell LLP, Providence, 1969—, mng. ptnr., 1986-94. Trustee First Night Providence, 1988-93, 2001—04, pres., 1991-93; bd. dirs. R.I. Philharm. Orch., 1985-2003, 04—, pres., 1993-95; trustee Providence Preservation Soc., 1990—, pres. 1996-99; trustee Providence Athenaeum, 2004—; mem. R.I. Com. on Jud. Tenure and Discipline, 1992-2000; bd. dirs. Providence YMCA, 1975-85, Blackstone Pk. Improvement Assn., 1979—, Nope's Island Conservation Assn., 1992-98, New Eng. Legal Found., 1994—, R.I. Legal Edn. Partnership, 2000-03, Grow Smart RI, 1998—, sec., 1998—; corporator R.I. Hosp., 1989—; bd. dirs. Friends of Blackstone Pk. and Blvd. 2001--, pres., 2001—; trustee Festival Ballet Providence, 2002—, v.p., 2003—. Fellow R.I. Bar Found.; mem. ABA, R.I. Bar Assn., Amherst Alumni Assn. R.I. (pres. 1980-91), Greater Providence C. of C. (bd. dirs. 1991-94). Home: 254 Irving Ave Providence RI 02906-5544 Office: Edwards & Angell LLP 2800 Financial Plz Providence RI 02903 Office Phone: 401-274-9200. E-mail: dsherman@edwardsangell.com.

SHERMAN, EDWARD FRANCIS, dean, law educator; b. El Paso, Tex., July 5, 1937; s. Raphael Eugene and Mary (Stedmond) S.; m. Alice Theresa hammer, Feb. 23, 1963; children: Edward F. Jr., Paul. BA, Georgetown U., 1959; MA, U. Tex., El Paso, 1962, 67; LLB, Harvard U., 1962, SJD, 1981. Bar: Tex. 1962, Ind. 1976. Aide to gov. Nev., state govt. fellow, Carson City, 1962; law clk. judge U.S. Dist. Ct. (we. dist.), El Paso, Tex., 1963; ptnr. Mayfield, Broaddus & Perrenot, El Paso, 1963-65; tchg. fellow Law Sch.

Harvard U., Cambridge, Mass., 1967-69; prof. Sch. Law Ind. U., Bloomington, 1969-77; Edward Clark Centennial prof. U. Tex., Austin, 1977-96; prof., dean Tulane U. Law Sch., 1996—. Fulbright prof. Trinity Coll., Dublin, 1973-74; vis. prof. Stanford Law Sch., 1977, U. London, 1989, Sch. Pub. Adminstrn., Warsaw, Poland, 1995, Chuo U., Tokyo, 1995, U. New South Wales, Australia, 2002; counsel Tex. County Jail Litigation, 1978-85; bd. dirs., officer Travis County Dispute Resolution, 1993—; mem. arbitrtor panel, course dir. Internat. Ctrs. Arbitration. Co-author: The Military in American Society, 1979, Complex Litigation, 1985, 3d edit., 1998, Processes of Dispute Resolution, 1989, 3d edit., 2002, Civil Procedure: A Modern Approach, 1989, 3d edit., 2000, Rau & Sherman & Shannon's Texas ADR and Arbitration Statutes, 1994, 3d edit., 1999. Capt. U.S. Army, 1965-67, lt. col. Res., 1970-90. Fellow Tex. Bar Found.; mem. ABA (reporter civil justice improvements project 1993, offer of judgement task force 1995, com. on pro bono and pub. svc. 1997—, chmn. task force class action legis. 2002-03), Am. Arbitration Assn. (arbitrator panel), AAUP (gen. counsel 1986-88), Am. Law Inst., Tex. State Bar Assn. (alternative dispute resolution com. 1985-96, chair pattern jury charge com. 1983-94, Evans award for excellence in dispute resolution 1998), Tex. Civil Liberties Union (gen. counsel 1985-91), La. Law Inst., La. State Bar (bd. govs. 1997-99, com. on codes of lawyer and jud. conduct 1999—, com. on multi-juris. practice 2000—); La. Bar Found. (jud. liason com. 1999—), Assn. Am. Law Schs. (chmn. Sect. Litigation 1999, chmn. Sect. ADR 1995, com. on clin. legal edn. 1999—. Office: Tulane Law Sch 6329 Freret St New Orleans LA 70118-6231 Home: 21 Newcomb Blvd New Orleans LA 70118

SHERMAN, ERIC, director, writer, educator; b. Santa Monica, Calif., June 29, 1947; s. Vincent and Hedda (Comorau) S.; m. Eugenia Blackiston Dillard, Apr. 1, 1978; children: Cosiimo, Rocky. BA cum laude, Yale U., 1968. Film prodr., dir., writer, photographer, editor. Pres. Film Transform; film tchr. Art Ctr. Coll. Design, Cal Arts, L.A. Film Sch., Pepperdine U., UCLA; guest lectr. Yale, Calif. Inst. Tech., U. So. Calif.; Andrew Mellon lectr. on arts Calif. Inst. Tech., 1977; chief cons. (motion picture industry) Gallup Orgn. Films include: Charles Lloyd-Journey Within, 1968; Paul Weiss-a Philospher in Process, 1972; Waltz, 1980; Inside Out, 1982; Measure of America, 1983; Michael Reagan's Assault on Great Lakes, 1983, Futures, 1990 (Peabody Broadcast award 1990), Pep Squad, 1998, Mystic Nights, 1998, After Freedom, 2000; represented in film festivals N.Y.C. Cine Golden Eagle, Melbourne, Australia, Bilbao, Spain, others; books include: (with others) The Director's Event, 1970; Directing the Film, 1976; Frame by Frame, 1987, Selling Your Film, 1990; contbr. numerous articles to film publs. and distbn. catalogues, book dedication; works include three oral h istories for Am. Film Inst. under Louis B. Mayer Found. grant. Trustee Am. Cinematheque; bd. dir. Film Forum. Mem. Soc. Motion Picture and TV Engrs. (assoc.), Assn. I nd. Video Filmmakers, Univ. Film Assn., Assn. Visual Communicators, Nat. Alliance Media Arts Ctrs. Home and Office: 316 N Maryland Ave Apt 208 Glendale CA 91206-3512 E-mail: ericsfilm@aol.com.

SHERMAN, ETHAN, contractor, publisher; b. N.Y.C., June 23, 1941; s. Frank Issac and Jean (Abel) S.; m. Irene Linder, Oct. 31, 1965; children: Adam Howard, Rachael Suzanne. BS, Rider U., 1963. With Style-Master, Poughkeepsie, N.Y., 1971—, pres., 1979—. Author, pub.: How I Straightened My Spine, 1991. Trustee The Ethan Sherman Found., Poughkeepsie, N.Y., 1995—. With USAF, 1969-71. Mem. Knights of Pythias (chancellor comdr. 1989, 2000). Avocations: sailing, camping, gardening. Home: 37 Hornbeck Rd Poughkeepsie NY 12603-1121 Office: Style-Master Home Products Inc 37 Hornbeck Rd Poughkeepsie NY 12603 Office Phone: 845-471-3950. Personal E-mail: ahern62@juno.com.

SHERMAN, EUGENE JAY, retired marketing executive, economist; b. N.Y.C., Jan. 10, 1935; s. Samuel and Sarah (Lavinsky) S.; m. Mary Eileen Van, Apr. 22, 1966; 1 child, Rebecca. BA, CCNY, 1956; MBA, NYU, 1959, postgrad., 1959-63. Economist Fed. Res. Bank N.Y., 1959-62, Chase Manhattan Bank, N.Y.C., 1962-65; v.p. Bank of N.Y., N.Y.C., 1965-72; sr. v.p., exec. dir., dir. rsch. Merrill Lynch and Co., N.Y.C., 1972-78; v.p., chief economist, mgr.internat. investment Internat. Gold Corp., N.Y.C., 1980-86; sr. v.p., chief economist Fed. Home Loan Bank N.Y., 1986-93; sr. v.p., dir. rsch. M.A. Schapiro & Co., Inc., N.Y.C., 1993-96. Gold cons., N.Y.C., 1986—; adj. prof. Touro Coll., N.Y.C., 1997-98; exec.-in-residence, adj. prof. Baruch Coll., N.Y.C., 1997—, mem. faculty senate. Author: Gold Investment: Theory and Application, 1986; contbr. articles to profl. jours. Recipient Tchg. Excellence award, Zicklin Sch., 2003. Mem. Money Marketeers (pres. 1971-72. honored fellow 1987), Downtown Economist Club (chmn. 1988-89), Forecasters (winner 1986, 95), Treasury Securities Luncheon (pres. 1995-96), Nat. Assn. Bus. Econs., N.Y. Assn. Bus. Econs. Avocations: mountain climbing, performing arts. Home: 115 E 9th St New York NY 10003-5414

SHERMAN, FLOYD F. construction executive; Chmn., CEO Triangle Pacific, Builders FirstSource, Dallas, 2001—. Office: Builders FirstSource 2001 Bryan St Ste 1666 Dallas TX 75201

SHERMAN, FRANCIS GEORGE HARRY, advertising agency executive; b. Croydon, Eng., Apr. 12, 1924; came to U.S. 1947, naturalized 1950. s. Frank Edward and Amelia Elizabeth (Oddy) S.; m. Barbara Opal Blick, May 3, 1947 (dec. 1975); children: Christopher Randolph, Dawn Madeline Ann; m. Elaine Roemisch Crane, Feb. 6, 1977; 1 child, Elizabeth Courtney Crane. Student, U. Durham, Eng., 1942-43, Harvard Coll., 1947-48; MBA, Harvard U., 1950. Sales rep. Eagle-Ottawa Leather Co., Grand Haven, Mich., 1951—55; automotive sales mgr. Detroit, 1955—58; regional mgr. Rogers Publ. Co., Pitts., 1958—59; exec. v.p. Penn & Hamaker, Inc., Cleve., 1959—71; v.p. mktg. Soc. Nat. Bank, Cleve., 1971—77, McKinney Great Lakes Advt., Cleve., 1977—79, pres., 1979—83; v.p. internat. ops. McKinney, Inc., Cleve., Chgo. and Phila., 1983—86, sr. v.p., 1986—89; pres. Ted Sherman Mktg. Comm., Inc., Willoughby Hills, Ohio, 1989—2002. Bd. dirs. Minority Econ. Developers Coun., Cleve., 1973-90, Breckenridge Village, Ohio Presbyn. Retirement Svcs., 2002-04; pres. West Shore Symphony Orch., Muskegon, Mich., 1955-56; pub. rels. com. Cleve. Orch., 1974-86; mktg. dir. Harvard Bus. Sch. 2001 Global Alumni Conf., 1998-2001; mktg. dir. Cleve. Coun. on World Affairs, 2002-. With RAF, 1947. Mem. Indsl. Marketers Cleve. (trustee 1980-83, best programs award 1981), Affiliated Advt. Agys. Internat. (trustee 1981-83), Am. Assn. Advt. Agys., Cleve. World Trade Assn. (bd. dirs. 1985-97, chmn. mktg. and communications com. 1985-92), Assn. Ohio Commodores (life mem.), Soc. Automotive Engrs., Lake County Profl. Communicators (trustee 1984-90, pres. 1988), Harvard Bus. Sch. Club Northeastern Ohio (pres. 1964-65, trustee 1965-66, 66-68, 75-79, 87-2001, trustee emeritus 2001—), Harvard U. Club Northeastern Ohio, Royal Air Force Club (London).

SHERMAN, FRED, biochemist, educator; b. Mpls., May 21, 1932; s. Harry and Ann (Kaufman) Sherman; m. Revina Freeman, July 25, 1958 (div.); children: Aaron, Mark, Rhea; m. Elena Rustchenko Bulgac, May 5, 2001. BA, U. Minn., Mpls., 1953; PhD, U. Calif., Berkeley, 1958, U. Minn., 2002. Postdoctoral fellow U. Wash., Seattle, 1959—60; 60postdoctoral fellow 61Lab. Genetique Physiol., Gif-sur-Yvette, France, 1960-61; sr. instr. U. Rochester, NY, 1961—62, asst. prof., 1962—66, assoc. prof., 1966—71, prof. dept. biochemistry Sch. Medicine & Dentistry, 1971—, chmn. dept. biochemistry, 1982—99. Instr. Cold Spring Harbor Lab., NY, 1970—87; Wander Meml. lectr., 1975; Wilson prof. U. Rochester, 1982. Co-author: Cold Spring Harbor Manual on Yeast Genetics and Molecular Biology, 1970—87; assoc. editor: Genetics, 1975—82, Molecular Cell Biology, 1979—88. Fellow NIH, 1959—61; grantee, 1963. Mem.: Am. Soc. Microbiology, Genetic Soc. Am. (bd. dirs. 1983—85), NAS (chmn. genet. sec. 2000—03), AAAS. Home: 69 Westminster Rd Rochester NY 14607-2223 E-mail: fred_sherman@URMC.Rochester.edu.

SHERMAN, FREDERICK SCOTT, pediatric cardiologist; b. Cambridge, Mass., Feb. 7, 1949; s. Henry Sherman and Doris Gimpelson; m. Kathryn Rich; children: Alexis, Nathaniel. AB, Harvard U., 1971; MD, Yale U., 1975; MBA, U. Pitts., 2002. Resident in pediatrics U. Va., Charlottesville, 1975-78; asst. surgeon U.S. Pub. Health Svc., New Canton, Va., 1978-80; fellow in cardiology Children's Hosp., Boston, 1981-84; asst. prof. in pediatrics U. Calif., San Diego, Calif., 1984-88; prof. of pediatrics U. Pitts., 1988—. Dir. perinatal cardiology Magee Women's Hosp., Pitts., 1988—. Bd. dirs. Children's Home, Pitts., 1990—, Opera Theater of Pitts., 1995—. Fellow Am. Coll. Cardiology, Am. Acad. Pediatrics; mem. The Pitts. Golf Club, Am. Heart Assn., Am. Soc. Echocardiography. Avocations: golf, squash, opera. Office: Magee Womens Hosp 300 Halket St Pittsburgh PA 15213-3180

SHERMAN, GEORGE M. manufacturing executive; b. N.Y.C., Aug. 6, 1941; s. Joseph B. and Fredericka (Hand) S.; m. Betsy Rae Bicknell, Nov. 26, 1966; children: Jonathan, David, Michael, Matthew. BS, L.I. U., 1963; MBA, U. Louisville, 1971. Product gen. mgr. Gen. Electric Co., Bridgeport, Conn., 1966-79; pres. Weed Eater div. Emersen Electric Co., Houston, 1979-80; pres. Skil Corp. div. Emerson Electric Co., Chgo., 1980-82; group v.p. U.S. power tools group Black & Decker Corp., Balt., 1985, sr. v.p., pres. power tools group, from 1986, then exec. v.p., pres. power tools group, until 1990; now chief exec. officer Danaher Corp, Washington, D.C., 1990—. Mem. adv. bd. Nat. Home Ctr. Show, Chgo., 1987; bd. dirs. D.I.Y. Research Inst., Lincolnshire, Ill., 1988. Bd. dirs. Ctr. Stage, Balt., 1988. Served with U.S. Army, 1964-66. Mem. Am. Mgmt. Assn. (mem. gen. mgmt. council 1988). Clubs: Center (Balt.); Hillendale Country (Phoenix, Md.). Avocations: flying, skiing, scuba diving, racquetball, golf. Office: Danaher Corporation 2099 Pennsylvania Ave NW Washington DC 20006-6800

SHERMAN, GERALD, nuclear physicist, financial estate adviser, financial company executive; b. Bklyn., Sept. 7, 1938; s. Saul and Claire S.; m. Annette Ellen Drasin, Aug. 29, 1965; children: Rochelle Heidi, Sondra Nicole. BA in Physics, UCLA, 1960, MS in Nuclear Physics, 1962; PhD in Physics, Columbia Pacific U., 1985. Cert. Nat. Assn. Securities Dealers, Series 6 and 63, Investment Co. Products/Variable Contracts, registered rep.; lic. in securities and health and life ins. Calif.; lic. Fed. Securities Series 7. Physics instr., lower divsn. Lab. UCLA, 1960-62, physics instr. upper divsn. nuclear physics, 1961-62; nuclear ion engine rocket physicist Rocketdyne, Canoga Park, Calif., 1961; sr. scientist Advanced Tech. Co., L.A., 1965-66; physicist, principle superconductivity investigator Northrop Space Sci. Lab., Hawthorne, Calif., 1966-70; pres. Sherman Ins. Agy., Inc., L.A., 1970-84; pres., CEO Sherman Fin. Svcs., Inc., Thousand Oaks, Calif., 1984—. Cons. TRW, 1970; spkr. sci. seminars for NASA, U.S. Air Force, Lockheed; speaker fin. seminars, 1972—; developer bus. plan between Bank of China and New USA-China Project; create internet interactive website bus. plan, 1998—. Author: Microwave Phenomenological Theory of Superconductivity, 1965, Superconductive Antennas, 1966, Estate Tax Savings of 90%, 1992, Financial Security for Life, 1993; creater original internet interactive ins. investment website bus. plan, 1998-99. Recipient AEC Time Reduction Analysis award Am. Electronics, 1960, Top Prodr. Nationwide award U.S. Life Ins. Co. Calif., 1978, Leading Disability Prodr. Nationwide award Chubb Life Ins. Co. Am., 1983-85, 90, Leading Combined Life and Disability Prodr. award Chubb, 1987, Leading Combined Disability and Life Ins. Producer award Chubb, 1989, Internat. Life and Health Ins. awards Chubb Corp./Summit Club Calif., 1979, 88, 89, 92, 94, Hawaii, 1982, 92, 94, Italy, 1984, 93, Greece, 1984, Bermuda, 1985, 72, 88, England, 1985, Scotland, 1985, Mex., 1986, Monaco 1987, Switzerland, 1987, Hong Kong, 1988, Thailand, 1988, France, 1989, Africa, 1989, Puerto Rico, 1990, 95, Ariz., 1991, Australia, 1992, Fla., 1993, Austria, 1994, Securities Acad. Award, 1997, Stock Option award Jefferson Pilot Fin., 1999, Locust Street Securities award, Hawaii, 1999, Summit award Jefferson Pilot Fin., Eng./Scotland, 1999; PhD Rsch. fellow UCLA, 1962-64. Mem. Calif. Assn. Life Underwriters, Westlake Art Guild, UCLA Physics Honor Soc. (v.p. 1959, exec. v.p. 1960), Sigma Pi Sigma. Achievements include created concept and experimentally performed the first superconductive short antenna for very low frequency communication; originated and performed first superconductive non-destructive test to determine aircraft titanium alloy strength; first to design the NASA crystal experiment for astronauts; research in planetary astrophotography. Avocations: art, music. Office: Sherman Financial Svcs Inc 2158 Calle Riscoso Thousand Oaks CA 91362-1141

SHERMAN, GERALD HOWARD, lawyer, educator; b. NYC, Aug. 29, 1932; s. Abraham and Jean (Rose) S.; m. Lola Barbara Kay, Mar. 19, 1961; children: Jonathan, Ann. BBA, CCNY, 1953; LLB, Harvard U., 1958. Bar: N.Y. 1959, D.C. 1960. Mem. firm Cooper & Silverstein, Washington, 1958-61; ptnr. Silverstein & Mullens, Washington, 1961-99; shareholder Buchanan Ingersoll, P.C., 2000—; gen. counsel Assn. Advanced Life Underwriting. Adj. prof. Georgetown U. Law Ctr., 1974-87, dep. tech. dir., adv. bd. tax mgmt., 1960—, BNA Pension Reporter, 1975-81. Bd. dirs., v.p. Jewish Found. for Group Homes, 1982-90; bd. dirs. Am. Digestive Disease Soc., 1983-87, Washington Conservatory Music, 1995-01. Mem. ABA, Bar Assn. D.C. Home: 3804 Klingle Pl NW Washington DC 20016-5433 Office: 1776 K St NW Washington DC 20006-2304

SHERMAN, IAN MATTHEW, lawyer; b. Chgo., Apr. 30, 1953; s. George and Vivian K. (Soffran) S.; m. Barbara Jan Smiley, Aug. 6, 1978; children: Wendy Joyce, Wesley Jacob, David Scott. AB, U. Ill., 1975; JD, Boston U., 1978. Bar: Ill. 1978, U.S. Dist. Ct. (no. dist.) Ill. 1978, U.S. Dist. Ct. (ea. dist.) Wis. 1995, U.S. Dist. Ct. (no. dist.) Ind. 2000, U.S. Ct. Appeals (7th cir.) 1984. Ptnr. Rooks, Pitts & Poust, Chgo., 1978—. Lectr. in field. Contbr. articles to profl. jours. Participant Youth Motivation Program Chgo. Pub. H.S., 1982; pro bono Am. Jewish Congress, Chgo., 1992—; vol. Legal Svcs. Inst., Chgo., 1982—; commr. Winnetka (Ill.) Park Dist., 2001—, v.p., 2002—03; bd. dirs. The Vol. Ctr., 1986—90, chmn. fin. com., 1986—87, sec., 1987—88, pres., 1988—89. Recipient Disting. Svc. award, Legal Svcs. Inst., 2003. Mem.: Chgo. Bar Assn. (chmn. med.-legal rels. com. 2001—02, cert. appreciation 1983, 2003), Ill. State Bar Assn., Ill. Assn. Healthcare Attys., Ill. Soc. Trial Lawyers, Phi Kappa Phi, Phi Beta Kappa. Home: 923 Oak St Winnetka IL 60093-2440 Office: Dykema Gossett Rooks Pitts PLLC 10 S Wacker Dr Ste 2300 Chicago IL 60606-7407 Office Phone: 312-876-1700. Business E-Mail: isherman@dykema.com.

SHERMAN, IRWIN WILLIAM, biological sciences educator; b. N.Y.C., Feb. 12, 1933; s. Morris and Anna (Ezaak) S.; m. Vilia Gay Turner, Aug. 25, 1966; children: Jonathan Turner, Alexa Joy. BS, CCNY, 1954; MS, Northwestern U., 1959, PhD, 1960. Asst. prof. U. Calif., Riverside, 1962-67, assoc. prof., 1967-70, prof. biology, 1970—, chmn. biology dept., 1974-79, dean Coll. Natural and Agrl. Scis., dir. agrl. expt. sta., 1981-88, exec. vice chancellor, 1993-94, chmn., Academic Senate, 1997—2004. Instr. marine biol. lab., Woods Hole, Mass., 1963-68; mem. study sect. tropical medicine NIH, 1970-73; cons. Agy. Internat. Devel., 1978-90; mem. ad hoc study group U.S. Army, 1975-78. Author: The Invertebrates: Function and Form, 1976, Biology: A Human Approach, 1989, Malaria: Parasite Biology, Pathogenesis, Protection, 1998, Chemotherapy of Malaria. Steering com. World Health Orgn., 1978-87. With U.S. Army, 1954-56. USPHS fellow Rockefeller Inst., 1960-62, Guggenheim fellow, 1967, NIH/Nat. Inst. Med. Rsch. fellow 1973-74, Walter and Eliza Hall Inst. for Med. Rsch. fellow, 1986; Wellcome Trust lectr. Brit. Soc. Parasitology, 1987, Scripps Rsch. Inst. fellow 1991, 2003-04. Mem. AAAS, Am. Soc. Tropical Medicine and Hygiene, Soc. Protozoology, Soc. Parasitology, Sigma Xi. Democrat. Jewish. Avocations: painting, reading. Office: U Calif Riverside Dept Biology Riverside CA 92521-0001 Office Phone: 951-787-5905. E-mail: sherman@mail.ucr.edu.

SHERMAN, JANANN MARGARET, history educator, writer; b. Mpls., Apr. 9, 1944; d. Melvin Albert and Jeanette Mary Stephenson; m. Charles Daniel Sherman, May 30, 1962. PhD, Rutgers U., 1993. Electronics technician Motorola Inc., Mesa, Ariz., 1965—73; assoc. prof. U. of Memphis, 1994—. Author: (biography) No Place for a Woman: A Life of Senator Margaret Chase Smith, (monograph) Interviews with Betty Friedan, The Perfect 36: Tennessee Delivers Woman Suffrage; dir.: (exhbn.) The Perfect 36. Bd. dirs. Women of Achievement, Memphis, 2001—03, Shelby County Hist. Commn., Memphis, 2002—03, Memphis Network, 1998—2003; Tenn. coord. Nat. History Day, Memphis, 1999—2003; pres. West Tenn. Hist. Soc., Memphis, 2002—. Named Woman of Achievement, Women of Achievement, 2001; recipient First Pl. award. for No Place for a Woman, Nat. Fedn. of Press Women, 2001, Excellence in Cmty. Svc. award, DAR, 1995. Avocations: travel, reading. Home: 3153 Dothan St Memphis TN 38118 Office: U Memphis Alumni St Memphis TN 38152 Personal E-mail: jsherma1@midsouth.rr.com. E-mail: sherman@memphis.edu.

SHERMAN, JEFFREY ALAN, dentist; b. Bklyn., June 16, 1947; s. Joseph G. and Gertrude P. S.; m. Roslyn B. Tillis, Aug. 15, 1970; children: Jodi Heather, Brett Andrew. BA, Adelphi U., 1969; DDS, Howard U., 1973. Diplomate Am. Bd. Oral Electrosurgery. Resident in gen. dentistry Del. State Hosp., 1974; pvt. practice, Oakdale, N.Y., 1975—. Mem. faculty Albert Einstein Coll. Medicine; vis. lectr. Tufts U.; dir. Greater L.I. Dental Meeting, 1990—. Author: Oral Electrosurgery: An Illustrated Clinical Guide, 1992, Oral Radiosurgery, 2d edit., 1997; contbr. to profl. publs. Fellow Internat. Coll. Dentists, Am. Coll. Dentists; mem. ADA (lectr. ann. meetings 1978—), Suffolk County Dental Soc. (bd. dels. 1989—, dental lab and trades com. 1989—; edn. com. 1989-91, photographer dental meeting 1990—, sec. 1997-98, pres. 2000—), Acad. Gen. Dentistry (membership com. 1992—, area v.p. 1991-92), Am. Acad. Dental Electrosurgery (co-editor, pres. 1987), N.Y. State Acad. Gen. Dentistry (pub. info. officer 1992). Office: 1237 Montauk Hwy Oakdale NY 11769-1434

SHERMAN, JEFFREY BARRY, retail executive; b. Passaic, N.J., June 25, 1948; s. Maxwell and Elinor (Richman) S.; m. Karin Lynn Swann, May 1, 1971; children— Erik, Brett, Peter, Kristin BS in Econs., CCNY, 1971; MBA, NYU, 1975. With Bloomingdale's, N.Y.C., 1971—, v.p. merchandising, 1982-83, sr. v.p., 1983-85, exec. v.p., 1985—, now pres. Avocations: skiing; sailing. Office: Bloomingdale's 59th St & Lexington New York NY 10022

SHERMAN, JEFFREY WAYNE, physician, clinical researcher; b. Chgo., Nov. 15, 1954; s. Ben and Stella (Kwiatkowski) S.; m. Mary Ann Bryan, Aug. 9, 1980; two children. BA, Lake Forest Coll., 1976; MD, Chgo. Med. Sch., 1981. Diplomate Nat. Bd. Med. Examiners; diplomate in internal medicine and infectious diseases Am. Bd. Internal Medicine. Intern, resident, chief resident internal medicine Northwestern Med. Ctr., Chgo., 1981-85; fellowship in infectious disease U. Calif., San Francisco, 1985-88, rsch. assoc. Howard Hughes Med. Inst., 1986-88; from asst. dir. to assoc. dir. clin. pharmacology The Squibb Inst. Med. Rsch., Princeton, N.J., 1988-90; dir. clin. rsch. The Bristol-Myers Squibb Pharm. Rsch. Inst., Princeton, 1990-92; from dir. clin. rsch. to exec. dir. clin. rsch. Searle/Monsanto, Skokie, Ill., 1992-99, head oncology global med. ops. Global Med. Mktg./Oncology Franchise, 2000; chief med. officer, exec. v.p. NeoPharm, Lake Forest, Ill., 2000—. Fellow: ACP; mem.: APHA, Am. Soc. Therapeutic Radiol. Oncology, European Assn. Neuro-Oncology, Am. Assn. Cancer Rsch., Soc. Neuro-Oncology, Am. Coll. Physician Execs., Am. Soc. Preventive Oncology, Soc. for Biol. Therapy, Am. Acad. Pharm. Physicians, Am. Coll. Gastroenterology, Am. Gastrointestinal Assn., Drug Info. Assn. (bd. dirs.), Am. Soc. Blood and Marrow Transplantation, Am. Soc. Clin. Oncology, Am. Soc. Hematology, European Soc. Med. Oncology, Infectious Disease Soc. Am., European Soc. Clin. Microbiology, Am. Soc. Microbiology, Am. Soc. Clin. Pharmacology and Therapeutics, Am. Fedn. Clin. Rsch., Am. Coll. Clin. Pharmacology (bd. dirs.), Internat. Soc. Antiviral Rsch., Am. Assn. Neuro-Surg. (assoc.). Office: 150 Field Dr Ste 195 Lake Forest IL 60045 Office Phone: 847-295-8678 x211. E-mail: jsherman@neophrm.com.

SHERMAN, JEROME KALMAN, retired anatomy educator; b. Bklyn., Aug. 14, 1925; s. Murray and Beatrice Freilich S.; m. Hildegard Schroeder, Dec. 26, 1952; children: Karen, Marc, Keith. AB, Brown U., 1947; MS, Western Res. U., 1949; PhD, U. Iowa, 1954. Teaching asst. Brown U., Providence, 1946-47; grad. asst. Western Res. U., Cleve., 1947-49; from rsch. asst. to rsch. assoc. U. Iowa, Iowa City, 1949-54; rsch. assoc. Am. Found. for Biol. Rsch., Madison, Wis., 1954-58; from asst. to assoc. prof. U. Ark. for Med. Sci., Little Rock, 1958-67, prof., 1967-92, prof. emeritus, 1992—; spl. chair prof. Nat. Chung Hsin U., Taichung, Taiwan, 1973-74; Fulbright prof. U. Munich, 1965-66. Cons. Animal Breeders Svc., 1956-57, Winrock Farm Semen Storage Project, 1960; sci. adv. Idant Corp., 1971-73; rsch. cons. Naval Med. Rsch. Unit II, Taipei, Taiwan, 1973-74, Dow Chemical Co., 1977-89; cons. Human Frozen Semen Banks (various states), 1972—. Contbr. articles to profl. jours., chpts. to books. Pres. Forest Heights Lions Club, Little Rock, 1978-79; bd. trustees Agudah Achim Synagogue, Temple B'Nai Israel, Little Rock, 1965, 76; chmn. adv. bd. Amelia Ives Day Care Ctr., Little Rock, 1970-90; vice-chmn. Nat. Med. Exploring Com. Boy Scouts Am., Dallas, 1978-81; bd. dirs. Cmty. Org. for Prevention of Poverty, 1993-98; mem. Douglas MacArthur Mil. Mus. Commn., 1995-2000. Lt. comdr. USN, 1943-46. Recipient Lederle Med. Faculty award Am. Cyanamid Co., 1961-64, Fulbright Sr. Rsch. award Fulbright Found., Munich, 1965-66, Nat. Sci. Coun. award Taiwan, Republic of China, 1973-74, Vol. Svc. Project Head Start award U.S. Dept. Health and Human Svcs., 1988, 89, Outstanding Vol. Svc. award V.A., 1989, 90, 91, Judge Gubow Nat. Americanism award Jewish War Veterans, 1991, Faculty Vol. Svc. award, Disting. Faculty award U. Ark. for Med. Sci., 1991, 92, Nat. Shofar award Boy Scouts Am., 1978, Whitney M. Young Svc. award, 1992, Golden Rule Cmty. Svc. award, 1995; named to Sr. Arkansas Hall of Fame, 1995. Mem. Am. Assn. Tissue Banks (founding, chmn. reproduction coun., bd. govs. 1976-93, Disting. Svc. award 1994), Soc. Exptl. Biology and Medicine, Am. Physiological Soc., Am. Soc. Anatomists, Am. Soc. Zoologists, Soc. for Cryobiology (charter, bd. govs. 1964-66), Soc. for Cryosurgery (hon.), Seven Sci. Soc., Sigma Xi (pres. Little Rock chpt. 1975-76). Democrat. Jewish. Avocations: fishing, camping, hiking, tennis, home repair. Home: 3012 N Grant St Little Rock AR 72207-2820

SHERMAN, JIMMIE LEE, mathematician, educator; b. LA, Feb. 15, 1944; s. Harold and Lillie (Lee) Sherman. Student, Compton Jr. Coll. Bus. mgr., reporter Watts (Calif.) Star Rev. Newspaper, 1965—66; publicity dir. Watts Happening Coffee House, 1965—67; screen writer Universal Studios, Universal City, Calif., 1967—68; creative dir., tchr. Watts Writers Workshop, 1987; cons., tchr. Compton (Calif.) Unified Sch. Dist., 1988—90, Nat. Coun. Negro Women, Pomona, Calif., 1997—98; tchr. math. Motivational Inst., LA, 2002—. Publ. Lesson Book Libr. Publ. Co., LA, 1979—; tchr., tutor Jimmie Shermans Literacy Campaign, LA, 1999—; cons. in field. Author: numerous poems, Principles of Immortality, 2003. With U.S. Army, 1961—64. Named Worlds' Best Tchr. award, God's Little Angels Pvt. Sch., 2000, Poet of Yr., Famous Poets Soc., 2003; recipient Quality of Life award, Sigma Gamma Rho, 1994, Breaking Barriers award, KJLH and LA Dodgers, 1997, Shakespeare Trophy of Excellence award, Famous Poets Soc., 2003. Mem.: Shermans Future Tchrs. Assn. (hon.). Avocations: painting, poetry, writing, reading. Home: 652 E 43rd St Los Angeles CA 90011 Office: Lesson Book Libr Publ Co 652 E 43rd St Los Angeles CA 90011 Office Phone: 323-846-6979. E-mail: jimmysherman@dslextreme.com.

SHERMAN, JOHN ERIC, plastic surgeon; b. NYC, 1951; m. Emily Sherman; 2 children. MD, NY Med. Coll., 1975. Internship & residency Montefiore Hospital Med. Ctr., NYC, 1975—78; chief resident plastic surgery Cornell Med. Ctr., 1978—80; fellowship reconstructive plastic surgery Memorial Sloan Kettering Cancer Ctr., 1979—80; plastic surgeon priv. practice, NYC, 1980—; attending plastic surgeon NY Hospital, Lenox Hill Hospital; clinical assist. prof. surgery Cornell U. Med. Coll. Author: Surgery of Facial Bone Fractures, 1987. Fellow: Am. Coll. of Surgeons; mem.: Am. Soc. of Maxillofacial Surgeons, Am. Soc. of Aesthetic Plastic Surgeons, Am. Soc. of Plastic & Reconstructive Surgeons. Avocation: golf. Office: 1016 5th Ave New York NY 10028

SHERMAN, JOHN FOORD, biomedical consultant; b. Oneonta, N.Y., Sept. 4, 1919; s. Henry C. and Ruth (Foord) Sherman; m. Betsy Deane Murray, Feb. 8, 1944; children: Betsy Deane, Mary Ann. BS, Albany Coll. Pharmacy/Union U., 1949, DSc, 1970; PhD, Yale U., 1953. With NIH, 1953—74; assoc. dir. extramural programs Nat. Inst. Neurol. Diseases and Blindness, 1961—62, Nat. Inst. Arthritis and Metabolic Disease, 1962—63; assoc. dir. for extramural programs Office Dir. NIH, 1964—68, dep. dir., 1968—74; v.p. Assn. Am. Med. Colls., Washington, 1974—91, exec. v.p., 1987—91, spl. cons., 1991—94. Bd. advisors Am. Bd. Internal Medicine, 1991—98; sr. advisor Rsch!Am., 1994—. Asst. surgeon gen. USPHS, 1964—68; spl. rsch. chemotherapy and neuropharmacology; panel on data and studies NRC, 1976—87;

biomed. libr. rev. com. NIH, 1981—98; bd. dirs. Spinal Cord Injury Edn. and Tng. Found., 1986—92, Musculoskeletal Transplant Found., 1987—2003. With U.S. Army, 1941—46. Decorated Bronze Star; recipient Meritorious Svc. award, USPHS, 1965, Disting. Svc. award, HEW, 1971, Sec.'s Spl. Citation award, 1973, Nat. Civil Svc. League award, 1973, Disting. Alumnus award, Union U.-Pharmacy Coll. Coun., 1974, Lifetime Achievement award, Nat. Assn. for Biomed. Rsch., 1990, Spl. Recognition award, Assn. Am. Med. Colls., 1996. Fellow: AAAS; mem.: Inst. Medicine NAS, Cosmos Club, Sigma Xi. Congregationalist. E-mail: johnfsherman@msn.com.

SHERMAN, JONATHAN HENRY, lawyer; b. Washington, Jan. 4, 1963; s. Gerald Howard and Lola (Kay) Sherman; m. Catherine Sara Foot, Nov. 4, 2000; 1 child, Benjamin Ashton. BA in History magna cum laude, U. Rochester, 1984; MA in History, Yale U., 1989; JD, Stanford U., 1991. Bar: N.Y. 1992, U.S. Dist. Ct. (so. dist.) N.Y. 1992, U.S. Supreme Ct. 1995, U.S. Dist. Ct. (ea. dist.) N.Y. 1996, U.S. Ct. Appeals (11th cir.) 1996, U.S. Dist. Ct. (we. dist.) N.Y. 1998, D.C. 2000. Assoc. Cahill Gordon & Reindel, N.Y.C., 1991-2000; ptnr. Boies, Schiller & Flexner LLP, Washington, 2001—. Lectr. Stanford U., Palo Alto, Calif., 1991, Yale Coll., New Haven, 1993; adj. assoc. prof. law Fordham Law Sch., N.Y.C., 1998-2001. Sponsor, mentor Student-Sponsor Partnership, N.Y.C., 1992-96; contbr. The Cornerstone Sch., Jersey City, 1994. Mem. ABA, N.Y. State Bar Assn. (media law com. 1997-99), Phi Beta Kappa. Office: Boies Schiller & Flexner LLP Ste 800 5301 Wisconsin Ave NW Washington DC 20015-2061 Home: 5725 Bradley Blvd Bethesda MD 20814-1033 E-mail: jsherman@bsfllp.com.

SHERMAN, JOSEPH OWEN, pediatric surgeon; b. Chgo., Aug. 15, 1936; s. Joseph Owen and Mary Elizabeth (Kelly) Sherman; m. June Marie Martin, Mar. 16, 1963; children: Brian William, Lee Ann. Student, U. Ill., 1955—58; BS, Northwestern U., 1959, MD, 1962. Diplomate Am. Bd. Surgery, Am. Bd. Pediatric Surgery, lic. physician Ill. Rotating intern Passavant Meml. Hosp., Chgo., 1963-64; resident in gen. surgery VA Rsch. Hosp., Chgo., 1964-65, 67-68; Am. Cancer Soc. clin. fellow Northwestern U. Med. Sch., Chgo., 1965-66, from instr. to assoc. prof. surgery, 1967—86, prof. clin. surgery, 1986—; resident in pediatric surgery Children's Meml. Hosp., Chgo., 1966, 68-69; resident in thoracic surgery Mcpl. Tb San., Chgo., 1967. Emeritus staff dept. surgery Children's Meml. Hosp., 1995—, Evanston (Ill.) Hosp., 1995—. Contbr. articles to profl. jours. With Ill. Army N.G., 1953—57, with Ill. Air N.G., 1966—67. Fellow: ACS; mem.: AMA, Ill. State Med. Soc., Ill. Pediat. Surg. Assn., Chgo. Surg. Soc., Chgo. Med. Soc., Assn. Acad. Surgery, Am. Pediat. Surg. Assn. Avocations: photography, computer programing, indoor and outdoor gardening. Personal E-mail: j.o.sherman@att.net.

SHERMAN, JUDITH DOROTHY, producer, recording company owner, recording engineer; b. Cleve., Nov. 12, 1942; d. William Paul and Laverne (Spoerke) Luekens; m. Kenneth Sherman, Aug. 1, 1964 Idiv. Aug. 1972); m. Max Wilcox, Jan. 1, 1981 (div. Jan. 1988); m. Curtis Macomber, Apr. 29, 1988. BA, Valparaiso U., 1964; MFA, SUNY, Buffalo, 1971. Rec. engr. Edward at the Moog, N.Y.C., 1971-72; producer-music dir. WBAI-FM, N.Y.C., 1972-76; owner-producer Judith Sherman Prodns., N.Y.C., 1976—. Rec. engr. Marlboro (Vt.) Music Festival, 1976-94; adminstrv. dir. La Musica di Asolo, Sarasota, Fla., 1986-88; vocalist Steve Reich and Musicians, 1971-72. Recipient Corp. Pub. Broadcasting award, 1976, two Grammy award nominations, 1991, Grammy award, Classical Prodr. of Yr., 1993, Grammy award nominations, 1994, 95, 97, 98. Mem. NAFE, Chamber Music Am. (bd. dirs. 2000—), NARAS. Democrat. Home and Office: 645 W 239th St Apt 2A Bronx NY 10463-1236

SHERMAN, KENNETH ELIOT, medicine educator, researcher; b. Long Branch, NJ, Dec. 21, 1955; s. Emanuel and Gertrude Sherman; m. Susan Nacht, Nov. 30, 1980; children: Marc, Amy. BS, Rutgers U., 1976, PhD, 1980; MD, George Washington U., 1985. Diplomate Am. Bd. Internal Medicine, Am. Bd. Gastroenterology. Commd. capt. U.S. Army, 1985, advanced through grades to lt. col., 1995; intern, then resident in medicine Tripler Army Med. Ctr., Honolulu, 1985-88; fellow in gastroentrology Fitzsimmons Army Med. Ctr., Aurora, Colo., 1989-91; gastroenterologist Fitzsimons Army Med. Ctr., Aurora, Colo., 1991-94, chief dept. clin. investigation, 1992-94; resigned, 1994; assoc. prof. medicine and pathology U. Cin. Med. Ctr., 1994—2002, dir. hepatology and liver transplant medicine, 1998—, Gould prof. medicine, 2002—. Adv. com. FDA, 2003—, dir. divsn. digestive diseases, 2003—. Author, editor: Viral Insecticides for Biological Control, 1985; reviewer Hepatology, 1993—, Am. Jour. Gastroentrology, 1994—; mem. editorial bd. Am. Jour. Gastroenterology, 1998—; contbr. articles to med. jours., chpt. to book; inventor composition and method. Asst. cubmaster Boy Scouts Am., Aurora, 1993-94. Recipient heroism award Kiwanis, 1982, rsch. award William Beaumont Soc., 1991; Busch predoctoral fellow Waksman Inst. Microbiology, 1976. Fellow ACP, Am. Coll. Gastroent.; mem. Am. Assn. for Study Liver Disease, Am. Soc. for Microbiology, Am. Gastroent. Assn., Am. Fedn. of Med. Rsch., Am. Soc. for Gastrointestinal Endoscopy, Am. Assn. of Transplantation, European Assn. for Study of the Liver. Avocations: skiing, camping, fishing. Office: U Cin Med Ctr Liver Unit Divsn Digestive Diseases Cincinnati OH 45267-0595

SHERMAN, LAWRENCE JAY, lawyer; b. Pitts., May 20, 1942; s. Ben E. and Leonora C. (Weill) S.; m. Iris Shapiro, Aug. 19, 1967; children: Rachel L., Jessica S. BA in Polit. Sci. with honors, U. Pitts., 1963; JD, U. Mich., 1966. Bar: D.C. 1967, Calif. 1967, Md. 1984, U.S. Dist. Ct. D.C., U.S. Dist. Ct. Md., U.S. Claims Ct., U.S. Ct. Appeals (D.C., 1st, 3rd, 4th, 5th and 6th cir.). Appellate atty. NLRB, Washington, 1966-69; assoc. Cohen & Berfield, Washington, 1969-70; exec. dir. Migrant Legal Action Program, Washington, 1970-75; assoc. Lichtman, Abeles, Anker & Nagle, P.C., Washington, 1975-77; pvt. practice Washington, 1977-81; ptnr. Sherman & Lapidus, Washington, 1981-86; counsel Deso, Thomas, Spevack, Weitzman & Rost PC, Washington, 1991-2000; ptnr. Brown & Sherman, LLP, Washington, 2001—02; prin. Law Offices of Lawrence J. Sherman, P.C., Washington, 2002—. Adj. prof. George Meany Ctr. for Labor Studies, Silver Spring, Md. 1988-2000; prin. Mng. Human Resources For 21st Century, Washington, 1990-99. Contbr. articles to profl. jours. Fellow Am. Bd. Trial Advocates; mem. D.C. Bar (labor and employment law sect., litig. sect., co-chmn. steering com., 1981-85, labor law sect. 1978-84, co-chmn. labor law sect. 1983-84, lawyers coord. com.), Met. Washington Employment Lawyers Assn., Md. Employment Lawyers Assn., Nat. Employment Lawyers Assn. Democrat. Avocations: tennis, racquetball, photography, travel, reading. Office: Lawrence J Sherman PC Ste 450 1625 Massachusetts Ave NW Washington DC 20036 Office Phone: 202-785-0384.

SHERMAN, LAWRENCE WILLIAM, criminologist; b. Schenectady, Oct. 25, 1949; s. Donald Lester and Margaret (Heckman) Sherman; m. Eva Fass Fass; children: Eliot, Katharine. BA, Denison U., Granville, Ohio, 1970; MA, U. Chgo., 1970; Diploma in Criminology, Cambridge U., Eng., 1973; PhD, Yale U., 1976; MA, U. Pa., 1999. Program rsch. analyst N.Y.C. Police Dept., 1971—72; asst. to assoc. prof. criminal justice SUNY, Albany, 1976—82; dir. rsch., v.p. Police Found., Washington, 1979—85; pres. Crime Control Ins., Washington, 1985—95; assoc. prof. to Disting. univ. prof and chair dept. criminology and criminal justice U. Md., College Park, Md., 1982—99; Albert M. Greenfield prof. human relations, dept. sociology, dir. Jerry Lee Ctr. of Criminology and dir. Fels Inst. of Govt. U. Pa., Phila., 1999—. Pres. Crime Control Rsch. Corp., Phila., 1981—; mem. panel on rsch. policies NRC-NAS, Washington, 2000—; lead co-chmn. transition com. on pub. safety Office of the Mayor, Phila., 1999—2000; lectr. FBI Acad., Quantico, 1980—2000; adj. prof. law and sci. dir. reintegrative shaming experiments Rsch. Sch. Social Scis., Australian Nat. U.,, Canberra, ACT, Australia, 1993—; dir. Justice Rsch. Consortium, Oxford, 2000—. Editor: (Book) Police Corruption: A Sociological Perspective, 1974; author: (book) Scandal and Reform: Controlling Police Corruption, 1978, Policing Domestic Violence: Experiments and Dilemmas, 1992 (Am.Sociological Assn. Disting. Scholarship award in Crime, Law and Deviance, 1973); co-author: Evidence Based Crime Prevention, 2002; contbr. articles to profl. jours. Recipient Bruce Smith award for disting. contbn. to criminal justice, Acad. of Criminal Justice Scis., 1994; fellow N.Y.C. Urban fellow, Alfred P. Sloan Foun., 1970—71. Fellow: Am. Soc. Criminology (pres. 2001—02, E.H. Sutherland Award for Disting. Contbn. to Criminology 1999); mem.: Acad. of Exptl. Criminology (pres. 1999—2001), Internat. Soc. Criminology (pres. sci. commn. 1995—99, pres. 2000—), Am. Acad. Polit. and Social Sci. (pres. 2001—). Home: 3507 Baring St Philadelphia PA 19104 Office: University of Pennsylvania 3814 Walnut St Philadelphia PA 19104 Personal E-mail: lws@sas.upenn.edu. Business E-Mail: lws@sas.upenn.edu.

SHERMAN, LOUIS ALLEN, biology professor, department chairman; b. Chgo., Dec. 16, 1943; s. Stanley E. and Sarah R. Sherman; m. Debra Meddoff, June 15, 1969; children: Daniel, Jeff. BS in Physics, U. Chgo., 1965, PhD in Biophysics, 1970. Postdoctoral fellow Cornell U., Ithaca, N.Y., 1970-72; asst. prof. U. Mo., Columbia, 1972-78, assoc. prof., 1978-83, prof., 1983-88, dir. biol. scis., 1985-88; prof., head dept. biol. scis. Purdue U., West Lafayette, Ind., 1989-2000, prof. biol. scis., 1989—. Contbr. articles to profl. jours. NIH fellow, 1965-72; Fulbright Hayes scholar, The Netherlands, 1979-80; NSF travel grantee, Fed. Republic Germany, Japan; grantee NIH, USDA, Dept. Energy. Fellow: AAAS, Am. Acad. Microbiology; mem.: AAUP, Plant Molecular Biology Soc., Biophys. Soc., Am. Soc. Plant Biologists, Am. Soc. Microbiology. Office: Purdue U Dept Biol Scis Lilly Hall West Lafayette IN 47907

SHERMAN, MARTIN PETER, lawyer; b. NYC, May 2, 1940; m. Susan Randall, Feb. 16, 1969; children: David, Timothy, Peter. BA, UCLA, 1961; JD, U. Chgo., 1964; LLM, U. So. Calif., 1969. Bar: Calif. 1965, Pa. 1972. Law clk. LA Superior Ct., 1964—65; dep. county counsel LA County, 1965—66; atty. antipoverty program Ventura, San Francisco and LA, Calif., 1966—69; counsel Atlantic Richfield Co., LA and Phila., 1969—73; asst. gen. counsel Ampex Corp., Redwood City, Calif., 1973—87; corp. counsel Amgen, Inc., Thousand Oaks, Calif., 1987—88; sr. atty. Intel Corp., Santa Clara, Calif., 1988—95; spl. counsel Tomlinson, Zisko, Morosoli & Maser, Palo Alto, Calif., 1995—97. Contbr. articles to profl. jours. Mem.: ABA. Office: 1310 Jones St # 1102 San Francisco CA 94109 E-mail: sherman2@ix.netcom.com., marty@shermanlegal.net.

SHERMAN, MARY ANGUS, public library administrator; b. Lawton, Okla., Jan. 3, 1937; d. Donald Adelbert and Mabel (Felkner) Angus; m. Donald Neil Sherman, Feb. 8, 1958; children: Elizabeth, Donald Neil II. BS in Home Econs., U. Okla., 1958, MLS, 1969. Br. head Pioneer Libr. System, Purcell, Okla., 1966-76, regional libr. Norman, Okla., 1976-78, asst. dir., 1978-80, dir., 1987—. Bd. dirs. McClain Bank, chair audit com., 1997—. Mem. bd. visitors U. Okla. Coll. Arts and Scis., 1998—; bd. dirs. U. Okla. Found., 2004—, Women's Resource Ctr., Norman, 1998—2003, pres., 2002. Named one of Disting. Alumni, Sch. Home Econs. U. Okla., 1980; recipient award of merit, Okla. Sch. Libr. and Info. Sci., 2000. Mem. ALA (councilor 1988-96, planning and budget assembly 1990-91, internat. rels. com. 1992-96, 2001—, internat. rels. round table 1989—, orientation com. 1998-99, mem. com. 1999-2000, chair sister libr. com. 2000-02, exec. bd. 2000-02), Pub. Libr. Assn. (divsn. of ALA, pres. pub. policy for pub. librs. sect. 1995-96, chmn. internat. rels. com., 2002-04), Tech. in Publ. Librs. Com. 2002-06, Internat. Fedn. Libr. Assns. (standing com. on pub. librs. 1999—), AAUW (pres. Okla. chpt. 1975-77, nat. bd. dirs. 1983-87, S.W. ctrl. region dir. 1983-85, v.p. nat. membership 1985-87, Woman of the Yr. Purcell chpt. 1982), Okla. Libr. Assn. (pres. 1982-83, interlibr. cooperation com. 1993-95, chair 1994-95, legis. com. 1998—, Disting. Svc. award 1986), Norman Soc. Internat. Affairs (v.p. 1998-99, pres. 1999-2001), Norman C. of C. (bd. dirs. 1988-96, pres. 1994-95), Rotary (program chair 1991-92, 1999-2001, bd. dirs. 1993-97, pres. 1995-96, Paul Harris fellow, group study exch. leader to Iceland 1998, dist. literacy chair 1998-2000, dist. group study exch. chair 2001—), Norman Assistance League Club (cmty. assoc.), Norman Sister City Com. 1994-98, Delta Gamma Mothers (pres. 1978-79), Kappa Alpha Theta (pres. Alpha Omicron House Corp. 1984-87, nat. dir. house corps. 1987-88), Beta Phi Mu, Phi Beta K Democrat. Methodist. Office: Pioneer Libr System 225 N Webster Ave Norman OK 73069-7133 Office Phone: 405-701-2642. E-mail: mary@pls.lib.ok.us.

SHERMAN, MICHAEL, lawyer; b. 1946; AB, U. Conn., JD, 1971. Bar: Conn. 1971. Asst. pub. def. Stamford Superior Ct., asst. pros.; asst. town atty. Town of Greenwich; ptnr. Sherman & Richichi, Stamford, Conn., 1971—. Mem.: ATLA, Conn. Trial Lawyers Assn., Nat. Assn. Criminal Def. Lawyers, Conn. Criminal Def. Lawyers Assn. (founding mem., officer, bd. mem., lectr.). Office: Sherman & Richichi 27 5th St Stamford CT 06905

SHERMAN, MICHAEL FRANCIS, professional football coach; b. Norwood, Mass., Dec. 19, 1954; m. Karen Sherman; children: Sarah, Emily, Matthew, Benjamin. Student, Ctrl. Conn. State U., 1974, 76-77. Coach U. Pitts., 1981-82, Tulane, 1983-84; offensive coord. Holy Cross, 1985-88; offensive line coord. Tex. A&M, 1989-93, 95-96, UCLA, 1994; tight ends/asst. offensive line Green Bay Packers, 1997-98, head coach, 2000—; offensive coord. Seattle Seahawks, 1999; exec. VP & gen. mgr. Green Bay Packers, 2001—. Office: care Green Bay Packers PO Box 10628 Green Bay WI 54307-0628 also: Green Bay Packers Inc 1265 Lombardi Ave Green Bay WI 54304

SHERMAN, MILDRED MOZELLE, music educator, vocalist, actress, opera director; b. Mt. Grove, Mo., Nov. 21, 1932; d. William Husley and Jessie Claire (Faulkner) Clark; m. Louis Leroy Sherman, Aug. 14, 1954; children: Clark Michael, Gayla Dawn. MusB, Bethany Coll., Lindsborg, Kans., 1953; MusM, Ind. U., 1955; PhD, U. Wis., 1971; postgrad., U. Wis., Stevens Point, Kans. U., Baylor U. Instr. music Kans. State U., Manhattan, 1962-66; prof. music Howard Payne U., Brownwood, Tex., 1973-80, Grand Canyon U., Phoenix, 1980-84; prof. ch. music, dir. ch. music, drama, theatre So. Bapt. Theol. Sem., Louisville, 1984-2001, founding dir. Ch. Music Drama Theatre, sr. prof. ch. music, 2001—. Instr., rep. Inst. Pan Americano, Panama City, 1955-56; vis. prof. Belem and Rio Bapt. Sems., Brazil; owner Sherman Svcs., 2000—, Ky. Opera Roster, 2001—; vis. lectr. Staley, Cambridge, Union, Furman, Stetson, and Fla. Bapt. univs., 1990-99. Performer, dir. over 1000 operas, musicals, and plays including Women of the Bible, 1986-97; author: The Vocal Technician, 1991, also short stories; translator Mozarts Obligation of the 1st Commandment, 1986, Debussy's Prodigal Son, 1987, Massenet's Herodiade, 1997, Two from Galilee prodn. kit, 1996; also monologues; contbg. author: New Christian Dictionary, 2001. Recipient Orpheus award Phi Mu Alpha Sinfonia, 1978; Lily Found. grantee, 1988-90; Baylor Univ. fellow, 1990-91. Mem. Nat. Opera Assn., Nat. Assn. Tchrs. Singing, Met. Opera Guild, Ch. Music Conf., DAR, Ea. Star, Christian Opera Assn. Bd., Sigma Alpha Iota. Baptist. Avocations: geneology, handwork, animals, travel. Home: 3602 Coronado Dr Louisville KY 40241-2611 Office: So Bapt Theol Sem 2825 Lexington Rd Louisville KY 40280-0001 Business E-Mail: msherman@sbts.edu.

SHERMAN, NANCY, philosophy educator; b. Passaic, N.J., June 20, 1951; d. Seymour and Beatrice (Hoffman) S.; m. Marshall Presser, June 22, 1980; children: Kala, Jonathan. AB in Philosophy magna cum laude, Bryn Mawr Coll., 1973; postgrad., Boston U., 1973; MLitt in Philosophy, U. Edinburgh, Scotland, 1976; PhD, Harvard U., 1982. Tchg. asst. in philosophy Harvard U., Cambridge, Mass., 1980-81; asst. prof. Yale U., New Haven, 1982-88, assoc. prof., 1988-89, Georgetown U., Washington, 1989-94, prof., 1994—, univ prof. Vis. rsch. scholar King's Coll., Cambridge (Eng.) U., spring 1978; vis. prof. Johns Hopkins U., Balt., spring 1995, U. Md., College Park, spring 1995, 96; cons. on ethics to undersec. Dept. Navy, 1994; vis. disting. chair of ethics U.S. Naval Acad., Annapolis, Md., 1997, 98; participant numerous confs., symposia, colloquia; lectr., spkr. in field. Author: The Fabric of Character: Aristotle's Theory of Virtue, 1989, paperback edit., 1991, Making a Necessity of Virtue: Aristotle and Kant on Virtue, 1996; editor: Aristotle's Ethics: Critical Essays, 1999; contbr. articles and revs. to profl. jours. Vans Dunlop scholar U. Edinburgh, 1974-76; Teschemacher fellow Harvard U., 1976-81, Newcombe fellow, 1981-82, fellow NEH, 1984-85, 96, Am. Coun. Learned Socs., 1987, Mellon fellow Yale U., 1988, Whitney Humanities fellow Yale U., 1987-88, fellow Kennedy Inst. Ethics, 1991-96, Mellon summer fellow, 1992, Georgetown U. summer fellow, 1990, 91, 94, 95; Am. Philos. Soc. fellow, 2002. Mem. APA (program com. ea. divsn. 1995-97), Soc. for Ancient Greek Philosophy, N.Am. Kant Soc., Am. Philos. Assn., Washington Psychoanalytic Found. Office: Georgetown U Dept Philosophy 224 New North St NW Washington DC 20057-0001

SHERMAN, NORMAN MARK, advertising agency executive; b. N.Y.C., June 19, 1948; s. Sol and Rhoda (Kaplan) S.; m. Michelle Petnov, Jan. 8, 1978; 1 child, Michael Isaac. BA, U. Buffalo, 1970; MBA, Columbia U., 1972. Cert. tchr., N.Y. Product mgr. RCA Records, N.Y.C., 1972-73; dir. mktg. Shelter Records, N.Y.C., 1973-74; account exec. Rosenfeld Sirowitz & Lawson, N.Y.C., 1974-76, Benton & Bowles, N.Y.C., 1976-78, v.p. account supr., 1978-81, sr. v.p., mgmt. supr., 1981-84; exec. v.p., dir. account mgmt. Avrett, Free & Ginsberg, N.Y.C., 1984-85; sr. v.p., group account dir. D'arcy, Masius, Benton & Bowles, 1985-93, mng. dir., bd. dirs., 1993-96, corp. exec. v.p., 1996-98; mng. dir. The Sr. Network, Stamford, Conn., 1998-99; pres. N.Am. Gundersen Ptnrs. LLC, N.Y.C., 1999—2001; exec. v.p., dir. healthcare Hill, Holliday, Connors, Cosmopulos, 2002—. Home: 330 W 72nd St New York NY 10023-2641 Office: Hill Holliday 622 Third Ave New York NY 10017 Office Phone: 212-905-7023. E-mail: nsherman@hhny.com.

SHERMAN, PATSY O'CONNELL, retired technical development administrator, chemist; b. Mpls., Sept. 15, 1930; d. James Patrick and Edna Fern (Stitzel) O'Connell m. Hubert Townsend Sherman, Aug. 15, 1953; children: Sharilyn Kay Sherman Loushin, Wendy Jane Sherman Heil. BA, Gustavus Adolphus Coll., 1952. Chemist 3M, St. Paul, 1952-67, rsch. specialist, 1967-73, tech. mgr., 1973-82, mgr. tech. devel., 1982—92; ret., 1992. Trustee GMI Engring. and Mgmt. Inst., Flint, Mich., 1986-92; bd. dirs., owner Advanced Optics Inc., Mpls. Contbr. numerous articles to profl. jours.; patentee in field. Trustee Gustavus Adolphus Coll., 1989-92. Recipient Disting. Alumni award Gustavus Adolphus Coll., 1975, Spurgeon award Boy Scouts Am., 1980; named to Minn. Inventors Hall of Fame, 1989, Nat. Inventors Hall of Fame, 2001. Mem. Am. Chem. Soc., Am. Soc. Tng. and Devel., Am. Soc. Engring. Edn. (dir. continuing profl. devel. div. 1986-89, chair 1989-90). Achievements include invention of Scotchgard (with Samuel Smith) in 1956. Home: 9401 Lyndale Ave S Apt 417 Bloomington MN 55420 Personal E-mail: patsherman@aol.com.

SHERMAN, PETER R. lawyer, educator; b. South Bend, Ind., Apr. 14, 1939; BS with distinction, Ind. U., 1961; JD, Georgetown U., 1964, ML in Trail Advocacy, 1966. Bar: DC. Law clk. to Hon. L. W. Youngdahl U.S. Dist. Ct. DC, 1965—66; ptnr. Sherman, Meehan, Curtin & Ain, P.C., Washington. Adj. prof. Washington Coll. Law Am. U., 1977—80, 1993—; pvt. bar rep. rules com. family divsn. Superior Ct. DC, mem. rules revision com., 1991—96. Bd. editors Georgetown Law Jour., 1963—64. Mem. Task Force Race and Ethnic Bias in DC Cts., 1990—91. Prettyman fellow, Georgetown U., 1965—66. Fellow: Am. Acad. Matrimonial Lawyers. Office: 1900 M St NW Ste 600 Washington DC 20036-3565

SHERMAN, RANDOLPH, plastic and reconstructive surgeon, educator; b. St. Louis, May 27, 1951; s. Leon and Pearl (Lichtenfeld) S.; m. Sandra Lee Wackerman, May 3, 1992; 1 child, Max Lassen. BA, U. Rochester, 1973; MD, U. Mo., 1977. Diplomate Am. Bd. Surgery, Am. Bd. Plastic Surgery (cert. added qualification in hand surgery). Intern in gen. medicine U. Wis., Madison, 1978; intern in surgery U. Calif., San Francisco, 1978-79, resident in surgery, 1979-81, SUNY, Syracuse, 1981-83; fellow in plastic and reconstructive surgery U. So. Calif., 1983-85, asst. prof. surger and orthopedics, 1985-91, assoc. prof. clin. surgery and orthopaedics, 1991-92, assoc. prof. clin. surgery, orthopaedics and neurol. surgery, 1992-96, chmn. divsn. plastic and reconstructive surgery, 1994—, prof. clin. surgery, orthopaedics and neurol. surgery, 1996—. Mem. cons. staff City of Hope Nat. Med. Ctr., Duarte, Calif., 1985-91, 94—, St. John's Hosp., Santa Monica, 1989—; mem. staff, med. dir. Microsurg. Ctr. Hosp. Good Samaritan, L.A., 1985-93; mem. plastic and reconstructive surgery staff Kenneth Norris Jr. Cancer Hosp., L.A., 1985—, L.A. County/U. So. Calif. Med. Ctr., L.A., 1985—; mem. staff St. Vincent Med. Ctr., L.A., 1986-92, Orthop. Hosp., L.A., 1986—; Shriner's Hosp. for Crippled Children, L.A., 1987-92, Children's Hosp. L.A., 1987—, Cedars Sinai Med. Ctr., L.A., 1987—, Estelle Doheny Eye Hosp., L.A., 1994—, numerous others; chief plastic and reconstructive surgery divsn. U. So. Calif. U. Hosp., L.A., 1991—; dir. Am. Bd. Plastic Surgery 2000--; lectr., rschr. in field. Editor: Orthopedic Clinics, 1993; assoc. editor Surg. Rounds, 1989—, Jour. Hand Surgery, 1992-96, Am. Jour. Reconstructive Microsurgery, 1995—; contbr. articles to profl. jours., chpts. to books. Founder L.A. chpt. Operation Smile Internat., 1993—. Recipient L.A. Humanitarian award Calif. Hosp., 1994; Microsurg. Devel. grantee Hosp. Good Samaritan, 1987-92, U. So. Calif. U. Hosp., 1992—; grantee Searle R&D, 1995-97, Cohesion Corp., 1997. Fellow ACS, Am. Assn. Plastic Surgeons, Am. Assn. Hand Surgeons (bd. dirs. 1991-95), Am. Soc. Hand Surgery, Am. Soc. Reconstructive Microsurgery (past pres.), Calif. Soc. Plastic Surgery; mem. Am. Soc. Plastic and Reconstructive Surgery, Am. Soc. Peripheral Nerve, Internat. Soc. Reconstructive Microsurgery, Calif. Med. Assn., Calif. Soc. Plastic Surgery, Assn. Acad. Chmn. Plastic Surgery, Plastic Surgery Rsch. Coun., Musculoskeletal Infection Soc., Undersea Med. Soc., Flying Physicians Assn., Wound Healing Soc. Avocations: flying, mountain climbing, scuba diving, jazz piano, gardening. Office: 1450 San Pablo St Ste 2000 Los Angeles CA 90089-0106 Business E-Mail: rsherman@surgery.usc.edu.

SHERMAN, RICHARD ALLEN, SR., lawyer; b. Atlanta, Mar. 16, 1946; s. Robert Hiram and Olivia Mae (Latham) S.; m. Mary Margaret Sawyer, June 23, 1973 (div. June 1994); children: Richard A. Jr., Jill Mary, James Warren. BA, Tulane U., 1968, JD, 1972. Bar: Fla. 1974, La. 1973, U.S. Ct. Appeals (5th cir.) 1978, U.S. Ct. Appeals (11th cir.) 1981, U.S. Supreme Ct. 1981. Ptnr., head appellate divsn. Wicker, Smith, Blomqvist, Davant, Tutan, O'Hara, McCoy et al, Miami, 1973-83; pvt. practice Ft. Lauderdale, Fla., 1983—; practice limited to handling appeals in Fla. Mem. ABA (vice-chmn. U.S. Ct. Appeals 5th cir. com. 1981), Fla. Bar Assn. (appellate rules com. 1979-81), Dade County Bar Assn. (chmn. appellate cts. com. 1982-83), Mensa, Pres. Club, Lauderdale Yacht Club, Upper Keys Sailing Club (bd. dirs.). Avocations: yacht racing, boating, scuba diving, travel, theater. Office: 1777 S Andrews Ave Ste 302 Fort Lauderdale FL 33316-2517

SHERMAN, ROBERT, broadcaster; b. NYC, July 23, 1932; s. Isaac Jacob and Nadia (Reisenberg) S.; m. Veronica Jean Bravo; children: Steven J., Peter M. BA, NYU, 1952; MA, Columbia U., 1953. Music dir. Sta. WQXR-FM, N.Y.C., 1960-70, program dir., 1970-85, exec. prodr., 1985-93, sr. cons., 1993—. Faculty The Julliard Sch., N.Y.C., 1988—, Manhattan Sch. Music, N.Y.C., 1995—, Fordham U., 2002—; artistic advisor Pulvermann Found., Rye, N.Y., 1993—; artistic dir. Beethoven Festival, 1985--; narrator West Point Band, Rye, 1994—; bd. dirs. Naumburg Found., The Mannes Coll. of Music.; pres. adv. coun. Pa. Acad. Music. Co-author: Nadia Reisenberg, 1986, Complete Idiot's Guide to Classical Music, 1997; contbr. reviews and articles The New York Times, 1964—. Bd. dirs. Tisch Ctr. for the Arts, 1996-97. With U.S. Army, 1953-56. Recipient Verdi medal Met. Opera Nat. Coun., 1987, Sanford medal Yale U., 1994, Appreciation award ASCAP, 1993, radio competition prizes N.Y. festivals, 1994. Home: 5 Tavano Rd Ossining NY 10562-3105 Office: WQXR 122 5th Ave New York NY 10011-5605 Office Phone: 914-762-6282. Personal E-mail: rsher762@aol.com.

SHERMAN, ROBERT B(ERNARD), composer, lyricist, screenwriter; b. N.Y.C., Dec. 19, 1925; s. Al and Rosa (Dancis) S.; student UCLA, 1943; BA, Bard Coll., 1949; MusD (hon.) Lincoln U., 1990; m. Joyce Ruth Sasner, Sept. 27, 1953; children: Laurie Shane, Jeffrey Craig, Andrea Tracy, Robert Jason. Popular songwriter, 1950-60, including Tall Paul, Pineapple Princess, You're Sixteen (Gold Record); songwriter Walt Disney Prodns., Beverly Hills, Calif., 1960-68, for 29 films including The Parent Trap, 1961, Summer Magic, 1963, Mary Poppins, 1964, That Darn Cat, 1965, Winnie The Pooh, 1965, Jungle Book, 1967, Bedknobs and Broomsticks, 1971; co-composer song It's A Small World, theme of Disneyland, Walt Disney World, Fla., Disneyland, Tokyo, Disneyland, Paris; composer, lyricist United Artists, Beverly Hills, 1969—, songs for film Chitty, Chitty, Bang, Bang, 1969, Snoopy, Come Home!, 1972; song scores Charlotte's Web, 1972, Cabbage Patch Kids, 1974, Little Nemo, 1992, The Mighty Kong, 1996, The Tigger Movie, 1999; composer for Walt Disney's Wonderful World of Color, TV, 1961—; co-producer NBC-TV spl. Goldilocks, 1970; v.p. Musi-Classics, Inc.; co-producer, composer, lyricist stage musical Victory Canteen, 1971; composer-lyricist Broadway show Over Here, 1975, Busker Alley, 1995; screenplay and song score Tom Sawyer, United Artists, 1972, Huckleberry Finn, 1974, The Slipper and the Rose, 1977,

The Magic of Lassie, 1978. Served with inf. AUS, 1943-45; ETO. Decorated Purple Heart; recipient 2 Acad. awards best score for Mary Poppins, 1964, best song for Chim Chim Cheree, 1964; Grammy award, 1965; Christopher medal, 1965, 74; nine Acad. award nominations; Acad. award nomination for song score Bedknobs and Broomsticks, 1971, for best song The Age of Not Believing, 1971, others; 16 golden, 4 platinum and one diamond record album, 1965-83; first prize best composer song score Tom Sawyer, Moscow Film Festival, 1973, B.M.I. Pioneer award, 1977; Golden Cassette awards for Mary Poppins, Jungle Book, Bed Knobs and Broomsticks, 1983, Mouscar award Disney Studios, Disney Legend award, 1990, BMI Richard Kirk Lifetime Achievement award, 1991. Mem. Acad. Motion Picture Arts and Scis. (exec. bd. music br. 12 yrs.), AFTRA, Nat. Acad. Rec. Arts and Scis., Composers and Lyricists Guild (exec. bd.), Dramatists Guild, Authors League. Office: 9030 Harratt St West Hollywood CA 90069-3858

SHERMAN, ROBERT LEE, JR., chemist, educator; b. Mt. Carmel, Ill., Dec. 24, 1974; s. Robert Lee and Nancy Joan Sherman; m. Crystal Lynn Kirby, July 26, 1997. BS in Chemistry, So. Ill. U., 1997, MS in Chemistry, 2000; postgrad., Okla. State U., 2000—. Lab. technician Ctrl. State Analytical Co., Evansville, Ind., 1996, 97; tchg. asst. dept. chemistry So. Ill. U., Carbondale, 1997-2000; tchg. asst. Okla. State U., Stillwater, 2000, rsch. asst. in chemistry, 2002—; rsch. asst. Okla. State U., Stillwater, 2002—. C. David Schmulbach tchg. scholar So. Ill. U., 1997-98. Mem. Am. Chem. Soc. (assoc.). Baptist. Avocations: U.S. Civil War history, models. Home: 608 Copp Ave Mount Carmel IL 62863-1716 Office: Okla State Univ Chemistry Dept Stillwater OK 74075 E-mail: rlschem@aol.com.

SHERMAN, ROGER TALBOT, surgeon, educator; b. Chgo., Sept. 30, 1923; s. Joseph Bright and Alice Elizabeth (Baur) S.; m. Ruth Kathryn Thieman, Aug. 23, 1952; children: Nann, Alice, Nina, John, Julie. AB, Kenyon Coll., 1946; MD, U. Cin., 1948. Diplomate Am. Bd. Surgery (mem.). Intern, fellow in pathology St. Luke's Hosp., Chgo., 1948-50; resident in surgery Cin. Gen. Hosp., 1950-56; chief dept. exptl. surgery Walter Reed Army Med. Ctr., 1956-59; asst. prof. to prof. surgery U. Tenn., Memphis, 1959-72; prof., chmn. dept. surgery U. South Fla., Tampa, 1972-82; prof. surgery Emory U. Sch. Medicine, Atlanta, 1983-93; chief surgery Grady Meml. Hosp., Atlanta, 1983-92; Whitaker prof. surgery Emory U. Sch. Medicine, Atlanta, 1993-97, prof. emeritus, 1997—; dir. surg. edn. Piedmont Hosp., Atlanta, 1993-97. Mem. editorial bd. Am. Surgeon, 1970-91, Jour. Trauma, 1970-93; contbr. articles to profl. jour., chpt. to books. Served to maj. M.C. AUS, 1956-59. Recipient Golden Apple Tchr. of the Yr. award, 1972, Williams Disting. Tchg. award Emory U., 1984, Curtis P. Artz award, 1988. Fellow ACS (gov.); mem. Am. Assn. Surgery of Trauma (pres. 1979), Am. Surg. Assn., So. Surg. Assn., Southeastern Surg. Congress (pres. 1985), Internat. Surg. Soc., Soc. Surgery of Alimentary Tract, Am. Burn Assn., Shock Soc., Am. Trauma Soc., Ga. Surg. Soc. (pres. 1997), Sigma Xi, Psi Upsilon, Alpha Omega Alpha. Home: 3747 Peachtree Rd NE Apt 813-814 Atlanta GA 30319-1352 *Surgery. The opening, exploration and repair of the living human body is an awesome responsibility afforded to only a few. To be privileged to be counted among those is a high honor, surpassed only by being trusted to teach others this demanding, and marvelous craft.*

SHERMAN, SANDRA BROWN, lawyer; b. Galesburg, Ill., May 14, 1953; d. Charles Lewis and Lois Maria (Nelson) Brown; m. Robert Sherman, June 10, 1979; children: Michael Wesley, Stephen Averill, Alexander Joseph. B of Music Edn., Ind. U., 1975; JD, U. Ill., 1979, LLM, 1981. Bar: Ill. 1979, Tex. 1982, N.J. 1984, U.S. Tax Ct. 1988, N.Y. 1997. Instr. law U. Ill., Champaign, 1979-81; assoc. Law Offices of William E. Remy, San Antonio, 1984, Gutkin Miller Shapiro & Selesner, Millburn, N.J., 1985-88, ptnr., 1989-91; counsel Riker Danzig Scherer Hyland & Perretti LLP, Morristown, N.J., 1991-95; ptnr. Riker Danzig Scherer Hyland & Perretti, LLP, Morristown, N.J., 1996—. Contbr. articles to profl. jours. Trustee, sec. Found. U. Medicine and Dentistry N.J., 1998—; trustee Jersey Battered Women's Svc., 1999—. Scholar Ind. U., 1971-75, U. Ill., 1977-79. Mem. ABA (probate and trust law divsn.), N.J. Bar Assn., Estate Planning Coun. No. N.J., Estate Planning Coun. N.Y.C., Park Ave. Club. Avocation: music. Home: 15 Hawthorne Dr New Providence NJ 07974-1111 Office: Riker Danzig Scherer Hyland & Perretti LLP Headquarters Plz 1 Speedwell Ave Morristown NJ 07961-1981 E-mail: ssherman@riker.com.

SHERMAN, SANDRA LYNN, auditor; b. Albany, N.Y., Apr. 22, 1967; d. Charles Franklin Sherman and Theresa Louise Clark; m. Jeffrey M. Zelka; children: Brandon Michael Mueller, Victoria Kathryn Mueller. BBA in Acctg., Siena Coll., 1999; MBA in Mgmt. of Info. Sys., SUNY, Albany, 2003. Bookkeeper N.Y. State Troopers PBA, Albany, 1989—96; office adminstr. E. Stewart Jones PLLC, Troy, NY, 1996—2003; auditor PriceWaterhouse Coopers, Albany, 2003—. Cons. N.Y. State Troopers PBA, Albany, 1996—97. Recipient Nat. Leadership award, Nat. Rep. Congl. Com., 2003. Mem.: NAFE, AICPA, Assn. Legal Adminstrs. (pres. Hudson Valley chpt. 2002—03). Roman Catholic. Avocations: gardening, golf, boating, fishing, running. Office: PriceWaterhouse Coopers 80 State St Albany NY 12207 E-mail: shermmba@hotmail.com.

SHERMAN, SIGNE LIDFELDT, portfolio manager, former research chemist; b. Rochester, N.Y., Nov. 11, 1913; d. Carl Leonard Broström and Herta Elvira Maria (Tern) Lidfeldt; m. Joseph V. Sherman, Nov. 18, 1944 (dec. Oct. 1984). BA, U. Rochester, 1935, MS, 1937. Chief chemist Lab. Indsl. Medicine and Toxicology Eastman Kodak Co., Rochester, 1937-43; chief rsch. chemist Chesebrough-Pond's Inc., Clinton, Conn., 1943-44; ptnr. Joseph V. Sherman Cons., N.Y.C., 1944-84; portfolio strategist Sherman Holdings, Troy, Mont., 1984—. Author: The New Fibers, 1946. Fellow Am. Inst. Chemists; mem. AAAS, AAUW (life), Am. Chem. Soc., Am. Econ. Assn., Am. Assn. Ind. Investors (life), Fedn. Am. Scientists (life), Union Concerned Scientists (life), Earthquake Engring. Rsch. Inst., Nat. Ctr. for Earthquake Engring. Rsch., N.Y. Acad. Scis. (life), Cabinet View Country Club. Office: Sherman Holdings Angel Island 648 Halo Dr Troy MT 59935-9415 E-mail: creative@libby.org.

SHERMAN, SPENCER E. ophthalmologist; b. Jersey City, Apr. 8, 1936; AB cum laude, Princeton U., Sigma XI, 1958; MD, Columbia Coll. Physicians & Surgeons, 1962. Diplomate Am. Bd. Ophthalmology. Intern Mt. Sinai Hosp., N.Y.C., 1962-63, attending ophthalmologist, 1968—, resident in ophthalmology, 1965-68; asst. clin. prof. ophthalmology NYU Sch. Medicine, N.Y.C.; staff Mt. Sinai Hosp., 1998—. Attending ophthalmologist Manhattan Eye & Ear Hosp., NYC, 1968—, Lenox Hill Hosp., NYC, 1968—, NY Eye and Ear Infirmary, Mt. Sinai Hosp., 1970—. Capt. USAMC, 1963-65. Named one of Best Drs. in NY, Castle Connolly Group, 1980—, Top Drs. in US, Ctr. for Study of Svc. Fellow ACS, Internat. Coll. of Surgeons, Am. Acad. of Ophthalmology (Honor and Svc. award); mem. AMA, Nat. Soc. Prevention Blindness, Found. Children with Learning Disabilities, Am. Soc. Refractive Surgeons, NY Acad. Medicine, NY Ophthalmologic Soc., Internat. Soc. Refractive Surgery, Am. Soc. Cataract & Refractive Surgery, Harmonie Club, Sunningdale Country Club, Maidstone Gun Club, Peconic Sportsman Club, East Hampton Tennis Club. Office: 166 E 63rd St New York NY 10021-7636 Fax: (212) 752-4285. E-mail: sesmdpc@aol.com.

SHERMAN, STEVEN S.J. architectural firm executive; Ptnr. Sherman, Carter, Barnhart Archs., Lexington, Ky. Office: Sherman Carter Barnhart Archs 2405 Harrodsburg Rd Lexington KY 40504-3329

SHERMAN, STUART, internist, gastroenterologist; b. New York, N.Y., Feb. 21, 1955; s. Sol and Rhoda (Kaplan) S.; m. Leslie Jane Derus, Oct. 5, 1991; children: Matthew, Benjamin. BA, SUNY, Binghampton, 1977; MD, Washington U., St. Louis, 1982. Diplomate Am. Bd. Internal Medicine. Resident in internal medicine U. Pitts., 1982-85, rsch. fellow, 1985-86; gastroenterology fellow Sch. of Medicine UCLA, 1986-89; therapeutic endoscopy fellow Sch. Medicine Ind. U., 1989-90; asst. prof. medicine and pancreaticobiliary endoscopy UCLA, 1990-92; asst. prof. medicine Ind. U., 1992-95, assoc. prof., 1995—, assoc. prof. radiology, 1996—. Cons. Bard Interventional Products Adv. Panel, Tewksbury, Mass., 1994—. Contbr. articles to profl. jours. Recipient Glaxo Award for excellence in gastroenterology Midwest Am. Fedn. Clin. Rsch., 1993, Young Scholars Rsch. award World Congress of Gastroenterology, L.A., 1994. Fellow Am. Coll. Gastroenterology (mem. editl. bd. Gastrointestinal Endoscopy); mem. ACP, Am. Soc. for Gastrointestinal Endoscopy, Am. Gastroent. Assn. Avocations: travel, skiing, tennis, golf. Office: Ind U Med Ctr 550 University Blvd Ste 2300 Indianapolis IN 46202-5149 E-mail: ssherman@induni.edu.

SHERMAN, SUSAN JEAN, writer, educator, editor; b. N.Y.C., Oct. 30, 1939; d. Monroe and Gertrude (Horn) S. BA, Sarah Lawrence Coll., 1969, MA in Lit., 1971. Tchr. English Dwight-Englewood, 1970-72, Riverdale Country Sch., NY, 1972-97; writer Riverdale, NY, 1997—. Author: Give Me Myself, 1961, (rec.) Promises to Be Kept, 1962; editor: Forward Into the Past, 1992, May Sarton: Among the Usual Days, 1993, May Sarton: Selected Letters, 1916-1954, 1997, To Bid Us Still Rejoice, 1998, Dear Juliette: Letters of May Sarton to Juliette Huxley, 1999, May Sarton: Selected Letters, 1955-1995, 2002, May Sarton: Catching Beauty, The Earliest Poems (1924-1929), 2002, May Sarton: At Fifteen: A Journal, 2002.

SHERMAN, WILLIAM, architecture educator; AB, Princeton U.; MArch, Yale U. Dir. grad. Venice program U. Va., Charlottesville, assoc. prof. dept. arch., assoc. dean for acads., chair dept. arch. and landscape arch. Contbr. articles to profl. jours. Office: Univ Va Sch arch 209 Campbell Hall PO Box 400122 Charlottesville VA 22904-4122*

SHERMAN, WILLIAM FARRAR, lawyer, former state legislator; b. Little Rock, Sept. 12, 1937; s. Lincoln Farrar and Nancy (Lowe) S.; m. Carole Lynn Williams, Sept. 2, 1967; children: John, Anna, Lucy. BA in History, U. Ark., 1960; LLB, U. Va., 1964. Bar: Ark. 1964, U.S. Supreme Ct. 1970. Assoc. Smith, Williams, Friday & Bowen, Little Rock, 1964-66; asst. U.S. atty. Ea. Dist. Ark., Little Rock, 1966-69, Ark. Securities Commr., Little Rock, 1969-71; ptnr. Jacoway, Sherman & Pence, Little Rock, 1971—. Legal counsel Voice of the Retarded, 1991-2001, BBB Ark., 1971-2001; mem. Ark. Ho. of Reps., 1974-84; spl. assoc. justice Supreme Ct., 1991; del. Constnl. Conv. Ark., 1979. With U.S. Army, 1960-61, now brig. gen. U.S. Army ret. Mem. ABA, Ark. Bar Assn., Pulaski County Bar Assn., Ark. Bar Found. Democrat. Methodist. Office: 221 W 2nd St Little Rock AR 72201-2505 Office Phone: 501-372-3148. E-mail: clsherman@aristotle.net.

SHERMAN, ZACHARY, civil engineer, aerospace engineer, consultant; b. N.Y.C., Oct. 26, 1922; s. Harry and Minnie (Schulsinger) Sherman; m. Bertha Leikin, Mar. 23, 1947; children: Gene Victor, Carol Beth. BCE, CCNY, 1943; MCE, Polytech. U. N.Y., Bklyn., 1953, PhD in Civil Engring. & Mechanics, 1969; MME, Stevens Inst. Tech., 1968. Registered profl. engr., N.Y., N.J. Stress analyst Gen. Dynamics, San Diego, 1943-45; sr. stress analyst Republic Aviation, Farmingdale, NY, 1945-47, 59-62; prof. civil engring. U. Miss., Oxford, 1954-59; lectr. Stevens Inst. Tech., Hoboken, NJ, 1962-67, CUNY, 1967-69; assoc. prof. aerospace engring. Pa. State U., State College, 1969-73; prin. Dr. Zachary Sherman Cons. Engrs., Santa Monica, Calif., 1973—; aerospace engr. FAA, N.Y.C., 1980-86. Designated cons. engr. rep. FAA, 1986—. Contbr. articles to profl. jours. NSF grantee, 1972. Fellow: ASCE; mem.: AIAA (v.p. Western Conn. chpt. 1977—78), N.Y. Acad. Scis., Sigma Xi. Achievements include development of beam/beam-column deck suspension bridge, prestressed aircraft wing; pothole problem. Home and Office: 2021 California Ave Apt 7 Santa Monica CA 90403-4531 Fax: 310-264-5990. Office Phone: 310-264-5990. Personal E-mail: aerozach@earthlink.net.

SHERN, STEPHANIE MARIE, investment company executive, accountant; b. Taylor, Pa., Jan. 7, 1948; d. Joseph and Stephanie (Malodovitch) Andrews; m. George Emil Shern, Sept. 25, 1971. AA, Keystone Jr. Coll., 1967; BS, Pa. State U., 1969. CPA, N.Y. Staff acct. to ptnr., nat. dir. consumer products industry Ernst & Young, N.Y.C., 1969—, ptnr., vice chmn., global and U.S. dir. R&CP markets. Dir. Met. Retail Fin. Execs., N.Y.C. Contbr. articles to profl. jours. Named Keystonian of Yr., Keystone Jr. Coll., 1984. Mem. AICPA, N.Y. State Soc. CPAs (bd. dirs. 1985—), Women's Econ. Round Table, Panther Valley Golf (Allamuch, N.J.), Beta Alpha Psi (mem. adv. forum 1984—). Republican. Ukrainian Orthodox. Home: 11 Green Briar Ct Little Falls NJ 07424-2307 Office: Ernst & Young 5 Times Sq New York NY 10036-6530

SHERONY, CHERYL ANNE, dietician; b. Lincoln, Nebr., Dec. 5, 1948; d. John Eugene and Hazel Ethel (Stites) Howe; m. Bruce Carl Sherony, Aug. 11, 1973; children: Thomas Carl, Michael Bruce. BS in Dietetics, U. Wis., Stevens Point, 1971, MS, 1979. Registered dietitian. Dietitian Marquette (Mich.) Gen. Hosp., 1979-80, self employed, 1980-85, 89-90, Alger Marquette C.C., Marquette, 1982-87, Upper Peninsula Home Nursing, Marquette, 1989-93; dietititian self employed, Marquette, 1989-93; dietitian, owner Superior Dietetic Svcs. of the Upper Peninsula Inc., Marquette, 1996-99; pvt. practice dietitian dietitian, Marquette, 1999—. Citizen amb. to China, People to People Program, 1995. Sect. reviewer Pediat. Manual of Clin. Dietetics, 1998. Capt. USAF, 1972-90. Mem. Am. Dietetic Assn., Mich. Dietetic Assn., Upper Peninsula Dietetic Assn. Roman Catholic. Avocations: reading, water-skiing, cross country skiing. Home and Office: 1781 M-28 East Marquette MI 49855

SHERPA, FRAN MAGRUDER, geography educator, animal scientist, small business owner; b. Midland, Tex., Aug. 20, 1952; d. Edwin Howard Magruder and Barbara June Cowden; m. Ang Kazi Sherpa; children: Sarah, Susie, Sonia, Tsowang. BS Geography, Tex. State U., 1995, M Applied Geography, 1998. Registered massage therapist. Owner, operator Himalayan Excursions, Nepal, 1983—85; investor, mgr. office Nepal Internat. Clinic, Nepal, 1989—91; adj. prof. geography U. Tex. Permian Basin, Odessa, Tex., 2000—; owner Bodywork, 2003—. Mem. Kathmandu Assn. Mothers and Babies Internat., 1989—93; sec. Am. Women of Nepal, Nepal, 1989—93; mem. United Nations Women's Orgn., Nepal, 1989—93; mem. audio visual acom. Road Users Nepal, Nepal, 1992—93. Mem.: Am. Assn. Geographers, U.S. Polo Assn. Avocations: polo, photography, travel. Home: 2201 Neely Midland TX 79705 E-mail: fransherpa@cox.net.

SHERR, CHARLES J. medical educator; MD, PhD in Immunology, NYU. Pathology resident Bellevue Hosp. Ctr., N.Y.C.; postdoctoral tng., leader rsch. group Nat. Cancer Inst.; mem. dept. genetics and tumor cell biology St. Jude Children's Rsch. Hosp. Investigator Howard Hughes Med. Inst., Chevy Chase, Md.; adj. prof. molecular scis. U. Tenn. Coll. Medicine, Memphis. Mem.: NAS. Office: U Tenn Med Sch 801 Molecular Sci Bldg 790 Madison Ave Memphis TN 38105

SHERRARD, JAMES E., III, retired military officer; BA in Biol., U. Miss., 1965; M in Pers. Mgmt., Troy State U., 1976; grad., Air War Coll., 1981. Commd. 2d. lt. USAF, 1965, advanced through grades to lt. gen., 2001; student flight tng. Moody AFB, Ga., 1965-66; instr. pilot Sheppard AFB, Tex., 1966-70; instr. pilot, C-130A/B, AC-130A, flight examiner, squadron ops. officer 919th Tactical Airlift Group, Duke Field, Fla., 1971-77; squadron ops. officer, C-130E instr. pilot 913th Tactical Airlift Group, Willow Grove Air Res., 1977-78; asst. dep. comdr., then dep. comdr. ops. 459 Tactical Airlift Wing, Andrews AFB, Md., 1978-81; comdr. 910th Tactical Airlift Group, Youngstown Mcpl. Airport, Ohio, 1981-84; dep. chief staff plans, programs, manpower Hdqs. Air Force Reserve, Robins AFB, Ga., 1984—86; comdr. 440th Tactical Airlift Wing, Billy Mitchell Field, Wis., 1986-88, 443rd Mil. Airlift Wing, Kelly AFB, Tex., 1988-90, 4th Air Force, McClellan AFB, Calif., 1990-93; vice comdr. Air Force Res., Robins AFB, Ga., 1993-94; comdr. 22nd Air Force, Dobbins Air Res. Base, Ga., 1994-95; vice comdr. Air Force Res. Command, Robbins AFB, 1995-98; comdr. 22nd Air Force, Dobbins Air Res. Base, Ga., 1998; chief, Air Force Res. Hdqs. USAF, Washington, 1998—2004. Decorated D.S.M., Legion of Merit, Meritorious Svc. medal with three oak leaf clusters, Air Force Commendation medal, Air Force Outstanding Unit award with six oak leaf clustes, Air Force Organizational Excellence award with two oak leaf clusters, Combat Readiness medal ational Def. Svc. medal with service star, Armed Forces Res. medal with hourglass device. Mem. Res. Officers Assn., Air Force Assn., Order of the Daedalians, Airlift/Tanker Assn.

SHERRATT, GERALD ROBERT, retired academic administrator; b. Los Angeles, Nov. 6, 1931; s. Lowell Heyborne and Elva Genevieve (Lamb) S. BS in Edn., Utah State U., 1953, MS in Edn. Adminstrn., 1954; PhD in Adminstrn. Higher Edn., Mich. State U., 1975. Staff assoc. U. Utah, Salt Lake City, 1961-62; dir. high sch. relations Utah State U., Logan, 1962-64, asst. to pres., 1964-77, v.p. for univ. relations, 1977-81; pres. So. Utah U., Cedar City, 1982-97; mayor Cedar City, UT, 2002—. Dir. Honeyville Grain Inc., Utah; mem. coun. pres. Utah Sys. Higher Edn., 1982-97; chmn. bd. Utah Summer Games, Cedar City, 1984-97; chmn. pres.'s coun. Rocky Mountain Athletic Conf., Denver, 1984-85 Author hist. pageant: The West: America's Odyssey, 1973 (George Washington Honor medal 1973); musical review: How the West Was Won, 1998. Chmn. Festival of Am. West, Logan, Utah, 1972-82; chmn. bd. Utah Shakespearean Festival, Cedar City, 1982-86; chmn. bd. dirs. Salt Lake City Br. of the Fed. Res. Bank of San Francisco, 1996-98; bd. trustees Salt Lake Organizing Com. Winter Olympics 2002. 1st lt. USAF, 1954-57. Recipient Editing award Indsl. Editors Assn., 1962, Robins award Utah State U., 1967, Disting. Alumnus award Utah State U., 1974, So. Utah U., 1991, Total Citizen award Cedar City C. of C., 1993, Minuteman award Utah Nat. Guard, 1997; named to Utah Tourism Hall of Fame, 1989; Centennial medal So. Utah U., 1997; Imperial Order Utah Shakespearean Festival, 1997; named to Hall of Honor Utah Summer Games, 1997, Utah Educators Hall of Fame, 1999. Mem. Am. Assn. State Colls. and Univs., Cache C. of C. (bd. dirs. 1980-82), Cedar City Civic Club (pres.), Phi Kappa Phi, Phi Delta Kappa, Sigma Nu (regent 1976-78) Mem. Lds Ch.

SHERREN, ANNE TERRY, chemistry professor; b. Atlanta, July 1, 1936; d. Edward Allison and Annie Ayres (Lewis) Terry; m. William Samuel Sherren, Aug. 13, 1966. BA, Agnes Scott Coll., 1957; PhD, U. Fla., Gainesville, 1961. Grad. tchg. asst. U. Fla., Gainesville, 1957-61; from instr. to asst. prof. Tex. Womans U., Denton, 1961-66; rsch. participant Argonne Nat. Lab., 1973-80, 93-94; assoc. prof. chemistry North Cen. Coll., Naperville, Ill., 1966-76, prof., 1976-2001, prof. emeritus, 2001—. Contbr. articles to profl. jours. Ruling elder Knox Presbyn. Ch., 1971—, clk. of session, 1976-94. Mem. Am. Chem. Soc., Am. Inst. Chemists, Sigma Xi, Delta Kappa Gamma (chpt. pres. 2002-2004), Iota Sigma Pi (nat. pres. 1978-81, nat. dir. 1972-78, nat. historian 1989—). Presbyterian. Office: North Ctrl Coll Dept Chemistry Naperville IL 60566 Business E-Mail: atsherren@noctrl.edu.

SHERRER, CHARLES DAVID, college dean, clergyman; b. Marion, Ohio, Sept. 21, 1935; s. Harold D. and Catherine E. (Fye) S. AB, U. Notre Dame, 1958, MA, 1965; S.T.L., Gregorian U., 1962; PhD, U. N.C., 1969; HHD, King's Coll., 1997. Ordained priest Roman Cath. Ch., 1961. Instr. English U. Portland, Oreg., 1963-64, asst. prof., 1969-74, prof., 1990—, chmn. dept., 1970-74, dean Grad. Sch., 1982-87, mem. Bd. Regents, 1986-87, acad. v.p., 1987-96; pres. King's Coll., Wilkes Barre, Pa., 1974-81. Bd. trustees Stonehill Coll., 1992-98; dir. studies Holy Cross Fathers, Ind. Province, 1979-88.

SHERRER, GARY, former state lieutenant governor, bank executive; m. Judy (Waller), 1965; children: Stuart and Nancy. Grad., Emporia State U. Sec. Kans. Dept. Commerce and Housing, 1995—2002; lt. gov. State of Kans., 1996—2003; exec. v.p. Gold Banc, Leawood, Kans., 2002—. Vice chmn. Governor's Cabinet. Recipient Disting. Alumni Award Emporia State U., 1994, Award of Excellence, 1995; Carl Perkins Humanitarian Award, 2000; Toll fellow, 1999. Mem. Nat. Conf. Lt. Govs. (chmn.). Republican.

SHERRICK, DANIEL NOAH, real estate broker; b. Greenup, Ill., Mar. 28, 1929; s. Conrad Donovan and Helen Lorene (Neeley) S.; m. Dora Ann Moore, Aug. 11, 1957; children: Renata Ann Sherrick McBride, Sherrie Dee Sherrick Sierra. BS in Edn., Eastern Ill. U., Charleston, 1956. Owner Midwest Ins. Agy., Greenup, 1956-60; supt. agys. Midwest Life Ins. Co., Lincoln, Nebr., 1960-62; asst. v.p. Gulf Life Ins. Co., Jacksonville, Fla., 1962-71; pres. Bank of Carbondale, Ill., 1971-74, Prescription Learning Corp., Springfield, Ill., 1974-76; exec. v.p. Imperial Industries, Inc., Miami Lakes, Fla., 1976-88, pres., chief exec. officer, 1988-90; broker, salesman Coldwell Banker Residential Real Estate, 1990-91, 93—; pres., bd. dirs. Palmer State Bank, Taylorville, Ill., 1991-93; broker-salesman Coldwell Banker Highlands Properties, 1993—. Pres. Alderman Park Civic Assn., Jacksonville, 1968, Heritage Hills Home Owners Assn., Carbondale, 1973. With USAF, 1948-52. Mem.: VFW, Greater Sebring C. of C., Am. Legion, Elks, Masons. Presbyterian. Home: 6228 Aquavista Dr Sebring FL 33876 Office: Coldwell Banker Highlands Properties 2521 US Hwy 27 S Sebring FL 33870-2127 Office Phone: 863-382-3157. Personal E-mail: dandora@strato.net.

SHERRICK, REBECCA LOUISE, academic administrator; b. Carthage, Ill., May 28, 1953; d. Otho Downing and Elizabeth (Potter) S. BA, Ill. Wesleyan U., Bloomington, 1975; PhD, Northwestern U., 1980. Asst. prof. Carroll Coll., Waukesha, Wis., 1980-85, assoc. prof., 1987—, dir. women's studies, 1988-89, dir. planning, 1989-90, v.p. planning, 1990-91, v.p. enrollment and planning, 1991-92, v.p. enrollment and student svcs., 1992-93, v.p. adminstrn., 1993—. Cons. Milw. dist. United Meth. Ch., 1990-92. Contbr. articles to profl. jours. Bd. dirs., pres. The Women's Ctr., Waukesha, 1981-89; bd. dirs. Waukesha County Hist. Soc., 1985-88, Gt. Blue Heron coun. Girl Scouts U.S., 1987-90; bd. dirs., v.p. Christoph Meml. YWCA, Waukesha, 1986-89. Recipient Woman of Distinction award Waukesha YWCA, 1991; Lincoln Acad. of Scholars awardee State of Ill., 1975; William Randolph Hearst fellow, 1976, 77. Mem. Alpha Lambda Delta, Phi Alpha Theta, Kappa Delta Pi, Phi Kappa Phi. Methodist. Avocations: swimming, running, gardening.

SHERRILL, H. VIRGIL, securities company executive; b. Long Beach, Calif., 1920; Grad., Yale U., 1942, JD, 1948. Sr. dir. Prudential Securities Inc., N.Y.C.

SHERRILL, THOMAS BECK, former state legislator, financial planner; b. Atlanta; s. Elie Beck and Vena Edele (Thomas) S.; m. Dianne Hutchins; children: Alison, Jessica. BA, Ga. State U., 1968; MA, U. Va., 1970. CFP. Chartered life underwriter Conn. Mut. Life, Atlanta, 1975-84; pres. Sherrill & Hutchins Fin. Advisory, Inc., Atlanta, 1984—; mem. Ga. Ho. of Reps., Atlanta, 1991-99. Bd. dirs. Parent to Parent Ga.; mem. Immaculate Heart of Mary Cath. Ch. Capt. U.S. Army, 1971-75. Recipient Guardian of Bus. award Nat. Fedn. Ind. Businesses, Atlanta, 1992, 94, Achievement award Alzheimer's Assn., Atlanta, 1992, Outstanding Legislator award Coun. on Aging, Atlanta, 1992, 94, 95, Leadership in Govt. award Common Cause, Atlanta, 1993, Legislative Svc. award Assn. County Commrs. of Ga., 1994, Legislative award Ga. Gerontology Soc., 1994; named Policymaker of Yr., Atlanta Alliance on Devel. Disabilities, 1995, Lawmaker of Yr., Ga. chpt. Autism Soc., 1995, Legislator of the Yr., Profl. Assn. Ga. Educators, 1995. Mem. Atlanta Hist. Soc., Greater Ga. Alzheimers Assn. (v.p. bd.), Fin. Planning Assn., Internat. Churchill Soc., Henderson Mill Civic Club (pres.). Democrat. Avocations: genealogy, history, golf, reading, civic and political activities.

SHERRILL, THOMAS BOYKIN, III, retired newspaper publishing executive; b. Tampa, Fla., Nov. 19, 1930; s. Thomas Boykin Jr. and Mary Emma (Addison) S.; m. Sandra Louise Evans, Dec. 27, 1969; children: Thomas Glenn, Stephen Addison. Circulation dir. Tampa (Fla.) Tribune, 1962—67, Sarasota (Fla.) Herald-Tribune, 1967—75; v.p. circulation The Dispatch Printing Co., Columbus, Ohio, 1975—78, v.p. mktg., 1978—97, bd. dirs., 1977—97; v.p., bd. dirs. Ohio Mag., Inc., Columbus, 1979—97; ret., 1997. Bd. dirs., past chmn. bd. dirs. Salvation Army; trustee, past chmn. bd. dirs. Better Bus. Bur. Ctrl. Ohio, Inc.; bd. dirs. Ctrl. Ohio Ctr. Econ. Edn.; v.p., trustee Columbus Dispatch Charities; exec. bd. mem. Simon Kenton coun. Boy Scouts Am.; past pres. Wesley Glen United Meth. Retirement Ctr.; pres.'s adv. bd. Meth. Theol. Sch. With USN, 1951-56. Recipient Disting. Svc. award Editor and Pub. Mag., 1978; named hon. pres. Troy State U., 1979, hon. Ky. Col., 1980, hon. lt. col. aide-to-camp to Gov. State of Ala., 1984. Mem. Internat. Circulation Mgrs. Assn. (pres. 1975, Pres's. award 1989), Internat. Newspaper Mktg. Assn., Ohio Newspaper Assn. (bd. dirs. 1984-97, pres. 1986-88, Pres.'s award 1990), So. Circulation Mgrs. Assn. (life; pres. 1967-68, sec. and treas., 1968-75, C.W. Bevinger Meml. award 1972), Audit Bur. Circulations (bd. dirs. 1980-90), Am. Advt. Fedn., Navy League, Ohio

Newspapers Found., Ohio Circulation Mgrs. Assn (life; Pres.' award 1989), Columbus Area C. of C., SAR, Internat. Platform Assn., Athletic Club of Columbus, Muirfield Village Country Club, Kiwanis Club of Columbus (life, pres. 1982, George F. Hixon fellow). Republican. Home: 5215 Hampton Ln Columbus OH 43220-2270

SHERRIS, DAVID ALLAN, surgeon, medical researcher, educator; b. Buffalo, N.Y., Feb. 1, 1961; s. Donald Allan Sherris and Doris Mary Jones; m. Lisa Ellen Dubiel, Apr. 11, 1993; children: David Jr., Matthew, Lara. BA, Middlebury Coll., 1984; MD, U. Rochester, 1988. Diplomate Am. Bd. Otolaryngology, Am. Bd. Facial Plastic and Reconstructive Surgery. Resident otolaryngology U. Rochester, NY, 1989—93; fellow facial plastic surgery, clin. instr. U. Wash., Seattle, 1993—94; asst. prof. otolaryngology Mayo Med. Sch., Rochester, Minn., 1994—2000, assoc. prof., 2000—03; cons. surgeon Mayo Clinic, Rochester, 1994—2003, chair facial plastic surgery, 2002—03; chair otolaryngology SUNY, Buffalo, 2003—; chief of svc. otolaryngology Kaleida Health, 2003—. Author: Basic Surgical Skills, 1999, Essential Surgical Skills, 2004; author, editor: The Principles of Facial Reconstruction, 1995, reviewer: Archives of Facial Plastic Surgery, 2000—, mem. editl. bd.: Rhinology Jour., 2002—; contbr. 70 articles to profl. jours. Fellow: Am. Rhinologic Soc., Am. Acad. Otolaryngology Head and Neck Surgery (home study course faculty 2001—), Am. Acad. Facial Plastic and Reconstructive Surgery (active surgeon Face to Face Domestic Violence Program 1994—, Sir Harold Delf Gilles award 1994); mem.: Am. Bd. Otolaryngology (examiner 1999—). Avocations: running, skiing. Office: Millard Gates Hosp 3 Gates Cir Buffalo NY 14209 Office Phone: 716-887-5101. E-mail: dsherris@buffalo.edu.

SHERROD, DANNY TROY, writer, educator; b. North Richland Hills, Tex., Apr. 27, 1963; s. Yvonne Boatman and Dan Sherrod. AA and Sci., El Centro Coll., 1983—86; B of Humanities, So. Meth. U., 1997—2002. Caseworker Tex. Dept. of Human Services, Dallas, 1991—95; libr. specialist So. Meth. U., 1996—2003; tchr. writing, history L.P. Cowart Sch., 2003—. Author: (short story) Div. When it Rains - pub. in Primavera; editor: (newsletter) Theatre Hist. Soc. of Am.; contbr. jour. Legacies. Mem.: Humane Soc. of the U.S., People for the Ethical Treatment of Animals, SPCA of Tex., Golden Key Nat. Honor Soc. (life). Democrat. Avocations: animal welfare issues, environ. issues. Home: 1119 Newport Ave Dallas TX 75224-1248

SHERROD, LLOYD BRUCE, nutritionist; b. Goodland, Kans., Mar. 5, 1931; s. Charles and Helen S.; m. Judith Harms Sherrod, Dec. 21, 1963; children: Donna J., Barbara E. BS, S.D. State U., Brookings, 1958; MS, U. Ark., Fayetteville, 1960; PhD, Okla. State U., Stillwater, 1964. Rsch. assoc. Okla. State U., Stillwater, 1963; asst. prof. U. Hawaii, Hilo, 1964-67; from assoc. prof to prof. Tex. Tech. U. Ctr., Pantex, 1967-79; nutrition-chemistry instr. Frank Phillips Coll., Borger, Tex., 1979-88; part-time nutrition instr. Amarillo (Tex.) Coll., 1989-95; ret., 1995. Rschr. in field. Contbr. articles to sci. jours. Served with U.S. Army, 1951-53. Mem. AAAS, Am. Soc. Animal Science, Am. Dairy Science Assn., Am. Soc. Agronomy, Am. Inst. Biol. Scis., Tex. Jr. Coll. Tchrs. Assn., Am. Men and Women of Sci., Plains Nutrition Coun., Sigma Xi, Phi Kappa Phi, Gamma Sigma Delta. Home: PO Box 1017 Panhandle TX 79068-1017

SHERROD, LONNIE RAY, foundation administrator, researcher, psychologist; b. Knoxville, Tenn., Sept. 7, 1950; s. Raymond O. and Jane L. (Lambdin) S.; m. Barbara A. Cornblatt, Jan. 31, 1981; 1 child, Sara Raye. BS, Duke U., 1972; MA, U. Rochester, N.Y., 1974, Yale U., 1976, PhD, 1978. Rsch. assoc. Yale U., New Haven, 1978; staff assoc. Social Sci. Rsch. Coun., N.Y.C., 1979-85; sr. program assoc. William T. Grant Found., N.Y.C., 1986-89, v.p. programs, 1990-94; exec. v.p., 1995—; asst. dean grad. faculty New Sch. for Social Rsch., N.Y.C., 1986-89. Mem. adj. faculty psychology dept. NYU, N.Y.C., 1980-85, grad. faculty, 1986-91. Co-author: Infant Social Cognition, 1981, Late Adolescence and the Transition to Adulthood, 1993, Stress, Risk and Resiliency in Childhood, 1994, Growing Up in a Global World: Youth Political Development, 1998; assoc. editor Human Nature, 1989—, Jour. Applied Devel. Sci., Internat. Jour. Behavioral Devel., Children's Svcs. & Rsch.; editor: Social Policy Reports, 2000—; contbr. articles to profl. jours. Mem. program com. Grantmakers of Children and Youth, 1990, fin. com., treas., 1998—, conf. com., 1997-98; mem. program com. N.Y. Regional Assn. of Grantmakers, 1991-94; evaluation com. Nat. Found. Collaboration on Violence Prevention, 1994—; mem. adv. bd. Ctr. Study of Child and Adolescent Devel., Pa. State U., 1992—; bd. dirs. Life Trends, Inc., 1992—, Timber Trails Comty. Assn., 1992—, v.p., 1994-97, pres. 1997—; bd. dirs. Grantmakers of Children, Youth and Families, 1997—. Fellow APA (co-chair internat. com. 1994—, exec. coun. APA divsn. 1997—, com. children, youth & families divsn. & liaison); mem. Am. Psychol. Soc., Soc. Study of Social Biology (sec., treas. N.Y.C. chpt. 1984-90), Internat. Soc. for Study of Behavior Devel., Soc. Rsch. on Adolescence, Soc. for Rsch. in Child Devel. (mem. com. on pub. policy, pub. info. and child devel., chmn. 1993—, chmn. subcom. on pub. info. 1992-94). Office: William T Grant Found 570 Lexington Ave New York NY 10022-6837

SHERRY, GEORGE LEON, political science educator; b. Lodz, Poland, Jan. 5, 1924; came to U.S., 1939, naturalized 1945; s. Leon G. and Henrietta (Mess) S.; m. Doris H. Harf, Mar. 6, 1947; 1 child, Vivien Gail Sherry Greenberg. BA summa cum laude, CCNY, 1944; MA, Columbia U., 1951, MA, cert. Russian Inst., 1955, PhM, 1959. Reporter, radio news writer The N.Y. Times, N.Y.C., 1944-46; editor, interpreter, then sr. interpreter UN, N.Y.C., 1946-59, from polit. officer to dir. and dep. to under sec.-gen. for spl. polit. affairs, 1959-84; asst. sec.-gen. for spl. polit. affairs UN (office in charge peacekeeping forces which won Nobel Peace Prize, 1988), N.Y.C., 1984-85; Stuart Chevalier prof. diplomacy and world affairs Occidental Coll., Los Angeles, 1985—. Dir. Occidental at-the-UN program, N.Y.C., 1986-2002; U.S. del. staff Dartmouth Soviet-Am. confs., 1961-94; assoc. seminar on problem of peace Columbia U., N.Y.C.; cons. UN dept. peacekeeping ops., 1992, 93; leader UN tech. mission to Ga., 1993; UN envoy to follow Russian elections, 1993; cons. Internat. Peace Acad., 1993-97. Author: The United Nations Reborn: Conflict Control in the Post-Cold War World, 1990; editorial adv. bd. Polit. Sci. Quar., N.Y.C., 1973-89; contbr. articles and revs. to profl. jours. Recipient Townsend Harris medal CCNY, 1993; UN Inst. for Tng. and Rsch. sr. fellow, 1985-93. Mem. Coun. on Fgn. Rels., Acad. Coun. on UN Sys., UN Assn.-USA. Democrat. Avocations: piano playing, skiing, sailing. Home: 185 E 85th St Apt 3-c New York NY 10028-2172

SHERRY, JOHN SEBASTIAN, lawyer; b. Homestead, Pa., Apr. 18, 1946; s. Sebastian John and Margaret Josephine (Coyne) Sherry; m. Joan Carol Paulsen, Aug. 9, 1969; children: Brendan P., Michael S., Conor J. BA, U. Dayton, 1968; JD, Duquesne U., 1971. Bar: Pa. 1971, U.S. Dist. Ct. (we. dist.) Pa. 1971, U.S. Supreme Ct. 1975, U.S. Ct. Appeals (3d cir.) 1976, U.S. Claims Ct. 1977, U.S. Ct. Internat. Trade 1977, U.S. Tax Ct. 1977, U.S. Ct. Mil. Appeals 1977. Pvt. practice, Pitts., 1971—; mng. atty. Travlers Ins. Co., Pitts., 1972-78; mng. trial atty. CNA Ins. Cos., Pitts., 1978-88, sr. mgr. staff counsel, 1988-94, mng. trial atty., 1994-96, asst. v.p. claims litigation, 1996-98; pvt. practice John S. Sherry & Assocs., Pitts., 1999—; prin. Sherry Dispute Resolution Svcs., Pitts., 2001—. Lectr. Trial Advocacy Found., Pitts., 1984, Nat. Inst. Trial Advocacy, 1997, 98. Assoc. opinion editor: Pitts. Legal Jour., 1977—78; editor: YLS newsletter, 1980. Chmn. bd. auditors, South Park, Pa., 1977—85. Fellow: Acad. Trial Lawyers Allegheny County (bd. govs. 1997—98); mem.: ABA, Western Pa. Trial Lawyers Assn., Pa. Bar Assn. (jud. adminstrn. com. 1992—, ADR com. 2001—), Pa. Trial Lawyers Assn., Allegheny County Bar Assn. (CLE com. 1978—, coun. civil litigation sect. 1985—87, treas. 1988—2001, vice chmn. 1989, chmn. civil litigation sect. 1990, civil procedure rules com. 1999—, ADR com. 2001—), South Park C. of C. (past pres.), Pine Lake Trout Club, Rivers Club, Lions. Democrat. Roman Catholic. Avocations: fishing, hunting, literature. Address: 1302 Grant Bldg Pittsburgh PA 15219 Home: 113 Stonegate Dr Mc Murray PA 15317-2766 E-mail: jsherryesq@msn.com.

SHERRY, PAUL HENRY, minister, religious organization administrator; b. Tamaqua, Pa., Dec. 25, 1933; s. Paul Edward and Mary Elizabeth (Stein) Sherry; m. Mary Louise Thornburg, June 4, 1957; children: Mary Elizabeth, Paul David. BA, Franklin and Marshall Coll., 1955; ThM, Union Theol. Sem., N.Y.C., 1958, PhD, 1969; D (hon.), Ursinus Coll., 1981, Elmhurst Coll., 1990, Defiance Coll., 1991, Lakeland Coll., Sheboygan, Wis., 1991, Reformed Theological Acad., Debrecen, Hungary, 1994, United Theol. Sem. Twin Cities, 1995, Eden Theol. Sem., St. Louis, 2000, Chgo. Theol. Sem., 2000. Ordained to ministry United Ch. Christ, 1958. Pastor St. Matthew United Ch. of Christ, Kenhorst, Pa., 1958—61, Community United Ch. of Christ, Hasbrouck Heights, NJ, 1961—65; mem. staff United Ch. Bd. Homeland Ministry, N.Y.C., 1965—82; exec. dir. Community Renewal Soc., Chgo., 1983—89; pres. United Ch. of Christ, Cleve., 1989—99, pub. policy cons., 2000—02. Mem. gen. bd. Nat. Coun. Chs., N.Y.C., 1989—99; mem. ctrl. com. World Coun. Chs., 1990—99; del. 8th Assembly, Harare, Zimbabwe, 1998, 7th Assembly, Canberra, Australia, 1991; cons. Ctr. for Cmty. Change, 2001—. Editor: The Riverside Preachers, Jour. Current Social Issues, 1968—80; contbr. articles to religious jours.; host (weekly programs local sta.), 1974—78, 1984—85, 1993—97. Bd. dirs., cons. Nat. Campaign for Jobs and Income Support, 2000—; bd. dirs. Nat. Interfaith Com. Worker Justice, 2000—. Democrat. Mem. United Ch. Of Christ. Avocations: reading, hiking, cultural events. Home and Office: Apt 10F 1590 Anderson Ave Fort Lee NJ 07024-2709 E-mail: psher973@aol.com.

SHERRY, WILLIAM F. airport executive; Asst. city mgr., Vero Beach, Fla.; mgr. Vero Beach Airport, 1987—; dir. aviation Fla. Dept. of Transp., 1996-97; mgr. airports Broward County, Ft. Lauderdale, Fla., 1997-98, aviation dir., 1998—. Office: Aviation Dept Ft Lauderdale/Hollywood Internat Airport 320 Terminal Dr Fort Lauderdale FL 33315

SHERTZER, BRUCE ELDON, education educator; b. Bloomfield, Ind., Jan. 11, 1928; s. Edwin Franklin and Lois Belle S.; m. Carol Mae Rice, Nov. 24, 1948; children: Sarah Ann, Mark Eldon. BS, Ind. U., 1952, MS, 1953, EdD, 1958. Tchr., counselor Martinsville (Ind.) High Sch., 1952-56; dir. div. guidance Ind. Dept. Pub. Instrn., 1956-58; assoc. dir. project guidance of superior students North Central Assn. Coll. and Secondary Sch., 1958-60; asst. prof. Purdue U., 1960—, assoc. prof., 1962-65, prof., 1965-95, head dept. ednl. studies, 1989-95, prof. emeritus of counseling, 1995—. Vis. prof. ednl. psychology U. Hawaii, 1967; Fulbright sr. lectr., Reading, Eng., 1967-68; vis. prof. U. So. Calif. Overseas Grad. Program, 1975, 82; chmn. Nat. Adv. Council for Career Edn., 1976 Author: Career Exploration and Planning 1973, 2d edit., 1976, Fundamentals of Counseling, 3d edit., 1980, Fundamentals of Guidance, 4th edit., 1981, Individual Appraisal, 1979, Career Planning, 3d edit., 1985, also articles. Chmn. bd. trustees Found. Am. Assn. of Counseling and Devel., 1986-87. With AUS, 1946-47. Mem. Am. Counseling Assn. (pres. 1973-74, Disting. Profl. Svc. award 1986). Home: 1620 Western Dr West Lafayette IN 47906-2236 Office: Beering Hall Purdue University West Lafayette IN 47907

SHERVA, DENNIS G. retired investment company executive; b. Mpls., Dec. 3, 1942; s. Garfield Theodore and Dorothy Genevive (Oberlander) S.; m. Cathleen Marybeth Tischer, Oct. 15, 1965 BA, U. Minn., 1964; MA, Wayne State U., 1965. Chartered fin. analyst. Fin. analyst 1st Nat. Bank, Mpls., 1965-67; fin. analyst Honeywell, Inc., Mpls., 1967; v.p. Smith, Barney & Co., N.Y.C., 1967-71, Baker, Weeks & Co., N.Y.C., 1971-77; mng. dir. Morgan Stanley & Co., Inc., N.Y.C., 1977—2000. Bd. dirs. Morgan Stanley Ventures, San Francisco, Morgan Stanley Venture Capital, N.Y.C., Morgan Stanley Asset Mgmt. Inc., N.Y.C. Recipient All-Am. Research Team 1st place award Instl. Investor Mag., 1979, 81, 83, 84, 85, 87 Mem.: Nat. Assn. Securities Dealers (instl. com. 1985—90), PGA West Club, Torrington Country Club. Home: 42 Old South Rd PO Box 30 Litchfield CT 06759-0030 Home (Winter): 80715 Weiskopf Way La Quinta CA 92253

SHERWIN, JAMES TERRY, lawyer; b. N.Y.C., Oct. 25, 1933; s. Oscar and Stella (Zins) S.; m. Judith Johnson, June 21, 1955 (div. Apr. 1984); children—Miranda, Alison, Galen; m. Hiroko Inouye, June 15, 1985. BA, Columbia U., 1953, LLB (Stone scholar), 1956. Bar: N.Y. 1956, U.S. Supreme Ct. 1963. Assoc. Kaye, Scholer, Fierman, Hays & Handler, N.Y.C., 1957-60; with GAF Corp., N.Y.C., 1960-83, 84-90, assoc. counsel, gen. mgr. European ops., 1969-71, group v.p. photography, 1971-74, exec. v.p. fin. and adminstrn., legal and investment svcs., 1974-83, vice chmn., chief adminstrv. officer Wayne, N.J., 1984-90; exec. v.p., CFO Triangle Industries, Inc., 1983-84, Hunter-Douglas N.V., 1991-99, bd. dirs., 1999—. Bd. dirs. Internat. Rescue Com., chmn. exec. com., v.p. to 1990; mem. coun. U. Bath, 2001—. Lt. comdr. USCGR, 1956-57. U.S. intercollegiate chess champion, 1951-53, N.Y. State champion, 1951, U.S. speed champion, 1956-57, 59-60, internat. master. Mem. U. Bath Coun., UK, Am. Chess Found. (pres., bd. dirs. to 1990), Marshall (N.Y.) Chess Club (pres. 1967-69, gov. to 1990), Phi Beta Kappa. Home: The Chase Winsley Nr Bradford-on-Avon Wiltshire BA15 2LX England Office Phone: 44 1225 722113. E-mail: jsherwin@thechase99.freeserve.co.uk.

SHERWIN, STEPHEN A. health products executive; BA in Biology, Yale U.; MD, Harvard U. Diplomate Am. Bd. Medicine, Am. Bd. Med. Oncology. Former mem. staff Nat. Cancer Inst.; with Genentech, Inc., 1983—90; CEO, bd. dirs. Cell Genesys, Inc., Foster City, Calif., 1990—, pres., 1990—2001, chmn. bd. dirs., 1994—. Chmn. bd. dirs. Ceregene, Inc.; bd. dirs. Abgenix, Inc., Neurocrine Bioscis., Inc., Rigel Pharms, Inc., Calyx Therapeutics.

SHERWOOD, ALLEN JOSEPH, retired lawyer; b. Salt Lake City, Sept. 26, 1909; s. Charles Samuel and Sarah (Abramson) Shapiro; m. Edith Ziff, Jan. 19, 1941; children— Mary (Mrs. John Marshall), Arthur Lawrence Student, UCLA, 1927-30; AB, LLB, U. So. Calif., 1933. Bar: Calif. 1933, U.S. Supreme Ct. 1944. Pvt. practice law, L.A., 1933-54, Beverly Hills, 1954-95; ret. Legal counsel Internat. Family Planning Rsch. Assn., Inc., 1970-76; bd. dirs. Family Planning Ctrs. Greater L.A., Inc., 1968-84, pres., 1973-76 Mem. editorial bd. So. Calif. Law Rev., 1932-33. Contbr. articles to profl. jours. Mem. Calif. Atty. Gen.'s Vol. Adv. Coun. and its legis. subcom., 1972-78 Mem. Med.-Legal Soc. So. Calif. (bd. dirs. 1966-74), ABA, L.A. County Bar Assn., Beverly Hills Bar Assn., State Bar of Calif., Am. Arbitration Assn. (nat. panel arbitrators 1965—), Order of Coif, Tau Delta Phi, Brentwood Country Club (L.A.), Masons. Home: 575 Moreno Ave Los Angeles CA 90049-4840

SHERWOOD, ANDREW, management consultant; m. Diane K. Wells; children: Whitney, Kristen. BBA with honors, Nichols Coll., 1964; student, Fairleigh Dickinson U., 1965—67. Cert. profl. certification Inst. Mgmt. Cons., 1995. Founder, chmn., CEO Goodrich & Sherwood Assocs., Inc., N.Y.C., 1970—90; mng. dir. Stanton Chase Internat., 1990—. Congl. advisor Reagan and Bush White House; head bus. task force, NY; chmn. Goodrich Capital Internat., 1997—; lectr. in field. Author: Breakpoints, 1986; contbr. numerous articles to profl. jours. Sr. mem. Nat. Ski Patrol; mem. exec. com. Think First Found., 2003—, bd. dirs., 2003. Mem.: CMC Inst. Mgmt. Cons. (cert. mgmt. cons. 1995), Mashomack Field and Game Club, Chief Exec. Orgn., World Pres.'s Orgn., Young Pres.' Orgn. (bd. dirs., chpt. chmn. elect), Safari Club Internat. (bd. dirs.), Madison Ave. Sports Car Driving Club, Porcupine Rod and Gun Club, The Greenwich Polo Club, Explorers Club, Univ. Club, The Econ. Club of N.Y. Avocations: gardening, physical fitness, hunting, riding, antiques. Office: GSA Internat 52 Vanderbilt Ave New York NY 10175

SHERWOOD, ARTHUR LAWRENCE, lawyer; b. L.A., Jan. 25, 1943; s. Allen Joseph and Edith S.; m. Frances Merele, May 1, 1970; children: David, Chester. BA magna cum laude, U. Calif., Berkeley, 1964; MS, U. Chgo., 1965; JD cum laude, Harvard U., 1968. Bar: Calif. 1969, US. dist. cts. (cen. dist.) Calif. 1968 (no. dist.) Calif. 1971 (so. dist.) Calif. 1973 (ea. dist.) Calif. 1973, U.S. Ct. Appeals (9th cir.) 1973, U.S. Ct. Appeals (D.C. cir.) 1991, U.S. Supreme Ct., 1980. Instr. UCLA Law Sch., 1968-69; assoc. Gibson, Dunn & Crutcher, L.A., 1968-75, ptnr., 1975-98; of counsel, 1998-; judge pro tem., L.A. Mcpl. and Superior Ct., 1980-98; instr. law, UCLA, 1968-69, arbitrator N.Y. Stock Exchange., Nat. Futures Assn. Co-author: Civil Procedure During Trial, 1995, Civil Procedure Before Trial, 1990; contbr articles to profl. jours. NASA fellow U. Chgo., 1964-65; chmn. Far Ea. Art Coun., L.A. County Mus. Art, 1992-97. Mem. Calif. Bar Assn., Phi Beta Kappa. Republican. Avocations: art, 18th century Am. history. Office: 300 N Swall Dr Beverly Hills CA 90211-4733

SHERWOOD, ARTHUR MORLEY, lawyer; b. Buffalo, Oct. 3, 1939; s. Frederick T. and Neva E. (Merrill) S.; m. Karen H. Hilstad, Apr. 2, 1964; children: Laurel Ann, Carolyn Margaret. BA, Harvard U., 1961; JD, U. Mich., 1964. Bar: Mich. 1965, N.Y. 1967, U.S. Supreme Ct. 1989. Law clk. to Hon. Ralph M. Freeman U.S. Dist. Ct. (ea. dist.) Mich., Detroit, 1964-66; pntr. Phillips, Lytle, Hitchcock, Blaine & Huber, Buffalo, 1971-99. Contbr. articles to Trusts and Estates, N.Y. State Bar Jour. and N.Y. Tax Svc. Mem. adv. com. N.Y. State Legislature on N.Y. Estates, Powers and Trusts Law, Surrogate's Ct. Procedure. Fellow Am. Coll. Trust and Estate Counsel, N.Y. Bar Found.; mem. N.Y. State Bar Assn. (chairperson trusts and estates law sect. 1987). Home: 3770 Windover Dr Hamburg NY 14075-6322 Office: Phillips Lytle Hitchcock Blaine & Huber 3400 HSBC Ctr Buffalo NY 14203-2887

SHERWOOD, CHARLES H. pharmaceutical executive; B in Chem. Engring., Cornell U.; certificate in Mgmt., Claremont Grad. Sch.; M in Polymer Sci. & Engring., U. M in Polymer Sci. & Engring., PhD in Polymer Sci. & Engring., U. Mass. Registered. With Lord Corp., Hughes Aircraft Co., IOLAB Corp., 1982—95; sr. dir. Chiron Vision, 1995; v.p. rsch., devel. & engring. Anika Therapeutics, Inc., Woburn, Mass., pres., COO. Mem. faculty Calif. State Polytechnic U., Pomona, Calif. Office: Anika Therapeutics Inc 236 W Cummings Park Woburn MA 01801

SHERWOOD, DEVON FREDRICK, lawyer; b. Hanibal, Mo., June 20, 1943; s. Malcolm and Virginia Dolores (Gresham) S.; m. Stephanie Jan Wanner, Dec. 26, 1963 (div. Feb. 1976); children: Leslie, Jennifer, Stuart; m. Wanda Lee Mullins, May 17, 1977. AB, U. Mo., 1965, JD, 1968. Bar: Mo. 1968, U.S. Dist. Ct. (we. dist.) Mo. Assoc. Lilley & Cowan, Springfield, Mo., 1968-69, Donald Bonacker, Springfield, 1969-72; sr. ptnr. Sherwood & Bruer, Springfield, 1972-77; sole practice, Springfield, 1977-80; sr. ptnr. Sherwood, Honecker & Bender, Springfield, 1980—; city atty. Fair Grove, Mo., 1973-76. Bd. editors Mo. Law Rev., 1967-68. Elder deacon National Avenue Christian Ch., Springfield, 1969-74; del. Springfield Area Council Chs., 1971-74. Recipient Lon O. Hocker Outstanding Trial Lawyers award Mo. Bar Found. Mem. ATLA, Mo. Bar Assn., Springfield Met. Bar Assn., Mo. Assn. Trial Lawyers, Phi Delta Phi. Republican. Office: Sherwood Honecker & Bender 155 Park Central Sq Springfield MO 65806-1322 Home: 2101 E Wornall Pl Springfield MO 65804-8007 E-mail: shb@pcis.net.

SHERWOOD, DONALD LEWIS, congressman; b. Nicholson, Pa., Mar. 5, 1941; s. Walter A. and Doris (Williams) S.; m. Carol Evans, 1973; children: Jesse, Dana, Maria. BA in Econs., Dartmouth Coll., 1963. Founder, pres. Sherwood Chevrolet, Tunkhannock, Pa., 1967—; mem. U.S. Congress from 10th Pa. dist., 1999—; mem. appropriations com. Expanded Sherwood Chevrolet to include Horlacher-Sherwood Forestry Equipment; ptnr. in Sun Auto Group, Clarks Summit, Sun Buick/Pontiac/GMC, Moosic. Appointed to Tunkhannock Area Sch. Bd., 1975; subsequently elected 6 times; served as pres., 1992-98. Pres. Wyoming County Indsl. Found., Wyoming County United Fund; bd. dirs. Triton Hose Fire Co. Fireman's Relief Assn., Wyoming County C. of C. Elected to Ho. Reps. Nov. 3, 1998, replacing Joseph M. McDade (R-Clarks Summit)who retired after 36 yrs. in Congress. 10th Congl. Dist. includes the counties of Bradford, part of Lackawanna, Montour, Northumberland, Pike, Snyder, Sullivan, Susquehanna, Union, Wayne, Wyoming, and parts of Luzerne and Lycoming counties. Served with U.S. Army, 1963—66. Dir. Pa. Chevrolet Dealers Area Mktg. Group; v.p. N.E. Pa. Chevrolet Dealers Assn.; mem. Pa. Hardwood Lumber Mfrs. Assn., Pa. Farmers Assn. Republican. Avocation: raises and shows belgian horses. Office: 1223 Longworth House Office Bldg Washington DC 20515-3810

SHERWOOD, GLORIA N. graphic and literary artist, genealogy researcher; b. Winfield, Kans. d. Edwin E. Schroeder and Anna Y. McClure; stepmother Vivian J. Schroeder; children: Christina Knueven, J.E. Jurey, Jeannette Thornhill. B CMT cert., foster parent cert. Pvt. home health care nurse, Eufaula, Okla., 1996—. Author: The Poetic Works of Gloria Sherwood Book 1 vol. 1, 2000, Poetic Work Book 1, vol. 2, 2002, Just Be 2000, Remember Me, 1999, Spiritual Wings, 2001, Awaited Healing, 2001; visual artist: New Trails, 1998, Deep Is the Soul, 2000, Out of Bondage, 2001. Recipient Award of Excellence in Christian Web sites Joyful Mom's Web site. Mem. NAFE, Nat. Home Gardening Club, Nat. Arbor Day Found., Angelwings, Nat. Audubon Soc., Nat. Wildlife Fedn., World Wildlife Fedn. Democrat. Avocations: performing arts, gardening, playing guitar, writing music, crafts.

SHERWOOD, JAMES ALAN, physician, scientist, educator; b. Oneida County, N.Y., Jan. 4, 1953; s. Robert Merriam and Sally (Trevett-Edgett) S. AB, Hamilton Coll., 1974; MD, Columbia U., 1978. Diplomate Nat. Bd. Med. Examiners, Am. Bd. Internal Medicine, Am. Acad. HIV Medicine. Intern Duke U. Med. Ctr., Durham, N.C., 1978-79; resident physician Strong Meml. Hosp., Rochester, N.Y., 1979-81; fellow U. Rochester Sch. Medicine and Dentistry, 1981-83, NIH, Bethesda, Md., 1983-86; rsch. investigator Walter Reed Army Inst. Rsch., Washington, 1986-92; vis. scientist Clin. Rsch. Ctr., Kenya Med. Rsch. Inst., Nairobi, 1987-92; physician Saradidi Rural Health Programme, Nyilima, Kenya, 1987-92; rsch. cons. Rockville, Md., 1992-93; physician St. Mary's Hosp., Waterbury, Conn., 1993—; clin. instr. Sch. Medicine, Yale U., 1993-98; pvt. practice Conn., 1998—. Founding donor Yale Univ.-Kazan State Med. U. Russian Fedn. fellow exch. program. Contbr. chpt. to book, articles to profl. jours. Cmty. svc. vol. The Door, N.Y.C., 1976-77; vol. physician Washington Free Clinic, 1985-87; charity Sisters of St. Joseph of Chambery, 1993-98, Mulago Hosp., Makerere U., Kampala, Uganda. Lt. col. M.C., USAR, 1986-92. Recipient Norton prize in chemistry, 1974, Underwood prize in chemistry, 1974. Fellow Am. Coll. Physicians; mem. Med. Soc. D.C., Am. Fedn. Clin. Rsch., Am. Soc. Tropical Medicine and Hygiene, Conn. State Med. Soc., New Haven County Med. Assn., Muthaiga Club, Phi Beta Kappa, Sigma Xi. Avocations: drawing, book collecting. Office: PO Box 850 Watertown CT 06795-0850

SHERWOOD, JAMES WEBSTER, III, author, limousine company owner; b. Hollywood, Calif., May 18, 1936; s. James Webster Sherwood Jr. and Vesta Graybeal Hughes; m. Valdi Hiesinger, Apr. 17, 1964 (div. 1972); m. Marylou Coddington Lemke, July 4, 1972 (div. 1989); m. Karyn Virginia Lindig, Mar. 18, 1990; children: Veronica E.C. Sherwood, Alexandra C.E. Sherwood Patterson, Roxanna Z.S.R., Christopher Michael De Santis, James Webster IV, George Marshall De Santis. Student, Choate Sch., U. Chgo., 1954—55; BL, U. Paris, 1963. Reporter, columnist San Mateo (Calif.) Times, Burlingame Advance, 1951-52; mng. editor Chgo. Rev. Mag., 1954-55; prodr. Myers-Sherwood Pictures, Inc., Chgo., 1955; editor Trans World Pictures, Inc., Chgo., 1955; editor, columnist Westchester News-Advertiser, LA, 1956-57; prodn. asst. Cecil B. DeMille-Paramount Pictures, Hollywood, 1957-59; v.p., gen. mgr. Smith Limousine, NYC, 1977-85; pres., owner Sherwood Justice & Barton Limousine Corp., NYC, 1985—; dir. Hamilton Mfg. Corp., Holland, Ohio. Prodr., dir. Sherwood Films, Hollywood, 1958-60; cons. on Tom Jones, 1961; adaptor The Sicilian Clan, 1966; producer After Laughter, 1968, others; founder, pub. Opus Books. Author: Dining on Thorns, 1996, Some Sonnets of Flame & Flower, 1998; syndicated columnist 11 western states for Christian Sci. Monitor, Hungry Horse (Mont.) News, Hellenic Rev., 1956-58; editor Popular Libr., 1970-72; biographic researcher Holt, Rinehart & Winston, 1970-72; journalist Ladies Home Jour., Village Voice, N.Y., 1972-73; author: (verse play) The Wooed Wife, 1957; author: 101 Sonnets of Sex, God, The Circus and Love, 2d edit., 1959, (novels) Stradella, 1961, Shakespeare's Ghost, 2001, Sun of Another Sky, 2003. Trustee Shakespeare Oxford Soc. Recipient Nat. Book award for best translation preface to (with Ralph Manheim) Castle to Castle, 1970, John Dos Passos award for Creative Writing, 1987. Republican. Episcopalian. Avocation: walking. Home: Grand Central Five Central Dr Plandome NY 11030-1408 Office: Sherwood Limousines PO Box 925 Plainview NY 11803-0925 E-mail: karyn05@aol.com.

SHERWOOD, JOAN KAROLYN SARGENT, retired career counselor; b. Wichita, Kans., July 11, 1934; d. James Wirth and Ann K. (Freeburg) Sargent; m. Howard Kenneth Sherwood, Jan. 26, 1956 (div. 1966); children: Diane Elizabeth, Karolyn Sherwood, David Matthew. BS, Kans. State U., 1956; MA, Wichita State U., 1964; PhD, U. Kans., 1978. Asst. dir. student fin. aid U. Kans., Lawrence, 1973-78, asst. vice chancellor/student affairs, 1978-81, U. Mo., Kansas City, 1981-84; v.p. student affairs Western Wash. U., Bellingham, 1984-87; pres./owner Corp. Tng. Assurance, Kansas City, 1987-95; career coord. Park Univ., Parkville, Mo., 1995-01; ret., 2001. Program chair Phi Delta Kappa, Lawrence, 1983-84; initiation chair Phi Kappa Phi, Kansas City, 1983-84; organizer Singles Connection, Kansas City, 1983-84; creator SummerStart, Bellingham, 1988-89. Contbr.: Theatre Companies of the World, 1986; female voice: (film) Junction City, 1973; editor Case Studies in the Governance of Higher Edn., 1982, Nat. Assn. of Student Personnel Adminstrs. Alcohol Policies and Practices Among Colls. and Univs., 1987. Long range planning coord. Ch. Redeemer, Kansas City, 1994; workshop facilitator South Side Jr. C. of C., Kansas City, 1991; presenter Centurians, Kansas City, 1982; spkr. Pi Lambda Theta, 1983; vol., resident mgr. Hillcrest Ministries, 1996-99. NDEA fellow, 1969. Mem. ASTD, Phi Kappa Phi, Democrat. Roman Catholic. Avocations: creative writing, reading, films. Home: Unit 2204 2421 Yellowstone Wichita KS 67215 Office: Vista Vols Cmtys in Schs Alcott Acad 3400 E Murdock Wichita KS 67208

SHERWOOD, LOUIS MAIER, physician, scientist, pharmaceutical company executive; b. N.Y.C., Mar. 1, 1937; s. Arthur Joseph and Blanche (Burger) S.; m. Judith Brimberg, Mar. 27, 1966; children: Jennifer Beth, Arieh David. AB with honors, Johns Hopkins U., 1957; MD with honors, Columbia U., 1961. Diplomate Am. Bd. Internal Medicine, Subsplty. Bd. in Endocrinology and Metabolism. Intern Presbyn. Hosp., N.Y.C., 1961-62, asst. resident in medicine, 1962-63; clin. assoc. research fellow Nat. Heart Inst., NIH, Bethesda, Md., 1963-66; NIH trainee endocrinology and metabolism Coll. Physicians and Surgeons, Columbia U., N.Y.C., 1966-68; assoc. medicine Beth Israel Hosp. and Harvard Med. Sch., Boston, 1968-69; chief endocrinology Beth Israel Hosp., 1968-72; asst. prof. medicine Harvard U., 1969-71, assoc. prof., 1971-72; physician-in-chief, chmn. dept. medicine Michael Reese Hosp. and Med. Ctr., Chgo., 1972-80; prof. medicine, div. biol. scis. Pritzker Sch. Medicine, U. Chgo., 1972-80; Ted and Florence Baumritter prof. medicine and biochemistry Albert Einstein Coll. Medicine, 1980-88, vis. prof. medicine, 1989—, chmn. dept. medicine, 1980-87; physician-in-chief Montefiore Hosp. and Med. Ctr., N.Y.C., 1980-87; adj. prof. medicine U. Pa., 1993—. Sr. v.p. med. and sci. affairs Merck, Sharp & Dohme Internat., 1987-89; exec. v.p. worldwide devel. Merck, Sharp & Dohme Rsch. Labs., 1989-92, sr. v.p. U.S. Med. and Sci. Affairs Merck Human Health, 1992-2002; pres. MEDSA, LLC, 2002—; Josiah Macy Jr. Found. fellow and vis. scientist Weizmann Inst., Israel, 1978-79; assoc. mem. bd. on subcom. endocrinology and metabolism Am. Bd. Internal Medicine, 1977-83; med. adv. bd. HPR, 1996-99; pres., chief med. officer Bone Measurement Inst., 1996-2002; mem. nat. rsch. adv. com. Dept. Vets. Affairs, 2000—, clin. rsch. roundtable Inst. Medicine, 2000—04. Editor: Beth Israel seminars New Eng. Jour. Medicine, 1968-71; mem. editorial bd. Endocrinology, 1969-73; assoc. editor Metabolism, 1970-85, Gen. Medicine B Study Sect., NIH, 1975-79; mem. editorial bd. Yr. in Endocrinology, 1976-86, Calcified Tissue Internat., 1978-80, Internal Medicine Alert, 1979-89; contbr. numerous articles on endocrinology, protein hormones, calcium metabolism and ectopic proteins to jours. Trustee Michael Reese Med. Ctr., 1974-77; vis. council CUNY Med. Sch., 1986-95; alumni council Columbia Coll. Physicians and Surgeons, 1986—; bd. dirs. Jewish Fedn. Phila., 1997—, Alliance on Aging Rsch., 1997-2002, Hormone Found., 2002—. Served as surgeon USPHS, 1963-66. Recipient Joseph Mather Smith prize for outstanding alumni rsch. Coll. Physicians and Surgeons, Columbia U., 1972, Sr. Class Tchg. award U. Chgo., 1976, 77, Spl. Achievement award Assn. Profs. Medicine, 2002; grantee USPHS, 1968-88. Master: ACP (Outstanding Contbn. to Internal Medicine award 1987); mem.: AAAS, Chgo. Soc. Internal Medicine, Assn. Program Dirs. Internal Medicine (coun. 1979—85, pres. 1983—84), Ctrl. Soc. Clin. Rsch., Mass. Med. Soc., Am. Soc. Hypertension (bd. dirs. 1992—97), N.Y. Acad. Medicine (bd. dirs. 1991—95), Am. Acad. Pharm. Physicians (trustee 2000—02, v.p. strategic alliances and planning 2000—03, sec. 2003—04, pres.-elect 2004—, Lifetime Achievement award in Pharm. Medicine 2001), Am. Physicians Fellowship for Medicine in Israel (pres. 1993—97, Disting. Med. Svc. award 1998), Endocrine Soc. (bd. dirs. Hormone Found. 2002—), Assn. Am. Physicians, Am. Soc. Clin. Investigation (pres. 1982—83), Am. Soc. Biol. Chemists, Am. Inst. Chemists, Am. Fedn. Clin. Rsch. (bd. dirs. Found. 1989—92, Spl. Recognition award 1992), Interurban Clin. Club, Alpha Omega Alpha, Phi Beta Kappa. Achievements include research in protein and polypeptide hormones: structure, function and regulation of secretion; molecular studies of hormone biosynthesis; clinical pharmacology, new drug development, outcomes research and disease management. Office: MEDSA 7598 Playa Rienta Way Delray Beach FL 33446 Personal E-mail: sherwool@earthlink.net. Business E-Mail: lou@medsa.org. *To be a highly successful leader, you must be willing to surround yourself with outstanding individuals, give them your full support and enjoy their growth and accomplishments.*

SHERWOOD, PATRICIA WARING, artist, educator; b. Columbia, SC, Dec. 19, 1933; d. Clark du Val and Florence (Yarbrough) Waring; widowed; children: Cheryl Sherwood Kraft, Jana Sherwood Kern, Marikay Sherwood Taitt. BFA magna cum laude, Calif. State U., Hayward, 1970; MFA, Mills Coll., Oakland, Calif., 1974; postgrad., San Jose State U., 1980-86. Cert. tchr., Calif. Tchr. De Anza Jr. Coll., Cupertino, Calif., 1970-78, Foothill Jr. Coll., Los Altos, Calif., 1972-78, West Valley Jr. Coll., Saratoga, Calif., 1978—. Artist-in-residence Centrum Frans Masereel, Kasterlee, Belgium, 1989. One-woman shows include Triton Mus., Santa Clara, Calif., 1968, 2002, RayChem Corp., Sunnyvile, Calif., 1969, Palo Alto (Calif.) Cultural Ctr., 1977, Los Gatos (Calif.) Mus., 1992, Stanford U. faculty club, Palo Alto, 1993, d.p. Fong Gallery, San Jose, Calif., 1995, 97, Heritage Bank, San Jose, 1997, City Jr. Coll., d.p. Fong Gallery, San Jose, 1997, City Coll., San Jose, Calif., 1997, West Valley Coll., Saratoga, Calif., 1998, Mus. West, Palo Alto, 2000-2001, Triton Mus., Santa Clara, 2001; exhibited in group shows at Tressider Union Stanford U., 1969, Oakland (Calif.) Mus. Kaiser Ctr., 1969, Sonoma (Calif.) State Coll., 1969, Bank Am., San Francisco, 1969, Alrich Gallery, San Francisco, U. Calif. Santa Clara, 1967, Charles and Emma Frye Mus., Seattle, 1968, Eufrat Gallery DeAnza Coll., Cupertino, 1975, San Jose Mus. Art, 1976, Lytton Ctr., Palo Alto, 1968 (1st award), Zellerbach Ctr., San Francisco, 1970, Works Gallery, San Jose, 1994, Inst. Contemporary Art, San Jose, 1997, Triton Mus. Art, Santa Clara, Calif., 1997, 98, San Jose Inst. Contemporary Art, 1998, San Jose City Coll. Artists Forum, 1998, West Valley Jr. Coll., Saratoga, Calif., 1998, Calvin Charles Gallery, Scottsdale, Ariz.; represented in permanent collections Mills Coll., Bank Am., San Francisco, Heritage Bank, San Jose, Stanford U., Palo Alto, Calif., San Jose U., Smithsonian Inst. Nat. Mus. Am. Art, Washington, Calrin Charles Gallery, Scottsdale, Ariz. Art judge student show Stanford U., Palo Alto, 1977; mem. d.p. Fong Gallery, San Jose, Calif., 1994, J.J. Brooking Gallery, San Francisco, Mus. West Gallery, Palo Alto, Calif., Gallery Ocean Avenue, Carmel, Calif., 2002, Bryant Street Gallery, Palo Alto, 2003, Calvin Charles Gallery, Scottsdale, Ariz., 1212 Gallery, Burlingame, Calif. Nat. Endowment for Arts/We. States Art Fedn. fellow, 1994. Mem. NEA, Calif. Print Soc., Womens Caucus for Arts, Internat. Platform Assn., Smithsonian Instn., Nat. Mus. Am. Art. Home: 1500 Arriba Ct Los Altos CA 94024-5956

SHERWOOD, ROBERT PETERSEN, retired sociology educator; b. Black Diamond, Wash., May 17, 1932; s. James Brazier and Zina (Petersen) S.; m. Merlene Burningham, Nov. 21, 1951; children: Robert Lawrence, Richard William, Rolene, RaNae. BS, U. Utah, 1956, MS, 1957; EdD, U. Calif., Berkeley, 1965. Tchr. Arden-Carmichael Sch. Dist., Carmichael, Calif., 1957-59, vice prin. jr. high, 1960-61, prin. jr. high, 1962-65; v.p., prin. San Juan Unified Sch. Dist., Sacramento, 1966-70; assoc. prof. Calif. State U., Sacramento, 1966-71; dir. outreach progs. Am. River Coll., Sacramento, 1971-73, acting assoc. dean of instrn., 1973-74, prof. sociology, 1970-92, chmn. sociology/anthropology dept., 1980-86, retired, 1992. Pres. acad. senate Am. River Coll., 1990-91. With USN, 1953-55. Recipient Merit Recognition award, Boy Scouts Am., 1989. Mem. NEA, Calif. Tchrs. Assn., Faculty Assn. Calif. Community Colls., Western Assn. Schs. and Colls., Calif. Fedn. Coll. Profs., Phi Delta Kappa (life). Mem. Lds Ch. Avocations: reading, writing, woodworking, travel. Home: 4053 Esperanza Dr Sacramento CA 95864-3069

SHERWOOD, ROD(ERICK), III, computer company executive; BA with hons. in Econs., Stanford U.; MBA, Harvard U. With Chrysler Corp., 1981—95; from corp. v.p., treas. to pres. Spaceway Broadband Svcs. Hughes Electronics, 1995—98, pres. Spaceway Broadband Svcs., 1998—99; sr. v.p., CFO BroadStream Corp., 1999—2000, Loudcloud Inc., 2000—02, Gateway Inc., Poway, Calif., 2002—03, exec. v.p., CFO, 2003—. Office: Gateway 14303 Gateway Place Poway CA 92064*

SHERZER, HARVEY GERALD, lawyer; b. Phila., May 19, 1944; s. Leon and Rose (Levin) S.; m. Susan Bell, Mar. 28, 1971; children: Sheri Ann, David Lloyd. BA, Temple U., 1965; JD with honors, George Washington U., 1968. Bar: DC 1970, U.S. Ct. Appeals (DC cir.) 1970, U.S. Ct. Fed. Claims 1970, U.S. Ct. Appeals (fed. cir.) 1970, U.S. Supreme Ct. 1974. Law clk. to trial judges U.S. Ct. Fed. Claims, Washington, 1968-69; law clk. to chief judge U.S. Ct. Appeals for Fed. Cir., Washington, 1969-70; assoc. Sellers, Conner & Cuneo, Washington, 1970-75, ptnr., 1975-80, McKenna, Conner & Cuneo, Washington, 1980-82, Pettit & Martin, Washington, 1982-85, Howrey & Simon, Washington, 1985-2000, Howrey Simon Arnold & White, Washington, 2000—01, Greenberg Traurig, McLean, Va., 2001—03, Dickstein Shapiro Morin & Oshinsky LLP, 2003—. Adv. bd. The Govt. Contractor, 1996-99. Author: (with others) A Complete Guide to the Department of Defense Voluntary Disclosure Program, 1996; contbr. articles to profl. jours. Office: Dickstein Shapiro Morin & Oshinsky LLP 2101 L St NW Washington DC 20037 E-mail: sherzerh@dsmo.com.

SHESTACK, ALAN, museum administrator; b. N.Y.C., June 23, 1938; s. David and Sylvia P. (Saffran) S.; m. Nancy Jane Davidson, Sept. 24, 1967. BA, Wesleyan U., 1961, DFA (hon.), 1978; MA, Harvard U., 1963. Mus. curator graphic art Nat. Gallery Art, Washington, 1965-67; assoc. curator prints and drawings Yale Art Gallery, New Haven, 1967-68, curator prints and drawings, 1968-71, dir., 1971-85; adj. prof. history of art Yale U., 1971-85; dir. Mpls. Inst. Art, 1985-87, Boston Mus. Fine Arts, 1987-93; dep. dir. Nat. Gallery of Art, Washington, 1994—. Mem. adv. com. Art Mus., Princeton, 1972-75; mem. vis. com. Harvard U. Art Mus., 1990-95, Davis Mus. Wellesley Coll., 1997—; mem. mus. panel Nat. Endowment for the Arts, 1974-77; mem. com. prints and illustrated books Mus. Modern Art, N.Y.C., 1972—; mem. Fed. Arts and Artifacts Indemnification Panel, 1979-83. Author: Fifteenth Century Engravings of Northern Europe, 1967, The Engravings of Martin Schongauer, 1968, Master LCZ and Master WB, 1971, Exhibitions Organized and Catalogued: Master E.S, 1967, The Danube School, 1969, Hans Baldung Grien, Prints and Drawings, 1981, (exhbn. catalog) Art for the Nation, 2000; contbr. articles to profl. jours. Woodrow Wilson fellow Harvard U., 1963, David E. Finley fellow, 1963-65. Mem. Print Coun. Am. (bd. dirs., v.p. 1970-71), Coll. Art Assn. (bd. dirs. 1972-76), Am. Assn. Mus., Am. Fedn. Arts (trustee 1981-94), Alpha Delta Phi, Phi Beta Kappa. Office: Nat Gallery Art 2000-B S Club Dr Hyattsville MD 20785 E-mail: A-Shestack@nga.gov.

SHESTACK, JEROME JOSEPH, lawyer; b. Atlantic City, N.J., Feb. 11, 1925; s. Isidore and Olga (Shankman) Shestack; m. Marciarose Schleifer, Jan. 28, 1951; children: Jonathan Michael, Jennifer. AB, U. Pa., 1944; LLB, Harvard U., 1949; LLD (hon.), Dickinson Coll. Law, 1997, Stetson Sch. of Law, 1998, Whittier Coll. Law, 1998. Bar: Ill. 1950, Pa. 1952. Tchg. fellow Northwestern U. Law Sch., Chgo., 1949—50; asst. prof. law, faculty editor La. State Law Sch., Baton Rouge, 1950—52; dep. city solicitor City of Phila., 1952, 1st dep. solicitor, 1952—55; ptnr. Schnader, Harrison, Segal & Lewis, Phila. and Washington, 1956—91, Wolf, Block, Schorr & Solis-Cohen, Phila., 1991—. Adj. prof. law U. Pa., 1956; U.S. amb. to UN Human Rights Commn., 1979—80; U.S. del. to ECOSOC, UN, 1980; sr. U.S. del. to Helsinki Accords Conf., 1979—80; mem. U.S. Commn. on Improving Effectiveness of UN, 1989—; chmn. Internat. League Human Rights, 1973—94, hon. chmn., 1994—; U.S. del. to CSCE Conf., Moscow, 1991; founder, chmn. Lawyers Com. Internat. Human Rights, 1978—80, Jacob Blaustein Inst. Human Rights, 1988—92; mem. nat. adv. com. legal svcs. OEO, 1965—72; bd. dirs., exec. com. Lawyers Com. Civil Rights; mem. coun. Holocaust Mus., 1999—2004, exec. com., chair com. on conscience. Editor (with others): Rights of Americans, 1971, Human Rights, 1979, International Human Rights, 1985, Bill of Rights: A Bicentennial View, 1991, Understanding Human Rights, 1992, Thomas Jefferson: Lawyer, 1993, Francis Scott Key, 1994, Abraham Lincoln, Circuit Lawyer, 1994, The Holocaust, 1997, Moral Foundations of Human Rights, 1997, The Philosophy of Human Rights, 1997, W.B. Yeats, Poet of Passionate Intensity, 1997. Mem. exec. com. Nat. Legal Aid and Defender Assn., 1970—80; trustee Eleanor and Franklin Roosevelt Inst., 1986—; bd. govs. Tel Aviv U., 1983—, Hebrew U., 1969—; chmn. bd. dirs. Am. Poetry Ctr., 1976—91; trustee Free Libr. Phila., vice chmn., 1989—96; v.p. Am. Jewish Com., 1984—89. With USNR, 1943—46. Fellow Rubin, Columbia U. Law Sch., 1984, hon., U. Pa. Law Sch., 1980. Mem.: ABA Ctr. for Human Rights (chair 2003—), ABA (ho. of dels. 1971—73, 1977—, jud. com. 1985—90, bd. govs. 1992—95, exec. com. 1994—95, pres.-elect 1996, pres. 1997—98, pres. ALI-ABA 1997—98), Nat. Conf. Bar Found. (bd. dirs. 1998—, pres. 2004), Internat. Assn. Jewish Lawyers and Jurists (Am. Soc. pres. 2000—02), Am. Acad. Appellate Lawyers, Am. Coll. Trial Lawyers, Am. Arbitration Assn. (bd. dirs. 1999—2003), Am. Law Inst., Am. Soc. Internat. Law (exec. com. 1993—, internat. com. jurists exec. com. 1998—2001, commr. 1999—), Internat. Acad. Trial Lawyers, Internat. Bar Assn. (chmn. com. on human rights 1990—94, chmn. com. profl. ethics 2000—04), Order of Coif. Home: Parkway House 2201 Pennsylvania Ave Philadelphia PA 19130-3513 Office: Wolf Block Schorr & Solis-Cohen 1650 Arch St Fl 20 Philadelphia PA 19103-2029 E-mail: jshestack@wolfblock.com.

SHETH, JAGDISH NANCHAND, finance educator; b. Rangoon, Burma, Sept. 3, 1938; arrived in U.S., 1961, naturalized, 1975; s. Nanchand Jivraj and Diwaliben Sheth; m. Madhuri Ratilal Shah, Dec. 22, 1962; children: Reshma J., Raju J. B.Com. with honors, U. Madras, 1960; MBA, U. Pitts., 1962; PhD, 1966. Rsch. assoc., asst. prof. Grad. Sch. Bux. Columbia U., 1963—65; asst. prof. M.I.T., Cambridge, 1965—66, Columbia U., N.Y.C., 1966—69; assoc. prof. bus. adminstrn. U. Ill., Urbana, 1969—71, acting head dept., 1970—72, prof. and rsch. prof., 1971—73, I.B.A. Disting. prof. and rsch. prof., 1973—79, Walter H. Stellner Disting. prof. and rsch. prof., 1979—83; Robert E Brooker Disting. prof. mktg. and rsch. U. So. Calif., L.A., 1983—91; Charles H. Kellstadt prof. mktg. Emory U., Atlanta, 1991—. Vis. prof. Indian Inst. Mgmt., 1968; vis. lectr. Internat. Mktg. Inst. Harvard U., 1969; Albert Frey vis. prof. mktg. U. Pitts., 1974; founder, dir. Ctr. Telecom. Mgmt. U. So. Calif., 1985—, Ctr. Relationship Mktg. Emory U., 1992; condr. seminars industry and govt.; cons. to industry. Author (with John A. Howard): The Theory of Buyer Behavior, 1969; author: (with S. P. Sethi) Multinational Business Operations: Advanced Readings, 4 vols., 1973; author: (with A.Woodside and P. Bennett) Consumer and Industrial Buying Behavior, 1977; author: (with Bruce Newman) A Theory of Political Choice Behavior, 1986; author: (with Dennis Garrett) Marketing Theory, 1986; author: (with S. Ram) Bringing Innovation to Market; author: (with Gary Frazier) Theories of Marketing Practice; author: (with Milind Lele) The Customer is Key; editor: Models of Buyer Behavior, 1964; editor: (with Peter L. Wright) Marketing Analysis for Societal Problems, 1974; editor: Multivariate Methods for Market and Survey Research, 1977, Winning Back Your Market, 1984; editor: (with David Gardener and Dennis Garrett) Marketing Theory: Evolution and Evaluation, 1988; editor: (with Abdol Reza and Goli Eslghi) 9 vols. on global bus., 1989—90; editor: (with Bruce Newman and Barbara Gross) Consumption Values and Choice Behavior, 1990; editor: (with Bruce Newman and B. Miltal) Customer Behavior: Consumer Behavior and Beyond, 1998; editor: (with Banwari Mittal) Value Space, 2001; editor: (with Rajendra Sisodia) The Rule of Three, 2002, with A. Sobel: Clients for Life, 2000;; editor: (with A. Parvatiyar) Handbook of Relationship Marketing, 2000; editor: Internet Marketing, 2000; series editor: Rsch. in Mktg., 1978—2000, Rsch. in Consumer Behavior, 1984—86; contbr. articles to profl. jours. Recipient Viktor Mataja medal, Austrian Rsch. Soc., 1976, Mktg. Educator award, Sales and Mktg. Execs. Internat., 1991, 1999, Charles Covlige Perlin award for Market Rsch., AMA, 2004; Mgmt. Program for Execs. fellow, S & H Green Stamps fellow, 1963—64, Disting. fellow, Internat. Engring. Consortium, 1997. Fellow: APA, Acad. Mktg. Sci. (Mktg. Educator award 1989, Disting. fellow 1996); mem.: Am. Mktg. Assn. (P. D. Converse award 1992, Richard D. Irwin Disting. Mktg. Educator 2004). Home: 1626 Mason Mill Rd NE Atlanta GA 30329-4133 Office Phone: 404-325-0757.

SHETLAR, DAVID JOHN, entomologist, educator, research scientist; s. Marvin Roy Shetlar and Clara Luann Shelton; m. R. Renee Rice, Feb. 25, 1966; 1 child, Norann R. Ricigliano. BS in Zoology, U. Okla., Norman, 1969, MS in Zoology, 1971; PhD in Entomology, Pa. State, State Coll., 1977. Asst. prof. entomology Pa. State, State Coll., 1977—83; rsch. scientist ChemLawn Corp. R & D, Delaware, Ohio, 1984—90; asst. prof. entomology Ohio State, Columbus, 1990—96, assoc. prof. entomology, 1996—. Author: Destructive Turf Insects, 2d edit. Mem.: Entomol. Soc. Am., Stretch Glass Soc. (co-pres. 1991—2001). Office: Ohio State Univ Entomology 1991 Kenny Road Columbus OH 43210

SHETLAR, JAMES FRANCIS, physician; b. Wichita, Dec. 26, 1944; MD, U. Kans., 1970. Resident in family practice Saginaw Cooperative Hosp., 1970-72; staff Covenant Hosp.; asst. clin. prof. Mich. State U. Mem. AMA, Am. Acad. Family Physicians, Mich. Acad. Family Physicians. Office: 163 Churchgrove Rd Frankenmuth MI 48734-1025

SHETTY, JAYAKARA, surgeon; b. India, 1949; MD, Mysore U., India, 1973. Diplomate Am. Bd. Surgery. Intern U. Rochester, N.Y., 1977-78, resident, 1978-79, Waterbury (Conn.) Hosp., 1979-82; fellow in vascular surgery United Hosp.-N.J. Sch. Medicine, Newark, 1982-83; pvt. practice Waterbury. Mem. staff WaterburyHosp, St. Mary's Hosp., Watrbury. Fellow ACS, Royal Coll. Surgeons (Can.). Office: Waterbury Med Arts Bldg 134 Grandview Ave Ste 209 Waterbury CT 06708-2507 E-mail: surgicalspecialists@yahoo.com.

SHETTY, KAUP RAJMOHAN, endocrinologist, educator; came to U.S., 1966; s. Muddanna and Girija M. Shetty; m. Vasanthi R. Shetty; children: Sandeep, Suparna. MB BChir, Mysore Med. Coll., Karnataka, 1965. Diplomate Am. Bd. Internal Medicine, cert. in internal medicine, endocrinology and metabolism, geriatric medicine. Resident in internal medicine VA Med. Ctr., Chgo. and Milw., 1967-70; fellow in endocrinology and metabolism Med. Coll. Wis. and Affiliated Hosps., Milw., 1970-72, attending physician in endocrinology and metabolism, 1972—; attending physician in geriatrics and gerontology VA Med. Coll., Milw., 1991—; assoc. prof. medicine Med. Coll. Wis., Milw., 1991-95, prof. medicine, 1995-2000, prof. medicine emeritus, 2000—. Contbr. 10 chpts. to books, articles and abstracts to profl. jours. Fellow ACP, Royal Coll. Physicians Can., Am. Coll. Endocrinology; mem. Endocrine Soc., Am. Geriatric Soc., N.Y. Acad. Scis. Achievements include research in hormones and aging, post-polio syndrome, metabolic accompaniments of inactivity. Office: VA Med Ctr 5000 W National Ave Milwaukee WI 53295-0001

SHETTY, MULKI RADHAKRISHNA, retired oncologist, consultant; b. Hiriadka, Karnataka, India, July 10, 1940; arrived in U.S., 1974; s. Sunderram and Kusumavati Shetty. MBBS, Stanley Med. Coll., Madras, 1964; DTM, U. Liverpool, Eng., 1968; LMCC, Med. Coun., Can., 1975. House surgeon and physician Bombay Hosp., 1965-66; sr. house officer Manor Pk. Hosp., Bristol, Eng., 1966-67, Torbay Hosp., 1967-68, St. Lukes Hosp., Huddersfield, 1969-70; sr. resident Gen. Hosp. Meml. U., New Foundland, 1971-72; intern Ottawa Gen. Hosp., 1972-73; fellow in chemotherapy Ont. Cancer Found., Ottawa, Can., 1973-74; fellow in clin. oncology U. Fla., Gainesville, 1974-75; attending oncologist N.W. Community Hosp., Arlington Heights, Ill., 1975-2000; ret., 2000. Cons. N.W. Cmty. Hosp., Arlington Heights, Ill., 1975—2000. Author: (book) Lung Cancer, 1980, Recent Advanced in Chemotherapy, 1985, Wildlife Adventures, 1997, Chicago, 1997, Quotes and Notes, 2003; contbr. chapters to books, articles to profl. jours.; coined new word calcifectomy. Recipient Cert. for Oustanding Svc., Am. Cancer Soc., 1982. Hindu. Achievements include Reached the North Pole by icebreaker YAMAL, Aug. 5, 2001.

SHETTY, TARANATH, neurologist, educator; b. Mangalore, India, Apr. 29, 1938; s. Shankar and Bhavani Shetty; m. Urmila Shetty, Dec. 1972; children: Neeta, Teena, Geema. MBBS, Madras U., 1962; MD, Lucknow U., 1965. Diplomate Am. Bd. Pediatrics; diplomate in neurology with spl. competence in child neurology Am. Bd. Psychiatry and Neurology; diplomate with added qualification in clin. neurophysiology Am. Bd. Electroencephalography. Resident in pediatrics Children's Hosp. Med. Ctr., Boston, 1967-68, fellow in neurology, 1968-69; rsch. fellow in neurology Harvard U., Boston, 1968-69, tchg. fellow, 1971-72; resident in neurology Boston City Hosp., 1969-72; instr. Brown U., Providence, 1973-74, asst. prof., 1974-79, clin. assoc. prof., 1979—; dir. pediatric neurology R.I. Hosp., Providence, 1976—. Fellow Am. Acad. Neurology, Royal Coll. Physicians Can., Univ. Cub (Providence). Hindu. Home: 80 Clarendon Ave Providence RI 02906-5826 Office: 120 Dudley St Providence RI 02905-2436 Personal E-mail: tara_shetty@hotmail.com.

SHEU, CHWEN, finance educator; b. Tainan, Taiwan, Dec. 21, 1956; arrived in U.S., 1983, naturalized, 2001; s. Hsing-ming Sheu and Su-jen Chen; m. Litzang Hsu; children: Scott, Shawn. PhD, Ohio State U., 1990. Prof. Kans. State U., Manhattan, 1990—. Author: (rsch. and tchg. materials) Introduction to Operations Management, 1999, (video course) Theory of Constraints - Introduction, 2000. Recipient Best Paper award, Acad. Mgmt. Ops. Divsn., 2001; fellow, Kans. State U., 1999. Mem.: Decision Scis. Inst. (Instrnl. Innovation award 2001), Alpha Delta (hon.). Office: Kans State U 101 Calvin Hall Manhattan KS 66506 Business E-mail: csheu@ksu.edu.

SHEU, JIUH-BIING, transportation engineer, educator; b. Taipei, Taiwan, Sept. 21, 1966; arrived in US, 1993; s. Chin-Hsung Sheu and Hsiu-Tzu Chang; m. Chin-Fung Chou, June 19, 1993; children: Cherry Y.Y., Cindy J.Y. PhD, U. Calif., Irvine, 1997. Asst. prof. Nat. Kaohsiung First U. of Sci. and Tech., Taiwan, 1999—2002; assoc. prof. Inst. Traffic and Transport. Nat. Chiao Tung U., Taipei, Taiwan, 2002—. Postdoctoral rschr. U. Calif., Irvine, 1997—98. Recipient Dr. Da-You Wu Meml. Award, Nat. Sci. Coun., Taiwan, 2003. Mem.: Inst. Ops. Rsch. Mgmt. Sci., IEEE. Home: 4F no21 Ln 8 Guanjou St Taipei 100 Taiwan Office: Nat Chiao Tung Univ Taiwan 4F 114 Sec1 Chung Hsiao W Rd Taipei 10012 Taiwan Office Fax: +886-2-2349-4953. E-mail: jbsheu@mail.nctu.edu.tw.

SHEVCHUCK, HARRY, retired image systems consultant; b. Jerome, Pa., Sept. 24, 1924; s. Nickolai and Anastana (Emilianovich) S.; (div.), remarried Joyce E. Shevchuck; children: Robert N., Gregory A., Cathleen E. (dec.), Susan D., Ivan P., Lisa M. BS in Geology, W.Va. U., 1949; AS in Electronics, Temple U., 1960. Warehouse supr. Owens Ill. Glass Co., Fairmont, W.Va., 1949-50; polymer structural analyst E.I. DuPont de Nemours & Co., Wilmington, Del., 1950-73, electronic imaging equipment specialist, 1973-86, cons., 1986—; now ret. Asst. to scout master Boy Scouts Am., Wilmington, 1960. Served with inf. U.S. Army, 1943-45, ETO, prisoner of war, Germany. Mem.: Ceasar Rodney. Roman Catholic. Home: 602 Stanton Rd Wilmington DE 19804-3636

SHEVIN, ROBERT LEWIS, judge; b. Miami, Fla., Jan. 19, 1934; s. Aaron and Pauline (Bott) S.; m. Myrna Bressack, Jan. 27, 1957; children: Laura Dawn, Hilary Beth, Harry Alan. BA, U. Fla., 1955; JD magna cum laude, U. Miami, 1957. Bar: Fla. 1957, U.S. Dist. Ct. (so. and mid. dists.) Fla. 1963, U.S. Supreme Ct. 1971, U.S. Ct. Appeals (5th cir.) 1971, U.S. Dist. Ct. (no. dist.) Fla. Ptnr. Shevin, Goodman and Holtzman, 1957-67, Shevin and Shevin, 1967-70; mem. Fla. Ho. of Reps., 1963-65, chmn. interim com. on crime and law enforcement, 1965; mem. Fla. State Senate, 1966-70, chmn. select com. to investigate organized crime and law enforcemnt, 1967, mem. interim study com. on urban affairs, 1968; atty. gen. State of Fla., 1971-79; ptnr. Sparber, Shevin, Rosen, Shapo & Heilbronner, Miami, 1979-87, Stroock & Stroock & Lavan, Miami, 1988-96; judge 3d Dist. Ct. Appeals, Miami, 1996—. Mem. Fla. Tax Reform Commn., 1968, Fla. Constl. Revision Commn., 1978; city

atty. City of Miami Beach, Fla., 1979-80; apptd. to Fla. Jud. Mgmt. Coun., 1999-2002, chmn. jury trial innovations com., 1999—; mem. Supreme Ct. Workload Study Commn., 2000. Chmn. Housing Fin. Authority Dade County, Fla., 1980-82, Fla. State Athletic Commn., 1984-87; mem. exec. com. Miami Citizens Against Crime; bd. dirs. Fla. Citizens Against Crime, 1985-90; mem. Fla. Senate's Sunshine Adv. Com., 1988; chmn. Ptnrs. for Safe Neighborhoods, 1994; vis. com. U. Miami Law Sch. Recipient Allen Morris award, 1969, Intergovtl. award HUD, 1969, Conservationist of Yr. awards Fla. Wildlife Fedn., 1973, Audubon Soc., 1974, Furtherance of Justice award Fla. Prosecuting Attys. Assn., 1974, Disting. Svc. award Fla. Sheriff's Assn., 1976, Peace award State of Israel, 1977, Jud. Cmty. Svc. award Greater Miami Jewish Fedn., 1998, Statewide Jud. Achievement award Acad. Fla. Trial Lawyers, 2000; named one of 10 Most Valuable Mems. Fla. Legislature Capital Press Corps, 1965, Fla. Freedom Info. Hall Fame, 1997. Mem.: ABA, Nat. Assn. Attys. Gen. (chmn. So. region 1981), Am. Judicature Soc., Dade County Bar Assn., Fla. Bar Assn., Internat. Bar Assn., Fla. Blue Key, Iron Arrow, Sertoma, Omicron Delta Kappa, Phi Kappa Phi, Pi Lambda Phi, Phi Delta Phi. Democrat. Jewish. Home: 7171 SW 56th St Miami FL 33155-5616 Office: Third Dist Ct of Appeal 2001 SW 117th Ave Miami FL 33175-1799

SHEVITZ, MARK H. sales promotion and marketing executive; b. Dioles, France, July 10, 1955; came to U.S., 1956; s. Arthur E. and Marilyn (Sigoloff) S. Student, U. Mo., 1973-75, Rockhurst Coll., 1983-84; MBA, Washington U., St. Louis, 1988. Program dir. KFMZ-FM, Columbia, Mo., 1974-81; mgmt. supr. Bernstein-Rein Advt., Kansas City, Mo., 1981-84; account supr. The Hermann Group, St. Louis, 1984-86; dir. promotions, food svc. products divsn. Seven-Up Co., St. Louis, 1986-87; pres. Landing Assocs., St. Louis, 1987-88, SJI, Inc., St. Louis, 1988-98, SJI Fulfillment, Inc., St. Louis, 1991—; CEO SJI Inc., St. Louis. Lectr. Washington U., St. Louis, 1988—, Bowling Green (Ohio) State U., 1977-89, Stephens Coll., Columbia, Mo., 1976-89, U. Mo., Columbia, 1975-81. Contbr. articles to profl. jours. Chpt. chmn. March of Dimes, mid.-Mo., 1978-81; mem. devel. bd. Cardinal Glennon Children's Hosp., St. Louis, 1984-88; event chmn. March of Dimes, St. Louis, 1990. Named Entrepreneur of Yr. St. Louis region, 1993. Mem. Assn. Promotion Mktg. Agys. Worldwide (sec./treas. 1998-2000), Porsche Club Am. (pres. St. Louis region 1986). Office: SJI Inc 23 Locust Saint Louis MO 63103 also: SJI Fulfillment Inc 2300 Locust St Saint Louis MO 63103-1512

SHEVLIN, MICHAEL W. retired cultural organization administrator; AA, Bucks County C.C., 1984. Asst. mgr. Solar Resources, Horsham, Pa., 1985; sales rep., estimator Gainor Home Improvement Co., Phila., 1986—90; founder, dir. Heaven Org, 1996—. Author: (book) Keepers of the Unpopular Truth, (poetry) Perfect Lover (Silver and Gold poetry awards, 1988, 1989, 1990); musician: (CD) Broken Hearts-Secrets That We Keep, Night's Song Compilation, Stilo Novo-In The New Style. Recipient Acknowledgment of Enlightenment, Enlightenment Zone, 1998. Mem.: Human Cloning Found. (corr.; cons. 1998—2003), Time Travel Rsch. Assn. (assoc.), New Civilization Network (assoc.), Foresight Inst. (assoc.), Soc. Advancement of Autodynamics (assoc.), Fraternal Order of Police (assoc.). Achievements include first to Nano Computing, extened life research, time theories and time messaging research. E-mail: ourheavenorg@yahoo.com.

SHEWMAKER, KENNETH EARL, history professor; b. L.A., June 26, 1936; s. James Virgil and Jeanette M. (Greenberg) S.; m. Elisabeth L. Spalteholz, June 12, 1960; children: Richard Glenn, Nancy Jeanette. BS, Concordia Tchrs. Coll., 1960; MA, U. Calif., Berkeley, 1961; PhD, Northwestern U., 1966. Instr. Northwestern U., Evanston, Ill., 1965-66; asst. prof. Coll. William and Mary, Williamsburg, Va., 1966-67; from asst. prof. to assoc. prof. Dartmouth Coll., Hanover, N.H., 1967-78, prof. history, 1978—, acting chair dept. history, 1985-86, chmn. dept. history, 1986-89. Author: Americans and Chinese Communists, 1927-45: A Persuading Encounter, 1971 (Stuart L. Bernath prize 1972); editor: Papers of Daniel Webster, Diplomatic Papers, Vol. 1, 1841-1843, 1983, Vol. 2, 1850-1852, 1987, Daniel Webster, The Completest Man, 1990; contbr. articles to profl. jours. Recipient Disting. Tchg. awards, Dartmouth Coll., 1986, 1996, 2004. Mem. N.H. Hist. Soc., Orgn. Am. Historians, Soc. Historians Am. Fgn. Rels. Lutheran. Avocations: fly fishing, fly tying. Office: Dept History Dartmouth Coll Hanover NH 03755 E-mail: shewmaker@dartmouth.edu.

SHI, DAVID E. academic administrator, historian; s. Joseph and Evelyn Shi; m. Susan Thomson, June 1974; children: Jason, Jessica. BA magna cum laude, Furman U., 1973; MA, U. Va., 1975, PhD, 1976; HHD (hon.), Ctr. Coll., 2002. From asst. prof. to Frontis W. Johnston prof., chmn. history dept. Davidson (N.C.) Coll., 1976—93; v.p. acad. affairs Furman U., Greenville, SC, 1993—94, pres., 1994—. Bd. dirs. Nat. Comerce Fin. Corp., Memphis. Author: Facing Facts: Realism in American Thought and Culture 1850-1920, 1995, In Search of the Simple Life: American Voices, Past and Present, 1986, The Simple Life: Plain Living and High Thinking in American Culture, 1985 (Editors Choice award), Matthew Josephson, Bourgeois Bohemian, 1981; author: (with George Tindall) America: A Narrative History, 4th edit., 1996; contbr. articles to profl. jours. Bd. dirs. Urban League, Greenville. Capt. USAR. Recipient Presdl. Leadership award, James L. Knight Found., 1998, Presdl. award, John Templeton Found., 1999; fellow, Nat. Humanities Ctr., 1982—83, NEH, 1982—83, 1991—92, Huntington Libr., 1986—87; grantee, NEH, 1980, 1986; Andrew Mellon Faculty fellow, 1978, Travel grant, NEH, 1988. Mem.: Greenville C. of C. (bd. dirs.), Commerce Club (bd. dirs.), Omicron Delta Kappa, Phi Beta Kappa. Home: 1209 Roe Ford Rd Greenville SC 29617 Office: Furman Univ 3300 Poinsett Hwy Greenville SC 29613

SHI, JIALAN, pathologist, educator; b. Harbin, China, Feb. 1, 1957; s. Ruyou and Jingzhen (Zhang) S.; m. Yingli Yang, Aug. 1, 1987; 1 child, Yinan. MD, Harbin Med. U., China, 1978-83; MS, Harbin Med. U., 1986-89; PhD, Tokyo Med. and Dental U., 1993-97. Tchg. asst. Harbin Med. U., China, 1983-88, asst. prof., 1988-91, dir., 1989-91; rsch. fellow Tokyo Med. & Dental U., 1991-93, tchg. asst., 1996-98; postdoctoral fellow Harvard Med. Sch., Boston, 1998—. Contbr. articles to profl. jours. Grantee, Japanese Govt., Tokyo, 1991; 3rd prize Acad. Sci., Harbin, China, 1991, 2nd prize Dept. Health, Harbin, 1991. Mem. Japanese Soc. Immunology, N.Y. Acad. Scis., Am. Assn. Advancemsnt Sci., Am. Soc. of Hematology, Am. Chem. Soc. Avocations: swimming, skiing, classical music, travel. Home: 56 Cypress St Apt 2 Newton MA 02459 Office: Brigham and Women's Hosp 75 Francis St Boston MA 02115-6110 Personal E-mail: shi_jialan@yahoo.com. Business E-Mail: jialan_shi@hms.harvard.edu. E-mail: jshi@rics.bwh.harvard.edu.

SHI, LIZHENG, health economist; s. Risheng Shi and Zeer Li; m. Huahong Qiang, May 0, 1995. BS, Shanghai Med. U., 1987—92; MSc, Peking Union Med. Coll., 1992—94; MA, U. of Southen Calif., 1996—98; PhD, U. of So. Calif., 1995—2001. Rsch. assoc. Chinese Acad. of Med. Sciences, Beijing, 1994—95; rsch. asst. U. of So. Calif., 1995—2000; sr. health outcomes scientist Eli Lilly and Co., Indpls., 2000—. Contbr. articles to profl. jours. Summer fellowship, U. of So. Calif., 1998, U. of So. Calif., Sch. of Pharmacy, 1997, Best Grad. of the Yr., Peking Union Med. Coll., 1994, RongLing fellow, Shanghai Med. U., 1992. Mem.: Internat. Soc. for Pharmacoeconomics and Outcomes Rsch. (assoc.), Drug Info. Assn. (assoc.), Internat. Soc. for Bipolar Disorders (ISBD) (assoc.). Independent. Achievements include research in development of dual-selection method in the evaluation of pharmacy formulary evaluation. Office: Eli Lilly and Company Lilly Corp Ctr DC 6314 Indianapolis IN 46285 E-mail: lshi@lilly.com.

SHI, WEI, engineering educator, researcher; arrived in U.S., 2001; s. Zengshun Shi and Aimin Feng; m. Zhenyu Zhang, Oct. 1, 1989; children: Jinglu, Ashley. BS, Shandong U., Jinan, China, 1986, MS, 1989, PhD, 2000—00. Assoc. prof. Ministry of Edn., China, 1998, U. tchr. Ministry of Edn., China, 1996. Assoc. prof. Shandong U., Jinan, China, 1989—2001; rsch. assoc. U. Ark., Fayetteville, 2001—02; project dir. ArkLight, Inc., Fayetteville, 2002—02; rsch. assoc. Lehigh U., Bethlehem, Pa., 2002—. Author research; contbr. scientific papers to profl. jours. Grantee, Edn. Com. Shandong Province, China, 1997; Pres. of Shandong U. scholarship, 1998—99, Excellent Grad. Student scholarship, Shandung Province, 1997—98, 1999—2000. Mem.: IEEE (licentiate), Am. Phys. Soc. (licentiate), Optical Soc. of Am. (licentiate). Achievements include discovery of new interferometric technique to sequentially measure piezoelectric and EO coefficient of poled polymer films; two critical conditions at which THz modes destructively interfere; design of THz waveguides for efficient parametric THz generation; invention of coherent source continuously-tunable in 58.2-3540 um based on DFG in GaSe crystal; direct measurement of resonance peaks of water, polystyrene foam, DNA's and protein; tunable coherent THz generation by using quasi-PM DFG in GaP crystal; coherent in the widest range of 2.7-28.7 um by PM-DFG in GaSe crystal; continuously tunable coherent radiation in the range of 77.6-300 um in ZnGeP2 through collinear PM-DFG; development of single-mode rib polymer waveguides; charge effects on poling and stability for corona-poled polymer films; optimizing the corona poling condition using in situ signal intensity probing; first to achieve coherent radiation in the range of 15-28 um in cadmium selenide crystal; new type of electro-optical polymer waveguide switches using self-imaging multi-mode interference couplers; patents in field. Avocations: basketball, travel, fishing. Office: Lehigh U Packard Lab 19 Memorial Dr West Bethlehem PA 18015

SHI, XIANGYANG, research scientist; b. Nanyang, Henan, China, Aug. 5, 1970; s. Dezhong Shi and Xiulan Qin; m. Mingwu Shen, July 14, 1997; 1 child, Daniel. BS, Henan Normal U., XinXiang, China, 1988—92; MS, Beijing Inst. Tech., 1992—95; PhD in Organic Chemistry, Inst. Photographic Chemistry, Chinese Acad. Scis., Beijing, 1998. Postdoctoral rsch. fellow Tsinghua U., Beijing, 1998—2000; vis. scholar Max Planck Inst. Colloids and Interfaces, Potsdam, Germany, 2000—01; postdoctoral rsch. assoc. Calif. State U., LA, 2001—02; rsch. fellow U. Mich., Ann Arbor, 2002—03, rsch. assoc. II, 2003—. Contbr. articles to profl. jours. Mem.: Am. Chem. Soc., Sigma Xi. Achievements include research in nanostructured materials, dendrimer systhesis and characterization, dendrimer nano composites and nanodevices, self-assembly, novel nanodevices for catalysis, biosensor, and optics.

SHI, YUN QING, electrical engineer; b. Chong Qing, Sichuan, China; s. Kong Wai and Wen (Su) S. MS, Shanghai Jiao Tong U., 1980, U. Pitts., 1983, PhD, 1987. Lectr. Shanghai Jiao Tong U., 1980—82; tchg. fellow U. Pitts., 1984—87; asst. prof. N.J. Inst. Tech., Newark, 1987—95, assoc. prof., 1995—2002, prof., 2002—. Reviewer Maths. Rev., 1987—99; co-gen. chair IEEE Internat. Workshop on Multimedia Signal Processing, 2002. Assoc. editor IEEE Transactions on Signal Processing, 1994-96, IEEE Transactions on Circuits and Sys. Part II, 2004—; author: Image and Video Compression for Multimedia, 1999; contbg. author: CRC Press Comprehensive Dictionary of Electrical Engineering, 1998; guest editor: (spl. issue on image sequence processing) Internat. Jour. Imaging Sys. and Tech., 1998; mem. editl. bd. Internat. Jour. Images and Graphics, 1999—. Mem.: IEEE (sr.; chair signal processing chpt., North Jersey sect. 1996—, Circuits & Sys. Soc (CASS) tech. com. visual signal processing & comm. 2001—, CASS tech. com. multimedia systems and application 2001—, CASS disting. lectr. 2002—03, Signal Processing Soc.(SPS) tech. com. multimedia signal processing 2003—). Achievements include research in robust stability of 1-D and M-D Systems, spectral factorization, M-D interleaving schemes, unified optical flow field theory and algorithms, optical flow determination, thresholding techniques in block matching, video compression and transmission, image processing and pattern recognition, video traffic modeling, and digital multimedia data hiding. Office: NJ Inst Tech University Heights Newark NJ 07102 Business E-Mail: shi@njit.edu.

SHI, ZHENGZHONG, finance educator; b. Wuhan, Hubei, China, Aug. 11, 1968; arrived in U.S., 1996; s. Huixian Shi and Huiming Liu. BS in Process Control in Chem. Engring., Zhejiang U., 1989, MS in Computer Simulation in Chem. Engring., 1994; PhD of Mfg. Mgmt., U. Toledo, 2001. Intern Process Control Zhenhai Refinery, 1987, Shanghai Gaoqiao Refinery, 1988; engr. Rsch. Inst. of Indsl. Control Tech. Zhejiang U., 1989—91; coord., programmer Acctg. Info. Sys. Design Quickware Electronic Sys. Co., Hangzhou, China, 1994—95, project mgr. Acctg. Info. Sys. Design, 1995—96; tchg. asst., rsch. asst., lectr. U. Toledo, 1996—2000; lectr., asst. prof. N.D. State U., Fargo, 2000—. Contbr. revs. profl. jours., articles to profl. jours. Mem.: Inst. Operation Rsch. and Mgmt. Sci., Assn. Info. Sys., Decision Sci. Inst., Sigma Iota Epsilon, Phi Kappa Phi. Home: 1501 48th St SW Apt 204 Fargo ND 58103 Office: North Dakota State Univ Putnam Hall Fargo ND 58105 Office Phone: 701-231-6533.

SHI, ZHI-QING, endocrinologist; b. Shanghai, July 19, 1951; came to US, 1996; s. Yu-Qi Shi and Ai-Yi Zou; m. Ai-Ping Xu, May 9, 1982; 1 child, Andrew Bei-Hong. MD, Shanghai No. 2 Med. U., 1975; PhD, McGill U., 1986. Resident surgeon Shanghai 9th Mcpl. Hosp., 1975-78; rsch. fellow Shanghai No. 1 Med. U., 1978-80; dir. surg. rsch. ctr. Zhong Shan Hosp., Shanghai, 1987-89; postdoct. fellow U. Toronto, 1989-93, asst. prof. physiology and surgery, 1993-96; rsch. scientist Amgen, Inc., Thousand Oaks, Calif., 1996—. Invited lectr. physiology Canadian Meml. Chiropractic Coll., Toronto, 1993-95. Contbr. more than 40 research articles to profl. jours., chpts. to books. Recipient Outstanding Young Med. Profl. award City of Shanghai, 1988. Mem. Am. Diabetes Assn. Avocations: western and oriental classical music, literature. Home: 819 Cayo Grande Ct Newbury Park CA 91320-1944 Office: Amgen Inc One Amgen Ctr Dr Thousand Oaks CA 91320

SHIBASAKI, YOSHIO, chemistry educator, researcher; b. Gyoda, Japan, Mar. 21, 1934; s. Reiji and Shige (Kobayashi) S.; m. Teiko Ishizuka Shibasaki, Apr. 15, 1967; children: Hideaki, Miki. BS, Saitama U., Japan, 1959; DSc, U. Tokyo, 1980. Tech. official U. Tokyo, Japan, 1960-63, asst., 1963-67; lectr. Saitama U., Urawa, Japan, 1967-70, assoc. prof., 1970-92, prof., 1992-99, ret., 1999. Inventor: Kobunshi Kagaku, 1964, J. Polymer Science, 1967, 80, 98, 99. Internat. Conf. Thermal Analysis & Calorimetry, Japan Soc. Calorimetry & Thermal Analysis. Mem. AAAS, N.Y. Acad. Sci. Avocation: appreciation of pictures. Home: 1642 Tsutsumine Gyoda 361-0035 Japan

SHICK, JOHN EARL, retired radiologist; b. Chgo., Feb. 24, 1926; BA, Harvard U., 1947; MD, Northwestern U., Chgo., 1951. Diplomate Am. Bd. Radiology. Intern St. Luke's Hosp., Chgo., 1951-52; resident in radiology Thomas Jefferson U. Hosp., Phila., 1954-55, Barnes Hosp., St. Louis, 1955-57; pvt. practice Henry Ford Hosp., Detroit, 1957-61, Grossmont Hosp., La Mesa, Calif., 1961-81; ret., 1981. Mem. AMA, Am. Coll. Radiology, Radiol. Soc. N.Am.

SHICK, RICHARD ARLON, finance educator; b. DuBois, Pa., July 17, 1943; s. Arlon Elmer and Melva Elizabeth (Bartell) S.; m. Linda B. Shick; children: Richard Arlon, Charles, Elizabeth. BS, SUNY, Buffalo, 1966, MBA, 1968, PhD, 1972. Asst. prof. banking and fin. U. Ga., Athens, 1970-75; assoc. prof. fin. St. Bonaventure (N.Y.) U., 1975-78, chmn. fin. dept., 1975-78, acting chmn. mktg. dept., 1976-99; assoc. prof. fin. Canisius Coll., Buffalo, 1978-99, prof. fin., 1999—, dean Richard J. Wehle Sch. Bus., 1979—2002. Bd. dirs. Better Bus. Bur., 1990-95, Statler Culinary program Emerson H.S., buffalo, 1992-98; sec., treas., bd. dirs. Chautauqua Brick Co., 1995—. Mem. editl. bd. Jour. Bus. Rsch., 1973-76, Jour. Fin. Rsch., 1977-81, Jour. Econs. and Bus., 1984-88, Fin. Rev., 1976-87, editor, 1981-82; contbr. articles to profl. jours. Chmn. mayor's rev. com. Buffalo Bd. Edn.; bd. dirs. Buffalo Alliance Edn., Old Ft. Niagara; bd. dirs. Buffalo Philharm. Orch., 1995-97, treas., 1996-97, chmn. devel. com.; mem. N.Y. State Com. to Promote Pub. Trust and Confidence in the Legal System, 1999; bd. dirs. Studio Arena Theatre, 2001—, v.p. bd., pres. NDEA fellow, 1966-68; U.S. Savs. and Loan League grantee, 1974, St. Bonaventure U. grantee, 1976, U.s. Govt. Title III grantee, 1999. Mem. Am. Fin. Assn., Jesuit Colls. and Univs. Deans of Bus. Schs. (treas. 1983-84, v.p. 1985-89, pres. 1987-88), Middle Atlantic Assn. Colls. and Schs. Bus. Adminstrn. (v.p. 1985-86, pres. 1986-87), Country Club Buffalo, Automobile Club Western N.Y. (bd. dirs. 1995-99, exec. com. 1998-99, 2001), Beta Gamma Sigma, Alpha Kappa Psi, Di Gamma, Alpha Sigma Lambda, Alpha Signa Nu. Republican. Home: 157 Crestwood Ln Buffalo NY 14221-1508 Office: Canisius Coll 2001 Main St Buffalo NY 14208-1035 Office Phone: 716-888-2660. E-mail: shick@canisius.edu.

SHICKLEY, MARGARET S. librarian; b. Armstrong County, Pa., Mar. 11, 1938; d. Oscar Henry and Ella Margaret (Titus) Fry; m. Roger Clair Storms, Aug. 24, 1963 (dec. 1980); children: Ethel Charis, Eric Malcolm; m. Nelson W. Shickley Sr., June 23, 1996. BA in Christian Edn., Eastern Coll., 1961; MSLS, Clarion U., 1991. Organist, pianist Lee Bapt. Ch., Maine, 1965-78; tchr. sewing Beth Eden Bapt. Sch., Wheatridge, Colo., 1978-81; organist, pianist Evang. Meth. Ch., Altoona, Pa., 1984-91; libr. Manahath Sch. Theol., Hollidaysburg, Pa., 1984-90; piano tchr. Altoona, Pa., 1986-90; cataloging libr. Lancaster (Pa.) Bible Coll., 1991—. Music libr. Blair Concert Chorale, Altoona, 1987-90; choir dir. Bapt. Ch., New Bethlehem, Pa., 1990-91. Nat. sec. Nat. Temperance and Prohibition Coun., 1983-89, del., sec. Prohibition Nat. Com., Denver, 1979-95; trustee Prohibition Trust Assn., 1992-2002. Mem. Am. Theol. Libr. Assn., Harmony Club (pres. 1977), Lee Lit Club (cmty. project chmn. 1976-77). Avocations: music, needlecrafts, sewing, knitting, reading. *The building of today is not finished. Each day influences the next. Yesterday was the foundation that set the general outline for today's framework of living—built with solid materials of learning, experiences, relationships and memories. The life materials of today include a possibility of change and involvement with others as essential to our life building. Today's building influences the interior decorating of Tomorrow and its beauty to be revealed. Thus God's blueprint will be made visible.*

SHIDELER, ROSS PATRICK, foreign language and comparative literature educator, writer, translator, poet; b. Denver, Apr. 12, 1936; BA, San Francisco State U., 1958; MA, U. Stockholm, 1963; PhD, U. Calif., Berkeley, 1968. Instr. in comparative lit. U. Calif., Berkeley, 1967-68; asst. prof. English Hunter Coll., NYC, 1968-69; asst. prof. Scandinavian lang. and comparative lit. UCLA, 1969-73, assoc. prof., 1973-79, prof., 1979—, chmn. program in comparative lit., 1979-86, 92-96, assoc. dean Grad. Divsn., 2003—. Author: (monograph) Voices Under the Ground: Themes and Images in the Poetry of Gunnar Ekelof, 1973, Per Olov Enquist-A Critical Study, 1984, Questioning the Father: From Darwin to Zola, Ibsen, Strindberg and Hardy, 1999; translator: (plays) The Night of the Tribades (Per Olov Enquist), 1977, The Hour of the Lynx (Per Olov Enquist), 1990; co-editor (with Kathleen L. Komar): Lyrical Symbols and Narrative Transformations, Essays in Honor of Ralph Freedman, 1998; U.S. assoc. editor Swedish Book Rev., 1984—. Fellow, Nat. Defense Fgn. Language, 1964—65; Fulbright-Hays fellow, 1966—67. Mem. MLA (exec. com. divsn. Scandinavian Langs. and Lits. 1993-97), Soc. Advancement Scandinavian Studies (exec. coun. 1985-89, v.p. 1997-99, pres. 1999-2001), Internat. Comparative Lit. Assn. (treas. 2004-). Office: UCLA Dept Comparative Lit Los Angeles CA 90024

SHIDELER, SHIRLEY ANN WILLIAMS, lawyer; b. Mishawaka, Ind., July 9, 1930; d. William Harmon and Lois Wilma (Koch) Williams; 1 dau., Gail Shideler Frye. LLB, Ind. U., 1964. Bar: Ind. 1964. Legal sec. Barnes, Hickam, Pantzer & Boyd, Indpls., 1953-63; assoc. Barnes & Thornburg, 1964-70, ptnr., 1971-92, of counsel, 1993—. Participant fund drives Indpls. Symphony, 1968-81, Indpls. Mus. Art, 1969-79, Marion County Libr. Restoration, 1985-88, Goodwill Industries, 1988-89; bd. dirs. Bus. Unit Gals Indpls. Mus. Art, 1973-80; bd. dirs. Indpls. Legal Aid Soc., 1982-93, Cmty. Hosp. Found., 1986-94, Ctrl. Newspapers Found., 1979-99. Fellow Am. Coll. Trust and Estate Counsel, 1981-96; mem. Ind. Bar Assn. (sec. 1975-76, chmn. probate, trust and real property sect. 1982), Nat. Conf. Bar. Founds. (trustee 1988-94), Indpls. Bar Assn. (bd. mgrs. 1968-72, v.p. charge affairs 1972), Ind. Bar Found. (bd. mgrs. 1980-92, sec. 1981-82, treas. 1981-86, v.p. 1986-88, pres. 1988-90), Indpls. Bar Found. (bd. mgrs. 1970-82, sec. 1972-77), Women's Rotary (pres. Indpls. club 1969-71, dir. 1968-79). Office: Barnes & Thornburg 11 S Meridian St Ste 1313 Indianapolis IN 46204-3535 Address: PO Box 5031 Indianapolis IN 46255-5031

SHIDLER, JAY H. real estate company executive; BBA, U. Hawaii. Founder, mng. ptnr. The Shidler Group (predecessor co. to First Indsl.); chmn. bd. dirs. First Indsl. Realty Trust, Inc., Chgo., 1993—. Bd. dirs. Primus Guaranty, Ltd.; chmn. bd. dirs. Corp. Office Properties Trust; mem. investment and spl. coms. First Indsl. Realty Trust. Office: First Indsl Realty Trust Inc Ste 4000 311 S Wacker Dr Chicago IL 60606*

SHIEBER, STUART MERRILL, natural sciences educator; b. St. Louis, Apr. 27, 1959; s. William and Hortense (Rader) S.; m. Cassia Wyner, June 19, 1993. AB in Applied Math. summa cum laude, Harvard U., 1981; PhD in Computer Sci., Stanford U., 1989. Rsch. fellow Ctr. for Study of Lang. and Info., Stanford U., 1983-89; rsch. computer scientist Artificial Intelligence Ctr., SRI Internat., 1981-89; asst. prof. computer sci. Harvard U., Cambridge, Mass., 1989-93, John L. Loeb assoc. prof. natural scis., 1993—. Founder Cartesian Products, Inc., 1991; vis. prof. U. Calif., Santa Cruz, summer 1991; founder, organizer The Computation and Lang. E-Print Archive. Author: An Introduction to Unification-Based Approaches to Grammar, 1986, Spanish transl., 1989, French transl., 1990; Constraint-Based Grammar Formalisms, 1992; (with Fernando C.N. Pereira) Prolog and Natural-Language Analysis, 1987, Italian transl., 1992; editor: (with Peter Sells and Thomas Wasow) Foundational Issues in Natural Language Processing, 1991; contbr. numerous articles to profl. jours.; mem. editl. bd. Computational Linguistics, 1990-93, Jour. Artificial Intelligence Rsch., 1993—. Named Presdl. Young Investigator, 1991-93; Presdl. Faculty fellow, 1993—. Mem. Assn. Computational Linguistics (mem. exec. com. 1993—), Phi Beta Kappa. Office: Harvard Univ Cambridge MA 02138

SHIEH, JOHN TING-CHUNG, economics professor, department chairman; b. 1935; BS, Chunghsing U., Taiwan, 1956; MS, Kans. State U., 1960; MA, U. Calif., Riverside, 1970; DBA, U. So. Calif., 1981. Asst. prof. Northwestern State Coll., Alva, 1964—67; asst. prof. econs. Calif. State Poly. U., Pomona, 1967—70, assoc. prof., 1970—81, prof., chmn. dept. econs., 1982—85, prof., 1981—98, prof. emeritus, 1999—; vis. prof. econs. and mgmt. Xian U., China, 2003—. Prof., dir. Inst. Mainland China Studies, 1994-98, dean student affairs, 1997-99, Nat. Dong-hua U., Hwalian, Taiwan, 1994-2001; cons. to small bus., So. Calif., Taiwan, 1975—; vis. prof. Tax Inst., U. So. Calif., L.A., 1977-84, U. Calif., Irvine, 1978-79, U. So. Calif., 1978-81, UCLA, 1983-1998. Contbr. rsch. articles to publs. in field. NSF fellow, 1965, 66, 67, 73, fellow seminars in econs. and math. U. Wyo., summer 1972. Mem. Am. Econ. Assn., Omicron Delta Epsilon, Omega Rho. Home: 10556 Ilona Ave Los Angeles CA 90064-2313

SHIELD, GENE, managed health care company executive; BSBA, The Citadel; MS in Systems Mgmt., U. So. Calif.; M in Health Care Adminstrn., Med. Coll. Va.; grad., USAF Squadron Officers Sch., Indsl. Coll. of the Armed Forces. Former chief managed care divsn. Office of Air Force Surgeon Gen.; former cons. to Surgeon Gen. on managed care, advisor for legis. and CHAMPUS benefits and policy issues; pres., CEO Humana Mil. Healthcare Svcs. Humana Inc., Louisville, 1994—2000, sr. v.p. govt. programs, pres./CEO Emphesys, 2000—. Office: Humana Inc 500 W Main St Louisville KY 40202

SHIELDS, ALLAN EDWIN, writer, photographer, retired educator; b. Columbus, Ohio, July 3, 1919; s. Richard Edwin and Eloessa (Smith) S.; m. Bernice Clark, Aug. 2, 1941; children— Allan Oakley, Richard Minter, Larry Michael, Catherine Marie AB, U. Calif.-Berkeley, 1941; MA, U. So. Calif., 1947, PhD, 1951. Prof. philosophy San Diego State U., 1949-68, 70-78; emeritus prof. San Diego State Coll., 1978—; dean Coll. Humanities and Fine Arts U. No. Iowa, 1968-70; owner, pub. Jerseydale Ranch Press, 1992-98. Seasonal ranger naturalist Nat. Park Service, Yosemite Nat. Park, 1955-60; freelance writer, photographer, 1978—; violinist-violist, frequent recitalist; mem., sometime concertmaster Merced Symphony Orch., Calif., 1979-91; founder, with wife, Jerseydale Ranch Press, 1992. Author: Guide to Tuolumne Meadows Trails, 1960, rev. edit., 1973, (with Herbert Searles) A Bibliography of the Works of F.C.S. Schiller, 1969, (with Richard Shields) Tuolumne Profile: Yosemite, 1967, (novella) The Tragedy of Tenaya, 1974, new version 1992, A Bibliography of Bibliographies in Aesthetics, 1974, (poetry) A Horse in the House, 1985, Mariposa Now and Then, 1993, Tuffy, an Angel Hid in a Cloud, 1994, What Animals Taught Me, 1995, (with Bernice Shields) Into the Valley: A Brief History of Jerseydale Ranch, 1995, (with John Sharsmith) Climb Every Mountain: A Portrait of Carl Sharsmith, 1996, The Spirit of

Rin-Tin-Tin, 2001, also numerous poems and articles; editor: A Yosemite Adventure in 1863, 1992, Wild Bill Neely and the Pagan Brothers' Golden Goat Winery, 1993, The Song of Sonora, 1993, O.S.S.: One Sad Sack—Pvt. Neely Disciplines the Military, 1994, A Yosemite Naturalist's Odyssey, 1994, Wilderness Treks by Foot, Canoe, and Adobe Rocket, and Father's Far-Flung Fables, 1995, Dream Temple and Other Visions, 1997; pub. various profl. jours. Bd. dirs. San Diego Symphony. Served with USAAF, 1942-45 Mudd fellow in philosophy U. So. Calif., 1948-49 Mem. Am. Soc. for Aesthetics (trustee), Phi Beta Kappa, Phi Kappa Phi, Phi Mu Alpha Sinfonia (hon.). Home: 2444 Beverly Ave Clovis CA 93611-5927 Personal E-mail: ashields@csufresno.edu. *My greatest satisfactions have come with tasks completed to the best of my abilities. Whether raising children, building a building, nurturing a marriage, learning the violin, or writing, all have inherent standards demanding recognition. Though there is always joy in the process of doing, joy can be transformed into satisfaction only in completion evaluated against the standards of worth for that kind of undertaking.*

SHIELDS, ANTHONY FRANK, oncologist, hematologist; b. Highland Park, Mich., 1952; MD, Harvard U., 1979; PhD, MIT, 1979. Diplomate Am. Bd. Internal Medicine, Am. Bd. Oncology, Am. Bd. Hematology. Intern U. Wash. Hosp., 1979-80, resident internal medicine, 1980-81; fellow hematology/oncology U. Wash., 1981-84; mem. staff VA Med. Ctr., Seattle, 1987-95, Harper Hosp., Detroit, 1995—, Karmanos Cancer Inst., Mich., 1995—; asst. prof. U. Wash., 1987-93, assoc. prof., 1993-95, Wayne State U., 1995-99, prof. medicine and oncology, 1999—. Mem. Am. Assn. Cancer Rsch., Am. Soc. Clin. Oncology, Am. Soc. Hematology, Soc. Nuc. Medicine. Office: Karmanos Cancer Inst 4100 John R St 4th Fl Detroit MI 48201 2097 E-mail: shieldsa@karmanos.org.

SHIELDS, BROOKE CHRISTA CAMILLE, actress, model;; 1 child. BA, Princeton U., 1987. Model for Ivory Soap commls. starting in 1966, later for Calvin Klein jeans and Colgate toothpaste commls.; actress: (films) Alice, Sweet Alice, 1975, Pretty Baby, 1977, King of the Gypsies, 1978, Wanda Nevada, 1978, Just You and Me Kid, 1978, Blue Lagoon, 1979, Endless Love, 1980, Sahara, 1983, Backstreet Strays, 1989, Brenda Starr, 1992, Seventh Floor, 1993, Running Wild, 1993, Freaked, 1993, Freeway, 1996, The Misadventures of Margaret, 1998, The Weekend, 1999, The Bachelor, 1999, Black & White, 1999. After Sex, 2000, Rent-A-Husband, 2004; (TV movies) The Prince of Central Park, 1977, After the Fall, Wet Gold, I Can Make You Love Me: The Stalking of Laura Black, 1993, Nothing Lasts Forever, 1995, What Makes a Family, 2001, Miss Spider's Sunny Patch Kids, 2003; (TV mini-series) Widows, 2002 (TV shows) The Tonight Show, Bob Hope spls., The Diamond Trap, 1988, Friends, 1996, Suddenly Susan, 1996-99, That 70's Show, 2004; appeared on Broadway in Grease, 1994-95.*

SHIELDS, CAROLE, foundation administrator; MBA, U. Miami. Pres. People For the Am. Way Found., Washington, 1996—. Bd. dirs. PFAWF, Fla. State Health and Rehab. Svcs., Dade Childrens Partnership; vice-chair Pub. Health Trust, Dade Co., Fla.; v.p. Hospice Care, Inc.; appearences on PBS NewsHour, CNN Inside Politics, Fox Cables Crier & Co., Hannity & Colms. Bd. dirs. Dade Cmty. Found., Forum Med. Ethics and Philosophy, U. Miami.; mem. Kettering Found., Lilly Endowment Found., Davis Found. Office: People Am Way 2000 M St NW Ste 400 Washington DC 20036-3397 E-mail: pfaw@pfaw.org.

SHIELDS, CRAIG M. lawyer; b. Oceanside, N.Y., Nov. 28, 1941; s. John Anderson and Lillian Ethel (Hagen) S.; m. Candia Atwater Shields, July 13, 1963 (div. 1985); children: Mark, Christopher, Evan; m. Norma Magor Peters, Apr. 25, 1998. BA, Lafayette Coll., 1963; JD, Fordham U., 1966. Bar: N.Y. 1967, U.S. Dist. Ct. (so. and ea. dists.) N.Y. 1967, U.S. Ct. Appeals (2d cir.) 1967, U.S. Supreme Ct. 1976. Assoc. Clark, Carr & Ellis, N.Y.C., 1966—69; ptnr. Borden & Ball, N.Y.C., 1969—76, Sage, Gray, Todd & Sims, N.Y.C., 1976—80; counsel Conboy, Hewitt, O'Brien & Boardman, N.Y.C., 1980—83; ptnr. Collier, Cohen, Shields & Bock, N.Y.C., 1983—92, Quinn & Suhr, White Plains, NY, 1992—95; v.p., gen. counsel United Vanguard Homes, Inc., Glen Cove, NY, 1992—2003; pvt. practice N.Y.C., 2003—. Contbr. articles to profl. jours. Bd. dirs. Group House of Port Washington (N.Y.) Inc., 1973-85, Children's House, Inc., Mineola, N.Y., 1985-89, Resources for Program Devel., Inc., Port Washington, 1982—; pres. Port Washington Community Action Coun., 1968-69; committeeman Dem. Party, Port Washington, 1967-71. Mem. Assn. of Bar of City of New York, N.Y.State Bar Assn. Democrat. Methodist. Home and Office: 103 E 86th St Apt 7A New York NY 10028-1058 Office Phone: 212-876-4234. E-mail: norma.peters@netzero.net.

SHIELDS, DAVID BRANDON, historian, educator; b. Norfolk, Va., Nov. 7, 1965; s. William David Shields and Mary Elizabeth Wood. BA, Va. Commonwealth U., 1988; MA, London Sch. Econs., 1991; cert. advanced tchg. qualifications, Royal Holloway, 1996; PhD, U. London, 1998; MS, Manhattanville Coll., 2003. Dir. facilities UNICCO, Boston/Washington, 1993—94; polit. cons. L.B.C. Radio, London, 1994—97; asst. dean studies Manhattanville Coll., Purchase, NY, 2000—03, vis. prof. hist., 2003—; asst. dean Wesleyan U. Grad. Sch., Middletown, Conn., 2003—. Fund raiser Friends of London Sch. Econs. N.Y., 2000—, Dem. Nat. Com., 2000—. John F. Kennedy Rsch. Fellow, Kennedy Libr., 1997. Mem.: Brit. Rocketry Oral History Project (adv.), Inst. Hist. Rsch. (rsch. adv.). Democrat. Avocation: skiing. Home: 23 Webatuck Rd Gaylordsville CT 06755 Office: Wesleyan U 284 High St Middletown CT 06459

SHIELDS, JAMES JOSEPH, academic administrator, educator, writer; b. Phila., Feb. 11, 1935; s. James Joseph and Lena Josephine (Dyer) Shields. BS in Polit. Sci., Saint Joseph's U., 1956; EdM, Temple U., 1959; EdD, Columbia U., 1963. Asst. dir. internat. studies Tchrs. Coll., Columbia U., N.Y.C., 1961, field rschr., Tchrs. East Africa Program N.Y.C., Kampala, Uganda, 1961-62; asst. prof. history and philosophy edn. SUNY, New Paltz, 1962-64; asst. prof. comparative and internat. edn. CUNY, N.Y.C., 1964-69, assoc. prof., 1969-75, prof., 1975-98, prof. emeritus, 1998, head Sch. Adminstrn. Program, 1983-85, chair dept. social and psychol. founds., 1988-90; dir. Japan Initiative, 1986-98; dir. projects Ctr. Edn. Outreach and Innovation, N.Y.C., 1998—. Vis. prof. Tchrs. Coll., Columbia U., 1965—67, 1993—95, 1998, 2000—02, Yale U., 1997; cons. Inst. Ednl. Devel., N.Y.C., 1968—71, Equitable Life Ins. Co., N.Y.C., 1981, N.Y.C. Bd. Edn. Dist. 4, 1996—97, Time Mag., 1998, Inst. Internat. Edn., 1998—99; evaluation bd. Nat. Coun. Accreditation Tchr. Edn., Washington, 1970—75; vis. rsch. prof. Tokyo Met. U., 1986—95; assoc. univ. seminar modern Japan Columbia U., N.Y.C., 1987—, chair, 1990—91. Author: Education in Community Development: Its Function in Technical Assistance, 1967, Problems and Prospects in International Education, 1968, Foundations of Education: Dissenting Views, 1974, Japanese Schooling: Patterns of Socialization Equality and Political Control, 1989, rev. edit., 1993; contbr. chapters to books, articles to profl. jours. Mem. task force restructed ednl. sys. Pub. Edn. Assn., N.Y.C., 1977—78, mem. task force tchr. selection, 1981; mem. N.Y. Urban Coalition, 1982—84; mem. alumni coun. Tchrs. Coll., Columbia U., 1993—99. With USAR, 1959—65. Recipient Youth Coun. award, Wyo. Gov., 1974, Higher Edn. award, Holy Family Coll., Phila., 1990, Ann. Gertrude Langsam Ednl. Reconstrn. award, Adelphi U., 1992; grantee, N.Y. State Edn. Dept., 1969—72, Japan-U.S. Friendship Commn., 1986—88, Japan Found. Ctr. Global Partnership, 1994, U.S.-Japan Found., 1994—96, Tokyo Found., 1998—2000; Rsch. Found. grantee, SUNY, 1964, Fulbright Travel grantee, 1964, Rsch. Found. grantee, CUNY, 1980—81, City Coll. Provost Fund grantee, 1988—90, postdoctoral fellow, Yale U., 1967—68. Fellow: Comparative and Internat. Edn. Soc. (hon.; N.E. region conf. coord. 1984, bd. dirs. 1992—95); mem.: Soc. Ednl. Reconstruction (exec. com. 1973—), Carnegie Coun. Ethics and Internat. Affairs (trustee 1998—2003, vice-chmn. 2001—03), Am. Ednl. Studies Assn. (exec. coun. 1970—75, pres. 1973—74, founder), Beaux Arts Alliance, Japan Soc. N.Y., N.Y. Athletic Club (N.Y.C.). Avocations: collecting long island painters (1850-1950), travel, gardening. Address: Trump Pl 200 Riverside Blvd Apt 11N New York NY 10069-0911 also: 42 Old Town Xing Southampton NY 11968-5015 Office Phone: 212-787-3326. E-mail: jshields11@juno.com.

SHIELDS, JERRY ALLEN, ophthalmologist, educator; b. Pride Station, Ky., June 9, 1937; s. Fendell Harris and Beulah Etta (Williams) S.; m. Carol Lally, Oct. 26, 1985; children: Jerry, Patrick, William, Margaret, John. BA, Murray State U., 1960; MD, U. Mich., 1964. Diplomate Am. Bd. Ophtalmology. Intern Denver Gen. Hosp., 1964-65; resident in ophthalmology Wills Eye Hosp., Phila., 1967-70, fellowship in retina, 1970, fellowship in pathology, 1971, dir. ocular oncology svc., 1973—; prof. ophthalmology Thomas Jefferson U. Hosp., Phila., 1980—. Author: Diagnosis and Management of Intraocular Tumors, 1983, Diagnosis and Management of Orbital Tumors, 1989, Intraocular Tumors: A Text and Atlas, 1991; contbr. articles to jours., chpts. to textbooks. Lt. MC, USN, 1965-67, Vietnam. Recipient Golden Apple award Sr. Residents Wills Eye Hosp., 1990; co-recipient award Brady Cancer Rsch. Inst., 1986. Mem. AMA, Am. Acad. Ophthalmology, Am. Assn. Rsch. Ophthalmology, Phila. Ophthalmic Club, Pa. Acad. Ophthalmology and Otolaryngology. Home: 617 Williamson Rd Bryn Mawr PA 19010-1932 Office: Wills Eye Hosp Dept Oncology 9th And Walnut St Philadelphia PA 19107-5599

SHIELDS, JOHN CHARLES, American studies and African American studies and literature educator; b. Phoenix, Oct. 29, 1944; s. Granville Blaine and Elizabeth Merle (Hartgraves) S. BA, U. Tenn., Knoxville, 1967, MA in Coll. Teaching, 1969, PhD, 1978; EdS, George Peabody Coll., 1975. Tchr. English Sevier County High Sch., Sevierville, Tenn., 1967-68; head dept. English Battle Ground Acad., Franklin, Tenn., 1969-71; dir. academics Brentwood Acad., Nashville, 1971-73, Columbia (Tenn.) Mil. Acad., 1973-74; instr. U. Tenn., Knoxville, 1978-79; asst. prof. Ill. State U., Normal, 1979-86, assoc. prof. English, 1986-93, prof. English, 1993—. Cons. Ency. Britannica, Oxford Companion to African Am. Lit., Norton Anthology African Am. Lit., others; project dir. conf. on Phillis Wheatley NEH, 1983-85; faculty advisor Native Am. Student Soc. Ill. State U., 1990; Coll. of Arts and Sci. Lectr., Ill. State U., 2003—; mem. doctoral dissertation com. Assoc. editor Style, DeKalb, Ill., 1988-90, guest editor, 1990—; editor: The Collected Works of Phillis Wheatley, 1988, paperback, 1989; selected to be a mem. of the Adv. Bd. of The Greenwood Ency. of Am. Poetry, (7 vol.) contbr., adv. editor, contbr. Oxford Companion to African Am. Lit., 1997—, Am. Nat. Biography, 24 vol., 1994—; contbr. New Dictionary of Nat. Biography, Great Britain, 1995—; author: The Am. Aeneas: Classical Origins of the American Self, Univ. of Tenn. Press, 2001 (nominated for Ralph Waldo Emerson prize, John Hope Franklin award, Susan M. Glasscoch Interdisciplinary Book prize and Lora Romero First Book prize); contbr. articles to lit. jour. and chpt. to books; manuscript reviewer various presses and jour. Spokesperson for Native Am. citizens, 1990—. Ford Found. fellow, 1968-69, Soc. for Humanities fellow Cornell U., 1984-85, NEH fellow, 1983, 84, 89, 93, John. C. Hodges Teaching Excellence award, 1969. Mem. MLA, Soc. Early Americanists, Internat. Soc. for 18th-Century Studies, Am. Studies Assn., Melville Soc., Coll. Lang. Assn., Phi Mu Alpha Sinfonia, Alpha Phi Omega, Sigma Nu. Unitarian Universalist. Avocations: piano, singing, native american culture, archaeology, rare book collecting. Home: 1412 Donegal Dr Normal IL 61761-5416

SHIELDS, LAWRENCE THORNTON, orthopaedic surgeon, educator; b. Boston, Oct. 2, 1935; s. George Leo and Catherine Elizabeth (Thornton) S.; m. Karen S. Kraus, Sept. 21, 1968; children: Elizabeth Coulter, Laura Thornton, Sarah Daly, Michael Lawrence. AB, Harvard U., 1957; MD, Johns Hopkins U., 1961. Diplomate Am. Bd. Orthopaedic Surgery. Intern Barnes Hosp., Washington U., St. Louis, 1961—62, resident, 1962—63; resident orthop. surgeon Children's Hosp. Med. Ctr., Boston, 1966—67, Mass. Gen. Hosp., Boston, 1967—68, Peter Bent Brigham, Robert Breck Brigham Hosps., Boston, 1968—69, Harvard Med. Sch., Boston, 1965—69, instr., 1969—; orthop. surgeon Peter Bent Brigham & Women's Hosp., Children's hosps., 1969—, Waltham (Mass.)-Weston Hosp. and Med. Ctr., 1969—, also chief orthop. surgery, pres. med. staff. Mem. Waltham-Weston Orthop. Assocs.; proprietor Boston Athenaeum; mem. staff Hahnemann Hosp., Boston, Newton-Wellesley (Mass.) Hosp.; cons. orthop. surgeon VA Hosp., Boston; mem. faculty Harvard Med. Sch.; vis. scholar Trinity Hall Cambridge U., 1987; hon. prof. New Eng. Coll., Henniker, NH, Sussex, England, 1995; bd. dirs. Wal-West Health Sys., 1986—; pres. Mass. Bay Investment Trust; dir. Waltham Investment Group. Contbr. articles to med. jours. Bd. dirs. Mass. Acad. Emergency Med. Technicians, Waltham Boys' Club; bd. of overseers Boston Lyric Opera, 1993—; trustee, exec. com. Waltham-Weston Hosp. and Med. Ctr. Lt. M.C. USNR, 1963-65. Fellow: ACS, Mass. Hist. Soc. Libr., Am. Acad. Orthop. Surgeons, Mass. Hist. Soc.; mem.: Thomas B. Quigley Sports Medicine Soc. (v.p., pres. 2001—), R. Austen Freeman Soc. (v.p.), Mass. Med. Soc. (v.p. 1982—83, councillor), Mass. Orthop. Assn. (sec. 1986—, bd. dirs.), Royal Soc. Medicine, N.Y. Acad. Scis., Cox & Co., Boston Lyric Opera (bd. overseers 1993), English Speaking Union (bd. dirs.), Academie Brillat-Savarin, Confrerie de La Chaine des Rotisseurs (elected 1996), Waltham Hist. Soc., Trollope Soc. (founding mem., bd. dirs., London), Thoreau Soc., Internat. Consular Corps (hon.), Charles River Dist. (pres. 1982—83, treas., exec. com.), Titanic Hist. Soc., Boston Opera Assn. (bd. dirs.), Harvard Mus. Assn., Emerson Soc., Handel and Hayden Soc. (bd. overseers), Les Amis d'Escoffier Soc., L'Ordre Mondial (elected 1999), St. Crisplin's Soc. Boston (pres. 1991—, founding mem.), USS Wasp CV-19 Assn., Theodore Roosevelt Assn. New Eng. (founding), East India, Devonshire Sports and Pub. Schs. Club (London), New Eng. Orthop. Club, Boston Orthop. Club, St. Botolph Club (Boston), Bull Dog Terries, Clover Club Boston, Union Club Boston, Harvard Club, Algonquin Club Boston (pres. 1990—, bd. dirs.), Rotary, Pi Eta (Harvard). Home: 9 Beverly Rd Newton MA 02461-1112 Office: 721 Huntington Ave Boston MA 02115-6010 also: 20 Hope Ave Ste 314 Waltham MA 02453-2717 Office Phone: 781-893-0700. E-mail: ltshields@mcb.harvard.edu.

SHIELDS, MARLENE SUE, elementary school educator; b. Denver, Apr. 7, 1939; d. Morris and Rose (Sniderman) Goldberg; m. Charles H. Cohen, Dec. 22, 1957 (dec.); children: Lee, Richard, Monica; m. Harlan Shields. BA magna cum laude, Met. State Coll., 1980; MA, U. No. Colo., 1986. Preschool tchr. Temple Emanuel, Denver, 1970-75; tchr. Kindergarten Temple Sinai, Denver, 1975-80; tchr. pre-Kindergarten St. Mary's Acad., Englewood, Colo., 1980-83; tchr. Beach Court Elem., Denver, 1983-86, Valverde Sch., Denver, 1984-85; tchr. third grade Brown Elem., Denver, 1985-86; tchr. learning disabilities Cowell Elem. Sch., Denver, 1986-87, Sabin Elem. Sch., Denver, 1987-88; tchr. second grade Sabin Elem., Denver, 1988—. Mem. curriculum com. Denver Pub. Sch., 1989—, pers. subcom., 2000-02; citizen amb. Spain joint tchr. conf., 1995. Mem. personal subcom. Sabin Elementary Sch., 2000. Mem. Colo. Coun. Internat. Reading Assn., Nat. Assn. for Young Children, Nat. Tchrs. Colo. Math., Internat. Reading Assn., Carousel of Intervention, Delta Kappa Gamma (sec., v.p., grade level chair), PRIDE (lang. curriculum com., math. curriculum com., impact com., CDM rep. 1994-95), Delta Kappa Gamma (state 1st v.p.). Home: 5800 Big Canon Dr Englewood CO 80111-3516

SHIELDS, PETER D. lawyer; BA with honors, SUNY; JD, Syracuse U. Bar: D.C., N.Y., U.S. Ct. Appeals (D.C. cir.), U.S. Supreme Ct. Ptnr. Wiley Rein Fielding, LLP, Washington. Named Pro Bono Atty. of the Yr., D.C. Bar, 1993—94. Mem.: Fed. Comm. Bar Assn. (pres. 2002—03, Disting. Svc. award 1997—98). Office: Wiley Rein & Fielding 1776 K St NW Washington DC 20006

SHIELDS, PORTIA HOLMES, academic administrator; m. William H. Lewis. BS in Edn., D.C. Tchrs. Coll.; MA in Edn., George Washington U.; PhD in Early Childhood and Elem. Edn., U. Md. Various tchg. positions primary and secondary edn.; dir. med. and biomed. comm. Howard U. Coll. Medicine, Washington, 1989-93, dean Sch. of Edn., 1993-96; pres. Albany (Ga.) State U., 1996—. Presenter and cons. in field. Active Albany Mus. Art, Albany Tomorrow, Inc., Albany/Dougherty Cmty. Partnership for Edn. and Dougherty, 2000; chair steering com. Am. Reads Program; mem. bd. regents U. Sys. Ga., 1997; bd. dirs. Cmtys. in Schs. Mem.: Albany C. of C. (bd. dirs.), Nat. Coun. for Accreditation Tchr. Edn. (bd. dirs.), Am. Coun. on Edn. (bd. dirs., mem. appeals com.), Orgn. Instnl. Affiliates (bd. dirs.), Am. Assn. Colls. for Tchr. Edn. (bd. dirs.), Am. Assn. State Colls. and Univs. (com. on cultural diversity and social change). Office: Albany State U 504 College Dr Albany GA 31705 E-mail: pshields@asurams.edu.

SHIELDS, ROBERT EMMET, merchant banker, lawyer; b. Ridley Park, Pa., May 18, 1942; s. Joseph Leonard and Kathryn J. (Walsh) S.; m. Mary Katherine Reid, July 22, 1967; children: Christopher D., David R., Kevin M., Kathleen. AB, Coll. Holy Cross, 1964; LLB cum laude, NYU, 1967. Bar: Pa. 1968. Mem. faculty Boalt Hall Sch. Law U. Calif., Berkeley, 1967-68; assoc. Drinker Biddle & Reath, Phila., 1968-74, ptnr., 1974-94, mng. ptnr., 1979-83, 85-94, head corp. and securities group, 1983-93, CFO, 1993-94; mng. dir., prin., ptnr., COO Questor Gen. Ptnr., L.P., 1995—2003, Questor Ptnrs. Funds, L.P. and Questor Mgmt. Co., 1995—2003; vice chmn. AlixPartners Holdings, Inc., Southfield, Mich., 2003—, Questor Ptnrs. Holdings, Inc., Southfield, 2003—, TK Aluminum, Ltd., Hamilton, Bermuda, 2003—. Sec. Wallquest Inc. Author: (with Eliot B. Thomas) Federal Securities Act Handbook, 4th edit, 1977; (with Robert H. Strouse) Securities Practice Handbook, 1987. Mem. ABA, Am. Law Inst., Pa. Bar Assn., Phila. Bar Assn. Office: AlixPartners Holdings Inc 2000 Town Ctr Ste 2400 Southfield MI 48075-1406 also: 1 Logan Sq Ste 2000 Philadelphia PA 19103-6933 Home: 13021 2nd Ave Stone Harbor NJ 08247-1056 E-mail: rshields@alixpartners.com.

SHIELDS, ROBERT FRANCIS, stockbroker; b. Chgo., Oct. 22, 1923; s. Francis Hugh and Adele Marie (Melcher) S., children: Debra, Cynthia, Judith. BS in Econs., St. Joseph's Coll., 1944; MBA in Fin., Governors' State U., 1970. Registered fin. cons., investment adviser. With instl. bonds dept. Bear Stearns & Co., Chgo., 1946-49; resident mgr. Reynolds & Co., Chicago Heights, Ill., 1952-62; v.p., resident mgr. Dempsey Tegeler & Co, Chicago Heights, 1962-70; sr. v.p., resident mgr. Stifel Nicolaus & Co., Chicago Heights, 1970-93; sr. v.p. Everen Securities (formerly known as Prin. Fin. Securities), Munster, Ind., 1993 , First Union Securities, Ind., Wachovia Securities (formerly First Union Securities), Munster, 2002— Maj. USMC, 1943-46, 50-52. Decorated Purple Heart. Mem. Olympia Fields Country Club. Roman Catholic. Office: Wachovia Securities 8317 Calumet Ave Munster IN 46321-1723 Office Phone: 219-836-2590.

SHIELDS, THOMAS CHARLES, lawyer; b. Evergreen Park, Ill., Apr. 26, 1941; s. Thomas James and Adelaide (McElligott) Shields; m. Nicoline M. Murphy, Sept. 14, 1974; children: Thomas James II, Nicoline M. E., Suzanne Adelaide, Kerry Anne. AB, Georgetown U., 1963; JD cum laude, Northwestern U., 1966. Bar: Ill. 1966, U.S. Dist. Ct. (no. dist.) Ill. 1966, U.S. Ct. Appeals (7th cir.) 1966, U.S. Tax Ct. 1968, U.S. Supreme Ct. 1977. Assoc. Hopkins & Sutter, Chgo., 1966-73, ptnr., 1973-93; mem., chair health law dept. Bell, Boyd & Lloyd, Chgo., 1994—; chief counsel Cath. Health Assn. U.S., St. Louis, 1994—. Lectr. Ill. Inst. Continuing Legal Edn., 1973; mem. adv. bd. Health Law Inst. Loyola U. Sch. Law, Chgo., 1984—89, Health Law Inst. DePaul U. Sch. Law, Chgo., 1985—96. Contbr. articles to profl. jours. Trustee Village of Riverside, Ill., 2001—; mem. Ill. Health Facilities Authority, 2000—03; governing mem. Chgo. Zool. Soc., Chgo., Cath. Charities Chgo.; bd. dirs. Cancer Rsch. Found., Chgo., 1987—, Brother Louie and Fannie Roncoli Found., 1994—. Mem.: Chgo. Bar Assn., Ill. Assn. Healthcare Attys. (bd. dir. 1983—89, pres. 1987—88), Ill. Bar Assn., Am. Hosp. Assn. (tax adv. group 1987—90), Am. Health Lawyers Assn. (bd. dir. 1983—91, pres. 1989—90), Mid-Am. Club Chgo. (bd. govs. 2001—), Order of Coif. Avocations: skiing, bicycling, golf, tennis. Office: Bell Boyd & Lloyd 3 First Nat Plz Ste 3200 Chicago IL 60602 Office Phone: 312-807-4232. E-mail: tshields@bellboyd.com.

SHIELDS, THOMAS WILLIAM, surgeon, educator; b. Ambridge, Pa., Aug. 17, 1922; s. John Jr. and Elizabeth (Flanagan) S.; m. Dorothea Ann Thomas, June 12, 1948; children: Thomas William, John Leland, Carol Ann. BA, Kenyon Coll., 1943, DSc (hon.), 1978; MD, Temple U., 1947. Resident surgery Northwestern U. Med. Sch., Chgo., 1949-55, prof. surgery, 1968-92, prof. Emeritus of surgery, 1992—; practice medicine specializing in surgery Chgo., 1956—; chief of surgery VA Lakeside Hosp., Chgo., 1968-87; chief thoracic surgery VA Lakeside Med. Ctr., Chgo., 1987-90. Editor: General Thoracic Surgery, 1972, 5th edit., 2000, 6th edit 2004, Bronchial Carcinoma, 1974, Mediastinal Surgery, 1991; assoc. editor Surgery, Gynecology and Obstetrics, Annals of Thoracic Surgery, 1993-2002; mem. editl. bd. Annals of Thoracic Surgery, Lung Cancer; contbr. articles to profl. jours. Served with U.S. Army, 1951-53. Mem. ACS, AMA, Am. Assn. for Thoracic Surgery, Soc. Thoracic Surgery, Central, Western Surg. Assns., Société Internationale de Chirurgie, Soc. for Surgery of Alimentary Tract, Internat. Assn. for Study Lung Cancer, Japanese Assn. Thoracic Surgery (hon.), Pa. Assn. Thoracic Surgery (hon.), Pan Pacific Surg. Assn., Phi Beta Kappa, Sigma Xi, Alpha Omega Alpha. Home: 10513 E Cinnabar Ave Scottsdale AZ 85258-4908 Office: Northwestern U Feinberg Sch Medicine Galter 3-150 201 E Huron St Chicago IL 60611

SHIELDS, V. SUE, federal magistrate judge; b. 1939; AB, Ball State U., 1959; LLB, Ind. U., 1961. Atty. Office of the Regional Counsel, IRS, 1961; dept. atty. gen. Office of the Atty. Gen. of Ind., 1962-64; judge Hamilton Superior Ct., 1965-78, Ind. Ct. Appeals, 1978-94; magistrate judge U.S. Dist. Ct. for So. Dist. Ind., Indpls., 1994—. Office: 256 US Courthouse 46 E Ohio St Indianapolis IN 46204-1903 Office Phone: 317-229-3670.

SHIELY, JOHN STEPHEN, manufacturing executive, lawyer; b. June 19, 1952; s. Vincent Robert and Mary Elizabeth (Hope) S.; m. Helen Jane Pauly, Aug. 29, 1981; children: Michael, Erin, Megan. BBA, U. Notre Dame, 1974; JD, Marquette U., 1977; M of Mgmt., Northwestern U., 1990. With Arthur Andersen & Co., Milw., 1977-79, Hughes Hubbard & Reed, Milw., 1979-83, Allen-Bradley Co., Milw., 1983-86, Rockwell Internat. Corp., Milw., 1985-86, Briggs & Stratton Corp., Milw., 1986—, gen. counsel, 1986-90, v.p., gen. counsel, 1990-91, pres., COO, 1994-2001, pres., CEO, 2001—03, chmn., pres., CEO, 2003—. Bd. dirs. Briggs & Stratton Corp., Marshall & Ilsley Corp., Milw., 1999—, Quad/ Graphics, Inc., Pewaukee, Wis., 1996—. Mem. Greater Milw. Com., 2000—; chmn. bd., dir. Children's Hosp. Wis., 1992—; mem. bd. regents Milw. Sch. Engring., 1995—; trustee Med. Coll. Wis., 2003—; mem. corp. bd. dirs. Rock and Roll Hall of Fame and Mus.; bd. dirs. Outdoor Power Equipment Inst. Mem.: Wis. Mfrs. and Commerce (bd. dirs. 2002—), Assn. for Corp. Growth (past pres., bd. dirs. Wis. chpt. 1988—). Office: Briggs & Stratton Corp PO Box 702 Milwaukee WI 53201-0702

SHIENTAG, FLORENCE PERLOW, lawyer; b. N.Y.C. d. David and Ester (Germane) Perlow; m. Bernard L. Shientag, June 8, 1938. BS, NYU, 1940, LLB, 1933, JD, 1940. Bar: Fla. 1976, N.Y. Law aide Thomas E. Dewey, 1937; law sec. Mayor La Guardia, 1939-42; justice Domestic Relations Ct., 1941-42; mem. Tchrs. Retirement Bd., N.Y.C., 1942-46; asst. U.S. atty. So. dist. N.Y., 1943-53; cir. ct. mediator Fla. Supreme Ct., 1992; pvt. practice N.Y.C., 1960—, Palm Beach, Fla., 1976—. Lectr. on internat. divorce; mem. Nat. Commn. on Wiretapping and Electronic Surveillance, 1973—, Task Force on Women in Cts., 1985-86. Contbr. articles to profl. jours. Candidate N.Y. State Senate, 1954; bd. dirs. UN Devel. Corp., 1972-95, Franklin and Eleanor Roosevelt Inst., 1985—; bd. dirs., assoc. treas. YM and YWHA; hon. commr. commerce, N.Y.C. Mem. ABA, Fed. Bar Assn. (exec. com.), Internat. Bar Assn., N.Y. Women's Bar Assn. (pres., dir., Life Time Achievement award 1994, special award 2002), N.Y. State Bar Assn., N.Y.C. Bar Assn. (chmn. law and art sect.), N.Y. County Lawyers Assn. (dir.), Nat. Assn. Women LAwyers (sec.). Home: 737 Park Ave New York NY 10021-4256 Address: 44 Cocoanut Row Palm Beach FL 33480 Office Phone: 212-861-8800. *Success is a product of self respect and hard work at what you do well.*

SHIER, GLORIA BULAN, mathematics professor; b. The Philippines; came to U.S., 1966. d. Melecio Cauilan and Florentina (Cumagun) Bulan; m. Wayne Thomas Shier; children: John Thomas, Marie Teresita, Anna Christina. BS, U. Santo Tomas; MA, U. Ill., 1968; PhD, U. Minn., 1986. Tchr. Cagayan Valley Coll., Cagayan, Philippines, St. Paul Coll., Manila, Manila Div. City Schs.; asst. prof. U. of East, Manila; rsch. asst. U. Ill., Urbana, 1968—69; instr. Miramar C.C., San Diego, 1974—75, Mesa C.C., San Diego, 1975—80, Lakewood C.C., St. Paul, 1984, U. Minn., Mpls., 1986—87, North Hennepin C.C., Brooklyn Park, Minn., 1987—. Cons. PWS Kent Pub. Co., Boston, 1989—. Chairperson Filipino Am. Edn. Assn., San Diego, 1978-79. Fulbright scholar U.S. State Dept., U. Ill., 1966-70; fellow Nat. Sci. Found., Oberlin Coll., 1967; recipient Excellence in Teaching award UN Ednl. Scientific Cultural Organ., U. Philippines, Cert. Commendation award The Gov. of

Minn., 1990, Outstanding Filipino in the Midwest Edn. Cat. award 1992, Cavite Assn., 1998, Gintong Pamana Found.; Outstanding Filipino-Am. in Edn. Mem.: Am. Statis. Assn., Minn. Math. Assn. of Two Yr. Colls., Minn. Coun. Tchrs. Math., Internat. Group for Psychology of Math. Edn., Am. Math. Assn. for Two Yr. Colls., Nat. Coun. Tchrs. Math., Philippine-Am. Acad. Sci. and Engring., Math. Assn. Am., Am. Math. Soc., Fil-Minnesotan Assn. (bd. dirs. 1991—), Cultural Soc. Filipino-Ams. (pres. 2001—), Sigma Xi, Phi Kappa Phi. Roman Catholic. Avocation: piano. Business E-Mail: gloria.shier@nhcc.mnscw.edu.

SHIER, SHELLEY M. production company executive; b. Toronto, Mar. 15, 1957; d. Harry Shier and Rosaline (Cutler) Sonshine; m. Hank O'Neal, May 14, 1985. Student, H.B. Studio, NYC, 1975-76, Stella Adler Conservatory, 1976-80. Company mem., actor Soho Artists Theater, NYC, 1976-81; casting dir. Lawrence Price Prodns., NYC, 1981-82; pres. Hoss, Inc., NYC, 1983—; v.p. Chiaroscuro Records, NYC, 1987—; pres. Broadway Bound, Inc., NYC, 1998—. Cons. Peter Martin Assocs., NYC, 1983, Norwegian Cruise Line, Miami, Fla., 1983-98, Floating Jazz Festival, 1983—,Oslo (Norway) Jazz Festival, 1986—, New Sch. Social Rsch., NYC, 1989—, Big Bands Sea, Rhythm & Blues Cruise, Dixieland Sea, 1991—, Blues Cruise, 1991—, Beacons Jazz Awards Ceremony, Tribute Music Bob Wills Texas Playboys, Mardi Gras Sea. Talent acquisition agt. Save Children, NYC, 1986, Tomorrow's Children, NYC, 1990, Barcelona Olympics, NBC, 1992, Royal Caribbean Internat., Miami, 1994-96, Ultimate Caribbean Jazz Spectacular, Country Music Festival Caribbean, CUNARD NYC, 1994—, Broadway Sea, 1996, Millennium Sea, 1999—, Broadway Bound, 1999—, others. Avocations: Karate, photography, riding, fishing, weightlifting. Office: HOSS Inc 830 Broadway New York NY 10003-4827 Office Phone: 212-674-8631. Business E-Mail: broadwayboundinc@aol.com.

SHIFF, RICHARD ALLEN, director, art historian; b. Bridgeport, Conn., May 15, 1943; s. Joe Warren and Matilda Cohen Shiff. BA magna cum laude with highest honors in archtl. sci., Harvard Coll., 1961—65; student, Harvard Grad. Sch. Design, 1965, Harvard Grad. Sch. Arts and Sci., 1966; MA, Yale Grad. Sch., 1966—71; PhD in history art, Yale U., 1973. Asst. prof. art Tyler Sch. Art, Temple U., 1971—74; asst. prof., dept. art, com. art and design, com. gen. studies in humanities U. Chgo., 1974—78; assoc. prof. art U. N.C., Chapel Hill, 1978—86, prof. art, 1986—88; dir. Ctr. Study Modernism U. Tex., Austin, 1989—, Effie Marie Cain regents chair art, 1989—. Vis. prof. history of art Yale U., 1985; Whitney Halstead vis. prof. Sch. Art Inst. Chgo., 1987; vis. prof. art history Emory U., 1994. Author: (book) Cézanne and the End of Impressionism; editor: Critical Terms For Art History; contbr. articles to profl. jours.; author: Bernett Newman: A Catalogue Raisonné, 2004. Fellow, Nat. Humanities Ctr., 1986; Mellon Fellow in Humanities, U. Penn., 1979—80, John Simon Guggenheim Found. fellow, Guggenheim Found., 1985—86, Sr. Rsch. grant, Getty Rsch. Ctr., L.A., 1996—97. Office: Univ Tex at Austin Dept Art 23rd and Trinity Austin TX 78712-1104 Office Phone: 512-471-7547.

SHIFFER, JAMES DAVID, retired utility executive, consultant; b. San Diego, Mar. 24, 1938; s. Kenneth Frederick and Thelma Lucille (Good) S.; m. Margaret Edith Rightmyer, Sept. 5, 1959 (div. July 1986); children: James II, Elizabeth, Russell; m. Esther Zamora, Sept. 13, 1986; stepchildren: Bryan Boots, Jeremy Hellier, Marisol Loughead. BS in Chem. Engring., Stanford U., 1960, MS in Chem. Engring., 1962. Registered profl. engr., Calif. Nuc. engr. Pacific Gas & Electric Co., Humboldt Bay Power Plant, Eureka, Calif., 1961-71; tech. mgr. Pacific Gas & Electric. Co., Diablo Canyon Power Plant, Avila Beach, Calif., 1971-80; mgr. nuc. ops. Pacific Gas & Electric Co., San Francisco, 1980-84, v.p. nuc. power generation, 1984-90, sr. v.p., gen. mgr. nuc. power generation bus. unit, 1990-91; exec. v.p. Pacific Gas & Electric, San Francisco, 1991-97; ret., 1997; pres., CEO PG&E Enterprises, San Francisco, 1994-95, also bd. dirs. Bd. dirs. Math., Engring., Sci. Achievement, 1992-2002. Mem. AIChE, Am. Nuc. Soc., Commonwealth Club of Calif. (bd. govs. 1992-97). Republican. Episcopalian. Avocations: golf, music. Home: 2550 Royal Oaks Dr Alamo CA 94507-2227 E-mail: jshiffer@msn.com.

SHIFFMAN, BERNARD, mathematician, educator; b. NYC, 1942; s. Max and Bella S.; m. Doris Judith Yaffe, July 11, 1965; children: Jonathan, Daniel. BS, MIT, 1964; PhD, U. Calif., Berkeley, 1968. C.L.E. Moore instr. MIT, 1968-70; asst. prof. math. Yale U., 1970-73; assoc. prof. Johns Hopkins U., Balt., 1973-77, prof., 1977—, chair dept. math., 1990-93. Mem. Inst. Advanced Study, Princeton, NJ, 1975, Math. Scis. Rsch. Inst., Berkeley, Calif., 1996, 99; series lectr. U. Kaiserslautern, West Germany, 1977, Inst. Math., Academia Sinica, Beijing, 1978, U. Paris VI, 1979, Nordic Summer Sch., Joensuu, Finland, 1981, U. Tokyo, 2000; mem. Inst. des Hautes Etudes Scientifiques, Bures-sur-Yvette, France, 1979; vis. prof. U. Paris VI, 1981, 85, U. Grenoble, 1992, 95, 2001, 03. Editor Forum Mathematicum, 1989-95; assoc. editor Am. Jour. Math., 1990-92, editor, 1992-93, editor-in-chief, 1993—; rschr. publs. in complex analysis. Hon. Woodrow Wilson fellow, 1964, NSF fellow, 1968, Alfred P. Sloan rsch. fellow, 1973-75; recipient Woodrow Wilson Faculty Devel. award, 1979. Mem. Am. Math. Soc. Office: Johns Hopkins U Dept Math Baltimore MD 21218

SHIFFMAN, DANIEL STEVEN, literature educator; b. N.Y.C., June 25, 1963; s. Irving and Cynthia Frances Shiffman; m. Jessica Mier Ertman, Sept. 1, 1994; children: Isaac, Emma. BA in English, Colby Coll., Waterville, Maine, 1986; MA in English, U. Wis., Madison, 1989, PhD, 1994. Vis. asst. prof., English Idaho State U., Pocatello, 1994—99; asst. prof., English Berry Coll., Mount Berry, Ga., 1999—. Author: (book) Rooting Multiculturism: The Work of Louis Adamic, 2003. Fellow, Princeton U. Libr., 1998. Avocations: running, travel. Home: 14 Benvenue Dr Rome GA 30161 Office: English Dept Berry Coll Mount Berry GA 30149 Business E-Mail: dshiffman@berry.edu.

SHIFFMAN, MICHAEL A. lawyer; b. Newark, July 23, 1941; LLB magna cum laude, Lincoln U., 1973. Bar: Calif. 1973, U.S. Dist. Ct. (no. dist.) Calif. 1973; lic. real estate broker. Atty. Lanahan & Reilley, San Francisco. Editor: Lincoln U. Law Rev., 1972-73. Mem. ABA, Internat. Bar Assn., State Bar Calif. Office: Lanahan and Reilley LLP 1 Market St San Francisco CA 94105-1521 E-mail: shifflaw@aol.com.

SHIFLETT, SHAWN ALLEN, writer, educator; b. Chgo., Ill., Dec. 7, 1954; m. Jacqueline Patricia Maher, May 4, 1991; children: Maggie Lee, Cole Patrick. BA with highest honors, Columbia Coll., Chgo., 1976; MA, Ctrl. State U., Okla., 1982. Master approach tchr. Story Workshop Inst., 2000. Prof. Columbia Coll. Chgo., Chgo., 1983—. Author: (novel) Hidden Place. Fellowship in Fiction Writing, Ill. Arts Coun. Home: 517 Bell Ave La Grange IL 60525 Office: Columbia Coll Chgo 600 S Mich Ave Chicago IL 60605 Office Phone: 312-344-7536. E-mail: sshiflett@colum.edu.

SHIFRIN, KENNETH STEVEN, financial service executive; b. N.Y.C., Apr. 16, 1949; s. Bernard and Frieda (Morgenstern) S.; m. Yvonne Barber, Mar. 4, 1959; children: Zachary, Joshua, Jacob. BS, Ohio State U., 1971, MBA, 1973. CPA, D.C., Tex. Mgmt. cons. Arthur Andersen & Co., Washington, 1973-76; mgr. forecasting Fairchild Industries, Inc., Germantown, Md., 1976-78; v.p. fin. and contracts Fairchild Aircraft Corp., San Antonio, 1978-85; chief fin. officer Am. Physicians Service Group, Austin, Tex., 1985-87, pres., 1987—, also bd. dirs. Bd. dirs., chmn. Am. Phys. Svc. Group, Inc., Prime Med. Svcs., Inc. Mem. Young Pres. Organ. With USAR, 1969-75. Mem. AICPA. Jewish. Home: 15801 Chateau Ave Austin TX 78734-2638 Office: Am Physicians Svc Group Inc 1301 Capital Tex Hwy # B220 Austin TX 78746

SHIGETOMI, KEITH SHIGEO, lawyer; b. Honolulu, Oct. 16, 1956; s. Samson Shigeru and Doris (Ogawa) S.; m. Ann Keiko Furutomo, Oct. 29, 1985; children: Samson Shigeru II, Marisa Mae. BSBA magna cum laude, Drake U., 1978; JD, U. Hawaii, 1983. Bar: Hawaii, 1983, U.S. Dist. Ct. Hawaii 1983, U.S. Ct. Appeals (9th cir.) 1986. Dep. pub. defender Office of Pub. Defender, Honolulu, 1983-88; pvt. practice, Honolulu, 1988-90, 94—; ptnr. Shigetomi & Thompson, Honolulu, 1990-94. Ind. grand jury counsel Cir. Ct., State of Hawaii, Honolulu, 1988-89. Finalist Three Outstanding Young Persons Hawaii Jaycees, 1994; named Criminal Def. Lawyer of Yr. Consumer Bus. Rev., 1996, 97, 99. Mem. Hawaii Bar Assn., Nat. Asian Pacific Bar Assn., Beta Gamma Sigma, Beta Alpha Psi, Phi Eta Sigma. Office: 711 Kapiolani Blvd Ste 1440 Honolulu HI 96813-5238 Office Phone: 808-596-0880.

SHIGYO, TETSUO TED, emergency physician; b. Newell, Calif., 1944; BA in Zoology, U. Calif., Santa Barbara, 1969; MD, U. Calif., San Francisco, 1973. Intern Valley Med. Ctr., Fresno, Calif., 1973-74, resident, 1974-76, asst. chief emergency medicine, 1976-78; emergency physician Fresno Cmty. Hosp. and Med. Ctr., 1978-80, St. Agnes Med. Ctr., Fresno, 1980—, ACLS med. dir., 1983-94, chmn. CME com., 1988-90, 92-94. Med. dir. paramedic program Fresno County, Calif., 1976-78. Fellow Am. Coll. Emergency Physicians; mem. Calif. Med. Assn. Office: 1303 E Herndon Ave Fresno CA 93720-3309 Personal E-mail: shigyo@earthlink.net.

SHIH, CHUAN-KANG, anthropologist; arrived in U.S., 1983, naturalized, 2002; m. Liping Wang; 1 child, Gerry Chia-hsi. PhD, Stanford U., 1993; BA in History, Yunnan U., China, 1982; MA in Anthropology, Stanford U., 1986. Post-doctoral fellow Ctr. for Chinese Studies U. Mich., Ann Arbor, 1993—94; vis. asst. prof. dept. anthropology U. Ill., Urbana-Champaign, 1994—95, asst. prof. dept. anthropology Urbana, 1995—2002, asst. prof. dept. East Asian Langs. and Cultures, 1997—2002, rsch. fellow Ctr. for East Asian and Pacific Studies Champaign, 2002—03; asst. prof. dept. anthropology and Asian studies program U. Fla., Gainesville, 2003—. Univ. hon. prof. Yunnan U., Kunming, 2000—; vis. scholar dept. demography U. Calif., Berkeley, Calif., 2001—02. Contbr. articles to profl. jours. Recipient Career award, NSF, 2000—; fellow, Stanford U., 1983—87, Inst. for Women and Gender Studies, Stanford U., 1989—90, Ctr. for Chinese Studies, U. Mich., 1993—94; grantee, Ctr. for East Asian Studies, Stanford U., 1985, 1987, Wenner-Gren Found. for Anthrop. Rsch., 1988, William and Flora Found., 1996, U. Ill. at Urbana-Champaign, 1997, 1998; Gen. Edn. Bd. Cultural Studies Course Devel. Grant, 1997. Mem.: Assn. for Asian Studies, Am. Anthrop. Assn. Office: U Fla Dept Anthropology PO Box 117305 Gainesville FL 32611

SHIH-CARDUCCI, JOAN CHIA-MO, cooking educator, biochemist, medical technologist, author, writer; b. Rukuan, Chunghua, Taiwan, Dec. 21, 1933; came to U.S., 1955; d. Luke Chiang-hsi and Lien-chin (Chang) Shih; m. Kenneth M. Carducci, Sept. 30, 1960 (dec. July 1988); children: Suzanne R., Elizabeth M. BS in Chemistry, St. Mary Coll., Xavier, Kans., 1959; intern in med. tech., St. Mary's Hosp., Rochester, N.Y., 1960. Med. rschr. Strong Meml. Hosp. U. Rochester, 1960-61; pharm. chemist quality control Strasenburgh Labs., Rochester, 1961-62; cooking tchr. adult edn. Montgomery County Pub. Schs., Rockville, Md., 1973-79; tchr. The Chinese Cookery Inc., Rockville, 1975-86, Silver Spring, Md., 1986—, pres., bd. dirs., 1975—; chemist NIH, Bethesda, 1987-2000; analytical chemist NIH/WRAIR, Rockville, Md., 1994-96. Author: The Chinese Cookery, 1981, Hunan Cuisine, 1984, Vegetarian Cuisine, 2000, The Art of The Chinese Cookery, 2001. Mem. Am. Chem. Soc., Internat. Assn. Cooking Profls. (Woman of Yr. 1994-2004). Republican. Roman Catholic. Avocations: piano, music, dance, flowers, vegetables. Home and Office: The Chinese Cookery Inc 14209 Sturtevant Rd Silver Spring MD 20905-4448 Office Phone: 301-236-5311.

SHIKINA, SEIJI, educator, consultant; b. Naha, Okinawa, Japan, Mar. 2, 1940; s. Seitoku and Kiku (Zukeran) S.; m. Shikego Inamine, Mar. 31, 1968; children: Alice Yuko, Helen Ai, Edward Tatsuji, Robert Tetsuo. BA in English Lit., U. of Ryukyus, Japan, 1965; BA in Social Welfare, U. Nebr., 1973; MA in English, N.W. Mo. State U., 1975; PhD in English, U. S.W. La., 1986. Translator U.S. Counterintelligence, Okinawa, Japan, 1965-67; writer, editor Today's Ryukyus, Okinawa, Japan, 1967-70; family counselor Cath. Diocese of Lafayette, La., 1978-79; mgr. St. Francis Found., Lafayette, La., 1976-85; human resources exec. T.S. Trim Industries, Columbus, Ohio, 1987-91; prof. English Alcorn State U., Lorman, Miss., 1985-87; acad. dean U. Rio Grande, Tokyo, Japan, 1992-93, provost, 1993-94, cons. to pres., 1994-95. Univ. ombudsman U. S.W. La., Lafayette, 1983-85; owner cons. Bilingual Columbus, Ohio, 1991-99. Author: Requiem for a Toddler, 1995. Scholarship to U.S. Coll., Miami Rotary Club, Okinawa, Japan, 1970. Mem. Am. Translators Assn. Roman Catholic. Avocations: shakuhachi, Karate, chess, golf, swimming. Home: 2985 Upton Rd E Columbus OH 43232-5241

SHIKUMA, EUGENE YUJIN, travel company executive; b. Tokyo, Nov. 18, 1948; arrived in U.S., 1957; s. Mitsuo and Yukiko (Kanaoka) Shikuma. BSEE, U. Hawaii at Manoa, Honolulu, 1971, MS in Computer Sci., 1975. Lab. test engr. and scientist McDonnell Douglas Astronautics, Inc., 1971-72; systems engr. Lear Siegler Astronics, 1972-73; jr. coord. Japan Travel Bur. Hawaii, Inc., Honolulu, 1978-83, sr. coord., 1983-84, supr., 1984-89, mgr., 1989—. Bd. dir. Maui United Way, Kahului, Hawaii, 1988—89, Maui Hui Malama, Waiulku, 1989—90; mem. Maui County Visitor Task Force, 1995—; adv. bd. mem. Maui Acad. Travel and Tourism; bd. dir. Maui Visitors Bur., 2003—; hon. chmn. bus. adv. coun. Hawaii Nat. Rep. Congl. Com., 2003; bd. dir., sec. Kamoa Views Apt. Owners Assn., 1991—96. Mem.: Maui Japanese C. of C., Maui C. of C. Avocations: swimming, coin collecting/numismatics, art, antique prints. Office Phone: 808-871-6600. Business E-Mail: eshikuma@jtb-hawaii.com.

SHILEPSKY, ARNOLD CHARLES, mathematics educator, computer consultant; b. Norwalk, Conn., Dec. 10, 1944; s. Morris Jacob and Rose (Pfeffer) S.; m. Carol Irene Carter, June 15, 1968; children: Lisa Ruth, Beth Carter. AB, Wesleyan U., Middletown, Conn., 1966; PhD, U. Wis., 1971. Asst. prof. Ark. State U., Jonesboro, 1971-74; asst. prof. dept. math. Wells. Coll., Aurora, N.Y., 1974-79, assoc. prof., 1979-85, prof., 1985—, Herbert E. Ives prof. of scis., 1985-91, John D. Wilson Presdl. prof., 2000—. Cons. Digicomp Rsch. Corp., 1992-2000. Pres. Cmty. Devel. Fedn., S.W. Cayuga County, N.Y., 1987-92. Mem. Am. Math. Soc., Math. Assn. Am., Assn. for Women in Math. Home: Main St 295 Aurora NY 13026 Office: Wells Coll Dept Math Aurora NY 13026

SHILLESTAD, JOHN GARDNER, financial services company executive; b. Oak Park, Ill., Oct. 31, 1934; s. John Nelson and Isabel Blanche (Gardner) Shillestad; m. Astri Cedervall; children: Christine C, Annette. BBA, Northwestern U., 1964, MBA, 1967. CLU, CPCU; ChFC. Mktg. dir. spl. plans CNA Ins., Chgo., 1958-66; asst. v.p. Montgomery Ward Life, Chgo., 1966-69; pres., CEO Fort Dearborn Life Ins. Co., Chgo., 1969-79; sr. v.p. Hartford Life Cos., Conn., 1979-85, also bd. dirs., 1985-87; pres. JGS Fin. Svcs., Inc., 1987—, Columbian Mut. Life Ins. Co., Binghamton, NY, 1987—. Chmn. Columbian Life Ins Co, Washington Nat. Life NY; with Golden Eagles Sales Corp., 1997—; bd. dirs. Reassure Am, Valley Forge Life Ins. Co., 2004. Mem Bd Educ, Dist 30, Northbrook, Ill., 1976—79; mem adv bd SUNY Sch Mgt, Binghamton, Kellogg Sch Bus, Northwestern Univ; bd dirs Salvation Army, Binghamton, Partnership 2000, Southern Tier Equity Fund. With U.S. Army, 1954—56. Mem.: Broome County CofC (bd dirs), Pelican Marsh Golf Club (Naples, Fla), Sunset Ridge Club (Northfield, Ill). Republican. Congregationalist. Home: 3 Regentwood Rd Northfield IL 60093-2728 also: Unit 304 1600 Clermont Dr Naples FL 34109 E-mail: sjackshil@aol.com.

SHILLING, A. GARY, economic consultant, investment advisor; b. Fremont, Ohio, May 25, 1937; s. A. Vaughn and Lettie E. (O'Harrow) S.; m. Margaret E. Bloete, Dec. 22, 1962; children: Geoffrey B., Andrew J., Stephen E., Jennifer E. AB in Physics magna cum laude, Amherst (Mass.) Coll., 1960; MA in Econs., Stanford (Calif.) U., 1962, PhD in Econs., 1965; LLD (hon.), Tiffin U., 1999. Economist Standard Oil Co. (N.J.), N.Y.C., 1963-67; chief economist Merrill Lynch, Pierce, Fenner & Smith, N.Y.C., 1967-71; rsch. dir. Estabrook & Co., N.Y.C., 1971-72; sr. v.p., chief economist White, Weld & Co., N.Y.C., 1972-78; chmn., pres., dir. A. Gary Shilling & Co., Inc., Springfield, N.J., 1978—; pres. Lakeview Econ. Svcs., Inc., Springfield, 1979—; owner Lakeview Svcs., Inc., Springfield, 1993—. Bd. dirs. Nat. Life Vt., Montpelier, Palm Harbor Homes, Am. Productivity and Quality Ctr., Houston; adv. dir. Austin (Tex.) Trust Co., 1988—; informal econ. advisor Former Pres. George Bush, 1978—; mem. Nat. Com. on Jobs and Small Bus., 1986-87. Author: Is Inflation Ending? Are You Ready?, 1983, The World Has Definitely Changed: New Economic Forces and Their Implications for the Next Decade, 1986, After the Crash: Recession or Depression? Investment and Business Strategies for a Deflationary World, 1988, Deflation: Why it's coming, whether it's good or bad, and how it will affect your investments, business, and personal affairs, 1998, Korean and Chinese edits., 2000, Deflation: How to Survive and Thrive in the Coming Wave of Deflation, 1999, Chinese edit., 2000, Letting Off Steam, 2003; creator bd. game The Deflation Game, 1989; columnist Forbes, 1983—, Nihon Keizai Shimbun Jour. Bd. dirs. Aim Packaging Inc., 1986-89, Episcopal Ch. Found., N.Y.C., N.Y., 1989-97; chmn. Episcopal Preaching Found., Springfield, N.J., 1988—; trustee Bates Coll., Lewiston, Maine, 1988-91, Kent Pl. Sch., Summit, N.J., 1983-89, Henry J. Kessler Found., 1987-95; bd. dirs. The Gen. Theol. Episcopal Sem., N.Y.C., 1988-2001, treas., 1994-2001; chmn. N.J. State Revenue Forecasting Adv. Commn., 1995—; bd. dirs. Am. Rep. Ins. Co. of N.Y., 1978-81, N.J. Shakespeare Festival, 1987-96, chmn., 1994-96. Named Wall St. Top Econs., Instl. Investor Mag., 1975, 76, Top Commodity Trading Advisor, Futures Mag., 1993, Third best Stockmarket Forecaster in the World, Money Sense Mag., 2003. Mem. Nat. Assn. Bus. Economics, N.Y. Soc. Security Analysts, Short Hills Club, Phi Beta Kappa, Sigma Xi. Republican. Episcopalian. Avocations: tennis, travel, gardening, hunting, fishing, beekeeping. Home: 33 Lakeview Ave Short Hills NJ 07078-2264 Office: A Gary Shilling & Co Inc 500 Morris Ave Springfield NJ 07081-1020 Office Phone: 973-467-0070. Business E-Mail: gary@agaryshilling.com.

SHILLING, JENNIFER, state official; b. Oshkosh, Wis., July 4, 1969; married. BA, U. Wis., 1992. State assemblywoman, Wis., 2000—. Mem. fin. instns. com.; mem. health com.; mem. ins. com.; mem. Minn.-Wis. Boundary Area Commn.; mem. personal privacy com. Congl. aide to U.S. Rep. Ron Kind; mem. La Crosse County Dem. Party, La Crosse County LWV. Democrat. Office: State Capitol PO Box 8953 Madison WI 53708-8953

SHILLING, KAY MARLENE, psychiatrist; b. July 1, 1953; d. Harrison Gene and Rose Marie (Allen) Herber. BS, U. Nebr., Lincoln, 1976; MD, U. Nebr., Omaha, 1980. Diplomate Nat. Bd. Med. Examiners. Resident in psychiatry U. Nebr. Med. Ctr., Omaha, 1981-84; pvt. practice Omaha, 1984—; med. dir., chief of staff La Plaza (Nebr.) Cmty. Health Ctr., 1999—, also bd. dirs. Bd. dirs. Indian Chicano Health Ctr., 1983—92, Omaha Symphony Guild, 1999—, encore chair, 2000—04, v.p. adminstrn., 2003—, mem. nominating com., 2002, chair Spring Fundraiser, 2004, exec. bd., 2003—04; mem. Henry Doorly Zoo Guild; chair ann. meeting Opera Omaha Guild, 2004—, chair Holiday meeting, 2004; mem. Fontenelle Nature assn. Guild, 1999—, Omaha Botanical Gardens Guild, 2001—, Opera Omaha Guild Bd., 2003—; chair spring fundraiser Omaha Symphony Music Cir., 2004, chair annual meeting, 2005; bd. dirs. Museo Latino Ferid, 2004—. Mem. AMA, Royal Soc. Medicine, Ctrl. Neuro Psychiat. Assn. (bd. dirs., pres. 1996-97), Am. Med. Women's Assn. (pres. Omaha chpt. 1986-88, Nebr. State dir. 1988-94, regional gov. 1993-95, bd. dirs. 1993-95, book reviewer for JAMWA, Outstanding Physician award 1989, 90-93, nat. cmty. svc. award 1990), Am. Psychiat. Assn., Met. Omaha Med. Soc., Nebr. Med. Assn., Kiwanis Internat., Alpha Xi Delta. Avocations: gardening, travel, gourmet cooking, interior decorating, house renovation. Home: 1103 S 80th St Omaha NE 68124-1419 Office: 7602 Pacific St Ste 302 Omaha NE 68114-5405

SHILLING, ROY BRYANT, JR., academic administrator; b. Enville, Okla., Apr. 7, 1931; s. Roy Bryant and Lila M. (Prestage) S.; m. Margaret Riddle, Oct. 16, 1952; children: Roy Bryant III, Nancy Gale. BA, McMurry U., 1951, HHD, 1982; BD, So. Meth. U., 1957; MS, Ind. U., 1966, PhD, 1967. Presdl. asst. McMurry U., Abilene, Tex., 1959-61; asst. to pres. Tenn. Wesleyan Coll., 1961-64; asst. in devel. Ball State U., 1964-65; rsch. assoc. Ind. U., 1965-67; dir. planning and rsch. Baldwin Wallace Coll., 1967-68; exec. v.p. Southwestern U., 1968-69, pres., 1981-2000, pres. emeritus, 2000—; pres. Hendrix Coll., 1969-81; interim pres. McMurry Univ., 2002. Mem. Nat. Commn. on United Meth. Higher Edn., 1975-77. Mem. Ark. Arts and Humanities Coun., 1970-76, chmn., 1974-75; bd. dirs. Ark. Children's Hosp., 1981; mem. bd. higher edn. and ministry United Meth. Ch., 1972-80, mem. univ. senate, 1980-88, v.p. 1983-84, pres., 1984-88; chmn. Gulf dist. Rhodes Scholarship Selection Com., 1992, Ark. chmn., 1973-74, Tex. chmn., 1985-91; mem. Young Pres. Orgn., 1975-81; mem. bd. visitors Air U., 1991-94. With U.S. Army, 1952-54. Recipient Disting. Alumnus award McMurry U., 1980, Perkins Disting. Alumnus award So. Meth. U., 1987, Owen B. Sherrill award for leadership in econ. devel. Georgetown, 1988; named one of Top 100 Most Effective Coll. Pres. in Nation, Bowling Green State U./Exxon Edn. Found., 1986. Mem. North Ctrl. Assn. Colls. and Schs. (vice chmn., chmn. elect 1980-81), Nat. Assn Schs. and Colls. of United Meth. Ch. (v.p. 1975-76, pres. 1976-77), Nat. Coun. Ind. Colls. and Univs. (bd. dirs. 1984-88), So. U. Conf. (exec. com. 1974-78), 79-86, sec.-treas. 1979-86, v.p. 1991-92, pres. 1992-93), Am. Coun. Edn. (bd. dirs. 1989-91; mem. commn. on govt. and pub. rels. 1999-2000, spl. counselor to the pres. 2000-01), Inst. for Humanities (bd. dirs. Salado, Tex. chpt. 1985-91, mem. internat. coun. advs. 1994), NCAA Divsn. III Pres.'s Coun., 1998-2000, Philos Soc. Tex., Rotary, Masons, Alpha Chi, Phi Delta Kappa. Office: 1405 Mesa Ridge Ln Austin TX 78735-1639 E-mail: shilling@southwestern.edu.

SHILLINGBURG, HERBERT THOMPSON, JR., dental educator; b. Mar. 21, 1938; s. Herbert Thompson and Stefi Marie (Schuster) Shillingburg; m. Constance Joanne Murphy, June 11, 1960; children: Lisa Grace, Leslie Susan, Lara Stephanie. Student, U. N.Mex., 1955-58, 65-66; DDS, U. So. Calif., 1962. Gen. practice dentistry, Albuquerque, 1964-67; asst. prof. fixed prosthodontics sect. UCLA Sch. Dentistry, 1967-70, chmn., 1970-72; chmn. dept. fixed prosthodontics U. Okla. Coll. Dentistry, Okla. City, 1972—2003, David Ross Boyd Disting. prof., 1983, prof. emeritus, 2003—. Cons. VA Hosp., Muskogee, Okla., 1975—84, Oklahoma City, 1977—93, U.S. Army Dental Activity, Ft. Knox, Ky., 1980—94. Author: (also in Japanese, German, Greek, Spanish, Italian, French, Portuguese, Polish, Korean, Chinese and Russian) Preparations for Cast Gold Restorations, 1974, Fundamentals of Fixed Prosthodontics, 1976, Fundamentals of Fixed Prosthodontics, 2d edit., 1981, Fundamentals of Fixed Prosthodontics, 3d edit., 1997, Guide to Occlusal Waxing, 1979, Guide to Occlusal Waxing, 2d edit., 1984, Guide to Occlusal Waxing, 3d edit., 2000, Restoration of the Endodontically Treated Tooth, 1984, Fundamentals of Tooth Preparations for Cast Metal and Porcelain Restorations, 1987; co-editor: Quintessence of Dental Technology, 1984—88. Capt. U.S. Army, 1962—64. Named Disting. Lectr., O U Assoc., 1989; recipient Award for tchg. excellence, UCLA Sch. Dentistry, 1969, 1972, 1973, Okla. Coll. Dentistry, 1976, 1978, 1982, 1987, 1993, 1994, 1st prize, Am. Med. Writers Assn., 1988, Award for tchg. excellence, Okla. Coll. Dentistry, 1997, La Mèdaille de la Ville de Paris (èchelon Argent), 1990, Outstanding Profl. Achievement award, O U Coll. Dentristy, 2003. Fellow: Am. Coll. Dentists; mem.: ADA, Okla. State Dental Assn., Internat. Assn. Dental Rsch., Am. Coll. Prosthodontists (hon.), Am. Acad. Restorative Dentistry, Am. Acad. Fixed Prosthodontics (George H. Moulton award 1998), Acad. Operative Dentistry, Phi Kappa Phi, Omicron Kappa Upsilon (Stephen H. Leeper award for tchg. excellence 2000). Independent. Episcopalian. Avocations: travel, photography. Home: 1312 Brixton Rd Edmond OK 73034-3314 Office: U Okla Coll Dentistry PO Box 26901 Oklahoma City OK 73190-0001

SHILLINGLAW, GORDON, accounting educator, consultant; b. Albany, N.Y., July 26, 1925; s. James McCombe and Margaret Blanche (Stephens) S.; m. Barbara Ann Cross, June 24, 1950; children— James McCombe, Laura Cross. AB magna cum laude, Brown U., 1945; MS, U. Rochester, 1948; PhD, Harvard U., 1952. Asst. prof. Hamilton Coll., Clinton, N.Y., 1951-52; cons. assoc. Joel Dean Assocs., Yonkers, N.Y., 1952-55; asst. prof. MIT, Cambridge, 1955-61; assoc. prof. Columbia U., N.Y.C., 1961-66, prof. acctg., 1966-90, prof. emeritus, 1991—. Vis. prof. Mgmt. Devel. Inst., Lausanne, Switzerland, 1964-65, 67-69; mem. U.S. Cost Acctg. Stds. Bd., 1978-80, U.S. R.R. Acctg. Prin. Bd., 1985-87; dir./trustee Scudder Funds, AARP Investment Program Funds, 1979-2000; cons. in field. Author: Managerial Cost Accounting, 1961, 5th edit., 1982, Accounting: A Managment Approach, 1964, 9th edit., 1993, Financial Accounting: Concepts and Applications, 1989; contbr. articles to profl. jours. Mem. bd. advisors Fund Directions, 1990-96; bd. dirs., treas. Feris Found. Am., Stamford, Conn., 1970-94. Served with U.S. Navy. 1943-46. Recipient Disting. Tchr. award, Columbia U., 1970, Lifetime Achievement

award, Instnl. Investor Newsletter, 2002. Mem. Am. Acctg. Assn. (v.p. 1966-67), Phi Beta Kappa, Beta Gamma Sigma. Avocations: tennis, travel, family history. Home: 115 Live Oak Ln Largo FL 33770-2657 Personal E-mail: gslive25@aol.com.

SHILLINGSBURG, MIRIAM JONES, English educator, academic administrator; b. Balt., Oct. 5, 1943; d. W. Elvin and Miriam R. Jones; m. Peter L. Shillingsburg, Nov. 21, 1967; children: Robert, George, John, Alice, Anne Carol. BA, Mars Hill Coll., 1964; MA, U. S.C., 1966, PhD, 1969; BGS, Miss. State U., 1994. Asst. prof. Limestone Coll., Gaffney, S.C., 1969, Miss. State U., 1970-75, assoc. prof., 1975-80, prof. English, 1980-96, assoc. v.p. for acad. affairs, 1988-96, dir. summer sch., 1990-96, dir. undergrad. studies, 1994-96; dean arts and scis. Lamar U., Tex., 1996-99; dean liberal arts and scis. Ind. U., South Bend, 2000—04. Disting. acad. visitor Mark Twain Ctr., 1993, 2001; Simms rsch. prof. U. S.C., 1998; vis. fellow Australian Def. Force Acad., 1989; Fulbright lectr. U. New South Wales, Duntroon, Australia, 1984-85. NEH fellow in residence, Columbia U., 1976-77. Author: Mark Twain in Australasia, 1988; editor: Conquest of Granada, 1988, The Cub of the Panther, 1997; mem. editl. bd. Works of W.M. Thackeray, Miss. Quar., So. Quar.; contbr. articles to profl. jours. and mags. Mem. South Cul. 18th Century Soc., Am. Lit. Assn., Pop Culture Assn., Sigma Tau Delta, Phi Kappa Phi, Simms Soc. (pres. 1996-97). Business E-Mail: mshillin@iusb.edu.

SHILOH, ALLEN, writer; b. Bastrop, La., May 24, 1947; s. Al and Rosia B (Davis) S.; children: Datoya Moneake Penn. Grad. high sch., Bastrop; student, Cal/Arts, 1966-68. Mail handler U.S. Postal Svc., Bell, Calif., 1972—. Author: (novels) The Brotherhood, Terror, 1973, Bayou Girl, 1990, (paperback) The Real First United States President, 1983, (short stories pub.) New Cosmic Star, 1968. Sgt. USAF, 1968-72, Vietnam. Avocations: photography, drawing. Home: 305 S Essey Ave Compton CA 90221-3417

SHILS, EDWARD B. finance educator, lawyer, arbitrator, mediator; b. Phila., May 29, 1915; s. Benjamin and Dinah (Berkowitz) Shils; m. Shirley Siegle, July 31, 1942; children: Ronnie Lois, Nancy Ellen, Edward Barry. BS in Econs., U. Pa., 1936, MA in Polit. Sci., 1937, PhD, 1940, JD, 1986, LLM, 1990, SJD, 1997; LLD (hon.), Phila. U., 1975; PhD (hon.), Tel-Aviv U., 1990. Bar: Pa. 1988, U.S. Dist. Ct. (ea. dist.) Pa. 1988. Rsch. assoc. FELS Inst. Local and State Govt. U. Pa., Phila., 1937—38, mem. faculty Wharton Sch., 1956—, assoc. chmn. mgmt. dept., 1960—63, prof. mgmt., chmn. mgmt dept., 1968—76, George W. Taylor prof. emeritus entrepreneurial studies, 1979, prof. emeritus polit. sci., 1985—, dir., founder Wharton Entrepreneurial Ctr., 1973—86, dir. Wharton Entrepreneurial Ctr., 1973—86, dir. emeritus, 1986—, jud. adminstr., 1986—90; rsch. assoc. Pa. Economy League, 1938—42; cons. job classification and wage adminstrn. Phila. City Coun., 1942—43; chief coordination and planning VA, Phila., 1947—48; dir. pub. edn. survey Greater Phila. Movement, 1950—51; sr. dept. head U.S. Wage Stabilization Bd., Phila., 1951; methods cons. Budget Office Gov. Pa., 1951—55; cons., dir. Dental Dealers Am., 1952—2001, dir. emeritus, cons., 2001—; cons. Phila. County Med. Soc., 1955—56; chmn. social sci. dept. C.C., Temple U., Phila., grad. lectr. pub. adminstrn., 1948—56; pvt. practice law Phila., 1988—; of counsel Sarner and Assocs., Phila.; disting. prof. entrepreneurial studies Tel Aviv U., 1991—95; atty., cons. Office Phila. Dist. Atty., 2001—. Pres. cons. Phila. Bd. Pub. Edn., 1946—75, cons. tchr. salary schedules, 1948—50, cons. labor rels., 1951—68; cons. dir. Knitted Outerwear Mfrs. Assn. Pa., 1952—, Fashion Apparel Mfrs. Pa., 1952—; dir. study to create Phila. C.C., 1956, St. Louis Jr. Coll. Sys., 1960; cons. Phila. Psychiatry Ctr., 1971—76, Am. Bd. Internal Medicine, 1973—77, Girard Coll., 1974, Royal Coll. Physicians and Surgeons Can., 1977—80; cons. econ. Phila. New Conv. Ctr., 1988—90; mgmt. advisor Phila. Dist. Atty., 1992—93; dir., chmn. audit com. Vishay Intertechnology, Inc., 1983—; cons. econs. Phila. Profl. Sports Consortium, 1983—89, profl. sports, Washington, 1986—87. Author: Finances and Financial Adminstration of Philadelphia's Public Schools 1923-1939, 1940, Automation & Industrial Relations, 1964, Teachers, Administrators & Collective Bargaining, 1968, Industrial Peacemaker: George W. Taylor's Contributions to Collective Bargaining, 1979; co-editor: Frontiers of Entrepreneurship Research, 1985, The Shils Report, Impact of Mega Retail Chains on Small Enterprise, 1997. Chmn. bd. dirs., hon. pres. Pathway Sch., Jeffersonville, Pa., 1970—84; pres. Philadelphians for Good Govt., 1991—93, hon. pres., 1992—95; v.p. Fedn. Jewish Agys. Phila., 1976—84, Life Trust Fedn. Jewish Agys., 1990—; life trustee, hon chmn. trustee com. edn. Phila. U. Officer Signal Corps U.S. Army, 1943—46. Named Edward B. Shils professorship in his honor, U. Pa. Law Sch., 1991, Edward B. and Shirley R. Shils Term Professorship in his honor, 2001; recipient Alumni award of Merit, U. Pa., 2001. Mem.: ADA (Edward B. Shils Ednl. Entrepreneurial Fund named in his honor 2003), Jewish Publs. Soc. Am. (pres. 1978—81, hon. pres. 1982—), Green Valley Country Club (Plymouth, Pa.), Faculty Club U. Pa. (pres. 1966—69, 1987—92, bd. govs. 1993—), Shriners, Masons (32 degree), Union League Pa. (pres. Wishbone Club 2003). Home: 335 S Woodbine Ave Narberth PA 19072-1525 Office: U Pa Wharton Sch Philadelphia PA 19104 Also: 123 S Broad St Philadelphia PA 19109-1029 Office Phone: 215-731-9982. Business E-Mail: shilse@wharton.edu.

SHILS, MAURICE EDWARD, physiologist, educator, research scientist; b. Atlantic City, Dec. 31, 1914; s. Samuel L. and Sarah (Harris) S.; m. Cylia Finkiel, Feb. 19, 1939 (dec. Sept. 1987); children: Loraine J., Jonathan R.; m. Betty Ann Bell, Sept. 24, 1988. BA, Johns Hopkins U., 1937, ScD, 1940; MD, NYU, 1958. Intern joint program Cornell divsn. Bellevue Hosp. and Meml. Hosp., N.Y.C., 1958-59; fellow in physiology Meml. Hosp., 1959-60; instr., asst. prof. nutrition Sch. Pub. Health Columbia U., N.Y.C., 1946-54; instr. biochemistry Sch. Hygiene Johns Hopkins U., Balt., 1940-42; head Ctrl. Metabolic Lab. Sloan Kettering Inst., N.Y.C., 1960-72; from asst. to assoc. attending physician Meml. Hosp., N.Y.C., 1962-72, attending physician, 1972-85; asst. prof. biochem. Sloan-Kettering divsn. Med. Coll. Cornell U., N.Y.C., 1959-62, from asst. prof. to prof. medicine Med. Coll., 1962-85, prof. emeritus, 1985—. Adj. prof. nutrition dept. pub. health scis. Wake Forest U. Sch. Medicine, Winston-Salem, N.C., 1989-94, cons., 1994-97. Author, sr. editor: Modern Nutrition in Health and Disease, 9th edit., 1998; contbr. more than 200 rsch. and review articles to profl. jours. Fellow Am. Coll. Physicians, N.Y. Acad. Medicine (Acad. Plaque award 1987), Soc. Nutritional Scis.; mem. AMA (chmn. nutrition adv. group 1974-77, Goldberger award 1983), Am. Soc. Clin. Nutrition (pres. 1985-86, Excellence in Med. Sch. award 1994), Am. Bd. Physician Nutrition Specialists, Phi Beta Kappa, Alpha Omega Alpha. E-mail: mshils@triad.rr.com.

SHILTS, NANCY S. automotive executive, lawyer; b. Clinton, Mass., Feb. 10, 1942; BA, Smith Coll., 1963; JD, U. Mich., 1980. Bar: Mich. 1980. Assoc. gen. counsel Fed.-Mogul Corp., Southfield, Mich. Mem. ABA, State Bar Mich. Office: Fed Mogul Corp 26555 Northwestern Hwy Southfield MI 48034-2199

SHIM, ELISABETH K. dermatologist, writer; b. Chgo., Ill. BS, Northwestern U., 1990; MD, Northwestern U., 1994. Assoc. clin. prof. U. So. Calif. Med. Ctr., L.A. Fellow: Am. Soc. for Dermatologic Surgery, Am. Coll. Mohs Micrographic Surgery, Am. Acad. Dermatology. Office: Ste 570 1301 20th St Santa Monica CA 90404

SHIM, LEEM SEOP, computer scinetist, educator, researcher; b. Seoul, Korea (South), Aug. 23, 1954; s. Sang Don Shim and Jung Hee Park; m. Jong Sook Kim, Dec. 15, 1957; children: David Jaewoo, Mijung. BSEE, Seoul Nat. U., 1978; MS in Computer Sci., Ill. Inst. Tech., 1987, PhD in Computer Sci., 1991. Engr. Hyundai Engring. & Constrn. Co., Ltd., 1980—82; adj. prof. Govs. State U., University Park, Ill., 1990—91; asst. to assoc. prof. Hanshin U., Osan-si, Republic of Korea, 1994—2000; assoc. prof. Trinity Christian Coll., Palos Heights, 2000—02, Ind. U. Pa., Indiana, 2002—. Com. mem. UNB Internat. Symposium Artificial Intelligence, Frederickton, New Brunswick, Canada, 1991, Joint Conf. Artificial Intelligence, Expert Sys., Neural Networks and Fuzzy, Seoul, 1992; dept. chairperson Info. Sci. and Telecom., Hanshin U., Osan-si, Kyunggi-do, 1994—97; v.p. faculty union Hanshin U., Osan-si, Kyunggi-do, 1996—98, dean student affairs, 1998—99. Contbr. articles to profl. jours. 1st lt. Army of Republic of Korea, 1978—80, Seoul. Mem.: Korea Elec. and Electronic Assn., Korea Info. Sci. Soc., Internat. Soc. Tech.n Edn., IEEE Computer Soc., Assn. Computing Machinery. Achievements include research in rehabilitation training system for developmental disable people using multimedia data; English tutoring system using multimedia data; intelligent tutoring system for cardiovascular system; intelligent traffic information system; satellite mobile communication system analysis. Home: 214 Whippoorwill St Indiana PA 15701 Office: Ind Univ of Pa 210 S Tenth St Indiana PA 15705-1087 Personal E-mail: lshim@hanmail.net. E-mail: shim@iup.edu.

SHIM, SANG KOO, mental health services professional; b. Tokyo, Oct. 1, 1942; arrived in U.S., 1968; s. Sang Taek and Kum Ryon (Bae) Shim; m. Jae Hee Lee, July 12, 1972; children: Tammy, David. BS, Seoul (Republic of Korea) Nat. U., 1967; MBA, No. Ill. U., 1970; MS, U. Wis., 1975. CPA Ill. Acct. Vaughn Mfg. Co., Chgo., 1970-72, Stewart-Warner Corp., Chgo., 1972-73; fin. cons. Cen. Acctg. Assn., New Baden, Ill., 1977-79; auditor Ill. Dept. Mental Health, Springfield, 1980-82, CFO, 1983-97; chief bur. gen. acctg. Ill. Dept. Human Svcs., Springfield, 1997—2002. Treas. Korean Assn. Greater St. Louis, 1982. Mem.: Assn. Govt. Accts. (cert. govt. fin. mgr.), Ill. CPA Soc., Korean-Am. C. of C. (v.p. Greater St. Louis chpt. 1994—95). Office: Shim & Co, CPA 1600 Lebanon Ave Belleville IL 62221 Home: PO Box 4187 Fairview Heights IL 62208-4187 Office Phone: 618-257-1788. E-mail: skshim@aol.com.

SHIM, SANG-YEUN, mathematician, researcher; arrived in U.S., 1995; PhD, N.Y. U., N.Y.C., 2000. Associated rsch. scientist N.Y.U., N.Y.C., 1999—2002; rsch. analyst Global Fixed Income, Citigroup, N.Y.C., 2003—. Contbr. articles to profl. jours. Recipient Silver medal First Physics Olympiad, Korean Phys. Soc., 1989, Nat. winner Tenth Math Competition, Korean Math. Soc., 1991. Mem.: Am. Math. Soc. Achievements include research in efficient computational methods in inverse scattering; new algebraic solution in matrix splitting; development of calibration of multi-factor BGM model; math. proof of selective decay principle in geophysical flows. Office: Citigroup 10th Fl 388 Greenwich St New York NY 10013

SHIMADA, HARUO, physical chemistry educator; b. Himeji, Hyōgo, Japan, Mar. 27, 1935; s. Shigeyoshi and Shige (Okamoto) S.; m. Ikuko Tanaka, Sept. 21, 1968; children: Yōko, Kenichiro. Grad., U. Tokyo, 1958, doctorate, 1968. Rschr. Yawata (Japan) Iron & Steel Co., 1958-72; sr. rschr. Nippon Steel Corp., Kawasaki, Japan, 1973-80, chief rschr., 1980-90; prof. Sci. U. Tokyo, Shinjuku, Japan, 1990—. Editorial mem.: (monthly jour.) Chem. Industry, 1972—; contbr. articles to profl. jours. Mem. AAAS, Nat. Assn. Corrosion Engrs., Internat. Tech. Inst. (life mem.). Avocations: jogging, swimming. Home: Chuō 5-3-5 Tokyo Ota 143-0024 Japan Office: Sci Univ Tokyo 1-3 Kagurazaka Shinjuku 1628601 Japan

SHIMADA, KATSUNORI, retired electrical engineer; b. Tokyo, Mar. 12, 1922; arrived in U.S., 1950; s. Katsujiro and Mume Shimada; m. Ikuko Ueno, Oct. 30, 1975; m. Kazuko Matsumoto; children: Karl, Keiko Shimada Stearns. BSEE, U. Tokyo, 1945; MSEE, U. Minn., 1954, PhD, 1958. Engr. Toshiba Japan, Kawasaki, Japan, 1945—50; instr. U. Minn., Mpls., 1950—58; asst. prof. engring. U. Wash., Seattle, 1958—64; supr. JPL, G&C Rsch. Group, Pasadena, Calif., 1964—80; mgr., Field Ctr. Integration JPL, Pasadena, Calif., 1980—85, supr. Celestial Sensors, 1985—89; ret., 1989. Cons. Boeing Co., Seattle, 1960—63, NASDA of Japan, L.A., 1987—91; invited prof. engring. U. Tokyo, 1973; invited lectr. NEDO of Japan, Tokyo, 1983. Contbr. articles to profl. jours., tech. reports and memoranda. Com. mem. Nat. Parents Day Coalition, L.A., 1996—99, RSVP of Pasadena, 1993—95, Assoc. Retirees of Caltech/JPL, Pasadena, 1998—. Fellow Resident rsch., JPL, 1963—64. Mem.: AIAA, IEEE (sr.), Sigma Xi, Eta Kappa Nu. Achievements include patents for Cavity Emitter for Thermionics, 1969; Thermionic Diode Switch, 1975; Solid State Power Converter, 1979. Avocations: photography, computers, golf, travel. Home: 3840 Edgeview Dr Pasadena CA 91107

SHIMBERG, ELAINE FANTLE, writer; b. Yankton, SD, Feb. 26, 1937; d. Karl S. and Alfreda (Edelson) Fantle; m. Mandell Shimberg, Oct. 1, 1961; children: Karen, Scott, Betsy, Andrew, Michael. BS, Northwestern U., 1958; LHD (hon.), U. South Fla., 2002. Co-hostess Women's Point of View talk show Sta. WFLA-TV, Tampa, Fla., 1976-81; tchr. Writing for Publication and Profit, Hillsborough C.C., Tampa, 1980-82. Author: How to be A Successful Housewife/Writer, 1979, Two for the Money: A Woman's Guide to a Double Career Marriage, 1981; contbg. author: The Complete Guide to Writing Non-Fiction, 1983, Coping with Kids and Vacation, 1986, Relief From Irritable Bowel Syndrome, 1988, Strokes: What Families Should Know, 1990, Depression: What Families Should Know, 1992, Gifts of Time, 1993, Living with Tourette Syndrome, 1995, How to Get Out of the Hospital Alive, 1997, Blending Families, 1999, Write Where You Live, 1999, Coping with Chronic Heartburn, 2001, Coping with Chronic Obstructive Pulmonary Disease, 2003, Another Chance for Love, 2004; contbr. articles to popular mags. Pub. info. com. Fla. divsn. Am. Cancer Soc., 1974—89; bd. dirs. United Way, 1986—89, St. Joseph's Hosp., Tampa, 1985—; chmn. bd. St. Joseph's-Bapt. Health Care Alliance, 2003—. Mem. Am. Soc. Journalists and Authors, Am. Med. Writers Assn., Fla. Med. Assn. (coun. ethical and jud. affairs 1993—). Office: 611 W Bay St Tampa FL 33606-2703 Office Phone: 813-259-9673.

SHIMELMAN, SUSAN FROMM, state policy administrator; b. NYC, May 5, 1942; BA, McGill U., Montreal, 1964; MS, Columbia U., 1970. Fellow Harvard U., Cambridge, Mass., 1964-65; Can. coun. fellow McGill U., Montreal, 1965-68; asst. dir. Yale-New Haven Hosp., 1970-80; exec. dir. New Haven Jewish Fedn., 1980-90; undersec. Office Policy and Mgmt., State of Conn., Hartford, 1991-94, sec., 1994—95, dir. presdl. debates, 1995; dir. spl. cts. jud. br. State of Conn., 1995—2001; dir. Office Fiscal Analysis, 2001—. Chair Prison and Jail Overcrowding Commn., Hartford, 1990—, Health Care State Conn., Hartford, 1992—, Exec. Com. Info. and Tech., Hartford, 1994; vice chair Cmty. Econ. Devel. Found., Hartford, 1994. Bd. dirs. Fedn. United Way, New Haven, 1970-94; alt. N.E. Regional Compact, N.J. and Conn., 1991-94; active A Conn. Party, Hartford, 1990-94. Recipient Pres. award New Haven Jewish Fedn., 1990; named Powerful Woman of Vision, YWCA, 1988. Democrat. Home: 4 Kensington Park Bloomfield CT 06002-2146

SHIMER, DANIEL LEWIS, treasurer; b. San Angelo, Tex., July 30, 1944; s. Lewis V. and Mary A. (Slick) S.; married. BS in Acctg. and Mktg., Ind. U., 1972; postgrad., Loyola U., New Orleans, 1977. CPA. Sr. acct. Peat, Marwick, Mitchell & Co., Indpls., 1973-75; asst. treas. LTV Corp., Dallas, 1975-79; v.p. fin. Stoller Chem. Co., Houston, 1979-81; v.p., CFO Petro-Silver, Inc., Denver, 1981-83; v.p., treas. FoxMeyer Corp., Denver, 1983-86; v.p., treas., sec. CoastAmerica Corp., Denver, 1986-88; exec. v.p. Bard & Co., Denver, 1989-90; pres. nat accounts divsn. I Can't Believe It's Yogurt/ Brice Foods, Inc., Dallas, 1991-93; exec. v.p., CFO COREStaff Inc., Houston, 1994-96; venture ptnr. Austin Ventures, Dallas, 1996—2004; vice-chmn. ePartners, Inc., Dallas, 1996—; pres. Shimer Capital Ptnrs., Inc., Dallas, 1996—. Methodist. Avocations: carpentry, fishing. Home: 7436 Glenshannon Cir Dallas TX 75225-2048

SHIMIZU, IRIS M. statistician, consultant; b. Ark. d. Curtis Howard and Edna M. Moore; m. Matti Shimizu, 1972; 1 child, Jesse. BS in Math., South Ark. U., 1965; MS in Math., U. Ark., 1967; PhD in Math. Stats., Fla. State U., 1971. Instr. U. Mo., Columbia, 1970—71; math. statis.-biomed. specialist Nat. Ctr. for Health Statis., Hyattsville, Md., 1971—. Cons., lectr. in field. Contbr. articles to profl. jours. Recipient Exemplary Svc. award, Office of Asst. Sec. for Health, 1983. Mem.: Washington Statis. Soc., Internat. Assn. Survey Statisticians, Am. Statis. Assn. Avocation: puzzles. Office: Nat Ctr for Health Statis 3311 Toledo Rd Hyattsville MD 20782

SHIMIZU, KAZUHIKO, education educator; b. Akeno, Japan, Jan. 20, 1952; s. Kazuyoshi and Toyoko S.; m. Tsurumi Tamagawa, March 30, 1979; children: Kazutaka, Kazuma, Kazuki. BA, Tokyo U. Edn., 1974, MA, 1976; PhD, U. Tsukuba, Japan, 1997. Rsch. fellow Japan Soc. for the Promotion of Sci., Tokyo, 1980-81; asst. prof. Seisen Women's Jr. Coll., Nagano, Japan, 1983-86, assoc. prof., 1986-88; asst. prof. U. Tsukuba, 1988-91, assoc. prof., 1991-99, prof., 1999—, asst. pres., 2004—, pres., assoc. provost, 2004. Vis. assoc. prof. U. Hiroshima, 1992-96; vis. scholar U. Pa., Phila., 1995-96, U. Minn., Mpls., 2002; spl. lectr. Yonsei U., Seoul, Korea, 1996; guest lectr. Nat. Edn. Commn., Beijing, 1998, East China Normal U., Shanghai, 2001. Author: Comparative and Hist. Study of Univ. Credit Sys. Between USA and Japan, 1998, Univ. Reform in Japan, 1999; author and editor: A Databook of Edn. Statistics, 2002, Development of University Evaluation, 2004. Mem. Coun. for Univ. Chartering and Sch. Judicial Person (Monbusho), 2000-02; mem. Japanese Univ. Accreditation Assn., 1994-2000; trustee Assn. for the Advancement of Colls. in Japan, 1994—; mem. Inter-Univ. Seminar House, Tokyo, 1997-2002. Recipient rsch. fund Assn. Internat. Edn., Japan, 1990, grant-in-aid for sci. rsch. Ministry of Edn., Sci., Sport and Culture (Monbusho), Tokyo, 1998, 2000, 01, 03, 04. Mem.: Japanese Assn. Higher Edn. Rsch. (editor 2000—02, trustee 2003—), Japan Soc. Ednl. Sys. and Orgn. (office dir. 1999—), Japan Assn. Lifelong Edn. (office dir. 1998—2000), Comparative and Internat. Edn. Soc. Avocation: gardening. Home: 9015 Uede 407-0204 Yamanashi-ken Japan Office: Faculty of Edn U Tsukuba 1-1-1 Tennodai 305-8572 Tsukuba-shi Japan Office Phone: 81-29-853-6740. E-mail: shimizuk@sakura.cc.tsukuba.ac.jp.

SHIMIZU, YOSHIAKI, art historian, department chairman; b. Tokyo, Feb. 27, 1936; came to U.S., 1953, naturalized, 1999; s. Mamoru and Michiko (Hayasaka) S.; children: Karen Akiko Marie, Kenneth Cuyler Norio, Katherine Kimie, Kei Robert. BA, Harvard U., 1963; MA, U. Kans., 1968; MFA, Princeton U., 1971, PhD, 1974. Asst. prof. dept. art and archaeology Princeton (N.J.) U., 1973-75, prof., 1984—, chmn. dept. art and archaeology, 1990-92, Marquand prof. art & archaeology, 1992—; asst. prof. U. Calif., Berkeley, 1975-78, assoc. prof., 1978-79; curator Japanese art Freer Gallery, Smithsonian Instn., Washington, 1979-84; guest curator Nat. Gallery Art, Washington, 1982-89; guest prof. U. of Heidelberg, 1993. Guest prof. Ritsumeikan U., 1996; vis. fellow dept. art history U. Tokyo, 1996; mem. art adv. com. Japan Soc. Gallery, 1984—, adv. com. Asia Soc. Galleries, N.Y.C., 1992—, chmn. adv. com., 1999—; vis. fellow dept. comparative culture Sophia U., Tokyo, 1993. Author: (with John M. Rosenfield) Masters of Japanese Calligraphy, 1984; editor: (with Carolyn Wheelwright) Japanese Ink Paintings, 1976; author, editor: Japan: The Shaping of Daimyo Culture 1185-1858, 1988; mem. editorial bd. Archives of Asian Art, 1979-89. Adv. bd. Asian Art, Smithsonian Inst., 1985-93; mem. vis. com. Arthur M. Sackler Gallery, Washington, 1984-94. Smithsonian Inst. fellow, 1967, Social Sci. Rsch. Coun./Am. Coun. Learned Socs. fellow, 1977-78, Asian Cultural Coun. fellow, 1995. Mem. Coll. Art Assn. (bd. dirs. 1987-91), Japan Art History Assn., Japan Soc. N.Y., Ctr. for the Study of Japanese Woodblock Prints (mem. internat. adv. bd. 1983—) Home: 2 College Rd Princeton NJ 08540-5108 Office: Princeton U Dept Art and Archaeology Princeton NJ 08540 E-mail: shimizu@princeton.edu.

SHIMKHADA, DEEPAK, art historian; b. Darkha, Nepal, Sept. 5, 1945; s. Ratna Prasad and Kausalya Shimkhada; m. Kanti Koirala, July 7, 1970; children: Leepi, Riti. BFA, U. Of Baroda, 1968; MFA, U. Of Baroda, Baroda, India, 1970; MA, U. Of So. Calif., 1974; PhD, Claremont u., 2001. Prof. Rio Hondo Coll., Whittier, Calif., 1995—96, Mt. San Antonio Coll., Walnut, Calif., 1997—98; asst. prof. Claremont Mckenna Coll., Claremont, California, Calif., 1999—. Pres. Found. For Indic Philosophy & Culture, Claremont, 2001—; vis. prof. Scripps Coll., Claremont, 1981—82. Contbr. exhibition catalog Usc Collects: A Sampling Of Taste, 1973; author: (exhibition catalog) NEPALI ART; Author, Man, Woman, and Nature in Asian Art, exhibition catalog, 1982, 1973; editor: (compilation) Original Buddhist Mantras In Sanskrit, 1985 (grantee N.Am. Buddhist Found., 1984), Himalayas At A Crossroads: The Portrait Of A Changing World, 1988; contbr. Woven Jewels, 1992. Founder Himalayan Arts Coun. of Pacific Asia Mus., Pasadena, Calif., 1986—94. Recipient Cert. award, Nepal Assn. of Fine Arts, 1966, 1969, Grad. Students Alumni Rsch. award, Ohio State U., 1980; fellow Fulbright fellow, U.S. Dept. Of State, 1972—74, Tuition fellowship, U. Of Chgo., 1974—77; grantee Sr. Cultural fellow, Govt. Of India, 1968—70, Jr. Rsch. fellow, Am. Inst. Of Indian Studies, 1978—79. Mem.: Am. Nepal Soc. Calif. (pres. 1998—2000), Art Hist. of So. Calif., South Asia Soc., Assn. For Asian Studies, Assn. for Asian Studies (grantee 1989). Home: 1682 Lowell Avenue Claremont CA 91711

SHIMKUS, JOHN MONDY, congressman; b. Collinsville, Ill., Feb. 21, 1958; s. Gene Louis and Kathleen (Mondy) S.; m. Karen Kay Muth; children: David, Joshua. BS, U.S. Mil. Acad., 1980; MBA, So. Ill. U., Edwardsville, 1997. Advanced through grades to capt. U.S. Army, 1980-86; stationed at U.S. Army Base, Columbus, Ga., 1980-81, 85, served at Bamberg, Germany, 1981-84, stationed at Monterey, Calif, 1985-86; tchr. Metro East Luth. H.S., Edwardsville, Ill., 1986-90; treas. Madison County, Edwardsville, 1990-96; mem. U.S. Congress from 19th Ill. dist., 1997—, mem. energy and commerce com. Liaison officer U.S. Mil. Acad., 1987-96; treas. So. Ill. Law Enforcement Commn., 1990-96. Bd. dirs. Sr. Citizen Companion Program, Belleville, Ill., 1991; trustee Collinsville Twp., Ill., 1989-93; Rep. precinct committeeman, Collinsville, 1988—. Maj. USAR. Mem. Nat. Assn. County Treas. and Fin. Officers (bd. dirs.), Ill. County Treas. Assn., Am. Legion Post 365. Republican. Lutheran. Home: 504 Sumner Blvd Collinsville IL 62234-1934 Office: US Ho of Reps 513 Cannon HOB Washington DC 20515-1320 also: 3130 Chatham Rd Ste C Springfield IL 62704

SHIMMIN, MARGARET ANN, women's health nurse; b. Forbes, N.D., Oct. 26, 1941; d. George and Reba S. Diploma in Nursing, St. Luke's Hosp. Sch. Nursing, Fargo, N.D., 1962; BSW, U. West Fla., 1978; cert. ob-gyn nurse practitioner, U. Ala., Birmingham, 1983, MPH, 1986. Lic. nurse, Fla., N.D., Ala. Head nurse, emergency room St. Luke's Hosps., Fargo, 1962-67; charge nurse, labor and delivery, perinatal nurse educator Sacred Heart Hosp., Pensacola, Fla., 1970-82; ARNP Escambia County Pub. Health Unit, Pensacola, 1983-89; cmty. health nursing cons. Dist. 1 Health and Rehab. Svcs., Pensacola, 1989-96; sr. cmty. health nursing supr. Escambia County Health Dept., Pensacola, 1996—. Capt. nurse corps U.S. Army, 1967-70, Japan. Mem. NAACOG (cert. maternal-gynecol.-neonatal nursing 1978, ob-gyn nurse practitioner 1983), Fla. Nurses' Assn., ANA, N.W. Fla. ARNP (past sec./treas.), Fla. Perinatal Assn., Nat. Perinatal Assn., Healthy Mothers/Healthy Babies Coalition, Fla. Pub. Health Assn., U. West Fla. Alumni Assn., U. Ala. at Birmingham Sch. of Public Health Alumni Assn., Phi Alpha. Republican. Presbyterian. Avocations: cooking, music, travel, photography, reading. Home: 8570 Olympia Rd Pensacola FL 32514-8029 Office: Escambia County Health Dept 1295 W Fairfield Dr Pensacola FL 32501-1107 Office Phone: 850-595-6524.

SHIMODA, JERRY YASUTAKA, retired national historic park manager; b. Haleiwa, Hawaii, Mar. 21, 1930; s. Tamotsu and Sasai Shimoda; m. Clara H. Segawa, Aug. 7, 1954; children: Karen Marie K., Randall T., Shaun T., Teri Ellen H., Jacqueline Y., David Y. BA in Govt., U. Hawaii, 1952, MA in Far Ea. Area Studies, 1957; postgrad., St. Louis U., 1957-59. Historian Jefferson Nat. Expansion Meml. Nat. Hist. Site, St. Louis, 1957-60; chief historian, in charge hist. rsch. and visitor svcs. Saratoga Nat. Hist. Park, Stillwater, N.Y., 1960-66; chief historian Home of Franklin D. Roosevelt Nat. Hist. Site and, Frederick Vanderbilt Nat. Hist. Site, Hyde Park, N.Y., 1966-69; instr. Nat. Park Svc. Stephen T. Mather Tng. Ctr., Harpers Ferry, W.Va., 1969-72; supt. Pu'uhonua o Honaunau (Hawaii) Nat. Hist. Park, 1972-96, Puukohola Heiau Nat. Hist. Site, Kawaihae, 1972-96; ret., 1996. Lectr. environ. edn. Pa. State U., U. W.Va., Shepard Coll., 1969—72; acting supr. Kaloko-Honokohau Nat. Hist. Pk., 1988—90; instr. environ. edn., interpretive and basic instructing techniques U. Hawaii, Hilo, Kapiolani C.C.; instr. Japanese culture U. Hawaii, Hilo, 1994; U.S. del. and translator U.S.-Japan Panel on Nat. Parks and Equivalent Res., 1968—97, World Conf. on Marine Parks, Tokyo, 1975; mem. internat. bd. dirs. Heritage Interpretation Internat., 1989—98; presenter in field. Author booklets on nat. parks, mgmt. and history; contbr. numerous articles to profl. publs., mags. and newspapers. Bd. dirs. Volcano Art Ctr.; mem. adv. com. Wailoa State Ctr.; mem. Hawaii Gov.'s Task Force on Ocean and Recreation; chmn. restoration com. St. Benedict's Ch., Honaunau, 1982-95; chmn. bd. dirs. Kahua Na'au 'Ao, 1996-97; vol. training cons. to Nat. Pk. Svc., 1996-2001; cons. Nat. Park Svc., 2001-. Recipient Spl. Achievement award Nat. Park Svc., 1964, 68, 70, resolution W.Va. Senate, 1971, Hawaii Ho. of Reps., 1982, sec.'s cert. Dept. Interior, 1971, Exec. of Yr.

award West Hawaii chpt. Profl. Secs. Internat., 1981, cert. Govt. of Japan, 1981, staff plaque Pu'uhonua o Honaunau Nat. Hist. Park, Puukohola Heiau Nat. Hist. Site and Kaloko-Honokohau Nat. Hist. Park, 1988, cert. Japan Nat. Parks Assn., 1989, cert. of appreciation South Kona Aloha Lions Club, 1990, Meritorious Svc. award Sec. Interior, 1996, others. Mem. Hawaii Mus. Assn. (bd. dirs. 1988-92), Kona Hist. Soc. (bd. dirs. 1988-92), Big Island Ocean Recreation and Tourism Assn. (exec. com.), Kona Judo Club (pres. 1977-96), Rotary (pres. Kona Mauka 1978-79, co-founder Volcano chpt. 2001, Paul Harris fellow 1991, Disting. Svc. award 1992). Avocations: writing, reading, travel, teaching.

SHIMOFF, PAUL MARTIN, lawyer; b. San Francisco, Nov. 1, 1947; s. Marcus and Louise Barbara (Jacobs) S.; m. Susan Louise Richmond, Aug. 27, 1972; children: Aaron, Jared. BA, UCLA, 1969; JD, U. Calif. Hastings Coll. Law, 1972. Bar: Calif. 1972, U.S. Dist. Ct. (so. and cen. dists.) Calif. 1972, U.S. Ct. Appeals (9th cir.) 1972, U.S. Tax Ct. 1973, U.S. Ct. Claims 1973, U.S. Supreme Ct. 2001; cert. specialist in taxation law, Calif. Shareholder McPeters, McAlearney Shimoff & Hatt, PC, Redlands, Calif., 1985—98; vice chmn. Inland Action, Inc., Redlands, 1998—. Bd. dirs. San Bernardino Legal Aid Soc., 1985-86; advisor San Bernadino Cmty. Law-Related Edn., 1985; bd. dirs. Inland Empire Symphony, San Bernadino, 1981; bd. dir., v.p. Inland Action Cmty. Hosp. San Bernardino; trustees, U. Calif., Riverside. Found. State Bar Calif.; pres. San Bernardino Valley Coll. Found. Fellow Am. Coll. Trusts and Estates Counsel; mem. San Bernardino County Bar Assn. (pres. 1985-86), Estate Planning Coun. San Bernardino County (pres. 1985-86), Calif. Bd. Legal Specialization (cert.). Home: 12912 Hilary Way Redlands CA 92373-7466 Office: 4 W Redlands Blvd Fl 2 Redlands CA 92373-4702 Office Phone: 909-792-8919. E-mail: pms@mmsh.net.

SHIMOKUBO, JANICE TERUKO, marketing professional; b. Chgo. d. Paul Kazuso and Tsugiye Jane (Fujii) Shimokubo; m. Ronald Theodore Spreigl, Jan. 3, 1982; 1 child, Elizabeth Shimokubo Spreigl. BA, U. Ill., 1973; MBA, Loyola U., Chgo., 1976. Sales rep. 3M Co., Rockford, Ill., 1976-79, mktg. coord. St. Paul, 1979-81, mktg. supr., 1981-83, mktg. mgr., 1983-88, sales and mktg. mgr., 1988-90; mktg. dir. U S WEST Comms., Inc., Phoenix, 1990-95, exec. dir. Denver, 1995—. Advisor Jr. Achievement, St. Paul, 1980-82; mem. 3M Women's Adv. Coun., St. paul, 1984-87. Commr. Colo. Civil Rights commn., Denver, 1997—; bd. dirs. Ariz. Kidney Found., Phoenix, 1994-95, Phoenix Fire Pals, 1990-92, Melpomene Women's Health, St. Paul., 1986, YWCA USA, 1998—. Recipient Unity award KWGN-TV, 1997; Asian Pacific Am. Women's Leadership Inst. fellow, 1996. Fellow Internat. Women's Forum, 1998-99; mem. Am. Mktg. Assn. (nat. bd. dirs. 1999—), Women in Cable and Telecomms., Japanese Am. Citizens League, U. Ill. Alumni Assn., Alpha Omicron Pi. Avocations: golf, yoga, travel, needlecrafts. Home: Apt 2507 440 N Wabash Avenue Chicago IL 60611-7640

SHIMP, KAREN ANN, accountant, municipal financial executive; b. Atlantic, Iowa, July 17, 1959; d. Emerson Arnold and Verna Louise (Schmeling) Fett; m. Philip Kenneth Shimp, Jan. 30, 1988 (div.); 1 child, Keith Emerson. BSBA, Drake U., 1981. Acct. Midwest Mut. Ins. Co., West Des Moines, Iowa, 1981-84; staff acct. Deborah J. Kent, CPA, Palm Desert, Calif., 1985; fin. analyst Massey Sand & Rock Co., Indio, Calif., 1986-88; supr. interline Greyhound Lines, Inc., West Des Moines, 1989-93; fin. dir. City of Pella, Iowa, 1994-2000; dir. fin. orgnl. svcs. Cedar Falls (Iowa) Utilities, 2000—. Coord. Drake U. Bus. Aid Soc., 1980; mem. Inland Soc. Tax Consultants, 1987-91. Treas. Luth. Women's Missionary League, Indio, 1986-88, sec., 1988-89; v.p. Aid Assn. for Lutherans, Indio, 1988-89; bd. dirs. After School Kid's Klub, 1995-97. State of Iowa scholar, 1977. Mem. Inst. Mgmt. Accts., Kiwanis Internat (treas. 1996-97). Democrat. Avocations: sewing, reading, aerobics, taxes. Office: CVU Utility Pkwy PO Box 769 Cedar Falls IA 60613 Home: 915 W 10th St Cedar Falls IA 50613-2401 E-mail: kshimp@cfunet.net.

SHIMPOCK, KATHY ELIZABETH, lawyer, writer; b. Mooresville, N.C., July 20, 1952; d. Charles Walter and Minna Ethel (McLean) S.; m. David Edward Vieweg, Sept. 3, 1983 (div. Mar. 1997); children: Jessica Kim Vieweg, Jayme Elise Kyung Vieweg. BA, Colo. Coll., 1973; JD, U. Wyo., 1977; MLL, U. Denver, 1979; MBA, Ariz. State U., 1992. Bar: Ariz. 1977. Asst. librarian Stanford (Calif.) U. Coll. Law, 1979—81; law librarian, asst. prof. law U. Bridgeport (Conn.) Coll. Law, 1982—83; dir. Law Libr. Adminstrv. Svcs., Mountain View, Calif., 1983—85; exec. asst. to dean Ariz. State U. Coll. Law, Tempe, 1985—87; dir. Law Libr. Adminstrv. Svcs., Mesa, Ariz., 1987—95; dir. libr. svcs. Jennings, Strouss & Salmon, Phoenix, 1988—89; dir. rsch. svcs. O'Connor, Cavanagh et al, Phoenix, 1989—95; pres. Juris Rsch., Mesa, 1998—; counsel Muchmore & Wallwork, Phoenix, 1995—98; pres. Juris Rsch., Tempe, 1998—; rsch. and legal info. mgr. Bryan Cave LLP, 2000—. Adv. bd. West Pub. Co., St. Paul, 1991-94; bd. dir. Dillon S.W., Scottsdale, Ariz.; mediator Alternative Dispute Resolution Program, Maricopa County, Ariz. Author: Business Research Handbook: Methods and Sources for Lawyers and Business Professionals, 1996—; co-author: Arizona Legal Research Guide, 1992; contbr. chpts. to books, articles to profl. jours.; bi-monthly columnist AzALL News, 1996-97, Legal Assistant Today, 1993-96; contbr. book revs. to Libr. Jour., Legal Info. Alert, 1993-98; editor Southwest Assn. Law Librs. Bull., 1990, Ariz. State U. Coll. Law Law Forum, 1986, Juris Rsch. E-line, 1999—. Rsch. atty. Comml. Law Project for the Ukraine, Phoenix, 1995-96. Mem. ABA (co-chair law practice mgmt. environ. divsn. 1996-99), Am. Assn. Law Librs. (chair 1994-95), Ariz. Assn. Law Librs. (pres. 1996-97, pres.'s award 1997, Disting. Mem. award 1998), State Bar of Ariz. (chair 1996-98, Cont. Legal Edn. award 1998), Ariz. Women Lawyers Assn. (steering com. 1998-2000). Democrat. United Meth. Avocations: reading, yoga, painting, drawing. Office: Juris Rsch PO Box 2157 Tempe AZ 85280-2157 E-mail: kshimpock@jurisresearch.com.

SHIMURA, GORO, mathematician, educator; b. Japan, 1930; DSc, U. Tokyo, 1958. Tchr. U. Tokyo, Osaka U.; vis. prof. Princeton U., 1962, mem. faculty, 1964, prof. emeritus, 1999—. Vis. mem. Inst. Advanced Study. Author: Introduction to Arithmetic Theory of Automorphic Functions, 1971, Abelian Varieties with Complex Multiplications and Modular Functions, 1997, Arithmeticity in the Theory, 2000, Collected Papers of Goro Shimura, 1954-1965, Vol. 1, 2002, Collected Papers, 1978-1988, Vol. 3, 2002, Collected Papers, 1989-2001, Vol. 4, 2002, Euler Products and Eisenstein Series, 1997, Collected Papers of Goro Shimura, 1966-1972, Vol. 2, 2002; co-editor: Geometry and Number Theory: A Volume in Honor of Andre Weil, 1983. Recipient Cole prize for number theory, Am. Math. Soc., 1976, Steele prize for lifetime achievement, 1996. Achievements include research in relations among diverse areas of number theory, geometry, and algebra. Office: Princeton U Math Dept Fine Hall Washington Rd Princeton NJ 08544-1000

SHIN, JOHN JOONGSUNG, mechanical nuclear engineer, consultant; b. Keuchang-Gun, Kyongnam, Korea, Feb. 27, 1941; came to U.S., 1966; s. Jong-Hyup and Hyunpoong (Kwak) S.; m. Sooky C. Shin, Apr. 22, 1972; children: Michael P., Eric P. BS, Korea Maritime U., Pusan, 1963, Hanyang U., Seoul, Korea, 1965; MS, Syracuse U., 1968; PhD, U. Del., 1974. Tchg. asst. Korea Maritime U., Pusan, 1965-66; rsch. asst. Syracuse (N.Y.) U., 1966-68; design engr. Sargent, Webster, Crenshaw, Syracuse, 1968-69; rsch. asst. U. Del., Newark, 1969-73; engr., sr. engr., prin. engr. Ebasco Svcs., Inc., N.Y.C., 1973-93; prin. engr., cons., sr. cons. Raytheon Nuclear, Inc., N.Y.C., 1993-2000; pres. Advanced Nucleartech, Kearny, N.J., 2000—. Tech. cons. Ebasco/Raytheon Nuclear, Inc., N.Y.C., 1973—; tech. cons., seminar Korea Atomic Energy Rsch. Inst., Taejon, 1993, Korea Power Engring. Co., Yongin, Korea, 1992—; condr. seminar Seoul Nat. U., Korea Advanced Inst. Sci. and Tech., Seoul and Taejon, 1992, 93; mem. adv. bd. Korea Next Generation Reactor Tech. Devel., 1992—. Contbr. articles to profl. jours. 2nd engring. officer on ocean going vessels Korea Maritime Bur. Recipient awards U.S. Dept. Energy, 1988, 93, shining star awards Ebasco Svcs., Inc., Entergy Ops., Inc., 1986, 97. Mem. ASME, Am. Nuclear Soc., Korean Scientists and Engrs. Am., Korea Maritime U. Alumni Assn. (pres. 1990-92, 96-98). Democrat. Achievements include research on passive containment cooling of new production reactor and advaned reactors following loss of coolant accident, advanced reactor analyses including incontainment refueling water storage tank during air bubble oscillation, condensation-oscillation and chugging; hydrogen generation, hydrogen distribution, steam and hydrogen explosion, corium-concrete interaction and recritcality analyses following severe reactor accident of 100% reactor core meltdown, universal passive containment protection analysis for inherently safe advanced light water reactor, advanced neutron source reactor analyses, hydrogen ignitor location analyses inside reactor containments, boiling water reactor suppression pool analyses following loss of coolant accident. Home: 314 Division Ave Hasbrouck Heights NJ 07604-1722 Office: Advanced Nucleartech 340 Kearny Ave Kearny NJ 07032

SHIN, PAULL HOBOM, investment company executive, state legislator; b. Kumchon, Korea, Sept. 27, 1935; came to U.S., 1955; adopted s. Ray and Eloise (Siddoway) Paull; m. Donna June Skaggs, June 12, 1963; children: Paull Y., Alisa M. BA, Brigham Young U., 1962; MPIA, U. Pitts., 1964; MA, U. Wash., 1972, PhD, 1978. Asst. prof. Brigham Young U., Laie, Hawaii, 1964-67; prof. Shoreline Coll., Seattle, 1969-72; pres. A.P.S. Investment Co., Seattle, 1982—; chmn. T.T.I. Telecom. Inc., Bellevue, Wash., 1992—; mem. Wash. Ho. of Reps., Olympia, 1992-94, Wash. Senate, Dist. 21, Olympia, 1998—. Commr., chmn. Office of Pres. Korea, Seoul, 1985-88. Mission pres. LDS Ch., Seoul, 1988-91; bd. dirs. Asian-Ams. for Political Action, Seattle, 1982-84, United Way, Snohomish County, 1992—; advisor internat. trade Office Gov., Wash. State, 1983-88, Boy Scouts Am., 1986-88. With U.S. Army, 1958-60. Recipient Outstanding Svc. award Pres. Korea, 1985. Mem. Wash. State Korean Assn. (pres. 1983-84, Community Svc. award 1983), Rotary Club. Avocations: reading, travel, fishing, youth activities. Home: 8910 189th Pl SW Edmonds WA 98026-5929 Office: 405 John Obrien Bldg Olympia WA 98504-0001 Address: Legis Bldg Rm 412B Olympia WA 98504-0001 E-mail: shin_pa@leg.wa.gov.

SHINAGAWA, LARRY HATIME, American studies educator; b. Tokyo, Jan. 15, 1958; came to U.S., 1963; s. Roy Yonori and Fusaco Shinagawa; m. Sun Shinagawa, May 25, 1980; children: Nathan, Chiharu, Mitchell, Grant. AB in Ethnic Studies, AB in Sociology, U. Calif., Berkeley, 1983, MA in Sociology, 1986, PhD in Sociology, 1994. Lectr. U. Calif., Berkeley, 1984-87; mgr., statistician Census Bur., Washington, 1988-89; prof. dept. Am. multicultural studies Sonoma State U., Rohnert Park, Calif., 1990—. V.p. U. No. Calif., Novato, 1999-2000, Four Winds Rsch., San Francisco, 1994—. Author: Atlas of American Diversity, 1998, Multiracial Japanese, 2000; editor: Critical Perspectives, 1984, Asian Americans, 1998. Bd. dirs. Visions 2001, Santa Rosa, Calif., 2001, Accium, Santa Rosa, 1990—, Asian Americans for Marin, Santa Rosa, 1996-99, JACL, Santa Rosa, 1990-93; mem. Human Rights Commn., Santa Rosa, 1998. Rsch. fellow Stanford Law Sch., 1996. Mem. Assn. Asian Am. Studies, Am. Sociol. Assn. Democrat. Buddhist. Office: Sonoma State U Dept Am Multicultural Study 1801 E Coleti Ave Rohnert Park CA 94928 Home: 907 Danby Rd Ithaca NY 14850-5719

SHINAGEL, MICHAEL, dean, English literature educator; b. Vienna, Apr. 21, 1934; came to U.S., 1941; s. Emanuel and Lilly (Hillel) S.; m. Ann Birdsey Mitchell, Sept. 1, 1956 (div. 1970); children: Mark Mitchell, Victoria Stuart; m. Rosa Joanne Bonanno, Dec. 6, 1973 (div. 1993); m. Marjorie Lee North, May 26, 1995. AB, Oberlin Coll., 1957; A.M., Harvard U., 1959, PhD, 1964; Doctorate (hon.), Internat. U. Ecuador, 1997; Doctorate (hon.), U. Argentina Empresa, 2003. Teaching fellow Harvard U., Cambridge, Mass., 1958-59, tutor in English, 1962-64, assoc. dir. career office, 1959-64, dean continuing edn., 1975—, lectr. extension, 1976—, sr. lectr. English, 1983—, master Quincy House, 1986—2001, univ. dean of continuing edn.; asst. prof. English, Cornell U., Ithaca, N.Y., 1964-67; prof., chmn. dept. English, Union Coll., Schenectady, N.Y., 1967-75. Bd. dirs. Harvard Coop. Soc., publ. Harvard Rev.; pres. bd. dirs. Ednl. Exch. Boston, 1982-87; editor Continuing Higher Edn. Rev., 1997—. Author: Defoe and Middle-Class Gentility, 1968; co-author: (handbook) Summer Institutes in English, 1965; editor: Concordance to Poems of Swift, 1972, Critical Edition of Robinson Crusoe, 1975 (revised 1993); co-editor: Harvard Scholars in English (1890-1990), 1991. With U.S. Army, 1952—54, Korea. Woodrow Wilson fellow, 1957; NEH grantee, 1965 Mem. Univ. Continuing Edn. Assn., Assn. Continuing Higher Edn., Mass. Hist. Soc., Old South Meeting House, The Johnsonians, The Saturday Club, Harvard Faculty Club (pres. 1985-87), Phi Beta Kappa. Avocations: reading, cooking, music, tennis. Home: 22 Grozier Rd Cambridge MA 02138 Office: Harvard U Divsn Continuing Edn 51 Brattle St Cambridge MA 02138-3701 Office Phone: 617-495-2930. Business E-Mail: shinagel@hudce.harvard.edu.

SHINDLER, DONALD A. lawyer; b. New Orleans, Oct. 15, 1946; s. Alan and Isolene (Levy) S.; m. Laura Epstein, 1969; children: Jay, Susan. BSBA, Washington U., St. Louis, 1968; JD, Tulane U., 1971. Bar: La. 1971, U.S. Dist. Ct. (ea. dist.) La. 1971, U.S. Tax Ct. 1974, Ill. 1975, U.S. Dist. Ct. (no. dist.) Ill. 1975; CPA, La.; lic. real estate broker, Ill. Assoc. Pope, Ballard, Shepard & Fowle, Chgo., 1975-78, Rudnick & Wolfe, Chgo., 1978-81, ptnr., 1981-99; gen. counsel America's Second Harvest Nat. Food Bank Network, 1998-2000; ptnr. Piper Marbury Rudnick & Wolfe, Chgo., 1999—2002, Piper Rudnick LLP, Chgo., 2002—. Seminar lectr. ABA, Chgo. Bar Assn., Ill. Inst. CLE, Profl. Edn. Sys., Inc., Internat. Assn. Corp. Real Estate Execs., Urban Land Inst., Am. Corp. Counsel Assn., Bldg. Owners and Mgrs. Assn., Internat. Assn. of Attys. and Execs. in Corp. Real Estate, Lorman Ednl. Svcs., others. Contbr. articles on real estate to legal jours. Trustee Glencoe (Ill.) Pub. Libr., 1981-87, pres., 1986-87; alumni bd. govs. Washington U., 1992-93; mem. Glencoe Zoning Commn./Bd. Appeals, 1994-2000; Glencoe Play Commn, 1986-87. Lt. JAGC, USNR, 1971-75. Fellow Am. Coll. Mortgage Attys.; mem. Ill. Leading Lawyers (comml. R/E & R/E fin.), ABA, La. State Bar Assn., Chgo. Bar Assn. (com. chmn. 1979-80, 83-84, 90-94, 96-99, editor land trust seminars 1984-96), Urban Land Inst. (mem. steering com. Chgo. dist. coun.), CoreNet Global (pres. Chgo. chpt. 1997-98, dir. 1991-2003), Internat. Assn. Attys. and Execs. in Corp. Real Estate (fall forum co-chair 2002, spring conf. co-chair, 2003, bd. dirs. 2003—), Union League Club (chair real estate group 1993-96), Order of Coif, Beta Gamma Sigma, Omicron Delta Kappa. Office: Piper Rudnick LLP Ste 1800 203 N La Salle St Ste 1800 Chicago IL 60601-1210 E-mail: donald.shindler@piperrudnick.com.

SHINDLER, DORMAN TRUETT, JR., writer, journalist, critic, photographer, cartoonist; b. Landstühl, Germany, Nov. 30, 1959; arrived in U.S., 1962; s. Dorman Truett and Margaret Anna Shindler; m. Marcia Ann Nelson, Sept. 13, 1989; 1 child, Anya; m. Cheryl Ann Archer. Student, Del Mar Univ., Corpus Christi, Tex., 1979, Univ. Tex., Austin, Tex., 1982, Univ. Md., Ramstein, Germany, 1987. Book critic Kans. City Star, Kans. City, Mo., 1994—99; columnist, book critic Des Moines Register, Des Moines, 1995—99; book critic Denver Post, Denver, 1995—; book critic, columnist St. Petersburg Times, St. Petersburg, Fla., 1996—2000; columnist, book critic Dallas Morning News, Dallas, 1996—2001; book critic Bloomsburg Review, Arvada, Colo., 1997—2000; contbr. writer Pub. Weekly, N.Y., 1999—. Contbr. writer Kans. City Mag., Kans. City, Mo., 1999—; columnist St. Louis post, St. Louis, 2000—; contbr. writer Pages, San Diego, 2002—. Contbr. articles pub. to profl. jour., including The Writer's Handbook, The Patricia Cornwell Companion; book critic, contbg. writer: Amazing Stories, 2004—. E-4 U.S. Army, 1984—88, Germany. Independent. Avocations: hiking, bicycling, sailing. Home: PO Box 9398 Kansas City MO 64133 Office: Freelance writer PO Box 9398 Kansas City MO 64133

SHINDLER, MERRILL KARSH, writer, radio personality; b. N.Y.C., July 2, 1948; s. Joseph and Miriam (Karsh) S. BA, CCNY, 1970; MFA, NYU, 1971. Entertainment editor San Francisco Bay Guardian, 1972-75; music editor Rolling Stone mag., San Francisco, 1976-79; film critic Los Angeles mag., 1979-89; restaurant critic L.A. Examiner, 1979-88; editor Zagat Los Angeles Restaurant Survey, 1986—; restaurant critic L.A. Reader, 1990-96, Daily Breeze, 1990—, Daily News, 1989-94, San Gabriel Valley Newspapers, 1994—. Author: Best Restaurants of L.A., 1989, Zagat, L.A. Restaurant Survey, 1986—, American Dish, 1996, El Cholo: A History, 1998; writer (radio shows) Am. Top 40, 1979-89, 98—, Casey's Top 40, 1989—, Casey's Biggest Hits, 1990—, USA Top 20, 1990—, (TV shows) Am. Top 10, 1980-93, Cinemattractions, 1990—, USA Music Today, 1990—; host radio show Feed Your Face with Merrill Shindler, KLSX-FM, 1988—; contr. to Gault-Millau Best of Los Angeles, 1988, Gault-Millau Best of Hong Kong, 1989; contbr. articles to jours. Avocations: restaurants, cooking, jogging, travel.

SHINDLER PRICE, SHERRY A. writer, educator; d. Jim Franklin and Norma Nadine Hurlock; m. Gary Lowell Price, May 15, 2000; children: Stacey Bishop Hill, Scott Evan Shindler. BA, Long Beach State Coll., 1964. Cert. elem. edn. tchr. Calif., 1964, lic. real estate broker Calif., 1981, cert. cmty. coll. tchr. Calif., 1985. Mem. adv. bd. Allied Bus. Schs., Laguna Hills, Calif., 2001—; bd. dirs. Calif. Real Estate Educators Assn. Author: (book) California Real Estate Principles, Escrow Principles and Practices, Real Estate Finance, Real Estate Practices. Mem.: Calif. Real Estate Educators Assn. (assoc.; dir. 2002—04). Office Phone: 800-542-5543. Personal E-mail: sshindler@aol.com.

SHINDURLING, JON J. judge; b. Idaho Falls, Idaho, Apr. 13, 1947; s. Boyd Thomas and Donna Marie (Fullmer) S.; m. Christine Moss, May 24, 1974; children: Melissa, Marianne, Amanda, Alison. BA in English, Ariz. State U., 1972; JD, U. Idaho, 1977. Bar: Idaho. Ptnr. May & May Law Offices, Twin Falls, Idaho, 1977-88, Wright Law Offices, Idaho Falls, 1990-93; field dir. Sch. of Urban and Wilderness Survival, Shoshone, Idaho, 1988-90; dep. prosecuting atty. Bonneville County, Idaho Falls, 1994-2000, chief dep., 1995-2000; dist. judge 7th Jud. Dist., 2000—. Mem. continuing legal edn. com. Idaho Law Found., Boise, 1985-88; mem. civil jury instns. com. Idaho Supreme Ct., Boise, 1987-89, 96—. Mem. coun. exec. bd. Boy Scouts Am.-Snake River Area, Twin Falls, 1979-90; bd. dirs. Magic Valley YFCA, Twin Falls, 1988-90, Idaho Falls Opera Theatre, 1993-99. Mem. Idaho State Bar (mem. bar examination com. 1979-82, chmn. com. 1980-82, mem. fee disputes resolution com. 1991—). Mem. Lds Ch. Avocations: reading, fishing, scouting. Office: Office Dist Ct 605 N Capital Ave Idaho Falls ID 83402-3582 E-mail: jshindurling@co.bonneville.id.us.

SHINE, DANIEL JOSEPH, JR., management consultant; b. Lawrence, Mass., Feb. 17, 1944; s. Daniel Joseph and Catherine Theresa (Mahoney) S.; Rosanne Marie Pingaro, Sept. 30, 1967; children: Matthew David, Jonathan Marc. BA in History, Merrimack Coll., 1965; MS in Fgn. Svc., Georgetown U., 1968. Intelligence officer CIA, Washington, 1967-76; mgr. Sanders Assocs., Nashua, NH, 1976-85; sr. v.p. Arthur D. Little, Inc., Cambridge, Mass., 1985-94; prin. EDS/Mgmt. Consulting, Plano, Tex., 1994-95; v.p./global practice leader A.T. Kearney, Inc., Chgo., 1995—. Chmn. bd. advisors Georgetown U. Admissions, Washington, 1976—; trustee Merrimack Coll., North Andover, Mass., 2001—. Home: 11 Granada Way Andover MA 01810-4201 Office: AT Kearney Inc 1 Memorial Dr Cambridge MA 02142-1346 E-mail: dan.shine@atkearney.

SHINE, DAVID BRUCE, lawyer; b. Boston, Aug. 11, 1938; s. Thomas Foss and Alice Matilda (Hudgins) S.; m. Elizabeth Magoffin, May 31, 1969; children: James Vincent, Edward Magoffin, David Bruce Jr. BSBA, Tusculum Coll., 1960; JD, Vanderbilt U., 1964; postgrad., Columbia U., 1964-65; LLD (hon.), Tusculum Coll., 1984; LLM, U. Leicester, Eng., 1999. Bar: Tenn. 1964, N.Y. 1966, D.C. 1975. Mem. legal dept. Broadcast Music, Inc., 1964-66; legis. asst. to U.S. Sen. Ross Bass, 1966; mem. Office of Spl. Counsel V.P. U.S., 1966-67; assoc. McLellan, Thatcher & Donoahue, Washington and Kingsport, Tenn., 1967-69; ptnr. Ferguson & Shine, Kingsport, 1969-83; pvt. practice Kingsport, 1983-88; ptnr. Shine & Mason, Kingsport, 1988—. Gen. counsel United Textile Workers Am. AFL-CIO, 1978—; adj. prof. law Appalachian Sch. Law, 2000; vis. fellow Internat. Maritime Law Inst., Malta, 2000—. Contbr. articles to profl. jours. Chmn. bd. trustees Tusculum Coll., 1977-88; bd. trustees Hiwassee Coll., 1994-98; mem. Dem. Nat. Com., 1972-76; commr. ADR, Supreme Ct. of Tenn., 1996—; hon. consul Republic of Malta for Tenn. and N.C., 2004—. Decorated Order of Merit (Italy). Fellow ABA, Tenn. Bar Found.; mem. Nat. Lawyers Club. Anglican Catholic. Avocations: canoeing, collecting toy soldiers. Home: 548A Fleetwood St Kingsport TN 37660-3493 Office: 433 E Center St Kingsport TN 37660-4803 Office Phone: 423-246-8433. E-mail: bruceshine@chartertn.net.

SHINE, KENNETH IRWIN, cardiologist, educator; b. Worcester, Mass., 1935; Grad., Harvard Coll., 1957; MD, Harvard U., 1961. Diplomate Am. Bd. Internal Medicine. Intern Mass. Gen. Hosp., 1961—62, resident, 1962—63, resident, 1965—66, fellow in cardiology, 1966—67; surgeon USPHS, 1963—65; instr. Harvard Med. Sch., 1968—; asst. prof. medicine UCLA Sch. Medicine, 1971—73, assoc. prof., 1973—77, prof., 1977—92, prof. emeritus, 1993—, dir. CCU, 1971—75, chief div. cardiology, 1975—79, vice chmn. dept. medicine, 1979—81, exec. chmn., 1981—86, dean, 1986—92; clin. prof. medicine Georgetown U. Med. Ctr., Washington, 1993—; provost for med. scis. UCLA Sch. Medicine, 1991—92; pres. Inst. of Medicine, Washington, 1992—2002; dir. RAND Center for Domestic and International Health Security. Mem.: Assn. Am. Med. Colls. (adminstrv. bd. coun. deans 1989—92, exec. bd. 1990—92, chmn. coun. deans 1991—92), Am. Heart Assn. (pres. 1986—87). Office: RAND Cntr 1200 S Hayes St Arlington VA 22202-5050

SHINE, NEAL JAMES, journalism educator, former newspaper editor, publisher; b. Grosse Pointe Farms, Mich., Sept. 14, 1930; s. Patrick Joseph and Mary Ellen (Conlon) Shine; m. Phyllis Theresa Knowles, Jan. 24, 1953; children: Judith Ann, James Conlon, Susan Brigid, Thomas Patrick, Margaret Mary, Daniel Edward. BS in Journalism, U. Detroit, 1952; PhD (hon.), Cleary Coll., 1989, Siena Heights Coll., 1995, U. Mich., 1995, U. Detroit Mercy, 1966, Ctrl. Mich. U., 1996. Mem. staff Detroit Free Press, 1950—95, asst. city editor, 1963—65, city editor, 1965—71, mng. editor, 1971—82, sr. mng. editor, 1982—89, pub., 1990—95; prof. journalism Oakland U., Rochester, Mich., 1995—. Host, moderator Detroit Week in Rev., Sta. WTVS-TV, 1981—89; host Neal Shine's Detroit, 1989—91. Bd. dir. Children's Hosp.; trustee, vice chmn. bd. trustees Youth for Understanding, 1973—75, chmn., 1975—78; mem. bd. for student publs. U. Mich.; bd. dir. Econ. Club Detroit, Detroit Renaissance, New Detroit, Inc., Detroit Symphony Orch., Detroit Inst. Arts, Detroit Hist. Soc., United Way of Southeastern Mich., Met. Detroit Conv. and Visitors Bur., Operation ABLE, Detroit Press Club Found. With U.S. Army, 1953—55. Named to Mich. Journalism Hall of Fame, 1990. Mem.: Soc. of Profl. Journalists, AP Mng. Editors, Mich. Press Assn. (bd. dirs. 1990—95), Am. Newspaper Pub. Assn., Am. Soc. Newspaper Editors, Neal Shine Fund for Ethics in Journalism, Inc. Soc. Irish-Am. Lawyers, Sons of Whiskey Rebellion (comdr.-in-chief 1979), Detroit Press Club (charter, bd. govs. 1966—89, sec. 1957—68, v.p. 1969—71, pres. 1971—73). Home: 11009 Harbor Place Dr Saint Clair Shores MI 48080-1527 also: Carraig Rinn 13240 Crystal Beach Rd Pointe aux Roches ON Canada N0R 1N0

SHINEFIELD, HENRY ROBERT, pediatrician; b. Paterson, N.J., Oct. 11, 1925; s. Louis and Sarah (Kaplan) Shinefield; m. Jacqueline Marilyn Walker; children: Jill, Michael, Kimberley Putzer, Melissa Strome. BA, Columbia U., 1945, MD, 1948. Diplomate Diplomate: Am. Bd. Pediat. (examiner, 1975—, bd. dirs., 1979-84, v.p., 1981-84). 1949Rotating intern Mt. Sinai Hosp., N.Y.C., 1948; pediatric intern Duke Hosp., Durham, N.C., 1949-50; asst. resident pediatrician N.Y. Hosp. (Cornell), 1950-51, pediatrician to outpatients, 1953-59, instr. in pediatrics, 1959-60, asst. prof., 1960-64, asso. prof., 1964-65, asst. attending pediatrician, 1959-63, asso. attending pediatrician, 1963-65; pediatrician to outpatients Children's Hosp., Oakland, Calif., 1951-53; chief of pediatrics Kaiser-Permanente Med. Center, San Francisco, 1965-89, chief emeritus, 1989—; co-dir. Kaiser-Permanente Vaccine Study Ctr., San Francisco, 1984—; assoc. clin. prof. pediatrics Sch. Medicine U. Calif., 1966-68, clin. prof. pediatrics, 1968—, clin. prof. dermatology, 1970—; asso. attending pediatrician Paterson (N.J.) Gen. Hosp., 1955-59; chief of pediatrics Kaiser Found. Hosp., San Francisco, 1965-86; attending Moffitt Hosp., San Francisco, 1967-88; practice medicine specializing in pediatrics Paterson, 1953-59. Cons. San Francisco Gen. Hosp., 1967—88, Children's Hosp., San Francisco, 1970—88, Mt. Zion Hosp., San Francisco, 1970—88; mem. rsch. grants rev. br. NIH, HEW, 1970—74; med. dir. USPHSR, 1969—; bd. dirs. San Francisco Peer Rev. Orgn., 1975—81, sec., exec. com., 1976—81; chmn. Calif. State Child Health Disability Bd., 1973—82; mem. Inst. Medicine NAS, 1980—; cons. Bur. Drugs FDA, 1970, NIH, HEW, 1974—85. Editl. bd. We. Jour. Medicine, 1968—80, Am. Jour. Diseases of Children, 1970—82; contbr. articles to profl. publs. Chmn. San Francisco Med. Adv. Com. Nat. Found. March of Dimes, 1969—80. Served USPHS, 1951—53. Fellow: Am. Acad. Pediat. (com. fetus and newborn 1969—76, com. on drugs 1978—82); mem.: AMA, Am. Pediatric Soc., We. Soc. Clin. Rsch., We. Pediatric Soc., Infectious Diseases Soc. Am., Soc. Pediatric Rsch.,

Phi Beta Kappa. Office: Kaiser Permanente 4131 Geary Blvd San Francisco CA 94118-3101 Home: 2240 Hyde St #2 San Francisco CA 94109-1509 Office Phone: 510-267-7531. Business E-Mail: henry.shinefield@kp.org.

SHINEMAN, EDWARD WILLIAM, JR., retired pharmaceutical executive; b. Canajoharie, N.Y., Apr. 9, 1915; s. Edward W. and Bertelle H. (Shubert) S.; m. H. Doris Thompson, Apr. 15, 1939; children: Edward T., Alan B. AB, Cornell U., 1937. With apparatus dept., acctg. dept. Gen. Electric Co., 1938-46, line auditor, 1942-46; with Beech-Nut, Inc. and predecessor cos., 1946-68, asst. treas., 1948-63, contr., 1959-63, treas., 1963-68; asst. sec.-treas. Squibb Corp., 1968-81. Bd. dirs. Taconic Farms, Inc. Trustee Arkell Hall Found.; mem. emeritus coun. Cornell U. Mem. Fin. Execs. Inst., Inst. Mgmt. Accts. Republican. Home: 420 E 51st St Apt 14E New York NY 10022-8022 E-mail: ESHINEMAN@AOL.com.

SHINGLETON, ARTHUR BRADLEY, lawyer; b. May 1953; m. Sherburne Laughlin; children: Bill, Matt. BA, Dickinson Coll.; JD, Duke U. Bar: D.C. 1982. Atty. Young, Moore, Henderson & Alvis, Raleigh, NC, 1982—86; gen. counsel Deutsche Telekon Inc., Washington, 1994—.*

SHINKLE, JOHN THOMAS, lawyer; b. Albany, N.Y., May 9, 1946; s. Robert Thomas and Margery Joan (Kneip) S.; m. Csilla Elizabeth Bekasy, Sept. 2, 1967; children: Reka, Ildiko. BA, Yale U., 1967; JD, Harvard U., 1970. Bar: D.C. 1971, N.Y. 1983, U.S. Supreme Ct. 1974. Law clk. U.S. Ct. Appeals for D.C. Circuit, Washington, 1970-71; assoc. Caplin & Drysdale, Washington, 1971-77, ptnr., 1977-80; assoc. dir. divsn. corp. fin. SEC, Washington, 1980-81, dep. gen. counsel, 1981-82; gen. counsel Salomon Bros. Inc., NY, 1982-94, v.p., 1982-87, dir., 1988-94, Asia Pacific legal and compliance head, 1995—2003; mng. dir. Salomon Bros., Hong Kong, 1996-97, Salomon Smith Barney, Hong Kong, 1997—2003; gen. counsel global transaction svcs. Citigroup, NY, 2003; v.p. and dep. gen. counsel Bristol-Myers Squibb Co., NY, 2003—04; mng. dir., sr. dept. gen. counsel, global corp., investment bank Citigroup, Inc., NY, 2004—. Contbr. articles to profl. jours. Mem. ABA, Assn. Bar City N.Y., Securities Industry Assn. (chmn. fed. regulation com. 1989-91), Futures Industry Assn. (dir. 1989-97). Home: 220 Riverside Blvd Apt 36-B New York NY 10069 Office: Citigroup 388 Greenwich St New York NY 10013

SHINN, CLINTON WESLEY, lawyer; b. Haworth, Okla., Mar. 7, 1947; s. Clinton Elmo and Mary Lucille (Dowdy) Shinn; m. Catherine Borne; children: Laura Kathryn, Clinton Wesley, Timothy Daniel. BS, McNeese State U., 1969; JD, Tulane U., 1972; LLM, Harvard U., 1973. Bar: La. 1972, U.S. Dist. Ct. (ea. dist.) La. 1975, U.S. Dist. Ct. (we. dist.) La. 1980, U.S. Ct. Appeals (5th cir.) 1981, U.S. Ct. Appeals (11th cir.) 1982, U.S. Tax Ct. 1982. Asst. prof. law Tulane U., New Orleans, 1973—75; assoc. Stone, Pigman et al, New Orleans, 1975—78, ptnr., 1979—97, Gill & Shinn, LLC, Covington, La., 1998—2000, of counsel, 2000—; assoc. prof. law Appalachian Sch. Law, 1999—2002, Miss. Coll. Sch. Law, 2002—. Co-founder, bd. dirs. Childhood Ctr. Families Network, 1987—90; co-founder Camp Challenge, 1988; team leader Campaign for Caring, Children's Hosp., New Orleans, 1989—91; bd. dirs. Greater New Orleans YMCA, 1989—98, 1999—2000, exec. com., 1991—98, asst. sec., 1994—95, sec., 1996—98, mem. fin. com., 1994—98, exec. dir. search com., 1996, 2d vice-chair, 1998, mem. Leadership Coun., 1997—98; active Indian Guides/Princesses; bd. dirs. West ST. Tammany YMCA, 1987—95, exec. com., 1988—95, chmn. bd. dirs., 1989—90, 1992—93; bd. dirs. La. Air & Waste Mgmt. Assn., 1993—99, chmn. corp. rels. com., 1992—93, vice chmn., 1996—97, chair, 1997—98, past chair, 1998—99; bd. dirs. Christ Episcopal Sch., Covington, 1988—91, chmn. long-range planning, 1990—91, mem. exec. com., 1989—91, chmn. legal com., 1989—91, chmn. admissions/recruitment com., 1988—90, mem. headmaster search com., 1993; bd. dirs. Christwood, 1992—2001, v.p. bd. dirs., 1997—99. Co-recipient Pals of the Yr. award, Greater New Orleans YMCA Indian Guides/Princesses, 1987—88; named Vol. of the Yr., West St. Tammany YMCA, 1990, 1992. Fellow: La. Bar Found., Am. Coll. Trust and Estate Counsel; mem.: ABA, Air and Waste Mgmt. Assn., New Orleans Estate Planning Coun., Nat. Wildlife Fedn. (life), La. Forestry Assn., La. Bar Assn., Nat. Assn. Securities Dealers (bd. arbitrators), Order Coif. Avocations: backpacking, gardening. Home: 101 Aspen Dr Madison MS 39110 Office: Miss Coll Law Sch 151 E Griffith Jackson MS Office Phone: 601-925-7141. Business E-Mail: shinn@mc.edu. *In all things be firm but fair.*

SHINN, DAVID HAMILTON, educator, author, former diplomat; b. Yakima, Wash., June 9, 1940; s. Guy Wilson and Ada Louise (Gelvin) S.; m. Judy Karen Rolfe, Sept. 9, 1961; children: Steven Hamilton, Christopher Rolfe. AA, Yakima Valley Coll., 1960; BA, George Washington U., 1963, MA, 1964, PhD, 1980; cert. African studies, Northwestern U., Evanston, Ill., 1969. With U.S. State Dept., 1964-2000; rotational officer U.S. Embassy, Beirut, Lebanon, 1964-66; polit. officer Nairobi, Kenya, 1967-68; desk officer East African affairs Washington, 1969-72; polit. officer Dar es Salaam, Tanzania, 1972-74; dep. chief of mission Nouakchott, Mauritania, 1974-76, Office of Mayor, City of Seattle, 1977-78; dep. coord. state and local govt. U.S. Dept. State, Washington, 1978-81; dep. chief of mission Yaounde, Cameroon, 1981-83, Khartoum, Sudan, 1983-86; U.S. ambassador Ouagadougou, Burkina Faso, 1987-90; diplomat-in-residence Southern U., Baton Rouge, La., 1990-91; diplomat State Dept., Washington, 1991-96; U.S. Amb. Addis Ababa, Ethiopia, 1996-99; diplomat-in-residence UCLA, 1999-2000. Adj. prof. George Washington U., 2001—. Co-author: Historical Dictionary of Ethiopia, 2004. Sr. assoc. Internat. Ctr. for Religion and Diplomacy; mem. Pacific Coun. Internat. Policy; bd. dirs. U.S. Cares for Ethiopia, People to People, Inc., Horn Relief. Recipient Superior Honor award State Dept., 1980, 85, 94, Alumnus of Yr. award Am. Assn. Cmty. Colls., 1994, Phi Theta Kappa, 1995. Mem. Internat. Studies Assn., Ethiopian Studies Assn., Am. Fgn. Svc. Assn., Sudan Studies Assn., Am. Philatelic Soc., Rotary Internat. Methodist. Avocations: philately, skiing, physical fitness, antiques. Address: 23 8th St SE Washington DC 20003

SHINN, GEORGE LATIMER, investment banker, consultant, educator; b. Newark, Ohio, Mar. 12, 1923; s. Leon Powell and Bertha Florence (Latimer) S.; m. Clara LeBaron Sampson, May 21, 1949; children: Deborah, Amy, Martha, Sarah, Andrew. AB, Amherst Coll., 1948; LLD (hon.), Denison U., 1975, Amherst Coll., 1982; MA, Drew U., 1990, PhD, 1992. Trainee Merrill Lynch, Pierce, Fenner & Beane, 1948-49; various exec. positions, 1949-75; pres. Merrill Lynch & Co., Inc., 1973-75; chmn. bd., chief exec. officer 1st Boston Corp., 1975-83; investment banking consultant, 1983—. Adj. prof. history Drew U., Madison, N.J., 1992—; mem. exec. com. President's Pvt. Sector Survey on Cost Control, 1982-84; exec.-in-residence Columbia U. Grad. Sch. Bus., 1983-85; bd. govs. Am. Stock Exch., 1970-74; bd. dirs., trustee Colonial Group Mut. Funds, 1983-98; bd. dirs. Kelso & Co., 1992—, N.Y. Stock Exch., 1975-83, vice chmn., 1979-83; bd. dirs. N.Y. Times Co., 1978-99, Philps Dodge Corp., 1983-95, N.Y. Life Ins. Co., 1983-94, Lehigh Press, 1983-91, Superior Oil Co., 1984-87, Congoleum Corp. Gen. chmn. United Hosp. Fund, N.Y.C., 1973-74; trustee Kent Pl. Sch., Summit, N.J., 1966-73, Carnegie Found. for Advancement Teaching, 1976-85, Pingry Sch., 1977-79, Lucille P. Markey Charitable Trust, 1985-97, Rockefeller Family Office Trust, 1989-97, N.J. Coun. for the Humanities, 1994-2000, Arts Coun. Morris Area, 1978-91, Philharmonic Symphony Soc. N.Y., 1983-91, Nat. Humanities Ctr., 1988-94; trustee emeritus Amherst Coll., 1968-82, chmn. bd. trustees, 1973-80; bd. dirs. Rsch. Corp., 1975-86. Capt. USMCR, 1943-52. Fellow Am. Acad. Arts and Scis., N.Y. Acad. Medicine, River Club, Century Assn.

SHINN, MICHAEL ROBERT, lawyer; b. Salem, Oreg., June 25, 1947; s. William Robert and Miriam Jean (Becke) S. BA, Willamette U., 1969, JD, 1973. Bar: Oreg. 1973, U.S. Dist. Ct. Oreg. 1973, U.S. Ct. Appeals (9th cir.) 1973. Law clk. to judge U.S. Dist. Ct., Portland, Oreg., 1974-75; pvt. practice Portland, 1975—. Lectr. Masters at Trial Oreg., We. Trial Lawyers Assn., Oreg. State Bar, Mont. State Bar, Oreg. Law Inst., Nat. Bus. Inst. Editor Trial Lawyer Quar., 1988; dir., editor, producer: (videotape) (with Gerry Spence) Spence in Trial, 1989-90; co-producer, dir.: (videotape) Spence in Trial, Series for Trial Lawyers; cons. NBC mini-series Dead By Sunset, 1995. Pres. W. Hills and Island Neighbors Assn., Portland, 1983-84; del. Citizen to Citizen Legal Amb. Dels. to China, 1988; mem., bd. dirs. adv. coun. Oreg. Hearing Rsch. Ctr., 1992; bd. dirs. Portland Civic Theater. Inducted Willamette U. Athletic Hall of Fame, 1998. Mem. Oreg. Trial Lawyers Assn., (pres. 1980-81, edn. dir. 1984-89, svc. award 1986, 87), Am. Inns. of Ct. (master barrister 1988). Avocations: writing, wind surfing, skiing, water-skiing, tennis, rugby. Office: 621 SW Morrison St Ste 1000 Portland OR 97205-3821 E-mail: michaelshinn@aol.com.

SHINNAR, REUEL, chemical engineering educator, industrial consultant; b. Vienna, Sept. 15, 1923; came to U.S., 1962; s. Abraham Emil and Rosa (Storch) Bardfeld; m. Miryam Halpern, June 22, 1948; children: Shlomo, Meir Diploma in Chem. Engring., Technion, Haifa, Israel, 1945, M.Sc. in Chem. Engring., 1954; Dr. Engring. Sci., Columbia U., 1957. Various position in chem. engring., Israel, 1945-58; adj. assoc. prof. Technion, Haifa, Israel, 1958-62; visiting research fellow Guggenheim Labs., Princeton (N.J.) U., 1962-64; prof. chem. engring. CCNY, 1964—, disting. prof., 1979—. Pinhas Naor lectr. Technion U., 1974; Wilhelm Meml. lectr. Princeton U., 1985, Kelly lectr. Purdue U., 1991; cons. to various oil and chem. cos. Contbr. numerous articles to profl. jours.; patentee in field. Fellow AICE (Founders award 1992, Alpha Chi Sigma award 1979), N.Y. Acad. Scis.; mem. AIAA, Am. Chem. Soc., Nat. Acad. Engring. Office: City Coll NY Dept Chem Engring 140th St and Convent Ave New York NY 10031

SHINNAR, SHLOMO, child neurologist, educator; b. Haifa, Israel, Nov. 11, 1950; s. Reuel and Miryam (Halpern) S.; m. Shoshana Ellen Cohen, Aug. 11, 1974; children: Ora Rivka, Aviva Batya, Avraham Ever. BA in Physics summa cum laude, Columbia Coll., 1971; PhD, Albert Einstein Coll. Medicine, 1977, MD, 1978. Diplomate Am. Bd. Pediat., Am. Bd. Psychiatry and Neurology, Am. Bd. Child Neurology and Clin. Neurophysiology. Intern, asst. resident in pediatrics, fellow Johns Hopkins Hosp., Balt., 1978-80, asst. resident, resident in neurology, fellow, 1980-83; from asst. prof. to prof. neurology and pediat. Albert Einstein Coll. Medicine, Bronx, 1983—; from asst. attending to attending neurology and pediat. Montefiore Med. Ctr., Bronx Mcpl. & North Ctrl. Bronx Hosps., 1983—; Hyman Climenko prof. neurosci. rsch. Montefiore Med. Ctr., Bronx, 2002—. Co-dir. Epilepsy Mgmt. Ctr. Montefiore Med. Ctr. Albert Einstein Coll. Medicine, Bronx, 1983-86, dir., 1986—; mem. adv. bd. Epilepsy Inst., N.Y.C., 1984—, chair 1996—, instnl. rev. bd. protection of human subjects Montefiore Med. Ctr., Bronx, 1985—, vice-chmn., 1989—, prof. of neuroscience rsch., 2002—; adj. sch. scientist Gertrude Sergievsky Ctr. Columbia Coll. Physicians and Surgeons, N.Y.C., 1985—, Sergievsky Scholar, 1986—; cons. in field. Field editor Epilepsy Advances, 1987-93; editl. bd. The Neurologist, 1993—, Epilepsia, 1994-2000, Pediatric Neurology, 1996—; contbr. articles to profl. jours. N.Y. State Regents scholar, 1967-71; Martin and Emily L. Fisher fellow, 1991— Fellow Am. Acad. Pediats., Am. Acad. Neurology; mem. Am. Epilepsy Soc. (chmn. childhood onset epilepsy com. 1993-95, councillor 1992-95, Rsch. Recognition award 1989), Child Neurology Soc., Eastern EEG Soc., Internat. Child Neurology soc., Nat. Assn. Epilepsy Ctrs., Soc. for Pediat. Rsch., Am. Neurol. Assn. Office: Montefiore Med Ctr 111 E 210th St Bronx NY 10467-2401 Office Phone: 718-920-4378. Personal E-mail: sshinnar@aol.com.

SHINNERS, STANLEY MARVIN, electrical engineer; b. N.Y.C., May 9, 1933; s. Earl and Molly (Planter) S.; m. Doris Pinsker, Aug. 4, 1956; children: Sharon Rose Cooper, Walter Jay, Daniel Lawrence. BEE, CCNY, 1954; MSEE, Columbia U., 1959. Equipment engr. Western Electric Co., N.Y.C., 1953-54; staff engr. electronics divsn. Otis Elevator Co., Bklyn., 1954-56; project engr. Consol. Avionics Corp., Westbury, N.Y., 1956-58; program mgr., fed. sys. Lockheed Martin Corp. (formerly Loral Corp., Unisys Corp.), Mitchel Field, N.Y., 1958-99. Adj. prof. engring. The Cooper Union, N.Y.C., 1966—, N.Y. Inst. Tech., Old Westbury, N.Y., 1972-92, Poly. Inst. Bklyn., 1959-72. Author: Control System Design, 1964, Techniques of Systems Engineering, 1967, A Guide to Systems Engineering and Management, 1976, Modern Control System Theory and Application, 1978, Modern Control System Theory and Design, 1992, 2d edit., 1998, Advanced Modern Control System Theory and Design, 1998. Recipient Career Achievement medal CCNY Alumni Assn., 1980. Fellow IEEE (life); mem. Am. Soc. for Engring. Edn., Eta Kappa Nu, Tau Beta Pi. Home: 28 Sagamore Way N Jericho NY 11753-2358 E-mail: shinnerssm@optonline.net. *I was very poor financially as a child, but I received an abundance of love and encouragement from parents and family. I have always tried to succeed and to help others succeed. Above all, I have always tried to do what is right whether the decision had to be made in the business world or in private and family matters.*

SHINOLT, EILEEN THELMA, artist; b. Washington, May 18, 1919; d. Edward Lee and Blanche Addie (Marsh) Bennett; m. John Francis Shinolt, June 14, 1956 (dec. Aug. 1969). Student, Hans Hoffman Sch Art, 1949, Pa. Acad. Arts, 1950, Corcoran Sch. Art, 1945-51, Am. U., 1973-77. Sect. chief Dept. Army, Washington, 1940-73, retired, 1973. One-woman shows include various locations, 1982, 83, 85, 90, 94, 96; group shows include Perlmutter & Co., 1981, Fitch Fox and Brown, 1986, Foundry Gallery, 1987, Ann. Add Arts, 1986, Westminster Gallery, London, 1995; represented in permanent collections Women's Nat. Mus., Washington, Cameo Gallery, Columbia, S.C., Strathmore Hall Arts Ctr., North Bethesda, Md., 1997, 98, 99, 2000, Internat. Monetary Fund Members Show, Washington, 2000. Mem. Woman's Nat. Dem. Club, Washington, 1980—. Mem. Am. Art League (editor newsletter 1985-86, 1st pl. 1987, 2d pl. 1986), Arts Club Washington (exhbn. com. 1985—, admissions com. 1987-88), Miniature Painters, Sculptors & Gravers Soc. (historian 1989—, editor newsletter 1986-89). Roman Catholic. Avocations: reading, studying art periodicals, art galleries. Home: 4119 Davis Pl NW Apt 203 Washington DC 20007-1254

SHINOZAKI, TAMOTSU, retired physician, anesthesiologist; b. Dairen, Japan, Mar. 18, 1934; s. Yuichi and Shizue Shniozaki; m. Kazuko Sakanaka Shinozaki, Feb. 14, 1940; children: Aritomo, Yuji, Emiko. MD, Okayama U., Japan, 1958, D in Med. Scis., 1963. Diplomate Am. Bd. Anesthesiology; fellow critical care medicine; cert. spl. qualifications in critical care medicine. Intern St. Luke's Internat. Hosp., Tokyo, 1958-59; resident in anesthesiology Mary Fletcher Hosp., 1964-67; attending anesthesiologist Med. Ctr. Hosp. of Vt., Burlington, 1967-99; asst. prof. Med. Sch. U. Vt., Burlington, 1967-72, assoc. prof., 1972-90, clin. prof., 1990-99, med. co-dir. surg. ICU, 1985-99, prof. emeritus, 2000—; adminstrv. dir. surg. ICU Fletcher Allen Healthcare, Burlington, 1997-99, attending emeritus, 2000—. Cons. med. divsn. Hewlett Packard Co., Waltham, Mass., 1972-77, Intelligent Med. System, Carlsbad, Calif., 1987. Recipient Quality Cup award, Excellance in the Quality Movement, 1994. Fellow Am. Coll. Critical Care Medicine; mem. Sigma Xi. Home: 335 Dorset Hts South Burlington VT 05403 Business E-Mail: tshinoza@zoo.uvm.edu.

SHIPBAUGH, CALVIN LEROY, physicist; b. Huntington, Ind., Aug. 28, 1958; s. Paul and Marguerite (Pinkerton) S. BA, Rice U., 1980; PhD, U. Ill., 1988. Rsch. asst. U. Ill., Champaign-Urbana, 1981-88; analyst RAND Corp., Santa Monica, Calif., 1988—. Mem. space and surface power panel RAND support to NASA Project Outreach, Santa Monica, 1990; vis. scientist Fermilab, Batavia, Ill.,1982-85; workshop leader biotech. group RAND; team mem. POET, Arlington, Va., 1989-92; mem. bioscis. panel AAN Workshop, 1997; sr. assoc. Inst. Molecular Manufacturing. Contbr. articles to Phys. Rev. Letters, Physics Letters, RAND Pub. Series, others. Mem.: IEEE, Internat. Meteoritical Soc., AM. Phys. Soc. Achievements include research to measure charm particles' decay and hadronic production properties; evaluation of proposals from the public to the Space Exploration Initiative; policy analysis of nanotechnology; analysis of rotorcraft markets. Office: The RAND Corp 1700 Main St Santa Monica CA 90401-3297

SHIPLER, DAVID KARR, journalist, correspondent, author; b. Orange, N.J., Dec. 3, 1942; s. Guy Emery Jr. and Eleanor (Karr) Shipler; m. Deborah S. Isaacs, Sept. 17, 1966; children: Jonathan Robert, Laura Karr, Michael Edmund. AB, Dartmouth Coll., 1964; LittD (hon.) (hon.), Middlebury Coll., 1988, Glassboro (N.J.) State Coll., 1988; AM (hon.) (hon.), Dartmouth Coll., 1994. News clk. N.Y. Times, 1966—67, news summary writer, 1968, reporter met. staff, 1968—73, fgn. corr. Saigon bur., 1973—75, fgn. corr. Moscow Bur., 1975—, bur. chief Moscow Bur., 1977—79, chief Jerusalem bur., 1979—84, corr. Washington bur., 1985—87, chief diplomatic corr., 1987—88; sr. assoc. Carnegie Endowment for Internat. Peace, Washington, 1988—90. Guest scholar Brookings Instn., 1984—85; adj. prof. Am. U. Sch. Internat. Svc., Washington, 1990; Ferris prof. journalism and pub. affairs Princeton U., 1990—91; Woodrow Wilson vis. fellow, 1990—; writer-in-residence U. So. Calif., 1998; Montgomery fellow, vis. prof. gov. Dartmouth Coll., 2003. Author: Russia: Broken Idols, Solemn Dreams, 1983 (Overseas Press Club award), revised, 1989, Arab and Jew: Wounded Spirits in a Promised Land, 1986 (Pulitzer prize for Gen. Nonfiction, 1987), revised, 2002, A Country of Strangers: Blacks and Whites in America, 1997, The Working Poor: Invisible in America, 2004; exec. prodr.: (documentaries) from Arab and Jew: Wounded Spirits in a Promised Land, 1989 (Alfred DuPont-Columbia U. award for Broadcast Journalism, 1990), Arab and Jew: Return to the Promised Land, 2002; contbr. articles to nat. mags. Trustee Dartmouth Coll., 1993—2003. With USNR, 1964—66. Co-recipient George Polk award, 1982; recipient award for disting. reporting, Soc. Silurians, 1971, award for disting. pub. affairs reporting, Am. Polit. Sci. Assn., 1971, award, N.Y. chpt. Sigma Delta Chi, 1973. Office: 4005 Thornapple St Chevy Chase MD 20815-5037 *I have been governed professionally by the conviction that an open society needs open examination of itself to survive. Defining problems, inspecting blemishes, probing wounds, and exposing injustice are the required pastimes of a free people. Nothing intelligent can come from ignorance. If information does not guarantee wisdom, it is at least a prerequisite, for the only wise course is through knowledge. To write about current affairs, then, is to play a small role in a great endeavor. It is to measure one's own performance continually against the highest standards of honesty, fairness, thoroughness, intelligence, to search every day for a bit of truth, then share it. These are the ingredients of happiness, for such a job involves a life of constant learning, perpetual self-education. It keeps a man whole.*

SHIPLEY, ALDEN PEVERLY, broadcaster, broadcasting executive; b. Phila., Nov. 27, 1946; s. Alden Peverly and Selma Nadine (Smith) S.; m. Rose Marie Welsh, Dec. 27, 1969. Account exec. Sta. WAKY Radio/Multimedia Broadcast, Louisville, 1974-78; sales mgr. Sta. WGAC/Beasley Broadcast, Augusta, Ga., 1978-80; regional sales mgr. Stas. WVCG-WYOR/Insilco Broadcast, Coral Gables, Fla., 1980-83; gen. mgr. Sta. WMAD Radio, Madison, Wis., 1983-84; gen. sales mgr. Sta. WKAT Radio-Hernstadt Broadcast, Miami Beach, Fla., 1984-85; cons. Advanced Broadcast Mgmt., Washington, 1983-85; v.p. ops. Network Media Comm., N.Y.C., 1985-86; founder ABCI Prodns., Prospect, Ky., 1986—; founder, owner, dir. Automated Broadcast Cons., Inc., Miami Beach, 1986—. Corp. cons. Word Broadcasting. Co-author software Automated Cable Billing Sys.; prodr. TV programs Dance TV, Miss Robins Dance Class, World's Greatest Dancers, No Way with Ned and Joan Way. With USNR, 1965-67. Republican. Roman Catholic. Avocation: photography. Home: 7901 Barbourmeade Rd Louisville KY 40241-2621 Office: ABCI Prodns PO Box 768 Prospect KY 40059-0768 Office Phone: 502-387-9020. Business E-Mail: aps@abcipro.tv.

SHIPLEY, DAN, architect; BArch, U. Tex., 1979. With HKS, Inc., Metro Archs., Thomas and Booziotis Archs.; founder, pres. DanShipley Arch., Inc., 1992—. Recipient Honor award, Tex. Soc. Archs., 1998, 2000, Addition/Renovation of the Yr. award, D Mag., 2002, Achievement award, Preservation Dallas, 2003. Mem.: AIA (Dallas Honor award 2000, Dallas Merit award 1997, 1996, 1993). Office: 6404 Patrick Dr Dallas TX 75214

SHIPLEY, DAVID ELLIOTT, dean, lawyer; b. Urbana, Ill., Oct. 3, 1950; s. James Ross and Dorothy Jean (Elliott) S.; m. Virginia Florence Coleman, May 24, 1980; 1 child, Shannon C. BA, Oberlin Coll., 1972; JD, U. Chgo., 1975. Bar: R.I. 1975. Assoc. Tillinghast, Collins & Graham, Providence, 1975-77; asst. prof. U. S.C. Sch. Law, Columbia, 1977-81, assoc. prof., 1981-85, prof., 1985-90, assoc. dean, 1989-90; dean U. Miss. Sch. Law, University, 1990-93, U. Ky. Coll. Law, Lexington, 1993-98; prof., dean Sch. Law U. Ga., Athens, 1998—. Vis. prof. Coll. William and Mary, Williamsburg, Va., 1983-84, Ohio State U. Coll. Law, Columbus, 1986-87. Author: South Carolina Administrative Law, 1983, 2d edit., 1989; co-author Copyright Law, 1992. Pres. Shandon Neighborhood Assn., Columbia, 1988-90. Named Prof. of Yr., U. S.C. Sch. Law, 1990, faculty scholar, 1989-90. Mem. ABA, R.I. Bar Assn., S.C. Bar Assn. (assoc.). Methodist. Avocations: running, yardwork, gardening, reading. Home: 475 River Bottom Rd Athens GA 30606-6430 Office: U Ga Sch Law Dean Office Athens GA 30602-6012

SHIPLEY, L. PARKS, JR., banker; b. Orange, N.J., Aug. 2, 1931; s. L. Parks and Emily Catherine (Herzog) S.; m. Micheline Genevieve Oltramare, Apr. 2, 1966; children: Christiane, Daniel, Alix BA, Yale U., 1953. Vol. Moral ReArmament, Europe, Africa, S.Am., 1954-64; participant in founding Up With People Inc., 1964-69; from internat. banking officer to v.p. Marine Midland Bank, N.Y.C., 1969-76; v.p. Irving Trust Co., N.Y.C., 1976-84, exec. v.p., 1984-89, Bank of N.Y., N.Y.C., 1989-90; pres. Ultramar Assoc., Inc., N.Y.C., 1990-91, Ultramar Group, Inc., 1991-92; U.S. rep., bd. advisor Banco Credito Argentino; pres. Shipley Assocs. Bd. dirs. Global Pvt. Equity Co.; mem. adv. bd. Northstar Group of Cos. Trustee Acad. Art Mus. Easton, Md. Home: 7214 Solitude Rd Saint Michaels MD 21663-2824 E-mail: lpshipley@aol.com.

SHIPLEY, LARRY, food products executive; Asst. to pres. IBP Inc., Dakota City, Nebr., 1989, sr. v.p. corp. devel., exec. v.p. corp. devel., CFO, 1997—; pres. IBP Enterprises, Dakota City, Nebr., 1997—. Office: IBP Inc Ste 830 800 Stevens Port Dr North Sioux City SD 57049

SHIPLEY, SAMUEL LYNN, advertising and public relations executive; b. Marlborough, Mass., Nov. 14, 1929; s. Clifford Lynn and Esther (Jacobs) S.; m. Sue Finucan, Sept. 5, 1955; children— Jeffrey Lynn, Beth Ann, Amy. Student, Charles Morris Price Sch. Advt. and Journalism, U. N.H., 1948-50. Exec. dir. Democratic Party N.H., 1953-56; pres., chmn. Shipley Assos., Inc., Wilmington, Del., 1962—; pres. Cable TV Advt. Inc., 1982—. Dir. Del. Devel. Dept., Dover, 1965-69; mem. bd. overseers Del. Coll. Art and Design. Nominee for U.S. Congress, 1976; pub. relations dir. Del. Democratic Com., 1964-68; chmn. Del. Dem. Com., 1982-90; bd. dirs. Blood Bank of Del., Jobs for Del. Grads., For Children; mem. Del. Heritage Commn.; trustee Grand Opera House; former chair Dem. State Com. With U.S. Army, 1951-53. Recipient Freedoms Found. Honor medal, 1966, Outstanding Grad. award Charles Morris Price Sch., 1974 Mem. Am. Advt. Fedn., Nat. Press Club, Wilmington Advt. Club, Masons. Home: 1196 Paper Mill Rd Newark DE 19711-2924 Office: 1300 Pennsylvania Ave Wilmington DE 19806-4311 E-mail: s.shipley@shipleyassociates.com. *The ingredients for success are good health, average intelligence, a giving spirit, positive thinking, good imagination, self-discipline, hard work, and persistence.*

SHIPLEY, TONY L(EE), software company executive; b. Elizabethton, Tenn., July 19, 1946; s. James A. and Edith J. (Crowder) S.; m. Lynda Anne Jenkins, Nov. 19, 1971; children: Blake Alan, Sarah Robyn. BS in Indsl. Engring., U. Tenn., 1969; MBA, U. Cin., 1975. Indsl. engr. Monsanto Co., Pensacola, Fla., 1969—72; mktg. mgr. SDRC, Cin., 1972—76; v.p. sales and mktg. Anatrol Corp., Cin., 1977—81; pres. Entek Sci. Corp., Cin., 1981—96; pres., CEO Entek IRD Internat. Corp., 1996—2000; founding mem. Queen City Angels. Bd. dirs. RM Waste, Ohio IT Alliance, CHMack, The Circuit, Voice Control Inc., The Grid. Named Small Bus. Person of Yr., Greater Cin. C. of C., 1994, Entrepreneur of Yr. in Cin., No. Ky. Region, 1996. Mem. ASME, Soc. Automotive Engrs., Greater Cin. Software Assn. (pres. 1996-97, chmn. 1997-99, bd. dirs.), Greater Cin. C. of C., Leadership Class XVIII, Terrace Park (Ohio) Country Club (bd. dirs., past pres.). Republican. Avocations: golf, family activities, fishing. Home: 7825 Calderwood Ln Cincinnati OH 45243-1319 Personal E-mail: tshipley@fuse.net.

SHIPLEY, WALTER VINCENT, retired bank executive; b. Newark, Nov. 2, 1935; s. L. Parks and Emily (Herzog) S.; m. Judith Ann Lyman, Sept. 14, 1957; children: Barbara, Allison, Pamela, Dorothy, John. Student, Williams Coll., 1954-56; BS, NYU, 1961. With Chem. Bank, N.Y.C., 1956-96; chmn., CEO, chmn. bd. dirs. Chase Manhattan Corp., N.Y.C., 1996-99; ret., 1999. Bd.

dirs. Exxon Mobil Corp., Verizon Comms., Wyeth. Mem. The Bus. Coun., Coun. Fgn. Rels., Links, Augusta Nat. Golf Club, Baltusrol Golf Club (Springfield, N.J.). Office: JPMorgan Chase & Co 270 Park Ave New York NY 10017-2070

SHIPLEY BIDDY, SHELIA, artist management executive; b. Scottsville, Ky., Oct. 2, 1952; d. Robert Shelby Davis and Pauline (Powell) Willoughby; 1 child, Michael; m. Ken Biddy. Student, U. Tenn., 1975-77, Nashville Tech. Inst., 1978-79. Adminstrv. asst. Monument Records, Nashville, 1976-79; promotion/sales coord. RCA Records, Nashville, 1979-83; dir. career devel. Hallmark Direction Co., Nashville, 1983-84; sr. v.p. nat. promotion MCA Records, Nashville, 1984-93; sr. v.p., gen. mgr. Decca Records, 1994-99; pres., CEO Shipley Biddy Entertainment, Inc., 1999—2003; exec. Vivaton Records, Nashville, 2003—. Author poetry. Pres. Leadership Music; bd. dirs. Acad. Country Music. Mem. NARAS, Country Music Assn., Acad. Country Music, Country Radio Bd. Dirs., Nat. Assn. Talent Buyers, Country Radio Broadcasters (v.p.), Source, Leadership Music, Leadership Nashville. Republican. Baptist. Office: Vivaton Records 702 18th Ave South Nashville TN 37203

SHIPMAN, ROSS LOVELACE, petroleum executive; b. Jackson, Miss., Nov. 20, 1926; s. William Smylie and Jeanette Scott (Lovelace) S.; m. Lois Pegrim, June 6, 1948; 1 dau., Smylie Shipman Anderson. BA, U. Miss., 1950. Registered profl. geologist, Ark., chartered geologist, U.K. Geologist Humble Oil & Refining Co., West Tex., 1950-55; petroleum cons. Midland, Tex., 1955-60, Corpus Christi, Tex., 1960-67; asst. exec. dir. Am. Geol. Inst., Washington, 1967-71; assoc. dir. U. Tex. Marine Sci. Inst., Austin, 1971-79; assoc. v.p. for research U. Tex., Austin, 1979-85; pres., chief exec. officer Live Oak Energy, Inc., 1985-86; prin. Petroleum Investments/Worldwide, 1975—. Dir. Indsl. Assocs. program Coll. Nat. Scis. U. Tex., Austin, 1986-89; mem. Tex. Coastal and Marine Coun., 1979-85; U.S.-Mexico Boundary Water Study Program, 1978-99; del. Argonne Univs. Assn., Chgo., 1982. Editor, pub. AGI Report newsletter, 1968-70; editor Profl. Geologist, 1975-76; contbr. articles to profl. jours. Served with U.S. Army, 1944-46, PTO. Fellow Geol. Soc. London; mem. Am. Inst. Profl. Geologists (cert. profl. geologist, Tex. pres. 1974, nat. editor 1975-76), Soc. Ind. Profl. Earth Scientists, Tex. Soc. SAR (pres., lectr. in Am. history), Soc. of Mayflower Descs. (gov. San Antonio colony), Petroleum Club of San Antonio, Jamestowne Soc. (gov. San Antonio co.), SCV (comdr. Hood's Tex. Brigade Camp), Order First Families Miss., Gen. Soc. Colonial Wars, Gov. Tex. Soc. Home: 1911 E Lawndale Dr San Antonio TX 78209-2043 Office Phone: 210-829-5003.

SHIPP, THETA WANZA, social service organization administrator, educator, consultant, minister; b. Miami, Fla., June 19, 1948; d. James Willie and Fredericka Wanza; m. Robert Glenn Shipp, June 28, 1970 (div. Aug. 1975); children: Tammi LaTrice, Eloria April Michelle. BA, Fisk U., 1970; MS, So. Ill. U., 1977; postgrad., Howard U. Ordained to ministry Christian Faith Ctrs., 1998. Asst. program dir. U. South Fla., Tampa, 1971-72; adminstr. City of Tampa, 1972-74; adminstrv. supr. Juvenile Svcs. Program, St. Petersburg, Fla., 1974-76; staff asst. City of Carbondale, Ill., 1976-77; tchg./rsch. asst., editl. asst. So. Ill. U., Carbondale, 1977-78; staff asst. U.S. Rep. Claude Pepper, Washington, 1978-82; legis./spl. asst. U.S. Rep. Mervyn M. Dymally, Washington, 1982-87; chief of staff U.S. Rep. Major R. Owens, Washington, 1987-88, U.S. Rep. Earl F. Hilliard, Washington, 1993-95; project dir. Nat. Assn. for Equal Opportunity in Higher Edn., Washington, 1998-99; asst. to v.p. for pub. policy Planned Parenthood Fedn. of Am., Washington, 2000—01; instr. D.C. Pub. Schs., 2001—. Ind. cons., 1989-03; part-time instr. dept. sociology Howard U., 1978-82. Campaign worker various congl. campaigns, 1976-2000, campaign fundraiser, 1978-97; mem. ministerial staff Michigan Park Christian Ch., Washington, 2000—; vol. Black Ch. Initiative, Religious Coalition for Reproductive Choice, Washington, 2000; ministerial cons. Soul Saving Sta., Miami, 1990—; campaign coord. Dem. Nat. Com. Office of African Am. Religious Outreach, Washington, 2000. Named one of Outstanding Young Women in Am.; recipient recognition United Negro Coll. Fund, Assn. Urban Univs., Southeastern Coun. on Ednl. Opportunity Assn., Internat. Bus. and Exec. Women, Women's Dept. Ministry of Help. Mem. NAACP, Nat. Urban League, Am. Sociol. Assn., Nat. Black Women's Agenda, Nat. Coalition on Black Civic Participation, Nat. Coalition for Black Voter Participation, Friends of Africa, Delta Sigma Theta, Alpha Kappa Delta, Phi Delta Lambda. Democrat. Avocations: reading, witnessing, movies, swimming, gardening. Home: 1441 N W 168th Terr Miami FL 33169

SHIPPEY, SANDRA LEE, lawyer; b. Casper, Wyo., June 24, 1957; d. Virgil Carr and Doris Louise (Conklin) McClintock; m. Ojars Herberts Ozols, Sept. 2, 1978 (div.); children: Michael Ojars, Sara Ann, Brian Christopher; m. James Robert Shippey, Jan. 13, 1991; 1 child, Matthew James. BA with distinction, U. Colo., 1978; JD magna cum laude, Boston U., 1982. Bar: Colo. 1982, U.S. Dist. Ct. Colo. 1985. Assoc. Cohen, Brame & Smith, Denver, 1983-84, Parcel, Meyer, Schwartz, Ruttum & Mauro, Denver, 1984-85, Mayer, Brown & Platt, Denver, 1985-87; counsel western ops. GE Capital Corp., San Diego, 1987-94; assoc. Page, Polin, Busch & Boatwright, San Diego, 1994-95; v.p., gen. counsel First Comml. Corp., San Diego, 1995-96; legal counsel NextWave Telecom Inc., San Diego, 1996-98; ptnr. Procopio, Cory, Hargreaves and Savitch, LLP, 1998—. Spkr. in field. Contbr. articles to profl. jours. Active Pop Warner football and cheerleading; bd. dirs. Southwestern Christian Schs., Inc., 2002—, San Diego Christian Found., 2001—. Mem. Calif. State Bar (uniform comml. code com.), Phi Beta Kappa, Phi Delta Phi. Republican. Mem. Ch. of Christ. Avocations: tennis, golf, photography. Home: 15839 Big Springs Way San Diego CA 92127-2034 Office: Procopio Cory Et Al 530 B St Ste 2100 San Diego CA 92101-4496 Office Phone: 619-515-3226. E-mail: sls@procopio.com.

SHIPWAY, JOHN FRANCIS, retired career officer; b. Cherry Valley, N.Y. m. Lynn Doe. MS in Chem. Engring., U. Louisville, 1965; attended, Basic Officer Nuclear Power, Bainbridge, Md., Naval Nuclear Power Tng. Unit, West Milton, N.Y., Naval Sub. Sch., Groton, Conn., Def. Syss. Mgmt. Coll., Ft. Belvoir, Va., 1988; grad., Navy War Coll., Newport, R.I. Commd. ensign USN, 1965; advanced through grades to rear admiral, 1994; communicator USS Cubera (SS 347), 1967; asst. damage control, main propulsion USS Von Steuben; exec. officer nuclear sub. NR-1, 1971-75; exec. officer USS Swordfish (SSN 579), 1971-78; asst. to program mgr. MK 48 torpedo acquisition program Naval Sea Sys. Cmd., 1978-81; comdr. USS Los Angeles (SSN 688), 1981-85; comdg. officer nuclear power tng. unit, 1985-87; acquisition profl., 1985; program mgr. SSN 688 attack sub. acquisition program, 1988-91; program mgr. Seawolf, 1991-92; program exec. officer Dept. of Navy, 1992-95; dep. comdr. subs. naval sea sys. cmd., 1995-98; comdr. Naval Undersea Warfare Ctr., 1995-98; dir. strategic system programs, 1998-2000. Decorated 4 Legion of Merit awards. Mem. Am. Soc. Naval Engrs., Assn. Scientists and Engrs., U.S. Naval Inst., Naval Sub. League. Office: Strategic Sys Dept Navy 3801 Nebraska Ave NW Washington DC 20393-0001

SHIRAI, SCOTT, communications executive; b. Honolulu, June 5, 1942; s. George Yoshio and Thelma Takeko (Tominaga) S.; m. Michelle M.; children: Todd, Kimberly, Lance, Lyle, April. MusB, U. Hawaii, 1983. Exec. dir. news, reporter Sta. KHON-TV, Honolulu, 1974—81; asst. gen. mgr. Vanguard Investments, Berkeley, Calif., 1976—79; newscaster Sta. KPOI, Honolulu, 1979—80; news dir. Sta. KGU, Honolulu, 1981—82; owner Visual Perspectives, 1980—; dir. pub. rels. Hawaiian Electric Co., Honolulu, 1982—90; dir. cmty. rels. Hawaiian Electric Industries, 1990—2000; chmn., dir. Colo. Pub. TV, Denver, 2000—; exec. dir. Japan Am. Soc. of Colo., 2000—02; dir. The Samaritan Inst., 2000—03; exec. dir. Combined Fed. Campaign, Mile High United Way, Denver, 2002—; sr. cons. Myerberg Shain & Assocs., 2004—. Instr. U. Hawaii, 1984-99; pres. Hawaii Cmty. TV, 1993-2000; dir. BBB of Hawaii, 1995-2000. Author: Karaoke: Sing Along Guide to Fun & Confidence, 1997; dir., prodr. Gridiron, 1998, 99, 2002-2004. Chair, dir. Hawaii Pub. TV Found., 1997-2000; bd. dirs., sec. Hawaii Com. for Freedom of Press, 1982-99; bd. dirs. Mental Health Assn. in Hawaii, 1981—, Moanalua Gardens Found., 1981-84, Health and Cmty Svcs. Coun., 1982-86, Friends of Father Damien, 1986; v.p. Mele Nani Singers, 1986—; mem. Mayor's Adv. Com. on Mcpl. TV, 1987, Office of hawaiian Affairs Pub. Rels. Adv. Com., 1987; sec., dir. Pro Geothermal Alliance, 1990-91. Recipient Jefferson award, Honolulu Advertiser, 1985, Gold award, Audio Visual Prodrs. Assn. Am., 1985, Audio Visual Dept. of Yr. award, Videography mag., 1986, Award of Excellence, Nat. Hospice Orgn., 1987, Intre award, Inst. Teleradial Atica P.R. Inc., 1988. Mem.: AFTRA (bd. dirs. 1980—83), ASTD, Hui Luna Club (bd. dirs. 1986—90), Hawaii Cmty. TV Assn. (pres. 1990—), Honolulu Cmty. Media Coun., Hawaii Film Bd., Hawaii Spkrs. Assn., Pub. Rels. Soc. Am. (past pres., nat. del. 1995—, sec., treas. Coll. of Fellows 2003, vice-chair Coll. of Fellows 2004, Pub. Rels. Profl. of Yr. award Hawaii chpt. 1999, Pub. Svc. award 2000, Paul M. Lund Pub. Svc. award 2000), Am. Film Inst., Internat. TV Assn. (pres. 1983—), Honolulu Press Club (bd. dirs. 1984—). Avocations: martial arts, singing. Office: Visual Perspectives 1083 W 124th Dr Westminster CO 80234 E-mail: shirai2@comcast.net.

SHIRAI, SHUN, law educator, lawyer; b. Tokyo, June 18, 1942; s. Kyo and Tomi Shirai; m. Junko Matsushita, Apr. 10, 1969; children: Akiko, Yuko, Jin. LLB, Hitotsubashi U., Tokyo, 1966, LLM, 1969. Cert. atty. at law. Asst. prof. criminal law Kokugakuin U., Tokyo, 1974-81, prof., 1981—, dean Grad. Sch., 1999-2001. Atty. Tokyo 2nd Bar Assn., 1992—. Author: Phenomenology of Crime, 1984, rev. edit., 1998, Thought on Criminal Law of Ancient India, 1985, Legal History on Criminal Law of Ancient India, 1990, Philosophy of Criminal Law in Ancient India, 1995, Phenomenology and Indian Philosophy for the Study on Ancient Indian Criminal Law, 1997, Prof. Shirai's Lectures on the Law of Criminal Procedure, 1998, Philosophy of Criminal Law in Bhagavad-gītā at Ancient India, 1998, Crime and Sorrowness of Human Being, 1999, Defence Lawyer's Statements in Criminal Court, 2000, Thoughts on Death Penalty in Ancient India, 2000, The Sanskrit, as a Legal Language, appearing in Judicial Documents of British India and Non-Violent Theory of Punishment, originated in Ancient India, 2000, Thought on Righteousness in Criminal Law, handed down by Tradition from Ancient India, 2002, On Basic Principles of Hindu Criminology, derived from Ancient Indian Criminal Law, 2002, Introduction to Study on Practice of Japanese Criminal Jurisdiction, 2003, Philosophy of Crime of Contemporary Indian Thought on Human Being, 2003—. Mem. Indian History Congress. Buddhist. Home: 703 Kinsen Bldg 2-16-1 Hanakawado Taito-ku Tokyo 111-0033 Japan Office: Kokugakuin U 4-10-28 Higashi Shibuya-Ku Tokyo 150-8440 Japan

SHIRAI, YASUHIRO, linguistic educator; s. Tatsuo and Masako Shirai. MA in Tchg. English as a Second Lang., UCLA, 1989, PhD in Applied Linguistics, 1991. From asst. to assoc. prof. of English linguistics Daito Bunka U., Tokyo, 1991—97; from asst. to assoc. prof. of linguistics Cornell U., Ithaca, NY, 1997—. Assoc. editor First Lang. jour., 2003—; editl. bd. mem. Studies in Second Lang. Acquisition jour., 2004—; vis. assoc. prof. Carnegie Mellon U., Pitts., 1995—96; plenary spkr. various internat. acad. confs. Author/editor (6 books in field). Named Outstanding Prof. or Rschr., U.S. Immigration and Naturalization Svcs., 1997; recipient Grant-in-Aid for Sci. Rsch., Japan Soc. for the Promotion of Sci., 1993—94, 1994—95, 1995—96, 1996—98, 1999—2001, Japan Found. Rsch. fellowship, Japan Found., 2001—02. Mem.: Japanese Soc. for Lang. Scis. (exec. bd. mem. 1999—2004). E-mail: ys54@cornell.edu.

SHIRCLIFF, JAMES VANDERBURGH, communications executive; b. Vincennes, Ind., Dec. 11, 1938; s. Thomas Maxwell and Martha Bayard (Somes) S.; m. Sally Anne Hoing, June 20, 1964; children: Thomas, Susan, Anne, Catherine, Caroline. AB, Brown U., 1961; postgrad., U. Va., 1963-64. Asst. gen. mgr. Pepsi Cola Allied Bottlers, Inc., Lynchburg, Va., 1964-65, v.p., divisional coord., 1966-68, v.p., dir. personnel, 1968-70; gen. mgr. First Colony Canners, Inc., Lynchburg, 1965-66; v.p., gen. mgr. GCC Beverages, Inc., Lynchburg, 1970-74, group v.p., 1974-75; corp. v.p. Gen. Cinema Corp., Beverage Divsn., 1976-77; owner/mgr. WLLL-AM, WGOL-FM, 1977-86; pres. Jamarbo Corp., 1977-88. Chmn. bd. SignWaves, Inc., pres., The Shircliff Partnership, Ltd., presdl. interchange exec., 1975-76; exec. dir. Nat. Indsl. Energy Coun., Dept. Commerce, Washington, 1975-76. V.p. JOBS, Lynchburg, 1970; dir. Ctrl. Va. Health Planning Coun., 1974-75; mem. Govs. Indsl. Energy Adv. Coun., 1976—; dir. Piedmont coun., Boy Scouts Am., 1972-73; mem. City of Lynchburg Keep Lynchburg Beautiful Commn., 1974-75, chmn. emergency planning bd., 1974-75, chmn. overall econ. planning coun., 1977-88; bd. dirs. Lynchburg Broadway Theatre, 1973-75, Acad. Music, 1973-74, United Fund, Lynchburg, 1966-67, Ctrl. Va. Industries, 1971-72, VA. Pub. Telecomm. Coun.; former trustee Culver Ednl. Found.; chmn. campaign United Way, 1982, pres., 1983; co-founder, chmn. Citizens for a Clean Lynchburg; campaign chmn. United Way of Ctrl. Va., Dir., 1996; chmn. Arts Coun. Ctrl. Va., 1990-93; mem. nat. adv. coun. U.S. Small Bus. Adminstrn., 1990-93; past trustee Va. Episc. Sch.; past mem. pres.' coun. Randolph-Macon Women's Coll., Ctrl. Va. C.C. Found. Bd.; past mem. Va-Israel Commn.; dir. Lynchburg Hist. Found., 1996-99. Lt. (j.g.) USN, 1961-63. Recipient Cloyd Meml. award for outstanding svc., Greater Lynchburg C. of C., 1975; Va. Soft Drink Assn. citation, 1970, 73, 74; NCCJ Brotherhood citation; Pub. Svc. award RAdio-TV Commn. of So. Bapt. Conf., NCCJ State Adv. Bd., Exec. Com. Swensen's Owners Coun., 1988, Centurian award for bus. moral and leadership C. of C., 1999. Mem. Va. Soft Drink Assn. (pres. 1973-74), Va. Pepsi Cola Bottlers Assn. (pres. 1970-73), Nat., Va. (dir. 1974, pres. 1985-86) assns. broadcasters, Lynchburg Advt. Club (v.p.), Va. AP Broadcasters Assn. (pres.), Lynchburg Fine Arts Ctr. (pres.), Va. C. of C. (dir. 1976-79), Greater Lynchburg C. of C. (dir., v.p. 1973-74, chmn. cmty. appearance task force 1977-79), Culver Academies Alumni Assn. (pres.), Culver Cum Laude Soc. (award 1996, hon.), Meansa, Boonsboro Country Club, Navy League, The Pavane Club, Knight Sovereign Mil. Order Malta Fedn. Assn., Rotary (past pres., Paul Harris fellow 1982, dist. gov. 1986-87). Roman Catholic.

SHIRE, DAVID LEE, composer; b. Buffalo, July 3, 1937; s. Irving Daniel and Esther Miriam (Sheinberg) S.; m. Talia Rose Coppola, Mar. 29, 1970 (div.); 1 child, Matthew Orlando; m. Didi Conn. Feb. 11, 1984; 1 child, Daniel Joshua. BA, Yale U., 1959. Film scores include The Conversation, 1974, The Taking of Pelham 1-2-3, 1974, Farewell, My Lovely, 1975, The Hindenburg, 1975, All the President's Men, 1977, Saturday Night Fever (adaptation and additional music), 1977, Norma Rae, 1979 (Acad. award for best original song It Goes Like It Goes), Only When I Laugh, 1981, The World According to Garp, 1982, Max Dugan Returns, 1983, 2010, 1984, Return to Oz, 1985, Short Circuit, 1986, 'Night, Mother, 1986, Vice Versa, 1988, Monkey Shines, 1988, Paris Trout, 1991, Bed and Breakfast, 1992, The Journey Inside (IMAX), 1993, One Night Stand, 1994, Ash Wednesday, 2002; TV scores include Raid on Entebbe, 1977 (Emmy nomination), The Defection of Simas Kudirka, 1978 (Emmy nomination), Do You Remember Love?, 1985 (Emmy nomination), Promise, 1986, Echoes in the Darkness, 1987, The Women of Brewster Place, 1989, The Kennedys of Massachusetts, 1990 (Emmy nomination), Common Ground, 1990, Sarah Plain & Tall, 1991, Last Wish, 1992, Broadway Bound, 1992, Skylark, 1993, Remember, 1993, The Companion, 1994, My Brother's Keeper, 1995, Serving in Silence, 1995, The Heidi Chronicles, 1995, My Antonia, 1995, The Streets of Laredo, 1995, Last Stand at Saber River, 1997, Rear Window, 1998 (Emmy nomination), Double Platinum, 1999, Small Vices, 1999, These Old Broads, 2001, Two Against Time, 2001; theatre scores include The Sap of Lie, 1961, Graham Crackers, 1962, The Unknown Soldier and His Wife, 1967, How Do You Do, I Love You, 1968, Love Match, 1970, Starting Here, Starting Now, 1977, Baby, 1983 (Tony nominee best mus. and best original score), Urban Blight, 1988, Closer Than Ever, 1989 (Outer Critics Circle award best off-Broadway musical and best score), Big, 1996 (Tony nominee best score); composer Sonata for Cocktail Piano, 1965; recorded songs include Autumn, 1959, Starting Here, Starting Now, 1965, What About Today?, 1969, Manhattan Skyline, 1977, The Promise, 1978 (Acad. award nomination), It Goes Like It Goes, 1979 (Acad. award), With You I'm Born Again, 1979; albums include Saturday Night Fever, 1977 (Grammy award 1978), Starting Here, Starting Now, 1977 (Grammy nomination 1977), Baby, 1984, Return to Oz, 1985, Closer Than Ever, 1990, David Shire at The Movies, 1991, Big, 1996. With Army N.G., 1960-66. Mem. Composers and Lyricists Guild Am., Am. Fedn. Musicians, Broadcast Music Inc., Acad. Motion Picture Arts and Scis., Nat. Acad. Rec. Arts and Scis., Nat. Acad. TV Arts and Scis., Dramatists Guild Am. (coun. mem.). Jewish. Office: Ste 304 16501 Ventura Blvd Encino CA 91436-2067 Personal E-mail: dshire@aol.com.

SHIRE, DONALD THOMAS, retired air products and chemicals executive, lawyer; b. Boston, Jan. 13, 1930; s. Thomas J. and Nellie M. S.; m. Anne Court Bither, Nov 21, 1953; children: Jennifer Anne, Andrew Carter, Daniel Orchard. BS in Bus. Adminstrn, Boston U., 1951, LL.B., 1953; postgrad., Harvard Bus. Sch., 1985; LLD (hon.), Muhlenberg Coll., 1997. Atty. Air Products and Chems., Inc., 1957-64, sec., atty., 1964-75, sec., asst. gen. counsel, 1975-78, v.p. energy and materials, 1978-85, v.p. human resources, 1986-90, sr. v.p. human resources and adminstrn., 1990-91, sr. v.p. adminstrn., 1991-93; ret., 1993; also bd. dirs. Air Products and Chems., Inc. Chmn. Air Products Found., 1991-93; bd. dirs. Lehigh Valley Bus./Edn. Partnership. Trustee Muhlenberg Coll. (life), 1976-95, Lehigh Valley Health Network., 1983-99, Lt. USNR, 1954-57. Mem. Am. Arbitration Assn. Home: 27 Drake Ln Scarborough ME 04074

SHIRE, HAROLD RAYMOND, law educator, writer; b. Denver, Nov. 23, 1910; s. Samuel Newport and Rose Betty (Herman) S.; m. Cecilia Goldhaar, May 9, 1973; children: David, Darcy, Esti, Donna, Margaret. MBA, Pepperdine U., 1972, LLD (hon.), 1975; JD, Southwestern U., L.A., 1974; M in Liberal Arts, U. So. Calif., 1977; PhD in Human Behavior, U.S. Internat. U., San Diego, 1980. Bar: Calif. 1937, U.S. Dist. Ct. (so. dist.) Calif. 1939, U.S. Supreme Ct. 1978. Dep. dist. atty. L.A. County, Calif., 1937-38; asst. U.S. atty. So. Dist. Calif., L.A. and San Diego, 1939-42; pvt. practice L.A., 1946-56; pres., chmn. bd. Gen. Connectors Corp., U.S. and Eng., 1956-73; prof. mgmt. and law Pepperdine U., Malibu, Calif., 1974-75, U.S. Internat. U., San Diego, 1980-83; dir. Bestobell Aviation, Eng., 1970-74. Author: Cha No Yu and Symbolic Interactionism: Method of Predicting Japanese Behavior, 1980, The Tea Ceremony, 1984. Patentee aerospace pneumatics; invented flexible connectors; designed, manufactured flexible integrity systems. Advisor U. S.C. Gerontology Andrus Ctr., pre-retirement tng., 1976-80; bd. dirs. Pepperdine U., 1974-80; nat. bd. govs. Union Orthodox Jewish Congregations Am., 1973—; mem. Rep. Nat. Com.; pres. Jewish Nat. Fund Legion of Honor, 1991—; mem. Presdl. Roundtable, Washington, 1989-97; mem. Inner Cir., Pres. Regan and Bush, 1989-92; life mem. Rep. Nat. Com. With U.S. Army, 1942-46. Decorated chevalier du vieux moulin (France); companion Royal Aero. Soc. (U.K.); recipient Tea Name Grand Master Soshitsu Sen XV Urasenke Sch., Kyoto, Japan, 1976, Medal of Honor Jewish Nat. Fund, Legion of Honor, 1991, U.S. Senate Medal of Freedom. Mem. ABA, Am. Welding Soc., Soc. Material and Process Engrs., Am. Legion (svc. officer China #1 Shanghai), Calif. Symphony Soc. (pres. 1998—), Masons (32 degree, Hiram award 1994), Royal Arch, Shrine, Legion of Honor Jewish Nat. Fund (nat. chmn. bd. 1999). Achievements include design and manufacture of fluidic systems flexible integrity for Saturn IV and welding in Apollo XI landing on moon, 1969. Office: PO Box 1352 Beverly Hills CA 90213-1352

SHIRE, LYDIA, food service executive; b. Brookline, Mass. Grad., Cordon Bleu Cooking Sch., London, 1970. Chef Maison Robert, Boston, Harvest, Cambridge, Mass.; restaurant chef Cafe Plaza; chef Parker's, 1981; opened with Jasper White Seasons Restaurant, exec. chef, Four Seasons Hotel on Beverly Hills, Calif., 1986—89; chef, owner Biba, Boston, 1989—, Pignoli, Boston, 1994—. Named Cafe Plaza as Best Dining Rm., Boston mag., One of Am.'s Ten Best Chefs, Food & Wine mag., Pignoli as One of Top Boston Dining Spots, Food & Wine, Biba as One of Top 15 Restaurants in U.S., Money mag., Biba as Best Restaurant in Boston, Boston mag.; recipient Four Stars for Cafe Plaza, Boston Globe, Ivy award. Mem.: Am. Inst. Wine and Food, James Beard Found. (Am.'s Best Chef of N.E., One of Top Chefs in Am.). Office: Biba 272 Boylston St Boston MA 02116

SHIRE, TALIA ROSE, actress; b. Jamaica, N.Y., Apr. 25, 1946; d. Carmine and Italia (Pennino) Coppola; m. David Lee Shire, Mar. 29, 1970 (div.); 1 son, Matthew Orlando; m. Jack Schwartzman, Aug. 23, 1979; children: Jason Francesco, Robert Coppola. Films include The Dunwich Horrors, 1971, The Christian Licorice State, 1971, Godfather, 1972, The Outside Man, 1973, Godfather II, 1974 (Oscar nominee for Best Supporting Actress), Rocky, 1976 (Oscar nominee for best actress, N.Y. Film Critics award for Best Supporting Actress), Old Boyfriends, 1979, Rocky II, 1979, Windows, 1980, Rocky III, 1982, Rocky IV, 1985, Bed and Breakfast, 1990, Gold Heaven, 1990, Godfather Part III, 1990, Rocky V, 1990, Cold Heaven, 1992, Bed & Breakfast, 1992, Deadfall, 1993, (Disney channel movie) Mark Twain, 1990, (HBO movie) getting there, 1991, She's So Lovely, 1997, Lured Innocence, 1998, Divorce: A Contemporary Western, 1998, Can I Play?, 1998, Palmer's Pick Up, 1999, Caminho dos Sonhos, 1999, Lured Innocence, 1999, The Visit, 2000; TV appearances include Foster & Laurie, 1975, Rich Man, Poor Man, 1976, Kill Me If You Can, 1977, Daddy, I Don't Like It Like This, 1978, Blood Vows, 1987, Mark Twain and Me, 1991, For Richer, For Poorer, 1992, Chatilly Lace, 1993, Born into Exile, 1997; prodr. Homo Sapien: People from Another Star, 1986, Lionheart, 1987; assoc. prodr.: The Landlady, 1998.

SHIREK, JOHN RICHARD, retired savings and loan executive; b. Bismarck, N.D., Feb. 5, 1926; s. James Max and Anna Agatha (Lala) S.; m. Ruth Martha Lietz, Sept. 22, 1950; children: Barbara Jo (Mrs. James A. Fowler), Jon Richard, Kenneth Edward. Student, U. Minn., 1944-46; BS with honors, Rollins Coll., 1978. Sports editor Bismarck (N.D.) Tribune, 1943-44; with Gate City Savs. and Loan Assn., Fargo, N.D., 1947-65, v.p., dir., 1960-65; exec. v.p., dir. 1st Fed. Savs. and Loan Assn., Melbourne, Fla., 1966-70; pres., dir. 1st Fed. Savs. and Loan Assn., Cocoa, Fla., 1970-82; exec. v.p., dir. The First F.A. (formerly 1st Fed. Savs. and Loan Assn. of Orlando), 1982-91. Interim pres. Freedom Savs. and Loan Assn., Tampa, Fla., 1987-88; trustee Savs. & Loan Found., Inc., 1980-84; dir. Fin. Trans. Syss., Inc., Magnolia Svcs. Corp., 1st Cocoa Corp., Magnolia Realty Co., 1982-91. Chmn., dir. United Fund, Fargo, N.D., 1962-65; dir., exec. bd. mem. Boy Scouts Am., 1960-70, mem. adv. bd. cen. Fla. coun., 1983-85, 91-95, exec. bd., 1985-91, v.p. long-range planning, 1989-91; bd. assocs. Fla. Inst. Tech., founding pres., 1968; moderator St. Johns Presbytery, 1979, chmn. adv. coun., 1980-81; chair local arrangements com. 1993 Gen. Assembly Presbyn. Ch.; moderator Synod of Fla., 1983, Ctrl. Fla. Presbytery, 1991, coordinating coun., 1992; coun. mem. Synod of South Atlantic, 2002-2003; mem. adv. bd. Brevard Art Ctr. and Mus., 1980-82; bd. dirs., founding chmn. devel. coun. Holmes Regional Med. Ctr., Melbourne, 1981-84; bd. dirs. Orlando Regional Med. Ctr. Found., 1982-85, Jr. Achievement Cen. Fla., 1989-91; mem. fin. com. Mayor's Task Force on Housing, 1983-84; chmn. spl. com. on Nat. Coun. Chs./World Coun. Chs. rels. Presbyn. Ch. in U.S.A., 1983-86; pres. Ecumenical Ctr. Inc., Orlando, 1985-91, bd. dirs., 2001—; chmn. Fla. adv. com. Ctr. Theol. Studies Columbia Theol. Sem., 1991-95. Lt. (j.g.) USNR, World War II. Mem. Fla. Savs. and Loan League (past dir.), Fla. Savs. and Loan Svcs. (past dir.), Savs. and Loan Found. (state membership chmn. 1976), Fla. Savs. and Loan Polit. Action Com. (dir. 1976-82), U.S. Savs. and Loan League (chmn. advt. and pub. rels. com. 1969-70, dir. S.E. conf. 1975-80), Downtown Melbourne Assn. (past pres.), Cocoa Rotary (pres. 1979), Masons, Shriners, Elks, Beta Theta Pi, Omicron Delta Epsilon. Republican. Home: PO Box 568831 Orlando FL 32856-8831 Personal E-mail: sjohnr@aol.com.

SHIREMAN, JOAN FOSTER, social work educator; b. Cleve., Oct. 28, 1933; d. Louis Omar and Genevieve (Duguid) Foster; m. Charles Howard Shireman, Mar. 18, 1967; 1 child, David Louis. BA, Radcliffe Coll., 1956; MA, U. Chgo., 1959, PhD, 1968. Caseworker N.H. Children's Aid Soc., Manchester, 1959-61; dir. research Chgo. Child Care Soc., 1968-72; assoc. prof. U. Ill., Chgo., 1972-85; prof. Portland State U., Oreg., 1985—2003, dir. PhD program, 1992-99; interim exec. dir. Partnership for Rsch., Tng. and Grad. Edn. in Child Welfare, 1994; prof. emerita Portland State U., Oreg., 2003—. Research cons. child welfare orgns., Ill., 1968-85, Oreg. 1985—; lectr. U. Chgo., 1968-72. Author: Critical Issues in Child Welfare, 2003; co-author: Care and Commitment: Foster Parent Adoption Decisions, 1985, Adoption: Theory, Policy and Practice, 1997; mem. editl. bd. Jour. Sch. Social Work, 1978-81, Social Work Rsch. and Abstracts, 1990-93, Children and Youth Svcs. Rev., 1990—, Jour. Social Work Edn., 1990-95; contbr. articles to profl. jours., chpts. to books. Bd. dirs. Oreg. chpt. Nat. Assn. for Prevention Child Abuse, 1985-87, Friendly House, Portland, 1991-97, 2002-03, Camp Fire U.S.A. Portland Metro Coun., 2002-04; mem. adv. com. Children's Svcs. divsn. State of Oreg., 1985-95. Grantee HEW, 1980-82, Chgo. Community Trust, 1982-86, Oreg. Children's Trust Fund, 1991-96. Mem. NASW, AAUP,

Acad. Cert. Social Workers, Coun. on Social Work Edn., Phi Beta Kappa. Home: 13584 SW Snowfire Dr Portland OR 97236 Office: Portland State U Grad Sch Social Work PO Box 751 Portland OR 97207-0751 E-mail: shiremanj@pdx.edu.

SHIRES, GEORGE THOMAS, surgeon, educator; b. Waco, Tex., Nov. 22, 1925; s. George Thomas and Donna Mae (Smith) S.; m. Robbie Jo Martin, Nov. 27, 1948; children: Donna Blain, George Thomas III, Jo Ellen. MD, U. Tex., Dallas, 1948. Intern Mass. Meml. Hosp., Boston, 1948—49; resident in surgery Parkland Meml. Hosp., Dallas, 1950—53; faculty U. Tex. Southwestern Med. Sch., Dallas, 1953—60, assoc. prof. surgery, acting chmn. dept., 1960—61, prof., chmn. dept., 1961—74; surgeon in chief surg. svcs. Parkland Meml. Hosp., 1960—74; prof., chmn. dept. surgery U. Wash. Sch. Medicine, Seattle, 1974—75; chief of svc. Harborview Med. Ctr., Seattle, Univ. Hosp., Seattle, 1974—75; chmn. dept. surgery N.Y. Hosp.-Cornell U. Med. Coll., 1975—91; dean, provost for med. affairs Cornell U. Med. Coll., 1987—91, prof. emeritus, 1996—; prof., chmn. surgery Tex. Tech. U., Lubbock, 1991—95, Canizaro disting. prof. surgery, 1995—97; prof. surgery U. Nev. Sch. Medicine, Las Vegas, 1997—. Cons. Surgeon Gen., U.S. Army, 1965—75, Jamaica Hosp., 1978—91, Inst. Medicine NAS, 1975—; metabolism and trauma com. NAS-NRC, 1964—71, com. trauma, 1964—71; rsch. program evaluation com., reviewer clin. investigation applications career devel. program VA, 1972—76; gen. med. rsch. program projects com. NIH NIH, 1965—69; mem. Surgery A study sect., 1970—74, chmn., 1976—78; mem. Nat. Adv. Gen. Med. Scis. Coun., 1980—84; cons. editl. bd. Jour. Trauma, 1968—88. Mem. editl. bd.: Year Book Med. Publs., 1970—92, Annals of Surgery, 1972—, Surg. Techniques Illustrated: An International Comparative Text, 1974—75, Am. Jour. Surgery, 1968—, Contemporary Surgery, 1973—89, assoc. editor-in-chief: Infections in Surgery, 1981, mem. editl. bd.: Jour. Clin. Surgery, 1980—82; editor: Surgery, Gynecology and Obstetrics, 1982—93. Lt. M.C. USNR, 1949—50, Lt. M.C. USNR, 1953—55. Fellow: Coll. Medicine South Africa (hon.); mem.: AMA, ACS (bd. regents 1971—82, chmn. bd. regents 1978—80, pres. 1981—82), James IV Assn. Surgeons (bd. dirs. 1980—81, sec. 1981—87, pres. 1987—91), Allen O. Whipple Surg. Soc., Western Surg. Assn., N.Y. Surg. Soc. (pres. 1981—82), So. Surg. Assn., Soc. Univ. Surgeons (chmn. publs. com. 1969—71), Soc. Surg Chairmen (pres. 1972—74), Soc. Clin. Surgery, Soc. Surgery Alimentary Tract, Pan Pacific Surg. Assn., Pan-Am. Med. Assn. (surgery coun. 1971), Am. Burn Assn., Internat. Surg. Soc. (sec. 1978—81, v.p. 1982—83, pres. U.S. chpt. 1984—85), Internat. Soc. Burn Injuries, Halsted Soc., Digestive Disease Found. (founding mem.), Am. Surg. Assn. (sec. 1969—74, pres. 1980), Am. Burn Assn., Am. Assn. Surgery Trauma, Dallas Soc. Gen. Surgeons (pres. 1972—74, pres.-elect), Am. Bd. Surgery (dir. 1968—74, chmn. 1972—74, diplomate), Surg. Biology Club (sec. 1968—70), Phi Beta Pi, Alpha Pi Alpha, Alpha Omega Alpha. Office: U Nev Sch Medicine 2040 W Charleston Blvd Ste 501 Las Vegas NV 89102-2207 Office Phone: 702-671-2338., 702-671-2297. Business E-Mail: gtshires@nvtrauma.com. E-mail: tshires@med.unr.edu.

SHIRES, LINDA M. English educator, writer; b. Providence, R.I., July 29, 1950; d. Philip Munroe and Helen English Shires; m. U. C. Knoepflmacher, Aug. 15, 1988; 1 child, Alexander stepchildren: Julie, Paul, Daniel. BA in Classics, Wheaton Coll., Norton, Mass., 1972; MA in Classics, Brown U., 1973; BA in English, Oxford (Eng.) U., 1977; MA/PhD in English, Princeton U., 1981. From asst. to assoc. prof. Syracuse (N.Y.) U., 1981—96, prof. English, 1996—. Referee presses, jours., univs., other orgns.; mem. adv. bd. Victorians Inst. Jour. U. N.C., 1995—; vis. assoc. prof. Princeton U., 1990—92. Author: British Poetry of the Second World War, 1985, Coming Home, 2003; co-author: Telling Stories, 1988, 5th edit., 2002; editor: Rewriting the Victorians, 1992; mem. editl. bd.: Nines, 2004—. Recipient directorship, NEH, 1993, 1995; fellow, Guggenheim Found., 1993—94. Mem.: MLA (elections com. 1990—92), Jewish Studies Assn., N.E. Victorians Assn. Jewish. Office: Syracuse U 401 Hall of Langs Syracuse NY 13244

SHIREY, JOHN FREDERICK, local government administrator; b. Muncie, Ind., July 10, 1949; s. John Mark and Chloie Marie Shirey; m. Marilyn Elaine Murden, Apr. 20, 1979; children: Jill Meredith, Gregory Mark, Elizabeth Anne. BSIE, Purdue U., 1971; MPA, U. So. Calif., 1973. Adminstrv. asst. City of Monterey Park, Calif., 1972-75; legis. analyst City of Long Beach, Calif., 1975-76, dir. intergovtl. rels., 1976-79, asst. city mgr., 1987-93; legis. counsel Nat. League Cities, Washington, 1979-82; asst. exec. dir. County of L.A. Cmty. Devel. Commn., Calif., 1982-85; asst. chief adminstrv. officer County of L.A., 1985-87; city mgr. City of Cin., 1993—2001; exec. dir. Calif. Redevelopment Assn., Sacramento, 2002—. Lectr. grad. ctr. for pub. policy and adminstrn., Calif. State U., Long Beach, 1977-79, 83-93, sch. pub. adminstrn. U. So. Calif, Los Angeles, 1986-93. Master track and field ofcl, USA Track and Field, So. Calif., 1974-93, Ohio, 1993-2002, Pacific, 2003—; bd. councilors Sch. Pub. Adminstrn., U. So. Calif., L.A., 1983-87, MPA adv. bd., 1998—, mem. adv. bd. Sacramento Ctr., 2002—; bd. dirs. Calif. Assn. Local Econ. Devel. Named Outstanding Young Man Am., U.S. Jaycees, 1980. Mem. Am. Soc. Pub. Adminstrn. (chpt. coun. 1978-79, 84-87, 94-2000, 2003—, nat. chmn. sect. on intergovtl. adminstrn. and mgmt. 1979-80, chpt. pres. 1988, 98, 2004, Seasongood Good Govt. award 2003), Internat. City Mgmt. Assn. (Program Excellence award for outstanding partneships 2001), Am. Soc. Assn. Execs., Internat. Econ. Devel. Coun., Mcpl. Mgmt. Assts. So. Calif. (pres. 1974-75), Urban Land Inst. Mem. Christian Ch. (Disciples of Christ, elder). Home: 7711 Rivers Landing Dr Sacramento CA 95831-5782 Office Phone: 916-448-8760.

SHIRILAU, MARK STEVEN, utilities executive; b. Long Beach, Calif., Dec. 13, 1955; s. Kenneth Eugene and Marrjorie Irene (Thorvick) Shirey; m. Jeffery Michael Lau, Nov. 25, 1984 (dec. Aug. 1993). BSEE, U. Calif., Irvine, 1977, MS in Bus. Adminstrn., 1980, PhD, 1988; M in Engring., Calif. Poly. State U., 1978; diploma in theology, Episc. Theol. Sch., Claremont, Calif., 1984; MA in Religion, Sch. Theology at Claremont, 1985. Ordained priest Ecumenical Cath. Ch., 1987, consecrated bishop, 1991; registered profl. engr., Calif., N.Y., Tex.; lic. contractor, Calif. Grad. asst. Electric Power Inst., 1977-78; pres., CEO M.S.E., Santa Ana, Calif., 1977-87; adminstrv. mgr. EECO Inc., Santa Ana, 1979-83; fin. engr. So. Calif. Edison Co., Rosemead, 1983-84, conservation engr., 1984-85, conservation supr., 1985-89; exec. v.p. Aloha Sys., Inc., Villa Grande, Calif., 1989-93, pres., 1993—, also bd. dirs.; lectr. engring. Citrus Coll., Glendora, Calif., 2000—. Bd. dirs. Ewing Consol. Corp., Outrider Trucking, Inc.; part-time instr. Santa Ana Coll., 1982-84, Citrus Coll., Glendora, Calif., 2000-; lectr. engring. West Coast U., Orange, Calif., 1984-91; bd. dirs. Am. Electronics Assn. Credit Union, Sweetwater Springs Water Dist., Heat Pump Coun. So. Calif., AIDS Interfaith Network Sonoma County. Author: Triune Love: An Insight into God, Creation, and Humanity, 1983, Salvation, Scripture and Sexuality, 1992, History and Overview of the Ecumenical Catholic Church, 1993, Power 101, A Basic Introduction to Electric Utility Power, 1998, The Five Fatal Fears, 2002. Archbishop, primate Ecumenical Cath. Ch.; chief chaplain svcs. Nolanville (Tex.) Police Dept., 1998-2000; chaplain Jonestown (Tex.) Police Dept., 2001—. Mem. IEEE (sr.), ASHRAE, Internat. Assn. Chiefs Police, Assn. Energy Mgrs. (sr.), Assn. Profl. Energy Mgrs. (bd. dirs.), Am. Soc. Nondestructive Testing, Assn. Energy Svcs. Profls. (bd. dirs., charter mem., exec. v.p.), Am. Soc. Safety Engrs., Nat. Assn. Chiefs Police, Pacific Bears Club (v.p.), Dignity Integrity (life), Eta Kappa Nu. Democrat. Home: 20 Lincoln Irvine CA 92604-1947 Office: 14801 Comet St Irvine CA 92604-2464 Office Phone: 949-851-2221. E-mail: archbishop@ecchurch.org., MarkS@alohasys.com.

SHIRLEY, AARON, pediatrician; b. Gluckstadt, Miss., Jan. 3, 1933; married; 4 children. BS, Tougaloo Coll., 1955; MD, McHarry Med. Coll., 1959, U. Miss., 1968. Intern Herbert Hosp., Tenn., 1959—60; gen. practice Vicksburg, 1960—65; project dir. Jackson-Hinds Comprehensive Health Ctr., Jackson, Miss., 1980—96; dir. cmty. health svcs. Jackson (Miss.) Med. Mall, 1996—; chmn. Jackson (Miss.) Med. Mall Found., 1996—. Mem. faculty medicine Tufts U. Medicine, Mass., 1968—73, U. Miss. Med. Sch., 1970—; head start cons. Am. Acad. Pediat., 1969—74; adv. bd. rural practice project Robert Wood Johnson Found., 1974—78; mem. Select Panel Prom. Child Health, Washington, 1979—81. Mem.: Inst. Medicine NAS (mem. coun. 1988—). Office: Jackson Med Mall Ste 615A 350 W Woodrow Wilson Ave Jackson MS 39213-7651*

SHIRLEY, BONNIE J. secondary school educator; d. John R. and Catherine G. Bartholomew; m. Alan D. Shirley, Nov. 26, 1966 (dec. 2003); 1 child, Scott A. BS in Sci., SUNY, Brockport, 1969, postgrad., 1974. Cert. tchr. N.Y. Tchr. Rochester (N.Y.) City Sch. Dist., 1967—2003, lead tchr., mentor, 1991—2003; tchr. Greece (N.Y.) Continuing Edn.; cons. Renaissance Learning, Madison, 2003—; asst. prof. Roberts Wesleyan Coll., Rochester. Mem. adv. bd. dept. edn. and human devel. SUNY, Brockport. Avocation: freelance writing. Home: 87 Ayer St Rochester NY 14615 Personal E-mail: bshirle1@rochester.rr.com.

SHIRLEY, DAVID ARTHUR, chemistry educator, science administrator; b. North Conway, NH, Mar. 30, 1934; m. Virginia Schultz, June 23, 1956 (dec. Mar. 1995); children: David N., Diane, Michael, Eric, Gail; m. Barbara Cerny, Dec. 26, 1995. BS, U. Maine, 1955, ScD (hon.), 1978; PhD in Chemistry, U. Calif.-Berkeley, 1959; D honoris causa, Free U. Berlin, 1987. With Lawrence Radiation Lab. (now Lawrence Berkeley Lab.), U. Calif., Berkeley, 1958-92, assoc. dir., head materials and molecular research div., 1975-80, dir., 1980-89, lectr. chemistry, 1959-60, asst. prof., 1960-64, assoc. prof., 1964-67, prof., 1967-92, vice chmn. dept. chemistry, 1968-71, chmn. dept. chemistry, 1971-75; sr. v.p. rsch., dean grad. sch. Pa. State U., University Park, 1992-96; dir. emeritus Lawrence Berkeley Nat. Lab., 1997—. Chair bd. overseers Fermilab. Contbr. over 400 rsch. articles. NSF fellow, 1955-58, 66-67, 70; recipient Ernest O. Lawrence award AEC, 1972, Humboldt award (sr. U.S. scientist); listed by Sci. Citation Index as one of the world's 300 most cited scientists for work published during 1965-78. Fellow Am. Phys. Soc.; mem. Nat. Acad. Scis., Am. Chem. Soc., AAAS, Am. Acad. Arts and Scis., Bohemian Club, Explorers Club, Sigma Xi, Tau Beta Pi, Sigma Pi Sigma, Phi Kappa Phi.

SHIRLEY, DONNA, museum director, former aerospace engineer; b. Wynnewood, Okla. 1 child, Laura. BS in Aerospace Engring., BA in Journalism, U. Okla.; MS in Aerospace Engring., U. So. Calif. With Jet Propulsion Lab., Pasadena, Calif., 1966—, Cassini project engr., mgr. exploration initiative studies, mgr. automation and robotics, mgr. Space Sta. program, mgr. mission design sect., project engr. for Mariner 10, mgr. Mars Pathfinder microrover Flight Experiment team, mgr. Mars exploration program; ret., 1998; pres. Managing Creativity, Norman, Okla.; assist. dean aerospace mechanical engrng. U. Oklahoma, 1999—2003; dir. Science Fiction Museum and Hall of Fame, Seattle, 2004—. Leader NASA-wide Sys. Engring. Working Group, 1990-93; leader NASA-wide team on program/project mgmt. NASA, 1991. Author: Managing Martians, 1998. Office: Science Fiction Museum and Hall of Fame 325 5th Ave N Seattle WA 98109*

SHIRLEY, GEORGE IRVING, tenor; b. Indpls., Apr. 18, 1934; s. Irving Ewing and Daisy (Bell) S.; m. Gladys Lee Ishop, June 24, 1956; children: Olwyn, Lyle. BS in Edn, Wayne State U., 1955, grad. student, 1955-56; H.D.H., Wilberforce U., 1967; LLD (hon.), Montclair State Coll., 1984; DFA (hon.), Lake Forest Coll., 1988. Tchr. music Detroit Bd. Edn., 1955-56; leading tenor Met. Opera, N.Y.C., 1961-73, Royal Opera, Covent Garden, London, 1967-79, Deutsche Opera, West Berlin, 1983—. Rec. sec. Am. Guild Mus. Artists, 1963-73; prof. voice U. Md., College Park, 1981-87, U. Mich., Ann Arbor, 1987—; artistic advisor New Sch. for Arts, Montclair, N.J.; prof. music U. Mich., 1987. Operatic debut in Die Fledermaus, Turnau Opera Players, Woodstock, N.Y., 1959, Teatro Novo, Milan; other appearances include Milan and Teatro Della Pergola, Florence, Italy, 1960, New Eng. Opera Theatre, 1961, Spring Opera, San Francisco, 1961, Festival of Two Worlds, Spoleto, Italy, 1961, Sante Fe Opera, 1961, N.Y.C. Opera, 1961, Met. Opera Co., 1961, Opera Soc. Washington, 1962, Teatro Colon, Buenos Aires, Argentina, 1964, La Scala, Milan, Italy, 1965, Glyndebourne Festival, Sussex, Eng., 1966, Scottish Opera, 1967, Royal Opera, Covent Garden, London, Eng., 1967, Amsterdam Festival, 1975, Netherlands Opera, 1976, Monte Carlo Opera, 1976, San Francisco Opera, 1977, Chgo. Lyric Opera, 1977, debut Deutsche Opera, W. Berlin, 1983. Winner Met. Opera Audition, 1961, Am. Opera Audition, 1960; recipient Nat. Arts Club award, 1960; winner Il Concorso di Musica e Danza Italy, 1960; named one of Disting. Scholar-tchr. U. Md., 1985-86 Mem. Nat. Assn. Tchrs. of Singing, Am. Guild Mus. Artists, AFTRA, Nat. Assn. Negro Musicians, Wayne State U. Alumni Assn. (award 1967), Alpha Phi Alpha, Phi Mu Alpha, Phi Kappa Phi, Omicron Delta Kappa, Pi Kappa Lambda. Office: care Ann Summers Internat Box 188 Sta A Toronto ON Canada M5W 1B2

SHIRLEY, GEORGE WILLIAM, retired music educator, farmer; b. May 30, 1922; s. William Aubry and Nell Gertrude (Harness) Shirley; m. Harriett Ellen Bunting. MusB, Ctrl. Coll., Fayette, Mo., 1944; MusM, U. Mich., 1950; postgrad., Ind. U., U. Tex. Asst. prof. music Ind. Ctrl. Coll. (now U. Indpls.), 1950—66, S.W. Mo. State U., Springfield, 1966—98. Sgt. U.S. Army, 1944—46. Mem.: Springfield Music Club. Baptist. Avocation: horseback riding. Home: 1938 S Dollison Ave Springfield MO 65807

SHIRLEY, GRAHAM EDWARD, management executive; b. Starkville, Miss., Jan. 4, 1943; s. Herman Milford and Helen (Lang) S.; m. Deborah Kay Long, 1996; children: Jennifer, Caryn, Tyler. BS, USAF Acad., 1966; MA, U. So. Calif., 1973. Commd. 2d lt. USAF, 1966, advanced through grades to brig. gen., 1988; ops. officer 393d Bomb Squadron, Pease AFB, N.H., 1977-78; comdr. 84th Fighter Interceptor Squadron, Castle AFB, Calif., 1978-80, 86th Tactical Fighter Wing, Ramstein Air Base, Germany, 1984-85, 20th Tactical Fighter Wing, RAF Upper Heyford, Eng., 1985-88; with Hdqrs. USAF, Washington, 1980-83, dir. regional plans, 1988-90; assigned to Air War Coll., Maxwell AFB, Ala., 1983-84; vice comdr. Air Force Intelligence Command, San Antonio, 1990-92; ret. brig. gen. USAF, 1992; pres. The Pegasus Group, Washington, 1992-97; sr. mgr. BearingPoint, LLC (formerly KPMG Cons.), San Antonio, 1997—. Decorated DSM, Legion of Merit, DFC, Air medal. Mem. Air Force Assn., Internat. Inst. for Strategic Studies (London), Air Force Acad. Assn. Grads., Daedalians. Avocations: flying, reading, hunting, fishing, travel. Home: 13746 Bluff Villas Ct San Antonio TX 78216-1940 Office: BearingPoint LLC 14100 San Pedro Ave #700 San Antonio TX 78232-4361 E-mail: ettington@msn.com., gshirley@bearingpoint.net. *An enlightened and progressive society cannot exist unless the leadership at all levels has compassion, integrity and courage. Compassion for the less fortunate—integrity to know what is right—courage to do what is right regardless of the personal consequences.*

SHIRLEY, VIRGINIA LEE, advertising executive; b. Kankakee, Ill., Mar. 24, 1936; d. Glenn Lee and Virginia Helen (Ritter) S. Student, Northwestern U., 1960-61. With prodn. control dept. Armour Pharm., Kankakee, 1954-58; exec. sec. Adolph Richman, Chgo., 1958-61; mgr. media dept. Don Kemper Co., Chgo., 1961-63, 65-69; exec. sec. Playboy mag., Chgo., 1964-65; exec. v.p. SMY Media inc., Chgo., 1969-96, CEO, chmn. bd., 1996-2000, CEO, 2000—. Mem. Tavern Club. Home: 1502-J S Prairie Ave Chicago IL 60605-2856 Office: SMY Media Inc 333 N Michigan Ave Chicago IL 60601-3901

SHIRLEY-QUIRK, JOHN, concert and opera singer; b. Liverpool, Eng., Aug. 28, 1931; arrived in US, 1990, naturalized, 2002; s. Joseph Stanley and Amelia (Griffiths) S.-Q.; m. Patricia May Hastie, July 1955 (dec. Feb. 1981); children: Kate, Peter; m. Sara Van Horn Watkins, Dec. 29, 1981 (dec. Dec. 1997); children: Benjamin, Emily (dec.), Julia. BSc, Liverpool U., 1953, MusD (hon.), 1977; D Univ., Brunel U., 1981. Asst. lectr. Acton Tech. Coll., London, 1956-60; vicar choral St. Paul's Cathedral, London, 1960-61; profl. singer, 1960—; joint artistic dir. Aldeburgh Festival, 1981-84. Mem. voice faculty Peabody Conservatory, Balt., 1991—; vis. artist Carnegie-Mellon U., Pitts., 1994-98. Numerous recs. and 1st performances, especially works of Benjamin Britten. Mem. ct. Brunel U., 1977-81. Flying officer RAF, 1952-55. Decorated comdr. Order of Brit. Empire. Mem. Royal Acad. Music (hon.). Business E-Mail: jssq@peabody.jhu.edu.

SHIRTLIFF, BRYAN, retail executive; m. Eve Shirtliff; 4 children. B, U. Montana. Various positions Am. Stores Co., 1983—96; v.p., health and beauty care and gen. merchandise Bruno's Inc.; dir. health care Rite Aid Corp., Camp Hill, Pa., 1998—99, dir., health care and seasonal, 1999—2000, v.p., seasonal and hardlines, 2000—03, sr. v.p., category mgmt., 2003—. Home: Rite Aid Corporation 30 Hunter Lane Camp Hill PA 17011

SHIRTUM, EARL EDWARD, retired civil engineer; b. Montague, Mich., Feb. 20, 1927; s. Earl Willard and Elizabeth Caroline (Boelke) S.; m. Martha Louise Wright, June 19, 1953. BS in Civil Engring., Ind. Tech. Coll., Ft. Wayne, 1950. Bridge design squad leader Mich. Dept. Transp., Lansing, 1952-63, transp. planning engr., 1963-96. Mem. Bridge Replacement and Rehab. Com., Lansing, 1967-94. With U.S. Army, 1945-46, ETO. Mem. Mich. Profl. Engring. Soc. (rep. engr. in govt. 1974-77), Lansing Engr. Club (bd. mem. 1980-84). Republican. Methodist. Avocations: fishing, bridge. Home: 1617 Victor Ave Lansing MI 48910-6511

SHIRVANI, ALIREZA, electrical engineer; b. Tehran, Iran, Jan. 9, 1975; s. Hassan Shirvani and Shahin Radfar; m. Negin Imani. BS in Elec. Engring., Sharif U. of Tech., Tehran, Iran, 1997; MS in Elec. Engring., Stanford U., Calif, 1999, PhD in Elec. Engring., 2003. Sr. mem. of tech. staff Tavanza Inc., Sunnyvale, Calif., 2000—02; staff design engr. Marvell Semiconductor, Sunnyvale, Calif., 2002—. Author: (book) Design and Control of RF Power Amplifiers, 2003; contbr. scientific papers to profl. confs. Mem.: IEEE (Jour. of Solid-State Circuits Best Paper award 2002). Achievements include research in in the area of radio-frequency power amplifiers; patents pending for several innovations in the area of radio-frequency integrated circuits. Office: Marvell Semiconductor 700 First Ave MS 209 Sunnyvale CA 94087 Personal E-mail: alireza@par.stanford.edu.

SHIRVANI, HAMID, architect, educator, author, administrator, philosopher; b. Tehran, Iran, Oct. 20, 1950; came to US, 1974, naturalized, 1986; s. Majid and Taji (Granpisheh) Shirvani; m. Fatemeh Shokrollahi, Oct. 4, 2002. Diploma in architecture, Poly. of Cen. London, 1974; MArch, Pratt Inst., 1975; MS, Rensselaer Poly. Inst., 1977; MLA, Harvard U., 1978; MA, Princeton U., 1979, PhD, 1980; LHD (hon.), Soka U., Japan, 2003. Project designer London Borough of Barnet, 1973-74; asst. prof. architecture Pa. State U., 1979-82; prof., dir. grad. studies SUNY, Syracuse, 1982-85; prof., dir. Sch. Urban Planning and Devel., U. Louisville, 1985-86; prof. architecture and urban design U. Colo., Denver, 1986-92, dean Sch. of Architecture and Planning, 1986-91; prof. philosophy, dean Coll. Arts and Scis. U. Mass., Lowell, 1992-95; v.p. grad. studies and rsch., prof. urban studies CUNY Queens Coll., Flushing, 1995-2000; provost, exec. v.p., Martha Masters prof. art/architecture Chapman U., Orange, Calif., 2000—. Vis. faculty So. Calif. Inst. Architecutre, U. So. Calif.; lectr. in field, including U. Tex., San Antonio, Lehigh U., U. Waterloo (Can.), U. Sydney (Australia), Mo. State U., Columbia U., NYC, Amsterdam Acad. Art, U. Venice (Italy), Chinese U. Hong Kong, So. China Inst. U., U. Calif., Irvine, Villanova U., Rutgers U., Ariz. State U., Duke U., U. Pa., Yale U., U. Colo., U. NC Author: Urban Design: A Comprehensive Reference, 1981, Urban Design Review, 1981, Urban Design Process, 1985, Beyond Public Architecture, 1990; editor Urban Design Rev., 1982-85, Urban Design and Preservation Quar., 1985-88; mem. editorial bd. Jour. Archtl. Edn., 1988-94, Avant Garde, 1988-93, Jour. Planning Edn. and Rsch., 1987-93, Art and Architecture, 1974-78, Jour. Am. Planning Assn., 1982-88. Recipient Gold medal in Architecture and Urbanism, Faculty Honor award, Acad. Leadership award, Faculty Rsch. award, Commendation award AIA, 2003, Justice award SGI, 2003. Fellow Am. Soc. Landscape Archs. (recognition award), Royal Geog. Soc., Royal Soc. Arts; mem. Am. Inst. Cert. Planners, Am. Planning Assn. (chmn. urban design divsn. 1987-89, Disting. award 1984, Urban Design award 1985), Sigma Xi, Omicron Delta Epsilon, Tau Sigma Delta (Silver medal in archtl. edn. 1988), Tau Beta Pi, Sigma Lambda Alpha. Office: Chapman U Orange CA 92866-1099 Fax: 714-997-6801. Office Phone: 714-997-6826. E-mail: ham@chapman.edu.

SHIRVINSKI, ADAM JOHN, management consultant; b. Mahanoy, Pa., Oct. 25, 1939; s. Adam F. and Louise Shirvinski; m. Jean Shirvinski, June 25, 1966; children: Adam Albert, Lisa Ellen, Lara Jean. BS engring., USCSA, 1961—88; MS quantitative analysis, US Naval Post Grad. Sch., Monterey, CA, 1970; MS fin., Am. U, Wash., DC, 1987. ASQ, CQE, CRE, CSQE. Group mgr.-product assurance EER Systems, Chantilly, Va., 1988—95; sailor- sea capt., acquisition project mgr. USCGC UNIMAK(Whec-379), (WMEC-270); QA/CM mgr., air & space div. Sentel Corp., Alexandria, Va., 1995—98; SR/QA specialist EDS Corp., Herndoh, Va., 1998—2001; QA/CM mgr. Intelli Dyne - LLC, Falls Church, Va., 2001—02. Pres.- CEO Adams' Quality, Inc., Potomac, Md., 1995—. Captain US Coast Guard, 1961—88. Mem.: Informs (assoc.), AFCEA (assoc.), IEEE (assoc.), US Naval Inst. (assoc.), Exec. Comm. Wash. DC Sec. ASQ (assoc.), Am. Soc. for Quality (sr.), Army Navy Club (assoc.). Republican. Roman Catholic. Avocations: tennis, hunting, fishing. Home: L26-B3-S2 Lake Shore Dr HC88 Box 386 Pocono Lake PA 18347 Office: Adams' Quality, Inc 1897 Milboro Dr Potomac MD 20854

SHIRZAD, FARYAR, federal agency administrator; married; 1 child. BS summa cum laude, U. Md.; JD, U. Va.; M in Pub. Policy, Harvard U. With Robins, Kaplan, Miller & Ciresi, Washington; internat. trade atty. Skadden, Arps, Slate Meagher & Flom, Washington; internat. trade counsel Senate Com. on Fin., 1997—2001; lead internat. trade policy coord. Bush-Cheney Transition Offices; asst. sec. for import adminstrn. U.S. Dept. of Commerce, Washington, 2001—.

SHISHKOFF, MURIEL MENDELSOHN, education writer; b. Chgo., Mar. 5, 1917; d. Henry Robert and Anita (Arnow) Mendelsohn; m. Nicholas Shishkoff, Aug. 26, 1946; children: Andrew, Debra. BA, U. Chgo., 1936; MA, Northwestern U., 1940. Founding dir. Women's Opportunities Ctr., U. Ext., U. Calif., Irvine, 1970-72, asst. dir. Office Rels. with Schs. and Colls., 1974-82, cons. edn. improvement programs, 1993-95. UCI cons. to ASSIST, 1985-90; cons. Prins. Conf. for Acad. Excellence in Effective Schs., 1985-91, Jacob Javits Gifted and Talented Students Edn. program, Sherman Intertribal Acad., 1990-92, CAPP Scholars in Tng./Curriculum Devel., 1991-92, Native Am. Intertribal U., 1992-94; cons. CPEC-Eisenhower Math and Sci. Leadership Tng., 1993-96. Author: Transferring Made Easy, 1991, (with Kogee Thomas and Barbara Al-Bayati) Dream Catchers: A Transfer Guide for Native American College Students with Special Assistance for Those from Tribal Colleges, 2000. V.p. LWV, Palos Verdes Peninsula, CAlif., 1963. Lt. USNR (W-VS), 1942-45. Grantee Reachout, Dept. Mental Hygiene, Sacramento, 1972. Mem. Nat. Mus. Women in Arts (charter). Democrat. Home: 19542 Sandcastle Ln Huntington Beach CA 92648-3069 E-mail: mms9999@socal.rr.com.

SHISHLO, ANDREI PETROVICH, physicist, researcher; s. Peter I. and Galina Shishlo; m. Galina N. Dudchenko, Sept. 30, 1993. PhD, St.-Petersburg State Tech. U., Russia, 1989. Assistant Professor Highest Certifying Bd., Russia, 1992. Staff mem. R&D ORNL, Oak Ridge, Tenn., 2002—03; advanced software engr. BNL, Upton, NY, 2000—02. Contbr. software development. Achievements include development of Parallel High Performance Computer Codes. Office: ORNL SNS-project MS-6473 701 Scarboro Rd Oak Ridge TN 37830 E-mail: shishlo@hotmail.com.

SHITABATA, PAUL KENT, pathologist; b. Fukuoka, Japan, Sept. 20, 1962; s. George Joji and Janet Aiko (Ikeda) S.; m. Evangeline Chan Uy, Aug. 30, 1997. BA, Pomona Coll., 1984; MD, U. Hawaii, 1988. Diplomate Am. Bd. Pathology, Am. Bd. Dermatopathology. Med. dir. South Bay Surgicenter, Torrance, Calif., 1994—99, Long Beach Doctor's Hosp., Calif., 1996—99; with Affiliated Pathologists Med. Group, Torrance, 1994—. Co-med. dir. Pathology Inc., 2003—; CEO, pres. The Doctor's Dr., 1999—. Contbr. articles to profl. jours. Mem.: Asian Am. Physicians Assn. (bd. dirs. 1999), Coll. Am. Pathologists (coun. plastic affairs 2003), Alpha Omega Alpha. Avocation: jazz. Office: Affiliated Pathologists Med Group 19951 Mariner Ave Ste 150 Torrance CA 90503

SHIU, BINGIEE, religious studies educator; b. Dallas, Oct. 12, 1961; s. Jimmie and Lai Shang Shiu; m. Cara Miller, May 25, 1985; children: Daniel, Nicholas. MusM, Sam Houston State U., 1987. Cert. lifetime tchg. Tex., 1984. Tchr., orch. condr. Labay Jr. H.S., Houston, 1988—93, Meml. H.S., 1993—; worship leader Cypress Bible Ch., 2001—02. Guest condr. various region & state orchs.; adjudicator various orchs. Arranger (string orch.) Preludium and Allegro, Four Pieces from Scenes from Childhood, Symphony IV. Ch. vol. work Cypress Bible Ch., Cypress, 1998—2004; alumni bd. St. Mark's Sch. Tex., Dallas, 2000—04; mem. Am. Festival Arts, Houston, 2002—04. Recipient Spotlight award, Cypress Fairbanks Ind. Sch. Dist., 1993, Denius award, U. Interscholastic League, Tex., 1995, Tchr. Yr., Meml. H.S., 1997, Leadership and Achievement award, Tex. Music Educators Assn., 1997, Young Alumnus Yr., Abilene Christian U., 2002, Crystal Tchr. award, Houston Chronicle and Spring Br. Edn. Found., 2004. Mem.: Tex. Orch. Directors Assn., Tex. Music Educators Assn. (Leadership and Achievement award 1997). Avocations: family, exercise, travel, music, youth. Office: Memorial High School Orchestra 935 Echo Lane Houston TX 77024 E-mail: shiub@springbranchisd.com.

SHIUE, WEN-TSONG, electrical and computer scientist, educator; b. Tounan, Yunlin, Taiwan, Feb. 18, 1965; s. Chun-Ming Hsueh and Jui-Jung Shen; m. Shu-Ching Tu; children: Vivian, Stephen. MS, Western Mich. U., 1991; PhD, Ariz. State U., 2000. Adj. prof. Tamkang U., Taipei, Taiwan, 1991—96; chief electronics officer China Airlines, Taoyuan, Taiwan, 1991—96; rsch. assoc. Ariz. State U., Tempe, 1997—2000; sr. staff scientist Motorola Inc., Austin, Tex., 1999—2000; lead software scientist Silicon Metrics Corp., Austin, 2000—01; prof. Oreg. State U., Corvallis, 2001—. Contbr. articles to profl. jours. Recipient Travel Grant award, Ariz. State U., 1999; grantee, IEEE/ACM 36th Design Automation Conf., 1999; scholar, Motorola Inc., 1999, 2000. Mem.: IEEE Computer Soc., Assn. Computing Machinery, IEEE Circuits and Sys. Soc., Am. Soc. Engring Edn., Gamma Beta Phi. Avocations: swimming, travel. Home: 3395 NW Poppy Dr Corvallis OR 97330 Office: Oreg State Univ Dept ECE Corvallis OR 97331 Personal E-mail: shiue@ieee.org. Business E-Mail: shiue@ece.orst.edu.

SHIVE, RICHARD BYRON, architect; b. Cleve., Jan. 16, 1933; s. Roy Allen and Mary Elizabeth (Thompson) S.; m. Patricia Butler, Aug. 28, 1954; children: Lisa Ann, Laura Mary, John Thompson, Nancy Butler. BS, Rensselaer Poly. Inst., Troy, N.Y., 1954; postgrad., Newark (N.J.) Coll. Engring., 1957, Rutgers U., 1960-63. Registered architect, N.J., N.Y., Pa., Vt.; lic. profl. planner, N.J. Field engr. Wigton-Abbott Corp., Plainfield, N.J., 1954-55, The Glenwal Co., Rochelle Park, N.J., 1955; asst. supt. Wigton-Abbott Corp., Plainfield, 1955-57; archtl. draftsman Raymond B. Flatt, Architect, Bloomfield, N.J., 1957-58, chief draftsman, 1958-60; project architect Scrimenti/Swackhamer/Perantoni Architects, Somerville, N.J., 1960-66, assoc., 1966-69; ptnr. Scrimenti, Shive, Spinelli, Perantoni Architects, Somerville, 1969-86, Shive/Spinelli/Perantoni & Assocs., Architects & Planners, Somerville, 1986-97; prin. emeritus SSP Archtl. Group, 1998—2002; pvt. practice Richard B. Shive, AIA, Architect, 2003—. Adv. com. First Fidelity Bank, Bound Brook, N.J., 1989-91; chmn. bd. Somerset Health Care Corp., 1987-91. Contbr. articles to profl. jours. Bd. dirs., exec. com. N.J. Hosp. Assn., Princeton, 1986-92, 93-95; chmn. bd. trustees Somerset Med. Ctr., Somerville, 1973-96; mem. Nat. Trust for Hist. Preservation; bd. dirs. Ctr. for Health Affairs, Inc., 1992-93; mem. Borough of Bound Brook Planning Bd., 2000—; chmn. Borough of Bound Brook Redevel. Adv. Com., 2000—; mem. Somerset County Econ. Devel. Incentive Adv. Com., 1997—. Recipient award James F. Lincoln Arc Welding Found., 1973, President's award for outstanding svc. Rolling Hills coun. Girl Scouts U.S.A., 1988, Trustee of Yr. award N.J. Hosp. Assn., 1993, Outstanding Citizen of Yr. award Somerset County C. of C., 1993, Spirit of Somerset award, 2000; Paul Harris fellow Bound Brook-Middlesex Rotary Club, 1993. Mem. AIA, ASTM, ASHRAE, ACI (chpt. bd. dirs. 1978-83), N.J. Soc. Architects, Illuminating Engring. Soc., Nat. Fire Protection Assn., Greater Somerset County C. of C. (v.p. 1985-86, 92-93, Outstanding Citizen of Yr. award 1993), Rotary (pres. 1969-70, Paul Harris fellow 1993), Wash. Campground Assn. (pres. 1975-76, v.p. 1977-78, sec. 1978-97), Chi Phi (sec. 1973). Republican. Congregationalist. Avocations: fishing, photography, skiing, canoeing, backpacking. Home and Office: 1786 Middlebrook Rd Bound Brook NJ 08805-1432 Office Phone: 732-469-2682. E-mail: rshive@verizon.net.

SHIVELY, DANIEL JEROME, retired transportation executive; b. Akron, Ohio, Sept. 2, 1924; s. Richard Miles and Josephine (Pellicer) S.; m. Pamela Marion Kurfess, July 31, 1954; children: Jennifer, Laurie, Thomas. Grad., U.S. Mcht. Marine Acad., King's Point, N.Y., 1945. Chief officer (tanker) Trinidad Corp., N.Y.C., 1946-51; co-owner, mgr. Shively Bros. Jersey Farm, Quaker City, Ohio, 1952-54; staff asst. Gulf Oil Corp., Phila., 1955-57; distbn. coord. Standard Oil Co., Cleve., 1957-73; budget coord. BP Oil Co., Wilmington, Del., 1973-79; mgr. mktg. budget and planning Standard Oil Co., Cleve., 1979-85; owner, mgr. Shively & Assocs., Cleve., 1985-88. Served to lt. (j.g.) USNR, 1945-61. Mem. Transp. Practitioners Assn. (exec. com. 1984-90, pres. local chpt. 1984-85), King's Point Club (treas. N.E. Ohio chpt. 1989-94, sec. 1999-2003), KC (chancellor 1986, dep. grand knight 1987-91). Republican. Roman Catholic. Avocations: farming, sailing. Home: 21347 Erie Rd Rocky River OH 44116-2133

SHIVELY, JOHN TERRY, business executive; b. Middletown, N.Y., July 1, 1943; s. Marvin Rathfelder and Esther (Manning) Westervelt; adopted child, Harold Eugene Shively. BA, U. N.C., 1965. Vol. worker VISTA, Bethel and Fairbanks, Alaska, 1965-68; health planner Greater Anchorage Area Cmty. Action Agy., 1968-69; health cons. Alaska Fed. Natives, Anchorage, 1969; dep. dir. Rural Alaska Cmty. Action Program, Anchorage, 1971-72; exec. v.p. Alaska Fedn. Natives, Anchorage, 1972-75; v.p. ops. NANA Regional Corp., Kotzebue, Alaska, 1975-77, NANA Devel. Corp., Anchorage, 1977-82; sr. v.p. NANA Regional Corp. Inc., 1986-92; pres. NANA Devel. Corp., 1992-94; commr. DNR, 1995-2000; chmn., CEO United Bar Corp., United Bank Alaska, 1987-88; sr. ptnr. Jade North, 2000—02; v.p. govt. and cmty. rels. Holland Am., 2002—. Dir. Unicorp. Inc., United Bank of Alaska, Resource Devel. Coun., exec. com., 2001—; dir. Alaska State C. of C., exec. com., 2003—. Mem. Greater Anchorage Area Comprehensive Health Plan Coun., 1969-75, chmn., 1969-75; founding mem. bd. dirs. Alaska Pub. Interest Rsch. Group, 1974-75, 86-90, chmn. 1987-90; mem. Gov.'s Rural Affairs Coun., 1971-76, Gov.'s Manpower Commn., 1971, Greater Anchorage Health Bd., 1969-75, Alaska Pipeline Edn. Com., 1973-74; bd. regents U. Alaska, 1979-83; bd. trustees Alaska Permanent Fund Bd., 1999-2000. Democrat. Episcopalian. Home and Office: 2301 Loren Cir Anchorage AK 99516 E-mail: jtshively@att.net.

SHIVELY, JUDITH CAROLYN (JUDY SHIVELY), contract administrator; b. Wilkinsburg, Pa., Jan. 30, 1962; d. John Allen and Edith (Crowell) S. BA in English, U. Nev., Las Vegas, 1984. Circulation aide Charleston Heights Libr., Las Vegas, 1979—86; asst. food editor Las Vegas Sun Newspaper, 1985—88, asst. horse racing editor, 1985—90, features writer, page editor, 1988—89, editor youth activities sect., 1989—90; racebook ticket writer, cashier Palace Sta. Hotel Racebook, Las Vegas, 1989—92; contract adminstr. nat. accts. Loomis, Fargo & Co., Las Vegas, 1992—2000; propr. Creative Computing, Las Vegas, 1996—; content prodn. Preference Techs., Inc., Las Vegas, 2000; data rsch. and processing PurchasePro.com, Las Vegas, 2000; adminstrv. asst. Uinta Bus. Systems, Las Vegas, 2001—02, Law Office of Frank Sorrentino, Las Vegas, 2003—. Horse racing historian, rschr., Las Vegas, 1985—; vol. rsch. asst. Dictionary of Gambling and Gaming, 1982-84; part-time clk. Hometown News, Las Vegas, 1994-96. Staff writer horse race handicaps, columns, articles, feature stories Las Vegas Sun Newspaper, 1985-90; freelance writer for monthly horse racing publ. Inside Track, 1992-94. Mem. Phi Beta Kappa. Republican. Avocations: collecting horse racing books, clippings, materials for personal library of horse racing, computers. Home: PO Box 26426 Las Vegas NV 89126-0426 Personal E-mail: racehors1@aol.com.

SHIVELY, MERRICK LEE, pharmaceutical scientist, consultant; b. Alamagordo, N.Mex., Dec. 12, 1958; s. Milton Lee and Dorothy Jean (Garlock) S.; m. Maureen Lynch, Dec. 28, 1985; 1 child, Sierra Lange. BS in Pharmacy, U. Conn., 1982, PhD in Pharmaceutics, 1986. Registered pharmacist, Colo., Mass. Sr. rsch. assoc. Baxter Healthcare, Morton Grove, Ill., 1985-87; asst. prof. U. Colo., Boulder, 1987-93; sr. rsch. scientist Atrix Labs., Inc., Ft. Collins, Colo., 1993-94; sr. scientist Nexagen, Inc., Boulder, 1994-96; founder, mng. ptnr. Drug Delivery Solutions LLC, Louisville, Colo., 1996—. Pharm. cons. Glaxo, Synergen, Chemex, Cell Tech., Lilly; del. U.S. Pharmacopeia, 1988-94. Contbr. articles to Pharm. Rsch., Jour. Colloid Interface Sci., Drug Devel. and Indsl. Pharmacy, Internat. Jour. Pharmaceutics, others. Mem. Denver Econ. Com., 1989. Richardson-Vicks fellow, 1982-85. Mem. Am. Assn. Pharm. Scientists, Soc. of Controlled Release, Am. Chem. Soc., Rocky Mountain Devel. Forum (treas. 1989—), Phi Kappa Phi, Rho Chi. Achievements include patents in field; discovery and method of manufacture of solid state emulsions; findings that the formation of multi-molecular inclusion compounds are responsible for unique properties. Home and Office: 10ll Turnberry Cir Louisville CO 80027-9594

SHIVELY, ROBERT WILLIAM, urban planner; b. Plainview, Nebr., Mar. 20, 1928; s. Samuel Burdette and Edna Angeline (Tutttle) Shively; married, Jan. 20, 1953; children: Steven Burdette, Susan Lee, Robert W. Jr. BS, U. Nebr., 1951. Mgr. Worland C. of C., Wyo., 1954—57; sales mgr. Puregas Svc. Co., Worland, 1957—62; mgr. Norfolk C. of C., Nebr., 1962—67, econ. develop. dir., 1986—90; area develop. mgr. Nebr. Pub. Power Dist., Columbus, 1967—74, mgr. mktg., 1974—86; dir. econ. develop. Peru (Nebr.) State Coll., 1990—93; econ. develop. cons. Ft. Collins, Colo., 1993—. Contbr. articles to profl. jours. Mem. econ. develop. coun. Larmer County, Ft. Collins, 1996—98; mem. Planning Commn., Columbus, 1980—86; pres. Young. Rep., Worland, Wyo., 1959—61. 1st lt. USN, 1951—54. Named Pub. Ofcl. of Yr., Assn. Retarded Citizens, Nebr., 1988, Man of Yr., Auburn C. of C., Nebr., 1992; recipient Dist. Svc. award, Jaycess, Norfolk, 1964. Mem.: Internat. Econ. Develop. Coun. Home: 1738 Centennial Rd Fort Collins CO 80525

SHIVELY, WILLIAM PHILLIPS, political scientist, educator; b. Altoona, Pa., Mar. 31, 1942; s. Arthur and Ruth Shively; m. Barbara Louise Shank, Aug. 29, 1964; children: Helen, David. BA, Franklin and Marshall Coll., 1963; PhD, U. N.C., 1968. Mem. faculty U. Oreg., Eugene, 1967-68, Yale U., 1968-71; mem. faculty U. Minn., Mpls., 1971—, prof. polit. sci., 1979—, provost arts, scis. & engring., 1995-97. Author: Craft of Political Research, 1974, 6th edit., 2004, Research Process in Political Science, 1985, Power and Choice, 1986, rev. edit., 1989, 9th edit., 2004, Comparative Governance, 1995, (with Christopher Achen) Cross-Level Inference, 1995; editor Am. Jour. Polit. Sci., 1977-79; contbr. articles on elections and voting to profl. jours. Home: 1572 Northrop St Saint Paul MN 55108-1322 Office: U Minn Dept Polit Sci 1414 Social Scis Tower Minneapolis MN 55455 E-mail: shively@polisci.umn.edu.

SHIVERS, MITCHELL EVERETT, retired investment advisor; b. NY, Nov. 19, 1947; s. Carl Everett and Mary Allison (Young) S.; m. Nancy Jane Shorsher; children: Mitchell Jr and Jane B. BS, Monmouth U., 1970; postgrad., New York U., 1975-77. Mgmt. exec. Merrill Lynch, NYC, Singapore, 1973—81; exec. dir. Samuel Montagu & Co., London, 1981—84; pvt. practice, 1984—85, 1992—93, 2003—; pres. Kleinwort Benson Inc., NYC, 1985—89, Fuji Securities, NYC, Chgo., 1989—92; mng. dir. Merrill Lynch, NYC, 1993—2001; ret., 2001; bus. cons., 2001—. Vice-chmn. Cultural Trust of NJ. Recipient Anniversary Cup, Am.'s Cup Jubilee, 2001, N.J. Disting. Svc. medal, State of N.J., 2002. Mem.: Internat. Guild Bankers, Internat. Securities Markets Assn. (bd. dirs. 2000—). Avocations: competitive sailing, jogging, golf, travel. Personal E-mail: mitchell_shivers@hotmail.com.

SHIVERY, CHARLES W. utilities executive; BA, BS, Johns Hopkins U.; MBA, U. Balt. With Balt. Gas & Electric Co., 1972—80, asst. treas., 1980—88, treas., asst. sec., 1988—89, v.p. corp. fin., 1989—93, v.p., CFO, 1993—97; chmn., pres., CEO Constellation Power Source, Inc., 1997—2002; CEO, pres. Constellation Enterprises, Inc., 1998—2002; pres., CEO Constellation Power Source Holdings, Inc., 2000—02; co-pres. Constellation Energy Group, Inc., 2000—02, 2000—02; pres., CEO NU Enterprises, Inc., 2002—04; interim pres. N.E. Utilities, Berlin, Conn., 2004, chmn., pres., CEO, 2004—. Office: Northeast Utilities 107 Seldon St Berlin CT 06037-1616*

SHIVES, PAULA J, lawyer; b. Monongahela, Pa., Sept. 28, 1950; BA, Western Ky. U., 1973; JD, U. Ky., 1979. Bar: Ky. 1979. Assoc. gen. counsel Long John Silver Restaurants, Inc., 1985—95; sr. v.p., gen. counsel, sec. Darden Restaurants, Inc., 1999—. Mem.: ABA, Ky. Bar Assn., Fayette County Bar Assn. Office: 5900 Lake Ellenor Dr Orlando FL 32809 Office Phone: 407-245-6566.

SHKLAR, GERALD, oral pathologist, periodontist, educator; b. Montreal, Que., Can., Dec. 2, 1924; came to U.S., 1950, naturalized, 1955; s. Louis and Ann (Schleifstein) S.; m. Judith Nisse, June 16, 1948 (dec. Sept. 18, 1992); children: David, Michael, Ruth; m. Se-Kyung Oh, July 13, 1997. BS, McGill U., 1947, DDS, 1949; MS, Tufts U., 1952; MA (hon.), Harvard U., 1971; D (hon.), U. Athens. Diplomate Am. Bd. Oral Pathology, Am. Bd. Periodontology. Asst. prof. oral pathology Sch. Dental Medicine Tufts U., Boston, 1953—59, assoc. prof. Sch. Dental Medicine, 1960—61, rsch. prof. peridontology Sch. Dental Medicine, 1961—71, lectr. oral pathology Sch. Dental Medicine, 1971—. Head dept. oral medicine and oral pathology Sch. Dental Medicine Harvard U., Boston, 1971-93, Charles A. Brackett prof. oral pathology, 1971-2000, Charles A. Brackett prof. oral pathology emeritus, 2000—; sr. clin. invesigator Forsyth Inst., Boston, 1994—; cons. oral pathology Children's Hosp. Med. Ctr., Brigham and Women's Hosp., Mass. Gen. Hosp. Author: Oral Cancer, 1984; co-author (with Edmund Cataldo and Henry Goldman): Oral Pathology: An Atlas of Microscopic Pathology, 1975; co-author: (with Philip L. McCarthy) The Oral Manifestations of Systemic Disease, 1976, Diseases of the Oral Mucosa, 2d edit., 1982; co-author: (with David Chernin) Libellus De Dentibus, 1563, of Bartholomaei Eustachii, 1999, A Sourcebook of Dental Medicine, 2002; co-author: (with Fermin Carranza) History of Periodontology, 2003; contbr. over 350 articles to profl. jours., chapters to books. Fellow AAAS, Am. Acad. Dental Sci., Am. Acad. Oral Medicine, Am. Acad. Oral Pathology, Am. Coll. Dentists, Internat. Coll. Dentists; mem. ADA, Internat. Assn. Dental Rsch., Am. Acad. Periodontology, Am. Cancer Soc., Am. Assn. Cancer Rsch., Am. Assn. Cancer Edn., Am. Acad. History Dentistry, History of Sci. Soc., Sigma Xi, Omicron Kappa Upsilon. Avocation: playing flute and harpsichord. Home: 154 Evelyn Rd Waban MA 02468-1042 Office: 188 Longwood Ave Boston MA 02115-5819 Business E-Mail: gerald_shklar@hms.harvard.edu.

SHLADOVER, STEVEN ELLIOT, transportation research professional; b. NYC, Feb. 15, 1950; s. Joel and Ida Shladover. SB, MIT, 1972, SM, 1974, ScD, 1978. Research asst. MIT, Cambridge, Mass., 1976-78, lectr., 1978; staff engr. Systems Control, Inc., Palo Alto, Calif., 1978-81; sr. engr. Systems Control Tech., Inc., Palo Alto, 1981-84, program mgr., 1984-86, dir. CAE systems, 1986-89, mgr., transp. systems engr., 1987-89; tech. dir. PATH Program, dep. dir. U. Calif., Berkeley, 1989—. U.S. Expert to Internat. Standards Orgn. (tech. com. 204, working group 14). Assoc. editor Jour. of Dynamic Systems, Measurement and Control, 1980-85; contbr. articles to profl. jours. Nat. mem. Met. Opera Guild, N.Y.C., 1973—; mem. San Francisco Opera Guild, 1979—, Mus. Soc., San Francisco, 1979—, Common Cause, Washington, 1983—. Named one of the Outstanding Young Men of Am., U.S. Jaycees, 1983; fellow NSF, 1972-75. Mem. SAE (ITS divsn. 1992—), Intelligent Transp. Soc. Am. (chmn. AVCS com. 1990-97), ASME (assoc. editor 1980-85, program chmn. dynamic systems and control div. 1986, honors com. 1988-91, sec. 1989-92, exec. com. 1992-97, chmn. 1996), Transp. Rsch. Bd. (com. new transp. systems and tech. 1988, com. on study advanced vehicle and hwy. techs. 1990-91, com. intelligent transp. systems 1992—, com. on vehicle hwy. automation 1997—), MIT Alumni Assn., Calif. Alliance for Adv. Transp. Sys. (bd. dirs. 1994—). Democrat. Avocations: opera critic, tennis, international travel. Office: U Calif PATH Program 1301 S 46th St Bldg 452 Richmond CA 94804-4600 E-mail: ses@its.berkeley.edu.

SHLAPAK, FRED, electronics executive; b. Canada; BSEE, MS, U. Waterloo, Can. Joined Motorola, Inc., 1970, applications engr., 1970, leader Can. semiconductor ops., 1976, head microsystems and digital divsn., 1982, leader European Semiconductor Group, asst. to pres. Semiconductor Products Sector, 1998—2000, exec. v.p. Semiconductor Products Sector, 2000, pres. Semiconductor Products Sector, exec. v.p., cons. to the office of the chmn., 2003—. Mem.: Semiconductor Industry Assn. (bd. dirs.). Office: Motorola 1303 E Algonquin Rd Schaumburg IL 60196

SHLAUDEMAN, HARRY WALTER, retired diplomat; b. L.A., May 17, 1926; s. Karl Whitman and Florence (Pixley) S.; m. Carol Jean Dickey, Aug. 7, 1948; children: Karl Frederick, Katherine Estelle, Harry Richard. BA, Stanford U., 1952. Joined U.S. Fgn. Svc., 1955; vice consul Barranquilla, Colombia, 1955-56; polit. officer Bogotá, Colombia, 1956-58; assigned lang. tng. Washington, 1958-59; consul Sofia, Bulgaria, 1960-62; chief polit. sect. Santo Domingo, Dominican Republic, 1962-64; officer charge Dominican Affairs State Dept., 1964-66; asst. dir. Office Caribbean Affairs, 1965-66; sr. seminar fgn. policy State Dept., 1966-67, spl. asst. to sec. state, 1967-69; dep. chief of mission Santiago, Chile, 1969-73; dep. asst. sec. state for Inter-Am. affairs Washington, 1973-75; amb. to Venezuela, 1975-76; asst. sec. state for Inter-Am. affairs, 1976-77; amb. to Peru, 1977-80; amb. to Argentina, 1980-83; exec. dir. Nat. Bipartisan Commn. on Central Am., 1983-84; spl. amb. to Cen. Am., 1984-86; amb. to Brazil, 1986-89; amb. to Nicaragua, 1990-92; ret., 1992. Served with USMCR, 1944-46. Recipient Disting. Honor award Dept. State, 1966, Pres. Disting. Svc. award, 1988, Brazil's Order of Cruzeiro Benementium, 1989, Pres. Medal Freedom, 1992. Mem. Am. Acad. Diplomacy, San Luis Obispo Golf and Country Club, Phi Gamma Delta. Home: 7006 Pebble Beach Way San Luis Obispo CA 93401-8916 Office Phone: 805-544-7539. E-mail: harrywal@aol.com.

SHMAVONIAN, GERALD S. philanthropist, art collector; b. L.A., June 26, 1945; s. Sergius Neshan and Berje-Lucia (der Hareutunyan) Shmavonian. Student, U. Calif., Berkeley, 1964-70. Leader archaeol. excavation team, Guatemala, Turkey, 1970-75; pub. City Mags., 1975-80; special advisor Bicentennial Commission, Washington, D.C., 1987; chmn. Am. Nationalities Coun., Stanford U., 1983-86; pres. Am. Talent, 1986—2000, Am. Documentary Film Acad., 2001—02; ptnr. Assembly Plant Ptnrs., 2001—. Recipient Intercollegiate Boxing Championship, 1965. Mem. Calif. Scholarship Fedn. (life, pres. 1963), Nat. Forensic League (pres. 1963, degree of honor). Home: 6219 N Prospect Ave Fresno CA 93711-1658

SHMUKLER, STANFORD, lawyer; b. Phila., June 16, 1930; s. Samuel and Tessye (Dounne) S.; m. Anita Golove, Mar. 21, 1951; children: Jodie Lynne Shmukler Girsh, Joel Mark, Steven David. BS in Econs., U. Pa., 1951, JD, 1954. Bar: D.C. 1954, Pa. 1955, U.S. Ct. Appeals (2d cir.) 1959, U.S. Supreme Ct. 1959, U.S. Ct. Appeals (3d cir.) 1960, U.S. Ct. Mil. Appeals 1966. Atty. U.S. Bur. Pub. Roads, 1954-55, cons., 1955-57; sole practice Phila., 1955—. Lectr. Temple U. Law Sch., 1975-78; mem., past sec., exec. dir. crminal procedural rules com. Pa. Supreme Ct., 1971-87; mem. lawyers adv. com. Ct. Appeals for 3d cir., 1977-80, selection com. Criminal Justice Act Panel, 1979-84; chmn. selection com. Phila. Bar Ct. Appointments, 1988-91. Contbr. articles to profl. jours. Bd. dirs. Ecumenical Halfway House, 1967-71; bd. mgrs. Alumni Assn., Ctrl. High Sch., Phila. Served to col. JAGC, USAR, from 1955 (ret.). Recipient Phila. Bar Assn. Criminal Justice Sect. award, 1977, Justice Thurgood Marshall award, 1992; Legion of Honor, Chapel of the Four Chaplains, 1983. Mem. ABA, Pa. Bar Assn., Phila. Bar Assn. (bd. govs. 1971-73, past chmn. criminal justice com. and mil. justice com.), Fed. Bar Assn. (past chmn. criminal law com. adminstrn. justice sect., co-chmn. criminal law com. Phila. chpt., Leadership award Phila. 1991, 94), Pa. Assn. Criminal Def. Lawyers, Nat. Assn. Criminal Def. Lawyers. Democrat. Jewish. Home: 1400 Melrose Ave Elkins Park PA 19027-3155 E-mail: SSESQ1@aol.com.

SHMUNES, EDWARD, dermatologist; b. Jacksonville, Fla., July 24, 1940; s. Nathan and Anne Lillian (Berg) S.; m. Sue Shmunes, Apr. 17, 1996; children: Stephanie, Marjorie, Jenifer. MD, U. Fla., 1965. Diplomate Am. Bd. Dermatology. Intern U.S. Pub. Health Hosp., New Orleans, 1965-66; epidemic intelligence officer svc. Ctr. for Disease Control, Atlanta, 1966-68; resident in dermatology U. Pa., Phila., 1968-71; ptnr. Columbia (S.C.) Skin Clinic, 1973—, pres., 1991—2000. Grantee NIH, 2 yrs., U. S.C., 1985. Mem. Greek Orthodox Ch. Office: Columbia Skin Clinic 3 Medical Park Rd Ste 500 Columbia SC 29203-6873 Office Phone: 803-779-7316.

SHNAYERSON, ROBERT BEAHAN, editor, consultant; b. N.Y.C., Dec. 8, 1925; s. Charles and Madalene (Griffin) Beahan; m. Lydia Conde Todd, Dec. 23, 1950 (dec. Sept. 1973); children: Michael, Kate; m. Laurie Platt Winfrey, June 9, 1980; children: Maggie, Bonnie. AB, Dartmouth, 1950. Reporter N.Y. Daily News, 1946; reporter Life mag., N.Y.C., 1950-54; corr. Time-Life News Svc., 1954-56; contbg. editor Time mag., 1957-59, edn. editor, 1959-64, law editor, 1964-67, sr. editor, 1967-71; editor-in-chief Harper's Mag., N.Y.C., 1971-76; editor, pub. Quest mag., N.Y.C., 1976-81, Technology mag., N.Y.C., 1981-82; editorial dir. Sci. Digest mag., 1986-87. Editl. cons. Lear's mag., 1987-90; cons. in mag. field; sr. advisor Travel Holiday mag., 1989-95. Author: Illustrated History of the Supreme Court, 1986; author, editor: Wordworks, 1995—; contbr. articles to various mags. With USNR, 1943-46. Home: 118 Riverside Dr New York NY 10024-3708 Office Phone: 212-787-4590.

SHNEIDERMAN, BEN ABRAHAM, computer science educator, writer; b. N.Y.C., Aug. 21, 1947; s. Samuel Leib and Eileen (Szymin) S.; m. Nancy Helman, Mar. 25, 1973 (div. Dec. 1994); children: Sara Beth, Anna Rose; m. Jennifer Preece, June 17, 2001. BS, CCNY, 1968; MS, SUNY, Stony Brook, 1972, PhD, 1973; hon. doctorate sci., U. Guelph, Ont., Can., 1995. Asst. prof. computer sci. Ind. U., Bloomington, 1973-76; asst. prof. U. Md., College Park, 1976-82, assoc. prof., 1982-89, prof., 1989—. Cons. Apple Computers, IBM, GE, Microsoft, Intel. Author: Software Psychology, 1980, Designing the User Interface, 1987, 2d edit., 1992, 3rd edit., 1998, 4th edit., 2004, Leonardo's Laptop, 2002, Hypertext Hands-On, 1989; co-author: Readings in Information Visualization, 1999, The Craft of Information Visualization, 2003; editor: Sparks of Innovation, 1992. Fellow ACM, AAAS. Avocation: skiing. Office: Univ Md Dept Computer Sci College Park MD 20742-0001 E-mail: ben@cs.umd.edu.

SHNEIDMAN, EDWIN S. psychologist, educator, thanatologist, suicidologist; b. York, Pa., May 13, 1918; s. Louis and Manya (Zukin) S.; m. Jeanne E. Keplinger, Oct. 1, 1944; children: David William, Jonathan Aaron, Paul Samuel, Robert James. AB, UCLA, 1938, MA, 1940; MS, U. So. Calif., 1947, PhD, 1948. Diplomate: Am. Bd. Examiners Profl. Psychology (past v.p.). Clin. psychologist VA Center, Los Angeles, 1947-50, chief research, 1950-53; co-dir. Central Research Unit for Study Unpredicted Deaths, 1953-58; co-dir. Suicide Prevention Center, Los Angeles, 1958-66; chief Center Studies Suicide Prevention NIMH, Bethesda, Md., 1966-69; vis. prof. Harvard U., 1969; fellow Ctr. Advanced Study in Behavioral Scis., 1969-70; clin. assoc. Mass. Gen. Hosp., 1969, Karolinska Hosp., Stockholm, 1978; prof. med. psychology UCLA, 1970-75, prof. thanatology, 1975-88, emeritus, 1988—. Vis. prof. Ben Gurion U. of Negev, Beersheva, 1983 Author: Deaths of Man, 1973, Voices of Death, 1980; Definition of Suicide, 1985, Suicide as Psychache, 1993, The Suicidal Mind, 1996, Comprehending Suicide, 2001, Autopsy of a Suicidal Mind, 2004; editor: Thematic Test Analysis, 1951; editor: (with N.L. Farberow) Clues to Suicide, 1957, The Cry for Help, 1961, Essays in Self-Destruction, 1967, (with M. Ortega) Aspects of Depression, 1969, On the Nature of Suicide, 1969, (with N.L. Farberow, L.E. Litman) Psychology of Suicide, 1970, Death and the College Student, 1972, Death: Current Perspectives, 1976, 80, 84, Suicidology: Contemporary Developments, 1976, Endeavors in Psychology: Selections From The Personology of Henry A. Murray, 1981, Suicide Thoughts and Reflections, 1981 Served to capt. USAAF, 1942-45. Recipient Harold M. Hildreth award Psychologists in Pub. Service, 1966; Louis I. Dublin award Am. Assn. Suicidology, 1969.

Mem. Am. Assn. Suicidology (founder, past pres.), Am. Psychol. Assn. (past div. pres., Disting. Profl. Contbn. to Pub. Svc. award 1987, Henry A. Murray award 1997), Melville Soc. Address: 11431 Kingsland St Los Angeles CA 90066-1329

SHNEIDMAN, J. LEE, historian, educator; b. N.Y.C., June 20, 1929; s. Bernard Wolf and Fannia Abramova (Raskin) S.; m. Conalee Levine, Sept. 3, 1961; children: Philip, Jack. BA, NYU, 1951, MA, 1952; PhD, U. Wis., 1957. Lectr. CCNY, 1956-57, U. Md. Overseas, 1957-58; asst. prof. Fairleigh Dickinson U., 1958-62; prof. history Adelphi U., 1963—2001, emeritus prof., 2001—. Chmn. seminar on hist., legal, and polit. thought Columbia U., 1985-2002. Author: Rise of the Aragonese-Catalan Empire, 2 vols, 1970, Spain and Franco, 1949-59, 1973, John F. Kennedy, 1974. Dem. N.Y. County committeeman, 1970—. Mem. Am. Hist. Assn., Medieval Acad. Am., Am. Philatel. Soc., Internat. Psychohist. Assn., Rossica Soc., China Soc. Jewish. Home: 161 W 86th St New York NY 10024-3411 Office: History Dept Adelphi University Garden City NY 11530 *Only by understanding from where we came can we understand where we are and where we are going.*

SHNEOUR, ELIE ALEXIS, biophysicist, researcher, historian, b. Neuilly-sur-Seine, France, Dec. 11, 1925; came to U.S., 1941, naturalized, 1944; s. Zalman and Salomea (Landau) S.; m. Polly H. Henderson, Sept. 7, 1990; children from previous marriage: Mark Zalman, Alan Brewster. BA, Columbia U., 1947; DSc (hon.), Bard Coll., 1969; MA, U. Calif., Berkeley, 1955; PhD, UCLA, 1958. Tchr. and rsch. fellow U. Calif., Berkeley, 1953-55, Am. Heart Assn. rsch. fellow, 1958-62, tchg. and rsch. fellow L.A., 1958; rsch. fellow Nat. Cancer Inst., 1956-57; Am. Heart Assn. rsch. fellow NYU, 1958-59; rsch. assoc. genetics Stanford U., 1962-65; assoc. prof. biology and neuroscis. U. Utah, 1965-69; rsch. neurochemist City of Hope Nat. Med. Ctr., Duarte, Calif., 1969-71. Dir. rsch. Calbiochem., 1971-75; pres. Biosystems Insts., Inc., 1975—; dir. Biosystems Rsch. Inst., 1979—; mem. steering com. Nat. Acad. Sci. Study Group on Biology and the Exploration of Mars, 1964; chmn. Western Regional coun. Rsch. in Basic Bioscis. for Manned Orbiting Missions, Am. Inst. Biol. Scis., NASA, 1966-69; fellow Com. Sci. Investigation Claims of Paranormal, 1996—. Author: Extraterrestrial Life, 1965, (with Eric A. Ottesen) National Academy of Sciences, National Rsch. Coun., 1966, (with S. Moffat) Life Beyond the Earth, 1966, The Malnourished Mind, 1974; contbr. numerous articles to sci. and lay jours. Chmn. citizens adv. coun. San Diego Pub. Schs., 1971-72, mem. adv. coun. Cousteau Soc., 1977-98; bd. dirs. Lunar Power System Coalition, 1993-2002, Transinnova S.A. France, 1990—; chmn. sci. adv. bd. County of San Diego, 1995-2002. With U.S. Army, 1944-45. Recipient William Lockwood prize, 1947. Mem. IEEE, AAAS (chmn. So. Calif. Skeptics soc. Pacific divsn. 1988-90), Am. Chem. Soc., N.Y. Acad. Scis., Am. Inst. Biol. Scis., Am. Soc. for Biochemistry and Molecular Biology (chmn. sci. advisors program 1973-75, mem. com. on pub. policy 1974-76, congl. liaison 1992—), Am. Soc. Neurochemistry (mem. coun. 1971-73), Soc. Neurosci., Internat. Soc. Neurochemistry, U.S. C. of C. (bd. dirs. 1993-98), La Jolla Chamber Music Soc. (bd. dirs. 1994-97), Internat. Coun. for Global Health Progress (N.Am. adv. bd. 1996—), Sigma Xi, Phi Sigma. Office: Biosystems Rsch Inst 700 Front St MS CDM 608 San Diego CA 92101-6085

SHNEYDER, ARTYOM V. science educator, researcher; b. Kharkov, Ukraine, Aug. 16, 1969; arrived in U.S., 1989; s. Vladimir I. Shneyder and Valeria M. Ranzer. BSc, Kharkov State U., 1989; MSc, Tenn. State U., 1995, EdD, 1996—. Sr. naturalist Kharkov Zoo, 1981—86; kennel asst. Murphy Rd. Animal Hosp., Nashville, 1990—91; clk. Capt. D's, Nashville, 1993—94; tchg. asst. Tenn. State U., Nashville, 1994—95, rsch. asst., 2000—; mailer Tennessean Newspaper, Nashville, 1995—99; nightman Super 8 Motel, Nashville, 1999. Author: Stereotypist Contradictionary, 1998, Close Fiend, 2002. Scholar, Kharkov State U., 1986—89; assistantship, Tenn. State U., 1994—95. Jewish. Achievements include discovery of w-reactivation in three Salmonella species; patents for feeding facility for fish; discovery of three new stamps that are consecutive on brilliant green apar. Avocations: Tae Kwon Do, chess, photography, drawing. Office: Tenn State U 3500 John A Merritt Blvd Nashville TN 37209 E-mail: a_shneyder@yahoo.com.

SHNIDER, BRUCE JAY, lawyer; b. Lansing, Mich., Oct. 16, 1950; s. Harold A. and Raynor (Seidner) Shnider; m. Patricia Lynn Strandness, Dec. 28, 1973; 1 child, Ruth Strandness. AB magna cum laude, Dartmouth Coll., 1972; MPP, JD magna cum laude, Harvard U., 1977. Bar: Minn. 1977, U.S. Dist. Ct. Minn. 1977, U.S. Tax Ct. 1978, U.S. Ct. Appeals (8th cir.) 1980, U.S. Supreme Ct. 1981. Asst. to dir. Mich. Dept. Commerce, Lansing, 1972-73; law clk. United Mineworkers Am. Health/Retirement Funds, 1975; summer assoc. Robins, Davis & Lyon, Mpls., 1976; assoc. Dorsey & Whitney, Mpls., 1977-82, ptnr., 1983—, chmn. diversity com., 1990-93, chmn. tax practice group, 1994-98. Bd. dirs. Minn. Justice Found., Mpls., 1989—91, Emergency Food Shelf Network, 2003—. Mem.: ABA, Hennepin County Bar Assn., Minn. State Bar Assn. Home: 1908 James Ave S Minneapolis MN 55403-2831 Office: Dorsey & Whitney 50 S 6th St Ste 1500 Minneapolis MN 55402-1498 Office Phone: 612-340-2862. Business E-Mail: shnider.bruce@dorsey.com.

SHO, JENNIFER YU-FEI, music educator, musician; b. Taipei, Taiwan, Oct. 2, 1976; d. Tung-Chiao Sho and Hsiu-Ching Chen; m. Steven Robert Ceprano, June 28, 2003. B in Piano Performance(hon.), San Francisco Conservatory of Music, 1993—97; M in Piano Performance, New Eng. Conservatory of Music, 1997—99, D in Musical Arts, 1999—. Pvt. piano tchr. Home Studio, Foster City, 1993—97, piano tchr. Boston, 1998—2002; pvt. piano instr. Edgewood Elem. Sch., Stoneham, 1998—2003; piano faculty The Ip Piano Sch., Boston, 1999—2002, Dana Hall Sch. of Music, Wellesley, Mass., 2002—; pvt. piano tchr. Home Studio, Melrose, 2002—03. Soloist Grand Piano Cable TV Program, Los Altos, Calif., 1989—92, Palo Alto Chamber Orch., Calif., 1990—92, The Twilight Outdoor Concert Series, United States, 1990, Santa Rosa Chamber Music Series, United States, 1992; guest soloist A Tribute to Adolph Baller- Stanford U. Honors Concert, United States, 1992; soloist Music in The Redwoods, Portolla Valley, Calif., United States, 1992—94, Stanford U. Alumni Music Series, United States, 1993—95; pianist San Francisco Conservatory Chamber Music Honors Concerts, 1994—96; soloist Chopin Found., San Francisco, 1995, Classical Philharm. Orch., Castro Valley, Calif., 1997; pianist New Eng. Conservatory- Chamber Music Gela, Boston, 1999; soloist New Eng. Conservatory Piano Dept. Festival, Boston, 1999, Sun-Ling Hall, Taichung, Taiwan, 2001; pianist Taipei Performing Arts Ctr., Taiwan, 2002, Nang Tu Performing Arts Ctr., Nang Tu, Taiwan, 2002, Taichung Performing Arts Ctr., Taiwan, 2002; guest artist, master class Longy Sch. of Music Prep. divsn., Cambridge, Mass., 2002; judge Bay State Contest of MMTA, 2003, MMTA Non-Competitive Evaluations, 2004. Mem.: Music Teachers Nat. Assn., Nat. Guild of Piano Teachers, Associated Bd. of Royal Schools of Music. Home: 26A Alton Pl Brookline MA 02446

SHOAFF, THOMAS MITCHELL, lawyer; b. Ft. Wayne, Ind., Aug. 21, 1941; s. John D. and Agnes H. (Hanna) S.; m. Eunice Swedberg, Feb. 7, 1970; children: Andrew, Nathaniel, Matthew-John. BA, Williams Coll., 1964; JD, Vanderbilt U., 1967. Bar: Ind. 1968. Assoc. Isham, Lincoln & Beale, Chgo., 1967-68; ptnr. Baker & Daniels, Ft. Wayne, Ind., 1968—. Bd. dirs. Weaver Popcorn Co., Inc., Ft. Wayne, Dreibelbiss Title Co., Inc., Ft. Wayne, Am. Steel Investment Corp., Ft. Wayne. Bd. dirs. McMillen Found., Ft. Wayne, Wilson Found., Ft. Wayne. Mem. ABA, Allen County Bar Assn., Ind. State Bar Assn. Presbyterian. Avocations: golf, sailing. Office: Baker & Daniels 111 E Wayne St Ste 800 Fort Wayne IN 46802-2603

SHOCHAT, STEPHEN JAY, pediatric surgeon; b. Balt., Dec. 17, 1938; s. Albert J. and Rose (Blechman) S.; m. Sheila Floam, July 1960 (div. July 1979); children: Francine Lynne, Alisa Joy; m. Carla Ann Centi, Jan. 26, 1980; children: David Robert, Sarah Elizabeth. BS, Randolph Mason Coll., 1959; MD, Med. Coll. Va., 1963. Surg. resident Washington U. Med. Ctr., St. Louis, 1963-68; pediatric surg. resident Boston Children's Hosp., 1968-70; thoracic surg. resident Queen Elizabeth Hosp., Birmingham, Eng., 1970, George Washington Hosp., Washington, 1972; chief pediatric surgery Hershey (Pa.) Med. Ctr., 1973-77, Stanford (Calif.) Med. Ctr., 1977-94; sr. surgeon Children's Hosp. Phila., 1994-96; surgeon-in-chief, chmn. dept. surgery St. Jude Children Rsch. Hosp., Memphis, 1996—; prof. pediats. and surgery U. Tenn., Memphis, 1996-98. Lt. col. USAF, 1970-72. Office: St Jude Children Rsch Hosp Dept Surgery Memphis TN 38105 Office Phone: 901-495-2911. Business E-Mail: stephen.shochat@stjude.org.

SHOCKED, MICHELLE, vocalist, songwriter; b. 1963; d. Bill Johnston. Student, U. Tex. Albums include The Texas Campfire Tapes, 1987, Short Sharp Shocked, 1988, Captain Swing, 1989, Arkansas Traveler, 1992, Kind Hearted Woman, 1995, Mercury Poise, 1988-95, 96. Office: care Mercury/Polygram Records Worldwide Plaza 825 8th Ave New York NY 10019-7416 also: Mercury Records 11150 Santa Monica Blvd Los Angeles CA 90025-3380

SHOCKEY, GARY LEE, lawyer; b. Casper, Wyo., Sept. 25, 1950; s. Bernis L. and Shirley E. (Diehl) Shockey; m. Dona K. Galles, June 1, 1979; children: Amber, Jeremy, Kimberly. AB in Polit. Sci. and Sociology, Yale U., 1973; JD, U. Wyo., 1976. Bar: Wyo. 1976, U.S. Dist. Ct. Wyo. 1976, U.S. Ct. Appeals (10th cir.) 1984, U.S. Ct. Appeals (9th cir.) 1988, U.S. Claims Ct. 1989, U.S. Supreme Ct. 1989, U.S. Ct. Appeals (fed. cir.) 1993, U.S. Dist. Ct. Ariz. 1994. Pub. defender State of Wyo. and City of Casper, 1976-78; pvt. practice Casper, 1976-79; assoc. Spence, Moriarity & Shockey, Casper and Jackson, Wyo., 1978-82, ptnr. Jackson, 1982—. Mem.: ATLA, ABA, Wyo. Trial Lawyers Assn. (bd. dirs. 1984—90), Wyo. State Bar (continuing legal edn. com. 1984—85, law and legis. reform com. 1986—88). Office: Spence Moriarity & Shockey PO Box 548 Jackson WY 83001-0548 E-mail: garyshockey@smswy.com.

SHOCKEY, JEREMY CHARLES, professional football player; b. Ada, OK, Aug. 18, 1980; s. Lucinda. Student, Northeast Oklahoma A&M Jr. College, 1999, Univ. of Miami, 2000—02. Tight end New York Giants, 2002—. Named NFL Rookie of the Yr., 2002; named to NFC Pro-Bowl team, 2002—03. Achievements include mem. NCAA Champion Miami Hurricanes, 2001. Office: c/o New York Giants Giants Stadium East Rutherford NJ 07073*

SHOCKEY, THOMAS EDWARD, real estate executive, engineer; b. Aug. 17, 1926; s. Verlie Draper and Margaret Ruth (Shuford) S.; m. Jacqueline McPherson, June 4, 1949; children: Cheryl Ann, Jocelyn Marie, Valerie Jean. BS, Tex. A&M U., 1950; postgrad., St. Mary's U., 1964, San Antonio Coll., 1972, Pacific Western U., 1981. With Petty Geophys. Survey, 1947-49, J.E. Ingram Equipment Co., 1950-51; co-owner, archtl. engr., realtor Moffett Lumber Co., Inc., San Antonio, 1952-76; cons. gen. contracting, gen. real estate, 1944—; retailer wholesale bldg. material, 1951—; v.p., 1959—. Real estate counselor, appraiser, 1972—; real estate appraiser Gill Appraisal Svc., San Antonio, 1977—; comml. loan appraiser, underwriter, analyst Gill Savs. Assn., Gill Cos., San Antonio, 1979; chief appraiser, underwriter, architect, engr., insp. Gill Cos., 1981, v.p., 1981-87, ret., 1987; v.p. La Hacienda Savs. Assn., 1988-91, ret., 1991. Fire chief Mico Vol. Fire Dept., 1993—95, tng. officer, 1996—2000. With inf. Signal Corps U.S. Army, 1944—46, ETO. Davidson fellow Tau Beta Pi. Mem. San Antonio C. of C., Nat. Lumber Dealers, Nat. Home Builders, Nat. Real Estate Bd., Nat. Inst. Real Estate Brokers, Internat. Soc. Real Estate Appraisers, Tex. Assn. Real Estate Insps., Real Estate Appraisers Tex., Nat. Assn. Rev. Appraisers and Mortgage Underwriters, Internat. Inst. Valuers, Internat. Platform Assn., State Firemen's and Fire Marshal's Assn. of Tex. Home: 126 County Road 2620 Mico TX 78056-5213

SHOCKLEY, ALONZO HILTON, JR., school system administrator; b. Milford, Del., Sept. 30, 1920; s. Alonzo Hilton Sr. and Elizabeth (Hilton) S.; m. Kay Marilyn Falke, Aug. 13, 1979; children: Novella Lela Shockley Randolph, Cheryl Emmelyn Shockley Durant, Alonzo Hilton III. BS, Del. State Coll., 1943; MA, Mich. State U., 1947; cert., NYU, 1956, postgrad., 1980, Queens Coll., 1961-62, U. Maine, 1963. Cert. tchr., N.Y., Pa., Del. Tchr. sci. Brooks High Sch., Prince Frederick, Md., 1948; prin. elem., jr. high schs. dept. public instrn., Dover, Del., 1948-58; rsch. assoc. Del. State Coll., Dover, 1958-60; elem. sch. tchr. Cen. Sch. Dist. 4, Plainview, N.Y., 1960-62; asst. elem. prin. Union Free Sch. Dist., Wyandanch, N.Y., 1962-64; assoc. adminstrn. official N.Y. State Edn. Dept., Albany, 1964-65; edn. coord. Nassau County Commn. Econ. Opportunity, Garden City, L.I., 1965-66; dir. state and fed. programs Freeport (N.Y.) Pub. Schs., 1966-85; coord. state and fed. programs Amityville Pub. Schs., L.I., N.Y., 1985-91, ednl. cons., 1988—. V.p. Internat. Rotary, Ronkonkoma, N.Y., 1997; v.p. Phi Delta Kappa of L.I. #1020. Contbr. articles in field of ednl. adminstrn. to profl. jours. Pres. mid L.I. chpt. UN Assn. of U.S., bd. dir. so. N.Y. divsn., mem. coun. pres. steeringcom., pres. Suffolk County chpt., 1995—; organizer of 1997 Mcpl. Elections Bill contbg. to the implementation of the Dayton Peace Accord, 1987; 6 time supr. for Bosnia/Herzegovia elections. Served with U.S. Army, 1942-45, NATOUSA; mem. NYU Alumni Chorus, 1980—, Huntington Men's Chorus, L.I., 1985—. Recipient Cert. of Merit for supervising registration in Bosnia and Herzegovia, Ctrl. Bosnia Canton 6, 1997. Mem. Am. Assn. Sch. Adminstrs., NEA, N.Y. State Tchrs. Edn., Assn. Childhood Edn. Internat., Assn. Supervision and Curriculum Devel., Nat. Assn. Elem. Prins., Amityville Sch. Dist. Adminstrs., Am. Acad. Polit. and Social Sci., NYU Alumni Assn. (bd. dirs., v.p.), Sch. Health, Edn. and Nursing Arts Professionals (pres.), Rotary (pres. Ronkonkomas, L.I.), Phi Delta (v.p. Long Island N.Y. chpt. 1994—). Home: 49 Gaymore Rd Port Jefferson Station NY 11776-1354

SHOCKLEY, EDWARD JULIAN, retired aerospace company executive; b. Augusta, Ga., Oct. 31, 1924; s. Julian P. and Margaret (Epps) S.; m. Dorothy Elizabeth Holley, Nov. 24, 1945; children: Edward J., Steven Holley. B.Aero. Engring., Ga. Inst. Tech., 1950; postgrad. (Sloan fellow), Stanford U. Grad. Sch. Bus., 1962-63. Flight test engr. Douglas Aircraft Co., 1950-53; with Lockheed-Ga. Co., 1953-80, dir. quality and safety, 1965-74, dir. mktg., 1974-78, v.p., 1978-80; pres. Lockheed Aircraft Service Co. div. Lockheed Corp., Burbank, Calif., 1980-86, sr. advisor to pres., 1986-87, ret., 1987; pres. Millimeter Wave Tech., Inc., Marietta, Ga., 1988-90, vice chmn. bd. dirs., 1991-92; ret., 1992. Dir. Aerosurge Mgmt. Cons., 1991-92; pres. Lockheed-Ga. Fed. Credit Union, 1971-74 Mem. bus. adv. coun. Ga. So. U.; mem. adv. coun. Sch. Bus. and Econs., Coll. of Charleston. Served with USN, 1941-46. Mem. Cherokee Town and Country Club. Republican. Methodist. Personal E-mail: eshock@charter.net.

SHOCKLEY, FLOYD WAYNE, research scientist; b. Richmond, Mo., Sept. 13, 1974; s. Daniel Paul and Deanna Kay Shockley; m. Shannon Elaine Myers, June 28, 1997. BA, Westminster Coll., 1996; MS, Univ. Mo.-Columbia, 2000; PhD, Univ. Ga.-Athens, 2001—. Lab tech. Westminster Coll., 1994—95, rsch. specialist, 1995—96; lab mgr. Univ. Mo., 1997—98, grad. rsch. asst., 1998—2000, rsch. specialist, 2000—01. Mem.: Entomol. Soc. of Am., Am. Assn. for the Advancement of Sci., Soc. the Study of Evolution, Soc. of Systematic Biologists, Coleopterists Soc., Am. Mus. Natural Hist., Am. Entomol. Soc., Pi Mu Epsilon, Beta Beta Beta. Republican. Office: Dept Entomol Univ Ga 413 Biological Sci Bldg Athens GA 30602-2603 Home: 165 Warren Way Athens GA 30605 Office Phone: 706-542-6187.

SHOCKLEY, MILTON M., JR., real estate brokerage executive; b. Greenville, S.C., Jan. 1, 1954; s. Milton M. and Bea W. Shockley; m. Laraine Davis, June 16, 1979; children: Ashley, Carrie, Megan. AD, North Greenville Coll., Tigerville, S.C., 1974; student, Furman U., 1976. Cert. residential specialist; cert. residential broker; grad. Realator Inst. Pres. Merrill Lynch/C. Dan Joyner, Greenville, 1972-79; founder, pres. M. Shockley Builders, Greenville, 1980; pres. Milton Shockley Co., Inc., Greenville, 1986—; prin. Young Concrete Co., Inc., Greenville, 1986—, SYS Assocs., Greenville, 1987—; pres. Century 21 Shockley Youngblood, Inc., Greenville, 1987—. Bd. dirs. YMCA, Greenville, Goodwill Industries, 1986-89; mem. adv. bd. Greenville Tech. Coll. Named Realtor of Yr., Greenville Bd. Realtors, 1987, Realtor of Yr., Greenville Assn. Realtors, 1996. Mem. Commerce Club (pres. 1987), Greenville Rotary (legis. chair 1991, state treas. 1990, chair young life com. 1981-85), Thornblade Club, Million Dollar Club (life; sec. 1987), New Bus. Breakfast Club, Metro Civitan Club (past pres.). Avocations: skiing, water-skiing, hunting, fishing, golf. Home: 212 Kilgore Cir Simpsonville SC 29681-4834 Office: Century 21/Shockley Youngblood PO Box 26537 333 Wade Hampton Blvd Greenville SC 29609-5738

SHOCKLEY, THOMAS V., III, electric power industry executive; BEE, Tex. A&I U.; MEE, U. Tex. Engr. Ctrl. Power and Light Co., Corpus Christi, Tex., 1970, various, 1970-87, pres., 1987-90; exec. v.p. Ctrl. and S.W. Corp., Dallas, 1990-97, pres., COO, 1997—. Office: American Electric Power 1 Riverside Plz Columbus OH 43215

SHOCKLEY-ZALABAK, PAMELA SUE, academic administrator; b. May 25, 1944; d. James William and Leatha Pearl (Cartwright) Shockley; m. Charles Zalabak, Dec. 30, 1975. BA in Comm., Okla. State U., 1965, MA in Comm., 1972; PHD in Orgnl. Comm., U. Colo., 1980. Instr. comm. Coll. Letters, Arts and Scis. U. Colo., 1976, from asst. to full prof., 1992, prof. comm., 1992—, vice chancellor for student success, interim chancellor, 2001—02, chancellor, 2002—. Cons. in field. Author 4 books; contbr. articles to profl. jours.; prodr.: (6 video documentaries). Recipient Disting. Svc. award, Colo. Speech Comm. Assn.; Lew Wentz Tri Delt scholar, 1961—65. Mem.: INternat. Comm. Assn., Speech Comm. Assn., Phi Kappa Phi. Democrat. Avocations: skiing, hiking, fly fishing. Home: 5905 Ridge Brook Ln Colorado Springs CO 80918-3416 Office: Univ Colorado Dept Communication PO Box 7150 Colorado Springs CO 80933-7150

SHOCKMAN, GERALD DAVID, microbiologist, educator; b. Mt. Clemens, Mich., Dec. 22, 1925; s. Solomon and Jennie (Madorsky) S.; m. Arlyne Taub, June 2, 1949; children— Joel, Deborah. BS, Cornell U., 1947; PhD, Rutgers U., 1950; Docteur (hon.), U. Liege, 1991. Predoctoral fellow Rutgers U., 1947-50; research asso. U. Pa., 1950-51; research fellow, research asso. Inst. Cancer Research, Phila., 1951-60; asso. prof. Temple U. Sch. Medicine, Phila., 1960-66, prof. dept. microbiology and immunology, 1966—, chmn. dept., 1974-90. Contbr. articles in field to profl. jours. Served with U.S. Army 1942-44. Recipient Research Career Devel. award NIH, 1965-70, Titular de la Chaire d'Actualité Scientifique U. Liège, Belgium, 1971-72; NRC fellow, 1954-55 Mem. Am. Soc. Biol. Chemists, Am. Acad. Microbiology, Am. Soc. Microbiology, AAAS, Sigma Xi. Home: 1919 Chestnut St Apt 2704 Philadelphia PA 19103-3449 Office: Temple U Sch Medicine 3400 N Broad St Philadelphia PA 19140-5104

SHOEMAKER, BOBBY JEAN (B.J. FOSTER), writer; d. Farris Lee and Grace Helen Foster; m. Leonard Wiley Shoemaker, June 1, 1958; children: Sharon Dawn, Walker. BA, Va. Intermont Coll., 1981. Cert. paralegal Nat. Ctr. for Paralegal Tng., Atlanta, 1985. Exec. v.p. Leonard W. Shoemaker & Assoc. Consulting Engrs., Houston, 1970—90; author Houston, 1990—. Author: Bayou Shadows, 2000 (named Book of Yr., High Country Writers, 2001). Mem.: Elk River Club. Presbyn. Avocations: horseback riding, golf, skiing, tennis, hiking.

SHOEMAKER, BOBBY LYNN, lawyer; b. Bay Springs, Miss., Jan. 1, 1952; s. Dewey O'Farrell and Doris Ann (Evans) S.; m. Lillous Faye Alexander, Jan. 1, 1971; children: Megan Leigh, Lillous Ann, Bobby Barr, Joanna Ophelia. BA in History and Polit. Sci., U. So. Miss., 1974; JD, U. Miss., 1977. Bar: Miss. 1977, U.S. Dist. Ct. (no. and so. dists.) Miss. 1977. Pvt. practice, Bay Springs, 1977—. Mem. adv. bd. First United Bank, Bay Springs, 1983-89; referee Jasper County Youth Ct., Bay Springs, 1984—, Jasper County Lunancy Ct., Bay Springs, 1984-88. Mem. ABA, ATLA, Miss. Bar Assn., Miss. Trial Lawyers Assn., Miss. Prosecutors Assn. (bd. dirs. 1980-83), Bay Springs C. of C. (pres. 1984-85), Rotary (sec. Bay Springs 1977, v.p. 1978, pres. 1979). Methodist. Office: PO Box 485 44 S 5th St Bay Springs MS 39422-0485 Office Phone: 601-764-3404.

SHOEMAKER, CAMERON DAVID JAMES, dean, educator; b. Honolulu, Dec. 15, 1940; s. John James and Belle Bird (Kellogg) S.; m. Catherine LaMoyne Prevost, May 23, 1966 (div. 1969); 1 child, David James; m. Leona Martha Wohlwend, May 18, 1972; 1 child, Jennifer Lee. BA in Polit. Sci., The Citadel, 1963; MA in History, San Jose State U., 1973; EdD, U. San Francisco, 1990. Commd. 2d lt. U.S. Army, 1963, advanced through grades to maj., 1971, fgn. area officer, 1972-84, ret., 1984; fin. cons. Merrill Lynch, Carmel, Calif., 1984-85; mgmt. analyst Def. Lang. Inst., Monterey, Calif., 1985, ednl. tech. project mgr., 1985-86, dir. info. resources mgmt., 1986-90; evening coll. adminstr., instnl. researcher Monterey Peninsula Coll., 1990-92; dean of bus. Sacramento (Calif.) City Coll., 1992-98; dean Vista Coll., Berkeley, Calif., 1999-2000; dir. ednl. svcs. Heald Coll., Roseville, Calif., 2000—01; project mgr. Little Hoover Commn. on Calif. State Govt. and Economy, 2002—04; project dir. Calif. Dept. Alcohol & Drug Programs, 2004—. Instr., Chapman Coll., Monterey, 1982-84, Monterey Inst., 1987; chmn. Asian Employment Program Com., Monterey, 1983-84; guest lectr., Naval Postgrad. Sch., Monterey, 1986-87; mem. Handicapped Individual Program Com., Monterey, 1986-90, treas., 1989-90. Contbr. articles to various publs. Pres., Creekside Cmty. Assn., Salinas, Calif., 1985-86; mem. County Svc. Area Adv. Bd., Salinas, 1985-87, Flood Control Dist. Planning Com., Salinas, 1986-87; active Leadership Monterey Peninsula, grad., 1992. Decorated Silver Star; recipient Comdrs. award for Civilian Svc. Dept. of Army, 1990; Carl D. Perkins fellow, 1993. Mem. Royal Asiatic Soc., Monterey Peninsula Scottish Soc. (treas. 1986-92), Los Rios Mgmt. Assn. (pres. 1995-96), Caledonian Club of Sacramento (treas. 1994-97, chief 1997-99). Republican. Roman Catholic. Home: 11577 Melones Cir Gold River CA 95670-7738 Office: Calif Dept Alcohol & Drug Programs 1700 K St Sacramento CA 95814 Personal E-mail: docshoe@comcast.net. *Personal philosophy: Always do what is right, regardless of the personal cost.*

SHOEMAKER, CAROLYN SPELLMAN, planetary astronomer; b. Gallup, N.Mex., June 24, 1929; d. Leonard Robert and Hazel Adele (Arthur) Spellmann; m. Eugene Merle Shoemaker, Aug. 18, 1951 (dec. July 1997); children: Christine Shoemaker Abanto, Patrick Gene, Linda Shoemaker Salazar. BA cum laude, Chico State Coll., 1949, MA, 1950; ScD, No. Ariz. U., 1990, St. Mary's U., N.S., Can., 2003. Vis. scientist Br. astrogeology U.S. Geol. Survey, Flagstaff, Ariz., 1980—; rsch. asst. Calif. Inst. Tech., Pasadena, 1981-85; rsch. prof. astronomy No. Ariz. U., Flagstaff, 1989—; mem. staff Lowell Obs., Flagstaff, 1993—. Guest observer Palomar Obs., Palomar Mountain, Calif., 1982-94; Ruth Northcott Meml. lectrs. R.A.S.C., 1995; co-McGovern lectr. Cosmos Club Found., 1995. Co-recipient Rittenhouse medal Rittenhouse Astron. Soc., 1988, Scientist of Yr. award ARCS Found., 1995, James C. Watson medal NAS, 1998; recipient Woman of Distinction award Soroptimists, 1994, 20th Anniversary Internat. Women's Yr. award Zonta and 99s, 1995, NASA Exceptional Scientific Achievement medal, 1996, Woman of Distinction award Nat. Assn. Women in Edn., 1996, Shoemaker award Am. Inst. Profl. Geologists, 1997, plaque Internat. Forest Friendship, Atchison, Kans., 1997, Robert Burnham Jr. award Western Regional Astron. League, 2000; named Disting. Alumna of the Calif. State U., Chico, 1996. Fellow AAAS, Am. Acad. Arts and Scis.; mem. Astron. Soc. of Pacific, Am. Geophys. Union, Meteoritical Soc. Achievements include discovery of 32 comets including Periodic Comet Shoemaker-Levy 9 which impacted Jupiter in July 1994, more than 500 asteroids including 44 Earth approachers and approximately 68 Mars crossers, meteorites at Veevers Crater, Australia and impactites at Wolfe Creek Crater, Australia. Home: 5231 Hidden Hollow Rd Flagstaff AZ 86001-3821 Office: Lowell Obs 1400 W Mars Hill Rd Flagstaff AZ 86001-4499

SHOEMAKER, ELEANOR BOGGS, television production company executive; b. Gulfport, Miss., Jan. 20, 1935; d. William Robertson and Bessie Eleanor (Ware) Boggs; m. D. Shoemaker, April 9, 1955 (div. 1987); children: Daniel W. III, William Boggs. Student in protocol, Southeastern U., 1952-53; student, George Washington U., Washington, 1953-56; BA in Communications and Polit. Sci. with honrs, Goucher Coll., 1981; postgrad., Villanova U. Feature writer Washington Times Herald, 1951-54; dir. Patricia Stevens Modeling Agy., Washington, 1955-56; free-lance model Julius Garfinkel, Woodward & Lothrop, Washington, 1951-56; research analyst Balt. County Council, Towson, Md., 1980-81; feature news reporter Sta. WGCB-TV, Red Lion, Pa., 1980-99; pub. speaker, protocol The Reliable Corp., Columbia, Md., 1982-86; media cons. The Enterprise Found., Columbia, Md., 1985-86; faculty, TV prodn. and communication St. Francis Prep Sch., Spring Grove, Pa., 1985-88; owner Windswept Prodns. Co., Felton, Pa., 1984—; mktg. svcs. coord. Yorktowne, Inc., Red Lion, Pa., 1993-95. Mem. conservation bd. Pa. Parks and Recreation Soc., 1984—; prodr. The Pa. County TV Prodn., 1981;

prodr., host Westar 4 Channel 9 half hour weekly news program Keystone Report. Prodr. The Pa. County TV Prodn., 1981, The Pa. County TV Prodn., 1981, documentary Human Rights: A Special Report, Sta. WGCB-TV, 1989; prodr., host Westar 4 Channel 9 half hour weekly news program Keystone Report, 1990. Bd. dirs. York (Pa.) County Parks and Recreation, 1972-87, YWCA, York, 1957-82, Hist. York, 1990—; mem. exec. com. York County Reps., 1972-82; accreditation adv. com. York Coll. of Pa.; instr. YWCA Women in Politics; founder, mem. Child Abuse Task Force, York, 1983—; mem. select com. Pa. Agrl. Zoning, 1988; mem. steering com. York Forum, 1989-96; co-chmn. Cross Mill Restoration, 1987—; mem. Displaced Homemaker's Bd., 1989—, pres., 1993—; bd. dirs. Hist. York, 1990-95; founder, host Old Rose Tree Pony Club, 1967—; chmn. camp com. U.S. Pony Club Inc., 1973-75; chair Spring Valley County Pk. Task Force, 1972; master of fox hounds Mrs. Shoemaker's Hounds, 1969—; master of beagles Mrs. Shoemaker's Weybright Beagles, 1988-96; edn. chair Jr. League of York, 1962-70. Recipient pro bono child legal representation grant Pa. Bar Assn., 1983, Pa. Tree Farmer of Yr. award, 1987, Outstanding Achievement in Broadcasting award Am. Women in Radio and TV, 1992, Lay Person of Yr. award Pa. Recreation and Parks Assn. and Gov. Thornburg, 1982, Jefferson award nominee, 1992, Matrix award Ctrl. Pa. Women in Comm., 1993, First pl. corp. video prodn. Ctrl. Pa. Women in Comm., 1993, Agrl. award C. of C., Cross Mill Restoration, 1999, Albright Care Found. Outstanding Vol. award, Ridge, Normandie, 1999, Daughters of Am. Revolution Outstanding Achievement award in preservation Nat. Resources, 2000, Game Commn. Recognition award farm game program, 2000, Albright Care Founders award; selected journalist for Novosti Press USSR-U.S. Press Exch. program, 1989. Mem. Am. Polled Hereford Assn., York Area C. of C., York County C. of C. (publicity com. 1985-90, agri. bus. com.), Masters of Foxhounds Assn. Episcopalian. Avocations: foxhunting, beagling. Home and Office: PO Box 167 Felton PA 17322-0167

SHOEMAKER, FRANK CRAWFORD, retired physicist; b. Ogden, Utah, Mar. 26, 1922; s. Roy Hopkins and Sarah Parker (Anderson) Shoemaker; m. Ruth Elizabeth Nelson, July 11, 1944; children: Barbara Elaine, Mary Frances. AB, Whitman Coll., 1943, DSc (hon.), 1978; PhD, U. Wis., 1949. Staff mem. Radiation Lab. MIT, 1943-45; instr. physics U. Wis., 1949-50; mem. faculty Princeton (N.J.) U., 1950-89, prof. physics, 1962—89, prof. emeritus, 1989—, dir. undergrad. physics dept., 1981—89; assoc. dir. Princeton U. Pa. Accelerator, 1962-66. Vis. scientist Rutherford High Energy Lab., 1965—66; main accelerator sect. head Nat. Accelerator Lab., 1968—69; prin. investigator Dept. of Energy High Energy Physics Contract, 1972—85. Fellow: Am. Phys. Soc.; mem.: Sigma Xi, Phi Beta Kappa. Home: 49 Meadow Lakes 03 Hightstown NJ 08520-3351 Office Phone: 609-258-6602. Business E-Mail: frankcs@princeton.edu.

SHOEMAKER, HAROLD LLOYD, infosystem specialist; b. Danville, Ky., Jan. 3, 1923; s. Eugene Clay and Amy (Wilson) S.; m. Dorothy M. Maddox, May 11, 1947 (dec. Feb. 1991). AB, Berea Coll., 1944; postgrad., State U. Ia., 1943-44, George Washington U., 1949-50, NYU, 1950-52. Rsch. physicist State U. Iowa, 1944-45, Frankford Arsenal, Pa., 1945-47; rsch. engr. N.Am. Aviation, L.A., 1947-49, Jacobs Instrument Co., Bethesda, 1949-50; assoc. head systems devel. group The Teletigister Corp., N.Y.C., 1950-53; mgr. electronic equipment devel. sect., head planning Hughes Aircraft Co., L.A., 1953-58; dir. command and control systems lab. Bunker-Ramo Corp., L.A., 1958-68; v.p. Data Systems, 1968-69, corp. dir. data processing, 1969-75; tech. staff R & D Assocs., Marina Del Rey, Calif., 1975-85; info. systems cons., 1985—. Patentee elec. digital computer. Served with AUS, 1945-46. Mem. IEEE, Ky. Cols. Home: PO Box 3385 Granada Hills CA 91394-0385 E-mail: haroldshoe@cs.com.

SHOEMAKER, HELEN E. MARTIN ACHOR, civic worker; b. Houston, Mar. 24, 1915; d. Earl L. and Blanche L. (Williams) Martin; m. Harold E. Achor, Oct. 11, 1935; children: Dianne Achor Johnston, Lana Achor Rainville; m. Robert N. Shoemaker, May 19, 1972. AB, Anderson (Ind.) Coll., 1960, LLD, 1978. Resident dir. Anderson Coll., 1967-69, dir. alumni svcs., 1969-72; legis. counsel Ind. Colls. and Univ. Ind., 1970-72; spl. asst. Ctr. Pub. Svc., Anderson, 1973-77, spl. asst. to dean for acad. devel., 1977-78. Sec.-treas. Ind. State Libr. and Hist. Bldg. Expansion Commn., 1973-78; mem. com. region VII, Girl Scouts U.S.A., 1958-66; adv. coun. fin. aid to students Office Edn. HEW, 1976-78; mem. Ind. Ho. of Reps. from Madison County, 1968-70; v.p. Ind. Fedn. Women's Rep. Clubs, 1945-46; treas. Nat. Fedn. Women's Rep. Clubs, 1947-51; Rep. precinct vice chmn. Madison County, 1946-68, vice chmn., Anderson, 1967-68; bd. dirs. Urban League Madison County, 1969-76; adv. com. Georgetown U. Grad. Sch. Acad. in Pub. Svc., 1976-83; mem. adv. com. on sex discrimination Ind. Civil Rights Commn., 1978-83; bd. dirs. Anderson Symphony Orch. Women's Guild, 1987, hon. mem.; trustee Anderson Coll., 1978-85; bd. dirs. Opportunities Industrialization Ctr., Inc., Madison County, 1980-84, Ind. Acad. Pub. Svc., 1981-83, Women's Alternatives Inc., Anderson, 1982-93 (Elizabeth Howard McMahan award 1987); mem. exec. com. devel. bd. St. John's Med. Ctr., Anderson, 1981-92; bd. dirs. life enrichment Park Place Ch. God, 1989-94; bd. dirs. Anderson Symphony Womens Guild. Recipient William B. Harper award Urban League Madison County, 1975; named Sagamore of Wabash, State of Ind., 1979. Mem. LWV (dir. Madison County 1973-76, 78-84, 87), Anderson Coun. Women, Anderson Fine Arts Ctr. (treas.). Mem. Ch. Of God. Home: 5801 W Bethel Ave Muncie IN 47304-9549

SHOEMAKER, INNIS HOWE, art museum curator; b. Reading, Pa. d. William Erety and Jean (Miller) S. AB, Vassar Coll., 1964; MA, Columbia U., 1968, PhD, 1975. Curator Vassar Coll. Art. Gallery, Poughkeepsie, N.Y., 1965-68, 73-76; asst. dir. Ackland Art Mus., U. N.C., Chapel Hill, 1976-82, dir., 1983-86; Audrey and William H. Helfand sr. curator prints, drawings and photographs Phila. Mus. Art, 1986—; adj. prof. U. Pa., 2001—. Fellow in art history Am. Acad. in Rome, 1971-73; adj. prof. U. N.C., Chapel Hill, 1983-86. Co-author: The Engravings of Marcantonio Raimondi, 1981, Paul Cézanne: Two Sketchbooks, 1989; author: Mad for Modernism: Earl Horter and His Collection, 1999, Jacques Villon and his Cubist Prints, 2001. Mem. vis. com. Lehman Loeb Art Ctr., Vassar Coll., 1993-. Mem. Coll. Art Assn. Am., Am. Assn. Mus., Print Coun. Am. (bd. dirs. 1986-89). Office: Phila Mus Art PO Box 7646 Philadelphia PA 19101-7646

SHOEMAKER, MARJORIE PATTERSON, textbook editor, consultant; b. Cleve., Aug. 8, 1933; d. Franklin J. and Marjorie (Kennel) Patterson; children: Stephanie A. Veith, Timothy R. BS, Bowling Green (Ohio) State U., 1955, MA, 1968; postgrad., U. Pitts., 1972-74; PhD, Syracuse (N.Y.) U., 1980. Cert. supr. curriculum and instrn. Tchr. high sch. history/govt. Vanlue (Ohio) Schs., 1955-57; jr. high sch. tchr. history/govt./English tchr. Crestline (Ohio) Schs., 1963-65; elem. tchr. Galion (Ohio) City Schs., 1965-67; reading supr. Anthony Wayne Schs., Whitehouse, Ohio, 1968-70; instr. reading, ednl. psychology Heidelberg Coll., Tiffin, Ohio, 1970-72; instr. reading Bowling Green (Ohio) State U., 1972-76; teaching fellow Syracuse U., 1976-79; reading cons. Macmillan Pub. Co., N.Y.C., 1980-88; editor Zaner-Bloser Ednl. Pub., Columbus, Ohio, 1988-90, sr. editor, 1990—, sr. curriculum editor, 1995, dir., 1995—. Cons. Ft. Wayne (Ind.) Schs., 1976-80, Las Cruces (N.Mex.) Schs., 1974-76; vis. prof. edn. N.Mex. State Coll., 1974, Ind.-Purdue U., 1976-80. Bd. trustees The Andrews Sch. for Girls, Willoughby, Ohio, 1978-81. Mem. Internat. Reading Assn. (editor newsletter 1974-76), Am. Soc. Curriculum and Devel., Edn. Press, Order Eastern Star.

SHOEMAKER, ROBERT MORIN, retired army officer, county government official; b. Almont, Mich., Feb. 18, 1924; s. Uriah Beebe and Pomala (Morin) S.; m. Mary Alice Rickard, July 17, 1948. BS, U.S. Mil. Acad., 1946; postgrad., U.S. Army Command and Gen. Staff Coll., 1959, Army War Coll., 1967. Commd. 2d lt. U.S. Army, 1946, advanced through grades to gen., 1978, platoon leader, bn. staff officer, co. comdr. 18th Inf., Fed. Republic Germany, 1947-50, co. comdr., regtl. S2, S3, 23d Inf., 1953-54, staff officer inf. br. DA, 1954-56, student, faculty officer U.S. Army Aviation Sch., 1959-62, project officer Army Concept Team, 1962-63, bn. comdr., asst. chief of staff, G-3, 11th Air Assault Div., 1963-65, bn. cmdr., squadron comdr. 1st Cav. Div., 1965-66, chief plans and programs Army Aviation DA, 1967-69, chief of staff, asst. div. comdr. 1st Cav., 1969-70, dep. comdr., chief. of staff III Corps and Ft. Hood, Tex., 1970, dept. comdr. MASSTER, 1971-72, comdr. 1st Cav., 1973-75, comdr. III Corps, 1975-77, dep. comdr. FORSCOM Ft. McPherson, Ga., 1977-78; comdr. U.S. Army Forces Command, 1978-82; ret., 1982; county commr. Bell County, Tex., 1987-94. Decorated D.S.M., Silver Star medal with oak leaf cluster, Legion of Merit, D.F.C., Bronze Star, Air medal with 48 oak leaf clusters, Army Commendation medal with oak leaf cluster, Croix de Guerre (France), Gallantry Cross with palm (Republic of Vietnam), RVN Honor medal 1st class; Robert M. Shoemaker H.S., Killeen, Tex. named in his honor, Aug. 2001; named Disting. Grad., West Point, 2004. Home: 111 Bluff Ln Belton TX 76513-9804

SHOEMAKER, ROBERT WILLOUGHBY, historian, educator; b. Chgo., Feb. 1, 1924; s. Robert Jay and Frances Ray Shoemaker; m. Caroline Louise Ferguson, June 14, 1947 (dec. Mar. 29, 1993); 1 child, Robert Thomas. BA with honors, U. Pa., 1947, MA, 1950, PhD in Am. Studies, 1951. Historian Independence Nat. Park, Phila., 1951—53; asst. prof. Rensselaer Poly. Inst., Troy, NY, 1953—60; assoc. prof. North Ctrl. Coll., Naperville, Ill., 1960—79, prof. emeritus, 1979—; sr. Fulbright prof. U. Koeln, Germany, 1973—74. Photography chief Chgo. Convention and Tourism Bur., 1978—80; testified before U.S. Senate Com. on Constn., Washington, 1969; vis. lectr. U. Ill., Chgo., 1961—62. Author: Origin and Meaning of Name Protestant Episcopal, 1959 (Keble award, 1959, Living Ch. award, 1959), Metric For Me, 1998; contbr. articles to profl. publs. With U.S. Army, 1942—45. Newberry fellow, Newberry Libr., Chgo., 1969. Mem.: Ind. Writers Chgo. Episcopalian. Avocation: photography. Home: 222 S Julian St Naperville IL 60540 Office Phone: 630-355-7180. E-mail: OpaRobert@aol.com.

SHOEMAKER, SANDRA KAYE, aerospace executive; b. Dallas, July 13, 1954; d. Vondyl Claud and Billie Juanita (Pritchett) Willis; m. Carl Vernon Shoemaker, Aug. 16, 1975; children: Regan Amanda, Ryan Adam. BBA, Baylor U., 1975. Fin. coord. Tex. A&M U., College Station, 1975-77; from engring. planner to mgr. adminstrv. support Gen. Dynamics Corp., Ft. Worth, 1977-90; dir. engring. adminstrn. Lockheed Ft. Worth Co., 1990-94, dir. rsch. & engring. svcs. & process support, 1994-96; dir. labs. and tech. support Lockheed Martin Tactical Aircraft Sys., 1996-97, dir. F-16 air vehicle, 1997-99, dir. and deputy ops. F-16 program, 1999-2000, dir. Aero Transition Team, 2000-01, dir. co. ops., 2001, v.p. integrated co. ops., 2001—03, v.p. program mgmt., 2003—. Republican. Baptist. Avocations: music, skiing, water-skiing, racquetball, snorkeling. Home: 5100 Dewdrop Ln Fort Worth TX 76123-1931 Office: Lockheed Martin Aeronautics Co PO Box 748 Fort Worth TX 76101-0748

SHOEMAKER, WILLIAM C. journalist; b. Simpson County, Miss., Nov. 19, 1931; s. William Ezra and Saleta (Roach) S.; m. Nell Slade, Apr. 12, 1957. Grad. high sch., Miss. Reporter Jackson (Miss.) Daily News, 1949-51, 54-65; editor, pub. The Star-Herald, Koscivsko, Miss., 1965-89; pres. Shoemaker Offset Inc., Koscivsko, Miss., 1989—, Scott County Times, Miss., 1983-89, Simpson County News, 1983-87, Pontotoc Progress, 1985-89, Bulldog Pubs., 1983-90. Bd. dirs. Merchants and Farmers Bank. Chmn. Miss. Econ. Coun., 1996-97; chmn. Miss. svc. delivery area U.S. Job Tng. Partnership Act, 1983-95. With U.S. Army, 1951-54. Mem. Rotary. Independent. Office: PO Box 457 Kosciusko MS 39090-0457

SHOEMAKER, WILLIAM EDWARD, financial executive; b. Charleston, W.Va., Sept. 17, 1945; s. Robert Edward and Janet Elizabeth (Hoglund) S.; 1 child, Marcus. BBA, U. Notre Dame, 1967. Assoc. buyer Proctor & Gamble, Cin., 1971; gen. mgr. Eastwind Inc., Anchorage, 1972-73; pres., operator Golden Horn Lodge, Inc., Bristol Bay, Alaska, 1973-79; treas. Hawley Resource Group, Inc., Anchorage, 1979-88; treas., chief fin. officer Golden Zone Resources, Inc., Campbell, Calif., 1988-90; ptnr. Resort Mgmt. Corp., Anchorage, 1987-90; pres. Discovery Holdings, Inc., Ft. Lauderdale, Fla., 1991—. Bd. dirs. Pacific Art & Design Cons., Inc. Bd. dirs. Anchorage Econ. Devel. Corp., 1988-90, 4 Children's Sake, 1997—; mem. exec. com. Broward Child Welfare Initiative, 2002—. Served to lt. (j.g.) USN, 1967-71. Republican. Avocations: boating, skiing, fishing. Office: Discovery Holdings Inc Ste 120 2400 E Las Olas Blvd Fort Lauderdale FL 33301-1529 Home: 1733 NE 8TH St Fort Lauderdale FL 33304-3474 Personal E-mail: weshoe@bellsouth.net.

SHOEMATE, CHARLES R. former food company executive; b. LaHarpe, Ill., Dec. 10, 1939; s. Richard Osborne and Mary Jane (Gillette) S.; m. Nancy Lee Gordon, Sept. 16, 1962; children: Steven, Jeffrey, Scott. BS, Western Ill. U., 1962; MBA, U. Chgo., 1973. Supr. Corn Products Co., Summit, Ill., 1962-72; comptr. Corn Products Unit of CPC Internat., Englewood Cliffs, NJ, 1972-74, plant mgr. Corpus Christi, Tex., 1974-76, v.p. ops. Englewood Cliffs, 1976-81; pres. Can. Starch Co., Montreal, Canada, 1981-83; v.p. Corn Refining divsn. CPC Internat., Englewood Cliffs, 1983-86, pres. Corn Refining divsn., 1986-88, corp v.p., 1983-88, pres., 1988-98, chmn., CEO, 1990-98; pres., chmn., CEO Bestfoods (formerly CPC Internat.), 1998—. Office: Unilever Bestfoods 700 Sylvan Ave Englewood Cliffs NJ 07632

SHOEN, EDWARD JOSEPH, transportation and insurance companies executive; s. Leonard and Anna (Carty) S. MBA, Harvard U. Pres., chmn. Amerco Nev. Corp., Phoenix; pres. U-Haul Internat., Inc., Phoenix. Office: Amerco 1325 Airmotive Way Reno NV 89502 also: Amerco 1325 Airmotive Way Reno NV 89502-3201

SHOENBERGER, ALLEN EDWARD, law educator; b. Waynesburg, Pa., Sept. 18, 1944; s. Allen Edward and Evelyn S.; m. Cynthia Grant (div. 1975); 1 child, Michael Grant; m. Caroline Orzac, Aug. 3, 1980; 1 child, Elisa Orzac. BA with honors, Swarthmore Coll., 1966; JD with honors, Columbia U., 1969; LLM, NYU, 1972. Bar: Ill. 1973, U.S. Dist. Ct. (no. dist.) Ill. 1973, U.S. Ct. Appeals (7th cir.) 1977, U.S. Supreme Ct. 1977. Vis. lectr. U. Nairobi, Kenya, 1969-71; fellow Internat. Legal Ctr., Nairobi, 1969-71; asst. prof. Loyola U., Chgo., 1972-77, assoc. prof., 1977-85, prof., 1985—, chmn. faculty coun., 1983—2000. Cons. Adminstrv. Conf. U.S., Washington, 1988; mem. Ill. A.G. Task Force for Handicapped, 1982—; chmn. adv. bldg. com. Cir. Ct. of Cook County, Chgo., 1988-93. Editor Spina Bifida publ., 1985-93, East African Law Reports, 1969-71, Jour. Nat. Assn. Adminstrv. Law Judges, 1996—; contbr. articles to profl. publs. Mem. Ill. Spina Bifida Assn., Chgo., 1980-93; hearing officer Ill. Pollution Control Bd., 1974-97, U.S. Dept. Energy, Ill., 1984-89. Recipient various grants, including NIE, 1973; fellow Ford Found., 1972, NEH, 1987. Mem. ABA, Fed. Bar Assn., Chgo. Bar Assn. (chmn. adminstrv. law com. 1985-86). Office: Loyola Sch of Law 1 E Pearson St Chicago IL 60611-2055

SHOGAN, ROBERT, news correspondent; b. N.Y.C., Sept. 12, 1930; s. Albert and Millie (Jacobs) S.; m. Ellen Shrewsbury, May 26, 1959; children: Cynthia Diane, Amelia Ford. BA, Syracuse U., 1951; postgrad., U. Mich. Inst. Pub. Adminstrn., 1951, Columbia U., 1952. Reporter Detroit Free Press, 1956-59; telegraph editor Miami (Fla.) News, 1959-61; asst. editor Wall St. Jour., N.Y.C., 1961-65; evaluation officer Peace Corps, Washington, 1965-66; corr. Newsweek, Washington, 1966-73; nation polit. corr. Los Angeles Times, Washington, 1973-99. Profl.-in-residence Annenberg Sch. Communication, U. Pa., 1993; adj. prof. Johns Hopkins U., Ctr. for Study of Am. Govt., Washington, 1999—. Author: Question of Judgement, 1972, Promises to Keep, 1977, None of the Above, 1982, The Riddle of Power, 1991, Hard Bargain, 1995, Fate of the Union, 1998, The Double-Edged Sword, 1998, Bad News, 2001, War Without End, 2002, The Battle of Blair Mountain, 2004; co-author: (with Tom Craig) The Detroit Race Riot, 1964. Served with U.S. Army, 1952-54. Recipient 1st prize Feature Writing, Mich. AP, 1959, Disting. Reporting Pub. Affairs award Am. Polit. Sci. Assn., 1969, Scribes Book award, 1972; rsch. grantee Harry S Truman Presdl. Libr., 1989, Lyndon B. Johnson Presdl. Libr., 1989, Gerald R. Ford Presdl. Libr., 1989; McCormick fellow Hoover Presdl. Libr., 1993; fellow Media Studies Ctr., 1998. Mem. Phi Beta Kappa Home: 3513 Raymond St Chevy Chase MD 20815-3227

SHOGEN, KUSLIMA, pharmaceutical executive; BS, Fairleigh Dickenson U., 1974, MS in Biology, 1976. Founder Alfacell Corp., Bloomfield, NJ, 1981, CFO, 1986—94, pres., 1986—96, CEO, 1986—, chmn., 1996—, acting CFO, 1999—. Cons. Lever Bros. Rsch. Group. Recipient 1st prize, Sigma Xi, 1974, Pinnacle award, Fairleigh Dickenson U., 1998. Mem.: Phi Beta Kappa. Office: Alfacell Corp 225 Belleville Ave Bloomfield NJ 07003

SHOHEN, SAUNDRA ANNE, health care communications and public relations executive; b. Washington, Aug. 22, 1934; d. Aaron Kohn and Malvina (Kleiman) Kohn Blinder; children: Susan, Brian. BS, Columbia Pacific U., 1979, MS in Health Svcs. Adminstrn., 1981. Adminstr. social work dept. Roosevelt Hosp., N.Y.C., 1978-79; adminstr. emergency dept. St. Luke's-Roosevelt Hosp. Ctr., N.Y.C., 1979-83, assoc. dir. pub. rels., 1983-87; pres. Saundra Shohen Assocs., Ltd., N.Y.C., 1987-92; v.p. Prism Internat., N.Y.C., 1988-91; bd. dirs. Tureck Bach Inst., N.Y.C., 1985—. Panelist ann. Emmy awards NATAS, N.Y.C., 1983, 84; tchr. healthcare mktg. Baruch Coll., N.Y.C., 1994. Author: Health Scripts for Radio, 1983, Voice of America, 1983 (Presdl. Recognition award, 1984); author: (with others) AIDS: A Health Care Management Response, 1987; author: EMERGENCY!, 1989. Mem. NATAS, Internat. Hosp. Fedn., Am. Soc. Hosp. Mktg. and Pub. Rels., Vols. in Tech. Assistance. Democrat. Jewish. Home: 240 Central Park S New York NY 10019-1413

SHOHET, JACK A. otolaryngologist; BS in Chemistry, U. Cin., 1986, MD, 1990. Resident in otolaryngology-head and neck surgery Vanderbilt U., Nashville, 1996; fellow in neurotology/skull base surgery Ear Found., Michael E. Glasscock, III, Nashville, 1996; dir. otology/neurotology U. Calif.-Irvine Med. Ctr., Orange, 1997—, assoc. clin. prof. dept head and neck surgery, 2002—. Office: 446 Old Newport Blvd Newport Beach CA 92663-3521 E-mail: jshohet@eardoctor.org.

SHOJI, HIROMU, orthopedic surgeon, educator; b. Chiba-Ken, Japan; Grad., Coll. Gen. Edn., 1959, U. Tokyo, Faculty Medicine, 1964. Diplomate Am. Bd. Orthopedic Surgery (examiner). Intern U. Tokyo Hosp., 1964-65, resident, 1965-67, Bklyn. Cumberland Med. Ctr., 1967-68, NYU Med. Ctr., 1968-69; Bone tumor clin. fellow Meml. Sloan-Kettering Med. Ctr., N.Y.C., 1969-70; orthopedic fellow Hosp. Spl. Surgery, N.Y.C., 1971-72; resident Bowman Gray Med. Sch., Winston-Salem, N.C., 1973-74; orthopedic surgeon pvt. practice, Sacramento, 1974-76, New Orleans, 1976-90, Riverside, Calif., 1990—. Mem. staff Parkview Hosp., Riverside Comty. Hosp., Corona Regional Hosp.; asst. prof. dept. orthopedic surgery U. Calif., Davis, 1974-76; assoc. prof. dept. orthopedic surgery La. State U. Med. Ctr., 1976-80, prof., 1980-90; clin. prof. Loma Linda U., 1990—. Contbr. numerous articles to profl. jours. Bone tumor clin. fellow Meml. Sloan-Kettering Med. Ctr., N.Y.C., 1966-70, orthopedic fellow Hosp. Spl. Surgery, N.Y.C., 1971-72. Mem. AMA, NAS, Am. Acad. Orthopaedic Surgeons, Am. Assn. Hip and Knee Surgeons, Japanese Orthopedic Assn., Orthopedic Rsch. Soc., Japanese Soc. Connective Tissue Rsch., Japanese Rehab. Assn., Am. Orthopedic Assn., So. Med. Assn., Am. Rheumatism Assn., Calif. Orthopedic Assn., Internat. Soc. Orthopedics and Traumatology, Knee Soc., Internat. Soc. Knee Surgery. Office: 3838 Sherman Dr Riverside CA 92503-4001 Office Phone: 951-354-7270. Personal E-mail: hiros65@aol.com.

SHOKEIR, MOHAMED HASSAN KAMEL, medical geneticist, educator; b. Mansoura, Egypt, July 2, 1938; emigrated to Can., 1969, naturalized, 1974; s. Hassan Sayed and Lolia Nora (Kira) S.; m. Donna Jean Nugent, Feb. 27, 1968; children: Marc Omar, Vanessa May. MB, BChir, Cairo U., 1960, D in Surgery, 1963, D in Surgery in Orthop., 1964; MS, U. Mich., 1965, PhD, 1969. Intern Cairo U. Hosps., 1960-61, resident, 1961-64; Fulbright rsch. scholar dept. human genetics U. Mich., 1964-69; asst. prof. pediat. U. Sask., Saskatoon, Can., 1969-71, assoc. prof., 1971-73, prof., 1977—, dir. divsn. med. genetics, 1975-97, head dept. pediat., 1979-96, Saskatoon Dist. Health Bd., 1993-96. Head sect. clin. genetics U. Man., Winnipeg, Can., 1973-75; mem. staffs Univ. Hosp., Saskatoon City Hosp., St. Paul's Hosp.; cons. Winnipeg Health Scis. Ctr., Regina Gen. Hosp. Contbr. articles to profl publs. Mem. Acad. Freedom and Tenure Com., Ottawa, Ont., Can., 1980-90, Queen Elizabeth II scientist, 1969-75. Med. Rsch. Coun. grantee, 1970-79; Can. Coll. Med. Geneticists Found. fellow, 1975— Fellow Can. Coll. Med. Geneticists, Can. Soc. Clin. Investigation (councillor 1974-76), Can. Med. Assn. (chmn., mem. adv. com. 1987-96); mem. APHA, Assn. Med. Sch. Pediat. Dept. Chairmen, Assn. Can. Univ. Dept. Chairmen, Am. Pediat. Soc., Soc. Pediat. Rsch., N.Y. Acad. Scis., Am. Geriat. Soc., Am. Fedn. Clin. Rsch., Mid-Western Soc. Pediat. Rsch., Western Pediat. Soc., Am. Soc. Human Genetics, Genetics Soc. Am., Genetics Soc. Can., Am. Genetic Assn. Home: 108 Riel Crescent Saskatoon SK Canada S7J 2W6 Office: U Sask Dept Pediatrics Saskatoon SK Canada S7N 0W8 E-mail: mshokeir@shaw.ca. *Never tried to imagine what the future will bring, found the present and its implications enough to occupy me. The overriding passions in my life have been the love of man and the pity for his suffering. I have come to accept the futility of eliminating bias, even prejudice— mine or others'; my hope now is to recognize it and shield one's actions from it. What the world needs is more tolerance. Always found praise a bit embarrassing, confusing and altogether inhibiting— the most lavish for the least deserved accomplishment. Always thought the world is, at best, approximate. I now realize that in life one cannot have all bases covered.*

SHOLL, JOHN GURNEY, III, physician; b. Phila., Mar. 6, 1915; s. John Gurney Jr. and Helen (Hare) S.; m. Marjorie Louise Hill, June 27, 1942 (dec. July 1999); children: John Douglas, Debora Sholl Humphreys, Robert Roy, David Gurney, Rebecca Sholl Baer. BS, Bucknell U., 1937; MD, Harvard U., 1941. Diplomate Am. Bd. Internal Medicine, cert. Nat. Bd. Med. Examiners. Intern Germantown Hosp., Phila., 1941-42; asst. resident in medicine Univ. Hosp., Cleve., 1942-43; pvt. practice in internal medicine Cleve., 1943-78; from demonstrator to assoc. clin. prof. medicine Case-Western Res. U., Cleve., 1943-78, assoc. prof. principles of medicine Dental Sch., 1965-76; dir. med. edn. U. Suburban Health Ctr., Cleve., 1973-78; chmn. edn. commn. Ohio Med. Assn., 1973-76; clin. prof. medicine U. Calif. San Diego, La Jolla, 1978-88, dir. internal medicine group, 1979-85; prof. clin. medicine St. Matthews U. Sch. Medicine MSA, Windham, Maine, 2003. Med. dir. E.F. Hutton Life Ins. Co., La Jolla, 1978-82; vol. cons. to med. staff Maine Vets. Homes, 1990-. Mem. editl. bd. Consultant mag., Greenwich, Conn., 1980-84, San Diego Physician, 1986-87. Capt. Army of US, 1944—46, ETO. Recipient Cert. of Lifetime Achievement award, Maine Health Care, 2003. Fellow ACP; mem. AMA (Cert. Merit 2003), Calif. Med. Assn., VFW (life), Am. Legion (life), U. Calif. San Diego Emeriti Assn., Rowfant Club (Cleve.). Republican. Am. Baptist. Avocations: writing, golf, reading. Home: 1 Huntington Common Dr Apt 200 Kennebunk ME 04043-6564

SHOLTIS, JOSEPH ARNOLD, JR., business owner, nuclear and aerospace engineer, consultant; b. Monongahela, Pa., Nov. 28, 1948; s. Joseph and Gladys S.; m. Cheryl Anita Senchur, Dec. 1970; children: Christian Joseph, Carole Lynne. BS in Nuc. Engring. Disting. Mil. Grad., Pa. State U., 1970; diplomas, Air Univ., 1975, 78; MS in Nuc. Engring., U. N.Mex., 1977, postgrad., 1978-80. Lic. sr. reactor operator NRC, 1980-84. Mathematician, statistician, mine safety analyst U.S. Bur. Mines, Pitts., 1968-70; commd. 2d lt. USAF, 1970, advanced through grades to lt. col., 1988, ret., 1993; nuc. rsch. officer Fgn. Tech. Divsn., Wright-Patterson AFB, Ohio, 1971-74; chief space nuc. sys. safety br. Air Force Weapons Lab., Kirtland AFB, N.Mex., 1974-78; mil. mem. tech. staff, project officer Sandia Nat. Labs., Albuquerque, 1978-80; chief radiation sources divsn., reactor facility dir. Armed Forces Radiobiology Rsch. Inst., Bethesda, Md., 1980-84; program mgr. SP-100 space reactor power sys. tech. devel. prog. Air Force Element U.S. Dept. Energy, Germantown, 1984—87; chief analysis and evaluation br. Air Force Safety Ctr., Kirtland AFB, N.Mex., 1987—91, chief nuc. power and sources divsn., 1991-92, chief nuc. energy sys., 1992-93; dir. rsch. and engring., gen. mgr. N.Mex. ops. Oakton Internat. Corp., Va., 1993-96; cons. in field, 1993-96; owner, prin. cons. Sholtis Engring. and Safety Consulting, Tijeras, N.Mex., 1996—. Tech. advisor Interagency nuc. safety rev. panel evaluations Viking 1 & 2, Lincoln Exptl. Satellites 8 & 9, Voyager 1 & 2 nuc.-powered space missions, 1974—77; space shuttle nuc. payload safety assessment officer Air Force Weapons Lab., Kirtland AFB, N.Mex., 1976—78; instr. med. effects nuc. weapons Armed Forces Radiobiology Rsch. Inst., Bethesda, Md., 1980—84, mem. reactor and radiation facility safety com., 1980—85; faculty lectr. Uniformed Svcs. U. Health Scis., 1982—87; U.S. del. and tech. advisor UN sci. and tech. subcom. and legal subcom. UN com. on peaceful uses outer

space and working group on nuc. power sources in outer space, 1984—87; mem. Schreiber-Spence award com. symposia on space nuc. power and propulsion U. N.Mex., 1987—91; chmn. Power Sys. Subpanel Interagency Nuc. Safety Rev. Panel risk assessments of Galileo and Ulysses nuc.-powered space missions, 1987—92; mem. Multimegawatt Space Reactor Power Project safety working group, 1988—91; mem. U.S. contingent U.S. and USSR discussions on nuc. space power sys. safety, 1989—90; Def. Dept. chmn. Interagy. Nuc. Safety Rev. panel evaluations of Ulysses and Cassini nuc.-powered space missions for Office of Pres., 1989—93; mem. adv. com. tech. program com. Space Tech. and Applications Internat. Forum U. N.Mex., 1989—; mem. NASA Space Exploration Initiative Nuc. Safety Policy Working Group, 1990—91, SP-100 Space Reactor Program safety adv. com., 1990—93; mem. safety com. USAF Thermionic Space Power Program, 1990—93; mem. Ind. Evaluation Group, Strategic Def. Initiative Orgn., 1991—93; lectr. N.Mex. Acad. Sci. Vis. Scientist Program, 1991—2000; mem. program com., reactor safety divsn. Am. Nuc. Soc., 1992—94; mem. ind. adv. safety assessment of TOPAZ-II space reactor power sys. U.S. Dept. Energy, 1993; mem. power sys. working group evaluation of Mars Pathfinder, Cassini and Mars Exploration Rover nuc.-powered space missions Interagency. Nuc. Safety Rev. Panel, 1993—2003; mem. NASA ind. rev. team recert. evaluation Cassini space mission Jet Propulsion Lab., 1994; mem. outstanding paper award com. Space Tech. and Applications Internat. Forum U. N.Mex., 1999—2000, 2003—, chmn., 2000—03; mem. coord. com. flight safety working group N.Mex. Office Space Commercialization, 1999—2003; mem. NASA rsch. award adv. bd. N.Mex. Space Grant Consortium U. N.Mex., 2000—; mem. reactor safeguards adv. com. U. N.Mex., 2002—; mem. What is an Engineer task force N.Mex. Soc. Profl. Engrs., 2002—; tech. cons. Boeing Rocketdyne for Jupiter Icy Moons Orbiter spacecraft and multi-mission radioisotope thermoelectric generator devel. efforts, 2003—. Author (with others): LMFBR Accident Delineation, 1980, Military Radiobiology, 1987, Power Systems Subpanel Reports for Galileo, Ulysses, Mars Pathfinder, Cassini and Mars Exploration Rover space missions, 1989—2003, Safety Evaluation Report for Ulysses space mission, 1990, A Critical Review of Space Nuclear Power and Propulsion 1984-93, 1994, Test Plan for Pu-238 Oxide Coated Particle Fuel and Fuel Forms for Space Radioisotopic Heater Units and Radioisotope Power Systems, 1999; contbr. over 100 papers to profl. publs. presented at nat. and internat. confs. Judge N.Mex. Sci. Fair, 1987—2000; charter mem. N.Mex. Edn. Outreach Com., 1989—93; vol. Bros. of the Good Shepherd food kitchen, Albuquerque, 1997—2000; pres. Tijeras Arroyo Golf Assn., Kirtland AFB, 1998—2000, v.p., 2000—03, mem. golf adv. com., 1998—2002; course evaluation panelist Golf Digest mag., 2000—. Decorated Def. Meritorious Svc. medal (2), Air Force Meritorious Svc. medal (2), Air Force Commendation medal (3), Nat. Def. Svc. medal (2), Air Force Svc. medal (5), Marksmanship medal, USAF Master Space Sys. badge, U.S. Army Reactor Comdr. badge, USAF Missileman badge; recipient NASA Achievement awards (3), Dept. Energy Achievement awards (3), Jet Propulsion Lab. Achievement awards (2), Congl. and White House citations. Fellow: AIAA (assoc.; edn. officer, career enhancement officer Albuquerque sect. 1997—2000); mem.: AAAS, ASME, Profl. Aerospace Contractors Assn. N.Mex., Nat. Orgn. Test, Rsch. and Tng. Reactors, Nat. Space Soc., Planetary Soc., N.Mex. Acad. Sci., Am. Nuc. Soc. (Best Paper 1977), Engring. Alumni Assn. U. N.Mex. (v.p. 1998—2000, pres. 2000—), Sun Country Amateur Golf Assn. N.Mex., West Tex. (chmn. long range planning com. 1999—2000, bd. mem.), U.S. Golf Assn. (course rating and rules ofcl. 1993—, regional affairs com. for N.Mex. 1996—), Sigma Xi. Republican. Achievements include origination of idea to advance and use coated particle fuel and fuel forms to enhance the design, performance, specific mass and volume, and safety of radioisotopic heaters and power systems for space and remote terrestrial applications, 1998. Office: Sholtis Engring & Safety Consulting PO Box 605 Tijeras NM 87059-0605 Office Phone: 505-281-4358. E-mail: sholtis@aol.com.

SHOMAKER, GORDON ALEXANDER, JR., poet, writer; b. Denver, Colo., Mar. 21, 1926; s. Gordon Alexander and Laura Louise Shomaker. BA, U.S.C., 1947; MA, U. Colo., 1952; postgrad., U. Paris/Sorvonne, 1948. Steel mill worker, Pueblo, Colo., 1951; instr. of various U. Theatres, 1957—67; instr. speech, English various univs., 1966—67; instr. Quinnipiac Coll., Hamden, Conn., 1953—57; appliance repair clerk Shomaker Electric Co., Pueblo, Colo., 1950—51; insp. Steel Mill, Pueblo, Colo., 1947. Treas., playwright Theatre Original Plays, Pueblo, Colo., 1980—85; bd. dirs. Colo. Outdoor, 2000—; summer stock stage mgr. NY Shakespeare, 1957. Playwright: plays Joshua, 1962, Literary Defectives, 1984, author poetry, short stories, one and two-act plays. Rschr. Conn. Pub., Hartford, 1952, Expenditure Coun., Inc., Conn. With U.S. armed forces, 1944—45, WWII. Mem.: Nature Conservancy, NAACP, Native Am. Rights Fund., Acad. Am. Poets. Avocations: walking, music. Home: 900 W Abriendo Apt # 1020C Pueblo CO 81004-1158

SHONK, ALBERT DAVENPORT, JR., advertising executive; b. L.A., May 23, 1932; s. Albert Davenport and Jean Spence (Stannard) S. BS in Bus. Adminstrn., U. So. Calif., 1954. Field rep. mktg. divsn. L.A. Examiner, 1954-55, asst. mgr. mktg. and field supr. mktg. divsn., 1955-56, mgr. mktg. divsn., 1956-57; account exec. Hearst Advt. Svc., L.A., 1957-59; account exec., mgr. Keith H. Evans & Assocs., San Francisco and Los Angeles, 1959-65; owner, pres. Albert D. Shonk Co., L.A., 1965-97; gen. ptnr. Shonk Land Co. Ltd., Charleston, W.Va., 1989-00; dir. Shonk, LLC, Del., 2001—. Pres. Signet Cir. Corp., Inc., 1977-81, dir., 1962-81, hon. life dir., 1981—, treas., 1989-2002, pres., 2002—. Founding chmn. Crittenton Assocs.; bd. dirs. Balboa Island Improvement Assn., 2000—, Balboa Island Mus. & Hist. Soc., 1999—, treas.; co-chair Centennial com. Florence Crittenton Ctr., 1992; c-chair reunion com. U.S.C. Class 1954, 2004; bd. dirs. Florence Crittenton Ctr., sec., 1978, 1st v.p., 1978—79, exec. v.p., 1979—81, pres., 1981—83, chmn. bd., 1983—85, hon. life dir., 1986—, treas., 1997, pres., 1997—2001, chmn. bd. dirs., 2002—03, pres., 2004—. Recipient Medallion of Merit Phi Sigma Kappa, 1976, Founders award, 1961, NIC Interfraternal award, 1989. Mem.: U. S.C. Class of 1954 Reunion Commn. (co-chmn. 2004), Jr. Advt. Club L.A. (hon. life, dir., treas., 1st v.p.), Nat. Assn. Pubs. Reps. (past v.p. West Coast 1981—83), Pubs. Rep. Assn. of So. Calif., Advt. Club L.A., Town Hall, Marshall Assocs. (bd. dirs. 1999—), World Affairs Coun., U. S.C. Assocs., U. So. Calif. Alumni Assn. (bd. govs. 2000—03), U. S.C. Marshall Sch. Bus. Alumni Assn. (nat. bd. 1991—99, treas. 1995—99), USC Cardinal and Gold, Trojan Club, Skull and Dagger, Rotary (Paul Harris fellow), Alpha Kappa Psi, Phi Sigma Kappa (dir. grand coun. 1962—70, 1977—79, grand pres. 1979—83, v.p. meml. found. 1979—84, chancellor 1983—87, pres. meml. found. 1984, found. trustee pres. 1984—95, chancellor 1990—91, recorder 1995—, found. trustee emeritus 1995—), Inter-Greek Soc. (v.p. 1976—79, pres. 1984—86, co-founder, hon. life, dir.). Home and Office: 225 Sapphire Ave Newport Beach CA 92662-1148 E-mail: adshonk@msn.com.

SHONKOFF, JACK P. dean, educator; AB, Cornell U., 1968; MD, NYU Sch. Medicine, 1972. Intern, asst. resident, sr. resident in pediatrics Bronx Mcpl. Hosp. Ctr., Albert Einstein Coll. Medicine, 1972-75; clin. trainee divsn. child psychiatry Albert Einstein Coll. Medicine, Bronx, 1974-75, rsch. asst. child developmental psychology unit, 1974-75; fellow in medicine developmental eval. clinic Children's Hosp. Med. Ctr. and Harvard Med. Sch., Boston, 1975-76; coord. developmental consultation svc. Martha Eliot Health Ctr., Jamaica Plain, Mass., 1975-76; cons. cmty. eval. and rehab. ctr. Wrentham (Mass.) State Sch., 1975-76; asst. in medicine Children's Hosp. Med. Ctr., Boston, 1976-79; attending pediatrician U. Mass. Med. Ctr., Worcester, Mass., 1979-94; pediatric coord. masters program Wheelock Coll., Boston, 1981-90; coord. early intervention study group U. Mass., Brandeis U., Wellesley Coll, Mass. Dept. Public Health, 1982-84; prin. investigator, project dir. early intervention collaborative study U. Mass. Med. Sch., 1984-94, Florence Heller Grad Sch. Brandeis U., Waltham, Mass., 1994-98, dean, 1994—. Instr. pediatrics Harvard Med. Sch., 1976-79, lectr. 1997—, Simmons Coll., Boston, 1976-79, instr. dept. early childhood edn. Wheelock Coll., Boston, 1979-80, adj. asst. prof. grad. sch., 1980-85, adj. assoc. prof. grad. sch., 1985-90; asst. prof. pediatrics U. Mass. Med. Sch., Worcester, Mass., 1979-85, assoc. prof. 1985-89, prof. 1990-94; Samuel F. and Rose B. Gingold prof. human devel. Brandeis U., Waltham, Mass., 1994—; adj. prof. family medicine and cmty. health Tufts U. Sch. Medicine, Boston, 1997—; chair bd. on Children, Youth and Families Inst. Medicine and Nat. Rsch. Coun./Nat. Acad. Scis., com. on integrating the science of early childhood devel. bd.; bd. dirs. Zero to Three: Nat. Ctr. for Infants, Toddlers and Families; Robert Wood Johnson vis. rsch. prof. U. Rochester Sch. Medicine and Dentistry, Rochester, N.Y., 1986; Arthur L. Tuuri Interdisciplinary lectr. Mott Children's Health Ctr., Flint, MI, 1986; vis. prof. Sistema Nacional para el Desarrollo Integral de la Familia, Mexico City, Mexico, 1986, U. Puerto Rico Sch. Medicine, San Juan, Puerto Rico, 1988, A.I. Dupont Inst., Wilmington, Del., 1989, U. Vermont Sch. Medicine, Burlington, 1990, Koret vis. prof. pediatrics Pacific Presbyn. Med. Ctr., San Francisco, Calif., 1990, Harrie R. Chamberlin lectr. and vis. prof. U. N.C., Chapel Hill, 1991, vis. prof. in pediatrics Children's Hosp., Oakland, Calif., 1991, Children's Nat. Med. Ctr., Washington, 1991, Omer H. Foust lectr. and vis. prof. Riley Hosp. for Children, Ind. U. Med. Ctr., Indpls., 1991, Dr. Louis W. Sauer lectr., vis. prof. Evanston Hosp., Ill., 1991, Sydney Rosen Commemorative lectr. Hosp. for Sick Children, Toronto, Ontario, 1992, vis. prof. Tel Aviv U., Israel, 1992, Felton Bequests' vis. lectr. Royal Children's Hosp. and Monash Med. Ctr., Melbourne, Australia, 1993, John B. Welsh Meml. lectureship and vis. prof. U. Calif. San Diego Med. Ctr., Calif., 1994, Warren Weiswasser lectr., vis. prof. Yale U. Sch. Medicine, New Haven, CT, 1995, Dr. Howard R. Rappaport Meml. lectureship, Mt. Sinai Sch. Medicine, N.Y.C., 1997, Raymond Keefe/Joseph Bellizzi Meml. lectr. St. Francis Hosp. and Med. Ctr., Hartford, Ct., 1998. Editl. bd.: Jour. Child Neurology, 1985-90, Jour. Early Intervention, 1989-94, Topics in Early Childhood Special Education, 1987-94, Infant Mental Health Jour., 1983-86; consulting editor: Child Development, 1983-90, Infant Mental Health Jour., 1993-95, Zero to Three, 1985—; assoc. editor: Infant Mental Health Jour., 19987-92, Rudolph's Pediatrics, 20th edit., 1993-94, 21st edit., 1998—; ad hoc manuscript review Am. Jour. Diseases of Children, Am. Jour. Pub. Health, Child Development, Clinical Pediatrics, Infant Mental Health Jour., Jour. of Am. Med. Assn., Jour. Child Psychology and Psychiatry, Jour. Devel. and Behavioral Pediatrics, Jour. Early Intervention, Jour. Division of Early Childhood, Jour. Special Edn., Pediatrics. Fellow W.K. Kellogg Found., 1980-83, Nat. Ctr. for Clin. Infant Programs, 1981-82; recipient Senator Gerard D'Amico award Mass. Early Intervention Consortium, 1986, award for Excellence Boston Inst. for Devel. of Infants and Parents, 1992, Disting. Contribution to Child Advocacy award APA Divsn. Child, Youth and Family Svcs., 1995; grantee in field. Mem. Am. Pediatric Soc. (elected mem.), Inst. Medicine (elected mem.). Office: Brandeis U Florence Heller Grad Sch PO Box 9110-MS 035 Waltham MA 02454-9110 Fax: (781) 736-3852. E-mail: shonkoff@brandeis.edu.

SHONS, ALAN RANCE, plastic surgeon, surgical oncologist, educator; b. Freeport, Ill., Jan. 10, 1938; s. Ferral Caldwell and Margaret (Zimmerman) S.; children: Lesley, Susan. AB, Dartmouth Coll., 1960; MD, Case Western Res. U., 1965; PhD in Surgery, U. Minn., 1976. Diplomate Am. Bd. Surgery, Am. Bd. Plastic Surgery. Intern U. Hosp., Cleve., 1965-66, resident in surgery, 1966-67; rsch. fellow transplantation immunology U. Minn., Mpls., 1969-72, asst. prof. plastic surgery, 1976-79, assoc. prof., 1979-84, prof., 1984; resident in surgery U. Minn. Hosp., 1972-74; resident plastic surgery NYU, 1974-76; dir. divsn. plastic and reconstructive surgery U. Minn. Hosp., St. Paul Ramsey Hosp., Mpls. VA Hosp., 1976-84; cons. plastic surgery St. Louis Park Med. Ctr., 1980-84; prof. surgery Case Western Res. U., Cleve., 1984-93, dir. divsn. plastic and reconstructive surgery, 1984-92; prof. surgery, assoc. dir. comprehensive breast program, H. Lee Moffitt Cancer Ctr. and Rsch. Inst. U. South Fla., Tampa, 1992—2003; surgeon pvt. practice, Great Neck, NY, 2004—. Examiner Am. Bd. Plastic Surgery, 1987-2000. Author: (with G.L. Adams and D. McQuarrie) Head and Neck Cancer, 1986; (with R. Jensen) Plastic Surgery Review, 1993. Capt. USAF, 1967-69. Fellow ACS (chmn. Minn. com. on trauma 1978-84); mem. AMA, Am. Soc. Plastic and Reconstructive Surgeons, Am. Assn. Plastic Surgeons, Minn. Acad. Plastic Surgeons (pres. 1981-82), Soc. Head and Neck Surgeons, Transplantation Soc., Plastic Surgery Rsch. Coun., Am. Soc. Aesthetic Plastic Surgery, Am. Soc. Maxillofacial Surgeons, Am. Assn. Immunologists, Soc. Exptl. Pathology, Am. Cleft Palate Assn., Am. Soc. Craniofacial Surg. Assn., Fla. Soc. Plastic and Reconstructive Surgeons, Sigma Xi. Office: 935 Northern Blvd Great Neck NY 11021

SHONTERE, JAMES G. construction executive; CFO, sec. JF Shea, Walnut, Calif. Office: JF Shea 655 Brea Canyon Rd Walnut CA 91789

SHOOK, ANN JONES, lawyer; b. Canton, Ohio, Apr. 18, 1925; d. William M. and Lura (Pontius) Jones; m. Gene E. Shook Sr., Nov. 30, 1956; children: Scott, William, Gene Edwin Jr. AB, Wittenberg U., 1947; LLB, William McKinley Law Sch., 1955. Bar: Ohio 1956, U.S. Dist. Ct. (no. dist.) Ohio 1961, U.S. Ct. Appeals (6th cir.) 1981. Cost acct. Hoover Co., North Canton, Ohio, 1947-51; asst. sec. Stark County Prosecutor's Office, Canton, Ohio, 1951-53; ins. adjuster Traveler's Ins. Co., Canton, 1953-56; ptnr. Shook & Shook, Toledo, 1958-62, North Olmsted, Ohio, 1962—. Mem. at large coun. Olmsted Community Ch., Olmsted Falls, Ohio, 1987-90; chmn. ways and means com. North Olmsted PTA, 1968; area chmn. United Way Appeal, North Olmsted, 1963; v.p. LWV, Toledo, 1960-62. Mem. Cleve. Bar Assn. Avocations: reading, boating, dance, exercise. E-mail: shooklaw@worldnet.att.net.

SHOOK, JAMES CREIGHTON, real estate executive; b. Lafayette, Ind., May 19, 1931; s. Charles Wheeler and Jane Creighton (Peffer) S.; m. Mary Weil, Apr. 12, 1958 (dec. Jan. 1987); children: James C. Jr., Kathryn S. Bates, Stephen H., Sara Sullivan; m. Janice Warren, Feb. 13, 1988. BS in Bus., Ind. U., 1952. Ptnr. The Shook Agy., Lafayette, 1954—86; pres. The Shook Agy., Inc., Lafayette, 1986—2000. Bd. dirs. Lafayette Union Rlwy. Pres. Greater Lafayette United Way, 1965-66, Lafayette Home Hosp., Inc., 1973-74; chmn. North Ctrl. Health Svc., 1989-91, 2003—. 1st lt. USAF, 1952-54. Mem. Ind. Acad., Ind. C. of C. (bd. dirs. 1975—), Lafayette Country Club (pres. 1969-70), Crystal Downs Country Club (Frankfort, Mich.), Bent Pine Golf Club (Vero Beach, Fla.). Republican. Avocations: golf, community activities, classic cars. Office: Coldwell Banker Shook Agy Inc 427 Main St Lafayette IN 47901-1369 E-mail: jshook5096@aol.com., jcshook@shook.com.

SHOOK, JOAN E. medical educator; b. Cleve., Mar. 27, 1954; m. Jeffery R. Starke, April 23, 1983; children: Nathan R., Matthew C., Hannah E. BA, Brown U., Providence, RI, 1976; MD, U. Cin., 1981; MBA, U. Houston, 1986. Asst. prof. pediat. Baylor Coll. Medicine, Houston, 1986-96, assoc. prof. pediat., 1996—2003, prof. pediat., 2003, head pediat. emergency medicine dept. pediat., 1993—; med. dir. emergency ctr. Tex. Childrens Hosp., Houston, 1986—, med. dir. short stay observation unit, 1994—, chief emergency med. svcs., 1994—, patient safety officer, 2002—; prof. pediat. Baylor, 2003—. Chair com. Am. Acad. Pediat. Nat. Orgn., 1995—; adj. prof. adminstrv. sci. Rice U., Houston, 1998—. Editor: Seminars in Pediatric Infectious Diseases, 1995, 1996; contbr. chpt. to book. Adv. bd. Houston C.C. Sys. Emergency, Med. Svc. Program, Houston, 1997—. Fellow Am. Acad. Pediat.; mem. Amulatory Pediat. Assn., Am. Coll. Emergency Physicians, Houston Soc. Emergency Medicine, Harris County Med. Soc., Am. Acad. Pediat. Nat. Orgn. (chair com. 1995—), Beta Gama Sigma. Office: Baylor College of Medicine Dept Pediatrics One Baylor Plaze Houston TX 77030 Office Phone: 832-824-2271.

SHOOP, GLENN POWELL, investment consultant; b. Gracemont, Okla., Sept. 1, 1920; s. Roy Alonzo and Myrtle Nancy (Goodfellow) S.; m. Louise Wilhelmina Vollmer, Mar. 19, 1943; children: Merilou Love, Paul, Nancy Caver. Student, U. Okla., 1938-42. Pilot Braniff Internat. Airways, Dallas, 1946-80. Cons. bd. dirs. Braniff Inc., 1984—88. Bd. dirs. 1st Bapt. Ch. Dallas, 1950-2000; mem. devel. bd. Golden Gate Bapt. Sem., San Francisco, Southwestern Bapt. Sem., Fort Worth. Maj. USAF, 1942-46, WWII. Republican. Achievements include first U.S. pilot to fly Concorde in U.S. scheduled service.

SHOOTER, ERIC MANVERS, neurobiology educator, consultant; b. Mansfield, Eng., Apr. 18, 1924; arrived in U.S., 1964; s. Fred and Pattie (Johnson) Shooter; m. Elaine Staley Arnold, May 28, 1949; 1 child, Annette Elizabeth. BA, Cambridge (Eng.) U., 1945, MA, 1949, PhD, 1950, ScD, 1986; DSc, U. London, 1964. Sr. scientist biochemistry Brewing Industry Rsch. Found., 1950—53; biochemistry lectr. Univ. Coll., London, 1953—63; assoc. prof. genetics Stanford U., 1963—68, prof. genetics and biochemistry, 1968—75, prof., chmn. neurobiology dept., 1975—87, prof. neurobiology, 1987—, chmn. Neurosci. PhD Program, 1972—82. Assoc. Neurosci. Rsch. Program, N.Y.C., 1979—89; mem. tchg. staff Internat. Sch. Neurosci., Praglia, Italy, 1987—93; sr. cons. Markey Charitable Trust, Miami, Fla., 1985—97; bd. dirs. Regeneron Pharm., Inc., Tarrytown, NY. Assoc. editor (book series) Ann. Rev. Neuroscis., 1984—2001; contbr. articles to profl. jours. Recipient Wakeman award, Duke U., 1988, Award for Disting. Achievement in Neurosci. Rsch., Bristol-Myers-Squibb, 1997; scholar, Josiah Macy Jr. Found., N.Y.C., 1974—75. Fellow: AAAS, Am. Acad. Arts and Scis., Royal Soc. (London); mem.: NAS, Am. Philos. Soc., Internat. Brain Rsch. Orgn., Internat. Soc. Neurochemistry, Am. Soc. Neurochemistry, Am. Assn. Biol. Chemists, Soc. for Neurosci. (Ralph W. Gerard prize 1995), Inst. Medicine of NAS, Alpha Omega Alpha (hon.). Avocation: travel. Home: 370 Golden Oak Dr Portola Valley CA 94028-7757 Office: Stanford U Sch Medicine Dept Neurobiology 299 Campus Dr Stanford CA 94305-5125 Business E-Mail: eshooter@cmgmz.stanford.edu.

SHOR, GEORGE G., JR., geophysicist, oceanographic administrator, engineer; b. N.Y.C., June 8, 1923; s. George Gershon and Dorothy (Williston); m. Elizabeth Louise Noble, June 11, 1950; children: Alexander Noble, Carolyn Elizabeth, Donald Williston. BS, Calif. Inst. Tech., 1944, MS, 1948, PhD, 1954. Joined Seismic Explorations, Inc., Houston, 1948, party chief, 1949-50; asst. research geophysicist to research geophysicist Scripps Inst. Oceanography, La Jolla, Calif., 1953-69, prof. marine geophysics, 1969-90, prof. emeritus, 1990—, assoc. dir., 1968-91; mgr. Calif. Sea Grant program, 1969-73. Mem. NAS-NRC panel on Mohole site selection, 1959; com. on underwater telecommunications, 1968, USN Marine Geophys. Survey Liaison Council, 1965-67; spl. adv. to Com. for Coordination of Joint Prospecting for Mineral Resources in Asian Offshore Areas, 1976-91; chmn. ship scheduling panel Univ. Nat. Oceanographic Lab. Systems, 1987-89; sci. leader oceanographic expdns. to various parts of Pacific and Indian oceans, 1955-82. Served to lt. (j.g.) USNR, 1943-46; now comdr. USNR Ret. Fellow Geol. Soc. Am., Am. Geophys. Union; mem. Soc. Exploration Geophysicists, Scholia Club, Am. Bamboo Soc. (pres. 1994-96). Home: 2655 Ellentown Rd La Jolla CA 92037-1147

SHOR, PETER W. mathematician, researcher; b. Aug. 14, 1959; BS, Calif. Inst. Tech.; PhD, MIT. Postdoc. fellow Mathematical Rsch. Ctr., Berkeley, Calif., 1985; mathematician AT&T Labs, Florham Park, N.J., 1986—. Contbr. articles to profl. jours. including Physics Rev. Letters, J. Combinational Theory, Algorithmica. Presenter at numerous conferences in field. Recipient King Faisal Inernat. prize Sci., 2002; fellow MacArthur Found. fellow, 1999. Office: AT & T Labs Rsch 180 Park Ave Rm C237 Florham Park NJ 07932-1004

SHORB, GARY SEYMOUR, hospital administrator; b. Memphis, Sept. 7, 1950; married. B, Clemson U., 1972; M, Memphis State U., 1985. Acting dir. Regional Med. Ctr., Memphis, 1986-87, pres., CEO, 1987-90, Meth. Hosps. of Memphis, 1990—2001, Meth. Healthcare, 2001—. Contbr. articles to profl. jours. Chmn. Memphis Shelby Crime Commn.; mem. U. Memphis Bd. Visitors; bd. mem. United Way of the Med-South, Tenn. Hosp. Assn., Goals for Memphis. Home: 360 Bluff Ridge Cv Cordova TN 38018-7617 Office: Meth Hosps Memphis 1265 Union Ave Memphis TN 38104

SHORE, ELEANOR GOSSARD, medical school dean; b. Ottawa, Ill., Aug. 11, 1930; d. Arthur Paul and Mary Catherine (Lineberger) Gossard; m. Miles Frederick Shore, July 4, 1953; children: Miles Paul, Rebecca Shore Lewin, Susanna Shore LeBoutillier. BA magna cum laude, Radcliffe Coll., 1951; MD, Harvard U., 1955, MPH, 1970. Diplomate Am. Bd. Preventive Medicine. Med. intern New Eng. Med. Ctr. Hosp., Boston, 1955-56; resident in occup. medicine Harvard U. Health Svcs., Cambridge, Mass., 1966-68; Macy scholar Radcliffe Inst., Radcliffe Coll., Cambridge, 1966-68; resident in preventive medicine Harvard Sch. Pub. Health, Boston, 1970-71; asst. physician Radcliffe Coll., 1959-61, Harvard U. Health Svcs., 1961-73; rsch. assoc. dept. microbiology Harvard U. Sch. Pub. Health, 1971-76; asst. to pres. Harvard U., 1972-81; assoc. dean for faculty affairs Harvard Med. Sch., 1978-89, mem. faculty, 1978—, dean for faculty affairs, 1989—. Mem. editl. bd. Harvard Med. Alumni Bull., 1976—; contbr. numerous articles to profl. jours. Bd. dirs. Mass.-Ukraine Citizens Bridge, Brockton, Mass., 1989-94, pres., 1991-92; bd. dirs. Needham (Mass.) Found. for Pub. Sch. Edn., 1990-94; bd. dirs. Mass. Health Rsch. Inst., Inc., 1990-99, sec., 1995-99; overseer Boston Mus. Sci., 1981—; trustee Schepens Eye Rsch. Inst., Boston, 1993—; mem. acad. coun. Real Colegio Complutense, Harvard U.; dep. dir. Harvard Med. Sch. Ctr. for Excellence in Women's Health, 1998-. Recipient Pres.'s Recognition award Am. Med. Women's Assn., 1996. Fellow Am. Acad. Preventive Medicine; mem. AAAS, APHA, Mass. Pub. Health Assn., Assn. Am. Med. Colls., Mass. Med. Soc., Aesculapian Club (treas. 1986-89, pres. 1990-91), Office: Harvard Med Sch 25 Shattuck St Bldg A Boston MA 02115-6027 E-mail: eleanor_shore@hms.harvard.edu.

SHORE, ERIC EUGENE, internist, consultant, lawyer; b. Phila., Feb. 12, 1948; s. Reuben and Mary (Osinoff) S.; m. Mona Diane Cherry, Oct. 23, 1977 (div. Dec. 1991); children: Brett Ian, Matthew Adam. Student, Temple U., 1965—67; BS in Biology, Widener U., 1969; DO, Phila. Coll. Osteo. Med., 1973; MBA, St. Joseph's U., 1997; postgrad in law, Widener U., 1999—2000; JD, Rutgers U., 2003. Med. diplomate Nat. Bd. Examiners, diplomate Am. Bd. Utilization Rev. and Quality Assurance. Intern Botsford Gen. Hosp., Farmington, Mich., 1973-74; resident Phila. (Pa.) Gen. Hosp., 1974; instr. in medicine Hahnemann Med. Coll., Phila., 1975-78; treas. med. staff West Park Hosp., Phila., 1986-87, chief of geriatrics, 1986-88; sec. of med. staff Jefferson Park Hosp., Phila., 1987-91, chief of family medicine, 1988-96; pres. Gen. Medicine Assocs., Ltd., Phila., 1987—, Bala Clin. Assocs., P.C., 1989—; asst. prof. medicine Phila. Coll. Osteopathic Medicine, Phila., 1987—; clin. asst. prof. medicine Med. Coll. Pa., Phila., 1991—2001, Drexel Coll. Medicine, Phila., 2002—. Med. dir. Fairmount Geriatric Ctr., Phila., 1985-88, Bala Nursing & Retirement Ctr., Phila., 1990-95; chmn. bd. UniMed Systems, Inc., Phila., 1989—, Am. Medigroup, Inc., 1997—; CEO, Am. MediGroup, Inc., 1996—; cons. medicine and geriatrics Phila. Psychiat. Ctr., Phila., 1987—. Med. officer Civil Air Patrol, Phila., 1976-78. Recipient Legion of Honor, Chapel of Four Chaplains, Phila., 1981. Fellow: Am. Coll. Legal Medicine, Am. Coll. Utilization Rev. Physicians, Am. Acad. Family Physicians; mem.: ATLA, AMA (physician's recognition award 1990, 1994, 1997, 1999, 2003), ABA, AAAS, Pa. Bar Assn. (Phila. chpt.), N.Y. Acad. Scis., Am. Coll. Physician Execs., Am. Health Lawyers Assn., Am. Geriatrics Soc., Royal Soc. Medicine. Avocations: music, flying, computers, sculpting, tennis. Home: 19 W Dartmouth Rd Bala Cynwyd PA 19004-2520 Office: Am MediGroup Inc Ste B 1100 N 63rd St Philadelphia PA 19151-2102 Business E-Mail: eshore@shoremedlaw.com.

SHORE, HARVEY HARRIS, business educator; b. Cambridge, Mass., Apr. 14, 1940; s. Jacob and Freda Edna (Pearlman) S.; m. Roberta Ann Rogers, Jan. 29, 1967 (div. Oct. 1999); children: Nina Ellen, Elissa Amy. BA cum laude, Harvard U., 1961; MS, MIT, 1963; DBA, Harvard U., 1966. Asst. prof. indsl. adminstrn. U. Conn., Storrs, 1966-72, assoc. prof. indsl. adminstrn., 1972-77, dir. Hartford MBA prog., 1977-82, assoc. prof. mgmt. Storrs, 1982-95, assoc. prof. emeritus, 1995—. Contbr. articles to profl. jours.; editor Cubic Rev., 1975-78; author: Arts Administration and Management, 1987. Chmn. bus. adv. com. Tunxis Community Coll., Farmington, Conn., 1983-85; bd. dirs. Temple Beth Sholom, Manchester, Conn., 1987-90. Mem. Coll. and Univ. Bus. Instrs. Conn. (pres. 1975-76), Greater Nashua Human Resources Assn. (treas. 1997-98, pres. 1998-2000), Masons. Democrat. Jewish. Avocation: tennis.

SHORE, HERBERT, writer, poet, educator; b. Phila, June 6, 1924; s. Meyer and Frances (Smiler) S.; m. Yen Lu Wong, Dec. 23, 1977; children: Norman Jon, Pia Wong, Maya Richards. BA, U. Pa., 1942; postgrad., Columbia U., 1946-48, Dramatic Workship New Sch., 1946-48; postgrad, Stanford U., 1948-53; MA, Stanford U., 1958; PhD, Internat. Coll., 1983. Writer, poet, dramatist and dramaturg, 1956—; dir. Council Tech. and Cultural Transformation, UNESCO, 1974-88; prof., assoc. dean Sch. of Theatre U. So. Calif., 1979-93, prof. emeritus Sch. Theatre, 1996, prof. profl. writing program, 1996-99; founding dir. TNR: The New Repertory, 1972—; provost Internat. Coll., 1983-86; writer-in-residence Blue Mountain Centre, 1985, 86; dir. plays for theatre and TV, author plays, also cantatas. Cons. UNESCO, 1974—;

disting. vis. fellow La Trobe U., Australia, 1990; artist in residence Eltham Coll., Australia, 1990; sr. affiliated scholar Multiethnic and Transnat. Studies, U. So. Calif., 1993—; fellow Mayibuye Ctr., South Africa, 1995; past mentor global studies Immaculate Heart Coll. Ctr.; bd. dir. Eduardo Mondlane Meml. Found., 1996; cons. Bent-Prop Film Project, 2002— founding dir. Sr. Readers Theatre, Urcad, 2001—. Author: Come Back Africa, 1970, Ashes Dark Antigone, 1972, Toward the World of Tomorrow, 1978, Cultural Policy, 1981, Cicada Images, Moulting, 1983, No Future Wrapped in Darkness, 1984; Seek to Be Human, 1985, Beginnings are Born in Memory, 1986, Shimé, 1986, Trees Die Standing, 1987, And the Dogs Are Silent, 1988, Should the Grain Perish, 1989, Namashawala, Santa Claus and the Bagamoyo Cock, 1990, South African Township Theatre, 1990, Southern Africa: A Dream Deferred, 1990, Apartheid's Waning and Dangerous Years, 1990, Sounds in the Wind, (poetry) 1991, Exile from El Salvador, Terra Infirma, 1992; co-author: (with George Houser) I Must Go Singing, An Oral History of Walter Sisulu, 1999; also articles, short stories, poems. Adv. coun. Internat. Symposium on Arts, Banff Centre, 1984—; exec. com. Internat. Inst. Audio-Visual Media, Vienna, 1985—; assoc. scholar Ctr. for African Studies, Eduardo Mondlane U., 1988—. Served with USMC, 1943-46. Named Herbert Shore Collection established, Immaculate Heart Coll. Ctr., 1991, Oberlin Coll., 1998, Jerome Lawrence Libr., 1995, Mayibuye Ctr., South Africa, 1995, Niebyl-Proctor Libr., Oakland, Calif., 1995, Calif. State U., Dominguez Hills, 1979, Photo Archives in Honor of Alvin Ailey, Alvin Ailey Am. Dance Found.; recipient Writers Digest prize for fiction, 1963, medal of Bagamoyo, Nat. Assembly, Mozambique, 1989; grantee, Ford. Found., 1978—79, 1996—97, Africa Fund, 1995—99, Rockefeller Found., 1966—67, NEH, 1979—81, Wurlitzer Found., 1958—60, Social Sci. Rsch. Coun., 1967—68, African and Am. Univs. Program, 1964—65, Kate Maremont Found., 1959—60, Centro Mexicano de Escritores, 1958. Mem. PEN Ctr. West, USA, LMDA, Assn. Theatre Higher Edn., Authors Guild, Acad. Am. Poets, Soc. Writers and Poets, African Studies Assn. E-mail: hshore@urcad.org.

SHORE, HOWARD LESLIE, composer; b. Toronto, Ontario, Canada, Oct. 18, 1946; s. Mac and Bernice (Ash) S.; m. Elizabeth Ann Cotnoir, Aug. 3, 1990; 1 child, Mae. Student, Berklee Sch. Music, 1965-67, Forest Hill Collegiate, Toronto, Ont., Can., 1961-64. Composer The Gorfaine/Schwartz Agy., Sherman Oaks, Calif. Composer film scores including I Miss You, Hugs and Kisses, 1978, the Brood, 1979, Scanners, 1981, Videodrome, 1983, Nothing Lasts Forever, 1984, After Hours, 1985, Belizaire the Cajun, 1987, Fire with Fire, 1986, The Fly, 1986, Nadine, 1987, The Local Stigmatic, 1987, Heaven, 1987, Moving, 1988, Dead Ringers, 1988 (Genie award), Big, 1988, She-Devil, 1989, An Innocent Man, 1989, Signs of Life, 1989, The Silence of the Lambs, 1991, A Kiss Before Dying, 1989, Naked Lunch, 1990, Prelude to a Kiss, 1992, Single White Female, 1992, (TV score) Scales of Justice, 1990, Guilty as Sin, 1993, Sliver, 1993, M. Butterfly, 1993, Mrs. Doubtfire, 1993, Philadelphia, 1993, The Client, 1994, Ed Wood, 1994, Nobody's Fool, 1994, Moonlight and Valentino, 1995, White Man's Burden, 1995, Seven, 1995, Before and After, 1996, The Truth About Cats and Dogs, 1996, Looking for Richard, 1996, Crash, 1996; music supr. Places in the Heart, 1984, Postcards From the Edge, 1990; music dir. Saturday Night Live, 1975-80, Striptease, 1996, That Thing You Do, 1996, Cop Land, 1997, The Game, 1997, Gloria, 1999, Analyze This, 1999, Dogma, 1999, High Fidelity, 2000. Mem. ASCAP, Lighthouse (founding mem.). Home: Wee Wah Lodge Tuxedo Park NY 10987 Office: The Gorfaine/Schwartz Agy 13245 Riverside Dr Ste 450 Sherman Oaks CA 91423-2172

SHORE, JAMES H(ENRY), psychiatrist; b. Winston-Salem, N.C., Apr. 6, 1940; s. James Henry and Ellen Elizabeth (Hayes) S.; m. Christine Lowenbach, Aug. 24, 1963; children— Ellen Ottilie, James Henry. MD, Duke U., 1965. Diplomate Am. Bd. Psychiatry and Neurology. Intern U. Utah Med. Ctr., 1965-66; resident in psychiatry U. Wash., 1966-69; chief mental health office Portland Area Indian Health Svc., Oreg., 1969-73; assoc. prof. psychiatry, dir. cmty. psychiatry tng. program U. Oreg. Health Sci. Ctr., 1973-75, prof., chmn. dept. psychiatry, 1975-85; from chmn. dept. psychiatry Health Sci. Ctr. to chancellor U. Colo., Denver, 1985—2004, chancellor, 2004—. Dir. Colo. Psychiatry Hosp., 1985-99; interim dir. U. Colo. Hosp., Denver, 1987-88, interim exec. vice chancellor, 1995-97, chancellor, 1998—; mem. exptl. and spl. edn. com. NIMH-Internal Rev. Group, 1976-80; cons. in field. Contbr. numerous articles to profl. publs. Mem. Various community bds. Served with USPHS, 1969-73. Decorated USPHS Commendation medal; various grants. Fellow Am. Psychiat. Assn., Am. Coll. Psychiatry (pres. 2003-04); mem. Am. Assn. Chmn. Depts. Psychiatry (pres. 1989), Am. Bd. Psychiatry and Neurology (dir. 1987—, pres. 1994), Residency Rev. Com. for Psychiatry (chmn. 1991-92). Office: U Colo Health Scis Ctr PO Box A 095 4200 E 9th Ave Denver CO 80262

SHORE, LEANN MARIE, small business owner, occupational therapist; b. Warren, Minn., Dec. 29, 1967; d. Larry H. and Diane H. Shore. BS, Colo. State U., 1989; MEd, St. Mary's U., Mpls., 2002. Lic. occupl. therapist Minn., registered Nat. Bd. for Cert. of Occupl. Therapists. Registered occupl. therapist Shakopee (Minn.) Pub. Schs., River Bend Edn. Dist., New Ulm, Minn.; traveling occupl. therapist Health Providers, Inc., Fort Lauderdale, Fla. Author: (handwriting test for children) Shore Handwriting Screening for Early Handwriting Development. Mem.: Minn. Occupl. Therapy Assn. Dfl. Achievements include Copyright Shore Handwriting Screening. Home: PO Box 225 Chaska MN 55318 Office: Shakopee Pub Schs 505 S Holmes St Shakopee MN 55379 Personal E-mail: leann.shore@mail.com. E-mail: lshore@shakopee.k12.mn.us.

SHORE, LISA, flight controller, trainer; BS in Aerospace Engring., U. Mich., 1985. With NASA Johnson Space Ctr. Shuttle and Station flight control and tng., Houston. Avocations: golf, softball, billiards, movies, pinball. Office: NASA Johnson Space Ctr Mailcode DX35 Houston TX 77058

SHORE, MILES FREDERICK, psychiatrist, educator; b. Chgo., May 26, 1929; s. Miles Victor and Margaret Elizabeth S.; m. Eleanor M. Gossard, July 4, 1953; children: Miles Paul, Rebecca M. Lewin, Susanna G. LeBoutillien. BA, U. Chgo., 1948; AB, Harvard U., 1950, MD, 1954. Intern U. Ill. Research and Edn. Hosp., Chgo., 1954-55; resident in psychiatry Mass. Mental Health Center, Beth Israel Hosp., Boston, 1956-61; asst. prof. psychiatry Tufts U. Sch. Medicine, Boston, 1964-68, assoc. prof., 1968-71, prof., 1971-75, prof. community health, 1972-75; founder, dir. Tufts Community Mental Health Center, 1968-74, asso. dean community affairs, 1972-75; mem. faculty Boston Psychoanalytic Inst., 1973—; Bullard prof. psychiatry Harvard Med. Sch., Boston, 1975—; supt. Mass. Mental Health Ctr., 1975-93; vis. scholar John F. Kennedy Sch. Govt. Harvard U., 1993—; cons. exec. edn. Harvard Med. Internat., 1999—, sr. cons., 2000—. Dir. program for chronic mental illness Robert Wood Johnson Found., 1985-92. Editl. bd. Psychat. Svcs. Jour., 1990; bd. editors Jour. Interdisciplinary History, 1975, Psycho History Rev., 1978; column editor Harvard Rev. Psychiatry, 1993; contbr. articles to profl. jours. Bd. dirs. Federated Dorchester Neighborhood Houses, Boston, 1975-78, tr. House, Boston, 1995—; bd. dirs. Med. Found., Boston, 1987—, chmn., 1999-2001; mem. Blue Ribbon Commn., Mass. Dept. Mental Health, 1979-80. Capt. U.S. Army, 1956-58. Community Mental Health Center grantee, 1964-75. Fellow Am. Psychiat. Assn. (life, joint commn. on pub. affairs, adminstrv. psychiatry award 1987), Am. Coll. Psychiatrists (chmn. fin. com. 1983-89, bd. regents 1988-90, 1st v.p. 1994, pres. 1996-97, Bowis award for svc. 1990, Arthur P. Noyes award 1994); mem. Assn. Am. Med. Colls. (coun. acad. socs. 1992—), Boston Psychoanalytic Soc. and Inst. (chmn. bd. trustees 1970-73), Mass. Psychiat. Soc. (pres. 1970-71), Mass. Hosp. Assn. (trustee 1980-85), Am. Hosp. Assn. (chmn. governing coun. for psychiat. and substance abuse svcs. 1992-93, ho. of dels. 1996—02, region I policy bd. 1997—2000), Roxbury Clinic Record Club, Aesculapian Club, Mass. Hist. Soc. Office: JFK Sch Govt 79 Jfk St Cambridge MA 02138-5801

SHORE, RICHARD ARNOLD, mathematics professor; b. Boston, Aug. 18, 1946; s. Philip M. and Miriam (Krensky) S.; m. Naomi J. Spiller, Aug. 3, 1969; children: Deena A., Aviva R. B in Jewish Edn., Hebrew Coll., 1966; AB, Harvard U., 1968; PhD, MIT, 1972. Instr. U. Chgo., 1972-74; asst. prof. Cornell U., Ithaca, NY, 1974-78, assoc. prof., 1978-83; asst. prof. U. Ill.-Chgo., 1977; vis. assoc. prof. MIT, Cambridge, 1980; vis. prof. Hebrew U., Jerusalem, 1982-83; prof. math. Cornell U., Ithaca, 1983—. Organizing com. Logic Yr. at MSRI, 1989-90, other internat. meetings. Author: (with A. Nerode) Logic for Applications; editor North-Holland, Studies in Logic and the Foundations of Mathematics, 1996—; cons. editor Jour. Symbolic Logic, 1980-83, editor, 1984-93, coord. editor, 1989-91; mng. editor: Bull. Symbolic Logic, 1993-2000; contbr. articles to profl. jours. V.p. for edn. Hillel Acad. Broome County, Binghamton, N.Y., 1985-89; treas. Beth David Synagogue, 1993-96; pres. Jewish Fedn. of Broome County, 1998-2000. NSF grantee, 1973-. Mem. Am. Math. Soc., Spl. Interest Group in Algorithms and Computation Theory, Assn. for Computing Machinery, Assn. for Symbolic Logic (coun. 1984—, pres. 2001-2004, bd. dirs. Project Euclid 2002-). Jewish. Home: 14 Kenwood Ave Newton MA 02459 Office: Cornell U Dept Math Malott Hall Ithaca NY 14853 Office Phone: 607-255-4081. E-mail: shore@math.cornell.edu.

SHORE, STEPHEN, photographer; b. N.Y.C., Oct. 8, 1947; m. Ginger Cramer Seippel, 1980; 1 child, Nicholas; 1 stepchild, Alex Seippel. Student, Minor White, Workshop, 1970. Photographer, 1953—. One-man shows, Met. Mus. Art, N.Y.C., 1971, Light Gallery, N.Y.C., 1972, 73, 75, 77, 78, 80, Phoenix Gallery, San Francisco, 1975, Mus. Modern Art, N.Y.C., 1976, Kunshalle, Dusseldorf, Germany, 1976, U. Akron, Ohio, 1978, Vision Gallery, Boston, 1978, La Photogaleria, Madrid, 1979, Ewing Gallery, Washington, 1979, Catskill Ctr. Photography, Woodstock, N.Y., 1980, Fraenkel Gallery, San Francisco, 1982, Mus. Arts and Scis., Daytona Beach, Fla., 1981, Polk Pub. Mus., 1982, ARCO Ctr. Visual Arts, L.A., 1982, N. Mex. State U. Art Gallery, Las Cruces, 1982, Art Inst. Chgo., 1984, Pace Wildenstein MacGill, N.Y.C., 1989, 95, Sprengel Mus., Hannover, 1995, Würt. Kunstverein, Stuttgart, 1995, Amerika Haus, Berlin, 1995, George Eastman House, Rochester, N.Y., 1996, Skstiftung Kultur, Koln, Germany, 1999, Spazio Oberdan, Milan, Italy, 1999, 303 Gallery, N.Y.C., 2000, 03, Galerie Conrads, Düsseldorf, 2001, 02, Sprueth Magers Lee, London, 2003; group shows include: Met. Mus. Art, N.Y.C., 1973, 82, 97, Internat. Mus. Photography, George Eastman House, 1975, Documenta 6, Kassel, W. Ger., 1977, Art Inst. Chgo., 1977, 79, 89, Mus. Modern Art, N.Y.C., 1978, 91, 2000, Corcoran Gallery, Washington, 1979, Kunsthaus, Zurich, Switzerland, 1980, U. Ariz. Mus. Art, Tucson, 1981, Nat. Gallery, Washington, 1989, Getty Mus., 1992, 97, Whitney Mus., N.Y.C., 1999, P.S. 1, N.Y.C., 1999, Victoria & Albert Mus., London, 1999, Sprenger Mus., Hannover, Germany, Uffizi Gallery, Florence, 2000, Tate Modern, London, 2003, Mus. Ludwig, Cologne, 2003; represented in permanent collections, Met. Mus. Art, N.Y.C., Mus. Modern Art, N.Y.C., Internat. Mus. Photography, George Eastman House, Rochester, N.Y., Mus. Fine Arts, Boston, Library of Congress, Washington, Art Inst. Chgo., Ctr. Creative Photography, U. Ariz., Tucson, Stedelijk Mus., Amsterdam, Netherlands, Neue Sammlung, Munich, W.Ger., Australian Nat. Gallery, Canberra; author: Andy Warhol, 1968, Uncommon Places, 1982, The Gardens at Giverny, 1983, Stephen Shore: Luzzara, 1993, Stephen Shore: Photographs 1973-1993, 1995, The Velvet Years, 1995, The Nature of Photographs, 1998, American Surfaces, 1999, Essex County, 2003, Uncommon Places: 50 Unpublished Photographs, 1973-1978, 2003, Uncommon Places: The Complete Work, 2004; portfolio 12 Photographs, 1976; contbr. articles to profl. jours. Nat. Endowment Arts grantee, 1974, 79; Guggenheim fellow, 1975, Am. Acad. (Rome) Spl. fellow, 1980, MacDowell Colony fellow, 1993. Mem. Century Assn.

SHOREMOUNT, PAUL ERIK, secondary school educator; b. Brooklyn, Ny, June 20, 1953; s. George Erik and Esther Shoremount; m. Tammy Sprouse, Oct. 5, 1985; children: Paul Danniel, Joseph Erik. MusM in edn., Shenandoah Conservatory, Winchester, Va., 1982—84. Cert. Collegiate Profl. Va., 2003. Tchr. Frederick County Pub. Schs., Winchester, Va., 1986—2002, Loudoun County Pub. Schs., Leesburg, Va., 2002—. Instr. jazz studies Performing and Visual Arts NW, Winchester, Va. Mem.: Va. Band and Orch. Dirs. Assn. (assoc.; instrumental rep. 1998—2002), Phi Beta Mu. Home: 1409 S Ox Rd Edinburg VA 22824 Office: Harmony Intermediate Sch 38174 W Colonial Highway Hamilton VA 20158 Business E-Mail: shoremo@loudoun.k12.va.us.

SHORENSTEIN, DOUGLAS W. corporate executive; BA, U. Calif., Berkeley; JD, Hastings Coll. Chair United Way of the Bay Area, 1998—. Office: Shorenstein 555 California St Ste 4900 San Francisco CA 94104*

SHORENSTEIN, ROSALIND GREENBERG, internist; b. N.Y.C., Jan. 14, 1947; d. Albert Samuel and Natalie Miriam (Sherman) Greenberg; m. Michael Lewis Shorenstein, June 18, 1967; children: Anna Irene, Claire Beth. BA in Chemistry, Wellesley Coll., 1968; MA in Biochemistry and Molecular Biology, Harvard U., 1970, PhD in Biochemistry and Molecular Biology, 1973; MD, Stanford U., 1976. Diplomate Am. Bd. Internal Medicine. Resident in internal medicine UCLA Med. Ctr., 1976-79; pvt. practice internal medicine Santa Cruz, Calif., 1979—. Mem. dept. internal medicine Dominican Hosp., Santa Cruz, 1979—; co-dir. med. svcs. Health Enhancement & Lifestyle Planning Systems, Santa Cruz, 1983—. Contbr. articles to profl. journals. Dir. Santa Cruz Chamber Players, 1993-94, pres., bd. dirs., 1994—. Recipient Charlie Parkhurst award Santa Cruz Women's Commn., 1989; NSF fellow, 1968-72, Sarah Perry Wood Med. fellow Wellesley Coll., 1972-76. Mem. Am. Soc. Internal Medicine (del. 1994, 95), Calif. Soc. Internal Medicine (trustee 1994—, sec.-treas. 1996-2000), Am. Med. Women's Assn. (Outstanding Svc. award 1987, br. #59 pres. 1986—), Calif. Med. Assn. (com. on women 1987-93), Santa Cruz County Med. Soc. (mem. bd. govs. 1993—, sec. 1997-99, pres. 2000-01, sec. 2002-), Phi Beta Kappa, Sigma Xi. Jewish. Office: 700 Frederick St Ste 103 Santa Cruz CA 95062-2239

SHORENSTEIN, WALTER HERBERT, commercial real estate development company executive; b. Glen Cove, N.Y., Feb. 23, 1915; m. Phyllis J. Finley, Aug. 8, 1945 (dec.); children: Joan (Dec.), Carole, Douglas. Student, Pa. State U., 1933-34, U. Pa., 1934-36; D in Econs. (hon.), HanYang U., Seoul, Republic of Korea, 1988. With property sales mgmt. depts. Milton Meyer & Co., San Francisco, 1946-51, ptnr., 1951-60, owner, chmn. bd. dirs., 1960—, Shorenstein Group, San Francisco, Shorenstein Co., San Francisco, 1960—. Appt. by Pres. Johnson adv. del. UN Econ. Commn. for Asia and Far East, 1967, Pub. Advisory Com. U.S. Trade Policy; apptd. Pres. Carter Com. for Preservation fo White House; appt. by Pres. Clinton bd. dirs. Corp. Nat. Svc., 1994-96, adv.com. U.S. Commerce Dept. Industry, 1995-96. Past chmn. bd. trustees Hastings Law Ctr., U. Calif., San Francisco; founding mem. exec. adv. com. Hubert H. Humphrey Inst. Pub. Affairs, U. Minn.; bd. visitors; past pres., hon. life bd. dirs. San Francisco Park and Recreation Commn.; chmn. Vietnam Orphans Airlift; bd. dirs. San Francisco Performing Arts Ctr.; trustee Asia Found.; fin. chmn. Dem. Nat. Conv., 1984; founder Joan Shorenstein Ctr. on Press, Politics and Public Policy, Harvard U., 1986; apptd. by Pres. Clinton to Nat. Svc. Commn., 1994, Bd. of Americorp, founding mem. WWII Nat. Monument com., Nat. Endowment Arts, White House Endowment Fund; apptd. by Pres. Carter chair White House Preservation Fund; apptd. by Mayor Frank Jordon chair Save the San Francisco Giants com.; personal advisor Pres. Johnson, Carter, Clinton; chmn. Pacific Rim Econ. Coun., San Francisco; bd. visitors Internat. Studies Bd. Stanford U.; co-founder Orpheum, Curran and Golden Gate Theatres, San Francisco; founder Johnson Presdl. Libr., Carter Ctr.; chmn. San Francisco U. N50 nat. com., 1995, also numerous polit. activities. Maj. USAF, 1940-45. Named Leader of Tomorrow, Time mag., 1953, Calif. Dem. of Yr., 1985; recipient Nat. Brotherhood award NCCJ, 1982, Disting. Svc. award Dem. Nat. Com., 1983, Golden Plate award Am. Acad. Achievement, 1991, Svc. to Youth award Cath. Youth Orgn., 1994, Lifetime Achievement award Dem. Party, 1997; inducted Real Estate Legends Hall of Fame, 1997, Bay Area Coun. Bay Area Bus. Hall of Fame, 1998; Shorenstein award named in his honor Dem. Nat. Com., 1999. Mem. Calif. C. of C. (past bd. dirs.), San Francisco C. of C. (past chmn. bd. dirs., life bd. dirs.). Office: Shorenstein Co 555 California St Ste 4900 San Francisco CA 94104-1714

SHORENSTEIN HAYS, CAROLE, theater producer; m. Jeffrey Hays; 2 children. Co-owner Curran Theatre, Golden Gate Theatre, Orpheum Theatre, San Francisco. Prodr.: (Broadway plays) Can-Can, 1981, Woman of the Year, 1981—83 (Tony nom. best musical, 1981), Oliver!, 1984, Fences, 1987 (Tony award best play, 1987), A Midsummer Night's Dream, 1996 (Tony nom. best revival of a play, 1996), The Old Neighborhood, 1997—98, The Chairs, 1998 (Tony nom. best revival of a play, 1996), Not About Nightingales, 1999 (Tony nom. best play, 1999), Closer, 1999 (Tony nom. best play, 1999), The Tale of the Allergist's Wife, 2000—02 (Tony nom. best play, 2001), Proof, 2000—03 (Tony award best play, 2001), The Goat, or Who Is Sylvia?, 2002 (Tony award best play, 2002), Topdog / Underdog, 2002 (Tony nom. best play, 2002), Take Me Out, 2003—04 (Tony award best play, 2003), Caroline, or Change, 2004— (Tony nom. best musical, 2004). Office: Curran Theatre 445 Geary St San Francisco CA 94102 also: Golden Gate Theatre P O Box 7110 San Francisco CA 94102*

SHORES, PEARL MARIE, health care company executive; b. Warsaw, N.Y., Aug. 29, 1946; d. Lawrence Dean and Mary Ellen (Sly) Arnold; m. Bruce Reid Dedrick, May 9, 1964 (div. 1966); 1 child, Dawn Aileen; m. James Lee Shores, Sept. 13, 1981. BBA cum laude, Nat. U., San Diego, 1979; MBA, Nat. U., 1981. Chief lab. technician Schoenfield Clin. Lab., Albuquerque, 1970-76, Allergy Med. Group, San Diego, 1976-78; chemstrip specialist BioDynamics/BMC, San Diego, 1978-80; sr. ter. mgr. Hollister, Inc., San Diego, 1980-84, dist. mgr. New Eng. dist., 1984-86; sales rep. E.R. Squibb/CONVATEC, San Diego, 1986-87; br. mgr. HOMEDCO, San Diego, 1987-89; dir. infusion therapy Spl. Solutions, 1989-90; territory mgt. Sween Corp., 1990-93; dir. Mercy Infusion Therapy, Escondido, Calif., 1993-96; regional sales cons. Dezinc Healthcare Solutions, 1996—; infusion therapy cons., accounts receivable mgr. Shores Enterprises, 1997—. Avocation: tennis. Fax: (760) 432-6618.

SHORS, CLAYTON MARION, cardiologist; b. Beemer, Nebr., June 10, 1925; s. Joseph Albert and Morva Edith (Clayton) S.; m. Arlene Towle, June 6, 1948; children: Susan Debra, Clayton Robert, Scott Towle BS, U. Nebr., 1950, MD, 1952. Diplomate Am. Bd. Internal Medicine (subspecialty cardiovascular disease). Intern Detroit Receiving Hosp., 1952-53, resident, 1953-56; practice medicine specializing in cardiology Detroit; chief cardiology St. John Hosp., Detroit. Bd. dirs. Sedona Acad.; mem. Sedona 30. Served with U.S. Army, 1943-46 Fellow Am. Coll. Cardiology, Internat. Coll. Angiology, Am. Heart Assn. Council on Clin. Cardiology; mem. Alpha Omega Alpha Home: 44 Rue De La Rose Sedona AZ 86336-5970 Office: 1785 W Highway 89A Sedona AZ 86336-5567 also: 6562 E Crested Saguaro Ln Scottsdale AZ 85262-7373

SHORS, JOHN D. lawyer; b. Ft. Dodge, Iowa, July 21, 1937; s. George A. and Catherine (Shaw) S.; m. Patricia Ann Percival, Oct. 7, 1967; children: John, Tom, Matt, Luke. BSEE, Iowa State U., 1959; JD, U. Iowa, 1964. Bar: Iowa, U.S. Supreme Ct. Assoc. then shareholder Davis, Brown, Koehn, Shors & Roberts, P.C., Des Moines, 1964—. Co-author: Closely Held Corporations in Business and Estate Planning, 1982. Pres. Mercy Hosp. Found., Des Moines, 1981-84; chair Iowa State U. Found., Ames, 1989-92; bd. dirs. Mercy Housing, Denver, 1992—. Cpl. U.S. Army, 1960-61. Recipient Iowa State U. Alumni medal, YLS Merit award Iowa State Bar Assn. Mem. Iowa State Bar Assn. (pres. 1992) Iowa Women Profl. Corp. (Good Guy award 1987), Iowa Rsch. Coun. (bd. dirs. 1994—), Am. Judicature Soc. (bd. dirs. 1974-79), Polk County Bar Assn. (pres. 1986), Rotary (Des Moines chpt.), DM Club, Glenoaks C.C. Republican. Roman Catholic. Office: Davis Brown Koehn Shors & Roberts PC 666 Walnut St Ste 2500 Des Moines IA 50309-3904 E-mail: johnshors@lawiowa.com.

SHORT, ALEXANDER CAMPBELL, lawyer; b. Washington, July 26, 1940; s. Joseph Hudson and Beth (Campbell) S.; m. Patricia Graves Thompson, Aug. 24, 1968; children: Joseph Graves, Ashley Campbell, Justin Owen. BA, Amherst Coll., 1963; MA, U. Pa., 1968; JD, U. Va., 1972. Bar: Conn. 1972, Md. 1973. Field and site rep. U.S. Dept. of HUD, Phila., 1963-69; assoc. Reid & Riege P.C., Hartford, Conn., 1972-73, Piper & Marbury, Balt., 1973-79, Miles & Stockbridge, Balt., 1979-81, ptnr., 1981-94; pvt. practice Balt., 1994-95; ptnr. Hooper, Kiefer & Cornell, LLP, Balt., 1995-96, Eastman & Short, LLP, Balt., 1996-2000; asst. atty. gen. State of Md., 2000—. Pres. Handel Soc. adv. bd. to Handel Choir, Balt., 1983-87; bd. dirs. Handel Choir, Balt., 1987-88, 2002-03, pres., 1987-88. Pres. North Balt. Neighborhood Coalition, 1996—2000; bd. dirs. Homeland Assn., Balt., 1984—85, Kernewood Assn., Balt., 1995—, Greater Homewood Cmty. Corp., 1997—2001; mem. bd. mgrs. Camp Dudley YMCA, 1991—96, 1998—2001. Mem. Md. Bar Assn. (real property planning and zoning sect., coun. 1981-88, 96-98, sec. 1982-84, chmn. elect 1984-86, chmn. 1986-88. Democrat. Presbyterian. Avocations: choral singing, scouting, gardening. Office: Office of Atty Gen Ednl Affairs Divsn 200 St Paul Pl Baltimore MD 21202 Office Phone: 410-576-6967. E-mail: ashort@oag.state.md.us.

SHORT, ELIZABETH M. internist, educator, retired federal agency administrator; b. Boston, June 2, 1942; d. James Edward and Arlene Elizabeth (Mitchell) Meehan; m. Michael Allen Friedman, June 21, 1976; children: Lia Gabrielle, Hannah Ariel, Eleanor Elana. BA in Philosophy magna cum laude, Mt. Holyoke Coll., 1963; MD cum laude, Yale U., 1968. Diplomate Am. Bd. Internal Medicine, Am. Bd. Med. Genetics. Resident in internal medicine Yale New Haven Hosp., 1968-70; postdoctoral fellow in human genetics Yale Med. Sch., 1970-72; resident U. Calif., San Francisco, 1972-73; sr. chief resident Stanford (Calif.) Med. Sch., 1973-75, asst. prof. medicine, 1975-83, assoc. dean student affairs, med. edn., 1978-83; dep. dir. acad. affairs, dir. biomed. rsch. Assn. Am. Med. Colls., Washington, 1983-88; dep. assoc. chief med. dir. for acad. affairs VA, Washington, 1988-92, assoc. chief med. dir. for acad. affairs, 1992-96; health policy cons. HHS, 1996—2001; ret., 2001. Vis. prof. human biology Stanford U., 1983-86; mem. Accreditation Coun. Grad. Med. Edn., 1988-97; mem. White House Task Force on Health Care Reform, 1993. Assoc. editor Clin. Rsch. Jour., 1976-79, editor 1980-84; contbr. articles to profl. jours. Mem. Nat. Child Health Adv. Coun., NIH, 1991-97; mem. com. edn. and tng. Office Sci. and Tech. Policy, White House, Washington, 1991-96. Recipient Maclean Zoology award; Munger scholar, Markle scholar, Sara Williston scholar Mt. Holyoke Coll., 1959-63, Yale Men in Medicine scholar, 1964-68; Bardwell Meml. Med. fellow, 1963. Mem. AAAS, Am. Soc. Human Genetics (pub. policy com. 1984-95, chmn. 1986-94), Am. Fedn. Clin. Rsch. (bd. dirs. 1973-83, co-chmn. com. status women 1975-77, editor Clin. Rsch. Jour., 1978-83, nat. coun., exec. com., pub. policy com. 1977-87), Western Soc. Clin. Investigation, Calif. Acad. Medicine, Phi Beta Kappa, Alpha Omega Alpha. Home and Office: 3535 Ranch Top Rd Pasadena CA 91107 E-mail: elizshort@aol.com.

SHORT, J. LINDSEY, JR., lawyer; b. Houston, Oct. 22, 1943; s. J. Lindsey and Roberta (Prince) S.; m. Agnes G. May, July 22, 1967; children: Ashley K., Shelley F., Sidney F. AB, Washington and Lee U., 1965; JD, U. Tex., 1967. Bar: Tex. 1967, U.S. Dist. Ct. (so. dist.) Tex. 1979, U.S. Ct. Appeals (5th and 11th cirs.) 1981, U.S. Supreme Ct., 2000. Assoc. Barrow, Bland and Rehmet, Houston, 1969-71; pvt. practice Houston, 1971-76; ptnr. Lilly and Short, 1976-80; pres. J. Lindsey Short Jr. and Assoc., Houston, 1980-87, Short and Little, P.L.C., Houston, 1987-88, J. Lindsey Short Jr. & Assocs., Houston, 1988—2000, Short & Jenkins, 2000—. Lectr. in field. Contbr. articles to profl. jours. Lt. (j.g.) USNR, 1967-70. Fellow Am. Acad. Matrimonial Lawyers (editor 1987-90, pres. 2001-02), Tex. Bar Found (life); mem. Internat. Acad. Matrimonial Lawyers, Am. Coll. Family Trial lawyers (founder), Tex. Bar Assn., Tex. Acad. Family Lawyers (past pres.), Family Law Adv. Commn., State Bar Tex. (bd. dirs.), Forest Club. Office: Short & Jenkins LLP 700 One Greenway Plz Houston TX 77027-7528 Office Phone: 713-626-0208.

SHORT, JAY MILTON, biotechnology company executive; b. Lebanon, Ind., Mar. 5, 1958; s. Roy Milton and Patricia Ann (Brewer) S.; m. Heidi Patrice Messinger, July 26, 1980; children: Ryan Milton, Cole Evan. BA in Chemistry with honors, Taylor U., Upland, Ind., 1980; PhD in Biochemistry, Case Western Res. U., 1985. Tchg. asst. Taylor U., 1978-80, Kent (Ohio) State U., 1981, Case Western Res. U., Cleve., 1981-85; staff scientist R & D, Stratagene Cloning Systems, La Jolla, Calif., 1985-88, sr. staff scientist, 1988-89, v.p. long term rsch. and biol. ops., 1989-92, v.p. long term rsch. and ops., 1992-94; pres. Stratcyte, Inc., La Jolla, 1992-94, Diversa Corp., San Diego, 1994—, CEO, 1994—, chief tech. officer, 1994—, bd. dir. Bd. dirs. Stressgen, Inc., Invitrogen, Synomyx, Chem. Engring. News, BioCom, Innovase, Zymetrics; reviewer human genome project and patenting DNA sequences U.S. Congl. Office Tech. Assessment; chmn., ofcl. Instnl. Animal Care and Use Com.; mem. peer rev. com. Nat. Inst. Environ. Health Scis., Molecular Biology, Microbiology, NAS, Genetic Analysis Techniques, Ana-

lytical Biochemistry, Nucleic Acids Rsch.; cons. on transgenic toxicology testing EEC, 1991-94; lectr. in field; mem. adj. faculty U. Calif., San Diego, 1991; lectr. Ctr. for Drug Evaluation and Rsch., FDA, 1992, others. Editor Mutation Rsch.; contbr. numerous articles and abstracts to sci. jours Recipient 1st place award for innovation and entrepreneurship in biotech. U. Calif., 1990, 91; named Entrepreneur of Yr., Ernst and Young, 2001; numerous grants including Nat. Inst. Environ. Health Scis., 1989-94, NIH, 1990-94, Nat. Cancer Inst., 1992-95. Mem. AAAS, Am. Soc. Biochemistry and Molecular Biology, Am. Soc. Microbiology, Environ. Mutagenesis Soc., Soc. Toxicology (chmn. corr. discussion group 1993), Japanese Environ. Mutagen Soc., N.Y. Acad. Scis. Achievements include patents in field. Avocations: flying, photography, collecting fossils, scuba diving. Office: Recombinant BioCatalysis Inc 10665 Sorrento Valley Rd San Diego CA 92121-1609

SHORT, JOEL BRADLEY, lawyer, software publisher; b. Birmingham, Ala., Dec. 27, 1941; s. Forrest Edwin and Laura Elizabeth (Bradley) S.; m. Georgianna Pohl, June 5, 1965 (div. Apr. 1973); m. Nancy Ann Harty, Dec. 17, 1977; children: Christopher Bradley, Matthew Douglas. BA, U. Colo., 1963, LLB, 1966, JD, 1968. Bar: Kans. 1966, U.S. Dist. Ct. Kans. 1966, U.S. Ct. Appeals (10th cir.) 1975, U.S. Supreme Ct. 1976. Ptnr. Short & Short, Attys., Fort Scott, Kans., 1966-77, Nugent & Short, Overland Park, Kans., 1977-83; pvt. practice J. Bradley Short & Assoc., Overland Park, Kans., 1983-91; ptnr. Short & Borth, Overland Park, Kans., 1991—; owner Bradley Software. Mem. tech. adv. com. Kans. Jud. Coun., Topeka, 1991-95. Contbg. author: Practitioner's Guide to Kansas Family Law, 1997-2002. 1st lt. U.S. Army, 1967-73. Fellow Am. Acad. Matrimonial Lawyers; mem. Johnson County Bar Assn. (ethics com. 1983-98, family law com. 1983—). Avocation: bonsai. Office: Short and Borth 55/500 Corporate Woods 9300 W 110th St Overland Park KS 66210-1405 Office Phone: 913-491-4400. Business E-Mail: brad@shortandborth.com.

SHORT, LINDA HUFFSTETLER, state legislator; b. Gastonia, N.C., July 9, 1947; d. Everett Rhyne and Violet Lucille (Kuykendall) Huffstetler; m. Paul E. Short, Jr., June 14, 1968; children: Lindy Lee, Melanie Lynne. BA in Psychology, Winthrop U., 1984. Mem. S.C. Senate, Columbia, 1993—, asst. majority whip, 1993—. Mem. edn. com. So. Legis. Conf., 1997, mem. edn. com., 1997-98; mem. health capacity task force Coun. State Govts., 1997, mem. health capacity task force, 1997-98; mem. bd. Status of Women in State Govt. Task Force, 1997; mem. adv. bd. women's network Nat. Conf. State Legislators, 1997; mem. Legis. Consumer Fin. Study Com., 1997-98. Mem. Chester County Sch. Bd., 1982-92, chmn., 1990-92; bd. dirs. Downtown Devel. Assn., 1989-93, Palmetto Leadership, 1990-91; bd. visitors Presbyn. Coll., 1990-93; mem. Chester County's Fall Affair, 1988-90; former coord. 6th Cir. Guardian Ad Litem Program; former jr. and sr. H.S. Sunday sch. tchr. Purity Presbyn. Ch., former pres. Presbyn. Women; former v.p. Providence Presbytery Presbyn. Women; mem. Children's Case Resolutions Sys. Panel, Joint Legis. com. Children and Families, 1992-95; state mem. nat. edn. policy focus Milken Family Found., 1997; co-chmn. Study Com. on Drug-Impaired Infants, 1997-98. Recipient S.C. Dept. Health and Environ. Control Bur. of Maternal and Child Health Legis.award 1995, Chester County's Econ. Devel. Efforts award 1995, Girl Scouts Women of Achievement award 1996, Ernestine C. Player Friend of Social Work award 1996. Mem. Bench Bar Com., Phi Kappa Phi, Delta Kappa Gamma. Democrat. Address: SC State Senate 502 Gressette Bldg PO Box 142 Columbia SC 29202-0142

SHORT, MARION PRISCILLA, neurogenetics educator; b. Milford, Del., June 12, 1951; d. Raymond Calistus and Barbara Anne (Ferguson) S.; m. Michael Peter Klein; 1 child, Asher Calistus Klein. BA, Bryn Mawr Coll., 1973; diploma, U. Edinburgh (Scotland), 1975; MD, Med. Coll. Pa., 1978. Diplomate Am. Bd. Psychiatry and Neurology, Am. Bd. Internal Medicine. Intern in internal medicine Hahnemann Med. Coll. Hosp., Phila., 1978-79; med. resident in internal medicine St. Lukes-Roosevelt Hosp., N.Y.C., 1979-81; neurology resident U. Pitts. Health Ctr., 1981-84; fellow in med. genetics Mt. Sinai Med. Ctr., N.Y.C., 1984-86; fellow in neurology Mass. Gen. Hosp., Boston, 1986-90, asst. neurologist, 1990-95; asst. prof. dept. neurology Harvard Med. Sch., Boston, 1990-95; asst. prof. dept. neurology, pediat. and pathology U. Chgo., 1995—97; program dir. genetics, transplantation and clin. rsch. AMA, Chgo., 1997—2002; fellow McLean Ctr. for Clin. Med. Ethics U. Chgo., 2002—03, sr. fellow McLean Ctr. for Clin. Med. Ethics, 2003—. Recipient Clin. Investigator Devel. award, NIH, 1988—93; fellow, Inst. Medicine, Chgo., 1999, McLean Ctr. for Clin. Med. Ethics, U. Chgo., 2002—. Mem. AMA, Am. Acad. Neurology, Am. Soc. for Human Genetics, Am. Coll. Med. Genetics. Office: Pediat Neurosurgery U Chgo MC 4066 5481 S Maryland Ave Chicago IL 60637-4325 Office Phone: 773-702-2475. Business E-Mail: mpshort@surgery.bsd.uchicago.edu.

SHORT, MARTIN, actor, comedian; b. Hamilton, Ont, Canada, Mar. 26, 1950; s. Charles Patrick and Olive Short; m. Nancy Dolman; children: Katherine, Oliver, Henry. Degree in social work, McMaster U., 1972. Actor: (feature films) Three Amigos, 1986, Innerspace, 1987, Cross My Heart, 1987, Three Fugitives, 1989, The Big Picture, 1989, Pure Luck, 1991, Father of the Bride, 1991, Captain Ron, 1992, We're Back! A Dinosaur's Story, 1993 (voice), Clifford, 1994, The Pebble and the Penguin, 1995 (voice), Father of the Bride 2, 1995, Mars Attack, 1996, Jungle 2 Jungle, 1997, The Fairy Godmother, 1997, A Simple Wish, 1997, Mumford, 1998, Akbar's Adventure Tours, 1998, (voice) Prince of Egypt, 1998, Get Over It, 2001, Jimmy Neutron: Boy Genius (voice), 2001, Treasure Planet (voice), 2001, Cinemagique, 2002; (TV series) The Associates, 1979, I'm a Big Girl Now, 1980-81, SCTV Network 90, 1982-84, Saturday Night Live, 1985-86, The Completely Mental Misadventures of Ed Grimley, 1988-89 (voice), The Martin Short Show, 1994, (miniseries) Merlin, 1998; (TV movies) The Family Man, 1979, Sunset Limousine, 1983, Alice in Wonderland, 1999, (Prince Charming, 2001; TV spls.) Martin Short's Concert for the North Americas, 1985, Really Weird Tales, 1987, I, Martin Short Goes Hollywood, 1989, The Martin Short Show (TV series), 1999-2000; also numerous revues and cabaret appearances with Second City comedy troupe, 1977-78, appeared on Broadway in The Goodbye Girl, 1993. Won 1999 Tony Award, Best Actor-Musical, Little Me. Office: William Morris Agency care Ames Cushing 1 William Morris Pl Beverly Hills CA 90212-2775

SHORT, RAY EVERETT, minister, sociology educator emeritus, author, lecturer; b. Coffeyville, Kans., Jan. 5, 1919; s. Franklin Marion and Jennie (Messersmith) S.; m. Jeannette Louise Stephens, June 12, 1954 (dec. Jan. 2000); children: Glenn Alan, Linda Louise, Kenneth Ray, Timothy Wesley, Karen Amy; 1 stepdau., Mary Jennings. AB, Willamette U., 1944; postgrad., U. Chgo., 1946; BD, Duke, 1948, PhD, 1961; postgrad., U. Idaho, 1950-51. Ordained to ministry Meth. Ch., 1946. Dir. Westminster Found., Duke, 1944-46; co-pastor Interracial Meth. Ch., Durham, N.C., 1947; asst. prof. religion, dir. chapel programs Fla. So. Coll., Lakeland, 1947-48; exec. dir. Fla. br. United World Federalists, 1948-51; dir. Intermountain Region, 1953-54, Wesley Found., U. Idaho, 1950-51; exec. dir. Student YMCA-YWCA, U. Denver, 1951-53; pastor Fairmont Meth. Ch., Lockport, Ill., 1954-56; grad. asst. sociology Duke, 1956-57; assoc. prof. religion, head divsn. religion and philosophy, chaplain Tenn. Wesleyan Coll., 1957-60; assoc. prof. sociology and religion, head dept. sociology U. Dubuque, Iowa, 1960-65, acting chmn. div. social sci., 1962-65; assoc. prof. sociology, head dept. sociology and anthropology U. Wis., Platteville, 1965-70, prof. sociology, 1966-87, prof. emeritus, 1987—; prof. sociology and anthropology Copenhagen Study Ctr. U. Wis., spring 1974, nat. lectr., 1975—. Chmn. Peace and World Order divsn. North Iowa Meth. Conf., 1963-69; rep. U.S. Jr. C. of C. in testimony before U.S. Senate Com. on Fgn. Rels., 1950; Midwest region rep. Nat. Coun. World Federalist Assn., 1964-73, pres. Midwest region, 1967-69, chmn. nat. coun., 1971-72, nat. v.p., 1991—; (with wife) WFA dels. to NGO Forum and 4th UN Conf. on Women, Beijing, 1995; D.C. hdqrs. WFA property named Ray and Jeannette Short Peacemakers Bldg., 1997 (Presdl. WFA award 1998, Nat. World Federalist of Month, June 2004); co-chmn. Grenville Clark Club; mem. spl. Wis. Conf. called with Pres.'s Comn. for Observance of 25th Anniversary of UN, 1970-87; mem. Wis. U. Meth. Bd. on Ch. and Soc., 1973-80, chmn. World Peace divsn., mem. exec. com., 1975-80. Author: Sex, Love or Infatuation: How Can I Really Know?, 1978, on videocassette, 1987, 2d edit. (Augsburg Bestseller), 11 fgn. edits., Sex, Dating and Love: Questions Most Often Asked, 1984, 2d edit., 1994, Sex, Love or Romance: You Can't Really Trust Your Heart?, 2004; contbr. articles to profl. jours. Nat. bd. Am. Freedom Assn.; nat. v.p. Campaign for UN Reform, 1983—87, 1st v.p., 1989—2004, exec. com., 1997—; bd. dirs. Dubuque Salvation Army, 1961—65; dir., founder Wis. Ann. World Peace Study Program, 1975—; Dem. candidate for Wis. 3d Dist. Congl. Seat, 1970, 1972; del. Dist. and State Convs., 1969—87, state platform com., 1975—87. Recipient Pick a Profl. award, 2003; NSF grantee Anthropology Inst., Fairmont State Coll., W.Va., 1962 Fellow Am. Sociol. Assn.; mem. AAUP, Nat. Coun. on Family Rels., Fedn. Am. Scientists, Nat. United Meth. Men (mem. peace adv. task force 1990—). Home: 505 S Miller Ave Lafayette CO 80026-1545 Office Phone: 303-666-5025. *Nuclear and chemical weapons, crises of environments. While my life has largely been spent helping others have a better future, I now know we have to help assure that they have a future at all by establishing limited democratic enforcible world law.*

SHORT, ROBERT, information technology executive; Graduate, CIT, Cork, Ireland; MS in Computer Sci., U. Wash. Sr. devel. mgr. Digital Equipment Corp.; from mem. devel. team to corp. v.p. Microsoft, Redmond, Wash., 1988, corp. v.p. windows core tech. Office: One Microsoft Way Redmond WA 98052-6399

SHORT, STEVE EUGENE, engineer; b. Crockett, Calif., Oct. 17, 1938; s. Roger Milton and Ida Mae (Mills) S.; m. Yumie Sedaka, Feb. 2, 1962; children: Anne Yumie, Justine Yumie, Katherine Yumie. BS in Gen. Engring. with honors, U. Hawaii, 1972, MBA, 1973; MS in Meteorology, U. Md., 1980. Registered profl. engr., Hawaii. With Nat. Weather Svc., NOAA, 1964—; pres. Short & Assocs., Inc., 1994—. Govt. exec. Silver Spring, Md., 1974-81, program mgr. ASOS,1981—, transition dir. 1991—; ind. tech. cons., 1994—; pres. Short & Assocs., Inc.; cons. engring. and mgmt.; cons. SBA. Contbr. articles to sci. jours. With USMC, 1956-60. Recipient Gold Medal award U.S. Dept. Commerce, 1992, Presdl. Meritorious Exec. award, 1992. Mem. VFW, Am. Meteorol. Soc., Japan-Am. Soc., Am. Soc. Pub. Adminstrn. Office: 3307 Rolling Rd Chevy Chase MD 20815-4033 E-mail: sshort@compuserve.com.

SHORT, THOMAS C. theatre union executive; s. Adrian Short, Jr. Mem. Internat. Alliance of Theatrical Stage Employes, Moving Picture Technicians, Artists and Allied Crafts U.S., AFL-CIO, 1968—, internat. v.p., 1988-94, gen. sec.-treas., 1993-95, internat. pres., 1994—. Bd. dirs. Motion Picture Industry Pension and Health Plans; trustee IATSE Nat. Pension Fund. Office: IATSE 1515 Broadway Ste 601 New York NY 10036-8901

SHORTAL, TERENCE MICHAEL, systems company executive; b. St. Louis, Oct. 13, 1937; s. Harold Leo and Catherine margaret S.; m. Linda Margaret Elias, May 29, 1965; children: Jennifer, Bradley Alexander. BSEE, U. Mo., 1961; MS, U.S. Naval Postgrad. Sch., 1966; grad. program execs., Carnegie Mellon U., 1979. Commd. ensign USN, 1961; advanced through grades to capt., 1980; ret., 1981; asst. officer in charge Engring. Duty Officer Sch., 1974-77; ship engring. mgr. AEGIS shipbldg. project Naval Ea Sys. Command, Washington, 1977-79; tech. dir. DDGX project, 1979-81; v.p., dir. Kastle Sys., LLC, 1981—. Trustee Cathedral Choral Soc., Washington, 1983-95, 97—, pres., 1986-88, 2000-2002; mem. vestry St. John's Episcopal Ch., McLean, Va., 1982-85; bd. dirs. Langley Sch., McLean, 1984-94, pres. 1986-88. Decorated Meritorious Svc. medal (2), Navy Commendation medal (2); recipient award of merit Cathedral Choral Soc., 1996. Mem. IEEE (br. award 1961), Am. Soc. Naval Engrs. (Flagship Sect. award 1979), Nat. Press Club (Washington), City Club, Gridiron Club (Washington), Sigma Xi, Phi Kappa Theta. Home: 858 Canal Dr Mc Lean VA 22102-1408 Office: 1501 Wilson Blvd Arlington VA 22209-2403 Business E-Mail: mike@kastle.com.

SHORTELL, STEPHEN MICHAEL, dean, health services researcher; b. New London, Wis., Nov. 9, 1944; BBA, U. Notre Dame, 1966; MPH, UCLA, 1968; MBA, U. Chgo., 1970, PhD in Behavioral Sci., 1972. Rsch. asst. Nat. Opinion Rsch. Ctr., 1969; instr., rsch. assoc. Ctr. Health Adminstrv. Studies, 1970—72; acting dir. grad. program hosp. adminstrn. U. Chgo., 1973—74, from asst. prof. to assoc. prof., 1974—79; prof. dept. health svc. Sch. Pub. Health and Cmty. Medicine, U. Wash., 1979—82; A.C. Buehler Disting. prof. health svc. mgmt. Northwestern U., Evanston, Ill., 1982—98; Blue Cross disting. prof. health policy and mgmt. Sch. Pub. Health, U. Calif., Berkeley, 1998—; dean Sch. Pub. Health, U. Calif. Berkeley, 2002—. Cons. VA, Robert Wood Found., Henry Kaiser Found.; asst. prof. Health Svcs. Orgn. U. Chgo., 1972—74; adj. asst. prof. dept. sociology U. Wash., 1975—76, dir. doctoral program dept. health svcs. Sch. Pub. Health and Cmty. Medicine, 1976—78; prof. sociology dept. sociology Northwestern U., 1982, prof. preventive medicine Sch. Medicine. Contbr. numerous articles to profl. jours. Recipient Baxter prize, Baxter-Allegiance Found., 1995, Honorary AHA Lifetime Mem. award, Gold Medal award, Amer. Coll. of Healthcare Exec., 1998, Dist. Investigator award, Assoc. for Health Services Research, 1998, Best Paper award, Acad. of Mgmnt., 1996, George R. Terry Book of the Year award, 1990. Fellow: Am. Coll. Healthcare Execs. (Gold medal 1998); mem.: Inst. Med.-NAS. Office: Univ Calif Berkeley Sch Pub Health 407 Warren Hl Berkeley CA 94720-0001

SHORTER, JAMES RUSSELL, JR., lawyer; b. NYC, June 10, 1946; s. James Russell and Helen (Ibert) S. AB, Columbia Coll., 1968; JD, Harvard U., 1975; LLM in Taxation, NYU, 1979. Bar: NY 1976, US Dist. Ct. (so. and ea. dists.) NY 1976, US Tax Ct. 1987. Assoc. Thacher Proffitt & Wood, NYC, 1975-84, ptnr., 1984—. Capt. USNR, 1968-98. Mem. ABA (tax, bus. law sect.), N.Y. State Bar Assn. (internat. law and practice sect.), Assn. Bar City N.Y., Internat. Fiscal Assn., Harvard Club (N.Y.C.), Down Town Assn. (N.Y.C.). Republican. Home: 345 E 80th St Apt 26C New York NY 10021-0671 Office: Thacher Proffitt & Wood LLP Two World Financial Ctr 28th Fl New York NY 10281 Office Phone: 212-912-7628. E-mail: jshorter@tpwlaw.com.

SHORTER, NICHOLAS ANDREW, pediatric surgeon; b. London, Oct. 14, 1953; came to the U.S., 1961; s. Roy Gerrard and Rhiannon (Morris) S.; m. Sally Jo Trued, Aug. 28, 1982; children: Timothy Anders, Brittain David, Jaime Elizabeth Rhiannon. AB, AM, Harvard U., 1975; MD, Johns Hopkins U., 1979. Diplomate in gen. surgery and pediat. surgery Am. Bd. Surgery. Intern The Johns Hopkins Hosp., Balt., 1979-80, jr. asst. resident in surgery, 1980-81, sr. asst. resident in surgery, 1981-82, 83-84, chief resident in surgery, 1984-85; rsch. fellow in surgery The Children's Hosp. Med. Ctr., Boston, 1982-83; asst. chief resident in pediatric surgery The Children's Hosp., Phila., 1985-86, chief resident in pediatric surgery, 1986-87; hosp. staff Duke U. Med. Ctr., Durham, N.C., 1987-91; chief pediatric surgery Children's Hosp. at Dartmouth, Dartmouth-Hitchcock Med. Ctr., 1991-99, exec. com., 1991-99; assoc. attending surgeon Meml. Hosp., N.Y.C., 1999—2002; attending surgeon SUNY-Downstate Med. Ctr., Bklyn., 2002—, chief divsn. pediat. surgery, 2002—. Tchg. fellow biology Harvard U., Cambridge, Mass., 1974-75; asst. instr. pediatric surgery U. Pa., Phila., 1985-87, Duke U., Durham, 1987-91, asst. prof. pediat. surgery and pediat.; asst. prof. pediat. Dartmouth Med. Sch., Hanover, N.H., 1991-94, asst. prof. surgery, 1991-94, assoc. prof. pediat., 1994-99, assoc. prof. surgery, 1994-99; hosp. staff The Children's Hosp., Phila., 1986-87, Dartmouth-Hitchcock Med. Ctr., Lebanon, N.H., 1991-99, Duke U. Med. Ctr., Durham, 1987-91, Meml. Hosp., N.Y., 1999-2002; dir. Kiwanis Affiliated Pediatric Trauma Ctr., Children's Hosp. at Dartmouth, Lebanon, 1993-99; mem. hosp. staff SUNY Downstate Med. Ctr., Bklyn., 2002—; assoc. prof. surgery Cornell U., N.Y.C., 2001-2002; vis. prof. surgery, SUNY, Bklyn., 2002-03, prof. clin. surgery, 2003—, prof. clin. pediat., 2003—. Referee Jour. Pediatric Surgery; contbr. chpts. to books and articles to profl. jours. Regular Clin. fellow Am. Cancer Soc., 1985-86. Fellow ACS, Am. Acad. Pediat., Southeastern Surg. Congress, Royal Soc. Medicine, Soc. Surg. Oncology; mem. Am. Pediatric Surg. Assn., Brit. Assn. Pediat. Surgeons, Internat. Soc. Pediat. Oncology, Internat. Pediatric Surg. Oncology, Am. Assn. for Cancer Rsch., Assn. for Acad. Surgery, N.Y. Acad. Scis., Royal Soc. Medicine, Cum Laude Soc., Phi Beta Kappa, Alpha Omega Alpha. Republican. Episcopalian. Avocation: collecting political memorabilia. Office Phone: 718-270-1986. Business E-Mail: nicholas.shorter@downstate.edu.

SHORTLIFFE, EDWARD HANCE, internist, medical educator, computer scientist; b. Edmonton, Alta., Can., Aug. 28, 1947; s. Ernest Carl and Elizabeth Joan Shortliffe. AB, Harvard U., 1970; PhD, Stanford U., 1975, MD, 1976. Diplomate Am. Bd. Internal Medicine. Trainee NIH, 1971—76; intern Mass. Gen. Hosp., Boston, 1976—77; resident Stanford Hosp., Palo Alto, Calif., 1977—79; asst. prof. medicine Stanford U. Sch. Medicine, Palo Alto, 1979—85, assoc. prof., 1985—90, chief divsn. gen. internal medicine, 1988—95, prof., 1990—2000; assoc. chair medicine Primary Care, 1993—95; assoc. dean info. resources and tech. Stanford U. Sch. Medicine, 1995—2000; prof., chair dept. biomed. informatics Columbia U. Coll. Physicians and Surgeons, N.Y.C., 2000—; deputy v.p. Info. Tech., Health Scis., Columbia U., N.Y.C., 2002—; bd. dirs. Medco Health Solutions, Inc., 2003—. Advisor Nat. Bd. Med. Examiners, Phila., 1987—93; pres. Symposium on Computer Applications in Med. Care, Washington, 1988—89; mem. Nat. Fed. Networking Adv. Coun., NSF, 1991—93; mem. computer sci. and telecomm. bd. NRC, 1991—96; bd. regents ACP-Am. Soc. Internal Medicine, 1996—2002; mem. Pres.'s Info. Tech. Adv. Com., 1997—2002; chmn. com. on healthcare and next generation internet NRC, 1998—2000; mem. Nat. Com. on Vital Health Stats., 2000—03. Editor: Rule-Based Expert Systems, 1984, Readings in Medical Artificial Intelligence, 1984, Medical Informatics: Computer Applications in Health Care, 1990, Medical Informatics: Computer Applications in Health Care and Biomedicine, 2d edit., 2000. Mem. com. Sci. and Engring. Pub. Policy NAS, 2001—03. Recipient Grace M. Hopper award, Assn. Computing Machinery, 1976, Young Investigator award, Western Soc. Clin. Investigation, 1987, Rsch. Career award, Nat. Libr. of Medicine, 1979—84; scholar, Kaiser Family Found., 1983—88. Fellow: Am. Coll. Med. Informatics (pres. 1992—94), Am. Assn. Artificial Intelligence; mem.: Am. Clin. and Climatol. Assn., Assn. Am. Physicians, Am. Med. Informatics Assn., Am. Soc. for Clin. Investigation, Inst. Medicine (mem. coun. 2000—03), Soc. for Med. Decisionmaking (pres. 1989—90). Achievements include development of several medical computer programs including MYCIN. Avocations: skiing, jazz. Office: Columbia U Med Ctr Vanderbilt Clinic Ste 550 622 W 168th St New York NY 10032-3720 Office Phone: 212-305-6896. Business E-Mail: shortliffe@dbmi.columbia.edu.

SHORT-MAYFIELD, PATRICIA AHLENE, business owner; b. Ft. Benning, Ga., Oct. 12, 1955; d. William Pressley and Ilse Marie (Hofmann) Short; m. Thomas Hicks Fort, June 2, 1973 (div. Jan. 1981); m. Michael Patrick Mayfield, Aug. 11, 1984; 1 child, William Zachary. Grad. high sch., Butler, Ga., 1973. Notary pub., Ga. Staff mem. Fairyland Day Care, Canton, Ga., 1973-74, Small World Child Care, Thomaston, Ga., 1974-77; nurses aide Kenneston Hosp., Marietta, Ga., 1978-80; staff worker Mental Health Ctr., Smyrna, Ga., 1980-81; dir. Kiddie Kollege, Marietta, 1981-85; bus. owner, mgr. Spiffy Clean by Mayfield, Marietta, 1985—95; lead cashier Petsmart, Kennesaw, Ga., 1994—. Choir staff Eastside Bapt. Ch., Marietta, 1988-89; vol. East Valley Elem. Sch., 1989-95, chorus vol., 1994-95; vol. East Cobb Middle Sch., 1995-98; active Nat. Congress Parents and Tchrs., Cobb County Humane Soc., 1991—. Mem. NAFE, Cobb County C. of C., Atlanta High Mus. Art, Dog Lovers Am. Republican. Baptist. Avocations: reading, walking, symphony, art, bicycling. Office: Spiffy Clean By Mayfield 2791 Georgian Ter Marietta GA 30068-3625

SHORTZ, RICHARD ALAN, lawyer; b. Chgo., Mar. 11, 1945; s. Lyle A. and Wilma Warner (Wildes) S.; m. Jennifer A. Harrell; children: Eric, Heidi. BS, Ind. U., 1967; JD, Harvard U., 1970. Bar: Calif. 1971, U.S. Supreme Ct. 1980. Assoc. Gibson, Dunn & Crutcher, L.A., 1970-73; sr. v.p., gen. counsel, sec. Tosco Corp., L.A., 1973-83; ptnr. Jones, Day, Reavis & Pogue, L.A., 1983-95, Rogers & Wells, L.A., 1995-97, Morgan Lewis & Bockius, L.A., 1997—. Mem. L.A. World Affairs Inst., 1983—, Town Hall L.A., 1983—. 2nd lt. U.S. Army, 1970-71. Mem.: Calif. Bar Assn., L.A. Bar. Assn., ABA, Merion Golf Club (Ardmore, Pa.), Loch Lomond Golf Club (Scotland), L.A. Country Club, Beach Club (Santa Monica, Calif.), Calif. Club. Republican. Episcopalian. Home: 1343 Pavia Pl Pacific Palisades CA 90272-4047 Office: Morgan Lewis & Bockius 300 S Grand Ave Ste 2200 Los Angeles CA 90071-3132 E-mail: rshortz@morganlewis.com.

SHORTZ, WILL, puzzle editor; b. Crawfordsville, Ind., Aug. 26, 1952; s. Lyle A. and Wilma Warner (Wildes) S. AB, Ind. U., 1974; JD, U. Va., 1977. Editor Penny Press, Stamford, Conn., 1977-78; assoc. editor Games Mag., N.Y.C., 1978-82, sr. editor, 1982-89, editor, 1989-93; crossword editor N.Y. Times, N.Y.C., 1993—. Founder, dir. Am. Crossword Puzzle Tournament, Stamford, Conn., 1978—, World Puzzle Championship, N.Y.C., 1992, Stamford, 2000; puzzlemaster Weekend Edit. Sunday, NPR, Washington, 1987—; U.S. team capt. Internat. Crossword Marathon, 1989-90, World Puzzle Championship, 1993-99; riddle writer Batman Forever, 1995; co-founder, chmn. World Puzzle Fedn., 1999--. Author: Brain Games, 1979, The American Quiz Book, 1979, Brain Games 2, 1980, The Bantam Great Masters Winning Crossword Puzzles, vol. 1-3, 1980, World Class Championship Crosswords, 1982, Brain Games 3, 1983, Games Mag. Book of Crossword Puzzles, 1985, American Championship Crosswords, 1990, Games Mag. Giant Book of Games, 1991, Will Shortz's Best Brain Busters, 1991, Games Mag. Best Pencil Puzzles, 1992, Brain Twisters from the First World Puzzle Championships, 1993, N.Y. Times Daily Crossword Puzzles, vol. 40-66, 1995—, The Puzzlemaster Presents, 1996, Will Shortz's Tournament Crosswords, 1997; N.Y. Times Sunday Crossword Puzzles, vol. 24-29, 1998—, Will Shortz's Favorite Crossword Puzzles, 2002, The Puzzlemaster Presents, vol. 2, 2004. Mem. Am. Antiquarian Soc., Am. Cryptogram Assn., Authors Guild, Nat. Puzzlers' League (pres. 1977, 81, historian 1992—). Avocations: ping pong/table tennis, book collecting. Office: NY Times 229 W 43rd St New York NY 10036-3959 Office Phone: 212-556-7435.

SHORTZ, WILMA WILDES, writer, utilities executive; b. Kansas City, Mo., Dec. 16, 1910; d. John Henry Jr. and Viola Alberta (Warner) Wildes; m. Lyle Alton Shortz, Sept. 16, 1939 (dec. Nov. 1994); children: April Irene, Richard Alan, William Frederic. Grad. ct. reporter, Gregg Coll., Chgo., 1931. Freelance ct. reporter, Chgo., 1930-43; freelance ct. reporter, Crawfordsville, Ind., 1951; supr. Montgomery County Soil & Water Conservation Dist., 1970—85, chair, 1981—85, assoc. supr., 1986—. Contbg. author: Montgomery County Legend and Lore, 1988; spkr. weekly program on horses Sta. WCVL, 1980-81; contbr. horse articles, stories and humor to mags. Mem. Presbyn. Ch. Women's Assn., 1955—, pres., 1963—64, Crawfordsville H.S. PTA, 1961—63; mem. organizing com. Montgomery County 4-H Horse and Pony Club, 1960—61, officer, 1961—65; mem. Current Events Club, 1959—, pres., 1966—67, 2000—01. Mem. LWV (pres. Montgomery County 1965-67). Presbyterian. Avocations: writing, contests.

SHOSKY, JOHN EDWIN, media consultant, speechwriter; b. Colorado Springs, Colo., Nov. 1, 1955; s. Alexander Matthew and Barbara Marie (Middlekamp) Shosky. BA in Polic. Sci., Colo. Coll., 1979; MA in Philosophy, U. Wyo., 1987; PhD in Philosophy, Am. U., 1992. Dep. dir. media and sports commns. White House Conf. for Drug Free Am., Washington, 1987—88; sr. policy analyst White House Office Pub. Affairs, 1988; cons. to sec. HHS, Washington, 1984—91, cons. to Surgeon Gen., 1991—92; cons. to office of nat. drug control policy Exec. Office of the Pres., Washington, 1992—93, cons. to sec. edn., 2003—; pres., sr. writer Roncalli Comm., 1991—; cons. to sec. Dept. Edn., 2003—. Speech writer for govt. ofcls., corp. execs., profl. athletes, congressmen, senators; lectr. in philosophy and internat. studies Am. U., 1987—, asst. prof. philosophy, 1996—97, asst. dir. honors program, 1999—2003; adj. prof. philosophy George Mason U., 1990—94; vis. sr. mem. Linacre Coll., Oxford, England, 1997—; vis. prof. Charles U., Prague, 1998; vis. scholar Ins. of Logic, Acad. Scis., Czech Republic, 1998; vis. fellow Acad. Scis., Czech Republic, 2002—04. Contbr. articles to profl. jours. and publs. Mem.: Mind Assn., Hume Soc., Am. Philos. Assn., Austrian Wittgenstein Soc., U. Wyo. Alumni Assn. Republican. Roman Catholic. Home: 1806 Rollins Dr Alexandria VA 22307-1613

SHOSS, CYNTHIA RENÉE, lawyer; b. Cape Girardeau, Mo., Nov. 29, 1950; d. Milton and Carroll Jane (Duncan) S.; m. David Goodwin Watson, Apr. 13, 1986; 1 child, Lucy J. Watson. BA cum laude, Newcomb Coll., 1971; JD, Tulane U., 1974; LLM in Taxation, NYU, 1980. Bar: La. 1974, Mo. 1977, Ill. 1978, N.Y. 1990. Law clk. to assoc. and chief justices La. Supreme Ct.,

New Orleans, 1974-76; assoc. Stone, Pigman et al, New Orleans, 1976-77, Lewis & Rice, St. Louis, 1977-79, Curtis, Mallet-Prevost, et al, N.Y.C., 1980-82; ptnr. LeBoeuf, Lamb, Greene & MacRae, L.L.P., N.Y.C., 1982—; mng. ptnr. London office LeBoeuf, Lamb, Leiby & MacRae, 1987-89. Assoc. editor Tulane Law Rev., 1972-74; frequent speaker before profl. orgns. and assns. Contbr. articles to profl. jours. Mem.: ABA, Assn. Life Ins. Counsels, Power of Atty., Inc. (chair bd. dirs.), Am. Mgmt. Assn. (ins. and risk mgmt. coun.). Office: LeBoeuf Lamb Greene Et Al 125 W 55th St New York NY 10019-5369 Office Phone: 212-424-8129. E-mail: cshoss@llgm.com.

SHOTKO, KURT JOSEPH, entrepreneur, music entertainer; b. Allentown, Pa., May 25, 1967; s. Karen Joy LaBella and Joseph Stanley Shotko. Student, Keystone Coll., 1985-87, East Stroudsburg U., 1989-90. Founder Hemp Expresses Rational Balance, Scranton, Pa., 1997—, An Idea Outlet, Moscow, Pa., 1996—, Earth Worship Nation, Scranton, Pa., 1997—. Founder Rhythm Against Rage, Scranton, 1997—. Contbr. articles to profl. jours. Green Party candidate 10th Dist. for U.S. Ho. Reps., Scranton, 1998, 2000, 2002; Green Party candidate for mayor, 2001; progressive activist, lobbyist Citizens for Common Sense, Scranton, 1995—; Lackawanna County chmn. for Ralph Nader, Green Party, 2000; candidate for Green Party Lackawanna County Commr., 2003. Named N.E. Pa. Best Activist The Electric City, 2000. Avocations: musician, poet, photographer, sculptor, painter, urban gardener. Office: An Idea Outlet 103 Van Brunt St Moscow PA 18444 Home: 106 Church St Moscow PA 18444-9021 E-mail: nation@epix.net.

SHOTT, SALLY RICHARD, otolaryngologist; b. Cin., 1956; Student, Williams Coll., 1974-76; BA, U. Chgo., 1978; MD, U. Cin., 1982. Diplomate Am. Bd. Otolaryngology. Resident in gen. surgery U. Cin. Hosps., 1982—83, resident in otolaryngology, 1983-87; fellow in pediatric otolaryngology Children's Hosp., Cin., 1987; mem. staff Children's Hosp. Med. Ctr., Cin.; clin. prof. U. Cin.; pvt. practice Cin. Mem.: S.E.N.T.A.C., AMA, Triologic Soc., Otolaryngol. Soc. N.Am., Am. Soc. Pediat. Otolaryngology, Am. Assn. Otolaryngology-Head and Neck Surgery. Office: 3333 Burnet Ave Bethesda and Elland Ave Cincinnati OH 45229 Office Phone: 513-636-4355. Business E-Mail: sally.shott@cchmc.org.

SHOTTS, EMMETT BOOKER, JR., microbiology educator, researcher; b. Jasper, Ala., Sept. 23, 1931; s. Emmett Booker and Will Laceye (Brown) Shotts; m. Martha C. Monroe, Sept. 7, 1997; children: Elizabeth, Dan, Evelyn, Georgia Alice Maria. BS, U. Ala., 1952; MS, U. Ga., 1958, PhD, 1966. Epidemic intellegence svc. Ctr. for Disease Control, Atlanta, 1959-61; rsch. microbiologist Ctrs. for Disease Control, Atlanta, 1962-64; rsch. assoc. U. Ga., Athens, 1957-59, prof., 1966—97, prof. emeritus, 1997—; dir. Nat. Fish Health Rsch. Lab. US Dept. Interior, 1997—2001; cons., 2001—. Contbr. 35 chpts. to books, 175 abstracts and 245 articles to profl. jours. With U.S. Army, 1954-56. Recipient Rsch. award Beecham Pharm., 1986, 87, Edwards award Am. Soc. for Microbiology southeastern br., 1990, Feeley award, 1992, Disting. Svc. award Wildlife Disease Assn., 1992, Sneiszko award Fish Health Am. Fisheries Soc., 1995. Fellow Am. Acad. Microbiology (specialist med. microbiology); mem. Am. Soc. Clin. Pathology (med. technologist), Am. Coll. Vet. Microbiology (hon. diplomate), Am. Vet. Epidemiology Soc. (hon. diplomate). Office: Dept Med Microbiology U Ga Athens GA 30602 Office Phone: 706-865-0621. E-mail: emshotts@alltel.net.

SHOTWELL, MALCOLM GREEN, retired minister; b. Brookneal, Va., Aug. 14, 1932; s. John Henry and Ada Mildred (Puckett) S.; m. LaVerne Brown, June 19, 1954; children: Donna (dec.), Paula. BA in Sociology, U. Richmond, 1954; MDiv, Colgate Rochester Div. Sch., 1957; D Ministry, Ea. Bapt. Theol. Sem., 1990; DD (hon.), Judson Coll., 1990. Ordained to ministry Am. Bapt. Ch. in U.S.A., 1957. Student asst. Greece Bapt. Ch., Rochester, N.Y., 1954-57; pastor 1st Bapt. Ch., Cuba, N.Y., 1957-62, sr. pastor Galesburg, Ill., 1962-71, Olean, N.Y., 1971-81; area minister Am. Bapt. Chs. of Pa. and Del., 1981-90; regional exec. minister Am. Bapt. Chs. of Great Rivers Region, Ill. and Mo., 1990-96; interim pastor First Bapt. Ch., Jacksonville, Ill., 2002, First Bapt. Ch., Galesburg, Ill., 2003. Mem. Midwest Commn. on Ministry Am. Bapt. Chs. U.S.A., 1990—96, mem. task force for So. Bapt. Am. Bapt. Chs. Relationships, 1990—96; cons. for ch. growth and planning. Author: Creative Programs for the Church Year, 1986, Renewing the Baptist Principle of Associations, 1990; contbg. writer Baptists in the Balance, 1997; rschr., writer, performer: (dramatic monologue) Our Neighbors, the Lincolns: A Clergyman Remembers, 1999—. Trustee No. Bapt. Theol. Sem., Lombard, Ill., 1993-96; mem. gen. exec. coun., 1990-96, regional exec. ministers coun., 1990-96; trustee Judson Coll., 1990-2003, trustee emeritus, 2003-, chmn., 1997-2000, chmn. presdl. search com., 1997-98; bd. dirs. Ctrl. Bapt. Theol. Sem., Kansas City, Kans., 1990-96, Old State Capitol Found.; sec. bd. dirs. Shurtleff Fund, Springfield, Ill., 1990-96; tchr., libr. Ctrl. Bapt. Ch., Springfield, 1997—; mem. Hist. Commn. Am. Bapts. Ill. and Mo., 1998-2002; retreat leader in stress mgmt., 1985—; conf., spkr., pulpit supply preacher Bapt. Ch.; mentor ILCS Elem. Sch., Old State Capital Reenactment of Lincoln-Douglas Debates, 1999-2001, 03—; tour guide Old State Capital, Springfield, 2003—. Walter Pope Binns fellow William Jewell Coll., 1995. Mem. Ministers Coun. Ill. and Mo., Coun. Ret. Execs., Abraham Lincoln Assn., Am. Bapt. Men of Ill. and Mo. (v.p., coord. disaster relief ministries).

SHOTWELL, SHEILA MURRAY, medical/surgical nurse; b. Alamance County, Dec. 27, 1963; d. Homer Banks and Betty Jane (Robertson) Murray; m. Tony Allen Shotwell, July 30, 1988; children: Brent Allen, Emily Beth. Diploma, Watt's Sch. Nursing, 1985. RN N.C., cert. case mgmt. . Staff nurse Durham (N.C.) County Gen. Hosp., 1985-91; home health nurse Home Care Providers, Burlington, N.C., 1992-98; utilization rev. case mgr. Jefferson Pilot Fin., Greensboro, N.C., 1998; disease mgr. Accordant Health Svcs., Greensboro, N.C., 1999—. Mem. Watt's Alumni Assn. Office: 4900 Koger Blvd Ste 300 Greensboro NC 27407-2710 E-mail: sshotwel@accordant.net.

SHOUN, ELLEN LLEWELLYN, retired secondary school educator; b. Germantown, Pa., Sept. 8, 1925; d. William Thomas and Ella (Hall) Llewellyn; m. Glenn Harte Shoun, June 25, 1949; children: Mary Deborah, Paul L., Eleanor C., Peter G., Elizabeth A. AB in Chemistry, Oberlin Coll., 1947; MA in Sci. Edn., Western Mich. U., 1972. Cert. libr. (ltd. profl.) Mich., secondary sch. tchr. Mich. Jr. chemist Am. Cyanamid, Stamford, Conn., 1947-49; Charles M. Hall Chem. instr. Oberlin (Ohio) Coll., 1949-51; br. libr. Bronson (Mich.) Pub. Libr., 1966-67; math. and sci. tchr. Bronson H.S., 1967-79; crew leader 1980 U.S. Census, Branch County, Mich., 1980; bus. mgr. Dr. C.F. Cole's Dental Office, Sturgis, Mich., 1982; reference aide Br. Dist. Libr., Coldwater, Mich., 1982-99; ret., 1999. Founder (with others) Bronson H.S. Cmty. Recycling Group, 1972—79. Trustee Bronson Pub. Libr., 1968—82, Housing Commn., 1975—, Bronson Cmty. Found., 2003—; instr. CPR Cmty. health Ctr., Coldwater, Mich., 1978—80; cmty. chorus Cmty. Found., 1987—; chair refugee family com. Bronson United Meth. Ch., 1974—82, ch. choir, 1967—, sec. adminstrv. bd., 1987—, chair adminstrv. bd., 1984—86; bd. dirs., treas., mgr. Food Pantry, 5 Ch. Coop., Bronson, 1993—. Named Hon. Grand Marshal, Polish Festival Parade, Bronson, 2002; recipient Cmty. Vol. of Yr. award, Gleaner Life Ins. Soc., 2001. Mem.: Phi Beta Kappa. Democrat. Avocations: photography, knitting, Scrabble.

SHOUP, ANDREW JAMES, JR., retired oil company executive; b. Monroe, La., Mar. 26, 1935; s. Andrew James Sr. and Ruth (Landis) S.; m. Sue Cowles, Sept. 12, 1959 (dec. May 1998); children: Catherine Shoup Collins, Andrew James III; m. Julia Conger Galloway, May 6, 2000. BS in Petroleum Engring., La. State U., 1957; M in Indsl. Adminstrn., Yale U., 1959. Registered engr., Tex. Prodn. engr. Continental Oil Co., Houston, 1959-65; v.p. DeGolyer and MacNaughton, Dallas, 1965-74; chmn., CEO Sabine Corp., Dallas, 1974-89; pres. Pacific Enterprises Oil Co. U.S.A, Dallas, 1989-90; pres., CEO The Wiser Oil Co., Dallas, 1991-2000; ret., 2000. 2nd lt. U.S. Army, 1959-60. Mem. Am. Petroleum Inst., Ind. Prodrs. Assn. Am., Soc. Petroleum Engrs. of AIME, Dallas Petroleum Club, Dallas Country Club. Avocations: skiing, jogging, tennis.

SHOUP, CHARLES SAMUEL, JR., chemicals and materials executive; b. Nashville, Dec. 10, 1935; s. Charles Samuel and Leola Ruth (Turner) S.; m. Frances Carolyn DiCarlo, June 7, 1958 (dec. Apr. 1999); children: Mark Steven, Elizabeth Ann Shoup Kehoe, Margaret Carol Shoup Meyer; m. Sara Jo Denkmann, May 5, 2001. AB, Princeton U., 1957; MS, U. Tenn., 1961, PhD, 1962. Rsch. chemist Oak Ridge (Tenn.) Natl. Lab., 1962-67; mgr. special projects Union Carbide Corp., N.Y.C., 1967-68; mgr. planning and controls Bell and Howell Co., Lincolnwood, Ill., 1968; v.p. Bell and Howell Sch. Inc., Chgo., 1968-69; mgr. tech. planning Cabot Corp., Boston and Cambridge, Mass., 1969-70, dir. corp. rsch., Mass., 1970-73, gen. mgr. E-A-R div., 1973-87, v.p., Indpls., 1984-87; pres. Alphaflex Ind. Inc., Indpls, 1987-88, bd. dirs., 1988, Cemkote Corp., Indpls., 1988-91. Chmn. bd. dirs. Blasterz Corp., Carmel, Ind., 1992-2001; mem. adv. bd. Technalysis, Inc., Indpls., 1996-99; bd. dirs. Exec. Svc. Corps, Indpls., 1993—2004, mem. exec. com., 1994-2003, vice chmn., sec., 1997-99, chmn. bd. dirs., 2001-03; mem. bd. visitors Coll. Arts and Scis., U. Tenn., Knoxville, 1994—; bd. dirs Nat. Exec. Svc. Corps, 2001-04. Contbr. articles to profl. jours. Treas. Oak Ridge Arts Ctr., 1965-67; pres. Sherborn Edn. Found., 1974-76; chmn. Met. Div. United Way, 1982; bd. trustees, Ind. Safety Equipment Assn. 1978-81. Fellow Am. Inst. Chemists; mem. AAAS, Am. Chem. Soc., Noise Control Products and Materials Assn. (trustee 1977-87, pres. 1982-84), Sigma Xi. Presbyterian. Home: 13045 Abraham Run Carmel IN 46033-8618

SHOUP, MICHAEL C. newspaper reporter, editor; b. Ringtown, Pa., July 17, 1940; s. Daniel George and Marie E (Fisher) S.; m. Mary Ellen Trimble, Jan. 2, 1965 (div. 1984); children: Rachael, Timothy; m. Mary Jo Crowley, July 23, 1988; stepchildren: David, Benjamin. BA, Moravian Coll., 1965; MS, Columbia U., 1966. Russian linguist intelligence svc. USAF, 1957-61; reporter, editor Phila. Bull., 1967-71; night city editor Phila. Inquirer, 1973, day city editor, 1974, mng. editor Phila. Inquirer Mag., 1975-79, travel editor, columnist, 1980-96; travel editor The Star-Ledger, Newark, 1996-97; free-lance journalist, 1998—. Travel columnist for Knight-Ridder newspapers, 1980-96. Avocations: bicycling, gardening. Office: PO Box 88 Millville PA 17846-0088

SHOURIE, RAJATH, venture capitalist, consultant; b. Bombay, Jan. 30, 1974; s. Deepak and Jyotsna Shourie; m. Moira G. Mayer, Apr. 17, 1998. BA, Harvard U., 1995, MBA, 2000. Bus. analyst McKinsey & Co., N.Y.C., 1995—97, assoc. Bombay, 1997—98, Goldman, Sachs & Co., N.Y.C., 2000—02; asst. v.p. Oaktree Capital Mgmt., L.A., 2002—. Scholar, Harvard U., 1991—95; John Harvard scholar, 1991, 1992, Richard Perkins Parker scholar, 1994, Baker scholar, Harvard Bus. Sch., 2000, Loeb scholar in fin., 2000. Office: Oaktree Capital Mgmt LLC 333 S Grand Ave 28th Floor Los Angeles CA 90071 Home: 13700 Marina Pointe Dr Unit 605 Marina Del Rey CA 90292-9260 Personal E-mail: rshourie@mba2000.hbs.edu. E-mail: rshourie@oaktreecap.com.

SHOWALTER, BUCK (WILLIAM NATHANIEL SHOWALTER III), major league baseball team manager; b. DeFuniak Springs, Fla., May 23, 1956; Student, Chipola Jr. Coll., Fla., Miss. State U. Player various minor league teams N.Y. Yankee orgn., 1977-83, minor league coach, 1984, minor league mgr., 1985-89; coach N.Y. Yankees, 1989—92, mgr., 1992-95, Ariz. Diamondbacks, 1998—2000, Texas Rangers, 2002—. Named N.Y.-Pa. League Mgr. of Yr., 1985, Eastern League Mgr. of Yr., 1989, Am. League Mgr. of Yr., 1994. Office: Texas Rangers 1000 Ballpark Way #400 Arlington TX 76011

SHOWALTER, DAVID SCOTT, accounting executive; b. Harrisonburg, Va., May 23, 1953; s. Harold Marvin and Martha (Myers) Showalter; m. Elizabeth Allison, June 1, 1974; children: Braxton, Allison, Mason. AS, Ferrum Coll., 1973; BSBA, U. Richmond, 1975. CPA Ill., 1994, Mo., 1997, Wis., 1995, Ind., 1988, NJ, 2003; cert. Gov. Fin. Mgr. 1994. Asst. to nat. dir. KPMG, N.Y.C., 1981-84, asst. to vice-chmn., 1986-88, ptnr., 1986—, area ptnr. in charge Indpls., 1993-96; nat. industry dir. state, local govts., Chgo., 1996-98; nat. mng. ptnr. Assurance & Adv. Svcs. Ctr., Montvale, NJ, 1998—2002, industry sector leader pub. sector, 2002—. Vis. prof. U. Ill.; vis. scholar Ind. U.; bd. dirs. KPMG Found., N.Y.C., co-founder Audit Com. Inst., co-founder Assurance Rsch. Inst.; spkr. in field. Editor: (newsletter) Govt Acct and Auditing Update. Pres Indianapolis Youth Hockey Asn, 1990—93; pres coun Boy Scouts Am, St Charles, Ill., 1995—97, chmn bd dirs, 1997—98, bd dirs, 1998—; mem. U.S. C. of C. Homeland Security Task Force; bd dirs Greater Indianapolis Rep Fin Comt, 1990—94. Named Ky Col, State of Ky, 1986, Sagamore of Wabash for Serv to State of Ind, 1990, D Scott Showalter Day named in his honor, City of Indianapolis, 1994; named one of Top 100 Most Influential in Acctg., Acctg. Today, 2001; recipient Silver Beaver Award, Boy Scouts Am, 1994, Dist Eagle Scout Award, 1998. Mem.: AICPA (mem. com.), Assn. Sch. Bus. Ofcls., Ill. CPA Soc., NJ CPA Soc., Am. Acctg. Assn (v.p. practice, auditing sect.), Govt. Fin. Officers Assn. (mem. com.). Presbyterian. Avocations: camping, jogging, backpacking, stamps. Home: 14 Forest Ridge Rd Upper Saddle River NJ 07458 Office: KPMG LLP 3 Chestnut Ridge Rd Montvale NJ 07645-1842 Office Phone: 201-505-5500. E-mail: dsshowalter@kpmg.com.

SHOWALTER, ELAINE, humanities educator; b. Cambridge, Mass., Jan. 21, 1941; d. Paul and Violet (Rottenberg) Cottler; m. English Showalter, June 8, 1963; children: Vinca, Michael. BA, Bryn Mawr Coll., 1962; MA, Brandeis U., 1964; PhD in English, U. Calif., Davis, 1970; LittD (hon.), Rutgers U., 2001. Teaching asst. English U. Calif., 1964-66, from instr. to assoc. prof., 1967-78; prof. English Rutgers U., from 1978, Princeton (N.J.) U., 1984—2003; Avalon Found. prof. humanities Princeton (N.J.) U., 1987—, prof. emeritus, 2003—. Vis. prof. English and women's studies U. Del., 1976-77; vis. prof. Sch. Criticism and Theory, Dartmouth Coll., 1986; prof. Salzburg (Austria) Seminars, 1988; Clarendon lectr. Oxford (Eng.) U., 1989; vis. scholar Phi Beta Kappa, 1993-94; numerous radio and TV appearances. Author: A Literature of Their Own, 1977, The Female Malady, 1985, Sexual Anarchy, 1990, Sister's Choice, 1991, Hystories, 1997, Inventing Herself, 2001, Teaching LIterature, 2002; co-author: Hysteria Beyond Freud, 1993; editor: These Modern Women, 1978, The New Feminist Criticism, 1985, Alternative Alcott, 1987, Speaking of Gender, 1989, Modern American Women Writers, 1991, Daughters of Decadence, 1993, Scribbling Women, 1997; also articles and revs. Recipient Howard Behrman humanities award Princeton U., 1989; faculty rsch. coun. fellow Rutgers U., 1972-73, Guggenheim fellow, 1977-78, Rockefeller humanities fellow, 1981-82, fellow NEH, 1988-89; Cotsen fellow Princeton U., 1998-2001; Mellon fellow, 2003—; Huntington fellow, 2004—. Mem. MLA (v.p. 1996-97, pres. 1998). Office: Princeton U Dept Of English Princeton NJ 08544-0001

SHOWALTER, ENGLISH, JR., French language educator; b. Roanoke, Va., May 14, 1935; m. 1963; 2 children. BA, Yale U., 1957, PhD in French, 1964. Asst. prof. French Haverford Coll., 1961-64, U. Calif.-Davis, 1964-66, Princeton U., N.J., 1966-74; assoc. prof. Rutgers U., Camden, N.J., 1974-78, prof., 1978-83, prof. II, 1985-2001, emeritus, 2001—; dir. MLA, N.Y.C., 1983-85. Author: The Evolution of the French Novel, 1641-1782, 1972, Voltaire et ses Amis, D'apres la Correspondance de Mme De Graffigny, 1975, Rousseau and Mme De Graffigny, 1978, Exiles and Strangers: A Reading of Camus's Exile and the Kingdom, 1984, Humanity and the Absurd: Camus' The Stranger, 1989, My Night at Maud's, 1993. Fellow NEH, 1977-78; Guggenheim fellow, 1982-83 Mem. MLA, Am. Assn. Tchrs. French, Am. Soc. 18th Century Studies, French Soc. 18th Century Studies Office: Rutgers U French Dept Camden NJ 08102 Home: 4620 N Park Ave Apt 405E Chevy Chase MD 20815-4579

SHOWALTER, JUDY, state representative; b. Dallas, Aug. 4, 1943; 4 children. BA in Nursing, BS in Nursing, Southwestern Coll. RN. Mem. Kans. Ho. of Reps., 1997—. Mem. Winfield City Commn., 1987—96; past chair Strother Field Indsl. Commn.; mayor Winfield, 1989—96; bd. dirs. Kans. League Mcpls. Named Woman of Yr., Bus. Profl. Women's Assn., 1989. Democrat. Presbyterian. Office: 273-W State Capitol 300 SW 10th Ave Topeka KS 66612 Home: 1917 Simpson Winfield KS 67156

SHOWALTER, MARILYN GRACE, state agency administrator; AB, Harvard U., 1972, JD, 1975. Bar: Wash. 1975. Dep. pros. atty. King County, Wash., 1975—81, counsel to gov., 1981—83; pvt. practice, 1985—89; counsel house appropriations com. Wash. State House of Reps., 1989—92, dep. chief clk., house counsel, 1992—93, chief clk., 1994—95, adv. Gov. Gary Locke, 1999, chairwoman, 1999—. Democrat. Office: Washington UTC PO Box 47250 Olympia WA 98504-7250 also: Washington UTC 1300 S Evergreen Park Dr SW Olympia WA 98504-7250 Office Phone: 360-664-1173. Business E-Mail: mshowalter@wutc.wa.gov.

SHOWALTER, SHIRLEY H. academic administrator; b. July 30, 1948; BA cum laude in English, Ea. Mennonite U., Harrisonburg, Va., 1970; MA in Am. civilization, U. Tex., Austin, 1974, PhD in Am. civilization, 1981. Tchr. English Harrisonburg (Va.) H.S, 1970—72; tchg. asst. English and Am. Studies depts. U. Tex., Austin, 1973—75, asst. instr. Am. Studies dept., 1976; dir. continuing edn. Goshen Coll., Ind., 1979—82, project dir. Title II tech. and liberal arts devel. grant, 1982—85, project dir. Consortium Advancemet of Pvt. Higher Edn. grant, 1985—86, asst. to prof. English, 1967—, pres., 1997—. Coord. Humanities program Harrisonburg (Va.) H.S., 1970—72; co-dir. Study-Svc. Term in Haiti Goshen Coll., 1981—82; rsch. asst. Consortium Advancement of Pvt. Higher Edn., Washington, 1986—87, interim v.p., 1987; chair English dept. Goshen Coll., 1990—93; sr. fellow Lilly Fellows program in Humanities and Arts Valparaiso U., Ind., 1993—94; co-dir. Study-Svc. Term in Ivory Coast Goshen Coll., 1993; lectr. and spkr. in humanities. Contbr. chapters to books, articles to profl. jours. Bd. mem. South Bend Symphony Assn.; mem. blue ribbon adv. group Boys and Girls Club; vice chair and mem. Hist. Com. of Mennonite Ch., 1984—88; co-sponsor Kid's Club No. Va. Mennonite Ch., 1987—88; chair curriculum com. Sojourner's Sunday Sch. class Coll. Mennonite Ch., 1987—88, mem. constn. revision com., 1988—92, tchr. H.S. age class, 1988—91, mem. worship commn., 1994—96; bd. mem. Coun. Christian Coll. and U., 2000—, Ind. Colls. of Ind., 1999—, Lantz Ctr. Christian Vocations, Indpls., 1998—; dir. Coun. Ind. Colls., 1999—; bd. dir. Mennonite Mutual Aid Trust; dir. Elkhart County Cmty. Found. Recipient Tchg. Excellence and Campus Leadership award, Sears Roebuck Found., 1990, Faculty Rsch., Goshen Coll., 1990, Knight Presdl. Leadership award, John S. and James L. Knight Found., 1999, 1999; fellow, George H. Gallup Rsch. Inst., 1999—2000, Coolidge Fellow, Yale U., Assn. Religion in Intellectual Life, 1996; grantee Faculty Rsch., Goshen Coll., 1977, 1982, Summer Stipend, Lilly Endowment, 1991. Mem.: AAUW, Am. Studies Assn., Am. Assn. Higher Edn. (Goshen Coll. rep. Forum on Exemplary Tchg. 1992, bd. dir. 1992—96), No. Ind. Partnership for the Arts, Willa Cather Pioneer Mem., Ind. Hist. Soc., Ellen Glasgow Soc., Blue Sky Assoc. Office: VP Programs Fetzer Inst 9292 West KL Ave Kalamazoo MI 49004-9398

SHOWELL, JEFFREY ADAMS, music educator, academic administrator, musician; s. John Sheldon and Florence Adams Showell; m. Denise Barbara Tritchel; children: David Christopher, Douglas Armitage Tritchel. German maj. (no degree), Stanford U., 1970—72; BM, Eastman Sch. of Music, 1972—74, M, 1974—76; DMA, Yale U., 1976—78. Peace Officer: Ariz. Peace Officers Standards Commn. 1982. Instr. Coll. of St. Benedict/St. Johns U., St. Joseph, Minn., 1978—80; prof. U. of Ariz., 1980—91, asst. dir., sch. of music, 1991—99; chair, music dept. U. of Ctrl. Ark., 1999—2004; dir. James Madison U., Sch. of Music, 2004—. Prin. violist Tucson Symphony Orch., 1982—90. Office: U of Ctrl Arkansas 201 Donaghey Conway AR 72035 E-mail: jshowell@mail.uca.edu.

SHOWEN JR. DONALD EUGENE, music educator; b. Charles Town, W.Va., Oct. 22, 1974; s. Donald Eugene and Carrie Alberta Showen; m. Tara Jenea Penick-Showen, Dec. 15, 2001. BA, Shepherd Coll., Shepherdstown, 1997. Coord. percussion studies Hancock H.S., Hancock, Md., 1993—94, Williamsport H.S., Williamsport, Md., 1994—98; asst. band dir. Jefferson H.S., Shenandoah Junction, W.Va., 1998—99; grad. asst. U. of Fla. Sch. of Music, Gainesville, Fla., 1999—2000; dir. bands Jefferson H.S., Shenandoah Junction, W.Va., 2000—. Bd. directors New Hopewell Dance Studio, Shenandoah Junction, W.Va., 2001—. Mem.: Music Educators Nat. Conf., Phi Mu Alpha Sinfonia Frat. (pres. 1993—95). D-Liberal. Achievements include Jefferson High Jazz band won National Championship in 1999 and was named best jazz band in the state in 1999, 2001 and 2002; Symphonic and jazz bands received first place in a national competition in Orlando, Florida. Avocations: golf, golf, golf. Office: Jefferson High School Band R1 1 Box 83 Shenandoah Junction WV 25442

SHOWER, ROBERT WESLEY, financial executive; b. Harvey, Ill., Sept. 5, 1937; s. Glenn Wesley and Chrissie Irene (Ford) S.; m. Sandra Marie Stough, June 27, 1959; children: David Wesley, Lynece Marie. BS, U. Tulsa, 1960; P.MD, Harvard Business Sch., 1972. Sr. auditor Arthur Andersen & Co., Tulsa, 1960-64; with The Williams Cos., Tulsa, 1964-86, asst. v.p., 1968-69, v.p. adminstrn., 1969-71, v.p., treas., 1971, v.p. fin., 1971-73, sr. v.p. fin., 1973-77, exec. v.p. fin. and adminstrn., dir., 1977-86; mng. dir. Shearson, Lehman, Hutton, Dallas, 1986-90; v.p. fin. Ameriserv Food Co., Dallas, 1990-91; sr. v.p. fin., CFO Seagull Energy Co., Houston, 1992-94, exec. v.p., CFO, 1994-96. Mem. Okla. Soc. CPAs, Lambda Chi Alpha, Delta Sigma Pi. Home: 2922 S Lakeview Dr Cedar Hill TX 75104-8262 Fax: (972) 291-4131. E-mail: rshower@attglobal.net.

SHOWERY, CHARLES GEORGE, JR., financial services company executive, consultant; b. El Paso, Tex., Sept. 28, 1951; s. Charles George and Mildred Marie (Romeu) S.; 1 child, Raelene Marie. Degree in med. microbiology, U. Tex., El Paso, 1976. Lab. mgr. Glass-Columbia Med., Conn., 1976-82; agt. Transamerica Life Cos., L.A., 1982-84; pres. Chico Enterprises, El Paso, 1984—. Instr. Life Underwriters Tng. Coun., L.A., 1982. Author: It's a Great Career But, 1974, (booklet) M.D. vs. M.T., 1974. Mem. Nat. Assn. Life Underwriters. Democrat. Roman Catholic.

SHOWS, RONNIE, former congressman; b. Moselle, Miss., Jan. 26, 1947; m. Johnnie Ruth, 1971; 4 children. BS, U. So. Miss., 1971. Tchr., coach various Jefferson County schs.; cir. ct. clk. Jefferson County, 1976-80; state senator, 1980-88; mem. So. Dist. Hwy. Commn., 1988—99, U.S. Congress from 4th Miss. dist., 1999—2003. Mem. transp. and infrastructure com., veterans affairs. com. In 1999 succeeded 5-term Rep. Mike Parker (Dem. turned Rep.); defeated Delbert Hosemann (R) for the seat in Congress. Democrat.

SHRADER, ALAN ROSS, editor, writer; s. Ross E. and Barbara W. Shrader; m. Patricia S. Shaw, Apr. 18, 1975; 1 child, Jessica K. AB, Antioch Coll., Yellow Springs, Ohio, 1967; PhD, U. of Calif., Berkeley, 1975. Lectr. Sci. U. of Malaysia, Penang, Malaysia, 1975—78; writer Oakland, Calif., 1979—83; mktg. dir. Jossey-Bass Pubs., San Francisco, 1983—88, sr. editor, 1989—94, exec. editor, 1994—99; dir. of acquisitions Consulting Psychology Press, Palo Alto, Calif., 1999—2001; mng. editor Leader to Leader, N.Y.C., 2002—. Prin. Shrader Pub. Svcs., Moraga, Calif., 2001—. Author: (novel) Satan's Chance; editor: (book) Be, Know, Do: Leadership the Army Way, Leader of the Future. Avocations: travel, political writing, swimming.

SHRADER, CHARLES REGINALD, historian; b. Nashville, July 3, 1943; s. Reginald Woodrow and Freda Olene (Presley) S.; m. Carole Anne Analore, Aug. 17, 1963; children: Peter Reginald, Sheila Lynne Shrader Bixby. BA cum laude, Vanderbilt U., 1964; MA History, Columbia U., 1970, M Phil, 1974, PhD History, 1976; Grad., U.S. Army Command/Gen. Staff, Coll., 1978, U.S. Army War Coll., 1982, NATO Def. Coll., 1984. Commd. 2d lt. U.S. Army, 1964, advanced through grades to lt. col., ret., 1987; asst. prof. history U.S. Mil. Acad., 1971-74; instr. European Divsn. U. Md., Pirmasens and Landstuhl, Germany, 1974-77; instr. U.S. Army Command and Gen. Staff Coll., 1977-80, U.S. Army War Coll., 1980-84; mem. staff NATO Def. Coll., Rome, 1984-85; independent historian, 1987—; exec. dir. Soc. for Mil. History, Carlisle, Pa., 1992-2000. Pres. Nat. Coalition Ind. Scholars, 2000-2002; adj. instr. Elizabethtown Coll., 1988-89, Penn State U.-Harrisburg, 1988-90; lectr. various Army svc. schs., CIA, U. Kans., U. Victoria/B.C., NATO Def. Coll. Mem. Carlisle

Mcpl. Authority, 1993—2003. Mem. Army and Navy Club, Phi Kappa Psi, Phi Beta Kappa. Roman Catholic. Home and Office: 910 Forbes Rd Carlisle PA 17013-1721 Office Phone: 717-249-5625. E-mail: heriger@aol.com.

SHRADER, DOUGLAS WALL, JR., philosophy educator; b. Grundy, Va., May 22, 1953; s. Douglas Wall and Audrey Anne (Looney) S.; m. Barbara Frances Donahoe, June 15, 1975; children: Callie Hannah, Sterling Douglas. BA, Va. Polytech. Inst., 1974; MA, U. Ill., Chgo., 1975, PhD, 1979. Asst. to dean grad. studies U. Ill., Chgo., 1974-79; instr. philosophy U. Wis., Parkside, 1979; asst. prof. philosophy SUNY, Oneonta, 1979-85, assoc. prof. philosophy, 1985-92, prof. philosophy, 1992-99, chair dept. philosophy, 1988-91, 93—, dean humanities and fine arts, 1991-93, disting. teaching prof. philosophy, 1999—. Cons. in field. Author: Pathways to Philosophy, 1996; editor: Seeds of Wisdom, 1997, Language, Ethics and Ontology, 1998, The Fractal Self, 2000, Ethics, Theory and Practice, 1996, Children of Athena, 1999, Philosophy and the Public Realm, 2001, Thinking Outside the Box, 2002, Philosophical Dreams, 2003, Self and Society, 2004; mem. editl. bd., editor-in-chief Oneonta Philosophy Studies, 1991—, Ashgate World Philosophies Series, 1999—; mem. editl. bd. Ednl. Change, 1995—, Eidos: Studies in Ancient and Medieval Philosophy, 1991—, East-West Connections, 2000—. Bd. dirs. Catskill Area Hospice, Oneonta, 1985-88; troop treas. Boy Scouts Am., Oneonta, 1994-98, cubmaster, 1991-94; judge Odyssey of the Mind, Oneonta, 1994—. Rsch. grantee W.B. Ford Found., 1995, 98, 99, 2000, Henry Luce Found., 1999, 2002 Chinese Minister of Edn., 2002; summer inst. fellow NEH, 1980, 85, 89, 95, 98; recipient Commendation for Acad. Excellence, SUNY-Oneonta Alumni Assn., 1995, Chancellor's award Excellence in Teaching, 1991 Mem. Soc. for Ancient Greek Philosophy, exec bd. mem., Soc. Comparative Study Civilizations, East-West Ctr. Assoc., N.Y. State Founds. Edn. Assn. Avocations: photography, music, construction, classic cars. Office: SUNY-Oneonta Ravine Pkwy Oneonta NY 13820-3414 Office Phone: 607-436-2456. E-mail: Shradedw@Oneonta.edu.

SHRADER, RALPH W. management consultant; BS in Engring., U. Pa.; MSEE, PhD in Elec. Engring., U. Ill. Chmn. Booz Allen & Hamilton, Mc Lean, Va., chmn., CEO, 1999—. Former chmn. bd. Armed Forces Comms. and Electronics Assn. Mem. adv. coun. Character Edn. Partnership; bd. dirs. Wolf Trap Found. Nat. Park for Performing Arts, Abilities, Inc. Office: Booz Allen & Hamilton Inc 8283 Greensboro Dr Mc Lean VA 22102

SHRADER, WILLIAM WHITNEY, radar consulting scientist; b. Foochow, China, Oct. 17, 1930; came to U.S., 1932; s. Ralph Raymond and Elizabeth Talmadge (Hand) S.; m. Natalie Lucinda Hutchinson, July 21, 1984. BSEE, U. Mass., 1953; MSEE, Northeastern U., 1961. Rsch. engr. Boeing Airplane Co., Seattle, 1953-56; cons. scientist, tech. dir. numerous radar systems developed Raytheon Co., Wayland, Mass., 1956-1994; pvt. practice radar cons. Shrader Assocs. Inc., Stow, Mass., 1994—. Author: (with others) Radar Handbook, 1970, 2d edit., 1990; contbr. articles to profl. jours.; holder 10 U.S. patents, numerous fgn. patents. Fellow IEEE. Avocation: sports car rallying. Home and Office: 144 Harvard Rd Stow MA 01775-1070 E-mail: shrader@prodigy.net.

SHRAUNER, BARBARA WAYNE ABRAHAM, electrical engineer, educator; b. Morristown, N.J., June 21, 1934; d. Leonard Gladstone and Ruth Elizabeth (Thrasher) Abraham; m. James Ely Shrauner, 1965; children: Elizabeth Ann, Jay Arthur. BA cum laude, U. Colo., 1956; AM, Harvard U., 1957, PhD, 1962. Postdoctoral researcher U. Libre de Bruxelles, Brussels, 1962-64; postdoctoral researcher NASA-Ames Rsch. Ctr., Moffett Field, Calif., 1964-65; asst. prof. Washington U., St. Louis, 1966-69, assoc. prof., 1969-77, prof., 1977—2003, sr. prof., 2003—. Sabbatical Los Alamos (N.Mex.) Sci. Lab., 1975-76, Lawrence Berkeley Lab., Berkeley, Calif., 1985-86; cons. Los Alamos Nat. Lab., 1979, 84, NASA, Washington, 1980, Naval Surface Weapons Lab., Silver Spring, Md., 1984. Contbr. articles on transport in semiconductors, hidden symmetries of differential equations, plasma physics to profl. jours. Fellow Am. Phys. Soc. (sr. divsn. plasma physics, exec. com. 1980-82, 96-98); mem. IEEE (sr.; sr. exec. com. of standing tech. com. on plasma sci. and applications 1996-98), AAUP (local sec.-treas. 1980-82), Am. Geophys. Union, Univ. Fusion Assn., Phi Beta Kappa, Sigma Xi, Eta Kappa Nu, Sigma Pi Sigma. Home: 7452 Stratford Ave Saint Louis MO 63130-4044 Office: Washington U 1 Brookings Dr Dept Elec Saint Louis MO 63130-4899 Office Phone: 314-935-6134. Business E-Mail: bas@ee.wustl.edu.

SHRECKHISE, ROBERT LYNN, minister, theology studies educator; s. Oliver Eugene Shreckhise and Roseva Cottingham; m. Paula Mary Ecker, June 28, 1969; children: Joseph Paul, Jeremy Andrew, Rachel Mara, Philip Joel. BA summa cum laude, Trinity Bible Coll., 1979; MDiv summa cum laude, Assemblies of God Theol. Sem., 1995; STM, Concordia Sem. Grad. Sch., 1998; postgrad., 2004. Cert. pastoral minister Colloquy Com., Luth. Ch. Mo. Synod, 1998. Min. of evangelism and visitation First Assembly of God, Elgin, Ill., 1979—80; pastor Athelstane (Wis.) Assembly of God, 1981—92; rschr. Concordia Hist. Inst., Saint Louis, 1995—2000; pastoral asst. Trinity Luth. Ch., Saint Charles, Mo., 2000—04. Guest lectr. Concordia Sem., St. Louis, 2001—. Composer: (songs) Fulness of Joy; co-author: (catechesis program) Here We Stand Together. Mem. adv. com. for sex edn. Wausaukee (Wis.) Sch. Dist., 1986—86. Petty officer USN, 1968—74. Grantee William Scheele fellowship Fund, Concordia Sem. Grad. Sch., 1999, 2000. Lutheran. Office: Exegetical Dept Concordia Seminary 801 De Mun Ave Saint Louis MO 63105

SHREEVE, JEAN'NE MARIE, chemist, educator; b. Deer Lodge, Mont., July 2, 1933; d. Charles William and Maryfrances (Briggerman) Shreeve. BA in Chemistry, U. Mont., 1953, DSc (hon.), 1982; MS in Analytical Chemistry, U. Minn., 1956; PhD in Inorganic Chemistry, U. Wash., 1961. From asst. prof. to assoc. prof. chemistry U. Idaho, Moscow, 1961—67, prof., 1967-73, 2000—, acting chmn. dept. chemistry, 1969-70, 1973, head dept. and prof., 1973-87, v.p. rsch. and grad. studies, prof. chemistry, 1987-99, Jean'ne M. Shreeve chemistry prof., 2004—. Mem. nat. com. Stds. Higher Edn., 1965—67, 1969—73; Lucy W. Pickett lectr. Mt. Holyoke Coll., 1976; George H. Cady lectr. U. Wash., 1993; chmn. Pres.'s Com. Medal Sci., 2003—. Mem. editl. bd. Jour. Fluorine Chemistry, 1970—, Jour. Heteroatom Chemistry, 1988—95, Accounts Chem. Rsch., 1973—75, Inorganic Synthesis, 1976—; contbr. articles to sci. jours. Mem. bd. govs. Argonne (Ill.) Nat. Lab., 1992—98. Named Hon. Alumnus, U. Idaho, 1972; named to Idaho Hall of Fame, 2001; recipient Disting. Alumni award, U. Mont., 1970, Outstanding Achievement award, U. Minn., 1975, Sr. U.S. Scientist award, Alexander Von Humboldt Found., 1978, Excellence in Tchg. award, Chem. Mfrs. Assn., 1980; NSF Postdoctoral fellow, U. Cambridge, Eng., 1967—68, U.S. Hon. Ramsay fellow, 1967—68, Alfred P. Sloan fellow, 1970—72. Mem.: AAUW (officer Moscow chpt. 1962—69), AAAS (bd. dirs. 1991—95), Idaho Acad. Sci. (Disting. Scientist 2001), Am. Chem. Soc. (bd. dirs. 1985—93, chmn. fluorine divsn. 1979—81, mem. adv. bd. Petroleum Rsch. Fund 1975—77, mem. women chemists com. 1972—77, Harry and Carol Mosher award Santa Clara Valley sect. 1992, Shirley B. Radding award Santa Clara Valley sect. 2003, Garvan medal 1972, award for creative work in fluorine chemistry 1978), Göttingen (Germany) Acad. Scis. (corr.), Phi Beta Kappa. Avocations: fishing, gardening. Office: U Idaho Dept Chemistry Moscow ID 83844-2343 Fax: 208-885-9146. Office Phone: 208-885-6215. Business E-Mail: jshreeve@kidaho.edu.

SHREM, CHARLES JOSEPH, metals corporation executive; b. Cairo, May 9, 1930; arrived in U.S., 1959; s. Joseph C. and Paula (Cadranel) S.; m. Vivian L. Chalom, Jan. 30, 1955; children: Jeff, Leslie Allen. Degree in bus. and economy, Coll. Français, Cairo, 1951. Export mgr. Stanton Ironworks U.K., Middle East, 1950-57; comml. mgr. Soc. Sovibor, Paris, 1957-59; purchasing dir. Montanore, Inc., N.Y.C., 1959-65; exec. v.p. Commonwealth Metal Corp., Englewood Cliffs, N.J., 1965-85, pres., CEO, 1985-2000, chmn., 2000—02; bus. cons. Pompton Plains, NJ, 2002—. Bd. dirs. Adult Edn., Pequannock, N.J., 1970-80; bd. govs. Nat. Grad. U., Arlington, Va., Coll. Democracy, Arlington. Mem. U.S. C. of C. (econ. coun., exec. com. U.S. Polish Coun./U.S. C. of C.). Office: 933 Rte 23 Pompton Plains NJ 07444

SHREMBEK, CAROL ROSE, claims consultant; b. Cleve., Oct. 27, 1957; d. Richard and Mary Rita Elchesen; m. David Edward Shrembek; 1 child, Nicole. BA, Kent State U., 1981; diploma in nursing, MetroHealth Sch. Nursing, Cleve., 1986. Cert. ACLS, legal nurse cons.; RN. Staff nurse Rainbow Babies and Childrens Hosp., Cleve., 1987—91, MetroHealth Med. Ctr., Cleve., 1986—87, 1991—93; asst. clin. mgr. Fairview Gen. Hosp., Fairview Park, Ohio, 1992—93; staff nurse S.W. Gen. Health Ctr., Middleburg Heights, 1993—96, StarMed Staffing Svcs., Independence, Ohio, 1996—98, Initial Health Care Svcs., Beachwood, Ohio, 1996—98; clin. nurse MetroHealth Med. Ctr., Cleve., 1998—2002; staff nurse MedSearch Staffing Svcs., Inc., Middleburg Heights, Ohio, 2002—04, St. John Westshore Hosp., Westlake, Ohio, 2003—; injury claim trainer State Farm, 2004—. Tchr. orientation classes Rainbow Babies and Childrens Hosp., Cleve., 1987—91, clin. preceptor, 1988—91; flight team MetroHealth Med. Ctr. Neonatal ICU, Cleve., 1991—93, clin. preceptor; workshop leader, spkr., cons. in field. Author: (novels) Cheri's Crossing, 2000, A Love Through Time, 2001. Roman Catholic. Avocations: gardening, reading, weightlifting. Personal E-mail: cshrembek@alltel.net.

SHRENSKY, DON STEVEN, accountant, consultant; b. Jersey City, N.J., Jan. 30, 1944; arrived in Israel, 1981; m. Joan L. Berman, Nov. 25, 1967; 2 children. BA, Rutgers State U., 1967; JD, Seton Hall U. Law Sch., 1971. Bar: N.J. 1972; CPA, N.Y., Israel. Ptnr. Gross, Manford & Reinschreiber, N.Y.C., 1970-81; chief acct. Mennen Medical Ltd., Rohovot, Israel, 1982-88; ptnr. Feldman Shrensky Brody & Co., Jerusalem, Israel, 1988-96; propr. Don Shrensky & Co., Jerusalem, 1997—. Speaker at conf., local groups and radio/TV. Treas. Assn. of Americans and Canadians in Israel, 1994-98, v.p., 1998-99; chmn. bd. Mercaz Harmony, 1985-95. Mem. AICPA, Inst. of CPAs in Israel, N.Y. Soc. CPAs, Assn. Ams. and Canadians in Israel, Jerusalem Rotary Club (bd. dirs., pres. 2003—), Jerusalem Rotary Found. (bd. dirs.). Office: Don Shrensky & Co PO Box 31570 Jerusalem 91001 Israel

SHREVE, ELIZABETH STEWARD, publishing executive; b. Charlottesville, Va., Feb. 19, 1970; d. Porter Gaylord Shreve Jr. and Susan Richards Shreve; m. Russell David Greiff; 1 child, Theo Oliver Greiff. BA, Kenyon Coll. Spl. asst. Corp. for Nat. Svc., Wash., DC, 1993—94; sr. pub., editor Counterpoint Books, Wash., 1995—96; publicity mgr. Dutton Publ., N.Y.C., 1996—97, Vintage Books, N.Y.C., 1997; v.p., dir. publicity Henry Holt & Co., N.Y.C., 1997—. Bd. dir. Publishers Publicity Assn., N.Y.C., 1998—2003, Am. Voices, Wash., 1995—. Mem.: Women's Media Group. Democrat. Avocations: cooking, singing. Office: Henry Holt and Co 115 W 18th St New York NY 10011 Office Phone: 212-886-9273.

SHREVE, GENE RUSSELL, law educator; b. San Diego, Aug. 6, 1943; s. Ronald D. and Hazel (Shepherd) S.; m. Marguerite Russell, May 26, 1973. AB with honors, U. Okla., 1965; LLB, Harvard U., 1968, LLM, 1975. Bar: Mass. 1969, Vt. 1981. Appellate atty. and state extradition hearing examiner Office of Mass. Atty Gen., 1968-69; law clk. U.S. Dist. Ct., Dallas, 1969-70; staff and supervising atty. Boston Legal Assistance Project, 1970-73; assoc. prof. Vt. Law Sch., Royalton, 1975-81; vis. assoc. prof. George Washington U., Washington, 1981-83; assoc. prof. law N.Y. Law Sch., N.Y.C., 1983-84, prof., 1984-87; vis. prof. law Ind. U., Bloomington, 1986, prof., 1987-94, Richard S. Melvin Prof. Law, 1994—. Author: A Conflict of Laws Anthology, 1997; co-author: Understanding Civil Procedure, 2d edit., 1994; mem. editl. bd. Am. Jour. Comparative Law, 1994-2003, Jour. Legal Edn., 1998-2001; contbr. numerous articles to legal jours. Mem. Am. Law Inst., Am. Soc. for Pol. and Legal Phil., Assn. Am. Law Schs. (civil procedure sect. chair 1997, conflict of laws sect. chair 1998). Democrat. Episcopalian. Office: Ind U Sch Law Bloomington IN 47405

SHREVE, SUSAN RICHARDS, writer, educator; b. Toledo, May 2, 1939; d. Robert Kenneth and Helen (Greene) Richards; children— Porter, Elizabeth, Caleb, Kate. BA, U. Pa., 1961; MA, U. Va., 1969. Prof. English lit. George Mason U., Fairfax, Va., 1976—. Vis. prof. Columbia U., N.Y.C., 1982—, Princeton U., 1991, 92, 93. Author: (novels) A Fortunate Madness, 1974, A Woman Like That, 1977, Children of Power, 1979, Miracle Play, 1981, Dreaming of Heroes, 1984, Queen of Hearts, 1986, A Country of Strangers, 1989, Daughters of the New World, 1992, The Train Home, 1993, Skin Deep: Women & Race, 1995, The Visiting Physician, 1995; (pseudonym Annie Waters) Glimmer, 1997, Plum & Jaggers, 2000; (children's books) The Nightmares of Geranium Street, 1977, Family Secrets, 1979, Loveletters, 1979, The Masquerade, 1980, The Bad Dreams of a Good Girl, 1981, The Revolution of Mary Leary, 1982, The Flunking of Joshua T. Bates, 1984, How I Saved the World on Purpose, 1985, Lucy Forever and Miss Rosetree, Shrinks, Inc., 1985, Joshua T. Bates In Charge, 1992, The Gift of the Girl Who Couldn't Hear, 1991, Wait for Me, 1992, Amy Dunn Quits School, 1993, Lucy Forever & the Stolen Baby, 1994, The Formerly Great Alexander Family, 1995, Zoe and Columbo, 1995, Warts, 1996, A Goalie, 1996, Joshua Bates in Trouble Again, 1997, Jonah, The Whale, 1997, Ghost Cats, 1999, The End of Amanda, The Good, 2000; co-editor: How We Want to Live: Narratives on Progress, 1996, (with Porter Shreve) Outside the Law: Narratives on Justice, 1997, How We Want to Live: Narratives on Progress, 1998, Tales Out of School: Narratives on Education, 1999, Blister, 2001, Trout & Me, 2002, Under the Watson's Porch, 2003; editor: Dream Me Home Safely, 2003. Recipient Jenny Moore award George Washington U., 1978; John Simon Guggenheim award in fiction, 1980; Nat. Endowment Arts fiction award, 1982. Mem. PEN/Faulkner Found. (pres.), Phi Beta Kappa. E-mail: srshreve@aol.com.

SHREVE, THEODORE NORRIS, construction company executive; b. St. Louis, Feb. 14, 1919; s. Truxtun Benbridge adn Beulah (Dyer) S.; m. Caroline Prouty, Jan. 7, 1943; children: Sara Ann Caile, Suzanne Shreve Foster, Theo Carol. BS, U. Colo., 1942. Registered profl. engr., Colo. Sec., treas. Trautman & Shreve, Inc., Denver, 1946-68, pres., 1965-86, chmn. bd., 1984—; pres. 4030 Corp., Denver, 1984—. Bd. dirs. Colo. U. Found., 1988—; rep. Country Assembly, 1962. Served with USNR, 1942-45. Mem. Colo. Soc. Profl. Engrs., Rotary, Gyro Club, Denver Country Club, Sigma Phi Epsilon. Republican. Episcopalian. Home: 420 S Marion Pkwy Apt 1403 Denver CO 80209-2549 Office: Trautman & Shreve 4406 Race St Denver CO 80216-3818 E-mail: tshreve333@aol.com.

SHRIBMAN, DAVID MARKS, editor; b. Salem, Mass., Mar. 2, 1954; m. Cindy Skrzycki, Sept. 9, 1978; children: Elizabeth, Natalie. AB summa cum laude, Dartmouth Coll., 1976, AM, 1993; LHD, Salem State Coll., 1995. Mem. city staff and Washington bur. Buffalo Evening News, 1977-80; mem. feature and nat. staff The Washington Star, 1980-81; with Washington bur. N.Y. Times, 1981-84; congl. reporter, nat. polit. corr. The Wall St. Jour., 1984-93; chief Washington bur., asst. mng. editor The Boston Globe, 1993—2003; exec. editor, v.p. Pitts. Post-Gazette, 2003—. Bd. visitors Nelson A. Rockefeller Ctr. for Social Scis. Dartmouth Coll.; panelist Washington Week in Rev. PBS; analyst BBC radio; lectr. in field. Trustee Dartmouth Coll. James B. Reynolds scholar Jesus Coll.; recipient Pulitzer Prize for beat reporting, 1995. Mem. Phi Beta Kappa. Office: Pittsburgh Post Gazette 34 Blvd of the Allies Pittsburgh PA 15222

SHRIER, ADAM LOUIS, investment firm executive, consultant; b. Warsaw, Mar. 26, 1938; came to U.S., 1943, naturalized, 1949; s. Henry Leon and Mathilda June (Czamanska) S.; m. Diane Kesler, June 10, 1961; children: Jonathan, Lydia, Catherine, David. BS, Columbia U., 1959; MS (Whitney fellow), MIT, 1960; D.Engr. and Applied Sci. (NSF fellow), Yale U., 1965; postdoctoral visitor, U. Cambridge, Eng., 1965-66; JD, Fordham U., 1976. With Esso Research & Engring. Co., Florham Park and Linden, N.J., 1963-65, 66-72, head. environ. scis. research area, 1969-72; coordinator pollution abatement activities, tanker dept. Exxon Internat. Co., N.Y.C., 1972-74; project mgr., energy systems Exxon Enterprises Inc., N.Y.C., 1974-75, gen. mgr. solar energy projects, 1975-77, pres. solar thermal systems div., 1977-81; corp. planning cons., sec. new bus. investments Exxon Corp., N.Y.C., 1981-82; div. mgr. supply and transp. Exxon Internat. Co., N.Y.C., 1983-86, mgr. policy and planning, 1986-88; mng. dir. Splty. Tech. Assocs., Washington, 1988-97; pres. Global Devel. Opportunities, LLC, Washington, 1997—. Adj. lectr. chem. egnring. Columbia U., N.Y.C., 1967-69; industry adv. bd. Internat. Energy Agy., 1984-88, Energy and Environ. Policy Ctr., Harvard U., 1986-88, Internat. Energy Program, Johns Hopkins U., 1987-88; sr. assoc. Global Bus. Forum, 1988—, Cambridge Energy Rsch. Assocs., 1988—, Internat. Exec. Svc. Corps, 2001—; adj. prof. internat. bus. Am. U., Washington, 2000—. Contbr. articles to profl. jours. Mem. AIChE, Internat. Assn. Energy Econs., Am. Chem. Soc., U.S. Energy Assn., Middle East Inst., Acad. Internat. Bus., Cosmos Club, Sigma Xi, Tau Beta Pi, Phi Lambda Upsilon. Achievements include patents in field. Office: 4000 Cathedral Ave NW Washington DC 20016-5249 Personal E-mail: alshrier@att.net.

SHRIER, DIANE KESLER, psychiatrist, educator; b. Mar. 23, 1941; d. Benjamin Arthur and Mollie (Wortman) Kesler; m. Adam Louis Shrier, June 10, 1961; children: Jonathan Laurence, Lydia Anne, Catherine Jane, David Leopold. BS in Chemistry/Biology magna cum laude, Queen's Coll., CUNY, 1961; postgrad., Washington U. Sch. Medicine, St. Louis, 1960-61; MD, Yale U., 1964. Diplomate Am. Bd. Psychiatry and Neurology. Pediat. intern Bellevue Hosp., N.Y.C., 1964-65; psychiat. resident Albert Einstein Coll. Medicine-Bronx Mcpl. Hosp. Ctr., 1966-68, child psychiatry fellow, 1968-70; staff cons. Family Svc. and Child Guidance Ctr. of the Oranges, Maplewood, Milburn-Orange, N.J., 1970-73, cons., 1973-79; pvt. practice Montclair, N.J., 1970-92, Washington, 1994—. Cons. Cmty. Day Nursery, East Orange, NJ, 1970—79, Montclair State Coll., 1976—78; psychiat. cons. Bloomfield (N.J.) pub. schs., 1974—75; clin. instr. Albert Einstein Coll. Medicine, 1970—73; clin. asst. prof. psychiatry U. Medicine and Dentistry N.J., 1978—82, clin. assoc. prof., 1982—89, prof. clin. psychiatry, 1989—92; vice-chmn., dir. clin. psychiat. svcs. dept. psychiatry Children's Nat. Med. Ctr., 1992—94, attending staff, 1994—; prof. psychiatry and pediats. George Washington U. Med. Ctr., 1992—94, clin. prof. psychiatry, behavioral scis. and pediat., 1994—; cons. Walter Reed Med. Ctr., 1994—. Contbr. articles to med. jours. Trustee Montessori Learning Ctr., Montclair, 1973-75. Regents scholar Queen's Coll., 1961. Fellow Am. Psychiat. Assn., Acad. Child Psychiatry; mem. Tri-County Psychiat. Assn. (exec. com., rec. sec. 1977-78, 2d v.p. 1978-79, 1st v.p. 1979-80, pres. 1977-81), N.J. Psychiat. Assn. (councillor 1981-84), Am. Acad. Child and Adolescent Psychiatry (councillor at large 1992-95), Phi Beta Kappa. Home: 4000 Cathedral Ave NW Apt 317B Washington DC 20016-5267 Office: Ste 104 1616 18th St NW Washington DC 20009-2521 Office Phone: 202-667-9005. Business E-Mail: diane.shrier.med.64@aya.yale.edu.

SHRINER, THOMAS L., JR., lawyer; b. Lafayette, Ind., Dec. 15, 1947; s. Thomas L. Sr. and Margaret (Kamstra); m. Donna L. Galchick, June 5, 1971; children: Thomas L. III, John H., Joseph P., James A. AB, Ind. U., 1969, JD, 1972. Bar: Wis. 1972, U.S. Ct. Appeals (7th cir.) 1972, U.S. Dist. Ct. (ea. dist.) Wis. 1973, U.S. Dist. Ct. (we. dist.) Wis. 1977, U.S. Supreme Ct. 1978, U.S. Ct. Appeals (8th cir.) 1989, U.S. Ct. Appeals (fed. cir.) 1990. Law clk to Hon. John S. Hastings U.S. Ct. Appeals (7th cir.), Chgo., 1972-73; assoc. Foley & Lardner, Milw., 1973-79, ptnr., 1979—. Chmn. bd. trustees Cath. Charities of Archdiocese of Milw., 2001—02. Fellow Am. Coll. Trial Lawyers; mem. 7th Cir. Bar Assn. (pres. 1993-94), Phi Beta Kappa. Republican. Roman Catholic. Office: Foley & Lardner LLP 777 E Wisconsin Ave Ste 3800 Milwaukee WI 53202-5306 Office Phone: 414-297-5601. E-mail: tshriner@foley.com.

SHRIVER, DONALD WOODS, JR., theology educator; b. Norfolk, Va., Dec. 20, 1927; s. Donald Woods and Gladys (Roberts) S.; m. Peggy Ann Leu, Aug. 9, 1953; children: Gregory Bruce, Lionel, Timothy Donald. BA, Davidson Coll., 1951; BD, Union Theol. Sem. Va., 1955; MST, Yale U., 1957; PhD, Harvard U., 1963; LHD (hon.), Ctrl. Coll., 1970; DD (hon.), Wagner Coll., 1978, Southwestern Coll., Memphis, 1983; LHD (hon.), Davidson Coll., 1984, Union Theol. Sem. Am., 1991, Jewish Theol. Sem., 1991; DD, DD, Colgate U., 1996. Ordained to ministry Presbyn. Ch., 1955. Pastor Linwood Presbyn. Ch., Gastonia, NC, 1956-59; univ. min., prof. religion NC State U., Raleigh, 1963-72, dir. univ. program on sci. and soc., 1968-72; prof. ethics and soc. Emory U., Atlanta, 1972-75; William E. Dodge prof. applied Christianity Union Theol. Sem., NYC, 1975-96, pres. faculty, 1975-91. Adj. prof. bus. ethics Sch. Bus. Adminstrn., Columbia U., prof. ethics Sch. Internat. Affairs, 1995-98; sr. fellow freedom forum Sch. Journalism, Columbia U., 1992-93; adj. prof. ethics, 1994—; lectr. Duke U., Va. State U., Ga. State U., numerous colls. and univs. in Can., Kenya, India, Japan and Korea. Author: How Do You Do and Why: An Introduction of Christian Ethics for Young People, 1966, Rich Man Poor Man: Christian Ethics for Modern Man Series, 1972, (with Dean D. Knudsen and John R. Earle) Spindles and Spires: A Restudy of Religion and Social Change in Gastonia, 1976, (with Karl A. Ostrom) Is There Hope for the City?, 1977, The Social Ethics of the Lord's Prayer, 1980, The Gospel, The Church, and Social Change, 1980, The Lord's Prayer: A Way of Life, 1983, An Ethic for Enemies: Forgiveness in Politics, 1995; co-author: Redeeming the City, 1982, Beyond Success: Corporations and Their Critics in the Nineties, 1991; editor: The Unsilent South, 1965, Medicine and Religion: Strategies of Care, 1979. Dir. Urban Policy Study NC State U., 1971-73; precinct chmn. Dem. Party, Raleigh, del. to nat. conv., 1968; mem. Mayor's Com. on Human Rels., Raleigh, 1967-71; chmn. Urban Policy Seminar, Ctr. for Theology and Pub. Policy, 1978-82. Served with Signal Corps U.S. Army, 1946-47. Recipient The Union medal, Union Theol. Sem., 1991; Rockefeller Doctoral fellow Harvard U., 1963; Kent fellow in religion, 1959; fellow Am. Acad. in Berlin, 1999. Mem. Am. Soc. Christian Ethics (pres. 1979-80), Soc. for Values in Higher Edn., Soc. for Health and Human Values, Soc. for Sci. Study of Religion, AAAS, Am. Sociol. Assn., Am. Soc. Engring. Edn. (chmn. liberal arts divsn. 1972-73), United Christian Youth Movement of Nat. Coun. of Chs. (nat. chmn. 1951-53), Coun. on Fgn. Rels. Home and Office: 440 Riverside Dr Apt 58 New York NY 10027-6830 Office Phone: 212-222-5112. Personal E-mail: dwshriver@aol.com. *Modern people need to recover connections between memory and hope. The past we applaud pre-enacts the future we hope for, and the past we deplore forms our obligation, in the present, to make a different future. In a time when young people find it hard to envision a long human future, the connections of history and ethics are indispensable. The forging of such connections is my vocation as an educator.*

SHRIVER, EUNICE MARY KENNEDY (MRS. ROBERT SARGENT SHRIVER JR.), foundation administrator, volunteer, social worker; b. Brookline, Mass., July 10, 1920; d. Joseph P. and Rose (Fitzgerald) Kennedy; m. Robert Sargent Shriver, Jr., May 23, 1953; children: Robert Sargent III, Maria Owings Shriver Schwarzenegger, Timothy Perry, Mark Kennedy, Anthony Paul Kennedy. BS in Sociology, Stanford U., Palo Alto, Calif., 1943; student, Manhattanville Coll. of Sacred Heart, LHD (hon.), 1963, D'Youville Coll., 1962, Regis Coll., 1963, Newton Coll., 1973, Brescia Coll., 1974, Holy Cross Coll., 1979, Princeton U., 1979, Boston Coll., 1990; LittD (hon.), U. Santa Clara, 1962, Yale U., 1996, Cardinal Strich U., 2002. With spl. war problems div. State Dept. Washington, 1943—46; sec. Nat. Conf. on Prevention and Control juvenile Delinquency, Dept. of Justice, Washington, 1947-48; social worker Fed. Penitentiary for Women, Alderson, W.Va., 1950, House of Good Shepherd & Juvenile Court, Chgo., 1951-54; exec. v.p. Joseph P. Kennedy, Jr. Found., 1956—; regional chmn. women's div. Community Fund-Red Cross Joint Appeal, Chgo., 1958; founder, CEO Spl. Olympics, 1968—90, founder, hon. chmn., 1990—. Cons. to Pres. John F. Kennedy's Panel on Mental Retardation, 1961; founder Community & Caring, Inc., 1981; mem. Chgo. Commn. on Youth Welfare, 1959-62; mem. bd. Special Olympics Internat. Editor: A Community of Caring, 1982, 85, Growing Up Caring, 1990. Co-chmn. women's com. Dem. Nat. Conv., Chgo., 1956. Decorated Legion of Honor; recipient Albert Lasker Pub. Svc. award, Lasker Found., 1966, Philip Murray-William Green award (with Sargent Shriver), AFL-CIO, 1966, Humanitarian award A.A.M.D., 1973, Nat. Vol. Service award, 1973, Phila. Civic Ballet award, 1973, Prix de la Couronne Française, 1974, Presdl. Medal of Freedom, 1984, Freedom From Want medal, Roosevelt Inst., 1993, Jewish Sports Hall of Fame Humanitarium award, 2000, Champion of Children award, Phoenix Found. for Children, 2000, Aetna Voice of Conscience award, 2002, Juanita Kreps award, 2002, Life award, Noel Found., 2002, Theodore Roosevelt award, NCAA, 2002; inducted into Nat. Women's Hall of Fame, 2002; appeared on Special Olympics World Summer Games silver commemorative coin, 1995. Office: Spl Olympics Internat & Joseph P Kennedy Jr Found 1325 G St NW Ste 500 Washington DC 20005*

SHRIVER, LOREN J. astronaut; b. Jefferson, Iowa, Sept. 23, 1944; m. Susan Diane Hane; children: Camilla, Melinda, Rebecca, Jered. BS in Aero. Engring., USAF Acad., 1967; MS in Astronautical Engring., Purdue U., 1968; grad., USAF Test Pilot Sch., 1975. Commd. 2d lt. USAF, 1967, advanced through grades to col.; acad. instr. pilot Vance Air Force Base, Okla., 1969—73; pilot Thailand, 1973—74; with 6512th Test Squadron, Edwards Air Force Base; test pilot F-15 Joint Test Force, Edwards Air Force Base; astronaut NASA, Houston, 1978—97, 1992, space shuttle program mgr., launch integration, 1993—, dep. dir. launch and payload processing John F. Kennedy Space Ctr., 1997—. Decorated DFC; recipient Flight Achievement award, Am. Astronautical Soc., 1990, Haley Space Flight award, AIAA, 1990. Achievements include logged over 6,200 hours in jet aircraft; logged 386 hours in space; pilot STS-51C (1985), STS-31 (1990) and STS-46 (1992). Office: Astronaut Office/CB NASA Johnson Space Ctr Houston TX 77058

SHRIVER, MARIA OWINGS, news correspondent; b. Chgo., Nov. 6, 1955; d. Robert Sargent and Eunice Mary (Kennedy) S.; m. Arnold Schwarzenegger, Apr. 26, 1986; children: Katherine, Christina, Patrick & Christopher. BA, Georgetown U. Coll. Am. Studies, Washington, 1977. News producer Sta. KYW-TV, 1977-78; producer Sta. WJZ-TV, 1978-80; nat. reporter PM Mag., 1981-83; news reporter CBS News, Los Angeles, 1983-85; news correspondent, co-anchor CBS Morning News, N.Y.C., 1985-86; co-host Sunday Today, NBC, 1987-90; anchor Main Street, NBC, 1987; co-anchor Yesterday, Today, and Tomorrow, NBC, 1989; anchor NBC Nightly News Weekend Edition, 1989-90, Cutting Edge with Maria Shriver, NBC, 1990, First Person with Maria Shriver, NBC, 1990—2004; First Lady of Calif., 2003—. Co-anchor summer olympics, Seoul, Korea, 1988; substitute anchor NBC News at Sunrise, Today, NBC Nightly News with Tom Brokaw; contbg. anchor Dateline, NBC, 1995-2004. Appeared in Last Action Hero, 1993; correspondent TV series The American Parade, 1984; author What's Heaven, 1999, Ten Things I Wish I'd Known Before I Went Into the Real World, 2000, What's Wrong With Timmy, 2001, What's Happening to Grandpa?, 2003. Recipient Christopher award for "Fatal Addictions", 1990, Exceptional Merit Media award Nat. Women's Political Caucus, first-place Commendation award Am. Women in Radio and TV, 1991, Emmy nomination, George Peabody Award, 1998. Democrat. Roman Catholic. Office: First Lady Maria Shriver State Capitol Bldg Sacramento CA 95814-4906*

SHRIVER, PAMELA H. retired professional tennis player, sports analyst; b. Balt., July 4, 1962; m. Joseph Shapiro, 1998. Profl. tennis player, 1979—; winner 21 career singles, 112 career doubles titles 21 career singles, 92 career doubles titles; winner 7 Australian Opens (with Martina Navratilova), 4 French Opens (with Navratilova), 5 Wimbledons (with Navratilova), 6 U.S. Opens, French Open mixed doubles (with Emilio Sanchez); analyst, commentator HBO, NBC, CBS, ABC, BBC, ESPN; part-owner Balt. Orioles baseball team; pres. Women's Sports Legends. Mem. U.S. Fedn. Cup Team, 1986, 87, 89, U.S. Wightman Cup Team, 1978-81, 83, 85, 87; co-winner 1998 Wimbledon 35 and Over Doubles title; mem. President's Coun. on Phys. Fitness and Sports, 1986-92; mem. Md. Fitness Commn.; v.p. Internat. Tennis Hall of Fame. Active ann. charity tennis exhbn. through Balt. Cmty. Found., also trustee; trustee McDonogh Sch.; hon. chmn. Balt. Tennis Patrons. Recipient Gold medal 1988 Olympic Games in doubles (with Zina Garrison), Player Who Makes a Difference award Family Circle mag., 1996. Mem. U.S. Tennis Assn. (bd. dirs. 1997—), Women's Tennis Assn. (pres. 1991-94, Corel Trou David Gray Svc. award 1998), Tour Players Assn. Address: PHS Ltd 401 Washington Ave Ste 902 Towson MD 21204-4835

SHRIVER, PHILLIP RAYMOND, academic administrator; b. Cleve., Aug. 16, 1922; s. Raymond Scott and Corinna Ruth (Smith) S.; m. Martha Damaris Nye, Apr. 15, 1944; children: Carolyn (Mrs. William Shaul), Susan (Mrs. Lester LaVine), Melinda (Mrs. David Williams), Darcy, Raymond Scott II. BA, Yale U., 1943; MA, Harvard U., 1946; PhD, Columbia U., 1954; LittD, U. Cin., 1966; LLD, Heidelberg Coll., 1966, Eastern Mich., 1972, Ohio State U., 1973; DH, McKendree Coll., 1973; DPS, Albion Coll., 1974; LHD, Central State U., 1976, No. Ky. State U., 1980, Miami U., 1984, U. Akron, 1988. Mem. faculty Kent (Ohio) State U., 1947-65, prof. Am. history, 1960-65; dean Coll. Arts and Scis., 1963-65; pres. Miami U., Oxford, Ohio, 1965-81, pres. emeritus, prof. Am. history, 1981-99. Pres. Ohio Coll. Assn., 1974-75; chmn. coun. pres.'s Mid-Am. Conf., 1971-77; chmn. Ohio Bicentennial Commn. for NW Ordinance and U.S. Constn., 1985-89, Ohio Tuition Trust Authority, 1989-92; chmn. coun. pres.'s Nat. Assn. State Univs. and Land Grant Colls., 1975-76, mem. exec. coun., 1976-78. Author: The Years of Youth, 1960, George A. Bowman: The Biography of an Educator, 1963, (with D.J. Breen) Ohio's Military Prisons of the Civil War, 1964, A Tour to New Connecticut in 1811: The Narrative of Henry Leavitt Ellsworth, 1985, Miami University: A Personal History, 1998, (with C.E. Wunderlin Jr.) The Documentary Heritage of Ohio, 2000, (with E.F. Puff) The History of Presbyterianism in Oxford, Ohio, 2000. Bd. dirs. Cin. Ctr. Sci. and Industry, 1965-70; trustee Ohio Coll. Library Center, 1968-74; chmn. bd. Univ. Regional Broadcasting, 1975-76, 78-79. Served to lt. (j.g.) USNR, 1943-46, PTO. Decorated Order of Merit (Grand Duchy of Luxembourg); recipient Disting. Acad. Svc. award AAUP, 1965, Gov.'s award 1969, A.K. Morris award, 1974, Ohioana Career medal, 1987, Converse award, 1990, award of merit Am. Assn. for State and Local History, 1993, Bjornson award Ohio Humanities Coun., 2001, John E. Dolibois History prize, 2003. Mem. Orgn. Am. Historians, Ohio Acad. History (pres. 1983-84, Disting. Svc. award 1991), Archaeol. Inst. Am., Ohio Hist. Soc. (trustee 1982-91, v.p. 1983-84, pres. 1984-86), Ohio Humanities Council (Bjornson award 2001), Am. Studies Assn., Mortar Board, Phi Beta Kappa, Omicron Delta Kappa, Phi Alpha Theta, Alpha Kappa Psi, Kappa Delta Pi, Phi Eta Sigma, Phi Kappa Phi, Kappa Kappa Psi, Alpha Lambda Delta, Beta Gamma Sigma, Sigma Delta Pi, Alpha Phi Omega, Delta Upsilon (Disting. Alumni Achievement award 1985) Clubs: Rotary. Presbyterian. Home: 5115 Bonham Rd Oxford OH 45056-1428 Office: Miami U Oxford OH 45056 E-mail: shrivepr@muohio.edu.

SHRIVER, ROBERT SARGENT, JR., lawyer; b. Westminster, Md., Nov. 9, 1915; s. Robert Sargent and Hilda Shriver; m. Eunice Mary Kennedy, May 23, 1953; children: Robert Sargent III, Maria, Timothy, Mark Kennedy, Anthony Paul Kennedy. Student, Canterbury Sch.; BA cum laude, Yale U., 1938, LLB, 1941; LLD, St. Procopius Coll., 1959, Notre Dame U., DePaul U., Seton Hall Coll., 1961, St. Louis U., Kansas State U., Brandeis U., 1962, St. Michael's Coll., Vt., Fordham U., Boston Coll., Yale U., Duquesne U., N.Y.U., Wesleyan U.; DCL, U. Liberia, 1963; HHD, Salem Coll., 1963, Bowling Green State U.; LHD, Springfield (Mass.) Coll., 1963, U. Scranton, Providence Coll.; D in Polit. Sci., Chulalongkorn U., Bangkok, Thailand, The Am. U. of Paris, 2002. Bar: N.Y. 1941, Ill. 1959, U.S. Supreme Ct. 1969, D.C. 1971. With Winthrop, Stimson, Putnam & Roberts, 1940—41; asst. editor Newsweek, 1945—46; assoc. Joseph P. Kennedy Enterprises, 1947—48; asst. gen. mgr. Merchandise Mart, Chgo., 1948—61; dir. Peace Corps., Washington, 1961—66, Office Econ. Opportunity, 1964—68; U.S. ambassador to France, 1968—70; spl. asst. to the Pres., 1965—68; sr. ptnr. law firm Fried, Frank, Harris, Shriver & Jacobson, N.Y.C., Washington, L.A., London, Eng., 1971—86, of counsel, 1986—; pres. Spl. Olympics, Washington, 1986—90, chmn., CEO, 1990—96, chmn. bd. dirs., 1996—, chmn. emeritus, 2003. Mem. Am. Com. on East-West Accord, 1978—, Ams. for SALT, 1979—. Author: Point of the Lance, 1964. Pres. Chgo. Bd. Edn., 1955—60; mem.-at-large Nat. Coun. Boy Scouts Am.; chmn. Internat. Orgn. Patrons on Israel Mus., 1972—75; bd. dirs. The Arms Control Assn., 1983—; Dem. candidate for v.p., 1972; ran for Dem. presdl. election, 1976; pres. Cath. Interracial Coun. Chgo., 1955—60. Lt. comdr. USNR, 1940—45. Named Lay Churchman of Yr., Religious Heritage Am., 1963; recipient Yale U. medal, 1957, Chgo. medal of merit, 1957, James H. Hoey award, Cath. Interracial Coun. N.Y., 1958, Golden Heart Presdl. award, Philippines, 1964, Laetare medal, U. Notre Dame, 1968, Franklin D. Roosevelt Freedom from Want award, 1993, Presdl. Medal of Freedom, 1994, Equal Justice award, Nat. Ctr. on Poverty Law, 1999, William O. Douglas award, Pub. Counsel Law Ctr., 1999. Mem.: Chgo. Coun. Fgn. Rels. (dir.), Yale U. Law Sch. Assn. (exec. com.), Navy League (life), Yale Club (N.Y.C.), Onwentsia Club (Lake Forest, Ill.), Execs. Club (Chgo.), Econ. Club, Serra Club, Racquet Club, Delta Kappa Epsilon. Roman Catholic. Achievements include extensive world travel to visit Peace Corps projects, 1961-1966. Office: Spl Olympics Internat 1325 G St NW Ste 500 Washington DC 20005-3104

SHRIVER, SARGENT, sports association executive; m. Eunice Kennedy Shriver; children: Robert Sargent Shriver III, Maria Owings Schwarzenegger, Timothy Perry, Mark Kennedy, Anthony Paul Kennedy. BS, Yale U.; JD, Yale Law Sch.; D (hon.), Brandeis U., Boston Coll., Yeshiva U., U. Liberia, Chulalongkom U. Organizer, dir. Peace Corps, 1961—66; amb. France, 1968—70; ptnr. Fried, Frank, Harris, Shriver and Jacobson, 1970—86; pres. bd. Spl. Olympics, Inc., Washington, 1984—90, chmn. bd., 1990—. Lt. comdr. USN. Named Nat. Father of Yr., 1964; recipient Vet. of Yr., 1956, Lay Churchman of Yr., 1963, Hannah G. Solomon award, Nat. Coun. Jewish Women, 1972, Order of Smile, 1989, Notre Dame Patriotism award, 1965, Nat. Brotherhood award, 1966. Mem.: KC, VFW, Navy League, Nat. Interreligious Task Force on Soviet Jewry, Nat. Cath. Conf. for Interracial Justice (James J. Hooey award N.Y. chpt. 1958). Office: Special Olympics Inc 1325 G St NW Ste 500 Washington DC 20005

SHRIVER, THOMAS L. park director; Supt. Hawks Nest State Park, Ansted, W.Va. Office: Hawks Nest State Park PO Box 857 Ansted WV 25812-0857

SHRIVER, TIMOTHY P. sports association executive; m. Linda Potter Shriver; 5 children. BS, Yale U.; M in Religion and Religious Edn., Cath. U.; DEd, U. Conn.; D (hon.), New Eng. Coll, Albertus Magnus Coll., Loyola U. Balt. Tchr. New Haven Pub. Schs., New Haven; supr. Pub. Schs. Social Devel. Project, New Haven, 1987—96; pres., CEO Spl. Olympics, Inc. Coprodr.(film): Amistad, 1997, The Loretta Claiborne Story, 2000. Bd. dirs. Compact for Learning and Citizenship, Frank Porter Child Devel. Ctr. at U. N.C.; co-chair Am.'s Promise Task Force on Youth Svcs., 1997—; chmn. Collaborative for Advancement of Social and Emotional Learning at U. Ill., 1994—; bd. dirs. John F. Kennedy Libr. Found., Boston. Recipient Medal of City of Athens, Order de Manuel Amador Guerrera, Pres. of Panama, Conn. Citizen of Yr.; fellow Yale Child Study Ctrs. Sch. Devel. Program, 1984. Office: Special Olympics NAm 1325 G St NW Ste 770 Washington DC 20005

SHRIVER, WILLIAM RUSSELL, secondary school educator; b. Garfield Heights, Ohio, Aug. 15, 1950; s. William Washington and Olive Elizabeth (Doutt) S.; m. Karen Ann Wolfe, June 20, 1987; children: Lauren, Matthew. BA, Coll. of Wooster, 1972; MA, U. Chgo., 1973; postgrad., Cleve. State U., 1973-74. Cert. tchr. Summer staff Philmont Scout Ranch, Cimarron, N.Mex., 1968-76; tchr. Mt. Vernon (Ohio) Sr. H.S., 1974—. Tchr. Kenyon Acad. Partnership Kenyon Coll./Mt. Vernon Sr. H.S., 1983—; vice chair state tchr. edn. cert. adv. commn. Ohio Bd. Edn., Columbus, 1991-99, state tchr. cert. standards revision com., 1992-95; mem. bd. examiners Nat. Coun. Accreditation of Tchr. Edn., Washington, 1993-02; mem. Ohio Gov.'s Commn. on Tchg. Success, 2001-03, Ohio Educators Stds. Bd., 2004—. Bd. of session First Presbyn. Ch., Mt. Vernon, 1980-87, 89-95, 2001—. Eagle Scout Boy Scouts Am., 1966. Mem. NEA (assembly del. 1983-99), Ohio Edn. Assn. (exec. com. 1987-93, 96-2002), North Ctrl. Ohio Edn. Assn. (pres. 1984-85, exec. sec. 1993-2004), Mt. Vernon Edn. Assn. (pres. 1976-78). Avocations: photography, geneology. Office: Mt Vernon HS 300 Martinsburg Rd Mount Vernon OH 43050-4246 E-mail: wshriver@mt-vernon.k12.oh.us.

SHROCK, ROBERT E. physicist, educator, research scientist; b. Boston, Feb. 10, 1950; s. Robert Rakes and Theodora Weidman Shrock; m. I-Hsiu Lee, July 30, 1983; children: Christine Lee, Ellen Lee. AB summa cum laude, Harvard Coll., Cambridge, MA, 1971; PhD in Physics, Princeton U., N.J., 1975. Postdoctoral rsch. assoc. in theoretical physics Fermi Nat. Accelerator Lab., Batavia, Ill., 1975—77; asst. prof. physics Princeton U., NJ, 1977—79, SUNY, Stony Brook, 1979—83, assoc. prof. physics, 1983—89, prof. physics, 1989—. Vis. prof. Supercomputer Computations Rsch. Inst., Tallahassee, 1989—90, DESY - German Electron Synchrotron Lab., Hamburg, 1989, Academia Sinica, Taiwan, 1986—99, U. Minn., Mpls., 1990, Max Planck Inst. Physics, Munich, 2003, Tri-U. Meson Physics Facility, Vancouver, Canada, 1980; adj. prof. Rockefeller U., N.Y.C., 1989—91; sabbatical Brookhaven Nat. Lab., Upton, NY, 1999—2000, Ohio State U., Columbus, 1985—86; referee on submitted manuscripts Phys. Rev. and Letters, 1974—, Nuc. Physics B, Physics Letters A, B, published by Elsevier Science Pub., Netherlands, 1976—, Physica A, Jour. of Statis. Physics, 1996—; referee on submitted proposals NSF, Dept. of Energy, Washington; vis. scientist European Coun. Nuc. Rsch., Geneva, 1977, Svc. Theoretical Physics, Saclay, France, 1977, Lawrence Berkeley Lab., Calif., 1979—83, Stanford Linear Accelerator Ctr., Calif., 1981, 92; vis. mem. program rev. com. Los Alamos Nat. Lab., N.Mex., 1986; supercomputer allocations com. Cornell U., Ithaca, NY, 1987—90; mem. working groups on neutrino factory and neutrino oscillation experiments Fermi Nat. Accelerator Lab., Batavia, Ill., 1999—; mem. neutrino working group Brookhaven Nat. Lab., Upton, NY, 2000—; advisor Gillman sub panel High Energy Physics Adv. Panel, Washington, 2000; organizer Conf. on Neutrinos and Implications for Physics Beyond the Std. Model, Stony Brook, NY, 2002; co-organizer NNN99 - Ultra Nucleon Decay and Neutrino Detector Conf., Stony Brook, NY, 1999, Soc. of Indsl. and Applied Math. Conf. on Graph Theory and Applications to Chemistry and Physics, 2003. Contbr. scholarly papers to profl. jours. Recipient Detur prize, Harvard Coll., 1968, Herschel prize, 1970, Proctor Award, Princeton U., 1971-1972; grantee Physics Rsch., U. S. Dept. of Energy, 1977-1979, NSF, 1979-present; Woodrow Wilson Fellowship, 1967. Fellow: Am. Phys. Soc., Am. Physics Soc. (life); mem.: Phi Beta Kappa (life). Achievements include research in theoretical physics including particle physics, quantum field theory, gauge theories, neutrino physics, statistical mechanics. Office: Yang Inst for Theoretical Physics SUNY at Stony Brook Stony Brook NY 11794 Office Phone: 631-632-7986.

SHROFF, GIDU K. computer company executive; b. India, Aug. 1945; Bachelor's in Metallurgy, Poona U., India, 1969; Master's in Material Sci., Stanford U., 1970; MBA, U. Santa Clara, 1975. With Signetics Memory Sys., Advanced Memory Sys., Fairchild Semiconductor; mfg. mgr. Fab 2 Intel Corp., Fab mgr., mgr. components contracting, 1990—97, v.p. and dir. materials, 1997—, corp. officer, 2002—. Office: 2200 Mission College Blvd Santa Clara CA 95052

SHRON, MARINA, playwright, scriptwriter; b. St. Petersburg, Russia, Mar. 25, 1964; arrived in US, 1991; d. Vadim and Galina (Kogan) Shron. MFA in Dramatic Writing, NYU, 1994. Prof. film and liberal arts Savannah (Ga.) Coll. Art and Design, 2002—; prof. film New Sch. U., N.Y.C., 2000—. Author: (play) King of Rats (NY Found. for the Arts fellowship in Playwriting, 1997), Christina (Jerome Fellowship in Playwriting, 1998), Time and the Beast (James Thurber Fellowship in Playwriting, 2001), The Guest (The Ministry of Culture of the Former USSR Best Play Award, 1990), (screenplay) The Silent Love of the Fish (The Hamptons Internat. Film Festival Hon. Mention, 2000), (non-fiction) Red Blues: Voices from the Last Wave of Russian Immigrants, 2002. Fellow, Ragdale Found., 1996; grantee fellow/resident, MacDowell Arts Colony, 2001;, 1998, Yaddo Colony, 1999, Walter E. Dakin fellow, Sewanee Writers' Conf., 2000, Fulbright Scholarship, 2004—05. Office: Savannah Coll Art and Design 217 ML King Blvd Savannah GA 31402 Home: 2437 Whitemarsh Way Savannah GA 31410 Personal E-mail: mshron@msn.com.

SHROPSHIRE, ASHAKI DJENABA-SERWAA, microbiologist; b. Washington, D.C., Dec. 1, 1972; d. Cheryl Wanda Shropshire. BS, N.C. A and T State U., Greensboro, 1990—94. Biol. sci. lab. technician U.S. Dept. Agr., Beltsville, Md., 1989—. Contbr. articles to profl. jours. Mem. Woodridge Civic Assn., Washington, 2000—04. Mem.: Am. Soc. for Microbiology. Independent. Achievements include discovery of a new bacterial species that kills pest insects of agricultural importance. Avocations: movies, travel, romance novels. Office: US Dept Agriculture 10300 Baltimore Ave Beltsville MD 20705-2350 E-mail: shropsht@ba.ars.usda.gov.

SHROPSHIRE, DONALD GRAY, hospital executive; b. Winston-Salem, N.C., Aug. 6, 1927; s. John Lee and Bess L. (Shouse) S.; m. Mary Ruth Bodenheimer, Aug. 19, 1950; children: Melanie Shropshire David, John Devin. BS, U. N.C., 1950; Erickson fellow postgrad., U. Chgo., 1958-59; LLD (hon.), U. Ariz., 1992; EdD (hon.), Tucson U., 1994. Personnel asst. Nat. Biscuit Co., Atlanta, 1950-52, asst. personnel mgr. Chgo., 1952-54; adminstr. Eastern State Hosp., Lexington, Ky., 1954-62; assoc. dir. U. Md. Hosp., Balt., 1962-67; adminstr. Tucson Med. Ctr., 1967-82, pres., 1982-92, pres. emeritus, 1992—; pres. Tucson Hosps. Med. Edn. Program, 1970-71, sec., 1971-86; pres. So. Ariz. Hosp. Council, 1968-69; bd. dirs. Ariz. Blue Cross, 1967-76, chmn. provider standards com., 1972-76; chmn. Healthways Inc., 1985-92. Mem. bd. La Posada at Park Centre, Inc., Green Valley, Ariz., 1996-2000, chmn. bd., 1996-99, mem. emeritus, 2000—. Bd. dirs. Health Planning Coun. Tucson, mem. exec. com., 1969-74; chmn. profl. divsn. United Way, Tucson, 1969-70, vice chmn. campaign, 1988, Ariz. Health Faciltities Authority, bd. dirs., 1992—; chmn. dietary svcs. com., vice chmn., 1988, Md. Hosp. Coun., 1966-67; bd. dirs. Ky. Hosp. Assn., 1961-62, chmn. coun. profl. practice, 1960-61; past pres. Blue Grass Hosp. Coun.; trustee Assn. Western Hosps., 1974-81, pres., 1979-80; mem. accreditation Coun. for Continuing Med. Edn., 1982-87, chair, 1986; bd. govs. Pima C.C., 1970-76, sec., 1973-74, chmn., 1975-76, bd. dirs. Found., 1978-82, Ariz. Bd. Regents, 1982-90, sec., 1983-86, pres., 1987-88; mem. Tucson Airport Authority, 1987—, bd. dirs., 1990-95, pres., 1995; v.p. Tucson Econ. Devel. Corp., 1977-82; founder, dir., bd. dirs. Vol. Hosps. Am., 1977-88, treas., 1979-82; mem. Ariz. Adv. Health Coun. Dirs., 1976-78; bd. dirs. Tucson Tomorrow, 1983-87, Tucson Downtown Devel. Corp., 1988-95, Rincon Inst., 1992-97, Sonoran Inst., 1992-97; dir. Mus. No. Ariz., 1988-2002, dir. emeritus, 2002—; nat. bd. advisors Eller Coll. Bus. U. Ariz., 1990—, mem. Dean's Bd. Coll. Fine Arts, 1992—, chmn., 1992-96, pres. Ariz. Coun. Econ. Edn., 1993-95; vis. panel Sch. Health Adminstrn. and Policy Ariz. State U., 1990-92; bd. dirs. Cmty. Found. So. Ariz., 1996-2001; mem. adv. bd. Steele Meml. Rsch. Ctr., U. Ariz. Coll. Medicine, 1996-2004. Named to Hon. Order Ky. Cols.; named Tucson Man of Yr. 1987, Tucson Father of Yr. 1997; recipient Disting. Svc. award Anti-Defamation League B'nai B'rith, 1989, Humanitarian award Arthritis Found. S.Am., 2001, Crystal Apple Lifetime Achievement award Tucson Metro Edn. Commn., 2004. Mem. Am. Hosp. Assn. (nominating com. 1983-86, trustee 1975-78, ho. dels. 1972-78, chmn. coun. profl. svc. 1973-74, regional adv. bd. 1969-78, chmn. joint com. with NASW 1963-64, Disting. Svc. award 1989), Ariz. Hosp. Assn. (Salisbury award 1982, bd. dirs. 1967-72, pres. 1970-71), Ariz. C. of C. (bd. dirs. 1988-93), Assn. Am. Med. Colls. (mem. assembly 1974-77), Tucson C. of C. (bd. dirs. 1968-69), Nat. League for Nursing, Ariz. Town Hall (bd. dirs. 1982-92, chmn. 1990-92, treas. 1985, Circle of Disting. Svc. award 2002), Pima County Acad. Decathlon Assn. (dir. 1983-85), The Rotary Club of Tucson (pres. 1993-94), U. Ariz. Alumni Assn. Coll. Nursing (hon. alumnus 1998). Baptist/Presbyterian (ch. moderator, chmn. finance com., deacon, ch. sch. supt., trustee, bd. dirs. ch. found.) Home: 6734 N Chapultepec Cir Tucson AZ 85750-1001 Office: Tucson Med Ctr 5301 E Grant Rd Tucson AZ 85712-2805 *It seems important to put something back into life - for all we take from it.*

SHROPSHIRE, WALTER, JR., biophysicist emeritus, pastor; b. Washington, Sept. 4, 1932; s. Walter and Mary Virginia (Anderson) S.; m. Audrey Marie McConkey, June 28, 1958; children— Janet Marie, Susan Lynn, Edward Allen. BS in Physics, George Washington U., 1954, MS in Botany, 1956, PhD in Plant Physiology, 1958; MDiv summa cum laude, Wesley Theol. Sem., 1990; postdoctoral fellow biophysics, Calif. Inst. Tech., 1957-59. Ordained to ministry United Meth. Ch., 1977. Physicist Smithsonian Instn., Washington, 1954—63; asst. dir. Smithsonian Environ. Rsch. Ctr., Washington, 1963-86; Gast prof. U. Freiburg, Germany, 1968-69; biophysicist, dir. Omega Lab., Cabin John, Md., 1986—. Professorial lectr. botany George Washington U., 1960-85; Gast prof. U. Zurich, Switzerland, 1985-86; part-time adj. prof. Practice Min. and Mission Wesley Theol. Sem., 1990—. Editor: Phytochrome, 1972, Joys of Research, 1981, Photomorphogenesis, Vol 16A, 16B, 1983, Photobiology, 1984-85; Contbr. 50 articles to profl. jours. Pastor, Foundry United Meth. Ch., Washington, 1991-2003. Recipient Smithsonian Outstanding Performance award, 1967, Smithsonian Research award, 1968, Merit award Soc. John Wesley, 1997, Templeton Sci. and Religion Course prize, 1999, 2002; NSF grantee, 1960-66. Fellow Explorers Club, Am. Solar Energy Soc. Office: Omega Lab PO Box 189 Cabin John MD 20818-0189 E-mail: wshrop@erols.com. *The world is an incredible place, rich with unexplored and unexplained interconnections between the biological and physical domains. I am fortunate to have been born when science has begun to unravel some of the mysteries of these interconnections and especially fortunate to have had teachers who shared their enthusiasm for learning. I also have benefited from mystical religious experiences of others and my own that enable me to work at the interface between science and religion. My belief is that the pursuit of both subjective and objective knowledge of ourselves and the universe we live in is necessary to enable humanity to develop to its fullest potential. This is an exciting pursuit I hope to continue to participate in a long time.*

SHROTRIYA, RAJESH C. medical company executive; BS in Chemistry, Agra U., Aligarh, India, 1962; M.B.BS, Armed Forces Med. Coll., Poona, India, 1967; Postgrad. Diploma in Chest Diseases, Delhi U., India, 1971; MD, Grant Med. Coll., Bombay, India, 1974; Cert. for Advanced Biomed. Rsch. Mgmt., Harvard U. Attending physician St. Joseph Hosp., Stamford, Conn.; with Hoechst Pharms., med. advisor; with Bristol-Myers Squibb Co., exec. dir. worldwide CNS clin. rsch.; v.p. med. affairs, v.p., chief med. officer MGI Pharma, Inc., 1994—96; exec. v.p., chief sci. officer SuperGen, Inc., 1996—2000, sr. v.p., spl. asst. to pres., 1996—97; pres., COO, dir. NeoTherapeutics Inc., Irvine, Calif., 2000—. Office: Neotherapeutics Inc 157 Technology Dr Irvine CA 92618

SHTENGOLD, YEFIM SHELICHOVICH, medical educator, researcher; b. Novograd Volinsk, Russia, Apr. 16, 1927; came to U.S., 1996; s. Shelik David and Basya (Grushko) S.; m. Liliya Nikitichna Vasilevskaya, Feb. 16, 1961; 1 child, Ekaterina Gribanova. MD, Med. Inst., Kishinew, Moldova, 1954; PhD, Inst. Clin. and Exptl. Surgery, Moscow, 1974. Intern in oncology Regional Med. Ctr., Grodno, Belarus, 1954-58; surgeon Regional Med. Ctr. Oncology, Moscow, 1958-62; anesthesiologist Inst. Child Surgery, Moscow, 1962-64; head Organ Preservation Lab., Inst. Clin. and Exptl. Surgery, Moscow, 1964-74; head Artificial Heart Lab., Inst. Transplantology and Artificial Organs, Moscow, 1974-80; head dept. biophysics, biomechanics and biomed. engring. Inst. Problems in Mechanics-Russian Acad. Sci., Moscow, 1980-96, prof., 1992—. Author: Mathematical Simulation of the Physiological Systems, 1971, Organ Preservation, 1975, Biomechanics of the Myocardial Muscle, 1981, Stress-Deformed Cardiovascular System and Hypertension, 1990; contbr. over 300 articles to sci. publs.; patentee in field. Home: 7549 Lexington Ave Los Angeles CA 90046-5563

SHTOHRYN, DMYTRO MICHAEL, librarian, educator; b. Zvyniach, Ukraine, Nov. 9, 1923; came to U.S., 1950; s. Mykhailo and Kateryna (Figol) S.; m. Eustachia Barwinska, Sept. 3, 1955; children: Bohdar O., Liudoslava V. Student, Ukrainian Free U., Munich, 1947-48, U. Minn., 1954; MA in Slavic Studies, U. Ottawa, Can., 1958, B.L.S., 1959, PhD in Slavic Studies, 1970. Slavic cataloger U. Ottawa, 1959; cataloger NRC Can., Ottawa, 1959-60; Slavic cataloger, instr. library adminstrn. U. Ill., Urbana, 1960-64, head Slavic cataloging, asst. prof. library adminstrn., 1964-68, head Slavic cataloging, assoc. prof., 1968-75, head Slavic cataloging, prof., 1975-85, lectr. Ukrainian lit., 1975-91, assoc. Slavic librarian, prof., 1985-95, prof. Ukrainian lit., 1991-95, prof. emeritus, 1995—. Vis. prof. Ukrainian lit. U. Ottawa, 1974; assoc. prof. Ukrainian lit. Ukrainian Cath. U., Rome, 1978—; prof. Ukrainian lit. Ukrainian Free U., Munich, 1983—, Ukrainian lang. and lit., U. Ill., 1991-95, Ukrainian culture, 1996—; chmn. Ukrainian Research Program U. Ill., 1984—. Editor: Catalog of Publications of Ukrainian Academy of Sciences, 1966, Ukrainians in North America: A Biographical Directory, 1975; author: Ukrainian Literature in the U.S.A.: Trends, Influences, Achievements, 1975, The Rise and Fall of Book Studies in Ukraine, 1986, Oleh Kandyba-Olzhych: Bibliography, 1992; editor: Bull. Ukrainian Libr. Assn. Am., 1982-88; mem. editl. bd. Ukrainian Historian, 1985-98, Ethnic Forum, 1985-95, Crossroads, 1986-97, Ukrainian Quar., 1993—, Ukrainian Problems,

1997—, Ukrainian Rev., 1997-99. Counselor Boy Scouts Am., Champaign, Ill., 1967-85; bd. dirs. Ukrainian-Am. Found., Chgo., 1978-87. Recipient Grant Future Credit Union Toronto, 1956, Grant U. Ill., 1977, 1982, Silver medal, Parliament of Can. Librarian, Ottawa, 1959, award, Glorier Soc. Can., 1959, citation plaque, Ukrainian Congress Com. Am., Chgo., 2000, Medal, V. Stefanyk Subcarpathian State U., 2001. Fellow Shevchenko Sci. Soc. (exec. com., M. Hrushevsky medal 1998); mem. ALA (chmn. Slavic and East European sect. 1968-69), Ukrainian Libr. Assn. Am. (pres. 1970-74, 82-87), Ukrainian Acad. and Profl. Assn. (charter, sec. 1985-89, pres. 1989—), I. Franko Internat. Soc. (founding mem., pres. 1978-79, 81-82), Ukrainian-Am. Assn. Univ. Profs. (exec. com. 1981-96), Ukrainian Hist. Assn. (exec. com. 1983-97), Ukrainian Acad. Arts and Scis. in U.S. (exec. com. 1993-98), Ukrainian Congress Com. of Am. Scholarly Coun., Ukrainian Writers' Assn. Slovo, Am. Assn. Ukrainian Studies, Libr. Congress Assocs. (charter mem.). Ukrainian Catholic. Home: 403 Park Lane Dr Champaign IL 61820-7729 Office: Dept Slavic Langs & Lits 3092 Fgn Langs Bldg U ill 707 S Mathews Ave Urbana IL 61801-3625 E-mail: shtohryn@uiuc.edu.

SHU, CHI-WANG, mathematics educator, researcher; b. Beijing, People's Republic of China, Jan. 2, 1957; arrived in U.S., 1982, naturalized, 1993; s. Kuang-Yao and Ding-Zhen (Shi) Shu; m. Din-Sui Loh, May 1, 1984; 1 child, Hai-Shuo. BS, U. Sci. and Tech. of China, 1982; PhD, UCLA, 1986. Rsch. assoc. U. Minn., Mpls., 1986—87; asst. prof. applied math. Brown U., Providence, 1987—91, assoc. prof., 1992—96, prof., 1996—, chmn., 1999—. Mng. editor: Math. of Computation, 2002—, co-chief editor: Jour. Sci. Computing, 2000—; contbr. Recipient Pub. Svc. Group Achievement award for pioneer work in computational fluid dynamics, NASA, 1992, First Feng Kang prize of Sci. Computing, Chinese Acad. Sci., 1995; grantee, NSF, NASA, Army Rsch. Office. Mem.: Soc. for Indsl. and Applied Math., Am. Math. Soc. Achievements include research in in numerical solutions for discontinuous problems. Home: 135 Woodbury St Providence RI 02906-3511 Office: Brown U Div Applied Maths 182 George St Providence RI 02912-9056

SHUART, CAREY CHENOWETH, farmer, volunteer; b. Houston, June 1, 1944; d. Robert Carey Chenoweth and Elizabeth Dorothy Smith; m. Willard Warren Shuart, Apr. 17, 1965 (dec. Mar. 1996); children: Nora Wellington Shuart-Faris, Sarah Espy Shuart Szymanski. Student, U. Tex., 1962—66, U. Houston, 1991—93, Glassell Sch. Mus. of Fine Arts, Houston, 1990—2001. Owner, cons. Bien Trouvé Art Gallery, Houston, 1979—85; rice farmer Shuart Farms, Houston. Mem. adv. bd. Blaffer Gallery U. Houston, 2002—. Editor: (newsletter) U Friends, 1992—98. Mem. alumni bd. St. John's Sch., Houston, 1973—75; sustainer Jr. League of Houston, 1975—2004; founder, pres. Pink Ladies-Eagle Lake Cmty. Hosp., 1967—72, Civic Garden Club, Eagle Lake, Tex., 1983—85; chmn. adv. bd. Friends of Women's Studies U. Houston, 2001—04; founder, patron Women's Archive and Rsch. Ctr. U. Houston; mem. photo subcom. Mus. Fine Arts, Houston, 2000—04; bd. dirs. Friends of Women's Studies U. Houston, 1992—2004, Honors Coll., U. Houston, 1992—95. Named Vol. of Yr., U. Houston U. Rels. Divsn., 1992, 1995, U. Houston, 1995, 1996; recipient Nat. CASE award, St. Johns Sch., Houston, 1982, Outstanding Alumni award, 1991. Mem.: Nat. Soc. Colonial Dames in State of Tex. (chmn. 1982—86, 2003—). Episcopalian. Avocations: photography, golf, social work. Office: Shuart Farms 2121 San Felipe #118 Houston TX 77019

SHUART, JAMES MARTIN, retired academic administrator; b. College Point, N.Y., May 9, 1931; s. John and Barbara (Schmidt) S.; m. Marjorie Strunk, Apr. 5, 1953; children: James Raymond, William Arthur. BA, Hofstra U., 1953, MA, 1962; PhD, NYU, 1966; D (hon.), L.I. U., 2000. Group rep. Home Life Ins. Co., 1955-57, N.Y. Life Ins. Co., 1957-59; adminstr. Hofstra U., Hempstead, N.Y., 1959-70, asst. dir. admissions, asst. dean faculty, asst. pres., exec. dean student services, assoc. dean liberal arts scis., trustee, 1973-75, v.p. adminstrv. svcs., 1975-76, pres., 1976-2001, pres. emeritus, 2001—. Mem. higher edn. adv. com. N.Y. State Senate, 1979-95; trustee Commn. on Ind. Colls. and Univs., N.Y. State, 1982-89, 92-95, chmn., 1988-89; mem. Am. Coun. on Edn.'s Labor/Higher Edn. Coun., 1983-88, Am. Coun. on Edns. Commn. on Leadership Devel., 1987-89, Peat Marwick Higher Edn. Pres.'s Adv. Com., 1988-96; bd. dirs. European Am. Bank, 1990-2001, Travelers-Solomon, Smith Barney World Funds, 1995-2000; chair Nassau County Property Tax Relief Commn., 1990-92; co-chair N.Y. State Temporary Commn. for L.I. Tax Relief, 1990-93; mem. nominating com. NASDQ, 2000—. Trustee Molloy Coll., 1973-77, L.I. (N.Y.) Power Authority, 2004—; mem. adv. bd. Adelphi U. Sch. Social Work, 1973-84; dep. county exec. Nassau County, 1973-75, commr. social svcs., 1971-73, commr. L.I. Reg. Planning Bd., 1978-83, chmn., 1981-83; bd. dirs L.I. Assn., 1986-90; trustee Uniondale (N.Y.) Pub. Libr., 1966-68, L.I. Hosp. Planning Coun., 1971-75; pres., bd. dirs. Health Welfare Coun. Nassau County, 1971-80; chmn. Nassau Bd. Social Svcs., 1971-73; bd. dirs. Winthrop U. Hosp., 1979-86; mem. Nassau County Charter Revision Commn., 1993-96. Decorated officer Order of Orange Nassau (The Netherlands); recipient Founders Day award NYU, 1967, Alumnus of Yr. award Hofstra U., 1973, George M. Estabrook Disting. svc. award Alumni Assn., 1974, Leadership in Govt. award C.W. Post coll., L.I. U., 1978, Man of Yr. award Hempstead C. of C., 1978, L.I. Pers. and Guidance Assn., award, 1977, Lincoln Day award Syosset-Woodbury Rep. Club, 1981, L.I. Bus. disting. Leadership award 1982, 96, Joseph Giacalone award 1986, Medal of Honor L.I. Assn., 1988, L.I. Achievement award Pub. Rels. Profls. of L.I., 1995, Award L.I. Bus. Devel. Coun., 1994, 98, WLIWCh21 Educator of the Yr. award, 1999, Lifetime Achievement award L.I. Assn., 2001, L.I. Software and Tech. Network award L.I. Software and Tech. Network, 2001; others; named to L.I. Hall of Fame, 1985, Lifetime Achievement award Met. Lacrosse Found., 2001. Home: 111 Cherry Valley Ave # M35 Garden City NY 11530-1570

SHUBART, DOROTHY LOUISE TEPFER, artist, educator; b. Ft. Collins, Colo, Mar. 1, 1923; d. Adam Christian and Rose Virginia (Ayers) Tepfer; m. Robert Franz Shubart, Apr. 22, 1950; children: Richard, Lorenne. AA, Colo. Women's Coll., 1944; grad., Cleve. Inst. Art, 1946; student, Western Res. U., 1947—48; BA, St. Thomas Aquinas Coll., 1974; MA, Coll. New Rochelle, 1978; student, Santa Fe C.C., 2001—03. Art tchr. Denver Mus., 1944—50; portrait painter, 1947—50; art tchr. adults and children Cleve. Recreation Dept., 1950—60; adult edn. art tchr. Nanuet Pub. Sch., NY, 1950-65, Pearl River Adult Edn., 1960—75. Rec. sec. Van Houten Fields Assn., West Nyack, NY, 1964—66. Exhibited in group shows at Hopper House, Rockland Ctr Arts, CWC, Cleve. Inst. Arts, Coll. New Rochelle, Rockland County Ann. Art Fair, Gonzalez Sr. Ctr.; co-author: (book and brochure) Van Houten Fields 1937-87, 1987; co-author, photographer: Windmills & Dreams, 1997; group show, Watercolor show, Santa Fe Cmty. Coll., 2003, exhibited in group shows at Santa Fe C.C. Leader 4-H Club, Nanuet, 1960—80, Girl Scouts US, 1961—68; mem. scholarship com., gen. com. PTA, 1964—68; rec. sec. Van Houten Fields Assn., West Nyack, NY, 1960—74; com. mem. Environ. Def. Fund, Union Concerned Scientists, Nat. Com. to Preserve Social Security and Medicare; capt., organizer Neighborhood Watch; campaign vol. Jim Baca for Gov., N.Mex., 1996, Gore for Pres., Santa Fe, 2000; bd. mem., mailings Friends of Santa Fe Libr., 2003—; vol. Santa Fe Libr., 1998—; com. mem. Eldorado Cmty. Improvement Assn.-Arterial Rd. Planning Com., 1992—94; campaign vol. Tom Udall for Congress, 1999—2003, 2003; mem. Eldorado Hist. Com., 1995—97; vol. Eldorado's Vista Grande Libr., 2001—03; mem. Eldorado chpt. Security Com., Eldorado Conservation Greenbelt Com., 1996—97, Shakespeare in Santa Fe Guild, 1998, Mil. Hist. Found., 2000—; vol. Cerro Grande Food Bank, 1998—. Gund traveling scholar, Cleve. Inst. Arts, 1946. Mem.: NOW, AAUW, Audubon Soc., Action on Smoking and Health, Union Concerned Scientists, Am. Dem. Action, Environ. Def. Fund, Wilderness Club, Phi Delta Kappa, Delta Tau Kappa. Democrat. Avocations: books, gardening, photography, bicycling, writing. Home: 122 Berkshire St Apt 2A Cambridge MA 02141-1426

SHUBB, WILLIAM BARNET, judge; b. Oakland, Calif., May 28, 1938; s. Ben and Nellie Bernice (Fruechtenicht) S.; m. Sandra Ann Talarico, July 29, 1962; children: Alisa Marie, Carissa Ann, Victoria Ann. AB, U. Calif., Berkeley, 1960, JD, 1963. Bar: Calif., 1964, U.S. Ct. Internat. Trade 1981, U.S. Customs Ct. 1980, U.S. Ct. Appeals (9th cir.) 1964, U.S. Supreme Ct. 1972. Law clk. U.S. Dist. Ct., Sacramento, 1963-65; asst. U.S. atty., Sacramento, 1965-71; chief asst. U.S. atty. (ea. dist.) Calif., 1971-74; assoc. Diepenbrock, Wulff, Plant & Hannegan, Sacramento, 1974-77, ptnr., 1977-80, 81-90; U.S. atty. Eastern Dist. Calif., 1980-81; judge U.S. Dist. Ct. (ea. dist.) Calif., 1990—, chief judge, 1996-2003; chmn. com. drafting of local criminal rules U.S. Dist. Ct. (ea. dist.) Calif., 1974, mem. speedy trial planning com., 1974-80; lawyer rep. 9th Cir. U.S. Jud. Conf., 1975-78; mem. faculty Fed. Practice Inst., 1978-80; instr. McGeorge Sch. Law, U. Pacific, 1964-66. Mem. ABA, Fed. Bar Assn. (pres. Sacramento chpt. 1977), Calif. Bar Assn., Assn. Def. Counsel, Am. Bd. Trial Advs., Sacramento County Bar Coun., Sacramento Rotary Club.

SHUBERT, GABRIELLE S. museum executive director; b. Phila., Apr. 28, 1955; d. Albert H. and Florence (Reiff) S. B in Music, Oberlin Coll., 1977; M in Public Adminstrn., N.Y.U., 1989. Asst. to v.p./dir. of sales Columbia Artist Mgmt., N.Y.C., 1979-80; artist rep. Herbert Barrett Mgmt., N.Y.C., 1980-81; dir. sales Sheldon Soffer Mgmt., N.Y.C., 1981-87; dir. work study program The Parks Coun., N.Y.C., 1987-88; mgr. arts for transit Met. Transp. Authority, N.Y.C., 1988-91; exec. dir. N.Y. Transit Mus., N.Y.C., 1991—. Guest lectr. N.Y.U., 1995, Yale U., New Haven, Conn., 1987; pub. art selection panel Dept. of Cultural Affairs, N.Y.C., 1992. Chmn. Concerned Citizens Upper Broadway, N.Y.C., 1983-85; fellow Coro Found. LEadership N.Y. program. Fellow Mus. Mgmt. Inst. Getty Mus., Berkeley, Calif., 1995, Mayor's Leadership Inst., N.Y.C., 1995. Fellow Mcpl. Art Soc. Office: NY Transit Museum 130 Livingston St Rm 9001 Brooklyn NY 11201-5106

SHUBERT, JOSEPH FRANCIS, librarian; b. Buffalo, Sept. 17, 1928; s. Joseph Francis and Lena M. (Kohn) Shubert; m. Dorothy Jean Whearty, Feb. 5, 1955 (div. Feb. 1980); children: Julia Ellen, Susan, Alan Joseph. BS, State U. Tchrs. Coll., Geneseo, N.Y., 1951; MA, U. Denver, 1957. Reference and ext. libr. Nev. State Libr., Carson City, 1951-57, libr. cons., 1957-59, state libr., 1959-61; asst. dir. internat. rels. office ALA, 1962-66; state libr. Ohio, 1966-77; sec., treas. chief officer state Libr. Agys. N.Y. State Edn. Dept., 1973-76, chmn., 1976-78, state libr., asst. commr. librs., 1977-96, state libr. emeritus, 1996—; mem. adv. coun. U.S. Pub. Printer, 1974-77; mem. adv. com. White House Conf. Libr. and Info. Svcs., 1977-79; chmn. steering com. survey state libr. agys. U.S. Nat. Ctr. Edn. Stats., 1992—2003. Trustee Ohio Coll. Libr. Ctr., 1976—78; Disting. Alumnus lectr. U. Denver, 1979; mem. adv. com. Ctr. for Book Libr. of Congress, 1979—82, mem. network adv. coun., 1981—96; mem. adv. coun. Sch. Libr. and Info. Sci., Pratt Inst., 1980—2000; bd. dirs. N.E. Document Conservation Ctr., 1980—82, treas., 1986—89; mem. design task force White House Conf. Libr. and Info. Svcs., 1985; chmn. chief officers State Librs. in N.E., 1987—89; bd. dirs. Capital Dist. Regional Info. Svc. Network State U. Albany, NY, 1994—97. Editor: The Bookmark, 1987—96; contbr. articles to periodicals. Dir. Friends N.Y. State Libr., Inc., 1998—; mem. adv. com. U. Wis. Inst. Edn., Federally Funded Literacy Program, 1992—94; co-chair 50th anniversary com. Coll. Geneseo, 2001. Named Disting. Alumnus, SUNY-Geneseo, 1985; named to Alumni Honor Roll, 1997; recipient Exceptional Achievement award, ALA Assn. Specialized and Coop. Libr. Agy. Assn., 1985, Disting. Pub. Svc. award, SUNY-Albany, Nelson A. Rockefeller Coll. Pub. Affairs and Policy, 1987, Hall of Fame award, Ohio Libr. Assn., 1991, Velma K. Moore award, N.Y. State Assn. Libr. Bds., 1996. Mem.: ALA (grass roots adv. 1996), Chief Officers State Libr. Agys. (chmn. 1977—78), N.Y. Libr. Assn. (hon. chair capital campaign 1999—2000, Outstanding Svc. award 1996), Meml. Libr. Assn., North Collins Libr. Assn., Nev. Libr. Assn. (pres.), Assn. Specialized and Coop. Lit. Agys. (pres. 1988—89), Task Force Pub. Libr. Stats. (mem. adv. com. 1990—96, chair steering com. NCES Survey State Libr. Agys. 1993—2003), Nat. Commn. Librs. and Info. Svcs., Nat. Ctr. Ednl. Stats., Nev. Congress Parents and Tchrs., Torch Club Albany. Roman Catholic. Home: 494 Madison Ave Albany NY 12208-3601 also: PO Box 1064 36 Lake Dr South Dennis MA 02660-2838 E-mail: jshubert@nycap.rr.com.

SHUBIK, MARTIN, economics professor; b. N.Y.C., Mar. 24, 1926; s. Joseph Louis and Sara S.; m. Julia Kahn, Aug. 11, 1970; 1 child, Claire Louise. BA, U. Toronto, 1947, MA, 1949; PhD, Princeton U., 1953. Rsch. asst. Princeton U., 1950—53, rsch. assoc., 1953-55; fellow Ctr. for Advanced Study in Behavioral Scis., Palo Alto, Calif., 1955-56; cons. mgmt. consultation svcs. Gen. Electric Co., 1956-60; adj. rsch. prof. Pa. State U., 1957-59; vis. prof. econs. Yale U., New Haven, 1960-61, prof. econs. of orgn., dept. adminstrv. sci., 1963-75, Seymour H. Knox prof. math. instl. econs., 1975—. Bd. dirs. Equity Strategies, Third Avenue Funds; mem. staff T.J. Watson Rsch. Labs., IBM Corp., 1961-63; vis. prof. Escuela de Estudios Económicos U. Chile, Santiago, 1965, Inst. Advanced Studies, Vienna, Austria, 1968, 70, U. Melbourne, Australia, 1973; cons. Rand Corp., Santa Monica, Calif., 1963; dir. Cowles Found. for Rsch. In Econs., Yale U., 1973-76; external faculty Santa Fe Inst., 1994—, sci. bd. 1996—; cons. in field. Author or co-author: numerous books, including The War Game, 1979, (with G. Brewer) The Aggressive Conservative Investor, 1979, (with M.J. Whitman) Market Structure and Behavior, 1980, (with R.E. Levitan) Game Theory in the Social Sciences, vol. 1, 1982, vol. 2, 1984, The Theory of Money and Financial Institutions, vols. 1 and 2, 1999; mem. editorial bd. Conflict Resolution; mem. editl. adv. bd. Internat. Studies Series; assoc. editor Mgmt. Sci, 1965-81; contbr. articles to profl. jours. Served to lt. Royal Can. Navy. Recipient Lanchester prize, 1983, Koopman prize mil. ops. rsch., 1996; named hon. prof. U. Vienna Fellow Econometric Soc., World Acad. Arts and Scis.; mem. Am. Acad. Arts and Scis., Conn. Acad. Arts and Scis. Home: 140 Edgehill Rd Hamden CT 06517-4011 Office: PO Box 208281 30 Hillhouse Ave New Haven CT 06520-8281 E-mail: martin.shubik@yale.edu.

SHUBROOKS, SAMUEL JOSEPH, JR., cardiologist; b. Phila., Nov. 4, 1939; s. Samuel J. and Edith L. (Dickson) Shubrooks; m. Gretchen A. Shubrooks, Jan. 15, 1993; children: Jeffrey A., Kimberly D. BS, Lebanon Valley Coll., 1961; MD, U. Pa., 1965. Diplomate Am. Bd. Internal Medicine, Am. Bd. Cardiovascular Disease & Interventional Cardiology. Attending staff Deaconess Hosp., Boston, 1974—96, Beth Israel Deaconess Med. Ctr., Boston, 1996—. Dir. cardiac catheterization Deaconess Hosp. Beth Israel, Boston, 1979—96; co-dir. cardiac catheterization lab. Beth Israel Deaconess Med. Ctr., Boston, 1996—; assoc. prof. Harvard Med. Sch., Boston, 2000—. Contbr. articles to profl. jours. Maj. USAF, 1969—72. Fellow: Am. Coll. Cardiology (bd. govs. and pres. Mass. chpt. 2004—), Am. Heart Assn. Office: Beth Israel Deaconess Med Ctr 1 Deaconess Rd Baker 4 Boston MA 02215 Office Phone: 617-632-9204.

SHUCART, WILLIAM ARTHUR, neurosurgeon; b. St. Louis, Oct. 23, 1935; s. Frank M. and Beatrice S.; m. Laura Huber, Dec. 16, 1971. AB, Washington U., 1957; MD, U. Mo., 1961. Diplomate Am. Bd. Neurol. Surgery. Intern U. Utah Hosp., Salt Lake City, 1961-62; resident in surgery Peter Bent Brigham Hosp., Boston, 1963-64; resident in neurosurgery Columbia-Presbyn. Hosp., N.Y.C., 1967-70, Hosp. for Sick Children, Toronto, Ont., Can., 1970-71; mem. faculty dept. neurosurgery Med. Sch. Tufts U., Boston, 1971-76, assoc. prof., 1976; prof., chmn. dept. neurosurgery SUNY, Downstate Med. Ctr., Bklyn., 1976-81; neurosurgeon Tufts-New England Med. Ctr., Boston, 1972-76, prof., chmn. dept. neurosurgery, 1981—; chief neurosurgery Beth Israel Hosp., Boston, 1996-97. Vis. prof. surgery Harvard Med. Sch., 1996-97. With U.S. Army, 1964-67. Mem. ACS, Am. Assn. Neurol. Surgeons, Soc. Neurol. Surgeons. Home: 100 Meadowbrook Rd Weston MA 02493-2406 Office: New England Med Ctr PO Box 178 750 Washington St Boston MA 02111-1526

SHUCK, EDWIN HAYWOOD, III, surgeon; b. Chattanooga, Tenn., 1948; MD, Washington U., St. Louis, 1973. Diplomate Am. Bd. Surgery, Am. Bd. Colon and Rectal Surgery. Intern Tulane U. Hosps., New Orleans, 1973-74, resident, 1974-78; fellow in colon and rectal surgery Carle Clinic, Urbana, Ill., 1978-79; priviliges Meml. Hosp., Chattanooga, Tenn.; pvt. practice Colon & Rectal Surg. Assocs. Asst. prof. clin. surgery U. Tenn. Fellow ACS, Am. Soc. Colon and Rectal Surgery. Office: Colon & Rectal Surg 2341 McCallie Ave #305 Plz Chattanooga TN 37404

SHUCK, JERRY MARK, surgeon, educator; b. Bucyrus, Ohio, Apr. 23, 1934; s. James Edwin and Pearl (Mark) S.; m. Linda Wayne, May 28, 1974; children: Jay Steven, Gail Ellen, Kimberly Ann, Lynn Meredith, Steven James. BS in Pharmacy, U. Cin., 1955, MD, 1959, DSc, 1966. Intern Colo. Gen. Hosp., Denver, 1959-60; resident in surgery U. Cin. Integrated Program, 1960-66; mem. faculty dept. surgery U. N.Mex., Albuquerque, 1968-80, prof., 1974-80; Oliver H. Payne prof. dept. surgery Case-Western Res. U., Cleve., 1980—, chmn. dept., 1980-2000, prof. anatomy, 1999—, interim v.p. for med. affairs, 1993-95, dir., assoc. dean grad. med. edn., 1999—. Cons. FDA, 1972-77 Contbr. articles to profl. jours. Served to capt. U.S. Army, 1966-68. Mem. ACS, Am. Surg. Assn., Am. Bd. Surgery (bd. dirs., chmn. 1993-94, residency rev. com. for surgery 1994-2000, vice chmn. 1997-2000), Soc. Univ. Surgeons, Am. Ass n. S urgery Trauma, Am. Trauma Soc. (founding mem.), Univ. Assn. Emergency Medicine (founding mem.), Am. Burn Assn. (founding mem.), We. Surg. Assn., Ctrl. Surg. Assn. (pres. 1996-97), Assn. Acad. Surgery, S.W. Surg. Assn., Cleve. Surg. Soc. (pres. 1988-89), Ohio Med. Assn., Acad. Medicine Cleve., Halsted Soc., Surg. Infection Soc. (founding mem.), B'nai B'rith, Jewish Cmty. Ctr. Club, The Temple Club. Democrat. Jewish. Office: Case Western Reserve U Dept Surgery 11100 Euclid Ave Cleveland OH 44106-2602

SHUCK, ROBERT F. financial executive; s. Robert F. II and Gertrude (Lehr) S.; m. Page Downe, May 30, 1969; children: Robert F. IV, Hollister A. BA in Acctg. with honors, S.E. Mo. Coll., 1959; MBA, Northwestern U., 1961. CPA, Ill.; cert. fin. planner. With Raymond James Fin., Inc., St. Petersburg, Fla., 1969—, vice chmn., 1991—. Bd. dirs. RJ Comm., Inc. Bd. dirs. Southeast Mo. Univ. Found.; trustee All Children's Hosp.; mem. long range devel. com. Fla. Coun. Econ. Edn.; mem. policy bd. Tampa Bay Partnership for Regional Econ. Devel.; mem. devel. found. St. Petersburg Jr. Coll.; stewardship chmn. Our Savior Luth. Ch., St. Petersburg. Mem. Securities Industry Assn. (sales and mktg. com.), Internat. Assn. for Fin. Planning (past bd. dirs.), Nat. Endowment for Fin. Edn. (trustee, mem. exec. com.). Office: Raymond James Fin 880 Carillon Pkwy Saint Petersburg FL 33716-1100

SHUE, ELISABETH, actress; b. Wilmington, Del., Oct. 6, 1963; m. Davis Guggenheim, 1994; 1 child: Miles. Student, Wellesley Coll.; grad., Harvard U.; studied with Sylvie Leigh, Showcase Theater. Appeared in Broadway plays including Some Americans Abroad, Birth and After Birth; appeared in films including The Karate Kid, 1984 (Young Artist award 1984), Link, 1986, Adventures in Babysitting, 1987, Cocktail, 1988, Body Wars, 1989, Back to the Future Part II, 1989, Back to the Future Part III, 1990, Soapdish, 1991, The Marrying Man, 1991, Twenty Bucks, 1993, Heart and Souls, 1993, Radio Inside, 1994, Blind Justice, 1994, The Underneath, 1995, Leaving Las Vegas, 1995 (Oscar nominee for Best Actress), The Trigger Effect, 1996, The Saint, 1996, Palmetto, 1997, Deconstructing Harry, 1997, Cousin Bette, 1997, Molly, 1998, Hollow Man, 2000, Tuck Everlasting, 2002; appeared in TV movies including Charles and Diana, Double Switch, 1987, Hale the Hero, 1992, Blind Justice; appeared in TV series Call to Glory, 1984, Amy & Isabelle, 2001. Office: Creative Arts Agy 9830 Wilshire Blvd Beverly Hills CA 90212-1804

SHUE, SHYH-PYNG JACK, aerospace engineer, researcher, electrical engineer, consultant; b. Taipei, Taiwan, China; came to U.S., 1991; s. Wan-Fung Shue and Chin Huan Lin; m. Wei-Chen Janus, Apr. 26, 1991; 1 child, Francis. BS in Marine Engring., Nat. Taiwan Ocean U., Keelung, China, 1986; MSME, Poly. U. Bklyn., 1992; PhD in Aerospace Engring., Wichita State U., 1997, PhD in Elec. and Computer Engring., 2000. Project engr. Even Fair Enterprise Co., Taipei, 1988-89; plant mgr. Casetek Internat. Co., Taipei, 1989-91; tech. support Hampel Techs. Inc., Tustin, Calif., 1992; rsch. asst. Wichita (Kans.) State U., 1993-98; rsch. assoc. Nat. Inst. Aviation Rsch., Wichita, 1997-98; engring. specialist Raytheon Aircraft Co., Wichita, 1998—2003; sr. engr. specialist Bell Helicopter Textron Inc., 2003—04. Contbr. more than 50 tech. papers to jours. Engring. fellow Wichita State U., 1995-96. Mem. AIAA (Best Paper 1995), Sigma Gamma Tau, Phi Kappa Phi. Avocations: golf, swim, fishing, boating, badminton. Home: 2809 Woodland Hills Dr Grapevine TX 76051-6431

SHUER, LAWRENCE MENDEL, neurosurgery educator; b. Toledo, Apr. 12, 1954; s. Bernard Benjamin and Estelle Rose (Drukker) S.; m. Paula Ann Elliott, Sept. 4, 1976; children: Jenna, Tammy, Nichole. BA with high distinction, U. Mich., 1975, MD cum laude, 1978. Diplomate Am. Bd. Neurol. Surgery, Nat. Bd. Med. Examiners. Fellow in neurology Inst. Neurology, London, 1979; intern in surgery Stanford (Calif.) U. Sch. Medicine, 1978-79, resident in neuropathology, 1980, resident in neurosurgery, 1980-84, clin. asst. prof. surgery and neurosurgery, 1984-90, assoc. prof., 1990—2002, acting chmn. dept. neurosurgery, 1992-95, 96—, assoc. dean, 1996—, chief of staff Stanford Health Sys., 1996—; chief of staff Stanford U. Hosp. and Clinics, 1999—, prof., 2002—. Numerous presentations in field. Contbr. articles and abstracts to med. jours., chpts. to books. Recipient Kaiser tchr. award Stanford U., 1993; James B. Angell scholar. Mem. AMA, Am. Assn. Neurol. Surgeons, Congress Neurol. Surgeons, Western Neurosurg. Soc., Calif. Assn. Neurol. Surgeons (bd. dirs., treas. 1995—98, 2nd v.p. 1998-99, 1st v.p. 1999-2000, pres.-elect 2000-01, pres. 2002-03), Calif. Med. Assn., Am. Heart Assn. (fellow stroke coun.), Santa Clara County Med. Assn., San Francisco Neurol. Soc., Alpha Omega Alpha. Avocations: skiing, swimming, travel. Office: Stanford U Med Ctr 300 Pasteur Dr R229 Palo Alto CA 94304-5327 Office Phone: 650-723-6093. Business E-Mail: lshuer@stanford.edu.

SHUEY, JOHN HENRY, diversified products company executive; b. Monroe, Mich., Mar. 14, 1946; s. John Henry and Bertha (Thomas) S.; children: Katherine, John Henry, John Joseph Satory. BS in Indsl. Engring., U. Mich., 1968, MBA, 1970. With Texas Instruments Co., Dallas, 1970-74; asst. treas. The Trane Co., La Crosse, Wis., 1974-78, treas., 1978-81, v.p., treas., 1981-83, v.p. fin., chief fin. officer, 1983-86; also v.p., group exec. Am. Standard; sr. v.p. and chief fin. officer AM Internat. Inc., Chgo., 1986-91; exec. v.p. Amcast Indsl. Corp., Dayton, Ohio, 1991-93, pres., COO, 1993-95, pres., CEO, 1995—, also chmn. bd. dirs., chmn. bd., pres., CEO, 1997—. Bd. dirs. Cooper Tire and Rubber Co., Findlay, Ohio, EMTEC. Bd. dirs. Wright State Univ. Found., 1996—; bd. trustees Dayton Ballet, 1996—, Ohio Found. of Ind. Colleges, 1994—. Mem. Fin. Execs. Inst. Congregationalist. Office: 7887 Washington Village Dr Dayton OH 45459-3900 also: Elkhart Products Corp 1255 Oak St Elkhart IN 46514-2277

SHUEY, RICHARD LYMAN, engineering educator, consultant; b. Chgo., May 7, 1920; s. Ralph Clement and Abbie Miriam (Strong) S.; m. Frances Barbara Fortier, Sept. 22, 1944; children: Roy Fortier, Marie Frances. BS in Engring., BSE in Math., U. Mich., 1942; PhD in Elec. Engring., U. Calif., Berkeley, 1950. Registered engr. N.Y., Calif. Engr. U. Calif. Radiation Lab., Berkeley, 1946-50; rsch. staff, br. mgr. GE Rsch. Lab., Schenectady, N.Y., 1950-84; adj. prof. Rensselaer Polytech. Inst., Troy, N.Y., 1985—; cons. Schenectady, 1985—. Author: The Architecture of Distributed Computer Systems, 1997; contbr. articles to profl. jours. Bd. dirs. Self Help for Hard of Hearing N.Y. Assn., 1996-2001. Sr. mem. IEEE (various coms., offices 1952-87, Donald McLellan Cmty. Svc. award, 3d Millennium medal), AAAS, Am. Auditory Soc., Soc. Mfg. Engrs., Assn. Computing Machines, Sigma Xi, Tau Beta Pi. Avocations: golf, bridge, photography. Office: Computer Sci Dept RPI Troy NY 12180 Home: 242 Glen Eddy Dr Schenectady NY 12309-4967 Personal E-mail: shueyrl@juno.com.

SHUFORD, HARLEY FERGUSON, JR., furniture manufacturing executive; b. Norfolk, Va., Oct. 7, 1937; s. Harley Ferguson Sr. and Nancy (Pope) S.; m. Helgi Kuuskraa; children: Linda, David. BA, U. N.C., 1959. Engr. Century Furniture Co., Hickory, N.C., 1959-60, mgr. data processing, 1960-63, v.p. mfg., 1964-67, pres., 1967-95; chmn. CV Industries (formerly Shuford Industries, Inc.), Hickory, 1994—. Bd. dirs. 1st Union Bank N.C., Charlotte. Trustee Catawba Meml. Hosp., Hickory, 1971-77, chmn., 1977-81; bd. dirs. U. N.C. Sys., Chapel Hill, 1975-83; bd. dirs. N.C. Citizens Bus. and Industry, Raleigh, 1982-95; chmn. N.C. Arts Coun., Raleigh, 1985-93. Mem. Am. Furniture Mfrs. Assn. (bd. dirs. 1968-92, pres., chmn. 1980-82), Catawba County C. of C. (pres. 1976), Phi Beta Kappa. Republican. Mem. United Ch. of Christ. Office: CV Industries PO Box 608 Hickory NC 28603-0608

SHUGART, HOWARD ALAN, physicist, researcher; b. Orange, Calif., Sept. 21, 1931; s. Howard Ancil and Bertha Elizabeth (Henderson) S.; m. Elizabeth L. Hanson, Feb. 6, 1971. BS, Calif. Inst. Tech., 1953; MA, U. Calif., Berkeley, 1955, PhD, 1957. Tchg. asst. physics U. Calif., Berkeley, 1953-56, assoc., 1957, lectr., 1957-58, acting asst. prof., 1958-59, asst. prof., 1959-63, assoc. prof., 1963-67, prof., 1967-93, prof. emeritus, 1993—, vice chmn., 1968—70, 1979—87, 1989—2001, acting chmn., 1979—81, 1983—84, 1987. Cons. Convair divsn. Gen. Dynamics Corp., 1960-61; mem. com. nuc. constants NRC, 1960-63; atomic beam group leader Lawrence Berkeley (Calif.) Nat. Lab., 1965-79, guest rschr., 1999—. Fellow Am. Phys. Soc. (acting sec. Pacific Coast 1961-64, exec. com. divsn. electron and atomic physics 1972-74), Nat. Speleological Soc. (gov. 1954-56); mem. Sigma Xi. Office: U Calif Dept Physics Berkeley CA 94720-7300

SHUGART, JILL, retired school system administrator, educational consultant; b. Dallas, July 15, 1940; d. Claude Ernest and Allie Merle (Hamilton) S. BA, Baylor U., 1962; MA, Tex. Woman's U., 1972, PhD, 1980. Middle sch. English tchr. Garland (Tex.) Ind. Sch. Dist., 1962-63, high sch. social studies tchr., 1963-76, high sch. asst. prin., 1976-79, dir. communications, 1979-82, asst. supt., 1982-85, supt., 1985—99; ret., 1999—; interim dir. Region X Edn. Svc. Ctr. Mem. legis. coun. U. Interscholastic League, Tex., 1989-99; chmn. Dist. III music com., Tex., 1989-99; adj. prof. Tex. Women's U., Denton, 1983; chmn. Region X ESC Adv. Coun., rep. to commr.'s supt.'s com., 1993-95; cons. Richardson and Carrollton-Farmers Br. Sch. Dists., 2000-04; coord. Region 10 ESC Supr.'s Acad., 2000-04. Gen. chmn. Boy Scouts Am. Scouting Night, Dallas, 1988-89; chmn. City of Garland Comty. Action Com., 1995-99; sec. Tex. Sch. Alliance, 1995-96, chmn., 1998-99; life mem. Tex. and nat. PTA; pres. Garland br. Am. Heart Assn., 1990-91; co-chmn. sustaining dr. Garland YMCA, 1995-96; mem. Adv. Com. to Gov. and State Legisture, 1998; mem. steering com. Garland Econ. Devel. Partnership, 1994-99, Tex. Fast Growth Sch. Coalition; chair Tex. Sch. Alliance, 1998—. Recipient Lamar award for excellence Masons, Award of Distinction, Tex. Ret. Tchrs. Assn.; named Top 100 Educators to Watch, Executive Educator mag., 1985, Finalist as Outstanding Tex. Sch. Supt., 1990, Woman of Distinction, Soroptimist Club; Paul Harris fellow. Mem. Quality Tex. Bd. Examiners, Garland Edn. Found. (bd. dirs. 1999-2004), Baylor Med. Ctr. Garland (bd. dirs. 2001-04). Republican. Baptist. Avocations: travel, lake activities.

SHUGHART, DONALD LOUIS, retired lawyer; b. Kansas City, Mo., Aug. 12, 1926; s. Henry M. and Dora M. (O'Leary) Shughart; m. Mary I. Shughart, July 25, 1953; children: Susan C. Hogsett, Nancy J. Goede. AB, U. Mo., Columbia, 1949, JD, 1951. Bar: Mo. 1951, U.S. Dist. Ct. (we. dist.) Mo. 1951, U.S. Tax Ct. 1979. With Shughart, Thompson & Kilroy, PC, Kansas City, Mo., 1951—. With AC, U.S. Army, 1944-47. Mem. Kansas City Bar Assn. (chmn. bus. orgns. com. 1990-91), Mo. Bar Assn. (chmn. corp. com. 1980-81, 82-83), Lawyers Assn. Kansas City, Am. Judicature Soc., Mo. Orgn. Def. Lawyers (pres. 1971-72), U. Mo. Law Soc., Phi Delta Phi, Sigma Chi. Republican. Roman Catholic. Home: 1242 W 67th Ter Kansas City MO 64113-1941 Office: Shug Thom Kilroy 12 Wyandotte Pla 120 W 12th St Kansas City MO 64105-1917

SHULA, DON FRANCIS, former professional football coach, team executive; b. Painesville, Ohio, Jan. 4, 1930; s. Dan and Mary (Miller) S.; children: David, Donna, Sharon, Anne, Michael; m. Mary Anne Shula. BS, John Carroll U., Cleve., 1951, H.H.D. (hon.), 1972; MA, Case Western Res. U., 1953; Sc.D. (hon.), Biscayne Coll., 1974, St. Thomas U., 1976, U. Miami, 1992, Fla. Atlantic U., 1999. Profl. football player Cleve. Browns, 1951-52, Balt. Colts, 1953-56, Washington Redskins, 1957; asst. coach U. Va., 1958, U. Ky., 1959, Detroit Lions, 1960-62; head coach Baltimore Colts, 1963-69, Miami (Fla.) Dolphins, 1970-96; vice chmn. Miami Dolphins, 1996—; owner, pres. Shula Enterprises. Author: The Winning Edge, 1972, (with Ken Blanchard) Everyone's A Coach, 1995. Fla. crusade chmn. Nat. Cancer Soc., 1975; co-chmn. Jerry Lewis March Against Dystrophy, 1975; nat. bd. dirs. Boy's Hope; mem. nat. sports com. Multiple Schlerosis Soc., Muscular Dystrophy Assn.; bd. dirs. Heart Assn. Greater Miami; established Don Shula Found., breast cancer rsch., 1991—; sponsor Don Shula Scholarship, 1978—. Coached 6 Superbowl teams, winning teams 1972, 73; recipient Coach of Yr. awards 1964, 66, 70, 71, 72, Coach of decade Profl. Football Hall of Fame, 1980, Pro Football's All-Time Winningest Coach, 1994, Brotherhood award Fla. region NCCJ, 1977, Light of Flames Leadership award Barry Coll., 1977, Concern award Cedars Med. Ctr., 1992, Solheim Lifetime Achievement award, 1992, Jim Thorpe award, 1993,Sportsman of Yr. Sports Illustrated, 1993, Horrigan award Pro Football Writers,1994, Horatio Alger award, 1995, Vince Lombardi Award of Excellence, 1999; named Balt. Colts Silver Anniversary Coach, 1977, elected to Pro Football Hall of Fame, 1997. Roman Catholic. Office: Shula Enterprises Inc 16 Indian Creek Is Miami Beach FL 33154-2904 *Success is never final; defeat is never fatal.*

SHULA, ROBERT JOSEPH, lawyer; b. South Bend, Ind., Dec. 10, 1936; s. Joseph Edward and Bertha Mona (Buckner) S.; m. Gaye Ann Martin, Oct. 8, 1978; children: Deirdre Regina, Robert Joseph II, Elizabeth Martin. BS in Mktg., Ind. U., 1958, JD, 1961. Bar: Ind. 1961. Ptnr. Bingham Summers Welsh & Spilman, Indpls., 1965-82, sr. ptnr., 1982-89; ptnr. Price & Shula, Indpls., 1989-91, Lowe Gray Steele & Darko, Indpls., 1991—2003; of counsel Norris Choplin and Schroeder, Indpls., 2003—. Mem. faculty Nat. Inst. Trial Advocacy; guest lectr. Brit. Medicine and Law Soc., 1979, Ind. U. Sch. Law; medico-legal lectr. Ind. U. Schs. Medicine, Dentistry, and Nursing. Bd. dirs. Arts Ind., Indpls., 1995-99; pres. Oriental Arts Soc., Indpls., 1975-79, Meridian Women's Clinic, Inc., Indpls.; trustee Indpls. Mus. Art, 1975-78, life trustee, 1984—; bd. dirs. Ind. Repertory Theatre, Indpls., 1982-92, chmn. bd. dirs., pres., 1985-89; pres. Repertory Soc., 1993-96; v.p., bd. dirs. Flanner House of Indpls., Inc., 1977-88, chmn., 1988-99; pres. Internat. Ctr. of Indpls., Inc., 1993-96. Maj. JAGC, USAFR, 1961—65. Recipient Gov.'s award of Sagamore of the Wabash, 1998. Master Am. Inns of Ct.; fellow Internat. Soc. Barristers; mem. ABA, FBA, Ind. Bar Assn., Indpls. Bar Assn. (diplomate), Am. Bd. Trial Advs. (pres. 2000), Am. Law Inst., Am. Coll. Legal Medicine, Def. Trial Counsel Ind. (diplomate), Confrerie Chevaliers du Tastevin, Woodstock Country Club. Democrat. Episcopalian. Home: 7924 Beaumont Green Pl Indianapolis IN 46250-1663 Office: 101 W Ohio St 9th Flr Indianapolis IN 46204-4213 Office Phone: 317-269-9330. E-mail: rshula@ncs-law.com.

SHULENBURGER, DAVID EDWIN, economics educator, university official; b. Salisbury, N.C., Sept. 19, 1945; s. Hubert Ray and Allie (Goodnight) S.; m. Carol Prentice, Aug. 10, 1994; children: Adam Anthony, Neal Gordon, Luke Nathan. BA, Lenoir-Rhyne Coll., 1967; MA, U. Ill., 1968, PhD, 1974. Instr. Clemson (S.C.) U., 1968-71; rsch. asst. U. Ill., Champaign, 1971-72, teaching asst., 1972-74; staff labor economist U.S. Dept. Labor, Washington, 1973; asst. prof. bus. adminstrn. U. Kans., Lawrence, 1974-77, assoc. prof. bus. adminstrn., 1977-83, prof. bus. adminstrn., 1983—, undergrad. dir., 1982-85, assoc. dean, 1985-88, assoc. vice chancellor, 1989-92, vice chancellor, 1993-96, provost, 1996—. Cons. Kans. Dept. Human Resources, Topeka, 1975-77, fact-finder, 1979—; panel arbitrator United Mine Workers and P&M Coal Co., Pitts., 1982—; earnings expert for numerous law firms, Kans., Mo., 1979-89. Contbr. articles to profl. jours. Chmn. troop com. Boy Scouts Am., Lawrence, 1984, asst. scoutmaster, 1985—; mem. Kansas City City Coun.; pres. Lawrence Bus./Edn. Partnership, 1995-96. Internat. Curriculum grantee U.S. Dept. Edn., 1987. Mem. AAUP (chpt. pres. 1981-82), Indsl. Rels. Rsch. Assn., Am. Econ. Assn., So. Econ. Assn., Swarthout Soc. (bd. dirs. 1989—). Avocations: travel, camping, gardening. Office: Office of Provost Strong Hall Lawrence KS 66045-7535

SHULER, ELLIE GIVAN, JR., retired military officer, military museum administrator; b. Raleigh, N.C., Dec. 6, 1936; s. Ellie Givan and Berta (Williams) S.; m. Annette Fontaine Maury, Mar. 22, 1961; children: Ellie Givan III, Franklin Maury, Gray Hays. BSCE, The Citadel, 1959; MS in Mgmt., Rensselaer Poly. Inst., 1967; grad., Squadron Officer Sch., Maxwell AFB, Ala., 1964; postgrad., Naval War Coll.; grad. command and staff course, Nat. War Coll., 1976; grad. cen. flight instr. course, Castle AFB, Calif. Engr. in tng., S.C. Commd. 2d lt. U.S. Air Force, 1959, advanced through grades to lt. gen., 1988, various positions and locations, 1959-68, F-4C pilot, asst. flight comdr. 558th Tactical Fighter Squadron, 1968-69, indsl. engr., then asst. dep. chief Engring. Mgmt. Div., Hdqrs. 2d Air Force Barksdale AFB, La., 1969-71; asst. exec. officer to comdr. in chief U.S. Air Force in Europe, Lindsey Air Sta., West Germany, 1972-73, base civil engr., comdr. 86th Civil Engring. Squadron Ramstein Air Base, Fed. Republic Germany, 1973-75; dir. ops. 3902d Air Base Wing, comdr. 3902d Ops. Squadron Offutt AFB, Nebr., 1976; dir. programs Office Dep. Chief of Staff for Engring. and Services SAC, Offutt AFB, Nebr., 1976-77, exec. to comdr. in chief, 1977-79; vice comdr., then comdr. 19th Bombardment Wing Robins AFB, Ga., 1979-80; comdr. 42d Bombardment Wing Loring AFB, Maine, 1980-81; comdr. 4th Air Div. F.E. Warren AFB, Wyo., 1981-84; comdr. 3rd Air Div. SAC, Andersen AFB, Guam, 1984-86; asst. dep. then dep. chief of staff, ops. SAC Hqrs., Offutt AFB, Nebr., 1986-88; comdr. 8th Air Force SAC, Barksdale AFB, 1988-91; retired, 1991; chmn. bd., CEO 8th Air Force Heritage Mus., 1992—98. Trustee, Longs Peak coun. Boy Scouts Am., 1983-84, chair bd. trustees, 1992-2004; trustee Falcon Found., USAF Acad., 8th Air Force Heritage Mus., 1992—. Decorated D.S.M. with oak leaf cluster, Legion of Merit with oak leaf cluster, D.F.C., Air medal with five oak leaf clusters, Air Force Commendation medal with oak leaf cluster. Mem. Soc. Am. Mil. Engrs. (chpt. pres. 1971), Am. Def. Preparedness Assn. (regional bd. dirs. 1981-84), Order of Dadaelians (hon. flight capt. 1981-85), Council on Am.'s Mil. Past, Mil. Order of World Wars, Kiwanis, Tau Beta Pi. Republican. Episcopalian. Avocations: numismatics, golf, hunting, fishing, military history. Office: 675 Willow Way W Alexander City AL 35010-6253

SHULER, JAMES MANNIE, health physicist; b. Orangeburg, S.C., Oct. 23, 1951; s. Ellie Grier Shuler and Gerdene Rickenbaker Shuler. BS in Botany, Clemson U., 1974; MA in Mgmt. and Supervision, Ctrl. Mich. U., 1977; MS in Radiation Sci., Georgetown U., 1988; MPA in Public Adminstrn., U. So. Calif., 1997, DPA in Public Adminstrn., 1999. Regstered radiation protection technologist, environ. profl., environ. mgr.; cert. hazard control mgr., hazardous materials mgr., environ. trainer transp. hazardous materials and waste occupl. health and safety. Health physics technician Allied-General Nuclear Svcs., Barnwell, S.C., 1975-79; supr. health physics Chem-Nuclear Sys., Inc., Barnwell, 1979, customer and compliance rep., 1979; radioactive materials enforcement specialist U.S. Dept. Transp., Washington, 1979-81, 83-88; radwaste/transp. specialist Applied Tech. of Barnwell, Inc., 1981-83; phys. scientist U.S. Dept. Energy, Germantown, Md., 1988-89, health physicist Aiken, S.C., 1989-93, from sr. health physicist to phys. scientist Washington, 1993-96, health physicist, 1996—. Assoc. staff instr. U.S. Dept. Transp./Transp. Safety Inst., Oklahoma City, 1981—89; vis. instr. Georgetown U., Washington, 1988—89; assoc. grad. faculty Ctrl. Mich. U., 2001—. Contbr. articles to profl. jours. and tech. publs. Mem. ASTM (sect. 6 leader radiation protection methods verification 1993-2003), Nat. Environ. Tng. Assn., Assn. of MBA Execs., Am. Nuclear Soc., Health Physics Soc. (environ. radiation sect., govt. sect. 1993—). Home: 12835 Locbury Cir Apt I Germantown MD 20874-3858 Office: US Dept Energy EM-24 CLOV-1081 Washington DC 20585-0001 Office Phone: 301-903-5513. E-mail: James.Shuler@hq.doe.gov.

SHULER, JON EMMETT, securities industry professional; b. Aiken, SC, Sept. 21, 1946; s. Cyril Ovierre and Elizabeth Carolina (Smith) S.; m. Virginia Rose Harris, Aug. 1, 1981; children: Jon Emmett Jr., Kline Martin. BA in Econs., Clemson U., 1968; MBA, U.S.C., 1970. CFP. Broker J.C. Bradford & Co., Spartanburg, S.C., 1972-81, br. mgr., 1981-88, Raymond James & Assocs., Spartanburg, S.C., 1988-94; owner, pres., reg. investment adv. Wealth Mgmt. Assocs., Inc., 1994—. Co-author: Getting to the Heart of the Matter, 1999. Bd. dirs. Habitat for Humanity, Spartanburg, 1990; mem. ARC State Pub. Support Com., Columbia, S.C., 1993; trustee Spartanburg Day Sch., 1997—; v.p. endowments Palmetto coun. Boy Scouts Am., 1999—2002. Mem. Rotary (pres. North Spartanburg chpt. 1990, Paul Harris fellow 1989), Soc. Mayflower Descendants. Republican. Presbyterian. Avocations: skiing, antique collecting, woodworking. Personal E-mail: jeshuler@hotmail.com.

SHULER, KURT EGON, chemist, educator; b. Nuremberg, Germany, July 10, 1922; came to U.S., 1937, naturalized, 1944; s. Louis and Donie (Wald) Schulherr; m. Beatrice Gwyn London, Nov. 11, 1944. BS, Ga. Inst. Tech., 1942; PhD, Cath. U. Am., 1949. Fellow Johns Hopkins U., 1949-51; sr. staff mem., asst. group supr., chem. physics group Applied Physics Lab., Johns Hopkins, 1951-55; supervisory phys. chemist Nat. Bur. Standards, 1955-58, cons. to dir., 1958-61, asst. dir., sr. research fellow, 1963-68; rsch. staff, sci. adviser to v.p. rsch. Gen. Motors Corp., 1958; spl. asst. to dir. rsch. Inst. Def. Analyses, 1961-63; vis. prof. chemistry U. Calif., San Diego, 1966-67, prof. chemistry, 1968-91, prof. emeritus, 1991—, chmn. dept., 1968-70, 84-87. Cons. in field; mem. Solvay Conf., 1962, 78; mem. adv. panel, chemistry div. NSF, 1973-75. Author, editor tech. books; assoc. editor: Jour. Math. Physics, 1963-66; bd. editors: Jour. Statis. Physics, 1968-80; mem. adv. bd.: Chem. Engring. News, 1967-70; contbr. articles to profl. jours. Served with U.S. Army, 1944-46. Recipient Distinguished Service award Nat. Bur. Standards, 1959, Gold medal award Dept. Commerce, 1968; Solvay Found. fellow, 1975 Fellow Am. Inst. Chemists, AAAS, Am. Phys. Soc., Washington Acad. Sci.; mem. Am. Chem. Soc., Washington Philos. Soc. Clubs: Rancho Santa Fe Golf. Home: PO Box 1504 Rancho Santa Fe CA 92067-1504 Office: Univ Calif San Diego Dept Chemistry La Jolla CA 92093

SHULER, SALLY ANN SMITH, retired media consultant; b. Mt. Olive, N.C., June 11, 1934; d. Leon Joseph and Ludia Irene (Montague) Simmons; m. Henry Ralph Smith Jr., Mar. 1, 1957 (div. Jan. 1976); children: Molly Montague, Barbara Ellen, Sara Ann, Mary Kathryn; m. Harold Robert Shuler, Aug. 2, 1987 (div. Mar. 1997). BA in Math., Duke U., 1956; student, U. Liège, Belgium, 1956-57; postgrad., Claremont Grad Sch., 1970-72. Mgr. fed. systems GE Info. Svcs. Co., Washington, 1976-78, mgr. mktg. support Rockville, Md., 1978-81; dir. bus. devel. info. tech. group Electronic Data Sys., Bethesda, Md., 1981-82, v.p. mktg. optimum systems div. Rockville, 1982-83, v.p. planning and comm. Dallas, 1983-84; exec. dir. comml. devel. U.S. West Inc., Englewood, Colo., 1984-90; v.p. mktg. devel. Cin. Bell Info. Sys. Inc., 1990-92; mgmt. cons. in mergers and acquisitions Denver, 1992-93, 1995—2002; v.p. major accounts U.S. Computer Svcs., Denver, 1993-95; ret., 2002. Bd. dirs. Rotary-Denver Tech. Ctr., 1999—2003, Seeking Common Ground, 2001—02. Recipient GE Centennial award, Rockville, 1978. Mem. Women in Telecommunications, Rotary (Found. fellow, prest. Denver Tech. Ctr. 1999-2000, amb. scholar 1956-57), Phi Beta Kappa, Tau Psi Omega, Pi Mu Epsilon, Sigma Kappa. Democrat. Presbyterian. Office Phone: 303-671-5950.

SHULER DONNER, LAUREN, film producer; BS in Film and Broadcasting, Boston U. Assoc. prodr.: (films) Thank God It's Friday, 1978; Mr. Mom, 1983; Ladyhawke, 1985; St. Elmo's Fire, 1985; Pretty in Pink, 1986; Three Fugitives, 1989; Radio Flyer, 1992; Dave, 1993; Free Willy, 1993; prodr.: (TV films) Amateur Night at the Dixie Bar and Grill, 1979; (films) Free Willy 2: The Adventure Home, 1995, You've Got Mail, 1998, Any Given Sunday, 1999, X-Men, 2000, X2: X-Men United, 2003, Timeline, 2003, Constantine, 2004; exec. prodr.: Assassins, 1995; Free Willy 3, 1997; Volcano, 1997; Out Cold, 2001; Just Married, 2003. Office: The Donners' Co Ste 420 9465 Wilshire Blvd Beverly Hills CA 90212

SHULEVITZ, URI, author, illustrator; b. Warsaw, Feb. 27, 1935; came to U.S., 1959, naturalized, 1965; Student, Tel-Aviv Art Inst., 1953-55; Tchrs. Cert., Tchrs. Coll. Israel, 1956; student, Bklyn. Museum Art Sch., 1959-61. Instr. illustrating and writing children's books The New Sch., 1970-86; dir. illustrating and writing children's books Hartwick Coll., 1974-92. Author, illustrator: The Moon In My Room, 1963, One Monday Morning, 1967, Rain Rain Rivers, 1969, Oh What a Noise, 1971, The Magician, 1973, Dawn, 1974, The Treasure, 1978, (Caldecott honor Book 1979), The Strange and Exciting Adventures of Jeremiah Hush, 1986, Toddlecreek Post Office, 1990, The Secret Room, 1993, Snow, 1998 (Caldecott Honor book 1999), What is a Wise Bird like you Doing in a silly tale like this?, 2000; author: Writing with Pictures: How to Write and Illustrate Children's Books, 1985; illustrator: The Mystery of the Woods, 1964, Charley Sang a Song, 1964, A Rose, A Bridge and A Wild Black Horse, 1964, The Second Witch, 1965, The Carpet of Solomon, 1966, Maximilian's World, 1966, The Silk Spinners, 1967, The Fool of the World and the Flying Ship, 1968 (Caldecott medal 1969), Runaway Jonah and Other Tales, 1968, The Twelve Dancing Princesses, 1966, Oh What A Noise!, 1971, Soldier and Tsar in the Forest, 1972, The Fools of Chelm, 1973, The Touchstone, 1976, Hanukah Money, 1978, The Lost Kingdom of Karnica, 1979, The Golem, 1982, Lilith's Cave: Jewish Tales of the Supernatural, 1988, The Diamond Tree, 1991, The Golden Goose, 1995, Hosni The Dreamer, 1997, others. Served with Israeli Army, 1956-59. Guggenheim fellowship, 1999. Mem Authors Guild. Address: PO Box 432 New York NY 10014 Office: care Farrar Straus & Giroux Inc 19 Union Sq W New York NY 10003-3304

SHULGASSER-PARKER, BARBARA, writer; b. Manhasset, N.Y., Apr. 10, 1954; d. Lew and Luba (Golante) S.; m. Norman Parker, Sept. 1999; 1 child: Atticus. Student, Sarah Lawrence Coll., 1973-74; BA magna cum laude, CUNY, 1977; MS, Columbia U., 1978. Feature writer Waterbury (Conn.) Rep., 1978-81; reporter, feature writer Chgo. Sun Times, 1981-84; film critic San Francisco Examiner, 1984-98; freelance book critic N.Y. Times Book Rev., N.Y.C., 1983—; film critic Chgo. Tribune, 1999—2001. Author: Funny Accent, 2001; co-author: (screenplay, with Robert Altman) Ready to Wear, 1994; freelance video columnist N.Y. Times Sunday Arts & Leisure, 1989, features for Vanity Fair, Glamour and Mirabella mags.

SHULL, CLAIRE, documentary film producer, casting director; b. NYC, Oct. 26, 1925; d. Barnet Joseph and Fannie (Florea) Klar; m. Leo Shull, Aug. 8, 1948; children: Lee Shull Pearlstein, David. Student, Am. Acad. Dramatic Arts, NYC, 1943—44, NYU, 1973—74. Editor, assoc. pub. Show Bus. Publs., NYC, 1957-85; owner, founder Claire/Casting, NYC and Miami, Fla., 1972—, Claire/Casting Film Prodns., NYC and Miami, 1978—; cons. dir., prodr., dir. film and TV The Bass Mus., Miami Beach, Fla., 1992—. Miami corr. film, TV, theatre Show Bus. Weekly, 1999—. Actress in The Front Page, USO European tour, 1945-46, (on Broadway) Tenting Tonight, 1947; prodr., dir. HBO TV series How To Break into Show Business, 1980-81, Cable-TV series, Join Us at the Bass, 1993-97. Recipient gold award and distinctive merit TV award Advt. Club. Hartford, Conn., 1984, Clio award, 1989. Mem.: Drama Desk, Actors Equity Assn., Ind. Casting Dirs. Assn. NY, Miami Internat. Press Club.

SHULL, HARRISON, chemist, educator; b. Princeton, N.J., Aug. 17, 1923; s. George Harrison and Mary (Nicholl) S.; m. Jeanne Louise Johnson, 1948 (div. 1962); children: James Robert (dec.), Kathy, George Harrison, Holly; m. Wil Joyce Bentley Long, 1962; children: Warren Michael Long, Jeffery Mark Long, Stanley Martin, Sarah Ellen. AB, Princeton U., 1943; PhD, U. Calif. at Berkeley, 1948. Assoc. chemist U.S. Naval Research Lab., 1943-45; asst. prof. Iowa State U., 1949-54; mem. faculty Ind. U., 1955-79, research prof., 1961-79, dean Grad. Sch., 1965-72, vice chancellor for research and devel., 1972-76, dir. Research Computing Center, 1959-63, acting chmn. chemistry dept., 1965-66, acting dean arts and scis., 1969-70, acting dean faculties, 1974; mem. faculty, provost, v.p. acad. affairs Rensselaer Poly. Inst., 1979-82; chancellor U. Colo., Boulder, 1982-85, prof. dept. chemistry, 1982-88; provost Naval Postgrad. Sch., 1988-95; asst. dir. rsch., quantum chemistry group Uppsala (Sweden) U., 1958-59; vis. prof. Washington U., St. Louis, 1960, U. Colo., 1963; founder, supr. Quantum Chemistry Program Exchange, 1962-79; chmn. subcom. molecular structure and spectroscopy NRC, 1958-63; chmn. Fulbright selection com. chemistry, 1963-67; mem. adv. com. Office Sci. Personnel, 1957-60; chmn. First Gordon Research Conf. Theoretical Chemistry, 1962; mem. com. survey chemistry Nat. Acad. Sci., 1964-65; mem. adv. panel chemistry NSF, 1964-67; mem. adv. panel Office Computer Activities, 1967-70, cons. chem. information program, 1965-71, mem. adv. com. for research, 1974-76; mem. vis. com. chemistry Brookhaven Nat. Lab., 1967-70; mem. adv. com. Chem. Abstracts Service, 1971-74. Dir. Storage Tech. Corp., 1983-99; chief of Naval Ops. Exec. Panel, 1984-88. Assoc. editor: Jour. Chem. Physics, 1952-54; editorial adv. bd.: Spectrochimica Acta, 1957-63, Internat. Jour. Quantum Chemistry, 1967—2001, Proc. NAS, 1976-81; contbr. articles to profl. jours. Trustee Argonne U. Assn., 1970-75, Asso. Univs., Inc., 1973-76, U. Rsch. Assn., 1984-89, Inst. Defense Analysis, 1984-96. Served as ensign USNR, 1945. NRC postdoctoral fellow phys. scis. U. Chgo., 1948-49; Guggenheim fellow U. Uppsala, 1954-55; NSF sr. postdoctoral fellow, 1968-69; Sloan research fellow, 1956-58 Fellow AAAS, Am. Acad. Arts and Scis. (v.p. 1976-83, chmn. Midwest Ctr. 1976-79), Am. Phys. Soc.; mem. Nat. Acad. Scis. (com. on sci. and pub. policy 1969-72, coun., exec. com. 1971-74, chmn. U.S.-USSR sci. policy subgroup for fundamental rsch. 1973-81, naval studies bd. 1974-79, 96-2001, chmn. Commn. on Human Resources, 1977-81, nominating com. 1978), Am. Chem. Soc., Royal Swedish Acad. Scis. (fgn. mem.), Royal Acad. Arts and Scis. Uppsala (corr. mem.), Cosmos Club (Washington), 1966-2003, Old Capital Club (Monterey), Phi Beta Kappa, Sigma Xi, Phi Lambda Upsilon. Home: 2 Cramden Dr Monterey CA 93940-4144

SHULL, MIKKI, media consultant; b. Cleve. d. Lois Biles; life ptnr. Jerome China. BS, Carnegie-Mellon U., 1983. Bus. transformation cons. PriceWaterhouseCoopers, N.Y.C., 1986-97; media and entertainment cons. IBM Global Svcs., N.Y.C., 1997—. Mem. Advt. Women N.Y. Republican. Office: IBM 590 Madison Ave New York NY 10022 Home: 180 Belmont Ave Jersey City NJ 07304-2002 E-mail: shull@us.ibm.com.

SHULMAN, ABRAHAM, otolaryngology educator, hospital administrator; b. N.Y.C., Feb. 24, 1929; s. Ben and Libby (Sarnoff) S.; m. Arlene P., Sept. 8, 1957; children: Rachel, Melanie. BS, CCNY, 1950; MD, U. Berne, Switzerland, 1955. Diplomate Am. Bd. Otolaryngology. Rotating surg. intern Queens County Gen. Hosp., 1955-56; resident in otolaryngology Kings County Hosp., Bklyn., 1957-60; clin. instr. Downstate Med. Ctr., SUNY, 1962-64, assoc. prof., 1975-89; prof. clin. otolaryngology SUNY Health Sci. Ctr., Bklyn., 1989—92, prof. emeritus clin. otolaryngology, 1992—; clin. instr. Albert Einstein Coll. Medicine, 1966-68, asst. clin. prof. otolaryngological surgery, 1968-75. Asst. surgeon Bklyn. Eye & Ear Hosp., 1966-69; otology cons. College Point chief of otolaryngology Lincoln Hosp., 1967-70, Bklyn. VA Med. Ctr., 1977-85, chief otolaryngology, staff attending otolaryngologist, 1985—, acting chief of otolaryngology, 1990-91; lectr., asst. attending otolaryngologist Mt. Sinai Hosp., 1974; chief otolaryngology Lincoln Hosp., 1967-1970; asst. attending otolaryngology Bronx Mcpl. Hosp., 1967-75; chief Otolaryngologist, asst. attending otolaryngologist, Kings County Hosp., 1962-64, dir. otolaryngology, 1975-92, attending otolaryngologist, 1975—, Brookdale Med. Ctr., 1982-86; chief otolaryngology Cath. Med. Ctr., Bklyn. and Queens, 1969-94, attending otololaryngologist St. John's Queens Hosp., 1969-94; chmn. Internat. Tinnitus Forum, 1982—; Martha Entenmann Tinnitus Rsch. Ctr., Inc., dir. otology neurotology 1994—. Editor (co-chief): Internat. Tinnitus Jour., 1994—; editor: (text) Tinnitus Diagnosis and Treatment, 1991—. Cons. Children's Devel. Ctr., 1975; med. cons. Office Vocat. Rehab., 1974; dir. med. svc. Lexington Sch. of the Deaf, 1972-74. Lt. comdr. USNR, 1960-62. Recipient Cert. of Appreciation, Am. Speech and Hearing Assn., 1989—, Hocks award, Am. Tinnitus Assn., 1990, Honor award, Am. Acad. Otolaryngology, 1994, Myrtle Reed award, Hadassah Zionist Orgn. Am., honoree, Neuro Equilibrimetric Soc., 1998. Fellow ACS, AMA, Am. Acad. Ophthalmology and Otolaryngology, Am. Neurotology Soc., Am. Audiology Soc., Am. Soc. Ophthalmologic and Otolaryngology Allergy, Am. Soc. Facial Plastic Surgery, Internat. Coll. Surgeons, Adam Politzer Soc.; mem. Am. Coun. Otolaryngology, Am. Soc. Contemporary Medicine and Surgery, Pan-Am. Assn. Otorhinolaryngology and Bronchoesophagology, N.Y. Acad. Sci., Soc. for Cryosurgery, Queens County Med. Soc., Soc. Univ. Otolaryngologists, Bklyn. Oncology Soc., Assn. for Rsch. in Otolaryngology, Neuroequilibrimetric Soc., Harvey Soc., Centurion Club, Sigma Xi. Office: SUNY Health Sci Ctr Bklyn Div Otolaryngology 450 Clarkson Ave Brooklyn NY 11203-2056

SHULMAN, ADLEY M. lawyer, educator; b. L.A., Aug. 28, 1931; s. Reuben and Dee (Rosenbaum) S.; m. Corinne S. Shulman, June 22, 1952; children: Gail Denise Feinberg, Susan Linda, Ogden, Nancy Ann Pullen, Barton Alan. BA with highest honors, UCLA, 1953, JD, 1958. Bar: Calif. 1958, U.S. Dist. Ct. (ctrl. dist.) Calif. 1958, U.S. Ct. Appeals (9th cir.) 1958, U.S. Supreme Ct. 1967. Ptnr. firm Shulman & Shulman, Beverly Hills, Calif., 1958-84, Shulman, Shulman & Siegel, 1984-2000, Shulman & Shulman, Hydesville, Calif., 2000—. Tchr. adult sch. L.A. Area Cmty. Schs., 1971-82; mem. faculty Humboldt State U., 1984-91. Mem. editl. staff UCLA Law Rev., 1956-58;

contbr. articles to profl. publs. Bd. dirs. Hospice of Humboldt, 1988-95; mem. joint commn. on social action United Synagogue of Am., L.A., 1963-66; mem. L.A. 5th Councilmanic Adv. Commn., 1968-73; mem. com. on law and legis. Jewish Fed. Coun., L.A., 1971-78; mem. Humboldt County Human Rights Commn., 1997-2001. Recipient 1st ann. Human Rels. award L.A. City Human Rels. Bur., 1970. Mem. Calif. State Bar Assn., Los Angeles County Bar Assn. (trustee 1982-83), Beverly Hills Bar Assn. (pres. 1983-84), Order of Coif, Phi Beta Kappa. Democrat. Jewish. Office: Shulman & Shulman PO Box 642 Hydesville CA 95547-0642

SHULMAN, ALIX KATES, writer; b. Cleve., Aug. 17, 1932; d. Samuel Simon and Dorothy (Davis) Kates; m. Martin Shulman, June 1959 (div. 1985); children: Ted, Polly; m. Scott York, Apr. 1989. BA, Case Western Res. U., 1953, LHD (hon.), 2001; MA, NYU, 1978. Instr. New Sch. for Social Rsch., N.Y.C., 1972-74, NYU Sch. of Continuing Edn., 1976-79, Yale U., New Haven, Conn., 1979-81, NYU, 1981-84; writer-in-residence U. Colo., Boulder, 1984-86; vis. writer-in-residence Ohio State U., Columbus, 1987; citizen's chair of lit. U. Hawaii at Manoa, Honolulu, 1991-92; vis. writer-in-residence U. Ariz., Tucson, 1994. Author: Bosley on the Number Line, 1970, Finders Keeper, 1971, Awake or Asleep, 1971, To the Barricades: The Anarchist Life of Emma Goldman, 1971, Memoirs of an Ex-Prom Queen, 1972, Red Emma Speaks, 1972, Burning Questions, 1978, On the Stroll, 1981, In Every Woman's Life..., 1987, Drinking the Rain, 1995, A Good Enough Daughter, 1999. Feminist activist Redstockings, NY, 1969-71, Carasa, NYC, 1971-82, No More Nice Girls, NYC and Honolulu, 1986-92, Women's Action Coalition, NYC, 1992-94, Vet. Feminists Am., 1998-04, Feminist Futures, NYC, 2001-04. Fellowship in fiction Nat. Endowment for the Arts, 1983, DeWitt Wallace/Reader's Digest fellow, 1979, MacDowell Colony for the Arts, 1975-77, 79, 81, Body Mind Spirit award of excellence, 1996, Rockefeller Found. Bellagio Ctr. resident, 1997. Mem. Poets Essayists Novelists (exec. bd. 1974-91, v.p. 1982-83), Nat. Writers Union, Author's Guild and Author's League, Columbia U. Seminar on Women and Soc. (exec. bd. 1980-82).

SHULMAN, ALLEN L. financial services company executive; BA in English, Rutgers Coll.; JD, Suffolk U. Mng. atty. Horvath & Lieber, Atlanta, 1983-96; CEO, gen. counsel, chief fin. officer United Refridgerated Svcs., Inc.; exec. v.p., chief fin. officer, gen. cons. Check Free Holdings, Inc., Norcross, Ga., 1997—. Office: Check Free Holdings Inc 4411 E Jones Bridge Rd Norcross GA 30092-1615

SHULMAN, ARTHUR, communications executive; b. N.Y.C., Mar. 4, 1927; s. Jacob and Sarah (Hochman) S.; m. Jan. 30, 1958; children: James, Karen. BA, Syracuse U., 1950. Asst. to pub. TV Guide Mag., Radnor, Pa., 1958-72; pub. Seventeen Mag., N.Y.C., 1972-73; dir. regional ops. TV Guide, 1974-82; dir. comm. B'nai B'rith Internat., Washington, 1983-93. Author: How Sweet It Was, 1966, The Television Years, 1972. Dir. Penn Wynne (Pa.) Civic Assn., 1965-66. S/Sgt. US Army, 1945-46, Japan. Mem. Radio & TV Execs. Soc., Nat. Press Club, Overseas Press Club, Nat. Acad. TV Arts & Scis. Jewish. Address: 4017 Jardin Ln Sarasota FL 34238-4504 Personal E-mail: artshulman@comcast.net.

SHULMAN, BARRY MARTIN, lawyer; b. Ithaca, N.Y., Dec. 31, 1939; s. Cecil and Shirley I. Shulman; m. Debrah Anne Roth, June 16, 1963; children— Marc-David Roth, Jennifer Suzanne, Allison Rebecca. B.S. in Econs., U. Pa., 1961; J.D., Cornell U., 1966. Bar: N.Y. 1966, U.S. Dist. Ct. (no. dist.) N.Y. 1966, U.S. Supreme Ct. 1970. Assoc., Mackenzie, Smith, Lewis, Mitchell & Hughes, Syracuse, N.Y., 1966-73, Axenfeld, Webb, Marshall, Bensani & Scolaro, Syracuse, 1973-78; ptnr. Shulman & Whitelaw, Syracuse, 1978-82, Scolaro, Shulman, Cohen & Whitelaw, Syracuse, 1981-82; ptnr., pres. Scolaro, Shulman, Cohen, Lawler & Burstein, P.C., Syracuse, 1982—; counsel N.Y. State Senate Judiciary Com., 1968-73; assoc. counsel N.Y. State Senator John H. Hughes; counsel to N.Y. State Senator Martin S. Auer, 1974; spl. counsel to minority leader N.Y. State Assembly, 1975-82; counsel Central N.Y. Regional Transp. Authority. Past counsel Jewish Home of Upstate N.Y., Huntington Family Ctr.; past gen. chmn. WCNY TV Auction; past chmn. United Way Attys. Drive; mem., bd. dirs. Syracuse Hebrew Day Sch.; hon. past pres. Temple Adath Yeshurun; mem., founding ptnr. counsel's sect. Am. Pub. Transit Assn.; bd. dirs. United Negro Coll. Fund; past pres. Liberty Republican Club; mem. Onondaga County Execs.' Com. on Hist. Sites; counsel to Cornell U. Central N.Y. Alumni Club; past bd. dirs. Hiawatha council Boy Scouts Am., Salt City Ctr. for Performing Arts, Easter Seal Soc.; bd. dirs., mem. exec. com., gen. campaign chmn. Syracuse Jewish Fedn., 1983-84. Served to 2d lt. U.S. Army, 1961-63. Mem. Onondaga County Bar Assn. (bd. dirs., organizer and panelist TV series), N.Y. State Bar Assn. (chmn. practical skills series). Home: 7800 Saint Charles Ave # C New Orleans LA 70118-3853 Office: Scolaro Shulman Cohen Lawler & Burstein PC 1064 James St Syracuse NY 13203-2704

SHULMAN, CAROLE KAREN, professional society administrator; b. Mpls., Nov. 25, 1940; d. Allen Eldon and Beulah Ovidia (Blomsness) Banbury; m. David Arthur Shulman, Mar. 26, 1962; children: Michael, Krista, Tracy, Robbyn. Student, Colo. Coll., 1958-61, California Coast U., 1983-84. Profl. instr. Rochester (Minn.) Figure Skating Club, 1962-84, dir. skating, 1964-79, cons., 1979—; exec. dir. Profl. Skaters Assn., Rochester, 1984—, master rating examiner, 1971—, world profl. judge, 1976, 79, 87-88. Editor Professional Skater mag., 1984—; prodr. U.S. Open Profl. Figure Skating Championships, 1987, 89—. Pres. Rochester Arts Council, 1983. Recipient Achievement award Rochester Arts Coun., 1983, Mayor's Medal of Honor, 1997; named triple gold medalist U.S. Figure Skating Assn., Colorado Springs, Colo., 1959, 63, Master Rated Coach Profl. Skaters Assn., 1970, Sr. Rated Coach in Dance Profl. Skaters Assn., 1970. Mem. Am. Harp Soc., Profl. Skaters Assn. (hon., Lifetime Achievement award 1989). Mem. Covenant ch. Avocations: harp, skiing. Office: Profl Skaters Assn Internat 3006 Allegro Park SW Rochester MN 55902-0886

SHULMAN, GERALD I. endocrinologist, educator, research scientist; b. Detroit, Feb. 8, 1953; BS with high honors and distinction, U. Mich., 1974; MD, PhD, Wayne State U., 1979; MA, privatim (hon.), Yale Univ., 1997. Intern Duke U., Durham, NC, 1979-80, residency, 1980-81; fellowship in endocrinology and metabolism Mass. Gen. Hosp., Boston, 1981-84; asst. prof. medicine Harvard U., Boston, 1985-87; assoc. prof. Sch. Medicine Yale U., New Haven, 1989-96; assoc. dir. Yale MD-PhD Program Sch. Medicine Yale U., New Haven, 1993—, prof. medicine, cellular and molecular physiology, 1996—. Vis. prof. Vanderbilt U., 1994, Albert Einstein Coll. Medicine, 1999, Washington U. Sch. Medicine, 2001, Cambridge U., 2002, U. Md., 2004; assoc. dir. Yale Diabetes Endocrine Rsch. Ctr., 1996—; investigator Howard Hughes Med. Inst., 1997—; program dir. Yale/New Haven Hosp. Gen. Clin. Rsch. Ctr.; Pfizer prof. U. Colo.; mem. NIH study sects.; lectr. in field. Mem. editl. bd. Diabetes Jour. Am., Am. Jour. Physiology, Diabetic Medicine, Jour. Clin. Investigation, Am. Jour. Medicine, Diabetologia, Internat. Jour. Molecular Medicine, Am. Jour. Physiology, Jour. Biol. Chemistry; mem. editl. bd.: Cell Metabolism, 2004—, PLoS Medicine, 2004—; contbr. articles to profl. jours. Recipient of the Outstanding Investigator award for Clinical Rsch. 1994, Young Investigator award Am. Fed. for Med. Rsch., 1997, Boehriger Mannheim/ Juvenile Diabetes Found. Internat., Diabetes Care Rsch. award, 1997, Young Investigator award in diabetes Novartis, 1999, Mary June Kugel award, Juvenile Diabetes Rsch. Found. Internat. 1999, E.H. Ahrens Jr. award, Assoc. for Patient-Oriented Rsch., 2001, Josiah Brown award in Diabetes, UCLA, 2002, Disting. Clin. Scientist award Am. Robotics Assn., 2004. Fellow ACP, Internat. Soc. Magnetic Resonance in Medicine, Am. Soc. Clin. Investigation; mem. Am. Diabetes Assn. (clin. rsch. grantee 1996, Outstanding Sci. Achievement Lilly Lectr. award 1997, Mentor award 1997, 99, Disting. Clin. Scientist award 2004); mem. Assn. Am. Physicians, Endocrine Soc., Am. Physiol. Soc., European Assn. for Study of Diabetes, Interurban Clin. Club. Office: Howard Hughes Med Inst Yale U Sch Medicine PO Box 9812 New Haven CT 06536-0812 Fax: 203-737-4059. E-mail: gerald.shulman@yale.edu.

SHULMAN, LAWRENCE EDWARD, biomedical research administrator, rheumatologist; b. Boston, July 25, 1919; s. David Herman and Belle (Tishler) S.; m. Pauline K. Flint, July 19, 1946; m. Reni Trudinger, Mar. 20, 1959; children: Kathryn Verena, Barbara Corina. AB, Harvard U., 1941, postgrad., 1941-42; PhD, Yale U., 1945, MD, 1949. Diplomate Nat. Bd. Med. Examiners. Intern Johns Hopkins Hosp., 1949-50, resident and fellow in internal medicine, 1950-53; dir. connective tissue div. Johns Hopkins U., 1955-75, assoc. prof. medicine, 1964—; assoc. dir. div. arthritis, musculoskeletal and skin diseases NIH, Bethesda, Md., 1976-86, dir., 1982-86, dir. Nat. Inst. Arthritis, Musculoskeletal and Skin Diseases, 1986-94, dir. emeritus, 1994—, emissary for clin. rsch., 1995—. Chmn. med. adminstrn. com. Arthritis Found., Atlanta, 1974-75, exec. com., 1972-77; dir. Lupus Found. Am.; med. adv. bd. United. Scleroderma Found., Watsonville, Calif., 1977-88; chmn. sci. group rheumatic diseases WHO, 1989; W.R. Graham meml. lectr., 1973; Cochrane disting. lectr., 1993; vis. prof. Imperial Coll., London, 2002. Discoverer: Eosinophilic Fasciitis, 1974, new med. sign friction rubs in scleroderma, 1961. Recipient Sr. Investigator award Arthritis Found., 1957-62, Disting. Svc. award, 1979, Heberden medal for rsch., London, 1975, Superior Svc. award USPHS, 1985, master Am. Rheumatism Assn., 1986, Spl. Recognition award Nat. Osteoprosis Found., 1991, Spl. award Am. Acad. Orthop. Surgeons, 1992, Presdl. citation for leadership Am. Acad. Dermatology, 1993, Leadership award Lupus Found. Am., 1994, Career Achievement award Am. Coll. Rheumatology, 1994, Outstanding Support Rsch. award Am. Soc. Bone Mineral Rsch., 1994, Gold medal Am. Coll. Rheumatology, 1995, 1995 Award of Merit, NASA, Johns Hopkins Medicine and Dean's Spl. Recognition award, 2004. Fellow ACP, AAAS; mem. Am. Rheumatism Assn. (pres. 1974-75), Pan-Am. League Against Rheumatism (pres. 1982-86, Morino Gold medal award 2002), Soc. Investigative Dermatology, Am. Soc. Bone Mineral Rsch. Home: Apt 7BC 3900 Watson Pl B NW Washington DC 20016 Office: NIH 9000 Rockville Pike Bethesda MD 20892-0003

SHULMAN, MADELYN R. SPATT, lawyer; b. NYC, Apr. 11, 1948; d. Max and Sarah (Rivin) Spatt; m. Michael Joel Shulman, Mar. 7, 1970; children: Jonathan, Jeremy. BA in Polit Sci., U. Mich., 1968; MA in Communications, Stanford U., 1976; JD, NYU, 1979, LLM in Tax Law, 1987. Bar: NY 1980. Assoc. Stroock & Stroock & Lavan, NYC, 1979-83, Hayt, Hayt & Landau, Great Neck, NY, 1984-87, Parker, Chapin, Flattau & Klimpl, Jericho, NY, 1987-89, Law Offices of Madelyn Spatt Shulman, Great Neck, NY, 1989-91; ptnr. Soberman, Shulman & Rosenberg, Lake Success, NY, 1991-99; of counsel Meltzer, Lippe, Goldstein, Wolf & Schissel P.C., Mineola, NY, 1999—2000; prin. Madelyn Spatt Shulman PC, Jericho, NY, 2000—. Bd. dir. Women Econ. Developers L.I., 1996—. Mem. ABA (lectr.), Nassau County Bar Assn. (chmn. corp. law com. 2002—, lectr.), NY State Bar Assn., Order of Coif. Democrat. Jewish. Office: Madelyn Spatt Shulman PC 350 Jericho Tpke Ste 101 Jericho NY 11753-1317 Office Phone: 516-942-5100. E-mail: msspc@optonline.net.

SHULMAN, MILDRED, artist; b. Perth Amboy, N.J., Aug. 13, 1927; d. Abraham and Estelle (Golub) S.; m. Ben Spina, Feb. 20, 1947 (div. Aug. 1954). Student, Sch. Indsl. Arts, N.Y.C., 1942—45, McDowell Sch. Art, 1946—47, NYU, 1961—62, Art Student's League, 1991—95. Contr. Continental Mdse. Co., Inc., N.Y.C., 1959-65, Famous Fashion Shops, N.Y.C., 1966-69; owner, pres. Luminere Creations, Inc., N.Y.C., 1969-91; self-employed artist N.Y.C., 1991—. Author: Barter*The Silent Giant, 1985. Mem.: New Art Ctr., Midtown West Art Assn., Am. Soc. Portrait Artists, Nat. Mus. Women in the Arts, Art Students League, Salmagundi Club. Achievements include patents for flexible screen partitions; electrical/sculptural lighting design; sculpturing method. Avocations: hiking, swimming. Fax: 212-242-2846.

SHULMAN, RICHARD, musician, composer, recording label owner; b. Niagara Falls, NY, May 11, 1951; s. Herbert and Celeste Shulman. BA in Music and Psychology, U. Rochester, 1973; MA in Music Composition, SUNY, Buffalo, 1978. Leader, pianist, composer Richard Shulman Group, Buffalo, N.Y.C. and Asheville, NC, 1979—2003; prin. composer Theatre of the Heart, N.Y.C., 1985—95; owner, primary rec. artist RichHeart Music, Woodstock, NY and Asheville, 1990—. Composer: jazz compositions with Richard Shulman Group, solo piano improvisations, synthesizer compositions for healing, background music for spoken word recordings, works for orch. and chamber groups. Recipient Coalition of Visionary Resources award, Camelot Reawakened CD, 2003; Composer Appearance grantee, Meet the Composer, N.Y.C., 1987—89. Mem.: Assn. for Ind. Music. Avocations: hiking, swimming, meditation, esoteric healing work. Office: RichHeart Music PO Box 6731 Scarborough ME 04070-6731 Office Phone: 888-699-3682. Business E-Mail: info@richheartmusic.com.

SHULMAN, ROBERT GERSON, biophysics educator; b. N.Y.C., Mar. 3, 1924; s. Joshua S. and Freda (Lipshay) S.; m. Saralee Deutsch, Aug., 1952 (dec. Oct. 1983); children: Joel, Mark, James; m. Stephanie S. Spangler, May 11, 1986. AB, Columbia U., 1943, MA, 1947, PhD, 1949. Rsch. assoc. Columbia U. Radiation Lab., N.Y.C., 1949; AEC fellow in chemistry Calif. Inst. Tech., Pasadena, 1949-50; head semicondr. research sect. Hughes Aircraft Co., Culver City, Calif., 1950-53; mem. tech. staff Bell Labs., Murray Hill, N.J., 1953-66, head biophysics rsch. dept., 1966-79; prof. molecular biophysics and biochemistry Yale U., 1979-94, dir. divsn. biol. scis., 1981-87, Sterling prof. molecular biophysics and biochemistry, 1994—2002, Sterling prof. emeritus molecular biophysics 2nd biochemistry, 2002—, sr. rsch. scientist dept. diagnostic radiology, 2002—. Rask Oersted lectr. U. Copenhagen, 1959; vis. prof. Ecole Normale Superieur, Paris, 1962; Appleton lectr. Brown U., 1965; vis. prof. physics U. Tokyo, 1965; Reilly lectr. U. Notre Dame, Ind., 1969; vis. prof. biophysics Princeton U., 1971-72; Regents lectr. UCLA, 1978 Lt. (j.g.) USNR, 1944-46. Guggenheim fellow in lab. molecular biology MRC Cambridge (Eng.) U., 1961-62; recipient Havinga medal Leiden U., 1983, Gold medal Soc. Magnetic Resonance in Medicine, 1984, Mem. Nat. Acad. Scis., Inst. Medicine. Achievements include research in spectroscopic techniques applied to physics, chemistry and biology. Office: Dept Diagnostic Radiology MRRC Yale U PO Box New Haven CT 06520-8043 E-mail: Robert.Shulman@Yale.edu.

SHULMAN, ROBERT JAY, pediatrician, educator, nutritionist; b. Newark; s. Irving Jack and Shirley Shulman; children: David Ian, Hannah Rachel. BA, Emory U., 1972; MD, Chgo. Med. Sch., 1976. Diplomate in pediatrics and pediatric gastroenterology Am. Bd. Pediatrics. Asst. prof. pediat. Baylor Coll. Medicine, Houston, 1982-89, assoc. prof., 1989-96, prof., 1996—; dir. nutritional support team Tex. Children's Hosp., Houston, 1982—; chair pediatric gastroenterology Tex. Children's Hosp. Found. Chmn. sub-bd. in pediatric gastroenterology Am. Bd. Pediatrics, 2003—. Author: Young Chef's Nutrition Guide and Cookbook, 1990, Keys to Child Nutrition, 1991; author: (with others) Pediatric Parenteral Nutrition, 1997, Principles and Practice of Pediatrics, 1998, Pediatric Gastroenterology and Nutrition in Clinical Practice, 2001; co-editor: Nutrition in Your Pocket, 2002; mem. editl. bd. Jour. Pediat. Gastroenterology and Nutrition, 1994—96. Fellow: Am. Acad. Pediat.; mem.: Soc. Pediat. Rsch., N.Am. Soc. Pediat. Gastoenterology and Nutrition (exec. coun. 1997—99), Am. Inst. Nutrition, Am. Soc. Patenteral and Enteral Nutrition (chmn. pediatric sect. 1997—99, pres. 1997—99), Am. Gastroent. Assn. Avocation: guitar. Office: Baylor Coll Medicine 1100 Bates Ave Houston TX 77030-2600

SHULMAN, RON E. lawyer; b. Boston, 1955; BA, Amherst (Mass.) Coll., 1977; JD, Rutgers U., 1981. Bar: N.Y. 1982, Calif. 1995. Ptnr. Fish & Neave, N.Y.C., 1981—95, Wilson Sonsini Goodrich & Rosati, Palo Alto, Calif., 1995—. Named one of Top Ten Jury Trial Lawyers in Country, The Nat. Law Jour., 2002. Office: Wilson Sonsini Goodrich & RosatiProfl Corp 650 Page Mill Rd Palo Alto CA 94304-1050*

SHULMAN, STEPHEN NEAL, lawyer; b. New Haven, Apr. 6, 1933; s. Harry and Rea (Karrel) S.; m. Sandra Paula Still, Aug. 14, 1954; children—Harry, Dean, John. BA, Harvard, 1954; LL.B. cum laude, Yale, 1958. Bar: Conn. 1958, D.C. 1960. Indsl. relations Bendix Aviation Corp., 1954-55; law clk. to Justice Harlan, U.S. Supreme Ct., 1958-59; vis. asst. pro. U. Mich. Law Sch., 1959; asso. firm Covington & Burling, Washington, 1959-60; asst. U.S. atty. Washington, 1960-61; exec. asst. to sec. labor, 1961-62; dept asst. sec. of def., 1962-65; gen. counsel U.S. Air Force, 1965-66; chmn. Equal Employment Opportunity Commn., 1966-67; mem. Kane, Shulman & Schlei, Washington, 1967-70; mem. firm Cadwalader, Wickersham & Taft, N.Y.C., also Washington, 1971-95, Freedman, Levy, Kroll & Simonds, Washington, 1995-99, O'Connor & Hannan, L.L.P., Washington, 1999—. Vis. prof. mgmt. U. Okla., 1965-66. Co-author: The Law of Equal Employment Opportunity, 1990; editor in chief Yale Law Jour., 1957-58. Mem. Book and Gavel, Order of Coif, Cum Laude Soc., Phi Alpha Delta. Home: 1332 Skipwith Rd Mc Lean VA 22101-1841 Office: O Connor & Hannan LLP 1666 K St NW Washington DC 20006-2803 Office Phone: 202-887-1442. E-mail: sshulman@oconnorhannan.com.

SHULMISTER, M(ORRIS) ROSS, lawyer; b. Atlanta, Jan. 6, 1940; s. Morris and Kathryn Sybella (Baker) S.; m. Benita Vee Rosin, Dec. 16, 1974. BEE, U. Fla., 1962, JD, 1973. Bar: Fla. 1973, U.S. Dist. Ct. (so. dist.) Fla. 1974, U.S. Dist. Ct. (mid. dist.) Fla. 1985, U.S. Ct. Appeals (5th and 11th cirs.) 1981. Pvt. practice, Broward County, Fla., Ft. Lauderdale, Fla., 1974—. Spl. master for code enforcement, Pompano Beach, Fla., 1991-92. Mem. Broward County Consumer Protection Bd., 1983-2001, chmn., 1999-2000; chmn. Charter Review Bd., Pompano Beach, Fla., 1994-97; dir. South Pompano Civic Assn., 1989-2000, v.p., 1989, pres., 1992-98. Lt. col. USAF, 1964-70, ret., USAFR, 1970-93. Mem. Fla. Bar (mem. constrn. law subcom., civil trial cert. 1984-99), Broward County Bar Assn. (bd. dirs. 2003—). Office: 590 SE 12th St Pompano Beach FL 33060-9409

SHULTIS, ROBERT LYNN, finance educator, cost systems consultant, retired professional association executive; b. Kingston, NY, June 30, 1924; s. Albert H. and Dorothy Elizabeth (Jenkins) S.; m. Bernice Elizabeth Johnson, Jan. 20, 1946; 1 son, Robert Lee. BS, Columbia Univ. Sch. Bus., 1949, postgrad., 1949-51. Staff acct. Price Waterhouse, N.Y.C., 1949-52; credit mgr., controller Organon, Inc., West Orange, N.J., 1952-68; v.p., treas., chief fin. officer Arwood Corp., Rockleigh, N.J., 1968-72; v.p., controller Technicon, Tarrytown, N.Y., 1972-80; exec. dir. Inst. of Mgmt. Accts., Montvale, N.J., 1980-86; faculty, exec. dir. Ctr. for Exec. Devel. Coll. William & Mary, Williamsburg, Va., 1987-91. Instr. Rutgers U., 1964-74, Fairleigh Dickinson U., 1967-68; mem. Fin. Acctg. Standards Adv. Coun., 1981-86; lectr., seminar leader, cons. on controllership, activity-based costing, cost mgmt., cost sys. design Boston U., U. Calif., Berkeley, U. Minn., Michigan State U., So. Meth. U., Baldwin Wallace Coll., George Mason U., James Madison U., U. N.C., Colo. State U., others, 1990—. Editor: Management Accountants' Handbook, and supplements, 1991-94; contbr. articles to profl. jours. Mem. bd. advs. U. Fla. Sch. Accountancy, James Madison U. Sch. Accountancy; mem. fin. and budget com. Kingsmill Cmty. Svcs. Assn.; interpreter Historic Jamestowne Island, 1997—. Served with USAF, 1943-45. Decorated Presdl. Unit Citation, ETO Ribbon, eight battle stars. Mem. AAUP, VFW, Am. Legion, Fin. Execs. Internat. (editl. adv. bd.), Inst. Mgmt. Accts., Assn. for Preservation of Va. Antiquities, Kingsmill Club, Beta Alpha Psi (adv. forum).

SHULTZ, BRIAN MICHAEL, diversified financial services company executive; s. Mike and Dee Shultz; m. Edineia Saccomandi, Sept. 8, 2001. MBA in Internanational Bus., Thunderbird Garun Sch. Internat. Mgmt., 1999. Intern Am. Embassy, Pretoria, South Africa, 1991, Sen. Lloyd Bentson, Austin, Tex., 1992; internat. trade program architect Lubbock (Tex.) C. of C., 1994; legis. aid Tex. Legis., Austin, 1995; dir. fin., gen. mgr. CellStar Internat., São Paulo, Brazil, 1995—98; dir. field ops. Fasturn Inc., Redwood City, Calif., 2000—03; mng. prin. Internat. Bus. Group, Dallas, 2003—. Spkr., lectr. in field. Rep. precinct chmn., Lubbock, 1994—95. Republican. Methodist. Avocations: rugby, travel, literature. Office: Internat Bus Group PO Box 12050 Dallas TX 75225 E-mail: bshultz@internationalbusinessgroup.com.

SHULTZ, DELRAY FRANKLIN (LUCKY SHULTZ), business and management consultant, coach; b. South Bend, Ind., Apr. 4, 1948; s. Jack Raymond and Georgina Martha (Johnston) S.; m. Catherine Elizabeth Yontz, June 6, 1970; children: Jeremy Frank, Eric Bruce, Jon Karl. BS, USAF Acad., 1970; MS, Air U., 1978. Commd. 2d lt. USAF, 1970, advanced through grades to capt., 1973, navigator, 1972—77, adminstrv. contracting officer L.A., 1978—81; mgr. purchasing, contracts supr. BP Exploration, Anchorage, 1981—92, internal cons. Bogotá, Colombia, 1992—93; mgr. contracts, internal cons. Alaska Petroleum Contractors, Anchorage, 1994—97; mgr. assurance and devel., internal cons. Natchiq Inc., Anchorage, 1997—2000; owner Pathways to Leadership, Seattle, 1999—2003, The Entrepreneur's Source, Seattle, 2002—03, Lucky Shultz & Assocs., 2003—; pres. IGC Assocs., Inc., 2003. Adj. prof. U. Alaska, Anchorage, 1989—96; edn. coord. Bus. Network Internat. (Mill Creek, Wash. chpt.), 2001—03; fin. aide Alaska State Senate Senator Fred Dyson, 2004. Bd. mem., vice chair bd. dirs. Family Connection, Inc., Anchorage, 1981-84; dir., bd. elders Bethany Christian Cmty., Anchorage, 1982-93; del. Rep. Party of Alaska, Anchorage, 1988, 96. Named Outstanding Young Men of Am., U.S. Jr. C. of C., 1978; recipient Silver medal Buckley Sch. Pub. Spkg., 1997. Mem. Nat. Contract Mgmt. Assn., Nat. Assn. Purchasing Mgrs., Am. Soc. for Quality. Avocations: commercial pilot, public speaker, personal development teacher/coach, musician. E-mail: ptlwest@aol.com.

SHULTZ, GEORGE PRATT, former government executive, economics educator; b. N.Y.C., Dec. 13, 1920; s. Birl E. and Margaret Lennox (Pratt) S.; children: Margaret Ann Shultz Tilsworth, Kathleen Pratt Shultz Jorgensen, Peter Milton, Barbara Lennox Shultz White, Alexander George; m. Charlotte Mailliard, Aug. 15, 1997. BA in Econs., Princeton U., 1942; PhD in Indsl. Econs., MIT, 1949; Hon. degree, Yeshiva U., U. Tel Aviv, Technion-Israel Inst. Tech., Keio U., Tokyo, Brandeis U., U. Notre Dame, Princeton U., Loyola U., U. Pa., U. Rochester, Carnegie-Mellon U., Baruch Coll., Northwestern U., Tblisi State U., Columbia U. Mem. faculty M.I.T., 1949-57; assoc. prof. indsl. relations MIT, 1955-57; prof. indsl. relations Grad. Sch. Bus., U. Chgo., 1957-68; dean sch. Grad. Sch. Bus. U. Chgo., 1962-68, fellow Ctr. for Advanced Study in Behavioral Scis., 1968-69; U.S. sec. labor, 1969-70; dir. Office Mgmt. and Budget, 1970-72; U.S. sec. treasury, also asst. to Pres., 1972-74; chmn. Council on Econ. Policy, East-West Trade Policy com.; exec. v.p. Bechtel Corp., San Francisco, 1974-75, pres., 1975-81, vice chmn., 1977-81; also dir.; pres. Bechtel Group, Inc., 1981-82; prof. mgmt. and pub. policy Stanford U., 1974-82, prof. internat. econs., 1989-91, prof. emeritus, 1991—; chmn. Pres. Reagan's Econ. Policy Adv. Bd., 1981-82; U.S. sec. of state, 1982-89; Thomas W. and Susan B. Ford disting. fellow Hoover Instn., Stanford, 1989—. Bd. dirs. Charles Schwab & Co., Bechtel Group, Inc., Gilead Scis.; mem. adv. coun. Bechtel Inc.; chmn. J.P. Morgan Chase Internat. Coun.; chmn. Accenture Energy adv. bd.; chmn. adv. coun. Inst. Internat. Studies, 1990-98; mem. Calif. Gov.'s Econ. Policy Adv. Bd., 1995-98, 2003-. Author: Pressures on Wage Decisions, 1950, (with Charles A. Myers) The Dynamics of a Labor Market, 1951, (with John R. Coleman) Labor Problems: Cases and Readings, 1953, (with T.L. Whisler) Management Organization and the Computer, 1960, (with Arnold R. Weber) Strategies for the Displaced Worker, 1966, (with Robert Z. Aliber) Guidelines, Informal Controls and the Marketplace, 1966, (with Albert Rees) Workers and Wages in the Urban Labor Market, 1970, Leaders and Followers in an Age of Ambiguity, 1975, (with Kenneth W. Dam) Economic Policy Beyond the Headlines, 1977, 2d edition, 1998, Turmoil and Triumph: My Years as Secretary of State, 1993; also articles, chpts. in books, reports, and essays. Served to capt. USMCR, 1942-45. Recipient Medal of Freedom, 1989, Seoul Peace prize, 1992, Eisenhower medal for Leadership and Svc., 2001, Reagan Disting. Am. award, 2002, Ralph Bunche award for diplomatic excellence, 2002. Mem. Am. Econ. Assn., Indsl. Relations Research Assn. (pres. 1968), Nat. Acad. Arbitrators. Republican. Office: Stanford U Hoover Instn Stanford CA 94305-6010

SHULTZ, JACK ELLSWORTH, education educator; b. Dec. 31, 1955; s. Emlyn Leslie Shultz and Florence Louise Schalles; m. Wendy Ellen Miller, June 21, 1986. BS, Bloomsburg Univ., Bloomsburg, Pa., 1979, MEd, 1983. Cert. instructional II-comm. & reading PA, 1987. Title I reading tchr. Del. Valley Sch. Dist., Matamoras, Pa., 1983—86, Warwick Sch. Dist., Lititz, Pa., 1986—89; reading & social studies tchr. Keystone Job Corps, Drums, Pa., 1990—2002; title I reading tchr. N.W. area sch. dist., Shickshinny, Pa., 2002—. Logo and cachet, Nescopeck Centennial, 1996; author: An Early

History of Nescopeck, 1996. Mem. Friends of Gettysburg, Gettysburg, Pa., 2004, Civil War Preservation Trust, Hagertown, Md., 2000—, Colonial Williamsburg Found., Williamsburg, Va., 2000—. Mem.: FCC (life restricted radiotelephone operator permit issued), Smithsonian Nat. Mus. of the Am. Indian (charter), Nat. Rifle Assn. (life), Nat. Muzzleloading Assn. Republican. Meth. Avocations: history, woodworking, hunting, fishing, drawing. Home: 834 First St Nescopeck PA 18635 Office Phone: 570-542-4126. E-mail: pejiwacipi2001@yahoo.com.

SHULTZ, JEANNE MARIE, training director, workforce improvement analyst; b. Detroit, Mich., Oct. 27, 1954; d. Raymond Vincent and Helen Frances (Towne) S. AA, Wayne State U., 1975, BA, 1978. Catering, sales dir. Maxwell's Plum, San Francisco, 1982-84; sales rep. Heath Sign Co., Hayward, Calif., 1984-87; sales assoc. Cornish & Carey Real Estate, San Jose, Calif., 1987-88, Fox & Carskadon/ Better Homes & Gardens, Danville, Calif., 1988-95; sales, telesales and conf. mgr. Coun on Edn. in Mgmt., Walnut Creek, Calif., 1995-98; tng. dir. No. Calif. Tng. Coun., Monterey, Calif., 1998—; workforce improvement analyst Pacific Grove, Calif., 1998—. Advisor, cons. Internat. Inst. of Rsch., London, 1995-97; assoc. Calif. Dept. Real Estate, 1987—. Author: (book) Telesales Encyclopedia, 1996, (tng. manual) Complete Sales Successes, 1985, rev. edit. 1990; (short story) in Ladies Home Jour.; contbg. editor Law Update Monthly; publisher, editor: (newsletter) Lines of Fortune, 1995-98; radio talk show host, prodr. Sta. KNRY/KIEZ, Monterey, Calif. Tech. advisor Jr. Achievement U.S., 1985-88; chair Bay Area Women in Bus., San Francisco, 1986-90; vol. Battered Women's Alternative, Contra Costa County, 1995-98, Monterey County Vols., 1988—, Friends of the Aquarium, Monterey, 1998; comm. coord City of Monterey, 1998; mem. Fairway Ptnrs. Salvation Army, Monterey County, Calif., 1998—. Mem. AAUW, Del Monte Women's Club, Toastmasters Group, Alliance on Aging Monterey County (sec.). Avocations: golf, martial arts. Office: No Calif Tng Ctr 651 Cannery Row Monterey CA 93940-1035

SHULTZ, JOHN DAVID, lawyer; b. L.A., Oct. 9, 1939; Student, Harvard Coll., 1960—61; BA, U. Ariz., 1964; JD, Boalt Hall, U. Calif., Berkeley, 1967. Bar: N.Y. 1968, Calif. 1978. Assoc. Cadwalader, Wickersham & Taft, N.Y.C., 1968—77; ptnr. Lawler, Felix & Hall, L.A., 1977—83, mem. exec. com., chmn. planning com., co-chmn. recruiting and hiring com.; ptnr. Morgan, Lewis & Bockius, L.A., 1983—, chmn. mgmt. com., mem. lateral entry com., chmn. profl. evaluation com., chmn. practice devel. com., chmn. recruiting com. Mem. adv. bd. Internat. and Comparative Law Ctr., Southwestern Legal Found., 1981—; active Practicing Law Inst. Adv. Bd., Corp. and Securities Law, 1992—; Trustee St. Thomas Ch., N.Y.C., 1969—72, Shore Acres Point Corp., Mamaroneck, NY, 1975—77. Mem.: N.Y. State Bar Assn., State Bar Calif., Assn. Bar City of N.Y., ABA. Office: Morgan Lewis & Bockius LLP 300 S Grand Ave Ste 22 Los Angeles CA 90071-3109

SHULTZ, LEILA MCREYNOLDS, botanist, educator; b. Bartlesville, Okla., Apr. 20, 1946; 1 child, Kirsten. BS, U. Tulsa, 1969; MA, U. Colo., 1975; PhD, Claremont Grad. Sch., 1983. Curator Intermountain Herbarium Utah State U., 1973-92, rsch. prof., 1994—; rschr. Harvard U., Cambridge, Mass., 1994—. Vis. prof., acting curator dept. botany U. Okla., 1992-93; bibliographer Gray Herbarium Index, Harvard U., Cambridge, 1994-95. Author: Atlas of the Vascular Plants of Utah, 1988; taxon editor, author: Flora of North America (7 vols.), 1993—. Office: Utah State U Logan UT 84322-5230

SHUMACKER, HARRIS B., JR., retired surgeon, educator, author; b. Laurel, Miss., May 20, 1908; s. Harris B. and Corinne (Teller) S.; m. Myrtle E. Landau, Dec. 1, 1933 (dec.); children: Peter D., James N.; m. Grace McConnel, Nov. 9, 1998. BS, U. Tenn., Chattanooga, 1927; A.M., Vanderbilt U., 1928; MD, Johns Hopkins U., 1932; D.Sc. (hon.), Ind. U., 1985. Diplomate Am. Bd. Surgery, Am. Bd. Thoracic Surgery. Asst. in surgery Johns Hopkins U., 1932-35, instr., 1938-41, asst. prof., 1941-46; asst. in surgery Yale U., 1936-37, instr., 1937-38, assoc. prof., 1946-48; prof. surgery Ind. U., 1948-70, chmn. dept., 1948-68, Disting. prof., 1970-78, Disting. prof. emeritus, 1978—. Prof., sr. advisor Uniformed Svcs. U. of Health Scis., Bethesda, Md., 1981-87, Disting. prof. surgery, 1988—; pres. Uniformed Svcs U. Assocs., 1987-88; hon. mem. surg. faculties in Peoples Republic of China, 1979-; dir. sect. cardiovascular-thoracic surgery St. Vincent Hosp., 1973-78, sr. surg. cons., 1978-81. Served from capt. to lt. col. M.C., U.S. Army, 1942-46; cons. surgeon gen., 1949-60 Recipient Roswell Park award, 1968, Medal of Honor, Evansville U., 1970, Disting. Alumus award U. Tenn. at Chattanooga, Curtis medal, 1970, Spl. Alumnus award Johns Hopkins U., 1973, Disting. Svc. award Am. Soc. Abdominal Surgery, letter of commendation Surgeon-Gen. USN, 1987, Disting. Svc. medal Uniformed Svc. U. Health Scis., 1988, René Leriche prize Soc. Internat. de Chir., 1993. Fellow Royal Coll. Surgeons Eng. (hon.); mem. Am. Assn. Surgery of Trauma, Am. Surg. Assn. (1st v.p. 1961, sec. 1964-68), So. Surg. Assn., Ctrl. Surg. Assn., Pan-Pacific Surg. Assn. (trustee 1961-64, v.p., 1964-75, pres. 1975-78), AMA (chmn. sect. gen. surgery), Internat. Surg. Soc., Internat. Soc. Cardiovasc. Surgeons (v.p. 1957-59, pres. N.Am. chpt. 1956-58), Soc. Clin. Surgery (pres. 1961-63), ACS (chmn. forum com. 1955-60, chmn. nat. TV com. 1964-68, Disting. Service award 1968), Soc. U. Surgeons (pres. 1951), Soc. for Vascular Surgery (pres. 1958-59, disting. fellow 2003), Am. Thoracic Surg. Assn., Soc. Thoracic Surgeons (hon.), Internat. Surg. Group (v.p. 1974-75, pres. 1975-76), Polish Surg. Assn. (hon.), Sociedad Cubana de Angiologia (hon.), Societa Italiana di Chirurgia (hon.), Internat. Surg. Group (hon.), Phi Beta Kappa, Sigma Xi, Alpha Omega Alpha.

SHUMADINE, ANNE BALLARD, financial advisor, lawyer; b. Norfolk, Va., Mar. 8, 1943; d. William Pierce Ballard and Helen Caulfield Ballard Hoffman; m. Conrad Moss Shumadine, Sept. 1, 1965; children: John Ballard, James Hunter. AB, Wellesley Coll., 1965; JD, Coll. William and Mary, 1983. Bar: Va. 1983. Assoc. McGuire Woods Battle & Boothe, Norfolk, 1983-88; ptnr. Shumadine & Rose, P.C., 1988-94, McCandlish Kaine & Grant, 1994—; pres. Signature Fin. Mgmt., 1994—. Bd. dirs. CENIT Bancorp, Norfolk; co-chmn. Old Dominion Tax Conf., Norfolk, 1992; mem. adv. coun. William and Mary Tax Conf., 1997—. Trustee William and Mary Law Sch. Found., 1992—; chmn. Tidewater Scholarship Found., Norfolk, 1995—; rector, bd. visitors Old Dominion U., 1996-97. Fellow Va. Law Found., 1999—; named Vol. of Yr., Downtown Norfolk Coun., 1995. Office: Signature Fin Mgmt 999 Waterside Dr Ste 2220 Norfolk VA 23510-3306

SHUMAN, CAROLYN RAE (THORBURN), psychologist, columnist, writer, nurse; d. Donald Spencer and Eileen Mary Thorburn; m. Gary H. Shuman, Nov. 22, 1975; m. Dennis Lee Atkin, June 15, 1963 (div. July 20, 1968); 1 child, Dennis Lee Atkin, Jr. PhD, Tex. A&M U., Commerce, 1985—96; MS, East Tex. State U., Commerce, 1985—90; BS, Bapt. Coll. of Charleston, SC, 1977—78; AA, Armstrong State Coll., Savannah, Ga., 1972—76. RN 1994. Owner Family and Children First, Cape Coral/ Ft. Myers, Fla., 2004—, Ctr. for Cognitive Therapy, Hamilton, Bermuda, 1999—2003; dir. USNAS-Bermuda, St David's, 1992—95; psychotherapist/psychologist Ashton Associates, Hamilton, 1994—99; clin. supr. USNAS-Bermuda, St. David's, 1991—94; adj. prof. Webster U., U. of Md., City Colleges of Chgo., USNAS-Bermuda, 1991—97. Cons. King Edward Hosp. VII EAP, Hamilton, 2001—03, Family Learning Ctr., Hamilton, 1994—96. Author: (book) Jenny Is Scared: When Sad Things Happen in the World (Psychology Grad. Faculty Scholarship, Tex. A&M-Commerce, 1987). Mem., spkr. Bermuda Chamber of Commerce, Hamilton, 2000—03; mem. Fairhaven Christian Care/ Nat. Drug Strategy/, Hamilton, 1998—2001. Recipient Journalism Enterprise, Ga. AP, 1972; scholar Honors Scholarship, Armstrong State Coll., 1973-1975, Grad. Faculty Honors, Tex. A&M Psychology Dept., 1987. Mem.: Nat. Writer Assn., Bermuda Psychol. Assn. (assoc.; pub. info. officer 2003—04), APA (life). Achievements include research in cross culture, health, cognitive behavior therapy, hardiness; death studies (Psychology Journal, 1992); presentations, Death & Dying, SWPA, 1993-1997. Avocations: writing, swimming, travel, music. Home: 1941 SE 26th Terrace Cape Coral FL 33904 Office: Family and Children First DelPrado Boulevard Cape Coral FL 33904 Office Phone: 441-505-5792. E-mail: drcshuman@datkin.net.

SHUMAN, EARL STANLEY, songwriter, music publisher; b. Boston, Aug. 2, 1923; s. Benjamin Morris and Mildred Judith (Kaplan) S.; m. Margaret Stein, Nov. 25, 1956; children: Cathy Elizabeth, Daniel James, Steven Lewis. BA, Yale U., 1947. Owner, pres. Earl/Peg Music Cos., N.Y.C., 1957—; pub. BMI, ASCAP, N.Y.C., 1977—. Composer (lyric writer) popular songs including Seven Lonely Days, 1953 (Country and Western award 1970), Hey There Lonely Girl, 1970 (Gold record), Banjo's Back in Town, Caterina, Clinging Vine, Close to Cathy, Hotel Happiness, Left Right Out of Your Heart, Most People Get Married, My Shy Violet, The River, Starry-Eyed, Theme For a Dream, Young New Mexican Puppeteer; lyricist (musicals) Secret Life of Walter Mitty, 1964 (award 1965), (country song) Leaves are the Tears of Autumn, 1968 (Country and Western award 1969), (TV themes) Coronet Blue, ABC TV, 1967, Confidence/NFL-CBS, 1967-76, (Movie Title Songs) The Disorderly Orderly, Judith, Situation Hopeless But Not Serious, Barrabas, Monica (love theme from The Carpetbaggers), Love Me Longer (love theme from Arrivederci Baby); pub. Bat Out of Hell album, 1977 (platinum award 1979). Capt. USMCR, 1943-46, 50-51. Mem.: ASCAP. Avocations: music, baseball. Home and Office: 111 E 88th St Apt 3B New York NY 10128-1158 Fax: (212) 722-3698. E-mail: earlmusic@earthlink.net.

SHUMAN, JAMES C. education educator; b. Des Moines, Apr. 6, 1945; s. Waymer Ruhl and Leora Elizabeth Shuman; m. Lauren Buys, June 14, 1996; children: Corey, Ryan stepchildren: John Holena, Daniel Holena, Elizabeth Holena. BA, Carleton Coll., Northfield, Minn., 1967; MS, W. Va. U., 1978, EdD, 1983; Cert. of Ordination, The New Sem., N.Y.C., 2000. Cert. tchr. sci. and math. Calif., 1970, Vt., 1987, sch. adminstr. Vt., 1987. Dir. edn. The Morton Arboretum, Lisle, Ill., 1978—79; vis. prof. W.Va. U., Morgantown, 1979—83; core faculty Goddard Coll., Plainfield, Vt., 1983—86; asst. prof. edn. Calif. State U., San Bernardino, 1986—87; sci. tchr. Champlain Valley H.S., Hinesburg, Vt., 1987—88; coord. tchr. edn. Middlebury Coll., Vt., 1988—89; chmn. dept edn., prof. edn. St. Lawrence U., Canton, NY, 1989—. Dir. Nat. Youth Sci. Camp, 1986—87. Bd. dirs. Nat. Youth Sci. Found., Charleston, W.Va., 1983—94. Recipient Mackey award for leadership, svc. and edn., N.Y. Assn. of Colls. of Tchr. Edn., 2003; grantee Rsch. grantee, NSF, 1993, Ind. Colls. Office, 2001, NSF, 2002. Mem.: Assn. of Tchr. Educators (del. 1995—98), N.Y. State Assn. Tchr. Educators (pres. 1996—98, bd. dirs. 1991—99). Home: 51 Farmer St Canton NY 13617-1163 Office: Saint Lawrence Univ Dept of Edn Canton NY 13617

SHUMAN, JOSEPH DUFF, lawyer; b. Pitts., Dec. 27, 1942; s. Joseph and Anna Jane (Phillips) D.; m. Ann Stewart McMillan, Nov. 9, 1969; children: David Stewart, Lauren Forbes. BA, Yale U., 1964; LLB, Harvard U., 1967. Bar: Pa. 1968, U.S. Dist. Ct. (we. dist.) Pa. 1968. Assoc. Thorp, Reed & Armstrong, LLP, Pitts., 1967-73, ptnr., 1974—, co-chmn., corp. and bus. law dept., 1990-94, chmn., 1994-97. Republican. Presbyterian. Office: Thorp Reed & Armstrong LLP One Oxford Ctr 301 Grant St 14th Fl Pittsburgh PA 15219-1425

SHUMAN, LARRY MYERS, soil chemist; b. Harrisburg, Pa., Apr. 3, 1944; s. Mark P. and Opal I. (Myers) Shuman; m. Catherine A. Yost, Mar. 21, 1970; children: Karen, Rebecca. BS, Pa. State U., 1966, MS, 1968, PhD, 1970. Asst. prof. soil chemistry U. Ga., Experiment, 1972-79, assoc. prof., 1979-91, prof., 1991—. USDA-OICD Exch. scientist to People's Republic of China, 1992. Co-editor, contbg. author Micronutrients in Agriculture, 1991; contbg. author: Zinc in Soils, 1979, Plant Environment Interactions, 1994, Methods of Soil Analysis, Part 3 - Chemical Methods, 1996; contbr. articles to profl. jours. Capt. M.S., U.S. Army, 1970-72. U.S. Aid grantee, 1980-81, USDA-CSRS grantee, 1992-94, Dept. Energy, 1995-96, U.S. EPA, 2000-04, NSF, 2000-04. Fellow Soil Sci Soc. Am. (soil chemistry divsn. chair 1994, assoc. editor jour. 1986-91, tech. editor jour. 2000—); mem. Am. Soc. Agronomy, Coun. Agrl. Sci. and Tech., Soc. Environ. Geochemistry and Health. Home: 447 Trice Rd Milner GA 30257-3427 Office: U Ga Griffin Campus 1109 Experiment St Griffin GA 30223-1797 Office Phone: 770-228-7276.

SHUMAN, R. BAIRD, academic program director, writer, English language educator, educational consultant; b. Paterson, N.J., June 20, 1929; s. George William and Elizabeth (Evans) S. AB (Trustees scholar), Lehigh U., 1951; M.Ed., Temple U., 1953; PhD (Univ. scholar), U. Pa., 1961; cert. in philology, U. Vienna, Austria, 1954. Tchr. Phila. Pub. Schs., 1953-55; asst. instr. English U. Pa., 1955-57; instr. humanities Drexel U., Phila., 1957-59; asst. prof. English San José (Calif.) State U., 1959-62; asst. prof. English, edn. Duke U., 1962-63, assoc. prof., 1963-66, prof. edn., 1966-77; prof. English, dir. English edn. U. Ill., Urbana-Champaign, 1977-85, dir. freshman rhetoric, 1979-84, coord. Univ. Associates in Rhetoric Program, 1978-84, dir. devel., 1988-93, acting dir. Ctr. for Study of Writing, 1989-90, prof. emeritus, 1993—. Vis. prof. Moore Inst. Art, 1958, Phila. Conservatory Music, 1958-59, Lynchburg Coll., 1965, King Faisal U., Saudi Arabia, 1978, 81, Bread Loaf Sch. English, Middlebury Coll., 1980, East Tenn. State U., Johnson City, 1980, Olivet Nazarene Coll., 1984, 86, 88, U. Tenn., Knoxville, 1987; cons. Ednl. Testing Svc., 1970—, Am. Coll. Testing Svc., 1975-82; cons. in lang. and lit. Coll. Engring., U. Ill., 1980-97, Worldwide Youth in Sci. and Engring., 1995-97; mem. William Inge Nat. Festival Com., 1989-95. Author: Clifford Odets, 1962, Robert E. Sherwood, 1964, William Inge, 1965, rev. edit., 1989, Strategies in Teaching Reading: Secondary, 1978, (with Robert J. Krajewski) The Beginning Teacher: A Guide to Problem Solving, 1979, Elements of Early Reading Instruction, 1979, The First R: Strategies in Early Reading Instruction, 1987, rev. edit., 1989, Classroom Encounters: Problems, Case Studies, Solutions, 1989, (with Eric Hobson) Reading and Writing in High School, (with Denny T. Wolfe Jr.) Teaching English Through the Arts, 1990, Resources for Writers, 1992, American drama 1918-1960, 1992, Georgia O'Keeffe, 1993; editor: Nine Black Poets, 1968, An Eye for an Eye, 1969, A Galaxy of Black Writing, 1970, Creative Approaches to the Teaching of English: Secondary, 1974, Questions English Teachers Ask, 1977, Educational Drama for Today's Schools, 1978, Education in the 80's—English, 1980, The Clearing House: A Closer Look, 1984, 70th anniversary issue The Clearing House, 1995, Great American Writers: 20th Century, 13 vols., 2002, Cyclopedia of Literary Places, 3 vols., 2003, The Clearing House: A Retrospective, 2004; exec. editor The Clearing House jour., 1976—; cons. editor Poet Lore, 1977-90, Cygnus, 1978-2001, Jour. Aesthetic Edn., 1978-82; contbg. editor Reading Horizons, 1975-85; editor quar. column Reading Horizons, 1975-85; editor Trends in English column Ednl. Leadership, 1989-96. Active Nat. Trust for Hist. Preservation. NEH researcher Trinity Coll., Dublin, Ireland, 1985 Mem. MLA, Nat. Coun. Tchrs. English (evaluator ERIC Clearing House, com. alt. careers for English profls.), Internat. Fedn. Tchrs. English, Internat. Coun. Edn. of tchrs., Nev. Coun. Tchrs. English, Conf. English Edn. (exec. com. 1976-79), Internat. Reading Assn. (coord. symposium on cultural literacy, Queensland, Australia 1988), Internat. Assn. Univ. Profs. English, Nat. Soc. Study Edn., Am. Fedn. Tchrs., Union Profl. Employees (editor newsletter 1988-92, exec. com. 1988-92). Democrat. Home: PO Box 27647 Las Vegas NV 89126-1647 E-mail: rbaird@intermind.net. *An education that does not produce people who are vibrantly alive, intoxicated with the wonder of existence, has fallen short. Joy of learning is the fulcrum upon which the human equation is balanced. I have always believed that emotion prevails over intellect and have led my life accordingly with the inevitable result of being extraordinarily happy for most of my days.*

SHUMAN, ROBERT Z. architect; BA (with distinction), Cornell U., 1973; B in Architecture (magna cum laude), Temple U., 1982. With Mitchell/Giurgola Architects, 1982—88, assoc., 1988—99, ptnr., 1999—, MGA Ptnrs., Phila., 1990—. Staff arch. Annenberg Sch. for Commns., U. of Pa., 1985, Columbia Ave. Subway Improvements, Phila., 1986; project arch. Treyffrin Pub. Libr. Renovations, Stratford, Pa., 1987, San Jose Conv. Ctr., 1989, Hilton Hotel, San Jose, 1991; project mgr. U.S. Fed. Courthouse, Camden, NJ, 1999, Annenberg Sch. for Commn., U. of Pa., 1999, Academic Facilities Masterplan, Bryn Mawr Coll., 2000, Student Residence, The U. of Arts, Phila., 2001, Hamilton Village, Low Rise Housing, U. of Pa., 2002, Theater/Neal Marshall Edn. Ctr., Ind. U., Bloomington, Ind., 2002. Curriculum com. Temple U. Coll. of Engring. and Architecture, 1983; vis. juror Temple U. and Drexel U. Adj. Faculty, 1992—95. Mem.: Bldg. Offcls. and Code Adminstrs. Internat., Am. Inst. of Archs. Phila. Chpt., Phi Beta Kappa. Office: MGA Ptnrs Architects 234 Market St Philadelphia PA 19106

SHUMAN, STANLEY S. investment banker; b. Cambridge, Mass., June 22, 1935; s. Saul A. and Sarah L. (Saxe) S.; m. Ruth H. Lande, 1967 (div. 1979); children: David Lande, Michael Adam; m. Sydney Roberts Gould, 1992. BA, Harvard U., Boston, 1956, JD, 1959, MBA, 1961. Bar: Mass. 1959, N.Y. 1991. Exec. v.p., mng. dir. Allen & Co., Inc., N.Y.C., 1961—. Bd. dirs. Bayou Steel Corp., Global Asset Mgmt. (USA), Inc., Hudson Gen. Corp. Ltd., News Corp. Ltd., News Am. Holdings Inc., Sesac Inc., News Am., Six Flags, Inc.; non-exec. dir. News Corp.; mem. Pres.'s Fgn. Intelligence Adv. Bd., 1995-2001. Mem. Fin. Control Bd., N.Y.C., 1977-97; active Channel 13 WNET, 1990—, Carnegie Hall, 1990—, Mus. TV and Radio, 1996—, N.Y. Law Sch., 1990-96, The Markle Found., 1992—, Nat. Pub. Radio Found., 1992—; chmn. Nat. Econ. Devel. and Law Ctr., 1978-83; chmn. adv. bd. Inst. Policy Scis. and Pub. Affairs Duke U., 1992-96; bd. advisors DeWitt Wallace Ctr. Comm. and Journalism, 1994—, Bertlesmann Found. Media Workshop, 1994—; mem. exec. com. Harvard Campaign, 1995—; mem. adv. bd. Ctr. Health Comm. Harvard Sch. Pub. Health, 1996—; chmn. adv. coun. Ctr. for N.Y.C. Law, 1996—; trustee The Dalton Sch., 1977-84, hon. trustee, 1984—; active Devel. Bd. Phillips Acad., Andover, Mass., 1972-80; pres. Wiliwyck Sch., 1971-78; v.p. exec. com. Jewish Guild for the Blind, 1973-80; trustee Jewish Publ. Soc., 1986-90; mem. Coun. on Fgn. Rels., 1995-2001, sect. corp. banking and bus. law, 1974—. Clubs: Harvard (Boston), Harvard (N.Y.C.), Quaker Ridge Golf, East Hampton Tennis. Office: Allen & Co Inc 711 5th Ave Fl 8 New York NY 10022-3111*

SHUMATE, JOHN PAGE, diplomat; b. El Paso, Tex., Sept. 18, 1934; s. John Page and Elizabeth (McWilliams) S.; m. Caroline Taylor, June 16, 1978. BA in Polit. Sci., UCLA, 1956; MAin Internat. Rels., U. So. Calif., 1970. Counsellor of Embassy, U.S. Embassy, Quito, Ecuador, 1970-72; dir. exec. tng. Fgn. Service Inst., Washington, 1972-75; dir. U.K. Affairs, Dept. State., 1975-78, exec. dir. Bur. Ednl. and Cultural Affairs, 1978-80, exec. dir. Bur. Adminstrn., Washington, 1981-84; staff dir. Sec. of State's Adv. Panel on Overseas Security, 1984-85; exec. v.p., CEO Am. Fgn. Svc. Protective Assn., 1986—, Assn. Fed. Health Orgns. (chmn. bd. dirs. 1992-97); co-pres. U.S.-Mexico Cultural Commn. com., 1978-80; exec. dir. sr. living found. Am. Fgn. Svcs. Recipient Superior Honor award U.S. Dept. State., 1981; Phi Kappa Phi Cert. of Honor, 1970. Mem. Am. Fgn. Service Assn., Nat. Assn. Sr. Living Industries, Phi Kappa Phi. Clubs: Ft. Meyer Officers, Fgn. Service, Dacor Bacon House, Bethany West Tennis. Office: Am Fgn Svc Protective Assn 1716 N St NW Washington DC 20036-2907 Business E-Mail: afspa@afspa.org.

SHUMWAY, ERIC, academic administrator; BA, Brigham Young U., 1964, MA, 1966; PhD, U. Va., 1973. Pres. Brigham Young U.-Hawaii, 1994—. Office: Brigham Young U-Hawaii 55-220 Kulanui St Laie HI 96762 Business E-Mail: shumwaye@byuh.edu.

SHUMWAY, NORMAN EDWARD, surgeon, educator; b. Kalamazoo, Mich., 1923; MD, Vanderbilt U., 1949; PhD in Surgery, U. Minn., 1956. Diplomate: Am. Bd. Surgery, Am. Bd. Thoracic Surgery. Intern U. Minn. Hosps., 1949-50, med. fellow surgery, 1950-51, 53-54, Nat. Heart Inst. research fellow, 1954-56, Nat. Heart Inst. spl. trainee, 1956-57; mem. surg. staff Stanford U. Hosps., 1958—, asst. prof. surgery, 1959-61, assoc. prof., 1961-65, prof., 1965—, head div. cardiovascular surgery Sch. Medicine, 1974—; Frances and Charles D. Field prof. Stanford U., 1976-2000, prof. emeritus, 2000—. Served to capt. USAF, 1951-53. Mem. AMA, Soc. Univ. Surgeons, Am. Assn. Thoracic Surgery, Am. Coll. Cardiology, Transplantation Soc., Samson Thoracic Surg. Soc., Soc. for Vascular Surgery, Alpha Omega Alpha Office: Stanford U Med Ctr Dept Cardiovascular Surgery CVRB Upper Level N Stanford CA 94305-5407

SHUNGU, DIKOMA CYRILLE, radiology educator; b. Wembo-Nyama, Congo Republic, Nov. 15, 1958; s. Wembi and Lutshumba Louise S. BA, Southwestern U., Georgetown, Tex., 1981; PhD, U. Ark., 1986. Postdoctoral rsch. fellow Milton S. Hershey Med. Ctr. of Pa. State U., Hershey, 1986-87, U. Fla. Health Sci. Ctr., Gainesville, 1987-89, Johns Hopkins U. Sch. of Medicine, Balt., 1989-92, rsch. assoc., 1992-93; asst. prof. radiology Columbia U., N.Y.C., 1993—. Grant rev. NIH, Bethesda; reviewer Magnetic Resonance in Medicine, Rockville, Md. Rsch. grantee NINDS/NIH, Bethesda, 1986, 1999, 2000. Mem. Internat. Soc. for Magnetic Resonance in Medicine, AAAS. Avocations: classical guitar, baroque recorder, photography. Office: Columbia U 710 W 168th St New York NY 10032-2603

SHUR, BARRY DAVID, cell biologist, researcher; b. Elizabeth, N.J., Jan. 3, 1950; m. Judith Jane Wishna, Nov. 11, 1949; 1 child, Emily Rachel. PhD, Johns Hopkins U., 1976. Fellow Sloan Kettering Cancer Inst., N.Y.C., 1976—78; from asst. prof. to assoc. prof. U. Conn. Sch. Medicine, Farmington, 1978—84; from assoc. prof. to prof., interim chmn. U. Tex. MD Anderson Cancer Ctr., Houston, 1984—96; prof., chmn. cell biology Emory U., Atlanta, 1996—. Contbr. articles to profl. jours. Recipient Endowed Professorships, U. Tex., Emory U., 1992—; Rsch. grantee, NIH, others, 1978—, Helen Hay Whitney Postdoctoral fellow, Helen Hay Whitney Found., 1976—78. Achievements include research in mechanisms of mammalian fertilization, basis of sperm-egg recognition. Office: Emory U Cell Biology 615 Michael St Rm 405E Atlanta GA 30322 Business E-Mail: barry@cellbio.emory.edu.

SHUR, MICHAEL, electrical engineer, educator, consultant; b. Kamensk-Uralski, Sverdlovsk, USSR, Nov. 13, 1942; came to U.S., 1976. s. Saul and Anna (Katz) S.; m. Paulina Gimmelfarb, Sept. 25, 1966; children: Luba, Natasha. MS, Leningrad Elec. Tech. Inst., 1965; PhD, Ioffe Inst., Leningrad, 1967; DSc, Ioffe Inst., St. Petersburg, 1992; Hon. Doctorate, St. Petersburg State Tech. U., 1994. Scientist Ioffe Inst., 1965-75; asst. prof. Wayne State U., Detroit, 1976-77, Oakland U., Rochester, Mich., 1978; prof. U. Minn., Mpls., 1979-92; John Marshall Money prof. U. Va., Charlottesville, Va., 1989-96; Patricia W. and C. Sheldon Roberts prof. Rensselaer Poly. Inst., 1996—; assoc. dir., prof. physics. and info. tech. Ctr. Integrated Electronics and Electronics Mfg., 1997—; dir. Ctr. for Broadband Data Transport Sci. and Tech., 2002—. Editor-in-chief Internat. Jour. High Speed Electronics and Systems, mem. hon. editl. bd. Solid State Electronics, Internat. Semiconductor Device Rsch. Symposium; contbr. over 700 articles to profl. jours., chapters to books; author: Gunn Effect, 1971, Physics of Semiconductor Devices, 1990, GaAs Devices and Circuits, 1991, Introduction to Electronic Devices, 1996, many others; co-author: Ferroelectrics and Antiferroelectrics, 1971, Gunn Effect, 1975, Semiconductor Device Modeling for VLSI, 1993, Introduction to Device Modeling and Circuit Simulation, 1998, Introduction to Solid State Lighting, 2002; co-editor: Semiconductor Technology: Processing and Novel Fabrication Techniques, 1997, Sensitive Skin, 2000, others. Recipient Van Der Ziel award, Internat. Semiconductor Device Rsch. Symposium, 1999, Humboldt Sr. Rsch. award, 2002, SOE Rsch. award, Rensselaer Poly. Inst., 2003, Compound SEMI Pioneer award, 2003. Fellow: IEEE (v.p. pubs. IEEE Sensor Coun., assoc. editor IEEE Trans. 1990—93, MTT Disting. Microwave lectr., EDS Disting. lectr.), Electrochem. Soc., Am. Phys. Soc.; mem.: ASEE, Humboldt Soc. Am., Materials Rsch. Soc., Sigma Xi, Tau Beta Pi, Eta Kappa Nu. Achievements include 30 patents on solid-state devices. Business E-Mail: shurm@rpi.edu. *When we were penniless refugees, the United States adopted me and my family with compassion and friendship, gave us work and citizenship. Our debt of gratitude to the American people who accepted us as their own we will never be able to repay.*

SHURBAJI, M. SALAH, pathologist; b. Cairo, 1957; came to U.S., 1984; BS with distinction, Am. U. Beirut, 1979, MS, 1981, MD with distinction, 1984. Diplomate Am. Bd. Pathology; cert. cytopathologist, anatomic and clin. pathologist; lic. physician Md., Tenn., Mich. Intern Am. U. Beirut Med. Ctr., 1983-84; resident pathology Johns Hopkins Hosp., Balt., 1984-87, resident dept. lab. medicine, 1987-89; clin. fellow dept. pathology Johns Hopkins U. Sch. Medicine, Balt., 1984-89, rsch. fellow dept. pathology, 1989-90; asst. prof. pathology East Tenn. State U., Johnson City, 1990-94, assoc. prof. pathology, 1994-2000; prof. pathology, 2000—; staff pathologist Univ. Physicians Practice Group, Johnson City, 1990—; staff pathologist Vets. Affairs Med. Ctr., Johnson City, 1990—, acting chief pathology and lab. medicine svc., 1993-94, chief pathology and lab. medicine svc., 1994—. Contbr. articles to profl. jours. Fellow Am. Soc. Clin. Pathologists, Coll. Am. Pathologists;

mem. A.P. Stout Soc. Surg. Pathologists, Am. Soc. Cytopathology, U.S. and Can. Acad. Pathology, Papanicolaou Soc. Cytopathology, Internat. Soc. Urologic Pathology, Sigma Xi, Alpha Omega Alpha. Achievements include contribution to understanding of certain factors that affect the prognosis of neoplasms especially prostate cancer. Office: East Tenn State U Coll Med Dept Pathology PO Box 70568 Johnson City TN 37614-1707

SHURDUT, JEFFREY HAYDEN, artist; b. L.I., Dec. 2, 1967; s. Howard Joseph and Florence (Moskowitz) Shurdut. BFA, NY, 1989. Artist, NY, 1967—; founder No Label Exptl. Performing Arts Records, 2003, Forever Music and the Arts (FMA), 2004, Music Life Orch., 2004. Artist in residence Sweden, Norway, Iceland, 1999. Exhibitions include 128 Rivington St., Lower East Side (with Billy Bang), N.Y.C., 2002, 157 W. 26 St., Chelsea, 2001, Avery Fisher Hall, Lincoln Ctr., 1994, film credit, The Documentary of Cecil Taylor, by Chris Felver, 2003, recording, Sounds of Shurdut Drawing, 2002. Grantee, Columbia U., 1993, N.Y. State Coun. Arts, 2002. Achievements include development of first series of jazz and exploratory music and sound recorded live in an artist's studio. Home: 175 East 74th St New York NY 10021 Personal E-mail: jeffreyhshurdut@hotmail.com.

SHURE, MYRNA BETH, psychologist, educator; b. Chgo., Sept. 11, 1937; d. Sidney Natkin and Frances (Laufman) Shure. Student, U. Colo., 1955; BS, U. Ill., 1959; MS, Cornell U., 1961, PhD, 1966. Lic. psychologist Pa. Asst. prof. U. R.I.; head tchr. Nursery Sch., Kingston, 1961-62; asst. prof. Temple U., Phila., 1966-67, assoc. prof., 1967-68; instr. Hahnemann Med. Coll., Phila., 1968-69, sr. instr. psychology, 1969-70, asst. prof., 1970-73, assoc. prof., 1973-80, prof., 1980—2002, Drexel U., Phila., 2002—. Spl. cons. PBS Children's TV Show The Puzzle Place; adv. bd. Parents Mag., 2004. Author (with George Spivack): Social Adjustment of Young Children, 1974; author: (with George Spivack and Jerome Platt) The Problem Solving Approach to Adjustment, 1976; author: (with George Spivack) Problem Solving Techniques in Childrearing, 1978; author: (child curricula manual) I Can Problem Solve, 1992; author: (trade book) Raising a Thinking Child, 1994; author: (audiotape, workbook, paperback) Raising a Thinking Preteen, 2000 (Parents' Choice award, 2001, Parent's Guide Classic award, 2001); author: Thinking Parent, Thinking Child, 2004. Recipient Lela Rowland Prevention award, Nat. Mental Health Assn., 1982, Sarah award, Women in Comm. (Phila. chpt., 1998, Psychology in the Media award, Pa. Psychol. Assn., 1999, award, Ctr. for Substance Abuse Prevention, 2001; grantee rsch. grant, NIMH, 1971—75, 1977—79, 1982—85, 1987, 1988—93. Fellow: APA (divsn. clin. psychology, child sect. 1994, Disting. Contbn. award divsn. cmty. psychology 1984, Task Force on Prevention award 1987, Task Force on Model Programs award 1994, U. Utah and Juvenile Justice Dept. of Delinquency Prevention award 1996, U.S. Dept. Edn. award 2001); mem.: Phila. Soc. Clin. Psychologists, Soc. Rsch. in Child Devel., Nat. Assn. Edn. Young Children, Nat. Assn. Sch. Psychologists. Home: 1500 Locust St Apt 3311 Philadelphia PA 19102-4323 Office: Drexel U Dept Psychology 245 N 15th St MS 626 Philadelphia PA 19102 Office Phone: 215-762-7205. Business E-Mail: mshure@drexel.edu.

SHURIN, SANDE, theater educator, director, writer; s. Sande Shurin and Mildred Cohen; m. Bruce Levy, May 20, 1980; 1 child, Stephanie Kaplan. At, Bklyn. Coll., N.Y. Theatrical dir., N.Y.C., 1970—; artistic dir. Sande Shurin Acting Studio, 1980—. On camera acting coach Faking It (Learning Channel), 2003; appearances on Oprah, 03; writer TV and radio. Author: Transformational Acting, 2002. Fundraiser AIDS Benefits, Dem. Party. Recipient Chekov award, 1999, Broadway Drama Guild award, 1995. Mem.: AFTRA, SSDC. Avocations: yoga, chanting meditation, reading, dance.

SHURLEY, JAY TALMADGE, writer, retired psychiatrist, medical educator, administrator, behavioral scientist, polar explorer, genealogist; b. Sonora, Tex., Dec. 20, 1917; s. Ira L. and Jewell L. (Choate) S.; m. Erwina Bode Cornelison, Dec. 20, 1986. BA in Zoology, U. Tex.-Austin, 1940; MD, U. Tex. Med. Br., Galveston, 1942. Diplomate Am. Bd. Psychiatry and Neurology. Intern. Ind. U.-Indpls. Med. Ctr., 1943; Rockefeller fellow in neuropsychiatry dept. mental and nervous disease Inst. for Mental Hygiene Pa. Hosp., Phila., 1944-47; pvt. practice medicine specializing in psychiatry and psychoanalysis Phila., 1947-51, Austin, 1951-52; pvt. practice medicine specializing in psychiatry San Antonio, 1952-54, Chevy Chase, Md., 1955-57; pvt. practice medicine specializing in psychiatry, psychoanalysis and sleep disorders medicine Oklahoma City, 1978-90; acting chief lab. adult psychiat. investigation, clin. investigations NIMH, NIH, Bethesda, 1955-57; chief psychiatry service and mental hygiene clinic VA Hosp., Oklahoma City, 1957-62; sr. med. investigator in psychiatry, research service, dept. medicine and surgery VA, 1962-76; founder and dir. behavioral sci. labs VA Med. Ctr., Oklahoma City, 1962-78; sci. dir. Oklahoma Mental Health Research Inst., Oklahoma Dept. Mental Health, 1988-89; cons.-liaison in geropsychiatry O'Donoghue Rehab. Inst., Okla. Med. Ctr., 1990-91; med. dir. emeritus Willow View Mental Health Ctr., Oklahoma City, 1985-87; prof. psychiatry Coll. Medicine U. Okla., Oklahoma City, 1957-77, prof. psychiatry and behavioral scis. Coll. of Medicine and Grad. Coll., 1977-81; prof. emeritus psychiatry and behavioral scis. U. Okla. Coll. Medicine, Oklahoma City, 1981—. Adj. prof. human ecology Coll. Health, U. Okla., 1967-81; mem. com. on polar rsch. NAS/NRC, 1970-74; U.S. rep. Working Group on Human Biology and Medicine XII Sci. Com. on Antarctic Rsch., Canberra and Melbourne, Australia, 1972; U.S. rep. Working Group on Human Biology and Medicine XIII Sci. Com. on Antarctic Rsch., Jackson Hole, Wyo., 1974; disting. vis. scientist program in human biology Acad. Scis. USSR, Moscow and Leningrad, 1972; Centennial Yr. vis. prof. dept. psychol. medicine U. Otago, Dunedin, N.Z., 1975; mem. Health Rsch. Com., Okla. Ctr. for Sci. and Tech., 1986-91, Okla. Alzheimer Rsch. Adv. Coun., 1990-92. Editor: Relating Environment to Mental Health and Illness: The Eco-psychiatric Data Base, 1979, Symposium on Man on the South Polar Plateau, 1970; mem. editorial bd. Jour. Clin. Psychology, 1970-80; contbr. more than 100 articles to sci. publs. Capt. M.C. U.S. Army, 1952-54. Recipient Antarctic Svc. medal NSF/NAS, 1970, Disting. Profl. Svc. award Okla. Psychol. Assn., 1972, Sustained Superior Achievement cert. VA, 1974, Disting. Psychiatrist award Mid-Continent Psychiat. Assn., 1986, Okla. Psychiat. Assn., 1990, Sealy Inc. prize Assn. Profl. Sleep Socs., 1991; Shurley Ridge, Pensacola Mountains Antarctica named in his honor. Fellow Am. Psychiat. Assn. (life), Am. Coll. Psychiatrists (life); mem. AMA, Oklahoma County Med. Soc., Okla. State Med. Assn. (life), Okla. Psychiat. Assn. (pres. 1968, chair ethics com. 1989-91), Faculty House Club, Sigma Xi, Alpha Omega Alpha, Alpha Epsilon Delta. Democrat. Address: 4127 E 48TH Pl Tulsa OK 74135-4740 E-mail: jshurl441@cox.net.

SHURN, PETER JOSEPH, III, lawyer; b. Queens, N.Y., Aug. 30, 1946; s. Peter J. Jr. and Vivienne M. (Tagliarino) Shurn; m. Ingrid Kelbert; children: Steven Douglas, Vanessa Leigh, David Michael. BSEE magna cum laude, Poly. Inst. Bklyn., 1974; JD magna cum laude, New Eng. Sch. Law, 1977; LLM in Patent and Trade Regulation Law, George Washington U., 1981. Bar: N.C. 1977, Va. 1979, Tex. 1982. Rsch. scientist GTE Labs., 1965—77; pvt. practice Raleigh, NC, 1977—78; assoc. Burns, Doane, Swecker & Mathis, Alexandria, Va., 1978—80; tech. advisor to judge U.S. Ct. Appeals (fed. cir.), 1980—81; ptnr. Arnold, White & Durkee, Houston, 1981—2000, Howrey, Simon, Arnold and White LLP, Houston, 2000—01. Adj. prof. S. Tex. Coll. Law, 1984—88, 2000—; invited mem. nat. panel neutrals Am. Arbitration Assn., 1993—; arbitrator Nat. Patent Bd., 1999—. Contbr. articles to profl. jours. With U.S. Army, 1966—68. Fellow: Coll. State Bar Tex., Houston Bar Found. (life); mem.: IEEE, ABA, ATLA, Houston Patent Law Assn., Am. Patent Law Assn. (Robert C. Watson award 1981), Houston Patent Law Assn., Sigma Xi. Office: 14138 Heatherfield Dr Houston TX 77079-6805 Office Phone: 281-496-0865. E-mail: pjshurn@ieee.org.

SHURTLEFF, AKIKO AOYAGI, artist, consultant; b. Tokyo, Jan. 24, 1950; d. Kinjiro and Fumiyo (Sugata) Aoyagi; m. William Roy Shurtleff, Mar. 10, 1977 (div. Jan. 1995); 1 child, Joseph Aoyagi. Grad., Women's Coll. Art, Tokyo, 1971; student, Acad. Art, San Francisco, 1991-92. Fashion designer, illustrator Marimura Co. and Hayakawa Shoji, Inc., Tokyo, 1970-72; co-founder, art dir. Soyfoods Ctr. consulting svcs., Lafayette, Calif., 1976-94; freelance illustrator, graphic designer. Lectr. U.S. Internat. Christian U., Tokyo, 1977, Japanese Tofu Mfrs. Conv., Osaka, 1978; presenter cooking demonstrations; tchr. cooking classes. Avocations: walking, running, dance, designing company logos. Office: PO Box 443 Lafayette CA 94549-0443 E-mail: akiko1717@aol.com.

SHURTLEFF, MALCOLM C. plant pathologist, consultant, educator, extension specialist; b. Fall River, Mass., June 24, 1922; s. Malcolm C. and Florence L. (Jewell) S.; m. Margaret E. Johnson, June 14, 1950; m. Freda L. Nothnagel, Aug. 1, 1998; children: Robert Glen, Janet Lee, Mark Steven. BS in Biology, U. R.I., 1943; MS in Plant Pathology, U. Minn., 1950, PhD in Plant Pathology, 1953. Asst. plant pathologist Conn. Agrl. Expt. Sta., New Haven, 1942, R.I. Agrl. Expt. Sta., Kingston, 1943; asst. extension prof. U. R.I., Kingston, 1950-54; assoc. extension prof. Iowa State U., Ames, 1954-61; prof. plant pathology U. Ill., Champaign-Urbana, 1961-92, prof. emeritus, 1992—; cons., writer Urbana, 1992-98. Adj. prof. Tex. A&M U., College Station, 1998—. Author: How To Control Plant Diseases, 1962, 66 (award Am. Garden Guild 1962, 66), How To Control Lawn Diseases and Pests, 1973, How To Control Tree Diseases and Pests, 1975, Controlling Turfgrass Pests, 1987, 97, 2002, A Glossary of Plant Pathological Terms, 1997, The Plant Disease Clinic and Field Diagnosis of Abiotic Diseases, 1997, Diagnosing Plant Diseases Caused by Nematodes, 2000; editor-in-chief Phytopathology News, 1966-69, Plant Disease, 1969-72; contbr. numerous articles to encys., profl. publs. and mags. Lt. (j.g.) USN, 1943-46, PTO. Recipient Disting. Svc. award USDA, Washington, 1986, E.C. Stakman award U. Minn., 2000. Fellow Am. Phytopathological Soc. (councilor at large 1970-71, Excellence in Extension Plant Pathology award 1991); mem. Internat. Soc. Plant Pathology (chmn. extension com. 1975-80), Am. Phytopathological Soc. (mem. various coms.). Avocation: photography. Home: 6730 Heron Ln Pearland TX 77584 6618 Personal E-mail: lmshurt@att.net.

SHURTLEFF, MARK L. state attorney general; BA, Brigham Young U.; JD, U. Utah. Officer, atty. JAG USN, 1985—90; pvt. practice in law Calif., 1990—93; asst. atty. gen. State of Utah, 1993—97; dep. county atty. Salt Lake County, 1997—98; commr. Salt Lake County Commn., 1999—2000, chmn., 2000; atty. gen. State of Utah, 2001—. Leader Boy Scout troops, 1980—; anti-drug lectr., at-risk youth mentor. Republican. Office: Office of the Attorney General East Office Building Ste 320 Salt Lake City UT 84114

SHURTLIFF, MARVIN KARL, lawyer; b. Idaho Falls, Idaho, Nov. 6, 1939; s. Noah Leon and Melba Dorothy (Hunting) S.; m. Peggy J. Griffin, Nov. 23, 1963; 1 dau., Jennifer Karyl. BA, Idaho State Coll., 1962; JD, U. Idaho, 1968. Bar: Idaho 1968. Tchr. pub. schs., Jefferson County, Idaho, 1964-65; atty. U.S. Dept. Justice, Washington, 1968-74; commr. Idaho Pub. Utilities Commn., 1974-75, pres., 1975-76; spl. asst., legal counsel Gov. of Idaho, Boise, 1977; U.S. atty. for Dist. of Idaho, Boise, 1977-81; practice law Boise, 1981—. Mem. Idaho Ho. of Reps., 1962-64 Mem. Idaho State Bd. Edn., 1990—95, Idaho Commn. on Redistricting, 2001. Mem. Idaho Bar Assn. Democrat. Home: 62 Horizon Dr Boise ID 83702-4419 Office: PO Box 1652 Boise ID 83701-1652 Office Phone: 208-343-2900.

SHUSHKEWICH, KENNETH WAYNE, structural engineer; b. Winnipeg, Man., Can., Sept. 22, 1952; m. Valdine Cuffe, Sept. 28, 1980. BSCE, U. Man., Winnipeg, 1974; MS in Structural Engring., U. Calif., Berkeley, 1975; PhD in Structural Engring., U. Alta., Edmonton, Can., 1985. Engr. Wardrop and Assocs., Winnipeg, 1974—78, Preconsult Can., Montreal, 1978—80; prof. U. Alta., 1981—85, U. Man., 1985—87; engr. T.Y. Lin Internat., San Francisco, 1988—90, H.J. Degenkolb Assocs., San Francisco, 1990—92, Ben C. Gerwick, Inc., San Francisco, 1993—94, J. Muller Internat., Chgo., 1994—95, T.Y. Lin Internat., San Francisco, 1995—99, KSI Bridge Engrs., San Francisco, 1999—. Prin. works include design of prestressed concrete segmental bridges; design mgr. for long-span west approach bridge of Northumberland Strait Crossing in Can.; contbr. articles to profl. jours. Recipient award for design of Vierendeel truss bridge, Man. Design Inst., 1977. Fellow ASCE; mem. Am. Concrete Inst., Prestressed Concrete Inst., Internat. Assn. Bridge and Structural Engrs. Achievements include invention of strutted box widening method for long-span bridge widening. Office: PO Box 3665 Bellevue WA 98009-3665

SHUSTER, ALVIN, journalist, newspaper editor; b. Washington, Jan. 25, 1930; s. Fred and Dora (Levy) S.; m. Miriam Schwartz, June 22, 1952; children: Fred, Jessica, Beth. AB, George Washington U., 1951. Reporter Washington Bur. N.Y. Times, 1952-61, asst. news editor, 1961-66, reporter London Bur., 1967-70; bur. chief Saigon, Vietnam, 1970-71, London, 1971-75, Rome, 1975-77; dep. editor editorial pages L.A. Times, 1977-83, fgn. editor, 1983-95, sr. consulting editor, 1995—. Pres. Fgn. Corrs. Assn., London, 1973-74; trustee Monterey (Calif.) Inst. Internat. Studies, 1983-99; chmn. Pulitzer Prize Jury Internat. Reporting, 1999. Editor: The Witnesses, 1964, Washington: The New York Times Guide to the Nations' Capital, 1967, International Press Institute Report, 1995-99; assc. editor Global Journalist, 1999-2004; contbg. author: The Kennedy Years, 1964; contbg. editor Columbia Journalism Rev., 1999-2004. Nieman fellow Harvard U., 1966-67. Mem. Reform Club (London). Office: Los Angeles Times 202 W 1st St Los Angeles CA 90012

SHUSTER, BUD, business executive, former congressman; b. Glassport, Pa., Jan. 23, 1932; s. Prather and Grace (Greinert) S.; m. Patricia Rommell, Aug. 27, 1955; children: Peg, Bill, Debbie, Bobby, Gia. BS, U. Pitts., 1954; MBA, Duquesne U., 1960; PhD in Econs. and Mgmt., Am. U., 1967. Nat. account mgr. Univac divsn. Sperry Rand, 1956, Univac divsn. Remington Rand Co. (now Sperry Rand), 1956-60; dist. mgr. Western Pa. RCA, 1960-62, mgr. ops., 1962-65, v.p. EPD divsn., 1965-68; pres. computer terminal co., 1968-72; mem. 93rd-106th Congresses from 9th Pa. dist., Washington, 1973-2001, former chmn. U.S. House Transp. Com., former ranking mem. U.S. House Select Com. on Intelligence; pres. Strategic Advisors, Everett, Pa., 2001—; chmn. Safe Extensions, Inc. Vis. prof. St. Francis U., Loretto, Pa., 2001. Author: Believing in America, 1983. Del. Rep. Nat. Conv., 1976, 80, 84, 88, 92, 96; co-chair Energy, Environment & Transp. Platform Subcom.; sr. transp. advisor Bush-Quayle Campaign; also mem. platform com.; chmn. Reagan-Bush Campaign in Western Pa.; sr. advisor to transition team for Dept. Transp., 1980-81; trustee J.F. Kennedy Ctr. for Performing Arts. With Counter-Intelligence U.S. Army, 1954—56. Recipient Watchdog of Treasury award, Guardian of Small Bus. award, Golden Age Hall of Fame award. Mem. Pa. Soc., Chowder and Marching Soc., Capitol Hill Club, Phi Beta Kappa, Omicron Delta Kappa, Sigma Chi (Significant Sig award).

SHUSTER, DIANA, former artistic director; Artistic dir. Am. Musical Theatre of San Jose, Calif., 1982—2002. Office: Am Musical Theatre 1717 Technology Dr San Jose CA 95110-1305

SHUSTER, FREDERICK, retired internist, gastroenterologist; b. Newark, Sept. 12, 1933; s. Ralph and Anne (Weinstein) S.; m. Jane B. Block, June 11, 1958; children: Alan R., Robert G. BS, Rutgers U., 1955; MD, U. Chgo., 1959. Diplomate Am. Bd. Internal Medicine, Am. Bd. Gastroenterology. Intern U. Mich. Hosp., Ann Arbor, 1959-60, resident internal medicine, 1960-62; resident gastroenterology VA Hosp. U. Miami, Fla., 1962-63; pvt. practice N. Miami Beach, Fla., 1963-97; from clin. instr. to assoc. prof. medicine U. Miami, Fla., 1963—; pvt. practice Aventura, Fla., 1997-98; ret., 1998. Chmn. dept. medicine Parkway Regional Med. Ctr., N. Miami Beach, 1967, 70, chief of staff, 1974-75, chief divsn. gastroenterology, 1976-77, chmn. pharmacy and therapeutics com., 1978-98. Chmn. med. advisory com. Crohn's and Colitis Found., S. Fla. chpt., Miami, 1979-81. Major U.S. Army, 1967-69. Recipient Physician's Recognition award in Continung Edn., AMA, Chgo., 1970—. Fellow Am. Coll. Physicians, Am. Coll. Gastroenterology, Alpha Omega Alpha. Jewish. Avocations: bowling, ballroom dancing, stock market research and investing. E-mail: fred991@att.net.

SHUSTER, MARGUERITE, minister, educator; b. Oxnard, Calif., Sept. 10, 1947; d. Carroll Lloyd and Grace Margaret (Hornbeck) S. BA with great distinction, Stanford U., 1968; MDiv, Fuller Sem., Pasadena, Calif., 1975; PhD, Fuller Grad. Sch. Psychology, Pasadena, 1977. Ordained to ministry Presbyn. Ch. (U.S.A.), 1980. From asst. to assoc. pastor Arcadia (Calif.) Presbyn. Ch., 1980-86; pastor Knox Presbyn. Ch., Pasadena, Calif., 1987-92; adj. asst. prof. preaching Fuller Sem., Pasadena, 1988-90; assoc. prof. preaching Fuller Theol. Sem., Pasadena, 1992-2001, prof. preaching, 2001. Del. gen. Assembly Mission Consultation Planning Team, 1984—85, Inst. Ecumenical and Cultural Rsch., Collegeville, Minn., 1985, Collegeville, 86; com. chair Gen. Assembly, 1988; Staley lectr. Sterling Coll., 2001; Harp lectr. Anderson Sch. Theology, 2004. Author: Power, Pathology, Paradox, 1987, The Fall and Sin: What We Have Become as Sinners, 2004; mem. editl. bd.: Theology, News and Notes, 1986—; contbr. articles sermons, and revs. in religious jours. and books; editor (contbr.): Perspectives on Christology, 1991, Who We Are: Our Dignity as Human, 1996. Bd. dirs. Sierra Madre Mountain Conservancy, 2002—. Named one of Outstanding Young Women in Am., 1979, 83. Mem. Presbytery of San Gabriel (chair, com. on ministry 1991, moderator, permanent jud. commn. 1993-95, moderator Presbytery 1996), Phi Beta Kappa. Home: 675 Mount Wilson Trl Sierra Madre CA 91024-1232 Office: Fuller Theol Sem 135 N Oakland Ave Pasadena CA 91182-0001 Office Phone: 626-584-5248. Business E-Mail: shuster@fuller.edu. *A goal: so to trust in Jesus Christ, especially in times of sorrow and disappointment, that others might find it easier rather than more difficult to believe in a loving, omnipotent God.*

SHUSTER, ROBERT G. electronics company executive, consultant; b. N.Y.C., June 1, 1927; s. Robert Chandler and Therese G. (Giraud); m. Marianne B. Lynski, Apr. 20, 1970 (div. Jan. 1987); m. H. Elizabeth Young, May 20, 1989 (div. Dec. 1995); m. Erika Megas, May 5, 2002. BSEE, CCNY, 1948; MSEE, Columbia U., 1955, postgrad., 1959-64. Test engr. Elec. Testing Labs., N.Y.C., 1948-50; project leader Sperry Gyroscope Co., Great Neck, N.Y., 1950-59; project mgr. RCA Advanced Communications Lab., N.Y.C., 1959-67; prin. scientist Tracor, Inc., Rockville, Md., 1967-75, v.p. electronics systems div., 1975-87; pres. Tracor Tech. Resources, Inc., Rockville, Md., 1984-90, RGS Assocs., McLean, Va., 1990—; v.p. C-Cubed Corp., Alexandria, Va., 1990-93, pres., 1993-95; sr. cons., 1996—. Mem. IEEE (sr.), N.Y. Acad. Scis. Avocations: photography, hiking.

SHUSTER, WILLIAM (BILL SHUSTER), congressman; b. McKeesport, Pa., Jan. 10, 1961; m. Rebecca Shuster; children: Ali, Garrett. BA, Dickinson Coll., Carlisle, Pa., 1983, MBA, American U., Washington, DC. Mgr. retail stores Goodyear Tire and Rubber Corporation; dist. mgr. Bandag Inc.; mem. U.S. Congress from 9th Pa., 2001—. Mem. com. on Transp. & Infrastructure and Small Bus., subcommittees on Highway & Transit, Water Resources & Environment, Aviation, Rural Enterprises, Agriculture and Tech. Republican. Office: US House Representatives 1108 Longworth House Office Building Washington DC 20515-3809

SHUSTERMAN, NATHAN, underwriter, financial consultant; b. Montreal, Que., Can., Aug. 27, 1927; arrived in US, 1950; s. Aaron and Annie (Nulman) S.; m. Norma Thalblum, Jan. 1950; children: Mark D., Claudia S. Student, Sir George Williams Coll., Montreal, 1944-47; grad., N.Y. Inst. Fin. CLU, chartered fin. cons. Retailing mgr. Jefferson Stores, Miami, Fla., 1950-65; gen. agt. Protective Life Ins. Co., Miami, 1965—. Chmn. emeritus field adv. coun., past pres. Protective Club; pres. Am. Fin. Counseling Corp., Miami; instr. estate and tax planning Am. Coll., Bryn Mawr, Pa., 1972—, U. Miami, Coral Gables, Fla., 1972—; registered rep. Pro Equity Services Inc.; cons. in field. Named Man of Yr., Gen. Agts. and Mgrs. Assn., Miami, 1965-67. Mem. North Dade-South Broward Estate Planning Coun., Million Dollar Round Table (life), Top of Table, Assn. Advanced Life Underwriting, Soc. Fin. Svc. Profls. (past pres. Miami chpt.), Nat. Assn. Ins. and Fin. Advisors (Nat. Sales Achievement award, Nat. Quality award), Fla. Assn. Ins. and Fin. Advisors, Miami Assn. Ins. and Fin. Advisors, Internat. Assn. Fin. Planners, Am. Soc. Pension Actuaries (assoc.), Optimists (pres. North Miami Beach, Fla. chpt. 1971), Masons, Shriners, B'nai B'rith (pres. Miami chpt 1950). Home: 2320 NE 196th St Miami FL 33180-2132 Office: Am Fin Counseling Corp 16121 NE 18th Ave Miami FL 33162-4749 Office Phone: 305-949-0906.

SHUSTERMAN, NEAL DOUGLAS, writer, screenwriter; b. N.Y.C., Nov. 12, 1962; s. Milton and Charlotte Ruth (Altman) S.; m. Elaine Gale Jones, Jan. 31, 1987; children: Brendan, Jarrod, Joelle, Erin. BA in Psychology and Drama, U. Calif., Irvine, 1985. Author, screenwriter, 1987—. Author: Guy Talk, 1987, The Shadow Club, 1988 (Children's CHoice award Internat. Reading Assn. 1989), Dissidents, 1989, Speeding Bullet, 1991 (Best Book for Teens award N.Y. Pub. Libr., nominated Calif. Young Reader Medal 1995-96), Kid Heroes, 1991, What Daddy Did, 1991 (Best Book for Young Adults award ALA, Outstanding Work of Fiction award So. Calif. Coun. Lit. for Children and Young People, Children's Choice award and Young Adult Choice award Internat. Reading Assn., Pick of the List award ABA, Best Book for Teens award N.Y. Pub. Libr., Okla. Sequoyah award 1994), The Eyes of Kid Midas, 1992 (ALA Best Book for Reluctant Readers), Darkness Creeping, 1993, Piggyback Ninja, 1994, Scorpion Shards, 1995 (N.Y. Pub. Libr. Best Book for the Teenaged), Darkness Creeping II, 1995, Mindquakes, 1996 (ALA YALSA Quick Pick), Mindstorms, 1996, Mindtwisters, 1997, The Dark Side of Nowhere, 1997 (ALA Best Book, ALA Quick Pick--Top 10 Book), Thief of Souls, 1999, Downsiders, 1999 (ALA Best Book, ALA Quick Pick), Mind-Benders, 2000, The Shadow Club Rising, 2002, Shattered Sky, 2002, Full Tilt, 2003 (Tex. Lonestar award), The Schwa Was Here, 2004; screenwriter: Double Dragon, 1992, Evolver, 1993; dir. Heart on a Chain, 1991 (Golden Eagle award CINE), What About the Sisters, 1993 (Golden Eagle award CINE), Games: How to Host a Teen Mystery, Hot Times at Hollywood High, 1994, Barbecue with the Vampire, 1997, Roswell that Ends Well, 1999, How to Host a Murder: Roman Ruins, 1996, The Good, the Bad and the Guilty, 1997, The Tragical Mystery Tour, 1998, The Maiming of the Shrew, 2000, Saturday Night Cleaver, 2000, An Affair to Dismember, 2003, (TV) Goosebumps: The Werewolf of Fever Swamp, 1996, Goosebumps: Night of the Living Dummy III, 1997, Animorphs (staff writer), 1998, Pixel Perfect, 2004. Mem. PEN, Writers Guild Am. West, Soc. Children's Book Writers and Illustrators. Avocations: swimming, tennis, storytelling. Office: PO Box 18516 Irvine CA 92623-8516 E-mail: NStoryman@aol.com.

SHUTE, RICHARD EMIL, government official, engineer; b. Bklyn., May 1, 1938; s. William Leonard and Doris S.; m. Linda Janan McElhiney, Mar. 7, 1960. BS in Mech. Engring., U. Miami, 1960; MBA, Fla. State U., 1970. Registered profl. engr., Fla. Engr. Pratt and Whitney Aircraft, West Palm Beach, Fla., 1960-62, Gen. Dynamics Corp., San Diego, 1962-64; aerospace engr. NASA/Kennedy Space Ctr., Fla., 1964-71; dir. planning and evaluation Fla. Dept. Health and Human Services, Tallahassee, 1971-76; dir. office program devel. Office Human Devel., HHS, Washington, 1976-87; dir. office of mgmt. and info. systems U.S. Dept. Commerce, Washington, 1987-90; pres. Richard E. Shute and Assocs. Mgmt. Cons., 1990—. Mem. Nat. Assn. Security Dealers (bd. arbitrators).

SHUTLER, MARY ELIZABETH, academic administrator; b. Oakland, Calif., Nov. 14, 1929; d. Hal Wilfred and Elizabeth Frances (Gimbel) Hall; m. Richard Shutler Jr., Sept. 8, 1951 (div. 1975); children: Kathryn Allice (dec.), John Hall, Richard Burnett. BA, U. Calif., Berkeley, 1951; MA, U. Ariz., 1958, PhD, 1967. Asst., assoc., full prof. anthropology, chmn. dept. San Diego State U., 1967-75; prof. anthropology, dept. chmn. Wash. State U., Pullman, 1975-80; dean Coll. Arts and Scis., prof. anthropology U. Alaska, Fairbanks, 1980-84; vice chancellor, dean of faculty, prof. anthropology U. Wis. Parkside, Kenosha, 1984-88; provost, v.p. for acad. affairs, prof. anthropology Calif. State U., L.A., 1988-94; provost West Coast U., L.A., 1994-97; dean Sch. of Arts and Scis. Nat. U., La Jolla, Calif., 1997—. Mem. core staff Lahav Rsch. Project, Miss. State U., 1975-92. Co-author: Oceanic Prehistory, 1975, Deer Creek Cave, 1964, Archaeological Survey of Southern Nevada, 1963, Stuart Rockshelter, 1962; contbr. articles to jours. in field. Mem. coun. Gamble House. Fellow Am. Anthropol. Assn.; mem. Soc. for Am. Archaeology, Am. Schs. for Oriental Rsch., Am. Coun. Edn., Am. Assn. for Higher Edn., Am. Assn. State Colls. and Univs., Delta Zeta. Republican. Roman Catholic. Avocations: travel, gardening, cats. E-mail: eshutler@nu.edu.

SHUTT, TIMOTHY BAKER, humanities educator, writer; b. Newark, Ohio, June 23, 1950; s. Richard Jack and Gratia Lucy Baker Shutt; m. Leslie Lynn Moran, Oct. 29, 1982; children: Whitt Talmadge Hanshaw, Doub Gil-Kelly Hanshaw, Pruitt Streeter Baker. BA, Yale U., 1972; MA, PhD, U. of Va., 1984. Instr. in english and history St. Mark's Sch. of Tex., Dallas, 1973—76, head swimming coach, 1973—76; asst. distance swimming coach U. of Va., Charlottesville, Va., 1980—83, fellow, 1984—86; asst. prof. of english integrated program in humane studies Kenyon Coll., Gambier, Ohio, 1986—94, assoc. prof. of english integrated program in humane studies, 1994—. Announcer NCAA, Indpls., 1986—; cons. and evaluator: faculty devel. Denison U., Granville, Ohio, 1992—; faculty asst. to pres. and provost Kenyon Coll., Gambier, Ohio, 1997—98. Author: Hebrews, Greeks, and Romans: The Foundations of Western Civilization, 2003; editor: Mil. History Mag., 1983—90, Monsters, Gods and Heroes, 2004. Named All-American in Swimming, NHSSCA, 1968; fellow, Mellon Found., 1984—86; grantee, Telluride Found., 1997. Avocations: reading, birding, astronomy, art, swimming. Home and Office: P O Box 789 Gambier OH 43022-0789 E-mail: shutt@kenyon.edu.

SHUTTLEWORTH, ANNE MARGARET, psychiatrist; b. Detroit, Jan. 17, 1931; d. Cornelius Joseph and Alice Catherine (Rice) S.; m. Joel R. Siegel, Apr. 19, 1959; children: Erika, Peter. AB, Cornell U., 1953, MD, 1956. Intern Lenox Hill Hosp., N.Y.C., 1956-57; resident Payne Whitney Clinic-N.Y. Hosp., 1957-60; practice medicine specializing in psychiatry Maplewood, N.J., 1960—. Cons. Maplewood Sch. System, 1960-62; instr. psychiatry Cornell U. Med. Sch., 1960; mem. Com. to Organize New Sch. Psychology, 1970. Mem. AMA (Physicians Recognition award 1975, 78, 81, 84, 87, 90, 93, 96, 99, 2002), Am. Psychiat. Assn., Am. Med. Women's Assn., N.Y. Acad. Scis., Acad. Medicine N.J., Phi Beta Kappa, Phi Kappa Phi. Office: 2066 Millburn Ave Maplewood NJ 07040-3715

SHUTZ, BYRON CHRISTOPHER, real estate executive; b. Kansas City, Mo., Feb. 16, 1928; s. Byron Theodore and Maxine (Christopher) S.; m. Marilyn Ann Tweedie, Mar. 30, 1957; children: Eleanor S. Gaines, Byron Christopher, Collin Reid, Allison S. Moskow, Lindley Anne Baile. AB in Econs, U. Kans., 1949. Ptnr. Herbert V. Jones & Co., Kansas City, Mo., 1953-72; pres. Herbert V. Jones Mortgage Corp., Kansas City, 1967-72, The Byron Shutz Co., Kansas City, 1973—. Dir. 1st Am. Financial Corp., Rothschild's, Inc., Bus. Men's Assurance Co., Faultless Starch, Bon Ami Co. Chmn. bd. trustees U. Kansas City, 1979-81; trustee Pembroke-Country Day Sch., 1974-77, Midwest Rsch. Inst., 1980-89; chmn., bd. govs. Kansas City Art Inst., 1960-62; chmn. bd. dirs. Ctr. for Bus. Innovation, Inc., 1985-87; bd. dirs. Kansas City Crime Commn. 1st lt. USAF, 1951-53. Mem. Mortgage Bankers Assn. Am. (bd. govs. 1966-74), Am. Inst. Real Estate Appraisers. Clubs: Kansas City Country, University, Mercury (pres. 1978-79); Fla. Yacht (Jacksonville), Ocean Reef (Key Largo, Fla.). Home: 1001 W 58th Ter Kansas City MO 64113-1159 Office: 800 W 47th St Kansas City MO 64112-1251 Personal E-mail: arrowrock3@sbcglobal.net.

SHVETSOV, ALEXANDER ANATOLIEVICH, biochemist, researcher; b. Orel, Russia, July 25, 1960; s. Anatoly Ivanovich and Anna Yakovlevna (Tsytsarkina) S.; m. Tatiana Vasilevna Orlova, Feb. 26, 1988; 1 child, Oksana. MS in Agronomy, Agrl. Acad., Orel, 1983; PhD in Biochemistry, Inst. Biochemistry, Moscow, 1992, postgrad., 1992-95. Jr. rsch. assoc. Inst. Agrl. Industry, Orel, 1986-88; sr. rschr. Inst. Biochemistry, 1995-98; sr. rsch. investigator Plant Physiology Inst., Moscow, 1998-2000; postdoctoral fellow UCLA, 2000—. Reviewer Nat. Rsch. Initiative Grants Program, Washington, 1996-99; sec. Internat. Symposium on Stress and Inorganic Nitrogen Assimilation, Moscow, 1996. Patentee in field; contbr. numerous articles to profl. jours. Lt. USSR Military Svc., 1983-85. Mem.: Am. Soc. for Cell Biology. Russian Orthodox. Avocations: music, philosophy, painting. Home: 48 Pepvomaiskaya Str Apt 14 303120 Orel Russia Office: UCLA Dept Chemistry 405 Hilgard Ave Los Angeles CA 90024-1569 E-mail: alexs@ucla.edu.

SHVIDLER, MARK JOSEPH, mathematician; b. Khmelnitsky, Ukraine, USSR, Mar. 25, 1931; s. Joseph Zuss and Lea Gersh (Gleyzer); m. Mariam Moses Mendelson, July 24, 1959; children: Irene, Eugene. MS in Applied Mechanics, Kiev State U., USSR, 1953; PhD, All-Union Rsch. Sci. Oil and Gas Inst., Moscow, 1958, DS, 1964. Scientist Sci. Rsch. Oil Inst., Ufa, USSR, 1953-58, dept. head, 1958-67; scientist All-Union Rsch.-Sci. Natural Gas Inst., Moscow, 1967-70; scientist, prof., dept. head All-Union Rsch.-Sci. Oil and Gas Inst., Moscow, 1970-91; scientist Lawrence Berkeley Nat. Lab., Berkeley, Calif., 1991-92. Vis. scientist Atomic Energy of Can. Ltd., Chalk River, Ont., Can., 1993, Lawrence Berkeley Nat. Lab., Berkeley, 1994-2004. Author: Filtration Flow in Heterogeneous Media, 1964, One-Dimensional Immiscible Flow Through Porous Media, 1970, Statistical Hydrodynamics of Porous Media, 1985; contbr. over 170 articles to profl. jours. Mem.: Am. Geophys. Union. Achievements include rsch. on statis. hydrodynamics of porous media and devel. of the theory. Home: 2550 Geary Blvd Apt 402 San Francisco CA 94115 Personal E-mail: shvidler@sbcglobal.net.

SHWARTZ, SIMA M. music educator; arrived in U.S., 1995; d. Michael Yakovlevich Shwartz and Sophia R. Leshchiner; m. Vladimir A. Shpachenko, June 7, 1975 (div. Oct. 1978); 1 child, Nadia Shpachenko. Grad., Music Sch. for Gifted Youth, Kharkov, 1964; MusM in Tchg. Piano, Accompanist, Performer, State Inst. Arts, Kharkov, 1969. Piano faculty Kharkov Music Schs., 1964—91; accompanist Kharkov State Philharm., 1964—91, Kharkov Inst. Arts, 1964—65; piano faculty Severodonetsk State Music Coll., 1969—72; founder, condr. Jewish Children Orch., Kharkov, 1990—91; piano tchr. Gilloh Dalled Sch., Jerusalem, 1992—95; founder, piano tchr. Sima's Music Club, Cambridge, Mass., 1996—2000; piano faculty The Music Sch., Providence, 1999—2000; founder, piano tchr. Shwartz Piano Sch., Marlborough, Mass., 2000—02; piano faculty Performing Arts Sch., Worcester, Mass., 2003—. Mem.: New Eng. Piano Tchrs. Assn., Music Tchrs. Nat. Assn. Avocations: walking, ping pong/table tennis, reading, theater.

SHWAYDER, ELIZABETH YANISH, sculptor; b. St. Louis; d. Sam and Fannie May (Weil) Yaffe; m. Nathan Yanish, July 5, 1944 (dec.); children: Ronald, Marilyn Ginsburg, Mindy; m. M.C. Shwayder, 1988 (dec.). Student, Washington U., 1941, Denver U., 1961; pvt. studies. One-woman shows include Woodstock Gallery, London, 1973, Internat. House, Denver, 1963, Colo. Women's Coll., Denver, 1975, Contemporaries Gallery, Santa Fe, 1963, So. Colo. State Coll. Pueblo, 1967, others; group shows include Salt Lake City Mus., 1964, 71, Denver Art Mus., 1961-75, Oklahoma City Mus., 1969, Joslyn Mus., Omaha, 1964-68, Lucca (Italy) Invitational, 1971, Denver Art Mus., Mus. Natural History, Mizel Mus., Eden Theatrical Workshop, Rose Hosp. Aux., Nat. Mus. Women in the Arts, Colo. Chpt. 8th Air Force Aux., Women's Art Ctr., others; represented in permanent collections including Colo. State Bank, Bmh Synagogue, Denver., Colo. Women's Coll., Har Ha Shem Congregation, Boulder, Colo., Faith Bible Chapel, Denver, others. Chmn. visual arts Colo. Centennial-Bicentennial, 1974-75; pres. Denver Coun. Arts and Humanities, 1973-75; co-chmn. visual arts spree Denver Pub. Schs., 1975; trustee Denver Ctr. Performing Arts, 1973-75; chmn. Concerned Citizens for the Arts, 1976; pres. Beth Israel Hosp. Aux., 1985-87; organizer Coat Drive for the Needy, Denver, N.Y.C., 1982-87, Common Cents penny drive for homeless, 1991-93; bd. dirs. Mizel Mus., Srs., Inc.; active Mayor's Com. on Cultural Affairs, Denver Art Mus., Mus. Natural History, Freedom Found. at Valley Forge, Hospice of Metro. Denver; bd. dirs. Rainbow Bridge; bd. dirs. Diabetes Found., Asian Arts Assn. Denver Art Mus., also pres.; historian Childrens Diabetes Found., Univ. Colo. Found. Inc. Humanities scholar Auraria Librs.-U. Colo.; recipient McCormick award Ball State U., Muncie, Ind., 1964, purchase award color Women's Coll., Denver, 1963, Tyler (Tex.) Mus., 1963, 1st prize in sculpture 1st Nat. Space Art Show, 1971, humanitarian award Milehi Denver Sertoma, 1994, The Gleitsman Found., 1994, svc. to mankind awards Freedom Found. at Valley Forge, Mile Hi Sertoma Club, Minoruyasui Found., Gleitsman Found. Mem. Denver Art Mus., Asian Arts Assn. (pres.). Home: Unit 503 2400 Cherry Creek South Dr Denver CO 80209-3259

SHYAMALAN, MANOJ NIGHT, film director; b. Pondicherry, Tamil-Nadu, India, Aug. 6, 1970; s. Jayalakshmi Shyamalan and Nelliate C; m. Bhavna Shyamalan, 1993; 2 children. Grad., NYU, 1992. Actor, dir., prodr., writer: (films) Praying with Anger, 1992, Unbreakable, 2000, Signs, 2002, The Village, 2004; Actor, dir., writer: (films) The Sixth Sense, 1999 (Bram Stoker Award for Best Screenplay, 1999, Golden Satellite Award for Best Original Screenplay, 1999, Visionary Award, Palm Springs Internat. Film Festival, 2000, Nebula Award for Best Script, Sci. Fiction and Fantasy Writers Am., 1999, nominated for Best Dir. and Best Original Screenplay, Acad. Awards 2000, Nominated for Best Screenplay, Golden Globes, 2000); dir., writer: (films) Praying Wide Awake, 1998; writer screenplay Stuart Little, 1999. Office: United Talent Agy Inc c/o Peter Benedek 9560 Wilshire Blvd Fl 5 Beverly Hills CA 90212-2400

SHYER, JOHN D. lawyer; b. Nashville, May 4, 1956; s. Michael and Hilda (Wertheim) S.; m. Marsha Anne Gisser, May 7, 1989; children: Allison Parcell, Michael Wertheim. AB, Princeton U., 1978; JD, Stanford U., 1981. Bar: N.Y. 1982, U.S. Ct. Appeals (2d cir.) 1983, U.S. Ct. Appeals (3d cir.) 1992. Assoc. Donovan, Leisure, Newton & Irvine, N.Y.C., 1981-85, Latham & Watkins LLP, N.Y.C., 1985-89, ptnr., 1989—. Trustee Princeton (N.J.) Broadcasting Svc., 1985—. Mem. Assn. Bar City N.Y., Employment and Labor Lawcast (bd. editl. advisors 1994—). Avocations: travel, hiking, reading. Office: Latham & Watkins LLP 885 3rd Ave Ste 1000 New York NY 10022-4834 Office Phone: 212-906-1200. Business E-Mail: john.shyer@lw.com.

SHYERS, LARRY EDWARD, mental health counselor, educator; b. Middletown, Ohio, Aug. 16, 1948; s. Edward and Ruth Evelyn (Davis) S.; m. Linda Faye Shearon, July 31, 1970; children: Jami Lynn, Karen Lindsey. BA, David Lipscomb Coll., Nashville, 1970; MA, Stetson U., Deland, Fla., 1973; MEd, U. Ctrl. Fla., 1981; PhD, U. Fla., 1992. Lic. mental health counselor, Fla.; nat. cert. counselor, psychologist, approved clin. supr.; diplomate Nat. Registry Neurofeedback Providers; ordained to ministry non-denom. Ch. of Christ, 1969. Minister Ch. of Christ, Ocala, Fla., 1970-75, Mt. Dora, Fla., 1975-80; tchr. Christian Home and Bible Sch., Mt. Dora, Fla., 1970-77, dir. guidance, 1977-86; pvt. practice individual and family counseling Mt. Dora, Fla., 1980—. Apptd. to state regulatory bd. for clin. social work, marriage, family therapy, mental heatlh counseling, 1987-95, vice-chmn., 1987-88, chmn., 1989-95, legis. liaison, 1988-95, probable cause panel, 1996—; adj. prof. Nova. U., 1986—, U. Ctrl. Fla., 1988—, psychology St. Leo Coll., 1985—, Rollins Coll., 1991—, Reformed Theol. Sem., 1995—; adj. instr. Lake Sumter CC, 1989—, Stetson U., 1990—; mem. individual manpower tng. sys. bd. Vocat.-Tech. Sch., Eustis, 1984-87; mem. adv. bd. US Achievement Bd., 1983—; cons. in field. Dir. edn. Mt. Dora Ch. of Christ, 1983-86; mem. Leadership Lake County Class of 1999. Mem. Fla. Mental Health Counselors Assn. (chmn. award and profl. devel. coms. 1985, chmn. govt. rels. com., pres. 1986-87), ACA (govt. rels. com. 1990-95, publs. rev. com. 1991—), Am. Mental Health Counselors Assn. (govt. rels. com. 1987-90, chmn. 1988-90, publs. com. 1991—, PP&I com. 1992-95), Am. Orthopsychiatric Assn., Am. Assn. Christian Counselors, Nat. Coun. Family Rels., Internat. Assn. Marriage and Family Counselors, Assn. of Assessment in Counseling, Am. Assn. Profl. Hypnotherapists, Lake Sumter Assn. for Counseling and Devel. (pres. 1987-88), Assn. for Applied Psychophysiology and Biofeedback, Mount Dora C. of C. (mem. youth com. 1984), Leadership Lake County Class of 1999, Kiwanis, Kappa Delta Pi, Pi Lambda Theta, Chi Sigma Iota. Republican. Avocations: amateur radio, target shooting. Office: 3750 Lake Center Loop Mount Dora FL 32757-2211 Office Phone: 352-383-2194. E-mail: larry@larryeshyers.com.

SHYY, WEI, aerospace and mechanical engineering researcher, educator; b. Tainan, Taiwan, China, July 19, 1955; arrived in U.S., 1979; s. Chiang-Chen and June-Hua (Chao) S.; m. Yuchen Shih; children: Albert, Alice, Andrew Chang, Kevin Chang. BS, Tsin-Hua U., Taiwan, 1977; MSE, U. Mich., 1981, PhD, 1982. Postdoctoral rsch. scholar U. Mich., Ann Arbor, 1982-83; rsch. scientist GE Corp. Rsch. and Devel. Ctr., Schenectady, NY, 1983-88; faculty mem. of aeronautics and astronautics Nat. Cheng-Kung U., Taiwan, 1987; assoc. prof. aerospace engring., mechanics and engring. sci. U. Fla., Gainesville, 1988-92, prof. aerospace engring., mechanics and engring. sci., 1992—, chmn. dept. aerospace engring., mechs. and engring. sci., 1996—2002, chmn. dept. mech. and aerospace engring., 2002—; dir. NASA URETI: Inst. for Future Space Flight, Gainesville, 2002—. Dir. Space Grant Consortium NASA, Fla., 1998—2000, dir. Univ. Rsch., Engring. and Tech. Inst. on 3rd Generation Reusable Launch Vehicle; cons. in field; lectr. in field. Editor: Recent Advances in Computational Fluid Dynamics, 1989; author: Computational Modeling for Fluid Flow and Interfacial Transport, 1994; co-author: Computational Fluid Dynamics with Moving Boundaries, 1996, Computational Techniques for Complex Transport Phenomena, 1997; editor: Fluid Dynamics at Interface, 1999; assoc. editor Jour. Applied Mechanis Rev., Computer Modeling in Engineering and Sciences, mng. editor Cambridge U. Press.: Aerospace Book Series, mem. editl. adv. bd. Numerical Heat Transfer Jour., Progress in Computational Fluid Dynamics, Internat. Jour. Numerical Methods for Heat and Fluid Flow; contbr. articles. Fellow AIAA (Pendray Aerospace Lit. award 2003), ASME; mem. Minerals, Metals and Materials Soc., Am. Phys. Soc., Combustion Inst. Office: U Fla Dept Mech and Aerospace Engring 231 Aero Bldg Gainesville FL 32611

SIA, CALVIN CHIA JUNG, pediatrician; b. Beijing, June 3, 1927; arrived in U.S., 1939; s. Richard Ho Ping and Mary Ling Sang Sia; m. Katherine Wai Kwan Li, June 3, 1951; children: Richard, Jeffrey, Michael. BA, Dartmouth Coll., 1950; MD, Western Res. U., 1955; PhD in Humanities (hon.), U. Hawaii, 1992. Intern William Beaumont Army Hosp., El Paso, Tex., 1955—56; pediat. resident Children's Hosp., Honolulu, 1956—58; pvt. practice pediat., 1958—96; clin. prof. dept. pediat. U. Hawaii Sch. Medicine, 1966—99, prof. pediat. dept. pediat., 1999—. Rschr. in field. Staff sgt. U.S. Army, 1945—47, 1st lt. U.S. Army, 1955—56. Recipient Pvt. Citizen award, Nat. Govs. Assn., 1997. Fellow: Am. Acad. Pediat. (chmn. Hawaii chpt. 1968—76, Clifford G. Grulee award 2001, Job Lewis Smith award 2001), Am. Bd. Pediat. (cert.); mem.: AMA (chmn. sect. coun. on pediat. 1983—, Benjamin Rush award 1998, Abraham Jacuri award 1992), Hawaii Med. Assn. (pres. 1976—77). Avocations: tennis, travel. Office: U Hawaii Dept Pediat 1319 Punahou St Honolulu HI 96826

SIAHPOOSH, FARIDEH TAMADDON, librarian; b. Eshghabad, Turkestan, Russia, Nov. 15, 1928; came to U.S., 1964; d. Hosane and Ghamar (Ramzi) Tamaddon; m. Ismail Siahpoosh, Nov. 30, 1958. BA, Tehran U., Iran, 1962; student, Columbia U., 1967; MLS, Queens Coll., Flushing, N.Y., 1972. Cert. librarian, N.Y. Reference libr. Queens Borough-Pub. Libr. Brs., N.Y.C., 1974-85, asst. br. mgr., 1985—94; part-time libr. Baha'i Internat. Cmty., N.Y.C., 1994—. Intern Baha'i World Ctr. Libr., Haifa, Israel, 1998; mem. L.I. Multi-Faith Forum. Mem. ALA. Mem. Baha'i Faith. Home: 19 Ridge Dr E Roslyn NY 11576-1443

SIAMBANES, DAVID, orthopedic surgeon; BS in Biology, U. Ill., Champaign, 1985—89. Cert. in osteopathic medicine Nat. Bd. Osteo. Med. Examiners, 1993. Gen. med. physician McNeal Outpatient Med. Ctr., Chgo., 1995—98; mem. of admissions com. Chgo. Coll. of Osteo. Medicine, 1997—98; v.p. Haider Spine Ctr. Med. Group, Inc., Riverside, Calif., 1999—; dir. of edn. Western U. Orthop. Residency, 2000—; pres., spine sect. Am. Osteo. Acad. Orthopaedics, 2003—04. Mem.: Osteo. Physicians and Surgeons of Calif., N.Am. Spine Soc., Am. Coll. Spine Surgery, Am. Osteo. Assn., Am. Osteo. Acad. Orthopedics, Sigma Sigma Phi, Alpha Epsilon Delta. Office: Haider Spine Ctr Med Group Inc 6276 River Crest Dr Riverside CA 92507 E-mail: dsiambanes@haiderspine.com.

SIANO, MARY ANN, art gallery director; b. N.Y.C., May 20, 1942; d. Antonio and Catherine Rinaldo; m. Anthony Siano, July 31, 1965; children: Suzanne, Michele. BA, CUNY, Bronx, 1989. Exec. sec. Erwin Wasey Ruthrauf & Ryan, N.Y.C., 1961—65; adminstrv. asst. Lehman Coll. Art Gallery, Bronx, 1989—93, 1993—. Mem.: Golden Key. Avocations: painting, reading, crafts.

SIAS, JOHN B. former multi-media company executive, newspaper publisher, publishing executive; b. 1927; AB, Stanford U., 1949. Group v.p. Metromedia Inc., 1962—71; with Capital Cities Comm., 1971—93; pres. Fairchild Pubs. Inc., 1971—75, exec. v.p., pres. pub. divsn., 1975—85; pres. ABC-TV Network Group, N.Y.C., 1986—93; also former exec. v.p. Capital Cities/ABC Inc. (parent), N.Y.C.; former pres., chmn Chronicle Pub. Co., San Francisco. Served with U.S. Army, 1945—46. Office: Chronicle Pub Co 901 Mission St San Francisco CA 94103-2905 also: Capital Cities ABC Inc 24 E 51st St New York NY 10022-6801

SIAS, MARY, university executive; b. Jackson, Miss., July 2, 1950; d. Augusta and Ada Lee (Hill) Evans; m. Shadrach Sherman Sias III, Mar. 20, 1976; 1 child, Adrienne Marie. BA, Tougaloo Coll., 1972; MS, U. Wis., 1974, PhD, 1980; MBA, Abilene Christian U., 1983. Instr. sociology Grambling (La.) State U., 1977-79; asst. prof. sociology U. Tex. at Dallas, Richardson, 1980-81, So. Meth. U., Highland Park, Tex., 1981-82; dir. women's resource ctr. YWCA Met. Dallas, 1982-83, asst. mgr. ctrl. br., 1983-84, exec. dir., 1984-95; sr. v.p. U. Tex., Dallas, 1995—2004; pres. Ky. State U., Frankfort, 2004—. Bd. dirs. Oaks Bank & Trust, Dallas Co-author: Planned Resettlement in Nepal's Terrain, 1976. Bd. dirs. King Found. Doctoral fellow Ford Found., 1972; recipient Maura award Women's Ctr., 1988, Trailblazer award South Dallas Bus. and Profl. Club, 1989, Outstanding Texan award State of Tex., 1989, She Knows Where She's Going award Girls, Inc., 1994, award of distinction Girl Scouts U.S.A., 1997, Women of Excellence award, 1998, Lance of Champions award, 2004, Profiles in Leadership award So. Meth. U., 2004. Mem. Nat. Assn. YWCA Execs., Greater Dallas C. of C., State Bar Tex. Avocations: reading, upholstering, refinishing furniture. Home: 201 Cold Harbor Dr Frankfort KY 40601-3009 Office: Ky State U Hume Hall 400 E Main St Frankfort KY 40601

SIBBALD, JOHN RISTOW, management consultant; b. Lincoln, Nebr., June 20, 1936; s. Garth E.W. and Rachel (Wright) S.; m. Kathryn J. Costick; children: Allison, John, Wright. BA, U. Nev., 1958; MA, U. Ill., 1964. Office mgr. Hewitt Assocs., Libertyville, Ill., 1964-66; coll. rels. mgr. Pfizer Inc., N.Y.C., 1966-69; pres., CEO Re-Con Systems, N.Y.C., 1969-70; v.p. Booz, Allen & Hamilton, N.Y.C., 1970-73, Chgo., 1973-75; pres., founder John Sibbald Assocs., Inc., Chgo., 1975. Mem. Nat. Advisory Coun., Nat. Club Assn. Author: The Career Makers, 1990, 92, The New Career Makers, 1995; pub. Club Leaders Forum; contbr. articles to profl. jours. Capt. AUS, 1958-64. Mem. Mid-Day Club Chgo., St. Louis Club. Episcopalian. Office: 7701 Forsyth Blvd Saint Louis MO 63105-1817 Office Phone: 314-727-0227. E-mail: jsibbald@sibbaldassociates.com.

SIBBERNSEN, RICHARD, telecommunications industry executive; b. Omaha; BA, Marquette U., 1971; grad., Creighton U., 1974. Various human resources positions Tenneco, Inc.; head corp. human resources TNT Ltd.; v.p. human resources Bellsouth Corp., Atlanta, 1997—. Office: Bellsouth Corp 1155 Peachtree St NW Atlanta GA 30309-3610

SIBILLA, SUZANNE ROSE, training and organizational development consultant; b. San Jose, Calif., Oct. 15, 1961; d. Susan Pilar Asuzano; m. Michael E. Coutches. BA, Westmont Coll., 1983; MA, Antioch U., 1989. Registered drama therapist Nat. Assn. Drama Therapists, lic. marriage, family, child counselor. Cons. tng. and orgnl. devel. Assn. Psychol. and Ednl. Counselors Asia, Thailand, Malaysia, Singapore; program dir. State of Oreg., Salem, 1988-93; cons. Hewlett Packard, Sun, Raychem, FEMA, CPC Hosps., San Jose, Fremont, Palo Alto, Calif., 1993-95; mgr. tng. and orgnl. devel. Tencor Instruments-KLA and TENCOR, Milpitas, Calif., 1995-97; mng. cons., tng. Sibilla & Assocs., Fremont, Calif., 1997—; orgnl. change specialist NEOPOST, 1998—; corp. tng. mgr. WebMD, 1999—2001; ind. cons. Hewlett Packard, 2001—, Compaq, 2001—, Right Mgmt. Cons., 2001—; cons. Sibilla and Assocs., 2001—. Initiator memtorship program Tencor, Palo Alto, 1997. Guest (film and TV program) People Are Talking, 1993, (TV series) Mornings on Two, 1994. Dir. mentorship program for girls YWCA, Daly City, 1993—95. Mem.: ASTD, NAFE, Women in Tech. Internat., Calif. Assn. Marriage, Family and Child Counselors (cert.), Assn. Psychol. and Ednl. Counselors Asia (cons. tng. and orgnl. devel. 1988—92, Key Presenter award 1992), Toastmasters, Menttium 100 (chairperson steering com. 1996—97). Avocations: acting, waterskiing, sailing, swimming, travel. E-mail: srsibilla@aol.com.

SIBLEY, JAMES MALCOLM, retired lawyer; b. Atlanta, Aug. 5, 1919; s. John Adams and Nettie Whitaker (Cone) S.; m. Karen Norris, Apr. 6, 1942; children: Karen Mariea, James Malcolm Jr., Jack Norris, Elsa Alexandria Victoria, Quintus Whitaker. AB, Princeton U., 1941; student, Woodrow Wilson Sch. Law, 1942, Harvard Law Sch., 1945—46. Bar: Ga. 1942. Assoc. King & Spalding, Atlanta, 1942-47, ptnr., 1947-91. Bd. dirs. Summit Industries, Inc.; exec. com., mem. pub. affairs com. Coca-Cola Co., 1979-91; chmn. exec. com. John H. Harland Co., 1963-91; chmn. exec. com., mem. compensation com. Trust Co. of Ga., 1975-92; mem. exec. com., mem. compensation com. SunTrust Banks, Inc., 1985-92. Trustee Joseph B. Whitehead Found., Lettie Pate Evans Found., A.G. Rhodes Home, Inc., Robert W. Woodruff Found., Inc. (formerly Trebor Found.), John H. and Wilhelmina D. Harland Charitable Found., Inc.; trustee emeritus Berry Coll., The Lovett Sch., Callaway Gardens Found., Emory U. With USAF, 1942—45. Mem. ABA, Ga. Bar Assn., Atlanta Bar Assn., Am. Coll. Probate Counsel, Am. Bar Found., Am. Law Inst., Piedmont Driving Club, Commerce Club. Episcopalian. also: King & Spalding 191 Peachtree St NE Ste 40 Atlanta GA 30303-1740 Home: 3045 Slaton Dr NW Atlanta GA 30305-2006

SIBLEY, JAMES SCARBOROUGH, career officer; b. Sardis, Tex., Feb. 20, 1930; s. Fred Scarborough Sibley and Gladys Nell Middleton; m. Nancy Ann Deisher, May 26, 1956 (dec. July 1975); children: Wayne Scarborough, Charles Patrick, Steven Emerson, James Francis, Kenneth Richards. AS, North Tex. Agrl. Coll., 1948; BS, U.S. Mil. Acad., West Point, N.Y., 1953; MS in Civil Engring., Calif. Inst. Tech., 1957. Registered profl. civil engr., La. Commd. 2nd lt. U.S. Army, advanced through grades to col.; with U.S. Army Corps of Engrs., 1953-79; civil engr. Hdqs. Pusan Mil. Post, Korea, 1954-55; co. comdr., aide de camp 6th Armored Divsn., Fort Leonard Wood, Mo., 1955-56; co. comdr. 91st Engr. Bn. Combat, Fort Belvoir, Va., 1957-58; civil engr. U.S. Army Engr. Dist. Eastern Ocean Goose Bay Labrador, 1959-61; math. instr. U.S. Mil. Acad., West Point, N.Y., 1961-63, asst. prof., asst. to dean, 1963-65; sr. advisor 20th Engr. Brigade ARVN, Pleiku, Vietnam, 1965-66; plans officer Hqrs. U.S. Army Pacific, Fort Shafter, Hawaii, 1966-68; comdr. 3rd Engr. Bn. Combat, Fort Riley, Kans., 1968-69; chief engring. divsn., chief Cons. Divsn. Hqrs. U.S. Army, Long Binh, Vietnam, 1969-70; chief base devel. planning sect. J4 CINCPAC, Camp Smith, Hawaii, 1970-73; dep. engr. U.S. Army Forces Command, Fort McPherson, Ga., 1973-77; dir. engring. and housing V Corps, Frankfurt, Germany, 1977—79; ret., 1979—. Author, pub. (2 vol. family genealogy): The Sibley Family in America, 1629-72, 2d edit., 1982. Precinct chmn. Republican Com., Ellis County, Tex., 1980-89; dir., sec.-treas. Sardis Cemetery Assn., Ellis County, Tex., 1988—, Sardis Lone Elm Water Supply Corp., Ellis County, 1982—; dir., sec. Ellis County Hist. Commn., 1984-2002; trustee Midlothian Ind. Sch. Dist., Tex., 1997-2000; Sunday sch. tchr. First United Meth. Ch., Midlothian, 1980—; host parent, area rep. Fgn. Exch. Student Program, Midlothian, 1991—. Decorated Legion of Merit, Bronze Star medal with oak leaf cluster, Commendation medal with oak leaf clusters, Air medal. Avocations: walking, biking, golf, tennis. Home: 2620 Mount Zion Rd Midlothian TX 76065-6357

SIBLEY, LYNN M. anthropologist, educator; b. Nashville, Tenn., Mar. 4, 1949; d. James G. and Peggy L. Middleton; m. George J. Armelagos, June 21, 1991; 1 child, Gabriel. PhD (Anthropology), U. of Colo., Boulder, Colorado, 1988—93; MS (Nursing), U. of Utah, Salt Lake City, Utah, 1978—80; BS (Nursing), U. of Colo., Denver, Colorado Health Sciences Center, 1970—73; MA (Anthropology), U. of Colo., Boulder, Colorado, 1986—87. Registered Nurse, Colo. State Bd. of Nursing, 1974, Certified Nurse Midwife, Am. Coll. of Nurse Midwives, 1980. Faculty U. of Colo. Sch. of Nursing, Denver, Colo., 1980—85; sr. tech. advisor Am. Coll. of Nurse-Midwives, Washington, 1995—; adj. asst. prof. of anthropology Emory U., Atlanta, Ga., 1995—; vis. clin. instr. Med. Coll. of Va., Richmond, Va. Cons. People's Clinic, Boulder,

Colo., 1983—83; co-organizer, nsf nasa conf. on remote sensing U. of Colo., Boulder, Colo.; cons., tech. consultation on attendance at birth: cmty. birth attendants UNICEF and World Bank, New York City, NY, 1997; consultant-,global tech. consultation on safe motherhood Global Safe Motherhood Inter-Agency Working Group, Colombo, Sri Lanka, 1997; cons. Nat. Summit on Safe Motherhood, Centers for Disease Control and others, Atlanta, 2001; co-chair, workshop on home based life saving skills Am. Coll. of Nurse Midwives, Tucson; cons. Johns Hopkins Sch. of Pub. Health, Baltimore, Md., 2002—. Author: (journal article) Journal of Nurse-Midwifery; co-author (journal article) Current Anthropology, Obstetrics and Gynecology, Medical Anthropology; author: (journal article) American Journal of Physical Anthropology, Journal of Nurse Midwifery, Quickening, Journal of Women's Health and Midwifery; co-author (training manual) Home Based Life Saving Skills. Recipient Sigma Theta Tau,, Gamma Rho Chpt., 1980, Phi Kappa Phi, U. of Utah Chpt., 1980, Nat. Dean's List, A Nat. Honor Soc., 1980; fellow Grad. Tchg./Rsch. Asst., U. of Colo., 1986-1988, Fulbright Dissertation Fellowship, Belize, US Fulbright Program, 1989-1990; grantee Nurse Traineeship, US HHS, 1978-1980, NSF Doctoral Grant for Improving Dissertation Rsch., NSF, 1989-1990. Mem.. Am. Assn. of Phys. Anthropologists, Am. Anthrop. Assn., APHA, Am. Coll. of Nurse Midwives. Achievements include development of Co-team leader for development of Home Based Life Saving Skills, an innovative community based stragety to reduce maternal and neonatal mortality in developing countries; research in Traditional Birth Attendant Training Effectiveness, a meta-analysis of global TBA training programs spanning 30 years of publicattions; Analysis of paleo-obstetrics in ancient Sudanese Nubia. Avocations: sea kayaking, sea kayaking, sea kayaking. Home: 1327 Peachtree St NE #504 Atlanta GA 30309 Office: American College of Nurse-Midwives 818 Connecticut Ave NW Suite 900 Washington DC 20006 Personal E-mail: antls#learnlink.emory.edu. E-mail: antls@learnlink.emory.edu.

SIBLEY, WILLIAM ARTHUR, academic administrator, physics educator, consultant; b. Ft. Worth, Nov. 22, 1932; s. William Franklin and Sada (Rasor) S.; m. Joyce Elaine Gregory, Dec. 21, 1957; children: William Timothy, Lauren Shawn, Stephen Marshall. BS, U. Okla., 1956, MS, 1958, PhD, 1960. Tchg., rsch. asst. U. Okla., 1956-60; postdoctoral rsch. in defect solid state Kernforschungsanlage Julich and Tech. U. Aachen, Germany, 1960-61; rsch. solid state divsn. Oak Ridge Nat. Lab., 1961-70; prof., head physics Okla. State U., Stillwater, 1970-76, dir. Sch. Phys. and Earth Scis., 1976-78, asst. v.p. rsch., 1978-88; v.p. acad. affairs U. Ala., Birmingham, 1990-96; program dir. NSF, Washington, 1988-89, acting dir. divsn. materials rsch., 1990, program dir., 1996-99, acting divsn. dir. rsch., evaluation and comm. divsn., 1998-99; pres. Okla. Ctr. for Advancement of Sci. and Tech., 2000—02; CEO, dir. Okla. Sci. and Tech. R & D, 2002—04. Mem. solid state sci. com. NAS, 1977-83; bd. dirs. Oak Ridge Assoc. Univs., 1982-88, Coun. on Govt. Rels., 1987-93, Okla. Ctr. for Advancement Sci. and Tech., 1987-88; trustee, chmn. materials rsch. counsel Southeastern Univ. Rsch. Assn., 1992-95; cons. univ. edn. and rsch. Author: University Management 2010, 1998; contbr. articles to profl. jours. Pres. Stillwater Indsl. Found., 1985-86. Served to lt. AUS, 1951-53. Maj. USAR, 1953-60, Korea. Fellow Am. Phys. Soc.; mem. Omicron Delta Kappa, Sigma Xi, Sigma Pi Sigma, Pi Mu Epsilon. Baptist. Home: 2517 Thunderwind Cir Edmond OK 73034-6880 E-mail: sibleybill@aol.com.

SIBLEY, WILLIS ELBRIDGE, anthropology educator, consultant; b. Nashville, Feb. 22, 1930; s. Elbridge and Elizabeth Reynolds (LaBarre) S.; m. Barbara Jean Grant, June 9, 1956; children: Sheila Katherine, Anthony Grant, Michael David. BA, Reed Coll., 1951; MA, U. Chgo., 1953, PhD, 1958. Instr. sociology and anthropology Miami (Ohio) U., 1956-58; asst. prof. anthropology U. Utah, 1958-60; from asst. prof. to prof. anthropology Wash. State U., 1960-71; prof. anthropology Cleve. State U., 1971—, chmn. dept., 1971-77, Cleve. (City) faculty fellow, 1987, interim chmn., 1989-90, prof. emeritus, 1990—; sr. program analyst EPA, Washington, 1977-78; Govtl. fellow Am. Coun. on Edn., 1978; Rockefeller Found. vis. prof. anthropology U. Philippines, Quezon City, 1968-69; postdoctoral fellow in society and tech. Carnegie-Mellon U., 1981-82. Fulbright grantee, 1954-55, 64; NIMH grantee, 1959-61; NSF grantee, 1964-71; Nat. Acad. Scis.-NRC travel grantee, 1966; Office Edn., HEW research grantee, 1967 Fellow AAAS, Assn. Profl. Anthropologists (pres. Washington chpt. 1999—), Am. Anthropol. Assn. (treas. 1989-91, com. on pub. policy 2000-2002), Soc. Applied Anthropology (sec. 1977-80, pres. 1981-82); mem. AAUP (treas. Wash. State U. chpt. 1962-63, v.p. 1963-64, pres. 1965-66, pres. Cleve. State U. chpt. 1979-80, treas. 1980-81, interim pres. 1989-90), ACLU (pres. Pullman chpt. 1963, 66), Ctrl. States Anthropol. Soc. (past mem. exec. bd., treas. 1986-89), Wash. Assn. Profl. Anthropologists, Edgewater Yacht Club (Cleve., commodore 1991), Chesapeake Yacht Club (Shady Side, Md.) (gov. 1999, 2000). Home: 1190 Cedar Ave Shady Side MD 20764 Office: Cleve State U Dept Anthropology Cleveland OH 44115 Office Phone: 301-261-9404. Personal E-mail: shadyside@aol.com.

SIBOLSKI, ELIZABETH HAWLEY, higher education administrator; b. Gt. Barrington, Mass., Aug. 18, 1950; d. William Snyder and Frances Harrington (Smith) Gallup; m. John Alfred Sibolski Jr., Aug. 15, 1970. BA, The Am. U., 1973, MPA, 1975, PhD, 1984. Acting dir. acad. adminstrn. Am. U., Washington, 1974, planning analyst, 1974—79, asst. dir. budget and planning, 1980—83, dir. instl. rsch., 1984—85, exec. dir. univ. planning and rsch., 1985—2000; exec. assoc. dir. Middle States Commn. on Higher Edn., Phila., 2000—. Trustee Mortar Bd. Nat. Found., 1989-95. Recipient Comencement award Am. U. Women's Club, 1973. Mem. Soc. Coll. and Univ. Planning (bd. dirs. 1995-2000, pres. 1998-99), Mortar Bd. (sect. coord. 1975-82), Pi Alpha Alpha, Phi Kappa Phi (chpt. officer 1986-92), Pi Sigma Alpha, Omicron Delta Kappa. Avocations: breed, raise and show morgan horses. Home: 565 Wayward Dr Annapolis MD 21401-6747 Office: Middle States Commn on Higher Edn 3624 Market St Philadelphia PA 19104-2614 E-mail: esibolski@msache.org.

SIBOLSKI, JOHN ALFRED, JR., educational association executive; b. Nov. 4, 1946; S. John A. and Isabelle Barcaster S.; m. Elizabeth Gallup, Aug. 15, 1970. AA in Data Processing, Andover Inst. Bus., 1966; BS in Tech. of Mgmt., Am. U., 1967; cert. in data processing, 1974, grad. cert. in data processing, 1978. With Automated Systems Corp., Washington, 1969-71, KMS Tech. Ctr., Arlington, Va., 1971-72; ind. cons., 1972-73, 74-76; with Law Enforcement Asst. Adminstrn., Dept. Justice, Washington, 1973-74; D.A. Lewis, Assocs., Clinton, Md., 1974; with Bur. Nat. Affairs, Inc., Washington, 1976-80; mgr. systems. devel. NEA, Washington, 1980-90, Saturn Corp., Cheverly, Md., 1990-91, FBI, Washington, 1991—. Recipient spl. achievement award Dept. Justice, 1974. Mem. Fata Processing Mgmt. Assn., Am. Soc. for Info. Sci. Home: 565 Wayward Dr Annapolis MD 21401-6747 Office: FBI 10th St And Pa Ave Washington DC 20535-0001 E-mail: jsibolski@comcast.net.

SIBUL, LEON HENRY, electrical engineer; b. Voru, Estonia, Aug. 30, 1932;, U.S.49; s. Aleksander and Helene Sibul; m. Hele Mall Mandel, July 29, 1961; children: Eric Allan, Christina Linda. BEE, George Washington U., 1960; MEE, NYU, 1963; PhD, Pa. State U., 1968. Field engr. Engleman & Co., Inc., Washington, 1958—60; mem. tech. staff Bell Telephone Lab., Holmdel, NY, 1960—64; rsch. asst./assoc. Applied Rsch. Lab. Pa. State U., University Park, 1964—81, prof., sr. scientist Applied Rsch. Lab., 1981—. Cons. NAS, Washington, 1972—74; sr. tech. adv. USN, Washington, 1978—82. Editor: Adaptive Signal Processing, 1987; mem. editl. bd.: Multidimensional Signal Processing; contbr. articles to profl. jours., chpts. to books. Faculty advisor Pa. State Sailing Club, University Park, 1974—. Republican. Lutheran. Achievements include development of adaptive array processing techniques for underwater systems, use of wavelet transforms in optimum detectors; first to use application of group theory to signal processing, use info. theoretic concepts for sensor fusion and blind source separation; research in stochastic operator theory. Avocations: sailing, golf, basketball, cross country skiing. Office: Pa State U Applied Rsch Lab PO Box 30 State College PA 16804-0030 E-mail: lhs2@psu.edu.

SICHERMAN, HARVEY, think-tank executive; BS in History, U. Scranton, 1966; PhD in Polit. Sci., U. Pa., 1971. Assoc. dir. for rsch. Fgn. Policy Rsch. Inst., Phila., 1978—80; spl. asst. Sec. of State Alexander M. Haig Jr., 1981—82; mem. policy planning staff Sec. of State James A. Baker III; cons. Sec. of the Navy John F. Lehman, Jr., 1982—87, Sec. of State George Schultz, 1988; pres., dir. Fgn. Policy Rsch. Inst., Phila., 1994—. Author: The Three Percent Solution and the Future of NATO, 1982, Palestinian Autonomy, Self-Government and Peace, 1993; co-author (with Alexander M. Haig Jr.): New Directions in U.S.-Chinese Relations, 1997; co-editor (with Murray Weidenbaum): The Chinese Economy: A New Scenario, 1999; co-editor: (with John Lehman) America the Vulnerable: Our Military Problems and How To Fix Them, 2002; contbr. articles to profl. jours. Office: Fgn Policy Rsch Inst Ste 610 1528 Walnut St Philadelphia PA 19102*

SICHERMAN, MARVIN ALLEN, lawyer; b. Cleve., Dec. 27, 1934; s. Harry and Malvina (Friedman) S.; m. Sue Kovacs, Aug. 18, 1957; children: Heidi Joyce, Steven Eric. BA, Case Western Res. U., 1957, LLB, 1960, JD, 1968. Bar: Ohio 1960. Mng. prin. Dettelbach, Sicherman & Baumgart, Cleve., 1971—. Editorial bd.: Case-Western Res. Law Rev, 1958-60; Contbr. articles to legal jours. Mem. Beachwood (Ohio) Civic League, 1972-92; mem. Beachwood Bd. Edn., 1978-86, pres., 1981, 85, v.p., 1984; trustee Beachwood Arts Council, 1977-84. Mem. Ohio Bar Assn. (lectr. truth in lending 1969, lectr. bankruptcy 1972, 81, 84, 99, 2000, 01, 02, 03, Meritorious Service awards 1971, 77, 78, 79, 83, 84, 85, 86, 87), Cleve. Bar Assn. (lectr. practice and procedure clinic 1960-80, 82-87, chmn. bankruptcy ct. com. 1971-73), Jewish Chautauqua Soc., Tau Epsilon Rho, Zeta Beta Tau. Jewish (trustee Temple brotherhood 1968-76, sec. 1971-73). Home: 24500 Albert Ln Cleveland OH 44122-2302 Office: Dettelbach Sicherman & Baumgart 1100 Ohio Savings Plz Cleveland OH 44114 Office Phone: 216-696-6000. Business E-Mail: msicherman@dsb-law.com.

SICHUK, GEORGE, entrepreneur, theoretical biologist; b. Butler Twp., Pa., May 10, 1933; s. Stephan Nicholas and Eva (Hawranick) Sichuk; m. Georgiana Nadya Stroyen, July 27, 1968. BA, Drew U., 1954; ScD, Rutgers U., 1962. Rsch. assoc. Sloan-Kettering Inst. Cancer Rsch., N.Y.C., 1961—71; asst. prof. biology Montclair State Coll., Upper Montclair, NJ, 1972—75, William Paterson Coll., Wayne, NJ, 1975; lectr. interdisciplinary studies Bloomfield (N.J.) Coll., 1976; sci. tchr. Eastside H.S., Paterson, NJ, 1988—93; entrepreneur author Lincoln Park, NJ, 1993—. Author: Gabriel's Voice, 1996, Uriel's Light, 1997, One Man's Testament, 1998, Common Sense Plus: Constitutional Imperatives for Rational Government, 2003; contbr. articles to profl. med. jours. Good will amb. U.S. Govt., Cuba, 1960; coach Police Athletic League, Lincoln Park, 1977—79; exec. and coach Orthodox Citizens' Club, NJ, 1980—90. Achievements include clarification of relationship of the endocrine and immune systems to cancer to direct attention to the nucleic acids (DNA and RNA); research in the role of sex hormones in thrombotic disease; clarification of transplantation immunology; research in dynamic relationship between dietary protein quality and function of adrenal cortex in mammals; proof that "butter yellow" a dibenzanthracene used to give margarine a yellow color is a carcinogen. Avocations: geo-politics, house maintenance engineering, golf, flying, music. Home: 18 Sewanois Ave Lincoln Park NJ 07035-1710

SICILIANI, ALESSANDRO DOMENICO, conductor; b. Florence, Italy; s. Francesco and Ambra Siciliani; 1 child, Giacomo Francesco. Student, Giuseppe Verdi Milano Cons., Rome, Santa Cecilia; studied with, Franco Ferrara. Music advisor Columbus Symphony Orch., 1991—, music dir., 1992—. Condr. Nat. Radio Orchs. of Rome and Naples, Symphony of Abruzzi, Palermo Symphony Orch., Cagliari Symphony Orch., Bari Symphony Orch., N.Y. City Opera, Opera Co. of Phila., New Orleans Opera, Ky. Opera, Teatro San Carlo, Naples, Italy, Teatro dell'Opera, Rome, Teatro Massimo, Palermo, Italy, Verdi, Pisa, Italy, also Barcelona, Spain, Marseille, France, Avignon, and Liege; condr. revivals Cavalleria Rusticana, Pagliacci, N.Y. City Opera's revival La Rondine, Am. premiere Schubert's Fierrabras; appeared with Pitts. Symphony, Nat. Symphony, Washington, D.C., Munich Symphony Orch., Cologne Symphony Orch., Dresden Symphony Orch., Stockholm Symphony Orch., Goteborg Symphony Orch., Hong Kong Symphony Orch., Nat. Arts Ctr. Orch. of Ottawa, English Chamber Orch., Symphonia Varsovia, Perugia Chamber Orch., Padova Chamber Orch.; participant festivals including Schleswig-Holstein, Panatenee Pompeiane, Printemps Festival of Praha, Spring Festival in Saratoga Springs, Sagra Musicale Umbra; prin. guest condr. Orch. Teatro Colon, Buenos Aires, Teatro Mcpl. Sao Paulo. Recipient Amerigo Vespucci award, 1992. Office: Columbus Symphony Orch/Ohio Theater 55 E State St Columbus OH 43215-4203

SICILIANO, ELIZABETH MARIE, secondary school educator; b. Mansfield, Ohio, Apr. 22, 1934; d. Samuel Sevario and Lucy (Sferro) S. BS in Edn., Ohio State U., 1957; MA in Edn., Ea. Mich. U., 1971; MFA, Bowling Green U., 1975. Cert. tchr., Mich. Instr. adult edn. The Toledo (Ohio) Mus. Art, 1972-81; tchr. art Monroe (Mich.) Pub. Schs., 1975-2001. Workshop facilitator; presenter in field; art tchr. computer graphics. Artist, working in oils, pastels and fabricating jewelry. Judge Monroe Bicentennial, Monroe Arts and Crafts League, other shows. Mem. NEA, Mich. Edn. Assn., Nat. Art Edn. Assn., Mich. Art Edn. Assn., Stratford Festival for the Arts, Toledo Craft Club, Toledo Fedn. Art Socs., Toledo Mus. Art. Avocations: swimming, skiing, classic cars, designing and creating jewelry, portraiture and landscape in oils. Home: 7179 Edinburgh Dr Lambertville MI 48144-9539 Office: Monroe High Sch 901 Herr Rd Monroe MI 48161-9744

SICILIANO, ROCCO CARMINE, institute executive; b. Salt Lake City, Mar. 4, 1922; s. Joseph Vincent and Mary (Arnone) S.; m. Marion Stiebel, Nov. 8, 1947; children: Loretta, A. Vincent, Fred R., John C., Maria. BA with honors, U. Utah, 1944; LL.B., Georgetown U., 1948; LHD, Hebrew Union Coll., Gettysburg Coll., 2000, U. Utah, 2001. Bar: D.C. bar 1949. Legal asst. to bd. mem. NLRB, Washington, 1948-50; asst. sec.-treas. Procon Inc., Des Plaines, Ill., 1950-53; asst. sec. labor charge employment and manpower Dept. Labor, Washington, 1953-57; spl. asst. to Eisenhower for personnel mgmt., 1957-59; ptnr. Wilkinson, Cragun & Barker, 1959-69; pres. Pacific Maritime Assn., San Francisco, 1965-69; undersec. of commerce Washington, 1969-71; pres., chmn. bd., chief exec. officer Ticor, Los Angeles, 1971-84, chmn., exec. com., 1984-85; of counsel Jones, Day, Reavis & Pogue, 1984-87; chmn. bd., chief exec. officer Am. Health Properties, Inc., 1987-88; chmn. Dwight D. Eisenhower World Affairs Inst., Washington, 1991-2001; apptd. mem. Eisenhower Meml. Commn., 2000, chmn., 2001—. Chmn. Ctr. for Govtl. Studies, 1992—; commr. Calif. Citizens Budget Commn.; mem. Fed. Pay Bd., 1971-73; trustee emeritus J. Paul Getty Trust. Past chmn. Calif. Bus. Roundtable; trustee Com. for Econ. Devel.; co-chmn. Calif. Commn. on Campaign Financing. 1st lt. AUS, 1943-46, MTO, ETO. Decorated Bronze Star, Valor Combat Infantryman's badge; Order of Merit (Italy). Mem. Nat. Acad. Pub. Adminstrn., Met. Club (Washington), L.A. Philharm. Assn. (life dir.), Calif. Club (L.A.). Home: 612 N Rodeo Dr Beverly Hills CA 90210-3208

SICK, WILLIAM NORMAN, JR., venture capital company executive; b. Houston, Apr. 20, 1935; s. William Norman and Gladys Phylena (Armstrong) S.; m. Stephanie Anne Williams, Sept. 14, 1963; children: Jill Melanie, David Louis. BA, Rice U., 1957, BSEE, 1958. With Tex. Instruments Inc., various locations, 1958-87; exec. v.p. Tex. Instruments, Inc., Dallas, 1982-87; pres. semicondr. products group Tex. Instruments Inc., Dallas, 1982-86; bd. dirs. Tex. Instruments, Inc., 1985-87; CEO Am. Nat. Can Co., Chgo., 1988-89; also bd. dirs. Am. Nat. Can. Co., Chgo., 1988-89; mem. exec. com. Pechiney, Paris, 1989; bd. dirs. Pechiney Internat., 1989; vice chmn., bd. dirs. Triangle Industries, N.Y.C., 1988—89; chmn., CEO, Bus. Resources Internat., Winnetka, Ill., 1989—; co-founder, mng. dir. Signature Capital Mgmt., LLC, Northfield, Ill., 1997—2003. Chmn. Acoustic Tech., Mesa, Ariz.; co-founder Metasolv, Dallas; bd. dir. VIRxSYS, Gaithersburg, Md.; former chmn. Aware, Bedford, Mass., Power Trends, Warrenville, Ill.; guest lectr. Sophia U., Tokyo, 1973. Trustee, past chmn. Shedd Aquarium, Chgo., 1990—; trustee Rice U., 1996—, Santa Fe Inst., 2000—. Mem. Chgo. Com., Exec. Club Chgo., Glenview Club, Sigma Xi, Tau Beta Pi, Sigma Tau. Episcopalian. Office: Bus Resources Internat PO Box 500 Winnetka IL 60093-0500

SICKLER, JOHN J. manufacturing executive; Former head corp. devel. Teleflex, Plymouth Meeting, Pa., pres. aerospace segment, 1986—90, vice chmn., 2000—, interim CFO, 2003—. Bd. dirs. PennEngring. Office: Teleflex 630 W Germantown Pike Plymouth Meeting PA 19462*

SICKLES, ROBIN C. economics and statistics educator, consultant; b. Pitts., Dec. 24, 1949; s. Walter E. and Georgene N. Sickles; m. Janet C. Meininger, July 3, 1981; children: Danielle L., David C. BS in Econs., Ga. Inst. of Tech., 1972; PhD in Econs., U. of N.C., 1976. Asst. prof. dept. of econs. George Wash. U., Washington, 1976—79; vis. prof. dept. of econs. U. of Pa., Phila., 1979—80, asst. prof. dept. of econs., 1980—85; faculty rsch. fellow Nat. Bur. of Econ. Rsch., Cambridge, 1984—92; assoc. prof. dept. of econs. Rice U., Houston, 1985—87, prof. dept. of econs., 1987—; vis. scholar dept. of econs. U. of Mich., Ann Arbor, 1992; vis. adj. prof. European Inst. of Bus. Adminstrn., Fontainebleau, France, 1992—94; vis. scholar Bd. Govs. Fed. Res. Sys., Washington, 1993; vis. prof. pure and applied math. Inst. of Stats. Univ. Catholique de Louvain, Louvain-la-Neuve, Belgium, 1999. Dir. Rice U. Ctr. for the Study of Institutions and Values, Houston, 1999—2002; dir. grad. program in econs. Rice U., Houston, 2000—; dir. Law and Econ. Cons. Group, Houston, 2002—. Author: (book) The Causes, Correlates and Consequences of Death Among Older Adults: Some Methodological Approaches and Substantive Analysis-Kluwer, Unlocking the Assets: Energy and the Future of Central Asia and the Caucasus: A Political, Economic, and Cultural Analysis-Palgrave, (book chpt.) Handbook of Population and Family Economics-North Holland, Handbook of Applied Economics, Volume II-Microeconometrics-Basil Blackwell, (jour. articles) Internat. Econ. Rev., Rev. of Econs. and Stats., Jour. of Econs., Jour. of Bus. and Econ. Stats., Jour. of Applied Econometrics, Am. Econ. Rev., Jour. of Productivity Analysis, Internat. Jour. of Indsl. Orgn., Econ. Jour.; editor (in chief): (profl. jour.) Jour. of Productivity Analysis; assoc. editor (profl. jour.) Jour. of Applied Econometrics, Comms. in Stats., So. Econ. Jour., Jour. of Bus. and Econ. Stats., Jour. of Econometrics, Empirical Econs., editl. bd. Jour. of Productivity Analysis. Mem. bd. dirs. Afton Oaks Civic Assn., Houston, 1988—94; coach Southwestern YMCA, Houston. Grantee, NSF, 1978—80, 1980—82, 1980—83, 1984—87, Nat. Bur. of Econ. Rsch., 1982, NIH, 1986—89, Baker Inst. for Pub. Policy, 1996—2002. Mem.: Am. Econ. Assn., Econometric Soc. Office: Dept of Econs Rice Univ 6100 S Main St MS-22 Houston TX 77005-1892 Office Phone: 713-348-4875.

SIDAMON-ERISTOFF, ANNE PHIPPS, community trust executive; b. N.Y.C., Sept. 12, 1932; d. Howard and Harriet Dyer (Price) Phipps; m. Constantine Sidamon-Eristoff, June 29, 1957; children— Simon, Elizabeth, Andrew. BA, Bryn Mawr Coll., 1954. Chmn. emerita Am. Mus. Natural History, N.Y.C.; dir.-at-large Black Rock Forest Consortium; mem. distbn. com. N.Y. Cmty. Trust. Trustee God Bless Am. Fund, Hudson River Found., Sept. 11th Fund; bd. dirs. Greenacre Found., Highland Falls (N.Y.) Libr.; trustee World Wildlife Fund, Storm King Art Ctr., Mountainville, NY; past bd. dirs. Scenic Hudson, St. Bernard's Sch., N.Y.C., Mus. Modern Art, N.Y.C., Mus. Hudson Highlands. Address: 120 E End Ave New York NY 10028-7552 E-mail: ananouri@aol.com.

SIDAMON-ERISTOFF, CONSTANTINE, lawyer; b. N.Y.C., June 28, 1930; s. Simon C. and Anne Huntington (Tracy) Sidamon-E.; m. Anne Phipps, June 29, 1957; children: Simon, Elizabeth, Andrew. BSE. in Geol. Engring, Princeton U., 1952; LL.B., Columbia U., 1957. Clk., then assoc. firm Kelley Drye Newhall Maginnes & Warren, N.Y.C., 1957-64; individual practice law N.Y.C., 1964-65, 74-77; exec. asst. to Congressman John V. Lindsay, 1964-65; city coordinator Lindsay Mayoral Campaign, N.Y.C., 1965; asst. to mayor City of N.Y., 1966, commr. hwys., 1967-68, transp. adminstr., 1968-73; ptnr. Sidamon-Eristoff, Morrison, Warren, & Ecker, N.Y.C., 1978-83; counsel Morrison & de Roos, 1984-88; pvt. practice N.Y.C., 1988-89; regional adminstr. Region II EPA, N.Y.C., 1989-93; of counsel Patterson, Belknap, Webb & Tyler, N.Y.C., 1993-99, Lacher & Lovell-Taylor, N.Y.C., 1999—. Mem. N.Y. State Met. Transp. Authority Bd., 1974—89; commr. N.Y. State Jud. Commn. on Minorities, 1987—91; mem. Gov.'s Coun. on Hudson River Valley Greenway, 1989; trustee United Mut. Savs. Bank, N.Y.C., 1979—82, Phipps Houses, N.Y.C., 1974—, chmn., 1986—2001, chmn. emeritus, 2001—. Trustee Am. the Beautiful Fund, Washington, 1985—97; chmn. Audubon N.Y., 1999—; trustee Allaverdy Found., N.Y.C., 1962—, Am. Farm Sch., Thessaloniki, Greece, 1973—79, Carnegie Hall, N.Y.C., 1967—92, Millbrook (N.Y.) Sch., 1971—89, hon. trustee, 1989—, Orange County (N.Y.) Citizens Found., 1974—81; bd. dirs., mem. exec. com. Mid-Hudson Pattern for Progress, Poughkeepsie, NY, 1975—89, chmn., 1981—85; bd. dirs. Coun. on Mcpl. Performance, N.Y.C., 1979—87, chmn., 1981—85, vice chmn., 1986—87; mem. Orange County (N.Y.) Planning Bd., 1997—; N.Y. State Rep. committeeman, 1980—89; bd. dirs. Tolstoy Found., N.Y.C., 1975—2002, chmn., bd. dirs., 1979—89, 1994—2001; bd. dirs. Caramoor Ctr. Music and Arts, Katonah, NY, 1961—80, Boyce Thompson Inst. for Plant Rsch., Ithaca, NY, 1994—. 1st lt. arty. AUS, 1952—54, Korea. Decorated Bronze Star; co-recipient Civic Leadership award (with wife), Citizens Union, 1997, Force for Nature award (with wife), Natural Resources Def. Coun., 1999, Environ. Leadership award (with wife), Nat. Audubon Soc., 2001; recipient Honor award, Kings County chpt. N.Y. State Soc. Profl. Engrs., 1969, Greater N.Y. coun. Girls Scouts U.S., 1973, Bd. Leadership award, Coun. Mcpl. Performance, 1984, Transp. Man of Yr. award, Greater N.Y. March of Dimes, 1985, award of excellence, Mid-Hudson Pattern for Progress, 1990, Honor award, Nat. and N.Y. Parks and Conservation Assn., 1992, Bronze medal, USEPA, 1993. Mem. ABA, N.Y. State Bar Assn., Assn. of Bar of City of N.Y., N.Y. County Lawyers Assn., Kent Moot Ct., AIME, Phi Delta Phi, Delta Psi. Clubs: Century Assn. (N.Y.C.), Knickerbocker (N.Y.C.), Racquet and Tennis (N.Y.C.). Eastern Orthodox. Office: Lacher & Lovell-Taylor 4th Fl 750 Lexington Ave New York NY 10022-8165 E-mail: cseristoff@lltlaw.com., ananouri@aol.com.

SIDAR, THOMAS WILSON, retail executive; b. New Brunswick, N.J., Nov. 21, 1949; s. Alexander George Jr. and Jean (Wilson) S.; m. Ellen Elizabeth Woods BA, Colby Coll., 1972; AMP, Harvard Bus. Sch., 2003. Sales rep. L.L. Bean, Inc., Freeport, Maine, 1975, retail buyer, 1976—82, asst. product mgr., 1982—85, product mgr., 1985—88, sr. product mgr., 1988—89, dir. product devel., 1990—, v.p. creative dept., 1991—98, sr. v.p., gen. mgr. of men's strategic bus. unit, 1998—2001, chief mktg. officer, mem. office of pres., bd. dirs., 2001—. With L.L. Bean Inc. Trustee, v.p. North Yarmouth Acad.; vice chair adv. commn., chair park use com. Acadia Nat. Park. Mem. Maine Inland Fisheries and Wildlife (adv. com. non-game), Leadership Maine (Maine Devel. Found.), Appalachian Mountain Club (bd. dirs., v.p., exec. com., chmn. capital campaign com., bd. advisors), Megantic Club, The Woodlands Club. Democrat. Episcopalian. Avocations: fly fishing, bird hunting, cross country skiing, mountain climbing, canoeing. Home: 91 Glen Rd Yarmouth ME 04096-8136 Office: LL Bean Inc Casco St Freeport ME 04033-0001

SIDDALL, DAVID L. gas industry executive, lawyer; b. Independence, Mo., Nov. 29, 1963; BA in Bus. Adminstrn. magna cum laude, Graceland U., 1985; JD with distinction, U. Iowa, 1987. Bar: Iowa 1987, Tex. 1988. Assoc. gen. counsel El Paso Corp., Houston, v.p., corp. sec., chief governance officer. Note and comment editor: Jour. Corp. Law, 1986—87. Mem.: ABA, State Bar Tex., Iowa State Bar. Office: El Paso Corp PO Box 2511 1001 Louisiana St Houston TX 77002-2511

SIDDALL, PAM, publishing executive; b. Phenix City, Ga. m. Greg Siddall; 2 children. B in Acctg., Columbus State U., 1991. CPA Ga. Sr. fin. analyst W.C. Bradley Co., Columbus, Ga., 1991—94; contr. lic. product divsn. Russell Corp., 1994—97; CFO Columbus Ledger-Enquirer, 1997—2001, v.p., gen. mgr., 2003—04, pres., pub., 2004—; CFO to v.p., CFO The Macon Telegraph, Ga., 2001—03. Office: Columbus Ledger-Enquirer 17 W 12th St Columbus GA 31902*

SIDDAYAO, CORAZON MORALES, economist, educator, consultant; b. Manila, July 26, 1932; came to U.S., 1968; d. Crispulo S. and Catalina T. (Morales) S. Cert. in elem. teaching, Philippine Normal Coll., 1951; BBA, U. East, Manila, 1962; MA in Econs., George Washington U., 1971, MPhil, PhD, 1975. Cert. Inst. de Francais, France. Tchr. pub. schs., Manila, 1951-53; exec.

asst. multinational oil corps., 1953-68; asst. pensions officer IMF, Washington, 1968-71; cons. economist Washington, 1971-75; rsch. assoc. Policy Studies in Sci. and Tech. George Washington U., Washington, 1971-72, teaching fellow dept. econs., 1972-75; natural gas specialist U.S. Fed. Energy Adminstrn., Washington, 1974-75; sr. rsch. economist, assoc. prof. Inst. S.E.A. Studies, Singapore, 1975-78; sr. rsch. fellow energy/economist East-West Ctr., 1978-81, project dir. energy and industrialization, 1981-86; vis. fellow London Sch. Econ., 1984-85; sr. energy economist in charge energy program Econ. Devel. Inst., World Bank, Washington, 1986-94, ret., 1994. Affiliate prof. econs. U. Hawaii, 1979—94; co-dir. UPecon Inst. Resource Studies, 1995—; vis. prof. econs. U. Montpellier, France, 1992, France, 1995—96, France, 1997—; vis. prof. pub. policy Duke U., 1997; lectr. pub. policy George Mason U., 2000; tchr. coord. English for Hispanic program Parish, 2002; cons., spkr. in field. Author or co-author: Increasing the Supply of Medical Personnel, 1973, The Offshore Petroleum Resources of Southeast Asia: Some Potential Conflicts and Related Economic Factors, 1978, Round Table Discussion on Asian and Multinational Corporations, 1978, The Supply of Petroleum Resources in Southeast Asia: Economic Implications of Evolving Property Rights Arrangements, 1980, Critical Energy Issues in Asia and the Pacific: The Next Twenty Years, 1982, Criteria for Energy Pricing Policy, 1985, Energy Demand and Economic Growth, 1986; editor, co-author: Energy Policy and Planning series, 1990-92, Energy Investments and the Environment, 1993; co-editor: Investissements Energetiques et Environnement, 1993; co-editor: (series) Energy Project Analysis for the CIS Countries (Russian), 1993, Politique d'Efficacité de l'Énergie et Environnement, Expérience pratiques, 1994, Matérial Pedagogique sur la Politique d'Efficacité de l'Energie et Environnement, 1994; contbr. chpts. to books, articles to profl. jours. Grantee in field; recipient Outstanding Alumni award Arellano Pub. H.S., 1998, Philippine Normal U., 2003 Mem.: Alliance Francaise, Internat. Assn. Energy Economists (charter 1986—2003), Am. Econ. Assn., Perpetual Adoration Soc. of St. Agnes (Arlington), John Carroll Soc., World Bank 1818 Soc. (bd. dirs. 1999—2000), Eucharistic Frat. 3d Order of St. P.J. Eymard, Chorale de St. Louis de France, Omicron Delta Epsilon. Roman Catholic. Office: 1201 S Eads St Ste 1712 Arlington VA 22202-2845 *Power and money were never the stimuli to my endeavors. Spiritual and intellectual challenges are what drive me. In the end, all our achievements mean nothing if we have not learned to appreciate them as gifts and shared what we can with others.*

SIDDIKOV, BAKHODIRZHON, mathematician, educator; b. Ferghana, Uzbekistan, Sept. 7, 1961; s. Musaffar and Kurvonbuvi Siddikov; m. Svetlana Siddikov, Aug. 13, 1983 (div. June 2001); children: Dilshod, Dilbar. BS in Applied Math., MS in Applied Math., Kiev (Ukraine) State U., 1983, PhD in Applied Math., 1989; PhD in Math., U. Wis., Milw., 2001. Rsch. mathematician Kiev State U., Ukraine, 1985—89; asst. prof. Ferghana Poly. Inst., 1990—91, Tashkent State Poly. U., Ferghana, 1992—93, 1994—95; fellow Marquette U., Milw., 1993—94; tchg. asst. U. Wis., Milw., 1996—2001; asst. prof. Ferris State U., Big Rapids, Mich., 2001—. Contbr. articles to profl. jours. Grantee, U. Wis., Milw., 1999, Ferris State U., Big Rapids, 2001. Mem.: Soc. for Indsl. and Applied Math., Am. Math. Soc. Avocations: tennis, soccer, swimming, reading, chess. Home: 521 W Fuller Ave #304D Big Rapids MI 49307 Office: Ferris State Univ Math Dept 820 Campus Dr ASC 2021 Big Rapids MI 49307

SIDDIQEE, MUHAMMAD WAHEEDUDDIN, electrical engineer; b. Lahore, Pakistan, Aug. 23, 1931; s. Muhammad Nazeeruddin and Ayesha Humaira Siddiqee; m. Sabiha Sultana Siddiqee, Dec. 24, 1961; 2 children. BA in Physics, Forman Christian Coll., Lahore, Pakistan, 1951; BSEE, Engring. Univ., Lahore, 1955; MSEE, U. Tenn., 1960; PhD in Control Sci., U. Minn., 1967. Elec. engr. Siemens Pakistan, Lahore, 1955—56, Siemens Germany, Erlangen, 1956—58; sr. elec. engr. Siemens Pakistan, Karachi, 1958—61; staff scientist Stanford Rsch. Inst., Menlo Park, Calif., 1967—82; info. systems specialist Lockheed Missiles and Space Co., Sunnyvale, Calif., 1982—93; tchr. Sunnyvale Sch. Dist., 1995—. Project leader Stanford Rsch. Inst., Menlo Park, Calif., 1976—82. Contbr. articles to profl. jours. Pres. United Muslims of Am., Calif., 1991—93, San Francisco Islamic Ctr., Calif., 1981—83, Pakistan Assn., San Francisco, 1975—77. Recipient Lockheed Pub. award, Lockheed Missiles and Space Co., Calif., 1988. Mem.: Assn. Ret. Am. Muslims (pres., founder 1996—). Avocation: Sitar player, cmty. activism in human rights. Home: 1733 Banff Dr Sunnyvale CA 94087

SIDDIQI, JAVED, neurosurgeon; HBSc, U. Western Ont., London, Can., 1983, MD, 1991; DPhil, Oxford (Eng.) U., 1987. Diplomate Am. Bd. Neurol. Surgery. Chief neurosurgery Arrowhead Regional Med. Ctr., Colton, Calif., 1999—, residency program dir., 1999—; chmn. dept. of clin. neurol. scis. Riverside County Regional Med. Ctr., Moreno Valley, Calif., 2001—. Temp. advisor WHO, Geneva, 1986; asst. prof. in polit. sci. U. Western Ont., 1991—95, asst. prof. in history of medicine, 1992—97; asst. prof. anatomy and surgery Western U. Health Sciences, Pomona, Calif., 1999—; presenter in field. Author: (book) World Health & World Politics, (photography book) In Their Hands; editor: (book) Multidisciplinary Critique of Phillip Rushton's Theory on Racial Ranking; photography exhibit, In Their Hands; contbr. book, articles to profl. publs. Scholar, Rhodes Trust, 1984—87, Med. Rsch. Coun. of Can., 1983; vis. scholar History of Medicine scholar, Hannah Inst. for the History of Medicine, 1988; Rsch. scholar, Natural Sciences and Engring. Rsch. Coun. of Can., 1982, Rhodes scholar, 1984—87, Logan Clendening Travelling fellow, U. Kans., 1988, Arts & Sciences Rsch. scholar, U. of Western Ont., 1989, Travel scholar, Couchiching Conf., 1990, CNS scholar, U. of Western Ont., 1994. Fellow: Royal Coll. Surgeons Can.; mem.: Am. Assn. Rhodes Scholars.

SIDDIQUE, MUHAMMAD, poultry pathobiologist; b. Faisalabad, Punjab, Pakistan, Jan. 1, 1950; s. Ghulam Ahmad and Naziran Begum; m. Farkhanda Jamil, Oct. 17, 1976; children: Amir, Imran, Hina. DVM, West Pakistan Agrl. U., Faisalabad, 1972; MSc with honors, U. Agr., Faisalabad, 1978; PhD, Inst. Agron. N.B., Bucharest, Romania, 1984; postgrad., U. Ga. Vet. officer L&DD, Lahore, Pakistan, 1973-74; lectr. in vet. pathology U. Agr., Faisalabad, 1975-86, asst. prof. vet. pathology, 1986-89, asst. prof. vet. microbiology, 1989-90, assoc. prof. vet. microbiology, 1990-99, chmn. dept. vet. microbiology, 1990-93, 96-98, prof. vet. microbiology, 1999—. Author: Current Situation of Poultry Industry in Pakistan, 1979; contbr. articles to profl. jours. Mem. Pakistan Vet. Med. Assn. (life, pres. 1987-89, mem. coun., Spl. award 1995), Pakistan Sci. Forum. Avocations: reading scientific treatises, quiz and mentor challenges. Home: 62 Rachna Town Faisalabad Punjab Pakistan Office: U Agr Vet Microbiology Faisalabad Punjab 38040 Pakistan

SIDDONS, ANNE RIVERS (SYBIL ANNE RIVERS SIDDONS), writer; b. Fairburn, Ga., Jan. 9, 1936; m. Heyward Siddons, 1966; 4 stepchildren. BA Auburn U., student Atlanta Sch. Art,, 1958. Mem. advt. dept. bank; sr. editor Atlanta mag., 1960. Author: (novels) John Chancellor Makes Me Cry, 1975, Heartbreak Hotel, 1976, Go Straight on Peachtree, 1977, The House Next Door, 1978, Fox's Earth, 1981, Homeplace, 1987, Peachtree Road, 1988, Kings Oak, 1990, Outer Banks, 1991, Colony, 1992, Hill Towns, 1993, Downtown, 1994, Fault Lines, 1995, Up Island, 1997, Low Country, 1998, Nora, Nora, 2000, Islands, 2003. Home: 60 Church St Charleston SC 29401-2558

SIDEBOTTOM, WILLIAM GEORGE, communications executive; b. Greeley, Colo., July 21, 1948; s. William Carroll and Florence Elaine (Krusenstjerna) S.; m. Rosemary Russell, May 16, 1981; children: Faith Ann, William Jeremiah. BS in Mgmt. cum laude, U. West Fla., 1975; MA in Pub. Policy magna cum laude, Regent U., 1985. Mgr. Mgmt. Recruiters, Internat., Pensacola, Fla., 1976-79, divsn. mgr. Virginia Beach, Va., 1979-81; dir. comm. Rock Ch., Virginia Beach, 1981-83; dir. devel., v.p. comm. Nat. Freedom Inst., Chesapeake, Va., 1983; pres. William G. Sidebottom & Assocs., 1986—, InterAct Response Comms., 1997—. Co-founder, pres., CEO Common Good, Inc., 2001—; pres. Sr.'s Alliance, 2003—; founder, mng. dir. Victor George Assoc., 2004—. Author: Who Owns the Children, 1985; sr. editor: The Perspective Papers, 1985, Essential Lectures, 1985. Cons. Am. Ctr. for Law and Justice, 1990-2002, Christian Advocates Serving Evangelism, 1995-2002, Christian Coalition, 1999-2003, Cathedral for the Nations Found., 2003—; sr. flight instr. U.S. Navy Aviation Tng. Ctr. Capt. USMC, 1970-76. Mem.: Pi Kappa Delta, Phi Kappa Phi. Mem. Charismatic Episcopal Ch. E-mail: wgsirc@earthlink.net.

SIDELSKY, PATRICIA LONEY, science educator; b. Hanover, N.H., Jan. 5, 1945; d. Charles Alexander and Mary (Zurbrugg) Loney; m. Richard W. Lippincott, Apr. 17, 1971 (div. Apr. 1980); 1 child, Richard Ryan; m. Michael G. Sidelsky, May 24, 1980; 1 child, Cory Charles. BS in Biology, Bucknell U., 1967; MS in Biology, Rutgers U., 1987; MAT, Mary Grove Coll., 2002. Cert. in comprehensive sci. tchr., N.J. Tchr. sci. Easton (Md.) Mid. Sch., 1972-79; med. technologist Easton Meml. Hosp., 1974-76; tchr. Easton Middle Sch., 1976-79; tchr. advanced placement biology and genetics Cherokee High Sch., Marlton, N.J., 1979—; med. technologist HIP of N.J., Medford, 1979-87, 90-92; lead tchr. Ctr. for Maths., Sci. and Computer Edn. Rutgers U., New Brunswick, N.J., 1988-93; lead tchr. Douglass Summer Sci. Inst., New Brunswick, 1988-92. Mem. Douglas Coll. Bd. for Women in Maths. & Sci., 1988-92. Co-author: Molecular Approaches to the Study of Gene Activity, 1987—. Recipient Outstanding Tchr. award, N.J., Nat. Assn. Biology Tchrs., 1989, Tandy Tchr. Scholar award, 1991; Access Excellence fellow Genentech, 1994; grantee Ptnrs. in Sci. Rsch. Corp., 1994-95; named Tchr. of Yr. Lenape Regional H.S. Dist., 1996. Mem. Biology Tchrs. Assn. N.J. (v.p. 1990, pres. elect 1991-92, pres. 1992—), Nat. Sci. Tchrs. Assn., N.J. Sci. Tchrs. Assn., Nat. Biology Tchrs. Assn., Am. Soc. Clin. Pathologists, Am. Soc. Microbiology. Episcopalian. Home: 8 Rockledge Ct Marlton NJ 08053-9774 Office: Cherokee High Sch Willowbend Rd Marlton NJ 08053

SIDEMAN, JILL, engineering executive; MA in Phys. and Inorganic Chemistry, Bryn Mawr (Pa.) Coll., 1963, PhD in Phys. and Inorganic Chemistry, 1965. Postdoctoral rschr. Nat. Bur. Standards; fellow Nat. Inst. Arthritis and Metabolic Diseases; chargee du rsch. Inst. Pasteur, Paris; rschr. U. Wash. Med. Ctr.; co-founder Shapiro and Assocs., Seattle, 1974—84, San Francisco, 1982—84, TRS Cons., San Francisco, 1984—86; from mgr. environ. planning San Francisco (Calif.) Bay Area to dir., v.p. CH2M HILL, 1986, dir. Englewood, Colo., v.p. Mem. Commn. Advancement Women and Minorities in Sci., Engring. and Tech. Fellow, NAS/NRC, NIH. Mem.: Nat. Assn. Women Sci. (bd. dir. 1995—). Office: CH2M HILL 9191 South Jamaica St Englewood CO 80112

SIDER, HARVEY RAY, retired minister, religious organization administrator; b. Cheapside, Ont., Can., June 20, 1930; s. Earl M. and Elsie (Sheffer) S.; m. Erma Jean Heise, July 20, 1957; children: Cheryl Sider Giles, Steven. BA, Western U., Ont., 1957; BD, Winona Lake Sch. Theology, Ind., 1962. Ordained to ministry Brethren in Christ Ch., 1953; cert. tchr., Ont. Pastor Brethren in Christ Ch., Toronto, Ont., 1957-61, missionary, adminstr. missions dept. Bihar, India, 1962-74, pastor Stayner, Ont., 1974-76; pres. Niagara Christian Coll., Ft. Erie, Ont., 1976-78; bishop Brethren in Christ Ch., Can., 1978-90, moderator, 1990-98.

SIDER, RONALD J. theology educator, author; b. Stevensville, Ont., Can., Sept. 17, 1939; m. Arbutus Lichti Sider, Aug. 19, 1961; children: Theodore Ronald, Michael Jay, Sonya Maria. BA with honors, Waterloo Luth. U., 1962; MA in History, Yale U., 1963, BD, 1967, PhD in History, 1969; DDiv (hon.), Westminster Coll., 1998. Lectr., asst. prof., then assoc. prof. Messiah Coll., 1968-78, acting dir., dean, 1971-75; assoc. prof. theology Ea. Bapt. Theol. Sem., Wynnewood, Pa., 1978-84, prof. theology and culture, 1984—2002, Ronald J. Sider prof. theology, holistic mission and pub. policy, 2002—; dir. Sider Ctr. on Ministry and Pub. Policy Eastern U., 2002—. Coord., chair, convenor workshops in field; coord. Internat. Consultation on Simple Lifestyle, London, 1980; lectr. in field. Editor: Preaching on Peace, 1982, Lifestyle in the Eighties: An Evangelical Commitment to Simple Life-Style, 1982, Evangelicals and Development: Toward a Theology of Social Change, 1982, Living More Simply, 1980, Cry Justice: The Bible on Hunger and Poverty, 1980, 91, For They Shall Be Fed, 1997, (with Diane Knippers) Toward an Evangelical Public Policy, 2004; author: Christ and Violence, 1979, Karlstadt's Battle with Luther: Documents in a Liberal-Radical Debate, 1978, 82, Evangelism, 1985, Rich Christians in an Age of Hunger: A Biblical Study, 1977, rev. edit., 1984, 90, 97, German edit., 1979, Dutch edit., 1980, Portuguese edit., 1984, Japanese edit., 1989, Chinese edit., 1998, Korean edit., 1998, Andreas Bodenstein Von Karlstadt, 1974, Genuine Christianity, 1996, (with Richard K. Taylor) Nuclear Holocaust and Christian Hope, 1982, English edit., 1984, (with Oliver O'Donovan) Peace and War: A Debate About Pacifism, 1985, (in Chinese) Evangelical Faith and Social Ethics, 1986, Completely Pro-Life, 1987, (with Michael A. King) Preaching About Life in Threatening World, 1988, (with Kathleen Hayes), JustLife/88: A 1988 Election Study Guide for Justice, Life and Peace, 1988, Testing the Limits of Nonviolence, 1988, One-Sided Christianity? Uniting the Church to Heal a Lost and Broken World, 1993, Cup of Water, Bread of Life: Inspiring Stories About Overcoming Lopsided Christianity, 1994, Good News and Good Works: A Theology for the Whole Gospel, 1999, Living Like Jesus, 1999, Just Generosity: A New Vision for Overcoming Poverty in America, 1999, (with Philip N. Olson and Heidi Rolland Unruh) Churches That Make a Difference: Reaching Your Community with Good News and Good Works, 2002, Doing Evangelism Jesus' Way, 2003; co-editor: Transformation mag., 1984-99; editor, contbr.: The Chicago Declaration, 1974; pub. Prism mag., 1993—, Green Cross, 1994-98, Creation Care, 1998-2002; contbr. numerous articles to profl. publs., chpts. to books. Head voter registration dr., New Haven, 1967; pres. Diamond St. Cmty. Ctr., 1986-91; exec. dir. Evangelicals for Social Action, 1987-92, pres., 1992—; exec. dir. Just Life, 1987-91, pres., 1991-94; bd. dirs. Bread for the World, 1978-84, Mennonite Ctrl. Com., 1978-80; co-chair Nat. Workshop on Race and Reconciliation, Atlanta, 1975. Malcolm Chase fellow, 1962-63, R.E. Darling fellow, 1963-64, fellow Yale U., 1967-68, Inst. for Advanced Christian Studies, 1976; co-chair Working Group on Human Needs and Faith-Based and Cmty. Initiatives II, 2002-03. Mem. Nat. Assn. Evangelicals (mem. social action commn. 1975—). Mennonite. Home: 312 W Logan St Philadelphia PA 19144-4120 Office: Ea Bapt Sem 6 E Lancaster Ave Wynnewood PA 19096-3430 Office Phone: 610-645-9354. Business E-Mail: ronsider@esa-online.org.

SIDEROW, NEIL, real estate company executive; BA, NYU; MBA, Pace U. Founding ptnr., COO Murray Hill Properties; vice chmn. TCN Worldwide, 2003—, also bd. dirs. Office: Murray Hill Properties INc 18th Fl 440 9th Ave New York NY 10001*

SIDES, JACK DAVIS, JR., lawyer; b. Dallas, Sept. 18, 1939; s. Jack Davis Sr. and Edith Eugenia (Lowrie) S.; m. Nancy Pauline Cantwell, July 22, 1967 (div. Sept. 1976); children: Mary Katharine, Jack Davis III; m. Laura Gail Miller, Aug. 2, 1979; children: Susan Ashley, Stacy Anne. BBA, U. Tex., 1962, JD with honors, 1963. Bar: Tex. 1963. Assoc. Jackson, Walker, et al, Dallas, 1963-67, White, McElroy, White, Sides & Rector, Dallas, 1968-78; sole practice Dallas, 1978—. Editor: U. Tex. Law Review, 1963. Trustee Highland Park Devel. Sch. Dist., 1996-2002; With USAFNG, 1963-69. Fellow Dallas Bar Found., Tex. Bar Found. (life); mem. ABA, Tex. Bar Assn. (grievance subcom. 1979-86), Dallas Bar Assn. (ethics com. 1973-77, jud. com. 1988—), Tex. Assn. Def. Counsel, Dallas Assn. Def. Counsel (sec. 1973-74). Clubs: Brook Hollow Golf (Dallas). Republican. Methodist. Avocations: reading, tennis, exercising.

SIDES, LARRY EUGENE, advertising executive; b. Albany, Ga., Nov. 14, 1946; s. Robert N. and Florine (Stewart) Sides; m. Kathy Ashworth, Aug. 13, 1950. BA in Radio and TV, U. La., 1970, MS in Communications, 1975. News reporter Sta. KATC-TV, Lafayette, La., 1970-71; account exec. Herbert S. Benjamin Assocs., Lafayette, La., 1971-76; pres. Sides & Assocs., Lafayette, La., 1976—. Vice-chmn. Crimestoppers, Lafayette, 1985; pres. Gateway Found., 1990; active Leadership La., 1989, 1990; mem. Coun. for Better La., 1991—94; bd. dirs. La. Coun. on Child Abuse, 1992—96; active Leadership Lafayette, 1995; mem. exec. com. Cristo en Cuba Coord. Coun.; bd. dirs. Episcopal Sch. Acadiana, Lafayette, 1987; mem. vestry Episcopal Ch. of Ascension, 2002—04, coord. Cuba project, 2001—, jr. warden, 2002; sr. warden Episcopal Diocese of We. La., 2003, chmn. Commn. on Internat. Missions, 2003; mem. Global Episcopal Mission Network, 2004; bd. dirs. Nat. Cristo En Cuba Coordinating Coun. Named Outstanding Young Men of Am., Lafayette Jaycees, 1976; recipient Disting. Alumni award dept. comms., U. La., 1995. Mem.: Acadiana Advt. Fedn., Pub. Rels. Soc. Am., Am. Soc. Hosp. Pub. Rels., Am. Assn. Advt. Agys. (pres. La. coun. 1989—90), Lafayette C. of C. (pres. 1989, bd. dirs. 2003, Entrepreneur of Yr. 1983), Beaver Club (pres. 1986, Outstanding Club Mem. award 1976), Sigma Nu (alumni pres. Lafayette chpt. 1977). Home: 1015 W Saint Mary Blvd Lafayette LA 70506-3420 Office: 404 Eraste Landry Rd Lafayette LA 70506-2324

SIDEY, HUGH SWANSON, correspondent; b. Greenfield, Iowa, Sept. 3, 1927; s. Kenneth H. and Alice Margaret (Swanson) S.; m. Alice Anne Trowbridge, Dec. 5, 1953; children: Cynthia Anne, Sandra, Bettina, Edwin. BS, Iowa State U., 1950. Reporter Adair County (Iowa) Free Press, 1950, The Nonpareil, Council Bluffs, Iowa, 1950-51, Omaha World-Herald, 1951-55; reporter Life mag., 1955-58; corr. Time mag., 1958-96; columnist The Presidency, Time mag., Life mag., 1966—; chief Washington Bur., Time mag., 1969-78, Washington contbg. editor, 1978-96. Contbr. Time mag., 1996—. Author: John F. Kennedy, President, 1963, A Very Personal Presidency, Lyndon Johnson in the White House, 1966, These United States, 1975, Portrait of a President, 1975, The Presidency, 1991, Portraits of the Presidents, 2000; co-author: 1,000 Ideas for Better News Pictures, 1956, The Memories, 1961—JFK—1963, 1973; contbr.: The Kennedy Circle, Prelude to Leadership, European Diary of John F. Kennedy, Summer 1945, 1995, Remembering Jack, 2003. Served with AUS, 1945-46. Mem. White House Hist. Assn. (chmn. 2000-03). Office: Time 555 12th St NW Ste 600 N Washington DC 20004-1200

SIDHU, JAY S. bank executive; b. India;, arrived in U.S. at age 18; MBA, Wilkes U. COO Penn Savings Bank, 1986—89; CEO, pres. Sovereign Bancorp (formerly Penn Savings Bank), Wyomissing, Pa., 1989—. Office: Sovereign Bancorp Inc PO Box 12646 1130 Berkshire Blvd Reading PA 19612*

SIDHU, SANJIV, information technology executive; married; 2 children. B in Chem. Engring., Osmania U., Hyderabad, India; M in Chem. Engring., Okla. State U.; postgrad. in Systems and Control Engring., Case Western U., Cleve. Software developer Tex. Instruments, Dallas; founder, CEO, chmn. i2 Techs., Inc., Dallas. Avocations: sailing (mem. India's nat. sailing team), surfing. Office: i2 Techs 1i2 Pl 11701 Luna Rd Dallas TX 75234

SIDJANSKI, DUSAN, economist, educator; b. Belgrade, Yugoslavia, Oct. 23, 1926; arrived in Switzerland, 1943; s. Vlastimir and Mara (Yankovitch-Petrovich) Sidjanski; m. Monique Foex Petrovich, Sept. 2, 1963 (dec. 1984); 1 child, Sacha; life ptnr. Clarina Firmenich. D. in Polit. Sci., U. Lausanne, Switzerland, 1954. From collaborator to asst. prof. Ctrl. U. Venezuela, 1950-53; head rsch. Intergovernmental Com. European Migrations, Geneva, 1956—57; head rsch., dir. Denis de Rougemont European Centre Culture, 1957—80; pvt. tchr. U. Geneva, 1959, from lectr. to prof. polit. sci. Inst. European Studies, 1963—68, prof., 1968—98, emeritus prof., 1995—, past dir. dept. polit sci. faculty econ. and social scis., former vice-dean faculty social and econ. scis. Former hon. advisor permanent del. Venezuela, Geneva. Author: (book) Fédéralisme amphictyonique, 1956, Partis politiques face à l'intégration européenne, 1961, Dimensions européennes de la science politique, 1963, Federative Aspects of the European-Community in Studies, in Conjecture, 1965, Décisions closes et décisions ouvertes, 1965, Dimensiones institucionales de la integracion latinamericano, 1967, Verso l'Europa Unita Gruppi di Promozione, 1968, The Federal Future of Europe, 2000, The Federal Approach to the European Union, 2001, others; contbr. articles to profl. jours. Bd. dirs. Latsis Found., 2003—. Mem.: EUSA, ECPR, Assn. Inst. Europe (gen. sec.), Hellenic Inst. Internat. Law (collaborator-corr.), French and Swiss Assn. Polit. Sci. (former pres.), European Cultural Ctr. (pres. 2003—), Internat. Assn. Polit. Sci. Avocations: music, sports, skiing, tennis, swimming. Home: 16 chemin de La Rippaz 1223 Cologny-Geneva Switzerland Office: Latsis Foundation 33 ch de l'Avanchet 1216 Geneva Switzerland E-mail: dusan.sidjanski@politic.unige.ch.

SIDLIK, THOMAS W. automotive executive; b. New Britain, Conn., Nov. 14, 1949; BS with hon. in Econ. & Fin., N.Y.U., 1971; MBA in Fin., U. Chgo., 1973. With controller's office car product devel. Ford Motor Co., 1973—80; mgr., car product fin. analysis Chrysler Corp., 1980, mgr., advanced product analysis, 1981, mgr., engring. and product devel. fin. control, 1982, controller, svc. and parts org., 1984, mgr., corp. fin. analysis, 1984, dir., engring. ops., 1987, gen. mgr. special projects engring., 1989, controller, product devel. group, 1989, group controller, product devel. & procurement, 1990, gen. mgr., sales & mktg. ops. planning, 1991, exec. dir., sales & mktg, planning and warranty programs, 1992, v.p., customer satisfaction and vehicle quality, 1992, v.p., chmn., Chrysler Fin. Corp., 1994, 1996, gen. mgr., small car ops., 1996; mem., bd. of mgmt. procurement & supply Chrysler Group DaimlerChrysler AG, 1998—, gen. mgr. Jeep Ops., 1998—. Mgmt. bd. Daimler Chrysler, 1998—; exec. sponsor Automotive Industry Action Group (AIAG). Vice-chmn. Nat. Minority Supplier Devel. Coun. (NMSDC); chmn. Coun. Exec. Com.; bd. overseers Leonard N. Stern Sch. of Bus., NYU. Office: Daimler Chrysler Corp 1000 Chrysler Drive Auburn Hills MI 48326-2766

SIDMAN, RICHARD LEON, neuroscientist, educator; b. Boston, Sept. 19, 1928; s. Manuel and Annabelle (Seltzer) Sidman; m. Ljiljana Lekic, 1974. AB, Harvard U., 1949, MD (Jeffries Wyman scholar), 1953. Intern in medicine Boston City Hosp., 1953—54; asst. resident in neurology Mass. Gen. Hosp., Boston, 1955—56; staff scientist NIH, Bethesda, Md., 1956—58; instr. to prof. neuropathology Harvard U. Med. Sch., Boston, 1959—69, Bullard prof., 1969—99, prof. emeritus, 1999—; chief div. neurogenetics New Eng. Regional Primate Rsch. Ctr. Harvard Med. Sch., Southborough, Mass., 1991—99; prof. neuropathology emeritus dept. neurosurgery Brigham and Womens Hosp., Boston, 1999—; sr. rsch. assoc. dept. neurology Beth Israel Deaconess Med. Ctr., Boston, 2001—. Chief dept. neurosci. Children's Hosp., Boston, 1972—88; 1st Richard Stearns Meml.ml. lectr. Albert Einstein Coll. Medicine, 1958; Bailey Meml. lectr. U. Sask., Canada, 1978; Waisman Meml. lectr. U. Wis. Author (with M. Sidman): Neuroanatomy - A Programmed Text, vol. 1, 1965; author: (with others) Catalog of the Neurological Mutants of the Mouse, 1965; author: (with R.D. Adams) Introduction to Neuropathology, 1968; author: (with others) Atlas of the Mouse Brain and Spinal Cord, 1971; contbr. numerous articles, book chpts., revs. on neuroembryology pathology and genetics to profl. publs. Mem. sci. adv. com. Retinitis Pigmentosa Found.; bd. sci. overseers Jackson Lab., Bar Harbor, Maine. Served with USPHS, 1956—58. Recipient Soma Weiss student rsch. prizes, Harvard U. Med. Sch., 1951—53, Boylston Soc. Essay prize, 1953; fellow Neurosci. Rsch. Program fellow, 1971—79; Harvard U. Mosley Travelling fellow, 1954—55. Fellow: Nat. Acad. Sci., Am. Acad. Arts and Scis.; mem.: AAAS, Tissue Culture Assn., Soc. Neurosci., Soc. Devel. Neurosci., Internat. Soc. Devel. Neurobiology, Soc. Devel. Biology, Internat. Brain Rsch. Orgn., Histochem. Soc., Am. Soc. Cell Biology, Am. Assn. Neuropathologists, Am. Assn. Anatomists, Am. Acad. Neurology. Office: Harvard Inst Medicine 855 77 Ave Louis Pasteur Boston MA 02115 E-mail: richard_sidman@hms.harvard.edu.

SIDMAN, ROBERT JOHN, lawyer; b. Cleve., Aug. 4, 1943; s. Charles Frances and Louise (Eckert) S.; m. Mary Mato, July 29, 1967; children: Christa Mary, Alicia Mary. BA, Benedictine Coll., 1965; JD, U. Notre Dame, 1968. Bar: Ohio 1968, U.S. Dist. Ct. (so. dist.) Ohio 1970, U.S. Ct. Appeals (6th cir.) 1971, U.S. Supreme Ct. 1971. Law clk. U.S. Dist. Ct. (so. dist.) Ohio, Columbus, 1968-70; assoc. Mayer, Tingley & Hurd, Columbus, 1970-75; judge Bankruptcy Ct. U.S. Dist. Ct. (so. dits.) Ohio, Columbus, 1975-82; ptnr. Vorys, Sater, Seymour & Pease, Columbus, 1982—. Prof. Ohio State U. Law Sch., Columbus, 1984, 85, 86. Mem. Nat. Conf. Bankruptcy Judges (bd. dirs. 1981-82), Assn. Former Bankruptcy Judges (bd. dirs. 1983-89, treas. 1986-87, pres. 1988-89). Office: Vorys Sater Seymour & Pease PO Box 1008 52 E Gay St Columbus OH 43215-3161 E-mail: rjsidman@vssp.com., rsidman843@aol.com.

SIDNAM, ALAN NORTHCOTE, retired advertising executive, venture capitalist; b. Kalamazoo, Mich., July 14, 1916; s. William Northcote and Esther Lulu (Humphrey) S.; m. Shirley S. Meeker, Dec. 31, 1947 (div. Sept. 1975); 1 child, Caroline; m. Gloria Delli-Bovi, Oct. 10, 1975. BA, Kalamazoo Coll., 1937. Apprentice Staake-Schoonmaker, Kalamazoo, 1937-38; acct. exec., copywriter Winternitz & Cairns, N.Y.C., 1938-39, Robert Winternitz, Advt., N.Y.C., 1939-42; acct. exec., exec. v.p. Benton & Bowles, Advt., N.Y.C., 1945-61; vice chmn. Ogilvy & Mather, N.Y.C., 1963-68, cons., 1968-70; venture capitalist N.Y.C., 1970—. Founding investor, dir. Lindblad Travel, N.Y.C., 1961-75; investor, dir. Kelley Oil Corp., Houston, 1970-87. Vestryman St. George's Episcopal Ch., N.Y.C., 1964-65; trustee Kalamazoo Coll., 1971-82, Ch. Heavenly Rest Day Sch., N.Y.C., 1973-79; bd. dirs. Mus. Tower, N.Y.C., 1999—. 1st lt. USAF, 1942-45, PTO. Mem. Univ. Club (coun. 1986-88), Waccabuc Country Club (pres. 1955-56). Republican. Episcopalian. Avocations: tennis, golf.

SIDRAN, MIRIAM, retired physics educator, researcher; b. Washington, May 25, 1920; d. Morris Samson and Theresa Rena (Gottlieb) S. BA, Bklyn. Coll., 1942; MA, Columbia U., N.Y.C., 1949; PhD, NYU, 1956. Rsch. assoc. dept. physics NYU, N.Y.C., 1950-55, postdoctoral fellow, 1955-57; asst. prof. Staten Island Community Coll., Richmond, N.Y., 1957-59; rsch. scientist Grumman Aerospace Corp., Bethpage, N.Y., 1959-67; prof. N.Y. Inst. Tech., N.Y.C., 1967-72; NSF rsch. fellow Nat. Marine Fisheries Svc., Miami, Fla., 1971-72; assoc. prof. then prof. physics Baruch Coll., N.Y.C., 1972-89, chmn. dept. natural scis., 1983-89, prof. emerita, 1990—. V.p. Baruch chpt. Profl. Staff Congress, 1983-89. Contbr. numerous articles to profl. and govtl. publs., chpts. to books. N.Y. State Regents scholar, 1937-41; NSF summer fellow, Miami, 1970. Mem. N.Y. Acad. Scis., Am. Assn. Physics Tchrs. Avocations: french and hebrew languages, music, bicycling, poetry. Home: 210 W 19th St Apt 5G New York NY 10011-4009

SIDRANSKY, DAVID, molecular biologist; b. El Paso, Tex., June 21, 1960; s. Julia and Amalia Sidransky; m. Lynn R. Clahr, Sept. 26, 1990; children: Elie M., Anina Libi, Yair S. BS in Chemistry, magna cum laude, with highest honors, Brandeis U., 1981; MD, Baylor U., 1984. Diplomate Am. Bd. Internal Medicine, Am. Bd. Med. Oncology. Intern in internal medicine Baylor Coll. Medicine, Houston, 1984-85, resident in internal medicine, 1985-87, clin. investigator Inst. Molecular Genetics, 1986-87, chief resident in internal medicine, 1987-88; sr. clin. fellow in oncology Johns Hopkins Hosp., Balt., 1988-89, rsch. fellow in oncology, 1989-92, asst. prof. oncology, 1992-94, asst. prof. otolaryngology, head and neck surgery, 1992-94, assoc. prof. oncology, 1994-98, dir. head and neck cancer rsch. divsn., 1994—, prof. otolaryngology, head and neck surgery, 1998—, prof. pathology, 1998—, prof. cellular and molecular medicine, 1998—, prof. urology, 1999—. Mem. external adv. bd. U. Calif., San Diego Cancer Ctr., U. Tex. M.D. Anderson Cancer Ctr., Houston; mem. sci. adv. coun. Israel Cancer Sch. Fund; mem. med. adv. coun. Israel Children's Cancer Found.; mem. devel. diagnostics com. Nat. Cancer Inst., 1996—, mem. cancer prevention and control com., 1996—, bd. sci. counselors, chmn. early detectin rsch. network. Contbr. articles to profl. jours. including Sci., Cancer Rsch., Sci., Nature Medicine; chmn., editl. bd. Internat. Jour. Cancer-Predictive Oncology; sr. editor Clin. Cancer Rsch.; assoc. editor Cancer Rsch., Jour. Nat. Cancer Inst., Oral Oncology. Recipient award Found. for the Promotion of Cancer Rsch., Japan, 1995, Sarstedt Internat. Rsch. prize German Soc. Clin. Chemistry, 1997, Cheng Suen Man Shook Found. award Hong Kong Cancer Inst., 1998, Walter Hubert award Brit. Assn. Cancer Rsch., 1998, Alton Ochsner award Relating Smoking and Health Am. Coll. Chest Physicians, 1998, award Internat. Union Against Cancer Role, 1999. Mem. AAAS, Am. Soc. for Head and Neck Surgery, Am. Assn. for Cancer Rsch., N.Y. Acad. Scis. Jewish. Avocation: racquetball. Office: Johns Hopkins U 720 Rutland Ave Ste 818 Baltimore MD 21205-2109*

SIDU, SANJIV, computer software executive; b. Hyderabad, India; BSCHemE, MSCHemE, postgrad., Case Western U. Lab. tech. Tex. Instruments; founder, CEO i2 Techs., Inc., Irving, then Dallas, 1988—. Co-recipient SE Asia sailing champsionship. Mem. Indian nat. sailing team. Avocation: avid sailor. Office: i2 Technologies Inc 11701 Luna Rd Dallas TX 75234-6072

SIDWELL, DAVID H. bank executive; BA, Cambridge (England) U., 1975. Chartered acct. With PricewaterhouseCoopers, 1975—84; from controller to CFO J.P. Morgan Chase & Co., N.Y., 1984—2004; CFO Morgan Stanley, 2004—. Office: c/o Morgan Stanley 1585 Broadway New York NY 10036*

SIDWELL, ROBERT WILLIAM, virologist, educator; b. Huntington Park, Calif., Mar. 17, 1937; s. Robert Glen and Eva Amalie (Gordy) S.; m. Rhea Julander, May 31, 1957; children: Richard Dale, Jeanette Kathleen, David Eugene, Cynthia Diane, Michael Jason, Robert Odell. BS, Brigham Young U., 1958; MS, U. Utah, 1961, PhD, 1963. Head serology, rickets and virus research Epizoology Lab., U. Utah, 1958-63; head virus div. So. Research Inst., Birmingham, Ala., 1963-69; head dept. virology ICN Nucleic Acid Research Inst., Irvine, Calif., 1969-72, head div. chemotherapy, 1972-75, dir. inst., 1975-77; prof. animal, dairy and vet. scis. Utah State U., Logan, 1977—; mem. faculty U. Ala. Med. Sch., 1968-69; dir. Inst. Antiviral Rsch. Utah State U., Logan, 1992—. Lectr. in field. Editor: ISAR News, 1992—; mem. editorial bd. Antimicrobial Agts. and Chemotherapy, 1972—, Chemotherapy, 1974—, Antiviral Research, 1980—, Internat. Antiviral News, 1992—; Contbr. articles to profl. jours. Mem. Nibley (Utah) City Planning and Zoning Commn., 1978-80; mem. steering com. Irvine Sch. Bd., 1972, chmn. health edn. awareness forum, 1975; chmn. basic rsch. subcommittee div. AIDS Nat. Inst. Allergy Infectious Diseases, NIH, 1990. Recipient E. Wynne Thorne Research award Utah State U., 1987, Silver Beaver award Boy Scouts Am., 1987; Gov.'s medal for Sci. and Tech., Utah State U., 1988; scholar Order of Eagles, 1954, Dept. Interior, 1954; named Coll. Agr. Prof. of Yr., 1989. Fellow Infectious Disease Soc. Am.; mem. AAAS, Am. Assn. Immunologists, Soc. Exptl. Biology and Medicine, Pan Am. Med. Assn., Internat. Soc. Chemotherapy (exec. com. 1991—), Inter-Am. Soc. Chemotherapy, Am. Soc. Microbiology, Am. Soc. Virology, Nat. Assn. Colls., Tchrs. in Agriculture, Am. Assn. U. Profs., Internat. Soc. Antiviral Rsch., Sigma Xi. Home: 162 Quarter Cir Logan UT 84321-6313 Office: Utah State U Inst Antiviral Rsch Logan UT 84322-0001

SIEBEL, MATHIAS PAUL, mechanical engineer, consultant; b. Witten, Germany, Mar. 6, 1924; arrived in U.S., 1957, naturalized, 1962; s. Franz and Marie-Luise Siebel; m. Katherine Elizabeth Jente, May 27, 1960. BSME, U. Bristol, Eng., 1949, PhD, 1952. From R&D engr. to asst. plant mgr. Tube Investments Ltd., Birmingham, England, 1952-57; rsch. assoc. Columbia U., N.Y.C., 1958-59; mgr. pressure equipment Pall Corp., Glen Cove, NY, 1959-64; v.p. ops. RDI Co., Westbury, NY, 1964-65; dir. mfg. engring. lab., then mem. sci. staff Marshall Space Flight Center, NASA, Huntsville, Ala., 1965-79; mgr. NASA Michoud Assembly Facility, New Orleans, 1979-87, cons., 1987—. Assoc. dean Coll. Engring. U. New Orleans, 1989—92, adj. prof. mech. engring., 1993—2001. Achievements include patents in field. Home: 5204 Janice Ave Kenner LA 70065-3238

SIEBEL, THOMAS M. software company executive; BA, MS in computer sci., MBA, U. Ill., Urbana-Champaign. Various positions including group v.p., gen. mgr. Oracle Corp.; CEO Gain Tech., until 1992, Siebel Systems, San Mateo, Calif., 1993—2004, chmn., 1993—. Author: Virtual Selling, Cyber Rules, Taking Care of eBusiness. Bd. advisors U. Ill., Coll. Engring., Stanford U. Grad. Sch. Bus., Stanford U. Law Sch. Named one of top 25 managers in the world, Business Week mag., 2000, 2001; recipient David Packard Award, Bus. Executives for Nat. Security, 2002, CEO of the Year, Industry Week mag., 2002. Office: Siebel Systems Inc 1855 S Grant St San Mateo CA 94402-7016*

SIEBENMORGEN, PAUL, retired family physician, lay church worker; b. Terre Haute, Ind., Sept. 16, 1920; s. Louis and Ruby E. (Curtis) Siebenmorgen; m. Jane Maxine Waggoner, June 20, 1948; children: Paul Stephen, Elizabeth Ann Siebenmorgen Brentlinger, Susan Lynn Siebenmorgen Amos. BS in Edn., Ind. State Teacher's Coll., 1941; MD, Ind. U., 1944. Pvt. practice, Terre Haute, 1947-2000; pres. med. and dental staff Terre Haute Regional Hosp., 1974-75, 96, trustee, 1975-81; assoc. clin. faculty Sch. Medicine, Ind. U., Inpls., 1975-2000. Deacon Cen. Christian Ch., Terre Haute, 1947, elder, 1948—2000, elder emeritus, 2001—, trustee, 1966—86, chmn. bd., 1957—59; mem. bd. Ind. Region Christian Ch. (Disciples of Christ), 1966—76, pres.-elect, 1972—74, moderator, 1974—76; mem. exec. com. Conf. Regional Mins. and Bd. Chmn., 1974—76; bd. dirs. Med. Assurance Ind., 1982—2001, chmn., 1986—91, pres., 1986—88; trustee Ind. State U., Terre Haute, 1975—83; mem. alumni coun. Ind. U. Sch. Medicine, 1989—97, pres., 1993, bd. dir. dean's coun., 1997—2001; mem. U. So. Ind. Found. Bd., 1976—86, Gov.'s Commn. for the United Way of Ind. Centennial Observance, 1986; sec. Vigo County Comprehensive Health Planning Coun.; bd. dir. So. Ind. Health Sys. Agy., 1975—78; mem. Ind. Statewide Health Coord. Coun., 1977—89, mem. exec. com., 1982—84; pres. Vigo County Heart Assn., 1967—68; hon. parade marshall Ind. State U. Homecoming, 1990; hon. mem. Ind. State U. Found. Bd., charter mem. Pres.'s Soc., 1990—; staff emeritus Union Hosp., Terre Haute, Ind., 2000—. Mem. Vigo County Bd. Health, 1967—82, pres., 1967—68, 1971—75, v.p., 1976—79; bd. dirs. Ind. Med. Polit. Action Com., 1988—94. Recipient Sustained Outstanding Svc. award, Scottish Rite Valley Terre Haute, 1972, Meritorious Svc. award, Ind. State U. Alumni Assn., 1972, Disting. Alumni award, Ind. State U., 1993, Hand Clasp award, Kiwanis Club Terre Haute, 1991, Disting. Alumni award, Ind. U. Sch. Medicine, 1994, Excellence in Health Care award, Columbia Terre Haute Regional Hosp. Found., 1997, Bowen award for Leadership, Ind. U., 1996, 50 Yr. Cert., Scottish Rite, 2002. Fellow: Am. Acad. Family Physicians (life; charter); mem.: AMA, Ind. Acad. Family Physicians (dist. pres. 1961, 1971, dir. 1973—82, pres. 1981, Lester Bibler award 1989), Aesculapian Soc. Wabash Valley, Vigo County Med. Soc. (pres. 1970), Ind. State Med. Assn. (chmn. bd. trustees 1981—84, pres., chmn. delegation to AMA Ho. Dels. 1985, named Ind. Family Physician of Yr. 1987), Terre Haute C. of C., Elks, Phi Rho Sigma, Kappa Delta Pi, Alpha Phi Omega, Sigma Alpha Epsilon. Home: 1241 Watertree Rd Terre Haute IN 47803-7712 *Though we have precious memories and lessons from the past, it is the future, a new frontier experienced by no one, that holds exciting new discoveries, challenges, opportunities, hope, and progress. Under God let us proceed with diligence and in confidence.*

SIEBER, DAWN, food service executive; Student in Psychology, U. Miami; grad., Balt. Internat. Culinary Arts Inst. Owner The Red Star, Balt.; from exec. sous chef to exec. chef Cheeca Lodge, Islamorada, Fla., 1988—. Featured in Am. Inst. Wine and Food weekend, Celebrity Chefs Eco-Challenge. Featured in Esquire, Food & Wine, Travel & Leisure and The Miami Herald, cooked at Masters of Food and Wine, Carmel, Calif., CBS Morning Show, Julia Child's gala birthday dinner (filmed for PBS). Office: Cheeca Lodge PO Box 527 Islamorada FL 33036

SIEBERT, CALVIN D. economist, educator; b. Hillsboro, Kans., Feb. 11, 1934; s. Ira and Margaret (Everett) S.; m. Valerie Dawn Nanninga, Feb. 18, 1960; children— Douglas Erik, Derek Christopher. BA, U. Kans., 1958, MA, 1960; PhD in Econs., U. Calif., Berkeley, 1966. Asst. prof. econs. U. Iowa, 1965-68, assoc. prof., 1968-75, prof., 1975—, chmn. dept., 1969-71, 75-79. Rockefeller Found. vis. asso. prof. U. Philippines, 1971-72 Contbr. articles to profl. jours. With U.S. Army, 1954-56. Ford Found. grantee, 1964-65 Mem. Am. Econ. Assn., Phi Beta Kappa. Home: 341 N 7th Ave Iowa City IA 52245-6003 Office: U Iowa Dept Econs S318 Pbb Iowa City IA 52242 E-mail: calvin_siebert@uiowa.edu.

SIEBERT, CHARLES, writer; b. Bklyn., Dec. 14, 1954; s. Charles John Siebert and Marion Agelina Valle; m. Rebecca Bex Brian, Nov. 26, 2002. B in Lit., SUNY, 1977; MFA, U. Houston, 1982. Prof. Marymount Coll., Tarrytown, NY, 1983; contbg. writer N.Y. Times Mag., NY, 1983—, Esquire Mag., NY, 1983—89, Harper's Mag., NY, 1990—94; prof. creative writing R.I. Coll., Providence, 1994. Author: (memoir) Wickerby: An Urban Pastoral, 1998, A Man After His Own Heart, 2004, (novels) Angus, 2000, The Best American Essays, 1970 (Notable Essay of Yr., 1990, 1991), 1991; contbr. poems, essays, articles to New Yorker, N.Y. Times Mag., Esquire, Outside. Grantee, N.Y. Found. Arts, N.Y.C., 1997. Mem.: PEN Am. Ctr.

SIEBERT, DIANE DOLORES, author, poet; b. Chgo., Ill., Mar. 18, 1948; m. Robert William Siebert, Sept. 21, 1969. RN. Author: Truck Song, 1984 (Notable Childrens Book award ALA 1984, Sch. Libr. Jour. one of Best Books 1984, Outstanding Childrens Book award NY Times Book Rev. 1984, Reading Rainbow Selection book 1991), Mojave, 1988 (Childrens Editors Choice 1988, Internat. Reading Assn. Tchr. Choice award 1989, others), Heartland, 1989 (award Nat. Coun. for Social Studies/Childrens Book Coun. 1989, on John Burroughs List Nature Book for Young Readers 1989, Ohio Farm Bur. Women award 1991), Train Song, 1990 (Notable Childrens Book award ALA, 1990, Redbook Mag. one of Top Ten Picture Books 1990, one of Best Books award Sch. Libr. Jour. 1990, others), Sierra, 1991 (Outstanding Sci. Trade Book for Children award NSTA 1991, Notable Childrens Trade Book in Field Social Studies award Nat. Coun. Social Studies 1991, Beatty award Calif. Libr. Assn. 1992), Plane Song, 1993 (Outstanding Sci. Trade Book for Children 1994, Reading Rainbow Selection book, Platinum award Oppenheim Toy Portfolio, Tchrs. Choice award Internat. Reading Assn. 1994), Cave, 2000 (Notable children's Book in the english Language Arts, 2001, Nat. Coun. of English Tchr., named to John Burroughs List of Nature Books for Young Readers 2000), Mississippi (named to John Burroughs List 2001), 2001, Motorcycle Song, 2002, Rhyolite, 2003. Avocations: environmental affairs, running, classical guitar, motorcycle, animals. Home: 9676 SW Jordan Rd Culver OR 97734-9567

SIEBERT, KARL JOSEPH, food science educator, consultant; b. Harrisburg, Pa., Oct. 29, 1945; s. Christian Ludwig and Katharine (Springer) S.; m. Sui Ti Atienza, Mar. 14, 1970; children: Trina, Sabrina. BS in Biochemistry, Pa. State U., 1967, MS in Biochemistry, 1968, PhD in Biochemistry, 1970. Chemist Applied Sci. Labs., State College, Pa., 1968-70; rsch. assoc. Stroh Brewery Co., Detroit, 1971, head R & D sect., 1971-73, mgr. R & D lab., 1973-82, dir. rsch., 1982-90; v.p. Strohtech, Detroit, 1986-90; prof. Cornell U., Geneva, NY, 1990—, chmn. dept. food sci. and tech., 1990-95, also assoc. dir. Cornell Inst. Food Sci. Ithaca, NY, 1990-95. Contbr. articles to profl. jours. Bd. visitors Oakland U. Biology Dept., Rochester, Mich., 1985-89; bd. dirs. Cornell Rsch. Found., 1990-96, Geneva Concerts Inc., 1991-98. Capt. USAR, 1967-75. Recipient Presdl. award Master Brewers Assn., 1986, 90; named hon. prof. Moscow State Acad. Food Prodn., 1996. Fellow NSF; mem. Am. Chem. Soc. (divsn. agrl. and food chemistry, computers in chemistry divsn.), Master Brewer Assn. Ams., Am. Soc. Brewing Chemists (chmn. tech. com. 1986-88, mem. editl. bd. 1983-91, 96—, Eric Kneen Meml. award 1998, 99, 2004, award of distinction 1999), Inst. Food Technologists (divsn. fruit and vegetable tech., food chemistry, food microbiology, sensory analysis), Internat. Chemometrics Soc. (N.Am. chpt.). Avocations: computers, electronics. Home: 9 Parkway St Geneva NY 14456-9765 Office: NY State Agrl Expt Sta Cornell U Dept Food Sci Geneva NY 14456 Office Phone: 315-787-2299. E-mail: kjs3@cornell.edu.

SIEBERT, MURIEL (MICKIE), brokerage house executive, former state banking official; b. Cleve., 1932; d. Irwin J. and Margaret Eunice (Roseman) Siebert. Student, Western Res. U., 1949-52; DCS (hon.), St. John's U., St. Bonaventure U., Molloy Coll., Adelphi U., St. Francis Coll., Mercy Coll., Coll. New Rochelle, St. Lawrence U., Manhattan Coll., Seton Hall Coll., Case Western Res. U., Marymount Manhattan Coll., Hofstra U. Security analyst Bache & Co., 1954-57; analyst Utilities & Industries Mgmt. Corp., 1958, Shields & Co., 1959-60; ptnr. Stearns & Co., 1961, Finkle & Co., 1962-65, Brimberg & Co., N.Y.C., 1965-67; individual mem. (first woman mem.) N.Y. Stock Exch., 1967; chmn., pres. Muriel Siebert & Co., Inc., 1969-77; trustee Manhattan Savs. Bank, 1975-77; supt. banks, dept. banking State of N.Y., 1977-82; dir. Urban Devel. Corp., N.Y.C., 1977-82, Job Devel. Authority, N.Y.C., 1977-82, State of N.Y. Mortgage Agy., 1977-82; chmn., pres. Muriel Siebert & Co., Inc., N.Y.C., 1983—. Assoc. in mgmt. Simmons Coll.; mem. adv. com. Fin. Acctg. Stds. Bd., 1981-84; adv. bd. Minority & Women-Owned Bus. Enterprise; guest lectr. numerous colls. Ran for Rep. nomination, U.S.Senate, 1982; former mem. women's adv. com. Econ. Devel. Adminstrn., N.Y.C.; former trustee Manhattan Coll.; v.p., former mem. exec. com. Greater N.Y. Area coun. Boy Scouts Am.; mem. N.Y. State Econ. Devel. Bd., N.Y. Coun. Economy; bd. overseers NYU Sch. Bus., 1984-88; former bd. dirs. United Way of N.Y.C.; former trustee Citizens Budget Commn., L.I. U.; mem. bus. com. Met. Mus., bus. com. of N.Y. State Bus. Coun.; advive Women's Campaign Fund.; bd. dirs. N.Y. Women's Agenda; bd. trustees Guild Hall Mus. EH; current appointee Commn. Jud. Nomination; founding mem. The Mus. Women-The Leadership Coun; founder, bd.dirs. The WISH List; Tokyo adv. com. Sister City Program N.Y.C. Recipient Spirit of Achievement award Albert Einstein Coll. Medicine, 1977, Women's Equity Action League award, 1978, Outstanding Contbns. to Equal Oppty. for Women award Bus. Coun. UN Decade for Women, 1979, Silver Beaver award Boy Scouts Am., 1981, Elizabeth Cutter Morrow award YWCA, 1983, Emily Roebling award Nat. Women's Hall of Fame, 1984, Entrepreneurial Excellence award White House Conf. on Small Bus., 1986, NOW Legal Def. and Edn. Fund award, 1981, Brotherhood award NCCJ. 1989, Women on the Move award Anti-Defamation League, 1990, Bus. Philanthropist of Yr. award So. Calif. Conf. for Women Bus. Owner's, 1990, award Borough of Manhattan, 1991, Benjamin Botwinick prize Columbia Bus. Sch., 1992, Women in Bus. Making History award Women's Bus. Coun. N.Y. C. of C., 1993, Disting. Woman of Yr. award Greater N.Y. Boy Scouts of Am., 1993, Corning Excellence award N.Y.C. Bus. Coun., 1993, Star award, N.Y. Women's Agenda, 1993, Woman of Yr. award Fin. Women's Assn. N.Y., 1994, Medal of Honor award Ellis Island, 1994, Star award N.Y. Women's Agenda, 1994, N.Y. Urban Coalition's Achievement award, 1994, Women of Distinction award Crohn's and Colitis Found., 1994, Entrepreneurial Leadership award Nat. Found. Tchg. Entrepreneurship, 1994, Athena award, 1997, USO Women of Yr. award, 1998, Sara Lee Frontrunner award, 1998, Mattel/Barbie Ambassador of Dreams award, 1999; inductee Nat. Woman's Hall of Fame, Seneca Falls, N.Y., 1994, Internat. Women's Forum Hall of Fame, 1994, Ohio Women's Hall Fame, 1994; N.Y. Univ.'s Stern Sch. Bus. 1st Woman Stovall fellow, 1992; Established Siebert Entrepreneurial Philanthropic Program, 1990. Mem. Women's Forum (founding mem., pres.), Com. 200, Fin. Women's Assn. (Cmty. Svc. award 1993), River Club, Doubles Club, Westchester Club, West Palm Beach Polo and Country Club, Nat. Assn. Women Bus. Owners (NAWBO's Veuve Clicquot Bus. Women of Yr. award 1992, Mayor's Lifetime Achievement award for Women Bus. Owners 1993), Econ. Club (exec. com.), Southampton Bath and Tennis Club (founding mem., bd. dirs.), Women's Campaign Fund, Fashion Group Internat., River Club, Doubles Club, Westchester County Club, West Palm Beach Polo and Country Club (former mem.); adv. coun. Women's Econ. Roundtable. Office: Muriel Siebert & Co Inc 885 3rd Ave Ste 1720 New York NY 10022-4834*

SIEBERT, THOMAS L. lawyer, former ambassador; b. Cleve., May 2, 1946; m. Deborah Simpson; 4 children. BA, JD, Georgetown U. Intern Rep. Robert E. Sweeney, 1965—66; vol. Senator Robert F. Kennedy, 1966—68; aide Senator Carl Hayden, 1968—70; assoc. Pittman, Lovett, Ford & Hennessey, Washington, 1971—78; ptnr. Lovett, Ford, Hennessey, Stambler & Siebert, 1978—87; of counsel Besozzi & Gavin, 1987—93, Besozzi, Gavin & Craven, Washington, 1993; U.S. amb. to Sweden Am. Embassy, Stockholm, 1994—98; mem. Patton Boggs LLP, Washington. Chmn. Plenipotentiary Conf., Internat. Telecom. Union, 1998; chmn., pres. U.S. Telemetry Corp., 1999—. Bd. regents Cath. U.; bd. visitors St. John's Coll., Georgetown U. Law Ctr.; mem. bd. visitors and govs. Washington Coll.; active U.S. Naval Acad. Midshipmen Program, Md. Hall for the Creative Arts. Mem.: ABA, Annapolis Assn., Fed. Comm. Bar Assn., D.C. Bar. Office: Patton Boggs LLP 2550 M St NW Washington DC 20037-1350

SIECK, ROBERT, aerospace engineer; Mem. Aerospace Safety Adv. Panel NASA, Washington; meteorologist USAF, 1960—64; Gemini spacecraft sys. engr. NASA, Kennedy Space Ctr., 1964—76, Apollo spacecraft test team project; engring. mgr. sulttle approach and landing tests Dryden Flight Rsch. Facility, Calif., 1976—78; chief shuttle project engr. NASA, Kennedy Space Ctr., 1978—83, shuttle flow dir., 1983—84, dir. launch and landing ops., 1984—92, dep. dir. shuttle ops., 1992—95, dir. shuttle processing; cons. Aerospace Adv. Panel NASA, Washington, 1999—. Office: Aerospace Safety Adv Panel NASA Hdqrs 300 E St SW Washington DC 20546

SIEDEL, GEORGE JOHN, III, law educator; b. Medina, Ohio, Feb. 17, 1945; s. George Joseph and Justine Elizabeth (Johnson) S.; m. Helen Louise Haeck, June 28, 1969; children: Joseph, Kathryn, John. BA, Coll. Wooster (Ohio), 1967; JD, U. Mich., 1970; DCLS, U. Cambridge, 1971. Bar: Mich. 1971, Fla. 1974, Ohio 1974, U.S. Supreme Ct. 1976. Assoc. Robertson, Bartlow and Des Chenes, Adrian, Mich., 1971-73; asst. prof. bus. law Bowling Green (Ohio) State U., 1973-74; prof. bus. law U. Mich., Ann Arbor, 1974—; assoc. dean, 1993—98; dist. chair in Humanities and Social Scis. Fulbright Program, 2001. Vis. fellow U. Cambridge, Eng., 1981, 89; vis. prof. Harvard U., Cambridge, Mass., 1998, Stanford U., Palo Alto, Calif., 1985, China U. Polit. Sci. and Law, 1992; Parsons fellow U. Sydney, Australia, 1991; Thurnau prof. U. Mich., 1992-95; Williamson family prof. bus. adminstrn. U. Mich., 1996—. Author: Business Law and the Legal Environment, 1992, Using the Law for Competitive Advantage, 2002, Real Estate Law, 2002, The Lawyer and Business, 1976; spl. editor Am. Bus. Law Jour., Athens, Ga., 1987-88; editor-in-chief Mich. Real Property Rev., 1976—. Corp. sec., dir. Medic Alert Found. Internat., Turlock, Calif., 1979-87; dir. William Davidson Inst., 1992—, AIESEC U.S., Inc., 1994-98. Recipient Excellence award Midwest Bus. Law Assn., 1982, Hoeber award Acad. Legal Studies in Bus., 1993; Ford Found. fellow, 1970-71, Ralph Bunche award, Acad. Legal Studies in Bus., Internat. Case Writing award, 2000. Fellow Mich. State Bar Found. (life); mem. ABA, Am. Corp. Counsel Assn. (bd. dirs. Mich. chpt. 1984-85), Am. Bus. Law Assn. Presbyterian. Office: U Mich Bus Sch 701 Tappan St Ann Arbor MI 48109-1234

SIEDLE, ROBERT DOUGLAS, management consultant; b. Canton, Ohio, Aug. 08; *Father Arnold D. Siedle, Lieutenant USNR (deceased), was one of the officers in charge of the United States Navy's highly classified WWII TDD program, the forerunner of today's UAV (unmanned aerial vehicle) and UCAV (unmanned combat air vehicle) programs.* BA in Econs., Hiram Coll., 1956; profl. cert. edn., Kent State U., Western Res. U., 1963. Tchr., prin. Ohio secondary schs., 1957-65; salesman, area rep. visual products divsn. 3M Co., 1966-68; mgr. market devel. and tng. AV divsn. Bell & Howell, 1968-69; Chgo. br. mgr. info. systems divsn. Am. Std., 1969-72; mgr. edn. systems divsn. Audiotronics Corp., 1972-76; gen. mgr. Niles Entertainment/Wardway Films, 1977-80; pres. The Ultimate Image, Lakeland, Fla., 1985—. *The youngest "passenger" to fly in the original prototype B-17 Flying Fortress (held on the lap of one of the test crew), his love for aviation was thus born leading to a life of participation and political involvement, both civilian and military. He actively supported and aided in getting both the Air Force Memorial and World War II Memorial projects underway. In 1999, his name was among the chosen to be inscribed on two microchips placed in the NASA Stardust Spacecraft, one to forever remain in space, one to return January 2006 in a capsule for museum placement following a 3.2 billion mile journey.* Prodr.: (films) New Dimensions in Learning II, 1969, District 65: The Exceptional Child, 1969, Career Exploration: Health, 1976, The Wide World of Work, 1976; author: Multisensory Learning: A Training Guide, 1973, Alphabet Zoo, 1973, City of Boston Young Adult Alternate Career Program, 1974, The Quick Job Hunt Guide, 1991; author, prodr., dir.: (multimedia rd. show) "Rap" With Students, 1975; prodr., editor: (film) Stampin' Ground, 1977; author poetry appearing in books and mags., 1991—; appeared on nat. radio and TV programs in U.S. and Can. Recipient Internat. Peace prize United Cultural Conv., 2002; named to Nat. Aviation and Space Exploration Wall of Honor Smithsonian Nat. Air and Space Mus. Dulles Ctr., 2000, VFW Patriot Corps award, 2004. Mem.: Smithsonian Instn., Profl. Football Rschrs. Assn., Nat. Space Soc., Aerospace Edn. Found., Smithsonian Air and Space Soc., Hat in the Ring Soc., Am. Air Mus. (Britain) (founding mem.), Exptl. Aircraft Assn. (life), World Nations Congress (life; senator), Navy League U.S. (life), U.S. Naval Inst. (life), Fla. Air Mus. Sun 'n Fun (life), Aircraft Owners and Pilots Assn. Safety Found. (life), Air Force Assn. (life), Aircraft Owners and Pilots Assn. (life), Naval Aviation Mus. Found. (life), Am. Assn. Individual Investors, Smithsonian Inst., Internat. Honour Soc. (charter mem.), Nat. Space Soc., Popular Rotorcraft Assn., Inc., Helper Soc. (St. Labre Indian Sch. Edn. Assn.), Century Soc. (St. Labre Indian Sch. Edn. Assn.), Soc. Prevention

Cruelty to Animals, Inc., Living Planet Soc. (world wildlife fund, Humanitarian award 2002), Defenders of Wildlife (pres.' coun.), Airship Assn. Ltd., Air Force Meml. Found. (charter sponsor), WW II Meml. Soc. (charter), Lighter-than-Air Soc. (life), Pituitary Network Assn. (life), Steamship Hist. Soc. (life), Great Lakes Hist. Soc. (life). Baptist. Office: The Ultimate Image PO Box 91388 Lakeland FL 33804-1388 Office Phone: 863-838-4621. E-mail: Office22@webtv.net., metalogenman@aol.com.

SIEDLECKI, PETER ANTHONY, English language and literature educator; b. North Tonawanda, N.Y., May 19, 1938; s. Anthony Paul and Mary Barbara (Litwin) S.; m. Rose Mary Murphy, June 25, 1960 (div. 1978); children: Christopher, Gregory, Jeffrey, William; m. Lynnette Noreen Mende, Apr. 26, 1980; children: Peter Emmanuel Mende-Siedlecki. BA, Niagara U., 1960, MA, 1966; PhD, SUNY, Buffalo, 1982. Tchr. English Lewiston-Porter Sr. H.S., Youngstown, NY, 1960—64, Grand Island (N.Y.) Sr. H.S., 1964—65; prof. English Rosary Hill Coll., Amherst, NY, 1965—74, Daemen Coll., Amherst, NY, 1974—, dean, divsn. arts and scis., 2001—, chair divsn. humanities and social scis., 1998—2001; prof. Am. Lit. Jagiellonian U., Krakow, Poland, 1982-84, Friedrich-Schiller U., Jena, 1988-89. Commentator pub. radio, 1995—. Author (poetry) Voyeur; contbr. articles to profl. jours. Fulbright Sr. lectr., Council for Internat. Exchange of Scholars, 1982-84, 88-89. Mem. MLA, Fulbright Alumni Assn. Democrat. Home: 249 Winspear Ave Buffalo NY 14215-1035 Office: Daemen College 4380 Main St Buffalo NY 14226-3592 E-mail: psiedlec@daemen.edu.

SIEDZIKOWSKI, HENRY FRANCIS, lawyer; b. Chester, Pa., Dec. 27, 1953; s. Henry W. and Virginia (Szymanski) S. BA cum laude, Juniata Coll., 1975; JD magna cum laude, Villanova U., 1979. Bar: Pa. 1979, U.S. Dist. Ct. (ea. dist.) Pa. 1979, U.S. Ct. Appeals (3d cir.) 1979, U.S. Ct. Appeals (8th cir.) 1981, U.S. Dist. Ct. (we. dist.) Pa. 1986, U.S. Dist. Ct. (mid. dist.) Pa. 1986. Assoc. Dilworth, Paxson, Kalish & Kauffman, Phila., 1979-86; ptnr. Baskin Flaherty Elliott & Mannino P.C., Phila., 1986—90, Elliott Bray & Riley, Phila., 1990—92, Elliott, Vanaskie & Riley, Blue Bell, Pa., 1992—94, Elliott, Reihner & Siedzikowski PC, Blue Bell, 1994—. Mem. hearing com. disciplinary bd. Supreme Ct. Pa., 1985—91. Mem. ABA (chmn. Lanham act subcom. of bus. torts com. of litigation sect. 1986—, rotating editor newsletter of antitrust sect. franchisee com.), Pa. Bar Assn., Phila. Bar Assn. (chmn. subcom. disciplinary rules for profl. responsibility com. 1984-90). Democrat. Roman Catholic. Office: Elliott Reihner et al 925 Harvest Dr Blue Bell PA 19422-1956 E-mail: hfs@elliottreihner.com.

SIEFERS, ROBERT GEORGE, banker; b. Pitts., Aug. 28, 1945; s. George Francis and Idella Alice (Eiler) S.; m. Janice Lynn Kirkpatrick, Mar. 25, 1970; children: Robert Scott, Jillian Stewart BA, Mt. Union Coll., 1967; MBA, Kent State U., 1971; JD, Cleveland Marshall Law Sch., 1976. Security analyst Nat. City Bank, Cleve., 1971-76, v.p., investment rsch. dir., 1976-80, v.p. adminstrn. and rsch., 1980-82; sr. v.p. corp. planning Nat. City Corp., Cleve., 1982-85; sr. v.p. corp. banking Nat. City Bank, Cleve., 1985-86; pres., chief exec. officer Ohio Citizens Bank (affiliate Nat. City Corp.), Toledo, 1986-90; vice chmn., CFO Nat. City Corp., Cleve., 1997—. Bd. dirs. HCR Corp. Bd. trustees Mt. Union Coll. Republican. Presbyterian Club: Chagrin Valley Country. Office: Nat City Corp 1900 E 9th St Cleveland OH 44114-3401 Home: 104 Partridge Ln Chagrin Falls OH 44022-4010

SIEFERT, DAVID MICHAEL, information technology executive, manufacturing executive; b. Dayton, Ohio, Apr. 8, 1951; s. Raymond Joseph and Laura Jayne (Blanford) S.; m. Rita Marlene Kuenle, Dec. 12, 1970; children: Christina Marie, Joel David, Jamie Michael, Matthew David, Caroline Marie. BA in Mgmt. Info. Sys., Capital U., 1988; MA in Bus., Antioch U., 1994. Cert. sys. profl., quality analyst; cert. assessment profl. Mgr. computer sys. ops. Koehring Bomag, Springfield, Ohio, 1974-77; gen. mgr. bus. ops. Mead Corp., Dayton, 1977-79, mgr. internat. support, 1979-81; sr. cons. computer applied sys. engring., lifecycle methodologies, software engring., edn. systems, software reliability and quality engring. NCR Corp., Dayton, 1981-86, mgr. advanced quality sys., 1986-89, dir. advanced quality tech., 1988-89, dir. strategic processes, 1990-91, program mgr. mergers and acquisitions, 1991, dir. rsch. and tech., 1992-94, dir. R&D corp. global adv. sys., 1996, dir. global learning strategy and arch., 1999—, dir. corp. learning tech., 1996-98. Inventor Continuous Learning Sys., VISIONet, Knowledge Ctr.; developer, reviewer internat. computer stds. Nat. Inst. Stds. and Tech.; founder NCR U., 1998, dir., asst. v.p. 2000—; dir. strategic programs Sinclair C.C.; program dir., prin. investigator NSF Grant; mgr. program dir. Nat. Found. IT grant; founder IT@Sinclair; mem. Nat. Blue Ribbon Panel, chmn. AIAA; mem. vis. com. Nat. Sci. Foun., Ky., Mass., Tenn., Fla. and W.Va.; cons. in field; profl. paper referee Nat. Computer Conf., 1983, 88, 89; disting. lectr. U.S. Commerce Dept., NIST. Author books on process management, grant management, software reliability, customer satisfaction and continuous improvement of software, knowledge mgmt., decision support systems, learning systems; contbr. articles to profl. jours.; 25 patents pending or issued. Vis. com. chmn. Ky. Nat. Sci. Found. Recipient invention disclosure awards AT&T, 1994, Eureka award for best patent, best patent award AT&T, NCR, 1997-99, Sinclair Visionary award, 2003. Mem. IEEE (sr., profl. paper reviewer IEEE Software Jour. 1988—, sr. mem. stds. com.), Assn. for Computing Machinery, Am. Soc. for Quality Control, Quality Assurance Inst., Nat. Sci. Found. Address: 831 Buckingham Rd Dayton OH 45419-3645 Office Phone: 937-643-2395. E-mail: siefer@att.net.

SIEFERT-KAZANJIAN, DONNA, corporate librarian; b. N.Y.C. d. Merrill Emil and Esther (Levins) S.; m. George John Kazanjian, June 15, 1974; 1 child, Merrill George. BA, NYU, 1969; MSLS, Columbia U., 1973; MBA, Fordham U., 1977. Asst. librarian Dun & Bradstreet, N.Y.C., 1969-73; research assoc. William E. Hill & Co., N.Y.C., 1973-76; sr. info. analyst Info. for Bus., N.Y.C., 1976-77; librarian Handy Assocs., N.Y.C., 1979-90; mgr. Infoserve Fuchs Cuthrell & Co., Inc., N.Y.C., 1991-94; info. specialist Heidrick & Struggles, Inc., N.Y.C., 1994-2001; learning media specialist St. Mary's Elem. Sch., Manhasset, NY, 2002—03; libr. I Manhasset Pub. Libr., 2003—. Mem. Am. Mensa Ltd. Roman Catholic.

SIEFKIN, WILLIAM CHARLES, investor, marketing/sales executive, consultant; b. Glendale, Calif., Jan. 15, 1946; s. Ernest Roosevelt and Violet May (Richardson) S.; m. Deborah Sue Olinger, Dec. 21, 1971; children: Barbra Anne, Katherine Marie, William Andrew. BBA, Calif. Polytech. U., San Luis Obispo, 1968; postgrad., U. Del., 1985; MS in Applied Tech. Tng. and Devel., U. North Tex., 1996. Tech. rep. photo products dept. DuPont Co., Houston and San Antonio, 1968-71, sr. tech. rep. photo products dept. Louisville, 1971-73, sr. export sales rep. photo products dept. internat. ops. div. Wilmington, Del., 1973-74, internat. planning mgr. photo systems and electronics dept., 1979-85, mktg. mgr. imaging systems dept., 1985-87, mgr. sales devel. corp. plans dept., 1987-91; dir. sales devel. Du Pont Corp. Plans, 1991-92; tech. sales mgr. internat. dept. Du Pont (Japan) K.K., Tokyo, 1974-79; pres. Montchanin Corp., Denton, Tex., 1981-97; v.p. customer growth Etheridge Printing Co., Dallas, 1992-93; realtor Ebby Halliday Realtors, Dallas, 1993-94; regional field trainer GTE Directories Sales Corp., Dallas-Ft. Worth Airport, 1994-98; v.p. sales Jobs.com, Inc., Irving, Tex., 1998-99; pres., CEO HyperGrowth Co., Denton, Tex., 1999-2000; sr. mgr. cons. svcs. high growth mid. market practice Ernst & Young, 2000-2001; sr. mgr. high growth CRM consulting CAP Gemini Ernst & Young US LLC, Irving, Tex., 2000—01; pres./CEO, CCO Internat., Denton, Tex., 2001—; new home sales cons. Robson Ranch, Robson Cmtys., Inc., 2002—. Mem. adv. bd. Calif. Poly. State U. Sch. Graphic Comm. Author numerous articles and books in field. Life mem. Rep. Nat. Com., Washington, 1985; dir., mem. exec. com. Jr. Achievement Del., Wilmington, 1986; mem. Dover Symphony, Brandywine Pops Orch. Recipient Bronze Nat. Leadership award Jr. Achievement, 1985, Silver award, 1990; named Honored Alumni of Yr., Calif. Poly. U. Sch. Bus., 1984. Mem. ASTD, Internat. Soc. Performance Improvement, Antique Automobile Club Am. (life), Mensa, Mercedes-Benz Club Am., Hon. Order Ky. Cols., Assn. Quality and Participation, Soc. Human Resource Mgmt. Republican. Methodist. Office: 10512 Countryside Dr Robson Ranch Denton TX 76207-6606

SIEG, ALBERT LOUIS, photographic company executive; b. Chgo., Mar. 25, 1930; s. Albert Fredrick and Louise Augusta (Strege) S.; m. Irma Alice Spencer, Sept. 3, 1955; children: Karen, Diane, Susan BS in Chemistry, U. Ill., 1951; PhD in Organic Chemistry, U. Rochester, 1954; P.MD, Harvard Bus. Sch., 1971. Supr. emulsion Eastman Kodak Co., Rochester, N.Y., 1970-72, corp. mgr. instant, 1972-76, mgr. paper mgmt., 1976-81, v.p., dir., 1981-84; pres. Kodak Japan K.K., Tokyo, 1984-89; pres., rep. dir. Eastman Kodak Japan, Tokyo, 1989-91, also bd. dirs.; pres., rep. dir. Eastman Chems. Japan Ltd., Tokyo, 1989-91; v.p., dir. strategic resources, sec. imaging bd. Eastman Kodak Co., Rochester, 1991-92, ret., 1992; prin., cons. Albert L. Sieg Assocs., Rochester, 1992—. Bd. dirs. Kodak Japan Industries, Ltd., XM Corp.; mem. adv. bd. Worldscape, Inc., 2001--; sr. lectr. U. Rochester, 1960-69 Co-author: 8th Here's How, 1972; co-author (with S. Bennett, Oliver Wight) Tokyo Chronicles, 1994; inventor in field. Bd. dirs., St. John's Home Found., 2000—; chmn. corp. gifts Rochester Philharm. Orch., 1982-84, corp. gifts Internat. Mus. Photography at George Eastman House, 1993, 94; pres. Reformation Luth. Ch., Rochester, 1978-83; bd. dirs. St. John's Home for the Aging, 1994-99, vice chmn. bd. dirs., 1997-99; bd. dirs. St. John's Nursing Home, 1994-99, vice chmn. bd. dirs., 1997-99, chmn., 1999-2001; bd. dirs. St. John's Sr. Svcs., 1997-2001, chair elect, 1997-99, chair, 1999-01, pres., 1997-01; bd. dirs. Found., 2001--. Served with Med. Svc. Corps, U.S. Army, 1955-57. Recipient George Eastman Medal Kodak Camera Clubs, 1980; Kiwanis Club Chgo. fellow, U. Ill., 1947-51; Am. Cyanamide fellow, 1953-54 Fellow Am. Inst. Chemists, Photog. Soc. Am. (v.p. 1969-84, Harold Lloyd award 1978, exec. v.p. 1995, progress medal 1995, pres. 1999-2003); mem. N.Am. Nature Photography Assn. (bd. dirs.), Am. Chem. Soc., Soc. Photog. Scientists and Engrs., AAAS, Rochester C. of C., Am. C. of C. in Japan (bd. govs. 1988-91, v.p. 1989-91), Internat. Stereoscopic Union (pres. 1993, 94), Photographic Soc. of Am. (bd. dirs. 1992—, exec. v.p. 1995-99, pres. 1999-2003). Clubs: American (Tokyo); Fgn. Correspondence. Republican. Avocations: skiing; photography; gardening. Home and Office: 159 Hillhurst Ln Rochester NY 14617-1938 E-mail: albert4182@aol.com.

SIEGAL, ALLAN MARSHALL, newspaper editor; b. N.Y.C., May 1, 1940; s. Irving and Sylvia Norma (Wrubel) S.; m. Gretchen M-P. Leefmans, May 31, 1977; children— Anna Marianita, Peter Bert Grad., NYU, 1962. With New York Times, 1960—, editor Pentagon Papers, 1971, asst. fgn. editor, 1971-76, asst. to exec. editor, 1976-77, news editor, 1977-87, asst. mng. editor, 1987—, standards editor, 2003—, founding editor nat. edit., 1980; tchr. journalism NYU, 1966, Columbia U., 1967-69. Juror Pulitzer Prize Nominating Com., 1987-89. Co-author: The New York Times Manual of Style and Usage, 1999. Mem. Century Assn., Am. Soc. Newspaper Editors. Office: NY Times Co 229 W 43rd St New York NY 10036-3959

SIEGAL, BURTON LEE, product designer, consultant, inventor; b. Chgo., Sept. 27, 1931; s. Norman A. and Sylvia (Vitz) S.; m. Rita Goran, Apr. 11, 1954; children: Norman, Laurence Scott BS in Mech. Engring., U. Ill., 1953. Torpedo designer U.S. Naval Ordnance, Forest Park, Ill., 1953-54; chief engr. Gen. Aluminum Corp., Chgo., 1954-55; product designer Chgo. Aerial Industries, Melrose Park, Ill., 1955-58; chief designer Emil J. Paidar Co., Chgo., 1958-59; founder, pres. Budd Engring. Corp., Chgo., 1959—. Dir. Dur-A-Case Corp., Chgo.; design cons. to numerous corps. Holder more than 125 patents in more than 40 fields including multimemory for power seats and electrified office panel sys., Piezo ink jet valves; contbr. articles to tech. publs. Mem. math., sci. and English adv. bds. Niles Twp. High Schs., Skokie, Ill., 1975-79; electronic cons. Chgo. Police Dept., 1964 Winner, Internat. Extrusion Design Competition, 1975; nominated Presdl. Medal Technology Sen. Paul Simon and Rep. Dan Rostenkowski, 1986; named Inventor of Yr. Patent Law Assn. Chgo., 1986. Mem. ASME, Soc. Plastics Engrs., Soc. Mfg. Engrs., Inventor's Coun., Soc. Automotive Engrs., Pres.'s Assn. Ill. Office: Skokie IL 60076 *A true professional can perform any time, any place, independent of his mood.*

SIEGAL, JUDY A. social services administrator; b. Chgo., July 28, 1947; d. Sidney and Carolyn Hedish Axelrod; m. Barry Preston Siegal, Dec. 29, 1968; children: Joshua, Kimberly, Marni. BA, U. Mich., 1969. Dir. coop. edn. Roosevelt U., Chgo., 1970—74; vol. coord. Resource Ctr. for Elderly, Arlington Heights, Ill., 1988—92; cmty. affairs coord. Sportmart, Inc., Wheeling, Ill., 1992—98; region dir. Women's Am. Ort, Northbrook, Ill., 1998—2000, Midwest dir. major gifts, 2000—02, Midwest dir. devel., 2002—. Mem. Chgo. Coun. on Planned Giving; bd. dirs. Congregation Bnai Tikvah, Deerfield, Ill. Recipient Pres.' award, Internat. Mass Retail Assn., Washington, 1996. Mem.: Women in Devel. North, Miriam's Path. Jewish. Avocations: reading, needlecrafts, singing. Office: Women's Am Ort 3701 Commercial Northbrook IL 60062 E-mail: jsiegal@waort.org.

SIEGAL, PEGGY, public relations executive; Owner Smith & Siegal Public Relations, The Peggy Siegal Co., Lizzie Grubman / Peggy Siegal Public Relations, 2000—01, Harriet Weintraub / Peggy Siegal Public Relations, 2001—. Co-prodr.(with Barbara Koppel): (films) The Hamptons, 2002. Office: Harriet Weintraub/Peggy Siegal PR 140 W 57th St New York NY 10019

SIEGAL, RITA GORAN, engineering company executive; b. Chgo., July 16, 1934; d. Leonard and Anabelle (Soloway) Goran; m. Burton L. Siegal, Apr. 11, 1954; children: Norman, Laurence Scott. Student, U. Ill., 1951-53; BA, DePaul U., 1956. Cert. elem. tchr., Ill. Tchr. Chgo. Public Schs., 1956-58; founder, chief exec. officer Budd Engring. Corp., Skokie, Ill., 1959—; founder, pres. Easy Living Products Co., Skokie, 1960—; pvt. practice in interior design, Chgo., 1968-73; dist. sales mgr. Super Girls, Skokie, 1976. Lectr. Northwestern U., 1983; guest speaker nat. radio and TV, 1979—. Contbr. to profl. jours. Mem. adv. bd. Skokie High Schs., 1975-79; advisor Cub Scouts Skokie coun. Boy Scouts Am., 1975; bus. mgr. Nutrition for Optimal Health Assn., Winnetka, Ill., 1980-82, pres., 1982-84, v.p. med./profl., 1985-93; leader Great Books Found., 1972; founder Profit Plus Investment, 1970; bd. dirs. Noha, Internat. Named Prominent Alumni, Sullivan H.S., 2001; recipient Cub Scout awards, Boy Scouts Am., 1971—72, Nat. Charlotte Danstrom award, Nat. Women of Achievement, 1988, Corp. Achievement award, 1988. Mem. North Shore Women in Mgmt. (pres, 1987-88), Presidents Assn. Ill. (bd. dirs 1990-94, membership chair 1991-93), Inventors Coun., Oriental Art Soc. Chgo. (publicity chair). Office: Skokie IL *Believe in yourself, if others can do it so can you. Prioritize so you are not overwhelmed by your responsibilities.*

SIEGAL, SUSAN E. biotechnology company executive; With Bio Red Lab., Bio Image/Kodak, E.I. DuPont, Amersham Pharmacia Biotech; sr. v.p. mktg. & sales Affymetrix, Inc., Santa Clara, Calif., 1998—99, pres., 1999—. Office: Affymetrix Inc 3380 Central Expwy Santa Clara CA 95051

SIEGAN, BERNARD HERBERT, lawyer, educator; b. Chgo., July 28, 1924; s. David and Jeannette S.; m. Sharon Goldberg, June 15, 1952 (dec. Feb. 1985); m. Shelley Zifferblatt, Nov. 19, 1995. AA, Herzl. Jr. Coll., Chgo., 1943, 46; Student, Roosevelt Coll., Chgo., 1946-47; JD, U. Chgo., 1949. Bar: Ill. 1950. Practiced in, Chgo.; partner firm Siegan & Karlin, 1952-73; pres., sec. various small corps. and gen. partner in partnerships engaged in real estate ownership and devel., 1955-70; weekly columnist Freedom newspaper chain, other papers, 1974-79. Cons. law and econs. program U. Chgo. Law Sch., 1970-73; adj. prof. law U. San Diego Law Sch., 1973-74, Disting. prof., 1975—; adj. scholar Cato Inst., Washington, 1991—, Heritage Found., 1992—; cons. windfalls and wipeouts project HUD, 1973-74; cons. FTC, 1985-86, U.S. Justice Dept., dir. constl. bibliog. project, 1986-88; keynote speaker 5th Internat. Conf. on Urbanism, Porto Alegre, Brazil, 1989; nominated by Pres. Reagan to U.S. Ct. Appeals (9th cir.) Feb. 2, 1987, confirmation denied July 14, 1988 by party line vote Senate Judiciary Com. Author: Land Use Without Zoning, 1972, Spanish edit., 1995, Other People's Property, 1976, Economic Liberties and the Constitution, 1980, The Supreme Court's Constitution: An Inquiry Into Judicial Review and Its Impact on Society, 1987, Drafting a Constitution for a Nation or Republic Emerging into Freedom, 1992, 2d edit., 1994, Portuguese, Ukrainian, Polish and Spanish edits., 1993, Property and Freedom: The Constitution, Supreme Court and Land Use Regulation, 1997, Adapting a Constitution to Protect Freedom and Provide Abundance (in Bulgarian), 1998, Property Rights: From Magna Carta to the Fourteenth Amendment, 2001; editor: Planning without Prices, 1977, The Interaction of Economics and the Law, 1977, Regulation, Economics and the Law, 1979, Government, Regulation and the Economy, 1980. Mem. pres.-elect's Task Force on Housing, 1980-81; mem. Pres.'s Commn. on Housing, 1981-82; mem. Nat. Commn. on bicentannial of U.S. Constn., 1985-91; chmn. adv. com. Affordable Housing Conf., San Diego, 1985, Rights of Regulated Conf., Coronado, Calif., 1976; chmn. Conf. on the Taking Issue, 1976; mem. Houston Regional Urban Design Team, Study of Houston, 1990; mem. U.S. team Bulgarian Econ. Growth and Transition Project, 1990; mem. devel. bd. Mingei Internat. Mus. World Folk Art, 1981-84. Served with AUS, 1943-46. Research fellow law and econs. U. Chgo. Law Sch., 1968-69; Urban Land Inst. research fellow, 1976-86; recipient Leander J. Monks Meml. Fund award Inst. Humane Studies, 1972, George Washington medal Freedom Founds. at Valley Forge, 1981, Spl. award Liberal Inst. of Rio Grande do Sul, Porto Alegre, Brazil, 1989, Thorsnes award for outstanding legal scholarship, 1998; named Univ. Prof., U. San Diego, 1997-98.

SIEGEL, ABRAHAM J. economics educator, academic administrator; b. N.Y.C., Nov. 6, 1922; s. Samuel J. and Dora (Drach) S.; m. Lillian Wakshull, Dec. 22, 1946; children: Emily Jean Siegel Stangle, Paul Howard, Barbara Ann Pugliese. BA summa cum laude, CCNY, 1943; MA, Columbia U., 1949; PhD, U. Calif., Berkeley, 1961. Instr. dept. econs. CCNY, 1947-49; research economist Inst. Indsl. Relations, U. Calif., Berkeley, 1952-54; instr. dept. econs. M.I.T., Cambridge, 1954-56, asst. prof., 1956-59, assoc. prof., 1959-64, prof. dept. econs. Sloan Sch. Mgmt., 1964-93, assoc. dean Sloan Sch. Mgmt., 1967-80, dean, 1980-87, prof. emeritus, sr. lectr., 1993—. Spl. lectr. Trade Union Program, Harvard U., 1961-64; vis. prof. Brandeis U., 1956-60; vis. prin. mem. div. Internat. Inst. Labour Studies, Internat. Labour Office, Geneva, 1964-65; asso. staff dir. Com. Econ. Devel., Study Group on Nat. Labor Policy, 1960-61; trustee, chmn. adminstrv. com. M.I.T. Retirement Plan for Staff Mems., 1970-91. Co-author: Industrial Relations in the Pacific Coast Longshore Industry, 1956, The Public Interest in National Labor Policy, 1961, The Impact of Computers on Collective Bargaining, 1969, Unfinished Business: An Agenda for Labor, Management and the Public, 1978. Bd. dirs. Whitehead Inst. Biomed. Rsch., Analysis Group, Inc., Internat. Data Group; mem. Framingham Sch. Com., South Middlesex Regional Dist. Vocat. Sch. Com., 1968-71. With USAF, 1943-46. Mem. Am. Econ. Assn., Indsl. Relations Research Assn., Nat. Acad. Arbitrators, Am. Arbitration Assn. (mem. various panels), Inst. Mgmt. Scis. Bus. Roundtable (exec. com.), Phi Beta Kappa. Office: MIT Sloan Sch Mgmt 50 Memorial Dr Cambridge MA 02142-1347 Home: 217 Del Pond Dr Canton MA 02021-2754

SIEGEL, ARTHUR HERBERT, finance company executive; b. N.Y.C., Jan. 5, 1938; s. Joseph Kenneth and Gertrude Sylvia (Hecker) Siegel; m. Eleanor Novick, June 5, 1960; children: Joan Aileen, Linda Beth, Mark Eric. AB, Columbia U., 1958, MBA, 1960. With Price Waterhouse, N.Y.C., 1960-97, mgr. L.I., 1961-72, ptnr. Boston, 1972-83, nat. dir. acctg. svcs. N.Y.C., 1984-88, vice chmn. bus. adv. and auditing svcs., 1988-95; mem. Fin. Acctg. Stds. Bd. Emerging Issues Task Force, 1985-88, Fin. Acctg. Stds. Adv. Coun., 1985-90; mem. adv. coun. Sch. Acctg., U. So. Calif., 1987-89. Exec. dir. Independence Stds. Bd., 1997—2001; bd. dirs., chmn. audit com. Rotech Healthcare, Inc., 2002—. Bd. dirs. Nat. Multiple Sclerosis Soc., treas., exec. com., chmn. fin. com., 1990—98. Mem.: AICPA (chmn. task force risks and uncertainties 1985—87, chmn. SEC practice exec. com. 1994—97), Mass. Soc. CPAs (pres.-elect 1983), N.Y. Soc. CPAs (Silver Medal award), Beta Gamma Sigma. Home and Office: Apt 3A 179 E 70th St New York NY 10021-5109 Office Phone: 212-327-0794. E-mail: ASiegs@ix.netcom.com.

SIEGEL, BARRY, reporter; b. St. Louis, Sept. 7, 1949; m. Marti Devore; 1 child, Alexandra Nicole. BA in English, Pomona Coll., 1971; MS in Journalism, Columbia U., 1972. Stringer L.A. bur. Newsweek, L.A., 1973; news editor West Coast Women's Wear Daily, 1973—76; writer View sect. L.A. Times, 1976—78, writer spl. assignment, 1979, corr. Nat., 1980—83, corr./sr. writer, 1983—. Vis. lectr. U. So. Calif., 1988. Author: A Death in White Bear Lake, 1990, Shades of Gray, 1992, The Perfect Witness, 1998, Actual Innocence, 1999; contbr. articles to profl. jours. Recipient USA West Lit. award in Journalism, PEN Ctr., 2000, USA West Journalism award, 1987, Silver Gavel award, ABA, 1985, Golden Medallion Media award, State Bar Calif., 1984, Paul Tobenkin Meml. award, 1997. Office: LA Times 202 W 1st St Los Angeles CA 90012

SIEGEL, BARRY ALAN, nuclear radiologist; b. Nashville, Dec. 30, 1944; s. Walter G. Siegel and Lillian B. Ivener; m. Pamela M. Mandel, Aug. 18, 1968 (div. Mar. 1981); children: Peter A., William A.; m. Marilyn J. Siegel, Jan. 29, 1983. AB, Washington U., St. Louis, 1966, MD, 1969. Diplomate Am. Bd. Nuc. Medicine, Am. Bd. Radiology. Intern Barnes Hosp., St. Louis, 1969-70; from resident in radiology to prof. Mallinckrodt Inst. Radiology Washington U., 1970—79, prof. radiology Mallinckrodt Inst. Radiology, 1979—, dir. divsn. nuc. medicine Mallinckrodt Inst. Radiology, 1973—, with Siteman Cancer Ctr. Mallinckrodt Inst. Radiology, 1996—. Dir. Am. Bd. Nuc. Medicine, L.A., 1985—90, sec., 1990; chmn. adv. com. on med. uses of isotopes NRC, Washington, 1990—96; chmn. radiopharm. drugs adv. com. FDA, Rockville, Md., 1982—85, radiol. devices panel, 1992—95; mem. U.S. Pharmacopeia Adv. Panel on Radiopharms., 1975—2000, Armed Forces Radiobiol. Rsch. Inst., Bethesda; coun. experts, chair radiopharm. expert com. U.S. Pharmacopoeial Conv., 2000—. Author, editor 33 books; contbr. articles to profl. jours., chpts. in books. Maj. USAF, 1974—76. Recipient Commr.'s Spl. citation U.S. FDA, 1988, Honor citation U.S. Pharmacopeial Conv., 1995, 2000. Fellow: ACP, Am. Coll. Nuc. Physicians, Am. Coll. Radiology (vice chmn. commn. on nuc. medicine 1981—93, editor-in-chief profl. self evaln. program 1988—2002); mem.: ACS (chmn. diagnostic imaging com. oncology group 1998—, mem. exec. com. 2000—), AMA, Acad. Molecular Imaging (chair inst. Clin. PET coun. 2001—02, bd. dirs. 2004—), Soc. Nuc. Medicine (trustee 1981—85, 1987—91, Georg Charles de Hevesy Nuclear Pioneer award 2003), Radiol. Soc. N.Am., Assn. Univ. Radiologists, Am. Roentgen Ray Soc. Office: Washington U Mallinckrodt Inst Radiology 510 S Kingshighway Blvd Saint Louis MO 63110-1016 Office Phone: 314-362-2809. Business E-Mail: siegelb@mir.wustl.edu.

SIEGEL, BENJAMIN, pediatrician; b. Boston, June 5, 1942; s. Max and Elaine Siegel; m. Jane Rosenberg, Sept. 25, 1965; children: Elizabeth Ellen, Rebecca Hope. BA, Boston U., 1963; MD, U. Chgo., 1967. Diplomate Am. Acad. Pediatrics. Intern to resident Boston City Hosp., Boston, 1967—69; resident Montefiore Hosp., Bronx, NY; dir. med. student edn. pediat. Boston U. Sch. Medicine, 1979—, prof. pediat. and psychiatry, 1991—. Sr. editor Ambulatory Pediat. Bd. dirs. City Wide Parents Coun., Boston, 1982—83, human svcs. collaborative, Boston pub., 1983—89; cons., mem. work group revision of state health curriculum frameworks, k-12 State Dept of Edn., Mass., 1998—98. Recipient Collegium Disting. Alumni award, Boston U. Coll. Liberal Arts, 1983. Mem.: Ambulatory Ped. Assn., Am. Acad. Ped., Psychoanalytic Couple and Family Inst. New Eng. (bd. dirs. 1998—), Am. Acad. Physician and Patient (bd. dirs. 1996—2002). Jewish. Avocations: classical music, reading, jogging, travel. Home: 148 West Canton St Boston MA 02118 Office: Boston Med Ctr 91 EConcord St Mat 417 Boston MA 02118 Business E-Mail: bsiegel@bu.edu.

SIEGEL, BERNARD LOUIS, lawyer; b. Pitts., Sept. 15, 1938; s. Ralph Robert and Frieda Sara (Stein) S.; m. Marcia Margolis, Sept. 3, 1961 (div. Aug. 1983); children: Jonathan, Sharon; m. Susan Erickson, Aug. 31, 1997 (div. June 2001). BA, Brandeis U., 1960; JD, Harvard U., 1963. Bar: Pa. 1964, U.S. Dist. Ct. (we. dist.) Pa. 1964, U.S. Dist. Ct. (ea. dist.) Pa. 1985, U.S. Ct. Appeals (3d cir.) 1985, U.S. Supreme Ct. 1985. Assoc. Silin, Eckert & Burke, Erie, Pa., 1963-66; ptnr. Silin, Eckert, Burke & Siegel, Erie, 1966-73; 1st asst. dist. atty. Erie County, 1972-76; dep. atty. gen. Pa. Dept. Justice, Phila., 1976-78; dep. dist. atty. Dist. Atty. of Phila., 1978-86; pvt. practice Phila., 1986—. Adj. prof. La Salle U., Phila., 1986—95; lectr. Fed. Law Enforcement Tng. Ctr., Glynco, Ga., 1986—97, Mercyhurst Coll., Erie, 1974—76, Nat. Coll. Dist. Attys., Houston, 1978—85; adj. prof. Temple U. law sch., 1995—; mem. criminal rules com. Pa. Supreme Ct., Phila., 1976—85; commr. Pa. Crime Commn., Harrisburg, 1976—79. Author: (with others) Pennsylvania Grand Jury Practice, 1983, By No Extraordinary Means, 1986. Mem.: ABA, Phila. Bar Assn. (chmn. criminal justice sect. 1990—91), Pa. Bar Assn. (chmn.

criminal law sect. 1988—91), Pa. Assn. Criminal Def. Lawyers (bd. dirs. 1988—, treas. 2002—04, v.p. 2004—), Nat. Assn. Criminal Def. Lawyers. Democrat. Jewish. Avocations: bicycling, reading, hiking. Office: 1515 Market St Ste 1915 Philadelphia PA 19102-1920 Office Phone: 215-751-9830. E-mail: blsesq@snip.net.

SIEGEL, BETTY LENTZ, university president; b. Cumberland, Ky., Jan. 24, 1931; d. Carl N. and Vera (Hogg) Lentz; m. Joel H. Siegel, June 6; children: David Jonathan, Michael Jeremy. BA, Wake Forest U., 1952; M.Ed., U. N.C., 1953; PhD, Fla. State U., 1961; postgrad., Ind. U., 1964-66; hon. doctorate, Miami U., 1985, Cumberland Coll., 1985, Ea. Ky. U., 1992, Morehead State U., 2002. Asst. prof. Lenoir Rhyne Coll., Hickory, N.C., 1956-59; assoc. prof., 1961-64; asst. prof. U. Fla., Gainesville, 1967-70, assoc. prof., 1970-72, prof., 1973-76, dean acad. affairs for continuing edn., 1972-76; dean Sch. Edn. and Psychology Western Carolina U., Cullowhee, N.C., 1976-81; pres. Kennesaw State U., Marietta, Ga., 1981—. Bd. dirs. Nat. Services Industries; cons. numerous sch. systems. Author: Problem Situations in Teaching, 1971, Becoming An Invitational Leader, 2002; contbr. articles to profl. jours. Bd. dirs. United Way Atlanta, Ga. Partnership for Excellence in Edn., Ga. Coun. Econ. Edn., Northside Hosp. Found., Atlanta Ballet; Ga. rep. so. growth policy bd. Commn. on Future of South, 1998. Recipient Outstanding Tchr. award U. Fla., 1969; Mortar Bd. Woman of Yr. award U. Fla., 1973, Mortar Bd. Educator of Yr., Ga. State U., 1983, CASE award, 1986, Alumna of Yr. award Wake Forest U., 1987, "Grad Made Good" award Fla. State U. Alumni Assn, Omicron Delta Kappa, 1991, Spirit of Life award City of Hope, 1992, Woman of Achievement award Cobb Chamber YWCA, 1992; named One of 100 Most Influential People in State of Ga., Ga. Trend Mag., Outstanding Alumni, Fla. State U. Coll. Edn. Alumni Assn., 1992, Cobb Citizen of the Yr. award, 1996, Ga. Woman of Yr. Ga. Commn. Women, 1997. Mem. Am. Psychol. Assn., Am. Assn. State Colls. and Univs. (bd. dirs., chmn. 1990), Am. Coun. Edn. (bd. dirs., bd. advisors), Am. Inst. Mng. Diversity (bd. dis.), Soc. Internat. Bus. Fellows, Internat. Alliance for Invitational Edn. (co-founder, co-dir.), Bus./Higher Edn. Forum, mem. exec. com.), Cobb C. of C. (chair 1996), Kiwanis (Atlanta chpt.), Phi Alpha Theta, Pi Kappa Delta, Alpha Psi Omega, Kappa Delta Pi, Pi Lambda Theta, Phi Delta Kappa, Delta Kappa Gamma. Baptist. Office: Kennesaw State Univ Office of the President 1000 Chastain Rd NW Kennesaw GA 30144-5591

SIEGEL, CAROLE ETHEL, mathematician; b. N.Y., Sept. 29, 1936; d. David and Helen (Mayer) Schore; m. Bertram Siegel, Aug. 18, 1957; children: Sharon, David. BA in Math., NYU, 1957, MS in Math., 1959, PhD in Math., 1963. With computer dept. Atomic Energy Commn., 1957-59; rsch. asst. Courant Inst. of Math. Sci., 1959-63; rsch. scientist dept. of engring. NYU, N.Y.C., 1963-64; rsch. math. Info. Scis. Div. Rockland Rsch. Inst., Orangeburg, N.Y., 1965-74; head Epidemiology and Health Svcs. Rsch. Lab Stat. Scis., Epidemiology divsn. Nathan S. Kline Inst. Psychiat. Rsch., Orangeburg, NY, 1974—2003, dir. stats. and rsch. div., 2003—. Adj. assoc. prof. Wagner Grad. Sch. Pub. Svc., NYU; rsch. prof. dept. psychiatry NYU, 1987—; dep. dir. WHO Collaborating Ctr., Nathan S. Kline Inst., 1987—; grant reviewer NIHM, 1988—; prin. investigator Ctr. for Study of Issues in Public Mental Health, NIMH, 1993—, prin. investigator, dir., 1995—. Editor: (with S. Fischer) Psychiatric Records in Mental Health Care, 1981; contbr. articles to profl. jours. Recipient Carl Taube award, mental health sect. APHA, 2001; grantee SAMHSA, CMHS, 1997—, NIMH, 1993—, 1988—91, Nat. Ctr. for Health Svcs. Rsch., 1979—82, Nat. Inst. Alcohol Abuse, 1978—82. Mem. Assn. for Health Svcs. Rsch., Am. Soc. Clin. Pharmacology and Therapeutics, Assn. Women in Math., Am. Statis. Assn. Avocations: pottery, gardening, cooking. Office: Nathan S Kline Inst Orangeburg NY 10962

SIEGEL, DAVID BURTON, lawyer; b. N.Y.C., Mar. 22, 1949; s. Henry and Ruth (Rosenzweig) S.; m. Barbara Joan Brown, Aug. 6, 1972; children: Jeffrey Spencer, Carolyn Rose, Laura Ellen. AB, Columbia Coll., 1971; JD, NYU, 1974. Assoc. atty. Kelley Drye & Warren, N.Y.C., 1974-77; corp. counsel W.R. Grace & Co., N.Y.C., 1977-87, asst. gen. counsel, 1987-91, assoc. gen. counsel Boca Raton, Fla., 1991-93, v.p., dep. gen. counsel, 1993-98, sr. v.p., gen. counsel and sec., 1998-2001, sr. v.p., gen. counsel, chief restructuring officer, 2001—. Mem. Econ. Coun. Palm Beach County, Fla., 1993-99; mem. bd. dirs. Edn. Partnership of Palm Beach County, 1994-96, treas., 1995-96. Home: 11150 Homewood Rd Ellicott City MD 21042-2807 Office: WR Grace & Co 7500 Grace Dr Columbia MD 21044-4029 E-mail: david.siegel@grace.com.

SIEGEL, EDWARD, lawyer; b. Asbury Park, N.J., Jan. 15, 1931; s. Nathan Albert and Fannie Siegel; m. Helen Dorothy Haber, Aug. 29, 1954; children: Sharon, Frances. BA, U. Fla., 1952, JD, 1955. Bar: Fla. 1955. Spl. asst. atty. gen. Office Atty. Gen. Fla., Tallahassee, 1955; ptnr. Adams, Rothstein & Siegel, Jacksonville, Fla., 1957-90. Author: How to Avoid Lawyers, 1969, Defend Yourself! The Moneysworth Legal Advisor, 1972, Just Like a Lawyer, 1993; mem. editorial bd. Fla. Bar Jour., 1979-86. Bd. dirs. Jacksonville Jewish Ctr., 1968-70; bd. dirs., v.p. Jewish Family and Children's Svcs., 1970-75; trustee Jacksonville Libr. Bd., 1978-82. Served as 1st lt. USAF, 1955-57. Mem. ABA, Fla. Bar Assn., Jacksonville Bar Assn. (chmn. fee arbitration com. 1976-77), Blue Key, Order of Coif, Phi Beta Kappa. Democrat. Home: 6855 San Sabastian Ave Jacksonville FL 32217-2731

SIEGEL, FREDERIC RICHARD, geology educator; b. Chelsea, Mass., Feb. 8, 1932; s. Louis and Eva (Minsky) S.; m. Felisa Matilde Puszkin, Mar. 3, 1962; children: Gabriela Davina, Galia Dinah. BA, Harvard U., 1954; MS, U. Kans., 1958, PhD, 1961. Prof. titular Universidad Nacional de Tucuman, Argentina, 1961-63; head geochemistry divsn. Kans. Geol. Survey, Lawrence, 1963-65; assoc. prof. geochemistry George Washington U., Washington, 1965-69, prof., 1969-99, prof. emeritus geochemistry, 1999—, dir. geochemistry program, 1965-99, chmn. dept. geology, 1976-86. Tech. cons. UN Devel. program, Havana, Cuba, 1980. Author: Applied Geochemistry, 1974, Geoquimica Aplicada, 1992, Natural and Anthropogenic Hazards in Development Planning, 1996, Environmental Geochemistry of Potentially Toxic Metals, 2001; co-author: Geochimica Ambientale, 2004; editor: Review of Research on Modern Problems in Geochemistry, 1979. With U.S. Army, 1954-56; ETO. Recipient Erasmus Haworth award Dept. Geology, U. Kans., 1958; Fulbright prof., 1970, Best Paper award Energy Minerals divsn. Am. Assn. Petroleum Geologists, 1989. Mem. Assn. Exploration Geochemists (councillor 1988-95), Geochem. Soc., Internat. Assn. Geochemists and Cosmochemists, Soc. Environ. Geochemistry and Health. Jewish. Home: 4353 Yuma St NW Washington DC 20016-2027 Office: George Washington U 2029 G St NW Washington DC 20052-4211 E-mail: nzkara@gwu.edu.

SIEGEL, GEORGE HENRY, international business development consultant; b. Bklyn., Oct. 8, 1926; s. Samuel S. and Sara Siegel; m. Lenore D. Greenberg, Oct. 28, 1951; children: Arthur B., Ellen S. BEE, CCNY, 1948; MS Indsl. Engring, NYU, 1951. Registered profl. engr., N.Y. From engr. to gen. mgr. Gen. Electric Corp., Syracuse, Utica and Binghamton, N.Y., 1951-74; v.p., gen. mgr. flight systems div. Bendix Corp., 1974-77, chief tech. officer, 1977-79, v.p., gen. mgr. diesel engine controls, 1979-82; v.p., group exec. Bendix Automation Co., Cleve., 1983-84; v.p. tech. Allied-Signal Internat., Morristown, N.J., 1984-90; v.p. Volt Tech. Svcs. Co., N.Y.C., 1991-93; pres. Point North Assocs., Inc., Madison, N.J., 1990—. Invited guest lectr. UCLA, 1960-63. Bd. visitors Oakland U., Rochester, Mich., 1977-83. Served with AUS, 1944-46. Mem. IEEE (sr., life, sect. chmn. 1965), Soc. Automotive Engrs. Office: Point North Assocs Inc PO Box 907 Madison NJ 07940-0907 E-mail: siegelgh@att.net.

SIEGEL, HARRIS G. managing editor; Grad., Syracuse U. Mng. editor design and photography Asbury Park Press, N.J., 1995—. Spkr. Am. Press Inst.; mem. news design desk Detroit Free Press. Mem. Soc. for News Design (spkr. 2 ann. internat. confs., 19th edit. coord. contest, Gold medal, 5 Silver medals, Judges Spl. Recognition award, others). Avocation: playing roller-hockey. Office: Asbury Park Press 3601 Hwy 66 Neptune NJ 07753-2694

SIEGEL, HERBERT BERNARD, management consultant; b. N.Y.C., Mar. 10, 1934; s. Jacob and Clara Dora (Goldgeier) S.; m. Joan Miriam Goodkin, Nov. 6, 1955; children: Jeffrey Roy, Lori Robin, Amy Hope, Jonathan Stuart. Degree, NYU, 1959, postgrad. in bus., 1960—63, Harvard U., 1975; PhD in Internat. Law, Columbia U., 1999; Internat. del. to, Coll. of Law of Eng. and Wales, 2003. Diplomate Am. Acad. Profl. Cons. and Legal Experts; cert. profl. mgmt. cons.; chartered cons., U.K.; accredited profl. cons. Pres. Emle Industries, Inc., N.Y.C., 1968-72; fed. pres. trustee Toys R Us, N.Y.C., 1973-78; pres. Nat. Silver Co., N.Y.C., 1973-78, F.B. Rogers Silver Co., N.Y.C., 1979-82; pres., chief exec. officer Quaker City Steel Co., 1980-86, Seal-Kap Packaging Co., N.Y.C., 1980-90, J. Ramsey Reese, Inc., Tarrytown, N.Y., 1980-87; pres. Deerhill Devel. Corp., 1980-87, Columbia Profl. Baseball Club, Inc., 1980-87; pres., CEO J.R. Reese Enterprises, Ltd. et al, 1989—91; prin. officer Whitestone Cons. Group, Ltd., 1991—; cons.-in-residence Magrill Bros., Inc., 2004—. Thesis examiner Grad. Sch. Banking, Rutgers U., 1963-64; chmn. Fin-Tec Corp.; lectr. Grad. Sch. Mgmt. and Orgn., Yale U.; bd. dirs. Swissco Industries, Inc., Fin-Tec Svc. Corp., Nat. Coin Entertainment Co. Inc., Corp. Fin. Internat., Motorcycle Malls of Am., Inc., Advanced Rehab. Ctrs., Inc., N.Y. Pacific Exch. Ltd., Silvergull Industries Inc., Havemeyer Equities, Inc., Lionville Packing Co., Coast-to-Coast Mktg. Am., Inc.; trustee Dime Savs. Bank of Williamsburg, N.Y.C., Neisner Bros. Dept. Stores, United Cerebral Palsey, Nassau; counsellor internat. bus. law. Author: A Trustee's View of Chapter Ten, 1981, Tomorrow's America, Made Today in the U.S.A., 1993, The Entropy of Government Deficits, 1995, Corporate Rehabilitation After Bankruptcy, 1995, The Masquerade of Cost Cutting, 1996, Market Economics for Multinational Corporations, 1997, International Trade and the Competitive Environment, 1997, Accounting Strategies for Multinational Corporations, 1998, Statistics That Measure the Wealth of Multinational Companies, 1998, Developments and Organizational Behavior in International Business Environments, 1998, Privatization: A Social Milestone or Millstone?, 1999. Served U.S. Army, 1955—57. Mem. ABA, Internat. Bar Assn., Am. Lawyers Expert Network, Internat. Studies Assn., Am. Mgmt. Assn., Am. Bankruptcy Inst., Am. Acad. Profl. Cons. and Experts, N.Y. Acad. Sci., NYU Alumni Club, Turnaround Mgmt. Assn., Soc. of Profls. in Dispute Resolutions, Prime Raters Fin. Club (pres.), Inst. Bus. Appraisers, Am. Mensa Soc., Am. Cons. League. Office Phone: 516-431-7300. E-mail: herb515@rcn.com.

SIEGEL, HERBERT JAY, communications executive, director; b. Phila., May 7, 1928; s. Jacob and Fritzi (Stern) S.; m. Ann F. Levy, June 29, 1950; children: John C., William D. BA in Journalism, Lehigh U., 1950. Sec., dir. Official Films, Inc., N.Y.C., 1951-54; v.p., dir. Bev-Rich Products, Inc., Phila., 1955-56; chmn. bd. Westley Industries, Inc., Cleve., 1955-58; v.p. Phila. Ice Hockey Club, Inc., 1955-60; chmn. bd. Fort Pitt Industries, Inc., Pitts., 1956-58, Seeburg Corp., 1958-60, Centlivre Brewing Corp., Ft. Wayne, Ind., 1959-61; dir. Baldwin Rubber Co., Pontiac, Mich., Mono-Sol Corp., Gary, Inc., 1959-62; chmn. bd. Baldwin-Montrose Chem. Co., 1960-67; pres., chmn. bd. Gen. Artists Corp., 1960-64, chmn., 1960-62; chmn. bd., pres. Chris-Craft Industries, Inc., 1968—2001; chmn. bd. BHC Comm. Inc., 1977—2001, pres., 1977-96; chmn. bd. dirs. United TV, Inc., 1982—2001, chmn. bd., 1982-96, CEO, 1983-90; bd. dirs. Warner Communications, Inc., 1984-89. Bd. dirs. Piper Aircraft Corp., 1971-77, Paramount Pictures, 1963-64, Harvard-Mahoney Neurosci. Inst., 2000. Bd. dirs. Friends of Israel Defense Forces, 1996—, Research to Prevent Blindness, 2000—, Phoenix House, 1978-81; bd. advisors Vets. Bedside Network, 1980-90; v.p. Friars Nat. Assn. Found., 1980—, Chas. A. Dana Found., Inc., 1996—; trustee Lehigh U., 1989-92, Blair Acad., 1985-92. Office: News America Inc 767 5th Ave Fl 46 New York NY 10153-0023

SIEGEL, HILDEGARDE JULIA, retired nursing educator; b. Wauwatosa, Wis., Mar. 20, 1923; d. Arthur Charles and Lillie Wilhelmena Siegel. BSPHN summa cum laude, Marquette U., Milw., 1961; MPH, U.Minn., Mpls., 1963, PhD, 1967. RN Wis. State Bd. of Nursing, 1961. Pub. health nurse Waukesha County Health Dept., Wis., 1959—61; dept. dir. Wis. Lung Assn., Milw., 1961—62; instr. and assoc. Marquette U., Milw., 1964—65, assoc. prof., 1967—69; prof. grads. U. Wis., Oshkosh, 1969—78; assoc. dean academic affairs Marquette U. Coll. of Nursing, Milw., 1978—88; prof. emeritus Marquette U., Milw., 1988—. Dept. dir. Wis. Lung Assn., 1961—62; dir. Peace Corps projects Marquette U., Milw., 1964—65; pres. Wis. League for Nursing, Milw., 1970—72, Wis. Nurses Assn., Madison, 1974—75; co-chair joint practice com. State Med. Soc. & Wis. Nurses Assn., Madison, 1972—78. Contbr. articles to profl. jours. Bd. mem. for home care Cmty. Meml. Hosp., Menomonee Falls, Wis., 1984; com. mem. for needs of older residents Village of Menomonee Falls, Menomonee Falls, Wis., 1968—73; mem. - feasibility study Linden Grove Care Ctr., Menomonee Falls, Wis., 1997. Grantee Grant, Nurses Ednl. Funds, NY, NY, 1967; scholar Nursing Edn., U.S. Dept. Pub. Health and Human Svcs., 1962-1965, Scholarship, Am. Jour. of Nursing, NY, NY, 1965-1966. Mem.: Soc. of Scholars, Nurses Ednl. Funds, Internat. Honor Soc. of Nurses (Hall of Fame 1997), Delta gamma chpt. Sigma Theta Tau. Republican. Achievements include Developed an innovative masters program preparing primary care nurse clinicians for joint practice with primary care physicians with special concern for underserved geographic areas. Home: N7890 Town Hall Rd Apt C153 Menomonee Falls WI 53051

SIEGEL, HOWARD JEROME, lawyer; b. Chgo., July 29, 1942; s. Leonard and Idele (Lehrner) S.; m. Diane L. Gerber; children: Sari D., Allison J., James G. BS, U. Ill., 1963; JD, Northwestern U., 1966. Bar: Ill. 1966, U.S. Dist. Ct. (no. dist.) Ill. 1967. Assoc. Ancel, Stonesifer & Glink, Chgo., 1966-70; ptnr. Goldstine & Siegel, Summit, Ill., 1970-75; sole practice Chgo., 1975-77; pres. Wexler, Siegel & Shaw, Ltd., Chgo., 1978-82; ptnr. Keck, Mahin & Cate, Chgo., 1982-95, Neal Gerber & Eisenberg, Chgo., 1995-99; counsel Fagel & Haber, Chgo., 1999—. Bd. dirs. various corps. Mem.: ABA, Chgo. Bar Assn., Ill. Bar Assn., Twin Orchard Country Club (Long Grove, Ill.). Office: FabelHaberLLC 55 E Monroe 40th Fl Chicago IL 60603 E-mail: hsiegel@fagelhaber.com.

SIEGEL, IRA T. publishing executive; b. N.Y.C., Sept. 23, 1944; s. David Aaron and Rose (Minsky) S.; m. Sharon Ruth Sacks, Sept. 5, 1965. BS, NYU, 1965; MBA, L.I. U., 1968. Bus. mgr. Buttenheim Pub. Co., N.Y.C., 1965-72; corp. v.p. rsch. Cahners Pub. Co. div. Reed Pub. USA, Boston, 1972-86; pres., COO, R.R. Bowker Pub. Co. div. Reed Pub. USA, New Providence, N.J., 1986-91; pres. Martindale-Hubbell div. Reed Pub. USA, New Providence, N.J., 1990-91; pres., CEO Reed Reference Pub. (includes R.R. Bowker Co., Martindale-Hubbell, Nat. Register Pub. Co., The Salesman's Guide, Marquis Who's Who), New Providence, N.J., 1991-95, Lexis-Nexis, Dayton, Ohio, 1995-97. Bd. dirs. Seisint (formerly eData.com), Boca Raton, Fla. Address: 16589 Senterra Dr Delray Beach FL 33484-6948

SIEGEL, JACK MORTON, retired biotechnology company executive; b. Sioux City, Iowa, June 11, 1922; s. Harry and Rose (Perlman) S.; m. Betty Virginia Collins, Feb. 22, 1946 (dec. Feb. 1986); children: Jennifer L. Mastricola, Marjorie G., Thomas A.; m. Dolores E. Williams Kinert, Dec. 20, 1991. BS in Chemistry, UCLA, 1944; PhD in Chemistry, Washington U., St. Louis, 1950. Chemist The Clinton Labs., Oak Ridge, Tenn., 1944-46; asst. prof. chemistry U. Ark. Sch. Medicine, Little Rock, 1950-55; chemist, v.p. P-L Biochems. Inc., Milw., 1955-82; v.p., gen. mgr. Pharmacia P-L Biochems. Inc., Milw., 1982-87, pres., 1987-89. Contbr. articles to profl. jours. Mem. AAAS, Am. Chem. Soc. Democrat. Jewish.

SIEGEL, JACOB STUART, writer, consultant, demographer, researcher, genentologist, statistician; b. Phila., July 25, 1921; s. Louis and Anna Siegel; m. Rose Varon Siegel, Jan. 3, 1953 (div.); 1 child, Lorise Varon. BA, U. Pa., 1941, MA, 1943. Demographic statistician US Bur. of Census, Washington, 1943—49, chief of estimates and forecasts unit, 1949—67, spl. asst. to chief, population div., 1967—74, sr. demographic statistician, 1974—82; cons. J. Stuart Siegel Demographic Svcs., North Bethesda, Md., 1975—. Expert witness, 1970—84; lectr. dept. demography Georgetown U., Washington, 1971—76, professorial lectr. dept of demography, 1976—95, sr. rsch. scholar, 1982—95; vis. prof. U. Conn., Storrs, Conn., 1977, U. So. Calif., LA, 1969, U. Calif., Berkeley, 1984, U. Calif., Irvine, 1995, Howard U., Washington, 1989—90, Cornell U., Ithaca, NY, 1988, U. Chile, 1962—63, UN, 1962—63. Co-author, co-editor: Methods and Materials of Demography Vols 1& 2; author: A Generation of Change: A Profile of America's Older Population, 1993, Applied Demography: Applications to Bus., Govt., Law, and Pub. Policy, 2002; co-author: Methods and Materials of Demography, condensed edit., 1976, Methods and Materials of Demography, rev. edit., 2004; contbr. articles to numerous profl. jours. Recipient Silver Medal, US Dept. Commerce, 1947, Gold Medal, 1979. Fellow: Gerontological Soc. Am., Am. Statististical Assn.; mem.: Internat. Union for Sci. Study of Population, Am. Sociological Assn., Population Assn. Am. (bd. mem. 1973—76, v.p. 1978, pres. 1980). Avocations: ballroom dancing, tennis. Home: 5809 Nicholson Ln #808 North Bethesda MD 20852 Office: J Stuart Siegel Demographic Svcs 5809 Nicholson Ln #808 North Bethesda MD 20852 E-mail: jstuartsiegel@cs.com.

SIEGEL, JEFFREY NORTON, lawyer; b. N.Y.C., Nov. 27, 1942; s. George Siegel and Rose (Friedman) Gerber; m. Judith Sharon Chused, June 11, 1966; children: Daniel, Linda. AB, Brown U., 1964; LLB, Harvard U., 1967. Bar: N.Y. 1968. Assoc., ptnr. Golenbock & Barell, N.Y.C., 1967—89; ptnr. Whitman & Ransom, N.Y.C., 1990—93, Shack Siegel Katz & Flaherty, P.C., N.Y.C., 1993—. Mem. bus. com. The Jewish Mus. Mem. ABA, Assn. Bar City N.Y. (com. securities regulation 1987-90, com. profl. responsibility 1979-84), Phi Beta Kappa. Home: 975 Park Ave New York NY 10028-0323 Office: Shack Siegel Katz & Flaherty PC 530 5th Ave New York NY 10036-5101

SIEGEL, JEREMY JAMES, finance educator, consultant; b. Chgo., Nov. 14, 1945; s. Bernard G. and Gertrude (Levite) S.; m. Ellen Ruth Schwartz, Jan. 14, 1980; children: Andrew M., Jeffrey Eric. BA, Columbia U., 1967; PhD, MIT, 1971. Asst. prof. bus. econs. Grad. Sch. Bus. U. Chgo., 1972-76; assoc. prof. fin. Wharton Sch. Bus. U. Pa., Phila., 1976—86, prof. fin. Wharton Sch. Bus., 1986—98, Russell E. Palmer Prof. Fin. Wharton Sch. Bus., 1998—. Macro-econs. coord. The Morgan Bank, (Now J.P. Morgan) N.Y.C., 1984-1999; acad. dir. Securities Industry Inst., 1987—; mem. adv. bd. Asian Securities Industry Assn., 1990—. Author: Revolution on Wall Street, 1993, Stocks for the Long Run, 1994, 98, 2002; contbr. numerous articles to profl. jours. NSF fellow, 1971-72; recipient Graham and Dodd award Assn. for Investment Mgmt., 1992; voted best bus. sch. prof., Bus. Week mag., 1994. Mem. Am. Econ. Assn., Am. Fin. Assn. Office: U Pa Wharton Sch Dept Fin Philadelphia PA 19104*

SIEGEL, JOEL STEVEN, television news correspondent; b. Los Angeles, July 7, 1943; s. Robert and Libby (Kantor) S.; m. Jane Kessler, Nov. 21, 1976 (dec. 1982); m. Melissa Nina De Mayo, Aug. 27, 1985 (div.); m. Ena Swansea, June 21, 1996; 1 child, Dylan. BA, UCLA, 1965, postgrad., 1966-67. Copywriter, producer Carson & Roberts Advt., Los Angeles, 1967-72; freelance writer Rolling Stone mag., Los Angeles Times, others, 1967-77; news anchorman Sta. KMET-FM, Los Angeles, 1972; corr. Sta. WCBS-TV, N.Y.C., 1972-76; corr., film critic Sta. WABC-TV, N.Y.C., 1976—, Good Morning America, N.Y.C., 1980—. Author: (Broadway mus.) The First, 1981 (Tony award nomination 1981). Dir. voter registration drive SCLC/Dr. Martin Luther King, Macon, Ga., 1965; joke writer Robert F. Kennedy, 1968. Served with USAR, 1967-73. Recipient 6 Emmy awards, numerous nominations Nat. Acad. TV Arts and Scis. (N.Y. chpt.), Freedom award B'nai Brith/Anti-Defamation League, 1976. Mem. AFTRA, Dramatists Guild, Drama Desk, Gilda's Club (founding pres.). Democrat. Jewish. Office: Good Morning Am 147 Columbus Ave New York NY 10023-5900

SIEGEL, KRISTI ELLEN, English educator; b. Breckenridge, Minn., Jan. 2, 1951; d. Dennis Elton and Cleo Ardell Hjalmer; m. Ronald Siegel, Sept. 30, 1978; children: Aaron, Adam, Ross, Elizabeth. PhD, U. Wis., Milw., 1991. Lectr. Mt. Mary Coll., Milw., 1992-99, asst. prof., 1999—2002, assoc. prof., 2002—, chair dept. English, 2003—, chair divsn. langs., lit. and comm. Author: Word 97 Fundamentals for the Workplace, 1998, Women's Autobiographies, Culture, Feminism, 1999, 2d edit., 2001, Excel 97/Power Point 97 for the Workplace, 1999; editor: Issues in Travel Writing: Empire, Spectacle, and Displacement, 2002, Gender, Genre and Identity in Women's Travel Writing, 2004; contbg. author: Special Needs Adoption Network: A Series on Adoption and Foster Care Issues, 2000. Mem.: MLA, AAUW (bd. dirs.), Internat. Soc. Travel Writing (steering com.), Soc. Tech. Comm., Autobiography Assn., Nat. Coun. Tchrs. English. Avocations: writing, music, tennis. Office: Mt Mary Coll 2900 N Menomonee River Pky Milwaukee WI 53222 Home: W223 N2257 Meadowood Ln Waukesha WI 53186-1182 Office Phone: 414-258-4810 ext 395. E-mail: siegelkr@mtmary.edu.

SIEGEL, LAURENCE B. investment research company executive, consultant; s. Atarah (Rosenthal) and Seymour Siegel; m. Connie O'Hara, Sept. 27, 1980; children: Joshua, Betsy. BA, U. Chgo., 1975, MBA, 1977. Researcher Am. Enterprise Inst., Washington, 1975—77, Marmon Group, Chgo., 1977—; cons. Ibbotson Assocs., Chgo., 1979—84, mng. dir., 1984—, also bd. dirs. Mem. Moody's Investors Svc., NYC, 1986—88; mem., editorial adv. bd. Journal of Portfolio Mgmt., 1986—; mem. adv. bd. Common Fund, Westport, Conn., 1987—; trustee Oberweis Emerging Growth Fund, 1993—94; mem. Household Personal Portfolios, Chicago, 1993—; mem. adv. bd. Rsch. Found. CFA Inst., 2000—. Author (book): Benchmarks and Investment Management, 2003; contbr. articles to prof. journals. Recipient Graham and Dodd award, Financial Analysts Jour., 1984. Mem.: Hawken Sch. Club, Chicago (class news editor 1984—), U. Chicago Met. Chicago, Nat. Soc. Rate Return Analysts, Am. Fin. Assn. Republican. Jewish. Avocations: folk and rock music, travel. Office: Ibbotson Associates 225 N Michigan Av Ste 700 Chicago IL 60601-7682 Office Phone: 212-573-5347. Business E-Mail: l.siegel@fordfound.org.

SIEGEL, LLOYD HARVEY, architect, real estate developer, consultant; b. NYC, Nov. 27, 1928; s. Saul M. and Lillian (Bell) Siegel; m. Margot Kopsidas Phillips, Oct. 25, 1987. BArch, Princeton U., 1949; MArch, MIT, 1953. Registered architect, N.Y., N.J., Conn., Ohio, Ill., Mich., cert. Nat. Coun. Archtl. Registration Bds. Designer Skidmore, Owings & Merrill, then I. M. Pei & Assocs., then Antonin Raymond, N.Y.C., 1955-60; assoc. Kelly & Gruzen, N.Y.C., 1960-66; dep. health svcs. adminstr. City of N.Y., 1966-70; dep. exec. dir. health and hosps. governing commn. Cook County, Chgo., 1970-76; prin. L.H.S. Cons. in Health Planning, Facility Design & Mgmt., Washington, 1976—, Siegel & Schroeder, P.C., Chgo., 1983-87; dir. Office Architecture & Engring. VA, Washington, 1987-94, dir. Facilities Quality Office, 1994-98, dir. Facilities Mgmt. Svc. Delivery Office, 1999-2001; dir. Facilities Strategic Mgmt. Office, 2001—. Prin. Yacht Harbor Devel. Co., South Haven, Mich., 1983—88, Siegel & Schroeder Developers Inc., Chgo., 1983—88; mem. adv. coms. HEW; mem. pub. adv. panels GSA; mem. adv. com. Legislature State of Ill.; mem. fellowship evaluation com. AIA-Am. Hosp. Assn.; mem. tech. adv. com. Northeastern Ill. Planning Commn.; chmn. Com. Architecture for Health, 1984. Author: (book) Hidden Asset? Interstitial Space, A Critical Evaluation, 1987; photography (permanent collections) Met. Mus. Art, N.Y.C., Mus. Modern Art, others; prin. works include N.Y. World's Fair Spanish Pavillion, N.Y.C. (N.Y. chpt. AIA award, 1964), Williams Meml. Residence, Flushing, N.Y. (Queens C. of C. award, 1964), Hebrew Home for Aged, Riverdale, N.Y. (Bronx C. of C. award, 1966). Recipient Presdl. Fed. Design Achievement award, Pres.'s award, Nat. Inst. Bldg. Scis., 2002; Fulbright fellow, Università di Roma, 1954, Politecnico di Milano, 1955. Fellow: AIA; mem.: Urban Land Inst., Univ. Club, Cosmos Club, Arts Club. Avocations: micology, micophagy, oenology. Home: 3133 Connecticut Ave NW Washington DC 20008-5147 Office: VA 810 Vermont Ave NW Washington DC 20420-0001

SIEGEL, LOUIS PENDLETON, forest products executive; b. Richmond, Va., Nov. 6, 1942; s. John Boschen Jr. and Francis Beale (Tyler) S.; m. Nancy Dicks Blanton, Apr. 10, 1974 (dec. July 1976); m. Nancy Northon, June 26, 1982; children: Kathryn Tyler. AB in Econs., Dartmouth Coll., 1967. Asst. cashier, security researcher First Nat. Citibank, N.Y.C., 1967-71; v.p. security rsch. Drexel Burnham Lambert, N.Y.C., 1971-79; with Potlatch Corp., San Francisco and Spokane, Wash., 1979—, sr. v.p. fin. and adminstrn. San Francisco, 1989, group v.p. wood products and corp. planning, 1989-92, group v.p. pulp and paperboard and corp. planning, 1992-93, exec. v.p. pulp-based ops. and corp. planning, 1993-94, pres., COO San Francisco and Spokane, Wash., 1994-99, also bd. dirs. Spokane, chair, CEO, 1999—. Bd. dirs. San Francisco Fed. Corp., 1985-96. Pres., bd. dirs. Bay Area Sci. Fair, San Francisco, 1989-90; trustee Am. Forest Found., 1999—, chmn. trustees, 2000—; bd. dirs. Nat. Coun. for Air and Stream Improvement, 1999—, chmn.

bd., 2003—; pres. Area One, Boy Scouts Am., 2003—. With USCG, 1964-65. Mem.: Am. Forest and Paper Assn. (bd. dirs. 1999—). Republican. Episcopalian. Avocations: golf, fishing. Office: Potlatch Corp 601 W Riverside Ave Ste 1100 Spokane WA 99201-0603 Office Phone: 509-835-1565.

SIEGEL, LUCY BOSWELL, public relations executive; b. N.Y.C., July 5, 1950; d. Werner Leiser and Carol (Fleischer) Boswell; m. Henry Winter Siegel, Nov. 11, 1979 (div.); children: David Alan Siegel, Joshua Adam Siegel. BA, Conn. Coll., 1972. Assoc. editor Conn. Western, Litchfield, Conn., 1972-73; assoc. editor, editor United Bus. Publ., N.Y.C., 1974—78; mgr. external communications Equitable Life Assurance Soc., N.Y.C., 1978—86; mgr. internat. affairs Cosmo Pub. Relations Corp., Tokyo, 1986-87, dir. internat. affairs, 1987-88; pres. Cosmo Pub. Rels. Corp., N.Y.C., 1988—90, Siegel Assocs. Internat., N.Y.C., 1990—; sr. v.p. Lobsenz Stevens, N.Y.C., 1997—99; sr. prin., mng. dir. Publicis Dialog, N.Y.C., 1999—2000, exec. v.p., group mng. dir., 2000—. Contbr. articles to jours. and mags. Bd. dirs., sec. N.Y.C. chpt. Am. Jewish Com., 1993—. Mem. Pub. Rels. Soc. Am. (treas., exec. com. bd., N.Y.C. chpt. 2001-, exec. bd. internat. sect.), Women Execs. in Pub. Rels. (bd. dirs. 1997-99). Democrat. Jewish. Home: 41 W 96th St Apt 12B New York NY 10025-6519 Office: 4 Herald Sq 950 Ave of the Ams New York NY 10001

SIEGEL, MARC MONROE, television and film producer, writer, director; b. N.Y.C., Dec. 8, 1916; s. Isaac and Annie N. (Natelson) S.; m. Anne Dorothy Fishman, Sept. 8, 1940; 1 son, Peter Kieve. BA, Washington Sq. Coll., 1936; MA, N.Y. U. Sch. Edn., 1938. Free-lance mag. writer, especially for: New Yorker mag, 1948-50; writer: Eternal Light radio series, NBC, N.Y.C., 1950-60; writer-dir-producer: Directions, ABC-TV, N.Y.C., 1961-78; exec. producer chief writer: Heritage: Civilization and the Jews, WNET, N.Y.C., 1978-84; author: feature screenplays A Child is Crying, 1961, The Young Adventurers, 1963; ABC News Bicentennial spls. Rendezvous With Freedom, 1973, The Right to Believe, 1975, The Will to Be Free, 1976; ABC News feature The Panama Canal, 1977 (Writers Guild award); (Recipient numerous awards, including: Edinburgh Film Festival award 1948, Venice Film Festival award 1962, Cannes Film Festival award 1964, Eternal Light award Jewish Theol. Sem. Am. 1969). Served with USAAF, 1943-45. Peabody award, 1979, 84; Gabriel award Nat. Assn. Catholic Broadcasters, 1979; Emmy award, 1984, Christopher award, 1984; also several awards Freedoms Found. Mem. Nat. Acad. TV Arts and Scis., Writers Guild Am. East (council 1972-73, 78-79, 84-88, awards 1959, 73, 78, 85, Jablow Meml. award 1988), Dirs. Guild Am. Democrat. Home: 75 Central Park W New York NY 10023-6011

SIEGEL, MARK BERNARD, surgeon; b. L.A., Dec. 19, 1948; Student, U. Calif., Berkeley, 1966-69; MD, UCLA, 1973. Diplomate Am. Bd. Surgery. Intern Barnes Hosp., St. Louis, 1973-74, resident in surgery, 1974-78; surgeon Grand Forks (N.D.) Clinic, 1978-97; med. dir. surg. svcs. Altru Health Sys., Grand Forks, 1997-99. Mem. staff Altru Hosp., Grand Forks, 1978—, chief of staff, 1991-93; clin. prof. U. N.D. Sch. Medicine. Mem. AMA, ACS, Southwestern Surg. Congress. Office: Altru Clinic 1000 S Columbia Rd Grand Forks ND 58201-4032

SIEGEL, MARVIN, newspaper editor; b. N.Y.C., June 23, 1935; s. Murray and Belle (Diamond) S.; 1 child, Joshua Murray. BA, U. Mich., 1957. Reporter The Record, Hackensack, N.J., 1957-59; free-lance writer Western Europe, 1960-62; reporter Fairchild Publs., N.Y.C., 1962-63; editor The World Telegram, N.Y.C., 1963-66; copy editor The N.Y. Times, 1966-67, asst. met. editor, 1967-76, founding editor Weekend sect., 1976-82; founding editor World of N.Y., 1982-86; founding editor Edn. Life The N.Y. Times, 1986, dep. editor Week in Rev., 1987, culture news editor, 1988-92, dep. editor Book Rev., 1992-95; asst. to mng. editor, 1995—. Co-author: The World of New York, 1985, The New York Times Great Lives of the 20th Century, 1988; editor: Deadly Sins, 1994, The Last Word: The New York Times Book of Obituaries and Farewells, 1997. Pfc. U.S. Army. Jewish. Office: NY Times Co 229 W 43d St New York NY 10036-3913

SIEGEL, MARY ANN GARVIN, writer; b. Louisville, Apr. 3, 1944; d. Samuel Hughes and Ann Wendell (Smith) Garvin; m. Charles Holladay Siegel, Sept. 2, 1967 (div.); children: Emily Hughes, Charles Holladay, Jr., Margaret Shafer. BA, Conn. Coll., 1966. Photog. rschr. Time Inc., NYC, 1966—67, Nat. Geog. Soc., Washington, 1967—68; content author and editor FundraisingIN-FO.com, 2000—01. Leadership Atlanta, 1993-94, exec. com., 1995-96. Trustee Conn. Coll., New London, 1985-90; chair Friends of Spelman Coll., Atlanta, 1990-92; active Atlanta/Fulton County adv. bd. United Way Met. Atlanta, 1994-96; Olympic Envoy to Republic of Nauru, Atlanta Com. Olympic Games, 1994-96; formerly active adv. bd. N.C. Outward Bound Sch., Asheville. Recipient Agnes Berkeley Leahy award Conn. Coll. Alumni Assn., 1991. E-mail: seagullwrite@yahoo.com.

SIEGEL, MAX LAURENCE, recording industry executive; b. 1964; s. William Siegel and Delores Frazier; m. Jennifer Satterfield-Siegel; children: Matthew, Max. BA in Psychology and Pre-Profl. Studies, U. Notre Dame, 1986; JD, Notre Dame U., 1992. Ptnr. Siegel Carter & Assocs.; co-head A&R ops., head gospel divsn. Tommy Boy Records; pres. Verity Records; v.p. Jive Records Urban A&R, 2001—. Named to, Crain's N.Y. Bus. "40 under 40", 2004. Office: Jive Records 137-139 W 25th St 9th Fl New York NY 10001*

SIEGEL, MICHAEL ALAN, dental educator; b. Balt., Feb. 6, 1953; s. Harold W. and Ellen Rosenbach Siegel; m. Sharon Crane, July 22, 1979; 1 child, Sarah Emily. BS, U. Md., College Park, 1975; DDS, Balt. Coll. of Dental Surgery, 1979; MS, U. Md., Balt., 1986. Diplomate Am. Bd. of Oral Medicine, 1988. Resident Walter Reed Army Hosp., 1980—82, intern in dentistry and gen. practice, 1982; assoc. prof. oral medicine Balt. Coll. of Dental Sugery, Balt., 1982—2002; assoc. prof. dermatology U. Md. Med. Sch., Balt., 1991—2002; assoc. faculty mem. Grad. Sch., U. Md., Balt., 2002; prof. and chmn. dept. of diagnostic scis. Nova Southeastern U. Coll. of Dental Medicine, Ft. Lauderdale, Fla., 2003—. Cons. Balt. VA Hosp., 1982—2002; mem. editl. bd. Oral Surgery, Oral Medicine, Oral Pathology, Oral Radiology and Endodontics, 1992—. Presenter (400+ continuing dental education courses) Current Concepts in Oral Medicine; author: (100+ articles, chapters and abstracts) Oral Medicine. Capt. U.S. Army Dental Corps, 1979—82, Washington, D.C. Fellowship, Acad. Gen. Dentistry, 1986. Fellow: Acad. Gen. Dentistry, Am. Acad. Oral Medicine (bd. trustees 1990—2003, pres. 2000—02); mem.: ADA (chmn. coun. sci. affairs 2002—03), Internat. Assn. for Dental Rsch., Omicron Kappa Upsilon (pres. 1999—2000). Achievements include research in Over One Million Dollars in Research Funding. Office: Nova Southeastern Univ 3200 S University Dr Fort Lauderdale FL 33328-2018 Office Phone: 954-262-4309. Business E-Mail: masiegel@nova.edu.

SIEGEL, MICHAEL ELLIOT, nuclear medicine physician, educator; b. N.Y.C., May 13, 1942; s. Benjamin and Rose (Gilbert) S.; m. Marsha Rose Snower, Mar. 20, 1966; children: Herrick Jove, Meridith Ann. AB, Cornell U., 1964; MD, Chgo. Med. Sch., 1968. Diplomate Nat. Bd. Med. Examiners. Intern Cedars-Sinai Med. Ctr., L.A., 1968-69, resident in radiology, 1969-70; NIH fellow in radiology Temple U. Med. Ctr., Phila., 1970-71; NIH fellow in nuclear medicine Johns Hopkins U. Sch. Medicine, Balt., 1971-73, asst. prof. radiology, 1972-76; assoc. prof. radiology and medicine U. So. Calif., L.A., 1976—, prof. radiology, 1989—, dir. divsn. nuclear medicine, 1982-99. Dir. Sch. Nuclear Medicine, Los Angeles County-U. So. Calif. Med. Ctr., 1976-99; dir. divsn. nuclear medicine Kenneth Norris Cancer Hosp. and Rsch. Ctr., L.A., 1983-99; dir. dept. nuclear medicine Orthopaedic Hosp., L.A., 1981—, Intercmty. Hosp., Covina, Calif., 1981—, U. So. Calif. Univ. Hosp., L.A., 1993—; clin. prof. radiology U. Calif., San Diego, 2000—. Author: Textbook of Nuclear Medicine, 1978, Vascular Surgery, 1983, 88, numerous other textbooks; editor: Nuclear Cardiology, 1981, Vascular Disease: Nuclear Medicine, 1983. Mem. Maple Ctr., Beverly Hills. Served as maj. USAF, 1974-76. Recipient Outstanding Alumnus award Chgo. Med. Sch., 1991. Fellow Am. Coll. Nuclear Medicine (sci. investigator 1974, 76, nominations com. 1980, program com. 1983, trustee 1993, disting. fellow, 1993, bd. reps. 1993—, bd. dirs. 1994—, treas. 1996—, chmn. ann. sci. program 1996—, pres.'s award 1997, v.p. 1997-98, pres. 1999—); mem. Soc. Nuclear Medicine (sic. exhbn. com. 1978-79, program com. 1979-80, Silver medal 1975), Calif. Med. Assn. (sci. adv. bd. 1987—), Radiol. Soc. N.Am., Soc. Nuclear Magnetic Resonance Imaging, Friars So. Calif., Alpha Omega Alpha. Achievements include research on development of nuclear medicine techniques to treat recurrent joint effusions, evaluate cardiovascular disease and diagnose and treat cancer; clinical utilization of video digital displays in nuclear medicine development; invention of pneumatic radiologic pressure system. Office: U So Calif Med Ctr Rm 5250 1200 N State St Los Angeles CA 90033-1029

SIEGEL, MORTON KALLOS, religious organization administrator, educational administrator; b. N.Y.C., Dec. 5, 1924; s. Samuel William and Esther (Sackin) S.; m. Pearl Fox, June 28, 1949; children: Deborah Siegel Eisenstadt, Daniel, Deenah Siegel Speiser. BA summa cum laude, Yeshiva U., 1945; MA in Philosophy and History, Columbia U., 1946, PhD, 1952. Ednl. dir. Laurelton Jewish Ctr., Queens, N.Y., 1945-49; ednl. dir., dir. educator placement United Synagogue Cons. Judaism, N.Y.C., 1949-51, dir. youth activities, 1951-64, exec. dir., 1970-75, ednl. dir., 1964-88, dir. regional and extension activities, 1988-98, sr. vp., 1998—. Adj. asst. prof. Sch. Edn., NYU, 1971-76; lectr. in field. Contbr. articles to profl. jours. Home: 43 Crossbow Ln Commack NY 11725-1214 Office: 155 5th Ave New York NY 10010-6802 Office Phone: 212-533-7800.

SIEGEL, NATHANIEL HAROLD, sociology educator; b. Bklyn., May 17, 1929; s. Victor and Yetta (Kogel) S.; m. Annabelle Replansky, Mar. 3, 1958; children— Anthony, Jennifer. AB, Bklyn. Coll., 1950; A.M., N.Y.U., 1952, PhD, 1956. Asst. prof. sociology Columbia, 1956-59; sociologist Hillside Hosp., Queens, N.Y., 1958-63; assoc. dir. behavioral research N.Y.C. Dept. Health, 1963-64; chief social sci. tng. sect. NIMH, 1964-67, cons., 1970-79; prof. sociology Queens Coll., 1967-79, chmn. dept., 1967-70, v.p., dean faculty, 1970-74, provost, 1974-77, acting pres., 1977-78; sr. v.p. acad. affairs SUNY Purchase, 1979-94; prof. sociology SUNY, 1979-2000. Served with M.C. AUS, 1950-51. Home: 8 Birchfield Rd Larchmont NY 10538-1505

SIEGEL, NED LAWRENCE, real estate developer; b. Newark, Sept. 26, 1951; s. Howard and Esther (Facher) S.; m. Stephanie Moak, Aug. 7, 1976; children: Justin, Joshua, Jillian. BA, U. Conn., 1973; JD, Dickinson Sch. Law, 1976. Law clk. U.S. Dist. Ct., Camden, N.J., 1976-77; assoc. Kimmelman, Wolff & Samson, Roseland, N.J., 1977-78; v.p. Howard Siegel Cos., Manalapan, N.J., 1978-80; pres. The Weingarten-Siegel Group, Manalapan, N.J., 1980-88, Weingarten Siegel Group of Fla., Inc., Boca Raton, Fla., 1985-91, Weingarten, Siegel, Fletcher Group, La Mesa, Calif., 1985-91, The Siegel Schoor Orgn. Fla., INc., Boca Raton, 1991-98. Pres. SGS Communities Inc., Manalapan, N.J., Boca Raton, 1992— (exec. com. Republican Jewish Coalition, 1995—), NLS Cmtys., Inc., 1996—; dir. Marietta Corp., 1996, Blue Lake Ltd., 1997—, Miami One Ctr., L.P., 1998—; chmn. The Siegel Group, 1997—, Siegel-Moskin Realty Group, 1998—; bd. dirs. Palm Beach Internat. Film Festival. Bd. govs. Solomon Schechter Sch., West Orange, N.J., 1986-88; mem. bd. adv. Pine Crest Sch. at Boca Raton, 1989-93, mem. bd. dirs. 1992—; bd. trustees Saint Andrew's Sch.; mem. task force City of Boca Raton Affordable Housing, 1995—; founding mem. Treve Brogan Ednl. Inst.; co-chmn. Palm Beach County Gov. George W. Bush Presdl. Exploratory com., Palm Beach County Jeb Bush for Governor Campaign, 1998, Palm Beach County Phil Gray for Pres., 1996. Named Bldr. of the Yr., N.J. Shore Bldrs. Assn., 1986. Mem. Nat. Assn. Homebuilders, Gold Coast Builder's Assn., Fla. Homebuilder's Assn., Internat. Coun. Shopping Ctrs., Found. Fla.'s Future (chmns. adv. bd.), Econ. Coun. Palm Beach County, The Beacon Coun. (Miami chpt.), Republican Eagles, Republican Party of Fla., N.J. Bldrs. Assn., N.J. Shore Bldrs. Assn. (v.p. 1986-88), Urban Land Inst., N.J. Bar Assn., Greater Miami C. of C., Greater Boca Raton C. of C., Phi Beta Kappa. Republican. Jewish. Avocations: tennis, sailing. Office: 5000 Blue Lake Dr Ste 150 Boca Raton FL 33431-4469

SIEGEL, PAUL, judge; b. Troy, NY, May 7, 1938; s. Benjamin and Mary (Silverman) S.; 1 child, Mark Aron; m. Janique Auvertin, Apr. 30, 1994. BS in Physics magna cum laude, U. Miami, 1958, LLB cum laude, 1962. Bar: Fla. 1963, DC 1964, U.S. Supreme Ct. 1967, U.S. Ct. Appeals (5th cir.) 1967, U.S. Ct. Appeals (11th cir.) 1982; cert. civil trial lawyer Fla. Bar. Mem. gen. counsel's office AEC, Washington, 1962-65; ptnr. Sinclair, Louis, Siegel, Heath, Nussbaum & Zavertnik, P.A., Miami, Fla., 1972-91; judge Dade County (Fla.) Cir. Ct., 1991—. Author: Florida Trial Objections, 2004; editor-in-chief, exec. editor: U. Miami Law Rev. Chmn. bd. dirs. Alliance Francaise of Dade County, 1983-87, pres., 1990-92; pres. Pro-Mozart Soc. Greater Miami, 1984-92. Home: 235 E San Marino Dr Miami FL 33139-1151 Office: Lawson E Thomas Courthouse Ctr 175 NW 1st Ave Ste 2019 Miami FL 33128 E-mail: psiegel@jud11.flcourts.org.

SIEGEL, RANDY, publishing executive; BA, Wesleyan U.; MBA, Yale U. Cons. Parade, 1999—2001, sr. v.p., 2001—03, assoc. publ., 2003, exec. v.p., pub., 2003—04, pres., pub., 2004—. Siegel's bus. experience includes the launches of Newsweek Interactive, HearSay mag. (a nat. coll. music publ.) and BrassRing.com, a joint venture among The Washington Post, Tribune Co. and Accel Ptnrs.; a major contbr. to Parade's strong positioning in the marketplace; led the sales, mktg. and comm. efforts for The Great Am. Bake Sale, a new program presented jointly by Parade and Share Our Strength, a leading nat. anti-hunger orgn.; he cemented a partnership with ESPN.com to create a program including sales, mktg. opportunities, and the All-Am. HS Sports program. Office: Parade Publ Inc 711 3rd Ave New York NY 10017-4014 Business E-Mail: randolph_siegel@parade.com.

SIEGEL, RICHARD DAVID, lawyer, former government official; b. Lewistown, Pa., Oct. 13, 1939; s. Robert and Pearl Eleanor (Nieman) S.; m. Marjorie Esther Greenwald, Mar. 13, 1966; children— Andrew, Jonathan, Michele BA, U. Pa., 1960; JD, Harvard U., 1963. Bar: Pa., D.C., U.S. Supreme Ct. Staff writer Phila. Inquirer, 1964-66; spl. asst. U.S. Rep. Richard Schweiker, Washington, 1966-69; legis. counsel U.S. Senator Richard Schweiker, Washington, 1969-71; assoc. minority counsel Senate Com. on Labor and Human Resources, Washington, 1971-73; sole practice Washington, 1978-79; mem. various firms, 1973-78, 80-81; dep. asst. sec. for natural resources and environment USDA, Washington, 1981-87; pvt. practice, Washington, 1987—. Contbr. articles to profl. jours. Treas. Com. for Senator Schweiker, Washington, 1974; mem. nat. coun. Am. Israel Pub. Affairs Com., Washington, 1974-77; v.p. Tifereth Israel Congregation, Washington, 1980-82, 93-99; sec.-treas. North Am.-Israel Hort. Found., 1987-95. With USCGR, 1963-64. Mem. ABA, FBA, Pa. Bar Assn., Assn. Former Senate Aides. Republican. Jewish. Home: 3141 Aberfoyle Pl NW Washington DC 20015-2325 Office: 1400 16th St NW Washington DC 20036-2220 E-mail: rsiegel@ofwlaw.com.

SIEGEL, RICHARD JAY, plastic surgeon, consultant; b. New York, Feb. 27, 1945; s. Beatrice P. Siegel; children: Brian R., Allison R. BA, Northwestern Univ., Evanston, IL, 1961—65. Cert. Am. Bd. of Plastic Surgery ABMS, 1976. Chief divsn. of plastic surgery Kaiser Hosp., Honolulu, 1975—; clin. prof. of plastic surgery John A. Burns Sch. of Medicine, U. of Hawaii, Honolulu, 1998—. Author Plastic Surgery, Splty. Eyelid Surgery. Fellow: Am. Assn. of Plastic Surgery. Office: Kaiser Hosp 3288 Moanalua Rd Honolulu HI 96819 Office Phone: 808-432-8276. Office Fax: 808-432-8155. Business E-Mail: richard.siegel@kp.org.

SIEGEL, RICHARD LAWRENCE, immunologist, allergist; b. Miami, Fla., Jan. 22, 1949; MD, Washington U., St. Louis, 1977; also PhD. Diplomate Am. Bd. Allergy and Immunology, Am. Bd. Diagnostic Lab. Immunology, Am. Bd. Pediats. Resident in pediats. Children's Hosp. Med. Ctr., Boston, 1977-79, fellow in allergy and immunology, 1979-81; allergist U. Comm. Hosp., Tampa, Fla. Fellow AIS, Am. Coll. Allergy, Asthma and Immunology; mem. Am. Acad. Pediats., Am. Acad. Allergy and Immunology. Office: 3450 E Fletcher Ave Ste 210 Tampa FL 33613-4600

SIEGEL, ROBERT, heat transfer engineer; b. Cleve., July 10, 1927; s. Morris and Mollie (Binder) S.; m. Elaine Jane Jaffe, July 19, 1951; children: Stephen, Lawrence. BS, Case Inst. Tech., 1950, MS, 1951; ScD, MIT, 1953. Heat transfer engr. GE, Schenectady, N.Y., 1953-54; heat transfer analyst Knolls Atomic Power Lab., Schenectady, 1954-55; rsch. scientist NASA Lewis Rsch. Ctr., Cleve., 1955-99; tech. cons., 1999—. Adj. prof. U. Toledo, 1981, 85, 95, adj. prof. mech. engring. U. Akron (Ohio), 1987, adj. prof. mech. engring. Cleve. State U., 1989, 91; mem. adv. coun. U. Akron, 1989-96. Author: Thermal Radiation Heat Transfer, 1972, 4th edit., 2002; tech. editor ASME, 1973-83, AIAA, 1986-98; author numerous sci. papers. With U.S. Army, 1945-47. Recipient Exceptional Sci. Achievement medal NASA, 1986, Space Act award, 1993, ASME-AIChE Max Jakob Meml. award, 1996. Fellow ASME (Heat Transfer Meml. award 1970, Max Jakob Bd. of award 1999-2002), AIAA (Thermophysics award 1993); mem. Sigma Xi, Tau Beta Pi. Jewish. Avocations: ballroom dancing, piano. Home and Office: 3052 Warrington Rd Shaker Heights OH 44120-2425

SIEGEL, ROBERT CHARLES, broadcast journalist; b. N.Y.C., June 26, 1947; s. Joseph and Edith Ruth (Joffe) S.; m. Jane Claudia Schwartz, June 17, 1973; children: Erica Anne, Leah Harriet. BA, Columbia U., 1968, postgrad. sch. journalism, 1969-70. Newscaster Sta. WGLI, Babylon, N.Y., 1968-69; reporter, news dir. Sta. WRVR-FM, N.Y.C., 1971-76; assoc. producer, editor Nat. Pub. Radio, Washington, 1976-78, sr. editor, 1976-79, dir. news and info., 1983-87, host All Things Considered, 1987—, sr. editor London, 1979-83. Host Ea. Europe: Breaking with the Past, The Learning Channel, Washington, 1990, Earth Scope, Arlington, Va., 1990-91. Editor: The NPR Interviews. Recipient DuPont-Columbia award Columbia U., 1984. Jewish. Avocations: reading, golf, baseball. Home: 1340 19th Rd S Arlington VA 22202-1637 Office: Nat Pub Radio All Things Considered 635 Massachusetts Ave NW Washington DC 20001-3753 E-mail: rsiegel@npr.org.

SIEGEL, ROBERT HAROLD, English literature educator, writer; b. Aug. 18, 1939; married; 3 children. Student, Denison U., 1957-59; BA in English, Wheaton Coll., 1961; MA, Johns Hopkins U., 1962; PhD in English, Harvard U., 1968. Instr. Dartmouth Coll., 1967-68, asst. prof., 1968-75; vis. lectr. Princeton (N.J.) U., 1975-76; poet-in-residence, McManes vis. prof. Wheaton (Ill.) Coll., 1976; asst. prof. U. Wis., Milw., 1976-79, assoc. prof. English, 1979-83, prof., 1983—99, prof. emeritus, 1999—. Poet on faculty Summer Writers' Inst., Wheaton Coll., 1980, Wesleyan U., 1982, 83, New Eng. Young Writers Conf., 2002-2004; vis. prof. J. W. v. Goethe U., Frankfurt, Fed. Republic Germany, 1985; lectr., reader various univs. Author: (fiction) Alpha Centauri, 1980, Whalesong, 1981, The Kingdom of Wundle, 1982, White Whale, 1991, The Ice at the End of the World, 1994; (poetry) The Beasts and the Elders, 1973, In A Pig's Eye, 1980, The Waters Under the Earth, 2004; contbr. poems to Atlantic Monthly, Sewanee Rev., other jours. Recipient Margaret O'Loughlin Foley award Am. mag., 1970, award Cliff Dwellers' Arts Found., 1974, Chgo. Poetry prize Soc. Midland Authors, 1974, Poetry prize Prairie Schooner, 1977, Jacob Glatstein Meml. prize Poetry mag., 1977, award Ingram Merrill Found., 1979, Gold medallion ECPA, 1981, Book of Yr. award Campus Life mag., 1981, 1st Pl. prize for juvenile fiction Coun. for Wis. Writers, 1981, 1st Pl. prize poetry Soc. Midland Authors, 1981, Matson award Friends of Lit., 1982, Golden Archer award Sch. Libr. Sci., U. Wis., Oshkosh, 1986; Dartmouth Coll. faculty fellow, 1971; Gilman fellow Johns Hopkins U., 1961-62; tchg. fellow Harvard U., 1965-67, Yaddo Artists' Colony, 1974, 75, Transatlantic Rev. fellow Bread Loaf Writers Conf., 1974, Nat. Endowment for Arts, 1980; grantee U. Wis., 1978, 84, 88-89, 96-97. Office: U Wis English Dept Milwaukee WI 53201 E-mail: siegelrh@uwm.edu.

SIEGEL, ROBERT JAMES, communications executive; b. N.Y.C., Feb. 26, 1929; s. Hiram and Regina (Goldstein) S.; m. Gonnie McClung, Jan. 8, 1953; children: William Laird, Richard Joseph. BS in Econs., Marietta Coll., 1950. With copy desk N.Y. Times, 1951-53; assoc. editor Lorain (Ohio) Jour., 1953-56; reporter Cleve. Press, 1956-61; with IBM, Armonk, N.Y., 1961—, data processing div. press rels. mgr., corp. info. mgr., corp. pub. affairs mgr., 1979—, dir. info., dir. internal communications, 1988-89; mng. dir., mktg. comm. agy. Metaphor, Inc., Atlanta, 1989-90; pres. Siegel Assocs., Communications Cons., Bal Harbour, Fla., 1991—. Mayor Key Colony Beach, Fla., 1995-98; bd. dirs. Fla. Keys Land and Sea Trust. Mem. Nat. Press Club, Overseas Press Club, Deadline Club of N.Y., Sigma Delta Chi. Home: 4427 SW 91st Dr Gainesville FL 32608-7137 E-mail: bobsiegel@att.net.

SIEGEL, SAMUEL, metals company executive; b. Elizabeth, N.J., Oct. 30, 1930; s. Morris and Anna (Fader) S.; m. Raenea Kershenbaum, Mar. 29, 1953; children: Daryl Lynn, Annie Roslyn. BBA, CUNY, 1952. CPA, N.Y. Cost accountant Seaporcel Metals, Inc., Long Island City, N.Y., 1955-56; asst. to controller Deltown Foods, Inc., Yonkers, N.Y., 1956-57; sr. accountant Touche Ross, N.Y.C., 1957-61; co-founder, vice chmn., chief fin. officer, treas., sec., dir. Nucor Corp., Charlotte, NC, 1961-99; ret., 2000. Mem. AICPA, Am. Soc. Corp. Secs., Fin. Execs. Inst. Office: 3421 Windbluff Dr Charlotte NC 28277-9850

SIEGEL, SHELDON C. pediatrician, allergist, immunologist; b. Mpls., Jan. 30, 1922; s. Carl S.; m. Priscilla Rikess, Mar. 3, 1946; children— Linda, Nancy. AA, Va. Jr. Coll., 1940; BA, BS, U. Minn., 1942, MD, 1945. Intern U. Minn. Hosp., 1946, resident in pediatrics, 1947-48; fellow in pediatric allergy Rochester, N.Y., 1949-50; practice medicine specializing in pediatric allergy and pediatrics St. Paul, 1950-52, San Antonio, 1952-54, Los Angeles, 1954—; clin. instr. pediatrics U. Rochester, 1949-50, U. Minn., 1950-51; asst. prof. pediatrics U. Tex., 1952-54; asst. clin. prof. U. Calif. at Los Angeles Med. Sch., 1955, clin. asso. prof., 1957-62, clin. prof., 1963—, co-chief pediatric allergy clinic, 1957—; mem. staff Harbor Gen. Hosp., Torrance, Calif., Daniel Freeman Hosp., Inglewood, Calif., Centinela Valley Community Hosp., Inglewood, Hawthorne (Calif.) Community Hosp. Editorial bd.: Jour. Allergy, 1973-75; contbr. articles to med. jours. Fellow Am. Acad. Allergy (pres. 1974), Am. Coll. Allergists, Am. Acad. Pediatrics; mem. AMA, Allergy Found. Am. (pres. 1976), Calif., Los Angeles County med. assns., Los Angeles Pediatric Soc., Calif., Los Angeles socs. allergy, Western Pediatric Research Soc., Am. Bd. Med. Specialists, Sigma Xi. Office: 11620 Wilshire Blvd Los Angeles CA 90025-1706 Office Phone: 310-312-5050.

SIEGEL, STANLEY, lawyer, educator; b. NYC, Mar. 2, 1941; s. David Aaron and Rose (Minsky) S. BS summa cum laude, NYU, 1960; JD magna cum laude, Harvard U., 1963. Bar: N.Y. 1963, D.C. 1964, Mich. 1970, Calif. 1976; CPA, Md. Atty. Office Sec. of Air Force, 1963-66; asst. prof. law U. Mich., Ann Arbor, 1966-69, assoc. prof., 1969-71, prof., 1971-74; ptnr. Honigman, Miller, Schwartz & Cohn, Detroit, 1974-76; prof. law UCLA, 1976-86, NYU, 1986—, assoc. dean, 1987-89. Vis. prof. Stanford Law Sch., 1973, Ctrl. European U., Budapest, 1993—2001, U. Konstanz, Germany, 1996, Tel Aviv U., 1998; fellow Max-Planck Inst., Hamburg, 1988; cons. reorgn. U.S. Postal Svc., 1969—71; exec. sec. Mich. Law Revision Commn., 1973; mem. bd. examiners AICPA, 1980—83. Author: (with Schulman and Moscow) Michigan Business Corporations, 1979, (with Conard and Knauss) Enterprise Organization, 4th edit., 1987, (with D. Siegel) Accounting and Financial Disclosure: A Guide to Basic Concepts, 1983, (with others) Swiss Company Law, 1996; mem. editl. bd. Lexis Electronic Author's Press, 1996-98. Served to capt. USAF, 1963-66. Mem. ABA, D.C. Bar Assn., Calif. Bar Assn., Assn. of Bar of City of N.Y., Am. Law Inst., AICPA. Office: NYU Law Sch 40 Washington Sq S New York NY 10012-1099

SIEGEL, STEPHEN, real estate company executive; Doctorate(hon.), Monmouth U., 2003, Baruch Coll., 2003. Chmn., CEO Insignia; global chmn. CB Richard Ellis, N.Y.C., 2003—. Named one of 100 Most Influential Bus. Leaders in N.Y.C., Crain's N.Y., 2003; recipient Humanitarian award, Found. Fighting Blindness, 1999, Urban Leadership award, NYU Real Estate Inst., 2000, Leadership Excellence award, Monmouth U. Real Estate Inst., 2001, Ellis Island Medal of Honor, Nat. Ethnic Coalition Orgn., 2002, Man of Yr. award, Crohns & Colitis Found., 2002. Office: CB Richard Ellis 16-19 Fls 200 Park Ave New York NY 10166*

SIEGEL, STEVEN DOUGLAS, oncologist; b. Mt. Vernon, N.Y., Oct. 26, 1950; s. Arthur Bernard and Edith Mildred (Kleinman) S.; m. Betsy Daniel, June 27, 1987; children: Zoe Elizabeth, Satchel Armond. BA, SUNY, Albany,

1972; MD, Loyola U., Maywood, Ill., 1983. Diplomate Am. Bd. Internal Medicine, Am. Bd. Med. Oncology. Physician North Fla. Hem. Onc. Assocs., Jacksonville, 1988—. Office: North Fla Hem Onc Assocs 1801 Barrs St Ste 800 Jacksonville FL 32204-4751

SIEGEL, STEVEN L. finance company executive, consultant; b. New Rochelle, NY, Feb. 21, 1962; s. Stuart A. Siegel and Stephanie (Kaplita); m. Elizabeth Ellen Starr, Dec. 12, 1987 (div. Jan. 1993). BS in Fin., MBA in Internat. Fin., Calif. Coast U.; D in Internat Fin. magna cum laude, U So. Calif. Fin. analyst Am. Express, Plantation, Fla., 1982-84; investment banker Kidder Peabody & Co., Ft. Lauderdale, Fla., 1985-87, Shearson Lehman Hutton, Boca Raton, Fla., 1987-89; pres. internat. divsn. Cabe Internat. Cons., Inc., Boca Raton, 1989-92; fin. and adminstv. dir. Ensec, Inc., Boca Raton, 1994-95, Art Collectors Internat., Miami, Fla., 1995-96; CFO, COO Enternet Entertainment Group, Inc., Ft. Lauderdale, 1996—97, S.L. Siegel and Assoc. Consulting Group, 1997—. Mng. dir. Fed. Group Ltd., 2001—02, bd. dir., Bought Deal, Inc.; pres., CEO Champion Accessories, 2002—03; bd. advisors Howa Telco, 1997—2002. Mem. Lambda Alpha Epsilon. Avocations: golf, sailing. Address: 2460 Deercreek CC Blvd Deerfield Beach FL 33442 Office Phone: 917-325-0114.

SIEGEL, STUART ELLIOTT, physician, pediatrics educator, cancer researcher; b. Plainfield, N.J., July 16, 1943; s. Hyman and Charlotte Pearl (Freinberg) S.; m. Linda Wertkin, Jan. 20, 1968; 1 child, Joshua. BA, MD, Boston U., 1967. Diplomate Am. Bd. Pediatrics, Am. Bd. Pediatric Oncology. Intern U. Minn. Hosp., Mpls., 1967-68, resident, 1968-69; clin. assoc. NIH, Bethesda, Md., 1969-72; asst. prof. pediatrics U. So. Calif. Sch. Medicine, L.A., 1972-76, assoc. prof., 1976-81, prof., 1981—, vice chmn. dept. pediat., 1994—; head div. hematology-oncology Childrens Hosp. L.A., 1976—, dep. physician-in-chief, 1987-90; dir. Childrens Ctr. for Cancer and Blood Diseases, L.A., 1996—. Mem. clin. cancer program project com. NIH, Nat. Cancer Inst., HEW, Bethesda, Md., 1978-82; pres. So. Calif. Children's Cancer Services, L.A., 1977-95. Bd. dirs. Nat. Leukemia Broadcast Coun., 1987—, Ronald McDonald Children's Charities, 1988-95, Make-A-Wish Found., 1987-95, Children's Hosp. L.A. Found., 1994-2000, Ronald McDonald House Charities, 1995—, L.A. Regional Coun. Am. Cancer Soc., 1996—, Nat. Childhood Cancer Found., 1995-2003; pres. Ronald McDonald House Charities So. Calif., 1996—; bd. trustees, Children's Hosp., L.A., 2000—; treas. Padres Contra El Cancer, 2003—. Surgeon USPHS, 1969-72. Fellow Am. Acad. Pediatrics. Office: Childrens Hosp LA Divsn Hematology Oncology MS#54 PO Box 54700 Los Angeles CA 90054-0700 Office Phone: 323-669-2205. Business E-Mail: ssiegel@chla.usc.edu.

SIEGELMAN, DON EUGENE, former governor; b. Mobile, Ala., Feb. 24, 1946; m. Lori Allen; c. Dana, Joseph. BA, U. Ala., 1968; JD, Georgetown U., 1972; postgrad., Oxford U., Eng., 1972-73. Bar: Ala. 1972. Sec. of state State of Ala., Montgomery, 1979-87, atty. gen., 1987-94, lt. gov., 1996-98, gov., 1999—2003. Democrat. Home: 3963 River View Dr Birmingham AL 35243-4711

SIEGENDORF, ARDEN M. judge; BBA, U. Miami, 1960, JD, 1963. Diplomate Fla. Acad. Profl. Mediators. Asst. atty. gen. State of Fla., 1963-71; county ct. and cir. judge, 1971-81; commr. City of Miami, 1971; pvt. practice, 1981-89; mediator, arbitrator, 1989—. Mem. Fla. Bd. Bar Examiners, 1970-71; past pres. Tallahassee Mediation Ctr., Inc., 1992-2000; spkr. in field. Contbr. articles to profl. jours. Named Outstanding Young Man of Miami, 1973; recipient excellence award Fla. Conflict Resolution Consortium, 2000. Fellow Am. Coll. Civil Trial Mediators; mem. Fla. Bar, Soc. for Profls. in Dispute Resolution, Tallahassee Bar Assn., Fla. Govtl. Bar Assn. (past v.p.), Iron Arrow Honor Soc., Bar and Gavel Legal Soc. (past pres., Roger Sorino award), Soc. of Wig and Robe, U. Miami Law Alumni Assn. (past pres.), Phi Alpha Delta, Phi Alpha Delta Alumni Assn. (past pres.), Omicron Delta Kappa. Address: 108 Lakeshore Dr #1139 North Palm Beach FL 33408 E-mail: asiegendorf@msn.com.

SIEGENTHALER, WALTER ERNST, internal medicine educator; b. Davos, Switzerland, Dec. 14, 1923; s. Walter and Anna Siegenthaler; m. Gertrud Siegenthaler, Dec. 31, 1957. MD, U. Zurich (Switzerland), l948; Dr.h.c., Martin Luther U., Halle, Germany, 1991. Chief resident in internal medicine, St. Gallen, Switzerland, 1954-58; prof. internal medicine, chmn. dept. U. Bonn, Fed. Republic Germany, 1969-71; asst. in pathology U. Zurich, 1949-50, asst. in internal medicine, 1950-54, chief resident, 1958-61, lectr., 1961-67, asst. prof., 1967-69, assoc. prof., 1971-91, chmn. dept., dean Med. Sch., 1978-80. Pres. Conf. Clinic Dirs., Zurich, 1980—91, 10th Internat. Congress Chemotherapy, Zurich, 1977, Swiss Rsch. Inst. for Climate and Medicine, Davos, 1992—; vis. prof. Baylor Med. Coll., Houston, 1981. Contbr. articles to profl. jours. Bd. dirs. EMDO Found., Zurich, 1974—, Jung Found., Hamburg, 1982—95, Opo Found., Zurich, 1994—2000, Swiss Found. for Promotion of Young People, 1995—2003, Walter and Gertrud Siegenthaler Found., 2003—, pres., 2003—. Col. Swiss Army, 1941—88. Named Acad. Naturforscher Leopoldina, 1981; recipient Ernst von Bergmann plaque, 1972, Ludwig Hellmeyer Gold medal, 1984, Sci. and Rsch. Gold medal, Jung Found., 1997, Crystal of Davos, 1998, Hon. Medal of Charitè, U. Berlin, 1999, Walter Siegenthaler award, German Med. Jour., 2000—04, Hippocrates award, Greek Soc. Internal Medicine, 2002. Fellow: Infectious Diseases Soc. Am. (corr.), Am. Acad. Microbiology (hon.); mem.: Soc. for Progress in Internal Medicine (bd. dirs., pres. 1990—), Assn. Am. Physicians (hon.), Swiss Soc. Infectious Diseases (hon.), Assn. German Internists (hon.), Paul Ehrlich Soc. (hon.; pres. 1969—71, 1973—75, 1975—77), Swiss Soc. Internal Medicine (hon.; bd. dirs. 1993), German Soc. Internal Medicine (hon.; pres. 1983—84, bd. dirs. 1992, Gustav von Bergman Gold medal 2000), Davos Tourism (hon.). Home: Forsterstrasse 61 CH-8044 Zurich Switzerland Office: Univ Hosp Rämistrasse 100 CH-8091 Zurich Switzerland Home Fax: 01141/1/252 2626.

SIEGER, DIANA R. foundation administrator; b. Detroit, Oct. 15, 1951; d. Robert R. and Rosemary F. Sieger; m. Thomas A VanTol, July 21, 1973 (div. Apr. 2, 1982). BA, Western Mich. U., 1973, MSW, 1978; DHL (hon.), Aquinas Coll., 1998, Grand Valley State U., 2000. Asst. program dir., svc. mil. families, vets. and disaster svcs. ARC, Kent County Chpt., Grand Rapids, Mich., 1974—77; assoc. exec. United Way Kent County; student asst. State of Mich., Dept. Labor and Governor's Office, Lansing, 1977—78; pres. Grand Rapids Cmty. Found., 1987—. V.p., cmty. founds. Coun. Mich. Founds., Grand Haven, 1999—, mem.,com. cmty. founds., 1988—; bd. dirs. Mich. Cmty. Founds. Venture Funds; chairperson, com. cmty. founds. Coun. Founds., Washington, 1995—2000. Com. mem. maj. corridor task force ITP, Grand Rapids, 2001—02; bd. chairperson, bd. mem. Leadership Grand Rapids, 1991—97; bd. mem. Butterworth Hosp., 1994—97; mem., regional issues com. Grand Rapids Area C. of C., 1990—2002; v.p. cmty. founds. Coun. Mich. Founds., 1999—2002; bd. mem. Mich. Cmty. Founds. Venture Funds, 1994—2002; mem. Kent County Family and Children's Coordinating Coun., 1995—, chairperson, 2001—03; mem., fellowship selection com. Transatlantic Cmty. Found. Fellowship German Marshall Fund, Washington, 2000—; chairperson, com. cmty. founds. Coun. Founds., 1995—2000, mem. stds. implementation com., 2001—; chmn. Mich. Cmty. Founds. Venture Funds, 1994—. Named Grantmaker of Yr., Nat. Soc. Fund Raising Profls., 1996, Disting. Cmty. Trustee, Leadership Grand Rapids, 2001, Outstanding Alumni Acad., Western Mich. U., 2002; named to Nat. Honor Soc. Pub. Affairs and Adminstrn., Pi Alpha Alpha Soc., 1998; recipient Tribute award, YWCA, 1995, Galaxy award, Nat. Kidney Found. Mich., 1999; fellow Transatlantic Cmty. Found. fellow, German Marshall Fund, C.S. Mott Found., King Baudoin Found., 2000. Mem.: Grand Rapids C. of C. Avocations: travel, art collecting, running, dancing - tap. Office: Grand Rapids Cmty Found 161 Ottawa NW #209-C Grand Rapids MI 49503

SIEGFRIED, DAVID CHARLES, retired lawyer; b. N.Y.C., Feb. 15, 1942; s. Charles Albert and Marjorie Claire (Young) S.; m. Meri Stephanie (Smith); children: Karin Elisabeth, Christine Elise. BA, Princeton U., 1964; JD, Harvard U., 1967. Bar: N.Y., 1970. Assoc. Milbank, Tweed, Hadley, and McCloy, N.Y.C., 1968-76, ptnr., 1977—98, resident ptnr. Hong Kong and Singapore, 1979-83, 85-88. Bd. dirs. Princeton Alumni Weekly; spkr. in field. Bd. dirs. Cmty. Agy. Corp. N.J., Inc., v.p. found. 1st lt. USAR, 1967-74. Mem.: ABA, Princeton U. (exec. com. alumni coun.), Millburn Short Hills Hist. Soc. (bd. dirs., past pres.), Millburn N.J. Hist. Preservation Commn. (vice chmn.), Assn. Bar City of N.Y., N.Y. State Bar Assn., Cricket Club, Tanglin Club (Singapore), Am. Club (Hong Kong and Singapore), Baltrusrol Golf Club, Short Hills (NJ) Club, Princeton Club. Congregationalist. Avocations: running, tennis, historic reading. Home: 30 Western Dr Short Hills NJ 07078-3230

SIEGFRIED, JOHN, association officer; BS, Rensselaer Polytechnic Inst., Troy, N.Y., 1967; MA, Pa. State U., 1968; PhD, U. Wis., 1972. Instr. in econs. Pa. State U., 1968-69; lectr. in econs. U. Wis., 1970-72; asst. prof. to full prof. econs. Vanderbilt U., Nashville, 1972-75, 81—, chmn. dept. econs., 1980-86; sec., treas. Am. Econ. Assn., 1997—. Vis. prof. U. Adelaide, South Australia, 1986, 91-92, 93-96, adj. prof. econs., 1996—; vis. prof. U. Leeds, Eng., 1987-88, Simon Fraser U., B.C., 1992; economist U.S. Fed. Trade Commn., Bur. of Econs., 1975-76; sr. staff economist, Pres.'s Coun. of Econ., 1976-77; econs. cons. numerous orgns. Bd. editors: The Quarterly Rev. of Econs. and Fin., 1985-97, Rev. of Indsl. Orgn., 1976-80, 83—, Jour. of Econ. Edn., 1990—; contbr. more than 140 articles to profl. jours. Recipient Marvin Bower award Nat. Coun. on Econ. Edn., 1995, Fulbright Sr. Scholar award/Australia, 1991-92, others. Mem. Nat. Bur. Econ. Rsch. (bd. dirs. 1997—), Am. Coun. Learned Socs. (mem. coun. adminstrv. officers 1997—), others. Office: Am Econ Assn 2014 Broadway Ste 305 Nashville TN 37203-2425 Fax: 615-343-7590.

SIEGFRIED, TOM, newspaper editor; b. Lakewood, Ohio, Dec. 23, 1950; s. Ivan T. and Marian (Griffin) S.; m. Anna Christine Beckelhymer, June 24, 1978. BA, Tex. Christian U., 1974; MA, U. Tex., 1981. Sci. editor Dallas Morning News. Author: The Bit and the Pendulum, 2000, Strange Matters, 2002. Office: The Dallas Morning News AH Belo Corp PO Box 655237 Dallas TX 75265-5237 E-mail: tsiegfried@dallasnews.com.

SIEGLE, DEL, education educator; b. Miles City, Mont., Jan. 22, 1954; s. Albert J. and Lorraine H. Siegle; m. D. Betsy McCoach, May 22, 1999. BA summa cum laude, Mont. State U., 1983, MEd, 1989; PhD, U. Conn., 1995. Prodn. mgr. Macek Photography, Billings, Mont., 1972—73; portrait photographer Lindstrom Photography, Helena, Mont., 1973—75; photojournalist The Terry (Mont.) Tribune, 1976—79; instr. gifted and talented Glendive (Mont.) Pub. Schs.; asst. prof. Boise (Idaho) State U., 1995—99; assoc. prof. ednl. rsch. U. Conn., Storrs, 1999—. Named Outstanding Alumni, Mont. State U., Billings, 1991, Adv. of Gifted and Talented Edn., Idaho Assn. for the Gifted, 1998, Outstanding Educator, Pi Lambda Theta Beta Sigma, 2001; U. Conn. Tchg. fellow, 2004. Mem.: Glendive Edn. Assn. (pres. 1990—91), Mont. Assn. Gifted and Talented Edn. (pres. 1988—89, Creation of the Del Siegle scholarship 1990), Am. Edn. Rsch. Assn. - Rsch. in Gifted Sig (exec. com. 2000—04), Nat. Assn. for Gifted Children (bd. dirs. 1998—, Early Leader 2001), Coun. for Exceptional Children - The Assn. for the Gifted (bd. dirs. 1997—2004). Office: Univ Conn 2131 Hillside Rd Unit 3007 Storrs CT 06269 Office Phone: 860-486-0616. E-mail: del.siegle@uconn.edu.

SIEGLER, MARK, internist, educator; b. N.Y.C., June 20, 1941; s. Abraham J. and Florence (Sternlieb) S.; m. Anna Elizabeth Hollinger, June 4, 1967; children:Dillan, Alison, Richard, Jessica. AB with honors, Princeton U., 1963; MD, U. Chgo., 1967. Diplomate Am. Bd. Internal Medicine. Resident, chief resident internal medicine U. Chgo., 1967-71; hon. sr. registrar in medicine Royal Postgrad. Med. Sch., London, 1971-72; asst. prof. medicine U. Chgo., 1972-78, assoc. prof. medicine, 1979-85, acting dir. div. gen. internal medicine, 1983-85, dir. MacLean Ctr. Clin. Med. Ethics, 1984—, prof. medicine, 1985—, Lindy Bergman prof., 1997-2000, Lindy Bergman Disting. Svc. prof., 2000—, dir. fellowship tng. program in clin. med. ethics, 1986—. Vis. asst. prof. medicine U. Wis., Madison, 1977; vis. assoc. prof. medicine U. Va., Charlottesville, 1981-82. Co-author: Clinical Ethics, 1981, 2d edit., 1986, 3d edit., 1992, 4th edit., 1998, 5th edit., 2002, An Annotated Bibliography of Medical Ethics, 1988, Institutional Protocols for Decisions About Life-Sustaining Treatment, 1988; co-editor: Changing Values in Medicine, 1985, Medical Innovations and Bad Outcomes, 1987; editl. bd.: Am. Jour. Medicine, 1979—94, 1997—, Archives Internal Medicine, 1979—90, Bibliography of Bioethics, Jour. Med. Philosophy, 1978—89, Jour. Med. Philosophy, 1978—89, Jour. Clin. Ethics, 1989—, Jour. Med. Ethics (London), 2002—; contbr. articles to profl. jours. Mem. adv. bd. Bioethics Inst., Madrid, Notre Dame Ctr. for Ethics and Culture. Grantee Andrew W. Mellon Found., Henry J. Kaiser Family Found., Pew Charitable Trusts, Field Found. Ill., Ira De Camp Found., Gaylord & Dorothy Donnelley Found.; Phi Beta Kappa vis. scholar, 1991-92, Chirone prize Italian Nat. Acad. Medicine, 1996; mem. NAS Cloning Panel, 2001-02, others. Fellow ACP (human rights com., ethics com. 1985-90), Hastings Ctr.; mem. ACS (ethics com. 1992—), Assn. Am. Physicians, Chgo. Clin. Ethics Program (pres. 1989-90). Office: Univ Chgo MC 6098 MacLean Ctr Clin Med Ethics 5841 S Maryland Ave Chicago IL 60637-1463

SIEGMAN, ANTHONY EDWARD, electrical engineer, educator; b. Detroit, Nov. 23, 1931; s. Orra Leslie and Helen Salome (Winnie) S.; married. AB summa cum laude, Harvard U., 1952; MS, UCLA, 1954; PhD, Stanford U., 1957. Faculty Stanford (Calif.) U., 1957—, assoc. prof. elec. engring., 1960-64, prof., 1964-98, prof. engring. emeritus, 1998—. Dir. Edward L. Ginzton Lab., 1978-83; cons. Lawrence Livermore Labs., Coherent Inc., GTE; mem. Air Force Sci. Adv. Bd.; vis. prof. Harvard U., 1965 Author: Microwave Solid State Masers, 1964, An Introduction to Lasers and Masers, 1970, Lasers, 1986; contbr. over 200 articles to profl. jours. Recipient Schawlow award Laser Inst. Am., 1991; Guggenheim fellow IBM Rsch. Lab., Zurich, 1969-70; Alexander von Humboldt Found. sr. scientist Max Planck Inst. Quantum Optics, Garching, Fed. Republic Germany, 1984-85. Fellow AAAS, IEEE (W.R.G. Baker award 1971, J.J. Ebers award 1977), Am. Phys. Soc., Laser Inst. Am., Optical Soc. Am. (R.W. Wood prize 1980), IEEE Laser Electro-Optics Soc. (Quantum Electronics award 1989), Am. Acad. Arts and Scis.; mem. NAS, NAE, AAUP, Phi Beta Kappa, Sigma Xi. Achievements include patents for microwave and optical devices and lasers, including the unstable optical resonator. Office: Stanford U Ginzton Lab MC 4085 Stanford CA 94305-4085

SIEJKA, GEORGE JOHN, artist; b. Vienna, June 24, 1946; came to U.S., 1950; Cert. Fine Arts, Sch. Visual Arts, N.Y.C., 1969; BS in Art Edn. cum laude, NYU, 1974, MA in Fine Arts, 1975. Represented by Nancy Hoffman Gallery, N.Y.C. Group exhbns. include Fitchburg (Mass.) Art Mus., Anchorage (Alaska) Mus. Art, Rockford (Ill.) Coll. Art Gallery, Chgo. Internat. Exposition, Nancy Hoffman Gallery, NY. Recipient Founders Day award NYU, 1974. Mem. N.Y. Artists Equity Assn.

SIEKERT, ROBERT GEORGE, neurologist; b. Milw., July 23, 1924; s. Hugo Paul and Elisa (Kraus) S.; m. Mary Jane Evans, Feb. 17, 1951; children: Robert G. Jr., John E., Friedrich A.P. BS, Northwestern U., 1945, MS, 1947, MD, 1948. Diplomate Am. Bd. Psychiatry and Neurology. Instr. anatomy U. Pa., Phila., 1948-49; fellow neurology Mayo Found., Rochester, Minn., 1950-54; cons. Mayo Clinic, Rochester, 1954-91, head neurology sect., 1966-76, bd. govs., 1973-80, prof. neurology med. sch., 1969-91, prof. emeritus neurology, 1991—. Chmn. Internat. Stroke Conf. Am. Heart Assn., 1976-80. Editor Mayo Clinic Procs., 1982-86; cons. editor Jour. Stroke, 1992-2001; contbr. articles to profl. jours.; described transient cerebral ischemic attacks. Trustee Mayo Found., Rochester, 1973-81, chmn. emeritus com., 1997-98. Served to lt. j.g. M.C., USNR, 1950-52. Recipient Disting. Achievement award, Am. Heart Assn., 1984, Merit award, 1989, Robert G. Siekert Young Investigator award Am. Heart Assn., 1986. Fellow Am. Coll. Physicians; mem. Am. Neurol. Assn., Northwestern U. Med. Sch. Alumni Assn. (Service award 1983), Swiss Neurol. Soc. (corr.), Alpha Omega Alpha. Avocation: stamp collecting/philately. Office: Mayo Clinic 200 1st St SW N-10 Rochester MN 55905-0002

SIEKMAN, THOMAS CLEMENT, lawyer; b. Somerville, Mass., Sept. 22, 1941; s. Aloysius C. and Estelle M. (Forte) S.; children: Michael T., James T., Amy K. BS in Engring., Merrimack Coll., 1963; JD, Villanova U., 1966. Bar: Mass. 1966, U.S. Dist. Ct. Mass. 1969. Patent atty. Bethlehem (Pa.) Steel, 1966-68, Mohawk Data Scis., Stoneham, Mass., 1968-72, Chittick, Thompson & Pfund, Boston, 1972-73; from patent atty. to v.p., gen. counsel Digital Equipment Corp., Maynard, Mass., 1973-98; Sr. v.p., gen. coun., sec. Compaq Computer Corp., 1998—2002; of counsel Skadden, Arps, Slate, Meagher & Flom LLP; chmn. Martha Stewart Living Omnimedia, Inc., 2004—. Bd. dirs., chmn. N.E. Legal Found; bd. dirs. Martha Stewart Living Omnimedia, Inc., 2003- Trustee Mass. Taxpayers Found., Merrimack Coll.; mem. New Eng. Legal Found.; mem. Houston cmty. adv. bd. Teach Am.; bd. dirs. Houston African-Am. Mus. Mem. ABA, Am. Corp. Counsel Assn., Assn. Gen. Counsel. Avocations: squash, skiing. Office: Skadden, Arps, Meagher & Flom LLP 1440 New York Ave, NW Washington DC 20005

SIEKMANN, DONALD CHARLES, accountant; b. St. Louis, July 2, 1938; s. Elmer Charles and Mabel Louise (Blue) S.; m. Linda Lee Knowles, Sept. 10, 1966; 1 child, Brian Charles. BS, Washington U., St. Louis, 1960. CPA, Ohio, Ga. Regional mng. ptnr. Arthur Andersen & Co., Cin., 1960-98. Columnist Cin. Enquirer, 1983-86, Gannett News Services, 1983-86; editor "Tax Clinic" column Tax Advisor mag., 1974-75. Mem. bd. Cin. Zool. Soc., 1985-88; officer, bd. dirs. Cin. Found. for Pub. TV, 1984-88, Cin. Symphony Orch., 1973-85, Cin. Ballet Co., 1973-88, Atlanta Symphony Orch., 1988-91, The Atlanta Opera, 1988-91, Cin. Theatrical Assn., Jewish Hosp., 1993—, Cin. Assn. for Performing Arts, 1992—, Cin. United Way, 1992-99, Cin. Pk. Bd. Found., 1995-98; pres. Greater Cin. Arts and Edn. Ctr., 1996-99; mem. Friends of Sch. for Creative and Performing Arts, 1996-99, Cin. Arts Festival, 1992-96, Ronald McDonald House, 1998—. Mem. AICPA, Ohio Soc. CPAs, Cin. Country Club (trustee 1983-88), Optimists Club (pres. Queen City chpt. 1986). Clubs: Cin. Country (trustee 1983-88). Lutheran. Home: 5495 Waring Dr Cincinnati OH 45243-3933 Office: Arthur Andersen LLP 720 E Pete Rose Way #400 Cincinnati OH 45202-3504 E-mail: dsiekmann@aol.com.

SIELICKI-KORCZAK, BORIS ZDZISLAW, political educator, investigative consultant; b. Wilno, Lithuania, Poland, Feb. 11, 1939; came to U.S., 1980; s. Wiltold and Antonina (Arciszewski) Sielicki-Korczak; m. Barbara Maria Kaniewski, May 29, 1971; children: Robert, Sandra. MSC, Warsaw U., 1964, Kunstindustriskole, Copenhagen, 1971; PhD, Basel (Switzerland) U., 1973. Pres. Impolex Ltd., Copenhagen, 1970-79; field operative Europe CIA, 1983-90; pres., educator Anti-Soviet Rsch. Ctr., McLean, Va., 1981-84; export dir. Worldwide Investment Ltd., Arlington, Va., 1985-87, pres. Amexim Internat. Co. Ltd., Arlington, 1986-89, BK & Assocs., Arlington, 1990—, Boris S. de Korczak, Inc., Fairfax Station, Va., 1986—. Pres. R.R. Internat. Ltd., Copenhagen, 1983-89; mng. dir. Securitas Inc., Arlington, 1986-87; multiple appearance on U.S. and fgn. TV shows as expert on terrorism, USSR and Russian intelligence and its ops.; crime scene analyst, 1986—. Author: A Man From Atlantis, 1976; designer anti-drug poster. Dir. Nat. Lyric Opera Co., Washington, 1981-91; chief investigator Nat. Police Def. Found., 1995-98; legis. asst. to Congl. James A. Traficant, U.S. Congress, 2001-2003; sr. analyst 17th Dist. Ohio Congl. Office, Washington. Independent. Avocations: chess, classic music, travel, art, history. Office: PO Box 7153 Fairfax Station VA 22039-7153 Business E-Mail: bkorczak@cox.net.

SIEMENS, ALBERT J. medical association administrator; Rsch. scientist Rsch. Inst. on Alcoholism, Buffalo, N.Y.; clin. product devel. staff Pfizer, Inc., N.Y.; v.p. rsch. Family Health Internat., until 1987; with Clin. Rsch. Internat., Inc.; CEO, vice chair bd. dirs. Family Health Internat., 1998—.

SIEMER, DEANNE CLEMENCE, lawyer; b. Buffalo, Dec. 25, 1940; d. Edward D. and Dorothy J. (Helsdon) S.; m. Howard P. Willens; 1 child, Jason L. BA, George Washington U., 1962; LLB, Harvard U., 1968. Bar: N.Y. 1968, D.C. 1969, Md. 1972. Economist Office of Mgmt. and Budget, Washington, 1964-67; assoc., then ptnr. Wilmer, Cutler & Pickering, Washington, 1968-77, 80-90; ptnr. Pillsbury, Madison & Sutro, Washington, 1990-95; mng. dir. Wilsie Co., Washington and Saipan, 1995—. Gen. counsel U.S. Dept. of Def., Washington, 1977—79; spl. asst. to sec. U.S. Dept. of Energy, Washington, 1979—80. Author: Tangible Evidence, 3d edit., 1996, National Security and Self-Determination: United States Policy in Micronesia, 1999, Corel Presentations for Litigators, 2000, PowerPoint for Litigators, 2000, Effective Use of Courtroom Technology: A Judge's Guide to Pretrial and Trial, 2001, An Honorable Accord: The Covenant Between the Northern Mariana Islands and the United States, 2001, Effective Use of Courtroom Technology: A Lawyer's Guide to Pretrial and Trial, 2002, Easy Tech: Cases and Materials on Courtroom Technology, 2002, The Patronus Technique: A Practical Proposal In Asbestos-Driven Bankruptcies, 2002, Power Point 2002 for Litigators, 2002, Basic Power Point Slides, 2003, Argument Slides, 2003, The Evidence Camera, 2004. Mem. Lawyers Com. for Civil Rights, Washington, 1973—; mediator D.C. Superior Ct., Washington, 1986—, U.S. Ct. Appeals, Washington, 1988—; trustee Nat. Inst. Trial Advocacy, 1989—, Am. Law Inst., 1988—; arbitrator Atty. Client Arbitration Bd., NASD; mem roundtable on sci. and security NAS. Recipient citation Air Force Assn., 1977, Dist. Pub. Svc. medal Sec. of Def., 1979, Commendation Pres. of U.S. 1981. Mem. ABA, D.C. Bar Assn., No. Marianas Bar Assn. Episcopalian.

SIEMON-BURGESON, MARILYN M. (MARILYN BURGESON), education administrator; b. Whittier, Calif., Nov. 15, 1934; d. John Roscoe and Louise Christina (Secoy) Mason; m. Carl J. Siemon, Aug. 18, 1956 (div. Oct. 1984); children: Timothy G., Melanie A. Siemon Imes; Troy M.; m. James K. Burgeson, Jan. 24, 1987. BA, U. Redlands, 1956; MA, Pacific Oaks Coll., 1975; postgrad., Point Loma Coll., 1979-80. Cert. adminstr., elem. and early childhood tchr. Tchr. Sierra Madre (Calif.) Cmty. Nursery Sch., 1970-77; tchr. parent edn. and music Pasadena (Calif.) Unified Schs., 1977-79, project coord., 1980-82, tchr. curriculum resource dept., 1982-83, adminstr. Washington Children's Ctr., 1983-99; endorsed trainer High Scope Found. Register, 1990—; cons. staff devel. and tng. Pasadena. Trainer Program for Infant/Toddler Caregivers; instr. Citrus Coll., 1996-98; conf. chair Calif. High Scope Educators, 1995—. Active Arcadia (Calif.) Bicentennial Commn., 1974-76; mem. policy coun. for cmty. housing svcs. Pasadena Head Start, 1992-95; life mem. Sierra Madre Sch. PTA; mem. Child Care Coalition, Pasadena; Altar Guild, lay Eucharistic minister St. Edmunds, San Marino, Calif., vestry mem., 2003—. Ednl. Professions Devel. fellow Pacific Oaks Coll., Pasadena, 1969. Mem.: AAUW (co-chair Math.-Sci. Conf. 1983, chair coll./univ. rels. 1988—, v.p. ednl. found. 1996—98, Calif. state divsn. program v.p. 2002—04, past pres., grantee 1982—83), Calif. Child Devel. Adminstrs. Assn. (bd. dirs.), Women's Ednl. Leadership (asst. program v.p.), Child Care Info. Svc. (chair parent edn. and family affairs 1986—, bd. dirs.), Nat. Assn. Edn. Young Children (grantee 1970), Pasadena Women's City Club (dir. membership 2000—02, chmn.), Coun. Women's Clubs (pres. 1995—98), Pasadena Coll. Women's Club (pres. 2000—02, pres. Scholarship Found. 2002—04), Delta Kappa Gamma (pres. Omicron chpt. 1986—88, 1992—94). Republican. Episcopalian. Avocation: music. Home: 2266 Kinclair Dr Pasadena CA 91107-1022 Personal E-mail: mburgeson@earthlink.net.

SIEMSEN, SUSAN ANNE, physician assistant; b. Monnett, Mo., Nov. 26, 1963; d. Norman Lee Snook and E. Avis Foster; m. Wayne Fredrick Siemsen, May 28, 1982; 1 child, Natalie Marie. B of Health Sci., Wichita State U., 1987. Nat. certified and state registered phys. asst. Phys. asst. to William Henderson, MD, Albuquerque, N.Y., 1988-89; subspecialty in pediatric GI/hematology/oncology KUMC Pediatrics, Kansas City, Kans., 1989-92; phys. asst. South Federal FP, Denver, 1992-97, Lawrence (Kans.) Family Practice Ctr., 1997—. Proctor for phys. asst. students, Colorado/Denver program, 1992-97, KUMC NP program, Lawrence, 1997—. Presbyterian. Avocations: golf, skiing, family. Home: 2820 Meadow Dr Lawrence KS 66047-3240 Office: Lawrence Fam Practice Ct 3510 Clinton Pkwy Ste 320 Lawrence KS 66047-2145

SIENA, JAMES, artist; b. Oct. 28, 1957; BFA, Cornell U., 1979. One-man shows include Pierogi 2000, Bklyn., 1996, Cristinerose Gallery, N.Y.C., 1997, Daniel Weinberg Gallery, San Francisco, 1998, L.A., 2000, one-woman shows include, 2002, one-man shows include Gorney Bravin & Lee, N.Y.C., 2000, 2001, 2003, San Francisco Art Inst., 2003, exhibited in group shows at Nova Zembla, Hertogenbosch, Holland, 1993, Exquisite Corpse Drawing Ctr., N.Y.C., 1993, Kunstverein Munich, Germany, 1994, Geoffrey Young Gallery,

Great Barrington, Mass., 1994, Lombard/Fried Fine Arts, N.Y.C., 1995, Chassie Post Gallery, 1995, Bklyn. Mus. Art, 1997, Phyllis Kind Gallery, N.Y.C., 1998, Nicholas Davies Gallery, 1998, San Francisco Mus. Modern Art, 1999, Am. Acad. Arts and Letters, N.Y., 1999, 2000 (award in art, 2000), Galerie Anne de Villepoix, Paris, 2000, Greater N.Y. PS1, L.I., 2000, New Editions Monoprints Pace/Prints, N.Y.C., 2002, 177th Ann. Nat. Acad. Design Mus., 2002, OSP Gallery, Boston, 2002—03, Represented in permanent collections Mus. Modern Art, N.Y.C., San Francisco Mus. Modern Art, Whitney Mus. Am. Art, N.Y. Named invited exhibitor, Whitney Mus. Am. Art, N.Y., 2004; recipient Biennal Competition award, Louis Comfort Tiffany Found., 1999; fellow in painting, N.Y. Found. for the Arts, 1994.*

SIEPI, CESARE, opera singer; b. Milan, Feb. 10, 1923; Operatic debut in Rigoletto, Schio, 1941, Il Nabucco, LaScala Opera, Milan, 1946, Don Carlo, Met. Opera, N.Y.C., 1950; soloist debut in, Carnegie Hall, N.Y.C., 1951; sang in Mozart and Verdi requiems, Edinburgh Festival, Albert Hall, London; leading bass at, Salzburg Festival, LaScala, Milan; appeared in: play Bravo Giovanni, 1962; appeared: play Vienna Staatsoper; made many opera recordings for, London Records. (Winner Nat. Singing Competition, Florence 1941, recipient Italy's Orfeo award 1956). Achievements include making operatic debut, Rigoletto, Schio, at age of 18. Home: 12095 Brookfield Club Dr Roswell GA 30075-1261

SIEPMANN, JAMES PATRICK, research company executive, retired physician; b. Rochester, Minn., Jan. 16, 1960; s. Richard James and Mary Margaret Siepmann; m. Victoria Lynn Ewert, Sept. 4, 1982; children: Jeffrey Michael (dec.), Justine Nicole, Jennifer Ashley, Jessica Raquel, Joelle Kristina, Jarett James. BA, U. St. Thomas, St. Paul, 1982; MD, Mayo Med. Sch., Rochester, Minn., 1986. Diplomate Am. Bd. Family Practice. Resident in family practice Mayo Grad. Sch. Medicine, Rochester, 1986—89; pvt. practice, Oshkosh, 1989—2000; founder, chmn. LightTime, Winnebago, Wis., 2000—. Med. dir. United Health Wis., Appleton, 1993-95; chmn. dept. family practice Mercy Med. Ctr., Oshkosh, 1992-94; team physician Lourdes H.S., Oshkosh, 1993-99. Editor Jour. Theoretics, 1999—. Founding pres. sch. bd. Oshkosh Area Cath. Sch. Sys. (now consol.), 1991-93 Mem. IEEE, AMA, Optical Soc. Am., Internat. Soc. Optical Enging., Wis. Med. Soc. (del. 1994-98, bd. dirs. polit. action com. 1994—99, Wis. Physician-Citizen of Yr. award 1993). Roman Catholic. Achievements include patents for humidifier and in the optoelectronic field. Avocations: inventing, theoretics, writing, computer science, collecting fine wines. Home: 2941 Prairie Wood Dr Oshkosh WI 54904-8478 Office: 375 City Ctr Oshkosh WI 54901 E-mail: siepmann@lighttime.com.

SIERACKI, ERIC P. diversified financial services company executive; BS in Econs., U. Pa. Mgr. Grant Thornton; sr. v.p. Countrywide Asset Mgmt. Corp., 1988—89; exec. v.p. corp. fin. Countrywide Fin. Corp., Calabasas, Calif., 1989—94, mng. dir., 1994—2002, sr. mng. dir. corp. fin., treas., 2002—. Office: Countrywide Fin Corp 4500 Park Granada Calabasas CA 91302-1613

SIERENS, GAYLE, newscaster; married; 3 children. BS in Mass Comm., Fla. State u. Reporter WFSU-TV, Tallahassee; weekend sports anchor, reporter WFLA-TV, Tampa, Fla., 1977—83, weekday sports anchor, 1983—85, sportscaster, news anchor, 1985—. Mem. adv. bd. Fla. Poison Info. Ctr. Found.; bd. dirs. Judeo-Christian Health Clinic. Appeared (weekly) NFL Live, NBC. Chairperson ann. Bowl for Kids' Sake fundraiser Boys and Girls Clubs of Greater Tampa, bd. dirs. Achievements include first woman to do play-by-play for an NFL game. Office: WFLA-TV PO Box 1410 Tampa FL 33601

SIERLES, FREDERICK STEPHEN, psychiatrist, educator; b. Bklyn., Nov. 9, 1942; s. Samuel and Elizabeth (Meiselman) S.; m. Laurene Harriet Cohn, Oct. 25, 1970 (div. Aug. 1990); children: Hannah Beth Alterson, Joshua Caleb. AB, Columbia U., 1963; MD, Chgo. Med. Sch., 1967. Diplomate Am. Bd. Psychiatry and Neurology. Intern Cook County Hosp., Chgo., 1967-68; resident in psychiatry Mt. Sinai Hosp., N.Y.C., 1968-69, Chgo. Med. Sch., 1969-71, chief resident, 1970-71; staff psychiatrist U.S. Reynolds Army Hosp., Ft. Sill, Okla., 1971-73; assoc. attending psychiatrist Mt. Sinai Hosp., Chgo., 1973-74; instr. psychiatry Chgo. Med. Sch., North Chicago, 1973—, asst. prof., 1974-78, assoc. prof., 1978-88; prof. Finch U. Health Scis., Chgo. Med. Sch., North Chicago, 1988—, vice chmn., 1990-94, acting chmn., 1994-95, chmn., 1995—2002, chmn. ednl. affairs com., 1983-85, 86-01, residency dir., 1999-2001. Cons. psychiatry Cook County Hosp., 1974-79, St. Mary of Nazareth Hosp., 1979-84, Gt. Lakes Naval Hosp., 1987-90, Jackson Park Hosp., 1987-89, Mt. Sinai Hosp., 1988—, Elgin Mental Health Ctr., 1997—; chief mental health clinic, North Chicago VA Hosp., 1982-85, chief psychiatry svc., 1983-85. Author: (wth others) General Hospital Psychiatry, 1985, Behavioral Science for the Boreds, 1987, rev. 2d edit., 1989, rev. 3d edit., 1993, USMLE Behavioral Science Made Ridiculously Simple, 1998; editor: Clinical Behavioral Science, 1982, Behavioral Science for Medical Students, 1993; mem. editl. bd. Acad. Psychiatry, 2000—; contbr. articles to profl. jours. Coach Glenview (Ill.) Youth Baseball, 1987-89, mgr. 1990 (age 10-12 Glenview World Series winner 1990), Glenview Tennis Club, 1986-90 (3.5 Men's Doubles League winner 1989-90). Maj. M.C., U.S. Army, 1971-73. N.Y.State Regents scholar, 1959-63; NIMH grantee, 1974-83, Chgo. Med. Sch. grantee, 1974-83; recipient Seymour Vestermark award NIMH/Am. Psychiat. Assn., 2003. Fellow Am. Psychiat. Assn. (coun. edn. and career devel. 1993-95, Disting. Fellow, 2003—); mem. Am. Coll. Psychiatrists, Ill. Psychiat. Soc. (fellowship com. 1985-99), Columbia Coll. Alumni Secondary Schs. Com., Assn. Dirs. Med. Student Edn. in Psychiatry (exec. coun. 1985-99, chmn. program com. 1987-88, treas. 1989-91, pres-elect 1991-93, pres. 1993-95, immediate past pres. 1995-99), Alliance for Clin. Edn., Am. Assn. Chmn. Depts. Psychiatry, Chgo. Consortium for Psychiat. Rsch. (sec. 1996-97, treas. 1997-99), Am. Assn. Dirs. Psychiat. Residency Tng. (exec. coun. 2000-03, chair workforce coalition 2000-03), Sigma Xi, Alpha Omega Alpha, Phi Epsilon Pi. Office: Finch U Health Sci Chgo Med Sch 3333 Green Bay Rd North Chicago IL 60064-3037 E-mail: sierlesf@finchcms.edu.

SIEROCKI, JOHN STANLEY, oncologist; b. New Haven, Conn., 1947; MD, Hahnemann U., 1973. Diplomate Am. Bd. Internal Medicine, Am. Bd. Med. Oncology. Intern Hahnemann U., Phila., 1973—74, resident in medicine, 1974—76; fellow in med. oncology Meml. Sloan-Kettering Cancer Ctr., N.Y.C., 1976—78; attending physician in medicine, hematology and med. oncology Med. Ctr. at Princeton, NJ, 1983—. Assoc. clin. prof. medicine U. Medicine and Dentistry N.J.-R.W. Johnson, 1985—. Named one of Top Drs. in N.Y. Metro Area, Castle Connolly, Top Drs. 2003, N.J. Monthly Mag. Office: Princeton Med Group 419 N Harrison St Princeton NJ 08540-3521

SIERRA-AMOR, ROSA ISABEL, health facility administrator; b. Tampico, Mex., Apr. 28, 1954; Licensure Degree in Clin. Biochemistry, Nat. Autonomous U. Mexico, 1979, MS, 1992, PhD, 1995; postgrad., U. Reading, Eng., 1986. Fellow dept. endocrinology and metabolism Jewish Hosp. and Washington U. Sch. Medicine, St. Louis, 1982; mem. staff dept. nephrology and mineral metabolism, assoc. investigator Nat. Inst. Nutrition Salvador Zubiran, Mexico City, 1978-90; dir. Mineral Metabolism Rsch. Lab., divsn. neonatology Children's Hosp.-U. Cin. Med. Ctr., 1990-96; lab. mgr. Pediat. Bone Rsch. Ctr. Children's Hosp. Med. Ctr., 1996—. Lectr. in field. Contbr. articles to profl. jours. Recipient Ames/Bayer L.Am. award, 1993, award Mexican Coll. Profls. in Chemistry, 1994. Mem.: Spanish Soc. Clin. Chemistry and Molecular Pathology, Iberoamerican Soc. for Rsch. on Bone Metabolism, Nat. Acad. Pharm. Scis. (Mexico), Mexican Assn. Clin. Biochemistry, Am. Assn. for Bone and Mineral Rsch., Am. Assn. for Clin. Chemistry (mem. internat. rels. com. 1992—94, chair OVS membership com. 1994, mem. internat. adv. panel 1994—96, chair exch. program in clin. chemistry OVS 1994—, chair Ohio Valley sect. awards com. 1997—, treas. pediat. materno-fetal divsn. 2002—, Internat. Fellowship award 1996, Bernard Katchman ann. award 2001), Mex. Assn. Clin. Biochemistry (chair continuing edn. com., chmn. sci. proc. 8th internat. congress on lab. automation, mem. sci. program), Internat. Fedn. Clin. Chemistry (alt. rep. to Mexican Assn. Clin. Biochemistry 1992—96, newsletter corr. and reviewer jour. 1992—, mem. sci. program XVII Internat. Congress in Clin. Chemistry 1996—, assoc. mem. com. in metabolic bone disease and bone markers sci. divsn 1996—, mem. at large 1997—99, mem. EB 2000—02, co-chmn. sci. com. XIX ICCC 2005). Office: Childrens Hosp Med Ctr B Rm 4315 ML 11011 3333 Burnet Ave Cincinnati OH 45229-3039 E-mail: rsierramor@hotmail.com.

SIESS, ALFRED ALBERT, JR., engineering executive, management consultant; b. Bklyn., Aug. 16, 1935; s. Alfred Albert and Matilda Helen (Suttmeier) S.; m. Gale Murray Scholes, Dec. 17, 1966; children: Matthew Alan, Daniel Adam. BCE, Ga. Inst. Tech., 1956; postgrad. in bus., Boston Coll., 1968; MBA, Lehigh U., 1972. With fabricated steel constrn. divsn. Bethlehem (Pa.) Steel Corp., 1958-76, project mgr., 1969-76, engr. projects and mining divsn., 1976-86; sr. cons. T.J. Trauner Assocs., Phila., 1986-87; assoc. S.T. Hudson Internat., Phila., 1987-90; dir. mktg. SWIN Resource Sys., Inc., Bloomsburg, Pa., 1989-90; mem. adj. faculty Drexel U., 1976-96. Weekly columnist Economic and Environmental Issues, East Pa. edit. The Free Press, 1981-86; co-patentee suspension bridge erection equipment. Founder S.A.V.E. Inc., Coopersburg, Pa., 1969, pres., 1970, 75, 81, bd. dirs. 1970—. Served with C.E., USN, 1956-58. Recipient Environ. Action award S.A.V.E., Inc., 1975. Mem. ASCE (chmn. environ. tech. com. Lehigh Valley sect. 1971-83, life), Lions, Chi Epsilon. Republican. Mem. United Church of Christ. Home: 6460 Blue Church Rd Coopersburg PA 18036-9371 Office: C E Resource Group PO Box 39 Coopersburg PA 18036-0039 E-mail: siess@quixnet.net.

SIESS, CHARLES P., JR., Pres. & CEO, Marathon Mfg. Co., Houston., chmn. Cabot Oil & Gas Corp., Houston. Office: Cabot Oil & Gas Corp PO Box 4544 Houston TX 77210-4544

SIEVENPIPER, DANIEL FREDERIC, engineer; s. Ladd and Laurie Sievenpiper; m. Dianne Elena Allen, June 20, 2001. PhD, U. Calif., L.A., 1999. Sr. rsch. staff engr. HRL Labs., Malibu, Calif., 1999—. Contbr. articles to profl. jours. Recipient Outstanding Inventor award, HRL Labs., 2000, 2002. Mem.: IEEE. Achievements include invention of Inventor of high impedance electromagnetic surfaces for low-profile and low-cost antennas and other applications; patents for currently hold 15 U.S. patents in various topics related to electromagnetics and antennas; first to Developed New Tunable Electromagnetic Structures For Low-Profile And Low-Cost Antennas, Including Microelectromechanical Structures And Other New Techniques.

SIEVER-HENDERSON, PATRICIA, history university educator; b. L.A., July 21, 1937; d. Raymond and Barbara Gammage; m. Daniel Siever, Sept. 22, 1969 (div. Apr. 1, 1991); 1 child, A. Joshua Siever; m. Dr. Luther L. Henderson, Jan. 1, 1995; children: Melanie, Robert, Stephanie Pinkard. BA, UCLA, 1971, MA, 1973. Rsch. tech. John Wesley Hosp., L.A., 1963; med. asst. Dr. Harry Breetwor, L.A., 1964-67; grad. tchg. asst. in history UCLA, 1971-73; prof. history L.A. Mission Coll., San Fernando, Calif., 1975-86, L.A. Pierce Coll., Woodland Hills, Calif., 1989—. Chair Commn. for Advancement of Tchg., 1986-88; pres. bd. dirs. Calif. Assn. C.C., Sacramento, 1989-90; pres. Dist. Acad. Senate, L.A. C.C. Dist., 1986-89; v.p. State Acad. Senate, Sacramento., 1991-92; mem. bd. Govt. Calif. Commn. Colls., Sacramento, 1997-2002, v.p. 2001-2002. Editor, creator: The Anvil and Quill, 1995-99, The Faculty Forum, 1977-85. Mem. AB3409 Task Force Calif. State Legis., Sacramento, 1986-87, Assn. Calif. C.C., L.A., 1977-85; treas. Calif. Black Faculty and Staff, L.A., 1980-82. Named Outstanding Black Educator Black Assn. Calif. C.C., Sacramento, 1989; recipient Golden Apple award Assoc. Student Orgn., L.A., 1989-99, Spl. Recognition, USA Today, 1994. Mem. United African Am. Student Assn. (faculty adv.), Asilomar Women's Leadership. Republican. Avocations: chess, tennis, dance. Office: LA Pierce Coll 6201 Winnetka Ave Woodland Hills CA 91371-0001 E-mail: sieverpg@aol.com.

SIEVERT, FREDERICK, insurance company executive; b. 1948; Sr. v.p., CFO N.Y. Life Ins. Co., N.Y.C., 1992-95, exec. v.p., 1995-97, vice chmn., 1997—. Office: NY Life Ins Co 51 Madison Ave New York NY 10010

SIEVERT, G. MICHAEL, marketing professional; BA in Econs., U. Pa. Program dir. IBM, 1996—98; v.p. mktg. E* Trade Group, Inc., Menlo Park, Calif., 1998—99; v.p., gen. mgr. Consumer Markets, 1999—2000, chief global mktg. and sales officer, 2000—01; chief mktg. officer AT&T Wireless Svcs., Inc., Redmond, Wash., 2002—. Bd. dirs. Harmonic Communications, 2002—. Office: AT&T Wireless Services Inc NE Bldg 1 7277 164th Ave Redmond WA 98052

SIEVERT, MARY ELIZABETH, small business owner, retired secondary school educator; b. Sioux City, Iowa, Sept. 28, 1939; d. Arthur Harry and Bertha Busboom Sievert. BS, Morningside Coll., 1960; MA, U. Nebr., 1962; postgrad., U. Iowa, Hope Coll., U. Calif., Irvine. Instr. chemistry lab. Morningside Coll., Sioux City, Iowa, 1959—60; tchr. chemistry Davenport Schs., Iowa, 1962—86, Blackhawk Coll., Moline, Ill.; admissions officer St. Luke's Hosp., Davenport; SSTP counselor U. Iowa, Iowa City; computer instr. Grinnell Coll., Iowa, 1983; P/K-12/A sci. coord. Davenport Schs., 1986—96, AGATE dept. chair, 1995—99; pres., CEO Memorabilia ExtraOrdinaire, Davenport, 1996—. Exchange tchr. Rowley Regis Coll., Birmingham, England, 1975; pres., CEO Quad Cities Sci. and Enging. Fair, Davenport, 1962—99; adv. evaluation coun. Antique Am., Davenport, 2000—01; antiques and collectibles lectr. Ea. Iowa C.C., Davenport, 2001—, Blackhawk Coll., Moline, Ill., 2002—. Contbr. articles to profl. jours. Fundraising v.p. Miss Iowa Bd., Davenport, 1999—2001; mem. plan and zone commn. City of Davenport, 1988—94; WelcomeAires mem. QC vol. bur. QC Internat. Airport, 2000—; charter mem. 1st in the Nation in Edn. Rschr. Found., 1986—97; 63 com. woman Scott County Rep. Party; handbell ringer, former dir. vacation Bible sch. Holy Cross Luth. Ch., Davenport; mem. bd. Christ Lutheran Ch., 2002—. Named Outstanding H.S. Chemistry Tchr. of Yr. in Iowa, Iowa Acad. Scis., 1969, Outstanding Young Educator, Davenport Jaycees, Centennial Tchr. of Yr. in Iowa, NIH, 1987; named to Iowa Sci. Tchrs. Hall of Fame, 2002; recipient Regional Catalyst award for outstanding chemistry tchr., Chem. Mfg. Assn., 1985, Golden Apple award for top educator, Scott County Edn. Orgn., 1998; fellow Woodrow Wilson fellow for outstanding H.S. chemistry tchrs., Princeton U., 1982; scholar NSF. Mem.: AAUW (past pres. local br. and Iowa State), NEA (life), U. Nebr. Alumni Assn. (life), Morningside Alumni Assn. (life), Delta Kappa Gamma (former local and state parliamentarian, mem. Hapke scholarship com.), Pi Lambda Theta (life; mem. charter alumni chpt.), Sigma Kappa (life). Avocations: bridge, gardening, travel, theater, symphony. Office: Memorabilia ExtraOrdinaire Inc 2707 East Hayes St Davenport IA 52803

SIEVING, PAUL A. federal agency administrator, ophthalmologist, educator; b. Ft. Wayne, Ind., 1948; BS in Physics and History with honors, Valparaiso U., 1970, DS (hon.), 2003; MS in Physics, Yale U., 1973; postgrad., Yale Law Sch., 1974; MD, U. Ill. Med. Sch., 1978; PhD in Bioengring., U. Ill. Grad. Sch., 1980. Diplomate Nat. Bd. Med. Examiners, 1978, Am. Bd. Ophthalmology, 1983. Med. resident in ophthalmology U. Ill. Eye and Ear Infirmary, 1978—82; post-doctoral fellow in retinal physiology U. Calif., San Francisco, 1982—84; clin. fellow in retinal degenerations Harvard, Berman-Gund Lab, Mass. Eye and Ear Infirmary, 1984—85; asst. prof. ophthalmology U. Mich., Ann Arbor, 1985—89, assoc. prof., 1989—94, prof., 1994—2001, Paul R. Lichter prof. of ophthalmic genetics, 1990—2001; dir. Nat. Eye Inst., NIH, 2001—. Chair Retinal Diseases NEI, Vision Rsch.: A Nat. Plan, 1999—2003. Named one of Best Doctors in Am., 1996, 1998, 2001; recipient Olga Keith Weiss scholar, 1989, Disting. Alumnus, Valparaiso U., 1991, Sr. Sci. Investigator award, 1998, Alcon Rsch. award, Alcon Rsch. Inst., 2000; James scholar, U. Ill. Med. Sch., 1978. Mem.: RP Found. Fighting Blindness (Sci. Adv. Bd. 1989—2001, vice-chair rsch. 1995—2001), Internat. Soc. Clinical Electrophysiology of Vision (tres. 1986—94), Am. Ophthal. Soc., Sigma Xi. Achievements include specializing in the treatment of human genetic retinal and macular degenerations and research to prevent blindness. Office: Nat Eye Inst Nat Inst Health 31 Ctr Dr Bldg 31 6A03 Bethesda MD 20892-2510

SIEWERT, ROBIN NOELLE, planning engineer; b. Heidelberg, Fed. Republic Germany, Dec. 14, 1956; (parents Am. citizens); d. Orville Ray and Norma Idella (Sprink) S. BSChemE, U. Tex., 1979; MA in Christian Edn., So. Bapt. Theol. Sem., 1993. Registered profl. engr. Start-up engr. Cen. Power and Light Co., Fannin, Tex., 1979-81, chem. engr. Corpus Christi, Tex., 1981-85, performance analysis engr., 1985-87, performance analysis supr., 1987-91; budget analyst Louisville Gas & Electric, 1992-93, chem. engr., 1994-2000, systems analyst, 2000—01, planning engr., 2001—. Republican. Baptist. Avocations: piano, singing, walking, travel, photography. Home: 9304 Smyrna Pkwy Louisville KY 40229-1418

SIFF, ANDREW, lawyer; Chief counsel to Rep. majority U.S. Senate Com. Rules and Adminstrn., Washington, 2001—02; counselor to sec. labor U.S. Dept. of Labor, Washington, 2002—. Office: US Dept Labor Frances Perkins Bldg 200 Constitution Ave NW Washington DC 20210 Business E-Mail: siff-andrew@dol.gov.

SIFF, MARLENE IDA, artist, designer; b. N.Y.C. d. Irving Louis and Dorothy Gertrude (Lahn) Marmer; m. Elmott Justin Siff, July 11, 1959; children: Bradford Evan, Brian Douglas. BA, Hunter Coll., 1957. Cert. tchr. elem. edn., N.Y., N.J. Tchr. Stewart Manor (N.Y.) Sch. Sys., 1957-59, Teaneck (N.J.) Sch. Sys., 1959-60; freelance interior designer Westport, Conn., 1966-70; designer Varo Inertial Products, Trumbull, Conn., 1970; designer signature collections J.P. Stevens & Co. Inc., N.Y., 1974-78, J.C. Penney Co., N.Y., 1978, C.R. Gibson Co., Norwalk, Conn., 1980. Corp. sec., treas., bd. dirs. Belmar Corp., Westport, 1972—; chmn. bd. Marlene Designs Inc., Westport, 1973-77; owner Marlene Siff Design Studio, Westport, 1978—; aesthetic cons. Alcide Corp., Norwalk, 1980-88. One-person shows include David Segal Gallery, N.Y.C., 1987, Conn. Pub. TV Gallery, Hartford, 1987, Paul Mellon Art Ctr., Choate Rosemary Hall, Wallingford, Conn., 1989, Conn. Nat. Bank Hdqs., Norwalk, 1990, Michael Stone Collection, Washington, 1992, Bergdorf Goodman Men, N.Y.C., 1993, Joel Kessler Fine Art, Miami Beach, Fla., 1994, Park Pl., Stamford, Conn., 1995, Westport Arts Ctr., 1995, Mitchells, Westport, 1998, NIH, Bethesda, Md., 1999, Durst Lobby Gallery, N.Y.C., 1999; represented in permanent collections B'nai Brith Klutznick Nat. Jewish Mus., Washington, 1997. Decorator Easter Seal Home Svc. Charity Ball, 1976; bd. dirs. United Jewish Appeal, Westport, 1982-86; com. mem. Levitt Pavillion of the Performing Arts, Westport, 1982-89; mem. art adv. coun. Herbert F. Johnson Art, Cornell U., Ithaca, N.Y. Recipient award for creating the most beautiful working environment in an indsl. facility in lower Conn., Lower Conn. Mfrs. Assn., 1970. Mem.: LVW, Art Adv. Coun. Herbert F. Johnson Mus. Art at Cornell U. NY, Anti Defamation League, Nat. Coun. Jewish Women, Kappa Pi. Jewish. Avocations: tennis, swimming, race walking, gardening. Home: 15 Broadview Rd Westport CT 06880-2303 Office Phone: 203-226-8557. Business E-Mail: marlene@marlenesiff.com.

SIFFERT, JOHN SAND, lawyer, educator, writer; b. NYC, Mar. 26, 1947; s. Robert Spencer and Miriam (Sand) S.; m. Goldie Alfasi-Siffert, June 1, 1975; children: David Alfasi, Matthew Alfasi. BA, Amherst Coll., 1969; JD, Columbia U., 1972. Bar: N.Y. 1973, U.S. Dist. Ct. (so. dist.) N.Y. 1974, (ea. dist.) N.Y. 1974, U.S. Ct. Appeals (2d cir.) 1974, U.S. Supreme Ct. 1979. Law clk. to Hon. Murray I. Gurfein U.S. Dist. Ct. (so. dist.) N.Y., 1972-74; asst. U.S. atty. (so. dist.) N.Y., 1974-79; ptnr. Fulop & Hardee and predcessor firm Barovick, Konecky et al, N.Y.C., 1979-83, Lankler & Siffert, N.Y.C., 1983-84, Lankler Siffert & Wohl LLP, N.Y.C., 1984—. Adj. prof. NYU, 1979—; adv. coun. procurement policy bd. City of NY, 1991-95; bd. dirs. NYC Off-Track-Betting, NYLPI, 1998-2004; mem. adv. bd. N.Y. Civil Rights Coalition, 1995-; spl. master First Dept. Appellate Divsn., 1999—; mem. divsn. first dept. Indigent Def. Orgn. Oversight Com., 2003-. Co-author: Business Crime, 1981, Modern Federal Jury Instructions-Criminal, Modern Federal Jury Instructions-Civil. Mem. adv. bd. N.Y. Civil Rights Coalition, 1995—. Fellow: Am. Coll. Trial Lawyers (chmn. com. on admission to fellowship 2001—04, chmn. downstate com. 2004—); mem.: ABA, Fed. Bar Coun. (pres. Inns of Ct. 2001—02), Assn. of Bar of City of N.Y. (chmn. fed. legis. com. 2003—), N.Y. State Bar Assn. Democrat. Jewish. Office: Lankler Siffert & Wohl 500 5th Ave Fl 33 New York NY 10110-3398 Office Phone: 212-921-8399. E-mail: jsiffert@lswlaw.com.

SIFFERT, ROBERT SPENCER, orthopedic surgeon; b. N.Y.C., June 16, 1918; s. Oscar and Sadye (Rusoff) Siffert; m. Miriam Sand, June 29, 1941; children: Joan, John. AB in Biology with honors, NYU, 1939, MD, 1943. Diplomate Am. Bd. Orthrop. Surgery, Nat. Bd. Med. Examiners. Intern Kings County Hosp., Bklyn., 1943; resident in orthop. surgery Mt. Sinai Hosp., N.Y.C., 1946-49, fellow in pathology, 1949-52, mem. staff, 1949—, dir. orthor. surgery, orthop. surgeon in chief, 1960-86, Lasker/Siffert Disting. Svc. prof., 1986—; pvt. practice N.Y.C., 1949—. Sr. orthop. cons. N.Y.C. Dept. Health, 1952—60; attending orthop. surgeon Blythedale Children's Hosp., Valhalla, 1960—86, cons., 1986—90; dir. dept. orthops. City Hosp., Elmhurst, 1965—86; prof., chmn. dept. orthrops. Mt. Sinai Sch. Medicine, 1966—86, Dr. Robert K. Lippman prof., 1983—86, acting chmn., 1993—94. Author (with J. F. Katz): (book) Management of Hip Disorders in Children, 1983; author: See How They Grow, 1985; contbr. articles to profl. jours. Bd. dirs., mem. profl. adv. com. Easter Seal Soc. Crippled Children and Adults, 1st v.p., 1977—79; mem. adv. bd. CARE-MEDICO, 1972—83, bd. dirs., chmn., 1981—83; bd. dirs. CARE, 1983—90; mem. adv. bd. Orthopaedics Overseas, 1981—93. Capt. USAAF, 1944—46, CBI. Decorated 4 Battle Stars; recipient Ann. award in medicine, N.Y. Pub. Health Assn., 1956, N.Y. Philanthropic League, 1959, Richman award for humanism in medicine, Mt. Sinai Sch. Medicine, 1989, Lifetime Achievement award, Arthritis Found., 2002. Fellow: APHA, ACS; mem.: N.Y. State Med. Soc. (chmn. orthrop. sect. 1967—68), N.Y. Acad. Medicine (fellow orthop. sect. 1952, sec. 1962—63, chmn. 1963—64), Orthop. Rsch. Soc., Internat. Skeletal Soc., Internat. Soc. Orthop. Surgery and Traumatology, Assn. Bone and Joint Surgeons, Am. Acad. Orthop. Surgery (chmn. com. care handicapped child), Am. Orthop. Assn., Century Assn. (N.Y.), Phi Beta Kappa, Alpha Omega Alpha. Office Phone: 212-288-2566.

SIFNEOS, PETER EMANUEL, psychiatrist, educator; b. Greece, Oct. 22, 1920; came to U.S., 1941, naturalized, 1944; s. Demitrios Z. and Mary E. (Lucas) S.; divorced; children: Ann Lucas Callahan, Peter Gray, Jean Coit Sifneos Schafer. B.Sc., Sorbonne, 1940; MD, Harvard U., 1946; PhD (hon.), U. Athens, Greece, 1998. Diplomate: Am. Bd. Psychiatry. Intern Boston City Hosp. and Harvard Med. Svc., 1946-47; resident in psychiatry McLean Hosp., Belmont, Mass., 1950-52; chief resident Mass. Gen. Hosp., Boston, 1952-53, mem. staff, chief psychiat. clinic, 1954-68; fellow Harvard U. Sch. Public Health, 1953-54; mem. faculty Harvard U. Med. Sch., 1952—, prof. psychiatry, 1973-91, prof. emeritus, 1991—; staff, assoc. dir. psychiatry dept. Beth Israel Hosp., Boston, 1968-94. Author: Ascent from Chaos, 1964, Short-Term Psychotherapy and Emotional Crisis, 1972, Short-Term Dynamic Psychotherapy Evaluation and Technique, 1979, 2d edit., 1987, Short-Term Anxiety Provking Psychotherapy, 1992, Escape?, 1998, 2d edit., 2002; editor-in-chief Psychotherapy and Psychosomatics, 1974-91; contbr. over 125 articles to profl. jours. Served with AUS, 1944-46, U.S. Army Med. Corp., Germany, 1947-50. Fellow: Am. Psychiat. Assn. (disting. life 2003); mem.: AMA, Am. Psychosomatic Soc., Italian Psychosomatic Soc. (hon.), Boston Psychoanalytic Soc. (life), Hellenic Psychosomatic Soc. (hon.), Internat. Fedn. Med. Psychotherapy (v.p. 1976—88, bd. dirs. 1988—94). Democrat. Home and Office: 59 Common St Belmont MA 02478-3022 Fax: 617-484-3496. Office Phone: 617-484-2701. E-mail: pesifneos@aol.com. *The principles which helped me most have been a belief in good education, a fierce sense of non-conformity, a strong sense of independence, an admiration of creativity and new ideas, a love of writing, teaching, reading, classic music, traveling, lecturing and conducting workshops, seminars all over North and South America and Europe, swimming, and luck in being healthy.*

SIFONTES, JOSE E. pediatrics educator; b. Arecibo, P.R. s. Jose E. and Josefa M. (Fontan) S.; m. Iris J. Sotomayor, Dec. 20, 1952; children: J. Jaime, Mariat, Iris, J. Roberto, Myrta, J. Ricardo, Beatriz. MD, Syracuse U., 1948. Diplomate Am. Bd. Pediatrics. Dir. USPHS TB Rsch., San Juan, Puerto Rico, 1958-66; dean U. Puerto Rico Sch. of Medicine, San Juan, 1966-71; chief of pediatrics U. Puerto Rico Sch. Medicine, San Juan, 1974-77, chief pediatric pulmonary program, 1960-66, prof. pediatrics, 1966—. Specializing in pulmonary pediatrics, San Juan, 1982—; cons. to many nat. and internat. health orgns. including WHO, UN, PAHO, CARE, 1954-82. Author: (Spanish

textbook) Neumologia Pediatrica, 1974; contbr. over 100 articles to profl. jours. and pediat. texts. Vol. Am. Thoracic Soc. ATS, ALA, 1953—. Surgeon USPHS, 1957-59. Grantee USPHS, NIH, 1954-82. Mem. Am. Acad. Pediatrics (fellow chest sect., nat. chmn. 1964-65), Am. Pediatric Soc., Alpha Omega Alpha. Roman Catholic.

SIFTON, CHARLES PROCTOR, federal judge; b. N.Y.C., Mar. 18, 1935; s. Paul F. and Claire G. S.; m. Susan Scott Rowland, May 20, 1986; children: Samuel, Tobias, John. AB, Harvard U., 1957; LL.B., Columbia U., 1961. Bar: N.Y. 1961. Assoc. Cadwalader, Wickersham & Taft, 1961-62, 64-66; staff atty. U.S. Senate Fgn. Rels. Com., 1962-63; asst. U.S. atty. N.Y.C., 1966-69; ptnr. LeBoeuf, Lamb, Leiby and MacRae, N.Y.C., 1969-77; judge U.S. Dist. Ct. (ea. dist.) N.Y., Bklyn., 1977—, chief judge, 1995-2000, sr. judge, 2000—. Mem.: Bar Assn. City of NY. Office: US Dist Ct US Courthouse 225 Cadman Plz E Rm 244 Brooklyn NY 11201-1818

SIFTON, DAVID WHITTIER, retired magazine editor; b. N.Y.C., Sept. 12, 1940; s. David William and Dorothy (Whittier) S. BA, Trinity Coll., Hartford, Conn., 1962; MA, Stanford U., 1967. Editor Inside Edn., N.Y. State Edn. Dept., 1968-70; adminstrv. editor Med. Econs., Oradell, N.J., 1970 72; editor Drug Topics, Oradell, 1972-75; editor in chief Current Prescribing, Oradell, 1975-78, RN mag., Oradell, 1978-83; dir. spl. editorial projects Med. Econs. Co., 1983-90; editor PDR Publs., Montvale, 1990—2003; ret., 2003. Founder Physicians' Desk Reference on CD-ROM, PDR's Drug Interactions and Side Effects Index, PDR's Indications Index, Pocket PDR (handheld electronic database), The PDR Family Guide to Prescription Drugs, The PDR Family Guide to Women's Health, The PDR Family Guide to Nutrition and Health, The PDR Family Guide to Lifelong Health, The PDR Family Guide Encyclopedia of Medical Care, The PDR Family Guide to Over the Counter Drugs, The PDR Family Guide to Natural Medicines and Healing Therapies, The PDR Family Guide to Common Ailments, The PDR Family Guide to Nutritional Supplements, The PDR Guide to Biological and Chemical Warfare Response, The PDR Drug Guide for Mental Health Professionals. Served to 1st lt. USAF, 1963-66. Decorated Air Force Commendation medal; grantee Ford Found., 1967 Mem. Am. Bus. Press (chmn. editorial com. 1975-76) Republican. Episcopalian. E-mail: david.sifton@verizon.net.

SIFTON, ELISABETH, book publisher; b. N.Y.C., Jan. 13, 1939; d. Reinhold and Ursula (Keppel-Compton) Niebuhr, m. Charles P. Sifton, 1962 (div. 1984); children: Peter Samuel, Charles Tobias, John Paul Gustav; m. Fritz R. Stern, 1996. BA magna cum laude, Radcliffe Coll., Cambridge, Mass., 1960; postgrad., U. Paris, 1960-61. Asst. to dep. asst. sec. of state U.S. Dept. of State, Washington, 1961-62; editorial asst., assoc. editor, editor, sr. editor Frederick A. Praeger Pubs., N.Y.C., 1962-68; editor, sr. editor, editor-in-chief The Viking Press, N.Y.C., 1969-83; v.p., pub. Elisabeth Sifton Books, Viking Penguin, N.Y.C., 1984-87; exec. v.p. Alfred A. Knopf, Inc., N.Y.C., 1987-92; sr. v.p. Farrar, Straus & Giroux, 1993—; pub. Hill & Wang, 1993—. Fulbright fellow, 1960-61 Democrat. Episcopalian. Home: 15 Claremont Ave New York NY 10027-6802 Office: Farrar Straus & Giroux 19 Union Sq W Fl 4 New York NY 10003-3304

SIGAI, A. GARY, engineer; b. Balt., Dec. 3, 1944; m. June E. McGrath, June 28, 1946; 1 child, Daniel Peter. BS in Chemistry, Rensselaer Poly. Inst., 1965, PhD in Chemistry, 1969. Mem. tech. staff RCA Labs., Princeton, NJ, 1969—72; sr. scientist Xerox Corp., Webster, NY, 1972—79; prin. mem. tech. staff GTE Labs., Waltham, Mass., 1979—92; pres. Lexington (Mass.) Tech. Group, 1992—93; chief materials scientist PolyVision, Wallingford, Conn., 1993—95; fellow engr. Philips Lighting Co., Salina, Kans., 1995—. Contbr. articles to profl. publs. Recipient Pres. award, GTE Corp. Mem.: Illuminating Engring. Soc., Electrochem. Soc., Am. Chem. Soc. Achievements include patents in field. Home: 2417 Brookwood Lane Salina KS 67401 Office: Philips Lighting Company Salina KS 67401 Office Phone: 785-822-1550.

SIGAL, GALE, literature educator; b. N.Y.C., Oct. 12, 1952; d. Max and Frieda Yetta Sigal; m. David Peter Weinstein, Apr. 21, 1949. BA, City Coll. of NY, 1975; MA, Fordham U., 1978; PhD, Grad. Ctr. City U. of NY, 1985. Adj. prof. City Coll. of NY, N.Y.C., 1982—86; vis. asst. prof. Yeshiva U., N.Y.C., 1986—87; asst. prof. Wake Forest U. NW, Winston-Salem, NC, 1987—92, assoc. prof., 1992—96, Zachary T. Smith prof., 1996—2000, prof., chair, 1998—. Vis. prof. St. Peter's Coll. Oxford U., Oxford, England, 2001—03. Author: Erotic Dawn-Songs of the Middle Ages, 1996; co-editor: Voices in Traslation: The Authority of 'Olde Books' in Medieval Literature, 1992. Recipient NEH Summer Inst. honor, Stanford U., 1991. Mem.: MLA. Office: Wake Forest U English Dept P O Box 7387 Winston Salem NC 27109

SIGALA, STEPHANIE CHILDS, art historian, librarian; b. Berkeley, Calif., Nov. 1, 1947; d. Henry Everett and Mary Elizabeth (Baeck) Childs. BA in Art History, UCLA, 1968, MA, 1970; MSLS, U. Ill., 1984. Instr. art dept. U. Wis., Whitewater, 1971-73, slide curator art history dept. Milw., 1973-74; asst. prof. dept. art Ill. State U., Normal, 1978-83; head libr. architecture and fine arts libr. Auburn (Ala.) U., 1984-85; head libr. Richardson Meml. Libr. St. Louis Art Mus., 1985—2000; acting dir. edn. pub. programs St. Louis (Mo.) Art Mus., 2000—02, mgr. gallery programs, 2002—. Adj. prof. sch. libr. and info. sci. U. Mo., Columbia, 1988-96; lectr. in art evening coll. U. Mo., St. Louis, 1990; instr. continuing edn. program Auburn U., 1985; mem. edn. com. St. Louis Regional Libr. Network, 1986-88; spkr. in field. Contbg. writer: A History of American Mass Market Magazines, 1990; editor, chief writer: The Museum Building: Inside and Out, Then and Now, 1990, Art of the Ancient World, 1989; editor: Art Documentation, 1996-2000; contbr. articles and revs. to profl. jours. Grantee Samuel H. Kress Found., 1969, NDEA Title II, 1970. Mem. ALA, Visual Resources Assn., Art Librs. Soc. N.Am. (collection devel. com. 1993-94, art documentation adv. com. 1989-92, vice chair Cen. Plains chpt. 1987-88, chair 1988-89, nat. exec. bd. 1995—97), Spl. Librs. Assn. (program com. chair St. Louis Metro chpt. 1993-94, dir.-at-large 1989-90), Archaeol. Inst. Am. (bd. local chpt. 1975-76), Beta Phi Mu, Phi Kappa Phi. Office: Saint Louis Art Mus 1 Fine Arts Dr Saint Louis MO 63110-1380 E-mail: athena@slam.org.

SIGAL-IBSEN, ROSE, artist; b. Bucharest, Romania, Aug. 22; arrived in U.S., 1957; d. Joseph and Tilly (Eckstein) Cohen; m. Albert D. Sigal, Dec. 25, 1941 (dec. May 1970); 1 child, Daniel M.; m. Joseph Ibsen, Oct. 1973 Diploma, Fashion Inst. Technology, N.Y.C., 1978; Parson, Sch. of Design, N.Y.C., 1985-86; student, Koho Sch. of Sumi-E, N.Y.C., 1979-90, Zhejiang Acad. Fine Arts, China, 1990. Curator Metro N.Y. Chpt. of Sumi-E Soc., 1990—, v.p., 1990—. One-woman shows include China-Gallery Weizhi Schubert, Hanover, Germany, 1991, Manhattan Savs. Bank, N.Y.C., 1993—94, Chem. Bank, 1993—95, N.Y. Pub. Libr., 1996, Bankers Fed., N.Y.C., 1996, Rep. Bank for Savs., 1996, Roumanian Cultural Found., Bucharest, 1998, World Fine Art Gallery, N.Y.C., 1998, Romanian Embassy, Washington, 2000, others, exhibited in group shows at China Nat. Acad. of Fine Arts, Hangzhou, 1994, Fourth World Conf. on Women, Beijing, 1995, Steinhardt Conservatory, Bklyn. Bot. Garden, 1996, Nat. Mus. of Women in the Arts, Washington, 1996, 80 Washington Square East Galleries, N.Y.C., 1996, Seton Hall U., South Orange, N.J., 1996, Golden West Coll. Fine Arts Gallery, Huntington Beach, Calif., 1995, Seton Hall Gallery, South Orange, N.J., 1996, Wesleyan U., Middletown, Conn., 1998, Taipei Gallery Chinese Info. and Culture Ctr. and the Chinese-Am. Arts Coun., 1998, Cork Gallery/Lincoln Ctr., N.Y.C., 1998, Pen and Brush, (All-sections award), Sumi-e Soc. Am., Inc., 1999, Japanese Am. Cultural & Cmty. Ctr. at Doizaki Gallery, 1999, Broome St. Gallery, N.Y.C., 1999, 2001—02, Nat. Mus. of Women in Arts, 1999, Asia Soc. Store, 1999, ASCA, 1999—2000, Japanese Cultural Ctr., L.A., 1999, Pen and Brush All Media Millennium Celebration, 2000, Pen and Brush Ann. Watercolor, 2000, Broome St. Gallery Invitational, 2000, Contemporary Artists Guild, 2000, Newark Mus. and Taiwan Art Edn. Inst., 2000, Sumi-e Soc. Am. Inc. at Courthouse Galleries of Portsmouth Va., 2001 (Hallie Hazen Meml. award, 2001), Pen and Brush Ann. Mixed Media, 2002, Korean Cultural Ctr., L.A., 2002, Japanese Artists Assn. N.Y., 2002, others; artwork Courage Card design, 1998. Recipient Manhattan Arts award Cover Art Competition, N.Y.C., 1992, 94, 95, 97, King Point award, Fla., 1991, Tenth Japanese Internat. Calligraphy Exhbn. award, N.Y.C., 1996, Manhattan Arts Internat. Showcase award, Emily N. Hatch Meml. award Pen and Brush, Inc., Spring Watercolor Exhbn., 1998, Hallie Hazen Meml. award Sumi-e Soc. Am., Inc., 2001. Mem. Nat. Mus. of Women in the Arts, Artist Equity of N.Y., Am. Soc. Contemporary Artists, Art of Ink in Am., The Oriental Brushwork Soc. of Am., Sumi-e Soc. (hon.). Avocations: sculptor in clay, dance. Home: One Irving Pl #222B New York NY 10003 9741

SIGALL, HAROLD FRED, psychology educator; b. N.Y.C., June 29, 1943; s. Walter and Regine (Goldenberg) S.; m. Brenda Ann Alpert, Aug. 8, 1965; children: Elana, Jennifer, Emily. BS, CUNY, 1964; PhD, U. Tex., 1968. Asst. prof. psychology U. Rochester, N.Y., 1968-72; assoc. prof. U. Md., College Park, 1972-78, prof., 1978—, dir. grad. program in social psychology, dir. grad. studies dept. Psyc., 2000—; cons. editor Jour. Applied Social Psychology, 1992—. Cons. social rsch. and decision making to numerous orgns., lectr. Smithsonian Inst., Washington, 1984, 85; vis. prof. U. Bologna, 1997, 2002. Editor Personality and Social Psychology Bull., 1977-81. Bd. dirs. Columbia (Md.) Jewish Congregation, 1985-87, Howard County (Md.) Jewish Cmty. Sch., Columbia, 1986-87; mem. Human Rights Commn., Howard County, 1994-99. NDEA fellow, 1967-68, Danforth Found. fellow, 1970-71. Fellow APA, Am. Psychol. Soc.; mem. Soc. Exptl. Social Psychology. Home: 5060 Castle Moor Dr Columbia MD 21044-1871 Office: U of Md Dept Psychology College Park MD 20742-0001 E-mail: hsigall@psyc.umd.edu.

SIGBAND, NORMAN BRUCE, management communication educator; b. Chgo., June 27, 1920; s. Max and Bessie S.; m. Joan C. Lyons, Aug. 3, 1944; children: Robin, Shelley, Betsy. BA, U. Chgo., 1940, MA, 1941, PhD, 1954; LHD (hon.), DePaul U., 1986. Asst. prof. bus. communication DePaul U., 1946-50, assoc. prof., 1950-54, prof., 1954-65; prof. mgmt. communication U. So. Calif., 1965—, chmn. dept. mktg., 1970-72, assoc. dean Sch. Bus., 1975 80, Disting. prof. emeritus, 1989 . Disting. Centennial lectr. U. Tex., Austin, 1986; cons. to industry; spkr., condr. workshops, seminars in field; scholar-in-residence Va. Commonwealth U., 1987, DePaul U., 1988; Borchard lectr., 2003. Author books including: Practical Communication for Everyday Use, 25th edit., 1954, Effective Report Writing for Business, Industry and Government, 1960, Communication for Management, 1970, Communicacion Para Directivos, 1972, Management Communication for Decision Making, 1972, Communication for Management and Business, 1976, Communication for Managers, 6th edit., 2001, Communicating in Business, 1987, 3d edit., 1989, in Spanish, 1993, in Chinese, 2001, Patient-Pharmacist Consultation: A Communication Skills Approach, 1993, Communication for Pharmacists and Other Health Professionals, 1995, 2d edit., 1996, (with J. Biles) The Status of American Universities: Challenges and Opportunities, 2003; movies include: Communication Barriers and Gateways, 2d edit., 1993, Listening: A Key to Problem Solving (award winnter), 2d edit., 1993, The Grapevine, The Power of a Minute, 1992; gen. editor books including: Harcourt Brace Jovanovich Bus. series; contbr. numerous articles to profl. jours., mags. Served to capt. AUS, 1942-46, ETO. Decorated Bronze Star; recipient recognition award City of L.A., 1985, hon. alumnus award U. So. Calif., 1991. Fellow Am. Bus. Communication Assn. (pres. 1964-65); mem. Internat. Communication Assn., Acad. Mgmt., Anti-Defamation League, Hadassah Assocs., Blue Key, Phi Kappa Phi, Alpha Kappa Psi, Beta Gamma Sigma. Democrat. Jewish. Home: 3109 Dona Susana Dr Studio City CA 91604-4355 Office: 1985 Zonal Ave Los Angeles CA 90089-0105 Office Phone: 323-442-1369.

SIGEL, MARSHALL ELLIOT, financial consultant; b. Hartford, Conn., Nov. 25, 1941; s. Paul and Bessie (Somer) S.; m. Sybil R. Miller, Nov. 23, 1995. BS in Econs., U. Pa., 1963; JD, U. Miami, 1982, LLM in Taxation, 1983. Exec. v.p. Advo-System div. KMS Industries, Inc., Hartford, 1963-69, pres., 1969-72; pres. Ad-Type Corp., Hartford, 1963-69, Ad-Lists, Inc., Hartford, 1963-69; fin. cons. Hartford, 1972-83, Boca Raton, Fla., 1987—; pvt. practice law, 1983-87. Bd. dirs. Wharton Sch. Club of South Fla. Mem. FOPA, World Pres.' Orgn., citizens bd. U. Miami, Boca Grove Club, 100 Club of So. Palm Beach County. Home and Office: PO Box 273408 Boca Raton FL 33427-3408

SIGELL, LEONARD TRITTACK, pharmacologist, educator; b. Portland, Oreg., Dec. 28, 1938; s. Edward Trittack and Rose (Lichtgarn) S. BS (RPh) Pharmacy, Oreg. State U., 1961; PhD in Pharmacology, U. Oreg., 1964. Reg. pharmacist, Oreg.; cert. prevention specialist. Registered pharmacist Fred Meyer Pharmacy, Portland, 1962-64; staff Oreg. Poison Ctr., Portland, 1962-64; mem. faculty dept. pharmacology, dept. medicine U. Cin., 1964-97; dir. Drug and Poison Info. Ctr., Cin., 1966-97; ret., 1997; prof. emeritus Dept. Pharmacology & Cell Biophysics Drug & Poison Info. Ctr., 1997—, dir. emeritus, 1997—. Former evaluator Law Enforcement Assistance Adminstrn., Open House Counseling Svc., Inc., Charlotte, N.C.; former mem. Nat. Adv. Panel to HEW Model Health Care Tech. Ctr. U. Mo., student rsch. awards com. Am. Assn. Poison Control Ctrs.; mem. profl. effectiveness program com. U. Cin., adv. com. Med. Ctr. Librs., past mem. admissions com. U. Coll. Medicine, Univ. Hosp.; mem. Cin. Health Dept. Pharmacy and Therapeutics com., Hamilton County Drug Abuse Coordinating Com.; past mem. steering com. Hamilton County Comty. Mental Health Bd.; former cons. multi-purpose Arthritis Ctr. for Tri-State area. Contbr. articles to numerous profl. jours; mem. edtl. bd. Poisindex, former mem. editors cons. panel Jour. Am. Med. Assn.; past book reviewer Archives Internal Medicine, past reviewer Am. Jour. Diseases of Children; reviewer Drug Intelligence and Clin. Pharmacy; past referee Am. Jour. Hosp. Pharmacy. Mem. Alcohol and Drug Abuse Prevention Assn. of Ohio, Assn. of Ohio Substance Abuse Programs; past mem. Citizens Against Substance Abuse; bd. dirs. Adolescent Clinic of Children's Hosp. Med. Ctr., U.S. Pharmacopoeia Conv. Recipient Oscar Schmidt Pub. Svc. award, U. Cin., 1990-91; grantee, Nat. Inst. Occupl. Safety and Health, Marion Merrell Dow, McNeil Consumer Products Co. Mem. Am. Assn. Poison Control Ctrs., Drug Info. Assn., Am. Soc. Hosp. Pharmacists (assoc.), Ohio Assn. Poison Control Ctrs. (pres.), Cin. Bar Assn./ Acad. Medicine Substance Abuse Task Force, Rho Chi, Kappa Psi. Personal E-mail: ltsnrjk@earthlink.net.

SIGERSON, CHARLES WILLARD, JR., insurance agency executive; b. Biloxi, Miss., Mar. 6, 1945; s. Charles Willard S.; m. Elizabeth Ann Moss, Dec. 9, 1967; children: Anthea Louise, Andrew Charles. B in Gen. Studies, U. Nebr., Omaha, 1971. Pres., owner Sigerson Ins. Agy., Inc., Omaha, 1973—. Pres. Floyd Rogers Diabetic Found., Lincoln, Nebr., 1981—; mem. state bd. dirs. Nebrasks Stroke Found., 2002—; chmn. Douglas County Rep. Com., Omaha, 1982-83, 90-93; mem. exec. com. Nebr. Rep. Com., Lincoln, 1982-83, 86-88, 90-2001, elected pres. Omaha City Coun., 2001; chmn. Nebr. Rep. Party, 1995-2001. Staff sgt. USAF, 1964-71. Recipient Cosmopolitan of Yr.award I-80 Cosmopolitan Club, 1982, Patrick hodgins award I-80 Cosmopolitan Club, 1983, Legion of Honor ward State Farm Ins. Co., 1984. Mem. Nat. Assn. Health Underwriters, Nat. Assn. Ins. and Fin. Advisors, Soc. Fin. Svc. Profls., Nat. Assn. Life Underwriters, Rotary Internat., Masons, Christian Missionary Alliance. Avocations: genealogy, antique book and newspaper collecting, coin collecting/numismatics. Home: 11435 Grand Cir Omaha NE 68164-2109 Office: Sigerson Ins Agy Inc 10766 Fort St Omaha NE 68134-1230

SIGERSON, MARJORIE LORRAINE, librarian; b. Pitts., June 11, 1923; d. Roy Allen and Myrtle Mae (Bering) Parke; m. David Kinley Sigerson, Apr. 9, 1943 (div. Dec. 1985); children: Diane Parke, David Kinley. Student, Carnegie Inst. Tech., 1941—42, U. Pitts., 1942—43. Libr. Mus. Arts and Scis., Daytona Beach, Fla., 1963—, trustee, 1978—, pres. Guild, 1978—79. Mem. com. Halifax Art Festival, 1963—99; mem. coun. Garden Clubs of Halifax Dist., 1965—67; charter mem. Ormond Beach (Fla.) Meml. Hosp. Aux., 1967—76; pres. Street Sch. P.T.A., New City, NY, 1958—59; leader Girl Scouts U.S.A., 1956—58. Recipient award for disting. svc., Mus. Arts and Scis., 1977, 1979—2003. Mem.: Guild of Mus. of Arts and Sci. (pres. 1978—79), Friendship Force of Daytona Beach, Cherry Laurel Garden Club (pres. 1966—67), Harvard Dames Club (sec. 1946—47). Presbyterian. Home: 210 Royal Dunes Blvd Ormond Beach FL 32176-4769 Office: Mus Arts & Scis 1040 Museum Blvd Daytona Beach FL 32114-4510

SIGETY, CHARLES BIRGE, investment company executive; b. NYC, Sept. 30, 1952; s. Charles Edward and Katharine Kinne (Snell) S.; m. Elizabeth Ross Pennington, Nov. 27, 1976; children: Austin Douglas, Katharine Colyer, Alexander Birge. BA in English Lit., Bates Coll., 1975. Lic. nursing home adminstr. Adminstr. in tng. Florence Nightingale Nursing Home, N.Y.C., 1972, asst. dir. facility ops., 1975, dir. facility ops., 1975-78, assoc. adminstr., 1978-81, exec. dir., 1981-82; pres., CEO Profl. Med. Products, Inc., Greenwood, S.C., 1982 96; dir. Upper Savannah Internat. Trade Assn., Greenwood, S.C., 1993-94, pres., 1993; CEO Bison Investments, Inc., Tampa, Fla., 1996—, Aerial Machine & Tool Corp., Vesta, Va., 1998—, Polyten Plastics, LLC, Washington, 1998-2000, Coeur Acquisition, LLC, Washington, NC, 1999, Polyten, LLC, Washington, NC, 2000—03. Mem. adv. bd. Liberty Mut. Ins. Cos. S.C., 1986—96, NationsBank (Bank of Am.), Greenwood, SC, 1984—96; vice chmn. Upper Savannah Bus. Group on Health Care, 1981—87, S.C. Bus. Roundtable for the Initiative for Work Force Excellence, Columbia, 1988—92; dir. exec. com. Osteo Am., Inc., 1993—96; bd. advisors Capital South Ptnrs., 2004—. Bd. visitors Med. U. S.C., 1988; treas. YPO HealthCare Focus Forum, 1997; active Soc. of Internat. Bus. Fellows, 1999—; bd. dirs. Stewards Found., 2003--. Mem. Health Industry Mfrs. Assn. (ofcl. rep. 1982-96, 99-2002), Upper Savannah Internat. Trade Assn. (pres. 1993), Young Pres.'s Orgn., Chief Execs. Orgn., World Pres.'s Orgn. Avocations: hunting, sailing. Office: Bison Investments Inc 3225 S Macdill Ave # 236 Tampa FL 33629-8171

SIGETY, CHARLES EDWARD, lawyer, consultant, family business consultant; b. N.Y.C., Oct. 10, 1922; s. Charles and Anna (Toth) S.; m. Katharine K. Snell, July 17, 1948; children: Charles, Katharine, Robert, Cornelius, Elizabeth. BS, Columbia U., 1944; MBA, Harvard U., 1947; LLB, Yale U., 1951; LHD (hon.), Cazenovia Coll., 1994. Bar: N.Y. 1952, D.C. 1958. With Bankers Trust Co., 1939-42; instr. adminstrv. engring. Pratt Inst., 1948; instr. econs. Yale U., 1948-50; vis. lectr. acctg. Sch. Gen. Studies Columbia U., N.Y.C., 1948-50, 52; rapporteur com. fed. taxation for U.S. coun. Internat. C. of C., 1952-53; asst. to com. fed. taxation Am. Inst. Accts., 1950-53; with Compton Advt. Agy., N.Y.C., 1954; vis. lectr. law Yale U., 1952; pvt. practice law N.Y.C., 1952-67; pres., dir. Video Vittles, Inc., N.Y.C., 1953-67; dep. commr. FHA, 1955-57; of counsel Javits and Javits, 1959-60; 1st asst. atty. gen. N.Y., 1958-59; dir., mem. exec. com. Gotham Bank, N.Y.C., 1961-63; dir. N.Y. State Housing Fin. Agy., 1962-63; chmn. Met. Ski Slopes, Inc., N.Y.C., 1962-65; pres., exec. adminstr. Florence Nightingale Health Ctr., N.Y.C., 1965-85; dir. Schaerer AG, Wabern, Switzerland, 1982-88; chmn. Kenbar Group, N.Y.C., 1997 , Internat. Bioimmune Sys., Inc., Great Neck, NY, 1999—2002. Professorial lectr. Sch. Architecture, Pratt Inst., N.Y.C., 1962-66; mem. Sigety Assocs., cons. in housing mortgage financing and urban renewal, 1957-67; ho. cons. Govt. of Peru, 1956; mem. missions to Hungary, Poland, Fed. Republic Germany, Malta, Czechoslovakia, Russia, Israel, Overseas Pvt. Investment Corp., 1990-92; owner, operator Peppermill Farms, Pipersville, Pa., 1956—. Bd. dirs., sec., v.p., treas. Nat. Coun. Health Ctrs., 1969-85; bd. dirs. Am.-Hungarian Found., 1974-76, Pritikin Rsch. Found., 1991—, Stratford Arms Condo Assn., 1992-93, 2002--, Global Leadership Inst., 1993—; founding mem., bd. dirs., Natl. Assn. for Continence, 1982, trustee Cazenovia (N.Y.) Coll., 1981-2002, Delaware Valley Coll. Sci. and Agr., Doylestown, Pa., 1998—; trustee, v.p. Woodmere Art Mus. Phila., 2000—, Navy Supply Corps Found., Athens, Ga., 2000—; del. White House Conf. on Aging, 1971, White House Conf. on Mgmt. Tng. and Market Econs. Edn. in Ctrl. and Ea. Europe, 1991; bd. visitors Lander Coll., U. S.C., Greenwood, 1982-84; mem. fin. com. World Games, Santa Clara, 1981, London, 1985, Karlsruhe, 1989, The Hague, 1993, Confrerie des Chevaliers du Tastevin, Confrerie de la Chaine des Rotisseurs, Wine and Food Soc., Wednesday 10. Lt. (j.g.) Supply Corps, USNR, 1942-46. Recipient President's medal Cazenovia Coll., 1990, George Washington laureate Am. Hungarian Found., 1996; named Prin. for Day, Townsend Harris H.S. N.Y.C. Bd. Edn., 1997-2001, Disting. Alumnus U.S. Navy Supply Corps Sch., Athens, Ga., 1998; Baker scholar Harvard U., 1947. Mem. DOCA (Defense Orientation Conf. Assn.). Presbyterian. Office: 7155 Old Easton Rd Box 156 Pipersville PA 18947-9701 E-mail: sigety@msn.com.

SIGETY, CORNELIUS EDWARD, family office manager; b. N.Y.C., June 6, 1958; s. Charles Edward and Katharine (Snell) Sigety; m. Virginia White, Oct. 28, 1995; children: Charles Edgar, Bradford Earle, Cornelia Ring. BA, U. Rochester, N.Y., 1980; MBA, Harvard U., Boston, 1985. Asst. adminstr. Florence Nightingale Health Ctr., N.Y., 1980-83; v.p. Profl. Med. Products, Greenwood, S.C., 1985-88; mng. dir. Kenbar Group, N.Y., 1988—. Bd. dirs. Heritage Conservancy. Mem. Union Club, Doylestown Country Club, Mantoloking Yacht Club. Presbyterian. Avocations: sailing, golf, skiing. Home: PO Box 369 Pipersville PA 18947-0369 Office: Kenbar Group 1760 3rd Ave New York NY 10029-6810 E-mail: cesigety@hotmail.com.

SIGINER, DENNIS A. mechanical engineering educator, university dean; b. Ankara, Turkey, July 10, 1946; came to U.S., 1976; s. Kazim Siginer and Emine Turkoz. BS, MS with honors, Tech. U. Istanbul, 1969, ScD, 1971; PhD, U. Minn., 1982. Rsch. assoc. U. Minn., Mpls., 1976-80; asst. prof. U. Ala., Tuscaloosa, 1981-83; assoc. prof. Auburn (Ala.) U., 1984-92, prof. mech. engring., 1992-97; prof., head dept. mech. engring. N.J. Inst. Tech., Newark, 1998-2000; dean Coll. Engring., Wichita (Kans.) State U., 2000—04. Organizer, chmn. several internat. and nat. confs.; invited spkr. several countries, fgn. and nat. instns., internat. and nat. meetings; reviewer for numerous profl. archival jours. and fed. and pvt. funding agys. including NSF; book reviewer pubs. in field. Editor procs. of 1st East-West Conf. on advances in structured and heterogeneous continua, Moscow, 1993; editor numerous books on devels. in non-Newtonian flows, electrorheol. fluids and fluid mechanics phenomena in microgravity, rheology and fluid mechanics of nonlinear materials; editor-in-chief: Advances in the Flow and Rheology of Non-Newtonian Fluids, 1999; assoc. editor Jour. of Applied Mechanics, 1997-2003, Jour. Fluids Engring., 2002—; guest editor Jour. Non-Newtonian Fluid Mechanics, 1999, Jour. Fluids Engring., 2003—, Jour. Applied Mechanics, 2003—; author books in field; contbr. more than 120 articles to profl. jours. Recipient 3 univ.-wide teaching awards; Summer faculty fellow NASA, 1991, 92. Fellow: Sci. and Tech. Rsch. Coun. Turkey, ASME (lectr. 2000, organizer 20 symposia, editor 20 procs. vols., svc. award 1993, 1995, 1996, 1997); mem.: N.Y. Acad. Scis., Soc. Engring. Sci., Am. Inst. Physics, Am. Acad. Mechanics, Soc. Rheology (organizer ann. meeting), Am. Soc. Engring. Edn. (rsch. award 1992), Sigma Xi, Pi Tau Sigma (hon.). Home: 13211 Edgewood Dr Wichita KS 67230 Office: Wichita State U Coll Engring Dept Mech Engring 1845 Fairmount Wichita KS 67260-0133 Office Phone: 316-978-6300. Business E-Mail: dennis.siginer@wichita.edu.

SIGLER, HOLLIS, artist, educator, author; b. Gary, Ind., Mar. 2, 1948; Studied in Florence, Italy, 1968-69; BFA, Moore Coll. Art, 1970, DFA (hon.), 1994; MFA, Sch. Art Inst. Chgo., 1973. Mem. faculty Columbia Coll., Chgo., 1978—, instr. painting and drawing, 1984—. One-woman shows include Akron (Ohio) Art Mus., 1986, S.W. Craft Ctr., San Antonio, 1989, Nat. Mus. Women Arts, Washington, 1991, 93, Printworks Gallery, Chgo., 1991, 93, Priebe Art Gallery, U. Wis., Oshkosh, 1992, Susan Cummins Gallery, Mill Valley, Calif., 1992, 94, Steven Scott Gallery, Balt., 1993, 94, Hartman Ctr. Gallery, Bradley U., Peoria, Ill., 1994, Mus. Contemporary Art, Chgo., 1994, Suburban Fine Arts Ctr., Highland Park, Ill., 1994, Lakeview Mus. Arts and Sci., Peoria, 1994, Decordova Mus. and Sculpture Park, Lincoln, Mass., 1994, Leedy-Voulkos Art Ctr. Gallery, Kansas City, Mo., 1995, Ark. Art Ctr., Little Rock, 1996, Elvehjem Mus. Art., U. Wis., Madison, 1997, Palo Alto Cultural Ctr., Calif., 1998, Carl Hammer Gallery, Chgo., 1998, Printworks Gallery, Chgo., 1999; exhibited in group shows Whitney Mus. Art, N.Y.C., 1981, Walker Art Mus., Mpls., 1982, Mus. Modern Art, N.Y.C., 1984, Corcoran Gallery Art, Washington, 1985, Chgo. Cultural Ctr., 1992, The Drawing Ctr., N.Y.C., 1993, The Contemporary Mus., Honolulu, 1994, Butler Inst. Am. Art, Youngstown, Ohio, 1995, Nat. Mus. Am. Art, Smithsonian, Washington, 1996, Corcoran Sch. of Art and U.S. Senate, Russell Rotunda Gallery, Washington, 1998; represented in permanent collections Mus. Contemporary Art, Chgo., Indpls. Mus. Art, Seattle Art Mus., Madison Art Ctr., High Mus. Art, Atlanta, Nat. Mus. Am. Art, Smithsonian, Nat. Mus. Women in the Arts, Washington, John D. and Catherine T. MacArthur Found., Johns Hopkins Hosp. Oncology Ctr., Balt.; pub.: Hollis Sigler's Breast Cancer Journal, 1999; also others. Recipient cash award Southwestern Ctr. for Contemporary Art, Winston-

Salem, N.C., 1987, Childe Hassam purchase award AAAL, 1988; grantee Ill. Arts Coun., 1986, Nat. Endowment for Arts, 1987. Office: Columbia Coll 600 S Michigan Ave Chicago IL 60605-1900 Home: 2040 Berkeley Rd Highland Park IL 60035-2743

SIGLER, LOIS OLIVER, retired secondary school educator; b. Piney Flats, Tenn., Sept. 8, 1923; d. Willie Campbell and Lillie (Brown) Oliver; m. William Virgil Sigler Jr., Aug. 25, 1962; 1 child, William Oliver. BS, East Tenn. State U., 1944; MS, U. Tenn., 1952; postgrad., Memphis State U., U. Tenn. Home econs. tchr. Buchanan (Va.) pub. schs., 1944-46; area supr. home econs. edn. and sch. lunch prog. State Dept. Edn., Commonwealth of Va., 1946-54; asst. nat. advisor Future Homemakers of Am./New Homemakers of Am., HEW, Washington, 1954-56, nat. advisor, 1956-63; family living coord. Ohio State Dept. and Columbus (Ohio) Pub. Schs., Columbus Met. Housing Authority, 1963; tchr. Millington (Tenn.) High Sch., 1966-92; ret., 1992. Mem. Pres. Kennedy's Food for Peace Coun., Pres. Eisenhower's Adv. Com. on Youth Fitness. Named Tenn. Home Econs. Tchr. of Yr., 1975, Woman of Yr., 1991, Twentieth Century award for achievement, 1991, One of Top 2000 Outstanding People of 20th Century, 1998. Mem. NEA, Am. Home Econs. Assn., Tenn. Home Econs. Assn., Am. Voc. Assn., Tenn. Voc. Assn., Nat. Voc. Home Econs. Tchrs. Assn., Tenn. Voc. Home Econs. Tchrs. Assn. (hon. 1992, past sec.-treas., Outstanding Svc. award 1986), W. Tenn. Home Econs. Edn. Assn. (past sec.), Tenn. Edn. Assn. (bd. dirs. 1977-80), W. Tenn. Edn. Assn., Shelby County Edn. Assn. (past sch. rep.), Future Homemakers Am. (nat. hon. 1956, state hon. 1991, master advisor award 1988, advisor mentor 1991), Omicron Nu, Pi Lambda Theta. Home: 4785 Rolling Meadows Dr Memphis TN 38128-4868

SIGMAN, STANLEY T. telecommunications industry executive; b. Lubbock, Tex. m. Gerry Lynn Sigman; 2 children. BBA, W. Tex. State U., 1970. Stockman Southwestern Bell Telephone, Hereford, Tex., 1965; exec. v.p. Southwestern Bell Mobile Sys., 1986—91, mng. dir., cellular and paging, SBC Comm., Teléfonos de México, 1991—93, v.p., gen. mgr., 1993—94, exec. v.p., 1994—95, pres., CEO, 1995—99, group pres., SBC opers., 1999; sr. exec. v.p., svcs. Southwestern Bell Telephone Co., CEO; pres., CEO Cingular Wireless, Atlanta, 2002—. Office: Cingular Wireless Glenridge Highlands Two 5565 Glenridge Connector Atlanta GA 30342*

SIGMON, J. LEWIS, JR., medical educator; b. Newton, NC, July 8, 1940; MD, U. N.C., 1966. Intern David Grant USAF Hosp., 1966-67; resident Charlotte (N.C.) Meml. Hosp., 1969-71; chmn. dept. family practice Carolinas Med. Ctr., Charlotte, 1984-95, clin. coord. Charlotte Ofcl Reg. Primary Care Edn., 1995—2001, sr. ind. cons. in grad. med. edn., fam. prac. and ins. med., 2001—, dir. family practice residency program Monroe, 1997—2001; prof. family medicine U. NC, 1993—2004, prof. emeritus, 2004—. Acad. coun. Nat. Inst. for Program Dir. Devel., Kansas City, Mo., 1999—2003; pres. Am. Bd. Family Practice Found., 2000—; residency rev. com. for family practice ACGME, 1997—2003, specialist site visitor for residency rev. com., 2004—. Mem. AMA, N.C. Acad. Family Physicians, Am. Acad. Ins. Medicine. Personal E-mail: sigmonjl@aol.com.

SIGMON, JOYCE ELIZABETH, professional society administrator; b. Stanley, NC, Oct. 4, 1935; d. Rome Alfred and Pearl Elizabeth (Beal) S. BS, U. N.C., 1971; MA, Loyola U., 1980. Cert. assn. exec. Dental asst. Dr. Paul A. Stroup, Jr., Charlotte, N.C., 1953-63; instr. Wayne Tech. Inst., Goldsboro, N.C., 1963-65, Ctrl. Piedmont CC, Charlotte, 1965—69; dir. Dental Assisting Edn. ADA, Chgo., 1971-85, asst. sec. Coun. Prosthetics Svcs., 1985-87, mgr. Office Quality Assurance, 1987—90, exec. dir. Aux., 1990-92; dir. adminstrv. activities Am. Acad. of Implant Dentistry, Chgo., 1993—; exec. sec. Am. Bd. of Oral Implantology/Implant Dentistry, 1993-99. Deacon 4th Presbyn. Ch., 1973-75, elder 1975-77, 88-91, 2002—, trustee, 1991-94; moderator Presbyn. Women in 4th Ch., 1987-91, Stephen min., 1997-99. Mem. Am. Soc. Assn. Execs., Chgo. Soc. Assn. Execs. (chair CAE com. 1991-92), Am. Dental Assts. Assn., N.C. Dental Assn. (pres. 1968-69), Charlotte Dental Assts. Soc. Presbyterian. Home: 260 E Chestnut St Chicago IL 60611-2401 Office: Am Acad Implant Dentistry 211 E Chicago Ave Chicago IL 60611-2637 Office Phone: 312-335-1550. Personal E-mail: jesigmon@aol.com.

SIGMON, SCOTT B. psychologist; b. Newark, Dec. 30, 1946; s. Henry and Shirley (Juffe) S. BA, Bloomfield Coll., 1973; MA, Montclair State Coll., 1975; profl. diploma in sch. psychology, Kean Coll., 1977; EdD, Rutgers U., 1985. Sch. psychologist Middlesex Borough Pub. Schs., N.J., 1976-77, Milton Sch., Millburn, N.J., 1977-78; sch. psychologist, chair child study team Irvington Pub. Schs., N.J., 1978-87; psychotherapist Family Svc. Bur. Newark, 1987; supr. child study East Orange (N.J.) Sch. Dist., 1987-88; sch. psychologist Elizabeth (N.J.) Pub. Schs., 1988-89; sch. psychologist, child study team chairperson Carlstadt-East Rutherford Regional H.S. Dist., N.J., 1989-2001; pvt. practice Union, N.J., 1991—. Adj. prof. grad. psychology, Kean Univ. N.J., 1986, adj. prof. grad. psychology and spl. edn. Seton Hall U. (N.J.), 1988-90; asst. prof. coun. svcs. program William Paterson U. of N.J., 1992-95. Author: Radical Socioeducational Analysis, 1985, Radical Analysis of Special Education: Focus on Historical Development and Learning Disabilities, 1987; author, editor: Critical Voices on Special Education: Problems and Progress Concerning the Mildly Handicapped, 1990; editor The N.J. Sch. Psychologist newsletter, 1986-88; contbr. articles to profl. jours. With USMC, 1966-69. Mem. APA, Nat. Acad. Neuropsychology, Internat. Sch. Psychology Assn., N.Am. Soc. of Sport Psychology and Phys. Activity, Assn. for the Advancement of Applied Sport Psychology, Am. Ednl. Rsch. Assn., N.J. Assn. Sch. Psychologists, N.J. Psychol. Assn. Office: 1945 Morris Ave Union NJ 07083-3526 Office Phone: 908-686-7555.

SIGMOND, CAROL ANN, lawyer; b. Phila., Jan. 9, 1951; d. Irwin and Mary Florence (Vollmer) S. BA, Grinnell Coll., 1972; JD, Cath. U., 1975. Bar: Va. 1975, D.C. 1980, Md. 1988, N.Y. 1990, U.S. Dist. Ct. (ea. dist.) Va. 1975, U.S. Dist. Ct. (so. and ea. dist.) N.Y. 1991, U.S. Ct. Appeals (4th cir.) 1976, U.S. Ct. Appeals (fed. cir.) 1987, U.S. Ct. Appeals (2d cir.) 2000. Asst. gen. counsel Washington Met. Area Transit Authority, 1978-85; acting assoc. gen. counsel for appeals and gen. law, 1985-86; assoc. Patterson, Belknap, Webb & Tyler, Washington, 1986-89, Berman, Paley, Goldstein & Kannry, N.Y.C., 1991-93; prin. Law Offices of Carol A. Sigmond, N.Y.C., 1993-97; of counsel Pollack & Greene, LLP, N.Y.C., 1998-2000; pvt. practice N.Y.C., 2000—03; ptnr. Kehl, Kilzun, & Sigmond, 2004—. Mem. Women's Nat. Dem. Club. Active Womens Nat. Dem. Club. Mem. ABA, D.C. Bar Assn., Arlington County Bar Assn., Va. State Bar Assn., Md. State Bar Assn., Assn. of Bar of City of N.Y. Democrat. Mem. Lds Ch. Avocations: piano, bridge. Office: 317 Madison Av 21st Fl New York NY 10017-5208 E-mail: CASigmond@KKSLegal.net.

SIGMOND, RICHARD BRIAN, lawyer; b. Phila., Dec. 7, 1944; s. Joseph and Jean (Nissman) S.; children: Michael, Catherine, Alina; m. Susan Helen Peteraf, Dec. 24, 1984. BS, Phila. Coll. Textiles & Sci., 1966; JD, Temple U., 1969. Bar: Pa. 1969, U.S. Supreme Ct. 1973, U.S. Dist. Ct. (ea. dist.) Pa. 1975, U.S. Ct. Appeals (3d cir.) 1975, N.Y. 1982, D.C. 1995. Atty. Pub. Defender Assn., Phila., 1969-70; ptnr. Meranze, Katz, Spear & Wilderman, Phila., 1970-84; sr. ptnr. Spear, Wilderman, Sigmond, Borish & Endy, Phila., 1985-89, Jennings Sigmond, Phila., 1989—; gen. counsel Internat. Brotherhood Painters and Allied Trades, 1997-2000. Chmn., bd. dirs. Gatehouse Phila., 1972-83; lectr. Pvt. Industry Coun., Phila., 1985—, labor studies div., Pa. State U., 1978-82, 85-86; gen. counsel Stabilization Agreement, Sheet Metal Industry Trust Fund, 1994—, Internat. Painters and Allied Trades Industry Pension Fund, 1997—. Mem. ABA (labor law com., litigation com.), AFL-CIO (lawyers coordinating com.), Pa. Bar Assn. (labor law com.), Phila. Bar Assn. (labor com.), Phi Alpha Delta. Avocations: sailing, writing. Office: Penn Mutual Towers 510 Walnut St Fl 16 Philadelphia PA 19106-3601 Office Phone: 215-351-0609. Business E-Mail: rsigmond@jslex.com.

SIGMUND, DIANE WEISS, judge; b. N.Y.C., Mar. 1, 1943; BS, Pa. State U., 1963; JD magna cum laude, Temple U., 1977. Bar: Pa. 1977. Atty. Blank, Rome, Cominsky & McCauley, Phila.; judge U.S. Bankruptcy Ct. (Pa. ea. dist.), 3rd circuit, Phila., 1993—, chief judge, 2004—. Mem. steering com. Ea. Dist. Pa. Bankruptcy Conf., 1995—, 3d Cir. Task Force Equal Treatment in Cts., Gender Commn., 1995-97; chmn. endowment edn. Nat. Conf. Bankruptcy Judges., 1996—, bd. govs., 1998—; mem. com. on automation and tech. Jud. Conf. U.S., 1997—. Fellow Am. Coll. Bankruptcy. Office: Robert NC Nix Courthouse 900 Market St Rm 203 Philadelphia PA 19107-4237

SIGNORILE, VINCENT ANTHONY, lawyer; b. Jersey City, Mar. 22, 1959; s. Ralph R. and Rita (DeRosa) S. BS, St. Peter's Coll., Jersey City, 1981; JD, Seton Hall U., 1985. Bar: N.J. 1985, Pa. 1985. Aide Jersey City Mcpl. Coun., 1980-81, Office of Mayor, City of Jersey City, 1981; law clk. Corp. Counsel Jersey City, 1981-85; law sec. Superior Ct. N.J. for Hudson County, Jersey City, 1985-86; assoc. atty. Jersey City, 1986-89; ptnr. Signorile & Saminski, Jersey City, 1989-97; atty. Jersey City Zoning Bd. Adjustment, 1994-97, Bayonne City Ethics Bd., 1995-97; judge Jersey City Mcpl. Ct., 1996—99, chief judge, 1999—. Elected mem. Hudson County Dem. Com., 1977-81, Jersey City Environ. Com., 1989-93, Jersey City Planning Bd. Com., 1991-93, Jersey City Ins. Fund Com., 1989-93; co-chmn. Hudson County Columbus Parade, 1984-85; elected to Mcpl. Coun. Jersey City, 1989-93. Mem. ATLA, ABA, N.J. Bar Assn., Pa. Bar Assn., Hudson County Bar Assn. (treas. Young Lawyer's Assn. 1987-88, scholar 1984-85). Roman Catholic. Home: 1691 John F Kennedy Blvd Jersey City NJ 07305-1841 Office: Jersey City Municipal Ct 365 Summit Ave Jersey City NJ 07306

SIGNOROVITCH, DENNIS J. communications executive; b. Norristown, Pa., July 23, 1945; s. James and Regina S.; m. Susan M. McLaughlin, 1968; children: James Edward, Sarah Elizabeth. BS in Fgn. Svc., Georgetown U., 1967; MA, Old Dominion U., 1972. Instr. U. Toledo, 1972-77; writer/editor Doehler Jarvis div. NL Industries, Toledo, 1977-78; mgr. pub. rels. Eltra Corp., N.Y.C., 1979, mgr. planning, 1980; various assignments AlliedSignal Corp., Morristown, N.J., 1980-92; v.p. pub. affairs AlliedSignal Inc., Torrance, Calif., 1992-98; v.p. mktg. and comm. AlliedSignal Aerospace, Torrance, 1998-99; v.p. comms. Honeywell Aerospace, 1999—. Mem. Exec. Comm. Forum. With U.S. Army, 1967-70. Decorated Bronze Star with oak leaf cluster. Mem. The Conf. Bd. (corp. comm. coun. 1991), Arthur W. Page Soc., San Francisco Acad. (trustee), Aerospace Industries Assn. (chmn. comms. coun. 2001—). Office: Honeywell Aerospace 2525 W 190th St Torrance CA 90504-6002

SIGUENZA, PETER CHARLES, JR., territory supreme court justice; b. Guam, July 1, 1951; s. Peter C. and Barbara L. (Bordallo) S.; m. Joleen Taitano Rios, Dec. 6, 1969; 1 child, Dawn. BA, Calif. State U., 1976; JD, U. of the Pacific, 1980. Bar: Calif. 1981, Guam 1981, U.S. Ct. Appeals (9th cir.), Commonwealth No. Marianas 1983. Pvt. practice Klemm, Blair & Barusch; staff atty. Guam Legal Svcs. Corp.; clk. Superior Ct. Guam; libr. Calif. Ct. Appeal; judge Guam Superior Ct., Agana, 1984-96; justice Supreme Ct. Guam, Agana, 1999—2001; chief justice Guam Supreme Ct., 1996—99, 2001—. Designated judge Dist. Ct. Guam, Supreme Ct. Federated States Micronesia; chair bd. trustees Father Duenas Meml. Sch., 1991; chair rules commn. Supreme Ct. Guam, 1993. Mem. ABA, Am. Judges Assn. Office: Supreme Ct Guam Judiciary Bldg Ste 300 120 W O'Brien Dr Hagatna GU 96910-5174

SIGULER, GEORGE WILLIAM, financial services executive; b. Cleve., Apr. 26, 1947; s. John Frederick and Helen Alice (Popp) S.; m. Pamela Ann Mallon, Oct. 31, 1981; children: George William Jr., Emily Ann, Charles Arthur, Mary Elizabeth, Andrew Cooper. AB, Amherst Coll., 1970; MBA, Harvard U., 1972. Ptnr. Harvard Mgmt. Co., Boston, 1974-83; chief of staff HHS, Washington, 1983-84; exec. v.p. Monarch Capital Corp., Springfield, Mass., 1984-87, vice chmn. bd., 1987-91; pres. Associated Capital Investor, San Francisco, 1990-91; mng. dir. Mitchell Hutchins Instl. Investors, Inc., N.Y.C., 1991-95; founder Siguler Guff & Co., 1995—. Assoc. treas. Harvard U., 1973-88; bd. dirs. Venture Lending and Leasing, Inc., Russia Ptnrs., L.P. Mem. vis. com. Harvard U. Med. Sch., Boston, 1986—; mem. nat. adv. com. on community health resources HHS, Washington, 1985-90; trustee Perkins Sch. for Blind, Watertown, Mass., 1976-83, New Eng. Aquarium, 1989-91, Bement Sch., 1999—. Recipient Disting. Svc. award HHS, 1984. Republican. Presbyterian. Office: Siguler Guff & Co 825 Third Ave 29th Fl New York NY 10022

SIH, CHARLES JOHN, pharmaceutical chemistry educator; b. Shanghai, Sept. 11, 1933; s. Paul Kwang-Tsien and Teresa (Dong) S.; m. Catherine Elizabeth Hsu, July 11, 1959; children: Shirley, Gilbert, Ronald. AB in Biology, Caroll Coll., 1953; MS in Bacteriology, Mont. State Coll., 1955; PhD in Bacteriology, U. Wis., 1958. Sr. research microbial biochemist Squibb Inst. for Med. Research, New Brunswick, N.J., 1958-60; mem. faculty U. Wis.-Madison, 1960—, Frederick B. Power prof. pharm. chemistry, 1978, Hilldare prof., 1987—. Recipient 1st Ernest Volwiler award, 1977; Roussel prize, 1980, Am. Pharm. Assoc. award 1987. Mem. Am. Chem. Soc., Soc. Am. Biol. Chemists, Acad. Pharm. Scis., Soc. Am. Microbiologists. Home: 10 Coyote Ct Madison WI 53717-2736

SIHLER, WILLIAM WOODING, finance educator; b. Seattle, Nov. 17, 1937; s. William and Helen Alice (Wooding) S.; m. Mary Elizabeth Unwin, Aug. 21, 1963; children: Edward Wooding, Jennifer Sihler Zysman. AB summa cum laude in Govt. (Sheldon traveling fellow), Harvard U., 1959, MBA with high distinction, 1962, DBA, 1965. Instr., asst. prof. Harvard U. Bus. Sch., 1964-67; assoc. prof. Darden Grad. Bus. Sch., U. Va., Charlottesville, 1967-72, prof., 1972-76, A.J. Morris prof., 1976-84; R.E. Trzcinski prof., 1984—; dir. D.B.A. Program, 1971-73; assoc. dean acad. affairs, 1972-77; exec. dir. BAFT/Ctr. for Internat. Banking Studies, 1977-91. Bd. dirs. Curtiss-Wright Corp.; pres. Southeastern Cons. Group, Ltd. Co-author: Financial Management: Text and Cases, 2d edit., 1991, The Troubled Money Business, 1992, Financial Service Organizations: Cases in Strategic Management, 1993, Cases in Applied Corporate Finance, 1994, Building Valve with Capital-Structure Strategies, 1998, Financial Turnarounds--Preserving Value, 2001; editor: Classics in Commercial Bank Lending, vol. 1, 1981, vol. 2, 1985; contbr. articles to profl. jours. Vis. com. Sch. Mgmt., Case Western Res. U., 1976-86, bd. overseers, 1980-86. Recipient DeL. K. Jay prize Harvard U., Disting. Prof. award U. Va. Alumni Assn., 1982; C.J. Bonaparte scholar Harvard U. Mem. Fin. Mgmt. Assn., Am. Econ. Assn., Am. Fin. Assn., Eastern Fin. Assn., Univ. Club (N.Y.C.), Harvard Club (N.Y.C.), Greencroft Club (Charlottesville), Phi Beta Kappa, Beta Gamma Sigma. Home: 3215 Heathcote Ln Keswick VA 22947-9160 Office: PO Box 6550 Charlottesville VA 22906-6550 Office Phone: 434-924-7489.

SIIROLA, JEFFREY JOHN, chemical engineer; b. Patuxent River, Md., July 17, 1945; s. Arthur Raymond and Nancy Ellen (Harris) S.; m. Sharon Ann Arnold, Apr. 24, 1971; childen: John Daniel, Jennifer Ann. BS in Chem. Engring., U. Utah, 1967; PhD, U. Wis., 1970. Rsch. engr. Eastman Chem. Co., Kingsport, Tenn., 1972-74, sr. rsch. engr., 1974-80, rsch. assoc., 1980-88, sr. rsch. assoc., 1988-95, tech. fellow, 1995—. Trustee CACHE Corp., Austin, Tex., 1983—. Co-author: Process Synthesis, 1973. Appalachian tr. maintenance Eastman Hiking Club, Kingsport, 1973—. With U.S. Army, 1970-72. Fellow AIChE (A.E. Marshall award 1967, Computing Practice award 1991, bd. dirs. 1999-2001, pres.-elect 2004); mem. Nat. Acad. Engring., Chem. Scis. Roundtable, Accreditation Bd. for Engring. and Tech., Am. Chem. Soc., Am. Soc. for Engring. Edn., Am. Assn. for Artificial Intelligence, Kingsport C. of C. Achievements include development of the AIDES chem. process flowsheet invention procedure. Home: 2517 Wildwood Dr Kingsport TN 37660-4748 Office: Eastman Chem Co 200 S Wilcox Dr PO Box 1972 Kingsport TN 37662-5150 E-mail: siirola@eastman.com.

SIKANDER, SHAHZIA, artist; b. Lahore, Pakistan, 1969; BFA, Nat. Coll. Arts, Lahore, 1992; MFA, RISD, Providence, 1995. One-woman shows include Barbara Davis Gallery, Houston, 1996, Hosfelt Gallery, San Francisco, 1997, Deitch Project, N.Y.C., 1997, Renaissance Soc. U. Chgo., 1998, Kemper Mus. Contemporary Art and Design, Kansas City, Mo., 1998—88, Hirshhorn Mus., Washington, 1999, exhibited in group shows at Rhotas Gallery, Islamabad, Pakistan, 1992, Pacific Asia Mus., Pasadena, Calif., 1994—95, Bradford (Eng.) City Mus., 1996, Glassell Sch. Art Mus. Fine Arts, 1996, 1997, Laing Gallery, Newcastle, Eng., 1997, Whitney Mus. Am. Art, 1997, Queens Mus. Art, Flushing Meadows, N.Y., 1997, Yerba Buena Gardens Ctr. Arts, San Francisco, Forum for Contemporary Art, St. Louis, 1998, Bard Coll., Annandale-on-Hudson, N.Y., 1998, Ludwig (Austria) Mus., 1998, Aldrich Mus. Contemporary Art, Conn., 1998, also exhbns. in Portugal, Johannesburg, South Africa, Mexico City, work represented in numerous newspapers and mags. Recipient Haji Sharif award for miniature painting, Shakik Ali award and Kipling award, Nat. Coll. Art, Lahore, 1993; grad. fellow, RISD, 1993—95, core fellow, Glassel Sch. Art Mus. Fine Arts, 1995—97, grantee, Louis Comfort Tiffany Found., 1997, Joan Mitchell grantee, 1998—99. Address: care Deitch Projects 76 Grand St New York NY 10013-2220

SIKER, EPHRAIM S. anesthesiologist; b. Port Chester, N.Y., Mar. 24, 1926; s. Samuel S. and Adele (Weiser) S.; m. m . Eileen Mary Bohnel, Aug. 5, 1951; children— Kathleen Ellen, Jeffrey Stephen, David Alan, Paul William, Richard Francis. Student, Duke U., 1943-45; MD, N.Y.U., 1949. Diplomate: Am. Bd. Anesthesiology (dir. 1971—, sec.-treas. 1974-82, pres. 1982-83) Nat. Bd. Med. Examiners. Intern Grasslands Hosp., Valhalla, N.Y., 1949-50, resident in anesthesia, 1950; resident dept. anesthesiology Mercy Hosp., Pitts., 1952-53, assoc. dir. dept., 1955-62, chmn., 1962-92; practice medicine, specializing in anesthesiology Pitts., 1954—; pres. Pitts. Anesthesia Assocs., Ltd., 1967-89; dir. anesthesia services Central Med. Ctr., Pitts., 1973-89. Courtesy staff St. Clair Meml. Hosp., Pitts., 1954—89; clin. prof. dept. anesthesiology U. Pitts. Sch. Medicine, 1968—; mem. exec. com. Am. Bd. Med. Spltys., 1978—81; Exch. cons. Welsh Nat. Sch. Medicine, Cardiff, 1955—56; mem. Pa. Gov.'s Commn. on Profl. Liability Ins., 1968—70; mem. adv. panel U.S. Pharmacopeia, 1970—76; mem. Am. Acupuncture Anesthesia Study Group NAS to Peoples Republic China, 1974; mem. adv. com. on splty. and geog. distbn. of physicians Inst. Medicine NAS, 1974—76; trustee Ednl. Coun. for Fgn. Med. Grads., 1980—82, Mercy Hosp. Found., 1983—95; bd. dirs., sec. Anesthesia Patient Safety Found., 1985—89, mem. exec. com., 1985—92, exec. dir., 1992—97. Author: (with F.F. Foldes) Narcotics and Narcotic Antagonists, 1964; sect. on narcotic: (with F.F. Foldes) numerous other publs. in med. lit. Ency. Brittanica. Served to lt. M.C. USNR, 1950-52. USPHS postdoctoral research fellow, 1954; hon. fellow faculty anaesthetists Royal Coll. Surgeons, Eng., 1974; hon. fellow faculty anesthetists Coll. Medicine South Africa, 1983; recipient Hippocratic award Mercy Hosp., 1982 Fellow Royal Coll. Surgeons Ireland, Faculty Anaesthetists (hon. 1988); mem. Am. Soc. Anesthesiologists (pres. 1973—, bd. dirs. Disting. Svc. award 1984), AMA (alt. del. 1962), Pa. Med. Soc., Allegheny County Med. Soc., Pa. Soc. Anesthesiologists (pres. 1965, Disting. Svc. award 1986), Royal Soc. Medicine (Eng.), Pitts. Acad. Medicine, Am. Coll. Anesthesiologists (bd. govs. 1969-71), World Fedn. Anesthesiologists (chmn. exec. com. 1980-84, v.p. 1984-88), Assn. Anesthesia Program Dirs. (pres. 1987-89), Japanese Soc. Anesthesiologists (hon.). Achievements include developing Siker Laryngoscope, 1956. Home: 185 Crestvue Manor Dr Pittsburgh PA 15228-1814 *If you have to tell someone who you are, then you probably aren't. People are measured by more than their deeds, and such estimations are frequently made on the basis of their inter-personal relationships. While achievement and effort usually bear a linear relationship to each other, the impact that the achiever has on society depends upon the impact he makes on individuals.*

SIKES, CYNTHIA LEE, actress, children's advocate, singer; b. Coffeyville, Kans., Jan. 2, 1954; d. Neil and Pat (Scott) S.; m. Alan Bud Yorkin, June 24, 1989. Student, Am. Conservatory Theater, San Francisco, 1977-79. Actor: (TV series) St. Elsewhere, 1981—83, L.A. Law, 1989, JAG, 2000—01, (TV movies) Oceans of Fire, 1986, His Mistress, 1990; prodr., actor: Sins of Silence, 1996; actor: (films) Man Who Loved Women, That's Life, Arthur on the Rocks, Love Hurts, 1988, Possums, 1998, Going Shopping, 2004, (Broadway musical) Into the Woods, 1988—89. Active Hollywood Women's Polit. Com.; apptd. Pres. Clinton's Adv. Com. on Arts John F. Kennedy Ctr. for Performing Arts, 1999. Recipient Gov.'s Medal of Merit, Kans., 1986. Democrat. Avocations: hiking, writing, reading.

SIKES, PAUL LEON, music educator; b. San Angelo, Tex., Aug. 8, 1971; s. David Ronnie Sikes and Mary Jan Black; m. Kristi Kaye Hood, June 6, 1996. MusB in Edn., Tex. Tech U., 1989—94; MusM, Baylor U., 1999—2001. Secondary Education Tex., 1994. Dir. of bands Midland Lee Freshman H.S., Tex., 1995—99; assoc. dir. of bands Tex. A&M U., 2001—. Contbr. articles The Southwestern Musician, Tex. Music Educator. Subsitute choir dir. Christ United Meth. Ch., College Station, Tex., 2003. Mem.: Nat. Band Assn., Coll. Band Directors Nat. Assn., Tex. Music Educators Assn., Golden Key Nat. Honor Soc., Pi Kappa Lambdq. Methodist. Avocations: gardening, travel. Office: Texas A&M Univ Bands 3153 Tamu College Station TX 77843-3153

SIKKA, KAMAL K. engineering executive; b. Jalandhar, Punjab, India, May 30, 1968; s. Satinder K. and Sundarbala Sikka; m. Aruna K. Katiyal, Dec. 28, 1993; 1 child, Katha K. BTech, Indian Inst. of Tech., Bombay, 1989; MS, Pa. State U., State College, 1991; PhD, Cornell U., 1997. Engr. IBM Microelectronics, Hopewell Junction, NY, 1997—2001, engring. mgr., 2002—. Contbr. articles to profl. jours. (Best Paper award ITHERM 96 Conf., 1996). Recipient Grad. Sch. fellowship, McMullen Found., 1995—96, Nat. Talent scholarship, NCERT, 1983. Achievements include patents for Efficient Cooling of Semiconductor Chips; Procedure and Method for Controlled Interface Gaps for Cooling Semiconductor Chips; development of a water-cooled thermal tester for thermal characterization of high-power electronic packages; package cooling designs for dual chip electronic modules with one high power chip; adhesive and controlled chip-cap thermal greae interface electronic packages for electronic cooling. Office: IBM Microelectronics Z/87P 2070 Rt 52 Hopewell Junction NY 12533 Personal E-mail: ksikka@att.net. E-mail: sikka@us.ibm.com.

SIKORA, BARBARA JEAN, library director; b. Passaic, N.J., Apr. 12, 1943; d. Stanley Francis and Jean (Sobczyk) S. BA in Edn., English, William Paterson Coll., 1969, MEd in Learning Disabilities, 1978; MLS, Rutgers U., 1978; Cert. in Fundraising Mgmt., Fairleigh Dickinson U., 1990. Profl. libr. N.J. Tchr. Clifton (N.J.) Pub. Schs., 1969-73; office mgr. Singer/TRW, Fairfield, N.J., 1974-76; prin. libr. Passaic Pub. Libr., 1978-88; asst. libr. dir. Pub. Libr. Livingston, N.J., 1989-90, libr. dir., 1991—. Adj. faculty William Paterson Coll., 1977-90; trustee Wayne Pub. Libr., 1986-88; bd. dirs. Polish and Slavic Fed. Credit Union, 1999—. Mem. Polish Heritage Festival Com., Holmdel, N.J., 1987—, gen. chmn., 1999; trustee, bd. dirs. Livingston Area C. of C., 1998—; pres. Libr. Pub. Rels. Coun., 1997; West Essex br. YMCA of the Oranges, 1997—; mem. Polish Children's Heartline, Inc. Grantee U.S. Dept. Edn. libr. literacy program, 1987, N.J. State Libr. Leadership Inst., 1988, Christopher Leadership Inst., 1997; Paul Harris fellow Rotary Internat., 1999. Mem. ALA (ethics com. 1995-99), AAUW, N.J. Libr. Assn., Nat. Spkrs.' Assn., Rotary (pres. Livingston chpt. 1994-96, 2000), Rutgers Sch. Comm. and Info. Libr. Studies Alumni Assn. (pres. 1991-94), Beta Phi Mu. Avocations: writing, speaking, adult education, psychology, leadership skills training. Home: The Mill 300 Main St Apt 314 Little Falls NJ 07424-1359 Office: Pub Libr Livingston 10 Robert Harp Dr Livingston NJ 07039 E-mail: sikora@bcols.org.

SIKORA, JAMES ROBERT, educational business consultant, financial analyst; b. Sacramento, July 8, 1945; s. George Robert and Marian Frances (Fears) S.; m. Marie Lynore Nyarady, June 22, 1968. BEE, U. Santa Clara, 1967; postgrad., U. Calif., Santa Cruz, 1979—98, personal fin. planning cert., 1998. Electronic engr. GTE-Sylvania, Santa Cruz, 1967-69, sys. analyst, 1969-71, sr. support analyst, 1971-73; coord. bus. sys. Santa Clara County Office Edn., San Jose, Calif., 1973-76, dir. dist. payroll, pers. svcs., 1976-85, dir. dist. bus. svcs., 1985-95; self-employed sch. bus. cons. Omniserve, Ben Lomond, Calif., 1995—; interim dir. fin. San Jose Unified Sch. Dist., 2001, spl. fiscal asst., 2001—02. Cons. Milpitas Unified Sch. Dist., 1995—97, San Jose Unified Sch. Dist., 1997, 2000, Santa Clara County Office of Edn., San Jose, 1997—2000, Los Altos Sch. Dist., 1998—99, Fairfield-Suisun Unified Sch. Dist., Fairfield, 1999, Burlingame Sch. Dist., 1999, San Lorenzo Valley Unified Sch. Dist., Felton, 2003; interim bus. mgr. Healdsburg Unified Sch. Dist., 1999—2000; interim dep. supt. adminstrv. svcs. Gilroy Unified Sch. Dist., 1999; interim bus. mgr. Moraga Sch. Dist., 1999; interim asst. supt. bus. svcs. Mountain-View/Los Altos Union H.S. Dist., Mountain View, 1997, Glenn County Office Edn., 2003; interim asst. supt. fiscal svcs. Cupertino Union Sch. Dist., 1997—98; interim CFO Union Sch. Dist., San Jose, 1998;

spl. asst. Milpitas Unified Sch. Dist., 1998—2000; interim bus. mgr. Los Gatos Sch. Dist., 1997; interim budget mgr. Saint Helena Unified Sch. Dist., 2000; interim AB1200 coord. Napa County Office Edn., 2000; vice-chmn. Edn. Mandated Cost Network Exec. Bd., 1991—95; mem. Schs. Fin. Svcs. subcom., 1987—94. Author, co-editor Howdy Rowdy Memorial, 1979. Active Ctr. Photog. Arts; treas. Mountain Parks Found., 1997—99; chmn. Unemployment Ins. Tech. Subcom., 1988—90; bd. dirs. Mountain Parks Found., 1997—2000. Mem.: Montalvo Assn., Santa Cruz Mus. Art and History, Am. Assn. Ret. Persons, Friends of Santa Cruz Pub. Librs., Nature Conservancy, Felton Cmty. Hall (supporter), Waddell Creek Assn. (sponsor), Point Lobos Natural History Assn., Calif. State Parks Found., Calif. Trout, Amnesty Internat., Wine Investigation for Novices and Oenephiles, Santa Cruz Fly Fisherman, Norwegian Elkhound Assn. (pres. 1977—79), Calif. Assn. Sch. Bus. Ofcls. (subsect. pres. 1984—85, risk mgmt. com. 1985—87, sect. bd. dirs. 1987—93, legis. com. 1989—2000, sect. pres. 1991—92, bd. dirs. 1991—92, schs. employer adv. com. rep. 1991—2004, state strategic planning com. 1994, risk mgmt. com. 1996—97, risk mgmt. com., bd. dirs., purchasing com. 1999—2002, state strategic planning com. 2001), Am. Diabetes Assn., Napa Valley Wine Libr. Assn. (life), Am. Assn. Individual Investors (life), Trout Unltd. (life), Friends of Long Marine Lab. Dirs. Cir. (charter), Am. Dog Owners Assn., Maui Arts and Cultural Ctr. Ohia Club, Quyana Club, Easter Seals Ctrl. Calif. Century Club, Sierra Club (life), Rotary San Lorenzo Valley (club svcs. dir. 2000—03, pres.-elect 2003—04, centennial pres. 2004—). Libertarian. Roman Catholic. Avocations: photography, travel, oenophilia, fishing, snorkelling. Home and Office: 400 Coon Heights Rd Ben Lomond CA 95005-9711

SIKORA, ROSANNA DAWN, emergency physician, educator; b. Weirton, W.Va., Nov. 16, 1955; d. Edward and Dorothy Ann (Wade) S.; m. Odus E. Brown, Nov. 25, 1994; stepchildren: Aza, Katherine, Hannah. AB in Biology, W.Va. U., 1978, MD, 1982. Cert. in emergency medicine; cert. in pediats., specialty in pediat. emergency medicine; cert. in internal medicine. Resident in pediat. internal medicine W.Va. U. Hosps. Inc., Morgantown, 1982-86, with. Assoc. prof. emergency medicine, pediats., internal medicine W.Va. U. Sch. Medicine, 1996—; mem. pediat. advanced life support subcom. Am. Heart Assn., Charleston, 1987-97, mem. pediat. advanced life support affiliate faculty, 1987-97. Physician men's/women's varsity swim/diving team W.Va. U., Morgantown, 1994 . Fellow Am. Coll. Emergency Physicians (bd. dirs. 1990—, sec.-treas. 1995-96, v.p. 1996-97, pres.-elect 1997-98); mem. AMA, ACP, Am. Acad. Pediats., Alpha Omega Alpha. Democrat. Roman Catholic. Office: W Va U Dept Emergency Medicine PO Box 9149 Morgantown WV 26506-9149

SIKORA, SHERYL L. application developer; b. Evergreen Park, Ill., May 23, 1971; d. Michael and Margaret (Vanderjack) Sikora. BS summa cum laude, Devry Inst. Tech., Chgo., 1997—99. Web developer USatWork.com, Rolling Meadows, Ill., 1999—2000; cons., level II New Resources Corp., Rolling Meadows, Ill., 2000; cons. Technium Consulting, Inc., Chgo., 2000; software test engr. InstallShield Software Corp., Schaumburg, Ill., 2001—02, software release engr., 2002—. Mem.: Assn. Info. Tech. Profls., Alpha Beta Gamma. Office: InstallShield Software Corporation 900 National Pkwy Schaumburg IL 60173 Personal E-mail: sls1971@yahoo.com. E-mail: ssikora@macrovision.com.

SIKORA, SUZANNE MARIE, dentist; b. Kenosha, Wis., Dec. 4, 1952; d. Leo F. and Ida A. (Dupuis) S. BS, U. Wis., Parkside, 1975; DDS, Marquette U., 1981. Assoc. Paul G. Hagemann, DDS, Racine, Wis., 1981-84; pvt. practice dentistry Racine, 1984—. Cons. Westview Health Care Ctr., Racine, 1981—89, Lincoln Luth. Home, Racine, 1981—2001, Becker-Shoop Ctr., Racine, 1981—2000, Lincoln Village Convalescent Ctr., Racine, 1986—2000, Lincoln Luth Cmty. Care Ctr., 1989—2000. Mem. ad hoc study com. County Health Dept., Racine, 1982—83. Mem.: ADA, Racine County Dental Soc. (pres.-elect 2001, v.p. 2002, pres. 2003, membership chairperson 2003—), Wis. Dental Assn. (coun. on access prevention and wellness com. 1984—86, impaired provider program intervenor 1990—2001, del. 1993—, Dental Care for Older Persons award 2000). Office: 1900 Lathrop Ave Racine WI 53405-3707 Office Phone: 262-632-0719.

SIKOROVSKY, EUGENE FRANK, retired lawyer; b. Jackson, Mich., Nov. 27, 1927; s. Frank Joseph and Betty Dorothy (Malik) S.; m. Patricia O'Byrne, July 11, 1953; children: Paul, Charles, Catherine, Elizabeth, Emily. BSEE, U. Mich., 1948; LLB, Harvard U., 1951. Bar: N.Y. 1952, Va. 1970, Ill. 1978. Assoc. predecessor firms Cahill, Gordon & Reindel, 1954-63, ptnr., 1964-68; v.p., gen. counsel, dir. Reynolds Metals Co., Richmond, Va., 1969-76; gen. counsel Gould Inc., Rolling Meadows, Ill., 1977-79, v.p., 1977-81; dep. gen. counsel Bell & Howell Co., Skokie, Ill., 1981-83, v.p., 1983-88, gen. counsel, 1983-92, sec., 1984-92, sr. v.p., dir., 1988-92. Lt. USNR, 1951-54. Mem. Ill. State Bar Assn., Tau Beta Pi, Eta Kappa Nu, Phi Eta Sigma, Phi Delta Theta. Episcopalian. Home: 720 Grandview Ln Lake Forest IL 60045-3953 E-mail: genesikor@earthlink.net.

SIKORSKI, JAMES ALAN, research chemist; b. Stevens Point, Wis., Nov. 9, 1948; s. John Paul and Florence Lucille (Wierzba) S.; m. Jeanne Delaney, Apr. 15, 1968 (div. 1975); 1 child, Christine René; m. Georgina Weber, Nov. 19, 1977. BS, Northeast La. State Coll., 1970; MS, Purdue U., 1976, PhD, 1981. With Monsanto Agrl. Co., St. Louis, 1976-91, sci. fellow, 1987-91, Monsanto Corp. Rsch., St. Louis, 1991-93; sci. fellow med. chem. G.D. Searle R&D, St. Louis, 1994-2000; sci. fellow med. chemistry Pharmacia Discovery Rsch., St. Louis, 2000—. Instr. organic chemistry St. Louis C.C., 1977-78; adj. prof. biochemistry Ctrl. Meth. Coll., 1995-97; invited spkr. tech. presentations and seminars. Contbr. chpts. to books, rev. articles, symposia-in-print and articles to profl. jours.; patentee and co-patentee in field. Mem. AAAS, Am. Chem. Soc. (St. Louis ACS award St. Louis Mo. sect. 1994, Kenneth A. Spencer award Kansas City Mo. sect. 1999, Internat. Soc. Heterocyclic Chemistry. Avocations: hiking, canoeing, skiing, photography, snorkeling. Office: Monsanto Pharmacia Corp 700 Chesterfield Pkwy W Chesterfield MO 63017-1732 E-mail: james.a.sikorski@pharmacia.com.

SILAK, CATHY R. lawyer, former state supreme court justice; b. Astoria, N.Y., May 25, 1950; d. Michael John and Rose Marie (Janor) S.; m. Nicholas G. Miller, Aug. 9, 1980; 3 children. BA, NYU, 1971; M in City Planning, Harvard U., 1973; JD, U. Calif., 1976. Bar: Calif. 1977, U.S. Dist. Ct. (no. dist.) Calif. 1977, D.C. 1979, U.S. Ct. Appeals (D.C. cir.) 1979, U.S. Dist. Ct. (so. dist.) N.Y. 1980, Idaho 1983, U.S. Dist. Ct. Idaho 1983, U.S. Ct. Appeals (2nd cir.) 1983, U.S. Ct. Appeals (9th cir.) 1985. Law clk. to Hon. William W. Schwarzer U.S. Dist. Ct. (no dist.), Calif., 1976-77; pvt. practice San Francisco, 1977-79, Washington, 1979-80; asst. U.S. atty. So. Dist. of N.Y., 1980-83; spl. asst. U.S. atty. Dist. of Idaho, 1983-84; pvt. practice Boise, Idaho, 1984-90; judge Idaho Ct. Appeals, 1990-93; justice Idaho Supreme Ct., Boise, 1993—2000; ptnr. Hawley, Troxell, Ennis, and Hawley, 2001—. Assoc. gen. counsel Morrison Knudsen Corp., 1989-90; mem. fairness com. Idaho Supreme Ct. and Gov.'s Task Force on Alternative Dispute Resolution; instr. and lectr. in field. Assoc. note and comment editor Calif. Law Rev., 1975-76. Land use planner Mass. Dept. Natural Resources, 1973; founder Idaho Coalition for Adult Literacy; bd. dirs. Literacy Lab., Inc.; mem. adv. bd. Boise State U. Legal Asst. Program. Recipient Jouce Stein award Boise YWCA, 1992, Women Helping Women award Soroptimist, Boise, 1993. Fellow Idaho Law Found (ann., lectr.); mem. ABA (nat. conf. state trial judges jud. adminstrn. divsn.), Nat. Assn. Women Judges, Idaho State Bar (corp./securities sect., instr.), Am. Law Inst., Fellows of the Am. Bar Found, Am. Judicature Soc. (bd. dirs.). Office: Hawley Troxell Ennis & Hawley PO Box 1617 Boise ID 83702-1617*

SILAS, CECIL JESSE, retired petroleum company executive; b. Miami, Fla., Apr. 15, 1932; s. David Edward and Hilda Videll (Carver) S.; m. Theodosea Hejda, Nov. 27, 1965; children: Karla, Peter, Michael, James. BSChemE, Ga. Inst. Tech., Atlanta, 1953. With Phillips Petroleum Co., Bartlesville, Okla., 1953-94, pres. Europe-Africa, Brussels and London, 1968-74, mng. dir. natural resource group Europe/Africa, 1974-76, v.p. gas and gas liquids div. natural resources group Bartlesville, 1976-78, sr. v.p. natural resources group, 1978-80, exec. v.p. exploration and prodn., minerals, gas and gas liquids, 1980-82, pres., chief operating officer, 1982-85, chmn., CEO, 1985-94. Bd. dirs. of Halliburton Co., Boys/Girls Clubs Am., Atlanta, parton councillor Atlantic Coun. of the U.S.; bd. dirs. Okla. Found. for Excellence, Ga. Tech. Found.; trustee Frank Phillips Found. Served to 1st lt. Chem. Corps, AUS, 1954-56. Decorated comdr. Order St. Olaf (Norway); inducted into Ga. Inst. Tech. Athletic Hall of Fame, 1959, recipient Former Scholar-Athlete Total Person award, 1988; inducted into Okla. Bus. Hall of Fame, 1989; named CEO of Yr., Internat. TV Assn., 1987. Mem. Am. Petroleum Inst., U.S. C. of C. (past chmn. bd. dirs.), 25 Yr. Club, Phi Delta Theta. Avocations: fishing, golf, hunting. Office: PO Box 2127 Bartlesville OK 74005-2127

SILAS, NANCY, small business owner; b. Gainesville, Fla., Sept. 7, 1943; d. Joseph N Simmons and Roberta (Thompson) Walker Simmons. BS, Fla. A&M U., Tallahassee, 1965; postgrad., U. South Fla., Tampa, 1969—77, Fla. Internat. U., Miami, 1978. Tchr. jr. and sr. high sch. Hillsborough County, Tampa, Fla., 1965—82; interior decorator Interior Show Rm., Tampa, Fla., 1986—89; self employed clothes/accessories, Tampa, Fla., 1989—93; bus. owner Source Innova Concepts Intl Inc, Gainesville, Fla., 2000—04, Fragrance Boutique (Nancy's Fancy and Fine Things), Gainesville, 2003—. Bd. dirs. Source Innova, Gainesville, Fla., 1999—; pres. exec. dir. Concepts Internat., Inc., Gainesville, 1999—; advocacy cons. For Youth /Women, Gainesville, Fla., 1999—; spkr. in field, seminar presenter. Author: (poetry book) Shapes of Human Forms, 2003. Vol. youth Weed And Seed Program, Gainesville, Fla., 2000—02. Grantee Bus. Grant, Gainesville, Fla., 2000. Mem.: Partners Cmty. (assoc.; parliamentarian 2002). Avocations: interior design, community projects, fine arts/crafts. Office: Source Innova Concepts Itl Inc # 23 2114 NW 55th Blvd Gainesville FL 32653

SILAS, PAUL, professional basketball coach; b. Prescott, Ariz. m. Carolyn Silas; children: Paula, Stephen. Student, Creighton U. Mem. St. Louis Hawks, 1964, Phoenix Suns, Boston Celtics, Denver Nuggets, Seattle Supersonics; head coach San Diego Clippers, 1980-83; asst. coach N.J. Nets, 1988-89, 92-95, N.Y. Knicks, 1989-92, Phoenix Suns, Charlotte Hornets, 1997-98, head coach, 1999—2003, Cleve. Cavaliers, 2003—. Host ann. corp. basketball tournament for Spl. Olympics, N.Y. Named NBA All-Star, NBA All-Defensive first team, 1975, 76, NBA All-Defensive second team, 1971, 72, 73. Achievements include rank of 14th on the all-time list with 12,357 career boards. Office: 1 Center Ct Cleveland OH 44115-4001

SILBER, JOHN ROBERT, retired academic administrator, law educator, philosophy educator; b. San Antonio, Aug. 15, 1926; s. Paul G. and Jewell (Joslin) S.; m. Kathryn Underwood, July 12, 1947; children: David Joslin (dec.), Mary Rachel, Judith Karen, Kathryn Alexandra, Martha Claire, Laura Ruth, Caroline Jocasta. BA summa cum laude, Trinity U., 1947; postgrad., Northwestern U., summer 1944, Yale Div. Sch., 1947-48, U. Tex. Sch. Law, 1948-49; MA, Yale, 1952, PhD, 1956; L.H.D., Kalamazoo Coll., 1970; many others. Instr. dept. philosophy Yale U., 1952-55; asst. prof. U. Tex., Austin, Austin, 1955-59, asso. prof., 1959-62, prof. philosophy, 1962-70, chmn. dept. philosophy, 1962-67, Univ. prof. arts and letters, 1967-70, chmn. (Comparative Studies Program), 1967, dean (Coll. Arts and Scis.), 1967-70; Univ. prof., prof. philosophy and law Boston U., 1971—, pres., 1971-96, prof. internat. rels., 1996—2003, chancellor, 1996—2003, prof. emeritus, 2003—. Vis. prof. Bonn U., 1960; fellow Kings Coll. U. London, 1963-64; bd. dirs. Mut. Am. Inst. Funds, Inc. Author: The Ethical Significance of Kant's Religion, 1960, Straight Shooting: What's Wrong With America and How to Fix It, 1989, Ist Amerika zu retten?, 1992; editor: Kant's Religion Within the Limits of Reason Alone, 1960, Works in Continental Philosophy, 1967—; assoc. editor: Kant-Studien, 1968-; contbr. to profl. jours. Chmn. Tex. Soc. to Abolish Capital Punishment, 1960-69; mem. Nat. Commn. United Meth. Higher Edn., 1974-77; exec. bd. Nat. Humanities Inst., 1975-78; trustee Coll. St. Scholastica, 1973-85, U. Denver, 1985-89, WGBH Ednl. Found., 1971-96, Adelphi U., 1989-97; bd. visitors Air U., 1974-80; bd. dirs. Greater Boston coun. Boy Scouts Am., 1981-93, v.p. fin., 1981-93, Silver Beaver award, 1989, Disting. Eagle, 1997; mem. Nat. Humanities Faculty, 1968-73, Nat. Captioning Inst., 1985-94; bd. advisors Matchette Found., 1969-70; mem. Nat. Bipartisan Commn. on Ctrl. Am., 1983-84, U.S. Strategic Inst., 1983-2001; Presdl. Adv. Bd. Radio Broadcasting to Cuba, 1985-92, v.p. 1984-98, vice chmn., 1998-2001; bd. dir. US Strategic Inst., 1983-2001, v.p., 1984-98, vice chmn., 1998-2001; adv. bd. Schurman Libr. of Am. Hist., Ruprecht-Karl U., Heidelberg, 1986—; mem. def. policy bd. U.S. Dept. Def., 1987-90; mem. internat. coun.advisors Inst. for Humanities at Salado, 1988—; bd. dirs. New Eng. Holocaust Meml. Com., 1989-95, Brit. Inst. of U.S., 1989—, Bette Davis Found., 1997—, Boston Police Found., 1997—; Dem. gubernatorial candidate of Mass., 1990; vice chmn. U.S. Strategic Inst.; bd. dirs., vice chmn. Americans for Med. Progress, 1992—, chmn., 1994-95, mem. exec. com. 1995—; chmn. Mass. Bd. Edn., 1996-99; bd. advisors Nat. Assn. Scholars. Recipient E. Harris Harbison award for disting. tchg. Danforth Found., 1966, Wilbur Lucius Cross medal Yale Grad. Sch., 1971, Outstanding Civilian Svc. medal U.S. Army, 1985, Disting. Pub. Svc. award Anti-Defamation League of B'nai B'rith, 1989, Horatio Alger award, 1992, Am.-Swiss Friendship award, 1991, Israel Peace medal, 1985, Ehrenmedaille U. Heidelberg, 1986, White House Small Bus. award for entrepreneurial excellence, 1986, Cross of Paideia, Greek Orthodox Archdiocese of North and South Am., 1988, Pro Bene Meritis award U. Tex., Austin, 1997; Fulbright rsch. fellow Germany, 1959-60; Guggenheim fellow Eng., 1963-64; decorated with Knight Comdr.'s Cross with Star of Order of Merit Fed. Republic of Germany, 1983; commandeur Nat. Order of Arts and Letters (France), 1985. Fellow Royal Soc. Arts; mem. Am. Philos. Assn., Am. Soc. Polit. and Legal Philosophy, Royal Inst. Philosophy, Am. Assn. Higher Edn., Nat. Assn. Ind. Colls. and Univs. (dir. 1976-81), Phi Beta Kappa. Office: Boston Univ 1 Sherborn St Boston MA 02215-1708

SILBER, JUDY G. dermatologist; b. Newark, July 26, 1953; MD, SUNY, Bklyn., 1978. Intern Brookdale Med. Ctr., Bklyn., 1978-79; resident in dermatology Kings County Hosp., Bklyn., 1979-82; pvt. practice dermatology. Affiliated with Meadowlands Med. Ctr., Secaucus, N.J. Fellow Am. Acad. Dermatology; mem. AMA, N.J. Med. Soc. Office: 952 Clifton Ave Clifton NJ 07013-3502

SILBER, NORMAN JULES, lawyer; b. Tampa, Fla., Apr. 18, 1945; s. Abe and Mildred (Hirsch) Silber; m. Linda Geraldine Hirsch, June 10, 1979; 1 child, Michael Hirsch. BA, Tulane U., 1967, JD, 1969; postgrad. in bus. adminstrn., NYU, 1970—72. Bar: Fla. 1970, U.S. Dist. Ct. (so. dist.) Fla. 1975, U.S. Tax Ct. 1975, U.S. Ct. Appeals (5th cir.) 1975, U.S. Ct. Appeals (11th cir.) 1981. With legal dept. Fiduciary Trust Co. N.Y., N.Y.C., 1969—72, asst. trust officer, 1971—72; exec. v.p. I.R.E. Fin. Corp., Miami, Fla., 1972—76; mng. atty. Norman J. Silber, P.A., Miami, 1973—85; ptnr. McDermott, Will & Emery, 1985—2001, Ruden, McClosky, Smith, Schuster & Russell, P.A., 2001—. Mem.: Fla. Bar (chmn. 11th jud. cir. grievance com. 1982—84). Republican. Jewish. Home: 1232 Palermo Ave Miami FL 33134-6327 Office: Ruden McClosky Smith Schuster & Russell PA 701 Brickell Ave Fl 19 Miami FL 33131 Business E-Mail: norman.silber@ruden.com.

SILBER, STEVEN A. lab administrator, physician; MD, Johns Hopkins U. Sch. Medicine, 1976. Resident, internal medicine U. Pa. Hosp., fellow, gen. internal medicine, chief resident; med. and regulatory affairs, clin. rsch. and devel. SmithKline Beecham; faculty mem. U. Pa., Phila.; pres. Premier Rsch., 2000—02; chief med. officer SCP Comm., Inc., N.Y.C., 2002—. Founder Info. Cos. of Am., Med. Broadcasting Co. Office: SCP Communications 134 W 29th St New York NY 10001*

SILBERBERG, DONALD H. neurologist; b. Washington, Mar. 2, 1934; s. William Aaron and Leslie Frances (Stone) S.; m. Marilyn Alice Damsky, June 7, 1959; children: Mark, Alan. MD, U. Mich., 1958; MA (hon.), U. Pa., 1971. Intern Mt. Sinai Hosp., N.Y.C., 1958-59; clin. assoc. in neurology NIH, Bethesda, Md., 1959-61; Fulbright scholar Nat. Hosp., London, 1961-62; NINDB spl. fellow in neuro-ophthalmology Washington U., St. Louis, 1962-63; assoc. neurology U. Pa., 1963-65, asst. prof., 1965-67, assoc. prof., 1967-71, prof., 1971-73, acting chmn. dept., 1973-74, prof., vice chmn. neurology, 1974-82, chmn., 1982-94, sr. assoc. dean, dir. internat. programs, 1994—2004. Active staff U. Pa. Med. Ctr., Phila.; cons. Children's Hosp., Phila.; pres., CEO Betasteron Found., Inc., 1994—. Contbr. articles to profl. jours., abstracts, chpts. in books. Recipient grants in study of multiple sclerosis. Mem.: Global Network for Rsch. on Mental and Neurol. Health (founding v.p.), World Fedn. Neurology, Phila. Neurol. Soc. (pres. 1978—79), Assn. Univ. Profs. Neurology (pres.-elect 1993), Nat. Multiple Sclerosis Soc. (trustee 1997—99, 2001—03), John Morgan Soc. U. Pa. (pres. 1974—75), Internat. Soc. Neurochemistry, Internat. Soc. Devel. Neuroscis., Coll. Physicians Phila., Am. Soc. Neurochemistry, Am. Neurol. Assn., Am. Acad. Neurology, Alpha Omega Alpha. Office: U Pa Med Ctr Dept Neurology 3400 Spruce St Philadelphia PA 19104-4206

SILBERBERG, RICHARD HOWARD, lawyer; b. NYC, Feb. 20, 1951; BA, U. Wis., 1972; JD, NYU, 1975. Bar: N.Y. 1976, U.S. Dist. Ct. (so. and ea. dists.) N.Y., 1976, U.S. Ct. Appeals (2d cir.) 1982, U.S. Ct. Internat. Trade 1983, U.S. Ct. Appeals (3d cir.) 1991, U.S. Supreme Ct. 1994, U.S. Ct. Appeals (11th cir.) 1996, U.S. Ct. Appeals (1st cir.) 1997. Assoc. Delson & Gordon, N.Y.C., 1975-83, ptnr., 1983-87, Dorsey & Whitney, N.Y.C., 1988—, mng. ptnr., 1994-97. Mem. panel arbitrators U.S. Dist. Ct. for Ea. Dist. N.Y., 1987—; mem. panel mediators U.S. Dist. Ct. for So. Dist. N.Y., 1992—; trustee Lawyers Com. for Civil Rights Under Law, 1992—; dir. Fund for Modern Cts., 1999—, High 5 Tickets to the Arts, 1999—. Mng. editor NYU Jour. Internat. Law and Politics, 1974-75. Mem.: Am. Arbitration Assn. (panel neutrals 1992—, bd. dirs.), NYU Law Alumni Assn. Office: Dorsey & Whitney LLP 250 Park Ave New York NY 10177-0001 Business E-Mail: silberberg.richard@dorseylaw.com.

SILBERFARB, PETER MICHAEL, psychiatrist, educator; b. Jersey City, Oct. 28, 1938; m. Anne Wagner, 1962; children: Benjamin, Leah S. BS, Bucknell U., 1960; postgrad., NYU, 1960-61; MD, Hahnemann Coll., 1965; MA (hon.), Dartmouth Coll., 1986. Diplomate Nat. Bd. Med. Examiners, Am. Bd. Psychiatry and Neurology (pres. 1998). Intern Hahnemann Med. Coll. Hosp., Phila., 1965-66; resident in internal medicine Dartmouth Affiliated Hosps., Hanover, N.H., 1966-68, resident in internal medicine and psychiatry, 1968-69, psychiatry resident, 1971-72, chief resident in psychiatry, 1972-73; instr. in psychiatry Med. Sch., Dartmouth Coll., Hanover, 1972-73, asst. prof. of psychiatry, 1973-77, dir. tng. and edn., 1976-86, assoc. prof. clin. psychiatry, assoc. prof. clin. medicine, 1977-80, dir. grad. edn. and residency tng., 1978-86, assoc. prof. psychiatry, assoc. prof. medicine, 1980-82, dir. tng. and edn., 1984—, prof. psychiatry, prof. medicine, 1986—, chmn. dept. psychiatry, 1986—, Raymond Sobel prof. psychiatry, 1993. Cons. psychiatrist Mary Hitchcock Meml. Hosp., Hanover, 1973—; dir. psychiat. in-patient svc. Dartmouth-Hitchcock Med. Ctr., 1973-75, dir. cancer psychiatry program Norris Cotton Cancer Ctr., 1975—, acting dir. psychiatry consultation svc., 1977-79, assoc. dir. cancer control Norris Ctr., 1981-86; sec. psychiatry com. Cancer and Leukemia Group B, 1976-79, vice chmn., 1979—; mem. grant rev. com. for cancer control Nat. Cancer Inst., 1979, 80, mem. spl. grant rev. com., 1981, 82, 85, cons. to bd. sci. counselors, 1982, mem. cancer control grant rev. com., 1986-90; vice chmn. adv. com. for psychosocial and behavioral rsch. Am. Cancer Soc., 1982-88, chmn., 1988-89; cons. collaborative ctr. for cancer pain relief WHO, Milan, 1985; mem. accreditation coun. for grad. med. edn. Appeals Bd. for Psychiatry, Chgo., 1983, specialist site visitor, 1985-90, mem. residency rev. com. for psychiatry, 1991—; dir. Am. Bd. Family Practice, 1996—; mem. exec. com. Am. Bd. Med. Specialties, 1996-99. Author chpts. to books; mem. editl. bd. Jour. Psychosocial Oncology, 1983-91, Internat. Jour. Psychiatry in Medicine, 1986-90, Contemporary Psychiatry, 1987-91, Psychooncology, 1991—; referee numerous manuscripts; contbr. articles to profl. jours. Surgeon USPHS, 1969-71. Fellow Am. Psychiat. Assn. (cons. to task force on treatment if psychiat. disorders 1989), Am. Coll. Psychiatrists; mem. AMA, Am. Soc. Psychiat. Oncology/AIDS, Am. Soc. Clin. Oncology, Am. Assn. Dirs. Psychiat. Residency Tng. (mem. curriculum com. 1979-88, mem. task force on med. students and residents, chmn. com. regional dirs. 1984-88, mem. exec. com. 1984-88), Am. Psychosomatic Soc., N.H. Psychiat. Soc. (chmn. membership com. 1974-76, chmn. continuing edn. com. 1977-79), N.H. Med. Soc., Assn. Rsch. in Nervous and Mental Disease, Assn. Acad. Psychiatry, Benjamin Rush Soc. Home: Bragg Hill Norwich VT 05055 Office: Dartmouth Coll Med Sch Dept Psychiatry Lebanon NH 03756-0001

SILBERGELD, ARTHUR F. lawyer; b. St. Louis, June 1, 1942; s. David and Sabina (Silbergeld) S.; m. Carol Ann Schwartz, may 1, 1970; children: Diana Lauren, Julia Kay. BA, U. Mich., 1968; M in City Planning, U. Pa., 1971; JD, Temple U., 1975. Bar: N.Y. 1976, Calif. 1978, D.C. 1983, U.S. Ct. Appeals (2nd cir.), U.S. Ct. Appeals (9th cir.), U.S. Ct. Appeals (D.C. cir.), U.S. Supreme Ct. 1999. Assoc. Vladeck, Elias, Vladeck & Lewis, N.Y.C., 1975-77; field atty. NLRB, L.A., 1977-78; ptnr., head employment law practice group McKenna, Conner & Cuneo, L.A., 1978-89; ptnr. Graham & James, L.A., 1990-96; labor ptnr. Sonnenschein Nath & Rosenthal, L.A., 1996-99; ptnr. Proskauer Rose LLP, L.A., 1999—. Instr. extension divsn. UCLA, 1981-89. Author: Doing Business in California: An Employment Law Handbook, 2nd edit., 1997, Advising California Employers, 1990-95 supplements; contbr. articles to profl. jours. Founding mem. L.A. Mus. Contemporary Art; bd. dirs. Bay Cities unit Am. Cancer Soc., Calif., 1981-85, Jewish Family Svc., L.A., 1981-85, So. Calif. Employers Roundtable, Leadership coun., So. Poverty Law Ctr., Leadership Task Force, Drs. Without Borders; pres. Mo. Valley Fedn. of Temple Youth, 1959-60; mem. Calif. com. south Human Rights Watch, 2003—; treas. L.A. Child Devel. Ctr., 2001—. Mem. L.A. County Bar Assn. (chair labor and employment law sect. 1999-2000, trustee 2000-01), Mus. Modern Art (N.Y.C.), Coll. of Labor and Employment Lawyers. Office: Proskauer Rose LLP 2049 Century Park E Fl 32 Los Angeles CA 90067-3101 Office Phone: 310-557-2900.

SILBERGELD, ELLEN KOVNER, environmental epidemiologist, researcher, toxicologist; b. Washington, July 29, 1945; d. Joseph and Mary (Gion) Kovner; m. Alan Mark Silbergeld, 1969; children: Sophia, Nicholas. AB, Vassar Coll., 1967; PhD, Johns Hopkins U., 1972. Kennedy fellow Johns Hopkins Med. Sch., Balt., 1974—75; scientist NIH, Bethesda, Md., 1975—81; chief toxics scientist Environ. Def. Fund, Washington, 1982—90; prof. epidemiology, toxicology and pharmacology U.Md., Balt., 1990—2001, affil. prof. environ. law, 1990—2001, dir. program in human health and environ., 1996—2000, prof. dept. pathology toxicology, 1995—2000, adj. prof. dept. pharmacology and exptl. therapeutics, 1995—2000; Prof. Environ. Health Scis. epidemiology, and health policy and mgmt. Bloomberg School of Public Health, Johns Hopkins U., Balt., 2001—. Mem. sci. adv. bd. EPA, 1983—89, 1993—99, Dept. Energy, 1994—95; mem. bd. on environ. sci. and toxicology NAS-NRC, 1983—89; mem. Com. Geosci. Environ. and Resources, 1994—98; mem. bd. biotech. and agr., 1999—; mem. bd. sci. counselors Nat. Inst. Environ. Health Scis., 1987—93; cons. Oil and Chem. Atomic Workers, 1970, NSF, 1974—75, OECD, 1987—90. Mem. editl. bd.: Neurobehavioral Toxicology, 1979—87, Am. Jour. Medicine, 1980—, Neurotoxicology, 1981—86, Environ. Rsch., 1983—, editor-in-chief:, 1994—. Mem. Homewood Friends Meeting. Recipient Wolman award, Md. Pub. Health Assn., 1991, Barsky award, APHA, 1992, Md. Gov. Excellence citation, 1990, 1993; scholar Baldwin scholar, Coll. Notre Dame; Fulbright fellow, London, 1967, Woodrow Wilson and Danforth fellow, 1967, NAS Exch. fellow, Yugoslavia, 1976, MacArthur Found. fellow, 1993—98. Mem.: APHA, AAAS, Soc. for Neurosci., Soc. Toxicology, Soc. for Occupl. and Environ. Health (sec.-treas. 1983—85, pres. 1987—89), Am. Soc. Tropical Med. Hygiene, Collegium Ramazzini (councillor), Phi Beta Kappa. Office: Bloomberg Sch Pub Health 615 N Wolfe St Baltimore MD 21205 Office Phone: 410-955-8678.

SILBERGELD, JEROME LESLIE, art historian, educator; b. Highland, Ill., Apr. 25, 1944; s. David and Sabina Silbergeld; m. Michelle DeKlyen, June 27, 1970; children: David, Emily. BA in History, Stanford U., 1966, MA in History, 1967; MA in Art History, U. Oreg., 1972; PhD in Art History, Stanford U., 1974. Vis. asst. prof. dept. art history U. Oreg., Eugene, 1974—75; from asst. prof. to prof. U. Wash., Seattle, 1975—2001, chmn. art history dept., 1988—92, dir. sch. art, 1992—96; Donald E. Petersen prof. arts, 2000—01; vis. prof. dept. fine arts Harvard U., Cambridge, Mass., 1996; P.Y. and Kinmay W. Tang prof. of Chinese art history Princeton U., 2001—, dir. Tang Ctr. for East Asian Art, 2001—. Author: Chinese Painting Style, 1982 (Soc. for Tech. Achievement award 1983), Mind Landscapes: The Painting of C.C. Wang, 1987, Contradictions: Artistic Life, the Socialist State, and the

Chinese Painter Li Huasheng, 1993 (among N.Y. Times Notable Books of 1993), China into Film: Frames of Reference in Contemporary Chinese Cinema, 1999, Hitchcock With a Chinese Face: Cinematic Doubles, 2004, Oedipal Triangles, 2004, China's Moral Voice, 2004; editor, translator: Chinese Painting Colors (Yu Fei'an) 1988; contbr. articles to profl. jours. Grantee Nat. Endowment for Humanities, 1981, 92, J. Paul Getty Trust, 1987. Mem. Assn. Asian Studies, Coll. Art Assn. Avocations: classical piano, long-distance running. Office: Princeton U Dept Art & Archaeology Princeton NJ 08544-0108 E-mail: jsil@princeton.edu.

SILBERMAN, ALAN HARVEY, lawyer; b. Chgo., Oct. 22, 1940; s. Milton J. and Mollie E. (Hymanson) S.; m. Margaret Judith Auslander, Nov. 17, 1968; children: Elena, Mark. BA with distinction, Northwestern U., 1961; LLB, Yale U., 1964. Bar: Ill. 1964, U.S. Dist. Ct. (no. dist.) Ill. 1966, U.S. Ct. Appeals (7th cir.) 1970, (5th and 9th cir.) 1977, (D.C. cir.) 1979, (4th cir.) 1980, (11th cir.) 1981, (3rd cir.) 1982, (8th and 10th cirs.) 1993, U.S. Supreme Ct. 1978. Law clk. U.S. Dist. Ct., Chgo., 1964-66; assoc. Sonnenschein Nath & Rosenthal, Chgo., 1964-71, ptnr., 1972—. Mem. antitrust adv. bd. Bur. Nat. Affairs, Washington, 1985—; mem. Ill. Atty. Gen. Franchise Adv. Bd., 1996—; bd. dirs., mem. exec. com. Mercaz, USA. Contbr. articles to profl. jours. Bd. dirs., v.p., sec. Camp Ramah in Wis., Inc., Chgo., 1966-86, pres., 1986-94; bd. dirs. Nat. Ramah Commn., Inc. of Jewish Theol. Sem. Am., N.Y.C., 1970—, v.p., 1986-94, pres., 1994-99, sr. v.p., 1999-2003; mem. U.S. del. 33d World Zionist Congress, Jerusalem, 1997, 34th World Zionist Congress, Jerusalem, 2002; bd. dirs., mem. exec. com. Masorti Olami/World Coun. of Synagogues, 2002—; bd. govs. Northwestern U. Libr., 2004-. Mem. ABA (chmn. antitrust sect. FTC com. 1981-83, chmn. nat. insts. 1983-85, mem. coun. antitrust sect. 1985-88, fin. officer 1988-90, sect. del. ho. of dels. 1990-92, chmn.-elect 1992-93, chmn. 1993-94), Ill. Bar Assn. (chmn. antitrust sect. 1975-76), Northwestern U. 1851 Soc. (chair 1994-97, regional vice-chair), Lex Mundi, Antitrust Competition and Trade Com. (1999-2003, internat. chair elect 2003-). Home: 430 Oakdale Ave Glencoe IL 60022-2113 Office: Sonnenschein Nath 233 S Wacker Dr Ste 8000 Chicago IL 60606-6491 Office Phone: 312-876-8103.

SILBERMAN, CHARLOTTE SCHATZBERG, retired lawyer, artist; b. N.Y.C., Oct. 15, 1918; d. Louis and Annie (Hammerman) Schatzberg; m. Bernard Silberman, Sept. 24, 1942 (dec. Mar. 1991); children: Adela Wagman, Margery Miller Moores. BA, Hunter Coll., 1938; LLB, JD, Bklyn. Law Sch., 1940; postgrad., SUNY, Albany, 1977-84, Fla. Atlantic U., 1984—. Bar: N.Y. 1941. Pvt. practice law, N.Y.C., 1940-43, Albany, N.Y., 1947-57; atty. State N.Y., Albany, 1957-63; assoc. counsel SUNY, Albany, 1963-74, dir. paralegal studies, 1975-77. Works exhibited Soc. of Four Arts, 1990, Cornell Mus., Delray Beach, Fla., 1994, 95. Home: 7076 Huntington Ln Apt 401 Delray Beach FL 33446-2554

SILBERMAN, DEBORAH F. general counsel; b. Washington, Feb. 27, 1952; m. May 30, 1974. BA (hons.), Clark U., 1974; JD, Cath. U. Am., 1981. Bar: D.C. 1981. Editor Urban Land Inst., Washington, 1974-75; law clerk, office mgr. Leo Resnick, Washington, 1975-82, atty. adv., 1982-86; special coun. Securities and Exchange Commn., Washington, 1986; dep. dir. corp. and securities divsn. Fed. Home Loan Bank Bd., Washington, 1986-89; asst. chief counsel bus. transactions divsn. Office of Thrift Supervision, Washington, 1990-94; from dep. gen. counsel to gen. counsel Fed. Housing Finance Bd., Washington, 1994-98, gen. counsel, 1998—. Recipient Special Act award Dept. Treasury, 1992, 94. Mem. ABA, FBA, Women in Housing and Finance, Conf. on Consumer Finance Law. Avocations: travel, singing, writing, reading. Office: Office of Gen Counsel Fed Housing Finance Bd 1777 F St NW Washington DC 20006-5210

SILBERMAN, EDWARD KENNETH, physician, educator; b. N.Y.C., Dec. 28, 1944; s. Alfred D. and Lillian J. (Simon) S.; m. Barbara Warnick, Sept. 21, 1975; children: Michael John, Peter Warnick. BA, Yale U., 1965; MD, Tufts U., 1974. Diplomate Nat. Bd. Med. Examiners, Am. Bd. Psychiatry and Neurology. Clin. assoc. NIMH, Bethesda, Md., 1977-82; resident in psychiatry Mass. Mental Health Ctr., Boston, 1974-77; clin. fellow in psychiatry Harvard Med. Sch., Boston, 1974-77; asst. to assoc. prof. psychiatry USUHS, Bethesda, 1982-86; dir. residency edn., assoc. prof. psychiatry Med. Coll. of Pa., Phila., 1986-92; dir. of residency edn., clin. prof. psychiatry Jefferson Med. Coll., Phila., 1992—. Editor: (book) Successful Psychiatric Practice; co-editor: Handbook of Psychiatric Education and Faculty Development, 1999; contbr. numerous articles to profl. jours., publs. and textbooks. Surgeon USPHS, 1977-82. Recipient Outstanding Svc. medal Uniformed Svcs. Univ. of the Health Scis., Bethesda, 1986. Fellow: Am. Psychiat. Assn. (disting.); mem.: Assn. for Acad. Psychiatry (pres. 2003), Am. Assn. of Dirs. of Residency Tng. in Psychiatry (mem. exec. coun. 1998—2001), Am. Coll. Psychiatrists. Home: 619 W Upsal St Philadelphia PA 19119-3627 Office: Jefferson Med Coll 1000 Sansom St Philadelphia PA 19107-5002 E-mail: edward.k.silberman@mail.tju.edu.

SILBERMAN, ENRIQUE, physics researcher and administrator; b. Buenos Aires, Dec. 9, 1921; came to U.S., 1966; m. 1949; 2 children. PhD in Engring., U. Buenos Aires, 1945. Investigator physics Argentina Atomic Energy Commn., Buenos Aires, 1953-58; head dept. Arg AEC, 1958-63; prof. U. Buenos Aires, 1963-66; prof. physics Fisk U., Nashville, 1966—; dir. photonic materials and devices NASA Ctr., 1992—. Guest prof. U. Notre Dame, 1963; cons. Arg Nat. Coun. Sci. Rsch., 1964; vis. prof. Vanderbilt U., 1967—. Mem. AAAS, Am. Assn. Physics Tchrs., Am. Phys. Soc., Arg Physics Assn. Office: Fisk U Dept Physics Nashville TN 37208-3051 Office Phone: 615-329-8620. Business E-Mail: esilber@fisk.edu.

SILBERMAN, H. LEE, public relations executive, editorial consultant; b. Newark, Apr. 26, 1919; s. Louis and Anna (Horel) S.; m. Ruth Irene Rapp, June 5, 1948; children: Richard Lyle, Gregory Alan, Todd Walter. BA, U. Wis., 1940. Radio continuity writer Radio Sta. WTAQ, Green Bay, Wis., 1940-41; reporter Bayonne (N.J.) Times, 1941-42; sales exec. War Assets Adminstrn., Chgo., 1946-47; copy editor Acme Newspictures, Chgo., 1947; reporter, editl. writer Wichita (Kans.) Eagle, 1948-55; reporter Wall St. Jour., N.Y.C., 1955-57, banking editor, 1957-68; 1st v.p., dir. corp. rels. Shearson-Hamill & Co., N.Y.C., 1968-74; N.Y. corr. Economist of London, 1966-72; from contbg. editor to editor in chief Finance mag., 1970-76; from v.p., dir. to exec. v.p. Fin. Svcs. Group, Carl Boyir & Assos., Inc., N.Y.C., 1976-86, exec. v.p., 1981-86; sr. counselor Hill & Knowlton, Inc., N.Y.C., 1986-93, sr. v.p., 1993-96, sr. mng. dir., 1996; pres. LSA Media Cons., 1997—. Cons. in field. Contbr. articles to profl. jours. Capt. C.E. AUS, 1942-46. Recipient Loeb Mag. award U. Conn., 1965; Loeb Achievement award for disting. writing on fin. Gerald M. Loeb Found., 1968 Mem. Soc. Profl. Journalists, Soc. Silurians, N.Y. Fin. Writers Assn., Deadline Club N.Y., Zeta Beta Tau. Republican. Home and Office: 475 E 2nd St Clayton NC 27520-2558

SILBERMAN, LAURENCE HIRSCH, federal judge; b. York, Pa., Oct. 12, 1935; s. William and Anna (Hirsch) S.; m. Rosalie G. Gaull, Apr. 28, 1957; children: Robert Stephen, Katherine DeBoer Balaban, Anne Gaull Otis. BA, Dartmouth Coll., 1957; LLB, Harvard U., 1961. Bar: Hawaii 1962, D.C. 1973. Assoc. Moore, Torkildson & Rice and Quinn & Moore, Honolulu, 1961-64; ptnr. Moore, Silberman & Schulze, Honolulu, 1964-67; atty. appellate divsn. gen. counsel's office NLRB, Washington, 1967-69; solicitor of labor U.S. Dept. Labor, Washington, 1969-70, undersec. labor, 1970-73; ptnr. Steptoe & Johnson, Washington, 1973-74; dep. atty. gen. U.S. Washington, 1974-75; amb. to Yugoslavia, 1975-77; mng. ptnr. Morrison & Foerster, Washington, 1978-79, 83-85; exec. v.p. Crocker Nat. Bank, San Francisco, 1979-83; judge U.S. Ct. Appeals (D.C. cir.), Washington, 1985—. Lectr. labor law and legis. U. Hawaii, 1962—63; adj. prof. adminstrv. law Georgetown U., Washington, 1987—94, 1997, 1999—2001, NYU, 1995, 96, Harvard U., 1998; adj. prof. labor law Georgetown U., Washington, 2001, disting. visitor from the Judiciary tchr. adminstrv. law and labor law; Pres.' spl. envoy on ILO affairs, 1976; gen. adv. com. on Arms Control and Disarmament, 1981—85; mem. Def. Policy Bd., 1981—85; vice-chmn. State Dept.'s Commn. on Security and Econ. Assistance, 1983—84. Bd. dirs. Com. on Present Danger, 1978-85, Inst. for Ednl. Affairs, 1981-85; mem U.S. Fgn. Intelligence Surveillance Act. Ct. of Rev., 1996-2003; cochmn. Commn. on Intelligence Capabilities of the U.S. Regarding Weapons of Mass Destruction, 2004—; vice chmn. adv. coun. on gen. govt. Rep. Nat. Com., 1977-80. With AUS, 1957-58. Am. Enterprise Inst. sr. fellow, 1977-78, vis. fellow 1978-85. Mem. Coun. on Fgn. Rels.

SILBERMAN, ROBERT A. S. lawyer; b. Lebanon, Pa., Mar. 4, 1945; s. Henry T. and Genevieve (Mensh) S.; m. Nancy D. Netzer, Nov. 10, 1974. BA magna cum laude, Yale U., 1967; JD, Harvard U., 1970. Bar: Mass. 1970, Pa. 1984. Assoc. Csaplar & Bok, Boston, 1970—78, ptnr., 1978—90, Gaston & Snow, Boston, 1990—91, Edwards & Angell, Boston, 1991—2000, Israel Silberman PC, Wellesley, Mass., 2000—. Mem. editl. bd. Managed Care Law Strategist, Am. Lawyer Media newsletter, 1999-2001. Citizens rev. com. United Way Mass. Bay, Boston, 1981-89; bd. dirs. All Newton (Mass.) Music Sch., 1994-96, v.p., 1995-96; bd. overseers Boston Baroque, 1998-2000, bd. dirs., chmn. bd. overseers, 2000-02, chmn. bd. dirs., 2003—. Mem. ABA (vice chmn. health law com. sect. bus. law 1992-95, chmn., 1995-99), Internat. Bar Assn., Boston Bar Assn., Nat. Health Lawyers Assn., Phi Beta Kappa. Office: Israel Silberman PC Ste 150 20 William St Wellesley MA 02481 Office Phone: 781-235-1500. Business E-Mail: rsilberman@israelsilberman.com.

SILBERSACK, MARK LOUIS, lawyer; b. Cin., Dec. 27, 1946; s. Joseph Leo and Rhoda Marie (Hinkler) S.; m. Ruth Ann Schwallie, Sept. 7, 1985. AB, Boston Coll., 1968; JD, U. Chgo., 1971. Bar: Ohio 1971, U.S. Dist. Ct. (so. dist.) Ohio 1973, U.S. Ct. Appeals (6th cir.) 1974, U.S. Supreme Ct. 1975. Atty. Dinsmore & Shohl, Cin., 1971—. Lectr. Ohio CLE Inst., Columbus, 1981-91. Co-author: Managed Care: The PPO Experience, 1990, Information Sharing Among Health Care Providers, 1994. Bd. dirs. United Way, Cmty. Chest, 1985-89, 2001—, chmn. pub. policy com., 1998—; vice-chmn. Ohio United Way, Columbus, 1989-94, chmn. bd. dir., 1994-96; pres. Hyde Park Neighborhood Coun., Cin., 1989-91, Hyde Park Ctr. for Older Adults, 1989-91; active Cin. Bd. Health, 1991-97, chmn., 1995-97; bd. dirs. Cath. Social Svc. of S.W. Ohio, 1998-2003; bd. dirs., Children, Inc., 2003-. Mem. ABA, Ohio State Bar Assn. (bd. govs., antitrust sect.), Cin. Bar Assn., Fed. Bar Assn., Hyde Park Golf And County Club. Republican. Roman Catholic. Avocations: reading, travel, theater. Home: 3465 Forestoak Ct Cincinnati OH 45208-1842 Office: Dinsmore & Shohl 1900 Chemed Ctr 255 E 5th St Cincinnati OH 45202-4700 Office Phone: 513-977-8243. Business E-Mail: mark.silbersack@dinslaw.com.

SILBERSTEIN, ALAN MARK, financial services executive; b. Munich, Dec. 22, 1947; came to U.S., 1949; s. Leon and Rose S.; m. Carol Krongold, Aug. 30, 1970; children: Eric, Adam, Meredith. BS in Engring., Columbia U., 1969; MBA, Harvard U., 1972. Design engr. Ford Motor Co., Dearborn, Mich., 1969-70; budget analyst N.Y.C. Bur. of Budget, 1972-74; various positions Chem. Bank, N.Y.C., 1974-88, exec. v.p., head Consumer Banking Group, 1990-92; exec. v.p. and dir. of retail banking Midlantic Corp., Edison, N.J., 1992-95; CEO claims divsn. Travelers Property Casualty Corp., Hartford, Conn., 1995-96, exec. v.p., 1997-98; pres. Silco Assocs., 1998—; pres., CEO Western Union Fin. Svcs., Inc., 2000—01. Bd. dirs. global Payments Inc., Capital Access Network, Debt Resolve, Inc. Trustee Tenafly Bd. Edn., N.J., 1983-86, Yeshiva U. Sy Syms Sch. Bus., 1989—; mem. consumer adv. coun. Fed. Res. Bd., 1989-91; bd. dirs. N.Y. State Tree Consortium Inc., 1990-92; mem. exec. No. N.J. Boy Scouts Am., 1992-2003; adv. coun. Columbia U. Sch. Engring., 1998-2004. Mem. Am. Bankers Assn. (chmn. retail banking exec. com. 1992—), Harvard Bus. Sch. Club N.Y. (sec. 1981-85, bd. dirs. 1982-83, 85-88), Coun. Fgn. Rels., Bus. Execs. for Nat. Security.

SILBERSTEIN, EDWARD BERNARD, nuclear medicine educator, oncologist, researcher; b. Cin., Sept. 3, 1936; s. Bernard Gumpert and Harriet Louise (Kahn) S.; m. Jacqueline Rose Mervis, Oct. 2, 1988; children: Scott, Lisa. BS magna cum laude, Yale U., 1958; MD, Harvard U., 1962. Intern Cin. Gen. Hosp., 1962—63, resident in internal medicine, 1963—64; resident Univ. Hosps. Cleve., 1966—67; NIH fellow in hematology New Eng. Med. Ctr., Boston, 1967—68; asst. prof. radiol. medicine U. Cin. Med. Ctr., 1968—72, assoc. prof. radiol. medicine, 1972—76, prof. radiol. medicine, 1976—, Eugene L. and Sue R. Saenger prof. radiol. scis., 1998—2000, prof. emeritus of radiology and medicine, 2000—. Assoc. dir. E.L. Saenger Radioisotope Lab., 1980—; chmn. Environ. Safety Health Com. Dept. Energy Fernald Facility, 1986-91; mem. U.S. Pharmacopeia Com. of Revision, 1990—; mem. Nat. Coun. on Radiation Protection and Measurement, 1997—; cons. Nuclear Regulatory Commn., 1988—; dir. divsn. nuclear medicine Jewish Hosp., 1976-95; cancer pain panel Agy. for Health Care Planning and Rsch., 1992-93. Author: Differential Diagnosis in Nuclear Medicine, 1984, Bone Scintigraphy, 1984, Diagnostic Patterns in Nuclear Medicine, 1998; contbr. articles to profl. jours. Active Race Rels. Commn. Greater Cin., 1995—2000; trustee Cin. Opera Assn., 1993—, v.p., 2003—; active Jewish Cmty. Rels. Coun., 1992—; trustee Isaac M. Wise Temple, 1992—2000, treas., 1997—2000; bd. dirs. Talbert House, 1969—, Air Pollution Control League, Cin., 1980—95. Capt. U.S. Army, 1964—66. Mem.: Am. Bd. Nuclear Medicine (chmn. 1999), Soc. Nuc. Medicine (sec. 1989—92, 1989—92, bd. dirs. 1989—99, pres. S.E. chpt. 1990—91, chair sci. program 1992—94, spkr. Ho. of Dels. 2002—04). Jewish. Avocations: tennis, history of art, archaeology, travel. Office: U Cin Med Ctr Mont Reid Pavilion G026 234 Goodman St Cincinnati OH 45219-2364 Office Phone: 513-584-9032. E-mail: silbereb@healthall.com.

SILBEY, ROBERT JAMES, chemistry educator, researcher, consultant; b. NYC, Oct. 19, 1940; s. Sidney Richard and Estelle (Mintzer) S.; m. Susan Sorkin, June 24, 1962; children: Jessica, Anna. BS, CUNY Bklyn. Coll., 1961; PhD, U. Chgo., 1965. From asst. prof. to assoc. prof. MIT, Cambridge, 1966-76, prof., 1976—, chmn. dept. chemistry, 1990-95, dir. ctr. for materials sci. and engring., 1998-2000, dean of sci., 2000—. Vis. prof. U. Utrecht, The Netherlands, 1972-73, 97, U. Grenoble, France, 1983; cons. Exxon Rsch., Clinton, N.J., 1984-98. Author: Physical Chemistry, 1991, 4th edit., 2004; editor: Conjugated Polymers, 1991; contbr. articles to profl. jours. Recipient Alexander von Humboldt Found. Sr. Scientist award, 1989, Max Planck award, 1992; Alfred P. Sloan fellow, 1968, John S. Guggenheim fellow, 1972; Dreyfus Found. Tchr.-Scholar grantee, 1969. Fellow AAAS, Am. Acad. Arts and Sci., Am. Phys. Soc.; mem. NAS. Avocations: swimming, sailing. Office: MIT Dept Chemistry 77 Mass Ave Cambridge MA 02139-4307 Office Phone: 617-253-8900. Business E-Mail: silbey@mit.edu.

SILBIGER, MARTIN L. radiologist, educator, dean; b. Ravenna, Ohio, Mar. 17, 1938; s. Alfred James and Evelyn Norma (Cheswick) Silbiger; m. Ruth Hope Steele, June 4, 1957; children: Martin, Eve, Jonathan, Holly, Wendy. BA, U. Pa., 1958; MD, Western Reserve U., 1962; MBA, U. South Fla., 1989. Diplomate Am. Bd. Radiology, Am. Bd. Nuc. Medicine. Intern Univ. Hosps. Cleve., 1962—63; resident Johns Hopkins Hosp., 1963—66; with NIH, 1966—68; radiologist Tampa (Fla.) Gen. Hosp., 1968—; prof. U. South Fla., Tampa, 1982—; chief of staff Tampa Gen. Hosp., 1978—80; chmn. dept. radiology U. South Fla. Coll. Medicine, 1982—95; dean coll. medicine U. South Fla., 1995—2000, v.p. health scis., 1995—2000. Founder Hillsborough County Med. Assn. Found., Tampa, 1992; treas. Cmty. Found. Tampa, 1993—95; bd. dirs. Moffitt Cancer Ctr., Tampa, 1985—2000, Moffitt Cancer Ctr. Found., 1994—2000. Avocations: reading, rollerblading, golf, tennis. Home: 1827 Bayshore Blvd Tampa FL 33606-3210 Office: 3301 Alumni Dr Tampa FL 33612-9413 also: 1209 Bruce B Downs Blvd PO Box 66 Tampa FL 33601-0066

SILCOX, FRANCES ELEANOR, museum and exhibits planning consultant; b. Orange, Calif., Sept. 26, 1956; d. William Henry and M. Eleanor (Saulpaugh) S.; m. David William Smith, June 21, 1986; children: Lena Celeste, Reid Whitney. BA in English, U. San Francisco, 1979; MA in Mus. Studies, George Washington U., 1984. Intern divsn. performing arts Smithsonian Instn., Washington, 1978; adminstrv. asst. exhibits dept. Calif. Acad. Scis., San Francisco, 1979-81; gallery coord. The George Washington U., Washington, 1981-83; intern art dept. aide Smithsonian Instn., Washington, 1983-84; asst. dir. Torpedo Factory Arts Ctr., Alexandria, Va., 1983-84; accreditation coord. Am. Assn. Mus., Washington, 1984-86; interpretive planner Design and Prodn. Inc., Lorton, Va., 1986-88; mus. planner West Office Exhbn. Design, San Francisco, 1988-91; ind. mus. and exhibits planner, owner Dallas, 1991—99; prin., owner ExhibiTree, Moraga, Calif., 2000—. Bd. mem. St. Gerard Circle, St. Rita Cath. Cmty., Dallas, 1995-98; contbr. numerous natural and cultural resources orgns. Scholar Nat. Endowment for the Arts-Am. Law Inst.-ABA, Washington, 1982. Mem. Am. Assn. for State and Local History, Am. Assn. Mus., Archaeol. Inst. Am., Internat. Coun. Mus., Nat. Assn. for Mus. Exhbn., Western Mus. Assn., Cultural Connections, Calif. Assn. Mus., World Monuments Fund. Democrat. Avocations: travel, correspondence, photography, reading, walking. Home and Office: 463 Fernwood Dr Moraga CA 94556-2119

SILCOX, GORDON BRUCE, executive coach; b. Takoma Park, Md., May 11, 1938; s. Walter Bruce and Ruth May (Davis) S.; m. Judith Andrea Smith, Mar. 7, 1970 (div. Apr. 1998); children: Andrea Davis, Jessica Lyn. AB, Princeton U., 1960; MBA, U. Pa., 1965. Trust investment officer Am. Security Bank, Washington, 1967—69; v.p., trust investment officer, head trust investment divsn. First Am. Bank, N.A., 1969—77; v.p., prin. Paul Stafford Assocs., Ltd., Washington, 1977-83; v.p., mgr. MSL Internat. Ltd., Washington, 1983-86; v.p. Manchester, Inc., Washington, 1987-91, sr. v.p., 1991—2003; prin. Words on Purpose, LLC, Washington, 2003—. Pres. Wash. Human Resource Forum, 1993-95. Treas. Princeton U. Class of 1960, v.p., 1980-85. Lt. (j.g.) USN, 1962-63. Mem. Univ. Club, Princeton Club (treas. Washington 1972-74, N.Y.C.). Methodist. Home and Office: 3159 Colchester Brook Ln Fairfax VA 22031-2609 Office Phone: 703-280-1041.

SILEN, WILLIAM, physician, surgery educator; b. San Francisco, Sept. 13, 1927; s. Dave and Rose (Miller) S.; m. Ruth Heppner, July 13, 1947; children: Stephen, Deborah, Mark. BA, U. Calif., Berkeley, 1946; MD, U. Calif., San Francisco, 1949; MA (hon.) (hon.), Harvard U., 1966. Diplomate Am. Bd. Surgery. Intern U. Calif., San Francisco, 1949—50, asst. resident gen. surgery, 1950—56, chief resident gen. surgery, 1956—57; asst. chief surgery Denver VA Hosp., 1957—59, chief surgery, 1959—60; asst. chief surgery San Francisco Gen. Hosp., 1960—61, chief surgery, 1961—66; surgeon-in-chief Beth Israel Hosp., Boston, 1966—94; instr. surgery, asst. prof. surgery U. Colo. Med. Sch., Denver, 1957—60; asst. prof. then assoc. prof. surgery U. Calif. Sch. Medicine, San Francisco, 1960—66; prof. surgery Harvard Med. Sch., Boston, 1966—, Johnson and Johnson prof. surgery, 1966—94, Johnson & Johnson disting. prof. surgery, 1994—, faculty dean faculty devel. & diversity, 1995—2000; adj. prof. biology Brandeis Univ. Dir. Harvard Digestive Diseases Ctr. NIH, Bethesda, Md., 1984—94; adj. prof. biology Brandeis U., 2000—. Author: Cope's Early Diagnosis of the Acute Abdomen, 1995, Conservative Management of Breast Cancer, 1983, Atlas of Techniques in Breast Surgery, 1995. With USAF, 1950—52. Mem.: ACS, AMA, H.C. Naffziger Surg. Soc., Soc. Univ. Surgeons, Phi Beta Kappa. Avocation: bonsai cultivation. Office: Harvard Med Sch Faculty Dev & Diversity 25 Shattuck St # A-151 Boston MA 02115-6027

SILER, EUGENE EDWARD, JR., federal judge; b. Williamsburg, Ky., Oct. 19, 1936; s. Eugene Edward and Lowell (Jones) Siler; m. Christy Dyanne Minnich, Oct. 18, 1969; children: Eugene Edward, Adam Troy. BA cum laude, Vanderbilt U., 1958; LLB, U. Va., 1963; LLM, Georgetown U., 1964; LLM, U. Va., 1995. Bar: Ky. 1963, Va. 1963, D.C. 1963. Pvt. practice, Williamsburg, 1964—65; county atty. Whitley County, Ky., 1965—70; atty. U.S. Atty., Ea. Dist., Lexington, 1970—75; judge U.S. Dist. Ct., Ea. and We. Dists., Ky., 1975—91; chief judge U.S. Dist. Ct., Ea. Dist., Ky., 1984—91; judge U.S. Ct. Appeals (6th cir.), 1991—. Trustee Cumberland Coll., Williamsburg, 1965—73, 1980—88; campaign co-chmn. Congressman Tim L. Carter, 1966, 5th Congl. Dist., U.S. Senator J.S. Cooper, 1966; 1st v.p. Ky. Bapt. Convention, 1986—87; bd. dirs. Bapt. Healthcare System Inc., 1990—. With USN, 1958—60, with USNR, 1960—83. Recipient Freedom's Found. medal, 1968; E. Barrett Prettyman fellow, 1963—64. Mem.: Va. State Bar, D.C. Bar Assn., Ky. Bar Assn. (Judge of Yr. 1992), Fed. Bar Assn. Republican. Baptist. Home: PO Box 129 Williamsburg KY 40769-0129 Office: US Ct Appeals 310 S Main Street Room 333 London KY 40741

SILER, SUSAN REEDER, communications educator; b. Knoxville, Tenn., May 31, 1940; d. Claude S. Jr. and Mary Frances (Cook) Reeder; m. Theodore Paul Siler Jr., Sept. 3, 1960; children: Mary Siler Walker, Theodore Paul III. BS in Communications and Journalism, U. Tenn., Knoxville, 1988, MS in Mass Comms., 1994, postgrad. 2d grade tchr. Lawton (Okla.) Pub. Schs., 1961-62, substitute tchr., 1963-64; with By Design, 1987-88; English tutor, 1991-95; adj. instr. comm. U. Tenn., 1994—, U. Tenn., Pellissippi State Tech. C.C., Knoxville, Tenn. Bd. dirs. Hlen Ross McNabb Mental Health Ctr., Knoxville. Tutor Episc. Ch. Ascension, Knoxville, 1990—; instr. United Meth. Ch., Knoxville, 1985-92; chmn. Dogwood Arts Festival, Knoxville, 1980-85; chmn. bd. Govs . of East Tenn. Presentation Soc., 1988-96, Dogwood Trails; chmn., sec. bd. dirs. YWCA, Knoxville, 1982-88, editor newsletter, membership chmn., placement adv., sec.; Knoxville Jr. League, 1979-95; bd. dirs. Knoxville Women's Ctr., 1993-94; spl. events chmn. St. Mary's Med. Ctr. Found., 1986-89; Pres. Knoxville area Literacy Assn., 1989-92, tutor Episcopal Ch. Literacy program, Knoxville, 1990-95. Mem. Internat. Mass Comm. Assn., Soc. Profl. Journalists, Am. Journalism Historians Assn., Assn. for Edn. in Journalism and Mass Comms., Kappa Tau Alpha, Golden Key. Home: 717 Kenesaw Ave Knoxville TN 37919-6662

SILETS, HARVEY MARVIN, lawyer; b. Chgo., Aug. 25, 1931; s. Joseph Lazarus and Sylvia Silets; m. Elaine L. Gordon, June 25, 1961; children: Hayden Leigh, Jonathan Lazarus (dec.), Alexandra Rose. BS cum laude, DePaul U., 1952; JD (Frederick Leicke scholar), U. Mich., 1955. Bar: Ill. 1955, U.S. Dist. Ct. (no. dist.) Ill. 1955, N.Y. 1956, U.S. Tax Ct. 1957, U.S. Ct. Mil. Appeals 1957, U.S. Ct. Appeals (7th cir.) 1958, U.S. Supreme Ct. 1959, U.S. Ct. Appeals (6th cir.) 1965, U.S. Ct. Appeals (2d cir.) 1971, U.S. Ct. Appeals (5th cir.) 1972, U.S. Ct. Appeals (11th cir.). Assoc. Paul, Weiss, Rifkind, Wharton & Garrison, N.Y.C., 1955-56; asst. atty. U.S. Dist. Ct. (no. dist.) Ill., 1958-60; chief tax atty. U.S. atty. No. Dist. Ill., Chgo., 1960-62; ptnr. Harris, Burman & Silets, Chgo., 1962-79, Silets & Martin, Ltd., Chgo., 1979-92, Katten Muchin Zavis Rosenman, Chgo., 1992—. Asst. advance tng. program IRS, U. Mich., 1952-53; law lectr. advance fed. taxation John Marshall Law Sch., 1962-66; adj. prof. taxation Chgo.-Kent Coll. Law, 1985—; gen. counsel Nat. Treasury Employees Union, 1968-92; mem. adv. com. tax litigation U.S. Dept. Justice, 1979-82; mem. Tax Reform Com., State of Ill., 1982-83; mem. Speedy Trial Act Planning Group U.S. Dist. Ct. (no. dist.) Ill., 1976-79; mem. civil justice reform act adv. com. U.S. Dist. Ct. (no. dist.) Ill., 1991-94; lectr. in field. Contbr. articles to profl. jours. Trustee Latin Sch., Chgo., 1970-76; active Chgo. Crime Commn., 1975-93, Gov.'s Commn. Reform Tax Laws, Ill., 1982-83. With AUS, 1956-58. Fellow Am. Coll. Trial Lawyers (chmn. com. on fed. rules of criminal procedure 1982-91, fed. rules of evidence com. 1988-93, jud. com., fed. criminal procedures com., Upstate Ill. com. chmn. 1990-91), Am. Coll. Tax Counsel, Internat. Acad. Trial Lawyers, Soc. Advanced Legal Studies (London, lectr. internat. symposium on econ. crime, Cambridge U. 1999-03); mem. ABA (active various coms.), Bar Assn. 7th Fed. Cir. (chmn. com. criminal law and procedure 1972-82, bd. govs. 1983-86, sec. 1986-88, v.p. 1989-90, pres. 1990-91), NACDL, FBA (bd. dirs. 1971—, pres. 1977-78, v.p. 1976-77, sec. 1975-76, treas. 1974-75, active various coms.), Chgo. Bar Assn. (tax com. 1958-66, com. devel. law 1966-72, 78-88, com. fed. taxation 1968—, com. evaluation candidates 1978-80, exec. com. tax sect. 1994—), Am. Bd. Criminal Def. Lawyers, Decalogue Soc. Lawyers, Bar Assn. N.Y. City, Standard Club, Chgo. Club, Phi Alpha delta, Pi Gamma Mu. Office: Katten Muchin Zavis Rosenman 525 W Monroe St Ste 1600 Chicago IL 60661-3693 Office Phone: 312-902-5511. E-mail: harvey.silets@kmzr.com.

SILICH, GREG, advertising executive; CFO Bcom3 Group, Chgo. Office: Bcom3 Group 35 W Wacker Dr Chicago IL 60601

SILICIANO, ROBERT F. immunologist, medical educator; b. Rochester, NY, 1952; BA in Chem., Princeton U., 1974; MD, Johns Hopkins U., 1978, PhD in Immunology, 1983. Fellow Johns Hopkins U., Dana-Farber Cancer Inst., Harvard U., 1983—86, pathology instr., 1986—88; asst. prof. Johns Hopkins U. Sch. Med., 1988—92, assoc. prof., 1992—98, prof. med. & molecular biology and genetics, 1998—. Investigator Howard Hughes Med.

Inst., Chevy Chase, Md., 2002—. Recipient Disting. Clin. Sci. award, Doris Duke Charitable Found., 2001. Office: Johns Hopkins U Sch Med 725 N Wolfe St 1049 Ross Baltimore MD 21205

SILIPIGNI, ALFREDO, opera conductor; b. Atlantic City, Apr. 9, 1931; s. Alfredo and Elisabeth (Calhoun) S.; m. Gloria Rose DiBenedetto, Apr. 11, 1953; children: Marisa, Elisabetta Luisa, Afredo Roberto. Student, Westminster Choir Coll., 1948, Juilliard Sch. Music, 1953; HHD (hon.), Kean Coll. N.J., 1978. Prin. condr., gen. dir., artistic dir. N.J. State Opera, Newark, 1965—, founder Young Artist Program, 1969—. Guest lectr. Glassboro (N.J.) State Coll. Carnegie Hall debut with Symphony of the Air, 1956; condr. NBC Symphony, Boston, Bklyn. and Conn. operas, Newark Symphony, Mascagni's Guglielmo Ratcliff, N.Y., 2003; guest condr. Vienna State Opera, 1976, Grand Liceo di Barcelona, Spain, 1976, London, 1977, also numerous cos. Eng., Venezuela, France, Italy, Mex. and Can. with frequent appearances at L'Opera de Montreal; made recs. of Zaza by Leoncavallo, "Adriana Lecouvrer" by Cilea; prin. guest condr. and advisor Bellas Artes, Mex., 1993-94; guest condr. Opera Colo., 1997-98, largest prodn. Aida anywhere in world, Shanghai, 2000. Decorated cavliere Order of Merit (Italy); recipient Centennial medal St. Peter's Coll., 1972, Disting. Svc. to Culture award City of San Remo, Columbia Found. award, Boys Town of Italy award, Music award N.J. Edn. Assn., 1988. Office: NJ State Opera 50 Park Pl Ste 10 Newark NJ 07102 E-mail: newjerseystateop@aol.com.

SILJAK, DRAGOSLAV D. engineering educator, researcher; b. Belgrade, Serbia, Sept. 10, 1933; came to U.S. 1964, naturalized; s. Dobrilo T. and Ljubica Z. (Zivanovic) S.; m. Dragana T. Todorovic, Sept. 28, 1967; children— Ana, Matija. BSEE, U. Belgrade, 1958, MSEE, 1961, ScD, 1963. Docent prof. U. Belgrade, 1963-64; assoc. prof. U. Santa Clara, Calif., 1964-70, prof. engring., 1970-84, B. and M. Swig Univ. chair, 1984—. Author: Nonlinear Systems, 1969, Large Scale Systems, 1978, Decentralized Control of Complex Systems, 1991; mem. editl. bd. Jour. Difference Equations, Nonlinear World, Comm. in Applied Analysis, Internat. Jour. Computer Rsch., Nonlinear Analysis: Theory, Methods and Applications, Dynamics of Cont., Disc. and Impulsive Systems, Math. Problems in Engring., Stability and Control: Theory and Applications. Disting. prof. Fulbright Found., 1984. Life fellow IEEE; mem. Serbian Acad. Scis. and Arts (hon.) Mem. Christian Orthodox Ch. E-mail: dsiljak@scu.edu.

SILK, ALVIN JOHN, business educator, management consultant; b. Winnipeg, Manitoba, Can., Dec. 31, 1935; came to U.S., 1959, naturalized, 1975; s. John Edward and Bertha Lena (Kirton) S.; m. Diane D. Wilson (dec. 2003); children: Jonathan, Andrea, Stephanie. BA, U. Western Ont., 1959; MBA, Northwestern U., 1960, PhD, 1968. Asst. prof. mgmt. UCLA, 1963-66; asst. prof. U. Chgo., 1966-68; from assoc. prof. to prof. Sloan Sch. Mgmt., MIT, Cambridge, 1968-88; dep. dean MIT Sloan Sch. Mgmt., Cambridge, 1981-87; Lincoln Filene prof. Grad. Sch. Bus. Adminstrn. Harvard U., Boston, 1988—. Vis. rsch. fellow Mktg. Sci. Inst., Cambridge, Mass., 1970-71, trustee, 1984-96, Disting. rsch. assoc., 2001–; Ford Found. vis. prof. European Inst. for Advanced Studies in Mgmt., Brussels, 1975-76, Harvard Bus. Sch., 1987—; bd. dirs. Reed and Barton, Inc., Taunton, Mass., AdPilot, Inc. Co-editor: Behavioral and Management Science in Marketing, 1978; assoc. editor: Mgmt. Sci., 1969-77; co-editor: Quantitative Mktg. Absracts, Social Sci. Rsch. Network; mem. editl. bd. Jour. Mktg. Rsch., 1969-73, Jour. Mktg., 1978-81, Mktg. Sci., 1980-93; author, co-author numerous articles to profl. jours. Mem. Am. Mktg. Assn. (O'Dell award 1983), INFORMS (Achievement award 1982, 83), Beta Gamma Sigma, Zeta Psi. Home: 464 Starboard Ln Osterville MA 02655-1432 Office Phone: 617-495-6036. Business E-Mail: asilk@hbs.edu.

SILK, FREDERICK C.Z. financial consultant; b. Pretoria, Transvaal, South Africa, July 29, 1934; arrived in Canada, 1964; s. Frederick Charles and Edythe D'Olier S.; m. Margaret Colbourne, May 12, 1962; children: Michael, Alison, Jennifer. BS, Rhodes U., Grahamstown, Republic South Africa, 1954; cert. acctg. theory, U. Witwatersrand, Johannesburg, Republic South Africa, 1957. Acct., cons. Deloitte, Plender, Haskins & Sells, Johannesburg, London and N.Y.C., 1954-64; mgmt. cons. P.S. Ross & Ptnrs., Montreal, Que, Can., 1964-68; v.p. fin. and adminstrn. J&P Coats Ltd., Montreal, Que, Can., 1968-74; treas. Standard Brands, Ltd., Montreal, Que, Can., 1974-75; asst. treas. Standard Brands, Inc., N.Y.C., 1975-78; treas. Harlequin Enterprises, Ltd., Toronto, Ont., Can., 1978-82; v.p., treas. Nabisco Brands, Ltd., Toronto, 1982-95; pvt. treas. cons. Toronto, 1995—. Fellow Inst. Chartered Accts. (Eng., Wales), Inst. Chartered Accts. (South Africa), Fin. Execs. Inst. Avocations: music, choral music, Gilbert and Sullivan operettas. Office: 80 Front St E Ste 602 Toronto ON Canada M5E 1T4 E-mail: fczsilk@hotmail.com.

SILKENAT, JAMES ROBERT, lawyer; b. Salina, Kans., Aug. 2, 1947; s. Ernest E. and Mildred R. (Iman) S.; children: David Andrew, Katherine Anne. BA, Drury Coll., 1969; JD, U. Chgo., 1972; LLM, NYU, 1978. Bar: N.Y. 1973, D.C. 1980. Assoc. Cravath, Swaine & Moore, N.Y.C., 1972-80; counsel Internat. Fin. Corp., Washington, 1980-86; ptnr. Morgan, Lewis & Bockius, N.Y.C., 1986-89, Morrison & Foerster, N.Y.C., 1989-92, Pillsbury, Winthrop, N.Y.C., 1992—2002, Arent Fox, N.Y.C., 2002—. Chmn. Council N.Y. Law Assocs., 1978-79, Lawyers Com. Internat. Human Rights, 1978-80. Editor ABA Guide to Fng. Law Firms, Moscow Conf. on Law Bilateral Econ. Rels., ABA Guide to Internat. Bus. Negotiations; contbr. articles to profl. jours. Capt. U.S. Army, 1972-73. Fellow NEH, 1977, U.S. Dept. State, 1981. Fellow Am. Bar Found.; mem. ABA (chmn. internat. law and practice sect. 1989-90, chmn. sect. officer's conf. 1990-92, mem. ho. of dels. 1989—, bd. govs. 1994-97). Office: Arent Fox 1675 Broadway New York NY 10019 Office Phone: 212-492-3318. E-mail: silkenat.james@arentfox.com.

SILL, GERALD DE SCHRENCK, hotel executive; b. Czech Republic, Dec. 11, 1917; arrived in U.S., 1948, naturalized, 1953; s. Edward and Margaret (Baroness von Schrenck-Notzing) S.; m. Maria Countess Draskovich, May 11, 1946; children: Susan, Gabrielle. BS, Budapest Tech. U., 1944. With econs. divsn. U.S. Hdqs., Vienna, 1945-48; exec. hotel positions N.Y.C., 1948-52; managerial positions with Hilton Hotel Corp., 1953-61; exec. v.p. Houston Internat. Hotels, Inc., 1961-72, pres., CEO, 1972-74, chmn. bd., 1984-86, v.p., bd. dirs., 1986-88; chmn. emeritus, adv. dir. Preferred Hotels Worldwide, 1989; pres., CEO GdSS Mgmt. and Cons., Inc., Houston, 1989—. Mem. Am. Arbitration Assn. (panel arbitrators), River Oaks Country Club (Houston), The Waldorf Disting. Alumni, Houston Breakfast Assn. Home: 2227 Pelham Dr Houston TX 77019-3530

SILL, MELANIE, editor; m. Bennett Groshong. Grad. in journalism, U. N.C., 1981. Mng. editor, 1998; asst. metro editor, 1988; with The Transylvania Times, Brevard, NC, United Press Internat., Raleigh; project editor Boss Hog; exec. editor, sr. v.p. The News & Observer, Raleigh, NC, 2002—. Recipient Pulitzer prize, Boss Hog, 1996; fellow Nieman, Harvard U., 1993—94. Office: 215 S McDowell St Raleigh NC 27601

SILLARS, MALCOLM OSGOOD, communication educator; b. Union City, N.J., Feb. 12, 1928; s. Malcolm Osgood and Dorothy Edna (Browning) S.; m. Charlotte Jane Grimm, June 1, 1948; children— Paul Louis, Bruce Malcolm, Alan Leslie. BA, U. Redlands, 1948, MA, 1949; PhD, U. Iowa, 1955. Asst. prof. communication Iowa State U., Ames, 1949-53; asst. prof. Calif. State U., Los Angeles, 1954-56, prof., dean Northridge, 1970-71, pres., 1969-70; prof. U. Mass., Amherst, 1971-74; prof. communication U. Utah, Salt Lake City, 1974-97, dean humanities, 1974-81, ret., 1998. Author: Speech: Content and Communications, 6th edit., 1991, Argumentation and Critical Decision Making, 6th edit., 2004, Communication Criticism, 2d edit., 2001; contbr. articles to profl. jours. Recipient Silver Beaver award Boy Scouts Am. Mem. ACLU, Nat. Comm. Assn. (pres.), We. States Comm. Assn. (pres.). Democrat. Home: 3508 Eastoaks Dr Salt Lake City UT 84124-3811

SILLER, STEPHEN I. lawyer; b. May 8, 1949; m. Helen Seewald, June 6, 1971. BA, Bklyn. Coll., 1970, JD cum laude, 1973; LLM, NYU, 1978. Bar: N.Y. 1974, U.S. Dist. Ct. (so. and ea. dists.) N.Y. 1974, U.S. Ct. Appeals (2d cir.) 1974. Assoc. Fried, Frank, Harris, Shriver & Jacobson, N.Y.C., 1973-78, Feit & Ahrens, N.Y.C., 1978-80, ptnr., 1981-87; founder, sr. ptnr. Siller Wilk LLP, N.Y.C., 1987—. Mem. ABA (partnership law com., negotiated acquisitions com.), Internat. Bar Assn., Assn. Bar City of N.Y. (transp. com. 1978—, U.S. in global economy com. 1996-97). Office: Siller Wilk LLP 675 3rd Ave Fl 9 New York NY 10017-5704 Office Phone: 212-421-2233. Business E-Mail: ssiller@sillerwilk.com.

SILLERUD, ARLEN ROGER, retired educator; b. Nov. 28, 1934; BS, Moorhead State U., 1958; postgrad., Bemidji State U., 1969-70, U. Minn., 1988-90. Tchr. Ada School Dist., Ada, Minn., 1958-90. Chmn. Norman County Reps., Ada, Minn., 1996—, county, dist., and state del., 1994-2000,, 2002—, state ctrl. del., 1997-2001, alt., 2000—; elder Zion Luth. Ch., Ada, 1994—, Gideon spkr., 1971—. Achievements include advancement of idea that heart fibrillation should not be considered fatal, but that the heart can be restarted by electric shock; creator five solutions to clean up oil spills. Home: 807 3rd Ave E Ada MN 56510-1120

SILLIMAN, JOHN PARKS, JR., national guard officer, engineering consultant; b. Rochester, Minn., Mar. 15, 1943; s. John Parks and Sylvia (Davidson) S.; m. Janet Marie English, July 10, 1971; children: Jennifer Sage, John Prks III. BA in Psychology, Hamline U., 1965. Admissions counselor Hamline U., St. Paul, 1965-68, dir. fin. aid, 1970-74; officer USAF, 1968-70; commd. 2d lt. Minn. Air N.G., 1968, advanced through grades to brig. gen., 1998, ops. officer, pilot 133d Airlift Wing, 1974—95, wing comdr., 1995—98; comdr., chief staff Hdqs. Minn. Air N.G., St. Paul, 1998—2001. Mem. air directorate fiedl adv. coun. Nat. Air N.G., Washington, 1995-98; mem. adv. bd. Starbase, MN, Inc., St. Paul, 1995—; cons. on human engring. design Litton Guidance and Control Sys., Northridge, Calif., 1998-2000, Boeing, Wichita, Kans., 2001-. Ordained elder North Como Presbyn. Ch., Roseville, Minn., 1998—; mem. vulcan krewe 2001 St. Paul Winter Carnival, 2000—. Decorated Legion of Merit. Mem. N.G. Assn., Air Force Assn., St. Paul Club (bd. dirs. 1997—). Avocations: golf, alpine skiing, sailing, mountain biking. E-mail: jpsillman@comcast.net.

SILLMAN, ARNOLD JOEL, physiologist, educator; b. N.Y.C., Oct. 10, 1940; s. Philip and Anne L. (Pearlman) S.; m. Jean Fletcher Van Keuren, Sept. 26, 1969; children: Andrea Jose, Diana Van Keuren. AB, UCLA, 1963, MA, 1965, PhD, 1968. Asst. prof. UCLA, 1969-73, U. Calif., Davis, 1975-78, assoc. prof., 1978-85, prof., 1985—; asst. prof. U. Pitts., 1973-75, interim dir. aquaculture and fisheries program, 1994—95, vice chair sect. neurobiology, physiology and behavior, 1998—, acting chair, 2001. Contbr. articles to profl. jours. USPHS trainee, UCLA, 1966-67; fellow NSF, 1967-68, Fight for Sight, Inc., 1968-69. Recipient Acad. Senate Disting. Tchg. award, 1996. Mem. Am. Physiol. Soc., Soc. Gen. Physiologists, Am. Soc. Zoologists, Assn. Rsch. in Vision and Ophthalmology, AAAS, N.Y. Acad. Sci. Jewish. Home: 1140 Los Robles St Davis CA 95616-4927 Office: U Calif Sect Neurobiology Physiology & Behavior Divsn Biol Scis Davis CA 95616 Office Phone: 530-752-3207. E-mail: ajsillman@ucdavis.edu.

SILLMANM, AMY, painter, art educator; b. Oct. 1955; Student, Beloit Coll., NYU; BFA, Sch. Visual Arts, Manhattan; MFA, Bard Coll. Milton Avery prof. arts, faculty Milton Avery Grad. Sch. Arts, Bard Coll., 1996—. One-man shows include Brent Sikkema Gallery, 2000, exhibitions include Casey Kaplan Gallery, Manhattan, N.Y., 1996, 1998, White Columns, 1996, Postmasters Gallery, N.Y.C., 1997, Sixth@Prince Fine Art, 1999, Exit Art, 2000. Named invited exhibitor biennial exhbn., Whitney Mus. Am. Art, N.Y., 2004; recipient Tiffany Found. award, 1999—2000; Guggenheim fellow, 2001—02.*

SILLS, BEVERLY (MRS. PETER B. GREENOUGH), performing arts organization executive, coloratura soprano; b. Bklyn., May 25, 1929; d. Morris and Sonia (Bahn) Silverman; m. Peter B. Greenough, 1956; children: Meredith, Peter B.; stepchildren: Lindley, Nancy, Diana. Student voice, Estelle Leibling; student piano, Paolo Gallico; student stagecraft, Desire Defrere; hon. doctorates, Harvard U., NYU, New Eng. Conservatory, Temple U.; degree (hon.), Harvard U., N.Y.U., Calif. Inst. Arts. Gen. dir. N.Y.C. Opera, 1979-1989; pres. N.Y.C. Opera Bd., 1989-90; mng. dir. Met. Opera, N.Y.C., 1991-94; chairwoman Lincoln Ctr. for Performing Arts, Inc., N.Y.C., 1994—2002; vice chairwoman Lincoln Ctr. for Performing Arts, N.Y.C., 2002—; chairwoman Met. Opera, N.Y.C., 2002—. Bd. dirs. Met. Opera, 1991-; cons. Nat. Coun. on Arts. Radio debut as Bubbles Silverman on Uncle Bob's Rainbow House, 1932; appeared on Major Bowes Capitol Family Hour, 1934-41, on Our Gal Sunday; toured with Shubert Tours, Charles Wagner Opera Co., 1950, 51; operatic debut Phila. Civic Opera, 1947; debut, N.Y.C. Opera Co. as Rosalinda in Die Fledermaus, 1955; debut San Francisco Opera, 1953; debut La Scala, Milan as Pamira in Siege of Corinth, 1969, Royal Opera, Covent Garden in Lucia di Lammermoor, London, 1971, Met. Opera, N.Y.C., 1975, Vienna State Opera, 1967, Teatro Fenice in La Traviata, Venice; appeared Teatro Colon, Buenos Aires; recital debut Paris, 1971, London Symphony Orch., 1971; appeared throughout U.S., Europe, S. Am. including Boston Symphony, Tanglewood Festival, 1968, 69, Robin Hood Dell, Phila., 1969; title roles in: Don Pasquale, Norma, Ballad of Baby Doe, Thais, La Traviata, Anna Bolena, Maria Stuarda, Lucia de Lammermoor, Barber of Seville, Manon, Louise, Tales of Hoffmann, Daughter of the Regiment, The Magic Flute, Elizabeth in Roberto Devereaux, I Puritana, Julius Caesar, Suor Angelica, Il Tabarro, Gianni Schicchi, Faust, La Loca, Merry Widow, Turk in Italy, Rigoletto, I Capuleti e I Montecchi, Lucrezia Borgia, Ariodante, Le Coq D'Or, others; recordings include The Art of Beverly Sills, Welcome to Vienna, Great Scores (with Placido Domingo); ret. from opera and concert stage, 1980; numerous TV spls; author: Bubbles:A Self-Portrait, 1976, Bubbles: An Encore, Beverly: An Autobiography. Active with March of Dimes, 1971- (Past chmn. bd., past nat. chmn. Mothers' March on Birth Defects); bd. dirs. Apollo Theatre Found., 1999-2001. Recipient Handel medallion, 1973, Pearl S. Buck Women's award, 1979, Emmy award for Profiles in Music, 1976, Emmy award for Lifestyles with Beverly Sills, 1978, Presdl. Medal of Freedom, 1980, Kennedy Ctr. Honors award, 1980, Heinz award in Arts and Humanities, 1995, Grammy award for Best Classical Vocal Soloist Performance, 1976, Best Opera Recording, 1978, Bess Wallace Truman award, March of Dimes, 1994, Juanita Kreps award, JC Penny Co., 1996, MS Hope award, Nat. Multiple Sclerosis Soc., 1998, Medal of the Order of Arts and Letters, Min. French Culture, 2000. Office: Met Opera Lincoln Ctr Performing Arts 140 W 65th St New York NY 10023*

SILLS, RICHARD REYNOLDS, scientist, educator; b. N.Y.C., Sept. 19, 1946; s. Leonard Harold and Carol (Rudin) S. BA, Boston U., 1968. Tchr. N.Y.C. Pub. Schs., 1968-70, 79-81; v.p. Plutronics, Inc., N.Y.C., 1981-85; pvt. practice N.Y.C., 1985—. Author: (children's book) Jonny the Jester, 1977; contbr. articles to profl. jours.; patentee method and apparatus for encoding and decoding signals, method and apparatus for modifying synthesized sound signals, analog processing system. Mem. Rep. Nat. Com., Washington, 1981—, Rep. Presdl. Task Force, Washington, 1982—, Rep. Senatorial Inner Cir., 1987—, Rep. Senatorial Trust, 1999—; founding mem. Chmn.'s Club, Ronald Reagan Presl. Found., 1997—. Named Educator of Decade, Found. for Universal Brotherhood Inc., 1978; recipient Rep. Senatorial Medal of Freedom, 1999. Mem. AAAS, N.Y. Acad. Scis., Union of Concerned Scientists. Avocations: running, weightlifting.

SILLS, WILLIAM HENRY, III, investment banker; b. Chgo, Ill, Jan. 2, 1936; s. William Henry II and Mary Dorothy (Trude) Sills; children: William Henry IV, David Andrew Henry. AB, Dartmouth Coll., 1958; MA, Northwestern U., 1961. Stockbroker Bache & Co., Chgo., 1961—64; co-founder, investment banker Chgo. Corp., Chgo., 1964—84, First of Mich. Corp., Chgo., 1984—86, Sills & Co., Inc., Zenda, Wis., 1986—. With Chgo. Harvard and Geneva Lake R.R. Co., 1962—, Wis. River Rail Transit Commn., 1995—; vice chmn., bd. dirs. Honduras-Am. Securities Ltd.; dir. Honduran-Am. Real Estate Programs; chmn. bd. dirs., pres. Cen. Am. Fund, Ltd., INVI, S.A., Honduras, San Pedro Sula, Cortes, 1990—; cons. in field; chmn., pres. Ferro Carreal Nacional de Honduras Acquiring Cmrp., 1993—; pres. PRC, U.S., Cen. Am. Transp. Co., 1988—. Commodore Sea Scout flotilla Ctrl. Region Boy Scouts Am., 1987—99, nat. vice commodore Nat. Sea Scout Fleet, 1992—; chmn. Geneva Lake (Wis.) Area Joint Transp. Commn., 1965—86, 1990—92, sec., 1992—. With USMC, 1955—61. Mem. Am. Soc. Traffic and Transp., Am. Short Line R.R. Assn., US Yacht Racing Union (sr. judge), Inland Lake Yachting Assn. (sr. judge), Lake Geneva Yacht Club (commodore), Lake Geneva Country Club, Skeeter Ice Boat Club. Republican. Forward In Faith Episcopal. Address: PO Box 40 Zenda WI 53195-0040

SILSBY, GRAHAM FORBES, mechanical engineer, consultant; b. Richmond, Va., Apr. 7, 1943; s. Howard Wiswell Silsby II and Eleanor Foltz Silsby; m. Louise R. Cianelli, May 12, 1979; 1 child, Jeffrey A. Shumate. BSME, Carnegie Tech., 1965; BSCE, Johns Hopkins U., 1977. EIT Pa., 1965. Mech. engr. Farrington, Inc., Springfield, Va., 1965—66, U.S. Army Nuc. Def. Lab., Edgewood Arsenal, Md., 1967—71, U.S. Army Rsch. Lab., Aberdeen Proving Ground, Md., 1972—. Lectr. Baldini Resource Assoc., Newton, NJ, 1987—2004. Various offices Webster United Ch. of Christ, Havre de Grace, Md., 1970—2004. With U.S. Army, 1966—68. Recipient Am. Spirit Honor Medal, Citizens Com. for the Army, Navy, and Air Force, Inc., 1967. Mem.: ASM, ASME, Lions. Mem.United Church Of Christ. Avocation: home improvement.

SILSBY, PAULA, prosecutor; U.S. atty. U.S. Dept. Justice, Maine, 2001—. Office: PO Box 9718 Portland ME 04104

SILVA, ALANA G, writer, speech professional; d. Frank and Gloria Silva. BA, Sonoma State U., Rohnert Park, Calif., 1967—70. Cmty. colls. instr. State of Calif., 1988, Adult Sch. tchng. credential Calif. Commn. on Tchr. Credentialing, 1997. Esl tchr. East Bay French-Am. Sch., Berkeley, Calif., 1984—2001; adult sch. esl tchr. West Contra Costa Adult Edn., Richmond, Calif., 1997 2000; reporter Post Newspaper Group, Oakland, Calif., 1999—2001, Uinta County Herald, Evanston, Wyo., 2001—03, Bridger Valley Pioneer, Lyman, Wyo., 2003—04; freelance reporter Casper Star-Tribune, Casper, Wyo., 2004—; spkr. self-employed, Lyman, Wyo., 2003—. Bus. leadership netwok adv. bd. Evanston Bus. Leadership Network, 2002—03; program chair Calif. Writers Club, Corte Madera, 2000—01; pub. rels. officer Toastmasters Internat., Richmond, 2000—01; preferred guest Nat. Speakers Assn. Utah Chpt., Salt Lake City, 2003—. Journalist (Bridger Valley Pioneer) Feature stories on edn. (Wyo. Edn. Assn. Sch. Bell Award, 2004), (newspaper articles) Uinta County Herald (Evanston Bus. Leadership Network Outstanding Employee, 2002), speaker (conf. spkr.) Mega Conf., Partners in Policymaking, writer (magazine article) Careers and the Disabled. Mem. Greater Bridger Valley C. of C., Lyman, 2003—04. Recipient Fgn. Lang. award, Bank of Am., 1966, Honors at Entrance, U. of Calif. at Davis, 1966. Mem.: Soc. of Profl. Journalists. Home: PO Box 404 Mountain View WY 82939 Personal E-mail: alanasilva@bvea.net.

SILVA, EUGENE JOSEPH, lawyer; b. Gloucester, Mass., May 23, 1942; s. Edward Joseph and Rose (Lebre) S.; m. Nancy Blue-Pearson, Jan. 8, 1972; children: Eugene Joseph II, Michael Joseph. BS with honors, Maine Maritime Acad., 1964; JD, U. Notre Dame, 1972. Bar: Calif. 1972, U.S. Dist. Ct. (so. and cen. dists.) Calif. 1972, Tex. 1977, U.S. Dist. Ct. (so. and ea. dists.) Tex. 1978, U.S. Ct. Appeals (5th, 9th, 2d and 11th cirs.) 1978, U.S. Supreme Ct. 1981; lic. Master Mariner. Assoc. Luce, Forward, Hamilton & Scripps, San Diego, 1972-77, Vinson & Elkins, Houston, 1977-79, ptnr., 1980—2003. Mem. adv. bd. Admiralty Law Inst. Tulane U., 1999—. Bd. dirs. Cabrillo Festival Inc., San Diego, 1974—77, San Jose Clinic, Inc., 1990—97, pres., 1993—95; bd. dirs. Portuguese Heritage Scholarship Found., 1995—, St. Joseph Hosp. Found., 1995—2000. Decorated knight grand cross Equestrian Order of Holy Sepulchre of Jerusalem; named one of Best Lawyers in Am., 1991—; recipient Outstanding Alumni award, Maine Maritime Acad., 1990. Mem. Houston Bar Assn., Calif. Bar Assn., Tex. Bar Assn., Internat. Bar Assn., Grays Inn U. Notre Dame Sch. Law (pres. 1970-72), Maritime Law Assn. U.S. (proctor in admiralty 1974—), Portuguese Union Calif. (bd. dirs. 1973-74), Portuguese Am. League San Diego (pres. 1974-75), Portuguese Am. Leadership Coun. U.S., Asia-Pacific Lawyers Assn., Notre Dame Club (pres. San Diego chpt. 1976-77). Roman Catholic. Home: 8 Smithdale Estates Dr Houston TX 77024-6600 Office: Vinson & Elkins 2300 First City Tower 1001 Fannin St Ste 3300 Houston TX 77002-6706

SILVA, JOSEPH, JR., dean, medical educator; BA in biol. scis., Rutgers U., 1962; MD, Northwestern U., 1966. Diplomate Am. Bd. Internal Medicine, 1972. Intern Johns Hopkins Hosp., Balt., 1962—66, asst. resident in medicine, 1967—68, sr. resident in medicine, 1968—69; fellow in infectious diseases U. Mich. Med. Ctr., Ann Arbor, 1969—70; asst. prof. internal medicine divsn. infectious diseases U. Mich., prof., 1980—82; prof. and chair. of internal med. U. Calif. Davis, 1982—97; dean U. Calif. Davis Sch. Medicine, 1997—; CEO U. Calif. Davis Health Sys.1, 1997—. Served 2 yrs. in USAF. Fellow: Royal Soc. Medicine, London, Infectious Diseases Soc. Am., ACP (regent); mem.: Sociedad Medica de Santiago, Chile (assoc. mem.), Internat. Immunocompromised Host Soc., Sacramento/Sierra Med. Soc., Western Assn. Physicians, Western Assn. Clin. Investigation, Soc. Intestinal Microecology and Disease, Soc. Hosp. Epidemiologists of Am., Sacramento/El Dorado Med. Soc. (affiliate), Reticuloendothelial Soc., Mich. Soc. Med. Rsch., Mich. Soc. Infection Control, Ctrl. Soc. Clin. Rsch., Calif. Acad. Medicine, Am. Soc. Tropical Medicine and Hygiene, Am. Soc. Internal Medicine, Am. Fedn. Clin. Rsch., Calif. Med. Assn., AMA, AAAS, Alpha Omega Alpha. Office: U Calif Sch Medicine Office of Dean 2315 Stockton Blvd Rm 1501 Sacramento CA 95817*

SILVA, LAWRENCE KEHINDE, physical education educator; b. Lagos, Nigeria, June 27, 1948; s. Jacob Olawumi and Leah Adetunmibi Rotimi-Silva; m. Moji Silva, Mar. 8, 1980; children: James, Emmanuel, Daniel, Grace. BS, Benedict Coll., 1976; MAT, U. S.C., 1978; PhD, Ahmadu Bello U., Zaria, Nigeria, 1987. Asst. edn. officer Ministry of Edn., Govt. of Nigeria, Kaduna, 1971-78; lectr. Ahmadu Bello U., Zaria, 1979-90; assoc. prof. Bowie (Md.) State U., 1990—. Chmn. phys. edn. dept. Advanced Tchrs. Coll., Zaria, 1982-86; phys. edn. specialist Inst. of Edn., Zaria, 1986-90; faculty athletic rep. Bowie State U., 1997-98. Author: Community and Public Health, 1988; contbr. articles to sci. and profl. jours. Mem. AAUP, AAHPERD, Md. Assn. for Health, Phys. Edn., Recreation and Dance, Internat. Coun. for Health, Phys. Edn. (aging commn. 1992—). Democrat. So. Baptist. Avocations: music, athletics, christian activities. Home: 9104 6th St Lanham Seabrook MD 20706 Office: Bowie State U 14000 Jericho Park Rd Bowie MD 20715 E-mail: lsilva@bowiestate.edu.

SILVA, LUIS M. marketing professional; b. San Juan, PR, July 1, 1963; s. Armando Silva and Vivian Cabrera; m. Mayra Muniz, Sept. 1, 1995; children: Rafael J., Sebastian A., Andrea P. BS in Gen. Sci. (cum laude), Bethany Coll., Santa Cruz, 1983. Area sales specialist AstraZeneca, San Juan, PR, 1997—98, managed care liaison, 1997—98, oncolgy care specialist, 1998, regional tng. coord. Atlanta, 1999—2000, dist. sales mgr. Boston, 2000—02, mktg. mgr. Wilmingotn, Del., 2002—. Faculty Strategic Rsch. Inst., 2003. Office: AstraZeneca 1800 Concord Pike 2B2-112 Newark DE 19713 E-mail: luis.silva@astrazeneca.com.

SILVA, YVONNE N. registrar; b. N.Y.C. d. Bartolo and Maria I. Almiral; m. Stephen Phillips, June 15, 1974 (dec. Aug. 1988); children: Michael Phillips, Natalie Phillips; m. Sergio P. Silva, Dec. 13, 1990; 1 child, Claudia. AS in Computer Programming, Midwestern State U., Wichita Falls, Tex., 1985; BS in MIS, Barry U., Miami Shores, Fla., 1997; MPA, Nova Southeastern U., Ft. Lauderdale, Fla., 1999; postgrad., Nova Southwestern U. Cert. adult educator Fla., dive master. Fin. aid technician St. Thomas/ECPT, Hialeah, Fla., 1991—94; fin. aid counselor Barry U., Miami Shores, 1993—94; fin. aid dir. Tech. Career Inst., Miami, 1994—96; comptroller, fin. aid dir. Miami Ad Sch., Miami Beach, 1996—98; fin. aid dir. Am. InterContinental U., Plantation, Fla., 1998—2000; dir. student fin. planning Fla. Met. U., Ft. Lauderdale, 2000—01; registrar Miami Ad Sch., Miami Beach, 2001—02. Bd. dirs. adv. com. Fla. Inst. Careers, Plexis Inst., Miami. Sgt. USAF, 1973—77. Mem.: NAFE. Republican. Baptist. Avocations: scuba diving, deep sea fishing, reading. Home: 2103 Nova Village Dr Davie FL 33317

SILVAGNI, ANTHONY JOSEPH, dean, osteopath; b. Atlantic City, Apr. 18, 1940; s. Anthony Serafino and Madeline (Valentino) S.; m. Marlene Scherr, Mar. 12, 1961 (div. July 1977); children: Paul, Michelle; m. Dianna Poole, Oct. 1, 1977. BS in Pharmacy, Phila. Coll. of Pharmacy and Sci., 1963, MS in Hosp. Pharmacy, 1966, PharmD, 1970; postgrad., Purdue U., 1963-64; DO, Phila. Coll. Osteo. Medicine, 1982. Resident in hosp. pharmacy Thomas Jefferson U. Hosp., Phila., 1965-66, assoc. dir. pharmacy services, 1969-73; chief pharmacist prescription div. cen. pharm. services Appalachian Regional Hosp., Williamson, W.Va., 1966-67, asst. dir. cen. pharm. services, 1967-68; dir. pharmacy services Presbyn. U. Pa. Hosp., Phila., 1968-69; dir. pharmacy programs Lake Area Health Edn. Ctr., Erie, Pa., 1973-74; assoc. dir. clin. pharmacy services Peter Bent Brigham Hosp., Boston, 1974-76; clin. pharmacist U. Ariz., Tucson, 1976-78; faculty Health Care Edn. Programs Am., Chestnut Hill, Mass., 1980-82; intern Tucson Gen. Hosp., 1982-83; physician Dakota Family Practice, Parkston, S.D., 1983—; dean Nova Southeastern Univ. Coll. of Osteopathic Med., 1998—. Instr. in clin. pharmacy Phila. Coll. Pharmacy and Sci., 1969-73; asst. profl clin. pharmacy U. Ariz., 1977-78; chmn. dept. clin. practice Mass. Coll. Pharmacy, Boston, 1974-76; cons. clin. pharmacy Tucson Gen. Hosp., 1977-78, dir. clin. pharmacy services, 1977-78, vis. cons. staff dept. medicine, 1978; vis. faculty hypertension, Smith, Kline & French, Phila., 1980-82; lectr. to nat., state, county and local health profl. orgns. Contbr. articles to profl. jours. Mem. curriculum com. Mass. Coll. Pharmacy, 1974-76, chmn. PharmD admissions com., 1975-76; mem. bldg. com. U. Ariz. Coll. Pharmacy, 1976-78, grad. thesis com., 1977-78, faculty voting rights com., 1978, chmn. grade grievance com, 1978. Served with U.S. Army, 1961-62. Pa. State U. grantee, VA grantee, Lakes Area Regional Med. Program grantee, Smith, Kline and French grantee; Merck Sharp and Dohme scholar, 1979, Nat. Student Osteo. Med. Assn. scholar, 1980. Fellow Am. Found. for Pharm Edn.; mem. AMA, Am. Acad. Gen. Practitioners, Am. Osteo. Assn. (grantee), Am. Pharm. Assn. (review panel for handbook 1975—, practitioner panel 1973—), Am. Soc. Hosp. Pharmacists (adv. panel on student membership 1975-76), Am. Pharm. Assn. Acad. of Pharmacy Practice (charter), S.D. Med. Assn., Dist. 6 Med. Soc., Kappa Psi, Phi Sigma Gamma, Rho Chi. Avocations: flying, skiing, motorcycling, camping. Office: Nova Southeastern Univ Coll Med 3200 S Univ Drive, Rm 1401 Terry Bldg Fort Lauderdale FL 33328

SILVER, ADAM, sports association executive; BA, Duke U.; JD, U. Chgo. Legis. aide Congressman Les AuCoin, Washington; law clk. Judge Kimba Wood Fed. Dist. Ct., N.Y.C.; litig. assoc. Cravath, Swaine & Moore, N.Y.; spl. asst. to commr. NBA, 1992—96; pres. NBA Entertainment, Secacus, NJ, 1997—2000, 2000—, COO, 2000—. Prodr.: Michael Jordan to the Max, 2000. Office: NBA Entertainment 450 Harmon Meadow Blvd Secaucus NJ 07904

SILVER, ALAN IRVING, lawyer; b. St. Paul, Sept. 17, 1949; s. Sherman J. Silver and Muriel (Bernstein) Brawerman; m. Janice Lynn Gleekel, July 8, 1973; children: Stephen, Amy. BA cum laude, U. Minn., 1971, JD cum laude, 1975. Bar: Minn. 1975, U.S. Dist. Ct. Minn. 1975, U.S. Dist. Ct. (ea. dist.) Wis. 1975, U.S. Ct. Appeals 8th and 10th cirs.) 1975. Assoc. Doherty, Rumble & Butler, P.A., St. Paul, 1975-80, ptnr. Mpls., 1980-99, Bassford, Remele (formerly called Bassford, Lockhart, Truesdell & Briggs, P.A.), Mpls., 1999—. Mem. 2d Jud. Dist. Ethics Com., St. Paul, 1985-88, 4th Jud. Dist. Ethics Com., Mpls., 1990-97. Author: Building a New Foundation: Torts, Contracts and the Economic Class Doctrine, 2000, other numerous continuing edn. seminar material. Vol. atty. Legal Assistance Ramsey County, St. Paul, 1975-82; mem. St. Louis Park (Minn.) Sch. Bd., 1993-99, chair, 1995-97; mem. St. Louis Park Human Rights Commn., 1987-91; chmn. site mgmt. coun. Susan Lindgren Sch., St. Louis Park, 1986-93; bd. dirs. Jewish Cmty. Rels. Coun., Anti-Defamation League Minn. and Dakotas, 1987-93, 97—, treas., 1992-93, v.p., 2003-. Mem. ABA, Minn. Bar Assn. (exec. bd. antitrust sect. 1984, litigation chair probate and trust sect.), Hennepin County Bar Assn. Avocations: running, guitar, reading. Home: 4320 W 25th St Minneapolis MN 55416-3841 Office: Bassford Remcle Ste 3800 33 S 6th St Minneapolis MN 55402-1501 E-mail: alans@bassford.com.

SILVER, BARNARD JOSEPH STEWART, mechanical and chemical engineer, consultant, inventor; b. Salt Lake City, Mar. 9, 1933; s. Harold Farnes and Madelyn Cannon (Stewart) S.; m. Cherry Bushman, Aug. 12, 1963; children: Madelyn Stewart Palmer, Cannon Farnes. BSME, MIT, 1957; MS in Engring. Mechanics, Stanford U., 1958; grad. Advanced Mgmt. Program, Harvard Grad. Sch. Bus., 1977. Registered profl. engr. Colo. Engr. aircraft nuclear propulsion divsn. GE Co., Evandale, Ohio, 1957; engr. Silver Engring. Works, Denver, 1959-66, mgr. sales and tech. svcs., 1966-71, pres., 1998-99, chmn. bd., 1999—; chief engr. Union Sugar divsn. Consol. Foods Co., Santa Maria, Calif., 1971-74; directeur du complex SODESUCRE Abidjan, Cote d'Ivoire, 1974-76; supt. engring. and maintenance U and I Inc., Moses Lake, Wash., 1976-79; pres. Silver Enterprise Denver, Moses Lake, 1971—, Silver Energy Systems Corp., Moses Lake, 1980-98, chmn. bd., 1998—; pres., gen. mgr. Silver Chief Corp., 1983—; pres. Silver Corp., 1984—; chmn. bd. Silver Pubs., Inc., 1986-87, 90—; exec. v.p. Cascadian Inulin L.L.C., Sedro-Wooley, Wash., 1996—99; mgr. Silver Inulin LLC, Moses Lake, 1996-98; dir. processing rsch. Inuloa, Wyo., 1999—2001; bd. mgrs. Inula, Wyo., Lovell; v.p. Barnard J. Stewart Cousins Land Co., 1987—88, 1992—2003; chmn. Mid. East Peace Inst., 1998—; founder Life Energy Foods, L.L.C., Holladay, 2000—. Dir. Isle Piquant Sugar Found., 1993-94; mem. steering com. World Botanical Inst., 1993-99; instr. engring. Big Bend C.C., 1980-81. Patentee in field, including patent for novel inulin fractions extracting soluable substances from subdivided solids, 1995. Explorer adviser Boy Scouts Am., 1965-66, 89-90, chmn. cub pack com., 1968-74, 94-96, chmn. scout troop com., 1968-74, vice chmn. Columbia Basin Dist., 1986-87; pres. Silver Found., 1961-87, v.p., 1987-97, sec., treas. 1997—; ednl. consclor MIT, 1971-89; pres. Chief Moses Jr. H.S. Parent Tchr. Student Assn., 1978-79; missionary Ch. of Jesus Christ of Latter-day Saints, Can., 1953-55, Hawaii, P.R., Ctrl. and South Am., Asia, 1959-68, West Africa, 1988, Cote d'Ivoire, 1988-89, Zaire, 1989, Holladay North Stakes, 1991, 95,-97, Cheyenne, 1998-99, Salt Lake Inner-City Project Mission, 2000-2003; dist. pres. No. B.C., No. Alberta, Yukon and N.W. Ters., 1955; stake high counselor, Santa Maria, Calif., 1971-72, Moses Lake Wash., 1977-79; presiding elder Cote d'Ivoire, 1974-76, 88; 2d counsleor Moses Lake Stake Presidency, 1980-88; bd. dirs. Columbia Basin Allied Arts, 1986-88; mem. Health Sci. Coun. U. Utah, 1991—; mem. Sunday sch. gen. bd. Ch. of Jesus Christ of Latter-Day Saints, 1991-93, com. for mems. with Disabilities, 1992-93, CHOICE adv. bd., 1993-95; emergency preparedness dir. Holladay North Stake, 1993-95. Served with Ordnance Corps., U.S. Army, 1958-59. Decorated Chevalier Ordre National (Repbulic of Cote d'Ivoire). Mem. ASME (life), Assn. Energy Engrs., AAAS, Am. Soc. Sugar Beet Technolgists, Internat. Soc. Sugar Cane Technologists, Am. Soc. Sugar Cane Technologists, Environ. Engrs. & Mgrs. Inst., Sugar Industry Technicians, Nat. Fedn. Ind. Bus., Utah State Hist. Soc. (life), Mormon Hist. Assn., G.P. Chowder and Marching Soc., Western Hist. Assn., Sons of Utah Pioneers (life), Univ. Archeol. Soc. (life), Kiwanis, Cannon-Hickley Study Group, Sigma Xi (life, sec., treas., Utah chpt. 1994-99), Pi Tau Sigma, Sigma Chi, Alpha Phi Omega. Republican. Mem. Lds Ch. also: Life Energy Foods LLC 4390 South 2300 East Holladay UT 84125-3651 also: Silver Pubs Inc 4390 S 2300 E Holladay UT 84124-3501 Office Phone: 801-278-9445. E-mail: bsilver@xmission.com.

SILVER, BRIAN QUAYLE, broadcast journalist, musician, educator; b. Denver, Sept. 8, 1942; s. Harold Farnes and Madelyn Cannon (Stewart) S.; m. Shubha Sankaran, Dec. 4, 1988; adopted children: Laila Benazir Robinson, Zain Ganapathi Ramdas Sankaran. BA, Harvard Coll., 1964; postgrad., Sch. Oriental and African Studies U. London, 1969-70; PhD., U. Chgo., 1980. Asst. prof. Urdu U. Minn., 1971-74; assoc. prof. Urdu & Indo-Muslim studies Harvard U., 1974-83; lectr. music U. Va., Charlottesville, 1995; dir. internat. house, asst. dean study abroad Duke U., 1983-86; exec. dir. Internat. Music Assocs., Washington, 1982—; chief, Urdu svc. Voice of Am., Washington, 1986—. Dir. internat. exchange programs Pan Orient Arts Found., Manchester, N.H., 1968—, exec. dir., 1994—; bd. dirs. Archive Rsch. Ctr. Ethnomusicology, New Delhi, India, 1993-98; South Asia coun. Assn. Asian Studies, Ann Arbor, Mich., 1983-86. Sitar performance in India, Pakistan, Bangladesh, Morocco, Rumania, England, Guatemala, Peru, Canada and U.S., 1966—; contbr. numerous publs. on South Asian Music and Urdu Lit. Dir. Durham Chpt. UNICEF, 1984-86. Named Khansahib, All-Pakistan Music Conf., Lahore, 1988; recipient Gold medal, 1989; grantee in aid D.C. Commn. for Arts and Humanities/Nat. Endowment for Arts, 1991-92, 96-97; Fulbright grantee Inst. Internat. Edn., India, 1964-66; Ford fellow Am. Coun. Learned Socs., England, Pakistan, India, 1969-71, Am. Inst. Indian Studies, India, 1982-83. Mem. Soc. Ethnomusicology (New England chpt. v.p. 1978-80), Assn. Asian Music, Internat. Coun. Tradition Mus., Asia Soc., Assn. Asian Studies, Folklore Soc. Greater Washington. Democrat. Avocations: cooking, gardening, films, travel. Home: 1730 C St NE Washington DC 20002-6661 Office: Internat Music Assocs PO Box 15526 Washington DC 20003-0526 E-mail: PanOrient@aol.com.

SILVER, CHARLES MORTON, communications company executive; b. New Haven, Sept. 22, 1929; s. Sam and Rose (Fischman) S.; m. Rose Charek, Mar. 27, 1960; children— Ronni Ellen, Suzanne Paula, Steven Mitchell. BS, U Conn., 1954. With Arthur Andersen & Co., N.Y.C., 1954-61, ITT, N.Y.C., 1961-88, ret. as v.p. and assoc. treas., 1988. Served with U.S. Army, 1947-48, 50-51. Mem. Roxbury Swim and Tennis Club. Home: 51 Akbar Rd Stamford CT 06902-1401 also: PO Box 420275 Summerland Key FL 33042-0275

SILVER, DAVID, lawyer; b. N.Y.C., Jan. 27, 1931; s. Sol and Fannie (Stein) S.; m. Meryl Young, Sept. 14, 1952 (dec.); children: Daniel, Matthew, Joshua; m. Ann Schwartz, June 4, 1993. BA, CCNY, 1953; LL.B. cum laude, Harvard U., 1958. Bar: N.Y. 1958, D.C. 1979. Pvt. practice law, N.Y.C., 1960-61; spl. counsel SEC, Washington, 1961-65; gen. counsel Investors Planning Corp., N.Y.C., 1965-66; asst. counsel Investment Co. Inst., Washington, 1966-69, gen. counsel, 1969-77, pres., 1977-91, ICI Mut. Ins. Co., Bethesda, Md., 1987-2001. Cons. securities regulation Govt. of India, 1964; mutual fund regulation Govt. of China, 1999; lectr. Law Sch. Boston U., 1995—98; mem. individual investor adv. com. N.Y. Stock Exch., 1994—99; dir. PGAM, Milan, 2001—. Served with U.S. Army, 1953-55. Mem. Fed. Bar Assn. (exec. coun. securities com., past chmn. investment co. com.). Home and Office: 9410 Brooke Dr Bethesda MD 20817-2110 E-mail: anndave@verizon.net.

SILVER, DIANE S. dermatologist; b. Passaic, N.J., Sept. 1, 1943; AB in Math., Rutgers U., 1965; MAT, Harvard U., 1966, postgrad., 1966—67, Tufts U., 1967—68; MD, U. So. Calif., 1971. Diplomate Am. Bd. Dermatology. Intern St. Mary's Hosp., San Fracisco, 1971—72; resident in dermatology Stanford U. Med. Ctr., Palo Alto, Calif., 1976—79; physician, head VD clinic, head family planning clinic Napa County Health Dept., Napa, Calif., 1972—76, VD contr., 1972—76; pvt. practice Napa, 1979—. Lectr. Stanford U., Palo Alto, 1977, Palo Alto, 78, Palo Alto, 79, U. Pacific Podiatry Sch., San Francisco, 1978. Contbr. articles to profl. jours. Mem.: Am. Acad. Dermatology, Sacramento Dermatologic Assn., Pacific Dermatologic Assn., Calif. Med. Assn., Napa County Med. Soc., Pi Mu Epsilon, Phi Beta Kappa. Home: 87 El Nido Dr Napa CA 94559 Mailing: PO Box 2099 Napa CA 94558 Office: 1100 Trancas St Napa CA 94558 Office Phone: 707-257-2888. Office Fax: 707-257-7655.

SILVER, DONALD, surgeon, educator; b. N.Y.C., Oct. 19, 1929; s. Herman and Cecilia (Meyer) S.; m. Helen Elizabeth Harnden, Aug. 9, 1958; children: Elizabeth Tyler, Donald Meyer, Stephanie Davies, William Paige. AB, Duke U., 1950, BS in Medicine, MD, 1955. Diplomate Am. Bd. Surgery, Am. Bd. Gen. Vascular Surgery, Am. Bd. Thoracic Surgery. Intern Duke Med. Ctr., 1955-56, asst. resident, 1958-63, resident, 1963-64; mem. faculty Duke Med. Sch., 1964-75, prof. surgery, 1972-75; cons. Watts Hosp., Durham, 1965-75, VA Hosp., Durham, 1970-75, chief surgery, 1968-70; prof. surgery, chmn. dept. U. Mo. VA Med. Ctr., Columbia, 1975-98, chmn. univ. physicians, 2002—. Cons. Harry S. Truman Hosp., Columbia, 1975—; mem. bd. sci. advisers Cancer Research Center, Columbia, 1975—; mem. surg. study sect. A NIH; dir surg. svcs. U. Mo. Health System, 2001-2003. Contbr. articles to med. jours., chpts. to books; editorial bds.; Jour. Vascular Surgery, Postgrad. Gen. Surgery, Vascular Surgery. Served with USAF, 1956-58. James IV Surg. traveler, 1977 Fellow ACS (gov. 1995-99), Deryl Hart Soc.; mem. AMA, AAAS, Mo. Med. Assn., Boone County Med. Soc., Internat. Cardiovascular Soc., Soc. Univ. Surgeons, Am. Heart Assn. (Mo. affiliate rsch. com.), Soc. Surgery Alimenatry Tract, Assn. Acad. Surgery, So. Thoracic Surg. Assn., Internat. Soc. Surgery, Soc. Vascular Surgery, Am. Assn. Thoracic Surgery, Am. Surg. Assn., Ctrl. Surg. Assn. (pres.-elect 1990-91, pres. 1991-92), Western Surg. Assn., Midwestern Vascular Surg. Soc. (pres. 1984-85), Ctrl. Surg. Assn. Found. (treas. 1992-93, 2d v.p. 1993-94, 1st v.p. 1994-95, pres. 1995-96). Home: 1050 W Covered Bridge Rd Columbia MO 65203-9569 Office: U Mo Med Ctr Dept Surgery N514 Columbia MO 65212-0001 Office Phone: 573-882-1612. Business E-Mail: Silverd@health.missour.edu.

SILVER, GEORGE, metal trading and processing company executive; b. Warren, Ohio, Dec. 17, 1918; s. Jacob and Sophie (Bradlyn) S.; m. Irene Miller, Aug. 5, 1945. Student, U. Ala., 1938; BA, Ohio U., 1940; postgrad. law sch., Ohio State U., 1940—41; grad., Adj. Gen. Sch., 1944. Pres. Riverside Indsl. Materials, Bettendorf, Iowa, 1947-70, Metalpel subs. Continental Telephone Co., Bettendorf, Iowa, 1970-71, Riverside Industries Inc., Bettendorf, Iowa, 1971—. Pres. Scott Resources Inc., Davenport, Iowa; v.p. Durbin Midwest, Davenport, 1987—90; mktg. dir. NAMCO Internat., Miami; cons. Waste Mgmt.-Non Ferrous Mktg., 1990—, Snyer Steel Casting, Iowa, Riverside Products, Ill., 1992—93, Tamron Internat. Ltd., Shanghai, 2002; founder Iowa Steel Mills (named changed to North Star Steel), Cargill and Wilton; mktg. dir. NAMCO Environ. Svcs. Corp., Miami, Fla., 1995—; bd. dirs. NAMCO Trading Co., Miami; cons. metal trading Cricket Club, Miami. Contbr. articles to profl. jours. Mem. Nat. UN Day Com., 1975-83. Capt. AC, USAF, 1941-46, 50-51, Korea. Named to Hon. Order Ky. Cols., 1991. Mem. Nat. Assn. Recycling Industries (co-chmn. nat. planning com., bd. dirs.), N.Y. Acad. Scis., Copper Club, Paper Stock Inst. Am. (exec. com.), Bur. Internat. de la Recuperation (chmn. adv. com.), Inter Global Trading Group (chmn. bd. dirs.), Mining Club N.Y.C., Outing Club, Hatchet Men's Chowder and Protective Assn., Copper Club, Jockey Club Miami, Williams Island Club, Rock Island Arsenal Officer's Club, Chemist Club (N.Y.C.), Crow Valley Country Club, Elks, Phi Sigma Delta.

SILVER, GEORGE ALBERT, preventive medicine physician, educator; b. Phila., Dec. 23, 1913; s. Morris M. and Sara (Tutelman) Silver; m. Mitzi Blieden, June 5, 1937; children: James David, Jane, Judith Ellen. BA, U. Pa., Phila., 1934; MD, Jefferson Med. Coll., Phila., 1938; MPH, Johns Hopkins U., Balt., 1948; MA (hon.), Yale U., New Haven, 1969. Diplomate Am. Bd. Preventive Medicine. Asst. demonstrator Jefferson Med. Coll., Phila., 1939—42; health officer Balt. City Health Dept., 1948—51; asst. prof. Johns Hopkins U., Balt., 1948—51; chief divsn. social medicine Montefiore Hosp., N.Y.C., 1951—65; assoc. prof. health adminstrn. Columbia U., N.Y.C., 1952—59; prof. social medicine Albert Einstein Coll. Medicine, N.Y.C., 1959—65; dep. asst. sec. health and sci. affairs HEW, Washington, 1965—68; health exec. Nat. Urban Coalition, Washington, 1968—71; prof. pub. health Yale U., New Haven, 1969—84, prof. pub. health emeritus, 1984—. Chmn. com. on health policy Fedn. Am. Scientists, 2000. Author: Family Medical Care, 1963, Spy in the House of Medicine, 1974, Child Health: America's Future, 1978. Maj. M.C. U.S. Army, 1942—46. Named to Soc. of Scholars, Johns Hopkins U., 1993; recipient Superior Svc. award, HEW, 1966; fellow Branford Coll., Yale U. Fellow: APHA, N.Y. Acad. Medicine, Inst. Medicine NAS (sr.); mem.: Elizabethan Club, Sigma Xi. Democrat. Jewish. Home: 8100 Connecticut Ave Chevy Chase MD 20815-1636

SILVER, GREGORY K. lawyer; b. Indpls., Oct. 16, 1946; s. David Mayer and Anita (Cohen) S.; m. Florence Ruekberg, Aug. 7, 1971; children: Sara Jennifer, Scott Henry. BA in Govt., Miami U., Oxford, Ohio, 1968; JD, Ind. U., 1972. Bar: Ind. 1972, D.C. 1975. Assoc. Eskenazi, Yosha & Hurst, Indpls., 1968-74; pvt. practice Indpls., 1974—. Cons. U.S. State Dept. Task Force on Population, 1994. Chmn. Indpls. Greenways Bd., 1996-2004; dir. Indpls. Clean City Com., 1975—; candidate Ind. State Senate, 1986, Indpls. City Coun., 1991; active Nat. Dem. Platform Com., Washington, 1984-8, Underground Storage Tank Bd., Ind., 1996-2003; bd. dirs. Indpls. Hebrew Cong. Recipient Sagamore of Wabash award, 1998. Mem. Sertoma, Indpls. Athletic Club, Broadmoor Country Club Indpls. Avocations: travel, basketball, children. Home: 8442 Oakwood Ct Indianapolis IN 46260-2355 Office: 342 Massachusetts Ave Ste 400 Indianapolis IN 46204-2132

SILVER, HARRY R. lawyer; b. Phila., Aug. 8, 1946; s. Jerome Benjamin Silver and Josephine Sandler (Steinberg) Furr; m. Jessica Dunsay, Nov. 23, 1972; children: Gregory, Alexander. BA, Temple U., 1968; JD, Columbia U., 1971. Bar: N.Y. 1972, D.C. 1973, U.S. Dist. Ct. D.C., U.S. Ct. Claims, U.S. Ct. Appeals (1st, 4th, 5th, 7th, 8th, 9th, 10th, fed. and D.C. cirs.), U.S. Supreme Ct. Law clk. to Hon. Harold R. Medina, U.S. Ct. Appeals (2d cir.), N.Y.C., 1971-72; assoc. Arent, Fox, Kintner, Plotkin & Kahn, Washington, 1972-74; atty. U.S. Dept. Justice, Washington, 1974-77, U.S. Dept. Energy, Washington, 1977-78; assoc. Akin, Gump, Strauss, Hauer & Feld, Washington, 1978-81, ptnr., 1981-88, Oppenheimer, Wolff & Donelly, Washington, 1988-91, Davis Wright Tremaine, Washington, 1991-94, Ober, Kaler, Grimes & Shriver, Washington, 1994—2004, Patton Boggs, Washington, 2004—. Mem. ABA, Fed. Bar Assn. Avocations: running, music, travel. Home: 6829 Wilson Ln Bethesda MD 20817-4948 Office: Patton Boggs 2550 M St NW Washington DC 20037 Office Phone: 202-457-6453. E-mail: hsilver@pattonboggs.com.

SILVER, HEIDI JAYE, nutritionist, educator, researcher; d. Leonard and Barbara (Levine) Silver; 1 child, Leonard Ross. BS cum laude, U. Mass., 1977; MS in Nutrition, Fla. Internat. U., 1991, PhD in Clin. Nutrition, 2001. Cert. nutrition support dietitian Am. Soc. for Parenteral and Enteral Nutrition, 1993, registered dietitian Am. Dietetic Assn., 1991. Nutrition support dietitian U. Miami (Fla.)/Jackson Meml. Med. Ctr., 1991—97; grad. tchg. asst. dept. dietetics and nutrition Fla. Internat. U., Miami, 1997—99; grad. rsch. assoc. Nat. Policy and Resource Ctr. on Nutrition and Aging, Miami, 1999—2001, assoc. dir. rsch., 2001—03; asst. prof. medicine Vanderbilt U., Nashville, 2003—. Convenor issue panel on dietary reference intakes Adminstrn. on Aging, Washington, 2001—; master's thesis advisor Dept. Dietetics and Nutrition Fla. Internat. U., Miami, 2001—; presenter in field. Contbr. articles to profl. jours. Parent chaperone South Fla. Youth Symphony, Miami; fundraiser Temple Beth Emet, Pembroke Pines, Fla., 1995. Grantee, NIH Agy. for Healthcare Rsch. and Quality, 2000—01, Nestles Clin. Nutrition, 2001—02; Florence Bayuk Found. fellow, Fla. Internat. U., 2000—01, Kraft Foods fellow, 2000—01. Mem.: Gerontol. Soc. Am. (poster presenter 2001—01), Am. Soc. on Aging (workshop presenter 2001—01), Am. Soc. for Nutritional Scis. (pres. Aging Rsch. Interest sect. 2004—), Am. Dietetic Assn. (reviewer Jour. Am. Dietetic Assn.). Avocations: bicycling, swimming, walking, reading. Office: Vanderbilt Univ Ctr for Human Nutrition Ste 514 Med Arts Bldg Nashville TN 37232-2713 Personal E-mail: nutrirose16@aol.com. E-mail: heidi.j.silver@vanderbilt.edu.

SILVER, JOAN MICKLIN, film director, screenwriter; b. Omaha, May 24, 1935; d. Maurice David and Doris (Shoshone) Micklin; m. Raphael D. Silver, June 28, 1956; children: Dina, Marisa, Claudia. BA, Sarah Lawrence Coll., 1956. Writer, dir. (movies) Hester Street, 1975 (Writers Guild best screenplay nomination), Chilly Scenes of Winter, 1981, (TV film PBS) Bernice Bobs Her Hair starring Shelly Du Vall, 1975; dir. (TV films HBO) Finnegan, Begin Again with Robert Preston and Mary Tyler Moore, Parole Board, A Private Matter with Sissy Spacek and Aidan Quinn, (TV film Showtime) In The Presence of Mine Enemies, 1997, (films) Between the Lines, 1976, Crossing Delancey with Amy Irving, 1988, Loverboy, 1989, Stepkids, 1991; dir. stage plays and musicals including Album, Maybe I'm Doing It Wrong, Off-Broaday prodn. A...My Name is Alice; prod. On The Yard, (radio) Great Jewish Stories from Eastern Europe and Beyond, 1995; dir. (feature film) A Fish in the Bathtub, 1998, (TV film Lifetime) Invisible Child, 1999, (TV film Showtime) Charms for the Easy Life, 2001, TV film LifeTime) Hunger Point, 2003. Office: Silverfilm Prodns Inc 510 Park Ave New York NY 10022-1105 Office Phone: 646-282-0312.

SILVER, JOEL, film producer; b. South Orange, N.J., July 14, 1952; Film producer: The Warriors, 1979, Xanadu, 1980, 48 Hours, 1982, Jekyll & Hyde...Together Again, 1982, Streets of Fire, 1984, Brewster's Millions, 1985, Weird Science, 1985, Commando, 1985, Jumpin' Jack Flash, 1986, Lethal Weapon, 1987, Predator, 1987, Action Jackson, 1988, Die Hard, 1988, Lethal Weapon 2, 1989, Roadhouse, 1989, The Adventures of Ford Fairlane, 1990, Die Hard 2, 1990, Predator 2, 1990, Hudson Hawk, 1991, Ricochet, 1991, The Last Boy Scout, 1991, Lethal Weapon 3, 1992, Demolition Man, 1993, Richie Rich, 1994, Demon Knight, 1995, Assassins, 1995, Fair Game, 1995, Executive Decision, 1996, Bordello of Blood, 1996, Father's Day, 1997, Conspiracy Theory, 1997, Lethal Weapon 4, 1998, Made Men, 1999, The Matrix, 1999, The House on Haunted Hill, 1999, Romeo Must Die, 2000, Dungeons and Dragons, 2000, Exit Wounds, 2001, Proximity, 2001, Swordfish, 2001, Thir13en Ghosts, 2001, Ghost Ship, 2001, Cradle 2 the Grave, 2003, The Matrix Reloaded, 2003; TV prodr.: W.E.I.R.D. World, 1995, Action, 1999, The Strip, 1999, Freedom, 2000, Jane Doe, 2001. Office: Silver Pictures care Warner Bros Pictures 4000 Warner Blvd Bldg 90 Burbank CA 91522-0001

SILVER, JOHN L. artist, educator, poet; s. Milton and Jane Grey (Gottshal) Silver; m. Ellen Margorie Gorlow, Jan. 27, 1973 (div. June 1984). BA in Art, Pa. State U., 1971; MFA, Pratt Inst., 1973. Spl. edn. tchr. NYC Sch. Sys., 1990—93; drawing instr. Yale U. Drama Sch., New Haven, 1993—94, Parsons Continuing Edn., 1993—2003. Host Tamarind Art & Poetry Mag., NYC, 1989—2001; curator art exhbn. Macelleria, NYC, 2003; adj. instr. portrait painting Parsons. One-man shows include Thompkins Sq. Libr., N.Y.C., 1983, NOHO Gallery, 1983, San Francisco Open Studio, 1985, 1986, Cafe NOBAR, N.Y.C., 1993—94, Maino-Viel 16 East 52nd St, 1995, Life Cafe, 1996, Westbeth Gallery, N.Y.C., 2001, exhibited in group shows at Heckscher Mus., Huntington, NY, 1981, Harbor Gallery, Cold Spring Harbor, NY, 1981, Hillwood Art Mus., C.W. Post Campus, Brookville, NY, 1991, Hoorn Ashby Gallery, 2000, numerous others;, author numerous poems. Active Westbeth Preservation, 2000—03. With USN, 1967. Fine Arts Recovery grant, NY Found. for the Arts, 2002—03. Mem.: Art Student's League (life). Buddhist. Avocations: sailing, canoeing, bicycling, hiking, meditation. Home: 55 Bethune St New York NY 10014 Personal E-mail: lance78@earthlink.net.

SILVER, MALCOLM DAVID, pathologist, educator; b. Adelaide, South Australia, Apr. 29, 1933; s. Eric Bertram and Stella Louisa (Riley) S.; m. Meredith May Galloway, Jan. 19, 1957; children: Stuart Faulkner, Claire Eleanor, Caryl Louise. MD, U. Adelaide; PhD, McGill U. Diplomate: Am. Bd. Pathology. Resident med. officer Royal Adelaide Hosp., 1957-58; resident in pathology Royal Victoria Hosp.-Pathol. Inst., McGill U., Montreal, Que., Can., 1958-63; research fellow dept. exptl. pathology John Curtin Sch. Med. Research, Australian Nat. U., Canberra, 1963-65; asst. prof. pathology U. Toronto, 1965-68, assoc. prof., 1968-74, prof., 1974—79, chmn. dept. pathology, 1985-95, prof. dept. laboratory medicine and pathobiology, 1997-98; staff pathologist Toronto Gen. Hosp., 1965-72, sr. staff pathologist, 1972-79; prof., chmn. dept. pathology U. Western Ont., London, Ont., Can., 1979-85; chief pathology Univ. Hosp., London, 1979-85; pathologist in chief Toronto Gen. Hosp., 1985-89, The Toronto Hosp. (Toronto Gen. and Toronto Western Divs.), 1989-91, sr. staff pathologist, 1991-98. Prof. emeritus U. Toronto, 1998—. Contbr. articles to profl. jours. Fellow Royal Coll. Pathologists Australasia, Royal Coll. Physicians and Surgeons Can.; mem. Can. Assn. Pathologists, Ont. Assn. Pathologists, Internat. Acad. Pathology, Can. Cardiovascular Soc.

SILVER, MARVIN S. lawyer; b. Portland, Maine, Nov. 21, 1951; BS, Syracuse U., 1974; JD, Boston U., 1977, LLM, 1981. Bar: Mass. 1977, U.S. Dist. Ct. Mass. 1978, U.S. Tax Ct. 1983. Atty. Seder & Seder, Worcester, Mass., 1977-82, Seder & Chandler, Worcester, 1983—. Bd. dirs. Jewish Cmty. Ctr. of Worcester, Inc., Mass., 1982-84; mem. fin. com. Town of Shrewsbury, Mass., 1986-93, vice chmn., 1987-88, chmn. 1988-89; bd. dirs. Children's Friend Inc., 1990-99; bd. dirs. Westborough Edn. Found., Inc., 1996--, pres. 1999-2002, treas. 1996-99. Fellow Am. Coll. Trust and Estate Counsel; mem. Mass. Bar Assn. (chmn. estate planning com. tax sect. 1982-84, mem. tax sect. coun. 1983-86, mem. bus. law sect., probate law sect., taxation sect.), Worcester County Bar Assn. (co-chmn. tax law sect. 1981-84, 86-87, 97-98,

bankruptcy and comml. law sect. 1987-88), Estate and Bus. Planning Coun. Worcester County (pres. 1990-91), Exch. Club of Tri-Towns, Inc. (pres. 1984-85) (Shrewsbury). Office: Seder & Chandler 339 Main St Ste 300 Worcester MA 01608-1585 Office Phone: 508-757-7721.

SILVER, MARY WILCOX, oceanography educator; b. San Francisco, July 13, 1941; d. Philip E. and Mary C. (Kartes) Wilcox; children: Monica, Joel. BA in Zoology, U. Calif., Berkeley, 1963; PhD in Oceanography, U. Calif., La Jolla, 1971. Asst. prof. biology San Francisco State U., 1971-72; prof. marine sci. U. Calif., Santa Cruz, 1972—, chmn. dept., 1992-95. Contbr. numerous articles on biol. oceanography to profl. jours. Recipient Bigelow medal, 1992, Mary Sears Woman Pioneer award, 2002; NSF grantee, 1979—. Mem. Am. Soc. Limnology and Oceanography, Am. Phycological Soc. Office: U Calif Dept Ocean Sci Santa Cruz CA 95064 Office Phone: 831-459-2908. E-mail: msilver@ucsc.edu.

SILVER, MICHAEL, education educator; b. Landsberg, Germany, Jan. 30, 1948; came to U.S., 1949; s. Norman and Esther Silver; m. Beverley Ann Moss, May 16, 1971; children: Sabina, Joseph. AB, Washington U., 1970, MEd, 1973, PhD, 1982. Cert. supt. Mo., Wash. Tchr. Normandy Sch. Dist., St. Louis, 1970-72, Parkway Sch. Dist., St. Louis, 1972-75, asst. prin., 1976-79, adminstrv. asst., 1979-83, asst. to supt., 1983-84, asst. supt., 1984-86; supt. Tukwila Sch. Dist., Seattle, 1986—2003; asst. prof. ednl. adminstrn. Seattle U. Bd. dirs. Cities in Schs., Seattle; mem. adv. bd. Sta. KCTS, Seattle, 1990—; vis. exec. Seattle U. Sch. Edn., 1995. Author: Values Education, 1976, Facing Issues of Life and Death, 1976. Pres. SeaTac Task Force, Seattle, 1989; bd. dirs. Anti-Defamation League, Seattle, 1987—; mem. City of Tukwila (Wash.) 2000 Com., 1988 90. Recipient A Plus award Wash. Coun. Econ. Edn., 1992, Excellence in Ednl. Leadership award Univ. Coun. for Ednl. Adminstrn., 1998, Art Tribute award, Wash. Art Edn. Assn., 2001; named Exec. Educator, 100 Exec. Educator Mag., 1985, 1996 Assoc. for Inst. for Ednl. Inquiry Leadership Program; named to Homework Ctrl.; 100 Most Influential People in U.S. Pub. Edn.; I/D/E/A fellow Charles F. Kettering Found., 1978, 88, Title VI fellow Washington U., 1971-73; named Supt. of Yr. Wash. Libr. Media Assn., 2000. Mem. ASCD, Am. Assn. Sch. Adminstrs., Wash. Assn. Sch. Adminstrs. (met. chpt., pres. 1989-90), King County Supts. (chmn. adv. com. 1989-90, 95-96), Southcenter Rotary Club (Paul Harris fellow 1994), Southwest King County C. of C., Phi Delta Kappa. Home: 14127 SE 50th St Bellevue WA 98006-3409 Office: Seattle U Sch Edn PO Box 222000 901 12th Ave Seattle WA 98812 Office Phone: 206-296-5798. Business E-Mail: silverm@seattleu.edu. E-mail: silver@eskimo.com.

SILVER, MORRIS, economist, educator; b. N.Y.C., July 9, 1931; s. Julius and Lilly Silver; m. Sondra P. Hartman, Jan. 26, 1958; children: Gerald David, Ronald Alan. BA, CCNY, 1958; PhD (Earhart Found. fellow, Ford Found. fellow), Columbia U., 1964. Mem. faculty City Coll. CUNY, 1964—, assoc. prof. econs., 1968—, prof., 1972—, chmn. dept., 1969-95. Rsch. assoc. Nat. Bur. Econ. RSch., 1967—71; cons. crime deterrence and offender career Nat. Ctr. Health Svcs. Rsch., 1970—, Hudson Inst., 1974. Author (with r. D. Auster): The State as a Firm, 1979; author: Affluence, Altruism, and Atrophy: The Decline of Welfare States, 1980, Prophets and Markets: The Political Economy of Ancient Israel, 1983, Enterprise and the Scope of the Firm, 1984, Economic Structures of the Ancient Near East, 1985, Foundations of Economic Justice, 1989, Taking Ancient Mythology Economically, 1992, Economic Structures of Antiquity, 1995. With U.S. Army, 1953—55. Mem.: Am. Econ. Assn. Jewish. Office: Dept Econs City Coll 133 D St New York NY 10031 E-mail: msilver12@nyc.rr.com.

SILVER, NEIL MARVIN, manufacturing executive; b. Bklyn., June 2, 1928; s. Jack and Rose (Eisenberg) S.; m. Leah Rebecca Coffman Silver, Sept. 4, 1949; children: Pamela Sue, Carole Beth. Student, U. Mich., 1945-46, 48-49; BS, Ind. U., 1951. Asst. mgr. Wolverine Parking Co., Lansing, Mich., 1951-54; treas. Capitol Parking Co., Indpls., 1955-60; controller, asst. to pres. Eberhart Steel Products, Inc., Mishawaka Tool & Die, Inc., Ind., 1961-63; PRES. Allied Quality Products, Inc., Mishawaka, Ind., 1964-67; treas. Allied Screw Products, Inc., Mishawaka, Ind., 1968-88, chmn., sec., 1989—. Bd. dirs. Ind. State Anti-Defamation League, 1955-57; bd. dirs., treas., pres., chmn. Fin. Commn., Family and Children's Ctr., Inc., Mishawaka, Ind., 1957-77; bd. dirs., treas. Family Svc. Assn. St. Joseph County, Ind., 1955-57. With U.S. Army, 1946-48. Mem. AIAA, Soc. Mfg. Engrs., SAE Internat., Internat. Computing Soc., ASM Internat., B'nai B'rith. Avocations: photography, travel. Office: Allied Screw Products Inc PO Box 543 815 E Lowell Ave Mishawaka IN 46545-6480

SILVER, PAUL ROBERT, marketing executive, consultant; b. Balt., Mar. 15, 1931; s. Harry and Frieda (Rosengarten) S.; m. Natalie Nessa Nechamkin, May 17, 1957; children; Geri Ellen, Steven Marc, Lawrence Alan. BA, U. Md., 1949; BS, U. Balt., 1958; postgrad., Eckerd Coll., 1984. Pres., CEO Sterling Prodns. Inc., Balt., 1950-51; advt. mgr. Hecht Co., Washington, 1951-53; pres., CEO Artists & Models, Inc., Washington and Balt., 1974-76, The Charles Agy. Inc., Washington and Balt., 1955-80, The Golden Triangle Agy., Clearwater, Fla., 1980-82; COO Bridgman Assocs. Inc., Annapolis, Md., 1985-86; dir. promotions Internat. Beverage Expn., Washington, 1986; pres., CEO Prasco Inc., Tampa, Fla., 1982—; CEO Kenaf Mktg. Worldwide, Tampa, Fla., 1994—, Ode Paper Mill & Kenaf Farms Ltd., Ghana, 1999—. Cons. Lewis and Ptnrs., Inc., San Francisco, Corp. Vision, Inc., L.A., Computer Response, Inc., Balt., Themes and Schemes, Inc., Dunedin, Fla., San Diego, 1984—, J&B Mgmt. Co., 1991, Alberee Products, Inc., 1992; v.p. Coupon Am., Bel Air, Md., 1987-88; dir. mktg. Miles Homes, Inc., Cheshire, Conn., 1993; CEO Universal Industries, Inc., 1994—; ptnr. Drakeford & Drakeford, PA, 1995-96; v.p. Chapman Security Inc., 1995-98; ptnr. Global Mktg. Internat., 1997, CEO, also chmn. bd. dirs. Stoppit! Corp., New Port Richey, Fl., 1999—. Active in Radio Free Asia, 1972, Pinellas County Heart Savers, Clearwater, 1981; campaign mgr. for candidates for Balt. City Coun., U.S. Senate and U.S. Congress, 1968, 88, Fla. Commr. Agr., 1990. With U.S. Army, 1953-55, 72. Democrat. Jewish. Avocations: writing, art. Office: Prasco Inc PO Box 24461 Tampa FL 33623-4461 E-mail: prscoinc@verizon.net .

SILVER, R. PHILIP, metal products executive; b. 1942; Grad., U. Mo., 1967. With Amour & Co., Atlanta, 1967—68, Boise Cascade Corp., Idaho, 1968—75; exec. v.p. Fla. Gas Co., Orlando, Fla., 1975—80; pres. Continental Can, Norwalk, Conn., 1980—87; pres., treas. Silgan Corp., Stamford, Conn., 1987—93; chmn., co-CEO Silgan Corp, Stamford, Conn., 1993—. Office: Silgan Corp 4 Landmark Sq Ste 400 Stamford CT 06901-2596

SILVER, RALPH DAVID, financial consultant and arbitrator; b. Chgo., Apr. 19, 1924; s. Morris J. and Amelia (Abrams) S.; m. Lois Reich, Feb. 4, 1951; children: Jay, Cappy. BS, U. Chgo., 1943; postgrad., Northwestern U., 1946-48; JD, DePaul U., 1952. Bar: Ill. bar 1952. Staff accountant David Himmelblau & Co. (C.P.A.'s), 1946-48; internal revenue agt. U.S. Dept. Treasury, 1948-51; practice in Chgo., 1952-55; atty. Lawrence J. West, 1952-55; exec. v.p.-fin., bd. dirs. Barton Inc., Chgo., 1955-92. Bd. dirs. Stone Fin. Corp., Stone Fin. II Corp., 1992-95; arbitrator N.Y. Stock Exch., Cir. Ct. of Cook County, Ill. Bd. dirs., pres. Ralph and Lois Silver Found. Lt. (j.g.) USNR, 1943-46. Mem. ABA, Chgo. Bar Assn., AICPA. Clubs: Green Acres Country. Home: 1124 Old Elm Ln Glencoe IL 60022-1235

SILVER, RICHARD TOBIAS, physician, educator; b. Jan. 18, 1929; m. Barbara Silver; 1 son, Adam Bennett. BA, Cornell U., 1950, MD, 1953. Diplomate Nat. Bd. Med. Examiners, Am. Bd. Internal Medicine, Am. Bd. Clin. Oncology. Intern N.Y. Hosp.-Cornell Med. Ctr., N.Y.C., 1953-54, asst. resident in medicine, 1956-57, resident in hematology, 1957-58; clin. assoc. gen. medicine br. Nat. Cancer Inst., NIH, Bethesda, Md., 1954-56; asst. in medicine Cornell U. Med. Coll., N.Y.C., 1956-58, instr. medicine, 1958-62, clin. asst. prof., 1962-67, clin. assoc. prof., 1967-73, clin. prof., 1973—2002; pres. N.Y. State Soc. Med. Oncologists and Hematologists, 1991—; asst. attending physician N.Y. Hosp., 1964-67, assoc. attending physician, 1967-73, attending physician, 1973—; dir. clin. oncology and chemotherapy rsch. N.Y. Hosp. Divsn. Hematology & Med. Oncology, 2000; prof. medicine, med. dir. Leukemia and Myeloproliferative Ctr., Weill Med. Coll. of Cornell U., 2002—. Asst. vis. physician 2d Cornell Med. div. Bellevue Hosp., N.Y.C., 1963-66; vis. Fulbright prof. U. Bahia Sch. Medicine, Brazil, 1958-59; vis. prof. Hershey Hosp.-Pa. State Hosp., 1976, Mayo Clinic, 1977, Upstate Med. Ctr., Binghamton, N.Y., 1977, Med. Coll. Va., 1979, Med. Sch. Colubia U., 1982, N.J. Coll. Medicine, New Brunswick, 1983, Meml. Med. Ctr. U. Ga., 1984, 86; invited lectr. Med. Coll. Shanghai and Chengchow, 1979, VIII Brazilian Hematology Congress, Salvador, 1981, 14th Internat. Congress Chemotherapy, Kyoto, Japan, 1985, XI Brazilian Congress of Cancerology, Florianopolis, Santa Catarina, 1987, 2d Internat. Conf. CML, Bologna, Italy, 1992, Internat. Symposium Myelo Proliferative Disorders, Mayo Clinic, Tochester Minn., 1994, 9th Internat. Symposium Molecular Biology Hematopolesis: Interferon in Myelo Proliferative Diseases, Genoa, Italy, 1995, The Myeloproliferative Dis. and Biol. Modifiers: Med. Grand Rounds, Sarasota Meml. Hosp. Fla., 1996, European and African Divsn., Durban, South Africa, 1999, Graz, Austria, 2003; chair 1st and 2d Internat. Congresses Myelproliferative and Myelodysplastic, 2001, 2003; vis. faculty curriculum Devel., Annenberg Ctr. Rancho Mirage, Calif., 1994—; mem. rev. bd. NIH, Nat. Cancer Inst.; cons. Cancer Chemotherapy Investigative Rev. Bd., 1980, clin. trials com., 1979-81; mem. Cornell U. Coun., 1987—; spl. site visitor medicine A Roswell Park Meml. Inst., NIH-Nat. Cancer Inst., 1976, mem. combined modality com. divsn. cancer treatment, 1977-79, clin. trials com., 1979-81, cons. cancer chemotherapy rev. bd., 1980; vis. Fulbright lectr. Sch. Medicine U. Bahia, Brazil, 1958-59; lectr., presenter in field. Thor: Morphology of the Blood and Marrow in Clinical Practice, 1970; co-author: (with R.D. Lauper, C.I. Jarowski) A Synopsis of Cancer Chemotherapy, 1977, 2ndedit., 1986, monographs; editor: Clinical Topics in Cancer: Diagnosis and Treatment, 1982, cons. editor Am. Jour. Medicine, 1974-84, mem. editl. adv. bd., 1984; editor, contbr.: Topics in Cancer, 1982; mem. editl. adv. bd. Cancer Investigation, 1983-94; ad-hoc rev. New Eng. Jour. Medicine, Annals of Internal Medicine, Mayo Clinic Proceedings, Blood, Cancer, Am. Jour. Hematology, Med. Rsch. Coun., Eng., others; contbr. chpts. to books and articles to profl. jours., to nat. and internat. profl. confs., seminars and workshops in medicine. Trustee Frances and Edwin Cummings Meml. Fund, 1985-92; med. dir. Rsch. for Blood Health, Inc., 1968-85, Arnold K. Krakower Hematology Found., 1966-75, Cancer Rsch. and Treatment Fund, 1985—. Recipient Pasmantier award, Timothy Gee award for outstanding tchr., clinician, inventor and humanist, 2001; N.Y. State scholar for profl. study of medicine. Fellow ACP; mem. N.Y. State Soc. Med. Hematologists and Oncologists (pres. 1991-2000), Cornell U. Med. Coll. Alumni Assn. (pres. 1973-76, sr. advisor 1976—), Am. Soc. Clin. Oncology (mem. com. clin. practice 1976, com. on pub. affairs 1981-83, chmn. program com. 1977), Internat. Soc. Hematology (chmn. bone marrow biopsy wokshop XV congress 1974, internat. adv. com. XX Congress 1984, lectr.), Am. Soc. Hematology (chmn., guidelines com.), Leukemia Soc. Am. (med. dir., v.p. N.Y.C. chpt. 1968-78), Chronic Myeloid Leukemia, Sass Found Hematologic Rsch. (bd. advs.), N.Y. Soc. Study of Blood, N.Y. County Med. Soc., N.Y. State Med. Soc. Oncologists and Hematologists (pres. 1991-93, mem. exec. com. 1991—), Harvey Soc., Am. Fedn. Clin. Rsch., Am. Assn. Cancer Rsch., Explorers Club (bd. dirs., chmn. sci. adv. com. 1987), Sigma Xi. Office: NY Presby Hosp Weill Cornell Med Ctr 525 E 68th St Box 581 New York NY 10021 Office Phone: 212-746-2098. E-mail: rtsilve@med.cornell.edu.

SILVER, RICK, marketing professional; Grad. cum laude, U. S.C., 1974. Pvt. practice as vice chmn., 1976—. Office: 1411 Gervais St Columbia SC 29201

SILVER, ROBERTA FRANCES (BOBBI SILVER), educator, writer; b. Sedalia, Mo., Oct. 11, 1941; d. Elvin Joshua and Hilda M. (Abrams) Gordon; m. Wayne E. Mason, July 19, 1959 (div. 1974); m. Burton B. Silver, June 3, 1989 (div. 1992); children: Lori Atkins, Philip A., Marc A. Mason. BA in Spl. Edn., Avila Coll., 1972; MA in Counselor Edn., U. Mo., 1974; MA in Spl. Edn., Santa Clara U., 1992. Cert. counselor, tchr., Calif.; specialist learning handicapped credential and multiple subject credential, 1992, C.L.A.D. Tchr. Learning Disabled Shawnee-Mission (Kans.) Sch. Dist., 1972-75; sch. counselor Hickman Mills Consolidated Sch. Dist. #1, Kansas City, Mo., 1975-77; tchr. Behavior Disorders Jefferson County Pub. Schs., Louisville, 1978-80; tchr. West Valley Ctr. for Edn. Therapy, Canoga Park, Calif., 1981-82, Ozanam Home for Boys, Kansas City, 1983-89; instr. in human svcs. and continuing edn. dept. Longview C.C., Lee's Summit, Mo., 1985-89; instr. learning handicapped Franklin-McKinley Sch. Dist., San Jose, Calif., 1990-95, chr. 2d grade, 1990—, lang. devel. tchr., art mentor. Writing and art mentor Gifted and talented (G.A.T.E.) program, coord. Author (as Roberta Gordon Silver) 3 novels; watercolorist; contbr. articles to pvt. in-house mag., poems to anthologies, short stories and articles to mags. Avocations: photography, painting, reading, hiking.

SILVER, ROSLYN OLSON, federal judge; b. Phoenix, Feb. 28, 1946; BA, U. Calif. Santa Barbara, 1968; JD cum laude, Ariz. State U., 1971. Bar: Ariz. 1971, U.S. Ct. Appeals (9th cir.) 1980, U.S. Supreme Ct. 1984. Law clk. Hon. Lorna E. Lockwood Ariz. Supreme Ct., Phoenix, 1971-72; advisor, litigator Navajo Nation Native Am. Rights Fund, Phoenix, 1974-76; legal labor counsel Dial Corp., Phoenix, 1976-78; ptnr. Logan and Aguirre, Phoenix, 1978-79; legal counsel EEOC, Phoenix, 1979-80; asst. U.S. Atty. Dist. Ariz., Phoenix, 1980-84; asst. atty. gen. Ariz. Atty. Gen.'s Office, Phoenix, 1984-86; acting 1st asst., chief criminal divsn. dist. Ariz. U.S. Atty. Office, Phoenix, 1986-94; judge Dist. Ariz. U.S. Dist. Ct., Phoenix, 1994—. Chair local rules com. Ariz. Dist. Ct.; mem. regional sect. panel Harry S Truman Scholarship Found. Contbg. editor: Rutter Group Practice Guide; contbr. articles to profl. jours. Mem. bd. visitors U. Ariz. Law Sch.; mem. adv. panel Lodestar Mediation Clinic, Ariz. State U. Law Sch. Named one of 100 Significant Women and Minorities in Ariz.'s Legal History, 2000. Mem. ABA, Fed. Bar Assn., Nat. Assn. Women Judges, Ariz. Bar Assn. (Pub. Lawyer of Yr. 1990), Ariz. Women Lawyers Assn. (outstanding legal practitioner award 1999), Ariz. State U. Alumni Assn. (outstanding alumnus award 1996). Office: US Dist Ct 401 W Washington SPC 59 Phoenix AZ 85003

SILVER, SHELDON, state legislator, lawyer; b. N.Y.C., Feb. 13, 1944; s. Nathan and Frieda (Bearman) S.; m. Rosa Mandelkern, June 25, 1967; children: Edward, Janine, Michelle, Esther. BA, Yeshiva U., 1965; JD, Bklyn. Coll., 1968. Bar: N.Y. l969, U.S. Dist. Ct. (so. and ea. dists.) N.Y. l970. Assoc. Schechter & Schwartz, N.Y.C., 1968-71; law sec. to Judge Francis Pecora N.Y.C., 1971-76; ptnr. Agri, Bilder & Silver, N.Y.C., 1976-81; pvt. practice N.Y.C., 1981—. Mem. N.Y. State Assembly, 1977—, chmn. ways and means com., 1992, speaker, 1994. Vice pres. Bialystoker Synagogue, Young Israel Synagogue. Named Man of Yr., Harry S. Truman Dem. Club, 1977, United Jewish Appeals, 1983, also others. Democrat. Office: 250 Broadway Ste 2301 New York NY 10007

SILVERBERG, DAVID STANLEY, financial consultant; b. Oelwein, Iowa, Mar. 3, 1936; s. Harold and Rose (Fishman) S.; m. Mary Ellen Silverberg, July 20, 1988; children: Laura, Sara, Stanley. Student, U. Minn.; LUTC, Life Underwriter Coll., Sioux City, Iowa, 1976; CFP, Coll. Fin. Planning, Denver, 1979. CFP. Fin. cons., 1st v.p. Smith Barney, Sioux City, 1978—. Instr. Western Iowa Tech. Coll., Sioux City, 1980-87, Inst. of Banking, Sioux City, 1990. Past pres. Sioux City Jewish Fedn., 1991-94; pres. Sioux City Jewish Cemetery Assn., 1990-2002; bd. dirs. Sioux City Symphony, 1991-2002, KWIT Pub. Radio Sta., 1997-2002. With U.S. Army, 1958-63. Recipient Young Leadership award Sioux City Jewish Fedn., 1984. Mem. Landmark Lodge AF&AM, Scottish Rite (32nd degree), Shriners, Sioux City Country Club. Avocation: golf. Home: 26 W 45th St Sioux City IA 51104-1002 Office: Smith Barney 600 4th St Sioux City IA 51101-1744 Office Phone: 712-277-3700.

SILVERBERG, LEWIS HENRY, legal consultant; b. L.A., Nov. 1, 1934; s. Milton Henry and Marjorie Vella (Coates) S.; children: Stephen, Richard, Donna; m. Alice Ellen Deakins, Mar. 9, 1979. BA, Pomona Coll., 1955; JD, UCLA, 1958. Bar: Calif. 1959, U.S. Supreme Ct. 1966. Pvt. practice, San Diego, 1959-89; bus. cons., 1993—. Active various pub., charitable and ednl. orgns. Office: 1515 Merritt Dr El Cajon CA 92020-7847 E-mail: lew@the-silverbergs.net.

SILVERBERG, MICHAEL BARRY, anesthesiologist; b. Bklyn., May 20, 1959; s. Norman and Florence (Berman) S.; m. Barbara Montana, Sept. 24, 1989. BA, Harvard U., 1979; MD, Yale U., 1983. Diplomate Am. Bd. Anesthesiology. Intern NYU Med. Ctr., N.Y.C., 1983-84, resident in internal medicine, 1983-86; resident in anesthesiology Hosp. U. Pa., Phila., 1986-89; anesthesia faculty Med. Coll. of Pa., 1989-91; anesthesia staff Staten Island U. Hosp., 1991—. Mem. staff Staten Island (N.Y.) U. Hosp. Mem. AMA, Am. Soc. Anesthesiologists, Internat. Anesthesia Rsch. Soc. Office: 475 Seaview Ave Staten Island NY 10305-3436 Office Phone: 718-226-9290. E-mail: msilverberg@siuh.edu.

SILVERBERG, MICHAEL JOEL, lawyer; b. Rochester, N.Y., Aug. 12, 1932; s. Goodman and Minnie (Krovetz) S.; m. Charlotte Goldman, June 19, 1955; children: Mark (dec. 1999), Daniel. BA, U. Rochester, 1954; JD, Columbia U., 1957. Bar: N.Y. 1958, U.S. Dist. Ct. (so. dist.) N.Y. 1965, U.S. Dist. Ct. (ea. dist.) N.Y. 1990, U.S. Ct. Appeals (2d cir.) 1975, U.S. Supreme Ct. 1967. Instr. Columbia U. Law Sch., N.Y.C., 1957—58; assoc. Phillips Nizer LLP (formerly Phillips, Nizer, Benjamin, Krim & Ballon), N.Y.C., 1960—67, ptnr., 1967—. Pres. Nat. Alliance Mentally Ill N.Y.C., Inc., 1997—2003; cons. sci. program com. Am. Psychiat. Assn., 2000—01. Bd. editors Columbia Law Rev., 1955—57. Bd. dirs. Nat. Alliance for Mentally Ill of N.Y. State, 1998—, pres., 1999—; mem. adv. bd. dept. psychiatry Columbia U.; mem. adv. bd. N.Y.C. Vis. Nurse Svc.; mem. nat. adv. coun. Columbia Teen Screen Program; mem. bd. editors Columbia Law Rev., 1955-57. Fulbright scholar U. Strasbourg, France, 1958-59. Mem. ABA, N.Y. State Bar Assn. (com. on internat. litigation), Assn. Bar City N.Y. Home: 205 W End Ave New York NY 10023-4804 E-mail: MSILVERBERG@PHILLIPSNIZER.COM.

SILVERBERG, ROBERT, author; b. N.Y.C., 1935; s. Michael and Helen (Baim) S.; m. Barbara Brown, 1956; m. Karen Haber, 1987. BA, Columbia U., 1956. Author: (novels) Thorns, 1967, The Masks of Time, 1968, Hawksbill Station, 1968, Nightwings, 1969, To Live Again, 1969, Tower of Glass, 1970, The World Inside, 1971, Son of Man, 1971, A Time of Changes, 1971, Dying Inside, 1972, The Book of Skulls, 1972, Born with the Dead, 1974, Shadrach in the Furnace, 1976, Lord Valentine's Castle, 1980, Majipoor Chronicles, 1982, Lord of Darkness, 1983, Valentine Pontifex, 1983, Gilgamesh the King, 1984, Tom O'Bedlam, 1985, Star of Gypsies, 1986, At Winter's End, 1988, To the Land of the Living, 1989, The New Springtime, 1990, (with Isaac Asimov) Nightfall, 1990, The Face of the Waters, 1991, (with Isaac Asimov) The Ugly Little Boy, 1992, Kingdoms of the Wall, 1993, (with Isaac Asimov) The Positronic Man, 1993, Hot Sky at Midnight, 1994, Mountains of Majipoor, 1995, Starborne, 1996, Sorcerers of Majipoor, 1997, The Alien Years, 1998, Lord Prestimion, 1999, The King of Dreams, 2001, The Longest Way Home, 2002, Roma Eterna, 2003, Phases of the Moon, 2004; (non-fiction) The Face of the Lost Cities and Vanished Civilizations, 1962, The Great Wall of China, 1965, The Old Ones: Indians of the American Southwest, 1965, Scientists and Scoundrels: A Book of Hoaxes, 1965, The Auk, the Dodo and the Oryx, 1966, The Morning of Mankind: Prehistoric Man in Europe, 1967, Mound Builders of Ancient America: The Archaeology of a Myth, 1968, If I Forget Thee, O Jerusalem: American Jews and the State of Israel, 1970, The Pueblo Revolt, 1970, The Realm of Prester John, 1971. Recipient Hugo award World Sci. Fiction Conv., 1956, 69, 87, 90; Nebula award Sci. Fiction Writers Am., 1970, 72, 75, 86, Grand Master Nebula award, 2004. Mem. Sci. Fiction Writers Am. (pres. 1967-68) Address: PO Box 13160 Oakland CA 94661-0160

SILVERBERG, STEVEN GEORGE, pathologist, educator; b. NYC, Nov. 30, 1938; s. Bertram P. and Esther (Weintraub) S.; m. Kiyoe Ono, Nov. 16, 1968. AB, Bklyn. Coll., 1958; MD, Johns Hopkins U., 1962. Diplomate Am. Bd. Pathology. Intern in medicine Bellevue/Meml. Hosp., NYC, 1962-63; resident in anatomic pathology Yale-New Haven Hosp., 1963-65; fellow in pathology Meml. Hosp. Cancer Allied Diseases, NYC, 1965-66; asst., assoc. prof. pathology Med. Coll. Va., Richmond, Va., 1968-72; assoc. prof., prof. pathology U. Colo., Denver, 1972-81; prof., dir. anatomic pathology George Washington U., Washington, 1981-96, U. Md., Balt., 1996—2004, clin. prof., 2004—. Exec. dir. Colo. Regional Cancer Ctr., Denver, 1976-80. Co-author: Pathology in Gynecology and Obstetrics, 1969, 4th edit., 1993; editor: Principles and Practice of Surgical Pathology, 1983, 3d edit., 1997; editor-in-chief Internat. Jour. Gyn. Pathology, 1984-92, Pathology Case Revs., 1995—; contbr. 220 articles to profl. jours. Capt. USAF, Japan, 1966-68. Jonas Salk scholar CUNY, 1958. Fellow Am. Soc. Clin. Pathologists (life, coun. 1977—, Disting. Svc. award 1991, H.P. Smith Disting. Pathology Educator award 1997); mem. Internat. Soc. Gyn. Pathologists (pres. 1998-2001), Assn. Dirs. Anatomic and Surg. Pathology (pres. 1998-2000), Internat. Soc. Breast Pathol. (pres. 2003-2005), Alpha Omega Alpha. Avocations: reading history, travel, collecting japanese edo period illustrated books, wine. Office: Dept Pathology U Md Med Sys 22 S Greene St Baltimore MD 21201-1544 Office Phone: 410-328-5072.

SILVERBERG, STEVEN MARK, lawyer; b. Bklyn., June 7, 1947; m. Arlene Leopold, July 4, 1971; 2 children. BA, Bklyn. Coll., 1969; JD, NYU, 1972. Bar: N.Y. 1973, U.S. Dist. Ct. (so. and ea. dists.) N.Y. 1974, U.S. Supreme Ct. 1976, U.S. Ct. Appeals (2nd cir.) 1978. Asst. dist. atty. Kings County Dist. Atty., Bklyn., 1972-75; dep. town. atty. Town of Greenburgh, N.Y., 1975-79; ptnr. Stowell, Kelly & Silverberg, White Plains, N.Y., 1979-83, Hoffman, Silverberg & Wachtell, Elmsford, N.Y., 1983-86, Hoffman, Silverberg, Wachtell & Koster, White Plains, N.Y., 1986-89; pvt. practice White Plains, 1989-92; ptnr. Kirkpatrick & Silverberg LLP, White Plains, 1993—2000, Wilson, Elser, Moskowitz, Edelman & Dicker LLP, White Plains, 2001—. Adj. assoc. prof. N.Y. Law Sch., 1990—93. Co-author: Wetlands and Coastal Zone Regulations and Compliance, 1993; contbr. to profl. publs. Counsel Greenburgh Housing Authority, 1979-84, Town of Mamaroneck, N.Y., 1984-96, Village of Mamaroneck, 1999-2003, planning and zoning bd. Town of Haverstraw, 2001—; bd. dirs. Temple Beth Torah, Upper Nyack, N.Y., 1977-89, 2000-03, pres. 1984-86; bd. dirs. N.J. West Hudson Valley Region Union of Am. Hebrew Congregations, 1986-88, Westchester Mcpl. Planning Fedn. Mem. ABA, N.Y. State Bar Assn., Westchester County Bar Assn. (chair environtl. law com. 1997—). Office: Wilson Elser Moskowitz Edelman & Dicker LLP 3 Gannett Dr White Plains NY 10604

SILVERMAN, AL, editor; b. Lynn, Mass., Apr. 12, 1926; s. Henry and Minnie (Damsky) S.; m. Rosa Magaro, Sept. 9, 1951; children: Thomas, Brian, Matthew. BS, Boston U., 1949, LittD, 1986. Assoc. editor Sport mag., 1951-52; sports editor True mag., 1952-54; asst. editor Argosy mag., 1954-55; free-lance mag. writer, contbr. Saturday Evening Post, Coronet, Pageant, This Week, Am. Weekly, Am. Heritage, Saturday Review, others, 1955-60; editor-in-chief Saga mag., Impact mag., Sport Library, Sport mag., 1960-72; exec. v.p., editorial dir. Book-of-the-Month Club, 1972—, pres., chief operating officer, 1981—, chmn., chief exec. office, 1985-88; v.p., contbg. editor Viking Penguin, 1989-92, sr. v.p., pub., editor in chief, 1992—, sr. v.p., editor-at-large, 1994-97, editl. advisor, 1998—. Author: Warren Spahn, 1961, Best from Sport, 1961, (with Phil Rizzuto) The Miracle New York Yankees, 1962, The World of Sport, 1962, Mickey Mantle, Master Yankee, 1963, World Series Heroes, 1964, (with Paul Hornung) Football and the Single Man, 1965, The Specialist in Pro Football, 1966, Sports Titans of the 20th Century, 1968, (with Frank Robinson) My Life is Baseball, 1968, More Sport Titans of the 20th Century, 1969, Joe DiMaggio, The Golden Year, 1969, I Am Third, (with Gale Sayers), 1970, Foster and Laurie, 1974; editor: The Book of the Month, 1986; co-editor: The 20th Century Treasury of Sports, 1992, It's Not Over 'Til It's Over, 2002. Mem. Authors Guild, PEN (bd. dirs.), The Merc. Libr. Home: 411 E 53rd St Apt 16H New York NY 10022

SILVERMAN, ALAN HENRY, lawyer; b. N.Y.C., Feb. 18, 1954; s. Melvin H. and Florence (Green) S.; m. Gretchen E. Freeman, May 25, 1986; children: Willa C.F., Gordon H.F. BA summa cum laude, Hamilton Coll., 1976; MBA, JD, U. Pa., 1980. Bar: N.Y. 1981, U.S. Dist. Ct. (so. and ea. dists.) N.Y. 1981, U.S. Ct. Internat. Trade 1981, D.C. 1986, U.S. Supreme Ct. 1990. Assoc. Hughes, Hubbard & Reed, N.Y.C., 1980-84; asst. counsel Newsweek, Inc., N.Y.C., 1984-86; v.p., gen. counsel, sec., dir. adminstrn. Cable One, Inc., Phoenix, 1986—. Contbr. articles to profl. jours. Mem. prevention adv. com.

Gov. Pa. Justice Commn., 1975-79; bd. dirs. Lawyers' Alliance for N.Y., 1982-85, N.Y. Lawyers Pub. Interest, 1983-85, Nat. Assn. JD-MBA Profls., 1983-85, Bus. Vols. for Arts, Inc., Phoenix, 1989-93, Ariz. Vol. Lawyers for the Arts, Inc., 1994-97, First Amendment Coalition Ariz., Inc., 1991—, Phoenix Falcons Fencing Club, Inc., 2003--; mem. Maricopa County Citizens Jud. Adv. Coun., 1990-93; mem. citizens' bond com. City of Phoenix, 2000. Mem. ABA, Assn. of Bar of City of N.Y., D.C. Bar Assn., Phi Beta Kappa. Home: 5833 N 30th St Phoenix AZ 85016-2401 Office: Cable One Inc 1314 N 3d St Phoenix AZ 85004 Office Phone: 602-364-6190. E-mail: alan.silverman@cableone.net.

SILVERMAN, ARNOLD, pediatrician, educator; b. N.Y.C., Feb. 15, 1933; s. Sol and Gertrude (Cohen) S.; m. Bonnie J. Fenson, Aug. 28, 1955; children: Jeffrey R., Paul A., David E. BA, U. Colo., 1954, MA, 1957, MD, 1961. Diplomate: Am. Bd. Pediatrics. Intern Colo. Gen. Hosp., Denver, 1961-62; resident in pediatrics U. Minn. Hosp., Mpls., 1962-64; fellow in pediatric gastroenterology U. Colo. Med. Center, Denver, 1964-65, mem. faculty, 1965—, assoc. prof. pediatrics, 1975-80; prof. U. Colo. Med. Ctr. (Health Sci. Ctr.), 1980-93, prof. emeritus, 1994—. Dir. grad. edn. Denver Children's Hosp., 1967-75, chief gastroenterology svc., 1967-75; dir. pediat. svc. Denver Gen. Hosp., 1975-92; cons. Surgeon Gen. Fitzsimons Army Med. Hosp., 1976-95; mem. Nat. Commn. Digestive Diseases, 1979-80. Author: (with C.C. Roy and D. Alagille) Pediatric Clinic Gastroenterology, 4th edit., 1995. Recipient Silver and Gold Med. Alumni award U. Colo. Med. Sch., 2000. Mem. Am. Acad. Pediatrics, Am. Gastroenterology Assn., Am. Pediatric Soc., Am. Gastroenterology Assn., N.Am. Soc. Pediatric Gastroenterology, Am. Assn. Study Liver Disease, Denver Med. Soc., Alpha Omega Alpha. Jewish. Home: 3335 S Newport St Denver CO 80224-2823

SILVERMAN, ARNOLD BARRY, lawyer; b. Sept. 1, 1937; s. Frank and Lillian Lena (Linder) S.; m. Susan L. Levin, Aug. 7, 1960; children: Michael Eric, Lee Oren. B of Engring. Sci., Johns Hopkins U., 1959; JD cum laude, U. Pitts., 1962. Bar: U.S. Dist. Ct. (we. dist.) Pa. 1963, Pa. 1964, U.S. Patent and Trademark Office 1965, U.S. Supreme Ct. 1967, Can. Patent Office 1968, U.S. Ct. Claims 1975, U.S. Ct. Appeals (3d cir.) 1982, U.S. Ct. Appeals (fed. cir.) 1985, U.S. Ct. Appeals (4th cir.) 2000. Patent atty. Alcoa, New Kensington, Pa., 1962-67, 68-72, sr. patent atty., 1972-76; ptnr. Price and Silverman, Pitts., 1967-68; v.p., gen. patent counsel Joy Mfg. Co., Pitts., 1976-80; ptnr. Murray Silverman & Keck, Pitts., 1980-81, Buell, Blenko, Ziesenheim & Beck, Pitts., 1984; ptnr. intellectual property dept. Eckert, Seamans, Cherin & Mellott, Pitts., 1984—, chmn., 1992—, chmn. info. tech. practice group, 1992-97; spl. asst. atty. gen. State of W.Va., 1985—; spl. counsel patents U. Pitts., 1975—. Spkr. on patents, trademarks, copyright, computer law; nat. panel of arbiters Am. Arbitration Assn., 1987—. Contbr. articles to profl. jours. Mem. Churchill CSC (Pa.), 1967-90, chmn., 1975-90; mem. Pitts. law com. Anti-Defamation League, 1981—, regional adv. bd., 1982—, ch-chmn. Pitts. region ann. dinner, 1983, mem. chmn. by-laws com., 1983; bd. govs. Slippery Rock U. Found., 1985-91; Pitts. steering com. MIT Enterprise Forum, 1986-87. With U.S. Army, 1963-64. Recipient Am. Spirit Honor medal, Ft. Knox, 1963; named Pa. Super Lawyer, 2004. Fellow: Mensa (lawyers in Mensa 1978—, nat. assoc. counsel patents and trademarks copyrights 1980—82, inventors' spl. interest group 1980—86); mem.: ASME, ABA, Assn. Corp. Patent Counsel (emeritus mem.), Intertel (treas. Pitts. Forum 1983—), Stratford Cmty. Assn. (v.p. 1966—67, gov. 1966—70, pres. 1967—68), Golden Panthers, U. Pitts. Law Alumni Assn. (bd. dirs. 1992—2004, treas. 1997—98, v.p. 1998—99, pres.-elect 1999—2000, pres. 2001—02), Johns Hopkins Soc. Engring. Alumni, Johns Hopkins U. Alumni Assn. (chmn. publicity com. 1963—66, exec. com. 1966—87, v.p. 1969—70, pres. 1971—72, nat. alumni coun. 1989—92, coun. mem. 2000—), Brit. Inst. Chartered Patent Agts. (fgn. mem.), Licensing Execs. Soc. (co-chmn. Pitts. chpt. 1994—96), Am. Chem. Soc. (chemistry and the law sect.), Nat. Assn. Coll. and Univ. Attys., Pa. Bar Assn. (co-chmn. sports/entertainment arts law com. 2001—03), D.C. Bar Assn., U.S. Trademark Assn. (chmn. task force on advt. agys. 1981, membership com. 1987—89), Am. Intellectual Property Law Assn. (membership com. 1985—88, pub. rels. com. 1994—), Pitts. Patent Law Assn. (chmn. pub. rels. com. 1968—69, chmn. patent laws com. 1970—72, chmn. legis. action com. 1972—75, chmn. nominating com. 1973, bd. mgrs., newsletter editor 1974—88, sec.-treas. 1976—84, v.p. 1984—85, pres. 1985—86, pub. rels. com. 1994—95, program com. 1995—96), Allegheny County Bar Assn. (chmn. pub. rels. com. 1978—80, vice-chmn. intellectual property sect. 1981—83, chmn. 1984—85), Robert Bruce Assn. Law Fellows (life), U. Pitts. Gen. Alumni Assn. (life; bd. dirs. 2001—03, exec. com. 2003—, sec. 2004—, 2004—), Duquesne Club, Order of Coif, Psi Chi, Tau Epsilon Rho. Republican. Jewish. Home: 2019 High Pointe Ct Murrysville PA 15668-8515 Office: 600 Grant St 44th Fl Pittsburgh PA 15219-2703 Office Phone: 412-566-2077. E-mail: arnie@telerama.com., abs@escm.com., asilverman@eckertseamans.com. *Welcome challenge and perform all tasks with enthusiasm, in a moral manner and to the very best of your ability.*

SILVERMAN, ARTHUR CHARLES, lawyer; b. Lewiston, Maine, June 13, 1938; s. Louis A. and Frances Edith (Brownstone) S.; BS in Elec. Engring., BS in Indsl. Mgmt., MIT, 1961; JD, Columbia U., 1964; m. Donna Linda Zolov, June 18, 1961; children: Leonard Stephen, Daniel Edward. Bar: N.Y. 1965, U.S. Supreme Ct. 1971. Engr., engring. asst. Gen. Electric Co., Pittsfield, Mass. and Phila., 1958-62; assoc. Baer & Marks, N.Y.C., 1965-68; assoc. Golenbock and Barell, N.Y.C., 1968-72, ptnr., 1972-89; ptnr. Reid & Priest LLP, N.Y.C., 1989-98, dep. chair, 1996-98; ptnr. Thelen Reid & Priest LLP, N.Y.C., 1998—. Treas., trustee Ramaz Sch., 1977-84, vice chmn., 1984-85, 86-88, chmn., 1988-92, hon. chmn., 1992—; bd. govs. MIT Hillel Found., 1979-84; mem. Bd. Jewish Edn. of City of N.Y., 1981-84; mem. exec. com. Nat. Jewish Ctr. for Learning and Leadership, 1984-90. Mem. IEEE, ABA, NSPE, N.Y. State Bar Assn., Fed. Bar Council, Assn. Bar City N.Y., N.Y. Soc. Architects, Internat. Bar Assn., Inter-Pacific Bar Assn., Constrn. Mgmt. Inst., Constrn. Specifications Inst. Home: 200 E 74th St New York NY 10021-3618 Office: Thelen Reid & Priest LLP 875 Third Ave New York NY 10022

SILVERMAN, BARRY G. federal judge; b. N.Y.C., Oct. 11, 1951; 1 child, Bagel Ann. BA summa cum laude, Ariz. State U., 1973, JD, 1976. Bar: Ariz. 1976, U.S. Dist. Ct. Ariz. 1976, U.S. Ct. Appeals (9th cir.) 1976, U.S. Supreme Ct. 1980. Asst. city prosecutor, Phoenix, 1976—77; dep. atty. Maricopa County, 1977—79; ct. commr., 1979—84; judge Superior Ct. Ariz. Maricopa County, 1984—95; apptd. magistrate judge U.S. Dist. Ct. Ariz., 1995—98; judge U.S. Ct. Appeals 9th cir., 1998—. Instr. constnl. law Coll. Law, Ariz. State U., 1983, adj. prof. advanced criminal procedure, 89; lectr. cmty. property BAR/BRI Ariz., Idaho and Nev. Bar Rev. Courses, 1989—. Recipient Exel award, Soc. Nat. Assn. Publs., 1992. Mem.: ABA, Maricopa County Bar Assn. (Henry Stevens award 1991), State Bar Ariz. Avocations: magic, beagles, baseball, wine tasting. Office: US Ct of Appeals 401 W Washington St SPC 78 Phoenix AZ 85003

SILVERMAN, BRUCE GARY, advertising executive; b. N.Y.C., Feb. 16, 1945; s. Edward E. and Lillian (Brill) S.; children: Jennifer, Matthew; m. Nancy Cole, 1996; children: Christen Cole, Larry Cole. BA, Adelphi U., 1965; JD, Albany Law Sch., 1967. Sr. v.p., exec. creative dir. Ogilvy & Mather Inc., N.Y.C., 1967-80; exec. v.p., exec. creative dir. Bozell & Jacobs Inc., Dallas, 1981-83, Batten, Barton, Durstine & Osborn Inc., L.A., 1984-85; exec. v.p., creative dir. Asher/Gould Advt. Inc., L.A., 1986-89, pres., chief creative officer, 1989-95, pres., COO, 1996-97; pres. Western Internat. Advocacy Group, L.A., 1997-98; exec. v.p., mng. dir. Initiative Media, L.A., 1998—; pres., CEO Initiative Ptnrs., USA, 1999—2002; pres. WONGDOODY Advt., L.A., 2003—. V.p., bd. dirs. L.A. Children's Mus., 1984-88; chmn. Resource Devel. com. Starbright Pavillion Found., 1993. Mem. Acad. TV Arts and Scis., Am. Assn. Advt. Agys. (bd. dirs., vice chmn. western region 2002). Home: 3168 Dona Mema Pl Studio City CA 91604-4264 Office: WONGDOODY Advt 9570 W Pico Blvd Los Angeles CA 90035

SILVERMAN, BURTON PHILIP, artist; b. Bklyn., June 11, 1928; s. Morris Daniel and Anne (Firstenberg) S.; m. Claire Guss, June 12, 1969; children: Robert Arthur, Karen Lila. BA, Columbia Coll., 1949. Freelance illustrator Life, Fortune, Esquire, Time, Newsweek, Sports Illus., New York, The New Yorkers mags., 1959—; instr. Sch. Visual Arts, N.Y.C., 1964-67. Co-author: Abel, 1968, A Portfolio of Drawings, 1968; author: Painting People, 1977, Breaking the Rules of Watercolor, 1983, Sight and Insight: The Art of Burton Silverman, 1999; contbr. articles and drawings to profl. jours.; one-man exhbns. include Davis Gallery, N.Y.C, 1956, 58, 62, Kenmore Galleries, Phila., 1963, 67, 70, FAR Gallery, N.Y.C., 1965, 70, 75, 77, Genesis Gallery, N.Y.C., 1979, Sindin Galleries, N.Y.C., 1983, Capricorn Galleries, Bethesda, Md., 1979, 91, Gallery 52, South Orange, N.J., 1967, 70, 77, Harbor Gallery, L.I., 1971, 74, U. Utah, 1967, Doll and Richards, Boston, 1980, Grand Ctrl. Galleries, N.Y.C., 1988, Cudahy's Gallery, N.Y.C., 1990, Joseph Keiffer, Inc., N.Y.C., 1993, Gerold Wunderlich & Co., N.Y.C., 1996, 97, Merrill Gallery, Denver, 1996, 98, Butler Inst. of Am. Art, 1999, Brigham Young Mus., Provo, 1999, Gallery Henoch, N.Y.C., 2001, 04; group exhbns. include Butler Inst. Am. Art, Youngstown, Ohio, 1954-71, 74, 76, 79, 88, 90, 93, 2002, NAD, N.Y.C., 1958-96, 98, 2001, 03, Am. Watercolor Soc., N.Y.C., 1978-82, 84-87, 89-91, 95-96, 97, 99, 2002, Pa. Acad. Fine Art, 1949, New Britain (Conn.) Mus. Am. Art, 1964, Wadsworth Atheneum, Hartford, Conn., 1961, Am. Acad. Arts and Letters, 1967, 74, 76, 79, N.Y. Hist. Soc., 1976, Pa. State Mus. Art, Portsmouth (Va.) Mus. Art, 1976, 79-80, 82 (Purchase prize, 1979, 82), Mexico City Mus. Art, 1990, Nat. Portrait Gallery, Washington, 1993, Hofstra Mus., N.Y.C., 1993, South Bend (Ind.) Mus. Art, 1994, Old Forge (N.Y.) Mus. and Gallery, 1994, Qgunquit Mus., 1997, Del. Art Mus., Wilmington, 2004. With AUS, 1951-53. Named to Hall of Fame, Soc. of Illustrators, N.Y., 1990, Pastel Soc. Am., 1992; named Artist of Am., 1991, 94, 2000; recipient Gold medal Nat. Portrait Soc., 2004. Mem. NAD (numerous awards and prizes including Joseph Isidor Gold medal 1992, Ranger Purchase prize 1962, 84, Benjamin Altman figure prize 1969), Am. Watercolor Soc. (numerous awards and prizes including Gold medal 1979, Silver medal 1984, 95, annuals), Pastel Soc. Am. (hon.). Home: 324 W 71st St New York NY 10023-3502 E-mail: bpsart@aol.com. *In art I am wary of things too facile, or appealing. My painting is rooted in a realist tradition that is equally concerned with objective facts and subjective realities. It is a visual language that allows me to explore the tensions and ambiguities engendered by this dual aspect of human experience. Art is my life and my life is in my art.*

SILVERMAN, CHARLOTTE, epidemiologist, educator; b. N.Y.C., May 21, 1913; d. Harry and Gussie (Goldman) S. BA, Bklyn. Coll., 1933; MD, Woman's Med. Coll. Pa., 1938; MPH, Johns Hopkins U., 1942, DrPH, 1948. Diplomate Am. Bd. Preventive Medicine. Intern Beekman Hosp., N.Y.C., 1939-40; resident Sea View Hosp., Staten Island, N.Y., 1940-41; asst. dir., dir. Bur. Tuberculosis Balt. City Health Dept., 1946-56; chief epidemiology, planning and rsch. Md. State Dept. Health, Balt., 1956-62; med. officer in various programs NIMH, Bethesda, Md., 1962-68; dep. dir. div. biol. effects and other positions Bur. Radiol. Health USPHS, Rockville, Md., 1968-83; assoc. dir. for human studies FDA, Rockville, 1983-92. Mem. faculty dept. epidemiology Johns Hopkins U. Sch. Hygiene and Pub. Health, Balt., 1950—. Author: Epidemiology of Depression, 1968; contbr. articles to profl. jours. Sr. Surg. USPHS, 1944-45. Recipient Mary Pemberton Nourse Meml. award AAUW, 1941-42, Merit award FDA, 1974, Alumni Life Achievement award Bklyn. Coll., 1994. Fellow APHA, Am. Coll. Preventive Medicine, Am. Orthopsychiat. Assn., Am. Coll. Epidemiology; mem. Delta Omega. Home: 501 Lincoln Ave Takoma Park MD 20912-5823

SILVERMAN, HARRY J. pizza delivery company executive; BA, U. Ill. CPA. With Grant Thornton, until 1985; regional contr. Domino's Pizza Inc., Chgo., 1985-88, nat. ops. contr. Ann Arbor, Mich., from 1988, divsnl. v.p. fin., CFO, v.p. fin. and adminstrn., 1993—, now exec. v.p. fin., CFO, treas. Office: 30 Frank Lloyd Wright Dr Ann Arbor MI 48105-9757

SILVERMAN, HENRY RICHARD, diversified business executive, lawyer; b. N.Y.C., Aug. 2, 1940; s. Herbert Robert and Roslyn (Moskowitz) S.; m. Susan H. Herson, June 13, 1965 (div. Jan. 1977); children: Robin Lynn, Deborah Leigh; m. Nancy Ann Kraner, Jan. 22, 1978; 1 child, Catherine Anne Grad. cum laude, Hackley Sch., Tarrytown, N.Y., 1957; BA with honors, Williams Coll., 1961; LL.B., U. Pa., 1964; postgrad. in corp. fin. and taxation, NYU, 1965. Bar: N.Y. 1965, U.S. Tax Ct. 1965, U.S. Ct. Appeals (2d cir.) 1965. Practice law, 1965-66; with White, Weld & Co., beginning 1966; then gen. ptnr. Oppenheimer & Co., until 1970; pres., chief exec. officer ITI Corp., 1970-72; founder, pres. Trans-York Securities Corp., 1972; exec. v.p., chmn. exec. com. Ladenburg, Thalmann & Co., 1973; pres., CEO Vavasseur Am. Ltd., subs. U.K. mcht. bank, 1974-75; gen. ptnr. Brisbane Ptnrs., 1976-77; prin. various investment groups, 1977—, Silverman Energy Co., N.Y.C., 1977—, NBC Channel 20, Springfield, Ill., 1977-83, ABC Channel 9, Syracuse, N.Y., 1977-81; prin., dir. Delta Queen Steamboat Co., New Orleans, 1977-86; also prin. outdoor advt., music pub., motion picture prodn., radio broadcasting & hardware mfg. cos.; pres., CEO Reliance Capital Corp., subs. Reliance Group Holdings, Inc., N.Y.C., 1982—; sr. v.p. bus. devel. Reliance Group Holdings, Inc., N.Y.C., 1982-90; chmn., CEO Days Inns Am., Inc., Atlanta, 1984-89; also dir.; pres., CEO Telemundo Group, Inc., N.Y.C., 1986-90; gen. ptnr. Blackstone Group, N.Y.C., 1990-91; chmn., CEO, pres. HFS Inc., N.Y.C., 1990—; chmn., pres., CEO Cendant Corp., N.Y.C., 1996—. Bd. dirs. N.Y. Univ. Hosp., N.Y.C., 1987—. Served to lt. USNR, 1965-73 Mem.: Harmonie (N.Y.C.). Republican. Jewish. Avocation: tennis. Office: Cendant Corp 9 W 57th St Fl 37 New York NY 10019-2701*

SILVERMAN, IRA NORTON, news producer; b. Bklyn., May 17, 1935; s. Joseph and Mildred (Axelrod) S.; m. Elizabeth Parsons Aspray, June 16, 1979; children by previous marriage: Gary, Bruce; stepchildren: Elizabeth, Aime, Alison. AB, Columbia U., 1957. Newspaper, mag. and book editor, 1957—67; prodr., writer NBC News, 1967—79; sr. prodr. spl. projects NBC Nightly News, Washington, 1977—95; contbr. The New Yorker, N.Y.C., 1995—, editl. cons., 1995—96; cons. NBC News, 1998, PBS, 1999, 2002. Co-author: The Pleasant Avenue Connection, 1976. Recipient Nat. Headliner award, 1977, 78, 81, 87, Alfred I. DuPont-Columbia U. award, 1983-84, 85-86, Emmy award for news and documentary, 1985, 87, award Overseas Press Club Am., 1987, 90, George Polk award L.I. U., 1988, Excellence in TV award Channels mag., 1990, George Foster Peabody award U. Ga., 1991, Citation for Excellence Overseas Press Club, 1992.

SILVERMAN, JANE ARESTY, not-for-profit organizational consultant; b. NYC, Apr. 5, 1945; d. Julian Joseph and Esther Bradford Aresty; m. Ira David Silverman, June 16, 1968 (dec. June 23, 1991); children: Jacob Louis, Rachel Emma, Sarah Julia. BA magna cum laude, Radcliffe Coll., 1967; MCP, U. Pa., 1970. Dir. of tng. The Harlan Co., N.Y.C., 1982—85; pres. Tng. Mgmt. Corp., Princeton, NJ, 1985—98; exec. dir. Assn. of Jr. Leagues Internat., N.Y.C., 1998—2002; pres. Jane Silverman and Assocs., LLC, Princeton, 2003—. Adv. com. Ctr. for Civil Soc., UCLA Sch. of Pub. Policy and Social Rsch., L.A., 1998—; nonresident fellow UCLA Sch. of Pub. Policy and Social Rsch., L.A., Calif., 1998—; mem. John W. Gardner leadership award jury Ind. Sector, Washington, 1999—2001. Editor: Housing: Supply and Affordability, Management and Control of Growth, vol. IV, 1978, vol. V, 1980. Trustee Opera Festival of NJ, Princeton, 1989—94, Princeton (NJ) Libr. Found., 2003—, Planned Parenthood Assn. of the Mercer Area, Trenton, NJ, 2003—; trustee, exec. com. Radcliffe Coll., Cambridge, Mass., 1994—99, Young Audiences of NJ, Princeton, 1986—94; internat. adv. com. New Israel Fund., 2003—; trustee Jewish Found. for Christian Rescuers (Thanks to Scandinavia), N.Y.C., 1989—93; officer Am. Jewish Com., NYC, 1996—. Recipient Nat. Disting. Leadership award, Am. Jewish Com., 2003, Phillip Forman Human Rels. award, Cen. N.J. chpt. Am. Jewish Com., 1999, Alumni award, Princeton Day Sch., 1994. Mem.: ASTD, N.J. Ctr. for Nonprofits, N.J. Soc. of Assn. Execs. (assoc.). Jewish. Avocations: travel, music, reading. Home: 118 Winant Rd Princeton NJ 08540 Office: Jane Silverman and Assocs LLC 118 Winant Rd Princeton NJ 08540 E-mail: silvermanjane@msn.com.

SILVERMAN, JONATHAN, actor; b. L.A., Aug. 5, 1966; s. Hillel Emanuel and Devora (Halaban) S. Student, U. So. Calif. Appearences include (films) Girls Just Want to Have Fun, 1985, Brighton Beach Memoirs, 1986, Caddyshack II, 1988, Stealing Home, 1988, Weekend at Bernie's, 1989, Class Action, 1991, Little Sister, 1992, Age Isn't Everything, 1992, Weekend at Bernie's II, 1993, Little Big League, 1994, Teresa's Tattoo, 1994, Two Guys Talking About Two Girls, 1994, 12 Bucks, 1998, Freak City, 1999, Just a Little Harmless Sex, 1999, Men Named Milo, Women Named Greta, 2000, The Medicine Show, 2000, The Cookout, 2004; (TV movies) Traveling Man, 1989, For Richer, For Poorer, 1992, Broadway Bound, 1992, 12:01, 1993, Hands That See, 1994, London Suite, 1996, The Inspectors, 1998, Inspectors 2: A Shred of Evidence, 2000, Bobbie's Girl, 2002, Deacons for Defense, 2003, Crazy Love, 2003, DeMarco Affairs, 2004; (TV series) Gimme a Break!, 1985-87, The Single Guy, 1995-97, (voice) Free for All, 2003; (plays) Brighton Beach Memoirs, Biloxi Blues, Broadway Bound (Helen Hays award 1988), The Illusion (Drama Lounge award 1990), Pay or Play (Drama League award), Sticks and Stones, 1994, Denial, 1998, The Odd Couple II, 1998, Freak City, 1999, Dirk and Betty, 1999, Denial, 1999. Co-founder Artists for a Free South Africa, L.A., 1989—. Mem. Young Artists United (hon. N.Y. and L.A. chpt. 1990, 91). Address: United Talent Agy Ste 500 9560 Wilshire Blvd Beverly Hills CA 90212 also: William Morris Agy 151 El Camino Dr Beverly Hills CA 90212*

SILVERMAN, JOSEPH, chemistry educator, scientist; b. N.Y.C., Nov. 5, 1922; s. Jakob and Mary (Chechick) S.; m. Joan Aline Jacks, Jan. 14, 1951; children: Joshua Henry, David Avrom. BA, Bklyn. Coll., 1944; A.M., Columbia U., 1948, PhD, 1951. Head research dept. Walter Kidde (nuclear labs.), Garden City, N.Y., 1952-54; v.p., tech. dir. RAI Research Corp., L.I. City, N.Y., 1954-59; assoc. prof. chemistry State U. N.Y., Stony Brook, 1959-60; prof. dept. materials and nuclear engring. U. Md., College Park, 1960-92, prof. emeritus, 1992—. Cons. Danish AEC, Indsl. Research Inst., Japan, Boris Kidric Inst., Yugoslavia, Bechtel Co., GPU Nuclear Corp., GE, IAEA, Vienna; disting. vis. prof. Tokyo U., 1974; gen. chmn. 2d Internat. Meeting on Radiation Processing, Miami, Fla., 1978, 3d Tokyo, 1980, hon. chmn. 6th, Ottawa, 1987; trustee Washington Inst. Values in Pub. Policy, 1981-87. Editor Internat. Jour. Applied Radiation and Isotopes, 1973-78, Trans. 1st Internat. Meetings on Radiation Processing, 1977, 3d edit., 1981; mem. editorial adv. bd. Radiation Physics and Chemistry, 1978-95. Served with AUS, 1944-46. Recipient Founders award 6th Internat. Meeting on Radiation Processing, 1987, Centennial medal U. Md. Coll. Engring., 1994; grad. rsch. fellow Brookhaven Nat. Lab., 1949-51; Guggenheim fellow, 1966-67. Fellow Nordic Soc. Radiation Chemistry and Tech., Am. Phys. Soc., Am. Nuclear Soc. (Radiation Industry award 1975); mem. Am. Chem. Soc., Sigma Xi. Home: 8101 Connecticut Ave Apt S407 Chevy Chase MD 20815-2839 Office: U Md Dept Materials Sci and Engring College Park MD 20742-2115 E-mail: jagman@umd.edu.

SILVERMAN, JOSEPH HILLEL, mathematics professor; b. N.Y.C., Mar. 27, 1955; s. Harry and Shirley (Seiner) S.; m. Susan Leslie Greenhaus, June 13, 1976; children: Deborah, Daniel, Jonathan. ScB, Brown U., 1977; MA, Harvard U., 1979, PhD, 1982. Moore instr. MIT, Cambridge, 1982-86; assoc. prof. Boston U., 1986-88; assoc. prof. math. Brown U., Providence, 1988-91, prof., 1991—, chmn., 2001—. Founder and v.p. rsch., NTRU Cryptosystems, Inc., 1997—. Author: Arithmetic of Elliptic Curves, 1986; editor: Arithmetic Geometry, 1987, Rational Points on Elliptic Curves, 1992, Advanced Topics in Arithmetic of Elliptic Curves, 1995, Diophantine Geometry (with M. Hindry), 2000. Fellow NSF, 1983-86, Sloan fellow Sloan Found., 1987, Guggenheim Found. fellow, 1998. Mem. Am. Math. Soc. Avocation: bridge. Office: Brown U Dept Math PO Box 1917 Providence RI 02912-1917 Office Phone: 401-863-1132.

SILVERMAN, KENNETH EUGENE, English educator, writer; b. NYC, Feb. 5, 1936; s. Gustave and Bessie (Goldberg) S.; children: Willa Zahava, Ethan Leigh. BA, Columbia U., 1956, MA, 1958, PhD, 1964. Instr. English U. Wyo., Laramie, 1958-59; preceptor in English Columbia U., NYC, 1962-64; prof. English, co-dir. The Biography Seminar NYU, NYC, 1964-2001. Adv. coun. Inst. Early Am. History and Culture, 1984-87. Author: Timothy Dwight, 1969, A Cultural History of the American Revolution, 1976, The Life and Times of Cotton Mather, 1984, Edgar A. Poe: Mournful and Never-ending Remembrance, 1991, Houdini!!! The Career of Ehrich Weiss, 1996, Lightning Man: The Accursed Life of Samuel F.B. Morse, 2003; editor: anthology Colonial American Poetry, 1968; compiler: Selected Letters of Cotton Mather, 1976; mem. editl. bd. Early Am Lit., 1969-72, 77-80, William and Mary Quar., 1984-87, Am. Lit. 1987-90. Recipient Bancroft prize in Am. history, 1985, Pulitzer Prize for biography, 1985, Edgar Allan Poe award Mystery Writers Am., 1992; grantee Bicentennial award NEH, 1972-74, Am. Philos. Soc., 1986, Am. Coun. Learned Socs., 1986; Guggenheim fellow, 1989-90. Mem. Am. Acad. Arts and Scis., Soc. Am. Historians, Am. Antiquarian Soc., Authors Guild, Soc. Am. Magicians. Jewish.

SILVERMAN, LEON, lawyer; b. N.Y.C., June 9, 1921; BA, Bklyn. Coll., 1942; LL.B., Yale U., 1948; postgrad., London Sch. Econs., 1948-49. Bar: N.Y. 1949. Assoc. firm Riegelman, Strasser, Schwartz & Spiegelberg, N.Y.C., 1949-53; asst. U.S. atty. So. Dist. N.Y., 1953-55; asst. dep. atty. gen. Dept. Justice, Washington, 1958-59, spl. prosecutor, 1981-82, ind. counsel investigating Sec. Labor, 1987; co-chmn. firm Fried, Frank, Harris, Shriver & Jacobson, N.Y.C., 1960—80, counsel to, 1980—. Counsel N.Y. Gov.'s Com. to Rev. N.Y. Laws and Procedure in the Area of Human Rights, 1967-68, Com. to Rev. Legis. and Jud. Salaries, 1972-73; mem. adv. com. on criminal rules to com. on rules of practice and procedure Jud. Conf. U.S.; mem. joint com. to monitor N.Y. drug laws; pres. N.Y. Legal Aid Soc., 1970-72, dir., 1966—; pres U.S. Supreme Ct. Hist. Soc., 1980-92, chmn. 1992-; spl. master Appellatte divsn. 1st dept. N.Y. Supreme Ct., 1984—. Trustee William Nelson Cromwell Found., 1983—; chmn. Legal Council for Soviet Jewery, 1987—. Recipient Judge Learned Hand Human Relations award, 1981, Emory Buckner Pub. Service medal, 1982, Judge Joseph M. Proskauer award, 1982. Mem. ABA, N.Y. State Bar Assn., Fed. Bar Assn., Am. Coll. Trial Lawyers (regent 1979—, pres. 1982-83), Am. Law Inst., Am. Judicature Soc., Practising Law Inst. (trustee), Assn. Bar City N.Y., Fed. Bar Council. Home: 16 Oak Dr Great Neck NY 11021-1810 Office: Fried Frank Harris Shriver & Jacobson 1 New York Plz 25th Fl New York NY 10004-1980

SILVERMAN, LESLIE E. federal agency administrator; b. Needham, Mass. Grad., U. Vt.; JD, Am. U.; M with distinction, Georgetown U. Bar: D.C., Mass. Law clk. U.S. Atty.'s Office; assoc. Keller and Heckman, 1990—97; labor counsel Senate Healtn, Edn., Labor and Pensions Com.; commr. Equal Opportunity Commn., Washington, 2002—. Office: EEOC 1801 L St NW Washington DC 20507

SILVERMAN, LESTER PAUL, economist, energy industry consultant; b. NYC, Feb. 28, 1947; s. Eli and Irene B. (Karp) S.; m. Janit Roslyn Smith, June 14, 1969 (dec.); children: Leigh, Stacy, Jenny; m. Patty Abramson, Jan. 7, 1995. BS in Adminstrn. and Mgmt. Sci., MS in Indsl. Adminstrn., Carnegie-Mellon U., 1969, PhD in Econs., 1973. Economist Ctr. for Naval Analyses, Arlington, Va., 1969-74; assoc. exec. dir. NAS, Washington, 1974-78; dir. policy analysis Dept. Interior, Washington, 1978-80; prin. dep. asst. sec. Dept. Energy, Washington, 1980-81; exec. v.p. Dist. Heat & Power, Inc., Washington, 1981-82; dir., head global nonprofit practice McKinsey & Co., Inc., Washington, 1982—. Author (with others) govt. report: Reducing U.S. Oil Vulnerability, 1981; editor: Population Redistribution and Public Policy, 1978; contbr. over 40 articles to profl. publs., op-ed pieces. Bd. dirs., v.p. Arena Stage, 1999—. Recipient Spl. Achievement award Dept. Interior, 1979, Outstanding Svc. award Dept. Energy, 1981. Mem. NAS (panel on natural gas stats., 1983-84, exploratory com. on future of nuclear power, 1984, alternative energy R&D com., 1989), Nat. Assembly of Health and Human Svc. Orgns. (bd. dirs., 2002-), Coun. on Excellence in Govt. (bd. dirs. 2003-), Omicron Delta Epsilon, Omicron Delta Kappa. Home: 3005 0 St NW Washington DC 20007 Office: McKinsey & Co Inc 600 14th St NW Washington DC 20005 Office Phone: 202-662-3150. Business E-Mail: les_silverman@mckinsey.com.

SILVERMAN, MARCIA, public relations executive; b. Lexington, Ky., Dec. 4, 1943; d. Harry and Rebecca (Green) S.; m. Stephen Regenstreif, Mar. 13, 1977; 1 child, Jacob Anthony. AB in Polit. Sci., U. Pa., 1965, MA in Econs., 1966. Reporter Nat. Jour., Washington, 1969-72; pub. rels. exec. J. Walter Thompson, N.Y.C., 1979-80, Ogilvy, Adams & Rinehart, Washington, 1981-95, pres., 1992-98, Ogilvy Pub. Rels. Worldwide, 1992—, pub. rels. exec., 1998—. Bd. dirs. Washington Internat Sch., 1994-95, Mex. Am. Legal Def. &

Edn. Fund, L.A., 1994-98, vice chair, 1997, Women's Campaign Fund, Washington, 1993-94. Recipient Pub. Rels. Star award Inside PR mag. Office: Ogilvy Pub Rels Worldwide 1901 L St NW Ste 300 Washington DC 20036-3506

SILVERMAN, MARK, publisher; Degree, U. Mass. Mng. editor Providence (RI) Jour.; exec. editor The Courier-Jour., Louisville, v.p. news; sr. mng. editor Gannett Suburban Newspapers, White Plains, NY, 1986—88; exec. editor Rockford (Ill.) Register Star, 1988—91, dir. Newspaper Divsn. NEWS 2000 program, 1991—96; pub., editor Detroit (Mich.) News, 1996—. Office: Detroit News 615 W Lafayette Blvd Detroit MI 48226-3197

SILVERMAN, MARTIN MORRIS BERNARD, secondary school educator; b. Boston, May 27, 1936; s. Joseph Lazarus and Sonya Lillian (Feldman) S.; m. Joseph Harvey. BS in Chemistry, U. Mass., 1960, MEd, 1962; EdM, Columbia U., 1974, EdD, 1985. Math. and sci. tchr. Northampton (Mass.) Pub. Schs., 1960-62, U.S. Dept. of Def., Korea and Bermuda, 1963-66; tchr. math, sci. N.Y.C. Bd. Edn., 1966-91. Rsch. scholar biophysics NYU, 1986—; biochemistry rsch. asst. Harvard U. Med. Sch., Boston, 1960, supr., dir. sci. fairs and competitions; cons. in field. Writer, musician, composer and performer; photographer Explorers Jour., U. Mo. Archives collection, Jour. Violin Soc. Am. Curator musical instrument collection, instrument restorer Abrons Arts Ctr., Henry Street Settlement, 2000—03. Internat. Ctr. Photography scholar, N.Y.C., 1975. Mem. Violin Soc. Am., Jour. Violin Soc. Am., Nat. Assn. Watch Clock Collectors Assn., Musical Box Soc. Internat., Mensa, Explorers Club. Home: 25 Montgomery St New York NY 10002-6557

SILVERMAN, MERVYN F. health science association administrator, consultant; BS cum laude, Washington and Lee U., 1960; MD, Tulane U., 1964; MPH, Harvard U., 1969. Cert. Am. Bd. Preventive Medicine. Physician Peace Corps, Thailand, 1965-67, regional med. dir. East Asia and the Pacific, 1967-68; spl. asst. to commr. FDA, Washington, 1969-70, dir. Office of Consumer Affairs, 1970-72; dir. health Wichita (Kans.)-Sedgwick County Dept. Cmty. Health, 1972-77; med. dir. Planned Parenthood Kans., Wichita, 1976-77; dir. health Dept. Health, San Francisco, 1977-85; health care cons. Mervyn F. Silverman & Assocs., Inc., 1985—; dir. AIDS health svcs. program Robert Wood Johnson Found., 1986-92; nat. spokesperson Am. Found. for AIDS Rsch., 1986-96, pres., also bd. dirs. Resident physician Sta. KPIX-TV, San Francisco, 1979-85; dir., prodr., host weekly health program Sta. KMPX Radio, 1980-82; sr. tech. advisor Acad. Ednl. Devel.-AIDSCOM, 1990-92; former med. advisor to bd. dirs. Golden Gate chpt. ARC, San Francisco; past vice chmn. Adv. Health Coun., State of Calif.; former assoc. clin. prof. Wichita State U.; former assoc. clin. prof. U. Hawaii; former adj. assoc. prof. Sch. Pub. Health and Tropical Medicine Tulane U.; former adj. prof. Inst. Health Policy Studies, Sch. Medicine, U. Calif., San Francisco; former mem. nat. adv. coun. Harvard AIDS Inst.; spkr., presenter in field. Author: (with others) Humanistic Perspectives in Medical Ethics, 1972, What to Do About AIDS, 1986, AIDS and Patient Management: Legal, Ethical and Social Issues, 1986, AIDS: Facts and Issues, 1986, AIDS in Children, Adolescents and Heterosexual Adults: An Interdisciplinary Approach to Prevention, 1988, others; contbg. and consulting editor Modern Medicine Publs., Mpls., 1970-75; contbg. editor Healthline, 1983-85; contbr. articles to profl. jours. Bd. dirs., vice-chmn. U.S.-China Ednl. Inst. Recipient Award for Courageous Leadership, San Francisco Found., Award of Excellence, KAIROS Support for Care Givers, Civic Achievement award Bay Area Non-Partisan Alliance, Heroes in Medicine award Internat. Assn. Physicians in AIDS Care, Pub. Health Hero award U. Calif., Berkeley, 2001; Wear Found. fellow Wichita State U., scholar Kans. Newman Coll. Mem. APHA, AMA, Omicron Delta Kappa, Delta Omega. Address: 9 Crolona Heights Dr Crockett CA 94525

SILVERMAN, MOSES, lawyer; b. Bklyn., Mar. 3, 1948; s. Bernard and Anne Silverman; m. Betty B. Robbins, Jan. 19, 1980; children: Benjamin, Rachel. AB, Colby Coll., 1969; JD, NYU, 1973. Bar: N.Y. 1974, U.S. Dist. Ct. (so. and ea. dists.) N.Y. 1974, U.S. Ct. Appeals (2d cir.) 1974, U.S. Ct. Appeals (D.C. cir.) 1977, U.S. Supreme Ct. 1977, D.C. 1982, U.S. Ct. Appeals (fed. cir.) 1985, U.S. Ct. Appeals (11th cir.) 2001, U.S. Dist. Ct. (D.C.) 2001, U.S. Ct. Appeals (9th cir.) 2002. Assoc. Paul, Weiss, Rifkind, Wharton & Garrison, NYC, 1973-81, ptnr., 1981—. Vol. U.S. Peace Corps., Istanbul, Turkey, 1969-70; bd. dirs. Legal Aid Soc., 1998; mem. bd. overseers Colby Coll., 2002—. Mem. ABA, N.Y. State Bar Assn., Assn. Bar City N.Y. Home: 7 Gracie Sq New York NY 10028-8001 Office: Paul Weiss Rifkind Wharton & Garrison 1285 Ave of Americas New York NY 10019-6028 Office Phone: 212-373-3355. Business E-Mail: msilverman@paulweiss.com.

SILVERMAN, NORMAN ALAN, cardiac surgeon; b. Boston, Dec. 19, 1946; BA, Dartmouth Coll., 1968; MD, Boston U., 1971. Prof. surgery U. Ill., Chgo., 1980-89; divsn. head Henry Ford Hosp., Detroit, 1989—; prof. surgery Case-Western Res. U., Cleve., 1992—. Contbr. 200 scientific articles to profl. jours. Lt. comdr. USPHS, 1973-75. Fellow Am. Coll. Surgeons, Am. coll. Cardiology, Am. Coll. Chest Physicians. Avocation: sailing. Office: Henry Ford Hosp 2799 W Grand Blvd Detroit MI 48202-2689 Office Phone: 313-916-2695. Business E-Mail: nsilver1@hfhs.org.

SILVERMAN, NORMAN HENRY, cardiologist, educator; b. Johannesburg, Sept. 29, 1942; came to U.S., 1972; s. Simon Cecil and Jean (Krawitz) S.; m. Heather Silverman. DSc in Medicine, U. Witwatersrand, Johannesburg, 1985, postgrad. Diplomate Am. Bd. Pediatrics. Asst. prof. pediatrics Stanford U., Palo Alto, Calif., 1974-75; asst. prof. pediatrics U. Calif., San Francisco, 1975, assoc. prof. radiology, 1979, prof., 1985—2002; prof. pediatrics Stanford U. Med. Ctr., 2002—. Co-author: Two Dimensional Echocardiography, 1982, Congenital Heart Disease, 1990; author: Pediatric Echocardiography, 1993; co-editor: Fetal Cardiology, 2003. Lt. South African Def. Force, 1968-69. Grantee March of Dimes, 1977-79, Am. Heart Assn., 1978-80, 90-92. Fellow Am. Coll. Cardiology, Coll. Physicians South Africa, Soc. Pediatric Rsch., Am. Pediatric Soc. Achievements include research in echocardiography of congenital heart disease in infants and children; fetal echocardiography and treatment. Office: Stanford U Med Ctr 750 Welch Rd #305 Palo Alto CA 94304 E-mail: norm.silverman@stanford.edu.

SILVERMAN, OZZIE, consulting strategist; b. Montreal, Que., Can., Jan. 30, 1939; s. Louis and Fanny (Black) S.; m. Sheela Marsha Zangwill, Aug. 22, 1962; children: Caroline, Marjorie. BSME, McGill U., Montreal, Que., 1963, diploma in mgmt., 1968, MBA, 1969. Cert. Que. Order of Engrs. Supr. quality control engrng. Pratt and Whitney, Montreal, 1964-68; sr. mktg. rschr. United Aircraft, Montreal, 1969-70; asst. chief internat. Dept. Industry, Trade and Commerce, Ottawa, Ont., Can., 1972-77; dir. industry projects Ministry of State for Sci. and Tech., Ottawa, 1978-85; dir. strategic techs. policy Industry, Sci. and Tech. Can., Ottawa, 1986-91; dir. gen. sci. strategy and innovation policy Industry Can., Ottawa, 1992-98; cons. ptnr. SECOR Cons., Inc., Ottawa, 1998—. Chmn. com. for sci. and tech. policy Orgn. for Econ. Coop. and Devel., Paris, 1995-98. Avocation: inuit and japanese graphic art. Home: 112 Pigeon Terr Ottawa ON Canada K1V 9H7 Office: 255 Albert St Ste 500 Ottawa ON Canada K1P 6A9 E-mail: osilverman@secor.ca.

SILVERMAN, RICHARD BRUCE, chemist, educator, biochemist; b. Phila., May 12, 1946; s. Philip and S. Ruth (Simon) S.; . Barbara Jean Kesner, Jan. 9, 1983; children: Matthew, Margaret, Philip. BS, Pa. State U., 1968; MA, Harvard U., 1972, PhD, 1974. From asst. prof. to prof. Northwestern U., Evanston, Ill., 1976—86, prof., 1986—, mem. Inst. Neurosci., 1990—. Mem. adv. panel NIH, Bethesda, Md., 1981, 83, 85, 87-91, 2001; expert analyst CHEMTRACTS; scientific adv. bd. Influx, Inc., 1998-2003, Protez Pharml., 2004—, Synchem, 2003—. NIGMS adv. coun., 2002; cons. in field. Mem. editl. bd.: Jour. Enzyme Inhibition, 1988—2002, Archives Biochem. & Biophys., 1993—, Jour. Medicinal Chemistry, 1995—2000, Enzyme Inhibition and Medicinal Chemistry, 2002—, Letters in Drug Design & Discovery, 2003—, Bioorganic & Medicinal Chemistry, 2003—, Bioorganic & Medicinal Chemistry Letters, 2003—, Current Enzyme Inhibition, 2004—. Mem. adv. bd. Ill. Math. & Scis. Acad., 1988. With U.S. Army, 1969-71. Recipient Career Devel. award USPHS, 1982-87, E. LeRoy Hall award for tchg. excellence, 1999, Northwestern Alumni Tchg. award, 2000; postdoctoral fellow Brandeis U., Waltham, Mass., 1974-76, DuPont Young Faculty fellow, 1976, Alfred P. Sloan Found. fellow, 1981-85; grantee various govt. and pvt. insts., 1976—. Arthur C. Cope. Sr. scholar ACS, 2003. Fellow: AAAS; mem.: Am. Chem. Soc. (nat. elected nominating com. divns. biol. chemistry 1993—96, long-range planning com. divsn. med. chem. 1999—2002), Am. Soc. Biochem. Molecular Biology, Am. Inst. Chemists. Avocations: family, golf. Office: Northwestern U Dept Chemistry 2145 Sheridan Rd Evanston IL 60208-3113

SILVERMAN, ROBERT ALAN, college official, historian; b. Phila., Dec. 22, 1947; s. Milton Edward and Rhoda (Pasternack) S.; m. Fran Stukelman, Mar. 30, 1969; 1 child, David. BS, Drexel U., 1969; MA, Harvard U., 1973, PhD, 1977. Fin. analyst Harvard U., Cambridge, Mass., 1977-78, v.p. Harvard real estate, 1978-84, dir. planning, 1984-88; sr. v.p. Watch Hill Co., 1988-89; mng. dir. Keystone Advisors, Inc., Cambridge, 1990-93; v.p. adminstrn. and fin. Emerson Coll., Boston, 1993—. Cons. in field. Author: Law and Urban Growth, 1981; editor: The Corporate Real Estate Handbook, 1987. With U.S. Army, 1969-72. Jewish. Office: Emerson Coll 120 Boylston St Boston MA 02116-4624

SILVERMAN, ROBERT JOSEPH, lawyer; b. Mpls., Apr. 4, 1942; s. Maurice and Toby (Goldstein) S.; 1 child, Adam Graham-Silverman; m. Suzanne M. Brown; 1 child, Thomas B. BA, U. Minn., 1964, JD, 1967. Bar: Minn. 1967. Assoc. Dorsey & Whitney, Mpls., 1967-72, of counsel, 1972—2001. Lectr. William Mitchell Coll. Law, St. Paul, 1977-78, Hamline Law Sch., St. Paul, 1990-96, Minn. Continuing Legal Edn., Mpls, 1985-01. Bd. dirs. Courage Ctr., Golden Valley, Minn., 1978-84, 85-95, v.p., 1983-86, pres., 1988-89. With USAR, 1967-73. Mem. ABA, Minn. Bar Assn., Hennepin County Bar Assn., Am. Coll. Real Estate Lawyers. Jewish. Office: Dorsey & Whitney 50 S 6th St Ste 1500 Minneapolis MN 55402-1498 E-mail: silverman.robert@dorseylaw.com.

SILVERMAN, SAM MENDEL, physicist, lawyer; b. NYC, Nov. 16, 1925; s. Moshe Aaron and Gitel (Korenbaum) S.; m. Jacqueline Greenberg, Sept. 12, 1948 (div. Apr. 1965); children: Ann, William, Nancy; m. Phyllis Rolfe, June 26, 1966; children: Gila, Aaron. BChE, CCNY, 1945; PhD, Ohio State U., 1952; JD, Suffolk U., 1982. Bar: Mass. 1982, U.S. Dist. Ct. Mass. 1982, U.S. Ct. Appeals (1st cir.) 1982, N.Y. 1983, U.S. Supreme Ct. 1986. Assoc. Ohio State U., Columbus, 1952-55; asst. prof. chem. physics U. Toledo, 1955-57; rsch. physicist Air Force Cambridge Rsch. Labs., Bedford, Mass., 1957-80, chief polar atmospheric processes br. and dir. geopole obs., 1963-74, cons., 1980—. Vis. rsch. assoc. Queens U., Belfast, 1963-64; vis. prof. Osmania U., Hyderabad, India, 1965-66; mem. adv. bd. Inst. Space and Atmospheric Studies, U. Sask. (Can.), 1965-69; sr. rsch. physicist Boston Coll., 1981-97; co-chmn. interdivisional commn. history Internat. Assn. Geomagnetism and Aeronomy, 1987-91; lectr. palliative care courses, Poland, 1993, 94, 2000. Contbr. articles to profl. jours. Mem. Town Meeting Lexington, Mass., 1973-79, 84—; elected mem. Lexington Dem. Town Com., 1996—; legal counsel Internat. Work Group on Death, Dying and Bereavement. With USAAF, 1945-46. Recipient Thurgood Marshall award, com. pub. counsel svcs. Mass. Pub. Defender's Agy., 2002. Fellow Am. Phys. Soc., Explorers Club; mem. Am. Geophys. Union (editor History of Geophysics newsletter 1983-91), Internat. Work Group on Death, Dying and Bereavement. Home: 18 Ingleside Rd Lexington MA 02420-2522 Office Phone: 781-861-0368. E-mail: smpr@rcn.com.

SILVERMAN, STANLEY WAYNE, chemical company executive; b. Phila., June 18, 1947; m. Ellen J. Seligsohn, June 7, 1970. BSChemE, Drexel U., 1969, MBA, 1974; AMP, Harvard U., 1989. Process engr. Atlantic Richfield Co., Phila., 1969-71, PQ Corp., Phila., 1971-74, mgr. oper. planning Valley Forge, Pa., 1974-76, product mgr., 1976-80, mktg. mgr., 1980-82, nat. sales mgr., 1982-84, pres. Nat. Silicates Ltd. subs. Toronto, Ont., Can., 1984-87, pres. ind. chem. group Valley Forge, 1987-90, exec. v.p., COO, 1990-99, pres., CEO, bd. dirs., 2000—; dir. C&D Techs., 2003—. Chmn. adv. coun. Drexel U. Coll. Engring, 1991-93, alumni bd. govs., 1998, bd. trustees, 2000—; bd. dirs. Phila. Acad., Inc., 1999—2004. Named among 100 most accomplished grads. Drexel U., 1992; recipient Alumni Achievement award Drexel U., 1995. Mem. Soap and Detergent Assn. (bd. dirs. 2004—, chmn. bd. 2004—), Am. Chemistry Coun. (bd. dirs. 2001—). Office: PQ Corp 1200 W Swedesford Rd Berwyn PA 19312-1078

SILVERMAN, VICTORIA LILLIAN, consultant, fundraiser, cultural organization administrator; b. St. Louis, July 2, 1961; d. Thomas and Eva Alice (Hasko) Schiff; m. Lloyd Alan Silverman, Dec. 31, 1995; children: Anyu Isabella, Emmanuelle Snow. BA, Washington U., 1983; postgrad., St. Louis U., 1985-86. Assoc. dir. devel. Jewish Cmty. Ctr., St. Louis, 1983-85; assoc. dir. engring. Washington U., 1986-89; dir. engring. fund Stanford (Calif.) U., 1989-92; dir. major gifts and planned giving U. Calif., Santa Barbara, 1992-95; v.p. devel., exec. dir. found. St. Francis Med. Ctr., Santa Barbara, 1995; dir. devel. Am. Film Inst., L.A., 1995—2001; v.p. external affairs St. Louis Symphony Orch., 2001—03; prin. VLS Strategies, Inc., 2003—; v.p. Internat. Mus. of Women, 2004—. Cons. Stanford Engring. Sch., 1992, COCA, St. Louis, 2002—03, various orgns. Bd. dirs. Santa Barbara Ballet, 1990-92; vol. fundraiser Walter Capps for Congress, Santa Barbara, 1991. Mem. Coun. Advancement Support Edn. (presentor 1992—, conf. dir. 1995). Democrat. Jewish. Avocations: percussionist, dance and film enthusiast. Office: Ste 460 101 Howard St San Francisco CA 94119 Office Phone: 415-543-4669.

SILVERMAN, WARREN, physician; b. N.Y.C., Nov. 16, 1954; s. Leon and Ruth S.; m. Jean Marie Ogburn, Apr. 11, 1981 (div. Sept. 1990); 1 child, Arone Yacov; m. Elena Gennadievna Kiyatkina, Oct. 13, 1997; children; Inessa, Danielle Nicole, Samantha Leah. BS in Biology, Rensselaer Polytech Inst., 1978; MD, Albany Med. Coll., 1978. Bd. cert. internal medicine, occupational medicine, forensic medicine, cert. med. invest. Med. dir. Ocrancoke (N.C.) Health Ctr., 1981-85; asst. prof. Albany Med. Coll., 1985-87; dir. emergency dept. Cmty. Hosp., Cobleskill, N.Y., 1989-91; med. dir. Workplace Health & Safety Assn., Latham, N.Y., 1986-95, dir., 1995-97, Access Case Mgmt. Svcs., Latham, N.Y., 1998—, Access Health Systems, Latham, NY, 1999—2002. Profl. adv. bd. Ctr. for Disabled, Albany, 1994-2000; med. review officer MROCC, 1996—, N.Y. Dept. of Labor, Safety and Health Consultation Code Rule 59; exec. dir. Northeast N.Y. Fed. Safety & Health Coun., Albany, 1998—; sr. aviation med. examiner FAA, Latham, 1989—; med. dir. N.Y.S. PPO Corvel Corp., 2000—; cons. in field. Editor Nat. Safety Data Sheets, 1989-91. Exec. dir. Theater Dance Network, Voorheesville, N.Y., 1998-2002; med. officer Civil Air Patrol, Albany, 1988-91; dir. Voohheesville Cmty. Sch. Found., 1990. Lt. comdr. USPHS, 1981-85. Fellow Am. Coll. Forensic Medicine, Am. Coll. Forensic Examiners; mem. Am. Coll. Occupational & Environ. Medicine, Internat. Soc. Police Surgeons, Am. Bd. Internal Medicine. Jewish. Home: 547 New Salem Rd Voorheesville NY 12186-4829 Office: Access Health Systems 776A Watervliet Shaker Rd Latham NY 12110-2296

SILVERS, GERALD THOMAS, retired publishing executive; b. Cin., Aug. 26, 1937; s. Steve Allen and Tina Mae (Roberts) S.; m. Ann Gregory Woodward, July 25, 1964. BA, U. Ky., 1960. Asst. rsch. svcs. mgr. Cin. Enquirer, 1963-72, rsch. svcs. dir., 1972-74, rsch. dir., 1974-90, v.p. mktg. svcs., 1990-94, v.p. market devel., 1994—2003; ret., 2003. Mem. U. Ky. Devel. Coun., Lexington, 1986—; trustee Neediest Kids of All, 1991—; mem. region 5 exec. com. Ohio Sch. to Work, 1997-2000; mem. corps. com. St. Elizabeth Med. Ctr. Found., 1998; mem. bd. overseers Taft Mus. Art, 1999—, treas., bd. govs., 2002--. 1st lt. U.S. Army, 1960-62. Recipient Thomas H. Copeland award of merit, 1991. Mem. U. Ky. Alumni Assn. Cin. Chpt. (pres. 1985), Newspaper Rsch. Coun. (pres. 1985,86), Internat. Newspaper Market Assn., Am. Mktg. Assn., Am. Art Soc. Cin. (pres. 1999-2001). Presbyterian. Home: 229 Watch Hill Rd Fort Mitchell KY 41011-1822

SILVERS, ROBERT B. editor; b. NY, Dec. 31, 1929; s. James J. and Rose (Roden) S. AB, U. Chgo., 1947; cert., Ecole de Sci. Politiques, Paris, 1956. Paris editor Paris Rev., 1954-59; asst. editor Harpers Mag., N.Y.C., 1959-63; co-editor N.Y. Rev. of Books, N.Y.C., 1963—. Editor: Writing in America, 1962, Hidden Histories of Science, 1995, Doing It: Five Performing Arts, 2001; co-editor: The Legacy of Isaiah Berlin, 2001, Striking Terror: America's New War, 2002. Trustee NY Pub. Libr., 1997—, Ditchley Found., 1996—, Am. Acad. in Rome, 1998-. Decorated Legion d'Honneur. Mem. Am. Acad. Arts and Scis., Coun. Fgn. Rels., Century Assn. Office: NY Rev of Books 1755 Broadway New York NY 10019-3743

SILVERS, SALLY, choreographer, performing company executive; b. Greeneville, Tenn., June 19, 1952; d. Herbert Ralston and Sara Elizabeth (Buchanan) S.; life ptnr. Bruce Erroll Andrews. BA in Dance and Polit. Sci., Antioch Coll., 1975. Artistic dir. Sally Silvers & Dancers, N.Y.C., 1980—. Mem. faculty Leicester Poly., 1986, 87, 89, summer choreography project Bennington Coll., 1988-92, Chisenhale Dance Space, London, 1989, 91, Am. Dance Festival, Durham, N.C., 1990, 92; guest tchr. European Dance Devel. Ctr., Arnhem, The Netherlands, 1992—. Choreographer (performances) Politics of the Body Microscope of Conduct, 1980, Social Movement, 1981, Connective Tissue, 1981, Less Time You Know Praxis, 1981, Don't No Do And This, 1981, Lack of Entrepreneurial Thrift, 1982, Celluoid Sally and Mr. E, 1982, Mutate, 1982, Being Red Enough, 1982, Disgusting, 1982, Bedtime at the Reformatory, 1982, Eat the Rich, 1982, They Can't Get It in the Shopping Cart, 1982, Blazing Forceps, 1982, And Find Out Why, 1983, Choose Your Weapons, 1984, Extend the Wish for Entire, 1985, No Best Better Way, 1985, Every All Which is Not Us, 1986, Swaps Ego Say So, 1986, Be Careful Now, You Know Sugar Melts in Water, 1987, Fact Confected, 1987, Both, Both, 1987, Tizzy boost, 1988, Moebius, 1988, Whatever Ever, 1989, Get Tough, Sports and Divertissement, 1989, Flap, 1989, Swan's Crayon, 1989, Fanfare Tripwire, 1990, Harry Meets Sally, 1990, Along the Skid Mark of Recorded History, 1990, Matinee Double-You, 1991, Grand Guignol, 1991, Dash Dash Slang Plural Plus, 1992, The Bubble Cut, 1992, Vigilant Corsage, 1992, Oops Fact, 1992, Small Room, 1993, Exwhyzee, 1993, Elegy, 1993, Now That It Is Now, 1994, Give Em Enough Rope, Swoon Noir, 1994, Radio Rouge, 1995, Braceletizing, 1995, Hush Comet, 1995, Bite the Pillow, 1995, Pandora's Cake Stain, 1996, Secrets Of, 1997, HUSHHUSH, Sugar Raised, 1998 Capture, Teddy Growl, 1999, Storming Heaven, 2000, Swaphot Trouble, 2001, Strike Me Lightning, 2002, Spaced Out, 2003, Dreams Do Come True, 2004, Dang Me, 2004; video and performance filmmaker: (films) Little Lieutenant, 1993 (Silver); N.Y. Dance on Camera Festival, Mechanics of the Brain, 1997; co-author: (book) Resurgant New Writings By Women, 1992; contbr. articles to profl. jours. Grantee Nat. Endowment Arts, 1987, 89, 90, 91, 98, Jerome Found., 1993, 1996, Meet the Composer N.Y. Found. for the Arts, 1995; Guggenheim Found. fellow, 1988; Found. Contemporary Performance Arts, 2001. Mem. Segue Found. (bd. dirs. Segue Performance Space 1992-2002). Avocations: reading, writing, art events, costume design. Home: 303 E 8th St Apt 4F New York NY 10009-5212

SILVERS, WILLYS KENT, geneticist; b. NYC, Jan. 12, 1929; s. Lewis Julian and Miriam Elizabeth (Rosenzweig) Silvers; m. Abigail M. Adams, Sept. 29, 1956; children: Deborah Elizabeth, Willys Kent. BA, Johns Hopkins U., 1950; PhD, U. Chgo., 1954. Assoc. staff scientist Jackson Lab., Bar Harbor, Maine, 1956-57; assoc. mem. Wistar Inst., Phila., 1957-65; mem. faculty U. Pa. Med. Sch., 1965—, prof. genetics, 1967-98, prof. emeritus, 1998—. Mem. allergy and immunology study sect. NIH, 1962—66, adv. bd. primate rsch. ctrs., 1968—71; mem. com. cancer immunobiology Nat. Cancer Inst., 1974—78; bd. sci. overseers Jackson Lab., Bar Harbor, 1980—89. Author: The Immunobiology of Transplantation, 1971, The Coat Colors of Mice: A Model for Mammalian Gene Action and Interaction, 1979; mem. editl. bd. Transplantation, 1963—71, Jour. Exptl. Zoology, 1965—70, 1981—86, Jour. Immunology, 1973—77, Jour. Reticuloendothelial Soc., 1974—77; contbr. articles to profl. jours. Mem.: Am. Genetic Assn. (coun. 1980—83, pres. 1983). Home: 210 Millcreek Rd Ardmore PA 19003-1506 Office: U Pa Dept Genetics Sch Medicine Philadelphia PA 19104 Personal E-mail: wsilvers@aol.com.

SILVERSTEIN, ARTHUR, publishing executive; Controller and CFO Advance Publs., Inc., S.I. Office: Advance Publs Inc 950 Fingerboard Rd Staten Island NY 10305-1453

SILVERSTEIN, BARBARA ANN, conductor, artistic director; b. Phila., July 24, 1947; d. Charles and Selma (Brenner) S.; m. Bernard J. Taylor II, Aug. 19, 1978. Student, Bennington Coll., 1965-67; BMus, Phila. Coll. Performing Arts, 1970; MA, U. Del., 1997. Assoc. music dir. Suburban Opera Co., Chester, Pa., 1967-75; asst. condr. Toledo Opera Assn., 1975-76; asst. condr., coach Curtis Inst. Music, Phila., 1973-77; asst. condr. Phila. Lyric Opera, 1971-74, Des Moines Opera Festival, Indianola, Iowa, 1974-78; music dir., condr. Savoy Co., Phila., 1977-80, Miss. Opera, Jackson, 1979-82; artistic dir., condr. Pa. Opera Theater, Phila., 1976-93; guest condr. Anchorage Opera, 1982, Opera Del., Wilmington, 1981, 83, Utah Festival Opera Co., 1993-96, Lyric Opera Kansas City, 1995—, Opera Roanoke, Va., 1995, 98, Hollins U., 1999; mng. editor Epotec Inc., 1999-2000, dir. comm., 2000—01; prof. English U. Del., Ursinus, 1996—. Recipient alumni award U. of Arts. Mem. Am. Fedn. Musicians, Jusic Fund Soc., Pa. Coun. on the Arts (adv. panel 1987-90, OPERA Am. (bd. dirs. 1987-93, exec. com. 1988-93). Jewish. Avocations: scuba diving, reading.

SILVERSTEIN, JONATHAN CHARLES, surgeon, researcher; s. Gerald Ellis and Mickie Silverstein; m. Tracey Anne Silverstein; children: Jacob Anthony, Jessica Lynn, Joshua Andrew. BS, U. Ill., 1986; MD, Wash. U., 1990; MS, Harvard Sch. Pub. Health, 1998. Cert. Am. Bd. Surgery, 1997. Dir. ctr. clin. info. U. Chgo. Hosps., 2001—; asst. prof. surgery U. Chgo., 2001—. Contbr. articles to profl. jours. Jr. bd. mem. Dystonia Med. Rsch. Found. Grantee, Nat. Libr. Medicine/NIH, 1998—2002, 2000, 2003—, The U. Chgo. Provost's Program for Academic Tech. Innovation, 2002—03. Fellow: ACS (mem. regents com. informatics 2001); mem.: Am. Med. Informatics Assn., Chgo. Surg. Soc., Assn Surg. Edn., Am. Med. Soc., Ill. Surg. Soc., Biomedical Libr. Informatics Rev. Com. Avocations: skiing, rowing, percussion. Office: The U Chgo Hosps 5841 S Maryland Ave MC 6051 Chicago IL 60637-1470 E-mail: silverstein@post.harvard.edu.

SILVERSTEIN, JOSEPH HARRY, conductor, musician; b. Detroit, Mar. 21, 1932; s. Bernard and Ida (Katz) S.; m. Adrienne Shufro, Apr. 27; children: Bernice, Deborah, Marc. Student, Curtis Inst. Music, 1945-50; D (hon.), Tufts U., 1971, R.I. U., 1980, Boston Coll., 1981, New Eng. Conservatory, 1986, Susquehanna, 1996, Brigham Young U., 1998. Violinist Houston Symphony Orch., Phila. Orch.; concertmaster Denver Symphony Orch., Boston Symphony Orch.; formerly chmn. string dept. New Eng. Conservatory Music; also chmn. faculty Berkshire Music Sch.; mem. faculty Boston U. Sch. Music, Yale U. Sch. Music; music dir. Boston Symphony Chamber Players, Boston U. Symphony Orch., Chautauqua (N.Y.) Instn., 1987—; interim music dir. Toledo Symphony Orch.; prin. guest condr. Balt. Symphony Orch., 1981; condr. Utah Symphony, music dir., 1983—, condr. laureate, 1998—; acting music dir. Fla. Philharm., 2001—. Mem. faculty Longy Sch., Curtis Inst.; artistic advisor Winnepeg and Aartford Symphonies. Recipient Silver medal Queen Elizabeth of Belgium Internat. contest, 1959, Naumber Found. award, 1960; named one of ten outstanding young men Boston C. of C., 1962. Fellow Am. Acad. Arts and Scis.; mem. Chamber Music Soc. Lincoln Ctr. (artist). Office: Box 1012 Stockbridge MA 01262 E-mail: joeyviolin@aol.com.

SILVERSTEIN, LARRY A. real estate developer; m. Klara Silverstein; children: Roger, Lisa, Sharon. Grad., NYU, 1952; JD, Brooklyn Law Sch. Bar: N.Y. Pres. Silverstein Properties, Inc., N.Y.C.; owner 529 Fifth Ave., 570 Seventh Ave., One River Place, Two River Place, 120 Wall St., 120 Broadway, Seven World Trade Ctr.; 99 year leaseholder World Trade Ctr., 2001—. Gov., past chmn. Real Estate Bd. N.Y.; founder, chmn. emeritus NYU Real Estate Inst.; chmn. Realty Found. Trustee NYU, vice chmn. bd. trustees; trustee South St. Seaport Mus., Mus. Jewish Heritage. Avocations: classical music, yachting. Office: Silverstein Properties Inc 521 Fifth Ave New York NY 10175*

SILVERSTEIN, LEONARD A. lawyer; b. Mobile, Ala., Apr. 18, 1958; s. Burton Howard and Fannye Mitchell Silverstein; m. Ellen Sue Frauenthal, May 25, 1986; children: Andrew, Laura, Anna. BA magna cum laude, Vanderbilt U., Nashville, 1980; JD, Vanderbilt U., 1983. Bar: Ga. 1983. Assoc./ptnr. Powell Goldstein Frazer & Murphy LLP, Atlanta, 1983—94; ptnr. McKenna Long & Aldridge LLP, Atlanta, 1994—. Mem. Ga. Biomed. Partnership, Atlanta, 2002—; mem., biosciences exec. com. Met. Atlanta C. of C., 2002—. Contbr. articles to profl. jours.; assoc. mng. editor, Vanderbilt Law Rev., 1982—83. Pres. Vanderbilt U. Alumni Club, Atlanta, 1991; co-pres. Bach n' Rollers, Divsn. of The Atlanta Symphony Assocs., 1992—93; bd. mem. and exec. com. mem. Zoo Atlanta, 1996—2001, bd. mem., 2003, Am.-Israel C. of C., S.E. Region, Atlanta, 1995—; bd. mem. and exec. com. mem. Am. Jewish Com., Atlanta, 1999—; bd. of trustees The Atlanta Symphony Assocs., 1992—93. Recipient IPO Rainmaker, IPO Counsel - The Corp. Fin. Inst., 1996. Mem.: Vanderbilt U. Alumni Assn. (bd. dirs. 1992—96), Ga. Bar Assn. (vice chair/chair elect of securities subcom. 2001—02), Atlanta Bar Assn. Achievements include patents pending for Reloadable Rights Plan for Preferred and Common Stock Rights Plans. Avocations: triathlons, golf. Office: McKenna Long & Aldridge LLP 303 Peachtree St Ste 5300 Atlanta GA 30308 Office Phone: 404-527-4390. Business E-Mail: lsilverstein@mckennalong.com.

SILVERSTEIN, LOUIS, art director, designer, editor; b. Bklyn., Oct. 10, 1919; s. Hyman and Yetta (Brodsky) S.; m. Helen Abby Becker, May 23, 1951; children: Jamie Richard (dec.), Anne Leith. B.F.A., Pratt Inst., Bkyln., 1940; MA credit, Inst. of Design, Chgo., 1948-50. Art. dir. Denhard & Stewart Advt., N.Y.C., 1942-43, 46-47; art. dir. Amerika (Russian lang. mag. distbn. USSR), Dept. State Publs., N.Y.C., 1947-48; promotion art dir. N.Y. Times, N.Y.C., 1952-67, corporate art dir., 1967-85, asst. mng. editor, 1969-85; cons. art director N.Y.C., 1985—; designer, cons. various newspapers, mags., U.S. and fgn. lectr. Am. Press Inst., Reston, Va., 1978-85; tchr. Sch. Visual Arts, N.Y.C., 1958-59; lectr. in field. Bd. dirs. Am. Inst. Graphic Arts, N.Y.C., 1958-59, Soc. Publ. Designers, 1976-78; cons. Toronto Star, 1988—; founder Louis Silverstein Design Assn.; lectr. Ctr. Ind. Journalism, Prague, Czechoslovakia, 1991; cons. art dir.-editor La Nación, Buenos Aires, 1997—; design cons. Coun. of Fgn. Rels., 1998—, Internat. Herald Tribune, Paris, 2000; designer, cons., editor Coun. on Fgn. Rels., N.Y.C., 1999—, The Nairobi (Kenya) Nation, 2000; cons., designer World Econ. Forum, Davos, Switzerland, 2000—, Agha Khan Found. Nation Newspaper Chain, Chantilly, France, Nairobi, Kenya, 2000—. Co-author: America's Taste, 1961; editor, art dir.: The Earth Times, 1993—, exec. editor, 1994—; exhibited in group shows and galleries, 1951—, Am. Fedn. Arts, 1963, USIA Exhbn., USSR, 1964; designer film strips Am. Fedn. Labor, 1950-52; one-man shows include Cooper Union, 1988, U. Montreal, 1988, Walker Art Ctr., Mpls.; author: Newspaper Design for the Times, 1989; design cons.: The Hill, 1994—, The American, 1996. Served with USAF, 1943-46 Recipient Spl. Gold award N.Y. Times Op-Ed Page, N.Y. Arts Dirs. Club, 1972, Hall of Fame, 1984, Gold Medal Lifetime Achievement award Soc. Publ. Designers, N.Y.C., 1984, Am. Inst. Graphic Arts Design Leadership award, Spl. medal for best design of Am. publs., 1989, Pulitzer prize nominee, 1984, 94, numerous awards Art Dir. Clubs, other profl. groups. Mem. Alliance Graphique Internationale, N.Y. Art Dirs. Club (bd. dirs. 1978-80, 82-84, 86—), Internat. Soc. Newspaper Designers (2001 Lifetime Svc. award), Am. Abstract Artists. Avocations: tennis; amateur poker. Home: 54 Remsen St Brooklyn NY 11201-2304 also: 36 Highland Rd Southampton NY 11968-3612 E-mail: helenabby7@aol.com.

SILVERSTEIN, MARTIN ELLIOT, surgeon, consultant, writer; b. N.Y.C., Sept. 6, 1922; s. Louis and Ethel (Statman) S.; m. Mabelle A. Cremer, Dec. 10, 1962. AB cum laude, Columbia U., 1945; MD, N.Y. Med. Coll., 1948; D of Mil. Medicine and Surgery (hon.), Uniformed Svcs. U. for Health Scis., 2003. Instr. bacteriology N.Y. Med. Coll., 1953-57, asst. to dean for clin. scis., 1953-58, instr. surgery, 1953-55, asst. dean, 1958, assoc. dean, 1959—62; asst. vis. surgeon Bird S. Coler Hosp., N.Y.C., 1953-57, assoc. vis. surgeon, 1957-60; asst. vis. surgeon Met. Hosp., N.Y.C., 1953-57, assoc. vis. surgeon, 1957-60; asst. attending surgeon Flower and 5th Ave. Hosps., N.Y.C., 1953-57; asst. attending surgeon Monorah Med. Ctr. U. Kans. Sch. Medicine, N.Y.C., 1963-65, exec. dir. Monorah Med. Ctr. Kansas City, 1963-65, exec. dir. Danciger Inst. for Health Scis., 1963-66, chmn. dept. exptl. surgery Danciger Inst. for Health Scis., 1963-66; chmn. dept. Surgery Menorah Med. Ctr. U. Kans. Sch. Medicine Affiliate, Kansas City, 1963-66; assoc. clin. prof. surgery U. Kans. Sch. Medicine, Kansas City, 1966-67; surgeon courtesy staff N.Y. Infirmary, 1969; surgeon Grand Canyon Med. Group and Hosp., 1969-70; chief sect. on surgery of trauma, dept. surgery U. Ariz. Coll. Med., Tucson, 1974-80, adj. assoc. prof. optical scis., 1979-83, assoc. prof. surgery, 1974-83, dir. quality assurance Univ. Hosp., 1983-84, rsch. prof. family and community medicine, internat. medicine, 1984-85, rsch. prof. surgical biology, 1984-85; sr. fellow in sci. and tch. Ctr. for Strategic and Internat. Studies Georgetown U., Washington, 1983-87. Pres. Claude Gips Found. Inc., N.Y.C., 1967-93; disting. vis. prof. Uniformed Svcs. U. Health Scis., 1984, adj. prof. surgery, 1999—; clin. prof. surgery F. Edward Hebert Sch. Medicine, 1984-99; disting. vis. prof. Tulane U. Med. Sch., 1984; mem. internat. adv. bd. Univ. Microfilms Internat. Collections on Terrorism, 1987—; internat. cons. Disaster Mgmt. and Disaster Medicine, Australia, India, others, 1983—; gov. emeritus Internat. Coun. for Computer Comm., 1996—, exec. com., v.p., 1972-92; bd. rep. Am. Coll. Nuclear Med., 2001—. Author: Disaster: Your Right to Survive, 1991; mem. editorial bd. Terrorism, 1976—, Prehosp. and Disaster Medicine, 1989—; assoc. editor Jour. Prehosp. Care, 1984-85; contbr. articles to profl. jours. With U.S. Army, 1943-45; lt. (j.g.) USNR, 1946-53. Fgn. fellow NSF, 1974. Fellow ACS (chmn. Ariz. State com. on trauma 1979-84), Am. Assn. for Surgery of Trauma, Am. Coll. Emergency Physicians, Am. Coll. Gastroenterology, Am. Coll. Nuc. Medicine (bd. reps. 2001—); mem. World Assn. for Emergency and Disaster Medicine (exec. com. 1987-92), Critical Care Soc., Internat. Coun. Computer Comm. (co-founder).

SILVERSTEIN, MARTIN J. ambassador; b. N.Y.C. married; 6 children. BA in Polit. Sci., Rutgers Coll., 1976; JD, Temple U., 1979. Bar: Pa., N.J., U.S. Ct. Internat. Trade, U.S. Ct. Customs and Patent Appeals. Founder Martin J. Silverstein and Assocs.; U.S. amb. to Uruguay Dept. State, Washington, 2001—. Mem. Fed. Jud. Nominating Commn., Pa. Active M.D. Anderson Cancer Ctr., Lower Merion Hist. Soc., U.S. Negro Coll. Fund, Phila. C. of C.; bd. mem. Vietnam Vets. Com. for Better Legislation. Recipient Citizens Commendation for Bravery, Phila. Police Dept. Mem.: Internat. Rep. Inst., Am. Fgn. Svc. Assn., Ctr. for Security Policy, Fgn. Policy Rsch. Inst., Am. Enterprise Inst., Heritage Found., World Affairs Coun. Office: DOS Amb 3360 Montevideo Pl Washington DC 20521

SILVERSTONE, ALICIA, actress; b. San Francisco, Oct. 4, 1976; d. Monty and Didi Silverstone. Stage debut in Carol's Eve at Met Theater, L.A.; starred in three Aerosmith videos, including Cryin', Amazing, Crazy; actress (films): The Crush, 1993, True Crime, 1995, Le Nouveau Monde, 1995, Hideaway, 1995, Clueless, 1995, The Babysitter, 1995, Batman & Robin, 1997, Blast from the Past, 1999, Love's Labour Lost, 2000, Scorched, 2002, Global Heresy, 2002, Scooby-Doo 2: Monsters Unleashed, 2004; actress, prodr.(film) Excess Baggage, 1997; exec. prodr. (TV Series) Braceface, 2001; appeared in TV programs including Torch Song, 1993, Scattered Dreams, 1993, The Cool and the Crazy, 1994; appeared in TV series: The Wonder Years, 1992, Braceface (voice only), 2001, Miss Match, 2003-. Office: c/o Innovative Artists 1999 Ave of the Stars #2850 Los Angeles CA 90067*

SILVERSTONE, DAVID EDWARD, ophthalmologist; b. NYC, Feb. 16, 1948; s. Sidney Milton and Estelle (Cohen) S.; m. Linda Carol Thalberg, June 19, 1969; 1 child, Scott; m. Barbara Lester Dunn, Dec. 5, 1999; children: Leonard, Meredith. AB, Columbia Coll., 1969; MD, NY Med. Coll., 1973. Cert. Ophthalmology, Am. Bd. Ophthalmology, 1977. Acad. internat. eye fellow Albert Schweitzer Hosp., Deschapples, Haiti, 1976; instr. dept. ophthalmology and visual scis. Yale Sch. Medicine, New Haven, Conn., 1976-77, asst. clin. prof. Dept. Ophthalmology and Visual Scis. Newhaven, Conn., 1977-86, assoc. clin. prof. Dept. Ophthalmology and Visual Scis., 1986-91, clin. prof. Dept. Ophthalmology and Visual Scis., 1991—; chief ophthalmology VA Hosp., West Haven, Conn., 1977-85; attending physician Yale-New Haven Hosp., New Haven, Conn., 1976—, asst. chief ophthalmology, 1988—. Dir. continuing edn. Am. Soc. Cataract and Refractive Surgery, Washington, 1991—; mem. Bd. Permanent Officers Yale Sch. Medicine, New Haven, 1991—. Author: Automated Visual Field Testing, 1986; contbr. articles to profl. jours. Recipient Med. Student Essay award Am. Sc. Pharmacology and Exptl. Therapeutics, 1971, Moshy Book award N.Y. Med. Coll., N.Y.C., 1973. Fellow Am. Acad. Ophthalmology (Honor award 1990); mem. New England Ophthalmological Soc., AMA (Physician's Recognition award 1976, 79, 82, 85, 96, 2000), ASCRS (dir. continuing edn. 1992—), Conn. State Med. Soc., Conn. Soc. Eye Physicians, New Haven County Med. Assn., Yale Alumni Ophthalmology, Assn. for Rsch. in Vision and Ophthalmology. Avocation: computers. Office: Eye Care Group 60 Temple St New Haven CT 06510-2716

SILVERTHORN, ROBERT STERNER, JR., lawyer; b. Dec. 22, 1948; Pres., bd. dirs. Windhurst Acres Homeowners Assn., St. Matthews, Ky., 1982-85; chmn. Louisville Armed Forces Com., 1986-88; active Louisville-Jefferson County Crime Commn., 1975-77. Lt. col. USAR, 1970-89. Mem. ABA (vice chmn. real property com. gen. practice sect.), Ky. Bar Assn., Louisville Bar Assn., Ky. Acad. Trial Attys., Hurstbourne Country Club, Jefferson Club, Masons, Delta Theta Phi, Sigma Chi. Home: 1724 Edenside Ave # 2 Louisville KY 40204-1520 Office: Silverthorn Law Offices 455 S 4th Ave Ste 1200 Louisville KY 40202-2512

SILVERTHORNE, MICHAEL JAMES, classics educator; b. Bristol, Eng., Dec. 20, 1941; emigrated to Can., 1966; s. Frederick J. and Freda (Fox) S.; m. Ann Frances O'Malley, Aug. 6, 1966; children: Christopher, Stephen, Katherine. BA, Oxford U., 1964, B.Litt., 1966, MA, 1967, D.Phil., 1973. Lectr. McGill U., Montreal, 1966-68, asst. prof., 1968-74, assoc. prof. dept. classics, 1974—2004, chmn. dept., 1981-86, 88-91, 94-97; hon. Univ. fellow Exeter U., 2002—; ret., 2004. Editor: On the Duty of Man and Citizen, 1991, On the Citizen, 1998, The New Organon, 2000, Natural Rights on the Threshold of the Scottish Enlightenment, 2002. Can. Council fellow, 1969-73; Social Sci. and Humanities Research Council Can. grantee, 1980-83, 92-95. Mem. Internat. Soc. Classical Tradition, Classical Assn. Can. (sec. 1991-95), Conf. Social and Polit. Thought. Home: 1 Chestnut Mews Feniton Honiton Devon EX14 3BA England Office: McGill U History Dept 855 Sherbrooke St W Montreal QC Canada H3A 2T7 Business E-Mail: michael.silverthorne@mcgill.ca. E-mail: mjsilverthorne@tiscali.co.uk.

SILVERTON, NANCY, food service executive; b. June 20, 1954; m. Mark Peel; three children. Student, Calif. State U., Cordon Bleu, London, Ecole Le Notre, France. Pastry chef Michael's Restaurant, Santa Monica, Calif.; 1st exec. pastry chef Spago, West Hollywood, Calif.; founder LaBrea Bakery, L.A., 1989, v.p. product devel., exec. v.p. Recipient Chef of Yr. award James Beard Found., Top 10 Chefs award Food and Wine Mag. Office: Campanile Restaurant 624 S LaBrea Ave Los Angeles CA 90036

SILVERTOOTH, ERIN J. preventive medicine physician; BA, Baylor U.; MD, U. Tex., 1998. Resident internal medicine and psychiatry Duke U., clin. assoc. depts. internal medicine and psychiatry, dir. assoc. program, psychiatry residency tng. program, asst. dir. psychiatry consultation and liaison svc. Mem.: AMA Found. (Excellence in Medicine Leadership award 2004). Avocations: reading, walking, drawing. Office: Duke U Med Ctr Psychiatry Dept Durham NC 27710

SILVESTRI, ALAN ANTHONY, film composer; b. N.Y.C., Mar. 26, 1950; s. Louis and Elizabeth (Clarke) S.; m. Sandra Dee Shue; children: Alexandra, Joseph, James. PhD in Music (hon.), Berklee Coll. Music, Boston, 1995. Film scores include The Doberman Gang, 1972, The Amazing Dobermans, Las Vegas Lady, 1976, Romancing the Stone, 1984, Par ou t'es rentre? On t'as vu sortir, 1984, Fandango, 1984, Cat's Eye, 1984, Back to the Future, 1985 (Grammy award nominations best instrumental composition and best album of original score for a motion picture, 1985), Summer Rental, 1985, Clan of the Cave Bear, 1986, The Delta Force, 1986, American Anthem, 1986, Flight of the Navigator, 1986, No Mercy, 1986, Critical Condition, 1987, Outrageous Fortune, 1987, Predator, 1987, Overboard, 1987, Who Framed Roger Rabbit?, 1988 (Grammy award nominations best instrumental composition and best album of original score for a motion picture, 1988), My Stepmother Is an Alien, 1988, Mac and Me, 1988, She's Out of Control, 1989, Downtown, 1989, The Abyss, 1989, Back to the Future II, 1989, Back to the Future III, 1990, Young Guns II, 1990, Predator II, 1990, Soapdish, 1991, Dutch, 1991, Ricohet, 1991, Shattered, 1991, Father of the Bride, 1991, Ferngully: The Last Rainforest, 1992, Death Becomes Her, 1992, Stop! Or My Mom Will Shoot, 1992, The Bodyguard, 1992, Cop and a Half, 1993, Sidekicks, 1993, Super Mario Bros., 1993, Judgment Night, 1993, Grumpy Old Men, 1993, Clean Slate, 1994, Blown Away, 1994, Forrest Gump, 1994 (Academy award nomination best original score, Grammy award nomination best instrumental performance for "Feather Theme from Forrest Gump," Golden Globe award nomination best original score), Richie Rich, 1994, The Quick and the Dead, 1994, The Perez Family, 1995, Judge Dredd, 1995, Father of the Bride II, 1995, Sgt. Bilko, 1995, Grumpier Old Men, 1995, Eraser, 1996, Long Kiss Goodnight, 1996, Fools Rush In, 1996, Volcano, 1997, Contact, 1997, Mousehunt, 1997, Odd Couple II, 1998, Parent Trap, 1998, Holyman, 1998, Practical Magic, 1998, Siegfried & Roy, The Magic Box, 1999, Stuart Little, 1999, Reindeer Games, 2000, What Lies Beneath, 2000, What Women Want, 2000, Castaway, 2000 (Grammy award winner for best instrumental composition for "Theme from Castaway"), The Mexican, 2001, What Women Want, 2000,The Mummy Returns, 2001, Serendipity, 2001, Showtime, 2002, Lilo & Stitch, 2002, Stuart Little 2, 2002; TV themes include CHiPs, 1978-83, Manimal, 1983. Recipient ACE award Nat. Acad. Cable Programming for Tales from the Crypt - All Through the House, 1990, Saturn award Acad. Arts and Sci. for fantasy and horror film, 1987, Grammy nominations for Back to the Future, 1985, Who Framed Rger Rabbit?, 1988, Forrest Gump, 1994, Castaway, 2001; nominated for Golden Globe, Forrest Gump, 1994.

SILVESTRI, GEORGE J., JR., retired thermodynamics engineer; b. Jessup, Pa., Aug. 3, 1927; m. Betty A. Huber, 1961 (dec. July 2002); children: Mary E. Silvestri Philbrick and Janet C. Silvestri Travis. BS, Drexel U., 1953, MS, 1956. Registered profl. engr., Fla., Pa. Devel. engr. Westinghouse Elec. Corp., 1953-69, fellow engr., 1969-72, 74, applications engr., 1972-73, adv. engr., 1974-94; project mgr. Elec. Power Rsch. Inst., 1973-74; ret., 1994. 59 patents in field. Mem. ASME (chmn. edn. and rsch. com. power divsn. 1982-85, 90-91, bd. rsch. and technol. devel. 1985-91, lectr. course on steam turbines power divsn. 1989-97, performance test code course on testing 1991-95, rsch. com. properties steam, James Harry Potter Gold medal 1993), Am. Nuclear Soc. Achievements include research in advanced power generation cycles, operation procedures to enhance steam turbine performance, low pressure turbine laboratory testing, improved steam property algorithms, steam turbine performance computer program. Address: 209 Robin Dr Souderton PA 18964-2160 E-mail: gjs803@verizon.net.

SILVESTRO, CLEMENT MARIO, museum director, historian; b. New Haven, Sept. 7, 1924; s. Joseph and Rose (Griego) S.; m. Betty C. Mack, June 26, 1950; 1 dau., Elizabeth J. Silvestro Casner. BS, Central Conn. State Coll., 1949; MS, U. Wis., 1951; PhD, 1959. Asst. to dir. Wis. Hist. Soc., 1956-57; dir. Am. Assn. State and Local History, 1957-64; editor History News, 1957-64; assoc. dir. Chgo. Hist. Soc., 1964-65, dir., 1965-74, sec., 1970-74; dir. Mus. of Our Nat. Heritage, Lexington, Mass., 1974-92. Mem. exec. com. Am. Assn. Museums, 1965-71, v.p., 1966-71; vis. lectr. Northeastern U., 1983-85 Co-author: A Decade of Collecting: Maps, 1985 Mem. Chgo. Archtl. and Landmark Com., 1968-74; mem. Ill. Historic Sites Adv. Council, 1970-74, U.S. ICOM, Nat. Com., 1970-74; chmn. Pres.'s Adv. Council on Historic Preservation, 1974-77; mem. adv. bd. Eleutherian Mills-Hagley Found., 1973-76; U.S. rep. to UNESCO Internat. Adv. Com. to Safeguard City of Venice, 1975; trustee U.S. Capitol Hist. Soc.; trustee, pres. Fruitlands Mus., 1982-85. Served with USAAF, 1943-45. Decorated Air medal with oak leaf clusters. Mem. Am. Assn. Mus., Orgn. Am Historians (chmn. hist. sites com. 1973-78), Chgo. Hist. Soc., Colonial Soc. Mass., Bostonian Soc., Mass. Hist. Soc. (resident), Union Club Boston, Masons. Home: PO Box 119 Hancock ME 04640-0119

SILVEY, ANITA LYNNE, editor; b. Bridgeport, Conn., Sept. 3, 1947; d. John Oscar and Juanita Lucille (McKitrick) Silvey. BS in Edn., Ind. U., 1965-69; MA in Comm. Arts, U. Wis., 1970. Editorial asst. children's book dept. Little Brown and Co., Boston, 1970-71; asst. editor Horn Book Mag., Boston, 1971-75; mng. editor, founder New Boston Rev., 1975-76; mktg. mgr. children's books, libr. svcs. mgr. trade divsn. Houghton Mifflin, Boston, 1976-84; editor-in-chief Horn Book Mag., Boston, 1985-95; v.p., pub. Children's Books Houghton Mifflin Co., Boston, 1995—2001. Editor: Children's Books and Their Creators, 1995, Help Wanted: Stories About Young People and Work, 1997, Essential Guide to Children's Books and their Creators, 2002, 100 Best Books for Children, 2004. Named one of 70 Women Who Have Made a Difference, Women's Nat. Book Assn., 1987. Mem.: ALA (chmn. children's librs., Laura Ingalls Wilder award 1987—89), Assn. Am. Pubs. (mem. libr. com.), Internat. Reading Assn. (mem. IRA Book award com. 1985—87), New Eng. Round Table (chmn. 1978—79). Office Phone: 781-329-5712. Personal E-mail: anitasilvey@aol.com.

SILVEY, MURL L. psychologist; b. Sanford, Tenn., June 25, 1941; s. William Lloyd and Evelyn Louise S.; m. Bev J., Oct. 25, 1963; children: Brian, Barbie. BA, Calif. State U., San Francisco, 1966; MS, Calif. State U., Fresno, 1975; PhD, Pacific U., 1986. Probation officer Merced County Probation Dept., Calif., 1966-77; psychologist Mt. Hood Counseling Svc., Sandy, Oreg., 1980—. Bd. dirs. Sandy Family Svcs., 1984-99. Mem. APA, Am. Counseling Assn., Oreg. Psychol. Assn. Office: Mt Hood Counseling Svc PO Box 1237 Sandy OR 97055-1237

SILVIA, DAVID ALAN, insurance broker; b. Taunton, Mass., Mar. 5, 1953; s. Edward J. and Loretta (Sousa) S.; m. Janet E. McMahon, Apr. 16, 1988 (div. Jan. 1996); 1 child, David. BA, Roger Williams U., 1975. Sales rep. New England Brass, Taunton, Mass., 1976-81; ins. agt. Prudential Ins., Raynham, Mass., 1981-82; owner, ptnr. CS Assocs., North Attleboro, Mass., 1982-86; asst. ice hockey coach New England Hockey Inst., 2002—. Independent. Office: 495 Somerset Ave North Dighton MA 02764-1809 Office Phone: 508-880-0650.

SIM, CRAIG STEPHEN, retired investment banker; b. Bklyn., Apr. 23, 1942; s. William Henry Craig and Lenore (Overton) S.; m. Susan Hart; children: Brandon Craig William, Stephanie Brooke. BA, Gettysburg Coll., 1965. Account exec. Francis I. duPont & Co., N.Y.C., 1969-72; v.p. E.F. Hutton & Co., N.Y.C., 1972-75; sr. v.p. Donaldson, Lufkin & Jenrette, N.Y.C., 1975-83; exec. v.p. Shearson Am. Express, N.Y.C., 1983-84; mng. dir. Donaldson, Lufkin & Jenrette, N.Y.C., 1984-2001, Credit Suisse First Boston, 2001—. Trustee Gettysburg Coll. Served to capt. USMC, 1965-69. Mem. Bond Club N.Y. (gov. 1979-80, 84-85, 90-93), Lawrence Beach Club (gov.), The Leash, India House, St. Andrew's Soc. (N.Y.C.), Burns Soc. City of N.Y. (trustee), L.I. Wyandanch Club, Seawanhaka Corinthian Yacht Club, Army and Navy Club (Washington), Union Club. Address: PO Box 57 Charlotte VT 05445

SIM, FRANKLIN H. orthopedic surgery educator; children: Leslie, Sheridan. MD, Dalhousie U. Med. Sch., 1960—64. Med. dr. MN, 1972. Prof. orthop. surgery Mayo Clinic, Rochester, Minn., 1972—. Chair, divsn. orthop. oncology Mayo Clinic, 2000—. Second lt Black Watch Rgt., 1961, Germany. Office: Mayo Clinic 200 First St SW Rochester MN 55905

SIMAAN, MARWAN, electrical engineering educator; b. July 23, 1946; m. Rita Simaan. MSEE, U. Pitts., 1970; PhDEE, U. Ill., 1972. Registered profl. engr., Pa. Rsch. engr. Shell Devel. Co., Houston, 1974-76; assoc. prof. elec. engring. U. Pitts., 1976-85, prof., 1985-89, Bell of Pa./Bell Atlantic prof., 1989—, chmn. dept. elec. engring., 1991—. Cons. Gulf Rsch. and Tech., Pitts., 1979-85, ALCOA, Pitts., 1986-89. Editor: Vertical Seismic Profiles, 1984, Two-dimensional Transforms, 1985, Artificial Intelligence in Petroleum Exploration, 1989, Expert Systems in Exploration, 1991, (series) Advances in Geophysical Signal Processing; co-editor jour. Multidimensional Sys. and Signal Processing; mem. editl. bd. profl. jours., including IEEE Procs., IEEE Transactions on Cirs. and Sys., IEEE Transactions on Geosci. and Remote Sensing, Jour. Optimization Theory and Applications, Integrated Computer-aided Engring. Jour., Jour. Cirs., Sys. and Computers; contbr. over 300 articles on signal processing and control to profl. publs. Grantee NSF, NIH, ONR, Def. Advance Rsch. Project Adminstrs., Ben Franklin, Westinghouse, Gulf, ALCOA; recipient Outstanding ECE Alumnus U. Ill. Fellow IEEE (Best Paper award 1985, 99), AAAS; mem. NAE, Am. Soc. Engring. Edn., Soc. Exploration Geophysics, Am. Assn. Artificial Intelligence, Eta Kappa Nu, Sigma Xi (Best Paper award ALCOA chpt. 1988).sec. of engring. sect. M of AAAS 2003—. Achievements include patent in application of signal processing technology in aluminum manufacturing. Office: Univ Pitts Dept Elec Engring Pittsburgh PA 15261-0001 Office Phone: 412-624-8099. E-mail: simaan@engr.pitt.edu.

SIMAI, MIHALY, economics and business educator; b. Budapest, Hungary, Apr. 4, 1930; s. Mátyas and Jolan (Rosenberg) S.; m. Vera Bence, Apr. 28, 1954; 1 child, Anna-Maria. MA, Budapest U. Econs., 1952, PhD, 1957. Asst. prof. Budapest U. Econs., 1952-57, assoc. prof., 1957-59, 61-64, prof., 1970—, dir. grad. studies, 1992—; staff mem. UN Econ.Commn. for Europe, 1959-60; staff mem., 1st officer UN Centre for Projections, N.Y.C., 1964-69; dir. Inst. World Econs., Budapest, 1987-91; Peace fellow U.S. Inst. Peace, Washington, 1991-92. Dir. World Inst. Devel. Econs. Rsch. of UN U., 1993-96; rsch. prof. Inst. World Econs., Hungarian Acad. Scis.; prof. internat. econ. and bus. studies, dir. grad. program on internat. econ. cooperation and bus. strategy Budapest U. Econ. Scis; mem., chmn. coun. UN Univ., Tokyo, 1986-92, dir. World Inst. for Devel. Econs, Helsinki, 1993-95; mem. adv. bd. UN Staff Coll; spl. advisor sec. gen. UN. Author: Interdependence and Conflicts in the World Economy, 1982, Power, Technology and the World Economy, 1990, The Future of Global Governance, 1994, The New Global Environment for the Development Process, 1995, Global Employment, The Future of Work, 2 vols., 1995, International Business Policy, 1996, The Democratic Process and the Market, 1999, The Reintegration of the Former Socialist Countries in Europe, China and Vietnam into the Global Economy, 2000, The Age of Global Transformations: The Human Dimension, 2001, others; contbr. articles to profl. jours.; mem. editl. bd. Transnational, Geneva, Global Governance, N.Y., Internat. Affairs, London, Devel. Studies, Geneva, Environment and Resource Econs., Amsterdam. Pres. World Fedn. UN Assns., Geneva, 1979-84, hon. pres., 1985-. Named to Order of the Flag of Hungarian Republic, Pres. of Republic of Hungary, Budapest, 1990. Mem. Hungarian Acad. Scis. (former dir. gen. Inst. World Econs.), Internat. Studies Assn. Avocations: hiking, skiing. Office: Inst World Econs Orszaghaz St 30 1014 Budapest Hungary Fax: 361 224 67-65. Office Phone: 361 224 67-62. E-mail: msimai@vki.hu.

SIMAKAJORNBOON, NARONG, physician; b. Bangkok; MD(hon.), Mahidol U., Thailand, 1992. Diplomate Am. Bd. of Pediat., 1996, Am. Sub-Board of Pediatric Pulmonology, 2000, Am. Bd. of Sleep Medicine, 2001. Med. dir. Tulane Sleep Disorders Ctr., New Orleans, 2001—; asst. prof. of pediat. Tulane U. Sch. of Medicine, New Orleans, 1999—; resident in pediat. Children Hosp. of Mich., Wayne State U., Detroit, 1993—96; fellowship in pediat. pulmonology Tulane U. Sch. of Medicine, New Orleans, 1996—99. Recipient Sheldon Brenner Resident Rsch. award, Children's Hosp. of Mich., Wayne State U., 1996, Young Investigator award, Annenberg Ctr. for Health Sciences, 2000; grantee, Am. Heart Assn., 2001—03. Fellow: Am. Acad. of Pediat., Am. Acad. of Sleep Medicine, Am. Physiol. Soc., Am. Coll. of Chest Physicians; mem.: Med. Coun. of Thailand, Am. Thoracic Soc., Sleep Rsch. Soc. Achievements include research in Sleep and respiratory control. Office: Tulane Univ Sch of Medicine 1430 Tulane Ave SL-37 New Orleans LA 70112

SIMANDLE, JEROME B. federal judge; b. Binghamton, N.Y., 1949; s. Paul R. Sr. and Mary F. Simandle; married; children: Roy C., Liza Jane. BSE magna cum laude, Princeton U., 1971; JD, U. Pa., 1976; diploma in Social Scis., U. Stockholm, 1974-75. Bar: Pa. 1977, N.J. 1978. Law clk. to Hon. John F. Gerry U.S. Dist. Ct., N.J., 1976-78; asst. U.S. atty. Dist. N.J., 1978-83; U.S. magistrate judge U.S. Dist. Ct., N.J., 1983-92, judge, 1992—. Mem. lawyers

adv. com. U.S. Dist. Ct., NJ, 1984—95; mem. ct. adminstrn. case mgmt. com. Jud. Conf. U.S., 1991—97; mem. joint adv. coun. of Adminstrv. Office of U.S. Cts., 2002—; mem. CPR Inst. for Dispute Resolution Commn. on Ethics and Stds. in Alternative Dispute Resolution, 1996—. Internat. grad. fellow Rotary Found., 1974-75. Master: Camden Inn of Ct. (program chmn. 1990 93, vice chmn. 1996—); fellow: Am. Bar Found.; mem.: Camden County Bar Assn., Am. Judicature Soc., Fed. Judges Assn. (bd. dirs. 1997—, treas. 2003—, co-editor In Camera 2004—). Office: Mitchell H Cohen US Courthouse Rm 6010 1 John F Gerry Pl Camden NJ 08101-0888

SIMAO, PAUL, news agency executive; Writer Reuters Am., Inc., $D, Can., bur. chief Atlanta Atlanta, 2000—. Office: Reuters America 3340 Peachtree Rd NE Ste 200 Atlanta GA 30326-1028

SIMECKA, BETTY JEAN, marketing executive; b. Topeka, Apr. 15, 1935; d. William Bryan and Regina Marie (Rezac) S.; m. Alex Pappas, Jan. 15, 1956 (div. Apr. 1983); 1 child, Alex William. Student, Butler County C.C., 1983—85. Freelance writer and photographer, L.A., also St. Marys, Kans., 1969-77; co-owner Creative Enterprises, El Dorado, Kans., 1977-83; coord. excursions into history Butler County C.C., El Dorado, 1983-84; dir. Hutchinson (Kans.) Conv. & Visitors Bur., 1984-85; dir. mktg. divsn. Exec. Mgmt., Inc., Wichita, 1985-87; exec. dir. Topeka Conv. and Visitors Bur., 1987-91, pres., CEO, 1991-96; pres. Internat. Connections, Inc., 1996-97, Simecka and Assoc., 1996-99, Pinnacle Prodns., L.L.C., 1997-99; pres., CEO Cultural Exhbns. and Events, L.L.C., 1999—2003; organizer Czars: 400 Years of Imperial Grandeur exhbn., 2002—; v.p. mktg. Sunflower Exhbns., L.L.C., 2003 ; mktg. cons., 2003 . Dir. promotion El Dorado Thunderboat Races, 1977-78. Contbr. articles to jours. and mags.; columnist St. Marys Star, 1973-79. Pres. El Dorado Art Assn., 1984; chair Santa Fe Trail Bike Assn., Kans., 1988-90; co-dir. St. Marys Summer Track Festival, 1973-81; chair spl. events Mulvane Art Mus., 1990, sec., 1991-92; membership chair, 1993-94, bd. dirs., 1995-96; bd. dirs. Topeka Civic Theater, 1991-96, co-chair spl. events, 1992; Kans. chair Russian Festival Com., 1992-93; vice-chair Kans. Film Commn., 1993-94, chair, 1994; bd. dirs. Kans. Expoctr. Adv. Bd., 1990-96, Brain Injury Assn. Greater Kansas City, Concerned Citizens Topeka, 1998-2000; pres. Kans. Internat. Mus., 1994-96. Recipient Kans. Gov.'s Tourism award Kans. Broadcaster's Assn., 1993, Disting. Svc award City of Topeka, 1995, Hist. Ward Meade Disting. award Topeka Parks & Recreation Dept., 1995; named Kansan of Yr., Topeka Capitol-Jour., 1995, Sales and Mktg. Exec. of Yr., 1995, Internat. Soroptomists, Topeka chpt., Woman of Distinction, 1996. Mem. Nat. Tour Assn., Sales and Mktg. execs. (bd. dirs. 1991-92), Internat. Assn. Conv. and Visitors Burs. (co-chair rural tourism com. 1994), Am. Soc. Assn. Execs., Travel Industry Assn. Kans. (membership chair 1988-89, sec. 1990, pres. 1991-92, Outstanding Merit award 1994), St. Marys C. of C. (pres. 1975), I-70 Assn. (v.p. 1989, pres. 1990), Optimists (social sec. Topeka chpt. 1988-89). Republican. Methodist. Avocations: writing, painting, photography. Holder Nat. AAU record for 100-yard dash, 1974. Office Phone: 785-357-6338. Personal E-mail: bettyj5@sbcglobal.net.

SIMENDINGER, THEODORE JOHN, writer, publishing executive; b. Phila., Oct. 6, 1954; s. Theodore John and Margaret Smith Simendinger; m. Bonita Ann Kolish; 1 child, Grace. BS, Jacksonville U., 1976. Founder, chmn. Pro Leisure Tour, Inc., Greenwood Village, Colo., 2000—; dir. profl. devel. We. Union, 2004—. Career devel. cons. Airplane Reader Pub., Greenwood Village, 2000—02. Author: Critters, Fish & Other Troublemakers, 1999, Rich Without Money, 2002, 12 Miles to Paradise, 2003, Searching for Tendulkar, 2004, Jurassic Trout, 2004. Founder, chmn. No Bats Baseball Club, Global Ambassadors for the Good of the Game, Greenwood Village, Colo., 1991—. Named Alumnae of the Yr., Jacksonville U., 2003. Avocations: reading, writing, comedy, fishing. Business E-Mail: theo@12milestoparadise.com.

SIMERAL, WILLIAM GOODRICH, retired chemical company executive; b. Portland, Oreg., May 22, 1926; s. Claire Cornelius and Geneva G. Simeral; m. Elizabeth Louise Ross, June 25, 1949; children: Linda Simeral McGregor, Karen Simeral Schousen, William Goodrich Jr., John David; m. Marion Poore Anderson, Nov. 3, 2001. BS in Physics, Franklin and Marshall Coll., Lancaster, Pa., 1948; PhD in Physics, U. Mich., 1953. With E.I. duPont de Nemours and Co., Inc., 1953-87, v.p., gen. mgr. plastics dept., 1974-76, v.p., gen. mgr. plastic products and resins dept., 1976-77, sr. v.p., dir., mem. exec. com., 1977-81, exec. v.p., dir., mem. exec. com., 1981-87; vice chmn. bd., chief operating officer Conoco Inc., 1984-85. Trustee Franklin and Marshall Coll., 1977—, chmn. bd., 1991-94; trustee, bd. dirs. Wilmington Med. Ctr., 1978-93, chmn. bd., 1982-86; bd. dirs. YMCA Wilmington and New Castle County, 1978-81. Mem. Chem. Mfrs. Assn. (vice chmn. bd. 1980-81, chmn. exec. com. 1981-82, chmn. bd. 1982-83), Am. Phys. Soc., Phi Beta Kappa, Sigma Xi, Wilmington Country Club.

SIMEROTH, DEAN CONRAD, chemical engineer; b. Marysville, Calif., Mar. 21, 1946; s. Raphael Conrad and Mary Beatrice (Watson) S.; m. Phyllis Deborah Minakowski, Feb. 7, 1971 (div. Nov. 1994); 1 child, Brian Conrad. BS in Chem. Engring., U. Calif., Davis, 1968. From air pollution specialist to chief engr. evaluation br. Calif. Air Resources Bd., Sacramento, 1969—87, chief criteria pollutant br., 1987—. Served in U.S. Army, 1969-71, Korea. Mem. AIChE, Air Waste Mgmt. Assn., Kiwanis (treas. Woodland, Calif. chpt. 1988-96). Democrat. Roman Catholic. Avocations: hunting, fishing, tennis, history. Office: Calif Air Resources Bd PO Box 2815 1010 I Street Sacramento CA 95814-4219 Office Phone: 916-322-6020. E-mail: dsimerot@arb.ca.gov.

SIMERVILLE, JAMES JASPER, pediatrician; b. Bend, Oreg., Sept. 15, 1939; s. George Melvin and Clara Louise (Jasper) S.; m. Carol Marie Smith, Dec. 26, 1961; children: Pamela Marie, Steven James, Jeffrey Alan. BS, Oreg. State U., 1961; MD, U. Oreg., 1965. Diplomate Am. Bd. Pediatrics; diplomate in occupational medicine Am. Bd. Preventive Medicine. Commd. 2d lt. USAF, 1964, advanced through grades to col., 1979; intern USAF Hosp. Travis, Travis AFB, Calif., 1965-66; resident USAF Hosp. Wilford Hall, Lackland AFB, Tex., 1966-68; chief pediatric svc. USAF, Westover AFB, Mass., Lakenheath, Eng., and Scott AFB, Ill., Eng., 1968-75; dir. med. edn. USAF Hosp. Scott, Scott AFB, 1975-84; cons. in pediatrics, then dep. comdr. U.S. Air Force Acad. Hosp., Colorado Springs, Colo., 1976-84; retired USAF, 1984; dir. Colorado Springs Sports Medicine Clinic, 1984-87, Colo. Ctr. Occupational Medicine, Colorado Springs, 1985-92; med. dir. Colorado Springs Health Ptnrs., 1992-96, Pacific Care, 1996—. Med. cons. sports medicine program, Chapman Coll., Colorado Springs, 1983-88. Fellow Am. Acad. Pediatrics; mem. Colo. Med. Soc., El Paso County Med. Soc. Roman Catholic. Avocations: walking, hiking, camping, golf, skiing. Office: Pacific Care 5755 Mark Dabling Blvd Ste 350 Colorado Springs CO 80919-2247

SIMES, DIMITRI KONSTANTIN, international affairs expert and educator; b. Moscow, Oct. 17, 1947; came to U.S., 1973; s. Konstantin M. and Dina (Kaminsky) S.; m. Anastasia Ryurikov, May 27, 1993; 1 child, Dimitri Alexander. MA, Moscow State U., 1969. Sr. research fellow Ctr. for Strategic and Internat. Studies, Washington, 1973-76, dir. Soviet studies, 1976-80; prof. Soviet studies, exec. dir. Soviet and East European research program Sch. Advanced Internat. Studies, Johns Hopkins U., Washington, 1980-83, lectr., 1983-90; sr. assoc. Carnegie Endowment for Internat. Peace, Washington, 1983-94; pres. The Nixon Ctr., Washington, 1994—; pub. The Nat. Interest, 2001—. Vis. prof. polit. sci. U. Calif., Berkeley, 1982; adj. prof. govt. Columbia U., N.Y.C., 1985, 92; cons. CBS News, N.Y.C., 1985-87, NBC News, 1987-94. Author: Detente and Conflict: Soviet Succession: Leadership in Transition, 1978, After the Collapse: Russia Seeks Its Place as a Great Power, 1999; columnist: Christian Sci. Monitor, Boston, 1983-87, L.A. Times Syndicate, 1987-89, Newsday, 1991—; contbr. articles to newspapers and jours. Mem. Coun. on Fgn. Rels. Office: The Nixon Ctr 1615 L St NW Ste 1250 Washington DC 20036-5651 E-mail: dsimes@nixoncenter.org.

SIMES, STEPHEN MARK, pharmaceutical products executive; b. N.Y.C., Nov. 23, 1951; s. Herbert H. and Mimi (Maurer) S.; m. Anita H. Herzog, Aug. 23, 1975. BS in Chemistry, Bklyn. Coll., 1973; MBA in Mktg., NYU, 1980. Sales rep. G.D. Searle and Co., N.Y.C., 1974-78, supr. sales tng. Chgo., 1978-79, dist. sales mgr. N.Y.C., 1979-81, product mgr. Chgo., 1981-82, sr. product mgr., 1982-83, dir. pub. affairs and communications, 1983-84; v.p. Gynex Inc., Chgo., 1984-88; dir. Gynex Pharms. Inc., Deerfield, 1985-93; pres., dir. Gynex Labs., Chgo., 1985-88; pres., CEO Contracap Inc., 1988-89, Gynex Pharms., Inc., Chgo., 1989-93, chmn., 1992-93; sr. v.p., dir. Bio-Technology Gen. Corp., 1993-94; pres., CEO, dir. Unimed Pharms., Inc., 1994-97; bd. dirs., CEO, pres. Simes Pharm. Cons., 1997-98. Vice chmn., CEO, pres., BioSante Pharms., Inc., Lincolnshire, Ill., 1998—. Mem.: iBio, Biotech. Industry Orgn., Menopause Soc., Endocrine Soc., Licensing Exec. Soc., Chgo. Coun. Fgn. Rels. Office: 111 Barclay Blvd Lincolnshire IL 60069

SIMÉUS, DUMAS M. food products executive; b. Pont-Sondé, Haiti, Sept. 11, 1939; Degree in Elect. Engring., Howard U.; MBA with honors, U. Chgo. Pres., CEO TLC Beatrice Internat. Foods, Mansfield, Tex., prior to 1996; chmn., CEO, controlling stockholder Siméus Foods Internat., Inc., Mansfield, Tex., 1996—. Mem. bd. dirs. TGIF. Pres. Dumas M. Siméus Found.; chmn. Caribbean Am. Leadership Coun.; pres. Dumas M. Siméus Found. to provide med. care, food and clothing to the less fortunate; active Haitian Am. Bus. Devel. Coun., Nat. Orgn. for Advancement of Haitians, Dallas Urban League, Inc., Dallas Together Forum, Dallas/Ft. Worth Minority Bus. Devel. Coun. Named Entrepreneur of Yr. for the Southwest Region by Ernst & Young, LLP; finalist Horatio Alger award. Mem. Internat. Foodservice Mfrs. Assn. (bd. dirs.), Caribbean/Am. Leadership Coun. (chmn.), Haitian/Am. Bus. Devel. Coun., Nat. Orgn. Advancement Haitians, Dallas Urban League, Inc., DF/W Minority Bus. Devel. Coun. Office: Siméus Foods Internat 812 S 5th Ave Mansfield TX 76063-2210 E-mail: dsimeus@simeusfoods.com.

SIMIC, CHARLES, English language educator, poet; b. Beograd, Yugoslavia, May 9, 1938; arrived in U.S., 1954, naturalized, 1971; s. George and Helen (Matijevich) Simic; m. Helen Dubin, Oct. 1964; children: Anna, Philip. BA, NYU, 1967. Editl. asst. Aperture, Quar. of Photography, N.Y.C., 1966—69; prof. English Calif. State U., Hayward, Calif., 1970—73, U. N.H., Durham, NH, 1973—. Author: What the Grass Says, 1967, Somewhere Among us a Stone is Taking Notes, 1969, Dismantling the Silence, 1971, White, 1972, Return to a Place Lit by a Glass of Milk, 1974, Biography and a Lament, 1976, Charon's Cosmology, 1977, Classic Ballroom Dances, 1980, Austerities, 1982, Weather Forecast for Utopia and Vicinity, 1983, Selected Poems, 1985, rev. edit., 1990, Unending Blues, 1986, The World Doesn't End, 1989 (Pulitzer Prize for poetry, 1990), The Book of Gods and Devils, 1990, Hotel Insomnia, 1992, A Wedding in Hell, 1994, Frightening Toys, 1995, Walking the Black Cat, 1996, Looking for Trouble, 1997, Selected Early Poems, 1999, Jackstraws, 1999, rev. edit., 2000, Night Picnic, 2001, Voice at 3 A.M., 2003, (novels) The Uncertain Certainty, 1985, Wonderful Words, Silent Truth, 1990, Dimestore Alchemy, 1992, The Unemployed Fortune Teller, 1994, Orphan Factory, 1998, A Fly in the Soup, 2000, Metaphysician in the Dark, 2003; translator (with C.W. Truesdale): Fire Gardens, 1970; translator: The Little Box, 1970; translator: (with Mark Strand) Another Republic, 1976; translator: Four Modern Yugoslav Poets, 1970, Homage to the Lame Wolf, 1979; translator: (with P. Kastmiler) Atlantis, 1987; translator: Roll Call of Mirrors, 1987, Some Other Wine and Light, 1989, Bandit Wind, 1991, The Horse Has Six Legs, 1992, Night Mail, 1992, Devil's Lunch, 1999, A Wake for the Living, 2002; contbr. Selected Poems of Tomaz Salamun, 1987, RollCall of Mirrors, 1987, poems to mags. and anthologies. With U.S. Army, 1961—63. Recipient PEN Internat. award for transl., 1970, 1980, Edgar Allan Poe award, Am. Acad. Poets, 1975, award, Nat. Inst. Arts and Letters, 1976, AAAL award, 1976, Harriet Monroe poetry award, U. Chgo., 1980, CiCastignola award, Poetry Soc. Am., 1980; fellow Guggenheim fellow, 1972—73, Nat. Endowment for the Arts, 1974—75, 1979—80, Fulbright Travelling fellow, 1982, Ingram Merrill fellow, 1983—84, Mac Arthur fellow, 1984—89. Mem.: Acad. Arts and Letters. Home: PO Box 192 Strafford NH 03884-0192 Office: U NH Dept English Durham NH 03824

SIMIS, THEODORE LUCKEY, investment banker, information technology executive; b. N.Y.C., June 17, 1924; s. Theodore William Ernest and Helen (Luckey) S.; m. Laura Cushman Ingraham, Sept. 8, 1946; children— Nancy Simis Ricca, Theodore Steven, Karen Simis Woods, June Simis Sobocinski BS, NYU, 1950, MBA, 1952. With Bell System, 1941-79; various positions to officer level with N.Y. Telephone Co., N.J. Telephone Co., and AT&T; v.p. Warner Amex Cable Co., 1980-81; sr. v.p. E.F. Hutton, Sarasota, Fla., 1982-87; vice chmn., bd. dirs. XMX Corp., Burlington, Mass., 1986-2000; pres. Pvt. Transatlantic Telecommunication System Inc., McLean, Va., 1987-89; chmn. Value Added Network System, Inc., Sarasota, Fla., 1990-91; vice-chmn., bd. dirs. OPIX Corp., Burlington, Ma., 2000—. Dir. Liebenzell Mission, Schooleys Mountain, N.J.; vis. Nieman fellow Harvard U., 1977. Mem. Republican Nat. Com., 1981—. 1st lt. U.S. Army, 1942-53, ETO Mem. N.Y. Acad. Scis., U.S. C. of C., NYU Club. Lutheran. Home: 6025 Manasota Key Rd Englewood FL 34223-9245 Fax: 941-475-1128. Office Phone: 941-474-8690. Personal E-mail: tlslns@cs.com.

SIMITIAN, JOE, state representative; BA, Colo. Coll.; MA in Internat. Policy Studies, Stanford U.; MA in City Planning, JD, U. Calif., Berkeley. Mem. Calif. Assembly, 2000—. Pres. peninsula divsn. League Calif. Cities; pres. Palo Alto Sch. Bd.; county supr. Santa Clara County, Calif.; chair Santa Clara County Intergovernmental Coun.; bd. dirs. Adolescent Counseling; stering com. Bay Area Coun.; mem. Calif. UN 50 Com.; bd. advisors Clara-Mateo Alliance, Inc.; pres. Friends Children's Theatre; bd. dirs. Silicaon Valley Network; trustee emeritus Jr. Statesmen Found.; former advisor Explorer Scouts; adv. team San Mateo County Svc. Learning Project; co-chair Silicon Valley Mfg. Group Housing Leadership Coun.; allocations com. United Way; mayor Palo Alto, Calif. Mem.: Santa Clara County Sch. Bds. Assn. (pres.). Office: PO Box 942849 Sacramento CA 95814 Address: 160 Town and Country Village Palo Alto CA 94301

SIMITIS, SPIROS, legal educator; b. Athens, Greece, Oct. 19, 1934; s. George and Fanny (Christopoulo) S.; m. Ilse Grubrich, Aug. 3, 1963. JD, U. Marburg, Fed. Republic Germany, 1956. Assoc. prof. U. Frankfurt, Fed. Republic Germany, 1963, prof., 1969, U. Giessen, Fed. Republic Germany, 1964-69; vis. prof. London Sch. Econs., U. Calif. - Berkeley, 1976, U. Pa., 1980, U. Strasbourg, France, 1987-88, Paris, 1990—, Yale U., New Haven, Conn., 1981—. Sec. gen. Internat. Civil Status Commn., 1966—80; chmn. Data Protection Experts Com. of the Coun. of Europe, Strasbourg, 1982—86; with Hesse Data protect commr., 1975—91; mem. rsch. coun. European Univ. Inst.; chmn. social rights com. European Commn., 1998; chmn. German Nat. Ethic Coun., 2000—. Contbr. numerous articles to legal publs. Mem.: Athens Acad. Scis., Nat. Bioethics Council (chmn.), German Coun. Pvt. Internat. Law, German Lawyers Assn. (bd. dirs. 1970—82). Office: Johann Wolfgang Goethe U Senckenberganlage 31 Postfach 111932 60054 Frankfurt Germany Office Phone: 0049-69-7982273. E-mail: simitis@jur.uni-frankfurt.de.

SIMITSES, GEORGE JOHN, retired engineering educator, consultant; b. Athens, Greece, July 31, 1932; came to U.S., 1951, naturalized, 1963; s. John G. and Vasilike (Goutoufas) S.; m. Nena Athena Economy, Sept. 11, 1960; children: John G., William G., Alexandra G. BS in Aerospace Engring., Ga. Tech. Inst., 1955, MS in Aerospace Engring., 1956; PhD in Aeronautics and Astronautics, Stanford U., 1965. From instr. to prof. engring. Ga. Inst. Tech., Atlanta, 1956-89; prof., head dept. aerospace engring., interim dean engring. U. Cin., 1989-2000, retired, 2000. Cons. Lockheed-Georgia Co., Marietta, Ga., 1965-70, King & Gavaris Engrs., N.Y.C., 1977-79, Ga. Power Co., Atlanta, 1971-72. Author: Stability of Elastic Structures, 1976, Dynamic Stability of Suddenly Loaded Structures, 1989; contbr. chpts. to books, articles to profl. jours. Cmty. rep. Am. Hellenic Inst., Washington, 1976-91; del. Ga. State Dem. Conv., Macon, 1969. Fellow AIAA (various coms. 1974—), ASME (coms. 1976—), Am. Acad. Mechs.; corr. mem. Acad. Athens; mem. Hellenic Soc. Theoretical and Applied Mechs. (founding hon. mem.), AHEPA (v.p. chpt. 1978-79, coms. 1975-90), Sigma Xi (Sustained Rsch. award 1980, Best Paper award 1985). Office: Ga Inst Technology Aerospace Engring Atlanta GA 30332-0150 Office Phone: 404-894-2770. E-mail: george.simitses@aerospace.gatech.edu.

SIMKANICH, JOHN JOSEPH, lawyer, civil engineer; b. Clairton, Pa., 1941; BSEE, Drexel Inst. Tech., 1964; MSEE, Purdue U., 1966; JD, George Washington U., 1972. Bar: U.S. Patent Office 1970, Pa. 1973, U.S. dist. Ct. (ea. dist.) Pa. 1977, U.S. Supreme Ct. 1977, U.S. Ct. Appeals (Fed. cir.) 1982, U.S. Ct. Appeals (3d cir.) 1992. Elec. engr. U.S. Steel Co., 1963-65; engr. Westinghouse Aerospace, Balt., 1966-69; sys. developer TRW Sys. Inc., Washington, 1969-70; patent atty. Burroughs Corp., Paoli, Pa., 1970-74, Johnson & Johnson, New Brunswick, NJ, 1974-77; pvt. practice intellectual property law Phila., 1977—. Adv. Soup, Inc., Washington, 1970-72; introducted to FTC truth-in-advt. law; presenter in field. Patentee in field; product developer and licensing; analog and digital computer designer, programmer. Mem. IEEE (sr.), Pa. Bar Assn., Bucks County Bar Assn., Phila. Intellectual Property Law Assn., Am. Intellectual Property Law Assn., Delta Theta Phi, Eta Kappa Nu. Roman Catholic. Republican. Office: Paul & Paul 2900 Two-Thousand Market St Philadelphia PA 19103

SIMKIN, PETER ANTHONY, internist, educator; b. Morgantown, W.Va., Nov. 22, 1935; s. William Edward and Ruth Helen (Commons) S.; m. Penelope Hart Payson, Aug. 9, 1958; children— Andrew, Caroline, Mary, Elizabeth. BA, Swarthmore Coll., 1957; MD, U. Pa., 1961. Intern N.C. Meml. Hosp., Chapel Hill, 1961-62, resident, 1962-63, Univ. Hosps. Cleve., 1965-66; fellow in medicine U. Wash., Seattle, 1966-69, asst. prof., 1969-74, assoc. prof., 1974-84, prof., 1984—. Mem. editorial bd.: Arthritis and Rheumatism, 1981-85, BIMR Rheumatology, 1980-84; contbr. articles to profl. jours. Bd. dirs. Wash. chpt. Arthritis Found., 1974-90, chmn. med. and sci. com., 1974-78. Served with U.S. Army, 1963-65. Mem. Am. Coll. Rheumatology (master), Osteoarthritis Rsch. Soc. Internat. Mem. Soc. Of Friends. Office: U Wash Rheumatology 356428 Seattle WA 98195-0001

SIMKO, JAN, English, foreign language and literature educator; b. Zlaté Moravce, Slovakia, Oct. 30, 1920; came to U.S., 1967; s. Simon Simko and Terezia Simkova; m. Libusa Safarikova, Dec. 20, 1950 (div. 1970, dec. 2004); children: Jan, Vladimir (dec.). Diploma in English, U. Bratislava, 1942, Diploma in German, 1943, PhD in English, 1944; MPhil in English, U. London, 1967. Tchr. English and German various bus. schs., 1942-45; asst. depts. English and German U. Bratislava, 1945-46; instr. English Econom U., 1946-47; faculty U. Bratislava, 1950-68, from asst. prof. to assoc. prof. English, 1957-68; prof. English Rio Grande Coll., Ohio, 1968-75. Instr. Shakespeare Georgetown U., 1982-84; vis. prof. English, scholar-in-residence W. Va. U., Parkersburg, 1989-90; instr. Slovak Fgn. Svc. Inst., Washington, 1974, 96, fed. govt., 1989, 91-93, IMF & World Bank, 1994-95; examiner critical langs. program Kent (Ohio) State U., 1974-91; feature writer Voice of Am., 1983-94; translator U.S. Dept. State, 1997—; bd. linguistics Slovak Acad. of Scis., 1957-67. Author: 3 English textbooks, 2 bilingual dictionaries, 1 linguistic monograph; editor: Lectures in the Circle of Modern Philology, 2 vols., 1965-66; chief consulting editor: textbooks of Slovak and Czech, 1993-96; contbg. writer: The Review, 1995-2002; Am./Can.-Slovak press; contbr. articles to profl. jours. With inf. Czecho-Slovak Army, 1946. Grantee Brit. Coun., 1947-49, Folger Shakespeare Libr./U.S. Dept. State, 1967-68; Internat. Rsch. and Exch. Bd., 1982, others; recipient awards W.Va. U., 1990, Bratislava U., 1995, medal Pres. of Slovakia, 2002. Mem. MLA (life), Slovak Studies Assn., Soc. for Scis. and Arts, Met. Opera Guild, Shakespeare Theater Guild, Nat. Symphony Orch. Assn., English-Speaking Union. Roman Catholic. Avocations: classical music, opera, theater, fine arts, hiking, swimming. Home: Apt 511 725 24th St NW Washington DC 20037

SIMMANG, CLIFFORD LILES, surgeon; b. Bryan, Tex., Dec. 6, 1953; s. Clifford Max and Elnora (Liles) S.; m. Karen Janette Black, May 19, 1979; children: Clifford Jonathan, Marc Alan. BS, Tex. A&M U., 1976, MS, 1978; MD, U. Tex. Med. Br., 1982. Diplomate Am. Bd. Surgery, Am. Bd. Colon and Rectal Surgery. Categorical surgery intern Brooke Army Med. Ctr., Ft. Sam Houston, Tex., 1981-82, resident in gen. surgery, 1982-87; resident in colon and rectal surgery Jewish Hosp.-Washington U., St. Louis, Mo., 1991-92; chief gen. surgery svc. Frankfurt Army Regional Med. Ctr., Germany, 1987-91; chief colon & rectal surg Madigan Army Med. Ctr., Tacoma, Wash., 1992-95; med. dir. aston surg. svcs., assoc. prof. surgery U. Tex. SW Med. Ctr., Dallas, 1995—, program dir. colon and rectal surgery residency. Surg. adv. bd. 3M Corp., St. Paul, 1993-95. Assoc. editor Diseases of the Colon and Rectum, 1997-2002. Decorated Meritorious Svc. medal with oak leaf cluster. Fellow ACS, Am. Soc. Colon and Rectal Surgeons (stds. task force 1994—, armed forces task force 1992-94); mem. AMA, Soc. Am. Gastrointestinal Endoscopic Surgeons, Soc. Surgery Alimentary Tract, S.W. Surg. Congress, Soc. for Surgery Alimentary Tract, Soc. Am. Gastrointestinal Endoscopic Surgeons, Southwest oncology Group, Tex. Soc. Colon and Rectal Surgeons, Dallas Soc. Gen. Surgeons, N.W. Soc. Colon and Rectal Surgeons, Midwest Soc. Colon and Rectal Surgeons (pres.), Soc. U.S. Army Flight Surgeons, Soc. for Surg. Oncology. Baptist. Avocations: parenting, water-skiing, skiing, golf, tennis. Office: U Tex SW Med Ctr 5323 Harry Hines Blvd Dallas TX 75390-9156 Office Phone: 214-648-3013.

SIMMON, VINCENT FOWLER, biotechnology executive; b. L.A., Aug. 9, 1943; s. Vincent Joseph and Gertrude (Fowler) S.; m. Carol Ann Lamboy, Dec. 28, 1963 (div. 1973); 1 child, Stacy Anne; m. Berniece Irene Yocum, Jan. 2, 1983 (dec. 1988); children: Vincent F. Jr., Geoffrey Hamilton; m. Susan Lynn Sweeten, Nov. 3, 1990; children: Marcus Wesley, Katlyn Shea. BA, Amherst Coll., 1964; MS, U. Toledo, 1966; PhD, Brown U., 1971. Postdoctoral fellow Stanford U., Palo Alto, Calif., 1971-73; rschr. SRI Internat., Menlo Park, Calif., 1973-75, mgr., 1975-77, asst. dir., 1977-79; dept. dir. Genex Corp., Rockville, Md., 1979-80, v.p., 1980-83, sr. v.p., 1984-85; v.p. rsch. divsn. W.R. Grace & Co., Columbia, Md., 1985-90; pres., CEO Alpha 1 Biomeds., Inc., Washington, 1990-94, Viral Techs. Inc., Washington, 1990-94, Prototek, Inc., Potomac, Md., 1994—; also chmn. bd. dirs. Prototech, Inc., Potomac, Md. Councilor Envirn. Mutagen Soc., 1977-79; bd. dirs. chem. Industry Ins. for Toxicology, Research Triangle Park, N.C., 1986-90, Viral Tecs., Inc., Alpha I Biomedics, Inc. Mem. AAAS, Am. Chem. Soc. Address: Prototek Inc 11902 Coldstream Dr Potomac MD 20854-3615 Office: Cortex Pharmaceuticals Inc 15241 Barranca Pkwy Irvine CA 92618

SIMMONDS, JIMMIE NEIL, theater educator; b. Battle Creek, Mich., Jan. 16, 1949; s. Deland M. and Frances J. S; divorced; 1 child, Jayme Allen. BS in Art Edn., Bowling Green (Ohio) State U., 1971, MA, 1989; MA in Christian Ministry, Internat. Sch. Theology, San Bernardino, 1986. Nat. dir. for drama Campus Crusade for Christ, San Bernardino, Calif., 1972-88; graphic artist Lamb's Theatre, N.Y.C., 1987-88; tchr. Union County H.S., Lake Butler, Fla., 1989-91; prof. Daytona Beach (Fla.) C.C., 1989-91; performing arts prof. Savannah Coll. of Art and Design, Ga., 2001—. Varsity foresica coach Bowling Green State U., 1988-89; regional selection team Am. Coll. Theatre Festival Kennedy Ctr. for Performing Arts, Washington, 2000. Actor, dir. many community plays. Arby Flynn Meml scholarship Kellogg C.C., 1968. Mem. Fla. C.C. Activity Assn. (dir. theatre divsn., adjudicator, dir. 1995-2001), Phi Kappa Delta. Office: Savannah Coll of Art and Design PO Box 8146 Savannah GA 31402 E-mail: simmondsj@bdcc.cc.fl.us.

SIMMONDS, RAE NICHOLS, musician, composer, educator; b. Lynn, Mass., Feb. 25, 1919; d. Raymond Edward and Abbie Iola (Spinney) Nichols; m. Carter Fillebrown, Jr., June 27, 1941 (div. May 15, 1971); children: Douglas C. (dec.), Richard A., Mary L., Donald E.; m. Ronald John Simmonds, Oct. 9, 1971 (dec. Nov. 1995). AA, Westbrook Coll., Portland, Maine, 1981; B in Music Performance summa cum laude, U. Maine, 1984; MS in Edn., U. So. Maine, 1989; PhD, Walden U., 1994. Founder, dir. Studio of Music/Children's Studio of Drama, Portsmouth, N.H., 1964-71, Studio of Music, Bromley, Eng., 1971-73, Bromley Children's Theatre, 1971-73, Oughterard Children's Theatre, County Galway, Ireland, 1973-74, Studio of Music, Portland, Maine, 1977-96, West Baldwin, Maine, 1997—; resident playwright Children's Theatre of Maine, Portland, 1979-81; organist, choir dir. Stevens Ave. Congl. Ch., Portland, 1987-95; field faculty advisor Norwich U., Montpelier, Vt., 1995. Field advisor grad. program Vt. Coll., Norwich U., 1995; cons./educator mus. tng. for disabled vets. VA, Portsmouth, N.H., 1966-69; show pianist and organist, mainland U.S.A., 1939-59, Hawaii, 1959-62, Rae Nichols Trio, 1962—; mus. dir. Theatre By the Sea, Portsmouth, N.H., 1969-70. Author/composer children's musical: Shamrock Road, 1980 (Blue Stocking award 1980), Glooscap, 1980; author/composer original scripts and music: Cinderella, If I Were a Princess, Beauty and the Beast, Baba Yaga - A Russian Folk Tale, The Journey - Musical Bible Story, The Perfect Gift -

A Christmas Legend; original stories set to music include: Heidi, A Little Princess, Tom Sawyer, Jungle Book, Treasure Island; compositions include: London Jazz Suite, Bitter Suite, Jazz Suite for Trio, Sea Dream, Easter (chorale), Rae Simmonds Jazz Trio Songbook Series, (CD) Fascinatin' Gershwin Rae Simmonds Jazz Trio, 2000; contbr. Maine Women Writers Collection. Recipient Am. Theatre Wing Svc. award, 1944, Pease AFB Svc. Club award, 1967, Bumpus award Westbrook Coll., 1980; Nat. Endowment for Arts grantee, 1969-70; Women's Lit. scholar, 1980, Westbrook scholar, 1980-81, Nason scholar, 1983; Kelaniya U. (Colombo, Sri Lanka) rsch. fellow, 1985-86. Mem. ASCAP, Internat. Soc. Poets, Internat. League Women Composers, Music Tchrs. of Maine, Am. Guild of Organists, Music Tchrs. Nat. Assn., Internat. Alliance for Women in Music, Doctorate Assn. N.Y. Educators, Inc., Delta Omicron, Phi Kappa Phi. Democrat. Episcopalian. Avocations: travel, stamp collecting/philately. Home: 230 Douglas Hill Rd West Baldwin ME 04091-9715

SIMMONDS, ROBERT MAURER, education educator; b. Beaver Falls, Pa., Apr. 16, 1947; s. Harold Maurer and Mary Simmonds; m. Deborah Lynne Carawan, June 25, 1977; children; Stephen Maurer, Kent Hayes. BS, Youngstown State U., 1972, MS, 1975; advanced cert. edn., Coll. William and Mary, 1983, EdD, 1985; grad. sr. exec. fellows program JFK Sch. Govt., Harvard, 2004. Regional planner Southeastern Va. Planning Dist. Commn., Norfolk, 1977-78; statis. rsch. analyst Nat. Ctr. for State Cts., Williamsburg, Va., 1978-82; assoc. prof. St. Leo Coll., Ft. Eustis, Va., 1982-85; ops. rsch. analyst U.S. Army Transp. Sch., Ft. Eustis, 1985-88; dept. chmn. sys. engring. dept. U.S. Army Logistics Mgmt. Coll., Ft. Lee, Va., 1988—. Cons. Dep. Chief of Staff for Tng., Ft. Monroe, Va., 1992, Picatinny Arsenal, N.J., 1994-96, Concepts and Analysis Agy., Washington, 1999-2001. Contbr. articles to profl. jours. Mem. bus. adv. coun. Chesterfield (Va.) Tech. Ctr., 1999—2002; bd. dirs. Terence M. Lynch Pediatric Arthritis and Other Related Diseases Assn., Inc. With USN, 1965—68. Avocations: walking, golf. Office: US Army Logistics Mgmt Coll 2401 Quarters Rd Fort Lee VA 23801-1705 Office Phone: 804-765-4607. Business E-Mail: simmondr@lee.army.mil. E-mail: orsasad1@comcast.net.

SIMMONS, ADELE SMITH, foundation executive, former educator; b. Lake Forest, Ill., June 21, 1941; d. Hermon Dunlap and Ellen T. (Thorne) Smith; m. John L. Simmons; children— Ian, Erica, Kevin BA in Social Studies with honors, Radcliffe Coll., 1963; PhD, Oxford U., Eng., 1969; LHD (hon.), Lake Forest Coll., 1976, Amherst Coll., 1977, Franklin Pierce Coll., 1978, U. Mass., 1978, Alverno Coll., 1982, Marlboro Coll., 1987, Smith Coll., 1988, Mt. Holyoke Coll., 1989, Am. U., 1992, Tufts U., 1994. Asst. prof. Tufts U., Boston, 1969-72; dean Jackson Coll., Medford, Mass., 1970-72; asst. prof. history, dean student affairs Princeton U., N.J., 1972-77; pres. Hampshire Coll., Amherst, Mass., 1977-89, John D. and Catherine T. MacArthur Found., Chgo., 1989—99; vice chair, sr. exec. Chgo. Metropolis 2020, 1999—; sr. assoc. Ctr. for Internat. Studies U. Chgo., 1999—. Bd. dirs. Marsh & McLennan Cos., N.Y.C., 1st Chgo. Corp./NBD, Synergos, Union Concerned Scientists, Synergos Inst., Environ. Def. Fund, Global Fund for Women, Field Mus., Chgo.; emeritus mem. bd. dirs. Rocky Mountain Inst.; cons. Ford. Found., Stockholm Internat. Peace Rsch. Inst., Radcliffe Coll.; former corr. in Mauritius and Tunisia for N.Y. Times, The Economist; high level adv. bd. UN, 1993—; mem. adv. com. World Bank Inst. Co-author: (with Freeman, Dunkle, Blau) Exploitation from 9 to 5: Twentieth Century Fund Task Force Report on Working Women, 1975; author: Modern Mauritius, 1982; contbr. articles on edn. and pub. policy in The N.Y. Times, Christian Sci. Monitor, The Bulletin of Atomic Scientist, Harper's, The Atlantic Monthly and others. Commr. Pres.'s Commn. on World Hunger, Washington, 1978-80, Pres.'s Commn. on Environ. Quality, 1991-92; mem. Commn. Global Governance; trustee Carnegie Found. for Advancement Teaching, 1978-86; chair Mayor Richard Daily's Youth Devel. Task Force, 1993-95. Named one of Chgos. 100 Most Influential Women, Crain's Chgo. Bus., 2004. Fellow Am. Acad. Arts and Scis.; mem. Phi Beta Kappa. Office: Chgo Metropolis 2020 30 W Monroe St Chicago IL 60603*

SIMMONS, ANNE L. federal official; b. Spencer, Iowa, Jan. 4, 1964; d. Donald Lewis and Lois Amber (Blass) S. B in Spl. Studies, Cornell Coll., 1986. Intern for Congressman Berkley Bedell, Washington, 1986; field staff Iowans for Clayton Hodgson, Sioux City, Iowa, 1986; exec. sec. Atomic Indsl. Forum, Bethesda, Md., 1986-87; staff asst. House Armed Svcs. Com., Washington, 1987; legis. asst. to Congressman Tim Johnson Washington, 1988-93; staff dir. gen. farms commodities subcom. House Agriculture Com., Washington, 1993, staff dir. environ., credit and rural devel. subcom., 1994, minority resource conservation rsch. and forestry subcom., 1995-96. Profl. Staff Ho. Com. on Agrl., 1997—. Music scholar Cornell Coll., 1982-86. Mem. Delta Phi Alpha. Democrat. Office: House Agriculture Com 1301 Longworth House Ofc Bldg Washington DC 20515-0001 E-mail: anne.simmons@mail.house.gov.

SIMMONS, BETTYE H. career officer; BSc in Nursing, Incarnate Word Coll.; MSc in Nursing, U. Tex. Commd. 2d. lt. U.S. Army, 1971, advanced through grades to brigadier gen.; instr., clin. staff nurse Brooke Army Med. Ctr.; army nurse corps. coun. U.S. Army Recruiting Command; head nurse Walter Reed Army Med. Ctr.; dep. chief Acad. Helath Scis.; chief nurse Bayne-Jones U.S. Army Cmty. Hosp.; cons. to surgeon gen. Nursing Adminstrn.; various assignments U.S. Army Med. Command; dep. comdr. U.S. Army Med. Dept. Ctr. and Sch.; dep. installation comdr. Fort Sam Houston, Tex.; chief Army Nurse Corps., 1995—; command surgeon U.S. Army Forces Command, 1997—. Decorated Legion of Merit with one oak leaf cluster, Meritorious Svc. medal with four oak leaf clusters. Mem. Order of Military Med. Merit.

SIMMONS, CARL KENNETH, cooperative executive; b. Kingman, Ind., Dec. 5, 1914; s. Claud Elmer and Sylvia Ethyl (Myers) Simmons; m. Allice Lucille Weaver, Dec. 16, 1939; 1 child, Erma Jane Simmons Barlow. Grad. exec. devel. program, Ind. U., 1959. Petroleum dept. mgr. Fountain County Coop., Veedersburg, Ind., 1936—40; dist. mgr. Ind. Farm Bur. Coop., Indpls., 1946—47; treas., mgr. Delaware County Coop., Muncie, 1940—46, 1948—86, emeritus gen. mgr., treas., 1986—. Pres., treas. Bi-County Line Farms, Inc., Kingman, 1980—. Mem. Mayor's Citizens Com., Muncie, 1982; bd. dirs. Delaware County Airport Authority, 1972—84, pres., 1983—84, CEO, 1984—. Mem.: Ind. Flying Farmers, Muncie Rifle Club, Masons (32 degree). Home: 225 E Centennial Ave Muncie IN 47303-2903 Office: 1100 W Carl Simmons Dr Muncie IN 47303 Office Phone: 765-747-5690.

SIMMONS, CLINTON CRAIG, human resources executive; b. Cleve., Nov. 25, 1947; s. Benjamin F. and Catharin (Thornton) R.; m. Cheryl LeRoy, June 16, 1973; 1 child, Eric. BBA, Miami U., Oxford, Ohio, 1969; grad. quality mgmt. course, Winter Park, Fla., 1986. Cert. quality edn. system instr. Specialist employee and cmty. rels. Euclid Lamp Plant, GE, Cleve., 1970-75; employee and indsl. rels. rep. Bailey Controls Co., Wickliffe, Ohio, 1975-78; mgr., coll. recruiting Gen. Tire and Rubber, Akron, Ohio, 1978-81, profl. staffing coord., 1981-82; regional human resource mgr. Gilbane Bldg. Co., Cleve., 1982-86, human resource mgr. Western regions, 1987-88; asst. v.p., dir. human resources St. Alexis Hosp. Med. Ctr. CA div. Sisters of St. Francis, 1988-90; corp. pers. mgr. MK-Ferguson Co., 1990-94, mgr. human resources, 1993-94; mgr. human resources engring., constrn. and environ. group Washington Group Internat., Cleve., 1994-2001, sr. mgr. human resources, 2001—; human resources cons. Key Source HCI, LLC, 2003—, Highbridge Assoc., 2003—. Author: (with w.J. McBurney Jr.) College Recruitment: Effective Programs and Practices, 1982. Past chmn. orgn. and extension com. Newton D. Baker Dist., Greater Cleve. coun. Boy Scouts Am., 1970-71; mem. Human Resource Com. for Greater Cleve. United Way, NAACP, Urban League of Cleve.; mem. pension and benefit coms. Greater Cleve. Hosp. Assn., 1988-90; Bd. Edn. commr. Villa Angela Acad. (pres., 1986-87, U.S. Edn. Dept. award 1987); founder, advisor Explorer Post, Gilbane Bldg. Co., Cleve., 1984-88; Cleve., 1988—; v.p. adv. bd. Cath. Social Svcs. Cuyahoga County, chmn. coun. advisors, 1992-93; mem. urban regional bd. Cath. Edn. Cleve., 1986; trustee Marotta Montessori Sch. of Cleve., 1993—, pres.-elect, 1993, pres., 1993-2000; founding trustee Harambee Svcs. Orgn. Cleve., 1987—; trustee Cath. Charities Svcs. Corp. N.E. Ohio, 1992—, Benedictine H.S.; mem. edn. commn. Villa Angela St. Joseph High Sch., 1990—, pres., 1993—; chmn. coun. advisors Cath. Social Svcs. Cuyahoga County, 1992—. Recipient commendation Nat. Alliance of Bus., Akron, 1979, Cmty. Svc. award WJW-Northwest Orient Airlines, 1975. Mem. Cleve. EEO Assn., Soc. Human Resources Mgmt., Soc. Am. Mil. Engrs., U.S. Naval Inst., Mid-West Coll. Placement Assn. (chmn. rubber industry com. 1979-81), Ctr. for Human Svcs. (v.p., trustee, vice chmn. bd. trustees), Internat. Human Resources Assn., Indsl. Rels. Rsch. Assn., Human Resources Systems Assn., Alpha Phi Alpha. Democrat. Roman Catholic. Home: 24400 Emery Rd Cleveland OH 44128-5614 Fax: 216-990-0898. E-mail: c.simmons@thekeysource.com., csimmons@highbridgeassociates.com.

SIMMONS, DEBORAH JO, pharmacy executive; b. Houston, July 31, 1953; d. Joe George Haskovec and Olga Norma (Clifton) Kirkland; m. Dennis Edwin Simmons, Mar. 24, 1979 (div. May 1988). BS, U. Tex., 1975. Registered pharmacist, Tex., Fla. Pharmacy intern Eckerd Drug Co., Dallas County, Tex., 1976, pharmacist, 1976-82, pharmacy area mgr. north Tex. Garland, 1982-86, pharmacy svcs. mgr. north Tex., 1986-90, pharmacy svcs. mgr. Largo, Fla., 1990-92; dir. pharmacy devel. Eckerd Corp., Largo, 1992—2002, sr. dir. pharmacy devel., 2002—. Dir. Eckerd Credit Union, Largo, 1993, 96, 98, vice-chair, 1994-95, 97. Mem. Am. Pharmacy Assn. (adminstrv. practice mem.-at-large 1997-99, chair-elect 2000, chair 2001, nominating com. 1999, 2000, publs. com. 1997-98, awards com. 2000, pharmacy practice com. 2001), Tex. Pharmacy Assn. (pub. affairs com. 1988-91, vice-chair ho. dels. 1990-91, chair 1991-92), Fla. Pharmacy Assn. (orgnl. affairs coun. 1999-2001, profl. affairs coun. 2001-03), Dallas County Pharmacy Soc. (pres. 1989-90), Am. Heart Assn. (bd. dirs. Pinellas County, 1999--, vice chmn. 2002-03, chmn. 2003-04). Avocations: travel, reading. Office: Eckerd Corp 8333 Bryan Dairy Rd Largo FL 33777-1230 E-mail: dsimm9@cs.com.

SIMMONS, DEBRA ADAMS, editor; m. Jonathan Simmons; children: Jacob, Jonathan. BA, Syracuse (N.Y.) U.; diploma in Advanced Exec. Program, Northwestern U. Reporter Syracuse (N.Y.) Herald-Jour., The Hartford (Conn.) Courant; metro editor The Virginian Post; asst. metro editor and reporter Detroit (Mich.) Free Press; dep. mng. editor The Virginian-Pilot, Norfolk, Va., 2000—03; mng. editor Akron (Ohio) Beacon Jour., 2003, editor, 2003—, v.p., 2003—. Office: Akron Beacon Journal 44 E Exchange St PO Box 640 Akron OH 44309-0640*

SIMMONS, DEIDRE WARNER, retired performing company executive, arts consultant; b. Easton, Pa., May 11, 1955; d. Francis Joseph and Irene Carol (Burd) Mooney; m. Robert D. Jacobson, June 27, 1981 (div. Mar. 1989); m. William Richard Simmons, Aug. 18, 1990; children: Caitlin Dawn, Abigail Patricia, Samantha Irene. BA in Music, Montclair State Coll., 1978. Music tchr. Warren Hills Regional Sch., Washington, NJ, 1978-80; devel. dir. N.J. Shakespeare Festival, Madison, 1981-83; dir. contbns. Parent Found., Lancaster, Pa., 1983-86; exec. dir. Fulton Opera House, Lancaster, 1986—2003, capital campaign counsel, 1990-95, dir. theatre advancement, 2000—03; arts cons., 2003—. Bd. dirs. WITF, 2000—. Vice chmn. bd. dirs. Ind. Eye, Lancaster, 1986—89; bd. dirs. Pa. Dutch Conv. and Visitors Bur., Lancaster Campaign; chair Destination Downtown. Recipient Exemplar award, Lancaster C. of C. and Industry, 2003. Mem.: League Hist. Theatres, Theatre Comm. Group. Avocations: piano, singing. E-mail: dwsimmons@comcast.net.

SIMMONS, EDWIN HOWARD, marine corps officer, historian; b. Paulsboro, N.J., Aug. 25, 1921; s. Edwin Lonsdale and Nettie Emma (Vankirk) S.; m. Frances Bliss, Apr. 25, 1962; children: Edwin Howard, Clarke Vankirk, Bliss, Courtney. BA, Lehigh U., 1942; MA, Ohio State U., 1955; postgrad., Amphibious Warfare Sch., 1949—50, Nat. War Coll., 1966—67. Commd. 2d lt. USMC, 1942, advanced through grades to brig. gen., 1967; asst. prof. NROTC, Ohio State U., 1952-55; with Hdqrs. Marine Corps, 1955- 59; naval attache Dominican Republic, 1959-60; with Hdqrs. Marine Corps and Joint Staff, 1962-65, 3d Marine Divsn., 1965-66, 1st Marine Divsn., Vietnam, 1970-71; dep. fiscal dir. Marine Corps, 1967-70; dir. Marine Corps history and museums USMC Hdqrs., Arlington, Va., 1971-95, dir. emeritus, 1996—. Pres. Am. Mil. Inst., 1979; v.p. U.S. Commn. Mil. History, 1979-83; exec. v.p. Marine Corps Hist. Found., 1979-96; pres. Coun. Am. Mil. Past, 1991-95. Author: The United States Marines, 1974, 76, 98, 2002, Marines, 1987, Dog Company Six, 2000, Frozen Chosin, 2002; editor: The Marines, 1998; mng. editor: Marine Corps Gazette, 1946-49; sr. editor: Publs. Group, Marine Corps Schs., 1960-61; Contbr. to numerous books, encys., mags., jours. and annuals. Decorated D.S.M., Silver Star, Legion of Merit with two gold stars, Bronze Star with gold star, Meritorious Svc. medal, Navy Commendation medal, Purple Heart; knight Nat. Order of Vietnam, Vietnamese Cross of Gallantry with 2 palms and silver star; recipient Centennial Disting. Grad. medallion Ohio State U., 1970. Fellow Co. Mil. Historians; mem. Am. Soc. Mil. Comptrollers (nat. v.p. 1967-69, pres. 1969-70), Nat. War Coll. Alumni Assn. (v.p. 1969-70, 74-75), Phi Beta Kappa, Omicron Delta Kappa, Phi Sigma Kappa. Home: 9020 Charles Augustine Dr Alexandria VA 22308-2822

SIMMONS, ELROY, JR., retired utility executive; b. Johnstown, Pa., Sept. 23, 1928; s. Elroy and Hazel Maria (Shomo) S. BS in Bus. Adminstrn., U. Pitts., 1951. With Pa. Electric Co., Johnstown, 1953, system treasury asst., 1969-71, system coordinator, treasury services, 1971-74, asst. treas., 1974-79, sec., treas., 1979-90; ret., 1990. Bd. dirs. Community Arts Ctr. of Cambria County, 1987-95. With CIC, U.S. Army, 1951-53. Mem. Pa. Electric Assn. (customer relations com. 1965-69), Nat. Corp. Cash Mgmt. Assn., Nat. Assn. Accts., Nat. Assn. Corp. Treas. Republican. Methodist. Home: 1023 Hillside Trl Johnstown PA 15905-1234

SIMMONS, EMMY B, federal agency administrator; b. Suring, Ws. m. Roger Simmons. B, U. Wis., Milw.; M Agrl. Econs., Cornell U. Vol. Peace Corps, agrl. rschr.; agrl. economist USAID, 1978—91, supv. program economist regional office East and So. Africa, 1991—94, sr. program officer mission in Moscow, 1994—97, deputy asst. adminstr., 1997—2002, asst. adminstr. bus. econ. growth, agrl. and trade, 2002—. Office: USAID RRB 1300 Pannsylvanis AVe NW Washington DC 20523-3900

SIMMONS, ENID BROWN, retired state agency administrator; b. Washington, June 6, 1947; d. Charles Mathews Brown and Susie (Nickens) Ludlow; m. Warren Simmons, Nov. 30, 1985; children: Stacey Arlene Herndon, Robert Eric Herndon, Nicholas Maxville Simmons. BA cum laude, Howard U., 1970, MA, 1973. With D.C. Pub. Schs., 1970-73; sr. evaluation cons. CTB/McGraw-Hill, Washington, 1973-79; sr. policy fellow Nat. Inst. Edn., Washington, 1979-80, sr. rsch. assoc.; rsch. area team leader Office Edn. Rsch. U.S. Dept. Edn., Washington, 1980-87; dep. assoc. dir. Office of Policy and Program Evaluation, Exec. Office Mayor, Washington, 1987-90; dir. office of policy and program evaluation Office of the Mayor, 1991—. Cons. Mid-Atlantic Equity Ctr., Am. U., Washington, 1988—. Author: Your Child and Testing, 1980, 89; exec. producer TV series Who's Keeping Score?, 1981. Bd. dirs. Lowell Sch., Community Prevention Partnership and Consortium and Univs. of Washington. Mem. Jack and Jill. Avocation: aerobics. Office: Govt of DC 441 4th St NW Washington DC 20001-2714

SIMMONS, GENE, musician; b. Haifa, Israel, Aug. 25, 1949; came to U.S., 1958, naturalized, 1963; A.BA, Sullivan Coll., SUNY, 1970; BA, Richmond Coll., CUNY, 1972. Singer, songwriter, actor, 1970—; founder, 1973 thereafter mem. group Kiss. Albums include: Alive, 1975, Kiss-The Originals, 1976, Destroyer, 1976, Rock & Roll Over, 1976, Love Gun, 1977, Alive II, 1977, Double Platinum, 1978, Gene Simmons, 1978, Dynasty, 1979, Unmasked, 1980, Music From the Elder, 1981, Creatures of the Night, 1982, Lick It Up, 1983, Animalize, 1984, Kiss, 1974, Hotter Than Hell, 1974, Dressed to Kill, 1975, Beth, 1976, I Was Made for Lovin' You, 1979, Asylum, 1985, Crazy Nights, 1987, Hot In The Shade, 1989, Smashes, Thrashes and Hits, 1989, Revenge, 1992, Alive III, 1993, MTV: Kiss Unplugged, 1996; film appearances include Kiss-Attack of the Phantom, 1978, Runaway, 1984, Never Too Young To Die, 1986, Trick or treat, 1986, Wanted: Dead or Alive, 1987, The Return of Bruno, 1988, Red Surf, 1990, Detroit Rock City, 1999. Winner 16 Gold Record Albums, 12 Platinum Record Albums, 2 Gold Single Records Mem. Am. Fedn. Musicians, AFTRA, ASCAP. Inventor of Axe bass guitar, 1980. Office: care Polygram Records Inc Worldwide Pla 825 8th Ave New York NY 10019-7416 *Listen to everyone around you, but do only what you believe.*

SIMMONS, GEOFFREY STUART, physician; b. Camp Gordon, Ga., July 28, 1943; s. Ted R. and Jane A. (Lavander) Simmons; m. Sherry Simmons, Sept. 7, 1985; children: Bradley, Anais. BS, U. Ill., 1965, MD, 1969. Diplomate Am. Bd. Internal Medicine. Intern U. So. Calif., L.A., 1969-70, resident, 1971-74; pvt. practice Astoria, Oreg., 1974-77, Eugene, Oreg., 1977—; chmn. internal medicine dept. Peace Health Med. Group, 1996-98, 2000—. Med. corres. KUGN Radio, 1993—95; chair Med. Res. Corps Coun., 2002—. Author: (book) The Z Papers, 1977, The Adam Experiment, 1978, Pandemic, 1980, Murdock, 1982, The Glue Factory, 1995, To Glue or Not to Glue, 1997, What Darwin Didn't Know, 2004; med. commentator KABC Radio, 1970. Mem.: Eugene Citizen Corps., Lane County Med. Soc. (chmn. task force for disaster preparedness 2001—03, chmn. bioterrorism task force, certs. trainer 2001—03, chair med. res. corps coun. Lane County 2002—03, pres. 2003—, bd. dirs.). Avocation: writing.

SIMMONS, GEORGE FINLAY, retired mathematics professor; b. Austin, Tex., Mar. 3, 1925; s. George Finlay and Armede Victoria (Hatcher) S.; m. Hope Bridgeford, Sept. 11, 1954; 1 child, Nancy Bingham. BS, Caltech, 1946; MS, U. Chgo., 1948; PhD, Yale U., 1957. Instr. U. Chgo., 1947-50, U. Maine, Orono, 1950-52, Yale U., New Haven, 1952-56; asst. prof. U. R.I., Kingston, 1956-58, Williams College, Williamstown, Mass., 1958-62; assoc. prof. math. Colo. Coll., Colorado Springs, 1962-65, prof., 1965-90, prof. emeritus, 1990—. Author: Introduction Topology and Modern Analysis, 1962, Differential Equations, 1972, 3rd edit., 2004, Precalculus Mathematics in a Nutshell, 1981, Calculus with Analytic Geometry, 1985, 2nd edit., 1995, Calculus Gems: Brief Lives and Memorable Mathematics, 1992. Mem. Math. Assn. Am. Avocations: travel, cooking, trout fishing, billiards. Home: 1401 Wood Ave Colorado Springs CO 80907-7348 Office: Colorado College Dept Math Colorado Springs CO 80903

SIMMONS, HARDWICK, stock exchange executive; b. Balt., June 8, 1940; s. Edward Ball and Margaret (Hardwick) S.; m. Sarah Bradlee Dolan, Sept. 9, 1962; children— Elizabeth, Huntington, Benjamin. BA, Harvard U., 1962, MBA, 1966. V.p. Hayden's Stone's Data Processing and Comm. Divsn., 1969, mgr., 1970, exec. v.p. retail and sales adminstrn., 1973; sr. exec. v.p. mktg. and sales Shearson/Am. Express, 1977; with Shearson Lehman Bros. Inc., 1966—, regional officer, 1972-75; vice chmn., dir. Shearson Lehman Hutton Inc. (formerly Shearson Lehman Bros. Inc.), NYC, 1975-90; chief exec. officer Prudential Securities Inc., NYC, 1991—2001; CEO, chmn. The Nasdaq Stock Market Inc., Washington, 2001—03. Dir. Chgo. Bd. Options Exchange. Served with USMCR, 1959-60. Served, 1960—66, U.S. Marine Corps Res. Mem. Bond Club N.Y.C. Republican.

SIMMONS, HENRY E. health care association executive; Undergrad. degree, MD, U. Pitts.; MPH, Harvard U. Dep. asst. for health Dept. Health, Edn. and Welfare, dir. Office Profl. Stds. Rev.; dir. Bru. of Drugs FDA; sr. v.p. J. Walter Thompson Co.; pres., CEO Hunterdon Med. Ctr., Flemington, N.J.; sr. v.p., dir. health care divsn. Sears World Trade, Inc.; dir. health and med. consulting divsn. Peat, Marwick, Mitchell & Co.; pres. Nat. Coalition on Health Care, 1988—. Vis. rsch. prof. Sch. Bus. and Govt., George Washington U.; faculty, cons. rheumatic diseases and internal medicine Tufts New Eng. Med. Ctr.; prof. cmty. and family medicine Rutgers U. Sch. Medicine; asst. clin. prof. medicine Georgetown U.; assoc. prof. medicine George Washington U. Sch. Medicine. Office: Nat Coalition on Health Care 1200 G St NW Ste 750 Washington DC 20005-6702

SIMMONS, HOWARD L. education educator; b. Mobile, Ala. BS in Secondary Edn., Spring Hill Coll., 1960; MAT in Slavic langs. and Lit., Ind. U., 1965; PhD in Design and Mgmt. of Postsecondary Edn., Fla. State U., 1975; LHD (hon.), Sojourner-Douglass Coll., 1995; HHD (hon.), King's Coll., 1998. Assoc. dir., asst. exec. sec. Commn. on Higher Edn. Middle States Assn. Colls. and Schs., Phila., 1974-95, exec. dir., 1988-95; prof. edn. leadership in higher edn. Ariz. State U., Tempe, 1996-2000, prof. emeritus, 2000—, assoc. dean, 1996-97; chair Dept. Adv. Studies, Leadership and Policy, 2003—; prof., coord. higher edn. doctoral program Morgan State U., Balt., 2001—. Vis. lectr. Russian Lafayette Coll., Easton, Pa., 1970—71; part-time Russian/Spanish instr. Clayton (Mo.) High Sch., 1965—67; dean instructional servs. Northampton C.C., Bethlehem, Pa., 1969—74; chmn. dept. fgn. lang. Forest Park C.C., Mo., 1964—69; sr. rschr. Ariz. State U., 1986—87, Nat. Ctr. Postsecondary Governance and Fin., 1986—87; cons. in field including cons./evaluator North Ctrl. Colls. and Schs., 1997—; prin. cons. Global Consults. in Higher Educ.; keynote speaker in field; rschr. on accreditation and blacks in higher educ.; app. Bd. Behavioral Health Examiners State Ariz., 1999; mem. commn. accreditation Coun. Chiropractic Edn., 2000; apptd. mem. Accreditation Com. on Acupuncture and Oriental Medicine, 2002—, APA Com. on Accreditation Adv. Coun., 2003—. Contbr. articles to profl. jours. Gov. apptd. mem. Bd. Behavioral Health Examiners. NDEA grantee Spring Hill Coll., 1958-60, grantee Japan-U.S. Friendship Commn., 1993-94; NDEA fellow Ind. U., 1963-64, Edn. Professions Devel. Act fellow Fla. State U., 1973-75, fellow Am. Coun. Edn., 1972-73; USIA Acad. Specialist grantee, Quito, Ecuador, 1996; ETS-HBCU rsch. scholar, 2003-04. Mem. Am. Ednl. Rsch. Assn., Am. Assn. for Cmty. and Jr. Colls. (assoc.), Assn. for Study of Higher Edn., Assn. Tchrs. Slavic and East European Langs., Assn. Caribbean Tertiary Instn., Am. Assn. for Higher Edn. (exec. bd. black caucus, nat. cultural diversity award by caucuses 1992), Lang. Labs. and Faculty Assn. Pres. (dir.), Phi Delta Kappa, Kappa Delta Pi. Home: 218 N Charles St Apt 604 Baltimore MD 21201 Office: Morgan State U Jenkins Hall 301 1700 E Cold Spring Ln Baltimore MD 21251 Office Phone: 443-885-1969. Business E-Mail: hsimmons@moac.morgan.edu. E-mail: simmons21@aol.com., simmons421@aol.com.

SIMMONS, JANET BRYANT, writer, publisher; b. Oakland, Calif., Apr. 22, 1925; d. Howard Pelton and Janet Horn (McNab) Bryant; m. William Ellis Simmons, May 17, 1944 (div. 1979); children: William Howard, Janet Margaret Simmons McAlpine. BA, San Jose State U., 1965; MA, U. San Francisco, 1979. Social worker Santa Clara County Social Svcs., San Jose, Calif., 1965-91; editor, pub. Enlightenment Press, Santa Clara, 1994—. Author: The Mystical Child, 1996. Mem. AAUW, Am. Booksellers Assn., Pubs. Mktg. Assn., Bay Area Ind. Pubs. Assn., Audubon Soc., Jacques Cousteau Soc. Avocations: playing piano, swimming, tai chi, travel, gardening. Office: Enlightenment Press PO Box 3314 Santa Clara CA 95055-3314 Office Phone: 408-248-3222. Personal E-mail: jntssimmons@aol.com.

SIMMONS, JOHN DEREK, retired financial consultant; b. Essex, Eng., July 17, 1931; arrived in U.S., 1952; s. Simon Leonard and Eve (Smart) Simmons; m. Rosalind Wellish, Mar. 5, 1961; children: Peter Lawrence, Sharon Leslie. BS, Columbia U., 1956; MBA, Rutgers U., 1959; postgrad., NYU, 1959-62. Chief cost acct. Airborne Accessories, Hillside, NJ, 1952-57; sr. cost analyst Curtiss-Wright Corp., Wood Ridge, NJ, 1957; sr. fin. analyst internat. group Ford Motor Co., Jersey City, 1958-60; rsch. assoc. Nat. Assn. Accts. (now Inst. Mgmt. Accts.), N.Y.C., 1960-64; asst. to v.p. fin. Air Reduction Co., Inc., 1965—67; mgr. corp. planning Anaconda Wire & Cable Co., N.Y.C., 1968; ind. fin. cons., 1968-71; assoc. cons. Rogers, Slade & Hill, Inc., N.Y.C., 1969-71; v.p., security analyst, economist Moore & Schley, Cameron & Co. (name now Fourteen Rsch. Corp.), 1972-81; v.p., security analyst Merrill Lynch Capital Markets, N.Y.C., 1981-88; security analyst Arnhold and S. Bleichroeder, Inc., 1988—89; v.p., security analyst, corp. fin. specialist Smith Barney, Harris Upham & Co., Inc., 1989—90; sr. cons. Carl Byoir & Assocs., 1991—94; assoc. mng. dir. Commonwealth Assocs., 1994—95; mng. dir. State St. Capital Markets Corp., 1996; v.p. GKN Securities Corp., 1996—97; dir. instnl. sales Gabelli & Co., Rye, 1997; assoc. Manning, Selvage & Lee, N.Y.C., 1998—2001; ret., 2001. Lectr. profl. socs. and confs.; lectr. econs., mgm., polit. sci. Rutgers U., 1957—64; lectr. fin. and bus. Marymount Manhattan Coll., N.Y.C., 2002—. Contbr. articles to U.S. and fgn. publs. Docent Asia Soc. and Mus., N.Y.C., 2002—. 1st lt. Brit. Army, 1950—52.

Grantee personal coat of Arms, by Queen Elizabeth II: manorial Lord of Ash, Suffolk, Eng. Mem.: Knight Templar Sovereign Mil. Order Temple of Jerusalem. Home: 360 E 72d St New York NY 10021-4753 E-mail: johnlordash@aol.com.

SIMMONS, LAWRENCE WILLIAM, healthcare company executive; b. Omaha, May 7, 1947; s. Albin Pachola and Leella Clarice (Franklin) S.; m. Leanna Carol McGee, Nov. 3, 1968; children: Scott, Anthony. Assoc. Gen. Studies, U. Nebr., 1977, B Gen. Studies, 1978. Pharm. sales rep. 3M Pharms., Omaha, 1972-83, dist. sales mgr. Chgo., 1983-89, regional sales mgr. midwest region St. Paul, 1989-92, group bus. mgr. pharm. and personal care Mexico City, 1992-95; group bus. dir. divsn. V health care 3M Mex., 1995-98; nat. mgr. managed care 3M Pharm., St. Paul, 1998—. Cluster mem. Xavier U., New Orleans, 1987—; minority outreach rep. 3M, St. Paul, 1987—. With U.S. Army, 1968-71, Vietnam. Mem. Kappa Alpha Psi (polemarch 1981-83, best chpt. award 1983). Office: 3M Center W-01 Bldg 275-3 Saint Paul MN 55144-0001

SIMMONS, LEE GUYTON, JR., zoological park director; b. Tucson, Feb. 20, 1938; s. Lee Guyton and Dorothy Esther (Taylor) S.; m. Marie Annette Geim, Sept. 6, 1959; children: Lee Guyton, Heather, Heidi. Student, Cen. State Coll.; DVM, Okla. State U. Resident veterinarian Columbus Zoo, Powell, Ohio, 1963-66, Henry Doorly Zoo, Omaha, 1966-70, dir., 1970—. Research cons. VA Hosp.; assoc. instr. U. Nebr. Med. Ctr., Omaha; assoc. clin. prof. Creighton U. Sch. Dentistry. Contbr. articles to profl. jours. Bd. dirs. Nebr. State Mus., Lincoln. Served with USAR. Recipient Nat. Idealism award City of Hope, 1979; named Man of Yr., Lions Club, 1978. Fellow AVMA, Am. Assn. Zool. Veterinarians (pres.), Am. Assn. Zool. Parks, Nebr. Vet. Med. Assn. (Veterinarian of Yr. 1979). Lodges: Rotary. Office: Henry Doorly Zoo Office of the Director 3701 S 10th St Omaha NE 68107-2200

SIMMONS, MARK, state representative; m. Joni Simmons; children: Lindy, Holly. With Boise Cascade, Oreg.; mem. Oreg. Ho. of Reps., 1997—, House Majority Whip, 1999, House Majority Leader, 1999, speaker, 2002—. Republican. Office: Speaker of the House 900 Court St NE Rm 269 Salem OR 97301

SIMMONS, MARSHA THRIFT, science and reading educator, musician; b. Brunswick, Ga., Jan. 18, 1953; d. James Russell II and Ouida (Tyre) Thrift; m. Samuel Leland Simmons, Aug. 2, 1975; 1 child, Natalie Renee. BA, Agnes Scott Coll., 1975; MEd, Coll. of Charleston, 1980; MA, Regent U., 2001. Cert. tchr., Tenn., postgrad. profl. lic., Va. Organist Epworth United Meth. Ch., Atlanta, 1975-76; tchr. 3d grade Hanahan (S.C.) Acad., 1976-77; grad. asst. Coll. of Charleston, S.C., 1977-78, sub. tchr. Early Childhood Devel. Ctr., 1978-79; owner, tchr. Marsha's Music (Studio and Store), S.C., Ga., Tex., Tenn., Va., 1979—; tchr. presch. Sykes Daycare, Lawrenceville, Ga., 1994; sub. tchr. Glynn County Schs., Brunswick, Ga., 1994; tchr. 6th grade sci. and reading Jackson (Tenn.)-Madison County Schs., 1995-97; sub. tchr. Virginia Beach (Va.) City Pub. Schs., Va., 1997—2000; doctoral intern Taylor Clinic, Brownwood, Tex. Treas. Kingwood (Tex.) Music Tchrs. Assn., 1985-87; mem. local sch. adv. com. Gwinnett County Bd. Edn., Lawrenceville, Ga., 1993-94; Odyssey of the Mind coord., coach N.E. Mid. Sch., Jackson, 1995-97; lead tchr. sci. stds. implementation Jackson-Madison County Schs., 1996-97; subst. tchr. Va. Beach City Schs., 1997-99; tchr. asst. Regent U., 2002-03; adminstrv. asst. U. Psychol. Svcs. Ctr., 2003—. Leader Girl Scouts Am., St. Simons Island, Ga., 1988-89; PTA v.p. and cultural arts chmn. Benefield Elem. Sch., Lawrenceville, 1991-93; chmn. cmty. outreach West Tenn. Music Tchr.'s Assn., Jackson, 1996-97. Recipient Spl. Svc. award Girl Scouts Am., 1989, Outstanding Woman in Bus. and Edn. award Parker Chapel Christian Meth. Episcopal Ch., Tenn., 1996, Lockheed Martin fellow Lockheed Martin Corp., 1997. Mem. ACA, Am. Guild Organists, Music Tchrs. Nat. Assn., Am. Assn. of Christian Counselors, Am. Psychol. Assn. Avocations: reading, cooking, sewing, crafts, drawing, painting. Home: 2413 Avenue E Brownwood TX 76801

SIMMONS, MARVIN GENE, geophysics educator; b. Dallas, May 15, 1929; s. Burt H. and Mable (Marshall) S.; m. Dorothy Richter; children by previous marriage: Jon Eric, Debra Lynn, Sandra Kay, Pamela Jean. BS, Tex. Agrl. and Mech. Coll., 1949; MS, So. Methodist U., 1958; PhD, Harvard U., 1962. Registered profl. geologist, N.H., Ky. Petroleum engr. Humble Oil Co., 1949-51; propr. gravel business, 1953-58; asst. prof. So. Meth. U., 1962-65; prof. geophysics MIT, 1965-89, prof. emeritus, 1989—; prin. Hager-Richter Geoscience Inc., 1989—. Cons. NASA, 1965-72; chief scientist NASA (Manned Spacecraft Center), Houston, 1969-71; cons. on siting of nuclear facilities; sec. Internat. Heat Flow Com., 1967-71; chmn. com. drilling for sci. purposes Nat. Acad. Scis., 1965; Mem. geophysics panel NSF. Served with USAF, 1951-53. NSF postdoctoral fellow, 1961-62 Fellow Geol. Soc. Am., Am. Geophys. Union; mem. ASTM (com. C-18 on dimension stone 1986—), Boston Geol. Soc. (pres. 1967-68), Soc. Exploration Geophysicists, Sigma Xi, Tau Beta Pi. Achievements include research on physical properties of materials, lunar exploration, marine geophysics, temperature of earth, regional geophysics, engineering geology and geophysics. Home: 180 N Policy St Salem NH 03079-1916 Office: 8 Industrial Way Unit D10 Salem NH 03079-2837

SIMMONS, MARY JANE, state legislator; b. Leominster, Mass., May 14, 1953; Mem. Mass. Ho. of Reps., Boston, 1993—. Office: Mass Ho of Reps State House Rm 146 Boston MA 02133 E-mail: rep.maryjanesimmons@hou.state.ma.us.

SIMMONS, MICHAEL ANTHONY, pediatrician; m. Margaret Clare Martindale (div.); children: Kristen Ann, Jeffrey Michael, Jennifer Clare Roe, Jason Davis. AB cum laude, Harvard Coll., 1963, MD, 1967. Diplomate Am. Bd. Pediatrics, Am. Bd. Neonatal-Perinatal Medicine. Intern Harriet Lane Svc., Johns Hopkins Hosp., Balt., 1967—68, asst. resident, 1968—69, sr. asst. resident, 1969; chief resident Dept. Pediatrics, U. Colo. Med. Ctr., Denver, 1971—72, rsch. fellow in perinatal medicine, 1972—74, clin. instr. in pediatrics, 1974—77, assoc. prof. pediatrics, 1977; assoc. prof. pediatrics and obstetrics Johns Hopkins U. Sch. Medicine, Balt., 1977—83; prof., chmn. dept. pediatrics U. Utah Sch. of Medicine, Salt Lake City, 1983—94; dean U. N.C. at Chapel Hill Sch. Medicine, 1994—97, prof. pediatrics, 1994—, interim chief, 1997. Adj. prof. dept. obstetrics and gynecology U. Utah Sch. of Medicine, Salt Lake City, 1984-94; co-dir. newborn svcs. U. Colo. Med. Ctr., Denver, 1974-77, Johns Hopkins Hosp., 1977-83; mem. staff Denver Gen. Hosp., 1976-77, Denver Children's Hosp., 1976-77; vice chmn. clin. affairs dept. pediatrics Johns Hopkins Hosp., 1981-83; chief of pediatrics U. Utah Med. Ctr., Salt Lake City, 1983-94; med. dir. Primary Children's Med. Ctr., 1983-94; bd. dirs. Triangle Univs. Licensing Consortium, U. N.C. Hosps. Contbr. numerous articles to profl. jours. Fellow Am. Acad. of Pediatrics (excellence in pediatric rsch. com. 1991—, coun. on govt. affairs 1992—); mem. Perinatal Rsch. Soc. (coun. 1982-84, pres.-elect 1985-87, pres. 1989), Western Soc. for Pediatric Rsch. (coun. 1985-86, pres.-elect 1987, pres. 1988), Soc. for Pediatric Rsch., Am. Bd. Pediatrics (sub-bd. of neonatal-perinatal medicine 1983-89, chmn. 1984-88). Office: UNC Health Care 101 Manning Dr Chapel Hill NC 27514 Office Phone: 336-832-6160. Personal E-mail: michael.simmons@mosescone.com.

SIMMONS, NORBERT A. entertainment company executive; BA, Tulane U.; JD, Boston U., 1972. Pres., CEO Belle of Orleans, New Orleans. Office: Belle of Orleans 25th Fl 201 Saint Charles Ave Fl 25 New Orleans LA 70170-1000

SIMMONS, PETER LAWRENCE, lawyer; b. NYC, May 1, 1965; s. John Derek and Rosalind (Wellish) S.; m. Corinne Ryan, Apr 7, 2001; children: Mark R., Matthew S. AB magna cum laude, Columbia U., 1985, JD, 1987. Bar: N.Y. 1987, U.S. Dist. Ct. (so. and ea. dists.) N.Y. 1988, U.S. Ct. Internat. Trade 1991, U.S. Spreme Ct. 1991, U.S. Ct. Appeals (2d cir.) 1992, U.S. Ct. Appeals (1st cir.) 1993, U.S. Ct. Appeals (6th cir.) 2001. Law clk. to Hon. Lawrence W. Pierce U.S. Ct. Appeals (2d cir.), N.Y.C., 1987-88; assoc. Fried, Frank, Harris, Shriver & Jacobson LLP, N.Y.C., 1988-94, ptnr., 1994—. Treas., sr. editor Columbia Law Rev., 1985-87. Harlan Fiske Stone scholar, 1985-87. Mem.: ABA, Assn. Bar City NY (profl. responsibility com. 1998—2001, civil rights com. 1989—92), NY Bar Assn., Fed. Bar Coun., Phi Beta Kappa. Home: 91 West Rd Short Hills NJ 07078 Office: Fried Frank Harris Shriver & Jacobson LLP 1 New York Plz Fl 22 New York NY 10004-1980 Office Phone: 212-859-8455. Business E-Mail: peter.simmons@friedfrank.com.

SIMMONS, RAYMOND HEDELIUS, lawyer; b. Salinas, Calif., May 27, 1958; s. Raymond Hedelius and Antoinette (Lynch) S. BA magna cum laude, U. Calif., San Diego, 1979; JD magna cum laude, U. Calif., San Francisco, 1982. Bar: Calif. 1982, U.S. Dist. Ct. (no. dist.) Calif. 1982, Ga. 1987. Assoc. Farella, Braun & Martel, San Francisco, 1982-85; atty., v.p. Barnett-Range Corp., Atlanta, 1985-86; counsel Nationwide Capital Corp. subs. HomeFed. Bank, Atlanta, 1986, HomeFed. Bank, San Diego, 1987-90; gen. counsel, sr. v.p., sec. ITT Fed. Bank, San Francisco, 1990-95; also ITT Residential Capital Corp., ITT Residential Capital Servicing Corp., San Francisco; pvt. practice, Newport Beach, Calif., 1995—. Mem.: ABA, Calif. Bar Assn., Calif. Scholarship Fedn. (life), Thurston Soc., Order of Coif. E-mail: rsimmons@simmonslawoffices.com.

SIMMONS, RICHARD DE LACEY, mass media executive; b. Cambridge, Mass., Dec. 30, 1934; s. Ernest J. and Winifred (McNamara) S.; m. Mary DeWitt Bleecker, May 20, 1961; children: Christopher DeWitt, Robin Bleecker Turner. Grad., 1951; AB, Harvard Coll., 1955; LLB, Columbia U., 1958. Bar: N.Y. 1959. V.p., gen. counsel Dun & Bradstreet Corp., N.Y.C., 1969-73, exec. v.p., 1976-79, vice chmn., 1979-81; pres. Moody's Investors Svc., N.Y.C., 1973-75, Dun & Bradstreet, Inc., N.Y.C., 1975; pres., chief oper. officer Washington Post Co., Washington, 1981-91; pres. Internat. Herald Tribune, Paris, 1989-96. Bd. dirs. Washington Post Co. Mem., dir. coun. White Burkett Miller Ctr. Pub. Affairs, U. Va. Office: 105 N Washington St Ste 202 Alexandria VA 22314-3022

SIMMONS, RICHARD L. surgeon; b. Boston, Feb. 23, 1934; s. Nathanial J. and Anne Dorothy (Levenson) S.; widowed (Feb. 1993); children: Nicole, Janine. AB in Biochem. Scis. magna cum laude, Harvard U., 1955; MD summa cum laude, Boston U., 1959. Diplomate Am. Bd. Surgery. Intern, resident in surgery Columbia Presbyn. Med. Ctr., N.Y.C., 1959-66; clin. and rsch. fellow Mass. Gen. Hosp., Boston, 1965; rsch. fellow in surgery Harvard Med. Sch., Boston, 1965; instr. surgery Columbia U. Coll. P&S, N.Y.C., 1965-68; from asst. prof. to assoc. prof. surgery U. Minn., Mpls., 1968-72, prof. surgery and microbiology, 1972-87; George V. Foster prof. surgery U. Pitts., 1987—98; chmn. dept. surgery U. Pitts. Med. Ctr., 1987-98; assoc. dean for clin. affairs Sch. Medicine U. Pitts., 1989-92, prof. molecular genetics and biochemistry, 1992—; med. dir. U. Pitts. Med. Ctr., 1996—. Chief of surgery Presbyn.-Univ. Hosp., Pitts., 1987—98. Author/co-author 11 books; contbr. more than 1200 articles to profl. jours. Recipient Disting. Svc. Prof. Surgery, 1994, other awards and grants. Mem. AMA, AAAS, ACS (pres. Southwestern Pa. chpt. 1992), NAS Inst. Medicine, Am. Soc. for Microbiology, Am. Soc. Transplant Physicians (pres. 1980-81), Am. Assn. Immunologists, Am. Assn. Pathologists, Am. Surg. Assn. (chmn. program com. 1990), Assn. for Acad. Surgery, Ctrl. Surg. Assn., Cell Transplant Soc., Halsted Soc., Infectious Diseases Soc. Am., Midwest Surg. Soc. (hon.), Reticuloendothelial Soc., Soc. for Leukocyte Biology, Soc. for Microbiology, Soc. Clin. Oncologists, Surg. Infection Soc. (pres. 1988), Soc. Surg. Chmn., Soc. Univ. Surgeons (exec. coun. 1973-81, pres. 1977-78), Allegheny County Med. Soc., Transplantation Soc. (councillor 1974-80), others. Office: U Pitts Sch Medicine 497 Scaife Hall Pittsburgh PA 15219

SIMMONS, RICHARD MILTON TEAGLE, physical fitness specialist, television personality; b. New Orleans, July 12, 1948; With Coty Cosmetics, beginning 1971; maitre d' Derrick's, Los Angeles; founder Ruffage and the Anatomy Asylum, Beverly Hills, Calif., from 1975; star The Richard Simmons Show, 1980-1984; owner nationwide chain of exercise salons, Simmons Richard Exercise Studio Slimmons, Beverly Hills, Calif., 1974-; sponsor, creator, Cruise to Lose Program, Carnival Cruise Lines; lectr. and supportor in the field; author: (with Suzy Kalter) Never-Say-Diet Book, 1980, Never-Say-Diet Cookbook, 1982, Richard Simmons' Better Body Book, 1983, Reach for Fitness, 1986, Richard Simmons' Never Give Up: Inspirations, Reflections, Stories of Hope, 1993, Farewell to Fat Cookbook, 1996, (autobiography) Still Hungry- After All These Years!; column Simmons Says, Soap Opera Digest, from 1981; contbr. articles to various publs.; album Reach, 1982; producer (videos) Sweatin' to the Oldies, 1988, Sweatin' to the Oldies II, 1990, Sweatin' to the Oldies III, 1991, Sweatin' to the Oldies IV, Sweat & Shout: An Aerobic Workout, 1992, Disco Sweat, 1995, Dance Your Pants Off, Groovin' In the House, Blast Off, Platinum Sweat; creator Deal-A-Meal Food Plan and FoodMover; appeared numerous commls., infomercials and QVC; guest numerous talk shows including Merv Griffin, Mike Douglas, Phil Donahue, Charlie Rose, AM Los Angeles, Rosie O'Donnell Show, David Letterman; Real People; cameo appearances: General Hospital, 1979-1983, All Star Salute to Mother's Day, 1981; appearances on: CHiPs, 1977, Fame, 1982, Biography, 1987, Saturday Night Live, 1994, "Whose Line Is It Anyway?", 1998, Arrested Development, 2003 appeared in movies: Satyricon, 1969, The Crowns, 1970; actor (voice) Rudolph the Red-Nosed Reindeer: The Movie, 1998, (voice) Hercules: Zero to Hero, 1999, (TV series) DreamMaker, 1999. Office: Good Times Entertainment 16 E 40th St New York NY 10016-0113 also: Simmons Richard Exercise Studio Slimmons 9306 Civic Center Dr Beverly Hills CA 90210

SIMMONS, RICHARD P. retired steel company executive; b. 1931; married. Grad., MIT, 1953. With Titanium Metals Corp. Am., 1957-59, Republic Steel, 1959-68, Allegheny Ludlum Steel Corp., Pitts., 1960-99, chief exec. officer, 1980-99, chmn., 1986-99; also dir. Allegheny Ludlum Corp. (formerly Allegheny Ludlum Steel Corp.), Pitts., formerly also pres.; chmn. Allegheny Teledyne Inc., Pitts., 1996-00, pres., CEO, 1997-00. Office: Allegheny Teledyne Inc 1000 6th PPG Pl Pittsburgh PA 15222-5479

SIMMONS, ROBERT J. treasurer; b. Provo, Utah, Aug. 5, 1962; BS magna cum laude, Brigham Young U., 1986; M in Mgmt., Northwestern U., 1989. Comml. banking officer Bank of Am., L.A., 1986-88; mgr. treasury ops. Oracle Corp., Redwood City, Calif., 1989-90, asst. treas., 1990—96; v.p., treas. Iomega Corp., Roy, Utah, 1996—99; exec. v.p., CFO Campus Pipeline, Salt Lake City, 1999—2001; CFO Consonus Inc., 2001; corp. treasurer E Trade Fin. Corp., 2001, CFO, 2004—. San Francisco Treasury Mgmt. Assn. (pres.). Avocations: golf, skiing, guitar. Office: E Trade 135 E 57th St New York NY 10022*

SIMMONS, ROBERT RUHL, congressman; b. N.Y.C., Feb. 11, 1943; s. Charles Herbert Jr. and Roxane Page (Ruhl) S.; m. Edith Heidi Paffard, June 22, 1974; children: Jane Adams, Robert Waldo Ruhl. BA, Haverford Coll., 1965; MPA, Harvard U., 1979; DHC (hon.), U. New Haven, 2003. Ops. officer CIA, Washington, 1969-79; legis. asst. U.S. Senator John H. Chafee, Washington, 1979-81; staff dir. intelligence com. U.S. Senate, Washington, 1981-85; vis. lectr. Yale U., New Haven, 1986—95; tchg. asst. U. Conn., 1988—91; mem. Conn. Gen. Assembly, Hartford, 1991—2001, 107th and 108th Congress from Conn. 2nd Dist., Washington, 2001—. Contbr. articles to profl. jours. Mem. Republican Nat. Com. Col. USAR, 1970-2003. Decorated Bronze Star with 1 oak leaf cluster, Meritorious Svc. medal, Army Commendation medal with 1 oak leaf cluster, Vietnam Svc. medal with four campaign stars, Nat. Def. medal, Army Res. Achievement medal, Vietnam Civilian Svc. medal; named to Infantry Officer Candidate Sch. Hall of Fame, 2003. Republican. Episcopalian. Avocations: chinese art, forestry. Office: 215 Cannon House Office Bld Washington DC 20515-0702 also: 2 Courthouse Square, 5th Floor Norwich CT 06360

SIMMONS, ROBERTA JOHNSON, public relations firm executive; b. St. Louis, June 28, 1947; d. Robert Andrew and Thelma Josephine (Bunch) J.; m. Clifford Michael Simmons, Aug. 10, 1968; children: Andrew Park, Matthew Clay, Jordan Michael. BA, Ind. U., South Bend, 1972. Lic. real estate broker, Ind.; accredited pub. rels. practitioner; mem. Inst. Residential Mktg. Account exec., supr. Juhl Advt., Inc., Mishawaka, Ind., 1971-74, pub. rels. dir., 1974-79, v.p., 1979, v.p., pub. rels. dir. Mishawaka and Indpls., 1984-89; v.p. E.L. Yoder & Assocs., Inc., Granger, Ind., 1979-80; pres. Simmons Communications, Inc., Mishawaka, 1981-82, v.p., gen. mgr. Juhl Bldg. Communications, Inc., South Bend, 1983-84; sr. v.p. Wyse Advt., Inc., Indpls., 1989-90; v.p., pub. rels. dir. Caldwell VanRiper, Inc., Indpls., 1990-94; v.p. Pub. Rels. Network, Indpls., 1995—. Contbr. articles to profl. publs. Mem. pub. rels. com. Ind. Adult Literacy Coalition, Indpls., 1989; chairperson pub. rels. com. Crossroads of Am. coun. Boy Scouts Am., Indpls., 1990-91; dep. community info. com. Indpls. C. of C. Infrastructure Study, 1990-91. Mem. PRSA (accredited, mem. counsellors acad., Hoosier chpt. job bank com. 1993—, Nat. Assembly Del., 1996—, v.p. programs, 1997), Nat. Sales Mktg. Coun. (trustee 1991-92), Inst. Residential Mktg. Elder Christian Ch. (Disciples of Christ). Avocations: travel, reading. Office: Pub Rels Network 111 Monument Cir Ste 882 Indianapolis IN 46204-5173

SIMMONS, ROY WILLIAM, banker, director; b. Portland, Oreg., Jan. 24, 1916; s. Henry Clay and Ida (Mudd) S.; m. Elizabeth Ellison, Oct. 28, 1938; children— Julia Simmons Watkins, Matthew R., Laurence E., Elizabeth Jane Simmons Hoke, Harris H., David E. Asst. cashier First Nat. Bank Layton, Utah, 1944-49; Utah bank commr., 1949-51; exec. v.p. Bank of Utah, Ogden, 1951-53; pres. Lockhart Co., Salt Lake City, 1953-64, Zion's First Nat. Bank, Salt Lake City, 1964-81, chmn. bd., 1965-98. Chmn., CEO Zion's Bancorp, 1965-91, chmn. bd., 1991—; chmn. bd. Zion's Savs. & Loan Assn., 1961-69; pres. Lockhart Co., 1964-87; bd. dirs. Ellison Ranching Co. Chmn. Utah Bus. Devel. Corp., 1969-80; Mem. Utah State Bd. Regents, 1969-81. Mem. Salt Lake City C. of C. (treas. 1964-65), Sigma Pi. Republican. Mem. Ch. of Jesus Christ of Latter Day Saints. Home: 817 Crestwood Rd Kaysville UT 84037-1712 Office: Zions Bancorp 10 E South Temple Ste 1000 Salt Lake City UT 84133-1112

SIMMONS, RUSSELL, recording industry executive; b. Queens, N.Y., Oct. 4, 1957; s. Daniel and Evelyn Simmons; m. Kimora Lee, 1998; children: Ming, Aoki Lee. Attended, CCNY. Co-founder, owner Def Jam Records, N.Y.C., 1983—; chmn., CEO, pres. Rush Communications, 1990—; owner Rush Artist Mgmt., PHAT Fashion, Rush Prodr. Mgmt.; partner Rush Model Mgmt. Represents Public Enemy, LL Cool J, others. Co-prodr.: (films) Krush Groove, 1985, The Funeral, 1996; prodr.: Tougher Than Leather, 1988, The Nutty Professor, 1996, How to Be a Player, 1997; exec. prodr.: Gridlock'd, 1997, The Addiction, 1995; prodr.: (TV special) Def Comedy Jam Primetime, 1994; (TV series) Def Poetry Jam, 2002; author: (autobiography) Life and Def, 2001. Founder Rush Philanthropic Arts Found. 10 gold albums, 6 platinum albums, 2 multiplatinum albums. Achievements include bringing hip-hop culture into the American mainstream. Office: Phat Fashions 512 Fashion Ave Rochester NY 14603-4603*

SIMMONS, RUTH J. academic administrator; b. Grapeland, Tex., July 3, 1945; d. Isaac and Fannie Stubblefield; m. Norbert Simmons, 1968 (div. 1989); children: Khari, Maya. Student, Universidad Internacional, Saltillo, Mex., 1965, Wellesley Coll., 1965—66; BA, Dillard U., 1967; postgrad., Universite de Lyon, 1967—68, George Washington U., 1968—69; AM, Harvard U., 1970, PhD in Romance Langs., 1973; LLD (hon.), Amherst Coll., 1995; LHD (hon.), Howard U., 1996, Dillard U., 1996; LLD (hon.), Princeton U., 1996, Lake Forest Coll., 1997; LHD (hon.), U. Mass., 1997; LLD (hon.), Dartmouth Coll., 1997, Mt. Holyoke Coll., 2001, U. Pa., 2001, Harvard U., 2002, George Washington U., 2002, Columbia U., 2002, Washington U., 2002, U. So. Calif., 2003, Boston U., Rensselaer Polytechnic Inst., N.Y. U., Northeastern. Interpreter lang. svcs. divsn. U.S. Dept. State, Washington, 1968—69; instr. French George Washington U., 1968—69; admissions officer Radcliffe Coll., 1970—72; asst. prof. French U. New Orleans, 1973—75, asst. dean coll. liberal arts, assoc. prof. French, 1975—76; adminstrv. coord. NEH liberal studies project Calif. State U., Northridge, 1977—78, acting dir. internat. programs, vis. assoc. prof. Pan-African studies, 1978—79; asst. dean grad. sch. U. So. Calif., 1979—82, assoc. dean grad. sch., 1982—83; dir. studies Butler Coll. Princeton U., NJ, 1983—85, acting. dir. Afro-Am. studies, 1985—87, asst. dean faculty, 1986—87, assoc. dean faculty, 1986—90, vice provost, 1992—95; provost Spelman Coll., 1990—91; pres. Smith Coll., Northampton, Mass., 1995—2001; pres Brown Univ., Providence, 2001—. Peer reviewer higher edn. divsn. NEH, 1980—83, bd. cons., 1981; mem. grad. adv. bd. Calif. Student Aid Commn., 1981—83; chair com. to visit dept. African-Am. studies Harvard U., 1991; mem. strategic planning task force N.J. Dept. Higher Edn., 1992—93; mem. nat. adv. commn. EQUITY 2000 Coll. Bd., 1992—95; mem. adv. bd. ctrl. N.J. NAACP Legal Def. Fund, 1992—95; mem. Mid. States Assn. Accreditation Team, Johns Hopkins U., 1993; chmn. accreditation team Bryn Mawr Coll., 1999; chair rev. panel for model instns. planning grants NSF, 1993; mem. Conf. Bd., 1995; bd. dirs. MetLife, JSTOR, Pfizer Inc., 1997—, COFHE, Com. Econ. Devel., Goldman Sachs, 1999—, Tex. Instruments, 1999—; mem. adv. coun. dept. Romance Langs. and Lit. Princeton U., 1996; trustee Carnegie Corp., 1999—; presenter, spkr. and panelist in field. Mem. editl. bd.: World Edn. series Am. Assn. Collegiate Registrars and Admissions Officers, 1984—86; contbr. articles to profl. jours. Named mem. Women's Progress Commemoration Commn. by Pres. Bill Clinton, 1999; mem. adv. coun. Bill and Melinda Gates Millennium Scholars Found.; mem. adv. bd. N.J. Master Faculty Program Woodrow Wilson Nat. Fellowship Found., 1987—90, bd. trustees, 1991—96; trustee Inst. Advances Study, 1995—98, The Clarke Sch. for Deaf, 1995—; chmn. bd. trustees Acad. Music, 1995—98; mem. adv. com. Healthy Steps for Young Children Program, 1996—98; mem. bd. advisors 1st Internat. Conf. on AIDS, Ethiopia, 1998. Named Women of Yr., CBS, 1996, Glamour Mag., 1996, Disting. Fulbright Alumna, Inst. Internat. Edn., 1997, Woman of World, NASA, 1998, Am. Best Coll. Pres., Time mag., 2001, Woman Yr., Ms. mag., 2002; named one of Newsweek Person to Watch, 2002; recipient Disting. Svc. award, Assn. Black Princeton Alumni, 1989, Dillard U., 1992, Pres.'s Recognition award, Bloomfield Coll., 1993, TWIN award, Princeton Area YWCA, 1993, Women's orgn. Tribute award, Princeton U., 1994, Leadership award, Third World Ctr. Princeton U., 1995, Tex. Excellence award, Leap Program, 1995, Benjamin E. Mays award, A Better Chance, 1995, Centennial medal, HArvard U. Grad. Sch. Arts & Scis., 1997, Achievement award, Nat. Urban League, 1998, Tchr. Coll. Medal for Disting. Svc., Columbia U., 1999, Pres. award, United Negro Coll. Fund, 2001, "Drum Major for Justice" Edn. award, So. Christian Leadership Conf./W.O.M.E.N., 2002, Fulbright Lifetime Achievement Medal, 2002, fellowship, DAAD; fellow, Danforth Found., 1967—73, Sr. Fulbright fellow, 1981; scholar, KYOK, 1963, Worthing Found., 1963—67, Fulbright scholar, U. de Lyon, 1967—68. Fellow: Am. Acad. Arts & Scis.; mem.: AAAS, Coun. Foreign Rels., Am. Philos. Soc. Office: Office of the President Brown University 1 Prospect Street, Campus Box 1860 Providence RI 02912 Mailing: Brown University President's Office Box 1860 Providence RI 02912-1860*

SIMMONS, SARAH R. lawyer; b. Ducktown, Tenn., Jan. 23, 1948; BA magna cum laude, U. Ariz., 1970, postgrad.; JD magna cum laude, U. Denver, 1973. Bar: Colo. 1974, Ariz. 1975. Mem. Molloy, Jones & Donahue, Tucson, Brown & Bain, P.A., Tucson, Lewis & Roca LLP. Trustee Tohono Club Park, 1995-2004, sec., 1997-99, v.p. 1999-2001, pres., 2001-03; trustee Tucson Airport Authority, 1996—; mem. Law Coll. Assn. Bd., 1996—, sec. 1998-99, pres. 2000-01; 4th R bd. Tucson Unified Sch., 1996—; bd. dirs. United Way of Tucson, 1995-2000, Family Advocacy Resource and Wellness Ctrs., Resources for Women, 1995-2000; bd. dirs. Ariz. Town Hall, 1998—; mem. adv. bd. Ariz. for a Drug Free Workplace, 1991—, So. Ariz. Sports Devel. Corp., U. Ariz. Social and Behavioral Scis., 1994-96; sec. So. Ariz. Minutemen, 1996-98; mem. bd. visitors Coll. Law, chair, 2002-04; v.p. Met. Tucson Conv. and Visitors Bur., 2003-04. Recipient Outstanding Alumni award U. Ariz. Coll. of Law, 1993, Tucson Woman of Yr. C. of C., 1994, Women on the Move award YWCA, 1995, Alice Truman Leadership award, 2003; named one of 100 Women and Minorities in the Law, 2000, Women Who Lead, U. Ariz. Women's Studies Adv. Coun., 2003. Fellow ABA, Ariz. Bar Assn.; mem. Nat. Assn. Bond Lawyers, State Bar Ariz. (bd. govs. 1987-95, sec.-treas. 1989-90, 2d v.p. 1990-91, 1st v.p. 1991-92, pres.-elect 1992-93, pres. 1993-94, employment law sect., profl. conduct com., fee arbitration com.), Ariz. Women Lawyers Assn. (charter), Colo. Bar Assn., Pima County Bar Assn. (bd. dirs. 1985-94), Am. Judicature Soc., So. Ariz. Legal Aid (bd. dirs. 1990-93),

Lawyers Against Hunger (bd. dirs., v.p. D-M 50 1996-98, pres. 1998-2000), Order St. Ives, Phi Beta Kappa, Phi Kappa Phi, Phi Alpha Theta, Kappa Beta Pi. Office: Lewis and Roca LLP 1 S Church Ave Ste 700 Tucson AZ 85701-1612 E-mail: sally_simmons@lrlaw.com.

SIMMONS, SCOTT MARTIN, information specialist; b. Albany, N.Y., Aug. 21, 1957; s. William Everett and Dorothy (McQueen) S.; m. Angela Koschelew, Feb. 14, 1985; children: Alexandra, Elizabeth. BS in Biology, U. Calif., Davis, 1978; MS in Zoology, U. Nev., 1981; MBA in Mgmt., So. Ill. U., 1985. Database adminstr. SAIC, O'Fallon, Ill., 1986-89; prin. cons. Sybase, Phoenix, 1989-95; prin. engr. Illustra, Denver, 1995; worldwide specialist Informix, Denver, 1996-98; prin. arch. Vitria, Denver, 1998-2000; dir. tech. solutions Extricity/Peregrine, Denver, 2000—02; bus. integration arch. IBM, Colo., 2002—. Grad. tchg. asst. U. Nev., Reno, 1979-81; presenter numerous speeches. Contbr. articles to profl. jours. Vol. EMT, Reno, 1979-81. Sgt. USAF, 1982-86. Mem. St. Louis Oracle Users Group (founder, pres. 1987-89), Beta Gamma Sigma. Avocations: guitar, skiing, hiking. E-mail: scottsim@starband.net.

SIMMONS, STEPHEN GREGORY, accountant; b. Milledgeville, Ga., Dec. 8, 1958; s. John Sidney and Glenda Faye Simmons; m. Mary Sue Simmons, Feb. 22, 1958; children: Melissa, Christopher, Matthew. BBA in Acctg., Ga. Coll., 1980. CPA, Ga. Staff acct. Powell, Booth & Thombley, P.C., Atlanta, 1980-83; mgr. Powell, Booth & Grace, P.C., Atlanta, 1983-87, ptnr., 1987-88; mgr. John S. Thombley P.C., Marietta, Ga., 1988-94; ptnr. Thombley & Simmons, P.C., Marietta, Ga., 1994—. Treas., bd. dirs. MUST Ministries, Inc., Marietta, Ga., 1998—. Mem. AICPA, Ga. Soc. CPAs, Delta Sigma Pi (life). Republican. Baptist. Avocations: golf, hunting, fishing, hiking. Home: 3305 Burnham Way Kennesaw GA 30152 Office: Thombley & Simmons PC 305 Lawrence St Ste 100 Marietta GA 30060 E-mail: sgs1258@bellsouth.net.

SIMMONS, STEPHEN JUDSON, lawyer; b. Columbus, Ohio, Feb. 19, 1946; s. Samuel A. and Jane A. (McGrath) S.; m. Claire Maxine Schriber, Aug. 15, 1970; children: Darren, Judson. BA, Ohio State U., 1968; JD, U. Cin., 1972. Bar: Ohio 1973, Tex. 1982. Sr. law clk. U.S. Dist. Ct. (ea. dist.) Tenn., Knoxville, 1972-74; asst. atty. gen. Office of Atty. of Ohio, Columbus, 1974-75; assoc. McGrath & Shirey, Columbus, 1975; corp. counsel Wendys, Inc., Columbus, 1975-79; sr. v.p., gen. counsel Precision Tune, Inc., Beaumont, Tex., 1979-87, also dir.; sr. v.p. adminstrn., dir. Kwik-Kopy Corp., Cypress, Tex., 1988-90; v.p. Deli Mgmt., Inc., 1990-94; pvt. practice Houston, 1994—. Bd. editors U. Cin. Law Rev., 1971-72. Mem. Tex. Bar Assn. Roman Catholic. Home: 13603 Balmore Cir Houston TX 77069-2703 Office: 3845 Fm 1960 Rd W Ste 250 Houston TX 77068-3548 Fax: 281-586-0088. Office Phone: 281-586-8500. E-mail: sjsimmons@aol.com.

SIMMONS, SUE, newscaster; d. John Simmons. Corr. WTNH-TV, New Haven, 1973-74, WBAL-TV, Balt., 1974, anchor, host Balt. at One, 1975—76; corr./anchor. WRC-TV, Washington, 1976—80; co-anchor Live at Five & News Channel 4 at 11/WNBC News Channel 4, N.Y.C., 1980—; host Images: A Year in Review, WNBC, 2002—. Recipient four Emmy awards, award for Outstanding Performance by a News Commentator, Barnabus McHenry, Vice-Chmn. Pres.'s Task Force on Arts and Humanities, 1981. Office: WNBC-TV 30 Rockefeller Plz New York NY 10112-0002

SIMMONS, SYLVIA JEANNE QUARLES (MRS. HERBERT G. SIMMONS JR.), university administrator, educator, executive; b. Boston, May 8, 1935; d. Lorenzo Christopher and Margaret Mary (Thomas) Quarles; m. Herbert G. Simmons, Jr., Oct. 26, 1957; children: Stephen, Alison, Lisa. BA, Manhattanville Coll., 1957; MEd, Boston Coll., 1962, PhD, 1990; DHL (hon.), St. Joseph's Coll., 1994; EdD (hon.), Merrimack Coll., 1999. Montessori tchr. Charles River Park Nursery Sch., Boston, 1970-76; registrar Boston Coll. Sch. Mgmt., Chestnut Hill, 1966-70; dir. fin. aid Radcliffe Coll., Cambridge, Mass., 1970-75, assoc. dean admissions and fin. aid, 1972-75, assoc. dean admissions, fin. aid and women's edn., 1975; assoc. dean admissions and fin. aid Harvard and Radcliffe, from 1975; assoc. v.p. for acad. affairs ctrl. adminstrn. U. Mass., Boston, 1976-79, spl. asst. to chancellor, 1979; v.p. field svcs. Am. Student Assistance, 1982-84, sr. v.p., 1984-93, exec. v.p., 1983-95, pres., 1996; mem. faculty Harvard U., 1970-77, pres. faculty, 1995-96; lectr. Boston U., 1991—. Cons. Mass. Bd. Higher Edn., 1973-77. Co-editor: Student Loans Riches and Realtities. Past bd. dirs. Rivers Country Day Sch., Weston, Mass., Simons's Rock Coll., Great Barrington, Mass., Wayland (Mass.) Fair Housing, Cambridge Mental Health Assn., Family Svcs. Greater Boston, Concerts in Black and White, Mass., Higher Edn. Assistance Corp.; chmn. bd. dirs. North Shore Cmty. Coll., 1986-88, mem. bd. dirs., 1985—; trustee and alumnae bd. dirs. Manhattanville Coll., 1986—; mem. adv. com. Upward Bound, Chestnut Hill Boston Coll., 1972-74, Women in Politics John McCormick Inst., 1994-2000; Camp Chimney Corners, Becket, Mass., 1971-77; bd. dirs. Am. Cancer Soc. Mass., 1987-89, Boston Coll., 1990-98, Merrimack Coll., 1992-2000, Mass. Found. for Humanities, 1990-92, Mass. Bay United Way, 1990-94, Grimes King Found., 1992—, St. Elizabeta's Hosp., 1991—, Anna Stearns Found., 1996—, Regis Coll., 1997—, Edn. Resources Inst., 1998—, Supreme Ct. Jud. Hist. Soc., 2001—, Newton Country Day Sch., 2002—, Shirley Eustes House, 2002—; overseer Mt. Ida Coll., 1990—, Exec. Svc. Corp., 1997—, Supreme Ct. Judicial Hist. Soc., 2001-, Newton County Day Sch., 2002-, Shirely Euestes House, 2002, The Edn. Resources Inst., 1998, Mus. Fine Arts, Boston, Mass., 2002—; chair Coll. Club Scholarship com., 1997. Recipient Educator of Yr. award Boston and Vicinity Club, 1989, Bicentennial medal Boston Coll., 1976, Achievement award Greater Boston YMCA, 1977, Human Rights awsard Mass. Tchrs. Assn., 1988, Pres'. award Mass. Ednl. Opportunity Assn., 1988, Archbishop Timothy Healy award, 1997, Outstanding Alumna award Girl's Latin Sch., 1998; named One of Ten Outstanding Yung Leaders, Boston Jr. C. of C., 1971, Sojourner's Daus.: 25 African women who have made a difference, 1991. Mem. Eastern Assns. Fin. Aid Officers (2st v.p. 1973), Coll. Scholarship Svc. Coun., Links (pres. local chpt. 1967-69), Nat. Inst. Fin. Aid Adminstrs. (dir. 1975-77), Jack and Jill Am. (pres. Newton chpt. 1972-74), Manhattanville Club (pres. Boston 1966-68), Delta Sigma Theta, Delta Kappa Gamma (pres. 1988-90). Home: 19 Clifford St Roxbury MA 02119-2120 Office: 330 Stuart St Boston MA 02116-5237 Personal E-mail: ssimm38414@aol.com.

SIMMONS, TED CONRAD, writer; b. Seattle, Sept. 1, 1916; s. Conrad and Clara Evelyn (Beaudry) S.; m. Dorothy Pauline Maltese, June 1, 1942; children: Lynn, Juliet. Student, U. Wash., 1938-41, UCLA and L.A. State U., 1952-54, Oxford (Eng.) U., 1980. Drama critic Seattle Daily Times, 1942; indsl. writer, reporter-editor L.A. Daily News, 1948-51; contbr. Steel, Western Metals, Western Industry, 1951—. Past poetry dir. Watts Writers Workshop; instr. Westside Poetry Center; asst. dir. Pacific Coast Writers Conf, Calif. State Coll. Los Angeles. Author: (poetry) Deadended, 1966; (novel) Middlearth, 1975; (drama) Greenhouse, 1977, Durable Chaucer, 1978, Rabelais and other plays, 1980, Dickeybird, 1981 (nominated TCG Plays-in-Progress award 1985), Alice and Eve, 1983, Deja Vu, Deja Vu, 1986, The Box, 1987, Ingrid Superstar, 1988, Three Quarks for Mr. Marks, 1989, Ingrid: Skier on the Slopes of Stromboli, 1990, A Midsummer's Hamlet, 1991, Hamlet Nintendo, After Hours, Dueling Banjoes, Viva el Presidente, Climate of the Sun, 1992, Nude Descending Jacob's Ladder, 1993, Almost an Opera, 1994, Landscape with Inverted Tree and Fred Astaire Dancing, 1995, O.J. Othello, Fast Track, Searching for Alice Liddell, Mr. Blue of Freaky Animals, Inc., 1997, Rosenstern & Guildencrantz II, 1997, Rosa/Rosa of the Centuries/Rosa of the Thorns, 1997, Joyce, 1997, Joyce-After Hours, 1997, Amadeus & da Cultchur Club, 1997, Wonderland: Alice's New Adventures, 1998, The Brilliant Life of an Intelligent Orchid-A Play About Ingrid Bergman, 1998, Chekhov Off-Broadway, The Premiere, Good Night Sweet Prince, The Scare, 1999, 18 Mini-Micro Dramas, BloomsDay, The Scream, The Bird, 2000, Will, Jean "n" Jim— A Play, 2001; writer short story, radio verse; book reviewer Los Angeles Times; contbr. poetry to the Am. Poet, Prairie Wings, Antioch Rev., Year Two Anthology; editor: Venice Poetry Company Presents, 1972. Served with USAAF, 1942-46. Grantee Art Commn. King County, 1993. Home and Office: 1340 Oak Knoll Dr Lake Forest IL 60045-3667

SIMMONS, VAUGHAN PIPPEN, medical consultant; b. Balt., Nov. 19, 1922; s. Harry S. and Sarah Jane (Pippen) S.; m. Marguerite Carolyn Massino, Dec. 27, 1947 (dec. 1990); children: Malynda Sarah, Jefferson Vaughan. Student, Ill. Inst. Tech., 1943-44; BS, U. Chgo., 1947, MD, 1949. Diplomate Am. Bd. Life Ins. Medicine. From instr. to asst. prof. Marquette U. Sch. Medicine, Milw., 1950-56; asst. med. dir. Northwestern Mut. Life Ins. Co., Milw., 1956-60; med. dir. Fidelity Mut. Life Ins. Co., Phila., 1961-73, v.p., 1968-73; v.p., med. dir. Colonial Penn Life Ins. Co., Phila., 1973-84. Vis. lectr. ins. medicine Temple U. Sch. Medicine, Phila., 1966-84; asst. prof. anatomy Jefferson Med. Coll., Phila., 1977-88, hon. asst. prof. anatomy, 1988—. Patentee in field (3); contbr. articles to profl. jours. Mem. ofcl. bd. St. Luke United Methodist Ch., Bryn Mawr, Pa., 1963-83, chmn. commn. membership and evangelism, 1963-71, trustee, 1968-83. Served with M.C., U.S. Army, 1943-45, as lt. (j.g.) USNR, 1952-54; Korea Fellow Coll. Physicians Phila. (chmn. pub. health sect. 1967-68, ins. medicine sect. 1970-72, planning com. 1981-82, adv. bd. Francis C. Wood Inst. History of Medicine 1984-88), Milw. Acad. Medicine, Am. Geriatrics Soc., N.Y. Acad. Medicine; mem. Am. Acad. Ins. Medicine (founding editor Ins. Medicine 1969-71, exec. coun. 1970-72, publs. com. 1967-75), Am. Life Ins. Assn. (sec. med. sect. 1974-77), Pa. Hist. Soc., Am. Assn. Automotive Medicine (dir. 1980-83), Am. Legion, Sigma Xi, Alpha Kappa Kappa. Clubs: Union League (bd. dirs. 1982-85, v.p. 1985-86), Sketch (Phila.). Avocations: photography, amateur radio, drawing, painting, medical research and writing. Home: 4665 S Landings Dr Fort Myers FL 33919-4683 E-mail: vaughanps@comcast.net.

SIMMONS, WILLIAM, physicist, retired aerospace research executive; b. Chgo., Apr. 24, 1932; s. Walter Garfield and Edna Dean (Winch) S.; m. Barbara Millet Haury, Oct. 4, 1954; children: Sheryl Lee, Cynthia Jane, Shelly Jean. BA in Physics, Carleton Coll., 1953; MS in Physics, U. Ill., 1955, PhD in Physics, 1960. Mem. tech. staff Space Tech. Labs., Redondo Beach, Calif., 1960-62; sr. rsch. scientist Gen. Tech., Torrance, Calif., 1962, TRW, Redondo Beach, 1962-71, dir. rsch., 1984-89, chief engr. spl. projects assigned to Lawrence Livermore (Calif.) Labs., 1989-92; engring. mgr. Lawrence Livermore Labs., 1972-84, rsch. reviewer, 1985-89; prof. engring. UCLA, 1968-72. Tech. panel mem. U. Calif., Berkeley, 1985; tech. reviewer Dept. Energy, Washington, 1986—, mem. rev. com., 1987—; cons. in field, 1992-99. Editor, reviewer 2 books, 1982, 83; contbr. numerous articles to profl. jours.; 10 patents for electro-optics devices. Named Disting. Engring. Prof. of Yr. UCLA, 1972, one of Top 100 Innovators in U.S.A, Sci. Digest, 1986; George F. Baker Found. scholar Carleton Coll., 1949-53. Mem. IEEE (sr., life, gen. chmn. symposia 1988, 89, Simon Ramo Major medal 1987), Laser Inst. Am., Laser Engring. and Optical Soc., Am. Phys. Soc., Soc. of Photographic and Instrumentation Engrs., U.S. Chess Club, Phi Beta Kappa, Sigma Xi. Republican. Avocations: chess, ping pong/table tennis, bridge. Office: Sys Solutions 1621 W 25th St Ste 231 San Pedro CA 90732-4300 Office Phone: 310-541-4140.

SIMMS, JACQUELINE KAMP, secondary school educator; Tchr. sci. Recipient Tandy Tech. Scholars prize Tandy Corp., 1994, Regional Catalyst award for Excellence in Chemistry Tchg. Chem. Mfrs. Assn., 1994, Presdl. award for Excellence in Sci. and Math. Tchg., 1994, Educator award Continental Cablevision, 1997. Office: Sandalwood High Sch 2750 John Prom Blvd Jacksonville FL 32246-3921

SIMMS, LOIS AVERETTA, retired secondary school educator; b. Charleston, SC, May 27, 1919; d. Jasper Simeon and Anna Inez (Ferguson) S. BA, Johnson C. Smith U., 1941; MA, Howard U., 1954. Cert. English and social studies educator, S.C. Directive tchr. Avery Normal Inst., Charleston, 1941-42; tchr. English and French Laing H.S., Mt. Pleasant, S.C., 1942-44; tchr. English and math. Henry P. Archer Sch., Charleston, 1944-45; tchr. social studies and English Burke H.S., Charleston, 1945-52; tchr. English Avery H.S., Charleston, 1952-54, Burke H.S., Charleston, 1954-73; tchr. English and history Charleston H.S., 1973-76; ret., 1976. Co-adviser Dramatic Club, Burke H.S., 1945-46, trainer section of chorus, 1945-47, chief advisor 1961 Bulldog Yearbook, 1960-61; advisor Crochet Club, Avery H.S., 1952-54, Charleston H.S., 1973-76. Author: Growing Up Presbyterian: Life in Presbyterian Colleges and Churches, 1991, Profiles of African American Females in Low Country of South Carolina, 1992, A Chalk and Chalkboard Career in Carolina, 1995, A History of Zion, Olivet, and Zion-Olivet Churches 1850-1985, 1989; editor The Scroll newsletter, 1984-94. Sec. exec. bd. YWCA of Greater Charleston, 1950s; active YWCA, SC Hist. Soc., SC ETV Endowment. Recipient plaque Zion-Olivet Presbyn. Ch., 1987, C.L. Campbell award Presbyn. Ch., 1988, plaque Staff of The Scroll, 1990. Mem. NAACP (Silver life, Trailblazer award 2002), Charleston County Ret. Educators Assn. Unit 2, Pres.'s Club (plaque 1991), Avery Inst. Afro-Am. History and Culture (editor The Bull. 1990-2000, Cert.), SC Soc., Assn. for Study of African-Am. Life and History, Johnson C. Smith U. Alumni Assn., Presbytn. Womens Assn. (chair com. qtrly. birthday celebration and grad. ceremony 1999-2003). Avocations: reading, playing music, playing scrabble, planting flowers, writing prose. Home: 28 Jasper St Charleston SC 29403-6006

SIMMS, MARIA KAY, writer, non-profit organization executive; b. Princeton, Ill., Nov. 18, 1940; d. Frank B. and Anna (Haurberg) S.; m. Neil F. Michelsen, Oct. 2, 1987 (dec. 1990); children: Shannon Sullivan Stillings, Molly A. Sullivan, Elizabeth Maria Jossick; m. James l. Jossick, July 12, 1998. BFA, Ill. Wesleyan U., 1962. Cert. cons. profl. astrologer; ordained min. L.A. Cmty. Ch. of Religious Sci. Elder priestess Covenant of the Goddess; art tchr. elem. and jr. high pub. schs., Dundee, Northbrook, Ill., 1962-65; H.S. art tchr. Danbury, Conn., 1975-76; freelance gallery painter various cities, 1962-77; free-lance comml. illustrator, 1972-74, 86-87; shop, gallery, café owner, 1976-79; art dir. ACS Pubs., Inc., San Diego, Calif., 1987-90; pres. Astro Comm. Svcs., Inc. (formerly ACS Pubs.), San Diego, 1990-98, dir., 1990-2000; acquisitions editor, 1998-2000; cons., 2000—. Bd. dirs. Omni Techs. Corp.; conf. lectr. Author: Twelve Wings of the Eagle, 1988, Dial Detective, 1989, 2d edit., 2001; co-author: Search for the Christmas Star, 1989, Circle of the Cosmic Muse, 1994, Your Magical Child, 1994, Future Signs, 1996, The Witch's Circle, 1996, Millenium: Fears, Fantasies and Facts, 1998, A Time for Magick, 2001; contbr. articles to popular mags.; columnist Moon Magick, www.starcraftsbob.com. High priestess Cir. of the Cosmic Muse; elder priestess Covenant of the Goddess, 2d officer Calafia Local Coun., 1995-96, pub. info. officer, 1996-98; mem. adv. bd. Kepler Coll., 1998—. Recipient numerous art awards. Mem. Nat. Coun. Geocosmic Rsch. Inc. (dir., pubs. dir. 1981-92, editor jour. 1984-92, chairperson bd. 1999—), Am. Fedn. Astrologers, Internat. Soc. Astrol. Rsch., New Age Pubs. Assn., Assn. for Profl. Astrologers Internat., Alpha Gamma Delta.

SIMMS, ROBERT D. former state supreme court justice; b. Tulsa, Feb. 6, 1926; s. Matthew Scott and Bessie L. (Moore) S.; m. Patricia C., Feb. 16, 1950; 1 son, Robert D. Student, Milligan Coll., Phillips U.; LLB, U. Tulsa. Bar: Okla. 1950. Pvt. practice law, Sand Springs, Okla., from 1950; asst. county atty. Tulsa County, 1953-54; chief prosecutor County Atty.'s Office, 1955-58, county atty., 1958-62; judge Okla. Dist. Ct., Dist. 14, 1962-71, Okla. Ct. Criminal Appeals, 1971-72; justice Okla. Supreme Ct., 1985—2000. Mem. Okla. Crime Commn. Mem. Gov.'s Spl. Com. on Drug Abuse, 1970; sponsor and coach Pee-Wee Baseball. Served with USN, 1943-46. Mem. Tulsa County Bar Assn., Okla. Bar Assn. (chmn. dist. atty. sect. 1959)

SIMOKAITIS, FRANK JOSEPH, air force officer, lawyer; b. St. Louis, Dec. 12, 1922; s. Frank and Constance (Ladish) S.; m. Mary Jane Feeny; children: Peggy, Mary, Frank (dec.). Student, Washington U., St. Louis, 1945-47; LL.B., St. Louis U., 1950, JD, 1970. Bar: U.S. Supreme Ct. U.S 1950, Mo. 1950, also other fed. cts. 1950. Commd. 2d lt. USAAF, 1943; advanced through grades to maj. gen. USAF, 1973; plans and ops. officer Hdqrs. Pacific Air Force, 1960-63; staff officer Hdqrs. USAF, Washington, 1963-69, exec. asst. to sec. air force, 1969-73; comdt. Air Force Inst. Tech., 1973-78; dir. Dept. Def. affairs Hdqrs. NASA, Washington, 1978-83, cons., 1983—. Bd. dirs. Dayton chpt. ARC, Greater Miami chpt., arbitrator Better Bus. Bur. Decorated D.S.M. with oak leaf cluster, Legion of Merit, Air medal with 4 oak leaf clusters, Air Force Commendation medal. Mem. Miami Air Force Assn. (bd. dirs.), Navy League (v.p. U.S. Miami coun.), Univ. Club of Washington D.C., Patrick AFB Officers Club. Home: 1594 Frontier Dr Melbourne FL 32940

SIMON, ABBEY, pianist; b. N.Y.C., Jan. 8, 1922; s. Solomon and Vera (Seldin) S.; m. Dina Levinson, July 28, 1942; 1 son, Jonathan Dean. Grad., Curtis Inst. Music, 1941. Mem. faculty music Ind., U., Juilliard Sch. Music, 1977—; Cullen Distinguished prof. U. Houston. Concert tours include, Australia, Europe, S. Am., Soviet Union, New Zealand, N.Am.; rec. artist, Philips, Epic, RCA, HMV, Vox. Recipient Walter Naumburg Found. award, Nat. Orchestral Assn. award, Fedn. Music Clubs award, Elizabeth Sprague Coolidge medal. Mem.: Lotos (N.Y.C.). Jewish. Office: Gurtman & Murtha Assocs 162 W 56th St New York NY 10019-3831

SIMON, ALBERT, physicist, engineer, educator; b. N.Y.C., Dec. 27, 1924; s. Emanuel D. and Sarah (Leitner) S.; m. Harriet E. Rubinstein, Aug. 17, 1947 (dec. June 1970); children: Richard, Janet, David; m. Rita Shiffman, June 11, 1972. BS, CCNY, 1947; PhD, U. Rochester, 1950. Registered profl. engr., N.Y. State. Physicist Oak Ridge Nat. Lab., 1950-54, assoc. dir. neutron physics divsn., 1954-61; head plasma physics divsn. Gen. Atomic Co., San Diego, 1961-66; prof. dept. mech. engring. U. Rochester, N.Y., 1966—, prof. physics, 1968—, chmn. dept. mech. engring., 1977-84. Mem. Inst. for Advanced Study, Princeton, 1974-75; sr. vis. fellow U.K. Sci. Rsch. Coun., Oxford U., 1975 Author: An Introduction to Thermonuclear Research, 1959; contbr. to: Ency. Americana, 1964, 74; editor Advances in Plasma Physics, 1967—. With USN, 1944-46. Recipient Univ. Mentor award, 1988-89; John Simon Guggenheim fellow, 1964-65. Fellow Am. Phys. Soc. (chmn. plasma physics divsn. 1963-64); mem. ASME, ASEE (chmn. nuc. engring. divsn. 1985-86). Home: 197 Brittany Ln Pittsford NY 14534 Office Phone: 585-275-4431. E-mail: simo@me.rochester.edu.

SIMON, ANDREW L. educational publishing executive; b. Bklyn., June 17, 1942; s. Sidney Simon and Ruth Kornblum; m. Andrea Judith Wollman, June 30, 1968; children: Alexandra, Rachel. BA, Washington U., 1963; MBA, Columbia U., 1965. Account exec. Ogilvy & Mather, N.Y.C., 1967-71, Benton & Bowles, N.Y.C., 1971-73; group product mgr. L'Oreal, N.Y.C., 1973-74, Norcliff-Thayer, Tuckahoe, N.Y., 1974-78; group head consumer products Lederle Labs., Pearl River, N.Y., 1978-79; v.p. Citibank, N.Y.C., 1980-83; v.p., divsn. head Bankers Trust, N.Y.C., 1983-86; cons. investor N.Y.C., 1986-94; chmn. bd., pres., CEO Touchstone Applied Sci. Assocs., Inc., Brewster, N.Y., 1994—. Bd. dirs. Hudson Valley Trust Inc., 2003—. Bd. govs. Washington U. Alumni, 1970-73; trustee City of Poughkeepsie (N.Y.) Partnership, 1987-93, The Harvey Sch., Katonah, N.Y., 1989-2000, Nat. Coun. Edn. & Human Devel., George Washington U., 2000—. With USNR, 1964-70. Avocations: tennis, riding, skiing. Home: 1905 Hunter Brook Rd Yorktown Heights NY 10598-6233 Office: Touchstone Appl Sci Assoc Inc PO Box 382 Brewster NY 10509-0382

SIMON, ANITA, psychologist; b. Phila., May 20, 1936; d. Harry and Bertha (Rosenberg) Mongin. BS summa cum laude, UCLA, 1962; MEd, Temple U., Phila., 1964, EdD with honors, 1966. Lic. psychologist, Pa. Program dir. Rsch. for Better Schs., Phila., 1966-73; dir. edn. The Restaurant Sch., Phila., 1973-80; psychologist in pvt. practice Phila., 1979—. Developer/trainer SAVI-System for Analyzing Verbal Behavior, Phila., 1965—. Author: The Parents Solution Book, 1983; editor: (anthology) Mirrors for Behavior, 1970; editor The Classroom Interaction Newsletter, 1964-68. Mem. APA, Systems Centered Therapy Network, Delaware Valley Gr. Psychotherapy Assn., Phi Beta Kappa. Avocations: writing, music, travel, bridge. Office: 1831 Chestnut St Ste 801 Philadelphia PA 19103-3700

SIMON, ARTHUR, pharmacologist, research laboratory executive; b. Bklyn., June 1, 1942; s. Harry and Ann S.; m. Sandra Goldberg, July 10, 1966; children— Brett David, Kira Denise BS in Biology, Phila. Coll. Pharmacy and Sci., 1965; MS cum laude, Fairleigh Dickinson U., 1969; PhD in Pharmacology (NIH fellow), U. Cin., 1972. Lab. technician La Wall and Harrisson Research Lab., Phila., 1962-63; research asst. toxicology dept. Wyeth Labs., Paoli, Pa., 1965-66; research assoc. pharmacology dept. Warner Lambert Research Inst., Morris Plains, N.J., 1966-69; research investigator Squibb Inst. for Med. Research, Princeton, N.J., 1972-74; sr. cardiovascular pharmacologist USV Pharm. Corp., Tuckahoe, N.Y., 1974-76; dir. cardiovascular clin. research Bristol Myers Co. Internat. Div., 1974-82; pres., chief exec. officer Research Testing Labs., Inc., Great Neck, N.Y., 1982—. Mem.: Regulatory Affairs Profl. Soc., Drug Info. Assn. Home: 52 Tamarack Ln Pomona NY 10970-2012 Office: Rsch Testing Labs Inc 255 Great Neck Rd Great Neck NY 11021-3308

SIMON, BERNECE KERN, retired social work educator; b. Denver, Nov. 27, 1914; d. Maurice Meyer and Jennie (Bloch) Kern; m. Marvin L. Simon, Feb. 26, 1939; 1 dau., Anne Elizabeth. BA, U. Chgo., 1936, MA, 1942. Social worker Jewish Children's Bur. Chgo., 1938-40, U. Chgo. Hosps. and Clinics, 1940-44; mem. faculty U. Chgo., 1944-81, instr., 1944-48, asst. prof., 1948-60, prof. social casework, 1960—, Samuel Deutsch prof. Sch. Social Service Adminstrn., 1960-81, emeritus, 1981—. Mem. bd. editors 17th Edit. Ency. Social Work, 1975-77, Social Svc. Rev., 1975-99; bd. editors: Social Work, 1978-82, book rev. editor, 1982-87; cons. editor Journal of Social Work Education, 1991-94; contbr. articles to profl. jours., book chpts., monographs. Mem. NASW, Coun. Social Work Edn. (mem. nat. bd., sec. 1972-74), Acad. Cert. Social Workers, Nat. Acads. Practice: Social Work Office: U Chgo Sch of Social Svc Administrn 969 E 60th St Chicago IL 60637-2677

SIMON, BOB, news correspondent, anchor; b. Bronx, May 29, 1941; m. Francoise Simon; 1 child. Degree in history, Brandeis U., 1962. Reporter CBS News, N.Y.C., London, Saigon, 1967-81, and Tel Aviv, Dept. State corr. Washington, 1981-82, nat. corr. N.Y.C., 1982-87, chief Mid.-Ea. corr., 1987—; contbr. 60 Mins., N.Y.C., 1996—; corr. 60 Mins. II, 1999—. Officer Am. Fgn. Svc., 1964-67. Recipient Emmy awards, Peabody award, Edward Weintal prize Georgetown U., 1997; Fulbright scholar, France, Woodrow Wilson scholar. Office: c/o 60 Minutes II 524 W 57th St New York NY 10019-2902

SIMON, CARLY, singer, composer, author; b. N.Y.C., June 25, 1945; d. Richard S.; m. James Taylor, 1972 (div. 1983); children: Sarah Maria, Benjamin Simon; m. James Hart, Dec. 23, 1987. Studied with Pete Seeger. Singer, composer, rec. artist, 1971—. Appeared in film No Nukes, 1980; albums include Carly Simon, 1971, Anticipation, 1972, No Secrets, 1973, Hotcakes, 1974, Playing Possum, 1975, The Best of Carly Simon, 1975, Another Passenger, 1976, Boys in the Trees, 1978, Spy, 1979, Come Upstairs, 1980, Torch, 1981, Hello Big Man, 1983, Spoiled Girl, 1985, Coming Around Again, 1987, Greatest Hits Live, 1988, My Romance, 1990, Have You Seen Me Lately?, 1990, Carly Simon, This Is My Life, 1992, Letters Never Sent, 1994; single records: You're So Vain/Nobody Does It Better, 1977, Let the River Run, 1988 (Academy award best original song, 1989), (with Frank Sinatra) In the Wee Small Hours of the Morning, 1993, Clouds in My Coffee, 1995, (with others) Come Upstairs, 1996, Film Noir, 1997, The Bedroom Tapes, 2000; recipient Grammy award as best new artist 1971; TV appearance: Carly in Concert: My Romance, 1990; created opera Romulus Hunt, 1993; composer various musical scores for films; author: (children's books) Amy the Dancing Bear, The Boy of the Bells, Fisherman's Song, The Nighttime Chauffeur. Office: Arista 6 W 57th St New York NY 10019-3999

SIMON, DAVID, real estate company officer; BS, Ind. U.; MBA, Columbia U. Assoc. First Boston Corp., N.Y.C.; CFO, COO Melvin Simon & Assocs., Inc.; v.p. Wasserstein Perella & Co., N.Y.C., til 1990; pres., CEO Simon Property Group, 1990-96; CEO Simon Propert Group, Inc., 1996—. 2d. vice-chmn. Nat. Assn. Real Estate Investment Trusts, Inc.; trustee Internat. Coun. Shopping Ctrs.; dir. 1st Health Corp. Mem. urban Land Inst. Office: Simon Property Group Inc 115 W Washington St Ste 1465 Indianapolis IN 46204-3464*

SIMON, DIANE MEYER, environmental services administrator, consultant; b. Nappanee, Ind., Apr. 2, 1946; d. Orlando Lott Meyer and Irene Elizabeth (Speheger) Best; m. N. Stuart Grauel, Aug. 2, 1969 (div. Nov. 1976); m. Herbert Simon, Nov. 25, 1981; children: Sarah, Rachel, Asher Benjamin. BA in Psychology, Butler U., 1968; postgrad., IUPUI. Press/media staff U.S. Senator Robert F. Kennedy, 1968; presdl. campaign adminstr. U.S. Senator Birch Bayh, Washington and Indpls., 1968-79; pres. Meyer Simon Group, Indpls., 1981-89; prin. ECO Ptnrs., Inc., Indpls., 1990—, ECO Educators, Indpls., 1990-94. Founder, pres. emeritus Global Green USA, Santa Monica, Calif., N.Y.C. and Washington, 1993—; exec. bd. Green Cross Internat., Geneva, 1993—. Bd. dirs. Hollywood Policy Ctr. Found., Calif., Sadat Peace Found., N.Y., Sundance Inst., Indpls. Children's Mus., Indpls. Symphony Orch., United Way Indpls., WFYI Channel 20 (PBS); co-founder Dialogue Today (Coalition of Black and Jewish Women); bd. sponsors Ind. Planned Parenthood; mem. Ind. U. Found., Indpls. Clean City Com., Indpls. Human Rels. Task Force; capital campaign co-chair Madame C.J. Walker Urban Life-Ctr.; bd. govs. Orchard Country Day Sch.; trustee YMCA; fin. chair Baron Hill for U.S. Senate, Ind.; mem. fin. com. Evan Bayh for Gov., Ind.; presdl. appointment to adv. com. on arts and JFK Ctr. for Performing Arts; committeewoman Dem. Nat. Com. Recipient Ind. State award for design ASID, Ind., 1986, Mary Mcleod Bethune award Nat. Coun. Negro Women, Ind., 1986, Wilma Rudolph Found. award, Indpls., 1988, King, Walker, Wilkins, Young award, Indpls., 1989, Millennium award Green Cross Internat., Geneva, 1997, Founders award Global Green USA, Santa Monica and Washington, 1997; named Woman of Yr., City of Indpls., 1985, Soroptomist Internat. Woman of Distinction for Environment, Indpls., 1988. Mem. Internat. Womens Forum. Jewish. Home: 1570 E Mountain Dr Montecito CA 93108-1407 also: 670 Alverna Dr Indianapolis IN 46260 Office: Global Green USA 227 Broadway Ste 302 Santa Monica CA 90401-2370

SIMON, DIANE ROSE, music educator, writer, poet; b. Appleton, Wis., Oct. 19, 1945; d. Raymond George and Violet Beatrice (Behnke) Rippl; m. Ronald Philip Simon, Sept. 18, 1938; children: David Clarence, Mary Anne. Saxophone student, Stevens Point State Tchrs. Coll., Wis., 1966; BMus, Ariz. State U., 1969, postgrad., 1971—94; saxophone student, Paris (France) Am. Acad., 1970, Union Coll., Schenectady, N.Y., 1970; student, Westminster Choir Coll., Princeton, N.J., 1979, Grand Canyon Coll., Phoenix, 1992, Inst. of Children's Lit., West Redding, Conn., 1998—2003, Poetry Laureate Program, Owings Mills, Md., 2002—04. Band dir., chorus, gen. music Wellton Elem. Sch. Dist., Ariz., 1969—70; saxophone instr. Ariz. Western Coll., Yuma, 1969—70; woodwind specialist Yuma Sch. Dist., 1970—72; band dir. Balsz Sch. Dist., Phoenix, 1972—76, Paradise Valley Sch. Dist., Phoenix, 1976—77; band dir., chorus, gen. music Mesa Pub. Schs., Ariz., 1978—94; ret., 1994. Saxophone clinician, adjudicator Ariz. Music Educators Assn., 1972—76, 2002—; dir. saxophone ensembles Yuma Sch. Dist. #1, 1970—72. Author: Expressions of the Heart, 1997, Family Treasures, 1998, With a Giggle and a Tear, 1998, Butterflies in the Meadow, 1999, Into the Millennium, 2000; pub. Beneath the Mesquite, 1999, Sunrise Over the Desert, 1999, poet (poetry) The Stain, 2003, Arm of Doom, 2003, poet pub. numerous anthologies (Editors Choice Award cert., 1996, 1997, 1998, 99, 2000, 2001, 2002, 2003); contbr. articles to profl. publs. Named one of Best Poets of 2002, Internat. Libr. Poetry, 2002; recipient The Muse of Fire trophy, medallion, The Famous Poets Soc., 2000. Mem.: Internat. Libr. of Poetry (Internat. Poetry Hall of Fame 1996), Internat. Soc. Poets (Disting. Membership 1996, Internat. Poet of Merit award Medallion and Commemorative Plaque 1996, 1998, Poet of Merit award medallion 2002, Silver award bowl trophy 2002, Poet of Merit award medallion 2004, Outstanding Achievement in Poetry Silver award cup 2004). Republican. Roman Catholic. Avocations: hiking, bicycling, tennis, cross stitch, embroidery. Home: 732 W Curry St Chandler AZ 85225

SIMON, DOLORES DALY, copy editor; b. San Francisco, Nov. 18, 1928; d. Francis Edward and Jeannette (Cooke) Daly; m. Sidney Blair Simon, Aug. 24, 1952 (div. Nov. 1955); children: John Roderick, Douglas Brian. BA in Journalism, Pa. State U., 1950. County editor Centre Daily Times, State College, Pa., 1950-51; soc. editor Bradford (Pa.) Era, 1951-52; copy editor Harper & Bros., Pubs., N.Y.C., 1955-60; copy chief Harper & Row, Pubs., N.Y.C., 1960-88; freelance editor, copy editor Warwick, N.Y., 1988—. Co-author: Recipes into Type, 1993 (Best Food Reference 1994). Mem. James Beard Found., Phi Mu. Democrat. Avocation: book collecting. Office: Editl Svcs 63 Blooms Corners Rd Warwick NY 10990-2403 Office Phone: 845-986-4442.

SIMON, DONALD JOHN, employee benefits administrator, insurance and investment broker; b. Chgo., July 16, 1947; s. Nicholas J. and Alice R. (Vaughan) S.; 1 child, Joshua K. BSBA, Oglethorpe U., 1969. CFP, CLU, ChFC. Sales rep. D. W. Shaw, Inc., Berlin, N.J., 1969-74; owner Simon Fin. Co., Vero Beach, Fla., 1975—. Mem. Nat. Assn. Ins. and Fin. Advisors, Indian River C. of C., Indian River Estate Planning Coun. Avocations: music, bicycling, boating. Home: 8080 24th St Vero Beach FL 32966

SIMON, ECKEHARD (PETER), foreign language educator; b. Schneidemühl, Germany, Jan. 5, 1939; came to U.S., 1955, naturalized, 1960; s. Herbert and Doris (Keiler) S.; m. Eileen Higginbottom, Dec. 19, 1959; children: Anders, Conrad (dec.), Matthew, Frederick. AB, Columbia U., 1960; A.M., Harvard U., 1961, PhD, 1964. Instr., German Harvard U., Cambridge, Mass., 1964-65, asst. prof., 1965-69, assoc. prof., 1969-71, prof., 1971—, Victor S. Thomas prof. Germanic langs. & lits., 1996—, head tutor and lang. coordinator, 1965-76, chmn. dept. German, 1976—82, 1996—99, chmn. com. on medieval studies, 1992—95, 2001—02. Author: Neidhart von Reuental: Geschichte der Forschung und Bibliographie, 1968, Neidhart von Reuental, 1975, The Türkenkalender (1454) Attributed to Gutenberg and the Strasbourg Lunation Tracts, 1988, Die Anfänge des weltlichen deutschen Schauspiels, 1370-1530, 2003; editor: The Theatre of Medieval Europe, New Research in Early Drama, 1991; mem. editorial adv. bd.: Dictionary of the Middle Ages, 1982-89; contbr. articles to profl. jours. Woodrow Wilson fellow, 1960-61; NEH Younger Scholar fellow, 1968-69; research fellow, 1977-78; Guggenheim fellow, 1968-69; Fulbright fellow U. Cologne, 1983; Sr. Exchange fellow Dumbarton Oaks, Washington, 2001. Mem. MLA, Am. Assn. Tchrs. German, Medieval Acad. Am. (asst. editor Speculum 1981-94, book review editor 1994-2000). Home: 11 Hayes Ave Lexington MA 02420-3521 Office: Harvard U Barker Ctr 345 Cambridge MA 02138-3879 Office Phone: 617-496-9359. Business E-Mail: simon2@fas.harvard.edu.

SIMON, ERIC JACOB, neurochemist, educator; b. Wiesbaden, Germany, June 2, 1924; came to U.S., 1938, naturalized, 1945; s. Joseph and Paula (Meyer) S.; m. Irene M. Ronis, Aug. 9, 1947; children: Martin A., Faye Ruth, Lawrence D. BS, Case Inst. Tech., Cleve., 1944; MS, U. Chgo., 1947, PhD, 1951; hon. doctorate, U. René Descartes Sorbonne, Paris, 1982. Postdoctoral trainee in biochemistry Columbia U. Coll. Physicians and Surgeons, 1951-53; lectr. in chemistry CCNY, 1952-59; research assoc. Cornell U. Med. Coll., 1953-59; asst. prof. medicine NYU Med. Center, 1959-64, assoc. prof. exptl. medicine, 1964-72, prof. exptl. medicine, 1972-80, prof. psychiatry and pharmacology, 1980—. Harry Williams Meml. lectr. Dept. Pharmacology Emory U., Atlanta, 1986; mem. initial rev. com. Nat. Inst. Drug Abuse, 1976-80, chmn. 1979-80, mem. Nat. Adv. Coun. on Drug Abuse, 1989-92; Sterling-Winthrop lectr. Albany Med. Coll., 1977; vis. prof. Coll. de France, Paris, 1990; vis. lectr. Shanghai and Beijing, 1985. Trustee Teaneck (N.J.) Bd. Edn., 1975-79. Served with U.S. Army, 1944-46. Recipient Rsch. Pace Setter award Nat. Inst. Drug Abuse, 1977, Louis and Bert Freedman Found. award N.Y. Acad. Scis., 1980, Nathan B. Eddy Meml. award Coll. on Problems of Drug Dependence, Lexington, Ky., 1983, Alumni Profl. Achievement award U. Chgo., 1986; Health Rsch. Coun. N.Y.C. career scientist, 1959-75 Fellow AAAS, N.Y. Acad. Scis. (trustee 1986-89); mem. Am. Soc. Biol. Chemists, Am. Soc. Neurochemistry, Am. Soc. Pharmacology, Internat. Soc. Neurochemistry, Am. Chem. Soc., Sigma Xi. Lodges: B'nai B'rith. Research, publs. on opiate receptors, endorphins, biochemistry of analgesic action, vitamin E metabolism, acyl-coenzyme A synthesis. Office: 550 1st Ave New York NY 10016-6402 E-mail: eric.simon@nyu.edu.

SIMON, EVELYN, lawyer; b. N.Y.C., May 13, 1943; d. Joseph and Adele (Holzschlag) Berkman; m. Fredrick Simon, Aug. 18, 1963; children: Amy Jocelyn, Marcie Ann. AB in Physics, Barnard Coll., 1963; MS in Physics, U. Pitts., 1964; JD, Wayne State U., 1978; LLB, Monash U., Melbourne, Australia, 1980. Bar: Mich. 1980, Victoria (Australia) 1981. Supr. engring. Chrysler Corp., Detroit, 1964-72; edn. and profl. mgr. Engring. Soc. Detroit, 1972-78; solicitor Arthur Robinson & Co., Melbourne, 1980-81; sr. atty. Ford Motor Co., Detroit, 1981-89; assoc. gen. counsel Sheller-Globe Corp., Detroit, 1989-90; v.p. planning, gen. counsel United Techs. Automotive Inc., Dearborn, Mich., 1991-94, v.p. bus. devel. and legal affairs, 1995-96, v.p. Asian bus. devel., 1997-98; pvt. practice, 1999—. Cons. internat. bus. devel., 1998—. Mem. Mich. Bar Assn. Office: 1787 Alexander Dr Bloomfield Hills MI 48302-1204 E-mail: evelynsimon@prodigy.net.

SIMON, GARY B. health care manager, investor; b. Honolulu, Oct. 15, 1960; s. Benedict Joseph and Frances (Seno) S.; m. Akemi Hata, July 9, 1993; 1 child, Seth Carlos Hisao. BS in Chemistry, U. Hawaii, 1985. Notary public, Hawaii. Vol. U.S. Peace Corps, Sierra Leone, 1985—87; exec. asst. to pres. Focus Techs., Inc., Washington, 1989—90; office mgr. St. Francis Hospice, Honolulu, 1990—95, bus. mgr., 1995—2004, dir., 2004—. Achievement award St. Francis Med. Ctr., 1998—, Mother Marianne award St. Francis Healthcare Sys. Hawaii, 2001. Mem. Health Care Info. Sys. Hawaii User Group (pres. 1996—). Republican. Office: St Francis Hospice 24 Puiwa Rd Honolulu HI 96817-1127 E-mail: GARYS@sfhs-hi.org.

SIMON, GARY LEONARD, internist, educator; b. Bklyn., Dec. 18, 1946; s. Bernard and Dorothy (Ligeti) Simon; m. Vicki Thiessen, Aug. 29, 1970; children: Jason, Jessica. BS, U. Md., 1968, MD, 1975; PhD, U. Wis., 1972. Diplomate Am. Bd. Internal Medicine, Am. Bd. Infectious Diseases. Resident in internal medicine U. Md. Hosp., Balt., 1975—78; fellow infectious diseases Tufts-New Eng. Med. Ctr., Boston, 1978—80; asst. prof. dept. medicine George Washington U., Washington, 1980-84, assoc. prof., 1984-89, assoc. chmn. medicine, 1984-97, prof., 1989—, dir. divsn. infectious diseases, 1993—, vice chmn. medicine, 1997—. Cons. on AIDS Assn. Am. Med. Coll., Washington, 1990—. Contbr. articles to profl. jours. Fellow: ACP (Laureate award 2000), Infectious Disease Soc.; mem.: Internat. AIDS Soc., Assn. Subspecialty Profs., Am. Soc. Microbiology. Office: George Washington U 2150 Pennsylvania Ave NW Washington DC 20037-3201 Office Phone: 202-741-2234. Business E-Mail: gsimon@mfa.gwu.edu.

SIMON, HAROLD, radiologist; b. Trenton, N.J., May 13, 1930; s. John and Rae B. Simon; m. Jane L. Ludwig, Feb. 25, 1956; children: Steven Gregg, John Gregory. MD, Duke U., 1955. Diplomate Am. Bd. Radiology, Am. Bd. Nuclear Medicine. Intern U.S. Naval Hosp., Chelsea, Mass., 1955-56; resident in radiology Mass. Gen. Hosp., Boston, 1958-61, Oak Ridge Inst. Nuc. Medicine, 1959; instr. radiology Med. Sch., Tufts U., Boston, 1961-63, clin. asst. prof., 1965, assoc. clin. prof., 1971-77, clin. prof., 1977-98; pvt. practice Newton Lower Falls, Mass., 1963-95; hon. mem. staff Newton (Mass.) Wellesley Hosp., assoc. chief radiology, 1977—, radiologist-in-chief, 1987-95. Dir. Sch. Nuc. Med. Tech.; bd. dirs., mem. CRC com., mem. audit com. Grove Bank, chmn. audit com., 1995—96; bd. dirs., treas. Newell Physicians, Inc., 1986—93; mem. staff Intracoastal Med. Sys., West Palm Beach, Fla., 1987—2001; bd. overseers Newell Health Corp.; cons. VA Hosp., Boston, 1996—, Charitas Norwood (Mass.) Hosp. Contbr. articles to profl. jours. With USNR, 1955—58, med. officer USN, 1956—58. Fellow: Am. Coll. Radiology; mem.: Mass. Radiology Soc., Mass. Med. Soc. (mem. ins. com. 1992—95), New Eng. Roentgen Ray Soc., Am. Roentgen Ray Soc., Radiol. Soc. N.Am., Banyon Country Club, Belmont Country Club, Pinebrook Country Club (pres. 1982—85), Phi Beta Kappa, Phi Eta Sigma. Home: 252 Atlantic Ave Palm Beach FL 33480-3709

SIMON, H(UEY) PAUL, lawyer; b. Lafayette, La., Oct. 19, 1923; s. Jules and Ida (Rogére) S.; m. Carolyn Perkins, Aug. 6, 1949 (dec. Dec. 1999); 1 child, John Clark. BS, U. Southwestern La., 1943; JD, Tulane U., 1947. CPA La., 1947; bar: La. 1947. Pvt. practice, New Orleans, 1947—; asst. prof. advanced acctg. and taxation U. Southwestern La., 1944-45; staff acct. Haskins & Sells (now Deloitte & Touche), New Orleans, 1945-53, prin., 1953-57; ptnr. Deutsch, Kerrigan & Stiles, 1957-79; sr. founding ptnr. Simon, Peragine, Smith & Redfearn, 1979—. Mem. New Orleans Bd. Trade. Author: Community Property and Liability for Funeral Expenses of Deceased Spouse, 1946, Income Tax Deductibility of Attorney's Fees in Action in Boundary, 1946, Fair Labor Standards Act and Employee's Waiver of Liquidated Damages, 1946, Louisiana Income Tax Law, 1956, Changes Effected by the Louisiana Trust Code, 1965, Gifts to Minors and the Parent's Obligation of Support, 1968; co-author: Deductions—Business or Hobby, 1975, Role of Attorney in IRS Tax Return Examination, 1978; assoc. editor: The Louisiana CPA, 1956-60; mem. bd. editors Tulane Law Rev., 1945-46, adv. bd. editors, 1992—; estates, gifts and trusts editor The Tax Times, 1986-87. Bd. dirs., mem. fin. com. World Trade Ctr., 1985-86; mem. New Orleans Met. Crime Commn., Coun. for a Better La., New Orleans Met. Area Com., Bur. Govtl. Rsch., Pub. Affairs Rsch. Coun.; co-chmn. NYU Tax Conf., New Orleans, 1976; mem. dean's coun. Tulane U. Law Sch. Fellow Am. Coll. Tax Counsel; mem. ABA (com. ct. procedure tax sect. 1958—), AICPA, La. Bar Assn. (com. on legis. and adminstrv. practice 1966-70, bd. cert. tax atty.), New Orleans Bar Assn., Internat. Bar Assn. (com. on securities issues and trading 1970-88), Am. Judicature Soc., Soc. La. CPAs, New Orleans Assn. Notaries, Tulane U. Alumni Assn., New Orleans C. of C. (coun. 1952-66), Tulane Tax Inst. (program com. 1960-96, emeritus 1997—), Internat. House (bd. dirs. 1976-79, 82-85), Internat. Platform Assn., City Energy Club, Press Club, New Orleans Country Club, Phi Delta Phi (past pres. New Orleans chpt.), Sigma Pi Alpha. Roman Catholic. Achievements include listed annually in the best lawyers in Am. 1985-. Home: 6075 Canal Blvd New Orleans LA 70124-2936 Office: 30th Fl Energy Ctr New Orleans LA 70163 Personal E-mail: hpsimon@aol.com. Business E-Mail: hpsimon@spsr-law.com. *Developing and maintaining consistency and constancy in feeling and showing genuine respect towards others, nourish and stimulate an individual to day by day become a better person. Whether alone or in the presence of others, one who abides by the guidance and rules he would advocate to others invariably finds the greatest reward of all--true respect for one's self.*

SIMON, J. STEPHEN, oil industry executive; BCE, Duke U.; MBA, Northwestern U., Evanston, Ill. With Exxon U.S.A., 1967, mgr. refinery; supply and transp. mgr. Esso Europe, Esso U.S.A.; exec. asst. to the pres. Exxon Corp.; gen. mgr. Esso Caribbean and Ctrl. Am.; pres. Esso Italiana; exec. v.p. Exxon Co. Internat., 1997—99; pres. ExxonMobil Refining and Supply Co., 1999—; v.p. ExxonMobil Corp., 1999—. Office: ExxonMobil Refining and Supply Co 3225 Gallows Rd Fairfax VA 22037

SIMON, JACK AARON, geologist, former state official; b. Champaign, Ill., June 17, 1919; s. Abraham and Lenore (Levy) S. BA, U. Ill., 1941, MS, 1946; postgrad., Northwestern U., 1947-49, D.Sc. (hon.), 1981. Tech. and research asst. Ill. State Geol. Survey, Urbana, 1937-42, asst. to assoc. geologist, 1945-53, geologist, head, coal sect., 1953-67, prin. geologist, 1967-74, asst. chief, 1973-74, chief, 1974-81, prin. scientist, 1981-83. Occasional cons.; asso. prof. dept. metallurgy and mining engring. U. Ill., 1967-74, prof., 1974-77, 80-85, adj. prof. dept. geology, 1979-86. Served with F.A. AUS, 1942-43, F.A., USAAF, 1943-45. Decorated Air Medal with 4 oak leaf clusters; recipient Disting. Svc. award So. Ill. U., Edwardsville, 1982, Coal Day award So. Ill. U., Carbondale, 1982, Alumni Achievement award U. Ill. dept. geology, 1994, Disting. Svc. award Assn. Am. State Geologists, 2004. Fellow AAAS (sect. E chmn. 1980), Geol. Soc. Am. (chmn. coal geology div. 1962-63, Gilbert H. Cady award 1975, mem. council and exec. com. 1979-81); mem. Am. Assn. Petroleum Geologists (ea. sect. Gordon M. Wood Jr. Meml. award 1991), AIME (chmn. Midwest coal sect. 1966, Percy W. Nicholls award 1981), Am. Inst. Profl. Geologists (v.p. 1973), Am. Mining Congress, Assn. Am. State Geologists (hon.), Ill. Mining Inst. (hon. life; exec. sec.-treas. 1963-68, v.p. 1980-81, pres. 1981-82), Ill. Soc. Coal Preparation Engrs. and Chemists, Ill. Geol. Soc., Ill. Acad. Sci., Soc. Econ. Geologists (councillor 1982-84), B'nai Brith, Sigma Xi. Clubs: Exchange (Urbana) (pres. 1969). Home: 101 W Windsor Rd # 4204 Urbana IL 61802-6697 E-mail: coaljack@hotmail.com.

SIMON, JACQUELINE ALBERT, political scientist, journalist; d. Louis and Rose (Axelroad) Albert; m. Pierre Simon; children: Lisette, Orville. BA cum laude, NYU, MA, 1972, PhD, 1977. Adj. assoc. prof. Southampton Coll., 1977-79; mng. editor Point of Contact, NYC, 1975-76; assoc. editor, US bur. chief Politique Internationale, Paris, 1979—. Sr. fellow Inst. French Studies, NYU, 1980—, adj. assoc. prof., 1982-85; assoc. prof. govt. Southampton Coll., 1982-83; frequent appearances French TV and radio. Contbg. editor Harper's mag., 1984-92; contbr. numerous articles to French mag., revs., books on internat. affairs. Bd. dir. Fresh Air Fund, 1984—. Mem. Women's Fgn. Policy Group, Overseas Press Club of Am. (bd. dirs., treas. 2000--), Phi Beta Kappa. Home: 988 5th Ave New York NY 10021-0143 E-mail: jasimon@ix.netcom.com.

SIMON, JAMES LOWELL, lawyer; b. Nov. 8, 1944; s. K. Lowell and Elizabeth Ann (Unholz) S.; m. RuthAnn Beck, July 4, 1997; children: Heather Lyn Small, Brandon James; stepchildren: Gary G. Mower, Richard M. Nazareth II, Juliet A. Nazareth. Student, U. Ill., 1962-63, JD with honors, 1975; BSEE magna cum laude, Bradley U., 1967. Bar: Fla. 1975, Utah 1999, Calif. 2002, U.S. Dist. Ct. (mid. dist.) Fla. 1976, U.S. Dist. Ct. Utah 1999, U.S. Dist. Ct. (no. dist.) Calif. 2002, U.S. Ct. Appeals (11th cir.) 1981, U.S. Patent Office 1983. Engr. Pan Am. World Airways, Cape Kennedy, Fla., 1967-68; assoc. Akerman, Senterfitt & Eidson, Orlando, Fla., 1975-80; ptnr. Bogin, Munns, Munns & Simon, Orlando, 1980-87, Holland & Knight, LLP, 1987-99; corp. counsel Agilent Technologies Inc., Palo Alto, Calif., 2000—. With Seminole County Sch. Adv. Coun., Fla., 1981-88, chmn., 1982, 83; with Forest City Local Sch. Adv. Com., Altamonte Springs, Fla., 1981-84, Code Enforcement Bd., Altamonte Springs, 1983-84, Cen. Bus. Dist. Study com., Altamonte Springs, 1983-85, Rep. Coun. of '76, Seminole County, 1982-87; mem. Seminole County Libr. Adv. Bd., 1989-92, sec., 1990, pres., 1991, Seminole County Citizens for Quality Edn., 1990-92; mem. Seminole County Sch. Dist. Strategic Planning Com., 1991-99, Leadership Orlando Alumni, 1992-99; bd. dirs. Found. for Seminole County Pub. Schs., Inc., 1992-95, chmn., 1993-94; bd. dirs. Greater Seminole C. of C., 1993; active Lake Brantley H.S. Band Boosters, 1995-2000, Lake Brantley H.S. PTSA, 1995-2000, Chorus Boosters, 1997, Leadership Club-Heart of Fla. United Way, 1997; sponsor concerts Orlando Philharm. Orch. for Boys and Girls Clubs. Cen. Fla., 1996-97; regional dir. region 5 Holocaust Remembrance Project, 1997-99. Capt. USAF, 1968-72. Mem. ABA, Am. Corp. Counsel Assn., Am. Intellectual Property Law Assn., Intellectual Property Owners Assn. (chair copyright law com. 2003—), U. Ill. Alumni Club, Phi Kappa Phi, Tau Beta Pi, Sigma Tau, Eta Kappa Nu. Republican. Home: 1675 Tupolo Dr San Jose CA 95124-4754 Office: M/S 26U-25 3500 Deer Creek Rd Palo Alto CA 94304-1317 Office Phone: 650-485-5672. E-mail: jim_simon@agilent.com., JimandRuthann@earthlink.net.

SIMON, JAMES M. federal agency administrator; Grad., U. Ala., So. Calif. Joined CIA, 1975—, asst. dir. adminstrn., 1998—. With U.S. Army. Office: CIA Office of Dir Washington DC 20505

SIMON, JIMMY LOUIS, pediatrician, educator; b. San Francisco, Dec. 27, 1930; s. Sylvain L. and Hilda H. (Netter) S.; m. Marilyn S. Wachter, June 21, 1953; children: Kent, Nancy. AB, U. Calif.-Berkeley, 1952; MD, U. Calif.-Berkeley, San Francisco, 1955. Diplomate Am. Bd. Pediats. Intern U. Calif., San Francisco, 1955-56; resident Grace-New Haven Hosp., 1956-57; sr. asst. resident Boston Children's Hosp., 1957-58; instr., asst. prof. pediats. U. Okla., Oklahoma City, 1960-64; asso. prof. U. Tex. Med. Br., Galveston, 1966-72, prof. pediatrics, 1972-74; prof., chmn. pediats. Bowman Gray Sch. Medicine, Wake Forest U., Winston-Salem, N.C., 1974-96; prof., chmn. emeritus Wake Forest U. Sch. Medicine, Winston-Salem, N.C., 1996—. With USAF, 1958-60. Mem. Am. Pediat. Soc., Am. Acad. Pediats., Am. Bd. Pediats., Ambulatory Pediat. Assn., Alpha Omega Alpha. Office: Wake Forest U Sch Medicine Dept Pediatrics Medical Center Blvd Winston Salem NC 27157-0001

SIMON, JOHN BERN, lawyer; b. Cleve., Aug. 8, 1942; s. Seymour Frank and Roslyn (Schultz) S.; children: Lindsey Helaine, Douglas Banning. BS, U. Wis., 1964; JD, DePaul U., 1967. Bar: Ill. 1967. Asst. U.S. atty. U.S. Justice Dept., Chgo., 1967-70, dep. chief civil div., 1970-71, chief civil div., 1971-74; spl. counsel to dir. Ill. Dept. Pub. Aid, Chgo., 1974-75; legal cons. to Commn. on Rev. of Nat. Policy Toward Gambling, Chgo., 1975-76; ptnr. firm Friedman & Koven, 1975-85, mem. exec. com., 1983-85; ptnr. firm Jenner & Block, 1986—. Spl. cons. to adminstr. DEA Dept. Justice, 1976-77; counsel to Gov.'s Revenue Study Commn. on Legalized Gambling, 1977-78; spl. counsel Ill. Racing Bd., 1979-80; lectr. tng. seminars and confs.; instr. U.S. Atty. Gen.'s Advocacy Inst., Washington, 1974; lectr. Nat. Conf. Organized Crime, Washington, 1975, Dade County Inst. Organized Crime, Ft. Lauderdale, Fla., 1976; faculty Cornell Inst. Organized Crime, Ithaca, N.Y., 1976, judge Miner Moot Ct. competition Northwestern U., 1971-73; mem. law coun. DePaul U., 1974-83, mem. alumni assn., 1984-85, chmn., 1975-79; adj. prof. DePaul U. Coll. Law, 1977, 81; faculty Practising Law Inst., Chgo., 1984. Contbr. articles to profl. jours. Bd. dirs. Lawyer's Trust Fund of Ill., 1998—, treas., 2000-01, v.p., 2002—, pres., 2003-2004, Cmty. Film Workshop of Chgo., 1977-90, Friends of Glencoe Parks, 1977-78, sec., 1978-79; mem. nominating com. Glencoe Sch. Bd., 1978-81, chmn. rules com., 1980-81; pres. Glencoe Hist. Soc., 1979-82; mem. Glencoe Zoning Bd. Appeals, Zoning Commn., Sign Bd. Appeals, 1981-86, chmn., 1984-86; mem. Ill. Inaugural Com., 1979, 83, 87, 95; bd. dirs., mem. exec. com. Chgo. World's Fair 1992 Authority, 1983-85; mem. Chancery divsn. task force Spl. Commn. on Adminstrn. of Justice in Cook County, 1985-87; trustee De Paul U., 1990, chair phys. plant and property com., 1992-94, vice chair, 1995-2004, chair, 2004—; commr. Ill. Racing Bd., 1990—; gen. trustee Lincoln Acad. Ill., 1993—, regent, 1999—, chancellor, 2001—; mem. Ill. Supreme Ct. Planning and Oversight Com. for Jud. Performance Evaluation Program, 1997-98, 2000—, Ill. Suprmee Ct. Rules Com., 2004—. Recipient Bancroft-Whitney Am. Jurisprudence award, 1965, 66, Judge Learned Hand Human Rels. award Am. Jewish Com., 1994, award for outstanding svc. to legal profession DePaul U. Coll. Law, 1996, Am. ORT Jurisprudence award, 1999. Mem. ABA (com. on liaison with the judiciary 1983-95), Fed. Bar Assn., Chgo. Bar Assn. (fed. civil procedure com. 1979-85, chmn. 1985-86, bd. mgrs. 1987-89, chmn. house com. 1989-90, treas. 1990-91, 2d v.p. 1991-92, 1st v.p. 1992-93, pres. 1993-94), Ill. State Bar Assn., Women's Bar Assn., Ill. Police Assn., Ill. Sheriffs Assn., U.S. Treasury Agts. Assn., Chgo. Bar Assn., DePaul U. Alumni Assn. (pres. 1985-87, chmn. spl. gifts com. campaign, chmn. Simon Commn. 1989-91, nat. chair for ann. giving 1991-94), Std. Club. Office: Jenner & Block One IBM Plz 42nd Fl Chicago IL 60611

SIMON, JOHN GERALD, law educator; b. N.Y.C., Sept. 19, 1928; s. Robert Alfred and Madeleine (Marshall) S.; m. Claire Aloise Bising, June 14, 1958; 1 son, John Kirby (dec.). Grad., Ethical Culture Schs., 1946; AB, Harvard U., 1950; LLB, Yale U., 1953; LLD (hon.), Ind. U., 1989. Bar: N.Y. 1953. Asst. to gen. counsel Office Sec. Army, 1956-58; with firm Paul, Weiss, Rifkind, Wharton & Garrison, N.Y.C., 1958-62; mem. faculty Yale Law Sch., 1962—, prof. law, 1967-76, Augustus Lines prof. law, 1976—2003, Augustus Lines prof. emeritus law, 2003—, dep. dean, 1985-90, acting dean, 1991; dir., co-chmn. program on non-profit orgns. Yale U., 1977-88. Author: (with Powers and Gunnemann) The Ethical Investor, 1972. Pres. Taconic Found., 1967—; trustee, sec. Potomac Inst., 1961-93; mem. grad. bd. Harvard Crimson, 1950—; chmn. bd. dirs. Coop. Assistance Fund, 1970-76, vice chmn., 1977—; mem. governing coun. Rockefeller Archives Ctr., 1982-86; trustee The Found. Ctr., 1983-92, Open Soc. Inst.-N.Y., 1996—. 1st lt. U.S. Army, 1953-5 6. Recipient Certificate of Achievement Dept. Army, 1956 Mem. Phi Beta Kappa. Office: Yale U Law Sch PO Box 208215 New Haven CT 06520-8215

SIMON, JOSEPH PATRICK, food services executive; b. Phila., Nov. 9, 1932; s. Joseph Patrick and Elizabeth Gertrude (McLaughlin) S.; m. Vera Cornelia Steiner, Sept. 15, 1956; children: Joseph Walter, Walter Joseph, Leslie Vera, Ernest William. BS, Cornell U., 1955. With Slater Systems, 1955-59; with ARA Services, Inc., Phila., 1959-72, regional v.p., 1964-66, area v.p., 1966-68, group v.p. and sr. v.p., 1968-70, pres. community and school food service div., 1970-71, gen. mgr., pres. internat. ops., 1971-72; v.p., gen. mgr. airline services div. Dobbs Houses Inc., Memphis, 1972-73; group

v.p. Service Systems Corp., Buffalo, 1973-79, pres., 1980-85, also nat. dir.; group v.p. P.J. Schmitt subs. Loblaw Ltd., 1984, sr. v.p., 1985-88, also bd. dirs., 1986, 87. Dist. chmn. Detroit United Fund, 1966-67, Nat. Alliance of Businessmen, 1969; mem. adv. bd. McComb Jr. Coll.; mem. council Cornell U., 1980-83; chmn. bd. Sheehan Emergency Hosp., Buffalo, 1984-85; trustee D'Youville Coll.; bd. dirs. United Fund, Buffalo, 1981-82, CODE Inc., 1986-87. Served as 1st lt. U.S. Army, 1955-56. Mem. Assn. Food Svc. Mgmt. (dir.), Nat. Automatic Merchandising Assn. (dir.), Buffalo C. of C. (dir. 1982-84), Cornell Hotel Soc. Mich. (pres.), Memphis Athletic Club, Detroit Athletic Club, Buffalo Club, Park County Club, The Meadows Country Club, Zeta Psi. Episcopalian. Home: 4422 Whisperwood Sarasota FL 34235-6924

SIMON, KEITH R. safety engineer, petroleum engineer, professional disc jockey; b. Lafayette, La., July 2, 1955; s. Jean Raymond and Ranelle T. (Touchet) S.; m. Martha Simon, Oct. 16, 1976 (div. Oct. 1979); 1 child, Jamie. BSN, BS, postgrad., U. La., 1980, student, 1981. Cert. in crane operation, first aid, CPR, offshore orientation, La. Ops. mgr. Boco of Lafayette, 1980-82, exec. v.p., 1982-84; pres., owner Silver Bullet Prodns. Inc., Silver Bullet Limousine, 1983—; founder Boco of La., 1980, ops. mgr., 1984-86; safety dir., corp. security Petro-Drive, Inc., Lafayette, 1989-91; v.p. Boco of La. Inc./Petro-Drive, Lafayette, 1991—; offshore internat. sector mgr. Sigma Coatings USA, 1998—. Engineered, developed new techs., methodologies for offshore oil drilling. Mem. ARC, 1986—. Named Coors Lite Nat. Disc Jockey, 1984, named in Men Achievement, 1991, 2000 Notable Am. Men, 1992, Personalities Am., 1993; recipient Silver Shield of Valor award, 1992, Lifetime Achievement award, 1993. Mem. Am. Soc. Safety Engrs. (profl.), Nat. Assn. Corrosion Engrs., Steel Structure Painting Coun., Nat. Safety Coun., ARC. Avocations: skiing, softball, football, disc jockey. Office: 1401 Destrehan Ave Harvey LA 70058-2436 Home: 104 Pomerol Pl Lafayette LA 70503-6527 E-mail: Keith.simon@sigmakalon.com.

SIMON, LATEEFAH, foundation administrator, director; Counselor Ctr. for Young Women's Devel., San Francisco, 1993—97, exec. dir., 1997—. Organizer and spokesperson Rock the Vote; adv. mem. San Francisco Youth Commn.; adv. panelist Juvenile Justice Commn. Recipient Leadership for a changing world award, Ford Found., 2001, Women who make a difference Honoree, The Nat. Coun. for Rsch. on Women, 2000; fellow MacArthur Found., 2003. Office: 1550 Bryant St Ste 700 San Francisco CA 94103-4876

SIMON, LEONARD SAMUEL, banker; b. N.Y.C., Oct. 28, 1936; s. Nathaniel and Lena (Pasternack) S.; m. Marion Appel, Sept. 1, 1957; children: Andrew, Jonathan. BS, MIT, 1958; MS, Columbia U., 1959, PhD, 1963. Mem. faculty Grad. Sch. Mgmt., U. Rochester, 1962-79, prof., 1974-79; v.p. Community Savs. Bank, Rochester, N.Y., 1969-74, sr. v.p., 1974-77, exec. v.p., 1977-83, Rochester Community Sav. Bank, 1983-84, chmn., chief exec. officer, 1984-97; chmn., CEO, pres. RSCB Fin., Inc., 1995-97; vice. chmn. charter One Financial Inc., 1997—; chmn. Captial Internet Grp., 1997—2000; vice chmn. Charter One Fin. Inc., 1997—. Bd. dirs. Gateway Am. Bank, Integrated Nano Tech., Inc.; chmn. Telephone Computing Svc. Corp., 1974—79; trustee Tchrs. Ins. Annuity Assn. Editor-in-chief, founding editor: Interfaces, 1970-76; Author books and articles in field. Past chmn. Rochester-Monroe County chpt. ARC, Rochester Area Ednl. TV Assn., Career Devel. Svcs. of Rochester; past trustee Ctr. for Govt. Rsch.; mem. Urban Policy Conf., Brookings Instn., 1972-73, 64th Am. Assembly; bd. dirs. Cmty. Preservation. Ford Found. grantee, 1964; recipient MIT Corp. Leadership award, 1987. Mem. Cmty. Bankers Assn. N.Y. State (bd. dirs.), Am.'s Cmty. Bankers, Genesee Valley Club, Beta Gamma Sigma.

SIMON, LOTHAR, publishing company executive; b. Wuppertal, Germany, Sept. 17, 1938; arrived in U.S., 1961, naturalized, 1973; s. Fritz and Erna (Backhaus) S.; m. Jeannine Rechtman, Oct. 30, 1964; 1 child, Charles. Mgr. book dept. Franz Bader Book Shop and Globe Book Shop, Washington, 1961-66; sales mgr. Humanities Press Inc., N.Y.C., 1966-73; pres. Longman Inc., N.Y.C., 1973-81; pub. cons., 1981-82; pres., CEO Sheridan House, Inc., Dobbs Ferry, NY, 1982—. Mem. Assn. Am. Pubs., Town Club (Scarsdale, N.Y.). Democrat. Office: Sheridan House Inc 145 Palisade St Dobbs Ferry NY 10522-1617

SIMON, LOU ANNA KIMSEY, academic administrator; V.p. acad. affairs, provost Coll. Human Medicine Mich. State U., 1993—. Office: Mich State U 438 Administration Bldg East Lansing MI 48824-1046

SIMON, MARC, communications executive; BS in Acctg., JD, U. Ill. CPA 1971. CFO, dir. APAC Customer Svcs. Inc. HA-LO Industries, Inc., Niles, Ill., 1995—98, vice chmn. APAC, 1998, exec. v.p., COO APAC Teleservices, Inc., 1998—2001, pres., CEO, 2001—. Office: Halo Ind 500 Lake Cook Rd Deerfield IL 60015-5609

SIMON, MARTIN STANLEY, commodity marketing company executive, economist; b. St. Louis, Sept. 6, 1926; s. Elmer Ellis and Bee Marion (Werner) S.; m. Rita Edith Scheinhorn, June 18, 1950; children: Deborah, Richard. BBA, CCNY, 1949; MA, NYU, 1953. Econ. statistician Indsl. Commodity Corp, N.Y.C., 1949-52; agrl. econ. statistician Dept. Agr., Washington, 1952-58; commodity analyst Connell Rice & Sugar Co., Inc., Westfield, NJ, 1958-62, asst. to pres., 1962-67, v.p., 1967-74; sr. v.p. Connell Rice & Sugar Co., Inc. (now The Connell Co.), Berkeley Heights, NJ, 1974-99; pres. Eureka Group, LLC, Westfield, NJ, 1999—, The Rice Econs. Group, LLC, Westfield, NJ, 1999—; cons. AID, Jamaica, 1963; mem. Rice Insp. Industry Adv. Com., Washington, 1971-72; adv. U.S. Del. to UN FAO Intergovtl. Meetings on Rice, 1981; export dir., bd. dirs. Assn. Administrn. Rice Quotas, Inc., 1997-99. Served with U.S. Army, 1944-46, ETO. Recipient Class of 1920 award for merit in econ. stats. CCNY, 1949 Mem. Am. Econ. Assn., Rice Millers Assn. (chmn. legis. options working group 1984-86, govt. programs com. 1986-87, chmn. PL480 subcom. 1988-90), Nat. Economists Club. Office: The Rice Econs Group LLC PO Box 2446 Westfield NJ 07091-2446 E-mail: rice.economics@prodigy.net.

SIMON, MELVIN I. molecular biologist, educator; b. N.Y.C., Feb. 8, 1937; s. Hyman and Sarah (Liebman) S.; m. Linda, Jan. 7, 1959; children— Joshua, David, Rachel BS, CCNY, 1959; PhD, Brandeis U., 1963. Postdoctoral fellow Princeton U., N.J., 1963-65; prof. biology U. Calif.-San Diego, La Jolla, 1965-82, Calif. Inst. Tech., Pasadena, 1982—, chmn., 1995-2000, prof., 2000—. Pres., dir. Agouron Inst., La Jolla, 1980— Contbr. articles to profl. jours. Mem. Nat. Acad. Scis. (Selman A. Waksman microbiology award 1991), Am. Soc. Microbiology

SIMON, MELVON, real estate company officer; married; 5 children. Leasing rep. Albert Frankel Co., Indpls.; co-founder Melvin Simon & Assocs., Indpls., 1960; co-chmn. bd. Simon Property Group, Inc., Indpls., 1993—; co-owner NBA Ind. Pacers. Prodr.: (films) Porky's. Office: Simon Property Group Inc National City Ctr 115 W Washington St Indianapolis IN 46204*

SIMON, MICHAEL RICHARD, allergist, immunologist, internist; b. NYC, Oct. 12, 1943; MD, NYU, 1969; MA, Stanford U., 1973. Diplomate Am. Bd. Allergy and Immunology, recert.; diplomate Am. Bd. Internal Medicine, recert.; diplomate Am. Bd. Med. Lab. Immunology. Intern SUNY-Downstate Med. Ctr., Bklyn., 1969-70; resident in internal medicine Wayne State U., Detroit, 1973-75; fellow in allergy and immunology U. Mich. Med. Ctr., Ann Arbor, 1975-77; chief sect. allergy and immunology VA Med. Ctr., Detroit, 1977-2000; assoc. prof. medicine Wayne State U., Detroit, 1990-98, assoc. prof. pediats., 1992-98, tng. program dir. allergy and immunology, 1991-2000, prof. pediat. and internal medicine, 1998—. Prof. pediatrics and internal medicine Wayne State U., Detroit, 1998—. Fellow ACP, Am. Acad. Allergy Asthma and Immunology, Am. Coll. Allergy Asthma and Immunology, Royal Coll. Physicians Can. Office: Henry Ford Health Sys Allergy and Immunology 1 Ford Pl Detroit MI 48202 Office Phone: 313-876-2662., 313-982-8272.

SIMON, MORDECAI, religious association administrator, clergyman; b. St. Louis, July 19, 1925; s. Abraham M. and Rose (Solomon) S.; m. Maxine R. Abrams, July 4, 1954; children: Ora, Eve, Avrom. BA, St. Louis U., 1947; MA, Washington U., St. Louis, 1952; MHL, Rabbi, Jewish Theol. Sem. Am., N.Y.C., 1952, DD (hon.), 1977. Ordained rabbi, 1952. Rabbi in, Mpls., 1952-56, Waterloo, Iowa, 1956-63; exec. dir. Chgo. Bd. Rabbis, 1963-80, exec. v.p., 1980-95, exec. v.p. emeritus, 1995—. Nat. chaplain Jewish War Vets., 1977-78. Host: (weekly program) What's Nu?, Sta. WGN-TV, 1973-92. With AUS, 1943-46. Recipient citation Jewish War Vets., 1967, Boy Scouts Am., 1966, 74, 88, Chgo. chpt. Am. Jewish Congress, 1973, Chgo. Conf. Jewish Women's Orgns., 1973, Chgo. Bd. Rabbis, 1973, Rabbinical Svc. award of Appreciation, Jewish Theol. Sem. Am., 1988, Raoul Wallenberg Humanitarian award, 1989, citation and commendation Ill. Ho. Reps., 1995, Order of Merit, The Equestrian Order of the Holy Sepulchre of Jerusalem, 1996; Rabbi Mordecai Simon Day proclaimed by Gov. James Edgar, State of Ill., 1995. Mem. Rabbinical Assembly. Home: 621 County Line Rd Highland Park IL 60035-5220 Office: 1 S Franklin St Chicago IL 60606-4609

SIMON, NEIL, playwright, screenwriter, television writer; b. Bronx, NY, July 4, 1927; s. Irving and Mamie Simon; m. Joan Baim, Sept. 30, 1953 (dec. 1973); children: Ellen, Nancy; m. Marsha Mason, 1973 (div. 1981); m. Diane Lander, 1987 (div. 1988); 1 child, Bryn; m. Diane Lander, 1990 (div. 1998); m. Elaine Joyce, 1999. Student, NYU, 1946; LLD (hon.), Hofstra U., 1981, Williams Coll., 1984. Sports editor Rev-Meter, Lowry Field, Colo., 1945—46; owner Eugene O'Neill Theatre, NYC. Author: materials for Tamiment (Pa.) revues, 1952—53, (Broadway plays) (with Danny Simon) Catch a Star, 1955, New Faces of 1956, 1956, (book for Broadway musical) Little Me, 1962 (Tony award nom. best book of a musical, 1963), Promises, Promises, 1970 (Tony award nom. best musical, 1969), They're Playing Our Song, 1980 (Tony award nom. best book of a musical, 1979), (Broadway plays) Come Blow Your Horn, 1961, Barefoot in the Park, 1964 (Tony award nom. best play, 1963), The Odd Couple, 1966 (Tony award best author, 1965, Writers Guild of Am. award best comedy, 1968), Sweet Charity, 1966 (Evening Standard Drama award, 1968, Tony award nom. best musical, 1966), The Star-Spangled Girl, 1967, Plaza Suite, 1969 (Tony award nom. best play, 1969), Last of the Red Hot Lovers, 1970 (Tony award nom. best play, 1970), The Gingerbread Lady, 1971, The Prisoner of Second Avenue, 1972 (Tony award nom. best play, 1972), The Sunshine Boys, 1973 (Tony award nom. best play, 1973), The Good Doctor, 1974 (Tony award nom. best score, 1974), God's Favorite, 1975, California Suite, 1977, Chapter Two, 1978 (Tony award nom. best play, 1978), I Ought to be in Pictures, 1981, Fools, 1982, Brighton Beach Memoirs, 1983 (NY Drama Critics Circle award best play, 1983), Biloxi Blues, 1986 (Tony award best play, 1986), The Odd Couple (female version), 1986, Broadway Bound, 1987 (Tony award nom. best play, 1987, Pulitzer prize nom. in drama, 1987), Rumors, 1990, Lost in Yonkers, 1991 (Tony award best play, 1991, Pulitzer prize in drama, 1991, Outer Critics Circle award outstanding play, 1991, Drama Desk award outstanding new play, 1991), Jake's Women, 1993, Laughter on the 23rd Floor, 1995, London Suite, 1995, Proposals, 1997, The Dinner Party, 2000, 45 Seconds From Broadway, 2001, (screenplay adaptations of plays) Come Blow Your Horn, 1963, Barefoot in the Park, 1967, The Odd Couple, 1968 (Acad. award nom. best adapted screenplay, 1969, Writers Guild of Am. award best comedy, 1969), Sweet Charity, 1969, Plaza Suite, 1971, The Star-Spangled Girl, 1971, Last of the Red Hot Lovers, 1972, The Prisoner of Second Avenue, 1975, The Sunshine Boys, 1975 (Writers Guild of Am. award best comedy adaptation, 1975, Acad. award nom. bext adapted screenplay, 1976, BAFTA award nom. best adapted screenplay, 1977, Golden Globe nom. best adapted screenplay, 1976), California Suite, 1978 (Acad. award nom. best adapted screenplay, 1979), Chapter Two, 1979, Brighton Beach Memoirs, 1986, Biloxi Blues, 1988, Broadway Bound, 1992, Lost in Yonkers, 1993; author & prodr. (screenplay adaptations of plays) Only When I Laugh (adapted from play The Gingerbread Lady), 1981, I Ought to be in Pictures, 1982; author: (screenplays) After the Fox, 1966, The Out-of-Towners, 1970 (Writers Guild of Am. award best comedy screenplay, 1970), The Heartbreak Kid, 1973 (Golden Globe nom. best screenplay, 1973), Murder by Death, 1976, The Goodbye Girl, 1977 (Golden Globe award best screenplay, 1977, Acad. award nom. best screenplay, 1978, BAFTA award nom. best screenplay, 1979), The Cheap Detective, 1978, Seems Like Old Times, 1980, The Lonely Guy (adaptation), 1984, The Sluggers Wife, 1984, The Marrying Man, 1991; author & prodr. (screenplays) Max Dugan Returns, 1983, The Odd Couple II, 1997; author: (TV series) Cavalcade of Stars, 1949—52, The Tallulah Bankhead Show, 1951, Stanley, 1956, The Sid Caesar Show, 1956—57 (Emmy award, 1956, 1957), The Phil Silvers Arrow Show, 1958—59 (Emmy award, 1958), The Garry Moore Show, 1959—60, The Odd Couple (based on play), 1970—75, also NBC spl. The Trouble with People, 1972, (TV films) Kibbe Hates Fitch, 1964, (teleplay) The Good Doctor, 1978, Sonny Boys, 1982, (teleplay) Jake's Women, 1996, London Suite, 1996, (autobiography) Rewrites: A Memoir, 1996. Cpl. USAF, 1945—46. Recipient Sam S. Shubert award, Shubert Found., 1968, Special Tony award for overall contribution to theater, 1975, Am. Comedy award for lifetime achievement, 1989, Drama League Unique Contribution to Theater award, 1991, Kennedy Ctr. Honors Lifetime Achievement award, 1995. Mem.: Writers Guild Am. (Laurel award 1979), Dramatists Guild. Address: c/o Albert DaSilva 502 Park Ave New York NY 10022-1108*

SIMON, NICHOLAS J., III, medical products executive; BS in Microbiology, U. Md.; MBA, Loyola Coll. Dir. bus. devel. Genentech, 1989—95, v.p. bus. and corp. devel., 1995—2000; founder, CEO Collabra Pharma, Inc., 2000—, dir., 1998—. Dir. Intermune, Inc., Predict, Inc., Genitope, Inc., BioStreet, Collabra Pharms., Inc. Office: Deltagen 700 Bay Rd Redwood City CA 94063-2469

SIMON, NORMA PLAVNICK, psychologist; b. Washington, Sept. 20, 1930; d. Mark and Mary Plavnick; m. Robert G. Simon, Dec. 18, 1949; children: Mark Allan, Susan. BA, NYU, 1952, cert. in psychoanalysis, 1977; MA, Columbia U., 1953, EdD, 1968. Diplomate Am. Bd. Profl. Psychology, 1988, Counseling Psychology, Psychoanalysis, 1997. Psychologist Queens Coll. Counseling Ctr., Flushing, N.Y., 1968-70, asst. dir., 1970-76, dir., 1976; gen. practice psychology N.Y.C., 1970—. Faculty, supr. New Hope Guild, Bklyn., 1976—, dir. child and adolescent tng. prog., 1988-98; adj. prof. clin. psychology Columbia U., N.Y.C., 1986—; supr. NYU Postdoctoral Prog. in Psychoanalysis, 1988—. Author: (with Robert G. Simon): Choosing a College Major: Social Science, 1981; co-author 3 book chpts. on licensure and ethics in psychology; mem. editl. bd. The Counseling Psychologist jour., 1986-89, Profl. Practice and Rsch. in Psychology, 1994-99, Jour. Infant, Child and Adolescent Psych Therapy, 1999—. Vice chair N.Y. State Bd. for Psychology State Edn. Dept., Albany, 1978-82, chair, 1982-88; bd. dirs. Pelham (N.Y.) Guidance Coun., 1980-83; pres.-elect Assn. State and Provincial Psychology Bds., 1990, pres., 1991. Recipient Karl Heiser award, 1993, Morton Berger award Assn. State and Provincial Psychology Bds., 1998, Outstanding Psychologist award Acad. Counseling Psychology, 2003. Fellow: APA (mem. bd. profl. affairs 1987—89, chair bd. profl. affairs 1989—90, policy and planning bd. 1991—93, mem. ethics com. 1995—98, vice chair ethics com. 1996—97, chair ethics com. 1997, workgroup on telehealth 1998—2000, mem. accreditation com. 2004—, John Black award 1994, Disting. Psychologist of Yr., Divsn. Ind. Practice 2004), Am. Bd. Counseling Psychology (bd. dirs. 1992—2000, pres.-elect 1999, pres. 2001—), Nat. Acads. of Practice (elected disting. practitioner), Am. Bd. Profl. Psychology (trustee 1998—2001, pres.-elect 2001—, pres. 2004—).

SIMON, PAUL, musician, composer; b. Newark, Oct. 13, 1941; s. Louis and Belle S.; m. Peggy Harper (div.); 1 son, Harper; m. Carrie Fisher (div.); m. Edie Brickell, 1992; 1 child, Adrian Edward. BA, Queens Coll.; postgrad., Bklyn. Law Sch. With mus. group Simon and Garfunkel, 1964-71; soloist, 1972—; songs recorded with Garfunkel include Mrs. Robinson (Grammy award), The Boxer, Bridge Over Troubled Water (Grammy award); albums with Garfunkel include Wednesday Morning 3 A.M, 1964, Sounds of Silence, 1966, Parsley, Sage, Rosemary and Thyme, 1966, The Graduate (soundtrack), 1968 (Grammy award), Bookends, 1968, Bridge over Troubled Waters, 1970 (Grammy award), Simon and Garfunkel's Greatest Hits, 1972, Concert in the Park, 1982; solo albums include Paul Simon, 1972, There Goes Rhymin' Simon, 1973, Live Rhymin', 1975, Still Crazy After All These Years, 1975 (Grammy award), Greatest Hits, Etc., 1977, One-Trick Pony, 1980, Hearts and Bones, 1983, Graceland, 1986 (Grammy award 1986, 87), Negotiations and Love Songs 1971-86, 1989, Paul Simon: Solo, 1990, The Rhythm of the Saints, 1990, 1964-93, 1993, Born at the Right Time, 1991, Collection, 1991, Paul Simon & Friends, 1993, Songs from the Capeman, 1998, In Concert/Live Rhymin, 1998; concerts include Central Park, 1991, Born at the Right Time tour, Johannesburg, South Africa, 1992, series with Art Garfunkel, Paramount, 1993; appeared in films Annie Hall, 1977, One-Trick Pony, 1980; appeared in Showtime prodn. Paul Simon's Graceland: The African Concert, 1987; author: (book) At the Zoo, 1991; (play) Capeman, 1998. Recipient Emmy award for Paul Simon Spl., NBC-TV, 1977; inducted into the Rock & Roll Hall of Fame, 1990.

SIMON, PAUL H. newspaper editor; Bur. chief AP, Omaha, 1978—. Office: 909 N 96th St Ste 104 Omaha NE 68114-2508

SIMON, PETER E. publishing executive; b. Bklyn., July 29, 1953; BA in English, CCNY, 1971; MA in Libr. Sci., Columbia U., 1980. Database mgr. R.R. Bowker, N.Y.C., 1982-84; v.p. R.R. Bowker/Reed Reference Pubs., 1984-93; sr. v.p. Reed Reference Pub., New Providence, N.J., 1993-95, exec. v.p., 1995-97; v.p. bus. devel. Nat. Info. Svcs./Lexis-Nexis, Horsham, Pa., 1997-98; v.p. new product planning and devel. The Gale Group, Farmington Hills, Mich., 1998—, v.p. product mgmt., 1999, v.p. bus. devel., 1999-2000; dir. content lic. The Deal, LLC, N.Y.C., 2000-2001; v.p. strategic devel. Digital Owl, Orlando, Fla., 2001—02; dir. new bus. devel. Nstein Techs. Corp., 2002—03; v.p. product mgmt. NewsBank, Inc., Naples, Fla., 2003—. Mem. Info. Industry Assn. (chmn. content divsn., bd. dirs.), Phi Beta Kappa.

SIMON, PETER J. editor; b. Bangor, Maine, July 10, 1967; s. John Joseph and Noreen (Thorne) Simon; m. Sylvia Diane Bachman, July 30, 1994 (div. Feb. 2001). BA, Grinnell Coll., 1990. Coll. rep. W.W. Norton & Co., N.Y.C., 1990—94, mktg. assoc., 1992—94, editor, 1994—. Editor: The Norton Anthology of Theory and Criticism, 2001. Mem.: Modern Lang. Assn., Phi Beta Kappa. Office: WW Norton & Co Inc 500 5th Ave New York NY 10110

SIMON, RALPH E. electronics executive; b. Passaic, N.J., Oct. 20, 1930; s. Paul and Sophie (Epstein) S.; m. Elena Schiffman, June 22, 1952; children: Richard L., David P., Michael A. BA, Princeton U., 1952; PhD, Cornell U., 1959. Mem. tech. staff RCA Labs., Princeton, N.J., 1958-67, dir., 1967-69; mgr. RCA Electronic Components, Lancaster, Pa., 1969-75; v.p. RCA Solid State Div., Lancaster, Pa., 1975-80; v.p. optoelectronics div. Gen. Instrument Corp., Palo Alto, Calif., 1980-84; pres. Lytel Inc., Somerville, N.J., 1984-87; pres., CEO QT Optoelectronics, Sunnyvale, Calif., 1989—. Dir. Xsirius Scientific, Inc., Marina Del Rey, Calif., 1988-91, Applied Electron Corp., Santa Clara, Calif., 1987—. Pres., mem. Lawrence Twp. Bd. Edn., Lawrenceville, N.J., 1964-69, Community Action Orgn., 1967-69. Recipient UK Zworykin prize IEEE, 1973. Office: QT Optoelectronics 3001 Orchard Pkwy San Jose CA 95134-2017

SIMON, ROBERT G. lawyer; b. N.Y.C., Feb. 21, 1927; s. Monroe and Claire S. S.; m. Norma Plavnick, Dec. 18, 1949; children: Mark A., Susan. BA, Cornell U., 1947; LLB, JD, Georgetown U., 1950; LLM, NYU, 1961. Bar: D.C. 1950, N.Y. 1951, U.S. Supreme Ct. 1955. Assoc. firms in, N.Y.C., 1950-52; legal sec. to judge U.S. Dist. Ct. So. Dist. N.Y., 1953-58; assoc. Jaffe & Wachtell, N.Y.C., 1958-61; legal adv. TV series The Verdict Is Yours, 1958-60; successively dir. bus. affairs, v.p., sr. v.p., mgr. bus. affairs dept. McCann-Erickson, Inc., N.Y.C., 1961-80; sr. broadcast atty. The Interpublic Group of Cos., N.Y.C., 1980-95. Adj. faculty Manhattan Community Coll., 1967, Baruch Coll., 1968, CCNY, 1968, New Sch. Social Research, 1972-73; speaker in field. Author: (with Norma Simon) Choosing a College Major: The Social Sciences, 1981; contbr. articles to profl. jours. Dem.-Liberal candidate for county clk. Westchester County, N.Y., 1952; chmn. Narcotics Guidance Coun., Pelham, N.Y., 1973; mem. Nat. Media Coun. on Disability, 1986-90; bd. dirs., gen. counsel Nat. Challenge Com. on Disability, 1986-88; mem. adv. bd. The Caption Ctr. WGBH Found., 1987—; mem. state bd. for podiatry N.Y. State Dept. Edn., 2000—. With USAAF, 1944-46. Mem.: NATAS (chpt. gov. 1972—85, treas. 1976—81, 1st v.p. 1981—83, nat. trustee 1981—85, pres. 1983—85, chpt. gov. 1996—97, nat. trustee 1996—98), Am. Assn. Advt. Agy.s (com. on broadcast adminstrn. policy 1985—93), N.Y. County Lawyers Assn. (com. on comms. and entertainment law 1990—, not-for-profit orgns., alternate dispute resolution com. 1998—), Hemlock Soc. N.Y. (bd. dirs. 2000—02).

SIMON, ROBERT STEPHEN, artist; b. Flushing, N.Y., Nov. 4, 1939; s. Benjamin and Clara (Helsel) S. BA, Ill. Wesleyan U., Bloomington, 1962; degree in Fine Arts, Arts Students League, N.Y.C., 1965. Landscape, portrait artist, N.Y.C., 1965-82; sports and portrait artist, 1983—. Sports artist: more than 500 paintings in last 10 yrs.; displayed in Baseball's Hall of Fame, Nat. Acad. Fine Art, Madison Sq. Garden, Downtown Athletic Club, Sports Immortals Mus., as well as in the personal collections of Mickey Mantle, Sylvester Stallone and Joe DiMaggio; The 70 Karat Diamond depicting 70 of baseball's greatest players on a diamond-shaped canvas will be displayed at the entrance of a baseball mus. that will open in Orlando, Fla., in 2001; recent completion of Masters of the Millenium a 50x50 oil painting depicting over 50 of the greatest golfers in history of game proving to be 1st of its kind. Sports Artist of Yr. U.S. Sports Acad. of Art, 1992; People's Choice 1st prize Broward Art Guild, 1997; 1st Prize Oil Norwood U., 1998; nominated for Disting. Alumni award Ill. Wesleyan U., 1999; Color Trend award for Disting. Artwork in Lithography, 1998. Mem. Nat. Soc. of Illustrators, Am. Soc. of Classical Realism, Internat. Soc. Artists, Allied Artists of Am., Salmagundi Club, Norton Mus. Fine Art Guild. Home: 2700 S Oakland Forest Dr Fort Lauderdale FL 33309-7527

SIMON, ROGER FRANK, law educator; b. Ft. Worth, Oct. 17, 1961; s. Richard Uriah Jr. and Bayla Handler Simon. BA, Rice U., 1984; MA, NYU, 1986; JD, U. Tex., 1997. Bar: Tex. 1997. Rschr. Am. Film Inst., L.A., 1989—90; dir. exhbns. Southwestern Alt. Media Project, Houston, 1991—93; briefing atty. Tex. Ct. Criminal Appeals, Austin, 1998, staff atty., 1999—2002; legal writing prof. Tex. Wesleyan U. Sch. Law, Ft. Worth, 2002—. Contbr. articles to profl. jours. Allen Lane Roberts Endowed Presdl. scholar, Austin, 1996-97; Tex. Law fellow, Austin, 1995. Mem. ABA, Tex. Bar. Home: 3720 Murray Ct Fort Worth TX 76107-6845 Office: Tex Wesleyan U Sch Law Legal Writing Dept Fort Worth TX 76102 E-mail: rsimon@law.tx.wes.edu.

SIMON, RONALD CHARLES, curator; b. Phila., Feb. 23, 1951; s. Samuel Charles and Emily (Luzenberg) Simon. BA, Dickinson Coll., 1973; postgrad., Brit. Film and TV Inst., Stirling, Scotland, 1973, Columbia U., 1973-75. Researcher NBC, N.Y.C., 1976—77; mgr. media prodn. 1st Boston Corp., N.Y.C., 1979; curator TV, Mus. TV and Radio, N.Y.C., 1979—. Adj. prof. Hunter Coll., CUNY, 1987—, Columbia U., N.Y.C., 1991—; cons., lectr. to mus. and colls. including Smithsonian Instn., Whitney Mus. Am. Art, NYU, Cooper Hewitt Mus., 1985—. Author: Worlds Without End: The Art and History of Soap Opera, 1997, The Tevevision of Dennis Potter, 1992. Mem. George Foster Peabody Awards Bd., 2003—. Decorated chevalier of Art and Sci. Ministry of French Culture; Metzger Conway Fellow, Dickinson Coll., 2002. Mem.: NATAS (panelist and juror for numerous awards 1985—, mem. editl. bd. TV Quar. 1987—), TV Ltd. (bd. dirs. 2000—). Home: 141 E 17th St New York NY 10003-3402 Office: Television & Radio 25 W 52nd St New York NY 10019-6104 Office Phone: 212-621-6680. Business E-Mail: rsimon@mtr.org. E-mail: ronsimonnyc@yahoo.com.

SIMON, RONALD I. financial executive; b. Cairo, Nov. 4, 1938; came to U.S., 1942; s. David and Helene (Zilkha) S.; m. Anne Faith Hartman, June 19, 1960; children: Cheryl, Eric, Daniel. BA, Harvard U., 1960; MA, Columbia U., 1962, PhD, 1968. V.p. Harpers Internat., N.Y.C., 1959-62; fin. analyst Amerace Corp., N.Y.C., 1965-66; v.p. Am. Foresight Inc., Phila., 1966-67; asst. to pres. Avco Corp., Greenwich, Conn., 1967-70; exec. v.p. Avco Community Developers Inc., La Jolla, Calif., 1970-73; pres. Ronald I. Simon Inc., La Jolla, 1973—99; pres., CEO Delta Data Systems Corp., Phila., 1980-81; exec. v.p. Towner Petroleum Corp., Houston, 1983-85; mng. dir., chief fin. officer The Henley Group Inc., La Jolla, 1986-90; pvt. practice fin. cons. La Jolla, 1990—2000. Vice-chmn. bd. dirs. Softnet Corp., San Francisco, 1998—2002, acting chmn. and CEO, 2001; CFO WingCast LLC, San

Diego, 2001—02; bd. dirs. Collateral Therapeutics, Inc., San Diego, 1999—2002; exec. v.p., CFO/bd. dirs. Western Water Co., San Diego, 1997—2000; bd. dirs. Am. Independence Corp., NY, 2002—, WFS Fin., Inc., Irvine, Calif., 2003—, BDI Investments, San Diego, 2003—. Bd. dirs. San Diego Opera Co., 1988-90, Univ. Art Gallery U. Calif., San Diego, 1991 95; bd. dirs., treas. Lyric Opera, San Diego, 2003—. Ford Found. fellow, 1963-65.

SIMON, ROSALYN MCCORD, public relations executive; BS in special edn., MA in edn. adminstrn.; PhD, U. Md. Sr. dir. customer advocacy/communications Amtrak, Washington. Mgmt. cons. Mass Transit Adminstrn., Baltimore; exec. dir. Project Accessible Transportation In Our Nation; Md. adv. com. Individuals with Disabilities. Recipient Chester Troy award for Outstanding Pub. Svc. to Persons with Disabilities, Md. Govs. Com. Employment People with Disabilities, Transportation Special Recognition award, Fed. Dept. Transportation. Office: Amtrak 60 Massachusetts Ave NE Washington DC 20002-4285

SIMON, SEYMOUR, lawyer, former state supreme court justice; b. Chgo., Aug. 10, 1915; s. Ben and Gertrude (Rusky) S.; m. Roslyn Schultz Biel, May 26, 1954; children: John B., Nancy Simon Cooper, Anthony Biel. BS, Northwestern U., 1935, JD, 1938; LLD (hon.), John Marshall Law Sch., 1982, North Park Coll., 1986, Northwestern U., 1987. Bar: Ill. 1938. Spl. atty. Dept. Justice, 1938-42; practice law Chgo., 1946-74; judge Ill. Appellate Ct., Chgo., 1974-80; presiding justice Ill. Appellate Ct. (1st Dist., 3d Div.), 1977, 79; justice Ill. Supreme Ct., 1980-88; ptnr. Piper Rudnick (formerly Piper Marbury Rudnick & Wolfe), Chgo., 1988—. Former chmn. Ill. Low-Level Radioactive Waste Disposal Facility Siting Commn.; former dir. Nat. Gen. Corp., Bantam Books, Grosset & Dunlap, Inc., Gt. Am. Ins. Corp. Contbr. articles to profl. jours. Mem. Cook County Bd. Commrs., 1961-66, pres., 1962-66; pres. Cook County Forest Preserve Dist., 1962-66; mem. Pub. Bldg. Commn., City Chgo., 1962-67; Alderman 40th ward, Chgo., 1955-61, 67-74; Democratic ward committeeman, 1960-74; bd. dirs. Schwab Rehab. Hosp., 1961-71, Swedish Covenant Hosp., 1969-75. With USNR, 1942-45. Decorated Legion of Merit; recipient Pub. Svc. award Tau Epsilon Rho, 1963, Hubert L. Will award Am. Vets. Com., 1983, award of merit Decalogue Soc. Lawyers, 1986, Judge Learned Hand award Am. Jewish Com., 1994, Frances Feinberg Meml. Crown award Associated Talmud Torahs of Chgo., 1995, Bill of Rights in Action award Constl. Rights Found., 1997, Civic Contbn. award LWV Chgo., 2000; named to Sr. Citizen's Hall of Fame, City of Chgo., 1989, Hall of Fame Jewish Cmty. Ctrs. Chgo., 1989, Laureate Lincoln Acad. Ill., 1997, Chgo. Coun. Lawyers and the Appleseed Fund Justice Commitment to Justice award, 1998, Lifetime Achievement award Ill. Judges Assn., 2002. Mem. ABA, Ill. Bar Assn., Ill. Judges Assn., Chgo. Bar Assn., Chgo. Hist. Soc., Decalogue Soc. Lawyers (Merit award 1986), Izaak Walton League, Am. Legion, VFW, Jewish War Vets., Chgo. Hort. Soc., Comml. Club Chgo., Std. Club, Variety Club, Order of Coif, Phi Beta Kappa, Phi Beta Kappa Assocs. Home: 1555 N Astor St Chicago IL 60610-1673 Office: Piper Rudnick 203 N La Salle St Ste 1800 Chicago IL 60601-1210 Office Phone: 312-368-7070.

SIMON, SHELDON WEISS, political science educator; b. St. Paul, Jan. 31, 1937; s. Blair S. and Jennie M. (Dim) S.; m. Charlann Lilwin Scheid, Apr. 27, 1962; 1 child, Alex Russell BA summa cum laude, U. Minn., 1958, PhD, 1964; MPA, Princeton U., 1960; postgrad., U. Geneva, 1962-63. Asst. prof., then prof. U. Ky., 1966-75; prof. polit. sci. Ariz. State U., 1975—, chmn. dept., 1975-79, dir. Ctr. Asian Studies, 1980-88. Vis. prof. George Washington U., 1965, U. B.C., Can., 1972-73, 79-80, Carleton U., 1976, Monterey Inst. Internat. Studies, 1991, 96, Am. Grad. Sch. Internat. Mgmt., 1991-92; cons. USIA Rsch. Analysis Corp., Am. Enterprise Inst. Pub. Policy Rsch., Hoover Instn., Orkand Corp.; cons., dir. S.E. Asian Projects, Nat. Bur. Asian Rsch., 1998—; Smithsonian Instn. lectr. on internat. politics for the Crystal and Radisson Cruise Lines, 2000—. Author: Asian Neutralism and U.S. Policy, 1975, The ASEAN States and Regional Security, 1982, The Future of Asian-Pacific Security Collaboration, 1988; editor: The Military and Security in the Third World, 1978, East Asian Security in the Post-Cold War Era, 1993, Southeast Asian Security in the New Millenium, 1996, The Many Faces of Asian Security, 2001; also others; contbr. articles to profl. jours., chpts. to books. Mem. Com. Fgn. Relations, Phoenix, 1976—; bd. dirs. Phoenix Little Theater, 1976-79 Grantee Am. Enterprise Inst., 1974, Earhart Found., 1979, 81, 92, 84, 88, U.S. Inst. Peace, 1994-96, 2000-01, Nat. Bur. Asian Rsch., 1998, W. Alton Jones Found., 2000; U.S. Pacific Command, 2002-03, Hoover Instn. fellow, 1980, 85. Mem. Am. Polit. Sci. Assn., Assn. Asian Studies, Internat. Studies Assn. (profl. ethics com. 1987-91, v.p. 1991-93), Asia Soc. (contemporary affairs com. 1987-92), U.S. Coun. for Asia-Pacific Security (exec. bd. 1998-2003), Phi Beta Kappa. Democrat. Jewish. Avocations: acting, singing, tennis. Home: 5630 S Rocky Point Rd Tempe AZ 85283-2134 Office: Ariz State U Polit Sci Dept Tempe AZ 85287 Office Phone: 480-965-1317. E-mail: shells@asu.edu.

SIMON, SHERYL JOY, writer, astrologer; b. Paris, Oct. 4, 1956; d. Morton and Arlene (Rogoff) Kranich; m. David Andrew Simon; child, Brenna. Student, Holy Family Coll., Atlantic C.C., Hunter Coll. Pres. Astro Depot, Fla., 1997—. Cons. HB Studio. Author: (children's books) Clean Your Room, Nancy Lee, 1997, Nancy Lee, 1997, (astrology book) Astro Star Kards, 1998. Recipient Mike Nichols Scholarship, 1989, 90, 91. Mem. Nat. Coun. Geocosmic Rsch., Am. Fedn. Astrologers. Avocations: acting, poetry, directing. Office: Astro Depot PO Box 167 Livingston NJ 07039 Fax: 973-243-9870. E-mail: Astrodepot@aol.com.

SIMON, THEODORE RONALD, physician, medical educator; b. Hartford, Conn., Feb. 2, 1949; s. Theologos Lingos and Lillian (Faix) S.; m. Marcia Anyzeski, Apr. 5, 1974; children: Jacob T., Theodore H., Mark G. BA cum laude, Trinity Coll., Hartford, 1970; MD, Yale U., 1975. Diplomate Am. Bd. Nuclear Medicine, Diplomate Nat. Bd. Med. Examiners; lic. Calif., Tex. Intern in surgery Strong Meml. Hosp., Rochester, N.Y., 1975-76; resident in diagnostic radiology U. Calif., San Francisco, 1976-78; resident in nuclear medicine Yale-New Haven Hosp., Conn., 1978-80, chief resident, 1979-80; asst. prof. nuclear medicine U. Tex. Southwestern Med. Ctr., Dallas, 1980-88, assoc. prof., 1990—. Cons. nuclear medicine St. Paul's Hosp., Dallas, 1981-88; cons. internal medicine Presbyn. Hosp., Dallas, 1981-88, 90, Med. City Hosp., Dallas, 1989—; cons. nuclear medicine VA Med. Ctr., Dallas, 1981-82, chief nuclear medicine svc., 1982-88; nat. dep. dir. nuclear medicine VA, 1985-88; dep. chief nuclear medicine NIH, Bethesda, Md., 1988-90; mem. del. Taiwan Atomic Energy, U.S. State Dept., 1990. Mem. editorial bd. Jour. History of Med. and Allied Scis., 1974-75; contbr. articles to Internat. Jour. Radiol. Applications, Jour. Nuclear Medicine, Am. Jour. Cardiology, Clin. Nuclear Medicine, Circulation, Yale Jour. Biol. Medicine, Radiology, Surg. Radiology, and others. Pres. Christ Lutheran Ch., University Park, Tex. Mem. Soc. Nuclear Medicine (treas. correlative imaging coun. 1988-90, mem. exec. com 1988—). Achievements include patent for Complex Motion Device to Enhance Single Photon Emission Computed Tomography Uniformity; research in single photon emission computed tomography as it related to substance abuse, schizophrenia, depression, neurotoxicity and chronic fatigue syndrome. Home and Office: 3902 Drexel St Dallas TX 75205-2622

SIMON, WILLIAM, biomathematician, educator; b. Pitts., May 27, 1929; m. Maxine Check, June 27, 1965; children: Robert, Steven, Alan. BS in Physics, Carnegie Inst. Tech., 1950; MA in Applied Physics, Harvard U., 1952, PhD, 1958. Staff physicist Comstock & Wescott, Inc. (cons. engrs.), Cambridge, Mass., 1951-53; head instruments sect. Spencer Kennedy Lab., Boston, 1953-57; sr. systems engr. Nat. Radio Co., Malden, Mass., 1957-59; chief physicist Image Instruments, Inc., Newton Lower Falls, Mass., 1959-60; mem. staff M.I.T. Lincoln Lab. and Center for Computer Tech. in Biomed. Scis., 1961-64; research asso. dept. physiology, dir. biomed. tech. cons. group Harvard U. Med. Sch., 1964-68; asso. prof., head div. biomath. U. Rochester Sch. Medicine and Dentistry, 1968-77, prof., head div. biomath., 1977-82, prof. biochemistry and biophysics, 1982—, prof. med. info., 1989. Vis. assoc. prof. dept. elec. engring. MIT, 1974-75 Author: Mathematical Techniques for Physiology and Medicine, 1972, Mathematical Techniques for Biology and Medicine, 1977; contbr. articles to profl. jours. Office: U Rochester Box BPHYS Rochester NY 14642 Business E-Mail: william_simon@urmc.rochester.edu.

SIMON, WILLIAM LEONARD, film and television writer and producer, writer; b. Washington, Dec. 3, 1930; s. Isaac B. and Marjorie (Felsteiner) S.; m. Arynne Lucy Abeles, Sept. 18, 1966; 1 child, Victoria Marie; 1 stepson, Sheldon M. Bermont. BEE, Cornell U., 1954; MA in Ednl. Psychology, Golden State U., 1982, PhD in Comm., 1983. Writer features and TV movies, documentary and indsl. films, TV programs, 1958—; lectr. George Washington U., Washington, 1968-70. Juror Coun. on Northeatrical Events Film Festival, 1975-90, Cindy Festival Blue Ribbon Panel, 1985—; jury chmn., bd. dirs. CINE film festival, 1988—. Author: more than 600 produced works for motion pictures and TV; author: (screenplays) Fair Woman Without Discretion, Majorca, Swindle, A Touch of Love, In the Shadows of Her Life; author: (teleplays and documentaries) From Information to Wisdom, Flight of Freedom II, Missing You; author: (home video) Star of India, Combat Vietnam series; writer, prodr. The Star of India: Setting Sail; co-author: Profit from Experience-The Story of Transformation Management, 1995, Lasting Change, 1997; author: Beyond the Numbers, 1996; co-author: On the Firing Line, My 500 Days at Apple Computer, 1998, High Velocity Leadership--The Mars Pathfinder Approach to Faster, Better, Cheaper, 1999, Driving Digital--What Microsoft is Learning from its Customers about Thriving in the Digital Revolution, 2000, The Afterlife Experiments--Breakthrough Scientific Evidence of Life After Death, 2002, The Art of Deception, 2002, In Search of Business Value, 2004. Pres. Foggy Bottom Citizens Assn., 1963-65, mem. exec. bd., 1965-69; v.p. Shakespeare Summer Festival, 1966-67, trustee, 1965-70; mem. interview com. Cornell U., 1987-88. Lt. USN, 1954-58. Recipient 12 Golden Eagle awards Cine Film Festival, gold medal N.Y. Internat. Festival, gold medal Freedoms Found., IFPA Gold Cindy; awards Berlin, Belgrade and Venice film Festivals, numerous others; named 30 Best Bus. Books of 1997 Exec. Book Summaries. Mem. Nat. Acad. TV Arts and Scis. (gov. D.C. chpt. 1970-73, gov. San Diego chpt. 1998-2002), Silver Ctr., Writers Guild Am., Rotary (bd. dirs., program chmn.), Eta Kappa Nu (chpt. pres. 1953-54), Tau Beta Pi. Republican. Avocations: crew member square-rigged brig Pilgrim, San Diego Museum ship Star of India, tennis. Home: 6151 Paseo Delicias PO Box 2048 Rancho Santa Fe CA 92067-2048 Office Phone: 858-756-1197.

SIMONAITIS, RICHARD AMBROSE, chemist; b. Chgo., Dec. 7, 1930; s. George Peter and Sofija Constance (Woijkiewicz) S.; m. Vera Sandra Hall, Sept. 17, 1960; children: Steven, Rachel, Laura. Student, Loyola U., Chgo., 1948-50; BS, U. Ill., 1952; MS, Ohio State U., 1957, PhD, 1962. Chemist Aerojet-Gen. Corp., Nimbus, Calif., 1962-64; rsch. chemist Gulf Oil Corp., Merriam, Kans., 1964-66; analytical chemist Gen. Electric Co., Liverpool, N.Y., 1966-69; rsch. chemist, rsch. leader, lead scientist Agrl. Rsch. Svc.-U.S. Dept. Agr., Savannah, Ga., 1970—. Abstractor Chem. Abstracts, 1965-85; contbr. articles to profl. jours. Bd. dirs. Savannah coun. Girl Scouts U.S.A., 1978-84, exec. com., 1980-84; neighborhood chmn. Oleander Neighborhood, 1980-89; booth chmn. Night in Old Savannah Ethnic Festival, 1977-91; usher Nativity of Our Lord Ch., 1974-2000, capt. ushers, 1977-2000, sec. Mens Club, 1976, Sunday sch. tchr., 1977-81; bd. dirs. Savannah Young Peoples Theater, 1980-85, treas., 1983-85; bd. dirs. Savannah Theatre Co., 1990-95, treas., 1991-95, house mgr., 1986-99. With U.S. Army, 1955-56. Mem. ASTM, Am. Chem. Soc. (exec. com. 1979-83, sec.-treas. 1979, chmn.-elect 1980, chmn. 1981, counselor 1981, Disting. Contbn. plaque 1978, Cert. Recognition Chem. Abstract Svc. 1975), Entomol. Soc. Am., Rsch. Soc. Am., Ga. Entomol. Soc., Assn. Ofcl. Analytical Chemists, Chem. Analysts Ctrl. N.Y., Wilmington Island Pleasure and Improvement Assn. (treas. 1975—), Tybee Light Power Squadron, KC, Sigma Xi, Phi Lambda Upsilon. Roman Catholic. Office: USDA Agrl Rsch Svc PO Box 22909 3401 Edwin Ave Savannah GA 31405-1607 E-mail: mrsimi@aol.com.

SIMONDS, CHARLES FREDERICK, artist; b. N.Y.C., Nov. 14, 1945; s. Robert and Anita I. (Bell) S. BA, U. Calif., Berkeley, 1967; MFA, Rutgers U., 1969. One man shows include Ctr. Nat. d'Art Contemporain, Paris, 1975, Mus. Modern Art, N.Y.C., 1976, Westfälischer Kunstverein, Munster, 1978, Mus. Ludwig, Cologne, 1979, Mus. Contemporary Art, Chgo., 1981, Phoenix (Ariz.) Mus. Art, 1982, Brooks Meml. Art Gallery, Memphis, 1982, Solomon R. Guggenheim Mus., N.Y., 1983, Leo Castelli Gallery, N.Y., 1984, Architekturmuseum, Bâle, 1985, Corcoran Gallery Art, Washington, 1988, Fundació "la Caixa," Barcelona, 1994, Galerie nat. Jeu Paume, Paris, 1994, retrospective IVAM, Valencia, Spain, 2003; exhibited in group shows Whitney Mus. Am. Art, N.Y., 1975, 77, Mus. d'Art moderne Ville de Paris, 1975, Stedelijk Mus., Amsterdam, 1978, Mus. Modern Art, N.Y., 1979, Hayward Gallery, London, 1980, Tate Gallery, London, 1983, Solomon R. Guggenheim Mus., N.Y., 1985, 87, 89; works included in publs. including Artforum, 1980, Art/Cahier, 1977, Sprache im Technischen Zeitalter, 1978, Art in America, 1983, Images and Issues, 1982, ARTnews, 1978, Beaux Arts, 1986. Fellow Am. Acad. Rome. Home: 26 E 22nd St New York NY 10010-6107 E-mail: simondsc@aol.com.

SIMONDS, JOHN EDWARD, retired newspaper editor; b. Boston, July 4, 1935; s. Alvin E. and Ruth Angeline (Rankin) S.; m. Rose B. Muller, Nov. 16, 1968; children— Maximillian P., Malia G.; children by previous marriage— Rachel F. Cobb, John B. BA, Bowdoin Coll., 1957. Reporter Daily Tribune, Seymour, Ind., 1957-58, UPI, Columbus, Ohio, 1958-60; reporter, asst. city editor Providence Jour. Bull., 1960-65, Washington Evening Star, 1965-66; corr. Gannett News Svc., Washington, 1966-75; mng. editor Honolulu Star Bull., 1975-80, exec. editor, 1980-87, sr. editor, editl. page editor, 1987-93; exec. Hawaii Newspaper Agy., Honolulu, 1993-99; reader rep. The Honolulu Advertiser, Honolulu, 1999—2002; ret., 2002. Served with U.S. Army, 1958. Mem. Am. Soc. Newspaper Editors, AP Mng. Editors, Soc. Profl. Journalists, Nat. Conf. Editl. Writers, Orgn. News Ombudsmen. Home: 5316 Nehu Pl Honolulu HI 96821-1941 Office: The Honolulu Advertiser 605 Kapiolani Blvd Honolulu HI 96813-5195 Office Phone: 808-373-3609. Personal E-mail: simondsj001@hawaii.rr.com.

SIMONDS, JOHN ORMSBEE, landscape architect; b. Jamestown, N.D., Mar. 11, 1913; s. Guy Wallace and Marguerite Lois (Ormsbee) S.; m. Marjorie C. Todd, May 1, 1943; children: Taye Anne, John Todd, Polly Jean, Leslie Brook. BS, Mich. State U., 1935, DSc hon.; MLandscape Architecture (Eugene Dodd medal), Harvard U., 1939. Landscape architect Mich. Dept. Parks, 1935-36; ptnr. Simonds and Simonds, Pitts., 1939-70, Collins, Simonds and Simonds, Washington, 1952-70, The Environ. Planning and Design Partnership, Pitts., also Miami Lakes, 1970-82, emeritus, 1983—. Cons. Dept. Pks., Collier County, Fla., 1986-90, Land and Nature Trust, Lexington, Ky., 1987-92, SW Fla. Water Mgmt. Dist., 1987-89; lectr., vis. critic urban and regional planning Carnegie-Mellon U., 1955-67; vis. critic Grad. Sch. Planning, also Sch. Architecture, Yale, 1961-62; Cons. Chgo. Cen. Area Com., 1962, Allegheny County Dept. Regional Pks., 1961-74; U.S. cons. community planning Inter-Am. Housing and Planning Ctr., Bogota, Colombia, 1960-61; mem. jury Am. Acad. Rome, 1963, 65, 66, 69; mem. jury projected pilgrim's reception Cultural Ctr., Mecca, 1995; mem. Nat. Adv. Com. on Hwy. Beautification; chmn. panel on pks. and open space White House Conf. on Natural Beauty; mem. Interprofl. Commn. on Environ. Design; mem. and report editor urban hwy. adv. bd. U.S. Bur. Pub. Rds., 1965-68; mem. landscape architecture adv. panel U.S. C.E., 1968-71, Pres.'s Task Force on Resources and Environ., 1968-70; mem. design adv. panel Operation Breakthrough, HUD, 1970-71; mem. Mid-Atlantic regional adv. bd. Nat. Park Svc., 1976-78; assoc. trustee U. Pa., 1962-66, mem. bd. fine arts, 1962-66; chmn. joint com. planning Carnegie-Mellon U. and U. Pitts., 1959-60; overseer's vis. com. Harvard Grad. Sch. Design, 1962-68, exec. coun. alumni assn., 1960-63; adv. com. Sch. Design, N.C. State U., 1965-67; mem. Fla. Gov.'s Task Force on Natural Resources, 1979-80, Chgo. Bot. Garden 25th Anniversary, 1991, keynote address, 1991, Internat. Fedn. Landscape Architects, Seoul, Korea, 1992; speaker keynote address Internat. Congress Urban Green, Geneva, 1986. Author: Landscape Architecture, the Shaping of Man's Natural Environment, 1961, 2d rev. edit., 1997, Earthscape, a Manual of Environmental Planning, 1978, revised edit. 1986, Garden Cities 21, Creating a Livable Urban Environment, 1994, Lessons, 1999; editor: Virginia's Common Wealth, 1965, The Freeway in the City, 1968, The Freeway in the City for Urban Advisors; contbr. sect. on urban design Ency. Architecture, 1990, sect. on landscape architecture Ency. Urban Planning, 1980, Lessons, 1999. Maj. works (with others) include master plans for Chgo. Bot. Garden, Mellon Sq., Pitts., Equitable Plaza, (Miami Lakes New Town, Va. I-66 Corridor, Fairfax and Arlington counties, Va., Pelican Bay Community, Fla., Weston New Town, Fla. Bd. dirs. Hubbard Ednl. Trust, 1974—. Recipient citation Top Men of Year Engring. News-Record, 1973, Sigma Lambda Alpha award Coun. Educators in Landscape Architecture, 1979, Charles L. Hutchinson medal Chgo. Hort. Soc., John R. Bracken medal Dept. Landscape Architecture, Pa. State U., 1985, Landscape Design award Am. Hort. Soc., 2004. Fellow Am. Soc. Landscape Architects (mem. exec. com. 1959-67, pres. 1963-65, pres. Found. 1966-68, recipient medal 1973, Centennial Pres.'s medal 1999), Royal Soc. Arts (Gt. Britain); mem. Nat. Acad. (US), Archtl. League N.Y., Royal Town Planning Inst. (hon. corr.), Landscape Arch. Found., Am. Soc. Landscape Archs., Am. Hort. Soc. (Landscape Design award 2004), AIA (hon. assoc. Pa. chpt.), Harvard-Yale-Princeton Club. Presbyterian (ruling elder). Home: 17 Penhurst Rd Pittsburgh PA 15202-1023 Office: The Loft 17 Penhurst Rd Pittsburgh PA 15202 Office Phone: 412-761-0983. *Perhaps the most important lesson in life is to learn to address oneself with intensity to each person, object and event. One may be with friends without awareness of either friend or friendship, live with family as an almost stranger, partake of food and drink without savor, pass burgeoning tree, splashing stream, or splendid view without appreciation . . . unless one learns to address all powers of perception-first consciously, and then by habit, to the subject at hand. Only thus may each experience be made rich and rewarding, and life, the sum of experience, be lived to the full.*

SIMONDS, RICHARD KIMBALL, investment executive; b. Detroit, June 7, 1927; s. Ralph Warner and Bernardine (Kimball) S.; M. Judith Holland, Jan. 27, 1956 (div. Nov. 1985); m. Barbara Wood, Oct. 4, 1986; children: Lisa, Todd. BS, U. Vt., 1952. Chartered fin. analyst. Pres. Baker Simonds & Co., Detroit, 1954-59, Investment Counsel Inc., Grosse Pointe, Mich., 1960-91. Contbr. articles to profl. publs. Bd. dirs. Boys Republic, Farmington Hills, Mich., 1961-73; trustee Liggett Sch., Grosse Pointe, 1962-71. Avocation: boating. Home: 19789 Wedgewood Dr Grosse Pointe Woods MI 48236-2732

SIMONDS, STEPHEN PAIGE, former state legislator; b. Franconia, N.H., Nov. 25, 1924; s. Stephen Moses and Gertrude Martha (Jesseman) S.; m. Judith Cole, Sept. 13, 1952; children: Scott, Mark, Laura, Jane. BA, U. N.H., 1948; MA in Social Svcs. Adminstrn., U. Chgo., 1953. Caseworker N.H. Dept. Pub. Welfare, Woodsville, 1950-51, dist. supr. Conway and Woodsville, 1953-56; field supr. Conn. Dept. Welfare, Hartford, 1958-60; dir. social welfare Maine Dept. Health and Welfare, Augusta, 1960-67; commr. Assistance Payments Adminstrn. HEW, Washington, 1967-69; commr. Cmty. Svcs. Adminstrn. HEW, Washington, 1968-71; founder, dir. Human Svcs. Devel. Inst., U. So. Maine, Portland, 1971-86, dir. Office Internat. Programs, 1986-92; mem. Maine Ho. of Reps., Augusta, 1990-94, mem. human resources com., edn. com. Past pres. World Affairs Coun. of Maine, Cmty. Counseling Ctr.; trustee SALT Inst. Documentary Studies, 1998—; past pres. Maine/Rio Grande do Norte, Ptnrs. of Ams. Recipient Disting. Svc. award World Affairs Coun. Maine, 1991; Fulbright scholar, Eng., 1957-58. Mem. Ptnrs. of Ams. (pres. 1997-2002), Chinese and Am. Friendship Assn. (co-founder). Democrat. Avocations: flying, boating, kayaking, gardening. Home: 18 Brentwood Rd Cape Elizabeth ME 04107-2210 Personal E-mail: ssimonds@maine.rr.com.

SIMONDS, VALERIE DEVERSE, healthcare educator; b. Greensburg, Pa., Jan. 23, 1943; d. John Young and Margaret (McCommons) Woods. Diploma in nursing, Shady Side Hosp., 1963; BS, Johns Hopkins U., 1976, MS with honors, 1979. RN, Md., Pa.; CEN NREMT-P. Health educator U. Md. Sch. of Pharmacy, Balt., 1979-80; EMT dept. chair Anne Arundel C.C., Arnold, Md., 1979-2000; health educator, cons. Johns Hopkins Inst. Policy Studies, Balt., 2000—03; health professions text editor/reviewer, 1990—. Developed and implemented 1st EMT-Paramedic program, Md.; mem. Md. Region III EMS adv. bd., Balt., 1986-98, advanced life support instr., Md. Fire Rescue Inst., 2003-. Recipient Disting. Program award Md. State Dept. of Edn., 1986. Home: 285 Laguna Cir Severna Park MD 21146-1360

SIMONE, ALBERT JOSEPH, academic administrator; b. Boston, Dec. 16, 1935; s. Edward and Mary (DiGiovanni) S.; m. Carolie Roberta Menko, Nov. 7, 1959; children: Edward, Karen, Debra, Laura. BA, Tufts U., 1957; PhD, MIT, 1962. Lectr. Coll. Bus. Adminstrn., Northeastern U., Boston, 1958-59; instr. econs. MIT and Tufts U., Boston, 1959-60; asst. prof. Northeastern U., Tufts U., 1960-63; assoc. prof. Coll. Bus. Adminstrn. Boston Coll., 1963-66, prof., dir. quantitative mgmt. program Coll. Bus. Adminstrn., 1966-68; prof., head dept. quantitative analysis Coll. Bus. Adminstrn. U. Cin., 1968-72, dean Coll. Bus. Adminstrn., 1972-83; v.p. acad. affairs U. Hawaii, Honolulu, 1983-84, acting pres., 1984-85; pres. U. Hawaii System, Honolulu, 1985-92; chancellor U. Hawaii at Manoa, 1985-92; pres. Rochester (N.Y.) Inst. Tech., 1992—. Mem., chair numerous univ. coms.; program chmn. 1970 Nat. Conf. of Am. Prodn. and Inventory Control Soc.; mem. accreditation com. Am. Assembly Collegiate Schs. Bus., 1978-83, visits to U. Ky., Carnegie-Mellon U., 1982; session chmn. various profl. confs.; cons. statis. forecasting, prodn. scheduling and sample design models various cos. including Cin. Gas & Electric Co., Cin. Milacron, Kroger Co.; econ. and mgmt. cons. Atty. Gen.'s Office, State of Mass.; mem. coun. econ. advisors to Gov., Commonwealth of Mass.; bd. dirs. Fed. Res. Bank N.Y.; adv. group M&T Bank. Author: Matematica Finita Con Aplicaciones A Las Ciencias Administrativas, 1969, Foundations of Contemporary Mathematics with Applications in the Social and Management Sciences, 1967, Probability: An Introduction with Applications, 1967; (with L. Kattsoff) Finite Mathematics with Applications in the Social and Management Sciences, 1965, (with R. Wessel and E. Willett) Statistics as Applied to Economics and Business, 1965; also articles. Bd. dirs. Greater Rochester Visitors Assn., Inc., Rochester/So. Region, United Way of Greater Rochester, Vis. Nurse Svc. of Rochester and Monroe County, Inc., High Tech. of Rochester, Greater Rochester Metro C. of C., past chair; bd. dirs. Indsl. Mgmt. Coun.; chmn. United Way Vol. Resources Divsn. Steering Com.; trustee George Eastman House; chmn. Commn. Indep. Colls. and Univs.; corp. mem. Hillside Children's Ctr. Fellow of grad. sch. U. Cin.; named Prof. of Yr., Delta Sigma Pi, Alpha Theta chpt., U. Cin., 1972, Citizen of Yr. Henrietta Commerce Network, 2000; recipient Tree of Life award Jewish Nat. Fund. Fellow Am. Inst. Decision Scis. (v.p. publs. 1969-70, v.p. and student liaison 1972, pres. 1974-75, founding editor and editor-in-chief jour. 1970-72, Disting. Svc. award 1972); mem. Acad. Mgmt., Am. Econ. Assn., Am. Inst. Indsl. Engrs., Am. Prodn. and Inventory Control Soc., Am. Statis. Assn., Assn. Computing Machinery, Univs. Rsch. Assn., Assn. of Ind. Tech. Univs., The Conf. Bd. RIT Rsch. Corp. (chmn., bd. dirs.), Nat. Commn. for Coop. Edn., N.Y. Commn. for Ind. Coll. and Univs. (chmn.), Rochester Area Coll. Consortium, Econometric Soc., Fin. Execs. Inst., Inst. Mgmt. Sci., Ops. Rsch. Soc. Am., Phi Beta Kappa, Phi Kappa Phi, Beta Gamma Sigma. Office: RIT George Eastman Bldg 2 Lomb Memorial Dr Rochester NY 14623-5604

SIMONE, JOSEPH, clergyman, educator; b. Bridgeport, Conn., Jan. 13, 1924; s. Dominic and Anna (Mastrianni) S.; B.A., Elon Coll., 1958; M.A., Andover Newton Theol. Sch., 1968; m. Viola Ruskay, June 27, 1953; children— J. Scott, Zachary D., Claudia A. Ordained to ministry Congl. Ch., 1960; pastor Congl. Ch., Chicopee Falls, Mass., 1958-61, 1st Congl. Ch., Farmington, N.H., 1961-63, Hope Congl. Ch., East Providence, R.I., 1963-65, All Souls Ch., Lowell, Mass., 1965-69; tchr. English, also guidance counselor, 1969-87 . Chmn. ecumenical commn. Greater Lowell Council Chs., 1967-68; founder Ecumenical Dialogue with Clergymen and Laymen, Lowell, 1966; Radio Ministry on Ecumenism, Lowell, 1966-69; chaplain Roger Hall Sch. for Girls, Lowell, 1965-69. Bd. dirs. Jewish-Arab Ednl. Fund, Lowell Served with AUS, 1942-45. Mem. Andover Assn. Ministers United Ch. of Christ (adv. com. 1966-87), Assn. Clin. Pastoral Edn., Am., Mass. sch. counselors assns., N.E.A., Nat. Vocational Guidance Assn., Am. Personnel and Guidance Assn., Sigma Mu Sigma (v.p. 1957). Mason. Home: 117 Jenkins Rd Andover MA 01810-2303

SIMONE, JOSEPH R. lawyer; b. N.Y.C., Jan. 7, 1949; m. Virginia E. Simone, May 29, 1971; children: Jacquelyn, Robert. BA cum laude, Queens Coll., 1971; LLM in Taxation, NYU, 1977; JD cum laude, Fordham U., 1974. Bar: N.Y. 1975, U.S. Dist. Ct. (so. dist.) N.Y. 1975, U.S. Ct. Appeals (2d cir.) 1975. Ptnr. Patterson, Belknap, Webb & Tyler, N.Y.C., 1982-88, Schulte, Roth & Zabel, N.Y.C., 1988—2002; spl. prof. law Hofstra U. Sch. Law, 1998—2003; of counsel Pitney Hardin LLP, N.Y.C., 2003—, ptnr., 2004—.

Author: (textbooks) Pension Answer Book, 5th edit., 1990, Essential Facts: Pension and Profit-sharing Plans, 1999; editl. advisor Jour. of Pension Planning. Mem. Am. Arbitration Assn. (panel on multiemployer pension plans), Am. Coll. Employee Benefits (counsel 2003—), Phi Beta Kappa. Office: Pitney Hardin LLP 7 Times Sq New York NY 10036 E-mail: jsimone@pitneyhardin.com.

SIMONE, JOSEPH VINCENT, physician, educator; b. Chgo., Sept. 19, 1935; s. Peter and Josephine (Casablanca) S.; m. Patricia Ann Sheahan, May 28, 1960; children: Patricia Marie, Julie Anne, Margaret Mary. Student, Loyola U., Chgo., 1953-56, MD, 1960. Diplomate: Am. Bd. Pediatrics (sub-bd. pediatric hematology-oncology), Am. Bd. Internal Medicine. Intern Presbyn.-St. Luke's Hosp., Chgo., 1960-61, resident in medicine, 1961-63; resident in pediatrics U. Ill. Research and Edn. Hosp., Chgo., 1965-66, fellow in pediatric hematology-oncology, 1963-66, instr. pediatrics, 1966-67; mem. staff St. Jude Children's Research Hosp., Memphis, 1967-77, 78—, asso. dir. clin. research, 1978-83, dir., 1983—; prof. pediatrics Stanford U., physician in chief Children's Hosp. at Stanford, Palo Alto, Calif., 1977-78; prof. pediatrics U. Tenn., 1978—. Editor: Clinics in Hematology, 1978; assoc. editor: Jour. Clin. Oncology, 1984—; contbr. articles on therapeutic research in childhood cancer to profl. jours. Mem. Am. Soc. Clin. Oncology (dir.), Am. Assn. Cancer Research, Am. Soc. Hematology, Soc. Pediatric Research, Am. Pediatric Soc. Roman Catholic. Office: St Jude Children's Rsch Hosp PO Box 318 332 N Lauderdale St Memphis TN 38105-2729

SIMONE, SAM PAUL, education educator, researcher; b. Savannah, Ga., May 7, 1945; s. Sam Paul Simone Sr. and Sara Josephine Simone; m. Linda Wilkinson Harris, June 21, 1978; children: Sara Leila, Rachael Felicity, Daniel Sam Hugh. BA, Dakota Wesleyan U., 1967; PhD, Brigham Young U., 1982. Tchr. U. Montevallo, Ala., 1989—, dir. theatre, 1989—2001, coord. of comm. studies, 1998—. Faculty senator U. Montevallo, 2002—, concert and lecture com. chmn., 1998—99. Author: Hitchcock as Activist; contbr. chapters to books. Active Ala. State Speech Academic Com., Montgomery, Ala., 1999—2002. With USN, 1969—74, sgt. N.G. USAR, 1983—87, with USAR. Mem.: Phi Kappa Phi. Mem. Lds Ch. Avocations: travel, writing. Home: 320 Vine St Montevallo AL 35115 Office: Univ Montevallo Station # 6210 Montevallo AL 35115 Business E-Mail: simones@montevallo.edu.

SIMONEAU, CYNTHIA LAMBERT, newspaper editor, journalism educator; b. Central Falls, R.I., May 18, 1958; d. Roland and L. Jean Simoneau; m. Paul E. Lambert, Oct. 24, 1981; children: Thomas S. Lambert, Marc S. Lambert. BA, U. R.I., 1980. Asst. news editor Newtown (Conn.) Bee, 1980-82; reporter Bridgeport (Conn.) Post & Telegram, 1982-83, bur. chief, 1983-91; editor Woman Wise Conn. Post, Bridgeport, 1991-97, asst. mng. editor, 1997—. Adj. prof. So. Conn. State U., New Haven, 1993—, Fairfield (Conn.) 2003—, Sacred Heart U., Fairfield, Conn., 2004. Eucharistic min., mem. parish adv. coun., former religious edn. tchr., St. Thomas Aquinas Ch., Fairfield, Conn. Mem. Soc. Profl. Journalists (bd. dirs. Conn. chpt. 1983-2003, treas. Conn. chpt. 1985-95, 2003—, pres. Conn. chpt. 1995-97, Journalism Excellence awards for news stories and columns, 2 Pres.'s award Conn. chpt., Women of Dist. award girl Scout Coun.). Avocation: reading. Office: Conn Post 410 State St Bridgeport CT 06604 E-mail: csimoneau@ctpost.com.

SIMONEAU, DANIEL ROBERT, accountant, watercolorist, educator, application developer; b. Lewiston, Maine, Aug. 3, 1962; s. Robert Eugene and Rolande Muriel (Plante) S. BFA, U. So. Maine, 1984. Reconciling specialist Fleet/Norstar Bank of Maine, Lewiston, 1981-84, acct., 1984-88, Sterling Engineered Products, Auburn, Maine, 1988-89; fin. analyst Pioneer Plastics Corp., Auburn, Maine, 1989-91; acct. Aeroquip Corp., New Haven, Ind., 1992, adminstrv. sys. coord. Maumee, Ohio, 1992-93, acct., 1993-94, Trinova Corp., Maumee, Ohio, 1994-96, chmn. employee activities com. ann. outing Toledo, 1995; fin. edn. specialist PeopleSoft, Inc., Westchester, Ill., 1996-98, master tech. instr., 2000—02; sr. cons. The Revere Group, Deerfield, Ill., 1998-2000, functional specialist, 2000; PeopleSoft developer Robert W. Baird, Milw., 2002—, asst. v.p., 2003—. Dir. Spectrum Gallery, 1995-96; pres. Pioneer Mgmt. Assn., 1991. Contbr. article to mag. Chmn. award winners show Spectrum Friends of Fine Art, Toledo, 1995. Recipient Recognition award Spectrum Friends of Fine Art, 1994, Com. award Spectrum Gallery, 1994, 3d pl. award Toledo Fedn. Art Socs., 1992, 3d Judge's award Lewiston Art Festival Com., 1988, 90, 91, Purchase award Portland Art Festival Com., 1981, 91. Mem. Northwestern Ohio Watercolor Soc., Coll. Art Assn., Friends of the Arts (Chgo.), Transparent Watercolor Soc. Am. (life, membership chair 2003—), Cream City Found. Milw. (treas. 2003—), Midwest Water Color Soc. (life). Office: Robert W Baird 777 E Wisconsin Ave Milwaukee WI 53201-0672 Home: 9507 74th St Kenosha WI 53142-8194

SIMONELLI, JOSEPH ARMAND, playwright; b. Brooklyn, NY, Nov. 1, 1957; s. Philip Leonard and Stella Simonelli; m. Denise E. Sorrano (div.); children: Nicholas Joseph, Kristen Elizabeth, Michael Mark. BS, St. Francis Coll. Author: (plays) Stocks and Blondes, Men are Dogs (Perry award, best new play, 2004), Heaven Help Me (Perry nomination, best new play, 2003), Roommates (Perry nomination, best new play, 2002), (musical) The Next Time Around (Perry nomination, best new musical, 2001). Mem.: Dramatist Guild of Am. (assoc.).

SIMONI, CHRISTOPHER, dean, law educator; AB in English, U. Mich., 1968; MA in English Lit., Marquette U., 1970, PhD in Am. Lit., 1977; JD, Northwestern U., 1980; MLIS, U. Tex., 1989. Prof. English Instituto Universitario Pedagogico Exptl. de Barquisimeto, Venezuela, 1973—75; from instr. to assoc. prof. Coll. Law Willamette U., 1980—85; with Tarlton Law Libr. U. Tex., Austin, 1987—90; assoc. dir., head pub. svcs. Law Libr. Northwestern U., Chgo., 1990—93, acting dir., 1993, assoc. dean libr. and info. svcs., prof. Sch. Law, 1996—; dir. Law Libr., asst. prof. Marquette U., 1994—96. Cons. Addis Ababa (Ethiopia) U. Law Faculty, 1997, U. Ghana Faculty Law, Legon, 2000. Assoc. editor: Scribes Jour. Legal Writing, 1990—92; mem. edit. bd. Perspectives: Tchg. Legal Rsch. Writing, 1994—2000. Mem.: ABA (mem law librs. com. 1999—), Chgo. Assn. Law Librs. (co-chair continuing edn. com. 1991—93), Oreg. State Bar, Am. Assn. Law Librs. (chair sect. librs. 1999—2000, mem. com. librs. and techs. 1999—2002, chair 2001—02, mem. law libr. jour. adv. com. 1996—99). Office: Northwestern U Sch Law Pritzker Legal Rsch Ctr 357 E Chicago Ave Chicago IL 60611 Business E-Mail: csimoni@law.northwestern.edu.

SIMONIAN, JOHN S. lawyer; b. Apr. 1965; s. Samuel and Mary Simonian. BA, U. R.I.; JD, Boston U. Bar: R.I., U.S. Dist. Ct. R.I. Sole practice, Cranston, RI, 1992—. State rep. R.I. Ho. of Reps., Providence, 1991-2002, dep. majority leader, 1993-2002, chmn. commn. on criminal justice, mem. house com. on fin., joint com. on veteran's affairs. Democrat. Apostolic. Home: 43 Eldridge St Cranston RI 02910-1810 Mailing: 273 Pontiac Ave Cranston RI 02910

SIMONIAN, SIMON JOHN, surgeon, scientist, educator, administrator; b. Antioch, French Ter., Apr. 20, 1932; arrived in U.S., 1965, naturalized, 1976; s. John Simon and Marie Cecile (Tomboulian) Simonian; m. Arpi Ani Yeghiayan, July 11, 1965; children: Leonard Armen, Charles Haig, Andrew Hovig. MD, U. London, 1957; BA in Animal Physiology, St. Edmund Hall, U. Oxford, Eng., 1964; MA in animal physiology, U. Oxford, 1969; MSc in nutrition, immunology & genetics, Harvard U., 1967, ScD in nutrition, immunology & genetics, 1969; DSc (hon.), Nat. Acad. Scis., Armenia, 1998. Diplomate Am. Bd. Surgery, 1977. Rsch. asst. smallpox vaccine lyophilization immunology unit Lister Inst. Preventive Medicine, Elstree, England, 1951—52; intern in medicine Univ. Coll. Hosp., London, 1957; intern in surgery Edinburgh (Scotland) Royal Infirmary, 1957-58, resident in surgery, 1961-62; clin. clk. Nat. Hosp. & Inst. of Neurology, 1958; resident Edinburgh Western Gen. Hosp., 1958-59, City Hosp., Edinburgh, Birmingham Accident and Burns Hosp., U. Birmingham, Eng., 1959-60; demonstrator dept. anatomy Edinburgh U., 1960-61; rsch. fellow in pathology Lab. Chem. Pathology Harvard U., Boston, 1965-68, trainee NIH, 1967; instr. immunology Harvard Med. Sch., Boston, 1966-70, instr., assoc. in surgery, 1968-70, surg. dir. course on transplantation, biology and medicine, 1968-70; vis. prof. Harvard Med. Sch., Mass. Gen. Hosp., Brigham and Womens Hosp., New Eng. Deaconess Hosp., 1982; dir. transplantation immunology unit, asst. in surgery Brigham and Womens Hosp., Boston, 1968-70; resident in surgery Boston City Hosp., 1970-74; attending surgeon in transplantation and gen. surgery services U. Chgo. Med. Ctr., 1974-77; asst. prof. surgery, mem. com. immunology U. Chgo., 1974-77; head div. renal transplantation Hahnemann U. Sch. Medicine and Hosp., 1978-87, prof. surgery, 1978-88, chmn. Transplantation Com., 1983-88, chmn. quality assurance of surgery com., 1986-88; dept. surgery coord. with joint commn. for accreditation of hosps. Hahnemann U. Sch. Medicine, 1986; chief and chmn. dept. surgery St. John Hosp. and Med. Ctr., Detroit, 1988-89, chmn. credentials com. of surgery and oper. rm. com., 1988-89, assoc. v.p. for med. affairs, 1989-90; pres., CEO Vein Inst. of Met. Washington, Inc., 1990—; assoc. Fairfax Hosp., Falls Church, Va., 1990-92, active faculty, 1992—; guest lectr., 1994, 99; clin. assoc. prof. surgery Georgetown U. Sch. Medicine, Washington, 1992-95, guest lectr., 1994—, clin. prof. surgery, 1995—. Vis. prof. Vanderbilt U., 1968, Cedars-Sinai Med. Ctr., UCLA, 1977, Addenbroke's Hosp., Cambridge U., 1977, Karolinska Inst., 1977, Huddinge Hosp., U. Stockholm, 1977, Med. Coll. Pa. and Hosp., 1980, 81, 85, Grad. Hosp., U. Pa., 1981, 85, U. Athens, 1981, U. Coll. Hosp., U. London, 1981, Western Gen. Hosp. Edinburg U., 1981, VA Hosp., Tufts U., 1982, John Radcliffe Hosp., U. Oxford, 1982, Nat. Acad. Scis., Yerevan, Armenia, 1995, St. Edmund Hall, U. Oxford, 1997, Christ Ch. Hosp., Chgo., 1974—77, South Chgo. Hosp., 1974—77, Del. Med. Ctr., Wilmington, 1977, Wilkes Barre (Pa.) Gen. Hosp., 1979, Robert Packer Hosp., Guthrie Clinic, Sayre, Pa., 1980, Brigham & Women's Hosp., Harvard Med. Sch., Boston, 1982, Abington Meml. Hosp., Phila., 1982, Crozer Chester Med. Ctr., Pa., 1982, St. Agnes Hosp. Med. Ctr., Phila., 1982, Sacred Heart Hosp., 1982, Riverview Hosp., Red Bank, NJ, 1983, Easton (Pa.) Hosp., Allentown, 1983, Newcombe Med. Ctr., Vineland, NJ, 1983, Cath. Med. Ctr., Manchester, NH, 1984, Burlington County Med. Ctr., Mount Holly, NJ, 1984; cons. Michael Reese Hosp., Chgo., 1976—77; cons. gen. surgery City of Phila., 1986—88; cons. vascular surgery Coll. Podiatry, Phila., 1986—88; cons. venous vascular surgery Podiatry Residence Program, No. Va. Med. Coll., Richmond, 1994—; cons. surgery John F. Kennedy Meml. Hosp., Stratford, NJ, 1982—86, St. Agnes Hosp. Med. Ctr., Phila., 1982—86; cons. Am.-Armenian Cultural Assn., 2001—; surgeon in chief, med. team support U.S. Pres. Ronald W. Reagan, 1988, George H. W. Bush, 1989, U.S. Presdl. visits to Detroit; vis. surgeon Inst. Vein Desease, Mich., 1989—90; vis. scientist Argonne (Ill.) Nat. Lab., 1969, 1974—77; mem. sci. bd. ctr. regenerative biology Ind. U., 2001—; invited spkr., panelist 8th Internat. Congress of Nephrology, Athens, 1981; bd. dirs., invited spkr. 1st Internat. Soc. for Edn. and Rsch. in Vascular Disease, San Diego, 1992; guest lectr., panelist 4th Internat. Dialogue Transition to Global Soc., U. Md., College Park, 1995; invited spkr. 3d Armenian Med. World Congress, Montreal, 1986, 4th Armenian Med. World Congress, LA, 1989; invited spkr., chairperson of session 5th Armenian Med. World Congress, Paris, 1992; invited spkr. 6th Armenian Med. World Congress, Boston, 1995, 7th Armenian Med. World Congress, Lyon, France, 1998, 8th Armenian Med. World Congress, Toronto, 2001; eminent scholar external assessor U. Zambia, Lusaka, 1994; mem. internat. consensus panel The Investigation Chronic Venous Insufficiency, Paris, 1997, Thromboembolism, Rhodes, Greece, 1999, Thrombophilia, Limasol, Cyprus, 2003; invited spkr., sci. advisor 8th Pan-Am. Congress Phlebology and Lymphology, Campo Grande, Brazil, 1998, 9th Pan-Am. Congress Phlebology and Lymphology, Cordoba, Argentina, 2000; hon. mem. Internat. Forum for Minisurgery of Varicose Veins, Frankfurt, Germany, 2000—, Korean Soc. of Phlebology, 2003. Co-author: Manual of Vascular Access Procedures, 1987; cons. to editl. bd. Dateline: Issues in Transplantation, 1985—87, mem. editl. bd. Phila. Medicine, 1988, Transplantation Procs., 1987—96, Jour. Transplantation Abstracts, 1969—70, Internat. Angiology, 1998—, assoc. editor Am. Coll. Phlebology Vein Line, 2000—, reviewer Jour. Oncology and Dermatologic Surgery, 1993, Jour. Dermatologic Surgery, 1997, Jour. Vascular Surgery, 2000—, The Surgeon Journal Royal College of Surgeons Edinburgh and Ireland, Venous Digest, 2002—; translator: Short Saphenous Vein issue, Jour. de Phlebologie, 1999; contbr. articles to profl. jours. and books; appeared in med. movie Giving. Co-founder Armenian Youth Soc., London, Eng., 1953, pres. 1953-54; Armenian Studies Program U. Chgo., 1975; bd. govs. Friends Sch., London, 1964-65; Mass. del., co-founder Armenian Assembly, Washington, 1970-74; fellow-trustee, co-founder Entry into Manhood of Armenian Youth at Age 13, 1981; co-founder Armenian Am. Health Assn. of Greater Washington, 1992, mem. pharms. com. 1992—, chmn. nominating com., 1993; sec., bd. dirs. Woodrock Inc., 1993-94; mem. Am. Friends of St. Edmund Hall, U. Oxford, 1992—, U.S. Campaign for St. Edmund Hall, 1995—, mem. bd. advisors, 1999-2003, mem. campaign steering bd., 2000—; mem. St. Mary's Armenian Apostolic Ch., Washington, guest preacher, 1994, 95, 96; guest spkr. Armenian Ch. Youth Orgn. Am., Washington, 1998; mem. Am. Friends State U. Armenia, Yerevan, 1994, bd. dirs. mammography unit and wellness ctr. State Med. U., Yerevan, Armenia, 1997-98; bd. dirs. Arlington (Va.) Symphony Orch., 1992-96, sci. com. Armenia-U.S.A., 1996—; mem. regional com. U.S. Campaign for Univ. Oxford, 1993; active amphitheatre endowment fund Boston City Hosp., 1994; dist. benefactor, fundraiser Eurasia Found., 1996; sci. advisor, chmn. session Internat. Union Plebology, World Congress, 11th, Monreal, Can., 1992, 12th, London, Eng., 1995, 13th, Sydney, Australia, 1998, 14th, Rome, 2001; sci. advisor, chmn. session Internat. Union Angiology World, Congress 17th, London, Eng., 1995, 18th, Tokyo, 1998, 19th, N.Y.C., 2001, 20th Rome, 2004. Turtle award, 1949, Harris award, 1949, Leadership award, 1949, Nairn scholar, 1949-52; Middlesex scholar, 1952-57; recipient Suckling prize, 1956, Brit. Med. Research Council award, 1962-64, NIH award, 1970, Alt prize, 1973, Thompson award, 1974-77, Johnson award, 1975-77, Guthrie lectr., Sayre, PA, 1980, Upjohn award, 1982, Presdl. Rep. Medal of Merit, 1982, U.S. Pres. Ronald W. Reagan Seal and Medal, 1988, Kabakjian award Armenian Student Assn. Am., 1986, Disting. Alumni award Med. Soc. St. Edmund Hall, U. Oxford, 1997, Kaken award, 1998, Vnus Lectr., Rhodes, Greece, 1999, STD award, 2000; named outstanding new citizen of Citizenship Coun. of Met. Chgo. and Dept. Justice, Washington, 1976-77, Jonathan E. Rhoads ann. orator, 1984; Businessman of Yr. Leadership award Nat. Rep. Congressional Com., 2003, Physician of Yr. Leadership award, 2003; Kwang Dong Lectr., Seoul, Korea, 2003; Diomed-Lectr., 2003, Venus Lectr., 2003, BSN-Jobst Lectr., San Diego, Calif., 2003; co-endowed The John and Marie J. Simonian Award, St. Nerces Sem., 1981, John R. Pfeifer, MD, Rsch. Award, Providence Hosp., Southfield, Mich., 1992; endowed Marie J. Simonian Prize, Georgetown U. Med. Sch., 1991 (prize com. 1991—); established The John N.D. Kelly Prize in Med. Studies St. Edmund Hall, U. Oxford, 1992, The Simon J. and Arpi A. Simonian Prize for scholastic excellence for doctoral candidates, Harvard U., 1992; recognized for philanthropy to Hahnemann U. by placques in med. sch. and hosp. lobbies., 1980—, Established Simon and Arpi Simonian plasma physics room Sch. of Humanities and Scis. U. Yerevan, Armenia, 1994, plaque in Cyrus Vesuna Auditorium and Conf. Ctr., Fairfax Hosp., Falls Church, Va., 1995; grantee U.S. Govt., industry cos., founds. Fellow: ACS (Phila., Mich. and Washington chpts.), Am. Coll. Phlebology, Phila. Acad. Surgery (Jonathan E. Rhoads ann. orator 1984—, Samuel D. Gross prize com. 1988), Royal Coll. Surgeons Edinburgh; mem.: APHA, AAAS, AMA, AAUP, Leadership Coun., Harvard Sch. Pub. Health (founding mem. 2003—), Phlebological Surgery Sect., Am. Coll. Phlebology (founding chair, bd. dirs. 2002—03, past chair 2003—), Ambulatory Phlebectomy Sect., Am. Coll. Phlebology (chmn. program com. and sec. treas. 1999—2001, sect. chair elect 2000—01, chair, bd. dirs. 2001—02), European Acad. Scis. and Arts (fgn.), Northern Va. Med. Soc., North Am. Soc. Phlebology, Chgo. Soc. Gastroenterology, Transplantation Soc. (membership com. 1980—82), Pa. Med. Soc., Phila. County Med. Soc. (rep. ctr. city br. 1981—83, pres. 1984, bd. dirs. 1985—87, chairperson long range planning com. 1986—98), Greater Del. Valley Soc. Transplant Surgeons (councilor 1978—80, pres. elect 1980—82, pres. 1982—85, councilor 1985—88), Phila. Acad. Scis. (co-chmn. membership com. 1982—88), Chgo. Soc. Gastroenterology, Assn. of Ill. Transplant Surgeons, Am. Venous Forum (co-chair session, ofcl. disscussant 10th ann. meeting 1999, chair Internat. Rels. Com. 2001—02), Am. Soc. Transplant Surgeons (co-founding mem. 1974, chair immunosuppression studies com. 1974—77, membership com. 1980—82), NY Acad. Scis., Samuel Hahnemann Surg. Soc., Am. Coll. Phlebology (curriculum devel. projects com. 1992—, co-chmn. symposiums and session 1992—, faculty 1993—, panelist 10th ann. congress 1996, membership com. 1998—, chmn. sci. program com. 13th ann. congress 1999, program chair 14th ann. congress 2000), Internat. Cardiovasc. Soc. (chair session 22d world congress 1995, N.Am. chpt.), European Soc. Organ Transplant, Am. Soc. Artificial Internal Organs, Am. Technion Soc., Wayne County Med. Soc., Greater Washington Telecomm. Assn. (pres.' club 1994), Am. Soc. Lymphology (nat. adv. bd., chair sci. com. 1999—, pres.-elect 2000—01, pres. 2001—03, re-elected pres. 2003—), Am. Fedn. Clin. Rsch., Transplantation Soc. Mich., Assn. Acad. Surgery, Armenian Med. and Dental Assn. Greater Phila. (co-founder 1983, pres. 1983—85, Outreach award 1986), Assn. for Study of Med. Edn., Physicians for Social Responsibility, Cancer Rsch. Assn. Boston, Am. Venous Found. (bd. dirs. 2002—), Brit. Med. Assn., Am. Armenian Med. Assn. (co-founder 1972, 25th anniversary co-founder award 1997), Nat. Assn. Armenian Studies and Rsch. (rep. Midatlantic region 1994—2003, bd. dirs. 2004—), Royal Coll. Physicians of London Licentiates, Med. Soc. Va., Fairfax County Med. Soc., Mich. State Med. Soc., Chgo. Assn. Immunologists, Detroit Surgical Assn., Detroit Acad. Surgery, Am. Coll. Physician Execs., Am. Assn. Vascular Surgery, Royal Coll. Surgeons of Eng., Nat. Acad. Scis. Armenia (fgn.), Organ Procurement Agy. Mich. (adv. bd. 1988—89), Armenian Gen. Benevolent Union (invited spkr. 1982, pres.' club 1990—), End Stage Renal Disease Network 24 (med. rev. bd. 1980—82, 1986—87), Soc. Brigham Surg. Alumni, Immunology Club Boston, Med. Club (Phila.), Sigma Xi. Mem. Soc. Of Friends. Achievements include bilateral lung reimplantation, reversal of renal allgraft rejection, prevention and treatment of massive gastroduodenal hemrrhage from hemorrhagic gastritis; co-discovery essential aminoacids phenylalanine and tryptphan are essential for antibody formation, participated in the lyophilization of the smallpox vaccine which was used by the WHO in 1966; to vaccinate everybody resulting in eradication of smallpox in 1977; co-discovery of immunogenetic control of antibody formation, rsch. advantages and disadvantages and pervention of splenectomy in renal transplant recipients; stage-enmasse cardiopulmonary reimplantation, zinc deficiency depresses the action of zinc dependent enzymes, priming the recipient with donor antigen improves kidney transplant survival; bonding protein carrier and cytotoxic agent for treatment of organ transplant rejection and cancer; combined surgery and sclerotherapy corrects; abnormal structure, function and aesthetics of leg varicose veins; pioneering conversion of arteriovenous shunt to arteriovenous fistula for hemodialysis, needle phlebectomy in USA; beaver microblade phlebectomy, bupivicaine wound infiltration in venous surgery wounds to minimize post operative pain; abolition of concurrent deep and perforator vein incompetence by surgical correction of superficial vein incompetence; treatment of the varicose giacomini vein; evolving concepts in mgmt. of accute superficial and deep thromboembolism, phlebolymphedema. Office: The Vein Inst 3301 Woodburn Rd Ste 202 Annandale VA 22003-6889

SIMONS, ALBERT, III, lawyer; b. Charleston, S.C., Nov. 22, 1950; s. Albert Jr. and Caroline Pinckney (Mitchell) S.; m. Theodora Bonnell Wilbur, Jan. 28, 1970; children: Albert IV, Charles A., Theodora B. BA, U. Va., 1972, JD, 1976. Bar: S.C. 1977, N.Y. 1978. Ptnr. Orrick, Herrington & Sutcliffe, N.Y.C., 1984—. Mem. S.C. Bar Assn., N.Y. State Bar Assn. Office: Orrick Herrington & Sutcliffe 666 5th Ave Rm 203 New York NY 10103-1798

SIMONS, ANNEKE PRINS, artist, educator; b. Amsterdam, The Netherlands, Feb. 15, 1930; arrived in U.S., 1940; d. Raphael Hugo and Charlotte Prins. BA, Vassar Coll., Poughkeepsie, NY, 1952; M.A.T., Harvard-Radcliffe, Cambridge, Mass., 1953; PhD, Pa. State U., Univ. Park, Pa., 1968; MA in Social Sci., Jersey City State Coll., Jersey City, NJ, 1975. Tchr., originator adult art edn. South End House, Boston, 1953—54; part-time asst. tchr. Boston Mus. Children's Rm., Boston, 1954—56; with Met. Mus. Art, NYC, 1957—61; tchr., art dir. Twin Pines, Oakland, Calif., 1961—62; grad. rsch. asst. tchr. art edn. Pa. State U., Univ. Park, Pa., 1962—64; prof. Jersey City U., 1967—2000; prof. emeritus. Senator-at-large Jersey City State Coll., mem. personnel com. art dept., dir. art program gifted H.S. students. One-woman shows include The Courtney Gallery, Jersey City State Coll., 1979, The Gallery, Jersey City, NJ, 1981, Stevens Inst. Tech., Hoboken, NJ, 1984, Jersey City Mus., 1996, exhibited in group shows at Gallery Stendhal, NYC, 1991, Jersey City State Coll., 1992, juried show, C.A.S.E. Mus., Jersey City, NJ, 1982, exhibitions include Lemmerman Gallery, NJ City U., 1999, City Spirit Cultural Arts Festival, Jersey City, NJ, 1981 (Best in Show, 1981), Visceglia Art Ctr. Caldwell Coll., Caldwell, NJ, 1994, The Rotunda Gallery City Hall, Jersey City, NJ, 1995, Viridian Gallery, NYC, 1997, numerous others; contbr. articles to profl. jours. Co-founder Genesis Project, Jersey City, 1986—. Recipient Martin Luther King, Jr. Cmty. Svc. award, Jersey City U., 1999; grantee Chinese Art Hist. Coll. Tchrs. summer seminar, Nat. Endowment Humanities, 1975; grad. sch. fellowship, Pa. State U., 1964—65. Mem.: Harvard Club NY, NJ.

SIMONS, CAROL LENORE, magazine editor; b. Bklyn., Feb. 2, 1942; d. Paul and Grace (Rotwein) Seiderman; m. Lewis M. Simons, Feb. 7, 1965; children: Justine, Rebecca, Adam. BA, Tufts U., 1963; MS, Columbia U., 1964. Rschr. Newsweek mag., N.Y.C., 1964-65, CBS News, N.Y.C. and Saigon, Vietnam, 1967-68; reporter Denver Post, 1965-67; editor Pres. Commn. on Marijuana and Drug Abuse, Washington, 1971-72; assoc. editor Smithsonian mag., Washington, 1978-82; dir. publs. Am. C. of C. in Japan, Tokyo, 1991-96; exec. editor AARP The Mag., Washington, 2003—. Office: AARP The Magazine 601 E St NW Washington DC 20049-0001

SIMONS, DENNIS, performing company executive; b. Port Alberni, B.C., Can., Apr. 05; Student, Royal Acad. Music, Eng. Conducter, coach, tchr. violin Chethams Sch. Music, Manchester, Eng., Royal No. Coll. Music, Manchester; founder, music dir. Altrincham Youth Chamber Orch.; concertmaster British Broadcasting Co. Philharmonic Orch., 1977-93; joint concertmaster London Philharmonic Orch.; artistic dir., conductor Saskatoon Symphony, 1993-97; music dir., conductor Shreveport (La.) Symphony, 1996—. Founder, leader Alberni String Quartet; preliminary juror Banff Internat. String Quartet Competition, 1995; juror for finals Banff Internat. String Quartet Competition, 1998. Guest conductor Toronto Symphony, Thirteen Strings of Ottawa, Victoria Symphony, Orch. London Ontario, Manitoba Chamber Orch.; recordings include Mozart Concert Arias; videos include The Maestro and the Diva. Fellow Royal Acad. Music. Office: Strand Theatre PO Box 205 Shreveport LA 71162-0205 E-mail: dsimons@aol.com.

SIMONS, DOLPH COLLINS, JR., newspaper executive and editor; b. Lawrence, Kans., Mar. 11, 1930; s. Dolph Collins and Marie (Nelson) S.; m. Pamela Counseller, Feb. 7, 1952; children: Pamela, Linda, Dolph Collins, Dan. AB, U. Kans., 1951; LLD (hon.), Colby Coll., 1972. Reporter Lawrence Jour.-World, 1953, asso. pub., 1957, pub., 1962—2004, editor, 1978—, pres., 1969—2004; reporter The Times, London, 1956, Johannesburg (South Africa) Star, 1958; chmn. World Co. Mem. Pulitzer Awards Jury, 1977, 78, 80, 81. Trustee, past pres. William Allen White Found.; trustee Midwest Rsch. Inst., Menninger Found., Nat. Parks Conservation Assn.; former mem. governing bd. Children's Mercy Hosp., Kansas City, Mo.; trustee, former chmn. U. Kans. Endowment Assn.; past bd. dirs. Greater Kansas City Cmty. Found., Commerce Bancshares, Kansas City, Mo.; former trustee The Freedom Forum, Kans. Nature Conservancy. Served to capt. USMRC, 1951-53. Recipient Elijah Parish Lovejoy award, 1972; Fred Ellsworth award for significant service to U. Kans., 1976; Disting. Service citation, 1980 Mem. Newspaper Advt. Bur. (past dir.), Am. Soc. Newspaper Editors, Inland Daily Press Assn. (past dir.), Kans. Press Assn. (past pres., dir.), AP (past dir.), Am. Newspaper Pubs. Assn. (past dir., past nat. sec.), Lawrence C. of C. (past pres., dir.), U. Kans. Alumni Assn. (past pres., dir.), Lawrence Country Club, Kansas City Country Club, Kansas City River Club, Masons, Rotary, Sigma Delta Chi, Phi Delta Theta. Republican. Episcopalian. Home: 2425 Vermont St Lawrence KS 66046-4761 Office: 609 New Hampshire St Lawrence KS 66044-2243 E-mail: dsimonsjr@ljworld.com.

SIMONS, ELIZABETH R(EIMAN), biochemist, educator; b. Vienna, Sept. 1, 1929; came to U.S., 1941, naturalized, 1948; d. William and Erna Engle (Weisselberg) Reiman; m. Harold Lee Simons, Aug. 12, 1951; children: Leslie Ann Mulert, Robert David. BChemE, Cooper Union, N.Y.C., 1950; MS, Yale U., 1951, PhD, 1954. Rsch. chemist Tech. Ops., Arlington, Mass., 1953-54; instr. chemistry Wellesley (Mass.) Coll., 1954-57; rsch. asst. Children's Hosp. Med. Ctr. and Cancer Rsch. Found., Boston, 1957-59, rsch. assoc. pathology, 1959-62; rsch. assoc. Harvard Med. Sch., 1962-66, lectr. biol. chemistry,

1966-72; tutor biochem. scis. Harvard Coll., 1971-94; assoc. prof. biochemistry Boston (Mass.) U., 1972-78, prof., 1978—, asst. dir. Office Med. Edn., 2000—. Contbr. articles to profl. jours. Grantee in field. Mem.: AAAS, Soc. for Neurosci., Biophys. Soc., Am. Soc. Hematology, Am. Soc. Cell Biology, Am. Soc. Biol. Chemists, Am. Chem. Soc. Office: Boston U Sch Medicine 80 E Concord St Roxbury MA 02118-2307 Office Phone: 617-638-4332. E-mail: esimons@bu.edu.

SIMONS, ELWYN LAVERNE, physical anthropologist, primatologist, paleontologist, educator; b. Lawrence, Kans., July 14, 1930; s. Verne Franklin and Verna Irene (Cuddeback) S.; m. Friderun Annursel Ankel, Dec. 2, 1972; children: Cornelia Verna Mathilde, Verne Franklin Herbert; 1 child by previous marriage: David Brenton. BS in Biology, Rice U., 1953; MA, Princeton U., 1955, PhD in Paleobiology, 1956; D.Phil., Oxford (Eng.) U., 1959; MA (hon.), Yale U., 1967; DSc, Oxford U., 1995. Demonstrator, exhibitor Oxford U., 1956-58; lectr. geology Princeton (N.J.) U., 1958-59; asst. prof. zoology U. Pa., Phila., 1959-61; vis. assoc. prof. geology, curator vertebrate paleontology Yale U., New Haven, 1960-61, head divsn. vert. paleontology, 1961-77, prof. paleontology, 1967; prof. geology, curator charge div. vertebrate paleontology Peabody Mus., 1965-77; prof. biol. anthropology, anatomy Duke U., Durham, NC, 1977-82, 1982, prof. zoology, dir. Duke Primate Center, 1977-91, sci. dir., 1991—2001, head, div. fossil primates, 2001—. Dir. Paleontol. Expdns., Egypt, 1961—68, Egypt, 1977—2002, sci. dir., Egypt, 1991—2002, dir., India, 1968—69, India, 1996, India, 98, India, 1999—2000; rsch. expdns. for fossil mammals, Wyo., 1960—96, Wyo., 1998—99, Iran, 1970, Spain, 71, Madagascar, 1983—2003; Barbour-Schramm Meml. lectr. U. Nebr., 1974; David French lectr. Claremont Coll., 1974; traveling lectr. French Bur. Fgn. Affairs, 1976; bd. dirs. Ctr. Tropical Conservation, NC. Author: Primate Evolution: An Introduction To Man's Place In Nature, 1972; co-editor: Macmillan Series in Physical Anthropology; A Simons Family History in England and America, 1975; contbr. numerous articles to profl. publs. Decorated chevalier Ordre Nat. (Madagascar); named hon. citizen, Fayum Province of Egypt, 1981; recipient Annadale Meml. medal, Asiatic Soc. Bengal, 1973, Sr. U.S. Scientist award, Alexander von Humboldt Found., 1975. Mem. AAAS, Am. Philos. Soc., Nat. Acad. Scis., Soc. Vertebrate Paleontology, Inst. Human Paleontology, Am. Assn. Zool. Parks and Aquariums (primate specialist group, advisor prosimian taxon group), Assn. Phys. Anthropology (Charles R. Darwin award 2000), Madagascar Fauna Group (bd. dirs.), Internat. Assn. Human Biologists, Sigma Xi. Democrat. Achievements include research in on early mammals, prosimians and primate and human evolution, with special interest in living prosimians, higher primate and human origin and evolution; discovery of 1st tarsiers and 1st marsupials in Africa; naming of earliest known ape Aegyptopithecus in Oligocene of Africa; discovery of Gigantopithecus in India, 1968; naming of earliest anthropoids Oligopithecus, 1962, Qatrania, 1983, Serapia and Arsinoea, 1992; discovery of and naming of new species of Propithecus: Golden Crowned Sifaka in Madagascar, 1989; conservation of lemurs and rain forest of Madagascar. Office: Duke Primate Ctr Divsn Fossil Primates 1013 Broad St Durham NC 27705 Fax: (919) 490-5394. E-mail: esimons@duke.edu.

SIMONS, ERIC WARD, financial executive; b. NYC, Sept. 21, 1958; s. Theodor Leonard and Jean Lenore (Farbman) S. BS in Mgmt. and Internat. Bus., NYU, 1980. Sales cons. Paris Health Club, N.Y.C., 1979-81; registered rep. First Investors Corp., N.Y.C., 1981-82; fin. courses instr. Learning Annex, NYC, 1981—2001; aquatics dir. West Side YMCA, N.Y.C., 1973—99; founder, pres. Simons Fin. Network, N.Y.C., 1982—; former exec. v.p. wealth mgmt. group Ramirez & Co. Adj. faculty NYU Sch. Cmty. Edn., 1997-98; treas. Rockville Dance Co., NYC, 1984-86. Spl. activities coord. West 83d St. Block Assn., NYC, 1970—76; trustee Temple of Universal Judaism, 2003—; bd. dirs. McBurney YMCA, 1996—98; chmn. bd. dirs. Found. in Motion, NYC, 1983—85. Named to Million Dollar Round Table, First Investors Corp., N.Y.C., 1982; recipient Highest Sales award Paris Health Club, N.Y.C., 1981. Mem. Fin. Planning Assn. (bd. dirs., officer 1988-99), Assn. Divorce Fin. Planners (co-founder, chmn. 1999-2001), Nat. Assn. Tax Prosecutors (bd. dirs. NY chpt. 2001—), NYU Tax Soc. (past bd. dirs.), Psi Upsilon (chmn. traditions and edn. com., Resolution of Appreciation exec. coun. 1987, bd. dirs. Delta chpt. 2001—). Jewish. Avocations: physical fitness, travel, Karate, numerology, yoga. Home: 175 W 93rd St Apt 1D New York NY 10025-9314 Office: Simons Fin Network 175 W 93d St New York NY 10025 E-mail: eric@simonsfinancialnetwork.com.

SIMONS, GAIL S. artist, educator, librarian; b. Elgin, Ill., Aug. 13, 1963; d. James Philip and Vivian Faith (Ewalt) S. Cert. Christian edn., Lincoln Christian Coll., 1986; BFA, Judson Coll., 1991. Tchg. asst. Pub. Sch. Dist. 300, Dundee, Ill., 1986-89; illustrator computer clip art Media Mktg. Svcs., St. Charles, Ill., 1989; computer data plant ops. Judson Coll., Elgin, Ill., 1990-91, watercolor painting instr., 1991—; libr. Dundee Twp. Pub. Libr., East Dundee, Ill., 1994—, staff artist, 1997—. Youth/adult choral dir. First Congl. Ch., Carpentersville, Ill., 1986-96; stop motion animator, Chgo., 1991. Exhibited works at Ruth M. Wendt Gallery, East Dundee, 1997-99, Agora Gallery, N.Y.C., 1999—, Incognito Gallery, Fox Lake, Ill., 2001, art-exchange.com, 2003; actress, asst. dir., set/prop designer various musicals and plays. Deaconess/Sunday sch. dir. Congl. Ch., Carpentersville, 1986-96; watercolor/craft tchr. Pub. Libr, East Dundee, 1997—; wildlife adv.; youth leader. Mem. Christians in the Visual Arts, N.W. Area Arts Coun., Dundee Twp. Fine Arts Coun., Alpha Chi Soc. Avocations: collecting, gardening, writing, entomology, old movies. Office: Dundee Twp Pub Libr Dist 555 Barrington Ave East Dundee IL 60118-1422

SIMONS, GALE GENE, nuclear and electrical engineer, educator; b. Kingman, Kans., Sept. 25, 1939; s. Robert Earl and Laura V. (Swartz) S.; m. Barbara Irene Rinkel, July 2, 1966; 1 child, Curtis Dean. BS, Kans. State U., 1962, MS, 1964, PhD, 1968. Engr. Argonne Nat. Lab., Idaho Falls, Idaho, 1968-77, mgr. fast source reactor, head exptl. support group, 1972-77; prof. nuclear engring. Kans. State U., Manhattan, 1977—, assoc. dean for rsch., dir. rsch. coun. Coll. Engring., 1988-97, emeritus prof., 2001—, bd. dirs. Rsch. Found., 1988-97, Presdl. lectr., 1983-96, career counselor, 1984-96. Cons. to pvt. and fed. agys., 1983—; bd. dirs. Kans. Tech. Enterprise Corp., Topeka; com. mem. Kans. Gov.'s Energy Policy Com., Topeka, 1992-97; numerous presentations in field; reviewer proposals fed. agys. Contbr. over 100 articles to sci. jours.; patentee radiation dosimeter. Expert witness State of Kans., Topeka, 1986. Fellow AEC, 1964-67; numerous grants from fed. agys., 1979—. Mem. AAAS, IEEE, Am. Nuclear Soc., Health Physics Soc., Am. Soc. for Engring. Edn., Masons, Rotary, Phi Kappa Phi, Tau Beta Pi, Pi Mu Epsilon. Home: 2395 Grandview Ter Manhattan KS 66502-3729

SIMONS, HELEN, school psychologist, psychotherapist, educator; b. Chgo., Feb. 13, 1930; d. Leo and Sarah (Shrayer) Pomper; m. Broudy Simons, May 20, 1956 (div. May 1972); children: Larry, Sheri. BA in Biol., Lake Forest Coll., 1951; MA in Clin. Psychology, Roosevelt U., 1972; D of Psychology, Ill. Sch. Profl. Psychology, 1980. Intern Cook County Hosp., Chgo., 1979-80; pvt. practice psychotherapist Chgo., 1980—; sch. psychologist Chgo. Bd. Edn., 1974-79, 80—. Faculty Internat. Soc. for Prevention of Child Abuse and Neglect; lectr., presenter at workshops. Contbr. articles to profl. jours. Mem.: APA, Internat. Sch. Psychologists Assn., Internat. Assn. Applied Psychology, Internat. Soc. for Prevention of Child Abuse and Neglect, Internat. Coun. Psychologists, Chgo. Sch. Psychol. Assn., Chgo. Psychol. Assn., Ill. Sch. Psychologists Assn., Nat. Sch. Psychologists Assn. Avocations: music, dance, reading. Home: 6145 N Sheridan Rd Apt 29D Chicago IL 60660-6855 Office: Gladstone Sch 1231 S Damen Ave Chicago IL 60608 E-mail: hpompers@aol.com.

SIMONS, JAMES, publishing executive; Chmn. Franklin Electronic Pub., Inc., N.Y.C., 1989—. Office: Franklin Electronic Pub Inc 800 3rd Ave Fl Dave33D New York NY 10022-7604

SIMONS, JAMES, technology company executive; BS, MIT; PhD in Math., U. Calif., Berkeley. Tchr. math. MIT and Harvard U., 1961—64; chmn. math. dept. SUNY, Stony Brook, 1968; pres., founder Renaissance Techs. Corp., East Setauket, NY, 1982—. Chmn. Stony Brook Found., 1989—; chmn. bd. dirs. Franklin Electronic Pubs., Segue Software; bd. dirs. Brookhaven Sci. Assocs. Recipient Oswald Veblen prize in Geometry, Am. Mathematical Society, 1976. Office: Renaissance Techs Corp 600 Route 25A East Setauket NY 11733-2841 also: Renaissance Techs Corp 800 3rd Ave Fl 33 New York NY 10022-7604*

SIMONS, JOHN S. food products executive; V.p., red meat bus. devel. Excel; pres., COO ConAgra Beef Co., Greeley, Colo., 1999—2002; pres., CEO Swift & Co. (formerly ConAgra Beef Co.), Greeley, Colo., 2002—. Office: Swift & Co 1770 Promontory Cir Greeley CO 80634

SIMONS, LAWRENCE BROOK, lawyer; b. N.Y.C., Oct. 19, 1924; s. Harry A. and Marion B. (Brook) Simons; m. Annalou Kadin, Aug. 24, 1947; children: Barbara Flexner, Kenneth. Student, Duke U., 1941-43, 46-47; JD, Columbia U., 1949. Bar: N.Y. 1949, U.S. Dist. Ct. (so. dist.) N.Y. 1949, DC 1984, U.S. Supreme Ct. 1987. Assoc. Spring & Eastman, N.Y.C., 1949-53; v.p., gen. mgr. Caribe Knitting Mills, San Juan, P.R., 1953-58; pres. LBS Constrn. Co. Inc., S.I., N.Y., 1958-77; asst. sec. housing FHA commn. HUD, Washington, 1977-81; ptnr. Powell, Goldstein, Frazier & Murphy, Washington, 1981—. Mem. task force quality life Dept. of Def., 1995. Chmn. bd. dirs. Nat. Housing Conf., 1981—; mem. Nat. Housing Task Force, 1988, Nat. Housing Trust, 1990—; trustee Bayley Seton Hosp., S.I., 1981—90, NHP Found., Inc., 1991—2003; chmn. bd. dirs. N.Y. State Urban Devel. Corp., 1975—77, Pa. Ave. Devel. Corp., 1981—87; trustee Affordable Housing Found., 1990—92, Ctr. Democracy, 1990—96; pres. Ctr. Housing Policy, 1992—96, bd. dirs., 1996—; commr. Beaufort (S.C.) Housing Authority, 1997—, Affordable Housing Commn., Hilton Head, SC, 1997—99. With U.S. Army, 1943—46, ETO. Named Man of the Yr., Nat. Housing Conf., 1985. Mem.: ABA, Nat. Assn. Home Builders (named to Housing Hall of Fame 2002), Sea Pines Country Club, Lambda Alpha. Democrat. Jewish. Avocation: golf. Home: 40 Plantation Dr Hilton Head Island SC 29928-4402 Office: Powell Goldstein Frazier Murphy 1001 Pennsylvania Ave NW Washington DC 20004-2505 E-mail: simonshhi@adelphia.net.

SIMONS, LEWIS MARTIN, journalist; b. Paterson, N.J., Jan. 9, 1939; s. Abram and Goldie (Fleisher) S.; m. Carol Lenore Seiderman, Feb. 7, 1965; children: Justine, Rebecca, Adam P.D. BA, NYU, 1962; MS, Columbia U., 1964. Corr. AP, Kuala Lumpur, Singapore, Saigon, Denver, 1965-70, Washington Post, Bangkok, New Delhi, Washington, 1971-82; bur. chief Knight-Ridder Newspapers, Tokyo and Beijing, 1982-95; fgn. policy corr. Time mag., 1996-97; freelance writer, 1997—. Author: Worth Dying For, 1987; contbg. author: Crimes of War, 1999, The World of Islam, 2001, Breach of Faith, 2002; contbr. to Nat. Geog. mag., Smithsonian mag., Atlantic Monthly, N.Y. Times. With USMC, 1962-64. Recipient Grand prize and Investigative Reporting award Am. Newspaper Guild, 1981, Citation for Excellence, Overseas Press Club Am., 1983, Jessie Meriton White award Friends World Coll., 1986, Investigative Reporters and Editors award U. Mo., 1986, Award of Excellence, World Affairs Coun., 1984, 86, 89, 92, Pulitzer Prize, 1986, George Polk award, 1985, Malcolm S. Forbes award Overseas Press Club Am., 1986, 92, Gerald Loeb award UCLA, 1993, Alumni award Columbia U. Grad. Sch. Journalism, 2004; Edward R. Murrow fellow Coun. of Fgn. Rels., 1970-71. Mem. Fgn. Corrs. Club Japan (bd. dirs. 1991-92, pres., 1993-94). E-mail: clsimons@ix.netcom.com.

SIMONS, LYNN OSBORN, educational consultant; b. Havre, Mont., June 1, 1934; d. Robert Blair and Dorothy (Briggs) Osborn; m. John Powell Simons, Jan. 19, 1957; children: Clayton Osborn, William Blair. Tchr. Midvale (Utah) Jr. H.S., 1956-57, Sweetwater county Sch. Dist. 1, Rock Springs, Wyo., 1957-58, U. Wyo., 1959-61, Natrona County Sch. Dist. 1, Casper, Wyo., 1963-64; credit mgr. Gallery 323, Casper, 1972-77; Wyo. state supt. pub. instrn. Cheyenne, 1979-91; sec.'s regional rep. region VIII U.S. Dept. Edn., Denver, 1993—2001; mem. Denver Fed. Exec. Bd., 1995-2001; mem. exec. bd. combined Fed. campaign, 1994—2001; ednl. cons., 2001—03; state planning coord. Capitol Bldg., Cheyenne, Wyo., 2003—. Mem. State Bds. Charities and Reform, Land Commrs., Farm Loan, 1979-91; mem. State Commns. Capitol Bldg., Liquor, 1979-91; Ex-officio mem. bd. trustees U. Wyo., 1979-91; ex-officio mem. Wyo. Community Coll. Commn., 1979-91; mem. steering com. Edn. Commn. of the States, 1988-90, 2003; mem. State Bd. Edn., 1971-77, chmn., 1976-77; advisor Nat. Trust for Hist. Preservation, 1980-86. Mem. LWV (pres. 1970-71). Democrat. Episcopalian. Office: Capitol Building Cheyenne WY 82003 E-mail: isimon@state.wy.us.

SIMONS, RICHARD DUNCAN, lawyer, retired judge; b. Niagara Falls, N.Y., Mar. 23, 1927; s. William Taylor and Sybil Irene (Swick) S.; m. Muriel (Penny) E. Genung, June 9, 1951 (dec. 1992); m. Esther (Esi) Turkington Tremblay, May 21, 1994; children: Ross T., Scott R., Kathryn E., Linda A. AB, Colgate U., 1949; LLB, U. Mich., 1952; LLD (hon.), Albany Law Sch., 1983. Bar: N.Y. 1952. Pvt. practice, Rome, N.Y., 1952-63; asst. corp. counsel City of Rome, 1955-58, corp. counsel, 1960-63; justice 5th jud. dist. N.Y. Supreme Ct., 1964-83, assoc. justice appellate divsn. 3d dept., 1971-72, assoc. justice appellate divsn. 4th dept., 1973-82; assoc. judge N.Y. Ct. Appeals, 1983—97, acting chief judge, 1992-93; counsel McMahon & Grow, Rome, NY, 1997-00; dir. N.Y. State Capital Defender Office, 1997-2000; chief judge Oneida Indian Nation, 1997—2003, chief trial judge, 2003—. Jurist in residence Syracuse U. Law Sch., 1998; mem. Law Sch. Admission Svcs., Bar Passage Study Com. Editorial staff: N.Y. Pattern Jury Instructions, 1979-83. Chmn. Republican City Com., 1958-62; vice chmn. Oneida County Rep. Com., 1958-62; bd. mgrs. Rome Hosp. and Murphy Meml. Hosp., 1953; trustee Rome Arts and Cmty. Ctr., 2003—, mem. chief judge's commn. fiduciary appointments, chief judge's com. promote trust and confidence in legal sys., N.Y. Fair Elections Project, Inc., Campaign for Effective Justice. Served with USN, World War II. NEH fellow U. Va. Law Sch., 1979 Fellow Am. Bar Found., N.Y. State Bar Found. (chmn. 1997-98); mem. ABA, N.Y. State Bar Assn. (chair task force on ct. reorgn. 1999-2003, chair spl. com. ct. structure and jud. selection 2004—, Disting. Svc. award 2000), Oneida County Bar Assn., Rome Bar Assn., Am. Law Inst., Inst. Jud. Adminstrn. Home: 6520 Pillmore Cir Rome NY 13440-7337 Office: McMahon & Grow 301 N Washington St Ste 4 Rome NY 13440-5152

SIMONS, ROBERT EDWARD, mechanical engineer, consultant; s. Stanley and Mary Simons; m. Miriam Freda Andros, Apr. 23, 1940; children: Anthony Robert, Gina Marie DaLatri, Lisa Marie Luber, Mark Edward. AAS, Dutchess C.C., Poughkeepsie, 1960; BSME, Pa. Mil. Coll., Chester, 1962; MS in Ops. Rsch. and Applied Stats., Union Coll., Schenectady, N.Y., 1985. Engr. GE Corp., Phila., 1962—66, IBM Corp., Poughkleepsie, 1966—69, project/devel. engr. Poughkeepsie, 1969—79, sr. engr., 1979—87, sr. tech. staff mem., 1987—93; cons. Electronics Cooling Applications, Poughkeepsie, 1993—97, IBM Corp., Poughkeepsie, 1997—. Guest editor IEEE Transactions (CHMT/CPT), N.Y.C., 1992—2002. Co-author: (packaging handbook chpt.) Heat Transfer in Electronic Packages; author: (book chpt.) Bibliography of Heat Transfer in Electronic Equipment: 1990-1994, Bibliography of Heat Transfer in Electronic Equipment, 1989, 1987, 1986; co-author: Recent Development in Thermal Technology for Electronic Packaging; author: Bibliography of Heat Transfer in Electronic Equipment, 1988. Recipient Semi-Therm Significant Contbr. award, IEEE Semiconductor Thermal Measurement and Mgmt. Symposium, 1995, Best Paper award, 2000, Semiconductor Thermal and Temperature Measurement Symposium, 1984, EDN Award for Excellence, EDN Mag., 1969. Achievements include co-invention of Thermal Conduction Module concept used to cool 3 generations of IBM mainframe computers; patents for cooling electronic packages and equipment; research in liquid cooling techniques for electronic equipment. Home: 16 Shamrock Cir Poughkeepsie NY 12603

SIMONS, ROSS B. environmental center director; b. Akron, Ohio, July 20, 1951; BA, Am. U., 1972. Special assistant to the US Secretary of State; joined Smithsonian Instn., Washington, 1972, dep asst. sec. scis., 1984-88, 90-93, dep. asst. sec. rsch., 1988-90, asst.provost sci., 1994-95; sr. advisor Nat. Mus. Natural History, Washington, 1996; acting dir. Smithsonian Environ. Rsch. Ctr., Edgewater, Md., 1997-98, dir., 1998—. Assoc. dir. rsch. & collections Nat. Mus. Natural History, Washington, 1998—. Bd. trustees Orgn. Tropical Studies, Coun. Am. Overseas Rsch. Ctr., Mpala Rsch. Trust, Chesapeake Rsch. Consortium. Office: Smithsonian Environ Rsch Ctr PO Box 28 Edgewater MD 21037-0028 E-mail: simons.ross@nmnh.si.edu.*

SIMONS, STEPHEN, mathematics educator, researcher; b. London, Aug. 11, 1938; came to U.S., 1965; s. Jack Isidore Simons and Ethel Esther (Littman) Harris; m. Jacqueline Mania Berchadsky, Aug. 13, 1963; 1 son, Mark. BA, Cambridge U., Eng., 1959, PhD, 1962. Instr. U. B.C., Vancouver, Can., 1962-63; asst. prof. U. BC., Vancouver, Can., 1964-65, U. Calif., Santa Barbara, 1965-67, assoc. prof., 1967-73, prof., 1973—2002, prof. emeritus, 2002—, chmn. dept., 1975-77, 88-89. Trustee Math. Scis. Rsch. Inst., Berkeley, Calif., 1988-94. Peterhouse rsch. fellow, Cambridge U., 1963-64. Mem. Am. Math. Soc. Office: Univ Calif Dept Math Santa Barbara CA 93106

SIMONS, THOMAS W., JR., history professor; b. Crosby, Minn., Sept. 4, 1938; s. Thomas Winston and Mary Jo (Enochs) S.; m. Margaret Eleanor Quinn, Dec. 23, 1963; children: Suzanne Deirdre, Benjamin Thomas. BA, Yale U., 1958, MA, Harvard U., 1959, PhD, 1963. Joined Fgn. Svc., Dept. State, 1963; sec. del., tech. sec. U.S. Del. to 6th round trade negotiation in GATT, 1964-67; consular officer, polit. officer Am. Embassy, Warsaw, Poland, 1968-71; Coun. on Fgn. Rels. fellow Hoover Instn., Stanford, Calif., 1971-72; internat. rels. officer Bur. Politico-Mil. Affairs, 1972-74, mem. policy planning staff, 1974-75; chief external reporting unit, polit. sect. Am. Embassy, Moscow, 1975-77, dep. chief of mission Bucharest, Romania, 1977-79, counselor for polit. affairs London, 1979-81; dir. for Soviet Union affairs Dept. State, 1981-85; mem. Sr. Seminar in Fgn. Policy, 1985-86; dep. asst. sec. for European and Can. affairs Dept. State, 1986-89; diplomat-in-residence, adj. prof. history Brown U., Providence, 1989-90; amb. extraordinary and plenipotentiary Poland, 1990-93. Coord. U.S. assistance to new ind. states of former Soviet Union, Washington, 1993-95; amb. extraordinary and plenipotentiary, Pakistan, 1995-98; cons. prof. history Stanford U., 1998-2002, Ctr. Internat. Security and Coop., Stanford U., 1998—; program dir. Davis Ctr. for Russian and Eurasian Studies, Harvard U., 2002—; vis. diplomat-scholar Wellesley Coll., 2002-2003. Author: The End of the Cold War?, 1990, Eastern Europe in the Postwar World, 2d edit., 1993. Office: 625 Massachusetts Ave Cambridge MA 02139

SIMONSON, DAVID C. retired newspaper association executive; b. N.Y.C., May 9, 1927; s. Simon and Rebecca (Coolman) S.; m. Lois E. Sneider, Nov. 1, 1952; children: Peter, Eric, John Frederick. BA, Hamilton Coll., 1948; postgrad., U. Vt., 1949, Art Student League of N.Y., 1949. Copywriter Forwell & Mart Advt., N.Y.C., 1949-50; reporter, editor Croton-Cortlandt News, Croton, N.Y., 1950-52; gen. mgr. Colony Publs., N.Y.C., 1952-54; editor, mgr. County Press Newspapers, Croton, 1955-59; promotion dir. Amcrete Corp., Peekskill, N.Y., 1959-60; various positions in mgmt. Patent Trader, Mt. Kisco, N.Y., 1960-72, pub., 1972-77; pres./pub. Pioneer Press Newspapers, Wilmette, Ill., 1977-86; exec. v.p., chief exec. officer Nat. Newspaper Assn., Washington, 1987-92; retired, 1992. Bd. dirs. Christian Herald Assn., N.Y.C., NY; lectr. Medill Sch. Journalism, Meridian House, U.S.A., numerous state press assns.; media cons.; seminar leader Ea. Europe for World Pres Freedom Com.; cons. to Slovenian publs. for U.S. Info. Agy., 1993—94; cons. to Slovakian publs. for USIA, 1995; cons. to African publs. for UNESCO, 95; cons. to Bulgarian Publs. for USIA, 96, 97; cons. to U.S. State dept. World Freedom Com., 2002—; cons. to Bulgarian Publs. for USIA Croatian Publs. for USIA, 1999; seminar leader Voice of Am. for Bulgarian Publs., 1997, Bosnian pubs., 2000, Albanian publs., 2000; U.S. rep. Media Conf., Prague, 2001; DUTV U.S. rep. with Chinese journalists, 01; participant Freedom Forum Roundtables; media panel cons. U.S. Dept. of State, 2003. Chmn. planning bd. Town of Croton-on-Hudson, N.Y., 1962-67, trustee, 1967, mayor, 1969. With USNR, 1945-46. Recipient Lesher award Suburban Newspapers of Am., 1998. Mem. Suburban Newspapers Am. (pres. 1984-85, bd. dirs. 1980-84), Ill. Press Assn (bd. dirs. 1980-84, 1st v.p. 1986), N.Y. Press Assn. (bd. dirs. 1966-76, 1st v.p. 1976), Nat. Newspaper Assn. (bd. dirs. 1985-86), Cook County Pubs. Assn. (pres. 1983-84). Avocations: painting, cartooning. Home: 1805 28th St S Arlington VA 22202-1536

SIMONSON, LEE STUART, broadcast company executive; b. Balt., July 3, 1948; s. Theodore and Sara (Silver) S.; m. Nancy Paula Levin, Mar. 25, 1973; children: Laura Todd, Michael Theodore. BA, U. Md., 1970. Acct. exec. WGMS-AM-FM (subs. RKO Gen.), Washington, 1971-73, retail sales mgr., 1973-76; sales mgr. WFYR-FM (subs. RKO Gen.), Chgo., 1976-80; v.p., gen. mgr. WRKS-FM (subs. RKO Gen.), N.Y.C., 1980-84, WOR-AM (subs. RKO Gen.), N.Y.C., 1984-88; vice chmn., COO, owner radio stas. Broadcasting Ptnrs., Inc., N.Y.C., 1988-95; chmn., CEO Broadcasting Ptnrs. Holdings, LP, N.Y.C., 1997-2000; pres. Simonson Assocs., 2000—. Bd. dirs. TheaterMania-.com, Findwhat.com. Bd. dirs. N.Y.C. chpt. March of Dimes, 1982—2002. With U.S. Army, 1970—76. Jewish. Office Phone: 201-767-9551. E-mail: SIMONSONLS@aol.com.

SIMONSON, SUSAN KAY, hospital clinical care coordinator; b. La Porte, Ind., Dec. 5, 1946; d. George Randolph and Myrtle Lucille (Opfel) Menkes; m. Richard Bruce Simonson, Aug. 25, 1973. BA with honors, Ind. U., 1969; MA, Washington U., St. Louis, 1972. Perinatal social worker Yakima Valley Meml. Hosp., Yakima, Wash., 1979-81, dir. patient support program, 1981—, dir. social svc., 1982-98; instr. Spanish, ethnic studies, sociology Yakima Valley Coll., Yakima, Wash., 1981—. Pres. Yakima Child Abuse Council, 1983-85; developer nat. patient support program, 1981. Contbr. articles to profl. jours. Mem. adv. council Robert Wood Johnson Found. Rural Infant Health Care Project, Yakima, 1980, Pregnancy Loss and Compassionate Friends Support Groups, Yakima, 1982—, Teen Outreach Program, Yakima, 1984—. Recipient NSF award, 1967, discharge planning program of yr. regional award Nat. Glasrock Home Health Care Discharge Planning Program, 1987; research grantee Ind. U., 1968, Fulbright grantee U.S. Dept. State, 1969-70; Nat. Def. Edn. Act fellowship, 1970-73. Mem. Soc. Med. Anthropology, Soc. Hosp. Social Work Dirs. of Am. Hosp. Assn. (regional award 1989), Nat. Assn. Social Workers, Phi Beta Kappa. Office: Yakima Valley Meml Hosp 2811 Tieton Dr Yakima WA 98902-3799 Office Phone: 509-575-8151.

SIMONTON, DEAN KEITH, psychology educator; b. Glendale, Calif., Jan. 27, 1948; s. Dean Clarence Simonton and Laverne (Merkobrad) Williams; m. Susan Youel, June 21, 1971; (div. 1982); m. Melody Boyer, Dec. 29, 1984 (div. 2004). BA in Psychology magna cum laude, Occidental Coll., 1970; MA in Social Psychology, Harvard U., 1973, PhD with distinction, 1975. Asst. prof. psychology U. Ark., Fayetteville, 1974-76; asst. prof. U. Calif., Davis, 1976-81, assoc. prof., 1981-85, prof., 1985—. Cons. Wissenschaftzentrun, Berlin, 1979, Ctr. for Creative Leadership, Greensboro, N.C., 1983, NATO, Brussels, Belgium, 1980-81, Dept. Def., Washington, 1983, Creative Problem Solving Inst., 1984, Arvin Perlmutter, Inc., 1992, Milken Family Found., 1994, Templeton Found., 2002. Author: Genius, Creativity and Leadership, 1984, Why Presidents Succeed, 1987, Scientific Genius, 1988, Psychology, Science, and History, 1990, Greatness, 1994, Genius and Creativity, 1997, Origins of Genius, 1999, Great Psychologists and Their Times, 2002, Creativity in Science, 2004; editor Jour. Creative Behavior, 1993-99; contbr. numerous articles to profl. jours. Recipient Excellence award Mensa Adn. and Rsch. Found., 1986, Francis Galton award Internat. Assn. Empirical Aesthetics, 1996. Fellow AAAS, Am. Psychol. Soc., Am. Assn. Applied and Preventive Psychology, Am. Psychol. Assn. (mem.-at-large 1979-82, pres. psychology and the arts divsn. 1985-86, Rudolf Arnheim award Outstanding Contbn. to Psychology and the Arts, 1996, George A. Miller award 1997); mem. Phi Beta Kappa, Sigma Xi. Home: 2903 Solito St Davis CA 95616-0274 Office: U Calif Dept Psychology Davis CA 95616 Office Phone: 530-752-1677. Business E-Mail: dksimonton@ucdavis.edu.

SIMPERS, MARY PALMER, state legislator; b. East Middlebury, Vt., Mar. 17, 1934; m. Harold J. Simpers Sr.; 2 children. BS, U. Vt., 1957. Mem. edn. com. Vt. Ho. of Reps., 1983-84, mem. health and welfare com., 1985-86, mem. mcpl. corp. com., 1987-88, mem. instnl. com., 1989-92, 95-98, mem., 1983-92, 95—; co-owner Poeseidon Breathing Air System, Colchester. Bd. dirs. Vt. Retail Assoc. Ins. Co-author: Looking Around Colchester and Milton.

Mem. Colchester Civil Bd. of Authority and J.P., 1970—; mem. Colchester Sch. Bd., 1978-85; bd. dirs. Lake Champlain Access TV. Mem. Zonta Club of Burlington (past pres.), Vt. Hist. Soc., Colchester & Chittenden County Hist. Soc.

SIMPKINS, HENRY, medical educator; BS in Chemistry, U. London, 1964, PhD in Biophys. and Molecular Biology, 1967; MD, U. Miami, 1975. Rsch. biologist U. Calif., San Deigo, 1967-69; head lab. molecular biology and biophys. Lady Davis Inst. Med. Rsch. of Jewish Gen. Hosp., Montreal, Can., 1969-75; asst. prof. dept. biochemistry U. Montreal, 1970-73, assoc. prof., 1973-75; resident U. Colo. Med. Ctr., Denver, 1975-78, instr. dept. pathology, 1976-78, asst. prof. dept. pathology, 1976-77, assoc. prof. dept. pathology, 1977-78, U. Calif., Irvine, 1978-81, prof. dept. pathology, 1981-85; prof. pathology SUNY, N.Y.C., 1985-91; prof., chmn. dept. pathology and lab. medicine Temple U. Med. Sch., Phila., 1991—. Head divsns. chem. pathology and hematopathology U. Calif., Irvine, 1978-81, head divsn. hematopathology, 1981-83, head divsn. hematopathology.blood bank, 1983-85, acting chmn. dept. pathology, 1984; cons. hematopathology Long Beach VA Hosp., 1979-85; dir. dept. pathology and lab. medicine U. Hosp. S.I., N.Y., 1985-91; presenter in field. Contbr. articles to profl. jours. Postdoctoral fellow King's Coll., London, 1964-67, U. Calif., San Diego, 1967-69; Ministry Edn. State scholar, Gt. Britain, 1961-64, Sci. Rsch. Coun. scholar, Gt. Britain, 1964-67; Can. MEd. Rsch. Coun. scholar, 1970-75. Mem. Am. Soc. Clin. Pathologists, Am. Assn. Blood Banks, Am. Soc. Hematology, Coll. Am. Pathologists, Internat. Acad. Pathology, The Pluto Club. Office: Temple U Sch Medicine Dept Pathology & Lab Med Rm 224 OPB 3307 N Broad St Philadelphia PA 19140-5101

SIMPKINS, WILLIAM B. federal agency administrator; BS in Bus. Adminstrn., Boston Coll., 1969; AS in Law Enforcement, Northeastern U., 1972. Police officer City of Newton, Mass., 1973—74; spl. agt. Drug Enforcement Adminstrn., 1974—86, resident agt. in charge West Palm Beach Resident Office, 1986, unit chief in planning and inspection divsn., spl. asst. to asst. adminstr. for planning and inspection, spl. asst. to the asst. adminstr. for intelligence, assoc. dep. chief insp., dep. chief insp., acting chief insp., asst. adminstr. for operational support, 1999—, acting dep. adminstr., 2001. Chmn. strategic mgmt. exec. coun. Drug Enforcement Adminstrn., bd. mem. survivor's benefit fund, mem. justice wireless comm. bd., mem. justice automated booking sys. and pub. safety wireless network exec. com.; mem. adv. com. Global Criminal Justice Info. Netowkr. Mem.: Internat. Assn. Chiefs of Police. Office: Drug Enforcement Adminstrn 2401 Jefferson Davis Hwy Alexandria VA 22301

SIMPLOT, JOHN R. agribusiness executive; b. Dubuque, Iowa, Jan. 4, 1909; m. Esther Becker; children: Richard, Don, Scott, Gay Simplot Otter. Founder, chmn. J.R. Simplot Co., Boise, Idaho, 1941—; bd. dirs. Micron Technology, First Security Corp., Continental Life and Accident Co., Morrison-Knudsen, Inc. Former chmn. bd. trustees Coll. Idaho. Avocations: skiing, horseback riding, hunting, fishing. Pioneer in commercial frozen french fries. Office: J R Simplot Co PO Box 27 1 Capitol Ctr Boise ID 83707

SIMPLOT, SCOTT R. diversified food products company executive; b. 1946; BA, U. Idaho; MBA, U. Pa. Exec. v.p., dir. J.R. Simplot Co., Boise. Office: J R Simplot Co PO Box 27 Boise ID 83707-0027

SIMPSON, ALAN KOOI, former US senator, lawyer; b. Cody, Wyo., Sept. 2, 1931; s. Milward Lee and Lorna (Kooi) S.; m. Ann Schroll, June 21, 1954; children— William Lloyd, Colin Mackenzie, Susan Lorna. BS, U. Wyo., 1954, JD, 1958; LLD (hon.), Calif. Western Sch. of Law, San Diego, 1983, Colo. Coll., Colo. Springs, 1986, Notre Dame U., South Bend, Ind., 1987, Am. U., Washington, D.C., 1989, Rocky Mountain Coll., Billings, Mont., 1996, U. Wyo., Laramie, 1999. Bar: Wyo. 1958, U.S. Supreme Ct. 1964. Asst. atty. gen. State of Wyo., 1959; city atty. City of Cody, 1959-69; ptnr. Simpson, Kepler, and Simpson, Cody, Wyo., 1959-78; mem. Wyo. Ho. of Reps., 1964-77, majority whip, 1973-75, majority floor leader, 1975-77, speaker pro tem, 1977; mem. U.S. Senate from Wyo., 1978-96, asst. majority or minority leader, 1984-94, chmn. vets. affairs com., chmn. fin. subcom. on Social Security and Family Policy, chmn. subcom. on Immigration and Refugee Policy; mem. Spec. Com. on Aging; dir. Inst. Politics Kennedy Sch. Govt. Harvard U., 1999—2000; ptnr. and shareholder Burg Simpson Eldredge Hersh Jardine and Simpson Kepler & Edwards PC, Cody, Wyo. Guest lectr. London exchange program Regent's Coll., London, 1987; vis. lectr. Lombard chair Shorenstein Ctr. for Press, Politics and Pub. Policy, Kennedy Sch. Govt., Harvard U., 1997-2000; bd. dirs. Am. Express Funds; former dir. Biogen; mem. Presdl. Debate Commn.; co-chair Continuity in Govt. Commn. Chmn. bd. trustees Buffalo Bill Hist. Ctr., Cody, trustee emeritus, Grand Teton Music Festival; former regent Smithsonian Inst., Washington; adv. bd. Folger Shakespeare Libr., Washington; mem. Am. Battle Monuments Commn. Recipient Nat. Assn. Land Grant Colls. Centennial Alumni award U. Wyo., 1987, Disting. Alumnus award, 1985, Lifetime Svc. award Vietnam Vets. Am., 1993, Thomas Jefferson award in Law U. Va., 1998. Mem. Wyo. Bar Assn., Park County Bar Assn., U. Wyo Alumni Assn. (pres. 1962, 63, Disting. Alumnus award 1985), VFW (life), Am. Legion, Amvets. (Silver Helmet award). Lodges: Eagles, Elks, Masons (33 deg., Order of Grand Cross), Shriners, Rotary. Republican. Office: Burg Simpson Eldredge Hersh & Jardine 1135 14th St PO Box 490 Cody WY 82414

SIMPSON, ALLAN BOYD, real estate company executive; b. Lakeland, Fla., Nov. 24, 1948; s. Alfred Forsythe and Ruth Jeanette (Coker) S.; m. Melody Elaine Mann; 1 child, Lauren Leigh. B in Indsl. Ingring., Ga. Inst. Tech., 1970; MBA, U. Pa., 1972. Cert. rev. appraiser; lic. realtor, Ga. Dir. mortgage banking Ackerman & Co., Atlanta, 1972-73; v.p. B.F. Saul & Co., Atlanta, 1973-79; pres. L.J. Hooker, Atlanta, 1979-88; also bd. dirs. Hooker/Barnes, Atlanta. Bd. dirs. Hooker Holdings (USA), Inc., Century Ins. Co., Hooker Internat. Devels. Ltd., Hooker Internat. Fin. BV, Charter Credit Corp. Ltd., Simpson Spring, Inc., Strategic Land, Inc., Dunwoody Retail, Inc., 750 Park Ave.; chmn., CEO The Simpson Orgn., Inc., Coker Capital Corp., 1989—. Bd. dirs. YES Atlanta, 1991—, Atlanta Coll. Art, Theatrical Outfit; bd. dirs., treas. Midtown Bus. Assn., 1979-88. Mem. Am. Inst. Indsl. Engrs., MBA Execs. Assn., Bldg. Owners and Mgrs. Assn., Nat. Assn. Realtors, U.S. C. of C., Atlanta C. of C., Internat. Coun. of Shopping Ctrs., Urban Land Inst., Nat. Assn. of Office and Indsl. Pks., Ctrl. Atlanta Progress, Amelia Island Club, Mystic Krewe of Ga. (capt.), Loch Lomond Golf Club, Pinehurst Country Club. Democrat. Methodist. Home: 750 Park Ave NE Atlanta GA 30326-3266 Office: 1401 Peachtree St Ste 400 Atlanta GA 30309-3607 Office Phone: 404-253-6350. E-mail: boyd@simpsonorg.com.

SIMPSON, ALLYSON BILICH, lawyer; b. Pasadena, Calif., Feb. 5, 1951; d. John Joseph and Barbaran Rita (Bessolo) Bilich; m. Roland Gilbert Simpson, Aug. 11, 1979; children: Megan Elise, Erin Marie, Brian Patrick. BS, U. So. Calif., L.A., 1973, JD, 1976. Bar: Calif. 1976. Staff atty. Gen. Telephone Co., Thousand Oaks, Calif., 1978-79; group staff atty., dir. legis. compliance Pacific Mut. Life Ins. Co., Newport Beach, Calif., 1980-86; corp. counsel and sec. Amicare Ins. Co., Beverly Hills, Calif., 1986; assoc. Leboeuf, Lamb, Leiby & MacRae, L.A., 1986-87; from assoc. to ptnr. Musick, Peeler & Garrett, L.A., 1988-94; ptnr. Sonnenschein Nath & Rosenthal, L.A., 1994-95; sr. v.p., sec., gen. counsel Fremont Compensation Ins. Group, Glendale, Calif., 1995—. Vis. pro. bus. law U. So. Calif., L.A., 1981. Trustee St. Anne's Maternity Home Found., L.A., 1991-97; bd. dirs. St. Anne's Maternity Home, L.A., 1993-97. Mem. Western Pension and Benefits Conf., Corp. Ins. Counsel, Am. Corp. Counsel Assn. Republican. Roman Catholic. Avocations: music, reading, family. Office: Fremont Compensation Ins Group 500 N Brand Blvd Ste 1100 Glendale CA 91203-3392

SIMPSON, ANDREA LYNN, communications executive; b. Altadena, Calif., Feb. 10, 1948; d. Kenneth and Barbara Simpson; 1 child, Christopher Ryan Myrdal. BA, U. So. Calif., 1969, MS, 1983; postgrad., U. Colo., Boulder Sch. Bank Mktg., 1977. Mktg. officer United Calif. Bank, L.A., 1969-73; asst. v.p. mktg. 1st Hawaiian Bank, Honolulu, 1973-78; v.p. corp. comms. Pacific Resources Inc., Honolulu, 1978-89, BHP Hawaii, Inc., 1989-98; v.p. corp. rels. Tesoro Petroleum Corp., San Antonio, 1998-2000; v.p. corp. comms. Edison Internat., Rosemead, Calif., 2000—01; pres. Simpson Comm., 2001—. Bd. dirs. Arts Coun., Hawaii, 1977-81, Hawaii Heart Assn., 1978-83, Coun. Pacific Girls Scouts USA, 1982-85, Child and Family Svcs., 1984-86, Honolulu Symphony Soc., 1985-91, Sta. KHPR Hawaii Pub. Radio, 1988-92, Kapiolani Found., 1990-95, Hanahauoli Sch., 1991-98, Hawaii Strategic Devel. Corp., 1991-98, Children's Discovery Ctr., 1994-98, Pacific Asian Affairs Coun., 1994-96, adv. dir. Hawaii Kids at Work, 1991-98, Hawaii MADD, 1992-96; bd. dirs., 2d v.p. Girl Scout Coun. Hawaii, 1994-96, mem. adv. bd., 1996-98; trustee Hawaii Loa Coll., 1984-86, Kapiolani Women's and Children's Hosp., 1988-97, Hawaii Sch. for Girls at LaPietra, 1989-91, Kapiolani Med. Ctr. at Pali Momi, 1994-98; bd. dirs. Aloha coun. Boy Scouts Am., 1998-2000, Alamo coun., Hawaii Pub. TV, 1998, bd. dirs., San Pedro Playhouse, 1999-2000; bd. dirs. Red Cross of San Antonio, 1999-2000; commr. Hawaii State Commn. on Status of Women, 1985-87, State Sesquecentennial of Pub. Schs. Commn., 1990-91. Named Advt. Woman of Yr., Honolulu Advt. Fedn., 1982, Pub. Rels. Profl. of Yr., Honolulu Pub. Rels. Soc., 1993, Communicator of Yr., Utilities Communicators Internat., 1983; recipient Silver Anvil award Pub. Rels. Soc. Am., 1983, 97. Mem. Internat. Pub. Rels. Assn. (Golden World award 1997), Am. Mktg. Assn., Pub. Rels. Soc. Am. (bd. dirs. Honolulu chpt. 1984-86, Silver Anvil award 1984, Pub. Rels. Profl. Yr. 1991), U. So. Calif. Alumni Assn. (bd. dirs. Hawaii 1981-83), Outrigger Canoe Club, Rotary (pub. rels. chmn. 1988-97, Honolulu chpt., bd. dirs. 1998), Rotary Club of San Antonio, Alpha Phi (past pres., dir. Hawaii), Hawaii Jaycees (Outstanding Young Person of Hawaii 1978).

SIMPSON, BERYL BRINTNALL, botany educator; b. Dallas, Apr. 28, 1942; d. Edward Everett and Barbara Frances (Brintnall) S.; children: Jonathan, Meghan. AB, Radcliffe Coll., 1964; MA, PhD, Harvard U., 1968. Rsch. fellow Arnold Arboretum/Gray Herbarium, Cambridge, Mass., 1969-71; curator Smithsonian Instn., Washington, 1971-78; prof. U. Tex., Austin, 1978—. Chmn. U.S. Com. to IUBS, 1985-88; co-pres. Internat. Congress Systematic and Evolutionary Biology, 1980-85. Author: Economic Botany, 1994, 3d edit., 2001; editor: Mesquite, 1977; contbr. over 160 articles and notes to profl. jours. Recipient Greenman award Mo. Bot. Garden, 1970. Fellow AAAS, Am. Acad. Arts and Sci.; mem. Soc. for Study Evolution (coun. 1975-80, pres. 1985-86), Bot. Soc. Am. (prs. 1990-91, Merit award 1992), Bot. Soc. Washington (v.p. 1975), Am. Soc. Plant Taxonomists (pres. 1994, Cooley award, Asa Gray award), Am. Inst. Biol. Scis. (bd. dirs. 1993-95), U.S.-Mex. Found. for Sci. (bd. govs.), Soc. Econ. Botany (pres. 1999). Office: 1 University Station A6700 Univ Tex Sect Integrative Biology Austin TX 78712

SIMPSON, CHAD W. pharmacist, educator; s. David Henry Simpson and Sharon Janine Park, Robert Frank Park, Jr. (Stepfather); life ptnr. C. S. Corning. BS in Pharmacy, Southwestern Okla. State U., 1996. Registered pharmacist Tex. Pharmacist Eckerd, San Antonio, 1996, Wal-Mart, 1996—98; pharmacy edn. coord. Bapt. St. Anthony's Health Sys., Amarillo, Tex., 1998—; instr. Amarillo Coll., 1999—2003. Mem. tech. adv. com. Amarillo Coll. Pharmacy, 1999—; bd. dirs. Tex. Soc. Health Sys. Pharmacists; mem. taskforce technician registration Tex. State Bd. Pharmacy. Author: (poster with abstract) Texas Society of Health System Pharmacists 53rd Annual Seminar, 2001. Mem.: Panhandle Soc. Health Sys. Pharmacists (pres. 2002—03), Tex. Soc. Health Sys. Pharmacists (vice-chair comm. coun. 2003—04, chair comm. coun. 2004—). Avocations: writing, cooking, reading. Office: Bapt Saint Anthony's Health Sys 1600 Wallace Blvd Amarillo TX 79106

SIMPSON, CHARLES R., III, judge; b. Cleve., July 8, 1945; s. Charles Ralph and Anne M. Simpson; married; 3 children. BA, U. Louisville, 1967, JD, 1970. Bar: Ky. 1970, U.S. Dist. Ct. (we. dist.) Ky. 1971, U.S. Cir. Ct. (6th cir.) 1985. With Rubin, Trautwein & Hays, Louisville, 1971-75, Levin, Yussman & Simpson, Louisville, 1975-77; judge U.S. Dist. Ct. (we. dist.) Ky., Louisville, 1986—; pvt. practice Louisville, 1977-86. Part-time staff counsel Jefferson County Judge/Exec., 1978-84; adminstr. Jefferson County Alcoholic Beverage Control, 1983-84; city clk. City of Rolling Fields, 1985-86. Roman Catholic. Office: We Dist Ct Ky 247 US Courthouse 601 W Broadway Louisville KY 40202-2238 E-mail: judgesimpson@kywd.vscourts.gov.

SIMPSON, CHARLES REAGAN, retired judge; b. Danville, Ill., June 16, 1921; s. Frank and Mamie (Moreland) S.; m. Ruth V. Thomason, June 5, 1948. BA with highest honors, U. Ill., 1944, JD with high honors, 1945; LL.M., Harvard U., 1950. Bar: Ill. 1945. Practiced in, Champaign, Ill., 1946-49; atty. OPS, 1951-52; with legislation and regulations div. Office Chief Counsel, IRS, 1952-65, dir. office, 1964-65; judge U.S. Tax Ct., 1965-88, ret., 1988. Teaching fellow Harvard Law Sch., 1950-51 Chmn. Champaign County chpt. Nat. Found. Infantile Paralysis, 1947-49; Mem. Ill. Gen. Assembly from 24th Dist., 1947-50. Recipient Justice Tom C. Clark award, Fed. Bar Assn., 1964. Mem. ABA, Am. Law Inst., Am. Judicature Soc., Phi Beta Kappa, Order of Coif, Phi Kappa Phi. Office: US Tax Ct 400 2nd St NW Washington DC 20217-0002 Personal E-mail: crsimpson2@comcast.net.

SIMPSON, CURTIS CHAPMAN, III, lawyer; b. Leonia, N.J., Apr. 19, 1952; s. Curtis Chapman Simpson Jr. and Marguerite (Johnson) Host; m. Joy D.; children: Ashley Blake, Curtis Chapman. BA, George Washington U., 1977; JD, Calif. Western U., 1980. Bar: Calif. 1981, U.S. Dist. Ct. (cen. dist.) Calif. 1983, U.S. Ct. Claims 1991. Pres. Curtis C. Simpson, III, P.C., Santa Barbara, Calif., 1981-84; assoc. Schurmer & Drane, Santa Barbara, 1984-90; prin. Curtis Simpson Law Offices, Santa Barbara, Oxnard, Calif., 1991—. Ct.-appointed arbitrator superior cts. Santa Barbara County, Ventura County, San Luis Obispo County, all Calif., 1991—; guest lectr. U. Calif., Santa Barbara, 1997. Contbr. to profl. jours. Co-chmn. youth group leader, coach Montecito YMCA, 1992, 97—; bd. dirs. Montecito Ednl. Found., 1993—; co-pres. Montecito Ednl. Found., 1994-97. Mem. Assn. Trial Lawyers Am., Consumer Attys. Calif. (cert. recognition 1991—), State Bar Calif., Santa Barbara County Bar Assn., Ventura County Bar Assn., Hon. Order Ky. Cols., Coral Casino Beach and Cabana Club. Episcopalian. Office: Ste 1-252 1187 Coast Village Rd Santa Barbara CA 93108-2761

SIMPSON, DANIEL H. ambassador; b. Wheeling, W.Va., July 9, 1939; married; 4 children. BA, Yale U., 1961; cert. in African studies, Northwestern U., 1973. Joined Fgn. Svc., U.S. Dept. State, Washington, 1966—, staff asst. Bur. Security and Consular Affairs, 1966-67, speech writer for asst. sec. state for African affairs, 1968, desk officer for Rhodesia, Botswana, Lesotho, and Swaziland, 1973-74; tng. officer USIA, Washington, 1967-68; polit., econ. and consular officer Am. Embassy, Bujumbura, Burundi, 1968-70, polit. officer Pretoria, Republic South Africa, 1970-72, dep. chief mission Beirut, until 1989; amb. to Cen. African Republic, Bangui, 1989-92; dep. comdr. Army War Coll., Carlisle, Pa., 1993-94; ambassador to Somalia Mogadishu, 1994-95; ambassador to Congo, 1995-98; v.p. Nat. Def. U., Washington, 1998-2000; regional dir. OSCE, Bosnia-Herzegovina, 2000—01; assoc. editor Pitts. Post-Gazette and Toledo Blade, 2001—. Address: Pitts Post-Gazette 34 Blvd of the Allies Pittsburgh PA 15222 Home: 112 Washington Pl #20A Pittsburgh PA 15219 E-mail: dsimpson@post-gazette.com.

SIMPSON, DANIEL REID, lawyer, mediator; b. Glen Alpine, N.C., Feb. 20, 1927; s. James R. and Margaret Ethel (Newton) S.; m. Mary Alice Leonard, Feb. 25, 1930; children: Mary Simpson Beyer, Ethel B. Simpson Todd, James R., II. BS, Wake Forest U., 1949, LLB, 1951. Bar: N.C. 1951, U.S. Dist. Ct. (we. dist.) N.C. 1951, U.S. Ct. Appeals (4th and 5th cirs.) 1980; cert. mediator. Former ptnr. Simpson Aycock PA, Morganton, N.C.; of counsel Simpson, Kuehnert, Vinay & Bellas, P.A., Morganton. Author: American Angels, 2001. Mem. N.C. Ho. of Reps., 1959-65; mem. N.C. Senate, 1984-96; del. Rep. Nat. Conv., 1968, 76; mem. N.C. Rep. Exec. Com. Served with AUS, 1943-45, PTO. Recipient Guardian Small Bus. award Order of Longleaf Pine; named to NRA Legion of Honor; sports complex named in his honor by Town of Glen Alpine, N.C. Mem. N.C. Bar Assn., Burke County Bar Assn., Masons. Baptist. Home: 2358 E Point Rd Nebo NC 28761-9694 Office: Simpson Kuehnert Vinay & Bellas PA 216 N Sterling St Morganton NC 28655 also: PO Box 1329 Morganton NC 28680-1329

SIMPSON, DAVID ALLEN, osteopath; b. Highland Park, Mich., Mar. 29, 1955; s. Fred Raymond and Mary Theresa (Rossi) S.; m. Anne M. Pawlak, Oct. 20, 1984. BS in Biology with distinction, Wayne State U., 1977, MS in Anatomy, 1979; DO, Kirksville Coll. Osteo. Medicine, 1983. Diplomate Am. Bd. Neurology and Psychiatry (examiner), Electrodiagnostic Medicine (examiner). Commd. 2d lt. U.S. Army, 1979, advanced through grades to maj., 1988; resident in neurology Botsford Gen. Hosp., Farmington Hills, 1988-91; staff neurologist Mich. Inst. for Neurologists, Farmington Hills, 1991—; asst. clin. prof. U. Mich., Mich. State U., 1991—. Dir. fellowship tng. in neuromuscular disease Mich. Inst. for Neurol. Disorder, U. Mich., MDA Clinic, Mich. State U.; co-dir. Muscular Dystrophy Clinic of Southeastern Mich., Mich. Inst. for Neurol. Disorders; physician Wheel-Chair Hockey League, 1999—; lectr. in field. Patentee in field; contbr. articles to profl. jours.; chief editor: Jour. of Am. Coll. of Neurologists and Psychiatrists. 2nd lt. USAR, 1979—84, with U.S. Army, 1988—97. Decorated Meritorious Svc. medal, DSM, Army Commendation medal, Humanitarian Svc. medal, Army Achievement medal, Good Conduct medal, Army Res. medal. Mem. Am. Osteo. Assn., Mich. Assn. Osteo. Physicians and Surgeons, Am. Coll. Neuropsychiatrists, Psi Sigma Alpha, Sigma Sigma Alpha. Roman Catholic. Avocation: golf. Home: 19550 Laurel Dr Livonia MI 48152-1141 Office: Mich Inst Neurologic Disord Dept Neurology Farmington Hills MI 48045 Office Phone: 248-553-0010. Personal E-mail: wchlphysician@msn.com.

SIMPSON, DAVID WILLIAM, artist, educator; b. Pasadena, Calif., Jan. 20, 1928; s. Frederick and Mary Adeline (White) S.; m. Dolores D. Debus, July 30, 1954; 1 stepchild, Gregory C. Vose; 1 child, Lisa C. B.F.A., Calif. Sch. Fine Arts, 1956; MA, San Francisco State Coll., 1958. Instr. art Am. River Jr. Coll., Sacramento, 1958-60, Contra Costa Jr. Coll., San Pablo, Calif., 1960-65; prof. art U. Calif., Berkeley, 1967-91, prof. emeritus, 1991—. Exhibited in one-man shows including Robert Elkon Gallery, NYC, 1961, 63, 64, San Francisco Mus. Art, 1967, Henri Gallery, Washington, 1968, Oakland Mus., 1978, Modernism, San Francisco, 1980-81, 84, 86, 2001, Sheldon Meml. Art Gallery, Lincoln, Nebr., 1990, Mincher/Wilcox Gallery, San Francisco, 1991, 92, 93, Angles Gallery, Santa Monica, Calif., 1991-92, 94, 99, Bemis Found., Omaha, Nebr., 1991, Anthony Ralph Gallery, NYC, 1992, John Berggruen Gallery, San Francisco, 1994, Charlotte Jackson Fine Art, Santa Fe, 1995, Laguna Art Mus., Laguna Beach, Calif., 1995 Haines Gallery, San Francisco, 1997, 99, 2004, Studio La Citta, Verona, Italy, 1998, 2002, Renate Schröder Gallery, Cologne, Germany, 2000-02, Artothek, Cologne, 2002, James Kelly Contemporary, Santa Fe, 2003; group shows include Mus. Modern Art, NYC, 1963, Carnegie Internat., Pitts., 1961-62, 66-67, LA Mus. Art, 1964, U. Ill., 1969, Expo '70, Osaka, Japan, 1970, Josly Art Mus., Omaha, 1970, John Berggruen Gallery, San Francisco, 1979, Angles Gallery, Santa Monica, 1988, 90, John Good Gallery, NY, 1992, John Berggruen Gallery, San Francisco, 1993, Cheryl Haines Gallery, San Francisco, 1996, Museo di Arte Moderna e Contemporanea, Trento, Italy, 1996, Studio La Citta, Verona, Italy, 1996, Llonja, Palma De Majorca, Spain, 1997, Museo Cantonale d'Arte, Lugano, Switzerland, 1997, Studio La Citta, Verona, Italy, 1997, Haines Gallery, San Francisco, 1997, Palazzo Ducale, Gubbio, Italy, 1999, Palazzo Ducale, Panza Della Gran Guardia, Verona, 2002; represented in permanent collections including Phila. Mus. Art, Nat. Collection Fine Arts, Washington, Seattle Art Mus., La Jolla (Calif.) Mus. Art, Mus. Modern Art, NYC, San Francisco Mus. Art, Oakland (Calif.) Mus., Panza Collection, Italy, Laguna Art Mus., Laguna Beach, Calif., U. Art Mus., Berkeley, Calif., Museo Cantonale d'Arte Lugano, Switzerland, Museo Di Arte Moderna e Contemporanea Di Trento e Roverato, Sassuolo, Panza Collection, Italy, Albright Knox Mus., Buffalo, N.Y. Home: 565 Vistamont Ave Berkeley CA 94708-1244 Office: U Calif Dept Art Berkeley CA 94720

SIMPSON, DENNIS DWAYNE, psychologist, educator; b. Lubbock, Tex., Nov. 9, 1943; s. Homer Arnold and Georgie Lee (Barrett) S.; m. Sherry Ann Johnson, Aug. 20, 1965; children: Jason Renn, Jeffrey Todd, Jennifer Lynn. BA, U. Tex., 1966; PhD, Tex. Christian U., 1970. Asst. prof. psychology Tex. Christian U., Ft. Worth, 1970-74, assoc. prof., 1974-79, prof., 1979-82, dir., prof., 1989—, S.B. Sells prof. psychology, 1992—; dir., prof. Tex. A&M U., College Station, 1982-89. Mem. sci. adv. bd. NICA Rsch. Ctrs., Washington, 1992—; mem. adv. bd. Nat. Drug Treatment Evaluation Studies, Washington, 1992—; cons. WHO, fgn. govts. regarding drug rsch. Mem. editl. bd. Am. Jour. Drug and Alcohol Abuse, Substance Abuse Treatment, Substance Use and Misuse; contbr. over 250 articles to profl. jours.; author: 9 books. Recipient Disting. Rsch. Achievement award Tex. Commn. on Alcohol and Drug Abuse, 1987; recipient numerous grants. Mem.: APA, Southwestern Psychol. Assn., Acad. for Health Svcs. Rsch. and Health Policy, The Coll. on Problems of Drug Dependence. Achievements include research emphasis on the process of treatment service delivery in relation to client attributes and how they related to retention rates, relapse and posttreatment outcomes; research in drug use in the workplace; organizational behavior and its role in transferring evidence-based innovations into practice in community-based treatment agencies as well as criminal justice settings; other areas. Office: Tex Christian U Inst Behavioral Rsch PO Box 298740 Fort Worth TX 76129-0001 Business E-Mail: ibr@tcu.edu.

SIMPSON, DOROTHY AUDREY, retired speech educator; b. Las Vegas, N.Mex., Feb. 29, 1944; d. Clyde Joseph and Audrey Shirley (Clements) Simpson; m. Gary Alan Beimer, May 13, 1972 (div. Apr. 1986); children: Laura Lea Beimer Mitchell, Rose Anne Colleen Beimer; m. Ian B. Croxton, Dec. 27, 1992 (div. Oct. 1993); m. Doyle W. Hauschulz, Feb. 23, 2001 (div. June 2003). BA, N.Mex. Highlands U., 1965; MS, U. Utah, 1968; EdD, U. N.Mex., 1989. Cert. secondary edn., N.Mex. Tchr. West Las Vegas (N.Mex.) H.S., 1966-67, Santa Rosa (N.Mex.) H.S., 1968-71, Questa (N.Mex.) Consol. Schs., 1972-73; prof. speech comm., assoc. dean coll. arts and scis. N.Mex. Highlands U., Las Vegas, 1975—2003, prof. emeritus, 2003—. Ednl. cons. Rancho Valmora, 2003—. Author: Hovels, Haciendas, and House Calls: The Life of Carl H. Gellenthien, M.D., 1986, Speaking for Life: A Speech Communication Guide for Adults, 1990, Wreck of the Destiny Train, 1993; From Pajarito to Lungchow, 2003. Active Calvary Bapt. Ch., Las Vegas, 1959—. Recipient Educator of Yr. award Pub. Svc. Co. of N.Mex., Albuquerque, 1990. Mem. P.E.O. Republican. Avocation: writing. Home: PO Box 778 Las Vegas NM 87701-0778

SIMPSON, FREDERICK JAMES, retired research administrator; b. Regina, Sask., Can., June 8, 1922; s. Ralph James and Lillian Mary (Anderson) S.; m. Margaret Christine Simpson, May 28, 1947 (dec. Apr. 2003); children: Christine Louise, Steven James, Leslie Coleen, Ralph Edwin, David Glen. B.Sc., U. Alta., Can., 1944, M.Sc. in Agr., 1946; PhD in Bacteriology, U. Wis., 1952. With Nat. Research Council Can., 1946-84; asst. dir. Atlantic Research Lab., Halifax, N.S., 1970-73, dir., 1973-84; sci. cons., 1985-90. Vis. scientist U. Ill., Urbana, 1955-56, vis. prof., 1964; mem. exec. council Atlantic Provinces Interuniv. Com. on Scis., 1976-79, chmn., 1981-84; pres. Fed. Inst. Mgmt., Halifax, 1981-82 Contbr. numerous articles to profl. jours. Treas. Lunburg Condominium Corp. No. 1, 1998—. Decorated Queen's Silver Anniversary medal. Fellow Royal Soc. of Arts (London); mem. Can. Soc. Microbiologists (hon., sec.-treas. 1969-70, v.p. 1971-72, pres. 1972-73), Nova Scotian Inst. Sci. (v.p. 1975-76, pres. 1977-78), Internat. Phycological Soc., Aquaculture Assn. Can., Sigma Xi. Mem. United Ch. of Canada.

SIMPSON, GEORGE TRUE, surgeon, educator; b. Aurora, Colo., Apr. 29, 1943; s. George True and Meryle Flora (Moore) S.; m. Sharon Louise Mason, Mar. 9, 1944; children: Amber-Louise Elizabeth, George True III. BA in History, LaSierra U., 1969; MD, Loma Linda U., 1973, MPH, 1975. Diplomate Am. Bd. Otolaryngology, Am. Bd. Laser Surgery, Nat. Bd. Med. Examiners. Surgery resident U. Ala. Hosp. & Clinics, Birmingham, 1973-75; surgeon Kalabo Hosp., Zambia, 1975; otolaryngology resident UCLA Head/Neck Surgery, L.A., 1975-78; pediatric otolaryngology fellow Children's Hosp, Boston, 1978-79; assoc. prof., acting chair Boston (Mass.) U., 1979-90; dir. dept. otolaryngology Boston (Mass.) City Hosp., 1979-90; otolaryngologist-in-chief U. Hosp., Boston, 1984-90; chmn. dept. otolaryngology SUNY, Buffalo, 1991-97, prof. otolaryngology, 1991—; chmn. dept. otolaryngology Sisters of Charity Hosp., Buffalo, 1991—96; pres. U. Head/Neck Surgery, Buffalo, 1991—96; chief head and neck surgery Buffalo VA Med. Ctr., 1995—. Cons. Ministry Pub. Health, State of Kuwait, 1976,

MIT, Cambridge, 1979—, Gillette Corp., Boston, 1984-90; pres. Boston City Hosp. Med. Staff, 1983, 85; bd. dirs. Voice Found. Sci. Adv., Phila.; chmn. otolaryngology sect. 10 Internat. Congress on Lasers in medicine and Surgery, Taipei, Taiwan, 1989; examiner Am. Bd. Otolaryngology, Chgo., 1992, 93, 94. Author: Lasers in Otolaryngology, 1985; author, editor: Textbook of General Medicine, 1987; editor: Lasers in Otolaryngology: OTOL Clinics of N.Am., 1990; contbr. articles to profl. jours. With U.S. Army, 1964-66. Recipient Caring Physician award Mass. Nursing Assn., Mass. Med. Assn., 1989. Fellow ACS, Am. Acad. Otolaryngology-Head/Neck Surgery (Honor award 1987), Am. Acad. Pediatrics, Am. Soc. Head/Neck Surgery, Am. Broncheosoph-agological, Am. Acad. Facial Plastic and Reconstructive Surgery, Am. Acad. Cosmetic Surgery, Royal Soc. Medicine, Am. Bd. Laser Surgery; mem. Am. Assn. Acad. Depts. Otolaryngology, Assn. for Rsch. in Otolaryngology, Soc. Univ. Otolaryngologist, Internat. Soc. for History Otolaryngology (sec./treas. 1984-87, v.p. 1987-89), Buffalo Otolaryngology Soc., Buffalo Canoe Club, Buffalo Club, Orchard Park Country Club, Alpha Omega Alpha. Avocations: medical history, personal computing, music, running, boating. Office: SUNY Buffalo-VA Med Ctr Dept Otolaryngology 3495 Bailey Ave Buffalo NY 14215-1129

SIMPSON, GERALD D. research scientist, consultant, educator; AB in Chemistry, U. Calif., Santa Barbara, 1964—66, PhD phys. chemistry, 1967—70. Rsch. assoc. Inst. of Molecular Biophysics, Fla. State U., Talla-hassee, 1970—73; mem. tech. staff Sci. Ctr., Rockwell Internat., Thousand Oaks, Calif., 1973—75; mem. tech. staff and acting mgr. laser physics & diagnostics Rocketdyne Divsn., Rockwell Internat., Canoga Park, Calif., 1975—80, Consulting rsch. scientist Cedars-Sinai Med. Ctr., Los Angeles, Calif., 1988—90. Author: (scientific research) Published in Journal of Chemical Physics, Molecular Photochemistry, Chemical Physics Letters, Optical Engineering, Clinical Chemistry, Journal of Analytical Toxicology, European Journal Clinical Chemistry Clinical Biochemistry. Mem.: Am. Assn. for Advancement of Sci. (AAAS). Green Party. Achievements include research in Carried out spectroscopy experiments on iodine molecule in collaboration with Professor Robert Mullikan, the theoretical chemist who received the Nobel Prize in Chemistry for molecular orbital theory; Experimental and theoretical contributions to excimer laser coronary artery angiolplasty program at Cedars-Sinai Medical Center Research Laboratories; Served as expert witness (pro bono) on more than 35 occasions, including a remand hearing for the New Jersey Supreme Court, 1989; development of ruby laser holography program at Rockewell Interat., 1977.

SIMPSON, H. RICHARD (DICK SIMPSON), retailer; b. Oct. 10, 1928; s. Bert M. and Violet K. (Mathias) S.; m. Marion Welty, 1950; children: Carla Sue, Barry Nelson, Richard Drew, Catherine Irene; m. Joan Rose Marshall, March 22, 1970; m. Charlotte S. Fox, Dec. 12, 1999. Student, U. Akron, 1949-50; BS, U. Md., 1955. Mgr. Tex. GMC, Detroit, 1959-62. Pres. Friendly Pontiac, Friendly Toyota, Derrick Chrysler, Simpson Oil Corp., Corp. S., Dick Tiger Homes, Austin, 1962-85, Simpson Hill Country Realty and Builders, 1989-2003. Served to lt. col. USAF, 1953-75; Korea. Decorated D.F.C., Air Medal. Mem. Soc. Automotive Engrs., Res. Officers Assn., Horseshoe Bay Yacht Club, Horseshoe Bay Country Club, Rotary Internat., Masons. Methodist. Office: PO Box 8186 Horseshoe Bay TX 78657-8186 Personal E-mail: dicksimpson_hsb@yahoo.com. E-mail: csinfinity@281.com.

SIMPSON, HUGH L. news correspondent, newswriter; b. Kingston, Jamaica, Jan. 17, 1942; s. Melville Herbert (Stepfather) and Aldina Poulton (Willis) Simpson; m. Stephanie Anna Harcken, Jan. 7, 1988; children: Star, Susan, Andrew(dec.). AA, Maui Cmty. Coll. Radio stringer WWRL, NYC, 1964; radio news reporter WMCA, NYC, 1964—68; press sec. for black media Robert F. Kennedy Presdl. Campaign, 1968; news writer WABC-TV, NYC, 1968; on-camera news reporter WCBS-TV, NYC, 1968—72; freelance Minn., SD and ND, 1973—. Mem.: Phi Theta Kappa.

SIMPSON, INDIA.ARIE, musician; b. Denver, Oct. 3, 1976; d. Ralph and Joyce Simpson, Gary Harris (Stepfather). Student, Savannah Coll. Art and Design. With Motown Records, 1999—. Musician: (recordings) Acoustic Soul, 1999 (Cert. Gold), (songs) Peaceful World (with John Mellencamp), Just Another Parade, Just Another Parade (with Cassandra Wilson), Good Man for film We Were Soldiers, (tour) Women in Hip-Hop and Soul, 2001, (recordings) Voyage to India (Gest R&B Album Grammy, 03); contbg. musician (compilation) Conceptions: Musical Tribute to Stevie Wonder, 2003. Nominee 7 Grammy awards, 2002; named Best New Artist, Vibe Mag., 2001, MTV2, 2001, Billboard Video Awards, 2001, Best R&B Female Artist, BET, 2002, Best Female R&B Artist, 2003; named one of Top 100 It Entertainers, Entertainment Weekly mag., 2001; recipient Essence award, 2002, Best Urban/Alternative Performance for Little Things, Grammy Awards, 2003. Office: Universal Music Enterprises Motown Records 2220 Colorado Ave Santa Monica CA 90404

SIMPSON, JACK BENJAMIN, medical technologist, business executive; b. Tompkinsville, Ky., Oct. 30, 1937; s. Benjamin Harrison and Verda Mae (Woods) S.; m. Winona Clara Walden, Mar. 21, 1957; children: Janet Lazann, Richard Benjamin, Randall Walden, Angela Elizabeth. Student, Western Ky. U., 1954-57; grad., Norton Infirmary Sch. Med. Tech., 1958. Asst. chief med. technologist Jackson County Hosp., Seymour, Ind., 1958-61; chief med. technologist, bus. mgr. Mershon Med. Labs., Indpls., 1962-66; founder, dir., officer Am. Monitor Corp., Indpls., 1966-77; founder, pres., dir. Global Data, Inc., Ft. Lauderdale, Fla., 1986—. Mng. ptnr. Astroland Enterprises, Indpls., 1968—, 106th St. Assocs., Indpls., 1969-72, Keystones Ltd., Indpls., 1970-82, Delray Rd. Assoc. Ltd., Indpls., 1970-71, Allisonville Assocs. Ltd., Indpls., 1970-82, Grandview Assocs. Ltd., 1977—, Rucker Assocs. Ltd., Indpls., 1974—; mng. ptnr. Raintree Assocs. Ltd., Indpls., 1978—, Westgate Assocs. Ltd., Indpls., 1978—; pres., dir. Topps Constrn. Co., Inc., Bradenton, Fla., 1973-91, Acrovest Corp., Asheville, N.C., 1980—; dir. Indpls. Broadcasting, Inc.; founder, bd. dirs. Bank of Bradenton, 1986-92; founder, CFO Biomass Processing Tech., Inc., West Palm Beach, Fla., 1996—; also bd. dirs. Mem. Am. Soc. Med. Technologists (cert.), Indpls. Soc. Med. Technologists, Fla. Soc. Med. Technologists, Am. Soc. Clin. Pathologists, Am. Assn. Clin. Chemistry, Royal Soc. Health (London), Internat. Platform Assn., Am. Mus. Natural History, Columbia of Indpls. Club, Harbor Beach Surf Club, Fishing of Am. Club, Marina Bay Club (Ft. Lauderdale), Elks. Republican. E-mail: jack_simpson@msn.com.

SIMPSON, JESSICA ANN, vocalist; b. Dallas, July 10, 1980; d. Joe and Tina Simpson; m. Nick Lachey, Oct. 26, 2002. Singer: (albums) Sweet Kisses, 1999, Irresistable, 2001, In This Skin, 2003; actor: (TV series) That '70s Show, 2003, Newlyweds: Nick and Jessica, 2003—; co-author: I Do: Achieving Your Dream Wedding, 2003; host: Saturday Night Live, 2004. Office: Top 40 Entertainment 156 West 56th St 5th Floor New York NY 10019

SIMPSON, JOANNE MALKUS, meteorologist; b. Boston, Mar. 23, 1923; d. Russell and Virginia (Vaughan) Gerould; m. Robert H. Simpson, Jan. 6, 1965; children by previous marriage: David Starr Malkus, Steven Willem Malkus, Karen Elizabeth Malkus. BS, U. Chgo., 1943, MS, 1945, PhD, 1949; DSc (hon.), SUNY, Albany, 1991. Instr. physics and meteorology Ill. Inst. Tech., 1946-49, asst. prof. 1949-51; meteorologist Woods Hole Oceanographic Instn., 1951-61; prof. meteorology UCLA, 1961-65; dir. exptl. meteorology lab. Nat. Oceanic & Atmospheric Adminstrn., 1965-74; prof. environ. scis. U. Va., Charlottesville, 1974-76. W.W. Corcoran prof. environ. scis., 1976-81; head Severe Storms br. Goddard Lab. Atmospheres, NASA, Greenbelt, Md., 1981-88, chief scientist for meteorology, 1988—; Goddard sr. fellow, earth scis. dir. Goddard Space Flight Ctr., NASA, 1988—; project scientist tropical rainfall measuring mission, 1986-98. Mem. Bd. on Atmospheric Scis. and Climate, NRC/NAS, 1990-93, 97-2000, Bd. on Geophys. and Environ. Data, 1993-96, com. on climate, ecosystems, infectious diseases and human health, 1998-2000; mem. sr. adv. bd. NOAA, 1998-2003. Author: (with Herbert Riehl) Cloud Structure and Distributions Over the Tropical Pacific Ocean; assoc. editor: Revs. Geophysics and Space Physics, 1964-72, 75-77; contbr. articles to profl. jours. Mem. Fla. Gov.'s Environ. Coordinating Coun., 1971-74. Recipient Disting. Authorship award NOAA, 1969, Silver medal Dept. Commerce, 1967, Gold medal, 1972, Vincent J. Schaefer award Weather

Modification Assn., 1979, Cmty. Headliner award Women in Comm., 1973, Profl. Achievement award U. Chgo. Alumni Assn., 1975, 92, Lifetime Achievement award Women in Sci. Engring. 1990, Exceptional Sci. Achievement award NASA, 1982, William Nordberg award NASA, 1994, NASA Medal Outstanding Leadership, 1998, I.M.O. prize World Meteorol. Orgn., 2002, U.S. Gov. Presdl. Rank award, 2003; named Woman of Yr. L.A. Times, 1963; Guggenheim fellow, 1954-55, Goddard Sr. fellow, 1988—. Fellow Am. Geophys. Union, Am. Meterol. Soc. (mem. coun. 1975-77, 79-81, mem. exec. com. 1977, 79-81, commr. sci. and tech. activities 1982-88, pres.-elect 1988, pres. 1989, publs. commr. 1992-98, hon. mem. 1995, Meisinger award 1962, Rossby Rsch. medal 1983, Charles Franklin Brooks award 1992, Charles E. Anderson award 2001), World Meterol. Orgn. (IMO prize 2002), Explorers Club, Nat. Acad. Engring.; mem. Royal Meteorol. Soc. (hon.), Cosmos Club, Phi Beta Kappa, Sigma Xi. Home: 540 N St SW Washington DC 20024-4557 Office: NASA Goddard Space Flight Ctr Earth Scis Greenbelt MD 20771-0001 Personal E-mail: nasajoanne@earthlink.net. Business E-Mail: simpson@agnes.gsfc.nasa.gov.

SIMPSON, JOE LEIGH, obstetrics and gynecology educator; b. Birmingham, Ala., Apr. 4, 1943; s. Robert S. and Winnie (Leigh) S.; m. Sandra A. Carson, May 6, 1978; children: Scott, Reid MD, Duke U., 1968. Diplomate Am. Bd. Ob-Gyn, Am. Bd. Med. Genetics. Fellow in ob-gyn Cornell Med. Coll., N.Y.C., 1968-73; clin. assoc. N.Y. Blood Ctr., N.Y.C., 1969-73; asst. clin. prof. ob-gyn U. Tex., San Antonio, 1973-75; assoc. prof., head ob-gyn Northwestern U. Med. Sch., Chgo., 1975-79, prof. ob-gyn, 1979-86; Faculty prof. chmn. dept. ob-gyn U. Tenn., Memphis, 1986-94; Ernst W. Bertner chmn. and prof. dept. ob-gyn., prof. dept. molecular and human genetics Baylor Coll. of Medicine, Houston, 1994—. Mem. genetics grant rev. and adv. bd. HHS, 1979-82; mem. clin. rsch. panel March of Dimes, 1986-94, chmn. adv. panel reproductive hazards, 1988-92; mem. sci. adv. bd., 1994—; mem. accreditation coun. grad. med. edn. Residency Rev. Com. Med. Genetics, 1993-98; mem. adv. com. Nat. Inst. Child Health and Devel., 1994-97. Author: Disorders of Sexual Development, 1976; author: (with others) Genetics in Obstetrics and Gynecology, 1982, 3d edit., 2003, Obstetrics: Normal and Problem Pregnancies, 1986, 4th edit., 2001; co-editor: Genetic Diseases in Pregnancy, 1981, Material Serum Screening for Fetal Genetic Disorders, 1992, Essentials of Prenatal Diagnosis, 1993; contbr. articles to profl. jours. and chpts. to books. Maj. U.S. Army, 1973-75. Recipient numerous awards Nat. Insts. Child Health and Devel., March of Dimes, Wyeth-Ayerest pub. recognition award Assn. Profs. Ob-Gyn, 1992. Fellow ACOG (chmn. genetics subcom. 1981-84), Am. Coll. Med. Genetics (treas. 1996-02), Royal Coll. Obstetricians and Gynecologists (hon.); mem. NAS, Inst. Medicine, Am. Gynecol. and Obstet. Soc. (mem. coun. 1997-99), Am. Soc. Reproductive Medicine (bd. dirs. 1984-87, pres. 1993-94), Soc. Gynecologic Investigation (pres. 1998-99, mem. coun., Pres.'s Achievement award 1986, Pres. Disting. Scientist award 2002), Soc. Advancement Contraception (pres. 1995-98), Am. Soc. Human Genetics (mem. program com. 1988-91), Internat. Soc. Prenatal Diagnosis (pres. 1994-98), Preimplantation Genetic Diagnosis Internat. Soc. (bd. dirs. 2003—). Office: Baylor Coll Medicine Dept Ob/Gyn 6550 Fannin St Ste 901 Houston TX 77030-2717

SIMPSON, JOHN AROL, retired government executive, physicist; b. Toronto, Ont., Can., Mar. 30, 1923; came to U.S., 1926; naturalized, 1938; s. Henry George and Verna Lavinia (Green) S.; m. Arlene Badel, Feb. 11, 1948; 1 child, George Badel. BS, Lehigh U., 1946, MS, 1948, PhD, 1951. Rsch. physicist Nat. Bur. Standards, Washington, 1948-62, supervisory physicist, 1962-69, dep. chief optical physics div., 1969-75, chief mechanics div., 1975-78, dir. Ctr. for Mfg. Engring. Gaithersburg, Md., 1978-91; dir. Mfg. Engring. Lab., Nat. Inst. Standards and Tech., Gaithersburg, 1991—; ret. Contbr. articles on electron optics to profl. jours. With U.S. Army, 1943-46. Recipient Silver medal Dept. Commerce, 1964, Gold medal, 1975; Allen V. Austin Measurement Sci. award, 1984; Disting. Exec. award Sr. Exec. Svc., 1985, Am. Machinist award, 1986. Fellow Am. Phys. Soc.; mem. NAE, Sigma Xi. Home: 312 Riley St Falls Church VA 22046-3310

SIMPSON, JOHN BARCLAY, academic administrator; b. Oakland, Calif., June 8, 1947; s. Barclay and Joan (Devine) S.; children: Matthew, Melissa. BA, U. Calif., Santa Barbar, 1969; MA, Northwestern U., 1972, PhD, 1973. Research assoc. U. Pa., Phila., 1973-75; from asst. prof. to prof. psychology U. Wash., Seattle, 1975—98, dir. physiology-psychology program, 1984-88, head of the physiological psychology area, 1986—90, assoc. dean for computing, rsch. and facilities, 1991—94, dean of College of Arts and Sciences, 1994—98; exec. vice chancellor, provost U. Calif., Santa Cruz, 1998—2003; president U. at Buffalo, SUNY, 2004—. Vis. researcher U. Calif., San Franicsco, 1976-80; vis. prof. Howard Florey Inst. U. Melbourne, Australia, 1983. Contbr. articles to profl. jours. Recipient Eugene NIH, 1974—. Mem. AAAS, Soc. for Neurosci., Soc. Study Ingestive Behavior. Avocations: mountain climbing, skiing, sailing, bicycling. Office: U at Buffalo 501 Capen Hall Buffalo NY 14260-1600

SIMPSON, JOHN M. lawyer; b. Ponca City, Okla., Sept. 26, 1950; AB, Harvard U., 1972; JD, Columbia U., 1978. Bar: D.C. 1979, N.C. 1988. Mem. Fulbright & Jaworski L.L.P., Washington. Office: Fulbright & Jaworski LLP Market Square 801 Pennsylvania Ave NW Washington DC 20004-2615 E-mail: jsimpson@fulbright.com.

SIMPSON, JOHN NOEL (VIRGINIA SIMPSON), healthcare administrator; b. Durham, N.C., Feb. 27, 1936; m. Virginia Marshall, June 27, 1959; children: John Noel, William M. Asst. adminstr. Riverside Health Sys., Newport News, Va., 1962-65, assoc. adminstr., 1965-70, Richmond (Va.) Meml. Hosp., 1970-74, sr. v.p., adminstr., 1974-77, exec. v.p., 1977-80, pres., 1980-85, Health Corp. Va., 1985-96; chmn. bd. Bon Secours-Richmond Health System, 1996-97, regional v.p., CEO, 1997-2000, divisional cons., 2000—. Preceptor Sch. Health Adminstrn. Duke U. and Med. Coll. Va., Washington U., St. Louis; bd. dirs. Sun Health, Inc./Sun Alliance, 1979-92, vice-chmn., 1984, chmn., 1985-87; vice-chmn. Med./Bus. Coalition, 1981-83; participant Leadership Met. Richmond; bd. dirs. Ctrl. Va. Health Sys. Agy., 1980-84, Richmond chpt. ARC, 1980-83; mem. Va. Bd. Med. Assistance, 1980-84; mem. joint subcom. studying Va. med. malpractice laws divsn. legal svcs. Gen Assembly of Comm. of Va., 1984; chmn. Va. Health Network, 1989-91; chmn. Hanover Bus. Coun., 1994-95; mem. Gov. Regional Econ. Devel. Adv. Coun., 1994-95. Served with Med. Svc. Corps U.S. Army, 1959-62. Fellow Am. Coll. Healthcare Execs. (Coun. of Regents 1976-82, Edgar C. Hayhow award 1976, bd. govs. 1990-94, regents award sr. exec. level 1995). Fellow Am. Coll. Healthcare Execs. (coun. of regents 1976-82, Edgar C. Hayhow award 1976, bd. govs. 1990-94, regents award sr. exec. level 1995); mem. Am. Hosp. Assn. (chmn. RPBIII 1994-97, del. 1989-93, mem. bd. trustees 1994-97, Va. Hosp. Assn. (chmn. 1984-85, Disting. Svc. award 1998), Va. Ins. Reciprocal (chmn. 1977-79), Met. Richmond C. of C. (bd. dirs.), Richmond Acad. Medicine (Disting. Svc. award 2000). Republican. Presbyterian. Office Phone: 804-379-2930. Personal E-mail: JSIMP22736@aol.com.

SIMPSON, JOHN S. former finance executive; Grad., U. Minn.; postgrad., Harvard U., U. Wis., U. Calif. Univ. Calif. Seco Electronics-Dana Corp., 1973-76; treas. Indsl. Power Transmission Divsn.-Dana Corp., 1976-78; contr. Perfect Circle Products Divsn.-Dana Corp., 1978-82; dir. internat. fin. Dana Corp., 1982-85; v.p. fin. Warner Electric, 1985-87; pres. Diamond Savs. & Loan, 1987-92, Dana Asia Pacific, 1992-96; v.p. fin., treas. Dana Corp., 1996-97, CFO, 1997-99; ret., 1999. Trustee Siena Heights Coll., Adrian, Mich. Mem. Fin. Execs. Inst. Office: Dana Corp PO Box 1000 Toledo OH 43697-1000

SIMPSON, JOHN WISTAR, energy consultant, former manufacturing company executive; b. Glenn Springs, S.C., Sept. 25, 1914; s. Richard Caspar and Mary (Berkeley) S.; m. Esther Slattery, Jan. 17, 1948; children: John Wistar, Carter B., Patricia A., Barbara J. Student, Wofford Coll., 1932-33, DSc, 1972; BS, U.S. Naval Acad., 1937; MS, U. Pitts., 1941; DSc (hon.), Seton Hill Coll., 1970. With Westinghouse Electric Corp., 1937-77; mgr. Navy and Marine switchboard engring., switchgear div., on leave as mgr. nuclear engring. Daniels pile group, Oak Ridge Nat. Lab., successively as Westing-

house Electric Corp. (Bettis Atomic Power div.), 1949-58; v.p. Westinghouse Electric Corp.; gen. mgr. Westinghouse Electric Corp. (Bettis atomic power lab.), 1958-59, v.p., gen. mgr. atomic power divs., 1959-62, v.p. engring. and research, 1962-63, v.p. electric utility group, 1963-69, pres. power systems, corp. exec. v.p., dir., 1971-77; chmn. bd. Internat. Energy Assocs. Ltd., 1976-80; pres. Simpson Bus. Services, Inc., 1980-86; v.p. Sea Pines Assocs., Hilton Head Island, S.C., 1989-91, also bd. dirs., 1987-91; bd. dirs. Sea Pines Real Estate Cos., Hilton Head Island, S.C., 1987-91. Pvt. energy cons.; mem. adv. bd. Lawrence Livermore Nat. Lab. Radiation, 1975-88; mem. Naval Tech. Mission to Japan, 1945; del. 1st Internat. Conf. on Peaceful Uses Atomic Energy, Geneva, Switzerland, 1955, Conf. on Peaceful Uses Atomic Energy (2d Internat. Conf.), 1958; chmn. Atomic Indsl. Forum, 1974-75; mem. energy research adv. bd. Dept. Energy, 1981-83; chmn. com. on outlook for fusion hybrid and tritium breeding fusion reactors NRC; mem. sci. adv. bd. Notre Dame, 1974-86. Author: Nuclear Power from Underseas to Outer Space, 1994. Mem. governing bd. Nat. Coun. Chs., 1979-81; trustee Seton Hall Coll., 1969-76, Point Park Coll., 1973—, Wofford Coll., 1973-87. Recipient Navy cert. of merit for civilian svc. in World War II, 1947, Gold medal for advancement of rsch. Am. Soc. Metals, 1973, Disting. Alumnus award U. Pitts., 1975. Fellow IEEE (Edison medal 1971), ASME (hon. mem., George Westinghouse Gold medal 1975), Am. Nuclear Soc. (pres. 1973, Henry Dewolf Smyth Nuclear Statesman award 1997); mem. Nat. Acad. Engring., Franklin Inst. (Newcomen Gold medal), Rolling Rock Club (Ligonier, Pa.), Daufuskie Island Club, Bear Creek Golf Club, Sea Pines Club (Hilton Head, S.C.). Home and Office: 36 E Beach Lagoon Rd Hilton Head Island SC 29928-5714 *The guiding principles of my career have been to work in an area I considered to be of major importance, to have the most competent people working for me, to know enough technically that I could properly evaluate performance and, as far as possible, always make my position clear to all.*

SIMPSON, LISA ANN, physician, educator; b. Lagos, Nigeria, Feb. 9, 1958; (parents Am. citizens); d. Howard Russell and Mary Alice (Turner) Simpson; m. Richard L. Wittenberg; children: Ethan Simpson Wittenberg, Sydney Simpson Wittenberg. MB, B of Surgery, Trinity Coll., Dublin, Ireland, 1981; MPH, U. Hawaii, 1986. Diplomate Am. Bd. Pediat. Resident in pediat. U. Hawaii, Honolulu, 1982-85; resident in preventive medicine U. NC, Chapel Hill, 1987-88; dir. Maternal and Child Health Bur. State Dept. Health, Honolulu, 1988-90, acting dir. family health svcs. divsn., 1990; policy advisor Office of Asst. Sec. for Health HHS, Washington, 1993-94; sr. advisor Agy. for Health Care Policy and Rsch. Rockville, Md., 1994-95, acting dep. adminstr. Agy. for Health Care Policy and Rsch., 1995-96, dep. adminstr. Agy. for Health Care Policy and Rsch., 1996-99, dep. dir. Agy. Healthcare Rsch. and Quality, 1999—2002; prof., All Children's Hosp. Guild endowed chair child health policy pediat. U. South Fla., St. Petersburg, 2003—. Mid-career fellow Inst. Health Policy Studies, San Francisco, 1991-93; adj. faculty dept. health policy and mgmt. Johns Hopkins U., Balt., 1995—; vis. prof. U. Wash., 2000, U. Mich., 2000. Mem. editl. bd. Future Children, Maternal and Child Health Jour., 1996-2003; contbr. articles to profl. jours. Recipient Preventive Medicine traineeship Pub. Health Svc., 1986, Sec. Disting. Svcs. award Dept. HHS, 2000, Dir. Disting. Svc. award AHRQ, 2001, Meritorious Rank SES Presdl. award, 2002. Fellow: Am. Acad. Pediat. (Excellence in Pub. Svc. award 2002); mem.: APHA (governing coun. 1994—96), Nat. Acad. for Social Ins., Ambulatory Pediat. Assn., Acad. Health. Avocations: hiking, cuisine, gardening. Address: 4321 Columbus Way S Saint Petersburg FL 33712-4124 Office Phone: 727-553-3672. Business E-Mail: lsimpso1@hsc.usf.edu.

SIMPSON, LOUIS A. insurance company executive; b. Chgo., Dec. 23, 1936; s. Irving and Lillian (Rubin) S.; m. Margaret Rowley, Dec. 16, 1959; children: Irving, Kenneth, Edward Student, Northwestern U., 1954-55; BA, Ohio Wesleyan U., 1958; AM, Princeton U., 1960. Instr. econs. Princeton U., 1961-62; assoc., ptnr. Stein Roe & Farnham, Chgo., 1962-69; v.p. Shareholders Mgmt., Los Angeles, 1969-70; sr. v.p., exec. v.p., pres. Western Asset Mgmt., Los Angeles, 1970-79; vice chmn. bd. Geico Corp., Washington, 1979-93, pres., chief exec. officer capital ops., 1993—. Bd. dirs. AT & T, Pacific Am. Income Shares, Western Asset Funds, Inc., HNC Software, ResMed, Inc. Mem. endowments com. Ohio Wesleyan U.; trustee Woodrow Wilson Nat. Fellowship, Cate Sch. Woodrow Wilson fellow, 1958 Mem. San Diego Soc. Fin. Analysts, Calif. Club, Arts Club Chgo., Chevy Chase Club, Met. Club. Episcopalian. Office: Geico Corp 1 Geico Plz Washington DC 20076-0005

SIMPSON, LOUIS ASTON MARANTZ, English educator, author; b. Jamaica, W.I., Mar. 27, 1923; s. Aston and Rosalind (Marantz) S.; m. Jeanne Claire Rogers, 1949 (div. 1954); 1 child, Louis Matthew; m. Dorothy Mildred Roochvarg, 1955 (div. 1979); children: Anne Borovoi, Anthony Rolf; m. Miriam Butensky Bachner, 1985 (div. 1998). Higher schols. certificate, Munro Coll., Jamaica, 1939; BS, Columbia U., 1948, A.M., 1950, PhD, 1959; D.H.L., Eastern Mich. U., 1977; DLitt, Hampden Sydney Coll., 1990. Editor Bobbs-Merrill Pub. Co., N.Y.C., 1950-55; instr. Columbia U., 1955-59; prof. English U. Calif., Berkeley, 1959-67, SUNY, Stony Brook, 1967-91, Disting. prof., 1991—. Author: (poems) The Arrivistes, 1949, Good News of Death, 1955, A Dream of Governors, 1959, At the End of the Open Road, 1963 (Pulitzer prize for poetry 1964), Selected Poems, 1965, Adventures of the Letter I, 1971, Searching for the Ox, 1976, Caviare at the Funeral, 1980, The Best Hour of the Night, 1983, People Live Here: Selected Poems 1949-83, 1983, Collected Poems, 1988, In the Room We Share, 1990, Jamaica Poems, 1993, There You Are, 1995, (translation) Nombres et poussière, 1996, Modern Poets of France, 1997, Kaviar på begravningen, 1998, François Villon: The Legacy and The Testament, The Owner of the House, New Collected Poems, 1940-2001, (prose) Riverside Drive, 1962, James Hogg: A Critical Study, 1962, North of Jamaica, 1972, Three on the Tower: The Lives and Works of Ezra Pound, T.S. Eliot and William Carlos Williams, 1975, A Revolution in Taste: Studies of Dylan Thomas, Allen Ginsberg, Sylvia Plath and Robert Lowell, 1978, A Company of Poets, 1981, The Character of the Poet, 1986, Selected Prose, 1989, Ships Going into the Blue, 1994, The King My Father's Wreck, 1995; editor: The New Poets of England and America, 1957, An Introduction to Poetry, 1967. Served with AUS, 1943-45. Decorated Purple Heart, Bronze Star with oak leaf cluster; Hudson Rev. fellow, 1957, Guggenheim fellow, 1962, 70; Am. Coun. Learned Socs. grantee, 1963; recipient Prix de Rome, 1957, Millay award, 1960, Distinguished Alumnus award Columbia U., 1960, medal for excellence Columbia U., 1965; American Acad. of Arts and Letters award in literature, 1976; Centenary medal Inst. of Jamaica, 1980, Jewish Book Coun. award for poetry, 1981, Elmer Holmes Bobst award, 1987, Harold Morton Landon award for translation, 1997. Fellow Am. Acad. in Rome. Home: PO Box 119 Setauket NY 11733-0119

SIMPSON, LYLE LEE, lawyer; b. Des Moines, Oct. 15, 1937; s. R. Clair and Martha B. (Accola) S. BA, Drake U., 1960, JD, 1963. Bar: Iowa 1963, U.S. Dist. Ct. (so. and no. dists.) Iowa 1963, U.S. Ct. Appeals (8th cir.) 1963, U.S. Tax Ct. 1963, U.S. Supreme Ct. 1970, U.S. Ct. Mil. Appeals 1972. Pvt. practice, Des Moines, 1963—; mem. Beving and Swanson, Des Moines, 1964-68; sr. ptnr. Peddicord, Simpson & Sutphin, Des Moines, 1968-83; pres. Dreher, Simpson & Jensen, PC, 1984—. Gen. counsel campaign com. Gov. Iowa, 1978-98. Contbr. articles to profl. jours. Chmn. bd. trustees Broadlawns Med. Ctr., 1974-80; mem. Iowa Inaugural Com., 1983, 87, 89, 91, 95; bd. dirs. YMCA Boys Camp, 1967-86, Home, Inc., 1981-85; Project H.E.L.P.E.R., 1983-87, Batten Found.; pres., bd. dirs. Polk County Health Svcs., 1972-88; chmn. Iowa Health Facilities Coun., 1988-93; pres. First Unitarian Ch., 1958-70, Iowa Humanities Bd., 1988-94, Humanist Found., 1980—, East High Alumni Found., 1992-2000; treas. Iowa Humanities Found., 1994-99; chmn. Iowa Health Found., 1993—; mem. investment com., fin. com. Iowa Health Sys., 2000—. Recipient Oren E. Scott award, Class of 1915 award in liberal arts Drake U., 1960. Mem. ABA, Iowa Bar Assn., Polk County Bar Assn., Am. Arbitration Assn., Am. Humanist Assn. (pres. 1979-89), Prairie Club (pres. 1992), Morning Club (pres. 1965), Le Chevaliers de vin Club (pres. 1976-85), YMCA Heritage Club (pres.), Masons, Scottish Rite (Shriner, 33 degree), Rotary. Republican. Congregationalist. Address: 222 Equitable Bldg 604 Locust St Des Moines IA 50309-3723 E-mail: lsimpson@dreherlaw.com.

SIMPSON, MARY MICHAEL, priest, psychotherapist; b. Evansville, Ind., 1925; d. Link Wilson and Mary Garrett (Price) S. BA, BS, Tex. Women's U., 1946; grad., N.Y. Tng. Sch. Deaconesses, 1949, Westchester Inst. Tng. in Psychoanalysis and Psychotherapy, 1976; S.T.M., Gen. Theol. Seminary, 1982. ordained priest Episcopal Ch., 1977. Missionary Holy Cross Mission, Bolahun, Liberia, 1950-52; mem. Order of St. Helena, 1952—; acad. head Margaret Hall Sch., Versailles, Ky., 1958-61; sister in charge Convent of St. Helena, Bolahan, 1962-67, dir. novices, 1968-74; pastoral counselor on staff St. John the Divine, N.Y.C., 1974-87, canon residentiary, canon counselor, 1977-87, hon. canon, 1988—. Pvt. practice psychoanalyst, 1974—; dir. Cathedral Counseling Svc., 1975-87; cons. psychotherapist Union Theol. Seminary, 1980-83; bd. dirs. Westchester Inst. Tng. in Psychoanalysis and Psychotherapy, 1982-84; priest-in-charge St. John's Ch., Wilmot, New Rochelle, N.Y., 1987-88; trustee Coun. Internat. and Pub. Affairs, 1983-87;interim pastor St. Michael's Ch., Manhattan, 1992-94; cons. Diocese of N.Y., 1990—. Author: The Ordination of Women in the American Episcopal Church: The Present Situation, 1981; contbg. author: Yes to Women Priests, 1978. Mem. Nat. Assn. Advancement of Psychoanalysis, N.Y. State Assn. Practicing Psychotherapists, N.Y. Soc. Clin. Psychologists. Home and Office: 151 E 31st St Apt 8H New York NY 10016-9502 Office Phone: 212-951-4316.

SIMPSON, MICHAEL, metals service center executive; b. Albany, N.Y., Dec. 10, 1938; s. John McLaren Simpson and Constance (Hasler) Ames; m. Barbara Ann Bodtke, Jan. 5, 1963; children: Leslie Ann, Elizabeth S. Wessel. BA, U. Mich., 1965, MBA, 1966. Product mgr. Armour & Co., Chgo., 1966-68; with A.M. Castle & Co., Franklin Park, Ill., 1968—, pres. Hy-Alloy Steels Co. divsn., 1974-79, v.p. Midwestern region, 1977-79, chmn. bd., 1979—2004, also bd. dirs., chmn. emeritus, 2004—. Trustee Rush U. Med. Ctr., Chgo., 1978—, mem. exec. com., 1980—, vice chmn., 1991—; trustee Oldfields Sch., Glencoe, Md., 1982-87, 95-2003, chmn. bd., 1998-2000; bd. dirs. Lake Forest (Ill.) Hosp. Found. and Lake Forest Hosp., 1998—; chmn. bd. overseers Rush U., Chgo., 1996-. Office: AM Castle & Co 3400 N Wolf Rd Franklin Park IL 60131-1319 Home: 30 N Western Ave Lake Forest IL 60045 E-mail: msimpson@amcastle.com.

SIMPSON, MICHAEL HOMER, dermatologist; b. Hamilton, Tex., Mar. 8, 1938; s. Edgar Randell and Lucille (Patterson) S.; m. Bertha Delia Meraz. BA, N. Tex. U., 1959; MD, U. Tex. S.W. Med. Sch., 1963. Diplomate Am. Bd. Dermatology. Intern Dallas VA Hosp., 1963-64; resident in dermatology U. Tex. Med. Br., Galveston, 1966-69; pvt. practice dermatology El Paso, Tex., 1970—. Capt. USAF., 1964-66. Office: 1501 Arizona Ave Ste 1A El Paso TX 79902-5089

SIMPSON, MICHAEL K. congressman; b. Burley, Idaho, Sept. 8, 1950; m. Kathy Johnson, 1971. Student, Utah State U.; DDS, Washington U., St. Louis, 1978. Dentist, Blackfoot, Idaho, 1978—; mem. from 2d Idaho dist. U.S. Ho. Reps., Washington, 1999—; mem. house approp. com. Serves on Agr., Resources, Transp. and Infrastructure and Veterans Affairs coms. Served as spkr. majority caucus chmn. and asst. majority leader in the Idaho Ho. Reps.Elected to U.S. Ho. Reps. in 1998, when 3-term Rep. Michael Crapo was elected to the U.S. Senate. Elected to Blackfoot City Coun., 1980, Idaho Ho. Reps., 1984; asst. majority leader, 1989-91; spkr. of the house, 1991-97. Mem. Idaho's Rep. Party Hall of Fame. Recipient Friend of Edn. award, 1994, Citizen of the Yr. award Idaho Family Forum, 1996, Boyd A. Martin award Assn. Idaho Cities. Mem. Idaho State Dental Assn. (Pres.'s award 1998), Am. Legis. Exch. Coun. (state chmn., nat. bd. dirs., Jefferson award 1994). Republican. Avocations: golf, chess, painting. Office: US Ho Reps 1339 Longworth Hob Washington DC 20515-0001

SIMPSON, MICHAEL MARCIAL, science specialist, consultant; b. Honolulu, Sept. 24, 1954; s. Marcial Tolentino and Beatrice (Martin) S. AB in Biol. Scis., U. Calif., Berkeley, 1976; MS in Biol. Scis., U. San Francisco, 1977; MS in Energy and Resources, U. Calif., Berkeley, 1979; PhD in Environ. Scis. and Engring., UCLA, 1986. Assoc. researcher NASA, Moffett Field, Calif., 1973; radio program host, producer Sta. KUSF-FM, San Francisco, 1976-78; rsch. asst. Lawrence Berkeley Lab., Berkeley, Calif., 1977-79; rsch. assoc. UCLA/U.S. Dept. Energy, 1979-81; congl. fellow, environ. health U.S. Congress, Washington, 1981-82; head biomed. policy sect. U.S. Congl. Rsch. Svc., Washington, 1982—, specialist in environ. techs., terrorism and life scis., environ. technologies and terrorism, 1982—. Adv. bd. Banbury Ctr., Cold Spring Harbor, N.Y., 1985—; adj. faculty The Washington Ctr., 1992—. Contbr. articles to profl. jours. Fellow AAAS (Named Congl. Sci. fellow 1981-82); mem. Washington Acad. Sci., Library of Congress Profl. Assn., UCLA in Washington (exec. steering com. 1986-92). Avocations: photography, bicycle touring, short story writing, travel. Office: US Congl Rsch Svc Crs Rsi Lm423 Washington DC 20540-7450 Business E-Mail: msimpson@crs.loc.gov.

SIMPSON, MIKE, talent agent; Co-head William Morris Agy., Beverly Hills, Calif. Office: William Morris Agy 151 S El Camino Dr Beverly Hills CA 90212-2775

SIMPSON, MINNIE PEACH, interior designer; b. Kinston, N.C., Apr. 8, 1949; d. Michael Joseph and Margie (Philips) Peach; m. John Wimberly Simpson, Aug. 1974 (div. Dec. 1980). BFA in Interior Design, U. Ga., 1973. Interior designer Hinson Galleries, Columbus, Ga., 1974-79; interior designer, sales rep. Crabapple Galleries, 1980-81; interior designer kitchen and bath design Larry Bussey, Inc., 1981-85; mem. staff sales/designer dept. Mansours, 1985-86; mgr. interior design/space planning AFLAC, 1986—2004; interior design cons., 2004—. Coord. March of Dimes, Columbus, 1993-96, Salisbury Fair, Columbus, 1996, Volunteers for Corta, Vol. for Allied Cats of Columbus, 2003. Mem. U.S. Tennis Assn., Am. Soc. Interior Designers, Internat. Interior Design Assn., Columbus Regional Tennis Assn. (mem. corta bd., 1999-2001). Avocations: tennis, crafts, antiquing. Home: 7157 Village Loop Columbus GA 31904

SIMPSON, MURRAY, electrical engineer, consultant; b. N.Y.C., July 27, 1921; s. George and Sonia (Vernov) Simpson; m. Ethel Gladstein, June 29, 1947; children: Anne Simpson Ozsan, David, Mindy, Jonathan. BEE, CCNY, 1942; MEE, Polytech. Inst. of N.Y., 1952. Engr. ITT, N.Y.C., 1942-44; sr. engr. Raytheon Co., Waltham, Mass., 1946-48; sect. mgr. Fairchild Guided Missles div., Farmingdale, NY, 1948-50; v.p. Maxson Elec. Co., N.Y.C., 1950-62; pres. SEDCO Sys. Inc. subs. Raytheon Co., Melville, NY, 1963-86; cons. M. Simpson Assocs., Ft. Lauderdale, Fla., 1986—. Former chmn. bd. dirs. Radyne Corp. Contbr. articles to profl. jours. Former bd. dirs. United Way, L.I., 1948—87. Served to lt. (j.g.) USNR, 1944—46, PTO. Fellow: IEEE (chmn. L.I. sect. 1963—64). Avocations: boating, skiing, golf, tennis. *Don't be afraid to take risk in the hope of great reward and satisfaction. The worst that could happen is that you may fail. A much greater loss is that you never tried and perhaps missed the great opportunity of your life.*

SIMPSON, PAMELA HEMENWAY, art historian, educator; b. Omaha, Sept. 8, 1946; d. Myrle E. and Leone K. (Cook) Hemenway; m. Henry H. Simpson III, Apr. 4, 1970; 1 child, Peter Stuart Hay. BA, Gettysburg Coll., 1968; MA, U. Mo., 1970; PhD, U. Del., 1974. Instr. art history Pa. State Extension Campus, Media, 1973, Washington and Lee U., Lexington, Va., 1973-74, asst. prof., 1974-79, assoc. prof., 1979-85, prof. art history, 1985—, Ernest Williams prof., 1993, chair art dept., 1987—, assoc. dean of coll., 1981-86. Chair co-edn. steering com. Washington and Lee Univ., Lexington, 1984-86; cons., head county survey Va. Hist. Landmarks Commn., Richmond, 1977-81. Author: Architecture of Historic Lexington, 1977 (Am. Assn. for State and Local History award 1977), The Sculptor's Clay: Charles Gafly, 1862-1929, 1996 (SECAC award), Cheap, Quick and Easy: Imitative Architectural Materials, 1870-1930, 1999; book reviewer Women's Art Jour., columnist, 1990—; contbr. articles to profl. jours. Officer Rockbridge Hist. Soc., Lexington, 1980—, Rockbridge Valley Nat. Orgn. for Women, Rockbridge County, Va., 1984—, Historic Lexington (Va.) Found., 1987—; founder, officer Rockbridge Area Coalition Against Sexual Assault, Lexington, 1990—; bd. dirs. Project Horizon, domestic violence, sexual assault, 1998—. Recipient Outstanding Faculty award State Coun. of Higher Edn., State of Va., 1995; grantee Nat. Endowment for Arts, 1974, NEH, 1975, 77, Glenn, Washington and Lee U., 1980-81, 91; NEH Summer Inst. scholar, 1989; Hagley-Winterthur Mus. fellow, 1991, 96. Fellow Nat. Humanities Ctr.; mem. Southeastern Soc. Archtl. Historians (bd. dirs. 1990-94, v.p. 1993-94, pres. 1994-95, editor Arris 1998—), Soc. Archtl. Historians (book rev. editor Am. section Jour. 1999—), Coll. Art Assn., Vernacular Architecture Forum (bd. dirs. 1982-84, 2d v.p. 1988-91, pres. 1997-99), Southeastern Coll. Art Conf. (pres. 1986-90, 2d v.p. 1994—, editor rev. 1979-82). Democrat. Episcopalian. Avocations: painting, reading mysteries. Office: Washington and Lee U Dupont Hall Lexington VA 24450

SIMPSON, RAVEN C. administrative assistant; b. Detroit, Sept. 17, 1979; d. Darron Donnell and Rita Coleman. AA, Prince Georges C.C., 2001; BA in Humanities, U. Md., 2003. Pharmacy tech. CVS Pharmacy, St. Pleasant, Md., 1996—97, head cashier Ft. Washington, 1997—99, shift supr., 1999—2000; teller Dunbar Cash Vault Svcs., Springfield, Va., 2000—02; tech. asst. CAF USA, Greenbeld, Md., 2001—03; program mgr. Naval Med. Rsch. Ctr., Silver Spring, 2003—. Author: The Way Life Came To Me, 2003.: 8322 Indian Head Way Apt B2 Fort Washington MD 20744-4513

SIMPSON, ROBERT GLENN, lawyer; b. Seattle, June 27, 1932; s. Harold Vernon and Anna Rondeau (McCabe) S.; m. Josephine Anne Heald, June 7, 1959; children: Jenifer Jane, Thomas Glenn, Mary Elizabeth. BS, U. Oreg., 1954; LLB, Willamette U., 1959. Bar: Oreg. 1959. Assoc. William B. Adams Law Office, Portland, Oreg., 1959-67; ptnr. Adams McLaughlin & Simpson, Portland, 1967-70, Schwabe Williamson & Wyatt, P.C., Portland, 1970—. Trustee, sec. Legacy Good Samaritan Hosp. and Med. Ctr., Portland, 1983-89, mem. cmty. bd., 1989-98; trustee, chancellor Episcopal Diocese of Oreg., Portland, 1988—. Mem. Oreg. State Bar (exec. com. health law sect. 1987-90), Am. Health Lawyers Assn. (program com. 1987-88), Oreg. Acad. Healthcare Attys. (pres. 1977-78, legis. com. 1989), Multnomah Athletic Club, Univ. Club. Home: 13345 SW Iron Mountain Blvd Portland OR 97219-9306 Office: Schwabe Williamson & Wyatt, PC 1211 SW 5th Ave Ste 1800 Portland OR 97204-3795

SIMPSON, ROBERT HOMER, meteorologist, consultant; b. Corpus Christi, Tex., Nov. 19, 1912; s. Clyde Robert and Annie Laurie (Rainey) S.; m. Mazie Houston, Dec. 22, 1935 (div. Dec. 1949); m. Joanne Gerould Malkus, Jan. 6, 1965; children: Peggy A., Lynn S.; stepchildren: David Malkus, Steven Malkus, Karen Malkus. *In February 2003, the American Meteorological Soc. uniquely honored Joanne and Robert Simpson jointly with a two-day symposium in recognition and extension of their professional contributions to tropical meteorology and hurricanes. In January 2004, they elected Robert Simpson Honorary Member, a distinction received by Joanne several years earlier.* BS, Southwestern U., Tex., 1932, DSc (hon.), 1963; MS, Emory U., 1935; PhD, U. Chgo., 1962. Cert. cons. meteorologist. Observer U.s. Weather Bur., Brownsville, Tex., 1940-42, forecaster New Orleans and Miami, Fla., 1942-45, exec. asst. to dep. chief Washington, 1946-48; established Pacific Region of U.S. Weather Bur., Honolulu, 1948-52; rsch. scientist U.S. Weather Bur., Washington, 1952-56, founding dir. Nat. Hurricane Rsch. Project West Palm Beach, fla., 1956-61, dep. dir. rsch. severe storms Washington, 1961-64; assoc. dir. ops. Nat. Weather Svc., NOAA, Washington, 1964-67, dir. Nat. Hurricane Ctr. Miami, 1967-74; founding dir. Simpson Weather Assoc., Inc., Charlottesville, Va., 1974—; rsch. prof. environ. sci. U. Va., Charlottesville, 1974-80. Established Mauna Loa Summit Obs., Hawaii, 1951. Author: (with Herbert Riehl) The Hurricane and Its Impact, 1981; chief editor: Hurricane: Coping with Disaster, 2002; contbr. articles to profl. jours. Recipient Gold medal Dept. Commerce, 1962, Profl. Achievement award U. Chgo. D.C. Alumni Group, 1998. Fellow Am. Meteorol. Soc. (hon. 1943, 2004, Cleveland Abbe award 1991), Explorers Club N.Y. Achievements include (with Herbert Saffir) creation and implementation of the Saffir-Simpson scale for hurricane damage potential; pioneering research flight in hurricane, Caribbean Sea, W. Pacific Ocean, first over-the-top flight in hurricane, Atlantic Ocean, 1947; many research penetrations of hurricane eyes. E-mail: r.h.simpson@verizon.net.

SIMPSON, ROBERT LEE, university official, biology educator; b. San Francisco, Apr. 3, 1942; s. Robert Lee and Valerie Brinley (Serrick) S.; m. Penelope Sue Flint, June 12, 1970; children: Robert Lee III, Elizabeth Jean. BA in Zoology, Fresno State Coll., 1965, MA in Biology, 1967; PhD in Limnology, Cornell U., 1971. Instr. Cornell U., Ithaca, N.Y., 1970; from asst. prof. to prof. biology Rider Coll., Lawrenceville, N.J., 1970-85, chairperson biology dept., 1972-80; acting dean sch. health professions and nursing William Paterson Coll., Wayne, N.J., 1986-87, prof. biology, 1985-91, dean sch. sci. and maths., 1985-91; provost, vice chancellor acad. affairs U. Mich., Dearborn, 1991—, prof. biology, 1991—. Adj. grad. prof. Rutgers U., Camden, N.J., 1976-91; vis. scientist Smithsonian Environ. Rsch. Ctr., Edgewater, N.J., 1977; mem. grad. degree adv. com. N.J. Dept. Higher Edn., Trenton, 1989-91. Editor: (with D. Whigham, R. Good) Freshwater Wetlands: Ecological Processes & Management Potential, 1978, (with M. Leck, V.T. Parker) Ecology of Soil Seed Banks, 1989; contbr. articles to profl. jours. Mem. N.J. Wetlands Mitigation Coun., Trenton, 1988-91; trustee Chilton Meml. Hosp., Pompton Plains, N.J., 1989-91; bd. dirs. Granville Acad., Detroit, 1991-93; chair acad. affairs affairs subcom. Pres. Coun. of State Univs. of Mich., 1997—. Rsch. grantee Office Water Rsch. & Tech., 1975, 79, U.S. EPA, 1976, 78, NSF, 1975, 80, U.S. Geol. Survey, 1983, Challenge to Excellence grantee N.J. Dept. Higher Edn., 1987. Mem. N.J. Acad. Sci. (pres. 1983-85, Outstanding Svc. award 1989), Ecol. Soc. Am., Brit. Ecol. Soc., Soc. Wetland Scientists, Am. Soc. Limnology and Oceanography, Sigma Xi. Home: 2470 Harness Dr West Bloomfield MI 48324-3733 E-mail: rlsumd@umich.edu.

SIMPSON, RUSSELL AVINGTON, retired law firm administrator; b. Greybull, Wyo., June 19, 1935; s. William Avington and Margaret E. (Draper) S.; m. Margarita A. del Valle, Dec. 19, 1960; children: Margaret E., Robert A., Alexandra P., Christina M. BS with honors, U. Wyo., 1957; LLB, Harvard U., 1965. Bar: Tex. 1965, Mass. 1966. Assoc. Bonilla, de Pena, Read & Bonilla, Corpus Christi, Tex., 1965-66; asst. dean, dir. admissions Harvard Law Sch., Cambridge, Mass., 1966-75, asst. dean, dir. fin. aid, 1972-78, asst. dean for fin. and gen. adminstrn., 1978-84; dir. adminstrn. Hill & Barlow, Boston, 1984-90; v.p., treas. The Archs. Collaborative, Cambridge, 1991-92, ret., 1992. Chmn. devel. com. Law Sch. Data Assembly Svc., 1969; pres. bd. dirs. Law Sch. Admissions Svcs., Newtown, Pa., 1979-80, bd. dirs., 1989-91; trustee Law Sch. Admission Coun., 1968-70, 72-78, 81-82, chmn. svcs. com. 1972-74, chmn. test devel. and rsch. 1976-78; founder Grad. and Profl. Sch. Fin. Aid Coun. Mem. Belmont (Mass.) Town Meeting, 1975-96, Belmont Sch. Com., 1977-83. Capt. USAF, 1957-62. Mem. Tex. Bar Assn., Rotary (bd. dirs. Belmont 1978-80), Phi Kappa Phi. Democrat. Home: 49 Elizabeth Rd Belmont MA 02478-3819 E-mail: russsmpsn@earthlink.net.

SIMPSON, RUSSELL GORDON, lawyer, former mayor, not-for-profit developer, consultant; b. Springfield, Mass., May 22, 1927; s. Archer Roberts and Maude Ethel (Gordon) S.; m. Bickley F. Flower, Sept. 11, 1954; children: Barbara G., Elisabeth Pires-Fernandes, Helen Blair. BA, Yale U., 1951; JD, Boston U., 1956; postgrad., Parker Sch. Internat. Law, 1962. Bar: Mass. 1956, U.S. Dist. Ct. (fed. dist.) Mass. 1957, U.S. Ct. Appeals (2d cir.) 1958, U.S. Supreme Ct. 1980. Advt. mgr. Burden Bryant Co., Springfield, 1951-53; assoc. Goodwin, Procter & Hoar, Boston, 1956-64, ptnr., 1965-87, of counsel, 1987—. Sr. advisor to pres. World Learning, Inc., Brattleboro, Vt., 1988-89, exec. v.p., 1989-90, sr. v.p., 1990-91, trustee, 1991—, exec. com., 1994—; trustee, mem. exec. com., Save the Children Fedn., Westport, Conn., 1995-2002; mem. exec. group Internat. Save the Children Alliance, Geneva, Switzerland and London, Eng., 1996—; dir., vice chmn., mem. exec. com., Cmty. Found. Palm Beach and Martin Counties, West Palm Beach, Fla., 1994-2000; counselor to not-for-profit orgns., 1991—. Author: The Lawyer's Basic Corporate Practice Manual, 1971, rev. edit., 1978, 84, 87. Mayor Jupiter Island, Fla., 1993-99; hon. consul New Eng. of Bolivia, 1958-82, mem. spl. com. to revise Mass. Corrupt Practices Act, 1961-62; bd. govs. Jupiter Island Club, 2000-2002; mem. blue ribbon commn. Martin County Fla. Econ. Coun. Named Outstanding Young Man of Greater Boston, 1963. Fellow Am. Bar Found., Mass. Bar Found.; mem. Mass. Bar Assn. (chmn. banking and bus. law sect. 1980-83, bd. dels., exec. com. 1983-87, v.p. 1985-87), ABA (corp. banking and bus. law sect., com. on law firms, co-chmn. com. on law firm governance, panel on corp. law ednl. programs), Hobe Sound Yacht Club (gov., sec. 2001-2002). Home: 1400 Sorolla Avenue Coral Gables FL 33134-3520

SIMPSON, SANDRA KAY, logistics management specialist; b. Rutland, Vt., Feb. 26, 1949; d. Freeman Edward and Ruth Gail (Smith) Campbell. BA, U. Vt., 1971; M of Pub. Adminstrn., Troy State U., Europe, 1988, MSc in Internat. Rels., 1991. Instr., trainer U.S. Govt., Ft. McClellan, Ala., 1975-79, asst. logistics officer Kitzingen, Germany, 1979-82, property acctg. officer Ft. Hood, Tex., 1982-86, Wiesbaden, Germany, 1986-93; exec. mgmt. asst. Sport and Sound, Mainz Kastel, Germany, 1993-94; maintenance mgmt. coord. U.S. Govt., Wiesbaden, 1994—, dep. dir. internal logistics, 1999—2002, theater level logistics mgr., 2002—03, def. logistics agy., 2003—. Cons. U.S. Govt., Heidelberg, Germany, 1994—. Served with U.S. Army, 1973—93. Mem. Women in Mil. Svc. to Am. Found. (charter mem.), USAREUR Retiree Coun., Wiesbaden/Mainz Retiree Coun. (sec. 1994—), Oxford Club. Avocations: photography, ultra-marathons. Home: Cmr 467 Box 1505 APO AE 09096-1505 Office Phone: 49-6134-604781.

SIMPSON, SHAWN MARIE, secondary school educator; b. Santa Rosa, Calif., Jan. 23, 1971; d. Linda Ellen and David Roy Simpson. Med, U. of Wash., Tacoma, 2001; BA, Pacific Luth. U., Tacoma, WA, 1993. Teacher Certificate Pacific Luth. U., Wash., 1993. Tchr. Eng. Todd Beamer H.S., Fed. Way, Wash., 2003—, disting. tchr., 2003—; tchr. Eng. Illahee Jr. H.S., Fed. Way, Wash., 1994—2003. Gates grant evaluation coord. Todd Beamer H.S., Federal Way, Wash., 2003—, testing coord., 2003—. Poet (poetry) Perseus at the Diner (Publ.: Celebrate Poets Speak Out: Teachers 2001, 2001). Participant Puget Sound Writers Project Inst., 2004. Scholar Sun Valley Writer's Scholarship, U. of Wash. & Frank Russell Co., 2000. Mem.: Nat. Coun. of Teachers of English (corr.), Coalition of Essential Schools (corr.). D-Liberal. Office: Todd Beamer High School 35999 16th Avenue South Federal Way WA 98003 Personal E-mail: shawnmaire34@comcast.net. E-mail: ssimpson@fwps.org.

SIMPSON, TERRY L. education educator, department chairman; b. Loudon, Tenn., Jan. 14, 1949; s. W. V. and Marjorie Simpson; m. Deborah L. Taylor, May 4, 1990; 1 child, Jennifer Simpson Mowdy. BA, U. Tenn., 1973, MS, 1984; MDiv, Southwestern Bapt. Sem., Ft. Worth, 1986; EdD, U. Tex. A&M, 1990. Social studies tchr. Cedar Bluff Mid. Sch., Knoxville, 1973—80; min. edn. Ridgecrest Bapt. Ch., Greenville, Tex., 1980—86; assoc. prof. Maryville (Tenn.) Coll., 1990—, chair divsn. edn., 1998—. Guest lectr. U.S. Embassy, Tallinn, Estonia, 2000. Co-author: Education in Estonia, 2001. Participant NEA Tchr. Exch. Program, China, 1987; dir. ch. constrn. Port Margo, Haiti, 1985. Named Alumni amb., Tex. A&M U. Commerce, 1999; fellow, Salzburg (Austria) Sem., 1998; Fulbright scholar, Tartu U. Estonia, 2000, Fulbright Sr. scholar, Ministry of Edn. Saudi Arabia, 2002. Mem.: Tenn. Coun. Social Studies (bd. dirs., newsletter editor), Phi Delta Kappa, Kappa Delta Pi (chpt. counselor 1996—). Home: 607 Court St Maryville TN 37803 Office: Maryville Coll 502 E Lamar Alexander Pky Maryville TN 37804 Office Phone: 865-981-8106. Office Fax: 865-981-8010. Business E-Mail: terry.simpson@maryvillecollege.edu.

SIMPSON, VI, state senator; b. L.A., Mar. 18, 1946; d. Lloyd M. and Helen (Chacon) Sentman; m. William D. McCarty; children: Jason, Kristina. Student, Ind. U., Indpls. Asst. to chmn. Com. on Status of Women, Calif., 1974-75; dir. pub. affairs Calif. Parks and Recreation Soc., Sacramento, 1975-77; county auditor Monroe County, Ind., 1980-84; mem. Ind. Senate, Indpls., 1984—; exec. dir. Heritage Edn. Found., Indpls., 1989—. Editor Equal Rights Monitor mag., 1974-76; syndicated newspaper columnist Know You Rights, 1975-76. Named Fresman Dem. Senator of Yr., Ind. Broadcasters Assn., 1985, Legislator of Yr., Ind. State Employees Assn., 1985, various legis. awards Sierra Club, Ind. Wildlife Fedn., Isaac Walton League, Ind. Parks and Recreation Assn. Mem. NAACP, AAUW. Methodist. Office: Heritage Edn Found 7821 W Morris St Indianapolis IN 46231-1364 also: Ind Senate Dist 40 200 W Washington St Indianapolis IN 46204-2728

SIMPSON, VINSON RALEIGH, manufacturing executive, director; b. Chgo., Aug. 9, 1928; s. Vinson Raleigh and Elsie (Passeger) S.; m. Elizabeth Caroline Matte, Sept. 9, 1950; children: Kathleen Simpson Zier, Nancy Simpson Ignacio, James Morgan. SB in Chem. Engring, MIT, 1950; MBA, Ind. U., 1955. With Trane Co., LaCrosse, Wis., 1950-75, mgr. mktg. services, 1957-64, mgr. dealer devel., 1964-66; mng. dir. Trane Ltd., Edinburgh, Scotland, 1966-67; v.p. internat. Trane Co., LaCrosse, Wis., 1967-68, exec. v.p., 1968-70; exec. v.p., gen. mgr. comml. air conditioning div., 1970-73; pres., dir., 1973-75, Simpson and Co., La Crosse, 1975-76; pres., chief operating officer, dir. Marathon Electric Mfg. Corp., Wausau, Wis., 1976-80; chmn., pres., chief exec. officer Marion Body Works, Inc., Wis., 1980-93, chmn., 1993—. Bd. dirs. Clintonville Area Found. Past trustee, treas. Fox Valley Tech. Coll.; bd. dir., past pres. Fox Valley Tech. Coll. Found.; past pres., bd. dir. Wausau Area Jr. Achievement; mem. Marion Minutemen; past 20 yr. trustee, chair endowment com., trustee emeritus Northland Coll.; past dir. Wis. Mfrs. and Commerce. Decorated Korean War Commendation ribbon. Mem. Am. Legion, Kappa Kappa Sigma, Alpha Tau Omega, Beta Gamma Sigma (dirs. table). Lodges: Masons, Shriners, Rotary (past. pres. Marion club, Paul Harris fellow). Congregationalist. Avocations: running, snorkeling, cross country skiing, playing the trombone. Home: 171 Fairway Dr Clintonville WI 54929-1071

SIMPSON, VIRGINIA See SIMPSON, JOHN NOEL

SIMPSON, WILLIAM ARTHUR, insurance company executive; b. Oakland, Calif., Feb. 2, 1939; s. Arthur Earl and Pauline (Mikalasic) S.; m. Nancy Doughery Simpson, Mar. 31, 1962; children— Sharon Elizabeth, Shelley Pauline BS, U. Calif.-Berkeley, 1961; postgrad. Exec. Mgmt. Program, Columbia U. C.L.U. V.p. mktg. Countrywide Life, L.A., 1973-76; v.p. agy. Occidental Life of Calif., L.A., 1976-79; pres., CEO Vol. State Life, Chattanooga, 1979-83; exec. v.p. Transam. Occidental Life Ins. Co., L.A., 1983-86, pres., 1986-88, pres., CEO, COO, 1988-90, also bd. dirs.; dir. USLIFE Corp., N.Y.C., 1990—; pres., CEO All Am. Life Ins. Co., Pasadena, Calif., 1990-94, USLIFE Life Ins. div. USLIFE Corp., 1994, USLIFE Corp., 1995-97. Chmn. Franklin Life Ins. Co. Pres. Chattanooga coun. Boy Scouts Am., 1982, bd. dirs., L.A., 1983, v.p., 1983-85, vice-chmn L.A. area, 1989, chmn., 1989; pres. bd. councillors L.A. County Am. Cancer Soc.; trustee Verdugo Hills Hosp. Found. 1st lt. U.S. Army, 1961-64, Ill. Symphony Orch.; bd. dirs. Abraham Lincoln coun. Boy Scouts Am. Mem. Am. Soc. CLUs, Life Ins. Mktg. and Rsch. Assn. (bd. dirs. 1986-89), Ctl. Ill. Ins. Co. (bd. dirs.). Lodges: Rotary. Republican. Presbyterian. Avocations: golf, skiing. Office: Franklin Life Ins Co 1 Franklin Sq Springfield IL 62713-0002

SIMPSON, WILLIAM KELLY, curator, Egyptologist, educator; b. NYC, Jan. 3, 1928; s. Kenneth Farrand and Helen L.K. (Porter) S.; m. Marilyn E. Milton, June 19, 1953; children: Laura Knickerbacker Simpson Thorn, Abby Rockefeller Simpson Mydland. BA, Yale U., 1947, MA, 1948, PhD, 1954; DHL (hon.), Am. U. in Cairo, 2001. Asst. in Egyptian art Met. Mus. Art, 1948-54; rsch. fellow Center Middle East Studies, Harvard U., 1957-58; faculty Yale U., New Haven, 1958—65, prof. Egyptology, 1965—2004, chmn. dept. Near Eastern langs., 1966-69; curator Egyptian and ancient Near Eastern art Mus. Fine Arts, Boston, 1970-86; ltd. partner Kin and Co., 1967-69; ltd. ptnr. Venrock, 1970—. Dir. editor of papers Penn-Yale Archaeol. Expdn. to Egypt, 1960—; mem. adv. council fgn. currency program Smithsonian Instn., 1966-69 Author: Papyrus Reisner I-Records of a Building Project, 1963, Hekanefer and the Dynastic Material from Toshka, 1963, Papyrus Reisner II-Accounts of the Dockyard Workshop, 1965, Papyrus Reisner III: Records of a Building Project in the Early Twelfth Dynasty, 1969, The Terrace of the Great God at Abydos, 1974, The Mastabas of Qar and Idu, 1976, The Offering Chapel of Sekhem-ankh-ptah, 1976, The Offering Chapel of Kayemnofnet in the Museum of Fine Arts Boston, 1992, The Inscribed Material from the Pennsylvania-Yale Excavations at Abydos, 1995, (with others) The Ancient Near East, A History, 2d edit., 1998, The Literature of Ancient Egypt, 1972,

The Mastaba of Queen Mersyankh III, 1994. Trustee Am. Sch. Classical Studies, Athens, Am. U. in Cairo; mem. internat. council Mus. Modern Art, N.Y.C.; pres. Wrexham Found., 1965-67. Fulbright fellow Egypt, 1955-57; Guggenheim fellow, 1965 Mem. Am. Oriental Soc., Am. Philos. Soc., Archaeol. Inst. Am., Internat. Assn. Egyptologists, Egypt Exploration Soc., Soc. française d'egyptologie, German Archaeol. Inst., Foundation egyptologique Reine Elisabeth. Clubs: Century (N.Y.C.), Met. Opera (N.Y.C.), University (N.Y.C.), Union (N.Y.C.), River (N.Y.C.); Bedford (N.Y.); Golf and Tennis. Home: 129 Katonah Woods Rd Katonah NY 10536-3846 Business E-Mail: william-simpson@yale.edu.

SIMS, BENNETT JONES, minister, educator; b. Greenfield, Mass., Aug. 9, 1920; s. Lewis Raymond and Sarah Cosette (Jones) S.; children: Laura (Mrs. John P. Boucher), Grayson, David. AB, Baker U., 1943, LHD (hon.), 1985; postgrad., Princeton Theol. Sem., 1946-47; B.D., Va. Theol. Sem., 1949, D.D., 1966, U. of South, 1972; Merrill fellow, Harvard U., 1964-65; postgrad., Cath. U., 1969-71. Ordained to ministry Episc. Ch. as deacon, 1949, priest, 1950. Rector Ch. of Redeemer, Balt., 1951-64; dir. continuing edn. Va. Theol. Sem., 1966-72; bishop of Atlanta, 1972-83; vis. prof. theology Emory U., Atlanta, 1980-88, founder Inst. for Servant Leadership, 1988—; priest-in-charge St. Alban's Ch., Tokyo, 1962, 69. Author: Invitation to Hope, 1976, Purple Ink, 1982, Servanthood: Leadership for the Third Millennium, 1997, Why Bush Must Go, A Faith Based Challenge, 2004. Trustee U. of South. With USNR, 1943-46. Named Young Man of Yr. Balt. C. of C., 1953; Disting. Alumnus of Yr., Baker U., 1972 Episcopalian. Office: Inst Servant Leadership 5 Macon Ave Asheville NC 28801-1522 E-mail: bennettsims@mchsi.com.

SIMS, BETTY, state legislator; b. St. Louis, Mo., Dec. 15, 1935; Mem. Mo. Senate from 24th dist., Jefferson City, 1994—. Active United Way, Girl Scout Coun., Jr. League Girls, Inc., 1972—. Office: Mo State Mems Rm 226 State Capitol Bldg Jefferson City MO 65101

SIMS, DOUGLAS D. bank executive; b. 1946; Grad., U. Ill., Urbana, 1968. With St. Louis Bank for Cooperatives, St. Louis, 1969-74; v.p. Ctrl. Bank for Coops., 1974-78; pres. St. Louis Bank for Coops., 1978-84; exec. v.p. Farm Credit Banks of St. Louis, 1984-86, pres., 1986-88, Nat. Bank for Cooperatives, Englewood, Colo., 1988-93; CEO CoBank, Englewood, 1994—. Office: CoBank 5500 S Quebec St Greenwood Village CO 80111-1914

SIMS, EDWARD HOWELL, editor, publisher; b. Orangeburg, S.C., May 29, 1923; s. Hugo Sheridan and Jesse Lucile (Howell) S.; m. Frances Dell Hartt, Jan. 5, 1946; m. Martha Lurene Bass, July 18, 1960; children— Edward H., Robert; m. Bente Thorlund Christensen, Oct. 4, 1969; children— Edward Christian, Frederik. AB, Wofford Coll., 1943; postgrad., Emory U., 1946-47. Mng. editor Orangeburg Times and Democrat, 1946, editor, 1952—; Washington corr., founder Washington bur. for number S.C. dailies, 1947. Dir. Sims Pub. Co., Orangeburg. Columnist: Looking South From Washington, 1948—; Washington Bur. chief: Editor's Copy syndicate, 1950-52; editor-pub., 1952—; radio news analyst: The News of The Week In Washington, 1951—; Author: American Aces, 1958, Greatest Fighter Missions, 1962, The Fighter Pilots, 1967, Fighter Tactics 1914-70, 1972, Aces Over the Oceans, 1987; contbr. articles to publs. White House corr. covering Pres.''s confs., 1948—; mem. Senate and House press galleries, 1947—; Am. consul Munich, Germany, 1963-65; cons. Exec. Office of White House, 1966-67; consul gen. Zurich, 1992; apptd. mem. Commn. to Preserve Am. Heritage Abroad, 1987. Served to 1st lt. USAF, World War II. Recipient Young Man of the Year award S.C. Jr. C. of C., 1959 Mem. White House Corrs. Assn., Am. Legion, V.F.W. Clubs: Rotary, Nat. Press; Metropolitan (Washington); R.A.F. (London). Methodist. Home: 3803 Pin Oaks St Sarasota FL 34232-1241 also: PO Box 400 Fairview NC 28730-0400 Office: PO Box 532 Orangeburg SC 29116-0532

SIMS, ELIZABETH LANEAL, association executive; b. Manila, Ark., May 22, 1948; d. Aaron Neal and Mary Elizabeth (Butler) Shedd; m. Jared Preston Sims, Aug. 31, 1968; children: Jared Neal, David Paul, Christopher Wayne. BA in English, James Madison U., 1974. Tchr. English Buffalo Gap H.S., Augusta County, Va., 1977—79, Wilson Meml. H.S., 1981—88, tchr., sponsor, high sch. yr. book The Hornet's Nest, 1981—88; vol. coord., case mgr. Family Children's Svc., Richmond, 1989—93, program adminstr. sr. svcs., 1993—98; exec. dir. Hanover Mental Health Assn., Inc., Ashland, 1998—. Pres. bd. dirs. Hanover Mental Health Assn., 1996-98; bd. dirs. Va. Coalition for Aging. Mem. adminstrv. bd. Ctr. United Meth. Ch., 1981—83; mem. staff/parish com. Duncan Meml. United Meth. Ch., 2002—, sec. to adminstrv. bd., 2003—; bd. dirs. United Way, Richmond, 1995—97, campaign cabinet, 1998—2000; v.p. bd. dirs. Urban League Greater Richmond, 1999—2004; bd. dirs. Urban League Found., 2002—04. Recipient Cert. of Appreciation, Urban League, 1998, United Way Svcs., 1997, 1999, 2000, Cert. of Appreciation for Profl. Excellence in Edn., Aug. Co., 1987. Mem. Internat. Assn. Psychosocial Rehab. Svcs., Mental Health Assn. Va. (bd. dirs. 1998—). United Methodist. Avocations: Boy Scout counselor, first aid and CPR instruction.

SIMS, EZRA, composer; b. Birmingham, Ala., Jan. 16, 1928; s. Ezra G. and Kathryn W. (Wallace) S. BA, Birmingham So. Coll., 1947; postgrad., Birmingham Conservatory Music, 1945-48; MusB in Composition, Yale U. Sch. Music, 1952; MA in Composition, Mills Coll., 1956. Librarian Harvard Music Library, Cambridge, Mass., 1958-62, 65-74; music dir. New Eng. Dinosaur Dance Theatre, Boston, 1968-78; instr. theory New Eng. Conservatory Music, Boston, 1976-78; instr. microtonal theory Mozarteum, Salzburg, 1992-93; freelance composer Cambridge, 1974—. Dir. Dinosaur Annex Music Ensemble, Cambridge, pres. 1977-2003; guest composer 23d Ann. Contemporary Music Festival, Ill. Wesleyan U., 1977; lectr. various colls. including Warwick U., Cleve. Inst. Music, Internat. Christian U., Westport Friends of Music, Schlumberger-Doll Rsch., Webster U., Mozarteum, Northwestern U., Hochschule für Musik, Hamburg. Composer over 100 works, predominantly microtonal music for various mediums including Chamber Cantata on Chinese Poems, 1954, Mass, 1955, Two Folk Songs, 1958, String Quartet, 1959, Sieben-Spencer Lieder, 1960, Sonate Concertanti, 1961, Third Quartet, 1962, Buchlein for Lyon, 1962, Cantata III, 1963, Octet for Strings, 1964, In Memoriam Alice Hawthorne, 1967, Antimatter: Three Dances for Toby, 1968, A Frank Overture: Four Dented Interludes and Coda, 1969, Pastorale, 1970, Clement Wenceslaus Lothaire Nepomucene, Prince Mettermich (1773-1859), In Memoriam, 1970, Real Toads, 1970, Interlope, 1971, Tango Variations, 1971, Museum Piece, 1972, Where the Wild Things Are, 1973, String Quartet #2 (1962), 1974, After Lyle or Untitled, 1975, When the Angels Blow Their Trumpets, 1976, Celebration of Dead Ladies, 1976, Elegie-nach Rilke, 1976, Collage XIII, 1977, Aeneas on the Saxophone, 1977, Come Away, 1978, Midorigaoka, 1978, 5 Songs, 1979, -And, As I Was Saying..., 1979, Two for One, 1980, Sextet, 1981, All Done From Memory, 1980, Phenomena, 1981, Solo After Sextet, 1981, Quartet, 1982, Pictures for an Institution, 1983, Tune and Variations, 1983, Brief Elegies, 1983, String Quartet #4, 1984, The Conversions, 1985, Wedding Winds, 1986, Quintet, 1987, Chase, 1987, Solo in four movements, 1987, AEDM in memoriam, 1988, Flight, 1989, Night Piece: IN Girum Imus nocte et Consuminur Igni, 1989, Concert Piece, 1990, Duo, 1992, Invocation, 1992, Stanzas, 1995, If I Told Him, 1996, Duo, 1996, 97, Encores: Three Parlor Songs, 2000, String Quartet #5, 2000, Musing and Recollection, 2003; contbr. articles to profl. jours. Served as pvt. U.S. Army, 1952-54. Recipient Composers Forum award, 1959, Koussevitzky Found. commn., 1983, Am. Acad. Arts and Letters award, 1985; grantee Cambridge Arts Coun., 1975, 76, Martha Baird Rockefeller Found., 1977; fellow Guggenheim Found., 1962, McDowell Colony, 1966, Nat. Endowment for Arts, 1976, 78, Mass. Artists Found., 1979, Djerassi Found., 1990, Fulbright Sr. Scholar, 1992, Wurlitzer Found., 1998, Camargo Found., 2000. Mem. Broadcast Music, Inc. Home and Office: 229 Hurley St Cambridge MA 02141-2133 Address: Rosalie Czlabuese Mgmt Box 20580 Park West St New York NY 10025-1521 Office Phone: 617-864-8781. E-mail: ezrsims@aol.com.

SIMS, HENRY P., JR., management educator; Prof. mgmt. U. Md., College Park. Author: The Thinking Organization: Dynamics of Organizational Social Cognition, 1986, SuperLeadership: Leading Others to Lead Themselves, 1989, The New Leadership Paradigm: Social Learning and Cognition in Organizations, 1992, Business Without Bosses: How Self-Managing Teams Are Building High-Performance Companies, 1993, Company of Heroes: Unleashing the Power of Self Leadership, 1996, Team Work and Group Dynamics, 1999, The New Superleadership: Leading Others to Lead Themselves, 2001. Office: U Md Van Munching Hall College Park MD 20742-0001 E-mail: hsims@rhsmith.umd.edu.

SIMS, JOHN R. lawyer; b. 1950; Bachelors, U. Mo., 1972, JD, 1975. V.p., dep. gen. counsel Federated Dept. Stores, Inc., Cincinnati, Ohio, 1990—2002; exec. v.p., gen. counsel Albertson's Inc., Boise, Idaho, 2002—. Mem.: Law Review, Phi Beta Kappa. Office: Albertsons Inc 250 Parkcenter Blvd Boise ID 83706

SIMS, JOHN ROGERS, JR., lawyer; b. Red Star, W.Va., Apr. 10, 1924; s. John Rogers and Myrtle (Hutchison) S.; m. Geraldine L. Bucklew, Oct. 8, 1966; children: John Rogers III, Joyce Rebecca. BS in Commerce, U. Va., 1950, LLB, 1952. Assoc. Dow, Lohnes & Albertson, Washington, 1953-57; gen. counsel D.C. Transit Sys., Inc., Washington, 1957-65; individual practice law Washington, 1965-68; ptnr. Wrape and Hernly, Arlington, Va., 1968-71, Sims, Walker & Steinfeld (and predecessor firm), Washington, 1972-95, pvt. practice Nellysford, Va., 1995—. Chmn. bd. dirs. John Sims Assocs., Inc., 1978-2000, Purnell Bros. Transport, Ltd., 1981-91; co-founder, bd. dirs., gen. counsel A Presdl. Classroom for Young Ams., Inc., chmn. bd. dirs., 1979-83; dir., v.p., gen. counsel, sec. SunWorld Internat. Airways, Inc., 1984-88; chmn. corp. bd. adv. Omniplex World Svcs. Corp., 1997—. Vice chmn. Falls Church (Va.) Planning Commn., 1958-64; pres. Falls Church Republican Party, 1961-62; bd. dirs. Heart Assn. No. Va., Inc., pres., 1963-64, bd. dirs., v.p., gen. counsel Commonwealth Doctors Hosp., Fairfax, Va., 1967-74; bd. dirs., vice chmn. Jefferson Area Bd. for Aging. Served with Armed Forces, 1943-45. Mem. ABA, W.Va. Bar Assn., D.C. Bar Assn., Va. State Bar, Motor Carrier Lawyers Assn. (nat. pres. 1971-72), Assn. for Transp. Law, Logistics and Policy, Va. Trial Lawyers Assn., Rotary, Masons (Shriner), Washington Golf and Country Club, Farmington Country Club (Charlottesville, Va.). Presbyterian. Home: 31 Sawmill Creek Dr Nellysford VA 22958-9538 also: PO Box 623 Nellysford VA 22958-0623 E-mail: sims@firstva.com.

SIMS, KATHLEEN MARIE EICHNER, nursing educator; b. Portland, Oreg., Mar. 27, 1942; d. Virgil Douglas and Viola Minnie (Roth) Eichner; m. Allen Grant Sims, Aug. 3, 1963; children: Vera Marie, Valerie Gwyn, Victoria Lyn. BS, U. Oreg., 1963; MS, Oreg. Health Scis. U., 1984; MA, George Fox U., Newberg, Oreg., 1992; PsyD in Psychology, George Fox U., 2000. RN Oreg. Staff nurse Univ. Hosp., Portland, 1963; office nurse Raglione & Diack, Surgeons, Portland, 1965—66; staff nurse maternity Multnomah County Hosp., Portland, 1966—68; nurse educator Good Samaritan Sch. Nursing, Portland, 1968—84; prof. nursing Linfield Coll., Portland, 1984—. Contbr. articles to profl. jours. Vol. Washington County Immunization Clinics, Beaverton, Oreg., Neighborhood Health Clinics, Portland, 1996—2002; vol. various schs. Portland, 1970—90. Recipient Award for Outstanding Rsch. Presentation, Children's Hosp., Calif., 1985; grantee Rsch. grantee, Xi Mu, Beta Psi, 1999—2000, Edn. grantee, Linfield Coll., 1990—99; Clin. fellow, Peterson Fund, 1988—92. Mem.: ANA, AAUW, AAUP (v.p. Portland campus 1999), Oreg. Nurses Assn. (v.p.), Sigma Theta Tau, Xi Mu (faculty counselor, newsletter editor 2000—). Avocations: sewing, reading history, reading biographies. Home: 18391 SW Burnsridge Ct Aloha OR 97007 Office: Linfield College Sch of Nursing 2255 NW Northrup Portland OR 97210 Office Phone: 503-413-7170. Business E-Mail: ksims@linfield.edu.

SIMS, KENT OTWAY, economist; b. Chickasha, Okla., Nov. 2, 1940; s. Jesse Otway and Mable Vela (Bear) S.; m. Jeanette McCollum, June 9, 1961; children: Marketa, Adam. BA, U. Colo., 1963, PhD, 1966. registered investment advisor. Economist Urban Renewal Authority, Denver, 1965-66, U.S. Dept. State mission to Pakistan, 1966-69, Fed. Res. Bank of San Francisco, 1969-71, asst. v.p., 1971-72, v.p., dir. research, 1972-74, sr. v.p., 1974-82, exec. v.p., chief fin. officer, 1982-85; fin. advisor, investment mgr., mgmt. cons. Theodore R. Seton, 1985-86; ptnr. C&K Partnership, 1987-89. Pres. Her Equal Share, Inc., 1986-89, San Francisco Econ. Devel. Corp., 1988-91; dir. econ. planning and devel. Mayor's Office, San Francisco, 1992-93, San Francisco Redevel. Agy., 1993-96; dir. spl. projects City Mgr.'s Office, Oakland, Calif., 1997; dep. dir. Com. Econ. Devel., Oakland, 1997-98; cons. Bay Area Life Scis. Alliance, 1999, San Francisco Planning and Urban Rsch. Assn., 2000, Golden Gate Restaurant Assn., 2001-03, San Francisco Small Property Owners, 2003, San Francisco Small Bus. Alliance, 2003, Burnham & Brown, Attys., 2003-04. Bd. govs. Econ. Lit. Coun. Calif., Long Beach, 1983-88; trustee Strybing Arboretum Soc. Golden Gate Park, San Francisco, 1983-96; bd. dirs. Jewish Community Mus., San Francisco, 1986-93, Design Coun. San Francisco Bay Area, 1989-90, Career Resources Devel. Ctr., 1991-92; adv. bd. St. Lukes Hosp., San Francisco, 1988-96. Mem. Am. Econs. Assn., Nat. Audubon Soc. Am. Clubs: Sierra. E-mail: kentsims@pacbell.net.

SIMS, LORENE JOY, music educator; d. Francis Steele Chandler and Rhoda May Nelson; m. Larry Jay Sims, Aug. 25, 1941; children: Lon, Lachelle, Lori, Lisa. BA in Elem. Edn., U. Wyo., 1967. Endorsement elem. music tchg. Piano and organ tchr., Laramie, Wyo., 1987—; tchr. Albany County Sch. Dist. #1, Laramie, 1994—2003. Leader Camp Fire USA, Laramie, 1982—. bd. mem., 1996—. Mem.: Wyo. Music Tchrs. Assn. (state treas. 2000—04), Music Tchrs. Nat. Assn., Relief Soc. (pres. 2003—), Beta Sigma Phi (sec. city coun. 2001—02, pres. 2003—04, treas. 2004—06). Republican. Mem. Lds Ch. Avocations: gardening, cross country skiing, church choir, family history librarian.

SIMS, MARTHA J. library director; b. Portsmouth, Va., Oct. 29, 1946; m. Hunter Sims; children: Hunter, Clara. BA in English, Mary Baldwin Coll., 1968; MS in Libr. Sci., U. N.C., 1969; MBA in Pub. Adminstrn., Old Dominion U., 1979. Reference asst. U. N.C., Chapel Hill, 1968-69; libr. art and music dept. Richmond Pub. Libr., 1969-71; br. libr. Virginia Beach Pub. Libr., 1971-74, asst. dir., 1974-76, dir., 1976—. Mem. adv. bd. New Va. Review, 1976-80. Contbr. articles to profl. jours. Bd. dirs. Va. Beach Arts Ctr., 1971-82, treas., 1974-75; mem. Va. Beach Bicentennial Commn., 1975-76, Jr. League Norfolk, Virginia Beach, 1976-82; sec. Tidewater Area Libr. Dir.'s Coun., 1984-85; bd. dirs. Boys Club Norfolk/Virginia Beach, 1986-90, Literacy Action South Hampton Roads, 1988—, Va. Ctr. for the Book, 1987—, pres. 1995—, Va. Literacy Found., 1989—; mem. steering com. Virginia Beach Roundtable, 1988-92; census chairperson Mayor's Complete Count Com. 1990, 1989-90; lead agt. region 12 literacy coord. com. State Office Adult Literacy, 1989-92; trustee, sec. Va. Beach Pub. Libr. Endowment Found., 1982—; mem. adv. bd. Tidewater Literacy Coun., 1984-90; tchr. Sunday sch. 1st Presbyn. Ch., 1988—; mem. steering com. Adult Literacy Lab, Adult Lng. Ctr. Va. Beach Pub. Schs., 1989—; keel divsn. leader United Way, 1991-92; bd. trustees Norfolk Acad., 1991—; keel club chairperson United Way, Virginia Beach, 1992-93; city chmn. United Way, Virginia Beach, 1995. Mem. ALA, Am. Soc. Pub. Adminstrs., Southeastern Libr. Assn., Va. Libr. Assn. (sec. 1976-78, legis. com. 1979-85, local arrangements 1982 conv. 1981-82, chmn. pub. libr. sect. 1982-84, state libr. bd. liaison com. 1984-88). Home: 1160 Cedar Point Dr Virginia Beach VA 23451-3864 Office: Virginia Beach Dept of Public Libraries Municipal Ctr Bldg 192nd Virginia Beach VA 23456-9115

SIMS, PAM, writer, minister; Attended Tulane Univ., Sch. Law seminars. Past pres. Ikebana Internat., Le Gals Inc.; pres. Titanic Bead Co. Taught legal secretarial classes. Prin. works include Ikebana design articles; contbr. articles to mags. Mem. Pensacola Camellia Club; former bd. mem. Women for Responsible Legis.; charter mem. Bush/Cheney 2004, Inc. re-election campaign, Arlington, Va.; mem. Pensacola Christian Women's Club. Recipient Cert. of Recognition, Rep. Nat. Com., signed by Pres. George Bush, 2002, Congl. Award of Merit, 2004, award, Fla. Fedn. Garden Clubs. Mem.: Nat. Notary Public Assn., Ikebana Internat. (past pres.), Fla. Notary Pub. Commn. Office: 4051 G Barrancas Ave PMB #286 Pensacola FL 32507

SIMS, PAULINE ANDRÉE VILLARICO, artist; b. Montreal, Que., Canada, Aug. 27, 1965; d. Remigio Condecido and Suzanne Bouvier (Massé) Villarico; m. Paul Michael Sims, Nov. 20, 1985. BA in Studio Art, Trinity U., San Antonio, 1986. Artist, Austin, 1965—; represented by Austin Galleries, 1998—. Artist AskArt.com, Kentfield, Calif., 2002—. Exhibition, Days in Old Republic, exhibitions include KLRU Auction, Austin, 1995, Tex. TFAA Mem. Exhibit, 1996, W.A.M. Art Gallery, Tex. KLRU Connoisseur Collection, Tex. Expressionism, 1998, Austin Galleries, Represented in permanent collections Tex. Gallery Lombardi, Austin. Personal E-mail: paintresse@msn.com.

SIMS, REBECCA GIBBS, accountant, certified fraud examiner, journalist, editor; b. Houston, Mar. 13, 1951; d. Shelton P. Gibbs and Elizabeth Gill Bisby; m. Morris Raymond Sims (div. 1977); children: Diana Elizabeth, Aaron Redding. BFA, U. Houston, 1977. Cert. fraud examiner. V.p. Lexley U.S.A., Inc., Houston and Mexico City, 1977-81; acct. self-employed, Houston, 1982-87, journalist/investigator, 1987—, fin. fraud investigator, 1991—; mng. ptnr. Boynton & Assocs., 1996—, expert witness, 1997—. V.p. Homa S.A., Texcoco, Mex., 1994—. Editor, rschr.: Mafia, CIA and George Bush, 1992, U.S. resident editor: Daily Hot News, 1998, screenwriter:, journalist: Bilanz mag., 1989—91. Childbirth instr. Houston Orgn. Parent Edn., Houston, 1974 77. Mem. Investigative Reporters and Editors, Nat. Writers Union, Assn. Cert. Fraud Examiners, Mensa. Democrat. Avocations: painting, gardening. Office: 6601 Kirby Dr Ste 671 Houston TX 77005-3943 E-mail: rebeccagsims@aol.com.

SIMS, RICHARD LEE, hospital administrator; b. Columbus, Ohio, Jan. 6, 1929; s. Dorwin Delos and Christine Anna (Hanstein) S.; m. Marilyn Lou Atkinson, June 2, 1951; children: John Christopher, Steven Paul. BS, Ohio State U., 1951. Pres. Doctors Hosp. Found., Columbus, 1977-95; preceptor faculty Ohio State U. Coll. Health Care Adminstrn.; past chmn. Hosp. Coun. Franklin County; ret., 1995. Past chmn. Hosp. Shared Svc. Inc. Past chmn. 1st Cmty. Village Bd.; past chmn. governing bd. 1st Cmty. Ch.; pres. Scioto Valley Health Systems Agy., 1999-2002; pres. Employment for Srs., 1999-2000, Probus, 2003; past chair Columbus area chpt. ARC, emeritus bd. dirs. Recipient Disting. Svc. award Columbus Jr. C. of C., 1960-63. Fellow Am. Coll. Healthcare Execs. (life), Am. Coll. Osteo. Healthcare Execs. (life); mem. Am. Osteo. Healthcare Assn. (chmn. 1988), Ohio Soc. of Assn. Execs. (past pres.), Ohio Hosp. Assn. (past chmn. bd.), Ohio Osteo. Hosp. Assn. (past pres.), Am. Legion (past post comdr.), Rotary (pres. 1978 79), Columbus Club, Sigma Chi (named Significant Sig 2003). Home: 1180 Kenbrook Hills Dr Columbus OH 43220-4941

SIMS, ROBERT BARRY, lawyer; b. N.Y.C., Aug. 20, 1942; s. Irving Zach and Laura (Levine) S.; m. Roberta Jane Donner, Nov. 17, 1973; children: Alexandra Lauren, Andrew Michael, Amanda Morgan. AB, Franklin and Marshall Coll., 1964; JD, George Washington U., 1967; MBA, NYU, 1969. Bar: N.Y. 1968, D.C. 1969, Conn. 1980, Tex. 1995, U.S. Dist. Ct. D.C. 1969, U.S. Dist. Ct. (so. and ea. dists.) N.Y. 1970, U.S. Dist. Ct. Conn. 1978, U.S. Dist. Ct. (we. dist.) Tex. 1997, U.S. Ct. Appeals (2d and D.C. cirs.) 1969, U.S. Ct. Appeals (5th cir.) 1997, U.S. Ct. Claims 1977, U.S. Ct. Customs and Patent Appeals 1978, U.S. Supreme Ct. 1979, U.S. Ct. Internat. Trade 1981, U.S. Ct. Appeals (5th cir.) 1997, U.S. Dist. Ct. (we. dist.) Tex. 1997. Assoc. Cahill, Gordon & Reindel, N.Y.C., 1967-69, Whitman & Ransom, N.Y.C., 1969-72; asst. counsel Gen. Signal Corp., N.Y.C., Stamford, Conn., 1972-76; v.p., sec., gen. counsel Raymark Corp. (formerly Raybestos-Manhattan, Inc.), Trumbull, Conn., 1976-82, dir., 1992—2002; assoc. gen. counsel Lever Bros. Co., N.Y.C., 1983; asst. to pres., corp. counsel Math. Applications Group, Inc., Elmsford, N.Y., 1984; sr. v.p., sec., gen. counsel Summagraphics Corp., Austin, Tex., 1984-95; atty. at law, mediator, pres. Counselcor LLC, Austin, 1995-2001; v.p., sec., gen. counsel. Novadigm, Inc., Mahwah, NJ, 2001—03; ptnr. ProHome LLC, 2003—. Mem. ABA, N.Y. State Bar Assn., Assn. Bar City N.Y., D.C. Bar Assn., Conn. Bar Assn., Corp. Bar Assn., Tex. Bar Assn. E-mail: rbsims@prohometristate.com.

SIMS, ROGER W. lawyer; b. Cleve., Aug. 3, 1950; BA with high honors, U. Fla., 1972, JD, 1974. Bar: Fla. 1975. Mem. Holland & Knight, Orlando, Fla. Mem. Moot Ct. U. Fla.; contbr. to profl mag. and jour. Mem. ABA (mem. standing com. on environ. law 2000-2003), Fla. Bar Assn. (chmn. environ., land use law sect. 1988-89), Phi Beta Kappa, Phi Kappa Phi, Omicron Delta Kappa, Phi Alpha Delta, Fla. Blue Key. Office: Holland & Knight PO Box 1526 200 S Orange Ave Ste 2600 Orlando FL 32801-3453

SIMS, VICTOR DWAYNE, lawyer; b. Middletown, Ohio, Aug. 1, 1959; s. Gerald Clifton and Ethel Ree (Bruce) S. Student, Am. U., 1980; BA, Heidelberg Coll., 1981; JD, Howard U., 1987. Bar: Ohio, 1989; U.S. Dist. Ct. (so. dist.) Ohio, 1990. Congl. intern U.S. Congress, Washington, 1980; fundraiser Telecommunications Rsch. and Action Ctr., Washington, 1984; assoc. Leslie I. Gaines & Assoc., Cin., 1989-91; pvt. practice Sims and Assocs., Cin., 1991—. Mng. atty. Leslie I. Gaines & Assoc., 1990—; ptnr. Sims and Asmah Law Firm. Author poetry. Mem. ABA, Ohio Bar Assn., Cin. Bar Assn. Avocations: writing, music, current events. Office: Centennial Plaza III #850 895 Central Ave Cincinnati OH 45202

SIMS, WILLIAM RONALD, advertising executive; b. Coffeyville, Kans., Jan. 1, 1937; s. William Long and Mary Eloise (Lambe) S.; m. Greta Helene, July 12, 1958; children: Scott, Christopher, Douglas, Mark. BS, Northwestern U., 1958. Account exec. N.W. Ayer, Chgo., 1963-67, Leo Burnett Co., Inc., Chgo., 1967-73, account supr., 1973-76, account dir., 1976-77, sr. v.p., 1977—, retired, 1997; mktg. cons., pres., 1998—. Mktg. cons., pres. Lower Wacker LLC, 1996; writer in field. Active Chgo. Crime Commn. Mem. Chgo. Yacht Club (bd. dirs.), John Evans Club Northwestern U. (chair bd. dirs), Sheridan Shores Yacht Club. Clubs: Chgo. Yacht, Chgo. Athletic Assn. Republican. Presbyterian. Avocation: sailing. E-mail: rgsims@att.net.

SIMS, WILSON, lawyer; b. Nashville, Dec. 24, 1924; s. Cecil and Grace (Wilson) S.; m. Linda Bell, Aug. 12, 1948; children: Linda Rickman, Suzanne, Wilson. BA, U. N.C., 1946; JD, Vanderbilt U., 1948. Bar: Tenn. 1948. Since practiced in, Nashville; ptnr. Bass, Berry & Sims; gen. counsel, dir. Baird Ward Printing Co., Southeastern Capital Corp., Martha White Foods, Synercon Corp., Forrest Life Ins. Co., Charter Co., The Bailey Co., Kenworth of Tenn., Inc. Chmn. Tenn. Commn. for Human Devel., Tenn. Commn. on Continuing Legal Edn.; mem. Tenn. Gen. Assembly, 1959-60; bd. dirs. Nashville YMCA, United Cerebal Palsy, Kidney Found., Matthew 25, McKendree Village; trustee Meharry Med. Coll., Webb Sch., Bell Buckle, Tenn.; adv. bd. Jr. League; mem. bd. visitors U. N.C. 1st lt. USMCR, 1942-45, 50-52. Fellow Am. Bar Found. (life), Nashville Bar Found.; mem. ABA, Tenn. Bar Assn. (past spkr. ho. of dels., past pres.), Nashville Bar Assn. (past pres., dir., Pub. Svc. award), Tenn. Bar Found. (past chmn.), Am. Judicature Soc., Am. Acad. Polit. Sci., Vanderbilt U. Law Alumni Assn. (past pres., Disting. Svc. award), Nashville C. of C. (2 terms bd. govs.), Belle Meade Country Club (bd. dirs.), High Hampton Colony Club (bd. dirs., pres.). Methodist. Home: 22 Foxhall Close Nashville TN 37215-1862 Office: Bass Berry & Sims AmSouth Ctr Ste 2700 315 Deaderick St Nashville TN 37238-3001

SIMS-CURRY, KRISTY, women's college basketball coach; b. Olla., La., 1967; m. Kelly Curry, 2 dau. BS in Health and Phys. Edn., N.E. La. U., 1988; MS in Kinesiology, Stephen F. Austin U., Nacogdoches, Tex., 1992. Coach Weston H.S., Mansfield H.S., La.; women's asst. basketball coach Tulane U., 1991-93, Stephen F. Austin U., 1993-94, Tex. A&M U., 1994-96; asst. coach La. Tech. U., 1996-99; head coach Purdue U., West Lafayette, 1999—. Office: care Women's Basketball 1790 Mackey Arena Rm 44 West Lafayette IN 47907-1790

SIMS IANNELLI, KIMBERLY, writer; b. Hereford, Tex., Mar. 9, 1964; d. Bob S. and Sue Hess Sims; m. Peter Carmine Iannelli, Sept. 6, 1997; 1 child, Sydney Iannelli. BS, Tex. A&M U., 1986, MPA, 1988, MA, 1999. Legis. aide, com. clk. Tex. Senate, Austin, 1993-95; dir. agr. and conservation policy Office of Gov. George W. Bush, Austin, 1995-97; exec. dir., sec. Tex. Water Found., Austin, 1998-2000; interim exec. dir. Environ. Edn. Found. Tex., Austin, 2000—01. Adj. faculty South Tex. C.C., McAllen, Tex., 2001—. Dir. Tex. Women's Alliance, Austin, 1995-2001; mem. adv. coun. Hidalgo County Hist.

Mus., Edinburg, Tex., 2000-2001; dir. Friends of Wildlife Corridor, McAllen, 2001. Mem. Tex. Agrl. Lifetime Leadership, Daus. of the King. Methodist. Avocations: travel, fine dining, reading, tennis, scrapbooking.

SIMSIC, JANET M. cardiologist; d. Carl and Eleanor Simsic. MD, E. Carolina U., 1992. Diplomate Am. Bd. Pediatrics, Am. Bd. Pediatric Cardiology. Pediatric cardiologist Med. U. S.C., Charleston, 1999—2003, Sibley Heart Ctr. Cardiology, Atlanta, 2003—. Med. mission team leader Heart Care Internat., 1999—; med. mission physician Children's Heartlink, 2000—. Office: Sibley Heart Ctr Cardiology 52 Executive Park S Ste 5200 Atlanta GA 30329 Office Phone: 800-542-2233.

SIMSON, BEVLYN, artist; b. Columbus, Ohio, Sept. 9, 1917; d. Amon and Fannie Florence (Gilbert) Thall; m. Theodore Richard Simson, Mar. 25, 1938; children: Sherran Blair, Douglas A. BFA, Ohio State U., 1969, MFA, 1972. Author, artist Prints and Poetry, 1969. One woman shows include J.B. Speed Art Mus., Louisville, 1970, Huntington Gallery, Columbus, Ohio, 1970, 73, United Christian Ctr., Columbus, 1970, Bodley Gallery, N.Y., 1971, 74, Gilman Galleries, Chgo., 1971, Gallery 200, Columbus, 1972, Hopkins Hall Gallery, Ohio State U., Columbus, 1972, Meth. Theol Sch., Deleware, Ohio, 1973, Columbus Public Lib., 1973, Garfinkels, Washington, 1973, City Hall, Mayor's Office, Columbus, 1974, 82, Capital U., Bexley, Ohio, 1977, Hillel Found., Ohio State U., 1978, Columbus Tech. Inst., 1979, Springfield (Ohio) Art Mus., 1980, Peace Luth. Ch., Gahanna, Ohio, 1981, Franklin U. Gallery, Columbus, 1981, Columbus Mus. Art Collectors Gallery, 1983; exhibited in juried and invitational shows at Columbus Mus. Art-Ohio Art League, 1968, 70, 71, 73, 74, 75, 77, 78, 79, 80, 86, Ohio Statehouse and State Office Tower, Columbus, 1968-78, Battelle Meml. Inst., Columbus, 1969-73, 75, 78, 81-82, Schumacher Gallery, Capital U., Columbus, 1969-85, 87, 88, Salles d'Exposition, Paris, 1969, Am. Cultural Ctr., Kyoto, Japan, J.B. Speed Art Mus. Collector's Gallery, Louisville, 1970-85, Studio San Guiseppe, Mt. St. Joseph Coll., Cin., 1971, Silver Anniversary Coll. Arts, 2nd Biennial Alumni Exhbn., Hopkins Hall Gallery, 1972, 2nd Internat. Art Exhbn., Paramaribo, Serinam, 1974, Mansfield (Ohio) Art Ctr., 1971, Collector's Showroom, Chgo., 1971-82, Gov.'s MansionState of Ohio, 1972, 74, Western Ill. U., 1972, Albatross Gallery, Rome, 1972, Palazzo Dell Exprizioni, Rome, 1972, Place-Allrich Gallery, San Francisco, 1973-75, Chautauqua Assn., N.Y., 1973, Butler Inst. Am. Art, Youngtown, Ohio, 1973, 76, Huntington Gallery, Columbus, 1973, 74, Gallery 200, Columbus, 1972-76, Columbus C. of C., 1974, 75, Zanesville (Ohio) Art Ctr., 1976, Columbus Inst. Contemporary Art, 1978, Nationwide Plaza Gallery, Columbus, 1980, Franklin U., Columbus, 1980, Ohio State U., 1993, Ohio Art League, 1987, Jeffrey Mansion, Bexley, Ohio, 1996, 10th Ann. Women Artists Expo Seal of Ohio Girl Scout Coun., Inc. Columbus, 1996, Financial Group Gallery, Worthington, Ohio, 1997, Ohio Art League, 1997, 4th Hall Gallery, Ohio State U., 1997, Concourse Gallery, Upper Arlington, Ohio, 1998, 13th Ann. Women Artists Expo Art in The Nation Wide Atrium, Columbus, Ohio, 1999, Bexley (Ohio) Art League, Jeffrey Mansion, 2000;(Ohio) Art League Mem. Curated Exhbn., Structure/Consequences, 1997, Fourth Biennial Alumni Exhbn.:ReSiDivist, Hopkins Hall Gallery, Ohio State U., 1997, Concourse Gallery, Arlington Ohio, 1998, Bexley Art League, Precision Concepts, Dublin, Ohio, 1999, Art in the Atrium, Columbus, Ohio, 1999, Art on Main Street, Schumacher Gallery, 2002, others; represented in permanent collections Columbus Mus. Arts, J.B. Speed Art Mus., Louisville, Capital U., Bexley, Fordham U., N.Y.C., Kyoto City U. Fine Arts, Springfield (Ohio) Art Mus., Tyler (Tex.) Mus. Art, Wichita (Kans.) Mus. Art, Zanesville (Ohio) Art Ctr., Ohio State U., Columbus, Meth. Theol. Sch., Delaware, Ohio, Yerke Mortgage Co., Columbus, Marcorp, N.Y., Kresge Co., Detroit, IBM, Columbus, Chase Manhattan Bank, N.Y.C., Chase Bank Ohio, Am. Bancorp., Columbus, Ohio Nat. Bank Plaza, Columbus, Pan Western Life Ins. Co., Columbus, First Investment Co., Columbus, Children's Hosp., Phila., Franklin County Crippled Children's Ctr., Columbus, Zenith East, N.Y.C., First Cmty. Bank, Columbus, First City Bank, Columbus, Ohio, Ronald McDonald House, Columbus, Columbia Gas of Ohio, Columbus, Midland Title Security Co., Columbus, Huntington Nat. Bank Ctr., Columbus, Lehman Bros., N.Y.C., Columbus Sch. for Girls, Grand Prix Assocs., Inc., Columbus, Grant Hosp. Med Ctr., Columbus, Libr. and Rsch. Ctr. Nat. Mus. Women in Arts, Washington, D.C., Ohio State U. Libr. Rare Books Room Collection, Laredo (Tex.) Pub. Libr.; represented in private collections. Mem. Nat. League Am. Pen Women, Nat. Artists Equity Assn., Bexley Art League, Columbus Mus. Art, Ohio Art League (bd. dirs. 1965-96, treas., sec., pres. 1977), Ohio State U. Alumni Assn., Pres.'s Club (Ohio State U.), Winding Hollow Country Club, Phi Sigma Sigma. Avocations: golf, theater, symphony, travel. Studio: Bevlyn Simson Studio 4300 E Broad St 1st Cmty Bank Bldg Columbus OH 43213-1243 Office Phone: 614-239-4600. E-mail: trsimson@netwalk.com.

SIMSON, GARY JOSEPH, law educator; b. Newark, Mar. 18, 1950; s. Marvin and Mildred (Silberg) S.; m. Rosalind Slivka, Aug. 15, 1971; children: Nathaniel, Jennie Anne. BA, Yale Coll., 1971; JD, Yale U., 1974. Bar: Conn. 1974, N.Y. 1980. Law clk. to judge U.S. Ct. Appeals 2d Cir., 1974-75; from asst. prof. law to prof. law U. Tex., 1975-80; prof. law Cornell U., Ithaca, NY, 1980—, assoc. dean, 1997—2004. Vis. prof. law Cornell U., Ithaca, 1979-80, U. Calif., Berkeley, 1986; chmn. adv. bd. law casebook series Carolina Acad. Press. Author: Issues and Perspectives in Conflict of Laws, 1985, 3d edit., 1997; contbr. articles to profl. jours. Mem. ABA, ACLU, Phi Beta Kappa. Office: Cornell U Law Sch Myron Taylor Hall Ithaca NY 14853 Office Phone: 607-255-3890. E-mail: simson@law.mail.cornell.edu.

SIMSON, JO ANNE, retired anatomy and cell biology educator, biologist, educator; b. Chgo., Nov. 19, 1936; d. Kenneth Brown and Helen Marjorie (Pascoe) Valentine; m. Arnold Simson, June 1961 (div.); 1 child, Maria; m. Michael Smith, Nov. 10, 1971 (div.); children: Elisabeth Smith, Briana Smith. BA, Kalamazoo Coll., 1959; MS, U. Mich., 1961; PhD, SUNY, Syracuse, 1969. Fellow Temple U. Health Sci. Ctr., Phila., 1968-70; asst. prof. Med. U. S.C., Charleston, 1970-76, assoc. prof., 1976-83, prof. anatomy and cell biology, 1983-96, prof. emerita, 1996—2001. With overseas program UMUC overseas divsn., 1999—2001; featured in Smithsonian exhibit Sci. in Am. Life, 1994—. Contbr. articles to profl. jours.; author short stories and poems. Active adult edn. Unitarian Ch., Charleston, 1973-75, social action, 1990-92. Grantee NSF, 1959-60, NIH, 1966-67, 72-87, 91-95. Mem. Am. Assn. Anatomists, Am. Soc. Cell Biology, Histochem. Soc. (sec. 1979-82, exec. com. 1985-89), Fogarty Internat. Fellowship Bioctr. (Basel, Switzerland, 1987-88), Amnesty Internat. (newsletter editor Group 168 1982-86), Phi Beta Kappa. Home: PO Box 80129 Charleston SC 29416-0129 Business E-Mail: joannesimson@hotmail.com. *In the end, it is only what a person has created and given to the rest of the world that endures.*

SIMSON, WILHELM, company executive; PhD in Bio-organic Compounds, U. Munich, 1968. Vis. dir. paint sector ICI Lacke-Farben, Slough, Eng., 1984; exec. dir. paints divsn. ICI, London, 1987; with SKW Trostberg AG, 1989-91, chmn. bd. mgmt., pers. dir., 1991-98; chmn. bd. mgmt. VIAG Aktiengesellschaft, Munich, 1998—; co-chmn. bd. mgmt., co-CEO E. ON AG, Dusseldorf. Chmn. supervisory bd. Bayernwerk AG, SKW Trostberg AG, Th. Goldschmidt AG, Essen, Germany; trustee Chem. Industry Fund, 1994. Mem. Assn. Chem. Industry, Fedn. German Chem. Industry (bd. dirs. 1997, chmn. com. for trade policy 1998—), German Paint Makers' Assn. (pres. 1982-86), others. Office: E ON AG Bennigsenplatz 1 D-40474 Düsseldorf Germany

SINAGRA, JACK G. air transportation executive; b. Queens, N.Y., Mar. 18, 1950; m. Eileen Cook, 1978; children: Jacklyn, Alexandra, Patrick. Grad., Emporia Coll., 1972. Mem. N.J. Senate, Dist. 18, Trenton, 1992—2002; chmn. Port Author. Board of NY and NJ, 2001—. V.p. Turtle & Hughes, Linden, N.J. Mem. Assn. for a Better Middlesex County. Office: 225 Park Ave S New York NY 10003 Home: PO Box 99 Trenton NJ 08625-0099

SINAI, ALLEN LEO, economist, educator; b. Detroit, Apr. 4, 1939; s. Joseph and Betty Paula (Feinberg) S.; m. Lee Davis Etsten, June 23, 1963; children: Lauren Beth, Todd Michael AB, U. Mich., 1961; MA, Northwestern U., 1966, PhD, 1969. From asst. prof. to assoc. prof. econs. U. Ill., Chgo., 1966-75; chmn. fin. info. group, chief fin. economist Data Resources, Lexington, Mass., 1971-83; chief economist, mng. dir. Lehman Bros. and Shearson Lehman Bros. Inc., N.Y.C., 1983-87; chief economist, exec. v.p. The Boston Co. Inc., 1988-93; pres., CEO The Boston Co. Econ. Advisors Inc., Boston and N.Y.C., 1988-93, Econ. Advisors, Inc., Boston, 1993-96; mng. dir., chief global economist, dir. global econs. Lehman Bros., N.Y.C., 1993-96; pres., CEO, chief global economist Decision Econs., Boston, N.Y., London, Tokyo, 1996—; chief global economist, vice-chmn. The WEFA Group, 1997-2000; global chief economist, exec. v.p. Global Insight, Inc., Lexington, Mass., 2001—. Cons. Laural Cons., Lexington and Evanston, Ill., 1966; vis. assoc. prof. econs. and fin. MIT, Cambridge, 1975-77; adj. prof. econs. Boston U., 1977-78, 81-83, NYU, 1984-88; adj. prof. econs. and fin. Lemberg Sch., Brandeis U., 1988-95; vis. faculty Sloan Sch., MIT, 1989-91; bd. dirs. Boston Pvt. Fin. Holdings, Inc., 1997-. Contbr. articles to profl. jours. and books. Mem. reducing the fed. budget deficit task force Roosevelt Ctr., Washington, 1984; bd. govs. Com. on Developing Am. Capitalism, 1984-96, chmn., 1990-95; bd. economists Time Mag., 1991—. Recipient Alumnus Merit award Northwestern U., 1985 Mem. Am. Econ. Assn., Econometric Soc., N.Am. Fin. Econ. Assn. (pres. elect 2003—), Ea. Econs. Assn. (v.p. 1988-89, pres. 1990-91, Otto Eckstein prize 1988, fellow 1994), Western Econ. Assn. (exec. com.), Econometric Soc. Jewish. Avocations: tennis, skiing. E-mail: asinai@pdeeco.com.

SINAISKY, NICHOLAS ALEKSEEVICH, mechanical engineer, researcher, consultant; b. Volgograd, Russia, Aug. 10, 1924; came to U.S., 1992; s. Aleksey Ivanovich and Klavdja Stepanovna (Krasukova) S.; m. Elizaveta Agapovna Kargina, Mar. 16, 1962 (div. Nov. 1984); children: Natalia, Nadezda, Julia; m. Valentina Alekseevna Pilgasova Pokrovskaya, Jan. 16., 1985. BME, Tomsk Poly. U., Russia, 1958; MME, USSR Acad. of Sci., Moscow, 1968; PhD in ME, USSR Acad. of Sci., Novosibirsk, Russia, 1980. Sr. designer combustion Siberian Sci. Rsch. Inst. for Aviation, Novosibirsk, Russia, 1958-60; lead engr. Inst. Theoretical and Applied Physics Siberian Dept. of USSR Acad. Sci., Novosibirsk, Russia, 1960-62, sci. worker Inst. for Physics and Chem., 1962-68, sr. rsch. assoc. Inst. for Solid Matter, 1968-74; adj. prof., sr. rsc. assoc. Inst. for Constn. & Clinker, Novosibirsk-Krasnoyarsk, 1974-85; top mgr. in environ. protection Sci. Rsch. Inst. for Energy & Cavitator Enterprise, Baku, Azerbaijan, 1985-92; prin. rschr., cons. Cavitator LLC, Portsmouth, NH, 1992—. Patentee low temperature plasma and cavitation; contbr. numerous articles to Russian and Am. profl. jours. Polit. prisoner, north camps USSR, 1947-50, Kazakhstan, 1950-54. Recipient Vet. of Labour medal Presidium of the Supreme Ct. of the USSR, 1983, Golden medal and diploma 26th Salon Int. of Inventions, Geneva, Switzerland, 1998, Inventors laureate, Russia, 2000; named laureate in ecology Georgia Energo USSR, Tbilisi, 1990, 500 Leaders of Influence Presdl. Seal of Honor, 2001, Outstanding Scientists of 20th and 21st Century, Companion of Honor, Internat. Order of Merit, 2000, Am. medal of honor Imminent Scientists of Today, 2002, World Lifetime Achievement award, 2002; named to Contemporary Hall of Fame, 2002. Mem.: Assn. Victims Unlawful Polit. Repressions, Libr. Russian Acad. Scis. (hon.). Achievements include work in ballistic missile reentry radiation analysis, demonstrating short wave excitomic decay photoeffect in wide-gap insulators; atomization with atoms/molecules excitation/radiation through plural cumulative shock in spray used by means of cavitator to reduce boiler fouling, NOx/CO/SO2carbon emission and improve fossil fuel saving, including oil, coal-water slurries and orimulsion, coal-water slurries; leader in heavy cavitation assisted oil/orimulsion burning for power generation by North American, European, and Russian electric utilities. Home and Office: Cavitator LLC 20 Islington St #205 Portsmouth NH 03801-4242 Fax: 603-436-9720.

SINAY, HERSHEL DAVID, publishing executive; b. Chgo., Mar. 15, 1938; s. Irving Paul and Gertrude (Drucker) S. BA, U. So. Calif., 1960. Account exec. Telecomm. and Cinema Wall St. Jour., L.A., 1961—63; account exec. R.J. Friedman Assocs., L.A., 1963—66; dir. sales Performing Arts Mag., L.A., 1966—72; pub. East, West Network, L.A., 1972—79, 1985—87; pres., pub. Calif. Bus. Mag., L.A., 1979—85; pub., editor-in-chief Ranch & Coast Mag., DelMar, Calif., 1987—88; pub. Am. Film. Mag., L.A., 1988—91; pres. Project Mktg. Custom Publ. Specialists divsn. Sinay Comm., Inc., L.A., 1991—. Recipient 32 Maggie awards Western Pub. Assn., 1979-2002. Mem. Am. Film Inst., Western Pub. Assn. (v.p., bd. dirs.), L.A. Advt. Club. Avocations: yachting, jogging, gardening, photography. Office: 810 S Hauser Blvd Los Angeles CA 90036-4726 Office Phone: 323-931-7400. E-mail: sinaycomm@comcast.net.

SINAY, JOSEPH, retail executive; b. Chgo., Dec. 5, 1920; s. Hyman and Ella S.; m. Ruth Milman, Mar. 7, 1961; 1 dau., Elise Sinay Spilker. Student, Herzl Jr. Coll., 1939. Gen. mgr. Fanchon & Marco Theatres, L.A., 1943-54; v.p., founder Interstate United, Chgo., 1953-56; ptnr. Josam Investment Co., L.A., 1956-97, Sinay Co. L.L.C., L.A., 1997—; pres., CEO R B Industries Inc., L.A., 1956-89, also chmn. bd. dirs., cons.; chmn. bd. dirs. Gorian Sinay Land Co., Inc., L.A., 1997—. Bd. dirs. Am. Acad. Dramatic Arts; pres. Variety Clubs Internat., 1985-87; gen. chmn. United Jewish Welfare L.A., 1976; pres. We. region Am. Friends Hebrew U., 1980; Calif. fin. chmn. Muskie for Pres., 1972; trustee Idyllwild Arts Found., 1968-73; bd. dirs. Constl. Rights Found., 1973-78. Mem. Nat. Home Furnishing Assn. Jewish. Office: Sinay Co LLC 1801 Century Park E Los Angeles CA 90067-2302

SINBAD, (DAVID ADKINS), actor, comedian; b. Benton Harbor, Mich. m. Meredith, 1985 (div. 1992); children: Paige, Royce. Student, U. Denver. Stand-up comedian various comedy clubs and concerts nationwide; regular on TV series A Different World, NBC, 1987-91, The Sinbad Show, 1993, (host) Vibe, 1997-98, Hollywood Squares, 1998, other TV appearances include Starch Search (winner stand-up comedian competition 1984), The Cosby Show, Keep on Cruisin, The Redd Foxx Show, Cosby, 1998, 99, Moesha, 2000; occasional co-host Showtime at the Apollo; toured with The Pointer Sisters, Anita Baker, Luther Vandross, Smokey Robinson; appeared in films including That's Adequate, 1989, Necessary Roughness, 1991, Meteor Man, 1993, Coneheads, 1993, Houseguest, 1994, Jingle All The Way, 1996, (voice) Homeward Bound II: Lost in San Francisco, 1996, First Kid, 1996, Good Burger, 1997, Crazy as Hell, 2002, (voice) Hansel & Gretel, 2002, Treading Water, 2002; TV movies: Ready to Run, 2000; author: Sinbad's Guide to Life. Active USAF, to 1983. Address: 12031 Ventura Blvd #3 Studio City CA 91604-2636*

SINCLAIR, ALASTAIR JAMES, geology educator; b. Hamilton, Ont., Can., Aug. 1, 1935; s. Burton Leslie and Grace (Isherwood) S.; m. Elizabeth Mary Sylvia Hill, June 13, 1964; children: Alison Trevena, Fiona Tamsin. BS, U. Toronto, Can., 1957, MS, 1958; PhD, U. B.C., Can., 1964. Asst. prof. U. Wash., Seattle, 1962-64, U. B.C., Vancouver, 1964-68, assoc. prof., 1968-74, prof., 1974-98, prof. emeritus, 1999—, head dept. geol. scis., 1985-90, dir. Geol. Engring., 1979-80, 81-82, 92-98. Pres. Sinclair Cons. Ltd., Vancouver, 1980—, Internat. Croesus Venture Corp., 2004—; dir. Tiger Pacific Mining, 2004—. Author (with G. Blackwell): Applied Mineral Inventory Estimation, 2002, Applied Ore Microscopy and Minerolography, 2003, Quality Control of Assay Data, 2004; contbr. numerous articles to profl. jours. Killam Sr. fellow, 1990—91. Fellow Geol. Assn. Can. (treas. mineral deposits divsn. 1978-89, Disting. Svc. award 2001), Soc. Econ. Geologists; mem. Assn. Profl. Engrs. B.C., Assn. Exploration Geochemists (councillor 1992-96), Can. Inst. Mining, Metallurgy and Petroleum (life, disting. lectr. 1999-2000, Robert Elver award 1991), Geol. Soc. Brazil (hon. mem. sci.-tech. commn. geochemistry 1982), Brazilian Geochem. Soc. (hon.). Avocations: classical music, skiing, golf. Home: 2972 W 44th Ave Vancouver BC Canada V6N 3K4 Office: U BC Dept Earth and Ocean Scis Vancouver BC Canada V6T 1Z4

SINCLAIR, BRIAN ROBERT, psychologist, architect, educator; b. Calgary, Alta., Can., June 29, 1957; came to U.S., 1998; s. David Hickey and Evelyn Irene Sinclair; m. Yuki Kurosawa; children: Julie, Rei, Lauren, Brianne, Brennen. BSc in Psychology, U. Calgary, 1979, MSc in Psychology, 1981, M of Environ. Design in Architecture, 1987. Pres. Uptown Ave. Design, Calgary, 1983-98; architect Pendergast Group Architects, Calgary, 1986-89; assoc. Arthur Erickson, AWA Architects, Vancouver, B.C., Can., 1989-92; asst. prof. U. Man., Winnipeg, Can., 1992-96, assoc. prof., 1996-98, dir. CADLAB, 1993-98; prof., chair dept. arch. Ball State U., Muncie, Ind., 1998—2003; dean coll. environ. design U. Calgary, Alberta, Canada, 2003—. Cons. Sinclair Cons., Winnipeg, 1992; adj. prof. arch. U. B.C., Vancouver, 1990-92; mem. Ctr. Plan adv. bd. City of Winnipeg, 1992-98; bd. dirs. Archtl. Rsch. Ctrs. Consortium, Washington, 1997—, Intersymp, Baden-Baden, Germany; design and planning advisor Nepal Engring. Coll. and Inst. Engring., Kathmandu, 1998—, King Mongkut U., Bangkok, Thailand; vis. scholar Internat. Inst. for Advanced Studies, Washington, 2002—; senator U. Calgary, 2003—. Sect. author Frank Lloyd Wright project Digital UnBuilt, 1999; editor procs. in field; contbr. articles to profl. publs. Pres. Can. Assn. Computers in Design Edn., Toronto, Ont., Can., 1996-98; devel. cons. Can. Internat. Devel. Agy., Ottawa, 1996-98; design sector cons. Human Resource Devel. Can., Ottawa, 1995-98; mem. continuing edn. com. Man. Assn. Architects, 1992-98. Recipient Best Paper award Internat. Inst. Advanced Studies, UN Edn., Sci. and Culture Orgn., 1997, Outstanding Scholarly Contbn. award, 1997, Culture of Peace Disting. Scholar award, 1998, Millennium medal and award, 2000. Mem. AIA, Royal Archtl. Inst. Can., Environ. Design Rsch. Assn., Assn. for Computer Aided Design in Architecture, Assn. Collegiate Schs. of Arch. (councilor 1992-98, chair Counterbalance, west ctrl. conf.), Archtl. Rsch. Ctrs. Consortium (bd. dirs. 1997—), Soc. Nepalese Architects, Toda Inst. Global Peace and Policy Rsch. (mem. internat. adv. bd.). Office: Univ Calgary Faculty Environ Design Calgary AB Canada t@n 326

SINCLAIR, CAROLE, publisher, editor, author; b. Haddonfield, N.J., May 13, 1942; d. Earl Walter and Ruth (Sinclair) Dunham; 1 child, Wendy. Student, U. Florence, Italy, 1963; BA in Polit. Sci., Bucknell U, 1964. Advt. copywriter BBD&O Advertising, N.Y.C., 1966-67; sales promotion mgr. Macmillan Pub. Co., N.Y.C., 1967-71; mktg. mgr. Doubleday & Co., Inc., N.Y.C., 1972-74, promotion dir., 1974-76, advt. mgr., sales and promotion, chmn. mktg. com., 1976-80; v.p. mktg., editorial dir. Davis Pubs., N.Y.C., 1980-83; founder, pub., editorial dir., sr. v.p. Sylvia Porter's Personal Fin. Mag., N.Y.C., 1983-90; pres. The Sylvia Porter Orgn., Inc., N.Y.C., 1980-91; founder, pres. Sinclair Media Inc., N.Y.C., 1990—. Mktg. dir. Denver Pub. Inst., summers 1975-78; lectr. Columbia U. Bus. Sch. and Sch. of Journalism, 1976; host nationally syndicated TV show, Sylvia Porter's Money Tips, syndicated daily radio show, Sylvia Porter's Personal Fin. Report, audio cassette series on fin. topics. Author: Keys for Women Starting and Owning a Business, 1991, Keys to Women's Basic Professional Needs, 1991, When Women Retire, 1992; contbg. editor Pushcart Prize, 1977; contbr. The Business of Publishing, 1980. Renaissance Art Program fellow, Florence, Italy, 1963; White House intern, 1962. Mem. Women's Forum, Intercorp. Communications Group, Mag. Pubs.' Assn., Advt. Women in N.Y., Spence Sch. Parent's League. Clubs: Pubs. Lunch. Presbyterian. Avocation: boating.

SINCLAIR, DAISY, casting executive; b. Perth Amboy, N.J., Mar. 22, 1941; d. James Patrick and Margaret Mary (McAniff) Nieland; m. James Pratt Sinclair, May 25, 1978; children: Duncan, Gibbons. BA, Caldwell Coll., 1962. Jr. copywriter Young & Rubican, N.Y.C., 1962-64; various positions in casting dept. Ogilvy & Mather, N.Y.C., 1964-90, sr. v.p., dir. casting, 1990—. Mem.: Drama League N.Y. (3d v.p. 1982—), Am. Assn. Advt. (talent agt. com. 1972—), N.Y. Yacht Club, Union Club, Tuxedo Club, Chapaquoit Yacht Club, Edgartown Yacht Club, Knickerbocker Greys (pres.). Republican. Episcopalian. Avocations: opera, theater, sailing, skiing. Home: 4 E 95th St New York NY 10128-0705

SINCLAIR, GAIL D. education educator; b. Lancaster, Wis., Aug. 27, 1956; d. Eugene H. and Marilyn J. Duvé; m. John V. Sinclair, May 29, 1977; children: J. Taylor, Kaley M. BE, Univ. Mo., Kanas City, Mo., 1977; MA, Univ. Mo., 1983; PhD English, Univ. So. Fla., Tampa, Fla, 1997. Tchr. Smith Cotton H.S., Sedalia, Mo., 1978—81, Marshall H.S., Marshall, Mo., 1981—85, Boone H.S., Orlando, Fla., 1985—99; vis. asst. prof. Univ. So. Fla., Tampa, Fla., 1999—2001, Rollins Coll., Winter Pk., Fla., 2001—. Site dir. Ernest Hemingway Soc. Named for 2004 Conf.; bd. dirs. F. Scott Fitzgerald Soc. Contbr. articles to profl. jour. Vol. Habitat for Humanity, Ctrl., Fla.; bd. trustees Maitland Art Ctr., Maitland, Fla., Dommerich Neighborhood Assn., Maitland, Fla. Mem.: Modern Language Assoc., F. Scott Fitzgerald Soc., Ernest Hemingway Soc. Home: 320 Seneca Trl Maitland FL 32751 Office: Rollins Coll 1000 Holt Ave Winter Park FL 32789 Office Phone: 407-691-1706.

SINCLAIR, GLENN BRUCE, mechanical engineering educator, researcher; b. Auckland, New Zealand, Mar. 7, 1946; came to U.S., 1969; s. Alan John and Piri (Vincent) S.; m. Della Jane Sutton, Dec. 23, 1972; children— Heidi Lee, Heather Ann, Hillary Colleen, Christopher Alan B.Sc., U. Auckland, 1967, B.E., 1969; PhD, Calif. Inst. Tech., 1972. J. Willard Gibbs instr. mech. engring. Yale U., New Haven, 1972-74; lectr. U. Auckland, 1974-77; asst. prof. Carnegie-Mellon U., Pitts., 1977-80, assoc. prof., 1980-82, prof., 1982-2000, head, 1986-92; vis. prof. Cambridge U., England, 1981; prof. La. State U., Baton Rouge, 2000—, chmn. dept. mech. engring., 2000—. Research scientist Dept. Sci. and Indsl. Research, Wellington, New Zealand, 1968-69; summer prof. Pratt & Whitney, Hartford, Conn., 1978, Aircraft Corp., West Palm Beach, Fla., 1979; cons. in field. Contbr. articles to profl. jours. Fulbright scholar, 1969-72. Mem. Am. Acad. Mechanics Office: La State U Dept Mech Engring Baton Rouge LA 70803 Office Phone: 225-578-5899. Business E-Mail: sinclair@me.lsu.edu.

SINCLAIR, JAMES BURTON, retired plant pathology educator, consultant; b. Chgo., Dec. 21, 1927; s. James Lawrence Sinclair and Helen Marie (Thompson) Owens. BSc, Lawrence U., 1951; PhD, U. Wis., 1955. Grad. rsch. asst. U. Wis., Madison, 1951-55, grad. rsch. assoc., 1955-56; from asst. prof. to assoc. prof. La. State U., Baton Rouge, 1956-65, prof., 1965-68, adminstrv. asst. to chancellor, 1966-68; prof. U. Ill., Urbana, 1968-96, dir. nat. soybean rsch. lab., 1992-96; ret. Co-author: Basic Plant Pathology Methods, 1985, 1995, Principles of Seed Pathology, 1987, 1997, Anatomy and Physiology of Diseased Plants, 1991; contbr. articles to profl. jours. Pres. bd. dirs. W.R. and C.V. Spurlock Mus., Urbana, 1998-2000; sec., editor Greater Cmty. AIDS Project, 1996-2000; mem. Econ. Devel. Com., Savoy, 2003—; mem. fin. planning com. Carle Hospice, 2001-02. Sgt. U.S. Army, 1946-47, mem. Coun. for the Krannert Art Mus. and Kincaid Pavilion, 1998- (docent). Recipient Soybean Rsch. Recognition award, Am. Soybean Assn., 1983, Prodn. Rsch. award, 1989, Paul A. Funk award, 1984, Disting. Svc. award, USDA, 1988, Phytopathol. Soc. (north ctrl. divsn.), 1991, Rsch. award, Land of Lincoln Soybean Assn., 1992, Lucia R. Briggs Disting. Achievement award, Lawrence U., 2001. Fellow Am. Phytopathol. Soc., Nat. Acad. Scis. (India); mem. Ill. Crop Improvement Assn. (hon.), Am. Soc. Agronomy (hon.), Rotary (chmn. internat. com. Savoy chpt. 1990-91, v.p. 1991-93, pres. 1993-94, chmn. club svc. conf. 2003-04). Home: 408 Arbours Dr Savoy IL 61874-9752 Business E-Mail: jsinclai@uiuc.edu.

SINCLAIR, LINDA DRUMWRIGHT, educational consultant; b. Norfolk, Va., Aug. 4, 1942; d. Raymond Edward and Evelyn Elizabeth (Edwards) Drumwright; m. Charles Armstrong Sinclair, Oct. 5, 1962; children: William, Dianne, Sandy. BS, U. S.C., 1974, MA, 1976, postgrad. Cert. tchr. in biology, chemistry, physics. Sci. tchr. Keenan H.S., Columbia, S.C., 1976-77; chemistry/physics tchr. Lexington (S.C.) H.S., 1977-93; talented/gifted tchr. U. S.C., Columbia, 1988; tchr. rsch. program Oak Ridge (Tenn.) Nat. Lab., 1989; rschr. Savannah River Ecology Lab., Aiken, S.C., 1991-92; state sci. edn. cons. S.C. Dept. Edn., Columbia, 1993—. Cons. Prentice Hall Pub., Princeton, N.J., 1992-93. Author: Operation Radon, 1993. Adv. bd. S.C. Forestry Commn., Columbia, 1993—, S.C. Environ. Coalition, Columbia, 1993—, S.C. Sci. Coun., Columbia, 1989—; mem., com. chair Lexington Woman's Club, 1986—; v.p. Lexington Garden Club, 1983—. Named S.C. Sci. Tchr. of the Yr., S.C. Acad. Sci., 1986, Sigma Xi, 1986, S.C. Chemistry Tchr. of the Yr., S.C. Chem. Soc., 1992; recipient Presdl. Award for Excellence in Sci. Teaching, NSF, 1993. Mem. S.C. Sci. Coun. (v.p., pres.), S.C. Chemistry Tchrs. Assn. (bd. dirs. 1987—), S.C. Acad. Sci. (bd. dirs. 1982—), S.C. Jr. Acad. Sci. (bd. dirs. 1980—), S.C. Environ. Edn. Assn. (bd. dirs. 1990—), Nat. Sci. Tchrs. Assn. (bd. dirs. 1992-94). Lutheran. Avocations: horseback riding, gardening, swimming, water sports. Home: 107 Hermitage Rd Lexington SC 29072-2221 Office: SC Dept Edn 801-H Rutledge Bldg 1429 Senate St Columbia SC 29201-3730 Office Phone: 803-734-0887. E-mail: lsinclair@sde.state.sc.us.

SINCLAIR, ROBERT EWALD, retired physician; b. Columbus, Ohio, Jan. 19, 1924; s. George Albert and Bertha Florence (Ewald) S.; m. Mary Almira Underwood, Mar. 31, 1945; children: Marcia Ann, Bonnie Sue. *Father George was a civil engineer and mother Bertha was a court clerk in Columbus, Ohio. Wife of 59 years, Mary A. Underwood Sinclair is a professional artist, genealogist, author and illustrator of books, four of which are located in the Library of Congress. Daughter, Marcia Ann Grauerholz, BA Humanities, is an Educational Consultant, Sprint Communications Co. L.P. at World Headquarters, Overland Park, Kansas. Daughter Bonnie Sue Parker Andrews, RN BSN, is a Clinical Decision Support Coordinator, Clinical Data Management, North Colorado Medical Center, Banner Health, Greeley, Colorado. Extended family includes five grandchildren, Robert, Charles and Elizabeth Parker, Jesselyn Grauerholz Neufeld, Zachary Grauerholz, and great grandchild Henry Alexander Neufeld.* BA, Ohio State U., 1948, MD, 1952. Lic. physician, Ohio, Colo., Ala., Kans. Intern Mt. Carmel Hosp., Columbus, 1952-53; resident in neurology and psychiatry Columbus State Hosp., 1964-66, chief psychiatric resident adolescent unit, 1965-66; pvt. practice medicine Columbus, 1953-57, Granville, Ohio, 1957-64; dir. student health svc., prof. health edn., team physician Denison U., 1957-64; dir. student health svc., team physician U. Cin., 1966-70; dir. Latene Student Health Ctr. and U. Hosp.; team physician Kans. State U., Manhattan, 1970-80; dir. Russell Student Health Ctr. and Hosp.; prof. medicine U. Ala., University, 1980-92, ret. Physician Westinghouse Electric Corp., Columbus, 1953-57; asst. zone chief Civilian Def., Columbus, 1954-57; mem. Licking County Bd. Health, Ohio, 1958-59. Bd. dirs. social health com. Cin. and Hamilton County, Ohio, 1967-70, drug abuse and edn. com., 1968-70. With USNR, 1943-46. Mem. AMA, Ohio Med. Soc., Kans. Med. Soc., Ala. Med. Soc., Columbus Acad. Medicine, Licking County Med. Soc. (Ohio), Riley County Med. Soc. (Kans.), Tuscaloosa County Med. Soc., Nat. Athletic Trainers Assn., Ohio Coll. Health Assn. (editor Newsletter 1968-70, pres. 1970-71), Central Coll. Health Assn. (pres. 1972-73), So. Coll. Health Assn. (pres. 1986), St. Andrews Soc., So. Medicine Assn., Delta Tau Delta (faculty advisor), Nu Sigma Nu, Nu Sigma Nu Alumni Assn. (pres. 1953-54), Kiwanis, Rotary. Home: 1 Rollingwood Tuscaloosa AL 35406-2261 Personal E-mail: unsink2@aol.com.

SINCLAIR, ROLF MALCOLM, retired physicist; b. N.Y.C., Aug. 15, 1929; s. Nathan and Elizabeth S.; m. Margaret Lee Andrews, June 13, 1959 (div. 1978); children: Elizabeth Ann, Andrew Caisley; m. Allyn J. Miner, July 29, 1991 (div. 1998); m. Sarah Richards, Mar. 18, 2004. BS, Calif. Inst. Tech., 1949; MA (Reade scholar), Rice U., 1951, PhD (Inst. fellow), 1954. Physicist, Westinghouse Research Labs., 1953-56; vis. scientist U. Hamburg, Germany, 1956-57, U. Paris, 1957-58, U.K. Atomic Energy Authority, Culham Lab., Eng., 1965-66; research physicist Princeton U., 1958-69; program dir. NSF, Washington, 1969-98; ret., 1998. Mem. Solstice Project, 1978-91; NSF rep. U.S. Solar Eclipse Expdn. to Can., 1979, to India, 1980, Amundsen-Scott South Pole Sta., 1995, 96; Disting. vis. prof. N.Mex. State U., 1985; vis. prof. No. Ariz. U., 1986; vis. scientist Los Alamos Nat. Lab., 1988-89, guest scientist, 1989—; cons. to industry, 1960-69, 98—; sr. advisor Centro de Estudios Cientificos, Valdivia, Chile, 1999—. Fellow Am. Phys. Soc. (panel pub. affairs 1976-77, nominating com. 1988-90), AAAS (sec. physics sect. 1972-2000, mem. coun. 1972-73, nominating com. 1982-83); mem. Soc. Am. Archaeology, Sigma Xi. Achievements include research and publs. on physics, archaeoastronomy, tech. and instrumentation. Home: 7508 Tarrytown Rd Chevy Chase MD 20815-6027 E-mail: rolf@santafe.edu.

SINCLAIR, VIRGIL LEE, JR., judge, writer; b. Canton, Ohio, Nov. 10, 1951; s. Virgil Lee and Thelma Irene (Dunlap) S.; children: Kelly, Shannon; m. Janet Brahler Sinclair. BA, Kent State U., 1973; JD, U. Akron, 1976; postgrad., Case Western Res. U., 1939. Adminstr. Stark County Prosecutor's Office, Canton, 1974-76; mem. faculty Walsh Coll., Canton, 1976-78; asst. pros. atty. Stark County, Canton, 1976-77; ptnr. Amerman Burt Bones Co. LPA, Canton, 1976-91, Buckingham, Doolittle and Burroughs Co., L.P.A., Canton, 1991-95; judge Stark County Common Pleas Ct., 1995—, adminstrv. judge, 1996, presiding judge, 1999. Mem. faculty Ohio Jud. Coll., 1991—, lead faculty, 1998—; mem. legal adviser Mayor's Office, City of North Canton, Ohio, 1978-79; referee Stark County Family Ct., Canton, 1981, Canton Mcpl. Ct., 1991—; spl. referee Canton Mcpl. Ct., 1985-86. Author: Law Enforcement Officers' Guide to Juvenile Law, 1975, Lawy Manual of Juvenile Law, 1976, Handling Capital Punishment Cases, 1998, Ohio Jury Institutions, Capital Punishment Approved, Jury Instructions, 2000; editor: U. Akron Law Rev.; contbr. to Ohio Family Law, 1983, also articles to profl. jours. Mem. North Canton Planning Comm., 1979-82; bd. mgrs. North Canton YMCA, 1976—, Camp Tippecanoe, Ohio, 1981—; profl. adviser Parents Without Partners, 1980—; spl. sep. Stark County Sheriff Dept., 1983—; trustee Palace Theatre Assn., Canton, 1983—. Recipient Disting. Service award U.S. Jaycees, 1984; named to Hall of Distinction, Plain Local Schs., 1999, Jud. Hall of Fame, U. Akron Sch. Law, 2000. Mem. ABA, Ohio Bar Assn., Stark County Bar Assn. (lects. 1984), Ohio Trial Lawyers Assn., Assn. Trial Lawyers Am., Nat. Dist. Attys. Assn., Akron Law Sch. Alumni Assn. (trustee), Jaycees, Elks, Eagles, Masons, Delta Theta Phi (bailiff 1976, nat. key winner 1975-76). Republican. Methodist. Office Phone: 330-451-7789.

SINCLAIR, WILLIAM DONALD, state legislator, former church official; b. LA, Dec. 27, 1924; s. Arthur Livingston and Lillian May (Holt) S.; m. Barbara Jean Hughes, Aug. 9, 1952; children: Paul Scott, Victoria Sharon. BA cum laude, St. Martin's Coll., Olympia, Wash., 1975; postgrad., Emory U., 1978-79. Commd. 2d lt. USAAF, 1944; advanced through grades to col. USAF, 1970; served as pilot and navigator Italy, Korea, Vietnam, Japan; ret., 1975; bus. adminstr. 1st United Mth. Ch., Colorado Springs, Colo., 1976-85, Village Seven Presbyn. Ch., 1985-87, Sunrise United Meth. Ch., 1987-89; vice chmn. coun. fin. and adminstrn. Rocky Mountain Conf., United Meth. Ch. U.S.A., 1979-83; mem. Colo. Ho. of Reps., Denver, 1996—, majority whip, 2001—. Bd. dirs. Chins-Up, Colorado Springs, 1983-86; chmn. bd. dirs. Pikes Peak Performing Arts Ctr., 1985-92; pres. Pioneers Mus. Found., 1985—; bd. dirs. Prostate Cancer Edn. Coun., 2001—; Rep. candidate for Colo. State Chmn., 1992-93. Decorated Legion of Merit with oak leaf cluster, DFC, Air medal with six oak leaf clusters, Dept. Def. Meritorious Svc. medal, Vietnam Cross of Gallantry with palms; named Legislator of Yr., Colo. Assn. Commerce and Industry, 1998—99, Colo. Sheriff's Assn., 2001; recipient Frying Pan award, Colo. Restaurant Assn., 1999, 2003, Guardian Small Bus. award, Nat. Fedn. Ind. Bus., 1999—2001, 2003, Disting. Legislator award, United Vets. Com. of Colo., 2002, Common Sense in the Courtroom award, Colo. Civil Justice League, 2003. Fellow Ch. Bus. Adminstrn. Nat. Assn. (nat. dir., regional v.p., v.p. 1983-85, pres. 1985-87, Ch. Bus. Adminstr. of Yr. award 1983, inducted into Hall of Fame 1995), Colo. Assn. Ch. Bus. Adminstrs. (past pres.), United Meth. Assn. Ch. Bus. Adminstrs. (nat. sec. 1978-81), Christian Ministries Mgmt. Assn. (dir. 1983-85), USAF Acad. Athletic Assn., Colorado Springs Country Club, Garden of Gods Club, Met. Club (Denver), Winter Night Club, Rotary (pres. Colorado Springs 1985-86), Order of Daedalians, Pinnacle Club (Denver). Home: 3007 Chelton Dr Colorado Springs CO 80909-1008

SINCLITICO, DENNIS J. lawyer; b. St. Louis, Jan. 9, 1947; BA, U. San Diego, 1968; JD cum laude, U. Wis., 1971. Bar: Wis. 1971, Calif. 1972, U.S. Dist. Ct. (cen. and so. dists.) Calif. 1972. Prof. Calif. Coll. Law, 1972; ptnr. Sinclitico & Burns PLC, Long Beach, Calif. Arbitrator spl. arbitration plan Los Angeles County Superior Ct., 1975—. Mem. Am. Bd. Trial Advocates (nat. exec. com. 1978—, pres. L.A. chpt., editor newsletter), State Bar Wis., State Bar Calif., Assn. So. Calif. Def. Counsel (program chmn. 1980-81, bd. dirs. 1980—), Cal-Abota (chair 1994), Phi Alpha Delta. Office: Sinclitico & Burns PLC 330 Golden Shore # 410 Long Beach CA 90802 Office Phone: 562-628-1919. Business E-Mail: dsinclitico@sin-burns.com.

SINCOFF, MICHAEL Z. human resources and marketing professional; b. Washington, June 28, 1943; s. Murray P. and Anna F. (Jaffe) S. m. Kathleen M. Dunham, Oct. 9, 1983. BA, U. Md., 1964, MA, 1966; PhD, Purdue U., 1969. Instr. U. Tenn., Knoxville, 1968; asst. prof. Ohio U., Athens, 1969-74, dir. Ctr. for Comm. Studies, 1969-76, assoc. prof., 1974-76; vis. prof. U. Minn., St. Paul, 1974; dir. personnel devel. Hoechst-Celanese Corp. (formerly Celanese Corp.), N.Y., 1976-79; dir. employee comm. MeadWestvaco (formerly The Mead Corp.), Dayton, Ohio, 1979-81, dir. edn., tng., 1981-83; assoc. dean Sch. of Bus. Adminstrn. Georgetown U., Washington, 1983-84; v.p. human resources ADVO Inc. (formerly ADVO-Sys.), Hartford, Conn., 1984-87; v.p. human resources, corp. officer DIMAC Direct Inc., St. Louis, 1987-88; sr. v.p. human resources and adminstrn., sr. corp. officer DIMAC Mktg. Corp. (parent of DIMAC Direct Inc.), St. Louis, 1988-97, also sec., asst. treas., exec. com., 1988-97; sr. v.p. human resources, exec. corp. officer Brooks Fiber Properties, Inc. (now Brooks WorldCom), St. Louis, 1997-98; pres., CEO Michaelson Group Ptnrs., Dayton, Ohio, 1969—. Vis. prof. Wright State U., Dayton, Ohio, 1999—; assoc. grad. faculty mem. Ctrl. Mich. U., Mt. Pleasant, 1999—2001, assoc. prof., 2001-. Author, editor human resources sect. Am. Mgmt. Assn. Mgmt. Handbook, 3d edit.; author approximately 50 books and articles; mem. edtl. adv. bd. Jour. Applied Comm. Rsch., 1991-97. Life mem. Internat. Comm. Assn. (bus. mgr.-exec. sec. 1969-73, fin. com. 1982-85); mem. Am. Mgmt. Assn. (human resources coun. 1990-2000), Printing Industries of Am. (employer resources group 1989-97).

SINCOSKIE, W. DAVID, computer engineer; Degree, U. Del. Rsch. scientist Bellcore; v.p. applied rsch. Internet Arch. Rsch. Lab. Telcordia Techs., Inc., Morristown, N.J. Cons. in field; adviser to Taiwan govt. on devel. of NII; mem. panel high performance computer and comm. initiative NRC; adj. prof. computer and info. sci. U. Del.; mem. adv. com. dean engring. U Pa. Fellow IEEE; mem. NAE, Internet Soc., Def. Advanced Rsch. Projects Agy., Info. Scis. and Tech. Com. Achievements include leading team that produced the experimental Sunshine ATM switch; building of ethernet-based packet telephones; inventor set of extensions to self-learning bridges known as VLANs. Office: Telcordia Techs 1 Telcordia Dr Piscataway NJ 08854-4151

SINDELKA, JOSEF, postal service and telecommunications administrator; b. Vienna, May 24, 1938; m. Martina Jammernegg; 1 child, Thomas. Student, Technologisches Gewerbemuseum, Vienna; JD, U. Vienna, 1964. Cert. in gen. mgmt. Engr., mem. bd. Post and Telecomm. Adminstrn., 1957-69, dep. gen. dir., 1985, gen. dir., 1985-96; chmn. bd. dirs. Post and Telecomm. Austria, 1996—; gen. dir. Post and Telecom Austria; with telephone law dept. Gen. Post and Telecomm. Directorate, 1969-75; with dept. 02 Gen. Post Directorate, 1975-79, head dept. 02, 1979-85. Sec. to Fed. Min. of Transport, 1977-79; bd. dirs. Austrian Postal Savings Bank. Contbr. articles to specialist jours. Avocations: reading, classical music, sports. Office: Post and Telecom Austria Postgasse 8 10 A 1010 Vienna Austria

SINDEN, HARRY, professional hockey team executive; b. Collins Bay, Ont., Can., Sept. 14, 1932; m. Eleanor Sinden; children: Nancy, Carol, Donna, Julie. Player Hull-Ottawa Eastern Pro League hockey team; player-coach Kingston team, from 1961; coach numerous teams Central League, until 1967; coach Boston Bruins, 1966-70, gen. dir., 1972—, pres., alt. gov., 1989—, gen. mgr., 1989-2000; TV hockey commentator, 1970-72; coach Team Can., 1973, Stanley Cup team, 1970. Office: Boston Bruins 1 Fleet Ctr Ste 250 Boston MA 02114-1389

SINDERBRAND, DAVID I. lawyer; b. Atlantic City, June 14, 1961; s. Saul Albert and Joyce Rita Sinderbrand; m. Jennifer M. Sinderbrand, June 24, 1995. BA, Ithaca Coll., 1983; JD, Calif. Western Sch. Law, San Diego, 1987. Bar: N.J. 1988, U.S. Dist. Ct. N.J. 1988; cert. civil trial atty. N.J. Supreme Ct., 2000. Lawyer Horn, Goldberg et al, Atlantic City, 1988-90, Manchel, Lundy & Lessin, Phila., 1990-92, Westmoreland, Vesper et al, Atlantic City, 1992—. Mem. Am. Trial Lawyers Assn., Atlantic County Bar Assn. Office: Westmoreland Vesper et al Bayport One Ste 500 Pleasantville NJ 08232

SINDLER, ALLAN JAY, chemical engineer, sculptor, educator; b. Bishopville, SC, Oct. 23, 1925; s. Frank and Pauline Ruth Sindler; m. Sophie Payeff Sindler, June 17, 1951; children: Robert, Marc, Michael. BS in Chemistry, U. S.C., 1944, BS in Chem. Engring., 1948, EdM in Pub. Sch. Adminstrn., 1951, postgrad., 1977—81, Stanford U., 1950, U. Del., 1962—64. Registered profl. engr., Del., S.C., 1967. Chem. engr., supr. Du Plan Corp., Winston-Salem, NC, 1948—49; tchr. Dreher H.S., Columbia, SC, 1949—52; chem. engr. E.I. duPont, Inc., Camden, SC, 1952—84, Newark, 1960—65; tchr. Camden H.S., 1984—87; cons., prof. sculptor S.C. Arts Commn., Columbia, 1987—99. Mem., v.p. S.C. Soc. Engrs.; bd. dirs. Fine Arts Ctr. Kershaw County, Camden. Pres. ARC-Kershaw County Chpt., 1967—68; mem. adv. bd. Kershaw County Detention Ctr., Camden, 2002—; campaign mgr., del. S.C. Dems., 1952—. 2d lt. U.S. Army, 1945—46, ETO. Named Outstanding Young Man in S.C., S.C. Jaycees, 1956; recipient Disting. Svc. award, Camden Jaycees, 1956, medal, Freedom Found., 1956. Mem.: Smithsonian Inst. Conf. (del., Kershaw County dept. chair 1990), Tri State Sculptors Guild (chair ann. show 1982—). Jewish And Unitarian. Avocations: swimming, diving, reading, writing, gardening. Home: 2006 N Brailsford Rd Camden SC 29020 Office: Sculptured Products Co 2006 N Brailsford Rd Camden SC 29020 Office Phone: 803-432-4865.

SINDU, PRADEEP, information technology executive; b. India, 1953; married; 2 children. BA in Electrical Engring., Indian Inst. Tech., Kampur, India; MA in Electrical Engring., U. Hawaii; PhD in Computer Sci., Carnegie Mellon U. Rsch. staff computer sci. lab Xerox Corp., Palo Alto, 1984—91, prin. scientist computer sci. lab, 1987—96, disting. engr. computer sci. lab, 1994—96; vice chmn., CTO, founder Juniper, 1996—. Bd. dirs. Infinera Corp. Achievements include work on design tools that lead to Sun Microsystems first high-performance memory multiprocessors. Mailing: 1194 N Mathilda Ave Sunnyvale CA 94089

SINE, WESLEY FRANKLIN, lawyer; b. Salt Lake City, Dec. 13, 1936; s. Ira F. and Dora Ann (Popp) S.; m. Barbara A. Belnap, June 6, 1958 (div. 1978); children: Barri Ann, Jeri Charlene, Wesley D., Anthony L.; m. Melva Carol Holmes, Dec. 30, 1978; children: Tammy Louise, Dorethea Ann, Christina Jean, Jared F., Katrina C., Joshua F., Kathryn M. JD, U. Utah, 1962. Bar: Utah 1962, U.S. Dist. Ct. Utah 1962, U.S. Ct. Appeals (10th cir.) 1962. Pvt. practice, Salt Lake City. Bd. dirs. Utah Hotel Motel Assn., Salt Lake City, 1963-79, pres. 1976; pres. Salt Lake Valley Inn, Salt Lake City, 1978, Utah Apt. Assn., 1977, Utah State Bowling Proprs., 1965, 83. Mem. Rep. Lincoln Day Club, Salt Lake City, 1985—. Mem.: Kiwanis (pres. Salt Lake City 1984—85, 1999—2000, dist. adminstr. collegiate orgn. Utah-Idaho dist. 1988—, lt. gov. divsn. 2 Utah 1989—90, George F. Hixon fellow award 2000). Mem. Lds Ch. Home: 451 Northmont Way Salt Lake City UT 84103-3322 Office Phone: 801-364-5125.

SINEATH, TIMOTHY WAYNE, library educator, university dean; b. Jacksonville, Fla., May 21, 1940; s. Holcombe Asbury and Christine Marcel (Cook) S.; m. Patricia Ann Greenwood, June 8, 1962; children: Philip Greenwood, Paul Byron. BA, Fla. State U., 1962, MS, 1963; PhD (Higher Edn. Act fellow), U. Ill., 1970. Reference librarian U. Ga., 1963-64, catalog librarian, 1964-66; acad. coordinator continuing edn. in library sci. U. Ill., 1966-68; asst. prof. library sci. Simmons Coll., 1970-74, coordinator doctoral program, 1974-77; prof., dean Coll. Libr. Sci. and Info. Sci. U. Ky., Lexington, 1977-87, prof., 1987-97, dir. sch. Libr. and Info. Sci., 1997—. Cons. to libraries, schs., chs., industry; mem. Lexington (Ky.) Public Library Bd., 1978— Author profl. reports; contbr. articles on library and info. sci., gen. info. mgmt., organizational and small group behavior to profl. jours. Mem. ALA, Am. Soc. Info. Sci. and Tech., Assn. for Libr. and Info. Sci. Edn. (pres. 1993). Episcopalian. Home: 3418 Bay Leaf Dr Lexington KY 40502-3804 Office: U Ky ML King Bldg Lexington KY 40506-0039 E-mail: tsineath@uky.edu.

SINEGAL, JAMES D. wholesale distribution executive; b. 1936; With Fed-Mart Corp., 1954-77, exec. v.p.; v.p. Builders Emporium, 1977-78; exec. v.p. Price Co., 1978-79; with Sinegal/Chamberlin & Assocs., 1979-83; pres., COO Costco Wholesale Corp., Issaquah, Wash., 1983—, CEO, 1988—, bd. dirs. Address: Costco Wholesale PO Box 34331 999 Lake Dr Ste 200 Issaquah WA 98027-8982

SINERIUS-RUPP-BLOOR, SHARON KAY, painter, photographer, sculptor; b. Deer-Lodge, Mont., Feb. 15, 1955; d. Ben and Larada Sinerius; children: Amity, Jason, Aaron, Matthew, Brian. BA, U. Great Falls, 1995. Mem.: Wash. State Arts Alliance (bd. legis. affairs 2000—02), Artist Trust (grant 1998), N.W. Women's Caucus for Art (v.p. N.W. chpt.). Avocations: painting, sculpting, photography, drawing, cats and dogs. Home: 2870 Cabela Ct Richland WA 99352 Personal E-mail: tbloor2b@charter.net.

SINES, RANDY DWAIN, business executive; b. Spokane, Jan. 16, 1948; s. Myron Jones and Paula Inez (Walls) S.; m. Irene Cheng, Mar. 18, 1981. Student, Wash. State U., 1966-67, U. Wash., 1968-69. Lic. water well contractor, Wash., Mont. With Boeing Co., 1967, Winchell's Donut House, Inc., Seattle, 1968-71; owner, mgr. bakeries Wash. and Mont., 1972-78; owner, mgr. Sonsine Inc., Great Falls, Mont., 1976-79; pres. Gardian Port Corp., Oxnard, Calif., 1980-82; pres., chmn. SNS Motor Imports, Inc., Oxnard, 1982-86; chmn. Karakal Corp. of Ams., Ventura, Calif., 1986-89; CEO, chmn. Steel Stix, U.S.A., 1990—; chmn. MITT U.S.A. Corp., 1991—; mng. ptnr. Sharps Internat., 1993—. CEO Casinovations Inc., 1995-96; founder, CEO Inven Corp., Spokane, Wash., 1996-97; chmn. Digideal Corp., Las Vegas, 1998-; chmn. eCardless Bancorp., Spokane, Wash., 2000-; CEO VeriCard, Inc., Spokane, Wash., 2000-. Holder more than 50 utility patents. Recipient alumni grant Wash. State U., 1967. Home: 4056 S Madelia St Spokane WA 99203-4227 E-mail: rsines@digideal.com, rds@mittusa.com.

SINFELT, JOHN HENRY, chemist; b. Munson, Pa., Feb. 18, 1931; s. Henry Gustave and June Lillian (McDonald) Sinfelt; m. Muriel Jean Vadersen, July 14, 1956; 1 child, Klaus Herbert. BS, Pa. State U., 1951; PhD, U. Ill., 1954, DSc (hon.), 1981. Research engr. Exxon Research Engring. Co., Linden, NJ, 1954—57, sr. research engr., 1957—62, research assoc., 1962—68, sr. research assoc., 1968—72, sci. advisor, 1972—79, sr. sci. advisor, 1979—96, sr. sci. advisor emeritus, 1996—. Vis. prof. chem. engring. U. Minn., 1969; Lacey lectr. Calif. Inst. Tech., 1973; Reilly lectr. U. Notre Dame, 1974; Frontiers in Chemistry lectr. Case Western Res. U., Cleve., 1978; Matthew Van Winkle lectr. U. Tex., 1979, disting. vis. lectr. in chemistry, 81; Francois Gault lectr. catalysis Coun. Europe Rsch. Group Catalysis, 1980; Mobay lectr. in chemistry U. Pitts., 1980; Robert Welch Found. lectr. Confs. on Chem. Rsch., 1981; Camille and Henry Dreyfus lectr. UCLA, 1982; Edward Clark Lee Meml. lectr. U. Chgo., 1983; Dow disting. lectr. in chemistry Mich. State U., 1984; Arthur D. Little lectr. Northeastern U., 1985; Vollmer W. Fries lectr. Rensselaer Poly. Inst., 1986; disting. lectr. Ctr. Chem. Physics U. Fla., 1988; David M. Mason lectr. Stanford U., 1995, cons. prof. dept. chem. engring., 1996—. Contbr. articles to profl. jours. Named to N.J. Inventors Hall of Fame, 1991; recipient Dickson prize, Carnegie-Mellon U., 1977, Internat. prize for new materials, Am. Phys. Soc., 1978, Nat. medal of sci., 1979, Perkin medal in chemistry, Soc. Chem. Industry, 1984, Disting. Alumnus award, Pa. State U., 1985. Fellow: AIChE (Alpha Chi Sigma award 1971, Profl. Progress award 1975), Am. Inst. Chemists (Chem. Pioneer award 1981, Gold medal 1984), Am. Acad. Arts and Scis.; mem.: NAE, NAS (award for indsl. application of sci. 1996), Am. Philos. Soc., Catalysis Soc. (Emmett award 1973), Am. Chem. Soc. (Carothers lectr. Del. sect. 1982, Petroleum Chemistry award 1976, Murphree award 1986). Methodist. Achievements include development of bimetallic clusters as catalysts; invention of polymetallic cluster catalysts used commercially in petroleum reforming. Home: PO Box 364 Oldwick NJ 08858

SING, BILL, editor; Bus. editor L.A. Times, 1996—2002, sr. editor, special sections, 2002—04, economics editor, 2004—. Office: Los Angeles Times 202 W 1st St Los Angeles CA 90012

SING, ROBERT FONG, physician; b. Camden, N.J., May 29, 1953; s. William Fong and Elizabeth (Maxwell) S.; m. Lauren McNamee, May 11, 1991. BS in Biology, Ursinus Coll., 1975; DO, Coll. Osteo. Medicine, Surgery, 1978. Intern Met. Hosp., Phila., 1978-79, resident in family practice, 1979-80; dir. emergency dept. Springfield (Pa.) Hosp., 1984—2000; dir. sports medicine Sports Sci. Ctr., 1987—; med. dir. Emergency Ambulance Svcs., Inc., 1994-95; owner J. Enright Jewelers, Inc., Swarthmore, Pa., 1995-97; owner, pres. Springfield Sports Emergency Med. Corp., 1999—. Owner, pres. Finish Line Sports, Inc., Phila., 1988-94; sch. and team physician Springfield Sch. Dist., 1989—, Rose Tree-Media (Pa.) Sch. Dist., 1987—; chief med. officer Kent Profl. Bicyling Tour of China, 1995, U.S. Olympic Cycling Trials, 1996. Author: Dynamics of the Javelin Throw, 1984. Med. dir. Springfield Ambulance Corp., 1988—. Named to Ursinus Coll. Athletic Hall of Fame, 1985. Fellow Am. Coll. Sports Medicine, Am. Osteo. Acad. Sports Medicine; mem. Am. Coll. Osteo. Emergency Physicians, Am. Coll. Emergency Physicians. Avocations: track and field, classical music, bicycling. Home: 1274 Gradyville Rd Glen Mills PA 19342-9614 Office: Sports Sci Ctr 166 Saxer Ave Springfield PA 19064-2335 Office Phone: 610-328-7262.

SING, WILLIAM BENDER, lawyer; b. Houston, Oct. 16, 1947; s. William Bender Sr. and Alice Irene S.; m. Doris Anne Spradley, Sept. 1, 1967; children: Erin Elaine, Emily Elizabeth. BS cum laude, U. Houston, 1968, JD magna cum laude, 1971; MLA, U. St. Thomas, 1995. Bar: Tex. 1971. Assoc. Fulbright & Jaworski, LLP, Houston, 1973-80, ptnr., 1980—. Elder, trustee St. Andrew's Presbyn. Ch., Houston; past pres., bd. dirs. St. Andrew's Presbyn. Sch., Houston; past pres. Houston C.C. Place Civic Assn. 1st lt. U.S. Army, 1971-73. Mem. ABA, Tex. Bar Assn., Houston Bar Assn., Order of the Barons Law Honor Soc., U. Houston Alumni Orgn. (life), Phi Delta Phi (life), Phi Kappa Phi, Omicron Delta Epsilon. Presbyterian. Avocation: reading history and literature. Office: Fulbright & Jaworski LLP 1301 Mckinney St Houston TX 77010-3095 Office Phone: 713-651-3709.

SINGER, ALAN DANIEL, artist; b. N.Y.C., June 19, 1950; s. Arthur B. and Edith (Goulfine) S.; m. Anna K. Sears, Sept. 1, 1979; 1 child, Nathaniel. BFA, Cooper Union, 1972; MFA, Cornell U., 1975; student, Yale U., 1971; postgrad., Pratt Inst., 1976-77. Artist, painter, freelance writer, educator, designer, illustrator and curator, 1974—; prof. dept. fine art Rochester Inst. Tech., 1987—; adult edn. instr. N.Y. Bot. Garden, 1985-88; instr. Asa Wright Nature Ctr., Trinidad, W.I., 1978-80. Designer program Franklin Mint Graphics for TDK/Impressions Illustration and Design Exhibits, Bklyn. Botanic Garden, 1987, designs and mechanicals for L.I. U. Brochures/N.C. Zool. Assn., 1986, others; designer, illustrator stamps U.S. Postal Svc., 1980-81. One-man shows include: Hobart William & Smith Coll., Geneva, N.Y., 2001, The Mill Art Ctr., Honeoye Falls, N.Y., 2001, Century Club, Rochester, 1999, Upstairs Gallery: Gallery Arabesque, Ithaca, N.Y., 1998, Germanow-Coffey Gallery, 1997, Angel Fire Gallery, Rochester, N.Y., 1993, 55 Mercer St. Gallery, N.Y.C., 1985, 1992, Hacnah-Kent Gallery, N.Y.C., 1991, Bali Miller Gallery, N.Y.C., 1988, Smithsonian Mus. of Natural History, Washington, 1987, Dyer Art Gallery, R.I.T., Rochester, N.Y., 2004, others; group shows include Everson Mus., Syracuse, N.Y., 1999, Norman Rockwell Mus., Stockbridge, Mass., 2000, Sonnenberg Gardens, Canandaigua, N.Y., 2000, Kew Gardens, Eng., 1997, Buffalo Mus. Sci., 1997, Monroe C.C., 1997, Meml. Art Gallery, Rochester, 1991, 93, Angel Fire Gallery, 1992, Rochester Inst. Tech., 1988, Nat. Acad. Design, N.Y.C., 1986, Cmty. Gallery, Bklyn. Mus., 1985, Coffey Germanow Gallery, 1995, Mill Art Ctr., Honeoye Falls, N.Y., 2003, Nat. Postal Svc. Mus., 2003, others; author: Wildlife Art, 1999, Botanica 2000, 2000—, Traveling the Erie Canal by Watercolor, 2001; author essays in mus. catalogs, newspapers and jours. Recipient cert. Merit Soc. Illustrators, 1985, Best of Yr. award Postal Commemorative Soc., 1983, Purchase award Nassau C.C., 1976, Pres.'s award Nat. Arts Club, N.Y.C., 1975; Rochester Inst. Tech. grantee, 1991, Faculty Devel. grantee, 1997. Mem. Rochester Print Club (pres.). Avocations: gardening, guitar, hiking. Office: Rochester Inst Tech One Lomb Memorial Dr Rochester NY 14623 E-mail: alan@singerarts.com.

SINGER, ALLEN MORRIS, lawyer; b. Mpls., Dec. 30, 1923; s. William and Ida (Simenstein) S. JD, U. Chgo., 1948; LLM, Harvard U., 1958. Bar: Ill. 1948, Calif. 1949. Pvt. practice, 1950-55, 59—; v.p., sec., gen. counsel ABM Industries, San Francisco, 1969-85. Assoc. prof. law U. Oreg., 1955-59; lectr. law Stanford (Calif.) U., 1960-62; of counsel Cooper, White & Cooper, San Francisco, 1970-97. Contbr. articles to profl. jours. Mem. U. Chgo. Nat. Alumni Cabinet, 1978-80. 2nd lt., USAAF, 1943-45. Mem. ABA, San Francisco Bar Assn., Calif. Bar Assn. Office: 1070 Green St Ste 703 San Francisco CA 94133-5414 Office Phone: 415-673-9149.

SINGER, ARMAND EDWARDS, foreign language educator; b. Detroit, Nov. 30, 1914; s. Elvin Satori Singer and Fredericka Elizabeth (Edwards) Singer Goetz; m. Mary Rebecca White, Aug. 8, 1940 (dec. Mar. 11, 2004); 1 child, Fredericka Ann Hill. AB, Amherst Coll., 1935; MA, Duke U., 1939, PhD, 1944; diploma, U. Paris, 1939; postgrad., Ind. U., summer 1964. Teaching fellow in sci. Amherst Coll., 1935-36; instr. French and Spanish, part-time Duke U., 1938-40; teaching fellow Romance langs. W.Va. U., Morgantown, 1940-41, instr., 1941-47, asst. prof., 1947-55, assoc. prof., 1955-60, prof., 1960-80, prof. emeritus, 1980—, chmn. program for humanities, 1963-72, chmn. dept. integrated studies, 1963, acting chmn. dept. religion and program for humanities, 1973, dir. ann. colloquium on modern lit. and film, 1976—80, 1985—86, 1996—97, 1999—2001. Author: A Bibliography of the Don Juan Theme: Versions and Criticism, 1954, The Don Juan Theme, Versions and Criticism: An Annotated Bibliography, 1965, Paul Bourget, 1975, The Don Juan Theme: A Bibliography of Versions, Analogues, Uses, and Adaptations, 1993, supplement, 2003, The Armand E. Singer Tibet, 1809-1975, 1995, supplement, 1998, The Armand E. Singer Nepal, 1772-1961 and Beyond, 1997, The Officials of Tibet, 1999, The Chinese Presence in Tibet, 2002, The Essays and Proofs of Tibet, 2004, (with J.F. Stasny) Anthology of Readings: Humanities I, 1966, Anthology of Readings: Humanities II, 1967, (with R.F. Gould) A Graded Catalog of Himalayan Mountaineering Correspondence, 2002; editor: West Virginia George Sand Conference Papers, 1981, (with Jürgen E. Schlunk) Martin Walser: International Perspectives, 1987, Doctor Faustus: Archetypal Subtext at the Millennium, 1999; editor W.Va. U. Philol. Papers, 1948-50, 53-55, editor-in-chief, 1951-52, 1955-2004; editor: 1001 Horny Limericks by Ward Marden, 1996, 500+ of Marden's Favorite Limericks, 2004; editor, contbr. Essays on the Literature of Mountaineering, 1982; bd. editors, The European Legacy, 2003-; contbr. numerous articles to profl. and philatelic jours. Bd. dirs. Cmty. Concert Assn., Morgantown, 1959-60, Humanities Found. W.Va., 1981-87. Recipient 4th Ann. Humanities award, W.Va. Humanities Coun., 1990, Armand E. and Mary W. Singer Professorship in Humanities named in honor of Armand Singer and wife Mary Singer, 1999. Mem. MLA (internat. bibliography com. 1956-59, nat. del. assembly 1975-78), So. Atlantic MLA (exec. com. 1971-74), Am. Assn. Tchrs. Spanish and Portuguese, Am. Philatelic Soc., Nepal and Tibet Philatelic Study Cir. (pres. 1999—), Nepal Philatelic Soc., Collectors Club of N.Y., Phi Beta Kappa. Republican. Home: 248 Grandview Ave Morgantown WV 26501-6925 *In an age of deteriorating standards, I want to be counted among those educators who stand against the tide. We ask too little of others, we ask too little of ourselves; others ask too little of us. When we constantly encounter shoddy construction, shoddy merchandise, shoddy performances, shoddy ethics, shoddy education, we may be tempted to forswear our standards. But through our hands pass tomorrow's leaders. As teachers we must help stop this erosion of our national pride. If we fail, make no mistake: it could well destroy us all.*

SINGER, BARBARA HELEN, photographer; b. NYC, Jan. 29, 1927; d. Robert and Rose (Kaplowitz) S.; m. Nat Herz, Jan. 15, 1956 (dec. Nov. 1964); m. Melvin C. Zalkan, Sept. 7, 1983 (dec. Nov. 1993). BA in Biology, NYU, 1947; studied with Eli Siegel, 1944-76. Radiographer, 1951-90; instr. Meth. Hosp. Sch. Radiologic Tech., Bklyn., 1968-72; asst. to Benedict J. Fernandez N.Y.C., N.Y., 1985-91; asst. to Lucien Clergue New Sch./Parsons, N.Y.C., 1989; photographer N.Y.C., 1983—. Lectr. NY Film Acad., NYC, 2000; panel mem. Phoenix Gallery, NYC, 1999, St. Francis Coll., NYC, 2001. Represented by John Stevenson Gallery, Bridgeman Art Library Internat. Ltd., photonica, workbookstock.com; exhibited in numerous group shows including most recently John Stevenson Gallery, N.Y.C., 1999, 2003, Pietra di Luna Gallery, Fla., 1999, 2000, Park Ave. Armory, N.Y.C., 1999, AIPAD, N.Y.C., 1999, George A. Spiva Ctr. for the Arts, Mo., 2000, Hist. Yellow Springs, Chester, Pa., 2000, Nat. League Am. Pen Women Art Exhbn., N.Y.C., 2000, AIR Gallery, NYC, 2000, Pietra di Luna Gall., Hollywood FL., 2000, St. Francis Coll., NYC, 2001, Modernage, N.Y.C., 2001, Ashforth-Warburg Downtown, N.Y.C., 2002, The Gallery in Stamford, Conn., 2003, WBENC Conf. and Bus. Fair, N.Y.C., 2003, Photo-Plus Expo, N.Y.C., 2003, APA, N.Y.C., 2003; CD-ROM Urbane Photography, 1996; photography published in The Murray Hill News, 1983, Profl. Women Photographers Newsletter, 1985, 95, Light and Shade, 1985, Best of Photography Annual 1990, Women of Vision, 1990, Tear Sheet, 1995, Wildlife Conservation Soc. Annual Report, Photonica 21, 1996, In Shape, 1996, Summer of Betrayal, Farrar Straus Giroux, 1997, Wildlife Conservation Mag., 1997, Worldcare Annual Report, 1997, Svenska Missions, 1997, Photonica 25, 1997, Fotophile, 1997, Photonica 34, 1998, Photonica 38, 44, 1999, 49, 2000, Shots, vol. 63, 1999, Photo Dist. News Online, 2003, How Success Happens, 2003, The Picture Professional, 2003, Women's Winners Circle, 2004; lit. published in PWP Newsletter, 2001, Tear Sheet, vol. 3, 1995, Today's Great Poems, 1994, Evangelism in America, 1988, Radiologic Tech., 1969, 71; editor, pub. The Impossible Landscapes of Nat Herz and Kurt Seligmann, 1999; appeared in website video, 2003, Manhattan Neighborhood, 2004. Photographers' Forum Finalist, 1990; recipient Photography award Beaux Arts Soc., 1994, fiscal sponsorship N.Y. Found. for the Arts, 2000, 2d pl. winner for poetry E.F.S. 1999 Ann. Writing Competition, 2000. Cert. by Women Pres. Ednl. Orgn., 2002, Cert. by the City of NY, 2004. Mem.: Poetry Soc. Am., Women Presidents Ednl. Orgn., Am. Soc. Media Photographers, Am. Soc. Picture Profls., Women's Bus. Enterprise Nat. Coun. Avocation: ballroom dancing. Office: Madison Sq Sta PO Box 1150 New York NY 10159-1150 Fax: 212-684-1051. Office Phone: 212-689-0395. E-mail: barbara@barbarasinger.com.

SINGER, BETH J. philosopher; b. Bklyn., N.Y., Oct. 27, 1927; BA, U. Wis., Madison, 1949; MA, Columbia U., 1957, PhD, 1967. Instr. Manhattanville Coll., Purchase, NY, 1966—67, asst. prof., 1967—72, CUNY, Bklyn., 1972—73, assoc. prof., 1974—78, prof., 1979—96, chair dept. philosophy, 1991—95, prof. emerita, 1996—. Author: The Rational Society: A Critical Study of Santayana'a Social Thought, 1970, Ordinal Naturalism: An Introduction to the Philosophy of Justus Buchler, 1983, Operative Rights, 1993, Pragmatism, Rights, and Democracy, 1999; editor (with Tom Rockmore) Antifoundationalism Old and New, 1992. Mem. Am. Philosophical Assn., Soc. Advancement Am. Philosophy (pres. 1986-88, Herbert W. Schneider award for Disting. Contbns. to Understanding and Devel. Am. Philosophy 1994), Concerned Philosophers for Peace (pres. 1998-99). Personal E-mail: bjs.105152@cs.com.

SINGER, CAROL ANN, librarian, researcher; b. Tarentum, Pa., Mar. 13, 1953; d. Richard Meade and Eleanor (Weir) S. BA, Bowling Green State U., 1975; MLS, Ind. U., 1979. Instr. info. svc. Wayne (Nebr.) State Coll., 1979-84; govt. documents libr. U. Nebr., Omaha, 1984-85, Kenyon Coll., Gambier, Ohio, 1985-91; sr. ref. libr. U.S. Dept. Energy, Washington, 1991-92; ref. libr. USDA, Washington, 1992-97; asst. libr. U.S. Dept. Justice, Washington, 1997-98; ref. libr. Bowling Green (Ohio) State U., 1998—. Temp. instr. Kent State U., Bowling Green, Ohio, 1999; researcher. Contbr. articles to profl. jours. Mem. ALA, Acad. Libr. Assn. Ohio, Ohio Govt. Documents Roundtable. Office: Bowling Green State U Jerome Libr Rm 152 Bowling Green OH 43403 Office Phone: 419-372-9412. Business E-Mail: singerc@bgnet.bgsu.edu.

SINGER, CECILE DORIS, bank executive, former state legislator; BA, Queens Coll.; DHL (hon.), Pace U., 1997. Past rep. Spl. Svcs. for Children, N.Y.C.; past exec. dir. N.Y. State Assembly Social Svcs. and Judiciary Coms., Joint Legis. Com. on Corps., Authorities and Commns.; past pub. rep. Yonkers (N.Y.) Emergency Control Bd.; past coord. Westchester County Assembly Dels.; past chief of staff for dep. minority leader; mem. N.Y. State Assembly, Albany, 1988—94, leadership sec. Rep. Conf., mem. assembly children & families com., mem. various other coms.; bd. dirs. Hudson Valley Bank; prin. Cecile D. Singer Cons. Past rep. Temp. Commn. to Revise Social Svcs. Law; mem. Presdl. Commn. on Privacy Conf., N.Y. State Senate Transp. Conf.; task force on substance abuse Am. Legis. Exch. Coun., task force on econ. devel., crime victims' rights, hosp. crisis, women's issues, com. on mass transit; sec. Rep. Conf. Nat. Adv. Panel Child Care Action Campaign; chmn. Westchester County Commn. on Pub. Financing of Campaigns; chmn. Lower Hudson Valley Adv. Com. N.Y. State Divsn. for Women.; past dir. commn. on poverty and pregnancy, Yonkers IDA, N.Y.; treas. Riverside Corp.; chair, N.Y. State Hudson Valley Coun.; pres. Women's Enterprise Devel. Ctr.; bd. dirs. Hudson Valley Bank, N.Y.; prin. Cecile D. Singer Cons. Chair adv. com. Westchester C.C. Found., Westchester 2000 Rsch., Womens Adv. Bd. Westchester County; task force on certiorari Westchester County Sch. Bds. Assn.; sch. and cmty. chmn. Yonkers PTA; bd. dirs. Yonkers chpt. United Jewish Appeal; v.p. Westchester Sr. Housing; chair Women's Networking, Women in Bus. and the Professions; v.p. Westchester Srs. Housing; trustee, treas. St. John Hosp. Recipient Jenkins Meml. award, Nat. PTA award, Bus. and Profl. award Yonkers C. of C.; inducted Women's Hall of Fame, 1996, Sr. Citizens Hall of Fame, 1996. Mem. Mental Health Assn. (bd. dirs., v.p., nominating and pub. affairs coms. Westchester County chpt., Steering award, Star award), Rotary. Office: 21 Scarsdale Rd Yonkers NY 10707-3204 Home: 1 Scarsdale Rd Tuckahoe NY 10707-3215

SINGER, CRAIG, entrepreneur, inventor, investor, consultant; b. N.Y.C., Aug. 13, 1947; s. Albert and Dorothy (Blackman) Singer; m. Ellen Rappaport, Aug. 31, 1969; children: Chad Adam, Cara Danielle. BS, Cornell U., 1969; JD, Columbia U., 1972. Bar: N.Y. 1973. Exec. Continental Wingage Co., Inc., N.Y.C., 1972-74, Integrated Resources, Inc., N.Y.C., 1974-87; pres. Westminster Fin. Group, Inc., Bedford Corners, NY, 1989—. Chmn. bd. dirs. Integrated Resources Funding Corp., AIM Capital Mgmt. Corp., 1983—87; bus. exec.; entrepreneur; inventor; cons., broker, investor, Bedford Corners, NY, 1988—; reporter. Former mem. editl. adv. bd. Bur. Nat. Affairs Housing and Devel.; former dir. Assn. Govt. Assisted Housing, Inc., 1976—84; former mem. exec. com. Coalition Low and Moderate Income Housing. Home and Office: 148 Meeting House Rd Bedford Corners NY 10549-4241

SINGER, DANIEL MORRIS, lawyer; b. Bklyn., Oct. 10, 1930; s. Samuel W. and Fannie G. (Sabloff) S.; m. Maxine Frank, June 15, 1952; children: Amy E., Ellen R., David B., Stephanie F. BA with honors, Swarthmore Coll., 1951; LLB, Yale U., 1954. Bar: N.Y. 1956, U.S. Dist. Ct. D.C. 1957, U.S. Ct. Appeals (D.C. cir.) 1957, U.S. Supreme Ct. 1959. Motions clk. U.S. Ct. Appeals for D.C. Circuit, Washington, 1956-57, law clk. to Judge George T. Washington, 1957-58; assoc. Fried, Frank, Harris, Shriver & Jacobson, Washington, 1958-64, ptnr., 1965-87, counsel, 1987—. Arbitrator complex comml. case and constrn. nat. panels; mediator US Dist. Ct., Washington; vol. atty. Lawyers Com. for Civil Rights Under Law, 1965, 66; mem. exec. com. Washington Lawyers Com. for Civil Rights Under Law, 1973—; spl. asst. corp. counsel, D.C., 1995-2000. Bd. mgrs. Swarthmore Coll., 1987—91; dir., sec.-treas. Coun. for a Livable World, 1962—64; dir. Am. Soc. for Protection of Nature in Israel, 1986—; mem. governing coun., mem. exec. com. Am. Jewish Congress, 1986—96, v.p., 1988—92; bd. dirs., sec.-treas. Nat. Com. Tithing in Investment, 1964—65; bd. dirs. D.C. Developing Families Ctr., 1999—, D.C. Appleseed Ctr., 1996—, chmn. bd., 2000—04. With Signal Corps U.S. Army, 1954—56. Mem.: ABA, D.C. Bar. Home: 5410 39th St NW Washington DC 20015-2902 Office: Fried Frank Harris Shriver & Jacobson 1001 Pennsylvania Ave NW Washington DC 20004-2596 E-mail: daniel.singer@ffhsj.com.

SINGER, DAVID MICHAEL, marketing and public relations company executive; b. Bklyn., Feb. 11, 1957; s. Seymour Allen and Ellen Sybil (Pavnick) S.; m. Pamela Rae Silton, July 20, 1986; children, Max!, Bobby. BA in History, NYU, 1978; MA in Comms., Syracuse U., 1979; MA in Media, New Sch. Social Rsch., 1983; JD, Yeshiva U., 1981. Cons. pub. rels. Burson-Marsteller, N.Y.C., 1979-81, The Haas Group, N.Y.C., 1981-84, Braff & Co., N.Y.C., 1987-89; pub., editor-in-chief Lodestone Pub., N.Y.C., 1984-87; chief oper. officer Pentagon Ltd., N.Y.C., 1989-91; v.p. pub. rels. Braff & Co., N.Y.C., 1991-92; v.p. G.S. Schwartz & Co., N.Y.C., 1993-97; v.p. mktg. comm. Imedia, Morristown, N.J., 1998-99; pres. S&S Mktg. Comms. Inc. Lectr. evening div. NYU, 1982-96; dir. media rels. Braff & Co. Contbr. articles and poems to profl. and consumer jours. and mags. Pres. Jewish Cultural Found., N.Y.C., 1976. Named to Outstanding Young Man of Am., Jaycees, 1977; recipient Cert. Recognition Am. Film Inst., 1982, ANDY Design award Advt. Club N.Y., 1983, Proclamation Bklyn. Borough Pres., 1987. Mem. Alpha Epsilon Pi (Bro. of Yr. 1976). Avocations: baseball, politics, ping-pong, films, theater.

SINGER, DINAH S. federal agency administrator, immunologist, researcher; MPhil, PhD, Columbia U. Sr. scientific officer Howard Hughes Med. Inst., 1998—99; dir. divsn. cancer biology Nat. Cancer Inst., 1999—. Mem.: Am. Assn. Immunologists. Office: Nat Cancer Inst Divsn Cancer Biology Executive Plaza North Ste 5000 Bethesda MD 20892*

SINGER, DONNA LEA, writer, editor, educator; b. Wilmington, Del., Oct. 6, 1944; d. Marshall Richard and Sara Emma (Eppihimer) S. BA in English cum laude, Gettysburg Coll., 1966; postgrad., Montclair State Coll., 1972-73, U. Birmingham, Eng., 1977; M of Letters, Drew U., 1985. Asst. to dir. student activities Fairleigh Dickinson U., Madison, crw., 1966-68; tchr., drama coach Morris Hills High Sch., Rockaway, N.J., 1968-84; free-lance editor Basic Books, Inc., N.Y.C., 1983-86; adj. instr. Fairleigh Dickinson U., Madison, 1986-87; free-lance writer, editor Visual Edn. Corp., Princeton, N.J., 1988—, Fact's on File, Bantam, Random House, Fodor's Travel Books, N.Y.C., 1990—, John Wiley & Sons, N.Y.C., 1990—; tchr. Sylvan Learning and Tech. Ctr., Sarasota, Fla., 1999—. Co-founder, co-dir. Traveling Hist. Troupe, Rockaway, 1976-78; tour leader Am. Leadership Study Groups, 1976, 78, 82; theatre studies participant Royal Shakespeare Co., Stratford, Eng., 1978, 79, 81; docent, lectr. acting co. Hist. Spanish Point, Osprey, Fla., 1989-2001. Contbg. author (poetry) Chasing Rainbows, 1987, An American Heritage, 1994, The Nitty Gritty, 1997, Doorways, 1997, The Best Poems of 1998, The Lasting Joy, 1998, Everlasting Dreams, 1998, America at the Millennium, 2000, The Sound of Poetry, 2001, (biography) Past and Promise: Lives of New Jersey Women, 1990, World Explorers and Discoverers, 1992, American Cultural Leaders, 1993, Structures That Changed the World, 1997, (fiction) Thema, 2000, Tapestry, 2002; contbr. articles to profl. jours. Big sister Big Bros./Big Sisters, Sarasota, Fla., 1990-98. Mem. Internat. Women's Writing Guild, West Coast Writers, Met. Mus. Art, Royal Shakespeare Company Assocs., Emerald Coast Writers, Travel Writers Internat. Network. Avocations: dance, theater, travel, antiquing. E-mail: shakesds@aol.com.

SINGER, EMEL, staffing industry executive; b. Gaziantep, Turkey, Apr. 7, 1944; came to U.S., 1960; d. Mehmet Resit and Nesrin (Kescioglu) Tuzun; m. James Michael Singer, Apr. 28, 1968 (dec. 1987); children: Justin Michael, Jodi Michelle. BBA, Bradley U., 1968. Adminstrv. asst. U. Ky. Med. Ctr., Lexington, 1968; exec. sec. Hoffman Products/Cortron Industries, Chgo., 1968-70; co-founder, adminstr. Banner Pers. Svc., Inc., Chgo., 1970-87, chmn., CEO, 1988—; co-founder Banner Temp. Svc., 1982—; founder Banner Tng. Ctrs., 1996—, Banner Acctg. and Fin., 1999—. Guest spkr. Chgo. Entrepeneurship Program, U. Ill., Chgo., 1993—; fund-raising co-chair U. Chgo., Divsn. Mid. Ea. Studies, 1993-95. Mem. parents bd. Bradley U., Peoria, Ill., 1989-90, assoc. trustee, 1992-93, alumni master, 1993, mem. Bradley coun., 1993-95, bd. trustees, 1995—. Listed in Crains Chgo. Bus. as a Top Woman-Owned Firm, 1989, 90, 91, Today's Chgo. Woman as one of 100 Women Making a Difference, 1997; named to Entrepreneurship Hall of Fame, 1993. Mem. ASTD, Chgo. Orgn. Data Processing Educators, Nat. Assn. Pers. Svcs., Nat. Assn. Temp. Svcs., Ill. Assn. Pers. Svcs., Ill. Assn. Temporary Svcs. Avocations: skiing, scuba diving, travel, sailing. Home: 3750 N Lake Shore Dr Chicago IL 60613-4238 Office: Banner Personnel Service Inc 125 S Wacker Dr #1250 Chicago IL 60606-4424

SINGER, ERIC T. investment banker; b. N.Y.C., 1952; s. Roger M. and Meredith Singer; m. Aet Paaro, Aug. 10, 1974; children: Brett A., Jamison P. BA, SUNY, Stony Brook, 1974; JD, Cornell U., 1977. Assoc. Barrett, Smith et al, N.Y.C., 1977-80; v.p. Smith Barney, N.Y.C., 1980-84; sr. v.p. PaineWebber, N.Y.C., 1984-88; exec. v.p. Metromedia Hotels, N.Y.C., 1988-90; exec. v.p., dir. corp. fin. Gerard Klauer Mattison, N.Y.C., 1990-99; mng. dir., pres. H.C. Wainwright & Co., Inc., N.Y.C., 1999—2003; mng. dir. Burnham Hill Ptnrs., LLC, N.Y.C., 2003—; mng. ptnr. Singer Fund and Singer Opportunity Fund, 2004—; founder, owner Singer Funds, 2004—. Mem. Cornell Law Rev. Mem. U.S. Maccabiah Squash Team, 1997, 2001. Mem. Heights Casino Club, Yale Club, Phi Beta Kappa. Home: 72 Hicks St Brooklyn NY 11201-1709 Office Phone: 212-259-2039.

SINGER, EZRA D. telecommunications industry executive; m. Cathy Singer; 1 child, Allison. B, Cornell U., 1975; JD, Hofstra U. Atty. GTE, 1982, pres., assoc. gen. counsel human resources, sr. v.p. human resources-compensation and benefits; exec. v.p. human resources Verizon Comm., Inc., 2000—. Office: Verizon Comm Inc 1095 Ave of Americas New York NY 10036-6797

SINGER, FREDERICK RAPHAEL, medical researcher; b. St. Louis, June 27, 1939; s. Meyer and Lee (Minkle) S.; m. Sandra Joy Barnes, Aug. 16, 1964; children: Stefanie, Jeffrey. Student, UCLA, 1956—59; BS, U. Calif., Berkeley, 1960; MD, U. Calif., San Francisco, 1963. Diplomate Am. Bd. Internal Medicine, Am. Bd. Endocrinology and Metabolism. Intern UCLA Affiliated Hosp., 1963-64; resident VA Hosp., L.A., 1964-65, 68-69; instr. in medicine Harvard U., Boston, 1971-72; asst. prof. medicine UCLA, 1972-73, U. So. Calif., L.A., 1973-74, assoc. prof., 1974-78, prof., 1978-89, prof. orthop. surgery, 1980-89; dir. Bone Ctr. Cedars-Sinai Med. Ctr., L.A., 1989-92, clin. prof. medicine, 1993—. Dir. Osteoporosis/Metabolic Bone Disease program St. Johns Hosp. and Health Ctr., Santa Monica, Calif., 1992—; dir. Skeletal Biology Lab, John Wayne Cancer Inst., Santa Monica, 1992—; mem. endocrine and metabolic drug adv. com. FDA, USPHS, Bethesda, Md., 1983-87. Author: Paget's Disease of Bone, 1977; contbr. numerous articles, revs. to profl. jours. Vice chmn. cmty. adv. com. Univ. H.S., L.A., 1984. Capt. USAF, 1965-67. Calif. State scholar, 1956-60; clin. investigator VA, 1971-73. Mem. Endocrine Soc., Am. Soc. Clin. Investigation, Am. Soc. Bone and Mineral Rsch. (chmn. pub. affairs 1981-86, coun. 1987, pres.-elect 1989, pres. 1990), Paget's Disease Found. (chmn. bd. dirs. 1990—). Office: John Wayne Cancer Inst 2200 Santa Monica Blvd Santa Monica CA 90404-2302 Personal E-mail: singerf@yahoo.com.

SINGER, GEORGE MILTON, clinical psychologist; b. Phila., Oct. 13, 1924; s. Benjamin and Bessie (Podlisker) S.; m. Carol Ann Horton, June 15, 1977; children: Elizabeth Carol, Susan Theresa, Sonnet Marie-Anne. BA, Temple U., 1950, AM, 1952, PhD, 1958. Grad. asst. exptl. psychology lab. Temple U., Phila., 1950-51, grad. asst. psychol. clinic, 1951-53, lectr., 1953-54; chief psychologist Phila. State Hosp., 1953-56; dir. psychol. services Pennhurst State Hosp., Spring City, Pa., 1958-61; clin. psychologist Kern County Mental Health Dept., Bakersfield, Calif., 1961-68; project dir., coordinator Kernview Community Mental Health Ctr., Bakersfield, 1968-70; pvt. practice clin. psychology Bakersfield, 1953—2001; ret., 2001. Mem. med. staff Kern View Mental Health Ctr. and Hosp., Bakersfield, Calif., 1988-92; mem. med. staff Meml. Ctr. for Behavioral Health, Bakersfield, 1992-97; affiliated med. staff Hoag Meml. Hosp., Newport Beach, Calif., 1972-73; cons. psychologist Pioneer Cmty. Hosp., 1976-83. Cons. editor Dictionary of Psychology, Corsini, 1999. Mem. Kern County Mental Health Adv. Bd., 1976-83, adv. bd. Patton State Hosp., 1979-85; bd. dirs. Orange County Child Guidance Clinic, 1973-74. Served with USAAF, 1943-46, ETO, MTO. Recipient Service award Psi Chi, 1952, Cert. of Achievement Southeast Pa. Mental Health Assn., 1956. Mem. AAAS, APA, Calif. Psychol. Assn., Am. Soc. Clin. Hypnosis, Kern County Soc. Clin. Psychologists (pres. 1993-94), Kern County Psychol. Assn. (pres. 1968-69), Internat. Soc. Hypnosis, Rotary of Spring City (pres. 1960-61). Home: 1805 Ridgewood Dr Bakersfield CA 93306-3829 Personal E-mail: geo99sin@cs.com.

SINGER, HERSH, marketing executive; Chmn. SMS Rsch. & Mktg. Svcs. Office: SMS Rsch & Mktg Svcs 1042 Fort St Mall Ste 200 Honolulu HI 96813-5698

SINGER, HOWARD JACK, biology professor, researcher; b. Newark, Sept. 4, 1940; s. Nat I. and Rose (Alboum) S.; m. Helena Liisa Niskanen, May 29, 1986; children: Jamie Alexander Niskanen-Singer. BA, Oberlin Coll., 1962; MS, U. Minn., 1966; PhD, Tufts U., 1970. Prof. biology N.J. City U. (formerly Jersey City State Coll.), Jersey City, 1970—. Cons. Proforma Base Corp., Jersey City, 1985-87, Instructivision, Inc., Livingston, N.J., 1988-89; researcher SUNY Downstate Med. Ctr., Bklyn., 1987-89. Contbr. articles to profl. jours. Pres. Van Vorst Pk. Assn., Jersey City, 1977-78; treas. Environ. Voters Alliance, N.J., 1984-90; dir. Hudson County (N.J.) Toxic Task Force, 1980-86; active Scientists Com. for Pub. Info., N.Y.C., 1976-80. Am. Chem. Soc. scholar, 1958-62; fellow NIH, 1966-70, NSF, 1961. Mem.: Am. Fedn. Tchrs. (membership chmn. 1989—), Theobald Smith Soc. (pres. 1996—97, alt. nat. councilor 1997—99, nat. councilor 2000—, alt. nat. councilor 2002—03, chmn. program com., nat. councilor 2003—), Am. Soc. for Microbiology. Avocations: skiing, art nouveau, scuba, tennis. Home: 297 York St Jersey City NJ 07302-4016 Office: NJ City U 2039 John F Kennedy Blvd Jersey City NJ 07305-1527 Office Phone: 201-200-3310. E-mail: hsinger@njcu.edu.

SINGER, IRVING, philosophy educator; b. N.Y.C., Dec. 24, 1925; s. Isidore and Nettie (Stromer) S.; m. Josephine Fisk, June 10, 1949; children— Anne, Margaret, Emily, Benjamin. AB summa cum laude, Harvard U., 1948, MA, 1949, PhD, 1952. Instr. philosophy Cornell U., 1953-56; asst. prof. U. Mich., 1956-59; vis. lectr. Johns Hopkins U., 1957-58; mem. faculty M.I.T., 1958—, prof. philosophy, 1969—. Author: Santayana's Aesthetics, 1957, The Nature of Love: Plato to Luther, 1966, rev. edit., 1984, The Goals of Human Sexuality, 1973, Mozart and Beethoven, 1977, The Nature of Love: Courtly and Romantic, 1984, The Nature of Love: The Modern World, 1987, Meaning in Life: The Creation of Value, 1992, The Pursuit of Love, 1994, The Creation of Value, 1996, The Harmony of Nature and Spirit, 1996, Reality Transformed: Film as Meaning and Technique, 1998, George Santayana: Literary Philosopher, 2000, Feeling and Imagination: The Vibrant Flux of our Existence, 2001, Sex: A Philosophical Primer, 2001, Explorations in Love and Sex, 2001, Three Philosophical Filmmakers: Hitchcock, Welles, Renoir, 2004. Served with AUS, 1944-46. Fellow Guggenheim Found., 1965, Rockefeller Found., 1970, Bollingen Found., 1966; grantee Am. Council Learned Socs., 1966; Fulbright fellow, 1955. Mem. Am. Philos. Assn. Office: MIT Rm 32D-808 Cambridge MA 02139 Office Phone: 617-253-2649.

SINGER, ISADORE MANUEL, mathematician, educator; b. Detroit, May 3, 1924; married; 5 children. BS, U. Mich., 1944; MS, U. Chgo., 1948, PhD in Math., 1950; ScD (hon.), Tulane U., 1981; LLD (hon.), U. Mich., 1989, U. Ill., Chgo. Moore instr. math. MIT, Cambridge, 1950—52, prof. math., 1956—70, Norbert Wiener prof., 1970—79, John D. MacArthur prof. math. (1st holder), 1983—, Inst. prof., 1987—; asst. prof. UCLA, 1952—54; vis. prof. math U. Calif., Berkeley, 1977—79, prof., 1979—83, Miller prof. math., 1982—83, prof. math., 1977—83. Vis. asst. prof. math. Columbia U., N.Y.C., 1954—55; mem. Inst. Advanced Study, 1955—56; past steering com. Ctr. for Non-Linear Scis., Los Alamos Nat. Labs.; adv. bd. Inst. Theoretical Physics, U. Calif., Santa Barbara; bd. dirs. Santa Fe Inst.; mem. various organizing coms.; editor procs. for confs. in field. Former editor profl. jours. Recipient Nat. medal of Sci., 1983, Steele prize Lifetime Achievement, 2000; fellow Alfred P. Sloan, 1959—62, Guggenheim, 1968—69, 1975—76. Mem.: NAS (past councillor, former mem. com. math. and phys. scis., other coms.), Internat. Congress Mathematicians (program com.; 1986, Wigner prize 1989), Am. Phys. Soc., Am. Math. Soc. (v.p. 1970—72, past exec. com., Bocher Meml. prize 1969, Pub. Svc. award 1993), Am. Acad. Arts and Scis., Am. Philos. Soc. Office: MIT Dept of Math Bldg 2 Rm 387 77 Massachusetts Ave Cambridge MA 02139-4307

SINGER, JEFFREY ALAN, surgeon; b. Bklyn., Feb. 2, 1952; s. Harold and Hilda (Ginsburg) S.; m. Margaret Sue Gordon, May 23, 1976; children: Deborah Suzanne, Pamela Michele. BA cum laude, Bklyn. Coll., 1973; MD, N.Y. Med. Coll., 1976. Diplomate Am. Bd. Surgery. Intern Maricopa County Gen. Hosp., Phoenix, 1976-77, resident, 1977-81, mem. teaching faculty, 1981-96; trauma cons. John C. Lincoln Hosp., Phoenix, 1981-83; pvt. practice Phoenix, 1981-87; group pvt. practice Valley Surg. Clinics, Ltd., Phoenix, 1987—, S.W. Surg. Clinics, P.C., Phoenix, 1996-97. Sec.-treas. med. staff Humana Desert Valley Hosp., Phoenix, 1987-89, chief surgery, 1985-87, 91-93, exec. com., 1993-95; adj. asst. prof. divsn. clin. edn. Ariz. Coll. Osteo. Med., Midwestern U., 1998—; mem. adj. clin. faculty Kirksville (Mo.) Coll. Osteo. Medicine. Assoc. editor Ariz. Medicine, 1994-2000, contbg. writer, 2001—. Rep. precinct committeeman, Phoenix, 1986-2000; mem. exec. com. bd. dirs. Goldwater Inst. for Pub. Policy Rsch., 2002—. Named Top Doc, Phoenix Mag., 1999. Fellow: ACS, Am. Soc. Abdominal Surgeons, South-

western Surg. Congress, Internat. Coll. Surgeons; mem.: Maricopa County Med. Soc. (v.p. 1998, bd. dirs. 1998—2002), Ariz. Med. Assn. (bd. dirs. polit. com. 1985—, legis com. 1986—, chmn. bd. dirs. polit. com. 1991—93, Walk the Talk award 2001), Ariz. Sch. Choice Trust (bd. dirs. 1998—2004, adv. bd. 2004—), Alpha Omega Alpha. Avocations: philosophy, politics, history, travel, underwater sports, writing. Office: Valley Surg Clinics Ltd 16601 N 40th St Ste 216 Phoenix AZ 85032-3353 Office Phone: 602-996-4747. Business E-Mail: ValleySurgClinic@aol.com.

SINGER, JON DOUGLAS, receptionist, writer; b. N.Y.C. s. Jerome Leonard and Dorothy Gottlieb Singer. BA, NYU, 1974, MA, 1978. Shelver libr. books Yale U. Med. Sch., New Haven, Conn., 1987-88, Wilbur Smith Assocs., New Haven, 1996; receptionist Fellowship Club, 2000—. Author: Lost Lands and Cities, 1987, Lost Lands and Cities Beneath the Sea, 1997, Ireland's Mysterious Lands and Sunken Cities, 2001. Campaign asst. Dem. Party, N.Y.C., 1980; mem. Rep. Nat. Com., 2003; mem. U.S. Naval Inst., 2003. Jewish. Avocations: archaeology, astronomy, quantum physics. Home: 305 Audubon Ct New Haven CT 06510

SINGER, KATHRYN J. assistant principal; d. Walter and Elinor Katyryniuk; children: Joseph, Kristine. AA, Centralia (Wash.) Coll., 1963; BA, U. Puget Sound, 1965; MEd, Lesley Coll., 1991. Lic. adminstrv. edn. Nev., Wash. Sci. dept. chair Clark County Sch. Dist., Las Vegas, 1994-97, dean of students, 1997-99, asst. prin., 1999—. Chairperson Profl. Devel. Com., Las Vegas, 2000—; cons. Chapman U. State of Nev., 1998-2000, prof., 1998—; adv. bd. Nev. Sci. Project, Las Vegas, 1995-99. Named Outstanding Sci. Tchr. Clark County Sci. Tchrs. Assn., 1995, 96. Mem. Nat. Assn. of Secondary Sch. Prins., Assn. of Secondary Curriculum Devel., Phi Delta Kappa. Avocations: hiking, walking, books. Home: 113 Clifton Heights Dr Las Vegas NV 89145

SINGER, KURT DEUTSCH, news commentator, writer, publisher; b. Vienna, Aug. 10, 1911; came to U.S., 1940, naturalized, 1951; s. Ignaz Deutsch and Irene (Singer) S.; m. Hilda Tradelius, Dec. 23, 1932 (div. 1954); children: Marian Alice Birgit, Kenneth Walt; m. Jane Sherrod, Apr. 9, 1955 (dec. Jan. 1985); m. Katherine Han, Apr. 8, 1989. Student, U. Zürich, Switzerland, 1930, Labor Coll., Stockholm, 1936; PhD, Div. Coll. Metaphysics, Indpls., 1951. Escaped to, Sweden, 1934; founder Ossietzky Com. (successful in release Ossietzky from concentration camp); corr. Swedish mag. Folket i Bild, 1935-40; founder Niemöller Com.; pub. biography Göring in Eng. (confiscated in Sweden), 1940; co-founder pro-Allied newspaper Trots Allt, 1939; corr. Swedish newspapers in, 1940; editor News Background, 1942; lectr. U. Minn., U. Kans., U. Wis., 1945-49; radio commentator Sta. WKAT, 1950; corr. N.Am. Newspaper Alliance, N.Y.C., 1953—; pres. Singer Media Corp., 1987—99. Dir. Oceanic Press Svc., San Clemente, Calif. Author, editor: underground weekly Mitteilungsblätter, Berlin, Germany, 1933; author: The Coming War, 1934, (biog.) Carl von Ossietzky, 1936 (Nobel Peace prize), Germany's Secret Service in Central America, 1943, Spies and Saboteurs in Argentina, 1943, Duel for the Northland, 1943, White Book of the Church of Norway, 1940, Spies and Traitors of World War II, 1945, Who are the Communists in America, 1948, 3000 Years of Espionage, 1951, World's Greatest Women Spies, 1952, (juvenile) Kippie the Cow, 1952, Polgar the Hypnotist, 1953, Gentlemen Spies, 1953, The Man in the Trojan Horse, 1954, World's Best Spy Stories, 1954, Charles Laughton Story; adapted TV, motion pictures, 1954, Spies Over Asia, 1955, More Spy Stories, 1955, My Greatest Crime Story, 1956, My Most Famous Case, 1957, The Danny Kaye Saga; My Strangest Case, 1958, Spy Omnibus, 1959, Spies for Democracy, 1960, Crime Omnibus Spies Who Changed History, 1961, Hemmingway-Life and Death of a Giant, 1961, True Adventures in Crime, Dr. Albert Schweitzer, Medical Missionary, 1962, Lyndon Baines Johnson-Man of Reason, 1964, Ho-i-man; juveniles, 1965; Kurt Singer's Ghost Omnibus, 1965; juvenile Kurt Singer's Horror Omnibus; The World's Greatest Stories of the Occult, The Unearthly, 1965, Mata Hari-Goddess of Sin, 1965, Daughter of Mata Hari, 1965, Lyndon Johnson-From Kennedy to Vietnam, 1966, Weird Tales Anthology, 1966, I Can't Sleep at Night, 1966, Weird Tales of Supernatural, 1967, Tales of Terror, 1967, Famous Short Stories, 1967, Folktales of the South Pacific, 1967, Tales of The Uncanny, 1968, Gothic Reader, 1968, Bloch and Bradbury, 1969, Folktales of Mexico, 1969, Tales of the Unknown, 1970, The House in the Valley, 1970, Hablan Los Artistas, 1970, Tales of the Macabre, 1971, Three Thousand Years of Espionage, 1971, El Mundo de Hoy, 1971, Cuentos Fantasticos del Mas, 1971, Aldous Huxley, El Camino al Infierno, 1971, Ghouls and Ghosts, 1972, The Unearthly, 1972, The Gothic Reader, 1972, Satanic Omnibus, 1973, The Plague of the Living Dead, 1973, Gothic Horror Omnibus, 1974, Dictionary of Household Hints and Help, 1974, Supernatural, 1974, They are Possessed, 1976, True Adventures into the Unknown, 1980, I Spied-And Survived, 1980, Great Adventures in Crime, 1982, The Oblong Box, 1982, Shriek, 1984, First Target Book of Horror, 1984, 2d, 1984, 3d, 1985, 4th, 1985, Solve A Crime, 1994, The Ultimate Quiz Book, 1994, The Complete Guide to Career Advancement, 1994, The Sex Quiz Book, 1994, The Marriage Quiz Book, The Psychology Quiz Book, The Teenage Quiz Book, Success Secrets, 1995, Conozcase Mejor y Triunfe, 1995, The Joy of Practical Parenting, 1995, Der Deutsche Widerstand gegen Hitlers Krieg - 1939-45, 2002; editor: UN Calendar, 1959-58; fgn. corres. German mags., 1996-2000; contbr. articles to newspapers, popular mags., U.S., fgn. countries, all his books and papers in Boston U. Libr.-Spl. Collections, Danish Peace Acad., 2001, Gandhi Centre Berlin, 2003, Awd Literatur Haus, Vienna, Austria. Mem. UN Speakers Rsch. Com., UN Children's Emergency Fund, Menninger Found. Mem. Nat. Geog. Soc., Smithsonian Assos., Internat. Platform Assn. (v.p.), United Sch. Assemblies (pres.), Danish Peace Acad. *In the sunset years of my life, I feel stronger than ever that the most important contribution one makes in a lifetime is to plant as many seeds as possible with many people, and perhaps many countries. Who knows where the seeds of ideas survive and expand?.*

SINGER, LEONARD S. chemist, research scientist, consultant; b. Middletown, Pa., Oct. 9, 1923; s. Isaac and Lena Singer; life ptnr. Margaret Gold; children: Ruth, Meredith Lugasy. BS in Chem. Engring., Pa. State U., 1943; PhD in Phys. Chemistry, U. Chgo., 1950; postgrad., Cornell U., 1950—51. Chem. engr. Celanese Corp. Am., Cumberland, Md., 1943—44; rsch. chemist U.S. Naval Rsch. Lab., Washington, 1951—55; rsch. scientist Union Carbide Corp., Parma, Ohio, 1955—74, corp. rsch. fellow, 1974—85; ret., 1985; cons., 1986—. Contbr. articles to profl. jours. With U.S. Army, 1944—46. Named to Polymer Processing Hall of Fame, U. Akron, 2001. Fellow: Am. Carbon Soc. (Charles E. Pettinos award 1977, George D. Graffin Lectureship 1983); mem.: Am. Chem. Soc. (emeritus), Sigma Xi. Achievements include patents in field of carbon and carbon fibers; development of process for producing high-modulus, high-strength carbon fibers from mesophase pitch. Avocation: music. Home: 33 Kendal Dr Oberlin OH 44074-1902

SINGER, MARCUS GEORGE, philosopher, author, educator; b. N.Y.C., Jan. 4, 1926; s. David Emanuel and Esther (Kobre) S.; m. Blanche Ladenson, Aug. 10, 1947; children: Karen Beth, Debra Ann. AB with high honors, U. Ill., 1948; PhD (Susan Linn Sage fellow), Cornell U., 1952. Asst. in philosophy Cornell U., Ithaca, N.Y., 1948-49, instr. philosophy, 1951-52, U. Wis.-Madison, 1952-55, asst. prof., 1955-59, assoc. prof., 1959-63, prof. philosophy, 1963-92, prof. emeritus, 1992—, chmn. dept. philosophy, 1963-68; chmn. philosophy dept. U. Wis. Center System, 1964-66; dir. pub. lectr. series Royal Inst. Philosophy, London, 1984-85. Vis. fellow Birkbeck Coll., U. London, 1962-63; rsch. assoc. U. Calif.-Berkeley, 1969; vis. Cowling prof. philosophy Carleton Coll., Northfield, Minn., 1972; vis. prof. humanities U. Fla., Gainesville, 1975; vis. fellow U. Warwick, 1977, 84-85; vis. Francis M. Bernardin disting. prof. humanities U. Mo., Kansas City, 1979; hon. rsch. fellow Birkbeck Coll., U. London, 1984-85; acad. visitor London Sch. Econs., U. London, 1984-85 Author: Generalization in Ethics, 2nd edit., 1971, Verallgemeinerung in der Ethik, 1975, The Ideal of a Rational Morality, 2002; editor: Morals and Values, 1977, American Philosophy, 1985, Reason, Reality, and Speculative Philosophy, 1996, Essays on Ethics and Method, 2000; contbr. Essays in Moral Philosophy, 1958, Limits of Liberty, 1966, Moral Philosophy, 1967, Indian Review of Philosophy, 1972, Etyka, 1973, Monist, 1974, Moral Philosophy: An Introduction, 1976, Ency. of Philosophy, 1967, Approaches to Ethics, 1969, Readings in Ethical Theory, 1970, Readings in Contemporary Ethical Theory, 1970, Law and Philosophy, 1971, Introduction to Moral Philosophy, 1973, Skepticism and Moral Principles, 1973, Introductory Readings in Ethics, 1974, Morals and Values, 1977, Zygon, 1980; contbr. Criminal Justice Ethics, 1983; contbr. Acad. Am. Ency., 1982, 1984, 1989, Gewirth's Ethical Rationalism, 1984, American Philosophy, 1985, Morality and Universality, 1985, New Directions in Ethics, 1986, The Handbook of Western Philosophy, 1988, Applying Philosophy, 1988, An Ency. of Philosophy, 1988, Moral Philosophy: Historical and Contemporary Essays, 1989, Conduct and Character: Readings in Moral Theory, 1989, Analisis Filosofico, 1990, Key Themes in Philosophy, 1990, Essays on Henry Sidgwick, 1992, Ency. of Ethics, 1992, 2001, A History of Western Ethics, 1992, A History of Western Ethics, 2nd edit., 2003, Ethics, 1993, Consequentialism, 1993, Cambridge Dictionary of Philosophy, 1995, 1999, Biographical Dictionary of Twentieth Century Philosophers, 1996, Pragmatism, Reason, and Norms, 1998, Ratio Juris, 2000; co-editor: Introductory Readings in Philosophy, 2nd edit., 1974, Reason and the Common Good, 1963, Belief, Knowledge and Truth, 1970, Legislative Intent and other Essays on Law, Politics and Morality, 1993; editor: numerous other essays and publs. Served with USAAF, 1944-45. Am. Philos. Assn. Western Divsn. fellow, 1956-57; Summer Rsch. grant Social Sci. Rsch. Coun., 1958; Guggenheim fellow, 1962-63; Inst. for Rsch. in Humanities fellow U. Wis., 1984. Mem. AAUP, Am. Philos. Assn. (v.p. Western divsn. 1984-85, pres. Ctrl. divsn. 1985-86, bd. officers 1991-94), Royal Inst. Philosophy, Charles S. Peirce Soc, Soc. for Advancement Am. Philosophy, Wis. Acad. Scis., Arts and Letters, N.Y. Acad. Scis., Sidgwick Soc. (exec. dir.), Phi Beta Kappa, Phi Kappa Phi. Home: 5021 Regent St Madison WI 53705-4745

SINGER, MARKUS MORTON, retired trade association executive; b. N.Y.C., Dec. 20, 1917; s. Isadore and Nettie (Stromer) S.; m. Phyllis Berger, June 26, 1945; children— Fredric L., Robert B. B.C.S., NYU, 1939; postgrad., George Washington U., 1951-55. With Nat. Food Brokers Assn., Washington, 1946—, v.p., 1961-65, exec. v.p., 1965-71, pres., 1972-83, pres. emeritus, 1983—, acting pres., chief exec. officer, 1987-88. Lifetime hon. trustee Nat. Food Brokers Assn. Edn. and Tng. Found. Served with AUS, 1942-45. Recipient Pres.'s award as Man of Yr. Can. Food Brokers Assn., 1976 Mem. European Food Brokers Assn. (hon. life), Frozen Food Industry Disting. Order of Zerocrats. Jewish.

SINGER, MARTIN H. Internet company executive; BA, U. Mich.; MA in Exptl. Psychology, PhD in Exptl. Psychology, Vanderbilt U. With Bell Labs., AT&T, Tellabs; v.p., gen. mgr. Wireless Access Bus. Devel. Divsn. Cellular Infrastructure Group Motorola, 1990—98; pres., CEO SAFCO, 1998—2001; CEO Pctel Inc., Chgo., 2001, chmn., 2001—. Achievements include patents in field. Office: Pctel Inc 8725 West Higgins Rd Ste 400 Chicago IL 60631*

SINGER, MAXINE FRANK, retired biochemist, scientific institute executive; b. N.Y.C., Feb. 15, 1931; d. Hyman S. and Henrietta (Perlowitz) Frank; m. Daniel Morris Singer, June 15, 1952; children: Amy Elizabeth, Ellen Ruth, David Byrd, Stephanie Frank. AB, Swarthmore Coll., 1952, DSc (hon.), 1978; PhD, Yale U., 1957, DSc (hon.), 1994, Wesleyan U., 1977, U. Md.-Baltimore County, 1985, Cedar Crest Coll., 1986, CUNY, 1988, Brandeis U., 1988, Radcliffe Coll., 2000, Williams Coll., 1990, Franklin and Marshall Coll., 1991, George Washington U., 1991, NYU, 1992, Lehigh U., 1992, Dartmouth Coll., 1993, Harvard U., 1994, Yale U., 1994, U. Nebr., 2004; PhD honoris causa (hon.), Weizmann Inst. Sci., 1995. USPHS postdoctoral fellow NIH, Bethesda, Md., 1956—58, rsch. chemist biochemistry, 1958—74; head sect. on nucleic acid enzymology Nat. Cancer Inst., 1974—79; chief Lab. of Biochemistry, Nat. Cancer Inst., 1979—87, rsch. chemist, 1987—88; pres. Carnegie Inst. Washington, 1988—2002. Regents vis. lectr. U. Calif., Berkeley, 1981; bd. dirs. Perlegen Sci., Inc. Mem. editl. bd.: Jour. Biol. Chemistry, 1968—74, Sci. mag, 1972—82, chmn. editl. bd.: Procs. of NAS, 1985—88; co-author (with Paul Berg): 3 books on molecular biology and a sci. biog.; contbr. articles to scholarly jours. Chmn. Smithsonian Coun., 1992—93; trustee Wesleyan U., Middletown, Colo., 1972—75, Yale Corp., New Haven, 1975—90; bd. govs. Weizmann Inst. Sci., Rehovot, Israel, 1978—; bd. dirs. Whitehead Inst., 1985—94, chmn. bd., 2003—. Named to Washington D.C. Hall of Fame, 2000; recipient award for achievement in biol. scis., Washington Acad. Scis., 1969, award for rsch. in biol. scis., Yale Sci. and Engring. Assn., 1974, Superior Svc. Honor award, HEW, 1975, Dirs. award, NIH, 1977, Disting. Svc. medal, HHS, 1983, Presdl. Disting. Exec. Rank award, 1987, U.S. Disting. Exec. Rank award, 1987, Mory's Cup, Bd. Govs. Mory's Assn., 1991, Wilbur Lucius Cross Medal for Honor, Yale Grad. Sch. Assn., 1991, Nat. Medal Sci., NSF, 1992, Pub. Svc. award, NIH Alumni Assn., 1995, Vannevar Bush award, Nat. Sci. Bd., 1999. Fellow: Am. Acad. Arts and Scis.; mem.: AAAS (Sci. Freedom and Responsibility award 1982), NAS (coun. 1982—85, com. sci., engring. and pub. policy 1989—91, chmn. 1999—), N.Y. Acad. Scis., Human Genome Orgn., Pontifical Acad. of Scis., Inst. Medicine of NAS, Am. Philos. Soc., Am. Chem. Soc., Am. Soc. Microbiologists, Am. Soc. Biol. Chemists. Home: 5410 39th St NW Washington DC 20015-2902 Office: Carnegie Inst Washington 1530 P St NW Washington DC 20005-1933

SINGER, MERLE ELLIOT, rabbi; b. Duluth, Minn., May 11, 1939; s. Samuel and Brenda (Naymark) S.; m. Myra Golden, Aug. 29, 1965; children: Jonathan, Jeremy, Michael, Mark. AB, U. Cin., 1961; BHL, MAHL, Hebrew Union Coll., Cin., 1966, DD (hon.), 1991; DHL, Gwynedd-Mercy Coll., 1978; D in Pub. Svc. (hon.), Fla. Atlantic U., 1999. Ordained rabbi. Rabbi Temple Sinai, Washington, 1966-71, Reform Congregation Beth Or, Phila., 1971-78; sr. rabbi Temple Beth El, Boca Raton, Fla., 1978—. Adj. prof. history, Judaic studies Fla. Atlantic U., Boca Raton,1978-79; adj. prof. Judaic studies Gwynedd Mercy Coll., Phila., 1975-78; instr. I.M. Wise div. Gratz Coll., Phila., 1971-76; chaplain Boca Raton Police Dept.; rabbinic and com. Camp Coleman, Union Am. Hebrew Congregations, Cleveland, Ga., 1978—; delegate to World Zionist Congress, Israel, 1997. Sponsor inter-faith and Holocaust seminars for the Sisters of Mercy, facuty and students of Gwynedd Mercy Coll., 1978; Jewish student affairs advisor Phila. Coll. of Textiles and Scis., 1976-77, Villanova U., 1976-77; Rabbinic bd. overseers Hebrew Union Coll., 1985—; campaign v.p. United Way of South Palm Beach County, 1986-87, pres., 1987-88; mem. adv. bd. Mae Volen Sr. Ctr., Boca Raton, 1981; clergy advisor Planned Parenthood of Palm Beach County, Inc., Boca Raton; bd. dirs. Edn. Found. Palm Beach County, Inc., 1986-88, Florence Fuller Child Devel. Ctr., Boca Raton, Am. Jewish Com., 1995—; past pres. Religious Leadres Assn. Boca Raton; mem. ethics com. Boca Raton Cmty. Hosp., 1992—; invitee Pres.'s Ann. Prayer Breakfast, Washington, 1996. Recipient nat. award for outstanding svc. Domestic Policy Assn./Nat. Issues Forum, 1985-86, Ben Gurion award for Israel bonds State of Israel, 1975, 85, Torch of Liberty Humanitarian award Anti-Defamation League, 1981, Cmty. Svc. award Boca Raton News, 1982, So Far award Boy Scouts Am., 1987, B'nai Avraham award Am. Jewish Com., 1991, citation Jewish Chautauqua Soc., 1993, Silver Medallion Brotherhood award NCCJ, 1992, Cmty. Svc. award Boys Town Jerusalem, 1993, Golden Shofar award Israel Bonds, 1997, Leading Man award Palm Beach County Cystic Fibrosis Found., 1998; named to Four Chaplains Legion of Honor, Phila., 1981; named Minister of Day, State of Fla., 1993; Merle E. Singer Day proclaimed in his honor, City of Boca Raton, 1991, 96; elected to Boca Raton's Walk of Recognition, 1999. Mem. South Palm Beach Bd. of Rabbis, Palm Beach Bd. of Rabbis (past. pres.), Union of Am. Hebrew Congregations (com. for winning the unaffiliated), Assn. Reform Zionists Am. (bd. dirs. 1983—), S.E. Ctrl. Conf. Am. Rabbis (pres. 1995—), Ctrl. Conf. Am. Rabbis (com. on relief, subvention and solicitation, nat. bd. 1995—), Israel Bonds (nat. rabbinic cabinet), Hebrew Union Coll. Inst. of Religion (presidents alumni assn. 1984—), Synagogue Coun. Am. (nat. bd. govs.). Office: Temple Beth El 333 SW 4th Ave Boca Raton FL 33432-5798

SINGER, MYER R(ICHARD), lawyer; b. Everett, Mass., Oct. 24, 1938; s. Nathan and Celia (Rudin) Singer; m. Elaine Doris Ginesky, June 17, 1962; children: Andrew L., Stephen D., Jocelyn G. BSBA, Boston U., 1960, LLB, 1963. Bar: Mass. 1963, U.S. Ct. Appeals (1st cir.) 1963. Atty. Boston Legal Aid Soc., 1963—64; pvt. practice Dennis Port, Mass., 1965—2001; ptnr. Singer & Singer, LLC, 2001—. Trustee, corporator, mem. bd. investment Cape Cod Five Cents Savs. bank, Harwich Port, Mass.; trustee Cape Cod Mus. of Natural History, 2001—; faculty Mass. Continuing Legal Edn., Inc., 1985, 1990—98; program chmn. Real Estate Devel. Cape Cod-Mass. Bar Inst., 1999; spkr. in field. Co-author: (book) Creation and Care of Condominiums, 1985, Everything You Need to Know about the Cape Cod Commission Act, 1990. Pres. Dennis Yarmouth Band Parents, 1986—87; mem. adv. bd. Cape Mus. Fine Arts, Dennis, 1988—96; former trustee Cape Cod Synagogue; mem., clk. Yarmouth (Mass.) Zoning Bd. Appeals, 1980—86; former bd. dirs. Cape Cod and Island chpt. of Mass. Heart Assn.; former pres. Legal Svcs. of Cape Cod and Island, Inc. Mem.: ABA, Barnstable County Bar Assn. (mem. exec. com. 1999—2003), Mass. Bar Assn. (chmn. bar assn. program real estate devel. Cape Cod 1999). Avocations: boating, photography. Home: 238 Greenland Circle East Dennis MA 02641-1302 Office: PO Box 67 26 Upper County Rd Dennis Port MA 02639-0067 E-mail: mrsinger@singer-law.com.

SINGER, NIKI, media consultant; b. Rochester, NY, Sept. 10, 1937; d. Goodman A. and Evelyn (Simon) Sarachan; m. Michael J. Sheets, 1973; children: Romaine Kitty, Nicholas Simon Feramorz. BA cum laude, U. Mich., 1959. Mgr. advt. sales promotion Fairchild Publ., NYC, 1959-67; acct. exec., acct. supr. Vernon Pope Co., NYC, 1967-69, v.p., 1969-71; pres. Niki Singer, Inc., NYC, 1971-93; sr. v.p. M. Shanken Comm., Cigar Aficionado, Wine Spectator, 1994—2002; founder Niki Singer, LLC, 2003—. Mem.: Les Dames d'Escoffier (bd. dirs.), Am. Inst. Wine and Food (bd. dirs.). Office: 1035 5th Ave New York NY 10028-0135 E-mail: sheets@nyc.rr.com.

SINGER, NORBERT, health services professional, educational consultant; b. Vienna, May 3, 1931; arrived in Eng., 1939; s. Salomon and Mina (Korn) S.; m. Brenda Margaret Walter, May 23, 1980. BSc in Spl. Chemistry, U. London, 1951, PhD in Phys. Chemistry, 1954; DSc (hon.), U. Greenwich, London, 1993. Project leader Morgan Crucible Co. Ltd., London, 1954-57; lectr., dep. head dept. chemistry No. Polytechnic, London, 1958-70; prof., head dept. life scis. Polytechnic of Cen. London, 1971-74; asst., dep. dir. Polytechnic of North London, 1974-78; vice chancellor U. Greenwich (formerly Thames Poly.), London, 1978—93; chmn. Oxleas NHS Health Trust, Bexley, 1993-2001, St. Peter's Primary CE Sch. Vis. prof. U. Westminster, 1996. Contbr. articles to profl. jours., including Jour. Chem. Soc. Chmn. Rose Bruford Coll., 1994-99. Decorated comdr. Order Brit. Empire; fellow Queen Mary and Westfield Coll., U. Coll., Northampton. Fellow Royal Soc. Chemistry. Home: Croft Lodge Bayhall Rd Tunbridge Wells TN2 4TP England

SINGER, PAULA NOYES, lawyer, software company executive; b. Portsmouth, N.H., Aug. 2, 1944; d. Paul Snowman and Grace Marion (Smith) Noyes; m. Wayne Allen Goodrich, Sept. 6, 1964 (div. 1973); 1 child, Beth Ann; m. Gary Philip Singer, June 1, 1976; 1 child, Samantha Anne. BA, U. Maine, Orono, 1966; JD, U. Maine, Portland, 1978. Bar: Maine 1978, Mass. 1978, U.S. Dist. Ct. Maine 1978, U.S. Dist. Ct. Mass. 1979, U.S. Tax Ct. 1985, U.S. Ct. Appeals (1st cir.) 1996, U.S. Supreme Ct. 1986. Programmer New Eng. Mut. Life Ins. Co., Boston, 1966-67; programmer to sr. systems analyst Union Mut. Life Ins. Co., Portland, 1968-77; tax specialist Peat, Marwick, Mitchell & Co., Portland, 1977-79; internat. personnel specialist Arthur D. Little, Cambridge, Mass., 1979-85; lawyer Vacovec, Miller & Rothenberg, Brookline, Mass., 1985-88; ptnr. Vacovec, Rothenberg, Mayotte & Singer, Newton, Mass., 1988-90, Vacovec, Mayotte & Singer, Newton, Mass., 1990—; co-founder, CEO Windstar Techs., Inc., 1994—; co-founder, pres. Windstar Publ., Inc., 2000—. Author: (6 books under the collective title) U.S. Tax Guide for Foreign Persons and Those Who Pay Them; contbr. articles pub. to profl.jour. Bd. dirs. U. Maine Law Sch. Alumni, 1989-95. Mem. ABA, Mass. Bar Assn., Boston Bar Assn., Am. Assn. Immigration Lawyers, Women in World Trade (bd. dirs. 1987-89), ADL Alumni Assn. (bd. dirs. 1987-95, clerk 1987—), Internat. Fiscal Assn., Phi Beta Kappa, Phi Kappa Phi. Democrat. Jewish. Avocation: reading. Office: Windstar Tech Inc 1400 Providence Hwy Bldg 3 Ste 3250 Norwood MA 02062-0800 also: Vacovec Mayotte & Singer 255 Washington St Ste 340 Newton MA 02458-1634 Office Phone: 781-551-5858.

SINGER, PHILIP CHARLES, environmental engineer, educator; b. Bklyn., Sept. 6, 1942; married Ellen Becker, 1965; children: Naomi, Elizabeth, Robert, Jennifer. BCE, Cooper Union, 1963; MS, Northwestern U., 1965; SM, Harvard U., 1965, PhD, 1969. Asst. prof. civil engring. U. Notre Dame, 1969-73; assoc. prof. environ. sci. and engring. U. N.C., Chapel Hill, 1973-78, prof., 1978—, dir. water resources engring., 1979-98, dir. drinking water rsch. ctr., 1999—. Mem. NAE, ASCE, Am. Chem. Soc., Am. Water Works Assn., Am. Acad. Environ. Engrs., Water Environment Fedn., Assn. Environ. Engring. Profs., Internat. Ozone Assn. Achievements include research on drinking water treatment, disinfection by-products formation and control, ozonation. Office: Univ North Carolina Dept Environ Sci & Engring CB7431 Chapel Hill NC 27599 E-mail: phil_singer@unc.edu.

SINGER, ROBERT, plastic surgeon; b. Buffalo, Oct. 22, 1942; s. Murray and Fay Singer; m. Judith Harris. Student, SUNY, Buffalo, 1960-63; MD, SUNY, 1967. Lic. physician, Calif.; diplomate Am. Bd. Plastic and Reconstructive Surgery. Resident in gen. surgery Stanford Med. Ctr., Palo Alto, Calif., 1967-69, Santa Barbara Cottage and Gen. Hosp., 1972-74; resident in plastic surgery Vanderbilt U., 1974-76; pvt. practice specializing in emergency and trauma San Diego, 1971-72; pvt. practice plastic, reconstructive and aesthetic surgery La Jolla, Calif., 1976—. Prior asst. clin. prof. plastic surgery U. Calif., San Diego; sr. staff, chief plastic surgery Scripps Meml. Hosp., La Jolla, 1980-86, vice chmn. dept. surgery, 1989-91. Contbr. articles to profl. jours. Active San Diego Opera, San Diego Mus. of Man, La Jolla Playhouse, Voices for Children, San Diego Zoo, Mus. Photog. Arts, KPBS, others. Fellow ACS; mem. AMA, Calif. Med. Assn., San Diego County Med. Soc., San Diego Internat. Soc. Plastic Surgeons (pres. 1988-89), Calif. Soc. Plastic Surgeons (pres. 1995-96), Am. Soc. Aesthetic Plastic Surgeons (pres. 1994-95), Internat. Soc. Clin. Plastic Surgeons, Am. Soc. Plastic and Reconstructive Surgeons (trustee 1996—, chmn. bd. trustees 1998-99), J.B. Lynch Soc., Royal Soc. Medicine, Am. Assn. for Accreditation of Ambulatory Surgery Facilities (pres. 1991-2000), San Diego Plastic Surgery Soc. (pres. 1989-90), Aesthetic Surgery Edn. and Rsch. Found. (pres., 2000—) Avocations: tennis, travel, pre-columbian art. Office: 9834 Genesee Ave Ste 100 La Jolla CA 92037-1214

SINGER, ROBERT W. metallurgist, company executive officer; b. 1937; m. Janet Singer. B, Tex. A&M U. V.p. mktg. KEYCON Industries, 1982-84; pres. wire divsn. Valhi, Inc., 1985-86; v.p. Contran Corp., 1986-88; pres., COO Keystone Consol. Industries, Inc., Dallas, 1988-97, pres., CEO, 1997—. Office: Keystone Consol Industries Inc Three Lincoln Centre 5430 LBJ Fwy Ste 1740 Dallas TX 75240 Fax: 972-458-8108.

SINGER, SARAH BETH, poet; b. N.Y.C., July 4, 1915; d. Samuel and Rose (Dunetz) White; m. Leon Eugene Singer, Nov. 23, 1938; children: Jack, Rachel. BA, NYU, 1934; postgrad., New Sch. Social Research, 1961-63. Tchr. creative writing Hillside Hosp., Queens, N.Y., 1964-75, Samuel Field YMHA, Queens, 1980-82. Mem. Pacific N.W. Writers Conf.; prin. reader Frye Art Mus., 1998, 2000, 01, 03. Author: Magic Casements, 1957, After the Beginning, 1975, Of Love and Shoes, 1987, The Gathering, 1992, contbr. poetry to anthologies, poetry mags. and quars. including Am. Women Poets, 1976, Yearbook Am. Poetry, 1981, The Best of 1980, 81, Filtered Images, 1992, the Croton Rev., The Lyric, Bitterroot, Judaism, Encore, The Jewish Frontier, Yankee, Hartford Courant, Poet Lore, N.Y.Times, Christian Sci. Monitor, Voices Internat., The Round Table, Orphic Lute, Brussels Sprout, Poetry and Medicine Column Jour. AMA, The Shakespeare Newsletter, Midstream (N.Y.C. Jewish Rev.), The Penwoman, Poets West, Showcase; cons. editor Poet Lore, 1975-81. Recipient Stephen Vincent Benet award Poet Lore, 1968, 71, Dellbrook award Shenandoah Valley Acad. Lit. and Dellbrook-Shenandoah Coll. Writers' Conf., 1978, 79, C.W. Post Poetry award, 1979-80, award for best poem Lyric quar., 1981, biennial award for achievement in poetry Seattle br. Nat. League Penwomen, 1988, award for traditional poetry Wash. Poets Assn., 1989, 95, 97, 98, Traditional Poetry award Wash. Poets Assn., 1995, 98, four honorable mentions for structured verse, 1998, 2000, cert. of merit Muse mag., 1990, Editor's Choice award for Haiku Brussels Sprout, 1992, Carlin Aden award for structured verse Washington Poets Assn., 2001, 02, Hon. Mention, 2001, 03, 2 Hon. Mentions, 2002, 03; poem chosen for Met. Bus. Poetry Project, Seattle, 1992, 96, hon. mention Wash. Poets Assn., 1997, 98, 2000; poem Upon My Demise translated into Russian, recorded 1st prize Marj McAllister award Voices Internat., 1993; poem chosen

in top ten of structured verse category Writer's Digest, 1999, three honorable mentions in structured verse category, 1999, two honorable mentions, 2000, 2 hon. mentions for structured verse category Writer's Digest Contest, 2000, 02, Lifetime Achievement award Poets/West, 2003. Mem. PEN, Poetry Soc. Am., Poets and Writers, Nat. League Am. Penwomen (poetry chmn. L.I. br. 1957-87, publicity chmn. 1990, sec. Seattle br. 1990, pres. 1992-94, v.p. 1994—, publicity chmn. State of Wash. 1992—, Marion Doyle Meml. award 1976, 3d place, 2000, 1st prize nat. poetry contest 1976, Drama award 1977, Poetry award 1977, 1st prize modern rhymed poetry 1978, Lectr. award 1980, Sonnet award Alexandria br. 1980, 81, Catherine Cushman Leach award 1982, 3d place, 2000; poetry award Phoenix br. 1983, Pasadena br. 1984, Alexandria br. 1985, 1st prize award Portland br. 1990, structured verse award Spokane br. 1992, Della Crowder Miller Meml. Petrarchan Sonnet award 1994, 2000, Della Crowder Meml. Free Verse award, 2000, Honorable Mention Anita Marie Boggs Meml. award 1994, 2000, Owl award and Ann. award for achievement in poetry Seattle br. 1994, Poet's Choice award Portland br. 1995, 2d prize Internat. Poetry Contest, Palomar br., 1996, 3d prize in internat. poetry 1997, Palomar Branch internat. poetry contest honorable mention, 1998, 1st prize Internat. Poetry Contest Palomar br., 1999, hon. mention, 1999, honorable mention Anne Marx Sestina award 2000, 3d pl. Catherine Cushman Leach Poetry award 2000, 3d pl. Marion Doyle Poetry award 2000, Della Crowder Meml. award for Petrarchan sonnet 2000, Della Crowder Meml. award for free verse 2000, 3d pl. Anne Marx Sestina award 2002), Poetry Soc. Am. (v.p. 1974-78, exec. dir. L.I., 1979-83, James Joyce award 1972, Consuelo Ford award 1973, Gustav Davidson award 1974, 1st prize award 1975, Celia Wagner award 1976), Wash. Poets Assn., Northwest Writer's Conf., Washington Poets Assn. Address: 900 University St Apt 6N Seattle WA 98101-2728 E-mail: sarahsing2@aol.com. *As a poet, I have sought never to compromise my standards as to what constitutes poetry, despite fads that come and go. My goal has been to achieve whatever perfection I can in my work, and to preserve enough humility to realize that the best is never good enough. My life has truly been enriched by vision and aspiration. As a poet, the important thing for me is to create something moving and beautiful. Publication is a welcome by-product, but in itself, is not the goal for which I strive.*

SINGER, S(IEGFRIED) FRED, geophysicist, educator; b. Vienna, Sept. 27, 1924; came to U.S., 1940, naturalized, 1944; s. Joseph B. and Anne (Kelman) S.; m. Candace Carolyn Crandall, 1990. BEE, Ohio State U., 1943, DSc (hon.), 1970; AM, Princeton U., 1944, PhD in Physics, 1948. Instr. physics Princeton, 1943-44; physicist, applied physics lab. Johns Hopkins, 1946-50; sci. liaison officer Office Naval Research, Am. embassy, London, 1950-53; asso. prof. physics U. Md., College Park, 1953-59, prof., 1959-62; dir. Nat. Weather Satellite Center, Dept. Commerce, 1962-64; dean Sch. Environ. and Planetary Scis., U. Miami, 1964-67; dep. asst. sec. for water quality and research Dept. Interior, Washington, 1967-70; dep. asst. adminstr. EPA, Washington, 1970-71; prof. environ. scis. U. Va., Charlottesville, 1971-87; chief scientist U.S. Dept. Transp., Washington, 1987-89; pres. Sci. and Environ. Policy Project, 1989—. Vis. rsch. prof. Jet Propulsion Lab., Calif. Inst. Tech., 1961-62; Fed. Exec. fellow Brookings Instn., 1971; vis. Sid Richardson prof. J.B. Johnson Sch., U. Tex., 1978; sr. fellow Heritage Found., 1982-83; vis. eminent scholar George Mason U., 1984-86, disting. rsch. prof., 1994—; Wesson fellow Hoover Instn., Stanford, 1992, 98; head sci. evaluation group astronautics and space exploration com. U.S. Ho. of Reps., 1958; cons. U.S. Treasury Dept., GAO, Office Tech. Assessment, U.S. Congress; mem. bd. Nat. Com. on Am. Fgn. Policy; mem. White House Panel on U.S.-Brazil Sci. and Tech. Exch., 1987; guest scholar Nat Air and Space Mus., Smithsonian Instn., 1991, Woodrow Wilson Internat. Ctr. for Scholars, 1991, Hoover Instn., 1992; disting. rsch. rpof. Inst. for Space Sci. and Tech., Gainesville, Fla., 1989-95; bd. dirs. AMREP Corp., Patent Enforcement Fund, Inc. Author: Geophysical Research with Artificial Earth Satellites, 1956, Manned Laboratories in Space, 1970, Global Effects of Environmental Pollution, 1970, Is There an Optimum Level of Population, 1971, The Changing Global Environment, 1975, Arid Zone Development: Potentialities and Problems, 1977, The Economic Effects of Demographic Changes, 1977, Energy, 1979, Price of World Oil, 1983, Free Market Energy, 1984, Global Climate Change, 1990, Origins of The Universe, 1990, The Ocean in Human Affairs, 1990, The Greenhouse Debate Continued, 1992, Hot Talk, Cold Science: Global Warming's Unfinished Debate, 1997, Climate Policy: From Rio to Kyoto, 2000; sci. adv. com. Dept State 1981; vice chmn. Nat. Adv. Com. Oceans and Atmosphere, 1981-86; contbr. articles on space, energy, environment and population problems to profl. publs. Served with USNR, 1944-46, USAFR, 1950-53. Recipient Presdl. commendation, 1958, gold medal for exceptional service Dept. Commerce, 1965; named Outstanding Young Man U.S. Jr. C. of C., 1959 Fellow AAAS (com. coun. affairs 1970), AIAA, Am. Geophys. Union, Am. Phys. Soc.; mem. Internat. Acad. Astronautics, European Acad. for Environ. Affairs, Pan Am. Med. Assn. (pres. sect. on environ. health scis. 1973-85), Cosmos Club (Washington), Colonnade Club (Charlottesville). E-mail: singer@sepp.org.

SINGER, SUZANNE FRIED, editor; b. N.Y.C., July 9, 1935; d. Maurice Aaron and Augusta G. (Ginsberg) Fried; m. Max Singer, Feb. 12, 1959; children: Saul, Alexander (dec.), Daniel, Benjamin. BA with honors, Swarthmore Coll., 1956; MA, Columbia U., 1958. Program asst. NSF, Washington, 1958-60; assoc. editor Bibl. Archaeology Rev., Washington, 1979-84, mng. editor, 1984-96, exec. editor, 1996-99, contbg. editor, 1999—; mng. editor Bibl. Rev., Washington, 1984-96, exec. editor, 1994-99, contbg. editor, 1999—; mng. editor Moment, Washington, 1990-99, exec. editor, 1999—, Archaeology Odyssey, 1998-99, contbg. editor, 1999—. Jewish. also: 1 Barak Jerusalem Israel 93502

SINGER, THOMAS KENYON, international business consultant, fruit grower; b. Wilson, N.Y., Jan. 30, 1932; s. Harold Thomas and Grace (Kenyon) S.; m. Jacqueline Germain Moulin, June 8, 1957; children: Marc Andre, Vivianne Grace Singer Scott, Claire Anne, Michele Moulin Singer Ross, Gail Kenyon Singer Watson. BS in Econs., U. Pa., 1954. Dir. mktg. Europe Kaiser Aluminum & Chem. Corp., London, 1959-66; v.p. Kaiser LeNickel subs., Oakland, Calif., 1967-73, div. mgr., 1973-75; v.p. govt. relations Kaiser Aluminum & Chem. Corp., Washington, 1975-81, corp. v.p. Oakland, Calif., 1982—86; pres. Kaiser Internat. Corp., Oakland, Calif., 1982-86, also dir.; chmn. Singer Farms LLC, Appleton, NY. Dir., pres. IBA Inc., 1986-2000. Trustee United Way of Niagara County, trustee The Nature Conservancy of Central and Western N.Y., trustee Niagara Area Found. Capt. USAF, 1955-57. Mem. Army and Navy Club (Washington), Niagara Frontier Country Club. Republican. Episcopalian. Home: 6627 Hummingbird Ln Appleton NY 14008-9693 Office: 6730 Lake Rd Appleton NY 14008-9673 E-mail: appletks@hotmail.com.

SINGERMAN, PHILLIP A. corporate executive; BA, Oberlin Coll.; MA in Polit. Sci., PhD in Polit. Sci., Yale U. Past dir. mayor's office policy devel. City of Phila.; past exec. asst. to devel. adminstr. City of New Haven; pres., CEO Ben Franklin Tech. Ctr., Pa., 1983-95; pres. Md. Tech. Devel. Corp. (TEDCO), Balt., 1999—; asst sec. econ. devel. U.S. Dept. Commerce, 1995-99. Past policy devel. dir. Conn. Conf. Municipalities; past instr. urban policy and regional devel. Barnard Coll., U. Pa., Yale U.; past mem. gov.'s task force tech. transfer. Vol. Peace Corps, Colombia, 1965-67; bd. dirs. Greater Balt. Tech. Coun., State Tech. Coun. Office: TEDCO 5575 Sternett Pl Ste 240 Columbia MD 21044 E-mail: psingerman@marylandtedco.org.

SINGH, BRAHMA NAND, pharmaceutical scientist; b. Varanasi, Uttar Pradesh, India, May 10, 1969; came to U.S., 1995; s. Parma Nand and Vidya (Rai) S.; m. Priya Roy, Dec. 1, 1995. BPharm, Banaras Hindu U., Varanasi, 1991, MPharm, 1993; MS in Pharm. Scis., S.D. State U., 1997; PhD in Pharm., St. John's U., 2003. Trainee pharmacist R&D formulation Alkem Labs. Ltd., Mumbai, India, 1993-94; prodn. officer dept. tablets and capsules Hoechst Marion Roussel Ltd., Ankleshwar, India, 1994-95; scientist Emisphere Tech., Inc., Tarrytown, NY, 2002—. Presenter in field. Jour. reviewer Am. Jour. Physiology, Clin. Pharmacokinetics, Pharmacology Rsch., Pharmaceutical Rsch., Drugs; contbr. articles to profl. jours. Recipient First in Handwriting award Personality Devel. Soc., 1985, Tech. Excellence Award Emisphere Technologies Inc., 2003; jr. rsch. fellow Banaras Hindu U., 1991-93; Doctoral fellow St. John's U., 1997-2002; Univ. Doctoral fellow St. John's U., 1999; rsch. prizes, Internat. Soc. Preventive Oncology, 2000, Am. Coll. Clin. Pharmacology, 2002. Mem. Am. Assn. Pharm. Scientists, Controlled Release Soc., Internat. Microencapsulation Soc., Rho Chi, Sigma Xi. Avocations: reading, swimming, watching indian and american movies. Office: 765 Old Saw Mill River Rd Tarrytown NY 10591 Fax: 914-347-2498. E-mail: BSingh@Emisphere.com.

SINGH, DALJIT, dean, business and public administration educator; b. Montgomery, Punjab, India, Apr. 13, 1942; came to U.S., 1960; s. Balwant Singh and Sant Kaur Dua; m. Katherine Lowe, Apr., 28, 1968; children: Nancy Kiran, John Norman Sher. BA, Calif. State U., 1965; PhD, Claremont U., 1970; LLM, Liecester U., 1997. Asst. prof. Adams State Coll., Alamosa, Colo., 1967-69; assoc. prof. Bemidji (Minn.) State U., 1969-72, Tuskegee (Ala.) U., 1972-75; chairperson polit. scis. dept. Fisk U., Nashville, 1976-79; dean, prof. U. Guam, Mangilao, 1979-96, prof. emeritus, 1996—; dean U. D.C., 1989—91; sr. mentor North Ctrl. U., Prescott, Ariz., 1998—. Sr. faculty mentor North Ctrl. U. Author: Government of Guam, 1981; editor: Small Business and Public Policy in America. Treas. dem. ctrl. com. Tulare County, Calif., 1998; mem. Dem. ctrl. com., Calif., 2000—; mem. affirmative action com. City of Visali, Calif., 1998, human resources adv. com., 1999. Recipient Ancient Order of Chamorri award Govt. Guam, 1996, Legis. Resolution award. Mem. Rotary (pres. 1984-85). Avocations: travel, tutoring, mentoring. Home: 1645 S Cedar St Visalia CA 93292 E-mail: deansingh2@yahoo.com.

SINGH, INDERJIT, nephrologist, internist, medical educator; b. Patiala, India, Oct. 17, 1962; arrived in U.S., 1987; s. Charanjit Singh and Pritinder Kaur; m. Toniya Cheema Singh, June 5, 1994; children: Kunaal Inder, Kabir Inder. MBBS, U. Delhi, 1986. Diplomate Am. Bd. Internal Medicine, Am. Bd. Nephrology. Cert. ACLS. Intern U. Delhi Affiliated Hosps., 1985-86, resident in internal medicine, 1986-87, Easton Hosp.-Hahnemann U. Hosp., 1990-92; rsch. assoc. in endocrinology U. Health Scis.-Chgo. Med. Sch., 1987-88; intern Nassau County Med. Ctr., N.Y., 1988-89; rsch. assoc. in med. transplantation Presbyn. Hosp.-U. Pitts., 1989-90; clin. fellow divsn. nephrology U. Mich., 1992-93, rsch. fellow, 1993-95; clin. asst. prof. internal medicine So. Ill. U. Sch. Medicine, Carbondale, 1995-97; clin. asst. prof. medicine St. Louis U. Sch. Medicine; with Metro Hypertension and Kidney Ctr.; staff nephrologist BMA Carbondale Dialysis Unit, 1995-97, Marion Nephroplex Dialysis Unit, 1996-97; assoc. med. dir. Jefferson County Dialysis, Festus, Mo., 1998—; med. dir. Washington County Dialysis, Potosi, Mo., 1999—. Med. dir. Arrowhead Point Med. Clinic, Harrisburg, Ill., 1995-97; staff nephrologist BMA Carbondale Dialysis Unit, 1995—, Marion (Ill.) Nephroplex Dialysis Unit, 1996—, Christian NE Hosp., St. Louis, DePaul Hosp., St. Louis, Jefferson Meml. Hosp., Crystal City, Mo., others; chmn. infection control com. Marion Meml. Hosp., 1995-97; instr. Washington U. Sch. Medicine. Contbr. articles to profl. jours., chpts. in books; presenter in field. Fellow ACP; mem. Am. Soc. Nephrology, Nat. Kidney Found., Am. Soc. Internal Medicine. Sikh. Avocations: travel, sports, tennis, opera, music, broadway. Home: 843 Courtwood Ln Ballwin MO 63011-5110 Office: Metro Hypertension and Kidney Ctr 11155 Dunn Rd Ste 315E Saint Louis MO 63136-6111 Office Phone: 314-741-1600. Personal E-mail: ijsinghmd@yahoo.com.

SINGH, JAI, online news executive; b. Agra, India; Exec. editor news InfoWorld, PC Week; head The Source; founding editor, v.p., editor-in-chief CNET News.com, 1996—. Named Most Influential Online Journalist, Marketing Computers Mag., 2001—04; recipient Nat. Mag. award, 2004. Mem.: South Asian Journalists Assn. Office: CNET News.com 235 Second St San Francisco CA 94105

SINGH, JYOTI SHANKAR, international organization executive; b. Pathalgaon, India, Apr. 15, 1935; arrived in U.S., 1972; s. Brijnath Kumar and Tirthmani (Singh) S.; m. Maria Luz Molares, 1962; children: Anil, Rajeev, Ajit. BA, Banaras U., India, 1952, MA, 1954, LLB, 1955; MA, NYU, 1979; D (honoris causa), Internat. Inst. Integration, Bolivia, 1980. Assoc. sec. coordinating secretariat, Leiden, The Netherlands, 1960-61; sec. gen. coordinating secretariat, 1961-64; programme cons. Internat. Youth Centre, New Delhi, 1965-66; sec. gen. World Assembly of Youth, Brussels, 1966-72; liaison officer Fund for Population Activities UN, N.Y.C., 1972-73, asst. exec. sec. World Population Yr., 1973-74, dep. chief info. and pub. affairs, 1975-80, dir. info. and external rels., 1980—90; dir. tech. and evaluation div. UN Population Fund, N.Y.C., 1990-95, dep. exec. dir., 1995-96; spl. adviser to exec. dir. UNFPA, N.Y.C., 1996-99; exec. coord. 23rd spl. session UN Gen. Assembly, 2000; exec. coord. World Conf. Against Racism, Geneva, 2000—01; pres. Population 2005, 1999—. Hon. prof. Ctrl. Am. U., Managua, Nicaragua, 1975; exec. coord. UN Internat. Conf. on Population, 1982-84, permanent observer to UN, Ptnrs. in Population and Devel., NY; exec. coord. Internat. Conf. on Population and Devel., 1992-94; chmn. The Earth Times, 1996-98. Author: Creating a New Consensus on Population, 1998; editor-in-chief Populi, 1980-90. Mem. U.S. Com. for UNFPA (bd. dirs.), Population Inst. (bd.dirs.). Home: 10 Waterside Plz Apt 26D New York NY 10010-2606 Office: 405 Lexington Ave 4th Fl New York NY 10174 Office Phone: 212-457-1877. E-mail: jyotissingh@hotmail.com.

SINGH, LOREN CHAN, writer, educator; b. Palo Alto, Calif., Sept. 10, 1943; s. Shau Wing and Anna Mae Chan; m. Frances Anastasia Chow, Apr. 19, 1975 (div. Jan. 1988); children: Karen Monique Chan, Pierre Benedict Chan, Marc Henri Chan; m. Sandra Marie Miner, Mar. 14, 2000. AB, Stanford U., 1965, AM, 1966; MS, Golden Gate U., 1988; PhD, UCLA, 1971. Tchg. asst. UCLA, 1968-69, tchg. assoc., 1969-70; lectr. in history Calif. State U., Northridge, 1970-71, San Jose (Calif.) State U., 1971-72, asst. prof. history, 1972-76, assoc. prof. history, 1976-80; lectr. history Calif. State U., Hayward, 1980-81; prodn. test technician Nicolet Paratronics Corp., Fremont, Calif., 1982; computer svc. technician Bell-No. Rsch., Mountain View, Calif., 1982-83, rsch. analyst, 1984-85, tech. writer, 1985-87; sr. tech. writer StrataCom, Inc., Campbell, Calif., 1987-88; tech. writer Sun Microsystems, Palo Alto, 1988-90, sr. tech. writer, 1990-2000; tech. editor Brocade Comms. Sys., Inc., San Jose, 2000—02; instr. adult edn. Santa Clara (Calif.) Unified Sch. Dist., 2002—03; bus driver Serendipity Land Yachts, Ltd., Santa Clara, 2002—. Author: Sagebrush Statesman, 1973, Collected Technical Support Notes, 1988, SPARCstation 1 Installation Guide, 1989, Desktop Storage Pack Installation Guide, 1989—90, SPARCstation 2 Installation Guide, 1990, SPARCstation 10 Installation Guide, 1992, SPARCstateion 10 Networking and Communication Guide, 1993, SPARCstateion 10SX VSIMMs Installation, 1993, SPARCstateion 20 HyperSPARC Module Upgrade, 1995, SPARCstateion 20 SuperSPARC-II Module Upgrade, 1995, Sun Ultra 1 Reference Material, 1995—96, Sun Ultra 2 Reference Manual, 1996, Sun Ultra 30 Installation Guide, 1997, SPARCstorage FlexiPack Removable Storage Tray Installation Guide, 1997, Sun StorEdge long Wave Gigabit Interface Converter Service Manual, 1999, Sun StorEdge PCI Dual Fibre Channel Host Adapter Installation, 2000; editor: Chinese-American History Reader, 1976; contbr. articles to profl. jours. Radio sta. trustee ARC, Menlo Park, Calif., 1975—80. Recipient Presdl. Sports award, Pres.'s Coun. Phys. Fitness and Sports, 1973. Mem.: Am. Radio Relay League, South Valley YMCA. Democrat. Sikh. Avocations: masters swimming, amateur radio, stamp collecting/philately. Home: 195 Blossom Hill Rd # 123 San Jose CA 95123-2348 Office: Serendipity Land Yachts Ltd 1051 Richard Ave Santa Clara CA 95050-9911

SINGH, MANMOHAN, orthopedic surgeon, educator; b. Patiala, Punjab, India, Oct. 5, 1940; came to U.S., 1969; s. Ajmer and Kartar Singh; m. Manjit Anand, Jan. 1, 1974; children: Kirpal, Gurmeet. MB, BS, Govt. Med. Coll., Patiala, 1964; CM, Panjab U., Chandigarh, India, 1968. Diplomate Am. Bd. Orthop. Surgery. Mem. vis. faculty Mayo Grad. Sch., Rochester, Minn., 1969; rsch. fellow Inst. Internat. Edn., Chgo., 1969-74; resident in orthop. surgery Michael Reese Hosp. and Med. Ctr., Chgo., 1974-78; pvt. practice Chgo., 1979—; mem. attending staff, dir. orthop. rsch. Michael Reese Hosp. and Med. Ctr., Chgo., 1979-94; fellow in orthop. oncology Mayo Clinic and Mayo Found., Rochester, 1979; assoc. prof. U. Ill., Chgo., 1996—. Founder Quantum Health Cir./Enterprises for Holistic Medicine. Developer x-ray method (Singh Index) and bone density method (Radius Index) for diagnosis of osteoporosis. Fulbright travel grantee, 1968. Fellow Am. Acad. Orthop. Surgeons, Am. Orthop. Foot and Ankle Soc.; mem. Orthop. Rsch. Soc., Am. Soc. for Bone and Mineral Rsch., Internat. Bone and Mineral Soc. Democrat. Sikh. Avocations: stamp collecting/philately, photography, meditation. Office: 110 Ridge Rd Munster IN 46321 E-mail: msingh@illianasurgery.com.

SINGH, PARBUDYAL, dean, educator; arrived in US, 1999; s. Katie (Ramdai) Singh; m. Nirmala Persaud, Dec. 24, 1992; 1 child, Amelia Devi. PhD, McMaster U., Ont., Can., 1998. Asst. prof. Sch. of Bus., U. of New Haven, West Haven, Conn., 1999—, asst. dean, 2001—. Dir. U. of New Haven, Assn. to Advance Coll. Sch. of Bus., West Haven, 2000—. Contbr. articles to profl. jours. Recipient Robert Joyner Doctoral prize. Mem.: Soc. for Human Resource Mgmt., Indsl. Rels. Rsch. Assn., Ea. Acad. of Mgmt., Acad. of Mgmt. Home: 167 Old Foxon Rd New Haven CT 06513 Office: U New Haven 300 Orange Ave West Haven CT 06516 Personal E-mail: psingh@newhaven.edu. Home E-mail: psingh@newhaven.edu.

SINGH, RAJENDRA, mechanical engineering educator; b. Dhampur, India, Feb. 13, 1950; came to U.S., 1973; s. Raghubir and Ishwar (Kali) S.; m. Veena Ghungesh, June 24, 1979; children: Rohit, Arun. BS with honors, Birla Inst., 1971; MS, U. Roorkee, India, 1973; PhD, Purdue U., 1975. Grad. instr. Purdue U., West Layfayette, Ind., 1973-75; sr. engr. Carrier Corp., Syracuse, N.Y., 1975-79; asst. prof. Ohio State U., Columbus, 1979-83, assoc. prof., 1983-87, prof., 1987—, Donald D. Glower chair in engring., 2001—. Adj. lectr. Syracuse (N.Y.) U., 1977-79; bd. dirs. Inst. of Noise Control Engring., 1994-96, 99—, v.p. tech. activities, 2000-02, pres., 2003; gen. chmn. Nat. Noise Conf., Columbus, 1985; leader U.S. delegation to India-U.S.A. Symposium on Vibration and Noise Engring., 1996; vis. prof. U. Calif., Berkeley, 1987-88; pres. Inter-Noise 2002 Congress; chmn. India-USA Symposium on Vibration and Noise, 2001; cons., lectr. in field. Author: Emerging Trends in Vibration and Noise Engineering, 1996; contbr. more than 300 articles to profl. jours.; guest editor jours. Recipient Gold medal U. Roorkee, 1973, R. H. Kohr Rsch. award Purdue U., 1975, Excellence in Tchg. award Inst. Noise Control Engring., 1989, Rsch. award Ohio State U., 1983, 87, 91, 96, 2001, Educator of Yr. award GM Tech. Edn. Program, 1998. Fellow ASME, Acoustical Soc. Am.; mem. Soc. Auto Engring., Inst. Noise Control Engring.(cert.), Am. Soc. Engring. Edn. (George Westinghouse award 1993). Achievements include patent for rolling door; development of new analytical and experimental techniques in machine dynamics, acoustics, vibration and fluid control. Home: 4772 Belfield Ct Dublin OH 43017-2592 Office: Ohio State U 206 W 18th Ave Columbus OH 43210-1189 Office Phone: 614-292-9044. Business E-Mail: singh.3@osu.edu.

SINGH, RONALD, social sciences educator, researcher; s. Heeraman and Rajmatti Singh; 1 child, Raymond Anthony D'Angelo. B in Social Sci., U. (Georgetown) Guyana, 1986; MS, Hunter Coll., 1999. Trained tchr.'s cert. Ministry Edn., Guyana, 1981. Tchr. St. Lawrence CC & Vreeden Hoop CH Schs., Parika, Vreeden Hoop, 1974—87; planner State Planning Commn., Georgetown, 1987—91; rsch. asst. Nat. Exptl. U. Guayana, Puerto Ordaz, Venezuela, 1991—92; pres., dir. Internat. Devel. Consulting, Caracas, Venezuela, 1993—98; rsch. assoc. Rsch. Inst. Study Caribbean Diaspora, Queens, 1999—; pres., dir. Liberty Tutoring Ctr., Queens, NY, 2000—; v.p. Millennium Photo Inc., Queens, 2002—. Advisor Nat. Econ. & Social Coun., Georgetown, 1987—91. Author: (poetry) Fragrance of a Dessert-Rose; contbr. articles and chpts. to books; exec. editor Caribbean Jour., Queens, 1999—. V.p. Guyana Venezuela Friendship Assn., Caracas, Venezuela, 1995—98; rschr., editor East Indian Diaspora, Inc., Queens, 1998—2002; pres. U. Guyana Assn. of NY, N.Y.C., 1999—2002. Named to Internat. Soc. Poets Hall of Fame, Wash., 1997; recipient Edn. Psychology prize, Cyril Potter Coll. Edn., 1981, Editor's Choice award, Nat. Libr. Poetry, 1995. Mem.: East Indian Diaspora (assoc.; asst. sec. 1999), Internat. Soc. Poets (life Internat. Poet of Merit award 1997), Liberty Knights Sports Club (pres. 2001). Avocations: cricket, travel, reading. Office: Liberty Tutoring Ctr & RISCD 91-08 Liberty Ave Queens NY 11417

SINGH, SEOPAUL, security firm executive; b. Georgetown, Guyana, Apr. 26, 1946; s. Mooni and D. Singh; m. Gloria Indrouti Birbal, Nov. 6, 1972 (div.); children: Shelly Valini, Paul Rabindranauth, Sharlene Charisma Padmini. Diploma in Pub. Adminstrn., U. Guyana, Georgetown, 1981. Cert. emergency mgr. Va.; ordained min. Internat. Gospels Assemblies, 1977, Assemblies of God, 1979; cert. profl. security mgr. John Jay Coll. N.Y., 2003. Office mgr. UN Urban Planning, Georgetown, 1977—78; trade intelligence exec. Ministry Trade and Consumer Protection, Georgetown, 1978—83, chief allocation distbn., 1978—83; exec. officer CD Commn., Georgetown, 1983—88; resource person Partners Americas, Georgetown, 1988—92; emergency mgmt. specialist UN Volunteers, Geneva, 1992—97; security supr. Morgan Stanley, N.Y.C., 1991—. Advisor emergency relief Nat. Relief Com., Georgetown, 1983—88; advisor emergency mgmt. Partners Americas, 1988—92, Miss., 1988—92; presbyter, missions dir. Assembly God, Georgetown, 1975—83. Author: (book of poetry) Changing Moods; contbr. articles to profl. jours. Co-founder, sec. Guyanese-Am. Assn., Queens, 1992; co founder, pub. rels. officer Assn. Arts & Writers, Queens, NY, 1998. Fellow, Ctrl. U.S. Earth Quake Consortium, 1992, Masonry Inst. Tenn., 1992, Harvard, 1994, Maj. Indsl. Accident Coun. Can. Mem.: NOAA, Assn. Contingency Planners, Internat. Assn. Emergency Mgrs. D-Conservative. International Gospel Assembly. Achievements include development of First Integrated Disaster Response Mechanism, Office of the Prime Minister, Georgetown, Guyana; received Citation for Professionalism in high rise rescue of individual trapped in an elevator; pioneered five churches in five years in Guyana. Avocations: pool, dominoes, chess, poetry reading, christian ministry camping. Home: 139-20 89th Avenue Jamaica NY 11435 Office: Association Artists & Writers 105-27 Liberty Avenue Ozone Park NY 11417 Personal E-mail: seopauls@aol.com.

SINGH, SHIWENDRA PRASAD, civil engineer; b. Mukrera, Bihar, India, July 5, 1937; came to U.S., 1969; s. Ramchandra and Dhanna (Devi) S.; m. Sita Singh, Mar. 7, 1962; children: Sarita, Sabita, Kavita, Saket. BSc in Civil Engring., Bihar Coll. Engring., Patna, India, 1961; MSc in Civil Engring., U. Calgary, Alta., Can., 1968. Registered profl. engr., Pa. Asst. bridge engr. Bihar Pub. Works Dept., Patna, 1962-66; sr. project mgr. Pa. Dept. Transp., Clearfield, 1969—. Recipient Gov.'s Meritorious award Pa. State Gov., 1977, Outstanding Managerial Ability award Pa. Dept. Transp., 1982, Sec. award for excellence Pa. Dept. Transp., 1990. Mem. NSPE, Am. Soc. Hwy. Engrs. Home: 2537 Meadow Rd Clearfield PA 16830-1140 Office: Pa Dept Transp 1924 Daisy St Clearfield PA 16830-3224

SINGH, SURENDRA P. agricultural economics professor, consultant; b. Chunar, India, Aug. 16, 1944; arrived in U.S., 1967; s. Dhani Ram and Devi Rama; m. Gita Singh, May 30, 1974; children: Vikas, Yojna. BSc, Agra U., Kanpur, India, 1963, MSc, 1965; PhD, Pa. State U., 1972. Rsch. assoc. Pa. State U., University Park, 1972; from rsch. assoc. to assoc. prof. Tenn. State U., Nashville, 1980—86, prof. agricultural econ., 1986—. Cons. United Nations Devel. Prog. (UNDP), India, 1991—92, ACDI/VOCA, Uganda, 1994; cons./PI USAID/USDA, 1991—. Author: Perspectives on the Small Farm, 1986; assoc. editor: So. Jour. Agrl. Econs., 1990—93; contbr. articles to profl. jours. Pres. Hindu Cultural Ctr. Tenn., Nashville, 1988—98, trustee, 1990—98. Recipient Fulbright Scholar award, 1989. Mem.: SAEA, AAEA, IAMA. Hindu. Home: 112 Montcastle Ct Nashville TN 37221 Office: Tenn State Univ 3500 John A Merritt Blvd Nashville TN 37209

SINGH, VIJAY, professional golfer; b. Lautoka, Fiji, Feb. 22, 1963; m. Andrena Seth Singh; 1 child, Qass Seth. Professional golfer PGA Tour, 1993—. Player The President's Cup, 1994, 96, 98, 2000, 03. Named Hon. Chairperson, National Golf Day, 1999. Achievements include 20 Career PGA Tour victories; winner PGA Championship, 1998, 2004, Masters Tournament, 2002. Avocations: snooker, cricket, rugby, soccer. Office: South Fla Sect PGA 10804 W Sample Rd Coral Springs FL 33065-2632*

SINGH, YESH PAL, mechanical engineering educator, consultant; b. Muzaffarnagar, India, Jan. 1, 1940; came to U.S., 1970; s. Chhatar and Gyandevi Singh; m. Veena Singh, Feb. 27, 1963; children: Sveta, Vinay. BSME, Roorkee (India) U., 1962; MSME, Youngstown State U., 1974; postgrad., SUNY, Buffalo, 1974-75; DEng, U. Wis., Milw., 1984. Design engr., asst. engr. H.E.C.

Ltd., Ranchi, India, 1962-70; design engr. Youjuralmashzavod, Orsk, USSR, 1964-65, Birdsboro (Pa.) Corp., 1970, 72-73; mech. engr. DES-ENG-Corp., Reading, Pa., 1971—72; engr. Allis-Chalmers Corp., Milw., 1975-77, sr. engr. I, 1977-84, sr. engr. II, 1984-85; assoc. prof. mech. engring. U. Tex., San Antonio, 1985—2003, prof. mech. engring. and biomech., 2003—. Chair mech. design group U. Tex., San Antonio, 1985—2000, chmn. mech. engring., 1993—96, chmn., advisor records mech. engring. grad. program, 1998—2001. Contbr. articles to profl. jours. Recipient Coll. Engring. and Applied Sci. Outstanding Alumni award U. Wis., Milw., 1996, Charles E. Balleisen Awd., 1999. Fellow ASME (treas. San Antonio sect. 1991-92, sec. 1992-93, vice-chmn. 1993-94, chmn. 1994-95, chair nomination and nat. agenda com. 1995-96, chair coll. rels. 1996-97, chair profl. practice 1997-98, Clifford H. Schumaker award Region X, 1998). Achievements include development of design procedures for very large spur and helical gears; of procedures and design programs for determining natural frequency and mode shapes of centrifugal pump systems; of designs for various units of high speed continuous slab casters; of finite element based design procedures for endodontic root canal instrument; of synthesis procedures for design of planar cam-link mechanisms. Home: 2615 Caravan Cir San Antonio TX 78258 Office: U Tex San Antonio 6900 N Loop 1604 W San Antonio TX 78249 0670 Office Phone: 210-458-5527. Business E-Mail: ysingh@utsa.edu.

SINGHAL, MEENA, education educator; b. New Castle, England, Apr. 1, 1968; d. Raj and Mohini Singhal; m. Walid Sabbagh, May 30, 2000. BA, BEd, U. Calgary, Canada, 1992; MEd, McGill U., Montreal, Canada, 1996; PhD, U. Ariz., 1999. Lectr. U. Calif., Irvine, 2000; instr. Long Beach (Calif.) City Coll., 2000—. Editor The Reading Matrix, Irvine, Calif., 2000—. Curriculum project Web-Based Reading Program for Composition Students (Milton Riepe award for Excellence in Tchg., 1999). Fellow, U. of Ariz., 1999, grantee Partnership for Excellence Grant-New Course Proposal, Long Beach City Coll., 2000, Devel. of Integrated Syllabus for Learning Communities Project, 2001, Faculty Devel. and Improvement of Academic Programs: Strengthening Academic Bridges & Support for Success-Methods to Increase Latino Student Retention, 2002. Mem.: Pi Lamba Theta (hon.). Achievements include research in computer-assisted langauge learning and reading. Office: Long Beach City Coll ESL Dept 1305 East Pacific Coast Hwy Long Beach CA 90806 Personal E-mail: msinghal@lbcc.edu. E-mail: msinghal@lbcc.edu.

SINGHAL, RAJAN, engineering executive, consultant; b. Saharanpur, Up, India, Oct. 15, 1954; s. Balmukand and Sonadevi Singhal; m. Uma Gangal, June 18, 1979; children: Ekta, Parul. BS in Engring. & Comm., Nat. Inst. Tech., 1976; LLB, Garhwal U., 1997; MBA, Richard Stockton Coll. N.J., 2004. Jr. scientist Solidstate Physics Lab., Delhi, 1976—77; sub divisional officer UP State Electricity Bd., Meerut, 1977—86, exec. engr. Dehradun, 1986—96, superintending engr., 1996—2000; dir. Hi-Tec Sys., Inc., Egg Harbor, NJ, 2000—01, dir. recruiting & placement, 2000—, sr. aviation engr., 2001—. Guardian Agarwal Com., Dehradun, 1996—2000. Mem.: IEEE (chair 2002—02, Engr. of Yr. 2002), Internat. Test & Evaluation Assn., Am. Inst. of Aeronautics & Astronautics, Internat. Toastmasters (v.p. 2001—02). Office Phone: 609-645-7777. Personal E-mail: rajansinghal@hotmail.com.

SINGHAL, VIVEK KUMAR, management consultant; b. Delhi, India, May 15, 1949; came to the U.S., 1970; s. Om Prakash Saraswati and Kirti Rani; m. Asha Garg; children; Ritu, Vikas. BSEE, Indian Inst. Tech., New Delhi, 1970; MSEE, U. Mich., 1971, MBA, 1973. Cert. mgmt. cons. Inst. Mgmt. Cons. Various positions Rockwell Internat., Troy, Mich., 1973-77; dir. strategic planning Sara Lee Corp., Chgo., 1977-84; v.p. Beatrice Cos., Chgo., 1984-85; founder, pres. Strategic Bus. Mgmt. Co., Oakbrook Terrace, Ill., 1986—. Founder, CEO Global Outsource Bids, Oakbrook Terrace, 2000; adj. prof. Lake Forest Grad. Sch. Mgmt. Exec. com. mem. Assn. Indians in Am., Chgo., 1993-95; treas. Midwest Club, Oakbrook, Ill., 1994-96, dir. Inst. Mgmt. Cons., Chgo. Mem. U. Mich. Alumni Assn., World Future Soc. (v.p. Greater Chicagoland Futurists). Avocations: reading, travel, public speaking. Office: Strategic Bus Mgmt Co 2 Mid America Plz Oakbrook Terrace IL 60181-4451 E-mail: vsingha1@hotmail.com.

SINGHVI, SURENDRA SINGH, finance and strategy consultant; b. Jodhpur, Rajasthan, India, Jan. 16, 1942; came to U.S., 1962, naturalized 1986; s. Rang Raj and Ugam Kanwar (Surana) S.; m. Sushila Bhandari, July 7, 1965; children: Seema, Sandeep. B in Commerce, Rajasthan U., 1961; MBA, Atlanta U., 1963; PhD, Columbia U., 1967. CPA; cert. mgmt. acct. Asst. prof. fin. Miami U., Oxford, Ohio, 1967-69, assoc. prof., 1969-70; adj. prof. fin., 1970-95; fin. mgr. ARMCO Inc., Middletown, Ohio, 1970-79, asst. treas., 1979-83, gen. fin. mgr., 1983-86; v.p. and treas. Edison Bros. Stores, Inc., St. Louis, 1986-90; pres. Singhvi & Assocs., Inc., Dayton, Ohio, 1990—. Bd. dirs. Columbia Indsl. Sales Corp., Hauer Music Co., Oasis Property Inc., Keystone Industries Ltd., Om Hospitality, Inc., Chester Hospitality Inc. Author: Planning for Capital Investment, 1980; co-editor: Frontiers of Financial Management, 4th edit., 1984, Global Finance 2000-A Handbook of Strategy and Organization (The Conference Board), 1996; contbr. over 90 articles to profl. jours. Bd. trustees South Ctrl. Ohio Minority Bus. Coun., 2000—. Recipient Chancellor's Gold medal Rajasthan U., Ahimsa (Non-Violence) award Fedn. Jaina Assns. in N.Am., 1999, 2003. Mem. Inst. Mgmt. Accts. (Bayer Silver medal 1978), Fin. Execs. Inst., Fin. Mgmt. Assn., Dayton Minority Supplier Devel. Coun. (dir. 1997—, chmn. 2000), Rotary (dir. internat. program Middletown chpt. 1973-86, Dayton chpt. 1995—, treas., dir. 2001—02), India Club (pres. Dayton chpt. 1980). Avocations: swimming, kanasta, travel, writing. Home and Office: Singhvi and Assocs Inc 439 Ridge Line Ct Dayton OH 45458-9546 Office Phone: 937-885-7414. E-mail: s.singhvi@yahoo.com.

SINGLE, THOMAS E. paper company executive; b. Gary, Ind., May 31, 1961; BSCE, BS in Pulp & Paper Tech., N.C. State U., 1984; MBA, U. N.C., 1988. Area mgr. Measurex, Atlanta, 1984—86; mgr. corp. fin. James River, Richmond, Va., 1988—91, dir. energy planning & devel., 1991—95, dir. energy procurement, 1995—98, dir. strategic sourcing & procurement, 1998—2000; v.p. cost reduction & productivity Fort James, Deerfield, Ill., 2000—01; v.p. strategic sourcing and procurement Ga. Pacific Corp., Atlanta, 2001—. Office: Ga Pacific Corp 133 Peachtree St NE Atlanta GA 30303

SINGLEHURST, DONA GEISENHEYNER, horse farm owner; b. Tacoma, June 19, 1928; d. Herbert Russell and Rose Evelyn (Rubish) Geisenheyner; m. Thomas G. Singlehurst, May 16, 1959 (dec.); 1 child, Suanna Singlehurst. BA in Psychology, Whitman Coll., 1950. With pub. rels. and advt. staff Lane Wells, L.A., 1950-52; staff mem. in charge new bus. Bishop Trust Co., Honolulu, 1953-58; mgr. Town & Country Stables, Honolulu, 1958-62; co-owner, v.p. pub. rels. Carol & Mary, Ltd., Honolulu, 1964-84; owner Stanhope Farms, Waialua, Hawaii, 1969—. Internat. dressage judge, sport horse breeding judge US Equestrian; sr. judge Can. Dressage Fedn. Chmn. ways and means com. The Outdoor Cir., Hawaii, 1958-64, life mem.; pres. emeritus Morris Animal Found., Englewood, Colo., 1988—, pres., 1984-88; bd. dirs., pres. Delta Soc., Renton, Wash., 1994-97, chmn. emeritus 1998—, N.Y.C.; mem. Jr. League of Honolulu; mem. devel. com. Honolulu Symphony. Recipient Best Friends award Honolulu Vet. Soc., 1986, Spl. Recognition award Am. Animal Hosp. Assn., 1988, Recognition award Am. Vet. Med. Assn. Mem. NAFE, AAUW, Hawaii Horse Show Assn. (Harry Hutaff award 1985, past pres., bd. dirs.), Hawaii Combined Tng. Assn. (past pres. bd. dirs.), Calif. Dressage Soc., U.S. Dressage Fedn., U.S. Equestrian Team (area chmn. 1981-85), Hawaiian Humane Soc. (life), U.S. Pony Clubs (dist. commr. 1970-75, nat. examiner 1970-75), Pacific Club, Outrigger Canoe Club. Republican. Episcopalian. Avocations: music, travel. Home and Office: Stanhope Farms PO Box 546 Waialua HI 96791 Office Phone: 808-637-5625.

SINGLETARY, PATRICIA ANN, minister; b. N.Y.C., Mar. 3, 1948; d. George and Minnie Juanita (Williams) Nickens; m. Edward Franklin Singletary, Feb. 5, 1966 (dec.); children: Erik Franklin, Don Andre. BTh, New World Bible Inst. & Sem., 1984, MRE, 1986; AS, BS, SUNY-Empire State Coll., 1991; AA, Va. Sem. and Coll., 1995; MDiv, New Brunswick Theol. Sem., 1995; DD, Tenn. Bapt. Sch. Religion, 1989. Sr. reorgn. underwriter Depository Trust Co., N.Y.C., 1968-90, acct. coord., 1990—98, security specialist, 1998—2003; ret., 2003. Nat. corr. sec. Nat. Bapt. Conv. U.S.A. Inc., 1984-87; vice chair Spiritual Life Commn. of Clergywomen, 1987—; assoc. minister Morning Star Missionsry Bapt. Ch. of Jamaica, N.Y. CEO, founder Adoni Econ. Enterprises, Inc., v.p. Queens County Young Pastors, Mins. Evangelist Ea. Bapt. Assn. Author: African-American Guide to Buying Stock Without a Broker; nat editor: Ekklesia, 1986. Pastor Elmendorf Reformed Ch., East Harlem, NY. Recipient Vol. Svcs. award City of N.Y., 1980. Mem. NAFE, Nat. Assn. Negro Bus. and Profl. Women, Interdenominational Bd. Clergywoman (gen. sec. 1985-91), Nat. Bapt. Women Ministers Conv. (bd. mgrs. 1983-91), Ea. Bapt. Assn. (instr. 1981-83, v.p. evangelistic unit 1982-83, gen. dir. women's aux. 1988-91), Nat. Coun. Women U.S., Internat. Platform Assn., Bronx Bapt. Ministers Evening Conf. Greater N.Y. and Vicinity, Queens Bapt. Mins. Conf. Greater N.Y. and Vicinity, Assn. Black Seminarians (pres. 1993-95).

SINGLETARY, SONJA EVA, surgeon, educator; b. Coward, S.C., Dec. 23, 1952; 1 child. BS, Clemson U., 1973; MD, U. S.C., 1977. Resident in gen. surgery U. Fla., 1977-83; surg. oncology fellow M.D. Anderson Cancer Ctr., Houston, 1983-85; faculty assoc. U. Tex. M.D. Anderson Cancer Ctr., Houston, 1985-86, asst. prof. surgery, 1986-91, assoc. prof. surgery, 1991-96, prof., 1996—. Author: Breast Cancer, 1999, Breast Cancer-M.D. Anderson Solid Tumor Oncology Series, 1999, Advanced Therapy of Breast Disease, 2004. Named one of Good Housekeeping's Best Doctors in Am., 1995—2004; recipient Women on the Move award, Tex. Exec. Women, 1998, Ptnrs. in Courage award, 1999, Cancer Fighters Eagle award, 1999. Office: U Tex MD Anderson Cancer Ctr Box 444 1515 Holcombe Blvd Houston TX 77030-4009 Office Fax: 713-792-2225. E-mail: esinglet@mdanderson.org.

SINGLETERRY, GARY LEE, investment banker; b. Seattle, May 10, 1948; s. Richard W. and Anita J. (Fowler) S.; m. Mary Beth Burtlend, Nov. 29, 1969; children: Douglas, Laura. AB, Harvard U., 1970; MBA, Stanford U., 1974. Assoc. Morgan Stanley & Co., N.Y.C., 1974-79, Wm Sword & Co., Princeton, N.J., 1979-80; v.p. Thomson, McKinnon & Co., N.Y.C., 1981-82; mng. dir. Dean Witter Reynolds, N.Y.C., 1983-85, Prudential-Bache Securities, N.Y.C., 1985-91; pres. Singleterry & Co., Summit, N.J., 1991—. Mem. FNMA Nat. Adv. Coun., 1991. Republican. Office: Singleterry & Co 57 Union Pl Ste 316 Summit NJ 07901-2568 Fax: 908-918-0232. Office Phone: 908-918-0023. E-mail: garysingle@aol.com.

SINGLETERRY, ROBERT CLAY, JR., aerospace technologist, physicist; b. Fayetteville, N.C., Jan. 4, 1961; s. Robert Clay and Phyllis Lea (Donovan) S.; m. Maria Star Groshner, May 18, 1984. BS in Nuclear Engring., U. Ariz., 1984, MS, 1990, PhD, 1993; postgrad., U. Idaho, 1986-91, Coll. of William and Mary, 1998—. Software-reactor engr. Ga. Power Co., Baxley, 1984-85; software engr. Energy Inc., Idaho Falls, 1985-89; grad. rsch. asst. U. Ariz., Tucson, 1989-93; rsch. asst. Argonne Nat. Lab., Idaho Falls, summers 1989-93, staff nuclear engr., 1993-97; prin. mem. Quantum Solutions, LLC, Idaho Falls, 1995-97; aerospace technologist, physicist NASA Langley Rsch. Ctr., Hampton, Va., 1997—; adminstr.'s fellow NASA/Prairie View A&M U., 2002—03, Star Bridge Sys., Inc., 2003—, U. N.Mex., 2003—. Adj. prof. dept. nuclear sci. and engring. Idaho State U., Pocatello, 1994-97; vis. scientist program coord. Idaho Acad. Sci., 1997. Contbr. articles to profl. jours. Vice-chair Young Women's Conf., Idaho Falls, 1993-94, chair, 1994-95. Mem. Am. Nuc. Soc. (chair tech. group on aerospace nuc. sci. tech.), Va. Acad. Sci. Avocations: golf, volleyball, teaching, community service. Office: NASA Langley Rsch Ctr Mail Ctr Stop 188B Hampton VA 23681-0001 Fax: 757-864-8094. E-mail: robert.c.singleterry@nasa.gov.

SINGLETON, ALVIN E. composer; b. Bklyn., Dec. 28, 1940; Student, NYU; graduate, Yale U., New Haven, Conn., 1971; studied with Goffredo Petrassi, Acad. Nat. Santa Cecilia, Rome, 1971. Composer-in-residence Atlanta Symphony Orch., 1985—88; resident composer Spelman Coll., Atlanta, 1988—91; UNISYS composer-in-residence Detroit Symphony Orch., 1996—97; vis. prof., composition Yale U. Sch. Music. Composer: compositions featured at Tanglewood, Aspen, Nat. Black Arts Festival, Atlanta, Vienna Summer Music Festival, Pro Musica Nova, Bremen, Styrian Autumn Festival, Graz, Brussels ISCM World Music Days, IRCAM, Paris, (albums) Shadows, A Yellow Rose Petal, After Fallen Crumbs. Recipient Kranischsteiner Musikpreis, City of Darmstadt, Germany, Musikprotokoll Kompositionpreis, Austrian Radio; Fulbright Scholar, 1971, Mayor's Fellowship in the Arts, City of Atlanta. Mem.: Nat. Artistic Directorate, Am. Classical Music Hall of Fame, Cin.*

SINGLETON, DONALD EDWARD, journalist; b. Morristown, N.J., Nov. 8, 1936; s. Edward Leslie and Charlotte (Angerbauer) S.; m. Maureen Ann McNiff, Aug. 8, 1959 (div. 1977); children: Nancy Ann, Mark Aram, Jill Susan. Student, Fairleigh Dickinson U., 1955-58. Reporter Dover (N.J.) Advance, 1959-61, Morristown Daily Record, 1961-63, Newark Eve. News, 1963-64; feature reporter-writer N.Y. Daily News, 1964—. Organizer Com. to Save Church Sq. Park, Hoboken, N.J.; vice chmn. Hoboken Environment Com.; mem. due process com. ACLU., Mem. bd. edn., City of Hoboken, 1974-77. Recipient Pub. Service award N.Y. Council Civic Affairs, 1967; President's Distinguished Service award N.Y.C. Council, 1969; Newspaper award merit Women's Press Club N.Y.C., 1970, 79; citation VFW, 1970; Heywood Broun Meml. award Am. Newspaper Guild, 1970; Silver medal for pub. service journalism N.Y. chpt. Pub. Relations Soc. Am., 1970; certificate merit Am. Bar Assn., 1971; Page One award Newspaper Guild N.Y., 1970; Feature award Newspaper Reporters Assn. N.Y., 1972; Consistent Excellence award Uniformed Firefighters Assn., 1991. Mem. Am. Newspaper Guild. Clubs: Press (N.Y.C.). Home: 366 Ogden Ave Jersey City NJ 07307-1115 Office: 220 E 42nd St New York NY 10017-5806 *In reporting, I try very hard to avoid gathering facts in such a way as to fulfill a preconception. I also attempt to force myself to review constantly my opinions about my subjects, and to keep my mind as open as possible. In writing, I try to ask myself the following questions regularly: "Is this what I really believe? Or am I simply writing this way because I believe that this is what some other person or group would like me to write?" Unless I can answer the first question in the affirmative, and the second in the negative, I am not satisfied with a particular story.*

SINGLETON, FRANCIS SETH, international educator; b. Phila., July 13, 1940; s. William Francis and Anna A. (Setian) S.; m. Margaret Neff, June 14, 1962 (div. 1983); children: William, Andrew; m. Charlotte T. Kennedy, Jan. 16, 1988. AB, Harvard U., 1962; MA, Yale U., 1963, PhD, 1968. Budget examiner Bur. of Budget, Washington, 1964-65; dean Pearson Coll. Yale U., New Haven, 1966-69; lectr. U. Dares Salaam, Tanzania, 1969-70; asst. prof. U. Alta., Edmonton, Can., 1970-71; from assoc. prof. to prof., chair politics and govt. Ripon (Wis.) Coll., 1972-83; rsch. assoc. Russian Ctr., Harvard U., Cambridge, Mass., 1983-84; dean arts and scis. Pacific U., Forest Grove, Oreg., 1984-91, prof. govt., 1991—; academic dean Espiritu Santo U., Guayaquil, Ecuador, 1994-97. Ampart lectr. U.S.I.A., Africa, 1983, Africa, 90; lectr. Ural U., Russia, 1991; cons. Russia Fedn. Govt., 1992; mem. Pacific Coun. on Internat. Policy, 1998—; chair nat. peer rev. com. for S.E. Asia Fulbright Scholars, 2001—04. Author: (book) Africa in Perspective, 1968, Introduction to Vietnam and Kue; contbr. articles to profl. publs., chpts. to books. Bd. dirs. Com. Fgn. Rels., Portland, 1989-92; mem. adv. com. Light Rail Tri-Met, Portland, Oreg., 1989-94. Grantee Rockefeller Found., 1969-70, Nat. Coun. Soviet and E. Europe Rsch., 1983-84; U.S. Fulbright scholar, Vietnam, 1999-2000. Avocations: sailing, outdoor activities. E-mail. Home: 39 Hall Quarry Rd PO Box 185 Mount Desert ME 04660-0185 E-mail: ssinglet@pacificu.edu., seth_singleton@unit.maine.edu.

SINGLETON, GREGORY HOLMES, historian, educator; b. Florence, Ala., Oct. 4, 1940; s. David Greene and Anne Rose Singleton; m. Jeannine Carol Jung, Aug. 11, 1995. BA, Calif. State U., Northridge, 1962; PhD, UCLA, 1970. Instr. history Northwestern U., Evanston, Ill., 1970—72; asst. prof. history Northeastern Ill. U., Chgo., 1972—77, assoc. prof. history, 1977—83, prof. history, 1983—2000, chair dept. and prof. history, 2000—. Contbg. author: Religion in the City of Angels: American Protestant Culture and Urbanization, Los Angeles 1850 - 1930, 1979, The New Urban History: Quantitative Explorations by American Historians, Victorian America, The New Urban History: Quantitative Explorations by American Historians, Victorian America; contbr. articles to profl. jours. Fellow, NEH, 1977—78, Inst. for the Advanced Study Religion, 1981—82. Mem.: Am. Soc. for Ch. History, Orgn. Am. Historians, Am. Hist. Assn. Democrat. Lutheran. Avocations: singing, guitar, photography. Home: 7401 N Sheridan Rd Chicago IL 60626 Office: Northeastern Ill Univ 5500 N St Louis Ave Chicago IL 60625 E-mail: g-singleton@neiu.edu.

SINGLETON, HARRY MICHAEL, lawyer; b. Meadville, Pa., Apr. 10, 1949; s. Getdins T. and Rose Ann (Fucci) S.; children: Harry M. Jr., Leah Rose DiFucci. BA, Johns Hopkins U., 1971; JD, Yale U., 1974. Bar: D.C. 1975, Pa. 1976, Calif. 1999, Md. 1999, U.S. Dist. Ct. D.C. 1975, U.S. Dist. Ct. Md. 2001, U.S. Ct. Appeals (D.C. cir.) 1975, U.S. Ct. Mil. Appeals 1975. Assoc. Houston & Gardner, Washington, 1974-75, Covington & Burling, Washington, 1976-77; atty. FTC, Washington, 1975-76; dep. minority counsel Com. on D.C./U.S. Ho. of Reps., Washington, 1977-79, minority chief counsel, staff dir., 1979-81; dep. asst. sec. U.S. Dept. Commerce, Washington, 1981-82; asst. sec. U.S. Dept. Edn., Washington, 1982-86; pres. Harry M. Singleton & Assocs., Washington, 1986-91; pvt. practice law Washington, 1991—; pres. Singleton Entertainment, LLC, Washington, 1999-2000; pres., gen. counsel Single Source Tech. Solutions, LLC, Washington, 2001—03. Legis. cons. Am. Enterprise Inst., Washington, 1975. Pres. bd. trustees Barney Neighborhood House, Washington, 1978-80; corp. bd. dirs. Children's Hosp. Nat. Med. Ctr., Washington, 1984-88; mem. crime com. Boys and Girls Clubs of Greater Washington, 1994-97; mem. D.C. Rep. State Com., 1991—2004, Rep. Nat. Com., 1992-2000, R.N.C. exec. coun., 1993-95, resolutions com., 1997-2000; mem. Rep. Nat. Hispanic Assembly Washington, 1991-92. Mem. Rep. Nat. Lawyers Assn. (bd. dirs. D.C. chpt. 1990-91), Coun. of 100 Black Reps. (bd. dirs. 1991-92), D.C. Black Rep. Coun. (chmn. 1992-93), Rep. Nat. African-Am. Coun. (nat. chmn. 1993-2001), D.C. Rep. Nat. African-Am. Coun. (chmn. 1993-2001). Republican. Presbyterian. Office: 2121 K St NW Ste 800 Washington DC 20037-1829 Office Phone: 202-261-3575.

SINGLETON, JAMES KEITH, federal judge; b. Oakland, Calif., Jan. 27, 1939; s. James K. and Irene Elisabeth (Lilly) S.; m. Sandra Claire Hoskins, Oct. 15, 1966; children: Matthew David, Michael Keith. Student, U. Santa Clara, 1957-58; AB in Polit. Sci., U. Calif., Berkeley, 1961, LLB, 1964. Bar: Calif. 1965, Alaska, 1965. Assoc. Delaney Wiles Moore and Hayes, Anchorage, 1963, 65-68, Law Offices Roger Cremo, Anchorage, 1968-70; judge Alaska Superior Ct., Anchorage, 1970-80, Alaska Ct. Appeals, Anchorage, 1980-90, U.S. Dist. Ct. for Alaska, Anchorage, 1990—, chief judge, 1995—2002. Chmn. Alaska Local Boundary Commn., Anchorage, 1966-69. Chmn. 3d Dist. Rep. Com., Anchorage, 1969—70. Mem. ABA, Alaska Bar Assn., Phi Delta Phi, Tau Kappa Epsilon. Office: US Dist Ct 222 W 7th Ave Unit 41 Anchorage AK 99513-7504

SINGLETON, JOHN, director, screenwriter; b. L.A., Jan. 6, 1968; s. Danny Singleton and Sheila Ward. BA, U. So. Calif., 1990. Writer, dir. Boyz N the Hood, 1991 (Acad. award nominee Best Dir. and Best Screenplay 1992), Shaft, 2000; writer, dir., prodr. Poetic Justice, 1993, Higher Learning, 1995; dir., prodr., screenwriter Michael Jackson's Remember the Time video, 1992, Rosewood, 1997, Woo, 1998. Achievements include being the first African-American and youngest person to be nominated for an Academy Award for Best Director. Office: Creative Artists Agy 1888 Century Park E Ste 1400 Los Angeles CA 90067-1718 also: New Deal Prodns 10202 Washington Blvd Culver City CA 90232-3119

SINGLETON, MARVIN AYERS, state legislator, otolaryngologist; b. Baytown, Tex., Oct. 7, 1939; s. Henry Marvin and Mary Ruth Singleton. BA, U. of the South, 1962; MD, U. Tenn., 1966. Diplomate Am. Bd. Otolaryngology. Intern City of Memphis Hosps., 1966-67; resident in surgery Highland Alameda City Hosp., Oakland, Calif., 1967-68; resident in otolaryngology U. Tenn. Hosp., Memphis, 1968-71; fellow in otolaryngic pathology Armed Forces Inst. Pathology, Washington, 1971; fellow in otologic surgery U. Colo. at Gallup (N.Mex.) Indian Med. Ctr., 1972; practice medicine specializing in otolaryngology/allergies Joplin, Mo., 1972—. Founder, operator Home and Farm Investments, Joplin, 1975—, staff mem. Freeman Hosp., St. John's Hosp., Joplin; cons. in otolaryngology Mo. Crippled Children's Service, Santa Fe R.R.; pres. Ozark Mfg. Co., Inc., Joplin. Mem. Internat. Arabian Racing Bd., 1983-88; mem. Mo. State Senate, 1990-2003; del. Rep. Nat. Conv., 1988, 92. Served with USNG, 1966-72. Fellow Am. Coll. Surgeons, Am. Acad. Otolaryngologic Allergy (past pres.), Am. Assn. Acad. Asthma, Allergy and Immunology; mem. AMA (Mo. del.), Mo. State Med. Assn., Sthn. Med. Assn., Jasper County Med. Assn., Coun. Otolaryngology, Mo. State Allergy Assn., Ear Nose & Throat Soc. Mo. (past. pres.), Joplin C. of C., Masons (32d degree), Sigam Alpha Epsilon, Phi Theta Kappa, Phi Chi. Republican. Methodist. Home: 4478 Five Mile Rd Seneca MO 64865-8357 Office: 1637 W Swain Rd Stockton CA 95207-4172 Office Phone: 209-476-5623. Personal E-mail: senatorsingleton@hotmail.com.

SINGLETON, ROBERT CULTON, graduate school administrator, Bible educator; b. Amarillo, Tex., Oct. 17, 1950; s. William Madison and Doris (Culton) S.; m. Stephanie Diane Lawrence, May 17, 1975; children: Kristin Michelle, Robert Culton Jr. BSEE, U. Tex., 1973; ThM in Bible Exposition, Dallas Theol. Sem., 1977; PhD in Higher Edn., U. Tex., 1993. Ordained to ministry Cmty. Bible Chapel, 1981. Campus staff Campus Crusade for Christ, Dallas, 1974-77; dean Nairobi (Kenya) Internat. Sch. Theology, 1978-83; grad. studies staff Campus Crusade for Christ, Austin, Tex., 1984-92; dean faculty East Asia Sch. Theology, Singapore, 1993-96; faculty The Orlando (Fla.) Inst., 1997—. Bd. dirs. Nairobi Internat. Sch. Theology, 1981-83. Contbr. articles to profl. jours. Mem. Kappa Delta Pi, Phi Kappa Phi. So. Bapt. Avocations: personal computers, tennis. E-mail: bsingleton@toi.edu.

SINGLETON, ROBERT M. theater educator, secondary school educator; b. Ancon, Panama, Feb. 26, 1945; BFA in Drama Edn., U. Tex., 1970, MFA in Drama Edn., 1972. English/theatre tchr. Travis H.S., Austin, Tex., 1972—73, Anderson H.S., Austin, 1973—77; theatre dept. chair, tchr. H.S. for the Performing and Visual Arts, Houston, 1977—. Summer theatre workshop U. Tex., Austin, 1970—2000; UIL-OAP critic judge U. Interscholastic League, Austin, 1990—2003; bd. mem. Nat. Bd. for Profl. Tchg. Stds. Author: (play adaptation) The Comedy of Errors, 1983, She Stoops to Conquer, 1990. Named Tchr. of the Yr., Rotary Club, 1999. Mem.: Tex. Ednl. Theatre Assn. (various offices and coms. 1972—). Office: HSPVA 4001 Stanford Houston TX 77006 Office Phone: 713-942-1966.

SINGLETON, WILLIAM DEAN, publishing executive; b. Graham, Tex., Aug. 1, 1951; s. William Hyde and Florence E. (Myrick) S.; m. Adrienne Casale, Dec. 31, 1983; children: William Dean II, Susan Paige, Adam Nicholas. Student, Tyler (Tex.) Jr. Coll., El Centro Coll., Dallas; BS, U. Tex., Arlington. Chmn. Denver Newspaper Agy.; vice chmn., CEO MediaNews Group Inc., Denver; chmn., pub. Denver Post, 2001—. Bd. dirs. Associated Press. Mem. Salvation Army, Am. Heart Assn. of Ft. Bend County. Mem. Newspaper Assn. Am. (bd. govs.), So. Newspapers Assn., New Eng. Newspaper Assn., N.J. Press Assn., Tex. Daily Newspaper Assn., Greater Houston Partnership Assn. Baptist. Office: Denver Post 1560 Broadway Denver CO 80202-1577

SINGLETON-WOOD, ALLAN JAMES, communications executive; b. Newport, Monmouthshire, Eng., Feb. 13, 1933; arrived in Can., 1968; s. Charles James and Violet Anne (Bond) S.-W.; m. Joan Davies, June 23, 1956; children: Ceri, Glendon. Student, London U., 1949-51. TV and radio musical dir., 1953-57; TV producer, 1957-61; freelance producer for BBC, 1962-64; indsl. advt. mgr. Western Mail, Cardiff, Wales, 1964; advt. dir. Voice of Brit. Industry Mags., London, 1966; mktg. svcs. exec. The Sun and The People, I.P.C. Newspapers, London, 1966-68; mktg. svcs. mgr. Fin. Post, Toronto, Ont., Can., 1969-71, rsch. mgr., 1971-76, nat. sales mgr., 1976-77; pub. Fin. Post Mag., 1978-79, dir. advt. sales Fin. Post divsn., 1980-83; pub. Small Bus. Mag., 1983-87; v.p. pub. Bedford House Ltd., Toronto, 1987-88; pub. Small Bus. mag., v.p. CB Media Ltd., Toronto, 1988—; v.p. pub. Can. Bus. and Small Bus. mags., Who's Who in Can. Bus., Who's Who in Can. Fin., 1989—; corp. pub., gen. mgr. Sentry Comm., Willowdale, Ont., 1991-92; group pub. Bus. Publs. divsn. MacLean Hunter Ltd., Toronto, 1992-93; pres. Can.

Productivity divsn. CB Media Ltd., Toronto, 1994-96; pres., CEO Singleton-Wood Comm. Inc., Victoria, Canada, 1996—. Lectr. at various univs.; cons. in field; pres., CEO, founder Can. Info. Productivity Awards, 1994—2001. Composer: contemporary music including title theme of Swing High, BBC nat. network series, 1953-57. Mem. Anglican Ch. Achievements include development of first computer media evaluation program for Canadian advertising industry.

SINGLEY, JOHN EDWARD, JR., retired environmental scientist, consultant; b. Wildwood, N.J., July 31, 1924; s. John Edward Singley and Dorothy Mae (Pfrommer) S.; children: Gladys, Ann, Margaret, Patricia; m. June Walden Calohan, Apr. 28, 2001; stepchildren: Daniel, Christopher Calohan. BS, Ga. Inst. Tech, 1950; MS, Ga. Inst. Tech., 1952; PhD, U. Fla., 1966. Chemist Redstone Arsenal, Huntsville, Ala., 1950-51; dir. tech. svs. Tenn. Corp., College Park, Ga., 1951-64; lectr. chemistry Ga. State U., Atlanta, 1954-64, assoc. prof., 1964-67; prof. environ. engring. sci. U. Fla., Gainesville, 1967-90, prof. emeritus, 1990—; dir. TREEO Ctr., Gainesville, 1978-86; v.p. James M. Montgomery, Cons. Engrs., Inc., Gainesville, 1984-93, Montgomery Watson Cons. Engrs. Inc., Gainesville, 1993-96; sr. v.p. Environ. Scis. Engring. Inc., Gainesville, 1977-84; prin. Water and Air Rsch., Gainesville, 1970-77; v.p. Metcalf & Eddy, Gainesville, 1996-99; ret., 1999. Cons. Carollo Engrs., Sarasota, Fla., Jones, Edmondson Assocs., Gainesville. Patentee in field of polymers. Mem. Fulton County Rep. Exec. Com., 1962-64; trustee Water for People, 1990-92. With USN, 1943-45. Recipient Donald R. Boyd award Met. Water Agys., 1992. Fellow Am. Inst. Chemists, Inst. Water and Environ. Mgmt.; mem. Am. Water Works Assn. (hon., life, bd. dirs. 1984-87, exec. com. 1986-87, 89-93, v.p. 1989-90, pres.-elect 1990-91, pres. 1991-92, Fuller award 1974, rsch. award 1983, Abel Wolman Excellence award 1995, Disting. Pub. Svc. award 1995, Water Industry Hall of Fame 2000), Fla. Water and Pollution Control Operators Assn. (Flanigan award 1979), Nat. Lime Assn. (Recognition award), Internat. Water Supply Assn., Nat. Assn. Corrosion Engrs., Internat. Ozone Assn. (bd. dirs. 1985-93). Clubs: Gainesville, Civitan (pres. 1972, lt. gov. Fla. dist. 1973-76). Presbyterian. Home: 1719 NW 23rd Blvd # Phe Gainesville FL 32605-3027 Office: 1719 NW 23rd Ave PHE Gainesville FL 32605-3079 E-mail: h20doceds@aol.com.

SINGSTOCK, DAVID JOHN, military officer; b. Oshkosh, Wis., July 19, 1940; s. Arnold William and Viola Rufine (Gerdener) S.; children: Susan, Brian, Elissa, Timothy. BS with distinction, Maine Maritime Acad., 1964; student, U.S. Merchant Marine Acad., 1959-62; BSBA with distinction, George Washington U., 1973, MS, 1975. Lic. profl. marine engr. Commd. ensign USN, 1964, advanced through grades to comdr., 1984, various sea assignments including combat duty in Vietnam, 1964-69, engr. officer USS Harold J. Ellison, 1969-71, ADP fin. mgr. Cinclantflt, 1971-73, planning and quality assurance officer supr. shipbuilding Portsmouth, Va., 1973-76, prodn./repair officer supr. shipbuilding Bath, Maine, 1976-79, ship maintenance mgr. chief naval ops. Washington, 1980-83, dir. fleet modernization program space/naval warfare systems command, 1983-86, program mgr. USS Stark restoration naval sea systems command, 1986-88, tech. dir. dep. asst. sec. Navy for internat. programs, 1988-93; ships program mgr. ROH, Inc., Arlington, Va., 1993-95; ship self def. mgr. Vitro, Corp., Arlington, 1996-97; theater ballistic missile def. R & D mgr. Tracor Sys. Techs., Inc., Arlington, 1998-99; theater ballistic missile def. mgr. Marconi Sys. Techs., Inc., Arlington, 1999—2001; dep. dir. Applied Ordnance Tech. Internat., Arlington, 1999—2001; tech. dir. Aegis Ballistic Missile Def. Anteon Corp., Arlington, 2001—. Sr. tech. advisor Royal Saudi Naval Forces Ops. Desert Shield and Desert Storm, 1990-91; sr. naval tech. mem. to Sec. of Def. chartered delegation of sr. U.S. ofcls., Saudi Arabia, 1991; retired U.S. Navy, 1993. Asst. scoutmaster Boy Scouts Am., Dumfries, Va., 1985-90; coach Youth Soccer, Maine, Va., 1976-84; active local property owners civic orgns., Va., Maine, 1970—; instr. ARC, Seattle, 1967-68. Decorated Navy Commendation medal, Navy Achievement medal, Vietnamese Cross of Gallantry, Meritorious Svc. Medal, Joint Svc. Commendation medal, Bronze Star, Purple Heart; recipient Cert. of Appreciation and Gratitude, Comdr. of Saudi Arabian Armed Forces. Mem. Am. Soc. Naval Engrs. (dep. com. chmn., speaker 1988), Nat. Contract Mgmt. Assn. (cert. contracts mgr.), Ret. Officers Assn., Nat. Eagle Scout Assn., Mason (32 degree), Scottish Rite, Shriner. Presbyterian. Avocations: sailing, jogging, camping, golf, music. Home: 1125 Portner Rd Alexandria VA 22314-1314 Office: Anteon Corp 2231 Crystal Dr Ste 1000 Arlington VA 22202-3742 Office Phone: 703-892-7966.

SINHA, AKHOURI A. geneticist, researcher, cell biologist, educator; b. Churamanpur, Bihar, India, Dec. 17, 1933; arrived in U.S., 1961; s. Akhouri Chandra B. and Bittan Devi Sinha; m. Dorothy Kay Pamer, Sept. 29, 1979. BSc, Allahabad (India) U., 1954; MSc, Patna (India) U., 1956; PhD, U. Mo., 1965. Lectr. Ranchi (India) U., 1956—61; asst. prof. U. Wis., Eau Claire, 1965—67; sr. scientist U. Minn., Mpls., 1967—69; rsch. scientist VA Med. Ctr., Mpls., 1969—. Prof. U. Minn., 1981—. Contbr. articles to profl. jours. Hindu. Avocations: riding, cross country skiing, photography, travel, reading. Office: Rsch Svcs One Veterans Dr Minneapolis MN 55417 Office Phone: 612-467-2846. E-mail: sinha001@tc.umn.edu.

SINHA, MANISHA, historian, educator; b. Patna, Bihar, India, Nov. 2, 1962; arrived in U.S., 1984; d. Srinivas Kumar and Premini Verma Sinha; m. Karsten R. Stueber; 1 child, Sheel K. Stueber. BA, Delhi U., 1984; MA, SUNY, Stony Brook, 1986; MPhil, Columbia U., 1988, PhD, 1994. Preceptor, instr. Columbia U., N.Y.C., 1988—92; fellow Harvard U., Cambridge, Mass., 1992—94, U. N.C., Chapel Hill, 1994—95; asst. prof. U. Mass., Amherst, 1994—2000, assoc. prof., 2001—. Manuscript reader Jour. So. History, Houston, 2000—, Civil War History, University Park, Pa., 2000—, Jour. Early Republic, Lafayette, Ind., 2000—. Author: The Counterrevolution of Slavery, 2000; co-editor: African American Mosaic: A Documentary History, 2004. Spkr. Mass. Found. for Humanities, Boston, 1997, Conn. Humanities Coun., Litchfield, 1999, Smithsonian Instn., Washington, 2001. Fellow, NEH, 2004—05; postdoctoral fellow, Harvard U., Cambridge, 1993—94, Rockefeller Found., Chapel Hill, 1994—95, rsch. grantee, Am. Philos. Soc., Phila., 1999. Mem.: Assn. Study of African Am. Life and History, So. Hist. Orgn., Orgn. Am. Historians (Disting. lectr.), Am. Hist. Assn. (local arrangements com. 2001). Democrat. Hindu. Home: 20 Whittemore Rd Sturbridge MA 01566 Office: Univ Mass 325 New Africa House Amherst MA 01003

SINHA, RAJ P. education educator, researcher; b. Pahsara, Bihar, India, Nov. 11, 1934; arrived in U.S., 1961; s. Kapilded P. and Kaushilya Sinha; m. Rani P. Sinha; children: Rajiv R., Nilu Sinha-Tiwari, Ena. BSc, Patna U., Bihar, India, 1957; MS, U. Wyo., 1963; PhD, U. Manitoba, Can., 1967. Fellow Carleton U., Ottawa, Canada, 1968—72; rsch. scientist Food Rsch. Inst., Ottawa, Canada, 1972—92; assoc. prof. Chgo. State U., 1992—. Contbr. articles to profl. jours. Recipient Provential Govt. Ontario award, 1980. Office: Chgo State Univ Dept Biology 9501 S King Dr Chicago IL 60628-1598 E-mail: rp.sinha@csu.edu.

SINHA, SUNIL K. engineer, educator; b. Patna, India, Mar. 1, 1962; s. Mahesh C. P. and Indu R. Sinha; m. Anju Singh, Jan. 15, 1970; 1 child, Sushruth. B in Engring., Birla Inst. of Tech., 1986; PhD, U. of Waterloo, Can., 2000; MA in Sci., U. Waterloo, 1997. Constrn. engr. PACS-MECON Consultants, Lagos, Nigeria, 1986—87; project engr. Govt. of Bihar, Patna, India, 1987—96; rsch. asst. U. of Waterloo, Canada, 1996—2000, post-doctoral fellow, 2000—01; asst. prof. Pa. State U., State College, Pa., 2001—. Contbr. articles to profl. jours. Mem. of adv. bd. Municipality of State Coll., State College, Pa., 2001—. Fellow Post-Doctoral fellowship, Nat. Sci. & Engring. Rsch. Coun. of Can., 2000; scholar U. Grad. Scholarships, U. of Waterloo, 1997, Doctoral Scholarship, Nat. Sci. & Engring. Rsch. Coun. of Can., 1998. Mem.: ASCE (life). Achievements include research in Development of Sustainable Civil Infrastructure Systems. Home: 145 Jay Ln State College PA 16801 Office: Pa State Univ 223 Sackett Bldg State College PA 16802 Personal E-mail: sunil@engr.psu.edu. E-mail: sunil@engr.psu.edu.

SINHA, SUNIL KUMAR, physicist; b. Calcutta, India, Sept. 13, 1939; came to U.S., 1965; s. Sushil Kumar and Romola Sinha; m. Lonny Linde Olsen, Jan. 27, 1962; children: Arjun, Ranjan. BA in Natural Scis., Cambridge U., Britain, 1960, PhD in Physics, 1964. Vis. scientist Bhabha Atomic Rsch. Ctr., Trombay, India, 1965; asst. prof. physics dept. Iowa State U., Ames, 1966-69, assoc. prof., 1969-71, prof. physics, 1972-75; sr. physicist Argonne (Ill.) Nat. Lab., 1975-82; sr. rsch. assoc. Corp. Rsch., Exxon Rsch., Annandale, NJ, 1982-95; sr. scientist and assoc. dir., exptl. facilities div. Argonne (Ill.) Nat. Lab., 1995-2001; prof. physics U. Calif., San Diego, 2001—. Chmn. U. Chgo. Rev. Com. for Materials Scis. Div., Argonne (Ill.) Nat. Lab., 1990; past chmn. Argonne Intense Pulsed Neutron Source Rev. Com., 1987-91; chmn. Div. Condensed Matter Physics Fellowship Com. of Am. Phys. Soc., 1990-91, Oak Ridge Nat. Small Angle Scattering Ctr. Rev. Com., 1986-89. Editor: Ordering in Two Dimensions, 1980, Spin Waves and Magnetic Excitations, 1990; contbr. articles to profl. jours. Recipient Dept. Energy Rsch. Achievement award, 1981, Ernest Orlando Lawrence Meml. award, 1996, Arthur H. Compton award Advanced Photon Source, 2000; Guggenheim fellow, 1982. Fellow AAAS, Am. Phys. Soc.; mem. Materials Rsch. Soc., Am. Crystallographic Assn. Achievements include rsch. in antiferromagnetism in High Tc materials by neutron diffraction; theory of diffuse X-ray scattering from surfaces. Office: U Calif San Diego Physics Dept 9500 Gilman Dr La Jolla CA 92093 E-mail: ssinha@physics.ucsd.edu.

SINHARAY, SANDIP, statistician, researcher; b. Kenna, India, May 18, 1972; arrived in U.S.A., 1997; s. Radhanath and Pushpamita Sinharay; m. Lopamudra Sinharay, Dec. 10, 2001. MS in Stats., Indian Stats. Inst., 1996; MS, Iowa State U., 1998, PhD, 2001. Rsch. asst. Iowa State U., 1997—2001, tchg. asst., 1998—99; assoc. rsch. scientist Ednl. Testing Svc., Princeton, NJ, 2001—04, rsch. scientist, 2004—. V.p. Iowa Stat-ers, 1999—2001; senator Grad. Student Senate Iowa State U., 2000—01. Contbr. articles and revs. to profl. jours. Mem.: Nat. Coun. Measurement Edn., Psychometric Soc., Am. Statis. Assn. Avocations: travel, running, tennis, badminton. Office: Educational Testing Service T133 Rosedale Road Princeton NJ 08541 Office Phone: 609-734-5079.

SINICKI, CHRISTINE, state official; b. Mar. 28, 1960; married; 2 children. Mgr. small bus.; state assemblywoman, 1998—; del. U.S. Presdl. Electoral Coll., 2000. Mem. children and families com.; mem. edn. com.; mem. edn. reform com.; mem. personal privacy com.; mem. Wis. Housing and Econ. Devel. Authority. Mem. Milw. Sch. Bd., 1991—98. Democrat. Office: State Capitol Rm 321F W PO Box 8953 Madison WI 53708-8953

SINICROPI, JOSEPH, manufacturing executive; CFO, sec. Synthetic Industries, Inc., Chickamauga, Ga., 1995—. Office: Synthetic Industries Inc 309 Lafayette Rd Chickamauga GA 30707-1710

SINISCALCO, GARY RICHARD, lawyer; b. N.Y.C., Aug. 14, 1943; BA in Econs., Le Moyne Coll., 1965; JD, Georgetown U., 1969. Bar: Calif. Regional counsel, sr. trial atty. EEOC, San Francisco, 1969-78; ptnr. Orrick, Herrington & Sutcliffe, San Francisco, 1978—, past co-chair employment law dept. Mem. adv. bd. Nat. Employment Law Inst.; lectr. in field. Co-author: Manager's Guide to Lawful Terminations, 1991; author: (with others) Employment Discrimination Law, 1979, 3rd edit., 1996; contbr. articles to profl. jours. Mem. ABA (mem. com. on internat. labor rels. and equal employment opportunity, mgmt. co-chairperson equal employment opportunity com. 1996-98), State Bar Calif., Bar Commonwealth Va., Am. Employment Law Coun. (founder). Office: Orrick Herrington 400 Sansome St San Francisco CA 94111-3143

SINISE, GARY, actor, director; b. Blue Island, IL, Mar. 17, 1955; Co-founder, artistic dir. Steppenwolf Theatre, Chgo. Appeared in (plays) The Indian Wants The Bronx, 1977, Getting Out, 1980 (Joseph Jefferson award), Of Mice And Men, 1980, Loose Ends, 1982, True West, 1983 (also dir., Obie award best dir. 1982-83), Balm in Gilead, 1984, Streamers, 1985, The Caretaker, 1986, Grapes of Wrath, 1990 (Tony award and Drama Desk), (TV films) The Final Days, 1989, My Name is Bill W., 1989, The Stand, 1994, (theatrical films) Miles from Home, 1988, Of Mice and Men, 1991 (also actor); (actor) Jack The Bear, 1991, A Midnight Clear, 1991, Forrest Gump, 1994 (acad. award nominee, 1994, Disabled Am. Veterans Nat. Commanders award, 1994), The Quick and the Dead, 1995, Apollo 13, 1995, (TV) Truman, 1995 (Cable Ace award 1996, Golden Globe, 1996, Screen Actors Guild Award, 1996,), Ransom 1996, Albino Alligator, 1996, (play) Buried Child, 1996 (Tony award nominee, Joseph Jefferson award, 1996), (TV) George Wallace, 1997 (Emmy award, 1998, Screen Actors Guild award, 1998, Cable ACE Award, 1997), Snake Eyes, 1998, That Championship Season, 1999, Being John Malkovich, 1999, Reindeer Games, 1999, Mission to Mars, 1999, Bruno, 1999, All the Rage, 1999, The Green Mile, 1999, A Gentleman's Game, 2001, Impostor, 2002, Made-Up, 2002, The Human Stain, 2003; (TV) Path to War, 2002; various TV appearances including Crime Story (also dir.), Hunter, True West, Grapes of Wrath; dir. (plays) Frank's Wild Years, Action, The Miss Firecracker Contest, Waiting for the Parade, Tracers, Orphans, Landscape of the Body, 1984, (TV tapes) thirtysomething, 1989, China Beach, 1991. Office: care CAA 9830 Wilshire Blvd Beverly Hills CA 90212-1804 also: Licker & Ozurovich 2029 Century Park E Ste 1060 Los Angeles CA 90067-2919

SINISGALLI, PETER F. financial company executive; b. 1956; CFO Nielsen Media Rsch. divsn. Dun and Bradstreet; sr. v.p., group fin. Dun & Bradstreet Corp., 94; v.p., CFO Dun & Bradstreet Software, 1994-96; v.p., COO Check Free Holdings Inc., Norcross, Ga., 1996-99, pres., COO, 1999—. Office: Check Free Holdings Inc 4411 E Jones Bridge Rd Norcross GA 30092-1615

SINK, JOHN DAVIS, chemist, clergyperson; b. Homer City, Pa., Dec. 19, 1934; s. Aaron Tinsman and Louella Bell (Davis) S.; m. Nancy Lee Hile, Nov. 9, 1956 (dec. Aug. 1961); 1 child, Lou Ann (dec. Aug. 1961); m. Claire Kaye Huschka, June 13, 1964 (div. Feb. 1987); children: Kara Joan, Karl John; m. Sharon Ferrando Padden, July 15, 1989; 1 child, Lisa Michelle Padden. BS in Animal/Vet. Sci., Pa. State U., 1956, MS in Biophys./Animal Sci., 1960, PhD in Biochem./Animal Sci., 1962; EdD in Higher Edn., U. Pitts., 1986; MDiv, Emory U., 2001. Adminstrv. officer, exec. asst. to sec. agr. State of Pa., Harriwburg, 1962; prof., group leader dept. food, dairy and animal sci. Inst. Policy Rsch. and Evaluation, Pa. State U., University Park, 1962-79; pres. Collegian, Inc., 1971-72; joint planning & evaluation staff officer Sci. & Edn. Adminstrn., U.S. Dept. Agr., Washington, 1979-80; prof., chmn. intercoll. program food sci. & nutrition U.W.Va., Morgantown, 1980-85; pres., CEO Pa. State U., Uniontown, 1985-92; pres. Sink, Padden & Assocs., Atlanta, 1992—; pastor Sardis United Meth. Ch., 1995—2003; prof. chemistry, biochemistry So. Polytech. State U., Marietta, Ga., 1997—. Dir. S.W. Inst. Uniontown, 1989-92; gen. mgr. Cavert Wire Co., Inc., Atlanta, 1993-97; exec. asst. naval rep. to gov. and adj. gen. State W.Va., Charleston, 1981-84; cons. Allied Mills Inc., Am. Air Lines, Am. Home Foods, Inc., Apollo Analytical Labgs., Armour Food Co., Atlas Chem. Industries, others. Author: The Control of Metabolism, 1974, Citizen Extraordinarire, 1993, On Atlanta's Holy Mountain, 2000; contbr. articles to profl. jours. Mem. nat. adv. bd. Am. Security Coun., 1981-91; mem. nat. adv. coun. Nat. Commn. Higher Edn. Issues, 1980-82; bd. dirs. W.Va. Cattleman's Assn., 1981-83, W.Va. Poultry Assn., 1980-83, Pembroke Welsh Corgi Club, 1969-71, Greater Uniontown Idnsl. Fund, 1986-91, Fayette County Econ. Devel. Coun., 1985-93, Westmoreland-Fayette coun. Boy Scouts Am., 1986-91, Westmoreland-Fayette hist. Soc., 1986-91, Fayette County Soil Conservation Dist., 1990-93, Pa. Youth Found., 1989-93, Fayette County Coop. Extension Bd., 1992-93, Pa. Masonic Found., 1993, Ga. Meth. Commn. on Higher Edn. and Campus Min., 2000—. Capt. USNR, 1985-86, ret. Decorated Army commendation medal; recipient Nat. Merit Trophy award nat. Block and Bridle Club, 1956, Darbarker prize Pa. Aca.d Sci., 1967, W.Va. Disting. Achievement medal, Disting. Leadership award Am. Security Coun. Found., 1983; Pa. Meat Packers Assn. scholar, 1958-62; hon. fellow in biochemistry U. Wis., 1965, NSF postdoctoral fellow, 1964-65; Sherman scholar, 1996-2001. Fellow AAAS, Am. Inst. Chemists, Inst. Food Technologists; mem. Am. Meat Sci. Assn. (pres. 1974-75), Pa. Air N.G. Armory (trustee 1968-80), Pa. Acad. Sci., U.S. Naval Inst., Res. Officers Assn., Armed Forces Comm. and Elecs. Assn., Acad. Polit. Sci. (world affairs coun. Pitts. chpt.), Am. Assn. higher Edn., Am. Assn. Univ. Adminstrs., Am. Chem. Soc., Am. Soc. for Biochemistry and Molecular Biology, Biophys. Soc., Am. Soc. Animal Sci., Inst. Food Technologists, Soc. Rsch. Adminstrs., Am. Cancer Soc. (bd. dirs. 1988-91), Greater Uniontown C. of C. (bd. dirs. 1989-93), Greater Connellsville C. of C. (pres., bd. dirs. 1989-91), North Fayette C. of C. (bd. dirs. 1986-89), Mon Valley Tri-State Network, Inc. (chmn. bd. dirs. 1989-92), Rotary (sec. State Coll. 1969-71, Paul Harris fellow 1991), Elks, Internat. Assn. Turtles, Consistory, Shriners, Masons, Alpha Zeta, Omicron Delta Kappa, Gamma Sigma Delta, Sigma Xi, Phi Lambda Upsilon, Gamma Alpha, Phi Tau Sigma, Phi Sigma, Phi Delta Kappa, Pi Sigma Phi. Republican. E-mail: jsink@spsu.edu.

SINKFIELD, GEORGANNA T. state legislator; m. Richard H. Sinkfield; 2 children. BS, Tenn. State U.; student law sch., Emory U. Mem. Ga. Ho. of Reps., Atlanta, 1982—. Chairperson children and youth com.; mem. appropriations com., edn. com. Mem. adv. bd. Spl. Audiences Inc., Martin Luther King Day Care, Applecorp. Recipient Friend of Children award Coun. on Children, Disting. Svc. award Atlanta. Democrat. Office: State Capitol Rm 416 Atlanta GA 30334

SINKFORD, JEANNE CRAIG, dental association administrator, retired dentist, retired dean, educator; b. Washington, Jan. 30, 1933; d. Richard E. and Geneva (Jefferson) Craig; m. Stanley M. Sinkford, Dec. 8, 1951; children: Dianne Sylvia, Janet Lynn, Stanley M. III. BS, Howard U., 1953, MS, 1962, DDS, 1958, PhD, 1963; DSc (hon.), Georgetown U., 1978, U. Med. and Dentistry of N.J., 1992, Detroit Mercy U., 1996. Instr. prosthodontics Sch. Dentistry Howard U., Washington, 1958—60, faculty dentistry, 1964—, rsch. coord., co-chmn. dept. restorative dentistry, assoc. dean, 1968—75, dean, 1975—91, prof. Prosthodontics Grad. Sch., 1977—91, dean emeritus, prof., 1991—; spl. asst. Am. Assn. Dental Schs., 1991—93, dir. office women and minority affairs, 1993—97, assoc. exec. dir., 1998—. Instr. rsch. and crown and bridge Northwestern U. Sch. Dentistry, 1963—64; cons. prosthodontics and rsch. VA Hosp., Washington, 1965—; resident Children's Hosp. Nat. Med. Ctr., 1974—75; cons. St. Elizabeth's Hosp.; mem. attending staff Freedman's Hosp., Washington, 1964—; adv. bd. D.C. Gen. Hosp., 1975—; mem. nat. adv. dental rsch. coun. Nat. Bd. Dental Examiners; mem. ad hoc adv. panel Tuskegee Syphilis Study for HEW; sponsor D.C. Pub. Health Apprentice Program; mem. adv. coun. to dir. NIH; adv. com. NIH/NIDR/NIA Aging Rsch. Coun.; mem. dental devices classification panel FDA; mem. select panel for promotion child health, 1979—80; mem. spl. med. adv. group VA; bd. overseers U. Pa. Dental Sch., Boston U. Dental Sch.; bd. advisors U. Pitts. Dental Sch.; mem. bd. visitors Temple U. Sch. Dentistry; mem. anat. rev. bd. D.C. NRC Governing Bd.; cons. FDA; mem. Nat. Adv. Dental Rsch. Coun., 1993—96; active NRC Governing Bd. Mem. editl. bd. Jour. Am. Coll. Dentists, 1988—. Mem. Mayor's Block Grant Adv. Com., 1982; mem. parents' coun. Sidwell Friends, 1983; adv. bd. United Negro Coll. Fund, Robert Wood Johnson Health Policy Fellowships; mem. women's health task force NIH; bd. dirs. Girl Scouts U.S.A., 1993—95; bd. visitors Temple U. Sch. Dentistry. Fellow Louise C. Ball fellow grad. tng., 1960—63. Fellow: Internat. Coll. Dentists (Merit award), Am. Coll. Dentists (sec.-treas. Wash. met. sect.); mem.: ADA (chmn. appeal bd. coun. on dental edn. 1975—82), Links Inc., Dean's Coun. (chair), Smithsonian Assocs., N.Y. Acad. Scis., Am. Soc. Dentistry for Children, Inst. Medicine of NAS (coun.), Nat. Dental Assn., Fed. Prosthodontic Orgn., Am. Prosthodontic Soc., Am. Pedodontic Soc., Leadership in Acad. Medicine (adv. bd.), Health Professions Partnership Initiative (adv. bd.), Assn. Am. Women Dentists, Wash. Coun. Adminstrv. Women, So. Conf. Dental Deans (chmn.), Inst. Grad. Dentists (trustee), Am. Inst. Oral Biology, Dist. Dental Soc., Internat. Assn. Dental Rsch., Am. Soc. for Geriatric Dentistry (bd. dirs.), North Portal Civic League, Golden Key, Beta Kappa Chi, Psi Chi, Omicron Kappa Upsilon, Phi Beta Kappa, Sigma Xi (pres.). Achievements include first female dental dean at Howard University.

SINKIN, FAY MARIE, environmentalist; b. N.Y.C., Mar. 24, 1918; d. Joseph E. and Amelia (Kronish) Bloom; m. William R. Sinkin, May 31, 1942; children: Richard, Lanny. BA, Syracuse U., 1938. Pres. LWV, San Antonio, 1947-51; pres., organizer Vis. Nurse Assn., San Antonio, 1952-54; pres. Brandeis U. Women's Com., San Antonio, 1954-56; recruiter, cons. U.S. State Dept. (A.I.D.), Washington, 1963-67; pres. Aquifer Protection Assn., San Antonio, 1974-80, Portrait of Am. Women, San Antonio, 1976-82; chair Bexar County/Edwards Underground Water Dist., San Antonio, 1983-89; chairwoman Edwards Aquifer Preservation Trust, San Antonio, 1990. Editor (pamphlet) Is Applewhite Necessary?, 1978. Named Woman of Yr. Express New Publ., 1964, Sunday Woman San Antonio Light, 1965, Mother of Yr. Avance, 1988; recipient WICI award Women in Comm., 1989, Spirit of Giving award J.C. Penney, 1993, Best and Brightest award U. Round Table, 1998; elected to Women's Hall of Fame, San Antonio, 1985. Mem. San Antonio 100, Tex. Internat. Woman's Forum, Bexar Audobon Soc. (Oustanding Cmty. Svc. award 2003), San Antonio Conservation Soc. (award for preservation of the environment 2002). Democrat. Jewish. Avocations: folk art museum, needlepoint, swimming, reading. Home: 7887 Broadway St Apt 303 San Antonio TX 78209-2537 E-mail: fay2646@aol.com.

SINN, JERRY L. army officer; m. Cheryl Parant; children: Jacob, Andrew. Grad., U. Mo., Rolla, Command and Gen. Staff Coll. Math. instr. U.S. Mil. Acad., West Point; enlisted U.S. Army, 1968, commd. 2d lt., 1969, advanced through grades to comdr.; dir. for ops. and and support, asst. to Sec. of Army for Fin. Mgmt. and Compt., 1995-97; divsn. engr. U.S. Army C.E., Bklyn., 1997-98, comdg. gen. North Atlantic divsn., 1998-99; dep. asst. sec. U.S. Army Budget Office, Washington, 1999—2003; mil. dep. for budget ASA (FM&C), 2003—. Decorated Legion of Merit with 3 oakleaf clusters, Bronze Star medal with V device, Purple Heart with oakleaf cluster, others. Office: ASA/DAS 109 Army Pentagon Rm 3a662 Washington DC 20310-0109*

SINNARD, ELAINE JANICE, painter, sculptor; b. Fort Collins, Colo., Feb. 14, 1926; d. Elven Orestes and Catherine (Bennet) S. Student, Art Students League, 1948, NYU, 1953, Sculpture Ctr., N.Y.C., 1954, Academie Grande Chaumiere, Paris, 1956. Painter, sculptor. Works exhibited Riverside Mus., N.Y.C., 1955, City Ctr., N.Y.C., 1954-56, Nat. Arts Club, N.Y.C., 1959-90, Lord & Taylor, N.Y.C., 1963-78, Bergdorf Goodman, N.Y.C., 1980-90, Zantman Art Galleries, Carmel-by-the-Sea, Calif., 1970-73, Chevy Chase Gallery, Washington, 1981-88; one woman shows and group exhbns. include: Bergdorf Goodman Nena's Choice Gallery, Sinnard Art Studios; tchr. open workshop for artists. Mem. Nat. Arts Club N.Y.C. Home: PO Box 304 New Hampton NY 10958-0304 Office Phone: 845-374-8128. Personal E-mail: sinnard@warwick.net.

SINNECK, MICHAEL, information technology executive; married; 3 children. BA in Math., St. Francis Coll. Various positions IBM Global Svc.; corp. v.p. Microsoft, Redmond, Wash., 2001—. Avocations: scuba diving, skiing, playing piano. Office: One Microsoft Way Redmond WA 98052-6399

SINNING, MARK ALAN, thoracic and vascular surgeon; b. Holton, Kans., Apr. 24, 1953; s. Henry Harold and Valere Madelene (Davey) S.; m. Kathy Diann Pugh, Sept. 25, 1982 (div.); m. Srinuan Williamson, Sept. 3, 2003; children: Sarah, Emily, Mark, Rachel, Walter. BA, U. Kans., 1975; MD, U. Kans., Kansas City, 1978. Diplomate Am. Bd. Surgery, Am. Bd. Thoracic Surgery. Gen. surgery resident St. Luke's Hosp., Kansas City, Mo., 1978-83, thoracic surgery resident, 1983-85; pvt. practice Coastal Surg. Specialists, PA, New Bern, N.C., 1986—. Attending staff Danbury (Conn.) Hosp., 1985-86, Craven Regional Med. Ctr., New Bern, 1986—; asst. clin. prof. East Carolina U., Greenville, 1992—. Fellow ACS, Am. Coll. Chest Physicians; mem. AMA, Soc. Thoracic Surgeons, So. Assn. Thoracic Surgery, N.C. Med. Soc., Phi Beta Kappa, Alpha Omega Alpha. Avocations: golf, skiing, music. Office: Coastal Surgical Specialists 800 Hospital Dr Ste 10 New Bern NC 28560-3489

SINNOTT, JOHN PATRICK, lawyer, educator; b. Bklyn., Aug. 17, 1931; s. John Patrick and Elizabeth Muriel (Zinkand) Sinnott; m. Rose Marie Yuppa, May 30, 1959; children: James Alexander, Jessica Michelle. BS, U.S. Naval Acad., 1953; MS, USAF Inst. Tech., 1956; JD, No. Ky. U., 1960. Bar: Ohio 1961, NY 1963, NJ 1970, Ga. 1970, US Patent Office 1963, US Supreme Ct 1977. Assoc. Brumbaugh, Graves, Donohue & Raymond, N.Y.C., 1961-63; patent atty. Bell Tel. Labs., Murray Hill, N.J., 1963-64, Schlumberger Ltd., N.Y.C., 1964-71; asst. chief patent counsel Babcock & Wilcox, N.Y.C.,

1971-79; chief patent and trademark counsel Am. Std. Inc., N.Y.C., 1979-92; of counsel Morgan & Finnegan, N.Y.C., 1992-99, Langdale & Vallotton, Valdosta, Ga., 2000—. Adj lectr NJ Inst Technology, Newark, 1974—89; adj prof Seton Hall Univ Sch Law, Newark, 1989—98. Author: (book) Counterfeit Goods Suppression, 1998, World Patent Law and Practice, Vols 2-2P, 1999, A Practical Guide to Document Authentication, 2004; contbr. articles to profl jours. Mem. local Selective Serv Bd., Plainfield, NJ, 1971; bd dirs New Providence Community Swimming Pool, NJ, 1970. Capt. USAF, 1953—61, col. AUS ret., 1977—91. Decorated Legion of Merit, others. Mem. N.Y. Intellectual Property Law Assn. (bd. dirs. 1974-76), Squadron A Assn., Cosmos Club, Valdosta Country Club. Republican. Roman Catholic. Home: 2517 Rolling Rd Valdosta GA 31602-1244 Office: Langdale & Vallotton 1007 N Patterson St PO Box 1547 Valdosta GA 31603 Fax: 229-244-9646. Office Phone: 229-244-5400. E-mail: specan23@aol.com.

SINNOTT, JOHN THOMAS, internist, educator; b. Reading, Pa., May 16, 1948; s. John Thomas and Josephine (Mallon) S.; m. Barbara Ballentine, May 30, 1970. BA, Columbus (Ga.) Coll., 1971; MA, U. South Fla., 1973; MD, U. South Ala., 1978. Diplomate Am. Bd. Internal Medicine, Am. Bd. Infectious Diseases. Resident in internal medicine U. South Fla. Coll. Medicine, Tampa, 1978-81, infectious disease resident, 1981-83, prof. and dir. infectious diseases, 1991-2000, James Cullsion prof. medicine, 2000—, assoc. prof., 1987-92, asst. prof., 1983-87; mem. med. exec. bd. Tampa Gen. Healthcare, 1992—, vice chief staff, 1992-94, chief staff, 1994-96, dir. epidemiology, 1985—. Dir. S.W. Fla. Tissue Bank, 1987—. Editor jour. Infections in Medicine, 1994—. Recipient hon. alumnus award U. South Fla. Coll. Medicine, 1998, Outstanding Clin. Prof. award, 1986-92; Humanism in Medicine award NBI Healthcare Found., 1998, award For AIDS Care Today, 1998; John T. Sinnott Outstanding Clin Prof. award named in his honor U. So. Fla. Coll. Medicine, 1992. Fellow ACP, Infectious Disease Soc. Am. (fin. com. 1998—); mem. Soc. Hosp. Epidemiology (fin. com. 1998—), Alpha Omega Alpha. Avocations: fishing, flying. Home: 9666 Oak St NE Saint Petersburg FL 33702-2610 Office: Tampa Gen Hosp Dept Infectious Disease Tampa FL 33601-1289 E-mail: jsinnott@tgh.org.

SINNOTT, LINDA JOHNETTEE, educational association administrator; b. Shreveport, La., Aug. 3, 1969; d. Lide Gordon Jeffus and Linda Diane Stephens; m. Dale Patrick Sinnott, Apr. 27, 1992; 2 children; 1 child from previous marriage, Mark Andrew Bleth. BS in Psychology, U. Md., 2001. Electronics technician USAF, 1988—94; office mgr., safety dir. Pete King Corp., Las Vegas, 1994—96; bookkeeper Shaheen Office Supply, Warner Robins, Ga., 1996—99; statis. technician Ctrl. State Hosp., Milledgeville, Ga., 1999—2000; coord. Children & Adults with Attendtion Deficit Hyperactivity Disorder (CHADD), Albuquerque, 2003—. Leader Weight Watchers, Albuquerque, 2002—. Fellow: S.W. Writers, Romance Writers of Am. Avocations: exercise, writing, reading, quilting. Home: 12016 Flat Rock Ct NW Albuquerque NM 87114 Personal E-mail: johnettee2@aol.com.

SINOFSKY, STEVEN J. information technology executive; BA with hon., Cornell U., 1987; MS in Computer Sci., U. Mass., 1989. From software engr. to sr. v.p. Microsoft, Redmond, Wash., 1989, sr. v.p. Microsoft Office. Vis. scholar Harvard U. Bus. Sch., Cambridge, Mass., 1998. Office: One Microsoft Way Redmond WA 98052-6399

SINOR, DENIS, Orientalist, educator; b. Kolozsvar, Hungary, Apr. 17, 1916; s. Miklos and Marguerite (Weitzenfeld) S.; m. Eugenia Trinajstic (dec.); children: Christophe (dec.), Sophie. BA, U. Budapest, 1938; MA, Cambridge (Eng.) U., 1948; doctorate (hon.), U. Szeged, Hungary, 1971. Attache Centre National de la Recherche Scientifique, Paris, 1939-48; univ. lectr. Altaic studies Cambridge U., 1948-62; prof. Uralic and Altaic studies and history Ind. U., Bloomington, 1962-81, disting. prof. Uralic and Altaic studies and history, 1975-86, disting. prof. emeritus Uralic and Altaic studies and history, 1986—, chmn. dept. Uralic and Altaic studies, 1963-1981, dir. Lang. and Area Ctr., 1963-88, dir. Asian studies program, 1965-67, dir. Asian Studies Rsch. Inst., 1967-79, dir. Rsch. Inst. for Inner Asian Studies, 1979-1981, 85-86. Sec. gen. Permanent Internat. Altaistic Conf., 1961—; rsch. project dir. U.S. Office Edn., 1969-70; sec. Internat. Union Orientalists, 1954-64; vis. prof. Institut Nat. des Langues et Civilizations Orientales, Paris, spring 1974; scholar-in-residence Rockefeller Found. Study Ctr., Bellagio, 1975; vice chmn. UNESCO Commn. for History Civilization Cen. Asia, 1981—, mem. consultative com. UNESCO Silk Rd. Project, 1990-97; summer seminar dir. NEH, 1988. Author: Orientalism and History, 1954, History of Hungary, 1959, Introduction a l'ètude de l'Eurasie Centrale, 1963, Aspects of Altaic Civilization, 1963, Inner Asia, 1968, Inner Asia and Its Contacts with Medieval Europe, 1977, Tanulmányok, 1982, Essays in Comparative Altaic Linguistics, 1990, Studies in Medieval Inner Asia, 1997; editor, contbr.: Modern Hungary, 1977, Studies in Finno-Ugric Linguistics, 1977, Uralic Languages, 1988, Essays on Uzbek History, Culture and Languages, 1993, Cambridge History of Early Inner Asia, Handbook of Uralic Studies, Jour. Asian History, Ind. U. Uralic and Altaic Series; mem. Am. editl. rev. bd. Britannica-Hungarica. Served with Forces Françaises de l'Intérieur, 1943-44; with French Army, 1944-45. NEH grantee, 1981, 87, 88; recipient Jubilee prize U. Budapest, 1938, Barczi Geza Meml. medal, 1981, Gold medal Permanent Internat. Altaistic Conf., 1982, 1996, Arminius Vambery Meml. medal, 1983, The Thomas Hart Benton Mural Medallion, Hungarian Order of Star, 1986, UNESCO Avicenna medal, 1998, medal of honor Am. Oriental Soc. Medicine, 1999, medal for outstanding svcs. U. Szeged, 2002; Am. Philos. Soc. Rsch. grantee, 1963; Am. Coun. Learned Socs. rsch. grantee, 1962; Guggenheim fellow, 1968-69, 1981-82. Fellow Körösi Csoma Soc. (hon.); mem. Royal Asiatic Soc. (hon. sec. 1954-64, Denis Sinor medal for Inner Asian Studies named in his honor 1992), Am. Oriental Soc. (pres. Midwest br. 1968-70, nat. pres. 1975-76, medal of honor 1999), Assn. Asian Studies, Am. Hist. Soc., Soc. Asiatique (hon.), Tibet Soc. (pres. 1969-74), Mongolia Soc. (pres. 1987-94), Correspondant de l'Académie des inscriptions et belles lettres (Paris), Hungarian Acad. Scis. (hon.), Acad. Europaea (fgn.), Deutsche Morgenlandische Gesellschaft, Suomalais-Ugrilaisen Seura (hon.), Soc. Uralo-Altaica (v.p. 1964-94, hon.), Internat. Union Oriental and Asian Studies (v.p. 1993—), Cosmos Club Washington, Explorers Club N.Y.C., United Oxford and Cambridge Club London. Home: 5581 E Lampkins Ridge Rd Bloomington IN 47401-8674 Office: Indiana U Dept Ctrl Eurasian Studies Goodbody Hall Bloomington IN 47405 E-mail: sinord@indiana.edu.

SINOR, HOWARD EARL, JR., lawyer; b. New Orleans, Sept. 6, 1949; s. Howard E. and Beverly M. (Bourgeois) S.; children: Sally, Vera Sue, Sarah, Sadie. BA with honors, U. New Orleans, 1971; JD cum laude, Harvard U., 1975. Bar: La. 1975, U.S. Supreme Ct. 1983, U.S. Ct. Appeals (3rd, 5th and 11th cir.), U.S. Dist. Ct. (ea., middle, we.) Dist. La. Ptnr. Jones, Walker, Waechter, Poitevent, Carrere & Denegre, 1975-98, Gordon, Arata, McCollam, Duplantis & Eagan, New Orleans, 1999—. Contbg. author: La. Appellate Practice Handbook, 1990, 97; editor: CLE Manual of Recent Developments, 1985; contbr. articles to profl. jours. Recipient Pres.'s award, La. State Bar Assn., 1987. Fellow La. Bar Found.; mem. ABA, FBA, La. State Bar Assn. (chmn. antitrust sect. 1987-89). Avocations: golf, hiking. Office: Gordon Arata et al 201 Saint Charles Ave Fl 40 New Orleans LA 70170-4000

SINSHEIMER, ROBERT LOUIS, retired academic administrator, educator; b. Washington, Feb. 5, 1920; s. Allen S. and Rose (Davidson) S.; m. Flora Joan Hirsch, Aug. 8, 1943 (div. 1972); children: Lois June (Mrs. Wickstrom), Kathy Jean (Mrs. Vandagriff), Roger Allen; m. Kathleen Mae Reynolds, Sept. 10, 1972 (div. 1980); m. Karen Current, Aug. 1, 1981. S.B., MIT, 1941, MS, 1942, PhD, 1948. Staff mem. radiation lab. MIT, Cambridge, 1942-46; assoc. prof. biophysics, physics dept. Iowa State Coll., Ames, 1949-55, prof., 1955-57; prof. biophysics Calif. Inst. Tech., Pasadena, 1957-77, chmn. div. biology, 1968-77; chancellor U. Calif., Santa Cruz, 1977-87, chancellor emeritus, 1987—, prof. Santa Barbara, 1988-90, prof. emeritus, 1990—. Editor: Jour. Molecular Biology, 1959-67, Ann. Rev. Biochemistry, 1966-72. Named Calif. Scientist of Year, 1968; recipient N.W. Beijerinck-Virologie medal Netherlands Acad. Sci., 1969 Fellow Am. Acad. Arts and Scis.; mem. Am. Soc. Biol. Chemists, Biophys. soc. (pres. 1970), AAAS, Nat. Acad. Scis. (mem. council 1970-73, chmn. bd. editors Proc. 1972-80), Inst. Medicine. Achievements include discovery of single-stranded DNA, circular DNA; co-investigator in first in vitro replication of infective DNA. Office: U Calif MCD Biology Santa Barbara CA 93106 Office Phone: 805-893-8038.

SINSHEIMER, WARREN JACK, lawyer; b. NYC, May 22, 1927; s. Jerome William and Elizabeth (Berch) S.; m. Florence Dubin, Mar. 30, 1950; children: Linda Ruth, Ralph David, Alan Jay, Michael Neal. Student, Ind. U., 1943-47; JD cum laude, NY Law Sch., 1950; LLM, NYU, 1957; MPhil, Columbia U., 1977; HLD (hon.), Drew U., 2002. Bar: NY bar 1950. Ptnr. Sinsheimer, Sinsheimer & Dubin, NYC, 1950-78, Satterlee & Stephens, NYC, 1978-86, Patterson, Belknap, Webb & Tyler, NYC, 1986-91; counsel Patterson Belknap Webb & Tyler, NYC, 1991-96; pres., bd. dirs. Neighborhood Bagel Corp., 1994—. Pres. Plessey, Inc., NYC, 1956-70, chmn., CEO, 1970-89; dir. oversees ops. devel. The Plessey Co., Ltd., Illford, Essex, Eng., 1969-70, dep. chief exec., dir., 1976-89; dir. Plessey, Inc.; trustee NYU Sch. Law, 1996—; pres., bd. dirs. Legal Svcs. Children, Inc., 1998—. Chmn. Com. of 68, 1964-67; Mem. Westchester County Rep. Com., 1956-73; chmn. Nat. Scranton Pres. Com., 1964; mem. NY State Assembly, 1965-66; Bd. visitors Wassaic State Sch., 1962-64; trustee Sch. Law, NYU, 1996—, bd. dirs. Shalom Hartman Inst., Jerusalem, 1991—, treas., 1996—; trustee Citi Bar Fund, 1998-2004. Served with USNR, 1944-45; with USAF, 1950-52. Mem. ABA, Assn. Bar City NY, Torch and Scroll, Century Club (Purchase, NY, gov., treas. 1997—), Century Assn. NYC, Univ. Club, Zeta Beta Tau. Jewish. Home: 22 Murray Hill Rd Scarsdale NY 10583-2828 Office: 271 Madison Ave New York NY 10016-1001 Business E-Mail: Sinsheimer@kidslaw.org.

SINTZ, EDWARD FRANCIS, librarian; b. New Trenton, Ind., Feb. 6, 1924; s. John and Edith E. (Rudicil) S.; m. Donna Norris, Apr. 12, 1952; children—Ann Kristin, Lesley Elizabeth, Julie Melinda. BA, U. Kans., 1950; MA in L.S. U. Denver, 1954; MS in Pub. Adminstrn, U. Mo., 1965. With Kansas City (Mo.) Pub. Library, 1954-66, asst. dir., 1964-66; asso. librarian St. Louis Pub. Library, 1966-68; dir. pub. libraries Miami-Dade Pub. Libr., 1968—89, ret. Instr. Washington U., St. Louis, 1966-67; library surveys for Mo. State Library, 1967-68; library bldg. cons., 1965—. Editor: Mo. Library Assn. Quar., 1956—58. Served with USAAF, 1942-45. Mem. ALA, Fla. Library Assn. (pres. 1975-76), Southeastern Library Assn. Clubs: Kiwanian. Home: 7105 Lakeside Dr Charlotte NC 28215

SIO, JIMMY ONG, embryologist; b. Manila, Philippines, Mar. 9, 1954; arrived in U.S., 1973; s. Vicente and SiokBee (Ong) Sio. Biology major, U. Philippines, 1971—73; BS in Biology, Calif. State Coll. Bakersfield, 1976; PhD of Cell Biology, U. Tex. Health Sci. Ctr., Dallas, 1985; MD, Emory U., 1985. Diplomate Nat. Bd. Med. Examiners, Am. Bd. Hosp. Physicians, Am. Coll. Ethical Physicians. Resident Anatomical Pathology Emory U., Atlanta, 1985—86; resident Internal Medicine Kem Med. Ctr., Bakersfield, Calif., 1990—93; physician Kaiser So. Calif. Permanente Med. Group, Bakersfield, 1993—. *Internet Associates: The leaders have influenced me by introducing me to the writings of various thinkers, motivational speakers, dreamers, and visionaries. One of them, Charles Jones, stated that one of the greatest thoughts he has heard is the following: "You will be the same in five years as you are today except for the people you meet and the books you read." Reading: A significant benefit that I have experienced from reading is stated wisely by Socrates as follows: "Employ your time in improving yourself by other people's writing so you shall come easily by what others have labored hard for."* Pvt. Philippine Armed Forces, 1971—73. Fellow: Am. Biog. Assn.; mem.: Internat. Biog. Ctr. (Dep. Dir. Gen.), Internat. Biog. Inst. (life), N.Y. Acad. Scis., Internat. Order of Merit, Order of Internat. Fellowship, InterNet Assocs. Avocation: reading. Home: 8604 Dinard Pl Bakersfield CA 93311 Office: Kaiser So Calif Permanente Med Group 8800 Ming Ave Bakersfield CA 93311 Office Phone: 661-664-3706.

SION, MAURICE, mathematics professor; b. Skopje, Yugoslavia, Oct. 17, 1928; came to Can., 1960; s. Max and Sarah (Alalouf) S.; m. Emilie Grace Chisholm, Sept. 15, 1957; children: Crispin, Sarah, Dirk. BA, NYU, 1947, MA, 1948; PhD, U. Calif., Berkeley, 1951. Mathematician Nat. Bur. Stds., Washington, 1951-52; instr. U. Calif., 1952-53; asst. prof. U. Calif., 1957-60; mem. Inst. for Advanced Study, Princeton, N.J., 1955-57, 62; asst. prof. U. B.C., Vancouver, Can., 1960, assoc. prof., 1961, prof., 1964-89, prof. emeritus, 1989—, head math. dept., 1984-86, dir. Quadra Inst. Math., 1970-89. Author: Introduction to Methods of Real Analysis, 1969, Theory Semi Group Valued Measures, 1973; contbr. articles to profl. jours. With U.S. Army, 1953-55. Mem. Am. Math. Soc., Can. Math. Soc. (v.p. 1972-74). Office: U BC Dept Math Vancouver BC Canada V6T 1Z2

SIPAHIOGLU, HATICE ELCIN, diplomat, interpreter/translator; b. Ankara, Turkey, Apr. 8, 1969; came to U.S., 1997; d. Vahdet and Nurten Sipahioglu. BA, Hacettepe U., Ankara, 1990; MA, Hacettepe U., 1995; MBA, U. St. Thomas, 2000. Translator, interpreter Turkish State Rlwys., Ankara, 1990-95; adminstrv. officer Ministry Fgn. Affairs, Ankara, 1995-97; adminstrv. attaché Turkish Consulate Gen., Houston, 1997—. Scholar INst. for PUb. Adminstrn. for Turkey and Mid. East, Ankara, 1996-97. Mem. Houston World Affairs Coun., Houston Masterworks Chorus. Avocations: music, photography, yoga, hiking, travel. Home: 623 E 11 1/2 St Houston TX 77008 Office: Turkish Consulate Gen 1990 Post Oak Blvd Ste 1300 Houston TX 77056-3833

SIPCHEN, BOB, reporter; b. Chgo., June 13, 1953; m. Pamela Jean Sipchen; children: Ashley Rose-Anna, Emily Sage, Robert John III. BA in English, U. Calif. Santa Barbara, 1976. Freelance writer, 1980—87; staff writer Orange County Edit. LA Times, 1987—88, staff writer, 1988—98, sr. editor Mag., 1998—2001, assoc. editor Editl. Pages, 2001—. Author: Baby Insane and the Buddha, 1993. Recipient Pulitzer prize, 2002. Mem.: PEN, Nat. Writers Union, Soc. Profl. Journalists, Sigma Delta Chi. Office: LA Times 202 W 1st St Los Angeles CA 90012

SIPES, CONNIE W. state legislator, educator; b. New Albany, Ind., Aug. 6, 1949; m. Stephen Sipes; children: Cassie, Zachary. BS, Ind. U.-S.E., 1971, MS in Edn., 1975, MS in Adminstrn., 1991. Prin. Fairmont Elem. Sch., New Albany, Ind., 1991—; mem. Ind. Senate from 46th dist., Indpls., 1997—; mem. edn. com., mem. pension and labor com.; ranking minority elections com.; mem. transp. and interstate coop. com. Mem. Dem. Women's Club. Recipient Woman of Achievement award BPW, 1986. Mem. LWV, Ind. State Prins. Assn., Nat. Assn. Elem. Prins. Avocation: running. Office: 200 W Washington St Indianapolis IN 46204-2728

SIPES, KAREN KAY, communications executive; b. Higginsville, Mo., Jan. 8, 1947; d. Walter John and Katherine Marie (McLelland) Heins; m. Joel Rodney Sipes, Sept. 24, 1971; 1 child, Lesley Katherine. BS in Edn., Ctrl. Mo. State U., 1970. Reporter/news editor Newton Kansan, 1973—76; sports writer Capital-Jour., Topeka, 1976—83, spl. sects. editor, 1983—85, editl. page editor, 1985—92, mng. editor/features, 1992—2002, asst. editl. page editor, 2002—03; dir. commn. Kans. Dept. Aging, Topeka, 2003—. Co-chair Mayor's Commn. on Literacy, Topeka, 1995-96; mem. Act Against Violence Com., Topeka, 1995-96, Mayor's Task Force on Race Rels., 1998; mem. planning com. Leadership Greater Topeka, 1997; Great Am. Cleanup, 1999-2001, ERC/Resource and Referral, 2001—; mem. Martin Luther King Living the Dream Bus. Ptnrs. Com., 2001—; mem. Centennial planning com. Family Svc. and Guidance Ctr., 2003-04; mem. Project Topeka Com., 2004—, Arthritis Walk Com., 2004, Faith in Action-No Place Like Home Coalition, 2003—; bd. dirs. Western Swing Music Soc. Kans., 2003--. Mem. Ctrl. Mo. State U. Alumni Assn. (bd. dirs. 1996-2002, v.p. 1999, pres. 2000). Avocations: music, gardening, art. Office: Kans Dept Aging New England Bldg 503 S Kans Ave Topeka KS 66603-3404 Office Phone: 785-296-6154. E-mail: critterkaren@aol.com., karen.sipes@aging.state.ks.us.

SIPIORA, LEONARD PAUL, retired museum director, art appraiser; b. Lawrence, Mass., Sept. 1, 1934; s. Walter and Agnes S.; m. Sandra Joyce Coon, 1962; children— Alexandra, Erika. AB cum laude, U. Mich., 1955, MA, 1956. Dir. museums, City of El Paso, Tex., 1967-90; ret. Co-founder, pres. El Paso Arts Council, 1969-71; sec.-treas. El Paso Council Internat. Visitors, 1968-71; trustee El Paso Mus. Art; bd. dirs. Tex. Com. Humanities, Assn. Southwestern Humanities Council; adv. bd. S.W. Arts Found.; expert Antiques Roadshow-U.S.A. Bd. dirs. Community Concert Assn. El Paso, El Paso Symphony Orch., El Paso Hist. Soc. Mem. Assn. Mus. Dirs., Mountain Plains Mus. Assn. (pres. 1978-79), Tex. Assn. Museums (pres. 1977-79), Appraisers Assn. Am., Knights of Malta (decorated Grand Cross), Prior of Tex., Kappa Pi. Republican. Lutheran. Home: 1012 Blanchard Ave El Paso TX 79902-2727

SIPORIN, DAVID, human resources specialist; b. Detroit, June 8, 1954; s. Erwin and Ruth (Haase) S.; m. Maureen Lynn Wertheim, Sept. 4, 1977; children: Kaylyn Nellie, Ariana Molly. BA in Anthropology, Mich. State U., 1976, M in Labor and Indsl. Rels., 1978. Orgn. planning splst. Amoco Corp., Chgo., 1979-81; human resources rep. Amoco Prodn. Co., Denver, 1981-84, Chgo., 1984-88, human resources mgr., 1988-92, Amoco Chem.-Polymers, Alpharetta, Ga., 1992-96; mng. dir. orgn. devel. Aristech Chem. Corp., Pitts., 1996-98, v.p. corp. svcs., 1999—2001; v.p. human resources Lord Corp., Cary, NC, 2001—. Mem. Soc. Human Resource Mgmt., Indsl. Rels. Rsch. Assn., Coun. Human Resource Execs. (conf. bd. 1997). Avocations: golf, skiing, gardening, excercise. Home: 109 Barkridge Ct Morrisville NC 27560-7069 Office: Lord Corp 111 Lord Dr Cary NC 27511

SIPOS, THOMAS M. writer; BFA, N.Y. U., N.Y., 1982. Author: (novels) Vampire Nation (Prometheus Award nominee, 2001), Manhattan Sharks, (collection) Halloween Candy, (plays) Power Chris (Grand Prize, Writer Digest Contest, 1992), (TV series) Washington Tricks: The Art of Politics (Winner, Writer's Found., America's Best Contest, 1999). Mem.: Ind. Feature Project, Am. Fedn. of TV & Radio Artists, SAG, Nat. Writers Union, Sci. Fiction & Fantasy Writers of Am., Horror Writers Assn. Libertarian. Catholic. Office: Na PO Box 1903 Santa Monica CA 90406-1903 Office Phone: 310-458-6048. Business E-Mail: tsipos@communistvampires.com.

SIPPEL, WILLIAM LEROY, lawyer; b. Fond du Lac, Wis., Aug. 14, 1948; m. Barbara Jean Brost, Aug. 23, 1970; children: Katharine Jean, David William. BA, JD, U. Wis. Bar: Wis. 1974, U.S. Dist. Ct. (we. dist.) Wis. 1974, Minn. 1981, U.S. Dist. Ct. Minn. 1981, U.S. Ct. Appeals (10th cir.) 1984, U.S. Ct. Appeals (8th cir.) 1985. Research assoc. dept. agrl. econs. U. Wis., Madison, 1974-75; counsel monopolics and comml. law subcom. Ho. Judiciary Com., Washington, 1975-80; spl. asst. to asst. gen. antitrust div. U.S. Dept. of Justice, Washington, 1980-81; from assoc. to ptnr. Doherty, Rumble & Butler, Mpls. and St. Paul, Minn., 1981-99; ptnr. Oppenheimer, Wolff & Donnelly, LLP, Mpls., 1999—. Bd. dirs. Music in the Park, Inc.; mem. adj. faculty antitrust William Mitchell Coll. Law, spring of 2000, 2001. Co-author: The Antitrust Health Care Handbook, 1988; contbg. author: ABA Energy Antitrust Handbook, 2002. Mem. program com. Minn. World Trade Assn., Mpls., St. Paul, 1985-86, bd. dirs., 1986, Minn.; former dir. Music in the Park, Mpls.; dir. Person to Person Inc.; chmn. antitrust mktg. orders com. Nat. Coun. Farmer Coops., 2001—. With USAR, 1971-77. Mem. ABA (vice chmn. ins. industry com. 1990-91, contbr. ABA Joint Ventures in Health Care), Minn. Bar Assn. (co-chmn. antitrust sect. 1986-88, internat. law sect. coun. 1986-89, treas. 1989-90, sec. 1990-91, vice chmn. 1995-96, chmn. 1996-97), Minn. Med. Alley Assn. (co-chmn. internat. bus. com. 1990-95, Hennepin County Office Internat. Trade (bd. dirs. 1988-93), Phi Beta Kappa. Roman Catholic. Avocations: reading, photography, computers. Home: 2151 Commonwealth Ave Saint Paul MN 55108-1730 Office: Oppenheimer Wolff Donnelly LLP Plaza VII 45 S Seventh St Ste 3400 Minneapolis MN 55402-1609

SIPPEY, ROGER BOYD, corporate executive; b. Zanesville, Ohio, Feb. 6, 1942; s. Walter Boyd and Ruth Lillian Sippey; m. Janet Elsa Hoehn, Nov. 24, 1943; children: Michael, Nancy Denenburg, Jason, Margarette. BS, Muskingum Coll., New Concord, Ohio, 1960—64. V.p. Feralloy Corp., Chgo., 1968—. Bd. dirs. Acero Prime Sa de Cv, San Louis Potosi, Mexico. Mem.: Steel Svc. Ctr. Inst., Racquet Club Chgo. Republican. Episcopalian. Avocations: boating, travel. Home: 1366 N Dearborn Pkwy Chicago IL 60610 Office: Feralloy Corp 5745 Higgins Road Chicago IL 60645 Office Phone: 773-380-1500. Home Fax: 773-380-1500; Office Fax: 773-380-1812. Business E-Mail: rsippey@feralloy.com.

SIPPRELL, GEORGE SIDNEY, engineering professional; b. Buffalo, Jan. 10, 1949; s. George Gilbert and Eleanor M. Sipprell; m. Kathleen Ann Meyer, July 22, 1972; children: Jeffrey David, Benjamin Daniel. BS in Aero. Engring., Rensselaer Poly. Inst., 1970, MEng in Aero. Engring., 1972. Joined Sikorsky Aircraft Corp., Stratford, Conn., 1972, propulsion sys. analyst, 1972—74, helicopter icin lead rsch. engr., 1974—76, UH-60A Black Hawk project engr., 1972—76, engring. mgr. USCG SRR/S76, 1976—79, sr. sys. analyst, LHX, 1979, program mgr., engring. mgr. UH60A Black Hawk ESSS, 1979—83, engring. mgr. LHX Program, 1983—90, engr. mgr. LHX simulation and SHADOW program, 1988—91, dep. program mgr. RAH-66 Comanche Helicopter Program, 1990—2002, chief engr. U.S. Army/DARPA Unmanned Combat Armed Rotorcraft program, 2002—03, dir. engring., sys. requirements and analysis and advanced concepts, 2003—04, ret., 2004; ind. aerospace systems engring. cons., 2004—. Recipient U.S. Army Chief of Staff award, 1993, AHS Grover Bell award, 1990, Bd. Dirs. Trophy award United Technologies Corp., 2001. Mem. Am. Helicopter Soc., Quarter Century Mem. Group, Sikorsky Ski Club (pres. 1980-82, Outstanding Member award 1982). Avocations: 0-gauge model railroading, skiing, automotive restoration, toy collecting, historic homes. Home and Office: 4 Featherbed Ln Branford CT 06405-6113 Office Phone: 203-481-4866. E-mail: gsipprell@excite.com.

SIPPRELLE, DUDLEY GENE, investor; b. Compton, Calif., July 6, 1935; s. Foster and Dolores Lee (Dudley) S.; m. Linda Dekum Mills, Feb. 1, 1957; children: Dwight, Keith, Scott, Mark. BA, U. Redlands, 1957; postgrad., UCLA, 1957-59, Stanford U., 1960. Diplomatic & consular officer U.S. Dept. of State, Washington, 1963-93; investor pvt. practice, Santa Barbara, Calif., 1994—. Diplomat in residence Lehigh U., Bethlehem, Pa., 1980-81. Recipient Presdl. Meritorious Svc. award U.S. Dept. State, Washington, 1986. Mem. Coun. Fgn. Rels. Avocations: travel, exercise. Home: 1349 Plaza Pacifica Santa Barbara CA 93108

SIPSKI, MARY LEONIDE, physician, healthcare administrator; b. Somerville, N.J., July 6, 1950; d. Joseph John and Sophia Barbara (Marcewicz) Sipski; m. Thomas Edward Lammertse, June 16, 1979; children: Meredith, Matthew, Evan. AB, Douglass Coll./Rutgers U., 1972; PhD in Phys. Biochemistry, Ohio U., 1976; MD, Ohio State U., 1979; M in Med. Mgmt., U. So. Calif., 2003. Diplomate Am. Bd. Phys. Medicine and Rehab., Am. Bd. Managed Care Medicine, cert. in med. mgmt. Am. Coll. Physician Execs. and U. So. Calif., 2001. Intern, resident in phys. medicine and rehab. Ohio State U. Hosps., 1979-83; dir. phys. medicine and rehab. Gaylord Hosp., Wallingford, Conn., 1983-90; dir. brain injury program, dir. outpatient svcs. Kessler Inst. Rehab., Chester, NJ, 1990-97; chief med. officer Consumer Health Network Solutions, South Plainfield, NJ, 1997—, Selective Ins. Managed Care Solutions, Hamilton, NJ, 2002—. Med. dir. Gaylord/Yale-New haven Ctr. at Long Wharf, 1989-90; asst. clin. prof. dept. orthopedics and rehab. Yale U., New Haven, 1989-90; cons. Bur. Disability Determination, Columbus, Ohio, 1982-83; pvt. practice cons. in brain injury, disability, and expert medico-legal testimony, Far Hills, 1991—. Fellow Am. Acad. Phys. Medicine and Rehab. (sec. Conn. soc.); mem. AMA, Am. Coll. Physician Execs., Am. Coll. Managed Care Medicine, Consumer Health Network Solutions. Office: Consumer Health Network Solutions 3525 Quakerbridge Rd Hamilton NJ 08619 Office Phone: 800-225-4246. E-mail: dr.sipski@chn.com.

SIPZNER, HOWARD M. real estate executive; MBA, Harvard U. Analyst mcpl. securities Merrill Lynch, 1983—85; v.p. real estate and lodging investment banking Chase Securities, Inc., 1987—89; CFO Equity One, Inc., North Miami Beach, 1999—. Office: 1696 NE Miami Gardens Dr North Miami Beach FL 33179

SIQUELAND, EINAR, psychology educator; b. Glasgow, Mont., Nov. 15, 1932; s. Harald and Anna Lydia (Kristensen) S.; m. Marian McGrail, Dec. 1960 (div. May 1970); children: Lynne Ruth, Beth Ann; m. Jillian E.A. Godfree, June 29, 1973. BA, Pacific Luth. U., 1954; MS, U. Wash., 1962,

PhD, 1963. Rsch. assoc. pharmacology U. Wash., Seattle, 1958-59; clin. intern psychology VA Mental Hygiene Clinic, Seattle, 1960-61; asst. prof. dept. psychology Brown U., Providence, 1965-69, assoc. prof., 1969-88, prof., 1988-99; rsch. scientist dept. Pediatrics Women's and Infants' Hosp., Providence, 1975-93; prof. emeritus Brown U., 1999—. Contbr. articles to profl. jours., chpts. to books. With U.S. Army, 1956-58, Korea. Predoctoral fellow USPHS, 1961-63, postdoctoral fellow, 1963-65. Fellow Am. Psychol. Soc.; mem. AAUP, APA, Soc. Rsch. in Child Devel., Sigma Xi. Office: Brown U Dept Psychology PO Box 1853 Providence RI 02912-1853 E-mail: siquel-e@cox.net.

SIRACUSANO, LOUIS H. communications company executive; b. N.Y.C., July 19, 1942; s. Luciano A. and Mafalda (Rossi) S.; m. Theresa Boegle, June 1, 1963; children: Marie, Louis H. Student, Bronx C.C., 1960-62. Electronics technologist Bendix Corp., Teterborough, N.J., 1962-68; broadcast engr. ABC Network, N.Y.C., 1968-70; field engr. AMPEX Corp., Hackensack, N.J., 1970-72, sales engr. Washington, 1972-75; pres., CEO Video Svcs. Corp., Northvale, N.J., 1975—. Mem. adv. bd. Key Bank, Westchester, N.Y., 1997; bd. dirs. Internat. Post Ltd., N.Y.C. Trustee Good Samaritan Hosp., Suffern, N.Y., 1988-94; chmn. Dem. Party, Washington Twp., N.J., 1969-75; bd. govs. CYO Youth Ministry, Newark, 1988-96. Recipient Medal of Honor, Good Samaritan Hosp., 1993, Outstanding Achievement awrd Vision Fund Am., 1992, Ellis Island Medal of Honor, 2000. Mem. KC (3d deg.). Roman Catholic. Avocations: golf, skiing. Home: 4 Concklin Ln Rockleigh NJ 07647 E-mail: usc.ceo@worldnet.att.net.

SIRAGUSA, CHARLES J. judge; BA, Lemoyne Coll., 1969; JD, Albany Law Sch., 1976. Judge U.S. Dist. Ct. (we. dist.) N.Y., 1997—. Office: 1360 US Courthouse 100 State St Rochester NY 14614-1350 Office Phone: 585-613-4050.

SIRBAUGH, NORA B. performing arts educator, vocalist; b. Ft. Jackson, N.C., Mar. 10, 1953; d. Wallace Randell Sirbaugh and Dolores Bujalski Patskin; m. Robert Crawford Holmes; children: Genevieve Sirbaugh Holmes, Aubrey Crawford Holmes. BA, SUNY Coll., Fredonia, N.Y., 1975; Mus M, Temple U., Phila., Pa, 1979; Mus D, Peabody Inst. Johns Hopkins U., Balt., Md., 1994. Artist faculty Coll. of NJ, Ewing, NJ, 1989—, Mercer County C.C., Trenton, NJ, 1985—; voice faculty Temple U. Ctr. City, Phila., 1985—90; instr. Peabody Inst. Johns Hopkins U., Balti., Md., 1991—94. Editor Mercer County Master Gardeners, Trenton, NJ, 2002—. Musician solo recitalist songs, Inaugural Recital of the Ivor Gurney Society, singer (soloist) Operas; contbr. articles pub. to profl. jour. 1st v.p. Master Gardeners of Mercer County, NJ, 2003; adult leader St. Matthew's LOGOS-youth group, Pennington, NJ, 1997. Recipient Inaugural Recital of the Ivor Gurney Soc., Three Choirs Festival, Gloucester, Eng., 1995, Award for Excellence, State of NJ Master Gardeners Assn., 2002; grantee Rsch., Peabody Inst. Johns Hopkins U., 1994. Mem.: Nat. Assn. of Tchrs. of Singing (chair, doris lenz scholarship 2003), Finzi Soc., Delius Soc. (U.S., Eng.), Ivor Gurney Soc., Alpha Mu Gamma, Phi Kappa Lambda. Democrat. Episcopalian. Avocations: gardening, environment, writing, family-soccer and swimming mom. Home: 2 Fanning Way Pennington NJ 08534 Office: Coll N J PO Box 7718 Ewing NJ 08628 Personal E-mail: sirbaugh@tcnj.edu. Business E-Mail: sirbaugh@tcnj.edu.

SIRES, ALBIO, legislative staff member, business owner; BA in Spanish, Mktg., St. Peter's Coll.; MA in Spanish, Middlebury Coll. Owner A.M. Title Agy., Inc.; mayor West N.Y., 1995—, gen. assembly, 2000—, acting gov., 2002, spkr., 2002—; Spkr. of Ho. State of N.J., Dist. 33, 2002—. Mem.: Legis. Svcs. Commn. Office: 303 58th St West New York NJ 07093

SIRES, NORMAN GRUBER, JR., lawyer; b. Charleston, S.C., Sept. 14, 1942; s. N. Gruber and Emily (Neese) S.; m. Ann Jackson, Oct. 3, 1964; children: N. Gruber III, David Brian. BS in Bus. Adminstrn., U. S.C., 1967, JD, 1971. Bar: S.C. 1971, U.S. Dist. Ct. S.C. 1974. Pvt. practice, Seneca, S.C., 1971—; pub. defender Oconce County, S.C., 1972—; city atty. City of Clemson (S.C.), 1981-95. Pres. Oconce County Bar, 1978; commr. S.C. Indigent Def. Commn., 1992—. Mem. House Dels., S.C. Bar Assn. With U.S. Army Security agency E-5, 1963-66. Coxswain USCG Aux, past vice Flotilla commdr., 1996. Mem. S.C. Bar Assn., Oconce County Bar Assn. Republican. Methodist. Office: Commons Sq 123 PO Box 1277 Seneca SC 29679-1277

SIRICA, ALPHONSE EUGENE, pathology educator; b. Waterbury, Conn., Jan. 16, 1944; s. Alphonse Eugene and Elena Virginia (Mascolo) S.; m. Annette Marie Murray, June 9, 1984; children: Gabrielle Theresa, Nicholas Steven. MS, Fordham U., 1968; PhD in Biomed. Sci., U. Conn., 1977. Asst. prof. U. Wis., Madison, 1979-84; assoc. prof. Med. Coll. Va., Va. Commonwealth U., Richmond, 1984-90, prof. of pathology, 1990—, divsn. chair exptl. pathology, 1992-99, divsn. chair cellular and molecular pathogenesis, 1999—. Vis. prof., Pa. State U. Coll. Medicine, 2000, chmn. symposium on Pathobiology of Neoplasia, Am. Soc. Investigative Pathology, Richmond, Va., 1993; regular mem. sci. adv. com. on carcinogenesis and nutrition Am. Cancer Soc., Atlanta, 1989-92, metabolic pathology study sect., NIH, Bethesda, 1991-95, ad hoc mem. study sect., 1997-2004; chmn. Fedn. Am. Socs. Expt. Biology Summer Rsch. Conf. on Growth Factor Receptor Tyrosine Kinases, Snowmass Village, Colo., 1999, 2001. Editor, author: The Pathobiology of Neoplasia, 1989, The Role of Cell Types in Hepatocarcinogenesis, 1992, Cellular and Molecular Pathogenesis, 1996; co-editor, author: Biliary and Pancreatic Ductal Epithelia: Pathobiology and Pathophysiology, 1997; mem. editl. bd. Pathobiology, 1990-99, Hepatology, 1991-94; rev. bd. In Vitro Cellular and Devel. Biology, 1987—, Exptl. and Molecular Pathology, 1999—; contbr. rsch. papers to Am. Jour. Pathology, Cancer Rsch., Hepatology, others. Mem.: AAAS, Internat. Soc. for Study of Comparative Oncology, Soc. Toxicology, Hans. Popper Hepatopathology Soc., Soc. Exptl. Biology and Medicine, NY Acad. Scis., Am. Gastroenterological Assn., Am. Assn. Study Liver Diseases, Am. Soc. Investigative Pathology (chair program com. 1994—96), Assn. Clin. Scientists, Soc. for In Vitro Biology, Am. Assn. Cancer Rsch. (chmn. Va. state legis. com. 1992—95), Am. Soc. Cell Biology. Achievements include development of collagen gel-nylon mesh system for culturing hepatocytes; first establishment and characterization of hyperplastic bile ductular epithelial cells in culture; research in hepato and biliary carcinogenesis, pathobiology of hepatocyte and biliary epithelial cells and molecular pathogenesis and experimental therapeutics of biliary cancer. Office: Med Coll Va Va Commonwealth U PO Box 980297 Richmond VA 23298-0297 Office Phone: 804-828-9549. E-mail: asirica@hsc.vcu.edu.

SIRICO, GENARO, actor; b. Bklyn., July 29, 1942; Actor: (TV series) The Soprano's, 1999—; (TV films) Perfect Witness, 1989, In the Shadow of a Killer, 1992, Gotti, 1996; (films) Hughes and Harlow: Angels in Hell, 1977, Fingers, 1978, The One Man Jury, 1978, Gangsters, 1979, Defiance, 1980, So Fine, 1981, Love and Money, 1982, Exposed, 1983, The Last Fight, 1983, The Pick-Up Artist, 1987, Hello Again, 1987, Cookie, 1989, White Hot, 1989, Goodfellas, 1990, Catchfire, 1990, 29th Street, 1991, Innocent Blood, 1992, Romeo is Bleeding, 1993, Bullets Over Broadway, 1994, The Search for One-eye Jimmy, 1994, Mighty Aphrodite, 1995, Dead Presidents, 1995, Dearly Beloved, 1995, Everyone Says I Love You, 1996, New York Cop, 1996, Cop Land, 1997, Deconstructing Harry, 1997, The Deli, 1997, Mob Queen, 1998, Celebrity, 1998, Mickey Blue Eyes, 1999, It Had to Be You, 2000, Smokin' Stogies, 2001, Turn of Faith, 2001. Office: c/o Arcieri & Assoc Inc Ste 2315 305 Madison Ave New York NY 10165*

SIRIGNANO, MONICA ANN, performing company executive, playwright; b. Princeton, N.J., May 18, 1971; d. William Alfonso and Molly Wilhelmina Sirignano. BA in English, Stetson U., 1993; postgrad., CUNY. Mng. editor Encore Mag., Miami, Fla., 1993—95; asst. mng. editor PC Mag., N.Y.C., 1995—2000; performer, playwright N.Y.C., 1995—; artistic dir., pres. Screaming Venus Prodns., N.Y.C., 1999—, also bd. dirs. Adjudicator Fringe NYC, 2000, 01; mem. adv. bd. Blue Allied Theatre Co., N.Y.C., 2002—. Contbr. articles to mags. Mem. membership com., mem. creative black tie invitation com. Am. Cancer Soc., Miami, 1993—94; mem. Habitat for Humanity, Ft. Lauderdale, Fla., 1994. Recipient award, Off-Off Broadway Rev., 2001; grantee, Harburg Found., 2000. Mem.: Theatre Comm. Group, Dramatists Guild. Avocations: photography, painting, graphic design. Office: Screaming Venus Prodns 29-22 Hoyt Ave S # 21 Astoria NY 11102

SIRIGNANO, WILLIAM ALFONSO, aerospace and mechanical engineer, educator; b. Bronx, N.Y., Apr. 14, 1938; s. Anthony P. and Lucy (Caruso) S.; m. Lynn Haisfield, Nov. 26, 1977; children: Monica Ann, Jacqueline Hope, Justin Anthony. B.Aero.Engring., Rensselaer Poly. Inst., 1959; PhD, Princeton U., 1964. Mem. research staff Guggenheim Labs., aerospace, mech. scis. dept. Princeton U., 1964-67, asst. prof. aerospace and mech. scis., 1967-69, assoc. prof., 1969-73, prof., 1973-79, dept. dir. grad. studies, 1974-78; George Tallman Ladd prof., head dept. mech. engring. Carnegie-Mellon U., 1979-85; dean Sch. Engring., U. Calif.-Irvine, 1985-94, prof., 1994—. Cons. industry and govt., 1966—; lectr. and cons. NATO adv. group on aero. rsch. and devel., 1967, 75, 80; chmn. nat. and internat. tech. congs.; chmn. acad. adv. coun. Indsl. Rsch. Inst., 1985-88; mem. space sci. applications adv. com. NASA, 1985-90, chmn. combustion sci. microgravity disciplinary working group, 1987-90; chmn. com. on microgravity rsch. space studies bd. NRC, 1991-94, Henry Samueli Edward chmn. engring, 2004-. Spl. issues editor: Combustion Sci. and Tech., 1969-70, 2000—; assoc. tech. editor Jour. Heat Transfer, 1986-92; contbr. articles to nat. and internat. profl. jours., also rsch. monographs. Recipient Disting. Alumni Rsch. award U. Calif. Irvine, 1992, Recognition award Am. Electronics Assn., 1994, Excellence award Orange County Engring. Coun., 1994; United Aircraft rsch. fellow, 1973-74. Fellow: AAAS, ASME (Freeman scholar 1992, Energy Systems award 2004), AIAA (Pendray Aerospace Lit. award 1991, Propellants and Combustion award 1992), Am. Phys. Soc.; mem.: NAE, Soc. Indsl. and Applied Math., Combustion Inst. (treas. internat. orgn., chmn. ea. sect., Alfred C. Egerton Gold medal 1996), Inst. Dynamics Explosives and Reactive Sys. (v.p. 1991—95, pres. 1995—99, Oppenheim award 1993). Office: U Calif Irvine Sch Engring S3202 Engring Gtwy Irvine CA 92697-3975 Office Phone: 949-824-3700. Business E-Mail: sirignan@uci.edu.

SIRIS, ETHEL SILVERMAN, endocrinologist; b. Clifton, N.J., Aug. 21, 1945; s. Irving A. and Gertrude (Gollop) Silverman; m. Samuel G. Siris, June 2, 1971; children: Benjamin A., Sara A. AB in Biology magna cum laude, Radcliffe Coll. Harvard U., 1963-67; MD, Columbia U. Coll. Physicians and Surgeons, 1967-71. Nat. Bd. of Medical Examiners, Diplomate Am Bd. Internal Medicine, Diplomate Am. Bd. Internal Medicine, Certification in Endocrinology and Metabolism. Intern, asst. resident dept. medicine Presbyn. Hosp., N.Y.C., 1971-74, asst. attending physician, 1977-84, assoc. attending physician, 1984-91, attending physician, 1991—; NIH guest worker Reproduction Rsch. Br. Nat. Inst. Child Health and Human Devel., NIH, 1974-75, NIH rsch. fellow, 1975-76; fellow in Endocrinology Columbia U. Coll. of Physicians & Surgeons and Presbyn. Hosp., N.Y.C., 1976-77. Bd. dirs. the Paget Found. for Paget's Disease of Bone and Related Disorders; bd. trustees Nat. Osteoporosis Found.; dir. programs in osteoporosis Ctr. for Women's Health, 1993—; asst. prof. dept. medicine Columbia U., 1977-84, assoc. prof. clin. medicine, 1984-91, prof. clin. medicine, 1991-96, Madeline C. Stabile prof. clin. medicine, 1996—, dir. Toni Stabile Ctr. for Prevention and Treatment of Osteoporosis, 1996—, course dir. phys. diagnosis dept. medicine, 1985-96; med. dir. Nat. Osteoporosis Risk Assessment, 1997—; mem. endocrinologic and metabolic drugs adv. com. FDA, 1992-95. Contbr. numerous articles to profl. jours. Recipient Upjohn award Columbia U. Coll. of Physicians and Surgeons, 1971, Mary Putnam Jacobi award for Clin. Rsch., 1979, Rsch. award The Paget's Disease Fdn., 1986, 87, John B. Johnson award, 2000. Am. Soc. for Bone and Mineral Rsch., Endocrine Soc., Am. Assn. of Clin. Endocrinologists, Phi Beta Kappa, Alpha Omega Alpha. Home: 60 Prescott St Demarest NJ 07627-1420 Office: Dept Medicine Columbia U Coll Phys & Surgeons 180 Fort Washington Ave New York NY 10032-3710

SIRIS, SAMUEL GIDDING, psychiatrist; b. Phila., Aug. 28, 1944; s. Sydney Milton and Charlotte (Gidding) S.; m. Ethel Martha Silverman, June 2, 1971; children: Benjamin Avram, Sara Ann. BA in Biology, Lehigh U., 1966, MS in Biology, 1967; MD, Columbia U., 1970. Diplomate Am. Bd. Psychiatry and Neurology; cert. in adminstrv. psychiatry Am. Psychiat. Assn. Com. on Adminstriv. Psychiatry. Med. intern Mt. Sinai Med. Ctr., N.Y.C., 1970-71; psychiat. resident N.Y. State Psychiat. Inst., N.Y.C., 1971-74; fellow in biol. psychiatry NIMH, Bethesda, Md., 1974-76; asst. prof. psychiatry Columbia U., N.Y.C., 1977-79, psychoanalytic tng., 1976-82; asst. prof. psychiatry Mt. Sinai Sch. Medicine, N.Y.C., 1979-84, assoc. prof. psychiatry, 1984-88; dir. adult psychiat. day programs Hillside Hosp./L.I. Jewish Med. Ctr., N.Y.C., 1988-97, dir. ambulatory psychiatry, 1995-97, dir. continuing psychiat. svcs. for schizophrenia and related conditions, 1997—; prof. psychiatry Albert Einstein Coll. Medicine, N.Y.C., 1989—. Contbr. articles to profl. jours., chpts. to books; reviewer jours. in field. Lt. comdr. USPHS, 1974-76. Grantee NIMH, Rockville, Md., 1981-90, Nat. Inst. Drug Abuse, Rockville, 1987-91, others. Fellow: Assn. Clin. Psychosocial Rsch., Am. Psychopathol. Assn., Am. Psychiat. Assn. (disting.); mem.: Am. Psychoanalytic Assn., Group for Advancement of Psychiatry, Collegium Internat. Neuro-Psychopharmacologicum, Am. Coll. Neuropsychopharmacology. Office: The Zucker-Hillside Hosp 75-59 263rd St Glen Oaks NY 11004-1150 Office Phone: 718-470-8138.

SIRKEN, MONROE GILBERT, statistician; b. N.Y.C., Jan. 11, 1921; s. Irving and Henrietta (Oram) S.; m. Blanche Skalak Hurwitz (div. 1960); children: Robert, Philip. BA, UCLA, 1946, MA, 1947; PhD, U. Wash., 1950. Lectr. Med. Sch. U. Wash., Seattle, 1949; fellow Stats. Lab. U. Calif., Berkeley, 1950; statistician Census Bur., Suitland, Md., 1951-54, Pub. Health Svc., Washington, 1954-60, Nat. Ctr. Health Stats., Hyattsville, Md., 1961—. Cons. NIH, 1980-85, Nat. Inst. Drug Addiction, 1976-80, NSF, 1986—, Health Care Fin. Adminstrn., 1989-90. Contbr. articles to Jour. Am. Statis. Assn., Biometrics, Demography, Jour. APHA, Pub. Health Reports, also others. Home: 3309 Claridge Ct Silver Spring MD 20902-2201 Office Phone: 301-458-4505. Business E-Mail: mgs2@cdc.gov.

SIRMAN, ROBERT, performing company executive; MA in Sociology, U. Toronto. Intern French Ministry of Culture, Paris; past speech writer Ont. Cabinet Min. Robert Welch; spl. asst., policy advisor Ont. Cabinet Min. Robert Welch, 1961—71; dir. ops. Ont. Arts Coun., Toronto, 1981—91; adminstrv. dir. The Nat. Ballet Sch., Toronto, Canada, 1991—. Chair bd. dirs. Peggy Baker Dance Projects, Toronto; adv. com.arts adminstrn. co-op program U. Toronto, Scarborough Campus. Chmn. bd. dirs. Toronto PWA Found. Office: The Nat Ballet Sch 105 Maitland Toronto ON M4Y 1E4 Canada

SIRO, RIK NEAL, lawyer; b. Bklyn., Dec. 31, 1957; s. Jack N. and Beatrice Siro; m. Teresa A. Woody, Aug. 9; children: Alexander Lewis, Lia Ann Xuesong. BA, U. Mo., 1979; JD, U. Calif., San Francisco, 1982. Bar: Mo., Calif., U.S. Dist. Ct. (we. dist.) Mo., U.S. Dist. Ct. (no. dist.) Calif., U.S. Ct. Appeals (7th, 8th, 9th, 10th cirs.). Assoc. Murphy, Pearson, Bradley & Feeney, San Francisco, 1982-84, Gage & Tucker, Kansas City, Mo., 1984-86; sr. ptnr. Siro & Moyer, Kansas City, 1986—. Bd. dirs., pres.-elect, pres. Big Bros., Big Sisters of Greater Kans. City, 1987—; bd. dirs., pres. Mattie Rhodes Counseling and Art Ctr., Kansas City, chair Art of the Mask Fundraising, 1993—. Mem. ATLA, Mo. Assn. Trial Attys. (bd. govs.), Nat. Employment Lawyers Assn., Kansas City Met. Bar Assn. Avocations: spanish, french, skiing, guitar, piano. Home: 3654 Belleview Ave Kansas City MO 64111-3860 Office: Blumer Nally & Siro 1621 Baltimore Ave Kansas City MO 64108-1347 Office Phone: 816-471-4881.

SIROIS, CHARLES, communications executive; b. Chicoutimi, Que., Can., May 22, 1954; children: François-Charles, Marie-Hèlène. Doctorate (hon.), U. Québec, Montréal, U. Ottawa (Can.), Concordia U., Montreal, Laval U., Que.; B Fin., Sherbrooke U., Qué.; M Fin., Laval U., Qué. Founder Telesystem Ltd., Montreal, 1984—, Nat. Pagette Ltd., Montreal, 1986-88; chmn., CEO BCE Mobile Comms. Inc., Montreal, 1988-90, Teleglobe Inc., Montreal, 1992-2000, Telesystem Ltd., Montreal, 1990—; chmn. Microcell Telecomms. Inc., 1993—, Telesys. Internat. Wireless, 1997—. Bd dirs Can Imperial Bank Commerce; mem Global Info Infrastructure Comn, Can Info Hwy. Co-author: (book) The Medium and the Muse, 1995, Organic Management-Creating a Culture of Innovation, 2000. Mem.: Knight Order nat du Que, Order Can (hon.). Office: Telesystem Ltd 38th Fl 1250 René Lévesque Blvd W Montreal QC Canada H3B 4W8 E-mail: csirois@telesystem.ca.

SIROTKIN, PHILLIP LEONARD, education administrator; b. Moline, Ill., Aug. 2, 1923; s. Alexander and Molly (Berghaus) S.; m. Cecille Sylvia Gussack, May 1, 1945; children— Steven Marc, Laurie Anne. BA (McGregor Found. scholar), Wayne State U., 1945; MA, U. Chgo., 1947, PhD (Walgreen Found. scholar, Carnegie fellow), 1951. Lectr. U. Chgo., 1949-50; instr. Wellesley Coll., 1950-52, asst. prof. polit. sci., 1953-57; asso. dir. Western Interstate Commn. Higher Edn., Boulder, Colo., 1957-60; exec. asst. to dir. Calif. Dept. Mental Hygiene, Sacramento, 1960-63; asst. dir. NIMH, 1964-66, asso. dir., 1967-71, cons., 1971-73; exec. v.p., acad. v.p. State U. N.Y. at Albany, 1971-76; exec. dir. Western Interstate Commn. Higher Edn., Boulder, Colo., 1976-90, sr. adviser, 1990—, Midwestern Legis. Higher Edn. Steering Com., Boulder, Colo., 1990-91; sr. cons. Midwestern Higher Edn. Commn., 1991—; mem. oversight com. Hispanic Agenda, Larasa, 1992-98. Cons. Nebr. Post-Secondary Edn. Commn., 1994; nat. adv. com. Soc. Coll. and Univ. Planning, 1976, adv. panel, rev. state system higher edn. in N.D., 1986, gov.'s com. on bi-state med. edn. plan for N.D. and S.D., 1988-90, Edn. Commn. States' Nat. Task Force for Minority Achievement in Higher Edn., 1989-91; cons. Bur. Health Manpower Edn., NIH, 1972-74, Nat. Ctr. Health Svcs. Rsch., 1975-85; spl. cons. AID, 1963-64; case writer Resources for the Future, 1954-55; mem. 1st U.S. Mission on Mental Health to USSR, 1967. Author: The Echo Park Dam Controversy and Upper Colorado River Development, 1959. Bd. dirs. Council Social Work Edn., 1959-60. 1st lt. AUS, 1943-46. Recipient Superior Svc. award HEW, 1967; Faculty Rsch. award Wellesley Coll., 1956 Home: 299 Green Rock Dr Boulder CO 80302-4745

SIROTKO, THEODORE FRANCIS, priest, retired military officer; b. Muskegon, Mich., Oct. 5, 1936; s. Theodore Felix and Dorothy Mary (Bray) S.; m. Phyllis Anne Bourziel, May 5, 1962; children: Mary Anne, Kathleen, Stephen, Michael. BS, Ferris State U., 1958; MDiv, Nashotah House Theol. Sem., 1965; D in Ministry, San Francisco Theol. Sem., 1982; MSA, U. Notre Dame, 1982. Ordained to ministry Episcopal Ch., 1965. Vicar St. Matthew Ch., Sparta, Mich., 1965-68; rector St. Mark Parish, Howe, Ind., 1968-70; sr. chaplain Howe Mil. Sch., 1968-70; with U.S. Army, 1959-61, 70-93, advanced through grades to lt. col., 1985, chaplain, 1970-93, chief parish, profl. devel. Europe, 1982-85, chief pastoral ministry, counselling Chaplain Ctr. and Sch., 1985-88, asst. dir. dept. mil. ministry, 1988-89, dir., 1989, chief resource mgmt. br., 1989—91, chief adminstrn./ops. br., dep. post chaplain, 1991—93; ret., 1993; rector St. Peter's-by-the-lake, Montague, Mich., 1993—2002. Exec. coun. Diocese Western Mich., 1995-97. Bd. dirs. LaGrange County Mental Health Assn., Ind., 1969-70, Sch. Opportunity, LaGrange, 1969-70; chaplain Montague Fire Dept., 1995—; mem. Montague City Planning Commn., 2000-01. Decorated Bronze Star with 1 bronze oak leaf cluster, Air medal with 3 bronze oak leaf clusters, Meritorious Svc. medal with 3 bronze oak leaf clusters, Army Commendation medal with 1 oak leaf cluster. Mem. DAV (life), U.S. Army Chaplain Mus. Assn. (bd. dirs. 1986-88), Am. Soc. Mil. Comptrollers, Mil. Officers Assn. of Am. (life), Mil. Chaplains Assn., Confrater Order of St. Benedict, Ferris State U. Alumni Assn., Nashotah House Theol. Sem. Alumni Assn., Torch Club Internat., Forward in Faith. Home: 4788 S Shore Dr Whitehall MI 49461

SIROTY, WILLIAM CHARLES, physician; b. NYC, June 9, 1951; s. Daniel Hirsch and Eileen (Gusman) S. BS, SUNY, Stony Brook, 1973; MD, Georgetown U., 1977. Diplomate Am. Bd. Internal Medicine, Am. Bd. Allergy-Immunology. Intern in internal medicine Beth Israel Med. Ctr., NYC, 1977-78, resident in internal medicine, 1977-78; fellow allergy and immunology NY Hosp.-Cornell U. Med. Ctr., 1980-82; pvt. practice NYC, 1982-94; staff physician Nashua (NH) Med. Group, 1994—. Mem. adv. bd. Cmty. Rsch. Initiative, 1990-94, HIV Arts Network, 1994-95. Editor: NH News Links, 2000—. Vol. Neighborhood Health Clinic; co-founder, first co-chair Gay People in Medicine Caucus Am. Med. Student Assn., 1976—77; active NH State Dem. Com., 1998—, Hillsborough County Dem. Com., NH, 1998—, vice-chmn., 2004—; del. Dem. Nat. Conv., 2000, 2004; bd. dirs. Elizabeth Streb Ringside, Inc., NH Civil Liberties Union. Mem. Am. Acad. Allergy, Asthma and Immunology, NH Med. Soc. Office: Nashua Med Group 173 Daniel Webster Hwy Nashua NH 03060-5224

SIROWER, BONNIE FOX, fundraising executive; b. Bklyn., Jan. 9, 1949; d. Stanley S. and Harriet (Fischer) Fox; m. Martin Alan Sirower, Sept. 20, 1970; children: Kenneth, Daniel. AB, Barnard Coll., 1970; MA, Columbia U., 1971. Tchr. United Cerebral Palsy, N.Y.C., 1970-73, Bergen County Bd. Spl. Svcs., Paramus, N.J., 1973-76; spl. events coord. Am. Heart Assn., Glen Ridge, N.J., 1979-81; dir. devel. Goodwill Industries, Astoria, N.Y., 1981-83; pres. Access Unltd., 1984-85; dir. devel. Cheshire Home, Inc., 1986-89, Barnert Hosp., Paterson, N.J., 1989-95; from dir. devel. to sr. v.p. United Way Passaic County, N.J., 1995-97; dir. devel. Cereral Palsy No. Jersey, N.J., 1997-99; dir. annual giving Union County Coll., Cranford, NJ, 1999—2001, Iona Coll., 2001—04; exec. dir. Cmty. Blood Svcs. Fedn., Paramus, NJ, 2004—. Commr. Paterson (N.J.) Coun. for Disabled, 1994; trustee YMCA, Paterson, 1991; founder Pride in Paterson, 1993—; chair Youth in Philanthropy, 1995—; Paterson rep. Pres. Summit for Am. Future, 1997; dir. ann. giving Union County Coll. Found., 1999-2001; bd. dirs. Westchester Assn. of Devel. Officers, 2002—. Recipient Accolades Bronze Medal award CASE R4gion III, 2001; named Outstanding N.J. Fundraiser, Nat. Soc. of Fundraising Execs. of N.J., 1995, Gold & Silver medal awards, 2003. Mem. Nat. Assn. Fund Raising Profls. (seminars chmn. 1998-2000, 3d v.p. 2001, Gold award), N.J. Soc. Fund Raising Execs. (bd. dirs. 1989, chmn. mentoring com., 3d v.p., nat. del., chmn. N.J. Conf. on Philanthropy 1994), Assn. Fund Raisers for Disabled (pres. 1981-83), N.J. Puzzlers' League (pres.), Westchester Assn. of Devel. Officers (bd. dirs. 2002-03, v.p. profl. advancement, 2003—), Barnard Coll. Class of '70 (pres. 1990-2000), Rotary Internat. (v.p. Paterson, past pres., asst. dist. sec., Outstanding fundraiser in N.J. 1995, bd. dir. New Rochelle chpt., 2003—), Cranford Rotary (bd. dirs.), Cranford N.J. C. of C. (bd. dirs. 1999-2001), Bergen Women of Accomplishment, Cranford C. of C. (bd. dirs. 1999-2001), Phi Beta Kappa, Rotary (internat. svc. chair New Rochelle club 2002—). Jewish. Home: 69 Godfrey Ter Glen Rock NJ 07452-3510 E-mail: Botzie@aol.com., bonnies@berbe.org.

SIS, PETER, illustrator, children's book author, artist, filmmaker; b. Brno, Czech Republic, May 11, 1949; came to U.S., 1982, naturalized, 1988; s. Vladimir and Alena (Petrvalska) S.; m. Terry Ann Lajtha, Oct. 23, 1990; children: Madeleine, Matej. BA, Acad. of Applied Arts, 1968—74; MA, Royal Coll. of Art, 1977. Author, illustrator: Rainbow Rhino, 1987 (Best Illustrated Book award NY Times, 1988), Waving, 1988, Going Up, 1989, Beach Ball, 1990 (Best Illustrated Book award N.Y. Times, 1990), Follow the Dream, 1991 (Best Illustrated Book award N.Y. Times, 1992), An Ocean World, 1992, A Small, Tall Tale from the Far Far North, 1992, Komodo!, 1993, The Three Golden Keys, 1994, Starry Messenger: Galileo Galilei, 1996 (Caldecott Honor Book, 1997), Tibet Through the Red Box, 1998, Madlenka's Dog, 2002, The Tree of Life, 2003; illustrator: Fairy Tales of the Brothers Grimm, 2 vols., 1976, 77, Hexe Lakritze and Buchstabenkonig, 1977, Zizkov Romances, 1978, Hexe Lakritze and Rhino Rhinoceros, 1979, Poetry, 1980, Baltic Fairy Tales, 1981, Little Singer, 1982, Bean Boy, 1983, Stories to solve, 1984, Whipping Boy, 1985 (Newberry medal 1987), Oaf, 1986, Three Yellow Dogs, 1986, Higgledy Piggledy, 1986, Jed and the Space Bandits, 1987, After Midnight, 1987, City Lights, 1987, Scarebird, 1988, Alphabet Soup, 1988, Halloween, 1989, The Ghost in the Noonday Sun, 1989, The Midnight Horse, 1990, More Stories to Solve, 1991, Rumpelstiltskin, 1993, The Dragons Are Singing Tonight, 1993, Still More Stories to Solve, 1994, The 13th Floor, 1995, Monday's Troll, 1996, Sleep Safe Little Whale, 1997; filmmaker: (TV series) Hexe Lakritze, 1982, (short films) Mimikry, 1975, Island for 6,000 Alarm Clocks, 1977, Heads, 1979 (Golden Bear award Berlin Film Festival 1980), Players, 1981 (Grand Prix Toronto Film Festival 1981), You Gotta Serve Somebody, 1983 (CINE Golden Eagle award 1983), Aesop's Fables, 1984, Twelve Months, 1985; artist one man shows include Gallery Martinska, Gallery Nerudova, Gallery Rubin, Prague, 1977-79, Gallery Klostermauer, St. Gallen, 1975, Gallery Ploem, Delft, 1977, Gallery Vista Nova, Zurich, 1980,

Gallery Medici, London, 1981, Sch. Art U. Ohio, Athens, 1990. Recipient MacArthur Fellowship, 2003. Office: Farrar, Straus & Giroux Books for Young Readers 19 Union Square West New York NY 10003*

SISCHY, INGRID BARBARA, editor, art critic; b. Johannesburg, Republic of South Africa, Mar. 2, 1952; came to U.S., 1967; d. Benjamin and Claire S. BS, Sarah Lawrence Coll., 1973; PhD (hon.), Moore Coll. Art, 1987. Assoc. editor Print Collector's Newsletter, N.Y.C., 1974-77; dir. Printed Matter, N.Y.C., 1977-78; curatorial intern Mus. Modern Art, N.Y.C., 1978-79; editor ArtForum Mag., N.Y.C., 1979-88; editor-in-chief Interview, N.Y.C., 1989—. Office: Interview Magazine 575 Broadway Fl 5 New York NY 10012-3230

SISCO, JOSEPH JOHN, management consultant, corporation director, educator, government official; b. Chgo., Oct. 31, 1919; m. Jean Churchill Head, Mar. 26, 1946; children: Carol Bolton, Jane Murdock. Student, Morton Jr. Coll., 1937-39; AB magna cum laude, Knox Coll., 1941; MA, U. Chgo., 1947, PhD, 1950. Newspaper reporter, 1936-40; with City News Bur., Chgo., 1937; high sch. tchr., 1941; govt. service, 1950-51; staff Dept. State, 1951-76; successivley fgn. affairs officer, specialist internat. orgnl. affairs, officer-in charge Gen. Assembly, Security Council affairs, fgn. service officer, officer-in-charge UN polit. affairs, 1951-58; dep. dir. Office UN Polit. and Security Affairs, 1958-60, dir., 1960-63; dep. asst. sec. Bur. Internat. Orgn. Affairs, 1963-65, asst. sec. state internat. orgn. affairs, 1965-69; asst. sec. state Near East-South Asia, 1969-74; under sec. state for polit. affairs, 1974-76; pres. Am. U., Washington, 1976-80, chancellor, 1980-81; ptnr. Sisco Assocs. (mgmt. cons.), Washington, 1981—; chmn. Am. Acad. Diplomacy. Mem. U.S. delegation UN Collective Measures Com., 1952, U.S. delegations to UN Gen. Assembly, 1952-68; U.S. del. Spl. UN Gen. Assembly, session of Mid East, 1967; exec. officer, 1954=57; polit. adviser U.S. delegation Internat. Atomic Energy Agy., 1959; lectr. Fgn. Svc. Inst. Contbr. articles on internat. orgn., fgn. affairs to publs. Served as 1st lt., inf. AUS, 1941-45. Recipient Top Ten Career Service award Civil Service League, 1966, Rockefeller pub. service award, 1971; Silver Helmet Peace award Am. Vets. Com., 1973 Mem. Am. Acad. Diplomacy (chmn. bd. dirs.), Coun. Fgn. Rels. (pvt. sector coun.). Clubs: Cosmos (Washington). Home: 5630 Wisconsin Ave Chevy Chase MD 20815-4450 Office: 5335 Wisconsin Ave NW Washington DC 20015-2030

SISE, KAREN H. acoustical engineer; AS, Full Sail, Winter Park, Fla., 1998. 1st asst. engr. SoundStream Media Svcs., Northampton, Mass., 1999—2002; office mgr. Klondike Sound Co., Greenfield, Mass., 2002—; owner One Hand Clapping Sound, Easthampton, Mass., 1998—2003. Mem.: Audio Engring. Soc.

SISK, ALBERT FLETCHER, JR., retired insurance agent; b. Easton, Md., Nov. 25, 1928; s. Albert Fletcher and Helen (Marvel) S.; m. Mary Douglass Tweedy, Jan. 8, 1955; children: Douglass Fletcher, Geoffrey Price. Student, Washington and Lee U., 1946—49. CLU. With Albert W. Sisk & Son, Preston, Md., 1950-66; ins. agt. Conn. Gen. Life Ins. Co., 1968-94; dir. emeritus Provident State Bank, Preston. Pres. Farrell & Sisk, Inc. Trustee Meml. Hosp., Easton, Md., 1965-71, sch. nursing com., 1969-98; bd. visitors Horn Point Labs. U. Md., 1987-93. With USN, 1952-54. Mem. NRA, Am. Soc. CLUs, Meml. Hosp. Assn., Chesapeake Bay Yacht Club. Home: 3009 Larkspur Run Williamsburg VA 23185-3766

SISK, DANIEL ARTHUR, lawyer; b. Albuquerque, July 12, 1927; s. Arthur Henry and Myrl (Hope) S.; m. Katharine Banning, Nov. 27, 1954; children: John, Sarah, Thomas. BA, Stanford U., 1950, JD, 1954. Bar: N.Mex. 1955, Calif. 1954. Ptnr. firm Modrall, Sperling, Roehl, Harris & Sisk, Albuquerque, 1954-70, 71—; justice N.Mex. Supreme Ct., Santa Fe, 1970. Chmn. bd. Sunwest Fin. Svcs., Inc., Albuquerque, 1975-90. Pres. Legal Aid Soc., Albuquerque, 1960-61; trustee Sandia Sch., 1968-72, Albuquerque Acad., 1971-73, A.T. & S.F. Meml. Hosps., Topeka, 1966-82; bd. dirs. N.Mex. Sch. Banking Found., 1981-85. Served with USNR, 1945-46, PTO; to capt. USMCR, 1951-52, Korea. Mem. N.Mex. Bar Assn., Albuquerque Bar Assn. (dir. 1962-63), ABA, State Bar Calif. Presbyn. (elder). Office: 500 4th St NW Albuquerque NM 87102-5324

SISK, FRED DEAN, retired cartographer; b. Johnson City, Tenn., May 26, 1940; s. Aubrey Mackenzie and Violet Mae (McCartt) S.; m. Martha Lynn Robinson, Aug. 25, 1963. BS, East Tenn. State U., 1962; MS, George Mason U., 1984. Cartographer Def. Mapping Agy., Brookmont, Md., 1965-79, sr. cartographer Ft. Belvior, Va., 1979-81, course mgr., 1981-88, dep. div. chief, 1983-88, new employees tng. coord. Bethesda, Md., 1988-89; tng. coord. Def. Mapping Agy. Reston (Va.) Ctr., 1989-90, security analyst, 1990-95. Mem. scholarship com. George Mason U. Alumni Assn., Fairfax, 1990, Republican Presdl. Task Force, Washington, 1990—, adv. com. House of Dels., 54th Dist., 1995-2002; officer of election City of Fredericksburg, 1995—, mem. pub. transit adv. bd., 1996—, chmn. memls. adv. commn., 2000-03; notary public, 1996—, security officer, 1996—; pres. Fox Run Homeowners Assn., 1996—. 1st lt. U.S. Army, 1962-64. Mem.: Internat. Freelance Photographers Orgn. (master photographer 2004—), Civil War Round Table, The Heritage Found. Baptist. Home: 18 Devonshire Dr Fredericksburg VA 22401-2100

SISK, GREGORY CHARLES, lawyer, educator; b. Des Moines, May 29, 1960; s. James Anderson and Roberta Jean (Thornburg) S.; m. Melinda Fay Gilchrist, June 14, 1981; 1 child, Caitlin Anne. Student, Western Mont. Coll., 1978; BA in Polit. Sci., Mont. State U., 1981; JD, U. Wash., 1984. Bar: Wash. 1985, Iowa 1992, US Ct. Appeals (3d cir. and 9th cir.) 1986, US Ct. Appeals (2d, 5th, 11th and DC cir.) 1987, US Ct. Appeals (4th, 8th and fed. cir.) 1988, US Ct. Appeals (1st cir.) 1989, US Supreme Ct. 1988. Legis. asst. US Senate, Washington, 1984-85; jud. clk. US Ct. Appeals (9th cir.), Seattle, 1985-86; appellate staff atty. civil div. US Dept. Justice, Washington, 1986-89; assoc. Karr, Tuttle & Campbell, Seattle, 1989-91; asst. prof. Drake U., Des Moines, 1991-94, assoc. prof., 1994-97, prof., 1997—2003, Richard M. and Anita Calkins disting. prof., 1999—2003; prof. U. St. Thomas, Mpls., 2003—. Mem. ABA, Am. Law Inst., Fed. Bar Assn., Christian Legal Soc., Order of Coif, Nat. Order of Barristers, Law and Soc. Assn., Am. Polit. Sci. Assn. Republican. Roman Catholic. Office: Univ St Thomas Sch Law 1000 La Salle Ave Minneapolis MN 55403-2005

SISKA, ROBERT JOHN, software engineer; b. Evergreen Park, Ill., May 28, 1949; s. Emil Thomas and Maria Clara Siska; m. Jane Suzan Dwyer, May 25, 1979; children: Johanna, Charlotte. BA, U. Mass., 1974. Advt. coord. Goldblatt Bros., Chgo., 1976-79; tech. writer Calif Fed., L.A., 1980-82; software engr. Informatics Gen. Corp., Canoga Park, Calif., 1982-84; software programmer Great We. Bank, Northridge, Calif., 1984-86; sr. software engr. Litton Computer Svcs., Woodland Hills, Calif., 1986-90; sr. software devel. Legent Corp., Woodland Hills, 1990-94; sr. systems programmer Nat. Computer Sys., Iowa City, 1994-97; sr. software devel. Storage Tek, Louisville, 1997—2003; sys. programmer State of Colo., Lakewood, 2003—. Cons. advisor Johnson County, Iowa City, 1996—97; creator, coord. Craven Maven Record Co., pres., 1995—. Cons. advisor Johnson County Computer Com., Iowa City, 1996—97. Mem.: Network and Sys. Profls. Assn., Johnson County Blues Soc., Colo. Blues Soc. Avocations: record company, marathon running, literature, music. Office: State of Colo Dept Info Tech 690 Kipling St Lakewood CO 80215 Office Phone: 303-239-4313. E-mail: bob.siska@state.co.us.

SISKE, ROGER CHARLES, lawyer; b. Starkville, Miss., Mar. 2, 1944; s. Lester L. and Helen S.; m. Regina Markunas, May 31, 1969; children: Kelly, Jennifer, Kimberly. BS in Fin. with honors, Ohio State U., 1966; JD magna cum laude, U. Mich., 1969. Bar: Ill. 1969. Assoc. Sonnenschein Nath & Rosenthal, Chgo., 1969-78, ptnr., 1978—. Chmn. nat. employee benefits and exec. compensation dept., mem. policy and planning com. Served to capt. U.S. Army, 1970—71. Decorated Bronze Star. Fellow Am. Coll. Employee Benefits Counsel (charter); mem. ABA (past chmn. tax sect. employee benefits com., past chmn. joint com. on employee benefits and exec. compensation and bus. law sect., employee benefits and exec. compensation com.), Chgo. Bar Assn. (past chmn. employee benefits com., mem. exec. coun. of tax com.), past chmn. employee benefits coun. ISBA, Order of Coif (editor law review), Phi Alpha Kappa. Republican. Office: Sonnenschein Nath Rosenthal 233 S Wacker Dr Ste 8000 Chicago IL 60606-6491 Office Phone: 312-876-8018.

SISKIN, EDWARD JOSEPH, engineering and construction company executive; b. Bklyn., Apr. 30, 1941; s. Haskell and Sylvia (Steckler) S.; m. Patricia Ann Moore, June 26, 1965 (div. Apr. 1990); children: Candice P. Howard, Cristin Jo; m. Jean Elizabeth Bowen, Dec. 17, 1994. BSE, U. Pa., 1963; cert., Bettis Reactor Engring. Sch., West Mifflin, Pa., 1965; postgrad., George Washington U., 1963—67. Registered profl. engr., Pa., Mass., N.Y., N.J., Ill., Mich., Fla., W.Va., Ind., S.C., Tex., La., Nebr., Calif., Ala. Engr. U.S. Atomic Energy Commn., Washington, 1963-67, field office mgr. Pitts., 1967-70, Groton, Conn., 1970-77; project mgr. Stone & Webster Engring. Corp., Boston, 1977-78, asst. engring. mgr., 1978-79, engring. mgr. N.Y.C., 1979-83, v.p., mgr., 1984-86, sr. v.p., mgr. Cherry Hill, NJ, 1987-88, exec. v.p., 1988-90, dir. Boston, 1985-90; gen. mgr. Superconducting Supercollider Lab., Dallas, 1990-94; pres. Enerjoin Svcs., Inc., 1994—. Mem. adv. com. Inst. of Nuc. Power Ops., Atlanta, 1987-90, adv. bd. Ctr. for Chem. Plant Safety, N.Y.C., 1988-90. Bd. dirs. PenJerDel Coun., Phila., 1987-90. Lt. USN, 1963-69. Sr. mem. IEEE; mem. Am. Nuc. Soc., Am. Philatelic Soc. (State College, Pa.). Office: PO Box 17 Haddonfield NJ 08033-0016

SISKIND, ARTHUR, lawyer, director; b. NY, Oct. 11, 1938; s. William and Sylvia (Schuman) S.; m. Mary Ann Silverman, Nov. 10, 1962; children: Laura, Julie, Kenneth. BA in Liberal Arts, Cornell U., 1960, LLB with distinction, 1962. Ptnr. Squadron, Ellenoff, Plesent & Lehrer, N.Y., 1970-91; sr. exec. v.p., group gen. counsel, mem. exec. com., office chmn., dir. The News Corp. Ltd., N.Y., 1991—; sr. exec. v.p., gen. counsel, dir. Fox Entertainment Grp. Inc., 1998—. Dir. Brit. Sky Broadcasting Group, PLC, Star TV Ltd., NDS plc. Active Cornell Law Sch. Adv. Coun., 1996—; nat. chmn. Cornell Law Sch. Alumni Fund, 1998-2001, Citizens Budget Commn. N.Y.C. Capt. U.S. Army, 1963-65. Mem. ABA, City Bar Assn., Cornell Club, Stockbridge Golf Club. Office: The News Corp Ltd Ste 300 1211 Avenue Of The Americas New York NY 10036-8795 E-mail: asiskind@newscorp.com.

SISKIND, DONALD HENRY, lawyer; b. Providence, Dec. 25, 1937; s. Samuel and Sadie (Wasserman) S.; m. Beth Mohel, July 15, 1962; children: Steven M., Edward M. BS, U. Pa., 1959; LLB, Columbia U., 1962. Bar: Mass. 1962, N.Y. 1963. Assoc. Marshall Bratter Greene Allison & Tucker, N.Y.C., 1962-69, ptnr., 1969-82, Katten Muchin Zavis Rosenman, 1982—99, of counsel, 1999—. Bd. dirs. Chgo. Title Ins. Co.; chmn. various seminars Practicing Law Inst., 1974—; vis. lectr. Columbia U. Sch. Law, 1993—; mem. exec. com. of adv. bd. Wharton Real Estate Ctr. Adv. bd. Real Estate Fin. Jour.; contbr. articles to profl. jours. Pres. Greenville Community Coun., 1974-76; pres. bd. edn. Union Free Sch. Dist., Scarsdale, N.Y., 1978-81 Mem. ABA, Am. Coll. Real Estate Lawyers (past pres.), Anglo Am. Real Property Inst. (pres.-elect), N.Y. State Bar Assn., Assn. of Bar of City of N.Y., Phi Alpha Psi. Home: 876 Park Ave New York NY 10021-1832 Office: Katten Muchin Zavis Rosenman 575 Madison Ave Fl 26 New York NY 10022-2585 E-mail: donald.siskind@kmzr.com.

SISLER, GLEN E. surgeon, educator; MD, NYU, N.Y.C., 1961. Diplomate Am. Bd. Thoracic Surgery, 1998. Intern Gen. Surgery NYU Bellevue Med. Ctr., N.Y.C., 1961—62; resident Surgery NYU Med. Ctr., N.Y.C., 1962—66; fellow Thoracic Surgery NYU, 1968—70; physician divsn. Thoracic Surgery Robert Wood Johnson U. Med. Group, New Brunswick, NJ, 1990—. Clin. assoc. prof. surgery Robert Wood U. Hosp., New Brunswick, NJ, 1991—. Office: Clin Acad Bldg 125 Paterson St New Brunswick NJ 08901-1977

SISLER, HARRY HALL, retired chemistry professor; b. Ironton, Ohio, Mar. 13, 1917; s. Harry C. and Minta A. (Hall) S.; m. Helen E. Shaver, June 29, 1940; children: Elizabeth A., David F., Raymond K., Susan C.; m. Hannelore L. Wass, Apr. 13, 1978. BSc, Ohio State U., 1936; MSc, U. Ill., 1937, PhD, 1939; Doctorate honoris causa, U. Poznan, Poland, 1977. Instr. Chgo. City Colls., 1939-41; from instr. to assoc. prof. chemistry U. Kans., Lawrence, 1941-46; from asst. prof. to prof. chemistry Ohio State U., Columbus, 1946-56; Arthur and Ruth Sloan vis. prof. chemistry Harvard, fall, 1962-63; prof., chmn. dept. chemistry U. Fla., Gainesville, 1956-68, dean Coll. Arts and Scis., 1968-70, exec. v.p., 1970-73, dean grad. sch., 1973-79, dir. divsn. sponsored rsch., 1976-79, Disting. Svc. prof. chemistry, 1979-85, Disting. Svc. prof. chemistry emeritus, 1985—. Indsl. cons. W.R. Grace & Co., Martin Marietta Aerospace, Naval Ordnance Lab., TVA; chemistry adv. panel, also vis. scientists panel NSF, 1959-62; cons. USAF Acad., Battelle Meml. Inst., chmn. interinstl. com. nuclear research, Fla., 1958-64; mem. Fla. Nuclear Devel. Commn. Teaching Sci. and Math., 1958; chemistry adv. panel Oak Ridge Nat. Lab., 1965-69; dir. sponsored rsch. U. Fla., 1976-79. Author: Electronic Structure, Properties, and the Periodic Law, 2d edit, 1973, Starlight-A Book of Poems, 1976, Of Outer and Inner Space—A Book of Poems, 1981, Earth, Air, Fire and Water-A Book of Poems, 1989, (with others) Gen. Chemistry: A Systematic Approach, 2d edit, 1959, Coll. Chemistry: A Systematic Approach, 4th edit, 1980, Essentials of Chemistry, 2d edit, 1959, A Systematic Laboratory Course in Chemistry, 1950, Essentials of Experimental Chemistry, 2d edit, 1959, Semimicro Qualitative Analysis, 1958, rev. edit., 1965, Comprehensive Inorganic Chemistry, Vol. V, 1956, Chemistry in Non-Aqueous Solvents, 1961, The Chloramination Reaction, 1977, Dying-Facing the Facts, 1988, Inorganic Reactions and Methods, Vol. 7, 1988, Encyclopedia of Inorganic Chemistry, Vol. 5, Nitrogen: Inorganic Chemistry, 1994, Autumn Harvest-A Book of Poems, 1996, Perspective-A Book of Poems, 1999; cons. editor: (with others) Dowden, Hutchinson & Ross, 1971-78; series editor: (with others) Phys. and Inorganic Textbook Series, Reinhold Pub. Corp, 1958-70; contbr. (with others) articles to profl. jours.; patentee in field. Decorated Royal Order North Star(Sweden); Named Outstanding Chemist in South, Am. Chem. Soc., 1969, Outstanding Chemist in Southeast, Am. Chem. Soc., 1960, James Flack Norris award Am. Chem. Soc., 1979; recipient Outstanding Centennial Achievement award Ohio State U., 1970. Mem. Am. Chem. Soc. (nat. chmn. div. chem. edn. 1957-58, exec. com. 1957-60, bd. publ. Jour. Chem. Edn. 1956-58), Phi Beta Kappa, Sigma Xi, Phi Delta Kappa, Phi Lambda Upsilon, Phi Kappa Phi, Alpha Chi Sigma. Methodist. Home: 6014 NW 54th Way Gainesville FL 32653-3265

SISLEY, BECKY LYNN, physical education educator; b. Seattle, May 10, 1939; d. Leslie James and Blanche (Howe) S.; m. Jerry Newcomb, 1994. BA, U. Wash., 1961; MSPE, U. N.C., Greensboro, 1964, EdD, 1973. Tchr. Lake Washington H.S., Kirkland, Wash., 1961-62; instr. U. Wis., Madison, 1963-65, U. Oreg., Eugene, 1965-68, prof. phys. edn., 1968—2004, women's athletic dir., 1973-79, head undergrad. studies in phys. edn., 1985-92. Co-author: Softball for Girls, 1971; contbr. articles to profl. jours. Mem. athletic adv. bd. Women's Sports Found., 1993-96. Named to Hall of Fame, U. Oreg. Athletics, 1998, N.W. Women's Sports Found., Seattle, 1981, Nat. Masters Track and Field Hall of Fame, 2001; recipient Honor award, N.W. Dist. AAHPERD, 1988, Nat. Assn. for Girls and Women in Sports, 1995, Disting. Alumni award, Sch. Health and Human Performance, U. N.C., Greensboro, 1996. Mem. AAHPERD, Oreg. Alliance Health, Phys. Edn., Recreation and Dance (hon. life mem.), Western Soc. for Phys. Edn. of Coll. Women (hon. mem., exec. bd. 1982-85), Oreg. High Sch. Coaches Assn., N.W. Coll. Women's Sports Assn. (pres. 1977-78), Oreg. Women's Sports Leadership Network (dir. 1987-97), Phi Epsilon Kappa, others. Office: U Oreg Phys Activity & Recreation Svcs Eugene OR 97403

SISLEY, EMILY LUCRETIA, retired psychologist, medical writer; b. North Charleroi, Pa., May 7, 1930; d. Frederick William and Harriet Watkins (Litman) S. PhD in Clin. Psychology, L.I. U., 1972. Diplomate Am. Bd. Med. Psychotherapists. Mng. editor Med. Jours., Harper & Row, N.Y.C., 1960-67; freelance med. writer-editor N.Y.C., 1967-95; supervising psychologist, dept. psychiatry Roosevelt Hosp., N.Y.C., 1972-77; clin. instr. Columbia Univ. Coll. Physicians and Surgeons, N.Y.C., 1975-77; chief psychologist Gramercy Park Inst., N.Y.C., 1978-84; staff therapist MedcoBehavioral Care Sys., N.Y.C., 1984-95; ret., 1995. Cons. Internat. Jour. Group Tensions, N.Y.C., 1968-72. Illustrator: You and Your Brain, 1963, Thomas Alva Edison award, 1963; co-author: The Vitamin C Connection, 1983; contbr. articles to profl. and lit. jours. Fellow Am. Bd. Med. Psychotherapists; mem. APA, N.Y. Acad. Scis. Democrat. Episcopalian. Avocations: music, golf, skiing, sailing.

SISLEY, NINA MAE, physician, public health service officer; b. Jacksonville, Fla., Aug. 19, 1924; d. Leonard Percy and Verna (Martin) S.; m. George W. Fischer, May 16, 1962 (dec. 1990). BA, Tex. State Coll. for Women, 1944; MD, U. Tex., Galveston, 1950; MPH, U. Mich., 1963. Intern City of Detroit Receiving Hosp., 1950-51; resident in gen. practice St. Mary's Infirmary, Galveston, Tex., 1951-52; sch. physician Galveston Ind. Sch. Dist., 1953-56; dir. med. svcs. San Antonio Health Dept., 1960-63, acting dir., 1963-64; resident in pub. health Tex. Dept. Pub. Health, San Antonio, 1963-65; dir. cmty. health svcs. Corpus Christi-Nueces County Dept. Health, Tex., 1964-67; dir. Tb control region 5 Tex. Dept. Health, Corpus Christi, 1967-73; chief chronic illness control City of Houston Health Dept., Rosenberg, 1973-78; dir. pub. health region 11 Tex. Dept. Health, Rosenberg, 1978-87; dir. Corpus Christi-Nueces County Dept. Pub. Health, 1987—2002. Lectr. Incarnate Word Coll., San Antonio, 1963-64; adj. prof. U. Tex. Sch. Pub. Health, Houston, 1980 ; adj. prof. Tex. A&M U., Corpus Christi, 1997 ; pvt. practice Galveston, Stockdale, Hereford and Borger, Tex., 1952-59; mem. adv. bd. Cmty. Adv. Coun.; clin. instr. U. Tex. Health Sci. Ctr., San Antonio, 1997—. Bd. dirs. Coastal Bend chpt. ARC, Corpus Christi, 1990-94, 2003—, pres., 1990-91; bd. dirs. United Way-Coastal Bend, Coastal Bend Coalition on AIDS, 1988-94; mem. Nueces County Child Fatality Rev. Com.; mem. adv. com. Nueces County Hosp. Dist.; mem. adv. bd. Alzheimers Assn.; mem. health adv. bd. Corpus Christi Ind. Sch. Dist.; bd. dirs. Charlie's Place Alcohol and Drug Rehab. Ctr. Fellow Am. Coll. Preventive Medicine; mem. Tex. Med. Assn., Nueces County Med. Soc. (pres. 1997 98), Tex. Assn. Pub. Health Physicians, Tex. Pub. Health Assn. (pres. 1991-92), Local Emergency Planning Assn., Long Term Health Assn. Episcopalian. Avocations: fishing, crossword puzzles, raising African violets. Home: 62 Rock Creek Dr Corpus Christi TX 78412-4214 Office: Corpus Christi-Nueces County Dept Health 1702 Horne Rd Corpus Christi TX 78416-1902 Personal E-mail: nms@ci.corpus.christi.tx.us.

SISSEL, GEORGE ALLEN, manufacturing executive, lawyer, engineer; b. Chgo., July 30, 1936; s. William Worth and Hannah Ruth (Harlan) S.; m. Mary Ruth Runsvold, Oct. 5, 1960; children: Jenifer Ruth, Gregory Allen. BSEE, U. Colo., 1958; JD cum laude, U. Minn., 1966. Bar: Colo. 1966, Ind. 1973, U.S. Supreme Ct. 1981. Assoc. Sherman & Howard, Denver, 1966-70; with Ball Corp., Broomfield, Colo., 1970—2002, CEO, 1995-2001, chmn. bd., 1996—2002, also bd. dirs. Bd. dirs. Ciber, Inc. Assoc. editor: U. Minn. Law Rev., 1965-66. Served with USN, 1954-65. Mem. Colo. Assn. Commerce & Industry, Order of Coif, MIT Soc. Sr. Execs. (bd. govs. 1987-95), Sigma Chi, Sigma Tau, Eta Kappa Nu. Lodges: Rotary. Methodist.

SISSOM, LEIGHTON ESTEN, engineering educator, dean, consultant; b. Manchester, Tenn., Aug. 26, 1934; s. Willie Esten and Bertha Sarah (Davis) S.; m. Evelyn Janelle Lee, June 13, 1953; children: Terry Lee, Denny Leighton. BS, Middle Tenn. State Coll., 1956; BS in Mech. Engring., Tenn. Technol. U., 1962; MS in Mech. Engring., Ga. Inst. Tech., 1964, PhD, 1965. Diplomate Nat. Acad. Forensic Engrs.; registered profl. engr., Tenn. Draftsman Westinghouse Electric Corp., Tullahoma, 1953-57; mech. designer ARO, Inc., Tullahoma, 1957-58; instr. mech. engring. Tenn. Technol. U., Cookeville, 1958-62, chmn. dept. mech. engring., 1965-79, dean engring., 1979-88, dean of engring. emeritus, 1988—; prin. cons. Sissom & Assocs., Cookeville, Tenn., 1962—. Bd. dirs. Accreditation Bd. Engring. and Tech., N.Y.C., 1978-86, treas., 1982-86. Author: (with Donald R. Pitts) Elements of Transport Phenomena, 1972, Heat Transfer, 1977, 1,000 Solved Problems in Heat Transfer, 1991; contbr. An Attorney's Guide to Engineering, 1986; contbr. articles to various publs. Fellow ASME (sr. v.p. 1982-86, gov. 1986-88, Golden medallion), Am. Soc. Engring. Edn. (bd. dirs. 1984-87, pres. 1991-92), Accreditation Bd. Engring. and Tech.; mem. NSPE, Soc. Automotive Engrs., Nat. Engring. Deans Coun. (chmn. 1984-87), Order of the Engr. (chmn. bd. govs. 1994-96), Tau Beta Pi (v.p. 1986-89, councillor 1986-89). Home and Office: 1151 Shipley Church Rd Cookeville TN 38501-7730 Office Phone: 931-526-9123.

SISSON, RAY L. retired dean, author; b. Pueblo, Colo., Apr. 24, 1934; s. William Franklin and Lillie Mae (Hall) S.; m. Dixie Lee McConnell, Oct. 5, 1952; children: Mark Lynn, Bryan Keith, Tammy Sue Ann. BSEE, U. Colo., 1960; MSEE, Colo. State U., 1966; AA, Pueblo Coll., 1958; EdD, U. No. Colo., 1973. Electronic technician TV Svcs. Co., Pueblo, 1958, Sid's Appliance Ctr., Tucson; from instr. engring. to asst. prof. So. Colo. State Coll., Pueblo, 1960-63, assoc. prof., 1963-76, engring., electronics dept. head, 1968-70; dean Sch. Applied Sci. and Engring. Tech. U. So. Colo., Pueblo, 1973-84, prof., 1976—, interim dean Coll. Engring. and Sci., 1984-85, dean Coll. Applied Sci. and Engring. Tech., 1985-96, dean, prof. emeritus, 1996—. Cons. Escuela Superior Politecnica del Litoral, Ecuador, 1979-82, SUNY, Alfred, Farmingdale, 1982, Moorhead U., 1985, N.Mex. Highlands U., 1985, 90, Kans. State U., Salina, 1994, Ministry Edn., Republic of Yemen, 1996, Min. Edn., State of Kuwait, 1998. Author: Pueblo Army Air Base 1942-46 A Chronological History, 2001. Bd. dirs. Colo. Transp. Inst., 1993-96; exec. dir. So. Colo. Bus. and Tech. Ctr., 1994-96. With USN, 1952-56. Recipient James H. McGraw award Am. Soc. Engring. Edn., 1990; NSF grantee, 1964, 65, 67, 68, 80-83. Mem. IEEE, ABET (tech. accreditation commn. 1990-96, chmn. definition com. 1991, vice chmn. tech. accreditation commn., 1993-96), Am. Soc. Engring. Edn. (active, spectrum com. 1989-90, chmn. definition com. 1991, fellow 1993), Engring. Tech. Leadership Inst. (founding mem., bd. dirs. 1983-88, chmn. 1984-85), Profl. Engrs. Colo. (So. chpt., assoc. mem., chair young engrs. 1969, scholarship, edn. com. 1969, chair state scholarship com. 1968), Pueblo Pachyderm Club (pres. 1986, 89, 98), Pueblo Hist. Aircraft Soc. (historian 1999—), Retirees Assn. (pres. 1998, 99), Phi Delta Kappa, Eta Kappa Nu, Tau Alpha Pi. Home: 403 Starlite Dr Pueblo CO 81005-2685 Business E-Mail: Ray.Sisson@colostate-pueblo.edu.

SISTI, MICHAEL BRIAN, neurosurgeon; b. Bklyn., June 24, 1955; B in engring., Cooper Union Sch. Engring., 1977; MD, Columbia U., 1981; neurol. surgery, Columbia Neurol., 1988. Asst. attending neurosurgeon NY Presbyn. Hosp., NYC, 1988—; asst. prof. clin. neurosurgery Columbia U., 1988—, asst. prof. clin. neurosurgery in otolaryn., head, neck, 1995—. Recipient Tau Beta Pi, 1946, Alpha Omega Alpha, 1980, Allen Whipple prize for excellence in surgery, 1981. Fellow: Am. Coll. Surgeons; mem.: Am. Assn. Neurol. Surgeons, Congress of Neurol. Surgeons. Office: NY Neurological Inst 710 W 168th St Rm 413 New York NY 10032 Office Phone: 212-305-1728. E-mail: mbs4@columbia.edu.

SISTLA, ARAVINDA PRASAD, computer scientist, educator; b. Guntur, Andhra Pradesh, India, Oct. 28, 1952; s. Purnananda Sastry and Nagalakshmi Sistla; m. Durga Nagamani Tadepalli, Aug. 29, 1985; children: Sandhya, Maitreyi. PhD, Harvard U., Cambridge, Mass., 1983. Systems analyst Tata Consultancy Svcs., Mumbai, India, 1976—79; asst. prof. U. Mass., Amherst, Mass., 1983—85; sr. mem. tech. staff GTE Rsch. Labs., Waltham, Mass., 1985—91; assoc. prof. U. Ill., Chgo., 1991—2000, prof., 2000—. Author: ACM Trans. on Programming Langs. and Sys., ACM Trans. on Software Engring. Methodologies; contbr. scientific papers to profl. jours. Recipient Rsch. award, Coll. of Engring., UIC, 2000, Highly cited, ISI; grantee Info. Tech. Rsch., NSF, 2002. Achievements include invention of model checking as an approach for concurrent program verification; symmetry based reductions for efficient model checking; research in multi-dimensional temporal logic for analysis process networks. Office: U Ill at Chgo M/C 152 851 S Morgan St Chicago IL 60607 Personal E-mail: sistla@ameritech.net. E-mail: sistla@cs.uic.edu.

SISTO, FERNANDO, mechanical engineering educator; b. La Coruña, Spain, Aug. 2, 1924; s. Fernando Cartelle and Clara (Reiss) S.; m. Grace Jeanette Wexler, June 27, 1946; children: Jane Caroll, Ellen Gail, Todd Frederic. Student, NYU, 1940-43; BS, U.S. Naval Acad., 1946; ScD, MIT, 1952; M Engring. (hon.), Stevens Inst. Tech., 1962. Registered profl. engr., N.J. Commd. ensign USN, 1946, service in the Pacific, ret., 1949; propulsion div. chief Curtiss-Wright Research, Clifton, N.J., 1952-58; prof. mech. engring. Stevens Inst. Tech., Hoboken, N.J., 1959-96, chmn. dept., 1966-79,

George Meade Bond prof., 1978-96, prof. emeritus, 1996—, dean of the grad. sch., 1993-94. Bd. dirs., trustee Am. Capital Mut. Funds, Houston, 1960—, chmn. bd., 1992-95; co-chmn. merged bd. Van Kampen Am. Capital, 1995-97, dir. emeritus, 2001—; bd. dirs. Dynalysis of Princeton; cons. UN Devel. Program at Nat. Aero. Lab., Bangalore, India, 1978. Co-author: (textbook) A Modern Course in Aeroelasticity, 1978, 3d edit., 1995. Lt. USN, 1943-49. R.C. DuPont fellow MIT, 1951-52. Fellow ASME; mem. Adirondack Mountain Club. Avocations: skiing, tennis, woodworking, sculling. Office: Stevens Inst Tech Dept Mech Engring Hoboken NJ 07030-5991 E-mail: gsandfs@aol.com.

SISULU, SHEILA VIOLET MAKATE, diplomat; m. Lungi Sisulu. BA, U. Lesotho; BE, Witwatersrand U. Various sr. positions South African Com. for Higher Edn., 1978-88; edn. coord. African Bursary Fund South African Coun. Chs., 1988-91; dir. Joint Enrichment Project, 1991-94; spl. advisor Min. Edn., 1994-97; consul-gen. South African Consulate-Gen., N.Y., 1997-99; amb. extraordinary and plenipotentiary to the U.S. South African Govt., 1999—2002; deputy exec. dir. U.N. World Food Programme, 2003—. Organizer, coord. several confs., workshops and seminars on youth and edn.; presenter in field. Mem. ANC Nat. Edn. Com., U.S.A./South Africa Leadership Tng. Program, Cmty. Bank Found.; coun. mem. U. Witwatersrand; trustee Equal Opportunity Found., Women's Devel. Found., Women's Devel. Bank, South African Broadcasting Cooperation. Office: via CG Viola 68 Parco Dei Medici 00148 Rome Italy Fax: 202-265-1607. E-mail: wfpinfo@wfp.org.

SIT, EUGENE C. investment executive; b. Canton, China, Aug. 8, 1938; s. Hom Yuen and Sue (Eng) S.; m. Gail V. Chin, Sept. 14, 1958; children: Ronald, Debra, Roger, Raymond, Robert, Richard. BSC, DePaul U., 1960; postgrad., Grad. Sch. Bus., 1962-65. CPA, Ill.; CFA. Fin. analyst Commonwealth Edison, Chgo., 1960-66, fin. asst. to chmn. finance com., 1966-68; assoc. portfolio mgr. Investors Stock Fund, Investors Diversified Svcs., Mpls., 1968-69; portfolio mgr. IDS New Dimensions, IDS Growth Fund., Mpls., 1972-76; pres. IDS Adv., Mpls., 1976-77, pres., CEO, 1977-81; CEO IDS Trust Co., 1979-81; chmn., CEO IDS Adv./Gartmore Internat. Ltd., 1979-81; chmn., CEO, global investment officer Sit Investment Assocs., Inc., Mpls., 1981—. Chmn. Sit/Kim Internat. Investment Assocs., Inc.; chmn., pres., dir. Sit Mut. Fund Group; bd. dirs. Corning, Inc., Smurfit Stone Container. Trustee Carleton Coll.; bd. visitors U. Minn. Med. Sch.; mem. internat. coun. U. Minn. Carlson Grad. Sch. Mgmt. Mem.: Minn. Hist. Soc. (hon. coun.), Spring Hill Golf Club, Rancho LaQuinta Country Club, World Trade Club (San Francisco), Edina Country Club, Mpls. Club, Chgo. Club, Univ. Club (N.Y.). Home: 6216 Braeburn Cir Minneapolis MN 55439-2548 Office: 3300 IDS Ctr 80 S 8th St Minneapolis MN 55402

SIT, HONG CHAN, minister; b. St. Louis, Nov. 25, 1921; s. Gan and Ying Foon (Wong) S.; m. Amy Wang, June 16, 1949; children: David, Daniel, Estelle Joy, Mary. BS summa cum laude, U. Ill., 1943; BD, STM, Faith Theol Sem., 1950; ThD, No. Bapt. Theol. Sem., 1957. Ordained to ministry Blue Ch., Springfield, Pa., 1950. Missionary China Inter-Varsity Fellowship, Shanghai, 1947; pastor Chinese Evang. Ch., N.Y.C., 1950-51, Chinese Bapt. Ch., Houston, 1953-56, Grace Chapel, 1956-90, missionary pastor, 1990—. Pres. Chinese Fgn. Missionary Union, 1974, Chinese Full Gospel Fellowship Internat., Hong Kong, 1983-98; mem. bd. govs. Network of Christian Ministries, 1990—. Author: Your Next Step With Jesus, 1977, My View From a Bridge: Autobiography of Hong Sit, 1999; contbr. articles to profl. jours. Mem.: Phi Lambda Upsilon, Phi Beta Kappa. Home and Office: Apt 8204 11900 Barryknoll Ln Houston TX 77024-4374 Office Phone: 713-827-7289. E-mail: pasit@Ev1.net.

SITA, MICHAEL JOHN, pharmacist, educator; b. Apr. 28, 1953; s. Julianne Gail Sita; m. Nora Ann Dillon, June 1, 1974 (div. 1996); children: Michael John, Paul Thomas, Julianne Joyce; m. Christine Elizabeth Nordmann, Aug. 22, 1997; children: Mary Elizabeth, April Christine. BS, St. Louis Coll. Pharmacy, 1976; MBA, So. Ill. U., 1983. Registered pharmacist Mo., Ill. Staff pharmacist Luth. Med. Ctr., St. Louis, 1976-78, asst. chief pharmacist, 1978-81, adminstrv. coord. pharmacy svcs., 1981-85; dir. pharmacy svcs. Jefferson Meml. Hosp., 1985-98; pharmacist Mo. Bapt. Hosp., 1998-2000, Walgreen's, 2000—. Instr. St. Louis Coll. Health Careers, 1983-86; adj. instr. pharmacy practice St. Louis Coll. Pharmacy, 1980-98; relief pharmacist Dolgins Apothecary, St. Louis, 1976-86, Best Pharmacy, 1986-88, Carraige Drugs, 1989-93, Medicine Shoppe, Festus, Mo., 1990-97, Otto (Mo.) Drug, 1997-2000. Author, editor: Pharmacy Capsule quar., 1977-85. Mem. St. Louis Soc. Hosp. Pharmacists (treas. 1985-87, pres. 1988-89, sec. 1990-92, Pharmacist of Yr. 1994-95), Mo. Soc. Hosp. Pharmacists, Hosp. Assn. Met. St. Louis (chmn. pharmacy tech. adv. com. 1985-86). Avocations: carpentry, rehabbing. Home: 111 Ward Ter Crystal City MO 63019-1707 Office: Walgreens 101 Twin City Mall Crystal City MO 63019 Office Phone: 636-937-3641.

SITARZ, ANNELIESE LOTTE, pediatrics educator, physician; b. Medellin, Colombia, Aug. 31, 1928; came to U.S., 1935; d. Hans and Elisabeth (Noll) S. BA cum laude, Bryn Mawr (Pa.) Coll., 1950; MD, Columbia U., 1954. Diplomate Nat. Bd. Med. Examiners, Am. Bd. Pediatrics., Am. Bd. Pediatric Hematology and Oncology. Intern Children's Med. Ctr., Boston, 1954-55; resident in pediat. Babies Hosp.-Columbia-Presbyn. Med. Ctr., N.Y.C., 1955-57; mem. faculty Columbia U., N.Y.C., 1957—, assoc. prof. clin. pediat., 1974-83, prof. clin. pediat., 1983-2000, prof. emerita clin. pediat., spl. lectr. in pediat., 2000—; attending in pediat. Babies and Children's Hosp., N.Y.C., 1983—. Cons. pediatrics, hematology and oncology Harlem Hosp., N.Y.C., 1967—72, Overlook Hosp., Summit, NJ, 1975—2001. Contbr. numerous articles to profl. jours. Pres. Mt. Prospect Assn., Summit, 1987—. Fellow Am. Acad. Pediatrics; mem. Am. Assn. Cancer Rsch., Am. Soc. Clin. Oncology, Am. Soc. Hematology, Internat. Soc. Hematology, Harvey Soc. Republican. Episcopalian. Avocations: gardening, sewing, skiing, hiking, stamp collecting/philately. Office: Childrens Hosp of NY Presbyn Irving Pavilion 161 Ft Washington Ave New York NY 10032-3710 Office Phone: 212-305-5808.

SITEK, ARKADIUSZ, physicist, consultant; b. Czestochowa, Poland, Dec. 17, 1968; s. Henryk and Anna Maria Sitek; m. Sylwia Legowik, Dec. 17, 2002. MSc, Warsaw U., Poland, 1987—94; PhD, U. B.C., Vancouver, Can., 1994—97. Rsch. assoc. U. Utah, Salt Lake City, 1998—2002; vis. scientist E.O. Lawrence Berkeley Nat. Labs., Calif., 2000—02. Office: Beth Israel Deaconess Med Ctr 330 Brookline Ave Boston MA 02215

SITES, RICHARD LOREN, lawyer, educator; b. Feb. 16, 1948; s. Loren Richard and Frances Mary (Tellaro) Sites; m. Karen Ann Heazlit, Oct. 6, 1979; children: Brian, David. BA, Coll. Wooster, 1970; JD, U. Denver, 1973, MS, 1975. Bar: Colo. 1973, Ohio 1975, U.S. Dist. Ct. 1973, U.S. Supreme Ct. 1977; cert. health care fin. mgmt. Ohio State U., 1984. Sole practice, Columbus, Ohio, 1973—; atty. HHS, Columbus, 1975—85, Ohio Hosp. Assn., Columbus, 1985—. Assoc. grad. faculty, academic adv. Ctrl. Mich. U., 1992—; faculty Franklin U., Ohio, 1999—2001, Wittenberg U., Ohio, 2002—; exec. dir. OHA Purchasing Solutions, 2004—; trustee Ohio for EDI, Inc., 2002—. Contbr. articles to profl. jours. Co-founder FAMOHIO, Inc., 1992, pres., 1996—98; v.p. LEGAL, 2002—; leader Boy Scouts Am., 1992—2002; alumni admissions rep. Coll. Wooster, Ohio, 1979—85, fund raiser, 1984; v.p. Sycamore Hills Residents Assn., Columbus, 1983, pres., 1984; chair hemophilia adv. coun. Ohio Dept. of Health, 1995—2000. Recipient Spl. Contbn. award, Ohio Soc. for Hosp. Engring., 1988, 1993, Ira Gaffin Meml. award, Famohio, Inc., 1999, Rosie Hass Adv. award, N.W. Ohio Hemophilia Found., 2002. Mem.: Ohio Dept. Health, Newborn Genetic Screening Adv. Coun. Office: Ohio Hosp Assn 155 E Broad St Fl 15 Columbus OH 43215-3609 Office Phone: 614-221-7614.

SITILIDES, JOHN, government relations executive, policy analyst; b. Jersey City, Feb. 8, 1962; s. Louis and Frances Sitilides; m. Angela Beth Johnson, Oct. 11, 1997. BA, Queens Coll., 1984; M of Internat. Affairs, Columbia U., 1986. Campaign dir. Maltese for State Senate, Maspeth, N.Y., 1988; exec. asst. for comms. and legis. affairs U.S. Senator Alfonse M. D'Amato, N.Y.C., 1986-93; pres. The Sitilides Group, Sacramento, 1993-98; exec. dir. The Western Policy Ctr., Washington, 1994—; pres. JS Assocs, Alexandria, Va., 1998—. Exec. editor The Strategic Regional Report. Policy advisor Dole/Kemp '96, Calif., 1996; policy advisor Hellenic Am. Rep. Assn., N.Y.C., 1997—. Mem. Am.-Israel Pub. Affairs Com., Am. Soc. Assn. Execs., World Affairs Coun. Washington, Ahepa (chmn. Cyprus and Hellenic affairs com. 1994—). Republican. Greek Orthodox. Avocations: reading history current events, baseball, entertainment industry, creative writing. Home: 41 Alexander St Alexandria VA 22314-3872

SITNYAKOVSKY, ROMAN EMMANUIL, scientist, writer, inventor, translator; b. Kiev, Ukraine, Jan. 5, 1934; arrived in U.S., 1988; s. Emmanuil I. and Yevgeniya N. (Glazova) S.; m. Bella Baram, Oct. 4, 1968 (div. Mar. 1992); 1 child, Art. MS in Mech. and Heat Engring., Polytech. Inst., Kiev, Ukraine, 1956; PhD in Heat Theory/Engring., USSR Acad. Scis., Minsk, Belarus, 1967. Project engr. Ural Turbomotor, Sverdlovsk, USSR, 1956-58; mech. engr. Engring Factory, Kiev, Ukraine, 1958-61; project engr. Design Inst., Kiev, Ukraine, 1961-63; sr. engr. Heat and Mass Transfer Inst., Minsk, Belarus, 1963-68; prin. engr. Thermophysics Inst., Kiev, Ukraine, 1968-87; project engr. Hirt Combustion Engring., Montebello, Calif., 1989-90. Cons. Socio-Econ. Sys., LA, 1988-93; translator, Kiev, 1979-87, LA, 1988—, journalist Panorama, LA, 1989-98. Author: I Disagree with Guberman, 1995, Chernobyl is our Fate, 2000, Mollify, not harass hearts, 2003, What is Love?, 2004, Democrats, Communists, Nationalists, Fascists, 2003, To the Point, 2004, Fundamentals, 2004; contbr. articles to profl. jours., newspapers and mags. Achievements include over 100 inventions; patentee in field; discovery of discreteness property of internal heat-mass transfer processes in three-phase media; wave nature of moisture transfer into wet bodies; resonances at heat-mass transfer in three-phase media. Office Phone: 323-654-7111.

SITOMER, SHEILA MARIE, television producer, director; b. Hartford, Conn., Aug. 25, 1951; d. George W. and Mary E. (Chaponis) Bowe; m. Daniel J. Sitomer, Aug. 25, 1985. BA, Smith Coll., 1973. Field producer, dir. Good Morning Am., ABC-TV, N.Y.C., 1981-86; field producer Evening Magazine, WWOR-TV, KDKA-TV, Pitts. and Secaucus, N.J., 1978-79, 88; supervising producer The Reporters, Fox Broadcasting, N.Y.C., 1988; producer Inside Edition, King World Prodns., N.Y.C., 1988-95; co-exec. prodr. Inside Edition and Am. Jour., 1995-98; exec. prodr. Extra, 1998-2000; exec. prodr. program devel. ABC News, N.Y.C., 2000—. Recipient Peabody award, Columbia Dupont award, AWRT Gracie award, 3 Emmys, New England chpt. TV Acad. Arts & Scis., 1975-78, 2 Emmys, N.Y. chpt. TV Acad. Arts & Scis., 1979, 89, recipient first prize Internat. Film & TV Festival N.Y., 1988, No. N.J. Press Club award, 1988, George Polk award, Sigma Delta Chi award, IRE award Nat. Headliners, Columbus Film Festival. Mem. Dirs. Guild Am., Actors Equity Assn. Office: ABC News 47 W 66th St New York NY 10023 E-mail: sheila.sitomer@abc.com.

SITTON, CLAUDE FOX, newspaper editor; b. Emory, Ga., Dec. 4, 1925; s. Claude B. and Pauline (Fox) S.; m. Eva McLaurin Whetstone, June 5, 1953; children: Lea Sitton Stanley, Clinton, Suzanna Sitton Greene, McLaurin. AB, Emory U., 1949, L.H.D., 1984. Reporter Internat. News Service, 1949-50; with U.P., 1950-55, writer-editor, 1952-55; information officer USIA, 1955-57; mem. staff N.Y. Times, 1957-68, nat. news dir., 1964-68; editorial dir. The News and Observer Pub. Co., Raleigh, N.C., 1968-90, dir., 1969-90, v.p., 1970-90; editor News and Observer, 1970-90; sr. lectr. Emory U., Atlanta, 1991-94. Active Pulitzer Prize Bd., 1985-94, chmn., 1992-93; bd. counselors Oxford Coll. Emory U., 1993-2001. Lay mem. Commn. on Evaluation of Disciplinary Enforcement, Ga. Supreme Ct., 1995-96; mem. Ga. First Amendment Found. Bd., 1994-97. With USNR, 1943-46, PTO. Recipient Pulitzer prize for commentary, 1983 Mem. Am. Soc. Newspaper Editors (dir. 1977-83). Home: PO Box 1326 Oxford GA 30054-1326

SITTON, WINDY, mayor; m. Frank Sitton, 1965; 1 child, John. BEd in History and English, N. Tex. U.; MA in Counseling, Tex. Women's U. Tchr. English, secondary schs. Dallas Bd. Edn., counselor; owner, mgr. Sitton Selections Co., Lubbock, 1992—; mayor Lubbock, Tex. Owner, mgr. Employee Imaging Co., Dallas, 1980-87. Chair major gifts Capital Campaign for Women's Protective Svcs. and YWCA; mem. Chancellor's Coun., Red Raider Club, Tex. Tech. U., Jr. League Comty. Adv. Com., Lubbock Symphony Guild; mem. Leadership Am., 2001—. Nominated Woman Entrepreneur of Yr., 1996; inducted Tex. Leaderhip Hall of Fame, 1996; recipient Disting. Alumni award Tex. Women's U., 1998. Mem. South Plains Assn. Govts. (bd. dirs.), Greater Lubbock C. of C., Lubbock C. of C., West Tex. Home Builders' Assn. Baptist. Avocations: volunteering, antiquing, golf, reading, collecting. Office: PO Box 2000 Lubbock TX 79457-0001 E-mail: wsitton@mail.ci.lubbock.tx.us.

SIU, WILLIAM M. computer company executive; b. Hong Kong, 1951; Bachelor of Applied Scis., Toronto, Ont., Can., 1973, Master of Applied Scis., 1975, PhD in Biomedical and Elec. Engring., 1978. Mem. sci. staff Bell-No. Rsch., Ottawa; asst. prof. biomedical engring. Case We. Res. U., Cleve.; device physicist Intel Corp., 1980, various positions in design, silicon tech. devel., and assembly/package tech. devel., v.p. Microprocessor Products Group, gen. mgr. Performance Microprocessor div., corp. v.p. Intel Arch. Group and gen. mgr. Desktop Platforms Group, 2001—. Office: 2200 Mission College Blvd Santa Clara CA 95052

SIV, SICHAN AUN, ambassador; b. Phnom Penh, Cambodia, Mar. 1, 1948; came to U.S., 1976; s. Chham and Aun (Chea) S.; m. Martha Pattillo, Dec. 24, 1983. Diplome du Professorat, U. Phnom Penh, Cambodia, 1972; B. en Droit, U. Phnom Penh, 1974, Lic. es Lettres, 1975; M. Internat. Affairs, Columbia U., 1981. Flight attendant Royal Air Cambodge, 1969-70; tchr. high sch. Phnom Penh, 1972-74; program assoc. Care-Cambodia, Phnom Penh, 1974-75; statistician Lower Eastside Svc. Ctr., N.Y.C., 1977-78; staff asst. Lutheran Immigration & Refugee Svc., N.Y.C., 1978-80; mgmt. assoc. Marine Midland Bank, N.Y.C., 1981-82; adminstr., fin. officer Episcopal Ch., N.Y.C., 1982-83; UN rep. Cambodian Non Communist Resistance, N.Y.C., 1983-87; Asia-Pacific mgr. Inst. Internat. Edn., N.Y.C., 1987-89; dep. asst. to The Pres. for pub. liaison The White House, Washington, 1989—93; U.S. repr. to econ. and social coun. of U.N. U.S. Dept. State, Washington, 2001—. Office: US Mission to the UN 799 United Nations Plaza New York NY 10017-3505

SIVAKUMARAN, KUMARASWAMY, civil engineer, consultant, lawyer; b. Inuvil, Sri Lanka, May 29, 1952; arrived in U.S., 1986; s. Thambipillai and Theivanayaki (Selliah) K.; m. Muthumanimoli Pakkirisamy, June 24, 1982; children: Karthikgeyan, Sathiyan. BS in Civil Engring., U. Sri Lanka, Moratuwa, 1976; MS in Civil Engring., U. Newcastle-upon-Tyne, Eng., 1985; PhD in Civil Engring., Colo. State U., 1989; JD, W.Va. U., 2001. Bar: W.Va. 2002. Irrigation engr. Irrigation Dept., Colombo, Sri Lanka, 1977-80; design engr. Group Engring. Consulting, Colombo, 1981; sr. project engr. Samek Constrn. Co. Ltd., Aba, Nigeria, 1981-84; rsch. asst. Colo. State U., Ft. Collins, 1986-89; guest scientist GKSS Rsch. Ctr., Geesthacht, Germany, 1990-91; assoc., sr. water resources engr. TAMS Consultants, Inc., N.Y.C., 1991—2002; pres. Sterling Legal Svcs. PLLC, 2002—. Adj. asst. prof. W.Va. U., Morgantown, 1998—; pres. Sterling Legal Svcs., PLLC. Travel grantee, Am. Pub. Works Assn., 1986. Mem.: ASCE, U.S. Com. on Large Dams. Home: 154 Edgewood Dr Weston WV 26452-8540 Office: Earthtech 655 3d Ave New York NY 10017 Office Phone: 304-622-5770. E-mail: kumarsivakumaran@aol.com.

SIVANANTHAN, SIVALINGAM, science educator; PhD. Dir., microphysics lab. U. Ill., 1994—. Pres. EPIR Technologies Inc., Boolingbrook, Ill., 2003. Author over 160 publications. Mem.: Adv. Bd. for Ill. Coll. of Tech., Nat. Adv. Bd. for Micro fabrication Applications Lab., Editl. Bd. of Jour. of Infrared and Millimeter Waves, Proceeding US workshop on the physics and chemistry of II-VI materials, SPIE (assoc.). Achievements include first to use mercury cadmium telluride (MCT) semiconductor materials in some devices. Office: Dept Physics- UIC 845 W Taylor Str (M/C 273) Room 2236 Chicago IL 60607

SIVASUBRAMANIAN, KOLINJAVADI NAGARAJAN, neonatologist, educator; b. Coimbatore, Madras, India, May 9, 1945; came to U.S., 1971; s. Kolinjavadi Ramaswamy and Sukanthi (Subramanian) Nagarajan; m. Kalyani Hariharier, Feb. 5, 1975; children: Ramya, Rajeev, Ranjan. BSc, Madras U., 1964, MD, 1969. Diplomate Am. Bd. Pediatrics and Neonatal-Perinatal Medicine. Intern in pediat. Jewish Hosp. and Med. Ctr., Bklyn., 1971-72; resident in pediat. U. Md. Hosp., Balt., 1972-74; fellow in neonatology Georgetown U. Hosp., Washington, 1974-76, attending neonatologist, 1976—, dir. nurseries, chief neonatology, 1981—, vice chair pediat., 1988-98, prof. pediat. and ob-gyn. Editor: Trace Elements/Mineral Metablolism During Development, 1993; editor pub. SIDS Series, 1985; editor jour. Current Concepts in Neonatology, India, 1990—; internat. editor Indian Jour. Pediat., India, 1988—. Chmn. Siva Vishnu Temple, Lanham, Md., 1981-91; mem. Fetus and New Born Com., Washington, 1988; founder, bd. dirs. Coun. of Hindu Temples U.S.A.; founder, coord. United Hindu Temples of Met. Washington; 1st v.p. Interfaith Conf., Washington; mem. D.C. bd. dirs. Nat. Youth Leadership Forum. Recipient "Preemies" cover article Newsweek, 1988; featured in "Washingtonian" jour., 1996. Fellow Am. Coll. Nutrition, Am. Acad. Pediat.; mem. AAAS, N.Y. Acad. Scis., Internat. Soc. for Trace Element Rsch. in Humans, Soc. for Bioethics Consultation, Am. Soc. Law, Medicine and Ethics. Hindu. Achievements include research in neonatology, trace elements kinetics, reduction in infant mortality, neonatal immunology, and bioethics. Office: Georgetown U Hosp 3 South Hospital 3800 Reservoir Rd NW Washington DC 20007-2113

SIVCO, DEBORAH LEE, research materials scientist; b. Somerville, N.J., Dec. 21, 1957; d. Lawrence M. Skurkay and Elizabeth J. McCulla; m. Gregory Charles Sivco, July 11, 1981; children: Scott Gregory, Michelle Elizabeth, Carolyn Suzanne, David Charles. BA in chem. edn., Rutgers Univ., 1980; MS in material sci., Stevens Inst., 1988. III-V processing tech. Laser Diode Labs, New Brunswick, N.J., 1980-81; materials scientist Bell Labs. Lucent Technologies, Murray Hill, N.J., 1981—. Contbr. articles to profl. jours.; 22 patents in field. Recipient Newcomb Cleveland prize AAAS, 1993-94, Electronics Letters premium Instn. Elec. Engrs. U.K., 1995, Group Achievement award NASA, 2000. Office: Bell Labs Lucent Technologies 600 Mountain Ave New Providence NJ 07974-2008 E-mail: dls@lucent.com.

SIVE, REBECCA ANNE, public affairs company executive; b. NYC, Jan. 29, 1950; d. David and Mary (Robinson) S.; m. Clark Steven Tomashefsky, June 18, 1972. BA, Carleton Coll., 1972; MA in Am. History, U. Ill., Chgo., 1975. Asst. to chmn. of pres.' task force on vocations Carleton Coll., Northfield, Minn., 1972; rsch. asst. Jane Addams Hull House, Chgo., 1974; instr. Loop Coll., Chgo., 1975, Columbia Coll., Chgo., 1975-76; dir. Ill. Women's History Project, 1975-76; founder, exec. dir. Midwest Women's Ctr., Chgo., 1977-81; exec. dir. Playboy Found., 1981-84; v.p. pub. affairs/pub. rels. Playboy Video Corp., 1985—85; v.p. pub. affairs Playboy Enterprises, Inc., Chgo., 1985-86; pres. The Sive Group, Inc., Chgo., 1986—. Instr. Roosevelt U., Chgo., 1977-78; dir. spl. projects Inst. on Pluralism and Group Identity, Am. Jewish Com.; trainer Midwest Acad. Contbr. articles to profl. jours. Commr. Chgo. Park Dist., 1986-88; del.-at-large Nat. Women's conf., 1977; mem. Ill. Human Rights Commn., 1980-87, Ill. coordinating com., Internat Womens Yr.; coord. Ill. Bicentennial Photog. Exhbn., 1977; mem. Ill. Employment and Tng. Coun.; bd dirs. Nat. Abortion Rights Action League and NARAL Found., Ill. div. ACLU, Midwest Women's Ctr. Recipient award for outstanding cmty. leadership YWCA Met. Chgo., 1979, award for outstanding cmty. leadership Chgo. Jaycees, 1988. Home: 1235 N Astor St Apt 3N Chicago IL 60610-5213 Office: The Sive Group Inc 1235 N Astor St Chicago IL 60610-5213

SIVERD, ROBERT JOSEPH, lawyer; b. July 27, 1948; s. Clifford David and Elizabeth Ann (Klink) S.; m. Bonita Marie Shulock, Jan. 8, 1972; children: Robert J. Jr., Veronica Leigh. AB in French, Georgetown U., 1970, JD, 1973; postgrad., The Sorbonne, Paris, 1969. Bar: N.Y. 1974, U.S. Dist. Ct. (so. and ea. dists.) N.Y. 1974, U.S. Ct. Appeals (2d cir.) 1974, U.S. Supreme Ct. 1980, U.S. Dist. Ct. (ea. dist.) Pa. 1984, U.S. Ct. Appeals (3d cir.) 1984, U.S. Ct. Appeals (6th cir.) 1985, Ohio 1991, Ky. 1992. Assoc. Donovan Leisure Newton & Irvine, N.Y.C., 1973-83; staff v.p., litigation counsel Am. Fin. Group, Inc., Greenwich, Conn., 1983-85, v.p. litigation counsel, 1986-87, v.p. assoc. gen. counsel Cin., 1987-92; sr. v.p., gen. counsel and sec. Gen. Cable Corp., 1992-94, exec. v.p., gen. counsel and sec., 1994—. Mem. Ky. Bar Assn. Republican. Office: Gen Cable Corp 4 Tesseneer Dr Newport KY 41076-9167 Business E-Mail: rsiverd@generalcable.com.

SIVERS, RICHARD HENRY, minister, writer; b. Oswego, NY, Dec. 10, 1947; s. Robert Foster and Laura Belle Sivers; m. Alice Isabel Fletcher, June 1, 1974; children: Jennifer Renee, Anne Elizabeth, Rachel Lynn. BA, SUNY Coll. at Oswego, 1966—70; MDiv, Union Theol. Sem. In NYC, 1976—79. Vista vol. VISTA, Estancia, N.Mex., 1970—71; reporter Palladium-Times, Oswego, NY, 1971—74; oswego county info. officer County of Oswego, Oswego, NY, 1974—76; prodn. editor Union Sem. Quar. Rev., New York, 1977—78; pastor Delta United Meth. Ch., Rome, NY, 1984—89, Stockbridge Charge United Meth. Ch., Munnsville, NY, 1989—91; editor/mng. editor Oswego Observer, Oswego, NY, 1992—95; pastor Palermo United Meth. Ch., NY, 1994—97, Minetto United Meth. Ch., Minetto, NY, 1997—. Oral history consultat Gen. Commn. on Christian Unity and Interrelgious Concerns, NYC, 1986—90. Author: (short stories) Little Teddy (Hon. Mention, Writer's Digest Writing Competition, 2002). Fellow: Fellowship of United Methodists in Music and Worship; mem.: Oswego Players, Inc. (pres. 1974—75), Oswego Opera Theater, Inc. (pres. 2002—04). United Methodist. Avocations: weaving, travel, cooking/baking. Home: PO Box 217 2431 Co Rt 8 Minetto NY 13115 Office: United Methodist Church P O Box 217 Minetto NY 13115

SIVERTSEN, LINDA JOYCE, writer, publishing consultant, editor; b. Stanford, Calif., Aug. 31, 1964; d. Alfred Eugene and Joanne Rose Tisch; m. Mark Duanne Sivertsen, Sept. 10, 1988; 1 child, Tosh. Student, U. So. Calif., 1984—87. Life coach, L.A., 1987—89; owner pet sitting bus. Beverly Hills, 1989—94; cons. writing, nat. and internat., 1995—; author Health Comms., Deerfield Beach, Fla., 1998—; West Coast editor Balance Mag., Ft. Lauderdale, Fla., 2002—. Book proposal writer Illiani Co., L.A., 1999—; ghostwriter, co-author Jodere Pub. Group, San Diego, 2001, San Diego, 03, individuals, 2001—; spkr. in field; tchr. Learning Annex, L.A., 2001—03. Author: Lives Charmed: Intimate Conversations with Extraordinary People, 1998 (Earth Island Jour. award, 2000); co-author: Will to Survive: A Mental and Emotional Survival Guide for Law Enforcement Professionals, 2003; contbr. columns in newspapers. Mem.: Nat. Assn. Women Bus. Owners, Delta Gamma (life). Avocations: tennis, gardening, hiking, painting, reading. Office: ILLIANI Co PO Box 41 1893 Los Angeles CA 90041

SIVINSKI, TINA M. human resources specialist; Grad. magna cum laude, Springfield Coll. V.p. Data Gen. Corp.; corp. v.p. mktg. and innovation Sci. Applications Internat. Corp.; v.p. strategic mktg., sales and bus. devel. GrandBasin; pres. Energy Global Industry Solutions, 2001—02; exec. v.p. human resources Elec. Data Systems, Plano, Tex., 2002—. Office: Elec Data Systems 5400 Legacy Dr Plano TX 75024-3199

SIVY, MICHAEL, journalist; b. N.Y.C., May 30, 1953; s. Michael and Mary Frances (Waller) S. BA, Columbia U., 1974, MA, 1977. Chartered fin. analyst. Journalist Time, Inc., N.Y.C., 1985—. Author: Michael Sivy's Rules of Investing, 1996. Mem. N.Y. Soc. Security Analysts, Assn. Investment Mgmt. and Rsch. Office: Money Edit Rm 32-10 1271 Ave of Americas New York NY 10020

SIX, FRED N. retired state supreme court justice; b. Independence, Mo., Apr. 20, 1929; AB, U. Kans., 1951, JD with honors, 1956; LLM in Judicial Process, U. Va., 1990. Bar: Kans. 1956. Asst. atty. gen. State of Kans., 1957-58; pvt. practice Lawrence, Kans., 1958-87; judge Kans. Ct. Appeals, 1987-88; justice Kans. Supreme Ct., Topeka, 1988—2003. Editor-in-chief U. Kans. Law Review, 1955-56; lectr. on law Washburn U. Sch. Law, 1957-58, U. Kans., 1975-76. Served with USMC, 1951-53; USMCR, 1957-62. Recipient Disting. Alumnus award, U. Kans. Sch. Law, 1994, Disting. Alumni Achievement award, U. Kans. Coll. Liberal Arts and Sci., 2000—01. Fellow Am. Bar Found. (chmn. Kans. chpt. 1983-87); mem. ABA (jud. adminstrn. divsn.), Am.

Judicature Soc., Kans. Bar Assn., Kans. Bar Found., Kans. Law Soc. (pres. 1970-72), Kans. Inn of Ct. (pres. 1993-94), Order of Coif, Phi Delta Phi. Address: 1180 E 1400 Rd Lawrence KS 66046

SIX, HANNAH L. communications executive, educator; b. San Francisco, Calif., Sept. 22, 1963; d. Richard W. Fiske and Bonnie L. Rollin, Walter J. Rollin (Stepfather); m. Christopher D. Six, Mar. 25, 2003. BA, U. Pa., 1991. Reporter The Pottstown Mercury, Pottstown, Pa., 1999—2001; owner/operator Quotable Cat Comm., Hyattsville, Md., 2002—; comm. assoc., writer, editor NASW, Washington, 2003—04; mktg. and commns. specialist Acad. Ednl. Devel., 2004—. Judge VFA Nat. Essay Contest, NJ, 1995; counselor, asst. tchr. Pre-Freshman Program U. Pa., Phila., 1986, reporter Daily Pennsylvanian, 1985—86; substitute tchr. Spearfish (S.Dak.) Sch. Dist., 1991; adj. prof. Reading (Pa.) Area C.C., 2002—03; staff writer Great Valley Pub. Co., Spring City, Pa., 2001—03. Contbr.: Writing Alone and With Others; contbr. articles to mags. Dir. pub. rels. Swing Fever Dance Band, 2001—03, U. TV, 1985—86; founder, pres. Spirit of Airwaves Players, 2002—03. Finalist Dominican Coll. Poetry awards, 1979; recipient Second Pl. award Spot News Coverage, Phila. Press Assn. Contest, 2001. Mem.: Assn. Writers and Writing Programs. Avocations: writing, travel, foreign languages, formula 1 auto racing, jazz.

SIZE, DENNIS MICHAEL, lighting and scenery designer; b. Scranton, Pa., Oct. 25, 1955; s. Michael Joseph and Virginia Mae (Nicholoff) S.; m. Patti McCormick; 1 child, Amanda Madison. BA in English, BA in Communications, U. Scranton, 1976; postgrad., Pa. State U., State Coll., 1976-79. Design Sta. WVIA-TV, Pittston, Pa., 1973-75; lighting designer White Birch Dinner Theater Co., Dalton, Pa., 1975-76; shop supr. dept. theater and film Pa. State U., State College, 1978-79; instr. theater design and prodn. U. Scranton, 1979-80; instr. theater Pa. State U., Scranton, 1980; lighting designer Disney/ABC-TV, N.Y.C., 1980-97; v.p. design Lighting Design Gp., N.Y.C., 1997—. Condr. master classes in lighting design for various colls., schs. and profl groups. Lighting designer numerous TV shows including All My Children, One Life To Live, Ryans Hope, As The World Turns, Oprah Winfrey Show, Ananda Lewis Show, Montel Williams Show, Dr. Joy Brown, Martha Stewart Living, Dick Clark's Rockin' New Year's Eve, Live With Regis & Kathie Lee, Gayle King Show, Good Morning America, several presidential convs., ABC Monday Night Football, Loving, 20/20; theatrical credits include CNN, Wall Street Week, Oxygen Network, My Old Friends with Imogene Coca, Ferocious Kisses, Dancing at Lughnasa; scenery designer: Peg O' My Heart, A Christmas Carol, The Time of Your Life, Philadelphia, Here I Come; columnist for TV Technology, 1984-85. Recipient Silver Screen award, Monitor award Internat. Teleproduction Soc., 1985, nomination, 1986, Emmy award nominations (6), Emmy award, 1989, 99, Axiem award, 1999-2001, 02, 03. Mem. United Scenic Artists, Internat. Alliance Theatrical Stage Employees, Nat. Assn. Broadcast Employees and Technicians, Nat. Acad. TV Arts and Scis., Illuminating Engrng. Soc., Soc. Motion Picture and TV Engrs., U.S. Inst. Theater Tech., Irish Am. Cultural Inst., Am. Film Inst., Internat. Assn. Lighting Designers. Roman Catholic. Avocations: architecture, photography, piano, dancing, fgn. traveling. Home: 163 Amsterdam Ave # 347 New York NY 10023-5001 Fax: 718-416-1964. E-mail: size@ldg.com.

SIZEMORE, DEBORAH LIGHTFOOT, writer, editor; b. Lamesa, Tex., Mar. 18, 1956; d. Glenn Billy and Francis Earlene (Cable) Lightfoot; m. O.E. Gene Sizemore, June 19, 1981. BS in Agrl. Journalism summa cum laude, Tex. A&M U., 1977. Writer Tex. Agrl. Extension, College Station, 1976—77; copy editor Abilene (Tex.) Reporter-News, 1978; customer svc. rep. Motheral Printing Co., Ft. Worth, 1978—79; prodn. coord. Graphic Arts, Inc., Ft. Worth, 1980—81; writer, editor Crowley, Tex., 1981—; freelance writer, editor Boy Scouts Am., Irving, Tex., 1981—; mng. editor Seven Rivers Pub., Crowley, 2003—. Author: The LH7 Ranch, 1991, 2000, Trail Fever, 1992, 2003, co-author: (with Simon W. Freese) A Century in the Works, 1994; contbg. writer New Handbook of Texas, 1996; contbg. editor Dairymen's Digest, Arlington, Tex., 1981-89, 95-97, Longhorn Scene, Ft. Worth, 1982-84, Lone Star Horse Report, Ft. Worth, 1985-86; acting assoc. editor Boy's Life mag., Boy Scouts Am., 1995; writer, photographer Harvest Times, Dallas, 1983-84, Simbrah World, Ft. Worth, 1985-87; contbr. photographs to mags.; contbr. articles to mags. Women's issues chmn., v.p. membership, pub. info. officer, newsletter editor, yearbook editor AAUW of Tarrant County, 1981-86, 90-92, vice chmn. devel. com. Friends of Ft. Worth Pub. Lib., 1991-93, bd. mem., 1994-97, v.p. 1995-97. Recipient Sr. Merit award in Agrl. Journalism Tex. A&M U., 1978, Thomas S. Gathright Acad. Excellence award, 1976, Cert. of Merit Livestock Publs. Coun., 1984, 86, 2d place Nonfiction Book award Tex.-Wide Writers' Competition, 1988, 89, Publication awards San Antonio Conservation Soc., 1993, History and Heritage award Tex. sect. Am. Soc. Civil Engrs., 1997, grand prize Laura Bower Van Nuys writing contest, 2002, finalist sci. fiction/fantasy novel S.W. Writers Contest, 2002. Mem. Authors Guild, Soc. Children's Book Writers and Illustrators (publicity dir. North Ctrl. Tex. chpt. 1991-92, program dir. 1994-95, newsletter designer 2002-03), Sci. Fiction and Fantasy Workshop, Tex. Folklore Soc., Phi Kappa Phi, Gamma Sigma Delta. Office: PO Box 682 Crowley TX 76036-0682 Office Phone: 817-297-1533. Personal E-mail: djls@djlightfoot.com.

SIZEMORE, HERMAN MASON, JR., newspaper executive; b. Halifax, Va., Apr. 15, 1941; s. Herman Mason and Hazel (Johnson) S.; m. Connie Catterton, June 22, 1963; children: Jill, Jennifer. AB in History, Coll. William and Mary, 1963; postgrad., U. Mo., 1965; MBA, U. Wash., 1985. Reporter Norfolk (Va.) Ledger-Star, summers 1961, 62, 63; copy editor Seattle Times, 1965-70, copy-desk chief, 1970-75, asst. mng. editor, 1975-77, mng. editor, 1977-81, prodn. dir., 1981-83, asst. gen. mgr., 1984, v.p., gen. mgr., 1985, pres., chief operating officer, 1985—. Vis. instr. Sch. Comms. U. Wash., 1972-78; bd. dirs. Times Comms. Co., Walla Walla Union-Bull, Inc., Yakima Herald-Republic, Blethen Maine Newspapers, Northwestern Mut. Life Ins. Co., 1993—, mem. policyowner examining com., 1985, chmn., 1986. Bd. dirs. Ctrl. Puget Sound Campfire Coun., 1985-91, pres., 1989-90; bd. dirs. Ptnrs. in Pub. Edn., 1987-88, Downtown Seattle Assn.; chmn. bd. dirs. United Way; adv. coun. Puget Sound Blood Ctr. and Program; adv. bd. USO-Puget Sound Area, U. Wash. Sch. Bus. Named Seattle Newsmaker of Tomorrow, 1978; recipient Alumni medallion Coll. William and Mary, 1998. Mem. AP Mng. Editors, Soc. Profl. Journalists, Pacific N.W. Newspaper Assn. (bd. dirs.), Newspaper Assn of Am. (vice-chair newsprint com.), Allied Daily Newspapers Washington, Coll. William and Mary Alumni Assn., Greater Seatt C. of C. (bd. dirs.), U. Wash. Exec. MBA Alumni Assn. (pres. 1988), Wash. Athletic Club (chmn. bd. dirs.), Rainier Club, Rotary. Methodist. Office: Seattle Times PO Box 70 Seattle WA 98111-0070

SIZEMORE, MICHAEL MAYNARD, architectural firm executive; b. Detroit, July 20, 1943; s. Arthur Logan and Evelyn (Willer) S.; m. Christine Wick, June 1, 1968; children: Christine Corsaut, James Gawne. BArch, Ga. Inst. Tech., 1966; MArch in Urban Design, Carnegie-Mellon U., 1968. Registered arch. Arch. Vincent King & Ptnrs., Phila., 1968-70, Heery Archs., Atlanta, 1970-72; project arch. Jova Daniels Busby, Atlanta, 1972-74; owner Sizemore & Assocs., Atlanta, 1974-76; v.p. CRS, Sizemore/CRS, Houston and Atlanta, 1976-78; sr. prin. Sizemore Floyd (now Sizemore Group), Atlanta, 1973—. Mem. bd. advisors dist. coun. Urban Land Inst.; trustee The Ga. Conservancy. Author: Energy Planning in Buildings, 1979; prin. works include redesign of hqrs. AIA, Washington, Emory U. Clinic, Hale Ctr. Theatre, Salt Lake City, Atlanta C. of C., master plan of Centennial Olympics, Atlanta, 1996, master plan, feasibility Centennial Olympic Park, hqrs. Atlanta Com. Olympic Games, Smyrna Town Ctr. Design and Devel. (Nat. award Urban Land Inst. 1997). Fellow AIA; mem. Atlanta C. of C. (bd. advisors). Office: 1700 Commerce Dr NW Atlanta GA 30318-3123

SIZEMORE, R. TOM, III, military officer, hospital administrator; b. Clay, W.Va. BS, U.S.Naval Acad., 1972; MD, W.Va. U., 1977. Lic. Calif., 1981. Commd. USN, 1972, advanced through grades to capt.; intern Naval Hosp., Oakland, Calif., 1977—78, resident in ophthalmology San iego, 1978—81, ophthalmologist, exec. officer, Phila., commdg. officer, Annapolis, Md.; fleet med. officer to comdr. in chief U.S. Naval Forces, Europe, 1998—2000; dep. comdr. Nat. Naval Med. Ctr., Bethesda, Md., 2000—. Decorated Legion of Merit (3), Meritorious Svc. medal, Def. Meritorious Svc. medal, Nat. Def. medal (2), NATO Svc. medal, numerous others. Fellow: Am. Acad. Ophthalmology, Am. Bd. Ophthalmology; mem.: Am. Coll. Physician Execs., Am. Coll. Healthcare Execs. (assoc.). Office: National Naval Med Ctr 8901 Wisconsin Ave Bethesda MD 20889-5600

SIZEMORE, WILLIAM CHRISTIAN, retired academic administrator, county official; b. South Boston, Va., June 19, 1938; s. Herman Mason and Hazel (Johnson) S.; m. Anne Catherine Mills, June 24, 1961; children: Robert C., Richard M., Edward S. BA, U. Richmond, 1960; BD, Southeastern Bapt. Theol. Sem., Wake Forest, N.C., 1963; MLS, U. N.C., 1964; MLS (advanced), Fla. State U., 1971, PhD, 1973; postgrad., Harvard U., 1989. Library asst. U. N.C., Chapel Hill, 1963-64; assoc. librarian, instr. grad. research Southeastern Bapt. Theol. Sem., 1964-66; librarian, assoc. prof. South Ga. Coll., Douglas, 1966-71, acad. dean, prof., 1971-80, dean coll., prof., 1980-83, acting pres., 1982-83; pres. Alderson-Broaddus Coll., Philippi, W.Va., 1983-94, William Jewell Coll., Liberty, Mo., 1994-2000, chancellor, 2000—02; dir. bus. expansion Clay County Econ. Devel. Coun., Kansas City, Mo., 2003—. Cons. Continental R&D, Shawnee Mission, Kans., 1987-92, So. Assn. Colls. and Schs., Atlanta, 1977, S.C. Comm. on Higher Edn., Columbia, 1975-76, State Coun. Higher Edn. for Va., Richmond, 1969-70, Software Valley Corp., 1989-94; adv. bd. Software Valley Found., 1991-94. Contbr. articles to profl. jours. Active Barbour County Devel. Authority, Philippi, 1984-94, Barbour County Emergency Food and Shelter Bd., 1985-94, Barbour County Extension Com., 1990-94; mem. exec. coun. Yellow Pine area Boy Scouts Am., Valdosta, 1974-76; pres. Satilla Librarians Ednl. Coun., Douglas, 1969-71; lectr., workshop leader on Bible studies various orgns., 1966—; bd. advisors Swatow Kakwang Profl. Acad., Peoples Republic China; pres. bd. dirs. W.Va. Inter-collegiate Athletic Conf., 1985-86, coun. of pres. Nat. Assn. Intercollegiate Athletics; bd. dirs., mem. exec. com. Broaddus Hosp., Philippi, 1983-94; chmn. W.Va. Productive Industry Efforts Found., 1989-92; mktg. com. W.Va. Life Scis. Park Found., 1989-94, Gov.'s Partnership for Progress, 1989-94; mem. adv. panel W.Va. Rural Health Initiative, 1991-94; gov. bd., bd. dirs. W.Va. Alliance of Hosps., 1991-94; bd. dirs. Clay-Platte Econ. Devel. Coun., 1996—; bd. dirs. ARC, Kansas City, 1996-2002, exec.com. 2000-02; adv. com. Mo. Conservation Heritage Found. Discovery Ctr. Campaign, 1998-2002; mem. Clay County Millennium Hist. Bd., 2002—; mem. Liberty HIstory Book Steering Com., 2001—. Joseph Ruzicka scholar N.C. Library Assn., 1963; recipient Douglas Pilot Club Edn. award, 1981, Good Citizenship medal Nat. Soc. Sons of Am. Revolution, 1999. Mem. ALA, Am. Assn. for Higher Edn., Am. Assn. Univ. Adminstrs., Nat. Coun. Instrnl. Adminstrs., W.Va. Assn. Coll. and Univ. Pres. (exec. com., v.p., pres. 1992), Mountain State Assn. Colls., W.Va. Found. for Ind. Colls. (dir. 1983-84, v.p. 1988-92), Mo. Colls. Fund (exec. com. 1997-98), Barbour County C. of C. (bd. dirs. 1988-94, v.p. 1988-90, pres. 1990-92, chmn. bd. 1992-94), Liberty Area C. of C. (bd. dirs. 1995-97), Kansas City Club. Democrat. Baptist. Avocations: woodworking, gardening. Home: 1417 Woodbury Dr Liberty MO 64068-1266 Office: Clay County Econ Devel Coun Office 110 NW Barry Rd Kansas City MO 64155

SIZEMORE, WILLIAM HOWARD, JR., journalist; b. South Boston, Va., Dec. 18, 1948; s. W. Howard and Genevieve T. (Walton) S.; m. Mary K. Lamont, Jan. 29, 1972; children: Justin, Jennifer, Julie. BA in Philosophy, Coll. William and Mary, 1971. Editor The Clarksville (Va.) Times, 1972-75; reporter The Roanoke (Va.) Times, 1975-76, The Times-Herald, Newport News, Va., 1976-81; editor, pub. The York Town Crier, Yorktown, Va., 1981-88; copy editor The Ledger-Star, Norfolk, Va., 1982-89, news editor, 1989-95; writer, editor The Virginian-Pilot, Norfolk, Va., 1995—. Recipient various Journalism awards Va. Press Assn., 1972-2004. Avocations: tennis, music, bicycling, camping. Home: 4704 Yarrow Ct Williamsburg VA 23188-2427 Office: Virginian-Pilot 150 W Brambleton Ave Norfolk VA 23510-2075 Office Phone: 757-446-2276. E-mail: bill.sizemore@pilotonline.com.

SIZER, PHILLIP SPELMAN, consultant, retired oil field services executive; b. Whittier, Calif., Apr. 11, 1926; s. Frank Milton and Helen Louise (Saylor) S.; m. Evelyn Sue Jones, Aug. 16, 1952; children: Phillip Spelman Jr., Ves Warner. BSME, So. Meth. U., 1948. Registered profl. engr., Tex. With Otis Engrng. Corp., Dallas, 1948-91, project engr., 1958-62, chief devel. engr., 1962-70, v.p. R & D, 1970-73, v.p. engrng. and rsch., 1973-76, sr. v.p., tech. dir., 1977-91, bd. dirs., 1975-91; pres. Sizer Engrng. Inc., 1992—; prin. Crawford-Sizer Devel. Co., 1996—. Bd. dirs. DHV Internat., Inc.; cons. in field; mem. exec. com. Offshore Tech. Conf., 1976-79. Patentee in field Mem. U. Tex. Mech. Engrng. Dept. Vis. Com., 1977-83. Named to Hall of Achievement Coll. Engrng., U. Tex., Arlington, 1983 Fellow ASME (chmn. exec. com. petroleum divsn. 1974-75, SPPE-1 chmn. main com. 1981-88, Engr. of Yr. award North Tex. sect. 1971, centennial medal 1980, OILDROP award petroleum divsn. 1982, Dedicated Svc. award 1985, Silver Patent award 1990, region x Clifford H. Shumaker award 1993); mem. Soc. Petroleum Engrs., S.W. Rsch. Inst. (trustee 1982—), Assn. Wellhead Eq. Mfrs. (pres. 1996), Petroleum Engrs. Club of Dallas, Rotary Internat., Kappa Sigma, Tau Beta Pi, Kappa Mu Epsilon. Home: 14127 Tanglewood Dr Dallas TX 75234-3851 Personal E-mail: sizer26@comcast.net.

SJOERDSMA, ALBERT, research institute executive; b. Lansing, Ill., Aug. 31, 1924; s. Sam and Agnes S.; m. Fern E. MacAllister, Dec. 2, 1950; children— Leslie, Ann, Albert, Britt. Ph.B., U. Chgo., 1944, BS, 1945, PhD, 1948, MD, 1949. Research asst. U. Chgo., 1947-49, NIH postdoctoral research fellow, 1950; intern U. Mich. Hosp., Ann Arbor, 1949-50; resident physician Michael Reese Hosp., Chgo., 1951; resident in internal medicine USPHS Hosp., Balt., 1951-53; sr. investigator, chief exptl. therapeutics br. Nat. Heart and Lung Inst., Bethesda, Md., 1953-71; v.p. Merrell Internat. Co., Strasbourg, France, 1971-78; v.p. pharm. research and devel. Richardson-Merrell Inc., 1978-81; v.p. pharm. research Merrell Dow Pharms., Cin., 1981-83; pres. Merrell Dow Research Inst., Cin., 1983-89, pres. emeritus, 1989-94; med. scis. cons., 1994—. Vis. spl. fellow Gen. Hosp., Malmo, Sweden, 1959-60; spl. lectr. George Washington U., 1959-71; Anton Julius Carlson lectr. U. Chgo., 1984; hon. chmn. 2d World Conf. on Clin. Pharmacology and Therapeutics, Washington, 1983; clin. prof. medicine U. Cin. Med. Ctr., 1986-91. Mem. AAAS (Theobold Smith award med. scis. 1958), Am. Soc. Pharm. and Exptl. Therapeutics (Harry Gold award in clin. pharmacology 1977, Exptl. Therapeutics award 1990), Am. Soc. Clin. Pharmacology and Therapeutics (Oscar B. Hunter Meml. award in therapeutics 1981), Internat. Soc. Hypertension, Coun. High Blood Pressure Rsch., Am. Heart Assn., Am. Fedn. Clin. Rsch., Am. Soc. Clin. Investigation, Am. Soc. Exptl. Biology and Medicine, Assn. Am. Physicians, Am. Coll. Neuropsychopharmacology. Home and Office: 263 N Dogwood Trail Kitty Hawk NC 27949-3138

SJOGREN, BENGT B, corporate financial executive; s. Bengt Ilson and Gerd E. Sjogren; m. Gerd Hawerman, May 26, 1973; children: Ebba, Hanna, Gustaf, Oscar. MBA, Stockholm Sch. of Econ., Stockholm, 1968—71. Vice chmn. and CEO Interverbum Group, Kista, Sweden, 1999—; mng. ptnr. InnoVisions Group, Chgo., 1998—; exec. v.p. Beloit Corp., Beloit, Wis., 1997—98; sr. ptnr. Slack Barshinger & Partners, Chgo., 1996—97; pres. & ceo Tetra Pak Inc., Chgo., 1991—96; group v.p. - internat. Tetra Pak Group, Lausanne, Switzerland, 1987—91; pres. Tetra Pak Pacific, Singapore, 1983—87; mng. dir. Tetra Pak Korea, Seoul, Republic of Korea, 1979—82. Dir. Munkeby Systems, Malmo, Sweden, 2002—. Chmn. Swedish Am. Chamber of Commerce, New York, NY, 1995—96; dir. Nat. Food Processors Assn., Washington, 1991—96; treas. Internat. Fedn. of Modern Penthalon, Monaco, Monaco, 1996—2000; chmn. Swedish Modern Penthalon Assn., Stockholm, 1989—2000; chmn. of long range planning com. Shedd Aquarium, Chgo., 1993; chmn. Swedish Am. Mus. Ctr., Chgo., 1998. Mem.: Swedish Am. C. of C. (dir. 1991—97, hon. dir. 1997—). Office: Interverbum 233 No Mich Ave #3050 Chicago IL 60601 Office Phone: 1-312-970 5800. Office Fax: 1-312-970 5850.

SJOSTRAND, FRITIOF STIG, biologist, educator; b. Stockholm, Nov. 5, 1912; s. Nils Johan and Dagmar (Hansen) S.; m. Marta Bruhn-Fahraeus, Mar. 24, 1941 (dec. June 1954); 1 child, Rutger; m. Ebba Gyllenkrok, Mar. 28, 1955; 1 child, Johan; m. Birgitta Petterson, Jan. 23, 1969; 1 child, Peter. MD, Karolinska Institutet, Stockholm, 1941, PhD, 1945; PhD (hon.), U. Siena, 1974, North-East Hill U., Shillon, India, 1989. Asst. prof. anatomy Karolinska Institutet, 1945-48, assoc. prof., 1949-59, prof. histology, 1960-61; research assoc. MIT, 1947-48; vis. prof. UCLA, 1959, prof. zoology, 1960-82, prof. emeritus molecular biology, 1982—. Author: Über die Eigenfluoreszenz Tierischer Gewebe Mit Besonderer Berücksichtigung der Säugetierniere, 1944, Electron Microscopy of Cells and Tissues, Vol. I, 1967, Deducing Function from Structure, Vols. I and II, 1990; also numerous articles. Decorated North Star Orden Sweden; recipient Jubilee award Swedish Med. Soc., 1959, Anders Retzius gold medal, 1967; Paul Ehrlich-Ludwig Darmstaedter prize, 1971 Fellow Royal Micros. Soc. (hon., London), Am. Acad. Arts and Scis.; mem. Electron Microscopy Soc. Am. (hon., Disting. Scientist award 1992), Japan Electron Microscopy Soc. (hon.), Scandinavian Electron Microscopy Soc. (hon.). Achievements include development technique for high resolution electron microscopy of cells, fluorescence microspectrography; inventor ultramicrotome. E-mail: fsjostra@ucla.edu.

SKAAR, ERIC CHRISTEN, education educator, consultant; b. Syracuse, N.Y., Dec. 26, 1947; s. Christen and Dorothy Arpert Skaar; m. Alice Emma Roden, Jan. 16, 1971; children: Alice Dorothy, Christen John, Eric Timothy. BS in Ceramic Engrng., Alfred Univ., Alfred, N.Y., 1970; PhD in Ceramic Engrng., MIT, Cambridge, Mass., 1977. Lic. P.E. #15322 S.C. Sr. staff scientist AC Sparkplug Divsn. of GM, Flint, Mich., 1977—79; staff scientist Gould, Inc., Cleve., 1980—81; assoc. prof. Clemson Univ., Clemson, SC, 1982—. Cons. ED&T, Columbia, SC, 1987—, Elan Tech., Midway, Ga., 2001—; disting. vis. prof. U.S.A.F. Acad., Colo. Springs, Colo., 2000—01. Author: (instrnl. video) Finite Elements in Action, 1996; dir.: (instrnl. video) Finite Elements in Action, 1996. Elder Oconee ARP Ch., Seneca, SC, 1998—2004; reading clk. 2nd Presbyn., Greenville, SC, 1994—2004 Capt. U.S. Army, 1970—73, Watertown, Mass. Mem.: Tau Beta Pi. Avocations: amateur radio, woodcarving, farming. Home: 216 Pea Ridge Rd Central SC 29630 Office: Clemson Univ PO Box 340971 Clemson SC 29634-0971 Office Phone: 864-656-5351.

SKAFF, JOSEPH JOHN, retired state agency administrator, army officer; b. Charleston, W.Va., June 13, 1930; s. Michael Joseph and Zahia S.; m. Maree A. Fleming, Aug. 4, 1957; children: Joseph M., Lynn M. Johnson, Gregory M., Nancy E. Kochman. BS, U.S. Mil. Acad., 1955; MS, George Wash. U., 1968. Commd. 2d. lt. U.S. Army, 1955; commd. 1/27 FA bn., 1968-69; mem. staff and faculty U.S. Mil. Acad., 1972-76; Vietnam's advance through grades to maj. gen.; dep. dir. internat. negotiations U.S. Army Joint Chiefs of Staff, Washington, 1979-81; also dep. commr. U.S. Del. Standing Consultative Commn., Geneva, 1979-81; dep. dir. ops. readiness and moblzn. hdqrs. U.S. Army, Washington, 1981-83, dep. comdr./chief staff, 1982-84; dep. commdg. gen., commdg. gen. 1st U.S. Army, Fort Devens, Mass., 1985-89; adj. gen. W.Va. U.S. Army, Fort Devens, Mass., 1989-95; cabinet sec. mil. affairs and pub. safety W.Va., 1989-97. Bd. dirs. Christian Internet Svc. Decorated DSM U.S. Army, Def. Superior Svc. medal, Legion of Merit, Bronze Star, Air medal, others; recipient Disting. W. Va. award. Mem. Assn. Grads. U.S. Mil. Acad., Assn. U.S. Army, Arty. Assn., Adj. Gens. Assn. U.S., N.G. Assn. U.S., Fellowship Christian Athletes (regional bd.). Eastern Orthodox. E-mail: jjskaff55@aol.com.

SKAGGS, BEBE REBECCA PATTEN, college dean, clergywoman; b. Berkeley, Calif., Jan. 30, 1950; d. Carl Thomas and Bebe (Harrison) P. BS in Bible, Patten Coll., 1969; BA in Philosophy, Holy Names Coll., 1970; MA in Bibl. Studies New Testament, Wheaton Coll., 1972; PhD in Bibl. Studies New Testament, Drew U., 1976; MA in Philosophy, Dominican Sch. Philosophy & Theology, 1990; postgrad., U. Calif., Berkeley, 1991-92. Ordained to ministry Christian Evang. Ch., 1963. Co-pastor Christian Cathedral, Christian Evang. Chs. Am., Inc., 1964—; assoc. prof. Patten Coll., Oakland, Calif., 1975-82, dean, 1977—, prof. N.T., 1982—. Presenter in field. Author: Before the Times, 1980, The World of the Early Church, 1990; contbg. author: Internat. Standard Bibl. Ency., rev. edit., 1983, Women's Study Bible, Pneuma Faculty Dialogue. Active Wheaton Coll. Symphony, 1971-72, Drew U. Ensemble, 1971-75, Young Artists Symphony, N.J., 1972-75, Somerset Hill Symphony, N.J., 1973-74, Peninsula Symphony, 1977, 80-81, Madison Chamber Trio, N.J., 1973-75. Named one of Outstanding Young Women of Am., 1976, 77, 80-81, 82; St. Olaf's Coll. fellow, 1990. Mem. AAUP, Am. Acad. Religion, Soc. Bibl. Lit., Internat. Biographical Assn., Christian Evang. Chs. of Am., Inc. (bd. dirs. 1964—), Inst. for Bibl. Rsch., Soc. for Pentecostal Studies (pres. 1998-99), Phi Delta Kappa.

SKAGGS, RONALD LLOYD, architect; b. Dallas, Nov. 7, 1942; s. Henry Lloyd and Willye Velle (Hill) S.; m. Sondra Lanette Garrett, June 25, 1965; children: David, Stephen, Jeffrey. BArch, Tex. A&M U., 1966, MArch, 1967. Registered architect, Tex., Ind., Kans., Minn., La., Ark., Tenn., Iowa, Ala., N.Mex., Mich., S.C., D.C., Idaho, Nebr. Architect/assoc. CRS Design assocs., Houston, 1970-73; architect HKS Architects, Dallas, 1973-74, assoc., 1974-75, sr. v.p., 1975-80, exec. v.p., 1980-88, chmn., CEO, 1988—2002, chmn., 2003—. Adv. bd. Constrn. Industry Pres.'s Round Table, Washington, 1993-96. Author: Architecture for Long Term Care Facilities, 1993; co-author: Building Type Basics for Healthcare Facilities; editor: The Architecture of Healing, 1994; contbr. articles to profl. jours. Bd. advisors Salvation Army, Plano, Tex., 1995—; bd. trustees Tex. Scottish Rite Hosp. for Children, Dallas, 1990—; bd. dirs. Priority One Internat., Dallas, 1986-95; chmn. arch. devel. coun. Tex. A&M U., College Station, 1991—; regent Am. Archtl. Found., Washington, 1993—; mem. exec. bd. Cir. Ten coun. Boy Scouts Am., 2002—; mem. Nat. Architectural Accrediting Bd., 2002—; mem. bd. dirs. Tex. A&M U. Assn. of Former Students, 2002—; mem. bd. dirs. Faith Bapt. Missions, 2001—; bd. dirs. Nat. Inst. Bldg. Scis., 2003--. Decorated Army Commendation medal; recipient numerous design awards; named Disting. Alumnus Tex. A&M U., Outstanding Alumnus Coll. of Architecture Tex. A&M U., SIR award Assoc. Gen. Contractors. Fellow AIA (bd. dirs. 1995-97, v.p. 1998, pres. elect 1999, pres. 2000), Health Facilities Inst., Am. Coll. Healthcare Archs.; mem. Forum for Health Care Planning (pres. 1992-93), Masons (Scottish Rite 33 degree), Tau Sigma Delta (Silver medal). Republican. Baptist. Avocations: music, reading, art collecting, skiing, water sports. Office: HKS Architects 1919 Mckinney Ave Dallas TX 75201-1768

SKAGGS, SANFORD MERLE, lawyer; b. Berkeley, Calif., Oct. 24, 1939; s. Sherman G. and Barbara Jewell (Stinson) Skaggs; m. Sharon Ann Barnes, Sept. 3, 1976; children: Stephen, Paula Ferry, Barbara Gallagher, Darren Peterson. BA, U. Calif., Berkeley, 1961; JD, U. Calif., 1964. Bar: Calif. 1965. Atty. Pacific Gas and Electric Co., San Francisco, 1964-73; gen. counsel Pacific Gas Transmission Co., San Francisco, 1973-75; ptnr. Van Voorhis & Skaggs, Walnut Creek, Calif., 1975-85, McCutchen, Doyle, Brown & Enersen, San Francisco and Walnut Creek, 1985—2002, Bingham McCutchen LLP, 2002—; dir. John Muir Mt. Diablo Health Sys., 1997—. Mem. Calif. Law Revision Commn., 1990—2001, chmn., 1993. Councilman City of Walnut Creek, 1972-78, mayor 1974-75, 76-77; bd. dirs. East Bay Mcpl. Utility Dist., 1978-90, pres., 1982-90. Mem.: Contra Costa County Bar Assn., Calif. State Bar Assn., Phi Delta Phi, Alpha Delta Phi, Lambda Alpha. Republican. Office: Bingham McCutchen 1333 N California Blvd Ste 210 Walnut Creek CA 94596-4585 Office Phone: 925-975-5310.

SKAGGS, TINA MARIE, accountant; b. Jackson, Miss., Dec. 11, 1959; d. George Garrel and Ernestine (Berry) Warren; m. David Layton, July 30, 1976 (div. 1978); 1 child, Amanda; m. Fred Lewis Skaggs, Aug. 10, 1991; children: Adam, Jonathan, Christopher, Timothy, Benjamin. B in Profl. Accountancy, Miss. State U., 1982. CPA, Calif., Tex.; cert. fraud examiner. Staff acct. Arthur Andersen & Co., Houston, 1982-85; sr. acct. Arthur Young, L.A., 1985-87, audit mgr., 1987-89; sr. audit mgr. Ernst & Young, L.A., 1989-92; pvt. practice expert witness Laguna Niguel, Calif., 1992-95; pvt. practice litigation cons. La Canada, Calif., 1995—. Mem. AICPA, Nat. Assn. Cert. Fraud Examiners. Mem. Lds Ch. Avocations: skiing, piano, biking.

SKAGGS, WAYNE GERARD, financial services company executive, retired; b. Bonneterre, Mo., Dec. 12, 1929; s. Jasper Pinkney and Lattie May (Duren) S.; m. Hana Kaneko, June 1, 1952; children: Robert Kenneth, Melody Jane, Joy Elizabeth. Student, Mo. Inst. Acctg. and Law, 1947-48, U. Mo., Columbia, 1954-55. With Advantage Capital Corp. (formerly Am. Capital Corp.), Houston, 1955-96, ret., 1996; pres., COO Mktg. Group of Cos.,

Houston, 1976-80, corp. v.p., cons., 1972-90. Served with USAF, 1950-54, Korea. Mem. Nat. Assn. Securities Dealers (nat. vice-chmn. 1977, dist. chmn. 1972), Nat. Bus. Conduct (gov., chmn. 1976), Investment Co. Inst., Am. Legion (life), VFW (life), Optimists (life, pres. 1966). Home: PO Box 726 Wimberley TX 78676-0726

SKALA, GARY DENNIS, management consultant; b. Bay Shore, N.Y, Oct. 15, 1946; s. Harry A. and Emily Skala. BS in Mgmt. Engring., Rensselaer Polytech. Inst., 1969; MA in Psychology, Hofstra U., 1972; postgrad., Chgo. Theol. Sem., 1996—. Engr. L.I. Lighting Co., Hicksville, NY, 1969-71, labor rels. coord., 1971-73; mgmt. cons. Gilbert/Commonwealth, N.Y.C., 1973-74; sr. mgmt. cons. Booz, Allen & Hamilton, San Francisco, 1974-78; mgr. utility cons. A.T. Kearney, Chgo., 1978-81; mng. cons. Cresap, div. Towers Perrin, Chgo., 1981-85; pres. Gary D. Skala & Assocs. Mgmt. Cons., Chgo., 1985—. Lectr. utility bus. issues Edison Electric Inst., Utility Exec. Mgmt. Com., Internat. Maintenance Conf., Assn. Rural Electric Coops., Inst. Indsl. Engrs.; subcontracting cons. Arthur D. Little, Inc., Liberty Cons. Group, Ernst & Young, Cresap, A. T. Kearney, Towers Perrin, Michael Paris Assocs. Ltd., Planmetrics. Contbr. articles to profl. jours. Trustee Samaritan Inst. for Religious Studies, 1995—97, chair instnl. advancement com., 1995; bd. dirs. Bailiwick Repertory Theater, 1999—, pres., 2001—02, chair mktg./pub. rels. com.; bd. dirs. Good Shepherd Parish Met. Cmty. Ch. of Chgo., 1995—99, vice moderator, 1996—97; mem. bd. Ordained Ministry of Gt. Lakes Dist. of Universal Fellowship Met. Cmty. Chs., 1996—99; vol. The Night Ministry of Chgo. Mem.: Am. Inst. Indsl. Engrs. (chmn. Midwest chpt. utility divsn. 1980—81), Inst. Indsl. Engrs. (sr.; mem. utility divsn. 1978—, charter). Office: Gary D Skala & Assocs PO Box 14838 Chicago IL 60614-0838 Office Phone: 773-935-1362.

SKALAGARD, HANS MARTIN, artist; b. Skuko, Faroe Islands, Feb. 7, 1924; came to U.S., 1942, naturalized, 1955. s. Ole Johannes and Hanna Elisa (Fredriksen) S.; m. Mignon Diana Haack Haegland, Mar. 31, 1955; 1 child, Karen Solveig Sikes. Pupil, Anton Otto Fisher, 1947. Joined U.S. Mcht. Marine, 1942, advanced through grades to chief mate, 1945; ret., 1965; owner, operator Skalagard Sq. Rigger Art Gallery, Carmel, Calif., 1966—; libr. Mayo Hays O'Donnel Libr., Monterey, Calif., 1971-73; painter U.S. Naval Heritage series, 1973—. Lectr., bd. dirs. Allen Knight Maritime Mus., 1973—, mem. adv. and acquisitions coms., 1973-77; spkr. in field. One-man shows include Palace Legion of Honor, San Francisco, 1960, J.F. Howland, 1963-65, Fairmont Hotel, San Francisco, 1963, Galerie de Tours, 1969, 72-73, Pebble Beach (Calif.) Gallery, 1963, Laguna Beach (Calif.) Gallery, 1969, Arden Gallery, Atlanta, 1970, Gilbert Gallery, San Francisco, Maritime Mus. of Monterey, 1993, 97, Rigger Art Gallery, Carmel, Stanton Ctr., Monterey, 1993, Monterey Maritime Mus., 1993, 1997, St. Francis Yacht Club, San Francisco, 1995, Ventura County Maritime Mus., Oxnard, Calif., 1998; exhibited in group shows at Am. Artists, Eugene, Oreg., Robert Louis Stevenson Exhibit, Carmel Valley Gallery, Biarritz and Paris, David Findley Galleries, N.Y.C. and Faroe Island, Maritime Mus., Calif., 1993, 94, 95, Pacific Coast Lumber Schooners, 1994,, San Francisco Art Expo, 2000, Herrschoff Marine Mus., Bristol, R.I., 2002, Cavalier Galleries, Inc., Nantucket, Mass., 2003, Cavalier Galleries, Inc., Greenwich, Conn., 2003, numerous others; represented in permanent collections Naval Post Grad. Sch. and Libr., Allen Knight Maritime Mus., Salvation Army Bldg., Monterey, Robert Louis Stevenson Sch., Pebble Beach, Anenberg Art Galleries, Chestlibrook Ltd., Skalagard Art Gallery, Carmel; work represented in numerous books including Modern Masters of Marine Art, 1993; featured artist KTEH-TV On-Air Art Auction, 1998; profiled in profl. jours.; subject of cover and article Palette Talk, 1980, Compass mag., 1980; artist (series of paintings) American Revolutionary War at Sea, 2003. Chairperson Mayor's Choice Exhibit, Carmel, 1993-95; co-founder Carmel Gallery Alliance, 2000--. Recipient Silver medal Tommaso Campanella Internat. Acad. Arts, Letters and Scis., Rome, 1970, Gold medal, 1972, Gold medal and hon. life membership Acad. Italia dell Arti e del Honoro, 1980, Gold medal for artistic merit Acad. d'Italia, Statue of Victory award Acad. d'Italia, 2003. Mem. Navy League (bd. dirs. Monterey), Internat. Platform Assn., Sons of Norway (cultural dir. 1974-75, 76-77), Am. Mcht. Marine Vets. Assn. (Goden Gate chpt.), Combat Mcht. Marine WWII Assn. (coun.), Mariners (San Francisco Bay area chpt.). Home: 602 Stony Point Rd Petaluma CA 94952-1048 Fax: 707-776-4889. Office Phone: 707-769-9340. E-mail: skalagard@aol.com.

SKALKA, ANNA MARIE, molecular biologist; b. N.Y.C., July 2, 1938; AB, Adelphi U., 1959; PhD in Microbiology, NYU, 1964. Am. Cancer Soc. fellow molecular biology genetics rsch. unit Carnegie Inst., 1964-66, fellow, 1966-69; asst. mem. dept. cell biology lab. molecular and biochemical genetics Roche Inst. Molecular Biology, 1969-71, assoc. mem., 1971-76, mem., 1976-80, head, 1980-87; now dir. Inst. Cancer Rsch., Phila., 1987—; sr. v.p. basic sci. Fox Chase Cancer Ctr., Phila., 1987—. Adj. prof. microbiology, Sch. Medicine, U. Pa., 1973—, Rockefeller U., 1975. Mem. AAAS, Am. Soc. Microbiology, Am. Soc. Biol. Chem., Assn. Women Sci., Sigma Xi. Achievements include research in the structure and function of DNA, host and viral functions in the synthesis of viral DNA and RNA, phage DNA as a vehicle for the amplification and study of eukaryotic genes, molecular biology of avian retroviruses. Office: Inst for Cancer Rsch Fox Chase Cancer Ctr 7701 Burholme Ave Philadelphia PA 19111-2412

SKALKA, HAROLD WALTER, ophthalmologist, educator; b. N.Y.C., Aug. 22, 1941; s. Jack and Sylvia Skalka; m. Barbara Jean Herbert, Oct. 2, 1965; children: Jennifer, Gretchen, Kirsten. AB with distinction, Cornell U., 1962; MD, NYU, 1966. Intern Greenwich (Conn.) Hosp., 1966-67; resident in ophthalmology Bellevue Hosp., Univ. Hosp., Manhattan VA Hosp., 1967-70; fellow in retinal physiology and ultrasonography, 1970-71; cons. in ophthalmology St. Jude's Hosp., Montgomery, Ala., 1971-73; asst. prof. ophthalmology U. Ala., Birmingham, 1973-75, assoc. prof., 1975-80, prof., 1980-81, assoc. prof. dept. medicine, 1980—, chmn. combined program in ophthalmology, 1981-97, Nathan E. Miles prof., 1986—. Acting chmn. combined program ophthalmology U. Ala., 1974-76; ophthalmologist Lowndes County Bd. Health Community Health Project, 1972. Contbr. articles to Am. Jour. Ophthalmology, Eye, Ear, Nose and Throat Monthly, Annals of Ophthalmology, Ophthalmic Surgery, Jour. Clin. Ultrasound, Jour. Pediatric Ophthalmology and Strabismus, The Lancet, AMA Archives of Ophthalmology, Jour. So. Med. Assn., Acta Ophthalmologica, Metabolic and Pediatric Ophthalmology, Applied Radiology, Brit. Jour. Ophthalmology, Blood, Neuro-Ophthalmology; mem. editl. bd. Ala. Jour. Med. Sci. Major USAFMC, 1971-73. Mem. AAAS, AMA, ACS, SIDUO, Ala. Sight Conservation Assn., Ala. Conservancy, Ala. Wildlife Fedn., Eye Bank Bd., Am. Acad. Ophthalmology, Am. Inst. Ultrasound in Medicine, Internat. Soc. for Clin. Electrophysiology of Vision, Internat. Soc. on Metabolic Eye Disease, Assn. for Rsch. in Vision and Ophthalmology, AAUP, Am. Intraocular Implant Soc., Am. Assn. Ophthalmology, Pan Am. Assn. Ophthalmology, So. Med. Assn., Rsch. to Prevent Blindness, Ala. Acad. Ophthalmology, Ala. Med. Assn., Jefferson County Med. Soc., Contact Lens Assn. Ophthalmologists, Ala. Ultrasound Soc., Royal Soc. Medicine, N.Y. Acad. Scis., Am. Soc. Standardized Ophthalmic Echography (charter exec. bd. mem.), Am. Coll. Nutrition. Office: Eye Found Hosp U Ala 700 18th St S Ste 200 Birmingham AL 35233-3800 Business E-Mail: hskalka@uabmc.edu.

SKAMAI, ROBERT WALTER, music educator; b. Kittanning, Pa., Sept. 4, 1952; s. George and Anna Jane Skamai; m. Marguerite Anne Palilla, July 5, 1986; children: Robert Michael, Kathryn Patrice, David John, Thomas Joseph, Anna Marie. BS, Ind. U. of Pa., 1974. Cert. music edn. tchr. Pa. Music tchr. Armstrong Sch. Dist., Ford City, Pa., 1980—; instrumental music educator Lenape Elem. Sch., Ford City, Pa., 1982—. Musician, Pa. Musician: (performance) Music Educators Nat. Conf. All Eastern Divsn. Conf. Cmty. choir dir. Rural Valley Ministerium, Pa. Mem.: Pa. Music Educators Assn. (assoc.). Democrat-Npl. Catholic. Avocations: walking, reading, gardening, performing music for weddings and dances, spending time with family. Home: Rd # 5 Box 187 E Kittanning PA 16201 Office: Lenape Elem Sch 2300 Center Ave Ford City PA Office Phone: 724-763-5299.

SKAMBIS, CHRISTOPHER CHARLES, JR., lawyer; b. Painesville, Ohio, Jan. 21, 1953; s. Christopher Charles and Anne (Haritos) S.; m. Susan Elaine Adrianson, Dec. 18, 1976 (div. Mar. 1997); m. Kathleen Louise Maloney, Feb. 1999; children: Adrianne Elaine, Christopher Roy. Student, U. Pa., 1970-72; BA, U. Conn., 1972-74; JD, Ohio State U. Coll. Law, Columbus, 1975-78. Bar: Fla. 1978, U.S. Dist. Ct. (mid. dist.), 1979, U.S. Dist. Ct. (no. and so. dists.) 1997, U.S. Ct. Appeals (5th and 11th cir.) 1981, U.S. Supreme Ct. 1989. Assoc. VandenBerg, Gay & Burke, Orlando, Fla., 1978-81, ptnr., 1982, VandenBerg, Gay, Burke, Wilson & Arkin, Orlando, Fla., 1982-85, Foley & Lardner, Orlando, Fla., 1985—95, Moran & Shams PA, Orlando, Fla., 1996-99, The Skambis Law Firm, Orlando, 2000—. Mem. Orange County Bar Assn., Orlando, Fla., 1978, Fla. Bar 9D Grievance Commn., Orlando, Fla., 1989; arbitrator Fla. Bar 9th Cir. Fee Arbitration Commn., Orlando, Fla., 1987; co-chair Federal and State Trial Practice Co., Orlando, Fla., 1992-93. Mem. Am. Judicature Soc., ABA. Avocation: amateur ham radio operator. Office: The Skambis Law Firm 715 Vassar St Orlando FL 32804-4920 Fax: (407) 649-0191. E-mail: cskambis@cfl.rr.com.

SKANDERA-TROMBLEY, LAURA ELISE, language professional, English; b. L.A., Nov. 1, 1960; d. John and Mary Ruth (Chaney) S.; m. Nelson Edmund Trombley, July 13, 1991. BA, Pepperdine U., 1981, MA, 1983; PhD, U. So. Calif., 1989. Asst. lectr. U. So. Calif., L.A., 1983-87; vis. prof. U. Eichstatt, Bavaria, Germany, 1985-87, Pepperdine U., Malibu, Calif., 1988-90; asst. prof. Potsdam Coll., SUNY, 1990—. Author: Mark Twain's Literary Marriage, 1992; editor: Poetry and Epistemology, 1986. Named Quarry Farm fellow Ctr. for Mark Twain Studies, 1988, Finklestein fellow U. Soc. Calif., 1988. Office: Potsdam Coll Dept Of English Potsdam NY 13676

SKANTZE, PAT, model, consultant; b. Birmingham, Ala. m. Lawrence A. Skantze; children: Lawrence Michael, Patricia Anne, Vanessa Maria. BA in Speech and Drama, Birmingham So. Coll. Tchg. fellow U. Ala. Model, cons., commentator major dept. stores, N.Y.C., Washington, L.A.; spkr., lectr. image improvement and success motivation; advisor fgn. nats. through mil. cmty. Personality, spokesperson variety shows, talk show hostess, sitcoms, documentaries and commls. Past pres. bd. assocs. Nat. Rehab. Hosp.; past pres. Women's Com. of Washington Ballet; active Salvation Army Women's Aux., Welcome to Washington, Lab. Sch. Washington, Neediest Kids, Nat. Mil. Family Assn.; bd. trustees Nat. Aviation Hall of Fame. Mem. Capitol Spkrs. Club (pres.), Tower Club (bd. govs.). Home: 1703 Chesterbrook Vale Ct Mc Lean VA 22101-3244 Personal E-mail: gen4las@aol.com.

SKARBEK, ANDREW ALEXANDER, investment advisor, artist; b. Munich, July 26, 1947; s. Anthony and Barbara C Skarbek; m. Jolanta Joanna Zablocka, Aug. 14, 1982; 1 child, Michelle Dianna. BA, Calif. State U., 1977, MA, 1985. Engr. No. Am. Phillips Corp., Santa Ana, Calif., 1981—91; stock broker Charles Schwab & Co., Phoenix, 1992—. Ednl. cons. EDART, Scottsdale, Ariz., 1998—2000. Author: (book) Human Rights Struggle Against, 1985, Twinkles, A Fairies Tale, 2002, (anthology) Day Break at Wycamp Lake, 2000. Mem. New Ch. Bldg. Fund, 1992. Democrat. Roman Cath. Avocations: painting, skiing, tennis. Home: 4111 E Woodstock Rd Cave Creek AZ 85331

SKARDA, LYNELL GRIFFITH, lawyer, banker; b. Clovis, N.Mex., Aug. 28, 1915; s. Albert S. and Bertha V. (Taylor) Skarda; m. Kathryn Burns Skarda, Dec. 25, 1939; children: Jeffrey J., Patricia Lyn, Katrina A., Gregory A.F. BS, U. Calif.-Berkeley, 1937; JD, Washington and Lee U., 1941. Bar: N.Mex. 1941. Sole practice, Clovis, N.Mex., 1941—. Chmn. bd. Citizens Bank of Clovis, 1968—; mem. Uniform Jury Instrn. Com., 1963—83. Capt. JAG Corps U.S. Army. Fellow: Am. Coll. Trust and Estate Counsel; mem.: ABA, Am. Judicature Soc., N.Mex. Bar Assn. Home: PO Box 400 Clovis NM 88102-0400 Office: Citizens Bank Bldg PO Box 400 Clovis NM 88102-0400 E-mail: lskarda@3lefties.com.

SKARDA, PATRICIA LYN, English language educator; b. Clovis, N.Mex., Mar. 31, 1946; d. Lynell Griffith and Kathryn Rose (Burns) S. Student, Sweet Briar Coll., 1964—67; BA, Tex. Tech. U., 1969; PhD, U. Tex., 1973. Prof. English Smith Coll., Northampton, Mass., 1973—. Edn. dir. Girls Nation, Washington, 1973-75, A.P. Inst. Leader, U. No. Colo., Greeley, 1988-91, 94-2003; cons. USCCB Bishop's Com. on Vocations, 1998—. Editor: The Evil Image, 1981, Smith Voices, 1990, 99, Textured Lives: Celebrating Ada Comstock Scholars at Smith College, 2000, Instrumentum Laboris for the Third Continental Congress of Vocations, 2001; contbr. articles to profl. jours. Dir. Girls State, N.Mex., 1973. Fellow in Acad. Adminstrn., Am. Coun. on Edn., 1978-79, NDEA grad. fellow, Disting. Vis. prof. USAF Acad., 1992-93. Mem. MLA, N.Am. Soc. Study Romanticism, Phi Beta Kappa, Sigma Tau Delta, Phi Kappa Phi. Democrat. Roman Catholic. Avocations: reading, swimming, playing piano, travel, praying. Office: Smith Coll Dept English Northampton MA 01063-0001 Office Phone: 413-585-3331. E-mail: pskarda@smith.edu.

SKARE, ROBERT MARTIN, lawyer, director; b. Jan. 13, 1930; s. Martin Samuel and Verna Adelle (Forseth) S.; m. Marilyn Hutchinson, Aug. 28, 1954; children: Randolph, Robertson, Rodger, Richard. Student, St. Olaf Coll., 1947-48; BS, U. Minn., 1951, JD, 1954. Bar: Minn. 1956. Clk. Minn. Supreme Ct., 1953-54; assoc. Best and Flanagan, Mpls., 1956-60, ptnr., 1960-90, sr. ptnr., 1970-90, of counsel, 1990—. Founder, dir., gen. counsel, v.p. Luth. Brotherhood-Thrivent Mut. Funds, Mpls., 1969—93; corp. mcpl. counsel City of Golden Valley, Minn., 1963—88; bd. dirs. Vesper Soc. Group, San Francisco, Son of Heaven, Seattle, Aspen Inst. Cmty. Forum, Nat. Coun. Search Inst. Youth Initiative, Venture Catalysts of Calif.; nat. pres. Luth. Human Rels. Assn. Am., 1977—79; founder, dir. Episc. Found. of Aspen, Vinland Nat. Ctr.; founder Westwood Luth. Found.; adv. bd. Venture Fin. Inst. Claremont Calif. U. P.F. Drucker Grad. Sch., 2003—. Trustee Am. Luth. Ch.; mem. bd. mgmt. U. Minn. YMCA. Officer Counter-Intelligence Corps U.S. Army, 1954—56. Recipient Pres. award Luth. Human Rels. Assn. Am., 1979, Presdl. award Search Inst., 1997, Disting. Svc. award Luth. Brotherhood, 1992; named Disting. Mil. Student Res. Officers Tng. Corps., U. Minn., 1954. Mem. ABA, Minn. State Bar Assn., Hennepin County Bar Assn., U. Minn. Alumni Club (charter), Mpls. Club, Torske Klubben, Sigma Alpha Epsilon (Disting. Alumni Svc. award 1978). Office: 4000 US Bank Pl Minneapolis MN 55402-4331 Home: Villa Sandia de Luz 47000 Box 1390 Fallbrook CA 92088 Office: 780 Mt Laurel Aspen CO 81611 E-mail: marskare@aol.com.

SKAU, MICHAEL W. English educator; b. Chgo., Jan. 6, 1944; s. Walter Francis and Martha Catherine (Marich) S. BA, U. Ill., 1965, MA, 1967, PhD, 1973. Rsch. asst. U. Ill., Urbana and Champaign, 1965-66, teaching asst., 1966-73; asst. prof. English U. Nebr., Omaha, 1973-78, assoc. prof. English, 1978-85, prof. English, 1985—. Jefferis chair, 1997—2000, dept. chair, 2001—. Author: Constantly Risking Absurdity: The Writings of Lawrence Ferlinghetti, 1989; Me and God Poems, 1990, A Clown in a Grave: Complexities and Tensions in the Works of Gregory Corso, 1999; author poems; contbr. articles to profl. jours. Mem. MLA, AAUP. Home: 4913 Chicago St Omaha NE 68132-2914 Office: U Nebr 60th & Dodge Sts Omaha NE 68182-0001 Office Phone: 402-554-3314. E-mail: mskau@mail.unomaha.edu.

SKAUEN, DONALD MATTHEW, retired pharmaceutical educator; b. Newton, Mass., May 14, 1916; s. Marcus and Mary A. (Duncan) S.; m. Rachel M. Burns, Oct. 25, 1942; children: Deborah Skauen Hinchcliffe, Bruce. BS, Mass. Coll. Pharmacy, 1938, MS, 1942; PhD, Purdue U., 1949. Dir. pharm. svc. Children's Hosp. Med. Ctr., Boston, 1940-46; teaching asst. Purdue U., West Lafayette, Ind., 1946-48; asst. prof. pharmaceutics U. Conn., Storrs, 1948-53, assoc. prof., 1953-59, prof., 1959-79, prof. emeritus, 1979—. Mem. del. of med. scientists to discuss biol. and pharm. uses of ultrasound Nat. Coun. U.S.-China Trade, People's Republic China, 1979. Co-author: American Pharmacy, 4th edit., 1955, 5th edit., 1961, 6th edit., 1966, Husa's Pharmaceutical Dispensing, 1959, 2d edit., 1966, Radioecology, 1963; contbr. numerous articles to Sci., Nature, Jour. Am. Pharm. Assn. Mem. Am. Pharm. Assn., Am. Soc. Hosp. Pharmacists, Sigma Xi. Achievements include research on effects of ultrasound on pharmaceutical and biological systems; radioecology, including gross beta levels in oysters and other organisms in Thames River, Connecticut, and zinc-65 levels in oysters. Home: 16 Storrs Heights Rd Storrs Mansfield CT 06268-2322

SKAVLEM, MELISSA KLINE, publisher; Pres. Hanser Gardner Pub., Cin. Office: Hanser Gardner Pub 6600 Clough Pike Cincinnati OH 45244-4028

SKEEN, DAVID RAY, systems engineer, consultant, engineering executive, educator; b. Bucklin, Kans., July 12, 1942; s. Claude E. and Velma A. (Birney) S.; m. Carol J. Stimpert, Aug. 23, 1964; children: Jeffrey Kent, Timothy Sean, Kimberly Dawn. BA in Math., Emporia State U., 1964; MS, Am. U., 1972; grad., Fed. Exec. Inst., 1983, Naval War Coll., 1984; DSc in Engring. Mgmt., George Washington U., 1998. Cert. office automation profl. Computer sys. analyst to comdr.-in-chief U.S. Naval Forces-Europe, London, 1967-70; computer sys. analyst Naval Command Sys. Support Activity, Washington, 1970-73; dir. data processing Office Naval Rsch., U.S. Navy Dept., Arlington, Va., 1973-78; dir. mgmt. info. sys. Naval Civilian Pers. Command, Washington, 1978-80; dep. dir. manpower, pers. tng. automated sys. Dept. Naval Mil. Pers. Command, Washington, 1980-85; dir. manpower, pers. tng. info. resource mgmt. Chief Naval Ops., Washington, 1985-91; assoc. dir. Office of IRM, USDA, Washington, 1992-96; dir. modernization of adminstrn. processes program, 1996-98; dep. dir. office of ops. USDA, Washington, 1998; sr. engring. manager, cons. Lockheed Martin, Washington, 1998—2004; sys. engring. cons. GCI, 2004—. Lectr. Inst. Sci. and Pub. Affairs, 1973-76; cons. Electronic Data Processing Career Devel. Programs, 1975—; detailed to Pres.'s Reorgn. Project for Automated Data Processing, 1978, spl. Navy IRM studies, SECNAV, 1991, USDA/Office of Mgmt. and Budget IRM, 1993, spl. USDA Field Structure Studies, 1997; adj. prof. Sch. Engring. and Applied Sci., George Washington U., 1985—; with Pres.'s Fed. Automated Data Processing Users Group, Washington, 1978-80. Contbr. articles to profl. jours. Capt. USNR, 1960-91. Recipient Outstanding Performance award Interagy. Com. Data Processing, 1976, Adminstrv. Staff Performance award, 1998, Sec.'s cert. Appreciation, 1998. Mem. IEEE, Internat. Coun. on Sys. Engring., Sr. Exec. Assn., Assn. Fed. IRM, Naval Res. Assn., Pres. Fed. Automated Data Processing Users Group. Home: 707 Forest Park Rd Great Falls VA 22066-2908 Personal E-mail: docskeen@earthlink.net. Business E-Mail: david.r.skeen@lmco.com.

SKEEN, KERRY B. airline executive; With Delta Airlines, 1978—; co-founder Atlantic Coast Airlines Holdings, Inc. divsn. WestAir Holdings, Inc., 1994; pres., CEO Atlantic Coast Airlines, Inc., 1995-99; chmn. bd. Atlatnic Coast Airlines Holdings, Inc. Office: Atlantic Coast Arlines Inc 515A Show Rd Dulles VA 20166

SKEES, WILLIAM LEONARD, JR., lawyer; b. Indpls., Jan. 26, 1947; s. William Leonard and Marian Catherine (Fagan) S.; children: Kristina Suzanne Carlsen, Elizabeth Ann Garrison; children: Catherine Fagan, William Leonard III (dec.), Samuel Jackson. BA, Ball State U., 1969; JD, Ind. U., 1971. Bar: Ind. 1971, Ky. 1981. Law clk. U.S. Dist. Ct. (no. dist.), Fort Wayne, Ind., 1971-72; assoc. Ice, Miller Donadio & Ryan, Indpls., 1972-80; mem. Frost Brown Todd, LLC, Louisville, 1981—. Contbr. articles to jours. in field. Mem. bd. visitors Ind. U. Sch. Law, 1975-91; bd. dirs., past pres. Louisville Housing Partnership, 1978—; bd. dirs. Stage One, Louisville Children's Theatre, pres., 1990-91; bd. dirs. Ky. chpt. Nat. SIDS Found.; grad. Leadership Ky., 1996. Mem. ABA, Ky. Bar Assn., Ind. Bar Assn., Louisville Bar Assn., Nat. Assn. Bond Lawyers. Office: Frost Brown Todd LLC 400 W Market St Fl 32D Louisville KY 40202-3346 E-mail: bskees@FBTLaw.com.

SKEETE, HELEN WATKINS, minister, counselor; b. Wallace, N.C., Mar. 2, 1938; d. James Edward Newkirk, Edith Newkirk; m. Paul Louis, Sr. Watkins, Aug. 31, 1958; children: Paul Jr. Watkins, Stella Ross Finch, Trina Joy Gatlin. BTh, Calvary Grace Inst., Columbus, Ohio, 1977. Cert. crisis counselor. Internat. evangelist Soul Saving Sta. Every Nation, N.Y.C., 1959—84; asst. adminstr., assoc. min. Grace Ch. All Nations, Boston, 1983—88; founder, CEO Love Unlimited Drug Rehab. Outreach Programs, Inc., Boston, 1988—; founder, dir. Love U God's Gang, Brookline, Mass., 1991—; founder, CEO, pastor Love Unlimited Outreach Ministries, Inc., Boston, 1991—; overseer Men & Women of Crossroads Ministries, Dorchester, Mass., 1996—, Gospel Truth Ministries. Mem. adv. bd. New Eng. Med. Ctr. Hosp., Boston, 1981—83, Boston Against Drugs, 1991—96, Living After Murder Program, Inc., Roxbury, Mass., 1993—95. Author: (plays) Life on the Streets in a World of Drugs, 1990 (Proclamation from Mayor Flynn of Boston, 1990), Matriac of Ministry, 2002, Official Resolution - Boston City Council, 2002; co-author: Boston Area Violence Prevention Resource Directory, 1993 (Hon. Cmty. Svc. award, 1993). Facilitator Healthy Boston, 1997—99; mem. AIDS Action Com., Boston, 1995—2001; counselor Boston Safe Neighborhood, 1990—97; mem. evaluation team Boston Against Drugs, 1993—97; dir. March Against Violence, 1991. Recipient Recognition of Achievement, Gov. Paul Cellucci of Mass., 1997, Ofcl. Resolution, Boston City Coun., Recognition of Achievement, Commonwealth of Mass. Ho. Reps., 1997, Letter of Recognition, U.S. Pres. George Bush, 1990, Letter of Appreciation, U.S. Pres. Bill Clinton, 1997, cert. of Appreciation, Boston Police Dept., 1997, Proclamation, City of Boston Mayor Menino, 1997, Letter of Recognition, U.S. Pres. Ronald Regan, 1983; grantee, Boston Safe Neighborhood, 1991. Mem.: Grandparents Raising Their Grandchildren (facilitator 1996—99, cert. of Appreciation 1997). Democrat. Avocations: travel, reading, sewing, singing, writing. Home: 99 Kent St Ste 7-317 Brookline MA 02445-7955 Office: Love Unlimited Drug Rehabilitation Out Brookline MA 02445-7955 Personal E-mail: revhelenwatkinsskeete@yahoo.com. Business E-Mail: revhelenwatkinsskeete@yahoo.com.

SKEFF, KELLEY MICHAEL, health facility administrator; b. Center, Colo., 1944; MD, U. Chgo., 1970. Diplomate Am. Bd. Internal Medicine. Intern Harbor Gen. Hosp., Torrance, Calif., 1970-71; resident in internal medicine U. Colo. Med. Ctr., Denver, 1974-75, Stanford (Calif.) U. Hosps., 1975-76, fellow in internal medicine, 1976; resident in internal medicine Stanford U., 1989—, assoc. prof. medicine. Recipient Alpha Omega Alpha award Assocs. Am. Med. Coll., 1994. Office: Stanford U Dept Med 300 Pasteur Dr Palo Alto CA 94304-2203

SKELLAND, ANTHONY HAROLD PETER, chemical engineering educator; b. Birmingham, Eng., Feb. 21, 1928; came to U.S., 1959; s. Harold and Hilda Skelland. BSChemE, U. Birmingham, 1948, PhD in Chem. Engring., 1952. Mgr. Procter and Gamble, Eng., 1954-56, R&D engr., 1956-59; asst. prof. Ill. Inst. Tech., Chgo., 1959-62; assoc. prof. U. Notre Dame, South Bend, Ind., 1962-66, prof., 1966-69; Ashland prof. U. Ky., Lexington, 1969-79; prof. Ga. Inst. Tech., Atlanta, 1979—. Cons. Monsanto, Babcock and Wilcox, Union Carbide, E.I. duPont de Nemours, FMC Corp., Westinghouse and others. Author: Non-Newtonian Flow and Heat Transfer, 1967, Diffusional Mass Transfer, 1974; contbr. over 80 articles to profl. jours. Fellow AIChE, Inst. Petroleum; mem. Royal Soc. Chemistry (Eng.), Inst. Chem. Engrs. (Eng.). Avocations: tennis, theater, dining out.

SKELLINGS, EDMUND, communications educator, poet; b. Ludlow, Mass., Mar. 12, 1932; s. Romeo Theodore Skellings and Lolita LaPlant; m. Louis Delores Noah, Aug. 17, 1962; 1 child, Sonnet. BA, U. Mass., 1957; PhD, U. Iowa, 1962; DFA (hon.), Internat. Fine Arts Coll., Miami, Fla. Dir., prof. Fla. Ctr. Electronic Comm., Fla. Atlantic U., Ft. Lauderdale, 1968—. Cons. IBM, Armonk, 1988-89. Author: Heart Attacks, 1976, Face Value, 1977, Showing My Age, 1978, Living Proof, 1985, Collected Poems, 1998; patent for computer colortext. Sgt. airborne divsn. U.S. Army, 1951-54, Ft. Bragg. Named Poet Laureate, Gov. of Fla. Avocation: computers. Office: Fla Atlantic U 111 E Las Olas Blvd Fort Lauderdale FL 33301 E-mail: skellings@bellsouth.net.

SKELLY, JOHN JOSHUA, retired clergyman, fundraiser; b. Central Falls, R.I., Oct. 25, 1932; s. Joshua Essa and Catherine (Hermiz) S.; m. Una C. Meadowcroft, June 21, 1959 (div.); children: Timothy John, Joan Louise, Steven Allan. BSBA, Pepperdine U., 1956; BD, San Francisco Theol. Sem.,

1959, DS in Theology, 1981; DD, Tarkio Coll., 1971. Asst. pastor First Presbyn. Ch., Granada Hill, Calif., 1959-61; pastor Port Hueneme (Calif.) Presbyn. Ch., 1961-65; v.p. devel. Pikeville (Ky.) Coll., 1967-69; sr. pastor Westminster Presbyn. Ch., Topeka, 1969-72; v.p. seminary rels. San Francisco Theol. Sem., 1972-83; pres. Pacific Homes Found., Woodland Hills, Calif., 1988-99; ret. Area counselor The Fifty Million Fund, United Presbyn. Ch., Kans.-Mo., 1965-67; mission devel. cons., 1967—; cons. Model Cities Program, Pikeville, 1968; campaign cons. United Way, L.A., 1986-87. V.p. student body Pepperdine U., L.A., 1955-56; pres. Hueneme-Oxnard Ministerial Assn., Port Hueneme, 1962; chmn. law enforcement com. Ventura County Grand Jury, 1964-65; chaplain of the day Ho. of Reps., State of Kans., 1970. Staff sgt. U.S. Army, 1950-52. Named Most Inspirational Player, Pepperdine Rugby Club, L.A., 1955, Outstanding Young Men of Am., U.S. Jr. C. of C., Port Hueneme, 1964. Democrat. Avocations: gardening, cooking middle eastern food, swimming, biking, golf. Home and Office: 7969 Sentinel San Diego CA 92127-2569

SKELTON, CAROL, member of parliament; b. Dec. 12, 1945; m. Noel Skelton; 3 children. Farmer, Harris, Canada; past coord. Can. Blood Svc.; mem. House of Commons, Ottawa, Canada, 2000—, dep. house leader ofcl. opposition, ofcl. opposition dep. critic health. Vice-chair leader's com. sr. issues Can. Alliance; adv. com. Min. of Health on Alcohol, Drugs and Youth, Saskatchewan; past bd. dirs. Saskatchewan Rsch. Coun., Can. 4-H Coun.; mem. mgmt. com. Saskatchewan Party. Can. Alliance Caucus. Office: House of Commons Rm 400 Justice Bldg Ottawa ON K1A 0A6 Canada Address: 940 E 22nd St E Saskatoon SK S7M 0S1 Canada E-mail: skelton@canadianalliance.ca.

SKELTON, DOUGLAS H. architect; b. Cottage Grove, Oreg., Apr. 17, 1939; s. Harry Edward and Mary Jane S.; m. Bonita L. Baker, June 17, 1961; children: Paul D., Cynthia J., Justin D. Student, Oreg. State U., 1957—59; degree in Architecture, U. Oreg., 1963. Registered arch., Oreg. Draftsman Payne & Struble Architecture, Medford, Oreg., 1965-66; intern Wayne Struble Arch., Medford, 1966-70, assoc. arch., 1973-78; project arch. William Seibert Arch., Medford, 1970-73; ptnr. Struble & Skelton Archs., Medford, 1978-83; owner Douglas Skelton Arch., Medford, 1983-89; ptnr. Skelton, Straus & Seibert Archs., Medford, 1989—. Design bldg. renovation (911 Mag. 1991, Excellence in Sch. Architecture AS&U mag. 1987); arch. Jacksonville, Oreg. Libr. (Best Contemp. Design, 2003). Mem. So. Oreg. Regional Econ. Devel. Inc.; bd. dirs. Rogue Valley Christian Ch., 1990—. Recipient Design Competition award Lake Creek Learning Ctr., 1998, Best Contemporary Bldg. Jacksonville Libr. award Hist. Arch. Rev. Commn., 2003. Mem. AIA (pres. So. Oreg. chpt.), AIA Oreg. (treas. 1989), Nation Trust for Hist. Preservation, Rotary (pres. Jacksonville/Applegate chpt. 1998-99), Medford/Jackson County C. of C. Avocations: camping, fishing, boating. Office: Skelton Straus & Seibert Architects and Planners LLP 26 Hawthorne Ave Medford OR 97504-7114

SKELTON, ISAAC NEWTON, IV, (IKE SKELTON), congressman; b. Lexington, Mo., Dec. 20, 1931; s. Isaac Newton and Carolyn (Boone) S.; m. Susan B. Anding, July 22, 1961; children: Ike, Jim, Page. AA, Wentworth Military Acad., 1951; AB, U. Mo., 1953, LLB, 1956. Bar: Mo. 1956. Pvt. practice, Lexington; pros. atty. Lafayette County, Mo., 1957-60; spl. asst. atty. gen., 1961-63; mem. Mo. Senate from 28th dist., 1971-76, 95th-107th Congresses from 4th Mo. Dist., 1977—, ranking minority mem. ho. armed svcs. com. Active Boy Scouts Am. Mem. Phi Beta Kappa, Sigma Chi, Masons, Shriners, Elks. Democrat. Mem. Christian Ch. Home: 6754 Towne Lane Rd Mc Lean VA 22101-2935 Office: US Ho of Reps 2206 Rayburn House Ofc Bldg Washington DC 20515-2876

SKELTON, WILLIAM DOUGLAS, physician; MD, Emory U., 1963. Sr. v.p. rsch. and health affairs Mercer U., Macon, Ga., 1985—2004; dist health dir. East Health Dists. 9-1 and 9-3, Savannah, Ga., 2004—. Office: East Health Dist 9-1 2011 Eisenhower Dr Savannah GA 31416-1257 Office Phone: 912-356-2233. E-mail: wdskelton@gdph.state.ga.us.

SKERKER, ARTHUR J. secondary school educator; Sci. tchr. Hartford (Conn.) Pub. H.S., 1995, computer resource tchr., 1995—. Named State Tchr. of Yr., Sci., Conn., 1993. Office: Hartford Public High Sch 55 Forest St Hartford CT 06105-3243

SKERRITT, TOM, actor; b. Detroit, Aug. 25, 1933; Student, Wayne State U., UCLA. Films: War Hunt, 1962, One Man's Way, 1964, Those Calloways, 1964, M*A*S*H, 1970, WIld Rovers, 1972, Fuzz, 1972, Big Bad Mama, 1974, Thieves Like Us, 1974, The Devil's Rain, 1975, The Turning Point, 1977 (Nat. Bd. Rev. Best Supporting Actor), Up In Smoke, 1978, Alien, 1979, Ice Castles, 1979, Silence of the North, 1981, A Dangerous Summer, 1981, Savage Harvest, 1981, Fighting Back, 1982, The Dead Zone, 1983, Top Gun, 1986, Space Camp, 1987, The Big Town, 1987, Wisdom, 1987, Opposing Force, 1987, Maid to Order, 1987, Poltergeist III, 1988, Steel Magnolias, 1989, Big Man On Campus, 1990, The Rookie, 1991, Blue Movie Blue, 1991, Poison Ivy, 1991, A River Runs Through It, 1992, Contact, 1997, The Other Sister, Texas Rangers, 2000, Tears of the Sun, 2003; TV shows: Ryan's Four, 1983, Contact, 1997, On The Edge, 1987, Cheers, 1987-88, Picket Fences, 1992-96 (Emmy award Outstanding Lead Actor in a Drama Series, 1993); guest star Will and Grace, 2003, West Wing, 2003; TV movies: The Bird Man, The Last Day, Maneaters Are Loose!, Calendar Girl Murders, Miles to Go, True Believer, Parent Trap II, A Touch of Scandal, Poker Alice, Nightmare At Bitter Creek, Moving Target, The Heist, Red King White Knight, The China Lake Murders, Child of the Night, In Sickness and In Health, Getting Up and Going Home, Divided By Hate, 1997, What the Deaf Man Heard, The Heart of the Unicorn Killer, 1999, Aftershock, 1999, American Daughter, 2000, High Noon, 2000, Jacqueline Bouvier Kennedy Onassis: Alife, 2000, Path to War, 2002. Office: Guttman Assocs 118 S Beverly Dr Beverly Hills CA 90212-3003

SKIDD, THOMAS PATRICK, JR., lawyer; s. Thomas Patrick and Anna Skidd; m. Judith Chase Roberts, Sept. 10, 1960; children: Suanne C., Sherry E., Thomas Patrick III, Jody E. BA in Econs. cum laude, Georgetown U., 1958; LLB, Yale U., 1961. Bar: Conn. 1961, U.S. Supreme Ct. 1963. Ptnr., prin. Cummings & Lockwood LLC, Stamford, Conn., 1961—. Mem. Conn. Bar Assn. (real estate sect. and land use sect.), Stamford-Norwalk Regional Bar Assn., Roton Point Club (Rowayton, Conn.). Roman Catholic. Avocation: phonograph record collector. Office: Cummings & Lockwood LLC 107 Elm St 11th Fl Stamford CT 06904-0120 Office Phone: 203-351-4409.

SKIDMORE, DONALD EARL, JR., government official; b. Tacoma, Apr. 27, 1944; s. Donald E. and Ingeborg (Johnsrud) S. BS, Evangel. Coll., 1968; grad., Bellevue (Wash.) Police Acad., 1992. With Dept. Social and Health Svcs. State of Wash., Yakima, 1967-74; quality rev. splst. Social Security Adminstrn., Seattle, 1974-76; program analyst Balt., 1976-79, Seattle, 1979-81; quality assurance officer, mgr. Satellite office Spokane, Wash., 1981-84; program analyst Seattle, 1984-90; mgmt. analyst, 1990—. V.p., trustee Norwood Village, 1987-90; vice chair ops. subcom., mem. citizen's adv. com. land use planning, Bellevue, Wash., 1988-90; pres., bd. dirs. Compton Ct. Condo Assn., 1980-81. Office: 701 5th Ave Seattle WA 98104-7097

SKIDMORE, JAMES ALBERT, JR., management, computer technology and engineering services company executive; b. Newark, June 30, 1932; s. James A. and Frances W. (Barker) S.; m. Peggy Ann Young, July 10, 1954; children: Jacqueline Sue, James Albert III. BA, Muhlenberg Coll., 1954; postgrad., Duke U., 1984. Customer sales rep. N.J. Bell Tel. Co., Newark, 1957-65, then dist. sales mgr., divsn. mktg. mgr.; asst. to pres. for pub. affairs Pepsi Co., Inc., N.Y.C., 1967—69; asst. to Pres. of U.S., 1968-69; v.p. Handy Assoc., N.Y.C., 1969—71, pres., 1972; pres., CEO Sci. Mgmt. Corp., Basking Ridge, N.J., 1972—; chmn. bd. dirs. Newark Brush Co., 1974-79. Bd. dirs. United Jersey Banks, United Jersey Bank, Franklin State Bank; mem. exec. com. UJB Fin.-Summit Bank, 1985-93, Blue Cross & Blue Shield N.J., Inc., Enterprise Holding Co., Inc.; exec. com., trustee Blue Cross of N.J., 1983—; dir. Coca Cola, N.Y., 1980-85, Mariner Comm., 1983-85, Horizon Blue Cross Blue Shield N.J., Pa., N.Y., Del., 1998—; mem., chmn. mktg. com. Seton Hall Commn., 1987; trustee Rutgers U. Grad. Sch. Mgmt., 1989—; trustee Pub. Affairs Rsch. Inst. N.J., 1988-99; lectr. U. Amsterdam, 1967, U. Toronto, U. Helsinki, 1967, Tokyo U. Guest columnist Rotary Internat. mag., 1966-68, Kiwanis mag., 1966-68, Japan Times on Cmty. Responsibility and Leadership, 1965-67. Mem. Nat. Commn. on Crime and Delinquency, 1965-66; mem. Nat. Commn. on Youth Employment, 1966-67; state chmn. N.J. Nat. Found. March of Dimes, 1966-73; mem. exec. bd. Watchung Area coun. Boy Scouts Am., 1972-77, dir. N.E. region, 1983-90; mem. Citizen's Adv. Bd. on Youth Opportunity, 1969-75; state chmn. United Citizens for Nixon-Agnew, N.J., 1968; nat. bd. govs. Alpha Tau Omega Found., 1967-73; treas. Jr. Chamber Internat., 1967-68; bd. dirs. Muhlenberg Coll., Allentown, Pa., 1980-92, 2001—, N.E. region Boy Scouts Am., 1983—; trustee Brick Twp. Hosp., Inc., Brick Town, N.J., 1976-80; bd. dirs. Am. Christmas Trains and Trucks, chmn., 1966-67; pres. Project Concern, San Diego, 1966-78; trustee The Scholarship Fund for Inner-City Children, 1997—, Ctr. for Analysis of Pub. Issues, 1999—. Served to capt. USMCR, 1954-57. Decorated Order of St. John (Eng.); recipient Internat. Understanding award, Brussels, 1966, Disting. Svc. award, St. Paul, 1966, Freedom Found. George Washington Medal of Honor award, 1965, Outstanding Achievement in Life award Muhlenberg Coll. Alumni, 1966, Amb. award U.S. Jaycees, 1977, Trinidad and Tobago award Prime Minister of Ireland, 1970, Human Rels. award Soc. Advancement of Mgmt., 1982, Statesman award N.J. Jaycees, 1983, Disting. Citizens award Boy Scouts Am., 1983, Pvt. Sector Initiative award Pres. Reagan, 1985; named among Am.'s Ten Outstanding Young Men, Look Mag. and U.S. Jaycees, 1968; inducted into U.S. Jaycees Hall of Leadership, 1983. Mem. N.J. State C. of C. (bd. dirs. 1984-2003), Jr. C. of C., Muhlenberg Coll. Alumni Assn., Alpha Tau Omega, Sky Club (N.Y.C.), Baltusrol Golf Club, Longboat Key Club. Home: 641 Ocean Ave Sea Girt NJ 08750 also: 1465 Gulf Of Mexico Dr Longboat Key FL 34228-3447 Office: Sci Mgmt Co LLC 745 US Hwy 202/206 Bridgewater NJ 08807-1760 Office Phone: 908-722-0300.

SKIDMORE, JOYCE THORUM, public relations and communication executive; b. Dec. 30, 1926; d. Rolla Arden and Alice Luetta (Fox) Thorum; m. E. Douglas Jacobsen, Mar. 20, 1956 (dec.); 1 child, Kelly Douglas Jacobsen; m. Clarence E. Skidmore Jr., Aug. 9, 1969. BS, U. Utah, 1950, postgrad., 1953-55, U. So. Calif., 1964, U. Calif., Irvine, 1973-74, Cambridge (Eng.) U., 1992. Sales and promotion devel. JBL Internat., L.A., 1959-69; press sec. Utah Auditor's Office, Salt Lake City, 1979-81; pres., owner Joyce Skidmore Cons./Snowflake Prodns., 1980—; pub. affairs officer Babcock Performing Readers, 2003—. Adminstrv. asst. world hdqs. Toastmasters Internat., Santa Ana, Calif., 1973; adj. prof. comms. Pepperdine U., 1974; developer human resources, Oran, Algeria, 1975; promotions coord. Utah Bicentennial Project, Salt Lake City, 1976; adj. prof. Westminster Coll., 1978-79, 92-93, Brigham Young U., 1978—; cons., pub. rels. health costs and tourism C. of C. of Salt Lake Area; adj. prof. mktg. and comm. dept. and theater/film dept. Colo. Mountain Coll., 1985-86; bus. cons., prof. mktg. and comms. Mountainwest Coll. Bus. and Brigham Young U., Salt Lake City; cons. Hema U.S.A., Westline and Bunell Inc.; guest dir., writer Cablevision, Newport Beach, Calif., 1975; initiated use of old copper from Utah Capitol dome as collector's item, 1980; lectr. in field; writer pub. svc. announcements. Author: Happy Holidays, 1968; assoc. editor Utah Symphony newsletter; newsletter editor Nat. Auditor's Assn., 1979-81, State Auditor's Assn., 1979-81, Utah Health Fairs, 1982-83; journalist The Butler Banner; editor: Saga Weekly Post, Children's Page, Stavanger and Bergen, Norway, 1976-78; playwright, dir., author book and lyrics: (musical) They Came to Union Fort; playwright, dir. hist. musicals Shadows, Danish Dreams, A Perfect Picture; contbr. weekly columns to The Rifle Telegram; contbr. articles to Calif., Colo., Norwegian and Utah newspapers; author nat. bus. newsletters and family history newsletters; owner/performer: Tell Me a Story. Actress Taylorsville Arts Coun. 2003, Taylorsville Tombstone Days, 2004, Babcock Theatre U. Utah, 2003; chair Playwright's Cir. Competition, 2004; Utah dir. Nat. Health Screening Coun. for Vol. Orgns., Bethesda, Md., 1982-83; guest dir. Westminster Theatre, 1974; organizer Stavanger Theatre Guild and Workshops, 1977, Bookcliffs Arts and Humanities Coun., 1984-86; originator, organizer Hurlburt Days, Grand Valley and Parachute, Colo.; initiator, dir. Reader's Theatre, Comty. Christmas Festival; dir. Storytelling Festival, Neil Simon Night; promoter Salt Lake Arts Festival, Am. Geneal. Lending Libr. World Hdqs.; appearance Japanese condr. in Salt Lake City; Sister-City exch. Salt Lake and Matsumoto, Japan; fundraiser Utah Symphony Guild; dir. theater Art Barn, Salt Lake City; mem. steering com. 1st nat. competition Utah Playwriting Conf., Sundance, 1979-80; mem. local econ. devel. coun.; polit. dist. del., 1986; initiated invitation from Bergen Internat. Festival to Utah Symphony, 1981; campaign mgr. Mayor Lake Valley City, Utah, 1982; cons. Cottonwood Heights (Utah) Coun., 1982-83; cons. to Utah pres. Instrumentation Soc. Am.; co-chair advt. Utah Symphony Guild; winter and summer fundraisers Carousel Ball and Taste of the Town, 1988-89; guest dir., historian MMB Reading Arts Soc., 1988-89; promoter Utah Arts Orgns.; missionary leader Ch. of Jesus Christ of Latter-day Saints; v.p. Pub. Awareness RP Found. Fighting Blindness; dir. Internat. First Night Festival, Salt Lake City, 1993-2001; bd. dirs. Utah Centennial Commn., The Found. Fighting Blindness, 1st Night Festival of the Arts; com. mem. Sister City, Dresden; storyteller August Cult. Arts Festival, 2004. Recipient Best Dir. statue, Colo., 2 Top Editor's awards Calif. Press Women, 1977, 4 writing awards 1977-78, Internat. Yr. of Child award Family Acad., San Francisco and Stavanger, 1979, Colo. Oscar award for Best Dir., 1986, Congl. Cup, Utah Polo Club; nat. Zeta Phi Eta scholar, 1948, So. Calif. Credit Assn. scholar, 1964; U. Utah fellow, 1953-55 Mem. LWV (dist. pres. 1976), Pub. Rels. Soc. Am. (student adv. 1980-82), Utah Press Women (6 writing awards 1979-81, 3d v.p. 1981-82), Instrument Soc. Am., Friendship Force Utah, MMB Reading Arts Soc. (v.p. devel.), Internat. Platform Assn., Daus. of Utah Pioneers (capt. Union Fort camp 1998-2000), Utah Polo Club (bd. dirs.), Japan-Am. Soc. (bd. dirs., with pub. affairs 1993-2000), Utah Storytelling Guild, UN Assn. Utah, Babcock Performing Readers (pres. 1996-2000, One-Act Play award 2002), Internat. Soroptomist Club (pub. affairs dir.), Fima Voyagers France. Avocations: historian, extensive genealogical research, global business and education research programs, screenwriting for film and tv. Home and Office: 2629 Oak Creek Dr Sandy UT 84093-6522 Office Phone: 801-942-2431.

SKIGEN, PATRICIA SUE, lawyer; b. Springfield, Mass., June 16, 1942; d. David P. and Gertrude H. (Hirschhaut) Skigen; m. Irwin J. Sugarman, May 1973 (div. Nov. 1994); 1 child, Alexander David Sugarman; m. Gary W. Guttman, May 2001. BA with distinction, Cornell U., 1964; LLB, Yale U., 1968. Bar: N.Y. 1968, U.S. Dist. Ct. (so. dist.) N.Y. 1969. Law clk. Anderson, Mori & Rabinowitz, Tokyo, 1966-67; assoc. Rosenman Colin Kaye Petschek Freund & Emil, N.Y.C., 1968-70, Willkie Farr & Gallagher, N.Y.C., 1970-75, ptnr., 1977-95; v.p., corp. fin. group legal dept. J.P. Morgan Chase & Co., N.Y.C., 1995—2002, mng. dir., assoc. gen. counsel, 2002—. Dep. supt., gen. counsel N.Y. State Banking Dept., N.Y.C., 1975-77, first dep. supt. banks, 1977; adj. prof. Benjamin Cardozo Law Sch. Yeshiva U., 1979. Contbr. articles to profl. jours. Cornell U. Dean's scholar, 1960-64, Regent's scholar, 1960-64, Yale Law Sch. scholar, 1964-68. Mem.: ABA (corp. banking and bus. law sect.), Assn. of Bar of City of N.Y. (chmn. com. banking 1991—94, long range planning com. 1994—96, audit com. 1994—2001), Phi Kappa Phi, Phi Beta Kappa. Office: JP Morgan Chase and Co 270 Park Ave Fl 40 New York NY 10017-2014

SKILES, JAMES JEAN, electrical engineer, computer engineer, educator; b. St. Louis, Oct. 16, 1928; s. Coy Emerson and Vernetta Beatrice (Maples) Skiles; m. Deloris Audrey McKenney, Sept. 4, 1948; children: Steven, Randall, Jeffrey. BSEE, Washington U., St. Louis, 1948; MS, U. Mo.-Rolla, 1951; PhD, U. Wis., 1954. Engr. Union Electric Co., St. Louis, 1948-49; instr. U. Mo., Rolla, 1949-51; instr. elec. engring. U. Wis., Madison, 1951—54, prof. elec. engring., 1954-89, prof. emeritus, 1989—, chmn. Dept. Elec. Engring., 1967-72, dir. Univ. Industry Rsch. program, 1972-75, dir. Energy Rsch. Ctr., 1975-95. Cons. in field. Contbr. articles to profl. jours. Mem. Monona Grove Dist. Sch. Bd., Wis., 1961—69; mem. adv. com. Wis. Energy Office, Madison, 1979—80, Wis. Pub. Svc. Commn., 1980—81. Recipient Kiekhofer Tchg. award, 1955, Wis. Electric Utilities Professorship in Energy Engring., U. Wis., 1975—89, Benjamin Smith Reynolds Tchg. award, 1980, Acad. Elec. Engring. award, U. Mo. - Rolla, 1982. Mem.: IEEE (sr.), Am. Soc. Engring. Edn. Home: 8099 Coray Ln Verona WI 53593-9073 Office: Univ of Wisconsin Dept Elec & Computer Engring 1415 Engineering Dr Madison WI 53706 1607 Personal E-mail: skiles@engr.wisc.edu.

SKILES, SCOTT ALLEN, professional basketball coach; b. LaPorte, Ind., Mar. 5, 1964; Profl. basketball player Milwaukee Bucks, 1986—87, Ind. Pacers, 1987—89, Orlando Magic, 1989—94, Wash. Bullets, 1994—95, Phila. 76ers, 1995—96; asst. coach Phoenix Suns, 1997-99, head coach, 1999—2002, Chgo. Bulls, 2003—. Office: c/o Chgo Bulls 1901 W Madison St Chicago IL 60612*

SKILLERN, FRANK FLETCHER, law educator; b. Sept. 26, 1942; s. Will T. and Vera Catherine (Ryberg) S.; m. Susan Schlaefer, Sept. 3, 1966; children: Nathan Edward, Leah Catherine. AB, U. Chgo., 1964; JD, U. Denver, 1966; LLM, U. Mich., 1969. Bar: Colo. 1967, Tex. 1978. Pvt. practice law, Denver, 1967; gen. atty. Maritime Adminstrn., Washington, 1967-68; asst. prof. law Ohio No. U., 1969-71, Tex. Tech U., Lubbock, 1971-73, assoc. prof. law, 1973-75, prof. law, 1975—, George W. McCleskey prof. water law, 1998—. Vis. prof. U. Tex. Law Sch., summer 1979, U. Ark. Law Sch., 1979-80, U. Tulsa Coll. Law, 1981-82; cons. and speaker in field. Author: Environmental Protection: The Legal Framework, 1981, 2d edit. published as Environmental Protection Deskbook, 1995, Regulation of Water and Sewer Utilities, 1989, Texas Water Law, Vol. I, 1988, rev. edit., 1992, Vol. II, 1991; contbr. chpts. to Powell on Real Property, Zoning and Land Use Controls, others; author cong. procs. and numerous articles. Mem. ABA (mem. publs. com. Sect. Natural Resources Law 1984—, vice chair internat. environ. law com. Sect. Natural Resources Law 1987). Office: Tex Tech U Sch Law PO Box 40004 Lubbock TX 79409-0004 Home: 2333 Table Rock Rd Boise ID 83712-7544

SKILLERN, FRANK L., JR., bank executive; Gen. counsel FDIC, 1979-81; law practice Dallas and Washington; with IDS, 1983-89; pres., CEO, Acuma Unit, Am. Express, London, 1989-91; chmn., pres. Am. Express Centurion Bank, N.Y.C., 1991—; exec. v.p. Optima Card and consumer lending svcs. Am. Express Travel Related Svcs. Co., Inc., N.Y.C., 1991—.

SKILLINGSTAD, CONSTANCE YVONNE, social services administrator, educator; b. Portland, Oreg, Nov. 18, 1944; d. Irving Elmer and Beulah Ruby (Aleckson) Erickson; M. David W. Skillingstad, Jan. 12, 1968 (div. Mar. 1981); children: Michael, Brian. BA in Sociology, U. Minn., 1966; MBA, U. St. Thomas, St. Paul, 1982. Cert. vol. adminstr.; lic. social worker; lic. real estate agt. Social worker Rock County Welfare Dept., Luverne, Minn., 1966-68, Hennepin County Social Svc., Mpls., 1968-70, vol. coord., 1970-78, St. Joseph's Home for Children, Mpls., 1978-89, mgr. cmty. resources, 1989-94; exec. dir. Mpls. Crisis Nursery, 1994-97; mem. cmty. faculty Met. State U., St. Paul and Mpls., 1980-97; faculty U. St. Thomas Ctr. for Non Profit Mgmt., 1990—2001; asst. adminstr. St. Joseph's Home for Children, Mpls., 1997-98; asst. dir. Cath. Charities of Archdiocese of St. Paul and Mpls., 1998-2000; dir. mem. svc. Minn. Coun. Founds., 2001—02; exec. dir. Prevent Child Abuse Minn., St. Paul, 2002—; pres. Golden Girl Homes, Inc., 2001—. Trainer, mem. adv. commn. Mpls. Vol. Ctr., 1978-90, cons., 1980—, chmn. Contbr. articles to Jour. Vol. Adminstrn. Mem. adv. bd. MADD, Minn., 1986-88, Stop It Now! Minn., 2003, Congregations Concerned for Children, 2002—; vice chmn., chmn. adminstrv. coun., lay leader Hobart United Meth. Ch.; lay rep. to Minn. Ann. Conf. of Meth. Chs., 1989-92; chmn. social concerns. commn. Pk. Ave. United Meth. Ch., 1992—; bd. dir. Ctr. for Grief, Loss and Transition; mem. Initiative for Violence Free Families, 1998—. Named one of Oustanding Young Women in Am., 1974, Woman of Distinction Mpls. St. Paul Mag./ Sta. KARE-TV, 1995. Mem. Minn. Assn. Vol. Dirs. (pres. 1975, sec., ethics chmn. 1987—), Assn. for Vol. Adminstrn. (v.p. regional affairs 1985-87, mem. assessment panel 1986-94, coord. nat. tng. team, cert. process for vol. adminstr. 1988-92, profl. devel. chair 1990-92), Minn. Social Svcs. Assn. (pres. 1981, 98-99, bd. dirs. 1996-2001, legis. com., Disting. Svc. award 1987). Mem. Dem.-Farmer-Labor Party. Methodist. Avocations: bridge, volleyball, accordion, travel, reading. Office: Prevent Child Abuse Minn Ste 202-S 1821 University Ave Saint Paul MN 55104 Home: 4906 Sycamore Dr Saint Paul MN 55123-4912 Office Phone: 651-523-0099. Business E-Mail: cskillingstad@pcamn.org. E-mail: cskillingstad@msn.com.

SKILLMAN, BECKY SUE, state legislator; b. Bedford, Ind., Sept. 26, 1950; d. Jack Delmar and Catherine Louise (Flinn) Foddrill; m. Stephen E. Skillman, 1969. Dep. recorder Lawrence County, 1971-76, county recorder, 1977-84; clerk Lawrence County crct. ct., 1985—; mem. Ind. Senate from 44th dist., 1992—. Co-dir. Lawrence County Young Reps., 1973-78; co-chmn. State Young Reps. Conv., 1975, 77; vice chmn. Lawrence County Rep. Ctrl. Com. Office: Ind Senate Dist 44 200 W Washington St Indianapolis IN 46204-2728

SKILLMAN, ERNEST EDWARD, JR., real estate sales and management executive; b. New Orleans, Oct. 3, 1937; s. Ernest Edward and Helen Cecilia (Klein) S BA, La. State U., 1960, postgrad. in law, 1960-61; postgrad., Southeastern La. U., 1973. intelligence work for USN, 1960—. Commd. USN, 1961—99, advanced through grades to admiral, ret., 1999; Engaged in real estate mgmt. Baton Rouge, 1964—; sales, 1969—. Sustaining mem. Republican Nat. Com., 1976—, life mem., 1980—, mem. congressional com., 1978—; mem. pres.'s club Democratic Nat. Com., 1979—; mem. Rep. Presdl. Task Force; mem. Jackson (La.) Assembly. Mem.: Grad. Realtors Inst., Rep. Senatorial Inner Circle (Washington), Feliciana C. of C., Mil. Order World Wars (life), U.S. Naval Inst. (life), La. Mem. Aviation Mus. Assn. (charter life), Submarine Force Library and Mus. Assn. (life), Res. Officers Assn. (life), Ret. Officers Assn. (life), Navy League U.S. (life), Am. Contract Bridge League (sr. master), Army and Navy Club (pres. comdr. USS Kidd DD661 Navy Club 1997—98, cmdr. 1997—98), Amvets (cmdr. 1985—87, pres. Foss-Landry Post #2 1985—87), Kiwanis, Am. Legion, Sigma Chi (life). Roman Catholic. Home: 753 Kenilworth Pky Baton Rouge LA 70808-5716 Office: 4150 Perkins Rd Baton Rouge LA 70808-3027 E-mail: ernies1937@aol.com.

SKILLMAN, WILLIAM ALFRED, consulting engineering executive; b. Lakehurst, N.J., Jan. 22, 1928; s. Wilbur Newton and Greta Alfreda (Ekman) S.; m. Anne Marie Cavender, Sept. 19, 1948; children: Thomas R., Gregory A., Karen L. BS in Engring. Physics, Lehigh U., 1952; MS in Physics, U. Rochester, 1954. Assoc. engr. Westinghouse Electric Corp., Balt., 1954-56, engr., 1956-58, sr. engr., 1958-61, supervisory engr., 1961-64, adv. engr., 1964-73, sr. adv. engr., 1973-85, cons. engr., 1986-93, cons. electronic systems group, 1993—. Author: Radar Calculations Using the TI-59 Programmable Calculator, 1983; author: (with others) Radar Handbook, 2d edit., 1990; patentee in field Served with USN, 1946-48. Fellow IEEE (life, Dennis J. Picard medal for radar technologies and applications 2003); mem. Aerospace and Electronic Sys. Soc. (Pioneer award 1995), Phi Beta Kappa. Republican. Methodist. Avocations: photography, travel, genealogy, programming. Home and Office: 605 Forest View Rd Linthicum Heights MD 21090-2819 E-mail: wskillman@aol.com.

SKILLRUD, HAROLD CLAYTON, minister, retired bishop; b. St. Cloud, Minn., June 29, 1928; s. Harold and Amanda Skillrud; m. Lois Dickhart, June 8, 1951; children: David, Janet, John. BA magna cum laude, Gustavus Adolphus Coll., 1950; MDiv magna cum laude, Augustana Theol. Sem., Rock Island, Ill., 1954; STM, Luth. Sch. Theology, Chgo., 1969; DD (hon.), Augustana Coll., 1978, Newberry Coll., 1988. Ordained to ministry Evang. Luth. Ch. in Am., 1954. Supply pastor Saron Luth. Ch., Big Lake, Minn., 1950-51; mem. staff 1st Luth. Ch., Rock Island, Ill., 1951-52; intern, organizer new mission Faith Luth. Ch., Syosset, N.Y., 1952-53; sr. pastor St. John's Luth. Ch., Bloomington, Ill., 1954-79, Luth. Ch. of the Redeemer, Atlanta, 1979-87; bishop Southeastern Synod Evang. Luth. Ch. in Am., Atlanta, 1987-95, regional rep. bd. pensions, 1995—. Del. to various convs. Luth. Ch. in Am., Luth. World Fedn. in Helsinki, 1963, mem. bd. publ., 1976-84, pastor-evangelist Evang. Outreach Emphasis program, 1977-79, mem. exec. bd. Ill. synod, 1977-79, pres. bd. publ., 1980-84, leader stewardship cluster Southeastern synod, 1983, mem. exec. bd. Southeastern synod, 1984-87; mem. exec. coun., Luth. Ch. in Am., 1984-87; mem. task force on new ch. design Commn. on New Luth. Ch., task force on ch. pub. house, 1985; del.

constituting conv. Evang. Luth. Ch. in Am., 1987, del. assemblies Evang. Luth. Ch. in Am., 1989, 91, 93, 95; mem. commn. on clergy confidentiality Luth. Coun. in USA, 1987; co-chair USA Luth.- Roman Cath. Dialogue, 1990-97; mem. Task Force on Theol. Edn. Author: LSTC: Decade of Decision, 1969; co-editor Scripture and Tradition, Lutherans and Catholics in Dialogue, 1995; mem. edtl. bd. Partners mag., 1978-80; contbr. articles and sermons to religious jours. Former bd. dirs. Augustana Theol. Sem.; bd. dirs. Augustana Coll., 1969-77, chmn. bd., 1976-77; bd. dirs. Kessler Reformation Collection, Newberry Coll., Luth. World Relief, Augsburg Fortress; chmn. bd. dirs. Luth. Sch. Theology, Chgo., 1962-69; mem. Leadership Atlanta, 1980-81, United Way, Atlanta, 1980-81; mem. Bishop's Commn. on Econ. Justice, 1985-86; pres. bd. dirs. Atlanta Samaritan House, 1986-87. Recipient Alumni award Luth. Sch. Theology, Chgo., 1976, award Leadership Atlanta, 1981, The Rev. John Bachman award, Luth. Theol. Sem., Columbia, S.C., 1996. Mem. Luth. Sch. Theology Alumni Assn. (pres. 1975-77), Conf. of Bishops, Kiwanis (pres. Midtown chpt. 1984-85). Lutheran. Avocations: travel, photography. Home: 368 E Wesley Rd NE Atlanta GA 30305-3824 E-mail: hcskillrud@aol.com.

SKINNER, ALASTAIR, retired accountant; m. Patricia Skinner; children: Lisa, Iain, James, Graeme. CA, Queens U., Kingston, Ont., Can., 1959; MBA, Harvard U., 1963. Cert. mgmt. cons. Served to maj. Can. Army Res., 1954-71; nat. mng. ptnr. MacGillivray & Co. (name now Grant Thornton), 1977-83; ptnr.-in-charge Toronto (Ont.) Office, Spicer MacGillivray (name now Grant Thornton), 1984-86, 88-91; ptnr. Grant Thornton, Toronto, 1991—2001, ret., 2001. Co-author: profl. manuals. Fellow Inst. Chartered Accts. of Ont. (pres. 1983-84), Soc. Mgmt. Accts. of Can. (bd. dirs.); mem. Inst. Mgmt. Cons. of Ont., Can. Tax Found. (bd. govs.), Pub. Accts. Coun. Ont. (pres. 1999-2000), Albany Club (Toronto), Devil's Glen Country Club (bd. dirs.). Avocations: skiing, bridge.

SKINNER, ANDREW CHARLES, history educator, religious writer; b. Durango, Colo., Apr. 25, 1951; s. Charles La Verne and Julia Magdalena (Schunk) S.; m. Janet Corbridge, Mar. 22, 1974; children: Cheryl Lyn, Charles Lon, Kelli Ann, Mark Andrew, Holly, Suzanne. BA with distinction, U. Colo., 1975; MA with distinction, Iliff Sch. Theology, Denver, 1978; ThM, Harvard U., 1980; PhD, U. Denver, 1986. Group mgr. May Co. Dept. Store, Denver, 1980-83; assoc. studio dir. Talking Books Pub. Co., Denver, 1984-88; instr. history Metro. State Coll., Denver, 1984-88; prof. history Ricks Coll., Rexburg, Utah, 1988-92; prof. ancient scripture Brigham Young U., Provo, Utah, 1992—, chmn. ancient scripture, 1997—, dean Coll. of Religious Edn., 2000—, dir. Religious Studies Ctr., 2000—. Vis. instr. ancient scripture Brigham Young U., 1987; vis. prof. Jerusalem Ctr. for Nr. Eastern Studies, Israel; cons. Univ. Without Walls, Loretto Heights Coll., Denver, 1985-88; mem. editl. staff Dead Sea Scrolls, publ. bd. Israel Antiquities Authority; gen. editor New Testament Commentary, Brigham Young U. Author chpts. numerous books including Gethsemane, 2002, Parables of the Latter Days, Golgotha, 2004; co-author: Jerusalem-The Eternal City, 1996, New Testament Apostles Testify of Christ, 1998, C.S. Lewis: The Man and His Message, 1999, Parables of the Latter Days, 2001, Discoveries in the Judaean Desert XXXIII-Qumran Cave 4; contbr. articles to profl. jours. Bishop Mormon Ch., Denver, 1986-88, Utah, 1996—; varsity scout leader Teton Parks coun. Boy Scouts Am., Rexburg, 1988-89; host Internat. Scholars Conf. on Holocaust and the Chs., 1995; bd. dirs. Children of Israel Found., 2001—, Inst. for Study and Preservation of Ancient Religious Texts, 2001—. Mil. history fellow U.S. Mil. Acad., 1989. Mem. Am. Hist. Assn., Soc. Bibl. Lit., Mormon History Assn., Phi Theta Kappa, Phi Alpha Theta. Mem. Lds Ch. Office: Brigham Young U Coll Religious Edn JSB 375-A Provo UT 84602

SKINNER, BRIAN JOHN, geologist, educator; b. Wallaroo, South Australia, Dec. 15, 1928; came to U.S., 1958, naturalized, 1963; s. Joshua Henry and Joyce Barbara Lloyd (Prince) S.; m. Helen Catherine Wild, Oct. 9, 1954; children: Adrienne Wild, Stephanie Wild, Thalassa Wild. B.Sc., U. Adelaide, Australia, 1950; A.M., Harvard U., 1952, PhD, 1955; D Engring. (hon.), Colo. Sch. Mines, 1998; DSc (hon.), U. Toronto, 1998. Lectr. U. Adelaide, 1955-58; research geologist U.S. Geol. Survey, 1958-62, chief br. exptl. geochemistry and mineralogy, 1962-66; prof. geology and geophysics, chmn. dept. Yale U., New Haven, 1966-73, Eugene Higgins prof., 1972—. Hugh Exton McKinstry Meml. lectr. Harvard U., 1978; Alex L. du Toit lectr. Combined Socs. South Africa, 1979; Cecil H. and Ida Green lectr. U. B.C., 1983; Thayer Lindsley Meml. lectr. Soc. Econ. Geologists, 1983; Soc. Econ. Geologists Overseas lectr., 1985; Hoffman lectr. Harvard U., 1986, Joubin-James lectr. U. Toronto, 1987; mem. exec. com. divsn. earth scis. NRC, 1966-69; chmn. com. mineral resources and the environ. Nat. Acad. Scis.-NRC, 1973-75; mem. Lunar Sample Analysis Planning Team, 1968-70, Lunar Sci. Rev. Bd., 1971-72, U.S. Nat. Com. for Geochemistry, 1966-67, U.S. Nat. Com. for Geology, 1973-77, 85-93, chmn., 1987-93, chmn. bd. earth scis. NRC, 1987-88, earth scis. and resources, 1989-90; mem. bd. Internat. Geol. Correlation Program, UNESCO-IUGS, 1985-89, 90-96, chmn., 1986-89; cons. Office Sci. and Tech. Policy, 1977-80, NSF, 1977-82; dir. Econ. Geology Pub. Co.; chmn. governing bd. Am. Jour. Sci., 1972—; pres. Econ. Geology Pub. Co., 1996-2000. Author: Earth Resources, 1969, 77, 86, Man and the Ocean, 1973, Physical Geology, 1974, 77, 87, Rocks and Rock Minerals, 1979, The New Iron Age Ahead, 1987, Resources and World Development, 1987, The Dynamic Earth, 1989, 92, 95, 2000, 03, The Blue Planet, 1995, 99, 2000, Environmental Geology, 1996, Geology Today, 1999, Oxford Companion to the Earth, 2000; editor: Econ. Geology, 1969-96, Oxford Univ. Press Monographs in Geological Sciences, 1979—, Internat. Geology Rev., 1995—2003; editl. bd. Am. Scientist, 1974-90, chmn., 1987-90. Trustee Hopkins Grammar Sch., 1978-83. Recipient Disting. Contbns. award, Assn. Earth Sci. Editors, 1979, medal, Geol. Assn. Can., 1998, Futer's medal, Inst. of Mining and Metallurgy, London, 2002; fellow, Guggenheim fellow, 1970. Fellow Geol. Soc. Am. (councillor 1976-78, chmn. spl. publs. com. 1980-81, chmn. com. on coms. 1983, pres. 1985); mem. Geochem. Soc. (pres. 1972-73), Conn. Acad. Sci. and Engring. (div. chmn. 1978-80, coun. 1982-87), Soc. Econ. Geologists (pres. 1995, Silver medal 1981, Marsden medal 2003). Home: PO Box 894 Woodbury CT 06798-0894

SKINNER, DANIEL THOMAS, language educator; b. Boston, May 1, 1916; s. Thomas Henson and Esther Hannetta (Jennings) Skinner; m. Vyna May Wingood, Oct. 15, 1944 (dec. Jan. 1995); children: David Edward, John Arnold. AB magna cum laude, Harvard U., 1938, PhD in Romance Lang., 1953; MA in Romance Lang., Boston Coll., 1939. Substitute instr. in French Va. State Coll., Ettrick, 1939—40; instr. in French and Spanish Dillard U., New Orleans, 1940—42; from asst. prof. to prof. French and Latin Morgan State Coll., Balt., 1946—81. Vis. prof. Tex. So. U., Houston, 1953—54, Houston, 1956, Towson State Coll., Balt., 1964; part-time prof. Sojourner-Douglass Coll., Balt., 1981—85, Coppin State Coll., Balt., 1985—90; mem. adv. bd. Directory of Am. Scholars, N.Y.C., 1970—80. Author: U.S. Teacher-Training Program: for France, 1959, Victor Hugo and L. Frechette, 1972, Ustaz Aswad (Black Professor), 1996. Pres. PTA, Balt., 1957. Named Rosenwald fellow, Rosenwald Found., Chgo., 1947—48, Fulbright prof. in France, Fulbright Found., Washington, 1956—57; recipient Nat. award, Urban League, Boston, 1949. Mem.: Frisby Hist. Soc. (fin. sec. 2001—02), Henson Family Soc., Phi Beta Kappa. Democrat. Roman Catholic. Avocations: movies, pinochle, sports, foreign travel. Home: 2033 Wheeler Ave Baltimore MD 21216-3225

SKINNER, ELLIOTT PERCIVAL, anthropology educator; b. Port-of-Spain, Trinidad-Tobago, June 20, 1924; came to the U.S., 1943; s. Joseph McDonald Skinner and Ettice Geraldine Frances; m. Thelma Garvin, Dec. 15, 1946 (div. Dec. 1976); children: Victor, Gail, Sagha, Touray; m. Gwendolyn Yolande Mikell, May 28, 1982; 1 child, Luce Mikell Remy. BA in Biology, NYU, 1951; MA in Anthropology, Columbia U., 1952, PhD in Anthropology, 1955; LLD (hon.), Lincoln (Pa.) U., 1990. Rsch. asst. anthropology Columbia U., N.Y.C., 1954-55, vis. asst. prof. anthropology, 1957-59, asst. prof. anthropology, 1959-63, 63-69, Franz-Boas prof. anthropology, 1969—, chmn. dept. anthropology, 1972-75. Tchr. Sunrise semester courses on Africa, NYU/WCBS-TV, 1960, 62; U.S. amb. to Upper Volta, Burkina-Faso, 1966-69; mem. rsch. adv. com. USAID, 1978-81; mem. black forum on fgn. policy TRANSAFRICA, 1996—; dir. Pre-Freshman Inst. on Pub. Policy and Diplomacy, Lincoln, 1993; lectr. and cons. in field. Author: The Mossi of Upper Volta: The Political Development of a Sudanese People, 1964, (with D. Chu) A Glorious Age in Africa, 1974 (Melville J. Herskovits prize for best book 1975), African-Americans and U.S. Policy Towards Africa, 1992. Bd. dirs. Fulbright Assn., Washington, 1990-95; trustee U. Bridgeport, Conn., 1995—. With U.S. Army, 1943-46, ETO. Recipient Commandeur de l'Ordre Nat. Voltaique, Pres. of the Republic of Upper Volta, 1968, Spl. Svc. award Faculty of the Borough of Manhattan C.C., 1974, Disting. Africanist award African Studies Assn., N.Y., 1986; named hon. citizen State of Tenn., 1983; Opportunity fellow John Hay Whitney Found., 1953, Columbia U. Traveling fellow, N.Y.C., 1954, Fulbright fellow U. Abidjan, Cote d'Ivoire, 1987. Fellow Internat. African Inst.; mem. Assn. Black Am. Ambs. (pres. 1988-92), Coun. on Fgn. Rels., Coun. Am. Ambs. Home: 700 New Hampshire Ave NW # 317 Washington DC 20037-2406 Office: Columbia Univ Dept Anthropology 460 Schermerhorn Ext New York NY 10027 E-mail: eps1@columbia.edu.

SKINNER, G(EORGE) WILLIAM, anthropologist, educator; b. Oakland, Calif., Feb. 14, 1925; s. John James and Eunice (Engle) S.; m. Carol Bagger, Mar. 25, 1951 (div. Jan. 1970); children: Geoffrey Crane, James Lauriston, Mark Williamson, Jeremy Burr; m. Susan Mann, Apr. 26, 1980; 1 dau., Alison Jane. Student, Deep Springs (Calif.) Coll., 1942-43; BA with distinction in Far Eastern Studies, Cornell U., Ithaca, N.Y., 1947, PhD in Cultural Anthropology, 1954; LLD (hon.), U. Hong Kong, 2001. Field dir. Cornell U. S.E. Asia program, also Cornell Research Center, Bangkok, Thailand, 1951-55; rsch. assoc. in Indonesia, 1956-58; asso. prof., then prof. anthropology Cornell U., Ithaca, N.Y., 1960-65; asst. prof. sociology Columbia, 1958-60; sr. specialist in residence East-West Ctr. Honolulu, 1965-66; prof. anthropology Stanford, 1966-89; Barbara Kimball Browning prof. humanities and scis., 1987-89; prof. anthropology U. Calif., Davis, 1990—. Vis. prof. U. Pa., 1977, Duke U., 1978, Keio U., Tokyo, 1985, 1988, U. Calif., San Diego, 1986, Hong Kong U., 2002; field rsch. China, 1949-50, 77, S.E. Asia, 1950-51, Thailand, 1951-53, 54-55, Java and Borneo, 1956-58, Japan, 1985, 88, 95; joint com. on contemporary China Social Sci. Research Coun.-Am. Acad. Learned Socs., 1961-65, 80-81, internat. com. on Chinese studies, 1963-64, mem. joint com. on Chinese studies, 1981-83; mem. subcom. rsch. Chinese Soc. Social Sci. Rsch. Coun., 1961-70, chmn., 1963-70; dir. program on East Asian Local Systems, 1969-71; dir. Chinese Soc. Bibliography Project, 1964-73; assoc. dir. Cornell China Program, 1961-63; dir. London-Cornell Project Social Rsch., 1962-65; mem. com. on scholarly communication with People's Republic of China, Nat. Acad. Scis., 1966-70, social scis. and humanities panel, 1982-83; adv. com. Ctr. for Chinese Rsch. Materials, Assn. Rsch. Libraries, 1967-70; bd. dirs. Nat. Ctr. for Geog. Info. and Analysis, 1989-92; policy and planning com. China in Time and Space, 1993-96; mem. mgmt. com. China Hist. GIS, 2000—. Author: Chinese Society in Thailand, 1957, Leadership and Power in the Chinese Community of Thailand, 1958; also articles; Editor: The Social Sciences and Thailand, 1956, Local, Ethnic and National Loyalties in Village Indonesia, 1959, Modern Chinese Society: An Analytical Bibliography, 3 vols, 1973, (with Mark Elvin) The Chinese City Between Two Worlds, 1974, (with A. Thomas Kirsch) Change and Persistence in Thai Society, 1975, The City in Late Imperial China, 1977, The Study of Chinese Society, 1979. Served to ensign USNR, 1943-46. Fellow Center for Advanced Study in Behavioral Scis., 1969-70, Guggenheim fellow, 1969, NIMH spl. fellow, 1970 Mem. NAS, AAAS, Am. Anthrop. Assn., Am. Sociol. Assn., Assn. Asian Studies (bd. dirs. 1962-65, chmn. nominating com. 1967-68, pres. 1983-84), Soc. for Cultural Anthropology, Internat. Union for Sci. Study of Population, Social Sci. History Assn., Am. Ethnol. Soc., Population Assn. Am., Siam Soc., Soc. Qing Studies, Soc. Econ. Anthropology, Phi Beta Kappa, Sigma Xi. Office: U Calif Dept Anthropology 1 Shields Ave Davis CA 95616-5270

SKINNER, JAMES E. corporate financial executive; Grad., Tex. Tech U. CPA. Ptnr. Ernst & Young, 1987—91; chief acctg. officer CompUSA, Dallas, 1991—94, CFO, exec. v.p., treas., 1994—2000; sr. v.p., CFO CapRock Comms. Corp., Dallas, 2000—01; CFO, sr. v.p. Neiman Marcus Group, 2001—. Office: Neiman Marcus Group 1618 Main St Dallas TX 75201*

SKINNER, JAMES LAURISTON, chemist, educator; b. Ithaca, N.Y., Aug. 17, 1953; s. G. William and Carol (Bagger) S.; m. Wendy Moore, May 31, 1986; children: Colin Andrew, Duncan Geoffrey. AB, U. Calif., Santa Cruz, 1975; PhD, Harvard U., 1979. Rsch. assoc. Stanford (Calif.) U., 1980-81; from asst. prof. to prof. chemistry Columbia U., N.Y.C., 1981-90; Hirschfelder prof. chemistry, dir. Theol. Chemistry Inst. U. Wis., Madison, 1990—. Vis. scientist Inst. Theol. Physics U. Calif., Santa Barbara, 1987; vis. prof. physics U. Jos. Fourier, Grenoble, France, 1987, U. Bordeaux (France), 1995. Contbr. articles to profl. jours. Recipient Fresenius award Phi Lambda Upsilon, 1989, Camille and Henry Dreyfus Tchr.-Scholar award, 1984, NSF Presdl. Young Investigator award, 1984, Humboldt Sr. Scientist award, 1993; NSF grad fellow, 1975, NSF postdoctoral fellow, 1980, Alfred P. Sloan Found. fellow, 1984, Guggenheim fellow, 1993. Mem. AAAS, Am. Chem. Soc., Am. Phys. Soc. Achievements include fundamental research in condensed phase theoretical chemistry. Office: U Wis Dept Chemistry Theoretical Chem Inst 1101 University Ave Madison WI 53706-1322

SKINNER, JAMES LISTER, III, English language educator; b. Emory, Ga., Sept. 24, 1938; s. James Lister and Josephine Norvell (Fry) S.; m. Ramona Ann York Skinner, Apr. 2, 1961; 1 child, James Lister Skinner IV. AB in English, N. Ga. Coll., Dahlonega, 1960; MA in English, U. Ark., Fayetteville, 1962, PhD in English, 1965. Comdr. Headquarters and Headquarters Battery 28th Artillery Group, Selfridge AFB, Mich., 1964-65; assoc. prof. English Presbyn. Coll., Clinton, SC, 1965-70, prof. English, 1970-92, Charles A. Dana prof. English, 1992—2003, chmn. The Russell Program, 1986-98, co-chmn. English dept., 1996-99, sr. faculty coun., 1995-98, chair sr. faculty coun., 1997-98, chair English dept., 1999-2001, Charles A. Dana prof. English emeritus, 2003—. NDEA fellow U. Ark., Fayetteville, 1960-63; NEH summer fellow Yale U., New Haven, Conn., 1976; hon. vis. fellow Leicester (Eng.) U., 1983; sec. Presbyterian Coll. Faculty, Clinton, S.C., 1995-98. Author: Boys Farm: A History, 2002; editor: The Autobiography of Henry Merrell: Industrial Missionary to the South, 1991, The Refugees: Roswell, 2004; co-editor: The Death of a Confederate, 1996. 1st lt. U.S. Army, 1963-65. Recipient Commendation medal U.S. Army, 1965; named Presbyterian Prof. of Yr. Presbyterian Coll., Clinton, S.C., 1991, State Prof. of Yr. Coun. for Advancement and Support of Edn., 1991, Gov's. Prof. of Yr., Gov. of S.C., Columbia, 1991, DAR History Award medal, 1998, Alumni Hall of Fame award No. Ga. Coll. and State U., 2004. Mem. Phi Beta Kappa, Omicron Delta Kappa, Alpha Psi Omega, Phi Alpha Theta, Sigma Tau Delta. Democrat. Presbyterian. Home: 108 E Maple St Clinton SC 29325-2836 Business E-Mail: jskinner@presby.edu.

SKINNER, JIM, food products executive; b. Davenport, IA; m. Kathleen Skinner; 1 child. Grad, Roosevelt U. Trainee, several positions with McDonald's Corp., 1971—; US zone v.p. McDonald's corp., 1987—92; sr. v.p., relationship ptnr., 1992—95; exec. v.p., internat. relationship ptnr. McDonald's Ctrl. Europe, Middle East, Africa, India, 1995—97; pres. McDonald's Europe, 1997—2001; pres., COO McDonald's Europe/Asia/Pacific and Middle East, 2001—02, McDonald's Restaurant Group, 2002—03; vice chmn. McDonald's Corp., 2003—. Adv. dir. (twice) McDonald's Corp. Bd. of Dirs. Bd. mem. Ronald McDonald House Charities. Office: McDonald's Corp McDonald's Plaza Oak Brook IL 60523

SKINNER, KNUTE RUMSEY, poet, English educator; b. St. Louis, Apr. 25, 1929; s. George Rumsey and Lidi (Skjoldvig) S.; m. Jeanne Pratt; 1953; divorced 1954; 1 child, Frank; m. Linda Kuhn, Mar. 30, 1961 (div. Sept. 1977); children: Dunstan, Morgan; m. Edna Kiel, Mar. 25, 1978. Student, Culver-Stockton Coll., 1947-49; BA, U. No. Colo., 1951; MA, Middlebury Coll., 1954; PhD, U. Iowa, 1958. Instr. English U. Iowa, Iowa City, 1955-56, 57-58, 60-61; asst. prof. English Okla. Coll. for Women, 1961-62; lectr. creative writing Western Wash. U., Bellingham, 1962-71, assoc. prof. English, 1971-73, prof. English, 1973-97; pres. Signpost Press Inc., nonprofit corp., 1983-95. Author: Stranger with a Watch, 1965, A Close Sky Over Killaspuglonane, 1968, 75, In Dinosaur Country, 1969, The Sorcerers: A Laotian Tale, 1972, Hearing of the Hard Times, 1981, The Flame Room, 1983, Selected Poems, 1985, Learning to Spell "Zucchini," 1988, The Bears and Other Poems, 1991, What Trudy Knows and Other Poems, 1994, The Cold Irish Earth: New and Selected Poems of Ireland, 1965-1995, 1996, An Afternoon Quiet and Other Poems, 1998, Greatest Hits, 1964-2000, 2001, Stretches, 2002; editor: Bellingham Rev., 1977-83, 93-95; contbr. poetry, short stories to anthologies, textbooks, periodicals. Nat. Endowment for the Arts fellow, 1975 Mem. Am. Conf. Irish Studies, Wash. Poets Assn. E-mail: knuteskinner@eircom.net.

SKINNER, MARGARET SHEPPARD, pathologist; b. Jamaica, N.Y., May 8, 1938; d. Benjamin Sheppard and Thelma Ruth Burns; divorced; children: Scott Renton, David Renton. Student, U. Miami, Fla., 1955-58; MD, Emory U., 1962. Diplomate Am. Bd. Pathology. Med. intern Emory U., Atlanta, 1962-63, resident in pathology, 1963-65; fellow Tulane U., New Orleans, 1965-67, asst. prof., 1968-71, assoc. prof., 1971-73; pathologist Daniel Seckinger MDPA, Miami, 1973-89, Palm Beach Pathology, West Palm Beach, Fla., 1989—2002. Mem. Fla. State Bd. Medicine, Tallahassee, 1986-90, 92-97, chmn., 1990; chmn. bd. dirs. COLA, Balt., 2000-02, vice chmn., 2002-03. Mem. med. adv. bd. Head Start, Palm Beach County, Fla., 1998-99; chmn. quality mgmt. com. Health Care Taxing Dist., Palm Beach County, 1998-2001. Mem. Coll. Am. Pathologists (bd. govs. 1997-2003, Pres. medal 1999); mem. Am. Soc. Investigative Pathology, Alpha Omega Alpha. Office: PO Box 32609 Palm Beach Gardens FL 33420-2609

SKINNER, MARY "HONEY" JACOBS, lawyer; b. 1957; m. Sam Skinner, Aug. 17, 1989; stepchildren: Thomas, Steven, Jane. BA cum laude, Harvard U., 1978; JD, Northwestern U., 1981. Bar: Ill. 1981, D.C. 1990, U.S. Supreme Ct. 1990. With Sidley Austin Brown & Wood, Chgo., 1981—, ptnr., 1989—; counsel to spkr. Ill. Ho. of Reps., Springfield, Ill., 1983—85. Intern White House, 1979. Former trustee RAdcliffe Coll.; participant leadership coun. Greater Chgo. Fellowship Program, 1984. Named One of Forty under 40 Most Outstanding Leaders in Chco., Crain's Chgo. Bus. Mem. Harvard Alumni Assn. (bd. dirs.), Radcliffe Coll. Alumni Assn. (past pres.). Office: Sidley Austin Brown and Wood Bank One Plz 10 S Dearborn St Chicago IL 60603

SKINNER, MIKE, professional race car driver; b. Ontario, Calif., June 28, 1957; m. Beth Skinner. Race car driver tracks in Nev., Calif.; race car driver Carolinas and Va.; race car driver NASCAR Winston Cup Series and Busch Series, 1986—; stock car driver Richard Childress Racing, Welcome, NC, 1994—. Named NASCAR Winston Cup Series Rookie of Yr., 1997. Achievements include 1995 NASCAR Craftsman Truck Series champion; winner Bud Poles, Daytona; winner 10 poles, 1995, numerous other pole positions. Avocations: golf, hunting, fishing, horseback riding, billiards. Office: c/o Richard Childress Racing PO Box 1189 Welcome NC 27374-1189

SKINNER, PATRICIA MORAG, state legislator; b. Glasgow, Scotland, Dec. 3, 1932; d. John Stuart and Frances Charlotte (Swann) Robertson; m. Robert A. Skinner, Dec. 28, 1957; children: Robin Ann, Pamela. BA, NYU, 1953. Mdse. trainee Lord & Taylor, N.Y.C.; adminstrv. asst. Atlantic Products, N.Y.C.; newspaper corr. Salem Observer, N.H., 1964-84; mem. N.H. Ho. of Reps., 1972-94, chmn. labor, human resources, and rehab. com., 1975-86, mem. House edn. com., 1987, chmn., 1989-94, exec. com. Nat. Conf. State Legislatures, 1987-90; chmn. N.H. Adv. Coun. Unemployment Compensation, 1984-94. Mem. State Libr. Adv. Coun., 2001—. Bd. dirs. Castle Jr. Coll., 1975, chmn. bd., 1988-96; v.p. bd. Swift Water coun. Girl Scouts U.S., v.p., 1987-92; N.H. Voc-Tech. Coll., Nashua, 1978-83; trustee Nesmith Libr., Windham, N.H., 1982—, chmn. bd. trustees, 1994-99; pres. N.H. Fedn. Rep. Women's Clubs, parliamentarian, legis. chmn., 1984-86, 94-96. Mem. Windham Woman's Club (pres. 1981-83), Order Ea. Star. Christian Scientist.

SKINNER, PETER GRAEME, publishing executive, lawyer; b. London, Ont., Can., July 27, 1944;, naturalized, U.S., 1952; s. George Woodley and Marjorie Grace S. AB, Princeton U., 1966; JD, MBA, Columbia U., 1970. Bar: (N.Y. 1971). Assoc. Patterson, Belknap, Webb & Tyler, N.Y.C., 1970-77, ptnr., 1977-85; gen. counsel, sec. Dow Jones & Co., N.Y.C., 1985—, v.p., 1985—89, sr. v.p., 1989—98, exec. v.p., 1998—. Mem.: ABA, Assn. Bar City N.Y., N.Y. State Bar Assn. Office: Dow Jones & Co Inc 200 Liberty St Fl 12 New York NY 10281-1003

SKINNER, ROBERT C., JR., retail executive; Pres. Oxford Shirt Group, 1987—99; v.p. Oxford Industries, 1999—2000; pres. Kellwood Menswear, 2000—02; from v.p. to pres., COO Kellwood Co., St. Louis, 2002—03, pres., 2003—, COO, 2003—. Bd. govs. Young Mens Assn. Office: Kellwood Co 600 Kellwood Pkwy Saint Louis MO 63178*

SKINNER, ROBERT EARLE, librarian, writer; b. Alexandria, Va., June 25, 1948; s. Earl Woodrow and Pearle Labar (Capper) S.; m. Linda Sue Long, June 12, 1970 (div. 1976); children: Christopher William, Kelly Sue; m. Patricia Ann Friedmann, Mar. 17, 1979 (div. 1996); children: Esme F., Werner H.; m. Bettye Jean Harrison, June 20, 2001. BA in History, Old Dominion U., 1970; MLS, Ind. U., 1977; postgrad. student, U. New Orleans, 1991-93. Search analyst Strughold Aeromed. Libr., Brooks AFB, Tex., 1977-79; from reference libr. to head med. edn. libr. La. State U. Med. Ctr., New Orleans, 1979-85; spl. cons. Robert L. Siegel & Assocs., New Orleans, 1985-87; univ. libr. Xavier U., New Orleans, 1987—; mng. editor Xavier Rev. Press, 1989—. Vis. lectr. in Am. studies U.S. Air Force Acad., 2002. Author: The Hard-Boiled Explicator, 1985, The New Hard-Boiled Dicks, 1987, rev. edit., 1995, Two Guns From Harlem, 1989, (with Michel J. Fabre) Chester Himes: An Annotated Primary and Secondary Bibliography, 1992, Fiction in Ellipsis, 1992, (with Thomas Bonner, Jr.) Above Ground, 1993, Immortelles, 1995, (with Michel J. Fabre) Plan B, 1993, (with Michel J. Fabre) Conversations with Chester Himes, 1995, Fiction in Hard Boiled, 1994, Fiction in Crime Yellow, 1994, Skin Deep, Blood Red, 1997, Cat-Eyed Trouble, 1998, Daddy's Gone-A-Hunting, 1999, Blood to Drink, 2000, Pale Shadow, 2001, The Righteous Cut, 2002; guest editor La. Lit., spring 1998, guest editor, contbr. Plots With Guns, 2002, 03; contbr. fiction to Xavier Rev., 2000, War, Literature and the Arts, 2001, (essay) Andre Dubus: Tributes, 2002; contbr. essays to Miss. Quar., Paradoxa, 2001. With USCG, 1970-74. Grantee Mellon Found., 1987-95, La. Divsn. of the Arts, 1993, 95, NEH, 1991—. Mem. ALA. Avocations: hiking, reading, book collecting, antique radios, shortwave listening. Office: Xavier Univ Libr 1 Drexel Dr New Orleans LA 70125-1056 Office Phone: 504-520-7303. E-mail: rskinner@xula.edu.

SKINNER, ROBERT EARLE, JR., civil engineer, engineering executive; b. Washington, Aug. 10, 1946; s. Robert Earle and Dorothy Inez (Ballance) S.; m. Dianne Lynette Sands; children: Martha, Jeffrey. BSCE, U. Va., 1969; MS in Civil Engring., MIT, 1971. Registered profl. engr., Va. Sr. assoc. PRC Voorhees, McLean, Va., 1971-79, v.p., 1979-83; sr. staff officer Transp. Rsch. Bd., Washington, 1983-86, dir. studies and info. svc., 1986-94, exec. dir., 1994—. Exec. com. Hwy. Innovative Tech. Evaluation Ctr., Washington, 1994—; adv. com. Ctr. for Transp. and the Environment, Raleigh, N.C., 1995—; bd. dirs. Innovation Pavement Rsch. Found., Washington, 1999-2002; mem. adv. bd. Ctr. for Urban Transp. Rsch., U. South Fla., 2003—; mem. vis. com. engirng. sys. divsn. MIT, 2004—. Contbr. articles to profl. jours.; mem. editorial bd. Jour. Trans. and Stats., 1996. Mem. adv. coun. U. Va., 1995—; mem. vis. com. Engring. Sys. Ctr., MIT, 2003—. With U.S. Army N.G., 1970-76. Mem.: ASCE. Methodist. Avocations: woodworking, tennis. Office: Transportation Research Bd of the Nat Acads 500 5th St NW Washington DC 20001-

SKINNER, THOMAS, broadcasting and film executive; b. Poughkeepsie, N.Y., Aug. 17, 1934; s. Clarence F. and Frances D. S.; m. Elizabeth Burroughs, June 22, 1957; children: Kristin Jon, Karin Anne, Erik Lloyd. BS, SUNY, Fredonia, 1956; MA, U. Mich., 1957, PhD, 1962. Instr. speech U. Mich., 1960; assoc. prof., exec. producer dept. broadcasting San Diego State U., 1961-66; asst. mgr. Sta. WITF-TV, Hershey, Pa., 1966-70; v.p. Sta. WQED-TV, Pitts., 1970-72; exec. v.p., COO QED Communications Inc. (WQED-TV, WQED-FM, Pittsburgh mag., WQEX-TV), 1972-93; founder, pres., exec. prodr. Windrush Assocs., 1993—; v.p. Programming Resolution Prodns., Burlington, Vt., 1996—; asst. dir. Inland Seas Edn. Assn., 2000—. Exec. prodr.: spls. and series including (for PBS) Nat. Geog. spls. Planet Earth, The Infinite Voyage, Conserving America, (for TBS) Pirate Tales, (for A&E) Floating Palaces,

California and the Dream Seekers, The Story of Money, (for Discovery) Battleship, The Secret World of Air Freight. Recipient award as exec. prodr. DuPont Columbia, 1979, Oscar award as dir. Acad. Motion Picture Arts and Scis., 1967, Emmy award as exec. prodr. Nat. Acad. TV Arts and Scis., 1979, 83-84, 86-87, Peabody award as exec. prodr., 1980, 86. Episcopalian. Office Phone: 231 271-3077. E-mail: ski361@aol.com.

SKINNER, THOMAS V. government agency administrator; Grad., Lawrence U.; JD, Northwestern U. Ptnr. Winston & Strawn, Chgo., 1991—99; dir. Ill. EPA, 1999—2001; regional adminstr. U.S. EPA, Chgo., 2001—. Office: US EPA Region 5 77 W Jackson Blvd Chicago IL 60604

SKINNER, WALTER JAY, federal judge; b. Washington, Sept. 12, 1927; s. Frederick Snowden and Mary Waterman (Comstock) S.; m. Sylvia Henderson, Aug. 12, 1950; 4 children. AB, Harvard, 1948; JD, 1952. Bar: Mass. 1952, U.S. Dist. Ct. 1954. Assoc. firm Gaston, Snow, Rice & Boyd, Boston, 1952-57; pvt. practice law Scituate, Mass., 1957-63; asst. dist. atty. Plymouth County, 1957-63; town counsel Scituate, 1957-63; asst. atty. gen., chief Criminal Div., Commonwealth of Mass., 1963-65; mem. firm Wardwell, Allen, McLaughlin & Skinner, Boston, 1965-74; judge U.S. Dist. Ct. of Mass., 1974—; sr. status, 1992 . Bd. dirs. Douglas A. Thom Clinic, 1966-70. Mem. Mass. Bar Assn., Boston Bar Assn. Office: US Dist Ct 1 Courthouse Way Boston MA 02210-3002

SKINNER, WILLIAM POLK, lawyer; b. St. Louis, Apr. 4, 1951; s. Edwin Lemoine Jr. and Grizelda Gilchrist (Polk) S.; m. Karen Kenny, Aug. 2, 1975; children: Suzanne, William. BA, Harvard U., 1972, JD, 1975. Bar: Mo. 1976, DC 1976. Assoc. Covington & Burling, Washington, 1976-83, ptnr., 1983—. Office: Covington & Burling 1201 Pennsylvania Ave NW Washington DC 20004

SKIPPER, JASON EDWARD, writer, educator; b. Worcester, Mass., July 15, 1975; s. Eugene Thomas and Kathy Darrell Skipper. BA, U. North Tex., 1999; MA, Miami U., Oxford, Ohio, 2001. Tchg. asst. English dept. Miami U., 1999—2001; doctoral assoc. English dept. Western Mich. U., Kalamazoo, 2001—03, asst. dir. creative writing program, 2004—. Fiction editor Ox Mag, Oxford, 1999—2001, Third Coast Lit. Jour., Kalamazoo, 2001—03, advising editor, 2003—. Contbr. short stories to lit. jours. Organizer Writers for Relief-A Benefit for 9/11 Victims, Kalamazoo, 2001, Third Coast Fiction Contest, Kalamazoo, 2003. Recipient Fiction award, Touchstone Lit. Jour., 2003, hon. mention, Zoetrope-All-Story, 2002; Irving Gilmore Emerging Artist grantee, Arts Coun. of Kalamazoo. Home: 224 Old Orchard Kalamazoo MI 49007

SKIRBOLL, LANA R. federal health policy director; b. Balt., Dec. 7, 1948; m. Leonard Taylor, Feb. 19, 1986; 2 children. BA, NYU, 1970; MS in Zoology and Physiology, Miami U., 1972; PhD in Pharmacology, Georgetown U., 1977. Postdoctoral tng. in psychiatry and pharmacology Yale U. Sch. Medicine, New Haven, 1977-79; vis. scientist dept. histology and neurobiology Karolinska Inst., Stockholm, 1979-81; chief electrophysiology unit NIMH, 1981—86; dep. sci. advisor Alcohol Drug Abuse and Mental Health Adminstrn., 1986—88, exec. asst. to administr., 1989-91, assoc. adminstr. for sci., 1990—92; dir. office of sci. policy and program planning NIMH, 1992-95, 95—. Cons. Ctr. Environ. Health and Human Toxicology, 1985-87. Author: Pharmacology of Biochemical Behavior, 1988, Neuroanatomical Tract-Tracing Methods II: 1981-86, 1990, (with T. Hokfelt, G. Foster, O. Johannsson et alCentral Phenylethanolamine N-Methyltransferase Immunoreactive Neurons: Distribution Projections, Fine Structure, Ontogeny and Co-Existing Peptides, 1988, (with G.Stoner, S. Werkman, D. Hommer) Effects of Caffeine on the Substania Nigra, Biological Psychiatry, 1988, (with J.A. Stivers, R. Long, J. Crawley) Anatomical Analysis of Frontal Cortex Sites at Which Carbachol Induces Moteor Seizures in the Rat, (with T. Hokfelt, B. Robertson) Retrograde Flourescent Tracers with Immunohistochemistry, (with M. Palkovits, E. Mezey, T. Hokfelt) Adrenergic Projections from the Lower Brainstem to the Hypothalamic Paraventricular Nucleus, the Lateral Hypothalamic Area and the Central Nucleus of the Amygdala in Rats, vol. 1020, 1992. Biol. Scis. fellow in in psychiatry NIMH, 1977-79, Fogarty fellow, Internat. fellow Swedish Med. Rsch. Coun., 1979-81. Mem. AAAS, Am. Coll. Neuropsychopharmacology (Mead Johnson award), N.Y. Acad. Scis., Nat. Com. Edn. (Potomac chpt. pres. 1988-89), European Neurosci. Soc., Soc. Neurosci. Office: HHS NIH 9000 Rockville Pike Bldg 1 Bethesda MD 20892-0001

SKIRDE, EDWARD GEORGE, academic administrator, consultant; s. Herbert William and Anna Irene Skirde; m. Priscilla Ann Christman, Dec. 20, 1969; children: Deborah Ann Gleeson, Kevin Edward. BA, St. John's U., 1963—67; MA, Pa. State U., 1967—69, PhD, 1969—72. Instr. of speech Pa. State U., U. Pk., 1969—72; asst. dean and chmn., divsn. of interdisplinary studies St. John's U., Jamaica, NY, 1972—78, dir. of alumni rels., 1978—82, adminstrative v.p., 1982—85, v.p. for instl. advancement, 1985—97; v.p. emeritus and exec. dir. of devel. St. John's U. Sch. of Law, 2000—. Cons. Skirde Enterprises, S.I., NY, 1997—. Trustee St. Elizabeth Ann Seton Rehab. Ctr. and Nursing Home, S.I., NY, 1998—2003; bd. of dir. Italian Cultural Ctr. of St. John's U., Jamaica, NY, 1995—2003; trustee St. Vincent's Med. Ctr., S.I., NY, 1988—97, Notre Dame Acad., S.I., NY, 1989—97. Recipient President's medal, St. John's U., 1997, Outstanding Alumni Achievement award, 1992, Outstanding Adminstrv. Achievement award, 1986, Pietas medal, 1981, Nat. Hon. Speech Soc., Delta Sigma Rho - Tau Kappa Alpha, 1970. Mem.: Assn. of Am. Law Schools, Coun. for Advancement and Support of Edn. Avocations: travel, golf. Office: St John's U Sch of Law 8000 Utopia Pkwy Jamaica NY 11439

SKIRNICK, ROBERT ANDREW, lawyer; b. Chgo., Apr. 23, 1938; s. Andrew and Stella (Sanders) S.; children: Rebecca, David; m. Maria Ann Castellano, Oct. 4, 1974; 1 child, Gabriella. BA, Roosevelt U., 1961; JD, U. Chgo., 1966. Bar: U.S. Dist. Ct. (no. dist.) Ill. 1966, U.S. Ct. Appeals (7th cir.) 1968, U.S. Supreme Ct. 1970, U.S. Ct. Appeals (5th and 9th cirs.) 1982, N.Y. 1989, U.S. Ct. Appeals (11th cir.) 1992, U.S. Dist. Ct. (so. dist.) Tex. 1992, U.S. Dist. Ct. Ariz. 1993, U.S. Ct. Appeals (4th, 6th and 8th cirs.) 2002. Atty. office gen. counsel honors program HEW, Washington, 1966-68; ptnr. Fortes, Eiger, Epstein & Skirnick, Chgo., 1975-77, Much, Shelist, Freed, Chgo., 1977-79, Wolf, Popper, Ross, Wolf & Jones, N.Y.C., 1979-87, Kaplan, Kilsheimer & Foley, N.Y.C., 1988-89, Wechsler, Skirnick, Harwood, Halebian & Feffer, N.Y.C., 1989-95, Lovell & Skirnick, LLP, N.Y.C., 1995-97, Meredith Cohen Greenfogel & Skirnick, P.C., N.Y.C., 1997—. Cons. Nat. Legal Aid and Def. Assn., Chgo., 1968—69; instr. NYU, 1979—80; spl. asst. atty. gen. Ill. Atty. Gen. Office, Chgo., 1972—73; spl. antitrust counsel State of Conn., 1976—77; mem. adv. bd. Small Bus. Legal Def. Commn., San Francisco, 1982—; lectr. Practicing Law Inst., N.Y.C., 1986—87; spl. master So. Dist. N.Y., 1988—91; ct. apptd. co-lead counsel NASDAQ market makers antitrust litigation, 1994—; sponsor Skirmick Fellowships for Pub. Interest Law Harvard Law Sch. Author: (with others) Federal Subject Matter Jurisdiction of U.S. District Courts, Federal Civil Practice, 1974, Antitrust Class Actions-Twenty Years Under Rule 23, 1986, The State Court Class Action-A Potpourri of Difference in the ABA Forum, Summer 1985; contbg. author: Multiparty Bargaining in Class Actions, Attorneys' Practice Guide to Negotiations, 2d edit., 1996; bd. editors Ill. Bar Antitrust Newsletter, 1969-73; topic and articles editor Jour. Forum Com. on Franchising, 1981-86. Atty. Office Gen. Counsel Honors Program, U.S. Dept. HEW, 1966-68; chmn. Ill. Legis. Com. Antitrust Section Ill. Bar., 1970-71; Topic and Articles Editor, Jour. Forum Com. on Franchising, 1981-86. Mem.: ATLA, ABA (co-chair securities law subcom. litigation sect. 1987, mem. com. on regulation of futures and derivative instruments, mem. forum com. on franchising, mem. com. on class actions and derivative suits, mem. internat. antitrust and fgn. competition laws com.), Nat. Assn. Pub. Interest Law (mem. fin. and investment com. 1998—, nomination and election com. 1998—99, chair nominations and elections com. 1999—2000, chair fin. and investment com. 2000—, bd. dirs. 1997—), Nat. Assn. for Pub. Interest Law Fellowships (mem. exec. com., mem. selection com., mem. investment and fin. com., bd. dirs. 1991—97, v.p. 1994—97, treas. 2000—, mem. budget com. 1998—, nomination and election coms. 1998—99, bd. dirs. 1997—), Ill. Bar Assn. (chmn. antitust sect. Ill. legis. com. 1970—71), N.Y. State Trial Lawyers Assn., N.Y. State Bar Assn. (mem. class action com.), Fed. Bar Coun. (mem. com. on second cir. cts. 1983—86), Navy League of U.S. (N.Y. coun., mem. jour. com. 1995—97), Plandome Country Club, Carlton Club. Office: Meredith Cohen Greenfogel & Skirnick 63 Wall St New York NY 10005-3001

SKJERVOLD, GERALDINE REID See REID, GERALDINE

SKLANSKY, JACK, electrical and computer engineering educator, researcher; b. NYC, Nov. 15, 1928; s. Abraham and Clara S.; m. Gloria Joy Weiss, Dec. 24, 1957; children: David Alan, Mark Steven, Jeffrey Paul. BEE, CCNY, 1950; MSEE, Purdue U., 1952; D in Engring. Sci., Columbia U., 1955. Research engr. RCA Labs., Princeton, NJ, 1955-65; mgr. Nat. Cash Register Co., Dayton, Ohio, 1965-66; prof. elec. and computer engring. U. Calif., Irvine, 1966—94; pres. Scanicon Corp., Irvine, 1980-89; prof. radiology Charles R. Drew U. of Medicine and Sci., LA, 1995—. Author: (with others) Pattern Classifiers and Trainable Machines, 1981; editor: Pattern Recognition, 1973, (with others) Biomedical Images and Computers, 1982; editor-in-chief: Machine Vision and Applications, 1987. Recipient best paper award Jour. Pattern Recognition, 1977, 2000; rsch. grantee NIH, 1971-84, Army Rsch. Office, 1984-91, NSF, 1992-96, Office of Naval Rsch., 1995-97, Naval Air Warfare Ctr., 1997-98, Calif. Breast Cancer Rsch. Program, 1997-99, US Army Med. Rsch. and Materiel Command, 1999-2004, Calif. Telehealth and Telemedicine Ctr., 2000-02. Fellow IEEE, Internat. Assn. for Pattern Recognition; mem. ACM. Office: Charles R Drew Univ Med Sci Dept Rad Los Angeles CA 90059 E-mail: sklansky@uci.edu.

SKLAR, ALAN CURTIS, lawyer; b. N.Y.C., Aug. 19, 1959; s. Jerry and Martha (Kolin) S.; m. Linda Susan Catalan, Dec. 26, 1982; twins: Daniel Jay and Jennifer Rachel. BA summa cum laude, U. Pa., 1980, JD, 1982. Bar: Calif., Nev. Assoc. Wolf Block Schorr & Solis-Cohen, Phila., 1980, 81, Rifkind & Sterling, Beverly Hills, Calif., 1982-84, Mitchell Silberberg & Knupp, L.A., 1984-86; mng. dir. Coastal Investment Group, Beverly Hills, 1986-89; ptnr. Warren Clark & Sklar (and predecessor), L.A., 1989—, Gordon & Silver, Las Vegas, Nev., 1991-95, Sklar Warren Conway & Williams LLP, Las Vegas, Nev., 1995—. Bd. dirs. Consolidated Mgmt., Inc., N.Y.C., L.A., Las Vegas. Author: Tactics and Techniques in Mergers and Acquisitions, 1985, Recent Developments in Mergers and Acquisitions, 1985, California Corporate Securities Laws, 1985, Corporate Law Overview, 1985, Secured Real Estate Transactions, 1993. Bd. trustees Las Vegas Bowl Organizing Com., 1995, 96, So. Nev. Housing Corp., 1995—; mem. U. Pa. Alumni Secondary Sch. Com., 1998—; counsel Chabad of So. Nev., Las Vegas, 1991-2000. Named Top Corp. Atty., Nev. Bus. Jour. Mem. ABA, State Bar Nev., State Bar Calif., TPC Summerlin Country Club, World Zionist Orgn., Phi Beta Kappa, Phi Alpha Theta. Democrat. Jewish. Office: 8363 W Sunset RD #300 Las Vegas NV 89113-2092 E-mail: asklar@sklar-law.com.

SKLAR, ALEXANDER, electric company executive; b. N.Y.C., May 18, 1915; s. David and Bessie (Wolf) S.; m. Hilda Rae Gevarter, Oct. 27, 1940; 1 dau., Carolyn Mae (Mrs. Louis M. Taff). Student, Cooper Union, N.Y.C., 1932-35; MBA, Fla. Atlantic U., 1976. Chief engr. Aerovox Corp., New Bedford, Mass., 1933-39; mgr. mfg., engring. Indsl. Condenser Corp., Chgo., 1939-44; owner Capacitron Inc., 1944-48; exec. v.p. Jefferson Electric Co., Bellwood, Ill., 1948-65; v.p., gen. mgr. electro-mechs. divsn. Essex Internat., Detroit, 1965-67. Advisor, bd. dirs. various corps.; vis. prof. mgmt. Fla. Atlantic U., Boca Raton, 1971-92, ret., 1993; lectr. profl. mgmt. UCLA, Harvard U. Grad. Sch. Bus. Adminstrn., U. Ill. Mem. Acad. Internat. Bus., Soc. Automotive Engrs. Address: 4100 Galt Ocean Dr #1505 Fort Lauderdale FL 33308-6030

SKLAR, FREDERICK H. neurosurgeon; b. Phila., 1945; m. Alice Sklar; 3 children. BS with highest honors, Pa. State U.; MD, Johns Hopkins U., 1970. Diplomate Am. Bd. Neurol. Surgery, Am. Bd. Pediat. Neurol. Surgery, lic. physician Tex. Halsted intern in surgery Johns Hopkins U., Balt., 1970—71; resident in neurosurgery Johns Hopkins Hosp., 1971—76; clin. assoc. prof. neurol. surgery U. Tex. Southwestern Med. Sch., Dallas; dir. pediat. neurosurgery Children's Med. Ctr. Dallas; founder Neurosurgeons for Children, 1985—. Cons. Tex. Scottish Rite Hosp. for Children, Parkland Meml. Hosp., Dallas. Contbr. articles to profl. jours. Mem.: Alpha Omega Alpha, Phi Beta Kappa. Office: Children's Med Ctr-Neurosurgery 1935 Motor St Dallas TX 75235

SKLAR, HOLLY L. nonfiction writer; b. N.Y.C., May 6, 1955; BA, Oberlin Coll., 1977; MA in Polit. Sci., Columbia U., 1980. Rschr. UN Ctr. Transnat. Corps., N.Y., 1978; writer, rschr. N. Am. Congress Latin Am., N.Y., 1981-82; exec. dir. Inst. New Communications, N.Y., 1982-84; writer, lectr. N.Y., Boston. Review panelist NEH, Washington, 1989; del. Soviet-Am. Women's Summit, N.Y., Washington, 1990; dir. MediaVision, Boston, 1997—. Author, co-author (books) Trilateralism, 1980, Poverty in the American Dream: Women and Children First, 1983, Washington's War on Nicaragua, 1988, Streets of Hope: The Fall and Rise of an Urban Neighborhood, 1994, Chaos or Community? Seeking Solutions, Not Scapegoats for Bad Economics, 1995, Shifting Fortunes: The Perils of the Growing American Wealth Gap, 1999, Raise the Floor: Wages and Policies that Work for All of Us, 2001. Mem. adv. bd. The Progressive Media Project, Polit. Rsch. Assocs.; bd. dirs. United for a Fair Economy, 1996-2000; mem. steering com. Caribbean Basin Info. Project, 1982-85; mem. working group on global econs. Am. Friends Svc. Com., 2002—. Recipient Outstanding Book award Gustavus Myers Ctr. for Study Human Rights in U.S., 1988, Assocs. award Polit. Rsch. Assocs., Cambridge, 1991-97; fellow Columbia U. Grad. Sch. Arts and Scis., 1978-80. Mem. Nat. Writers Union, Acad. Polit. Sci. Office: 52 Parley Ave Boston MA 02130-1857 E-mail: Mediavi@aol.com.

SKLAR, KATHRYN KISH, historian, educator; b. Columbus, Ohio, Dec. 26, 1939; d. William Edward and Elizabeth Sue (Rhodes) Kish; m. Robert A. Sklar, 1958 (div. 1978); children: Leonard Scott, Susan Rebecca Sklar Friedman; m. Thomas L. Dublin, Apr. 30, 1988. BA magna cum laude, Radcliffe Coll., 1965; PhD, U. Mich., 1969. Asst. prof., lectr. U. Mich., Ann Arbor, 1969-74; assoc. prof. history UCLA, 1974-81, chmn. com. to administer program in women's studies Coll. Letters and Sci., 1974-81, prof., 1981-88; Disting. Prof. history SUNY, Binghamton, 1988—, co-dir., Ctr. Hist. Study of Women and Gender, 1998—. Pulitzer juror in history, 1976; fellow Newberry Libr. Family and Community History Seminar, 1973; active Calif. Coun. for Humanities, 1981-85, N.Y. Coun. for Humanities, 1992—. Author: Catharine Beecher: A Study in American Domesticity, 1973 (Berkshire pri e 1974); editor: Catharine Beecher: A Treatise on Domestic Economy, 1977, Harriet Beecher Stowe: Uncle Tom's Cabin, or Life Among the Lowly: The Minister's Wooing, Oldtown Folks, 1981, Notes of Sixty Years: The Autobiography of Florence Kelley, 1849-1926, 1984, (with Thomas Dublin) Women and Power in American History: A Reader (2 vols.), 1991, (with Linda Kerber and Alice Kessler-Harris) U.S. History as Women's History: New Feminist Essays, 1995, Women's Rights Emerges within the Antislavery Movement: A Short History with Documents, 1830-1870, 2000; co-editor: The Social Survey Movement in Historical Perspective, 1992, Florence Kelley and the Nation's Work: The Rise of Women's Political Culture, 1830-1900, 1995 (Berkshire prize 1996). Social Justice Feminists in the United States and Germany: A Dialogue in Documents, 1885-1933, 1998; mem. editl. bd. Jour. Women's History, 1987—, Women's History Rev., 1990—, Jour. Am. History, 1978-81; contbr. chpts. to books. Fellow Woodrow Wilson Found., 1965-67, Danforth Found., 1967-69, Radcliffe Inst., 1973-74, Nat. Humanities Inst., 1975-76, Rockefeller Found. Humanities, 1981-82, Woodrow Wilson Internat. Ctr. for Scholars, 1982, 1992-93, Guggenheim Found., 1984, Ctr. Advanced Study Behavioral and Social Scis., Stanford U., 1987-88, AAUW, 1990-91; Daniels fellow Am. Antiquarian Soc., 1976, NEH fellow Newberry Library, 1982-83; Ford Found. faculty rsch. grantee, 1973-74; grantee NEH, 1976-78, UCLA Coun. for Internat. and Comparative Studies, 1983. Mem. Am. Hist. Assn. (chmn. com. on women historians 1980-83, v.p. Pacific Coast br. 1986-87, pres. 1987-88), Orgn. Am. Historians (exec. bd. 1983-86, Merle Curti award com. 1978-79, lectr. 1982—), Am. Studies Assn. (coun. mem.-at-large 1978-80), Berkshire Conf. Women Historians, Am. Antiquarian Soc., Phi Beta Kappa. Avocation: photography. Office: SUNY Dept History Binghamton NY 13902

SKLAR, LOUISE MARGARET, computer company executive; b. L.A., Aug. 12, 1934; d. Samuel Baldwin Smith and Judith LeRoy (Boughton) Nelson; m. Edwynn Edgar Schroeder, Mar. 20, 1955 (div. July 1975); children: Neil Nelson Schroeder, Leslie Louise Schroeder Grandclaudon, Samuel George Schroeder; m. Martin Sklar, Oct. 17, 1983. Student, U. So. Calif., 1952-54, UCLA, 1977-79. Acct. Valentine Assocs., Northridge, Calif., 1976-78, programmer, 1978-79; contr. Western Monetary, Encino, Calif., 1979-81; pres. Automatic Computer Composition, Reno, 1984—. Mem.: DAR, New England Hist. Genealogical Soc., So. Calif. Assistance League, Conn. Soc. Genealogists, Greater L.A. Zoo. Assn., Am. Contract Bridge League (bd. govs. 1993—99, mem. nat. charity com. 1982—, mem. nat. goodwill com. 1994—), Assn. Los Angeles County Bridge Units (bd. dirs. 1990—2000, sec. 1984—86), Ky. Hist. Soc., Safari Club Internat., Zeta Tau Alpha. Republican. Avocations: tournament bridge, travel. Office: Automatic Computer Composition Inc Reno NV 89511

SKLAR, MARTIN A. recreational facility executive; m. Leah Sklar. Grad., UCLA. Asst. news editor Media Agy. Clients Publs.; with Walt Disney Co., Burbank, Calif., 1956—; v.p. concepts/planning Walt Disney Imagineering, Walt Disney Co., Burbank, Calif., 1974—79, v.p. creative devel., 1979—87, pres., 1987—96, vice chmn., prin. creative exec., 1996—. One of founders Ryman Program for Young Artists. Contbr. articles to Showman of the World films. Mem. bd. edn. Anaheim City Sch. Dist., 1969, 1973; pres. Orange County, Calif. Sch. Bds. Assn.; commr. Anaheim City; founding chmn. Michael L. Roston Creative Writing Awards. Recipient Cmty. Svc. award for Anaheim, Cypress Coll., 1977, Lifetime Achievement award, Themed Entertainment Assn., 1995; inducted into, Hall of Fame, Internat. Assn. Amusement Pks. and Attractions, 2002. Office: Walt Disney Co 500 S Buena Vista St Burbank CA 91521-9722

SKLAR, RICHARD LAWRENCE, political science educator; b. N.Y.C., Mar. 22, 1930; s. Kalman and Sophie (Laub) S.; m. Eva Molineux, July 14, 1962; children: Judith Anne, Katherine Elizabeth. AB, U. Utah, 1952; MA, Princeton U., 1957, PhD, 1961. Mem. faculty Brandeis U., U. Ibadan, Nigeria, U. Zambia, SUNY-Stony Brook, UCLA; now prof. emeritus polit. sci. UCLA. Mem. fgn. area fellowship program Africa Nat. Com., 1970-73; Simon vis. prof. U. Manchester, Eng., 1975, Fulbright vis. prof. U. Zimbabwe, 1984; Lester Martin fellow Harry S. Truman Rsch. Inst., Hebrew U. Jerusalem, 1979; fellow Africa Inst. of South Africa, 1994—. Author: Nigerian Political Parties: Power in an Emergent African Nation, 1963, Corporate Power in an African State, 1975, African Politics in Postimperial Times, 2002; co-author: Postimperialism: International Capitalism and Development, 1987, African Politics and Problems in Development, 1991; co-editor: Postimperialism and World Politics, 1999; contbr. articles to profl. jours. Served with U.S. Army, 1952-54. Rockefeller Found. grantee, 1967 Mem. Am. Polit. Sci. Assn., African Studies Assn. (dir. 1976-78, 80-83, v.p. 1980-81, pres. 1981-82), AAUP (pres. Calif. Conf. 1980-81) Home: 1951 Holmby Ave Los Angeles CA 90025-5905

SKLAR, STANLEY LAWRENCE, judge; b. N.Y.C., Jan. 25, 1932; s. Julius and Rebecca (Skerker) S.; m. Margot Algase, Dec. 10, 1972; 1 child, Deborah. BA, Columbia U., 1953, LLB, 1956. Bar: N.Y. 1957, U.S. Supreme Ct. 1967. Assoc. Zipser & Levitt, N.Y.C., 1957-60, Wolf, Popper, Ross, Wolf & Jones, N.Y.C., 1960-64, Rubin, Baum, Levin, Constant & Friedman, N.Y.C., 1964-67, ptnr., 1967-76; judge N.Y.C. Civil Ct., 1977-78; acting justice N.Y. State Supreme Ct., N.Y.C., 1978-85, justice, 1986—. Author: Shoplifting: What You Need to Know About the Law, 1982; contbr. articles to profl. jours. Mem. Assn. Bar City N.Y., Am. Judicature Soc., Assn. Justices of the Supreme Ct. of City of N.Y. (pres. 2000-01), Bd. of Supreme Ct. Justices N.Y. County (chair 2001—). Office: NY Supreme Ct 60 Centre St Fl 5 New York NY 10007-1402

SKLAREW, ROBERT JAY, biomedical research educator, consultant; b. N.Y.C., Nov. 25, 1941; s. Arthur and Jeanette (Laven) S.; m. Toby Willner, July 15, 1970; children: David Michael, Gary Richard. BA in Zoology, Cornell U., 1963; MS, NYU, 1965, PhD in Biology, 1970. Assoc. rsch. scientist NYU Sch. Medicine, N.Y.C., 1965-70, rsch. scientist, 1971-73, sr. rsch. scientist, 1973-79; rsch. asst. prof. pathology Goldwater Meml. Hosp. Sch. Medicine, N.Y.C., 1979-87, rsch. assoc. prof. pathology, 1987-88; dir. cytokinetics and imaging lab. NYU rsch. svc. Goldwater Meml. Hosp., N.Y.C., 1980-88; prof. cell biology, anatomy and medicine N.Y. Med. Coll., Valhalla, 1988-98. Rsch. assoc. dept. pathology Lenox Hill Hosp., N.Y.C., 1981-88; pres., CEO R.J. Sklarew Imaging Assoc., Inc., Larchmont, N.Y., 1990—2003; chmn. consensus panel for diagnostic cancer imaging Nat. Cancer Inst., 1994. Author: Microscopic Imaging of Steroid Receptors, 1990; sr. author: Cytometry, Jour. Histochem. Cytochem., Cancer, Exptl. Cell Rsch. Mem. Beth Emeth Synagogue, Larchmont, 1974—; group leader Boy Scouts Am., Larchmont, 1978-80; mem., bd. dirs. Pinelake Park Coop, 1998-2001. Grantee Am. Cancer Soc., Nat. Cancer Inst./NIH Conc. for Tobacco Rsch., R.J. Reynolds Industries Found., NYU; recipient Shannon award Nat. Cancer Inst., 1991. Mem. AAAS, Cell Kinetics Soc. (sec. 1983-85, 85-87, v.p. 1987-88, pres. 1988-89, chmn. nominations 1991, 93), N.Y. Acad. Sci., Soc. for Analytic Cytology, Soc. for Cell Biology, Tissue Culture Assn., Union Concerned Scientists, Kappa Delta Rho. Democrat. Achievements include development of methodology, algorithms and Receptogram analytic software for application of microscopic imaging in medical research and in pathodiagnosis of cancer, imaging methods for simultaneous densitometry and autoradiographic analysis; research in diagnostic imaging of steroid receptors, oncogenes and DNA ploidy in cancer, proliferative patterns and cell cycle kinetics of human solid tumors. Home: 8 Vine Rd Larchmont NY 10538-1247 Office: RJ Sklarew Imaging Assoc Inc 8 Vine Rd Larchmont NY 10538-1247 Personal E-mail: rjsklarew@aol.com.

SKLARSKY, CHARLES B. lawyer; b. Chgo., June 13, 1946; s. Morris and Sadie (Brenner) S.; m. Elizabeth Ann Hardzinski, Dec. 28, 1973; children: Jacob Daniel, Katherine Gabrielle, Jessica Leah. AB, Harvard U., 1968; JD, U. Wis., 1973. Bar: Wis. 1973, Ill. 1973, U.S. Dist. Ct. (no. dist.) Ill. 1973, U.S. Ct. Appeals (7th cir.) 1978, U.S. Ct. Appeals (2nd cir.) 1986. Asst. states atty. Cook County, Chgo., 1973-78; asst. U.S. atty. U.S. Dist. Ct. (no. dist.) Ill., Chgo., 1978-86; ptnr. Jenner & Block, Chgo., 1986—. Mem. ABA, Am. Coll. Trial Lawyers, Chgo. Bar Assn. Office: Jenner & Block One IBM Plz Chicago IL 60611-3586

SKLENAR, HERBERT ANTHONY, industrial products manufacturing company executive; b. Omaha, June 7, 1931; s. Michael Joseph and Alice Madeline (Spicka) S.; m. Eleanor Lydia Vincenz, Sept. 15, 1956; children: Susan A., Patricia I. BSBA summa cum laude, U. Omaha, 1952; MBA, Harvard U., 1954; LLD (hon.), Birmingham-So. Coll., 1996. CPA, W.Va. V.p., comptr. Parkersburg-Aetna Corp., W.Va., 1956-63; v.p., dir. Marmac Corp, Parkersburg, 1963-66; mgr. fin. control Boise-Cascade Corp., Idaho, 1966-67; exec. v.p. fin. and adminstrn., sec. Cudahy Co., Phoenix, 1967-72; chmn. emeritus Vulcan Materials Co., Birmingham, Ala., 1972-97, chmn. bd. dirs. emeritus, 1997—. Author: (with others) The Automatic Factory: A Critical Examination, 1955 Trustee Leadership Birmingham, Leadership Ala., Birmingham-So. Coll. Recipient Alumni Achievement award U. Nebr.-Omaha, 1977, cert. merit W.Va. Soc. CPAs, Elizah Watts Sells award AICPA, 1965, Brotherhood award NCCJ, 1993; inductee Ala. Acad. Honor, 1997. Mem.: Phi Eta Sigma, Birmingham Country Club, Shoal Creek Club, Phi Kappa Phi, Omicron Delta Kappa, Delta Sigma Pi. Republican. Presbyterian. Home: 2809 Shook Hill Cir Birmingham AL 35223-2618 Office: Vulcan Materials Co 1200 Urban Center Dr Birmingham AL 35242-2545

SKLOVSKY, ROBERT JOEL, naturopathic physician, pharmacist, educator; b. N.Y. BS, Bklyn. Coll., 1975; MA in Sci. Edn., Columbia U., 1976; PharmD, U. of Pacific, 1977; D in Naturopathic Medicine, Nat. Coll. Naturopathic Medicine, 1983. Intern Tripler Army Med. Ctr., Honolulu, 1977;

pvt. practice Milwaukie, Oreg., 1983—. Recipient Bristol Labs. award, 1983. Mem.: N.Y. Acad. Sci. Avocations: classical and jazz music, art, gardening, acting, painting. Office: 6910 SE Lake Rd Milwaukie OR 97267-2101

SKOCHELAK, SUSAN E. college dean; BS, Mich. Tech. U., 1975, MS in Biol. Sci., 1977; MD, U. Mich., 1981; MPH, U. N.C., 1986. Diplomae Am. Bd. Family Medicine. Intern, resident family medicine U. N.C.-N.C. Meml. Hosp., Chapel Hill, 1977-81; assoc. dean Academic Affairs U. Wis., Madison, 1993—. Cons. in field; assoc. prof. U. Wis. Author: (with others) Preceptor Education Project, Handbook for Clerkship Directors. Mem. Wis. Rural Health Dev. Council, Consortium Primary Care in Wis.; co-dir. Wis. Area Health Edn. Sys. Recipient National award Patient Care mag., 1997. Mem. AMA, Soc. Tchrs. Family Medicine, Assn. Am. Med. Colls., Am. Med. Women's ssn., ACPHE. Office: Univ Wiscónsin Med School 1300 University Ave Madison WI 53706-1510

SKOCPOL, THEDA RUTH, sociology and political science educator; b. Detroit, May 4, 1947; d. Allan Earnest and Jennie Mae (Becker) Barron; m. William John Skocpol, June 10, 1967; children: Michael Allan. BA in Sociology, Mich. State U., 1969; MA in Sociology, Harvard U., 1972, PhD in Sociology with distinction, 1975; DSc (hon.), Mich. State U., 1997. Asst. prof. sociology Harvard U., Cambridge, Mass., 1975—78, assoc. prof. sociology, 1978—81, prof. sociology, 1986—94, prof. govt./sociology, 1995—, dir., Ctr. for Am. Polit. Studies, 2000—; assoc. prof. sociology and polit. sci. U. Chgo., 1981—84, prof. sociology and polit. sci., 1984—86, dir. Ctr. for Study of Indsl. Socs., 1982—85. Mem. Sch. for Social Sci., Inst. for Advanced Study, Princeton, 1980—81; vis. disting. prof. Amsterdam Sch. for Social Science Rsch., Netherlands, 1997. Author: States and Social Revolutions: A Comparative Analysis of France, Russia and China, 1979, edits. in Italian, 1981, Korean, 1980, French, 1985, Spanish, 1985, Portuguese, 1985 (Wright Mills award Soc. Study of Social Problems, 1979, Am. Sociol. Assn. award, 1980), Protecting Soldiers and Mothers: The Political Origins of Social Policy in the U.S., 1992 (Woodrow Wilson Found. award, 1993, J. David Greenstone award, 1993, Best Book award Am. Sociol. Assn., 1993, Allan Sharlin Meml. award Soc. Sci. History Assn., 1993, Ralph Waldo Emerson award Phi Beta Kappa, 1993), Boomerang: Clinton's Health Security Effort and the Turn Against Govt. in the U.S., 1996, Diminished Democracy: From Membership to Mgmt. in American Civil Life, 2003; author: Social Revolutions in the Modern World, 1994, Japanese edit., Iwanami, 1997, Social Policy in the U.S.: Future Possibilities in Hist. Perspective, 1995; author: (with Kenneth Finegold) State and Party in America's New Deal, 1995; author: Boomerang: Health Reform and the Turn Against Govt., paperback edit., 1997, The Missing Middle: Working Families and the Future of Am. Social Policy, 2000; editor: Vision and Method in Hist. Sociology, 1984, Japanese edit. by Bokutakusha, 1995, Democracy, Revolution, and History, 1998, Turkish edit. by Tarih Vakfi Yayinlari, 1999; co-editor, with Peter Evans and Dietrich Rueschemeyer: Bringing the State Back In, 1985;; co-editor: (with Margaret Weir and Ann Shola Orloff) The Politics of Social Policy in the U.S.; co-editor: (with John L. Campbell) Am. Soc. and Politics: Institutional, Hist., and Theoretical Perspectives, 1994; co-editor: (with Dietrich Rueschemeyer) States, Social Knowledge, and the Origins of Modern Social Policies, 1996; co-editor: (with Stanley B. Greenberg) The New Majority: Toward a Popular Progressive Politics, 1997; co-editor: (with Morris P. Fiorina) Civic Engagement in Am. Democracy, 1999; contbr. articles to profl. jours. Fellow Danforth Found., 1969—74, Woodrow Wilson Found., NSF, 1969—72, John Simon Guggenheim Found., 1990; grantee Russell Sage Found., 1983—84, 1990—92, Ford Found., 1986—87; sr. vis. scholar, Russell Sage Found., 1984—85, Nat. Merit scholar, 1965—69. Fellow: Nat. Acad. of Arts and Sci.; mem.: Nat. Acad. Social Ins., Social Sci. History Assn. (pres. 1996), Am. Sociol. Assn., Am. Polit. Sci. Assn. (pres. politics and history sect. 1991—92, coun. mem. 1994—96, chair Hubert Humphrey award com. 1995, pres. 2002—03), Sociol. Sci. Rsch. Assn. (founder, co-chair 1985—94), Phi Beta Kappa. Democrat. Home: 66 Huron Ave Cambridge MA 02138-6708 Office: Harvard U 233 Littauer Cambridge MA 02138

SKODON, EMIL MARK, diplomat; b. Chgo., Nov. 25, 1953; s. Emil John and Anne (Soltes) S.; m. Dorothea Shaffer, Mar. 6, 1982; children: Catherine Marie, Christine Louise. BA, U. Chgo., 1975, MBA, 1976. Consular officer Am. Embassy, Bridgetown, Barbados, 1977-79, econ. officer East Berlin, Germany, 1979-81; econ. officer Office So. African Affairs, Dept. State, Washington, 1982-84; econ. officer Am. Embassy, Vienna, 1984-88, Kuwait City, Kuwait, 1989-91; consul gen. Am. Consulate Gen., Perth, Australia, 1991-94; dep. chief mission Am. Embassy, Singapore, 1995-98; dir. office Australia, New Zealand, Pacific Island Affairs Dept. State, Washington, 1998-2000, polit. advisor to USAF chief of staff, 2000—02; deputy chief of Mission Am. Embassy, Rome, 2002—. Recipient of U.S. Air Force decoration for exceptional civilian svc. Mem. Nat. Trust for Hist. Preservation. Avocations: visiting historic sites, good food, spending time with family. Office: US Embassy Rome Via Veneto 119A 00187 Rome Italy

SKOGEN, HAVEN SHERMAN, investment company executive; b. Rochester, Minn., May 8, 1927; s. Joseph Harold and Elpha (Hemphill) S.; m. Beverly R. Baker, Feb. 19, 1949; 1 child, Scott H. BS, Iowa State U., 1950; MS, Rutgers U., 1954, PhD, 1955; MBA, U. Chgo., 1970. Registered profl. engr., Wis. Devel. engr. E.I. duPont, Wilmington, Del., 1955—57; prof. Elmhurst (Ill.) Coll., 1957—58; chief engr. Stackpole, St. Marys, Pa., 1958—62; plant mgr. Magnatronics, Elizabethtown, Ky., 1962—65; mgr. Allen-Bradley, Milw., 1965—70; v.p. Dill-Clithrow, Chgo., 1970—74; oil co. exec. Occidental Oil Co., Grand Junction, Colo., 1974—92; ptnr. H&B Investment Co., 1992—. Author: Synthetic Fuel Combustion, 1984; inventor radioactive retort doping, locus retorting zone. Naval Rsch. fellow, 1951-55. Fellow Am. Inst. Chemists; mem. Internat. Platform Assn., Masons, Elks, Sigma Xi, Phi Beta Kappa, Phi Lambda Upsilon. Republican. Avocations: fly fishing, travel, reading, teaching. Home: 3152 Primrose Ct Grand Junction CO 81506-4147

SKOGLUND, MARILYN, state supreme court justice; b. Chgo., Aug. 28, 1946; BA, So. Ill. U., 1971; clerkship, 1977-81. Bar: Vt. 1981, U.S. Dist. Ct. Vt. 1981, U.S. Ct. Appeals (2d cir.) 1983. Asst. atty. gen. Civil Law Divsn., 1981—89, chief, 1988—93, Pub. Protection Divsn., 1993-94; judge Vt. Dist. Ct., 1994-97; assoc. justice Vt. Supreme Ct., 1997—. Office: Vt Supreme Ct 109 State St Montpelier VT 05609-0001

SKOGSBERGH, JAMES H. health facility administrator; BS, Iowa State U.; M in health admin., U. Iowa. Exec. v.p. Iowa Health Sys., Des Moines; pres, CEO Iowa Meth. Med. Ctr., Iowa Luth. Hosp., Blank Children's Hosp.; admin. resident to exec. v.p., chief oper. officer Mem. Health Sys., South Bend, Ind., 1982—91; exec. v.p. Iowa Meth. Med. Ctr., 1991; chief operating officer Advocate Health Care, Oak Brook, Ill., 2001—02, pres., CEO, 2002—. Fellow: Am. Coll. Healthcare Exec.; mem.: Ill. Hosp. Assoc. Advocacy Coun., Metro. Chgo. Healthcare Coun., Young Pres. Organ., Chgo. Econ. Club. Office: Advocate health Care 2025 Windsor Dr Oak Brook IL 60523-1586

SKOL, MICHAEL, anti-corruption and counter-money laundering consultant; b. Chgo., Oct. 15, 1942; s. Ted and Rebecca (Williams) S.; m. Claudia Serwer, Sept. 29, 1973. BA, Yale U., 1964. U.S. fgn. svc. officer Dept. State, 1965-96; polit. officer U.S. Embassy, Buenos Aires, 1966-67, Saigon, Viet Nam, 1968-70; desk officer Dept. State, Washington, 1970-72; comml. attache U.S. Embassy, Santo Domingo, Dominican Republic, 1972-75; econ. comml. officer U.S. Consulate Gen., Naples, Italy, 1975-76; comml. attache U.S. Embassy, Rome, 1976-78, polit. counselor San Jose, Costa Rica, 1978-82; dep. dir. policy planning Inter-Am. Affairs Bur. Dept. State, Washington, 1982-85; dep. chief of mission U.S. Embassy, Bogota, Colombia, 1985-87; dir. Andean affairs Dept. State, Washington, 1987-88; dep. asst. sec. state for S.Am. U.S. Dept. of State, Washington, 1988-90; amb. U.S. Embassy, Caracas, Venezuela, 1990-93; prin. dep. asst. sec. for Latin Am./Caribbean Dept. State, Washington, 1993-96; sr. v.p. Diplomatic Resolutions, Inc., Washington, 1996-97; pres. Skol & Assoc. Inc., N.Y., Washington, Bogota, 1998—; chmn. US Colombian Bus. Ptnrshp., 1996-99; mng. dir. L.Am. Decision Strategies, N.Y.C., 1998—. Pres. Skol, Ospina & Serna, N.Y.C., Washington ahd Bogota, 2001—03. Mem.: Coun. on Fgn. Rels., Yale Club of N.Y. Office: Skol & Assocs Inc 33 E 33d St 4th fl New York NY 10019

SKOLDBERG, PHYLLIS LINNEA, music educator, musician; d. August Theodore Skoldberg and Esther Amanda Carlson. MusB with honors, New Eng. Conservatory, 1955, MusM, 1957; M in Music Edn. with high distinction, Ind. U., 1964, Mus D in Performance, 1967. Violinist Houston Symphony Orch., 1957—59, Cin. Symphony Orch., 1959—62; assoc. instr. Ind. U., Bloomington, 1962—64; prof. music SUNY, Oswego, 1964—77; asst. dean fine arts Ariz. State U., Tempe, 1977—84, prof. music, 1977—2001, prof. emeritus, 2001—. Vis. artist Paris Conservatoire, 1973; vis. prof., cons. Australian String Tchrs. Assn., Brisbane and Sydney, 1984, Shanghai Conservatory Music, 1984; artist-in-residence U. Hong Kong, 1984; adj. prof., coord. string dept. Mesa (Ariz.) CC, 2001—. Author: The Strings: A Comparative View, Vol. I, 1981, Vol. 2, 1982; performer: (solos) Reston (Va.) Music Festival, 1972, 1973, Charles Ives Music Festival, 1975, 1976, Western Music Festival, 1980, (1st violin) Concert Quartet, 2003. Named winner performance competition, Seattle Philharm. Orch., 1952; recipient Boston Civic Music award, 1954. Mem.: Music Tchrs. Nat. Assn., Am. String Tchrs. Assn. (Ariz. pres. 1984—86, adv. bds. 1970—84). Home: 12002 S Tuzigoot Ct Phoenix AZ 85044-3467 Office: Mesa CC 1833 W Southern Ave Mesa AZ 85202 E-mail: phyllis.skoldberg@asu.edu.

SKOLER, CELIA REBECCA, retired art gallery director; b. Sioux City, Iowa, Apr. 7, 1931; d. Jacob and Flora (Gorchow) Stern; m. Louis Skoler, Aug. 24, 1952; children: Elisa Anne, Harry Jay. BFA in Art and Music magna cum laude, Syracuse U., 1976. Fin. planner Architects' Partnership, Syracuse, NY, 1969-71; bus. mgr. Skoler & Lee Architects P.C., Syracuse, 1971-89; owner, dir. New Acquisitions Gallery, Syracuse, 1981-95, 1995—2003; ptnr. Gallery Metro, Syracuse, 1991-93, mng. ptnr., 1992-93; contbg. writer Syracuse Herald and Syracuse Newtimes, Syracuse, 1989-91; ret., 2003. Art cons. Costello, Cooney & Fearon, Syracuse, 1981—83, IBM Hdqs., Syracuse, NY, 1983, Rochester, NY, 84, Albany, NY, 86, Menter, Rudin & Trivelpiece, Syracuse, 1987—88, Blue Cross/Blue Shield, Ctrl. N.Y., Syracuse, 1990, Syracuse Newspapers, 1992—94, GTE Svcs. Corp., Syracuse, 1995; gallery supr. of sudent interns Syracuse U., 1981—93; dir. mayoral portrait City of Syracuse, 1983; dir. Gelling Meml. portrait U. Coll., 1984; dir. Levine Meml. Commn. Temple Concord, 1984; TV producer Syracuse U. Friends of Art, 1979—80; panelist for art critique Everson Mus. Art, Syracuse, 1989; lectr. on gallery mgmt. Syracuse U. Sch. of Art, 1989; juror fine art N.Y. State Fair, 1982, 89; panelist Cultural Resources Coun., Onondaga County, NY, 2001—. One-man shows include Camillus Plaza, 1972, The Associated Artists Gallery, Syracuse, 1973, Libr. Fayetteville, N.Y., 1974; exhibited in group shows at N.Y. State Fair (1st prize 1974), U. Coll, 1967, 69, 71, Rochester Meml. Gallery, 1969-72, 74, The Associated Artists, 1971-72, Cen. N.Y. Art Open, 1970, 71, (Purchase prize 1970, 71), Munson Williams Protor Inst, Utica, N.Y., 1971, 72, Cayuga Mus., Auburn, N.Y., 1972, Oneida (N.Y.) Art Festival, 1969, (1st prize), Jewish Community Ctr., Syracuse, 1968 (1st prize 1969), St. David's Invitational, Dewitt, N.Y., 1970-75, Cooperstown Art Inst., Nat. Show, 1973, 74, Arena Nat. Show, Binghamton, N.Y., 1975 (Purchase prize 1975); prodr.: (autobiographical CD-ROM) In Rehearsal, 1997; represented in permanent collection at Savannah (Ga.) Coll. Art and Design & Syracuse U. Peer counselor Univ. Coll., Syracuse, 1980-85; Tel-auc auctioneer Sta. WCNY-TV, Liverpool, N.Y., 1982; mem. steering and implementation com. Gelling Meml. Lounge U. Coll., 1984-85; exec. bd. Syracuse U. Friends of Art, 1977-80; fine art juror Downtown Com., Syracuse, 1982, Oswego (N.Y.) Art Guild, 1984. Recipient Purchase prize Marine Midland Bank, 1974, Crouse-Irving Hosp., 1971, 1974; named to Sioux City Ctrl. High Roster Hall of Fame, 1998. Mem. Everson Mus. Art (corp.) mem. Phi Kappa Phi, Alpha Sigma Lambda (pres. 1980-81). Home and Office: 213 Scottholm Ter Syracuse NY 13224-1737

SKOLER, LOUIS, architect, educator; b. Apr. 5, 1920; s. Harry and Etta (Mitkoff) S.; m. Celia Rebecca Stern, 1952; children: Elisa Anne, Harry Jay. BArch, Cornell U., 1951. Maj. designer Sargent, Webster, Crenshaw & Folley, Syracuse, N.Y., 1951-59; design critic Cornell U., Ithaca, N.Y., 1956-57; pvt. practice arch. Syracuse, 1956-69; faculty Sch. Arch. Syracuse U., 1959-92, prof. emeritus, 1990—. Head of arch. masters program, 1980-82, head undergrad. program, 1989-90, arch. programs abroad, London, 1977, Scandinavia, 1985, Japan, 1988; ptnr. Arch. Partnership, Syracuse, 1969-71; pres. Skoler & Lee Archs., P.C., Syracuse, 1971-89; lectr. Nanjing Inst. Tech., China, summer 1986. Named Best in Residential Design, Design-in-Steel, 1968-69. Mem.: AIA. Home: 213 Scottholm Ter Syracuse NY 13224-1737 *A guiding principle over many years of teaching and practice, is the interrelationship of theory and work-of idea and circumstance, of imagination and the forces generated by day to day life.*

SKOLFIELD, MELISSA T. public relations executive, government official; b. New Orleans, June 25, 1958; m. Frank W. Curtis. BA in Econ. and Behavioral Sci., Rice U., 1980; MA in Pub. Affairs, George Washington U., 1986. Account exec. McDaniel & Tate Pub. Rels., Houston, 1981-84; press sec. Rep. Michael Andrews of Tex., 1985-87; press. sec. Senator Dale Bumpers of Ark., 1987-93; dep. asst. sec. for pub. affairs for policy and strategy Dept. Health and Human Svcs., Washington, 1993-95, asst. sec. pub. affairs, 1995—2001; sr. v.p., dir. healthcare practice group Golin/Harris Internat., Washington, 2001—03; comm. counsel Dem. Leader Nancy Pelosi U.S. House of Reps., Washington, 2003—. Press asst. Dem. Nat. Com., Dem. Nat. Conv., 1988, Clinton Pres. Campaign, Dem. Nat. Com., 1992. Mem. Senate Press Secs. Assn. (pres.), Assn. Dem. Press Assts., Pub. Rels. Soc. Am. Office: US Ho of Reps Office Dem Leader Washington DC 20515

SKOLL, JEFFREY, philanthropist, Internet company executive; BSEE, U. Toronto, 1987; MBA, Stanford U., 1995; LLD (hon.), U. Toronto, 2003. Founder Skoll Engring., 1987, Micros on the Move Ltd., 1990; mgr. distbn. channels online news info. Knight-Ridder Info.; co-founder, pres., v.p. strategic analysis and planning eBay Inc., San Jose, Calif., 1995. Bd. dirs. e-Bay Found., 1998—; founder, chmn. Skoll Found., 1999—; bd. dirs. Cmty. Found. Silicon Valley; mem. advisory bd. Stanford Grad. Sch. Bus. Named one of the most innovative philanthropists of the past decade, BusinessWeek, 2002, 2003; recipient Leafy award, 1999, Visionary award, Software Development Forum, 2001, Outstanding Philanthropist award, Silicon Valley chapter Assn. Fundraising Professionals, 2002, Internat. Assn. Fundraising Professionals, 2003. Office: Skoll Foundation 250 University Ave Ste 200 Palo Alto CA 94301 Office Phone: 650-331-1031. Office Fax: 650-331-1033.

SKOLNICK, JEROME H. law educator; b. 1931; BBA, CCNY, 1952, MA, 1953; PhD, Yale U., 1957. Rsch. assoc. Yale U., New Haven, 1956-60, asst. prof., 1960-62, U. Calif.-Berkeley Law Sch., 1962-67, prof., 1970—; Claire Clements deans prof. law emeritus Jurisprudence and Social Policy, 1970—; disting. prof. sch. of law NYU, 1997—. Vis. assoc. prof. NYU, 1966; vis. prof. U. Denver, 1967; assoc. prof. U. Chgo., 1967-69; prof. U. Calif.-San Diego, 1969-70; dir. Ctr. Study of Law and Soc., 1972—; cons. Bd. dirs. Pres.'s Commn. on Causes and Prevention of Violence, 1968-69; disting. vis. prof. John Jay Coll. Criminal Justice, 1995-96; adj. prof., co-dir. Ctr. for Rsch. in Crime and Justice NYU Sch. Law, 1996-97; chmn. com. on law and justice NRC, 1994-97. Author: (with D. Bayley) The New Blue Line, 1986, Justice Without Trial, 1966, House of Cards, 1978, (with R.D. Schwartz) Society and the Legal Order, 1970, (with J. Fyfe) Above the Law, 1993, (with J. Kaplan and M. Feeley) Criminal Justice. Carnegie fellow, 1956-66, Guggenheim fellow, 1980; Rockefeller Found. fellow, Bellagio, 1991. Mem. Am. Sociol. Assn. (bd. dirs. 1971-74), ACLU, Am. Soc. Criminology (pres.), Law and Soc. Assn. (trustee). Office: NYU Sch Law 40 Washington Sq S New York NY 10012-1005

SKOLNICK, LAWRENCE, neonatologist, medical administrator; b. N.Y.C., July 29, 1947; s. Harry and Sylvia Skolnick; m. Tamar Tumarkin, Apr. 7, 1970; children: Daniel, Michael, Rachel. BS, CUNY, 1968; MD, NYU, 1972; MPH, U. N.C., 1980. Dir. newborn medicine Hosp. of Albert Einstein Coll. Medicine, Bronx, N.Y., 1977-80; dir. neonatology Morristown (N.J.) Meml. Hosp., 1980—, Overlook Hosp., Summit, NJ, 1999—, Atlantic Health Sys., 1999—; assoc. prof. med. pediat. UNDNJ-N.J.Sch. medicine, 2001—. E-mail: larry.skolnick@ahsys.org.

SKOLNICK, MARILYN, civic worker; b. N.Y.C., Jan. 17, 1925; d. Max and Annie Ruth (Stern) Kassel; n. Herbert Skolnick, Aug. 2, 1948; 1 child, Tamara. BA, Bklyn. Coll., 1946; MA, U. Okla., 1948; postgrad., State U. Iowa, 1948-52. Host, prodr. cable TV program Focus on Issues, 1983—; chair citizen participation com. Transp. Rsch. Bd., Nat. Acad. Sci., 1987-94; sec. local transp. fin. com., 1987—. Bd. dirs. Port Authority of Allegheny County, 1982-95; pres. Allegheny County Transp. Coun., 1997-99, v.p., 1999—; mem. Pa. Small Bus. Compliance Adv. Com., 1992—. Chair Monroeville Planning Commn., 1983-85; bd. dirs. Pa. Planning Assn., 1983-85; mem. Allegheny County Hazardous Waste Task Force, 1983-85; bd. dirs. Group Against Smog and Pllution; mem. Pa. Transp. Adv. Com., 1983-86; mem. air pollution ctrl. adv. com. Allegheny County Health Dept., 1985—; mem. Allegheny County Local Emergency Planning Com., 1987—. Mem. LWV (former bd. dirs.), N.Y. Acad. Scis., Pa. Acad. Scis., Sierra Club (bd. dirs. Pa. chpt. 1986—, chair Allegheny Group 1988-91), Sigma Xi. Home: 109 Southridge Dr Monroeville PA 15146-4739

SKOLNICK, S. HAROLD, lawyer; b. Woonsocket, R.I., June 17, 1915; s. David and Elsie (Silberman) S.; m. Shirley Marshall. AB cum laude, Amherst Coll., 1936; JD, Boston U., 1940. Bar: R.I. 1940, U.S. Supreme Ct. 1946, D.C. 1947, Fla. 1952, U.S. Dist. Ct. (so. dist.) Fla. 1953, U.S. Ct. Appeals (5th cir.) 1960, U.S. Ct. Appeals (11th cir.) 1981. Atty. Dept. of War, Washington, 1940-42; asst. gen. counsel, asst. chief legal dept. Office Chief Ordnance, Dept. of Army, Washington, 1947-50; assoc. Francis I. McCanna, Providence, R.I., 1951-52; ptnr. French & Skolnick, Miami, Fla., 1953-60; sole practice Miami, Fla., 1961—. Served to lt. col. U.S. Army, 1942-47. Mem. ABA, Am. Judicature Soc., Nat. Def. Indsl. Assn. (life), R.I. Bar Assn., D.C. Bar Assn., Dade County Bar Assn., Estate Planning Coun. Greater Miami, Masons, Shriners. Home and Office: 6521 SW 122d St Miami FL 33156-5550

SKOLNIK, BARNET DAVID, retired lawyer; b. N.Y.C., Feb. 8, 1941; s. Jack and Edythe (Savitz) S.; m. Patricia L. Krohn; children: Sarah, Deborah, Daniel, Joseph, Benjamin, Rebecca, Zachary. AB in Am. Govt. cum laude, Harvard U., 1962, LLB, 1965. Bar: D.C. 1966, Md. 1984, Maine 1991. Atty. criminal div. U.S. Dept. Justice, Washington, 1966-68; asst. U.S. atty. for Dist. Md., Balt., 1968-78; chief public corruption unit U.S. Atty.'s Office, Balt., 1973-78; pvt. practice law Balt. and Washington, 1978—91, Portland, Maine, 1991—94; ret. Tchr., lectr. on trial practice, white collar criminality, pub. corruption. Recipient Spl. Achievement award Dept. Justice, 1972, 74, Spl. Commendation for Outstanding Svc., Dept. Justice, 1978, Younger Fed. Lawyer award Fed. Bar Assn., 1974, Atty. Gen.'s Disting. Service award, 1974, Legal award Assn. Fed. Investigators, 1977 E-mail: bskolnik@megalink.net.

SKOLNIK, MERRILL I. electrical engineer; b. Balt., Nov. 6, 1927; s. Samuel and Mary (Baker) S.; m. Judith Magid, June 4, 1950; children: Nachama, Martin Allen, Julia Anne, Ellen Charlotte. BEng, Johns Hopkins U., 1947, MSEng, 1949, DEng, 1951. Research scientist Johns Hopkins U., Balt., 1947-54, vis. prof., 1973-74; engring. specialist Sylvania Electric, Boston, 1954; staff mem. MIT Lincoln Lab., Lexington, Mass., 1954-59; research mgr. Electronic Communications, Timonium, Md., 1959-64, Inst. Def. Analyses, Arlington, Va., 1964-65; supr. radar divsn. Naval Research Lab., Washington, 1965-96, radar sys. cons., 1996—. Mem. bd. visitors Duke U. Engring. Sch., Durham, N.C., 1976-93; disting. vis. sci. Jet Propulsion Lab., 1990-92; mem. Md. Gov.'s Exec. Adv. Com., 1993-95. Author: Introduction to Radar Systems, 1962, 3d edit., 2001, Radar Handbook, 1970, 2d edit., 1990; editor: Radar Applications, 1988. Recipient Heinrich Hertz premium Instn. Electronic and Radio Engrs., London, 1964, Disting. Alumnus award Johns Hopkins U., 1979, Disting. Civilian Svc. award USN, 1982, Meritorious Exec. award Sr. Exec. Svc., 1986, Johns Hopkins Engring. and Applied Sci. Excellence in Tchg. award, 1998; named to Soc. of Scholars, Johns Hopkins U., 1975. Fellow IEEE (editor Proceedings 1986-89, Harry Diamond award 1983, Centennial medal 1984, Dennis J. Picard medal for radar technologies and applications 2000); mem. Nat. Acad. Engring. Home: 8123 McDonogh Rd Baltimore MD 21208-1005 Office: Naval Rsch Lab Washington DC 20375-5320 E-mail: skolnik@radar.nrl.navy.mil.

SKOLNIK, RICHARD ALAN, plastic surgeon; b. N.Y.C., Jan. 7, 1951; BA in Biology summa cum laude, C.W. Post Coll., 1972; MD, Cornell U., 1976. Cert. Am. Bd. Plastic and Reconstructive Surgery. Resident gen. surgery Mt. Sinai Med. Ctr., N.Y.C., 1976-79, resident plastic surgery, 1979-82; clin. instr. Mt. Sinai Sch. Medicine, N.Y.C., 1982-84, asst. clin. prof., 1985—; assoc. attending Mt. Sinai Med. Ctr., N.Y.C., 1982—, Beth Israel Med. Ctr., N.Y.C., 1984—; courtesy staff Beth Israel North (Doctor's Hosp.), N.Y.C., 1987—. Fellow cleft lip and palate Children's Hosp., Lima, Peru, 1982; vis. prof. Reconstructive Surgery Found., Maceo, Brazil, 1990, Pune, India, 1994, Beijing, China, 1998. Fellow ACS; mem. Am. Soc. of Plastic and Reconstructive Surgeons, N.Y. Regional Soc. Plastic and Reconstructive Surgeons, AMA, Barsky Soc., N.Y. State Med. Soc. Avocations: ceramics, cooking, golf, tennis. Office: 21 E 87th St New York NY 10128-0506

SKOLNIKOFF, EUGENE B. political science educator; b. Phila., Aug. 29, 1928; s. Benjamin H. and Betty (Turoff) S.; m. Winifred S. Weinstein, Sept. 15, 1957; children: Matthew, Jessica. BS, MS, MIT, 1950, PhD, 1965; BA, Oxford (Eng.) U., 1952, MA, 1955. Registered profl. engr. Rsch. asst. in elec. engring. Uppsala U., Sweden, 1950; prof. polit. sci. emeritus M.I.T., 1965—, chmn. polit. sci. dept., 1970-74; dir. Center for Internat. Studies, 1972-87. Vis. rsch. prof. Carnegie Endowment for Internat. Peace, Geneva, 1969-70; vis. fellow Balliol Coll., U. Oxford, 1989; vis. scholar Yale U., 1997; systems analyst Inst. for Def. Analyses, Washington, 1957-58; mem. White House staff Office Spl. Asst. to Pres. for Sci. and Tech., Washington, 1958-63; adj. prof. Fletcher Sch. Law and Diplomacy, Tufts U., Medford, Mass., 1965-72; sr. cons. White House Office of Sci. and Tech. Policy, 1977-81, also vice chmn. adv. com. on sci., tech. and devel.; mem. policy rev. com. on nat. low-level nuclear waste mgmt., 1980-86; cons. Dept. State, Office of Tech. Assessment, AID, OECD, Resources for the Future, Am. Soc. Internat. Law, Ford Found., Inst. Def. Analyses; chmn., pres. Sci. and Public Policy Studies Group, 1967-73; mem. Internat. Council Sci. Policy Studies; Montague Burton vis. prof. U. Edinburgh, 1977, mem. several Nat. Rsch. Coun. coms.; chmn. bd. UN U. Inst. on New Tech. (INTECH), Maastricht, Holland, 1998—; Michael Dukakis vis. prof. pub. policy Am. Coll. Thessaloniki, Greece, 2000. Author: Science, Technology and American Foreign Policy, 1967, International Imperatives of Technology, 1972, The Elusive Transformation: Science, Technology, and the Evolution of International Politics, 1993; co-editor: World Eco-Crisis, 1972, Visions of Apocalypse, End or Rebirth?, 1985, The Implementation and Effectiveness of International Environmental Commitments, 1998; contbr. articles to publs.; chmn. editorial bd. Pub. Sci., 1971-75; mem. editorial bd. Tech. Rev., 1976-78, Social Studies of Sci., 1970-75, Internat. Orgn., 1974-80, Internat. Rels. of Asia Pacific, 2000--; patentee hybrid circuits. Trustee German Marshall Fund, 1979-87, chmn., 1980-86; trustee UN Rsch. Inst. for Social Devel., 1979-85; bd. dirs. Saco Def., 1984-86; mem. Overseas Devel. Coun.; mem. U.S. del. UN Commn. for Social Devel., 1979; mem. State Dept. Adv. Com. on Sci. and Tech., 1987-90. Served with U.S. Army Security Agy., 1955-57. Rhodes scholar, 1950-52; Rockefeller Found. fellow, 1963-65; decorated Comdr.'s Cross Fed. Republic Germany, Order of Rising Sun, Golden Rays, Neck Ribbon, Japan. Fellow Am. Acad. Arts and Scis. (councillor 1973-77), AAAS (sec. sect. K 1967-69, mem. com. on sci. and pub. policy 1973-74, com. on sci., engring. and pub. policy 1984-89); mem. UN Assn., Fedn. Am. Scientists, (coun. 1981-85), Coun. Fgn. Rels., Am. Assn. Rhodes Scholars, Soc. for Social Studies of Sci., Sigma Xi, Tau Beta Pi, Eta Kappa Nu. Home: 3 Chandler St Lexington MA 02420-3601 Office: MIT E53-366 77 Massachusetts Ave Cambridge MA 02139-4307 E-mail: ebskol@mit.edu.

SKOLOVSKY, ZADEL, concert pianist, educator; b. Vancouver, B.C., Can. came to U.S., 1923, naturalized, 1929; s. Max and Kate (Jones) S.; m. Alice Maffett Glass, July 29, 1947 (div. 1953). Diploma, Curtis Inst. Music, 1937; studied piano with, Isabelle Vengerova and Leopold Godowsky; conducting with, Fritz Reiner and Pierre Monteux; violin with, Edwin Bachmann. Prof. music Ind. U., 1975-87, prof. emeritus, 1987—; juror NYU Internat. Tchaikovsky Piano Competition, 1978, 3d Latin Am. Teresa Carreno Piano Competition, Caracas, Venezuela, 1978, U. Md. Internat. Piano Competition, 1981, Joanna Hodges Internat. Piano Competition, Palm Desert, Calif., 1983; tchr. master classes; concert tour of U.S., S. Am. and Far East, 1989-90. Debut at Town Hall as winner of the Walter W. Naumburg award, 1939; appearances in recitals in Carnegie Hall, N.Y.C., 1939—, ann. concert tours U.S.A. and Can., 1939—, biennial tours Europe, Israel, S.Am., Far East, also condr. master classes, 1986—; soloist with N.Y. Philharmonic Symphony Orch.; soloist under condrs. Dimitri Mitropoulos, Charles Munch, Leonard Bernstein, Lorin Maazel, Erich Leinsdorf, Jan Kubelik, Paul Kletzki, Arthur Rodzinski, Paul Paray; appeared as a soloist Lewishohn Stadium, N.Y. and Robin Hood Dell, Phila., under condrs. Vladimir Golschmann, Pierre Monteux, Alexander Smallens; soloist with NBC Orch., Nat. Orch. Assn., Phila. Orch., Nat. Orch., Washington, San Francisco Symphony, Israel Philharmonic, Residentie Orch. at The Hague, L'Orchestre Nat. de Belgique, B.B.C. Scottish Orch., orchs. of Luxembourg, Lisbon, Portugal, Hilversum Radio, Holland, Paris, London, Ravinia, Chgo., N.Y.C.; also appeared on TV; first performance Second Piano Concerto by Prokofieff with N.Y. Philharmonic Orch. under Charles Munch, 1948; world premier Concerto No. 4 of Darius Milhaud with Boston Symphony, 1950; 1st extensive European tour, 1953; appeared with Residency Orch. of the Hague, 2d tour, appeared as soloist with Israel Philharmonic Orch. at opening concert World Festival Music, 1954, appeared in Mexico, 1965, European tour, Eng., Holland, Scandinavia, Belgium, 1965-66, 67, recital, Queen Elizabeth Hall, London, Eng., 1971, 73, recitals, B.C., 1975; concert tour of, S. Am., 1978, U.S., Can. and Europe, 1981-82, Can., 1991; 1st concert tour of Far East, 1983; mus. films for TV., recorded for Columbia Masterworks Records, Philips Records; transcontinental Can. tour, 1991, U.S.A, 1991; annual concert tours U.S.A., Can., Europe, 1992-93. Recipient prizes from Nat. Fedn. Music Clubs, 1943, Nat. Music League, 1940, Robin Hood Dell Young Am. Artists award 1943; recipient Walter W. Naumburg award, 1939. Mem.: Lotos (N.Y.C.). Democrat. Jewish. Avocations: tennis, chess, literature, theater.

SKOMAL, EDWARD NELSON, aerospace company executive, electromagnetic environments consultant; b. Kansas City, Mo., Apr. 15, 1926; s. Edward Albert and Ruth (Bangs) S.; m. Elizabeth Birkbeck, Mar. 4, 1951; children: Susan Beth, Catherine Anne, Margaret Elaine; m. Joan Kerner, Apr. 9, 1988. BA, Rice U., Houston, 1947, MA, 1949. Engr., Socony Rsch. Labs., Dallas, 1949-51; asst. sect. head Nat. Bur. Standards, Washington, 1951-56; project engr. Sylvania Research Lab., Palo Alto, Calif., 1956-59; mgr. applications engrng., chief applications engr. Motorola Solid State Systems Div., Phoenix, 1959-63; dir. communications dept. Aerospace Corp., El Segundo, Calif., 1963-86, ret., 1986; mem. Presdl. Joint Tech. Adv. Com. on Electromagnetic Compatibility, Washington, 1965-70, 71-75. Author: Man Made Radio Noise, 1978, Automatic Vehicle Locating Systems, 1980; Measuring the Radio Frequency Environment, 1985; contbr. articles to profl. jours. Patentee in field of radio systems, solid state devices, radar cross sect. reduction of ballistic rentry vehicles and sold state microwave components. Elder Riverside Presbytery. With USN, 1944-6. Fellow IEEE (asst. editor Trans. Electromatic Compatibility 1978-86, chmn. tech. adv. com. 1982-86, chmn. tech. com. electromagnetic environments 1976-82, standards com. 1980-86, fellow nominating com. 1980-83, nat. com. standards coordinating com. on definitions 1986—, Richard A. Stoddart award 1980, cert. of Achievement 1971, Paper of Yr. award 1970); mem. IEEE Electromagnetic Soc. (life), Am. Phys. Soc., Internat. Union Radio Scientists, Friends A.H. Smiley Pub. Libr., Sigma Xi. Republican. Presbyterian. Home: 1802 Morning Dove Ln Redlands CA 92373

SKONEY, SOPHIE ESSA, educational administrator; b. Detroit, Jan. 29, 1929; d. George Essa and Helena (Dihmes) Cokalay; m. Daniel J. Skoney, Dec. 28, 1957; children: Joseph Anthony, James Francis, Carol Anne. PhB, U. Detroit, 1951; MEd, Wayne State U., 1960, EdD, 1975; postgrad., Ednl. Inst. Harvard Grad. Sch., 1986—. Tchr. elem. sch. Detroit Bd. Edn., 1952-69, remedial reading specialist, 1969-70, curriculum coord., 1970-71, region 6 article 3 title I coord., 1971-83, area achievement specialist, 1984-88; adminstrv. asst. Office Grant Procurement and Compliance, 1988-2000. Mem. dean's adv. coun. Coll. Edn. Wayne State U., 1995—; cons. in field. Editor newsletter Alliance to the Mich. Dental Assn., 1993-2000. Recipient Disting. Alumni award Wayne State U., 1993. Mem. ASCD, Wayne State U. Edn. Alumni Assn. (pres. bd. govs. 1979-80, newsletter editor 1975-77, 80—), Macomb Dental Aux. (pres. 1969-70), Mich. Dental Aux. (pres. 1980-81), Alliance Mich. Dental Assn. (pres. 1998-2000), Am. Assn. Sch. Adminstrs., Wayne State U. Alumni Assn. (dir., v.p. 1985-86), Internat. Reading Assn., Mich. Reading Assn., Mich. Assn. State and Fed. Program Specialists, Profl. Women's Network (newsletter editor 1981-83, pres. 1985-87, Anthony Wayne award for leadership 1981), Retirees Orgn. Sch. Adminstrs. and Suprs. (pres. 2003—), Anthony Wayne Soc., Delta Kappa Gamma, Beta Sigma Phi, Phi Delta Kappa (v.p. 1988-90, pres. 1990-91, Educator of Yr. 1985, 91, 96, 2000). Roman Catholic. Home: 20813 Lakeland St Saint Clair Shores MI 48081-2104 Personal E-mail: skoneys@aol.com.

SKOOG, DONALD PAUL, retired pathologist, educator; b. Sioux City, Iowa, Sept. 29, 1931; m. Mary Ann Bunn, 1955; children: Robert Eugene, David Alan (dec.), Kristin Marie. BA magna cum laude, Midland Lutheran Coll., Fremont, Nebr., 1953; MD cum laude, U. Nebr., 1958; DSci (hon.), Midland Luth. Coll., 1993. Diplomate Am. Bd. Pathology. Intern, then resident in pathology Bishop Clarkson Meml. Hosp., Omaha, 1958-62; resident in pathology Parkland Meml. Hosp., Dallas, 1962-63; fellow in pathology U. Tex. Southwestern Med. Sch., Dallas, 1962-63; practice medicine specializing in pathology Omaha, 1963-92. Pathologist Bishop Carlson Meml. Hosp., 1963-88, chmn. dept. pathology, 1978-80, dir. dept., 1986-87, chmn. med. edn. com., 1978-83, sec.-treas. med. staff, 1982-87; prof. pathology and microbiology U. Nebr. Coll. Med., 1977-93, mem. dean's faculty adv. coun., 1977-79, mem. grad. and continuing edn. com., 1980-85, mem. coun. for affilitated instns., 1981-83, mem. admissions com., 1986-91, sr. cons. pathology and microbiology, 1993—; assoc. med. dir. ARC Blood Svcs., Midwest Region, Omaha, 1988, med. dir./dir. 1989-91, dir./prin. officer, 1991-92, mem. computer sys. selection com., 1991; med. affairs com. ARC Blood Svcs., Washington, 1991-92; mem. exec. com., chmn. loan com. Nebr. Med. Edn. Fund, 1983-91, sec., treas., 1984-91; mem. comm. com., credentials and quality improvement com. Pvt. Practice Assocs., Omaha, 1998—. Mem. editl. bd. Lab. Medicine, 1979—2003; contbr. articles to med. jours. Councilman Luther Meml. Luth. Ch., Omaha, 1966-72, 87-91, vice chmn., 1969-72; trustee Midland Luth. Coll., 1968-87, chmn., 1973-75. Recipient Alumni Achievement award Midland Luth. Coll., 1972, Disting. Svc. award Sch. of Allied Health Program, U. Nebr. Med. Ctr., 1990, Disting. Alumnus award U. Nebr. Coll. Medicine Alumni Assn., 1998. Fellow Am. Soc. Clin. Pathologists (hematology profl. self-assessment com. 1972, 75,78, adv. coun. 1972-78, chmn. coun. hematology 1978-81, editor Hematology Check Sample 1983-88, Disting. Svc. award Commn. on Continuing Edn. 1985, mem. bd. censors 1987-89, mem. nat. meeting activities com. 1989-92, chmn. 1990-92, Israel Davidsohn disting. svc. award 1993), Coll. Am. Pathologists (hematology resource com. 1981-86, vice chmn. 1982-85); mem. AMA, Nebr. Assn. Pathologists, Nebr. Med. Assn., Met. Omaha Med. Soc. (coun. on grievances and profl. ethics 1983-91), Midland Luth. Coll. Alumni Assn. (pres. 1969-70), Alpha Omega Alpha (pres. U. Nebr. chpt. 1976-77, counsellor 1984-90). Home: 706 S 96th St Omaha NE 68114-4918 Personal E-mail: dpsmd@cox.net.

SKOOG, DOUGLAS ARVID, retired chemistry educator, writer; b. Willmar, Minn., May 4, 1918; s. Arvid C. and Hilma E. (Erickson) S.; m. Judith Bone, Oct. 10, 1942; children: James Arvid, Jon Douglas. BS, Oreg. State U., 1940; PhD, U. Ill., 1943. Research chemist Standard Oil Co. of Calif., Richmond, Calif., 1943-47; asst. prof. chemistry Stanford (Calif.) U., 1947-53, assoc. prof., 1953-62, prof., assoc. exec. head dept. chemistry, 1963-76, prof. emeritus, 1976—; writer Stanford, 1976—. Author: Fundamentals of Analytical Chemistry, 8th rev. edit., 2003, Principles of Instrumental Analysis, 1998, 5th rev. edit., 1992, Analytical Chemistry, 7th rev. edit., 2000; contbr. articles to profl. jours. Fellow AAAS; mem. Am. Chem. Soc. (pres. Santa Clara Valley sect. 1962, Fisher award in analytical chemistry 1999), Sigma Xi, Phi Kappa Phi, Alpha Chi Sigma. Clubs: Bohemian (San Francisco). Avocations: flying, skiing. Home: 401 Webster St Apt 302 Palo Alto CA 94301-1249 Personal E-mail: skoog@stanford.edu.

SKOOG, GERALD DUANE, science educator; b. Sioux City, Iowa, Feb. 27, 1936; s. Paul and Mary Ann Skoog; m. Elizabeth Ann Lee, Dec. 28, 1962; children: Jeffrey, John, Sarah. BS, U. Nebr., 1958; MA, U. No. Iowa, 1963; Ed.D., U. Nebr., 1969. Tchr. various schs., Nebr., Ill., 1958-69; instr. U. Nebr., Lincoln, summer 1969; asst. prof. curriculum and instrn. Tex. Tech U., Lubbock, 1969-72, assoc. prof., coordinator program, 1972-74, assoc. prof., chmn. secondary edn., 1976-80, prof., chmn. secondary edn., 1980-90, prof., chmn. curriculum and instrn., 1990-97, Helen DeVitt Jones prof., 1997-2001, pres. faculty senate, 1986-87, Paul Whitfield Horn prof., 2000—, dean Coll. Edn., 2002—03. Vis. prof. Western Ill. U., summer 1972; lectr. in field; participant, facilitator numerous workshops; cons. Contbr. numerous articles to profl. jours., also reviewer articles and papers; co-author secondary sch. science textbooks. Bd. dirs. Gloria Dei Luth. Ch., Lubbock, 1971-74, 92-93; bd. dirs. Luth. Coun. Cmty. Action, 1970-71, Good Neighbor Ministry, 1982-84; leader Boy Scouts Am., 1978-79; foster parent Luth. Social Svcs. Tex.; bd. dirs. Triangle Coalition for Sci. and Tech., 1986-95. Recipient Pres.'s Faculty Achievement award Tex. Tech. U., 1986, Disting. Leadership award, 1996, Award of Excellence, U. Nebr., Lincoln Tchrs. Coll. Alumni Assn., 2003; named Notable Alumnus, U. Nebr., Lincoln, Tchrs. Coll., 1998; named to Tex. Sci. Hall of Fame, 2000. Fellow AAAS; mem. ASCD, Nat. Sci. Tchrs. Assn. (life, bd. dirs. 1977-79, pres. 1985-86, various coms., Disting. Svc. to Sci. Edn. award 1994, Robert H. Carleton award 2004), Nat. Assn. Rsch. Sci. Teaching, Assn. Edn. Tchrs. Sci., Sci. Tchrs. Assn. Tex. (hon. mem., past pres., Skoog Cup award, Robert H. Carleton award 2004), Nat. Assn. Biology Tchrs., Soc. Study Edn., Phi Delta Kappa. Home: 3214 67th St Lubbock TX 79413-6206 Office: Tex Tech U Coll Edn Lubbock TX 79409 Office Phone: 806-742-1998.

SKOOG, WILLIAM ARTHUR, former oncologist, educator; b. Culver City, Calif., Apr. 10, 1925; s. John Lundeen and Allis Rose (Gatz) Skoog; m. Ann Douglas, Sept. 17, 1949; children: Karen, William Arthur, James Douglas, Allison. AA, UCLA, 1944; BA with great distinction, Stanford U., 1946, MD, 1949. Intern in medicine Stanford Hosp., San Francisco, 1948-49, asst. resident in medicine, 1949-50, N.Y. Hosp., N.Y.C., 1950-51; sr. resideit in medicine Wadsworth VA Hosp., L.A., 1951, attending specialist in internal medicine, 1962-68; pvt. practice internal medicine Los Altos, Calif., 1959-61; pvt. practice hematology and oncology, Santa Monica, Calif., 1971-72; pvt. practice med. oncology, San Bernardino, Calif., 1972-94. Assoc. staff Palo Alto-Stanford Med. Ctr., 1959-61, U. Calif. Med. Ctr., San francisco, 1959-61; assoc. attending physician UCLA Hosp. and Clinics, 1961-78; vis. physician in internal medicine Harbor Gen. Hosp., Torrance, Calif., 1962-65, attending physician, 1965-71; cons. in chemistry Clin. Lab., UCLA Hosp., 1963-68; affiliate cons. staff St. John's Hosp., Santa Monica, 1967-71, courtesy staff, 1971-72; courtesy attending med. staff Santa Monica Hosp., 1967-72; staff physician St. Bernardine (Calif.) Hosp., 1972-94, hon. staff, 1994—; staff physician San Bernardino Cmty. Hosp., 1972-90, courtesy staff, 1990-94; chief sect. oncology San Bernardino County Hosp., 1972-76; cons. staff Redlands(Calf.) Cmty. Hosp., 1972-83, courtesy staff, 1983-94, hon. staff, 1994—; asst. in medicine Cornell U. Med. Coll., N.Y.C., 1950-51; jr. rsch. physician UCLA Atomic Energy Project, 1954-55; instr. medicine, asst. rsch. physician dept. medicine UCLA Med. Ctr., 1955-56, asst. prof. medicine, asst. rsch. physician, 1956-59; clin. assoc. in hematology VA Ctr., L.A., 1956-59; co-dir. metabolic rsch. unit UCLA Ctr. for Health Scis., 1955-59, 61-65; co-dir. Health Scis. Clin. Rsch. Ctr., 1965-68, dir., 1968-72; clin. instr. medicine Stanford U., 1959-61; asst. clin. prof. medicine, assoc. rsch. physician U. Calif. Med. Ctr., San Francisco, 1959-61; lectr. medicine UCLA Sch. Medicine, 1961-62, assoc. prof., 1962-72, assoc. clin. prof., 1973—. Contbr. articles to med. jours. Active duty USNR, 1943—46, lt. M.C. USNR, 1951—53. Fellow: ACP, Am Soc. Internal Medicine; mem.: AMA, San Bernardino County Med. Soc., Am. Soc Clin. Oncology, L.A. Acad. Medicine, Am. Fedn. Clin. Rsch., Western Soc. Clin. Rsch., So. Calif. Acad. Clin. Oncology, Calif. Med. Assn., Redlands Country Club, Alpha Omega Alpha, Sigma Xi, Phi Beta Kappa, Alpha Kappa Kappa. Episcopalian (vestryman 1965-70). Home: 1119 Kimberly Pl Redlands CA 92373-6786 Home Fax: 909-798-5016. Personal E-mail: wasredarrow@aol.com.

SKOOR, JOHN BRIAN, art educator, art consultant; b. Mount Vernon, Wash., Dec. 14, 1939; s. George Nephi and Marie Elizabeth (Collins) S.; m. Susan Diane Waugh, June 17, 1972; children: Marie Elizabeth, Christine Elaine. AA in Edn., Graceland Coll., Lamoni, 1960; BA in Art, Cen. Wash. U., 1962, BA in Edn., 1965, MA in Art, 1969. Art instr. Delta (Mich.) Coll., Saginaw, 1977-79; instr. Renton (Wash.) Vocat. Tech. Inst., 1981-83; art instr. Green River (Wash.) Community Coll., Auburn, 1988—; cons. staff and development instr. various Seattle sch. dists., 1988—; art instr. Higline Community Coll., Seattle, 1990—. Adj. faculty Cen. Wash. U., 1984—, Seattle Pacific U., 1986—; dir. sr. programs Highline C.C., 1992—, instr. sr.'s making art program, 1998—; guest speaker Wash. Art Educators Assn. Conv., 1990. Illustrator of religious curriculum texts, 1978-80; exhibited acrylic theol. paintings show, Independence, Mo., 1980. Guest speaker Alma (Mich.) Art Dept., 1977, Nat. Camping Assn., Detroit, 1979, Wash. Art Tchrs. Assn., 1990; coord. sr. programs Highline C.C., 1992-99; elder Reorganized Ch. of Jesus Christ of Latter Day Saints, Seattle, 1966—, pastor, 1987—, bd. dirs. creative arts festival, Mich., 1977; art instr. Srs. Making Art, Greater Puget Sound area. Mem. Wash. Alliance for Arts Edn. (commn. chmn. 1987—), Richland Art Tchrs. Assn. (pres. 1965-66), Tri-City Art Tchrs. Assn. (pres. 1966-67), Nat. Art Educators Assn. Avocations: public speaking, graphic design, calligrapher, performing artist, ministry. Home: 8506 Daimler Way Sacramento CA 95828-5855

SKOPIL, OTTO RICHARD, JR., federal judge; b. Portland, Oreg., June 3, 1919; s. Otto Richard and Freda Martha (Boetticher) Skopil; m. Jane Rae Lundy, July 27, 1956; children: Otto Richard III, Casey Robert, Shannon Ida, Molly Jo. BA in Econs., Willamette U., 1941, LLB, 1946, LLD (hon.), 1983. Bar: Oreg. 1946, U.S. Dist. Ct. Oreg., U.S. Ct. Appeals (9th cir.), U.S. Supreme Ct. 1946. Assoc. Skopil & Skopil, 1946—51; ptnr. Williams, Skopil, Miller & Beck (and predecessors), Salem, Oreg., 1951—72; judge U.S. Dist. Ct., Portland, 1972—79, chief judge, 1976—79; judge U.S. Ct. Appeals (9th cir.), Portland, 1979—85, sr. judge, 1986—. Chmn. com. adminstrn. of fed. magistrate sys. U.S. Jud. Conf., 1980—86; co-founder Oreg. chpt. Am. Leadership Forum; chmn. 9th cir. Jud. Coun. Magistrates Adv. Com., 1988—91; chmn. U.S. Jud. Conf. Long Range Planning Com., 1990—95. Hi-Y adviser Salem YMCA, 1951—52; appeal agt. SSS Marion County (Oreg.) Draft Bd., 1953—66; master of ceremonies 1st Gov.'s Prayer Breakfast for State Oreg., 1959; citizens adv. com. City of Salem, 1970—71; Gov.'s Com. on Staffing Mental Instns., 1969—70; pres., bd. dirs. Marion County Tb and Health Assn., 1958—61; bd. dirs. Willamette U., 1969—71; elder Mt. Park Ch., 1979—81; bd. dirs. Willamette Valley Camp Fire Girls, 1946—56, Internat. Christian Leadership, 1959, Fed. Jud. Ctr., 1979. Lt. USNR, 1942—46. Recipient Oreg. Legal Citizen of Yr. award, 1986, Disting. Alumni award, Willamette U. Sch. Law, 1988. Mem.: ABA, Internat. Soc. Barristers, Assn. Ins. Attys. U.S. and Can. (Oreg. rep. 1970), Def. Rsch. Inst., Oreg. Assn. Def. Counsel (bd. dirs.), Am. Judicature Soc., Marion County Bar Assn., Oreg. Bar Assn. (bd. dirs.), Prayer Breakfast Movement (fellowship coun.), Illahe Hills Country Club (pres., bd. dirs. 1964—67), Exchange Club (pres. 1947), Salem Club. Office: Sr Circuit Judge 827 US Courthouse 1000 SW 3rd Ave Portland OR 97204-2930

SKORA, SUSAN SUNDMAN, lawyer; b. Chgo., Jan. 5, 1947; d. Gordon Manley and Julia Walker (Firebaugh) Sundman; m. Alan Patrick Skora, May 1, 1977. AB, U. Ill., Chgo., 1970; JD, Ill. Inst. Tech., 1980. Bar: Ill. 1980, Mich. 1983, U.S. Dist. Ct. (we. dist.) Mich. 1983. Dir. Chgo. programs U. Ill. Found., 1973—79; asst. dir. bus. affairs U of Ill., Chgo., 1980—81, exec. asst. to exec. v.p., 1981—83; 2d v.p. Nat. Bank of Detroit, Grand Rapids, 1983—88; v.p., dept. head bus. devel. NBD Grand Rapids Bank, 1985—88; v.p., trust divsn. head, mem. exec. com. First Bank, Davenport, Iowa, 1988—91; v.p., trust Firstar Bank, Davenport, Iowa, 1992—97; asst. prof. dept. bus. adminstrn. Black Hawk Coll., 1992; v.p. pvt. client svcs. Wells Fargo Bank, Davenport, Iowa, 1998—2004; pres., CEO Cmty. Found. of Gt. River Bend, Davenport, Iowa, 2004—. Author: Cuneen Linguist, 1975. Mem. Scott County Osteo. Physicians and Surgeons Aux., 1988-99, treas., 1989, 91-99, v.p., 1990; v.p. West Mich. U. Ill. Alumni Club, 1983-86; mem. Quad City Osteo. Found., 1988—, bequest and fin. com. mem., 1988-95, 97-2004, bd. dirs., 1992-95; lead gift com. mem. Davenport Mus. Art, 1988, endowment com. mem. St. Ambrose U., 1988, Quad City Arts, 1992-94; devel. and fin. com. CASI, 1998-2004, bd. govs., 1992-98, chair trustees com., 1994-98; bd. dirs. Cmty. Found. of the Great River Bend, 1998-2003, chair major gifts com., 1998, 2d v.p. 1998-2000, 1st vice chair, 2001, chair, 2002-03; bd. dirs. Quad City Planned Giving Coun., 1998—, pres., 2000; mem. capital campaign com. Luth. Social Svcs., 1994; mem. Quad City Estate Planning Coun., 1988—; planned giving com. Am. Cancer Soc., 2000-03. Mem. U. Ill. Alumni Assn. (various offices to sec. 1989-91, exec. com. bd. dirs. 1985-91, nominating com. 1991), Quad City Employee Benefits Group (treas. 1993-95, 96-99), Davenport C. of C. (mem. com. 1996-97), Davenport Country Club (fin. com. 1996-2000), Pi Alpha Tau. Avocations: gardening, reading, golf, auctions. Home: 1139 Brookview Dr De Witt IA 52742-9290 Office: Cmty Found of the Gt River Bend 111E 3d St Davenport IA 52801-1977 Office Phone: 563-326-2840. E-mail: SusanSkora@mail.com.

SKORA, WAYNE PHILIP, retired air force officer; b. Chgo., Jan. 16, 1944; s. Felix Anthony Skora and Lillie (Goshko) St. Thomas; m. Dorothy Mae Barrett, June 13, 1966; children: Tanya Christine, Christopher Michael. BS in Engring. Sci., USAF Acad., 1966; MS in Human Resource Mgmt., U. Utah, 1976. Commd. 2d lt. USAF, 1966, advanced through grades to col., 1988, F-4 pilot, 1967-69, 71-79; flight safety officer Hdqrs. Tactical Air Command, Langley AFB, Va., 1979-82; chief safety, A-10 pilot 23d Tactical Fighter Wing, England AFB, La., 1982-84; chief Office Mil. Cooperation, Am. Embassy, Manama, Bahrain, 1984-87; asst. chief logistics 507th Tactical Air Control Wing, Shaw AFB, S.C., 1987-88; dep. comdr. for ops. So. Air Div., Howard AFB, Panama, 1988-90; dep. for safety Air Force Devel. Test Ctr., Eglin AFB, Fla., 1990-92; pres. Skora Enterprises, Inc., Colorado Springs, Colo., 1994—. Decorated Legion of Merit, DFC with oak leaf cluster, Air medal with 21 oak leaf clusters, Def. Meritorious Svc. medal, AF Meritorious Svc. medal with oak leaf cluster, AF Commendation medal with oak leaf cluster. Mem. Order of Daedalians (sec. 1988-90), Sertoma. Roman Catholic. Home: 24 Luxury Ln Colorado Springs CO 80921-3300 E-mail: wayne@skorateam.com.

SKORIKOV, VLADIMIR B. researcher, educator; b. Moscow, Apr. 6, 1959; s. Boris A Skorikov, Vladimira G Petrenko. PhD in Psychology, State Academy of Management, Moscow, Russia. Prof. State Acad. Mgmt., Moscow, 1982—91; instr. Pa. State U., University Park, Pa., 1993—97; prof. U. Hawaii, Hilo, 1997—. Mem. editl. bd. Career Devel. Quar., 1997—2003; reviewer 4th Natl. Counseling Psychology Conf., Houston, 2001; ad hoc reviewer Jour. Adolesent Rsch., Health, Internat. Jour. Behavioral Devel., Jour. Adolescence, Jour. Res. Adolescence, 1997—2004, Jour. Adolescence, 1997—2004, Jour. Early Adolescence, 1997—2004; prin. investigator NIH. Contbr. articles to profl. jours. Mem.: Am. Psychol. Soc., Soc. for Rsch. on Identity Formation, Soc. Vocational Psychology, Soc. Rsch. on Adolescence, Nat. Career Devel. Assn. Avocation: tennis, skiing, swimming. Office: U Hawaii at Hilo 200 West Kawili St Hilo HI 96720 Office Phone: (808) 974-7373. Business E-Mail: skorikov@hawaii.edu.

SKORTON, DAVID JAN, academic administrator; b. Milw., Nov. 22, 1949; s. Samuel and Pauline (Millstein) Skorton; 1 child, Joshua Samuel. BA, Northwestern U., 1970; MD, Northwestern U., Chgo., 1974. Diplomate Nat. Bd. Med. Examiners, Am. Bd. Internal Medicine, Am. Bd. Cardiovascular Disease. Resident UCLA, 1974—77, fellow in cardiology, 1977—80, chief resident in medicine, 1978—79, adj. asst. prof., 1978—80; instr. medicine U. Iowa, Iowa City, 1980—81, asst. prof., 1981—82, asst. prof. elec. and computer engring., 1982—84, assoc. prof. medicine and elec. and computer engring., 1984—88, prof. medicine, elec. and computer engring. and biomed. engring., 1988—; acting dir., then dir. div. gen. internal medicine U. Iowa Coll. Medicine, Iowa City, 1985—89, assoc. chmn. for clinical programs, 1989—92, v.p. for rsch. and external rels., 1992—2002; pres. U. Iowa, 2003—. Dir. echocardiology lab. VA Med. Ctr., Iowa City, 1980—89; mem. internat. and coop. projects study sect. NIH, 1988—92, chmn., 1990—92; lectr. in field numerous sci. sessions, nat. and internat. meetings; manuscript reviewer maj. jours. in field. Editor: (book) Cardiac Imaging and Image Processing, 1986, Cardiac Imaging, 1990, Cardiac Imaging, 2d edit., 1996; contbr. articles and abstracts to profl. jours., chapters to books. Named Intern-of-Yr., UCLA, 1975; recipient Rsch. Assoc. Career Devel. award, VA, 1981—84, Rsch. Career Devel. award, Nat. Heart Lung & Blood Inst., 1984—89; scholar Regents', UCLA, 1967—68. Fellow: ACP, Am. Physiol. Soc., Am. Heart Assn., Am. Coll. Cardiology; mem.: AAAS, Internat. Soc. Adult Congenital Cardiac Disease, Assn. Univ. Cardiologists. Jewish. Office: U Iowa Office of Pres 101 Jessup Hall Iowa City IA 52242-1316 E-mail: david-skorton@uiowa.edu.

SKOTHEIM, ROBERT ALLEN, retired college and museum administrator; b. Seattle, Jan. 31, 1933; s. Sivert O. and Marjorie F. (Allen) S.; m. Nadine Vail, June 14, 1953; children— Marjorie, Kris, Julia. BA, U. Wash., 1955, MA, 1958, PhD, 1962; LLD (hon.), Hobart and William Smith Colls., Geneva, N.Y., 1975; LittD (hon.), Whitman Coll., 1988; LHD (hon.), Coll. Idaho, 1988, Occidental Coll., 1989, Ill. Wesleyan U., 1990; DFA (hon.), Willamette U., 1989, Whittier Coll., 2000, Gustavus Adolphys Coll., 2000. Prof. history U. Wash., 1962-63; prof. history Wayne State U., Detroit, 1963-66; prof. UCLA, 1966-67, U. Colo., Boulder, 1967-72; provost, dean faculty Hobart and William Smith Colls., 1972-75; pres. Whitman Coll., Walla Walla, Wash., 1975-88, Huntington Libr., Art Collections & Bot. Gardens, San Marino, Calif., 1988-2001; ret., 2001. Author: American Intellectual Histories and Historians, 1966, Totalitarianism and American Social Thought, 1971; Editor: The Historian and the Climate of Opinion, 1969; co-editor: American Social Thought: Sources and Interpretations, 2 vols, 1972. Guggenheim fellow, 1967-68 Mem. Phi Beta Kappa (hon.)

SKOV, ARLIE MASON, petroleum engineer, consultant; b. Perry, Okla., Sept. 21, 1928; s. Arnold and Mary (Mason) S.; m. Luella Luticia Sloan, July 31, 1951; children: Gregory Morgan, Jeffrey Markham, Tamara Kay. BS in Petroleum Engring., U. Okla., 1956; postgrad., U. Va., 1966. Engr., Sohio Petroleum Co., Pauls Valley, Oklahoma City, Okla., 1958-66, mgr. spl. projects Oklahoma City, 1966—76; mgr. prodn. planning BP Alaska Inc., San Francisco, 1977-80; project advisor Sohio Gas Pipeline Co., San Francisco, 1980-81; mgr. new tech. devel. Sohio Petroleum Co., San Francisco, 1981-83; dir. prodn. tech. Sohio Petroleum Co. and Standard Oil Prodn., Dallas, 1983-88; sr. cons. BP Exploration, Inc., Houston, 1989-92; owner Arlie M. Skov, Inc. Petroleum Consulting, Houston, 1993—2001. Chair Santa Barbara City Water Commn., 2003—. Recipient Disting. Svc. award Okla. Petroleum Coun. 1973. Mem. AIME (bd. dirs. 1977-79, trustee 1990-92, 95-97) Soc. Petroleum Engrs. (hon.; bd. dirs. 1972-74, exec. com. 1990-92, pres. 1991, pres. Found. 2003-04, Disting. Mem.), Santa Barbara Club, Cosmopolitan Club of Santa Barbara. Avocations: reading, travel. Office Phone: 805-965-5101. E-mail: askov@earthlink.com.

SKOVE, THOMAS MALCOLM, retired manufacturing company financial executive; b. Cleve., June 27, 1925; s. Thomas Malcolm and Ethel C. (Rush) S.; m. Helen Busing, June 12, 1948; children: Margaret, Thomas, Richard, Marcie, Douglas. BS, Bucknell U., 1949. Controller, treas. Cleve. Twist Drill Co., 1949-68; treas. Acme-Cleve. Corp., 1968-81, dep. treas., 1981-86, treas., 1986-88. Councilman, City of Aurora, Ohio, 1977-83; chmn. Aurora Meml. Library Trust, 1984-89. Served with USN, 1943-46. Mem. Sugar Mill Country Club (pres. 1993-94). Republican. Home: 209 Bromely Cir New Smyrna Beach FL 32168-2006 E-mail: tombuz209@yahoo.com.

SKOWRONSKI, VINCENT PAUL, concert violinist, classical recordings producer; b. Kenosha, Wis., Jan. 22, 1944; MusB, Northwestern U., 1966, MusM, 1968. V.p. Eberley-Skowronski, Inc., Evanston, Ill., 1973-92; internat. dir. mktg. and pub. rels. Vincent Skowronski: Producer of Classical Recordings, Evanston, 1993—. Internat. broker rare instruments Strings & Things, Evanston, 1973-92; owner Vincent Skowronski: Fine Violins, Evanston, 1993—; internat. dir. mktg. and pub. rels. EB-SKO Prodns., Evanston, 1978-92; dir. media comm. E-S Mgmt., Evanston, 1985-92; instr. violin Northwestern U., 1969-71; asst. prof. violin U. Wyo., 1971-72; pvt. violin tchr., chamber music coach, lectr., master classes. Solo violinist debut Chgo. Youth Orch., 1959; soloist Chgo. Civic Orch., 1968, guest solo artist Am. Artist Gala, Nat. Puerto Rican TV, 1960, guest solo artist Peninsula Music Festival, Fish Creek, Wis., 1965, 66; guest solo artist Young Am. Musicians Sta. WKAR-TV Mich. State U., 1966, N.Am. premiere R. Nanes' Rhapsody Pathetique for violin and orch., Chgo. Cultural Ctr., 1994, Beijing, 1994, DePaul U. Ctr., Chgo., 1994, Skowronski in Recital: 20 Years Remembered, Northwestern U., Evanston, Ill., 1994, IV Internat. Tchaikovsky Competition Commemorative Recital-Moscow Remembered: 1970-95, Evanston, Ill., 1995, J.L. Kellogg Sch. Mgmt. Recital Northwestern Univ., Ill., 1996; featured solo artist Artist Showcase, Sta. WGN-TV Chgo., 1966-71; featured soloist Honors Concert-Northwestern U., 1966, guest solo artist A.M. Am., Sta. ABC-TV, 1977—; numerous concerts and recitals in Europe and U.S.; solo guest artist radio appearances include Continental Bank Concerts, Sta. WFMT-FM Chgo., 1983, 85-86, 88, 90, United Airlines Presents, Live!, Sta. WFMT-FM Chgo., Schumann, 1986, Szymanowski, 1987, Bloch, 1988, Saint-Saens, 1989, Grieg, 1991, Excursions in Music: The Artistry of Vincent P. Skowronski, Sta. KQED-FM San Francisco, 1979, Skowronski: Musical Giant, Interlake Profiles, Sta. WFMT-FM Chgo., 1980, Skowronski at 50: A Birthday Celebration Sta. WNIB-FM, Chgo., 1994; guest solo artist Chgo. Musicians Sta. WNIB-FM, 1996-97; Skowronski at 55: A Birthday Celebration, Station WNIB-FM, Chgo., 1999; guest solo artist, producer, annotator for LPs Separate But Equal, 1976, All Brahms, 1977; solo artist, exec. producer, annotator for LPs Gentleman Gypsy, 1978, Strauss and Szymanowski, 1979, Franck and Szymanowski, 1982; CDs Skowronski Alone, 1996, Skowronski Plays, Strauss and Szymanowski, 1998, Skowronski Plays, Live in Concert, 2000, Skowronski Plays! Franck, Szymanowski, Bacewicz and Saint-Saens, 2002, Skowronski Plays! Gentleman Gypsy, 2003, Skowronski Plays Beethoven, Live in Concert, 2003, Skowronski Plays, Avec et Sans, Live in Concert, 2004; producer, annotator for LPs Opera Lady I, 1978, Eberley Sings Strauss, 1980, American Girl, 1983, Opera Lady II, 1984; guest performances numerous TV stas. Bd. dirs. Chgo. Youth Orch., 1973-77, v.p., 1974-77; artistic cons. Classical and Protege Symphony Orchs., Chgo., 1994—; spl. cons. Beck Inst. for Arts, Schaumburg, Ill., 1998-2000; adjudicator ice skating shows and competitions Wilmette (Ill.) Park Dist., 1985-89; guest panelist classical performance-career forum Sch. of Music, Northwestern U., Evanston, 1992, 94; guest cons. career symposium Edwin G. Foreman High Sch., Chgo., 1989; mem. mayor's founding com. Evanston Arts Coun., 1974-75; pres. Vincent Skowronski Music Found., Evanston, 1997—. Recipient Excellence in Performance award Northwestern U., 1958, 59, 60, Nat. H.S. Inst., 1958-60, Roy Harris award Inter-Am. U., San German, P.R., 1960, award Am. Fedn. Musicians, 1961, award Soc. Am. Musicians, 1961, McCormick Found. award Chgo. Tribune, 1965, Wade Fetzer award for excellence in performance Northwestern U., 1966, award Crescendo Musical Club, 1967; selected as one of 7 violinists to represent U.S. in IV Internat. Tchaikovsky Competition, Moscow, 1970; Grammy award entry list Best Chamber Music Performance, 2001, 04—; guest dignitary Papal Audience, The Vatican, 1995. Mem. Internat. Platform Assn. (voting mem.), Nat. Acad. Arts and Scis., Sigma Nu Office Phone: 847-491-9155. E-mail: skowviolinstudio@ameritech.net., skowronskirecordings@ameritech.net.

SKRAMSTAD, HAROLD KENNETH, JR., museum consultant; b. Washington, June 3, 1941; s. Harold K. and Sarah (Shroat) S.; m. Susan Chappelear, Dec. 28, 1963; children: Robert, Elizabeth. AB, George Washington U., 1963, PhD, 1971. Asst. dir. Am. studies program Smithsonian Instn., Washington, 1969-71, spl. asst. to dir. Nat. Mus. Am. History, 1971, chief spl. projects Nat. Mus. Am. History, chief exhibit programs Nat. Mus. Am. History, 1971-74; dir. Chgo. Hist. Soc., 1974-80; pres. Henry Ford Mus. and Greenfield Village, Dearborn, Mich., 1981—96; mus. cons., 1996—. Mem. Nat. Coun. on Humanities, 1994; mem. mus. mgmt. adv. com. J. Paul Getty Trust, L.A., 1984-90; mem. presdl. commn., action plan, Nat. Mus. African Am. Hsitory and Culture, 2003. Chmn. bd. Met. Detroit Conv. and Visitors Bur., 1993, chmn., mem. exec. com., 1985—; trustee Coll. Art and Design, Detroit, 1981—; mem. Mich. Travel Commn., 1989—. Recipient Charles Frankel prize Nat. Endowment for the Humanities, 1992. Mem. Am. Assn. Mus. (v.p. 1984-88, accreditation commn. 1982, ethics commn. 1992-93), Smithsonian Instn. Nat. Air and Space Mus. (pub. programming adv. com. 1990—), Nat. Coun. on the Humanitites, 1994, Greater Detroit and Windsor Japan-Am. Soc. (bd. dirs. 1989—), Detroit Club, Cosmos Club (Washington).*

SKRETNY, WILLIAM MARION, federal judge; b. Buffalo, Mar. 8, 1945; s. William S. and Rita E. Skretny; m. Carol Ann Skretny; 3 children. AB, Canisius Coll., 1966; JD, Howard U., 1969; LLM, Northwestern U., 1972. Bar: Ill. 1969, U.S. Dist. Ct. (no. dist) Ill. 1969, N.Y. 1972, U.S. Ct. Appeals (7th cir.) 1972, U.S. Dist. Ct. (we. dist.) N.Y. 1973, U.S. Ct. Appeals (2d cir.) 1976, U.S. Supreme Ct. 1980. Asst. U.S. atty. Office of U.S. Atty. No. Dist. Ill., Chgo., 1971-73, Office of U.S. Atty. We. Dist. N.Y., Buffalo, 1973-81, 1st asst., 1975-81; gen. ptnr. Duke, Holzman, Yaeger & Radlin, Buffalo, 1981-83; 1st dep. dist. atty. Office Dist. Atty Erie County, Buffalo, 1983-88; with Gross, Shuman, Brizdle and Gillfillan, PC, Buffalo, 1988, Cox, Barrell, Buffalo, 1989-90; judge U.S. Dist. Ct. (we. dist.) N.Y., Buffalo, 1990—. Mem. jud. conf. com. on security and facilities, 1994; chair subcom. on planning and space mgmt.; com. liaison for long range planning; spl. counsel U.S. Atty. Gen.'s Advocacy Inst., 1979; staff atty., Office of Spl. Prosecutor U.S. Dept. Justice, 1980. Named Citizen of Yr. Am Pol Eagle Newspaper, 1977, 90, Disting. Grad. Nat. Cath. Edn. Assn. Dept. Elem. Sch., 1991, Disting. Alumnus Canisius Coll., 1993; named to Wall of Fame Law Sch. Northwestern U. Mem. ABA, Fed. Judges Assn., Bar Assn. of Erie County, Di Gamma, Phi Alpha Delta, Alpha Sigma Nu. Republican. Roman Catholic. Office: US District Court 68 Court St Rm 507 Buffalo NY 14202-3405

SKRINE, BRUCE E. retired lawyer; Sr. v.p., gen. counsel, sec. John Hancock Mutual Life Ins. Co., Boston, 1996-97, sr. v.p., dep. gen. counsel, 1997-2000, ret., 2000. Office: John Hancock Mut Life Insur Co PO Box 111 Boston MA 02117-0111

SKRIP, LINDA JEAN, nurse; b. Neenah, Wis., Apr. 16, 1963; d. Donald Charles and Kathryn Amelia Patrikus; m. Stephen Michael, May 21, 1988. BSN, U. Wis., 1986. RN Va. Staff nurse U. Hosp. Ill., Chgo., 1986-87; asst. clin. nurse mgr. Northwestern Meml. Hosp., Chgo., 1987-88; nursing coord. Pitt County Meml. Hosp., Greenville, N.C., 1988-91; nursing supr. Chesapeake (Va.) Gen. Hosp., 1991-92, case mgmt. coord., 1992—2000, cert. case mgr., 1993-2000, dir. care mgmt., 2000—02. Roman Catholic. Avocations: tennis, travel. Home: 1253 Smokey Mountain Trail Chesapeake VA 23320-8187 E-mail: ljsccm@msn.com.

SKROBELA, KATHERINE CREELMAN, music producer; b. N.Y.C., Jan. 18, 1941; d. George Douglas and Marjorie Ethel (Broer) Creelman; m. Paul John Skrobela, May 23, 1970 (dec. Feb. 1999). AB, Vassar Coll., 1962; MLS, Columbia U., 1964. Music cataloger Bklyn. Coll., 1964-71; music libr. Middlebury (Vt.) Coll., 1971-80; programmer ADT Co., N.Y.C., 1981-83; sr. cons. Marathon Software & Svcs. Inc., 1983-90; sr. programmer analyst Chase Manhattan Bank, 1990-2000; dir. info. tech. Brown Harris Stevens, 2003—. Pres. Miranda Music, Inc., 1995—. Editor Music Cataloging bull., 1970-75; prodr. Blame It On My Youth: Berri Blair Sings Ballads, 1999, Karen Oberlin: My Standards, 2000, Christopher Gines: The Way It Goes, 2001, Karen Oberlin: Secret Love: the Music of Doris Day, 2002, John Wallowitch & Bertram Ross: Wallowitch & Ross, 2002; contbg. author: Legacy: 50 years of Dance and Song; composer Magnificat. Treas., bd. dirs. Middlebury Farmers Market, 1979; dir. St. Stephen's Motet Choir, Middlebury, 1975-78; membership chair Bklyn. Bot. Garden Aux,; treas. Vassar Class of 1962. Mem. ALA, Music Libr. Assn. (chmn. com. on cataloging, rep. to ALA catalog code revision com.), Music OCLC Users Group, UFO-Cobol/XE Internat. Users Group (v.p. 1989-91), Country Dance and Song Soc. Am., Manhattan Assn. Cabarets and Clubs. Home: 234 Lincoln Rd Brooklyn NY 11225-3432 Office: Brown Harris Stevens 150 Montague St Brooklyn NY 11201 Office Phone: 718-875-1289 x205. Personal E-mail: ceo@mirandamusic.com.

SKROCH, LARRY EUGENE, railway conductor; b. Oakes, N.D., Nov. 24, 1955; s. Peter Carl and Opal May (Peters) S. AS in Pre-law, N.D. State Sch. Sci., 1982; BA in Social Sci., U. N.D., 1984, MA in History, 1988. Warehouse laborer Internat. Multifoods, Forman, N.D., 1978-80; laborer Chicago Bridge and Iron, Grand Forks, N.D., 1987-88; brakeman, switchman Burlington No. Santa Fe, Grand Forks, 1988-90, condr., 1990—. Co-publ. Valley Heritage Press, Grand Forks, 1994—. Co-author: (regional history books) Looking for Candles in the Window: The Tragic Red River Valley Blizzard of March 15, 1941, 1992, The Raging Red: The 1950 Red River Valley Flood, 1996. With U.S. Army, 1975-78, N.D. Nat. Guard, 1978-91. Mem. United Transp. Union local 525. Democrat. Avocations: avid reader, book collector, creating scrapbooks on political cartoons, old west collectibles, playing softball. Home: 1918 Drees Dr Grand Forks ND 58201-8137 Office: Valley Heritage Press PO Box 12872 Grand Forks ND 58208-2872

SKROMME, LAWRENCE H. consulting agricultural engineer; b. Roland, Iowa, Aug. 26, 1913; s. Austin G. and Ingeborg B. (Holmedal) S.; m. Margaret Elizabeth Gleason, June 24, 1939; children: Cherlyn Sue Granrose, Inga Jean Hill, Karen Ann Sequino. BS with honors, Iowa State U., Ames, 1937. Registered profl. engr., Pa. Design and test engr. Goodyear Tire and Rubber Co., Akron, Ohio, 1937-41; project engr., asst. chief engr. Harry Ferguson Inc., Detroit, 1941-51; chief engr. Sperry New Holland div. Sperry Corp., New Holland, Pa., 1951-61, v.p. engring., 1961-78; cons. agrl. engr. Lancaster, Pa., 1978—. Mem. adv. bd. U.S. Congresss Com. on Sci. and Tech., 1989—93; cons. AID, World Bank, others, 1978—85, Saudi Arabia, 1985—86. Patentee; contbr. articles to profl. jours. Dir., pres. Farm and Home Found., Lancaster County, 1968—90, Lancaster County Agrl. Land Preservation Bd., 1978—2002, sec.-treas., 1989—99, dir. emeritus, 2002—; rsch. adv. com. U.S. Dept. Agr., Washington, 1964—68; gov.'s com. agr. and land preservation Gov. of Pa., 1969; bd. dirs. awards com. Engrs. Joint Coun., N.Y.C., 1967—75. Fellow: Am. Soc. Agrl. Engrs. (v.p. 1952—55, pres. 1959—60, Gold medal 1974); mem.: NAE (peer and membership com. 1978—82), Am. Soc. Engring. Edn., Internat. Assn. Agrl. Engrs. (v.p. 1974—79, pres. farm machine divsn.), Nat. Soc. Profl. Engrs., Tau Beta Pi, Alpha Zeta, Phi Kappa Phi. Republican. Methodist. Avocations: collecting old tools and antiques, farm machinery history. Office Phone: 717-392-6127. E-mail: lhsae@aol.com.

SKROWACZEWSKI, STANISLAW, conductor, composer; b. Lwow, Poland, Oct. 3, 1923; came to U.S., 1960; s. Pawel and Zofia (Karszniewicz) S.; m. Krystyna Jarosz, Sept. 6, 1956; children: Anna, Paul, Nicholas. Diploma faculty philosophy, U. Lwow, 1945; diploma faculties composition and conducting, Acad. Music Lwow, 1945, Conservatory at Krakow, Poland, 1946; L.H.D., Hamline U., 1963, Macalester Coll., 1972; L.H.D. hon. doctorate, U. Minn. Guest condr. in, Europe, S.A., U.S., 1947—; Composer, 1931—; pianist, 1928—; violinist, 1934—; condr., 1939—; permanent condr., music dir. Wroclaw (Poland) Philharmonic, 1946-47, Katowice (Poland) Nat. Philharmonic, 1949-54, Krakow Philharmonic, 1955-56, Warsaw Nat. Philharmonic Orch., 1957-59, Minnesota Orch., 1960-79; prin. condr., mus. adviser Halle Orch., Manchester, Eng., 1984-91; musical advisor St. Paul Chamber Orchestra, 1986-87. First symphony and overture for orch. written at age 8, played by Lwow Philharm. Orch., 1931. Composer: 4 symphonies Prelude and Fugue for Orchestra (conducted first performance Paris), 1948, Overture, 1947 (2d prize Szymanowski Concours, Warsaw 1947); Cantiques des Cantiques, 1951, String Quartet, 1953 (2d Prize Internat. Concours Composers, Belgium 1953), Suite Symphonique, 1954 (first prize, gold medal Composers Competition Moscow 1957), Music at Night, 1954, Ricercari Notturni, 1978 (3d prize Kennedy Center Friedheim Competition, Washington), Concerti for Clarinet and Orch., 1980, Violin Concerto, 1985, Concerto for Orch., 1985, Fanfare for Orch., 1987, Sextett for Oboe, Violin, Viola, Orchestra, 1980, String Trio for Violin, Viola, 1990, Triple Concerto for Violin, Clarinet, Piano, Orchestra, 1992, Fantasie per Tre (Flute, Oboe, Cello), 1993, Chamber Concerto, 1993, Passacaglia Immaginaria for Orch., 1995, Musica a Quattro for Clarinet, Violin, Viola, Cello, 1998, Concerto for Piano left hand and Orch., 2002, Symphony, 2003; also music for theatre, motion pictures, songs and piano sonatas, English horn concerto; rec. by Mercury, Columbia, RCA, Albany, Victor, Vox, EMI, Angel. Decorated comdrs. cross Polonia Restituta; recipient nat. prize for artistic activity Poland, 1953, 1st prize Santa Cecilia Internat. Concours for Condrs., Rome, 1956, Cannes Festival award for best rec. of 19th century symphonic music, 2002, Disting. Artist award McKnight Found., 2004. Mem. Union Polish Composers, Internat. Soc. Modern Music, Nat. Assn. Am. Composers-Condrs., Am. Music Center. Office: Orch Hall 1111 Nicollet Mall Minneapolis MN 55403-2406

SKRUPKY, ELAINE CHARLOTTE, art educator; b. Amery, Wis., Nov. 11, 1927; d. Herbert Roy Peterson and Nina Louise Olson; m. Hartferd Gay Elaine Charlotte Peterson, June 24, 1950 (dec. Aug. 2, 1982); children: Lynn, Jenene, Van(dec.), Renée, Shawndel(dec.). BSc in Art and English, River Falls U., 1949. Art supr. Rice Lake (Wis.) Schs., 1949—50; art tchr. U. Wis. Ctr., Rice Lake, 1968—69, VIII Pk., Jensen Beach, Fla., 1993—. Author: Poetry Guild Anthology, 1996 (Editors Choice award, 1996), The Best Poems of the 90's, 1997 (named Internat. Poet of Merit, Internat. Soc. Poetry, 1997), Of Moonlight and Wishes, 1997, A Celebration of Poets, 1998, sound of Poetry, 1998. Chmn. and organizer Aquafest Art Show, Rice Lake, 1960—75; chmn. state fine arts Wis. Fedn. Women's Clubs, 1972—74, state drama chmn., 1974—76, dist. art chmn., 1976; pres. Daubers Guild, Rice Lake, 1976—77; chmn. Am. Cancer Dr., Rice Lake, 1979—80, Heart Drive, Rice Lake, 1980; organizer The Red Barn Theatre, Rice Lake. Named Outstanding Woman in Arts, Wis. Federated Woman's Club, 2000; named to Internat. Hall of Fame, Internat. Soc. Poetry, 2000; recipient State Art award, Rural Artists Wis., 1979, State Achievement award, Wis. Federated Woman's Club, 2000, 2001. Mem.: Art League, Alpha Psi Omega, Art Gallery Coop, Poetry Club. Avocations: painting, writing, piano, singing, acting. Home: 10701 S Ocean Drive Jensen Beach FL 34957 Home (Summer): 2834 A 28 11/16 Ave Birchwood WI 54817

SKRZYPCZAK, JOZEF ALEKSANDER, education educator; b. Poznan, Poland, Mar. 1, 1938; s. Franciszek and Bronislawa (Kolodziejczyk) S.; m. Alina Sokolowska, Aug. 30, 1964 (div. 1980); 1 child, Liliana; m. Teresa Maresch, July 10, 1980; 1 child, Lidia. MA in Chemistry, Adam Mickiewicz U., Poznan, Poland, 1964, PhD in Chemistry, 1970, degree in Humanities, 1979. From asst. dept. magnetic chemistry to prof. Adam Mickiewicz U., 1964—89, prof., 1989—, vice head inst. pedagogy, 1978—82, head dept. adult edn., 1983—. Mem. sub-com. adult edn. Polish Acad. Sci., Warszawa, Poland, 1983—; mem. Univ. Senate, 1993—; expert Minister Edn. & Sport, 1995—; pres. Tech. Coll. Health & Beauty Treatment, Poznan, 2000—. Author: Model Assumptions of Audio-Visual Manual in Chemistry, 1977 (Ministry of Edn. award 1978), Didactic Film in Higher Education 1985 (Ministry of Edn. award 1986), Theoretical and Practical Problems of Research Methodology of a School Book, 1985 (Ministry of Edn. award 1986), Adult Education Strategies, 1991, Selected Aspects of Adult Education, 1991, 2d edit., 1993, The Construction and Evaluation of Handbooks, 1996 (Ministry of Edn. award 1996), Popular Encyclopaedia of Mass Media, 1999, School Book-Demands, Estimation, Apply, Evaluation, 2003. Mem. Solidarity, 1980-89. Recipient The Gold Cross of Merit, Pres. Poland, 1984, Medal of Com. of Nat. Edn., Minister of Edn., 1995. Mem. Polish United Workers Party, Poznan, 1970-89. Avocations: films, chess, tourism, reading, videos. Home: Osiedle Boleslawa Chrobrego 11 m 224 60-681 Poznan Poland Office: Adam Mickiewicz U Szamarzewskiego 89 60-569 Poznan Poland Fax: 0048 (61) 8292295. Office Phone: (048) 618225482. Business E-Mail: andrago@amu.edu.pl.

SKULE, JOHN L. pharmaceutical company executive; B.S. in Economics, Univ. Minn. V.p. Squibb Corp., Bristol-Myers Squibb, v.p. Public Affairs, Corporate Staff, 1993—97, sr. v.p. corp. and environ. affairs, 1998—. Office: Bristol-Myers Squibb Co 345 Park Ave New York NY 10154-0004

SKULINA, THOMAS RAYMOND, lawyer; b. Cleve., Sept. 14, 1933; s. John J. and Mary B. (Vesely) S. AB, John Carroll U., 1955; JD, Case Western Res. U., 1959, LLM, 1962. Bar: Ohio 1959, U.S. Supreme Ct. 1964, ICC 1965. Ptnr. Skulina & Stringer, Cleve., 1967-72, Riemer Oberdank & Skulina, Cleve., 1978-81, Skulina, Fillo, Walters & Negrelli, 1981-86, Skulina & McKeon, Cleve., 1986-90, Skulina & Hill, Cleve., 1990-97; atty. Penn Ctrl. Transp. Co., Cleve., 1960-65, asst. gen. atty., 1965-78, trial counsel, 1965-76; with Consol. Rail Corp., 1976-78; pvt. practice Cleve., 1997—. Tchr. comml. law Practicing Law Inst., N.Y.C., 1970; practicing labor arbitrator Fed. Mediation and Conciliation Svc., 1990—; arbitrator Mcpl. Securities Rulemaking Bd., 1994-98, N.Y. Stock Exch., 1995—, NASD, 1996—; mediator NASD, 1997—, AAA Comml., 1997—; mediator vol. panel EEOC, 1997-99, contract panel, 1999-2000, v.p., 2001—; arbitrator Better Bus. Bur., 2000—. Contbr. articles to legal jours. Income tax and fed. fund coord. City of Warrensville Heights, Ohio, 1970—77; spl. counsel City of North Olmstead, Ohio, 1971—75; spl. counsel to Ohio Atty. Gen., 1983—93, Cleve. Charter Rev. Commn., 1988, referee, 1986—; fact-finder State Employees Rels. Bd., Ohio, 1986—; hearing officer Human Resource Commn., Summit County, Ohio, 2000—03. With U.S. Army, 1959. Mem. ABA (R.R. and motor carrier com. 1988-96, jr. chmn. 1989-96, alt. dispute resolution com. 1998—), FBA, Assn. Conflict Resolution, Cleve. Bar Assn. (grievance com. 1987-93, chmn. 1997-98, trustee 1993-96, ADR com. 1997—), Ohio Bar Assn. (bd. govs. litigation sect. 1986-98, negligence law com. 1989-96, ethics and profl. responsibility com. 1990-91, alt. dispute resolution com. 1996—), Am. Arbitration Assn. (practicing labor arbitrator 1987—), Nat. Assn. R.R. Trial Counsel, Internat. Assn. Law and Sci., Pub. Sector Labor Rels. Assn., Internat. Indsl. Rels. Rsch. Assn. Democrat. Roman Catholic. Home: 3162 W 165th St Cleveland OH 44111-1016 Office: 24803 Detroit Rd Cleveland OH 44145-2553 Office Phone: 440-899-1911. E-mail: tskulina@msn.com.

SKUPINSKI, BOGDAN KAZIMIERZ, artist; b. Poland, July 16, 1942; came to U.S., 1971, naturalized, 1976; s. Kazimierz Stanislaw and Jrena Lucja (Kanar) S. BA, Acad. Fine Arts, Krakow, Poland, 1969, MA, 1971; cert., Ecole Nationale Superieure de Beaux Arts, Paris, 1971. Pres. Bogdan & Assoc., N.Y.C. Graphic artist: painting Proclamation, 1968, Escape, 1968, Return, 1969, Good Journey, (permanent collection N.J. State Mus., 1971, The Stable, (permanent collection Library of Congress), 1971, Nouvel Ordre, 1970 (annual prize Ministry of Cultural Affairs of France), Gare du Nord, 1970 (award Commn. Fine Arts. Paris), anti-war themes, 1969-76; life and work of John F. Kennedy and Albert Michelson, 1969-76. Recipient Grand Prix, Nat. Salon Young Artists, 1968, People's Choice award 2d Nat. Graphic Rev., Karkow, 1969, ann. Bartoczek and Babrowski award Polish Ministry Art and Culture, 1970, lst prize for prints and drawings Nat. Conn. Acad. Exhbn., Hartford, 1971, medal Internat. Exhbn. Graphic Art, Frechen, Fed. Republic Germany, 1976, Presdl. Medal of Merit, 1990; fellow Ecole Nat. Superieure Beaux Arts. Fellow Pratt Inst.; mem. NAD (Cannon prize for graphics 1971), Kosciuszko Found., Rep. Presdl. Task Force. Roman Catholic. Home: Cathedral Sta PO Box 849 215 W 104th St New York NY 10025-4297 E-mail: bogdanart@worldnet.att.net.

SKURA, MEREDITH ANNE, English educator; b. Bklyn., May 11, 1944; d. George and Esther (Ruth Feld) Skura.; m. Martin Joel Wiener, May 17, 1981; chdren: Rebecca, Vivian. BA, Swarthmore Coll., 1965; PhD, Yale U., 1971. With English dept. U. Bridgeport, Conn., 1968-69, 70-73, Yale U., New Haven, 1973-78, Rice U., Houston, 1978—. Author: The Literary Use of the Psychoanalytic Process, 1981, Shakespeare the Actor and the Purposes of Playing, 1993. Grantee Guggenheim Found., 1982-83, NEH, 1989-90, Folger Shakespeare Libr., 1998-99, Am. Coun. Learned Socs., 1981. Mem. MLA, Shakespeare Assn. Am. (v.p. 1999-2000, pres. 2000—). Jewish. Avocations: drawing, travel. Office: 6100 Main St Houston TX 77005-1827

SKURLA, LAURUS See LAURUS

SKURZYNSKI, GLORIA JOAN, writer; b. Duquesne, Pa., July 6, 1930; d. Aylmer Kearney and Serena Elizabeth (Decker) Flister; m. Edward Joseph Skurzynski, Dec. 1, 1951; children: Serena Nolan, Janine Skurzynski-Mahoney, Joan Alm, Alane Ferguson, Lauren Thliveris. Student, Carlow Coll., 1948-50. Author: The Magic Pumpkin, 1971, The Remarkable Journey of Gustavus Bell, 1973, The Poltergeist of Jason Morey, 1975, In a Bottle with a Cork on Top, 1976, Two Fools and a Faker, 1977, Bionic Parts for People, 1978 (Golden Kite Honor Bk. award Soc. Children's Bk. Writers), Martin by Himself, 1979, What Happened in Hamelin, 1979 (telecast on Storybreak, CBS, 1987, Christopher award, Reviewer's Choice award, Horn Bk. Honor List, ALA Booklist), Honest Andrew, 1981, Safeguarding the Land, 1981, Three Folktales, 1981, Manwolf, 1981 (Best Bks. for Young Adults award ALA, Reviewer's Choice award ALA Booklist, Bks. of Yr. award Child Study Assn., Notable Children's Trade Bk. in Field of Social Studies), Lost in the Devil's Desert, 1982 (Utah Children's Bk. award), The Tempering, 1983 (Golden Kite award Soc. Children's Bk. Writers, Best Bks. for Young Adults award ALA, Best Bks. of Yr. award Sch. Libr. Jour., Children's Bks. of Yr. award Libr. Congress, Bks. of Yr. award Child Study Assn.), Trapped in the Slickrock Canyon, 1984 (Golden Spur award Western Writers Am., Am. Booksellers Pick of the List, Jr. Lit. Guild Selection), Caught in the Moving Mountains, 1984, Swept in the Wave of Terror, 1985, The Minstrel in the Tower, 1988, Dangerous Ground, 1989, Robots, 1990 (100 Children's Bks. award N.Y. Pub. Libr. 1990, Outstanding Science Trade Bk. for Children award NSTA/CBC 1991), Almost the Real Thing, 1991 (Children's Sci. Bk. award Am. Inst. Physics 1992), Here Comes the Mail, 1992, Good-Bye, Billy Radish, 1992 (Best Bks. of Yr. award Sch. Libr. Jour., Jefferson Cup Hon. award Va. Libr. Assn., Judy Lopez Meml. Hon. Bk., Women's Nat. Bk. Assn.), Get the Message, 1993 (Outstanding Sci. Trade Bks. for Children award NSTA/CBC 1994, Bks. for the Teen Age award N.Y. Pub. Libr. 1994), Know the Score, 1994 (Bks. for the Teen Age award N.Y. Pub. Libr. 1995), Zero Gravity, 1994 (Outstanding Sci. Trade Bks. for Children award NSTA/CBC 1995, Children's Bk. of Yr., Bank Street Coll. Child Study Com.), Cyberstorm, 1995, Caitlin's Big Idea, 1995, Waves, the Electromagnetic Universe, 1996, Virtual War, 1997, (with Alane Ferguson) The Mystery of the Spooky Shadow, 1996, The Mystery of the Vanishing Creatures, 1996, Wolf Stalker, 1997, Rage of Fire, 1998, Discover Mars, 1998, Cliff-Hanger, 1999, Spider's Voice, 1999, Deadly Waters, 1999, On Time, 2000, Ghost Horses, 2000, The Hunted, 2000, Over the Edge, 2001 (Ind. Children's Choice award), Valley of Death, 2001, Rockbuster, 2001 (Western Writers Am. award), Escape From Fear, 2002, Out of the Deep, 2002, Running Scared, 2002, Buried Alive, 2003, Are We Alone: Scientists Search for Life in Space, 2004, The Virtual War Chronologs, Book One, Virtual War, 2004, Book Two, The Clones, 2004. Mem. Soc. of Children's Book Writers and Illustrators, Utah Women's Forum, Internat. Women's Forum. Home and Office: 5898 W Riverbend Ln Boise ID 83703-6249 E-mail: gloriabooks@qwest.net.

SKUTA, GREGORY LOUIS, ophthalmologist, educator; b. Benton, Ill., June 22, 1956; s. Richard Louis and Jacquelyn Gail (Weaver) S.; m. Anne Marie (Phelan), May 26, 1984; children: Jonathan Richard, Catherine Anne, Matthew Gregory. BS, U. Ill., 1977, MD, 1981. Intern St. Joseph Mercy Hosp., Ann Arbor, Mich., 1981—82; ophthalmology resident U. Wis., Madison, 1982—85; glaucoma fellow Bascom Palmer Eye Inst., Miami, Fla., 1985—87; asst. prof. ophthalmology U. Mich., Ann Arbor, 1987—92; James P. Luton clin. prof. Dean A. McGee Eye Inst., U. Okla. Coll. Medicine, Okla. City, 1992—. V.p., pres. elect Am. Glaucoma Soc., 2003-04; dir. Am. Bd. Ophthalmology 2001-; sec. Ophthalmic Knowledge Am. Academy Ophthalmology, 2001-. Contbr. chpts. to books and articles to profl. journals. Fellow Am. Acad. Ophthalmology; mem. AMA, Assn. Rsch. Vision and Ophthalmology, Pan Am. Assn. Ophthalmology, Am. Glaucoma Soc., Okla. State Med. Soc., Okla. Academy Ophthalmology, Am. Eye Study Club, Glaucoma Soc. of Internat. Congress of Ophthalmology, Phi Beta Kappa, Phi Kappa Phi, Alpha Omega Alpha. Methodist. Avocations: music, theater, tennis, travel. Home: 1516 Sweetbriar Ct Edmond OK 73034-6555 Office: Dean A McGee Eye Inst 608 Stanton L Young Blvd Oklahoma City OK 73104 Office Phone: 405-271-7806.

SKVORECKY, JOSEF VACLAV, English literature educator, novelist; b. Nachod, Czechoslovakia, Sept. 27, 1924; arrived Can., 1969; s. Josef Karel and Anna (Kurazova) S.; m. Zdenka Josefa Salivarova, Mar. 30, 1958 PhD, Charles U., Czechoslovakia, 1951, SUNY, 1986, Masaryk U., 1991, U. Calgary, 1992, U. Toronto, 1992. Vis. lectr. U. Toronto, Ont., Can., 1969-70, writer-in-residence, 1970-71, assoc. prof., 1971-75, prof. English, 1975-90; prof. emeritus, 1990—. Lectr. on lit. topics Voice of Am., 1973—; adv. to Pres. Vaclav Havel, 1990. Editor: Sixty Eight Publ. Corp., 1972—; author: The Cowards, 1958, The End of the Nylon Age, 1967, Republic of Whores, 1969, The Miracle Game, 1972, The End of Lieutenant Boruvka, 1980, The Engineer of Human Souls, 1984, Miss Silver's Past, 1985, Dvorak in Love, 1986, The Bride of Texas, 1992, Headed for the Blues, 1996, The Two Murders in My Double Life, 1996, An Inexplicable Story, 2002; author: (with Z. Salivarova) Brief Encounter, With Murder, 1999; author Brief Encounter After Many Years with Murder, 2000, Brief Encounter at the End of an Era, With Murder, 2001, Brief Encounter in the White Lady, With Murder, 2003, Pulchra, 2003, (short story collections) The Menorah, 1964, The Life of High Society, 1965, The Mournful Demeanor of Lieutenant Boruvka, 1966, A Babylonian Story, 1967, The Bitter World, 1969, Sins for Father Knox, 1973, Oh, My Papa!, 1972, The Edenvale Stories, 1996, When Eve Was Naked, 2001, (plays) The New Men and Women CBC Radio, 1977, God in Your House, 1980 (1st prize Multicultural Theatre Festival Hamilton, 1980), (films) The Tank Battalion, 1991, The Swell Season, 1994, Eine Kleine Jazzmusik, 1996, Poe and the Death of a Beautiful Girl, 1997, The Legend of Emoke, 1998, The Detective Agency, 2000, (essays) Reading Detective Stories, 1965, They-Which is We, 1968, All the Bright Young Men and Women, 1972, Working Overtime, 1979, Talkin' Moscow Blues, 1989. Decorated Order of the White Lion; apptd. mem. Order of Can., 1992; recipient Neustadt Internat. prize for lit., U. Okla., 1980, Gov. Gen. Can.'s award, 1985, lit. prize Echoing Green Found., 1990, Czech Republic's State Prize for Lit., 1999, Pangea prize 2001. Fellow Royal Soc. Can.; mem. Can. Writers' Union, Authors' League Am., Crime Writers Can., Mystery Writers Am., The Internat. PEN Club, Can. br. Czechosolovak Nat. Assn. Can., Order of Can. Progressive Conservative. Roman Catholic Avocation: swing music. Home: 487 Sackville St Toronto ON Canada M4X 1T6

SKWARA, ERICH WOLFGANG, novelist, poet, educator, literary critic; b. Salzburg, Austria, Nov. 4, 1948; came to U.S., 1975, naturalized, 1981. s. Alois Gaigg and Hermine Maria Skwara; m. Victoria Anne Dufresne, July 10, 1974 (div. Mar. 1978); m. Gloria Elaine Winniski, June 8, 1978; children: Gabriella Maria, Alexandra Felicitas. BA, U. Paris VII, 1970; MA, Salzburg U., 1972; PhD, N.Y. State U., Albany, 1985. Instr. U. Md., Balt., 1975-77; freelance author Balt. and Paris, 1977-82; vis. lectr. Georgetown U., Washington, D.C., 1982-84; freelance author Salzburg, 1984-86; prof. humanities, comparative lit. and German San Diego State U., 1986—. Dep. editor-in-chief for cultural affairs Die Welt, Berlin, 1993; cultural and lit. corr. for a number of German and Austrian newspapers and media, 1979—; worldwide readings and lecture tours. Author: (novels) Black Sails, 1979, 99, The Cool Million, 1990, Tristan Island, 1992, Die Heimlichen Könige, 1995, Plague in Siena, 1994, 95, Ice on the Bridge, 1997, Versuch einer Heimkehr, 1998, Nach dem Norden, 1998, The Angel of Death, 1998, Anruf aus Rom, 1999, Pest in Siena, 2001, Zerbrechlichkeit, 2002, Träumeerzählen, 2002 others; translated (from English and French to German) works by T. Williams, Thomas Wolfe, J.J. Rousseau, Gustave Flaubert, others; own works translated into English, French, Japanese, Arabic, others. Recipient Hermann-Lenz-Preis, Germany, 2002; awarded title of prof., Republic of Austria, 2003. Mem. Internat. PEN Club, PEN Ctr. of German Speaking Authors Abroad (bd. dirs. 1985—), PEN Ctr. of Austria, PEN Ctr. of France. Roman Catholic. Avocations: fine wines, travel, walking. Office: San Diego State U Dept Classics Humanities San Diego CA 92182 also: Suhrkamp Verlag Linden Str 29-35 D60325 Frankfurt am Main Germany also: 264 rue Saint Honore F75001 Paris France E-mail: poetskwara@aol.com.

SKWARCZYNSKI, HENRYK ADAM (HENRYK SKWAR), writer; b. Lódź, Poland, Aug. 13, 1952; came to U.S., 1980; s. Zdzislaw and Stanislawa Ewa (Laszczyk) S.; m. Eglé Juodvalkis, Sept. 2, 1989 MA, U. Warsaw, 1977; postgrad., Polish Acad. Sci., 1978-80, Sorbonne U. Free-lance writer, N.Y.C., 1980-81, Voice of Am., Washington, 1981-82; instr. Defense Lang. Inst., Monterey, Calif., 1982-84; staff writer Libertas, Paris, 1984-86; free-lance writer Radio Free Europe, Munich, 1987-95; writer Chgo., 1995—. Author: Man in a Cleft, 1979, The Anguish of Becoming American, 1989, Sweeney Among the Nightingales, 2000, The Straw Sea, 2002, A Rose and the Moon in a Coat-of-Arms, 2004; editor-in-chief: Ephemeron, 1974—75; contbr. short stories to mags. Activist Solidarity Movement, 1980-89. Rotary Club grantee, 1982, Hoover Inst. grantee, 1985. Avocation: travel in Africa.

SKWERES, THOMAS A. real estate company executive; s. Thomas W. Skweres. BS in Bus. Mgmt. and Adminstrn., Bradley U., 1974. Cert. mgr. cmty. assns. Cmty. Assns. Inst. Sales rep., merchandising mgr. Tobey-Peoria (Ill.) Paper Co., 1974—78; asst. v.p. sales Darling & Co., Chgo., 1978—83; pres., gen. mgr. ABC Property Mgmt., Inc., Darien, Ill., 1982—88; v.p. property mgmt. Draper & Kramer, Inc., Chgo., 1988—98; v.p. mktg. and edn. Brouwer Bros. Steamatic, Alsip, Ill., 1998—2001; v.p. condo. divsn. Habitat Co., 2001—. Instr. Coll. of DuPage, Glen Ellyn, Ill., 1987—. Contbr. articles to profl. jours. Pres. Darien Youth Club, 1983—; sch. bd. mem. Cass Dist. # 63, Darien, 1994—, mem. facility mgmt. com.; former mem. City of Darien Zoning Bd. of Appeals, Darien Pub. Libr. Bd.; former dir. Hinsdale (Ill.) South H.S. Booster Club; former bd. dirs. Hinswood Cmty. Assn., Portsmouth Condo. Assn.; former precinct committeeman Downers Grove (Ill.) Twp. Mem.: AAHPERD, Nat. Assn. Youth Sports, Cmty. Assns. Inst., Internat. Facility Mgmt. Assn., Inst. Real Estate Mgmt. Home: 17W504 Waltham Pl Darien IL 60561

SKWERES, THOMAS W. entrepreneur, writer, poet, investor, consultant, advertising executive; b. Chgo., May 11, 1929; s. Marion John and Sophie Regina (Rataiczyk) Skweres; children: Thomas Allan, Pamela Charmaine, Patricia Ann. AA, Wright C.C., Chgo., 1949; student, Northwestern U., Chgo., 1949—51, student, 1953—56. Prodn. mgr. Reincke, Meyer & Finn, Chgo., 1953—55; v.p., account exec. Hanson and Stevens, Chgo., 1955—61; v.p. sales, gen. mgr. Ross & White, Wheeling, Ill., 1961—84; sales mgr. Graphics Plus, Lisle, Ill., 1984—89, Essig Printing, Lisle, Ill., 1989—91; CEO Tomco Enterprises, Lisle, Ill., 1991—. Staff sgt. U.S. Army, 1951—53, Europe. Achievements include patents and innovations in design and engring. for a wide scope of light and heavy transp. vehicles and sys; experienced in various aspects aviation, chem., metals, R.R. products, automotive fields, printing, art direction, real estate, mfg. and fin. industries. Avocations: travel, gardening, guidance, conservative gambling, teaching. Home: 5613 Snowdrop Lisle IL 60532 Office: Tomco Printing & Enterprise PO Box 475 Lisle IL 60532

SKWIERSKY, PAUL, accountant; b. N.Y.C., Aug. 14, 1925; s. Abraham and Dora (Rainer) S.; m. Gloria Evelyn Lederman, Dec. 27, 1947; children: Janet S., Denise C. Skwiersky Cohen. BS, NYU, 1948. CPA, N.Y., N.J. Mng. ptnr. Benjamin Nadel & Co., N.Y.C., 1942-87, Skwiersky, Alpert & Bressler, N.Y.C., 1987—. Bd. dirs. Philip & Janice Levin Found., North Plainfield, N.J., Darcy Found., Inc., N.Y.C., 1980-87, Levin Mgmt. Corp., North Plainfield, Allstate Constrn. Corp., North Plainfield; panelist, arbitrator Am. Arbitration Assn., N.Y.C. Dir. Birchwood Park Civic Assn., Syosset, N.Y., 1962. Sgt. U.S. Army, 1943-46. Mem. Fiber Producers Credit Assn., Textile Distbrs. Assn., Inc., N.Y. Credit & Fin. Mgmt. Assn., N.Y. State Soc. CPAs, Masons (master 1977-79), Fountains of Palm Beach Country Club. Avocations: reading, travel, golf. Office: Skwiersky Alpert Bressler LLP 462 7th Ave New York NY 10018-7606

SKYES, GREGORY, food products executive; New products mktg. mgr. Hillshire Farm & Kahn's, 1984; pres., CEO Ball Park Brands, 1995; mgr. State Fair Foods, Best Kosher; v.p. Sara Lee Foods, Chgo.; pres., CEO Sara Lee Foods Retail, Chgo. Office: Sara Lee Corp 3 First National Plz Chicago IL 60602-4260

SLAATTÈ, HOWARD ALEXANDER, minister, philosophy educator; b. Evanston, Ill., Oct. 18, 1919; s. Iver T. and Esther (Larsen) S.; m. Mildred Gegenheimer, June 20, 1951; children: Elaine Slaatte Quaddur, Mark, Paul. AA, Kendall Coll., 1940; BA cum laude, U. N.D., 1942; B.D. cum laude, Drew U., 1945, PhD, 1956; Drew fellow, Mansfield Coll., Oxford (Eng.) U., 1949-50. Ordained to ministry Meth. Ch. as elder, 1943. Pastor Detroit Conf. United Meth. Ch., 1950-65; assoc. prof. systematic theology Temple U., 1956-60; vis. prof., prof. philosophy and religion McMurry Coll. (now named McMurry U.), 1960-65; prof. dept. philosophy Marshall U., Huntington, W.Va., 1965-89, prof. emeritus, 1989—, chmn. dept., 1966-81, mem. grad. council, 1970-73, mem. research bd., 1974-76, mem. acad. standards and policy com., 1975-77, research grantee, 1976, 77; mem. bd. Campus Christian Center, 1973-75; prof. ethics St. Leo (Fla.) Coll., 1993. Lectr. Traverse City (Mich.) State Hosp., 1966-71, Am. Ontoanalytical Assn. internat. conf., Acapulco, Mex., 1970, World Congress Logotherapy, San Diego, 1980, other orgns. Author: Time and Its End, 1962, Fire in the Brand, 1963, The Pertinence of the Paradox, 1968, The Paradox of Existentialist Theology, 1971, Modern Science and the Human Condition, 1974, The Arminian Arm of Theology, 1977, The Dogma of Immaculate Perception, 1979, Discovering Your Real Self, 1980, The Seven Ecumenical Councils, 1980, The Creativity of Consciousness, 1983, Contemporary Philosophies of Religion, 1986, Time, Existence and Destiny, 1988, Critical Survey of Ethics, 1988; co-author: The Philosophy of Martin Heidegger, 1983, Religious Issues in Contemporary Philosophy, 1988, Our Cultural Cancer and Its Cure, 1995, A Re-Appraisal of Kierkegaard, 1995, Plato's Dialogues and Ethics, 1999, A Purview of Wesley's Theology, 2000; contbr. Analecta Frankliana, 1981; gen. editor: (series) Contemporary Existentialism; contbr. to theol. and philos. jours. Mem. W.Va. Conf. United Meth. Ch., 1966-87, ret., 1987; bd. dirs. Inst. for Advanced Philos. Research, 1979-90; chmn. bd. dirs. Salvation Army of Huntington, W. Va.; courtesy prof. U. South Fla., 1993-99. Recipient Outstanding Educators of Am. award, 1975, Profl. Excellence award Faculty Merit Found., State of W.Va., 1986, U. N.D. Found. award, 2000; named to Honorable Order of Ky. Colonels, W.Va. Ambassador of Good Will; named Internat. Man of Yr., 1993; NSF fellow, 1965, Benedum Found. rsch. grantee, 1970, NSF rsch.-grantee, 1965, 71. Mem. W.Va. Philos. Assn. (pres., 1966-67, 83-84), Am. Philos. Assn., AAUP, Am. Acad. Religion. Home: 203N Foliage Cir Cary NC 27511 *Most knowledge is relative, a balanced existential position with empirical implications, except for the divine Absolute encountered by faith in existence. The revealed principles opened up thereby, especially the ultimacy of sacrifical love (Agape), give basis and motivation for vital morality and a healthy culture. True freedom springs from commitment to these principles.*

SLABACH, STEPHEN HALL, lawyer; b. Nov. 15, 1934; s. Carl Edward and Alvine A. Slabach; m. Elizabeth Havard Cartwright, Feb. 15, 1958; children: Elizabeth Slabach Schmit, Stephen Edward, William Cartwright. BSME, Northwestern U., 1957; postgrad., George Washington U. Sch. Law, 1957—59; LLB, Stanford U, 1961. Bar: Calif., U.S. Dist. Ct. (no. dist.) Calif. 62, U.S. Ct. Appeals (9th cir.) 73, U.S. Supreme Ct. 76. Law clk. to judge Calif. First Dist. Ct. Appeal, San Francisco, 1961—62; assoc. Cooley, Corwley, Gather, Godward, Castro & Huddleson, San Francisco, 1962—65, Cushing, Cullinan, Hancock & Rothert, San Francisco, 1965—73, ptnr., 1973—75; sole practice Burlingame, Calif., 1975—88, San Mateo, Calif., 1988—. Legal aid vol. San Mateo County; trustee San Mateo County Law Libr. Com., 1993—2002, v.p., 1998—2002; pres. Pacific Locomotive Assn., 1988—90, gen. counsel, 1980—. Mem.: ABA, State Bar Calif., Kiwanis. Republican. Episcopalian. Office: 520 S El Camino Real Ste 700 San Mateo CA 94402-1720 Office Phone: 650-347-7776.

SLACHTA, GREGORY ANDREW, urologist; b. Paterson, N.J., Mar. 17, 1946; s. Andrew Gregory and Mary Catherine (Shimko) S.; children: Gregory Andrew, Lara Ann, Andrea; m. Patricia A. Albano, Nov. 7, 1981. BS, Pa. State U., 1966; MD, Jefferson Med. Coll., 1968. Diplomate Am. Bd. Urology. Intern Lankenan Hosp., Phila., 1968-69; resident in urology Temple U. Hosp., Phila., 1969-70, 1973-75; pvt. practice, Springfield, Mass., 1975—97, Hilton Head (S.C.) Med. Group, 1997—99. Author: Inflammatory Diseases of the Male Genital Tract, 1982. Mem. City Council Com. for Health Ins., Springfield, 1984, Springfield Planning Bd., 1991. Maj. U.S. Army, 1971-73. Fellow ACS; mem. AMA, Am. Urol. Assn. (chmn. socioecon. com. 1986-91, del. to AMA 1991—), Mass. Med. Soc. (alt. del. to AMA 1986-91, vice chmn. legis. and nat. legis. affairs com. 1987-89), Hampden Dist. Med. Soc. (pres. 1986-88), Mass. Assn. Practicing Urologists (pres. 1985-87), Beaufort County med. Soc. (pres. 1998-2001). Republican. Roman Catholic. Avocation: golf. Office: Hilton Head Clinics Med Office Bldg 25 Hospital Center Dr Ste 300 Hilton Head Island SC 29926-2730

SLACK, DONALD CARL, agricultural engineer, educator; b. Cody, Wyo., June 25, 1942; s. Clarence Ralbon and Clara May (Beightol) S.; m. Marion Arline Kimball, Dec. 19, 1964; children: Jonel Marie, Jennifer Michelle. BS in Agrl. Engring., U. Wyo., 1965; MS in Agrl. Engring., U. Ky., 1968, PhD in Agrl. Engring., 1975. Registered profl. engr., Ky., Ariz. Asst. civil engr. City of Los Angeles, 1965; research specialist U. Ky., Lexington, 1966—70, agrl. engring. advisor Tha Phra, Thailand, 1970—73, rsch. asst. Lexington, 1973—75; from asst. prof. to assoc. prof. agrl. engring. U. Minn., St. Paul, 1975—84; prof. U. Ariz., Tucson, 1984—, head dept. agrl. and biosystems engring., 1991—. Mem. Mid. East and Mediterranean Desert Devel. Program, 1997—; vis. prof. dept. atmospheric sci. Fed. U. Paraiba, Campina Grande, Brazil, 1997; vis. prof. dept. irrigation Chapingo Autonomous U., Mexico, 2000; tech. adv. Ariz. Dept. Water Resources, Phoenix, 1985—, Tucson active mgmt. area, 1996—; cons. Winrock Internat., Morrilton, Ark., 1984, Water Mgmt. Synthesis II, Logan, Utah, 1985, Desert Agrl. Tech. Sys., Tucson, 1985—, Portek Hermosillo, Mexico, 1989—, World Bank, Washington, 1992—, Malawi Environ. Monitoring Project, 1996, Mex. Inst. for Water Tech., 1997, Nat. Agrl. Rsch. Inst., La Serena, Chile, 1997; cons. F.J. Hansen Inst. for World Peace San Diego State U., 1997—; dep. program support mgr. Rsch. Irrigation Support Project for Asia and the Near East, Arlington, Va., 1987—94; mem. adv. team Cearan Found. for Meteorology and Hydrology, Fortaleza, Brazil, 1995—; mem. internat. adv. panel Matrou Resources Mgmt. Project, World Bank, Egypt, 1996—2000; bd. dirs. Sonoita Vineyards, Ltd., Watershed Mgmt. Group, Inc. Contbr. articles to profl. jours. Fellow ASCE (Outstanding Jour. Paper award 1988), Am. Soc. Agrl. Engrs. (Ariz. sect. Engr of Yr. 1993); mem. Am. Geophys. Union, Am. Soc. Agronomy, Soil Sci. Soc. Am., U.S. Com. on Irrigation and Drainage (life), Am. Soc. Engring. Edn. (program evaluator accreditation bd. for enring. and tech., 2001—), SAR, Brotherhood of Knights of the Vine (master knight), Rocky Mountain Elk Found. (life), Sigma Xi, Tau Beta Pi, Alpha Epsilon, Gamma Sigma Delta. Democrat. Lutheran. Achievements include 3 patents pending; developer of infrared based irrigation scheduling device. Home: 9230 E Visco Pl Tucson AZ 85710-3167 Office: U Ariz Agrl Biosystems Engring Tucson AZ 85721-0001 Office Phone: 520-621-7230. Business E-Mail: slackd@email.arizona.edu. *Personal philosophy: Don't take yourself too seriously and don't take anyone else too seriously either.*

SLACK, VICKIE, human services administrator; b. Monroe, La., Mar. 27; d. Rufus J. and Minnie (Starr) S. BS, Sacramento State U., 1988; MPA, Golden Gate U., 1989. Phys. therapy asst. Easter Seals, Sacramento, 1983-84; intern aide to Congresswoman Barbara Boxer, Vallejo, Calif., 1986-87; phys. therapist asst. U. Calif.-Davis Med. Ctr., Sacramento, 1984-85; adminstrv. asst. St. Luke Hosp., San Francisco, 1987-88; ins. rep. Am. Nat. Ins. Co., Vallejo, 1988-89; health info. specialist Solano County Health Dept., Vallejo, Calif., 1990-93; supr., health educator, dir. tobacco edn. programs Bay Area Urban League, Oakland, Calif., 1993-95, health and human svc. dir., 1995—. Mem. Housing and Redevel. Commn., Cultural Commn., Commn. on Aging and Sister City Assn., City of Vallejo. Mem. NAFE, NAACP, Nat. Assn. Pub. Adminstrs., Nat. Council Negro Women, Delta Sigma Theta. Democrat. Baptist. Office: Bay Area Urban League 2201 Broadway Ste 100A Oakland CA 94612-3039 Home: #120 55 Springstowne CTR Vallejo CA 94591-5566

SLADE, BERNARD, playwright; b. St. Catharines, Ont., Can., May 2, 1930; s. Frederick and Bessie (Walbourne) Newbound; m. Jill Florence Hancock, July 25, 1953; children: Laurel, Christopher. Ed., Caernarvon Grammar Sch. Eng. Actor: Garden Ctr. Theatre, Vineland, Ont., Crest Theatre, Toronto, CBC-TV, Citadel Theatre, Edmonton, Alta.; screenwriter of over 20 hour TV plays for CBC, CBS, ABC, NBC, 1957—; writer/creator (TV series) Love on a Rooftop, The Partridge Family, The Flying Nun, The Girl with Something Extra, Bridget Loves Bernie; story editor, writer 15 episodes of TV series Bewitched; writer/creator (plays) A Very Close Family, 1962, Same Time Next Year (Drama Desk award 1975, Tony award nomination 1975), Tribute, 1978, Romantic Comedy, 1979, Special Occasions, 1981, Fatal Attraction, 1984, Return Engagements, 1986, Sweet William, 1987, An Act of the Imagination, 1987, I Remember You, 1991, You Say Tomatoes, 1993, Everytime I See You, 1994, Same Time, Another Year, Fling!, 2000; feature films: Same Time, Next Year, 1977, Tribute, 1978, Romantic Comedy, 1979, Shared Laughter-a memoir, 2000, (film biography) Comedic Genius of Bernard Slade, 2003. Recipient Acad. award nomination Motion Picture Arts and Scis., 1978. Mem. Dramatists Guild Am., Writers Guild Am. (award nomination), Acad. Motion Picture Arts and Scis. (Acad. award nomination 1978), Soc. Authors and Artists (France). Avocation: tennis. Address: Apt 1201 1100 Alta Loma Rd West Hollywood CA 90069-2439 *I am a prisoner of a childhood dream: to write for the theatre. The fulfillment of that dream has lived up to all my expectations. I believe the theatre should be a celebration of the human condition and that the artist's job is to remind us of all that is good about ourselves. I feel privileged to be given a platform for my particular vision of life, and, whether my plays succeed or fail, I am always grateful for the use of the hall.*

SLADE, BERNARD NEWTON, electronics company executive; b. Sioux City, Iowa, Dec. 21, 1923; s. William Charles and Katherine Gertrude Slotsky; m. Margot Friedlein, Aug. 18, 1946; children: Steven P., Eric J. BSEE, U. Wis., 1948; MS, Stevens Inst. Tech., 1954. Devel. engr. tube divsn. RCA, Harrison, NJ, 1948-55; devel. engr. RCA Labs., Princeton, NJ, 1955-56; mgr. tech. program IBM, Poughkeepsie, NY, 1956-60, mgr. product ops. Hopewell Junction, NY, 1960-64; mgr. mfg. tech. IBM World Trade Corp., Armonk, NY, 1964-65; corp. dir. of mfg. tech. IBM Corp., Armonk, 1965-84; sr. cons. Arthur D. Little, Inc., Cambridge, Mass., 1984-86, Gemini Cons., Morristown, NJ, 1986-93; founder, v.p., bd. dirs. Yieldup Internat. Corp., 1993-97; bd. dirs. V3 Semiconductors, 1996—2003, Anon, Inc. Co-author: Winning the Productivity Race, 1985; author: Compressing the Product Develop. Cycle, 1992; contbr. articles to profl. jours.; patentee in field; contbg. author: Transistors, 1956, Handbook of Semiconductor Electronics, 1962. 2nd lt. AUS, 1943-46. Mem.: IEEE (sr.), Sigma Xi. Home: 12 Merry Hill Rd Poughkeepsie NY 12603-3214

SLADE, JOHN DANTON, lobbyist; b. Balt., Apr. 5, 1939; s. Eldon and Marie (Smith) S.; m. Dale Iris Walden, Mar. 14, 1964 (dec. Dec. 1965); 1 child, Kenyatta Conrad; m. Deborah Faye Douglas, Dec. 11, 1987. BA in Sociology, Morgan State U., 1964; MA in Sociology, CUNY, 1966. Mgmt. trainee IBM, N.Y.C., 1966-69; producer, dir. WBAL-TV, Balt., 1969-71, WGBH-TV, Boston, 1971-73, KPIX-TV, San Francisco, 1973-75; announcer KEST Radio, San Francisco, 1975-76; gen. mgr. Channel 8 Access TV, San Francisco, 1975-79; owner Swansbriar Plantation, Cumberland, Va., 1979-85; asst. prof. military sci., dept. chmn. Howard U., Bowie State U., Georgetown U., Washington, 1985-88; acting chief Nat. Guard Bur., Washington, 1988-92; exec. dir. Assn. Reserve Minority Svc. Members, Inc., Washington, 1992—; founder Iota Phi Theta, Inc. Talk show host WOL Radio, Washington; bd. dirs. Meridian Distributors, St. Thomas, V.I.; guest lectr. Stanford (Calif.) U., Northeastern U., Boston, Morgan State Coll., Balt., Merritt Coll., Oakland, Calif., U. Mass., Amherst; mem. spl. com. San Francisco Chronicle; mem. Balt. Community Rels. Commn.; mem. N.G. Drug Reduction Bd., 1990-91. Author: Last Testament of an American, 1993, Flight of an Angel, 1993, The Founding and Ascendancy of Iota Phi Theta, 1994; Man-Made (Guide to Single Mothers Raising Black Boys Alone), 1994, Iota Phi Theta (Ascending to the Next Millenium), 1999; film producer Breaking the Chains of Bondage, 1972. Lt. col. U.S. Army, 1985-92. Recipient Roy Wilkens Renown Svc. award, 1991, Award of Honor, NAACP, Balt., Community Svc. award Les Hommes Civic and Social Club, Hampton, Va., 1991. Mem. Iota Phi Theta (founding mem., bus. mgr. 1963-64). Republican. Office: ARMS 1401 Madison St NW Washington DC 20011-6805

SLADE, MARGOT, editor; Various positions N.Y. Times, 1981—2001; editor, sr. dir. Consumer Reports, 2001—. Office: Consumer Reports 101 Truman Ave Yonkers NY 10703-1044

SLADE, ROY, artist, college president, museum director; b. Cardiff, U.K., July 14, 1933; came to U.S., 1967, naturalized, 1975; s. David Trevor and Millicent (Stone) S. N.D.D., Cardiff Coll. Art, 1954; A.T.D., U. Wales, 1954; D of Arts, Art Inst. So. Calif., 1994. Tchr. art and crafts Heolgam High Sch., Wales, 1956-60; lectr. art Clarendon Coll., Nottingham, Eng., 1960-64; sr. lectr. fine art Leeds Coll. Art, Eng., 1964-67; prof. painting Corcoran Sch. Art, Washington, 1967-68, assoc. dean, 1969-70, dean, 1970-77; dir. Corcoran Gallery of Art, Washington, 1972-77; pres., dir. Cranbrook Acad. Art, Bloomfield Hills, Mich., 1977-94, now dir. emeritus. Sr. lectr. Leeds Coll. Art, England, 1968—69; vis. Boston Mus. Fine Arts, 1970; dir. emeritus Cranbrook Art Mus., 2000—. Exhibited one-man shows Howard Roberts Gallery, Cardiff, Wales, 1958, New Art Ctr., London, 1960, U. Birmingham, 1964, 69, Herbert Art Gallery and Mus., Coventry, 1964, Va. State Art League, 1967, Mus. of Arts and Crafts, Columbus, Ga., 1968, Jefferson Place Gallery, Washington, 1968, 70, 72, 73, Park Sq. Gallery, Leeds, 1969, St. Mary's Coll., Md., 1971, Guelph U., Ont., Can., 1971, Hood Coll., 1974, Pyramid Gallery, Washington, 1976, Robert Kidd Gallery, 1981, 92, Herman Miller, Inc., Mich., 1985; group shows in U.K., Washington, Can.; represented in permanent collections Arts Council Gt. Brit., Contemporary Art Soc., Nuffield Found., Ministry of Works, Eng., Brit. Embassy, Washington, Brit. Overseas Airways Corp., U. Birmingham, Wakefield City Art Gallery, Clarendon Coll., Cadbury Bros., Ltd., Eng., Lord Ogmore, Local Edn. Authorities. Mem. D.C. Commn. on Arts.; bd. dirs. Artists for Environment Found., Nat. Assn. Schs. Art; chmn. Nat. Council Art Adminstrs., 1981. Served with Brit. Army, 1954-56. Decorated knight 1st class Order of White Rose (Finland), Royal Order of Polar Star (Sweden); recipient award Welsh Soc., Phila., 1974, Gov.'s Arts Orgn. award, 1988; Fulbright scholar, 1967-68. Mem. Nat. Soc. Lit. and Arts, AIA (hon. Detroit chpt.), Assn. Art Mus. Dirs. (hon.). Home: 31 Island Way Apt 801 Clearwater FL 33767-2206 E-mail: roy.slade@worldnet.att.net.

SLADEK, LYLE VIRGIL, mathematician, educator; b. Pukwana, S.D., Oct. 13, 1923; s. Charles Frank and Emma Margaret (Swanson) S.; m. Patricia Knotts, Sept. 12, 1948; children: Susan, Ann, Laura, Karen. BS, S.D. State U., 1948; MA, U. S.D., 1949, Stanford U., 1963; PhD, UCLA, 1970. Tchr. high sch., Mitchell, S.D., 1950-56; asst. prof. math. Black Hills State Coll., S.D., 1957-62; prof. math. Calif. Luth. Univ., Thousand Oaks, 1963-94, prof. emeritus, 1994—. Lectr. history WWII. Contbr. short stories, poems to mags. and newspapers. Pres. congregation Our Savior's Lutheran Ch., Spearfish, S.D., 1961. Served as officer U.S. Army, 1943-46, PTO, ETO. Shell Merit fellow, 1956; NSF fellow, 1956-57, 62-63; recipient Meritorious Achievement award edn. S.D. Mines and Tech., 1957; Fulbright-Hays lectr. Bahamas, 1980-81 Mem. Math. Assn. Am., Blue Key, Pi Kappa Delta, Phi Delta Kappa Home: 3243 Pioneer St Thousand Oaks CA 91360-2730 E-mail: patlyle@hotmail.com. *I learned from my parents during the dust bowl years that adversity often can be overcome through patience and determination, and that problems provide challenges that add spice to life. I have sought to return full measure to society for all the opportunities and joys of life that have come my way.*

SLADEK, RONALD JOHN, physics educator; b. Chgo., Sept. 19, 1926; s. James Joseph and Rose (Vachulka) S.; m. Jeanne T. McFadden, Sept. 19, 1953; children: Linda, James, Frances, Stephen, Rosemarie, Edward. PhB, U. Chgo., 1947, SB, 1949, SM, 1950, PhD, 1954. Rsch. physicist Westinghouse Rsch. Labs., Pitts., 1953-60, fellow scientist, 1960-61; assoc. prof. physics Purdue U., West Lafayette, Ind., 1961-66, prof., 1966-91, prof. physics emeritus, 1992—, acting head dept. physics, 1969-71, assoc. dean sci., 1974-87. Vis. scientist Sci. Center, N.Am. Rockwell Corp., Thousand Oaks,

Calif., summer 1967; sabbatical scientist Xerox Rsch. Ctr., Palo Alto, Calif., 1976-77 Contbr. articles to profl. jours. With USNR, 1945-46. AEC fellow U. Chgo., 1952-53. Fellow Am. Phys. Soc. Home: 963 Ridgeview Dr Reno NV 89511-8506

SLADKUS, HARVEY IRA, lawyer; b. Mar. 5, 1929; s. Samuel Harold and Charlotte Dorothy Sladkus; m. Harriet Marcia Barske, Nov. 26, 1967 (div.); children: Steven David, Jeffrey Brandon; m. Roberta Frances Pope, Oct. 24, 1986. AB, Syracuse U., 1950; JD, NYU, 1961. Bar: NY 1962, U.S. Supreme Ct. 1967, Conn. 1981. Assoc. Morris Ploscowe, NYC, 1961-66; pvt. practice NYC, 1968—95, 1997—; ptnr. Dweck & Sladkus and Feiden, Dweck & Sladkus, NYC, 1968-95, Dweck & Sladkus, LLP, NYC, 1996. Small claims arbitrator Civil Ct. City of NY, 1977—; adj. prof. law Benjamin N. Cardozo Sch. Law, 1994—95; lectr. family and matrimonial law. Co-author: (book) Practice Under New York's Matrimonial Law, 1971—79; editor-in-chief: Family Law Practice, 1982, contbg. columnist: It's the Law, Suffolk Times, 1999—2002, Bottom Line, 2000—; contbr. articles to profl. jours. 1st lt. U.S. Army, 1952—53, Korea. Decorated Bronze Star, War Svc. medal Korean Govt.; named Arbitrator of Yr., NY Civil Small Claims Ct., 2002, Civil Ct. NY County, 2002; recipient George Washington Honor medal, Freedoms Found., Valley Forge, 1953. Mem.: Suffolk County Bar Assn., Am. Arbitration Assn. (nat. panel arbitrators), Internat. Acad. Matrimonial Lawyers, Am. Acad. Matrimonial Lawyers, Assn. Bar City of NY, NY State Bar Assn. Jewish. Office: 425 Park Ave New York NY 10022-3506 Office Phone: 212-754-9400. E-mail: hisatty@nyc.rr.com. *Notable cases include: Burns vs. Burns, first to constitute a tenant in occupancy to subscribe to shares of an apt. corp. going coop.; Brown vs. Brown, case of first impression reclause in agreement of ex-wife living with another man.*

SLAFF, ALLAN PAUL, naval officer, university administrator, educator, entrepeneur; b. Mt. Vernon, N.Y., Feb. 2, 1923; s. Frank Alfred and Augusta Raye (Scher) S.; m. Mary Lee Schaeffer; children: Randolph Elliott, Valerie Anne. BS, U.S. Naval Acad., 1944; postgrad., U.S. Naval Post Grad Sch., 1949-50, U.S. Naval War Coll., Newport, R.I., 1959-60, Harvard U., 1967. Commd. ensign USN, 1944, advanced through grades to capt., 1965, WWII Battleship Mass. Fast Carrier TF, 1944-46, personal aide to CNO Adm. Arleigh Burke, 1950-51, spl. security officer commd. in Korean War Navy, comdr. USS Lester, Davis, Luce, Albany, 1957-70, sr. naval advisor to Vietnam Navy, 1967-68, ret., 1970; dean, mem. faculty Bus. Sch. Harvard U., Boston, 1970-80; chmn. Luzerne Co. News Co., Wilkes Barre, Pa., 1980-86, LABSPHERE, Inc., N. Sutton, N.H., 1983-94. Cons. Harvard Bus. Sch., 1980-84. Author: (book) A Sailor's Story, 2004; contbr. numerous articles to profl. jours. and mags. Bd. dirs. numerous schs., clubs, corps., civic and polit. orgns. Decorated Legion of Merit, Bronze Star, Nat. Order of Vietnam, numerous other decorations U.S. Navy, 1941-70; recipient Disting. Grad. award Wyoming Sem., Kingston, Pa., 1990. Mem. Port Royal Club (sec. bd. dirs.), The Naples Yacht Club (treas., bd. dirs.), Royal Poinciana Golf Club, Port Royal Property Owners Assn. (bd. dirs.), Lake Sunapee Yacht Club, Baker Hill Golf Club. Republican. Episcopalian. Avocations: golf, travel, photograprhy, gardening. Home: 4151 Gulf Shore Blvd N # 601 Naples FL 34103-2292 also: PO Box 1836 27 Highland Rdg New London NH 03257-4321 E-mail: allanslaff@aol.com.

SLAFKA, KRISTI LYNNE, journalist; b. McKeesport, Pa., Aug. 18, 1978; d. Kenneth Edward and Debra Lynne Slafka. BA, Washington and Lee U., 2000; web prodr. cert., Georgetown U., 2002. Assoc. editor Hotline, Washington, 2000—; stringer People mag., Washington, 2002. Mem.: Radio & TV News dirs. assn., Soc. Profl. Journalists, Kappa Delta. Office: The Hotline The Watergate 600 New Hampshire Ave NW Washington DC 20037

SLAGELL-GOSSEN, REONNA RICHELE, science educator, researcher; b. Weatherford, Okla., Sept. 12, 1965; s. Harold Joseph and Ella M. Slagell; m. Bryan Jay Gossen, Mar. 2, 1996. BS in Biol. Scis., Okla. State U., 1989, MS in Natural and Applied Sci., 1997. Electron microscopy cert., cert. tchr. Okla. Sci. tchr. Corn (Okla.) Bible Acad., 1989—94; grad. tchg. asst. Okla. State U., Stillwater, 1994—96; asst. plant pathologist Am. Sunmelon, Hinton, Okla., 1997; lead instr. Redlands CC, El Reno, Okla., 1998—. Facilitator Leadership Devel. Inst., Oklahoma City, 2003; mem. nursing adv. com., mem. global edn. com. Redlands CC, El Reno, 2003—. Judge Okla. Future Farmers Am. Assn., 1999—; mem. Canadian County Coalition Children and Families, 1999—2001, Leadership Canadian County Class X. Recipient Tchg. Excellence award, Nat. Inst. for Staff and Orgnl Devel, 2001; grantee, Okla. Ctr. Advancement Sci. and Tech., Redlands CC and USDA-ARS, 2000—02. Mem.: Nat. Inst. for Staff and Orgnl. Devel., Okla. Microscopy Soc., Okla. Acad. Sci., Nat. Assn. Biology Tchrs., Nat. Sci. Tchrs. Assn., Gt. Plains RC&D Assn., Phi Kappa Phi, Delta Kappa Gamma. Republican. Mennonite. Avocations: cooking, water-skiing, gardening, music, NASCAR. Home: 205 Luella Dr Corn OK 73024 Office: Redlands CC 1300 S Country Club Rd El Reno OK 73036 Office Fax: 405-422-1200. Business E-Mail: rslagellgossen@juno.com.

SLAGER, DONALD W. waste management executive; Various mgmt. positions Gen. Waste Svcs., 1985—90, gen. mgr., 1990—92; dist. mgr. Chgo. metro dist. Allied Waste Svcs., 1992—96, regional v.p. west region, 1996—97, asst. v.p. ops., 1997—98; v.p. ops. Allied Waste Industries, 1998—2001, sr. v.p. ops., 2001—03, exec. v.p., COO, 2003—; pres., CEO Browning-Ferris Industries Inc, Houston. Office: Allied Waste Industries Ste 100 15880 N Greenway-Hayden Loop Scottsdale AZ 85260*

SLAGLE, LARRY B. human resources specialist; b. Templeton, Pa., Dec. 17, 1934; s. William Harry and Luella (Armstrong) S. AB, Wabash Coll., 1956; postgrad., Am. U., 1967-71. Dep. admistr. for mgmt. and budget USDA Animal & Plant Health Inspection Svc., Washington, 1978-88, assoc. adminstr., 1988-90; dir. pers. USDA, Washington, 1990-94; pvt. practice human resources and orgnl. cons., 1994—. With U.S. Army, 1957-59, Korea. Named Meritorious Exec. President Reagan, 1985, President Bush, 1991. Avocation: bicycling. Home and Office: 208 6th St SE Washington DC 20003-1134 Office Phone: 202-257-9612. Personal E-mail: lbslagle@comcast.net.

SLAIGHT, GARY, broadcast executive; b. Edmonton, Alta., Can., 1951; married; 2 children. BA in English, U. Western Ont. Media estimator McLaren Advt., 1973; promotion mgr. Quality Records, 1974-75, WEA Records, 1975; account exec. Q107, 1977, program dir., 1978, v.p., gen. mgr., 1982, MIX 99.9, 1987-2000; pres., CEO Std. Radio. Inc., Toronto, 1987—, Std. Broadcasting Corp., Ltd., 2000—; gen. mgr. CFRB, Toronto, 1987-2000. Bd. dirs. Can. Acad. Recording Arts and Scis. Bd. dirs. Walk of Fame, Moontaxi, Hosp. for Sick Children. Recipient ann. music industry awards Gen. Mgr. of Yr., 1986, Program Dir. of Yr., 1987, Broadcast Exec. of Yr., 1992, 93, 96, 98. Office: Standard Radio Inc 2 St Clair Ave W Toronto ON Canada M4V 1L6

SLATE, FLOYD OWEN, retired engineering educator; b. Carroll County, Ind., July 26, 1920; s. Ora George and Gladys Marie (Miller) Slate; m. Margaret Mary Magley, Oct. 14, 1939; children: Sally Lee Slate McEnteer, Sandra Kay Slate Miller, Rex Owen. BS, Purdue U., 1941, MS, 1942, PhD, 1944. Chemist Manhattan Project, Columbia U., N.Y.C. and Decatur, Ill., 1944-46; asst. prof. civil engring. Purdue U., Lafayette, Ind., 1946-49; v.p., dir. Geotechnics & Resources Inc., White Plains, NY, 1959-63; prof. engring. materials Cornell U., Ithaca, NY, 1949-87; prof. emeritus, 1987. Internat. lectr.; cons. concrete, low-cost housing. Author; contbr. articles to profl. jours. Recipient Excellence in Engring. Tchg. award, Cornell U., 1976; sr. fellow, East-West Ctr., 1976, rsch. grantee, NSF, 1960—86. Fellow: Am. Inst. Chemists, Am. Concrete Inst. (hon. Wason Rsch. medal 1957, 1965, 1974, 1986, Anderson award 1983); mem.: ASTM, ASCE, Am. Chem. Soc. Achievements include research in internal structure of concrete vs. properties; chemistry applied to engineering problems and low-cost housing for developing countries. Home: 255 The Esplanade N Apt 306 Venice FL 34285-1518 *Think positively and be optimistic. Be considerate of others, try to help others, and enjoy life.*

SLATE, JOE HUTSON, psychologist, educator; b. Hartselle, Ala., Sept. 21, 1930; s. Murphy Edmund and Marie (Hutson) S.; m. Rachel Holladay, July 1, 1950; children: Marc Allan, John David, James Daryl. BS, Athens Coll., 1960; MA, U. Ala., 1965, PhD, 1970. Mem. faculty Athens (Ala.) State Coll., 1965-92, prof. psychology, 1974-92, chmn. behavioral scis., 1974-92; pvt. practice psychology Athens, 1970-92, Hartselle, 1992—; v.p. Slate Security Systems, Hartselle, Ala., 1984—. Author: Psychic Phenomena, 1988, Self-Empowerment, 1991, Psychic Empowerment, 1995, Psychic Empowerment for Health and Fitness, 1996, Astral Projection, 1998, Aura Energy for Health Healing, and Balance, 1999, Rejevenation: Strategies for Living Younger, Longer and Better, 2001, Psychic Vampires, 2002. Named hon. prof. U. Montevallo, 1973, prof. emeritus Athens State U., 1992. Mem. APA, Am. Soc. Clin. Hypnosis, Inst. Parapsychol. Rsch. (founder), Coun. for Nat. Register Health Svc. Providers in Psychology, NEA, Ala. Edn. Assn., Delta Tau Delta, Phi Delta Kappa, Kappa Delta Pi. Home: 1807 Highway 31 NW Hartselle AL 35640-4442 Office: 310 E Main St Hartselle AL 35640 E-mail: joehslate@aol.com.

SLATE, JOHN BUTLER, biomedical engineer; b. Schenectady, N.Y., Sept. 27, 1953; s. Herbert Butler and Violet (Perugi) S. BSEE, U. Wis., 1975, MEE, 1977, PhDEE, 1980. Spl. fellow of cardiovascular surgery U. Ala., Birmingham, 1980-81, dept. biomed. research engr., 1981-82; microbiology fellow, 1981-82; sr. research engr. IMED Corp., San Diego, 1982-83, sr. research scientist, 1983-86; sci. dir. Pacesetter Infusion Ltd. (dba MiniMed Technologies), Sylmar, Calif., 1986-87; v.p. tech. MiniMed Technologies, Sylmar, Calif., 1987-91; v.p. R & D Siemens Infusion Systems, Sylmar, Calif., 1991-93; v.p. tech. devel. Via Med., San Diego, 1993-94; pres. Slate Engring., San Diego, 1997—2003, Avant Drug Delivery Sys., Inc., San Diego, 1997—2002; v.p. ops. Avant Med. Corp., San Diego, 2002—, pres., 2002—. Mem. IEEE (IEE Ayrton award), Sigma Xi. Office: Avant Med Corp 10225 Barnes Canyon Rd Ste A113 San Diego CA 92121 Office Phone: 858-202-1560. E-mail: jslate@avantmedical.com.

SLATER, BRIAN (RAUEN SLATE), writer; b. Arlington Heights, Ill., June 19, 1973; s. Robert Vincent and Kathe Lynn Slater; m. Debra Renee Staudt (div. Feb. 27, 2002). Prin. Slate Raven Novels, Ill., 1993—. Author: (novels) Civilized War 2023, 2000, Fresh Start, 2001. Mem.: Knights in Shining Leather (life; swordfighting trainer 1991—2002). Avocations: swimming, martial arts, sword collecting. Office Phone: 847-359-2894.

SLATER, CARMEN ROCHELLE, elementary school educator; b. Fort Worth, Tex., Mar. 3, 1973; d. Carl Leslie, Sr. and Billie Faye Slater. BA in Communication & Elem. Edn., BA in English & Elem. Edn., U. Tex., Arlington, 1991—96. Cert. Elem. Sch. tchr. Tex. State Bd. Edn., 1996, Elem. Speech Comm. tchr. Tex. State Bd. Edn., 1996, Early Childhood Edn. tchr. Tex. State Bd. Edn., 2000. Kindergarten tchr. Paul L. Dunbar Elem. Sch., Dallas, 1996—. Reading/lang. arts rep. (K-3), Campus Intrnl. Leadership Team Paul L. Dunbar Learning Ctr., Dallas, 1999—, grade level chair, 1999—, campus early childhood rep., 1999—, new tchr. mentor, 2000—03, campus headstart liaison, 2001—, kindergarten sponsor, Benjamin Banneker Math Club, 2001—. Mem.: Internat. Reading Assn., Am. Fedn. Tchrs., Delta Sigma Theta, Phi Delta Kappa (xinos sponsor 1999—2003). Conservative. Baptist. Avocations: reading, singing, travel. Home: 5509 Kilpatrick Ave Fort Worth TX 76107 Personal E-mail: crslater73@hotmail.com.

SLATER, DORIS ERNESTINE WILKE, business executive; b. Oakes, N.D.; d. Arthur Waldemar and Anna Mary (Dill) Wilke; m. Lawrence Bert Slater, June 4, 1930 (dec., 1960). Grad. high sch. Sec. to circulation mgr. Mpls. Daily Star, 1928-30; promotion activities Lions Internat. in U.S., Can., Cuba, 1930-48; exec. sec. parade and spl. events com. Inaugural Com., 1948-49; exec. sec. Nat. Capital Sesquicentennial Commn., 1949-50, Capitol Hill Assos., Inc., 1951, Pres.'s Cup Regatta, 1951; adminstrv. asst. Nat. Assn. Food Chains, 1951-60; v.p., sec.-treas. John A. Logan Assos., Inc., Washington, 1960—; v.p., sec.-treas. Logan, Seaman, Slater, Inc., 1962—; mng. dir. Western Hemisphere, Internat. Assn. Chain Stores, 1964— . With pub. relations div. Boston Met. chpt. ARC, 1941-42; mem. Nat. Cherry Blossom Festival Com., 1949—; mem. Inaugural Ball Com., 1953, 57, 65. Methodist. Lion. Home and Office: 2500 Wisconsin Ave NW Washington DC 20007-4504

SLATER, EVE, federal agency administrator; 2 children. Grad., Vassar Coll. Cert. internal medicine and cardiology. Intern and resident Mass. Gen. Hosp., chief resident medicine; chief hypertension unit, asst. prof. medicine Harvard Med. Sch., 1977—82; sr. dir. biochem. endocrinology Merck Rsch. Labs., 1983—88, sr. v.p. external policy, v.p. corp. pub. affairs; asst. sec. for health Dept. HHS, Washington, 2002—. Chmn. Internat. Conf. on Harmonization Com. on the Structure and Content of Clin. Studies Reports; chmn. regulations adv. bd. Ctr. for Medicine Rsch.; mem. Keystone Nat. Policy Dialogue on HIV; founder Forum for HIV Rsch. Mem.: Phi Beta Kappa. Avocation: flute. Office: Dept HHS Pub Health and Sci 200 Independence Ave SW Washington DC 20201

SLATER, GARY, retail executive; Pres., CEO BW Techs., Calgary, Canada. Office: BW Tech 2840 2d Ave SE Calgary AB Canada T2A 6T7

SLATER, JAMES ALEXANDER, entomologist, educator; b. Belvidere, Ill., Jan. 10, 1920; s. Ray Alvin and Gladys (Banks) S.; m. Elizabeth Thackston, Feb. 20, 1943; children: James Alexander, Jacquelyn, Samuel, Lydia. BA, U. Ill., 1942, MS, 1947; PhD, Iowa State U., 1950. Asst. prof. Iowa State U., Ames, 1950-53, U. Conn., Storrs, 1953-55, assoc. prof., 1955-60, prof., 1960-87, head dept zoology and entomology, 1961-67, emeritus prof., 1987—, head sect. systematics, evolutionary biology, 1970-82. State ornithologist, Conn., 1955-80; commr. Conn. Geol. and Natural History Survey, 1960s; mem. Conn. Accrediting Bd. Higher Edn., 1960s. Contbr. articles to profl. jours., chpts. to books. Served to lt. USNR, 1943-46. Recipient Faculty Rsch. award, U. Conn. Alumni Assn., 1972, Founder's Meml. ESA award, 1996, Thomas Say award, ESA, 1996, citation of merit, Conn. State Assembly, 2001. Fellow Entomol. soc. Am. (L.O. Howard Disting. Rsch. award 1986); mem. Royal Entomol. Soc. London, Entomol. Soc. South Africa, Assn. Gravestone Studies (Harriet Forbes Meml. award 1981), Nat. Milk Glass Collectors Soc. (pres. 1987-91), Soc. Systematic Zoology (pres. 1983-85). Democrat. Avocation: antique glass collecting. Home: 373 Bassetts Bridge Rd Mansfield Center CT 06250-1305 Office: U Conn Life Sci U 43 Storrs Mansfield CT 06269-0001 Office Phone: 860-486-2227.

SLATER, JAMES MUNRO, radiation oncologist; b. Salt Lake City, Jan. 7, 1929; s. Donald Munro and Leone Forestine (Fehr) S.; m. JoAnn Strout, Dec. 28, 1948; children: James, Julie, Jan, Jerry, Jon. BS in Physics, U. Utah, Utah State U., 1954; MD, Loma Linda U., 1963; PhD (hon.), Andrews U., Berrien Springs, Mich., 1996. Diplomate Am. Bd. Radiology. Intern Latter Day Saints Hosp., Salt Lake City, 1963-64, resident in radiology, 1964-65; resident in radiotherapy Loma Linda U. Med. Ctr., White Meml. Med. Center, L.A., fellow in radiotherapy, 1967-68, U. Tex.-M.D. Anderson Hosp. and Tumor Inst., Houston, 1968-69; dir. radiation oncology sect. Loma Linda U. Med. Ctr., Calif., 1970—79, dir. dept. nuc. medicine, 1975—79, chmn. dept. radiation scis., 1978—90, chmn. dept. radiation medicine, 1990—2001, dir. Cancer Inst., 1993—97, treas., 1995-96, exec. v.p., 1994—95; founder, dir. Loma Linda U./NASA Radiation Biology Lab., Calif., 1997—. Co-dir. cmty. radiology oncology program L.A. County-U. So. Calif. Comprehensive Cancer Ctr., 1978-83; mem. cancer adv. coun. State of Calif., 1980-85; clin. prof. U. So. Calif., 1982—; founding mem. Proton Therapy Coop. Group, 1985—, chmn. 1987-91; cons. charged particle therapy program Lawrence Berkeley Lab., 1986-94; cons. R&D monoclonal antibodies Hybritech Inc., 1985-94, bd. dirs., 1985-94; cons. Berkeley lab., 1986-94; mem. panel cons. Internat. Atomic Energy Agy. UN, 1994—; cons. Sci. Applications Internat. Corp., 1979, 89-91. Bd. dirs. Am. Cancer Soc., San Bernardino/Riverside, 1976—, exec. com., 1976—; pres. Inland Empire chpt., 1981-83. NIH fellow, 1968-69; recipient exhbn. awards Radiol. Soc. N.Am., 1973, exhbn. awards European Assn. Radiology, 1975, exhbn. awards Am. Soc. Therapeutic Radiologists, 1978, Alumnus of Yr. award, 1993-94. Fellow Am. Coll. Radiology; mem. AAAS, AMA, ACS (liaison mem. to commn. on cancer 1976-84), Am. Radium Soc., Am. Soc. Clin. Oncology, Am. Soc. Therapeutics Radiologists, Assn. Univ. Radiologists, Soc. for Clinical Trials, N.Y. Acad. Scis., Calif. Med. Assn., Calif. Radiol. Soc., Gilbert H. Fletcher Soc. (pres. 1981-82), Loma Linda U. Med. Sch. Alumni Assn., Radiol. Soc. N.Am., Bernardino County Med Soc., Soc. Chairmen Of Acad. Radiation Oncology Programs, Alpha Omega Alpha. Achievements include development of world's first proton accelerator system for treating patients with cancer and some benign diseases in a hospital environment; development of world's first computer assisted radiation treatment planning system utilizing patient's digitized anatomic images with overlying radiation distribution images. Office: Loma Linda U Med Ctr Radiation Medicine 11234 Anderson St Loma Linda CA 92354-2804 E-mail: jmslater@dominion.llumc.edu.

SLATER, JESS EVERETT, artist; b. Westfield, Mass., Dec. 31, 1910; s. Jess G. and Eva M. (Warman) S.; m. Helen E. Kozlowski, Sept. 1956. Grad. H.S., Westfield, Mass.; studied with Marco Zim, N.Y.C. Indsl. artist Hamilton Std., Windsor Locks, Conn., 1954-68. Group shows include Nat. Exhbn., Old Forge, N.Y., 1987, 89, 93, 97, New Eng. Water Color Soc. (Merit award), Water Color USA, Nat. Soc. Acrylic Painters; represented in numerous permanent collections. Mem. Midwest Water Color Soc. (Members award 1989). Democrat. Home: 42 Pomeroy Meadow Rd Southampton MA 01073-9410 E-mail: bracreto@javanet.com.

SLATER, JIM, sportswriter, journalist; b. Williamsburg, Va., May 31, 1961; s. James and Iva Slater. BA in Journalism and Sociology, Ind. U., Bloomington, 1982. Sports journalist UPI, Indpls., 1983—91, Watertown Daily Times, NY, 1991—93; sports editor Agence France-Presse, Washington, 1993—. Recipient Second pl. nat. sports news writing/circulation 50, 000 and under, AP, 1992, 1993, Hon. Mention sports features and in-depth investigative sports reporting/circulation 50, 000 or less, 1992, 1993. Office: Agence France-Presse Ste 500 1015 15th St NW Washington DC 20005

SLATER, LORI ANNETTE, project manager; b. Houston, Aug. 8, 1964; d. Ted Gerald Patterson, JoAnn Patterson. AAS in Bus., Blinn Coll., 1984; BA in Applied Behavioral Sci., Nat. Louis U., 2000. Cert. profl. project mgr. Sec. Century Coating, Houston, 1984—85; asst. Ted's Pool Svc., Houston, 1985—88; sec. Freestone County Attorney's Office, Fairfield, Tex., 1989—90; dispatcher Tex. Instruments, Inc., Houston, 1990—93, Hewlett Packard Co., Atlanta, 1993—95; global accounts tech. adminstr. Hewlett Packard Co., Atlanta, 1995—98; bus. process analyst Hewlett Packard Co., Atlanta, 1998—2000, project/program mgr., 2000—. Mem. Friends of the Ctr. So. Poverty Law Ctr., Montgomery, 2001—, founding mem. Nat. Campaign for Tolerance, 2001—. Mem.: Project Mgmt. Inst. Avocations: reading, tennis, watching old movies. Business E-Mail: lori.slater@hp.com.

SLATER, MICHAEL, communications executive; Founder MicroDesign Resources, 1997—. Lectr. Stanford U., Santa Clara U., Nat. Technol. U.; seminars in field. Author: Microprocessor Based Design; co-author: Practical Microprocessors; editl. dir., pub. Microprocessor Report; dir. Microprocessor Forum. Office: MicroDesign Resources PMB92 708 Gravenstein Hwy N Sebastopol CA 95472-2808

SLATER, RALPH EVAN, lawyer; b. Bklyn., July 14, 1948; s. Ralph Groff and Silvia Helen (Montanelli) S.; m. Cynthia Elaine Mahn, Aug. 29, 1970; children: Robert Evan, Andrew Montgomery, Steven Edward. AB, Princeton U., 1970; JD, U. Pa., 1973. Bar: Conn. 1973, U.S. Dist. Ct. Conn. 1984, U.S. Tax Ct. 1984, U.S. Supreme Ct. 1987. Assoc. Gregory & Adams, Wilton, Conn., 1973-79, ptnr., 1980-93; prin. Gregory & Adams P.C., 1994—, pres., 1996—. Chmn. bd. The Wilton Bank, 1986—; atty. Planning and Zoning Commn., Zoning Bd. Appeals, Ridgefield, Conn., 1979-81. Chmn. bd. edn. 1st Congl. Ch., Ridgefield, Conn., 1982-84, chmn. bd. trustees, 1985-87. Mem. Conn. Bar Assn. (exec. com. estates and probate sect. 1984-86, 93-99), Western Conn. Estate and Tax Planning Coun. Inc. (dir. 1992-96). Republican. Mem. Ch. of Christ. Home: 30 Strawberry Ridge Rd Ridgefield CT 06877-6019 Office: Gregory & Adams 190 Old Ridgefield Rd Wilton CT 06897-4023 E-mail: rslater@gregoryandadams.com.

SLATER, RODNEY E. former federal official, lawyer; b. Tutwyler, Miss., Feb. 23, 1955; m. Cassandra Wilkins; 1 child. BS, Ea. Mich. U., 1977; JD, U. Ark., 1980. Asst. atty. gen. State of Ark., 1980-82; spl. asst. for community and minority affairs Gov. of Ark., 1983-85, exec. asst. for econ. and community programs, 1985-87; dir. intergovernmental rels. Ark. State U., 1987-93; adminstr. fed. hwy. adminstrn. U.S. Dept. Transp., Washington, 1993-97, sec., 1997-2001; ptnr. Patton Boggs LLP, Washington, 2001—. Mem. Ark. State Hwy. and Transp. Commn., 1987-93, chair, 1992-93; dep. campaign mgr., sr. traveling advisor Clinton for Pres. Campaign, 1992; dep. to chair Clinton/Gore Transition Team, 1992-93; bd. dirs. Africare, 2001—, Joint Ctr Polit. and Econ. Studies, 2001— Ark. liaison Martin Luther King, Jr. Fed. Holiday Commn., 1983-87; mem. Ark. Sesquicentennial Commn., 1986. Mem. Ark. Bar Assn. (sec.-treas. 1989-93), W. Harold Flowers Law Soc. (pres. 1985-92). Democrat. Office: Patton Boggs 2550 M St NW Washington DC 20037

SLATER, STEWART EUGENE, theatre producer; b. San Antonio, Jan. 18, 1943; s. Oliver Eugene and EvaB (Richardson) S. BFA, Southwestern U., Georgetown, Tex., 1965; postgrad., U. Tex., 1971. Mem. faculty Gladewater (Tex.) Ind. Sch. Dist., 1965-67, Alamo Heights Ind. Sch. Dist., San Antonio, 1967-69; instr. Baylor U., Waco, 1971-72; tech. dir. Everyman Players, Pineville, Ky., 1973-75; asst. adminstrv. dir. Actors' Theatre of Louisville, 1973-76; bus. mgr. Ind. Repertory Theatre, Indpls., 1976-78; gen. mgr. Am. Conservatory Theatre, San Francisco, 1978-79, San Jose (Calif.) Civic Light Opera, 1980-84, exec. prodr., 1984-95, Am. Mus. Theatre San Jose, 1995-99, pres., exec. prodr., 1999—. Actor Everyman Players, New Orleans, 1973; adj. faculty San Joaquin Delta Coll., Stockton, Calif., 1980; dir. Nat. Alliance Mus. Theatre, NYC, 1985-98, pres., 94-96; bd. dirs. Arts Coun. Silicon Valley, San Jose, 1987-97; founding mem. San Jose Arts Round Table, 1983—, chmn, 1985-87, 2001-02. Exec. prodr. over 80 live musical prodns. Bd. dirs. Jt. Agencies Trust, Los Altos, Calif., 1998—. Named one of Outstanding Young Men in Am., 1970. Mem.: Rotary. Office: Am Mus Theatre San Jose 1717 Technology Dr San Jose CA 95110 Fax: 408-453-7123. E-mail: sslater@amtsj.org.

SLATER, THOMAS BOWIE, minister, educator; b. Magnolia, Ark., July 28, 1952; s. Thomas Jefferson and Thelma Lee (Bowie) S.; m. Renea Denise Bush, Dec. 27, 1986. BA in Journalism with honors, Ark. Tech. U., 1974; ThM, So. Meth. U., 1978, D of Ministry in Christian Edn., 1981; postdoctoral studies, U. Va. Ordained to ministry United Meth. Ch. Assoc. pastor St. James A.M.E. Temple, Dallas, 1975-76; min.-in-tng. El Paso (Tex.) Wesley Found./St. James-Myrtle United Meth. Ch., 1976-77; assoc. pastor Greater Garth Chapel A.M.E. Ch., Dallas, 1978-79; campus min. Greater Dallas Commmunity of Chs., 1978-80; pastor Conner Chapel A.M.E. Ch., Little Rock, 1980-83; acad. dean Jackson Theol. Sem., North Little Rock, Ark., 1980-83; assoc. dir. John Wesley United Meth. Parish, Little Rock, 1983-84; pastor Haden's Chapel United Meth. Ch., Palmyra, Va., 1985-86; teaching asst. dept. religious studies U. Va., 1986-87; instr. dept. religion U. Ga., Athens, 1988—, undergrad. advisor, 1989-91. Learning assoc. student devel. and programs dept. Mountain View Coll., Dallas, 1979-80; instr. Bible Perkins Sch. Theology, So. Meth. U., 1980-88. Contbr. articles to religious jours. Bd. dirs. Wesley Found., U. Va., 1985-88, U. Ga., 1990—. Mem. Soc. Bibl. Lit., Alpha Phi Omega. Home: 509 Watson Pl SE Gainesville GA 30501-4541 Office: U Ga Dept Religion Peabody Hall Athens GA 30602

SLATER, THOMAS GLASCOCK, JR., lawyer; b. Washington, Mar. 15, 1944; s. Thomas G. and Hylton R. S.; m. Scott Newell Brent, Aug. 31, 1996; children: Thomas Glascock, Tacie Holden, Andrew Fletcher. BA, Va. Mil. Inst., 1966; LLB, U. Va., 1969. Bar: Va. 1969, D.C. 1980, U.S. Dist. Ct. (ea. dist.) Va. 1970, U.S. Dist Ct. (we. dist.) Va. 1979, U.S. Ct. Appeals (4th cir.) 1975, U.S. Ct. Appeals D.C. 1980, U.S. Supreme Ct. 1981. Assoc. Hunton & Williams, Richmond, Va., 1969-76, ptnr., 1976—. Bd. dirs. Tredegar Industries. Pres. VMI Found., 1995—97, VMI Bd. Visitors, 2003—. Fellow: ABA, Am. Coll. Trial Lawyers; mem.: Richmond Bar Assn. (pres. 1989—90), D.C.

Bar Assn., Va. State Bar Coun. (exec. com.), 4th Cir. Jud. Conf., Va. Law Found., Va. Mil. Inst. Alumni Assn. (past pres.). Office: Hunton & Williams Riverfrnt Plaza East Tower 951 E Byrd St Richmond VA 23219-4074 Office Phone: 804-788-8475. Business E-Mail: tslater@hunton.com.

SLATER, VALERIE A. lawyer; b. Passaic, N.J., Oct. 13, 1952; BA magna cum laude, Allegheny Coll., 1974; JD, Cath. U. Am., 1977. Bar: D.C. 1977, U.S. Ct. Appeals (D.C. cir.) 1978, U.S. Dist. Ct. (D.C. dist.) 1982, U.S. Ct. Internat. Trade 1984, U.S. Ct. Appeals (fed. cir.) 1984. With Akin, Gump, Strauss et al., Washington. Mem. Phi Beta Kappa. Office: Akin Gump Strauss Hauer & Feld Ste 400 1333 New Hampshire Ave NW Washington DC 20036-1564 Business E-Mail: vslater@akingump.com.

SLATER, WANDA MARIE WORTH, property manager; b. Thurston, Ohio, Feb. 18, 1927; d. Daniel Harrison and Grace Marie (Neel) Worth; m. Charles Edwin Slater; children: Margaret Grace(dec.), Daniel Worthington(dec.), Donald Edwin. Student, Denison U., 1941-45, Bethany Coll., 1945-46. Recipient certs. Ohio Ho. Reps. and Senate, 116th Ohio Assembly, Creative Living, Columbus. Sub. tchr. Licking County Schs., Union Twp., Ohio, 1946; clerical typist Farm Bur. Ins. Co., Columbus, Ohio, 1947-49; salesperson Avon Co., Clyde, Ohio, 1954-63; dep. registrar Sandusky County, Ohio, 1960-64; notary pub. State of Ohio, Clyde, 1965-78, Hebron-Buckeye Lake, Ohio, 1978-98. Owner, mgr. rental property. Editor OFWC Buckeye mag., 1970-74, 88-98. Pres. Welcome Wagon, Clyde, 1957, Clyde Jr. League of Women, 1966, Leads-Licking County Cmty. Action Com., 1988, 94, 2000-01. Recipient Disting. Leadership award 1992, certificate of appreciation CARE. Mem.: Twentieth Century Club (pres. 1976—77), Order Eastern Star (worthy matron Clyde chpt. 1965, 1978, Hebron Eagon chpt. 1989, 1994, 2001), Mut. and Civic Improvement Club (pres. 1994—), Ohio Fedn. Women's Clubs (pres. 1986—88), Gen. Fedn. Women's Clubs Marionettes (pres. 1988—). Republican. Avocations: monologues, flower arranging, travel, crafts. Home and Office: 36 Worth Dr Hebron OH 43025-9760

SLATER, WILLIAM ADCOCK, retired social services organization executive; b. Kiangsu, People's Republic China, July 26, 1933; (parents U.S. citizens); s. Paul Raymond and Daisy Roberta (Butcher) S.; m. Karen C. Crutchfield, Sept. 4, 1956; children: Kathleen Ann, Bryan Paul. BA in Sociology and History, Wichita State U., 1958; MSW, Denver U., 1960. Juvenile probation officer Hennepin County Dept. Ct. Svcs., Mpls., 1960-63, program dir., 1963-65, dir. social svcs., 1965-67; clin. dir. St. Cloud (Minn.) Children's Home, 1967-70; exec. dir. Gillis Ctr., Women's Christian Assn., Kansas City, Mo., 1970-88, mng. exec. dir., 1988-95; ret., 1995. Team leader Coun. on Accreditation Svcs. for Families and Children, Washington, 1975—; presenter various child welfare confs., Okla., Kans., Mo., 1980-88; mem. Mo. Residential Treatment Task Force, Mo. Licensing Standards Task Foprce; mem. levels of care com. Kans. Dept. Social Svcs.; mem. EEO panels Fed. Exec. Bd., 1978, 79; mem. mental health tour People to People, People's Republic China, 1990. Contbr. articles to profl. jours. Mem. spkr.'s bur. United Way Kansas City, 1970—, chmn. agy. rels. com., agys. div., mem. homeless com.; mem. adv. bd. Bingham Jr. High Sch., Kansas City, 1984-86; mem. Kansas City-Xiao Sister City Com. With U.S. Army, 1953-55. Mem. NASW, Acad. Cert. Social Workers, Mo. Assn. Social Welfare, Mo. Child Care Assn. (bd. dirs. 1972-74, 84-88), Kans. Assn. Lic. Pvt. Child Care Agys., Children's Residential Treatment Assn. Kansas City (chmn.), Child Welfare League Am. (steering com. midwest region, nat. adv. coun. to exec. dir. 1976-80), U.S.-China Peoples Friendship Assn. (Kansas City chpt., bd. dirs. Midwest Region), Waldo Bus. Assn. (v.p.), Alpha Kappa Delta. Mem. Christian Ch. (Disciples Of Christ). Avocations: history, photography. Home: 9328 Woodson Dr Shawnee Mission KS 66207-2437

SLATKIN, LEONARD EDWARD, conductor, music director, pianist; b. LA, Sept. 1, 1944; s. Felix and Eleanor (Aller) Slatkin; m. Linda Hohenfeld, Mar. 29, 1986. Began violin study, 1947; piano study with, Victor Aller and Selma Cramer, 1955; composition study with, Castelnuovo-Tedesco, 1958; viola study with, Sol Schoenbach, 1959; conducting study with, Felix Slatkin, Amerigo Marino and Ingolf Dahl; student, Ind. U., 1962, L.A. City Coll., 1963, Juilliard Sch.; student (Irving Berlin fellow in musical direction), beginning 1964; student of, Jean Morel and Walter Susskind. Condr. laureate St. Louis Symphony; music dir. Nat. Symphony Orch., Washington, 1996—; chief condr. BBC Symphony Orch., 2000—. Condr. St. Louis Symphony Orch., 1968—96, musical dir., 1979—96, condr. laureate, 1996—; founder, music dir., condr. St. Louis Symphony Youth Orch., 1969—, mus. advisor, 1979—80; with ICM Artist, Ltd., Harold Holt, Ltd., Konzertdirektion/Schmidt; founder, dir. Nat. Conducting Inst. Composer: The Raven, Dialogue for Two Cellos and Orchestra, Ext. 1, 2, 3, 4. Recipient 2 Grammy awards, Prokofiev Symphony No. 5 with St. Louis Symphony, 1985, Declaration of Honor in Silver, Austrian Govt., 1986. Mem.: NARAS (bd. govs. Chgo. chpt.). Office: BBC Symphony Orchestra Maida Vale Studios Deleware Rd London W9 2LG England also: Nat Symphony Orch 2700 F St NW Washington DC 20566*

SLATNER, THOMAS ALLEN, bookseller; b. Marple, Cheshire, Eng., May 1, 1940; arrived in U.S., 1947; s. Hugo and Edith (Elsner) S.; m. Eve Naomi Silberberg, Aug. 11, 1961; children: Nicole, Claude, Genevieve. BA, CCNY, 1961. Mgr. Richard Abel & Co., London, 1968-73; dir. Thomas Slatner & Co., London and N.J., 1978—. Home: 2 Wellfield Ave London N10 2EA England Office: 1127 Kennedy Blvd North Bergen NJ 07047-1839

SLATON, DANIELLE VICTORIA, professional soccer player; b. San Jose, Calif., June 10, 1980; Majored in psychology, Santa Clara U., Calif., 1998—2001. Capt. U.S. Under-16 Nat. Team, 1996—97; mem. U.S. Under-21 Nat. Team, 1999, starter, Nordic Cup championship team, 1999; soccer player, defender U.S. Women's Nat. Team, 1999—; mem. U.S. soccer team Summer Olympics, Sydney, Australia, 2000; team mem. Carolina Courage, WUSA. Finalist Mo. Athletic Club award, 2000, 2001, Hermann trophy, 2001; named third team All-Am., NSCAA, 1998, first team All-Am., 1999, 2001, 2002. Office: US Soccer Fedn 1801 S Prairie Ave Chicago IL 60616

SLATOPOLSKY, EDUARDO, nephrologist, educator; b. Buenos Aires, Dec. 12, 1934; (parents Am. citizens); married, 1959; 3 children. BS, Nat. Coll. Nicolas Avellaneda, 1952; MD, U. Buenos Aires, 1959. Postdoctoral renal USPHS, renal divsn., Dept. Internal Medicine Washington U. Sch. Medicine, 1963-65, instr. med. nephrology, 1965-67, from asst. prof. to assoc. prof. medicine dept. nephrology, 1967-75; dir. Chromalloy Am. Kidney Ctr., Washington U. Sch. medicine, St. Louis, 1967-97, co-dir. renal divsn., 1972-97, prof. medicine, nephrology dept., 1975—, Joseph Friedman Prof. renal disease medicine, 1991—. Adv. mem. regional med. program, renal program sch. medicine Washington U., 1970-75; chmn. transplantation com. Barne Hosp., 1975—; fellow com. Kidney Found. Ea. Mo. and Metro.-E., 1978; mem. adv. com. artificial kidney-chronic uremia program NIH, 1978-90, rep. Latin-Am. nephrology, 1983-88; mem. study sect. Gen. Med., NIH, 1984-88. Recipient Frederick C. Bartter award 1991. Mem. AAAS, Am. Fedn. Clin. Rsch., Internat. Soc. Nephrology, Am. Soc. Nephrology, Endocrine Soc., Sigma Xi. Achievements include pathogenesis and treatment of secondary hyparathyroidism and bone disease in renal failure; studies conducted at both levels: clinical, on patients maintained on chronic dialysis and on animals with experimentally induced renal feilure; detailed studies of the effects of calcitriol on PTH MRNA and the extra-renal production of calcitriol by macrophages; vitro studies in primary culture of bovine parathyroid cells used to understand the mechanisms that control the secretion of PTH. Office: Washington U Chromalloy Am Kidney Ctr PO Box 8126 Saint Louis MO 63156-8126

SLATTERY, CHARLES WILBUR, biochemistry educator; b. La Junta, Colo., Nov. 18, 1937; s. Robert Ernest Slattery and Virgie Belle (Chamberlain) Tobin; m. Arline Sylvia Reile, June 15, 1958; children: Scott Charles, Coleen Kay. BA, Union Coll., 1959; MS, U. Nebr., 1961; PhD, 1965. Instr. chemistry Union Coll., Lincoln, Nebr., 1961-63; asst. prof., assoc. prof. chemistry Atlantic Union Coll., South Lancaster, Mass., 1963-68; rsch. assoc. biophysics MIT, Cambridge, Mass., 1967-70; asst. prof., then prof. biochemistry Loma Linda U., Calif., 1970-80; prof. biochemistry-pediatrics, 1980—; chmn. dept., 1983-99. Vis. prof. U. So. Calif., L.A., 1978-79. Contbr. articles to profl. jours. NIH grantee, 1979-82, 86-89, AHA (Calif.), 1981-83, 83-84. Mem. AAAS, Am. Chem. Soc. (biochemistry divsn.), Am. Dairy Sci. Assn., N.Y. Acad. Scis., The Protein Soc., Am. Soc. Biochemistry and Molecular Biology, Sigma Xi. Office: Loma Linda U Sch Medicine Dept Biochemistry Loma Linda CA 92350-0001

SLATTERY, JAMES JOSEPH (JOE SLATTERY), actor; b. Memphis, Feb. 7, 1922; s. James Joseph and Katie May (Carlin) S.; m. Mary Margaret Costello, May 23, 1944 (dec. Aug. 1987); children: James Joseph, John P., Ann, Mary, Nancy; m. Marilyn Daus, Sept. 16, 1989. AB, Hendrix Coll., Conway, Ark., 1947. Pres. Am. Fedn. TV and Radio Artists, 1976-79. Actor. Served with USAAF, 1942-46; to lt. col. USAF (ret.) Recipient Disting. Grad. award Hendrix Coll., 1986. Mem. Screen Actors Guild. Roman Catholic. Address: 5 The Court Of Bayview Northbrook IL 60062-3201 E-mail: jslats@sbcglobal.net.

SLAUCITAJS, ANDREW PAUL, videographer, video producer; b. Denver, Nov. 10, 1959; s. Andis Slaucitajs and Shirley Ann Jordan; one child, Matthew Lurz, one brother, John Robert. TV instr. Rogers State Coll., Claremore, Okla., 1981-83; ind. video graphic artist Strata Prodn., Tulsa, Okla., 1983-85; TV prodr. Okla. Ednl. TV Authority, Tulsa, Okla., 1985-86; broadcast sales staff Tulsa Electronic Sys., Okla., 1986-87; ind. video graphic artist Mediamax, Tulsa, Okla., 1987-89; ind. video graphic artist, video cons., lectr., rsch. Slaucitajs Media, Tulsa, Okla., 1989—. Prodr. numerous shows; sculptor outdoor steel sculpture, "Earth and Sky". Mem. Okla. Anthrop. Soc. Republican. Avocations: archaeology, auto racing, photography, art. Home and Office: 4525 E 33rd St Tulsa OK 74135-2061 E-mail: andys@amsiweb.com.

SLAUGH, LYNN H. chemist; With Shell Devel. Co., Houston. Author 152 patents; inventor two indsl. processes; contbr. articles to profl. jours. Recipient Indsl. Chemistry award Am. Chem. Soc., 1995. Achievements include 160 patents. Office: Shell Chem Comp PO Box 1380 Houston TX 77251-1380

SLAUGHTER, ALEXANDER HOKE, lawyer; b. Charlottesville, Va., Nov. 24, 1937; s. Edward Ratliff and Mary (Hoke) S.; m. Virginia Borah, 1964 (div.); 1 child, David A.; m. Mary Peeples, 1971. BA, Yale U., 1960; LLB, U. Va., 1963. Ptnr. McGuire, Woods, Richmond, Va., 1969—. Episcopalian. Home: 3016 Rugby Rd Richmond VA 23221-3936 Office: McGuire Woods One James Ctr 901 E Cary St Richmond VA 23219-4030 Office Phone: 804-775-4346. E-mail: aslaughter@mcguirewoods.com.

SLAUGHTER, DJUANIQUE NATÉ, healthcare analyst, project manager, consultant; BS in Criminal Justice, Grambling State U., 1993; MPA, Calif. State U., Dominguez Hills, 1998. Med. clinic asst. Green Clinic, Ruston, La., 1993; pub. health intern Dept. Health and Human Svcs., Long Beach, Calif., 1997; project mgmt. specialist Scan Health Plan, Long Beach, 1998; adminstrv. asst. Salick Health Care, L.A., 1998—99; managed care report analyst Health Care Ptnrs., Torrance, Calif., 1999—2000; healthcare analyst, cons., project mgr. Salice Healthcare, L.A., 1999; project mgr. Ops. Health Care Ptnrs., Torrance, 2000—03; project mgr. claims adminstrn. Kaiser Permanente, Pasadena, Calif., 2003—. HIV/AIDS peer counselor Campus Awareness Prevention, Grambling, La., 1993. Mem. Reach 2010, Reach 2010 Project, 2001—. Am. scholar Grambling State U. Mem.: ASPA, Nat. Assn. Health Svcs. Execs., Women in Health Adminstrn. E-mail: deedee@pacbell.net.

SLAUGHTER, EDWARD RATLIFF, JR., lawyer; b. Raleigh, N.C., Sept. 15, 1931; s. Edward Ratliff and Mary McBee (Hoke) S.; m. Anne Limbosch, July 25, 1957; children: Anne-Marie, Hoke, Bryan. AB, Princeton U., 1953; postgrad. (Rotary Found. fellow), U. Brussels, 1955-56; LLB, U. Va., 1959. Bar: Va. 1959, D.C. 1981. Assoc. firm McGuire, Woods & Battle (now McGuire Woods) and predecessors, Charlottesville, Va., 1959-64; ptnr. McGuire, Woods & Battle and predecessors, 1964-79, head dept. litig., 1964-79, spl. asst. for litig. to atty. gen. U.S., 1979-81; ptnr. firm Whitman & Ransom, Washington, 1981-84; prin. Slaughter & Redinger, P.C., Charlottesville, 1984-95, Slaughter, Izakowitz, Clarke & Nunley, P.C., 1995-96, Woods, Rogers & Hazlegrove, P.L.C., 1996—2002, of counsel, 2002—03, Michie, Hamlett, Lowry, Rasmussen, & Tweel, P.C., 2003—. Vis. lectr. trial advocacy U. Va., 1970-77, Va. procedure, 1986-91; disting. lectr. U. Tunis, 1996; mem. standing com. on commrs. of accounts Jud. Coun. of Va., 1993—, chmn., 1995-2001. Chmn. Albemarle County (Va.) Dem. Com., 1969-73; pres. Charlottesville-Albemarle United Way, 1972; commr. accounts Albemarle County, 1986—; trustee Lime Kiln Arts, Inc., 1992-98. Served with USNR, 1953-55. Recipient William J. Brennan award U. Va. Trial Advocacy Inst., 1996. Fellow Am. Bar Found., Am. Coll. Trial Lawyers; mem. D.C. Bar, Charlottesville-Albemarle Bar Assn. (pres. 1976-77), Va. Bar Assn. (pres. 1978), Va. State Bar (bd. govs. internat. practice sect. 1992-2000), Thomas Jefferson Inn Ct. (pres. 1995-96), Farmington Country Club. Home: 200 Tuckahoe Farm Ln Charlottesville VA 22901-5531 Office: Michie Hamlett Lowry Rasmussen & Tweel 500 Court Sq Ste 300 PO Box 298 Charlottesville VA 22902-0298 E-mail: eslaughter@mhlrt.com.

SLAUGHTER, FREEMAN CLUFF, retired dentist; b. Estes, Miss., Dec. 30, 1926; s. William Cluff and Vay (Fox) S.; m. Genevieve Anne Parks, July 30, 1948; children: Mary Anne, Thomas Freeman, James Hugh. Student, Wake Forest U., 1944, Emory U., 1946-47; DDS, Emory U. Sch. of Dentistry, 1951. Lic. real estate broker. Practice gen. dentistry, Kannapolis, N.C., 1951-89; ret. Mem. N.C. State Bd. Dental Examiners, 1966-75, pres., 1968-69, sec.-treas., 1971-74; chief dental staff Cabarrus Meml. Hosp. (now N.E. Med. Ctr.), Concord, N.C., 1965-66, 75; mem. N.C. Adv. Com. for Edn. Dental Aux. Pers.-N.C. State Bd. Edn., 1967-70; advisor dental asst. program Rowan Cabarrus C.C., 1974-76; Duke Med. Ctr. Davison Century Club. Trustee N.C. Symphony Soc., 1962-68, pres. Kannapolis chpt., 1961; mem. Cabarrus County Bd. Health, 1977-83, chmn., 1981-83, acting health dir., 1981; vice chmn. Kannapolis Charter Commn., 1983-84; mem. City Coun. Kannapolis, 1984-85; Mayor protem, Kannapolis, 1984-85; past active Boy Scouts Am., Eagle scout with silver palm. Served with USN, 1944-46, WW II, ETO, MTO. Recipient Kannapolis Citizen of Yr. award, 1982. Fellow Am. Coll. Dentists (life); mem. ADA (life), Am. Legion, Kannapolis Jr. C. of C. (v.p. 1952), Toastmasters Internat. (pres. Kannapolis chpt. 1963-64), Am. Assn. Dental Examiners (Dentist Citizen of Yr. 1975, v.p. 1977-79, Recognition plaque, 1980), So. Conf. Dental Deans and Examiners (v.p. 1969), N.C. Dental Soc. (resolution of commendation 1975), N.C. Dental Soc. Anesthesiology (pres. 1964), Southeastern Acad. Prosthodontics, So. Acad. Oral Surgery, Am. Soc. Dentistry for Children (pres. N.C. unit 1957), Internat. Assn. Dental Rsch., Cabarrus County Dental Soc. (pres. 1953-54, 63-64, 69), N.C. Assn. Professions (dir. 1976-80), Kannapolis Music Club (pres. 1962-63), Masons, Shriners, Rotary (dir. 1977-80), Omicron Kappa Upsilon, Alpha Epsilon Upsilon.

SLAUGHTER, JOHN BROOKS, professional society administrator; b. Topeka, Mar. 16, 1934; s. Reuben Brooks and Dora (Reeves) S.; m. Ida Bernice Johnson, Aug. 31, 1956; children: John Brooks, Jacqueline Michelle. Student, Washburn U., 1951-53; BSEE, Kans. State U., 1956, DSc (hon.), 1988; MS in Engring., UCLA, 1961; PhD in Engring. Scis, U. Calif., San Diego, 1971; D Engring. (hon.), Rensselaer Poly. Inst., 1981; DSc (hon.), U. So. Calif., 1981, Tuskegee Inst., 1981, U. Md., 1982, U. Notre Dame, 1982, U. Miami, 1983, U. Mass., 1983, Tex. So. U., 1984, U. Toledo, 1985, U. Ill., 1986, SUNY, 1986; LHD (hon.), Bowie State Coll., 1987; DSc (hon.), Morehouse Coll., 1988, Kans. State U., 1988; LLD (hon.), U. Pacific, 1989; DSc (hon.), Pomona Coll., 1989; LHD (hon.), Alfred U., 1991, Calif. Luth. U., 1991, Washburn U., 1992. Registered profl. engr., Wash. Electronics engr. Gen. Dynamics Convair, San Diego, 1956-60; with Naval Electronics Lab. Center, San Diego, 1960-75, div. head, 1965-71, dept. head, 1971-75; dir. applied physics lab. U. Wash., 1975-77; asst. dir. NSF, Washington, 1977-79, dir., 1980-82; acad. v.p., provost Wash. State U., 1979-80; chancellor U. Md., College Park, 1982-88; pres. Occidental Coll., Los Angeles, 1988-99; co-chair Calif. Citizens Commn. on Higher Edn., 1996-99; ret., 1999. Res., pres, CEO NACME, Inc., N.Y.C.; bd. dirs., vice chmn. San Diego Transit Corp., 1968-75; mem. com. on minorities in engring. Nat. Rsch. Coun., 1976-79; mem. Commn. on Pre-Coll. Edn. in Math., Sci. and Tech. Nat. Sci. Bd., 1982-83; bd. dirs. Solutia, Inc., ARCO, Avery Dennison Corp., IBM, Northrop Grumman Corp.; chmn. advancement com. Music Ctr. of L.A. County, 1989-93. Editor: Jour. Computers and Elec. Engring., 1972—. Bd. dirs. San Diego Urban League, 1962-66, pres., 1964-66; mem. Pres.'s Com. on Nat. Medal Sci., 1979-80; trustee Rensselaer Poly. Inst., 1982; chmn. Pres.'s Com. Nat. Collegiate Athletic Assn., 1986-88; bd. govs. Town Hall of Calif., 1990; bd. dirs. L.A. World Affairs Coun., 1990. Recipient Engring. Disting. Alumnus of Yr. award UCLA, 1978, UCLA medal, 1989, Roger Revelle award U. Calif.-San Diego, 1991, Disting. Svc. award NSF, 1979, Svc. in Engring. award Kans. State U., 1981, Disting. Alumnus of Yr. award U. Calif.-San Diego, 1982, Martin Luther King Jr. Nat. award, 1997; Naval Electronics Lab. Ctr. fellow, 1969-70; elected to Topeka High Sch. Hall of Fame, 1983, Hall of Fame of Am. Soc. Engring. Edn., 1993; named Kansan of Yr. by Kans. Native Sons and Daus., 1994. Fellow IEEE (chmn. com. on minority affairs 1976-80), Am. Acad. Arts and Scis.; mem. NAE, Nat. Collegiate Athletic Assn. (chmn. pres. commn.), Am. Soc. for Engring. Edn. (inducted into Hall of Fame 1993), Phi Beta Kappa (hon.), Tau Beta Pi, Eta Kappa Nu. Office: NACME Inc 440 Hamilton Ave White Plains NY 10601-1813

SLAUGHTER, LOUISE MCINTOSH, congresswoman; b. Harlan County, Ky., Aug. 14, 1929; d. Oscar Lewis and Grace (Byers) McIntosh; m. Robert Slaughter, 1956; children: Megan Rae, Amy Louise, Emily Robin. BS, U. Ky., 1951, MS, 1953. Bacteriologist Ky. Dept. Health, Louisville, 1951-52, U. Ky., 1952-53; market researcher Procter & Gamble, Cin., 1953-56; mem. staff Office of the Lt. Gov. N.Y., Albany, 1978 82; state rep. N.Y. Gen. Assembly, Albany, 1983-86; mem. U.S. Congress from 28th N.Y. dist., Washington, 1987—; mem. Ho. rules com. Del. Dem. Nat. Conv., 1972, 76, 80, 88, 92, 96; mem. Commn. on Security and Coop. in Europe, Nat. Ctr. for Policy Alternatives Adv. Bd., League of Women Voters, Nat. Women's Polit. Caucus. Democrat. Office: US Ho of Reps Office of House Mems 2469 Rayburn Bldg Washington DC 20515-3228*

SLAUGHTER, RICHARD ARTHUR, political scientist, economist, educator; b. Twin Falls, Idaho, Nov. 20, 1943; s. Walter Arthur and Mary Viola Slaughter; m. Susan Kay Clark, Aug. 11, 1966; children: Scott, Ryan. BA in Polit. Sci., U. Idaho, 1966; MA in Internat. Rels., U. Denver, 1968, PhD in Internat. Politics, 1974. Asst. prof. polit. sci. West Ga. Coll., Carrollton, 1972-76; economist divsn. fin. mgmt. State of Idaho, Boise, 1976-80, chief economist, 1980-84; pres. Richard Slaughter Assocs., Boise, 1984—; dir. Martin Inst. for Peace Studies U. Idaho, 1996—2000; internat. economist Cen. Asia, 1998—2001; cons. economist Climate Impacts Group, U. Wash., 2000—. Vol. exec. dir. Boise Com. on Fgn. Rels.; mem. adv. bd. Martin Inst. Peace Studies, 1990-96; co-founder Am. Coms. on Fgn. Rels., treas. 1995-2001. Editor Idaho Econ. Forecast jour., 1977-84; author articles on Third World econ. devel. and nation-bldg., global climate change policy. Bd. dirs. Capitol Youth Soccer Assn., Boise, 1980-89, soccer commr., 1983-86. Mem. Coun. Fgn. Rels. Home and Office: 907 Harrison Blvd Boise ID 83702-4079 Office Phone: 208-850-1223. Business E-Mail: rboise@rsaboise.com.

SLAUGHTER, ROCHELLE DENISE, elementary school educator; b. Kansas City, Kans., Jan. 3, 1956; d. Theodore and Barbara Jean (Williams) Hall; m. Eddie Slaughter, Nov. 1, 1997. AA, Penn Valley C.C., Kansas City, Mo., 1976; BA, U. Mo., Kansas City, 1978, MA, 1985; Edn. Specialist Degree, U. Mo., 1992. Cert. specialist in reading, Mo. Tchr. Kansas City Sch. Dist., 1979-85, reading resource tchr., 1985-95, tchr. 1st grade, 1995—2000, tchr. 3d grade, 2000—; S.T.A.R.R. tchr., 2002. Del. Literacy and Lang. Arts Instrn. Delegation to Peoples Republic of China, 1995. Supt. Sunday sch. Emmanuel Bapt. Ch., 1992—; del. lang. arts & literacy delegation People to People Citizen Amb. Progra, China, 1995; vol. for adult basic edn. program; tutor Laubach Literacy Coun. Kansas City, 1996-97. Recipient IMPACT Reading award Kansas City Reading dept., 1990. Mem. ASCD, NAACP, Internat. Reading Assn. (chpt. v.p. 1994-95, pres.-elect 1995-97, pres. 1997-99), Phi Delta Kappa (youth advisor 1993-99). Democrat. Baptist. Avocations: reading, computer work, sewing. Office: 5306 Holmes Kansas City MO 64110

SLAUGHTER ANDREW, ANNE, lawyer; b. Evansville, Ind., Sept. 23, 1955; d. Owen L. and Marjorie (Specht) Slaughter; m. Joseph J. Andrew, Sept. 9, 1989. BA, Georgetown U., 1977; JD cum laude, Ind. U., 1983. Bar: Ind. 1983, U.S. Dist. Ct. (so. dist.) Ind. Ptnr. Baker & Daniels, Indpls. Adj. prof. environ. law Ind. U. Sch. Law, Indpls. Editor-in-chief Ind. U. Law Rev., 1982-83; contbr. articles to profl. jours. Bd. dirs. Nature Conservancy, 1997—, Ind. Natural Resources Found., 1994—; mem. Indpls. Pub. Sch. Found. Com., 1997—; mem. Brownfield Remediation Adv. Com., 1997—. Mem. ABA (chair state and regional environ. coop. com. 1996-98), Ind. Bar Assn. (chair environ. law sect. 1992-93), Ind. C. of C. (govt. affairs commn.). Office: Baker & Daniels 300 N Meridian St Ste 2700 Indianapolis IN 46204-1782

SLAUGHTER-DEFOE, DIANA TRESA, education educator; b. Chgo., Oct. 28, 1941; d. John Ison and Gwendolyn Malva (Armstead) S.; m. Michael Defoe (div.). BA, U. Chgo., 1962, MA, 1964, PhD, 1968. Instr. dept. psychiatry Howard U., Washington, 1967-68; rsch. assoc., asst. prof. Yale U. Child Study Ctr., New Haven, 1968-70; asst. prof. dept. behavioral scis. and edn. U. Chgo., 1970-77; asst. to assoc. prof. edn. and African Am. studies and Ctr. for Urban Affairs and Policy Rsch. (now Inst. for Policy Rsch.) Northwestern U., Evanston, Ill., 1977-90, prof., 1990-97; Constance E. Clayton prof. urban edn. Grad. Sch. Edn. U. Pa., 1998—. Nat. adv. bd. Fed. Ctr. for Child Abuse & Neglect, 1979-82, coord. Human Devel. and Social Policy Program, 1994-97; nat. adv. bd. Learning Rsch. and Devel. Ctr. U. Pitts., Ednl. Rsch. & Devel. Ctr., U. Tex., Austin; formerly chmn., dir. public policy program com. Chgo. Black Child Devel. Inst., 1982-84; dir. Ill. Infant Mental Health Com., 1982-83; res. adv. bd. Chgo. Urban League, 1986-97. Contbr. articles to profl. jours. Fellow APA (mem. divsn. ethnic and minority affairs, com. on children, youth and families, devel. psychology, sch. psychology, bd. sci. affairs 1995-97, bd. advancement psychology pub. interest 2003-, assoc. editor, mem. edtl. bd. Child Devel. 1995-98, Disting. Contbn. to Rsch. in Pub. Policy award 1993, bd. for advancement of psychol. in the pub. intrest 2003—); mem. Soc. for Rsch. in Child Devel. (governing coun. 1981-87), Am. Ednl. Rsch. Assn. (editl. bd. Rev. Ednl. Rsch.), Nat. Assn. Edn. Young Children, Assn. Study African Ams. and History, Nat. Head Start (past R & E adv. bd.), Nat. Acad. Scis. (com. on child devel. and publ. policy 1987-93), Delta Sigma Theta. Office: U Pa Grad Sch Edn 3700 Walnut St Philadelphia PA 19104-6216 Office Phone: 215-573-3947. Business E-Mail: dianasd@gse.upenn.edu.

SLAVENS, THOMAS PAUL, library science educator; b. Cincinnati, Iowa, Nov. 12, 1928; s. William Blaine and Rhoda (Bowen) S.; m. Cora Hart, July 9, 1950; 1 son, Mark Thomas. BA, Phillips U., 1951; MDiv, Union Theol. Sem., 1954; MA, U. Minn., 1962; PhD, U. Mich., 1965. Ordained to ministry Christian Ch., 1953. Pastor First Christian Ch., Sac City, Iowa, 1953-56, Sioux Falls, S.D., 1956-60; librarian Divinity Sch., Drake U., Des Moines, 1960-64; teaching fellow Sch. Info., U. Mich., Ann Arbor, 1964-65; instr. U. Mich., Ann Arbor, 1965-66, asst. prof., 1966-69, assoc. prof., 1969-77, prof., 1977—. Vis. prof. U. Minn., 1967, U. Coll. of Wales, 1978, 80, 93; vis. scholar U. Oxford, Eng., 1980; adv. bd. Marcel Dekker Inc., N.Y.C., 1982—; cons. Nutrition Planning Abstracts-UN, N.Y.C., 1977-79. Author-editor: Library Problems in the Humanities, 1981, (with John F. Wilson) Research Guide to Religious Studies, 1982, (with W. Eugene Kleinbaur) Research Guide to History of Western Art, 1982, (with Terrence Tice) Research Guide to Philosophy, 1983, Theological Libraries at Oxford, 1984, (with James Pruett) Research Guide to Musicology, 1985, The Literary Adviser, 1985, A Great Library through Gifts, 1986, The Retrieval of Information, 1989, Number One in the U.S.A.: Records and Wins in Sports, Entertainment, Business, and Science, 1988, 3d edit., 2004, Doors to God, 1990, Sources of Information for Historical Research, 1994, Introduction to Systematic Theology, 1992, Reference Interviews Questions and Materials, 3d edit., 1994, Using the Finance and Business Literature, 2004. Served with U.S. Army, 1946-48. Recipient Warner Rice Faculty award U. Mich., 1975; H.W. Wilson fellow, 1960; Lilly Endowment fellow Am. Theol. Libr. Assn., 1963. Mem. Assn. Libr. and Info. Sci. Edn. (pres. 1972), Beta Phi Mu.

SLAVICK, ANN LILLIAN, retired art educator; b. Chgo., Sept. 29, 1933; d. Irving and Goldie (Bernstein) Friedman; m. Lester Irwin Slavick, Nov. 21, 1954 (div. Mar. 1987); children: Jack, Rachel. BFA, Sch. of Art Inst. of Chgo., 1973, MA in Art History, Theory, Criticism, 1991. Dir. art gallery South Shore Commn., Chgo., 1963-67; tchr. painting, drawing, crafts Halfway House, Chgo., 1972-73; tchr. studio art Conant H.S., Hoffman Estates, Ill., 1973-74; tchr. art history and studio arts New Trier H.S., Winnetka and Northfield, Ill., 1974-80; tchr. 20th century art history New Trier Adult Edn. Program, Winnetka, 1980-81; tchr. art adult edn. program H.S. Dist. 113, Highland Park, Ill., 1980-81; rschr., writer Art History Notes McDougall-Littel Pub., Evanston, Ill., 1984-85; tchr. art and art history Highland Park and Deerfield (Ill.) H.S., 1980-2000; tchr. art history Coll. of Lake County, Grayslake, Ill., 1986-88; ret., 2000. Faculty chair for visual arts Focus on the Arts, Highland Park H.S., 1981-85, faculty coord. Focus on the Arts, 1987—; panelist Ill. Arts Coun. Arts Tour, 1999, Evanston Arts Coun., 2000-02, Ill. Arts Coun. Multidisciplinary Grant Awards, 2001-03; reader advanced placement art history exams, 2003. One woman show Bernal Gallery, 1979, U. Ill., Chgo., 1983, Ann Brierly Gallery, Winnetka, 1984; exhibited paintings, drawings, prints and constrns. throughout Chgo. area; work represented by Art Rental and Sales Gallery, Art Inst. Chgo., 1960-87, Bernal Gallery, 1978-82; group shows at Bernal Gallery; work in pvt. collections in Ill., N.Y., Calif., Ariz., Ohio. Recipient Outstanding Svc. in Art Edn. award Ea. Ill. U., 1992, Mayors award for contbn. to the arts, Highland Park, 1995. Mem.: Ill. Art Edn. Assn., Nat. Art Edn. Assn. Avocations: cooking, reading, theater. Home: 5057 N Sheridan Rd Chicago IL 60640-3127 Office: Highland Park High Sch 433 Vine Ave Highland Park IL 60035-2099

SLAVIN, ALEXANDRA NADAL, artistic director, educator; b. Port-au-Prince, Haiti, Oct. 26, 1943; came to U.S., 1946; d. Pierre E. and Marie Therese (Clerié) Nadal; m. Eugene Slavin, Dec. 24, 1967; 1 child, Nicholas V. Grad. high sch., Chgo. Dancer Ballet Russe de Monte Carlo, N.Y.C., 1960-61, Chgo. Opera Ballet and N.Y.C. Opera Ballet, 1961-64, Am. Ballet Theatre, N.Y.C., 1965-66, Ballet de Monte Carlo, 1966-67, The Royal Winnipeg (Can.) Ballet, 1967-72; artistic dir. Ballet Austin, Tex., 1972-89; owner, dir. The Slavin Nadal Sch. Ballet, Austin, 1989—. Recipient Achievement in the Arts award Austin chpt. YWCA, 1987. Roman Catholic. Avocation: gardening. Office: Slavin-Nadal Sch Ballet 5521 Burnet Rd Austin TX 78756-1603

SLAVIN, ARLENE, artist; b. N.Y.C., Oct. 26, 1942; d. Louis and Sally (Bryck) Eisenberg; m. Neal Slavin, May 24, 1964 (div. 1979); m. Eric Bregman, Sept. 21, 1980; 1 child, Ethan. BFA, Cooper Union for the Advancement of Sci. and Art, 1964; MFA, Pratt Inst., 1967. One-woman shows include Fischbach Gallery, N.Y., 1973, 1974, 2003, Brooke Alexander Gallery, 1976, Alexander Milliken Gallery, N.Y.C., 1979, 1980, 1981, 1983, U. Colo., 1981, Pratt Inst., N.Y.C., 1981, Am. Embassy, Belgrad, Yugoslavia, 1984, Heckscher Mus., Huntington, N.Y., 1987, Katherine Rich Perlow Gallery, 1988, Chauncey Gallery, Princeton, N.J., 1990, The Gallery Benjamin N. Cardoza Sch. Law, 1991, Norton Ctr. for Arts, Danville, Ky., 1992, Kavesh Gallery, Ketchum, Idaho, 1993, exhibited in group shows at Bass Mus. Art, Fla., Whitney Museum of Art, 1973, The Contempory Arts Center, Cin., 1974, Indpls. Mus. Art, 1974, Madison (Wis.) Art Ctr., Santa Barbara (Calif.) Mus., Winnipeg (Can.) Art Gallery, Gensler Assocs., San Francisco, 1986, Eliane Benson Gallery, Bridgehampton, N.Y., 1987, 1989, 1991, 1993, 2004, City of N.Y. Parks and Recreation Central Park, N.Y.C., 1989, Benton Gallery, Southampton, N.Y., 1991, Parish Mus., Southampton, 1991, Michele Miller Fine Art, 1993, Dillon Gallery, N.Y.C., 1998, Hebrew Union Coll., 2000—01, Fischbach Gallery, 2003, Am. Inst. Archs., 2003, Represented in permanent collections Met. Mus. of Art, N.Y.C., Fogg Art Mus., Cambridge, Mass., Hudson River Mus., Yonkers, N.Y., Heckscher Mus., Huntington, N.Y., Cin. Art Mus., Readers' Digest, Pleasantville, N.Y., pub. commns., N.C. Zoo, 1999, N.Y.C. Parks and Recreation, 1999, NJ Transit, Hoboken Terminal and Middletown Station, NJ, 1999—2002, Forest City Ratner, Ct. St Devel., 2000, Assunpink (N.Y.) Wildlife Ctr., 2004; subject: bibliography Arlene Slavin: Mediating Public Space, 2001; pub. commns., Town of Chapel Hill, N.C., 2002, PS 89, NYC, 2003, Assunpink Wildlife Preserve, N.J., 2004, one-woman shows include Fischbach Gallery, N.Y., 2003; artist mem. design team Hillsborough Area Regional Transit, Tampa, Fla., 2003—05. Grantee Nat. Endowment for Arts, 1977-78, Threshold Found., 1991. Home: 119 E 18th St New York NY 10003-2107 Office Phone: 212-777-3042. E-mail: slavin@arleneslavin.com.

SLAVIN, KONSTANTIN VLADIMIROVICH, neurosurgeon; b. Baku, Azerbaijan, USSR, Aug. 20, 1969; s. Vladimir Leonidovich and Frangiz Mirzoevna (Gull) S.; m. Ekaterina Yurievna Shashina, Aug. 3, 1990; children: Mikhail Konstantinovich, Svetlana Konstantinovna. MD, Azerbaijan State Med. Inst., Baku, 1988. Nurse Rep. Neurosurg. Hosp., Baku, 1985-88; clin. coord. Postgrad. Inst., Moscow, 1988-90, aspirant neurosurgeon, 1990-92; rsch. fellow U. Ill., Chgo., 1992-94, resident in neurosurgery, 1994-2001, instr. dept. neurosurgery, 2000-01, asst. prof. dept. neurosurgery, 2001—; fellow in stereotactic and functional neurosurgery OHSU, 1998—99; dir. Am. Soc. Stereotactic and Functional Neurosurgery, 2003—. Asst. to editor Surg. Neurology jour., 1993-2003; contbr. articles to profl. jours., chpts. to books. Recipient Lenin scholarship Azerbaijan Med. Inst., 1987, 88. Mem. AMA, Am. Assn. Neurol. Surgeons, Congress Neurol. Surgeons, Am. Pain Soc., Am. Soc. Stereotactic Functional Neurosurgery (bd. dirs. 2003—). Avocations: computers, collecting stamps. Office: U Ill Chgo 912 S Wood St Chicago IL 60612-7325 Office Phone: 312-996-4842. Business E-Mail: kslavin@uic.edu.

SLAVIN, PETER L. hospital administrator; AB, Harvard U., 1979, MD, 1984, MBA, 1990. Sr. v.p., chief med. officer Mass. Gen. Hosp., Boston, 1994—97; pres. Barnes-Jewish Hosp., St. Louis, 1997-99; med. dir. Mass. Gen. Physicians Orgn., Boston, chair., CEO, 1999—2003; pres. Mass. Gen. Hosp., Boston, 2003—. Office: Mass Gen Hosp 55 Fruit St Boston MA 02114-2622 Office Phone: 617-724-9300.

SLAVIN, RAYMOND GRANAM, allergist, immunologist; b. Cleve., June 29, 1930; s. Philip and Dinah (Baskind) S.; m. Alberta Cohrt, June 10, 1953; children: Philip, Stuart, David, Linda. AB, U. Mich., 1952; MD, St. Louis U., 1956; MS, Northwestern U., 1963. Diplomate Am. Bd. Internal Medicine, Am. Bd. Allergy and Immunology (treas.). Intern U. Mich. Hosp., Ann Arbor, 1956-57; resident St. Louis U. Hosp., 1959-61; fellow in allergy and immunology Northwestern U. Med. Sch., 1961-64; asst. prof. internal medicine and microbiology St. Louis U., 1965-70, assoc. prof., 1970-73, prof., 1973—, dir. divsn. allergy and immunology, 1965—. Mem. NIH study sect., 1985-89; cons. U.S. Army M.C. Contbr. numerous articles to med. publs.; editl. bd.: Jour. Allergy and Clin. Immunology, 1975-81. Chmn. bd. Asthma and Allergy Found. Am., 1985-88. With M.C., U.S. Army, 1957-59. Grantee NIH, 1967-70, 84—, Nat. Inst. Occupl. Safety and Health, 1974-80. Master: ACP; fellow: Am. Acad. Allergy and Immunology (exec. bd., historian, pres. 1983—84, Disting. Svc. award 1995, Disting. Clinician award 2005); mem.: AAAS, Ctrl. Soc. Clin. Rsch., Am. Assn. Immunologists. Democrat. Jewish. Home: 631 E Polo Dr Saint Louis MO 63105-2629 Office: 1402 S Grand Blvd Saint Louis MO 63104-1004 Office Phone: 314-977-8829. Business E-Mail: slavinrg@slu.edu.

SLAVIN, THOMAS JOHN, industrial hygienist, director; b. Bad Axe, Mich., Mar. 27, 1947; s. Stanley and Eleanor Mary Slavin; m. Rosetta Murray, Apr. 18, 1970; 1 child, Brian David. BS, Zoology, U. of Ill., Urbana, 1967—69; MS, Occupl. and Environ. Health, Wayne State U., Detroit, Mich., 1977—79; MBA, U. of Chgo., 1981—83. Cert. safety profl. Bd. of Cert. Safety Professionals, Ill., 1975, indsl. hygienist Am. Bd. of Indsl. Hygiene, Mich., 1979, profl. environ. auditor, health and safety Bd. of Environ., Health & Safety Auditor Certifications, Fla., 2001, safety and health mgr. Inst. for Safety and Health Mgmt., Mo., 1999. Loss prevention/indsl. hygienist Liberty Mut. Ins. Co., Southfield, Mich., 1969—77; coord., indsl. hygiene Motor Vehicle Manufacturers Assn., Detroit, 1977—79; indsl. hygienist Internat. Harvester, Chicago, 1979—84; mgr., occupl. safety and health Internat. Truck and Engine Corp, Warrenville, Ill., 1984—. Dir. Nat. Safety Mgmt. Soc., Walnut Creek, Calif., 1994—, Inst. for Safety and Health Mgmt., Columbia, Mo., 2003—; steering com. mem. ORC Worldwide, Washington, 1995—2000; occupl. safety and health steering com. mem. Automotive Industry Action Group, Southfield, Mich., 2002—, NAM, Washington, 2000—; mem., musculoskeletal team Nat. Inst. for Occupl. Safety and Health, Nat. Occupl. Rsch. Agenda, Washington, 1998—; mem. Am. Nat. Standards Inst. Z10 Com. on Occupl. Health and Safety Mangement Systems, New York, 2000—. Contbr. book, booklet, journal article (US Pub. Health Svc. Engring. Lit. Award, 2003), book. Treas. Internat. Truck and Engine Good Govt. Com., Warrenville, Ill., 2002—03. Recipient Childress-Loebler Lifetime Achievement Award, Am. Foundry Soc., 2002. Mem.: ASTM (chmn. e34.20 foundry safety and health 2002—03), Human Factors and Ergonomics Soc., Soc. Automotive Engrs., Nat. Fire Protection Assn., Am. Soc. Safety Engrs., Am. Foundry Soc. (chmn. 10q safety and health com. 1996—2003). Achievements include contbg. articles to various journals. Avocations: gardening, golf, travel. Office: International Truck and Engine Corp 4201 Winfield Rd Warrenville IL 60555 Office Phone: 312-836-3929. E-mail: tom.slavin@nav-international.com.

SLAVIT, DAVID HAL, otolaryngologist; b. N.Y.C., Sept. 5, 1960; s. Leonard S. and Barbara H. (Levine) S.; m. Robin E. Feldman, July 31, 1983; children: Danielle, Evan, Roni. BS, Cornell U., 1982; MD, Mt. Sinai U., 1986. Cert. in otolaryngology. Intern Mayo Clinic, Rochester, Minn., 1986-87, resident in otolaryngology, 1987-91; with Lenox Hill Hosp., N.Y.C. Asst. prof. Health Sci. Ctr.-SUNY Downstate; cons. Juilliard Sch. Music, N.Y.C., 1994-99; dir. Ames Vocal Dynamics Lab., N.Y.C., 1998-2001. Author, editor: (book) Essentials of Otolaryngology, 1993; author: (books) Voice Disorders, 1995, Rhinologic Diagnosis and Treatment, 1996, Systemic Disease of the Nasal Airway, 1993; contbr. articles to profl. jours. Fellow ACS; mem. AMA, Am. Acad. Otolaryngology-Head and Neck Surgery, Am. Acad. Facial Plastic and Reconstructive Surgery, Am. Rhinologic Soc.

SLAVITT, BEN J. lawyer; b. Newark, Dec. 31, 1934; s. Arthur and Berdie (Goodman) S.; children: Lauri, Julie, Donna, John. BA, Bucknell Univ., 1956; JD, Univ. Va., 1959. Bar: N.J., 1959, U.S. Dist. Ct. N.J., 1959, U.S. Supreme Ct., 1973. Ptnr. Slavitt and Cowen, PA and predecessors, Newark, 1959—. Served in U.S. Army, 1959-60. Mem. N.J. Bar Assn. Democrat. Jewish. Office: Slavitt and Cowen 17 Academy St Ste 415 Newark NJ 07102-2905 Office Phone: 973-622-6418. Business E-Mail: slavitt_cowen@yahoo.com.

SLAVITT, DAVID WALTON, retired lawyer; b. Chgo., Mar. 15, 1931; s. Isaac and Fay (Goldstein) S.; m. Roberta Chelnek, July 26, 1953; children: Steven, Denise, Howard. BS, UCLA, 1952, JD, 1955. Bar: Calif. 1956; C.P.A., Calif. Since practiced in Los Angeles; pres. Slavitt & Borofsky (P.C.), 1969-87. Moderator continuing edn. programs. Author articles in field. Served with USNR, 1955. Mem. Am. Assn. Atty.-C.P.A.s (pres. 1964), ABA, State Bar Calif., Calif. Assn. Atty.-C.P.A.s (pres. 1963), Beverly Hills Bar Assn. (vice chmn. continuing edn. of bar 1970, asst. chmn. law practice mgmt. com. 1973).

SLAVKIN, HAROLD CHARLES, dean, biologist; b. Chgo., Mar. 20, 1938; m. Lois S. Slavkin; children: Mark D., Todd P. BA in English lit., U. So. Calif., 1961, DDS, 1965; Doctorate (hon.), Georgetown U., 1990, U. Paris, 1996, U. Md., 1997. Mem. faculty U. So. Calif. Sch. Dentistry, L.A., 1968—, mem. faculty gerontology inst., 1969, chmn. dept. biochemistry and nutrition, 1969—75, prof., 1974—, chmn. grad. program in craniofacial molecular biology, 1975-85, founding dir. Ctr. for Craniofacial Molecular Biology, 1989-95, George & Mary Lou Boone prof. craniofacial molecular biology, 1989-95, dean, 2000—, G. Donald and Marian James Montgomery Dean's Chair in Dentistry, 2000—; dir. Nat. Inst. Dental and Craniofacial Rsch., NIH, Bethesda, Md., 1995—2000. Vis. prof. Israel Inst. Tech., Haifa, 1987-88; cons. U.S. News and World Report, 1985-95, L.A. Edn. Partnership, 1983-95, Torstar Books, Inc., 1985-95. Contbr. articles to profl. jours. Mem. sci. adv. bd. Calif. Mus. Sci. and Tech., 1985-95. Rsch. scholar U. Coll. London, 1980. Mem. AAAS, Am. Assn. Anatomists, Am. Inst. Biol. Scis., Am. Soc. for Cell Biology, Am. Assn. for Dental Rsch. (pres. 1993-94), N.Y. Acad. Scis., Inst. Medicine of NAS, Internat. Coll. Dentistry, Am. Coll. Dentistry, Los Angeles County Art Mus. Assocs. Office: 925 W 34th St Los Angeles CA 90089*

SLAVNEY, PHILLIP RICHARD, psychiatrist; b. Madison, Wisconsin, Sept. 13, 1940; s. Coleman Mordecai and Ann Sarah S.; m. Jacqueline Lillian (Smith), Apr. 15, 1966. BA, U. Wis., 1962; MD, Albert Einstein Coll. Medicine, 1966. Diplomate Am. Bd. Psychiatry and Neurology. Asst. prof. psychiatry U. Oreg. Sch. Medicine, Portland, 1973—76; attending psychiatrist Johns Hopkins Hosp., Balt., 1976—; asst. prof. psychiatry Johns Hopkins U. Sch. Medicine, Balt., 1976—80, dir. psychiat. residency edn., 1977—93, assoc. prof. psychiatry, 1980—93, prof. psychiatry, 1993—; dir. gen. hosp. psychiatry Johns Hopkins Hosp., Balt., 1993—; Eugene Meyer III prof. psychiatry and medicine Johns Hopkins U. Sch. Medicine, Balt., 1993—. Cons. psychiatrist Johns Hopkins Oncology Ctr., Balt., 1994-. Author: Psychiatric Polarities: Methodology and Practice, 1987, Perspectives on "Hysteria", 1990, Psychiatric Dimensions of Medical Practice: What Primary Care Physicians Should Know About Delirium, Demoralization, Suicidal Thinking, and Competence to Refuse Medical Advice, 1998; co-author: The Perspectives of Psychiatry, 1983, 98. Sr. asst. surgeon, USPHS, 1967-69. Avocations: art history, travel. Office: Johns Hopkins Hosp Osler 320 600 N Wolfe St Baltimore MD 21287-5371 Office Phone: 410-955-6767. Business E-Mail: slavney@jhmi.edu.

SLAWSKY, DONNA SUSAN, librarian, singer; b. N.Y.C., Jan. 18, 1956; d. Samuel Slawsky and Lillian (Freizer) Alexander. BA, City Coll. N.Y., 1977; M of Infor. Libr. Sci., Pratt Inst., 1998. Coord. NYNEX Market Info. Ctr., White Plains, NY, 1985—87; dir. Info. Ctr./Archives, exhbns. curator HarperCollins Pubs., N.Y.C., 1988—99; singer N.Y.C., 1987—; dir. content devel. BuyerWeb, Inc., N.Y.C., 1999—2000; founder Info Diva, N.Y.C., 2001—02; mgr. indexing for digital archive Scholastic, Inc., N.Y.C., 2002—. Contbr. articles to profl. jours.; co-founder (quartet women's voices) Rose Ensemble debut Weill Recital Hall, Carnegie Hall, 1997. Pres. Assn. HarperCollins Employees, N.Y.C., 1990-94; dir. Tenants Assn., N.Y.C., 1994. Recipient Schubertiade Lieder Competition award 92d St. Y, N.Y.C., 1990. Mem.: Am. Soc. Info. Sci. and Tech., Assn. Inst. Info. Profls., Profl. Women Singers Assn. (treas. 1992—96, mem.-at-large 1997—, webmaster 2001—), Spl. Librs. Assn., Beta Phi Mu. Avocations: bicycling, theater, jewelry designing. Office: Scholastic Inc 568 Broadway Rm 1045 New York NY 10012 Office Phone: 212-343-7716. E-mail: dslawsky@scholastic.com.

SLAWTER, JOHN DAVID, JR., oil company and manufacturing executive; b. Winston-Salem, N.C., May 11, 1917; s. John David and Carrie Wess (Linville) S.; children: Suzanne Marie, Sheila Margaret; m. Joan Margaret Pirek, July 7, 1966. Student, U. N.C., 1935-37, 38-40. V.p. B&B Gas and Petroleum, Corpus Christi, Tex., 1950-59; exec. v.p. Cal-O-Tex Oil, Columbus, Ohio, 1959-65; pres. Atlantic Internat. Oil, Charleston, W.Va., 1966-73; CEO Interstate Hotels, Inc., 1975, Pacific Internat. Prodn. Holding Co. for Activated Carbon Corp. Am., Dallas, 1989, Mid-Continent Oil, 1974—, OFG Corp., 1995—, EMTEC, 1997—, HTS, 1999—. Chmn. adv. bd. Cal-O-Tex, 1966—, Atlantic Internat. Oil, 1974—, Pacific Internat., 1974—, Black Diamond Coal Co., 1978—, Southwest Interstate Support Sys., 1985—, Activated Carbon Corp., 1989—; vice chair AIOC Trust, Slawter Trust (lifetime). Author: (patents and copyrights) purification and desalination sys., 1991, pumping unit tech., 1995, oil field gen., 1996, oil field mobile remote control unit, 1998, heat transfer sys., 1999. Mem. Rep. Nat. Nom. Com., Washington, 1994-2000. Maj. Engrs. 1941-45, WWII, PTO. Decorated Purple Heart, Silver Star, Bronze Star with oak leaf cluster, Presdl. Citation, 4 Battle Stars. Mem. internat. petroleum clubs, Geneva Exec. Club (v.p. 1970-78), Chi Phi. Avocations: aviation, golf. Office: Pacific Internat Prodn/Subs Ste 8108 4350 Trinity Mills Rd Dallas TX 75287-7037 also: PO Box 795273 Dallas TX 75379-5273 Office Phone: 972-380-5560. E-mail: joslawter2@earthlink.com.

SLAWTER, MARK, professional golfer; b. Winston-Salem, NC, Dec. 12, 1973; married. Student, NC State U. Profl. golfer Can. Profl. Golf Tour, 1996—. Named winner, Eagle Creek Classic, 2001. Mem.: Heritage Country Club. Office: Canadian Tour 212 King St W Ste 203 Toronto ON Canada M5H 1K5

SLAY, BRANDON, Olympic athlete; b. Amarillo, Tex., Oct. 14, 1975; s. Doug and Becky Slay. BS in Econs., U. Pa., 1998. Male Athlete of Yr. U. Pa., 1998; Nat. Champion, Outstanding Wrestler Olympic Tng. Ctr., Colorado Springs, Colo., 2000; Olympic Gold medalist in wrestling, 2000. Mem.: Alpha Tau Omega (v.p. 1997—98, sec. 1996—97, rush chmn. 1995—96).

SLAY, FRANCIS G. mayor; b. St. Louis, Missouri; s. Francis R. and Anna Slay; m. Kim Slay; children: Francis Jr., Katherine. Law degree, Saint Louis U. Sch. Law, 1980; postgrad in political sci., Quincy Coll., Ill., 1977. Mayor City of St. Louis, 2001—; pvt. lawyer 20 yrs.; law clerk Judge Paul J. Simon, Mo. Court Appeals, 1981; ptnr. Guilfoil, Petzall & Shoemake. Mem. St. Louis Bd. Alderman, 1995, elected pres. Office: City Hall Rm 200 1200 Mrk St Saint Louis MO 63103

SLAYDEN, JAMES BRAGDON, retired department store executive; b. Seattle, Sept. 28, 1924; s. Philip Lee and Ruth Alwin (Bragdon) S.; m. Barbara Marie McBride, May 7, 1955; children: Tracy Anne, James Bragdon. BA, U. Wash., 1948; MBA, U. So. Calif., 1949. Buyer Frederick & Nelson, Seattle, 1949-59, div. mdse. mgr., 1959-65; gen. mgr. Bullocks Westwood, Los Angeles, 1965-69. Exec. v.p., gen. mdse. mgr. May D&F Co. dept. store, Denver, 1969-72; pres., CEO J. W. Robinson dept. store, L.A., 1972-78; exec. v.p. ops. Marshall Field & Co., Chgo., 1978-80; gen. mgr. Bullocks Del Amo, 1980-85; lectr. mktg. U. So. Calif., 1985-93. Active United Crusade United Way, L.A., 1973-78, Chgo. Heart Assn., 1978-79; chmn. Pvt. Industry Coun., 1982-95; cons. Internat. Exec. Svc. Corps., 1987—, traffic comm. Rancho Palos Verdes, 1994-97, planning commn., 1997-2000, view restoration com., 2000—04. With U.S. Army, 1943-45. Mem. Phi Kappa Psi. Republican. Christian Scientist. Home: 37 Mela Ln Palos Verdes Peninsula CA 90275-5086

SLAYMAKER, GENE ARTHUR, public relations executive; b. Kenton, Ohio, Sept. 15, 1928; s. Edwin Paul and Anna Elizabeth (Grable) S.; divorced; children: Jill Brook, Scott Wood, Leslie Beth; m. Julie Ann Graff, Feb. 3, 1979; 1 adopted child, Peter Fredric Bannon II; stepchildren: Jennifer Elizabeth Nash, David Frank Nash. BA in Radio Journalism, Ohio State U. Announcer, reporter WLWC-TV, Columbus, Ohio, 1951-52; anchor, reporter WKBN-AM-FM-TV, Youngstown, Ohio, 1952-56, KYW-TV, Cleve., 1956-60; editor news Sta. WFBM-AM-FM-TV, Indpls., 1960-68; pres., founder Slaymaker & Assocs. Pub. Rels., 1969—; dir. news, sports, pub. affairs WTLC-FM and WTUX-AM, Indpls., 1976-92; community rels. liaison Marion County Pros. Atty. Office, Indpls., 1993. Pres., founder Slaymaker and Assocs., Indpls., 1969—. Mambo dancer (movie) Going All the Way, 1996. Past bd. dirs. Park-Tudor Father's Assn.; mem. Meridian Kessler Neighborhood Assn., pres., 1968-69. Recipient Disting. Service award (2). Mem. Ind. AP Broadcasters Assn. (awards), UPI (awards), Nat. Fedn. Press Women, Soc. Profl. Journalists (awards Ind. chpt., bd. dirs., chpt. pres. 1991-92, Radio-TV News Dirs. Assn. (region bd. dirs. 1987-91), Indpls. Press Club, Woman's Press Club Ind., Players Club, Lambs Club (pres. 2000—). Clubs: Nat. Headliners, Unity. Democrat. Avocations: writing, painting, singing, gardening, tennis. Home: 5161 N Washington Blvd Indianapolis IN 46205-1071 Office: Slaymaker Assoc 5161 N Washington Blvd Indianapolis IN 46205-1071

SLAYMAKER, OLAV, geography educator; b. Swansea, Wales, Jan. 31, 1939; came to Can., 1968; s. Arthur J. and Astri H. (Breen) S.; m. Margaret A. Rapson, Apr. 8, 1967; children— Karen M., Paul O., Sarah J., Heidi R. BA, King's Coll., Cambridge, Eng., 1961; AM, Harvard U., 1963; PhD, Cambridge U., 1968. Asst. lectr. U. Coll. Wales, Aberystwyth, 1964-66, lectr., 1966-68; asst. prof. geography U.B.C., Vancouver, Can., 1968-70, assoc. prof., 1970-81, prof., 1981—, head dept., 1982-91, assoc. v.p. rsch., 1991-95, prof. geography. Cons. water quality br. Inland Waters, Vancouver, 1976—; dir. Liu Ctr. Study of Global Issues. Editor: Mountain Geomorphology, 1972, Field Experiments, 1978, High Mountains, 1981, Extreme Landforming Events, 1983, Geomorphology and Land Managment, 1986, Erosion Budgets and Their Hydrologic Basis, 1986, Canada's Cold Environments, 1993, Steepland Geomorphology, 1995, Geomorphic Hazards, 1996, Physical Geography and Global Environmental Change, 1998, Geomorphology, Human Activity and Global Environmental Change, 2000. Senate mem. Vancouver Sch. Theology, 1973-75; bd. dirs. Regent Coll., Vancouver, 1975-78, U. B.C., 1984-87; gov. Internat. Devel. Rsch. Ctr., Ottawa, 1994-2002. Rsch. grantee Natural Sci. and Engring. Rsch. Coun., Ottawa, Ont., Can., 1968-98. Mem. Can. Assn. Geographers (pres. 1991-92), Am. Geophys. Union, Internat. Geog. Union (commn. chmn., sec., chmn. Can. nat. com. 1984-88), Internat. Assn. Geomorphologists (v.p. 1993-97, pres. 1997-2001), Faculty Club (Vancouver). Anglican. Avocations: mountain hiking, stamp collecting/philately. Office: Univ BC Dept Geography 1984 West Mall Vancouver BC Canada V6T 1Z2 E-mail: olav@geog.ubc.ca.

SLAYMAN, CAROLYN WALCH, geneticist, educator; b. Portland, Maine, Mar. 11, 1937; d. John Weston and Ruth Dyer (Sanborn) Walch; m. Clifford L. Slayman; children: Andrew, Rachel BA with highest honors, Swarthmore Coll., 1958; PhD, Rockefeller U., 1963; DSc (hon.), Bowdoin Coll., 1985. Instr., then asst. prof. Case Western Res. U., Cleve., 1967; from asst. prof. to prof. genetics Yale U. Sch. Medicine, New Haven, 1967—, Sterling prof. genetics, 1991—, chmn. dept. genetics, 1984-95, dep. dean acad. and sci. affairs, 1995—. Mem. genetic basis of disease rev. commn. NIH, 1981—85, nat. adv. gen. med. scis. coun., 1989—93; bd. dirs. J. Weston Walch Pub., Portland, Maine, Applera Corp.; mem. sci. rev. bd. Howard Hughes Med. Inst., 1992—97. Mem. editl. bd. Jour. Biol. Chemistry, 1989-94; contbr. articles to sci. jours. Trustee Foote Sch., New Haven, 1983—89, Hopkins Sch., New Haven, 1988—93; bd. overseers Dartmouth Med. Sch., 1997—. Woods Hole Oceanographic Instn., 1997—, Bowdoin Coll., Brunswick, Maine, 1976—88, trustee, 1988—2001. Recipient Deborah Morton award Westbrook Coll., 1986. Mem. Am. Soc. Biol. Chemists, Genetics Soc. Am., Soc. Gen. Physiologists, Am. Soc. Microbiology, Inst. Medicine, Phi Beta Kappa Office: Yale U Sch Medicine Dept Genetics 333 Cedar St New Haven CT 06510-3289

SLAYMAN, CLIFFORD LEROY, biophysicist, educator; b. Mt. Vernon, Ohio, July 7, 1936; s. Clifford Leroy and Ethel May (Stantz) S.; m. Carolyn Ruth Walch, Dec. 26, 1959; children: Andrew Lowell, Rachel Whitehouse. AB, Kenyon Coll., 1958; PhD, Rockefeller Inst., 1963; DSc (hon.), Kenyon Coll, 1991. NSF fellow Cambridge (Eng.) U., 1963-64; asst. prof. Western Res. U., Cleve., 1964-67; from asst. prof. to prof. physiology Yale U., New Haven, 1967—. Mem panel on pre-doctoral fellowships NSF, Washington, 1969-71; DOE-DOA-NSF panel on Plant Sci. Ctrs., Washington, 1988. Editor: Electrogenic Ion Pumps, 1982; contbr. articles to profl. jours. and revs.; editorial bd. Bio Sci. Jour., 1985-88, Jour. Membrane Biology, 1982—. Mem. Hamden (Conn.) Neighborhood Preservation Com., 1980-82. Grantee NIH, 1964-91, 2000-04, NSF, 1979-82, DOE, 1985-2000. Mem. AAAS, Am. Physiol. Soc., Am. Soc. Plant Physiologists, N.Y. Acad. Scis., Soc. Gen. Physiologists, Conn. Acad. Arts and Scis. Avocations: antique house restoration, conservation, nature watching. Office: Yale Sch Medicine 333 Cedar St New Haven CT 06510-3289 E-mail: clifford.slayman@yale.edu.

SLAYTON, GUS, foundation administrator; b. Pocahontas, Ark., Jan. 20, 1937; s. Alvin M. and Eula Inis (Milam) S.; m. Ruth Virginia Furr, May 27, 1961 (dec. Nov. 1989). BA, U. Md., College Park, 1973. Enslited U.S. Army, 1957, commd. 2nd lt., 1963, advanced through grades to lt. col., 1978; various operational and research and devel. assignments, including The Pentagon, 1974-78; ret., 1980; exec. dir. Assn. of Old Crows, Alexandria, Va., 1980-92, AOC Ednl. Found., 1992—. Decorated Legion of Merit (2), Bronze Star (2) Republican. Avocation: real estate investment. Home: 152 Mill Cove Ln Ponte Vedra Beach FL 32082-4135 E-mail: slaytonag@earthlink.net.

SLAYTON, JOHN ARTHUR, electric motor manufacturing executive; b. St. Joseph, Mo., Aug. 12, 1918; s. Ernest Roy and Cora Belle (Hutchison) S.; m. Elizabeth Van Horn Duerr, Aug. 15, 1942; children: Richard, Elizabeth, Jane, James, Robert, Sarah, Mary. BS, U. Mo., 1940. Salesman Burroughs Co., Chgo., 1940-42; acct. Standard Brands, Green Bay, Wis., 1945-48; exec. v.p. Marathon Electric, Wausau, Wis., 1948-88, pres., vice chmn., 1988-97, ret., 1997. Pres. C. of C. Found., Wausau, 1981-89, Woodson YMCA Found.,

1977—; bd. dirs. Wausau Hosp. Ctr., 1976-82, North Ctrl. Mental Health Found., 1980-85, Wausau Area Vol. Exch., 1983-89, Wasau Health Found., 1975—; pres., bd. dirs. Grant Theatre Found., 1985—; bd. dirs., treas., pres. Lehigh Yawkey Woodson Art Mus., 1985—, pres., 1996—; trstuee, elder 1st Presbyn. Ch., 1960-65. Served in USN, 1942-44. Recipient Citation of Merit U. Mo., Columbia, 1976, Wausau Disting. Cmty. Service award, 1983, Wis. Gov.'s award, 1986; Paul Harris fellow, 1977; Legacy award established in his honor Wausau Hosp., 1999. Mem. Wausau Area C. of C. (pres., dir. 1977-81) Clubs: Wausau Country (pres., dir. 1958-61), Wausau, YMCA (pres., dir. 1961-67). Lodges: Rotary (pres., dir. 1960-63). Republican. Home: 1115 Wildwood Ln Naples FL 34105-3236

SLAYTON, JOHN HOWARD, lawyer, trust company executive; b. Sparta, Wis., July 6, 1955; s. Rex Gordon and Elizabeth (Ward) S.; m. Judith Hughes. BA in Polit. Sci. cum laude, Marquette U., 1977; JD cum laude, George Washington U., 1980, MBA in Fin., 1982; LLM in Taxation, Georgetown U., 1986. Bar: D.C. 1981, U.S. Ct. Appeals (D.C. cir.) 1981, U.S. Dist. Ct. D.C. 1981, Va. 1993. Assoc. Metzger, Shadyac & Schwarz, Washington, 1980—83, Pillsbury, Madison & Sutro, Washington, 1983—87, Leland & Assocs., Inc., Washington, 1987—95; cons. Gordon Getty Family trust, Washington, 1995—96; pres., CEO The Trust Co. of the South, Burlington, 1996—. Instr. real estate syndication, Arlington (Va.) County Continuing Edn./Realty Bd., 1982; mem. Joint Commn. N.C. Bankers Assn. and N.C. Bar Assn. Contbr. articles to profl. jours. Mem.: N.C. Bar Assn. (chmn. legis. com. of estate planning com., chmn. uniform trust code subcom. of estate planning legis. com.), D.C. Bar Assn., Va. Bar Assn., ABA (chmn. trusts and investments subcom. of banking com., com. fed. regulation of securities). Roman Catholic. Office: The Trust Co of the South 3041 S Church St Burlington NC 27215-5154 Business E-Mail: jslayton@tcts.com.

SLAZBERG, BARRY, accounting firm executive; Undergraduate degree in acctg., Bklyn. Coll.; JD, Bklyn. Law Sch.; LLM in taxation, NYU Sch. Law. US dep. mng. ptnr.; mng. ptnr. Deloitte & Touche Tohmatsu USA LLP, 2003—; bd. dirs. Deloitte & Touche, mem. global tax mgmt. group, mem. US firm's mgmt. and exec. com. Recipient CEO Diversity Leadership award, Bus. Women's Network, 2004. Mem.: NYSSCPA, AICPA, NY County Lawyers Assn. Office: Deloitte Global Office 1633 Broadway New York NY 10019-6754 Office Phone: 212-489-1600. Office Fax: 212-489-1687.

SLEDGE, CLEMENT BLOUNT, orthopedic surgeon, educator; b. Ada, Okla., Nov. 1, 1930; s. John B. and Mollie D. (Blount) Sledge; m. Georgia Kurrus, Apr. 13, 1957; children: Margaret, John, Matthew, Claire. MD, Yale U., 1955; MA (hon.), Harvard U., 1970; ScD (hon.), U. The South, 1987. Diplomate Am. Bd. Orthopedic Surgery. Intern Barnes Hosp., St. Louis, 1955—56; resident in orthopedic surgery Harvard U., 1960—63; fellow in orthopedic pathology Armed Forces Inst. Pathology, 1963; vis. scientist Strangeways Research Lab., Cambridge (Eng.) U., 1963—66; asst. prof. orthopedic surgery Harvard U., 1963—67, assoc. prof., 1967—70, prof. orthop. surgery MIT div. health & tech., 1970—; chmn. Brigham and Women's Physician Hosp. Orgn., 1995—97. Chmn. dept. orthopedic surgery Brigham and Women's Hosp., 1970—96. Editor: Textbook of Rheumatology, 1981, 1985, 1989, 1993, 1997; contbr. Active Arthritis Found.; adv. bd. Nat. Arthritis Found., 1978—80. Served with M.C. USNR, 1956—58. Fellow, Med. Found. Boston, 1963—66, Gebbie Rsch. fellow, 1968; grantee, NIH, 1967. Mem.: The Hip Soc. (pres. 1985), Nat. Acad. Sci., Inst. of Medicine, Am. Rheumatism Assn., Orthopedic Rsch. Soc. (pres. 1978—80), Am. Acad. Orthopedic Surgeons (pres. 1985—86), Interurban Orthopedic Club. Episcopalian. Office: Harvard U Dept Orthop Surgery Boston MA 02115*

SLEE, VERGIL N. healthcare informatics executive, physician, author; b. Eaton Rapids, Mich., Sept. 24, 1917; s. William Willey and Matilda Elizabeth Slee; m. Beth Stoke, June 10, 1941; children: Dan, Sara Slee Brown, David, Debora. BA, Albion Coll., 1937; MD, Washington U., St. Louis, 1941; MPH, U. Mich., 1947. Diplomate in pub. health Am. Bd. Preventive Medicine. Intern in internal medicine Barnes Hosp., St. Louis, 1941, resident, 1942; dir. Barry County Health Ctr., Hastings, Mich., 1947-56; dir., founder Commn. on Profl. and Hosp. Activities, Ann Arbor, Mich., 1956-71, pres., until 1980, pres. emeritus, 1980—; dir., mem. faculty Estes Park Inst., Englewood, Colo., 1981—; CEO The Tringa Group, Brevard, N.C., 1982—. Non-resident lectr. U. Mich. Sch. Pub. Health, Ann Arbor, 1947-78; dir., founder profl. activity study Southwestern Mich. Hosp. Coun., Hastings, 1953-55; chmn. Health Commons Inst., Portland, Maine, 1992—; pres. Coun. on Clin. Classifications, Ann Arbor, 1976-80. Author: Slee's Health Care Terms, 1986, 4th edit., 2001, The Endangered Medical Record: Ensuring Its Integrity in the Age of Informatics, 2000; editor: International Classification of Diseases, 9th revision, Clinical Modification, 1978. Trustee Transylvania Cmty. Hosp., Brevard, 1988—. Flight surgeon USAAC, 1942-46. Recipient Key award Mich. Hosp. Assn., 1968, spl. citation, 1980; resolution of commendation Southwestern Mich. Hosp. Assn., 1978, Am. Hosp. Assn., 1980; award of merit Am. Assn. Healthcare Cons., 1988, Disting. Svc. award Am. Health Info. Mgmt. Assn., 1993; Vergil N. Slee disting. professorship healthcare quality mgmt. established by U.N.C., Chapel Hill, 1998; Jackson Johnson scholar Washington U. Sch. Medicine, 1937-41; Edwin L. Crosby fellow Am. Hosp. Assn., 1980. Mem. ACP (Richard and Hinds Rosenthal award 1982), APHA, AMA, Alpha Omega Alpha, Phi Kappa Phi, Delta Omega, Phi Gamma. Office Phone: 828-884-6508. E-mail: vslee@juno.com.

SLEED, JOEL, columnist; b. N.Y.C., Jan. 29, 1929; m. MaryLou Kalwara, Nov. 15, 1983; children: Jodie, Jill, Jeffrey, Kristin Kalwara, Karen Hepler. Former travel editor The Star-Ledger, Newark, Newhouse News Svc., Washington; columnist travel sect. Sunday Rep., Springfield, Mass.; travel editor Palm Beach Soc. mag. Office: Newhouse Newspapers 711 Third Ave New York NY 10017 E-mail: joelsleed@msn.com.

SLEEMAN, DONALD GEORGE, construction executive, contractor; BS in Acctg., Miami U. CFO, exec. v.p., treas. Turner Corp. Office: The Turner Corporation 901 Main St Ste 4900 Dallas TX 75202 Office Phone: 214-915-9600.

SLEET, GREGORY M. lawyer, judge; b. N.Y.C. m. Mary Sleet; children: Moneta, Kelsi. BA in Polit. Sci. cum laude, Hampton U., 1973; JD, Rutgers U., 1976. Bar: Del., N.Y., Pa., U.S. Dist. Ct. (ea. dist.) Pa., U.S. Dist. Ct. (ea. dist.) Del., U.S. Ct. Appeals (3d cir.). Pvt. practice, Phila.; dep. atty. gen. State of Del.; in-house counsel Hercules Inc.; dep. atty. gen. U.S. Dist. Ct., Del.; U.S. atty. U.S. Dist. Ct. (ea. dist.), Del., 1994—, judge, 1998—. Mem. Atty. Gen. Janet Reno's adv. com., 1995-97, vice-chair, 1996—. Bd. overseers Widener U. Sch. of Law. Recipient Disting. Svc. award NAACP, 1994. Office: US Courthouse Lockbox 19 844 King St Wilmington DE 19801-3519

SLEETER, JOHN WILLIAM HIGGS, retired physician, health service administrator; b. Toledo, Iowa, Feb. 16, 1917; s. Charles Elmer and Meta DeLad (Higgs) S.; m. Betti Deming, Aug. 28, 1943 (div. Mar. 1963); m. Patricia C. Parker, July 1963 (dec. Oct. 1986); m. Patricia Catherine Parrillo, July 8, 1989; children: John William, Marilee Ann, Thomas David. BA, Cornell Coll., Mt. Vernon, Iowa, 1942; MD, U. Iowa, 1945. Pres. San Gabriel Primary Care, Arcadia, Calif., 1952-62, L.A. County Acad. GP, Calif., 1965-66; inst. paramedic care St. Terisita Hosp., Duarte, Calif., 1970-75; pres., chief operating officer Profsnl. Rev. Area 21, 1970-75; 1st pres. L.A. County Paramedic Commn., 1974-75; pres., CEO, dir. pvt. practice assn., Arcadia, 1984-2000; ret., 2000. Capt. AUS, 1945-49. Mem. Balboa Bay Club, Masons (32d degree). Republican. Avocation: golf. Home: 2467 Calle Villada Cir Duarte CA 91010-2158

SLEICHER, CHARLES ALBERT, chemical engineer; b. Albany, N.Y., Aug. 15, 1924; s. Charles Albert and Beatrice Eugena (Cole) S.; m. Janis Jorgensen, Sept. 5, 1953; children— Jeffrey Mark, Gretchen Gail. BS, Brown U., 1946; MS, M.I.T., 1949; PhD, U. Mich., 1955. Asst. dir. M.I.T. Sch. Chem. Engring.; Practice Bangor, Maine, 1949-51; research engr. Shell Devel. Co., Emeryville, Calif., 1955-59; assoc. prof. chem. engring. U. Wash., Seattle, 1960-66, prof., 1966-92, prof. emeritus, 1993—, dept. chmn., 1977-89. Cons. Westinghouse-Hanford Co.; profl. photographer, 1994—. Contbr. articles on extraction, heat transfer, fluid mechanics, pesticide transport to profl. jours.; contbr. photos to mags., books & calendars. Served with USN, 1943-47. NSF postdoctoral fellow, 1959-60; SEED grantee, 1973-74; research grantee NSF; research grantee Chevron Research Corp.; research grantee Am. Chem. Soc. Fellow AIChE (program and awards coms.), AAAS; mem. Am. Chem. Soc., N.Am. Nature Photography Assn., Photographic Soc. Am., Sigma Xi. Achievements include chem. reactor design patents, nat. photography awards, co-founder Columbia Winery. Home: 5002 Harold Pl NE Seattle WA 98105-2809 Office: U Wash Dept Chem Engring PO Box 351750 Seattle WA 98195-1750

SLEIGH, SYLVIA, artist, educator; b. Llandudno, North Wales; came to U.S., 1961; d. John Harold and Katherine Amy (Miller) S.; m. Lawrence Alloway, June 28, 1954. Student, Sch. Art, Brighton, Sussex, Eng., 1932-36; diploma, U. London Extra-Mural Dept., 1947. Vis. asst. prof. SUNY-Stony Brook, 1978; instr. New Sch. Social Research, N.Y.C., 1974-77, 78-80; Edith Kreeger Wolf disting. prof. Northwestern U., Evanston, Ill., 1977; vis. artist Baldwin Seminar Oberlin Coll., Ohio, 1982, New Sch. Social Rsch., N.Y.C. One person shows include Bennington (Vt.) Coll., 1963, Soho 20 Art Gallery, N.Y.C., 1974, 76, 80, 82, A.I.R. Gallery, N.Y.C., 1974, 76, 78, Ohio State U., Columbus, 1976, Matrix, Wadsworth Atheneum, Hartford, Conn., 1976, Marianne Deson Gallery, Chgo., 1990, G.W. Einstein, Inc., N.Y.C., 1980, 83, 85, U. Mo., Saint Louis, 1981, Zaks Gallery, Chgo., 1985, 95, Milw. Art Mus., Butler Inst., Youngstown, Ohio, 1990, Stiebel Modern, N.Y.C., 1992, 94, Gallery 609, Denver, Canton (Ohio) Art Inst., Soho 20 Gallery, 1999, Deven Golden Fine Arts, N.Y., 1999, The Art of Sylvia Sleigh and Lawrence Allway Phila. Art Alliance, Phila., 2001; exhibited in group shows Newhouse Gallery, S.I., N.Y., Stamford (Conn.) Mus., 1985, Albany (N.Y.) Inst. Art, Cin. Art Mus., New Orleans Mus. Art, Denver Art Mus., Pa. Acad. Fine Arts, 1989, Carlsten Art Gallery, Stevens Point, Wis., 1993, Stiebel Modern, N.Y.C., 1994, Soho 20, N.Y.C., 1993, 96, Katzen Brown Gallery, N.Y.C., 1989, Zaks Gallery, Chgo., 1986, Steinbaum Krauss Gallery, 1997, Deven Golden Fine Arts, Ltd., N.Y.C., 1997, Rutgers U., New Brunswick, N.J., 1984, 86, RioArriba Gallery, Abiquiu, N.Mex., 1996, Milw. Art Mus., 1996, Steinbaum Krauss Gallery, 1997, N.Y. Mus. exhbn. traveling until 2001, David and Alfred Smart Mus., Chgo., Broome St. Gallery, N.Y.C., Deven Golden Fine Arts, N.Y.C., A.I.R. Gallery, N.Y.C., Apex Art Co., N.Y.C., 1998, McKee Gallery, N.Y.C., 1998, Royal Coll. Art, London, 1998, Heckscher Mus. Art, Huntington, N.Y., 1999, Printworks Gallery, 2000, others. Panelist Creative Artists Pub. Service Program, N.Y.C., 1976. Nat. Endowment for Arts grantee, 1982, Pollock-Krasner Found. grantee, 1985. Home: 330 W 20th St New York NY 10011-3302 E-mail: ssleigh@mindspring.com.

SLEIGHT, ARTHUR WILLIAM, chemist, educator; b. Ballston Spa, NY, Apr. 1, 1939; s. Hollis Decker and Elizabeth (Smith) S.; m. Betty F. Hilberg, Apr. 19, 1963; children: Jeffrey William, Jeannette Anne, Jason Arthur. AB, Hamilton Coll., 1960; PhD, U. Conn., 1963. Faculty U. Stockholm, Sweden, 1963-64; with E.I. du Pont de Nemours & Co., Inc., Wilmington, Del., 1965-89, rsch. mgr. solid. state/catalytic chemistry, 1981-89; Harris Chair prof. materials sci. Oreg. State U., Corvallis, 1989—; dir. Ctr. for Advanced Materials Rsch., 1995—. Adj. prof. U. Del., 1978-89. Editor: Materials Rsch. Bull., 1994—; editorial bd. Inorganic Chemistry Rev., 1979—, Jour. Catalysis, 1986—, Applied Catalysis, 1987—, Solid State Scis., 1987—, Chemistry of Materials, 1988—, Materials Chemistry and Physics, 1988—, Jour. of Solid State Chemistry, 1988—; patentee in field; contbr. articles to profl. jours. Mem. Presdl. Commn. Superconductivity, 1989. Recipient Phila. chpt. Am. Inst. Chemists award, 1988, Gold Medal award Nat. Assn. Sci. Tech. and Soc., 1994. Mem. Am. Chem. Soc. (award Del. sect. 1978, Chemistry of Materials award 1997). Home: PO Box 907 Philomath OR 97370-0907 Office: Oreg State U Dept Chemistry 153 Gilbert Hall Corvallis OR 97331-8546 Office Phone: 541-737-6749. E-mail: arthur.sleight@oregonstate.edu.

SLEIGHT, GARTH HESSEN, language educator, dean; b. Wiesbaden, Hessen, Germany, Aug. 29, 1955; s. Lynn Goochey and Dolores Peterson Sleight; m. Carilee Draper, Apr. 17, 1980; children: Raylynn, Grant, Camille, Lena. BA, Brigham Young U., 1980, MA, 1982. Instr. Spanish Missionary Tng. Ctr., Provo, Utah, 1977—81; instr. ESL Eng. Lang. Ctr., Provo; instr. Spanish and comm. Miles C.C., Miles City, Mont., 1986—, dean arts and sci., 1996—. Mem. lang. arts curriculum com. Miles City Unified Sch. Dist., 1990—91; mem. humanities sub. com. Mont. U. Sys. Core Curriculum Com., Helena, 1990—96. Contbr. articles to profl. jours. Scoutmaster Boy Scouts Am., Miles City, 1993—95; bishop Ch. Jesus Christ of LDS, Miles City, 1997—2002. Mem.: Am. Assn. C.C. Republican. Mem. Lds Ch. Avocations: reading, ice skating, volunteering. Home: 501 S Lake Miles City MT 59301 Office: Miles Cmty Coll 2715 Dickinson Miles City MT 59301 E-mail: sleightg@milescc.edu.

SLEIK, THOMAS SCOTT, lawyer; b. La Crosse, Wis., Feb. 24, 1947; s. John Thomas and Marion Gladys (Johnson) S.; m. Judith Mattson, Aug. 24, 1968; children: Jennifer, Julia, Joanna. BS, Marquette U., 1969, JD, 1971. Bar: Wis. 1971, U.S. Dist. Ct. (we. dist.) Wis. 1971. Assoc. Hale Skemp Hanson Skemp & Sleik, La Crosse, 1971-74, ptnr., 1975—. State pres. Boy Scouts Am., 1981—83, bd. dirs. Gateway Area Con., 1973—99, pres., 1980—81; trustee La Crosse Pub. Libr., 1981—; bd. dirs. Children's Mus. of La Crosse, 1997—2002, Greater La Crosse Area United Way, 1985—92, campaign chmn., 1986, pres., 1987; mem. Sch. Dist. La Crosse Bd. Edn., 1973—77, v.p., 1977; festmaster Oktoberfest (LaCross Festivals Inc.), 2001, trustee, 2001—. Fellow Am. Acad. Matrimonial Lawyers (pres. Wis. chpt. 1999-2000); mem. ABA, State Bar Wis. (bd. govs. 1987-94, pres. 1992-93, spkr. litigation sect. and family law seminars), La Crosse County Bar Assn. Roman Catholic. Home: 4082 Glenhaven Dr La Crosse WI 54601-7503 Office: Hale Skemp Hanson Skemp & Sleik 505 King St Ste 300 La Crosse WI 54602-1927 E-mail: tss@haleskemp.com.

SLEMMONS, ROBERT SHELDON, architect; b. Mitchell, Nebr., Mar. 12, 1922; s. Matthew Garvin and K. Fern (Borland) S.; m. Dorothy Virginia Herrick, Dec. 16, 1945; children: David (dec.), Claire, Jennifer, Robert, Timothy. AB, U. Nebr., 1947, BArch, 1948. Draftsman Davis & Wilson, Archs., Lincoln, Nebr., 1947-48; chief designer, project arch. Office of Kans. State Arch., Topeka, 1948-54; assoc. John A. Brown, Arch., Topeka, 1954-56; ptnr. Brown & Slemmons, Arch., Topeka, 1956-69; v.p. Brown-Slemmons-Krueger, Archs., Topeka, 1969-73; owner Robert S. Slemmons, A.I.A. & Assocs., Archs., Topeka, 1973—. Cons. Kans. State Office Bldg. Commn., 1956-57; lectr. in design U. Kans., 1961; bd. dirs. Kaw Valley State Bank & Trust Co., Topeka, 1978-92. Prin. archtl. works include Kans. State Office Bldg., 1954, Topeka Presbyn. Manor, 1960-74, Meadowlark Hills Ret. Cmty., 1979, Shawnee County Adult Detention Facility, 1985. Bd. dirs. Topeka Civic Symphony Soc., 1950-60, Midstates Ret. Cmtys., Inc., 1986-92, Topeka Festival Singers; cons. Ministries for Aging, Inc., Topeka, 1984-97; mem. Topeka Bd. Bldg. and Fire Appeals, Kans., 1977-97, Com. for Employer Support of the Guard and Res. With USNR, 1942-48. Mem. AIA (Topeka pres. 1955-56, Kans. dir. 1957-58, com. on housing, com. for hist. resources), Internat. Conf. Bldg. Ofcls., Topeka Art Guild (pres. 1950), Am. Corrections Assn., Kans. Coun. Chs. (dir. 1961-62), Shawnee County Hist. Soc., Greater Topeka C. of C. (sr. coun., pres.), Downtown Topeka Inc. (v.p. 1992-99), Topeka, Shawnee County Libr. (dir. friends of the libr.), St. Andrews Soc. (pres.), SAR (pres. state soc., pres. chpt.), Soc. of Antiquaries of Scotland (fellow), U. Nebr. Alumni Assn. (life), Band Alumni Assn., Kiwanis (pres. 1966-67), Topeka Knife and Fork Club. Presbyterian (elder, deacon, chmn. trustees). Office: Slemmons Assocs Archs 534 S Kansas Ave Ste 140 Topeka KS 66603-3473 Personal E-mail: rdslem@hotmail.com.

SLEMON, GORDON RICHARD, electrical engineering educator; b. Bowmanville, Ont., Can., Aug. 15, 1924; s. Milton Everitt and Selena (Johns) S.; m. Margaret Jean Matheson, July 9, 1949; children: Sally, Stephen, Mark, Jane. BASc., U. Toronto, 1946, MASc., 1948; D.I.C., Imperial Coll. Sci., London (Eng.) U., 1951, PhD, 1952; D of Engring. (hon.), Meml. U. Nfld., 1994. Asst. prof. elec. engring. N.S. Tech. Coll., Can., 1953-55; assoc. prof. U. Toronto, Ont., Can., 1955-63, prof., 1964-90, chmn. dept. elec. engring., 1966-76, dean of faculty of applied sci. and engring., 1979-86, prof. emeritus, 1990—. Colombo plan adviser, India, 1963-64; pres. Elec. Engring. Consociates, 1976-79; bd. dirs. Inverpower Controls Ltd., Innovations Found. Author: (with J.M. Ham) Scientific Basis of Electrical Engineering, Magnetoelectric Devices, (with A. Straughen) Electric Machinery; (with S.B. Dewan, A. Straughen) Power Semiconductor Drives, Electric Machines and Drives; contbr. articles to profl. jours. Chmn. Innovations Found., 1980-93, vice chmn., 1993—97; chmn. Microelectronics Devel. Ctr., 1983-88. Decorated officer Order of Can.; recipient excellence in tchg. award Western Electric, 1965, Can. Centennial medal, 1967, Ross medal, 1978, 83, Gold medal Jugoslav Union of Nikola Tesla Socs., Engring. Alumni medal, Educator of Yr. award Can. Engrs., 1992, Hall of Distinction award U. Toronto, 1992, Achievement award IEEE Magnetics Soc., 1997, Arbor award U. Toronto, 1997. Fellow Can. Acad. Engring. (pres. 1998-99), Engring. Inst. Can., Instn. Elec. Engrs. (hon. fellow 1995), IEEE (Centennial medal 1984, Nikola Tesla award, Millennium medal 2000); mem. Am. Soc. Engring. Edn., others. Achievements include patents in field. Home: 40 Chatfield Dr Don Mills ON Canada M3B 1K5 Office: U Toronto Fac Applied Sci and Engring Toronto ON M5S 3G4 Canada E-mail: g.slemon@utoronto.ca.

SLEMONS, GREGORY L. communications executive; With McCaw Cellular; v.p. Wireless Network Svcs. AT&T Wireless Svcs., Inc., Redmond, Wash. Office: AT&T Wireless Services Inc 7277 164th Ave NE Bldg 1 Redmond WA 98052

SLEPIAN, DAVID, mathematician, communications engineer; b. Pitts., June 30, 1923; s. Joseph and Rose Grace (Myerson) S.; m. Janice Dorothea Berek, Apr. 18, 1950; children: Steven Louis, Don Joseph, Anne Marie. Student, U. Mich., 1941-43; MA, Harvard U., 1947, PhD, 1949; postdoctoral studies, Cambridge U., Eng., 1949, Sorbonne, Paris, 1950. With AT&T Bell Labs., Murray Hill, N.J., 1950-82, head math. studies dept., 1970-82. Prof. elec. engring. U. Hawaii, Honolulu, 1970-81; McKay prof. elec. engring. U. Calif., Berkeley, 1957-58, Regents lectr., 1977. Editor, author: Development of Information Theory, 1973; contbr. articles to profl. jours.; patentee in field. Served with U.S. Army, 1943-46, ETO. Von Neumann lectr. Soc. for Indsl. and Applied Math., 1982; Parker fellow in physics Harvard U., 1949-50. Fellow IEEE (editor Procs. 1969-70, Alexander Graham Bell award 1981), AAAS, Inst. Math. Stats.; mem. NAS, NAE, Am. Acad. Arts and Scis. Avocations: music, travel, languages. Home: 7 Sunningdale Ct Maplewood NJ 07040 E-mail: dslepian@comcast.net.

SLESINGER, DORIS PEYSER, sociology educator; b. N.Y.C., Dec. 26, 1927; d. Harold L. and Helene (Fantel) Peyser; m. Jonathan Avery Slesinger, Feb. 2, 1950 (div. 1976); children: Jeffrey, David, Paul Avery; m. Edward Wellin, Aug. 6, 1976. AB, Vassar Coll., 1949; MA, U. Mich., 1960; Phd, U. Wis., 1973. Various rsch. and editl. positions U. Wis.-Milw., U. Mich., Ann Arbor, 1951—69; co-dir. Applied Population Lab., dept. rural sociology U. Wis., Madison, 1975—87; co-dir. Wis. State Data Ctr. U. Wis.-Extension, 1979—87; asst. prof. dept. rural sociology U. Wis., Madison, 1974—80, assoc. prof., 1980—84, prof., 1984—98, chair dept., 1987—91, emerita prof., 1998—, ombuds, 2003—. Mem. com. on health and safety implications of child labor Nat. Rsch. Coun., 1997-98; mem. health svcs. devel. grants rev. com., agy. for health care policy and rsch. U.S. Dept. HHS, 1991-94. Author: Mothercraft and Infant Health: A Sociodemographic and Sociocultural Approach, 1981; author software; contbr. chpts. to books, articles to profl. jours. Bd. dirs. Group Health Coop. of South Ctrl. Wis., Inc., 1984-87, Wis. Coun. Hum;n Concerns, 1984-88, 88-92; mem. Wis. Gov.'s Adv. Cou. on Migrant Labor, 1998—. Recipient numerous grants and fellowships. Mem. APHA, Nat. Rural Health Assn., Population Assn. Am., Am. Sociol. Assn. (com. on regulation of rsch. 1980-83), Rural Sociol. Soc. (v.p. 1989-90, chair endowment com. 1992-93, Disting. Rural Sociol. award 2002). Office: U Wis Dept Rural Sociology 1450 Linden Dr Madison WI 53706-1522 E-mail: slesinger@ssc.wisc.edu.

SLICHTER, CHARLES PENCE, physicist, researcher; b. Ithaca, N.Y., Jan. 21, 1924; s. Sumner Huber and Ada (Pence) S.; m. Gertrude Thayer Almy, Aug. 23, 1952 (div. Sept. 1977); children: Sumner Pence, William Almy, Jacob Huber, Ann Thayer; m. Anne FitzGerald, June 7, 1980; children: Daniel Huber, David Pence AB, Harvard U., 1946, MA, 1947, PhD, 1949; DSc (hon.), U. Waterloo, 1993; LLD (hon.), Harvard U., 1996. Rsch. asst. Underwater Explosives Rsch. Lab., Woods Hole, Mass., 1943-46; faculty U. Ill., Urbana, 1949—, prof. physics, 1955-97, prof. Ctr. for Advanced Study, 1968-97, prof. chemistry, 1986-97, rsch. prof. physics, 1997—, prof. emeritus, 1997—. Morris Loeb lectr. Harvard U., 1961; mem. Pres.'s Sci. Adv. Com., 1964-69, Com. on Nat. Medal Sci., 1969-74, Nat. Sci. Bd., 1975-84, Pres.'s Com. Sci. and Tech., 1976 Author: Principles of Magnetic Resonance, 1963, 3d edit., 1989; Contbr. articles to profl. jours. Former trustee, mem. corp. Woods Hole Oceanog. Instn.; mem. Harvard Corp., 1970-95. Recipient Langmuir award Am. Phys. Soc., 1969, Buckley prize, 1996; Alfred P. Sloan fellow, 1955-61. Fellow AAAS, Am. Phys. Soc., Internat. Electron Paramagnetic Resonance Soc.; mem. NAS (Comstock prize 1993), Am. Acad. Arts and Scis., Am. Philos. Soc., Internat. Soc. Magnetic Resonance (pres. 1987-90, Trienniel prize 1986). Home: 61 Chestnut Ct Champaign IL 61822-7121

SLICKER, FREDERICK KENT, lawyer; b. Tulsa, Aug. 21, 1943; s. James Floyd and Lucille Geneva (Nordling) S.; children: Laura, Kipp. BA, U. Kans., 1965, JD with highest distinction, 1968; LLM, Harvard U., 1973. Bar: Kans. 1968, U.S. Ct. Mil. Appeals 1968, U.S. Supreme Ct. 1972, Tex. 1973, Okla. 1980. Prin. founder Slicker Law Firm, P.C., 2000—. Author: A Practical Guide to Church Bond Financing, 1985, Angels All Around, 1999, Seeking God's Heart, 2004. Capt. U.S. Army, 1965—72. Mem. ABA, Okla. Bar Assn., Order of Coif. Democrat. Methodist. Avocation: Christian men's ministries. Office: 4444 E 66th Ste #201 Tulsa OK 74136-4206 Office Phone: 918-496-9020. E-mail: fslicker@swbell.com.

SLIFE, BRENT DONALD, psychologist, educator, author; b. Ames, Iowa, Dec. 7, 1953; s. Leo Nathan and Phyllis (Bryant) S.; m. Karen Somerville, May 22, 1976; children: Conor Merchant, Nathan Matthew, Jacob Tristan. BA, William Jewell Coll., Liberty, Mo., 1976; MS, Purdue U., 1977, PhD, 1981. Lic. clin. psychologist and psychotherapist. Intern Palo Alto (Calif.) VA Med. Ctr., 1980-81; asst. prof. Santa Clara (Calif.) U., 1981-84, Baylor U., Waco, Tex., 1984-87, assoc. prof., 1987-93, prof. psychology, 1993-94, Brigham Young U., Provo, Utah, 1994—, chmn. theoretical program, 1998—. Author: Taking Sides: Clashing Views on Controversial Psychological Issues, 1980, 2002, Time and Psychological Explanation, 1993, What's Behind the Research, 1995, Toward a Unified Psychology: Incommensurability, Hermeneutics and Morality, 2000, Critical Issues in Psychotherapy, 2001; editor: Jour. Theoretical and Philos. Psychology, 1989—98; assoc. editor Jour. Theoretical and Philos. Psychology, 1998—, mem. edit. bd., assoc. editor Jour. of Mind and Behavior, 1990—, Theory and Psychology, 1990—94, Methods, 1999—. Bd. dirs., treas. Sunny View Manor Retirement Facility, 1982-84; psychol. counselor Caritas Food and Care Coalition, Waco, 1990-94; chmn. com., asst. scoutmaster Boy Scouts Am., Waco, Tex., 1984-93; Lindon, Utah, 1994-98; elder Presbyn. Ch., American Fork, Utah, 1996—. Recipient Circle of Achievement award Baylor U., 1992, Karl G. Maesar award for outstanding rsch., 2002—; named Outstanding Rsch. Prof., Baylor U., 1991, Tchr. of Yr., Brigham Young U., 1997, Most Outstanding Prof., Brigham Young U. Psi Chi, 2000; Elisa R. Snow fellow, 2000-2002. Fellow APA (pres. divsn. 24, 1999-2000, Disting. Contbn. award 1998). Avocations: banjo, piano, organ. Office: Brigham Young U 1072 SWKT Dept Psychology Provo UT 84602

SLIFKA, ALFRED A. oil corporation executive; b. Boston, June 3, 1932; s. Abraham and Sonya Slifka; m. Gilda Koritz; children: Adam, Jennifer, Eric. Grad. high sch., Boston, 1949. Pres., dir., co-owner Global Petroleum Corp., Waltham, Mass., CEO. Bd. dirs. New England Fuel Inst., 1974—, Better Hom Heat Coun., Petroleum Inst. Rsch. Found., N.Y.C.; past bd. dirs. U.S. Trust Co., Boston. Contbr. articles to profl. jours. Vice chmn. Hebrew Rehab. Ctr., Boston; trustee Combined Jewish Philanthropies, Boston; bd. dirs. Griffith Consumers Co., Cheverly, Md. Mem.: N.Y. Mcht. Exch., Pine Brook Country Club (past gov. 1985—89). Avocations: jogging, golf, tennis. Office: 800 South St Waltham MA 02453-1478

SLIFKIN, LAWRENCE MYER, physics educator; b. Bluefield, W.Va., Sept. 29, 1925; s. Isaac L. and Eva (Baden) S.; m. Miriam Kresses, July 4, 1948; children: Anne, Rebecca, Merle, Naomi. BA, NYU, 1947; PhD, Princeton U., 1950. Rsch. assoc., rsch. asst. prof. U. Ill., Urbana, 1950-54; asst prof. U. Minn., Mpls., 1954-55; asst. prof., then prof. physics U. N.C., Chapel Hill, 1955-91, Bowman Gray prof., 1979-82, Alumni Disting. prof., 1983-91, prof. emeritus, 1991—. Rsch. fellow Oxford U., 1962-63; liaison sci. U.S. Office Naval Rsch., London, 1969-70; collaborateur étranger, CEN-Saclay, France, 1975-76. Editor: (with J. H. Crawford): Point Defects in Solids, vol. I, 1972, vol. II, 1975; contbr. more than 125 articles to profl. jours. and books. With U.S. Army, 1944-46, PTO. Fellow Am. Phys. Soc. (exec. com. div. condensed matter physics 1978-80, Jesse Beams award rsch. excellence S.E. Sect. 1977), Soc. Photographic Scientists and Engrs.; mem. Am. Assn. Physics Tchrs. Democrat. Jewish. Avocations: music, travel, reading, grandfathering. Home: 313 Burlage Cir Chapel Hill NC 27514-2703 Office: U NC Cb 3255 Phillips Hall Chapel Hill NC 27599-3255 Personal E-mail: mslifkin@bellsouth.net.

SLIGER, BERNARD FRANCIS, academic administrator, economist, educator; b. Chassell, Mich., Sept. 30, 1924; s. Paul and Hazel (MacLauchlin) S.; m. Greta Taube, Sept. 1, 1945; children: Nan, Paul, Greta Lee, Sten. BA in Econs. with high hons., Mich. State U., 1949, MA, 1950, PhD, 1955; postgrad., U. Minn., 1961-62. Mem. faculty La. State U., 1953-61, prof. econs., 1961, head dept., 1961-65, vice chancellor, dean academic affairs, 1965-68; sec. adminstrn. State of La., 1968—69; sec.-treas. La. Office Bldg. Corp., 1969-72; organizer, exec. dir. La. Coordinating Council Higher Edn., 1969-72; prof. econs. Fla. State U., Tallahassee, 1973—2003, prof. econ. emeritus, 2003—, exec. v.p., 1972-76, chief acad. officer, 1973-76, pres., 1977-91, interim pres., 1993, dir. univ.'s London Study Ctr., 1975, pres. emeritus, 1992—2003; ret., 2003. Mem. staff sci. and tech. com. Fla. Ho. of Reps., 1979; mem. V.P. Mondale's Select Com. on Sci. and Tech., 1980; mem. bd. dirs. Fed. Res Bank of Atlanta, 1983-88; cons. econ. theory and pub. fin. to pvt. and pub. commns., orgns.; mem., chief cons. Gov. La.'s tax study com., 1968; formerly La. commr. adminstrn. and chief budget officer; mem. NCAA pres.'s commn., 1987-91. Author: (text) Public Finance, 1964, rev. edit., 1970, (with others) Municipal Finance Administration, 1976, rev.; contbr. to profl. publs. Vol. economist Tallahassee C. of C., 1977, Fla. C .of C., 1978; mem. Acad. Task Force for Review of the Ins. and Tort Systems, 1986-88; trustee The Nature Conservancy, 1986—; trustee Am. Coll. Testing Corp., 1981-87, chmn. 1985-87; ex-officio mem. Fla. Coun. 100. With C.E., U.S. Army, 1943-46. Named Dir. Practical Politics La. Ho. of Reps., 1969; Bernard F. Sliger Eminent scholar Chair in Econ. Edn. created in his name by Fla. State U., 1987, Bernard F. Sliger Bldg. dedicated at univ.-related rsch. park, Bernard F. Sliger Tower in Univ. Ctr. Bldg. dedicated, 1999. Mem. Kiwanis, Phi Beta Kappa, Omicron Delta Kappa, Phi Kappa Phi, Omicron Delta Epsilon, Alpha Kappa Psi, Beta Gamma Sigma, Phi Eta Sigma. Presbyterian. Home: 3341 E Lakeshore Dr Tallahassee FL 32312-1440 Office: Gus A Stavros Ctr Adv Free Enterprise & Economic Edu 250 S Woodward Ave Tallahassee FL 32306-4220 Office Fax: 850-644-9866. E-mail: sliger@mailer.fsu.edu/sliger@garnet.acns.fsu.edu.

SLIGER, HERBERT JACQUEMIN, JR., lawyer; b. Urbana, Ill., Nov. 21, 1948; s. Herbert Jacquemin and Marina (Mantia) S.; m. Sandra Ann Ratti, May 3, 1996; children: Lauren Christine, Matthew Ryan, Nicholas Adam, Claire Nicole, Adam Gregory. BS in Fin., U. Ill., 1970; JD, U. Ariz., 1974. Bar: Ariz. 1974, Ill. 1975, U.S. Supreme Ct. 1983, Okla. 1984, U.S. Ct. Appeals (7th cir.) 1980, U.S. Tax Ct. 1980; CPA, Okla. Lawyer Charles W. Phillips Law Offices, Harrisburg, Ill., 1974—75; trust counsel Magna Trust Co., F/K/A Millikin Nat. Bank, Decatur, Ill., 1976—80, First of America Trust Co., Springfield, Ill., 1980—83; trust counsel personal fin. svcs. group First Interstate Bank Okla. NA, Oklahoma City, 1983—86; mgr. employee benefits trust dept. First Interstate Bank of Okla., NA, Oklahoma City, 1986—89; v.p., pension counsel Star Bank, NA, Cin., Cin., 1989—90; asst. gen. counsel Bank One Ariz. Corp., Phoenix, 1990—95; asst. gen. counsel, nat. practice group head Banc One Corp., Columbus, Ohio, 1995—98, state gen. counsel Phoenix, 1996—97; sec. of bd. and cashier Bank One, Ariz. NA, 1996—97; sec. of bd. and statutory agt. Banc One Ariz. Corp., 1996—97; sec. bd. Bank One Trust Co. N.A., Columbus, 1996—; asst. gen. counsel, trust counsel practice group head law dept. Bank One Corp., Chgo., 1999—2003, sr. counsel, 2003—04, J.P. Morgan Chase & Co., 2004—. Co-chmn. Nat. Conf. Lawyers and Corp. Fiduciaries, 1992-94; instr. Chaminade U. Hawaii, Hawaii Tax Inst., 1999. Contbr. articles to profl. jours. Mem. ABA (sect. bus. law, banking law com., trust and investment svcs. subcom. 1991-99, sect. real property, probate and trust law 1974—, fiduciary income taxation subcom. 1994—, fiduciary environ. problems com. 1993-99, sect. of taxation, employee benefits com. 1991-2001), State Bar of Ariz. (mem. exec. coun., probate and trust sect., chmn. ethics com., mem. subcom. uniform laws 2002—), Okla. Bar Assn., Am. Bankers Assn. (chmn. trust counsel com. 1992-94, mem. and head of fiduciary law dept. Nat./Grad. Trust Sch. Bd. of Faculty Advisors 1994-95, faculty mem. teaching "fiduciary duties under ERISA" Nat. Employee Benefit Trust Sch. 1994-96, spokesman Environ. Risk Task Force 1994-95, mem. trust and investment divsn. exec. com. 1992-94, mini-adv. bd. chairperson trusts and estates 1995-99), Nat. Conf. Lawyers and Corp. Fiduciaries (co-chmn. 1992-94), Am. Corp. Counsel Assn. Roman Catholic. Avocation: phys. fitness.

SLIM, MICHEL S. surgeon, educator, health facility administrator; b. Nov. 18, 1929; s. Saliba and Julia Slim; m. Norma Gebara, Sept. 4, 1958; children: Julie, Lina, Nayla. MD, Am. U., Beirut, Lebanon, 1954. Diplomate Am. Bd. Surgery, Am. Bd. Pediatric Surgery, Am. Bd. Thoracic Surgery. Chief pediatric surgery, prof. surgery Am. U., Beirut, 1963-86; prof. N.Y. Med. Coll., N.Y.C., 1986—; attending Westchester Med. Ctr., Valhalla, 1986—, chief pediatric trauma, 1991—, chief pediatric surgery, 1994—2002. Editl. cons. Pediatric Surg. Internat., 1985—; reviewer Ann. Thoracic Surgery, Jordan Med. Jour.; contbr. articles to profl. jours. Evarts Graham Traveling fellow Am. Assn. Thoracic Surgery, 1970-71. Fellow ACS, Am. Acad. Pediat., Am. Coll. Chest Physicians; mem. Am. Pediatric Surgery Assn., Brit. Assn. Pediatric Surgery, Internat. Soc. Surgery. Office: NY Med Coll Munger Pavilion Valhalla NY 10595 E-mail: mslimpedsurg@hotmail.com.

SLINEY, DAVID HAMMOND, medical physicist; b. Washington, Feb. 21, 1941; s. David Xavier and Ida Lee (Echols) S.; m. Carol Ann Scott, Feb. 19, 1966 (div.); children: Sean S., D. Scott, Stephen P.; m. Judith Sarkany, Sept. 22, 2002. BS in Physics, Va. Poly. Inst., 1963; MS in Physics, Emory U., 1965; PhD in Biophysics, U. London, 1991. Pres. David H. Sliney, Consulting Physicist, Fallston, Md., 1972—; chief laser branch U.S. Army Environ. Hygiene Agy., Aberdeen Proving Ground, Md., 1965-94; assoc. Johns Hopkins Sch. Pub. Health, 1987—; program mgr. laser/optical radiation program U.S. Army Ctr. for Health Promotion and Preventive Medicine, 1994—. Chmn. Gordon Rsch. conf. on Lasers in Medicine and Biology, Meriden, N.H., 1976, 84; mem. com. on phys. agt. TLVs, Am. Conf. Govtl. Indsl. Hygienists, 1966-97, 2003—, chmn., 1986-96; cons. div. environ. health WHO, Geneva, 1976—; vis. lectr. UNESCO, Beijing, 1987. Author: Safety with Lasers and Other Optical Sources, 1980, Medical Lasers: Their Safe Use, 1992; editor Health Physics Jour., 1976-86, Lasers in the Life Scis.; mem. editl. bd. Lasers in Surgery and Medicine, Lasers and Light in Ophthalmology, 1985-2000, Ophthalmic Laser Therapy; contbr. articles to profl. jours. Mem. (apptd.) tech. electronic product radiation safety com. FDA, Rockville, Md., 1982-85; mem. panel on impact of video viewing Nat. Rsch. Coun., Washington, 1981-83; Internat. Electrotech. Commn., Geneva, 1976—; dir. Div. 6, Photobiology, Commn. Internat. de l'Eclairage, 1991-2003, v.p., 2003—. Capt. U.S. Army, 1965-67. Fulbright fellow U.S. Govt., Herceg-Novi, Yugoslavia, 1976. Fellow: Soc. Photo-Optical Instrumentation Engrs. (symposia chair), Laser Inst. Am. (bd. dirs. 1974—88, 1994—, pres. 1997), Am. Soc. for Lasers in Medicine and Surgery (com. chair 1981—82, bd. dirs. 1989—); mem.: Assn. Rsch. in Vision and Ophthalmology, Am. Acad. Ophthalmology (laser safety com.), Am. Soc. for Photo-biology (mem. governing coun. 2002—), Optical Soc. Am., Internat. Commn. on Occupational Health, Internat. Commn. on Non-Ionizing Radiation Protection, Internat. Radiation Protection Assn. (internat. non-ionizing radiation com.), Nat. Coun. Radiation Protection and Measurements. Unitarian Universalist. Avocation: photography. Home: 406 Streamside Dr Fallston MD 21047-2806 Office: Laser/Optical Radiation Pgm USACHPPM Bldg E-1950 Aberdeen Proving Ground MD 21010-5403 E-mail: david.sliney@att.net.

SLINGER, MICHAEL JEFFERY, law library director; b. Pitts., Apr. 12, 1956; s. Maurice and Mary Helen (Kengerski) S.; m. Cheryl Blaney, Apr. 19, 1980; children: Rebecca, Sarah. BA, U. Pitts., 1978; M Librianship, U. S.C., 1979; JD, Duquesne U., 1984. Reference libr. Duquesne U. Sch. Law, Pitts., 1983-84; rsch. libr. U. Notre Dame (Ind.) Sch. Law, 1984-85, head rsch. svcs., 1985-86, assoc. dir. pub. svcs., 1986-90; law libr. dir., assoc. prof. law Suffolk U. Sch. Law, Boston, 1990-93, law libr. dir., prof. law, 1994-95; law libr. dir., prof. law, assoc. dean Cleve. State U., 1995—. Contbr. articles to profl. jours., chpt. to book. Mem. ABA, ALA, Am. Assn. Law Librs. (vice char, chair-elect acad. spl. interest sect., 2004-), Am. Assn. Law Schs. (exec. bd. sect. on law librs. 1993-94), New Eng. Law Libr. Consortium (treas. 1992-95), Ohio Regional Assn. Law Librs. (v.p. 1987-88, pres. 1988-89, Pres. award 1989). Avocations: reading, sports, family. Office: Cleveland-Marshall Coll Law Law Libr 1801 Euclid Ave Cleveland OH 44115-2223 Office Phone: 216-687-3547. Business E-Mail: michael.slinger@law.csuohio.edu.

SLIPMAN, CURTIS W. rehabilitation medicine physician; b. Pittsburgh, Okla., Oct. 10, 1958; s. Max Joseph and Betty Lubel Slipman; 1 child, Jared Clay Slipman. BA, SUNY, Stony Brook, 1979; MD with honors, Baylor U., 1983. Resident Columbia Presbyn. Ctr., N.Y.C., 1983-86; chief resident, chronic pain and sports Miss. Meth. Rehab. Ctr., Jackson, 1986-88; pvt. practice, 1988-92; dir., U. Pa. Spine Ctr. Hosp. U. Pa., Phila., 1992—; asst. prof. rehab. medicine U. Pa., Phila., 1992—. Named Top Doc, Phila. Mag., 1994, Best Docotr in Am., 96. Fellow Internat. Assn. Study of Pain; mem. Internat. Injection Soc., Am. Acad. Phys. Medicine and Rehab. (Rosanthal lectr. 1999), Am. Pain Soc., Am. Acad. Physiatric Assn. Spine Sports and Occupl. Rehab. (bd. dirs. 1993-97, nom. com. 1998), Phila. Coll. Physicians. Home: 529 Pine St Philadelphia PA 19106-4110 Office: Hosp U Pa 3400 Spruce St Philadelphia PA 19104-4206

SLIPSAGER, HENRIK C. human resources specialist; CFO ISS Internat. Svc. Sys., Inc., 1984-85, exec. v.p., COO, 1985-88, pres., CEO, 1988-94; exec. v.p. janitorial svcs. Am. Bldg. Maintenance Industries Inc., San Francisco, 1994-99, sr. v.p., 1997-99, pres. Am. Bldg. Maintenance Co., 1999-2000, CEO, pres., 2000—. Office: ABM Industries 160 Pacific Ave San Francisco CA 94111

SLIVE, SEYMOUR, museum director, fine arts educator; b. Chgo., Sept. 15, 1920; s. Daniel and Sonia (Rapoport) S.; m. Zoya Gregorevna Sandomirsky, June 29, 1946; children: Katherine, Alexander, Sarah. AB, U. Chgo., 1943, PhD, 1952; MA (hon.), Harvard U., 1958, Oxford (Eng.) U., 1972. Instr. fine arts Oberlin (Ohio) Coll., 1950-51; chmn. art dept. Pomona (Calif.) Coll., 1952-54; mem. faculty Harvard U., Cambridge, Mass., 1954—, prof. fine arts, 1961—, Gleason prof. fine arts, 1973-91, Gleason prof. fine arts emeritus, 1991—, chmn. dept. fine arts, 1968-71, dir. Fogg Art Mus., 1975-82; Elizabeth and John Moors Cabot dir. emeritus Harvard art museums, 1982. Exchange prof. Leningrad (USSR) U., 1961; Ryerson lectr. Yale U., 1962; Slade prof. Oxford (Eng.) U., 1972-73 Author: Rembrandt and His Critics, 1630-1730, 1953, The Rembrandt Bible, 1959, Catalogue of the Paintings of Frans Hals, 1962, Drawings of Rembrandt, 1965, (with Jakob Rosenberg and E.H. ter Kuile) Dutch Art and Architecture 1600-1800, 2nd edit., 1978, Rembrandt's Drawings, 1965, Frans Hals, 3 vols., 1970-74, Jacob van Ruisdael, 1981, Frans Hals, 1989, Dutch Painting: 1600-1800, 1995, 2d edit., 1998, Jacob van Ruisdael: A Complete Catalogue of His Paintings, Drawings and Etchings, 2001. Trustee Solomon R. Guggenheim Found., 1978—, Norton Simon Mus., 1989-91; bd. dirs. Burlington mag. Found., 1987—. Lt. (j.g.) USNR, 1943-46, PTO. Decorated officer Order Orange Nassau Netherlands, 1962; Fulbright fellow Netherlands, 1951-52; Guggenheim fellow, 1956-57, 78-79; Fulbright research scholar Utrecht (Netherlands) U., 1959-60 Fellow Am. Acad. Arts and Scis.; mem. Karel van Mander Soc. (hon.), Coll. Art Assn. (dir. 1958-62, 65-69), Renaissance Soc., Dutch Soc. Scis. (fgn. mem.), Brit. Acad. (corr. fellow). Office: Harvard U Sackler Art Museum Cambridge MA 02138

SLJIVIC-SIMSIC, BILJANA B. Slavic and Baltic languages educator; b. Belgrade, Yugoslavia, Jan. 20, 1933; came to U.S., 1962; d. Branko M. and Radoyka (Pesic) S.; m. Branislav S. Simsic, Jan. 21, 1953 (div. 1963); 1 child, Violet Ljubica. Diploma, U. Belgrade, 1955; MA, Harvard U., 1963, PhD, 1966. Asst. lectr. U. Belgrade, 1957-62; vis. lectr. U. Clermont-Ferrand, France, 1959-61, UCLA, 1964-65, vis. asst. prof., 1965-66; asst. prof. U. Ky., Lexington, 1966-67, U. Pa., Phila., 1967-73; vis. lectr. Princeton (N.J.) U., 1967-69; assoc. prof. U. Ill., Chgo., 1973-86, head of dept., 1981—96, prof. dept. Slavic and Baltic langs. and lit., 1986—. Exch. prof. U. London and Cambridge (Eng.) U., 1989—90, U. Amsterdam, 2000, 02; cons., panelist U.S. Dept. Edn., Fulbright Fellowship, Washington; sr. writer Ohio State U., summers, 1983, 84, 85, 86, 88. Co-author: Serbo-Croatian-English Dictionary, 1972 (grant), Judeo-Spanish Ballads in Bosnia, 1972 (grant); author: Serbo-Crotian, Just For You, 1985 (grant 1983-84); major author 8 vols. of Serbo-Crotian Textbooks for Individualized Studies, 1983-88. Grantee, U. Pa., Phila., 1972; scholar, Radcliffe Coll., 1962—63, Harvard U., 1963—64. Mem. Am. Assn. for the Avancement of Slavic Studies(AAASS), N.Am. Soc. Serbian Studies (sec.-treas. 1976-82, pres. 1982-84, mem. exec. bd. 1984-86), Assn. Serbian Writers, Chgo. Hort. Soc., Harvard and Radcliffe Clubs Chgo. Serbian Orthodox. Avocations: photography, travel, grandchildren, gardening. Office: U Ill Chgo Dept Slavic & Baltic Langs & Lit 601 S Morgan St Chicago IL 60607-1716 Office Phone: 312-996-4412. Business E-Mail: bibi@uic.edu.

SLOAN, ALBERT, college president; b. Atlanta, Sept. 24, 1942; s. Albert John Hicks and Addie Cannon S.; m. Emma Lillian Lee, Aug. 29, 1970; children: Ashaki Nicole, Ashante Denise, Alescia Alexandria. BA, Albany State U., 1965; MDiv, Interdenominational Theol., Ctr., Atlanta, 1968; JD, Miles Law Sch., 1982; DDiv, Faith Grant Coll., 1998; LLD, Tex. Coll., 1999. Counselor Upward Bound Program/Ala. State U., Montgomery, 1969-71; team tchr. Huntsville (Ala.) Space Ctr., 1974-75; prof. religion and philosophy Miles Coll., Fairfield, 1972-89, asst. to the pres., 1972-73, dean of chapel, 1971-89, dean of students, 1987-89, pres., 1989—. Pres. Fairfield Bd. Edn., 1978-93, Birmingham Civil Rights Inst.; mem. Jud. Coun. C.M.E. Ch., Birmingham; assoc. justice C.M.E. Ch. Religious editor: Atlanta Enquirer, 1969-70; contbr. articles to religious publs. Mem. Birmingham Personnel Bd., Leadership Birmingham, 1992—, Fairfield C. of C., 1992—. Recipient Nat. Hist. Preservation award Ala. Hist. Commn., 1994. Mem. Nat. Bar Assn., Omega Psi Phi, Phi Delta Kappa, Delta Theta Pi. Avocations: swimming, singing, public speaking. Office: Miles Coll PO Box 3800 Birmingham AL 35208-0800

SLOAN, ALLAN HERBERT, journalist; b. Bklyn., Nov. 27, 1944; s. Samuel and Doris (Shanblott) S.; m. Nancy Nolan, June 29, 1969; children: Sharon R., Susan M., Dena A. BA, Bklyn. Coll., 1966; MS, Columbia U., 1967. Reporter Charlotte (N.C.) Observer, 1968-72, Detroit Free Press, 1972-79; assoc. editor, staff writer Forbes Mag., N.Y.C., 1979-81; staff writer Money Mag., N.Y.C., 1982-84; sr. editor Forbes Mag., N.Y.C., 1984-88; columnist N.Y. Newsday, N.Y.C., 1989-95; Wall St. editor Newsweek Mag., N.Y.C., 1995—. Author: Three Plus One Equals Billions: The Bendix-Martin Marietta War, 1982. Recipient Loeb award for fin. journalism Loeb Found., 1974, 84, 91, 93, 98, Hancock award for fin. journalism Hancock Found., 1992, Loeb Lifetime Achievement award, 2001, Disting. Achievement award Am. Bus. Editors and Writers, 2001. Office: Newsweek 251 W 57th St New York NY 10019-1802

SLOAN, DANIEL KAY, electrical engineer; b. Walla Walla, Wash., Oct. 20, 1944; s. James Lester and Bertha Louise (Ulstrup) S.; m. Janice Kay Christensen, Jan. 31, 1965 (dec.); m. Patrica Ann Purdy, Feb. 8, 2003. BSEE, Wash. State U., 1967. Product line controls engr. Beloit (Wis.) Corp., 1967-72, product line mgr.-controls, 1972-79; elec. engr. U & I Inc., Kennewick, Wash., 1979-81; elec. project engr. Boise-Cascade, Wallula, Wash., 1981-86; sr. elec. project engr. Simpson Tacoma (Wash.) Kraft Co., 1986—. Staff sgt. U.S. Air Guard, 1967-73. Mem. IEEE, Instrumentation, Systems and Automation Soc., Elks. Office: Simpson Tacoma Kraft Co 801 Portland Ave Tacoma WA 98421-3098

SLOAN, DAVID EDWARD, retired finance company executive; b. Winnipeg, Man., Can., Mar. 29, 1922; s. David and Annie Maud (Gorvin) S.; m. Kathleen Lowry Craig, Dec. 26, 1947; children: Pamela Jane, John David, Kathleen Anne. B.Commerce, U. Man., 1942. With Monarch Life Assurance Co., Winnipeg, 1946-47, Can. Pacific Ltd., 1947-88, treas., 1969-88; pres. and chief exec. officer Can. Pacific Securities Ltd., 1985-88. Mem. adv. com. Can. Pension Plan, Can. Govt., 1967-76, chmn., 1974-76. Lt. Royal Can. Army Service Corps, 1942-45. Mem. Fin. Exec. Inst. Can. (past pres. Montreal chpt.), Toronto Soc. Fin. Analysts, Soc. Internat. Treas. (internat. chmn. 1985-86, mem. coun. advisors 1978-87), Assn. Investment Mgmt. and Rsch., U. Man. Alumni Assn., The Toronto Hunt Club. Mem. United Ch. Can. Home: 316 Rosemary Rd Toronto ON Canada M5P 3E3

SLOAN, DENISE MAY, psychology educator; d. William Sloan; m. Brian P. Marx, Feb. 28, 1967; 1 child, Colin Sloan Marx. PhD, Case Western Res. U., 1998. Lic. clin. psychology Pa. Rsch. fellow U. of Fla., Gainesville, 1998—2000; asst. prof. Temple U., Phila., 2000—. Contbr. articles to profl. jours. (Scholar award, 2000). Recipient rsch. grant, Alcohol Beverage Med. Rsch. Found., 2004—06. Mem.: Soc. for Psychophysiological Rsch. (membership co-chair 2002—04), Soc. for a Sci. of Clin. Psychology (sec.-treas. 2002—04). Office: Temple Univ Dept Psychology Weiss Hall 1701 13th St Philadelphia PA 19122 Personal E-mail: dsloan@temple.edu. E-mail: dsloan@temple.edu

SLOAN, DONNIE ROBERT, JR., lawyer; b. Nashville, July 24, 1946; s. Donnie R. Sr. and Mary Catharine (Willis) S. BS in Indsl. Engring., Ga. Inst. Tech, 1968; JD cum laude, U. Ga., 1971; LLM, Harvard U., 1975. Bar: Ga. 1971, U.S. Dist. Ct. (no. dist.) Ga. 1971, U.S. Ct. Appeals (11th cir.). Atty. Southwire Co., Carrollton, Ga., 1971-74; assoc., ptnr. Hyatt & Rhoads, P.C., Atlanta, 1975-89; pvt. practice, 1989-96; ptnr. Davidson, Fuller & Sloan, LLP, 1996—. Instr. legal rsch. U. Ga., Athens, 1970-71; instr. music law Ga. State U., Atlanta, 1976. Mem. editl. bd. Ga. Law Rev., 1969-71. Treas. Ga. Wheelchair Athletic Assn., Atlanta, 1981-84; pres., treas. Dixie Wheelchair Athletic Assn., Atlanta, 1984-87. Recipient Appreciation award Ga. Wheelchair Sports and Recreation Assn., 1979; named one of Outstanding Young Men of Am., 1981; named to Dixie Wheelchair Athletic Assn. Hall of Fame, 1990. Mem. Am. Judicature Soc., Phi Kappa Phi, Alpha Phi Mu, Ga. Tech. Club, Harvard Club. Presbyterian. Avocations: skiing, jogging, swimming. Home: 820 Saddlehill Rd Roswell GA 30075 Office: 11330 Lakefield Dr Ste 250 Duluth GA 30097-1578 E-mail: drsloan@dfslaw.com.

SLOAN, EARLE DENDY, JR., chemical engineering educator; b. Seneca, S.C., Apr. 23, 1944; s. Earle Dendy and Sarah (Bellotte) S.; m. Marjorie Nilson, Sept. 7, 1968; children: Earle Dendy III, John Mark. BSChemE, Clemson U., 1965, MSChemE, 1972, PhD in Chem. Engring., 1974. Engr. Du Pont, Chattanooga, 1965-66, Seaford, Del., 1966-67, cons. Parkersburg, W.Va., 1967-68, sr. engr. Camden, S.C., 1968-70; postdoctoral fellow Rice U., 1975; prof. chem. engring. Colo. Sch. Mines, Golden, 1976—, dir. Ctr. for Rsch. on Hydrates and Other Solids, 1990—, Gaylord and Phyllis Weaver dist. prof. chem. engring., 1992—. Inaugural pres. faculty senate Colo. Sch. Mines, 1989-90, disting. lectr., 1997-98, appointed senator, 1998; Tokyo Electric Power Co. chair Keio U., Japan, 1996; Erskine fellow U. Canterbury, Christchurch, N.Z., 2002. Author: Clathrate Hydrates of Natural Gases, 1990, 2d edit., 1998, Hydrate Engineering, 2000; chmn. pub. bd. Chem. Engring. Edn., 1990—. Scoutmaster local Cub Scouts, 1978-81; elder Presbyn. Ch., Golden, Colo., 1977-79, 92-94; elder Ctrl. Presbyn. Ch., Denver, 1999—. Recipient Donald L. Katz award for rsch., Gas Processors Assn. Fellow AIChE (chmn. area Ia thermodynamics and transport 1990-93); mem. Am. Soc. for Engring. Edn. (chmn. ednl. rsch. methods divsn. 1983-85, chmn. chem. engring. divsn. 1984), Am. Chem. Soc., Soc. Petroleum Engrs. (Disting. Lectr. 1996-97). Avocations: bicycling, cello, philosophy. Office: Colo Sch of Mines Ctr for Hydrate Rsch Golden CO 80401 Personal E-mail: edendysloan@comcast.net. Business E-Mail: esloan@mines.edu.

SLOAN, FRANK ALLEN, economist, educator; b. Greensboro, N.C., Aug. 15, 1942; s. Harry Benjamin and Edith (Vortrefflich) Sloan; m. Paula Jane Rackoff, June 22, 1969; children: Elyse Valerie, Richard Matthew. AB, Oberlin Coll., 1964; PhD, Harvard U., 1969. Rsch. economist Rand Corp., Santa Monica, Calif., 1968—71; asst. prof. econs. U. Fla., Gainesville, 1971—73, assoc. prof., 1973—76; prof. econs. Vanderbilt U., Nashville, 1976—84, Centennial prof. econs., 1984—93, chmn. dept., 1986—89; J. Alexander McMahon health policy and mgmt., prof. econs. Duke U., Durham, NC, 1993—, prof. health policy and mgmt., 1994—, dir. Ctr. for Health Policy, Law and Mgmt., 1998—. Dir. Health Policy Ctr. Vanderbilt U. Inst. Pub. Policy Studies, 1976—93; mem. Inst. Medicine, Washington, 1982—, mem. prospective payment rev. commns., 1996—; mem. Nat. Coun. Health Care Tech., Washington, 1979—81, Nat. Allergy and Infectious Disease Coun., Washington, 1971—74; cons. adv. coun. Social Security, Washington, 1983. Co-author: Private Physicians and Public Programs, 1978, Hospital Labor Markets, 1980, Insurance, Regulation and Hospital Costs, 1980, Uncompensated Hospital Care: Rights and Responsibilities, 1986, Insuring Medical Malpractice, 1991. Mem.: Western Econ. Assn., Soc. Econ. Assn., Am. Econ. Assn. Office: Duke University Ctr for Health Policy PO Box 90253 Durham NC 27708-0253

SLOAN, F(RANK) BLAINE, law educator; b. Geneva, Nebr., Jan. 3, 1920; s. Charles Porter and Lillian Josephine (Stiefer) S.; m. Patricia Sand, Sept. 2, 1944; children: DeAnne Sloan Riddle, Michael Blaine, Charles Porter. AB with high distinction, U. Nebr., 1942, LLB cum laude, 1946; LLM in Internat. Law, Columbia U., 1947. Bar: Nebr. 1946, N.Y. 1947. Asst. to spl. counsel Intergovtl. Com. for Refugees, 1947; mem. Office Legal Affairs UN Secretariat, N.Y.C., 1948—78; gen. counsel Relief and Works Agy. Palestine Refugees, Beirut, 1958—60; dir. gen. legal divsn., dep. to legal counsel UN Legal Office, N.Y.C., 1966—78, rep. of Sec. Gen. to UN Commn. Internat. Trade Law, 1969—78, rep. to Legal Sub-com. on Outer Space, 1966—78; rep. UN Del. Vietnam Conf., Paris, 1973, UN Conf. on Carriage of Goods by Sea, Hamburg, 1978; prof. internat. law orgn. and water law Pace U., 1979—87, prof. emeritus, 1987—. Law lectr. Blaine Sloan Internat., 1988—. Author: United Nations General Assembly Resolutions in Our Changing World, 1991; contbr. articles to legal jours. Cons. UN Office of Legal Affairs, 1983-84, UN Water Resources Br., 1983; supervisory com., Pace Peace Ctr.; legal advisor Korean Missions, 1951, 53, UNTSO, Jerusalem, 1952, UNEF I, Gaza, 1957-58; prin. sec.UN Commn. to investigate Sec.-Gen. Hammarskjold's crash, 1961-62. Navigator AC, U.S. Army, 1943-46 Decorated Air medal. Mem. Am. Soc. Internat. Law, Am. Acad. Polit. and Social Sci., Am. Arbitration Assn., Order of Coif, Phi Beta Kappa, Phi Alpha Delta (hon.). Republican. Roman Catholic. Home: HCR-68 Box 72 Foxwind-Forbes Park Fort Garland CO 81133 Office: 78 N Broadway White Plains NY 10603-3710 also: 375 Soubry Pl Forbes Park Fort Garland CO 81133

SLOAN, HERBERT ELIAS, physician, surgeon; b. Clarksburg, W.Va., Oct. 10, 1914; s. Herbert Elias and Luella (Dye) S.; m. Doris Edwards, May 3, 1943; children: Herbert, Ann, Elizabeth, John, Robert. AB, Washington and Lee U., 1936; MD, Johns Hopkins U., 1940. Diplomate Am. Bd. Surgery, Am. Bd. Thoracic Surgery (bd. dirs. 1966-86, v.p. 1971-73, sec.-treas. 1973-86). Resident in surgery Johns Hopkins Hosp., 1941-44; instr. dept. surgery Johns Hopkins U., 1943-44; resident in thoracic surgery U. Mich. Hosp., Ann Arbor, 1947-49, instr. thoracic surgery, 1949-50; asst. prof. U. Mich., Ann Arbor, 1950-53, assoc. prof., 1953-62, prof. surgery, 1962-87, head sect. thoracic surgery, 1970-85; chief clin. affairs U. Mich. Hosps., Ann Arbor, 1982-86, med. dir. operating room, 1986-87, prof. emeritus surgery, 1987—; med. dir. managed health care U. Mich., Ann Arbor, 1989-96, Herbert Sloan Collegiate Professorship in cardiac surgery, 2003. Mem. staff VA Hosp., Ann Arbor, 1953—, cons., 1968—. Author: The American Board of Thoracic Surgery: A Fifty Year Perspective, 1998, (with Marvin M. Kirsh) Blunt Chest Trauma, General Principles of Management, 1977; editor Annals of Thoracic Surgery,

1969-85; contbr. (with Marvin M. Kirsh) chpts. to books, articles to profl. jours. Served to maj. M.C. U.S. Army, 1944-47. Recipient Bruce Douglas award in thoracic diseases, 1974, Med. Alumni Svc. award Johns Hopkins Sch. Medicine, 1973, Disting. Svc. award Johns Hopkins U. Sch. Medicine, 1983, Disting. Svc. award Mich. Med. Ctr. Alumni Soc., 1988, Herbert Sloan Collegiate Prof. Cardiac Surgery award, 2003. Mem. ACS, Am. Surg. Assn., Am. Heart Assn., Am. Assn. Thoracic Surgery (pres. 1979-80), Soc. Thoracic Surgeons (pres. 1974-75, Disting. Svc. award 1981), Central Surg. Assn., Soc. Univ. Surgeons, So. Thoracic Surgery Assn. (hon.), Thoracic Soc. Gt. Britain (hon.), John Alexander Soc., Western Thoracic Surg. Assn. (hon.), Cardiovascular Surgeons Club, Detroit Heart Club, Am. Trudeau Soc., Mich. Heart Assn., Mich. Trudeau Soc., Am. Acad. Pediatrics, Soc. Vascular Surgery, Frederick A. Coller Surg. Soc., U. Mich. Med. Alumni Soc. (Disting. Svc. award 1988), U. Mich. James Angell Soc., Rsch. Club, Phi Beta Kappa, Alpha Omega Alpha, Omicron Delta Kappa, Sigma Xi. Clubs: Ann Arbor Figure Skating (pres. 1965-66). Home: 471 Barton North Dr Ann Arbor MI 48105-1017 Office: Taubman Health Care Ctr Sect Thoracic Surgery PO Box 344 Ann Arbor MI 48106-0344 E-mail: hsloan@umich.edu.

SLOAN, HUGH WALTER, JR., automotive executive; b. Princeton, N.J., Nov. 1, 1940; s. Hugh Walter and Elizabeth (Johnson) Sloan; m. Deborah Louise Murray, Feb. 20, 1971; children: Melissa, Peter, Jennifer, William. AB in History with honors, Princeton U., 1963. Staff asst. to Pres. U.S. White Ho., Washington, 1969-71; treas. Pres. Nixon's Re-election Campaign, Washington, 1971; spl. asst. to pres. Budd Co., Troy, Mich., 1973-74, exec. asst. internat., 1974-77, mgr. corp. mktg., 1977-79; pres., gen. mgr. Budd Can. Inc., Kitchener, Canada, 1979-85; pres. automotive Woodbridge Group, Troy, 1985-98, dep. chmn., 1998—. Bd. dirs. Woodbridge Foam Corp., Mfrs. Life Ins. Co., Wescast Industries, Virtek Vision Internat. Inc. Trustee Cranbrook Ednl. Cmty.; bd. dirs. Cmty. House, Beaumont Found., Deerwood Found. Lt. USNR, 1963—65. Recipient Outstanding Bus. Leader award, Wilfrid Laurier U., 1987. Mem.: Automotive Market Rsch. Coun. (past pres.), Originial Equipment Suppliers Assn. (past dir.), Am. Soc. Employers (dir., past chmn., pres.), Automotive Parts Mfrs. Assn. (past chmn.), World Pres. Orgn., Bloomfield Hills (Mich.) Country Club. Republican. Office: Woodbridge Group 2500 Meijer Dr Troy MI 48084-7146

SLOAN, JAMES PARK, novelist, biographer, educator, investment adviser; b. Greenwood, S.C., Sept. 22, 1944; s. James Park and Alice Catherine (Gaines) S.; m. Jeanette Carol Pasin, July 25, 1968 (div. 1987);; children: Eugene Blakely, Anna Jeanette; m. Athena Dadjou Uslander, June 2, 2001. BA, Harvard U., 1968. Mem. faculty U. Ill., Chgo., 1972—, assoc. prof. English, 1976-94, prof., 1994—, chmn. program for writers, 1976-79, 89-93. Lectr. in field, 1972— Author: War Games, 1971 (Best First Novel award Gt. Lakes Colls. Assn. 1971), (Peggy McPhaul award Midwestern Writers Assn. 1971), The Case History of Comrade V, 1972 (Friends of Lit. award 1972), The Last Cold-War Cowboy, 1987, Jerzy Kosinski: A Biography, 1996 (biography award Soc. Midland Authors 1996); also book revs.; contbg. editor: Am. Pen Quar., 1974—. Served with USAR, 1964-67, Vietnam. Decorated Army Commendation medal; recipient Cliff Dwellers award Chgo., 1977 Mem. PEN Midwest (bd. dirs. 1987—, chmn. 1993—). Office: U Ill Dept English 601 S Morgan St Chicago IL 60607 E-mail: jim@frugaladviser.com.

SLOAN, JEANETTE PASIN, artist; b. Chgo., Mar. 18, 1946; d. Antonio and Anna (Baggio) Pasin; children: Eugene Blakely, Anna Jeanette. BFA, Marymount Coll., Tarrytown, N.Y., 1967; MFA, U. Chgo., 1969. Exhibited in one-woman shows G.W. Einstein Gallery, N.Y.C., 1977-85, Landfall Press Gallery, Chgo., N.Y.C., 1978, 87, Roger Ramsay Gallery, Chgo., 1987, 89, 92, Tatischeff Gallery, Santa Monica, Calif., 1989, Steven Scott Gallery, Balt., 1989, Butters Gallery, Portland, Oreg., 1989, 91, 94, 96, 99, Tatistcheff & Co. Inc., 1995, 97, 99, Ouartet Editions, N.Y.C., 1995, Elliot Smith Gallery, St. Louis, 1994, Peltz Gallery, Milw., 1994-95, 99, Gerhard Wurzer Gallery, Houston, 1997, 2001, Cline Fine Arts Gallery, Santa Fe, 1998, 2001, J. Cacciola Gallery, N.Y.C., 2004; represented in permanent collections Art Mus. Chgo., Cleve. Mus. Art, Ill. State Mus., Indpls. Mus. Art, Canton (Ohio) Art Inst., Ball State Bus., Mpls., Inst. Art, Fogg Mus. Harvard U., Yale U. Art Gallery, Snite Mus. U. Notre Dame, Met. Mus. Art, N.Y.C., Herbert F. Johnson Mus. Cornell U., Ithaca, N.Y., Valpariaso (Ind.) Mus. Art, Nat. Gallery Art, Washington; exhibited in group shows; subject of book by Gerritt Henry, Jeanette Pasin Sloan, 2000; subject of book, The Prints of Jeanette Pasin Sloan, by James Yood, 2003. Studio: 301 Loma Arisco Santa Fe NM 87501 Personal E-mail: jeanettepasin@aol.com.

SLOAN, JERRY (GERALD EUGENE SLOAN), professional basketball coach; b. McLeansboro, Ill., Mar. 28, 1942; m. Bobbye (dec. 2004); 3 children: Kathy, Brian, Holly. Student, Evansville (Ind.) Coll., 1965. Professional basketball player, Baltimore, 1965-66, Chicago Bulls, NBA, 1966-76; head coach Chicago Bulls, 1979-82; scout Utah Jazz, NBA, Salt Lake City, 1983-84, asst. coach, 1984-88, head coach, 1988—. Player 2 NBA All-Star games; named to NBA All-Defensive First Team, 1969, 72, 74, 75. Office: c/o Utah Jazz Delta Ctr 301 W South Temple Salt Lake City UT 84101-1216

SLOAN, JUDI C. former physical education educator; b. Kansas City, Mo., July 17, 1944; d. Oscar H. Wilde and Florance (Janes) Wilde Graupner; m. Richard J. Sloan; children: Blake, Tracy. BS in Phys. Edn., No. Ill. U., 1966, postgrad.; MS in Phys. Edn., Ind. U., 1970; postgrad., U. Ill., DePaul U., Loyola U., Nat. Louis U. Tchr. phys. edn., coach Niles West High Sch., Skokie, Ill., 1966-99. Former coach gymnastics, tennis; coach cross-country; coop. tchr.; creator, dir. Galibo Gymnastics Show, 1968-75; founder, co-chair staff wellness com., Niles Township Sch. Dist., 1988—, curriculum coun., 1988-91; creator phys. mgmt. course, sophomore health and fitness program, evening children's, summer girls' gymnastics programs; co-dir. Indian Cross Country Invitational, Niles West Gymnastics Invitational; adv. com. cross country Ill. High Sch. Assn. Recipient All-Am. High Sch. Gymnastics Coach award U.S. Gymnastics Fedn., 1981, award of Honor Nat. Sch. Pub. Rels. Assn., 1990, Ill. Disting. Educator award, 1992; Named Ill. Tchr. Yr., 1992-93. Mem. AAHPERD, Am. Fedn. Tchrs., Nat. Assn. Secondary Physical Edn., Nat. Coaches Fedn., Ill. Fedn. Tchrs., Ill. Assn. Health, Phys. Edn., Recreation, Dance (Outstanding Phys. Edn. award 1986), Nat. Assn. Girls' and Women's Sports, Ill. Track and Cross Country Coaches Assn., Ill. Girls' Coaches Assn. Office: Niles West High Sch 5701 Oakton St Skokie IL 60077-2681

SLOAN, L. LAWRENCE, publishing executive; b. N.Y.C., 1947; Grad., UCLA. Chmn. Price Stern Sloan, Inc., West Hollywood, Calif. Pres. Sloan Co. Office: 11150 W Olympic Blvd Los Angeles CA 90064-1817

SLOAN, LUCINDA HECK, music educator; b. Lakewood, Ohio, June 13, 1950; d. Stephen Wendell and Margaret Catherin Heck; m. Dana Hugh Sloan, Sept. 5, 1971; children: Ryan Todd, Ashley Kristin. MusB, U. Ill., 1971; MA, Radford U., 1973; D of Music, U. Ill., 1985. Prof. music Midland Luth. Coll., Fremont, Nebr., 1980—; instr. music Dana Coll., Blair, 1981—97, U. Nebr., Omaha, 1989—92. Artist Opera Omaha; soloist Omaha Symphony; recitalist. Author: The Influence of Rhetoric on Rameau's Solo Vocal Cantatas and Tratise of 1772, 1990. Fellow, Radford U.; scholar, Ohio State U., U. Ill. Mem.: Nat. Assn. Tchrs. Music.

SLOAN, MACEO KENNEDY, lawyer, investment company executive; b. Phila., Oct. 18, 1949; s. Maceo Archibald and Charlotte (Kennedy) S.; m. Melva Iona Wilder, July 3, 1971; children: Maceo S., Malia K. BA, Morehouse Coll., 1971; MBA with honors, Ga. State U., 1973; JD with honors, N.C. Cen. U., 1979. CFA. Investment analyst N.C. Mut. Life Ins. Co., Durham, 1973-77, asst. to treas., 1977-78, asst. v.p., 1978-83, treas., 1983-85, v.p., treas., 1985-86; pres. NCM Devel. Group subs. N.C. Mut. Life Ins. Co., Durham, 1985-86; of counsel Moore & Van Allen, Durham, 1985-86; pres., CEO NCM Capital Mgmt. Group, Inc., Durham, 1986-91, chmn., pres., CEO, 1991—, Sloan Fin. Group, Inc., Durham, N.C., 1991—. Adj. vis. prof. N.C. Ctrl. U., Durham, 1978-86, workshop rev. leader Study Seminar for Fin. Analysts, Windsor, Ont., Can., 1980—; bd. dirs. Mechanics & Farmers Bank, Durham, 1979—, chmn. trust com., 1979-93; networking leader Black Enterprise mag., 1987—; bd. trustees Coll. Retirement Equities Fund, 1991—, ERISA Adv. Coun. U.S. Dept. Labor, 1991-93; bd. dirs. News and Observer Pub. Co. Bd. dirs. United Way, Durham, 1980-87, Urban Ministries, Durham, 1983-88, Internat. Found. Edn. and Self Help, 1993—, N.C. Air Cargo Airport Authority, 1993—; bd. visitors N.C. Ctrl. U. Sch. Law, Durham, 1979-86, U. N.C., Chapel Hill, 1990— Recipient Outstanding Svc. award Better Bus. Bur., 1980, Freedom Guard award Durham Jaycees, 1982, Outstanding Leadership award United Way Durham, 1984, Resolution in Appreciation Durham City Coun., 1983. Fellow Life Mgmt. Inst.; mem. ABA, Fin. Analysts Fedn., N.C. Soc. Fin. Analysts (v.p. 1977-78), N.C. State Bar Assn., Durham C. of C., Nat. Investment Mgrs. Assn. (founder, chmn.), Nat. Assn. Securities Profls., Treyburn Country Club (Durham), Univ. Club (Durham), The George Town (Washington). Democrat. Baptist. Avocations: reading, jogging, weight training, golf, tennis. Home: 24000 S Lowell Rd Bahama NC 27503-9693 Office: Sloan Fin Group Inc 103 W Main St Fl 4 Durham NC 27701-3638 also: NCM Mgmt/Sloan Financial 2634 Durham-Chapel Hill Blvd Ste 206 Durham NC 27707-1958

SLOAN, MARY JEAN, retired media specialist; b. Lakeland, Fla., Nov. 29, 1927; d. Marion Wilder and Elba (Jinks) Sloan. BS, Peabody Coll., Nashville, 1949; MLS, Atlanta U., 1978, SLS, 1980. Cert. libr. media specialist. Music dir. Pinecrest Sch., Tampa, Fla., 1949-50, Polk County Schs., Bartow, Fla., 1950-54; pvt. music tchr. Lakeland, 1954-58; tchr. Clayton County Schs., Jonesboro, Ga., 1958-59; media specialist Eastualley Sch., Marietta, Ga., 1959-89; ret., 1989. Coord. conf. Ga. Libr. Media Dept., Jekyll Island, 1982-83, sec., Atlanta, 1982-83, com. chmn. ethnic conf., Atlanta, 1978, pres., 1984-85, state pres., 1985-86; program chmn. Ga. Media Orgns. Conf, Jekyll Island, 1988. Contbr. to bibliographies. Recipient Walter Bell award Ga. Assn. Instrnl. Tech., 1988, Disting. Svc. award, 1991. Mem. ALA (del. 1984, 85, 90), NEA, Southeastern Libr. Assn., Am. Assn. Sch. Librs., Soc. for Sch. Librs., Internat., Ga. Assn. Educators (polit. action com. 1983), Beta Phi Mu, Phi Delta Kappa. Republican. Methodist. Home: 797 Yorkshire Rd NE Atlanta GA 30306-3264

SLOAN, MICHAEL DANA, information systems specialist; b. Santa Monica, Calif., Sept. 30, 1960; s. Avery and Beverly Rae (Krantz) S.; m. Barbara Rogers; 1 child, Ashley Harrison. BS in Bus. Adminstrn., Calif. State U., Northridge, 1983; MBA, Pepperdine U., 1987. Programmer/analyst TICOR, Inc., L.A., 1979-80; data processing analyst Deluxe Check Printers, Inc., Chatsworth, Calif., 1980-83; fin. systems analyst Wismer & Assocs., Inc., Canoga Park, Calif., 1983-84; sr. systems analyst Coast Savs. & Loan, Granada Hills, Calif., 1984-86; microcomputer systems specialist Litton Industries, Woodland Hills, Calif., 1986-87; systems mgr., info. resources mgr. TRW, Inc.- Space and Def., Redondo Beach, Calif., 1987-93; project mgr. Health Net, Woodland Hills, 1993-95; mgr. fin. and sales systems Merisel Ams. Inc., El Segundo, Calif., 1995-97; sr. mgr. web tech. & devel. Ingram Micro Inc., Santa Ana, Calif., 2000—01; with Ptnrs. Cons. Svcs., Inc., Laguna Beach, Calif., 2001—02, Consulting Solutions, Inc., Calabasas, Calif., 2002—. Cons. Data Most, Inc., Chatsworth, 1982—83, Home Savs. & Loan, North Hollywood, Calif., 1987, Micro Tech., L.A., 1987, TRW, Inc.-Space and Def., Redondo Beach, Calif., 1993—2000, Pacificare Health Systems, Inc., 1997, Nissan North America (formerly Nissan Motor Corp., USA), 1998—99, Prosum Info. Techs., Inc., 2000—01, Am. Honda Motors, Inc., 1999—2000, Toyota Fin. Svcs., 2001—02, Warner Bros. Studios, 2002—. Mem. IEEE Computer Soc., Salle Gascon Fencing Club, U.S. Fencing Assn., Delta Sigma Pi. Republican. Avocations: fencing, comedy improvisation, tennis, volleyball, travel, sailing. Office: Consulting Solutions Inc 23901 Calabasas Rd Ste 2009 Calabasas CA 91302 Office Phone: 818-977-4265.

SLOAN, O. TEMPLE, JR., automotive equipment executive; b. Sanford, N.C., Feb. 21, 1939; s. Orris Temple and Thelma (Hamilton) S.; m. Carol Carson; children: C. Carson Henline, O. Temple Sloan III, Mark H. Sloan. BA in Bus. Adminstrn., Duke U., 1961. Founder, chmn., CEO Gen. Parts Inc., Raleigh, NC, 1961—. Chmn. bd. dirs. Highwoods Properties Inc., Raleigh; bd. dirs. So. Equipment Co., Raleigh, CARQUEST Corp., Raleigh, Al Smith Buick Inc., Bank of Am., Charlotte, Morguard, Toronto, Lowe's Cos., Inc., Golden Corral. Trustee Boys and Girls Homes N.C., Lake Waccamaw, 1973—; mem. adv. bd. Salvation Army, Raleigh, 1973-87, chmn., 1976-77; exec. bd., v.p., treas. Occoneechee coun. Boy Scouts Am., 1967—; bd. visitors Peace Coll., Raleigh, 1985-87, trustee, 1987-97, vice chmn.; bd. dirs. Rex Hosp. Found., 1989-90; campaign chmn. Wake County United Way, 2001; elder Presbyn. Ch.; mem. Centennial Authority, Raleigh, 1995—. Recipient Silver Beaver award Boy Scouts Am., Disting. Eagle Scout award Boy Scouts Am., Disting. Svc. citation Automotive Hall of Fame, 1997; named Northwood U. Outstanding Bus. Leader, 1999. Mem. Automotive Warehouse Distbrs. Assn. Inc. (dir. 1969—, chmn. 1976-77, Scholarship award 1977, Automotive Man of Yr. award 1989), The Fifty Group (bd. dirs. 1983-88, pres. 1986-87), Greater Raleigh C. of C. (bd. dirs. 1989-91), Carolina Country Club (Raleigh). Avocations: fishing, hunting, ranching. Home: 3026 Randolph Dr Raleigh NC 27609-6942 Office: Gen Parts Inc PO Box 26006 Raleigh NC 27611 E-mail: licanipe@gpi.com.

SLOAN, REBA FAYE, dietitian, consultant; b. South Bend, Ind., Feb. 5, 1955; d. Kenneth and Ruby Faye (Long) Lewis; m. Gilbert Kevin Sloan, May 22, 1976. BS, Harding U., 1976; MPH, Loma Linda U., 1989; Cert. Tng. in Child/Adolescent Obesity, U. Calif., San Francisco. Registered dietitian; lic. dietitian and nutritionist; cert. advanced clin. tng. adolescent obesity. Dietetic intern Vanderbilt U. Med. Ctr., Nashville, 1978, rsch. dietitian, 1979-80; therapeutic dietitian Bapt. Hosp., Nashville, 1981-85; staff dietitian Nautilus Total Fitness Ctrs., Nashville, 1983-86; cons. dietitian Nashville Met. Govt., 1986-95, Bapt. Hosp. Ctr. for Health Promotion, Nashville, 1987-91, Parkwest Eating Disorder Clinic, Nashville, 1989-91; nutrition therapist, pvt. practice Nashville, Tenn., 1992—. Adj. prof. Vanderbilt U., 1995—; nutrition cons. The Nashville Striders, 1979-81; cons. nutritionist; mem. Vanderbilt U. Eating Disorder Com.; founding mem. Eating Disorder Coalition of Tenn. Vol. Belmont Ch. Ministries, Nashville, 1981-97; spkr. Am. Heart Assn., Nashvile 1990—; founder Dietetic Scholarship Fund, Harding U.; founding mem., bd. dirs. Eating Disorder Coalition of Tenn. Recipient cert. of appreciation Am. Heart Assn., 1990, Disting. Lectr. cert. Harding U.; Leaders fellow YMCA. Mem. Am. Dietetic Assn., Sports and Cardiovascular Nutritionists, Cons. Nutritionists, Am. Coll. Sports Medicine, Am. Running and Fitness Assn., Nashville Dist. Dietetic Assn. (contbr. diet manual 1984), Nat. Assn. for Chrisian Recovery, Alpha Chi. Avocations: travel, running, exercise, reading. Home: 1817 Shackleford Rd Nashville TN 37215-3525 Office: 121 21st Ave N Ste 208 Nashville TN 37203-6402

SLOAN, ROBERT BRYAN, JR., university president; b. Coleman, Tex., 1949; m. Sue Collier; children: Charissa, Bryan, Eraina, Michael, Alathea, Sophia, Paul. BA cum laude, Baylor U., 1970; MDiv magna cum laude, Princeton Theol. Sem., 1973; doktor der theologie insigni cum laude, U. Basel, 1978. Faculty Hardin-Simmons U., Abilene, Southwestern Bapt. Theol. Sem., Fort Worth; faculty dept. religion Baylor U., George W. Truett chair, dean Truett Sem., pres., CEO, 1995—. Mem. Cooper Found. Bd., Compass Bank Adv. Bd.; pastor, interim pastor over 20 chs., Tex., Okla., N.J., Germany; mem., treas. Big 12 Exec. Com.; bd. dirs. Salado Inst. for the Humanities. Inducted Little League Hall of Excellence. Mem. Studiorum Novi Testamenti Societas, Soc. of Bib. Lit., Inst. for Bib. Rsch.

SLOAN, ROBERT D. energy executive; b. 1947; BA, U. Mich.; JD, Harvard U. V.p., dir. Sovereign Credit Mgmt. Divsn. 1st Nat. Bank Chgo.; ptnr. Pepper, Hamilton and Sheetz Law Firm, Washington, 1989—92; mng. ptnr. Brussels office McKenna and Cuneo LLP, 1993—98; v.p., gen. counsel GE Indsl. Sys., 1998—2003; sr. v.p., gen. counsel, sec. Entergy Corp., New Orleans, 2003—. Office: Entergy Corp PO Box 61000 New Orleans LA 70161

SLOAN, SAUNDRA JENNINGS, real estate company executive; b. Prosperity, S.C., June 30, 1961; d. Denny Jennings and Kay Hyler Green; m. Lowell Evan Sloan, Mar. 14, 1998. Student, Midlands Tech. Coll., Airport Location/Columbia, 1979—82. Lic. real estate. Pres. Southpark Svcs., Inc., Columbia, SC, 1990—95; mgr. sales and leasing Foster, Saad & Co., Columbia, SC, 1995—. Pres. BNI Midlands Chpt., Columbia, SC, 1999—2000. Recipient Gold Club award, Bus. Network Internat., 2001. Avocations: dance, travel, sewing. Office: Foster Saad & Co Ste 2A 1201 Hampton St Columbia SC 29201 Business E-Mail: SaunJenSloan@aol.com.

SLOAN, WILLIAM MARSHALL, lawyer; b. Omaha, May 30, 1930; s. William McKinley Sloan and Marguarette (Marshall) Esther; m. Joan Arlene Dennis, Aug. 18, 1957; children: Valerie, Michael, Bonnie, Kathryn. BS, U. Oreg., 1952, LLB, 1956. Bar: Oreg. 1956, US Dist. Ct. Oreg. 1956. Assoc. Johnson & Telfer, Grants Pass, Oreg., 1956—58; ptnr. Johnson, Telfer & Sloan, Grants Pass, 1958—67, Johnson, Sloan & Jordan, Grants Pass, 1968—76, Sloan, Hawkins & Neufeld, Grants Pass, 1977—80, Sloan & Hull, Grants Pass, 1981—85. Circuit judge pro-tem, 2003—. Legal counsel Oreg. State Jaycees, 1961—62; patrolman Nat. Ski Patrol Svc., Mt. Ashland, 1963—72; chmn. bldg. fund Josephine County Park Bd., Oreg., 1980—93, Bd. of Four Way Cmty. Found., 1994—2000, chmn., 1996—97; Advisor, committeeman Trahern for State Rep., Grants Pass, 1982; chmn. bldg. fund Bethany Presbyterian Ch., Grants Pass, 1962; pres. Josephine County Cancer Assn., Grants Pass, 1961. 1st lt. U.S. Army, 1952—54, Korea. Decorated Bronze Star. Mem.: Josephine County Bar Assn. (pres. 1963—64), Jaycees (pres. 1962—63, Disting. Svc. award 1962), Caveman Coin Club (Grants Pass) (pres. 1959—60), Elks, Phi Delta Phi. Republican. Presbyterian. Home: 16 Big Sky Ln Sunriver OR 97707 Office: 130 NW D St PO Box 1476 Grants Pass OR 97528-0332 Personal E-mail: williamjoan@juno.com.

SLOAN, W(ILSON) KEITH, actuary; b. Red Oak, Iowa, Mar. 11, 1924; s. Francis Asbury and Inez Claire (Snyder) S.; m. Mary Kay Kirby, July 9, 1945; children: Karen Osborne, Kirby Bartlett Sloan. BS, U. Mich., 1949. Underwriter Commonwealth Life Ins. Co., Louisville, 1951-55; asst. sec. Bankers Security Life Ins. Soc., Washington, 1955—57; agt. Penn Mut. Life Ins. Co., Louisville, 1957; chief underwriter, agy. sec. Consumers Nat. Life Ins. Co., Evansville, Ind., 1957-60; gen. mgr. Early Am. Life Ins. Co., Evansville, Ind., 1960-61; actuary, asst. sec., dir. Pioneer Ins. Co., Lincoln, Nebr., 1961-63; group actuarial adminstr. Life & Casualty Ins. Co. Tenn., Nashville, 1963-67; chief actuary Tenn. Dept. Ins. & Banking, Nashville, 1967-71; v.p., acutary Am. Family Life Ins. Co. Columbus (Ga.), 1971-74; life & health actuary Ark. Ins. Dept., Little Rock, 1974-78; asst. actuary Kemper Group, Long Grove, Ill., 1978-81; chief life & health actuary Ky. Dept. Ins., Frankfort, 1981-82; v.p. actuary Citizens Security Life Ins. Co., Frankfort, 1982-88; cons. actuary Bryan, Pendleton, Swats & McAllister, Nashville, 1989-97; retired. Lectr. fin. U. Ark., Little Rock, 1977-78; cons. in field. Co-author: Patchwork: An Uncommon Quilt of Words, 2000, Writings from the Heart, An Anthology, 2004; articles to profl. jours. With U.S. Army, 1942-46. Fellow Conf. Cons. Actuaries; mem. Am. Acad. Actuaries, Tenn. Writers Alliance, Wordsmiths, Inc., Southeastern Actuaries Club, Nashville Actuarial Club (past pres.), Faculty Actuaries Students Soc. (life). Avocation: writing. Home: 1506 Teil Dr Franklin TN 37064-6832 E-mail: wks37064@earthlink.net.

SLOANE, BEVERLY LEBOV, writer, consultant; b. N.Y.C., May 26, 1936; d. Benjamin S. and Anne (Weinberg) LeBov; m. Robert Malcolm Sloane, Sept. 27, 1959 (dec. May 16, 2002); 1 child, Alison Lori Sloane Gaylin. AB, Vassar Coll., 1958; MA, Claremont Grad. U., 1975, postgrad., 1975-76; cert. in exec. mgmt., grad. exec. mgmt. program, UCLA Grad. Sch. Mgmt., 1982; grad. intensive bioethics course Kennedy Inst. Ethics, Georgetown U., 1987, advanced bioethics course, 1988; grad. sem. in Health Care Ethics, U. Wash. Sch. Medicine, Seattle, summer 1988-90, 94; grad. Summer Bioethics Inst., Loyola Marymount U., summer 1990; grad. Annual Summer Inst. on Teaching of Writing, Columbia U. Tchrs. Coll., summer 1990; grad. Annual Summer Inst. on Advanced Teaching of Writing, Columbia Tchrs. Coll., summer 1993; grad. Annual Inst. Pub. Health and Human Rights, Harvard U. Sch. Pub. Health, 1994; grad. pub. course profl. pub., Stanford U., 1982; Ethics Fellow, cert. clin. intensive biomedical ethics, Loma Linda U. Med. Ctr., 1989; grad. exec. refresher course profl. pub., Stanford U., 1994; cert Exec. Mgmt. Inst. in Health Care, U. So. Calif., 1995; cert. in ethics corps tng. program, Josephson Inst. of Ethics, 1991; cert. advanced exec. program Grad. Sch. Mgmt., UCLA, 1995; grad. Women's Campaign Sch., Yale U., 1998. Circulation libr. Harvard Med. Libr., Boston, 1958-59; social worker Conn. State Welfare, New Haven, 1960-61; tchr. English Hebrew Day Sch., New Haven, 1961-64; instr. creative writing and English lit. Monmouth Coll., West Long Branch, NJ, 1967-69; writer, cons., 1970—. V.p. coun. grad. students, Claremont Grad. U., 1971-72, adj. dir. Writing Ctr. Speaker Series, 1993-2000, spkr., 1996-98, Claremont Grad. U.; mem. Strategic Planning Task Force Com. Campaign Pre-eminence. 1986-87, Alumni Coun., bd. dirs. Alumni Assn., 1993-96; mem. Vol. Devel. Com., 1994-96, Alumni Awards Com., 1993-96; bd. visitors Claremont Grad. U. Ctrs. for Arts and Humanities, 2001—; adv. coun. tech. and profl. writing Dept. English, Calif. State U., Long Beach, 1980-82; adv. bd. Calif. Health Rev., 1982-83; mem. Foothill Health Dist. Adv. Coun. L.A. County Dept. Health Svcs., 1987-93, pres., 1989-91; vis. scholar Hastings Ctr., 1996; spkr. N.Y. State Task Force on Life and the Law, 1996; panel spkr. Annual Conf. Am. Assn. Suicidology, 1998. Author: From Vassar to Kitchen, 1967, A Guide to Health Facilities: Personnel and Management, 1971, 2nd edit., 1977, 3d edit., 1992, Introduction to Healthcare Delivery Organization: Functions and Management, 4th edit., 1999. Co-chmn. Vassar Christmas Showcase Vassar Club, New Haven, 1965—66; pub. rels. bd. Monmouth County Mental Health Assn., 1968—69; co-chmn. Vassar Club So. Calif. Annual Book Fair award Vassar Coll., 1970—71; chmn. creative writing group Calif. Inst. Tech. Woman's Club, 1975—79; mem. task force edn. and cultural activities City of Duarte, 1987—88; class rep. Vassar Coll. Alumnae Assn., 1989; chmn. creative writing group Yale U. Newcomers, 1965—66; dir. creative writing group Yale U. Women's Orgn., 1966—67; mem. Exec. Program Network UCLA Grad. Sch. Mgmt., 1987—2000; trustee Ctr. Improvement Child Caring, 1981—83; mem. League Crippled Children, 1982—, treas. for gen. meetings, 1990—91, chmn. hostesses com., 1988—89, pub. rels. com., 1990—91; del. Task Force on Minorities in Newspaper Bus., 1987—89; rep. cmty. County Health Network Tobacco Control Program, 1991; mem. NY Citizens Com. Health Care Decisions, Vassar Coll. Class Gift Com., 1998; chmn. 1st ann. Rabbi Camillus Angel Interfaith Svc. Temple Beth David, 1978, v.p., 1983—86; cmty. rels. com. Jewish Fedn. Coun. Greater L.A., 1985—87; bd. dirs. League Crippled Children, 1988—91; ethics com., human subjects protection com. Jewish Home for Aging, Reseda, Calif., 1994—97; various positions and coms. Claremont Grad. U., 1986—; bd. visitors Claremont Grad. U. Ctr. Arts and Humanities, 2001—; bd. dirs. L.A. Commn. Assaults Against Women, 1983—84; class corr. Vassar Coll. Quar. Alumnae Mag., 1993—98; class of 1958 coms. Vassar Coll., class v.p., 1998—2000, class co-pres., 2000—01, class pres., 2001—03, program chmn. 40th reunion, 1998. Recipient cert. of appreciation City of Duarte, 1988, County of L.A., 1988, Ann. Key Mem. award L.A. Dept. Health Svcs., 1990, cert. of appreciation Alumni Coun. Claremont Grad Sch., 1996; Coro Found. fellow, 1979, Ethics fellow Loma Linda U. Med. Ctr., 1989; named Calif. Communicator of Achievement, Woman of Yr. Calif. Press Women, 1992. Fellow: Am. Med. Writers Assn. (Pacific S.W. del. to nat. bd. 1980—87, dir. 1980—93, chmn. nat. book awards trade category 1982—83, chmn. Nat. Networking Luncheon 1983—84, nat. chmn. freelance sect. 1984—85, workshop leader, Nat. Ann. Conf. 1984—89, gen. chmn. Asilomar Western Regional Conf. 1985, workshop leader, Asilomar Western Regional Conf. 1985, nat. exec. bd. dirs. 1985—86, nat. adminr. sects. 1985—86, pres.-elect Pacific Southwest chpt. 1985—87, chmn. gen. session nat. conf. 1986—87, chmn. Walter C. Alvarez Mem. Found award 1986—87, program co-chmn. 1987, program chmn. nat. conf. 1987, moderator gen. session. nat. conf. 1987, pres. Pacific S.W. chap. 1987—89, workshop leader, Asilomar Western Nat. Conf. 1988, spkr. Pacific S.W. chpt. 1988—89, program co-chmn. 1989, workshop leader, Asilomar Western Nat. Conf. 1989, Pacific Southwest deleg. to nat. bd. 1989—91, immediate past pres. 1989—91, workshop leader, Nat. Ann. Conf. 1990—92, bd. dirs. 1991—93, workshop leader, Nat. Ann. Conf. 1995, chmn. conv. coms., Appreciation award for outstanding leadership 1989, named to Workshop Leaders Honor Roll 1991); mem.: AAUP, APHA, AAUW (creative writing chmn. 1969—70, books and plays chmn. Arcadia Br. 1973—74, 1st v.p. program dir. 1975—76, legis. chmn. Arcadia Br. 1976—77, networking chmn. 1981—82, spkr. 1987, chmn. task force promoting individual liberties 1987—88, pres.-elect 1998—99, educ. equity chmn. 1998—99, chmn. deleg. to national conv. 1999, chmn. Technical Trek Sci. Camp Scholarship for Girls 1999, Career Day 1999, pres. Arcadia br. 1999—2000, writer in res Calif. State Am. Assn. Univ. Women 1999—2000, diversity chmn. Arcadia br.

2000—01, LA Interbr. Coun. Arcadia br. repr. 2000—02, program vice-chmn. LA County Interbr. Coun. 2000—02, Calif. State diversity com. 2000—02, Woman of Achievement Arcadia br. 1986, cert. of appreciation 1987), Calif. State AAUW (program co-v.p. 2002), Town Hall Calif. (vice chmn. cmty. affairs sect. 1982—87, faculty-instr. Exec. Breakfast Inst. 1985—86, Exec. Breakfast Inst. spkr. 1986), Pasadena Athletic, Claremont Cols. Faculty House, Women's City (Pasadena), Nat. Writer's Union, Authors Guild, Assn. Writing Programs, NY Acad. Medicine (met. NY Ethics Network), Soc. Health and Human Values, Kennedy Inst. Ethics, Technical Comt., Nat. Fedn. Press Women (chmn. state women of achievement comt. 1986—87, nat. co-chmn. task force recruitment minorities 1987—89, del. 1987—89, bd. dirs. 1987—93, nat. dir. spkrs. bur. 1989—93, Plenary past pres. state 1989—, workshop leader, spkr. annual nat. conf. 1990, editor spkrs. bur. directory 1991—92, editor spkrs. bur. addendum dir. 1992, cert. of appreciation 1991, 1st runner up, Nat. Communicator of Achievement 1992, cert. of appreciation 1993), Hastings Cent. (vis. scholar 1996), Ind. Writers So. Calif. (bd. dirs. corp. 1988—89, bd. dirs. 1989—90, dir. specialized groups 1989—90, dir. at large 1989—90, dir. speech writing group 1991—92), NY Acad. Scis., Calif. Press Women (v.p. programs L.A. chpt. 1982—85, pres. 1985—87, state pres. 1987—89, immediate past state pres. 1989—91, chmn. state speakers bur. 1989—95, deleg. nat. bd. 1989—95, dir. family literacy day Calif. 1990, moderator, ann. spring conv. 1990, chmn. nominating comt. 1990—91, Calif. literacy dir. 1990—92, dir. state literacy com. 1990—92, moderator, ann. spring conv. 1992, Cert. of Appreciation 1991, Calif. Communicator of Achievement 1992), Am. Soc. Law, Medicine, Ethics, AAUW Calif. State Comns. Comt. (writer in residence 1999—2000), Coro Nat. Alumni Assn. (bd. dirs. 1999—, continuing edn. com. 2003—), Am. Assn. Higher Edn., Women in Comm. Inc. (N.E. area rep. 1980—81, bd. dirs. 1980—82, v.p. cmty. affairs 1981—82, chmn. awards banquet 1982, chmn. LA chpt. Agnes Underwood Freedom Info. Awards banquet 1982, nominating com. 1982—83, seminar leader, spkr., ann. nat. profl. conf. 1985, program adv. com. L.A. chpt. 1987, com. Women of the Press awards luncheon 1988, bd. dirs. 1989—90, v.p. activities 1989—90, Recognition award 1983), Duarte Rotary Club. Home and Office: 1301 N Santa Anita Ave Arcadia CA 91006-2419

SLOANE, CARL STUART, educator and management consultant; b. N.Y.C., Feb. 9, 1937; s. George and Dorothy (Cohen) S.; m. Toby Tattlebaum, Dec. 27, 1958; children: Lisa Beth, Amy Rachel, Todd Cowan. BA, Harvard U., 1958, MBA, 1960. Asst. to pres. Revlon, Inc., N.Y.C., 1960-62; mgmt. cons. Harbridge House, Inc., Boston, 1962-69; pres., CEO, chmn. Temple, Barker & Sloane, Inc., Lexington, Mass., 1970—91; prof. bus. adminstrn. Harvard Grad. Sch. Bus. Adminstrn., Lexington, 1991—2001. Policyholders' examining com. N.W. Mut. Life Ins. Co.; bus. adv. com. Transp. Ctr., Northwestern U., 1984-91; adv. com. Ctr. for Sci. and Internat. Affairs, Kennedy Sch. Govt., Harvard U., 1984-94; bd. dirs. Rayonier, Inc., Brinks Co., MedSource Techs. Bd. dirs. Harvard-Radcliffe Hillel, Cambridge, Mass., 1987-98, chmn., 1994-98; bd. dirs., trustee Beth Israel Deaconess Med. Ctr., Boston, 1993—, vice-chmn., 1996-2002, chmn. 2002—; nat. fund chmn. Harvard . Bus. Sch., 1987-89, vis. com. Mem. Assn. Mgmt. Cons. Firms (chmn. 1984-86), Harvard U. Bus. Sch. Alumni Assn. (v.p. 1989, pres. 1989-91), Boston Yacht Club (Marblehead), Kernwood County Club (Salem), Harvard Club N.Y.C. Home: 9 Sargent Rd Marblehead MA 01945-3744 Office: Harvard Bus Sch Soldiers Fld Boston MA 02163-1317

SLOANE, JAMES ROBERT, chemical engineer; b. Pitts., June 14, 1942; s. Paul Guyer Sloan and Mildred Catherine Reuter; m. Susan Richards (div. May 1992); children: Michelle Karin(dec.), James Robert Jr., Jonathan Westby; m. Judy Southerland, Dec. 6, 1997. BSChemE, Pa. State U., 1994; MPA, U. Ctrl. Fla., 2001. Registered profl. engr., Fla. Engr. Westinghouse Electric Corp., 1964, Graver Water Cond. Co., 1967; sales engr. Datum Co., Houston, 1971; charter pilot, aircraft sales mgr. W. Houston Airport, 1972; flight supr. Embry-Riddle Aero. U., Daytona Beach, Fla., 1973; project mgr. Russell and Axon Engrs., Daytona Beach, 1974; sr. project mgr. Briley, Wild and Assocs. Inc., Ormond Beach, Fla., 1986, McKim and Creed Engrs., Daytona Beach, 1994; dep. pub. works dir., city engr. City Daytona Beach, 1998. Mem. AOPA, ASPA, Am. Pub. Works Assn., Fla. Engr. Soc. Methodist. Avocations: flying, aircraft, water-skiing. Home: 630-635 Lake Winnemissett Dr Deland FL 32724-4817 Office: The City Daytona Beach PO Box 2451 Daytona Beach FL 32115-2451 Office Phone: 386-671-8610. E-mail: JRSloane@aol.com.

SLOANE, JAMES R.W. academic administrator, writer; b. N.Y., May 8, 1953; s. James Ross and Helen (Stuart) Sloane; m. Elizabeth Davidson, June 6, 1981; children: Phoebe, James Jr. BA, Williams Coll., 1976; MBA, Yale U., 1984. Mng. dir. Aetna Life and Casualty, Hartford, Conn., 1984—95; ptnr. Handles Internat., Boston, 1996—98; COO Barin, Asset Mgmt., Boston, 1998—99; CEO Katapult, Inc., Cambridge, Mass., 1998—2001; CFO U. Hawaii, Honolulu, 2001—. Mem. tech. adv. bd. Phillips Exeter Acad., dir. alumni coun.; dir. Yale Sch. Mgmt. Alumni Assn. Contbr. essays to radio. Mem. Bd. Edn., West Hartford, Conn., 1998—. Fellow, Am. Leadership Forum, 1992. Avocations: skiing, cross country skiing, piano, surfing. Home: 2302 Sonoma St Honolulu HI 96822 Office: Univ Hawaii 2444 Dole St Honolulu HI 96822

SLOANE, J.P. television producer, writer, entertainer, theologian; b. Hollywood, Calif., Sept. 6, 1942; s. Jimmy Jackson and Anita (Thibodeaux) Barrios. Cert. in TV prodn., Purdue U., 1981; grad., Oral Roberts U.; diploma, Inst. Jewish-Christian Studies, Dallas; grad., Moody Bible Inst., Chgo.; student, IBEX Campus, Abu Ghosh, Israel, 2001; BA summa cum laude, Master's Coll., 2003, MA, 2004. Biblical scholar and lectr.; appeared on major Christian networks. Guest Art Linkletter's House Party (age 5), CBS Radio Network; played Billy Kettle in Ma and Pa Kettle movie series; appeared on Memory Lane TV show, Hollywood; recorded High on a Mountain, 1960, Linda Darling, 1960; lead singer The Brothers Grim, 1965-68; featured act with Charlie Rich; mem. J.P. Sloane & Co. group, 1973-78; albums include Solid Gold; tv and radio prodr. Recipient Excellence in Media Angel awards for Outstanding TV Prodr., Outstanding Male Vocalist and Outstanding Music Video, Medal of Merit, Pres. Ronald Reagan; named Hon. Sheriff, L.A. County, Hon. Ky. Col., Hon. Lt. Gov. State of Ind., Hon. Citizen, Tulsa, Met. Nashville, 22d Internat. Angel award best multiple character voices, 1999, others; nominee Cleo award, 1980; key to cities Nashville and New Orleans, others. Mem.: Nat. Scholars Honor Soc. (life). Office: Angeles Crest Productions Ste 407 2219 E Thousand Oaks Blvd Thousand Oaks CA 91362-2930 Business E-Mail: jp@jpsloane.com.

SLOANE, MARSHALL M. banker; b. Somerville, Mass., 1926; s. Jacob and Rose (Jacobson) S.; m. Barbara Gluck, Mar. 7, 1954; children: Barry Richard, Jonathan Gary, Linda Ruth. Chmn. bd., CEO, founder Century Bank & Trust Co., Somerville, 1969—. Chmn. bd., pres. Century Bancorp Inc., Somerville, 1972—, Sloane Furniture Co., 1952-68. Chmn. bd. visitors Boston U.; citizens adv. bd. Medford Telecom Commn.; bd. trustees Boston U.; exec. bd. Boy Scouts Am., trustee Nat. Mus. Boy Scouts Am.; trustee Cath. Found. Archdiocese Boston, Boston Regional Office Cath. Charities; active Mass. Gen. Hosp. Coun., Corp. Ptnrs. Health Care Sys., Inc., Corp. Perkins Sch. for Blind. With USN. Named Baden Powell inductee, World Scout Found. Boy Scouts Am., 1989, decorated Knight St. Gregory The Great, by Pope John Paul II, 1994; recipient good scout award, Greater Boston Boy Scouts Am., 1983, Shofar award, Nat. Jewish Relationships Coun. Boy Scouts Am., 1984, commendation, Nat. Bapt. Relationships Boy Scouts Am., 1984, Mortimer Schiff award, Jewish Relationships Com. Boy Scouts Am., 1985, Silver Beaver award, Boy Scouts Am., 1979, Silver Antelope, 1983, Silver Buffalo award, 1988, Allah-O-Akbar award, Nat. Islamic Com. on Scouting, 1985, Theo. Storer award svc. to Boston cmty., 1986, Israeli Peace medal, 1987, St. George medal, Nat. Cath. Cmty. Boy Scouts Am., 1990, Bus. and Profl. award, Religious Heritage, 1991, Sword of Hope award, Am. Cancer Soc., 1992, Somerville pride award, 1997, alumni award, Boston U. Sch. Mgmt., 1998—, Israei Bonds Salvador Dali Menorah award, 2000. Mem. Mass. Bankers Assn., Exec. Club, Algonquin Club, Pinebrook Club, Masons. Jewish. Office: Century Bancorp Inc 400 Mystic Ave Medford MA 02155-6316

SLOANE, NEIL JAMES ALEXANDER, mathematician, researcher; b. Beaumaris, Wales, Oct. 10, 1939; came to U.S., 1961; s. Charles Ronald and Jessie (Robinson) S.; m. Susanna Stevens Cuyler, Mar. 8, 1980. BA with honors, U. Melbourne, Australia, 1959, BEE, 1960; MS, Cornell U., 1964, PhD, 1967. Asst. prof. Cornell U., Ithaca, N.Y., 1967-69; mem. tech. staff AT&T Bell Labs., Murray Hill, N.J., 1969-96; prin. mem. tech. staff AT&T Rsch. Labs, 1996—, fellow, 1998. Author: Handbook of Integer Sequences, 1973; co-author: (with F.J. MacWilliams) Theory of Error-Correcting Codes, 1977, (with J.H. Conway) Sphere-Packings, Lattices and Groups, 1988, 32d edit., 1998, (with A.D. Wyner) Claude Elwood Shannon:Collected Papers, 1993, (with S. Plouffe) Encyclopedia of Integer Sequences, 1995, (with A.S. Hedayat and J. Stufken) Orthogonal Arrays, 1999, (with P. Nick) Rock Climbing New Jersey, 2000. Fellow IEEE (editor in chief Trans. Info. Theory jour. 1978-80); mem. NAE, Math. Assn. Am. (Chauvenet prize 1979, Earle Raymond Hedrick lectr. 1984), Am. Math. Soc., Am. Stat. Assn. Avocation: rock climbing. Office Phone: 973-360-8415. E-mail: njas@research.att.com.

SLOANE, RICHARD, legal educator, librarian; b. 1916. B.S. in Social Sci., CCNY, 1937; B.S. in Library Sci., Columbia U., 1940. Bar: N.Y. 1962. Assoc., Cravath, Swaine & Moore, N.Y.C., 1962-71; prof. law, Biddle law librarian U. Pa. Law Sch., Phila., 1971-84; library planning cons., 1984—; mem. edn. adv. com. to index legal periodicals, H.W. Wilson Co. Mem. Bus. Libraries Commn., ABA. Editor: Recommended Law Books, 1969; co-author: Manual of Procedures for Private Law Libraries, 1962; (with Marke) Coordinated Law Research, 1977; (with Wallace) Private Law Library: 1980 and Beyond, 1979; (with Marke) Legal Research and Law Library Management, 1982; (with Dorland) Annotated Medical Legal Dictionary, 1987. Office: U Pa Law Sch 3400 Chestnut St Philadelphia PA 19104-6204

SLOANE, THOMAS O. speech educator; b. West Frankfort, Ill., July 12, 1929; s. Thomas Orville and Blanche (Morris) S.; m. Barbara Lee Lewis, Nov. 1, 1952; children— Elizabeth Alison, David Lewis, Emily. BA, So. Ill. U., 1951, MA, 1952; PhD, Northwestern U., 1960. Instr. English, Washington and Lee U., 1958-60; asst. prof. speech U. Ill., 1960-65, assoc. prof., 1965-70, assoc. head dept., 1967-68, asst. dean liberal arts and scis., 1966-67; prof. rhetoric, chmn. rhetoric dept. U. Calif., Berkeley, 1970-92, pres.'s chair, 1987-90. Dir. Nat. Endowment Humanities Summer Seminar for Coll. Tchrs., 1979 Editor: The Oral Study of Literature, 1966, The Passions of the Minde in Generall (Thomas Wright), 1971, (with Raymond B. Waddington) The Rhetoric of Renaissance Poetry, 1974, (with Joanna H. Maclay) Interpretation, 1972; Donne, Milton and the End of Humanist Rhetoric, 1985, On the Contrary, 1997, (with Peter Oesterreich) Rhetorica Movet, 1999; editor in chief: Encyclopedia of Rhetoric, 2001; contbr. articles to profl. jours. Served to lt. USNR, 1952-55. Faculty research fellow, 1964; U. Ill. instructional devel. awardee, 1965; Henry H. Huntington Library research awardee, 1967; U. Calif. humanities research fellow, 1974; Guggenheim fellow, 1981-82 Office: U Calif Berkeley CA 94720-0001 E-mail: tos@berkeley.edu.

SLOAT, BARBARA FURIN, cell biologist, educator; b. Youngstown, Ohio, Jan. 20, 1942; d. Walter and Mary Helen (Maceyko) Furin; m. John Barry Sloat, Nov. 2, 1968; children: John Andrew, Eric Furin. BS, Denison U., 1963; MS, U. Mich., 1966, PhD, 1968. Lic. and cert. emergency med. technician, paramedic. Lab. asst. U. Ghent, Belgium, 1964; tchg. fellow, lectr. U. Mich., Ann Arbor, 1964-66, 68-70, asst. rsch. biologist Mental Health Rsch. Inst., 1972-74, vis. asst. prof., lectr. Ann Arbor and Dearborn, 1974-76, dir. women in sci. Ann Arbor, 1980-84, assoc. dir. honors, 1986-87, rsch. scientist, 1976—, lectr. Residential Coll., 1984—, assoc. Inst. Humanities, 1991—. Author: Laboratory Guide for Zoology, 1979, Summer Internships in the Sciences for High School Women (CASE Silver medal, 1985, Excellence in Edn. award, U. Mich., 1993). Recipient Acad. Women's Caucus award, U. Mich., 1984, Grace Lyon Alumnae Award, Denison U., 1988; grantee NSF, U.S. Dept. Edn., Warner Lambert Found., others. Mem. AAAS, Am. Soc. Cell Biology, N.Y. Acad. Scis., Nat. Assn. Women Deans, Adminstrs. and Counselors, Assn. for Women in Sci. (councilor 1988-90, pres. elect 1990, mentor of yr. award Detroit area chpt. 1994), Phi Beta Kappa, Sigma Xi. Avocations: hiking, yoga, tibetology, Tibetan medicine. Home: 240 Indian River Pl Ann Arbor MI 48104-1825 Office: U Mich Residential Coll 216 Tyler East Quad Ann Arbor MI 48109-1245 Business E-Mail: bsloat@umich.edu.

SLOAT, JANE ROBERTS DEGRAFF, government official, civic worker, consultant; b. N.Y.C., Dec. 31, 1939; d. John Wayne and Agnes (Murton) Roberts; m. Elliott Dodd DeGraff, June 28, 1959 (div.); children: Pamela DeGraff Porter, Jill Katherine; m. Jonathan Welsh Sloat, June 19, 1983 (dec.). Active Hospitality Info. Svc., Washington, 1964-70, sec. bd., 1971-73; spl. asst. to ambassador-at-large for cultural affairs Dept. State, Washington, 1981; spl. asst. to U.S. refugee affairs Washington, 1982-85; coord. conf. on Ethical Issues and Moral Principles in U.S. Refugee Policy, 1983; real estate broker Samuel P. Pardoe Real Estate, Washington, 1986—98. Tour lectr. Corcoran Gallery Art, Washington, 1965-70. Vice chmn. UN Concert, Washington, 1971, 50th Jubilee Nat. English Speaking Union, 1971; spl. asst. to chmn. United Givers fund, Washington. 1971-72; chmn. ball Opera Soc., Washington, 1972; bd. dirs. Jr. League, 1970-71, Nat. Ballet Soc., 1972-74, Washington Performing Arts Soc., 1972-75, The Washington Opera, The Nat. Arboretum; mem. D.C. Mayor's Com. on Internat. Visitors, 1972-77; trustee Hosp. for Sick Children, Washington, 1973-76; chmn. Washington Antiques Show, 1972-75; mem. D.C. Rep. Fin. Com., 1972-75; trustee Meridian House Internat. Ctr., founder, chmn. Meridian House Ball, Washington, 1964-82, sec. 1974-75, vice chmn. bd., 1976-82, adv. bd.; mem. bd. advisers D.C. Lung Assn., 1975—; mem. fund-raising drive for Washington Cathedral, 1976; chair assocs. bd. IONA Sr. Svcs.; bd. dirs. Washington Home for Incurables, 1976-89, Nat. Eye Found., 1976-78, Childrens Hosp. Nat. Rsch. Found., 1978-81, D.C. chpt. ARC, 1976-84, Travelers Aid Soc., 1976-90; chmn. Washington Antiques Show, 1976-78, Washington Cathedral Flower Mart; dir. fin. devel. YWCA of Nat. Capital Area, 1979; vice chmn. Reagan Bush Inaugural, Washington, 1981; mem. transition team for Reagan Bush for NEA, 1981; bd. dirs. Family Stress Services, 1981-84; founder, chmn. Entertaining People, 1982-91; bd. dirs. All Hallows Guild, Washington br. English Speaking Union, 1987-90, brd. Washington Opera, 1997-2003, Nat. Arboretum; bd. dirs., chair Woodrow Wilson House, 1990-02, Washington; chrm. adv. brd. Iona Senior Services; chmn. Bush-Quayle Inaugural Ball, 1989, Am. Franklin Friends Com., 1992-95; fundraiser Ann. Fund Kennedy Ctr. Performing Arts, 1987, 90; v.p. bd. Washington Home, 1990-92; apptd. mem. Pres.'s Commn. Arts & Humanities, 1990-94; chmn. Am. Friends Fund-Inst. for U.S. Studies, U. London, bd. The Washington Opera 1996-2003; chief of protocol Rep. Convention, Phila., 2002; mem. Endowment Fund Coord. for State Dept., 2003—. Mem.: Million Dollar Club, Chevy Chase Club, Sulgrave Club (bd. dirs. 2003—). Episcopalian. Avocations: art, design, tennis, opera, fly fishing. Personal E-mail: JaneSloat@aol.com.

SLOBODCHIKOFF, CONSTANTINE NICHOLAS, biologist, educator; s. Nicholas and Valerie Slobodchikoff; m. Judith Kiriazis, May 30, 1993; children: Michael, Katherine. BS, U. Calif., Berkeley, PhD, 1971. Asst. prof. of biology No. Ariz. U., Flagstaff, Ariz., 1971—79, assoc. prof. biology, 1979—83, prof. of biology, 1983—; vis. prof. Kenyatta U., Nairobi, Kenya, 1983—83. Editor: (scientific book) The Ecology of Social Behavior, A New Ecology, Concepts of Species. Grantee Fullbright fellow, Washington D.C., 1983. Mem.: Animal Behavior Soc. Achievements include research in Decoding animal language; Understanding ecological factors of sociality. Office: No Arizona U Dept BiolScis Flagstaff AZ 86011 Office Phone: 928-523-7231. Business E-Mail: con.slobodchikoff@nau.edu.

SLOBODIEN, HOWARD DAVID, surgeon, educator; b. Perth Amboy, N.J., July 25, 1923; s. Albert Leo and Anna Frances (Sontag) S.; m. Sally Doris Yerkes, May 9, 1950; children: David, Donald, Daniel, Douglas. Diplomate Am. Bd. Surgery. Intern Morrisania City Hosp., N.Y.C., 1947-48, resident, 1948-52; practice medicine specializing in surgery Perth Amboy, 1955-96; pres. John F. Kennedy Med. Ctr., Edison, N.J., 1967-70, dir. surgery, 1975-79, dir. Breast Ctr., 1997—. Attending surgeon Gen. Hosp., Perth Amboy, dir. surgery, 1970-74; chief gen. surgery, past pres. med. staff Roosevelt Hosp., Edison; cons. surgery Meml. Hosp., South Amboy; clin. asst. prof. surgery Rutgers U. Med. Sch., 1971-84, mem. adv. council Office Consumer Health Edn., 1973-81; mem. adv. council Middlesex County Coll., 1968-78; v.p. Regional Health Facilities Planning Council, 1970-73. Editor N.J. Medicine, 1988-99. Pack committeeman Cub Scouts, 1960-64; active steering com. Metuchen YMCA, 1962. With USNR, 1943-45, USAF, 1952-54. Fellow ACS; mem. AMA, World, Pan-Am. med. assns., N.J. (trustee 1972-84, chmn. pub. rels. coun. 1973-76, pres. 1982-83), Middlesex County (pres. 1970-71) med. socs., Pan-Pacific Surg. Assn., Royal Soc. Health, Am. Acad. Med. Adminstrs., Royal Soc. Medicine, N.J. Acad. Medicine (trustee 1974-78), Middlesex County Med. Assts. Assn. (county med. advisor 1973-80), N.J. Soc. Surgeons, Phi Beta Kappa, Metuchen Country Club. Home: 34 Linden Ave Metuchen NJ 08840-1418

SLOBOZHANIN, LEV ARKADIEVICH, fluid mechanics researcher; b. Nylga, Russia, Sept. 1, 1941; arrived in US, 1995; s. Arkadii Alexandrovich and Iraida Stepanovna (Vlasova) S.; divorced; children: Andrei L., Darya L. Degree in mech. engrng. with honors, Kharkov (Ukraine) Aviation Inst., 1963; PhD in Physics and Math., Inst. for Low Temperature Physics and Engrng., Kharkov, 1968; cert. sr. rsch. scientist, Acad. Scis. of Ukraine, 1975; DSc in Physics and Math., Lavrentyev Inst. Hydrodynamics, Novosibirsk, Russia, 1989. Engr. B. Verkin Inst. Low Temperature Physics and Engrng. Nat. Acad. Scis. of Ukraine, Kharkov, 1963-66, sr. engr., 1966-69, jr. scientist, 1969-71, sr. scientist, 1971-89, leading scientist, 1989-98. Sr. tchr. Kharkov Aviation Inst., 1969—71, prof., 1989—90; vis. prof. Madrid Poly. U., 1993—94; vis. scholar U. Ala., Huntsville, 1995—2002; vis. rschr. Case Western Res. U., Cleve., 1999—2002, prin. rschr., 2002—. Co-author: Fluid Mechanics of Weightlessness, 1976, Low-Gravity Fluid Mechanics, 1987, Solution Methods for Fluid Mechanics Problems Under Weightlessness Conditions, 1992; contbr. articles to profl. jours. Chmn. trade union com. B. Verkin Inst. for Low Temperature Physics and Engring., 1986-89. Mem.: Am. Phys. Soc. Office: Case Western Res U 414 Glennan Bldg 10900 Euclid Ave Cleveland OH 44106-7222 Office Phone: 216-368-6453. Business E-Mail: lion@mae.cwru.edu.

SLOCA, STEVEN LANE, lawyer; b. Plainfield, N.J., Dec. 18, 1944; s. Charles and Maureen (Rushmore) S.; children: Lee M. H., Andrew C. BA summa cum laude with highest distinct, Dartmouth Coll., 1966; LLB, Yale U., 1969. Bar: Calif. 1970, U.S. Dist. Ct. (cen. dist.) Calif. 1970, U.S. Ct. Appeals (9th cir.) 1976, U.S. Ct. Appeals (3d cir.) 2003. Assoc. Irell & Manella, L.A., 1969-77, ptnr., 1977—2000; mng. ptnr. Cybermate Webservices, LLC, 2000—. Instr. trial advocacy Yale U., New Haven, 1968-69. Editor: Yale Law Jour., 1967-69. Served to capt. U.S. Army, 1970-71, Vietnam. Mem. State Bar Calif., Dartmouth Lawyers Assn., Order of Coif, Phi Beta Kappa. Democrat. Home and Office: 12 W Averstone Dr Washington Crossing PA 18977

SLOCUM, DONALD HILLMAN, product development executive; b. Flushing, N.Y., Jan. 6, 1930; s. John G. and Frances H. S.; m. June Manning, Sept. 22, 1952 (dec. 1976); children: Richard, Mark, Carol; m. Barbara M. Ruane, Nov. 1, 1985. BS, Davis and Elkins Coll., 1951; MS, U. Vt., 1956; PhD, Ohio State U., 1958; LLD, Fla. Tech. Inst., 1968; MBA, Rider Coll., 1971; Dr. Profl. Studies, Pace U., 1974; ScD, Davis and Elkins Coll., 2000. Rsch. chem. Charles Pfizer, Inc., Bklyn., 1954; rsch. scientist Procter & Gamble, Cin., 1958—60; mgr. product devel. E.I. DuPont de Nemours & Co., Wilmington, Del., 1960-68; dir. new ventures N.L. Industries, N.Y.C., 1968-71; dir. fin. planning Hoffmann LaRoche, Nutley, N.J., 1971-74; v.p. Curtiss-Wright Corp., Woodridge, N.J., 1974-78; sr. v.p. Masonite-USG/Internat. Paper, Chgo., 1978-85; pres. Doner-Viking Corp., Madison, N.J., 1985-87, Woodtec, Inc. subs. Masco, Taylor, Mich., 1987-96, Versitec Industries, 1996—. Author: New Venture Methodology, 1974; contbr. articles to tech. and bus. publs.; patentee in field. Lt. U.S. Army, 1951-54, Korea, Col. Res., ret. Achievements include patent of DuPont Corian. Home: 61 Chimney Ridge Dr Morristown NJ 07960-4722 Office: SRA 3400 Bee Ridge Rd Sarasota FL 34239-7223

SLOCUM, DONALD WARREN, chemist; m. Laurel Hopper, 1990 (dec. May 1997); children from previous marriage: Warren, Matthew. BS in Chemistry, BA in English, U. Rochester; PhD in Chemistry, NYU, 1963. Postdoctoral rsch. assoc. Duke U., Durham, N.C., 1963-64; asst. prof. chemistry Carnegie Inst. Tech., Pitts., 1964-65; from asst. to assoc. prof. chemistry So. Ill. U., Carbondale, 1965-72, prof., 1972-81, adj. prof., 1981-84; program dir. chem. dynamics sect., chemistry div. NSF, Washington, 1984-85; program leader div. edn. programs, sr. scientist chem. tech. div. Argonne (Ill.) Nat. Lab., 1985-90; head dept. chemistry Western Ky. U., Bowling Green, 1990-95, prof. chemistry, 1995—. Sr. scientist Gulf Rsch. and Devel. Co., Pitts., 1980-82; vis. prof. U. Ill., 1970, U. Bristol, Eng., 1973, U. Cin., 1976; vis. fellow U. Bristol, 1972; vis. lectr. Carnegie-Mellon U., 1983-84, U. Pitts., 1983-84; organizer symposia on organometallic chemistry and catalysis; bd. dirs. Ctrl. States Univs., Inc., 1986-88, Arts at Argonne, 1988-90; cons. in field; mem. nat. organizing com. XVth Internat. Conf. on Organometallic Chemistry Wayne State U., Detroit, 1990; mem. internat. adv. bd. XVth Internat. Conf. on Organometallic Chemistry, Warsaw, 1992; mem. NSF/EPSCoR subcom., Ky., 1993-94; mem. coun. on undergrad. rsch. Instnl. Liaison Rep. to Western Ky. U., 1995—. Co-editor: Advances in Chemistry Series of Am. Chem. Soc., Vol. 230, 1992, Methane and Alkane Activation (Plenum), 1995; contbr. over 70 articles to profl. jours., chpts. to books; mem. editl. bd. Synthesis and Reactivity in Inorganic and Metal-Organic Chemistry, 1971—; regional editor Letters in Organic Chemistry, 2004-. Recipient Rsch./Creativity award Ogden Coll. of Sci., Technology and Health, Western Ky. U., 1996, Sci. award honoring Brian Andreen, Cottrell Coll. Sci., 1999. Mem. Am. Chem. Soc. (sec. gen. elect catalysis and surface sci. secretariat 1992, sec. gen. 1993, organic divsn. rep. to catalysis and surface sci. secretariat, 1993-98, co-chmn. symposium, San Diego, 1994), Chem. Soc. Gt. Britain, Catalysis Soc., Bowling Green Chamber Singers, Sigma Xi. Avocations: music, literature, sports. Office: Western Ky U Dept Chemistry Bowling Green KY 42101 Office Phone: 270-745-5239. Business E-Mail: Donald.Slocum@wku.edu.

SLOCUM, RICHARD COPELAND (R.C. SLOCUM), university athletic coach; b. Oakdale, La, Nov. 7, 1944; Asst. football coach Tex. A&M U. Aggies, 1972-80, 82-89, U. So. Calif., 1981; head football coach Tex. A&M U. Aggies, 1989—. Office: Texas A&M Univ Dept Athletics PO Box 30017 College Station TX 77843-3017

SLOCUM, ROBERT BIGNEY, retired librarian; b. Brockton, Mass., Apr. 6, 1922; s. George Weeden and Florence Alice (Heustis) S.; m. Christine Stanfield, Aug. 23, 1953; children: Robert Stanfield, Kathryn Slocum Goodwin. BA, Boston U., 1946; MA, Columbia U., 1947; BSLS, Simmons Coll., 1949. Libr. intern Libr. of Congress, Washington, 1949-50; asst. to dir. librs. Simmons Coll., Boston, 1950-51; libr. cataloger, instr. U. Ill. Libr., Urbana, 1951-54; assoc. catalog libr. Cornell U. Libr., Ithaca, N.Y., 1954-88. Author: Sample Catalog Cards, 1962, Biographical Dictionaries and Related Works, 1967-78, 2d edit., 1986, Sample Cataloging Forms, 1968, rev. edit., 1980; editor Manual of Cataloging Procedures, 1959, rev. edit., 1969, New England in Fiction, 1994; contbr. articles to profl. jours. Active Am. for Dem. Action, Pub. Citizen, Am. Farmland Trust, steering bd. Cornell U. Retirees Vols. in Svc.; co-chmn. Dryden Bicentennial Com. With U.S. Army, 1942-45, ETO. Mem. AAUP, ALA, AARP, Am. Hist. Assn., Common Cause, Smithsonian Assocs., Dryden Hist. Soc., Sane/Freeze, Libr. Congress Assocs., NY State Hist. Assn., Newark Valley Hist. Soc., Cornell Assn. Profs. Emeriti, Cornell U. Libr. Assocs., Drake Group. Presbyterian. Avocations: hiking, movie research, victorian literature, early americana. Home: 92 W Main St Dryden NY 13053-9706 E-mail: rbs8@cornell.edu.

SLOCUM, ROSEMARIE, physician services consultant, recruiter; b. Port Arthur, Tex., Dec. 19, 1948; d. Edly and Ella (McNeely) Raccard; m. James Rubenstein; 1 child from previous marriage, Blair Ashton. BS, La. State U., Baton Rouge, 1971; MA in Bus. Comm., Jones Internat. U., Englewood, Colo., 1999. Cert. tchr. La. Edn. specialist La. Dept. Occupl. Stds., Baton Rouge, 1971-74; account exec. Uarco, Inc., 1974-77; owner, broker Rosemarie Slocum Real Estate, 1977—85; physician recruiter MSI, New Orleans, 1985-86; assoc. dir. physician recruitment Physician Svcs. Cons., Fairfax, Va., 1986-88; spl. cons. Caswell/Winters Physician Search Cons., Milw., 1988-89; v.p. U.S. Med. Search, Inc. subs. of Caswell/Winters, 1988-89; dir. physician

recruitment/mktg. East Range Clinics, Ltd., Virginia, Minn., 1989-91; pres. RSI Physician Svcs. Cons., Mpls., 1991—. Office: RSI Physician Svcs Cons 3622 W 44th St Minneapolis MN 55410-1366 Office Phone: 612-703-0410. E-mail: rsrsi@earthlink.net.

SLOGOFF, STEPHEN, dean, anesthesiologist, educator; b. Phila., July 7, 1942; s. Israel and Lillian (Rittenberg) S.; m. Barbara Anita Gershman, June 2, 1963; children: Michele, Deborah. AB in Biology, Franklin and Marshall Coll., 1964; MD, Jefferson Med. Coll., 1967. Diplomate Am. Bd. Med. Examiners, Am. Bd. Anesthesiology (jr. assoc. examiner 1977-80, sr. assoc. examiner 1980-81, bd. dirs. 1981-93, pres. 1989-90, joint coun. on in-tng. exams, vice chmn. 1983-86, chmn. 1986-92). Intern Harrisburg (Pa.) Hosp., 1967-68; resident in anesthesiology Jefferson Med. Coll. Hosp., 1968-71; chief anesthesia sect. U.S. Army, Brooke Army Med. Ctr., Fort Sam Houston, Tex., 1971-74; staff anesthesiologist Baylor Coll. Medicne, Houston, 1974-75; attending cardiovascular anesthesiologist U. Tex. Health Sci. Ctr., Houston, 1974-93, clin. asst. prof., 1977-81, clin. assoc. prof., 1981-85, clin. prof., 1985-93; prof., chmn. dept. anesthesiology Loyola U., Chgo., 1993—; sr. v.p. for clin. affairs Loyola U. Health Sys., 1999—; dean, Strich Sch. Medicine Loyola U., Chgo., 1999—. Chmn. rsch com., co-dir. rsch. labs Tex. Heart Inst., Houston, 1990-93. Contbr. articles to profl. jours. Trustee Loyola U. Health Sys., Chgo., 1996—; chmn. Loyola U. Physicians Found., 1995-99. Mem. Am. Soc. Anesthesiologists, Alpha Omega Alpha. Avocations: tennis, jogging. Office: Loyola U Med Ctr Office of Dean 2160 S 1st Ave Maywood IL 60153-3304

SLOMA, ROBERT J. business process consultant; m. Laura J. Novak, June 23, 1989; children: Michael S., Benjamin J. BSME, U. of Cin., 1987; MBA in Fin., U. of Toledo, Ohio, 1993. Mech. engr. Libbey-Owens-Ford Co., Toledo, 1987—89, product engr., 1989—91; computer graphics mgr. Modern Tools, Inc., Toledo, 1992—97; bus. process cons. Self-Employed working exclusively with Pilkington N.Am., Toledo, 1997—. Mem.: Soc. of Automotive Engrs. (assoc.), ASME (assoc.), Beta Gamma Sigma Bus. Honor Soc. (life), Phi Delta Theta (life; warden 1986—87). Achievements include patents for Application of Primer Coating. Home: 20720 Carter Rd Bowling Green OH 43402-8895

SLOMAN, MARVIN SHERK, lawyer; b. Fort Worth, Apr. 17, 1925; s. Richard Jack and Lucy Janette (Sherk) S.; m. Margaret Jane Dinwiddie, Apr. 11, 1953; children: Lucy Carter, Richard Dinwiddie. BA, U. Tex., 1948; LLB with honors, 1950. Bar: Tex. 1950, N.Y. 1951. Assoc. Sullivan & Cromwell, N.Y.C., 1950-56, Carrington, Coleman, Sloman & Blumenthal LLP and predecessor, Dallas, 1956-60, ptnr., 1960-97; sr. counsel, 1998—. Office: Carrington Coleman Sloman & Blumenthal LLP 200 Crescent Ct Ste 1500 Dallas TX 75201-1848

SLOMANSON, LLOYD HOWARD, architect, musician, photographer; b. N.Y.C., July 31, 1928; s. Albert Jerome and Dorothea (Jacobson) S.; m. Joan Barbara Kanel; children: Peter, Eric. BArch, Syracuse U., 1949. Registered architect, 18 states including N.Y. and N.J.; NCARB; registered profl. planner, N.J. Archtl. draftsman Rich & Conn Architects, Bklyn., 1949-50; project architect Fordyce & Hamby/Raymond Loewy, N.Y.C., 1951-53; project architect, assoc. ptnr. Serge P. Petroff, Architect, N.Y.C., 1953-58; project dir. Robert W. Hegardt, Architect, N.Y.C., 1959-60; project architect, ptnr. Fordyce & Hamby Assocs., N.Y.C., 1960-67; ptnr. Fordyce, Hamby & Kennerly, N.Y.C., 1967-69, Hamby, Kennerly & Slomanson, N.Y.C., 1969-72, Kennerly, Slomanson & Smith, N.Y.C., 1972-81; mng. ptnr. Slomanson, Smith & Barresi, N.Y.C., 1981-99; pvt. practice, 1999—. Arbitrator Am. Arbitration Assn. and NASD Dispute Resolution, N.Y.C. Author articles. Served with U.S. Army, 1950-51. Recipient 1st prize for design S.I. C. of C., 1967, 84. Mem. AIA, N.Y. Soc. Architects (Store of Yr. award 1985, Design award 1993), N.Y. State Assn. Architects, Bldg. Ofcls. Conf. Am., Univ. Club, The Players. Avocations: playing music with a big band, photography. Office: 137 W 78th St New York NY 10024-6702 E-mail: woodpics@aol.com.

SLONAKER, MARY JOANNA KING, columnist; b. Richmond, Ind., July 18, 1930; d. Claiborn F. and Carlyle (Diffendenfer) King; divorced; children: Mary Sue Hosey, Steven, Allis Ann Fox. Student, Earlham Coll., 1948-49; BS, Ball State U., 1969; MA in Teaching, Ind. U., 1974. Cert. residential child care worker. Home econs. tchr. Lewisville (Ind.) Sch., 1978-79, Morton Meml. Sch., Knightstown, Ind., 1970-83; town coun. mem. Cambridge City, Ind., 1991-2001. Mem. Ind. U. Chancellor's Medallion Dinner Com., 2001. Recipient Kiwanis Cmty. award, 1983-84, 95, Appreciation award Am. Bus. Women, 1985, Appreciation award Waseda U. Japanese Exch. Program, 1986-88. Mem. AAUW, Soc. Profl. Journalists, Ind. U. Alumni Club, Ind. U. Varsity Club, The Woman's Club, Psi Iota Xi, Alpha Delta Kappa, Pi Beta Phi. Democrat. Presbyterian. Avocations: basketball, football, harness racing, walking, gardening. Home: 36 W Church St Cambridge City IN 47327-1615 Office: 127 N Foote St Cambridge City IN 47327-1144

SLONAKER, NORMAN DALE, lawyer; b. Havre, Mont., Sept. 16, 1940; s. Frederick and Agnes (Monson) S.; m. Helen Bogumil, Aug. 29, 1964. BS, U. Wash., Seattle, 1962; LLM, Harvard U., 1965. Bar: NY 1966. Assoc. Sidley Austin Brown & Wood, LLP, NYC, 1965—72, ptnr., 1973—. Office Phone: 212-839-5356.

SLONE, RICCA C, state representative; b. Ottawa, Ontario, Feb. 19, 1947; m. William Berkman; children: Zachary Berkman, Sydney Berkman, Seth Berkman. BA, Wash. Univ., St. Louis, 1968; MA, Univ. of Calif., Los Angeles, Calif., 1970, Ohio State Univ., Ohio, 1978; JD, Univ. of Ill, Coll. of Law, Ill., 1990. Atty. self employed, 1991—96; free lance writer/cons., 1981—86; sr. rsch. assoc. US Dept. of Housing and Urban Develop., 1979—81, Ohio Legis. Svc. Comm., 1975—79; assoc. US Office of Mgmt. and Budget; Rep., Dist. 92 US State Rep., Ill., 1996—. Ill. State House of Rep., 1996—; mem. Peoria City-County Landfill Comm., 1994—96. Mem.: Growth Task Force, 1998-1999, Ill. House Smart (chair), Ill. Growth Task Force (Vice chair 2001—02), Bd. of Visitors, Univ. of Ill. Coll. of Law, Regional Conference, Law and the Great Lakes: Into the Twenty-First Century (planning chair), Ill. State Bar Assoc., Environ. Law Sect. Coun. (former chair 1994—95), Ill. State Bar Assoc., 1990-pres., Am. Bar Assoc., Sect. on Natural Resources, Energy and Environ. Law. Democrat. Jewish. Office: 256-W Stratton Office Bldg Springfield IL 62706 Mailing: 456 Fulton Suite 150 Peoria IL 61602 Home: 1904 Grandview Terr Peoria IL 61614

SLONE, SANDI, artist; b. Boston, Oct. 1, 1939; d. Louis and Ida (Spind) Sudikoff; children: Erric Solomon, Jon Solomon. Student, Boston Mus. Fine Arts Sch., 1970-73; BA magna cum laude, Wellesley Coll., 1974. Sr., grad. painting faculty Boston Mus. Fine Arts Sch./Tufts U., 1975—; instr. grad. program Sch. Visual Art, N.Y.C., 1989-90; lectr. painting Harvard U., Cambridge, Mass., 1982. Vis. artist Triangle Artists Workshop, N.Y., 1982, 87, 90; co-founder, dir. Art/Omi Internat. Artists Found., N.Y.C., 1992—. One-woman shows include ICA, Boston, 1977, Harcus Krakow Gallery, Boston, 1978, 79, 80, 82, 84, 86, Acquavella Contemporary Art, N.Y., 1977, 79, 80, 82, 84, Stephen Rosenberg Gallery, N.Y., 1988, Levinson Kane Gallery, Boston, 1989, Smith Jariwala Gallery, London, 1990, Jersey City Mus., 1996, The Artists Mus., Lodz, Poland, 1997, Cristinerose Gallery, N.Y.C., 1999, Savage Gallery, Portland, Oreg., 2001; exhibited in group shows at Mus. Fine Arts, Boston, 1977, Corcoran Gallery of Art 35th Biennial, Washington, 1977, Edmonton Art Mus., 1977, 85, Hayden Gallery MIT, Cambridge, Mass., 1978, New Generation Andre Emmerich Gallery, N.Y., 1980-81, Am. Ctr., Paris, 1980-81, Amerika Haus, Berlin, 1980-81, Carpenter Ctr., Harvard U., Ctr. de la Cultura Contemporania, Barcelona, 1987, Federated Union of Black Artists, Johannesburg, South Africa, 1989, Jan Weiss Gallery, N.Y., 1990, Olympia Internat. Art Fairs, London, 1991, Gallery Korea, N.Y., 1992, Klarfeld Perry Gallery, N.Y., 1994, Out of the Blue Gallery, Edinburgh, Scotland, 1994, Gallery One, Toronto, 1996, Fine Arts Ctr., U. R.I., Kingston, 1996, Crieger Dane Gallery, Boston, 1996, Visual Arts Gallery, N.Y., 1997, TransHudson Gallery, N.Y., 1997, Butler Inst. of Am. Art, Youngstown, Ohio, 1998, 45th Biennial Corcoran Mus. Art, Washington, 1998, Lombard-Freid Fine Arts, N.Y., 1999, 2000, Cristinerose Gallery, N.Y., 2001, Savage Gallery, Portland, Oreg., 2004, others; represented in permanent collections Mus. Modern Art, N.Y.C., Mus. Contemporary Art, Barcelona, Mus. Fine Arts, Boston, Hirshhorn Mus., Washington, Corcoran Gallery & Mus. Art, Washington; artist-in-residence City Hall, Barcelona, 1987, 89. Mus. Fine Arts Boston fellow, 1977, 81; Ford Found. grantee, 1979; internat. artists residency East-South Project, Poland, 1997. Studio: 13 Worth St New York NY 10013-2922

SLOSBERG, MIKE, advertising executive; b. Phila., Aug. 29, 1934; s. Sam. M. and Florence (Frank) S.; m. Joan Shidler, Aug. 29, 1957 (div. 1984); children: Sydney Ellen, Robert Morton; m. Janet Cohn, June 10, 1987. BSBA, U. Denver, 1960. With Young & Rubicam, Inc., N.Y.C., 1960-78; pres. Wunderman, Rocotta & Kline, N.Y.C., 1978-83; exec. v.p., exec. creative dir. Marsteller, Inc., N.Y.C., 1983-84, Bozell Jacobs, Kenyon & Eckhardt, N.Y.C., 1984-86, pres. direct mktg. div., 1986-87; exec. creative dir. Bronner Slosberg Humphrey, Boston, 1987-96; vice chmn., chief creative officer Digitas (formerly Bronner Slosberg Humphrey), Boston, 1996-2000; co-founder Digitas, Inc. Author: The August Strangers, 1978. Mem. Friars Club. Avocation: writing novels. Office: Digitas 355 Park Ave S New York NY 10010

SLOSBURG-ACKERMAN, JILL ROSE, artist, educator; b. Omaha, Aug. 28, 1948; d. Harold Walter and Marion (Gill) Slosburg; m. James Sloss Ackerman, Aug. 8, 1987; 1 child, Jesse August. Diploma, Boston Mus. Sch., 1971; BFA, Tufts U., 1971, MFA, 1983. Prof. art Mass. Coll. of Art, Boston, 1973—; vis. artist Cranbrook Acad. of Art, Bloomfield, Mich., Spring 1993. One-woman shows include Harcus-Krakow Gallery, Boston, 1978, 80, Helen Shlien Gallery, Boston, 1980, 82, Cohen Arts Ctr., Tufts U., Medford, Mass., 1982, Van Buren/Brazelton/Cutting Gallery, Cambridge, Mass., 1985, Genovese Gallery, Boston, 1995, Manwaring Gallery Cumings Art Ctr., Conn. Coll., New London, 1995, Rose Art Mus., Brandeis U., Waltham, Mass., 1996, Atrium Gallery/U. Mass., Dartmouth, 1999, Judy Ann Goldman Fine Art, Boston, 1999, Judy Goldman Fine Art, Boston, 2004; exhibited in group shows including Naga Gallery, Boston, Boston, 1980, DeCordova Mus., Lincoln, Mass., 1980, Jewett Art Ctr., Wellesley, Mass., 1982, Helen Shlien Gallery, Boston, 1982, Cherry Stone Gallery, Wellfleet, Mass., 1984, Quadrum Gallery, Chestnut Hill, Mass., 1985, Fed. Res. Gallery, Boston, 1986, Danforth Mus., 1986, Conseil de la Sculpture, Montreal, 1986, North Hall Gallery, Boston, 1987, Artists Found. Gallery, Boston, 1990, Mus. Decorative Arts, Prague, 1991, Nancy Margolis Gallery, NYC, 1991, Bellevue (Wash.) Art Mus., 1992, Artwear, NY, 1992, Genovese Gallery, Albany, NY, 1992, Judy Ann Goldman Fine Art, Boston, 1997, 2002, Mills Gallery, Boston, 1997-98, 2003, Boston Mus. Fine Arts, 1999, DeCordova Mus., Lincoln, Mass., 2000, Forest Hills Cemetery, Boston, 2002, 04; represented in permanent collections J.L. Brandeis & Sons, Omaha, Mass. Coll. Art, Boston, Boston Pub. Libr., City of Cambridge, also pvt. collections; contbr. articles to profl. jours. Founder, mem. Boston Women's Action Coalition; bd. dirs. Cambridge (Mass.) Multi-Cultural Ctr., Gallery at Green St., 1993. Recipient Patricia Jellinek Hallowell prize for jewelry, 1984, Disting. Svc. award Mass. Coll. of Art, 1980, 4th prize sterling silver design competition Nat. Guild of Sterling Silversmiths, 1970; fellow Haystack Mountain Sch. Crafts, Deer Isle, Maine, 1972, 76, Nat. Endowment Arts, 1974, 86, The Artists Found., Boston, 1984, Mary Ingraham Bunting Inst., 1985-86; Mass. Coll. Art profl. devel. grantee, 1987, Polaroid Corp. photography grantee, 1988, Sch. Boston Mus. Fine Arts traveling scholar, 1998, New Eng. Found. for the Arts fellow, 1998; Mass. Cultural Coun. Artist's grantee, 1999, grantee Artist's Resource Trust, 2001. Jewish. Home: 12 Coolidge Hill Rd Cambridge MA 02138-5510 Studio: One Fitchburg St Apt C415 Somerville MA 02143-2128 Office Phone: 617-625-4056. Personal E-mail: jackerman86@comcast.net.

SLOSS, MERLE, shoe company executive; b. Atlantic City, N.J., Feb. 26, 1948; d. Ralph and Annette (Nemirosky) S.; m. Matthew Barry Smith, June 10, 1973. BA in Chemistry, U. Pa., 1970; MBA, Boston U., 1972. Asst. product mgr. Gen. Foods Corp., White Plains, N.Y., 1972-73, assoc. product mgr., 1974-75, product mgr., 1976-78, group product mgr., 1979-82; dir. mktg. Bally of Switzerland, New Rochelle, N.Y., 1982-83, v.p. mktg., 1984, exec. v.p., gen. mgr., 1985-92, also bd. dirs., pres. and CEO, 1992-93; pres. of licensing Anne Klein, New York, NY, 1995-96; pres. Ralph Lauren Footware; pres. of licensing Anne Klein, 2000—. Mem. Women in Mgmt., Phi Lamda Upsilon, Beta Gamma Sigma. Democrat. Jewish. Avocations: photography, art history, travel. Office: Anne Klein 11 W 42nd St New York NY 10036-8002

SLOSSON, CONSTANCE SWEET, retired music educator; b. New Brighton, Pa., Jan. 31, 1942; d. W. Coburn, Jr. and Nancy McIlwain Sweet; m. George F. Slosson, Aug. 15, 1964; children: Deborah Tilmont, Sharon Bucks, Barbara Boulerice, Ronald. BS in Christian edn., Baldwin-Wallace Coll., Berea, Ohio, 1959—63; MS in music edn., SUNY, Potsdam, 1963—66. Cert. Music Edn. K-12 NY State Edn. Dept., 1966. Music tchr. Cumberland Head Elem. Sch., Plattsburgh, NY, 1963—67; elem. music tchr. St. Mary's Acad., Champlain, NY, 1983—85; music tchr. Northside Elem. Sch., Peru, NY, 1986—89, Plattsburgh City Sch. Dist., 1989—97; pvt. music instrn. Slosson Music Studios, Plattsburgh, 1997—. Ch. organist Glenville Presbyn. Ch., Cleve., 1957—60, Plattsburgh AFB Chapel, 1963—66, First Meth. Ch., 1968—71; asst. choir dir. Ch. Nazarene, 2001—. Mem., com. chmn. Plattsburgh Mothers Club, 1968—74; music chmn., gen. co-chm. BiCentennial Celebration 1976, Chazy, 1974—76; co-chairman West Chazy BiCentennial Field Days, 1974—76; girl scout troop leader Chazy Jr. Girl Scout Troop, NY, 1974—82; tchr. Congl. Ch., Berea, Ohio, 1961—63; ch. sch. tchr., supt. Chazy Presbyn. Ch., 1974—81; ch. sch. tchr. Ch. Nazarene, 1986—89; mem., officer West Chazy Grange #979, 1964—90. Mem.: AAUW (rec. sec. 1968—71), Am. Orff Schulwerk Assn., Clinton County Music Educators Assn. (corresponding sec. 1965—68), Music Educators Nat. Conf., NY State Sch. Music Assn., NY State Ret. Tchrs. Assn. (life). Avocations: singing, swimming, travel, mentoring. Home: 76 Slosson Rd West Chazy NY 12992

SLOTKIN, TODD, holding company executive; b. Detroit, Mar. 19, 1953; s. Hugo and Babette Slotkin; m. Judy Scavone, Jan. 30, 1988; children: Matthew, William, Thomas, Peter. BS, Cornell U., 1974, MBA, 1975. With Citicorp, 1975-92, sr. credit officer, 1984-92, head divsn. corp. fin., 1988-90, sr. mng. dir., 1990-92; with MacAndrews & Forbes Holdings, Inc., N.Y.C., 1992—, sr. v.p., 1992-98, exec. v.p., 1998—, CFO, 1999—; dir. Century Bus. Svc., Inc., 2003—. Dir. Food Allergy Initiative, 1999—. Home: 888 Park Ave Apt 12 B New York NY 10021 Office: MacAndrews & Forbes Holding 35 E 62nd St New York NY 10021-8032

SLOTNICK, BARRY IVAN, lawyer; b. N.Y.C., June 18, 1939; s. Meyer and Rose Ann (Hurwitz) S.; m. Donna Miriam Auerbach, July 12, 1968; children: Stuart Philip, Melissa Lynne, Deborah Anne-Shoshana, Melanie Judith-Chani. BA, CCNY, 1959; JD, NYU, 1961. Bar: N.Y. 1961, U.S. Ct. Appeals (2d cir.), U.S. Dist. Ct. (ea. dist., so. dist.) N.Y., U.S. Supreme Ct., 1966. Pvt. practice, N.Y.C., 1966-68; sr. ptnr. Slotnick & Baker, N.Y.C., 1986-94, Slotnick & Shapiro, LLP (now Slotnick, Shapiro & Crocker LLP), N.Y.C., 1994—. Adj. prof. in trial practice Cardozo Law Sch., N.Y.C., 1983—; judge moot ct. competition NYU and Bklyn. Law Sch., 1978—. Contbr. articles to profl. jours. Recipient Anti-defamation and Anti-discrimination award Italian Am. Civil Rights League, 1970, Honor plaque Jewish Def. League, 1973, Champion of Youth award B'nai B'rith, 1973, Masada award Jewish Identity Ctr., 1978, AMMY award for best criminal lawyer Am. Lawyer, 1981, Humanitarian award Crime Victims' Profl. Platform, 1982, Award on Behalf of Crime Victims N.Y. Supreme Ct. Officers Assn., 1983, Israel Leadership Peace award Greater Westchester Div., 1984; named Man of Yr. Young Israel Scarsdale, 1982. Mem. N.Y. State Bar Assn. (criminal justice sect.-Outstanding Practitioner award 1987, fed. judiciary com.), Fed. Bar Assn., Inter-Am. Bar Assn., Assn. of Bar of City of N.Y., N.Y. County Lawyer's Assn., Bronx County Bar Assn., P.R. Bar Assn. (assoc. selective svc. examiner 1968-70, spl. dep. atty. gen. 1972). Clubs: Atrium, Downtown Athletic (N.Y.). Republican. Avocation: boating. Office: Slotnick Shapiro & Crocker LLP 100 Park Ave 35th Fl New York NY 10017

SLOTNICK, MORTIMER H. artist; b. N.Y.C., Nov. 7, 1920; s. Max S. and Sarah B. S.; m. Phyllis June Gluckin, July 26, 1953; children: Debra Jan, Mark Stuart. BSS, CCNY, 1942; MA, Tchrs. Coll., Columbia U., 1942. Tchr. visual arts, public schs., New Rochelle, N.Y., 1946-64; supr. arts and humanities City Sch. Dist., 1964-72; prin. Davis Elem. Sch., 1972-84. Adj. prof. art CCNY, 1964-72; prof. art Coll. New Rochelle, N.Y., 1972-78; adj. prof. edn. Pace U., 1988-93. One-man shows include Ada Ahrtz Galleries, N.Y.C., 1959, Westport (Conn.) Art Gallery, 1986, New Rochelle Coun. on the Arts, 1989, exhibited in group shows Nat. Acad. N.Y., World Trade Ctr., N.Y.C., Lever House, N.Y.C., Am. Artists Profl. League, Nat. Arts Club, Salmagundi Club, Kent (Conn.) Art Gallery; represented in permanent collections Nat. Mus. Am. Art, Smithsonian Instn., New Britain Mus. Am. Art, Johnson Mus. Art Cornell U., Nat. Archives, Washington, Truman Home, Independence, Mo., F.D.R. Mus., Hyde Park, N.Y.; also pvt. and corp. collections; works published in Artists of Am. Calendar. Mem. City Art Commn. New Rochelle, 1977-80. Served with AUS, 1942-46, ETO, PTO. Mem. N.Y. Artists Equity Assn., Allied Artists Am., Am. Artists Profl. League, Coll. Art Assn., Nat. Assn. Humanities Edn., Art. Pub., Am. Artists Group, Bernard Picture Co., McLeery-Cumming Co., Donald Art. Co., Scafa-Tornabene Art Publ., A. B. Franklin Gallery, Internet, Masons. Home and Office: 43 Amherst Dr New Rochelle NY 10804-1814 E-mail: Phyllmor@gateway.net. *An artist must respect the totality of his art. His work must express his integrity, his honesty and his wish to communicate with the viewer. It must strive toward the sublime. Anything less is unworthy of being called art.*

SLOTNICK, ROBERT D, food products executive; B in bus. adminstrn., Fairleigh Dickinson U. Systems analyst to mgr. of distbn. systems Warner-Lambert Co., 1980—85; MIS dir. AFI, 1985, v.p. ops., 1987, gen. mgr., 1992, co-pres., 1997; sr. v.p. Performance Food Group, 2003—, CIO, 1999—. Office: Performance Food Group P O Box 29269 Richmond VA 23242

SLOTSVE, GEORGE AARON, economist, educator, consultant; b. Estevan, Saskatchewan, Can., Sept. 5, 1959; s. Stanley and Mary Elizabeth Slotsve. BA (with honors), Queen's U., Kingston, Ont., Can., 1981; MA in Econ., U. Western Ont., London, Can., 1982; MS in Econ., U. Wis., 1985, PhD in Econ., 1989. Prof. Vanderbilt U., Nashville, 1988—96, No. Ill. U., DeKlab, 1996—. Vis. prof. Queen's U., Kingston, Ont., Canada, 1992, U. Philippines, Quezon City, 1999. Author: (book) Are We Becoming Two Societies?: Income Polarization and the Myth of the Declining Middle Class in Canada. Office: Northern Ill Univ Dept Econ Zulauf Hall Dekalb IL 60115 Personal E-mail: gslotsve@niu.edu. E-mail: gslotsve@niu.edu.

SLOUGH, MAJOR CARL, lawyer, writer; b. Cin., Aug. 11, 1918; s. Carl Paul and Elizabeth Lucille (McAuley) S.; m. Adele Benero, July 27, 1950; children— Robert Bernero, James Anthony. A.B., Columbia U., 1938; J.D., Ind. U., 1941. Bar: Ind. 1941, Kans. 1965, U.S. Supreme Ct. 1971. Assoc., Kivett & Kivett, Indpls., 1941-46; prof. law U. Kans., Lawrence, 1946-57, dean Sch. Law, 1957-60; prof. law U. Tex., Austin, also judge Mcpl. Ct., St. Marys, Kans., 1961-72; judge pro tem Dist. Ct. Kans., 1970; ptnr. Wagner, Leek & Mullins, Shawnee Mission, Kans., 1961—; lectr. U. Kans. Med. Sch., Menninger Found. Mem. Gov.'s Adv. Com. Constl. Revision, Gov.'s Adv. Com. State Mental Instns., 1957-60. Served to lt. USNR, 1942-46. Mem. ABA, Kans. Bar Assn., Order of Coif, Phi Delta Phi. Republican. Roman Catholic. Club: Kansas City. Author: Kansas Civil Code, 1960; Obscenity and Constitutional Freedom, 1964; Privacy Freedom and Responsibility, 1969; Obscenity Freedom and Responsibility, 1976; contbr. articles law and med. jours.

SLOVIK, SANDRA LEE, retired art educator; b. Elizabeth, N.J., Mar. 22, 1943; d. Edward Stanley and Frances (Garbus) S. BA, Newark State Coll., 1965, MA, 1970. Cert. art tchr. Art tchr. Holmdel (N.J.) Twp. Bd. Edn., 1965-99, ret., 1999. Computer art in-sv. tng. Holmdel Bd. Edn., 1990; computer art workshop Madison (N.J.) Bd. Edn., 1991; presenter Nat. Edn. Computer Conv., 1999. Charter supporter, mem. Statue of Liberty/Ellis Island Found., 1976—; charter supporter Sheriffs' Assn. N.J., 1993—; mem. PTA, Holmdel, 1965—. Recipient Curriculum award N.J. ASCD, 1992; grantee Holmdel Bd. Edn., 1989, 90, N.J. Bus., Industry, Sci., Edn. Consortium, 1990. Mem. NEA, Nat. Art Edn., Assn., N.J. Art Educators Assn., N.J. Edn. Assn., Monmouth County Edn. Assn., Holmdel Twp. Edn. Assn. (sr. bldg. rep. 1977-79). Avocations: travel, sports. Office: Village Sch 67 Mccampbell Rd Holmdel NJ 07733-2299 E-mail: sslovik@hotmail.com.

SLOVIS, THOMAS LAURENCE, radiologist; b. Passaic, N.J., June 16, 1941; BA, Hobart Coll., 1963; MD, U. Pa., 1967. Diplomate Am. Bd. Pediats., Am. Bd. Radiology; cert. added qualification in pediat. radiology. Pediat. resident U. Colo. Med. Ctr., Denver, 1967-70; radiology resident Columbia Presbyn. Hosp. Babies Hosp., N.Y.C., 1972-75; prof. radiology and pediats. Wayne State U. Sch. Medicine, Detroit, 1984—; chief pediat. imaging Children's Hosp. Mich., 1987—2003; mng. editor Pediatric Radiology, 2003—. Author: Imaging of Pediatric Urinary Tract, 1989; editor: Caffey's Pediatric Diagnostic Imaging, 10th edit.; contbr. 200 articles to profl. jours. Maj. USAF, 1970-72. Mem. Soc. Pediat. Radiology (pres. 1999-2000, chmn. bd. 2000-2001). Office: Children's Hosp Mich 3901 Beaubien Detroit MI 48201

SLOVITER, DOLORES KORMAN, federal judge; b. Phila., Sept. 5, 1932; d. David and Tillie Korman; m. Henry A. Sloviter, Apr. 3, 1969 (dec. May 2003); 1 child, Vikki Amanda. AB in Econs. with distinction, Temple U., 1953, LHD (hon.), 1986; LLB magna cum laude, U. Pa., 1956; LLD (hon.), Dickinson Sch. Law, 1984, U. Richmond, 1992, Widener U., 1994. Bar: Pa. 1957. From assoc. to ptnr. Dilworth, Paxson, Kalish, Kohn & Levy, Phila., 1956—69; mem. Harold E. Kohn PA, Phila., 1969—72; from assoc. prof. to prof. Temple U. Law Sch., Phila., 1972—79; judge U.S. Ct. Appeals (3rd cir.), Phila., 1979—, chief judge, 1991—98. Bd. overseers U. Pa. Law Sch., 1993—99; bd. trustees Nat. Constitution Ctr., 1998—; mem. Jud. Conf. of U.S., 1991—98. Chair Pa. Rhodes Scholarship Selection Com., 2003—; mem. S.E. region Pa. Gov.'s Conf. on Aging, 1976—79, Com. of 70, 1976—79; U.S. com. Bicentennial Constn., 1987—90; com. on Rules of Practice and Procedure, 1990—93; trustee Jewish Publ. Soc. Am., 1983—89. Recipient Juliette Low medal, Girl Scouts Greater Phila., Inc., 1990, Honor award, Girls High Alumnae Assn., 1991, Jud. award, Pa. Bar Assn., 1994, James Wilson award, U. Pa., 1996, Cert. of Honor award, Temple U., 1996; Disting. Fulbright scholar, Chile, 1990. Mem.: ABA, Phila. Bar Assn. (gov. 1976—78, Sandra Day O'Connor award 1997), Am. Judicature Soc. (bd. dirs. 1990—95), Nat. Assn. Women Judges, Am. Law Inst., Fed. Judges Assn., Fed. Bar Assn., Order of Coif (pres. U. Pa. chpt. 1975—77), Phi Beta Kappa. Office: US Ct Appeals 18614 US Courthouse 601 Market St Philadelphia PA 19106-1713

SLOWIAK, JAMES, theater director, educator; b. Stanley, Wis., Mar. 26, 1955; s. Raymond and Yvonne Slowiak; life ptnr. Jairo Cuesta. BA in Anthropology, French, and Dramatic Arts, Macalester Coll., 1977; MFA in Directing, U. Calif., Irvine, 1985. Founder, artistic dir. At Random Theatre Ensemble, St. Paul, 1978—82; asst. Focused Rsch. Program in Objective Drama, Irvine, Calif., 1983—92, Workcenter of Jerzy Grotowski, Pontedera, Italy, 1986—89; prof. of theatre U. Akron, Ohio, 1989—; co-artistic dir. New World Performance Lab., Akron, Ohio, 1992—. Conducted workshops Internationally. Dir.(playwright): (performance) Winesburg, Ohio (ACTF Regional Festival, 2004), Love in the Time of Lunatics, Hamletmachine, Woyzeck (Fragments from a Morality Play as Performed by the Prodigies of Dr. Somnus' Freak Show (No. Ohio Live Achievement nomination, 1998), The Book of Saints and Martyrs, Mother's Work, (of performances at numerous festivals internationally). Office: Univ Akron Theatre Program Akron OH 44325-1005 Office Phone: 330-972-5909. Personal E-mail: nwpl@eudoramail.com. E-mail: nwpl@lycos.com.

SLOWIK, RICHARD ANDREW, air force officer; b. Detroit, Sept. 9, 1939; s. Louis Stanley ad Mary Jean (Zaucha) S; 1 stepchild, Amber Dawn Evans. BS, U.S. Air Force Acad., 1963; BS in Bus. Adminstrn., No. Mich. U., 1967; LLB, LaSalle Extension U., 1969; MBA, Fla. Tech. U., 1972; MS in Adminstrn., Ga. Coll., 1979; MA, Georgetown U., 1983; postgrad. cert., Va. Poly. Inst. and State U., 1986. Commd. 1st lt. U.S. Air Force, 1963, advanced through grades to lt. col; pilot Craig AFB, Ala., 1963-64, Sawyer AFB, Mich., 1964-68; forward air contr. Pacific Air Forces, South Vietnam, 1968-69; pilot SAC, McCoy AFB, Fla., 1969-71; asst. prof. aerospace studies Va. Poly. Inst.

and State U., Blacksburg, 1972-76; br. chief current ops. br. Robins AFB, Ga., 1976-80; asst. dep. chief ops. group Hdqrs Air Force, Pentagon, Washignton, 1980-82; Western Hemisphere and Pacific Area desk officer Nat. Mi. Command Ctr., Pentagon, Washington, 1982-83; mil. rep Ops. Ctr., Dept. State, Washington, 1983-85; ops. officer 97th Bombardment Wing, Blytheville AFB, Ark., 1985-87; chief base ops. and tng. divsn. 97th Combat Support Group, Blytheville AFB, Ark., 1987-88; chief airfield mgmt. divsn. Eaker AFB, Ark., 1988-91; freelance writer, 1991—. Contbr. articles to profl. jours. Group ops. officer CAP, Marquette, Mich., 1967-67, Orlando, Fla., 1970-72, sr. programs officer, Blacksburg, 1972-76, Warner Robins, Ga., 1976-80, wing plans and programs officer, Washington, 1980—. Decorated Def. Meritorious Svc. medal, 10 Air medals, 3 Air Force Meritorious Svc. medals, 2 Commendation medals, Corss of Gallantry with palm, Presdl. Legion of Merit, Presdl. Medal of Merit (3), Presdl. Achievement award (3), others; recipient Bill Baker Short Story award Miss. County Writers Guild, 1995. Mem. Acad. of Mgmt., Air Force Assn., Cato Inst., Heritage Found., Mil. Order World Wars, Am. Def. Preparedness Assn., Am. Security Coun., Order of Daedalians. Roman Catholic. Home and Office: 1708 N Broadway St Blytheville AR 72315-1320 E-mail: slowik@blyonline.com., ras6@georgetown.edu.

SLOYAN, GERARD STEPHEN, religious studies educator, priest; b. N.Y.C., Dec. 13, 1919; s. Jerome James and Marie (Kelley) S. AB, Seton Hall U., 1940; S.T.L., Cath. U. Am., 1944, PhD, 1948; DLitt, Seton Hall U., 1984; HHD, St. Ambrose U., 1995. Ordained priest Roman Cath. Ch., 1944. Asst. pastor in, Trenton, Maple Shade, N.J., 1947-50; mem. faculty Cath. U. Am., Washington, 1950-67, chmn. dept. religion, 1957-67; prof. N.T. studies Temple U., Phila., 1967-90, chmn. dept. religion, 1970-74, 84-86. Disting. lectr. Georgetown U., 1997—; vis. prof. Cath. U. Am., Washington, 1992—, Iowa State U., 1995. English editor: N.T., The New American Bible, 1970; author: Jesus on Trial: Development of the Passion Narratives, 1973, Historical Atlas of the Religions of the World, 1974, Is Christ the End of the Law?, 1978, Jesus in Focus, 1983, 2d edit., 1993, The Jesus Tradition, 1986, John: "Interpretation" Commentary, 1988, Jesus, Redeemer and Divine Word, 1989, What Are They Saying About John?, 1991, rev. edit., 2004, Walking in the Truth: 1, 2, and 3 John, 1995, The Crucifixion of Jesus, History, Myth, Faith, 1995, Open Catholicism, The Tradition at Its Best, 1997, Holy Week and Easter, 1999, What Men Owe to Women, Men's Voices from World Religions, 2001, Preaching from the Lectionary: An Exegetical Commentary, 2003, Why Jesus Died, 2004. Recipient Pro Ecclesia et Pontifice medal, 1970, Johannes Quasten medal Cath U. Am., 1985, Michael Mathis award Notre Dame Ctr. Pastoral Liturgy, 1994. Mem. AAUP, Cath. Bibl. Assn., Soc. Bibl. Lit., Cath. Theol. Soc. Am. (John Courtney Murray award 1981, pres. 1993-94), Coll. Theology Soc. (pres. 1964-66), Liturg. Conf. (pres. 1962-64, v.p. 1970-71, 75-88, chmn. bd. dirs. 1980-88), N.Am. Acad. Liturgy (Berakah award 1986). Democrat. E-mail: cua-religed@cua.edu.

SLOYAN, PATRICK JOSEPH, journalist; b. Stamford, Conn., Jan. 11, 1937; s. James Joseph and Annamae (O'Brien) Sloyan; m. Phyllis Hampton, Nov. 19, 1960; children: Nora, Amy, Patrick, John. BS, U. Md., 1963. Reporter Albany (N.Y.) Times-Union, 1957—58, Balt. News Post, 1958—60, UPI, Washington, 1960—69, Hearst News Svc., Washington, 1969—74, Newsday, Washington, 1974—81, bur. chief London, 1981—86, Washington, 1986—88, sr. corr., 1988—2001; assoc. editor Digital Journalist.org, 2002—. Dir. Fund for Investigative Journalism, Washington, 1987—. With U.S. Army, 1955—57. Recipient Best Writing award, Am. Soc. Newspaper Editors, 1982, War Reporting award, George Polk Awards, 1992, Pulitzer Prize for internat. reporting, 1992, Raymond Clapper award, 1996; Alicia Patterson Found. fellow, 2000. Mem.: Gridiron Club. Roman Catholic. Avocations: gardening, swimming, tennis. Home: 17115 Simpson Cir Paeonian Springs VA 20129-1735

SLUBERSKI, THOMAS RICHARD, international educator, journalist, theologian; b. Jersey City, Dec. 7, 1939; s. Walter and Anna Louise (Gall) S. BA with honors, Concordia U., 1962; MDiv with high honors, Concordia Sem., 1966; postgrad., U. Vienna, Austria, 1966, U. Erlangen-Nuremberg, Fed. Republic Germany, 1966-68; MA in English Lit., Washington U., 1970; ThD with honors, U. Heidelberg, Fed. Republic Germany, 1973, NYU, 1978. Ordained to ministry Luth. Ch.-Mo. Synod, 1969. Vicar Zion Luth. Ch., Wausau, Wis., 1964-65; asst. to dean chapel., lectr. dept. theology Valparaiso (Ind.) U., 1969-70; prof. English, religion, humanities Concordia Univ. Sys., Bronxville, N.Y., 1972—, Duda chair in religion, 2000—; pastor St. Matthew's Luth. Ch., Hastings-on-Hudson, N.Y., 1977-87; exec. dir. Am. Luth. Publicity Bur., 1987-89; guest prof. ULBRA U., Canoas, Brazil, 2004—. Rsch. asst., editor Luth. World Fedn., Geneva, 1968—69; judge Nat. Physique com., 1983—87, Russian Fedn. Body Builders, 1992—94; coord. 9th and 10th Inter-Luth. forums, 1988—90; bd. dirs. Luth. Soc. Worship, Music and Arts, 1971—73; lectr. U. St. Petersburg, U. Omsk, Merchant Marine Acad., Vladivostok, Russia, U. Khabarovsk, U. Vladivostok, Alexander von Herzen U., Russia; staff Russian-Am. Press Ctr.; warden U.S. Consulate at St. Petersburg; coord. vols. St. Petersburg Goodwill Games, 1994; tchr. sports mktg. Sports Couns. of Singapore, Hong Kong and Kuala Lumpur, Malaysia, 1995; prof. Russian Luth. Sem., 1992—94, Deacon's Tng. Sch., 1992—94; instr., bd. mem. Ben Weider Coll. Bodybldg., St. Petersburg, 1993—94; advisor Internat. Shaping Fedn., 1992—94; mem. exec. bd. 15th Ann. Workshop on Jewish Christian Rels., Stamford, Conn.; bd. dirs. Peterschule, St. Petersburg, 1993—94. Asst. editor Seminarian jour., 1965-66; lit. survey editor, rsch. asst. Luth. World Fedn., Geneva, Switzerland, 1968-69; judge (TV) Emmy's, 1995—; contbr. articles to profl. jours. Juror Am. Film Festival, N.Y.C., 1976-87; mem. nat. faculty of U.S. Sports Acad., Daphne, Ala., 1995—. Austrian State scholar, 1966; Bavarian State scholar, 1966-67; World Coun. Chs. fellow, 1967, Nat. Merit scholar, 1958, Luth. World Fedn. scholar, 1967, Deutscher Akademischer Austauschdienst fellow, 1970-72, Ctr. for Creative Persons fellow, 1975, 76; Aid Assn. for Luths. Faculty Study grantee, 1972. Fellow Christian Writers Inst.; mem. Nat. Acad. TV Arts and Scis., Polish Inst. Arts and Scis., Am. Film Inst., Soc. Arts, Religion and Culture. Office: ULBRA U Canoas Brazil Home: 529 Bastogne Dr Akron OH 44303-1606 E-mail: sluberski@aol.com.

SLUDIKOFF, STANLEY ROBERT, publisher, writer; b. Bronx, N.Y., July 17, 1935; s. Harry and Lillie (Elberger) S.; m. Ann Paula Blumberg, June 30, 1972; children: Lisa Beth, Jaime Dawn, Bonnie Joy. B.Arch., Pratt Inst., 1957; grad. student, U. So. Calif., 1960-62. Cert. planner Am. Inst. Cert. Planners. Project planner Robert E. Alexander, F.A.I.A. & Assos., Los Angeles, 1965-66, Daniel, Mann, Johnson & Mendenhall (City and Regional Planning Cons.), Los Angeles, 1967-70; pres., editor, pub. Gambling Times Inc., also Two Worlds Mgmt., Inc., Los Angeles, 1971—2003; v.p. Prima Quality Farms, Inc., P.R.; chmn. Creative Games, Inc., 1992—. Pres. Las Vegas TV Weekly, also Postal West, Las Vegas, 1975-79; founder Stanley Roberts Sch. Winning Blackjack, 1976; instr. city and regional planning program U. So. Calif., 1960-63; founding mem. Mfrs. Direct, 1996. Author: (under pen name Stanley Roberts) Winning Blackjack, 1971, How to Win at Weekend Blackjack, 1973, Gambling Times Guide to Blackjack, 1983; author: The Beginner's Guide to Winning Blackjack, 1983, Begin to Win at Blackjack, 1997, Begin to Win at Video Poker, 1997, Begin to Win at Craps, 1997; also monthly column, 1977—; creator & tournament dir. The World Casino Games; editor/pub. Poker Player Newspaper, 1982-88, 2003—; inventor Daily Digit lottery game, Straight Out casino game; founder www.gamblingtimes.com, 1995—; patentee in field. Mem. Destination 90 Forum, Citizens Planning Group, San Fernando Valley, Calif., 1966-67, Rebuild L.A. land use com., 1992—. Served to lt. col. U.S. Army, now Res. ret. Recipient commendation from mayor Los Angeles for work on model cities funding, 1968 Mem. AIA, Am. Planning Assn., Am. Inst. Cert. Planners, Internat. Casino Assn. (sec. 1980-), Res. Officers Assn. (life), Mensa (life) Achievements include invention of Straight Out gambling game. Home: 10035 Laramie Ave Chatsworth CA 91311-3912 Office: 3883 W Century Blvd Inglewood CA 90303-1003 E-mail: srs@gamblingtimes.com. *The challenge of being alive lies in the development of one's maximum potential. To do less is to fly in the face of the gifts of creation, to shorten the aspect of one's life and to deny the fullness of existence. "The weakness of the flesh" prevents anyone's full development from reaching fruition but the personal and societal loss lies in giving up too soon, before we have fully tested our limits.*

SLUMAN, JEFF (JEFFREY GEORGE SLUMAN), professional golfer; b. Rochester, New York, Sept. 11, 1957; m. Linda; 1 child, Kathryn Doreen. BA in Fin., Fla. State U., 1980. Professional golfer, 1980—. Professional golfer, mem. PGA, winner PGA Championship, 1988; Tucson Chrysler Classic, 1997; Greater Milwaukee Open, 1998; Sony Open in Hawaii, 1999. Office: c/o PGA Tour 112 Tpc Blvd Ponte Vedra Beach FL 32082-3046

SLUSHER, KIMBERLY GOODE, researcher; b. Benham, Ky., Oct. 4, 1960; d. Herschel James and Nevelyn Faye (Hayes) Goode; m. Joe Allan Slusher, May 1, 1985; children: Tarah Rena, Preston Cole. BS in Agr., Ea. Ky. U., 1982; MS in Agr., U. Tenn., 1989. Rsch. asst. U. Tenn., Knoxville, 1983-89; info. analyst Oak Ridge (Tenn.) Nat. Lab., 1989—, tchr., cons. sci. honors program, 1993. Author: (army study) Drinking Water Contamination Study, 1995; contbr. chpt.: Teratogens: Chemicals Which Cause Birth Defects, 1993. Methodist. Avocations: gardening, piano. Office: Human Gene Info Analysis Sect 1060 Commerce Park Dr # Ms6480 Oak Ridge TN 37830-8043 E-mail: Kfg@ornl.gov.

SLUSS, DOROTHY LOUISE, education educator, researcher; b. Hurley, Va., Aug. 2, 1951; d. Monroe Irvin and Mildred A. Dotson Justus; m. James Roger Sluss, Sr., Aug. 5, 1969; 1 child, James Roger II. BS, U. of Va., 1978; MS (magna cum laude), Va. Tech., 1983, PhD, 1995. Commonwealth of Va. Postgrad. Profl. Cert. Va. State Dept. of Edn., 1983. Elem. tchr. Coeburn Primary and Mid. Schs., Va., 1978—92; adj. prof. Va. Tech., Blacksburg, 1993—94; vis. prof. Emory & Henry Coll., Va., 1994—95; asst. prof. East Tenn. State U., Johnson City, 1995—2000, assoc. prof., program coord., 2000—01; assoc. prof. Clemson U., SC, 2001—. V.p. Va. Assn. for the Edn. of Young Children, 1994—95; dir. project ties East Tenn. State U., Johnson City, SC, 1996—2001; panel chair, grants reviewer U.S. Dept. of Edn., Washington, 2000; pres. The Assn. for the Study of Play, 2000—01; adv. bd. Playing for Keeps, Wilmette, Ill., 2003—. Author: (book chpt.) Block play among preschool children, Project TIES Training Manual; editor (guest editor for rsch.): (play policy and practice newsletter) National Newsletter; editor: (newsletter) The Association for the Study of Play. Clk. of the session, elder Castlewood Presbyn. Ch., Va., 1985—99. Recipient Darden Soc. award, U. of Va. at Wise, 1978, W.D. Richmond award in Edn., 1978; grantee Towards Inclusion in Edn. Project (TIES), U.S. Office of Edn., 1996—2002. Mem.: Soc. for Rsch. in Child Devel. (assoc.), Kappa Omicron Nu (treas. 1993—94), Phi Delta Kappa (assoc.; sec. 2002—03), Phi Kappa Phi (assoc.). Office: Clemson U 406 Tillman Hall Clemson SC 29634 Personal E-mail: djsluss@charter.net. E-mail: djsluss@clemson.edu.

SLUSSER, EUGENE ALVIN, electronics manufacturing executive; b. Denver, Mar. 13, 1922; s. Jesse Alvin and Grace (Carter) S.; m. Anne L. Longley, Oct. 2, 1943; children: Robert, Jon, Carolyn. BS in Physics, U. Denver, 1947. Registered profl. engr., N.H. Mem. staff MIT Radiation Lab., Cambridge, 1942-45; project engr. Heiland Rsch. Co., Denver, 1945-47; cons. Gen. Telephone Sys., N.Y.C., 1947-51; project engr. Airborne Inst. Lab., Mineola, N.Y., 1951-53; v.p. N.E. Electronics Corp., Concord, N.H., 1953-58; pres. Aerotronic Assocs., Inc., Contoocook, N.H., 1958-84, N.H. Automatic Equipment Corp., Concord, N.H., 1962-90, N.H. Realty Corp., Concord, N.H., 1990-96, E.A. Slusser & Assocs., Concord, N.H. Patentee electronics field. Chmn. Hopkinton (N.H.) Water Bd., 1962-69, Hopkinton Planning Bd., 1971-77, Hopkinton Precinct Bd. Adjustment, 1977. Mem. Aircraft Owners and Pilots Assn., Captiva Island (Fla.) Yacht Club (past commodore), Wharf Rat Club, Anglers Club, Pacific Club (Nantucket, Mass.), Masons (32 degree). Office: 232 Putney Hill Rd Concord NH 03301 E-mail: easlusser@aol.com.

SLUSSER, MICHAEL, theology studies educator, department chairman, priest; BA, St. Paul Sem., Minn., 1962; MA, Cath. U. Louvain, Belgium, 1965, STB, 1966; DPhil in Theology, U. Oxford, Eng., 1975. Prof. theology Duquesne U., Pitts., 2000—, chair, dept. theology. Mem.: Assn. Internat. d'Etudes Patristiques (gen. sec.), Coll. Theology Soc., North Am. Patristics Soc., Soc. of Bibl. Lit., Cath. Theol. Soc. Am. Office: Duquesne U Dept Theology Pittsburgh PA 15282 Office Phone: 412-396-5716. E-mail: slusser@duq.edu.

SLUSSER, ROBERT WYMAN, aerospace company executive; b. Mineola, NY, May 10, 1938; s. John Leonard and Margaret McKenzie (Wyman) S.; m. Linda Killeas, Aug. 3, 1968. BS, MIT, 1960; MBA, U. Pa., 1962; ERC, Ft. Belvior Def. Sys. Mgmt. Sch., 1977; AMP, Claremont, 1982. Assoc. adminstr.'s staff NASA Hdqrs., Washington, 1962-65; with Northrop Corp., Hawthorne, Calif., 1965-96; adminstr. Space Labs., 1965-68; mgr. bus. and fin. Warnecke Electron Tubes Co. divsn., Chgo., 1968-71; mgr. bus. adminstrn. YF-17 Program Aircraft Divsn., 1971-75, mgr. adminstrn. F-18/Cobra programs, also mgr. F-18 design to cost program, 1975-79, mgr. engring. adminstrn., 1980-82, acting v.p. engring., 1982, v.p. info. resources, 1983-91, mgr. long range planning, 1991-93, program mgr.-bus. F/A-18E/F program, 1994-96, cons., 1996—. Bd. dirs., CFO So. Calif. Hist. Aviation Found., 1987-90, chmn. of bd., pres., 1990-97; treas. Flight Path Learning Ctr. of So. Calif., 1996-2001; bd. dirs., contracting officer, PDES, 1988-91; mem. dirs. adv. bd. S.C. Rsch. Authority, 1991-95. Grumman Aircraft Engring. scholar, 1956-60. Fellow AIAA (assoc., membership chmn. L.A. sect. 1996-98); mem. So. Calif. Soc. Info. Mgmt. (mem. exec. com. 1987-91), Northrop Mgmt. Club (bd. dirs. 1992-93, Man of Yr. 1991-92). Avocation: private pilot. Home: 7270 Berry Hill Dr Palos Verdes Peninsula CA 90275-4402

SLUSSER, WILLIAM PETER, investment banker; b. June 20, 1929; s. Eugene and Thelma (Donovan) S.; m. Joanne Eleanor Briggs, June 20, 1953; children: Kathleen E., Martin E., Wendelin M., Caroline E., Sarah A. BA cum laude, Stanford U., 1951; MBA, Harvard U., 1953. Mgr. spl. situations dept. Dean Witter & Co., N.Y.C., 1955-60; ptnr., sr. v.p. in charge corp. fin. dept. Shields & Co., N.Y.C., 1960-75; co-mgr., investment banking divsn., sr. v.p. Paine Webber, Inc., N.Y.C., 1975-80; mng. dir., head merger and acquisitions dept. Blyth Eastman Paine Webber, Inc., N.Y.C., 1980-88; pres. Slusser Assocs., Inc., N.Y.C., 1988—. Bd. dirs. Ampex Corp., Sparton Corp., Willaim D. Witter, Inc., Magellan Group Ltd.; underwriter or fin. cons. Square D Co., Times Mirror co., Ashland Oil, Inc., Ga. Pacific, TRW, Inc., Avon Products, TransAm, Realty Investors, Atex, Inc. subsidiary of Eastman Kodak Co., Perini Corp., Downey Savs. & Loan, Booth Newspapers, Inc., Holly Hill Lumber Co., Stanhome, Inc., Santee Portland Cement Co., Grow Group, Orion Rsch., Inc., Crown Cork & Seal Co., Dr. Pepper Co. of So. Calif., Houghton Mifflin Co., Sparton Corp., Mission West Properties, Inc., San Jose Water Co., ADT Ltd., Cap Gemini Ernst & Young, Ltd., London, De La Rue, PLC, London, VNU Inc., Haarlem, The Netherlands, Bertlesmann Pub. Co., Fed. Republic Germany, ADT Ltd., London, Bank of Guam, Pacific Holding co., vice chmn., 1969-73. Contbr. articles to profl. jours. Founding. stockholder Assoc. Mortgage Cos.; bd. fin. advisors Columbia U. Bus. Sch., Calif. Senate Commn. on Local Govt. Investments; mem. Calif. Senate Commn. on Corp. Governance. Served to 1st lt. USAF, 1953-55. Mem. Investment Assn. N.Y., So. Calif. Pioneers, Knickerbocker Club, Stanford Assocs., Harvard (N.Y.C.) Club, Lawrence Beach Club, Stanford of N.Y. Club, Alpha Delta Phi (exec. coun. 1956-62, treas. 1961). Home: 901 Lexington Ave New York NY 10021-5924 also: Slusser Ranch Windsor CA 95492 Office: Slusser Assocs Inc 1 Citicorp Ctr Ste 5100 153 E 53d St New York NY 10022-4611

SLUTSKY, LORIE A(NN), foundation executive; b. N.Y.C., Jan. 5, 1953; d. Edward and Adele (Moskowitz) S. BA, Colgate U, 1975; MA in Urban Policy and Analysis, New Sch. for Social Rsch., N.Y.C., 1977. Program officer N.Y. Cmty. Trust, N.Y.C., 1977-83, v.p., 1983-87, exec. v.p., 1987-89, pres., CEO, 1990—. Former mem. and chmn. bd. Coun. on Founds., Inc., Washington, 1986-95. Trustee emerita, former chmn. budget com. Colgate U., Hamilton, N.Y., 1989-98; former mem. bd. dirs. Found. Ctr., Inc., N.Y.C., L.A. Wallace Fund for Met. Mus. Art, N.Y.C., D. Wallace Fund for Meml. Sloan Kettering, United Way of N.Y.C.; bd. dirs. BoardSource; chmn. Alliance Capital; trustee New Sch. U. Office: NY Community Trust 2 Park Ave Fl 24 New York NY 10016-9301

SLY, RIDGE MICHAEL, pediatrician, educator, allergist, immunologist; b. Seattle, Nov. 3, 1933; s. Ridge Joseph and Eva Jean (Ruddell) S.; m. Ann Turner Jennings, June 12, 1957; children: Teresa Ann Perper, Cynthia Marie Schattenfield. AB, Kenyon Coll., 1956; MD, Washington U., St. Louis, 1960. Diplomate Am. Bd. Pediat., Am. Sub-Bd. Pediat. Allergy, Am. Bd. Allergy and Immunology. Intern, resident in pediat. St. Louis Children's Hosp, 1960—62; chief resident in pediat. U. Ky. Med. Ctr., Lexington, 1962—63; fellow in allergy and immunology UCLA Med. Ctr., 1965—67; from asst. prof. to prof. pediat. La. State U. Med. Ctr., New Orleans, 1967—78; head sect. allergy and immunology Children's Nat. Med. Ctr., Washington, 1978—; prof. pediat. George Washington U., Washington, 1978—. Author: Textbook of Pediatric Allergy, 1985; mem. editl. bd. Annals of Allergy, Asthma, & Immunology, 1982-98, 99-2002, Jour. Asthma, 1982-93, Clin. Revs. in Allergy, 1982-2001, Pediat. Asthma, Allergy, & Immunology, 1987—; assoc. editor Annals of Allergy, Asthma, & Immunology, 1989-90, editor, 1990-98; contbr. articles to profl. jours. Served to capt. USAF, 1963-65 Recipient La. plaque Am. Lung Assn. of La., 1978 Fellow Am. Acad. Allergy, Asthma & Immunology (chmn. com. on drugs 1981-87), Am. Acad. Pediats. (sect. on allergy com. 1972-75), Am. Coll. Allergy, Asthma, and Immunology (Disting. Fellow award 1993, Bela Schick award 1997, chmn. ethics com. 1997-99); mem. Am. Thoracic Soc., Assn. for Care of Asthma (pres. 1980-81, dir. postgrad. courses 1980—, Peshkin Meml. award 1983), Ctr. for Bioethics and Human Dignity, Phi Beta Kappa. Republican. Baptist. Avocations: music, piano. Office: Children's Nat Med Ctr 111 Michigan Ave NW Washington DC 20010-2970

SLY, WILLIAM S. biochemist, educator; b. East St. Louis, Ill., Oct. 19, 1932; MD, St. Louis U., 1957. Intern, asst. resident ward medicine Barnes Hosp., St. Louis, 1957-59; clin. assoc. nat. heart inst. NIH, Bethesda, Md., 1959-63, rsch. biochemist, 1959-63; dir. divsn. med. genetics, dept. medicine and pediatrics, sch. medicine Washington U., St. Louis, 1964-84, from asst. prof. to prof. medicine, 1964-78, from asst. prof. to prof. pediatrics, 1967-78, prof. pediatrics, medicine and genetics, 1978-84; prof. biochemistry and pediat. St. Louis U., 1984—, chmn. Edward A. Doisy dept. biochemistry-molecular biology, 1984—. Vis. physician Nat. Heart Inst., 1961-63, pediatric genetics clinic U. Wis., Madison, 1963-64; Am. Cancer Soc. fellow lab. enzymol Nat. Ctr. Sci. Rsch., Gif-sur-Yvette, France, 1963, dept. biochemistry and genetics U. Wis., 1963-64; attending physician St. Louis County Hosp., Mo., 1964-84; asst. physician Barnes Hosp., St. Louis, 1964-84, St. Louis Children's Hosp., 1967-84; genetics cons. Homer G. Philips Hosp., St. Louis, 1969-81; mem. genetics study sect. divsn. rsch. grants NIH, 1971-75; mem. active staff Cardinal Glennon Children's Hosp., St. Louis, 1984—; mem. med. adv. bd. Howard Hughes Med. Inst., 1989-92. Recipient Merit award NIH, 1988; elected to Nat. Acad. Sci., 1989; named Passano Found. laureate, 1991. Mem. NAS, AMA, AAAS, Am. Soc. Human Genetics (mem. steering com. human cell biology program 1971-73, com. genetic counseling 1972-76), Am. Soc. Clin. Investigation, Am. Chem. Soc., Genetics Soc. Am., Am. Soc. Microbiology, Soc. Pediatric Rsch., Sigma Xi. Achievements include research on lysosomal enzyme replacement in storage diseases, inherited carbonic anhydrase deficiencies, and hereditary hemochromatosis. Office: St Louis U Med Sch Dept Biochemistry 1402 S Grand Blvd Saint Louis MO 63104-1004

SMAGALSKI, CAROLYN M, publishing executive, webmaster, director; b. Philadelphia, Pa., Aug. 28, 1952; d. Raymond L and Mary K Hanisco; children: Michael M, Tyler A. BA Cum Laude, Temple U., Philadelphia, 1971—75. Lic. private pilot SEL with IFR rating and Complex Aircraft Rating US Dept. of Transp./Fed. Aviation Adminstrn., 1996. Account mgr. Brown Printing Co., East Greenville, Pa., 1996—; exec. dir./author/webmaster/internetwork marketer CQ Web Wide LLC, Harleysville, Pa., 2002—. Webmaster/ graphic designer/author (website/articles) cqwebwide.com. Recipient 475 donated vacation hours from Brown Printing Co. employees for use during son's accident recovery in 2002., Brown Printing Co., 2002. Mem.: Better Internet Bur., Internat. Assn. of Home Bus. Entrepreneurs, Internat. Orgn. of Women Pilots, Aircraft Owners & Pilot's Assn. Achievements include aiding in the extraordinary recovery of my 15-year-old son, who suffered multiple skull fractures and traumatic brain injury, the result of an auto accident in August, 2002. Avocations: information technology, aviation, psychology of brain & socio-emotional challenges, gourmet cookery, public relations & travel. Home: 805 Continental Drive Harleysville PA 19438 Office: CQ Web Wide LLC 805 Continental Drive Harleysville PA 19438 Office Phone: 215-541-2723. Personal E-mail: carolsmagalski@comcast.net.

SMAGORINSKY, PETER, education educator; b. Princeton, N.J., Oct. 24, 1952; s. Joseph and Margaret (Knoepfel) Smagorinsky; m. Anne O'Gorman, July 10, 1982 (dec. Aug. 1982); m. Jane E. Farrell, Oct. 12, 1985; children: Alysha, David. BA, Kenyon Coll., 1974; MA in Tchg., U. Chgo., 1977, PhD, 1989. English tchr. Westmont (Ill.) H.S., 1977-78, Barrington (Ill.) H.S., 1978-85, Oak Park (Ill.) and River Forest H.S., 1985-90; asst. prof. U. Okla., Norman, 1990-95, assoc. prof., 1995-98, U. Ga., Athens, 1998-2001, prof., 2001—. Author: Standards in Practice, 1996; co-author: How English Teachers Get Taught, 1995, The Language of Interpretation, 1995; co-editor: Rsch. Tchg. English, 1996—2003, Reading Rsch. Quar. Rev. Ednl. Rsch., Am. Jour. Edn., Written Comm., Reading and Writing Quar. Recipient Steve Cahir award for Rsch. in Writing, Am. Ednl. Rsch. Assn., 1991, Raymond B. Cattell award for Disting. Programmatic Rsch., 1999. Mem.: Nat. Coun. Tchrs. English (chair standing com. rsch. 1995—96, co-chair assembly rsch. 1996, trustee rsch. found. 1997—2003, chair 2000—03, pres. nat. conf. rsch. lang. and literacy 2001, English Jour. Writing award 1989, Edwin M. Hopkins award 2000, Janet Emig award 2003). Home: 175 Emerald Dr Athens GA 30605-4106 Office: U Ga 125 Aderhold Hall Athens GA 30602 Business E-Mail: smago@coe.uga.edu.

SMAIL, LAURENCE MITCHELL, lawyer, educator; b. May 2, 1937; s. Samuel Percy and Kathryn Jeanette (Mitchell) S.; m. Katherine Sylvia Carr, Nov. 30, 1964; 1 child, Leslie Anne. BA, Washington and Lee U., 1959, JD, 1962; MBA, Coll. William and Mary, 1973. Bar: Va. 1964, U.S. Ct. Claims 1967, U.S. Supreme Ct. 1968, U.S. Ct. Appeals (Fed. cir.) 1982; cert. profl. contracts mgr. Assoc. Hoyle & Short, Newport News, Va., 1965-66; atty. advisor USAAV Labs., Ft. Eustis, Va., 1966-74; counsel SUPSHIP, Newport News, 1974, U.S. Army Aviation Applied Tech. Directorate, Ft. Eustis, 1974-99; dir. 1st advantage Fed. Credit Union, Ft. Eustis, 1973—. Adj. prof. Fla. Tech., 1976—, asst. prof. mgmt., 1999—; pres. Med. Security Card, Inc., Newport News, 1995—99, dir. Ret. Sr. Vol. Program, 2002—; chmn. legal issues com. Fed. Lab. Consortium, 1993—94. Contbr. articles to profl. jours. Pres. Brentwood Civic League, 1969; chmn. Newport News Taxpayers Assn., 1973; dir. VA Fin. Network Ptnrs., 2002--. Served to capt. U.S. Army, 1962-65. Fellow Nat. Contract Mgmt. Assn. (nat. v.p. 1979-80), Am. Helicopter Soc., Fed. Bar Assn., Va. Bar Assn., Phi Delta Phi, Phi Gamma Delta, Warwick Yacht Club, Pegasus Club (past pres.). Republican. Presbyterian. Home: 507 Beech Dr Newport News VA 23601-3109 Office: Fla Tech Hampton Rds Grad Ctr Bldg 1708 Fort Eustis VA 23604 E-mail: l-smail@cox.net.

SMALDONE, EDWARD MICHAEL, composer; b. Wantagh, N.Y., Nov. 19, 1956; m. Karen Ajamian, Aug. 5, 1979; children: Laura, Gregory, Julia. BA in Music, Queens Coll., 1978, MA in Music, 1980; PhD in Music, CUNY, 1986. Lectr. SUNY, Purchase, 1986-90; adj. asst. prof. Hofstra U., Hempstead, N.Y., 1988-90; vis. asst. prof. New Sch. for Social Rsch., N.Y.C., 1988; adminstrv. dir. Speculum Musicae, N.Y.C., 1988-89; artistic dir. Sounds for the Left Bank, Rego Park, N.Y., 1985-92; asst. prof. Copland Sch. of Music, CUNY, Flushing, 1990-99; assoc. prof., 1999—. Composer in residence N.Y.C. Pub. Schs., 1994, 95; Carlisle Project Choreographer and Composer Collaboration Commn., 1994; assoc. composer Atlantic Ctr. Arts, 1999, vis. fac., Univ. Coll. Chichester, Eng., 1999. Composer: Two String Quartets, 1980, 86, Dialogue for orch., 1987, Double Duo (flute, clarinet, violin, cello), 1987, Transformational Etudes (solo piano), 1990, Rhapsody for piano and orch., 1992, Suite for violin and piano, 1993, Three Scenes from "The Heartland" for solo piano, 1994, Saxophone Quartet, 1995, Rituals: Sacred and Profane for flute, cello and piano, 1996, American Spiritual Fantasy for string orch., 1997, Psalm of the Phoenix for Shakuhachi and cello, 1998, Suite for violin and 12 instruments, 2000, Letters from Home, mezzo soprano, flute, clarinet, and piano, 2000, String Quartet No. 2, 2001, Life Imagined, Life Engaged for

piccolo and chamber orch., 2001; dance compositions: The Chair, The Table and Tatyana's Letter (choreography by Yin Mei), 1999; albums include Scenes from the Heartland Recipient Standard award ASCAP, 1986—, Creative Incentive award CUNY Rsch. Found., 1992, 95, 97; residency fellow Yaddo Corp., 1986, 87, Composer's fellow Charles Ives Ctr. for Am. Music, 1990, residency fellow MacDowell Colony, 1994, Goddard Lieberson fellow Am. Acad. Arts and Letters, 1993; prize winner Percussive Arts Soc., 1994. Home: 228 Manhasset Ave Manhasset NY 11030-2220 Office: Copland Sch of Music Queens College Flushing NY 11030

SMALE, JOHN GRAY, diversified industry executive; b. Listowel, Ont., Can., Aug. 1, 1927; s. Peter John and Vera Gladys (Gray) S.; m. Phyllis Anne Weaver, Sept. 2, 1950; children: John Gray, Jr., Catherine Anne, Lisa Beth, Peter McKee. BS, Miami U., Oxford, Ohio, 1949; LLD (hon.), Kenyon Coll., Gambier, Ohio, 1974, Miami U., Oxford, Ohio, 1979; DSc (hon.), DePauw U., 1983; DCL (hon.), St. Augustine's Coll., 1985; LLD (hon.), Xavier U., 1986. With Vick Chem. Co., N.Y.C., 1949-50, Bio-Rsch., Inc., N.Y.C., 1950-52; asst. brand mgr. Procter & Gamble Co., 1952-54, brand mgr., 1954-58, assoc. advt. mgr., 1958-63, mgr. advt. dept. toilet goods divsn., 1963-66, mgr. toilet goods divsn., 1966-67, v.p. toilet goods divsn., 1967-68, v.p. bar soap and household cleaning products divsn., 1968-69, v.p. packaged soap and detergent divsn., 1969-70, v.p. group exec., 1970-72, mem. bd. dirs., 1972, exec. v.p., 1973-74, pres., 1974-81, pres., chief exec., 1981-86, chmn. of bd., chief exec., 1986-90, chmn. exec. com. of bd. of dirs., 1990-95; chmn. GM, 1992-95, chmn. exec. com., 1995-2000, chmn. bd. dirs., 1996-2000, chmn. exec. com., 1996-2000, also bd. dirs.; ret., 2000. Emeritus trustee Kenyon Coll. With USNR, 1945-46. Mem. Comml. Club, Queen City Club, Cin. Country Club. Office: Procter & Gamble PO Box 599 Cincinnati OH 45201-0599

SMALES, FRED BENSON, corporate executive; b. Keokuk, Iowa, Oct. 7, 1914; s. Fred B. and Mary Alice (Warwick) S.; m. Constance Brennan, Dec. 11, 1965; children: Fred Benson III, Catherine (Mrs. Jonathan Christensen); children by previous marriage: Nancy (Mrs. Bruce Clark). Student public schs., Los Angeles. With U.S. Plywood Corp., 1933-68, successively San Francisco mgr., 1938-44, Los Angeles, Western div. mgr., 1944-55, v.p. Western sales div., 1955-65, v.p., regional dir., 1965-68, pres. Lewers & Cooke, Inc. div., 1966-68; chmn. Securities of Am., Inc., 1968-70; chmn., pres., dir. Hawaiian Cement Co., 1970-84; pres. Transpacific Cons., 1984-94; owner Plywood Hawaii, 1995—. Trustee Hawaii-Pacific U., Hawaii Maritime Ctr. Recipient Disting. Citizen award Nat. Govs. Assn., 1986. Mem. C. of C. Hawaii (past chmn.), So. Calif. Yachting Assn. (sr. staff commodore), Balboa Yacht Club (Corona del Mar, Calif, sr. staff commodore), Transpacific Yacht, Waikiki Yacht (staff commodore), Pacific Club (past pres.), Sequoia Yacht Club (Redwood City, Calif., sr. staff commodore). Home: 46-422 Hulupala Pl Kaneohe HI 96744-4243 Office: 1062 Kikowaena Pl Honolulu HI 96819-4413

SMALES, JOEL ROBERT, music educator; b. Binghamton, NY, June 8, 1967; s. Robert and Karen Smales; m. Athena Ficchi, June 9, 1990; children: Jacob, Nathan, Mariah, Elaina. MusB, SUNY Potsdam Crane Sch. of Music, 1985—89; MusM, Binghamton U., 1989—2001. Cert. Music Teacher NY, 1998. Percussionist Binghamton Philharm. Orch., Binghamton, NY, 1993—; prin. percussion Tri-Cities Opera Orch., Binghamton, 2003; dir. of bands Binghamton H.S., 1997—, Binghamton H.S. Rod Serling Sch. of Arts, 1997—. Nys v.p. Percussive Arts Soc., NYC, 2004—; percussion chair NY State Sch. Music Assn., 2004—, music adjudicator, 1995—, percussion chair, 2004—, music adjudicator, 1991—. Composer: (book) Linear Drumming; author (with Dr. Steven Porter): Teaching Music at the Secondary Level; composer: Warm Ups and Mind Reading for the Smart Percussionist, (music ensemble) Another One for Steel Drum Band, (percussion solos) Whisper for Marimba, Forward Motion for Multiple Percussion, Snare Drum Solo Collection; contbr. articles. Fellow: Percussive Arts Soc.; mem.: Music Educators Nat. Conf. Home: 84 Trim St Kirkwood NY 13795 Office: Binghamton High School 31 Main St Binghamton NY 13905 Office Phone: 607-762-8229. Personal E-mail: joeldrum@aol.com.

SMALKIN, FREDERIC N. federal judge; BA, Johns Hopkins U., 1968; JD, U. Maryland, 1971. Atty. office of judge advocate gen. Dept. Army, 1972-74, asst. to gen. counsel, 1974-76; pvt. practice Monkton, Md., 1976; magistrate U.S. Dist. Ct. Md., Balt., 1976-86, judge, 1986—. Lectr. comml. law U. Md., Balt., 1978—, SMH bar rev., Balt., 1985-86, 93-95, BRI/Modern Bar Rev. Course, Inc., Balt., 1980-81; panel spkr. on Utilization of Magistrates at the 1985 fourth cir., Jud. Conf. Capt. U.S. Army, 1968-76, lt. col. CAP (USAF Auxiliary). Mem. Fed. Bar Assn., Order of Coif, Phi Beta Kappa. Office: US Dist Ct 101 W Lombard St Ste 3A Baltimore MD 21201-2605

SMALL, BERTRICE W. writer; b. N.Y.C., Dec. 9, 1937; d. David Roger Williams, Doris Melissa (Maud) Steen; m. George Sumner Small, Oct. 5, 1963; 1 child, Thomas David. Student, Western Coll. for Women, Oxford, Ohio, Katherine Gibbs Sectl. Sch., N.Y.C., 1959. With Young & Rubicon, N.Y.C., 1959—60, Weed Radio & TV, N.Y.C., 1960—61, Edward Petry & Co., N.Y.C., 1961—63. Author: The Kadin, 1978, Sky O'Malley, 1980, All The Sweet Tomorrows, 1984, Amount In Time, 1991, Betrayal, 1998, The Innocent, 1999, Rosamund, 2002, 25 others. Vestrywoman Redeemer Episc. Ch., Mattituck, NY, 1998—2001. Recipient Career Achievement Reviewers Choice award, Romantic Times Mag., 1983, 1988, 1995, 2001. Mem.: L.I. Romance Writers (bd. dirs. 1999—2001), Romance Writers of Am., Authors Guild. Episcopalian. Avocation: gardening. Mailing: PO Box 765 Southold NY 11971

SMALL, DONALD MACFARLAND, biophysics educator, department chairman, gastroenterologist, researcher; b. Newton, Mass., Sept. 15, 1931; s. Grace (MacFarland) S.; m. Elisabeth Chan, July 8, 1957 (div. 1979); children: Geoffrey, Philip; m. Kathryn Ross, July 26, 1986 (div. 1999); 1 child, Samuel. BA, Occidental Coll., 1954; MA (hon.), Oxford (Eng.) U., 1964; MD, UCLA, 1960. Intern, asst. resident in medicine Mass. Meml. Hosps., Boston, 1960-62; sr. resident Boston City Hosp., 1962-63, vis. physician med. svcs., 1965—90; asst. prof. medicine Boston U. Sch. Medicine, 1968-69, assoc. prof. medicine and biochemistry, 1969-73, prof., 1973—, prof. biophysics, chmn. dept., 1989-2000, dir. Biophysics Inst., 1972—, prof. chmn. dept. physiology and biophysics, 2000—. Spl. tng. in phys. chemistry of lipids Inst. Pasteur, Paris, 1963-65; mem. adv. bd. Gladstone Found Labs., San Francisco, 1980—; George Lyman Duff Meml. lectr. Coun. Arteriosclerosis, Am. Heart Assn., 1986; cons. Nat. Inst. Arthritis and Metabolic Diseases, NIH, 1968-72, mem. task force Nat. Heart, Lung and Blood Inst., 1990; also others. Author, editor: Physical Chemistry of Lipids, 1986; mem. editl. bd. Gastroenterology, 1967-74, Arteriosclerosis, Thrombosis and Vascular Biology, 1980-2002, Jour. Biol. Chemistry, Current Opinions in Structural Biology, 1990—, Structure, 1992-98; sub-editor: Jour. Lipid Rsch., 1974-78, editor, 1979-83; editor: (with R. Havel) Advances in Lipid Rsch., 1989-99; mem. internat. bd. editors Jour. Nutritional Biochemistry, 1989—; contbr. articles and revs. to profl. jours.; author: (with A. Adams) The Healthy Meateaters Cookbook, 1991. Recipient Eppinger prize IV Internat. Congress on Liver Disease, 1976, Disting. Achievment award Modern Medicine, 1978, Disting. Alumni award UCLA Sch. Medicine Alumni Assn., 1988; Marshall scholar Magdalen Coll., Oxford, 1956-58, Aesculapian scholar UCLA, 1958-60, Markle scholar, 1966-70; others. Mem. AAAS, Am. Heart Assn. (fellow coun. arteriosclerosis, chmn. program com. 1988-90, chmn. coun. 1992-94), Am. Assn. Physicians, Am. Soc. Biol. Chemists, Biophys. Soc., Am. Soc. Clin. Investigation, Am. Gastroent. Assn. (Ann. Disting. Achievement award 1972, Beaumont prize 2000), Am. Oil Chemists Soc. (Alton E. Bailey award 1998), Am. Fedn. Clin. Rsch., Am. Chem. Soc., Mass. Med. Soc., Suffolk Dist. Med. Soc., Phi Beta Kappa, Alpha Omega Alpha, Sigma Xi. Achievements include patents for on method for making meat products having a reduced saturated fat and cholesterol content. Office: Boston U Sch Medicine Dept Physiology and Biophysics 715 Albany St W302 Boston MA 02118-2526 Office Phone: 617-638-4001. E-mail: dmsmall@bu.edu.

SMALL, ELISABETH CHAN, psychiatrist, educator; b. Beijing, July 11, 1934; came to U.S., 1937; d. Stanley Hong and Lily Luella (Lum) Chan; m. Donald M. Small, July 8, 1957 (div. 1980); children Geoffrey Brooks, Philip Willard Stanley; m. H. Sidney Robinson, Jan. 12, 1991 (div. 2001). Student, Immaculate Heart Coll., L.A., 1951-52; BA in Polit. Sci., UCLA, 1955, MD, 1960. Intern Newton-Wellesley Hosp., Mass., 1960-61; asst. dir. for venereal diseases Mass. Dept. Pub. Health, 1961-63; resident in psychiatry Boston State Hosp., Mattapan, Mass., 1965-66, Tufts New Eng. Med. Ctr. Hosps., 1966-69, psychiat. cons. dept. gynecology, 1973-75, asst. clin. prof. psychiatry Sch. Medicine Tufts U., 1973-75, assoc. clin. prof., 1975-82, asst. clin. prof. ob-gyn, 1977-80, assoc. clin. prof. ob-gyn, 1980-82; from assoc. prof. to prof. psychiatry U. Nev. Sch. Med., Reno, 1982-95; practice psychiatry specializing in psychological effects of bodily changes on women, 1969—; emeritus prof. psychiatry and behavioral scis. U. Nev. Sch. Medicine, Reno, 1995—, from assoc. prof. to clin. assoc. prof. ob-gyn, 1982-88; mem. staff Tufts New Eng. Med. Ctr. Hosps., 1977-82, St. Margaret's Hosps., Boston, 1977-82, Washoe Med. Ctr., Reno, Sparks (Nev.) Family Hosp., Truckee Meadows Hosp., Reno, St. Mary's Hosp., Reno; chief psychiatry svc. Reno VA Med. Ctr., 1989-94. Lectr., cons. in field; mem. psychiatry adv. panel Hosp. Satellite Network; mem. office external peer rev. NIMH, HEW; psychiat. cons. to Boston Redevelopment Authority on Relocation of Chinese Families of South Cove Area, 1968-70; mem. New Eng. Med. Ctr. Hosps. Cancer Ctr. Com., 1979-80, Pain Control Com., 1981-82; reproductive sys. curriculum com. Tufts Univ. Sch. Medicine, 1975-82. Mem. editorial bd. Psychiat. Update Am. (Psychiat. Assn. ann. rev.), 1983-85; reviewer Psychosomatics and Hosp. Community Psychiatry, New Eng. Jour. of Medicine, Am. Jour. of Psychiatry Psychosomatic Medicine; contbr. articles to profl. jours. Immaculate Heart Coll. scholar, 1951-52, Mira Hershey scholar UCLA, 1955; fellow Radcliffe Inst., 1967-70. Fellow Am. Coll. Psychiatrists (sci. program com. 1989-98); mem. AMA, Am. Psychiat. Assn. (rep. to sect. com. AAAS, chmn. ad hoc com. Asian-Am. Psychiatrists 1975, task force 1975-77, task force cost effectiveness in consultation 1984—, caucus chmn. 1981-82, sci. program com. 1982-88, courses subcom. chmn. sci. program com. 1986-88), Nev. Psychiat. Assn. (life), Assn. for Acad. Psychiatry (fellowship com. 1982), Washoe County Med. Assn., Nev. Med. Soc. Avocations: skiing, culinary arts. Home and Office: 825 Caughlin Crossing Reno NV 89509-0647

SMALL, GARY W. academic administrator, psychiatrist, educator; b. L.A., July 28, 1951; s. Max Sidney and Gertrude (Axelrod) S.; m. Giselle Vorgan, May 28, 1989; children: Rachel, Harrison. BA summa cum laude, U. Calif., L.A., 1973; MD, U. So. Calif. Sch. Medicine, L.A., 1977; resident, clinical fellow psychiatry, Mass. Gen. Hosp., Harvard Med., Boston, 1981. Lic. Calif.; diplomate Am. Bd. Psychiatry & Neurology. Chief Geriatric Psychiatry Program West L.A. VA Med. Ctr., 1990-96; assoc. investigator UCLA Dept. Energy Lab. of Structural Biology & Molecular Med, L.A., 1997—; dir. Imaging & Genetics Core UCLA Alzheimer's Disease Ctr., L.A., 1997—; prof. Dept. Psychiatry & Behavioral Scis. UCLA, 1995—; attending psychiatrist UCLA Neuropsychiatric Hosp., L.A., 1993—; assoc. prof. Dept. Psychiatry & Behavioral Scis. UCLA, 1990-95; dir. UCLA Ctr. on Aging, 1997—. Mem. Mental Disorders of Aging Review NIMH, 1993-97; mem. editl. bd. Alzheimer Disease & Associated Disorders, 1985—. Co-author: Parentcare, 1988. Recipient Parlow-Solomon Professorship on Aging UCLA Sch. Medicine, 1998, Zenith award Alzheimer's Assn. 1998. Fellow Gerontological Soc. Am.; mem. APA (Jack Weinberg award Geriatric Psychiatry 2000), Am. Assn. Geriatric Psychiatry (bd. dirs. 1991-96, Sr. Investigator award 2000), Am. Coll. Neuropsychopharmacology, Internat. Psychogeriatric Assn. (Rsch. award 1987), Phi Beta Kappa, Alpha Omega Alpha. Avocations: crossword puzzles, classical music, cinema. Office: UCLA Neuropsychiatric Inst 760 Westwood Plz Los Angeles CA 90095-8353

SMALL, GEORGE LEROY, geographer, educator; b. Malden, Mass., Mar. 27, 1924; s. George Arthur and Alice Mildred (Weston) S.; m. Geraldine H. Koepke, July 4, 1970; 1 dau., Elizabeth Mary. BA, Brown U., 1950; M.I.A., Columbia U., 1952, PhD, 1968. French tchr. pvt. schs., Ariz., 1955-62; instr. geography Hunter Coll., 1964-68; asso. prof. geography Coll. S.I., CUNY, 1968—. Cons. problems of whaling to environ. groups. Author: The Blue Whale, 1971. Served with U.S. Army, 1942-46. Recipient Nat. Book award, 1972; Rotary Found. fellow, 1952-53 Mem. Assn. Am. Geographers. Office: CUNY Coll Staten Is New York NY 10314

SMALL, HAMISH, chemist; b. Newtown Crommelin, No. Ireland, Oct. 5, 1929; s. Johnston and Jean (Wilson) S.; m. Beryl Maureen Burley, Mar. 27, 1954; children: Deborah Jane, Claire Leslie. BS, Queens U., Belfast, Northern Ireland, 1949, MS, 1953. Chemist U.S. Atomic Energy Authority, Harwell, England, 1949-55; rsch. scientist Dow Chem. Co., Midland, Mich., 1955-83; chemist ind. rsch. and consulting, 1983—. Author: Ion Chromatography, 1990; contbr. articles to profl. jours. Recipient Albert F. Sperry award Instrument Soc. Am., 1978, A.O. Beckman award, 1983, Herbert H. Dow Gold Medal Dow Chem. Co., 1983, Stephen Dal Nogare award, 1984, Am. Chem. Soc. award in Chromatography, 1991. Mem. Am. Chem. Soc. Achievements include patents in field. Avocations: painting, sketching. Home: 4176 Oxford Dr Leland MI 49654-9716 E-mail: montalto29@aol.com.

SMALL, JONATHAN ANDREW, lawyer; b. N.Y.C., Dec. 26, 1942; s. Milton and Teresa Markell (Joseph) S.; m. Cornelia Mendenhall, June 8, 1969; children: Anne, Katherine. BA, Brown U., 1964; student, U. Paris, 1962-63; LLB, Harvard U., 1967; MA, Fletcher Sch. of Law and Diplomacy, 1968; LLM, NYU, 1974. Bar: N.Y. 1967. VISTA vol., Washington and Cambridge, Mass., 1968; law clk. to judge U.S. Ct. Appeals (2d cir.), 1968-69; assoc. Debevoise & Plimpton, N.Y.C., 1969-75, ptnr., 1976-99; pres. Nonprofit Coord. Com. N.Y., 2000—. Cons. Spl. Task Force of N.Y. State Taxation, 1976; bd. overseers Fletcher Sch. Law and Diplomacy Tufts U., 2003—. Trustee Brearley Sch., 1985-95; bd. dirs. Nonprofit Coordinating Com. of N.Y., 1985—, Muscular Dystrophy Assn., 1986-88, Human Svcs. Coun. N.Y.C., Inc., 2000—, Investor Responsibility Rsch. Ctr., Inc., 2000—, Lawyers Alliance for N.Y., 2000—, U.S. Com. to the UN Population Fund, 2000—. Mem. ABA, Am. Law Inst., N.Y. State Bar Assn. (chmn. tax sect. com. exempt orgns. 1980-82, co-chmn., 1995), Assn. Bar City N.Y., Nonprofit Forum, Phi Beta Kappa. Home: 60 E End Ave New York NY 10028-7907 Office: Nonprofit Coord Com of NY 1350 Broadway Rm 1801 New York NY 10018-7718

SMALL, JOYCE GRAHAM, psychiatrist, educator; b. Edmonton, Alta., Can., June 12, 1931; came to U.S., 1956; d. John Earl and Rachel C. (Redmond) Graham; m. Iver Francis Small, May 26, 1954; children: Michael, Jeffrey. BA, U. Sask., Saskatoon, Can., 1951; MD, U. Man., Alta., Can., 1956; MS, U. Mich., 1959. Diplomat Am. Bd. Psychiatry and Neurology, Am. Bd. Electroencephalography. Instr. in psychiatry Neuropsychiat. Inst. U. Mich., Ann Arbor, 1959-60; instr. in psychiatry med. sch. U. Oreg., Portland, 1960-61, asst. prof. in psychiatry med. sch., 1961-62; asst. prof. in psychiatry sch. of medicine Washington U., St. Louis, 1962-65; assoc. prof. in psychiatry sch. of medicine Ind. U., Indpls., 1965—69, prof. psychiatry sch. of medicine, 1969—2004, prof. emeritus psychiatry, 2004—, prof. emeritus, 2004—. Mem. initial rev. groups NIMH, Washington, 1972-76, 79-82, 87-91; assoc. mem. Inst. Psychiat. Rsch., Indpls., 1974—. Mem. editl. bd. Quar. Jour. Convulsive Therapy, 1984-2000, Clin. EEG, 1990—, and more than 200 publs. in field; contbr. articles to profl. jours. Rsch. grantee NIMH, Portland, Oreg., 1961-62, St. Louis, 1962-64, Indpls., 1967-95, Epilepsy Found., Dreyfus Found., Indpls., 1965; recipient Merit award NIMH, Indpls., 1990, Career award EEG and Clin. Neurosci. Soc., 2003. Fellow Am. Psychiat. Assn., Am. EEG Soc. (councillor 1972-75, 1982); mem. Soc. Biol. Psychiatry, Cen. Assn. Electroencephalographers (sec., treas. 1967-68, pres. 1970, councillor 1971-72), Sigma Xi. Business E-Mail: jgsmall@iupui.edu.

SMALL, KENT WILSON, ophthalmologist, educator; b. New Orleans, La., Oct. 19, 1956; s. George Wilson Small and Barbara Jane Dabareiner; m. Frances Culler Small, Dec. 12, 1957; children: Natalie, Leslie. Student, La. State U., 1977; MD, Tulane U., 1981. Cert. bd. cert. Asst. clin. prof. Duke U., Durham, NC, 1988—90; asst. prof. Med. U. S.C., Charleston, 1991; assoc. prof. U. Fla., Gainesville, 1992—94; prof. UCLA, 1994—. Founder, CEO Molecular Insight LLC, Fla., 2000—; spkr. in field. Editor: (electronic jour.) Molecular Vision, 1998—; jour. reviewer: sci. jours., mem. editl. bd.: Molecular Vision Electronic Jour., 1999—; contbr. articles to profl. jours. Mem. steering com. Youth Ministry Bel Air Presbyn. Ch., L.A., 2001; vol. eye surgeon Rotary Internat., Indonesia, 2001. Recipient Jacob Javits fellowship, NIH, 1989—91, 6 rsch. grants, 1994—, Found. Fighting Blindness grant, 1994—. Fellow: Am. Ophthalmol. Soc., Am. Acad. Opthalmology (Achievement award 1988). Avocations: sailing, swimming. Office: U Calif 200 Stein Plz Los Angeles CA 90095-0001 E-mail: small@jsei.ucla.edu.

SMALL, LAWRENCE M. museum executive; b. NY, Sept. 14, 1941; m. Sandra Small; 2 children. BA, Brown U., 1963; JD (hon.), Morehouse Coll. Vice chmn. bd., chmn. exec. com., dir. Citicorp, N.Y.C., 1964-91; pres., COO Fannie Mae, Washington, 1991-2000; CEO., sec. Smithsonian Instn., Washington, 2000—. Bd. dirs. Chubb Corp., Marriott Internat. Trustee emeritus Brown U., Morehouse Coll., Atlanta, 1973-99, Mt. Sinai-NYU Med. Ctr., Nat. Bldg. Mus.; bd. dirs. Spanish Repertory Theatre, Fannie Mae Found. Office: Smithsonian Instn 1000 Jefferson Dr SW Washington DC 20560-0009

SMALL, MARY E. state legislator; b. Bath, Maine, Sept. 12, 1954; d. Donald Nichols and Marguerite (Brown) S. Grad., Green Mountain Coll., 1973; MA, U. So. Maine, 1976. Mem. Maine Ho. of Reps., Augusta, 1979-94, mem. edn. com.; mem. dist. 19 Maine Senate, Augusta, 1995—. Campaign coord. Re-election U.S. Rep. David Emery, 1976. Mem. Delta Zeta. Home: 175 Oak St Bath ME 04530-2431 Office: Maine State Senate 3 State House Sta Augusta ME 04333-0003

SMALL, MELVIN, history educator; b. N.Y.C., Mar. 14, 1939; s. Herman Z. and Ann (Ashkinazy) S.; m. Sarajane Miller, Oct. 23, 1958; children: Michael, Mark. BA, Dartmouth Coll., 1960; MA, U. Mich., 1961, PhD, 1965. Asst. prof. history Wayne State U., Detroit, 1965-68, assoc. prof., 1968-76, prof., 1976—, chmn. dept. history, 1979-86, disting. prof., 2004—. Vis. prof. U. Mich., Ann Arbor, 1968, Marygrove Coll., Detroit, 1971, Aarhus (Denmark) U., 1972-74, 83, Windsor (Ont., Can.) U., 1977-78. Author: Was War Necessary, 1980, Johnson, Nixon and the Doves, 1988, Covering Dissent, 1994, Democracy and Diplomacy, 1996, The Presidency of Richard Nixon, 1999, Antiwarriors, 2002; co-author: Wages of War, 1972, Resort to Arms, 1982; editor: Public Opinion and Historians, 1970; co-editor: International War, 1986, Appeasing Fascism, 1991, Give Peace a Chance, 1992; mem. editl. bd. Internat. Interactions, 1987-91, Peace and Change, 1989—; restaurant critic Detroit Metro Times, 1982-95; history book reviewer Detroit Free Press, 1988-95. Mem. hon. bd. Swords into Plowshares Mus., 1992—; bd. dirs. Abraham Lincoln Brigade Archives, 1998—, Ctr. on Peace and Liberty, 2003—, David S. Wyman Inst. for Holocaust Studies, 2003—. Recipient Disting. Faculty award Mich. Assn. Governing Bds., 1993; Am. Coun. Learned Socs. fellow, 1969; Stanford Ctr. for Advanced Study fellow, 1969-70; grantee Am. Coun. Learned Socs., 1983, Johnson Libr., 1982, 88, Can. Govt., 1987; NATO rsch. fellow, 1996. Mem. Coun. on Peace Rsch. in History (nat. coun. 1986-90, pres. 1990-92), Am. Hist. Assn., Atlantic Coun. (acad. assoc.), Orgn. Am. Historians, Soc. for Historians of Am. Fgn. Rels. (Warren Kuehl prize 1989). Home: 1815 Northwood Blvd Royal Oak MI 48073-3919 Office: Wayne State U Dept History 3119 Fab Detroit MI 48202 Office Phone: 313-577-6138. E-mail: M.Small@Wayne.edu.

SMALL, MELVIN D. physician, educator; b. Somerville, Mass., May 22, 1925; s. Sidney J. and Ida (Gelbsman) Small; m. Judith Nogee, Dec. 23, 1962; children: Michael Dorian, Michele. AB, U. Wis., 1953; MD, Duke U., 1959; studied under Dr. Gregory Pincus, Worcester Found. Exptl. Biol. and Medicine, 1950-53; studied under Prof. Brian Abel-Smith, London Sch. Econs, 1986-90, MPhil, 1988. Lic. physician Fla., Md., DC, Va. Intern Georgetown U. Med. Ctr., Washington, 1959-60, resident, 1960-61, chief gastrointestinal rsch., 1961-64, instr. medicine, 1961-66, asst. prof., 1966-67, asst. clin. prof., 1967-81, 93—; chief gastroenterology sect. Georgetown divsn. DC Gen. Hosp., 1964-68. Chief animal experimentation cancer rsch. under Dr. Sidney Farber Children's Med. Ctr., Boston, 1948—50; rsch. asst. Boston U. Sch. Medicine, 1956—57; lectr. hygiene and preventive medicine Peace Corps groups, Ethiopia, Turkey, Brazil, and Columbia Georgetown U., 1961—62; active staff Fairfax (Va.) Hosp., 1961—73, Arlington (Va.) Hosp., 1961—85, Cir. Terr. Hosp., Alexandria, 1965—85, Commonwealth Drs. Hosp., Fairfax, 1969—74, Mt. Vernon Hosp., Alexandria, 1976—85; attending physician DC Gen. Hosp., 1961—68, Georgetown U. Hosp., 1961—81, 1993—, Mt. Sinai Hosp., Miami Beach, Fla., 1992—; cons. Children's Hosp., Washington, 1962—66; chmn. dept. medicine Alexandria Hosp., 1974—75, hon. staff mem., 1985—89, 1992—; founder, chmn. No. Va. Consortium Continuing Med. Edn., 1974—86; chmn. emeritus No. Va. Consotium Continuing Med. Edn., 1986; witness subcom. small bus. U.S. Senate, 1967; lectr in field; founder, chmn. Nat. Coun. State Coms. Continuing Med. Edn., 1977—79. Author: publs. in field. Nominated candidate Palm Beach (Fla.) Town Coun., 1995—96; trustee Jefferson Meml. Hosp., 1965—74, mem. founding group, 1965, chmn. pharmacy com., 1965—76, co-chmn. tissue com., 1965—74. Fellow, Mallory Inst. Pathology, 1953—59, Gastroenterology Rsch., Evans Meml. Hosp., 1951—53. Mem.: ACP, AMA, Palm Beach County Med. Soc., Fla. Med. Soc., Royal Soc. Medicine, Alexandria Med. Soc. (v.p. 1979—80), Med. Soc. Va. (chmn. commn. continuing med. edn. 1978—81), DC Med. Soc., Am. Soc. Gastrointestinal Endoscopy, Am. Physiol. Soc., Am. Inst. Nutrition, Am. Gastroent. Assn., Am. Coll. Gastroenterology. Home: 47 Saint George Pl Palm Beach Gardens FL 33418 Personal E-mail: drmelv5@aol.com.

SMALL, MICHELE GESLIN, English studies and modern languages educator; b. Port-Vila, Vanuatu, South Pacific, June 16, 1944; 1 child, Jonathan Michael. Licence d'anglais, U. Nice, 1967; MA in English, SUNY, Albany, 1969; PhD in Social, Psychol. and Philos. Edn., U. Minn., Mpls., 1983. French instr. SUNY, Albany, 1969-72; asst. prof. English and French Northland Coll., Ashland, Wis., 1975-81, assoc. prof. English and French, 1981-85, prof. English and modern langs., 1985—. Recipient Tchg. Excellence award Sears Roebuck Found., 1991. Office: Northland Coll 1411 Ellis Ave Ashland WI 54806-3925

SMALL, NATALIE SETTIMELLI, pediatric mental health counselor; b. Quincy, Mass., June 2, 1933; d. Joseph Peter and Edmea Natalie (Bagnaschi) Settimelli; m. Parker Adams Small, Jr., Aug. 26, 1956; children: Parker Adams III, Peter McMichael, Carla Edmea. BA, Tufts U., 1955; MA, EdS, U. Fla., 1976, PhD, 1987. Cert. child life specialist. Pediatric counselor U. Fla. Coll. Medicine, Gainesville, 1976-80, Shands Hosp.-U. Fla., Gainesville, 1980-87, supr. child life dept. patient and family resources, 1987—2003; pres. Small Group Cons.com, 2003—. Adminstrv. liaison for self-dir. work teams, mem. faculty Ctr. for Coop. Learning for Health and Sci. Edn., Gainesville, 1988-2003, assoc. dir., 1996, supr. pastoral svcs., 1998-2003; cons. and lectr. in field. Author: Parents Know Best, 1991; co-author team packs series for teaching at risk adolescent health edn. Building Strong Families, 1998. Bd. dirs. Ronald McDonald House, Gainesville, 1980—, mem. exec. com., 1991—; bd. dirs. Gainesville Assn. Creative Arts, 1994—; mem. health profl. adv. com. March of Dimes, Gainesville, 1986-96, HIV prevention planning partnership, 1995-96; mem. Teen Pregnancy Prevention Action Com., 1998-2000, exec. com. Children's Hosp., 1998-2003. Boston Stewart Club scholar, Florence, Italy, 1955; grantee Jessie Ball Du Pont Fund, 1978, Children's Miracle Network, 1990, 92-95, 97, 2000, 2001-2003; recipient Caring and Sharing award Ronald McDonald House, 1995, Appreciation award March of Dimes, 1996. Mem. ACA, Nat. Bd. Cert. Counselors. Roman Catholic. Avocations: travel, reading, swimming. Home: 3454 NW 12th Ave Gainesville FL 32605-4811 E-mail: smallgroup2@aol.com.

SMALL, PARKER ADAMS, JR., pediatrician, educator; b. Cin., July 5, 1932; s. Parker Adams and Grace (McMichael) S.; m. Natalie Settimelli, Aug. 26, 1956; children: Parker Adams, Peter McMichael, Carla Edmea. Student, Tufts U., 1950-53; MD, U. Cin., 1957; BS extraordinem, 1986. Med. intern Pa. Hosp., Phila., 1957-58; rsch. assoc. Nat. Heart Inst. NIH, Washington, 1958-60; rsch. fellow St. Mary's Hosp., London, 1960-61; sr. surgeon NIMH, Washington, 1961-66; prof. immunology and med. microbiology U. Fla., 1966-95, chmn. dept., 1966-75, prof. pediat., 1979—2003, prof. emeritus, 2003—, prof. pathology, 1995—2003, prof. emeritus, 2003—, adj. clin. prof. large animal sci., 1999—2003; pres. PigVax Inc., 2000—01. Dir. Ctr. for Coop. Learning for Health Sci. Edn., U. Fla., 1988-2003; vis. prof. U. Lausanne, Switzerland, 1972, U. Lagos, Nigeria, 1982, Al Hada Hosp., Saudi Arabia, 1983; vis. scholar Assn. Am. Med. Colls., Washington, 1973; assoc.

life scis. panel Nat. Acad. Scis., 1981-88, co-chmn., 1982-83; bd. dirs. Biol. Sci. Curriculum Study, 1984-90, exec. bd., 1987-90; mem. edn. adv. com. Nat. Fund Med. Edn., 1984-87; mem. study com. Nat. Bd. Med. Examiners, 1983-85, mem. nat. vaccine adv. com., 1987-91, chmn. subcom. on new vaccines, 1987-91; v.p. smallgroupconsultants.com, 2003—; cons. in field. Creator patient oriented problem solving system/POPS, for tchg. immunology and coop. learning to med. students and Team Packs for tchg. K-12 & coll. students health edn. and coop. learning; co-dir. Fla. Ptnrs. in Prevention of Substance Abuse, 1997-2003; editor: The Secretory Immunologic System, 1971; mem. editl. bd. Infection and Immunity, 1974-76, Jour. Med. Edn., 1978-80; cons. editor Microbios, Cytobios; patentee in field; contbr. more than 150 articles to profl. jours. Sec., treas. Oakmont, Md., 1964-65, mayor, 1965-66; chmn. Citizens for Pub. Schs. Gainesville, Fla., 1969-70; mem. Teen Pregnancy Prevention Action Com., 1998-2000. With USPHS, 1958-60, 61-66. Named Tchr. of Yr. U. Fla. Coll. Medicine, 1978-79, Disting. Lectr. AMA, 1986; recipient Presdl. medallion U. Fla., 1987, Nat. Basic Sci. Disting. Tchg. award Alpha Omega Alpha, 1993, Jacob Ehrenzeller award, 1995, Pres.'s Faculty Humanitarian award U. Fla., 1996, Pep award U. Fla., 1998, Lifetime Achievement award U. Fla. Coll. Medicine, 2003; NIH spl. fellow, 1960-61, rsch. grantee, 1966-91, U. Fla. Tchr./Scholar and commencement spkr., 1987; invited lectr. Assn. Am. Med. Colls., 1992. Mem. AAAS, Am. Assn. Immunologists (edn. com. 1983-86), Physicians for Social Responsibility, Fla. Med. Assn., Phi Beta Kappa, Sigma Xi, Alpha Omega Alpha, Theta Delta Chi. Home: 3454 NW 12th Ave Gainesville FL 32605-4811 Office: U Fla Coll Med PO Box 100275 Gainesville FL 32610-0275 Business E-Mail: small@pathology.ufl.edu.

SMALL, PARKER ADAMS, III, investment banker; b. Phila., Feb. 1, 1958; s. Parker Adams Jr. and Natalie (Settimelli) S.; m. Katherine Currier, Aug. 24, 1985; children: Margaret Edmea, Elizabeth Parker. BA, Dartmouth Coll., 1980; MBA, Harvard U., 1985. Account exec. Leo Burnett Advt., Chgo., 1980-83; assoc. Merrill Lynch-Becker Paribas, N.Y.C., 1984; product mgmt. The Gillette Co., Boston, 1985-86; mgmt. cons. Arthur D. Little Inc., Cambridge, Mass., 1986-89; v.p. Butler Capital Corp., N.Y.C., 1989-92. Pres. S.R.S. Sera Co., Gainesville, Fla., 1976-91; bd. dirs. Julius Koch USA Inc., Strine Printing Co., Lancaster Press Inc. Author: Understanding Immunology, 1976; producer Dartmouth Coll. video, 1980. Reunion chmn. Dartmouth Coll., 1990, mem. alumni coun., 1999; bd. dirs. Wellesley Edn. Found. Avocations: skiing, tennis, scuba diving. Home: 11 Westwood Rd Wellesley MA 02482-7015

SMALL, RAY, university administrator; b. Winters, Tex., Aug. 2, 1915; s. George Norman Small and Etta Thompson; m. Dollee Georgia Meyer, Aug. 6, 1938 (div. Jan. 1981); children: Marilynn, Andra; m. Maria Victoria De Leon, Aug. 14, 1998. BA, West Tex. A&M, 1937; MA, U. Tex., 1941, PhD, 1958. Prin. Quail (Tex.) Pub. Sch., 1937-38; tchr. Wayside (Tex.) Sch., 1938-40, prin., 1940-41; tchr. Horace Mann Sch., Amarillo, Tex., 1941—47; prof. Amarillo Coll., 1946; prof., asst. to pres. Tex. Western Coll., El Paso, 1961-63; prof., dean U. Tex., El Paso, 1963-79, acting dir. student publication, 1985-90, editl. advisor-student publs., 1990-95, acad. advisor-comms., 1995—. Emeritus dean liberal arts U. Tex., 1979, emeritus prof. English, 1981, emeritus prof. comm., 1995. Served to comdr. USN, 1943—75. Presbyterian. Home: 603 E Baltimore Dr El Paso TX 79902 Office: U Tex at El Paso 500 W University El Paso TX 79968

SMALL, RICHARD DONALD, travel company executive; b. West Orange, N.J., May 24, 1929; s. Joseph George and Elizabeth (McGarry) S.; m. Arlene P. Small; children: Colleen P., Richard Donald, Joseph W., Mark G., Brian P. AB cum laude, U. Notre Dame, 1951. With Union-Camp Corp., N.Y.C. and Chgo., 1952-62; chmn. Alumni Holidays, Inc., 1962—. AHI Internat. Corp., 1962—; pres. All Horizons, Inc., 1982—. Chmn. AHI, Inc., 1982-89; bd. dirs. French Cruise Lines, Des Plaines, Ill., Russian Cruise Lines, Alumni Campus Abroad, 1994—. Recipient Munich Ptnr. award, 1989. Mem.: Carlton Club (Chgo.), Univ. Club Chgo. Home: Water Tower Pl 180 E Pearson St # 3306 Chicago IL 60611-6730 also: Wailea Golf Estates 3954 Waakaula Pl Wailea HI 96753 Office: 6400 Shafer Ct Rosemont IL 60018 Business E-Mail: royals@hawaii.rr.com., rds@AHITravel.com.

SMALL, STEPHEN BRADLEY, lawyer; b. St. Louis, 1960; BA, U. Mo., 1981; JD, U. Mo., Kansas City, 1985; diploma, Mo. Auction Sch., Kansas City, 1994. Bar: Mo. 1985, Kans. 1986, U.S. Dist. Ct. Kans. 1986, U.S. Dist. Ct. Mo. 1985, U.S. Ct. Appeals (8th cir.) 2000, U.S. Supreme Ct. 2000. Pvt. practice Small Law Office, Kansas City, Mo., 1986—; auctioneer Kansas City, Mo., 1994—. Mem. ATLA, ABA, Mo. Bar Assn., Kans. Bar Assn., Kansas City Metro Bar Assn. (fee dispute com., mng. poster com.), Mo. Trial Lawyers Assn., Am. Legal Svcs. Assn., Nat. Auctioneers Assn., Mensa. Avocations: antiques, automated musical instruments, poker, Egyptian Arabian horses. Office: Small Law Office PO Box 414678 Kansas City MO 64141-4678

SMALL, WILLIAM C. religious organization administrator; s. James Small and Samellar Terrell. PhD in Bibl. Studies, Ross Coll., 2003. Police officer Buffalo Police Dept., 1993—99; pres., CEO Beautiful Feet Ministries, Inc, 1998—. Adv. bd. mem. NY State Child and Family Services, Buffalo, 2001—. Author: A Multitude of Counsel on Strengthening the Family, Healing the Wounded Woman; contbr. periodical. With U.S. Army, 1976—96. Avocations: coach/officiate: basketball, coach/officiate: football, teach bible studies, host seminars, host twice weekly radio broadcast. Office: Beautiful Feet Ministries PO Box 99 Buffalo NY 14209-0099 E-mail: beautifulfeet@worldnet.att.net.

SMALL, WILLIAM EDWIN, JR., association and recreation executive; b. Jackson, Mich., Jan. 18, 1937; s. William Edwin and Lena Louisa (Hunt) S.; m. Ruth Ann Toombs, Mar. 28, 1959; children: Suzanne Marie, William Edwin III, Bryan Anthony. AS, Jackson C.C., 1959; BS in Geology, Mich. State U., 1961, MA in Journalism, 1964. Reporter Sci. Svc., Washington, 1961-62; writer sci. U. Chgo., 1963-64; sci. info. officer Pa. State U., State College, 1964-66; corr. McGraw-Hill, Washington, 1966-69; staff com. pub. works U.S. Senate, 1969—71; founding editor Biomed. News, 1969-71; dir. pub. info. Nat. Bur. Standards, Washington, 1972-76; editor Am. Pharmacy Jour., 1979-82; dir. media and info. svcs. AMA, Washington, 1982-86; exec. dir. Nat. Found. Infectious Diseases, Washington, 1986-91, Assn. Biotech. Cos., 1991-93; CEO, Bioconfs. Internat., Bethesda, Md., 1993-95, WESmall & Assocs., Assn. Execs., Louisa, Va., 1976—. Owner recreation resort Small Country Campground, Louisa, 1976—; exec. dir. Va. Biotech. Assn., 1996-2000; exec. dir. Va. Campground Assn., 2001-03. Author: Third Pollution, 1971. With Security Agy., AUS, 1955-59. Recipient Superior Accomplishment award U.S. Dept. Commerce, 1974. Fellow AAAS; life mem. Nat. Assn. Sci. Writers. Office: PO Box 343 Louisa VA 23093-0343

SMALLBECK, AMANDA, music educator; d. Jeffrey and Anita Capp; m. Christopher Smallbeck. MusB in edn., U. of ND, 1998—2002. Specialist 188th Army N.G. Band, Fargo, ND, 1998—; band dir. Grafton Pub. Schools, Grafton, ND, 2003—. Mem.: NEA, Music Educators Nat. Conf.

SMALLEY, CHRISTOPHER JOSEPH, pharmaceutical company professional; b. Phila., June 26, 1953; s. Charles Wilfred and Verna May (Coulter) S.; m. Maria Visnikie, Aug. 9, 1974; children: Christa Maria, Mark Charles, Lora Loray. BS, Phila. Coll. Pharmacy and Sci., 1976; MBA, Temple U., 1982; PhD, LaSalle U., 1991. Ordained elder, Presbyn. ch., 1992. Mfg. pharmacist supr. McNeil Labs., Fort Washington, Pa., 1976-77; mfg. pharmacist group supr. McNeil Consumer Products Co., 1978-79, mfg. pharmacist mgr., 1980-85; tech. svcs. mgr. Janssen Pharmaceutica, 1985-88, plant mgr., 1988-94; quality assurance dir. Sanofi rsch. divsn. Sanofi Pharms., Inc., Malvern, Pa., 1994-98; dir. validation compliance Wyeth-Ayerst Pharms., St. Davids, Pa., 1998—. Mem. Rep. Nat. Com., 1979—. With USNR Med. Corps., 1986-95, with USAF, 1995—. Mem. Am. Pharm. Assn., Assn. Mil. Surgeons of U.S., Am. Assn. Pharm. Scientists, Internat. Soc. Pharm. Engrs., Aerospace Med. Assn., Am. Acad. Med. Adminstrs., Assn. Med. Svc. Corps Officers, Pa. Pharm. Assn., Inst. Environ. Scis., Eastern Assn. GMP Trainers, Parenteral Drug Assn. (chmn. tng. com.), Pharm. Mfrs. Assn. (prodn. sect.), Phila. Pharm. Forum, USN Inst., NRA, Kappa Psi. Presbyterian. Home: 816 Kenmara Dr West Chester PA 19380-2022 Office: 240 N Radnor Chester Rd Saint Davids PA 19087-5106

SMALLEY, DAVID VINCENT, lawyer; b. N.Y.C., Mar. 27, 1935; s. Vincent R. and Ethel A. (Sullivan) S.; m. Patricia Doyle Tolles, Nov. 28, 1964; children: Brian W., Gregory T. BA, Hamilton Coll.; LLB, Harvard U. Bar: N.Y. 1960. Assoc. Debevoise & Plimpton, N.Y.C., 1959-67, ptnr., 1968-99. Mem. Assn. Bar City N.Y. Home: 10 Wildwood Cir Larchmont NY 10538-3427 Office: Debevoise & Plimpton 919 Third Ave New York NY 10022

SMALLEY, RICHARD ERRETT, chemistry and physics educator, researcher; b. Akron, Ohio, June 6, 1943; s. Frank Dudley and Virginia (Rhoads) Smalley; m. Judith Grace Sampieri, May 4, 1968 (div. July 1979); 1 child, Chad; m. Mary Lynn Chapieski, July 10, 1980 (div. Nov. 1994); m. JoNell Marie Chauvin, Mar. 1, 1997 (div. June 1998); 1 child, Preston. BS in Chemistry, U. Mich., 1965; MA in Chemistry, Princeton U., 1971, PhD in Chemistry, 1973; PhD (hon.), U. Liege, Belgium, 1991; DSc (hon.), U. Chgo., 1995. Assoc. The James Franck Inst., Chgo., 1973—76; from asst. prof. to prof. William Marsh Rice U., Houston, 1976—82, Gene & Norman Hackerman prof. chemistry, 1982—; prof. dept. physics Rice U., Houston, 1990—, univ. prof., 2002—. Chmn. Rice Quantum Inst., Houston, 1986—96; dir. Rice Ctr. for Nanoscale Sci. and Tech., 1996—2002. Contbr. numerous articles to profl. jours. Recipient Franklin medal, Franklin Inst., Phila., 1996, Nobel Prize in chemistry, 1996. Fellow: Am. Phys. Soc. (divsn. chem. physics, Irving Langmuir prize 1991, Internat. New Materials prize 1992); mem.: Am. Acad. Arts and Scis., Materials Rsch. Soc., Am. Chem. Soc. (divsn. phys. chemistry, William H. Nichols medal 1993, S.W. regional award 1992, Harrison Howe award Rochester sect. 1994, Madison Marshall award North Ala. sect. 1995), NAS, AAAS, Sigma Xi. Office: Rice Univ Ctr Nanoscale Sci and Tech 6100 Main St # Ms100 Houston TX 77005-1892

SMALLEY, ROBERT MANNING, government official; b. Los Angeles, Nov. 14, 1925; s. William Denny and Helen (McConnell) S.; m. Lois Louisa Williamson, Nov. 28, 1948 (div.) m. Rosemary Sumner, Jan. 4, 1957; children— Leslie Estelle, David Christian. Student, UCLA, 1946-48. Radio news editor Mut. Radio Broadcasting System, Los Angeles, 1950-55; mgr. Agrl. Info. Inc., Sacramento, 1957-59; with Whitaker & Baxter, San Francisco, 1956-57, 59-61; sec. Mayor, San Francisco, 1961-63; asst. dir. pub. relations Republican Nat. Com., 1964; press sec. Republican vice presdl. candidate William E. Miller, 1964; dir. pub. relations Republican Nat. Com., 1965; v.p. Whitaker & Baxter, San Francisco, 1966-68; asst. press sec. Republican vice presdl. candidate Spiro Agnew, 1968; spl. asst. Sec. Commerce, Washington, 1969-72; adminstrv. asst. U.S. Senator Robert P. Griffin, Washington, 1972-73; dir. corp. affairs Potomac Electric Power Co., Washington, 1973-75; U.S. rep. devel. assistance com. O.E.C.D., Paris, 1975-77; spl. asst. U.S. Senator Robert P. Griffin, Washington, 1977-78; asst. to campaign mgr. Reagan for Pres. Com., Washington, 1979; sr. advisor mgmt. communications IBM, 1979-82; dep. asst. sec. of state pub. affairs Dept. of State, Washington, 1982-87, U.S. amb. to Kingdom of Lesotho, 1987-89; lectr. in U.S. politics and pub. policy. Author: (book) The Admiralities at War 1944-45, 2002. Campaign mgr. Senator Robert P. Griffin, MIch., 1966, 72. Served with USN, 1944-46, PTO. Republican. Episcopalian. Home: Breton Bay Landing 40439 Breton View Dr Leonardtown MD 20650 E-mail: rsmalley@gmexpress.net.

SMALLMAN, BEVERLEY N. retired biology professor; b. Port Perry, Ont., Can., Dec. 11, 1913; s. Richard Benjamin and Ethel May (Doubt) S.; m. Hazel Mayne, Dec. 11, 1937 (dec. 1962); 1 child, Sylvia Gail; m. Florence Hazel Cook, July 27, 1965 BA, Queens U., Kingston, Ont., 1936; M.Sc., Western U. Ont., Can., 1938; PhD, U. Edinburgh, Scotland, 1941; LL.D.(hon.), Trent U., Ont., 1982. Mem. staff Stored Grain Insect Investigations Bd. of Grain Commnrs., Winnipeg, 1941-45; officer-in-charge Stored Products Lab., Agrl. Can., Winnipeg, 1945-50; head entomol. sect. rsch. inst. Agrl. Can., London, 1950-57, chief entomol., rsch. dir. entomology, plant pathology Ottawa, 1957-63; prof., head dept. biology Queens U., Kingston, Ont., Can., 1963-73, prof. biology, 1973-78, prof. emeritus biology, 1979—. Vis. scientist Nat. Inst. Med. Rsch., London, Eng., 1954-56, CSIRO Labs., Brisbane, Australia, 1970-71, 76; apiary insp. Province of Ont., 1981-91; cons., lectr. in field. Prin. author: Agricultural Science in Canada, 1970, Queen's Biology, 1992; co-author: Good Bye Bugs, 1983. Contbr. articles to profl. jours. Fellow Royal Soc. Can.; mem. Entomol. Soc. Can., Zool. Soc. Can., Entomol. Soc. Man. (founding pres. 1945), Entomol. Soc. Ont. Avocation: reading. Home: 364 Emerald St Kingston ON Canada K7P 3E1

SMALLWOOD, CAROL, writer; b. Cheboygan, Mich., May 3, 1939; d. Lloyd Gouine and Lucille Drozdowska; m. T.M. Smallwood, 1963 (div. 1976); 2 children. BS, Ea. Mich. U., 1961, M in History, 1963; MLS, We. Mich. U., 1976. Tchr. Redford Union High Sch., Livonia, Mich., 1961-62, Flat Rock (Mich.) Jr. High Sch., 1963-64; grad. asst. Western Mich. U., Kalamazoo, 1975-76; Title I libr. cons. Northland (Mich.), Grand Traverse (Mich.) Library Systems, 1976-77; head media dir. Pellston (Mich.) Pub. Schs., 1977—97; writer, libr. cons. Mt. Pleasant, 1998—. Asst. dir. Northland Libr. System, Alpena, Mich., 1977; developer, operator ednl. materials clearinghouse, 1981-83; adult edn. tchr. Cheboygan Area Schs., 1985-86. Author: Free Michigan Materials for Educators, 1980, 2nd edit., 1986, Free Materials Resource Disk, 1983, Exceptional Free Library Resource Materials, 1984, Free Resource Builder, 1985, 2d edit., 1992, A Guide to Selected Federal Agency Programs and Publications for Librarians and Teachers, 1986, Health Resource Builder, 1988, An Educational Guide to the National Park System, 1989, Current Issues Builder, 1989, Library Puzzles and Word Games, for Grades 7-12, 1990, Reference Puzzles and Word Games for Grades 7-12, 1991, Michigan Authors, 1993, Helpful Hints for the School Library, 1993, Recycling Tips for Teachers and Librarians, 1995, An Insider's Guide to Libraries, 1997, Free or Low-Cost Health Information, 1998, (with S. McElmeel) WWW Almanac, 1999; columnist Detroit News, 1983-85, Morning Sun, 2003—, Catch: The Entertainment News, 1988-89, Essential Resources for Schools and Libraries, 1997-2003, Morning Sun, 2003—; contbr. to lit., poetry and fiction mags., anthologies, 2001—. Charter bd. mem., publicity chmn. Cheboygan Area Arts Coun.; founder, pres. Cheboygan County Humane Soc.; co-founder Humane Animal Treatment Soc. Mem.: Poetry Soc. Am., Doris Day Animal Found. Home: 543 S Whiteville Rd Mount Pleasant MI 48858-9761 E-mail: csmallwo@edcen.ehhs.cmich.edu.

SMALLWOOD, FRANKLIN, political science educator; b. Ridgewood, N.J., June 24, 1927; s. J. William and Carolyn (Linkroum) S.; m. Ann Logie, Sept. 8, 1951; children: Susan, Sandra, David, Donald. AB, Dartmouth Coll., 1951, A.M. (hon.), 1968; M.P.A., Harvard U., 1953, PhD, 1958. With AEC, 1953-57; asst. to pres. Dartmouth Coll., 1957-59, mem. faculty, 1959-92, prof. govt., 1967-92, Nelson A. Rockefeller prof. govt. emeritus, 1992—; U. Vt., Burlington, 1989—; chmn. city planning and urban studies program Dartmouth Coll., 1965-72, chmn. social sci. div., 1968-72, asso. dean faculty, 1968-72, acting dean, 1972, v.p. student affairs, 1975-77, chmn. policy studies program, 1977-83, dir. Nelson A. Rockefeller Center for Social Scis., 1983-86. Chmn. Vt. Gov.'s Commn. Higher Edn., 1973-80, Vt. Adv. Commn. on Intergovtl. Relations, 1985-86, Vt. Legis Apportionment Bd., 1990—; fenceviewer Norwich, Vt., 1976-90. Author: Metro Toronto: A Decade Later, 1963, Greater London: The Politics of Metropolitan Reform, 1965, Free and Independent, 1976, The Politics of Policy Implementation, 1980, The Other Candidates, 1983, Thomas Chittenden, Vermont's First Statesman, 1997, The UVM Presidents, 1997. Mem. Vt. Senate, 1973-75; trustee Vt. State Colls., 1967-73, chmn., 1973. Served with AUS, 1945-46. Recipient Superior Achievement award AEC, 1957, Dartmouth Presdl. Leadership medal, 1991; fellow Inst. Pub. Adminstrn., 1960; Dartmouth Coll. Faculty fellow, 1962-63; Nuffield Coll. (Oxford U.), vis. fellow, 1981, 86-87. Mem. Phi Beta Kappa. Office: 804 Wake Robin Dr Shelburne VT 05482

SMALLWOOD, GLENN WALTER, JR., utility marketing management executive; b. Jeffersonville, Ind., Oct. 12, 1956; s. Glenn Walter and Darlene Ruth (Zeller) S. BSBA, S.E. Mo. State U., 1978; MA in Bus., Webster U., 1992, MBA, 1993. Cert. econ. developer Inst. Econ. Devel. Cert., counselor, energy mgr. Customer svc. advisor Union Electric Co., Mexico, Mo., 1979—95, Cape Girardeau, Mo., 1995—97; cmty. devel. exec. Ameren Svcs., Cape Girardeau, 1997—98, bus. devel. exec., 1998—. Instr. Mexico Vo-Tech Sch., 1981; panelist on home design Mo. Extension Svc., 1984; co. advisor Mo. Bus. Week. Coord. local United Way, 1984; mem., chair Gt. Rivers coun. Boy Scouts Am., chair Shawnee dist. Eagle Scout advancement com., 1999-2001, chair Shawnee Dist. com., 2002--; panelist Mo. Freedmon Forum, 1990; charter mem. class Mo. Leadership; chmn. Leadership Mexico Program; coordinating advisor Jr. Achievement, Mexico H.S.; committeeman, chmn. Republican Party of Audrain County; bd. dirs. Mo. Rep. Grassroots Caucus, S.E. Mo. Univ. Found., 1998— chmn. Cape Girardeau Planning and Zoning Commn., 2004—. Named among Ten Outstanding Young Missourians, Mo. Jaycees, 1993; recipient Disting. Svc. award Mexico, Mo. Jaycees, 1993. Mem. Am. Mktg. Assn. (profl.), Nat. Eagle Scout Assn. (bd. dirs. St. Louis coun.), Cooper Dome Soc., Boy Scouts Am. Alumni Family, Mexico Area C. of C. (bd. dirs. 1993-95), Cape Girardeau C. of C. (chair govtl. affairs com.), S.E. Mo. U. Alumni Assn., Inst. Cert. Profl. Mgrs. (cert. mgr.), Assn. Energy Engrs. (cert. energy mgr.), Adminstrv. Mgmt. Soc., Optimists (Youth Appreciation award 1974), Kiwanis (cert. appreciation 1984), Mexico Noon (bd. dirs. 1990, treas. 1990-91, v.p. 1991-92, pres. 1993-94), Audrain County Pachyderm Club (bd. dirs., 2d v.p. 1990-92, pres. 1993), S.E. Mo. Univ. Found. (bd. dirs.), S.E. Mo. Pachyderm Club (founder, pres. 1997-98), Mo. Fedn. Pachyderm Clubs (bd. dirs.), Honorable Order Ky. Cols. (commd. Ky. col. 1995), Sons of Confederate Vets., Disting. Hoosier Com. (State of Ind. 1999), Rotary. Republican. Avocations: music, spectator sports, baseball, basketball, tennis. Office: Ameren Svcs 340 Silver Springs Rd Cape Girardeau MO 63703 E-mail: gsmallwood@ameren.com.

SMALLWOOD, ROBERT ALBIAN, JR., secondary education educator; b. Phila., Oct. 3, 1946; s. Robert Albian and Mildred May (Miller) S.; m. Geraldine Ann Boozan, May 27, 1972; children: Amy Lynn, Daniel James. BSC, Rider Coll., 1969, MA, 1976; EdS, Rutgers U., 1986. Cert. social studies tchr., secondary sch. prin., supr. curriculum and instrn., Pa.; cert. social studies and gen. bus. tchr., prin., supr., sch. bus. adminstr., asst. supt. bus., sch. adminstr. (supt.) N.J. Tchr. social studies Trenton Bd. Edn., 1973-76, tchr. bus. edn., 1975-76, sch. disciplinearian, 1976-84, 94-97; acting asst. prin. Jr. High Sch. 2, 1980-83, tchr. U.S. history, 1983-87, chmn. social studies dept., 1984-85; acting asst. prin. Carroll Robbins Elem. Sch., Jr. High Schs. #1 and #5, 1987-88; tchr. gifted and talented social studies Dunn Jr. High Sch., 1989-93, social studies tchr., 1997-99, whole sch. reform site facilitator, 1999—. Mem. Dist.'s Affirmative Action Adv. Council; mem. Nat. Tchr. Corps Project, Trenton Area; fin. advisor M.S. Prin., 1998—. Asst. ops. officer Trenton CD Unit, 1974-76, asst. disaster analysis officer, 1976, disaster analysis officer, 1976-79; trustee N.J. Coun. for Alcohol/Drug Edn., 1983-99, mem. exec. com., 1985-95, 96-99, chmn. nominating com., 1985, 86, treas., 1987-95, acting exec. dir., 1994-95, v.p., 1996-98, pres. 1998-99. With U.S. Army, 1969-72. Decorated Bronze Star, Army Commendation medal with oak leaf cluster, Joint Svc. Commendation medal. Mem. NEA, Vietnam Vets. Am., Va. Geneal. Soc., Md. Geneal. Soc., Md. Hist. Soc., Geneal. Soc. Pa., Nat. Geneal. Soc., Assn. Profl. Genealogists, Phi Delta Kappa. Home: 2 Leese Ave Trenton NJ 08609-1828

SMALLY, DONALD JAY, consulting engineering executive; b. Cleve., 1922; s. Daniel James and Alice (Rohrheimer) S.; m. Ruth Janet Glasser, July 8, 1944; children: Alan Jon, Leonard Arthur. BME, U. Cin., 1949. Prodn. engr. N. Ransohoff, Inc., Cin., 1949-50; chief engr. Mosby Engring. Assocs., Sarasota, Fla., 1952-55; prin. Smally, Wellford & Nalven, Inc., Sarasota, 1956-91. Mem. tech. adv. com. Manatee Community Coll., Sarasota, 1965-90; mem. adv. com. Vocat.-Tech. High Sch., Sarasota, 1968-80 V.p. Sarasota YMCA, 1968-71, Sarasota Opera Assn., 1975-88, pres., 1988-89; chmn. Sarasota Vol. Talent Pool, 1973-76; sec.-treas. Civitan Found., 1965-79; bd. dirs. Suncoast Heart Assn., 1976; mem. Fla. Coordinating Coun. for Vocat. and Adult Edn., 1984-95, chmn., 1987-88; chmn. Sarasota Hist. Preservation Bd., 1988-91; pres. Sarasota County Rd. Improvement Task Force, 1990-93; mem. Sarasota County Pub. Sch. Found., 1990-95, chmn., 1990-91; v.p. Hist. Soc. Sarasota, 1990-91, Children's Haven and Adult Cmty. Svcs., 1983-99, pres., 1991-94; pres. John Ringling Ctr. Found., 1991-98; mem. Plymouth Harbor Bd., 1994-99. Recipient Good Citizenship award SAR, 1975, Disting. Alumni award U. Cin. Engring. Coll., 1985, Outstanding Svc. award Myakka Chpt. Fla. Engring. Soc., 1993; named Citizen of Yr. Sarasota Civitan Club, 1975, Engr. of Yr. Sarasota-Manatee Engrs. Soc., 1976. Fellow Am. Coun. Engring. Cos. (treas. 1980-82), Fla. Engring. Soc. (pres. Sarasota-Manatee chpt. 1956-58); mem. Sarasota County C. of C. (past dir., v.p. 1983), Cons. Engrs. Council Fla. (pres. 1968), Fla. Soc. Profl. Land Surveyors (chpt. pres. 1973), Am. Water Works Resources Assn. (pres. Fla. Soc. 1981), Sarasota-Manatee Engring. Soc.

SMARDON, RICHARD CLAY, landscape architecture and environmental studies educator; b. Burlington, Vt., May 13, 1948; s. Philip Albert and Louise Gertrude (Peters) S.; m. Anne Marie Graveline, Aug. 19, 1973; children: Regina Elizabeth, Andrea May. BS cum laude, U. Mass., 1970, MLA, 1973; PhD in Environ. Planning, U. Calif., Berkeley, 1982. Environ. planner, landscape architect Wallace, Floyd, Ellenzweig, Inc., Cambridge, Mass., 1972-73; assoc. planner Exec. Office Environ. Affairs, State of Mass., Boston, 1973-75; environ. impact assessment specialist USDA extension svc. Oreg. State U., Corvallis, 1975-76; landscape architect USDA Pacific S.W. Forest and Range Expt. Sta., Berkeley, 1977; rsch. landscape architect U. Calif., Berkeley, 1977-79; prof. landscape architecture, sr. rsch. assoc. SUNY Coll. Environ. Sci. and Forestry, Syracuse, 1979-86, prof. environ. studies, 1987—, dir. Inst. for Environ. Policy and Planning, 1987-95, chair faculty of environ. studies, 1996—. Co-dir. Gt. Lakes Rsch. Consortium, Syracuse, 1986—; guest lectr. numerous univs.; adj. asst. prof. U. Mass., Amherst, 1974-75, dir. R.G. Pack Environment Inst., 1996—; Sea Grant trainee Inst. for Urban and Regional Devel., Berkeley, 1976; condr., presenter numerous seminars and workshops; cons. to numerous orgns.; mem. com. on environ. design and landscape Transp. Rsch. Bd.-NAS, 1985-95; mem. tech. adv. bd. Wetlands Rsch., Inc., Chgo., 1985; mem. adv. bd. Wetlands Fund, N.Y., 1985; v.p. Integrated Site, Syracuse, 1990-2002. Co-editor: Our National Landscape, 1979, spl. issue Coastal Zone Mgmt. Jour., 1982, The Future of Wetlands, 1983, Foundations for Visual Project Analysis, 1986, The Legal Landscape, 1993, Protecting Floodplain Resources, 1995, Adirondacks and Beyond, 1998, Environmental Knowledge, 2001; mem. editl. bd. Northeastern Environ. Sci. Jour., 1981-85, Landscape and Urban Planning, 1991—, Environ. Sci. and Policy, 1999—, The Sci. World, 2001—; contbr. over 100 articles to profl. jours. Bd. dirs. Sackets Harbor Area Hist. Preservation Found., Watertown, N.Y., 1984-90; pres. Save the County, Inc., Fayetteville, N.Y., 1986-88, 2002—; apptd. to Great Lakes (N.Y.) Adv. Commn., chmn., 1993-98, Great Lakes Legal Found., 1999, NY State Wetlands Forum Bd., 2000. Recipient Beatrice Farrand award U. Calif., 1979, Am. Soc. Landscape Architects award, 1972, Pub. Svc. award in edn., 1990, Progressive Architecture mag. award 1992, Pres.'s Pub. Svc. award 1994. Mem. AAAS, NAEP, N.Y. Acad. of Sci., Am. Land Resource Assn. (charter), Internat. Assn. for Impact Assessment, Coastal Soc., Alpha Zeta (life), Sigma Lambda Alpha. Avocations: folk guitar, hiking, skiing, travel. Office: SUNY Faculty Environ Studies Syracuse NY 13210 Office Phone: 315-470-6576.

SMARDZ, ZOFIA JADWIGA, editor, writer; b. Reinbek, Germany, Oct. 20, 1950; arrived in U.S., 1950; d. Stanislaw Kostka and Krystyna Maria Smardz; m. Daniel Felix Arnaud, Oct. 11, 1975 (div. 1984); m. Charles Anson Franklin, Feb. 27, 1987; children: Andrew, Roman. BA, Vassar Coll., 1972; M Journalism, U. Calif., Berkeley, 1975. Reporter Washington Star, 1976—81; fgn. corr. Newsweek, Bonn, Germany, 1981—84, corr. Washington, 1984—86; editor Washington Post, 2000—. Freelance editor, cons., Washington, 1986—2000. Co-author: Special Trust, 1994; writer, editor: Awakening Intuition, 1997. Bd. edn. Our Lady of Victory Sch., Washington, 1997—99. Fellow, Alicia Patterson Found., Washington, 1986; scholar, Woodrow Wilson Ctr., Washington, 1986; Fulbright fellow, 1972. Republican. Roman Catholic. Avocations: music, voice, piano, flute, gardening. E-mail: smardzz@washpost.com.

SMART, ALLEN RICH, II, retired lawyer; b. Chgo., July 3, 1934; s. Jackson W. Smart and Dorothy (Byrnes) Bowles. Student, Deerfield Acad., 1949-52; AB magna cum laude, Princeton U., 1956; LLB, Harvard U., 1959. Bar: Ill. 1961. Assoc. Bell Boyd & Lloyd, Chgo., 1961-69, ptnr., 1970-91, of counsel, 1992—2001. Bd. dirs. Rec. for Blind, Inc., Chgo., 1984-95, vice-chmn., 1987-90; co-chmn. zoning com. Old Town Triangle Assn., Chgo., 1987-94; bd. dirs. Lawrence Hall Sch. for Boys, 1965-70, Old Masters Soc., Art Inst., 1987—; governing mem. Orchestral Assn. Lt. USNR, 1956-58. Mem.: ABA, Chgo. Opera Theater (dir. 2002—), Renaissance Soc. Chgo. (bd. dirs. 1988—), Inst. for Psychoanalysis (dir. 2001—), Friends of the Pks. Chgo. (bd. dirs. 1986—), Infant Welfare Soc. Chgo. (bd. dirs. 1971—95, pres. 1982—86), Racquet Club Chgo., Arts, Lawyers Econ. Clubs of Chgo., Univ. Club (bd. dirs. 1986—89). Home: 1732 N North Park Ave Chicago IL 60614-5710 Office: Bell Boyd & Lloyd 3200 Three First Nat Pl Chicago IL 60602

SMART, ANN CATHERINE, dean; b. Anderson, Ind., Nov. 27, 1946; d. Edward Vernon and Virginia Ruth (Hersberger) Dillie; m. Houston Wynnlee Crisp, Aug. 17, 1968 (div. 1980); m. William H. Smart, Aug. 16, 1987. BS in Edn., Ball State U., 1969; postgrad., U. Alaska, 1971—73; M in Home Econs., Oreg. State U., 1975, PhD, 1991. Youth nutrition specialist U. Alaska, Fairbanks, 1970—73, extension mgmt. info. coord., 1972—73; specialist nutrition edn. Oreg. State U., Corvallis, Oreg., 1975; parent edn. and home econs. coord. Linn-Benton C.C., Albany, NY, 1975—77, Albany (N.Y.) Ctr. dir., 1977—79, Benton Ctr. dir., 1979—85, cmty. edn. divsn. dir., 1985—89, spl. asst. to v.p. bus. affairs, 1987, interim v.p. instrn., 1989—90, dean student svcs. and extended learning, 1991—94, dean extended learning and info. svcs., 1994—; ret. Rsch. assoc. Western Oreg. State Coll., Monmouth, Oreg., 1983; chmn. task force Cmty. Edn. Dirs., Oreg., 1983. Author: Anotated Bibliography Nutrition Education Resources, 1975, Program Planning Activities Nutrition for Elderly, 1975; co-prodr.: (films) Alaskan Food Choices, 1973; contbr. articles to bulls. Founding pres. Oreg. Coast C.C. Svc. Dist., Newport, Oreg., 1987—88; chmn. task force Charting the Future of Corvallis, 1988—89; mem. UN Forum 85, Nairobi, Kenya, 1985; sec. Benton County United Way, 1984—87, pres., 1991—92, Zonta Svc. Found. Corvallis, 1991—92, treas., 1994—. Named Leader of the 80s, League Innovation in Cmty. Colls., 1982. Mem.: LWV, Oreg. Cmty. Edn., Am. Assn. Women in C.C., Oreg. C.C. Assn., Nat. Coun. Cmty. Svcs. and Continuing Edn. (Oreg. rep. 1994—, Regional Person of Yr. award 1993), Am. Assn. Adult and Continuing Edn. (v.p. region VIII 1987—89), Oreg. Home Econs. Assn. (sec. 1979—81, mem. joint bds. articulation commn. 1992—95, named Disting. Leader 1984), N.W. Adult Edn. Assn. (pres. 1984—85, named Adult Educator of Yr. 1987), Corvallis C. of C. (bd. dirs.), Rotary, Albany (N.Y.) Club, Zonta Club (pres. Corvallis club 1982—83, internat. del. 1982, alt. 1984, African study tour 1985, named Zontian of Yr. 1994), Phi Kappa Phi, Phi Theta Kappa, Sigma Zeta. Democrat. Office: Linn-Benton Community Coll 6500 Pacific Blvd SW Albany OR 97321-3755

SMART, EDITH MERRILL, civic worker; b. Sept. 10, 1929; d. Edwin Katte and Helen Phelps (Stokes) Merrill; m. S. Bruce Smart, Jr., Sept. 10, 1949; children: Edith Minturn Smart Moore, William Candler, Charlotte Merrill Smart Rogan, Priscilla Smart Schwarzenbach. Student, Smith Coll., 1947—49, Barnard Coll., 1949—50. Tchr. elem. schs., Gibson Island, Md., 1959—60; guide, instr. Mill River Wetlands Com., Fairfield, Conn., 1967—85; treas. Near and Far Aid Assn., Fairfield, 1970—75, v.p., 1975—77, pres., 1977—79, Nature Ctr. of Environ. Activities, Westport, Conn., chmn., 1981—85; trustee Fairfield U., 1987—93; leader No. Cook county coun. Girl Scouts Am., Kenilworth, Ill., 1962—64; chmn. Southport-Westport Antiques Show, 1974—76; trustee Conn. chpt. Nature Conservancy, 1981—91, Va. chpt. Nature Conservancy, 1992—. Guide Nat. Aquarium, 1985—90; dir. Piedmont Child Devel. Ctr., 1991—97, Land Trust of Va., 2002—. Vestryman St. Timothy's Ch., Fairfield, 1976—79. Mem.: MFH The Fairfax Hunt Club, Upperville Garden Club. Republican. Episcopalian. Home: 20561 Trappe Rd Upperville VA 20184-3021

SMART, MARY-LEIGH CALL (MRS. J. SCOTT SMART), civic worker; b. Springfield, Ill., Feb. 27, 1917; d. S(amuel) Leigh and Mary (Bradish) Call; m. J. Scott Smart, Sept. 11, 1951 (dec. 1960). Diploma, Monticello Coll., 1934; student, Oxford U., 1935; BA, Wellesley Coll., 1937; MA, Columbia U., 1939, postgrad., 1940-41, NYU, 1940-41; painting student, with Bernard Karfiol, 1937-38. Dir. mgmt. Cen. Ill. Grain Farms, Logan County, 1939—; owner Lowtrek Kennel, Ogunquit, Maine, 1957-73, Cove Studio Art Gallery, Ogunquit, 1961-68; art collector, patron, publicist, 1954—. Cons. in field. Editor: Hamilton Easter Field Art Found. Collection Catalog, 1966; originator, dir. show, compiler of catalog Art: Ogunquit, 1967; Peggy Bacon-A Celebration, Barn Gallery, Ogunquit, 1979. Program dir., sec. bd. Barn Gallery Assoc., Inc., 1958-69, pres., 1969-70, 82-87, asst. treas., 1987-92, hon. dir., 1970-78, adv. trustee, 1992-94, v.p., 1994-2003; curator Hamilton Easter Field Art Found. Collection, 1978-79, curator exhbn., 1979-86, chair exhbn. com., 1987-94; acquisition com. DeCordova Mus., Lincoln, Mass., 1966-78; chancellor's coun. U. Tex., 1972—; pres. coun. U. NH, 1978—; bd. dir. Ogunquit C. of C., 1966, treas., 1966-67, hon. life mem., 1968—; bd. overseers Strawbery Banke, Inc., Portsmouth, NH, 1972-75, 3d vice chmn., 1973, 2d vice-chmn., 1974; bd. advisors U. Art Galleries, U. NH, 1973-89; pres., 1981-89; bd. dir. Old York Hist. and Improvement Soc., York, Maine, 1979-81, v.p., 1981-82; adv. com. Bowdoin Coll. Mus. Art Invitational exhibit, 1975, '76 Maine Artists Invitational Exhbn., Maine State Mus., Maine Coast Artists, Rockport, 1975-78, All Maine Biennial '79, Bowdoin Coll. Mus. Art juried exhbn.; mem. jury for scholarship awards Maine com. Skowhegan Sch. Painting & Sculpture, 1982-84; nat. com. Wellesley Coll. Friends of Art, 1983—; adv. trustee Portland Mus. Art, 1983-85, fellow, 1985—; mus. panel Maine State Commn. on Arts and Humanities, 1983-86; adv. com. Maine Biennial, Colby Coll. Mus. Art, 1983; coun. advisors Farnsworth Art Mus., Rockland, Maine, 1986-98; collections com. Payson Gallery, Westbrook Coll., Portland, 1987-91; dir. Greater Piscataqua Cmty. Found., NH Charitable Fund, 1991-97; com. to establish artist's advancement grant, 2001; mem. corp. Ogunquit Mus. Am. Art, 1988-90, 95-2000; active Maine Women's Forum, 1993—; mem. art com. York Pub. Libr., 2002—; pres. Class of 1937, Wellesley Coll., 2001—. Lt. (j.g.) WAVES, 1942-45. Recipient Deborah Morton award Westbrook Coll., 1988, Friend of the Arts award Maine Art Dealers Assn., 1993. Mem. Springfield Art Assn., Jr. League Springfield Ill., Western Maine Wellesley Club. Episcopalian. Address: 30 Surf Point Rd York ME 03909-5053

SMART, STEPHEN BRUCE, JR., business and government executive; b. N.Y.C., Feb. 7, 1923; s. Stephen Bruce and Beatrice (Cobb) S.; m. Edith Minturn Merrill, Sept. 10, 1949; children: Edith Minturn Smart Moore, William Candler, Charlotte Merrill Smart Rogan, Priscilla Smart Schwarzenbach. Student, Milton Acad.; AB cum laude, Harvard U., 1945; SM, MIT, 1947. Sales engr. Permutit Co., N.Y., 1947-51; various sales, gen. mgmt. positions Continental Group, Inc. (formerly Continental Can Co.), N.Y.C., 1953-85, v.p. Central metal divsn., 1962-65, v.p. marketing and corporate planning, 1965-67, v.p., asst. gen. mgr. paper ops., 1967-69, group v.p. paper ops., 1969-71, exec. v.p. paper ops., 1971-73, vice chmn. bd. dirs., 1973-75, pres., 1975-85, chmn., CEO, 1981-85; undersec. for internat. trade U.S. Dept. Commerce, Washington, 1985-88; cons. U.S. Dept. State, Washington, 1988-89; sr. fellow World Resources Inst., Washington, 1989-95, bd. dirs., 1992-2001. Author: Beyond Compliance: A New Industry View of the Environment, 1992, Indian Summer--A Memoir, 1999, A Community of the Horse: Partnerships, 2003. Trustee, vice chmn. Smith Coll., 1976-86; gov., vice chmn. The Nature Conservancy, 1979-85; bd. dirs. League of Conservation Voters, Va. Thoroughbred Assn., 2001—; chmn. bd. dirs. Notre Dame Acad., Middleburg, Va., 1996-98. Mem.: Sigma Xi. Home and Office: 20561 Trappe Rd Upperville VA 20184-3021

SMARTSCHAN, GLENN FRED, educational consultant; b. Allentown, Pa., Dec. 11, 1946; s. Fred Gotfred and Joyce Isabel (Hensinger) S.; m. Linda Susan Bastinelli, Mar. 18, 1972; children: Erin Joy, Lauren Nicole. BS in Edn., Kutztown State Coll., 1968; MS in Edn., Temple U., 1972; EdD in Ednl. Adminstrn., Lehigh U., 1979. Cert. tchr. history and comprehensive social studies, secondary prin., supt., Pa. Tchr. 8th grade social studies South Mountain Jr. H.S., 1968-76; adminstrv. asst. to prin. to prin. Raub Jr. H.S., 1976-80, dist. dir. curriculum, 1980-84, asst. to supt. for curriculum and cmty. svcs., 1984-86; supt. schs. Brandywine Hts. Area Sch. Dist., Topton, Pa., 1986-90, Mt. Lebanon Sch. Dist., Pitts., 1990—2003. Adj. prof. Cedar Crest Coll., 1986-88, Duquesne U., 1997, U. Pitts., 2001; CEO Ednl. Dynamics Cons.; spkr. and cons. Multiple Client Feedback (MCF), Pay for Performance Plans, Match of Written, Taught and Tested Curriculum, Criterion Referenced Testing, Strategic Planning; rsch. assoc. U. Pitts; ednl. planner Burt Hill Kosar Rittelmann, 2003—; cons. Tri-State area study coun. Univ. Pitts for planning and accountability, 2003—. Bd. dirs. Alternative House, Inc., Bethlehem, Pa., 1976-81, chmn. program com., 1977-78, v.p., 1979, pres., 1980; adv. com. Lehigh County (Pa.) Hist. Mus., 1980-86; bd. dirs. Girls Club Allentown, 1983-86, v.p., 1985. Mem. ASCD, Pa. Assn. Supervision and Curriculum Devel. (exec. com., registrar ea. regional meeting, v.p. Ea. region, pres. 1988), Am. Assn. Sch. Adminstrs. (Pa. State Supt. of Yr. 1999), Pa. Assn. Sch. Adminstrs. (pres. 1996), Pa. Sch. Bds. Assn., Juvenile Diabetes Assn. (bd. dirs.), Alumni Coun. Lehigh U. (pres. 1986), Phi Delta Kappa, Fleetwood Club, Rotary (charter mem. Allentown club, exec. com. 1985). Roman Catholic. Home: One Spalding Cir Pittsburgh PA 15228 Office Phone: 412-344-8663. Business E-Mail: edcsmartschan@adelphia.net.

SMARTT, BILL, air courier company executive; CFO DHL Airways Inc., Redwood City, Calif.; exec. v.p., CFO, chief administrv. officer DHL Worldwide Express, Redwood City, Calif. Office: DHL Worldwide Express 50 California St Ste 500 San Francisco CA 94111-4608

SMARTT, JOHN MADISON, lawyer; b. Smartt, Tenn., Feb. 24, 1919; s. Robert White and Sarah Alma (Roggli) Smartt; m. Harriet Chapin, June 9, 1943; children: John Madison, Jane Stroud, Douglas A., Robert W. III. BS, U. Tenn., 1942, JD, 1948. Bar: Tenn. 1948, U.S. Dist. Ct. (ea. dist.) Tenn. 1969. Dir. alumni U. Tenn., Knoxville, 1948—69; ptnr. Fowler & Robertson, Knoxville, 1969—83; counsel Ambrose, Wilson, Grimm & Durand, Knoxville, 1983—. Coord. Tenn. Law Inst., Knoxville, 1972—97. Bd. dirs. United Way of Greater Knoxville, 1984; life mem. 5th Cir. Jud. Conf. Capt. AUS, 1942—46, lt. col. USAR. Mem.: Tenn. Bar Found., Great Smokey Mt. Conservation Assn. (pres. 1978), Kiwanis, Phi Delta Phi. Democrat. Presbyterian. Avocations: hiking, running, singing. Home: 4603 Holston Hills Rd Knoxville TN 37914-5007 Office: Ambrose Wilson Grimm & Durand PO Box 2466 Knoxville TN 37901 2466

SMASON, IVAN, psychologist, writer; b. New Orleans, Apr. 13, 1963; BS, Syracuse U., 1985; MA, Trinity U., 1987; PhD, U. N.Mex., 1992; JD, U. Pacific, 1999. Cert. psychologist Calif. Bd. Psychology, 1997. Pvt. practice, L.A., 1997—. Prodr.: (CD) Marijuana, 2002; author: Jazz Boy, 2003. Mem.: Acad. Am. Poets, Internat. Neuropsychol. Soc. Avocations: piano, reading, exercise, walking.

SMATHERS, JAMES BURTON, medical physicist, educator; b. Prairie du Chien, Wis., Aug. 26, 1935; s. James Levi and Irma Marie (Stindt) S.; m. Sylvia Lee Rath, Apr. 20, 1957; children— Kristine Kay, Kathryn Ann, James Scott, Ernest Kent. B.Nuclear Enging., N.C. State Coll., 1957, MS, 1959; PhD, U. Md., 1967. Diplomate Am. Bd. Radiology, Am. Bd. Health Physics, Am. Bd. Medical Physics; cert. in radiation oncology physics; registered profl. engr., D.C., Tex., Calif. Research engr. Atomics Internat., Canoga Park, Calif., 1959, Walter Reed Army Inst. Research, Washington, 1961-67; prof. nuclear engring. Tex. A. and M. U., College Station, 1967-80, prof., head bioengring., 1976-80; prof., head med. physics, dept. radiation oncology UCLA, 1980-2001, prof. emeritus, 2001—. Cons. U.S. Army, Dept. Energy, also pvt.; industry. Served with U.S. Army, 1959-61. Recipient Excellence in Teaching award Gen. Dynamics, 1971; Excellence in Research award Tex. A. and M. U. Former Students Assn., 1976 Mem. Health Physics Soc., Am. Assn. Physcists in Medicine, Am. Soc. Enging. Edn. (Outstanding Tchr. award in nuclear engring. div. 1972), Sigma Xi, Sigma Pi Sigma, Phi Kappa Phi. Home: 18229 Minnehaha St Northridge CA 91326-3427 E-mail: smathers@ucla.edu.

SMAY, CONNIE R. educational media specialist, educator; b. Benton Harbor, Mich., May 27, 1953; d. Victor Wier and Lois Reynolds; m. James Robert Smay, Aug. 11, 1979; children: Robert James, Thomas Victor, Rebekah Josephine. Student, Western Mich. U., Kalamazoo, 1975, 76; BS in Edn., Ctrl. Mich. U., Mt. Pleasant, 1975; MS in Edn. with honors, No. Ill. U., DeKalb, 1979. Tchr.'s aide Coloma (Mich.) Migrant Program, 1971, 73-76, tchr., 1977; factory prodn. line worker Voice of Music, Benton Harbor, 1972; student tchr. Wyoming (Mich.) Sch. Dist., 1975; libr., media specialist Cmty. Sch. Dist. 300, Dundee, Ill., 1975-79, Cmty. Sch. Dist. 115, Oquawka, Ill., 1980; children's libr. Warren County Pub. Libr., Monmouth, Ill., 1980-81; ednl. media specialist Parsippany Troy Hills (N.J.) Bd. Edn., 1990—. Computer liaison Parsippany Troy Hills Bd. Edn., 1993-98, insvc. trainer for dist., 1995—, integrator of technology and NJ Core Content Stds. into content curriculum areas, 1990—; Internet trainer, 1997—, coord. NetDay, 1997-98. Grantee EBSCO Pub., Ipswich, Mass., 1996-97; recipient dist. mini-grant Sci. Is for Everyone, 1996, Hit the Nail on the Head, 1997, Integrating Core Curriculum Stds. in Sci. and Math. Mem. DAR, ALA, Am. Assn. Sch. Libr., NJ Reading Assn., NJ Statewide Systemic Initiative, NJ Edn. Assn., Parsippany Tech. Com. (sci. standing com., learning resources and media svcs. com.), Ednl. Media Specialists Assn., Ednl. Media Assn. NJ, Morris County Media Specialist Assn., Disting. Flying Cross Soc. (assoc.). Methodist. Home: 152 Orben Dr Landing NJ 07850-1828 Office: Parsippany Troy Hills Sch Dist care Ctrl Mid Sch Parsippany NJ 07054 also: Brooklawn Mid Sch Parsippany NJ 07054

SMEAD, KENNETH WILLIAM, music educator; s. Edward L. and Lucille Alma Smead; m. Mary Nicole Naccarato, Sept. 26, 1958; children: Michael Anthony, Kathryn Elizabeth. MusB in edn., James Madison U., 1976—80. Microsoft Office User Expert Microsoft, Va., 2002. Choral dir./asst. band dir. Galax City Pub. Schools, Va., 1980—81; vocal musician USN, 1981—2001; youth choir dir. Francis Asbury United Meth. Ch., Va. Beach, 1992—2001; adj. instr. Tidewater C.C., Va. Beach, 1998—; choral dir./tchr. Va. Beach City Pub. Schools, 2001—. Cons. Princess Anne H.S. Fabulous Marching Cavaliers, Va. Beach, 2001—; a.p.p.l.e. instr. Va. Beach City Pub. Schools, 2001—; presenter Va. Soc. for Tech. in Edn., 2000, Tech. Symposium, Arlington, Va., 2000. Chief musician USN, 1981—2001. Decorated Navy Commendation medal USN, Navy Achievement medal, Armed Forces Sch. of Music Sailor of the Yr.; recipient Recommended for Tchr. of the Yr., Larkspur Mid. Sch., 2003, Tagged by the Supt., Va. Beach City Pub. Schools. Mem.: Va. Choral Director's Assn., Va. Music Educator's Assn., Music Educators Nat. Conf., Va. Soc. for Tech. in Edn., Chief Petty Officers Assn. (life). Avocation: music technology. Office: Larkspur Middle Sch 4696 Princess Anne Rd Virginia Beach VA 23462 E-mail: kwsmead@vbcps.k12.va.us.

SMEAL, ELEANOR CUTRI, civil rights executive; b. Ashtabula, Ohio, July 30, 1939; d. Peter Anthony and Josephine E. (Agresti) Cutri; m. Charles R. Smeal, Apr. 27, 1963; children: Tod, Lori. BA, Duke U., 1961, LLD (hon.), 1991; MA, U. Fla., 1963. Mem. bd. Upper St. Clair (Pa.) chpt. LWV, 1968-72, sec.-treas. Allegheny County Council, 1971-72; mem. NOW, 1971—; convenor, 1st pres. S. Hills (Pa.) chpt. NOW, 1971-73, 1st pres., state coordinator, 1972-75; nat. bd. dirs. NOW, 1973-75, chairwoman bd., 1975-77, pres., 1977-82, 85-87, mem. bd. Legal Def. and Edn. Fund, 1975—, chairwoman ERA Strike Force, 1977—; pres. Fund for Feminist Majority, Arlington, Va., 1987—. Mem. 1st nominating com., founding conf. Nat. Women's Polit. Caucus, 1971; bd. dirs. Allegheny County Women's Polit. Caucus, 1971-72; co-founder, bd. dirs. S. Hills NOW Day Nursery Sch., 1972—; mem. Nat. Commn., Observance of Internat. Women's Year, 1977; mem. exec. com. Leadership Conf. on Civil Rights, 1979—; mem. Nat. Adv. Com. on Women, 1978 Named One of 25 Most Influential Women in U.S. World Almanac, 1978 Office: The Feminist Majority 1600 Wilson Blvd Ste 801 Arlington VA 22209-2513

SMECK, WILLIAM H. computer scientist; b. Chester, Pa., Sept. 1, 1945; s. William H. and Dolores M. S.; m. Barbara Nunan, Aug. 1, 1970; 1 child, Gregory. BA in English Lit., Widener U., 1977; MEd in Tech., Edn., Rosemont Coll., 1995. Computer ops. shift supervisor Certain-Teed Products Co., Valley Forge, Pa., 1969-73; asst. computer ops. mgr. Wawa (Pa.) Food Markets, 1973-77; computer programmer Clement Pub., Concordville, Pa., 1977-79; sr. programmer, analyst Scott Paper Co., Phila., 1979-93; project adminstr. Computer Sci. Corp., Ft. Worth, 1993-95; project leader Lockheed Martin Aircraft Corp., Valley Forge, Pa., 1995-97; project mgr. CAI, Inc., Wilmington, Del., 1997—. Referee coll. and h.s. track and cross country meets. Sgt., U.S. Army, 1963-66. Mem. Project Mgmt. Inst., Rosemont Coll. Alumnae (bd. dirs., grad. sch. rep. 1997—), St. James Cath. H.S. Boys Alumni Assn. Roman Catholic. Avocations: long distance running, history. Home: 514 Wheatsheaf Rd Springfield PA 19064 Office: Computer Aid Inc 901 Market St Wilmington DE 19801

SMEDLEY, CHARLES VINCENT, sociology educator; b. Washington, Sept. 1, 1955; s. Frederick Joseph Smedley and Ruth (Bouknight) McGee; m. Sue Marie Prosser, Aug. 28, 1976; 1 child, Sarah Jane. BS cum laude, U. S.C., 1978; MA, U. Ill., 1980, PhD, 1986. Asst. prof. U. Charleston, W.Va., 1986-88, Charleston (S.C.) So. U., 1988—. Mem. editorial adv. bd. Roxbury Pub. Co., 1989—, Collegiate Press, 1991—; editor Behavioral Sci. update Charleston So. U., 1989—. Mem. 1st Scots Presbyn. Ch., Charleston, 1990—. Fellowship U. Ill., 1978-79, 85 Fellow Soc. Applied Anthropology; mem. AAAS, Am. Sociol. Assn., Am. Anthropol. Assn., N.Y. Acad. Scis., Am. Acad. Polit. and Social Sci., Soc. for Advancement of Socio-econs., Soc. Psychol. Study Social Issues, Soc. Southeastern Social Psychologists, Archaeol. Inst. Am., S.C. Social Assn., Soc. Applied Anthropology, Mo. Archaeol. Soc., Nat. Trust for Historic Preservation, U. S.C. Alumni Assn., U. Ill. Alumni Assn., U. S.C. Gamecock Club, Berkeley County Soc. for Prevention of Cruelty to Animals, Phi Beta Kappa, Phi Kappa Phi, Pi Gamma Mu, Alpha Kappa Delta. Republican. Home: 111 Dominion Cir Goose Creek SC 29445-5512 Office: Charleston So U PO Box 118087 Charleston SC 29423-8087

SMEDLEY, LAWRENCE THOMAS, retired organization executive; b. Lorain, Ohio, Sept. 2, 1929; s. Robert E. and Gerda Sofia (Johnson) S.; m. Carmen Nancy Suarez, June 29, 1962; children: Lorraine, Robert, Lawrence, Richard. BA, Bowling Green State U., 1952; MA, U. Mich., 1957; PhD, Am. U., 1972. Analyst Social Security dept. AFL-CIO, Washington, 1962-65, asst. dir. dept., 1965-73, assoc. dir. dept. occupation safety-health-social security, 1973-88; exec. dir. Nat. Coun. Sr. Citizens, Inc., Washington, 1988-96. Former mem. numerous presdl. task forces and coms. on older Ams. and disabled; mem. planning and adv. coms. White House Conf. on Aging, 1971, 81; former mem. adv. coun. on employee welfare and pension plans Dept. Labor, also former mem. spl. task force examining policies relating to asset reversions from over-funded pension plans; bd. dirs. Nat. Coun. Sr. Citizens. Co-chmn. Leadership Coun. Aging Orgns., Washington, 1988-95; mem. exec. bd. Com. for Nat. Health Ins., WAshington, 1989—; mem. policy conv. White House Conf. on Aging, 1995; chair Montgomery County Com. Aging. With M.I., U.S. Army, 1952-55, Korea. Recipient Svc. award Commn. on Accreditation of Facilities of Rehab., 1975, Dedicated Svc. award White House Conf. on Handicapped, 1977, award of honor Industry-Labor Coun., 1981, Outstanding Svc. award Pres.'s Com. on Employment of Handicapped, 1987. Democrat. Lutheran. Home: 1616 Winding Waye Ln Silver Spring MD 20902-1456 Personal E-mail: ltsmed@aol.com.

SMEDS, EDWARD WILLIAM, retired food company executive; b. Chgo., Feb. 15, 1936; s. Sigvard A. and Ida S.; m. Alice J. Lawler, Jan. 26, 1957; children: Ellen R., Brad W. BS, Carthage Coll., 1957; MS, U. Ill., 1959; grad. advanced mgmt. program, Harvard U., 1977. With Borg Warner Corp., 1958-61, Kraft Foods div. Kraft Inc., 1961-75, v.p., dir. personnel, ops. group, 1976-78, v.p. human resources, 1978-79, sr. v.p. human resources, 1979-80, sr. v.p. fin. and adminstrn., 1980-84; pres. Kraft Asia Pacific, 1984-88; chmn. Kraft Foods Ltd., Australia, 1984-88; pres. Kraft Ltd. Can., 1988-89; sr. v.p. ops. and logistics Kraft Gen. Foods, Glenview, Ill., 1990-94; pres. customer svc. and ops. Kraft, Northfield, Ill., 1993-94, ret., 1994. Chmn. bd. Thrivent Mut. Funds. Chmn. bd. trustees Carthage Coll., Cornerstone Fund. Mem. Econ. Club of Chgo., Sunset Ridge Country Club, Club at Pelican Bay, Olde Fla. Home: 10 Regentwood Rd Northfield IL 60093-2728 also: 6814 Pelican Bay Blvd Naples FL 34108-8218 E-mail: esmeds@comcast.net.

SMEEKES, FRANK, executive recruiter, consultant; b. Breda, Netherlands, Jan. 19, 1959; s. Maria Kruyssen and Martin Smeekes; m. Mirjam Ottenhoff, June 2, 1990; children: Beatrijs, Isabelle, Maxime. BS, Midden Brabant Higher Edn., Breda, The Netherlands, 1983; MBA, Newport U., Utrecht, The Netherlands, 1990. Mgmt. cons. Fokker Aircraft, Amsterdam, 1983—85; sr. cons. External Mgmt. Ptnrs., Zeist, Netherlands, 1985—90; mktg. & sales mgr. Unigrant, The Hague, 1990—91; mgr., retail ops. An Wb, The Hague, 1991—93; sr. cons. A.T. Kearney Exec. Search, Amsterdam, 1993—94, v.p., 1994—97, Chgo., 1997—. Bd. dirs. Orchard Village, Chgo., 2001—; spkr. in field. Mem. World Bus. of Chgo., 1999, Coun. on Fgn. Rels. of Chgo., 2003. Office: AT Kearney Inc 222 W Adams St Chicago IL 60606 Office Phone: 312-223-6282.

SMEETON, THOMAS ROONEY, governmental affairs consultant; b. Evanston, Ill., Sept. 26, 1934; s. Cecil Brooks, Jr. and Florence Mary (Rooney).; m. Susan Diane Tollefson, Feb. 23, 1963; children: Sean, Timothy, Shannon, Brendan, Colin. BS in History, Marquette U., 1958; postgrad., U. Notre Dame, 1958-59; grad., Armed Forces Staff Coll., 1972. Intelligence officer U.S. CIA, Langley, Va., 1962-73; vp., gen. mgr. Nowicki Fla. Devel. Corp., Ft. Lauderdale, 1973-75; cons. spl. projects com. on fgn. affairs U.S. House Reps., Washington, 1975-86, minority counsel permanent select com. on intelligence, 1986-92, minority staff dir. Iran/Contra com., 1987-88, exec. dir. Rep. policy com., 1993-94; adminstr., chief investigator House Judiciary Com., Washington, D.C., 1995-96; govtl. affairs cons., 1996—. Contbg. author: (with Hyde) For Every Idle Silence, 1985. Bd. dirs. Sylvan Beach Found. With U.S. Army, 1959-62. Recipient Agy. Seal medallion CIA, 1993. Mem. Assn. Former Intelligence Officers, Ctrl. Intelligence Retirees Assn., Am. Legion, Notre Dame Club Washington (vice chmn. 1982-84), Amelia Island Club, Capitol Hill Club. Republican. Roman Catholic. Avocation: golf. Home and Office: PO Box 8029 Fernandina Beach FL 32035-8029

SMEGAL, THOMAS FRANK, JR., lawyer; b. Eveleth, Minn., June 15, 1935; s. Thomas Frank and Genevieve (Andreachi) S.; m. Susan Jane Stanton, May 28, 1966; children: Thomas Frank, Elizabeth Jane. BS in Chem. Engring., Mich. Technol. U., 1957; JD, George Washington U., 1961. Bar: Va. 1961, D.C. 1961, Calif. 1964, U.S. Supreme Ct. 1976. Patent examiner U.S. Patent Office, Washington, 1957-61; staff patent atty. Shell Devel. Co., San Francisco, 1962-65; patent atty. Townsend and Townsend, San Francisco, 1965-91, mng. ptnr., 1974-89; sr. ptnr. Graham and James, San Francisco, 1992-97; pres., ptnr. Knobbe, Martens, Olson & Bear, San Francisco, 1997—. Mem. U.S. del. to Paris Conv. for Protection of Indsl. Property; mem. adv. com. Ct. of Appeals for Fed. Cir., 1992-96. Contbr. articles to profl. jours. Pres. bd. dirs. Legal Aid Soc. San Francisco, 1982-84, Youth Law Ctr., 1973-84; bd. dirs. Nat. Ctr. for Youth Law, 1978-84, San Francisco Lawyers Com. for Urban Affairs, 1972—, Legal Svcs. for Children, 1980-88; bd. dirs., presdl. nominee Legal Svcs. Corp., 1984-90, 1993-2003. Capt. Chem. Corps, U.S. Army, 1961-62. Recipient St. Thomas More award, 1982. Mem. ABA (chmn. PTC sect. 1990-91, ho. of dels. 1988-2000, mem. standing com. Legal Aid and Indigent Defendants 1991-94, 2004—, chair sect. officer conf. 1992-94, bd. govs. 1994-97, standing com. on Pro Bono and Pub. Svc. 1997-2001, standing com. on Gavel awards 2001-04, commn. on racial and ethnic diversity in the profession), Intellectual Property Law Assn. (chmn. nat. coun. 1989), Nat. Inventors Hall of Fame (pres. 1988), Calif. Bar Assn. (v.p. bd. dirs. 1986-87), Am. Patent Law Assn. (pres. 1986), Internat. Assn. Intellectual Property Lawyers (pres. 1995-2001), Bar Assn. San Francisco (pres. 1979), Patent Law Assn. San Francisco (pres. 1974), World Trade Club, Olympic Club, Golden Gate Breakfast Club, Claremont Club (Berkeley). Republican. Roman Catholic. Office: Knobbe Martens Olson & Bear One Sansome Ste 3500 San Francisco CA 94104 Home: 107 King Ave Piedmont CA 94610 Office Phone: 415-217-8383. E-mail: tsmegal@kmob.com.

SMELSER, NEIL JOSEPH, sociologist; b. Kahoka, Mo., July 22, 1930; s. Joseph Nelson and Susie Marie (Hess) S.; m. Helen Thelma Margolis, June 10, 1954 (div. 1965); children: Eric Jonathan, Tina Rachel; m. Sharin Fateley, Dec.

20, 1967; children: Joseph Neil, Sarah Joanne. BA, Harvard U., 1952, PhD, 1958; BA, Oxford (Eng.) U., 1954, MA, 1959; grad., San Francisco Psychoanalytic Inst., 1971. Mem. faculty U. Calif., Berkeley, 1958-94; prof. sociology, 1962—, asst. chancellor ednl. devel., 1966-68; assoc. dir. Inst. of Internat. Studies, Berkeley, 1969-73, 80-89; prof. sociology U. Calif., Berkeley, 1972-94; prof. emeritus, 1994—; dir. edn. abroad program for U. Calif., Berkeley, 1977-79, spl. advisor Office of Pres., 1993-94, dir. Ctr. for Advanced Study in Behavioral Scis., 1994-2001. Bd. dirs. Social Sci. Rsch. Coun., chmn., 1971-73, com. econ. growth, 1961-65; trustee Ctr. for Advanced Study in Behavioral Scis., 1980-93, 94-, chmn., 1984-86; trustee Russell Sage Found., 1990-2000; subcom. humanism Am. Bd. Internal Medicine, 1981-85, 89-90, adv. com., 1992-99, chmn. adv. com., 1995-99; chmn. sociology panel Behavioral and Social Scis. survey NAS and Social Sci. Rsch. Coun., 1967-69; com. on basic rsch. in behavioral and social scis. NRC, 1980-89, chmn., 1984-86, co-chmn., 1986-89; chmn. com. of selection Guggenheim Found., 1996-; chmn. Commn. for Behavioral and Social Scis. and Edn. (NAS/NRC), 1996-2003, German-Am. Acad. Coun., 1999-2000. Author: (with T. Parsons) Economy and Society, 1956, Social Change in the Industrial Revolution, 1959, Theory of Collective Behavior, 1962, The Sociology of Economic Life, 1963, 2d edit., 1975, Essays in Sociological Explanation, 1968, Sociological Theory: A Contemporary View, 1971, Comparative Methods in the Social Sciences, 1976, (with Robin Content) The Changing Academic Market, 1980, Sociology, 1981, 2d edit., 1984, 3d edit., 1987, 4th edit., 1991, 5th edit., 1995, Social Paralysis and Social Change, 1991, Effective Committee Service, 1993, Sociology, 1994, Problematics of Sociology, 1997, The Social Edges of Psychoanalysis, 1999; editor: (with W.T. Smelser) Personality and Social Systems, 1963, 2d edit., 1971, (with S.M. Lipset) Social Structure and Mobility in Economic Development, 1966, Sociology, 1967, 2d edit., 1973, (with James Davis) Sociology: A Survey Report, 1969, Karl Marx on Society and Social Change, 1973, (with Gabriel Almond) Public Higher Education in California, 1974, (with Erik Erikson) Themes of Work and Love in Adulthood, 1980, (with Jeffrey Alexander et al) The Micro-Macro Link, 1987, Handbook of Sociology, 1988, (with Hans Haferkamp) Social Change and Modernity, 1992; (with Richard Munch) Theory of Culture, 1992; (with Richard Swedberg) The Handbook of Economic Sociology, 1994; (with Jeffrey Alexander) Diversity and Its Discontents, 1999; (with William Julius Wilson and Faith Mitchell) American Becoming: Racial Trends and their Consequences, 2001, (with Paul B. Baltes) International Encyclopedia of the Social and Behavioral Sciences, 2001; editor Am. Sociol. Rev., 1962-65; adv. editor Am. Jour. Sociology, 1960-62. Rhodes scholar, 1952-54; Jr. fellow Soc. Fellows, Harvard U., 1955-58, fellow Russell Sage Found., 1989-90. Mem. Am. Sociol. Assn. (coun. 1962-65, 67-70, exec. com. 1963-65, pres. elect 1995-96, pres. 1996-97), Pacific Sociol. Assn., Internat. Sociol. Assn. (exec. com. 1986-94, v.p. 1990-94), Am. Acad. Arts and Scis. (hon.), Am. Philos. Soc. (hon.), Nat. Acad. of Scis. (hon.). Business E-Mail: nsmelser@uclink.berkeley.edu.

SMELT, RONALD, retired air transportation executive; b. Houghton Le Spring, Durham, Eng., Dec. 4, 1913; arrived in U.S., 1948, naturalized, 1955; s. Henry Wilson and Florence (Bradburn) Smelt; m. Marie Anita Collings, Nov. 2, 1940 (dec. May 1964); 1 child, David; m. Jean Stuart, Jan. 15, 1965. BA, Cambridge (Eng.) U., 1935, MA, 1939; PhD, Stanford U., 1961. With Royal Aircraft Establishment, 1935-48, chief high speed flight, 1940-45, chief guided weapons dept., 1945-48; dep. chief aeroballistic research dept. USN Ordnance Lab., 1948-50; chief gas dynamics facility ARO, Inc., Tullahoma, Tenn., 1950-57; dir. research and devel. missile sys. divsn. Lockheed Aircraft Corp., Sunnyvale, Calif., 1958-59, mgr. Discoverer Satellite sys., 1959-60, chief scientist, 1960-62, v.p., gen. mgr. space programs divsn., 1962-63, v.p., chief scientist, 1963-78; ret., 1978. Gugenheim lectr. Internat. Congress Aero. Sci., 1978; mem. com. space vehicle aerodynamics NASA, 1965—66, chmn. rsch. adv. com. space vehicles, 1966—73, chmn. rsch. and tech. adv. coun., 1973—77; chmn. tech. adv. bd. Dept. Transp., 1970—74; mem. engring. adv. com. Stanford U., 1988—89; mem. adv. com. NASA-Stanford Ctr. Turbulence Rsch. Fellow: AIAA (hon.; dir.-at-large 1966—68, pres. 1969, 1970), Am. Astronautical Soc., Royal Aero. Soc. (London), Cambridge Philos. Soc.; mem.: Nat. Acad. Engring. Home: PO Box 149 Oakland OR 97462-0149

SMELTZER, DEBRA JEAN, botanist; b. Camden, Ark., Oct. 13, 1953; d. William Dewey and Frankie Jean (Braswell) S.; m. James Richard Ziesler, Sept. 1, 1984. Cert. in interior design, Bauder Fashion Coll., Arlington, Tex., 1973; BA in Botany, U. Tex., 1985. Biol. rsch. asst. U.S. Dept. Interior, Everglades Nat. Park, Fla., 1980; biologist, surveyor Great Lakes Dredge and Dock, Miami Beach, Fla., 1981-82, 1984, biologist, surveyor, drafter Port Everglades, Fla., 1984; biologist, lab. tech. J.B. Reark and Assocs., Miami, 1982-84; fisheries biologist Kathryn Chandler and Assocs., Alexandria, Va., 1981-84; pres. Greensleeves, Inc., Miami and San Juan, P.R., 1985—, San Juan, P.R., 1991-95. Bd. govs. Nat. Coun. for Interior Hort. Cert., Columbus, Ohio, 1989-92; licensee Interior Landscape Internat. Corp., Dade, Monroe, Caribbean, 1990-92. Eucharistic min. St. Timothy Cath. Ch. Recipient Best Project award Interiorscape Mag., 1989, 1996, State Award of Excellence Fla. Nurserymen and Growers Assn., 1989, award of recognition, 1999. Mem. Associated Landscape Contractors Am. (award of Distinction 1989, 91, 92, Grand award 1990, 2001), South Fla. Interior Landscape Assn. (ednl. com. 1987-89, bd. dirs. 1986-87, author newsletter articles 1986-89, founder 1986), Coral Gables C. of C. (trustee coun.), Calif. Internior Plantscape Assn. (judges award, 2001, Distinction award 2001, 02). Republican. Avocations: waterskiing, skiing, scuba diving, photography.

SMERDON, ERNEST THOMAS, engineering educator; b. Ritchey, Mo., Jan. 19, 1930; s. John Erle and Ada (Davidson) S.; m. Joanne Duck, June 9, 1951; children: Thomas, Katherine, Gary. BS in Engring., U. Mo., 1951, MS in Engring., 1956, PhD in Engring., 1959, DSc (hon.), 2003. Registered profl. engr., Ariz. Chmn. dept. agrl. engring. U. Fla., Gainesville, 1968-74, asst. dean for rsch., 1974-76; vice chancellor for acad. affairs U. Tex. System, Austin, 1976-82; dir. Ctr. for Rsch. in Water Resources U. Tex., 1982-88; dean Coll. Engring. and Mines U. Ariz., Tucson, 1988-92, vice provost, dean Engring. 1992-97; sr. edn. assoc. NSF, Arlington, Va., 1997-00; prof. civil engring. and hydrology U. Ariz., Tucson, 2000—01, dean emeritus, 2001—. Mem. bd. sci. and tech. for internat. devel. NRC, 1990-94, mem. com. on plannin and remediation for irrigation-induced water quality problems, 1990-96, chair com. Yucca Mountain peer rev., 1995, mem. com. study of rsch.-doctorate programs in U.S., 1991-95, com. on Missouri River Ecosystem Sci., 1999-2001; chair com. Water Resources Mgmt. Instream Flow and Salmon Survival in the Columbia River, 2002—; others. Editor: Managing Water Related Conflicts: The Engineer's Role, 1989. Mem. Ariz. Gov.'s Sci. and Tech. Coun., Tucson, 1989-98; bd. dirs. Greater Tucson Econ. Coun., Tucson, 1990-95. Recipient Disting. Svc. in Engring. award U. Mo., 1982, Lifetime Achievement award Environ. and Water Resources Inst., 2002. Fellow: NAE (peer com., 1986-90, 2002—, acad. adv. bd. 1989—95, tech. policy options com. 1990—91, chair com. on career-long edn. for engrs. 1997—2000, acad. adv. bd. 1998—99, vice-chmn. sect. 12 2002—04, peer com. 2002—05, steering com. on engr. of 2020, policy com. on Engr. of 2020), ASCE (hon. Outstanding Svc. award irrigation and drainage divsn. 1988, Royce Tipton award 1989); mem.: Ariz. Soc. Profl. Engrs. (Engr. of Yr. award 1990), Univ. Coun. on Water Resources, Am. Geophys. Union, Am. Soc. Engring. Edn. (chmn., bd. dirs. engring. dean's coun. 1995—97, pres. 1998—99), Am. Water Resources Assn. (Icko Iben award 1989), Am. Soc. Agrl. Engrs., Pi Mu Epsilon, Tau Beta Pi, Phi Kappa Phi, Sigma Xi. Avocations: hiking, golf, scuba diving, painting. Office: U Ariz Rm N521 Tucson AZ 85721-0001

SMERGE, RAYMOND G. mortgage company executive; b. Portales, NM; m. Patricia Smerge; children: Paul, Jessica, Mark. BS, Northern Ill. U., 1967; JD, De Paul U. Law, Chgo., 1971. Closing officer Centex Corp., 1968-72, v.p., gen. counsel, 1972-85, v.p., 1985—93, chief legal officer, 1985—, sec., 1993—, exec. v.p., 1997—. Mem.: Dallas Bar Assn., ABA. Office: Centex Corp 2728 N Harwood St Ste 200 Dallas TX 75201-1591 Office Phone: 214-981-6530. E-mail: rsmerge@centex.com.

SMETANA, MARK, food products executive; CFO Eby-Brown Co., Naperville, Ill. Office: 280 Shuman Blvd Ste 280 Naperville IL 60563-2578

SMETHERAM, HERBERT EDWIN, management consultant; b. Seattle, Sept. 9, 1934; s. Francis Edwin and Grace Elizabeth (Warner) S.; m. Beverly Joan Heckert, Sept. 7, 1963; children: Alice, Helen, Charles. BA, U. Wash., 1956; diploma, Naval Intelligence Sch., 1962; MA, U. Md., 1971; diploma in Swedish, U.S. Fgn. Svc. Inst., 1978; MBA, Rollins Coll., 1991. Ensign USN, 1956, advanced through grades to capt., 1976; comdr. USS Lind (DD-703), 1971-73; attache to Sweden USN, Stockholm, 1978-81; comdr. Naval Adminstrn. Command, Orlando, Fla., 1981-84; ret. USN, 1984; strategic planner electronics, info. and missiles group Martin Marietta Corp., Orlando, 1985-93; exec. dir. re-use com. Naval Tng. Ctr., Orlando, 1993-97, mil. base closure cons., 1991-98. Mgmt. cons., ZHA, Inc., 1998—. Mem. ARC Ctrl. Fla.; mem. Ctrl. Fla. coun. USO, Orlando, 1981—93, pres., 1991—93; mem. steering com. U.S. Congressman McCollum for Re-election, 1992—96; mem. U.S. Senator Hawkins Naval Acad. Nominating Com., Orlando, 1982—86, Fla. Gov.'s Def. Reinvestment Task Force, 1992—93; treas. St. Mathews Episcopal Parish, Orlando, 2000—03; bd. dirs. Episcopal Diocese Ctrl. Fla., 2002—, exec. com. Decorated Royal Order of North Star (Sweden). Mem. SAR, Electronics Industry Assn. (requirements com. 1985-93), Nat. Assn. Installation Developers (southeast regional dir. 1996-97, treas. 1996-2000, bd. dirs. 1996-2000), Fla. Def. Alliance, Ret. Officers Assn., Fla. Econ. Devel. Coun., Navy League, Univ. Club of Winter Park, Fla. (bd. dirs. 2003—), U.S. Tennis Assn., Fla. Tennis Assn., Army Navy Country Club, Orlando Tennis Ctr., Royal Lawn Tennis Club Stockholm, Winter Park (Fla.) Tennis Ctr., Delta Kappa Epsilon. Republican. Episcopalian. Avocation: tennis. Home: 3985 Lake Mira Dr Orlando FL 32817-1643 E-mail: hesmetheram@msn.com.

SMETHURST, E(DWARD) WILLIAM, JR., investment manager; b. Newark, Apr. 15, 1930; s. Edward William and Helen Lea (Wiener) S.; m. Ludlow Bixby, June 30, 953; children: James, Andrew, Katherine. AB, Amherst Coll., 1952; MBA, Harvard U., 1958. Credit analyst Chase Manhattan Bank, N.Y.C., 1958-60; mgr. securities Irwin Mgmt. Co., Columbus, Ind., 1961-64; ptnr. Wertheim & Co., N.Y.C., 1965-79; sr. v.p. Cyrus J. Lawrence Inc., N.Y.C., 1980-87; mng. dir. Wertheim Schroder & Co. Inc., N.Y.C., 1988-95; pres., chief investment officer Schroder Wertheim Investment Svcs., N.Y.C., 1990-96; chmn., trustee Wertheim Series Trust, N.Y.C.; retired, 1996; mng. dir. Byram Capital Mgmt., Greenwich, Conn., 2002—. Trustee Mount Holyoke Coll., South Hadley, Mass., 1982—98. Lt. USN, 1952—55. Episcopalian. Home: 861 Bingham Rd Ridgewood NJ 07450-2111 Office: Byram Captial Mgmt 41 West Putnam Ave Greenwich NY 06830 Office Phone: 203-869-5570 x225.

SMIALEK, WILLIAM, musicologist; b. Fall River, Mass., June 9, 1952; s. Jacob Joseph and Amelia Mary (Skrzypiec) Smialek; m. Molly McCoy, Dec. 30, 1978; children: Andrew Jacob, Adam Roger. MusB, U. R.I., 1974; MusM, No. Tex. State U., 1976, PhD, 1981. Asst. prof. music Jarvis Christian Coll., Hawkins, Tex., 1981—86, assoc. prof. music, 1986—91, prof. music, 1991—99, dean acad. affairs, 1995—99; v.p. acad. affairs, dean faculty Midway Coll., Ky., 1999—2004; exec. v.p. Jarvis Christian Coll., Hawkins, Tex., 2004—. Choir dir. South Elkhorn Christian Ch., Lexington, 1999—2002; faculty woodwind recital Jarvis Christian Coll., 1988; chorister Christ Episc. Ch., Tyler, 1983—98, First Presbyn. Ch., Tyler, 1980—82; proposal evaluator NEH, 1998—; bd. dirs. Midway Renaissance Inc., 2000—02; accreditation evaluator So. Assn. of Colleges and Schools, 2000—. Author: The Symphony in Poland, 1982, Polish Music: A Research and Information Guide, 1989, Ignacy Feliks Dobrzynski and Musical Life in Nineteenth-Century Poland, 1991, Frédéric Chopin, Composer Resource Manual, 2000; contbr. articles to profl. jours.; reviewer Jour. on Excellence in Coll. Tchg., 1999—. Bd. dirs. Tyler Civic Chorale, 1981—91, Boy Scouts Am., 1992—. Grantee East European Lang. Tng. grantee, Am. Coun. Learned s., 1991, Summer Assoc. grantee, Russian and East European Ctr., U. Ill., 1988—2003; Fulbright scholar, 1979—80, Kosciuszko Found. grantee, 1978—79, 1980—81. Mem.: Am. Assn. for the Advancement of Slavic Studies, Polish Inst. of Arts and Scis., Music Libr. Assn., Coll. Music Soc., Am. Musicol. Soc. Mailing: PO Box 1071 Big Sandy TX 75755 Office: Jarvis Christian Coll PO Box 1470 Hawkins TX 75765 Home: 1209 E Eighth St Tyler TX 75701 Office Phone: 903-769-5755.

SMIALOWSKI, JOSEPH A. finance company executive; b. 1949; BA in Philosophy, Merrimack Coll., Andover, MA; MS in Computer Sys. Mgmt., Rochester Inst. Technology, NY. Mgr. Xerox Corp., 1974—83, Dennison Mfg., 1983—84; ptnr. Price Waterhouse, 1984—93; v.p., chief info. officer Sears, Roebuck & Co., 1993—95, sr. v.p., 1995—98; exec. v.p. BankBoston, 1998—99; vice chmn., tech. and ops. FleetBoston Fin. Corp., Boston, 1999—2002, exec. v.p., 2002—. Mem. Rochester Inst. Tech. Presdl. Roundtable, Banking Info. Tech. Secretariat, Pvt. Sector Coun. Active mem. United Way of Mass. Bay. Named a Premier 100 IT Leader, Computerworld Mag., 2000; named one of Top 25 People To Watch, 1998. Office: FleetBoston Fin Corp 100 Federal St Boston MA 02110

SMICK, SUSAN SCHNEE, manufacturing executive, tile designer, marketing professional; b. Bklyn., July 12, 1947; d. Henry and Rhoda (Noskin) Schnee; m. Edward Lewis Smick, Feb. 5, 1972 (separated 1994); 1 child, Joshua Henry. BA with honors, C.W. Post Coll., 1970; postgrad., NYU, 1970-71. Cert. tchr., N.Y. Customer svc. and campus rep. Trans World Airlines, N.Y.C., 1966-71, strategic airline mktg. planner, 1971-72, fleet planning analyst, 1972-73; propr. Sailor's Valentine, Chatham, Mass., 1974-76; ednl. and corp. tour developer Crimson Travel, Cambridge, Mass., 1977-80; propr., tile designer, mfr. Cape Cod Tile Co., 1986-97; founding ptnr. TileGraphics, Weston, Mass., 1994-97; founding ptnr., tile designer, mfr. Great Am. Tile Works, Weston, Mass., 1997—. Cons. U.S. Dept. Transp., 1975. Author (ednl. tours) The Flying Classroom, 1977-80; ceramic artist; author mktg. software. Friends of McLean, McLean Hosp., Belmont, Mass., 1997; mem. Mass. Horticulture Soc., 1995—; bd. dirs. Women's Cmty. League of Weston, 1999, chmn. ways and means com., 2000; chmn. of events Pub. Action for the Arts, 1999, adv. bd. mem., 2000. Recipient Howard Gold Polit. Sci. scholarship Howard Gold Meml. Fund, 1965, acad. scholarship C.W. Post Coll., 1967-70, Nat. Profl. Devel. Act fellowship NYU Grad. Sch. Edn. and History, 1970. Mem. Soc. Glass and Ceramic Decorators, Pi Gamma Mu, Phi Beta Kappa. Avocations: fundraising, Am. folk art, interior design, fashion design, horticulture. Office: Great Am Tile Works PO Box 363 Weston MA 02493-0002 Home: 199 Coolidge Ave Apt 513 Watertown MA 02472-1572 E-mail: ssmick@mediaone.net.

SMIDDY, JOSEPH CHARLES, retired academic administrator; b. Jellico, Tenn., June 20, 1920; s. Joseph F. and Sara Nan (Tye) Smiddy; m. Reba Graham, Sept. 6, 1985; children: Joseph F., Elizabeth Lee. BA, Lincoln Meml. U., 1948, LHD, 1970; MA, Peabody Coll., 1952; LLD, U. Richmond, 1975; LHD, Coll. William and Mary, 1986; DAm, Cumberland Coll., 1993. Tchr. Jonesville HS, 1948-51, prin., 1951-52; sec.-treas. Powell Valley Oil Co., Big Stone Gap, Va., 1952-53; prof. biology Clinch Valley Coll., U. Va., Wise, 1956—57, dean, 1957—68, dir., 1968—85, chancellor, 1968-85, chancellor emeritus, 1985—. Mem. Charter Day Award Emory and Henry Coll., 1980; mem. Commonwealth Day Award James Madison U., 1985. Musician, singer. Trustee Lincoln Meml. U. With U.S. Army, 1942—45, PTO. Recipient Laurel Leaves award, Appalachian Consortium, 1995, Kanto Ednl. award, Wise County, 1995. Mem.: Bapt. Gen. Assn. Va. (pres. 1974—), Kiwanis, Shriners, Masons. Home: Ridgefield Acres Wise VA 24293 Office: PO Box 3160 Wise VA 24293-3160

SMIETANA, ROBERT E. real estate company executive; V.p., devel. mgr. Palmer Group Ltd., 1985—; COO Fifield's (now FC&S) , exec. v.p. FC&S Mgmt. Co., pres., 1993—94; pres., asset mgmt. group, prin. Hiffman Shaffer, 1994—; pres., COO Hiffman Shaffer/HSA Comml., 1995—2004; vice chmn., CEO HSA Comml., Chgo., 2004—. Former dir. Great No. Savs. Bank. Mem. exec. com., bd. dirs. Chgo. Commons; dir., v.p. U. Ill. Real Estate Alumni Forum. Office: HSA Comml Ste 500 180 N Wacker Dr Chicago IL 60606*

SMIETANA, WALTER, educational research director; b. New Bedford, Mass., Nov. 8, 1922; s. Stanislaw and Frances (Wojtal) S. AB in Edn., U. Mich., 1948; MS, Boston U., 1956, EdD, 1965; ScD (hon.), U. Mass., Dartmouth, 1975. Cert. tchr., Mich. Tchr. sci. and math. Somerset (Mass.) Pub. Schs., 1948-65; prof. edn. Elmhurst (Ill.) Coll., 1965-69, Alliance Coll., Cambridge Springs, Pa., 1969-87, chmn. divsn. social sci., pres., 1971-72; dir. rsch. SYLLAGENES, New Bedford, 1987—. Liaison Study of Undergrad. Experience in Am., Carnegie Found. for Advancement of Teaching, Alliance Coll., 1984; participant Pa. Dept. Edn. ETS, Tchr. Cert. Test Devel., 1986-87; develop and accredite new tchr. edn. programs, state, regional and nat. levels, 1965-87; develop and evaluate year abroad and exch. programs Alliance Coll./Jagiellonian U., Cracow, Poland in coop. with U.S. Office Edn., 1969-85. Chmn. city com. Rep. Party, New Bedford, 1953-58; mem. citizens adv. com. Heritage State Park, New Bedford, 1989-93; chmn. bd. trustees Inst. Tech., New Bedford, 1963-64; chmn. adv. com. The Rsch. Found., New Bedford, 1962-64. Recipient Cert. of Merit for non-English Lang. Resources Rsch., Yeshiva U., 1981; U.S. Office Edn./ERIC grantee, 1969. Mem. World Future Soc., Inst. for Global Ethics, Nat. Space Soc., Inst. Noetic Scis., Libr. of Congress Assocs. (charter mem.). Republican. Roman Catholic. Avocations: astronomy, photography. Home and Office: 84 Ellen St New Bedford MA 02744-1521

SMIGEL, IRWIN, dentist; b. NYC, Oct. 9, 1924; m. Lucia Shvetz, Sept. 30, 1956; children: Bellanca Smigel Rutter, Robert. WSC, DDS, NYU, 1950. Diplomate Am. Bd. Aesthetic Dentistry. Dentist pvt. practice, N.Y.C., 1950—. Vis. prof. Pitts. Dental Sch., 1980-83, Case Western U., 1990—; lectr. SUNY Buffalo, U. Mo., Kansas City, U. Minn.; cons., lectr. in field. Author: Dental Health, Dental Beauty, 1978; contbr. editor Dentistry Today, 1980-, dental adv. bd.; contbr. articles to dental jours. With INF., 1943-45. Irwin Smigel Chair in Aesthetic Dentistry established NYU Sch. Dentistry, 1996, Smigel Prize; recipient Outstanding Contbrn. to Aesthetic Dentistry award, Am. Acad. Cosmetic Dentistry, 1994 Fellow Am. Soc. Dental Aesthetics (founder, pres. 1979—); mem. Am. Dental Assn., Acad. Gen. Dentistry, Fedn. Dentaire, First Dist. Dental Soc. Achievements include invention of the Supersmile Whitening brand mouthrinse, toothpaste, floss and brush, tooth bonding technique. Avocations: reading, tennis, racewalking, art, music. Office: 635 Madison Ave New York NY 10022-1009*

SMILES, RONALD, management educator; b. Sunderland, Eng., June 15, 1933; s. Andrew and Margaret (Turns) S.; m. Evelyn Lorraine Webster, Apr. 12, 1959 (div. June 1981); children: Tracy Lynn, Scott Webster, Wendy Louise; m. Linda Janet Miller, June 23, 1990. Assoc. in Bus. Adminstrn., U. Pa., 1968; BSBA, Phila. Coll. Textiles & Sci., 1969; PhD, Calif. Western U., 1977; MA, U. Tex., Arlington, 1985, PhD, 1987. V.p. Liquid Dynamics Corp., Southampton, Pa., 1968-71; pres., gen. mgr. Internat. Election Systems Corp., Burlington, N.J., 1971-76; plant mgr. Rack Engring. Co., Connellsville, Pa., 1977-80; v.p. Ft. Worth (Tex.) Houdaille, 1980-85; chmn. grad. sch. bus. Dallas Bapt. U., 1987-92, prof., 1987—, assoc. dean Coll. Bus., 1996-97. Author: Impact on Legislation of Competition in the Voting Machine Industry, 1978, A Study of Japanese Targeting Practices and U.S. Machine Tool Industry Responses, 1985, Occupational Accident Statistics: An Evaluation of Injury and Illness Incidence Rates, 1987. Mem. Burlington County (N.J.) Selective Svc. Bd., 1974-76. Served with Royal Arty., 1951-53. Mem. Greater Connellsville C. of C. (v.p. 1979-80), Night Watch Honor Soc., Sigma Kappa Phi, Alpha Delta Epsilon (award 1968). Office: Dallas Bapt Univ Dallas TX 75211

SMILEY, CAROL ANNE, home health administrator, sculptor; b. Cedar Rapids, Iowa, Sept. 11, 1937; d. Ralph Derold and Mary C. Miller; m. Donald Victor Smiley, June 29, 1956 (div. Aug. 1970); children: Donald Victor Jr., Julie Ann, Joseph Charles, Thomas Wayne; m. Douglas Brewster Reed, Aug. 6, 1976 (div. Jan. 1988); 1 child, Brook (dec.). Co-founder, v.p., sec., treas. Anvic Enterprise, Cedar Rapids, 1963-70; co-founder, dir. Yankee Horse Trader, Bennington, Vt., 1984-86; organic farmer Solon, Iowa, Argyle, N.Y., 1970-86; fiber sculptor, 1970-86; tchr. Solon H.S., 1973-74; caregiver, coord. Home Health Care and Hospice, Brattleboro, Vt., 1986—. Sculpture shows include Green Mt. Collaborative, Bennington, 1974-78, Woman Art Gallery, N.Y.C., 1977-78, Lincoln Ctr. Group Show, N.Y.C., 1978; exhbns. various group shows. Mem. GOP ctrl. com. for Johnson County, Iowa, 1971-72. Mem.: ACLU. Office: Home Health Care Hospice 142 Green St Brattleboro VT 05301

SMILEY, DAVID BRUCE, administrative director; b. Pitts., Aug. 6, 1942; s. Alan Gary and Sarah Marie (Frank) S.; m. Eleanor Gayle Houk, Feb. 10, 1966 (dec.); children: Linda Marie, Jonathan David; m. Peggy N. Dannar, June 24, 1995. BS in Edn., Ind. State Coll., 1964; MBA, St. Louis U., 1975. Commd. 2d lt. U.S. Army, 1964, advanced through grades to lt. col., 1981, ret., 1984; dir. adminstrn. Sherman, Wickens, Lysaught & Speck, P.C., Kansas City, Mo., 1984-86, Armstrong Teasdale LLP, Kansas City, Mo., 1986—. Decorated Bronze Star medal. Mem. Assn. Legal Adminstrs. (pres. Kansas City chpt. 1990, 99—). Republican. Methodist. Avocations: stamp collecting/philately, reading, jogging. Office: Armstrong Teasdale LLP 2345 Grand Blvd Ste 2000 Kansas City MO 64108-2617

SMILEY, FREDERICK MELVIN, education educator, consultant; b. Yuba City, Calif., Apr. 13, 1943; s. Lester Boomer and Claire Leone (DeChesne) S. AA, Yuba Coll., 1963; BA, Chico State U., 1966; MA in Edn., Chapman Coll., 1973, MA in English, 1978, MA in Spl. Edn., 1982; PhD, U. Santa Barbara, 1982; EdD, Okla. State U., 1992. Tchr., coach, v.p. McDermitt (Nev.) High Sch., 1978-80; resource specialist Eagle Mt. (Calif.) High Sch., 1980-81; instr. spl. edn. Mary Stone Sch., San Mateo, Calif., 1981-86; dept. leader Quaezar Corp., Bridgeport, Conn., 1986-87; cons., researcher Multi-functional Resource Ctr., Stillwater and Norman, Okla., 1988-91; prof. edn. Cameron U., Lawton, Okla., 1991—. Contbr. articles to profl. jours.; contbg. editor Think!, The Writing Teacher, Okla. Assn. Tchr. Eductors Jour., ATE Jour. Mem. AAUP, Am. Assn. for Teaching and Curriculum, Am. Soc. Curriculum Devel., Am. Coun. Rural Spl. Edn., Am. Assn. Colls. for Tchr. Edn., Coun. for Exceptional Children, Okla. Assn. Tchr. Educators (pres. 2001—), Soc. Educators and Scholars, Kappa Delta Pi, Phi Delta Kappa, Phi Kappa Phi. Democrat. Lutheran. Avocations: reading, writing, racing, tennis, golf. Office: Cameron U 2800 W Gore Blvd Lawton OK 73505-6377 Home: 2001 Alford Park Dr Kenosha WI 53140-1929 E-mail: freds@cameron.edu.

SMILEY, JANE GRAVES, author, educator; b. L.A., Sept. 26, 1949; d. James La Verne and Frances Nuelle (Graves) S.; m. John Whiston, Sept. 4, 1970 (div.); m. William Silag, May 1, 1978 (div.); children: Phoebe Silag, Lucy Silag; m. Stephen Mark Mortensen, July 25, 1987; 1 child, Axel James Mortensen. BA, Vassar Coll., 1971; MFA, U. Iowa, 1976, MA, PhD, U. Iowa, 1978. Asst. prof. Iowa State U., Ames, 1981-84, assoc. prof., 1984-89, prof., 1989-90, Disting. prof., 1992-96. Vis. asst. prof. U. Iowa, Iowa City, 1981, 87. Author: (fiction) Barn Blind, 1980, At Paradise Gate, 1981 (Friends of American Writers prize 1981), Duplicate Keys, 1984, The Age of Grief, 1987 (Nat. Book Critics Cirle award nomination 1987), The Greenlanders, 1988, Ordinary Love and Goodwill, 1989, A Thousand Acres, 1991 (Pulitzer Prize for fiction 1992, Nat. Book Critics Cirle award 1992, Midland Authors award 1992, Amb. award 1992, Heartland prize 1992), Moo: A Novel, 1995; (non-fiction) Catskill Crafts: Artisans of the Catskill Mountains, 1987, The All-True Travels and Adventures of Lidie Newton, 1998, Horse Heaven, 2001, Good Faith, 2003. Grantee Fulbright U.S. Govt., Iceland, 1976-77, NEA, 1978, 87; recipient O. Henry award, 1982, 85, 88. Mem. Author's Guild, Screenwriters Guild. Avocations: cooking, swimming, playing piano, quilting. Office: c/o Molly Friedrich Dept English 708 3rd Ave Fl 23 New York NY 10017-4201

SMILEY, MARILYNN JEAN, musicologist; b. Columbia City, Ind., June 5, 1932; d. Orla Raymond and Mary Jane (Bailey) S. BS (State scholar), Ball State U., 1954; MusM, Northwestern U., 1958; cert., Ecoles d'Art Americaines, Fontainebleau, France, 1959; PhD (Grad. scholar, Delta Kampa Gamma scholar), U. Ill., 1970. Public sch. music tchr., Logansport, Ind., 1954-61; faculty music dept. SUNY-Oswego, 1961—, Disting. Teaching prof., 1974—, chmn. dept., 1976-81. Presenter papers at confs. Contbr. articles to profl. jours. Bd. dirs. Oswego Opera Theatre, 1978—, Oswego Orch. Soc., 1978—, Penfield Libr. Assocs., 1985—. Recipient Chancellor's award for Excellence in Tchg., 1973; SUNY Rsch. Found. fellow, summers, 1971, 1972, 1974, NEH grantee, 1990—91. Mem.: AAUW (grantee 1984, pres. Oswego br. 1984—86, br. coun. rep. dist. III, N.Y. State divsn. 1986—88, br. coun. coord. N.Y. State

divsn. 1988—90, N.Y. divsn. area intererst rep. cultural interests 1990—92, N.Y. divsn. diversity dir. 1993—96, Oswego br. diversity chair 1995—, N.Y. divsn. historian 2000—), NOW, Oswego County Hist. Soc., Early Music Am., Am. Recorder Soc., Soc. Am. Music (membership chair 1998—2003), Renaissance Soc. Am., Coll. Music Soc., Music Libr. Assn., Medieval Acad. Am., Am. Musicol. Soc. (chmn. N.Y. chpt. 1975—77, chpt. rep. to AMS coun. 1993—96, bd. dirs. N.Y. State-St. Lawrence chpt. 1993—96, mem. status of women com. 1997—2000), Oswego Recorder Consort, Ontario Singers, Heritage Found. of Oswego, Phi Kappa Phi, Kappa Delta Pi, Sigma Tau Delta, Sigma Alpha Iota, Pi Kappa Lambda, Delta Phi Alpha, Phi Delta Kappa, Delta Kappa Gamma (music chair State of Ind. 1961, music chair State of N.Y. 1968). Methodist. Office: SUNY Dept Music Oswego NY 13126 Office Phone: 315-312-3054. Business E-Mail: smiley@oswego.edu.

SMILEY, RICHARD WAYNE, researcher; b. Paso Robles, Calif., Aug. 17, 1943; s. Cecil Wallace and Elenore Louise (Hamm) S.; m. Marilyn Lois Wenning, June 24, 1967; 1 child, Shawn Elizabeth. BSc in Soil Sci., Calif. State Poly. U., San Luis Obispo, 1965; MSc in Soils, Wash. State U., 1969, PhD in Plant Pathology, 1972. Asst. soil scientist Agrl. Rsch. Svc., USDA, Pullman, Wash., 1966-69; rsch. asst. dept. plant pathology Wash. State U., Pullman, 1969-72; soil microbiologist Commonwealth Sci. and Indsl. Rsch. Orgn., Adelaide, Australia, 1972-73; rsch. assoc. dept. plant pathology Cornell U., Ithaca, N.Y., 1973-74, asst. prof., 1975-80, assoc. prof., 1980-85; supt. Columbia Basin Agr. Rsch. Ctr., 1985-2000; prof. Oreg. State U., 1985—. Vis. scientist Plant Rsch. Inst., Victoria Dept. Agr., Melbourne, Australia, 1982-83. Author: Compendium of Turfgrass Diseases, 1983, 2d edit., 1992; contbr. more than 200 articles to profl. jours. Postdoctoral fellow NATO, 1972. Fellow Am. Phytopath. Soc. (sr. editor APS Press 1984-87, editor-in-chief 1987-91); mem. Coun. Agrl. Sci. and Tech., Rotary (pres. Pendleton chpt. 1991-92, Paul Harris fellow 1993). Achievements include discovery of the etiology of a serious disease of turfgrasses, which led to a redefinition of studies and disease processes in turfgrasses. Office: Oreg State U Columbia Basin Agr Rsch Ctr PO Box 370 Pendleton OR 97801-0370 Business E-Mail: richard.smiley@oregonstate.edu.

SMILEY, ROBERT WILLIAM, JR., investment banker; b. Lansing, Mich., Nov. 17, 1943; s. Robert William Sr. and Rebecca Lee (Flint) S. AB in Econs., Stanford U., 1970; postgrad., San Fernando Valley Coll. Law, 1973 75; MBA in Corp. Fin., City U. L.A., 1979; LLB, LaSalle U., 1982. Bar: Calif. 1984. Sr. v.p. mktg. Actuarial Systems Inc., San Jose, Calif., 1972-73; founder, chmn. Benefit Systems Inc., L.A. and S.E. Nev., 1973-84, Brentwood Sq. Savs. and Loan, L.A., 1982-84; chmn., CEO The Benefit Capital Cos. Inc., L.A. and S.E. Nev., 1984—. Lectr. U. Calif. Ext., L.A. and Berkeley, 1977—; instr. Am. Coll. Life Underwriters. Editor, contbg. author: Employee Stock Ownership Plans: Business Planning, Implementation, Law and Taxation, 1989, 2d edit. 1998; contbg. author: The Handbook of Employee Benefits, 1984, 6th edit., 2000; contbr. articles to profl. jours. Mem. nat. adv. coun., trustee Reason Found., L.A., 1983-91; bd. dirs. Nat. Ctr. for Employee Ownership, Oakland, Calif.; trustee The Employee Ownership Found., Washington, 2000-04. With USN, 1961-64, Vietnam. Recipient Spl. Achievement award Pres.' Commn. on Pension Policy, 1984. Fellow Life Mgmt. Inst.; mem. Employee Stock Ownership Plan Assn. (founder, pres., bd. dirs., lifetime dir.), Assn. for Corp. Growth, Western and SW Pension Confs., Nat. Assn. Bus. Economists, ABA, Calif. Bar Assn. Office: The Benefit Capital Cos Inc PO Box 542 Logandale NV 89021-0542 Office Phone: 702-398-3222.

SMILEY, STANLEY ROBERT, lawyer; b. Feb. 19, 1947; s. Arthur and Rose Smiley; m. Anita Kape, June 28, 1970; children: Wayne Alan, Lori Patricia. BA, State Univ. N.Y., Buffalo, 1968; JD, St. John's Univ., 1971. Bar: N.Y. 1971, U.S. Tax Ct. 1972, U.S. Ct. Mil. Appeals 1972, Calif. 1977, U.S. Dist. Ct. (Ctrl. Dist.) Calif. 1978, U.S. Ct. Appeals (9th Cir.) 1979, U.S. Dist. Ct. (No., So., and Ea. Dist.) Calif. 1979. Atty. Office of Chief Counsel, IRS, Newark, 1971—72, LA, 1976—78; ptnr. McLaughlin and Irvin, LA, 1978—95, St. John, Smiley, and Zamost, LA, 1995—97; of counsel St. John, Wallace, Brennan, and Folan, Torrance, Calif., 1997—2001; sr. v.p. adv. markets ING Adv. Network, Torrance, Calif., 2001—. Guest instr. Univ. Md., Madrid, 1974—76. Assoc. editor St. John's Law Rev., 1969—71. With JAGC USAF, 1972—76. Mem.: Bar Assn. San Francisco, LA County Bar Assn., Phi Delta Phi.

SMIRNOV, ALEXEI VLADIMIROVICH, research scientist, consultant; s. Vladimir Fedorovich Smirnov and Iraida Izmailovna Smirnova; m. Svetlana Georgievna Kadysheva; children: Ivan, Anna Smirnova, Ilya, Sergey, Anastasia Smirnova. Masters cum laude(hon.), Moscow Engring. Physics Inst., 1982, postgrad., 1985; PhD, Supreme Certifying Com., 1986. Tchr., lectr. math. Moscow Inst. Radio-Electronics and Automatics, 1990—91; reviewer dissertations and projects Russian Rsch. Ctr. Kurchatov Inst., Moscow, 1992—98; IBM network product mgr. UNIT Group Internat., Moscow, 1995—96; cons. head analytical dept. GI Cons., Moscow, 1996—99; patent expert Patent Inst., Moscow, 1998—99; tech. reviewer manuscripts DULY Rsch. Inc., Rancho Palos Verdes, Calif., 2001—02, scientist, 1999—. Contbr. articles to profl. jours., including Am. Inst. Phys. Procs.; author: The Role of Consulting in Enterprise Restructuring, 1998. Trade union mgr. dept. Russian Rsch. Ctr. Kurchatov Inst., Moscow, 1986—90. Named Winner contest Young Scientists and Engrs.-Rschrs., I.V. Kurchatov Inst. Atomic Energy, 1990; recipient prize Best Engring. Devel., Sci. Coun. Russian Rsch. Ctr., Kurchatov Inst., 1995; grantee, Internat. Sci. Found., Soros Found., 1993, 1994, Internat. Sci. Found., 1995. Mem.: American Physical Society APS. Achievements include invention of section of resonant accelerator of charged particles, system for waveguide cooling, method for determination of radio-frequency parameters of accelerating structures; linear electron accelerator with RF-energy compression, planar electromagnetic undulator, linear accelerator of electrons with RF energy compression and an RF device. Home: 1934 Trudie Dr Rancho Palos Verdes CA 90275 Office Phone: 310-548-0290.

SMISEK, JEFFERY A. airline company executive; b. Washington, Aug. 17, 1954; married; 2 children. AB, Princeton U., 1976; JD, Harvard U., 1982. Bar: Mass., 1982, Tex. 1983. Ptnr., exec. v.p. Vinson & Elkins, LLP, Houston, 1983-95; sr. v.p., gen. counsel Continental Airlines, Inc., Houston, 1995—96, exec. v.p., gen. counsel and sec., 1996—2001, exec. v.p., corp., 2001—03, exec. v.p., 2003—. Bd. dirs. Varco Internat., Inc., Orbitz, Inc. Office: Continental Airlines Inc 1600 Smith St Dept Hqseo Houston TX 77002-7362

SMISKO, NICHOLAS RICHARD, bishop, educator; b. Perth Amboy, N.J., Feb. 23, 1936; s. Andrew and Anna (Totin) S. BTh, Christ the Saviour Sem., 1959; BA, U. Youngstown, 1961; Lic. in Theology, Halki (Greece) Sch. Theology, 1965. Ordained priest Carpatho-Russian Orthodox Greek Cath. Ch., 1959; elevated to rank of met. bishop, 1997. Pastorate Sts. Peter and Paul Ch., Windber, Pa., 1959-62; prefect of discipline Christ the Saviour Sem., Johnstown, Pa., 1963-65; pastor Sts. Peter and Paul Ch., Homer City, Pa., 1965-71, St. Michael's Ch., Clymer, Pa., 1971-72; pastorate St. Nicholas Ch., N.Y.C., 1972-77; abbot Monastery of the Annunciation, Tuxedo Park, N.Y., 1978-83; bishop of Amissos Carpatho-Russian Orthodox Diocese, 1983—. Mem. del. Ecumenical Patriarchate World Coun. Chs. 6th Gen. Assembly, Vancouver, B.C., Can.; mem. standing conf. Canonical Orthodox Bishops in Ams.; active Orthodox-Cath. Consultation of Hierarchs. Mem. Halki Alumni Assn. Am., Christ the Saviour Sem. Alumni Assn., Am. Soc. Constantinople. Carpatho-Russian Orthodox. Home and Office: 312 Garfield St Johnstown PA 15906-2122

SMISKO, RICHARD G. See NICHOLAS

SMIST, JULIANNE MARIE, chemist, educator; b. Springfield, Mass., Aug. 14, 1950; d. Abel Alves and Mary Gloria DaSilva; m. Stephen Francis Smist, June 29, 1974; 1 child, Jennifer. BA, Elms Coll., 1972; MS, Boston Coll., 1974; PhD, U. Conn., 1996. Cert. tchr. chemistry, math., Mass. Tchr. chemistry Cathedral H.S., Springfield, 1975-77; instr. chemistry Am. Internat. Coll., Springfield, 1977-79, Springfield Coll., Springfield, 1981-88, asst. prof. to assoc. prof., 1988—. Author: Experiments for Chemistry Survey, 2000. Mem. parish coun. Sacred Heart Ch., Feeding Hills, Mass., 1998—. Gelbrich fellow U. Conn., 1996. Mem. Am. Chem. Soc., Nat. Sci. Tchrs. Assn., Am. Ednl. Rsch. Found., Beta Beta Beta. Avocation: singing. Office: Springfield Coll Bemis Hall Springfield MA 01109 E-mail: jsmist@spfldcol.edu.

SMITH, A. ROBERT, editor, author; b. York, Pa., Feb. 13, 1925; s. Arthur R. and Inez (Dunnick) S.; m. Yvonne Franklin, 1945 (div. 1965); 1 child, Dana C.; m. Elizabeth McDowell Morgan, 1967 (div. 1988); children: Philip S. Morgan IV, Edward A. M. Morgan, Elizabeth A. Morgan; m. Jane Dreifus, 1993 (dec. 1999). BS, Juniata Coll., 1950; postgrad., George Washington U., 1950. Reporter Huntingdon (Pa.) Daily News, 1947, Evening Star, Washington, 1950; Washington corr. Eugene (Oreg.) Register-Guard, 1951-78, Portland Oregonian, 1952-72, King Broadcasting, 1976-78; assoc. editor Virginian-Pilot, Norfolk, 1978-83; editor Venture Inward, Assn. Rsch. and Enlightenment mag., Virginia Beach, Va., 1984—2003. Author: The Tiger in the Senate, 1962, Hugh Lynn Cayce: About My Father's Business, 1988, The Lost Memoirs of Edgar Cayce, 1997, Misdiagnosed: Was My Wife a Casualty of America's Medical Cold War?, 2001; co-author: (with Eric Sevareid and Fred J. Maroon) Washington: Magnificent Capital, 1965; (with James V. Giles) An American Rape, 1975. With USNR, 1943-46, PTO. E-mail: abob@cox.net.

SMITH, AARON, retired research director, clinical psychologist; b. Boston, Nov. 3, 1930; s. Harry and Anne (Gilgoff) S.; m. Sept. 7, 1952 (div.); children: Naomi E., Jeffrey O., David G., Andrew H.; m. D. Sharon Casey, Jan. 7, 1972. AB, Brown U., 1952; PhD, U. Ill., 1958. Co-dir. N.E. Psychol. Clinic, Phila., 1959-75; dir. rsch. Haverford State Hosp., Pa., 1962-73, asst. hosp. dir., 1973-75; assoc. rsch. prof. U. Nev., Reno, 1975-2001; dir. rsch. VA Med. Ctr., Reno, 1975-2001; exec. dir. Sierra Biomed. Rsch. Corp., Reno, 1989-2001. Chmn. Nev. Legislature Mental Health Task Force, Carson City, 1978; sci. adviser Gov.'s Com. on Radiation Effects, Carson City, 1979-82. Co-author: Anti-depressant Drug Studies 1956-66, 1969, Medications and Emotional Illness, 1976; co-editor: Goal Attainment Scaling: Application, Theory, and Measurement, 1994; contbr. chpts. to books and articles to profl. jours. Grantee Squibb Inst. med. Rsch., 1965-69, NIMH, 1965-69, Smith Kline & French Labs., 1968-69, VA Health Svcs. Rsch., 1976-93. Mem.: APA. Home: 1516 Diamond Country Dr Reno NV 89521-6149

SMITH, ABBIE OLIVER, college administrator, educator; b. Augusta, Ga., Jan. 31, 1931; d. Rowland Sheppard and Abigail Seabrook (Hanahan) Oliver; m. William Parkhurst Smith, Jr., July 2, 1953; children: William Parkhurst Smith, III, Oliver Hamilton. BS, George Washington U., 1953, MEd, 1958, EdDin Higher Edn., 1986. Tchr. St. Mary's Acad., Monroe, Mich., 1954-55; tchr., coach Washington-Lee H.S., Arlington, Va., 1955-58; homemaker, cmty. vol. Bethesda, Md., 1959-64; asst. professorial lectr. George Washington U., Washington, 1965-69, adminstr. continuing edn., 1969-80, asst. dean, dir., 1981-89, acting dean divsn. continuing edn., 1989-93, asst. v.p., asst. to dean institutional advancement, 1993—. Panelist TV series WETA, Washington; mem. exec. bd., newsletter editor Tng. Officers Conf., 1989—, chair charter expansion 1992—. Co-author: (workbook) Developing New Horizons for Women, 1975, Manual for Counselors for Developing New Horizons for Women, 1975. Mem. adv. bd. Washington Bd. Trade, 1975-77, women's branch adv. bd. State Nat. Bank, Bethesda, Md., 1978-81; collegiate adv. bd. Episcopal Diocese of Washington, 1977-79. Recipient Leadership in Adult Edn. award, 1976, GW award for outstanding contbn. to univ. life Office of GW Pres., 1991, Washington Women of Achievement, Washington Edn. TV Assn., 1980. Mem. Nat. U. Continuing Edn. Assn. (awards chair divsn. women's edn. 1977-78, nat. chair 1977-78, chair-elect divsn. part-time students program 1984-86, nat. chair 1984-86, chair coun. human resources 1985-86, nat. spl. com. on couns. and divsn. 1984-86, nat. exec. bd. 1984-86, nat. bd. dirs. 1984-98, nat. charters and bylaws coms. 1987-89, sec.-elect divsn. cert. and nontraditional degree programs 1987-89, chair-elect 1989-90, nat. chair 1990-91, nat. ann. planning coms. 1987, 92, sec. region II 1989-90, chair-elect, ann. conf. chair, single host instn. ann. conf. region II 1990-91, chair region II 1991-92, awards com. chair 1992, Walton S. Bittner Svc. Citation 1994, hon. mention for program catalog nat. divsn. mktg. 1988, Floyd B. Fisher Leadership award 1996), Phi Delta Kappa Internat. (G.W. chpt., v.p. for programs 1995-96, pres. 1996-97, newsletter editor 1977—, Newsletter Award Merit 1998-99, Outstanding Newsletter award 1999-2000, 2000-01). Democrat. Episcopalian. Avocations: writing, painting, swimming, dance, travel. Home: 3751 Jocelyn St NW Washington DC 20015-1836 Office: George Washington U 2134 G St NW Washington DC 20037-2797 E-mail: asmith@gwu.edu.

SMITH, ADA L. state legislator; b. Amherst County, Va. d. Thomas and Lillian Smith. Grad., CUNY. Dep. clk. N.Y.C.; state senator N.Y. Legislature, Albany, 1988—, mem. various coms., ranking corp. commn. and authorities, 1994, minority whip, 1994—2003, chair Senate Dem. Conf., 2003—. Mem. Senate Minority Puerto Rican and Hispanic Task Force; chair Senate Minority Task Force on Privatization of Kennedy and Laguardia Airports. Trustee, life dir. Coll. Fund Baruch Coll. Recipient Outstanding Alumni award Baruch Coll. Mem. African Am. Clergy and Elected Ofcls., Inc., N.Y. Assn. of State Black and Puerto Rican Legislators, Baruch Coll. Alumni Assn. (pres., Disting. Svc. award, Outstanding Achievement award). Office: NY State Senate Rm 808 Legis Office Bldg Albany NY 12247 also: Queens Dist Office 11643 Sutphin Blvd Jamaica NY 11434-1526

SMITH, ADAM See GOODMAN, GEORGE JEROME WALDO

SMITH, ADRIAN DEVAUN, architect; b. Chgo., Aug. 19, 1944; s. Alfred D. and Hazel (Davis) S.; m. Nancy L. Smith, Aug. 17, 1968; children: Katherine, Jason. Student, Tex. A&M U., 1962-66; BArch, U. Ill., Chgo., 1969. Registered architect, Ill., Mass., Fla. Design ptnr. Skidmore, Owings, & Merrill, Chgo., 1967—2003, CEO, 1994-96, cons. ptnr., 2004—. Vis. faculty Sch. Architecture, U. Ill., Chgo., 1984, 1986, U. Ill. Sch. Archtl. Alumni Assn., AIA Jury on Inst. Honors; adv. jury AIA gold metal and architecture firm award, 2000; chmn. nat. AIA awards jury for architecture and 25 yr. award, 2004; chmn. Skidmore Owings Merrill Found., 1990-95; pres. Chgo. Ctrl. Area, 1998-99; bd. dirs. Greater State Street Coun. trustee; bd. govs. Sch. Art Inst. Chgo., 1999—; cons. and lectr. in field. Designer numerous projects including Burj Dubai Tower, Jin Mao Tower (World's Tallest Mixed-Use Project), Shanghai, China (Nat. AIA award for interior architecture 2000), Trump Tower Chgo., Banco de Occidente, Guatemala City (CCAIA Interior Architecture award 1981, NAIA Honor award 1982), United Gulf Bank, Manama, Bahrain (Progressive Architecture award 1984, CCAIA Disting. Bldg. award 1988, NAIA Honor award 1988, CCAIA Disting. Detail Honor award 1989), 222 N. LaSalle, Chgo., (Disting. Bldg. award CCAIA 1988), Art Inst. Chgo. 2d Fl. Galleries (CCAIA Disting. Bldg. award 1987), Rowes Wharf, Boston (Build Am. award 1988, Build Mass. award 1989, ULI award 1989, PCI Profl. Design award 1989, CCAIA Hon. award 1998, Nat. AIA Honor award 1994), AT&T Corp. Ctr., Chgo. (recipient Gold Metal Ill. Ind. Masonry award), NBC Tower (Chgo. Sun Times Bldg. of Yr. award 1989, CCAIA Disting. Bldg. award 1990, PCI Design award 1989), 75 State St. Boston (Archtl. Woodwork Inst. award 1989, Nat. Comml. Builder's Coun. Merit award 1990, Bldg. Stone Inst. Tucker Archtl. award 1990), Arthur Anderson Tng. Ctr. (Masonry award 1988), St. Charles, Ill., USG Hdqs., Chgo., Heller Internat. Tower, Chgo., State St. Renovation (spl. achievement award 1997, AIA honor award urban design 1998) designer numerous other fgn. projects including: Monterey Cultural Ctr., Mex., 1978; Hdqs. Canary Wharf Fin. Ctr., London, Eng., 1988, 10 Ludgate (CCAIA 1994 Honor award, Brit. Civil Trust award), 100 Ludgate, London, 1992, Aramco Hdqs. Dharan Saudi Arabia, Tower Palace III, Seoul, Korea, 7 South Dearborn Tower, Chgo., McGraw Hill European Headquarters, Canary Wharf (DS4), CSFB European Headquarters, Canary Wharf (DSI), Morgan Stanley Headquarters for Europe (HQI), Canary Wharf; author: Monograph of Adrian P. Smith, 2002; contbr. articles to profl. jours.; subject numerous pubs. in architecture. Mem. com. Task Force for New City Plan, Chgo., Light Up Chgo., Ctrl. Area Com. Task Force Chgo.; chmn. Senator Richard A. Newhouse Bldg. Competition Jury, 1982, Progressive Architecture Design Jury, 1985; bd. dirs. State St. Coun. Recipient U. Ill. Alumni Achievement award. Fellow AIA (mem. Young Architects Award Design July, 1987, Mich. Jury 1988, chmn. nat. jury arch. and 25 yr. award 2004, Disting. Bldg. award 1990), Royal Inst. Brit. Architects, Archtl. Registration Coun., U.K., Nat. Coun. Archtl. Registration Bds., Architecture Soc. of Art Inst. Chgo., Chgo. Arch. Found., Chgo. Archtl. Club, Urban Found. (bd. trustees) University Club, Arts Club. Home: 1100 W Summerfield Dr Lake Forest IL 60045-1545 Office: Skidmore Owings & Merrill LLP 224 S Michigan Ave Ste 1000 Chicago IL 60604-2592

SMITH, ADRIAN J.R. management company executive; b. Liverpool, Eng. married; 4 children. Grad., Liverpool Law Sch., 1966. With Procter & Gamble Ltd., 1966-79; v.p. European consumer ops. Ecolab Inc., Minn., 1979-90; pres. Ecolab Can. Ltd.; with Arthur Andersen and Co., 1990-96; CEO Grant Thornton LLP, Chgo., 1996. Mem. Am. Bus. Conf. Bd. dirs. March of Dimes, Chgo., Montessori Sch., Lake Forest, Chgo. Sinfonietta. Office: 800 One Prudential Plz 244 Ave Ste 1000 Chicago IL 60604

SMITH, ADRIAN M. state legislator, real estate agent; b. Scottsbluff, Nebr., Dec. 19, 1970; BS in Mktg. Edn., U. Nebr., 1993, postgrad., Portland State U. Legis. page Nebr. Legislature, 1992; mem. Nebr. Legislature from 48th dist., Lincoln, 1998—; staff internat., mktg. specialist Nebrs. Gov.'s Office, 1992; rsch. asst. U. Nebr. Found., 1992-93; educator, staff devel. project mgr. Ednl. Svc. Unit 13, 1994-97; real estate agt., mktg. specialist Buyers Realty, 1997—. Mem. Scotts Bluff County Bd. Realtors. Mem. Gering City Coun., 1994-98, We. Nebr. Regional Airport Ops. Bd., Scotts Bluff County Visitors Adv. Com., 1995-96, N. Platte Valley Hist. Soc., Riverside Zool. Soc., Wyo-Braska Mus. Natural History, Calvary Meml. Evang. Free Ch., Farm and Ranch Mus. Assn.; chmn. land use task force Vision 2020; bd. dirs. Twin Cities Devel. Mem. Scottsbluff Kiwanis Club (bd. dirs. Camp Kiwanis). Office: State Capitol Dist 48 PO Box 94604 Rm 1523 Lincoln NE 68509 Home: 3321 Avenue I #1 Scottsbluff NE 69361-4587

SMITH, AGNES EYVONDA, writer; b. Nashville, Tenn., Apr. 24, 1959; d. Robert Jackson and Agnes Marieo Odom; m. Harold Haywood Smith, Aug. 3, 1999; m. James G. Parker, Dec. 12, 1982 (div. Apr. 25, 1993); children: Tangla S. Odom, Gary J. Parker, Steven J. Parker. At sch. of nursing, Tenn. State U., 1979. Cert. Nashville Area Vocat. Sch., 1980. LPN Carriage Ho., Nashville, 1980—92; coach operator Metro. Transit Authority, Nashville, 1992—2000; writer T.H.A.T. Pub., Nashville, 1999—. Author: (books) Wonderful Soul Food, 2001, Entering into the Unknown, 2002. Bd. mem. Amalgamated Transit Union, Nashville, 1991—2003. Mem.: Ea. Star, Sarai Chpt. 419 (worthy matron 2002—03). Home: 1111 S Douglas Ave Nashville TN 37204 Office: THAT Publisher PO Box 40781 Nashville TN 37204 E-mail: 0957@bellsouth.net.

SMITH, AGNES MONROE, history professor; b. Hiram, Ohio, Aug. 8, 1920; d. Bernie Alfred and Joyce (Messenger) Monroe; m. Stanley Blair Smith; children: David, Doris, Darl, Diane. BA, Hiram Coll., 1940; MA, W.Va. U., 1945; PhD, Western Res. U., 1966. Social sci. tchr. Freedom (Ohio) High Sch., 1940-44; instr. of history W.Va. U., Morgantown, 1945; instr. of social sci. Hiram Coll., 1946; inst. history and social sci. Youngstown (Ohio) State U., 1964-66, asst. prof. to prof. of history, 1966-84, prof. history emeritus, 1984—; vis. prof. history Hiram Coll., 1988-90. Co-editor: Bourgeois, Sans Culottes and other Frenchmen, 1981; contbr. articles to profl. jours. Mem. Ohio Acad. History, Delta Kappa Gamma, Phi Alpha Theta, Pi Gamma Mu. Mem. Christian Ch. (Disciples Of Christ). Home: 16759 Main Market Rd West Farmington OH 44491-9608

SMITH, AIDA MARISSA, medical reference librarian; b. Takoma Park, Md., Sept. 1971; d. Burton Floyd and Ida Tucker; m. James Lynwood Smith, Nov. 1969; 2 children. BA in History, So. Coll., Collegedale, Tenn., 1993; MLIS, San Jose State U., 1995. Cert. secondary sch. history tchr. Tenn., 1993. Reference libr., Del E. Webb Meml. Library Loma Linda U., Loma Linda, Calif., 1995—. Health info. adv. bd. Medicine on the Net, Santa Barbara, Calif.; book reviewer Libr. Jour., N.Y., NY, 1997—; reviewer Biomed. Digital Librs. Contbr. articles to profl. jours. Mem.: Med. Libr. Assn. Office: Loma Linda U 11072 Anderson St Loma Linda CA 92350

SMITH, AKILI, professional football player; b. Aug. 21, 1975; Student, U. Oreg. Football player Cin. Bengals, 1999—. Avocations: weightlifting, Bible reading. Office: 14654 Lyons Valley Jamul CA 91935

SMITH, ALBERT ALOYSIUS, JR., electrical engineer, consultant; b. Yonkers, N.Y., Dec. 2, 1935; s. Albert Aloysius and Jean Mary (Misiewicz) S.; m. Rosemarie Torricelli, Apr. 4, 1964 (dec. 1982); children: Denise, Matthew. BSEE, Milw. Sch. Engring., 1961; MSEE, NYU, 1964. Staff engr. Adler/Westrex, New Rochelle, N.Y., 1961-64; adv. engr. IBM, Kingston, N.Y., 1964-78, sr. engr. Poughkeepsie, N.Y., 1978-85, Kingston, 1985-91; cons., 1991—. Author: Coupling of External Electromagnetic Fields to Transmission Lines, 1977, Measuring the Radio Frequency Environment, 1985, Radio Frequency Principles and Applications, 1998. Com. chmn. Woodstock Boy Scout Troop 34, 1978-79; com. chmn. Woodstock Cub Pack 34, 1976-78. Served with USN, 1953-56. Recipient Outstanding Alumnus award Milw. Sch. Engring., 1981; Invention Achievement awards IBM, 1979, 90, Div. award, 1981. Fellow IEEE (tech. com. on electromagnetic environments, assoc. editor Trans. on EMC); mem. Am. Nat. Standards Com. Roman Catholic. Home: 4507 Burnett St Valatie NY 12184-2516

SMITH, ALBERT CROMWELL, JR., investment company executive, writer; b. Norfolk, Va., Dec. 6, 1925; s. Albert Cromwell and Georgie (Foreman) Smith; m. Laura Thaxton, Oct. 25, 1952; children: Albert, Elizabeth, Laura. BSCE, Va. Mil. Inst., 1949; MS in Govtl. Adminstrn., George Washington U., 1965; MBA, Pepperdine U., 1975; PhD in Bus. Adminstrn., LaSalle U., 1994. Enlisted man USMC, 1944, advanced through grades to col., 1970, comdr. inf. platoons, cos., landing force; assigned to staffs, U.K. Joint Force, U.S. Sec. Navy, Brit. Staff Coll., Marine Staff Coll., U.K. Staff Coll. and Latimer Staff Coll.; advisor, analyst amphibious sys. USMC; ret., 1974; pres. A. Cromwell-Smith, Ltd., Charlottesville, Va., 1973; head broker, cons. A. Cromwell Smith, Investments, La Jolla and Coronado, Calif., 1975—. Author: The Individual Investor in Tomorrow's Stock Market, 1977, The Little Guy's Stock Market Survival Guide, 1979, rev. edit., 2000, Wake Up Detroit: The EVs are Coming, 1982, The Little Guy's Tax Survival Guide, 1984, Little Guy's Real Estate Success Guide, 1990, Little Guy's Stock Market Success Guide, 1992, Little Guy's Stock Market Future Effectiveness, 1994, The Little Guy's Sailboat Success, 1996, The Little Guy's Business Success, 1997, Business Success, 1997, Stock Market Success, 1998, Semper Fidelis in Peace and War, 1999, revised edit., 2003, Sailboat Success, 1999, Tax Survival Guide, 1999, The EVs are Coming, 1999, Real Estate Success, 2000; contbr. articles to profl. jours. Bd. dirs. La Jolla Reps., 1975—76; vestryman St. Martin's Episcopal Ch., 1971—73. Decorated Legion of Merit with oak leaf cluster with V device, Bronze Star with V device with oak leaf cluster, Air medal with two oak leav clusters, Purple Heart, Vietnamese Galantry Cross with gold star. Mem.: VFW, SAR, ASCE, So. Calif. Options Soc., Stockbrokers Soc., Coronado Bd. Realtors, San Diego Bd. Realtors, Calif. Assn. Realtors, Nat. Assn. Realtors, Mil. Order Purple Heart. Address: 1810 Ave del Mundo Coronado CA 92118 Office Phone: 619-435-1928.

SMITH, ALBERT E. college president; b. Sioux Falls, S.D., Oct. 24, 1932; s. Calvert and Ethel (Johnson) S.; m. Sadie Burris, Jan. 27, 1956; children: Albert Clayton, Robbin Renae, Angela E. BS, N.C. A&T State U., 1956; MS, George Williams Coll., Downers Grove, Ill., 1963; PhD, U. Pitts., 1984. Boy's program dir. YMCA of Met. Chgo., unit dir.; dir. student ctr., head baseball coach Knoxville (Tenn.) Coll.; dir. Intercollegiate Athletics and Meml. Student Union N.C. A&T State U., Greensboro, vice chancellor devel. and univ. rels.; exec. asst. dir. Intercollegiate Athletics, lectr. U. Pitts.; dir. Intercollegiate Athletics, assoc. prof. edn. Ea. Mich. U., Ypsilanti; pres. S.C. State Coll., Orangeburg, 1986-93, Fla. Meml. Coll., 1993—. Bd. dirs. 1st Nat. Bank of Orangeburg. Chmn. coun. pres.'s S.C. State Colls. and Univs.; mem. adv. com. Office of Advancement for Pub. Black Colls.; adv. bd. Gov.'s Agrl. and Rural Econ. Devel. Task Force; commr. Commn. on Future of S.C.; bd. dirs. S.C. Heart Assn., City Indsl. Devel. Commn., S.C. Bus. Week. 2d lt. U.S. Army. Recipient 2d Ann. Golden Achievement award Afro-Am. Hist. Club George Washington Carver High Sch.; inducted into N.C. A&T Sports Hall of Fame, Hall of Fame Mid-Eastern Athletic Conf. Mem. NEA, Nat. Sickle Cell Anemia

Found., United Way Orangeburg and Calhoun Counties, Rotary, Phi Delta Kappa, Alpha Phi Alpha. Office: Florida Memorial Coll Office of Pres 15800 NW 42nd Ave Opa Locka FL 33054-6155

SMITH, ALBERT E. areonautics company professional; BSEE, Northeastern U., Boston. With CIA, Washington, 1972—85, Lockheed Martin Missiles & Space, 1985-96; pres. electronics systems sector Harris Corp., 1996-98; pres. Sanders Divsn. Lockheed Martin Aerospace Electronics Systems, 1998-99; exec. v.p. Lockheed Martin Space Systems, 1999—2003; exec. v.p., integrated Systems and Solutions (IS&S) Lockheed Martin Corp., 2003—. Mem. Security Affairs Support Assn., Assn. of U.S. Army, Assn. of Old Crows, Armed Forces Comms. and Electronics Assn. Office: Lockheed Martin Corp 6801 Rockledge Dr Bethesda MD 20817-1836

SMITH, ALDO RALSTON, JR., brokerage house executive; b. Yonkers, N.Y., Mar. 19, 1947; s. Aldo Ralston Sr. and Maggie (Allen) S.; m. Linda McKenney Davila, Oct. 15, 1983; children: Damian Allen, Caitlin Victoria McKenney. BA in Psychology summa cum laude, Talladega Coll., 1973; postgrad., CUNY, 1973-76. Account exec. trainee Advest Inc., N.Y.C., 1978-79; account exec. Merrill, Lynch, Pierce, Fenner & Smith, N.Y.C., 1979-80, Lehman Brothers Kuhn Loeb, N.Y.C., 1980-82; fin. cons. Shearson Am. Express, N.Y.C., 1982-84; v.p. instl. mcpl. bond sales A.L. Haven Securities, N.Y.C., 1984; v.p. Prescott Ball & Turben, Inc., N.Y.C., 1984-85; v.p. instl. sales Baird Patrick & Co Inc., N.Y.C., 1985-91, Lincoln Pvt. Bank, 1991—; account exec. North Fork Bank Corp., 1995. Bd. dirs. Hale House for Human Potential, N.Y.C., 1978-80, Yonkers Family Svc. Assn., 2002—, Lower Hudson Valley Legal Svcs.; v.p.r Yonkers Family Svc. Assn.; mem. Mayor's Citizens Adv. Budget Com., 1993; chmn. Yonkers Police Citizens Profl. Standards Adv. Com., 1992. With U.S. Army, 1967-70. Named Outstanding Young Men of Am. Nat. Jr. C. of C., 1981. Mem. Yonkers Lions Club (bd. dirs. 1985—, pres. 1991-92, zone chmn. 1992-93), Masons (dist. dep. grand master 4th Manhattan dist.), Alpha Chi. Republican. Episcopalian. Avocations: scuba diving, photography, horticulture, cooking. Home: 96 Edgecliff Ter Yonkers NY 10705-1609

SMITH, ALEXANDER WYLY, JR., lawyer; b. Atlanta, June 9, 1923; s. Alexander Wyly and Laura (Payne) S.; m. Betty Rawson Haverty, Aug. 31, 1946; children— Elizabeth Smith Crew, Clarence Haverty, Laura Smith Brown, James Haverty, Edward Kendrick, Anthony Marion, William Rawson. Grad., Marist Sch., 1941; student, Holy Cross Coll., 1941-42; BBA, U. Ga., 1947, LL.B. cum laude, 1949. Bar: Ga. 1948. Practiced in, Atlanta, 1948-98; ret. ptnr. Smith, Gambrell & Russell and predecessor, 1994—. Bd. dirs. Our Lady of Perpetual Help Free Cancer Home; bd. dirs., planning and devel. coun. Cath. Archdiocese Atlanta, Marist Sch., Atlanta, John and Mary Franklin Found. Served with USAAF, 1943-46. Mem. Ga. Bar Assn., Atlanta Bar Assn., Phi Delta Phi, Chi Phi, Piedmont Driving Club Atlanta, Peachtree Golf Club Atlanta (pres. 1989-91). Home: 2771 Peachtree Rd #5 Atlanta GA 30305-3523 Office: 3100 Promenade II Atlanta GA 30309-3574 Office Phone: 404-815-3507.

SMITH, ALFRED GOUD, anthropologist, educator; b. The Hague, Netherlands, Aug. 20, 1921; s. William G. and Joan (Wraslouski) S.; m. Britta Helen Bonazzi, May 30, 1946. AB, U. Mich., 1943; postgrad., Princeton U., Yale U., 1943; MA, U. Wis., 1947, PhD, 1956. Far East analyst OSS and Dept. State, Washington, 1944-46; asst., instr. philosophy and anthropology U. Wis., 1946-50; supr. linguistics, Pacific area specialist Trust Ter. Pacific Islands and Dept. Interior, Micronesia and Washington, 1950-53; asst. prof. anthropology Antioch Coll., Yellow Springs, Ohio, 1953-56; asst. prof., assoc. prof. anthropology Emory U., Atlanta, 1956-62; assoc. prof., prof. anthropology, cmty. svc. and pub. affairs. U. Oreg., Eugene, 1962-73; dir. Ctr. for Communication Rsch., U. Tex., Austin, 1973-78; prof. anthropology and comm. studies Sch. Communication, U. Tex., 1973—. Cons. Ga. Dept. Pub. Health, 1956-60, Peace Corps, 1965-69, Job Corps, 1968-70, USIA, 1972-79, 82; U.S. State Dept. specialist, Mex., 1978; cons. on problems of comm. and anthropology to state and fed. agys., industry, museums, instns. of higher learning; staff mem. AID Comm. Seminars, 1966-81; lectr. in field, Eng., Mex., Venezuela, Germany, and Can. Author: Communication and Culture, 1966, Cognitive Styles in Law Schools, 1979; mem. editl. bd. Communication and Info. Scis., Info. and Behavior, Progress in Communication Scis.; contbr. articles to profl. jours., chpts. to books; further reprintings and revs. Served to 1st lt. AUS, 1942-45. Simon Mandlebaum scholar, U. Mich., 1943, Am. Coun. Learned Socs. fellow in Oriental Langs., 1943. Fellow Am. Anthrop. Assn., AAAS; mem. Internat. Communication Assn. (pres. 1973-74, dir.), Town and Gown Club, Sigma Xi, Alpha Kappa Delta, Phi Kappa Phi. Home: 1801 Lavaca St Austin TX 78701-1341 Office: U Tex Coll Communication Austin TX 78712 Business E-Mail: mcdagsbbs@mail.utexas.edu.

SMITH, ALISON LEIGH, lawyer; b. Brownsville, Tex., Sept. 24, 1952; d. Arthur Lee and June (Allen) Smith; m. Dean A. Burkhardt, Apr. 24, 1981. B in Journalism summa cum laude, U. Tex., 1974, JD cum laude, 1977. Bar: Tex. 1977, U.S. Dist. Ct. (so. dist.) Tex. (1978), U.S. Ct. Appeals (5th cir.) 1981, U.S. Dist. Ct. (no. dist.) Tex. 1987, U.S. Ct. Appeals (D.C. cir.) 1989. Assoc. Vinson & Elkins LLP, Houston, 1977-84, ptnr., 1984-89, 91—; dep. asst. atty. gen. antitrust divsn. U.S. Dept. Justice, Washington, 1989-91; ptnr. Dewey Ballantine LLP, Houston, 2004—. Adj. prof. law U. Tex., Austin, 1992-93. Alternate del. Rep. Nat. Conv., New Orleans, 1988; mem. ethics com. City of Houston, 1988-89. Mem. ABA (antitrust law sect., chair transp. industry com., 1992-95, co-chmn. pvt. antitrust litig. com. 2001-), Am. Law Inst., Tex. Bar Found., Houston Bar Assn. Home: 2125 Bolsover St Houston TX 77005-1617 Office: Dewey Ballantine LLP 700 Louisiana Ste 1900 Houston TX 77002-2725 Office Phone: 713-445-1590. Business E-Mail: asmith@deweyballantine.com.

SMITH, ALLIE MAITLAND, engineering educator; b. Lumberton, N.C., June 9, 1934; s. Allie McCoy and Emma Hattie (Wright) S.; m. Sarah Louise Whitlock, June 16, 1957; children: Sara Leianne, Hollis Duval, Meredith Lorren. BME with honors, N.C. State U., Raleigh, 1956, MS, 1961, PhD, 1966. Assoc. engr. Martin Co., Balt., 1956-57; devel. engr. Western Electric Co., 1957-60; mem. tech. staff Bell Tel. Labs., Burlington, N.C., 1960-62; instr., then asst. prof. extension N.C. State U., 1958-62; rsch. project engr. Rsch. Triangle Inst., Durham, N.C., 1962-66; rsch. supr. Sverdrup/ARO, Inc., Arnold Air Force Sta., Tenn., 1966-79; adj. prof. U. Tenn., Tullahoma, 1967-79; prof. mech. engring. U. Miss., University, 1979—, dean Sch. Engring., 1979—2000. Bd. dirs., mem. scholarship bd. Miss. Mineral Resources Inst.; exec. chmn. 14th conf. Southeastern Conf. on Theoretical and Applied Mechanics, mem. exec. com. 13th through 16th confs., mem. ops. com. and policy com., 1990-99, session chair, 1994; mem. organizing com., internat. sci. adv. bd., plenary session presiding officer Internat. Conf. on Hydrosci. and Engring., 1993, 95; mem. organizing com., plenary session chair Conf. on Mgmt. of Landscapes Disturbed by Channel Incision, 1997; keynote lecture and plenary sessions chair, Third Internat. Conf. on Hydrosci. and Engring., Berlin, 1998. Author: Fundamentals of Silicon Integrated Device Technology, Vol. I: Oxidation, Diffusion and Epitaxy, 1967, also articles, revs.; editor: Radiative Transfer and Thermal Control, 1976, Thermophysics of Spacecraft and Outer Planet Entry Probes, 1977, Fundamentals and Applications of Radiation Heat Transfer, 1987, Developments in Theoretical and Applied Mechanics, Vol. XIV, 1988, Radiation Heat Transfer: Fundamentals and Applications, 1990, Fundamentals of Radiation Heat Transfer, 1991, Radiative Heat Transfer: Theory and Applications, 1993, Solution Methods for Radiative Heat Transfer in Participating Media, 1996, Radiative Heat Transfer, 1997. Fellow AIAA (chmn. thermophysics tech. com. 1975-77, ASME (aerospace heat transfer com. 1975—; chmn. radiative heat transfer I and II sessions, Pitts. 2000, chmn. radiation heat transfer II session, St. Louis, 2002), chmn. terrestrial energy sys. tech. com. 1979-81, chmn. confs. 1975, 79, assoc. editor jour. 1975-77, 1986—, nat. publ. com. 1979-83, Nat. Thermophysics award 1978, Hermann Oberth award 1984-85, Space Shuttle Flag Challenger plaque 1984, supernumerary dir. Ala.-Miss. sect. 1994—); mem. AAUP, NSPE (pres. N.E. Miss. chpt. 1990-91), Am. Soc. Engring. Edn. (host Nat. Engring. Deans' Inst. 1991), N.Y. Acad. Scis., Sigma Xi, Phi Kappa Phi, Tau Beta Pi, Pi Tau Sigma, Upsilon Pi Epsilon, Sigma Pi (scholar 1955), Order of the Engr., Rotary Club. Achievements include discovery of anomalous refraction maxima phenomenon. Home: PO Box 1857 University MS 38677-1857 Office: U Miss 205 Carrier Hall University MS 38677 Office Phone: 662-915-5842. E-mail: enas@olemiss.edu.

SMITH, ALMA WHEELER, state legislator; b. Aug. 6, 1941; BA, U. Mich. Legis. coord. Senator Lane Pollack; mem. Mich. Senate from 18th dist., Lansing, 1995—; mem. appropriations com. Mem. South Lyon (Mich.) Bd. Edn.

SMITH, ANDREW ALFRED, JR., urban planner; b. Lynchburg, Va., Oct. 3, 1947; s. Andrew Alfred and Josephine (Vaughan) S. BArch (cum laude), Howard U., 1972; M in City Planning, MIT, 1980. Archtl. designer The Architects Collaborative Inc., Cambridge, Mass., 1972-76; archtl. coordinator Fay, Spofford & Thorndike Inc., Boston, 1977-79; assoc. city planner N.Y.C. Planning Commn., 1980—. Active Briarwood (N.Y.) Community Assn., 1985—, Jamaica YMCA, Queens, N.Y.; Newark Area Planning Assn., 1968, Peoples Involvement Corp., Washington, 1971-72, Mission Hill Planning Commn., Boston, 1978-80. HUD grantee, 1978-80; recipient Hallmark medal, 1989. Mem. Am. Planning Assn., Inst. Urban Design, Nat. Assn. Housing and Redevel. Ofcls. (exec. v.p. N.Y. Met. chpt. 1996—), Urban Land Inst. (assoc.), Howard U. Alumni Assn. (regional rep. 1978-79, 82-86, pres. L.I. chpt. 1983-85), Sierra Club, Nat. Travel Club, Mpcl. Art Soc. Democrat. Avocations: scuba diving, horseback riding, travel photographing, fundraising, arts and crafts collecting. Home: 84-55 Daniels St Apt 6L Briarwood NY 11435-2014 Office: NYC Planning Commn 22 Reade St New York NY 10007-1216 E-mail: asmith1@planning.nyc.gov.

SMITH, ANGELE LEORA, school nurse practitioner, poet, artist; d. Vernon Kenneth and Julie Stephanie Hartlen; m. Stephen Smith, Oct. 18, 1986; 1 child, Nathaniel Alden. ASN, Excelsior Coll., 1986. CPR/BLS/ACLS, 2004. Sch. nurse Upper Conn. Valley Hosp., Colebrook, NH, 2000—. Author: (poems) Houdini's Nook (William Falkner Creative Writing Competition finalist, 2002), Bestseller (Northern New England Review award, 2004), Crimson Eyes (Anne Rice Create-A-Vampire Contest by Alfred A. Knopf winner), Ode to Grampa, Vagabond (William Faulkner Creative Writing Competition semi-finalist, 2002). Bd. dirs. North Country C. of C., Colebrook, 2003—04.

SMITH, ANN DELORISE, municipal official; b. Union, S.C., June 26, 1941; 1 child. BS in Social Svc., Ea. Mich. U., 1962, postgrad., 1992-93. Planner III demonstration agy. City of L.A., 1970-75, sr. grants mgmt. specialist cmty. devel. dept., 1975-83, sr. mgmt. analyst I dept. aging, 1983-94, gen. mgr. dept. aging, 1994—. Del. White House Conf. on Aging, 1995; tchr. h.s. social studies, Flint and Ecors, Mich., 1962-63, grant cons., 1964-69, L.A./Detroit. Mem. adv. bd. Roybal Inst., Drew/RAND Ctr. on Health and Aging, KCET; mem. L.A. Urban League; mem. bd. dirs. Delta Sigma Theta HeadStart/State Presch.; involved in fed. grant programs including War on Poverty, 1960's. Mem. Am. Soc. on Aging, Nat. Ctr. and Caucus on Black Aging, Nat. Assn. of Area Agencies on Aging, Calif. Assn. of Area Agencies on Aging, Nat. Coun. on Aging, Gerontol. Soc. Am., Delta Sigma Theta. Home: 3803 S Dunsmuir Ave Los Angeles CA 90008-1016 also: 3580 Wilshire Blvd #300 Los Angeles CA 90010-2501

SMITH, ANNA DEAVERE, actress, educator, playwright; b. Balt., Sept. 18, 1950; d. Deavere Young and Anna (Young) S. BA, Beaver Coll., Pa., 1971, D hon., 1973; MFA, Am. Conservatory Theatre, 1977; D hon., U. N.C., 1995; hon. degree, Wheelock Coll., 1995, Colgate U., 1997, Sch. Visual Arts, 1997, Wesleyan U., 1997, Northwestern U., 1997, Coll. of the Holy Cross, 1997. Ann O'Day Maples prof. arts and drama Stanford U. Artist-in-residence Ford Found., 1997. Playwright, performer one-woman shows On the Road: A Search for American Character, 1983, Aye, Aye, Aye, I'm Integrated, 1984, Piano, 1991 (Drama-Logue award), Fires in the Mirror, 1989 (Obie award 1992, Drama Desk award 1992, N.Y. Drama Critics spl. citation 1993-94), Twilight: Los Angeles 1992 (Obie award, 2 Tony award nominations, Drama Critics Cir. spl. citation, Outer Critics Cir. award, Drama Desk award, Audelco award, Beverly Hills, Hollywood NAACP theatre awards), House Arrest, 1997; writer libretto for Judith Jamison, performer Hymn, 1993; appeared in (films) Dave, 1993, Philadelphia, 1993, The American President, 1995, Twilight: Los Angeles, 2000. Founding dir. The Inst. on Arts and Civic Dialogue Harvard U., 1998. Named One of Women of Yr., Glamour mag., 1993; fellow Bunting Inst., Radcliffe Coll.; genius fellow The MacArthur Found., 1996. Office: 1460 4th St Ste 212 Santa Monica CA 90401-3414 also: Stanford U Dept Drama Memorial Hall Stanford CA 94305

SMITH, ANNA NICOLE (VICKIE LYNN HOGAN), television personality, model; b. Mexia, Tex., Nov. 28, 1967; m. Billy Smith, 1985 (div. 1987); 1 child, Daniel; m. J. Howard Marshall II, Jun. 27, 1994 (dec.). Model for Guess? jeans. Spokesperson Trim Spa, 2003—. Appeared in films Naked Gun 33 1/3: The Final Insult, 1994, The Hudsucker Proxy, 1994; (TV series) The Anna Nicole Smith Show, 2002-; guest TV appearance, Ally McBeal; cover model Playboy, 1992 (Playmate of the Yr. 1993). Office: Alein Souliers 121 Madison Ave New York NY 10016-7033*

SMITH, ANNICK, writer; b. Paris, May 11, 1936; came to U.S., 1937; d. Stephen and Helene Deutch; m. David James Smith (dec. 1974); children: Eric, Stephen, Alex, Andrew. Student, Cornell Univ., 1954-55, U. Chgo., 1955-57; BA, U. Wash., 1961. Editor U. Wash. Press, Seattle, 1961-64, Montana Bus. Quarterly, U. Montana, Missoula, 1971-72; founding bd. mem. Sundance Film Inst., Sundance, Utah, 1981-85; founding mem. Ind. Film Project, N.Y.C., 1981-84; acting dir. Montana Com. for the Humanities, Missoula, 1983-84; devel. dir. Hellgate Writers, Inc., Missoula, 1986-96; creative dir. Yellow Bay Writers Workshop, U. Montana Continuing Edn. Dept, Missoula, 1987-98. Freelance filmmaker, producer, arts administrator, writer, Mont., 1974—; past H.S. tchr., cmty. organizer, environ. worker. Exec. prodr. Heartland, 1981; co-prodr. A River Runs Through It, 1992; co-editor: (with William Kittredge) The Last Best Place; author: Homestead, 1994, Big BlueStem A Journey into the Tall Grass, 1996, In This We Are Native, 2001; contbr. to anthologies including Best Am. Short Stories, 1992. Recipient Western Heritage award Cowboy Hall of Fame, 1981; Mont. Humanites award Mont. Com. for Humanities, 1988, Okla. Book award, 1997, Bancroft Prize Denver Pub. Libr., 1998. Mem. Trout Unlimited, Blackfoot Challenge. Democrat. Office: HC70 Box 173 Bonner MT 59823

SMITH, ANTHONY L. utilities executive; Grad. with honors, Whittier Coll.; MBA, M in Bus. Taxation, U. So. Calif.; grad. pub. utility exec. program, U. Mich.; grad. exec. fin. program, U. Pa. Joined Edison Internat., 1970, mgmt. trainee, various mgmt. and supervisory positions, dir. taxes, asst. contr., 1988, v.p., dir. tax So. Calif. Edison subs., v.p., dir. tax, 1999—. Former chair Calif. Taxpayer's Assn.; mem., former chair taxation com. and tax analysis and rsch. subcom. Edison Electric Inst. Mem.: Internat. Tax Inst., Tax Execs. Inst., Calif. Assessor's Assn. Office: Edison Internat 2244 Walnut Grove Ave Rosemead CA 91770 Office Phone: 626-302-2004. E-mail: anthony.smith@sck.com.

SMITH, ARTHUR B., JR., lawyer; b. Abilene, Tex., Sept. 11, 1944; s. Arthur B. and Florence B. (Baker) S.; m. Tracey L. Truesdale, 1999; children: Arthur C., Sarah R. BS, Cornell U., 1966; JD, U. Chgo., 1969. Bar: Ill. 1969, N.Y. 1976. Assoc. Vedder, Price, Kaufman & Kammholz, Chgo., 1969-74; asst. prof. labor law N.Y. State Sch. Indls. and Labor Rels., Cornell U., 1975-77; ptnr. Vedder, Price, Kaufman & Kammholz, Chgo., 1977-86; founding mem. Murphy, Smith & Polk, Chgo., 1986-98; shareholder Ogletree, Deakins, Chgo., 1999—. Guest. lectr. Northwestern U. Grad. Sch. Mgmt., 1979, Sch. Law, spring 1980; mem. hearing bd. Ill. Atty. Registration and Disciplinary Commn. Author: Employment Discrimination Law Cases and Materials, 5th edit., 2000, supplement, 2004, Construction Labor Relations, 1984, supplement, 1993; co-editor-in-chief: 1976 Annual Supplement to Morris, The Developing Labor Law, 1977; chpt. editor: The Developing Labor Law, 4th edit., 2000, supplement, 2004; contbr. articles to profl. jours. Recipient award for highest degree of dedication and excellence in tchg. N.Y. State Sch. Indsl. and Labor Rels., Cornell U., 1977; listed in The Best Lawyers in Am., 2003—. Fellow Coll. Labor and Employment Lawyers; mem. ABA (co-chmn. com. on devel. law under Nat. Labor Rels. Act, Sect. Labor Rels. Law 1976-77), N.Y. State Bar Assn., Phi Eta Sigma, Phi Kappa Phi, Chgo. Athletic Assn., Mid-Day Club. Presbyterian. Office: Ogletree Deakins et al 2 First National Plz Fl 25 Chicago IL 60603 Office Phone: 312-558-1230. Business E-Mail: Arthur.Smith@odnss.com.

SMITH, ARTHUR KITTREDGE, JR., academic administrator, political science educator; b. Derry, N.H., Aug. 15, 1937; s. Arthur Kittredge and Rena Belle (Roberts) S.; m. June Mary Dahar, Nov. 28, 1959; children: Arthur, Valerie, Meredith. BS, U.S. Naval Acad., 1959; MA, U. N.H., 1966; PhD, Cornell U., 1970. Vis. prof. El Colegio de Mexico, Mexico City, 1968-69; asst. prof. polit. sci. SUNY-Binghamton, 1970-74, assoc. prof., 1974-84, prof., 1984-88, provost for grad. studies and research, 1976-83, v.p. for adminstrn., 1982-88; prof. govt. and internat. studies U. S.C., Columbia, 1988-91, exec. v.p. for acad. affairs, provost, 1988-90, 91, interim pres., 1990-91; pres., prof. polit. sci. U. Utah, Salt Lake City, 1991-97; chancellor U. Houston Sys., 1997—; pres., prof. polit. sci. U. Houston Main Campus, 1997—. Author: (with Claude E. Welch, Jr.) Military Role and Rule: Perspectives on Civil-Military Relations, 1975; contbr. articles to profl. jours. With USN, 1959-65. Lehman fellow, 1966-69, NDEA fellow, 1969-70 Mem. Am. Polit. Sci. Assn., L.Am. Studies Assn., Inter-Univ. Sem. on Armed Forces and Soc., Am. Coun. on Edn., World Affairs Coun. (pres. Binghamton chpt. 1976-76), Bus.-Higher Edn. Forum, Phi Beta Kappa, Pi Sigma Alpha, Omicron Delta Kappa, Phi Delta Kappa, Beta Gamma Sigma, Phi Kappa Phi. Office: U Houston Sys Office Of The Chancellor Houston TX 77204-0001 E-mail: aksmith@uh.edu.

SMITH, ARTHUR LEE, lawyer; b. Davenport, Iowa, Dec. 19, 1941; s. Harry Arthur Smith and Ethel (Hoffman) Duerre; m. Georgia Mills, June 12, 1965 (dec. Jan. 1984); m. Jean Bowler, Aug. 4, 1984; children: Juliana, Christopher, Andrew, Wendy. BA, Augustana Coll., Rock Island, Ill., 1964; MA, Am. U., 1968; JD, Washington U., St. Louis, 1971. Bar: Mo 1971, DC 1983. Telegraph editor Davenport Morning Democrat, 1962-64; ptnr. Peper Martin Jensen Maichel & Hetlage, 1971-95, Husch & Eppenberger, St. Louis, 1995—. Arbitrator Nat Asn Security Dealers, 1980—, Am Arbit Asn, 1980—. Columnist: St Louis Lawyer, syndicated columnist: Technolawyer.com and other publications. Dir. P. Buckley Moss Found. for Children's Edn., 2001—03. Lt USN, 1964—68. Mem.: ABA (co-chair electronic discovery subcom.), St. Louis Bar Found. (dir. 2004—), Bar Assn. Met. St. Louis (chmn law mgt comt 1993—96, chair technology comt 1996—99, Pres.'s award Exceptional Service 1995, 2003), P. Buckley Moss Soc. (dir 1994—, v.p. 1998—2000, exec vpres 2001—02, pres. 2002—), Mo. Bar Assn. (vice-chair ins programs comt 1981—83, vice-chair antitrust comt 1981—83, chair admin law comt 1995—97), D.C. Bar Assn. (chmn law practice mgt 1990—91), Order of Coif. Office: Husch & Eppenberger Ste 600 190 Carondelet Plz Saint Louis MO 63105-3441 Office Phone: 314-480-1500. E-mail: arthur.smith@husch.com.

SMITH, BAKER ARMSTRONG, management executive, lawyer; b. Oct. 3, 1947; s. William Armstrong and Priscilla (Baker) S.; m. Deborah Elizabeth Ellis, Nov. 13, 1982; children: Ellis Armstrong, Elizabeth Anne, Everett Baker, Emery Manning. BS, U.S. Naval Acad., 1969; MBA, Northeastern U., 1975; JD cum laude, Suffolk U., 1977; LLM in Labor, Georgetown U., 1981. Bar: Ga. 1977, D.C. 1978, U.S. Supreme Ct. 1980; cert. turnaround profl., 1994; fellow Family Firm Inst. Commd. ensign USN, 1969, advanced through grades to lt., 1974; exec. dir., founder Ctr. on Nat. Labor Policy, Inc., North Springfield, Va., 1977-81; asst. to sec., dir. labor rels. U.S. Dept. HUD, Washington, 1981-83; exec. v.p. U.S. Bus. and Indsl. Coun., Nashville, 1983-84; pres. Am. Quality Builders, Inc., Nashville, 1984-86; v.p. Hopeman Bros., Inc., Waynesboro, Va., 1986-88; pres. Morris, Anderson, Atlanta, 1988—. Sec., founder U.S. Constnl. Rights Legal Def. Fund, Inc., Atlanta, 1983—; trustee Leadership Inst., Springfield, Va., 1978—; v.p., 1998—; dir. Turnaround Mgmt. Assn., Chgo., 1994-2003, v.p., 1998-99; pres. Assn. Cert. Turnaround Profls., Boston, 1997-98; mem. Coun. for Nat. Policy, Washington, 1981—, Civil Rights Reviewing Authority U.S. Dept. Edn., Washington, 1984-88; transition team leader Office of the Pres.-Elect of the U.S., NLRB, Occupl. Safety and Health Rev. Commn., Fed. Mediation and Conciliation Svc., Nat. Mediation Bd., Fed. Labor Rels. Authority, Washington, 1980-81; instr. law, faculty sec. No. Va. Law Sch., Alexandria, Va., 1980-83; instr. law D.C. Law Sch., Washington, 1978-80. Contbg. author: Mandate for Leadership, 1981; contbr. articles to profl. jours. Recipient Outstanding Contbn. to the Turnaround Profession award, 1999. Fellow Family Firm Inst.; mem. ABA (Nat. Law Day chmn. 1976-77, Silver Key award 1977), St. George's House, Windsor Castle (assoc.), Phila. Soc., U.S. Supreme Ct. Hist. Soc., Federalist Soc., Beta Gamma Sigma, Phi Delta Phi (pres. 1989-91), Capitol Hill Club (Washington), Piedmont Club (Winston-Salem). Republican. Presbyterian. Home: 3360 E Terrell Branch Ct Marietta GA 30067-5164 Office Phone: 770-984-3262. Business E-Mail: bsmith@morris-anderson.com.

SMITH, BARBARA, food service executive, model; b. Everson, Pa., Aug. 24, 1949; m. Dan Gasby; 1 stepdaughter. Owner B. Smith Restaurant Group; former model. Mem. adv. bd. Culinary Inst. Am., 1995—. Author: B. Smith's Cooking and Entertaining for Friends, 1995; host (syndicated weekly TV show) B. Smith With Style; founder B. Smith Style mag. Mem.: Screen Actors Guild, Feminist Press (founding bd. mem.), NY Women's Found. (founding bd. mem.), Times Sq. Bus. Improvement Dist. (founding bd. mem.). Achievements include appeared in over 100 radio, print, and TV ads; First African Am. woman elected to bd. trustees Culinary Inst. Am. Avocation: family activities. Mailing: 320 W 46th St New York NY 10036

SMITH, BARBARA ANNE, health facility administrator, consultant; b. N.Y.C., Oct. 10, 1946; d. John Allen and Lelia Maria (De Silva) Santoro; m. Joseph Newton Smith, Feb. 5, 1966 (div. Sept. 1984); children: J. Michael, Robert Lawrence. Student, Oceanside/Carlsbad Coll. Real estate agt. Routh Robbins, Inc., Washington, 1973-75; gen. mgr. Mall Shops, Inc., Kansas City, Kans., 1975-80; regional mgr. FAO Schwarz, N.Y.C., 1980-84; clin. adminstr. North Denver Med. Ctr., Thornton, Colo., 1984-88; adminstrv. dir. Country Side Ambulatory Surgery Ctr., Leesburg, Va., 1989-91; pres. SCS Healthcare Mgmt. Inc., Washington, 1991—. Bd. dirs. Franz Carl Weber Internat., Geneva, 1982-84; mng. dir. Nat. Healthcare Consortium, 1997—; mng. assoc. Monarch Assocs. in Healthcare. Pres. Am. Women Chile, 1968; v.p. Oak Park Assn., Kansas City, 1977-78, pres., 1978-79; vol. Visitor Info. and Assn. Reception Ctr. program Smithsonian Instn., Washington. Mem. NAFE, Network Colo., Profl. Bus. Women Assn., Med. Group Mgmt. Assn., Federated Ambulatory Surgery Assn.

SMITH, BARBARA BARNARD, music educator; b. Ventura, Calif., June 10, 1920; d. Fred W. and Grace (Hobson) S. BA, Pomona Coll., 1942; Mus.M., U. Rochester, 1943, performer's cert., 1945; DMus (hon.), Pomona Coll., 2001. Mem. faculty piano and theory Eastman Sch. Music, U. Rochester, 1943-49; mem. faculty U. Hawaii, Honolulu, 1949—, assoc. prof. music, 1953-62, prof., 1962-82, prof. emeritus, 1982—; sr. fellow East-West Center, 1973. Lectr., recitals in Hawaiian and Asian music, U.S., Europe and Asia, 1956—; field researcher Asia, 1956, 60, 66, 71, 80, Micronesia, 1963, 70, 87, 88, 90, 91, Solomon Islands, 1976. Contbr. articles to profl. jours. Mem. Internat. Soc. Music Edn., Internat. Musicol. Soc., Soc. Ethnomusicology, Internat. Coun. for Traditional Music, Am. Mus. Instrument Soc., Coll. Music Soc., Soc. for Asian Music, Music Educators Nat. Conf., Pacific Sci. Assn., Phi Beta Kappa, Mu Phi Epsilon. Home: 1314 Kalakaua Ave Apt 1403 Honolulu HI 96826-1929

SMITH, BARBARA JEAN, lawyer; b. Washington, Jan. 9, 1947; d. Harry Wallace and Jean (Fraser) S.; m. Philip R. Chall, July 13, 1991; children: Brian C.S. Brown, Craig F.S. Brown, Amy E. Spiers, Carrie A. Chall. BA, Old Dominion Coll., 1968; MBA, Pepperdine U., 1974; JD, Case Western Res. U., 1977. Bar: Ohio 1977. Assoc. Squire, Sanders & Dempsey, Cleve., 1977-88, ptnr., 1988-93; shareholder McDonald, Hopkins, Burke & Haber Co., L.P.A., Cleve., 1993—. Bd. editors Health Law Jour. of Ohio, 1989-95; contbr. articles to health jours. and periodicals. Trustee Urban Community Sch., Cleve., 1984-86, Alzheimer's Assn. Greater Cleve., 2000—. Mem. Ohio Women's Bar Assn. (pres. 1994-95), Cleve. Bar Assn. (pres. 1998-99, trustee 1992-95, chair health law sect. 1991-92), Am. Health Lawyers Assn., Ohio

State Bar Assn. (health law com. 1991—), Soc. Ohio Hosp. Attys. Democrat. Mem. United Ch. of Christ. Avocations: reading, hiking. Home: 416 Fairway Vw Chagrin Falls OH 44023-6718 Office: McDonald Hopkins Burke & Haber 2100 Bank One Ctr 600 Superior Ave E Cleveland OH 44114-2653 E-mail: bsmith@mhbh.com.

SMITH, BARBARA JEANNE, retired librarian; b. Jersey Shore, Pa., Apr. 14, 1939; d. Moyer Emmerson and Mary Kathryn (Ebner) S. BS in Edn. (Biology), Pa. State U., 1961, DEd in Higher Edn., 1981; MS in Edn. (English), SUNY, Oswego, N.Y., 1967; MLS, U. Pitts., 1970. Reference libr. Pa. State U. Librs., University Park, 1970-75, commonwealth campus coord., 1975-82, asst. dean librs., head commonwealth campus librs. divsn., 1982-89; dir. Smithsonian Instn. Librs., Washington, 1989-98. Gen. sci. tchr., Binghampton (N.Y.) City Schs., 1961-62; English tchr., North Syracuse (N.Y.) Ctrl. Schs., 1970-75; mem. Smithsonian Instn. Rsch. Info. Svc. (chair 1993-95), Planning Adv. Group, 1989-93; chair Internet Implementation Com., Smithsonian Instn. Librs. User Adv. Com., 1989-97; founding dir. Chesapeake Info. and Rsch. Libr. Alliance, 1996-98. Contbr. articles to profl. jours.; speaker in field. UCLA Grad. Sch. of Libr. and Info. Sci. Sr. fellow, 1982. Mem. AAUW, ALA (mem. coun. 1987-91), Cosmos Club (Washington), Centre County (Pa.) Hist. Soc. (life), U. Pitts. Alumni Assn. (bd. dirs. 1991-94), Ctr. Hills Country Club, Beta Phi Mu. E-mail: bsmith5598@pennswoods.net.

SMITH, BARBARA RODERICK, health and social services administrator, nursing consultant; b. Peoria, Ill., Mar. 5, 1948; d. Fremont August and Jessie May (Burdess) Roderick; m. Ronald Nelson Smith, June 18, 1976; children: Yvette, Roderick, Jennifer. Student, Peoria Sch. Practical Nursing, 1967-68; assoc., Ill. Cen. Coll. Registered Nursing, 1971; BS, Coll. St. Francis, Joliet, 1981; postgrad., U. Ill., 1985-90, U. Iowa, Bradley U., 1991-93; MS in Nursing, Columbia State U., 1995, PhD in Social Work, 1997. Cert. sch. nurse; lic. local Meth. Pastor; cert. social worker. Med. coord. Covenant Children's Home, Princeton, Ill.; cons. Donna Home Care, Bartonville, Ill.; nursing cons. Rose Shelter, Peoria; adminstr. health svc. Cath. Social Svc., Peoria; dir. Alzheimer unit Americana Health Care Manor Corp.; mem. faculty Ill. Cen. Coll., East Peoria, 1992—. Guest spkr. St. Francis Coll. Nursing; cons. Ill. Dept Children Family Svcs. Health Svc. Mgmt. Health Policy Divsn., implementation managed health care sys.; nurse cons., genetics, newborn screening, lead, child safety program Ill. Dept of Health; adminstr. detox, nursing programs White Oaks Detox Ctr.; exec. dir. Rural Peoria County COun. on Aging. Mem. subcom. on nursing Forward Peoria; adv. coun. Native Am. Child Welfare. Mem. Ill. Nursing Assn. (bd. dirs.), Ill. Assn. Maternal Child Health (bd. dirs.), Am. Indian Coun. of Ill.; Sigma Theta Tau. Home: PO Box 1521 Peoria IL 61655-1521

SMITH, BARNARD ELLIOT, management educator; b. Mpls., May 6, 1926; s. Sheldon Strong and Jessie (Gould) S.; m. Betty Lou Strohschein, Aug. 28, 1949; children: Carolyn Louise, Eileen Elizabeth. BS in Mech. Engring. with distinction, U. Minn., 1949, MS, 1950; PhD, Stanford U., 1961; MA (hon.), Dartmouth Coll., 1971. Asst. prof. mech. engring. U. N.D., 1950-51; mfg. specialist A.O. Smith Co., Milw., 1951-54; asst. prof. indsl. engring. Oreg. State Coll., 1954-58, Stanford U., 1958-61; asso. prof. mgmt. Sloan Sch. Mgmt., MIT, 1961-68; prof. mgmt. Indian Inst. Mgmt., Calcutta, 1965-68; prof. engring. Thayer Sch. Engring. Dartmouth Coll., 1968-71; dean Stuart Sch. Mgmt. and Finance, Ill. Inst. Tech., 1971-75, prof. mgmt., 1975-80; David M. French disting. prof. mgmt. U. Mich., Flint, 1980-89, emeritus, 1989; pres. Vineyards of the Acad., 1989, The Acad. of Wine of Oreg. Inc., 1993—. Cons. in field. Served with USNR, 1944-46. Mem. Phi Tau Sigma, Beta Gamma Sigma. Home: 18200 Highway 238 Grants Pass OR 97527-8631 E-mail: academy3@earthlink.net.

SMITH, BARRY HAMILTON, foundation administrator, physician; b. Orange, N.J., Oct. 6, 1943; s. Kenneth Wright and Harriet (Barr) S.; m. Carley Eldredge, Dec. 13, 1969; children: Christopher, Sara. BA, Harvard U., 1965; PhD, MIT, 1968; MD, Cornell U., 1972. Intern, resident N.Y. Hosp., N.Y.C., 1971-75; resident Mass. Gen. Hosp., Boston, 1975-78; program dir. Neuroscis. Rsch. Program MIT, Boston, 1975-78; dep. dir. Surg. Neurology Br. NIH, Bethesda, Md., 1978-83; sci. & med. dir. Dreyfus Med. Found., N.Y.C., 1983-88; dir. Dreyfus Health Found., N.Y.C., 1988—. Sr. v.p. Rogosin Inst., 1998—; prof. surgery Cornell U. Editor Ency. Neurosci.; contbr. articles to profl. jours. Bd. dirs. Desmond Tutu Peace Found., 1999—, Kornfeld Found., 2002—, N.Y.C. Rescue Mission, 1995—. Comdr. USPHS, 1978-83. Recipient Commendation Medal award, USPHS, 1982, EEO award, 1983. Mem. AMA, AAAS, Soc. Neurosci., Am. Pain Soc. (audit com. 1983-85), Nat. Coun. Internat. Health (governing bd. 1990-95, chair 1993-95), Phi Beta Kappa, Sigma Xi, Alpha Omega Alpha. Avocations: sailing, writing. Home: 1192 Park Ave Apt 10B New York NY 10128-1314 Office: Dreyfus Health Found 205 E 64th St Rm 404 New York NY 10021-6635 Office Phone: 212-750-5075. E-mail: bsmith@dhfglobal.org.

SMITH, BARRY SAMUEL, physiatrist; b. Windber, Pa., Jan. 15, 1947; MD, Jefferson Med. Coll., 1969. Diplomate Am. Bd. Phys. Medicine and Rehab. Intern Reading (Pa.) Hosp., 1969-70; resident in phys. medicine and rehab. Inst. Phys. Med. Rehab., Louisville, 1970-73; now with Baylor U. Med. Ctr., Dallas, chief in phys. medicine and rehab. Mem. AMA, Am. Acad. Phys. Medicine and Rehab., Am. Congress Rehab. Medicine, Assn. Acad. Physiatrists, Am. Assn. Electrodiagnostic Medicine, Nat. Bd. Med. Examiners (diplomate). Office: Baylor U Med Ctr Dept Phys Medicine and Rehab 3500 Gaston Ave Dallas TX 75246-2096

SMITH, BERNADINE M. radio announcer, filmmaker, writer, producer, director; d. Bernice and Dudley Smith; 1 child, Evan Dudley. Student, Am. Internat. Coll., Springfield, Mass., 1971—73. Founder/owner Every Woman Filmworks, Bklyn., 1990—, Queen Bee Multi-Media Advt. & Consulting Agy., Bklyn., 1988—; mgr. Nat. Amusements, Bklyn., 1998—2000; founder/owner GGTG WORLDWIDE Media, 2002—. Editor: (religious programming) Holiness is Right; writer/dir. (play) Sweet Pea's Place of Prayer, LUPUS, (feature film) Bad Kids, writer/dir. They Mines; dir.: (book) How He Made A Woman Out of Me/LIFE 101.da real skool; author: Bushwhackers from Texas...A Political Essay; playwright: 3 Women and a Man, Comin' Out, BROKEN; author: (songs) (radio drama) From the Table to the Heart, (sit-com) Max Warlock P.I. Chairperson, incorporator Big Sisters of Hampden County, Springfield, Mass., 1981—82; mem. Mt. Sinai Cathedral Ch. of God in Christ, 2000—. Recipient awards prodn. value and prodn. content, N.Am. Women in Cable, 1995, First Time Film Maker's Camera Package, Panavision Corp., 2001; prodn. grantee, The Endowment Channel, 1996. Democrat. Pentacostal. Avocations: writing, producing, teaching, mentoring. Office: Every Woman Filmworks Queen Bee Media 63 Lafayette Ave Brooklyn NY 11217 Office Phone: 917-202-6972. E-mail: blkonblk99@aol.com.

SMITH, BERNALD STEPHEN, retired airline pilot, aviation consultant; b. Long Beach, Calif., Dec. 24, 1926; s. Donald Albert and Bernice Merrill (Stephens) S.; m. Marilyn Mae Spence, July 22, 1949; children: Lorraine Ann Smith Foute, Evelyn Donice Smith DeRoos, Mark Stephen, Diane April (dec.). Student, U. Calif., Berkeley, 1944-45, 50-51. Cert. airline transport pilot, flight engr., FAA. Capt. Transocean Air Lines, Oakland (Calif.) and Tokyo, 1951-53, Hartford, Conn., 1954-55; 1st officer United Air Lines, Seattle, 1955, San Francisco, 1956-68, tng. capt. Denver and San Francisco, 1961-68, capt. San Francisco, 1968-86, 2d officer, 1986-93, ret., 1993. Founder, v.p. AviaAm., Palo Alto, Calif., 1970-72, AviaInternat., Palo Alto, 1972-74; cons. Caproni Vizzola, Milan, 1972-84; prin., cons. Internat. Aviation Cons. and Investments, Fremont, Calif., 1985—; instr. aviation Ohlone Coll., Fremont, 1976; founder Pacific Soaring Coun.; founder, trustee AirSailing, Inc., 1970—, Soaring Safety Found., 1985—. Author/editor: American Soaring Handbook, 1975, 80; contbr. articles to profl. jours. Trustee Nat. Soaring Mus., 1975-2001 (Gold medal, 2002, Barnaby Lecturer, 2003), pres. 1975-78; active RTCA, SSA del., 1992—, FAI del., 1996-. Comdr. USNR. Fellow Internat. GPS Svc. for Geodynamics; mem. AIAA (pub. bd. 1977-94), Soaring Soc. Am. (pres. 1969-70, chmn. pub. bd. 1971-84, ins. com. 1975-93, bd. dirs. 1963-97, Warren Eaton Meml. trophy, 1977, 97, Exceptional Svc. award 1970, 75, 82, 88, 91, Exceptional Achievement award 1996, named to Hall of Fame 1984, hon. vice-chmn. bd. dirs. 2000—, Schweizer Lifetime Svc. award 2003), Nat. Aero. Assn., Exptl. Aircraft Assn., Aircraft Owners and Pilots Assn., Airline Pilots Assn., Seaplane Pilots Assn., Orgn. Scientifique et Technique Internat. du Vol a Voile (hon., bd. dirs., U.S. del. 1981-97), Fedn. Aeronatique Internat. (environ. commn. v.p. and U.S. del. 1995—, airspace mgmt. group 1998—, del. environ. com. 2002—, Paul Tissandier diploma 1992, Lilienthal medal 1993, Bronze medal, 2003), Commn. de Vol A Voile (U.S. del. 1970-71, 78, 85-97, v.p. 1988-96), U. Calif. Alumni Assn. (life), Inst. Navigation, Civil GPS Svc. Interface Com. Democrat. Methodist. Office: Internat Aviation Cons Investments PO Box 3075 Fremont CA 94539-0307

SMITH, BERT KRUGER, retired mental health services professional; b. Wichita Falls, Tex., Nov. 18, 1915; d. Sam and Fania (Feldman) Kruger; m. Sidney Stewart Smith, Jan. 19, 1936; children: Sheldon Stuart, Jared Burt (dec.), Randy Smith Huke. BJ, U. Mo., 1936; MA, U. Tex., 1949; DHL (hon.), U. Mo., 1985. Soc. and entertainment editor Wichita Falls Post, 1936-37; freelance writer Juneau, Alaska, 1937; assoc. pub. Coleman Daily Dem. Voice, 1950-51; assoc. editor Jr. Coll. Jour., Austin, Tex., 1952-55; spl. cons., exec. Hogg Found. for Mental Health, Austin, Tex., 1952—2001, ret., 2001. Founder, chmn. Austin Groups for the Elderly, 1985—; mem. ethics com. St. David's Hosp.; panelist Nat. Assn. Southwest Conf. Mental Health and Aging; instr. mental health info., special edn., gerontology U. Tex., Austin; mem. com. Geriatric Rsch., Edn. Clin. Ctr. and Aging Rsch. and Edn. Ctr., U. Tex. Health Sci. Ctr., San Antonio. Author: No Language But A Cry, 1964, Your Non-Learning Child, 1968, A Teaspoon of Honey, 1970, Insights for Uptights, 1973, Aging in America, 1973, The Pursuit of Dignity, 1977, Looking Forward, 1983; contbr. numerous articles to profl. jours. Bert Kruger Smith professorship Sch. Social Work U. Tex., 1982; recipient Disting. Svc. award City of Austin, 1988, Cert. of Appreciation, Tex. Dept. Human Svcs., 1989, Ann Bert Smith award Sr.'s Respite Svc., 1989, S.W. Found. Founders' Spirit award, 1990, Tex. Leadership award Ann. Tex. Joint Conf. on Aging, 1992, Tex. Leadership award Tex. Dept. on Aging, 1992, Tex. Long-Term Care Vol. award, Women in Comm. Lifetime Achievement award, Mental Health Assn. Cmty. Svc. award, Internat. Tng. in Comm. Founder's Day Woman of Yr. award, Most Worthy Citizen award, Golden Rule award Memento, J.C. Penney, Inc., Disting. Svc. award City of Austin, Amazing Aging award Jewish Family Svcs., U. Tex. Sch. Social Work, Founder's award Holt House, 1998; named Woman of Distinction, Girl Scouts U.S., 2002; named to Tex. Women's Hall of Fame, 1988. Mem. Conf. Southwest Founds. (founder's spirit award, archives, film, & video com.), Adult Svcs. Coun. and Family Eldercare (bd. dirs.), Found. Religious Studies Tex. (bd. trustees), Timely Solutions (adv. bd.). Jewish. Avocations: walking, reading. Home: 5818 Westslope Dr Austin TX 78731-3633 Fax: 512-453-8400.

SMITH, BETTY, writer, nonprofit foundation executive; b. Bonham, Tex., Sept. 16; d. Sid and Gertrude (Dearing) S. Student, Stephens Coll.; BJ, U. Tex. Women's editor Daily Texan; pres. Hope Assocs. Corp., N.Y.C.; pres., owner Betty Smith Assocs., N.Y.C. Author: A Matter of Heart, 1969. Bd. dirs. Melchior Heldentenor Found., N.Y.C., 1968—, pres., 1987-97; pres., CEO Gerda Lissner Found., 1994—; CEO Herman Lissner Found., 1990—. Mem. Author's Guild. Home: 322 E 55th St New York NY 10022-4157 Office: care Lissner Found 135 E 55th St 8th Fl New York NY 10022-4049 Office Phone: 212-826-6100.

SMITH, BETTY DENNY, county official, administrator, fashion executive; b. Centralia, Ill., Nov. 12, 1932; d. Otto and Ferne Elizabeth (Beier) Hasenfuss; m. Peter S. Smith, Dec. 5, 1964; children: Carla Kip, Bruce Kimball. Student, U. Ill., 1950-52; student, L.A. City Coll., 1953-57, UCLA, 1965, U. San Francisco, 1982-84. Freelance fashion coordinator, L.A., N.Y.C., 1953-58; tchr. fashion Rita LeRoy Internat. Studios, 1959-60; mgr. Mo Nadler Fashion, L.A., 1961-64; showroom dir. Jean of Calif. Fashions, L.A., 1965—. Freelance polit. book reviewer for community newspapers, 1961-62; staff writer Valley Citizen News, 1963. Bd. dirs. Pet Assistance Found., 1969-76; founder, pres., dir. Vol. Services to Animals L.A., 1972-76; mem. County Com. To Discuss Animals in Rsch., 1973-74; mem. blue ribbon com. on animal control L.A. County, 1973-74; dir. L.A. County Animal Care and Control, 1976-82; mem. Calif. Animal Health Technician Exam. Com., 1975-82, chmn., 1979; bd. dirs. L.A. Soc. for Prevention Cruelty to Animals, 1984-94, Calif. Coun. Companion Animal Advocates, 1993-97; dir. West Coast Regional Office, Am. Humane Assn., 1988-97; CFO Coalition for Pet Population Control, 1987-92; trustee Gladys W. Sargent Found., 1997—, Coalition to End Pet Overpopulation, 1998—; cons. Jungle Book II, Disney Studios, 1997; mem. Coalition to Protect Calif. Wildlife, 1996-97, Spl. Commn. Spay/Neuter City L.A., 1998-99; adv. com. La. Dept. of Animal Reg. 2000; mem. Calif. Rep. Cen. Com., 1964-72, mem. exec. com., 1971-73; mem. L.A. County Rep. Cen. Com., 1964-70, mem. exec. com., 1966-70; chmn. 29th Congl. Cen. Com., 1969-70; sec. 28th Senatorial Cen. Com., 1967-68, Dept. Animal Reg., 2000-, Calif. Dept. Fish & Games Animal Care Advisory Com., 2003-; mem. speakers bur. George Murphy for U.S. Senate, 1970; campaign mgr. Los Angeles County for Spencer Williams for Atty. Gen., 1966; mem. adv. com. Moorpark Coll., 1988-97; mem. adv. bd. Wishbone Prodn., 1995-97, Dept. of animal Reg., 2003; mem. L.A. County Art Mus., Calif. Dept. of Fish & Games Animal Care Adv. Com., Calif. Rep Ctr., L.A. Libr. Assn. Mem. Internat. Platform Assn., Mannequins Assn. (bd. dirs. 1967-68), Motion Picture and TV Industry Assn. (govt. rels. and pub. affairs com. 1992-97), Lawyer's Wives San Gabriel Valley (bd. dirs. 1971-74, pres. 1972-73), L.A. Athletic Club, Town Hall. Home: 1766 Bluffhill Dr Monterey Park CA 91754-4533

SMITH, BETTY GENE, physical education educator; b. Pitts., Tex., July 17, 1947; d. Billy Gene and Betty Louise (Blakestead) S. BS, Okla. State U., 1969. Camp counselor, program dir. YWCA camp, Va. Beach; instr. physical edn. Tulsa Pub. Schs., 1969—. Bldg. coord. Tulsa Run, Tulsa Pub. Schs., Am. Heart Assn.; chair Sports Days in track and field, volleyball, gymnastics, synchronized swimming, cross country and fitness pentathlon Tulsa Pub. Schs., also coach; mem. Save our Schs. com. Tulsa Pub. Schs.; workshop presenter Tulsa Pub. Schs. Co-author handbooks, ednl. guides; photographer, editor videos. Coach basketball, track, volleyball Okla. Spl. Olympics; summer camp Tulsa Assn. Retarded; physical edn. coord. Autistic summer camp; swim instr. ARC; presentor Tulsa Great Expectations summer camp; worker Doenges Bros. Triathlon; coach in-sch. bowling program Am. Bowling Alliance; league and divsn. coord. Tulsa Women's Amateur Softball Assn. Recipient Cert. of Excellence Tulsa Bd. Edn., 1992, 93, Middle Sch. Physical Edn. Tchr. of the Yr. Nat. Assn. for Sport and Physical Edn., 1993. Mem. NEA, Okla. Edn. Assn. (Instrnl. Excellence in Edn. award 1993), PTA, Am. Alliance for Health, Physical Edn., Recreation and Dance, Okla. Alliance Health, Physical Edn., Recreation and Dance (Educator of Yr. 1992, legis. fitness day, conv. arrangements com., program presenter), So. Dist. Am. Alliance Health, Recreation and Dance (Middle Sch. Educator of Yr. 1992, Middle Sch. Physical Educator of Yr. 1993, gen. arrangements com.), Tulsa Classroom Tchrs. Assn. (bldg. del./alternate, re-write com. drug policy, chair middle sch. com.), Nat. Assn. Sport and Physical Edn., N.Am. Fisherman's Assn. Avocations: fly fishing, wood working, creative writing. Home: 9061 E 33rd St Tulsa OK 74145-1617 Office: Whitney Middle Sch 2177 S 67th East Ave Tulsa OK 74129-2007

SMITH, BETTY L. results coach, seminar leader; b. Trinidad, Colo., Oct. 17, 1932; d. Howard Melvin and Annabelle (Eastwood) Wade; m. Earl Gilbert Smith, Nov. 26, 1950; children: Wayne David, Christine E. Thomann, Clifford Todd. Student, CalistogaCalif.) Coll., 1961-63. Owner, founder Gilbert's Gallery Frame Shop, Santa Rosa, 1964-84; ind. rep., regional sales dir. Simplex, Santa Rosa, 1984-91; owner, transformation coach Betty Smith Results Coaching, Santa Rosa, 1992—. Author: Secrets of Living Life Abundantly, 1995, (poetry biography) Here I Am, There I Went, 1968; contbr. articles to profl. jours. Art commr. City of Santa Rosa, 1967-68; mem. steering coun. Earth Elders, treas., 1999-2001; mem. Sustainable Sonoma County. Democrat. Avocation: environmental education. Home and Office: 2319 Olympia Dr Santa Rosa CA 95405-8119

SMITH, BETTY W. librarian; b. Lincoln, Nebr., June 29, 1919; d. Clem and Edith Margaret (Stanley) Wilder; m. Dulaney Dale Smith, Mar. 20, 1946; children: Douglas D., Diane E., Richard W. BA, Wayne U., 1940; BS, U. Minn., 1941; MA, Mich. State U., 1955. Cert. libr. Br. libr. Pub. Libr., Park Ridge, Ill., 1941-42, reference libr. Dearborn, Mich., 1942-44; U.S.C.G. SPAR, libr. asst. U.S.C.G. Acad., New London, Conn., 1945-46; reference libr. Libr. Hawaii, Honolulu, 1946-47; libr. Hawaiian Econ. Found., Honolulu, 1947-49; reference libr. Lansing Pub. Libr., Mich., 1967-86, substitute libr., 1986-98. Mem. Citizens for Actions in Mental Health, 1980—86; steering com. Long-Range Planning Mich. Dept. Mental Health, 1986—90; bd. dirs. Tri-Co. Cmty. Mental Health, Lansing, 1992—98; founding and exec. com. mem. Alliance for Mentally Ill, Mich., 1985—2003, now v.p.; adv. coun. Mich. Forensic Ctr., 1988—, Lafayette Clinic, Detroit, 1986—92. Mem. LWV, Mental Health Assn., Mich. Assn. Emotionally Disturbed Children (bd. dirs. 1963-68), Mich. Mental Health (adv. coun. 1986-90), Phi Alpha Theta. Home: 1782 Eifert Rd Holt MI 48842-1976

SMITH, BEVERLY ANN EVANS, management consultant, small business owner; b. Massillon, Ohio, Apr. 12, 1948; d. Louie Edward and Willa (Dumas) Evans; m. Stephen John Smith, Aug. 1971; children: Brian Stephen, Stacy Nicole. MEd, Kent State U., 1973; BS in Edn., Bowling Green State U., 1970; diploma exch. edn. program, Babson Coll., 1987. Tchr. Garfield High Sch., Akron, Ohio, 1971-72; fin. aids officer, Upward Bound dir. Kent (Ohio) State U., 1971-76; dean student affairs Ga. State U., Atlanta, 1971-76; varied mgmt. positions So. Bell, Atlanta, 1976-84; dist. mgr. AT&T, Atlanta, 1984-96. Cons. in field; bd. advisors Riverside Bank, 1998-99. Bd. dirs., chmn. United Way, Cobb County, Ga., 1991, bd. dirs. Girls Inc., Cobb County; appointee Ga. Clean and Beautiful Commn., Atlanta, 1984-88; mem. Leadership Cobb, 1988—, mem. governing bd., 1993—, co-chair, 1997-98; cert. Stephen (lay) min. Episc. Ch., 1991—; mem. alumni bd. dirs. Bowling Green State U., 1999. Named Cobb County Ga. Woman of Yr. in Bus., Marietta (Ga.) Girls Club, 1984, Outstanding Young Profl., Washington, D.C. Bus. Exch., Outstanding Sr. Woman, Bowling Green State U., 1970, Outstanding Freshman Woman, 1967, recipient Disting. Svc. award, 1970; named one of Outstanding Young Women of Am., 1971, 80. Mem. Omicron Delta Kappa, Delta Sigma Theta (1st v.p. local chpt. 1986-88, nat. exec. dir. 1988-90, exec. bd. 2000--). Avocations: classical piano, writing non fiction. Home: 1152 Clarendon Dr Marietta GA 30068-2161 E-mail: thehrgroup@mindspring.com.

SMITH, BILL, city manager; b. NYC, June 24, 1940; s. Harry John and Catharine Marie (Wheeler) S.; m. Judith Ann Carroll, Mar. 18, 1961; children: Shawn, Kevin, Susan, Kurt, Eric. BA, Iona Coll., 1962; MS, USN Postgrad. Sch., 1971; MPA, Golden Gate U., 1982. Credentialed city mgr. ICMA, credentialed spl. dist. mgr. Calif. Spl. Dist. Assn. Adminstrv. analyst City of Monterey (Calif.), 1982-84; city adminstr. City of Sonora (Calif.), 1984-86; asst. city mgr. City of Monterey, 1986-90; city mgr. City of Manhattan Beach (Calif.), 1990-94, City of Westminster, Calif., 1994-97; gen. mgr. Ventura (Calif.) Regional Sanitation Dist., 1997—. Instr. USN Postgrad. Sch., Monterey, 1979-82; adj. prof. Golden Gate U., San Francisco, 1984-90. Contbr. articles to profl. jours. Bd. dirs. Monterey County AIDS Project, 1987-90. Lt. col. USMC, 1962-82. Decorated Silver Star, Bronze Star, PurpleHeart, Joint Svc. Commendation medal. Mem. Am. Soc. Pub. Adminstrn. (chpt. pres. 1983-84),Internat. City Mgrs. Assn., Retired Officers Assn., Disabled Am. Vets., VFW, Am. Legion. Home: 261 Cherry Hills Ct Thousand Oaks CA 91320-4171 Office: Ventura Regional Sanitation Dist 1001 Partridge Dr Ste 150 Ventura CA 93003-0704 E-mail: judy_billy@msn.com.

SMITH, BILL, advertising and marketing executive; V.p. advt. and mktg. Meijer, Inc., Grand Rapids, Mich., 1987—. Office: Meijer Inc 2929 Walker Ave NW Grand Rapids MI 49544-9428

SMITH, BOB, lawyer, state senator, educator; b. Scranton, Pa., Mar. 25, 1947; s. Philip and Ruth (Delmar) S.; m. Ellen Theresa Foster; children: Karen Elizabeth, Lisa. BA in History, U. Scranton, 1969, MS in Chemistry, 1970; MS in Environ. Sci., Rutgers U., 1973; JD, Seton Hall U., 1981. Bar: N.J. 1981. Sci. tchr. Lourdesmont H.S., Clark Summit, Pa., 1968-70; environ. health sci. curriculum coord. Middlesex County Coll., Edison, N.J., 1972-73, adminstrv. asst. to dean sci., 1974-77, instr., 1970-74, asst. prof., 1974-76, assoc. prof., 1976-79, prof. chemistry and environ. sci., 1979-86; law clk. N.J. Dept. Environ. Protection, Trenton, 1980; prin., pvt. practice law Bob Smith and Assocs., Piscataway, N.J., 1981—. Prosecutor East Brunswick, 1997—, South Brunswick, 1998—. Contbg. author Jour. Air Pollution Control Assn., 1976, Environ. Health Sci., 1975; co-editor: New Jersey State Wastewater Treatment Operations Manual, 1979. Mayor of Piscataway Twp., 1981-86; N.J. assemblyman N.J. 17th Legis. Dist., 1986-2001, mem. appropriations com. and environ. quality com., assembly select com. on ocean pollution, 1988, assembly energy and hazardous waste com. policy and rules, 1994; mem. N.J. State Senate, 2002—, chmn. environ. com., 2004—, mem. jud. com. and environment com.; parliamentarian Assembly Dem. Caucus, 1988-90, chmn. task force on environment, 1987; chmn. Piscataway Dem. Orgn., 1981-90; counsel N.J. State Dem. Platform Com., 1987, 89; chmn. Middlesex County Dem. Orgn., 1991-92; Assembly Dem. Dept. Minority Leader, 1993-95; councilman-at-large Piscataway Twp., 1977-80, pres. coun., 1979, v.p., 1978; mem. Middlesex County Transp. Coordinating Com., 1980-86; chmn. Piscataway Planning Bd, 1981-86, sec., 1975, chmn., 1976; bd. dirs. N.J. Conf. Mayors, 1984-86; mem. tech. adv. com. air pollution Middlesex County Planning Bd., 1973-74; mem. Greenbrook Basin com. Area 208 Mgmt. Planning Program, 1975-76; mem. commr.'s adv. com. N.J. Dept. Environ. Protection, 1972-86. Recipient Disting. Citizen award Piscataway Jewish Congregation B'nai Shalom, 1982; named Legis. of Yr. Eden Inst., N.J. State VFW, 1998, Environ. Legislator of Yr., N.J. Environ. Fedn., 1990; U. Scranton Presdl. scholar, 1965-69. Mem. Middlesex County Bar Assn. Roman Catholic. Office: 216 Stelton Rd B-1 Piscataway NJ 08854-3284 also: 216 Stelton Rd E-5 Piscataway NJ 08854-2600

SMITH, BONNIE GENE, historian, educator; b. Bridgeport, Conn. d. William Wallace and Harriet Amanda (Howard) Sullivan; m. Donald R. Kelley, June 30, 1979; children: Patrick W., Patience H.; 1 stepchild, John R. Kelley. AB, Smith Coll., 1962; PhD, U. Rochester, 1976. Asst. prof. history U. Wis.-Parkside, Racine, 1977-81; from asst. to full prof. U. Rochester, 1981-90; prof. history Rutgers U., New Brunswick, NJ, 1990—, dir. Inst. Rsch. Women, 1998—2001, bd. govs., disting. prof., 2002—. Dir. Susan B. Anthony Ctr. U. Rochester, 1988-90; chair advanced placement com. Coll. Bd./Educational Testing Service, N.Y.C. and Princeton, 1988-94; vis. prof. history U. Calif., Irvine, 1984, Ecole des Hautes Etudes, Paris, 1993-94, U. Bielefeld, Germany, 1993, Princeton U., 1995, 98. Author: Ladies of the Leisure Class, 1981, Confessions of a Concierge, 1985, Changing Lives: Women in European History, 1989, Gender of History, 1998, Imperialism, 2000, Women in Postwar Europe, 2000, Global Feminisms Since 1945, 2000; co-author: What is Property, 1994, Challenge of the West, 1995, Making of the West: Peoples and Cultures, 2001; co-editor: History and the Texture of Modern Life, 2001; gen. editor (book series) Women's and Gender History in Global Perspective, Am. Hist. Assn., 1996—, Gendering Disabiliy, 2004, Oxford World History; contbr. articles to profl. jours. Fellow Am. Coun. Learned Socs., N.Y., 1979-80, 84-85, Nat. Humanities Ctr., N.C., 1984, Shelby Cullom Davis Ctr., Princeton U., 1992-93, John Simon Guggenheim Found., N.Y., 1992-93. Mem. Am. Hist. Assn., Soc. for French Hist. Studies (bd. editors 1986-89, William Koren Jr. award 1997). Office: Rutgers Univ Dept History 16 Seminary Pl New Brunswick NJ 08901-1108

SMITH, BRADFORD LEE, information technology executive; m. Kathy Surace-Smith; 2 children. AB. summa cum laude, Princeton U., 1981; JD, Columbia U., 1985; student, Grad. Inst. Internat. Studies, Geneva, Switzerland. Former ptnr. Covington & Burling, Washington; mgr. European Law & Corp. Affairs group, Paris, 1993—96; dep. gen. counsel for worldwide sales Microsoft, Redmond, Wash., 1996—2001, sr. v.p., gen. counsel for law and corp. affairs, 2001—. Contbr. articles. Office: Microsoft One Microsoft Way Redmond WA 98052-6399*

SMITH, BRADLEY E. anesthesiologist; b. Cedar Vale, Kans., Jan. 4, 1933; MD, U. Okla., 1957. Diplomate Am. Bd. Anesthesiologists. Resident U.S. Naval Hosp., NYC, 1957-60; fellow Columbia Presbyn. Hosp., NYC, 1960—61; faculty Yale U., 1962-63, U. Miami, 1963-69; chmn., prof. dept. anesthesiology Vanderbilt U., Nashville, 1969-93, prof., 1993—2004, prof. emeritus, 2004—. Mem.: AMA, ACOG (assoc.), Am. Soc. Anesthesiologists. Office: Vandy Med Ctr Rm 209 Oxford House Nashville TN 37232-4125

SMITH, BRADLEY WILLIAM, criminal justice educator; s. Freddy C. and Darleen L. Smith; m. Sheryl Hansen Smith, Mar. 26, 1969. BS, Ea. Mich. U., 1993; MS, U. of Cin., 1995, PhD, 1999. Asst. prof. of criminal justice Wayne State U., Detroit, 1999—. Asst. editor Policing: An Internat. Jour., Cin., 1997—99. Contbr. articles and reports to scholarly jours. Recipient Grad. Rsch. fellowship, Nat. Inst. of Justice, 1998—99. Mem.: Midwestern Criminal Justice Soc., Acad. of Criminal Justice Scis., Am. Soc. of Criminology. Office: Wayne State Univ 2305 Faculty/Adminstrv Bldg Detroit MI 48202 E-mail: ag3416@wayne.edu.

SMITH, BRADLEY YOULE, lawyer; b. N.Y.C., Feb. 11, 1948; s. Bradley and Christine (Brown) S.; m. Anne Barre, Dec. 31, 1986; children: Evelyn McLaren, Andrew Robert, Lauren Barre, Timothy James, Lynden Eleanor, Christina McLaren. BA in History cum laude, Yale U., 1970; JD, NYU, 1974. Bar: N.Y. 1975, U.S. Dist. Ct. (so. dist.) N.Y. 1975, U.S. Ct. Appeals (2d cir.) 1975. With Davis Polk & Wardwell, N.Y.C., 1974—, ptnr., 1980—. Trustee Royal Coll. Surgeons Found., Inc. Mem. ABA (chmn. subcom. secured transactions 1983-87, moderator and panelist com. banking law and uniform comml. code), Am. Law Inst., N.Y. State Bar Assn. (mem. banking law com.). Office: Davis Polk & Wardwell 450 Lexington Ave New York NY 10017-3982 E-mail: bradley.smith@dpw.com.

SMITH, BRANSON M. computer technology company executive; BSc in Bus. Adminstrn., U. Ariz. Prin. Southwest Automation; from v.p. distbn. and sr. v.p. fulfillment svcs. Insight Direct USA, Inc. to pres. Insight Enterprises, Inc., Tempe, Ariz., 1992—2001, pres., 2001—. Office: Insight Enterprises Inc 1305 W Auto Drive Tempe AZ 85284

SMITH, BRIAN, lawyer; V.p., gen. counsel The Southland Corp., Dallas, 1992-97, sr. v.p. gen. counsel, 1997—. Office: The Southland Corporation PO Box 711 2711 N Haskell Ave Ste B10 Dallas TX 75204-2946

SMITH, BRIAN DAVID, lawyer, educator; b. Fayetteville, Ark., Oct. 29, 1953; s. Samuel Charles and Janelle (McCaskill) S.; children: Garrett Walker, Brian Austin, Marshall David; m. Teri Hill Smith. JD, La. State U., 1977. Bar: La. 1978, U.S. Dist. Ct. (we. dist.) La. 1979, U.S. Tax Ct. 1980, U.S. Ct. Appeals (5th cir.) 1980, U.S. Supreme Ct. 1990, Tex. 1993. Law clk. to presiding justice 1st Jud. Cir. Ct. La., Shreveport, La., 1978—79; assoc. Nelson, Hammons & Johnson, Shreveport, 1979—84, Lunn, Irion, Johnson, Salley & Carlisle, Shreveport, 1984—90, Ungarino & Eckert, Shreveport, 1990—. Instr. legal asst. cirriculum La. State U., Shreveport, 1984-87. Bd. dirs. YMCA of Shreveport-Bossier City, 1996-98. Mem. La. Bar Assn., La. Assn. Def. Counsel, State Bar Tex., Mensa, Shreveport Country Club. Methodist. Avocations: golf, running, shooting. Home: 5706 Lake Side Dr Bossier City LA 71111-5508 Office: Ungarino & Eckert 831 Kings Highway Ste 201 Shreveport LA 71104

SMITH, BRIAN RICHARD, hematologist, oncologist, pathologist; b. Glen Cove, N.Y., May 7, 1952; s. Frank C. and Gloria R. S.; m. Keiren Donovan, Apr. 17, 1993. AB in Chemistry summa cum laude, Princeton U., 1972; MD, Harvard U., 1976; MA (hon.), Yale U., 1997. Diplomate Am. Bd. Internal Medicine, HEmatology and Med. Oncology, Am. Bd. Pathology Hematopathology. Resident/fellow Harvard U., Brigham and Women's Hosp., 1976-80; instr. medicine Harvard Med. Sch., 1981—84; assoc. physician Brigham & Women's Hosp., Children's Hosp., Dana-Farber Cancer Ins, Boston, 1981-88; asst. prof. medicine Harvard Med. Sch., 1985-88; assoc. prof. medicine, lab. medicine & pediatrics sch. med. Yale U., New Haven, 1988-96, prof. medicine, lab medicine & pediatrics, 1996—, dir. immunohematology; vice chmn. dept. lab. medicine Yale Med. Sch.-Yale New Haven Hosp., 1997—; DeCamp lectr. biomed. ethics Princeton U., NJ, 1992. Contbr. over 140 articles to med. publs. Trustee Richard D. Frisbee III Found.; chair study sect. Am. Heart Assn. Recipient George A. Howe prize Princeton U., 1976; Am. Cancer Soc. fellow, 1981-84, Leukemia Soc. fellow, 1982-88; Leukemia Soc. Am. scholar, 1989, Stohlman scholar, 1993, Nat. Blood Found. scholar, 1996. Fellow ACP, Coll. Am. Pathologists; mem. NIH (recombinant DNA adv. com. 1992-97), Acad. Clin. Lab. Physicians and Scientists (exec. coun. 2000—), Phi Beta Kappa, Sigma Xi, Alpha Omega Alpha. Roman Catholic. Office: Yale U Sch Med PO Box 208035 333 Cedar St New Haven CT 06520-8035

SMITH, BRIAN WILLIAM, lawyer, former government official; b. N.Y.C., Feb. 3, 1947; s. William Francis and Dorothy Edwina (Vogel) S.; m. Donna Jean Holverson, Apr. 24, 1976; children: Mark Holverson, Lauren Elizabeth. BA, St. John's U., N.Y.C., 1968, JD, 1971; MS, Columbia U., 1981. Bar: N.Y. 1972, D.C. 1975, U.S. Dist. Ct. (ea. and so. dists.) N.Y. 1975, U.S. Supreme Ct. 1976, U.S. Dist. Ct. D.C. 1986. Atty. Am. Express Co., N.Y.C., 1970-73, CIT Fin. Corp., N.Y.C., 1973-74; assoc. counsel, mng. atty. Interbank Card Assn. (named changed to Master Card Internat., Inc.), N.Y.C., 1974-75, sr. v.p., corp. sec., gen. counsel, 1975-82; chief counsel Compt. of Currency, Washington, 1982-84; ptnr. Stroock & Stroock & Lavan, Washington, 1984-92, mng. ptnr., 1986-92; ptnr. Mayer, Brown, Rowe & Maw, LLP, Washington and N.Y.C., 1992—2004, Latham & Watkins LLP, Washington, 2004—. Lectr. fin. industry. Editor: E-Commerce, 2003, Financial Products and Services, 2004. Capt. USAR, 1970—78. Mem. ABA, N.Y. State Bar Assn., D.C. Bar Assn., Assn. Bar City N.Y., Fed. Bar Assn., N.Y. Athletic Club, Met. Club (N.Y.), Met. Club (Washington). Home: 35 W Lenox St Chevy Chase MD 20815-4208 Office: Latham & Watkins LLP 555 11th St NW Washington DC 20004-1304 Office Phone: 202-637-2288.

SMITH, BRUCE, professional football player; b. Norfolk, Va., June 18, 1963; Student, Va. Tech. U. Defensive end Buffalo Bills, 1985-99, Washington Redskins, 1999—. Player Super Bowl XXV, 1990, XXVI, 1991, XXVII, 1992, XXVIII, 1993. Recipient Outland trophy, 1984; named to Pro-Bowl, 1987-90, 92, 93, 95, 96, Sporting News All-Pro team, 1987-88, 90, 92-95. Office: Washington Redskins 21300 Redskin Park Dr Ashburn VA 20147-6100

SMITH, BRUCE ALFRED, oil industry executive; b. Coffeyville, Kans., Oct. 12, 1943; s. George Alfred and Isabel (Andrews) S.; m. Cynthia Denton Doughat, Aug. 7, 1969 (div. Jan. 1987); children: Denton Todd, Bruce Chandler, John Paul, Joseph Willimas, Charles Pinson Smith; m. Gail Hutchison, Nov. 10, 1990. BA, Westminster Coll., 1965; MBA, U. Kans., 1967; postgrad., U. Chgo., 1971. With Ford Motor Co., Dearborn, Mich., 1967-69; banking officer met. divsn. Continental Ill. Nat. Bank and Trust Co. Chgo., Chgo., 1971-73, 2nd v.p. multinat. divsn., 1973-75, v.p. mining divsn., 1975-77, v.p., sect. mgr. Chgo. and London, 1977-80, v.p., mgr. internat. energy divsn. Chgo., 1980-82, v.p., mgr. S.W. group, comml. banking Houston, 1983-86; corp. v.p., treas. Valero Energy Corp. and Valero Natural Gas Ptnrs., San Antonio, 1986-92; v.p. Tesoro Petroleum Corp., San Antonio, 1992-93, CFO, 1992-95, exec. v.p., 1993-95, exec. v.p. Tesoro Exploration and Prodn. Co., 1993-95, exec. v.p., COO, dir., 1995, pres., CEO, 1995-96, chmn., CEO, 1996—. Bd. dirs. San Antonio Sports Found. With U.S. Army, 1969-71. Mem. Fin. Execs. Inst. (past pres. San Antonio chpt.). Home: 400 Elizabeth Rd San Antonio TX 78209-5935 Office: Tesoro Petroleum Corp 300 Concord Plaza Dr San Antonio TX 78216-6903

SMITH, BRUCE I. state legislator; b. Harrisburg, Pa., Feb. 19, 1934; s. Bruce I. and Margaret M. (Zerbe) S.; m. Patricia A. Ninkovich; children: Rhonda J., Renee N. BA, Elizabethtown Coll., 1956; MEd, Pa. State U., 1961. Chmn. Newberry Twp. (Pa.) Recreation Bd., 1971-77, Newberry Twp. Bd. Supr., 1978-83; mem. Pa. Ho. of Reps., Harrisburg, 1980—. Chmn. game and fisheries com., 1995—, agrl. and rural affairs com., 1993-94; chmn. Ctrl. Pa. Rep. Caucus, 1995—. Rep. committeeman, 1976-80; active Newberry Twp. Planning Commn., 1978-80; tchr. Cedar Cliff H.S., West Shore. Sgt. USAR, 1958-64. Named Conservation Legislator of Yr., York County, Pa., 1987, 1994—98, Conservationist of Yr., York County, 1999, Pa., 2001, Legislator of Yr., Pa. Trappers Assn., 2001, Sportmens Legislator of Yr., Pa. Fedn. Sportsmen's Clubs, 2002. Mem. Shrine Club, Pinchot Par Isaac Walton League (charter). Address: Fairview Indsl Pk 540B Industrial Dr Lewisberry PA 17339-9534 Office Phone: 717-783-8783.

SMITH, BRUCE R. English language educator; b. Jackson, Miss., Mar. 21, 1946; Student, U. Birmingham, England, 1966-67; BA magna cum laude in English with honors, Tulane U., 1968; MA, U. Rochester, 1971, PhD with distinction, 1973. From asst. prof. to assoc. prof. English Georgetown U., Washington, 1972-87, prof. English, 1987—2003, U. So. Calif., 2003—04, Coll. Disting. prof. English, 2004—; faculty Bread Loaf Sch. English, Middlebury Coll., 1994—. Seminar dir. Folger Inst., 1994, 98-99. Author: Ancient Scripts and Modern Experience on the English Stage 1500-1700, 1988, Homosexual Desire in Shakespeare's England: A Cultural Poetics, 1991, Roasting the Swan of Avon: Shakespeare's Redoubtable Enemies and Dubious Friends, 1994, The Acoustic World of Early Modern England, 1999, Shakespeare and Masculinity, 2000; editor: Shakespeare, Twelfth Night: Text and Contexts, 2001; editl. bd. Shakespeare Quar., 1995—, PMLA, 2000-02, Studies in English Lit., 2003—; contbr. chpts. to books, articles to profl. jours. Summer grantee Georgetown U. Acad. Rsch., 1976, 84, 87, 89, 91, 92, 99; grantee Intercultural Curriculum Devel., 1982, Agecroft Assn., 1991; Mellon fellow Huntington Libr., 1996, jr. fellow Folger Inst., 1979, 85, fellow, 1990, 96, ACLS fellow, 1979-80, NEH fellow, 1987-88, 99, Va. Found. Humanites fellow, 1989, Internat. Globe fellow Shakespeare's Globe, London, 1997, Guggenheim fellow, 2001-02; recipient Roland Bainton pize for lit. 16th Century Studies Assn., 2000, Disting. Scholar award U. Rochester, 2002. Mem. MLA, Soc. Study Early Modern Women, Renaissance Soc. Am., Shakespeare Assn. Am. (pres. 1994-95), Com. for Lesbian and Gay History. Office: U So Calif Dept English Taper Hall 420 Los Angeles CA 90089-0354

SMITH, C. D. civil engineering educator; Cons. hydraulic engr., prof. civil engrng. U. Sask., Saskatoon, Can., to 1991, prof. emeritus civil engrng., cons. hydraulic engr., 1991—. Author: two books; contbr. to over 70 profl. jours. Recipient C. Dagenais award Can. Soc. Civil Engring., 1986, T.C. Keefer medal, 1991, Engring. Achievement Silver medal Profl. Engrs. of Sask., 1991,Engr. of Yr., Saskatoon Engring. Soc., 1993, Julian Smith medal Engring. Inst. Can., 2000. Mem. Can. Soc. Civil Engring. (past pres.). Home: 120 7th St E Saskatoon SK Canada S7H 0W8 E-mail: cds.hyd.eng@shaw.ca.

SMITH, C. GRANT, scriptwriter, film producer; b. Saint Louis, Mar. 1, 1967; s. Lynwood M. and Peggy M. Smith; m. Hannah King, June 17, 1971; 1 child, Samuel Owen; 1 child, Caroline K. Student in Comm./Writing, Webster U., 1995—2000; Cert., Am. Film Inst., L.A., 1997—98. Cert. Acctg., Sanford Brown Bus. Coll., 1988. Merchant developer Maritz, Inc., Fenton, Mo., 1995—97; flight attendant coord. TWA, Saint Louis, 1999—2001; ip law, info. tech. support Pfizer, Inc., Saint Louis, 2001—; co-owner BlackSmith Pictures, Inc. Co-writer/prodr.: screenplay Hunting Ground, co-author: screenplay Jersey Shore (finalist L.A. Screenwriting Expo., 2003), Hawkins. Democrat. Achievements include development of screenwriting application through MS Office 2000/Access. Home: 5446 Murdoch Ave Saint Louis MO 63109 Office Phone: 314-713-6872. Personal E-mail: cgsgrant@sbcglobal.net.

SMITH, C. LEMOYNE, publishing company executive; b. Atkins, Ark., Sept. 15, 1934; s. Cecil Garland and Salena Bell (Wilson) S.; m. Selma Jean Tucker, May 23, 1964; 1 child, Jennifer Lee BS, Ark. Tech. U., 1956; M.Ed., U. Ark., 1958. Tchr. pub. schs., Little Rock, 1956-58; instr. bus. adminstrn. Ark. Tech. U., Russellville, 1958-60; sales rep. South-Western Pub. Co., Cin., 1960-67, editorial staff, 1967-82, pres., chief exec. officer, 1982-90, chmn., 1990-91, ret., 1991. Bd. dirs. Cin. Council on World Affairs, 1983-95. Mem. Nat. Bus. Edn. Assn., Delta Pi Epsilon Republican. Presbyterian. Avocations: bridge, travel, golf. Office: South-Western Pub Co 5191 Natorp Blvd Mason OH 45040-7980

SMITH, C. THOMAS, JR., hospital administrator; b. Little Rock, Apr. 10, 1938; s. Carl Thomas and Mary Elizabeth (Singleton) S.; m. Martha Nell Fincher, June 24, 1961; children: Laura, Adam. BA, Baylor U., 1960; MBA, U. Chgo., 1962; DSc (hon.), U. Bridgeport, 1986; DHL (hon.), Quinnipiac Coll., 1988. Asst. to chmn. dept. psychology Baylor U., Waco, Tex., 1959-60; adminstrv. extern Ark. Bapt. Med. Ctr., Little Rock, summer 1958, acting personnel dir., summer 1960; adminstrv. extern Bapt. Meml. Hosp., Memphis, summer 1959, adminstrv. resident, 1961-62, adminstrv. asst., 1962-63, adminstrv. assoc., 1963-67; assoc. dir. U. Minn. Hosp., Mpls., 1967-71; coordinator health scis. planning U. Minn., Mpls., 1969-71; assoc. exec. dir. Henry Ford. Hosp., Detroit, 1971-74, v.p., exec. dir., 1974-77, trustee, 1974-77; pres. Yale-New Haven Hosp., 1977-91, trustee, 1978-91; pres. Yale-New Haven Health Svcs. Corp., 1983-91, also bd. dirs.; pres., CEO VHA Inc., Irving, Tex., 1991—2003. Lectr. health care adminstrn. U. Minn., 1969-71; lectr. dept. epidemiology and pub. health Sch. Medicine, Yale U., 1977-91; lectr. Sch. Orgn. and Mgmt., Yale U., 1979-91; preceptor grad. programs in hosp. and health care adminstrn. Yale U., 1977-91; speaker in field; trustee Nat. Com. Quality Health Care, 1978-98, Hosp. Rsch and Ednl. Trust, 1987-94; bd. dirs. Hosp. Rsch. and Devel. Inc., 1983-89; bd. dirs., exec. com. Vol. Hosps. Am., Inc., 1983—; U.S. del. King Edward's Hosp. Fund for London, 1983-88; mem. coun. on health care tech. Inst. Medicine, NAS, 1986-88; bd. dirs. Vol. Hosps. Am. of So. New Eng., 1985-91, Vol. Hosps. Am. Enterprises, 1988-91; bd. dirs. Genetech, Inc., 1986-99, New Haven Savs. Bank, 1978-91, others. Mem. editorial bds. Jour. Med. Edn., 1974-78, Health Care Mgmt. Rev., 1982-88, Health Services Research, 1984-88 Bd. dirs. United Way Greater New Haven, 1984-89, campaign chmn., 1986; bd. dirs. Sci. Pk. Devel. Corp., New Haven, 1983-91; trustee U. Bridgeport, 1987-89. Mem. Am. Hosp. Assn. (trustee 1987-92, chmn. 1991), Assn. Am. Med. Colls. (adminstrv. bd. council teaching hosps. 1982-86, chmn. 1986), Am. Coll. Healthcare Execs., Conn. Hosp. Assn. (trustee 1982-86). Presbyterian. Home: 17703 Cedar Creek Canyon Dr Dallas TX 75252-4969 Office: VHA Inc 220 Las Colinas Blvd E Irving TX 75039-5500

SMITH, CARL DEAN, JR., rehabilitation services professional, young adult advocate; b. Denver, Sept. 12, 1949; m. Patricia Ann O'Donnell, Aug. 18, 1973; children: Amanda Paige, Grant Carlton. BA, Springfield Coll., 1972; postgrad., Goethe Inst., Munich, 1972-73, Gordon Conwell Theol. Sem., Hamilton, Mass., 1986-88; MEd, Cambridge Coll., 1993. Bus. analyst Dun & Bradstreet, Inc., Boston, 1974-77; Western U.S. credit mgr. Salomon/N.Am., Inc., Peabody, Mass., 1977-81; regional credit mgr. Stride Rite Corp., Cambridge, Mass., 1981-82; sales mgr., franchisee V.R. Bus. Brokers of Chestnut Hill, Mass., 1982-85; pres. C.D. Smith Assocs., Wakefield, Mass., 1985-90; cons. Swampscott, 1990-94; crisis clinician Ctr. for Mental Health, Lexington, Mass., 1994-97; therapist HRI Counseling, Woburn, Mass., 1994-97, The Salvation Army Boston Adult Rehab. Ctr., Saugus, Mass., 1997—2004; cons., dir. Take It To The Next Level Ministries, Rowley, Mass., 2004—, Ponte Vedra Beach, Fla., 2004—. Adv. bd. The Salvation Army, Boston, 2004—. Class agt. Brewster Acad., 1968-96; asst. basketball coach Nth Shore C.C., Danvers, Mass., 1997-2000; mem. Park St. Ch., Boston Common, Mass. Mem.: Fellowship Cos. Christ (coord. New Eng. chpt. 1986—90). Avocations: golf, tennis. Home and Office: 314 Forest Ave Swampscott MA 01907-2109

SMITH, CARL MICHAEL, federal agency administrator, lawyer; b. Oklahoma City, Oct. 11, 1944; s. Carl W. Jr. and Nina (Furr) S.; m. Sharon Kay Lewis, June 5, 1971. BA, U. Okla., 1966, JD, 1969. Bar: Okla. 1969, U.S. Dist. Ct. (we., no. and ea. dists.) Okla. 1971, U.S. Ct. Appeals (10th cir.) 1976, U.S. Supreme Ct. 1976. Mem. firm Lawrence, Smith & Harmon, Oklahoma City, 1977-80; pres. Red Rock Exploration, Inc., Oklahoma City, 1980-83; mem. firm Lawrence & Ellis, P.A., Oklahoma City, 1983—; asst. secy. fossil energy U.S. Dept. Energy, Washington, 2002—. Mem. Blue Ribbon Commn. on Natural Gas, Oklahoma City, 1982; chmn. Okla. Polit. Action Com., Oklahoma City, 1986-90; mem. Okla. Legis. Interim Task Force on Environ. Regulation, Oklahoma City, 1991-92; sec. Okla. Energy Resources Bd., 1992-94; mem. Okla. Sec. of Energy, 1995—. Capt. U.S. Army, 1969-71, Vietnam. Mem. Okla. Ind. Petroleum Assn. (pres. 1994-95). Office: US Dept Energy Fossil Energy 1000 Independence Ave SW Washington DC 20585-0301

SMITH, CAROL ANN, academic administrator; b. Waterbury, Conn., Dec. 22, 1941; d. Prosper Mark and Emma Edna (Dumschott) Zailskas; m. Gordon B. Jobe; children from previous marriage: Amy, Christian, Meghan. BSN, Boston Coll., 1965; MSN, Boston U., 1971, PhD in Adminstrn., 1977. Chmn. grad. nursing dept. Boston Coll. Sch. Nursing, 1973—78; coord. Harvard Med. Sch. program Boston Coll., 1975—78; dir. baccalaureate nursing program Coll. of Our Lady of Elms, 1978—80; dean sch. nursing Duquesne U., 1980—83, acting acad. v.p., 1983—85; vis. v.p. for acad. affairs Carnegie-Mellon U., 1985—86; acad. v.p. Marshall U., Huntington, W.Va., 1985—89; pres. Mater Dei Coll., Ogdensburg, NY, 1989—. Field reader US Dept. Edn., 1990—91. Exec. com. Sisters of St. Joseph Consortium, 1990—; bd. dirs. Commn. Ind. Colls. and Univs., 1990—, Boys and Girls Club, A. Barton Hepburn Hosp. Found. Mem.: LWV, St. Lawrence C. of C. (bd. dirs.), Boston Coll. Club, Rotary, Delta Gamma Kappa, Phi Delta Kappa, Sigma Theta Tau, Delta Kappa Gamma. Roman Catholic. Office: Mater Dei College PO Box 794 Ogdensburg NY 13669-0794

SMITH, CAROL E. judge; b. Balt., July 30, 1946; 1 child, Ellen Elizabeth. BA, Coll. Notre Dame Md., 1970; JD, Cath. U. Am., 1975. Staff atty. domestic law unit, staff atty. and chief atty. housing law unit, chief atty. mental health law project Legal Aid Bur. Inc., 1975—80; with Matricciani & Smith, 1980—83; pvt. practice., 1983—85; assoc. judge Dist. Ct. Md., 1984—93, Cir. Ct. Balt. City, 1993—. Trustee Bryn Mawr Sch., 1997—; mem. adv. bd. Mercy Med. Ctr., Women's Ctr. for Health and Medicine, 1993—96, Girl Scouts Beyond Bars, 1993—97; coach Balt. City Dept. of Recreation and Parks, North Harford Recreation Ctr. Basketball Program, 1992—93. Recipient Bd. Dirs. award, Girl Scouts of Cen. Md., 1994. Mem.: Nat. Assn. Women Judges (pres. Md. chpt. 1993—95, chair women in prison task force 1995—97). Office: 111 N Calvert St Baltimore MD 21202

SMITH, CAROLE DIANNE, retired lawyer, editor, writer, product developer; b. Seattle, June 12, 1945; d. Glaude Francis and Elaine Claire (Finkenstein) S.; m. Stephen Bruce Presser, June 18, 1968 (div. June 1987); children: David Carter, Elisabeth Catherine. AB cum laude, Harvard U., Radcliffe Coll., 1968; JD, Georgetown U., 1974. Bar: Pa. 1974. Law clk. Hon. Judith Jamison, Phila., 1974—75; assoc. Gratz, Tate, Spiegel, Ervin & Ruthrouff, Phila., 1975—76; freelance editor, writer Evanston, Ill., 1983—87; editor Ill. Inst. Tech., Chgo., 1987—88; mng. editor LawLetters, Inc., Chgo., 1988—89; editor ABA, Chgo., 1989—95; product devel. dir. Gt. Lakes divsn. Lawyers Coop. Pub., Deerfield, Ill., 1995—96; product devel. mgr. Midwest Market Ctr. West Group, Deerfield, Ill., 1996—97; mgr acquisitions, bus. and fin. group CCH, Inc., Riverwoods, Ill., 1997—2002; ret. Author Jour. of Legal Medicine, 1975, Selling and the Law: Advertising and Promotion, 1987; (under pseudonym Sarah Toast) 79 children's books and stories, 1994-2002; editor The Brief, 1990-95, Criminal Justice, 1989-90, 92-95 (Gen. Excellence award Soc. Nat. Assn. Pubs. 1990, Feature Article award-bronze Soc. Nat. Assn. Pubs. 1994), Franchise Law Jour., 1995; mem. editl. bd. The Brief, 1995-2000. Dir. Radcliffe Club of Chgo., 1990-93; mem. parents coun. Latin Sch. Chgo., 1995-96; trustee Winnetka-Northfield Libr., 2003—; mem. Winnetka Plan Commn.2003—, Winnetka Forestry Commn., 2004—. Mem. ABA (editl. bd., tort trial and ins. practice sect. 1995-2000, mem. publs. editl. bd., 2002—).

SMITH, CARSON CLAY, business executive; b. Rushville, Ind., June 12, 1955; s. Merritt W. and Sally Smith; m. Patricia Jane Dice, Mar. 31, 2001; children: Sara Kathryn, Alexander, Elizabeth. BA in Religious Studies, Ind. U., 1977. Indsl. sales rep. Exotic Automation & Supply, Indpls., 1995—. Account mgr. Daimler Chrysler, Ford, GM, Subaru Ind. Automotive, Delco Remy Am., Delphi Guide, Visteon, ZF Transmission, Honda Engine and Transmission, Behr Thermal Products. Author: History of the Scottish Society of Indianapolis, Biography of Thomas H. (Tommy) Thompson, the History of the Kirkin' O' the Tartan, The Table Grace of the Scottish Society of Indianapolis, The Biography of Compatriot Clarence A. Cook, Scots and Freeasonry; contbr. articles to populcar mags.; participant in creation and revision Constn. and Bylaws; ofcl. Insignia and Flag Scottish Soc. Ind.; contbr. to AM radio programs. Pres. Kingsway Christian Sch. Bd. Dirs., 1990. Fellow: Soc. Antiquaries of Scotland, Samuel Victor Constant Soc.; mem.: SAR (pres. Indpls. chpt. 1991, 2003—, Patriot medal 1994, Meritorious Svc. medal 1994, Good Citizenship medal 1994), Ind. Soc. SAR (pres. 1993—95), Clan MacPherson (life), Scottish Soc. Indpls. (life; editor The Thistle newsletter 1985—86, 1990—92, pres. 1991—92, 2000—03, charter), Clan Chattan Assn. (life), Coun. of Scottish Clans and Assns., Soc. Colonial Wars (Ind. sec. treas. 2001—03), Scottish Soc. Greater Bloomington, Scottish Soc. of Louisville, Caledonian Soc. of Cincinnati, Ind. U. Alumni Assn. (life), Masons (Master, Royal Arch, Cryptic Rite), Sigma Chi (life; chpt. editor Lambda Larynx newsletter 1974, Outstanding Pledge 1974). Avocations: running, browsing bookstores, attending concerts, Scottish festivals and games. Home: 2207 Van Ness Pl Indianapolis IN 46240-4703 Office: Exotic Automation & Supply 8227 Northwest Blvd Ste 270 Indianapolis IN 46278-1386 Office Phone: 317-319-3712. Personal E-mail: carsonsmith@aol.com.

SMITH, CECE, venture capitalist; b. Washington, Nov. 16, 1944; d. Linn Charles and Grace Inez (Walker) S.; m. John Ford Lacy, Apr. 22, 1978. BBA, U. Mich., 1966; M in Liberal Arts, So. Meth. U., 1974. CPA, Tex. Staff acct. Arthur Young & Co. (CPAs), Boston, 1966-68; staff acct., then asst. to contr. Wyly Corp., Dallas, 1969-72; contr., treas. subs. Univ. Computing Co., Dallas, 1972-74; contr. Steak and Ale Restaurants Am., Inc., Dallas, 1974-76, v.p. fin., 1976-80, exec. v.p., 1980-81, Pearle Health Services, Inc., 1981-84, pres. Primacare divsn., 1984-86; gen. ptnr. Phillips-Smith-Machens Venture Ptnrs., 1986—; pres. Le Sportsac Dallas, Inc., 1981-87. Bd. dirs. Brinker Internat. Inc., Michaels Stores, Inc.; chmn. Fed. Res. Bank Dallas, 1994—96; past v.p., dir. IWF-Dallas; mem. pres. adv. group U. Mich. Former co-chmn. pres.'s rsch. coun. U. Tex. S.W. Med. Ctr. Dallas; former mem. vis. com. U. Mich. Bus. Sch.; exec. bd. So. Meth. U. Cox Sch. Bus.; former v.p., bd. dirs. Jr. Achievement Dallas; past pres. Charter 100; past treas. Dallas Assembly. Mem.: Com. of 200. Home: 3710 Shenandoah St Dallas TX 75205-2121 Office: 5080 Spectrum Dr Ste 805 W Addison TX 75001-4648 Office Phone: 972-387-0725.

SMITH, CECILIA MAY, hospital official; b. Oakland, Calif., Feb. 18, 1933; d. Frederick Arthur and Inez Calista Small; m. Harold Joseph Smith, June 17, 1957 (dec. June 18, 1966); children: Harold Frederick, Estelle Marie. BS, Holy Name Coll., 1956; MS, U. Calif., San Francisco, 1966; postgrad., U. Calif., Berkeley, 1972. RN Calif. Asst. prof. U. Nev., Reno, 1966-69; instr. U. Wash., Seattle, 1972-74; dir. continuing edn. Wash. State Nurses Assn., Seattle, 1974-78; pres., ptnr. World of Continuing Edn., Seattle, 1975-85; continuing edn. specialist U. Calif., San Francisco, 1979-82; asst. adminstr. Cordilleras Mental Health Ctr., Redwood City, Calif., 1984-86, adminstr., 1986-90; dir. psychiat. svcs. St. Luke's Hosp., San Francisco, 1990—. Mem. ANA Nat. Accreditation Bd., Kansas City, 1974-7; sec., workshop leader Nat. Staffing Systems, San Francisco, 1981-82; cons. WHO, New Delhi, 1985. Editor ind. study courses for nurses and nursing home adminstrs., 1975-85; author AIDS ind. study courses, 1984; contbr. articles to Jour. of Continuing Edn. Recipient Marie Durocher scholarship Coll. of Holy Name, 1952, NIMH traineeship U. Calif. San Francisco, 1963, Nursing Rsch. fellowship U. Calif. Berkeley, 1969-71. Mem.: Sigma Theta Tau. Office: St Luke's Hosp 3555 Cesar Chavez San Francisco CA 94110-4403 E-mail: ceciliams33@hotmail.com.

SMITH, CHARLES ANTHONY, business executive; b. Santa Fe, Sept. 16, 1939; s. Frances (Mier) Vigil; m. Paula Ann Thomas, June 26, 1965; 1 child, Charlene Danielle. Student various adminstrv. & law courses. Circulation mgr. Daily Alaska Empire, 1960-63; agt. Mut. of N.Y. Life Ins. Co., Juneau, Alaska, 1964-65; mng. ptnr. Future Investors in Alaska and Cinema Alaska, Juneau, 1961-62; SE Alaska rep. K & L Distbrs., 1966-68; mgr. SE Alaska Alaska Airlines Newspapers, 1969; dep. Alaska Retirement Sys., Juneau, 1970-71;

apptd. dir. hwy. safety, gov.'s hwy. safety rep. Juneau, 1971-83; pres. Valley Svc. Ctr., I Nc., 1984-94; chmn. S.E. Alaska Employee Support of the Guard and Reserve, 1992—; pres. 3-S Corp., 1995—. Apptd. chmn. S.E. Alaska for ESGR, 1995; apptd. Alaska state dir. Selective Svc., 1996—. Author various hwy. safety manuals and plans. Alaska pres. Muscular Dystrophy Assn. Am.; pres. SE Alaska Emergency Med. Svcs. Coun., 1965-72; state dir. Selective Svc., 1996. Served to maj. Army N.G., 1964-88. Named Alaska Safety Man of Yr., 1977. Mem. Am. Assn. Motor Vehicle Adminstrs., Alaska Peace Officers Assn., Nat. Assn. Gov.'s Hwy. Safety Reps., N.G. Assn., Internat. Platform Assn., Elks (Juneau). Roman Catholic. Home: PO Box 32856 Juneau AK 99803-2856

SMITH, CHARLES COURTLAND, JR., lawyer, state legislator; b. Edgewood, Md., Feb. 27, 1946; s. Charles Courtland and Nell Jeanette (Martin) S.; m. Patricia Arlene Cassens, Aug. 31, 1974; children: Brian Courtland, Joel McQuarrie. BA, U. Ga., 1968, JD, 1973. Ptnr. Nichols, Lavigao, Smith & Rice, Conyers, Ga., 1973-74, Smith & Floyd, St. Marys, Ga., 1976—; trial asst. dist. atty. Fulton County Dist. Atty., Atlanta, 1974-76; rep. Ga. Gen. Assembly, Atlanta, 1993—2003, adminstrn. fl. leader, 1999—2003. City atty. City of St. Marys, 1979-81. Chmn. bd. dirs. St. Marys United Meth. Ch., 1983. Fellow Kiwanis Internat.; mem. USN League (life), Am. Numis. Assn., Am. Radio Relay League (life), Camden-Kings Bay Navy League (charter), Camden-Kings Bay C. of C. (charter), St. Marys Kiwanis Club (pres. 1979). Democrat. Avocations: instrument pilot, scuba diving, skiing, amateur radio (extra class lic.), woodturning. Office: Smith & Floyd PO Drawer 766 1815 Osborne Rd Saint Marys GA 31558-9140

SMITH, CHARLES EDWIN, computer science educator; b. Columbia, Mo., Apr. 15, 1950; s. William Walter and Nelletha Pearl (Lavendar) S.; m. Mary L. Davis, July 27, 1991. AA, Edison C.C., Ft. Myers, Fla., 1971; BS, Troy State U., 1979; MA, Webster U., St. Louis, 1989. Adj. instr. Manatee C.C., Venice, Fla., 1989-90, Edison C.C., Punta Gorda, Fla., 1989-92, prof. computer sci., 1992—, Charles O'Neill endowed chair astronomy, 1997-2001. Cons. Charles E. Smith Consulting, North Port, Fla., 1989-91; owner SmithTech Dental Handpiece Repair. Served to maj. USAF, 1975-79, USAFR, 1979-96. Mem. Air Force Assn. Mem. Fla. Assn. C.C.s, Mil. Officers Assn. Am., Am. Legion, USGA. Avocations: reading, fishing, boating, astronomy, golf. Office: Edison C C 26300 Airport Rd Punta Gorda FL 33950-5748

SMITH, CHARLES HADDON, geoscientist, consultant; b. Dartmouth, N.S., Can., Sept. 3, 1926; s. Albion Benson and Dora Pauline (McGill) S.; m. Mary Gertrude Saint, Sept. 5, 1949; children: Charles Douglas, Richard David, Alan Michael, Timothy McGill. B.Sc. and Diploma in Engring, Dalhousie U., Can., 1946, M.Sc. in Geology, 1948; MS, Yale U., 1951, PhD in Econ. Geology, 1952. Instr. Dalhousie U., Halifax, N.S., 1946-48; geologist Cerro de Pasco Copper Corp., Morococha, Peru, 1949, Geol. Survey of Can., Ottawa, Ont., 1952-64, chief petrological scis. div., 1964-67, chief crustal geology div., 1967-68; sci. adviser Sci. Council Can., Ottawa, 1968-70; dir. planning Dept. Energy Mines and Resources, Ottawa, 1970-71, asst. dep. minister sci. and tech., 1971-75, sr. asst. dep. minister, 1975-81; pres. Charles H. Smith Cons., 1982-94. Mem. adv. coun. dept. geology and geophysics Princeton U., 1967-76; sci. advisor Can. Commn. for UNESCO, 1983-89; exec. dir. Can. Nat. Com./World Energy Conf., 1983-90; bd. govs. Can. Inst. Radiation Safety, 1983-86; hon. mem. Energy Coun. Can., 1991—; coord. 150th anniversary Geol. Survey Can., 1990-93. Mem. editl. bd. Am. Jour. Sci., 1967-72, Mineralium Deposita, 1968-83, Jour. Petrology, 1966-70, Econ. Geology, 1966-70; contbr. articles to profl. jours. Fellow Royal Soc. Can. (fgn. sec. 1986-90), Mineral. Soc. Am., Soc. Econ. Geologists (v.p. N.Am. 1968-70), Canadian Acad. Engring.; mem. Can. Inst. Mining and Metallurgy (life mem., v.p. 1982-84), Assn. Profl. Engrs. Ont., Geol. Assn. Can., Can. Geosci. Coun. (pres. 1984), Rotary.

SMITH, CHARLES ISAAC, geology educator; b. Hearne, Tex., Feb. 9, 1931; s. Walter Lee and Nellie Lucille (Clearwater) S.; m. Anita Lou Howell, Aug. 22, 1961; children: Lanita Maylene, James Emmett, Timothy Stephen, Sheila Nell. BS, Baylor U., 1952; MA, La. State U., 1955; PhD, U. Mich., 1966. Geologist Shell Devel. Co., Houston, 1955-60, 62-65; prof. geology U. Mich., Ann Arbor, 1965-77, chmn. dept., 1970-77; prof. geology U. Tex., Arlington, 1977-93, prof. emeritus, 1994—, chmn. dept., 1977-89, cons. geologist, 1993—. Contbr. articles to profl. jours. Home: 3814 Tridens Trl San Angelo TX 76904-7223 Office: Univ Tex Dept Geology Arlington TX 76019-0001

SMITH, CHARLES NATHANIEL, academic administrator; b. Nov. 17, 1953; BS in Psychology, Va. Commonwealth U.; EdD, Va. Polytech. & State U. Dis. spl. svcs., asst. prof. St. Paul's Coll.; dir. spl. svcs., assoc. prof. psychology Gulf Coast C.C.; dir. minority student affairs, spl. asst. to provost George Mason U.; asst. vice provost, dean student devel. Chgo. State U.; v.p. enrollment mgmt. & student affairs Del. State U., assoc. v.p. student affairs and intercollegiate athletics. Office: Del State U Grossley Hall #109 Dover DE 19901 Home: 102 Gardengate Rd Camden Wyoming DE 19934-9648

SMITH, CHARLES OLIVER, engineer; b. Clinton, Mass., May 28, 1920; s. Oliver E. and Flora (Small) S.; m. Mary J. Boyle, Feb. 9, 1946; children: Mary J., Charles M., John P., Susan M., Peter G., Robert A., Katherine M. BS in Mech. Engring., Worcester Poly. Inst., 1941; SM, MIT, 1947, ScD in Metallurgy, 1951. Instr. mech. engring. Worcester Poly. Inst., 1941-43; instr., then asst. prof. Mass. Inst. Tech., 1946-51; research engr. Alcoa Research Lab., 1951-55, Oak Ridge Nat. Lab, 1955-65; prof. engring. U. Detroit, 1965-76, U. Nebr., 1976-81, Rose-Hulman Inst. Tech., 1981-86. Author: Product Liability: Are You Vulnerable?, Nuclear Reactor Materials, Science of Engineering Materials, Introduction to Reliability in Design; also numerous papers on materials, design, product liability, engring. edn. Served with USNR, 1943-46. Recipient St. George award Boy Scouts Am. Fellow ASME (Triodyne Safety award 1992, Machine Design award, 1993), Am. Soc. Engring. Edn. (Fred Merryfield award 1981); mem. AIME, Am. Soc. Metals, Sigma Xi, Tau Beta Pi, Pi Tau Sigma, Phi Kappa Theta. Home: 1717 Homewood Blvd Apt 156 Delray Beach FL 33445-6899

SMITH, CHARLES Z. retired state supreme court justice; b. Lakeland, Fla., Feb. 23, 1927; s. John R. and Eva (Love) S.; m. Eleanor Jane Martinez, Aug. 20, 1955; children: Carlos M., Michael O., Stephen P., Felica L. BS, Temple U., 1952; JD, U. Wash., 1955. Bar: Wash. 1955. Law clk. Wash. Supreme Ct., Olympia, 1955-56; dep. pros. atty., asst. chief criminal div. King County, Seattle, 1956-60; ptnr. Bianchi, Smith & Tobin, Seattle, 1960-61; spl. asst. to atty. gen. criminal div. U.S. Dept. Justice, Washington, 1961-64; judge criminal dept. Seattle Mcpl. Ct., 1965-66; judge Superior Ct. King County, 1966-73; former assoc. dean, prof. law U. Wash., 1973—83; justice Wash. Supreme Ct., Olympia. Mem. adv. bd. NAACP, Seattle Urban League, Wash. State Literacy Coun., Boys Club, Wash. Citizens for Migrant Affairs, Medina Children's Svc., Children's Home Soc. Wash., Seattle Better Bus. Bur., Seattle Foundation, Seattle Symphony Orch., Seattle Opera Assn., Community Svc. Ctr. for Deaf and Hard of Hearing, Seattle U., Seattle Sexual Assault Ctr., Seattle Psychoanalytic Inst., The Little Sch., Linfield Coll., Japanese Am. Citizens League, Kawabe Meml. Hous, Puget Counseling Ctr, Am. Cancer Soc., Hutchinson Cancer Rsch. Ctr., Robert Chinn Found.; pres. Am. Bapt. Chs. U.S.A., 1976-77, U.S. Commn. on Internat. Religious Freedom, 1999-2000. lt. col. ret. USMCR Mem. ABA, Am. Judicature Soc., Washington Bar Assn., Seattle-King County Bar Assn., Order of Coif., Phi Alpha Delta, Alpha Phi Alpha. Mailing: PO Box 146 Olympia WA 98507-0146 Office Phone: 360-273-0964. E-mail: czsmith@usa.net.

SMITH, CHERYL T. pharmaceutical executive, public relations executive; BA, MA, Pa. State U. Systems analyst U.S. Ho. of Reps., Washington, 1975—78; various positions Ernst & Young, Honeywell, Verizon, 1978—85; chief info. officer Keyspan Techs., N.Y.C., 1985—2002; sr. v.p., chief info. officer McKesson Corp., San Francisco, 2002—. Office: McKesson Corp Hdqtrs One Post St San Francisco CA 94104

SMITH, CHESTER, broadcast executive; b. Mar. 29, 1930; s. Louis L. and Effie (Brown) Smith; m. Naomi L. Crenshaw, July 19, 1959 (div. 2002); children: Lauri, Lorna, Roxanne; m. Ann Lesley Huntington, Dec. 2003. Country western performer Capitol Records, TV, Radio, 1947-61, Sta. KLOC, Ceres-Modesto, Calif., 1963-81, Sta. KCBA-TV, Salinas-Monterey, Calif., 1963-81; owner, gen. ptnr. Sta. KCSO-TV, Modesto-Stockton-Sacramento, Calif., 1966-97, Sta. KCVU-TV, Paradise-Chico-Redding, Calif., 1986—, Sta. KBVU-TV, Eureka, Calif., 1990—, KNSO-TV, Merced-Fresno, Calif., 1996—2003, KCSO-LP, Sacramento, 1996—, KRVU-LP, Redding, Calif., 1997—, Univision, Chico, Calif., KMUV-LP, Monterey-Salinas, Calif., Sta. KUCO-LP, Chico, Calif., Sta. K46HI, Redding, Calif., Sta. K08NH, Oroville, Calif., Sta. K38FQ, Anderson and Central Valley, Calif., Sta. K17EH, Eureka, Calif., Sta. K31EW, Eureka, Calif., Sta. K33FN, Eureka, Calif., Sta. K52FK, Eureka, Calif., Sta. K67GU, Eureka, Calif., KKEY-LP, Bakersfield, Calif., 2004. Original rec. Wait A Little Longer Please Jesus in Country Music Hall of Fame, Nashville, 1955, album California Blend (with Merle Haggard), 2001. Inductee Western Swing Hall of Fame, Sacramento, 1988, Nat. Traditional Country Music Assn. Hall of Fame, 2003; recipient cert. of recognition for 50 years of cmty. svc. Calif. Assembly, 1997, Lifetime Achievement award Modesto Area Musicians Assn., 2002, Broadcaster of Yr. Calif. Broadcasters Assn., 2003. Mem.: Calif. Broadcasters Assn. Republican. Mem. Christian Ch. Address: Sainte Partners II L P PO Box 4159 Modesto CA 95352-4159 E-mail: csmith@sainte.tv.

SMITH, CHRISTOPHER ALLEN, technology company executive, finance professional; b. Rockford, Ill., Nov. 16, 1961; s. Robert Lee and Martha Ann (Moody) S.; m. Mary G. Meany, Apr. 13, 1991. BA, postgrad., Ind. U., 1983; Golden Gate U., 1986—87; MA, U. Phoenix, 2003. Rates analyst North American Van Lines, Ft. Wayne, Ind., 1984-85; mgr., investor rels. BRAE Corp., San Francisco, 1985-87; fin. analyst CIS Corp., San Francisco, 1987-89; dir., corp. devel. Affiliated Computer Systems, Inc., San Francisco, 1989-96; v.p. Sci. Applications Internat. Corp., San Francisco, 1996—. Contbr. articles to profl. jours. Vol. Rep. Party, Foster City, Calif., 1988; apptd. dir. Pvt. Industry Coun. Contra Costa County. With USMCR, 1982-83. Mem. Equipment Leasing Assn. Am. (Jour. award 1991), Ind. U. Alumni Assn. Republican. Roman Catholic. Avocations: freelance writing, photography, gardening. Office: Sci Applications Internat Corp 2000 Powell St Ste 1090 Emeryville CA 94608-1895 Office Phone: 510-652-7302. Business E-Mail: christopher.a.smith-2@saic.com.

SMITH, CHRISTOPHER HENRY, congressman; b. Rahway, N.J., Mar. 4, 1953; s. Bernard Henry and Katherine Joan (Hall) S.; m. Marie Hahn, July 2, 1977; children: Melissa, Christopher, Michael, Elyse. Student, Worcester Coll., Eng., 1973-74; BA in Bus. Adminstrn., Trenton State Coll., 1975. Exec. dir. N.J. Right to Life Com., 1976-78; dir. instl. sales Leisure Unltd. Inc., Woodbridge, N.J., 1978-80; mem. U.S. Congress from 4th N.J. dist., Washington, 1981—; vice chmn. internat. rels. com., mem. internat. ops. and human rights subcom.; sr. mem. subcom health, chmn. vets. affairs com.; co-chmn. Helsinki com., 1995. U.S. rep. to UN internat. conf. immunizing world's children. Active human rights movements Romania, China, former Soviet Union, Vietnam; co-chmn. House Pro-Life Caucus, 2002; mem. Alzheimer's Task Force and Autism Caucus. Named Legislator of Yr. VFW, Legislator of Yr. Internat. Assn. Chiropractors, Legislator of Yr. KC, 1989, Legislator of Yr. JWV of Am., 1996, Leader of the Yr., N.J. State Postal Workers Union, 2002, William Wilberforce award, 2002; recipient Leader for Peace award Peace Corps. Mem. Nat. Fedn. Ind. Bus. Republican. Roman Catholic. Office: 2373 Rayburn Ho Office Bldg Washington DC 20515-0001

SMITH, CHRISTOPHER M. music educator; b. Brewton, Ala., Nov. 10, 1971; s. James A. and Jane W. Smith. B in Music Edn., Troy State U., 1994, EdM, 1995. Asst. band dir. Bacon County H.S., Alma, Ga., 1995—96; band dir. Cottonwood (Ala.) H.S., 1996—. Adjudicator, clinician in field, 1995—; exec. dir. Houston County Honor Band, Dothan, Ala., 1997—; asst. color guard instr. Troy (Ala.) State U. Summer Band Camp, 2001—03. Writer (marching band shows). Prin. horn TSUD Cmty. Band, Dothan, 1999—; site coord. amendment HCBE-Cottonwood Sch., 2003. Named Outstanding Young Man Am., Outstanding Young Ams., 1996, 1998. Mem.: Ala. Band Masters Assn., Ala. Edn. Assn., Music Educators Nat. Conf. Avocations: reading, travel, online gaming, outdoor recreation. Office: Cottonwood HS 663 Houston St Cottonwood AL 36320 Office Phone: 334-691-2587 7. E-mail: chsbandal@yahoo.com.

SMITH, CLAIRE, chef; Grad., Calif. Culinary Acad., San Francisco; grad. in art and art history, Rice U. Chef Green, Oliveto, San Francisco Bay area, The Daily Review Cafe, Houston, 1994—. Office: 3412 W Lamar Houston TX 77019

SMITH, CLARA JEAN, retired nursing home administrator; b. Berwick, Pa., Aug. 31, 1932; d. Barton Fredrick and Evelyn Miriam (Bomboy) Hough; m. Robert W. Smith, June 7, 1958. BS in Nursing Edn., Wilkes Coll., Wilkes-Barre, Pa., 1960; MS in Edn., Temple U., Phila., 1968. RN, Pa. From staff nurse to DON Retreat State Hosp., Hunlock Creek, Pa., 1953-80; dir. long term care facility Danville (Pa.) State Hosp., 1980-82; ret., 1982. Dir. accreditation coordination and quality assurance, 1980—; spkr., instr. in field. Author tng. and ednl. programs. Mem. Pa. State Employees Retirement Assn. (pres. Luzerne/Columbia County chpt., regional v.p. northeastern Pa.), Pa. Assn. Ret. State Employees Assn., Williamsport Hosp. Sch. Nursing Alumni, Sunshine Club, Town Hill Hobby Group, Town Hill Over 50 Group. Methodist. Home: PO Box 999 Berwick PA 18603-0699 also: 1006 Roslyn Dr Berwick PA 18603

SMITH, (FLOYD) CLAYTON, state legislator, business owner; b. Trumann, Ark., Mar. 12, 1959; m. Mary Kim Boone. AS in EE, So. Ark. U. Mem. Miss. Ho. of Reps., 1998—; mem. conservation and water resources, judiciary A coms.; mem. fees and salaries com. Republican. Baptist. Home: 126 Dogwood Cir Brandon MS 39047-6611 Office: State Capitol Bldg PO Box 1018 Jackson MS 39215-1018 E-mail: fcsmith@mail.house.state.ms.us.

SMITH, CLODUS RAY, retired academic administrator; b. Blanchard, Okla., May 15, 1928; s. William Thomas and Rachel (Hale) S.; m. Pauline R. Chaat; children: Martha Lynn, William Paul, Paula Diane. Assoc. degree, Cameron State Coll., 1948; BS in Agrl. Edn., Okla. A & M Coll., 1950; MS in Vocat. Edn., Okla. State U., 1955; EdD in Vocat. Edn., Cornell U., 1960. Grad. asst. Cornell U., 1957-59; asst. prof. U. Md., 1959-62, assoc. prof., 1962-63, dir. Summer Sch., 1963-72, adminstrv. dean, 1972-73; spl. asst. to pres. Cleve. State U., 1973-74, v.p. for univ. rels., 1974-83; pres. Rio Grande Coll. and Rio Grande Community Coll., Ohio, 1983-86, Lake Erie Coll., Painesville, Ohio, 1986-92, Okla. Ind. Coll. Found., Oklahoma City, 1993-96, Okla. Assn. Ind. Colls. and Univs., 1993-96. Cons. NEA, Naval Weapons Lab., Dehlgren, Va.; researcher Personal and Profl. Satisfactions; contract investigator Nat. Endowment for Humanities; dir. Human Resources and Community Devel., Prince George's County, Md. Author: Planning and Paying for College, 1958, Rural Recreation for Profit, 1971, A Strategy for University Relations, 1975, State Relations for the 1980 Decade, 1982. Amb. Natural Resources, Ohio, 1984, chmn. dept.; founder N.Am. Assn. of Summer Schs., 1979. Recipient Rsch. award Nat. Project in Agrl. Communications, 1959, Edn. award Prince George's C. of C., 1971, Disting. Alumni award Cameron U. Mem. Am. Assn. U. Adminstrs., Am. Assn. for Higher Edn., Nat. Soc. for Study Edn., Coun. for Support and Advancement Edn., Am. Alumni Coun., Al Koran Hunter's Club, Shriners. Methodist. Avocations: volunteering on international religious missions, hunting, fishing, volunteering. E-mail: clodus@sbcglobal.net.

SMITH, CLYDE M. engineering and construction executive; CFO, v.p. BE&K, Inc., Birmingham, Ala. Office: BE&K Inc 2000 International Park Drive Birmingham AL 35243 also: BE&K Inc 2000 International Park Dr Birmingham AL 35243-4221

SMITH, CLYDE RAY, dean; b. Bassett, Va, Apr. 21, 1935; s. William Henry and Ava I. (Roberson) S.; m. Phyllis Jane Watkins, Mar. 25, 1959; children: Anthony William, Cheryl Ann, Theresa Jane. BA, Bridgewater Coll., 1956; MBA, U. Va., 1958; D in Bus. Adminstrn. (hon.), Bridgewater Coll., 2004. Instr. U. Va. - Darden, Charlottesville, Va., 1961-64, asst. prof., 1964-67, assoc. prof., 1967-72, prof., 1972—, assoc. dean MBA program, 1972-94, assoc. dean exec. edn., 1994-97, interim dean, 1997-98; exec. dir. Darden Sch. Found., 1998—2003; prof. emeritus U. Va. - Darden, Charlottesville, Va., 2003—. Adminstrv. dir. Inst. Chartered Fin. Analysts, Charlottesville, 1962-69; bd. trustees Bridgewater Coll. Co-author: (books) Executive's Guide to Mgmt. Accounting and Control Sys., 1998, Fin. Accounting for Mgmt., 1981. Capt. (res.) US Army, 1958-68. Named Disting. Alumnus Bridgewater Coll., Va., 1991. Mem. AICPA, Am. Real Estate Soc., Colonade Club, Farmington Country Club, Raven Soc., Beta Gamma Sigma, Omicron Delta Kappa. Home: 39 Canterbury Rd Charlottesville VA 22903-4700 Office: Univ Va - Darden Sch PO Box 6550 Charlottesville VA 22906-6550 Office Phone: 434-924-4799. E-mail: crs6n@virginia.edu.

SMITH, CONNIE, hospital administrator; b. Moline, Ill., Feb. 7, 1947; d. Phillip and Betty (McSparin) Warrick. Diploma, Moline Pub. Sch. Nursing, 1969; BSN, U. Iowa, 1975; MSN, Rush U., 1981. Cert. nurse operating rm. Staff nurse operating rm. Moline (Ill.) Pub. Hosp., 1969-70; head nurse operating rm./recovery Resurrection Hosp., Chgo., 1970-72; staff nurse operating rm. Mennonite Hosp., Bloomington, Ill., 1973-74; instr. Franciscan Hosp. Sch. Nursing, Rock Island, Ill., 1975-77; staff nurse intensive care unit Moline Luth. Hosp., 1977-79; MICU staff nurse, unit leader operating rm., univ. faculty mem. Rush Presbyn-St. Luke's Med. Ctr., Chgo., 1979-85; dir. operating rm. Albert Einstein Med. Ctr., Phila., 1985-88; dir. operating rm. svcs. St. Joseph Hosp., Houston, 1988-90; regional dir. surg. svcs. Sharp HealthCare, San Diego, 1990-93; surg. svcs. cons. Coast Assocs., 1993-99; dir. Fountain Valley (Calif.) Surgery Ctr., 1999—. Presenter in field.

SMITH, CORLIES MORGAN, publishing executive; b. Phila., Mar. 31, 1929; s. Charles Ross and Mary Howard (Stewart) S.; m. Sheila de Peyster Carey, June 17, 1950; children: Mark, Nicholas, Peter, Baylies, Timothy. BA, Yale U., 1951. Assoc. editor J.B. Lippincott Co., Phila., 1955-62; sr. editor The Viking Press, N.Y.C., 1962-83; editorial dir. Ticknor & Fields, N.Y.C., 1984-89; editor in chief Harcourt Brace & Co., N.Y.C., 1990-94, editorial con., 1995—. Home and Office: 1435 Lexington Ave New York NY 10128-1625

SMITH, CRAIG, medical company executive; BS in Metallurgical Engring., U. Wash., 1966; PhD in Materials Sci., Carnegie Mellon U., 1971. With Gen. Atomic Co.; v.p. engring. CarboMedics, Inc.; v.p. R&D Intermedics; pres. Encore Med. Corp., Austin, Tex., 1992—. Office: Encore Med Corp 9800 Metric Blvd Austin TX 78758-5445

SMITH, CRAIG BENNETT, lawyer; b. Wilmington, Del., Oct. 16, 1943; s. Wilfred Winter and Louetta Beatrice (Bennett) S.; m. Charlotte Anne Boucheron, May 27, 1967; 1 child, Stuart Evan. BA in English, Carleton Coll., 1966; MA in Creative Writing, Syracuse U., 1969, JD summa cum laude, 1975. Bar: U.S. Dist. Ct. Del. 1975. Assoc. Morris, Nichols, Arsht & Tunnell, Wilmington, 1975-83; ptnr. Biggs & Battaglia, Wilmington, 1983-84, Lassen, Smith, Katzenstein & Furlow, Wilmington, 1984-91, Smith, Katzenstein & Furlow, L.L.P., Wilmington, 1992—. Mem. adv. bd. Bur. Nat. Affairs Corp. Practices Series, Washington, 1988—. Co-author: State Limited Partnership Laws, 1987, Guide to the Takeover Law of Delaware, 1988, Limited Partnerships: Legal Aspects of Organization, Operation and Dissolution, 1992 (book chpts.) New York and Delaware Business Entities, 1997; mem. editorial bd. State Ltd. Partnership Laws-Prentice Hall Law & Bus., 1987—; sr. notes and comments editor Syracuse Law Rev., 1974-75; contbr. articles to profl. jours. Mem. Del. Gov's High Tech. Task Force, Wilmington, 1986, com. bus. & indsl. devel. cos. Del. Econ. Devel. Office, Wilmington, 1988. Named to Justinian Soc., 1974. Fellow ABA (litigation sect. 1985—, bus. law sect. 1975—); mem. Del. State Bar Assn. (corp. law sect. coun. 1987-90, 93—, com. Del. Revised Uniform Ltd. Partnership Act 1984—, chancery ct. fiduciary rules adv. com. 1986-89), Order of Coif. Republican. Avocations: classical guitar playing, sculpturing. Home: 318 Spalding Rd Wilmington DE 19803-2422 Office: Smith Katzenstein & Furlow LLP The Corporate Plaza 800 Delaware Ave Wilmington DE 19801-1322

SMITH, CRAIG R. medical equipment company executive; m. Cynthia Smith; 2 children. Grad., U. So. Calif. With Owens & Minor, Glen Allen, Va., 1989—, divsn. v.p., group v.p., sr. v.p. distbn. and info. sys., exec. v.p., COO, 1995—. Office: Owens & Minor 4800 Cox Rd Glen Allen VA 23060-6294

SMITH, CRAIG RICHEY, thoracic surgeon; b. Cleve., Nov. 17, 1948; AB, Williams Coll., 1970; MD, Case Western Res. U., 1977. Diplomate Am. Bd. Thoracic Surgery, Am. Bd. Surgery. Intern U. Rochester (N.Y.) Hosp., 1977-78, resident, 1978-82; fellow in cardiothoracic surgery Columbia-Presbyn. Med. Ctr., N.Y.C, 1982-84, chief, divsn. cardiothoracic surgery N.Y.C., 1996—; prof. surgery Columbia U. Coll. Physicians & Surgeons, 1997—2001, Calvin F. Barber prof. surgery, 2001—. Assoc. prof. surgery Columbia U. Hosp., N.Y.C. Mem. AMA, ACS, Am. Assn. Thoracic Surgery, Am. Heart Assn., Am. Surgical Assn., Internat. Soc. for Heart Transplantation, Am. Coll. Cardiology, NY Soc. for Thoracic Surgery, Assn. for Academic Surgery. Office: 177 Fort Washington Ave New York NY 10032-3713*

SMITH, CULLEN, lawyer; b. Waco, Tex., May 31, 1925; s. Curtis Cullen and Elizabeth (Brient) S.; m. Laura Risher Dossett, Mar. 6, 1948; children: Sallie Smith Wright, Alethea Risher Smith Gilbert, Elizabeth Brient Smith. Student, Emory U., 1943-44, Duke U., 1944; BBA, Baylor U., 1948, JD, 1950. Bar: Tex. 1950. Ptnr. firm Smith, McIlheran & Smith, Weslaco, Tex., 1950-53, Naman, Howell, Smith & Lee LLP, Waco, 1953—. Lectr. law Baylor U. Sch. Law, 1964-72 Contbr. articles to legal publs. Mem. standing com. Episcopal Diocese of Tex., 1960-63, 74-75; trustee Episcopal Theol. Sem. of S.W., 1962-67; mem. Waco City Coun., 1983-86; chmn. bd. Vanguard Sch., 1975; bd. dirs. G.H. Pape Found., 1993-94; bd. dirs., vice chmn. Tex. Ctr. for Legal Ethics and Professionalism, 1994-99; mem. adv. coun. Baylor U. Coll. Arts and Scis., 1998-2003. 1st lt. USMCR, 1943-46. Named One of 5 Outstanding Young Texans Tex. Jr. C. of C., 1957, Baylor Lawyer of Yr., 1980; recipient Disting. Alumnus award Waco Ind. Sch. Dist. Edn. Found., 2002. Fellow Am. Bar Found., Tex. Bar Found. (chmn. bd. 1973-74, 50 Yr. Lawyer award 2000), fellow Coll. of Law Practice Mgmt.; mem. ABA (chmn. standing com. econs. law practice 1965-69, chmn. spl. com. on law book pub. practices 1970-72, chmn. gen. practice sect. 1973-74, mem. house of dels. 1974-81), Am. Law Firm Assn. (chmn. 1989-90), Waco-McLennan County Bar Assn. (pres. 1956-57), Mont. Bar Assn. (hon.), State Bar Tex. (pres. jr. bar 1957-58, chmn. profl. econs. com. 1959-61, chmn. spl. com. on revision Tex. Canons Ethics 1969-71, dir. 1971-74, pres. 1978-79), Philos. Soc. Tex., Baylor U. Law Alumni Assn. (pres. 1962-63), Order of Coif, Delta Sigma Phi, Phi Delta Phi, Am. Inns Ct. (master), Ridgewood Country Club (pres. 1965), Hedonia Club (pres. 1957), Rotary. Avocation: photography. Home: Oak Grove Farm 447 Meandering Way China Spring TX 76633-2905 Office: Naman Howell Smith & Lee LLP Tex Ctr PO Box 1470 Waco TX 76703-1470

SMITH, CURTIS DAVID, lawyer; b. Freeport, Ill., Oct. 16, 1951; s. David Logan and Patricia Lou (Scott) S.; m. Terrie Lee Grant, Sept. 25, 1981; children: Grant, Megan, Gavin. BA, U. Ill., 1973; JD, Wm. Mitchell Coll. of Law, St. Paul, 1979. Bar: Minn. 1979, U.S. Dist. Ct. Minn. 1979, U.S. Tax Ct. 1980. Atty. Wiese & Cox, Ltd., Mpls., 1979-85; shareholder Moss & Barnett, Mpls., 1985—. Dir. Am. Subcontractors Assn. of Minn., St. Paul, 1992—. Coach White Bear, Minn. Hockey Assn., 1989-99. Mem. ABA, Minn. State Bar Assn., Hennepin County Bar Assn. Home: 6160 Woodchuck Cir White Bear Lake MN 55110-1045 Office: Moss & Barnett 4800 Wells Fargo Ctr Minneapolis MN 55402 Office Phone: 612-347-0285. E-mail: smithc@moss-barnett.com.

SMITH, CYNTHIA S. writer; b. N.Y.C., Dec. 29, 1934; d. Harry and Sarah (Cohen) Sharfin; m. David Smith, May 21, 1953 (dec. May 1985); 1 child, Hillary Smith Pannier. BA, Hunter Coll., 1954. Advt. dir. Joshua Meier Co., Inc., N.Y.C., 1955-65; pres. C/D Smith Advt., Inc., Rye, N.Y., 1966-01; assoc. adj. prof. Mgmt. Inst. NYU, 1992—. Author: How to Get Big Results from a Small Advertising Budget, 1978, Doctors' Wives, 1981, Step by Step

Advertising, 1985, Seven Levels of Marriage, 1988, Why Women Shouldn't Marry, 1990, What Has She Got?, 1995, Woman's Guide to Starting Business, 1996, Noblesse Oblige, 1996, Misleading Ladies, 1997, Impolite Society, 1997, Silver and Guilt, 1998, Royals and Rogues, 1998. Mem. Authors' Guild, Mystery Writers of Am., Sisters in Crime, Internat. Assn. Crime Writers. Avocations: tennis, chorale singing. E-mail: cynthiassmith@earthlink.net.

SMITH, D. ADAM, congressman; b. Washington, June 15, 1965; s. Ben Smith; m. Sara Bickle-Eldridge, Aug. 1993; 1 child, Kendall Charlotte. BA, Fordham U., 1987; JD, U. Wash., 1990. Driver United Parcel Svc., 1985-87; mem. Wash. State Senate, 1990-96; atty. Cromwell Mendoza Belur, 1991—92; asst. prosecuting atty. City of Seattle, 1993—95; pro tem judge, 1996; mem. 106th Congress from 9th dist. Wash., 1997—; mem. armed scvs. com., internat. rel. com. Mem. Kent Drinking Driver Task Force, Highline Citizens for Schs., Kent Meridian H.S. Site-Based Coun.; bd. mem. Judson Park Retirement Home. Mem.: Kiwanis Internat. Democrat. Office: 227 Cannon, US House Reps Washington DC 20515

SMITH, D. BROOKS, federal judge; b. 1951; BA, Franklin and Marshall Coll., 1973; JD, Dickinson Sch. Law, 1976. Pvt. practice Jubelirer, Carothers, Krier, Halpern & Smith, Altoona, Pa., 1976-84, mng. ptnr., 1981—83; judge Ct. Common Pleas of Blair County, Pa., 1984-88, U.S. Dist. Ct. (we. dist.) Pa., 1988—2002, chief judge, 2001—02; judge U.S. Ct. Appeals 3d Cir., Johnstown, Pa., 2003—. Asst. dist. atty. Blair County, part-time, 1977-79, spl. prosecutor, 1981-83, dist. atty. part-time, 1983-84; instr. Pa. State U., Altoona campus, 1977—, St. Francis Coll., 1986—; adv. com. on criminal rules U.S. Jud. Conf., 1993-99. Trustee St. Francis Coll., 1992—2004. Mem. Am. Law Inst., Pa. Bar Assn., Am. Judicature Soc., Pa. Soc., Amen Corner, Blair County Game, Fish and Forestry Assn., Fed. Judges Assn. (bd. dirs. 1993-97, 2002—), Inns of Ct., Allegheny County Bar Assn., Pi Gamma Mu. Office: Allegheny Profl Ctr 1798 Old Rte 220 N Ste 203 Duncansville PA 16635

SMITH, D(AISY) MULLETT, publisher; b. Washington, Aug. 17, 1948; d. Gordon Hunt and Suzanne Myrick (Mullett) Smith. BA, Am. U., 1970; cert. computer programming, U. So. Calif., Arlington, Va., 1986; cert. in records mgmt., Assn. Records Mgrs. Am., Prairie Village, Kans., 1987. Christian Sci. practitioner The First Ch. of Christ, Scientist, Boston, 1970-86; clk. Fifth Ch. of Christ, Scientist, Washington, 1971-74; Christian Sci. campus counsellor The Am. U., Washington, 1976-81; editor, computer specialist, desktop pub. Mullett-Smith Press, Washington, 1984-89, owner, pub., author, 1989—, music copyist, pub. on computer, 1990—, web weaver, 1996—. Computer cons. and pub. spkr. in field; guest participant divsn. children in trouble White House Conf. on Children, 1970. Author, editor, pub.: AB Mullett, His Relevance in American Architecture, 1990 (Printers award 1990); editor: AB Mullett, Architect Engineer 1862-90, 1985; contbr. articles to profl. jours.; desktop pub. musical scores by Richard Henry Lee, 1991—; art pamphlets by Suzanne M. Smith, 1999—. Participant White House Conf. on Children, 1970; active Save Pioneer Post Office, Portland, Oreg., 1996—; fund raiser com. U.S. Treasury Bill Restoration Fund, 1998-2000; libr. Christian Sci. Reading Rm., 1999-2002; renovator TH-7, 2003; spkr. JCPASH, 2003, Charlestown, Va., 2003, commrs. Jefferson County, W.Va., 2003; interviewer PBS radio, saving Jefferson County Jail . Recipient Key to the City, Mayor Lincoln, Nebr., 1989. Mem. Nat. Soc. Arts and Letters (editor/pub. directory 1971-88, 89-91, 92—, treas. 1988-90, web weaver 1996—), Nat. Trust for Hist. Preservation, Assn. Records Mgrs. and Adminstrs., Assn. for Info. and Image Mgmt. Internat., U.S. Treasury Hist. Assn. (spkr. 1992-96), U.S. Capitol Hist. Soc. Avocations: art, design, teaching and playing classical guitar, windsurfing, computers. E-mail: mspress@mullett-smithpress.com.

SMITH, DAN F. oil company executive; With Atlantic Richfield Co, Los Angeles, Calif., 1967—88; CFO, former v.p., dir. Lyondell Petrochemical Co.; now pres. & CEO Lyondell Chem. Co., Houston. Office: Lyondell Chemical Co 1221 Mckinney St Ste 700 Houston TX 77010-2015

SMITH, DANIEL, oncologist, gynecologist; b. Cushing, Okla., Feb. 12, 1946; MD, Harvard Med. Sch., 1972. Diplomate Am. Bd. Surgery, Am. Bd. Obstetrics and Gynecology with subspecialty in gynecologic oncology. Intern Mass. Gen. Hosp., Boston, 1972—73, resident, 1973—75, 1978, L.A. County/U. So. Calif. Med. Ctr., L.A., 1975—78; fellow Meml. Sloan-Kettering Cancer Ctr., 1979—81; oncologist, ob-gyn. Columbia Presbyn. Med. Ctr., N.Y.C., 1981—; assoc. prof. ob-gyn. Columbia Coll. Physicians and Surgeons. Office: 161 Fort Washington Ave New York NY 10032-3713

SMITH, DANIEL C. finance educator; PhD, U. Pitts., 1988. Asst. prof. Sch. Bus., U. Wis., Madison; asst. to assoc. prof. Joesph M. Katz Grad. Sch. Bus., U. Pitts.; joined faculty Kelley Sch. Bus., Ind. U., 1996, MBA program chair, 1998—2001, Clare W. Barker chair mktg., 2002—, assoc. dean acads., 2003—, interim dean, 2004—. Editl. review bd.: Jour. Mktg. (Outstanding Reviewer award, 1999), Jour. Acad. Mktg. Sci., Jour. Market-Focused Mgmt., Jour. Competitive Intelligence. Avocation: fly fishing. Office: Ind Univ Kelley Sch Bus 1309 E Tenth St Bloomington IN 47405 Office Phone: 812-855-8489. Business E-Mail: dansmith@indiana.edu.

SMITH, DANIEL CLIFFORD, lawyer; b. Cin., Aug. 9, 1936; s. Clifford John and Vivian Aileen (Stone) S.; m. Carroll Cunningham; children: Edward, Andrew, Scott. BS, Ariz. State U., 1960; postgrad., George Washington U., 1961—62; JD, Am. U., 1965. Bar: D.C. 1965, U.S. Ct. Appeals (D.C. cir.) 1966, U.S. Ct. Appeals (Fed. cir.), U.S. Dist. Ct. D.C. 1966, Va. 1967, U.S. Supreme Ct. 1969, U.S. Ct. Appeals (4th, 5th, 6th, 7th, 9th and 11th cirs.), U.S. Ct. Claims, U.S. Ct. Customs and Patent Appeals, U.S. Tax Ct. Assoc. Alpern & Feissner, Washington, 1963-66; atty. FTC, Washington, 1966-70; ptnr. Arent, Fox, Kintner, Plotkin & Kahn, Washington, 1970-93, Canfield & Smith, Washington, 1993—. Pres., dir. Country Pl. Citizens Assn., Inc., 1974-77; bd. dirs. Sea Watch Condominium, Ocean City, Md., 1978—, treas., 1982-86, pres. 1986—; active Supreme Ct. Hist. Soc., The Federalist Soc., Smithsonian Inst. Assocs., Ariz. State Soc. Served with USMC. Mem. D.C. Bar Assn. (bd. dirs. 1974-76, chmn. consumer protection com. 1972-74, chmn. D.C. affairs sect. 1975-76), Va. State Bar Assn., Fed. Bar Assn., Assn. Trial Lawyers Am., Nat. Field Selling Assn. (gen. counsel), Ariz. State U. Alumni Assn., Rotary Club (pres. 1987-88, 96-97), Optimist (pres. 1972-73), Internat. Town and Country Club (dir. 1969-73), Masons, Delta Theta Phi. Office: Canfield & Smith Ste 800 910 17th St NW Washington DC 20006-2606

SMITH, DANIEL L. electronics executive; b. Cheboygan, Mich., 1952; m. Patricia Smith; 2 children. BA, Chapman U., Orange, Calif.; MBA, Chapman U. Dir. submarine electronics Lockheed Martin; mgr. programs for US Navy ships Raytheon Co., 1996—98, v.p., gen. mgr. naval and maritime integrated systems, 1998—2002, v.p. integrated def. systems, 2002—. Lt. comdr. USN. Office: Raytheon Co 50 Apple Hill Dr Tewksbury MA 01876

SMITH, DANIEL LYNN, lawyer; b. Ottawa, Kans., June 22, 1952; s. Daniel H. and Mary K. (Lynn) S.; m. Alana A. Windhorst, Aug. 15, 1981; children: Tricia, Lauran, Alexa. BA, U. Kans., 1973; JD, Duke U., 1976. Bar: Kans. 1976, U.S. Dist. Ct. Kans. 1976, U.S. Ct. Appeals (10th cir.) 1977, U.S. Tax Ct. 1977. Assoc. Bronston Law Offices, Overland Park, Kans., 1976-78; ptnr. Oliver, Smith & Oliver, Overland Park, 1978-80, Bronston and Smith, Overland Park, 1981-92, Ankerholz & Smith, Overland Park, Kans., 1992—; pvt. practice Westwood, Kans., 1980-81. Mem. Kans. Bar Assn., Kans. Trial Lawyers Assn. (bd. govs. 1981—), Civil War Roundtable Kansas City, Phi Beta Kappa. Home: 10075 Goodman Dr Shawnee Mission KS 66212-3432 Office: Ankerholz & Smith 6900 College Blvd Overland Park KS 66211-1547

SMITH, DANIEL SCOTT, history educator, historian; b. Galesburg, Ill, Sept. 24, 1942; s. Charles Edward and Mildred (McCloud) Smith; m. Yvonne Neu Smith, Mar. 25, 1967 (div. Oct. 5, 2000); children: Jason Scott, Sarah Elizabeth. BA(hon.), U of Fl, Gainesville, Fl, 1963; MA, U of Calif., Berkeley, CA, 1965, PhD, 1973. Cert. demography Office of Population Rsch., Princeton U, 1974. Asst. prof., instr. Dept. of Hist., U of CN, Conn., 1971—74; asst. prof., 1974—77; assoc. dir. Family and Cmty. Hist. Ctr., Newberry Libr., Chgo., 1974—82; assoc. prof., 1977—83; prof. Dept. of Hist., U of Ill, Chgo., 1983—. Mem. editl. bd. Soc. Sci. Hist., 1977—84; editor Hist. Methods, 1979—90; mem. editl. bd. Continuity and Change, 1986—90, Hist. Methods, 1992, Am. Hist. Rev., 1994—97, Soc. Sci. Hist., 1994—2001, The Hist. of the Family: An Internat. Quar., 1996—. Author: (articles) numerous scholarly articles in the fields of Am. social, demographic,and family hist. Recipient Univ. Scholar, U of Ill, 1985—88; fellow Population Coun., Princeton U, 1973—74, Rsch., Am. Coun. of Learned Soc., 1977—78, NEH Sr., Newberry Lib., 1983—84, Fulbright, U of Lund,Sweden, 1984, Inst. Humanities Fellowship, U of Ill, 1986—87, Advanced Study in the Behavioral Sciences, Stanford Ctr., 1990—91, Inst. Humanities Fellowship, U of Ill, 2001—02, Nat. Endowment for the Humanities, 2002; grantee Am. Philol. Soc., 1976, rsch., Nat. Inst. on Aging, 1977—79, Am. Assoc. for State and Local Hist., 1983—84, rsch., Nat. Inst. of Child Health and Human Devel., 1988—92, Inst. for the Study of Am. Evang., 1989—91, Am. Philol. Soc., 2002—03. Mem.: Social Sci. Hist. Assoc. (assoc.), Population Assoc. of Am. (assoc.), Econ. Hist. Assoc. (assoc.), Am. Hist. Assoc. (assoc.), Social Sci. Hist. Assoc. (assoc.; pres. 1987—88, VP 1986—87). Home: 228 N Oak Park Ave Oak Park IL 60302-2170 Office: Univ of Ill 921 Univ Hall 601 S Morgan St Chicago IL 60607-7109

SMITH, DANIEL TIMOTHY, lawyer; b. Denver, July 20, 1948; s. Harold Kennedy and Dorothy (Gannon) S. BA, Duke U., 1970; JD, U. Denver, 1973. Bar: Colo. 1973, U.S. Dist. Ct. Colo. 1973, U.S. Ct. Appeals (10th cir.), U.S. Supreme Ct. 1979, U.S. Ct. Claims 1979. Dep. dist. atty. Denver Dist. Atty. Office, 1973-74; spl. asst. atty. gen. Colo. Atty. Gen.'s Office, Denver, 1973-74; asst. U.S. atty. Dist. of Colo., Denver, 1974-76; ptnr. Wiggins & Smith P.C., Denver, 1977-87; pvt. practice Denver, 1987—. Chmn. fundraising Am. Cancer Soc., Denver., 1992-93; mem. golf com. Am. Heart Assn., Denver, 1988—. Mem. ABA, Colo. Criminal Def. Bar (sec. 1979-81). Avocation: golf. Office: 1900 Grant St Ste 580 Denver CO 80203-4346

SMITH, DAVID A. medical services executive; Public acctg., 1983—87; regional mgr., gen. mgr., sales mgr. and opers. mgr. PSS/World Medical Inc., Jacksonville, Fla., 1987—93, v.p., 1992—96, bd. dirs., 1993—, exec. v.p., 1996—2000, pres., 2000—, CFO, 1992—2002, CEO, 2002—. Office: PSS World Med Inc 4345 Southpoint Blvd Jacksonville FL 32216

SMITH, DAVID BRUCE, lawyer; b. Moline, Ill., May 9, 1948; s. Neal Schriever and Barbara Jean (Harris) S.; children: Neal, Stephanie. BSME, U. Iowa, 1970; JD, U. Tex., 1973. Bar: Tex. 1973, Wis. 1975. Patent examiner U.S. Patent and Trademark Office, Washington, 1973—74; atty., intellectual property practice coord. Michael Best & Friedrich, Milw., 1978—. Co-chair Intellectual Property Com. of Lex Mundi. Pres. Milw. County coun. Boy Scouts Am., Milw., 1994-95. Mem. ABA, Am. Intellectual Property Law Assn., State Bar Wis., Wis. Intellectual Property Law Assn., Ozaukee Country Club, Milw. Club. Office: Michael Best & Friedrich 100 E Wisconsin Ave Ste 3300 Milwaukee WI 53202-4108 E-mail: dbsmith@mbf-law.com.

SMITH, DAVID BURNELL, lawyer; b. Charleston, W.Va., Apr. 8, 1941; s. Ernest Dayton and Nellie Dale (Tyler) S.; m. Rita J. Hughes, Sept. 25, 1967. BA, U. Charleston, 1967; JD, U. Balt., 1972; MJS, U. Nev., 1995. Bar: Colo. 1972, Md. 1972, U.S. Supreme Ct. 1980, Ariz. 1983, U.S. Dist. Ct. Md. 1972, U.S. Dist. Ct. Colo. 1972, U.S. Ct. Appeals (4th Cir.) 1972, U.S. Ct. Appeals (9th cir. 1972, U.S. Ct. Appeals (10th cir.) 1983. Sales rep. Gulf Oil, Washington, 1967-72; pvt. practice Littleton, Colo., 1972-83, Glendale, Ariz., 1983-86, Phoenix, 1986-88, Scottsdale, Ariz., 1988—. Pro-tempore judge Wickenburg Mcpl. Ct., 1986—; presiding judge Peoria (Ariz.) Mcpl. Ct., 1987-94, Cave Creek Mcpl. Ct., 1995-98. Appeared as actor in movie Dead Girls Don't Tango, 1990. V.p. South Jefferson County Reps., Lakewood, Colo., 1979, pres., 1990; candidate Dist. 6 for Congress; 2nd vice-chmn. Dist. 7 Rep. Party, pres. Ariz. Rep. Assembly Dist. 28, bd. dirs. Scottsdale (Ariz.) Constitution Commemorative Com., 1995-2003, pres., 2002—; Rep. candidate for Ho. Dist. 7. With USCG, 1959-66. Mem. ATLA, ABA (vice-chmn. family law 1983), Nat. Assn. Criminal Lawyers, Am. Judicature Soc., Nat. Assn. Criminal Def. Attys., Ariz. Magistrates Assn., Colo. Bar Assn., Ariz. Bar Assn., Scottsdale (Ariz.) Bar Assn. (sec. 2001-2002, v.p. 2002-2003, pres., 2003-2004), Md. Bar Assn., Colo. Trial Lawyers Assn., Maricopa County Bar Assn., Scottsdale Bar Assn. (bd. dirs., sec. 1996—, pres.), Masons, Shriners, Elks. Home: PO Box 5145 36418 N Wildflower Rd Carefree AZ 85377-5145 Office: 4310 N 75th St Scottsdale AZ 85251-3578 Personal E-mail: dbsatt@earthlink.net.

SMITH, DAVID CLARK, research scientist; b. Owensboro, Ky., Feb. 8, 1937; s. Robert Emmitt and Mary Margaret (Flaherty) S.; m. Kathleen Sue Kohne, June 27, 1964; children: Christine, Jennifer, Paula. BSME, U. Dayton, 1959; MS, Northwestern U., 1961, PHD, postgrad., Northwestern U., 1964. Rsch. scientist United Techs. Rsch. Ctr., East Hartford, Conn., 1965-67, sr. rsch. scientist, 1967-68, prin. scientist, 1968-80, mgr. exptl. optics, 1980-82, mgr. optical physics, 1982-91; cons. DCS Assoc., Inc., 1992-99, Conn. Tech. Assocs., 1992—, DCS Lasers/Optics LLC, 1997—. Author: (with G. Bekefi) Principles of Laser Plasmas, 1976; contbr. articles to profl. jours. Chmn. Youth and Family Resource Ctr. Commn., 1979-84; bd. dirs. Glastonbury A Better Chance, Conn., 1970-78; mem. Glastonbury Energy Com., 1979-83; tutor YMCA Read to Succeed Literacy; vol. Habitat for Humanity. Recipient Outstanding Svc. award, 1985, Glastonbury, Conn., United Techs. Outstanding Svc. award, 1987; named Man of Yr., Friends of Glastonbury Youth, 1984. Fellow: Am. Soc. Laser Medicine and Surgery; mem.: SPIE, IEEE, AIAA, AAAS, Am. Phys. Soc., Sigma Xi. Democrat. Roman Catholic. Achievements include patentee in field. Home: 44 Candlelight Dr Glastonbury CT 06033-2537 Office: DCS Lasers & Optics LLC PO Box 167 East Glastonbury CT 06025-0167 Office Phone: 860-657-9982. E-mail: kohne@aol.com.

SMITH, DAVID EDWARD, small business owner, aerospace engineer, aerospace scientist; b. Battle Creek, Mich., Sept. 16, 1939; s. Hebdin Leslie and Dureatha Rosella (Stephens) S.; m. Margaret Eugenia Clark, June 13, 1964; 1 child, Wendy Leigh. Student, Kellogg Community Coll., 1957-58; BS in Mech. Engring., Mich State U., 1962; MS in Real Estate Investing (hon.), Meta U., Salt Lake City, 1992. Engr., scientist Douglas Aircraft Co., Santa Monica, Calif., 1962-63, McDonnell Douglas Astronautics Co., Cape Kennedy, Fla., 1963-78; broker salesman Cape Kennedy Realty, Inc., Cape Canaveral, Fla., 1978-87; pres., founder Cash Flow Seminars, Merritt Island, Fla., 1979—, Cash Flow Systems, Inc., Merritt Island, Fla., 1983—; prof. fin. Meta U., Salt Lake City, 1992-94. Lectr. fin. convs. and orgns. including Fed. GSA, Pub. Bldg. Svc., Am. League of Savs., Fin. Instns. Mktg. Assn., Acad. Real Estate, Am. Congress Real Estate; prof. fin. Meta U., Salt Lake City, 1992-94; distbr. Hewlett Packard Corp., 1985-88; dir. comml. investment divsn. CKBOR, Merritt Island, 1978-79; adv. bd., lectr. Fin. Freedom Report, Nat. Inst. Fin. Planning, both Salt Lake City, 1985-92; instr. Fla. Real Estate Commn., La. Real Estate Commn., Fla. Bd. Accountancy, Am. Inst. Real Estate Appraisers. Author: Turbo-Diesel, The Time Value of Money, Creative Financing Techniques; contbr. articles to profl. jours. and mags. Mem.: Gold Wing Rd. Riders Assn., Internat. Platform Assn., Fla. Real Estate Exchangors. Republican. Avocations: flying, transcontinental bicycling, motorcycle touring. Office: Cash Flow Seminars PO Box 540634 Merritt Island FL 32954-0634

SMITH, DAVID ELVIN, physician; b. Bakersfield, Calif., Feb. 7, 1939; s. Elvin W. and Dorothy (McGinnis) S.; m. Millicent Buxton; children: Julia, Suzanne, Christopher Buxton-Smith, Sabree Hill-Smith. Intern San Francisco Gen. Hosp., 1965; fellow pharmacology and toxicology U. Calif., San Francisco, 1965-67; clin. prof. U. Calif., San Francisco Med. Ctr., 1967—, dir. psychopharmacology study group, dir. Inst. of Health, 1966-70, assoc. clin. prof., rsch. physician Med. Sch.; clin. prof. U. Calif., San Francisco; practice specializing in toxicology/addiction medicine San Francisco, 1965—. Physician Presbyn. Alcoholic Clinic, 1965—67, Contra Cost Alcoholic Clinic, 1965—67; dir. alcohol and drug abuse screening unit San Francisco Gen. Hosp., 1967—68; co-dir. Calif. drug abuse info. project U. Calif. Med. Ctr., 1967—72; founder, pres., med. dir. Haight-Ashbury Free Med. Clinic, San Francisco, 1967—; rsch. dir. Merritt Peralta Chem. Dependency Hosp., Oakland, Calif., 1984—; med. dir. Drug Abuse Scis., 1999, Calif. Alcohol and Drug Programs, U. Calif. San Francisco Substance Abuse Policy Ctr., 1999; assoc. med. dir., med. rev. officer Betty Ford Ctr. Profl. Recovery Program; chmn. Nat. Drug Abuse Conf., 1977, Calif. Gov.'s Commn. on Narcotics and Drug Abuse, 1977—; nat. health adviser to former U.S. Pres. Jimmy Carter; mem. Pres. Clinton's Health Care Task Force on Addiction and Nat. Health Reform, 1993; with Office Drug Abuse Policy, White House Task Force Physicians for Drug Abuse Prevention; dir. Benzodiazepine Rsch. and Tng. Project, Substance Abuse and Sexual Concerns Project, PCP Rsch. and Tng. Project; med. editor AlcoholMD.com, OpiateMD.org, Alcohol MD (CD-ROM); vis. assoc. prof. U. Nev. Med. Sch., 1975—; clin. prof. U. Calif. San Francisco Med. Ctr.; v.p. corp. med affairs Hythiam; cons. in field. Author: Love Needs Care, 1970, The New Social Drug: Cultural, Medical and Legal Perspectives on Marijuana, 1971, The Free Clnic: Community Approaches to Health Care and Drug Abuse, 1971, Treating the Cocaine Abuser, 1985, The Benzodiazepines: Current Standard Medical Practice, 1986, Physicians' Guide to Drug Abuse, 1987; co-author: It's So Good, Don't Even Try it Once: Heroin in Perspective, 1972, Uppers and Downers, 1973, Drugs in the Classroom, 1973, Barbiturate Use and Abuse, 1977, A Multicultural View of Drug Abuse, 1978, Amphetamine Use, Misuse and Abuse, 1979, PCP: Problems and Prevention, 1981, Sexological Aspects of Substance Use and Abuse, Treatment of the Cocaine Abuser, 1985, The Haight Ashbury Free Medical Clinic: Still Free After All These Years, Drug Free: Alternatives to Drug Abuse, 1987, Treatment of Opiate Dependence, Designer Drugs, 1988, Treatment of Cocaine Dependence, 1988, Treatment of Opiate Dependence, 1988, The New Drugs, 1989, Crack and Ice in the Era of Smokeable Drugs, 1992, Clinical Guide to Substance Abuse, 2001, others; also drug edn. films; founder, editor Jour. Psychedelic Drugs (now Jour. Psychoactive Drugs), 1967—; co-author: Clinical Guide to Substance Abuse; contbr. over 300 articles to profl. jours. Mem. Physicians for Prevention White House Office Drug Abuse Policy, 1995; pres. Youth Projects, Inc.; founder, chmn. bd., pres. Nat. Free Clin. Coun., 1968-72; med. dir. Calif. Alcohol and Drug Programs, 1998, U. Calif. Drug Policy Ctr., San Francisco, 1998—, Drug Abuse Scis., 1998—. Named one of Best Doctors in U.S., 1995, 1996, 1997, 2002; recipient Rsch. award, Borden Found., 1964, AMA Rsch. award, 1977, Cmty. Svc. award U. Calif., San Francisco, 1974, Calif. State Drug Abuse Treatment award, 1984, Vernelle Fox Drug Abuse Treatment award, 1985, UCLA Sidney Cohen Addiction Medicine award, 1989, U. Calif. San Francisco medal of honor, 1995, Lifetime Achievement award for sr. workers, Gov. of Calif., 2003. Mem. AMA (alt. del.), Calif. Med. Assn. (alt. del.), Am. Soc. on Addiction Medicine (bd. dirs., pres. 1995), San Francisco Med. Soc., APHA, Calif. Soc. on Addiction Medicine (pres., bd. dirs.), Am. Soc. Addiction Medicine, Sigma Xi, Phi Beta Kappa. Methodist. Home: 289 Frederick St San Francisco CA 94117-4051 Office: Haight Ashbury Free Clinics 612 Clayton St San Francisco CA 94117-2927 Office Phone: 415-487-3688. E-mail: dsmith4619@aol.com.

SMITH, DAVID ENGLISH, pathologist, educator; b. San Francisco, June 9, 1920; s. David English and Myrtle (Goodin) S.; m. Margaret Elizabeth Bronson, June 9, 1948; children: Ann English Smith Elbert, David Bronson, Mary Margaret. AB, Central Coll. Mo., 1941; MD cum laude, Washington U., St. Louis, 1944. Intern, resident pathology Barnes Hosp., St. Louis, 1944-46; instr. pathology Washington U. Med. Sch., 1948-51, asst. prof., 1951-54, asst. head dept., 1953-54, assoc. prof., 1954-55; prof. pathology U. Va. Sch. Medicine, 1955-73, chmn. dept., 1958-73; dir. div. U. Va. Sch. Medicine (Cancer Studies), 1972-73; prof. pathology Northwestern U. Sch. Medicine, 1974-75, U. Pa. Sch. Medicine, 1976-80, Tulane U. Sch. Medicine, 1980-85, assoc. dean, 1980-85; prof. pathology U. Tex. Med. Br., 1986—. Assoc. dir. Am. Bd. Med. Spltys., 1974-75; v.p., sec., dir. undergrad. evaluation Nat. Bd. Med. Examiners, 1975-80; trustee Am. Bd. Pathology, 1966-73, v.p., 1973; mem. Nat. Bd. Med. Examiners, chmn. pathology test com., 1966-72; chmn. test com. Ednl. Commn. for Fgn. Med. Grads., 1979-91; eligibility & due process com. Nat. Commn. Cert. Physician Assts., 1990-2001. Editor: Survey of Pathology in Medicine and Surgery, 1966-70; contbr. articles to profl. publs. Pres. Va. div. Am. Cancer Soc., 1967-69. Served from 1st lt. to capt. M.C. AUS, 1946-48. Named Disting. Alumnus, Wash. U. Med. Sch., 2004; recipient Preclin. Tchr. award, U. Tex. Med. Br., 1999; Paul Brindley Disting. scholar, 1997. Mem. Va. Soc. Pathology (pres. 1960), Am. Assn. Pathologists, Internat. Acad. Pathology (council 1956-59, pres. 1964-65), Am. Soc. Clin. Pathologists (co-dir. self assessment program 1970-75, Path Educator award 2000), AMA, Am. Assn. Neuropathologists, AAAS, Sigma Xi, Alpha Omega Alpha, Phi Beta Pi, Alpha Epsilon Delta. Home: 59 Colony Park Cir Galveston TX 77551-1737 E-mail: descolpkga@aol.com.

SMITH, DAVID EUGENE, business administration educator; b. Boise, Idaho, Dec. 14, 1941; s. Roy Arthur and Anna Margaret (Fries) S.; m. Patricia Stroy, Aug. 4, 1973; 1 child, Zachary Adam. BS in Applied Stats., San Francisco State Coll., 1964, MS in Mgmt. Sci., 1966; MBA, PhD in Bus. Adminstrn., U. Santa Clara, 1969. Asst. to dir. mgmt ctr. Grad. Sch. Bus., U. Santa Clara, Calif., 1966-69, lectr. mktg., 1968; asst. prof. bus. adminstrn. dept. mktg./decision Scis. San Jose State U., Calif., 1969—71, assoc. prof. bus. adminstrn. dept. mktg./decision Scis., 1971—76, prof. bus. adminstrn. dept. mktg./decision Scis., 1976—, chmn. dept. mktg./decision Scis., 1986—89. Author: Quantitative Business Analysis, 1977, Internat. Edit., 1979, 1982; contbr. articles to profl. jours. Mem.: DSI, INFORMS, Beta Gamma Sigma, Phi Kappa Phi. Republican. Avocations: tennis, fishing, skiing. Home: 22448 Tim Tam Ct Los Gatos CA 95033-8521 Office: San Jose State U Mktg/Decision Scis One Washington Sq San Jose CA 95192

SMITH, DAVID HORTON, retired social sciences educator; b. L.A., May 2, 1939; s. Paul Roosevelt Smith and Helen Ethel (Frechem) Mitchell; divorced; children: Gregory David, Laura Ghislaine. AB magna cum laude, U. So. Calif., 1960; MA, Harvard U., 1962, PhD, 1965. Asst. prof. U. So. Calif., L.A., 1966-68; assoc. prof. Boston Coll., Chestnut Hill, Mass., 1968-76, prof., 1976—2004. Rsch. fellow, lectr. Harvard U., 1965-66; cons. to govt. agys. and nonprofit orgns., including Nat. Ctr. for Voluntary Action, Brit. Nat. Vol. Ctr., Ctr. for Voluntary Soc., Filer Commn. on Pvt. Philanthropy and Pub. Needs, Union of Internat. Assns. Author: Latin American Student Activism, 1973, Grassroots Associations, 2000; co-author: Becoming Modern, 1974 (award 1975), Voluntary Sector Policy Research Needs, 1974, Participation in Social and Political Activities, 1980, Why People Recreate, 1987; editor: Voluntary Action Research, 1972, 73, 74, Volunteerism, Voluntary Assns. and Devel., 1981, Internat. Perspectives on Voluntary Action Rsch., 1983; contbr. numerous articles to profl. jours., chpts. to books; founding editor-in-chief Jour. Voluntary Action Rsch. (now Nonprofit and Voluntary Sector Quar.), 1971-76. Founding bd. dirs. Nat. Com. for Responsive Philanthropy, 1976-78, Alliance for Volunteerism; dir. rsch. Ctr. for Voluntary Soc., Washington, 1970-74. NSF grad. fellow, 1960-63; Woodrow Wilson Hon. fellow, 1960. Mem. Assn. Rsch. on Non-Profit Orgns. and Voluntary Action (founder, pres. 1971-73, Lifetime Achievement award 1993), Authors Guild, Sarasota Fiction Writers, Harvard Club of Sarasota, Phi Beta Kappa, Phi Kappa Phi, Ch. of the Cross. Avocations: reading, photography, fiction writing, jazz, foreign travel. Office: Boston Coll Sociol Dept 140 Commonwealth Ave Chestnut Hill MA 02467-3800 E-mail: dhortonsmith@hotmail.com.

SMITH, DAVID I. German language educator; s. Morris and Shirley Smith; m. Julia C Griffiths, Aug. 20, 1988; children: Nathaniel D, Miriam C, Amy C. BA with honors in modern lang., U. Oxford, Eng., 1988; post grad. cert. in edn., U. Nottingham, Eng., 1989; MPhil, Inst. for Christian Studies, Can., 1997; PhD in curriculum studies, U. London, Eng., 1997—2000. Rschr. The Stapleford Ctr., Nottingham, England, 1997—2000; asst. prof. german Calvin Coll., Grand Rapids, Mich., 2000—; dir. Kuyers Inst. for Christian Tchg. and Learning, 2004—. Editor various scholarly jours.; co-author: The Gift of the Stranger: Faith, Hospitality and Foreign Language Learning, The Bible and the Task of Teaching; author: The Spirit of the Foreign Language Classroom. Mem.: North Am. Christian Fgn. Lang. Assn. (jour. editor 2001). Office: Calvin Coll 3201 Burton St Grand Rapids MI 49546

SMITH, DAVID JAMES, corporate lawyer; b. 1955; BS, Western Ill. U.; JD, John Marshall Law Sch. Asst. sec. Archer Daniels Midland, Decatur, Ill., 1988-97, asst. gen. counsel, 1995-97, v.p., sec., gen. counsel, 1997—2001, sr. v.p., sec., gen. counsel, 2002—03, exec. v.p., sec. and gen. counsel, 2003—. Office: Archer Daniels Midland Co 4666 E Faries Pkwy Decatur IL 62526-5666*

SMITH, DAVID JEDDIE, American literature educator; b. Portsmouth, Va., Dec. 19, 1942; s. Ralph Gearld and Catherine Mary (Cornwell) S.; m. Deloras Mae Weaver, Mar. 31, 1966; children: David Jeddie, Lael Cornwell, Mary Catherine. BA, U. Va., 1965; MA, So. Ill. U., 1969; PhD, Ohio U., 1976. Staff creative writing Bennington (Vt.) Coll. summer prog., 1980-87; instr. English We. Mich. U., Kalamazoo, 1973-74; asst. prof. English Cottey Coll., Nevada, Mo., 1974-75; assoc. prof. English U. Utah, Salt Lake City, 1976-80; vis. prof. English SUNY, Binghamton, 1980-81; assoc. prof. English U. Fla., Gainesville, 1981-82; prof. Am. lit. Va. Commonwealth U., Richmond, 1982-89; prof. Am. Lit. La. State U., 1990-96, Hopkins P. Breazle Found. Prof. English, 1997-98; Boyd prof. of English, 1998—. Lectr. in field; cons. in field. Author: Local Assays, 1985, The Roundhouse Voices: Selected and new Poems, 1985, The Morrow Anthology of Younger American Poets, 1985, Gray Soldiers, 1984, Southern Delights, 1984, In the House of the Judge, 1983, The Pure Clear Word: Essays on the Poetry of James Wright, 1982, Onliness, 1981, Homage to Edgar Allan Poe, 1981, Cuba Night, 1990, Night Pleasures: New and Selected Poems (England), 1992, Fate's Kite: Poems 1991-1995, 1996, Floating on Solitude: Three Books of Poems, 1996, The Wick of Memory: New and Selected Poems 1970-2000, 2000, others; editor New Va. Rev., 1987, The Back Doors: A Poetry Mag., Southern Rev., 1990; contbr. articles to profl. jours. Recipient Va. Prize in Poetry, 1988, Prairie Schooner poetry prize, 1980, Portland Rev. poetry prize, 1979, Sou'wester poetry prize, 1973, others; Guggenheim fellow, 1981, Lyndhurst fellow, 1987, 88, 89, others. Mem. MLA, So. MLA, Poetry Soc. Am., Poetry Soc. Va., PEN, Nat. Book Critics Cir., Assn. Writing Progs., Acad. Am. Poets, Fellowship of So. Writers. Office: La State U So Rev 43 S Allen Hall Baton Rouge LA 70803-0001 also: 14 E Bishops Rd Baltimore MD 21218-2312

SMITH, DAVID JOHN, physicist, researcher; b. Melbourne, Australia, Oct. 10, 1948; arrived in U.S., 1984; s. Arthur and Agnes Frances S.; m. Gwenneth Paula Bland, Sept. 18, 1971 (div. 1992); children: Heather F., Marion J. BSc with honors, U. Melbourne, Australia, 1970, PhD, 1978, DSc, 1988. Post-doctoral rsch. asst. Cavendish Lab. U. Cambridge, Eng., 1976-78, sr. rsch. assoc., 1979-84; assoc. prof. Ariz. State U., Tempe, 1984-87, prof., 1987—, regents prof., 2000—, dir. Ctr. for Solid State Sci., 2001—04. Dir. Cambridge U. High Resolution Electron Microscope, 1979-84, NSF Ctr. for High Resolution Electron Microscopy, Tempe, 1991-96. Author 15 chpts. in books; editor 15 conf. procs.; contbr. over 400 articles to profl. jours. Recipient Faculty Achievement award Burlington Resources Found., 1990. Fellow Inst. Physics (U.K., Charles Vernon Boys prize 1985), Am. Phys. Soc.; mem. Material Rsch. Soc., Microscopy Soc. Am. Office: Ariz State U Ctr Solid State Sci Tempe AZ 85287 Office Phone: 480-965-4540. Business E-Mail: david.smith@asu.edu.

SMITH, DAVID JOHN, JR., plastic surgeon; b. Indpls., Feb. 20, 1947; s. David John and Carolyn (Culp) S.; m. Nancy Loonsten, June 7, 1975; children: Matthew, Peter, Hadley. BA, Wesleyan U., 1969; MD, Ind. U., 1973. Diplomate Am. Bd. Plastic Surgery. Resident Emory U.-Grady Hosp., Atlanta, 1973-78; resident Ind. U. Med. Ctr., Indpls., 1978-80; Christine Kleinert fellow in hand surgery, 1979; asst. prof. surgery Ind. U. Sch. Medicine, 1980-84; assoc. prof. of surgery Wayne State U. Sch. Medicine, 1984-87; assoc. prof. plastic surgery, surgery sect. head U. Mich. Med. Ctr., Ann Arbor, 1987-92, prof. surgery sect. head, 1992—2001; prof. surgery Coll. Medicine U. South Fla., 2004—, chmn. surg. oncology, 2004—, dir. Divsn. Plastic and Reconstructive Surgery, 2004—. Mem. Residency Rev. Com. for Plastic Surgery, 1992-2000, vice chmn., 1994, chmn. 1996-99; vis. prof. Ctr. Cutaneous Rsch. Queen Mary U., London, Eng., 2004—, Anglia Polytech. U., Cambrige, Eng., 2004—. Mem. editl. bd. Jour. of Surg. Rsch., 1989-95, Annals of Plastic Surgery, 1992-2002, assoc. editor, 1994-2002, Yearbook of Hand Surgery, 1989—; guest reviewer Surgery, 1988—, Plastic and Reconstructive Surgery, 1988—; contbr. articles to profl. jours. Recipient numerous grants. Fellow ACS (many coms.), Soc. Univ. Surgeons, Am. Assn. Plastic Surgeons, Am. Surg. Assn., Am. Bd. Plastic Surgeons (vice chmn. 1997-98, chair-elect 1998-99, chmn. oral exam 1995-97, chmn. 1999-2000), Assn. for Acad. Surgery, Western Surg. Assn., Ctrl. Surg. Assn., Am. Soc. for Surgery of the Hand, Am. Soc. Plastic Surgeons, Plastic Surgery Ednl. Found. (bd. dirs. 1988-99, treas. 1994, v.p., pres.-elec., pres., chair nominating com. 1997-98), Plastic Surgery Rsch. Coun., Am. Burn Assn. (chmn. com. on organization and delivery of burn care 1995-98), Am. Burn Life Support Nat. Faculty, Am. Assn. for Hand Surgeons (pres. 1994), Assn. Acad. Chmn. Plastic Surgery (pres.-elect 1997, pres. 1998-99, chmn. nominating com. 1999-2000). Home: 3107 Prospect Rd Tampa FL 33629 Office: USF Dept Surgery 4 Columbia Dr Ste 650 Tampa FL 33606

SMITH, DAVID KINGMAN, retired oil company executive, consultant; b. Malone, N.Y., June 5, 1928; s. Ernest DeAlton and Louisa Kingman (Bolster) S.; m. Lois Louise Wing, June 13, 1959; children: Mara Louise, David Andrew. BS in Engring., Princeton U., 1952. Registered profl. engr., Tex. Civil engr., supt. Raymont Internat. Inc., N.Y.C., 1952-55, asst. v.p., 1970-71, v.p., 1971-74, group v.p. Houston, 1974-80; mgr. Raymond-Brown and Root, Maracaibo, Venezuela, 1955-70; sr. engring. assoc. Exxon Prodn. Rsch. Co., Houston, 1980-81, supr., 1982-95; cons. project mgmt., 1995—. Pres. Yorkshire Civic Assn., Houston, 1979-80, trustee, 1985-97. With U.S. Army, 1946-48, PTO. Mem. ASCE, NSPE, Soc. Petroleum Engrs. (continuing edn. com. Gulf Coast chmn. 1989-93, treas. 1987-88, nat. continuing edn. com. 1991-93, dir. Gulf Coast sect. 1994-95), Tex. Soc. Profl. Engrs., Men's Garden Club Houston, Am. Legion, Princeton Alumni Assn. (dir. Houston sect.), Cen Ners In Square Dance Club (pres. 1996-97). Republican. Methodist. Avocations: photography, gardening, tennis, golf, square dancing. Home: 611 W Forest Dr Houston TX 77079-6915 Personal E-mail: smithdktx@aol.com.

SMITH, DAVID LEE, newspaper editor; b. Shelby, Ohio, Apr. 4, 1939; s. Ferris Francis and Rita Ann (Metzger) S.; m. Betty Stewart Walker, Sept. 10, 1960; children: Stacie Lynn, Stefanie Linn, David Lee, II (dec.). Student, Pontifical Coll. Josephinum, Worthington, Ohio, 1953-56, Ohio State U., Mansfield, 1961. Sports writer Mansfield News-Jour., 1960-61; sports editor Ashland (Ohio) Times-Gazette, 1961-63, Miami (Fla.) News, 1963-67, Ft. Lauderdale (Fla.) News, 1967-70, Boston Globe, 1970-78, Washington Star, 1978-81; dep. mng. editor, exec. sports editor Dallas Morning News, 1981—, sports dir. AH Belo pub. and new media divsns., 1998—2003, v.p., 2003—. Condr. seminars. Mem. adv. bd. Dallas Stars Found., Dallas Alliance for the Mentally Ill, SMU Athletics, Jesuit Sch. Found.; bd. dirs. Field Scovell Scholarship Found., Doak Walker Nat. Running Back Award, GTE-SMU Athletic Forum. With USMC, 1957—60. Mem. AP Sports Editors Assn. (1st pres. 1974-75), Baseball Writers Assn. (Red Smith award for major contbns. to sports journalism 1990), Football Writers Assn., Golf Writers Assn., SMU Athletic Forum (bd. dirs.), Bent Tree Country Club, Salesmanship Club of Dallas. Roman Catholic. Home: 12312 Marbrook Dr Dallas TX 75230-2244 Office: Dallas Morning News Communications Center Dallas TX 75265 E-mail: studie_dave@yahoo.com.

SMITH, DAVID MARTYN, retired forestry educator; b. Bryan, Tex., Mar. 10, 1921; s. John Blackmer and Doris (Clark) S.; m. Catherine Van Aken, June 16, 1951; children: Ellen, Nancy. BS, U. R.I., 1941; postgrad., NYU, 1942; MF, Yale U., 1946, PhD, 1950; DSc (hon.), Bates Coll., 1986, U. R.I., 1993. From instr. to prof. Sch. Forestry and Environ. Studies, Yale U., 1946-90, asst. dean, 1953-58; Morris K. Jesup prof. silviculture Yale U., 1967-90, Morris K. Jesup prof. emeritus, 1990—. Vis. prof. U. Munich, 1981; bd. dirs. Connwood Foresters, Inc. Author: Practice of Silviculture, 1954, 4th edit., 1997. Capt. Weather Svc., USAAF, 1942-45. Fellow Soc. Am. Foresters (Disting. Svc. New Eng. sect. award 1969, 93); mem. Am. Forests (Disting. Svc. award 1990), Nat. Acad. Forest Scis. Mex. (corr.), Ecol. Soc. Am., Conn. Forest and Park Assn. (dir.), Sigma Xi, Phi Kappa Phi. Mem. United Ch. of Christ. Home: 200 Leeder Hill Dr Apt 425 Hamden CT 06517-2728 E-mail: david.m.smith@yale.edu.

SMITH, DAVID ROBERT, higher education administrator, minister, writer; b. Quanah, Tex., Apr. 17, 1952; s. William Ingram and Genevieve (Gushee) S.; m. Jacalyn Ann Rainwater, June 8, 1974; children: Timothy, Alida. Edn. Doctorate, Peabody Coll. of Vanderbilt U., Nashville, TN, 1985—92; MDiv, Southwestern Bapt. Theol. Sem., Fort Worth, TX, 1975—78; BA, Hardin-Simmons U., Abilene, TX, 1970—74. Ordained to ministry Bapt. Ch., 1978. Admissions counselor Hardin-Simmons U., Abilene, TX, Tex., 1974—77; pastor Thornberry Bapt. Ch., Wichita Falls, Tex., 1975—78, First Bapt. Ch., Flora Vista, N.Mex., 1978—81; dir. of admissions Hardin-Simmons U., Abilene, Tex., 1981—85; dean of admissions Belmont U., Nashville, Tenn., 1985—92, asst. v.p. for denom. support, 1992—94; v.p. for u. advancement Wayland Bapt. U., Plainview, Tex., 1994—98; pres. Brewton-Parker Coll., Mount Vernon, Ga., 1998—. Bapt. student union dir. San Juan Coll., Farmington, N.Mex., 1978-81; sem. extension dir. San Juan Bapt. Assn., Farmington, 1978-81; cons. Together We Build fund raising program, Abilene, 1982-85. Author: (doctoral dissertation) Effects of Perceived Goal Congruence Upon Fund Raising at Selected Christian Colleges (Pub. Dissertation, 1992), (peer-reviewed article) More Than Just a Pretty Picture: Ethics in Promotional Literature (Presented at Ann. AMA Meeting; Pub. in Mktg. Of Higher Edn., 1991), (religious educational curriculum) Various Sunday School Lessons for Baptist Sunday School Board and Lifeway Services. Coach T-Ball, Abilene, 1985, Western Am. Little League Baseball, Nashville, 1987; den leader Boy Scouts of Am., Nashville, 1986-89; tchr. Harpeth Hts. Bapt. Ch., 1985-94. Recipient Outstanding Young Men of Am., OYMA Bd., 1977, 1981-1984, Who's Who in the SW, Marquis' Who's Who, 1997, Who's Who in the SE, 1999—2003. Mem. Hardin-Simmons U. Alumni Assn. (NM chpt. pres. 1980), Southwestern Bapt. Theol. Sem. Alumni Assn. (N.Mex. chpt. pres. 1981), (Ga. chpt. pres. 2002). Independent. Southern Baptist. Avocations: tennis, outdoor sports, reading. Home: BPC Box 2001 Mount Vernon GA 30445 Office: Brewton-Parker College BPC Box 2001 Mount Vernon GA 30445 Personal E-mail: smithdr@bpc.edu. E-mail: smithdr@bpc.edu.

SMITH, DAVID SHIVERICK, lawyer, former ambassador; b. Omaha, Jan. 25, 1918; s. Floyd Monroe and Anna (Shiverick) S.; m. June Noble, Dec. 8, 1945 (div. 1968); children:Noble, David Shiverick, Jeremy T., Bradford D.; m. Mary Edson, Feb. 14, 1972. Degre Superieur, Sorbonne, Paris, 1938; BA magna cum laude, Dartmouth Coll., 1939; JD, Columbia U., 1942. Bar: N.Y. 1942, Conn. 1950, D.C. 1954. Asso. Breed, Abbott & Morgan, N.Y.C., 1946-48; legal dept. ABC, N.Y.C., 1948-50; partner Chapman, Bryson, Walsh & O'Connell, N.Y.C. and Washington, 1950-54; spl. asst. to undersec. Dept. State, Washington, 1954; asst. sec. Air Force, 1954-59; founder, dir. internat. fellows program Columbia U., 1959-75, coordinator internat. studies, 1960-75, asso. dean sch. internat. affairs, 1960-74; cons. AEC, 1959-60; ptnr. Baker & McKenzie (and predecessor), N.Y.C. and Washington, 1960-75, Martin & Smith (and predecessors), Washington, 1975-76, 77-88, cons., 1988—; ambassador to Sweden, 1976-77. Dir. United Svcs. Life Ins. Corp., Internat. Bank, USLICO Corp., Liberian Svcs., Inc.; mem. Coun. Fgn. Rels.; dir. Fgn. Policy Assn.; mem. adv. coun. Sch. Advanced Internat. Studies, Johns Hopkins U., 1962—; pres., dir. Ctr. for Inter-Am. Rels., N.Y.C., 1969-74. Author: Reviewing the Years, 2003; adv. and contbg. editor: Jour. Internat. Affairs, 1960-74; editor: The Next Asia, 1969, Prospects for Latin America, 1970, Concerns in World Affairs, 1973, From War to Peace, 1974. Chmn. bd. George Olmsted Found., 1977-2001; advisor emeritus Nat. Trust Hist. Preservation; active in past various charitable orgns. Lt. USNR, 1942-54; PTO; col. USAFR, 1955-75. Decorated Purple Heart. Mem. ABA, Am. Soc. Internat. Law, Am. Fgn. Law Assn., N.Y. State Bar Assn., Conn. Bar Assn., Fed. Bar Assn. (v.p. for N.Y., N.J. and Conn.), Pilgrims of U.S., France-Am. Soc., English Speaking Union, Asia Soc., Coun. on Foreign Rels., Hudson Inst., Washington Inst. Fgn. Affairs, Coun. Fgn. Rels., Coun. Am. Ambs. (founder, bd. dirs., sec.), Soc. Mayflower Descs., Soc. Cin. (hon. mem.), Brook Club (N.Y.C.), Met. Club (Washington), Chevy Chase Club, Bathing Corp. of Southampton (N.Y.), Meadow Club (Southampton), Soc. Four Arts, Bath and Tennis Club, Everglades Club (Palm Beach), The Crocodiles, Old Guard Soc. Palm Beach Golfers, Phi Beta Kappa. Home: 525 S Flagler Dr Apt 20C West Palm Beach FL 33401-5925

SMITH, DAVID STUART, anesthesiology educator, physician; b. Detroit, May 29, 1946; s. Philip and Eleanor (Bishop) S.; m. Suzanne Wanda Zeleznik, Aug. 17, 1969; children: Katherine Michele, Lisa Anne. BA, Oakland U.; MD, PhD, Med. Coll. Wis., 1975. Intern dept. medicine Med. Coll. Wis., Milw., 1975-76; resident dept. anesthesia U. Pa., Phila., 1976-78, fellow dept. anesthesia, 1978-80; dir. divsn. neuroanesthesia Hosp. U. Pa., Phila., 1982-2001, attending anesthesiologist, 1980—; asst. prof. U. Pa., Phila., 1980-89, assoc. prof., 1989—. Co-editor: Anesthesia and Neurosurgery, 3d edit., 1994, 4th edit., 2001; mem. editl. bd. Jour. Neurosurg. Anesthesia, N.Y.C., 1987-97; author and co-author of numerous sci. papers, revs., and book chpts. Sr. fellow, Nat. Rsch. Svc. award, Phila., 1985-87. Fellow Coll. Physicians Phila.; mem. Am. Soc. Anesthesiologists, Soc. Neurosurg. Anesthesia and Critical Care (sec., treas. 1987-89, v.p. 1989-90, pres. elect 1990-91, pres. 1991-92), Assn. U. Anesthesiologists, Internat. Soc. Cerebral Blood Flow and Metabolism. Jewish. Office: Hosp U Pa Dept Anesthesia 3400 Spruce St Philadelphia PA 19104-4206

SMITH, DAVID WAYNE, psychologist, educator; b. Ind., Apr. 16, 1927; s. Lowell Wayne and Ruth Elizabeth (Westphal) S.; m. Marcene B. Leever, Oct. 20, 1948; children: David Wayne, Laurreen Lea. BS, Purdue U., 1949; MS, Ind. U., 1953, PhD, 1955. Diplomate Am. Bd. Psychol. Specialities. Prof. rehab., dir. Rehab. Center; asso. dean, later asst. v.p. acad. affairs Ariz. Health Scis. Center, U. Ariz., Tucson, 1955-80; research prof. rehab., adj. prof. medicine, cons. in research S.W. Arthritis Center, Coll. Medicine, 1980-87; prof. rehab. and rheumatology, dept. medicine U. Ariz., 1987—, also dir. disability assessment program. Pres. allied health professions sect. Nat. Arthritis Found.; bd. dirs. Nat. Arthritis Found. (S.W. chpt.); nat. vice chmn. bd. dirs.; mem. NIH Nat. Arthritis Adv. Bd., 1977-84; also chmn. subcom. community programs and rehab.; mem. staff Ariz. Legislature Health Welfare, 1972-73; Mem. Gov.'s Council Dept. Econ. Security, 1978-85; pres., bd. dirs. Tucson Assn. for Blind, 1974-86; chmn. Gov.'s Council on Blind and Visually Impaired, 1987—; active Gov.'s Coun. on Arthritis and Musculoskeletal Disease, 1987—, Gov.'s State wide Coun. on Rehab., 1998—, Am. Bd. Forensic Examiners, 1997—. Author: Worksamples; contbr. chpts. to books and articles to profl. jours. Mem. Gov.'s State Rehab. Coun., 1998—, commr. Commn. on Civil Rights, Az., 2002. Recipient Gov.'s awards for leadership in rehab., 1966, 69, 72, 73; awards for sci. and vol. services Nat. Arthritis Found., 1973, 75; 1st nat. Addie Thomas award Nat. Arthritis Found., 1983, Benson award, 1989, Govt. Affairs award, 1989; Arthritis Found. fellow, 1983. Mem. Am. Psychol. Assn. (div. 17 counseling psychology), Am. Coll. Forensics, Assn. Schs. Allied Health Professions, Nat. Rehab. Assn., Ariz. Psychol. Assn. Home: 5765 N Camino Real Tucson AZ 85718-4213 Office: U Ariz Arizona Health Scis Ctr Tucson AZ 85724-0001

SMITH, DEAN, communications advisor, arbitrator; b. N.Y.C., Aug. 10, 1925; s. Franklin Grant and Anna Lucille (Kranebell) S.; m. Andree Marie Praileur, Aug. 9, 1947; children: David F., Christopher P. Student, NYU, 1945-46, Columbia U., 1946-47, N.Y. Sch. Printing, 1946-47. Editor ShowBill Mag., N.Y.C., 1945-47; news editor Boulder City (Nev.) Daily News, 1947-49; owner, pub., editor Tucson Sun-News, N.Y.C., 1949-51; dir. radio and TV news Sta. WBEN/WBEN-TV, Buffalo, 1951-53; dir. pub. svc. and promotion Indpls. Times, Buffalo, 1953-56; v.p., gen. mgr Kendall Assocs., Inc., N.Y.C., 1956-60; dir. Office Publs. and Info., Commerce Dept., Washington, 1961-70, dir. publs. div., 1970; asst. dir. Nat. Tech. Info. Svc., Springfield, Va., 1971-81, dir. office of market devel., 1982-83; assoc. dir. NTIS, Springfield, Va., 1984-85, self-employed communications advisor, 1986—. Chmn. for fed. mail list policy Vice Pres.'s Com. on Right of Privacy; chmn. presdl. domestic policy rev. work group on fed. acquisition of fgn. tech., 1979; bd. dirs. Commerce Fed. Credit Union. Served with AUS, 1943-45 Decorated Silver Star with oak leaf cluster, Bronze Star, Purple Heart with oak leaf cluster; recipient award Ariz. Newspaper Assn., 1950, Ind. Photo Journalism award, 1954 Mem. Am. Arbitration Assn. (panelist), Washington Book Pubs., Soc. Mayflower Descs., Sons of Revolution (treas.), Flagon and Trencher, Soc. for the Descs. of the Colonial Clergy, Soc. Descs. of Founders of Hartford, Oldest Inhabitants of DC., St. Nicholas Soc. of N.Y.C. Democrat. Home and Office: 2325 49th St NW Washington DC 20007-1002 E-mail: deansmith@aol.com.

SMITH, DEAN EDWARDS, university basketball coach; b. Emporia, Kans., Feb. 28, 1931; s. Alfred Dillon and Vesta Marie (Edwards) S.; m. Linnea Weblemoe, May 21, 1976; children: Sharon, Sandy, Scott, Kristen, Kelly. BS in Math. and Phys. Edn., U. Kans., 1953. Asst. basketball coach USAF Acad., 1955-58; asst. basketball coach U. N.C., 1958-61, head basketball coach, 1961-97. Mem. U.S. and Canadian Basketball Rules Com., 1967-73; U.S. basketball coach Olympics, Montreal, Que., Can., 1976; lectr. basketball clinics, Germany, Italy. With USAF, 1954-58. Named Coach of Year, Atlantic Coast Conf., 1967, 1968, 1971, 1976, 1977, 79, Nat. Basketball Coach of Year, 1977, Nat. Coach of Yr., U.S. Basketball Writers, 1979, one of Top 5 Coaches of the 20th Century, ABC-TV and ESPN; named to Naismith Basketball Hall of Fame, 1982 Mem. Nat. Assn. Basketball Coaches (Nat. Basketball Coach of Yr. 1976, dir. 1972—, pres. 1981-82), Fellowship Christian Athletes (dir. 1965-70) Baptist. Office: U NC Office Basketball Coach PO Box 2126 Chapel Hill NC 27515-2126

SMITH, DEBRA A. insurance company executive; d. Larry Lee Smith DO and Lola V. BA in internat. econ., Youngstown State U., 1989; DO, Nova Southeastern U., 1993; M in internat. health mgmt., Thunderbird - AGSIM, Glendale, AZ, 1996; MBA in internat. mgmt., treas. mgmt., Thunderbird - AGSIM, 1996. Cert. Am. Osteo. Bd. of Preventive Medicine, 2000, Med. Rev. Officer Certification Coun., 2001, Am. Bd. of Ind. Med. Examiners, 2001, diplomate Am. Bd. of Quality Assurance & Utilization Rev. Physicians, 2001, Am. Bd. Preventive Medicine, 2004. Corp. med. dir. Highmark Life & Casualty Group, Pitts., 2001—. Mem. Coun. on Internat. Osteo. Med. Edn. of the Am. Osteo. Assn., Chicago, Ill., 2000—; bd. of trustees Am. Osteo. Coll. of Occupl. & Preventive Medicine, 2003—. Recipient Econ. Honor Soc., Omicron Delta Epsilon, 1988; grantee Stipend for Fgn. Students Studying in Austria, Austrian Ministry of Sci. and Rsch., 1992; scholar YSU Found. Scholarships, Youngstown State U., 1986-1989. Fellow: Am. Coll. Preventive Medicine, Am. Osteopathic Coll. Ocpl. and Preventive Medicine. Personal E-mail: drdebraasmith@zoominternet.net.

SMITH, DENNIS (EDWARD SMITH), author, publisher; b. N.Y.C., Sept. 9, 1940; s. John and Mary (Hogan) S.; m. Patricia Ann Kearney, Aug. 24, 1963 (div. May 1988); children: Brendan, Dennis, Sean, Deirdre and Aislinn (twins); m. Katina Arts Meyer, Dec. 25, 1997. BA, NYU, 1970, MA, 1972. Adj. asst. prof. Coll. New Rochelle, 1973-74; fireman City of N.Y., 1963-80; founder, pub., editor in chief Firehouse Mag., N.Y.C., 1976-89. Author: Report from Engine Co. 82, 1972, Final Fire, 1975, Firehouse, 1977, Dennis Smith's History of American Firefighting, 1978, Glitter and Ash, 1980, The Aran Islands—A Personal Journey, 1980, Steely Blue, 1985, Firefighters, Their Lives in Their Own Words, 1988, The Little Fire Engine That Saved the City, 1990, A Song for Mary, 1999, Report From Ground Zero, 2002. Mem. bd. advisors Boys and Girls Clubs Am., N.Y.C., The New York Fire Safety Found.; bd. dirs. Kips Bay Boys and Girls Club, N.Y.C., N.Y. Police & Fire Widows' & Children's Benefit Fund; bd. dirs., chmn. emeritus N.Y. Acad. Art; bd. dirs., pres. Found. for Am. Firefighters. With USAF, 1957-60. Recipient Christopher award for non-fiction, 1973. Mem. Century Assn. Club. Democrat. Roman Catholic. Home and Office: 1 W 67th St New York NY 10023

SMITH, DENNIS B. neurologist, educator; b. Albany, N.Y., Sept. 6, 1939; s. Bernard Y. and Virginia Shultel Smith; m. Bonnie Winburn Smith, July 6, 1984; children: Kimberly, Kendall, Jennifer. BA, Wesleyan U., 1961; MD, Albany U., 1965. Cert. neurology, Am. Bd. Clinical Neurophysiology (CNP). Asst. prof. U. Vt., Burlington, 1970—74; assoc. prof. to prof. Med. Coll. Ga., Augusta, 1974—84; chief of staff VA Hosp., Hampton, Va., 1984—86; assoc. dean Ea. VA Med. Sch., Norfolk, Va., 1984—86; dir. Oreg. Epilepsy Program Legacy Health Sys., Portland, Oreg., 1986—91; assoc. undersec. for health Dept. VA, Washington, 1991—94; prof. neurology Oreg. Health Scis. U., Portland, 1994—. Dir. Office of Stds. in Human Studies Rsch. Dept. VA, Washington, 1994—2000; cons., adv. bd. Oreg. Mus. Sci. and Industry, Portland, 2000—; cons. Nat. Ctr. Auditory Rsch. Dept. VA, Portland, 1997—. Editor: (books) Undergraduate Neurol Education, 1974, Epilepsy, Dx and Rx, 1990, Neurobehavioral Problems in Epilepsy, 1991. Mem. profl. adv. bd. exec. com. Epilepsy Found. Am., Washington, 1987—90; cons., advisor Exec. Office of the Pres., Washington, 1994; bd. dirs. Epilepsy Assn. Oreg., Portland, 1990, 1991. Fellow: Am. Acad. Neurology (edn. chair 1985—90); mem.: So. EEG Soc. (pres. 1984—85), Am. Neurol. Assn., Am. Epilepsy Soc. (exec. bd. 1991—94), Am. Coll. Healthcare Execs. Democrat. Avocations: sailing, painting. Home: 827 NW 25th Ave Portland OR 97210 Office: Oreg Health Scis U Sam Jackson Rd Portland OR 97201 E-mail: smithden@ohsu.edu.

SMITH, DENNIS G. federal agency administrator; married; 4 children. B in Polit. Sci., Ill. State U.; MPA, George Mason U. Mem. Senate Fin. Com., 1996; dir. dept. med. assistance svcs. Commonwealth of Va., 1998—2001; chief liaison to Bush-Cheney transition team U.S. Dept. Health and Human Svcs., dir. Ctr. for Medicaid and State Ops., Ctrs. for Medicare and Medicaid Svcs., 2001—03, acting adminstr. Ctrs. for Medicare and Medicaid Svcs., 2003—. Office: US Dept HHS Ctrs for Medicare and Medicaid Svcs 200 Independence Ave SW Washington DC 20201

SMITH, DEREK ARMAND, information technology executive; b. Hamilton, Ont., Can., Sept. 2, 1953; came to U.S., 1981; s. Alastair A.G. and Jessie Mead (Maben) S.; m. Rebecca Oldfield, Oct. 10, 1981; 1 child, Alastair Maben Oldfield. BCom., U. Toronto, 1976. Chartered acct.; CPA, Mass. Staff acct. Office of Auditor Gen., Ottawa, 1976-78; chartered acct. Peat Marwick Thorne, Ottawa, 1978-79; v.p. fin. adminstrn. Can. Dry Bottling Ltd., Kingston, Ont., 1979-81; supervising sr. Peat Marwick, Boston, 1981-82; mgr. corp. reporting Warren, Gorham & Lamont, Inc., Boston, 1981-82, asst. contr. N.Y.C., 1982-84, sr. v.p., CFO, 1988-90, Penguin Books USA Inc., N.Y.C., 1990-96; exec. v.p., 1995-96; exec. v.p., CFO Addison Wesley Longman Inc., Reading, Mass., 1996-98; v.p., chief adminstrv. officer Orgnl. Dynamics, Inc., Burlington, Mass., 1998-2000; CFO First Knowledge Ptnrs. Inc., Boston, 2000—02; CFO, v.p. adminstrn. Castel, Inc., Beverly, 2002—. Pres. Trinity Coll. Sch. Fund, Beverly, Mass., 1992; bd. govts. Trinity Coll. Sch., Port Hope, Ont., 1992-2003, trustee, 2003—. Trustee John Hart Hunter Ednl. Found., N.Y.C., 1992. Mem. AICPA (bd. examiners 1998-2003), Assn. Chartered Accts. U.S. Ltd. (treas. 1990-93, dir. 1989-94, hon. dir. 1994—), Kappa Alpha Soc. (exec. com., v.p. 1991-93, pres. 1993-95). Episcopalian. Avocations: skiing, sailing, tennis, paddle tennis, golf. Office: Castel Inc 100 Cummings Ctr Ste 157H Beverly MA 01915

SMITH, DEREK V. risk management consultant; Various positions Equifax, 1981, v.p., corp. v.p., treas., 1990-91, sr. v.p., CFO, 1991-93, v.p., group exec. ins. svcs. group, 1993; chmn., pres., CEO ChoicePoint, 1997—. Office: ChoicePoint 1000 Alderman Dr Alpharetta GA 30005-4199

SMITH, DIANA MARIE, business educator; b. Des Moines, Oct. 25, 1940; d. Nathan Henry and Helen (Hall) Kitchen; m. Robert Nelson Smith, Jan. 26, 1971; 1 child, Stephen. BA, Drake U., 1968, MA, 1971. Cert. tchr., Iowa. Stenographer Polk County Welfare Dept., Des Moines, 1960-67; typist Polk County Auditor, Des Moines, 1968, Cen. Life Assurance Co., Des Moines, 1976-79; computer oper. IRS, Des Moines, 1988; lead specialist II Norwest Bank, Des Moines, 1978—2002; sec. Shive-Hattery Engrs., Des Moines, 1976-90; adult edn. instr. Des Moines Ind. Dist., 1969—2001; tchr. bus., computers Des Moines Pub. Schs., 1968—2000; instr. computers St. Paul Ch. and Saks Inc., Des Moines, 2000—. Ind. computer cons.; instr.-authorized tng. assoc. program for Word Perfect, 1994; Mary Kay beauty cons., 1993—. Chair meml. com. Burns United Meth. Ch., Des Moines, 1988—, Sunday sch. tchr., 1961-83, 92-98, sec. adminstrv. bd. Democrat. Avocations: reading, computers. Office: Saks Inc 701 Walnut Des Moines IA 50309

SMITH, DON, communications executive; BS in Engring., Imperial Coll., London. Engr. BT Rsch. Labs., Canada; exec. v.p. Mitel, 1981; pres. AIT Corp.; founder, pres., CEO Cambrian Sys. Corp., 1996; CEO Mitel Networks Corp., Kanata, Canada, 2001—. Office: Mitel Networks Corp 350 Leggett Dr PO Box 13089 Kanata ON Canada K2K 2W7

SMITH, DON ALAN, history professor; b. Athens, Tenn., Feb. 7, 1936; s. Maurice Clifton S. and Frances Ellen Higgins. BA, Vanderbilt U., 1957, Oxford U., England, 1959, MA, 1968; PhD, Yale U., 1965. Instr. history Yale U., New Haven, Conn., 1963-66, asst. prof. history, 1966-70; assoc. prof. history Grinnell (Iowa) Coll., 1970-75, prof. history, 1975—, L.F. Parker prof. history, 2000—. Vis. prof. history Nanjing U., China, 1993—. Presdl. elector State of Iowa, 1992. Rhodes scholar, 1957-59. Mem. N.Am. Conf. Brit. Studies, Fortnightly Club (pres. 1988-89). Democrat. Avocations: politics, music, contract bridge. Home: 1420 Summer St Grinnell IA 50112-1256 Office: Grinnell Coll 1213 Sixth Ave Grinnell IA 50112-1670 E-mail: smithd@grinnell.edu.

SMITH, DONALD ARCHIE, religion business executive, consultant; b. Dayton, Ohio, Feb. 23, 1934; s. Archie Ford and Catherine Rosella (Rabold) S.; m. Joan Sandra Speedie, May 18, 1955; children: Douglas Alan, Keith Cameron, Deirdre Lynn, Neal Ramsey. BA in Sci. and Math., Harvard U., 1956; cert., Indsl. Coll. of Armed Forces, 1971. Mgmt. Acct., 1977, Enrolled Agt., 1996. Nuclear rsch. and project engr. N.Am. Aviation Co., 1956-62; fin. software specialist Nat. Cash Register, 1962-63; mgr. sys. engring. N.Am. Aviation, 1963-67; mgr. bus. planning, mktg. svcs. and pub. rels. N.Am. Rockwell, Columbus, Ohio, 1967-72, mgr. internat. sales and mktg., 1968-73; mgr. strategic planning Rockwell Internat. Corp., Columbus, 1973-76, program mgr. Condor weapons sys., 1976-77, dir. guided bomb programs, 1977-78, dir. bus. devel. and legis. liaison, 1978-80; v.p. fin. applied tech. group Arvin Industries, Columbus, Ind., 1980-84; v.p. fin. Calspan Corp., Columbus, Ind., 1980-82, v.p. fin. and adminstrn., 1982-84, CFO, treas., dir., 1983-84; bus. dir. Franklin United Meth. Home, 1984-86; dir. fin. and adminstrn. North Ind. Conf. of the United Meth. Ch., 1986-92; sr. assoc. gen. sec. health benefits/gen. bd. of pensions United Meth. Ch., 1992-96; staff devel. cons. logal ednl. software, 1996-2000; pres. Kid Solve, Inc., 1999—. Ops. rsch. cons., 1962-64; instr. math. Sinclair Coll., Dayton, Ohio, 1961-63; mem. U.S.-U.K. Bipartite Com. on Nuclear Weapons, 1958-61; industry chmn. Mil. Specifications and Stds. Rev. Com,. 1972-79; mgmt. cons., 1984—. Author: Financial Recordkeeping Handbook for Local Churches. Past pres., treas., trustee Players Theatre of Columbus, 1975—80; v.p. Ohio Assn. U.S. Army, 1979—80; dist. commr. Boy Scouts Am., 1970—73, cubmaster, 1965—70; squadron comdr. CAP, 1976; treas., dir. Franklin United Meth. Home, 1982—84; auditor First United Meth. Ch., 1981—84; ch. adminstr. Greenwood United Meth. Ch., 1997—2002; dir., treas. South Ind. United Meth. Found., 2002—; pres., trustee Columbus Arts Guild, 1980—83; mem. audit and rev. com. Gen. Coun. on Fin. and Adminstrn., 1988—92; chmn. Commn. on Racism in Columbus Pub. Schs., 1972; trustee Indpls. East Dist. United Meth. Ch., 2002—. Recipient Nat. award Jr. Achievement, Inc,. 1954; Letters of Commendation govt. agys., Am. Def. Preparedness Assn., Boy Scouts Am., 1958-78; Leadership award Nat. Mgmt. Assn., 1979. Mem.: NAEA, NAA, NRA, SAR, AIA (nat. chmn. soc. and aerospace tech. com. 1980—83, nat. pub. policy com.), AARP (state chmn. Ill. 1993—95, mem. nat. tech. com. 1996—98, state adminstr. Ind. 1996—2003), Nat. Mgmt. Assn. (v.p., trustee), Royal Inst. Nav., Nat. Tng. Com. (chmn. 1998—2003, Gt. Lakes regional coord. 2003—), Army and Navy Club, Harvard Club (Ind.), Palatines to Am., Shriners, Masons. Home and Office: 7 E Hill Valley Dr Indianapolis IN 46227-2624 E-mail: don@kidsolve.com.

SMITH, DONALD CAMERON, preventive medicine physician, educator; b. Peterborough, Ont., Can., Feb. 2, 1922; arrived in U.S., 1952, naturalized, 1960; m. Jean Morningstar, Sept. 11, 1946. MD, Queen's U., 1945; MSc in Medicine, U. Toronto, Ont., 1948, DPH, 1949. Diplomate Am. Bd. Preventive Medicine, Am. Bd. Pediatrics. Intern Victoria Hosp., London, Ont., 1945-46; fellow in physiology U. Toronto, 1947—49; med. officer health Kent County (Ont.) Health Unit, 1950—52; Commonwealth Fund fellow in pediat. U. Mich. Hosp., 1952-55; prof. maternal and child health Sch. Pub. Health U. Mich., prof. pediat. Med. Sch., 1961-79, chmn. dept. health and human devel., 1961-79; prof. psychiatry and behavioral scis. Northwestern U. Med. Sch., Chgo., 1979-85. Chmn. Medicaid Adv. Coun., 1969—72; vis. prof. maternal and child health Harvard U., 1969—72; prin. advisor health and med. affairs to gov., Mich., 1972—78; dir. Mich. Dept. Mental Health, 1974—78; chmn. State Pub. Health Adv. Coun., 1982—90; chmn. health care policy bd. Mich. Dept. Corrections, 1986—91; med. dir. Sisters Mercy Health Corp., 1981—91. Surgeon lt. Royal Can. Navy, 1946—47. Address: # 408 807 Asa Gray Dr Ann Arbor MI 48105 Business E-Mail: leelo@umich.edu.

SMITH, DONALD E. broadcast engineer, manager; b. Salt Lake City, Sept. 10, 1930; s. Thurman A. and Louise (Cardall) S.; m. Helen B. Lacy, 1978. BA, Columbia U., 1955; BS, U. Utah, 1970; postgrad., U. So. Calif., U. Utah, Harvard U.; PhD (hon.), Columbia U., 1985. Engr. Iowa State U. (WOI-TV), 1955-56; asst. chief engr. KLRJ-TV, Las Vegas, 1956-60; studio field engr. ABC, Hollywood, Calif., 1960; chief engr. Teletape, Inc., Salt Lake City, 1961; engring. supr. KUER, U. Utah, Salt Lake City, 1962-74, gen. mgr., 1975-85. Freelance cinematographer, 1950—; cons. radio TV (mgmt. engr. and prodn.), 1965—. Mem. Soc. Motion Pictures and TV Engrs., Lambda Chi Alpha. Home: 2233 S 500 E Unit #115 Salt Lake City UT 84106-1485 E-mail: donald.smith2@comcast.net.

SMITH, DONALD EUGENE, healthcare facility management administrator owner; b. Mishawaka, Ind., Oct. 15, 1936; s. Ernest Hartmann and Lucile Emma (Krumanaker) S.; m. Nancy Mae Jaffke, Sept. 2, 1961; children: Adam, Reid, Lynn. AB, Wabash Coll., 1959; MBA, U. Chgo., 1963. Adminstrv. resident Ind. U. Med. Ctr., 1960-61; assoc. dir. Ind. U. Hosps., 1966-72; pres. Henderson & Smith Corp., Indpls., 1978—. Lectr. in health adminstrn. Ind. U., 1965-66, adj. asst. prof. in health adminstrn., 1966-78; ptnr. Carmel (Ind.) Care Ctr., Countryside Manor, Anderson, Ind., Dearborn Enterprises, Lawrenceburg, Ind., Rawlins House, Pendleton, Ind., Manor House of Carmel, Ind.; chmn. Ind. State Bd. Registration and Edn. Health Facility Adminstrs., 1969-82. Bd. dirs. Ind. U. Med. Ctr. Fed. Credit Union, 1965-68, Ind. Blue Cross, 1966-71; med. ctr. chmn. United Fund Drive, 1962-65; sec. Carmel (Ind.) Classic, 1979, v.p., 1981, pres., 1982-83; bd. trustees Wabash Coll., 1986—, mem. exec. com., 1986—, chmn. capital campaign drive, 1987-91, mem. long range planning com., 1985; active Hamilton County Rep. Fin. Com., 1990—. Fellow ACHS; mem. Am. Health Care Assn., Ind. Health Care Assn., Wabash Coll. Alumni Assn., U. Chgo. Hosp. Adminstrn. Alumni Assn., Woodland Country Club, Vero Beach Country Club. Office: Henderson & Smith Corp 10333 N Meridian St Ste 250 Indianapolis IN 46290-1144

SMITH, DONALD F. dean; b. Picton, Ont., Can., Nov. 25, 1949; DVM with distinction, U. Guelph, Can., 1974. Diplomate Am. Coll. Vet. Surgeons. Intern, resident U. Pa.; mem. faculty Cornell U., Ithaca, NY, 1977—82, asst. prof. surgery, 1977, mem. faculty, 1987—, prof. surgery, chair dept. clin. svcs., 1987; tchr., rschr. U. Wis.-Madison Sch. Vet. Medicine, 1982—87, chair dept. surg. svcs., 1986; assoc. dean for acad. programs Cornell U. Coll. Vet. Medicine, Ithaca, NY, 1990, acting dean, 1997, dean, 1997—. Mem. Nat. Acad. of Practices; chmn. Zweig Memorial Fund. Com. Mem.: Am. Coll. Vet. Surgeons (diplomate), Nat. Acad. Practices. Office: Cornell U Coll Vet Medicine Box 44 Ithaca NY 14853-6401*

SMITH, DONALD G. metal products executive; m. Barbara Smith; children: Donald G. Smith Jr., Bonnie S. Longworth, Rebecca S. Wirt, Edward. With Roanoke Elec. Steel Corp., Va., 1957—85, pres., CEO, 1985—89, chmn., CEO, 1989—. Bd. dirs. Am. Elec. Power, Carillon Roanoke Meml. and Cmty. Hosps., First Union Nat. Bank-Mid-Atlantic Region. Bd. dirs. Richfield Retirement Cmty., YMCA. Mem.: Va. State C. of C. (bd. dirs.), Steel Mfrs. Assn. (bd. dirs.). Avocations: golf, tennis. Office: PO Box 13948 Roanoke VA 24038-3948

SMITH, DONALD RAYMOND, librarian; b. Highland, Ill., Sept. 25, 1946; s. Raymond Stanley and Gladys Loraine (Martin) S.; m. Elaine Marie Neudecker, Apr. 12, 1969; 1 child, Benjamin Christopher. BA, So. Ill. U., 1968, MA, 1972, MS, 1978; MLS, U. Mo., 1976. Acad. adv. So. Ill. U., Edwardsville, 1970-73, libr. instr., 1973-78, edn. libr., 1978-82; assoc. dir. pub. svc. and collection devel. U. Tulsa, 1982-88, assoc. dir. gen. svcs., 1988-93; dir. libr. N.E. La. U., Monroe, La., 1993-96; dean info. svcs. U. La., Monroe, 1996—2003, dean libr., 2003—. Cons. Hayner Pub. Libr., Alton, Ill., 1977-82, Tulsa City County Libr., 1984; cons. facilitator Tulsa Area Libr. Coop., 1987-88, 90; collection evaulator Okla. Jr. Coll., Tulsa, 1984. Author: Newspaper Indexing Handbook, 1981; editor and compiler newspaper index, 1976-77. Cataloger Our Lady Queen of Peace Sch., Belleville, Ill., 1979-82; campaign worker Dem. Party, Belleville, 1972; chair bd. dirs. Tulsa Area Libr. Coop., 1991-93. With U.S. Army, 1969-70. Recipient Millicent C. Palmer award Friends of Lovejoy Library, So. Ill. U., 1974, H.W. Wilson scholar, 1974, Higher Edn. Coordinating Act grantee Ill. State Library, 1980-81, Workshop award U. Okla. Sch. Library Sci., 1984. Mem.: ALA, La. Libr. Network Commn., Tech. Consortium Tchr. Edn., Trailblazer Libr. Dirs. Bd. and Commn., La. Acad. Libr. Info. Network Consortium (at-large exec. bd. dirs. 1994—96, chmn. rsch. and devel. com. 2001—03), La. Assn. Coll. and Rsch. Librs. (automation and tech. com. 2000—, v.p., pres.-elect 2003—), La. Libr. Assn. (sec. scholarship trust 1994—, co-chair ann. conf. 2003—04, network commn. 2004—), Okla. Libr. Assn. (chmn. contg. edn. com. 1985—86, chmn. adminstrn. roundtable 1989—90, chair automation roundtable 1991—92), Assn. Coll. and Rsch. Librs., NOTIS Users Group, Phi Delta Kappa, Phi Kappa Phi. Roman Catholic. Avocations: travel, history, reading. Office: U La Univ Libr 700 University Ave Monroe LA 71209-0720 Office Phone: 318-342-1050.

SMITH, DONALD VAUGHAN, artist, educator; b. Pascagoula, Miss., Dec. 4, 1954; s. Arthur V. and Doris (Megehee) S. B in Engring., U. Miss., 1978; BFA in Sculpture, William Carey Coll., 1997, MEd, 2000; workshops with, Jere Allen, Paul Soldner, Kouji Sugie, Peter Seabridge, Toshiko Takaezu. Art tchr. Vancleave H.S. Works represented in pub. and pvt. collections, galleries; prin. works include busts displayed at Trent Lott Mid. Sch., William Carey Coll.; artist (CD cover art) 3 Doors Down, (textbook cover art) Beginning Sculpture; actor in 6 feature films. Home: 906 Sarrazin Ave Pascagoula MS 39567-4955 Personal E-mail: donzart@hotmail.com.

SMITH, DOROTHY BRAND, retired librarian; b. Beaumont, Tex., Oct. 4, 1922; d. Robert and Lula (Jones) Brand; m. William E. Smith, June 15, 1941; children: Wilson B., Lurinda. BS in Social Sci., Lamar U., 1954; MLS, U. Tex., 1971. Tchr. Beaumont Ind. Sch. Dist., 1954-62, Austin (Tex.) Ind. Sch. Dist., 1962-66; libr. Galindo Elem. Sch., Austin, 1966-94; ret., 1994. Cons. Edn. Svc. Ctr., Austin, 1974, 83; workshop leader Austin Ind. Schs., 1980; China del. Citizen Amb. Program People Internat., 1993. Author: Texas in Children's Books, a Bibliography, 1974. Recipient Siddie Joe Johnson award, Children's Roundtable of Tex. Libr. Assn., 1984. Mem. ALA, AAUW, Tex. Libr. Assn. (life), Tex. State Tchrs. Assn. (life), Delta Kappa Gamma, Phi Delta Kappa. Presbyterian. Home: 6108 Mountainclimb Dr Austin TX 78731-3824 Personal E-mail: dorries@aol.com.

SMITH, DOROTHY OTTINGER, jewelry designer, civic worker; b. Indpls., 1922; d. Albert Ellsworth and Leona Aurelia (Waller) Ottinger; m. James Emory Smith, June 25, 1943 (div. 1984); children: Michael Ottinger, Sarah Anne, Theodore Arnold, Lisa Marie. Student, Herron Art Sch. of Purdue U. and Ind. U., 1941-42. Comml. artist William H. Block Co., Indpls., 1942-43, H.P. Wasson Co., 1943-44; dir. Riverside (Calif.) Art Ctr., 1963-64; jewelry designer Riverside, 1970—; numerous design commns. Adviser Riverside chpt. Freedom's Found. of Valley Forge; co-chmn. fund raising com. Riverside Art Ctr. and Mus., 1966-67, bd. dirs. Art Alliance, 1980-81; mem. Riverside City Hall sculpture selection panel Nat. Endowment for the Arts, 1974-75; chmn. fundraising benefit Riverside Art Ctr. and Mus., 1973-74, trustee, 1980-84, chmn. permanent collection, 1981-84, co-chmn. fund drive, 1982-84, trustee, 1998—; chmn. Riverside Mcpl. Arts Commn., 1974-76, Silver Anniversary Gala, 1992; juror Riverside Civic Ctr. Purchase Prize Art Show, 1975; mem. pub. bldgs. and grounds subcom., gen. plan citizens com. City of Riverside, 1965-66; mem. Mayor's Commn. on Civic Beauty, Mayor's Commn. on Sister City Sendai, 1965-66; bd. dirs., chmn. spl. events Children's League of Riverside Community Hosp., 1952-53; bd. dirs. Crippled Children's Soc. of Riverside, spl. events. chmn., 1952-53; bd. dirs. Nat. Charity League, pres. Riverside chpt., 1965-66; mem. exec. com. bd. trustees Riverside Arts Found., 1977-91, fund drive chmn., 1978-79, project rev. chmn., 1978-79, advisor Eveing for the Arts, 1998, juror Gemco Charitable and Scholarship Found., 1977-85; mem. bd. women deacons Calvary Presbyn. Ch., 1978-80, elder, 1989-92; mem. incorporating bd. Inland Empire United Fund for the Arts, 1980-81; bd dirs. Hospice Orgn. Riverside County, 1982-84; trustee Riverside Art Mus., 1998—; mem. Calif. Coun. Humanities, 1982-86. Recipient cert. Riverside City Coun., 1977, plaque Mayor of Riverside, 1977, Spl. Recognition Riverside Cultural Arts Coun., 1981, Disting. Svc. plaque Riverside Art Ctr. and Mus., Jr. League Silver Raincross Community Svc. award, 1989, Cert Appreciation Outstanding Svc. to the Arts Community Riverside Arts Found., 1990, Top Dog award Riverside Art Mus., 1999. Mem. Riverside Art Assn. (pres. 1961-63, 1st. v.p. 1964-65, 67-68, trustee 1959-70, 80-84, 87-92), Art Alliance of Riverside Art Ctr. and Museum (founder 1964, pres. 1969-70). Address: 3979 Chapman Pl Riverside CA 92506-1150

SMITH, DOUGLAS LARUE, marketing executive; b. Madison, Minn., July 25, 1917; s. Julius Waldo and Blanche (LaRue) S.; m. Jean Hefty, Feb. 8, 1941 (dec. 1979); children: Pamela Jean (Mrs. Robert Graham), and Gregory Douglas.; m. Annice Kerwin, Mar. 20, 1982. BA, U. Minn., 1948. Employed with U.S. Gypsum Company, Chicago, Ill., 1938-42; account exec. Melamed-Hobbs, Inc. (advt.), Mpls., 1946-49; product mgr. Swift & Co., Chgo., 1949-53; account exec. Batten, Barton, Durstine & Osborn, 1953-55; advt. mgr. Johnson's Wax Co., Racine, Wis., 1955-56, dir. advt. and mktg., 1956-64; sr. v.p. Lennen & Newell, Inc., N.Y.C., 1965-70; also dir., mem. exec. com.; sr. v.p. On-Line Decisions, Inc. (became Planmetrics, Inc. 1975), N.Y.C., 1970—; exec. v.p. Planmetrics, Inc., N.Y.C., 1981-88. Lectr. and author, 1988—; chmn. bd. dirs. Assn. Nat. Advertisers, N.Y.C., 1965; bd. dirs. Advt. Fedn. Am., 1961—, Advt. Assn. West, 1962— Author: Winged Foot Story, 1984, 94; editor Footnotes, Winged Foot's Historian, 1984—. Mem. exec. com. Rep. Party N.Y.C.; founder German-Am. Peace Monument, 1994. Maj., inf. AUS, 1942-46, ETO. Decorated Bronze Star with bronze oak leaf cluster, Purple Heart. Mem. Am. Assn. Advt. Agys. (gov. Ea. divsn.), Internat. Radio and TV Soc. (dir., treas.), Univ. Club (N.Y.C., Chgo.), Mid-Am. Club (Chgo.), Winged Foot Golf Club. Home: 209 Ivy Hill Ln Rye Brook NY 10573-1607 Office: care Winged Foot Golf Club Fenimore Rd Mamaroneck NY 10543 *Give-but never give up! For there is always a solution.*

SMITH, DOUGLAS V. manufacturing executive, heavy; b. 1943; BS Mech. Engring., Clemson U.; MS Mech. Engring., U. Ky.; MBA, Harvard Bus. Sch. Pres., CEO, dir. Lufkin (Tex.)Industries, Inc., 1993—. Office: 601 S Raguet St Lufkin TX 75904-3951

SMITH, DURET S. physician, medical educator; b. Palo Alto, Calif. m. Dorothy Hughes; children: Darrah, Erica. Grad. magna cum laude, Syracuse U., 1973; MD, SUNY, Buffalo, 1977. Resident in gen. and orthop. surgery SUNY Health Scis. Ctr., Syracuse; fellow in hand surgery U. N. Mex., Tucson; pres. med. staff Lakewood (Ohio) Hosp., chmn. dept. orthop. surgery; pvt. practice Cleve. Mem. faculty Case Western Res. U. Sch. Medicine, Uniformed Svcs. U. Health Scis. Bd. trustees Lakewood Hosp. Rear adm. M.C., USNR.

SMITH, DWIGHT L., III, academic administrator; b. St. Louis, Aug. 18, 1955; s. Dwight L. and Charlotte (Gerlach) S.; m. Janna K. Homann, June 18, 1977; children: Corey, Chelsea. BA, Blackburn Coll., 1977; MS, So. Ill. U., 1979; EdD, Rutgers U., 1990. Program advisor Tex. A&M U., College Station, 1979-81; dir. campus programs S.W. Tex. State U., San Marcos, 1981-83; assoc. dean students Rutgers Coll., New Brunswick, N.J., 1984-90; dir. admissions Blackburn Coll., Carlinville, Ill., 1990-91; asst. for acad. programs So. Ill. U., Edwardsville, 1991-98, asst. provost for planning, 1998—, adj. asst. prof., 1999—. Mem. AQIP evaluation team Higher Edn. Learning Commn. of North Cen. Assn. Chair curriculum/staffing com. O'Fallon (Ill.) Econ. Devel. Coun., 1994; chair student achievement com. O'Fallon (Ill.) Elem. Dist., 1994; team evaluator Middle States Comm. Higher Edn., 2000—; evaluator AQIP Commn. on Higher Edn. of North Ctrl. Assn. Schs. and Colls.; mem. Ill. Bd. Higher Edn. Academic Program (Approval and Redesign team), 1998—2002. Mem. Am. Assn. for Higher Edn., Am. Ednl. Rsch. Assn., Ill. Edn. Rsch. Coun. Adv. Bd., 2003-. E-mail: dwsmith@siue.edu.

SMITH, DWIGHT MORRELL, chemistry professor, academic administrator; b. Hudson, N.Y., Oct. 10, 1931; s. Elliott Monroe and Edith Helen (Hall) S.; m. Alice Beverly Bond, Aug. 27, 1955 (dec. 1990); children— Karen Elizabeth, Susan Allison, Jonathan Aaron; m. Elfi Nelson, Dec. 28, 1991. BA, Ctrl. Coll., Pella, Iowa, 1953; PhD, Pa. State U., 1957; ScD (hon.), Cen. Coll., 1986; LittD (hon.), U. Denver, 1990. Postdoctoral fellow, instr. Calif. Inst. Tech., 1957-59; sr. chemist Texaco Rsch. Ctr., Beacon, N.Y., 1959-61; asst. prof. chemistry Wesleyan U., Middletown, Conn., 1961-66; assoc. prof. Hope Coll., Holland, Mich., 1966-69, prof., 1969-72; prof. chemistry U. Denver, 1972—, chmn. dept., 1972-83, 99-01, vice chancellor for acad. affairs, 1983-84, chancellor, 1984-89; pres., bd. trustees Hawaii Loa Coll., Kaneohe, 1990-92. Mem. Registry for Interim Coll. and Univ. Pres.; mem. adv. bd. Solar Energy Rsch. Inst., 1989—91; mem. vis. com. Zettlemoyer Ctr. for Surface Studies Lehigh U., 1990—96; dept. chemistry and geochemistry Colo. Sch. Mines; mem. sci. adv. bd. Denver Rsch. Inst.; sr. advisor Rocky Mountain Ctr. Homeland Def. Editor Revs. on Petroleum Chemistry, 1975-78; editl. adv. bd. Recent Rsch. Devels. in Applied Spectroscopy, 1998—; contbr. articles to profl. jours.; patentee selective hydrogenation. Chmn. Chs. United for Social Action, Holland, 1968-69; mem. adv. com. Holland Sch. Bd., 1969-70; bd. commrs. Colo. Adv. Tech. Inst., 1984-88, Univ. Senate, United Meth. Ch., Nashville, 1987-88, 91-93; mem. adv. bd. United Way, Inst. Internat. Edn., Japan Am. Soc. Colo., Denver Winter Games Olympics Com.; mem. ch. bds. or consistories Ref. Ch. Am., N.Y., Conn., Mich., United Meth. Ch., Colo. DuPont fellow, 1956-57, NSF fellow Scripps Inst., 1971-72; recipient grants Research Corp., Petroleum Research Fund, NSF, Solar Energy Research Inst., Camille & Henry Dreyfus Found., Inc. Mem. AAAS, Am. Assn. Aerosol Rsch., Am. Chem. Soc. (chmn. Colo. 1976, sec. western Mich. 1970-71, joint coun. and bd. com. on sci. 1997-98, award Colo. sect. 1986), Soc. Applied Spectroscopy, Mile High Club, Sigma Xi. Home: 1931 W Sanibel Ct Littleton CO 80120-8133 Office: U Denver Dept Chem & Biochem Denver CO 80208-0001 Office Phone: 303-871-2938.

SMITH, DWIGHT RAYMOND, ecology and wildlife educator, writer; b. Sanders, Idaho, July 28, 1921; s. Andrew Leonard and Effie Elizabeth (Simons) S.; m. Carol Elizabeth Breclaw (dec. 1983); children Alan Dwight (dec.), Sharon Lee Smith Dequine, Gary Robert, Mark Jonathan (dec.). BS in Forestry, U. Idaho, 1949, MS in Wildlife Mgmt., 1951; PhD in Ecology, Utah State U., 1971. Rsch. biologist Idaho Fish and Game Dept., Salmon, 1950-52, area game mgr., 1953-56; range scientist U.S. Forest Svc., Ft. Collins, Colo., 1957-61, wildlife rsch. biologist, 1962-65; asst. prof. Colo. State U., Ft. Collins, 1965-70, assoc. prof., 1971-75, prof., 1975-83, prof. emeritus, 1983—. Nature photographer Alan Landsburg Prodns., Hollywood, Calif., 1971; energy cons. CF&I Steel, Pueblo, Colo., 1981. Author: Above Timberline: A Wildlife Biologist's Rocky Mountain Journal, 1981; writer/photographer (film) Research in the Rockies: A Scientist Explores the Alpine, 1973; contbr. articles to profl. jours. Served to 2d lt. (via battlefield comm.) inf. U.S. Army, 1942-45, PTO, ETO. Decorated Bronze Star; rsch. grantee, fellow U.S. Fish and Wildlife Svc., 1949-50, Wildlife Mgmt. Inst., 1950, Nat. Wildlife Fedn., 1954-55. Fellow Explorers Club; mem. Toastmasters (ednl. v.p. local chpt. 1960-62, pres. 1963), Xi Sigma Pi, Sigma Xi, Gamma Sigma Delta, Phi Kappa Phi. Democrat. Roman Catholic. Home: 2211 W Mulberry #257 Fort Collins CO 80521 E-mail: drsmithy@lamar.colostate.edu. *Do not be afraid of enthusiasm. You can do nothing effectively without it.*

SMITH, E. BERRY, television and radio consultant; b. Daytona Beach, Fla., Feb. 21, 1926; s. Samuel Rogers and Rosemary (Berry) S.; m. Mary Terese Hoffman, Apr. 3, 1948 (dec.); children: Kevin B., Martin J. BS, Butler U., 1949. Account exec. Sta. WIRE Radio, Indpls., 1949-54; dir. advt. and pub. relations Franklin Fin. Co., Hartford City, Ind., 1954-56; account exec. CBS Radio Network, Detroit, 1956-57; v.p. Sta. WFIE-TV, Evansville, 1957-61, Sta. WFRV-TV, Green Bay, Wis., 1961-62; exec. v.p. Sta. WLKY-TV, Louisville, 1962-64; pres. Sta. WTVW-TV, Evansville, 1964-80, Sta. WSBT, South Bend, Ind., 1981-89; sr. v.p. Schurz Comm. Inc., South Bend, 1989-2001, cons., 2001—. Dir. adv. bd. CBS-TV Affiliates Assn., 1984-87, sec., treas., 1988-90, chmn., 1990-91. Dir. Goodwill Industries, South Bend, 1984-85, Jr. Achievement Michiana, South Bend, 1984-91. Served to 1st lt. U.S. Army, 1944-46, PTO. Recipient Silver medal Am. Advt. Fedn., Evansville, Ind., 1973; named to Ind. Broadcasters Assn. Hall of Fame, 1989; appointed Sagamore of the Wabash, 1993. Mem. South Bend C. of C. (bd. dirs. 1988-92), Ind. Soc. Chgo., Nat. Press Club, Mensa, Notre Dame U. Club, Elks. Roman Catholic. Home: 5182 Finch Dr South Bend IN 46614-5491 Office: Schurz Comm Inc 5182 Finch Dr South Bend IN 46614-5491 Office Phone: 574-291-9664.

SMITH, EARL CHARLES, nephrologist, educator; b. Pitts., Mar. 1, 1936; s. Mose and Irene Smith. BS, Tufts U., 1957; MD, U. Pitts., 1961. Diplomate in internal medicine and nephrology Am. Bd. Internal Medicine. Intern Montefiore Hosp., Pitts., 1961-62; resident, fellow Cleve. Clinic, 1964-68; physician Cook County Hosp., Chgo., 1968-71; chief nephrology divsn. Mt. Sinai Hosp., Chgo., 1971—, pres. med. staff, 1985-87, vice chair medicine, 1987—; chief nephrology divsn. Chgo. Med. Sch., 1994—, prof. medicine, 1995—. Cons. Internat. Jour. Artificial Organs, Milan, 1986—; med. adv. bd. Kidney Found. Ill., Chgo., 1980—. Co-author: Medical Exam Book-Nephrology, 1976, Self Assessment in Internal Medicine, 1980; assoc. editor Kidney jour., 1991—; contbr. articles to profl. jours. Chair hypertension com. Chgo. Heart Assn., 1973-75. Capt. USAF, 1962-64. Recipient Meritorious Svc. award Chgo. Heart Assn., 1975. Fellow Am. Coll. Physicians, Am. soc. Nephrology; mem. Am. Soc. Artificial Internal Organs, Am. Soc. Hypertension Specialist in Clin. Hypertension, Internat. Soc. Nephrology, Phi Beta Kappa, Alpha Omega Alpha, Sigma Xi. Office: Mount Sinai Hosp 15th and California Ave Chicago IL 60608

SMITH, EDGAR BENTON, dermatologist; b. Houston, June 2, 1932; s. Burt Benton and Lela Elizabeth (Grant) S.; m. Francis Elaine Newton, Aug. 1, 1953; children— Sheri Elaine Smith Dinehart, Robin Marie Smith Fredrickson. Student, Rice U., 1950-53; BA, U. Houston, 1956; MD, Baylor U., 1957; diploma clin. medicine of the tropics, U. London, 1967. Intern Walter Reed Gen. Hosp., Washington, 1957-58; resident Brooke Gen. Hosp., Ft. Sam Houston, Tex., 1960-63; asst. prof. dermatology U. Miami Sch. Medicine, 1967-68, Baylor Coll. Medicine, Houston, 1968-71; asso. prof. medicine (dermatology) U. N.Mex. Sch. Medicine, Albuquerque, 1971-75, prof., 1975-78; prof., chmn. dept. dermatology U. Tex. Med. Br., Galveston, 1978-99; prof. dermatology U. N. Mex., Albuquerque, 1999—. Contbr. articles in field to profl. jours. Served with U.S. Army, 1956-66. Recipient Khatali award U. N.Mex. Sch. Medicine, 1976; Fulbright scholar London Sch. Hygiene and Tropical Medicine, 1966-67; Alfred Stengel travelling scholar ACP, 1967 Mem. AMA, Am. Acad. Dermatology (bd. dirs. 1978-82, pres.-elect 1988, pres. 1989, Sulzberger internat. lectr. 1992, Gold medal 2003), Assn. Profs. Dermatology (sec.-treas. 1979-82), Am. Dermatol. Assn. (bd. dirs. 1994-99), Southwestern Dermatol. Soc. (sec. 1974-77, pres. 1978, sec.-treas. 2002—), South Ctrl. Dermatol. Congress (sec.-gen. 1973-76, pres. 1976-81), N.Mex. Dermatol. Soc. (sec.-treas. 1972-78, v.p. 2002, pres. 2003), Tex. Dermatol. Soc. (trustee 1986), So. Med. Assn. (chmn. dermatology sect. 1988), Baker Street Irregulars, Alpha Omega Alpha. Democrat. Methodist. Home: 3918 Solano Pl NE Albuquerque NM 87110-5636 Office: U NMex Dept Dermatology 1021 Medical Arts Ave NE Albuquerque NM 87131-5231 E-mail: esmith@salud.unm.edu.

SMITH, EDGAR EUGENE, biochemist, university administrator; b. Hollandale, Miss., Aug. 6, 1934; s. Sam and Augusta Lillie (McCoy) S.; m. Inez Oree Wiley, May 27, 1955; children— E. Donald, Anthony R., Stephen S., Gregory S. BS, Tougaloo Coll., 1955; MS, Purdue U., 1957, PhD, 1960; degree (hon.), Morehouse Sch. Medicine, 1989, U. Mass., 2000, Tongalo Coll., 2002. Rsch. fellow in surgery (biochemistry) Harvard Med. Sch., Boston, 1959-61, rsch. assoc., 1961-68; assoc. in surg. rsch. Beth Israel Hosp., Boston, 1959-68; asst. prof. surgery (chemistry) Boston U. Sch. Medicine, 1968-70, assoc. prof. biochemistry, 1970-74, U. Mass. Med. Sch., Worcester, 1974-80, prof. emeritus biochemistry and molecular biology, 1991—, assoc. dean acad. affairs, 1974-77, provost, 1975-83; asst. dean minority affairs, prin. investigator Bur. Health Manpower Spl. Project grant Boston U. Sch.

Medicine, 1972-74; v.p. acad. affairs U. Mass. System, 1983-91; v.p. Nellie Mae, 1990-93; acting pres. Tougaloo Coll., 1995, edn. cons., 1996-98; sr. advisor to pres. Toogaloo Coll., 2002—; dir. AHEC program U. Miss. Med. Ctr., 1998-2000. Mem. governing bd. Robert Wood Johnson Health Policy Fellowship Program, Inst. Medicine, NAS, 1978-85. Contbr. writings to sci. publs. Chmn. bd. overseers Sch. Medicine Morehouse Coll.; trustee Tougaloo Coll., Metco Scholarship Fund, Lexington, Mass.; bd. dirs. Dimock Community Health Center, Boston, New Urban League of Greater Boston, So. Edn. Found., 1976-79; chmn. Boston Com. for Nat. Med. Fellowships, Inc. Recipient research career devel. award Nat. Cancer Inst., 1969-74, award for outstanding achievement in biochemistry Nat. Consortium for Black Profl. Devel., 1976, human relations award Mass. Teachers Assn., 1977, health award NAACP, 1977; Robert Wood Johnson Health Policy fellow Inst. Medicine, Nat. Acad. Scis., 1977-78; named Alumnus of Yr. Tougaloo Coll., 1969, Disting. Alumnus Nat. Assn. for Equal Opportunities in Higher Edn., 1979, 92, Old Master Purdue U., 1978 Fellow Am. Inst. Chemists; mem. Am. Soc. Biol. Chemists, Am. Chem. Soc. (div. biol. chemists), AAAS, N.Y. Acad. Scis., Am. Assn. for Cancer Research, Boston Cancer Research Assn., Am. Polit. Sci. Assn., Am. Soc. Biol. Chemists (com. on minorities 1980-83), Josiah Macy, Jr. Found. Scholarship Com. Marine Biol. Lab., Woods Hole, Mass., Sigma Xi, Phi Lambda Upsilon, Alpha Phi Alpha. Home: 5934 Paddock Pl Jackson MS 39206-2135 E-mail: Esmithahec@aol.com.

SMITH, EDWARD JOHN, geophysicist, physicist; b. Dravosburg, Pa., Sept. 21, 1927; married, 1953; 4 children. BA, UCLA, 1951, MS, 1952, PhD in Physics, 1960. Rsch. geophysicist Inst. Geophysics UCLA, 1955-59; mem. tech. staff Space Tech. Labs., 1959-61, Jet Propulsion Lab, 1961— . Recipient medal Exceptional Sci. Achievement NASA. Mem. AAAS, Internat. Sci. Radio Union, Am. Geophys. Union, Am. Astron. Soc., Sigma Xi. Achievements include research in planetary magnetism, space physics, interplanetary physics, wave-particle interactions in plasmas, propagation of electromagnetic waves, solar-terrestrial relations. Office: Calif Inst Tech Jet Propulsion Lab 4800 Oak Grove Dr M/S 169-506 Pasadena CA 91109-8001 E-mail: edward.j.smith@jpl.nasa.gov.

SMITH, EDWARD PAUL, JR., lawyer; b. Westbury, N.Y., Jan. 13, 1939; s. Edward Paul Sr. and Margaret (Eisenhauer) S.; m. Mary Elizabeth Neagle, Mar. 29, 1980; children: Nora, Edward, Brian, Thomas, Brendan. BA, Coll. of the Holy Cross, 1960; LLB, Columbia U., 1963. Bar: N.Y. 1964, Fla. 1966. Assoc. Chadbourne & Parke, N.Y.C., 1964-75, prin., 1975—. Corp. sec. Am. Bur. Metal Statis., N.Y.C., 1978—. Author: Regulation of Employee Benefit Plans, Under Erisa, 1990. Capt. USAF, 1964-67. Mem. N.Y. State Bar Assn., Fla. Bar Assn. Roman Catholic. Home: 36 Avon Rd Bronxville NY 10708-1614 Office: Chadbourne & Parke 30 Rockefeller Plz Fl 31 New York NY 10112-0129 Office Phone: 212-408-5100. Business E-Mail: esmith@chadbourne.com.

SMITH, EDWARD REAUGH, retired lawyer, retired cemetery/funeral home executive; b. Flora, Ill., Sept. 23, 1932; m. Jo Anne Myers, Sept. 10, 1954; children: Mark and Michael (twins), Jillian. BS, Midwestern U., 1953; LLB, So. Meth. U., 1957. Bar: Tex. 1957, U.S. Dist. Ct. (so. dist.) Tex. 1957, U.S. Dist. Ct. (no. dist.) Tex. 1961, U.S. Tax Ct. 1961, U.S. Ct. Appeals (5th cir.) 1971, U.S. Ct. Claims 1971, U.S. Supreme Ct. 1982; CPA, Tex. Atty. Vinson, Elkins, Weems & Searls, Houston, 1957-59, Nelson, McCleskey & Harringer, Lubbock, Tex., 1959-61; pvt. practice Lubbock, 1961-62; ptnr. Smith, Baker, Field & Clifford Inc. (formerly Smith & Baker Inc.), Lubbock, 1962-84; chmn., CEO Resthaven Funeral Home and Cemetery, Lubbock, 1979-93; cons. Svc. Corp. Internat., Lubbock, 1993—98. Bd. dirs. Briercroft Savs. Assn., 1962-84, Tex. Cemetery Assn., 1986-87, 90-91; pres., bd. chmn. Resthaven Funeral Home, 1965-69, Resthaven of Lubbock, Inc., 1979-93, Lakeview Meml. Gardens, 1978-86; lectr. profl. meetings on taxes and estate planning; bd. visitors So. Meth. U. Law Sch., 1968-71; chmn. estate planning seminar for women Tex. Tech. Found., 1971; pres. South Plains Trust and Estate Coun., 1963-64, others. Author: The Burning Bush, 1997, The Incredible Births of Jesus, 1998, The Disciple Whom Jesus Loved, 2000, David's Question "What is man?", 2001, The Soul's Long Journey, 2003; featured author SteinerBooks Catalogue, 2003-; contbr. articles to profl. jours. Mem. Lubbock Planning and Zoning Commn., 1964-65, chmn., 1966, budget divsn. United Fund; co-chmn. profl. divsn. United Way, 1981; tchr., bd. dirs. First Meth. Ch., Lubbock, 1963-88; pres. Haynes Elem. Sch. PTA, 1968-69; past mem. pres.'s adv. bd. Lubbock Christian Coll.; bd. dirs. Tex. Tech. U. Found., 1968-89, sec., 1969-76, vice-chmn., 1976-78, chmn., 1978-81, chmn. fund raising com., 1979-81; bd. dirs. Tex. Tech. U. Med. Sch. Found., 1970-78, vice-chmn., 1972-73, chmn., 1973-74; mem. chancellor's coun. Tex. Tech. U., 1978—; mem. adv. bd. Sophia Found. of N.Am., 2000—; spkr. ann. banquet Flora Acad. Found., Flora H.S., 1991, N.Y. Open Ctr., 1999, Anthrop. Soc. Conf., 2000; bd. dirs. Lubbock Symphony Orch., 1996-. Mem. Am. Acad. Religion/Soc. Biblical Lit., Am. Anthroposophical Soc., Tex. Cemeteries Assn. (hon. life), Alpha Chi. Avocations: mountain trails, research, writing, concert pianist.

SMITH, EDWIN ERIC, lawyer; b. Louisville, Sept. 29, 1946; s. Lester Henry and Nancy Joy (Heyman) S.; m. Katharine Case Thomson, Aug. 16, 1969; children: Benjamin Clark, George Lewis, Andrew Laurence. BA, Yale U., 1968; JD, Harvard Law Sch., 1974. Bar: Mass. 1974, U.S. Dist. Ct. Mass. 1974. Assoc. Bingham McCutchen LLP, Boston, 1974-81, ptnr., 1981—. Lectr. in field; Mass. commr. on uniform state laws; mem. uniform comml. code articles 5 and 9 drafting com.; chmn. uniform comml. code payments article divsn. drafting com.; U.S. del. to receivables assignment working group UN Commn. on Internat. Trade Law. Trustee Uniform Law Found. Lt. USNR, 1969-71. Recipient Achievement Medal USN, 1971. Mem. ABA (chmn. uniform comml. code com. bus. law sect. 1995-99, advisor to the permanent editl. bd. uniform comml. code 1999—), Am. Law Inst. (Uniform Comml. Code article 9 study com.), Am. Coll. Comml. Fin. Lawyers (pres. 2002-03), Assn. Comml. Fin. Attys., Nat. Bankruptcy Conf. Home: 4 Chiltern Rd Weston MA 02493-2714 Office: Bingham McCutchen LLP 150 Federal St Boston MA 02110-1713 Office Phone: 617-951-8615. Business E-Mail: edwin.smith@bingham.com.

SMITH, EDWIN O. real estate executive, state legislator; b. Brattleboro, Vt., Sept. 12, 1945; s. Orson G. and Eleanor (Stearns) S.; m. Sharron Holmes, Aug. 21, 1969; children: Dwight H., Jason E. Grad., Northampton (Mass.) Jr. Coll., 1968. With Peerless Ins. Co., Keene, N.H., 1968-70; ind. agt. Colton Ins. Agy., Hinsdale, N.H., 1970-88; real estate broker River Valley Realty Inc., Hinsdale, 1987—; mem. N.H. Ho. of Reps. (dist. 6), Concord, 1992—. Asst. majority whip N.H. Ho. of Reps.; trustee, vice chmn. Rescue Inc., Brattleboro, Vt., 1981—; mem. Hinsdale Budget Com., 1971-86, also chmn. Mem. Masons, Elks, Lions (pres., dir.). Republican. Home: PO Box 26 Hinsdale NH 03451-0026

SMITH, ELAINE DIANA, foreign service officer; b. Glencoe, Ill., Sept. 15, 1924; d. John Raymond and Elsie (Gelbard) S. BA, Grinnell Coll., 1946; MA, Johns Hopkins U., 1947; PhD, Am. U., 1959. Commd. fgn. svc. officer U.S. Dept. State, 1947; assigned to Brussels, 1947-50, Tehran, Iran, 1951-53, Wellington, New Zealand, 1954-56, Dept. State, Washington, 1956-60, Ankara, Turkey, 1960-69, Istanbul, Turkey, 1969-72, Dept. Commerce Exch., 1972-73; dep. examiner Fgn. Svc. Bd. Examiners, 1974-75; Turkish desk officer Dept. State, Washington, 1975-78. Consul gen., Izmir, Turkey, 1978-. Author: Origins of the Kemalist Movement, 1919-1923, 1959. Recipient Alumni award Grinnell Coll., 1957. Mem. U.S. Fgn. Svc. Assn., Phi Beta Kappa. Home: The Plaza 800 25th St NW Apt 306 Washington DC 20037-2207

SMITH, ELAINE E. school system administrator; b. Gooding, Idaho; m. Rich L. Smith, June 8, 1968; children: Camille, Kirk, Brenda. BA in Secondary Edn., Idaho State U. Cert. secondary tchr. Coord. vol. svcs.-bus. and edn. partnerships Sch. Dist. # 25, Pocatello, Idaho, 1985—. Coord. Expanding Your Horizons Conf., S.E. Idaho, 1986—. Past pres. Community Svcs. Coun., Pocatello; active Bannock County Youth at Risk, Pocatello, 1988—; mem. Pocatello Area Foster Grandparents Adv., Pocatello, 1989—; bd. dirs. YWCA of Ea. Idaho, 1990—; mem. Idaho West Point Parents Club, 1990-95; active United Way of S.E. Idaho; mem., coord. Portneuf Cropwalk. Recipient Friend of Edn. award Pocatello Edn. Assn., 1990, Disting. Young Woman of Yr. Jaycees, 1980. Mem. AAUW (past state pres.), Nat. Assn. Ptnrs. Edn., Nat. Coalition for Sex Equity Edn., Assn. Vol. Adminstrs., Greater Pocatello C. of C. (K-12 edn. com 1985—, state issues com. 1985—), Soroptimists (Women Helping award 1993 Pocatello chpt.), Alpha Omicron Pi, Delta Kappa Gamma. Office: Sch Dist # 25 3115 Poleline Rd Pocatello ID 83201-6119

SMITH, ELBERT BENJAMIN, historian, educator; b. Benham, Ky., May 1, 1920; s. Elbert Benjamin and Margaret Gladys (Huffaker) S.; m. Jean Frances Smith, Dec. 26, 1944; children: Randall, Stephen, Amy, Scott, Robert. AB, Maryville Coll., 1940; AM, U. Chgo., 1947, PhD, 1949. Assoc. prof. Youngstown (Ohio) U., 1949-57; assoc. prof., then prof. Iowa State U., Ames, 1957-67; prof. U. Md., College Park, 1968-90, prof. emeritus, 1990—. Vis. prof. U. Wis., Madison, 1967-68; vis. Fulbright prof. U. Tokyo, 1954-55, Moscow State U., 1976, 82, Leningrad (USSR) U., 1991; exch. prof. Beijing U., 1983, 88; lectr. cruise ships, 1989-2003. Author: Magnificent Missourian: Life of Thomas Hart Benton, 1958, 71, The Death of Slavery, 1967, 71, 73, The Presidency of James Buchanan, 1975 (Phi Alpha Theta award), Francis Preston Blair, 1980 (Phi Alpha Theta award), The Presidencies of Zachary Taylor and Millard Fillmore, 1988; contbr. articles to profl. jours. Dem. candidate U.S. Senate, 1962, 66; mem. U.S. Bd. Fgn. Scholarships, Washington, 1979-81; founding pres. DC chpt. Fulbright Assn., 1984, nat. pres., 1989-90. Lt. (j.g.) USNR, 1942-45. Recipient Disting. Alumni citation, Maryville Coll., 1981. Mem. Am. Assn. UN (chmn. Iowa Spkr. Bur. 1961-65), Am. Hist. Assn., Orgn. Am. Historians. Presbyterian. Avocations: sailing, travel, athletics, lecturing on cruise ships. Home: 6647 Chesapeake Ter Tracys Landing MD 20779-2521 E-mail: ebs@wam.umd.edu.

SMITH, ELDON, cardiologist, physiologist, educator; MD, Dalhousie U., Halifax, N.S., Can., 1967. From asst. prof. to assoc. prof. medicine and physiology Dalhousie U., 1973—80; prof. medicine and physiology and biophysics U. Calgary, Canada, 1980—, chief divsn. cardiology, 1980—86, chair dept. medicine, 1985—90, assoc. dean, clin. prof., 1990—92, dean faculty of medicine, 1992—97; trustee Alta. Heritage Found. for Med. Rsch., Canada, 2000—; dir., pres. Peter Lougheed Med. Rsch. Found., 1999—, mem. Premier's adv. coun. of health, 2000—02, mem. health professions adv. bd., 2002—. Corp. dir. Vasogen, Inc., Can. Natural Resources, Ltd., Pheromone Scis. Corp. Editor-in-chief: Can. Jour. Cardiology, 1997—. Fellow: Am. Heart Assn., Internat. Acad. Cardiovasc. Scis., Am. Coll. Cardiology, Royal Coll. Physicians and Surgeons Can. Office: U Calgary Faculty Medicine 3330 Hosp Dr Calgary AB Canada T2N 4N1 E-mail: esmith@ucalgary.ca.

SMITH, ELDRED GEE, church leader; b. Lehi, Utah, Jan. 9, 1907; s. Hyrum Gibbs and Martha E. (Gee) S.; m. Jeanne A. Ness, Aug. 17, 1932 (dec. June 1977); children: Miriam Smith Skeen, Eldred Gary, Audrey Gay Smith Vance, Gordon Raynor, Sylvia Dawn Smith Isom; m. Hortense H. Child, May 18, 1978; stepchildren: Carol Jane Child Burdette (dec.), Thomas Robert Child. Employed with sales div. Bennett Glass & Paint Co., Salt Lake City, 6 years; mech. design engr. Remington Arms Co., 2 years; design engr., prodn. equipment design Tenn. Eastman Corp., Oak Ridge, Tenn., 3 years; now presiding patriarch Ch. Jesus Christ of Latter-day Saints. Mem. Lds Ch. Home: 2942 Devonshire Cir Salt Lake City UT 84108-2526 Office: 47 E South Temple Salt Lake City UT 84150-9701

SMITH, ELDRED REID, library educator; b. Payette, Idaho, June 30, 1931; s. Lawrence E. and Jennie (Reid) S.; m. Judith Ausubel, June 25, 1953; children: Steven, Janet. BA, U. Calif.-Berkeley, 1956, MA, 1962; M.L.S., U. So. Calif., 1957. Aquisition reference librarian Long Beach State Coll. Library, 1957-59; reference librarian San Francisco State Coll. Library, 1959-60; bibliographer U. Calif.-Berkeley Library, 1960-65, head search div. acquisition dept., 1966-69, head loan dept., 1969-70, asso. univ. librarian, 1970-72, acting univ. librarian, 1971-72; dir. libraries, also prof. SUNY, Buffalo, 1973-76; univ. librarian U. Minn., 1976-87, prof., 1976-96. Lectr. Sch. Library Sci., U. Wash., 1972; bd. dirs. Center for Research Libraries, 1975-77 Author: The Librarian, The Scholar, and the Future of the Research Library, 1990; contbr. articles to libr. jours. Council on Library Resources fellow, 1970 Mem. ALA, Assn. Research Libraries (dir. 1979-85, pres. 1983-84), Assn. Coll. and Research Libraries (pres. 1977-78, dir. 1976-79, com. on academic status 1969-74, chmn. univ. libraries sect. 1974-75) Home: 100 Bay Pl Apt 401 Oakland CA 94610-4402

SMITH, ELEANOR JANE, retired university chancellor, consultant; b. Circleville, Ohio, Jan. 10, 1933; d. John Allen and Eleanor Jane (Dade) Lewis; m. James L. Banner, Aug. 10, 1957 (div. 1972); 1 child, Teresa M. Banner Watters; m. Paul M. Smith Jr. BS, Capital U., 1955; PhD, The Union Inst., Cin., 1972. Tchr. Columbus (Ohio) Pub. Schs., 1956-64, Worthington (Ohio) Pub. Schs., 1964-72; from faculty to administrator U. Cin., 1972-88; dean Smith Coll., Northampton, Mass., 1988-90; v.p. acad. affairs, provost William Paterson Coll., Wayne, N.J., 1990-94; chancellor U. Wis.-Parkside, Kenosha, 1994-97, ret., 1997; ind. cons. in higher edn. Dir. Afrikan Am. Inst., Cin., 1977-84; adv. bd. Edwina Bookwalter Gantz Undergrad. Studies Ctr., Cin.; mem. Gov.'s Tobacco Tax adv. coun. Performances include (concert) Black Heritage: History, Music and Dance, 1972—. Spl. Arts Night Com., Northampton, 1988-89; bd. dirs. Planned Parenthood No. and Ctrl. Ariz., Am. Lung Assn. Ariz./N.Mex. Named career woman of achievement YWCA, Cin., 1983. Mem. AAUW, Nat. Assn. Women in Higher Edn., Am. Assn. for Higher Edn., Leadership Am. (bd. dirs., treas. 1993-95), Nat. Assn. Black Women Historians (co-founder, co-dir. 1979-82), Am. Coun. on Edn. (mem. com. on internat. edn. 1994-97, bd. dirs. 1995-97), Am. Assn. State Colls. and Univs. (mem. com. on policies and purposes 1994-97). Avocations: music, pen and ink drawing, travel, reading. Home: 24823 S Lakestar Dr Sun Lakes AZ 85248-7465

SMITH, ELISE FIBER, international non-profit development agency administrator; b. Detroit, June 14, 1932; d. Guy and Mildred Geneva (Johnson) Fiber; m. James Frederick Smith, Aug. 11, 1956 (div. 1983); children: Gregory Douglas, Guy Charles; life ptnr. Jac Smit, 1990. BA, U. Mich., 1954; postgrad., U. Strasbourg, France, 1954-55; MA, Case Western Res. U., 1956. Tchr. U.S. Binat. Ctr., Caracas, Venezuela, 1964-66; instr. English Am. U., 1966-68; prof. lang. faculty Catholic U., Lima, Peru, 1968-70; coord. English lang. and culture program, lang. faculty El Rosario U., Bogota, Colombia, 1971-73; lang. specialist, mem. faculty Am. U., English Lang. Inst., 1975-78; exec. dir. OEF Internat. (name formerly Overseas Edn. Fund), Washington, 1978-89, bd. dirs.; dir. Global Women's Leadership Program Winrock Internat., 1989-98, sr. policy advisor on gender, 1998—. Founder, pres. Women's EDGE, 1997—; v.p. Pvt. Agys. Collaborating Together, NYC, 1983-89; trustee Internat. Devel. Conf., Washington, 1983-2001, exec. com., 1985-90; hon. com. for Global Crossroads Nat. Assembly, Global Perspectives in Edn., Inc., NYC, 1984, Washington, 1984-92, gen. assembly, 1992; nat. com. Focus on Hunger '84, LA; ofcl. observer UN Conf. on Status Women, 1980, UN 3rd World Conf. on Women, 1985, del. NGO Forum, UN 4th World Conf. on Women, del. NGO Forum, 1995; mental health adv. com. Dept. State, 1974-76; U.S. del. planning seminar integration women in devel. OAS, 1978; participant Women, Law and Devel. Forum; exec. com., chair commn. advancement women Interaction (Am. Coun. for Vol. Internat. Action), 1994-97, co-founder, 1985-88, chmn. bd.; bd. dirs. Sudan-Am. Found.; adv. bd. Global Links Devel. Edn., Washington, 1985-86; adv. coun. Global Fund for Women, 1988-93; U.S. del. Vital Voices Conf. Women and Democracy, Iceland, 1999; U.S. del. Women in Democracy Conf., Lithuania, 2000; U.S del Baltic Women in Democracy Conf., Estonia, 2003. Co-editor: Toward Internationalism: Readings in Cross-cultural Communication, 1979, 2d edit. 1986. Bd. dirs. Internat. Ctr. Rsch. on Women, 1992-2001; adv. com. on vol. fgn. aid US AID, 1994—; women and conservation adv. com. World Wildlife Fund, 1998-2002; mem. State Dept. Adv. Com. US Internat. Econ. Policy, 2000—. Rotary Internat. ambassadorial scholar Strasbourg, France, 1954-55; grantee Dept. State, 1975. Mem. Assn. Women in Devel., UNIFEM, Coalition Women in Internat. Devel. (co-founder 1979, chair 1993-96),pvt. Agys. in Internat. Devel. (co-chmn. 1980-82, pres. 1982-85), Nat. Assn. Fgn. Student Affairs (grantee 1975), U. Mich. Alumni Assn., Women's Fgn. Policy Group, Rotary Internat. (mem. global com. Women in Future Soc. 1996). Unitarian Universalist. Home: 4701 Connecticut Ave NW Apt 304 Washington DC 20008-5617

SMITH, ELMER, telecommunications industry executive; Grad., Tulane U. Numerous positions The Berry Co.; pres., CEO The Berry Co. (now Bellsouth Corp.); pres. advt. and pub. Bellsouth Corp., Atlanta, 2001—. Mem.: Assn. Directory Mktg. (bd. dirs.), Yellow Pages Integrated Media Assn. (chmn. 2003—04). Office: Bellsouth Corp 1155 Peachtree St NE Atlanta GA 30309-3610

SMITH, ELOUISE BEARD, restaurant owner; b. Richmond, Tex., Jan. 8, 1920; d. Lee Roy and Ruby Myrtle (Foy) Beard; m. Omar Smith, Nov. 27, 1940 (dec. July 1981); children: Mary Jean Smith Cherry, Terry Omar, Don Alan. Student, Tex. Womens U., 1937-39. Sec. First Nat. Bank, Rosenberg, Tex., 1939-41; owner Smith Dairy Queen chains, Bryan, Tex., 1947—. Author: The Haunted House, 1986; editor The College Widow, 1986. Omar and Elouise Beard Smith chair named in her honor Tex. A&M U., College Station, 1983, Elouise Beard Smith Human Performance Labs. named in her honor Tex. A&M U., 1984, Elouise Beard Smith Girls H.S. Viking Girls Softball Field named in her honor, Bryan, Tex., 1989. Charter Mem. AAUW. Republican. Baptist. Avocations: genealogist, restoring old cemeteries, exploring England. Home: 411 Crescent Dr Bryan TX 77801-3712 Office: Metro Ctr 3833 S Texas Ave Bryan TX 77802-4039

SMITH, ELWIN EARL, mining and oil company executive; b. Ellicottville, N.Y., Sept. 30, 1922; s. Henry B. and Beatrice M. (Spellman) S.; m. Mary Ellen Kirchmaier, Nov. 4, 1944; children: Peter E., Michael E., Timothy E. Student, U. Ala., 1941-43, NYU, 1954, Harvard Bus. Sch., 1962. Sales engr. Cities Service Oil Co., N.Y.C., 1949-55; gen. sales mgr. Climax Molybdenum Co., N.Y.C., 1955-64; exec. v.p., dir. Lithium Corp. Am., Gastonia, N.C., 1964-69, pres., CEO, 1969-77; v.p., dir. Gulf Resources & Chem. Co., Houston, 1970-77; pres., dir. Asia Lithium Corp., Osaka, Japan, 1970-77; pres. Amax Iron Ore, Greenwich, Conn., 1977-80, corp. v.p., group exec. for indsl. minerals and resources group, 1978-80; exec. v.p. Amax Inc., Greenwich, 1981-82, sr. exec. v.p., 1982-85; prin. Elwin Smith Internat. Sales Engrs., Darien, Conn., 1986—. Bd. dirs. Am. Metal & Coal Co., Greenwich, Ct., Ethanol Corp., Sydney, Australia, First Dynasty Mines, Denver, IMR Industries, Ltd., London; chmn. Seven Seas Cinema, Stamford, Conn., 1985-95. 1st lt. U.S. Army Paratroopers, 1943-48. Decorated Combat Inf. badge, Bronze Star, sr. parachute badge. Mem. AIME, Am. Petroleum Inst., Am. Chem. Soc., Am. Australian Assn., Japan Soc., Asia Soc., Mining and Petroleum Club of Sydney, Copper Club N.Y., Weeburn Country Club, Masons. Republican. Home and Office: 7 Tokeneke Trl Darien CT 06820-6126

SMITH, EMIL L. biochemist, educator; b. N.Y.C., July 5, 1911; s. Abraham and Esther (Lubart) S.; m. Esther Press, Mar. 29, 1934; children— Joseph Donald, Jeffrey Bernard BS, Columbia U., 1931, PhD, 1936. Instr. biophysics Columbia U., N.Y.C., 1936-38; John Simon Guggenheim fellow Cambridge U., Eng., 1938-39, Yale U., New Haven, 1939-40; fellow Rockefeller Inst., N.Y.C., 1940-42; biophysicist, biochemist E. R. Squibb & Sons, New Brunswick, N.J., 1942-46; assoc. prof. to prof. biochemistry U. Utah, Salt Lake City, 1946-63; prof. biol. chemistry Sch. Medicine UCLA, 1963-79, prof. emeritus, 1979—. Cons. NIH, Am. Cancer Soc., Office Naval Research Author: (with others) Principles of Biochemistry, 7th edit., 1983; also numerous articles Recipient Stein-Moore award Protein Soc., 1987. Mem. NAS, Am. Acad. Arts and Scis., Am. Philos. Soc., Am. Soc. Biochemistry and Molecular Biology, Am. Chem. Soc., Protein Soc., Acad. Scis. Russia (fgn.). Office: UCLA Sch Medicine Los Angeles CA 90095-1737

SMITH, EMMITT J., III, professional football player; b. Pensacola, Fla., May 15, 1969; s. Emmitt Jr. and Mary Smith. Student, U. Fla. With Dallas Cowboys, 1990—2003, Ariz. Cardinals, 2003—. Player Pro-Bowl, 1990—95, 1998—99, Super Bowl XXVII, 1992, Super Bowl XXVIII, 1993; owner Emmitt Inc. Named Running Back, Sporting News Coll. All-Am. team, 1989, Offensive Rookie of Yr., 1990, Running Back, Sporting News NFL All-Pro team, 1992, 1993, NFL Player of Yr., Sporting News, 1993; named to Pro-Bowl, 1993, 1995; recipient MVP award for season, 1993, MVP, award for Super Bowl, 1993. Achievements include NFL's all-time leading rusher, 2002; led NFL in rushing, 1991-93, 95; led NFL running backs in scoring, 1992, 95. Office: Ariz Cardinals PO Box 888 Phoenix AZ 85001-0888

SMITH, EMORY CLARK, lawyer, financial advisor; b. Denton, Tex., Nov. 2, 1910; s. James Willis and Julia (Miller) S.; 1 child, Cynthia Smith O'Brien. BA, U. North Tex., 1929; MA, U. Tex., 1933; JD, So. Meth. U., 1937; SJD, George Washington U., 1954. Bar: Tex. 1937, Okla. 1937, U.S. Supreme Ct. 1954, U.S. Ct. Mil. Appeals 1955, U.S. Ct. Claims 1956, U.S. Ct. Customs and Patent Appeals 1956. Pvt. practice, Oklahoma City, 1937-42; commd. USN, 1942-72, advanced through grades to capt., chief U.S. pros. atty., staff Gen. Douglas MacArthur, 1946—48; chief counsel USN Oceanographic Office U.S. Civil Svc., Washington, 1972-73; cons. antitrust atty. Foster Assocs., Washington, 1973-84; pvt. practice Washington, 1994; ret., 1995. Adj. prof. internat. law Am. U., Washington, 1977-84; energy cons. Foster Assocs., 1973-84; fin. advisor Friday Music Found., Washington, 1988-94; lectr. in field. Author: Law of the Sea, 1954; contbr. articles to profl. jours. Vestryman St. Alban's Ch., Washington, 1957-59, St. Paul's Within the Walls, Rome, 1967-68. Named Disting. Alumnus U. North Tex., 1972. Fellow N.Y. Explorers Club, Fed. Bar Assn., Inter-Am. Bar Assn. (natural resources com. chmn. 1973-76), Masons. Republican. Episcopalian. Avocation: farming. Office: 175 Keller RD Gettysburg PA 17325-8188

SMITH, EPHRAIM PHILIP, academic administrator, former university dean, educator; b. Fall River, Mass., Sept. 19, 1942; s. Jacob Max and Bertha (Horvitz) S.; m. Linda Sue Katz, Sept. 3, 1967; children: Benjamin, Rachel, Leah. BS, Providence Coll., 1964; MS, U. Mass., 1965; PhD, U. Ill., 1968. Chmn. dept. acctg. U. R.I., Kingston, 1972-73; dean Sch. Bus. Shippensburg State Coll., Pa., 1973-75; dean Coll. Bus. Adminstrn. Cleve. State U., 1975-90; dean Sch. Bus. Adminstrn. and Econ. Calif. State U., Fullerton, 1990-98, v.p. acad. affairs, 1998—. Co-author: Principles of Supervision: First and Second Level Management, 1984, Federal Taxation-Advanced Topics, 1995; contbr. articles to profl. jours. Mem. Am. Acctg. Assn., Am. Taxation Assn., Am. Inst. for Decision Scis., Fin. Execs. Inst., Beta Gamma Sigma, Beta Alpha Psi. Office: Calif State Univ VPAA Office MH-133 800 N State College Blvd Fullerton CA 92831-3599 Business E-Mail: esmith@fullerton.edu.

SMITH, ERIC PARKMAN, retired railroad executive; b. Cambridge, Mass., Mar. 23, 1910; s. B. Farnham and Helen T. (Blanchard) S. AB, Harvard U., 1932, MBA, 1934. Staff fed. coord. transp., Washington, 1934; with traffic and oper. dept.s N.Y. New Haven & Hartford R.R., Boston and New Haven, 1934-53; with Maine Ctrl. R.R., Portland, 1953-82, sec. adv. bd. retirement trust plan, 1958-82, asst. treas., dir. cost analysis, 1970-82, bd. dirs., 1981-82. Author: Verses on an Icelandic Vacation, 1965, The Church in Concord and its Ministers, 1971, In All That Dwell Below the Skies, 1972; contbr. The Meeting House on the Green, 1985. Trustee parish donations 1st Parish in Concord, Unitarian-Universalist Ch., 1960-96, trustee emeritus, 1996—. Mem. New Eng. R.R. Club (hon.; pres. 1973-74), Louisa May Alcott Meml. Assn. (dir. 1984-99, treas. 1987-99), The Thoreau Soc. (dir. 1987-95, treas. 1987-95). Home and Office: 35 Academy Ln Concord MA 01742-2431

SMITH, ERNEST KETCHAM, electrical engineer; b. Peking, China, May 31, 1922; (parents Am. citizens); s. Ernest Ketcham and Grace (Goodrich) S.; m. Mary Louise Standish, June 23, 1950; children: Priscilla Varland, Nancy Smith Johnson, Cynthia Jackson. BA in Physics, Swarthmore Coll., 1944; MSEE, Cornell U., 1951, PhD, 1956. With Mut. Broadcasting Sys., 1946-49, chief plans and allocations engr., 1949; with radio propagation lab. Nat. Bur. Stds., Boulder, Colo., 1951-65, chief ionosphere rsch. sect., 1957-60, divsn. chief, 1960-65; dir. aeronomy lab. Environ. Sci. Svcs. Adminstrn., Boulder, 1965-67; dir. Inst. Telecom. Scis., 1968, dir. univ. rels., 1968-70; assoc. dir. Inst. Telecom. Scis. Office of Telecom., Boulder, 1970-72, cons., 1972-76; tech. staff Jet Propulsion Lab. Calif. Inst. Tech., Pasadena, 1976-87; adj. prof.

dept. elec. and computer engring. U. Colo., Boulder, 1987—. Vis. fellow Coop. Inst. Rsch. on Environ. Scis., 1968; assoc. Harvard Coll. Obs., 1965-75; adj. prof. U. Colo., 1969-76; internat. vice-chmn. study group 6, Internat. Radio Consultative Com., 1958-70, chmn. U.S. study group, 1970-76; mem.-at-large U.S. nat. com. Internat. Sci. Radio Union, 1985-88; convenor Boulder Gatekeepers to the Future, 1990—. Author: Worldwide Occurrence of Sporadic E, 1957; (with S. Matsushita) Ionospheric Sporadic E, 1962. Contbr. numerous articles to profl. jours. Editor: Electromagnetic Probing of the Upper Atmosphere, 1969; assoc. editor for propagation IEEE Antennas and Propagation Mag., 1989—. Mem. 1st Congl. Ch., moderator, 1995-97. Recipient Diplôme d'Honneur, Internat. Radio Consultative Com., Internat. Telecom. Union, 1978; named to Gallery of Disting. Scientists, Engrs. and Adminstrs., Nat. Bus. Stds., Nat. Inst. Stds. and Tech., Gaithersburg, Md., 2003. Fellow IEEE (fellow com. 1993, 94, 95), AAAS; mem. Am. Geophys. Union, Electromagnetics Acad., Svc. Club, Kiwanis, Athenaeum (Pasadena), Boulder Country Club, UN Assn. of U.S. (convenor Boulder chpt. 1994. treas. 1994—), Sigma Xi (pres. U. Colo. chpt. 1994-95, v.p. 95-98). Home: 350 Ponca Pl Boulder CO 80303-3802 Office: U Colo Dept Elec & Computer Engring Campus Box 425 Boulder CO 80309-0425 Personal E-mail: n6hqkek@aol.com. Business E-Mail: ernest.smith@colorado.edu. *A weakness of many large organizations is that it is difficult for senior administrators to step down after peaking in their 40s. I'm grateful for a crisis at age 50 which resulted in my taking early retirement at age 54 and then accepting a more modest job until age 65.*

SMITH, ESTHER THOMAS, communications executive; b. Jesup, Ga., Mar. 13, 1939; d. Joseph H. and Leslie Thomas; m. James D. Smith, June 2, 1962; children: Leslie, Amy, James Thomas. BA, Agnes Scott Coll., 1962. Staff writer Sunday women's editor Atlanta Jour.-Constn., 1961-62; mng. editor Bull. of U. Miami Sch. Medicine, 1965-66; corr. Atlanta Jour.-Constn. and Fla. Times-Union, 1964, 67-68; founding editor Bus. Rev. of Washington, 1978-81; founding editor, gen. mgr. Washington Bus. Jour., 1982; pres., bd. dirs. TechNews, Inc., 1986-96, CEO, 1995-96; founder, editor-at-large Washington Tech., 1986-97, Tech. Transfer Bus. Mag., 1992-95; co-chair editl. bd. TechCapital Mag., 1997-99; prin. Poretz Group Investor Rels., McLean, Va., 1998—2000; ptnr. Qorvis Comm. LLC (successor to Poretz Group), McLean, 2000—. Bd. dirs. Provant Inc., Women Connect.com, telezoo inc., World Affairs Coun. Washington, The Atlantic Coun., Netpreneur Program Morino Inst., 1996—2002; mem. internat. adv. bd. Kilby Awards Found.; mem. MIT Enterprise Forum of Washington/Balt., 1981—82, Internat. Women's Forum, 1981—, No. Va. Bus. Round Table, exec. com., 1993—98; mem. adv. bd. Va. Math Coalition, 1991—94; commr. NACD Blue Ribbon Commn., 2001; trustee Ctr. for Excellence in Edn., 1993—96; bd. dirs., trustee Capital Region Technology Investors Conf.; bd. advisors George Washington U., Va., 1996—99; trustee George Mason U. Found., 2004—. Named to, Washington Bus. Hall of Fame, 2002; recipient Lifetime Achievement award, Women in Tech., 2000. Mem.: Md. High Tech. Coun., No. Va. Tech. Coun. (sr. adv. bd. 1998—2000, exec. com., bd. dirs., Earle C. Williams Leadership award 1999), Assn. Tech. Bus. Couns. (chmn. bd. advisors 1989—94). Office: Qorvis Comm LLC 8484 Westpark Dr 8th Fl Mc Lean VA 22102 Office Phone: 703-744-7800. Business E-Mail: esmith@qorvis.com.

SMITH, ETHEL FARRINGTON, retired social worker, genealogist, writer; b. Arlington, Mass., Mar. 26, 1910; d. Leander Morton and Blanche Emeline (Clough) Farrington; m. Harland Willard Hawes, Mar. 27, 1951 (dec. 1958); m. John Eldredge Smith, 1959 (dec. 1973); four stepchildren. AB, Smith Coll., 1931; MS, Columbia U., 1942. Cert. genealogist. Case worker N.H. State Dept. Pub. Welfare, Manchester, 1934-35; welfare worker City Dept. Welfare, Rochester, N.Y., 1935-36; placement interviewer N.H. State Employment Svc., Nashua, 1936-37; med. social worker Columbia Presbyn. Med. Ctr., N.Y.C., 1938-47, March of Dimes, Asheville, N.C., 1948-49, Boise, Idaho, 1948-49, Easter Seal Soc., Billings, Mont., 1949-50. Author: Adam Hawkes, 1980, Colonial American Doctresses, 2003; rschr.: Colonial Doctors and Doctresses 1975-2003; editor: Colonial Tavernkeepers, Vols. 10-12; editor Hawkes Talks, 1969-93; contbr. articles to New Eng. Historic and Genealog. Register vol. 142, 143, 149, 150. Active Girl Scouts U.S., past vol. tng. dir. Palm Glades coun., bd. dirs.; nat. bd. dirs. Daus. of Founders and Patriots of Am., 1973-90, past pres. Fla. chpt. Mem. Nat. League Am. Pen Women, Nat. Soc. Genealogists, New England Hist. Geneal. Soc. (trustee 1986-89, life, named trustees room the Ethel Farrington Smith Trustees Room 1993), Smith Coll. Club of the Palm Beaches (past pres.), Ancient and Hon. Artillery Co. of Mass. (past state officer women's divsn.), Soc. Mayflower Descs. (past state officer Fla.), Hull Mass. Hist. Soc. (hon. life). Avocations: travel, writing, lecturing, photography, music.

SMITH, EUGENE WILSON, retired university president and educator; b. Forrest City, Ark., June 10, 1930; s. Milton Saumel and Frank Leslie (Wilson) S.; m. Rebecca Ann Slaughter, May 27, 1956; children: Lucinda Anne, Bradley Eugene. BA, Ark. State U., 1952; M.Ed., U. Miss., 1955, Ed.D., 1958. Mem. faculty Ark. State U., State University, 1958-92, prof. edn., 1971-92, v.p. adminstrn., 1968-71, dean Grad. Sch., 1971-84, interim pres., 1980, sr. v.p., 1980-84, pres., 1984-92, 94-95; pres. emeritus Ark. State U., State University, 1992—, interim pres., 1994-95. Pres. Jonesboro Indsl. Devel. Corp., 1983-94; mem. exec. com. Conf. So. Grad. Schs., 1973-74, Ark. State Coun. on Econ. Edn., 1987-90; pres. Am. South Athletic Conf., 1987-89; dir. Mercantile Bank of Jonesboro, Union Planters Bank of Northeast Ark. Alderman, City of Jonesboro, 1982-84. Served to 1st lt. AUS, 1952-54, Korea. W.K. Kellogg Found. rsch. fellow, 1954-58 Mem. Ark. Adv. Council Elem. and Secondary Edn., Jonesboro C. of C. (dir. 1967-69, 80-85, v.p. 1981-82, pres. 1982-83), Phi Kappa Phi, Phi Delta Kappa, Kappa Delta Pi. Clubs: Rotary (pres. 1974-75). Home: 407 Lynne Ct Jonesboro AR 72401-8807

SMITH, EUGENIA SEWELL, funeral home executive; b. Albany, Ky., Oct. 24, 1922; d. Leo Matheny and Marjorie (Warinner) Sewell; m. James Frederick Smith, June 25, 1948; 1 child, Bryson Sewell (dec.). Student Berea Coll., 1937-41, Bowling Green Coll. Commerce, 1944-45. Owner, operator Sewell Funeral Home, Albany, 1977—; bd. dir. Citizens Bank of Albany, Ky., 1989—. Sec. Albany Woman's Club, 1950-54; den mother Cub Scouts, Boy Scouts Am., 1958-62; pres. Clinton County Homemakers, Albany, 1968-70, Modern Homemakers, 1992-98; mission action chmn. Missionary Baptist Ch., 1965-91; v.p. Modern Homemakers Club of Albany, 1990-92, pres., 1994-98. Democrat. Lodge: Demolay Mother's (pres. Albany club 1966-67), Order Eastern Star (former assoc. conductress, former Martha and Esther). Home: RR 5 Box 104 Burkesville Rd Albany KY 42602-9310 Office: Sewell Funeral Home 115 Cross St Albany KY 42602

SMITH, EVELYN ELAINE, language educator; b. Waco, Tex., July 25, 1952; d. Walstein Bennett and Evelyn Dougherty (Box) S. BA, Baylor U., 1974, MA, 1979; PhD, Tex. Christian U., 1995. Cert. secondary tchr., Tex. Grad. asst. Baylor U., Waco, Tex., 1975, proofreader, 1980, rsch. assoc., 1981-86; reporter Killeen (Tex.) Daily Herald, 1981; writing tchr. Waco (Tex.) Ind. Sch. Dist., 1989-90; grad. asst. Tex. Christian U., Ft. Worth, 1992-93; adj. prof. English McLennan C.C., Waco, Tex., 1993-94; adj. instr. English Tex. State Tech. Coll., Waco, 1993-94, 97; instr. English Hill Coll., Hillsboro, Tex., 1997, Ctrl. Tex. Coll., Killeen, 1997, So. Meth. U., Dallas, 1997, El Centro Coll., Dallas, 1998, North Ctrl. Tex. Coll., Lewisville, 1998. Adj. lectr. Ctrl. Tex. Coll., Killeen, 1997, So. Meth. U., Dallas, 1997; adj. instr. El Centro Coll., Dallas, 1998, North Ctrl. Tex. Coll., Lewisville, 1998; vis. asst. prof. Idaho State U., Pocatello, 1998—. Contbr. articles to profl. jours. Bd. dirs., newsletter editor Historic Waco Found., 1981-85, sec., exec., mem. nominating coms., 1994-96. Mem. MLA, South Ctrl. MLA, S.W./Tex. PGA/ACA, Nat. Conf. Tchrs. English, Conf. Coll. Composition and Comm. Democrat. Mem. So. Bapt. Ch. Avocation: historical preservation. Office: Idaho State U Dept English & Philosophy PO Box 8056 Pocatello ID 83209-0001

SMITH, F. CURTIS, health facility executive; b. 1931; BA, St. Lawrence; MBA, Northeastern; MPH, Harvard Med. Sch. Sr. adminstr. Harper-Grace Hosp., Inc., Detroit Med. Ctr.; sr. v.p. New England Deaconess Hosp., Boston; exec. v.p. Mass. Eye and Ear Infirmary, Boston, pres., 1992—. Bd. dirs. Greater Boston Chamber, 2004—. Office: MA Eye and Ear Infirmary 243 Charles St Boston MA 02114-3096

SMITH, F. D. (RICKY SMITH), rail transporation executive; Pres. Stevedoring Svcs. Am., Seattle, 1979-81, CEO, chmn., 1981—. Office: 1131 SW Klickitat Way Seattle WA 98134-1108

SMITH, FAYE, state legislator; b. Greenville, S.C. m. Tommy Smith; 4 children. Grad., Truett McConnell Coll., 1966; Bachelor's, U. Ga., 1968; MEd, Ga. Coll., 1975. Ret. tchr.; mem. 25th dist. Ga. State Senate, 1999—, sec. retirement com. Democrat. Office: Rm 421 State Capitol Atlanta GA 30334-9003 Office Phone: 404-656-0044.

SMITH, FERN M. judge; b. San Francisco; children: Susan, Julue. AA, Foothill Coll., 1970; BA, Stanford U., 1972, JD, 1975. Bar: Calif. 1975. Assoc. Bronson, Bronson & McKlinnon, San Francisco, 1975-81, ptnr., 1982-86; judge San Francisco County Superior Ct., 1986-88, U.S. Dist. Ct. (no. dist.) Calif., 1988—. Dir. Fed. Jud. Ctr., Wash., 1999—; mem. adv. com. on Jud. Conf. U.S., Rules of Evidence, 1993-96, chair, 1996-99; rep. standing com. Jud. Conf. Com. Rules of Practice and Procedure, 1996-99; mem. exec. com. Ninth Cir. Jud. Conf., 1994-96, Ninth Cir. State-Fed. Jud. Coun., 1990-93, Calif. Jud.Coun. 1987-88, 92— (mem. adv. Task Force on Gender Bias, 1988-90), hiring, mgmt. and pers. coms., active recruiting various law schs.; faculty Inst. Study and Devel. Legal Sys., 1992, Egypt & Bolivia, 1994, Mexico and Tunisia, 1995, Israel, Jordan, Greece and Egypt, 1996, India, 1998, Jordan and Italy, 1998, ISDLS Rule of Law Conf., Berkeley, Calif.; bd. vis. Law Sch. Stanford U., 1990-92, 99—. Contbr. articles to legal publ. Mem. ABA, Queen's Br. Nat. Assn. Women Judges, Calif. Women Lawyers Assn., Bar Assn. San Francisco, Fed. Judges Assn., 9th Cir. Dist. Judges Assn., Am. Judicature Soc., Calif. State Fed. Jud. Coun., Phi Beta Kappa.

SMITH, FLOYD LESLIE, insurance company executive; b. Silver Creek, N.Y., Nov. 12, 1931; s. Harry Lee and Fanny Diem (Arnold) S.; m. Jane Kathryn Elters, Feb. 18, 1956; children: Keith Arnold, Bruce Erik. AB, Oberlin Coll., (Ohio), 1953; MBA, NYU, 1962. Investment analyst Mut. of N.Y., N.Y.C., 1953-64, dir. investments, 1964-66; asst. v.p. securities investment Mut. of. N.Y., N.Y.C., 1966-69; 2d v.p. securities investment Mut. of N.Y., N.Y.C., 1969-74, v.p. securities investment, 1974-78, sr. v.p., 1978-81, chief investment officer, 1981-83, exec. v.p., chief investment officer, 1983-89, vice chmn., chief investment officer, 1989-91; trustee The Mut. Life Ins. Co. of N.Y., 1988-91; dir. MONY Series Fund, 1983—, Empire Fidelity Investments Life Ins. Co., 1994—. Trustee MONY Real Estate Investors, N.Y.C., 1981-90; bd. dirs., chmn. exec. com. Ins. Systems Am., Atlanta, 1974-82. Trustee Friends Sem., N.Y.C., 1975-84, Village of Saltaire, 1984-87; dir. St. Maarten Condo. Assn., Naples, Fla., 1993—; mem. Saltaire (N.Y.) Zoning Bd. Appeals, 1982-84; mem. fin. com. N.Y. Quarterly Meeting Soc. of Friends, 2004—. With Signal Corps, U.S. Army, 1954-56. Mem. Ft. Worth Boat Club, Edgewater Club.

SMITH, FLOYD RODENBACK, retired utilities executive; b. San Francisco, June 25, 1913; s. Floyd M. and Elizabeth (Rodenback) S.; m. Marion LaFrae Blythe, Oct. 5, 1935; children: Marion Katherine Smith White, Virginia Helene. Student, Long Beach (Calif.) Jr. Coll., 1931-33; BS, N.Mex. State U., 1935; postgrad., Harvard Bus. School, 1962. Registered profl. engr., Tex. With Gulf States Utilities Co., Beaumont, Tex., 1935-78, dir., 1965-78, v.p. Baton Rouge div., 1965-67, v.p. div. ops., 1967-69, exec. v.p., 1969, pres., 1970-73, prin. exec. officer, 1970-78, chmn. bd., prin. exec. officer, 1973-78. Pres. S.W. Atomic Energy Assocs., 1971-77; mgmt. cons., 1978-85. Bd. dirs., past chmn. Beaumont chpt. ARC; bd. dirs. Central City Devel. Corp., 1971-81, YMCA, 1980-83; trustee United Appeals, pres., 1975; pres. Tex. Atomic Energy Research Found., 1976-78. Named Disting. Alumnus Engring. Sch., N.Mex. State U., 1977 Mem. Tex. Atomic Energy Rsch. Found. (bd. dirs. 1970-78, pres. 1976-78), Southeastern Elec. Exch. (pres. 1975-76, bd. dirs. 1970-78), Tex. Rsch. League (bd. dirs. 1970-78), Assn. Electric Cos. of Tex. (chmn. 1978-79), Utility Shareholders Assn. of Tex. (chmn. 1986-93), Beaumont C. of C. (bd. dirs. 1970-76), Beaumont Country Club, Beaumont Club (bd. dirs. 1974-76). Presbyterian. Home: 21 Cheska Holw Beaumont TX 77706-2750

SMITH, FRANK EARL, retired association executive; b. Fremont Center, N.Y., Feb. 4, 1931; s. Earl A. and Hazel (Knack) S.; m. Caroline R. Gillin, Aug. 14, 1954; children: Stephen F., David S., Daniel E. BS, Syracuse U., 1952. With Mellor Advt. Agy., Elmira, N.Y., 1954-55; asst. mgr. Elmira Assn. of Commerce, 1955-56; retail dept. mgr. C. of C., Binghamton, N.Y.; mgr. Better Bus. Bur., Broome County, N.Y., 1956-60; exec. v.p. C. of C., Chemung County, Elmira, 1960-65, Schenectady County (N.Y.) C. of C., 1965-69, Greater Cin. C. of C., 1969-78; pres. Greater Detroit C. of C., 1978-95. Dir. Presbyn. Devel. Corp. Detroit, Inc. 1995—. Served to 1st lt. USAF, 1952-54. Named Young Man of Yr. Jr. C. of C. Elmira, 1964. Mem. C. of C. Execs. Mich., Am. C. of C. Execs. (past chmn.), N.Y. State C. of C. Execs. (past pres.), Ohio C. of C. Execs. (past pres.), C. of C. of U.S. (past bd. dirs. Ctr. Internatl Pvt. Enterprise, past chmn. nat. bd. regents, Inst. for Orgn. Mgmt.). Presbyterian. Home: 173 Windwood Pointe Dr Saint Clair Shores MI 48080

SMITH, FREDERICK COE, retired manufacturing executive; b. Ridgewood, N.J., June 3, 1916; s. Frederick Coe and Mary (Steffee) S.; m. Ruth Pfeiffer, Oct. 5, 1940; children: Frederick Coe, Geoffrey, Roger, William, Bart. BS, Cornell U., 1938; MBA, Harvard U., 1940. With Armstrong Cork Co., Lancaster, Pa., 1940-41; with Huffy Corp., Dayton, Ohio, 1946-86, pres., chief exec. officer, 1961-72, chmn., chief exec. officer, 1972-76, chmn., 1976-78, chmn. exec. com., 1979-86. Former chmn. Sinclair C.C. Found.; past chmn. nat. bd. dirs. Planned Parenthoo Fedn.;former dir. Internat. Parenthood Fedn.; past chmn. Dayton Found.; trustee emeritus Alan Gutmacher Inst., Ohio United Way; past chmn. employment and tng. com. Gov.'s Human Investment Coun. Lt. col. USAAF, 1941-46. Decorated Legion of Merit. Fax: 937-223-1441.

SMITH, FREDERICK ORVILLE, II, wood products manufacturer, retired naval officer; b. Cambridge, Mass., July 17, 1934; s. Harry Francis and Dorothy Spaulding (Zeller) S.; m. Mabel Roxy Moore, June 6, 1965; children: Sarah Zeller, Jennifer Joy, Erika Hildred. BA, Bowdoin Coll., 1956; MA in Polit. Sci., U. Vt., 2000. Deck officer, 1st lt. USN, 1957-59; officer US Naval Sta., Adak, Alaska, 1959-60; clk. & exec. Fred O. Smith Mfg. Co., New Vineyard, Maine, 1960-71, pres., treas., 1971—; res. officer Naval Res. Tng. Ctr., Augusta, Maine, 1960-69, Bangor, Maine, 1970-79 (ret.). Co-owner Sugarwood Gallery, Inc., 2000—. Editor: New Vineyard, Maine 1802-2002, Its Settlement, Its People, Its History, A New Vineyard Historical Society Document, 2002. Notary pub., 1978—; chair, mem. nat. com. Young Reps., Maine, 1960—68, pres. New Eng. coun., 1962—64; chmn. Franklin County (Maine) Rep. Com., 1976—80, v.p. state conv., 1994; mem. Maine Rep. State Com., 1980—86, 1992—94, 1998—2002; mem. state com. ASCO, 1998—2002; town chmn. Rep. Com., New Vineyard, 1972—86, Farmington, Maine, 1992—. Paul Harris fellow Farmington Rotary Club, 1996. Mem.: Franklin County Arts and Crafts (v.p. 2002—), Up Country Artists (bd. dirs. 1996—2003, v.p. 1997, pres. 1998—2000, bd. dirs. 2000—03), Shriners, Masons, Kora Temple Shrine. Congregationalist. Avocations: photography, cabinet making & design, skiing, hiking, writing. Home: 127 Anson St Farmington ME 04938-5734 Office: Fred O Smith Mfg Co PO Box 248 New Vineyard ME 04956-0248 Fax: 207-779-0716. Office Phone: 207-778-4177. E-mail: fosmith@somtel.com.

SMITH, FREDERICK WALLACE, delivery service executive; b. Marks, Miss., Aug. 11, 1944; s. Frederick Smith; m. Diane Avis., div. BS in econ., Yale U., 1966. Cert. comml. pilot. Owner Ark Aviation, 1969-71; founder FedEx Express Corp., Memphis, 1971—, pres., 1971—75, CEO, 1977—98, chmn. bd., 1975—; chmn. bd., pres, CEO FedEx Corp., 1998—. Served with USMC, 1966-70, co-chmn. WWII Memorial Campaign. Recipient Eagle of Aviation award, Embry-Riddle Aeronautical award, 2001, Champion of Workplace Learning and Performance award, Amer. Soc. for Training and Devel., 2002. Office: FedEx Corp 942 S Shady Grove Rd Memphis TN 38120-4117*

SMITH, FREDRICA EMRICH, rheumatologist, internist; b. Princeton, N.J., Apr. 28, 1945; d. Raymond Jay and Carolyn Sarah (Schleicher) Emrich; m. Paul David Smith, June 10, 1967. AB, Bryn Mawr Coll., 1967; MD, Duke U., 1971. Intern, resident U. N.Mex. Affiliated Hosps., 1971-73; fellow U. Va. Hosp., Charlottesville, 1974-75; pvt. practice, Los Alamos, N.Mex., 1975—. Chmn. credentials com. Los Alamos Med. Ctr., 1983—, chief staff, 1990, 2003; bd. dirs. N.Mex. Physicians Mut. Liability Ins. Co., Albuquerque. Contbr. articles to med. jours. Mem. bass sect. Los Alamos Symphony, 1975—; mem. Los Alamos County Parks and Recreation Bd., 1984-88, 92-96, Los Alamos County Med. Indigent Health Care Task Force, 1989—; mem. ops. subcom. Aquatic Ctr., Los Alamos County, 1988—. Fellow ACP, Am. Coll. Rheumatology; mem. N.Mex. Soc. Internal Medicine (pres. 1993-96), Friends of Bandelier. Democrat. Avocations: swimming, music, reading, hiking. Office: Los Alamos Med Ctr 3917 West Rd Los Alamos NM 87544-2275 Office Phone: 505-662-9400.

SMITH, GARDNER WATKINS, physician; b. Boston, July 2, 1931; s. George Van Siclen and Olive (Watkins) S.; m. Susan Elizabeth Whiteford, Sept. 6, 1958; children: Elizabeth Whiteford, Rebecca Tremain, George Van Siclen II. Grad., Phillips Acad., 1949; MD, Harvard U., 1956; AB, Princeton U., 1969. Diplomate: Am. Bd. Surgery, Am. Bd. Thoracic Surgery. Intern Johns Hopkins Hosp., Balt., 1956-57, asst. resident, 1958-59, fellow, 1957-58, asst. in surgery, 1957-59, prof. surgery, 1970-96, emeritus prof. surgery, 1996—, dep. dir. dept. surgery, 1978-85. Asst. resident U. Va., Charlottesville, 1959-61, resident, 1961-62, asst. in surgery, 1959-63, cardiovascular resident, 1962-63, instr., 1963-65, asst. prof., 1965-68, assoc. prof., 1968-70, surgeon, 1963-70; chief surgery Balt. City Hosp., 1970-79, vis. surgeon, 1979-85; chmn. sect. surg. scis. Johns Hopkins Bayview Med. Ctr., 1985-96; bd. dirs. Blue Hill Meml. Hosp. Found., 1998--, chair, 1999-2000; bd. dirs. Blue Hill Meml. Hosp., 1998--, chair, 2000--; cons. Greater Balt. Med. Ctr., 1970-91, Loch Raven VA Hosp., Balt., 1971-92, Walter Reed Army Med. Ctr., 1976-90, Nat. Naval Med. Ctr., 1984-90. Contbr. articles to med. jours. Mem. Soc. U. Surgeons, Am., So. surg. assns., A.C.S., Am. Gastroenterol. Assn., Assn. for Acad. Surgery, Balt. City Med. Soc., Halsted Soc., Med. and Chirurgical Faculty of Md., Soc. Surgery Alimentary Tract, Soc. Vascular Surgery, Internat. Cardiovascular Soc., So. Soc. Clin. Surgeons, Southeastern Surg Congress, So. Assn. Vasular Surgery, Va. Surg. Assn., Cum Laude Soc., Alpha Omega Alpha, Nu Sigma Nu. Home and Office: PO Box 565 Deer Isle ME 04627-0565 E-mail: gwsmith@direcway.com.

SMITH, GARY, marketing executive; b. 1943; Sr. v.p., dir. mktg. Safeway, Inc., Pleasanton, Calif., 1995—. Office: Safeway Inc 5918 Stoneridge Mall Rd Pleasanton CA 94588-3229

SMITH, GARY W.H. retired sales executive; s. Howard Frederick and Violet Irma Smith; m. Donna Jean Schallert, July 28, 1962; children: Darren H.F., Brian R.A., Garrick D.S. Student, Phoenix Coll., 1959—62, Fresno City Coll., 1963—64; BS in Psychology, Edgewood Coll., 2001. Regional mktg. dir. Berven Carpets Corp., Fresno, Calif., 1962—69; terr. mgr. Phila. Carpet Co., Dalton, Ga., 1969—75; pres., owner G. Wentworth Smith, Inc., Columbus, Wis., 1975—2003; v.p. ops., CEO Royal Impex Corp., Watertown, Wis., 1978—79; v.p. sales and mktg. Jaeckle Wholesale, Inc., Madison, Wis., 1985—86; pres., CEO Simuwear Corp., Columbus, 1995—2003; ret., 2003. Con. Human Movement Disorders Lab. U. Pitts. Sch. Medicine, 1990—2003. Editor-in-chief: Comml. Carpet Digest, 1979—92, columnist: Gralla Pubs. Trade Press, 1990. Chmn. Dane County Rep. Party Campaign Sch., Madison, 1980; campaign mgr. Rep. Party, Wis., 1982, del. various state conventions; cons. gubernatorial, congl. and legis. candidates. Recipient J.B. Campbell award, Dane County Rep. Party, 1980. Mem.: Masons (jr. warden 1979). Republican. Mem. Congregational Ch. Achievements include patents for foot force simulator. Avocations: writing, singing, composing. Home: 913 Vernon Ave Madison WI 53714

SMITH, GENE MARCUS, mental health services professional; b. Kitzmiller, Md., Mar. 5, 1946; s. James and Marie Strachan (Moon) Smith; m. Juanita Maria Mondeanado, Dec. 29, 2000; m. Rosemary Gail Moyers, Feb. 2, 1969 (div. 1998); children: Sean Marcus Wesley, Derek Gene. BA in hist. and polit. sci., Regents Coll., 1980. Tng. officer USN, Va. Beach, Va., 1964—87; counselor Graydon Manor, Lees Burg, Va., 1987—91; supr. U.S. Coast Guard Ops. Ctr., Martinsburg, W.Va., 1991—92; residential asst. Medsource, Frederick, Md., 1992—2003. Mem. Va. Beach Crime Prevention Steering Com., Va. Beach, 1986. Author: (book) Essay, Thinking of the Edge, 1993, Orphans of the Wind, 2004; Song, Silver Mine, 1972. Chief petty officer USN, 1964—87, U.S. Recipient Letter of Appreciation, World Peace Prayer Soc., 1993, Navy Achievement medal, Sec. of the USN, 1987. Fellow: Internat. Soc. for Philosophical Enquiry. Avocations: gardening, travel, keyboards. Home: 8989 Leetown Rd Kearneysville WV 25430

SMITH, GEORGE, marketing professional; Field sales rep. Elec. Components, Avnet, Inc., 1978—80, gen. mgr., 1980—84, Boston, 1984—88; N.E. regional v.p. Avnet, Inc., 1989—91; ea. area mgr. Avnet Computer Mktg., 1991; sr. v.p. sales North Am. Avnet Computer Mktg. Group, 1992—94; exec. v.p. Avnet Computer, 1994; exec. v.p. Hall-Mark Computer Products Avnet, Inc., 1995, pres. Hall-Mark Computer Products, 1996; regional pres. Avnet Computer Mktg. Europe, 1997; pres. Avnet Electronics Mktg. EMEA, Phoenix, 1998—2003; pres. computer mktg. Europe Avnet Computer Mktg.-Avnet Applied Computing, 2001—03; pres. Avnet Computer Mktg.-Avnet Applied Computing, Asia, 2003—; v.p. Avnet, Inc., 1996—. Office: Avnet Inc S 47th St Phoenix AZ 85034

SMITH, GEORGE BUNDY, state appeals court judge; b. New Orleans, Apr. 7, 1937; m. Alene L. Smith; children: George, Jr., Beth Beatrice. Cert. Polit. Studies, Institut d'Etudes Politiques, Paris, 1958; BA, Yale U., 1959, JD, 1962; MA in Polit. Sci., NYU, 1967, PhD, 1974; M of Jud. Process, U. Va., 2001. Staff atty. NAACP, 1962-64; law sec. to Hon. Jawn Sandifer, 1964-67; law sec. to Hon., Edward Dudley, 1967-71; law sect. to Hon. Harold Stevens, 1972-74; adminstr. model cities City of N.Y., 1974-75; interim judge Civil Ct. N.Y.C., 1975-76, judge, 1976-79, N.Y. State Supreme Ct., 1980-86, assoc. justice appellate divsn., 1st dept., 1987-92; assoc. judge N.Y. State Ct. Appeals, N.Y.C., 1992—. Apptd. mem. N.Y. State Ethics Commn. Unified Ct. System, 1989-90; adj. prof. law Fordham U., 1981—. Author: (with Alene L. Smith) You Decide: Applying the Bill of Rights to Real Cases; contbr. articles to profl. jours. Trustee Grace Congl. Ch., Harlem, N.Y., Horace Mann-Barnard Sch., Bronx, N.Y., 1977-99; bd. dirs. Harlem-Dowling Westside Ctr. for Children and Family Svcs., N.Y.C.; former alumni trustee Phillips Acad., Andover, Mass. Mem. Met. Black Bar Assn. (founding, former pres. Harlem Lawyers Assn., bd. dirs., chmn. 1984-88), Assn. of Bar of City of N.Y. (v.p. 1988-89), Judicial Friends. Office: NY Court Appeals 29th Fl 61 Broadway Rm 2900 New York NY 10006-2802 also: Ct of Appeals Hall 20 Eagle St Albany NY 12207-1009

SMITH, GEORGE CURTIS, judge; b. Columbus, Ohio, Aug. 8, 1935; s. George B. and Dorothy R. Smith; m. Barbara Jean Wood, July 10, 1963; children: Curtis, Geoffrey, Elizabeth Ann. BA, Ohio State U., 1957, JD, 1959. Bar: Ohio 1959, U.S. Dist. Ct. (so. dist.) Ohio 1987. Asst. city atty. City of Columbus, 1959-62; exec. asst. to Mayor of Columbus, 1962-63; asst. atty. gen. State of Ohio, 1964; chief counsel to pros. atty. Franklin County, Ohio, 1965-70; pros. atty., 1971-80; judge Franklin County Mcpl. Ct., Columbus, 1980-85; judge, sr. judge Franklin County Common Pleas Ct., 1985-87. Mem. 2003 Ohio Bicentennial Com.; mem. Historical Marker com., 2003; mem. Ohio Supreme Ct. Coun. on Victims Rights; judge in residence Law Sch. U. Cin.; chair Fed. Ct. Case Settlement Svc.; faculty Ohio Jud. Coll., Litig. Practice Inst.; chmn., Fed. Bench-Bar Conf.; lectr. ABA Anti-Trust Sec.; alumni spkr. law graduation Ohio State U.; pres. Young Rep. Club; chmn. Perry Group, 2004; exec. com. Franklin County Rep. Party, 1971-80. Elder Presbyn. Ch. Recipient Superior Jud. Svc. award Supreme Ct, Ohio; recipient Outstanding Pub. Svc. award Fr. Co. Rep. Orgn., 2001. Mem. Ohio Pros. Attys. Assn. (pres., Ohio Pros. of Yr. Award of Hon. Leadership award),

Columbus Bar Assn., Columbus Bar Found., Columbus Athletic Club (pres., dir.), Lawyers Club of Columbus (pres.), Masons (33d degree), Shriners. Office: 85 Marconi Blvd Columbus OH 43215-2823 Office Phone: 614-719-3220.

SMITH, GEORGE DRURY, publisher, editor, collagist, writer; b. Dayton, Ohio, Mar. 10, 1927; s. Martin Jefferson and Viola (Haas) S.; m. Anne Liard Jennings, Apr. 1967 (div. 1977), Leston Chandler Buell, 1996. AB cum laude, Marietta Coll., 1953; Diplome de Phonetique, U. Grenoble, 1950; student, U. Madrid, 1950-51, Heidelberg U., 1951-52, U. Minn., 1953-55, U. Calif.-Berkeley, 1965, UCLA, 1968. CFO Argonaut newspaper, 1972—. Editor: Beyond Baroque, 1968-80, NewLetters, 1969-75, (book series) NewBooks, 1976-78. Founder Beyond Baroque Found., Venice, Calif., 1968, chmn., 1968-80, chmn. emeritus, 1980—; mem. Mcpl. Arts Adv. Bd., L.A., 1980-82; chmn. Save Westminster Auditorium Com., Venice, 1977-80. With U.S. Army, 1945-47. Grantee Nat. Endowment for Arts, 1973-80, Calif. Arts Coun., 1977-80, Mcpl. Arts Commn., 1977-80, Coordinating Coun. Lit. Mags., 1974-80. E-mail: georgedrurysmith@yahoo.com. *I believe that if we have faith we can live without fear; that the universe is benevolent if we can love unconditionally; that we can live righteously and prosper if we are honest and seek divine guidance; and that our mission is to enjoy life and strive for beauty.*

SMITH, GEORGE LARRY, analytical and environmental chemist; b. Beloit, Kans., Oct. 11, 1951; s. Richard Bailey and Vonda Ellene (Cox) S.; m. Charlene Janell Musgrove, Sept. 4, 1973; 1 child, Brian Lawrence. BA, Augustana Coll., 1973. Lab. technician Sanitary Dist. of Hammond, Ind., 1973; chemist Federated Metals Corp., Whiting, Ind., 1973-77; rsch. technician Air Pollution Tech., Inc., San Diego, 1978-80, environ. chemist, 1980-81, sr. tech. asst., 1981; staff chemist I Occidental Rsch. Corp., Irvine, Calif., 1981-82, receiving chemist, 1982-84; processing chemist Chem. Waste Mgmt., Inc., Kettleman City, Calif., 1984-87, analytical chemist, 1987-89, wet analytical chemistry group leader, 1989-90, inorganic lab. supr., 1990-94, quality assurance/quality control specialist, 1994-96; lab. mgr. Bolsa Rsch. Assocs., Inc., Hollister, Calif., 1996—; lab. mgr., chemist Tri Cal-Bolsa Rsch. Assocs., Inc., Hollister, Calif., 1999—. Lab. analyst for published article in environ. sci. and tech., 1981. Bd. dirs. Apostolic Christian Missions, Inc., San Diego, 1978—82. Mem.: Analytical Lab. Mgrs. Assn., Assn. Ofcl. Analytical Chemists Internat., Nat. Geog. Soc., Am. Chem. Soc., Planetary Soc., Sierra Club. Avocations: coin collecting/numismatics, drawing, photography, reading about science, history and religion. Home: 991 Meridian St Hollister CA 95023-4130 Office: Bolsa Rsch Assocs Inc 8770 Hwy 25 Hollister CA 95024 E-mail: gsmith@trical.com.

SMITH, GEORGE PATRICK, II, lawyer, educator; b. Wabash, Ind., Sept. 1, 1939; s. George Patrick and Marie Louise (Barrett) S. BS, Ind. U., 1961, JD, 1964; certificate, Hague Acad. Internat. Law, 1965; LLM, Columbia U., 1975; LLD, Ind. U., 1998. Bar: Ind. 1964, U.S. Supreme Ct. 1968. Kannert teaching fellow Ind. U. Sch. Law, 1964-65; instr. law U. Mich. Sch. Law, 1965-66; practiced in Ind. and Washington, 1965—; legal adviser Fgn. Claims Settlement Commn., Dept. State, Washington, 1966; asst. prof., asst. dean State U. N.Y. at Buffalo Law Sch., 1967-69; vis. asst. prof. law George Washington U., Nat. Law Center, summer 1968; assoc. prof. law U. Ark., 1969-71; spl. counsel EPA, Washington, 1971-74; adj. prof. law Cath. U. Law Sch., Washington, 1973-74, prof., 1977—. Adj. prof. law Georgetown U. Law Ctr., 1971-75; assoc. prof. law U. Pitts. Sch. Law, 1975-78; Commonwealth fellow in law, sci. and medicine Yale U., New Haven, 1976-77; vis. prof. law U. Conn., 1977; disting. vis. scholar Kennedy Bioethics Inst., Georgetown U., 1977-81; vis. scholar Cambridge (Eng.) U., summer 1975, spring 1978-79, Hoover Inst. on War, Revolution and Peace Stanford (Calif.) U., summer 1983, Inst. Soc., Ethics and Life Scis., Hastings Ctr., N.Y., 1981, Lilly Rare Books Libr., Ind. U., July 1981, The Kinsey Inst. for Rsch. in Sex, Gender and Reproduction, U. Ind., July 1981, Am. Bar Found., Chgo., 1986, 87, Vatican Libr., Rome, July, 1989; Rockefeller Found. resdl. scholar, Bellagio, Italy, 1980; lectr. Sch. Medicine, Uniformed Svcs. U. Health Scis., Bethesda, Md., 1979-87; cons. environ. legislation Govt. of Greece, 1977; spl. counsel to Gov. Ark. for environ. affairs, 1969-71; cons. Ark. Planning Commn., 1970-71; mem. Ark. Waterway Commn., 1970-71; chmn. Ark. Com. on Environ. Control, 1970-71; mem. com. on hwy. rsch. NRC, NAS, 1971-81; life mem. Ind. U. Found.; univ. fellow Columbia U. Law Sch., 1974-75; fellow Max Planck Inst., Heidelberg, Fed. Republic of Germany, summer 1983; mem. Pres. Reagan's Pvt. Sector Survey on Cost Control, 1982; vis. fellow Clare Hall Cambridge U., 1983-84, summer 87, law, sci. and medicine Hughes Hall, Cambridge (Eng.) U., 1989, also vis. mem. law faculty, Apr.-Aug., 1989; Fulbright vis. prof. U. New South Wales, Syndey, Australia, 1984, vis. prof., vis. fellow Ctr. for Law and Tech., 1987; vis. fellow Inst. Advanced Study, Ind. U., 1985; vis. prof. law U. Notre Dame, 1986; vis. scholar Am. Bar Found., Chgo., 1986, 87; sr. vis. fellow U. Singapore, 1987; vis. fellow McGill U. Ctr. for Medicine, Ethics and Law, Montreal, 1988, Ctr. for Biomed. Ethics U. Va. Health Scis. Ctr., Charlottesville, 1990, Ctr. for Bioethics Monash U., Melbourne, Australia, 1990, Working Ctr. Studies in German and Internat. Med. Malpractice Law Free U. Berlin, 1992; vis. rsch. fellow Ctr. for Advanced Study of Ethics Georgetown U., Washington, 1990-91; rsch. fellow Divinity Sch. Yale U., New Haven, 1991; assoc. Med. Inst. for Law Faculty, Cleve. Clinic Ctr. Creative Thinking in Medicine Cleve. State U., 1991; vis. prof. rsch. U. Auckland Law Faculty, 1991, U. Sydney Law Faculty, 1991, U. Victoria Law Faculty, B.C., Can., 1992, Trinity Coll., 1992, Dublin U., Ireland, 1992, Wolfson Coll. Cambridge U., 1992, Ind. U. Sch. Public and Environ. Affairs, 1992, Queensland U. Faculty Law, Australia, 1993; vis. scholar Ctr. Biomed. Ethics U. Minn. Med. Sch., Mpls., 1991, Ctr. for Socio-Legal Studies Oxford U., July 1992, Princeton (N.J.) Theol. Sem., 1993, Ctr. Med. Ethics Pritzker Sch. Medicine U. Chgo., 1993; vis. fellow Ctr. for Internat. Malpractice Law Free U. Berlin, Jan. 1992, King's Coll. Ctr. for Med. Law and Ethics U. London, June 1992; vis. sr. fellow Ctr. for Study Aging and Human Devel. Duke U. Med. Ctr., 1994; vis. prof. Rsch. U. Otago, 1994; faculty of law, vis. fellow U. Bioethics Rsch. Ctr., Dunedin, New Zealand, 1994; vis. scholar Poynter Ctr. for Study of Ethics Am. Instns., Ind. U., Bloomington, 1994, law, medicine and ethics Schs. Medicine and Pub. Health Boston U., 1995, Ctr. Law and Health Ind. U., Indpls., 1995; vis. fellow U. Pa. Sch. Medicine, Phila., 1996, Inst. Study Applied & Profl. Ethics, Dartmouth Coll., Hanover, N.H., 1996, Cambridge (Eng.) U. Rsch. Ctr. Internat. Law, 1996; vis. scholar Vanderbilt U. Divinity Sch., Nashville, 1996, Northwestern U. Med. Sch., Med. Ethics & Humanities Program, Chgo., 1997, Hoover Instn., Stanford U., Palo Alto, Calif., 1997, Sch. Medicine U. Wash., 1997; vis. prof. Ind. U. Sch. Medicine Program Med. Ethics, Indpls., 1997; vis. prof. law Ind. U. Law Sch., Bloomington, 1997; Parson vis. prof. faculty law U. Sydney, 1998; vis. rsch. scholar Ctr. Clin. Bioethics, Georgetown U. Med. Sch., Washington, 1998-99, Ctr. Theology and Natural Scis. U. Calif., Berkeley, 1999; Quarter Century fellow Emmanual Coll., Cambridge U., Eng., 1999, fellow Crowley Program in Human Rights, Fordham U. Law Sch., 1999; vis. fellow faculty divinity U. Cambridge, 2001; vis. prof. law U. New South Wales, Australia, 2001; vis. fellow Johns Hopkins Program on Law and Pub. Health, Washington, D.C., 2001-02, Australian Inst. Ethics and the Professions, U. Queensland, Brisbane, Australia, 2003; Parsons vis. prof. law U. Sydney, Australia, 2003; vis. scholar Ctr fro Study of Sci. and Religion, Columbia U., 2002, Reilly Ctr. for Sci., Tech. and Values, Notre Dame U., 2002, Cardiff U. Law Sch., Wales, 2002, Ctr. for Ethics in Culture, Notre Dame U., 2003; vis. fellow Inst. for Health Law, Loyola U. Sch. Law, Chgo., 2004. Author: Restricting the Concept of Free Seas, 1980, Legal, Ethical and Social Issues of the Brave New World, 1980, Genetics, Ethics and the Law, 1981, Medical-Legal Aspects of Cryonics, 1983, The New Biology, 1989, Final Choices: Autonomy in Health Care Decisions, 1989, Bioethics and the Law, 1993, Legal and Healthcare Ethics for the Elderly, 1996, Family Values and the New Society: Dilemmas of the 21st Century, 1998; Human Rights and BioMedicine, 2000, The Christian Religion and Biotechnology, 2004; contbr. articles to profl. jours. U. Ark. del. Pacem In Maribus Conf., Malta, 1970. Recipient Disting. Alumni award Ind. U. Bd. Trustees, 1985, citation for Path-Breaking Work; establishment of George P. Smith II Disting. Professorship of Law, Ind. U., Bloomington, 1986. Mem. ABA (rep. UN Conf. on Human Environ., Stockholm 1972, rep. Law of Sea Conf., UN, N.Y.C. 1976, Switzerland 1979, cons. UNESCO Declaration on the Production of the Protection of the Human Genome, Paris 1995-97), Am. Law Inst., Soc. Ind. Pioneers, Am. Friends of Cambridge U., Order of St. John Hospitaller, Alpha Kappa Psi, Phi Alpha Delta, Sigma Alpha Epsilon, Order of Omega. Clubs: Cosmos (Washington). Republican. Business E-Mail: smithg@law.edu. *Think big, work hard and, above all, have a dream: these are the simple guideposts for a fulfilling life.*

SMITH, GEORGE S., JR., former entertainment company executive; b. Newark, Dec. 8, 1948; m. Pamela Smith. BS in Acctg., Hiram Scott Coll., Scottbluff, Nebr., 1971. Cash mgr. Diamondhead Corp., N.Y.C., 1971-75, Texasgulf Inc., N.Y.C., 1975-77; dir. fin. svcs. Viacom Internat. Inc., N.Y.C., 1977-79, dir. fin. planning, 1979-81, controller radio div., 1981-83, v.p. fin. and adminstrn. broadcast group, 1983-85, v.p., controller, 1985-87; sr. v.p., CFO Viacom Inc., N.Y.C., 1987-2000. Bd. dirs. Nat. Corp. Theater Fund, 1998—. Mem. Broadcast Cable Fin. Mgmt. Assn., Fin. Execs. Inst.

SMITH, GEORGE THORNEWELL, retired state supreme court justice; b. Camilla, Ga., Oct. 15, 1916; s. George C. and Rosa (Gray) S.; m. Eloise Taylor, Sept. 1, 1943 (dec.). Grad., Abraham Baldwin Agrl. Coll., 1940; LLB, U. Ga., 1948. Bar: Ga. 1947. Assoc. Cain & Smith, Cairo, Ga., 1947-71; city atty. Cairo, 1949-58; atty. Grady County, 1950-59; solicitor Cairo City Ct., 1951-59; mem. Ga. Ho. of Reps., 1959-67, speaker of the house, 1963-67; lt. gov. State of Ga., 1967-71; city atty. East Point, Ga., 1973-76; judge Ga. Ct. Appeals, 1976-81; justice Ga. Supreme Ct., Atlanta, 1981-91, presiding justice, 1990-91; of counsel Browning & Smith LLC, Marietta, Ga., 1992—. Past mem. exec. com. Nat. Conf. Appellate Judges; vice chmn. Nat. Conf. Lt. Govs. Trustee Nat. Arthritis Found. Lt. comdr. USN, 1940-45. Only person in the state's history to serve in an elective capacity in all 3 brs. of govt. Mem. State Bar Ga., Cobb County Bar Assn., Lawyers Club Atlanta, Am. Legion, VFW, Moose, Kiwanis. Avocations: hunting, golf. Office: Browning & Smith 31 Atlanta St Ste 201 Marietta GA 30060 Office Phone: 770-424-1500.

SMITH, GEORGE VINAL, librarian; b. Chgo., May 14, 1943; s. Earl Wesley and Frances (Kenney) S.; m. Chrystal Jean Stillings, Jan. 29, 1966; children: Rebecca Tyson, Morgen Elizabeth. BA, Whitman Coll., 1965; MA, Wash. State U., 1967; PhD, No. Ill. U., 1974; MS, U. Ill., 1975. Reference libr. Illinet/U. Ill., Urbana, 1975-76; info. svcs. cons. Lincoln Trail Libr. System, Champaign, Ill., 1977-79; circular and network svcs. supr. Oreg. State Libr., Salem, 1979-81, adminstr. of libr. devel., 1983-85; dir. Canby (Oreg.) Pub. Libr., 1981-82, Woodburn (Oreg.) Pub. Libr., 1982-83; dep. dir. Alaska State Div. of Librs., Archives and Mus., Juneau, Alaska, 1985—91, acting dir., 1991—92, dep. dir., 1992—2002, acting dir., 2002—. Vol. Peace Corps, Thailand, 1967-69; vis. asst. prof. Grad. Sch. Libr. Sci., U. Ill., 1977-78; instr. Chemekata C.C., Salem, 1980-83, Marylhurst Coll., Lake Oswego, Oreg., 1982; course mentor Grad. Sch. Libr. Sci., U. Ariz., Juneau, Alaska, 1992-94; mem. State of Alaska Personnel Reinvention Com., 1996; Library Fellow to Bulgaria, US State Dept., 2000. Author: The Dutch in 17th-Century Thailand, 1977; co-editor and author: Contributions to Asian Studies, 15, 1980. Pres., bd. dirs., coach Juneau Soccer Club, 1992-94; dir., adminstrv. staff Arctic Winter Games/Team Alaska, Fairbanks, 1992—; coach, referee, referee trainer, Juneau Parks and Recreation Dept., 1986—; vol., patron Alaska Folk Festival, 1986—. NDEA fellow No. Ill. U., 1972-73; recipient Gov.'s Mgmt. Recognition award, Gov. Oreg., 1985. Mem. ALA (Libr. fellow to Nat. Libr. Cambodia 1994-95), Pacific N.W. Libr. Assn. (pres., v.p. 1987-89), Alaska Libr. Assn., Oreg. Libr. Assn. (pres., v.p. 1984-85). Avocations: fishing, hiking, backpacking, soccer coaching and refereeing, home brewing. Home: 124 Behrends Ave Juneau AK 99801-1457 Office: Alaska State Libr/Archives PO Box 110571 Juneau AK 99811-0571*

SMITH, GEORGE WOLFRAM, physicist, researcher; b. Des Plaines, Ill., Sept. 19, 1932; s. Murray Sawyer and Alice Lucile (Wolfram) S.; m. Mary Lee Sackett, Sept. 7, 1956; children— Dean, Grant. BA, Knox Coll., 1954; MA, Rice U., 1956, PhD, 1958. Welch Found. fellow Rice U., 1958-59; sr. rsch. physicist GM, Warren, Mich., 1959-76, dept. rsch. scientist, 1976-81, sr. staff rsch. scientist, 1981-87, prin. rsch. scientist, 1987-99; retired, 1999. Lectr. physics and astronomy Cranbrook Inst. Sci., Bloomfield Hills, Mich., 1963-87, mem. sci. adv. com., 1989—; instr. Lawrence Inst. Tech., 1963-65; vice chmn. Gordon Rsch. Conf. on Orientational Disorder in Crystals, 1976, chmn., 1978; co-chmn. Internat. Symposium on Particulate Carbon, 1980; mem. rev. com. Liquid Crystal Inst., Kent (Ohio) State U., 1984-85; mem. adv. com. Conf. on Electrorheological Fluids, 1991, 93; mem. adv. bd. NSF Sci. and Tech. Ctr. for Advanced Liquid Crystalline Optical Materials, 1996-2000; physics co-chair Internat. Sci. and Engring. Fair, 2000. Co-editor: Particulate Carbon: Formation During Combustion, 1981; editl. cons. Ency. Applied Physics, 1988-2000; contbr. Handbook of Chemistry and Physics; contbr. articles to sci. and tech. jours.; patentee on temperature measuring device, liquid crystal device tech., dielectric heating, graphite fiber growth, polymer-dispersed liquid crystals. Mem. Mich. Regtl. Civil War Roundtable, 1965—, pres., 1971-72. Recipient Knox Coll. Achievement award 1977, John M. Campbell Research award, 1980, Charles L. McCuen Achievement award, Gen. Motors, 1985. Fellow Am. Phys. Soc. (com. on applications of physics 1988-91, chmn. 1991, chmn. com. on tutorials 1991, mem. Pake Prize Com. 1993-94); mem. Soc. Info. Display (program com. 1990-93), Detroit Zool. Inst. (docent 2001-03, sr. docent 2003—), Phi Beta Kappa, Sigma Xi (chpt. pres. 1980-81), Phi Delta Theta, Alpha Delta. Home: 1882 Melbourne St Birmingham MI 48009-1163

SMITH, GERALDINE, historic site administrator; Supt. Jean Lafitte Nat. Hist. Park and Preserve, New Orleans. Office: Jean Lafitte Nat Hist Park and Preserve 365 Canal St Ste 2400 New Orleans LA 70130-1142

SMITH, GERARD PETER, neuroscientist; b. Phila., Mar. 24, 1935; s. Stanley Alward and Agnes Marie (McLarney) S.; m. Barbara McInnis, May 12, 1962; children: Christopher, Mark, Hilary, Maura. BS, St. Joseph's U., Phila., 1956; MD, U. Pa., 1960, U. Camerino, Italy, ScD (hon.), 2002. Intern, resident N.Y. Hosp., 1960-62; with dept. neuroendocrinology Walter Reed Army Inst. Rsch., 1962—64; asst. prof. physiology U. Pa. Sch. Medicine, Phila., 1964-68; from asst. to assoc. prof. Cornell U., N.Y.C., 1968—, prof. psychiatry (behavioral neurosci.), 1973—. Vis. prof. MIT, 1973—74, Rockefeller U., 1979—80, adj. prof., 1982—86; cons. NIH; Curt Richter lectr. Johns Hopkins U., 1976; Leon lectr. U. Pa., 1990, Stellar lectr., 93; Rushton lectr. Fla. State U., 1992; Merck, Sharpe, and Dohm prof. neurosci. U. Flinder, Australia, 1992; Loucks lectr. U. Wash., 1995; dir. Eating Disorders Inst. N.Y. Hosp.-Cornell Med. Ctr., 1984—88. Recipient Rsch. Scientist, USPHS, 1982, Myers Lifetime Achievement award, Internat. Behavioral Neurosci. Soc.; grantee, NIH. Mem. AAAS, Am. Physiol. Soc., Soc. for Neurosci., Soc. for Study Ingestive Behavior (pres.), Internat. Behavioral Neurosci. Soc. (pres.), Alpha Omega Alpha, Alpha Sigma Nu. Office: NY Presbyn Hosp Westchester Divsn EW Bourne Behavioral Rsch Lab 21 Bloomingdale Rd White Plains NY 10605-1504 E-mail: gpsmith@mail.med.cornell.edu.

SMITH, GERRIT BRUCE, foreign language educator; b. Munich, Bavaria, Germany, Oct. 17, 1971; came to the U.S., 1988; s. Bruce Alan Smith and Gerlinde Karolina Ward. AA magna cum laude, Coll. William and Mary, 1993, BA magna cum laude, 1995; MA in German, U. Hawaii, 1999; MPA, U. Okla., 2000; student in Law, Ohio State U., 2002—. Cert. sales assoc. Army Air Force Exch. Svc., Ft. Lee, Va., 1991-96; tchg. asst. German U. Hawaii at Manoa, Honolulu, 1997-99; German tchr. Kaimuki Cmty. Sch. for Adults, 2000—. Substitute tchr. City of Colonial Heights Pub. Schs., Va., 2002—. Campaign/poll worker Re-election Campaign Stacy Stafford Clk. of Cir. Ct., Colonial Heights, Va., 1990; part-time vol. adminstrv. and rsch. asst. Judiciary of the State of Hawaii, Honolulu, 1997-99. Presdl. scholar Richard Bland Coll., Petersburg, Va., 1992-93. Mem. ASPA, Dem. Nat. Com., Hawaii Kai Opera Guild, German Nat. Honor Soc. (U. Hawaii chpt. treas. 1997-99), Phi Theta Kappa. Avocations: chess, stamp collecting/philately, opera, reading, weight training. E-mail: gerrit@hawaii.edu.

SMITH, GLADYS ANN, counselor, military medic; b. Leland, Miss., July 19, 1960; d. Gladys Rose. B in Healthcare Mgmt., So. Ill. U., 1993; M in Health Sci., Washington U., St. Louis, MO, 1997; MEd, U. Mo., 2001. Lic. substance abuse counselor, advanced substance abuse counselor, provisional lic. counselor. Mental health counselor Webster U., St. Louis, 2001—, petty officer, 1984—. Counselor, educator St. Louis County Corrections. Recipient Navy Achievement awards, 1992, 1997, 2001. Mem.: Nat. Counselors Assn., Nat. Assn. Drug Abuse Counselors (none), Coalition of 100 Black Women. Democrat. Mem. A.M.E. Ch. Avocations: dance, running, reading. Home: 7006 Stanford Saint Louis MO 63130 Office: Webster U 470 E Lockwood Saint Louis MO 63119 Personal E-mail: GSmith2222@aol.com. Business E-Mail: gasmith@webster.edu.

SMITH, GLEE SIDNEY, JR., lawyer; b. Rozel, Kans., Apr. 29, 1921; s. Glee S. and Bernice M. (Augustine) S.; m. Geraldine B. Buhler, Dec. 14, 1943; children: Glee S., Stephen B., Susan K. AB, U. Kans., 1943, JD, 1947. Bar: Kans. 1947, U.S. Dist. Ct. 1951, U.S. Supreme Ct. 1973, U.S. Ct. Mil. Appeals 1988. Ptnr. Smith Burnett & Larson, Lanred, Kans., 1947—. Of counsel Barber, Emerson et al., Lawrence, Kans., 1992—, Kans. state senator, 1957-73, pres. Senate, 1965-73; mem. Kans. Bd. Regents, 1975-83, pres., 1976; bd. govs. Kans. U. Law Soc., 1967—; mem. Kans. Jud. Coun., 1963-65; county atty. Pawnee County, 1949-53; mem. bd. edn. Larned, 1951-63; Kans. commr. Nat. Conf. Commn. on Uniform State Laws, 1963—; bd. dirs. Nat. Legal Svcs. Corp., 1975-79. Served to 1st lt. U.S. Army Air Corps, 1943-45. Recipient disting. svc. award U. Kans. Law Sch., 1976; disting. svc. citation U. Kans., 1984. Fellow Am. Coll. Probate Counsel, Am. Bar Found.; mem. ABA (bd. of govs. 1987-90, chmn. ops. com. 1989-90, exec. com. 1989-90, chmn. task force on solo and small firm practitioners 1990-91, chmn. com. on solo and small firm practitioners 1992-94, chmn. task force on applying fed. legis. to congress 1994-96), Kans. Bar Assn. (del. to ABA ho. of dels. 1982-92, bd. govs. 1982-92, leadership award 1973, medal of distinction 1993), Southwest Kans. Bar Assn., Am. Ind. Soc., Kiwanis, Masons, Rotary. Republican. Presbyterian. Home: 4313 Quail Pointe Rd Lawrence KS 66047-1966

SMITH, GLENN A. lawyer; b. Oakland, Calif., July 11, 1946; BA, Pomona Coll., 1968; JD, U. Calif., Berkeley, 1971; LLM in Taxation, NYU, 1973. Bar: Calif. 1972, D.C. 1975. Law clerk to Hon. William M. Drennen U.S. Tax Ct., 1973-75; ptnr. Heller, Ehrman, White & McAuliffe, Palo Alto, San Francisco, Calif., 1977—. Office: Heller Ehrman White & McAuliffe 525 University Ave Ste 900 Palo Alto CA 94301-1907

SMITH, GLORIA RICHARDSON, nursing educator; b. Chgo., Sept. 29, 1934; BSN, Wayne State U., 1955; MPH, U. Mich., 1959; cert., UCLA, 1971; MA in Anthropology, U. Okla., 1977; PhD, Union for Experimenting Colls. and Univs., 1979; D Honoris Causa (hon.), U. Cin., 1992. Pub. health nurse Detroit Vis. Nurse Assn., 1955-56, sr. pub. health nurse, 1957-58, asst. dist. office supr., 1959-63; asst. prof. nursing Tuskegee Inst. Sch. Nursing, Ala., 1963-66, Albany (Ga.) State Coll., 1966-68; cons. nurse home health care Okla. State Health Dept., 1968-70, medicare nurse cons., 1970-71; asst. prof. U. Okla. Coll. Nursing, Oklahoma City, 1971-73, assoc. prof. and interim dean, 1973-75; state health dir. Mich. Dept. Pub. Health, 1983-88; prof., dean Coll. Nursing Wayne State U., 1988-91; coord., program dir. in health WK Kellogg Found., 1991-95, v.p. programs in health, 1995—. Chair Mich. Task Force on Nursing Issues, 1989-90, Nat. Commn. on Nursing Shortage, 1990-91; cons. on nursing Colo. Commn. Higher Edn., 1990, U. N.C., 1990; mem. adv. com. nursing Okla. State Regents for Higher Edn., 1973-83; cons. VA Hosp., 1975-77, HEW, 1977-78, U. Mich. External Rev. Sch. Nursing, 1980. Contbr. articles on health care and nursing edn. to profl. pubs. Mem. Mayor's Com. to Study In-Migrants, Detroit, 1963; bd. dirs. St. Peter Claver Cmty. Credit Union, 1961-63, YMCA, Oklahoma City, 1972-76, Better Homes Found. for Homeless, 1986—; mem. steering com. Kellogg Fellowship Internat. Program in Health, 1985-89; mem. study com. health care for homeless Inst. Medicine, 1987-88. Recipient Outstanding Svc. award Franklin Settlement, 1963, Disting. Alumni award Wayne State U., 1984, Disting. Scholar award Am. Nurses Found., 1987—. Mem. Nat. League Nursing (dir. from 1979), Am. Nurses Assn. (mem. commn. on nursing edn. 1978-82), Okla. League Nursing, Midwest Alliance in Nursing (dir. 1977-80), Black Pers. (exec. com. 1974-76), Am. Assn. Colls. Nursing (exec. com. from 1976), Nat. Black Nurses Assn. (dir. 1972-78), Okla. State Nurses Assn. (Nurse of Yr. 1972), Am. Assn. for Higher Edn., Okla. State Assn. for Black Pers. in Higher Edn. (rec. sec. 1976-78), Am. Acad. Nursing (governing coun. 1983-85), Assn. State and Territorial Health Officers, Am. Pub. Health Assn., Okla. Pub. Health Assn., Sigma Gamma Rho (Outstanding Sigma of Yr. 1963), Sigma Theta Tau.

SMITH, G(ODFREY) T(AYLOR), retired academic administrator; b. Newton, Miss., Nov. 12, 1935; s. Taylor and Edna (Blanton) S.; m. Joni Eaton, Sept. 1, 1956; children: Paul Brian, Sherry Lynn. BA, Coll. of Wooster, 1956; MPA with distinction, Cornell U., 1960; LLD (hon.), Bethany Coll., 1979. Assoc. dir. devel. Cornell U., Ithaca, N.Y., 1960-62; dir. devel. Coll. Wooster, 1962-66, v.p., 1966-77; pres. Chapman U., Orange, Calif., 1977-88, pres. emeritus, 1988—; exec. dir. Talaris Rsch. Inst., Seattle, 2001—03. Lectr. in field. Contbr. numerous articles to profl. publs. Bd. dirs. Wayne County (Ohio) Indsl. Devel. Corp., 1966-72, World Affairs Coun. Orange Coun., Calif., 1978-89, Orange County chpt. NCCJ, 1979-86, Orange County coun. Boy Scouts Am., 1980-85, Coun. Ind. Colls., 1985-87; bd. dirs. div. higher edn. Christian Ch. (Disciples of Christ), 1980-86, chmn., 1984-86; bd. dirs., mem. exec. com. Ind. Colls. So. Calif., 1979-88, pres., 1981-82; mem. exec. com. Assn. Ind. Calif. Colls. and Univs., 1980-88, treas., 1982-87. Recipient Steuben Apple award for tchg. excellence Coun. for Advancement and Support Edn., 1984, Disting. Alumnus award Coll. of Wooster, 1991, Faith and Reason award Christian Ch. (Disciples of Christ), 1993, Laureate award for Lifetime Achievement Inst. for Charitable Giving, 1997; Smith Hall dedicated at Chapman U., 1988; Alfred P. Sloan fellow Cornell U., 1960. Presbyterian. Home: 20703 Pelton Pl Leavenworth WA 98826 *If we treat people as they are, they will stay as they are. But if we treat them for what they might be and might become, they will become those better selves.*

SMITH, GOFF, industrial equipment manufacturing executive; b. Jackson, Tenn., Oct. 7, 1916; s. Fred Thomas and Mabel (Goff) S.; m. Nancy Dall, Nov. 28, 1942 (dec. 1972); children: Goff Thomas, Susan Knight; m. Harriet Schneider Oliver, June 23, 1973 (dec. 1998). BSE, U. Mich., 1938, MBA, 1939; MS, MIT, 1953. Trainee Bucyrus Erie, South Milwaukee, Wis., 1939-40; mem. sales staff Amsted Industries, Chgo. and N.Y.C., 1946-55, subsidiary pres. Chgo., 1955-60, v.p., 1960-69, pres., dir., 1969-74, pres., CEO, dir., 1974-80, chmn., 1980-82. Pres. Village of Winnetka, Ill., 1967-69; pres., bd. dirs. United Way Chgo., 1976-85; bd. dirs. Rehab. Inst., Chgo., 1979-99, Chgo. Theol. Sem., 1979-99, Presbyn. Home, Evanston, Ill., 1979—; trustee Sigma Chi Found., 1977-99. Maj. U.S. Army, 1940-46. Sloan Fellow MIT, 1952-53. Republican. Avocations: hunting, fishing, golf.

SMITH, GORDON, finance company executive; Sr. v.p. Am. Express Co., Phoenix, 1997—. Office: Am Express Co 20022 N 31st Ave Phoenix AZ 85027-3900

SMITH, GORDON H. civil engineer, consultant, forensic engineer consultant; b. N.Y.C., Mar. 17, 1936; s. Henry and Theodora (Augenstern) S.; m. Norma Kaplan, Feb. 28, 1960; children: Randy Smith Aberg, Robin Smith. B in Engring., Yale U., 1957. Registered profl. engr., Mich., N.Y. V.p., chief engr. Albro Metal Products Corp., N.Y.C., 1957-69, pres., 1969-75, Gordon H. Smith Corp., N.Y.C., 1975—, Gordon H. Smith PE, PC, N.Y.C., 1998—. Guest lectr. Yale U. Sch. Arch., MIT, Am. Inst. Archs., Constrn. Specification Inst., Nat. Glass Assn., Glass Assn. N.Am.; protective glazing coun. N.Y. Inst. Tech. Contbr. articles to Archtl. Record, Progressive Arch., ASTM, Chgo. High Rise Com. Mem. NSPE, ASTM, ASCE, AIA (Inst. Honors 1994, 2003), Nat. Assn. Archtl. Metal Mfrs. (v.p., pres., bd. dirs.), Archtl. Aluminum Mfrs. Assn. (v.p., bd. dirs.), Nat. Assn. Miscellaneous, Ornamental and Archtl. Metal Mfrs. (bd. dirs.), Constrn. Specifications Inst. Office: Gordon H Smith Corp 200 Madison Ave New York NY 10016-3903 Office Phone: 212-696-0600. Business E-Mail: ghsmith@gordonsmithcorp.com.

SMITH, GORDON HAROLD, senator; b. Pendleton, Oreg., May 25, 1952; s. Milan Dale and Jessica (Udall) S.; m. Sharon Lankford; children: Brittany, Garrett, Morgan. BA in History, Brigham Young U., 1976; JD, Southwestern U., 1979. Law clk. to Justice H. Vern Payne N.Mex. Supreme Ct.; pvt. practice

Ariz.; owner Smith Frozen Foods; mem. Oreg. State Senate, 1992-95, pres., 1995-96; senator from Oreg. U.S. Senate, 1997—. Mem. budget com., chair subcom. water and power, mem. subcom. forests and pub. land mgmt., mem. subcom. energy rsch., devel., prodn. and regulation, mem. energy and natural resources com., chair subcom. European affairs, mem. subcom. Near Eastern and South Asian affairs, mem. fgn. rels. com., mem. subcom. on East Asian and Pacific affairs. Republican. Office: US Senate 404 Russell Senate Off Bldg Washington DC 20510-0001

SMITH, GORDON HOWELL, lawyer; b. Syracuse, N.Y., Oct. 26, 1915; s. Lewis P. and Maud (Mixer) S.; m. Eunice Hale, June 28,1947; children: Lewis Peter, Susan S. Rizk, Catherine S. Maxson, Maud S. Daudon. BA, Princeton U., 1932-36; LL.B., Yale U., 1939. Bar: N.Y. 1939, Ill. 1946. Asso. Lord, Day & Lord, N.Y.C., 1939-41, Gardner, Carton & Douglas, Chgo., 1946-51; partner Mackenzie, Smith & Michell, Syracuse, 1951-53, Gardner, Carton & Douglas, 1954-57, 60-85, of counsel, 1986-96, retired ptnr., 1996—. Sec., dir. Smith-Corona, Inc., 1951-54, v.p., Syracuse, 1957-60 Bd. dirs. Rehab. Inst. Chgo., chmn., 1974-78, 83-86; bd. dirs. United Way Met. Chgo., 1962-85. Served to lt. comdr. USNR, 1941-46. Mem. Am. Soc. Corporate Secs., Am., Ill., Chgo. bar assns. Clubs: Comml., Law, Econ., Legal, Chgo., Old Elm (Chgo.). Home: 1302 N Green Bay Rd Lake Forest IL 60045-1108 Office: 191 N Wacker Dr Chicago IL 60606

SMITH, GORDON PAUL, management consultant; b. Salem, Mass., Dec. 25, 1916; s. Gordon and May (Vaughan) S.; m. Daphne Miller, Nov. 23, 1943 (div. 1968); m. Ramona Chamberlain, Sept. 27, 1969; children: Randall B., Roderick F. BS in Mgmt., U. Mass., 1947; MS in Govt. Mgmt, U. Denver (Sloan fellow), 1948; postgrad. in polit. sci, NYU, 1948-50; DHL (hon.), Monterey Inst. Internat. Studies, 1994. With Econ. Rsch. Tax Found., Inc., N.Y.C., 1948—51, Booz, Allen & Hamilton, 1951-70, partner, 1959-62, v.p., 1962-67, mng. pntr. Western U.S., 1968-70; ptnr. Harrod, Williams and Smith, San Francisco, 1962—69; dir. fin. State of Calif., Calif., 1967—68; pres. Gordon Paul Smith & Co., Mgmt. Cons., 1968—; pres., CEO Golconda Corp., 1972—74, chmn. bd., 1974-85. Pres. Cermetek Corp., 1978-80; adviser task force def. procurement and contracting Hoover Commn., 1954-55; spl. asst. to pres. Republic Aviation Corp., 1954-55; cons., Hawaii, 1960-61, Alaska, 1963; cons. Wash. Hwy. Adminstrn., 1964, Am. Baseball League and Calif. Angels, 1960-62, others; bd. dirs. Monterey Coll. Law; chmn. Ft. Ord Econ. Devel. Adv. Group, 1991; chmn. Coalition on Rsch. and Edn., 1993—97; spkr. in field. Contbr. articles to profl. jours. Mem. Calif. Select Com. on Master Plan for Edn., 1971—73; mem. alumni coun. U. Mass., 1950—54, bd. dirs. alumni ass., 1964—70; chmn. West Coast Cancer Found., 1976—87, Coalition Rsch. and Edn., 1993—, Jim Tunney Youth Found., 1994—; trustee, chmn. Monterey Inst. Internat. Studies, 1978—92, trustee emeritus, 1995—; trustee Northfield Mt. Hermon Sch., 1983—93, Robert Louis Stevenson Sch., 1993—; mem. devel. coun. Cmty. Hosp. of Monterey Peninsula, 1983—84; sr. advisor Pres. Calif. State U., Monterey, Calif., 1998—; mem. 15 bds. and commns. State of Calif., 1967—72; bd. dirs. Alumni Assn. Mt. Hermon Prep. Sch., 1963; bd. dirs. Stanford Med. Ctr., 1960—62, pres., chmn., 1962—66; bd. dirs. Friends of the Performing Arts, 1985—, Monterey County Symphony Orch., 1991—96, Monterey Bay Futures Project, 1992—, Ctr. for Nonproliferation of Weapons of Mass Destruction, 1998—, Calif. Inst. for Local Self Govt., 2000—. Recipient spl. commendation Hoover Commn., 1955, Alumni of Yr. award U. Mass., 1963, Trustee of Yr. award Monterey-Peninsula, 1991, Monterey-Peninsula Outstanding Citizen of Yr. award, 1992, Laura Bride Powers Heritage award, 1991, U.S. Congl. award, 1992, Calif. Senate and Assembly Outstanding Citizen award, 1992, Wisdom award of honor Wisdom Soc., 1992; permanent Gordon Paul Smith Disting. Chair for Internat. Studies established at Monterey Inst. Internat. Studies; Gordon Paul Smith Scholarship Fund named in his honor Northfield Mt. Hermon Sch.and Robert Louis Stevenson Sch.; named to Honorable Order of Ky. Cols. Mem. Monterey History and Art Assn. (bd. dirs. 1987-92, pres. 1985-87, chmn. 1987-92, hon. lifetime dir. 1992—), The Stanton Heritage Ctr. (chmn. 1987-92, chmn. emeritus 1992—), Salvation Army (bd. dirs., chmn. hon. cabinet), Monterey Peninsula Mus. Art, Carmel Valley (Calif.) Country Club, Monterey Peninsula Country Club, Old Capitol Club, Edgartown Yacht Club. Home: 253 Del Mesa Carmel CA 93923 E-mail: gp1225@aol.com. *If the quest for personal success is only for an accumulation of prestige, power or wealth, then personal failure will be assured. Genuine personal success can surely be found, however, through a significant and lasting contribution toward helping the progress of others and raising the human worth. This is the true mark of leadership.*

SMITH, GRANT WARREN, II, university administrator, physical sciences educator; b. Kansas City, Mo., Jan. 21, 1941; m. Constance M. Krambeer, 1962; 1 child, Grant Warren III. BA, Grinnell Coll., 1962; PhD, Cornell U., 1966, postgrad., 1967. Asst. prof. chemistry Cornell U., Ithaca, N.Y., 1966-68, vis. prof. Am. Coun. on Edn. fellow, 1973-74; assoc. prof. U. Alaska, Fairbanks, 1968-77, prof., 1977-78, head dept. chemistry and chem. engring., 1968-73, acting head dept. gen. sci., 1972-73; pres. univ. assembly U. Alaska Sys., 1976-77; prof. phys. scis., dean Sch. Scis. and Tech., U. Houston, Clear Lake, 1979-84; prof. chemistry Southeastern La. U., Hammond, 1984-95, honors prof. arts and scis., 1995-97, v.p. acad. affairs, 1984-86, pres., 1986-95, Slippery Rock U., 1997—. Bd. dirs. Houston Area Rsch. Ctr., 1982-83, Penn-Northwest Devel. Corp., 1998—, Cmty. Devel. Corp. Butler County, 1998—, 3 Rivers Connect, 2000—; violinist, pres. exec. bd. Clear Lake Symphony, 1980-84. NIH fellow, 1963-66, DuPont fellow, 1967. Fellow Royal Soc. Chemistry (London, chartered chemist), Explorers Club; mem. Am. Assn. Higher Edn., Am. Assn. Univ. Adminstrs. (bd. dirs. 1982-88, 99—, v.p. 1988-90), AAAS, The Coll. Bd., Am. Chem. Soc., Internat. Assn. Univ. Pres., Internat. Soc. Ethnopharmacology, Am. Soc. Pharmacognosy, Internat. Soc. of Ethnobiology, Nat. Speleological Soc., Am. Spelean History Assn., Am. Bot. Coun., Arctic Inst. N.Am., Soc. for the History of Discoveries, Leadership Pitts. XV, Hammond C. of C. (bd. dirs. 1988-90), World Future Soc., Rotary, Sigma Xi, Phi Kappa Phi, Beta Gamma Sigma, Phi Eta Sigma. Office: Slippery Rock U Office of Pres Old Main Slippery Rock PA 16057-1326 E-mail: gwsmith@sru.edu.

SMITH, GRANT WILLIAM, English language educator, civic fundraiser; b. Bellingham, Wash., July 26, 1937; s. George Whitfield and Hazel (Speirs) S.; m. Lelia Dickinson, June 9, 1961; children: Kathryn, Gavin. BA, Reed Coll., 1964; MA, U. Nev., 1966; PhD, U. Del., 1975. Asst. prof. Eastern Wash. U., Cheney, 1968-76, assoc. prof., 1976-79, prof., 1979—. Faculty pres. Eastern Wash. U., Cheney, 1976-77, chair English dept., 1978-84, acting vice provost, 1987-88, coord. humanities, 1979—, dir. cultural outreach, 1995-97; host Pub. TV, Here's Shakespeare, 1980, 81; guest editor: NAMES, 1989. Editor Proceedings of the Am. Name Soc., 1997, 98, 99; contbr. articles to profl. jours. and conf. procs. Chair devel. Spokane Symphony, 2000—01; program chair Coun. Geo. Names Authorities, 1999; pres. Center Stage, 2004; moderator Cheney United Ch. of Christ, 1982—84. With U.S. Army, 1957—60. Grantee U.S. Geol. Survey, State Humanities Commn., NEH, others. Mem. MLA, AAUP, Placename Survey U.S. (chair 1990—), Connoisseur Concerts Assn. (pres. 1992-95), Am. Dialect Soc. (regional sec. 1982-98), Rocky Mountain MLA (program chair 1987, 95), Internat. Coun. Onomastic Scientists (exec. bd. dirs. 1999—, v.p. 2002—, editl. bd. ONOMA 2000—,), Internat. Soc. Dialectology and Geolinguistics, Am. Name Soc. (v.p. 1996-98, pres. 1999-2001), Wash. Bd. Geo. Names (guest editor 1989), others. Avocations: jogging, reading, singing. Home: 905 Gary St Cheney WA 99004-1341 Address: Eastern Wash Univ 250 Patterson Hall Dept of English Cheney WA 99004-2430 Office Phone: 509-359-6023. Business E-Mail: gsmith@ewu.edu.

SMITH, GREGORY ALLGIRE, college administrator; b. Washington, Mar. 31, 1951; s. Donald Eugene and Mary Elizabeth (Reichert) Smith; m. Susan Elizabeth Watts, Oct. 31, 1980; 1 child, David Joseph Smith-Watts. BA, The Johns Hopkins U., 1972; MA, Williams Coll., Williamstown, Mass., 1974. Adminstrv. asst. Washington Project for the Arts, 1975; intern Walker Art Ctr., Mpls., 1975—76; asst. devel. officer The Sci. Mus. of Minn., St. Paul, 1977; asst. dir. Akron (Ohio) Art Inst., 1977—80; asst. to dir. Toledo Mus. Art, 1980—82, asst. dir. adminstrn., 1982—86; exec. v.p. Internat. Exhbns. Found., Washington, 1986—87; dir. The Telfair Mus. Art, Savannah, Ga., 1987—94, Art Acad. of Cin., 1994—98, pres., 1998—. Trustee Greater Cin. Consortium of Colls. and Univs., vice chmn., 2001—03, chmn., 2003—; trustee Assn. Ind. Colls. of Art and Design; grad. Leadership Savanah, 1990—92, Leadership Cin., 2003—04. Mem.: Coll. Art Assn., Ohio Found. on the Arts (v.p. 1981—83, trustee 1981—84), Assn. Art Mus. Adminstrs. (founder 1984—85), Am. Assn. Mus., Rotary (dir. Cin. club 2000—01, sec.-treas. 2001—02, pres. 2002—03), Univ. Club. Avocation: collecting arts and crafts movement objects, landscape design, gardening. Home: 8380 Springvalley Dr Cincinnati OH 45236-1356 Office: Art Acad of Cin 1125 Saint Gregory St Cincinnati OH 45202-1799 E-mail: gasmith@artacademy.edu.

SMITH, GREGORY C. automotive executive; b. Toledo; BS in Mech. Engring., Rose-Hulman Inst. Tech.; MBA, Ea. Mich. U. With truck ops. Ford Motor Co., 1973—85, truck and powertrain mktg. plans mgr. Ford div., 1985—87, mgr. car mktg. plans Ford div., 1987—89, regional mktg. mgr. Ctrl. Region, 1989, dist. ops. mgr. Lincoln-Mercury div., 1989—90, dir. strategy and advanced planning for car product devel., 1990—93, exec. dir. strategic planning and external affairs Ford Fin. Svcs. Group, 1993—94, v.p. new bus. devel. diversified ops. Ford Motor Credit Co., 1994—95, exec. v.p. internat. financing ops. Ford Motor Credit Co., 1995—2002, chmn. and CEO Ford Motor Credit Co., 2002—04, group v.p., 2002—04, exec. v.p., 2004—, pres., The Americas, 2004—. Bd. dirs. Detroit Investment Fund. Mem. dean's adv. coun. Kelley Sch. Bus. Ind. U.; bd. dirs. Jr. Achievement S. Ea. Mich. Mem.: Am. Fin. Svcs. Assn. (past chmn.). Office: Ford Motor Co One American Rd Dearborn MI 48126

SMITH, GREGORY WHITE, writer; b. Ithaca, N.Y., Oct. 4, 1951; s. William R. and Kathryn (White) S. BA, Colby Coll., 1973; JD, Harvard U., 1977, MEd, 1980. Bar: Mass., 1980. Fellow Thomas J. Watson, 1973-74; pres. Woodward/White, Inc. Author: (with Steven Naifeh) Moving Up in Style, 1980, Gene Davis, 1981, How to Make Love to a Woman, 1982, What Every Client Needs to Know About Using a Lawyer, 1982, The Bargain Hunter's Guide to Art Collecting, 1982, Why Can't Men Open Up?: Overcoming Men's Fear of Intimacy, 1984, The Mormon Murders: A True Story of Greed, Forgery, Deceit, and Death, 1988, Jackson Pollock: An American Saga, 1989 (Nat. Book award nomination for nonfiction 1990, Pulitzer Prize for biography 1991), Final Justice: The True Story of the Richest Man Ever Tried for Murder, 1993, A Stranger in the Family: A True Story of Murder, Madness, and Unconditional Love, 1995, On a Street Called Easy, In a Cottage Called Joye: A Restoration Comedy, 1996, Making Miracles Happen, 1997; editor: (with Naifeh) The Best Lawyers in America series, The Best Doctors in America series. Chmn. Aiken Historic Preservation Commn. Office: Woodward/White 129 First Ave SW Aiken SC 29801 E-mail: gsmith@bestlawyers.com.

SMITH, GRIFFIN, editor; b. Fayetteville, Ark., June 29, 1941; s. Griffin and Mildred Smith; m. Mary Elizabeth Routh, Sept. 1, 1979. BA in History, Rice U., 1963; MA in Polit. Sci., Columbia U., 1965; postgrad. in philosophy, Oxford U., 1966; JD, U. Tex., 1969. Bar: Tex. 1969, U.S. Dist. Ct. (ea., we., no. and so. dists.) Tex. 1969, Ark. 1981, U.S. Dist. Ct. (ea. and we. dists.) Ark. 1981. Spl. asst. to Senator Fulbright U.S. Senate, Washington, 1968-69; atty. estate and gift tax div. IRS, Houston, 1970; rsch. dir. Tex. gubernatorial campaign Paul Eggers, 1970; chief counsel constl. amendments com. Tex. Senate, 1971, chief counsel drug law reform com., 1971-73; editor natural areas survey Lyndon B. Johnson Sch. Pub. Affairs U. Tex., Austin, 1973-77; speech writer Pres. of U.S., 1977-78; ptnr. Smith & Nixon (formerly Smith, Smith, Nixon & Duke), Little Rock, 1984-92. Author: (book) A Consumer Viewpoint on Taxation, 1971, Marijuana in Texas, 1972, The Best of Texas Monthly, 1978, Texas Monthly's Political Reader, 1978, 1980, Journey into China, 1982, Forgotten Texas: A Wilderness Portfolio, 1983, The Great State of Texas, 1985; sr. editor: Tex. Monthly Mag., 1973—77, exec. editor: Ark. Dem. Gazette Newspaper, 1992—. Fellow Woodrow Wilson, 1964. Mem.: Tex. Inst. Letters (award for best work of journalism in Tex. 1974, 1976), State Bar Tex. Episcopalian-Reformed. Office: Ark Dem Gazette 121 E Capitol Ave Little Rock AR 72201-3819

SMITH, GROVER C(LEVELAND), English language educator; b. Atlanta, Sept. 6, 1923; s. Grover C. and Lillian Julia (McDaniel) S.; m. Phyllis Jean Snyder, June 19, 1948 (div. 1965); children: Alice Elizabeth, Charles Grover; m. Dulcie Barbara Soper, Dec. 29, 1965; children: Stephen Kenneth, Julia Margaret. BA with honors, Columbia U., 1944, MA, 1945, PhD, 1950. Instr. English Rutgers U., 1946-48, Yale U., 1948-52, Duke U., 1952-55, asst. prof., 1955-61, assoc. prof., 1961-66, prof., 1966-93, prof. emeritus, 1993—. Mem. summer faculty CUNY, 1946, 47, 48, Columbia U., 1963, 64, NYU, 1963, Wake Forest U., 1966, vis. lectr., 1963, 64; instr. coll. entrance exam bd. Summer Inst. Commn. on English, 1962. Author: The Poems of T.S. Eliot 1909-1928: A Study in Symbols and Sources, 1950, T.S. Eliot's Poetry and Plays: A Study in Sources and Meaning, 1956 (Poetry Chapbook award) rev. edit., 1974, Archibald MacLeish, 1971, Ford Madox Ford, 1972, The Waste Land, 1983, T.S. Eliot and the Use of Memory, 1996; editor: Josiah Royce's Seminar, 1913-1914: As Recorded in the Notebooks of Harry T. Costello, 1963, Letters of Aldous Huxley, 1969. Mem. Christian Gauss Award com., 1973-75; mem. com. of sponsors Sir Julian Huxley Tribute, NY Soc. for Ethical Culture, 1975. With U.S. Army, 1943. Alexander M. Proudfit fellow Columbia U., 1945-46; Guggenheim fellow, 1958; Am. Philos. Soc. grantee, 1965; Am. Learned Socs. grantee, 1965; NEH grantee, 1979, fellow, 1980. Mem. T.S. Eliot Soc. (hon., Eliot Meml. Lectr. 1986, bd. dirs. 1986-94, 96-99, v.p. 1986-88, editor News and Notes, 1987-88, 90-91, pres. 1989-91, supr. elections 1992-94, sec. 1996-99), Am. Lit. Assn. (rep. to coun.of Am. Author Socs. 1990-91), Nat. Assn. Scholars. Home: 2 Silver Maple Ct Durham NC 27705-5642

SMITH, H. MORGAN, environmental scientist, educator; b. Orlando, Fla., Dec. 31, 1926; s. Claude Earle Smith and Pearl Adelaide Morgan; m. Marjori Blank (div. 1962). BS in Anthropology, Fla. State U., 1953; postgrad., U. Ala., Troy State U.; PhD (hon.), U. Peru, Iquitos, 2002. Prof. environ. sci. State of Ala., U. USAF; rsch. scientist, tchr., adminstr. fed. svc.; ret., 2001. Lectr. univs., schs., profl. and civic groups; conductor security, survival tng. people, India, Australia, Europe, and U.S., 2001—; tchr. rainforest ecology workshops ethnobotany, Peruvian Amazon, Panama; vol. prof. environ. sci. Selwyn Sch., Denton, Tex. *Mr. Smith's teaching experience uses an experiential education technique that is world wide. His principal area of interest has been the U.S. and Latin America. Mr. Smith is bilingual, speaking both Spanish and English. He is particularly adept in teaching across cultural barriers. His graduate work at the University of Alabama and Troy State was in education, psychology, and Spanish. Mr. Smith's is considered a world authority on tropical rainforests and the people who live them. He is the subject-matter expert for synergistic management exercises on rain forest, jungle, and ocean survival. Mr. Smith is also a skilled photographer, who uses his photos to augment his reports and lectures.* Author various articles; scriptwriter (5 major ednl. videos cross-cultural comm. and emergency survival). Office: 3333 University Dr W Denton TX 76207 Office Phone: 940-891-1133.

SMITH, H. PETE, retired oil industry executive; CFO Ultramar Diamond Shamrock Corp., San Antonio, 1996-2000, ret., 2000. Office: Ultramar Diamond Shamrock Corp PO Box 696000 San Antonio TX 78269-6000

SMITH, HAMILTON OTHANEL, molecular biologist, educator; b. N.Y.C., N.Y., Aug. 23, 1931; s. Bunnie Othanel and Tommie Harkey S.; m. Elizabeth Anne Bolton, May 25, 1957; children: Joel, Barry, Dirk, Bryan, Kirsten. Student, U. Ill., 1948-50; AB in Math, U. Calif., Berkeley, 1952; MD, Johns Hopkins U., 1956. Intern Barnes Hosp., St. Louis, 1956-57; resident in medicine Henry Ford Hosp., Detroit, 1959-62; USPHS fellow dept. human genetics U. Mich., Ann Arbor, 1962-64, rsch. assoc., 1964-67; asst. prof. molecular biology and genetics Sch. Medicine Johns Hopkins U., Balt., 1967-69, assoc. prof., 1969-73, prof., 1973—, now emeritus prof. molecular biology and genetics; scientist Celera Genomics. Asso. Inst. für Molekularbologie der U. Zurich, Switzerland, 1975-76; assoc. Rsch. Inst. Molecular Pathology, Vienna, 1990-91; trustee The Inst. for Genomic Rsch. Contbr. articles to profl. jours. Served to lt. M.C. USNR, 1957-59. Recipient Nobel prize in physiology or medicine, 1978; Guggenheim fellow, 1975-76. Mem. Am. Soc. Microbiology, AAAS, Am. Soc. Biol. Chemists, Nat. Acad. Sci.*

SMITH, HARMON LEE, JR., clergyman, moral theology educator; b. Ellisville, Miss., Aug. 23, 1930; s. Harmon Lee Sr. and Mary (O'Donnell) S.; children: Pamela Lee, Amy Joanna, Harmon Lee III. AB, Millsaps Coll., 1952; BD, Duke U., 1955, PhD, 1962. Ordain to priest Episcopal Ch., 1972. Asst. dean Duke U. Divinity Sch., Durham, N.C., 1959-65, asst. prof. Christian ethics, 1962-68, assoc. prof. moral theology, 1968-73, prof. moral theology, 1973-99, prof. community and family medicine, 1974-99, ret., 1999, prof. emeritus moral theology and cmty. family medicine. Cons. med. ethics; vis. prof. U. N.C., 1964, 70, 72, U. Edinburgh, Scotland, 1969, U. Windsor, Ont., 1974 Author books on Christian theology, ethics and med. ethics; sr. editor Social Science and Medicine, 1973-89; contbr. articles on Christian ethics to various publs. Lilly Found. fellow, 1960; Gurney Harris Kearns Found. fellow, 1961; Nat. Humanities Ctr. fellow, 1982-83 Mem. Am. Assn. Theol. Schs., Am. Soc. Christian Ethics, Am. Acad. Religion, Soc. for Religion in Higher Edn., Soc. Health and Human Values. Home: 3510 Randolph Rd Durham NC 27705-5347 E-mail: orare@aol.com.

SMITH, HAROLD B. manufacturing executive; b. Chgo., Apr. 7, 1933; s. Harold Byron and Pauline (Hart) S. Grad., Choate Sch., 1951; BS, Princeton U., 1955; MBA, Northwestern U., 1957. With Ill. Tool Works, Inc., Chgo., 1954—, exec. v.p., 1968-72, pres., 1972-81, vice chmn., 1981, chmn. exec. com., 1982—, also bd. dirs. Bd. dirs. W.W. Grainger, Inc., No. Trust Corp Mem. Rep. Nat. Com., 1976-99; chmn. Ill. Rep. Com., 1993-99; del. Rep. Nat. Conv., 1964, 76, 88, 92, 96, 2000; bd. dirs. Adler Planetarium, Boys and Girls Clubs Am., Northwestern U., Rush U. Med. Ctr., Newberry Libr. Mem.: Chicago, Commercial, Commonwealth, Economic, Northwestern, Princeton (Chgo.). Office: Ill Tool Works Inc 3600 W Lake Ave Glenview IL 60026-1215

SMITH, HAROLD CHARLES, private pension fund executive; b. N.Y.C., Jan. 11, 1934; s. Harold Elmore and Hedwig Agnes (Gronke) S. BA cum laude with honors, Ursinus Coll., 1955; MBA, NYU, 1958; M in Div., Union Theol. Sem., N.Y.C., 1958; DD (hon.), 1993; DD (hon.), Ursinus Coll., 1997; DHum (hon.), Springfield Coll., 1998. CFA; ordained minister United Ch. Christ, 1959. V.p. YMCA Retirement Fund, Inc., N.Y.C., 1958-69, portfolio mgr., 1960—, assoc. sec., 1969-77, v.p., 1977-80, exec. v.p., 1980-82, pres. elect, 1982-83, pres., 1983-2000; assoc. prof. bus. and fin. L.I. U., 1969-71. Trustee Bank Mart, Bridgeport, Conn., 1983-91; bd. dirs. Y Mut. Ins. Co., treas. 1988—. Author: Getting It All Together in Retirement, 1977. Trustee YWCA Greater Bridgeport, 1975—79, Pension Funds United Ch. of Christ, 1968—, Springfield Coll., Mass., 1983—, United Ch. Found., 1968—, vice chmn., 1995—98, chmn., 1998—99; pastor 1st E&R Ch., Bridgeport, Conn., 1958—88, Unity Hill United Ch. of Christ, 1988—2000, 1st Congl. Ch., Union, NJ, 2001—02, River Edge, NJ, 2002—03; treas. United H. Homes of N.J. Inc., 2001—; exec. coun. UCC, 2000—; bd. dirs. United Ch. Residencies, 1962—65, YMCA Greater N.Y., 2002—, 1983—97, Bridgeport Area Found., 1989—2000, Ursinus Coll., Pa., 1994—, Coun. of Chs. Greater Bridgeport, 1995—96, Silver Bay Christian Conf. Ctr., 1997. Mem. Am. Econs. Assn., N.Y. Soc. Security Analysts, Fin. Analysts Fedn., Masons, Order Ea. Star. Personal E-mail: hcsmith1@email.msn.com.

SMITH, HAROLD HASKEN, university administrator; b. Cin., Mar. 16, 1942; s. Harold C. and Ruth V. (Hasken) S.; m. Karen A. Willis, Dec. 20, 1969; children: Amy Elizabeth, Andrew David, Anne Cameron. AB, Centre Coll., 1964; MBA, Am. U., 1968. Admissions counselor Centre Coll., Danville, Ky., 1964-66, assoc. dir. admissions, 1968-70, dir. admissions, 1970-73, dean admissions, 1973-80, v.p., den students, 1980-83, lectr. econs. mgmt., 1973-80; v.p. devel. Muskingum Coll., New Concord, Ohio, 1983-97; pres. Pikeville (Ky.) Coll. and Coll. Osteo. Med., Ky., 1997—. Cons. in edn. Dir. Boyle-Mercer County (Ky.) YMCA, 1979-83; mem. bd. trustees S.E. Ohio Regional Med. Ctr., 1987-97; bd. dirs. Southeast Ohio Symphony Orch., 1983-97, Renew Environment of New Concord, 1983-97; active Leadership Ky., 2000. Recipient Disting. Chmn. award Rotary Found., 1981-82. Mem. Ctr. Coll. Athletic Hall of Fame, 1994, Council Ind. Ky. Colls. and Univs., Nat. Assn. Student Personnel Adminstrs., Am. Coll. Personnel Assn., Cambridge C. of C. (bd. dirs. 1984-97), Nat. Assn. Coll. Admissions Counselors, Rotary (pres. 1979-80, dist. gov.'s rep. 1981-82), Zanesville Country Club, Green Meadow Country Club. Office: Pres's Office Pikeville Coll Pikeville KY 41501 E-mail: halsmith@pc.edu.

SMITH, H(AROLD) LAWRENCE, lawyer; b. Evergreen Park, Ill., June 27, 1932; s. Harold Lawrence and Lorna Catherine (White) Smith; m. Madonna Jeanne Koehl, June 9, 1956 (div. 1968); children: Lawrence Kirby, Sandra Michelle, Madonna Clare Galloway; m. Nancy Leigh Baum, May 2, 1970 (dec. 1983); m. Louise Fredericka Jeffrey, Nov. 2, 1984 (div. 1994); m. Marianne Lorraine Laug, Apr. 19, 1997. BS, US Naval Acad., 1956; JD, John Marshall Law Sch., 1965. Bar: Ill. 1965, Mich. 1986, U.S. Dist. Ct. (no. dist.) Ill. 1965, U.S. Ct. Appeals (7th cir.) 1967, U.S. Ct. of Customs and Patent Appeals, 1976, U.S. Ct. Appeals (fed. cir.) 1982, U.S. Patent and Trademark Office 1968. Asst. prof. naval sci. U. Notre Dame, 1960-61; tech. asst. Langner, Parry, Card & Langner, Chgo., 1961-65, assoc., 1965-69; patent atty. Borg-Warner Corp., Chgo., 1970-74; sr. patent atty. Continental Can Co., Inc., Chgo. and Oak Brook, Ill., 1974-82, asst. gen. counsel Stamford and Norwalk, Conn., 1982-86; ptnr. Varnum, Riddering, Schmidt & Howlett, Grand Rapids, Mich., 1986-96, counsel, 1996-97; ptnr. Rader, Fishman, Grauer & McGarry, Grand Rapids, 1997—2001; of counsel McGarry Bair LLP, Grand Rapids, 2001—03; cons., 2003—. Adj. prof. patent law Cooley Law Sch., 1991—. Served to lt. USN, 1956-61. Fellow Mich. State Bar Found.; mem. Intellectual Property Law Assn. Chgo., Chartered Inst. Patent Agts. (London 1971-2003), World Affairs Coun. Western Mich. (bd. dirs. 1996-2002, treas. 1998-2000. E-mail: hls@mcgarrybair.com.

SMITH, HAROLD RAYMOND, neurologist, sleep medicine specialist, educator; b. Detroit, Dec. 15, 1953; s. Raymond Harold Smith and Veronica Bernice Zawacki; m. Margaret Mary Demaria, May 20, 1977. BS, U. Mich., 1975, MD, 1979. Diplomate Am. Bd. Neurology, Am. Bd. Sleep Medicine. Intern in internal medicine Henry Ford Hosp., Detroit, 1979-80; resident, chief resident U. Calif.-Irvine, Orange, 1980-83, attending faculty mem., 1983—, fellow in sleep medicine, 1984-85, mem. clin. faculty, 1983-86, asst. clin. prof., 1986-94, assoc. clin. prof., 1994-99, clin. prof., 1999—, med. dir., sleep medicine, 2003—, pres. exec. com.; pvt. practice neurology Irvine, 1983—. Clin. polysomnographer Hoag Hosp. Sleep Ctr., Newport Beach, Calif., 1986—. Contbr. chpts. to textbooks, articles to profl.jours. Fellow Am. Acad. Sleep Medicine, Am. Acad. Neurology (founding mem. sleep sect., chmn. edn. com. 1999—, mem. exec. com. 1999—); mem. Am. Assn. Electrodiagnostic Medicine, Am. Coll. Sports Medicine, Clin. Faculty Assn. U. Calif. Irvine (exec. com. adminstrv. coun. 2000—, pres.-elect 2002-2004, pres. 2004—), Irvine C. of C. Avocation: competitive long distance running. Office: U Calif-Irvine 4199 Campus Dr Ste 350 Irvine CA 92612-8603

SMITH, HARRI ANNE, state legislator; b. Houston County, Ala., Jan. 20, 1962; m. Charlie Smith. BS, Troy State U. Mem. Ala. State Senate, Montgomery, 1999—, chmn. small bus. and econ. devel. com., vice chmn. agr. and forestry com., banking and ins. com., indsl. devel. and recruitment com., commerce, transp. and utilities com. V.p. Slocomb Nat. Bank. Bd. dirs. Geneva County United Way; previously mayor pro-tem, Slocomb; mem. city coun., Slocomb, 1989—. Mem. So. Ala. Reg. Coun. Aging (bd. dirs.), State of Ala. Agribus. Coun., Dothan Area C. of C., Cmty. Bankers Assn., Ala. Bankers Assn. Republican. Baptist. Office: Ala State House 11 S Unio St Montgomery AL 36130-0001

SMITH, HARRISON HARVEY, journalism consultant; b. Wilkes-Barre, Pa., Oct. 24, 1915; s. Ernest Gray and Marjorie (Harvey) S.; m. Joanne Christopher, June 7, 1940 (div.); children: Barbara DeWitt, Marjorie Harvey, Susan C. (dec. 1999); m. Margaret Simons, July 18, 1947 (dec. May 1978); children: Rosanne Jameson, Elizabeth Simons; m. Dorothy Wright Welborn, June 22, 1989. Diploma in lit., Wyoming (Pa.) Sem., 1936; postgrad., Northwestern U., 1937-38. Asst. to pub. Wilkes-Barre Times-Leader, 1938-39, v.p., asst. sec., 1939-46, pres., 1946-79; editor Wilkes-Barre Record, 1962-72; newspaper cons. Key Biscayne, Fla., 1979—. Dir. emeritus 1st Ea. Bank Wilkes-Barre; pres. Pa. AP, 1953. Chmn. Wyoming Valley ARC, 1954-55; v.p. bd. dirs. Wilkes-Barre Gen. Hosp., 1954-76. With U.S. Army, 1945-46, Korea.

Mem. Am. Soc. Newspaper Editors, Nat. Conf. Editl. Writers, Soc. Profl. Journalists, Pa. Newspaper Pubs. Assn. (mem. exec. com. 1954-62), Wyoming Valley Hist. Soc. (pres. 1971-74), Newcomen Soc., Am. Legion, VFW, Poor Richard Club (Phila.), Mirador Club (Geneva), Westmoreland Club, Sankaty Head Golf and Beach Club (Nantucket Island, Mass.), Country Club Coral Gables, Key Biscayne Yacht Club, Masons (33 degree). Republican. Presbyterian. Home and Office: 177 Ocean Lane Dr Apt 811 Key Biscayne FL 33149-1427 also: 10 Lyons Ln PO Box 180 Siasconset MA 02564-0180

SMITH, HARRY, newscaster; b. Lansing, Ill., Aug. 21, 1951; m. Andrea Joyce; 2 children. BA in Comm. and Theater, Central Coll., Pella, Iowa. With KHOW and KIMN (radio), Denver, 1973—81, WLW (radio), Cin., Ohio, 1973—81, KRMA-TV, Denver, 1981—82; reporter, anchor KMGH-TV, Denver, 1982—85; reporter CBS News, Dallas, 1986, anchor, corr., featured contbr., 1986—99; corr. CBS Evening News, Dallas, 1987; co-anchor CBS This Morning, 1987—96; host Biography, 1999—; anchorman The Early Show, 2002—. Co-host, weekday morning coverage Olympic Winter Games CBS Sports, Albertville, France, 1992, Lillehammer, Norway, 94; substitute anchor, corr. CBS News Sunday Morning; anchor, contbr. CBS News documenaries, 48 Hours; contbr. CBS Evening News With Dan Rather. Office: CBS News 524 W 57th St New York NY 10019

SMITH, HARRY BUCHANAN, JR., graphic designer, painter, photographer, writer; b. Springfield, Ill., Aug. 30, 1924; s. Harry Buchanan and Cordelia Warren (Birchall) S.; divorced; 1 child, Mark Savolainen. B of Design, U. Mich., 1947; MS, ITT Inst. Design, 1948. Designer Chgo. Plan Commn., 1948-49, Warren Wetheral & Assocs., Chgo., 1949-50; dir. design Dekovic-Smith Design Orgn., Chgo., 1951-58; prin. H.B. Smith & Assocs., Chgo., 1959-87. Author: Contemporary Fables, 1988; works include graphic design (with Mortimer Adler) Encyclopaedia Britannica, 15th edit., 1975, 176 exhibitions, 1951-87; redesigned YMCA internat. symbol, numerous corporate identity programs, publs.; photographer Objects in Crisis (series); artist numerous mixed media. Lt. (j.g.) USNR, 1943-47, PTO. Mem. Am. Inst. Graphic Arts, Am. Ctr. for Design (steering com.). Home and Office: 2960 N Lake Shore DR Apt 3108 Chicago IL 60657-5664 E-mail: aristotl@runchicago.com.

SMITH, HARRY LEROY, securities firm executive; b. Waukegan, Ill., Nov. 7, 1909; s. Thomas William and Louise (Krantz) S.; m. Laura Sloo Johnson, Apr. 21, 1938; children: Harry Leroy, William Bridges. Student diplomatic studies, Ecole libre des scis. polit., Paris, 1930—31; BS, Georgetown U., 1933; MA, George Washington U., 1933, postgrad., 1939; LLB, Southeastern U., 1936. Bar: D.C. 1936. With Dist. Nat. Bank, Washington, 1928-29, U.S. Dept. Treasury, Washington, 1929-30, FBI, Washington, 1930, Dept. State, Washington, 1931-32; chief editl. sect. procurement divsn. U.S. Dept. Treasury, Washington, 1934-36, planning officer, 1936-40, chief surplus property divsn., 1940-41, chief econ. analysis divsn., 1941; gen. staff officer, chief G-2 dissemination and functional intelligence Army Gen. Staff, 1941—44, cons., 1947-48; asst., acting mil. attache Am. Embassy, Chile, 1944-46; exec. asst., dir. materials supply program Housing Expeditor's Office, 1946-47; commd. fgn. svc. officer Dept. State, 1948; consul Shanghai, 1948-49, Hong Kong, 1949-51; first sect., consul, comml. attache Am. Embassy, Baghdad, Iraq, 1951-53, first sect., consul Athens, Greece, 1953-56; internat. economist Dept. of State, Washington, 1956-58. Bd. chmn., CEO Halaro Products, Inc., Silver Spring, 1982-85, H.L. Smith Co., Silver Spring, 1959-84, investment securities, 1985—; chmn. bd. Smith & Lawrence Co., Arlington, Va., 1984-85; prof. econs. Southeastern U., Washington, 1956-64, asst. dean jr. coll., 1960-64; gen. agt. Std. Life of Ind., Silver Spring, 1960-70; mem. various presdl. commns. and joint Army-Navy coms. Contbr. articles to profl. jours. With USMC, 1929—32, served to col. U.S. Army, 1941—46. Mem. Pi Gamma Mu (pres. 1931-33), Delta Phi Epsilon. Episcopalian. Home and Office: 3708 Scenic Dr Cibolo TX 78108-2229

SMITH, HARRY MENDELL, JR., science educator; b. Wichita, Kans., Aug. 19, 1943; s. H. Mendell and Sevilla Mae (Cooper) S.; m. Cecile Marie Adams, Sept. 19, 1964; children: Jeff, Shauna, Noelle. AA, Pasadena Coll., 1966; BA, Calif. State U., L.A., 1970; Vocat. Credential, UCLA, 1979. Tchr. Glendora (Calif.) Unified Schs., 1970-80; instr. Citrus Coll., Azusa, Calif., 1978-82; mgr. Christian Chapel, Walnut, Calif., 1980-82; pres. Whitmore Printing, Inc., La Puente, Calif., 1982-85; mgr. Evang. Free Ch., Fullerton, Calif., 1985-87; chair dept. electronics & comp. tech. Mt. San Antonio Coll., Walnut, 1993—2000, prof., 1985—, chair dept. electronics and computer tech., 2003—; instr. sci. Biola Star program. Dir. Faculty Senate, Mt. San Antonio Coll., 1989-91; assoc. dean applied tech. and health sci., Mt. San Antonio Coll., summer 2000. Author: Electronic Devices and Circuits Lab Book, 1994, Experiments in DC/AC Circuits, 1998, Technical Applications in Microcomputers Using Microsoft Office, 2000, Experiments in Introductory Electronic Devices and Circuits, 2002. Treas. Sojourner Evangelical Free Ch., Fullerton, 1996-98. Chancellor's Office Electronic Tech. grantee, 1990. Mem. Nat. Assn. Radio and Telecommunications Engrs., Home Bldrs. Fellowship (pres. 1990-92), Skills USA-VICA (nat. advisor 2001—), Vocat. Indsl. Clubs Am. (region 3 coord. post secondary 1997—), Calif. Coun. Electronics Instrs. (sec. to bd. dirs. 1997-2000). Republican. Avocations: music, coin collecting/numismatics, electronics, physical fitness, solar energy. Home: 6373 Carter St Chino CA 91710-5390 Office: Mt San Antonio Coll 1100 N Grand Ave Walnut CA 91789 E-mail: hsmith@mtsac.edu.

SMITH, HARVEY ALVIN, mathematics educator, consultant; b. Easton, Pa., Jan. 30, 1932; s. William Augustus and Ruth Carolyn (Krauth) S.; m. Ruth Wismer Kolb, Aug. 27, 1955; children: Deirdre Lynn, Kirsten Nadine, Brinton Averil. BS, Lehigh U., 1952; MS, U. Pa., 1955, AM, 1958, PhD, 1964. Asst. prof. math Drexel U., 1960-65; mem. tech. staff Inst. Def. Analyses, Arlington, Va., 1965-66; assoc. prof. math Oakland U., 1966-68; ops. research scientist Exec. Office of Pres., Washington, 1968-70; prof. math. Oakland U., 1970-77; prof. Ariz. State U., Tempe, 1977—2003, prof. emeritus, 2003—; cons. Inst. Def. Analyses, 1967-69, Exec. Office Pres., 1967-73, U.S. Arms Control and Disarmament Agy, 1973-79, Los Alamos Nat. Lab., 1980-93. Author: Mathematical Foundations of Systems Analysis, 1969. NSF fellow, 1964-65; recipient Meritorious Service award Exec. Office of Pres., 1970 Mem. Soc. Indsl. and Applied Math., Am. Math. Soc., AAAS, Sigma Xi Home: 18 E Concorda Dr Tempe AZ 85282-3517 Office: Ariz State U Dept Math Tempe AZ 85287-1804 Office Phone: 480-968-6813. E-mail: hsmith@math.asu.edu.

SMITH, HEATHER LYNN, psychotherapist, recreational therapist; b. Modesto, Calif., May 31, 1956; d. Gary Fremont and Marilyn Rae (Brown) S. BS, Calif. State U., Fresno, 1979; MA, U. San Francisco, 1989. Lic. marriage, family and child counselor, Calif. Recreational therapist Casa Colina Rehab. Hops., Pomona, Calif., 1979-82; evaluator developmentally delayed, coord. family edn. Cath. Charities, Modesto, 1982-87; bereavement counselor Hospice, Modesto, 1983-87; high risk youth counselor Ctr. Human Svcs., Modesto, 1987—; pvt. practice, family therapist Modesto, 1988—. Program dir. chemically dependent treatment program Stanislaus County Juvenile Hall, 1990—; program adminstr. First Step, 1999—. Named Outstanding Young Woman of Stanislaus County, 1986, Citizen of Yr., Civitan, 1986, Outstanding Individual award Stanislaus County, 1992. Mem. Calif. Assn. Marriage and Family Therapists, Kappa Kappa Gamma. Republican. Episcopalian. Avocations: skiing, running, backpacking, tennis. Home: 806 Claratina Ave Modesto CA 95356-9610 Office: PO Box 577456 Modesto CA 95357-7456 Office Phone: 209-521-7254. E-mail: serenity.mft@aol.com.

SMITH, HEDRICK LAURENCE, journalist, television producer, correspondent, author, lecturer; b. Kilmacolm, Scotland, July 9, 1933; s. Sterling L. and Phebe (Hedrick) S.; m. Ann Bickford, June 29, 1957 (div. Dec. 1985); children: Laurel Ann, Jennifer Laurence, Sterling Scott, Lesley Roberts; m. Susan Zox, Mar. 7, 1987. BA, Williams Coll., 1955, LittD (hon.), 1975; postgrad. (Fulbright scholar), Balliol Coll., Oxford, Eng., 1955-56; LittD (hon.), Wittenburg U., 1985, N.H. Coll., 1991; LHD (hon.), Columbia Coll., 1992; LittD (hon.), Amherst Coll., 1992; LHD (hon.), U. S.C., 1992; LittD (hon.), Furman U., 1996. With U.P.I., Memphis, Nashville, Atlanta, 1959-62; with N.Y. Times, 1962-88, 1962-63, Vietnam, 1963-64; Middle East corr. N.Y. Times, Cairo, U.A.R., 1964-66, diplomatic news corr. Washington, 1962-64, 66-71, Moscow Bur. chief, 1971-74, dep. nat. editor, 1975-76, Washington Bur. chief, 1976-79, chief Washington corr., 1980-85; Washington correspondent N.Y. Times mag., 1987-88. Vis. journalist Am. Enterprise Inst., 1985-87; fellow Fgn. Policy Inst., Johns Hopkins U. Sch Advanced Internat. Studies, 1989-97; panelist Washington Week in Rev., PBS, 1969-95. Author: The Russians, 1975 (Overseas Press Club award, 1976), The Power Game: How Washington Works, 1988, The New Russians, 1990 (Overseas Press Club citation, 1991), Rethinking America, 1995; co-author: The Pentagon Papers, 1972, Reagan the Man, the President, 1981, Beyond Reagan: The Politics of Upheaval, 1986, Seven Days That Shook the World, 1991, (TV documentaries) Star Wars, 1985, Moscow Jews, 1986, Space Bridge, Chernobyl: Three Mile Island, 1987, 4-part Power Game series, PBS, 1989, Countdown to White House: The Bush Transition, 1989, 4-part series Inside Gorbachev's USSR, 1990 (George Polk award, Gold Baton award Columbia-DuPont), Guns, Tanks and Gorbachev (Frontline), 1991, Soviets, 1991 (George Peabody award), After Gorbachev's USSR (Frontline), 1992, 4-part series PBS, Challenge to America, 1994 (Cine Golden Eagle award, Rias award), Across the River pub. TV program, 1995 (Hillman award), The People and the Power Game, 1996 (Silver award Houston Film Festival), Surviving the Bottom Line, 1998 (Cine Golden Eagle award, Flagstaff Film Festival Bronze award), Seeking Solutions, 1999 (nat. award for pub. svc. Sigma Delta Chi, spl. gold medal Houston Film Festival), Duke Ellington's Washington, 2000 (N.Y. Film Festival Bronze prize), Critical Condition, 2000 (Emmy nomination), Dr. Solomon's Dilemma (Frontline), 2000 (Chris award), Juggling Work and Family, 2001, Rediscovering Dave Brubeck, 2001, Inside the Terror Network (Frontline), 2002 (co-winner Columbia-Dupont Gold Baton), Bigger Than Enron (Frontline), 2002 (Cine Gold Eagle), The Wall Street Fix (Frontline), 2003 (Emmy award, Cine Gold Eagle, Chris award), Tax Me If You Can (Frontline), 2004. Trustee Williams Coll., 1982-97; mem. Aspen Inst. Domestic Strategy Group, 1997-2002; bd. dirs. New American Schs., 1996-2004; mem. steering com. Concerned Dems., 2001—. With USAF, 1956-59. Recipient Pulitzer prize for pub. svc. Pentagon Papers Series, 1972, for internat. reporting from Soviet Union and Ea. Europe, 1974, William Allen White award U. Kans., 1996; Nieman fellow Harvard U., 1969-70. Mem. Gridiron Club, Phi Beta Kappa. Office Phone: 301-654-9848. Personal E-mail: hsmithprod@aol.com.

SMITH, HEIDI, political organization administrator; Political worker Goldwater for Pres. Campaign; pres. Oreg. Fedn. Rep. Women, Reno Club Fedn. Rep. Women; 2nd v.p. Nev. Fedn. Rep. Women; chairwoman Oreg. Women Reagan Campaign; treas., dir. region 9 Nat. Fedn. Rep. Women, Alexandria, Va., mem. exec. com. Mgr. Smith Ins. Agy.; tchr. genealogy. Planning commr., parks commr., fair bd. dirs., ct. apptd. spl. advocate, candidate mem. for Nat. State Assembly; events chmn. Truckee Meadows Habitat for Humanity; active The Gift of Life. Mem. No. Nev. Assn. Life Underwriters (exec. dir.). Office: Nat Fedn Rep Women 124 N Alfred St Alexandria VA 22314-3011 Fax: 703-548-9836. E-mail: ssmith@aci.net.

SMITH, HENRY CHARLES, III, symphony orchestra conductor; b. Phila., Jan. 31, 1931; s. Henry Charles Jr. and Gertrude Ruth (Downs) S.; m. Mary Jane Dressner, Sept. 3, 1955; children— Katherine Anne, Pamela Jane, Henry Charles IV. BA, U. Pa., 1952; artist diploma, Curtis Inst. Music, Phila., 1955. Solo trombonist Phila. Orch., 1955-67; condr. Rochester (Minn.) Symphony Orch., 1967-68; assoc. prof. music Ind. U., Bloomington, 1968-71; resident condr., ednl. dir. Minn. Orch., Mpls., 1971-88; prof. music U. Tex., Austin, 1988-89, Frank C. Erwin Centennial Prof. of Opera, 1988-89; music dir. S.D. Symphony, Sioux Falls, 1989-2001; prof. Ariz. State U., Tempe, 1989-93, prof. emeritus, 1993—. Vis. prof. U. Tex., Austin, 1987-88; founding mem. Phila. Brass Ensemble, 1956—; music dir. World Youth Symphony Orch., Interlochen, Mich., 1981-96. Composer 5 books of solos for trombone including Solos for the Trombone Player, 1963, Hear Us As We Pray, 1963, First Solos for the Trombone Player, 1972, Easy Duets for Winds, 1972; editor 14 books 20th century symphonies lit. Served to 1st lt. AUS, 1952-54. Recipient 3 Grammy nominations, 1967, 76, 1 Grammy award for best chamber music rec. with Phila. Brass Ensemble, 1969. Mem. Internat. Trombone Assn. (dir.), Am. Symphony Orch. League, Music Educators Nat. Conf., Am. Guild Organists, Am. Fedn. Musicians, Tubist Universal Brotherhood Assn., Acacia Fraternity. Republican. Congregationalist. Home: 8032 Pennsylvania Rd S Bloomington MN 55438-1135

SMITH, HILARY CRANWELL BOWEN, investment banker; b. Balt., Nov. 1, 1937; s. Henry Bowen and Clayton (Cranwell) S.; m. Janet Simmons, June 9, 1962. BA, Colgate U., 1960; MBA, U. Va., 1967. V.p. Goldman, Sachs & Co., N.Y.C., 1969-74, E. F. Hutton & Co., N.Y.C., 1974-77; sr. v.p. Blyth Eastman Dillon, N.Y.C., 1977-79; mng. dir. Salomon Bros., N.Y.C., 1979-90, UBS, N.Y.C., 1990—2004. Bd. dirs. Forest & Market. Trustee Wheaton Coll., 1997-2003, Chesapeake Maritime Mus., 1998-2004. Lt. USN, 1960-63. Office: UBS 299 Park Ave Fl 36 New York NY 10171-0002 Office Phone: 212-389-1500.

SMITH, HOWARD ALAN, editor, publishing executive; b. Ames, Iowa, Nov. 14, 1950; s. Delbert Dean and B Mildred (Nelson) Smith; m. Valle Jo Loving, June 2, 1973; children: Nathan A, Erin M, Cara L. BA in social studies, Graceland Coll., 1972; MA, Iowa State U., 1977. Reporter Red Oak Express, Red Oak, Iowa, 1972—75; bus. mgr. Iowa State U., 1975—77; gen. mgr. Dinsmore Pub. Inc., Fremont, Iowa, 1977—80; reporter Mount Ayr Record News, Iowa, 1980, editor/pub., 1981—. Pres./bd. mem. Iowa Newspaper Found., 1990—96; bd. mem. Iowa Newspaper Assn., 2000—. Author: (book) Our Heritage of Humor, 1978. Dist. study com. Mount Ayr Cmty. Sch. Dist., 2003—; dir. Family Ch. Camp, 2001—; mem. Mount Ayr C. of C.; presiding elder/asst. presiding elder Ch. of Jesus Christ, Mount Ayr, Iowa, 1983—. Recipient master editor/pub., Iowa Newspaper Assn., 1999. Mem.: Mount Ayr Lions Club (past pres.). Avocations: reading, photography, writing. Home: 607 E Madison Mount Ayr IA 50854 Office: Mount Ayr Record News 122 W Madison Mount Ayr IA 50854

SMITH, H(OWARD) DUANE, zoology educator; b. Fillmore, Utah, June 25, 1941; s. Howard Martell and Mary Ellen (Mitchell) S.; m. Dahnelle Bower, Dec. 18, 1961; children: Cory, Neichol. BS, Brigham Young U., 1963, MS, 1966; PhD, U. Ill., 1969. From asst. prof. to prof. Brigham Young U., Provo, Utah, 1969—; pvt. practice Orem, Utah, 1973—; dir. Monte L. Bean Life Sci. Mus., Provo, Utah. Dir. Life Sci. Mus. Co-author: Special Publications-Mammalogy, 1994; contbr. articles to profl. jours. State chair Mule Deer Found. Mem. Am. Soc. Mammalogists (sec. 1987-1992), Wildlife Soc., Rocky Mountain Elk Found., Mule Deer Found. (state chair), Safari Club Internat., Sigma Xi (pres. 1996-97). Republican. Mem. Lds Ch. Avocations: hunting, fishing. Office: Brigham Young Univ 290 MLBM Provo UT 84602-1049 E-mail: Duane@Museum.BYU.EDU.

SMITH, HOWARD I. insurance company executive; with BBA in Acctg., CCNY. CPA, N.Y. In charge N.Y. office ins. practice, N.Y.C.; with Coopers & Lybrand LLP, 19 yrs; comptr. Am. Internat. Group, Inc., N.Y.C., 1984—, v.p., 1984-87, sr. v.p., 1987-95, exec. v.p., 1995—, CFO, 1996—, vice chmn., 2002—, chief admin. officer, 2002—, also mem. bd. dirs. Mem. AICPA, N.Y. Soc. CPA's, Fin. Execs. Inst. Office: Am Internat Group Inc 70 Pine St New York NY 10270-0002

SMITH, HOWARD THOMPSON, manufacturing executive; b. Camden, Ark., Apr. 30, 1937; s. Howard Thompson and Pauline Virginia (Rogers) S.; m. Ann Monroe; children: Paul R., Elizabeth M. BS, Tulane U., 1960; postgrad. studies, La. State U., 1961-63; EPBA, Columbia U., 1978. Dir. planning Ethyl Corp., Baton Rouge, La., 1970-76; exec. v.p., gen. mgr. William Bonnell Co. subs. Ethyl Corp., Newman, Ga., 1976-81; pres. Steelcraft, Cin., 1981-84; v.p., group exec. Am. Standard, Cin., 1984-89, sr. v.p. N.Y.C., 1989-94, also bd. dirs., 1989—; pres., CEO The Trane Co., N.Y.C., 1989-94; mng. ptnr. Septa Assocs., 1994—; gen. ptnr. Rutledge Capital, 2000—. Pres. Thompson Smith Found., 1993—; chmn. bd. dirs. Trinity Mother Francis Health Sys., 1996—, Adobe, 2000—, Framed Picture Enterprises, 1999-,; bd. dirs. CROM Corp. Bd. dirs. Salvation Army, 1988—, Tex. Rsch. League, Austin, 1989, U. Tex., Tyler, 1990—, Mother Francis Hosp. Found., 1991—; chmn. bd. dirs. East Tex. Communities Found., 1993—; elder, trustee 1st Presbyn. Ch.; trustee U. Tex., Tyler, East Tex. Pres. Found., Union Theol. Sem., 1994— Mem. Tex. Assn. Taxpayers (dir.), Smith County C. of C. (bd. dirs. 1988-91), Tyler Petroleum Club, Hollytree Country Club, Willowbrook Country Club, Sawgrass Country Club. Republican. Presbyterian. Avocations: golf, tennis. Home: 6110 Covey Ln Tyler TX 75703-4507 Office: The Trane Co PO Box 9010 Tyler TX 75711-9010 also: 819 Spinnakers Reach Dr Ponte Vedra Beach FL 32082-3408

SMITH, HOWARD WELLINGTON, education educator, dean emeritus; b. Granby, Mo., Jan. 19, 1929; s. Howard W. and Margaret L. (Sanderson) S.; m. Margaret E. Bell, Mar. 1, 1953; 1 child, Christopher Alan. BS, S.W. Mo. State U., 1954; MEd, U. Mo., 1955, EdD, 1959. Tchr. Newton County (Mo.) Pub. Schs., 1948-51; instr. U. Mo., Columbia, 1955-59; asst. prof. So. Meth. U., Dallas, 1959-61; from asst. to full prof. U. North Tex., Denton, 1961-97, dean emeritus. Assoc. dean Coll. Edn. U. North Tex., 1972-76, assoc. v.p. acad. affairs, 1976-79, v.p. acad. affairs, 1979-82, interim dean, 1994-97; interim chancellor U. North Tex. Coll. Osteo. Medicine, Denton and Ft. Worth, 1981; sr. cons. Am. Assn. State Colls. and Univs., Washington, 1982; cons. Srinakharinwirot U., Thailand, 1986, Tex. Internat. Edn. Consortium, Austin, 1992, sr. author Operation Manual Al Akhawayn U., 1993; vis. prof. Shanxi Ednl. Coll. Taiyuan, China, 1993. Contbr. articles to ednl. jours. Prin. investigator Micro Tchg. Lab., 1967—69; chair Ret. Instrs., Pers. and Spouses U. North Tex., 2001; accreditation cons. Art Inst. Dallas, 2001—; chair Denton County Hist. Soc., 1999—; mem. adv. bd. Coll. Edn. U. North Tex., 1997—, mem. adv. bd. Bill J. Priest Ctr. for C.C. Edn., 1999—; pres. bd. dirs. Tex. Lakes Trail, 2002. With USAF, 1951—53. Democrat. Presbyterian. Avocations: travel, reading. Office: U North Tex Coll Edn PO Box 311337 Denton TX 76203-1337

SMITH, HUGH CADHAM, cardiovascular diseases physician; b. Winnipeg, Manitoba, Canada, July 14, 1939; BS, U. Manitoba, Winnipeg, MD, 1965. Intern U. Maitoba, 1965, resident in internal med., 1966—68; fellow in pulmonary disease U. Wash. Hosps., Seattle, 1968—70; resident in cardiology Mayo Clinic, Rochester, Minn., 1970—73, staff mem., 1970—. Chair bd. govs. Mayo Clinic, 1999—, prof. med.; v.p., mem. bd. trustees Mayo Found. Office: Mayo Clinic 200 First St SW Rochester MN 55905

SMITH, HUGH ELMORE, retired obstetrician and gynecologist; b. Mullins, S.C., Jan. 27, 1925; s. Howard Buchanan and Ruth (Bethea) S.; m. Martha Elizabeth Meares, June 21, 1947; children: Bonnie Raney, Hugh E. Jr., Jeff H., Brian B. Student, The Citadel, U. Miss.; MD, Med. Coll. S.C., 1950. Diplomate Am. Bd. Ob-Gyn. Intern Roper Hosp., Charleston, S.C., 1950-51, resident in ob-gyn., 1951-54; pvt. practice Orangeburg, S.C., 1954-83; ret., 1983. With USN, 1943-46. Fellow ACOG, Am. Fertility Soc.; mem. South Atlantic Assn. Ob-Gyn., South Central Ob-Gyn. Soc. (pres. 1982), S.C. Ob-Gyn. Soc. Methodist.

SMITH, IAN CORMACK PALMER, biophysicist; b. Winnipeg, Man., Can., Sept. 23, 1939; s. Cormack and Grace Mary Smith; m. Eva Gunilla Landvik, Mar. 27, 1965; children: Brittmarie, Cormack, Duncan, Roderick. BS, U. Man., 1961, MS, 1962; PhD, Cambridge U., England, 1965; Filosophie Doktor (hon.), U. Stockholm, 1986; DSc (hon.), U. Winnipeg, 1990, Brandon U., 2001; diploma in tech. (hon.), Red River Coll., 1996. Fellow Stanford U., 1965-66; mem. rsch. staff Bell Tel. Labs., Murray Hill, NJ, 1966-67; rsch. officer divsn. biol. scis. NRC, Ottawa, Canada, 1967-87, dir. gen., 1987-91, Inst. Biodiagnostics, Winnipeg, Canada, 1992—. Adj. prof. chemistry and biochemistry Carleton U., 1973—90, U. Ottawa, 1976—92; adj. prof. biophysics U. Ill., Chgo., 1974—80; adj. prof. chemistry, radiology, physics and anatomy U. Man., 1992—; allied scientist Ottawa Civic Hosp., 1985—98, Ottawa Gen. Hosp., 1989—98, Ont. Cancer Found., 1989—91, St. Boniface Hosp., 1992—, Health Scis. Ctr., 1993—, Econ. Tech. Innovation Coun., Man., 1994—98, mem. exec. com., Man., 1996—98, Man. Health Rsch. Coun., 1996—98, chmn., 1998—2002; mem. adv. bd. Loeb Inst., Ottawa, 1999—2001, Keystone Ventures, 1999—2002, Western LIfe Scis. Fund, 2002—, Novadaq, 2004—; bd. dirs. ENSIS Growth Fund, DIASPEC Holdings, IMRIS Inc., Magnetic Resonance Vets., Photonics Rsch. Ont., Spectex Pty., Biomed. Commercialization Can., Rover Imaging Inc., Ontario Centres of Excellence. Contbr. chapters to books, articles to profl. jours. Mem. Premier's Econ. Adv. Bd., 2001—, exec. com., 2004—; mem. adv. bd. Smart Winnipeg, 2000—03; bd. govs. U. Man., 2000—. Recipient Barringer award, Can. Spectroscopy Soc., 1979, Herzberg award, 1986, Organon Teknika award, Can. Soc. Clin. Chemists, 1987, Sr. Scientist award, Sigma Xi, 1995, Queen's Jubilee medal, 2003. Fellow: Soc. Magnetic Resonance Medicine (mem. exec. com. 1989—94), Royal Soc. Can. (Flavelle medal 1996), Chem. Inst. Can. (Merck award 1978, Labatt award 1984); mem.: Internat. Union Pure and Applied Biophysics (mem. coun. 1993—, v.p. 1996—99, 2002—), Biophysical Soc. Can. (pres. 1992—94), Can. Biochem. Soc., Biophysical Soc., Internat. Coun. Sci. Unions (mem. gen. com. 1989—94), U. Man. Alumni Assn. (bd. dirs. 1994—2000, v.p. 1997—98, pres. 1998—99). Office: Inst Biodiagnostics Winnipeg MB Canada R3B 1Y6 E-mail: ian.smith@nrc-cnrc.gc.ca.

SMITH, IRVING, gerontologist; b. Washington, June 4, 1948; s. Alfonso Marcellus and Nannie (Hunter) S.; children: Bryan, Rashard, Irving, Nevada, Ryan. M Human Svcs., grad. cert. advanced gerontology, Lincoln U., Pa., 1995; PhD in Health and Human Behavior, Walden U., 2002. Lic. profl. counselor Wash. Dir. Sr. Ctr. Md.-Nat. Capital Park and Planning Commn., Prince George's County, Md., 1969-71, 89—; prof. psychology Grad. Sch. Internat., nat. forum spkr. on leisure and aging issues; founder Prince George's County Centenarian Celebration; prin. investigator Prince George's County, Md. Centenarian Rsch. Study; bd. dirs., regional dir. Leisure and Aging. Mem. Nat. Recreation and Park Assn. (state rep. leisure and aging, bd. dirs. leisure and aging sect., dir. Mid-Atlantic region), Pi Gamma Mu. Democrat. Baptist. Home: 4311 23rd Pky #505 Temple Hills MD 20748 Personal E-mail: lsmith@starpower.net.

SMITH, ISABEL FRANCIS, financial planner; b. Detroit, May 21, 1935; d. Edward Hugh and Isabel (Winegar) Francis; m. Lawrence Smith, June 7, 1958; children: Mark, Hugh, Claire. Student, Newton Coll., 1953-54; BA, U. Mich., 1957, MA, 1958, postgrad., 1975-76. Registered investment adviser. Tchr. Edison Sch., Hazel Park, Mich., 1958-61, Warren Valley Sch., Dearborn Heights, Mich., 1958-61; counselor Riverside HS, Dearborn Heights, 1961-62; pres. Isabel Francis Smith Ltd., Farmington Hills, Mich., 1980—, Integrated Fin. Strategies Ltd., Farmington Hills, 1980—. Registered rep., dist. mgr. Investors Diversified Svcs., Oak Park, Mich., 1978—80; instr. Oakland CC, 1979—; cons. to women's orgns.; dir. pres. Oakland County Fin. and Estate Planning Coun., 1988—94; writer, profl. radio and TV personality. Lectr., trustee Bloomfield Twp. Libr., 1978—99, Interlochen Ctr. Arts, 1989—; founder Interlochen Friends, Vol. Network for Women. Recipient Heart of Gold award, United Found., 1976, Outstanding New Rep. award, Investors Diversified Svcs., 1979. Mem.: AAUW, Inst. Cert. Fin. Planners (nat. dir. 1980—86, dean retreat 1987, 1989, past regional dir., mem. leadership devel. com., cert. fin. planner), Internat. Assn. Fin. Planners (past pres. S.E. Mich. chpt.), Nat. Assn. Women Bus. Owners, U. Mich. Alumni Assn., Interlochen Alumni Founder Assn. (past pres., award), Village Club, Mut. Svcs. Corp. (pres. club 1992—2002, Outstanding Rep. award 1981—90), Women's Econ. Club, Phi Beta Kappa (nat. chmn., past pres., mem. exec. com. Pres. award Detroit assn.). Home: 7110 Paterese Dr Bloomfield Hills MI 48301-3764 Office: 31884 Northwestern Hwy Farmington Hills MI 48334-1628 Office Fax: 248-932-9345. Business E-Mail: isabel@ifs-ltd.com.

SMITH, J. GORDON, automotive executive; BA in Acctg., U. Mass.; grad., GE Fin. Mgmt. Program. Chief fin. officer comml. fin. units GE, 1990—2003; sr. v.p., chief fin. officer Asbury Automotive Group, Stamford, Conn., 2003—. Office: Asbury Automotive Group 3 Landmark Sw Stamford CT 06901

SMITH, J. KELLUM, JR., foundation executive, lawyer; b. N.Y.C., June 18, 1927; s. James Kellum and Elizabeth Dexter (Walker) S.; m. Sarah Tod Lohmann, July 22, 1950 (div. 1993); children: Alison Andrews, Timothy Kellum, Jennifer Harlow, Christopher Lohmann; m. Angela Marina Brown, Feb. 3, 1995. Grad., Phillips Exeter Acad., 1945; AB magna cum laude,

Amherst Coll., 1950; LL.B., Harvard, 1953. Bar: N.Y. 1955. Assoc. Lord, Day & Lord, N.Y.C., 1953-59; asst. sec. John Simon Guggenheim Meml. Found., 1960-62; mem. staff Rockefeller Found., 1962-74, asst. sec., 1963-64, sec., 1964—74; v.p., sec. Andrew W. Mellon Found., N.Y.C., 1974—89, sr. fellow, 1989-92; sr. advisor, 1992-98; pvt. practice cons. and writer. Trustee Nat. Sculpture Soc., 1955-71, Nat. Ins. Archtl. Edn., 1961-69, St. Bernard's Sch., N.Y.C., 1968-78, Found. for Child Devel., 1968-74; trustee Brearley Sch., N.Y.C., 1964-80, pres., 1973-78; trustee Am. Acad. in Rome, 1964-95, treas., 1965-66, 2d v.p., 1968-72, 84-88, sec., 1973-84, 89-95. With USAAF, 1945-46. Mem. Phi Beta Kappa. Clubs: Century Association (N.Y.C.). Home: 550 Number 37 Rd Saranac NY 12981-2956

SMITH, J. LEA, education educator, researcher; d. Delbert W. and Leah L. Smith. BA, Alberston Coll. Idaho; MEd, U. Idaho; MA, Stanford U.; PhD, U. Idaho. Assoc. prof. literacy edn. U. Louisville, Ky. Author: Dramatic Literacy, 2001. Office: Univ Louisville Dept Early and Mid Childhood Edn Louisville KY 40292 Office Phone: 502-852-0587. Office Fax: 502-852-0726. Business E-Mail: jlsmith01@louisville.edu.

SMITH, JACK C. supermarket executive; b. Aug. 21, 1925; Ptnr. Smith Realty, Grundy, Va., 1955—; chmn. K-VA-T Food Stores, Abington, Va. Office: 201 Trigg St Abingdon VA 24210-3470

SMITH, JACK CARL, foreign trade consultant; b. Cleve., Sept. 11, 1928; s. John Carl and Florence Agnes (O'Rourke) S.; m. Nannette June Boyd, Dec. 1, 1962; 1 dau., Colleen Wentworth. *Daughter, Colleen Wentworth Jones, attorney counselor-at-law, member American Bar Association, earned a Bachelor of Arts from Northwestern University; Juris Doctor from Marquette University Law School; Master of Law, Corporate Law, from Loyola University School of Law; Rogahn Law Offices through October 2003. November 2003 became principle of Wentworth Jones Law Firm LLC with Rod Rogahn of council. She is licensed in Wisconsin and Illinois. At Northwestern Colleen was president of The Equestrian Club, team captain and coach of intercollegiate riding competition; at Marquette was co-president of the International Law Society and lead advocate in their inter-collegiate moot court competition.* Student, Baldwin Wallace Coll., 1948-51, postgrad., 1958; BA, Ohio U., 1954. Rep. Flying Tiger Line, Inc., Los Angeles, 1958-61; prin. Pub. Rep. bus., Cleve., 1961-64; pub. Penton Pub., Cleve., 1964-90; spl. advisor Am. Fgn. Policy Coun., Washington, 1990—. Dir. Central Cleve. Corp., Nat. Distbn. Terminals; graduated Air Tng. Command Intelligence Officer Sch., served from 1958-62 AFR. Trustee Presdl. task force, Rep. Senatorial Inner Circle, Coun. of Logistics Mgmt., U.S. Bus. and Indsl. Coun. With USAF, 1954-58. Mem. Am. Mgmt. Assn., Material Handling Inst., Am. Trucking Assn., Nat. Council Phys. Distbn. Mgmt., Family Motor Coach Assn., Recreation Vehicle Industry Assn., Am. Bus. Press, Mag. Pubs. Assn., Sci. Research Soc., Internat. Platform Assn., Sigma Xi, Sigma Chi Clubs: Wings (N.Y.C.). Home: 457 Devonshire Ct Bay Village OH 44140-3009 Office: Am Fgn Policy Coun 1521 16th St NW Washington DC 20036-1463 *Do your best and God will forgive you the rest.*

SMITH, JACK DAVID, lawyer; b. Honolulu, Jan. 4, 1946; s. Jack David and Gloria June (Slater) S.; m. Mary Elizabeth Zasadny, Sept. 17, 1977; children: Amy Elizabeth, Amanda Marie. BA in Polit. Sci., George Washington U., 1968, JD, 1971. Bar: Va. 1971, U.S. Ct. Mil. Appeals 1971, U.S. Ct. Appeals (1st and D.C. cirs.) 1975, U.S. Ct. Appeals (2d and 7th cirs.) 1976, U.S. Supreme Ct. 1976, D.C. 1986. Atty. litig. div. FCC, Washington, 1974-81, dept. chief common carrier bur., 1981-83, chief common carrier bur., 1983-84, gen. counsel, 1984-86; dep. gen. counsel Fed. Home Loan Bank Bd., Washington, 1986-89, Fed. Deposit Ins. Corp., Washington, 1989—. Served to capt. USMC, 1971-74. Mem. Va. Bar Assn., D.C. Bar Assn. Avocations: tennis, running, skiing. Home: 7636 Kingsbury Rd Alexandria VA 22315-4157 Office: Fed Deposit Ins Corp 550 17th St NW Washington DC 20429-0002 E-mail: jsmith@fdic.gov.

SMITH, JACLYN, actress; b. Houston, Oct. 26, 1947; d. Jack and Margaret Ellen S.; m. Dennis Cole (div. 1981); m. Tony Richmond, Aug. 4, 1981; 1 dau., Spencer Margaret. Student, Trinity U., San Antonio. Worked as model. Motion picture appearances include The Adventurers, 1970, Bootleggers, Deja Vu; TV film appearances include Bogen County, 1977, The Users, 1978, Rage of Angels, 1980, Nightkill, 1980, Jacqueline Bouvier Kennedy, 1981, Sentimental Journey, 1984, George Washington (miniseries), 1984, Florence Nightingale, 1985, The Night They Saved Christmas, 1986, Wind Mills of the Gods (miniseries), 1988, The Bourne Identity, 1988, Settle the Score, 1989, Danielle Steele's Kaleidoscope, 1990, Lies Before Kisses, 1991, The Rape of Dr. Willis, 1991, In The Arms Of A Killer, 1992, Love Can Be Murder, 1992, Family Album, 1994, Cries Unheard: The Donna Yaklich Story, 1994, My Very Best Friend, 1996, Married to a Stranger, 1997, Before He Wakes, 1998, Three Secrets, 1999, Freefall, 1999; one of prin. roles TV series Charlie's Angels, 1976-80, (ABC Saturday Night Movie) Christine Cromwell, 1989-90; other TV appearances include Get Christy Love, McCloud, The Rookies, Love Boat, Switch, Navigating the Heart, 2000, The District, 2000; appeared in numerous TV commls. Mem. AFTRA. Office: ICM 8942 Wilshire Blvd Beverly Hills CA 90211-1934*

SMITH, JAMES A. lawyer; b. Akron, Ohio, June 11, 1930; s. Barton H. and Myrna S. (Young) S.; m. Melda I. Perry, Jan. 17, 1959; children: Hugh, Sarah Louise. AB, Western Res. U., 1952; postgrad., Columbia U., 1954-56, LLB, 1961; postgrad., Yale U., 1956-58. Bar: Ohio 1961, U.S. Dist. Ct. (no. dist.) Ohio 1963, U.S. Ct. Appeals (6th cir.) 1973, U.S. Supreme Ct. 1974, U.S. Ct. Appeals (11th cir.) 1983, U.S. Ct. Appeals (D.C. cir.) 1984. Assoc. Squire, Sanders and Dempsey, Cleve., 1961-70, ptnr., 1970-91, counsel, 1991-96; adj. prof. Case Western Res. U. Sch. Law, 1997-98, ret., 1994. Mem. spl. adv. com. Nat. Conf. Commrs. on Uniform State Laws, 1972-74. Trustee Chagrin Falls Park Cmty. Ctr., 1968-78, Greater Cleve. Neighborhood Ctrs. Assn., 1973-78, Legal Aid Soc. Cleve., 1977-80, Cleve. Inst. Music, 1994—; mem. Charter Rev. Commn., Chagrin Falls, 1966. Lt. (j.g.) USNR, 1952-54. Fellow Am. Coll. Trial Lawyers; mem. ABA, Ohio Bar Assn., Cleve. Bar Assn. (trustee 1988-92), U.S. Ct. Appeals for 6th Cir. Jud. Conf. (life), Ohio Ct. Appeals for 8th Jud. Dist. Conf. (life), Ct. of Nisi Prius (clk. 1975-76, judge 1994-95), Phi Beta Kappa, Omicron Delta Kappa, Delta Sigma Rho. Democrat.

SMITH, JAMES ALBERT, lawyer; b. Jackson, Mich., May 12, 1942; s. J. William and Mary Barbara (Browning) S.; m. Lucia S. Santini, Aug. 14, 1965; children: Matthew Browning, Aaron Michael, Rachel Elizabeth. BA, U. Mich., 1964, JD, 1967. Bar: Mich. 1968, U.S. Dist. Ct. (ea. dist.) Mich., U.S. Ct. Appeals (6th and D.C. cirs.), U.S. Supreme Ct. Assoc. Bodman, Longley & Dahling, Detroit, 1967-75, ptnr., 1975—. Mem. panel Atty. Discipline Bd., Wayne County, Mich., 1987—; arbitrator Am. Arbitration Assn., 1975—; mem. Banking Commrs. com. on Contested Case Adminstrn., 1978. Mem. pro bono referral group Call For Action, Detroit, 1982—. Mem. ABA, State Bar Mich., Detroit Bar Assn. Roman Catholic. Avocations: sailing, travel. Office: Bodman Longley & Dahling 100 Renaissance Ctr Ste 34 Detroit MI 48243-1001

SMITH, JAMES C. entrepreneur; B, Northeastern U., 1963. Sales exec. Tex. Instruments; founder ARC Mgmt.; pres., CEO First Health; chmn. Concentra, 2000—. Mem.: Northeastern U. Gov. Bd., Internat. Found. Employee Benefit Plans (chmn. strat. planning and devel. com., adv. dir., mem. edn. com.), Health Ins. Assn. Am. (mem. bd. dirs.), Healthcare Leadership Coun. (treas., mem. exec. com.). Office: 3200 Highland Grove Downers Grove IL 60515-1282

SMITH, JAMES CLOUDIS, secretary of state, former state attorney general; b. Jacksonville, Fla., May 25, 1940; s. John Albert and Elizabeth F. (West) S.; m. Carole Ann Clark, Dec. 29, 1962; children: Kathryn Elizabeth, Robert Scott, James Clark. BA, Fla. State U., 1962; JD, Stetson U., 1967, LLD (hon.), 1987. Bar: Fla. 1967. Deputy sec. of state Fla. Sec. of State, Tallahassee, 1969-71; exec. asst. to lt. gov. Fla., 1971; dep. to Sec. of Commerce State of Fla., Tallahassee, 1971, sr. staff asst. to Gov., 1971-72, atty. gen., 1979-87, chief of staff Office of Gov., 1987, sec. of state of Fla., 1987—95; ptnr. Smith, Ballard & Logan, P.A., Tallahasse, Fla., 1998—2002; sec. of state of Fla. State of Fla., 2002—. Chmn. Gov.'s Adv. Com. on Corrections; mem. Article V Rev. Commn., Fla. Coun. on Criminal Justice, Sentencing Guidelines Study Commn., Commn. on Bail Bond Reform, Fla. Law Revision Comm. Mem. bd. overseers Stetson Coll. Law; trustee Univ. Found., Fla. State U.; mem. adv. bd. Nat. Fedn. Parents for Drug-Free Youth. Served to capt. U.S. Army, 1962-64. Named Conservationist of Yr. Fla. Audubon Soc.; recipient Disting. Alumnus award Stetson U., award for effectiveness in drug enforcement Dept. Justice. Mem. ABA (criminal law com.), Fla. Bar Assn., Tallahassee Bar Assn., Am. Judicature Soc. Republican. Methodist. Office: Office Sec of State PL-02 The Capitol Tallahassee FL 32399-0250

SMITH, JAMES FINLEY, economist, educator; b. Dallas, Nov. 4, 1938; s. Emerson Russell and Achsah Elizabeth (Foster) S.; children: Carter Emerson, Jamie, Curtis Noel, Marshall Edward; m. Linda M. Topp, Aug. 5, 2001. BA, So. Meth. U., 1961, MA, 1964, PhD, 1971. Math. analyst Sears, Roebuck & Co., Oak Brook, Ill., 1965-68, adminstrv. asst. to v.p. and treas. Chgo., 1968-69, dir. econometric rsch., 1969-75; sr. economist Bd. Govs. FRS, Washington, 1975-77; dir. credit rsch. Sears, Roebuck & Co., Chgo., 1977-80; chief economist Union Carbide Corp., Danbury, Conn., 1980-85; dir. regional svcs. and U.S. cons. Wharton Econometric Forecasting Assocs., Phila., 1986; dir., chief economist Bur. Bus. Rsch. U. Tex., Austin, 1987-88; prof. fin. U. NC, Chapel Hill, 1988—, sr. fellow Kenan Inst. Pvt. Enterprise, 2002—; chief economist Nat. Assn. Realtors, Washington, 1999—2000; dir. Ctr. for Bus. Forecasting, U. N.C., 2002—; chief economist Soc. Indsl. and Office Realtors, Washington, 2002—. Econ. adv. bd. U.S. Dept. Commerce, 1977-80, 83-93; cons. Pres.'s Coun. of Econ. Advisers, Washington, 1978-83; pres. Nat. Bus. Econ. Issues Coun., N.Y.C., 1981-83; dir. Nat. Bur. Econ. Rsch., Cambridge, Mass., 1992-95; bd. advisors Thurston Arthritis Rsch. Ctr., Chapel Hill, N.C., 1994-99. Author: (quarterly) UNC Business Forecast, 1988—, (with others) Economic Growth and Investment in Higher Education, 1987, The New Texas Economy, 1988, (with Elsie Echeverri-Carroll) The Economic Impact of Travel on Texas Counties: 1986, 1988; contbr. articles to profl. jours. Served to lt. U.S. Army, 1961-62. Fellow NDEA, 1962—65. Fellow Nat. Assn. Bus. Econ. (v.p. 1988-89, pres. 1989-90, dir. 1980-92); Nat. Economists Club (bd. govs. 1984-87), Am. Econ. Assn., Economists Group Switzerland, Fin. Mgmt. Assn., Bus. Economists U.K. Methodist. Home: 201 Bolinwood Dr Chapel Hill NC 27514 Office: U NC Kenan Flagler Bus Sch Dept Fin McColl Bldg Campus Box 3490 Chapel Hill NC 27599-3490 Office Phone: 919-968-9995. Business E-Mail: j_smith@unc.edu.

SMITH, JAMES FREDERICK, securities executive; b. N.Y.C., Jan. 6, 1944; s. James Arthur and Agnes Rose (Kollenz) S.; m. Joan Ann Kelly, June 18, 1966; children: James Patrick, John Michael. BBA in Accountancy Practice, Pace U., 1970. CPA, N.Y.; registered fin. & operational prin., registered rep. Mgmt. trainee Chase Manhattan Bank, N.Y.C., 1965-67; internal auditor MW Kellogg & Co., N.Y.C., 1967-69; sr. acct. Price Waterhouse, N.Y.C., 1969-72; asst. treas. and contr. Henderson Bros. Inc., N.Y.C., 1972-80; pvt. practice Clearwater, Fla., 1980-82; sr. audit mgr. Price Waterhouse, N.Y.C., 1982-84; v.p. & contr. Integrated Resources, N.Y.C., 1984-86; pres., CFO, Freeman Securities, Jersey City, 1986—. With USN, 1961-65. Mem. AICPA, Internat. Soc. CEBS (charter mem.), N.Y. State Soc. CPA, Securities Industry Assn., The Bond Market Assn., Wall St. Tax Assn. Avocation: carpentry. Home: 328 Oaklake Ln Niceville FL 32578 Office: Freeman Securities 30 Montgomery St Ste 1300 Jersey City NJ 07302-3893 also: 1st Summit Capital Mgmt 8044 Montgomery Rd Cincinnati OH 45236-2919

SMITH, JAMES LAWRENCE, research physicist; b. Detroit, Sept. 3, 1943; s. William Leo and Marjorie Marie (Underwood) S.; m. Carol Ann Adam, Mar. 27, 1965; children: David Adam, William Leo. BS, Wayne State U., 1965; PhD, Brown U., 1974. Mem. staff Los Alamos (N.Mex.) Nat. Lab., 1973-82, fellow, 1982-86, dir. ctr. materials sci., 1986-87, fellow, 1987—; chief scientist Superconductivity Tech. Ctr., 1988-99; N.Am. editor Philos. Mag., 1990-95; editor Philos. Mag. B., 1995—2002, Philos. Mag., 2003—. Scientific editor: Los Alamos Rsch. Quar., 2002-03; contbr. articles to profl. jours. Recipient E.O. Lawrence award, 1986, Disting. Alumni award Wayne State U., 1993. Fellow Am. Phys. Soc. (internat. prize for new materials 1990); mem. AAAS, Materials Rsch. Soc., Minerals Metals Materials Soc., Am. Crystallographic Assn., Brown Alumni Assn. (bd. govs. 1998-2000), Phi Beta Kappa. Achievements include patents for design of magnetic field and high-strength conductors. Office: Los Alamos Nat Lab Mail Stop G770 Los Alamos NM 87545-0001

SMITH, JAMES PATRICK, economist; b. Aug. 3, 1943; s. James P. and Winefred (Harrison) S.; m. Sandra Berry, Oct. 25, 1983; children: Gillian Clare, Lauren Theresa. BS, Fordham U., 1965; PhD, U. Chgo., 1972. Rsch. assoc. Nat. Bur. Econ. Rsch., N.Y.C., 1972-74; sr. economist Rand Corp., Santa Monica, Calif., 1974—, dir. of rsch. labor and population, 1977-93. Bd. mem. Occupl. Safety and Health Standards State Calif. Editor: Female Labor Supply, 1980, The New Americans, 1997, The Immigration Debate, 1998, Wealth, Work, and Health, 1999; bd. editors: Am. Econ. Rev., 1980-83; author articles in field. Recipient Merit award NIH, 1995—. Mem. NIA (monitoring com., health and retirement survey, chair NAS panel on immigration, prin. investigator New Immigrant Survey), Am. Econ. Assn., Phi Beta Kappa. Office: RAND PO Box 2138 Santa Monica CA 90407-2138 Office Phone: 310-451-6925. Business E-Mail: smith@rand.org.

SMITH, JAMES ROBERT, airport terminal executive; married; 3 daus. BA in Aviation Mgmt., Auburn U., 1967; MS in Transp., U. S.C., 1974. Adminstrv. asst. to airport mgr. Norfolk Regional Airport Norfolk (Va.) Port and Indsl. Authority, 1967-70; asst. airport dir. Columbia (S.C.) Met. Airport, 1970-75; ops. mgr. Portland (Oreg.) Internat. Airport Port of Portland, 1975-77; dep. dir. aviation City of Phila., 1977-79; airport mgr. Sarasota-Bradenton (Fla.) Airport, 1979-80; mem. Civil Aeronautics Bd., Washington, 1980-84; cons. policy and internat. aviation FAA, Washington, 1985, dir. airport capacity program office, 1985-89, dep. dir. office of sys. capacity and requirements, 1989-92; exec. dir. Newport News/Williamsburg Internat. Airport Peninsula Airport Commn., Newport News, Va., 1992—. Mem. Am. Assn. Airport Execs., Internat. Aviation Club, Aero Club Washington. Office: Newport News/Williamsburg International Airport Newport News VA 23602

SMITH, JAMES W., JR., state supreme court chief justice; b. Louisville, Miss., Oct. 28, 1943; BS, U. So. Miss., 1965; JD, Jackson Sch. Law, 1972; MEd with honors, Miss. Coll., 1973. Bar: Miss. 1972, U.S. Dist. Ct. (no. and so. dists.) Miss. 1973, U.S. Ct. Appeals (5th cir.) 1974. Pvt. practice, Pearl, Miss., 1972-78, Brandon, Miss., 1979-80; pros. atty. City of Pearl, 1973-80; prosecutor Rankin County, Miss., 1976; dist. atty. 20th Jud. Dist., Miss., 1977-82; judge Rankin County, 1982-92; Supreme Ct. justice Ctrl. Dist., 1993—. Instr. courtroom procedure and testifying Miss. Law Enforcement Tng. Acad., 1980-91. With U.S. Army, 1966-69. Named Wildlife Conservationist of Yr. Rankin County, 1988; recipient Outstanding Positive Role Model for Today's Youth award, 1991, Child Forever award Miss. Voices of Children and Youth, 1992, You've Made a Difference award, 1995, Alumnus of Yr. award Hinds C.C., 1996. Fellow Miss. Bar Found. (bd. dirs. 1998); mem. Miss. State Bar Assn., Rankin County Bar Assn. Office: Carroll Gartin Justice Bldg PO Box 117 Jackson MS 39205-0117 Office Phone: 601-359-2093.

SMITH, JAMES WALKER, lawyer; b. S.I., N.Y., May 11, 1957; s. James Patrick and Ann Catherine (Sullivan) S.; m. Erin Patricia Murphy, Aug. 15, 1982; children: Patrick James, Daniel Timothy, Meghan Kathleen, James John. BA magna cum laude, Fordham U., 1979, JD, 1982; LLM, NYU, 1988. BAr: N.Y. 1983, N.J. 1984, Pa. 1993, U.S. Supreme Ct. 1994. Assoc. Mendes & Mount, N.Y.C., 1982, Costello Shea & Gaffney, N.Y.C., 1982-86; ptnr. Anderson Kill Olick & Oshinsky P.C., N.Y.C., 1986-96, Smith Abbot, LLP, N.Y.C., 1996—. Arbitrator N.Y.C. (N.Y.) Civil Ct., 1987-89; faculty chairperson hosp. law Fordham Law Sch., N.Y.C., 1989-93; mediator U.S. Dist. Ct. (so. dist.) N.Y., N.Y.C., 1992-96. Author: Hospital Liability, 1985—; editor-in-chief: New York Practice Guide, 1993-97; contbg. editor: Medical Malpractice Law and Strategy, 1993—; bd. editors Fordham Urban Law Jour., 1981-82. Mem. N.Y. County Lawyer's Assn. (com. on tort law 1993-95), Assn. of the Bar of the City of N.Y. (com. on tort law 1990-92, com. on state cts. 1994—). Roman Catholic. Avocations: golf, coaching youth basketball. Home: 15 Flagg Ct Staten Island NY 10304-1157 Office: Smith Abbot LLP 100 Maiden Ln New York NY 10038-4818

SMITH, JAMES WARREN, pathologist, educator, microbiologist, parasitologist; b. Logan, Utah, July 5, 1934; s. Kenneth Warren and Nina Lou (Sykes) S.; m. Nancy Chesterman, July 19, 1958; children: Warren, Scott. BS, U. Iowa, 1956, MD, 1959. Diplomate Am. Bd. Pathology. Intern Colo. Gen. Hosp., Denver, 1959-60; resident U. Iowa Hosps., Iowa City, 1960-65; asst. prof. pathology U. Vt., Burlington, 1967-70; prof. pathology Ind. U., Indpls., 1970-98, chmn. dept. pathology and lab. medicine, 1992-98, Nordshow prof. of lab. medicine, 1997-98, prof. emeritus, 1998—. Contbr. articles to profl. jours. Served to lt. comdr. USN, 1965-67. Recipient Outstanding Contbn. to Clin. Microbiology award South Ctrl. Assn. Clin. Microbiology, 1977. Fellow Coll. Am. Pathologists (chmn. microbiology resource com. 1981-85); mem. AMA, Infectious Disease Soc. Am., Am. Soc. Investigative Pathology, Royal Soc. Tropical Medicine and Hygiene, Am. Soc. Clin. Pathology, Am. Soc. Microbiology, Am. Soc. Tropical Medicine and Hygiene, U.S.-Can. Acad. Pathology, Assn. Pathology Chairs, Binford Dammin Soc. Infectious Disease Pathologists, Soc. Protozoologists. Home: 4375 Cold Spring Rd Indianapolis IN 46228-3327 Office: Ind U Med Ctr 635 Barnhill Dr Rm A128 Indianapolis IN 46202-5126

SMITH, JANE SCHNEBERGER, retired city administrator; b. Chgo., Aug. 9, 1928; d. Frank R. and Marion (Durante) Schneberger; m. Z. Erol Smith Jr., Oct. 28, 1950 (div. 1974); children: Suzan MacKenzie Smith, Tracy Smith Cawley, Cameron Farley, Z. Erol III, Kimberly Van Den Elzen, Scott. BA in Chemistry, U. Colo., 1950; MA in Comm., Mich. State U., 1978, PhD in Ednl. Adminstrn., 1987. Chemist Kellogg Switchboard, Chgo., 1950-51; v.p. South Cook County Girl Scouts, Harvey, Ill., 1967-69, staff advisor, 1970-72; tchr. Crab Orchard Sch., Palos Heights, Ill., 1969-70; program and tng. dir. Mich. Capitol. Coun. Girl Scouts, Lansing, Mich., 1972-75; dir. svc. learning ctr. Mich. State U., East Lansing, 1975-81; city clk. City of Ashland, Wis., 1981-89, interim city adminstr., 1989-90; ret., 1990; acting city clk. City of Ashland, 2003. Cons. vol. adminstrn., Mich., Wis., 1975—. Co-editor: Looking Backward Moving Forward, 1987, Roots and Wings, 2002; contbr. articles to profl. jours. V.p. Mich. Capitol Girl Scout Coun., Lansing, 1976-78; bd. dirs. Lansing RSVP, 1976-81, Ashland Mus., 1985-87, Ptnrs. in Recovery, 1985-87; v.p. Friends of the Libr., 1992-97, pres., 1997-99; sec. New Horizons, 1985-90, New Day Shelter, 1990-99, v.p., 1993-95, pres., 1995-97, sec., 1997-99; pres. LWV of Ashland Bayfield County, 1992-93, 96-98; sec. No. Wis. History Ctr., 1992-94; commr. Ashland Water and Wastewater Utility, 1993-96; mem. Ashland Beautification Com., 1993—, Big Top Chautauqua, 1996-2003, vice chair Alliance for Sustainability, 1994-99; v.p. GFWC/Ashland Monday Club, 1994-98, pres., 1998-2000, 1st v.p. 10th Dist. GFWC-W1, 2000-02; mem. Ashland County Human Svcs. Bd., 1998—, vice chair, 2003-04, Restore the Depot Com., 2001—; co-chair comprehensive plan update com., 2002—, tree bd. City of Ashland, 2002—, planning commn., 2004—. Recipient cert. appreciation Mich. Capitol Girl Scout Coun., 1975, Thanks Badge, 1972, Tribute to Excellence award LWV of Wis., 1999. Mem. Internat. Assn. Mcpl. Clks., Wis. Mcpl. Clks. Assn. (dist. dir. 1984-86), Am. Bus. Women's Assn. (scholarship chmn. 1985), Zonta (pres. 1979-81), Ashland Hist. Soc. (bd. dirs.). Roman Catholic. Avocations: stained glass, gardening, stamp collecting/philately, genealogy. Home: 700 MacArthur Ave Ashland WI 54806-2903 Personal E-mail: snowmont@cheqnet.net.

SMITH, JANET HUGIE, lawyer; b. Logan, Utah, Aug. 1, 1945; BA magna cum laude, Utah State U., 1967; MA cum laude, Stanford U., 1969; JD, U. Utah, 1976. Bar: Utah 1976, U.S. Supreme Ct. 1992, U.S. Ct. Appeals (10th cir.) 1977. Shareholder, exec. com. Ray, Quinney & Nebeker, Salt Lake City, 1983—. Mem. ABA (labor and employment law sect.), Utah State Bar (labor and employment law sect.), CUE (labor lawyers adv. coun.), Am. Law Coun., Am. Coll. Trial Lawyers, Aldon J. Anderson Am. Inns of Ct. Office: Ray Quinney & Nebeker 36 S State St Ste 1400 Salt Lake City UT 84111-1431 E-mail: jhsmith@rqn.com.

SMITH, JANET MARIE, sports and entertainment executive; b. Jackson, Miss., Dec. 13, 1957; d. Thomas Henry and Nellie Brown (Smith) S. BArch, Miss. State U., 1981; MA in Urban Planning, CCNY, 1984. Draftsman Thomas H. Smith and Assocs. Architects, Jackson, 1979; mktg. coord. The Eggers Group, P.C. Architects and Planners, N.Y.C., 1980; program assoc. Ptnrs. for Livable Places, Washington, 1980-82; coord. asst. Lance Jay Brown, Architect and Urban Planner, N.Y.C., 1983-84; coord. architecture and design Battery Park City Authority, N.Y.C., 1982-84; pres., chief exec. officer Pershing Sq. Mgmt. Assn., L.A., 1985-89; v.p. stadium planning and devel. Balt. Orioles Oriole Park at Camden Yard, 1989-94; v.p. sports facilities Turner Properties, Atlanta, 1994-97; v.p. planning and devel. Atlanta Braves, Braves, 1994—; pres. TBS Sports Devel., Inc., 1997-2000; with Struever Brothers, Eccles & Rouse, Inc., Balt., 2000—. Bd. dirs. Assn. Collegiate Schs. Architecture, Washington, 1979-82, Assn. Student Chpts. AIA, Washington, 1979-82. Guest editor: Urban Design Internat., 1985; assoc. editor: Crit, 1979-82; contbr. articles to profl. jours. Named Disting. Grad., Nat. Assn. State Univs. and Land Grant Colls., 1988, One of Outstanding Young Women of Am., 1982; recipient Spirit of Miss. award, Sta. WLBT, Jackson, 1987, Disting. Grad. award Nat. Assn. State Univs., 1988, Outstanding Alumni award Miss. State U., 1994, Andrew White medal Loyola Coll., 1997, Ptnrs. Livable Cmtys. award, 1998, City Coll. N.Y. award, 1998. Mem. AIA (assoc.), Urban Land Inst. Democrat. Episcopalian. Office: Struever Brothers Eccles & Rouse Inc 519 N Charles St Baltimore MD 21201-5099

SMITH, JANET SUE, systems specialist; b. Chgo., Jan. 15, 1945; d. Curtis Edwin and Margaret Louise (Yost) Smith. BA, Ind. U., 1967. Sales mgr. Marshall Field & Co., Chgo., 1968-70, programmer, 1970-72; sr. programmer, analyst Trailer Train Co., Chgo., 1972-75; mgr. data base and systems devel. Railinc-Assn. Am. R.R., Washington, 1975-85, asst. v.p., corp. sec., 1985-93, asst. v.p. strategic systems, 1994-98; exec. dir. Interline Svc., 1998-99, asst. v.p. bus. svc., 1999—2001; self-employed JSSmith Consulting LLC, 2002—. Nat. student v.p. YWCA, 1966-67; bd. dir., v.p. planning and fin. Guide Internat.; advisor Jr. Achievement; pres. Homeowner's Assn.; mem. alumni bd. dir. Ind. U. Coll. Arts and Scis., co-chair Ind. U. Colloquium for Women. Mem.: Woodburn Guild, Am. Coun. R.R. Women, Ind. U. Alumni Assn. (life). Home and Office: JSSmith Cons LLC 903 N Columbia St Chapel Hill NC 27516-1824

SMITH, JANICE M. poet, artist; b. Binghamton, N.Y., Jan. 26, 1967; d. Richard J. and Donna H. Yudin;; children: Cassandra, Donna. Student, Broome C.C., Binghamton, 1991—. Poet Secrets of the Soul, 1998, Eternal Songs, 2000, Colors of the heart, 2004. Mem.: ACLU, Student Nurses Orgn., Phi Theta Kappa. Republican. Avocations: travel, literature, nature, wildlife, theater.

SMITH, JARED RUSSELL WILLIAM, research executive, research scientist, consultant, poet; b. Cleve., Mar. 24, 1950; s. Russell Floyd William Smith and Mary Wiltrude Lee; m. Deborah Jane Parriott; children: Russell Jared Webster, Heather Frances. BA cum laude, NYU, 1973, MA, 1976. V.p. The Energy Bur., Inc., N.Y.C., 1976-86; assoc. dir. Inst. Gas Tech., Des Plaines, Ill., 1986-99; spl. appointee Argonee (Ill.) Nat. Lab., 1999—2000; cons., 2001—. Adj. faculty NYU, N.Y.C., 1974-76; mem. adv. bd. La. State U., Baton Rouge, 1999—; adviser to Pres.'s Commn. on Critical Infrastructure Protection, Washington, 1997—; bd. dirs., adviser N.Y. Quar. Literary Found., N.Y.C., 1986. Author: (poetry books) Song of the Blood, 1983, Dark Wing, 1986, Keeping the Outlaw Alive, 1988, Walking the Perimeters of the Plate Glass Window Factory, 2000, Lake Michigan adapted to stage by David Lightner, 2003; editor: (books) Integrating Microelectronics into Gas Distribution, 1987, Gas, Oil and Coal Biotechnology, 1990. Election dist. leader Dem. Party, White Plains, N.Y., 1972; chmn. nominating com. Sch. Dist. 181,

Hinsdale, Ill., 1993. Mem. Chgo. Poets Club, Poets and Patrons (pres.), Ill. State Poetry Soc. Democrat. Avocations: literature, fishing, hiking, painting, music. Home: 2630 Longview Dr Lisle IL 60532 E-mail: smithjrw@comcast.net.

SMITH, JAY, publishing executive; Pres. Cox Newspapers Inc., Atlanta. Office: Cox Newspapers Inc 1400 Lake Hearn Dr NE Atlanta GA 30319-1464

SMITH, JAY LAWRENCE, planning company executive; b. Detroit, June 10, 1954; s. Paul Edward Smith and Gloria D. Lawrence; m. Janice Irene Acheson, May 21, 1978; children: Kevin Hamilton, Travis Jay. Student, Oakland U., 1972-75. CFP. Asst. tng. dir. Equitable Cos., Troy, Mich., 1978-81; pres. JLS Fin. Planning Corp., Oxford, Mich., 1978—. Adj. faculty Oakland U., Rochester, Mich., 1986-87; commentator TV show Your Money and You, 1987. Cons. Practicing Fin. Planning, 1990; contbr. articles to profl. jours. Mem. Internat. Assn. Fin. Planning (v.p. 1985-87, bd. dirs. 1987-89), Inst. Cert. Fin. Planners (bd. dirs. 1988-90), Inst. Cert. Fin. Planners-Mich. (pres. 1992-93), Fin. Profl. Adv. Panel, Internat. Bd. Cert. Fin. Planners, Rotary (bd. dirs. 1984-86, treas. 1985-87, pres. Oxford 1992-93). Republican. Methodist. Avocations: skiing, music, raquetball. Office: Investment Mgmt & Rsch Inc PO Box 4 28 S Washington St Oxford MI 48371-4985

SMITH, JEAN KENNEDY, former ambassador; b. Brookline, Mass., Feb. 20, 1928; d. Joseph P. and Rose Kennedy; m. Stephen E. Smith (dec. 1990); 4 children. BA, Manhattanville Coll.; Degree (hon.), NYU, Fordham U., Nat. U. Ireland, Dublin City U. Founder, dir., chair Very Spl. Arts, 1974—; amb. to Ireland Dublin, 1993-98. Author: (with George Plimpton) Chronicles of Courage, 1993; contbr. articles on the disabled to profl. jours. Trustee Joseph P. Kennedy, Jr. Found., 1964—, John F. Kennedy Ctr. Performing Arts. Recipient Sec.'s award Dept. Vets. Affairs, Vol. of Yr. award People-to-People Com. Handicapped, Margaret Mead Humanitarian award Coun. Cerebral Palsy Auxs., Jefferson award Am. Inst. Pub. Svc., Spirit of Achievement award Yeshiva U., Humanitarian award Capital Children's Mus., Irish Am. of Yr. award Irish Am. Mag., 1995, Rotary One Internat. award Rotary Club Chgo., 1997, Terence Cardinal Cooke Humanitarian award, 1997.*

SMITH, JEAN WEBB (MRS. WILLIAM FRENCH SMITH), civic worker; b. LA; d. James Ellwood and Violet (Hughes) Webb; m. George William Vaughn, Mar. 14, 1942 (dec. Sept. 1963); children: George William Vaughn, Merry Vaughn; m. William French Smith, Nov. 6, 1964. BA summa cum laude, Stanford U., 1940. Mem. Nat. Vol. Svc. Adv. Coun. (ACTION), 1973—76, vice chmn., 1974—76; dir. Beneficial Std. Corp., 1976—85; bd. dirs. Cmty. TV So. Calif., 1979—93. Bd. dirs. United Way, Inc., 1973—80, Nat. Symphony Orch., 1980—85; nat. bd. dirs. Boys' Club Am., 1977—80; mem. Pres.'s Commn. White House Fellowships, 1980—90, Nat. Coun. Humanities, 1987—90, Calif. Arts Commn., 1971—74, vice chmn., 1973—74; bd. dirs. The Founders, Music Ctr., LA, 1971—74; bd. dirs. costume coun. Los Angeles County Mus. Art, 1971—73; bd. dirs. LA chpt. NCCJ, 1977—80, LA World Affairs Coun., 1990, LA chpt. ARC, 1994—95; mem. adv. bd. Salvation Army, 1979—; bd. overseers Hoover Instn. War, Revolution and Peace, 1989—94; bd. govs. Calif. Cmty. Found., 1990—; bd. dirs. Hosp. Good Samaritan, 1973—80, mem. exec. com., 1975—80; bd. fellows Claremont U. Ctr. and Grad. Sch., 1987—; bd. regents Children's Hops. LA, 1993—. Named Woman of the Yr. for Cmty. Svc., LA Times, 1958; recipient Citizens of the Yr. award, Boys Clubs Greater LA, 1982, Life Achievement award, LA Coun. Boy Scouts Am., 1985. Mem.: Kappa Kappa Gamma, Assn. Jr. Leagues Am. (dir. region XII 1956—58, pres. 1958—60), Jr. League LA (pres. 1954—55, Spirit of Volunteerism award 1996), Phi Beta Kappa. Home: 11718 Wetherby Ln Los Angeles CA 90077-1348

SMITH, JEFFREY CARLIN, lawyer; b. Chgo., Aug. 1, 1951; s. Robert Frederick and Marjorie (Carlin) S.; m. Phyllis Stagias, Oct. 7, 1978; children: Alex, Carlin. BS, Lewis and Clark Coll., 1974; JD, U. Calif., San Francisco, 1978; MBA, Pepperdine U., 1989. Bar: Calif. 1979, Md. 1989, D.C. 1989. Assoc. Gibbons, Stoddard & Lepper, Walnut Creek, Calif., 1978-81, Hyde & Drath, San Francisco, 1981-85; sr. staff counsel Times Mirror Co., L.A., 1985-88, assoc. gen. counsel, 1993-94, v.p. planning and devel., 1994-97; gen. counsel Balt. Sun, 1988-93; sr. v.p. gen. counsel IXC Comm., Austin, Tex., 1997-99; chief legal and adminstrv. officer Broadwing Inc., Austin, 1999-2001, chief human resources officer, gen. counsel, corp. sec., 2001—03; gen. counsel, corp. sec., and chief human resources officer Cin. Bell, Inc., 2003; gen. counsel, sec., and sr. v.p. human resources Worldspan, 2004—. Dir. Md., Del., D.C. Press Assn., Balt., 1990-93. Author: (with others) Fair Housing Advertising, 1992, Handbook Fair Housing Compliance, 1993. Dir. Pre-Columbian Art Rsch. Inst., San Francisco, 1983—; trustee Robert Louis Stevenson Sch., 1982-85, 87-90; mem. cmty. adv. bd. Helping Hand Home for Children, 2001-04. Mem. St. Francis Yacht Club, Bohemian Club. Office: 300 Galleria Pkwy NW Ste 2105 Atlanta GA 30339-3196

SMITH, JEFFREY CHIPPS, art educator; MA, Columbia U., 1975, MPhil, 1977, PhD, 1979. Kay Fortson chair in European art U. Tex., Austin, 1979—. Author: Nuremberg, A Renaissance City, 1500-1618, 1983, German Sculpture of the Later Renaissance, c. 1520-1580: Art in an Age of Uncertainty, 1994, Sensuous Worship: Jesuits and the Art of Early Catholic Reformation in Germany, 2002, The Northern Renaissance, 2004; editor: New Perspectives on the Art of Renaissance Nuremberg: Five Essays, 1985, Renaissance Quar., 2003—; contbr. articles to profl. jours.; reviewer in field, —. Alexander von Humboldt-Stiftung fellow, Bonn, Germany, ACLS grantee, NEH grantee, Getty Found. grantee, Guggenheim Found. grantee, Kimbell Art Found. grantee, Zentralinstitut Kunstgeschicht fellow. Mem.: Renaissance Soc. Am. (bd. dirs. 2000—, editor Renaissance Quarterly 2003—), Coll. Art Assn. (bd. dirs. 1996—2000). Office: U Tex Dept Art and Art History Austin TX 78712 Office Phone: 512-232-2609. Business E-Mail: chipps@mail.utexas.edu.

SMITH, JEFFREY E. pharmaceutical executive; b. 1947; BS, Fairleigh Dickinson U., 1968. CPA. With Coopers & Lybrand, CPAs, 1972-82; treas., contr. LCP Chemicals and Plastics, Inc., 1983-84; v.p. finance, CFO A.L. Labs., Inc., Ft. Lee, N.J., 1984-91, exec. v.p., CFO, 1991—. Office: Alpharma Inc 1 Executive Dr Fort Lee NJ 07024-3309

SMITH, JEFFREY GREENWOOD, industry executive, retired army officer; b. Ft. Sam Houston, Tex., Oct. 14, 1921; s. Henry Joseph Moody and Gladys Adrienne (Haile) S.; m. Dorothy Jane Holland, June 2, 1948; children: Meredith B. Exnicios, Jennifer H. Smith, Jeffrey Greenwood, Tracy E. McDonald, Melissa A. Deutsch, Ashley A. Pollock. BS in Civil Engring, Va. Mil. Inst., 1943; MS in Mech. Engring, Johns Hopkins U., 1949; MA in Internat. Affairs, George Washington U., 1964. Commd. 2d lt. U.S. Army, 1944, advanced through grades to lt. gen., 1975; service in CBI; comdr. 2d Inf. Div., Korea, 1971-73; dep. chief staff ops. Hdqrs. Army Forces Command, Ft. McPherson, Ga., 1973-74, chief staff, 1974-75; comdr. 1st U.S. Army, Ft. Meade, Md., 1975-79; ret., 1979; dir. govt. rels. Ethyl Corp., Washington, 1980—, v.p. govt. rels., 1992—, ret., 1994. Decorated D.S.M., Silver Star, Legion of Merit with 3 oak leaf clusters, D.F.C., Bronze Star with V device and 2 oak leaf clusters, Air medal with 12 oak leaf clusters, Army Commendation medal with oak leaf cluster, Purple Heart with oak leaf cluster, Combat Inf. badge (2); breast Order Yun Hui Republic China; Order Security Merit Korea; Gallantry Cross with silver and gold stars (Vietnam) Army Distinguished Service Order Mem. Assn. U.S. Army, Mil. Order Carabao, U.S. Cavalry Assn., Kappa Alpha, Tau Beta Pi. Clubs: Army and Navy. Home: 3000 Sevor Ln Alexandria VA 22309-2221 E-mail: genjeffrey@aol.com.

SMITH, JEFFREY MICHAEL, lawyer; b. Mpls, July 9, 1947; s. Philip and Gertrude E. (Miller) S.; 1 son, Brandon Michael. Student, U. Malaya, 1967-68; BA summa cum laude, U. Minn., 1970, JD magna cum laude, 1973. Bar: Ga. 1973. Assoc. Powell, Goldstein, Frazier & Murphy, 1973-76; ptnr. Rogers & Hardin, 1976-79, Bondurant, Stephenson & Smith, 1979-85, Arnall, Golden & Gregory, 1985-92, Katz, Smith & Cohen, 1992-98; prin. shareholder Greenberg Traurig, 1998—. Vis. lectr. Duke U., 1976-77, 79-80, 89-93; adj. prof. Emory U., 1976-79, 81-82; lectr. Vanderbilt U., 1977-82. Co-author: Preventing Legal Malpractice, 1999, Legal Malpractice, 1999. Bd. visitors Law Sch. U. Minn., 1976-82. Mem. ABA (vice-chmn. com. profl. liability 1980-82, mem. standing com. lawyers's profl. liability 1981-85, chmn. 1985-87, standing com. lawyer competency 1993-95), State Bar Ga. (chmn. profl. liability and ins. com. 1978-89, trustee Inst. Cont. Legal Edn. in Ga. 1979-80), Order of the Coif, Phi Beta Kappa. Home: 145 15th St NE Unit 811 Atlanta GA 30309-3559

SMITH, JEFFREY ROBERT, historian, educator; b. New London, Conn., Dec. 12, 1966; s. L. Glenn and Joan Karen Smith BA, Rice U., 1989; MA, U. Ill., 1991, PhD, 1997. Prof. history Northwestern State U., Natchitoches, La., 1998—. Author: World War I and the Cultures of Modernity, 2000. German Acad. Exchange Svc. rsch. grantee, 1993-94; U. Ill. history fellow, 1994-95. Mem. Am. Hist. Assn., Phi Alpha Theta, Phi Kappa Phi. Avocation: golf. Office: Dept Social Scis Northwestern State U Natchitoches LA 71497 E-mail: smithj@nsula.edu.

SMITH, JEFFRY ALAN, health administrator, physician, consultant; b. L.A., Dec. 8, 1943; s. Stanley W. and Marjorie E. S.; m. Jo Anne Hague. BA in Philosophy, UCLA, 1967, MPH, 1972; BA in Biology, Calif. State U., Northridge, 1971; MD, UACJ, 1977. Diplomate Am. Bd. Family Practice. Resident in family practice WAH, Takoma Park, Md., NIH, Bethesda, Md., Walter Reed Army Hosp., Washington, Children's Hosp. Nat. Med. Ctr., Washington, 1977-80; occupational physician Nev. Test Site, U.S. Dept. Energy, Las Vegas, 1981-82; dir. occupational medicine and environ. health Pacific Missile Test Ctr., Point Mugu, Calif., 1982-84; dist. health officer State Hawaii Dept. Health, Kauai, 1984-86; asst. dir. health County of Riverside (Calif.) Dept. Health, 1986-87, regional med. dir. Calif. Forensic Med. Group, Monterey, Calif., 1987-94; med. dir. Cmty. Human Svcs., Monterey, Calif., 1987-94, Colstrip (Mont.) Med. Ctr., 1994-97; cons. San Bernadino County, Riverside County, Riverside, Calif., 1998—; regional med. dir. Point Loma Healthcare Med. Group, Inc., San Diego, 1997-99; med. dir., CEO So. Calif. Mobile Physician Svcs., Riverside, Calif., 1997—. Fellow Am. Acad. Family Physicians; mem. AMA, Am. Occupational Medicine Assn., Flying Physicians, Am. Pub. Health Assn. Avocation: pvt. pilot. Office: Ste 71-448 5225 Canyon Crest Dr Riverside CA 92507-6301

SMITH, JEROME, not-for-profit developer, film producer, writer; b. Birmingham, Ala., Sept. 10, 1956; s. Herny Horace and Susie Govan Smith. BS in Edn., Daniel Payne Coll., Birmingham, Ala., 1979. Cert. tchr. Ala., Ohio. Tchr. Birmingham Bd. of Edn., Ala., 1979—84, Cleve. Bd. of Edn., 1984—95; CEO Poise Entertainment Edn., Cleve., 1999—. Ednl. prodr. Urban League, Cleve., 2001—03, United Black Fund, Cleve., 2000—03, Rock and Roll Hall of Fame, Cleve., 1999—, dir. cmty. svc., 2003—; songwriter Hilltop Records, Hollywood, Calif., 2004—; TV host You Can Do It Program. Author: Poise Entertainment Edn. Co.'s "You Can Do It Program", 2004; host, prodr. Poise Entertainment Edn. Co.'s "You Can Do It Program" Hall of Fame and Mus. Named to Nat. Dean's List; recipient Best Song honors, Hilltop Records, Best Songwriter honors, Americord, Cmty. Svc. award, Help Educate for Svc.; grantee, Urban League, 2002, United Black Fund, 2003, Ward 7 City of Cleve., 2004. Baptist. Avocations: songwriting, horseback riding. Home: 3819 E 151 St Cleveland OH 44128 Office: Poise Entertainment Edn Co 15115 Elm Ave Cleveland OH 44112 Office Phone: 216-644-7130.

SMITH, JERRY EDWIN, federal judge; b. Del Rio, Tex., Nov. 7, 1946; s. Lemuel Edwin and Ruth Irene (Henderson) Smith; m. Mary Jane Blackburn, June 4, 1977; children: Clark, Ruth Ann, J.J. BA, Yale U., 1969, JD, 1972. Bar: Tex. 1972. Law clk. to judge U.S. Dist. Ct. (no. dist.) Tex., Lubbock, 1972—73; assoc. then ptnr. Fulbright & Jaworski, Houston, 1973—84; dir. Harris County housing auth., Tex., 1978—80; special asst. office of atty. gen., Tex., 1981—82; Chmn. Houston Civ. Svc. Comm., 1982—84; city atty. City of Houston, 1984—87; cir. judge U.S. Ct. Appeals (5th cir.), Houston, 1988—. Chmn. Harris County Rep. Party, Houston, 1977—78; committeeman State Rep. Exec. Com., Tex., 1976—88. Mem.: Houston Bar Assn., State Bar Tex. Methodist. Office: US Ct Appeals Bob Casey US Courthouse 515 Rusk St Rm 12621 Houston TX 77002-2698

SMITH, JESSE GRAHAM, JR., dermatologist, educator; b. Winston-Salem, NC, Nov. 22, 1928; s. Jesse Graham and Pauline Field (Griffith) S.; m. Dorothy Jean Butler, Dec. 28, 1950; children: Jesse Graham, Cynthia Lynn, Grant Butler. BS, Duke U., 1962, MD, 1951. Diplomate: Am. Bd. Dermatology (dir. 1974-83, pres. 1980-81). Intern VA Hosp., Chamblee, Ga., 1951—52; resident in dermatology Duke U., 1954—56, assoc. prof. dermatology, 1960—62, prof., 1962—67; resident U. Miami, 1956—57, asst. prof., 1956—60; prof. dermatology Med. Coll. Ga., 1967—91, chmn. dept. dermatology, 1967—91, acting chmn. dept. pathology, 1973—75, acting v.p. devel., 1984—85; chief staff Talmadge Meml. Hosp., Augusta, Ga., 1970—72; chief divsn. of dermatology U. South Ala., Mobile, 1991—98, prof. dermatology, 1991—99, prof. emeritus, 1999—. Mem. advisory council Nat. Inst. Arthritis, 1975-79 Editorial bd. Archives of Dermatology, 1963-72, Jour. Investigative Dermatology, 1966-67, Jour. AMA, 1974-80; editorial bd. So. Med. Jour., 1976-2000, assoc. editor, 1991-92, editor, 1992-2000; editor Jour. Am. Acad. Dermatology, 1978-88; contbr. chpts. to books, articles to profl. jours. Served with USPHS, 1952-54. Recipient Disting. Alumnus award Duke U. 1981 Fellow ACP, Royal Soc. Medicine; mem. Am. Acad. Dermatology (hon., dir. 1971-74, 78-88, pres.-elect 1988-89, pres. 1989-90, master 2003), Can. Dermatol. Assn. (hon.), Am. Dermatol. Assn. (hon. sec. 1976-81, pres. 1981-82), Soc. Investigative Dermatology (dir. 1964-69, pres. 1979-80), S.E. Dermatol. Assn. (sec. 1970-71, pres. 1975-76), Ga. Soc. Dermatology (pres. 1979-80), So. Med. Assn. (chmn. sect. dermatology 1973-74), Assn. Profs. Dermatology (dir. 1976-77, 80-82, pres. 1984-86), Med. Rsch. Found. Ga. (bd. dir. 1967-91, pres. 1974-75), Alpha Omega Alpha. Home: 4272 Bit and Spur # 4 Mobile AL 36608 Office: Diagnostic and Med Clinic 1700 Spring Hill Ave Mobile AL 36604-1407 E-mail: skeesmith@mindspring.com.

SMITH, JESSIE P. DOWLING, retired social services administrator; b. Sturgills, NC, June 15, 1918; d. Rohe V. and Stella Pennington (Eller) Smith; m. F. P. Smith, July 22, 1983. AB, Berea Coll., 1939; MSW, Columbia U., 1945. Social work assignments WPA, Ky., 1939—43; social worker ARC, New Orleans, 1943—45, Bklyn., 1943—45, Huntington, W.Va., 1946—56, Washington, 1946—56; instr. Sch. Social Work W.Va. U., Morgantown, 1953—54; cons. W.Va. Dept. Mental Health, Charleston, 1954—55; program supr. USPHS Clin. Ctr., Bethesda, Md., 1956—62; cons., social work NIMH, Chgo., 1962—66, NYC, 1962—66; assoc. regional health dir. Mental Health Programs, NYC, 1966—81; ret., 1981; v.p. adv. bd. Mental Retardation Substance Abuse Programs Davidson County Mental Health, NC, 1987—89, pres., 1988—89. Mem.: NASW (exec. bd. 1968—70, pres. Washington Met. Area chpt., pioneer steering com. 1999—), Columbia U. Alumni Fedn. Bd., Columbia U. Sch. Social Work Alumni Assn. (pres. 1979—81), Columbia U. Sch. Social Work (adv. coun.), Social Casework (editl. adv. bd. 1968—70), NC Coun. of Cmty. Mental Health Programs (adv. bd. 1987—92). Home: Apt 703 1330 Massachusetts Ave NW Washington DC 20005-4154

SMITH, JIMMY, JR., professional football player; b. Detroit, Feb. 9, 1969; m. Sandra; 1 child, Jimmy Lee III. BS in Bus. Mgmt., Jackson State, 1992. Wide receiver Dallas Cowboys, 1992-94, Philadelphia Eagles, 1994, Jacksonville Jaguars, 1995—. Active Wolfson Children's Hosp., Jimmy Smith Scholarship Fund; personalized and signed child-sized chair to raise funds for re-design of Neonatal Intensive Care Unit, critical rsch. in asthma, and expansion of Bone Marrow Transplant Unit, hon. chmn. Chairs that Care fundraiser; Jaguars' 1999 NFL-United Way co-spokesman; ptnr. with Am. Lung Assn. Fla. for asthma awareness campaign; pub. svc. announcement with Jacksonville Mayor John Delaney; anti-tobacco pub. svc. announcement Jaguars Found. Named to Pro Bowl, 1997, 98, 99; named second-team All-Pro, AP, 1998, 99, Football News, Coll. and Pro Football Newsweekly, 1999, All-AFC, Pro Football Weekly, Football News, 1999; recipient Mackey award, 1996. Office: One ALLTEL Stadium Pl Jacksonville FL 32202

SMITH, JO ANN COSTA, retired comptroller; b. Houston, Dec. 19, 1937; d. Joseph Anthony and Anna Lois (Grice) Costa; m. Alton Paul Smith, Mar. 3, 1957; children: Robert Carlton, Rex Alan. Grad. high sch., Navasota, Tex. Bookkeeper Our Lady of Victory Ch., Paris, Tex., 1968-69; asst. office mgr. Ayres Dept. Store, Paris, 1969-71; cashier, clk. Mid South Electric Co-op, Navasota, 1971-77; owner, mgr. The Gift Shop, Navasota, 1977-97; v.p., comptroller Smith Bros. Impl. Co. Inc., Navasota, Tex., 1998—2001; ret., 2001. Pack mother Cub Scouts, Paris, 1965-67; v.p. Grimes County United Way, 1988-89, pres., 1989-90, bd. dirs., 1987—. Mem. Grimes County C. of C. (2d v.p. 1986, pres. 1987-88), Ciara Study Club (pres. 1969-70), Brazos Valley Bus. and Profl. Womens Club (charter, chmn. pub. rels. com. 1989-90). Democrat. Roman Catholic. Home: PO Box 70 Navasota TX 77868-0070 Office: Smith Bros Impl Co Inc PO Box 112 Navasota TX 77868-0112

SMITH, JO ANNE, writer, retired educator; b. Mpls., Mar. 18, 1930; d. Robert Bradburn and Virginia Mae S. BA, U. Minn., 1951, MA, 1957. Wire and sports editor Rhinelander (Wis.) Daily News, 1951-52; staff corr., night mgr. UPI, Mpls., 1952-56; interim instr. U. N.C., Chapel Hill, 1957-58; instr. U. Fla., Gainesville, 1959-65, asst. prof. journalism, communications, 1965-68, assoc. prof., 1968-76, prof., 1976-88, disting. lectr., 1977, prof. emeritus. Author: JM409 Casebook and Study Guide, 1976, Mass Communications Law Casebook, 1979, 3d edit., 1985. Active, Friends of Libr., Alachua County Humane Soc. Recipient outstanding Prof. award Fla. Blue Key, 1976; Danforth assoc., 1976-85. Mem. Women in Communications, Assn. Edn. in Journalism, Phi Beta Kappa, Kappa Tau Alpha. Democrat. Unitarian Universalist. Home: 208 NW 21st Ter Gainesville FL 32603-1732

SMITH, JOBAN JONATHAN, security consultant; b. Albuquerque, New Mex., Mar. 7, 1962; s. William Oswalt and Lou Ella (Agan) Hernandez; 1 child, Connor Nigel Smith. Student, Pensacola Christian Coll., 1980-81, Bradley U., 1981-82; BA in Psychology, Fellowship U., 1985; AA in Alcohol and Drug Counseling, SIPI, Albuquerque, 1990. Underwater demolitions trainer Dept. Defense, Pensacola, Fla., 1980-81, courier, escort Peoria, Ill., 1982-86, U.S. Consulate, N.Y.C., 1987-88; security cons. Atlantic Record Co., L.A., 1988; recreation therapist Indian Health Svc., Isleta, New Mex., 1990-91, Manor Care Nursing Home, Albuquerque, 1991—; owner, CEO Med. Security Corp., 1999—. Owner Joban Smith & Assocs., Albuquerque, 1990—; cons. S.W. Fun & Lesiure, Albuquerque, 1991—, McGartland & Assocs., 1991—. Mem. NRA, Nat. Assn. Security Cons., New Mex. Activities Assn. Avocations: scuba diving, fishing, track and field.

SMITH, JOE DORSEY, JR., retired newspaper executive; b. Selma, La., Apr. 6, 1922; s. Joe Dorsey and Louise (Lindsay) S.; 1 child, Lawrence Dorsey. BA, La. Coll. Pineville, 1939-43. Gen. mgr. Alexandria Daily Town Talk, La., 1958—, pub., 1965—; pres. McCormick & Co., Inc., 1968—, chmn., 1990-96. Served with USAF, 1942-45. Mem. Alexandria Golf and Country Club, Boston Club, New Orleans Club. Democrat. Episcopalian. Home: 2804 Georges Ln Alexandria LA 71301-4723 Office: Ste 1003 Hibernia Bldg 934 3rd St Alexandria LA 71301-8383 Office Phone: 318-448-3598. Personal E-mail: smith7462@aol.com.

SMITH, JOEL B. environmental analyst; b. Woburn, Mass., June 14, 1957; s. Warner L. and Amely B. Smith; m. Sarah J. Larson, Aug. 2, 1987; children: Rachel W., Rebecca E. BA, Williams Coll., 1979; M of Public Policy, U. Mich., 1982. Analyst U.S. EPA, Washington, 1984—87, dep. dir., climate change divsn., 1987—92; prin. Hagley Bailly Inc., 1992—98; v.p. Stratus Consulting, Boulder, Colo., 1998—. Office: Stratus Consulting Inc PO Box 4059 Boulder CO 80306-4059 E-mail: jsmith@stratusconsulting.com.

SMITH, JOHN BREWSTER, library administrator; b. Bryan, Tex., June 26, 1937; s. Elmer Gillam and Sara Roland (Lull) S.; m. Ida Hawa, Dec. 28, 1963; children: Susan Helen, Rona Esther. BA, Tex. A & M U., 1960; MS, Columbia U., 1963, cert. advanced librarianship, 1984, DLS, 1991. Asst. law librarian Columbia U., N.Y.C., 1963-66; asst. library dir. for pub. services Tex. A & M U., College Station, 1966-69, dir. libraries, 1969-74; dir. libraries, dean library scis. SUNY, Stony Brook, 1974-96, dir. library and info. sci. tchg. program, 1996-97; chief libr. Bronx Cmty. Coll., CUNY, 1997-2000, cons. on libr. mgmt., 2000—. Named Librarian of Year Tex. Library Assn., 1972 Mem. ALA. Home and Office: 108 Inverness Dr Montgomery TX 77356-5877

SMITH, JOHN EDWIN, philosophy educator; b. Bklyn., May 27, 1921; s. Joseph Robert and Florence Grace (Dunn) S.; m. Marilyn Blanche Schulhof, Aug. 25, 1951; children: Robin Dunn, Diana Edwards. AB, Columbia U., 1942, PhD, 1948; BD, Union Theol. Sem., N.Y.C., 1945; MA, Yale U., 1959; LL.D., U. Notre Dame, 1964. Instr. religion and philosophy Vassar Coll., 1945-46; instr., then asst. prof. Barnard Coll., 1946-52; mem. faculty Yale U., 1952—, prof. philosophy, 1959—, chmn. dept., 1961—, Clark prof. philosophy, 1972-91, Clark prof. philosophy emeritus, 1991—. Vis. prof. Union Theol. Sem., 1959, U. Mich., 1958; guest prof. U. Heidelberg, Germany, 1955-56; Fagothey chair of philosophy U. Santa Clara, 1984, vis. prof. Boston Coll., 1992; Dudleian lectr. Harvard, 1960; lectr. Am. Week, U. Munich, Germany, 1961; Suarez lectr. Fordham U., 1963; pub. lectr. King's College, Univ. London, 1965; Aquinas lectr. Marquette U., 1967; Warfield lectr. Princeton Theol. Sem., 1970; Fulbright lectr. Kyoto U., Japan, 1971; Sprunt lectr. Union Theol. Sem., Va., 1973; Mead-Swing lectr. Oberlin Coll., 1975; H. Richard Niebuhr lectr. Elmhurst Coll., Ill., 1977; Merrick lectr. Ohio Wesleyan U., 1977; Roy Wood Sellars lectr. Bucknell U., 1978; O'Hara lectr. U. Notre Dame, 1984; Hooker disting. vis. prof. Mc Master U., 1985; mem. adv. com. Nat. Humanities Inst., New Haven, 1974, dir., 1977-80. Author: Royce's Social Infinite, 1950, Value Convictions and Higher Education, 1958, Reason and God, 1961, The Spirit of American Philosophy, 1963, 2d edit., 1983, The Philosophy of Religion, 1965, Religion and Empiricism, 1967, Experience and God, 1968, revised edit., 1995, Themes in American Philosophy, 1970, Contemporary American Philosophy, 1970, The Analogy of Experience, 1973, Purpose and Thought: The Meaning of Pragmatism, 1978, America's Philosophical Vision, 1992, Jonathan Edwards, Puritan, Preacher, Philosopher, 1992, Quasi-Religions: Humanism, Marxism, Nationalism, 1994, Reason, Experience, and God, 1997; translator: (R. Kroner): Kant's Weltanschauung, 1956; editor: (Jonathan Edwards): Religious Affections, Vol. 2, 1959, An Edwards Reader, 1995; gen. editor, Yale edit.: Works of Jonathan Edwards, 1965-91, gen. editor emeritus, 1992—; Editorial bd.: Monist, 1962—, Jour. Religious Studies, Philosophy East and West, Jour. Chinese Philosophy, The Personalist Forum, Jour. Faith and Philosophy, Jour. Speculative Philosophy. Named Hon. Alumnus, Harvard Div. Sch., 1960; recipient Herbert W. Schneider award Soc. for Advancement of Am. Philosophy, 1990, Founder's medal Metaphys. Soc. Am., 1996; Am. Coun. Learned Socs. fellow, 1964-65. Mem. Culinary Inst. Am. (dir. New Haven affiliate), Am. Philos. Assn. (v.p. 1980, pres. 1981), Am. Theol. Soc. (pres. 1967-68), Metaphys. Soc. Am. (pres. 1970-71, founder's medal, 1996), Hegel Soc. Am. (pres. 1971), Charles S. Peirce Soc. (pres. 1992). Home: 300 Ridgewood Ave Hamden CT 06517-1428 Office: PO Box 201562 New Haven CT 06520-1562 E-mail: john.smith@yale.edu.

SMITH, JOHN FRANCIS, materials science educator; b. Kansas City, Kans., May 9, 1923; s. Peter Francis and Johanna Teresa (Spandle) S.; m. Evelyn Ann Ross, Sept. 1, 1947 (dec. July 1994); children— Mark Francis, Letitia Ann Smith Harder; m. Eileen R. Ross, Apr. 12, 1997. BA with distinction, U. Mo.-Kansas City, 1948; PhD, Iowa State U., 1953. Grad. asst. Iowa State U., Ames, 1948-53, faculty and research scientist, dept. chmn., div. chief Ames Lab., 1966-70, prof. emeritus, 1988. Cons. Tex. Instruments, Inc., Dallas and Attleboro, Mass., 1958-63, Argonne Nat. Lab., Ill., 1964-70, Iowa Hwy. Commn., Ames, Los Alamos Nat. Lab., N.Mex., 1984-88, bur. standards Nat. Inst. Standards and Tech., Gaithersburg, Md., 1988-91, Sandia Nat. Lab., Albuquerque, N.M., 1991-92, ASM Internat., Cleve., 1992—. Patentee ultrasonic determination of texture in metal sheet and plate, lead-free solder; author: Phase Diagrams of Binary Vanadium Alloys; Hellcats Over the Philippine Deep; co-author: Thorium: Preparation and Properties, 1975; editor: Calculation of Phase Diagrams and Thermochemistry of Alloy Phases, 1978; editor Jour. Phase Equilibria and Diffusion, 1988—; contbr. articles to profl. publs. Mem. former comdr. Ames-Boone Squadron CAP, 1970-75. With USN, 1942-46, PTO, comdr. USNR, 1946-64. Decorated Air medal with star; recipient Disting. Svc. award CAP, Maxwell AFB, Ala., 1979, faculty citation Iowa State U. Alumni Assn., Ames, 1977. Fellow Am. Inst. Chemists, ASM (chmn. Des Moines chpt. 1966); mem. AIME, Materials Rsch. Soc., Am.

Legion, Silent Knights, Inc. (trustee 1980-96), Exptl. Aircraft Assn., Alpha Sigma Mu (trustee 1984-86). Roman Catholic. Avocation: flying. Home: 2919 S Riverside Ames IA 50010-9520 Office: Iowa State U Ames Lab 136F Wilhelm Hall Ames IA 50010 Office Phone: 515-232-3013.

SMITH, JOHN FRANCIS, JR., retired automobile company executive; b. Worcester, Mass., Apr. 6, 1938; s. John Francis and Eleanor C. (Sullivan) S.; children: Brian, Kevin; m. Lydia G. Sigrist, Aug. 27, 1988; 1 stepchild, Nicola. BBA, U. Mass., 1960; MBA, Boston U., 1965. Fisher Body div. mgr. Gen. Motors Corp., Framingham, Mass., 1961-73, asst. treas N.Y.C., 1973-80, comptroller Detroit, 1980-81, dir. worldwide product planning, 1981-84; pres., gen. mgr. Gen. Motors Can., Oshawa, Ont., Can., 1984-85; exec. v.p. Gen. Motors Europe, Glattbrugg, Switzerland, 1986-87, pres., 1987-88; exec. v.p. internat. ops. Gen. Motors Corp., Detroit, 1988-90, vice chmn. internat. ops., 1990, bd. dirs., mem. fin. com., 1990-98, pres., COO, 1992-98; CEO, pres., 1992-98; chmn. bd., CEO, pres. Gen. Motors Corp., Detroit, 1996-98; chmn. bd., CEO Gen Motors Corp., Detroit, 1998-2000; chmn. bd General Motors Corp., Detroit, 1996—2003. Pres.'s coun. Global Strategy Bd.; mem. Bus. Roundtable Policy Com.; mem. U.S. Japan Bus. Coun., Am. Soc. Corp. Execs.; mem. Bd. of Detroit Renaissance; bus. coun. Meml. Sloan-Kettering Cancer Ctr.; bd. dirs. Procter & Gamble Co., Delta, Swiss Re Mem. chancellor's exec. com. U. Mass., dir.; trustee United Way S.E. Mich., New Am. Revolution, Boston U. Mem. Am. Soc. Corp. Execs., Am. Auto Mfrs. Assn. (bd. dirs.), Econ. Club Detroit (bd. dirs.), Beta Gamma Sigma (pres.), Dirs. Table. Roman Catholic. Office: GM 100 Renaissance Ctr Detroit MI 48265-0001

SMITH, JOHN FRANCIS, III, lawyer; b. White Plains, N.Y., Sept. 24, 1941; s. John Francis and Mary Dake (Mairs) S.; m. Susan Brown; children: John, Stephen, Peter. AB, Princeton U., 1963; LLB, Yale U., 1970. Bar: Pa. 1970, U.S. Supreme Ct. 1985. Assoc. Dilworth, Paxson, Kalish & Kauffman, Phila., 1970-75, ptnr., 1975-86, sr. ptnr., 1986-91; sr. litigation ptnr. Reed Smith LLP, Phila., 1991—, mem. exec. com., 1993—2004. Mem. exec. com. Employment Discrimination Referral Project, 1971-74; pres. Society Hill Civic Assn., 1975-76, Phila. Chamber Ensemble, 1977-80; bd. govs. Pa. Economy League (ea. divsn.), 1983—, sec. 1995-97; vice chair Health Care Task Force, 1993-96; bd. dirs. World Affairs Council Phila., 1983-87, chmn. program com., 1986-87; Burn Found., 1987-95, Internat. House of Phila., 2003—; moderator Main Line Unitarian Ch., 1986-89, 2000—; founder and pres. Found. for Individual Responsibility and Social Trust (FIRST), 1995—. Served to lt. (j.g.) USNR, 1963-67; Vietnam. Fellow Am. Bar Found.; mem. ABA, Phila. Bar Assn., Unitarian Universalist Assn. (pres.'s coun.), Yale Law Sch. Alumni Assn. (exec. com. 1982-88, sec. 1987-88), Princeton Club (Phila.). Office: Reed Smith LLP 2500 One Liberty Pl Philadelphia PA 19103 Office Phone: 215-241-7920. E-mail: jfsmith@reedsmith.com.

SMITH, JOHN KERWIN, lawyer; b. Oct. 18, 1926; 1 child, Cynthia. BA, Stanford U.; LLB, Hastings Coll. Law. Ptnr. Haley, Purchio, Sakai & Smith, Hayward, Calif. Bd. dirs. Berkeley Asphalt, Mission Valley Ready-Mix, Coliseum Found., Mission Valley Rock, Rowell Ranch Rodeo, Hastings Coll. Law (alumnus of yr. award 1989). Gen. ptnr. Oak Hills Apts., City Ctr. Commercial, Creekwood I and II Apts.; Road Parks commn. 1957; city coun. 1959-66, mayor 1966-70; chmn. Alameda County Mayors conf. 1968, revenue taxation com. League Calif. Cities, 1968; vice chmn. Oakland-Alameda County Coliseum; vol. Hastings 1066 Found. (pres., vol. svc. award 1990), Martin Kauffman 100 Club; bd. dirs. Hastings Coll. of Law, 1999—, pres. bd. dirs. Mem. ABA, Calif. Bar Assn., Alameda County Bar Assn., Am. Judicature Soc., Rotary. Office: Haley Purchio Sakai & Smith 22320 Foothill Blvd Ste 620 Hayward CA 94541-2700 Office Phone: 510-538-6400. E-mail: hpssckb@aol.com.

SMITH, JOHN MARVIN, III, surgeon, educator; b. San Antonio, July 31, 1947; s. John M. and Jane (Jordan) S.; m. Jill Jones, Aug. 1, 1981. MD, Tulane U., 1972. Diplomate Am. Bd. Surgery, Am. Bd. Thoracic Surgery. Intern U. Tex. Southwest Med. Sch., Dallas, 1972-73; resident in surgery U. Tex., San Antonio, 1973-77; resident in thoracic and cardiovascular surger Tex. Heart Inst., Houston, 1977-79; practice medicine specializing in cardiovasc. surgery San Antonio, 1979—. Mem. Staff Bapt. Med. Ctr., S.W. Tex. Meth. Hosp., Santa Rosa Med. Center, Met. Hosp., Nix Meml. Hosp.; clin. prof. surgery U. Tex. Health Sci. Ctr., San Antonio, 1979—; bd. mgrs. Bexar County Hosp. Dist.; chmn. bd. dirs. Tex. Ranger Assn., San Antonio Med. Found., World Affairs Coun. Served to maj. USAF, 1979-81. Fellow Am. Coll. Cardiology, Am. Coll. Surgery; mem. AMA, Tex. Med. Assn., Bexar County Med. Soc. (pres. 1998—), Denton A. Cooley Cardiovascular Surg. Soc. (pres. 1988-90), Cooley Hands, J. Bradley Aust. Surg. Soc., Soc. Air Force Clin. Surgeons, San Antonio Surg. Soc., San Antonio Cardiology Soc., Soc. Thoracic Surgeons, Tex. Surg. Soc., Tulane Med. Alumni Assn. (bd. dirs.), Tex. Hist. Soc., Sigma Alpha Epsilon, Nu Sigma Nu, Tex. Cavaliers, San Antonio Country Club, The Argyle Club, Giraud Club, Order Alamo, German Club, Christmas Cotillion, Rolling Rock Club, Sons Rep. Tex., San Antonio Gun Club, The Pilon Club. Episcopalian. Home: 204 Zambrano Rd San Antonio TX 78209-5459 Office: 4330 Medical Dr Ste 300 San Antonio TX 78229-3380 Fax: 210-616-0231. E-mail: jmsiii204@pol.net.

SMITH, JOHN STANLEY, lawyer, arbitrator, mediator; b. Albany, N.Y., Nov. 15, 1946; s. Robert Stanley Smith and Sylvia Rose Murgia Neary; m. Lourdes Umandap; children from previous marriage: Jon Jeffrey, James Michael, Brian Matthew, Melissa Marie. BA, St. Bernardine of Siena Coll., Loudonville, N.Y., 1968; JD, U. Balt., 1986. Bar: Md. 1986, U.S. Dist. Ct. Md. 1987, D.C. 1988. Commd. U.S. Army, 1968, advanced through grades to lt. col., comdr. assault helicoptor platoon, 1970-71, comdr. A Btry 3d Bn. 38th Field Artillery, 1972-74, comdr. 132 Assault Support Helicopter Co. Hunter Airfield, 1975, ops. officer 145th Aviation Bn., 1976-78, divsn. artillery aviation officer 25th Divsn. Artillery Schofield Barracks, 1979-80; dep. dir. Directorate of Res. Forces, Ft. Meade, Md., 1981-82; dep. chief Unit Tng. Br. First U.S. Army, 1982-84; divsn. chief Concepts Analysis Agy., Bethesda, Md., 1984-87; exec. officer war plans Dept. of Army, Washington, 1987-90; ptnr. Dziennik & Smith, Glen Burnie, Balt., 1990-92; v.p., gen. counsel Academy Title Group, Glen Burnie, 1992-93; pvt. practice Glen Burnie, 1992—; owner Smith Mediation Svcs., Glen Burnie, 1992—. Pres. Lorimar Title Corp., Glen Bunnie, 1995—. Author: Mid Range Forces Study 88-92, 1985, Mid Range Forces Study 90-94, 1986, Mid Range Forces Study 90-97, 1987. Bd. dirs. No. Anne Arundel County Rep. Club, 1994-95. Decorated Legion of Merit, Bronze Star, Air Medal, Purple Heart. Mem. ABA, Md. Bar Assn., Anne Arundel County Bar Assn., Balt. City Bar Assn., Acad. Family Mediators, No. Anne Arundel County C. of C. (pres. 1996), K.C. Roman Catholic. Avocations: running, bowling, basketball, hiking, camping. Office: 5 Crain Hwy N Glen Burnie MD 21061-2803

SMITH, JOHN W(ESLEY), JR., data processing executive, consultant; b. Bklyn., Jan. 6, 1946; s. John Wesley and Eunice (Davis) S.; m. Carolyn Ferrebbee, Aug. 19, 1971 (div. 1980); children: John Wesley III, Janine Carol. Student, NYU, 1989—. Supr. computer ops. Shearson Lehman Stone, Inc., N.Y.C., 1967—70; sr. ops. analyst Fin. Data Svcs., Inc., N.Y.C., 1970—77; coord. tng. program Chem. Bank, N.Y.C., 1977—78; sr. hardware analyst ADP, Clifton, NJ, 1978—79; adminstr. data base Depository Trust Co., N.Y.C., 1979—81; mgr. data ctr. ops. Leviton Mfg. Co., Littleneck, NY, 1981—83; dir. corp. info. svcs. Reed Robert's Assocs., Inc., Uniondale, 1983—86; dir. prodn. planning and control Human Resource Adminstrn., N.Y.C., 1986—87; mgmt. cons. Asbach/Sci., Inc., N.Y.C., 1987—. Mem. Data Processing Mgmt. Assn., Am. Soc. Notaries, Am. Mgmt. Assn., Am. Arbitration Assn. (comml. panel 1983—), Inst. Certification Computer Profls. (cert systems profl.). Avocation: real estate. Office: Smith Wesley Assocs Inc 1072 Barbey St Brooklyn NY 11207-9202 Office Phone: 718-272-0240.

SMITH, JONATHAN DAVID, medical educator; b. Cleve., Jan. 10, 1955; BS, U. Calif., Santa Cruz, 1978; PhD, Harvard U., 1984. Postdoctoral Lab. Biochem. Genetics and Metabolism The Rockefeller U., N.Y.C., 1984-89, asst. prof., 1989-96, assoc. prof., 1996—. Contbr. articles to profl. jours. Recipient Nat. Rsch. Svc. award NIH, 1985-87, Program Project award, 1995—. Mem. AAAS, Am. Heart Assn. (Investigatorship award N.Y.C. affiliate 1989-92, Grant-in-Aid 1989-92, 92-95, Established Investigator 1994—). Achievements include identification of genes that regulate atherosclerosis; development of animal models useful for testing therapies to proevent atherosclerosis; characterization of novel functions of apolopoprotein E which are relevant to Alzheimer's disease, cardiovascular disease and longevity. Home: 22687 Westchester Rd Shaker Heights OH 44122-2976

SMITH, JOSEPH A., JR., bank commission official; b. Charleston, WV, Nov. 9, 1949; m. Elizabeth Marion; children: Joseph A. 3rd, Matthew M. BA in history, Davidson Coll., 1971; JD, U. Va., 1975. Bar: NY 1975, NC 1989. Assoc. atty. pub. fin. Brown, Wood, Ivey, Mitchell & Petty (now Sidley Austin Brown & Wood), N.Y.C., 1975—79; corporate counsel PepsiCo, Inc., Purchase, NY, 1979—84; asst. gen. counsel Emery Air Freight Corp., Wilton, Conn., 1984—88; ptnr. Poyner & Spruill, Raleigh, NC, 1988—91; gen. counsel, sec. Centura Banks, Inc., Rocky Mount, NC, 1991—2000; atty. Thacher Proffitt & Wood, Washington, 2000—02; commr. of banks NC Banking Commn., 2002—. Mem. steering com. UNC Law Sch. Ctr. Banking & Finance. Office: 4309 Mail Svc Ctr Raleigh NC 27699-4309*

SMITH, JOSEPH PHELAN, film company executive; b. N.Y.C., 1911; s. John William and Margaret Mary (Phelan) S.; m. Madelyn Eleanor Davis, Jan. 17, 1942; children: Kevin, Karen, Margaret, Lisa. BS, Columbia U. Former salesman Van Alstyne Noel & Co., N.Y.C., RKO Radio Pictures, Inc., Boston, Omaha, div. mgr., Los Angeles, Portland, Oreg., San Francisco, 1938-47; former exec. v.p. Lippert Prodns., Hollywood, Calif.; former v.p., gen. mgr. sales Telepictures, N.Y.C.; founding pres. Cinema Vue Corp.; now chmn. Pathe News Inc., N.Y.C., 1995—, Pathe Pictures Inc., N.Y.C., 1995—. Served with U.S. Army. Mem. Motion Picture Pioneers, Am. Film Inst., Elks. Republican. Office: Pathe News Inc 630 9th Ave Ste 305 New York NY 10036-3708

SMITH, JULIA LADD, medical oncologist, hospice physician; b. Rochester, N.Y., July 26, 1951; d. John Herbert and Isabel (Walcott) Ladd; m. Stephen Slade Smith; 1 child. BA, Smith Coll., 1973; MD, N.Y. Med. Coll., 1976. Diplomate Am. Bd. Internal Medicine, Am. Bd. Med. Oncology, Am. Bd. Hospice and Palliative Medicine. Intern in medicine N.Y. Med. Coll., N.Y.C., 1976-77; resident in medicine Rochester Gen. Hosp., 1977-79; internist Genesee Valley Group Health, Rochester, 1979-80; oncology fellow U. Rochester, 1980-82, asst. prof. oncology in medicine sch. medicine and dentistry, 1986—; oncologist Med. Ctr. Clinic, Ltd., Pitts., 1982-83; oncologist, internist Rutgers Community Health Plan, New Brunswick, N.J., 1983-86; med. dir. Genesse Region Home Care Assn./Hospice, Rochester, 1988—; med. oncologist Genesee Hosp., Rochester, 1996—2001, chief hematology/oncology, 1996—2001; med. oncologist Rochester Gen. Hosp., 2001—. Bd. dirs. Am. Cancer Soc., Monroe County, 1988-92. Nat. Cancer Inst. rsch. grantee, 1993-95. Fellow Acad. Hospice Physicians; mem. ACP, Am. Soc. Clin. Oncology. Unitarian-Universalist. Avocations: sailing, reading, movies, bridge. Address: Lipson Blood and Cancer Ctr 1425 Portland Ave Rochester NY 14621 Office Phone: 585-922-4020.

SMITH, JULIAN CLEVELAND, JR., chemical engineering educator; b. Westmount, Que., Can., Mar. 10, 1919; s. Julian Cleveland and Bertha (Alexander) S.; m. Joan Elsen, June 1, 1946; children: Robert Elsen, Diane Louise Smith Brook, Brian Richard. B.Chemistry, Cornell U., 1941, Chem. Engr., 1942. Chem. engr. E. I. duPont de Nemours and Co., Inc., 1942-46; mem. faculty Cornell U., 1946—, prof. chem. engring., 1953-86, prof. emeritus, 1986—, dir. continuing engring. edn., 1965-71; assoc. dir. Cornell U. (Sch. Chem. Engring.), 1973-75, dir., 1975-83. Vis. lectr. U. Edinburgh, 1971-72; cons. to govt. and industry, 1947-2001; UNESCO cons. Universidad de Oriente, Venezuela, 1975 Author: (with W. L. McCabe and P. Harriott) Unit Operations of Chemical Engineering, 1956, 6th edit., 2000, also articles; sect. editor: Perry's Chemical Engineers' Handbook, 1963. Fellow Am. Inst. Chem. Engrs.; mem. Am. Chem. Soc., Ithaca Country Club, Savage Club, Sigma Xi, Tau Beta Pi, Phi Kappa Phi, Alpha Delta Phi. Home: 427 Savage Farm Dr Ithaca NY 14850-6507 Business E-Mail: jcs29@cornell.edu.

SMITH, JULIOUS PERRY, JR., lawyer; b. Richmond, Va., Jan. 10, 1943; s. Julious Perry and Mary Inez (Whitlow) S.; m. Sherrill Marie Poehler, July 28, 1967; children: Julious P. III, S. Hayes, Sarah Graham. BS, Hampden-Sydney (Va.) Coll., 1965; LLB, U. Va., 1968. Bar: Va. 1968, U.S. Dist. Ct. (ea. dist.) Va. 1969. Assoc. Williams Mullen, Richmond, 1968-73, shareholder, 1973—, pres., 1983—99, chmn., CEO, 1999—. Bd. dirs. Quarles Petroleum, Inc., Mut. Assurance Soc. of Va., LandAm. Fin. Group, Inc., Hilb Rogal and Hobbs Co.; spkr. Joel A. Rose Conf. on Law Firm Mgmt., 1995, 98, 2000, 04. Chmn. profl. divsn. United Way, 1990—92, campaign chmn., 1994—95, de Tocqueville Chair, 2000; Va. state chair U.S. Olympic Com., 1996—2000; trustee Hampden-Sydney Coll., 1996—, vice chmn., 2004—; bd. dirs. Theater Va., pres., 2001—02; chair Multiple Sclerosis Dinner, 2002, CCA-Fin.-Am. Cancer Soc. Golf Championship, 2004; mem. sch. bd. St. Bridget's Cath. Ch., Richmond, 1981—88, chmn. capital fund raising campaign, 1991. Recipient Micheli award Richmond Touchdown Club, 1981, Patrick Henry award Hampden-Sydney Coll., 2003; named to Salvation Army Boys and Girls Club Hall of Fame, 1997. Fellow: Va. Law Found., Am. Coll. Trust and Estate Coun.; mem.: ABA, Soc. Internat. Bus. Fellows (Va. chair 1996—97), Richmond Bar Assn. (chmn. young lawyers sect. 1973—74, bd. dirs. 1985—87, 1989—92, pres. 1995—96), Va. Bar Assn., Kinloch Golf Club, Farmington Country Club, Forum Club, Country Club Va., Commonwealth Club (bd. govs. 1997—2000, 2004—). Roman Catholic. Avocations: reading, sports, travel. Office: Williams Mullen 2 James Center PO Box 1320 Richmond VA 23218-1320 Office Phone: 804-783-6408. E-mail: jsmith@williamsmullen.com.

SMITH, KAREN ANN, visual artist; b. Trenton, NJ, May 25, 1964; d. James Roy and Clara Patricia (Walton) S. A in Comml. Art, Art Inst. Phila., 1984; BFA in Graphic Design and Art Therapy, U. Arts, Phila., 1989; grad. in graphic design, Basel Sch. for Design, 1991; MA in Expressive Therapies, Lesley Coll., 1993. Graphic designer Mercer County C.C., Trenton, 1984-86; mural painter, supr. Anti-Graffiti Network, Phila., 1988; tchr. drawing and set design Chestnut Hill (Mass.) Sch., 1995, 96; freelance graphic designer Swiss Fed. Rys., Bern, 1993-95; tchr. drawing Wentworth Inst. Tech., Boston, 1996, 97; tchr. design Northeastern U., Boston, 1997. Fireworks crew Pyrotech. Inc., Boston, 1997; apprentice Johnson Atelier Tech. Inst. of Sculpture, Trenton, 1997-99; artist Airtex Interiors, Fallsington, 2000-03, Midnight Kiwi Design, Newtown, Pa., 2003—; artist, activities asst. Pennswood Village, Newtown, 2003—; visual artist. One-woman shows include Contempo Galerie, Bern, Switzerland, 1994, Boston Archtl. Ctr. Atelier, 1997, George Sch., Newtown, Pa., 1997, exhibited in group shows at Howard Yezerski Gallery, Boston, 1994, Kingston Gallery, 1995, Phillips' Mill, New Hope, Pa., 1997, Woodmere Art Mus., Chestnut Hill, Pa., 1998, Princeton (NJ) Day Sch., 1999, Trenton City Mus., 1999, Vorpal Gallery, N.Y.C., 2000—02, Artsbridge, Prallsville Mills, N.J., 2000, Riverbank Arts, Stockton, N.J., 2000—, iTheo.com, San Francisco, 2000—01, Nat. Bottle Mus., Ballston Spa, N.Y., 2001, Artsbridge Photography Exhbn., Lamberville, NJ, 2003, Artists at the Farm, Langhorne, Pa., 2003—; author numerous poems. Scholar Women in Graphic Arts, 1987-89; grantee Mystic Studios Trust, 1994-97, Artists at the Farm, Langhorne, Pa., 2003—. Mem. Coll. Art Assn., Boston Athenaeum, Origami USA, Artsbridge.

SMITH, KAREN B. educational consultant; b. Monahans, Tex., Oct. 15, 1946; d. Ralph J. and Christine W. Barnes; m. Jack W. Smith, July 19, 1997. BS, No. Tex. State U., Denton, 1965—68; postgrad., Angelo State U., San Angelo, Tex., 1970—73. Provisional Tchg. Cert. 1968. Tchr. Fort Worth ind. sch. dist., Tex., 1968—70; tchr. and vocat. adjustment coord. San Angelo ind. sch. dist., Tex., 1973—91; site base com. mem. Ctrl. H.S., San Angelo, Tex., 1990—91; vocat. adjustment coord. San Angelo ind. sch. dist., Tex., 1997—. Instr. displaced workers Concho Valley Coun. Govts., San Angelo, Tex., 1994—97; v.p. of bd. dirs. Candlelight Apts., Inc., Concho Resource Ctr.; bd. dirs. Promised Wisdom Learning Ctr., com. chair. Active Tom Green County Rep. Women, San Angelo, Tex., 1982—90; past pres. C. of C. Concho Cadre, San Angelo, Tex., 1992—; exhibits com. mem. San Angelo Stock Show and Rodeo, Tex., 1990—; com. mem. Concho Valley Alliance for Transition, San Angelo, Tex., 1999—, Concho Valley Social and Health Resources Coalition, San Angelo, Tex., 2000—; transition task force mem. Mental Svcs. for Concho Valley, San Angelo, Tex., 2001—; vice chair Make a Wish Found., San Angelo, Tex., 1983—84; chair membership Mayor's Com. for Persons with Disabilites, San Angelo, Tex., 1984—86; GROW com. Glen Meadows Baptist Ch., San Angelo, Tex., 2001—; active San Angelo Mus. Fine Arts, 2000—01; vol. Fort Concho Nat. Hist. Landmark and Miss Hattie's Mus., San Angelo, Tex., 1991—. Named Pub. Employee of Yr., Mayor's Com. for Disabled Persons, 1988, Cadre Person of Yr., San Angelo C. of C., 1996; recipient Cmty. Accessibility Recognition award, Shannon Rehab. Ctr., 2002, 2003. Mem.: Guardianship Alliance (nomination com. mem. and bd. dirs. 2001—03), Ctrl. H.S. PTA, Tex. Assn. Vocat. Adjustment Coords., Tex. Classroom Tchrs. Assn. Baptist. Home: 219 Dellwood San Angelo TX 76903 Office: San Angelo Ctrl HS 100 Cottonwood San Angelo TX 76901

SMITH, KATHERINE TERESA, history educator; b. New Orleans, Apr. 30, 1946; d. Gerald Alfred and Margaret Mary (Murphy) S. BA in History, Nazareth Coll., 1967, BS in Elem. Edn., 1970; MA in History, SUNY, Genesco, 1975. Cert. Elem. Educator. Tchr. Rochester (N.Y.) Cath. Schs., 1969-70, Rush-Henrietta (N.Y.) Schs., 1970—. Mem. Henrietta Planning bd., 1975-82; membership com. Rochester Orchestra, 1982-85; treas., sec. Henrietta Dem. com., 1969-2000; bd. dirs. Riverton, sec., treas., 1973-74, 82-85; sec., treas. PTA R-H, 1970-2000. Recipient Citizenship award Henrietta Planning bd., 1982, Svc. award Riverton Cmty. Assn., Henrietta, 1985. Mem. Rush-Henrietta Educators Assn. (v.p. 1974-84, gold apple award 1984, delegate NEX, AFT, NYSUT). Democrat. Roman Cath. Home: 292 Countess Dr West Henrietta NY 14586-9416 Office: Rush Henrietta Schs 5509 E Henrietta Rd Rush NY 14543-9755

SMITH, KATHERYN JEANETTE, music educator; b. Siloam Springs, Ark., July 6, 1944; d. Charlie H. and Victoria Virginia (Jameson) Porter; m. Curtis Barth Smith, Jan. 10, 1975; 1 child, Melody Jeanette. B in Music Edn., So. Nazarene U., 1966; M in Music Edn., Kent (Ohio) State U., 1970. Gen. music tchr. Duncan (Okla.) Jr. H.S., 1966-68; elem. music tchr. Akron (Ohio) Pub. Schs., 1971-72; music prof. MidAm. Nazarene U., Olathe, Kans., 1972—. Clinician Lillenas Music Confs., Olathe, Kans., 1994, 96, 97. Keyboard accompanist Coll. Ch. of the Nazarene, 1973—. Mem. Music Educators Nat. Conf., Music Tchrs. Nat. Assn., MidAm. Nazarene Univ. Women's Aux. (chairperson 1973-74, 94-98). Avocation: whale collection. Office: MidAm Nazarene Univ 2030 E College Way Olathe KS 66062-1831 E-mail: ksmith@mnu.edu.

SMITH, KATHLEEN TENER, bank executive; b. Pitts., Oct. 19, 1943; d. Edward Harrison Tener Jr. and Barbara Elizabeth (McCormick) Tener; m. Roger Davis Smith, May 30, 1970 (dec.); children: Silas Wheelock, Jocelyn Tener, Luke Ewing Taft. BA summa cum laude, Vassar Coll., 1965; MA in Econs., Harvard U., 1968. Rsch. assoc. Harvard U. Grad. Sch. Bus., Cambridge, Mass., 1967-69; from assoc. economist to 2d v.p. Chase Manhattan Bank, NYC, 1969—72, v.p., 1973—98, treas. Global Bank, 1990—91; network ptnr. Smith Barney, Citigroup Global Markets, 1999—. Editor: Commodity Derivatives and Finance, 1996. Trustee Eleanor Roosevelt Ctr. Val-Kill, 2000—03, chmn. fin. com., 2001—03; mem. subcom. on edn. Chase Manhattan Found., N.Y.C., 1985—90; trustee Huguenot Hist. Soc. New Paltz, 1999—2002, chair fin. com., 1999—2002, trustee, JEBGA, 2000—; mem. working com. Huguenot Heritage, 1999—; chair Pyramid Soc. Vassar Coll., Poughkeepsie, 2001—, trustee, 1979—91, mem. exec. com., 1987—91, class pres., 2000—. Fellow, NSF, 1965—67. Mem.: Yale Club, Phi Beta Kappa. Republican. Episcopalian. Address: PO Box 129 New Paltz NY 12561-0129

SMITH, KATIE (KATHERINE MAY SMITH), professional basketball player; b. Logan, Ohio, June 4, 1974; d. Don Smith. Degree in zoology, Ohio State U., 1996. Profl. basketball player Columbus Quest, ABL, 1997—98, Minn. Lynx, WNBA, 1999—, Lotos VBW Clima, EuroLeague, Gdynia, Poland, 2001—02. Named Ohio State Female Athlete of the Century, Columbus Touchdown Club, 2002; named to ABL All-Star Team, 1997, 1998, All-ABL First Team, 1998, WNBA All-Star Team, 2000, 2001, 2002, 2003, All-WNBA First Team, 2001, 2003. Achievements include mem., Columbus Quest ABL Championship Team, 1997, 98; mem., US Women's Basketball Gold Medal Team, FIBA World Championships, 1998, 2002; mem., US Women's Basketball Gold Medal Team, Sydney Olympics, 2000; mem., US Women's Basketball Team, Athens Olympics, 2004; first female in history of Ohio State U. to have number retired, Jan. 21, 2001. Office: Minn Lynx 600 First Ave North Minneapolis MN 55403*

SMITH, KEITH, protective services official; Fire chief City of Indpls.; liaison 2001 World Police & Fire Games, Indlpls. Office: 2001 World Police & Fire Games 39 Jackson Pl Indianapolis IN 46225-1050

SMITH, KENNETH ALAN, chemical engineer, educator; b. Winthrop, Mass., Nov. 28, 1936; s. James Edward and Alice Gertrude (Walters) S.; m. Ambia Marie Olsson, Oct. 14, 1961; children: Kirsten Heather, Edward Eric, Andrew Ian Beaumont, Thurston Garrett. S.B., MIT, 1958, S.M., 1959, Sc.D., 1962; postgrad., Cambridge (Eng.) U., 1964-65. Asst. prof. chem. engring. MIT, 1961-67, assoc. prof., 1967-71, prof., 1971—. Edwin R. Gilliland prof. chem. engring., 1989—, acting head dept., 1976-77, assoc. provost, 1980-81, assoc. provost, v.p. rsch., 1981-91, dir. Whitaker Coll. Health Sci. and Tech., 1989-91. Cons. chem. and oil cos. NSF fellow, 1964-65, Overseas fellow, Churchill Coll., (Eng.), 1993, 01. Mem. Am. Inst. Chem. Engrs., Nat. Acad. Engring., Am. Chem. Soc., AAAS, Sigma Xi, Phi Lambda Upsilon, Tau Beta Pi. Episcopalian. Home: 32 School St Manchester MA 01944-1336 Office: MIT Bldg 66-540 Cambridge MA 02139 Office Phone: 617-253-1973.

SMITH, KENNETH DALE, civil engineer, consultant; s. Zella and Butler Barker Smith; m. Hayrunisa Palanci, June 1988; children: Ethan, Logan. BS in civil engring., BS in land surveying, Purdue U., West Lafayette, Ind., 1990—95. Cert. profl. engr., Ind., 2000. Dir. ops., civil engring. Fanning/Howey Assocs., Inc., Lafayette, Ind., 1996—. Cons. Fanning/Howey Assocs., Inc., Lafayette, Ind., 1996—. Author: A Study of the Purdue Linear Compactor. Water com. Lafayette C. of C., Ind., 2003. Staff sgt. U.S. Army, 1983—90, Fort Campbell, Kentucky, Germany. Decorated Army Commendation Medal, Meritorious Svc. U.S. Army. Mem.: Ind. Soc. Profl. Land Surveyors (assoc.). Conservative. Home: 3421 Covington St Lafayette IN 47906 Office: Fanning/Howey Assocs Inc 8 N 3rd Str Ste 402 Lafayette IN 47901 E-mail: ksmith@fhai.com.

SMITH, KENNETH JUDSON, JR., chemist, theoretician, educator; b. Raleigh, N.C., Sept. 4, 1930; s. Kenneth Judson and Irene (Strickland) S.; m. Dorothy Margaret Ratcliffe, Mar. 6, 1953; children: Patricia Lynne Smith Pittman, Pamela Jean. AB, East Carolina U., 1957; MA, Duke U., 1959, PhD, 1961. Research chemist Chemstrand Research Center, Durham, N.C., 1961-65, sr. research chemist, 1965-68; asst. prof. polymer research SUNY Coll. Environ. Sci. and Forestry, Syracuse, 1968-70, assoc. prof., 1970-73, prof., 1973-95, emeritus prof., 1995—, asst. dir. Polymer Research Center, 1971-79, acting dir., 1979-83, dir. Organic Materials Sci. Program, 1971-75, chmn. dept. chemistry, 1972-84. Vis. prof. Instituto di Chimica Industriale, U. Genoa, Italy, 1979; cons. U.S. Army Materials and Mechanics Rsch. Ctr., Watertown, Mass., 1973-75, cert. of appreciation 1973, NRC, Washington, 1980-87; mem. adv. coun. Syracuse Met. Transp. Coun., 1975-84; mem. adv. bd. confs. in polymer sci. and tech. SUNY, New Paltz, 1977-85; mem. rsch. found. joint com. on procedures SUNY, Albany, 1974-81; cons. Hong Kong Rsch. Coun., 1995—. Contbr. articles to profl. jours. Served with USMC, 1951-54. Recipient cert. Appreciation U.S. Army Materials and Mechanics Rsch. Ctr., 1973. Mem. AAAS, Am. Chem. Soc. (dir. Syracuse sect. 1977-79, chmn. 1978, councilor 1979-82), Am. Phys. Soc. (com. on internat. freedom of scientists, small coms.), Am. Inst. Chemists, Soc. Plastics Engrs., Math. Assn. Am., N.Y. Acad. Scis., Sigma Xi, Phi Lambda Upsilon, Kappa Delta Pi. Achievements include research on statistical mechanics, mechanical properties and theoretical studies of polymers; rubber elasticity and thermoelasticity;

crystallization of networks; structure-property relationships; ultimate properties of fibers; thermodynamic theory of polymer fiber properties; thermodyanic theory of fiber strength. Office: Coll Environ Sci and Forestry Suny Syracuse NY 13210

SMITH, KENNETH RODGER, university dean, economics educator; b. Vancouver, B.C., Can., May 12, 1942; arrived in US, 1962; s. John Douglas and Marion (Cannon) S.; m. Esther J. Davenport, July 26, 1977; children from previous marriage: Morgen Jennifer, Jason Andrew BA, U. Wash., 1964; PhD, Northwestern U., 1968. Vis. research fellow Universite Catholique de Louvain, Belgium, 1968-69; asst. prof. econs. Health Econs. Research Ctr., U. Wis., Madison, 1969-71, assoc. prof. econs., 1971-75; prof., program dir. Grad. Sch. Mgmt., Northwestern U., Evanston, Ill., 1975-79; Eller Disting. Svc. Prof. of Econs., Eller Coll. Mgmt. U. Ariz., Tucson, 1980—, dean, Eller Coll. Mgmt. and Coll. Bus. and Pub. Adminstrn., 1980—95, vice provost, 1992—95, interim dean, Eller Coll. Mgmt., 2004—. Vis. assoc. prof. U. Calif.-San Diego, 1971-72; bd. dirs. The FINOVA Group, Apache Nitrogen Products, Ventana Corp. Co-author: Hospital Cost Containment Programs: A Policy Analysis, 1978 Bd. dirs. Jr. Achievement of Tucson, 1980-88, St. Joseph Hosp., Tucson, 1980-83; vice chmn. Ariz. Commn. on Long Term Care, 1983-84; mem. nat. adv. com. Robert Wood Johnson Found. Program for Prepaid Health Care, 1983-88. Mem. Assn. to Advance Collegiate Schs. Bus. (bd. dirs., 1990-96, pres., 1994-95). Office: U Ariz Dept Econs PO Box 210108 Tucson AZ 85721-0108

SMITH, KENT ASHTON, scientific and technical information executive; b. Boston, Sept. 3, 1938; s. Kent Wooliscroft and Dorothy Patten Smith; m. Mary Margaret Gaffney; children: Holly L. Smith, Kent W. BA, Hobart Coll., 1960; MBA, Cornell U., 1962; postgrad., Am. U., 1978-79. Mgmt. analyst Office of Sec., HEW, Washington, 1962-65; adminstrv. officer divsn. rsch. facilities and resources NIH, Bethesda, Md., 1965-67, asst. exec. officer divsn. rsch. facilities and resources, 1967-68, exec. officer divsn. rsch. resources, 1968-71, asst. dir. adminstrn. Nat. Libr. Medicine, 1971-78, dep. dir., 1978—, PHS spl. expert-info. scientist, 2000—. Mem. exec. bd. and bur. Internat. Coun. Sci. and Tech. Info., Paris, 1983—2001; v.p. U.S. Nat. Com. of UNESCO-PGI, Washington, 1983—85; mem. exec. adv. bd. Fed. Libr. and Info. Ctr. Com., Washington, 1984—89; exec. com. CENDI-Info. Consortia, Washington, 1985—; exec. bd. Nat. Fed. Abstracting and Info. Sci., Phila., 1985—90; treas. Internat. Coun. Sci. and Tech. Info., Paris, 1986—89, Nat. Fed. Abstracting and Info. Sci., Phila., 1986—88; chmn. Info. Policy Com., 1988—89; pres. elect Nat. Fed. Abstracting and Info. Sci., Phila., 1989; mem. US Nat. Commn. for CODATA, 1990—2001; pres. Internat. Coun. Sci. and Tech. Info., Paris, 1990—94; chmn. CENDI-Info. Consortia, Washington, 2001—04; mem. panel on Dept. Energy Info. Infrastructure NAS, 2000; reviewer study digital strategy for Libr. Congress NRC, 2000; mem. panel on Nat. Tech. Info. Svc. Nat. Commn. Libr. and Info. Sci., 2000; mem. Science.gov Alliance, 2002—04. Contbr. articles to profl. jours., chpt. to book: Management of Federally Sponsored Libraries, 1995. Mem. Citizens Com. for Pub. Libr. Montgomery County, Bethesda, 1981-82; fin. dir. Christ Ch., Rockville, Md., 1990-91. Recipient Asst. Sec. for Health Exceptional Achievement award USPHS, 1978, Sr. Exec. Svc. award, 1996, 97, 98, 99, HEW Superior Svc. medal 1974, Nat. Fedn. Abstracting Info. Sci., 1998, Miles Conrad hon. lectureship, Hammer award V.P. US, 1999. Fellow Nat. Fedn. Abstracting and Info. Svcs.; mem. ASPA (vice chmn. 1971-72), AAAS, Int. Assn. Sci. Tech. and Med. Pubs., Am. Mgmt. Assn., Am. Soc. Info. Svc., Med. Libr. Assn. (Pres. award 1997, ICSTI Disting. Svc. award 2001, chair Alfred Zipf fellowship com. 2001-04), Assn. Rsch. Librs., Cosmos Club. Episcopalian. Avocations: golf, baseball, genealogy, theater, birdwatching, antiques. Home: 17903 Gainford Pl Olney MD 20832-1657 Office: Nat Libr Medicine 8600 Rockville Pike Bethesda MD 20894-0002 Office Phone: 301-496-6661.

SMITH, KENT ERNEST, non-profit organization executive; b. Oak Park, Ill., May 21, 1939; s. James Paul and Jane Louise (Gardner) S.; m. Pamela Ann Streich, Sept. 11, 1965; children: Julie Ellen, Stephen Paul. BS in Journalism, U. Ill., 1961. Prodr., writer pub. svc. programming Sta. WLW-TV, Cin., 1965-67; radio/TV news writer prodr. Sta. WGN, Chgo., 1967-69; TV news prodr., writer, project planner Sta. WLS-TV, Chgo., 1969-78; exec. dir. Spina Bifida Assn., Chgo., 1978-86, Cmty. Counseling Svc. Co. Inc., Chgo., 1986-89, Ill. Spina Bifida Assn. Am., Chgo., 1989-91; v.p. resource devel. Lifelink/Bensenville (Ill.) Home Soc., 1991-95; dir. devel. Luth. Child & Family Svcs. Ill., River Forest, 1995-2000; chief devel. officer Ada S. McKinley Cmty. Svcs., Inc., Chgo., 2000—. Chmn. bd. Coun. Disability Rights, Chgo. Served in U.S. Army, 1961-65. Mem. Am. Soc. Assn. Execs., Nat. Soc. Fund Raisers, Chgo. Soc. Assn. Execs., Chgo. Headline Club, Rotary (Elmhurst). Mem. United Ch. Christ. Home: 472 Prairie Ave Elmhurst IL 60126-4022 Office: 725 S Wells St Ste 1A Chicago IL 60607-4507 Office Phone: 312-385-2013. Business E-Mail: ksmith@adasmckinley.org.

SMITH, K(ERMIT) WAYNE, computer company executive; b. Newton, N.C., Sept. 15, 1938; s. Harold Robert and Hazel K. (Smith) S.; m. Audrey M. Kennedy, Dec. 19, 1958; 1 son, Stuart W. BA, Wake Forest U., 1960; MA, Princeton U., 1962, PhD, 1964; postgrad., U. So. Calif., 1965; LLD (hon.), Ohio U., 1992; LHD (hon.), Ohio State U., 1998. Instr. Princeton U., 1963; asst. prof. econs. and polit. sci. U.S. Mil. Acad., 1963-66; spl. asst. to asst. sec. def. for sys. analysis Washington, 1966-69; program mgr. def. studies RAND Corp., Santa Monica, Calif., 1969-70; dir. program analysis NSC, Washington, 1970-72; group v.p. planning Dart Industries, L.A., 1972-73, group pres. resort devel. group, 1973-76; exec. v.p. Washington Group, Inc., 1976-77; mng. ptnr. Coopers & Lybrand, Washington, 1977-80, group mng. ptnr., 1980-83; chmn., CEO World Book, Inc., 1983-86; prof. Wake Forest U., 1986—88, 2001—; CEO OCLC Online Computer Libr. Ctr., Inc., Dublin, Ohio, 1989-98, pres. emeritus, 1998—. Sr. cons. Dept. Def., Dept. State, NSC, NASA, Dept. Energy, OMB, GAO; bd. dirs. Nat. City Bank, K. Wayne Smith and Assocs., OCLC Info Dimensions, Inc.; con. prof. (hon.) Tsinghua U., Beijing, 1996; chmn. Rainbow Care For Kids Found., 1999-2000. Author: How Much is Enough? Shaping the Defense Program, 1961-69, 1971; editor: OCLC 1967-97: Thirty Years of Furthering Access to the World's Information, 1998; contbr. articles to profl. jours. Mem. vis. com. Brookings Instn., Washington, 1971-79; mem. bd. visitors Wake Forest U., 1974-78, 82-90, chmn. bd. visitors, 1976-78, trustee, 1991-95, 96-2000, 2001—; mem. bd. visitors Def. Sys. Mgmt. Coll., 1982-85, Lenoir Rhyne Coll., 1988-94, Mershon Ctr. Ohio State U., 1990-92, Columbus Assn. for Performing Arts, 1991-95, U. Pitts. Sch. Libr. and Info. Sci., 1992-95; mem. bd. visitors Bowman Gray Bapt. Hosp. Med. Ctr., 1992-95, chmn. bd. visitors, 1993-95. Danforth fellow, Woodrow Wilson fellow Princeton U., 1962-64. Mem. ALA (hon., life), Coun. Fgn. Rels., Internat. Inst. Strategic Studies, Int. Internat. Edn., Coun. Higher Edn., Am. Assn. Higher Edn., Chgo. Club, Lakes Golf and Country Club, Capital Club, Phi Beta Kappa, Omicron Delta Kappa, Kappa Sigma. Methodist. Home: 2606 Sigmon Dairy Rd Newton NC 28658-8607 Office: Online Computer Libr Ctr Inc 6565 Frantz Rd Dublin OH 43017-5308

SMITH, KERRY CLARK, lawyer; b. Phoenix, July 12, 1935; s. Clark and Fay (Jackson) S.; m. Michael Waterman, 1958; children: Kevin, Ian. AB, Stanford U., 1957, JD, 1962. Bar: Calif. 1963, U.S. Supreme Ct. 1980. Assoc. Chickering & Gregory, San Francisco, 1962-70, ptnr., 1970-81, Pettit & Martin, San Francisco, 1981-95, Hovis, Smith, San Francisco, 1995-99; pvt. practice San Francisco, 1999—. Mem. editl. bd. Stanford Law Rev., 1961-62. Lt. USN, 1957-60. Mem. ABA (bus. law sect.), Calif. Bar Assn., San Francisco Bar Assn., Orinda County Club, Palms Golf Club, La Quinta Citrus Golf Club, San Francisco World Trade Club. Office: Smith Law Offices 601 California St Ste 1600 San Francisco CA 94108-2821 E-mail: kerrysmith50965@msn.com.

SMITH, KEVIN, film director, writer, actor; b. Red Bank, NJ, Aug. 2, 1970; m. Jennifer Schwalbach; 1 child. Dr. Humane Letters(hon.), Illinois Wesleyan University. Owner Jay and Silent Bob's Secret Stash Comic Book Store, Red Bank, NJ, View Askew Productions, 1996—. Dir., writer, actor (films): Clerks, 1994, Mall Rats, 1996, Chasing Amy, 1997, Dogma, 1999; dir., writer, actor: Jay and Silent Bob Strike Back, 2001; exec. prodr.: Good Will Hunting, 1997, Vulgar, 2000; dir., producer, writer (films): Jersey Girl, 2004; screenwriter: (TV film) Roadside Attractions, 2002; dir., screenwriter: (TV film) The Flying Car, 2002; writer, actor, exec. prod. (TV series) Clerks, 2000; appeared in film: Scream 3, 1999, Daredevil, 2003. Office: Endeavor Agy 9701 Wilshire Blvd Fl 10 Beverly Hills CA 90212-2010

SMITH, KIKI, artist; b. Nuremberg, Germany, 1954; One-woman shows include The Kitchen, N.Y.C., 1982, Fawbush Gallery, 1988, 1992, 1993, Galerie René Blouin, Montreal, 1989, 1991—92, 1994, Dallas Mus. Art, 1989, Ezra and Cecile Zilkha Gallery Ctr. for the Arts Wesleyan U., Middletown, Conn., 1989, Tyler Gallery Tyler Sch. Art Temple U., Phila., 1990, Ctr. d'Arte Contemporaine, Geneva, 1990, Inst. Art and Urban Resources The Clocktower, Long Island, N.Y., 1990, Inst. Contemporary Art, Amsterdam, 1990, Mus. Modern Art, N.Y.C., 1990—91, Shoshana Wayne Gallery, Santa Monica, Calif., 1991, 1992, 1992—93, MAK Galerie, Vienna, 1991, U. Art Mus., Berkeley, Calif., 1991, Art Awareness, Inc., Lexington, N.Y., 1991, Corcoran Gallery Art, Washington, 1991, Greg Kucera Gallery, Seattle, 1991, Rose Art Mus. Brandeis U., Waltham, Mass., 1992, Österreichisches Mus. angewandte Kunst, Vienna, 1992, Moderna Mus., Stockholm, 1992, Bonner Kunstverein, Bonn, 1992, Galerie M & R Fricke, Düsseldorf, Germany, 1992—93, Williams Coll. Mus. Art, Williamstown, Mass., 1992—93, Ohio State U., Columbus, 1992—93, Anthony d'Offay Gallery, London, 1993, 1995, Phoenix Art Mus., 1993, U. Art Mus., Santa Barbara, Calif., 1994, La. Mus. Modern Art, Humlebaek, Denmark, 1994, The Israel Mus., Jerusalem, 1994, Barbara Gross Galerie, Munich, 1994, Laura Carpenter Fine Art, Santa Fe, 1994, Pace Wildenstein, N.Y., 1994, Royal LePage Gallery, Toronto, 1994—95, Barbara Krakow Gallery, Boston, 1994—96, Whitechapel Art Gallery, London, 1995, numerous others, exhibited in group shows at Brooke Alexander Gallery, N.Y., 1980, 1991, White Columns, N.Y., 1981, 1983, 1990, Artists Space, 1981, 1990, Barbara Gladstone Gallery, 1982, Hallwalls, Buffalo, N.Y., 1983, Susan Caldwell Gallery, N.Y., 1984, 1987, Galerie Engstrom, Stockholm, 1984, Art City, N.Y., 1985, Moderna Mus., Stockholm, 1985, Cin. Art Mus., 1985, Bklyn. Mus., 1986, 1989, Curt Marcus Gallery, N.Y., 1986, Fawbush Gallery, 1987, 1989, 1990, Mus. Modern Art, N.Y.C., 1988, 1992, IBM Gallery, N.Y., 1988, Arch Gallery, Amsterdam, 1988, Tom Cugliani Gallery, 1989, Simon Watson Gallery, N.Y., 0190, Mus. Fine Arts, Boston, 1990, Hunter Coll. Art Gallery, 1991, Milw. Art Mus., 1992, Paula Cooper Gallery, 1993, Serpentine Gallery, London, 1994, PaceWildenstein, N.Y., 1995, 1997, 1998, Ace Gallery, Mex., 1997, Yale U. Art Gallery, New Haven, Conn., 1998, numerous others. Office: c/o Pace Wildenstein 32 E 57th St New York NY 10022-2513

SMITH, KIRK ROBERT, environmental health sciences educator, researcher; b. Calif., Jan. 19, 1947; MPH, U. Calif., Berkeley, PhD in Biomed. & Environ. Health Scis., 1977. Founder, leader energy program East-West Ctr., Honolulu, 1978-85, sr. fellow, program area coord. environ. risk, 1985—; prof. environ. health scis. U. Calif., Berkeley, 1995—; dep. dir. Inst. Global Health, 2000—, Brian and Jennifer Maxwell chair in pub. health, 2003—. Author: 8 books; contbr. numerous articles to profl. jours. Named One of Am.'s 100 Brightest Young Scientists, Sci. Digest, 1984, Alumnus of Yr., U. Calif. Sch. Pub. Health, 1989. Mem. NAS. Achievements include research on pollution in developing countries. Office: U Calif Sch Pub Health Environ Health Scis Warren Hall Berkeley CA 94720-7360 E-mail: KRKSmith@uclink.berkeley.edu.

SMITH, L. DENNIS, former academic administrator; b. Muncie, Ind., Jan. 18, 1938; s. Thurman Lewis and Dorothy Ann (Dennis) S.; m. Suzanne F. Mctcalfe; children: Lauren Kay, Raymond Bradley. AB, Ind. U., 1959, PhD, 1964; DSc (hon.), Purdue U., 2000. Asst. embryologist Argonne (Ill.) Nat. Lab., 1964-67, assoc. biologist, 1967-69; assoc. prof. Purdue U., West Lafayette, Ind., 1969-73, prof. biology, 1973-87, assoc. head dept. biol. scis., 1979-80, head dept., 1980-87; prof. dept. devel. and cell. U. Calif., Irvine, 1987-94, dean Sch. Biol. Scis., 1987-90, exec. vice chancellor, 1990-94; pres. U. of Nebr., 1994—2004, pres. emeritus, prof. biol. scis., 2004—. Instr. embryology Woods Hole (Mass.) Marine Biology Lab., 1972-74, mem. Space Studies Bd., Washington, 1986-91; chmn. Space Biology and Medicine, space sci. bd., 1986-91; cell biology study sect. NIH, Bethesda, Md., 1971-75; chmn., 1977-79, bd. sci. counselors Nat. Inst. Child Health and Human Devel., 1990-95, chmn. 1992-95; space biology peer rev. bd. AIBS, 1980-85. Mem. Bus. Higher Edn. Forum, 1995—, chair, 2000—02; bd. dirs. Nebr. Arts Coun., Nebr., Nebr. Indsl. Competitiveness Alliance. Fellow Guggenheim, 1987; Sci. Freedom and Responsibility award, AAAS, 2002. Mem. AAAS, Am. Soc. Biochemistry and Molecular Biology, Internat. Soc. for Devel. Biology, Soc. for Devel. Biology, Am. Soc. Cell Biology, Am. Soc. for Microbiology. Office: Alex West Ste 135 312 No 14th St Lincoln NE 68588-0430 Office Phone: 402-472-7154.

SMITH, LAMAR SEELIGSON, congressman; b. San Antonio, Nov. 19, 1947; s. Campbell and Eloise Keith (Seeligson) S.; m. Elizabeth Schaefer, Mar. 20, 1992; children: Nell Seligson, Tobin Wells. BA, Yale U., 1969; JD, So. Meth. U., 1975. Mgmt. intern SBA, Washington, 1969-70; bus. writer The Christian Sci. Monitor, Boston, 1970-72; assoc. Maebius & Duncan, Inc., San Antonio, 1975-76; chmn. Rep. Party of Bexar County, San Antonio, 1978-81; state rep. Dist. 57-F, San Antonio, 1981-82; county commr. Precinct 3 Bexar County, 1983—85; mem. U.S. Congress from 21st Tex. dist., 1987—; mem. jud. com.; mem. joint econ. com.; mem. sci. com. Ptnr. Lamar Seeligson Ranch, Premont, Tex., 1975—. Republican. Christian Scientist. Office: US Ho of Reps 2231 Rayburn Ho Office Bldg Washington DC 20515-0001

SMITH, LANTY L(LOYD), lawyer, business executive; b. Sherrodsville, Ohio, Dec. 11, 1942; s. Lloyd H. and Ellen Ruth (Newell) S.; m. Margaret Hays Chandler, June 11, 1966; children: Abigail Lamoreaux Presson, Margaret Ellen Smith-Rhee, Amanda Prescott Lacoff. BS in Math. with honors, Wittenberg U., Springfield, Ohio, 1964; LLB with honors, Duke U., 1967. Bar: Ohio 1967. Assoc. Jones, Day, Cockley & Reavis, Cleve., 1967-73; ptnr. Jones, Day, Reavis & Pogue, Cleve., 1974-77; exec. v.p., sr. gen. counsel Burlington Industries, Inc., Greensboro, N.C., 1977-86, pres., 1986-88; chmn. Precision Fabrics Group Inc., Greensboro, 1988—, The Greenwood Group, Inc., Raleigh, N.C., 1992—, Soles Brower Smith & Co., 1998—. Bd. dirs., chmn. exec. com., lead ind. dir. Wachovia Corp.; bd. dirs. Wikoff Color, Renfro Corp.; pres., CEO MediWave Star Tech. Inc., 1999—. Mem. exec. com. Greensboro Devel. Corp.; bd. visitors Duke U. Sch. Law; bd. trustees The Duke Endowment; bd. dirs., exec. com. Duke U. Mgmt. Co.; mem. exec. com. The Ridge YMCA Retreat. Mem.: NC Inst. Medicine. Episcopalian. Home: 1401 Westridge Rd Greensboro NC 27410-2912 Office: Soles Brower Smith & Co Wachovia Tower Ste 925 Greensboro NC 27401-2167 E-mail: lsmith@solesbrower.com.

SMITH, LARRY G. career military officer; b. Bonneville, Miss., Aug. 11, 1944; Commd. 2d lt. U.S. Army; advanced through grades to maj. gen. comdr. gen. U.S. Army Security Assistance Command, 1997—. Office: US Army Security Assistance Command 5001 Eisenhower Ave Rm 5E22 Alexandria VA 22333-0001

SMITH, LAUREN ASHLEY, lawyer, journalist, clergyman, physicist; b. Clinton, Iowa, Nov. 30, 1924; s. William Thomas Roy and Ethel (Cook) S.; m. Barbara Ann Mills, Aug. 22, 1947; children: Christopher A., Laura Nan Smith Pringle, William Thomas Roy II. BS, U. Minn., 1946, JD, 1949; postgrad., U. Chgo., 1943-49; MDiv, McCormick Theol. Sem., 1950; postgrad., U. Iowa, 1992. Bar: Colo. 1957, Iowa 1959, Ill. 1963, Minn. 1983, U.S. Supreme Ct. 1967; ordained to ministry Presbyn. Ch., 1950. Pastor Presbyn. Ch., Fredonia, Kans., 1950-52, Lamar, Colo., 1952-57, Congl. Ch., Clinton, 1975-80; editor The Comml., Pine Bluff, Ark., 1957-58; ptnr. Schoenauer Smith & Fullerton ASP, Clinton, 1995—. CEO LASCO Pub. Group, Clinton, 1995—; CEO, founder Interlink for the Internet Generation; internat. conferee Stanley Found., Warrenton, Va., 1963—72; legal observer, USSR, 1978; co-sponsor All India Renewable Energy Conf., Bangalore, 1981; law sch. conferee U. Minn., China, 1983; lectr. law, religion, physics, nat. policy U. Wis., 2001, Spl. lectr. contemporary physics and religion, 01. Author: (jurisprudence treatise) Forma Dat Esse Rel, 1975, (monograph) First Strike Option, 1983; co-author: India On to New Horizons, 1989; columnist Crow Call, 1968—; co-editor Press and News of India, 1978-82; pub. Crow Call; pseudonym Christopher Crow, 1981—; writer BBC World Svc., London; editor Asian Econ. Cmty. Jour.; contbr. articles to religious publs. Minister-at-large Presbyn. Ch. U.S.A., Iowa, 1987—; bd. dirs. Iowa divsn. UN Assn. U.S.A., Iowa City, 1970-85; fellow Molecular Nanotechnology Foresight Inst., Palo Alto, Calif.; Franciscans United Nations Non Govt. Orgn.; assoc. Westar Inst. (The Jesus Seminar), Santa Rosa, Calif., 1997; active Quad City Estate Planning Coun.; founder, CEO Interlink relating quantum mechanics and religion; founding dir. Project 67/74, Road Map for the World; assoc. Cath. Order of St. Francis. Recipient World Wide Essay Contest award, Radio China Internat., 2003—04. Mem. Iowa Bar Assn., Ill. Bar Assn., St. Andrews Soc., Clinton County Bar Assn. (pres. 1968, Best in Iowa citation), Clinton Ministerial Assn., Samaritan Health Systems Chaplain Corps. (pres.), European Soc. for Study of Sci. and Religion, Quad City Estate Planning Coun., Quaker Internat. Yokefellow, Nat. Network for New Spiritual Formation Presbyn. Ch. USA, Franciscans Internat., Parish Without Walls (founding dir.), City Club of Quad Cities (bd. dirs.).

SMITH, LAURIE HYSON, lawyer; b. Palmerton, Pa., July 7, 1953; d. James Donaldson and Mary Ann (Hyson) Smith; m. Donald James Gerber, Aug. 1976 (div. May 1981); m. Witold Kaczanowski, Dec. 11, 1993 (div. Feb. 2002); 1 child, Wit Thomas Kaczanowski. BS, Pa. State U., 1975; MSW, U. Denver, 1981; JD, Northeastern U., 1989. Adminstrv. staff, resource coord., vol. coord., counselor Women in Crisis, Lakewood, Colo., 1977-79; program adminstr. Big Sis. of Colo., Life Choices Program, Denver, 1979-80; legis. coord., lobbyist Common Cause, Denver, 1980-81; social work advocate Denver Legal Aid Soc., 1982-86; legis. analyst Nat. Conf. State Legis., Denver, 1987; mediator, intake coord. Harvard Law Sch., Cambridge, Mass., 1988; law clk. Supreme Jud. Ct. State Mass., Boston, 1988-89; legis. staff Rep. Patricia Schroeder, U.S. Congress, Washington, 1989; ptnr. Pfaff & Smith Family Law Clinic, Denver, 1990—91; asst. city atty., sr. atty., founder alternative resolution program, dir. cmty. justice program Denver City Attys. Office, Denver, 1991—. Mem.: Denver Bar Assn., Colo. Bar Assn., Colo. Women's Bar Assn. Presbyterian. Home: 3216 E 6th Ave Denver CO 80206-4407 Office: Denver City Attys Office 201 W Colfax Ave 12th fl Denver CO 80204-2623 E-mail: lauriesmithk@msn.com.

SMITH, LAVENSKI R. (VENCE SMITH), federal judge; m. Trendle Smith; 2 children. BA, U. Ark., 1981, JD, 1987. Law clerk Hall, Wright & Morris, 1985—87; staff lawyer Ozark Legal Svcs., 1987-91; pvt. practice Springdale, 1991-94; asst. prof. John Brown U., 1994-96; regulatory liaison Ark. Gov. Off., 1996—97; interim assoc. justice Ark. State Supreme Ct., 1999—2000; commr. Ark. Pub. Serv. Commn., 2001; judge U.S. 8th Circuit Court, 2002—. Bd. dirs. N.W. Ark. Christian Justice Ctr.; trainer Ptnrs. for Family Tng., 1993-96; chmn. Ark. Pub. Svc. Commn., 1996-98. Republican. Office: Fed Bldg Rm 316 35 E Mountain St Fayetteville AR 72702

SMITH, LAWRENCE A. lawyer; BA, U. Bridgeport, 1969; JD, Bklyn. Law Sch., 1976. Bar: N.Y. 1976. Corp. counsel Grumman Allied Industries, 1980-83; sr. v.p. legal The Home Depot, Inc., Atlanta, 1987—. Office: Home Depot Inc 2455 Paces Ferry Rd SE Atlanta GA 30339-4024

SMITH, LAWRENCE BERK, economist, educator; b. Toronto, Ont., Canada, Nov. 10, 1939; s. Isadore E. and Ruth (Berk) Smith; m. Tracey Tremayne-Lloyd; 1 stepchild, Brooke; children from previous marriage: Cynthia Joy, Ilyse Jan, Natalie Jill. BCom, U. Toronto, Can., 1962; AM, Harvard U., 1964, PhD, 1966. Tchg. fellow Harvard U., Cambridge, Mass., 1964—66, instr., 1966—69; from asst. prof. to assoc. prof. U. Toronto, 1966—72, prof., 1972—98, prof. emeritus, 1998—, dir. econs., assoc. chair dept. polic. economy, 1975—79. Pres. High Value Cons. Ltd., 1970—; cons. Bank Can., Ministry of Urban Affairs, Salomon Bros., Inc., others. Co-editor: (book) Canadian Economic Problems and Policies, 1970, Issues in Canadian Economics, 1974, Public Property: The Habitat Defense Continued, 1977; author: The Postwar Canadian Housing and Residential Mortgage Markets and the Role of Government, 1974, Anatomy of a Crisis: Canadian Housing Policy in the Seventies, 1977; co-author: Government in Canadian Capital Markets: Selected Cases, 1978; mem. editl. bd. Fraser Inst., 1975—, Jour. Real Estate Fin. and Econs., 1987—, Jour. Housing Econs., 1990—, mem. editl. rev. bd. Real Estate Econs., 1980—93; contbr. articles to profl. jours. Dep. chair Fed. Task Force Can. Mortgage and Housing Corp., 1979; trustee United Way Greater Toronto, 1989—92, Cmty. Info. Toronto, 1992—2002; bd. dirs. Fair Rental Policy Orgn. Ont., Canada, 1990—; trustee Bernard Betel Ctr. Cmty. Living, 1995—, pres., 1998—. Vis. scholar, Grad. Sch. Mgmt., UCLA, 1973—74, Grad. Sch. Bus. Adminstrn., U. Calif., Berkeley, 1981—82; Woodrow Wilson fellow, 1962—63, Can. Coun. fellow, 1963—64, Ford Motor Co. Internat. fellow, 1964—65, others. Mem.: Am. Fin. Assn., Am. Econs. Assn., Am. Real Estate and Urban Econs. Assn., Can. Econs. Assn. (exec. 1977—80, 1980—83). Avocations: tennis, sailing, yoga, bridge. Office: 121 Harbord St Toronto ON Canada M5S 1G9

SMITH, LAWRENCE S. communications executive; Grad., Ithaca Coll., 1969. Former CFO Advanta Corp.; former tax ptnr. Arthur Anderson & Co., Phila.; exec. v.p. Comcast, Phila., 1988—. Bd. dirs. E! Entertainment Television, Inc., QVC, Inc. Bd. dirs. Meadowood Corp., Perkomen Sch., YMCA of Greater Phila. Office: Comcast Corp 1500 Market St Philadelphia PA 19102-2100

SMITH, LAWRENCE SHANNON, lawyer; b. Dallas, Oct. 6, 1943; s. Lawrence Shannon and Joan Smith. BA, U. Tex., 1965, JD, 1970. Bar: Tex. 1970, U.S. Supreme Ct. 1974. Shareholder Small, Craig, & Werkenthin, Austin, Tex., 1970—95; ptnr. Smith, Majcher & Mudge, Austin, 1995—. 1st lt. U.S. Army, 1966—68, Korea. Office: Smith Majcher & Mudge LLP 816 Congress Ave Ste 1270 Austin TX 78701-2476

SMITH, LEE ELTON, surgery educator, retired military officer; b. Ventura, Calif., July 19, 1937; s. Raymond Elroy and Edith Irene (Jordan) S.; m. Carole Sue Smith; children: Justine Diane, Alexander Loren. BS, U. Calif., Berkeley, 1959; MD, U. Calif., San Francisco, 1962. Diplomate Am. Bd. Surgery, Am. Bd. Colon and Rectal Surgery (pres. 1992-93). Commd. ens. USN, 1960, advanced through grades to capt., 1977; intern U. Utah, Salt Lake City, 1962-63; resident USN, San Diego, 1966-70, staff surgeon Bremerton, Wash., 1970-72; resident colorectal surgery U. Minn., Mpls., 1972-73; dir. colorectal surgery Nat. Naval Med. Ctr. USN, Bethesda, Md., 1973-82, ret., 1983, 1982; clin. prof. surgery Uniformed Svcs. U., Bethesda, 1976—; prof. surgery George Washington U., Washington, 1983-96, Georgetown U., Washington, 2001—; dir. sect. of colon and rectal surgery Washington Hosp. Ctr., 1996—. Pres. Am. Bd. Colon and Rectal Surgery, 1993-94. Editor: Practical Guide to Anorectal Physiology, 1990, 2d edit., 1995; assoc. editor Diseases of the Colon and Rectum, 1984-96, Perspectives in Colon and Rectal Surgery, 1989-2000. Mem. ACS (pres. Met. Washington chpt. 1993-94), Soc. Am. Gastrointestinal Endoscopic Surgeons (pres. 1989-90), Am. Cancer Soc. (v.p. D.C. chpt. 1985-93), Am. Soc. Colon & Rectal Surgeons (pres. 1998-99). Home: 7512 16th St NW Washington DC 20012 Office: Washington Hosp Ctr 106 Irving St NW Washington DC 20010-2975 Office Phone: 202-877-8484.

SMITH, LEILA HENTZEN, artist; b. Milw., May 20, 1932; d. Erwin Albert and Marian Leila (Austin) Hentzen; m. Richard Howard Smith, Sept. 12, 1959; 1 child, Jennie. BFA, Miami U., 1955; cert., Famous Artists Schs., 1959. Quilting tchr. Milw. Pub. Schs., 1975-79. One-woman shows include Boerner Bot. Gardens, Whitnall Park, Wis., 1995, 2 person show, Firefly Gallery, Wauwatosa, Wis., 2003, exhibited in group shows at Milw. Art Ctr., 1961, West Bend (Wis.) Gallery Fine Arts, 1963, Wustum Mus. Art, Racine, Wis., 1966, Mapledale Sch. Gallery, Bayside, Wis., 1977, 1981, Mount Mary Coll., Milw., 1969—77, Artist's World Gallery, Cedarburg, Wis., 1975, Mount Mary Coll., Milw., 1979—2001, Ozaukee Art Ctr, Cedarburg, Wis., 1982—86, John Michael Kohler Arts Ctr., Sheboygan, Wis., 1984, 1987, 1989—2002, Cedarburg Cultural Ctr., 1988—2001, West Bend Gallery Fine Arts, 1993, Ozaukee Art Ctr, Cedarburg, Wis., 1993, Rahr-West Art Mus., Manitowoc, Wis., 1994, West Bend Gallery Fine Arts, 1996, Gallery 110 North, Plymouth, Wis., 1996, Rahr-West Art Mus., Manitowoc, Wis., 1997, Cardinal Stritch U., 1998—2003, West Bend Gallery Fine Arts, 1999, 2002, Represented in

permanent collections Milw. County Art Commn. Women's aux. vol. Salvation Army, Milw.; mem. dean's adv. coun. U. Wis. Milw. Sch. Arts. Recipient Honorable Mention for painting Bayshore Merchants Assn, 1969, Delta Gamma Art Fair, 1981, Best of Show for painting John Michael Kohler Arts Ctr., 1988. Mem. AAUW, Cedarburg Artists Guild, Wis. Watercolor Soc., Seven Arts Soc. Milw. (pres. 1967-68, painters group chmn. 1962-63), DAR (Milw. chpt. Holiday Folk Fair chmn. 1965-76, libr. historian 1974-77, corr. sec. 1977-80, dir. 1983-86, rec. sec. 1992-95, regent 1995-98, Outstanding Jr. Mem. 1966), Wis. Soc. Daus. of Founders and Patriots of Am. (pres. 1964-66, 2d v.p. 1966-68, 70-73, corr. sec. 1976-79), Wis. Ct. Assts., Nat. Soc. Women Descendants Ancient and Hon. Arty. Co. Boston, Wis. Soc. Mayflower Descendants (sec. 1999-02), Delta Zeta. Congregationalist. Avocations: quilting, needlecrafts, swimming.

SMITH, LEON G. physician, educator; b. N.Y.C., Dec. 3, 1929; s. George and Pheobe (Besharo) S.; m. Margaret Davis, June 10, 1958; children: Leon, Michele, Stephen, Ann, Marshall. BA, NYU, 1951; MD, Georgetown U., 1956. Asst. prof. N.J. Med. Sch., Newark, 1962-70, prof. of medicine and rsch. medicine, 1970—; chmn. of medicine, info. dir. St. Michael's Med. Ctr., Newark, N.J., 1962—. Cons. Pub. Health Svc., Staten Island, N.Y.C., 1963-70. Republican. Roman Catholic. Avocations: sports, gardening, politics. Office: 306 King Blvd Newark NJ 07102-2011

SMITH, LEONARD GLENN, artist, educator, hypnotherapist; b. Runnels County, Tex., May 20, 1939; s. Leonard Frank Smith and Letha Bowen; m. Joan Karen Johnsos, 1971 (div. 1992); 1 child, Jeffrey Robert. BS in Edn., Abilene Christian Coll., Tex., 1957—60; MS, Trinity U., San Antonio, 1961—63; PhD, U. Okla., Norman, 1964—67. Cert. Hypnotherapist Nat. Guild of Hypnotists, 2002. Tchr. Eisenhower Jr. H.S., San Antonio, 1960—61, Rogers Jr. H.S., San Antonio, 1962—63; social sci. dept. chmn. Okla. Christian Coll., Oklahoma City, 1963—64; spl. instr. of edn. U. Okla., Norman, 1966—67; asst. prof., assoc. prof., prof. Coll. Edn., Iowa State U., Ames, 1967—84; prof., assoc. dean for grad. studies and rsch. U. Houston, Clear Lake City, 1984—85; prof. and chair, dept. of leadership and ednl. policy studies No. Ill. U., DeKalb, 1985—2003. Pres. Coun. of Learned Societies in Edn., 1992—93; exec. coun. Nat. Coun. for the Accreditation of Tchr. Edn., Washington, 1993—94. Contbr. chapters to books. Mem.: Nat. Guild of Hypnotists. Personal E-mail: lglenns@comcast.net.

SMITH, LEONORE RAE, artist; b. Chgo. d. Leon and Rose (Hershfield) Goodman; m. Paul Carl Smith, Apr. 17, 1943; children: Jill Henderson, Laurie Christman. Student, Chgo. Art Inst., 1935-40, U. Chgo., 1939—. Performer in many Broadway shows, with Met. Opera Quartet, Carnegie Hall, nat. concerts; portrait, landscape painter; signature artist Oil Painters of Am., Chgo., 1992-2000, Am. Acad. of Women Artists, 1997-98; ofcl. artist U.S. Coast Guard, Washington, 1989-2000; cert. artist Am. Portrait Soc., Huntington Harbor, Calif., 1985; nat. adv. bd. The Portrait Club, N.Y.C., 1983. Pres. Pacific Palisades Rep. Women, Calif. Named one of Master Artists of the World, Internat. Artist Mag., 1996; recipient Best of Show awards, Salamagundi U.S. Coast Guard, 1989, Pacific Palisades Art Assn., 1987, 1st prize in oils, Greater L.A. Art Competition, Santa Monica, Calif., 1995, prize, The Artist's Mag., 1995, Internat. Soc. Artists, 1977, 1st pl. award, Dream Studio competition, 1996, 1st pl. in portrait, O.P.A. Nat. Show, 2001, award, Northlight Art Mag., 2002, Internat. Artist Mag., 2002, several awards, Calif. Art Club, shown at Nat. Mus. Naval Aviation, Carnegie Mus., Frederick Weisman Mus., Malibu, Calif. Mem. Am. Acad. Women Artists (signature), Salmagundi Club, Pacific Palisades Art Assn. (past pres.), Calif. Art Club, Oil Painters of Am. (signature, 1st Pl. 2001), Am. Portrait Soc. (cert.). Avocations: singing, acting, poetry. Office Phone: 310-454-4223.

SMITH, LESLIE ROPER, hospital administrator, health facility administrator; b. Stockton, Calif., June 20, 1928; s. Austin J. and Helen (Roper) S.; m. Edith Sue Fincher, June 22, 1952; children: Melinda Sue, Leslie Erin, Timothy Brian. AB, U. Pacific, 1951; MS in Pub. Adminstrn, U. So. Calif., 1956. Adminstrv. asst. Ranchos Los Amigos Hosp., Downey, Calif., 1953-57; asst. adminstr. Harbor Gen. Hosp., Torrance, Calif., 1957-65; adminstr. Harbor UCLA Med. Ctr., 1966-71; acting regional dir. Los Angeles County Coastal Health Services Region, 1973; pres. San Pedro Peninsula Hosp., San Pedro, Cal., 1974-86; exec. dir. Los Angeles County/U. So. Calif. Med. Center, 1971-73; adminstr. Long Beach (Calif.) Hosp., 1965-66; assoc. clin. prof. community medicine and pub. health, also emergency medicine U. So. Calif., 1968-78; instr. U. So. Calif. (Sch. Pub. Adminstrn.), 1968; preceptor hosp. adminstrn. UCLA Sch. Pub. Health, 1964—; chief exec. officer French Hosp. Med. Ctr. and Health Plan, 1986-87; dir. health care services McCormack & Farrow, 1987—. Lectr. in field, 1963—; cons. emergency health services HEW, 1970-73; chmn. com. disaster preparedness Hosp. Council So. Calif., 1966-72, sec., 1971—, pres., 1973; mem. Calif. Assembly Com. on Emergency Med. Services, 1970, Calif. Emergency Med. Adv. Com., 1972-75, Los Angeles County Commn. on Emergency Med. Services, 1975-83, Los Angeles Health Planning and Devel. Agy. Commn., 1980-83; bd. dirs. Blue Cross of So. Calif.; mem. hosp. relations com. Blue Cross of Calif.; mem. adv. com. on emergency health services Calif. Dept. Health, 1974-75; bd. dirs., mem. exec. com. Truck Ins. Exchange of Farmers Ins. Group, 1977-82; bd. dirs. Hosp. Council of So. Calif., 1966-76, 81-86, Health Resources Inst., 1985-86; chmn. Preferred Health Network, 1983-86 Mem. goals com., Torrance, 1968—; pres. Silver Spur Little League, Palos Verdes, 1969-70. Served with AUS, 1946-48. Recipient Silver Knight and Gold Knight award Nat. Mgmt. Assn., 1970, 85, Walker Fellowship award, 1976 Fellow Am. Coll. Health Care Execs. (life); mem. Am., Nat. mgmt. assns., Am. Hosp. Assn. (chmn. com. on community emergency health services 1973), Calif. Hosp. Assn. (chmn. com. emergency services 1965-70, trustee 1973-76, bd. dirs. Calif. Ins. Service Group 1980-82), County Suprs. Assn. Calif. (chmn. joint subcom. on emergency care 1970) Presbyn. (elder, trustee). Home: 27 Marseille Laguna Niguel CA 92677-5400 Personal E-mail: leslie.smith@cox.net.

SMITH, LEWIS MOTTER, JR., retired advertising and direct marketing executive; b. Kansas City, Mo., Nov. 4, 1932; s. Lewis Motter and Virginia (Smith) S.; m. Alice Allen, June 28, 1975; children: Katherine Allen, Patience Allen. Student, Kenyon Coll., 1951-53, Columbia U., 1956-58. Copywriter mail order divsn. Grolier Soc., Inc., N.Y.C., 1957-59; free lance copywriter Santa Fe, N.M., 1960-61; v.p. creative svcs. Grolier Enterprises Inc., N.Y.C., 1962-67; v.p., creative planning dir. Wunderman, Ricotta & Kline, Inc., N.Y.C., 1968-72; exec. v.p., creative dir., 1972-79; exec. v.p. Young & Rubicam Direct Mktg. Group, 1980; sr. v.p., dir. mktg. Book-of-the-Month Club, Inc., 1980-84, dir., 1981-84; exec. v.p., creative dir. SSC&B: Vos Direct Inc., N.Y.C., 1985-87; pres., dir. creative services Lintas: Direct Inc. (formerly SSC&B: Vos Direct Inc.), N.Y.C., 1987-89; pres. Lew Smith & Assocs., Inc., Hyde Park, NY, 1989—2001. Bd. dirs. Young Concert Artists, Inc., N.Y.C., 1966-67, Harlem Sch. Arts, 1967-68. Served with U.S. Army, 1953-56. Mem. Delta Phi. Episcopalian. Home: 215 East Dr Hurley NY 12443

SMITH, LINDA A. retired congresswoman; m. Vern Smith; children: Sheri, Robi. Office mgr.; former mem. Wash. State Ho. of Reps.; mem. Wash. State Senate; congresswoman, Wash. 3rd Dist. U.S. House Reps., Washington, 1995-98; mem. resources com., small bus. com.; founder, dir. Shared Hope Internat., Vancouver, Wash., 1998—. Republican. Home: 10009 NW Ridgecrest Ave Vancouver WA 98685-5159 Office: Shared Hope Internat PO Box 65337 Vancouver WA 98665

SMITH, LINDA GENE, legislative staff member; BA, Brigham Young U., 1964, MA, 1966; postgrad., Denver U., U. Nat. Mexico, Mexico City. TV script writer, prodr., on-camera tchr. WETA, 1974; press sec., legis. asst. Rep. Allan Howe, 1975-76; spl. asst. Rep. Teno Roncalio, Wyo., 1977-78; press sec. Rep. Gillis Long, La., 1978-85, Ho. Dem. Caucus, 1981-85; chief of staff U.S. Rep. Tim Wirth, Colo., 1985-86, U.S. Rep. Howard L. Berman, Washington, 1986—. Office: 2330 Rayburn Ho Office Bldg Washington DC 20515-0001

SMITH, LIZ (MARY ELIZABETH SMITH), newspaper columnist, broadcast journalist; b. Ft. Worth, Feb. 2, 1923; d. Sloan and Sarah Elizabeth (McCall) S. B.J., U. Tex., 1948. Editor Dell Publns., N.Y.C., 1950-53; assoc. producer CBS Radio, 1953-55, NBC-TV, 1955-59; assoc. Cholly Knickerbocker newspaper column, N.Y.C., 1959-64; film critic Cosmpolitan mag., 1966; columnist Chgo. Tribune-N.Y. Daily News Syndicate (now Tribune Media Services), 1976-91; TV commentator WNBC-TV, N.Y.C., 1978-91; commentator Fox-TV, N.Y.C., 1991—; columnist Newsday, L.A. Times Syndicate, 1991—, Family Circle mag., 1993—; freelance mag. writer; commentator Gossip Show E! Entertainment, 1993—; columnist N.Y. Post, N.Y.C., 1995—, 1995—. Author: The Mother Book, 1978. Home and Office: 160 E 38th St New York NY 10016-2651 *A career in Journalism? Any career at all? I say learn to type. Read a lot. Keep on keeping on. Work is its own reward and success is loving your work. And remember, never give up. After the Middle Ages comes the Renaissance.*

SMITH, LLOYD, musician; b. Cleve., Dec. 1, 1941; s. Thomas George Russell and Anita May (Speer) S.; m. Rheta R. Naylor, Mar. 30, 1967 (div. Nov. 1994); 1 child, Peter Eldon; m. Nancy R. Bean, June 6, 1995. MusB, Curtis Inst. Music, 1965. Tchr. Settlement Music Sch., 1970-72, 92—. Cellist Pitts. Symphony, 1965-67, Phila. Orch., 1967—, asst. prin. cello, 1988-2002, acting assoc. prin. cello, 2002-2003, ret., 2003; soloist Indpls. Symphony, 1958, 68, Garden State Philharm., 1964, Lansdowne Symphony, 1965, West Jersey Chamber Orch., 1991, Haverford-Bryn Mawr Symphony, 1992, The Phila. Orch., 1994, Ocean City Symphony, 2001, The Brn Athym Orch., 2003; mem. Huntingdon Trio, 1974-93, Wister quartet, 1988—; composer Sonata for cello and piano, Op. 1, 1997, Quintet, Op. 2 for Saratoga Chamber Music Festival, 1998, duet for cello Four Hands, 1999, "You're Invited" for string quartet and violin, 1999, Suite for accordion and strings, Op. 4, 2000, String Quartet Op. 3, 2000, Full Circle for cello Op. 5, 2003, Ceremonial, Op. 6 for 8 cellos, 2004, Trio for cellos, Op. 7, 2004. Alumni rep. Curtis Inst. Music Bd. Trustees, chmn. Parents' Com., 1989-90; bd. dirs. Phila. Youth Orch., 1987-91, Community Out Reach Partnership, 1988-90. Recipient C. Hartman Kuhn award for outstanding achievement, Phila. Orch., 2002. Mem. Am. Soc. Ancient Instruments (asst. artistic dir. 1975-77, music dir. 1977-80), Curtis Inst. Music Nat. Alumni Assn. (treas., bd. dirs. 1989-90), 1807 & Friends (bd. dirs. 1994—). Home and Office: 5639 E Wister St Philadelphia PA 19144-1522 E-mail: frnd1807@verizon.net.

SMITH, LLOYD HOLLINGSWORTH, physician; b. Easley, S.C., Mar. 27, 1924; s. Lloyd H. and Phyllis (Page) S.; m. Margaret Constance Avery, Feb. 27, 1954; children— Virginia Constance, Christopher Avery, Rebecca Anne, Charlotte Page, Elizabeth Hollingsworth, Jeffrey Hollingsworth. AB, Washington and Lee U., 1944, D.Sc., 1969; MD, Harvard, 1948. Intern, then resident Mass. Gen. Hosp., Boston, 1948-50, chief resident physician, 1955-56; mem. Harvard Soc. Fellows, 1952-54; asst. prof. Harvard Soc. Fellows (Med. Sch.), 1956-63; vis. investigator Karolinska Inst., Stockholm, 1954-55, Oxford (Eng.) U., 1963-64; prof. medicine, chmn. dept. U. Calif. Med. Sch., San Francisco, 1964-85, assoc dean, 1985-2000. Mem. Pres.'s Sci. Adv. Com., 1970-73 Bd. overseers Harvard, 1974-80. Served to capt., M.C. AUS, 1950-52. Mem. Am. Acad. Arts and Scis., Am. Soc. Clin. Investigation (pres. 1969-70), Western Soc. Clin. Rsch. (pres. 1969-70), Assn. Am. Physicians (pres. 1974-75), Am. Fedn. Clin. Rsch. Achievements include special research genetic and metabolic diseases. Home: 309 Evergreen Dr Kentfield CA 94904-2709 Office: U Calif San Francisco Med Ctr San Francisco CA 94143-0001 E-mail: lloydhsmith@aol.com.

SMITH, LOIS ANN (L.A. SMITH), foundation administrator, consultant; b. Chattanooga, Nov. 30, 1944; d. W. and Rose C. (Tucker) Hicks; divorced; 1 child, Tony A. Student, Lemoyne-Owen Coll., 1962-64; BA in Sociology and Bus. Adminstrn., Howard U., 1976, postgrad., 1977-78. Cert. notary pub., Md., Ga. Field underwriter, sales trainer N.Y. Life Ins. Co., Franklin Life Ins. Co., 1979-82; pres., gen. mgr. Lotona Enterprises, Inc., Washington, 1979-85; mktg. coord. Montgomery County Dept. Transp., Md., 1985-87; fund raising and tng. cons. Princess Ann & Co., Washington, 1987-91; grant/contract adminstr. coll. medicine Howard U., NIH, Washington, 1991-92; founder, exec. dir. Good News & Give Aways, Inc., Tucker, Ga., 1989—. Pub. speaker Princess Ann & Co., Md., Ga., 1970-94, seminar presenter, 1985-94; radio host Managing Your Income & Personal Budget; freelance writer, 1975—; counselor in various fields, 1977—. Author: The Most Precious Moments, 1973, Let's Consider, A Sociological View of Employment, 1976, (play) A Reversible Oreo, 1974; pub., editor newsletter Good News & Give Aways, Inc., 1989-93; author, speaker (audio cassette tapes) I Care . . ., 1989, 90. Speaker, soloist various ednl., religious and civic orgns., 1960—; coord. Up the Hill Gang, 1979—; treas. Faith Cmty. Bapt. Ch., 1986-87; pub. speaker, vol. Dekalb Responds/Dekalb Econ. Opportunity Authority, Decatur, Ga., 1993-94. Recipient Disting. Svc. award Sta. WNOO, 1979. Mem. Ga. Coll. Counselors Assn., Bus. & Profl. Women's Club (charter, editor newsletter 1980-82, Woman of Yr. honoree 1980), Kappa Delta Pi, Phi Beta Lambda. Avocations: singing, fund raising. Office: Good News & Give Aways Inc PO Box 1495 Suitland MD 20752-1495

SMITH, LOIS ARLENE, actress, writer; b. Topeka, Nov. 3, 1930; d. William Oren and Carrie D. (Gottshalk) Humbert; m. Wesley Dale Smith, Nov. 5, 1948 (div. 1973); 1 child, Moon Elizabeth. Student, U. Wash., 1948-50; studied with Lee Strasberg, Actor's Studio, N.Y.C., 1955—. Guest dir. Juilliard Sch., 1987; Clarence Ross fellow Am. Theater Wing at Eugene O'Neill Theater Ctr., 1983; mem. adv. panel program fund Pub. Broadcasting Service, 1981-82; hon. founder Harold Clurman Theatre Artists Fund, Ctr. for Arts, SUNY-Purchase, 1981 Author: play All There Is, 1982; debut in Time Out for Ginger, 1952; actress Broadway and off-Broadway prodns., 1952—; stage appearances include Theater of the Living Arts, Mark Taper Forum, Long Wharf Theater, Balt. Centerstage and Steppenwolf Theater Co.; appears on network and pub. TV programs; stage appearances include, The Young and the Beautiful, 1955, The Glass Menagerie, 1956, Blues for Mr. Charlie, 1964, Orpheus Descending, 1957, Miss Julie, 1966, Uncle Vanya, 1965, 69, The Iceman Cometh, 1973, Harry Outside, 1975, Hillbilly Women, 1979, 81, the Vienna Notes, 1985, The Stick Wife, April Snow, 1987, The Grapes of Wrath, 1988-89, 90, Measure for Measure, Beside Herself, 1989, Escape from Happiness, 1993, Buried Child, 1995-96, Defying Gravity, 1997, Impossible Marriage, 1998, Mrs. Warren's Profession, 1999, Give Me Your Answer, Do, 1999, Mother Courage, 2001; films include East of Eden, 1955, Five Easy Pieces, 1970, Next Stop Greenwich Village, 1975, Resurrection, 1980, Green Card, 1990, Fried Green Tomatoes, 1991, Falling Down, 1993, How to Make an American Quilt, 1995, Dead Man Walking, 1995, Larger than Life, 1996, Twister, 1996, Tumbleweeds, 1998, Minority Report, 2002, The Laramie Project, 2002, Iron-Jawed Angels, 2004, Best Thief in the World, 2004, P.S., 2004. Named Best Supporting Actress for Five Easy Pieces, Nat. Soc. Film Critics, 1971; recipient Tony nominations for Grapes of Wrath, 1990, Buried Child, 1996; named to Filmdom's Famous Fives for East of Eden, Failm Daily mag., 1955, Steppenwolf Ensemble Nat. Medal of Arts, 1998. Mem. SAG, AFTRA, Actors Equity Assn., Dramatists Guild, Actors Studio, Ensemble Studio Theater, Steppenwolf Theatre Co. Ensemble, Acad. Motion Picture Arts and Scis.

SMITH, LONNIE MAX, diversified industries executive; b. Twin Falls, Idaho, July 28, 1944; s. Lonnie E. and Christie (Stuart) S.; m. Cheryl Diane Smith, June 10, 1968; children: Kristen, Maryam, Rebecca, Michael, Catherine. BSEE, Utah State U., 1967; MBA, Harvard U., 1974. Engr., mgr. field services, mgr. tech. services to asst. to v.p. plans and control IBM Corp., San Francisco, Palo Alto, Calif., and White Plains, N.Y., 1967-74; mgr., corp. strategy, then cons. Boston Cons. Group, 1974-76; exec. v.p. Am. Tourister, Inc., Warren, R.I., 1978-81; sr. v.p. corp. planning Hillenbrand Industries, Inc., Batesville, Ind., 1977-78, sr. exec. v.p., 1982-97, also bd. dirs., 1997; pres., CEO Intuitive Surgical Inc., Mountain View, Calif., 1997—. Pres. Biosite Diagnostics, Lozion Corp. Served to 1st lt. U.S. Army, 1969-72. Mem. Lds Ch. Avocations: tennis, skiing. Office: Intuitive Surg 950 Kifer Rd Sunnyvale CA 94086-5206

SMITH, LORAN BRADFORD, education educator; b. Medford, Mass., July 23, 1946; s. Gordon T. and Edith A. S. BA, Salem State Coll., 1968; MA, Okla. State U., 1971; PhD, U. Nebr., 1980. Instr. Black Hills State Coll., Spearfish, S.D., 1971-74, Augustana Coll., Sioux Falls, S.D., 1974-77; asst. prof. Mo. So. State Coll., Joplin, 1980-82, Washburn U., Topeka, Kans., 1982-86, assoc. prof., 1988-92; grad. faculty U. Kans., Lawrence, 1988-89; prof. Washburn U., 1992—. Election analyst KSNT-TV, Topeka, 1984-92. Contbr. articles to profl. jours. Chair pilot task force City of Topeka, 1983-84, mem. charter rev. com., 1999; chair Univ. Coun.; mem. coll. faculty coun., chair CAS curriculum com., social sci. divsn. Mem. Am. Polit. Sci. Assn., Am. Soc. Pub. Adminstrs. (Kans. chpt. v.p. 1985-87, pres. 1987-88), Urban Affairs Assn., Kansas Delta Alumni Corp., Sigma Phi Epsilon (Disting. Alumnus award 1997). Home: 4301 SW 15th St Apt 309 Topeka KS 66604-4311 Office: Washburn U 1700 SW College Ave Topeka KS 66621-0001 Office Phone: 785-231-1010 2026.

SMITH, LOREN ALLAN, federal judge; b. Chgo., Dec. 22, 1944; m. Catherine Yore; children: Loren Jr., Adam (dec.). BA in Polit. Sci., Northwestern U., 1966, JD, 1969; LLD (hon.), John Marshall Law Sch., 1995, Capital U. Law Sch., 1996, Campbell U., 1997. Bar: Ill. 1970, U.S. Ct. Mil. Appeals 1973, U.S. Ct. Appeals (D.C. cir.) 1974, U.S. Supreme Ct. 1974, U.S. Ct. Claims, 1985, U.S. Ct. Appeals (fed. cir.) 1986, U.S. Ct. Fed. Claims. Host nightly radio talk show What's Best for America?, 1972; cons. Sidney & Austin, Chgo., 1972-73; gen. atty. FCC, 1973; asst. to spl. counsel to the pres. White House, Washington, 1973-74; spl. asst. U.S. Atty., D.C., 1974-75; chief counsel Reagan for Pres. campaigns, 1976, 80; prof. Del. Law Sch., 1976-84; dep. dir. Office Exec. Br. Mgmt. Presdl. Transition, 1980-81; chmn. Adminstrv. Conf. U.S., 1981-85; appointed judge U.S. Ct. Fed. Claims, Washington, 1985, designated chief judge, 1986-2000; sr. judge, 2000—. Prof. law Del. Law Sch., 1976-84; adj. prof. Internat. Law Sch., 1973-74, Disting. lectr. Columbus Sch. Law, Cath. U. Am., 1996—; Disting. adj. prof. law George Mason U. Sch. Law, 1998—; past mem. Pres.'s Cabinet Coun. on Legal Policy, Pres.' Cabinet Coun. on Mgmt. and Adminstrn.; chmn. Coun. Ind. Regulatory Agys.; served as disting. jurist in residence U. Denver; Allen chair U. Richmond Sch. Law, 1995. Co-author: Black America and Organized Labor: A Fair Deal?, 1979; contbr. articles to profl. jours. Adv. bd. mem. WETA Pub. Radio Cmty. Adv. Bd. Recipient Presdl. medal Cath. U. Am. Law Sch., 1993, Romanian medal of justice Romanian Min. of Justice, 1995, Ronald Reagan Pub. Svc. award Nat. Property Rights Conf., 1997. Mem. Bar Assn. D.C. (hon. mem., judicial honoree award 1997), Univ. Club (Washington, named club mem. of the yr. 1991, chmn. entertainment com., centennial com.). Republican. Jewish. Office: US Ct of Fed Claims 717 Madison Pl NW Suite 328 Washington DC 20005

SMITH, LORETTA MAE, civilian military officer; b. Washington Twp., Pa., May 25, 1939; d. Irvin Calvin and Viola Mary (Deibler) Shambaugh; 1 child, Miriam Estella Smith. B in Humanities, Pa. State U., 1984. Bookkeeper Harrisburg (Pa.) Nat. Bank, 1957-62; contract specialist USN, Mechanicsburg, Pa., 1987—2001; ret., 2001. Founder Telecare, Harrisburg, Pa., 1972-82. Active ARC, instr. CPR, 1982—; active Girl Scouts U.S.A., trainer, 1972—. Recipient Hemlock award Hemlock coun. Girl Scouts U.S., Harrisburg, 1981; Merit scholar Hall Found., 1982. Mem. Nat. Contract Mgmt. Assn., Mensa. Avocations: walking in woods, birding, swimming, making music.

SMITH, LOUIS, sports association administrator; m. Sharon Smith; 4 children. BSEE, U. Mo., Rolla; MBA, Rockhurst Coll.; postgrad., U. Kans. Assoc. engr. to asst. gen. mgr. AlliedSignal Inc., Kansas City, Mo., 1966-86, v.p. prodn. ops. Bendix Aerospace Sector Arlington, Va., 1986-88; v.p. mfg. AlliedSignal Aerospace Co., Torrance, Calif., 1988-89; asst. gen. mgr., adminstrn. AlliedSignal Inc., Kansas City, 1989-90, pres., 1990-95; pres., COO, bd. dirs. Ewing Marion Kauffman Found., Kansas City, 1995—. Bd. dirs. Western Resources, Commerce Bank Kansas City. Bd. dirs. Kansas City Royals, Greater Kansas City C. of C., Midwest Rsch. Inst., Civic Coun. Greater Kansas City, The Learning Exch.; mem. exec. com. Kansas City Area Devel. Coun., Rockhurst Coll. Bd. Trustees; mem. numerous coms. U. Mo.-Rolla, U. Kans.;past chmn. corp. devel. coun., mem. Acad. Elec. Engring. U. Mo.-Rolla; adv. bd. U. Kans. Sch. Engring. On Board of Directors of KC Royals since 1992. Office: Kansas City Royals Kauffman Stadium PO Box 419969 Kansas City MO 64141-6969

SMITH, LOWNDES A. (LON), insurance company executive; Grad. cum laude, Babson Coll. Cert. mgmt. acct. Various fin. positions Mo. Fidelity Life, St. Louis, Conn. Gen. Life Ins. Co. (now CIGNA); dir., corp. acctg., contr., group contr. Hartford, 1968—; sr. v.p. Hartford Fin. Svcs. Group Inc., 1987, vice chmn., pres., CEO, 1996—. Mem.: Am. Coun. Life Inst. (bd. dirs.). Office: Hartford Plz 690 Asylum Ave Hartford CT 06105-3845

SMITH, LYLE MATTHEW, web producer, writer; b. Perth Amboy, NJ, May 3, 1968; s. Lyle Matthew and Agnes Catherine Smith. BA, Villanova U., 1990. Copy editor Morristown Daily Record, Parsippany, NJ, 1990—93; editor Echoes Sentinel, Stirling, NJ, 1993—94, Florham Pk. Eagle, Madison, NJ, 1994—95, IEEE, Piscataway, NJ, 1995—96, documentation specialist, 1996—99, web prod., 2000—03. Author: (plays) Killing Time, 1991, Fire in the Hole, 1993, Diggin the Boneyard, 2002. Recipient Jasper award silver, Jersey Shore Pub. Rels. Assn., 2002, 2d Pl. award for Pub. Svc., NJ Press Assn., 1993, Spl. Sect. award, 1994.

SMITH, MAGGIE CARROLL See SMITH, MARGARET A.

SMITH, M(AHLON) BREWSTER, retired psychologist, educator; b. Syracuse, N.Y., June 26, 1919; s. Mahlon Ellwood and Blanche Alice (Hinman) S.; m. Jean Dresden Schwartz, June 1942 (div. 1945); m. Deborah Anderson, June, 1947; children: Joshua H., T. Daniel, Rebecca M., J. Torquil. Student, Reed Coll., Portland, Oreg., 1935- 38; AB, Stanford U., 1939, AM, 1940; PhD, Harvard U., 1947. Rantoul scholar Harvard U., 1940-41; jr. analyst Office Coordinator of Information, U.S. Govt., 1941; Social Sci. Research Council fellow Harvard U., 1946-47; asst. prof. social psychology Harvard U. (Dept. Social Relations), 1947-49; prof. psychology, chmn. dept. Vassar Coll., 1949-52; staff Social Sci. Research Council, 1952-56; prof. psychology NYU, 1956-59, U. Calif. at Berkeley, 1959-68, dir. Inst. Human Devel., 1965-68; prof., chmn. dept. psychology U. Chgo., 1968-70; prof. psychology U. Calif. at Santa Cruz, 1970-88, prof. emeritus, 1988—, vice chancellor social scis., 1970-75, ret. Fellow Center Advanced Studies Behavioral Scis., 1964-65; Vice pres. Joint Commn. Mental Illness and Health, 1955-61 Author: Social Psychology and Human Values, 1969, Humanizing Social Psychology, 1974, Values, Self and Society, 1991, For a significant Social Psychology, 2003; co-author: The American Soldier, 1949, Opinions and Personality, 1956; editor: Jour. Social Issues, 1951-55, Jour. Abnormal Soc. Psychology, 1956-61; contbr. articles to profl. jours. Served from pvt. to maj. Adj. Gen. Div. AUS, 1942-46; research officer Information and Edn. div. War Dept., 1943-46; research asso. spl. com. on soldier attitudes Social Sci. Research Council 1946. Decorated Bronze Star medal.; NIMH fellow, 1964-65, NEH fellow, 1975-76; Belding scholar Found. for Child Devel., 1982-83; Gold medal award lifetime contbn. to psychology in pub. interest Am. Psychol. Found., 1992. Fellow AAAS, APA (pres. 1978, Disting. Contbn. to Pub. Interest award 1988, Henry A. Murray award in personality psychology 1993); mem. Soc. Psychol. Study Social Issues (pres. 1959, Kurt Lewin Meml. award 1986), Western Psychol. Assn. (pres. 1986, Lifetime Contbn. award 1996), Psychologists for Social Responsibility (pres. 1987-90), Internat. Soc. Polit. Psychology (Harold Lasswell award 1993), Internat. Assn. Applied Psychology (pres. divsn. polit. psychology 1994-98), Cosmos Club (Washington), Soc. for Study of Peace, Conflict and Violence (Lifetime Contbn. to Peace Psychology award 1999), Phi Beta Kappa, Sigma Xi. Democrat. Home: 316 Escalona Dr Santa Cruz CA 95060-2607 Office Phone: 831-459-2337. Business E-mail: brsmith@cats.ucsc.edu.

SMITH, MALCOLM BARRY ESTES, philosophy educator, lawyer; b. Houston, Oct. 24, 1939; s. Fairleigh Estes and Norna Barry (McNab) S.; m. Patricia Sweetser; children: Malcolm, Eric. BA, Va. Mil. Inst., 1961; PhD, Cornell U., 1969; JD, U. Calif., Berkeley, 1984. BarL Mass. 1985, U.S. Supreme Ct. 1992. Instr. philosophy Smith Coll., Northampton, Mass., 1967-69, asst. prof. philosophy, 1969-74, assoc. prof., 1974-79, prof., 1979—2002, prof. emeritus, 2002—. Served to capt. USAR, 1964-66. Mem. Mass. Bar Assn., Am. Philos. Assn. Home: 9 Park St Northampton MA 01062-1236 Office: Smith Coll Dept Philosophy PO Box 839 Northampton MA 01061-0839 Office Phone: 413-586-0679. E-mail: mbsmith@smith.edu.

SMITH, MALCOLM BERNARD, investment company executive; b. Lynn, Mass., May 27, 1923; s. Philip and Ida (Zenis) S.; m. Betty Booth, June 20, 1948; children: Eric, Daniel. BA summa cum laude, Dartmouth Coll., 1944; MA in Econs., Harvard U., 1948; hon. degree, New Sch. for Social Rsch., 1995. Sec. Gen. Am. Investors Co., N.Y.C., 1956-57, treas., 1957-59, v.p., 1958-61, pres., 1961-89, vice chmn., 1989-97; sr. cons., 1997—. Chmn. fin. com. N.Y. Found., 1973—82, treas., 1979—82, trustee, 1973—89; chmn. N.Y. Found., 1982—85; chmn. New Sch. for Social Rsch., N.Y.C., 1985—95, trustee, 1982—, treas., 1982—84, chmn. ednl. policy com., 1984—85, chmn. exec. com., 1985—95; mem. investment com. Phi Beta Kappa Found., 1987—96; bd. dirs. Learning Smith, Inc., 1992—93, Cybersmith, Inc., 1994—97; mem. investment com. Fedn. Jewish Philantrophies, NY, 1975—96; bd. dirs. Human Rights Watch, 1993—2001, emeritus, 2001—; trustee John Simon Guggenheim Meml. Found., 1982—95, chmn. fin. com., 1985—95; mng. trustee Permanent Fund of MLA, 1987—. With U.S. Army, 1943—46. Mem. AAAS (chmn. investment and fin. com. 1975—), Investment Co. Inst. (bd. govs. 1987-95), Assn. Publicly Traded Investment Funds (bd. dirs. 1970-87, chmn. 1971-79, Coun. on Fgn. Rels., N.Y. Soc. Security Analysts, Harvard Club (bd. mgrs. 1984-86), Century Assn. N.Y.c. (treas., bd. mgrs. 1999-2003), Phi Beta Kappa Fellows (adv. com. 1984-93, bd. dirs. 1993—), Phi Beta Kappa. Home: PO Box 358 Pound Ridge NY 10576-0358 Office: 1150 Park Ave New York NY 10128-1244

SMITH, MALCOLM SOMMERVILLE, bass; b. Rockville Centre, N.Y., June 22, 1933; s. Carlton Newell and Margaret (Sommerville) S.; m. Margaret Yauger, Oct. 4, 1975. B Music Edn., Oberlin Coll., 1957, B.Mus., 1960; MA in Edn1. Adminstrn, Columbia Tchrs. Coll., 1958; student, Ind. U. Sch. Music, 1960 62. Dir. choral music Ramapo Regional H.S., Wyckoff, NJ, 1958—60. Bass: Lyric Opera, bass soloist: Russian tour, Robert Shaw Choral, 1962; leading bass N.Y.C. Opera, 1965—70, Deutsche Oper Am Rhein, Dusseldorf, Germany, 1971—, Vienna State Opea, 1973—74, 86 Met. Opera, Japan tour, 1975, Met. Opera, N.Y.C., 1975—77, Paris Opera, 1978, Barcelona Opera, 1978, Sao Paulo, Brazil, 1978, Mexico City, 1979, 80, Berlin Opera, 1979, 80, Montreal Symphony, 1979, 80, 81, 82, Hamburg Opera, 1981, Koln Opera, 1980, Stuttgart Opera, 1980, Frankfurt Opera, 1980, Rome Opera, 1980, Trieste (Italy) Opera, 1981, Berlin Staatsoper, 1982, 85, Lyric Opera Phila., 1982, L.A. Philharm. at Hollywood Bowl, 1984, Mannheim Opera, Germany, 1986, Turin Opera, Italy, 1986, 88, Bordeaux, France, 1987, Dresden Opera, Germany, 1987, Staats Opera Berlin Japan tour, 1987, Polish TV, 1989, Oslo Opera, 1987, Paris Radio, 1988-89, Orange Festival, France, 1988, Penderecki Festival, Krakow, Poland, 1988, maj. soloist Schleswig Holstein Festival, Germany, 1989, Krakow Philharmonic, Poland, 1988, Maggio Musicale, Florence, Italy, 1988, Boston Symphony, Minn., Cin., Houston, Utah, Seattle, Chgo., Phila., Balt. Symphony, 1993, Mex. Nat. Symphony, 1993, nat. symphonies, also Cin. Summer Opera, Central City (Colo.), Summer Opera, Festival of Two Worlds, Spoleto, Italy, Saratoga Festival, 1985, debut La Scala, Milan, Italy, 1982, Salzburg Festival, 1986, Athens Festival, 1987, Bordeaux (France) Opera, 1987, Ft. Worth Opera, 1988, Orange Festival, France, 1988, Staatsoper Munich, 1990, Bastille Opera, Paris, 1991, Heidelberg Summer Festival, 1991, 92, Brussels Opera, 1992, 93, 94, 97, Opera Nice, France, 1992, Opera Montpelier, France, 1992, Cin. Opera, 1994, 2000, Dusseldorf Opera, 1994, Japan tour, 1994, Bregenz (Austria) Festival, 1996, Honolulu Opera, 1996, 98, Balt. Opera, 1996, Prague Autumn Festival, 1997, Cin. Opera, 1998, 2000, Grand Rapids Opera, 2000, Dusseldorf Opera, 2001, 2002, Portland Opera, 2001, Portland Symphony, 2002, recorded War and Peace, 1986, Penderecki Requiem, 1990, Aspen Music Festival, 1997; musician: Portland Symphony Orch., 2002, Schwerin Opera Festival, 2003. Served with AUS, 1954-56. Recipient Kämmersanger title Dusseldorf (Germany) Opera, 1996. Congregationalist. Office: care Thea Dispeker Artists Rep 59 E 54th St New York NY 10022-4211 *Hard work and a sense of humor.*

SMITH, MARCIA JEAN, accountant, tax specialist, financial consultant; b. Kansas City, Mo., Oct. 19, 1947; d. Eugene Hubert and Marcella Juanita (Greene) S. Student, U. Nebr., 1965-67; BA, Jersey City State Coll., 1971; MBA in Taxation, Golden Gate U., 1976, postgrad., 1976-77; MS in Acctg., Pace U., 1982; cert. of completion, Cours Commerciaux de Geneve, 1985-86. Cert. practitioner in taxation; cert. govt. fin. mgr.; accredited tax advisor. Legal intern Port Authority, N.Y., N.J., N.Y.C., 1972; legis. aide to Senator Harrison A. Williams Washington, 1973; tax accountant Bechtel Corp., San Francisco, 1974-77; sr. tax accountant Equitable Life Assurance Soc. U.S., N.Y.C., 1977, sec., 1977-79; tax sr. Arthur Andersen & Co., N.Y.C., 1979-82; pres. M.J. Smith Co., N.Y.C., 1983-85; prin. owner MJS Cons. Svcs. Internat. Tax Cons., Boston, Mass., 1988-93; gen. auditor dept. fin. Fulton County Govt., Atlanta, 1993-95; auditor State of Georgia, Dept. Med. Assistance, Atlanta, 1995-97; pres. ExecuTax, Inc., Chgo., 1997—. Cons. U.N., specialized agys., Geneva, 1985-87, CNA Fin. Corp., Chgo., 1998-99, CNA Ins. (Corp. Tax), 2000—; asst. sec. Equico Lessors, Inc., Mpls., 1977-78, Equitable Gen. Ins. Group, Ft. Worth, 1977-79, Heritage Life Infield Assurance Co., Toronto, Ont., Can., 1978-79, Informatics, Inc., L.A., 1978-79; sec. Equico Capital Corp., N.Y.C. 1977-79, Equico Personal Credit, Inc., Colorado Springs, Colo., 1978-79, Equico Securites, Inc., N.Y.C., 1977-79, Equitable Environ. Health, Inc., Woodbury, N.Y., 1977-79; tax cons., real estate salesperson. Spl. advisor U.S. Congl. Adv. Bd.; human rights chmn. YWCA, Lincoln, Nebr., 1966-67; mem. Atlanta Women's Network. Spl. advisor U.S. Congl. Adv. Bd.; human rights chmn. YWCA, Lincoln, Nebr., 1966-67; mem. Atlanta Women's Network. Mem. AAAS, AAUW, NAA (Swiss Romande chpt.), ACLU, Am. Mgmt. Assn., Nat. Soc. Pub. Accts., Am. Econs. Assn., Inst. Mgmt. Accts., Am. Acctg. Assn., Internat. Assn. Fin. Planners, Internat. Fin. Mgmt. Assn., Am. Women's Club of Geneva, Nat. Assn. Women Bus. Owners, Am. Assn. Individual Investors, Inst. Internal Auditors, N.Y. Acad. Scis., Nat. Hist. Soc., Nat. Assn. Tax Practitioners, Assn. Managerial Economists, Postal Commemorative Soc., Am. Mus. Natural History, Nat. Trust Historic Preservation, Ga. Govt. Fin. Officers Assn., Internat. Tax Inst., Calif. Soc. CPAs, Fla. Inst. CPAs, N.Y. State Soc. CPAs, Ga. Soc. CPAs, Ill. CPA Soc., Assn. Cert. Fraud Examiners, Assn. Govt. Accts., UN Assn. USA, Chgo. Coun. Fgn. Rels., EDP Auditors Assn., Mass. Soc. Ind. Accts., Acad. Legal Studies in Bus., Internat. Platform Assn., Nat. Assn. Cert. Valuation Analysts, U.S. Senatorial Club. Office: 151 N Michigan Ave Ste 1908 Chicago IL 60601-7566 Address: EXECU-Tax Incorporated Amoco Finance Facility PO Box 81049 Chicago IL 60681-0049 E-mail: executax@juno.com.

SMITH, MARCIA K. government agency administrator; b. Yakima, Wash., Dec. 7, 1953; d. Richard C. Stewart and Joyce M. Gardner; m. Jerry D. Smith, Mar. 18, 2001; children: Brittany M. Palmer, Benjamin T., Alysia D. AAS, Spokane (Wash.) C.C., 1974. Author: (novel) The Goddess Speaks, (poetry) My Son (Golden Poets award Writers Guild, 1992, 1993, 1994). Area rep. Coun. Magical Arts, Austin, Tex., 1992—2003; denom. svc. leader US Army, Fort Hood, Tex., 1996—98. Sgt. US Army, 1974—80. Mem.: ACLU. Libertarian. Achievements include first to 1st Druid High Priestess of US Mil.'s 1st officially sanctioned and federally protected Pagan Open Circle. Avocations: writing, art. Home: 228 Rosemont Belton TX 76513-4885 Personal E-mail: silth_elentari@yahoo.com.

SMITH, MARGARET, state legislator; b. Chgo. m. Fred J. Smith; 2 sons, (dec.). Student, Tenn. State U. Mem. Ill. Ho. of Reps., 1981-83, Ill. Senate dist. 12, 1983—. Trustee Chgo. Bapt. Inst. Democrat. Office: State Senate State Capital Rm 103A Springfield IL 62706-0001 Address: 4949 N Melvina Ave Chicago IL 60630-2907

SMITH, MARGARET A. (MAGGIE CARROLL SMITH), community volunteer; b. Akron, Ohio, Nov. 2, 1928; d. John Raymond Seiler and Helen Joseph Roach; m. Richard C. Carroll, Feb. 1, 1958 (div.); children: Stephan, Christopher, Daniel, John, Michael; m. Wiley Smith, Jr., May 3, 1985. Grad., St. Vincent H.S., Akron, Ohio, 1947. Interviewer Ohio Bur. of Employees Svcs., Akron, 1949-53; sales agt. Boebinger Realtors, 1979-86; lectr. on mental health, Akron U., Kent State U., Summit County Paramedics, Akron Police Dept., others; developer spl. mental health crisis intervention tng. program for Akron Police and Fire Dept., Ohio, 2000. Editor: (newsletter) National Alliance for the Mentally Ill of Summit County, 1987-99. Founding pres. Nat. Alliance/Mentally Ill of Summit County, Akron, 1986; pres. Nat. Alliance/Mentally Ill of Ohio, Columbus, 1988; steering com. for redesigning cmty. mental health system, 1986. Recipient Heart of Gold award Mental Health Assn. of Summit County, 1989, Recognition for Advocacy, Alcohol, Drug, and Mental Health, Summit County, 1996, Vol. of Yr. award We. Res. Psychiat. Hosp., Summit County, 1988, Solid Gold Mem. award Alliance for the Monthly Ill of Ohio, Columbus, 1991; Maggie C Smith House Residential Facility named in her honor, Ohio, 2000. Avocation: gardening. Office: Nat Alliance/Mentally Ill PO Box 462 Cuyahoga Falls OH 44222-0462

SMITH, MARGARET TAYLOR, volunteer; b. Roanoke Rapids, N.C., May 31, 1925; d. George Napoleon and Sarah Luella (Waller) T.; m. Sidney William Smith Jr., Aug. 15, 1947; children: Sarah Smith, Sidney William Smith III, Susan Smith, Amy Smith. BA in Sociology, Duke U., 1947. Chair emeritus bd. trustees Kresge Found., Troy, Mich., 1985—; chmn. Nat. Coun. for Women's Studies Duke U., N.C., 1986—, chmn. Trinity Bd. Visitors, 1988-98; chair emeritus. Chmn. bd. visitors Wayne State U. Med. Sch., 1993; bd. dirs., mem. exec. com. Detroit Med. Ctr.; mem. bd. govs. Detroit Med. Ctr. Recipient the Merrill-Palmer award Wayne State U., Detroit, 1987, Zimmerman award Gtr. Detroit Health Coun., Athena award C. of C., 1998, Women of Achievement award Mich. Women's Fedn., 1999, disting. svc. award Wayne State U., 1999; named disting. alumna award Duke U. Mem. The Village Club, Internat. Women's Forum, Pi Beta Phi, Phi Beta Kappa. Methodist. E-mail: sidmyth@aol.com.

SMITH, MARIE B. college president; BA, San Francisco State U.; MA in Biology, Sonoma State U.; DEdn, U. San Francisco. Biology instr. to acting pres. Indian Valley Coll., Novato, Calif., 1974; dean Coll. at Life Chiropractic Coll. West San Lorenzo, 1985; staff to dean instrn. Coll. of Alameda, 1990, pres., 1991-94, Am. River Coll., 1995—. Chair planning team McClennan AFB Privatization and Reuse adv. com.; co-chair strategic planning teams Los Rio C.C. Dist. Mem. Grant Joint Union H.S. Dist. Vol. Integration Cmty. adv. coun.; mem. Golden Gate U. Women's Leadership Inst., Calif. Ctr. for Health Improvement, Life College West, San Lorenzo, Calif.; pres. ARC. Mem. Biol. Field Svc. Assn. Office: Am River Coll 4700 College Oak Dr Sacramento CA 95841-4217

SMITH, MARIE EDMONDS, real estate agent, property manager; b. Quapaw, Okla., Oct. 5, 1927; d. Thomas Joseph and Maud Ethel Edmonds; m. Robert Lee Smith, Aug. 14, 1966 (dec. 1983). Grad. vocat. nurse, Hoag Hosp., Costa Mesa, Calif., 1953; BA, Vanguard U., 1955; MS, U. Alaska, 1963. Lic. vocat. nurse, Calif.; cert. sci. tchr., Alaska. Nurse Calif. Dept. Nurses, Costa Mesa, 1952-60; tchr. Alaska Dept. Edn., Aniak and Anchorage, 1955-60; tchr. sci. Garden Grove (Calif.) Sch. Dist., 1960-87; property mgr. Huntington Beach, Calif., 1970—; agent Sterling Realtors, Huntington Beach, 1988—. Author: Ocean Biology, 1969. Bd. dirs., tchr. Newport Mesa Christian Ctr., Costa Mesa, 1983-2001; com. chmn. Garden Grove Unified Sch. Dist. PTA, 1977. NSF grantee, 1960-62. Mem. AAUW, Vanguard U. Alumnae Assn. Republican. Avocations: skin diving, travel. Home: 8311 Reilly Dr Huntington Beach CA 92646 Office: L8153 Brookhurst St Fountain Valley CA 92708

SMITH, MARIE F. small business owner, writer; b. Kahakuloa, Hawaii; Dir. manpower mgmt. and orgn. planning Social Security Adminstrn.; realtor assoc., 1987—; small bus. owner, 1987—; freelance writer, 1987—; commr. State of Women Gov. Hawaii; chair Nat. Legis. Coun. AARP, Washington, spokesperson Women's Initiative Program, mem. audit and fin. com., 2000—02, mem. exec. dir. search com., 2000—02, treas. found. bd. dirs., 2000—02, pres., 2004—. Active Interfaith Vol. Caregivers; sec. bd. dirs. Maui Adult Day Care Ctr.; pres. bd. dirs. Maui Vol. Ctr. Recipient Woman of Excellence award, Commn. on the Status of Women, Circle of Women award, County Commn. on the Status of Women. Mem.: Nat. Assn. Ret. Fed. Employees (pres.), African Am. Heritage Found. Maui (pres.). Office: AARP 601 E St W Washington DC 20049

SMITH, MARILYN NOELTNER, retired science educator; b. LA, Feb. 14, 1933; d. Clarence Frederick and Gertrude Bertha (Smith) Noeltner; m. Edward Christopher Smith, Sept. 11, 1971 (dec. Oct. 1999). BA, Marymount Coll., 1957; MA, U. Notre Dame, 1966; MS, Boston Coll., 1969. Cert. tchr.; cert. community coll. tchr., Calif.; cert. adminstr., Calif. Tchr., chmn. sci. dept. Marymount High Sch., Santa Barbara, Calif., 1954-57, LA, 1957-58, 69-79, tchr., chmn. sci. and math. depts. Palos Verdes, Calif., 1959-69; tchr., chmn. math. dept. Corvallis High Sch., Studio City, Calif., 1958-59; instr. tchr. tng. Marymount-Loyola U., LA, 1965-71, instr. freshman interdisciplinary program, 1970-71; tchr. math. Santa Monica (Calif.) HS, 1971-72; instr. math., chemistry, physics Santa Monica Coll., 1971—79; tchr. sci. Beverly Vista Sch., Beverly Hills, Calif., 1972—2002; ret., 2002. Cons. Calif. State Sci. Framework Revision Com., LA, 1975; chmn. NASA Youth Sci. Congress, Pasadena, Calif., 1968-69, Hawaii, 1969-70; participant NASA Educators Conf. Jupiter Mission, Ames Research, San Francisco, 1973, NASA Educators Conf. Viking-Mars Ames Project, San Francisco, 1976-77, NASA Landsat Conf., Edward's AFB, Calif., 1978, NASA Uranus Mission, Pasadena, Calif., 1986, NASA Uranus-Voyager Mission, Pasadena, 1989, NASA Neptune-Voyager Mission, Pasadena, 1989; test scoring com. Calif. Learning Assessment System, U. Santa Barbara, 1993, writing com. Trainers Manual, 1993. Author books and computer progs. including NASA Voyager-Uranus Sci. Symposium for Educators, 1989, NASA Voyager 2 Neptune Encounter Conf., 1989, others; contbr. articles to profl. jours. Sponsor Social Svc. Club, Palos Verdes, 1959-69, moderator, sponsor ARC Youth Svc. Chmn., Beverly Hills, 1974-77, judge L.A. County Sci. Fair, 1969—, blue ribbon com. NATAS, 1971—; bd. dirs. Children First, Beverly Hills, 1990-91; vol. sch. initiative, Beverly Hills, 1989-90; steering com. on tech. Beverly Vista Sch., 1994-95; del. Congress of Am. Women Scientists to Cuba, People to People Amb. Program, 2001; active U. Notre Dame Badin Guild, 1989—. Recipient Commendation in Teaching cert. Am. Soc. Microbiology, 1962, Salute to Edn. award So. Calif. Industry Edn. Council, 1962, Outstanding Teaching citation Cons. Engrs. Assn. Calif., 1967, Cert. Honor, Silver Plaque Westinghouse Sci. Talent Search, 1963-68, Tchr. award Ford-Future Scientists of Am., 1968, Biomed. award Com. Advance Sci. Tng., 1971, Outstanding Tchr. award LA County Sci. Fair Com., 1975-76, Contbns. to Youth Service citation ARC, 1976-77, Outstanding Tchr. award Kiwanis, Beverly Hills, 1987, NAST Pres'. award, 1990, Woman of Yr. award, 1990, cert. appreciation Profl. Leadership and Support for Advancing Sci. Edn. Calif. Dept. Edn., 1992-93, Outstanding Tchr. Gifted Students award Johns Hopkins U., 1999-2000. Mem. We. Assn. Schs. and Colls. (vis. com. 1968, writing com. 1969—), Assn. Advancement Biomed. Edn. (pres. 1970-71), 1st Internat. Sci. Tchrs. Conf. (presider, evaluator 1977), Nat. Sci. Tchrs. Assn. (presider, evaluator 1976, chmn. contributed papers com. 1977-78, presenter 1990), Beverly Hills Edn. Assn. (pres. faculty coun. 1980-81, 85-86, sch. rep. 1990—, Ann. WHO award 1995, 96), Chemist's Club, Calif. Statewide Math. Adv. Com., So. Calif. Industry Edn. Council, Calif. Assn. Chemistry Tchrs. (program chmn. 1960), Calif. Sci. Tchrs. Assn., Am. Chem. Soc., AAAS, South Bay Math. League (sec. 1967-68, pres. 1968-69, 72, 1969-70), Calif. Math. Council, Nat. Assn. Biology Tchrs., U. Notre Dame Sorin Soc. Republican. Roman Catholic. Avocations: stone age architecture, Gaelic, Irish fisheries population samplings and contributions to data bank. Home: 3934 Sapphire Dr Encino CA 91436-3635 Office: Beverly Vista Sch 200 S Elm Dr Beverly Hills CA 90212-4011

SMITH, MARION PAFFORD, avionics company executive, retired; b. Waycross, Ga., Dec. 12, 1925; s. Rossa Elbert and Lillian Solee (Pafford) S.; m. Esther Pat Davis, Nov. 23, 1952; children: Bryan P., Danton D., Patricia Anne. Student, Okla. State U., 1944, Yale U., 1945; BS in EE, La. State U., 1949; postgrad., U. So. Fla., 1966-70. Engr. Bell Telephone Co., Baton Rouge, 1949-51; mgr. engring. Vitro Labs., Silver Spring, Md., 1952-57; design engring. mgr. dept. design and constrn. flight hand contrs. Space Shuttle and Space Sta. Honeywell Avionics Div., Clearwater, Fla., 1957-98. Vice chmn., bd. dirs. First Union, Largo, Fla., 1985-93; cons. U.S. Army Mgmt. Engring. Tng. Agy., 1975-79; U.S. Del. Internat. Elec. Tech. Commn., 1965-85, chmn. chief U.S. tech. adviser com. on reliability and maintainability, 1975-85, v.p., exec. com. U.S. nat. com., 1975-84; U.S. del. NATO Quality Conf., 1973; mem. White House Summit Conf. on Inflation, 1975; del. White House Conf. on Handicapped, 1977; mem. nat. adv. coun. on devel. disabilities HEW, 1974-78, Fla. Devel. Disabilities Coun., 1974-78; pres. Fla. Advocacy Ctr. for Persons with Disabilities, Inc., 1997-2000; commr. State of Fla. Occupl. Access Commn., 2000-2002; mem. devel. coun. Morton Plant Hosp., Clearwater, 1971-74. 1st lt. Signal Corps, AUS, 1944-45, 51-52. Served to 1st lt. Signal Corps AUS, 1944-45, 51-52. Recipient McDonald award Fla. Rehab. Assn., 1968; Bilgore award Citizen of Year Clearwater, Fla., 1969; Outstanding Service award Am. Soc. Quality Control, 1968-69; United Comml. Travelers award Most Outstanding Service Retarded Fla., 1970; named Engr. of Year Fla. W. Coast, 1970; Service to Mankind award Sertoma Clubs, 1977 Fellow IEEE (dir., Nat. Reliability award 1979); mem. Assn. Retarded Citizens USA (pres. 1973-75, nat. govt. affairs chmn. 1975-83), Am. Assn. Mental Deficiency, Nat. Symposium Reliability Quality Control (gen. chmn.), Sigma Chi. Presbyterian elder. Club: Kiwanis (Marion P. Smith award established in his honor). Home: 1884 Oakdale Ln N Clearwater FL 33764-6441 *True turning points in life are sometimes difficult to recognize, but for those who have become parents of a handicapped child, particularly a mentally retarded child, then that turning point is easy to recognize. After the difficult period of adjustment, one becomes aware of a realization that all persons have human dignity and worth and can make a contribution to humanity and to society.*

SMITH, MARJORIE AILEEN MATTHEWS, museum director; b. Richmond, Va., Aug. 19, 1918; d. Harry Anderson and Adelia Charlotte (Howland) Matthews; m. Robert Woodrow Smith, July 23, 1945 (dec. Mar. 1992). Pilot lic., Taneytown (Md.) Aviation Svc., 1944, cert. CAA navigation ground sch. instr., 1945. Founder, editor, pub. Spinning Wheel, Taneytown, 1945-63; v.p. Antiques Publs., Inc., Taneytown, 1960-68, pres. Prism Inc., Taneytown, 1968-78; mus. dir. Trapshooting Hall of Fame, Vandalia, Ohio, 1976-2000, mus. dir. emeritus, 2001—, sec., 1993-99. Co-author: Handbook of Tomorrow's Antiques, 1954; contbr. articles to profl. publs. Sec. Balt. area coun. Girl Scouts USA, 1950. Named to All-Am. Trapshooting team Sports Afield mag., 1960, 61; inductee Trapshooting Hall of Fame, 1998. Mem. Nat. League Am. Pen Women, Amateur Trapshooting Assn. (life), Internat. Assn. Sports Mus. and Halls of Fame (bd. dirs. 1993-94, W.R. Schroeder Disting. Svc. award 1999). Lutheran. Avocations: duplicate bridge, trapshooting, antiques collecting.

SMITH, MARJORIE K. state legislator; b. Feb. 22, 1944; d. Harold E. and Rose (Rothstein) Kester; m. Peter Sheridan Smith, 1966; children: Abigail, Douglas. BA, Beaver Coll., 1961, MPA, 1962. Mem. N.H. Ho. of Reps. (dist. 8), Concord, 1996—. Trustee Dunham Pub. Libr., 1997—. Office: NH State Legis State House Concord NH 03301

SMITH, MARK ALAN, management consultant; b. Lafayette, Ind., May 15, 1934; s. Mark Andrew and Sarah Fredissa (Palin) S.; children by previous marriages: Michelle Renee, Janene Marie. BA in Mus. Edn., BS in French, Ind. State U., 1957; MS in Adminstrn., George Washington U., 1976; postgrad., U. Pa. Wharton Sch., U. Denver Coll Law, U. Md. Coll. Law. Tech. writer Douglas Aircraft Co., Santa Monica, Calif., 1961-62; editor Copyright Law Office, Library Congress, Washington, 1963-64; asst. dir. pers. Holy Cross Hosp., Silver Spring, Md., 1964-65, dir. pers. adminstrn., 1965-80, dir. human resources adminstrn., 1980-82, asst. v.p., 1982-88; pres. HRM Assocs., Rockville, Md., 1989—. Instr. pers. mgmt. and labor rels. Strayer U., Washington, 1970-73, bus. adminstrn. Ctrl. Mich. U. Grad. Sch., Washington extension, 1975-80; vis. lectr. George Washington U. Grad. Sch. Bus. Adminstrn., Washington, 1969, 70, 76; cons. to various hosps. in Md., Va. and Washington, Am. Hosp. Assn. and other nat. profl. assns., 1975—; bd. dirs. Potomac Employers' Roundtable, 1991—, dir. membership, 1992—. Contbr. articles on orgn. devel. to profl. jours. Served with CIC, U.S. Army, 1957-60. Mem. Am. Hosp. Assn., Am. Soc. for Hosp. Pers. Dirs. (mem. labor rels. com. 1970), Soc. for Human Resource Mgmt. (cert., sr. prof. in human resources, mem. pub. affairs com. 1975), Am. Mgmt. Assn., Washington Pers. Assn., Hosp. Coun. of Nat. Capital Area (pres. pers. dirs. divsn. 1969, 71), Md. Hosp. Pers. Adminstrn. Assn., Am. Soc. Law and Medicine, Phi Delta Kappa, Phi Mu Alpha Sinfonia, Blue Key. Home and Office: 872 New Mark Esplanade Rockville MD 20850-2750 Fax: 301 340-2889. E-mail: hrmpros@msn.com.

SMITH, MARK D. foundation administrator; Pres., CEO Calif. Health Care Found., Oakland, Calif., 1999—. Office: Calif Health Care Found 476 Ninth St Oakland CA 94607 E-mail: msmith@chcf.org.

SMITH, MARK HALLARD, architect; b. Detroit, June 28, 1955; s. John Hallard and Barbara Ruth (Hinkle) S.; m. Janee Lynne Batey, July 18, 1981; children: Elizabeth Anne, Jacquelyne Ruth. BS, Ga. Inst. Tech., 1977, MArch, 1979. Registered architect, Fla.; cert. Nat. Coun. Archtl. Registration Bds. Draftsman Kirkland/Ogram Architects, Atlanta, 1979-80; project mgr. Bailey Vrooman Allegret, Atlanta, 1980-81, Rabun Hatch and Dendy, Atlanta, 1981; project architect C. Randolph Wedding & Assocs., St. Petersburg, Fla., 1981-83, Stearman Architects, St. Petersburg, 1983-90, Carl Abbott Arch. FAIA PA, Sarasota, Fla., 1990-94; prin. Smith Architects, Sarasota, 1994—. Panelist Ringling Mus. Art, Sarasota, 1991. Asst. editor Centerline, 1990. Chmn. Sarasota Design Conf., 1994, 96, 98; mem. steering com. John Ringling Ctr. Found., Sarasota, 1995; pres. Men's Club, St. Michael The Archangel Ch., 1993-96. Mem. AIA (archtl. juror Palm Beach chpt. 1993, pres. Fla. Gulf Coast chpt. 1994-95, v.p. Fla. chpt. 2000-02, Fla. award of excellence 1993, Fla. bd. dirs. 1995-99, Fla. Pres. award 1994), Nat. Trust for Hist. Preservation, Tiger Bay Club. Republican. Roman Catholic. Avocation: tennis. Home: 5562 Cape Aqua Dr Sarasota FL 34242-1804 Office: Smith Architects PA 5032 Calle Minorga Sarasota FL 34242-1519

SMITH, MARK LEE, architect; b. L.A., Nov. 16, 1957; s. Selma (Moidel) Smith. BA in History of Architecture, UCLA, 1978, MA in Architecture, 1980. Registered architect Calif., Nev., Oreg., Wash., Tenn., Colo., N.Y., Ohio. Designer, drafter John B. Ferguson and Assocs., L.A., 1976-83, architect, 1983; pvt. practice architecture L.A., 1984—. Mem. Los Angeles County Archtl. Evaluation Bd., 1990—; spkr. Western Pool and Spa Show, 1997—. Author: A Bridge Across the Continents, 2003; essay columnist AIA/SFV monthly, 1997—; founding editor ARCHimpressions.org mag., 2003—; contbr. articles to profl. jours. Bd. govs. UCLA John Wooden Ctr., 1978-80; judge Bank Am. Achievement Awards, 1998—, chair, 1999-2000. Regents scholar, U. Calif., Berkeley, UCLA, 1975-78; UCLA Grad. Sch. Architecture Rsch. fellow, 1979-80. Mem. AIA (treas. San Fernando Valley chpt. 1986, bd. dirs. 1986—, v.p. 1987, pres. 1988, Design award 1988, 89, 90, 91, 99, chmn. Design awards 1994, bd. dirs. Calif. coun. 1989-94, v.p. 1991-94, chmn. continuing edn. 1991-93, chmn. 1992 conf.), Phi Beta Kappa. Office: 18340 Ventura Blvd Ste 225 Tarzana CA 91356-4278

SMITH, MARK P. foundation executive; b. Charleston, W. Va., July 27, 1949; s. Bernard Henry and Josephine S. (Polan) Smith; m. Jane Stephens, May 6, 1978; children: Stephen Noblew, Allison Baxter. BA, Princeton U., 1971; JD, Yale U., 1978. Asst. to exec. dir. ABA, Chgo., 1976—79; v.p. Ctr. Am. and Internat. Law, Richardson, Tex., 1989—; dir. Inst. for Transnational Arbitration, 1993—98, Mcpl. Legal Studies Ctr., 1998—; sec. W. Va. Legal Svc. Plan, Inc., Charleston, 1987—88; treas. F; lectr. U. Tex., Dallas, 1990—94. Sec. W.Va. Legal Svcs. Plan, Inc., Charleston, 1987—88; treas. Found. for Youth and Govt., Charleston, 1983—88; lectr. U. Tex., Dallas, 1990—94. Pres. Saigling Elem. Sch. PTA, 1991—92; pres. bd. dirs. Kanawha County Coalition for Homeless, 1986—87; sec. W.Va. Coalition for the Homeless, 1986—87; pres. Vol. Ctr. Collin County, 2001—; mem. bd. Vol. Ctr. North Tex., 2001—. Mem.: Nat. Assn. Bar Exec. (chmn. continuing ed. com. 1981—82, mem. exec. com. 1984—86), Found. Youth and Govt. (treas.), Nat. Assn. Bar Exec. (chmn. continuing edn. com. 1981—82, mem. exec. com. 1984—86), Vo. Ctr. No. Tex., Vol. Ctr. Collin County (pres. 2001—, mem. bd. 2001—), Coalition for Homeless (pres., bd. dir. 1986—87, sec. 1986—87), Saigling Elem. Sch. PTA (pres. 1991—92). Office: Ctr Am and Internat Law PO Box 799030 Richardson TX 75379-9030

SMITH, MARK W. management consultant; BA in Acctg., Hillsdale (Mich.) Coll. CPA AICPA. Mgr. Arthur Andersen; various fin. positions Ryder Sys., Inc., Miami; from v.p. fin. to CFO Spherion Corp., Ft. Lauderdale, Fla., 1997—2003, CFO, 2003—. Mem.: Mich. Assn. CPAs and Fin. Execs. Internat. Office: Spherion corp 2050 Spectrum Blvd Fort Lauderdale FL 33309*

SMITH, MARKHAM H. architectural firm executive; BA, Tulane U. Sch. of Arts and Scis., 1979; B in Architecture, Tulane U. Sch. of Architecture, 1979. Lic. NCARB, Ga., 1987, La., 1983, Mich., 1989, Mo., 1996. With Arthur Cotton Moore & Assocs., Washington, 1979—81, Labouisse & Waggonner Archs., New Orleans, 1982, E. Eean McNaughton & Assocs., New Orleans, 1983—87, Smith Dalia Archs., Atlanta, 1987—. Mem., former bd. dirs. Atlanta Preservation Ctr.; adv. bd. Legal Environ. Assistance Found. Mem.: Ga. Trust for Hist. Preservation, Nat. Hist. Trust. Office: Smith Dalia Archs Ste C-140 621 N Ave NE Atlanta GA 30308

SMITH, MARSHA H. state agency administrator, lawyer; b. Boise, Idaho, Mar. 24, 1950; d. Eugene F. and Joyce (Ross) Hatch; m. Terrell F. Smith, Aug. 29, 1970; 2 children. BS in Biology/Edn., Idaho State U., 1973; MLS, Brigham Young U., 1975; JD, U. Wash., 1980. Bar: Idaho, U.S. Dist. Ct. Idaho, U.S. Ct. Appeals (9th cir.), U.S. Ct. Appeals (D.C. cir.). Dep. atty. gen. Bus./Consumer Protection Divsn., Boise, 1980-81, Idaho Pub. Utilities Commn., Boise, 1981-89, dir. policy and external rels., 1989-91, commr., 1991—, pres., 1991-95. Mem. Harvard Electricity Policy Group, Nat. Coun. on Competition and The Electric Industry; chair com. for regional electric power coop. Western Interstate Energy Bd. Legis. dist. chair Ada County Democrats, Idaho, 1986-89. Mem. Nat. Assn. Regulatory Utility Commrs. (chair electricity com.). Office: Idaho Pub Utilities Commn PO Box 83720 Boise ID 83720-0074

SMITH, MARSHALL SAVIDGE, foundation executive; b. East Orange, NJ, Sept. 16, 1937; s. Marshall Parsons and Ann Eileen (Zulauf) S.; m. Carol Goodspeed, June 25, 1960 (div. Aug. 1962); m. Louise Nixon Claiborn, Aug. 1964; children: Adam, Jennifer, Matthew, Megan. AB, Harvard U., 1960, EdM, 1963, EdD, 1970. Systems analyst and computer programmer Raytheon Corp., Andover, Mass., 1959-62; instr., assoc. prof. Harvard U., Cambridge, Mass., 1966-76; asst., assoc. dir. Nat. Inst. Edn., Washington, 1973-76; asst. commr. edn. HEW, Washington, 1976-79, chief of staff to U.S. Dept. Edn. sec., 1980; prof. U. Wis., Madison, 1980-86, Stanford (Calif.) U., 1986—2003, dean Sch. Edn., 1986-94; under-sec. edn. U.S. Dept. Edn., 1993-2000, acting dep. sec. edn., 1996-2000; program dir. Hewlett Found., 2001—. Task force, chmn. Clinton Presdl. Transition Team, 1992-93; chmn. PEW Forum on Ednl. Reform; chmn. bd. internat. com. studies in edn. NAS, 1992-93. Author: The General Inquirer, 1967, Inequality, 1972; contbr. several articles to profl. jours, chpts. to books. Pres. Madison West Hockey Assn., 1982-84. Mem. Am. Ednl. Rsch. Assn. (chmn. orgn. instl. affiliates 1985-86), Nat. Acad. Edn. Democrat. Avocations: environmental issues, philanthropy. Home: 1256 Forest Ave Palo Alto CA 94301 Office: Wm & Flora Hewlett Found Menlo Park CA Office Phone: 650-234-4500.

SMITH, MARTHA A. academic administrator; b. Bradford, Pa., Aug. 31, 1948; BA, Slippery Rock State U., Pa., 1970; EdM, U. Hawaii, 1972; EdD, U. No. Colo., 1974. Dir. Hawaii Open program U. Hawaii, 1975—77; v.p. student affairs Coll. of St. Theresa, 1977—81; dean of students Dundalk CC, 1982—87, acting pres., 1987, pres., 1988—94, Anne Arundel CC, Arnold, Md., 1994—. Mem. pres.'s adv. coun. St. John's Coll.; mem. Gov.'s Workforce Investment Bd.; mem. commn. on higher edn. Mid. States Assn. of Coll. and Sch.; bd. dir. Inst. CC Devel. at Cornell U.; commr. Am. Assn. of CC Workforce Devel.; mem. Md. Partnership Tchg. and Learning K-16; co-chair K-16 Std. Competency Assessment Team. Campaign chair Anne Arundel County United Way, 1999, mem. partnership bd., 1999; bd. dir. Anne Arundel Med. Ctr., Anne Arundel County Trade Coun., Harundale Youth Ctr. Named Bus. Leader of Yr., Anne Arundel Trade Coun., 1998; named one of Md.'s Top 100 Women, Daily Record, 1998, 2000; recipient First Women award, YECA of Annapolis and Anne Arundel County, 1995, Tribute to Women in Industry award, YMCA, 1995, Cmty Trustee award, 2001, Leadership Anne Arundel, 2001, Inside the Field Nat. Leadership award, Nat. Coun. Continuing Edn., 2001, CC of Yr. award, Nat. Alliance of Bus., 2001. Mem.: Md. Coun. of CC Pres., Rotary Club of Annapolis. Office: Anne Arundel CC 101 College Pkwy Arnold MD 21012-2222

SMITH, MARTHA VIRGINIA BARNES, retired elementary school educator; b. Camden, Ark., Oct. 12, 1940; d. William Victor and Lillian Louise (Givens) Barnes; m. Basil Loren Smith, Oct. 11, 1975; children: Jennifer Frost, Sean Barnes. BS in Edn., Ouachita Bapt. U., 1963; postgrad., Auburn U., 1974, Henderson State U., 1975. Cert. tchr., Mo. 2d and 1st grade tchr. Brevard County Schs., Titusville and Cocoa, Fla., 1963-65, 69-70; 1st grade tchr. Lakeside Sch. Dist., Hot Springs, Ark., 1965-66, Harmony Grove Sch., Camden, 1972-76; 1st and 5th grade tchr. Cumberland County Schs., Fayetteville, N.C., 1966-69; kindergarten tchr. Pulaski County Schs., Ft. Leonard Wood, Mo., 1970-72; 3d grade tchr. Mountain Grove (Mo.) Schs., 1976-99; ret., 1999. Chmn. career ladder com. Mountain Grove Dist., 1991-99. Children's pastor 1st Bapt. Ch., Vanzant, Mo., 1984-88. Mem. NEA (pres.-elect Mountain Grove chpt. 1995-97, pres. Mountain Grove chpt. 1997-99), Kappa Kappa Iota. Avocation: antique and classic cars.

SMITH, MARTIN BERNHARD, journalist; b. San Francisco, Apr. 20, 1930; s. John Edgar and Anna Sophie (Thorsen) S.; m. Joan Lovat Muller, Apr. 25, 1953; children: Catherine Joan, Karen Anne. AB, U. Calif., Berkeley, 1952, M Journalism, 1968. Reporter, city editor Modesto (Calif.) Bee, 1957-64; reporter, mng. editor Sacramento Bee, 1964-75; polit. editor, columnist McClatchy Newspapers, Sacramento, 1975-92; ret., 1992. Episcopalian. Personal E-mail: Joan_and_Marty@msn.com.

SMITH, MARTIN HENRY, retired pediatrician; b. Gainesville, Ga., Nov. 3, 1921; s. Charles E. and Mamie Mae (Emmett) S.; m. Mary Gillis, Feb. 25, 1950; children: Susan, Margaret, Mary MD, Emory U., 1945. Diplomate Am. Bd. Pediatrics. Intern City Hosp. System, Winston-Salem, N.C., 1945-46; fellow in infectious diseases Grady Meml. Hosp., Atlanta, 1948-49; resident Henrietta Egleston Hosp., Atlanta, 1949-50, Children's Hosp., Washington, 1950-51; practice medicine, specializing in pediatrics Gainesville, Ga.; ret., 1988; clin. asst. prof. Emory U. Hosp., Atlanta; chief of staff Hall County Hosp., Gainesville, 1965-66. Mem. Nat. Vaccine Adv. Commn., 1990—, chmn., 1991. Contbr. articles to profl. jours. Chmn. Nat. Vaccine Adv. Com., 1991—. Capt. M.C., U.S. Army, 1946-48 Fellow Am. Acad. Pediatrics (chpt. chmn. 1966-69, dist. chmn. 1977-83, pres.-elect 1984-85, pres. 1985-86); mem. Hall County Med. Soc. (pres. 1960), Ga. Pediatric Soc. (pres. 1965-66), Med. Assn. Ga., AMA, Alpha Omega Alpha Clubs: Chattahoochee Country (Gainesville); Piedmont Driving (Atlanta). Episcopalian.

SMITH, MARTIN JAY, advertising and marketing executive; b. N.Y.C., Feb. 1, 1942; s. Nathan and Helen (Schwartz) S.; m. Ellen Susan Chadakoff, Dec. 20, 1964; children: Hilary, Nancy. BA, U. Pitts., 1963. With sta. clearance dept. ABC Radio Network, N.Y.C., 1965-66; asst. account exec. Norman Craig & Kummel, N.Y.C., 1966-67, account exec., 1967-68, Gotham, Inc., N.Y.C., 1968-72, account supr., 1972-74, v.p., 1974-78, sr. v.p., 1978-80, exec. v.p., 1980-84, vice chmn., 1984—. Sgt. USAR, 1963-69. Mem. Am. Advt. Assn. Am. (mem. mgmt. com. 1987). Avocations: flying, tennis, golf. Home: 920 Park Ave New York NY 10028-0208 Office: Gotham Inc 100 5th Ave Fl 16 New York NY 10011-6996

SMITH, MARTIN JAY, physician, biomedical research scientist; b. Bklyn., May 21, 1934; s. I. Richard and Marilyn (Bernard) S.; m. Joyce Ellen Gleason, June 26, 1960 (div. Nov. 1968); children: Danielle, Robert, Alexander; m. Ruby Helen Rhodes, Apr. 7, 1972. BA, Hofstra Coll., 1955; MD, Columbia U., 1959. Diplomate Am. Bd. Internal Medicine, Am. Bd. Internal Medicine in Hematology, Am. Bd. Pathology in Clin. Pathology, Am. Bd. Pathology in Immunopathology. Intern Meth. Hosp., N.Y.C., 1959-60, resident in medicine, 1960-61, Montefiore Hosp., N.Y.C., 1963-64; rsch. fellow in medicine Harvard Coll., Cambridge, Mass., 1964-66; clin. and rsch. fellow in medicine Mass. Gen. Hosp., Boston, 1964-66; physician Gundersen Clinic and Luth. Hosp., La Crosse, Wis., 1966-99, chmn. dept. internal medicine, 1971-73; dir. spl. hematology lab. Gundersen Clinic, La Crosse, 1967-99, chmn. dept. lab. medicine, 1973-96; dir. lab. medicine Luth. Hosp., La Crosse, 1973-96. Dir. rsch. Gundersen Med. Found., 1975-88; med. dir. Med. Lab. Tech. Program Western Wis. Tech. Inst., 1978-99. Contbr. articles to New Eng. Jour Medicine, Jour. Lab. Clin. Medicine, Blood, Ann. Internal Medicine, Biochim, Biophys. Acta, Jour. Infectious Diseases, Clin. Chemistry. Capt. USNR, ret. Fellow ACP, Coll. Am. Pathologists (inspector labs. 1983-99); mem. Am. Assn. for Cancer Rsch., Am. Soc. Hematology, Internat. Soc. Hematology, Assn. Med. Lab. Immunologists, Phi Beta Kappa. Home: 1428 Main St La Crosse WI 54601-4225 Office: Gundersen Clinic Ltd 1836 South Ave La Crosse WI 54601-5494

SMITH, MARTIN LANE, biomedical researcher; b. Seattle, Mar. 15, 1959; s. Melvin Dale and Rosemary (Nations) Smith. BA, Austin Coll., 1981; PhD, Emory U., 1990. Assoc. U. Pitts. Sch. Medicine, 1990-93, NIH, Bethesda, Md., 1993-98; asst. prof. Ind. U. Sch. Medicine, Indpls., 1998—2004, assoc. prof., 2004—. Instr. biology Emory U., Atlanta, 1985—89. Contbr. articles to profl. jours. Recipient Am. Cancer Soc. award, 1992, 1998, 2002; grantee NIH, 1991—93. Mem.: AAAS, Radiation Rsch. Soc., Am. Assn. Cancer Rsch., Sigma Xi. Avocations: coin collecting/numismatics, hiking, travel.

SMITH, MAURA ABELN, lawyer; b. Reading, Pa., Oct. 3, 1955; d. Henry Joseph and Lynn (Blashe) Abeln; children: Gwendolyn Casebeer, Karl Casebeer; m. Steven A. Smith, Dec. 18, 1999. AB, Vassar Coll., 1977; M Philosophy, Oxford U., 1979; JD, U. Miami, 1982. Bar: Fla. 1982, Ohio 1999. Assoc. Steel, Hector & Davis, Miami, 1982—87; ptnr. Baker & McKenzie, Miami, 1987-91; v.p., gen. counsel GE Co./Plastics, Pittsfield, Mass., 1991-98; sr. v.p., gen. counsel, sec. Owens Corning, Toledo, 1998-2000, chief restructuring officer, sr. v.p., gen. counsel, sec., 2000—03, bd. dirs.; sr. v.p., gen. counsel, sec. Internat. Paper, Stamford, Conn., 2003—. Rhodes scholar, Oxford, Eng., 1977-79; John M. Olin fellow in law and econs., Olin Found., 1979-82. Mem.: Phi Beta Kappa. Avocations: skiing, horseback riding, tennis, golf.

SMITH, MAURY DRANE, lawyer; b. Samson, Ala., Feb. 2, 1927; s. Abb Jackson and Rose Drane (Sellers) S.; m. Lucile West Martin, Aug. 15, 1953; children: Martha Smith Vandervoort, Sally Smith Legg, Maury D. Smith, Jr. BS, U. Ala., 1950, LLB, JD, 1952. Bar: Ala., 1952; U.S. Dist. Ct. (mid., no. and so. dists.) Ala. 1953; U.S. Ct. Appeals, 1957, U.S. Supreme Ct., 1957. Asst. atty. gen. State of Ala., Montgomery, 1952-55; asst. dist. atty. Montgomery County, 1955-63; ptnr. Balch & Bingham LLP, Montgomery, 1955—. Chmn. lawyers adv. com. Mid. Dist. Ala., Montgomery, 1990—; mem. U.S. Ct. of Appeals 11th cir. adv. com. on rules, Montgomery, 1990—, U.S. Dist. Ct. Mid. Dist. civil justice reform act adv. com., Montgomery, 1991—. Pres. Montgomery Area United Way, Ala., 1987; mem. Leadership Montgomery, 1994. Fellow Am. Coll. Trial Lawyers, Am. Bar Found.; mem. Univ. Ala. System (bd. trustees 1991-97, trustee emeritus 1997—), Ala. Law Inst. (mem. coun.), ABA (mem. litigation sect.), Montgomery County Bar Assn. (pres. 1976), Montgomery Area C. of C. (pres. 1984), Ala. State Bar (chmn. jud. bldg. task force 1987-94). Avocations: farming, tennis. Home: 2426 Midfield Dr Montgomery AL 36111-1529 Office: Balch & Bingham LLP PO Box 78 Montgomery AL 36101-0078

SMITH, MAXWELL PAUL, retired lawyer; b. Elyria, Ohio, Jan. 8, 1924; s. Maxwell P. and Hilma Lillian (Holmgren) Smith; m. Vaunceil Hulda Tiarks, Nov. 10, 1928; children: Mark Paul, Terri Smith Lindvall, Amy Szwabowicz, Laura Eckstein. JD, Valparaiso U., 1950. Bar: Ind. 1950, US Dist. Ct. (no. dist.) Ind. 1950, US Dist. Ct. (so. dist.) Ind. 1950, US Ct. Appeals (6th cir.) 1982. Pres. Krueckeberg and Smith, PC, Ft. Wayne, Ind., 1982—90, M.P. Smith & Assocs., PC, Ft. Wayne, 1990—2004; ret., 2004. Contbg. author: Professional Corporations, 1978, Indiana Continuing Legal Education Forum, 1983. Pres. bd. trustees, elder First Presbyterian Ch., Ft. Wayne; pres. Neighbors, Inc., Ft. Wayne; bd. dirs. Samaritan Counseling, Inc. 1st lt. JAGC U.S. Army, 1952—53. Decorated Army Commendation medal. Mem.: Ind. State Bar Assn. (citation 1982), Allen County Bar Assn., Wildwood Racquet Club (Ft. Wayne). Office: 622 S Calhoun St Fort Wayne IN 46802-1708

SMITH, MERRITT ROE, history professor; b. Waverly, N.Y., Nov. 14, 1940; s. Wilson Niles and Mary Eleanor (Fitzgerald) S.; m. Bronwyn M. Mellquist, Aug. 24, 1974. AB, Georgetown U., 1963; MA, Pa. State U., 1965, PhD, 1971; LHD (hon.), Rensselaer Poly. Inst., 1997. Asst. prof. history Ohio State U., Columbus, 1970-74, assoc. prof., 1974-78; vis. prof. history and sociology of sci. U. Pa., Phila., 1976; prof. history tech. program in sci., tech. and society M.I.T., Cambridge, 1978—, Metcalfe prof. engring. and liberal arts, 1989-92, dir. progam in sci., tech. and society, 1992—96, 2000—02, Leverett and William King Cutten prof., 1993—. Author: Harpers Ferry Armory and the New Technology, 1977, Military Enterprise and Technological Change, 1985, Science, Technology and the Military, 2 vols., 1988, Does Technology Drive History?, 1994, Major Problems in the History of American Technology, 1998, Inventing America, 2002; mem. editorial bd. Tech. and Culture, 1973-91, Bus. History Rev., 1978-85, MIT Press, 1986-91, Archimedes, 1995—2001. Mem. Mass. Hist. Soc.; bd. advisors MIT Mus. Recipient Cert. of Commendation Am. Assn. State and Local History, 1978, Disting. Tchg. award Ohio State U., 1978, Founders Day award Charles River Mus. Industry, 2003; grantee Ohio State U., 1972, Am. Philos. Soc., 1974, Harvard Bus. Sch., 1974-75, Eleutherian Mills-Hagley Found., 1978-79, Alfred P. Sloan Found., 1994-2002; Guggenheim fellow, 1983-84, Regents fellow Smithsonian Instn., 1984-85. Mem. AAAS, Am. Acad. Arts and Scis., Soc. History Tech. (mem. exec. coun., Dexter Prize com., Da Vinci medal 1994, mus. com., v.p., pres. 1989-91), Orgn. Am. Historians (Frederick Jackson Turner award 1977, Disting. lectr. 2004—), Bus. History Conf., Am. Antiquarian Soc., Newcomen Soc. N.Am., Soc. Indsl. Archeology, History Sci. Soc. (Pfizer award 1978), Phi Kappa Phi, Phi Alpha Theta. Home: 17 Longfellow Rd Newton MA 02462-1505 Office: MIT Rm E51-185 Cambridge MA 02139 E-mail: roesmith@mit.edu.

SMITH, MICHAEL, college president; b. St. Joseph, Mo., Jan. 30, 1941; s. Walton Joseph and Margaret Dorothy (Chubb) S.; m. Connie Stanton, Oct. 27, 1965; children: Jeffrey, Timothy. AD, Mo. Western Community Coll., 1960; BS, N.E. Mo. State U., 1967; PhD, U. Nebr., 1975. Ins. investigator Retail Credit Co., St. Joseph, Mo., 1963-65; instr. Havana (Ill.) High Sch., 1967-68, West Bend (Iowa) High Sch., 1968-70, U. Nebr., 1972-75; asst. prof. English Albany (Ga.) Jr. Coll., 1975-78; chmn. arts and scis., dir. internat. programs U. Minn., Crookston, 1978-80; chief exec. officer, coll. dean N.D. State U., Bottineau, 1980-87; provost, dean of faculty Richard Bland Coll., Coll. William and Mary, 1987-89; chancellor La. State U., Eunice, 1989-95; pres. Our Lady of the Lake Coll., Baton Rouge. Commr. North Cen. Assn. Colls. and Schs., 1984-, accreditation cons./evaluator, 1982-87, vis. prof. English, U. New Orleans, 1995-98. With U.S. Army, 1960-63. Office: Our Lady of the Lake Coll 7434 Perkins Rd Baton Rouge LA 70808-4374 Office Phone: 225-768-1710. E-mail: msmith@ololcollege.edu.

SMITH, MICHAEL ALAN, retired insurance industry analyst; b. Schenectady, NY, Mar. 5, 1947; s. Norman Leslie and Margaret (Gleeson) S.; m. Denise Pagliaro, July 27, 1972 (separated Dec. 1989); children: James Michael, Dawn Susan. BS in Agrl. Econs., Cornell U., 1970; MBA in Fin., Fairleigh Dickinson U., 1978. Methods analyst Liberty Mut. Ins. Co., Boston, 1970-71; mktg. rep. Texaco Inc., Washington, 1972-74; sec. underwriting divsn. Palisades Life Ins. Co., Orangeburg, NY, 1974-76; sr. planning officer Home Ins. Group, NYC, 1976-83; v.p. planning Ideal Mut. Ins. Co., NYC, 1983-85; sr. v.p., ins. industry analyst Lehman Bros. Inc., NYC, 1985-96; dir., sr. ins. analyst Salomon Bros., NYC, 1996-97; mng. dir. Bear Stearns & Co., 1998—2003; ret., 2003. Contbr. articles to profl. jours. Mem. Assn. Ins. and Fin. Analysts. Avocations: youth coach, skiing, go-kart racing.

SMITH, MICHAEL ERNEST, archaeologist, educator; b. Olongapo Zambales, The Philippines, Sept. 12, 1953; came to U.S., 1954; s. Dudley Burcham and Esther Lucille (Oyler) S.; m. Cynthia M. Heath, Jan. 19, 1979; children: April Nicole, Heather Colleen. BA in Anthropology, Brandeis U., 1975; MA in Anthropology, U. Ill., 1978, PhD of Anthropology, 1983. Prof. Loyola U., Chgo., 1982-90, SUNY, Albany, 1991—. Dir. Inst. Mesoam. Studies, Albany, 1994-99, Archaeol. Excavations, Cuernavaca, Mex., 1985-2001; Archaeol. Rsch., Tolaco, Mex., 2002-; cons. U.S. Libr. Congress, 1997-2002. Author: The Aztecs, 1996, 2d edit., 2003, Aztec Imperial Strategies, 1996, Archaeological Excavations at Aztec Sites, 1992; editor: Economies and Politics in Aztec Realm, 1994, Ancient Civilizations of Mesoamerica: A Reader, 1999, The Postclassic Mesoamerican World, 2003; editl. bd. mem. Ancient Mesoam., 1990—; book rev. editor Latin American Antiquity, 1998-2002. Rsch. grantee NSF, 1995, 86, 89, 92, 2002, 03, Nat. Geog. Soc., 1994, Nat. Endowment Humanities, 1992. Mem. Soc. Am. Archaeology, Am. Anthropol. Assn., Sigma Xi. Office: Dept Anthropology State Univ NY Albany NY 12222-0001 E-mail: mesmith@albany.edu.

SMITH, MICHAEL JAMES, industrial engineering educator; b. Madison, Wis., May 12, 1945; s. James William and Ruth Gladys (Murphy) S.; m. Patricia Ann Bentley, June 22, 1968; children: Megan Colleen, Melissa Maureen. BA, U. Wis., 1968, MA, 1970, PhD, 1973. Rsch. analyst Wis. Dept. Industry Labor, Madison, 1971-74; rsch. psychologist Nat. Inst. for Occupational Safety and Health, USPHS, Cin., 1974-84; prof. U. Wis., Madison, 1984—. Owner, prin. M.J. Smith Assocs. Inc., Madison, 1991—. Contbr. articles to profl. jours. Mem. APA, Inst. Indsl. Engrs. (sr.), Human Factors Soc., Assn. Computer Machinery, Am. Soc. Testing and Measurement. Avocation: tennis. Home: 6719 Shamrock Glen Cir Middleton WI 53562-1144 Office: U Wis Dept Indsl Engring Human Factors Rsch Lab 1513 University Ave Madison WI 53706-1539 Office Phone: 608-263-6329. E-mail: mjsmith@engr.wisc.edu.

SMITH, MICHAEL L. transportation company executive; b. 1948; BA, DePauw U., 1970. V.p. Coll. Mktg. & Rsch. Corp., 1968-70; with Arthur Andersen & Co., 1970-75; div. contr. Mayflower Group, Carmel, Ind., 1975-77, group v.p., warehouse div., 1977, then exec. v.p., now pres., chief oper. officer, 1989—, also bd. dirs.; with Mayflower Transit Co. subs. Mayflower Group, Carmel, 1975—, then sr. v.p., chmn., CEO, 1989—, also bd. dirs. Office: Mayflower Contract Svcs 5360 College Blvd Shawnee Mission KS 66211-1641

SMITH, MICHAEL PETER, social science educator, researcher; b. Dunkirk, N.Y., Aug. 2, 1942; s. Peter Joseph and Rosalie Barbara (Lipka) S.; m. Patricia Anne Lendway, Aug. 21, 1965. BA magna cum laude, St. Michael's Coll., 1964; MA in Polit. Sci., U. Mass., 1966, PhD in Polit. Sci., 1971. Instr., asst. prof. dept. govt. Dartmouth Coll., Hanover, NH, 1968—71; asst. prof. dept. polit. sci. Boston U., 1971—74; assoc. prof., prof. dept. polit. sci. Tulane U., New Orleans, 1974—86; prof. cmty. studies U. Calif., Davis, 1986—, chmn. dept. applied behavioral scis., 1986—91, chmn. cmty. studies and devel. program, 2001—. Vis. prof. pub. policy U. Calif., Berkeley, 1981, city planning U. N.C., Chapel Hill, 1982, city planning U. Calif., Berkeley, 1985; vis. scholar in govt. U. Essex, Eng., 1979; vis. scholar polit. and social sci. U. Cambridge, Eng., 1982; vis. scholar Inst. Urban and Regional Devel., U. Calif., Berkeley, 1990, 94 Internat. Ctr. for Advanced Studies, NYU, 1998. Author: The City & Social Theory, 1979, City, State and Market, 1988, Transnational Urbanism, 2001; co-author: Restructuring the City, 1983, California's Changing Faces, 1993; editor: Cities in Transformation, 1984, Breaking Chains, 1991, After Modernism, 1992, Marginal Spaces, 1995, Comparative Urban & Community Research, 1986—; co-editor: The Capitalist City, 1987—, The Bubbling Cauldron, 1995, Transnationalism from Below, 1998, City and Nation: Rethinking Place and Identity, 2001; mem. editl. bd. U. Press Am., 1976—. Office: Dept Human & Cmty Devel Univ Calif Davis CA 95616 Office Phone: 916-752-2243. E-mail: mpsmith@ucdavis.edu.

SMITH, MICHAEL ROBERT, electro-optical engineer, physicist; b. Tela, Honduras, Aug. 24, 1937; s. Ike Morgan and Edith Helen (Hudson) S.; m., div., remarried Lorraine L. Smith, Apr. 26, 2002; children: Stephen, Monica, Meryl. BME, Ga. Inst. Tech., 1959, MS in Nuclear Engring., 1961; PhD, Case Inst. Tech., 1965. Mem. tech. staff Hughes Rsch. Labs., Malibu, Calif., 1965-68; v.p., dir. rsch. Britt Corp., L.A., 1968-73; sr. staff engr. Singer/Librascope divsn., Glendale, Calif., 1973-78; pres. Exocor Tech., Newbury Park, Calif., 1978-95; asst. prof., head physics program Calif. Luth. U., Thousand Oaks, 1990-96; design leader LIGO project Calif. Inst. Tech., Pasadena, 1996—. Contbr. articles to profl. jours.; inventor emergency vehicle warning and traffic control sys., emergency vehicle warning sign, flat electro-optic display panel, high power mirror, laser recording film with opaque coating, pulsed gas laser with radiation cooling, infrared laser photocautery device; 8 U.S. patents; 9 fgn. patents. Greek folk dance tchr. Arts Coun., Thousand Oaks, Calif., 1991-97. Mem. IEEE, Laser Electro-Optic Soc. (chair 1995-97), Sigma Xi, Pi Tau Sigma. Republican. Home: 1611 N Roosevelt Ave Pasadena CA 91104-1927 Business E-Mail: smith@ligo.caltech.edu.

SMITH, MICHAEL W. lawyer; b. Detroit, Apr. 23, 1943; s. Clarence William and Mary Drane (Corbett) S.; m. Sandra Lea Bartel, Dec. 17, 1967; children: Dominick, Jordan, Sloan. BBA, U. Mich., 1965; JD, U. Wis., 1968. Bar: Wis. 1968. Staff atty. Wis. Legis. Coun., Madison, 1968-70; assoc. Sieker, Reynolds & Peckham, Madison, 1970-72; pvt. practice Lodi, Wis., 1973—. City atty. City of Lodi, 1973—. Pres. Lodi Sch. Bd., 1983-89, Lodi Optimist Club, 1973. Mem. State Bar of Wis., Columbia County Bar Assn. Avocations: reading, skiing, bicycling, kayaking. Office: Law Offices Michael W Smith 154 S Main St Lodi WI 53555-1119

SMITH, MIEKO KOTAKE, education educator; b. Osaka, Japan, Sept. 19, 1941; arrived in U.S., 1968; d. Kohei and Toshiko Kotake; m. James Allen Smith; 6 children. BA, Tsuda Coll., Tokyo, Japan, 1964; MA, Ednl. Specialist Degree, Kent State U., 1972; PhD, Case Western Res. U., 1980. LCSW ind. social worker Ohio. Student activities coord., internat. student advisor Cleve. State U., 1972—78; rsch. assoc. Case Western Res. U., 1978—81; dir. aftercare Murtis H. Taylor Multi-Svcs. Ctr., 1981—82; dir. rsch. and tng. Hill House Mental Health Rehab. and Rsch., Inc., 1982—87; ind. cons. Beachwood, Ohio, 1987—90; asst. prof. Cleve. State U., 1990—93, assoc. prof., 1993—2000, prof., 2000—. Cons. Summit County Children Svcs. Bd., Akron, Ohio, 1988—90. Contbr. chapters to books, articles to profl. jours. Bd. dirs., v.p., pers. com. chair Cleve. YWCA, 1975—87; bd. dirs., edn. chair Women's City Club of the Greater Cleve., 1991—96; trustee Help Found., Cleve., 1994—96; chairperson Women Celebrating the Bicentennial, Cleve., 1994—97; trustee, com. chair Women's Cmty. Found., Cleve., 1991—97; bd. governance, chair Multi-Cultural Tng. Inst., Cleve., 1993—98; trustee Phoenix Soc., Cleve., 1996—98; bd. govs., first vice chair, program planning and policy com. chair Cuyahoga County Cmty. Mental Health Bd., Cleve., 1998; bd. dirs. Univ. Christian Movement, Cleve., 1992—94. Recipient Rsch. Recognition award, Ohio Program Evaluators' Group, 1992; grantee, Ohio Dept. Mental Health, 1985, 1990, 1999, U.S. Dept. Edn., 1999, City of Cleve., 1999, 2000, 2001, U.S. Dept. Health and Human Svcs., 2000. Mem.: AAUP, NASW, Am. Evaluation Assn. D-Liberal. Presbyterian. Avocation: reading.

SMITH, MIGNON C. publishing executive; AA, Briarcliff Jr. Coll., Briarcliff Manor, N.Y., 1952. Bur. chief Washington/Ala. News Reports, Washington, 1980—. Office: Washington/Ala News Reports PO Box 58058 Washington DC 20037-8058

SMITH, MILTON CLARK, JR., lawyer; b. Dallas, Apr. 5, 1940; s. Milton C. and Virginia (Terry) S.; m. Carol Ann Brinsmade, Aug. 23, 1963; children: Mollye Catherine, Patricia Clark. BBA, U. Tex., 1963, JD, 1966. Bar: Tex. 1966, U.S. Dist. Ct. (so. dist.) Tex. 1966, U.S. Dist. Ct. (no. dist.) Tex. 1972. Jr. ptnr. Cox, Wilson, Duncan & Clendenin, Brownsville, Tex., 1966-68; assoc. Wade & Thomas, Dallas, 1968; v.p. Bonanza Internat. Devel. Co., Dallas, 1968-71; corp. counsel Steak and Ale Restaurants Am., Inc., Dallas, 1971-72; ptnr. Johnson, Blakeley, Johnson, Smith & Clark, Dallas, 1972—88, Johnson

& McElroy, LLP, 1988—2002; sole practioner Dallas, 2002—. Fellow Tex. Bar Found.; mem. State Bar Tex., Dallas Bar Assn. Republican. Episcopalian. Home: 4226 Tomberra Way Dallas TX 75220 Office: 4516 Lovers Ln Ste 257 Dallas TX 75225-6993

SMITH, MIMI, artist; b. Brookline, Mass., May 13, 1942; BFA, Mass. Coll. Fine Arts, 1963; MFA, Rutgers U., 1966. Sculpture, Steel Wool Peignoir, Spencer Mus., Lawrence, Kans., 1966, TV and Easy Chair, Newark Mus., NJ, 1974, book, Technical Error 31, Mus. Modern Art, NYC, 1990; author: (book) This is a Test, 1983. Grantee NEA artist grant, 1978, NY Found. of Arts fellow., 1986, Joan Mitchell Found. grant, 1998. Studio: 451 W Broadway New York NY 10012

SMITH, MIRANDA CONSTANCE, writer, educator; b. Denver, June 19, 1944; d. Duncan Campbell and Mabel Elsie (Roller) Clark; m. Charles Ellsworth Smith, May 3, 1963 (div. 1967); m. Armand Cecil Lepage, July 9, 1979 (div. 1982); children: Tagore Duncan Smith, Simone Michelle Lepage. BA in Writing and Lit., Burlington (Vt.) Coll., 1992. Employment counselor San Jose (Calif.) Employment Agy., 1966-68; adminstrv. asst. to pres. Rochdale Coll., Toronto, Ont., Can., 1968-70; tchr. Mylora Farms, Richmond, B.C., Can., 1972; asst. dir. campaign save whales Greenpeace East, Montreal, Can., 1973-74; tchr., grower Rooftop Gardens, Montreal, 1974-76; dir. urban agrl. Inst. Local Self Reliance, Washington, 1976-78; group leader agrl., waste and recycling Nat. Ctr. Appropriate Tech., Butte, Mont., 1978-79; horticultural dir. Coolidge Farms, Topsfield, Mass., 1981-82; farmer, tchr. Hardwick (Vt.) Organic, 1985-86; cons. Memphremagog Group, Newport, Vt., and Can., 1979-88; writer, tchr. Vt., Mass., 1989-97, tchr. horticulturalist Sullivan Diagnostic Treatment, Harris, N.Y., 1997-99; sr. editor, gardening Creative Home Press, Upper Saddle River, N.J., 1999—. Author: Advanced Home Gardening, 2001, Your Backyard Herb Garden, 1996, 200 Tips for Growing Vegetables in the Northeast, 1995, 200 Tips for Growing Flowers in the Northeast, 1995, Rodale's Pest and Disease Problem Solver, 1995, Backyard Fruits and Berries, 1994, The Real Dirt, Farmers Tell about Organic and Low-Input Farming in the Northeast, 1994, The Expert's Book of Garden Hints, 1993, Rodale's All-New Encyclopedia of Organic Gardening, 1992, The Chemical Free Yard and Garden, 1991, Rodale's Garden Insect, Disease and Weed Identification Guide, 1988, Greenhouse Gardening, 1985. Organizer Lampson Brook Food Group, Belchertown, 1996-97. Mem. New Eng. Small Farm Inst. (bd. dirs. 1976-97, 2001—). Office: 24 Park Way Upper Saddle River NJ 07458

SMITH, MOLLY D. theater director; b. Yakima, Wash. d. Kay. BA, Cath. U.; MA in Theatre, Am. U., PhD (hon.), 2001. Founder Perserverance Theatre, Juneau, Alaska, 1979—98; artistic dir. Arena Stage, Washington, 1998—. Creative advisor Sundance Inst. New Plays; lit. advisor Banff Playwright's Colony, Canada; bd. dir. Theatre Comms. Group; panelist Ctr. Internat. Theatre Devel.; spkr. in field; prof. Arts, Music and Theatre Dept. Georgetown U.; judge Susan B. Blackburn Prize. Dir.: (plays). Named Artist of Yr., Alaska State Coun. Arts; named one of 100 Most Powerful Women, Washingtonian Mag., 2001; recipient Cmty. Leader award, U. Alaska Southeast. Office: Arena Stage 1101 6th St SW Washington DC 20024

SMITH, MORTON EDWARD, ophthalmology educator, dean; b. Balt., Oct. 17, 1934; BS, U. Md., 1956, MD, 1960. Bd. cert. Ophthalmology Bd.; lic. physician Mo., Md., Wis. Rotating intern Denver Gen. Hosp., 1960-61; resident, nat. inst. of neurol. diseases and blindness fellow in opthalmology Washington U. Sch. Medicine-Barnes Hosp., 1961-63; NIH spl. fellow in ophthalmic pathology Armed Forces Inst. of Pathology, Washington, 1964; chief resident, instr. ophthalmology Washington U. Sch. Medicine, St. Louis, 1965-66, instr. ophthalmology, 1966-67, asst. prof. ophthalmology and pathology, 1967-69, assoc. prof. ophthalmology and pathology, 1969-75, prof. ophthalmology and pathology, 1975—, asst. dean, 1978-91, assoc. dean, 1991-96, prof. emeritus, assoc. dean emeritus, 1996—; prof. ophthalmology U. Wis., Madison, 1995-2001. Vis. scholar Eye Inst., Columbia Presbyn. Med. Ctr., N.Y.C., 1966; prof./lectr. Montefiore Hosp., Pitts., 1969, U. Ark., 1970, 77, 80, 82, 84, 86, 88, U. Fla., 1972, 81, U. Tex. and Lackland AFB, San Antonio, 1973, U. Colo., 1974, 82, U. Mo., 1974, 79, 80, 88, So. Ill. U., Springfield, 1974, U. Md., 1975, Montreal (Can.) Gen. Hosp., 1975, U. Wis., 1976, 87, 93, U. Pitts., 1977, 83, 87, U. Iowa, 1977, 87, Cleve. Clinic, 1978, Colo. Ophthalmol. Soc., 1978, Brooke Army Hosp., San Antonio, 1979, Wills Eye Hosp., Phila., 1980, USPHS Hosp., San Francisco, 1981, U. Calif., Davis, 1981, Sinai Hosp., Balt., 1985, 89, 94, U. Calif., San Diego, 1985, Tufts U., Boston, 1985, Cornell U., N.Y.C., 1988, U. Wash., Seattle, 1990, Brown U., Providence, 1990, Vanderbilt U., Nashville, 1991, Duke U., Durham, N.C., 1992; Chandler lectr. Harvard U., 1988; The Lois A. Young-Thomas Meml. lectr. U. Md., 1991; Braley lectr. U. Iowa, 1993; Havener Meml. lectr. Ohio State, 1994. Editor pathology sect.: Perspectives in Ophthalmology, 1977; mem. editl. bd. Ophthalmic Plastic & Reconstructive Surgery, 1986-90; contbr. articles to profl. jours. With USAR M.C., 1958-66. Scholar U. Md., 1958, 59. Fellow Am. Acad. Ophthalmology (ophthalmic pathology com. 1977-83, chmn. ophthalmic com. 1979-83, Honor award for svc. 1981, Sr. Honor award 1992); mem. AMA, Am. Bd. Ophthalmology (diplomate, bd. dirs. 1992—), Assn. for Rsch. in Vision and Ophthalmology (chmn. sect. pathology ann. meeting 1971), Am. Assn. Ophthalmic Pathologists (pres. 1977-80), Assn. Am. Med. Colls. (group med. edn. 1985—), Mo. Med. Assn., Mo. Ophthalmol. Soc., Verhoeff Soc., Theobald Soc., St. Louis Med. Soc., St. Louis Ophthalmol. Soc., Soc. Med. Coll. Dirs. for Continuing Med. Edn., Alpha Omega Alpha (sec.-treas. chpt. 1993-95, councillor 2003—). Home: 1275 Castle Gate Dr Saint Louis MO 63132-1989 Office: Campus Box 8096 660 S Euclid Ave Saint Louis MO 63110-1093 Business E-Mail: smithm@vision.wustl.edu.

SMITH, MORTON HOWISON, religious organization administrator, educator; b. Roanoke, Va., Dec. 11, 1923; s. James Brookes and Margaret Morton (Howison) S.; m. Lois Virginia Knopf, July 7, 1925; children: Samuel Warfield, Susanne Rochet Margaret. BA, U. Mich., 1947; BD, Columbia Theol. Sem., 1953; ThM, ThD, Free U., Amsterdam, The Netherlands, 1962. Ordained to ministry Presbyn. Ch., 1954. Pastor Springfield-Roller Presbyn. Chs., Carroll County, Md., 1954; prof. bible Belhaven Coll., Jackson, Miss., 1954-63; guest lectr. Westminster Theol. Sem., Phila., 1963-64; prof. Reformed Theol. Sem., Jackson, 1964-79; stated clk. gen. assembly Presbyn. Ch. in Am., Decatur, Ga., 1973-88; prof. systematic theology Greenville Presbyn. Theol. Sem., 1987—, dean faculty, 1987-98. Moderator gen. assembly Presbyn. Ch. Am., 2000-01; advisor to bd. dirs. Greenville (S.C.) Presbyn. Theol. Sem., 1986-98, bd. dirs.; mem. bd. dirs. Presbyn. Jour., Asheville, N.C., 1965-87; lectr. on theology Republic of So. Africa, June-July, 1988, Riga, Latvia, 1992, Budapest, Hungary, 1994, Prague, Czech Republic, 1994, 95, Trinidad and Tobago, 1995, Zlin, Czech Republic, 1998, 99, on missions, Republic of Korea, June-July, 1989, Munkton, Can., 1998, 99, Recife, Brazil, 1998, 2002, Reformed Sem., St. Petersburg, Russia, New Zealand, 2003. Author: Studies in Southern Presbyterian Theology, 1962, 2d edit. 1987, How Is the Gold Become Dim, 1973, republished 1998, (pamphlet) Reformed Evangelism, 1970, Testimony, 1986, Commentary on the Book of Church Order, 1990, Harmony of the Westminster Confession and Catechisms, 1990, Systematic Theology, 1994; contbr. articles to Reformed Theology in Am., 1985, Did God Create in Six Days?, Written for our Instruction: The Sufficiency of Scripture for All of Life. Trustee Covenant Coll., Lookout Mountain, Tenn., 1982-90. 1st lt. USAAF, 1942-45. Fulbright fellow U.S. Govt., 1958. Mem. N.Am. Presbyn. and Reformed Coun. of Chs. (sec. 1977-92). Presbyterian. Avocations: flying, travel, genealogy. Office: Greenville Presbyn Theol Sem PO Box 690 Taylors SC 29687-0014

SMITH, MURRAY THOMAS, transportation company executive; b. Hudson, S.D., 1939; s. Rex D. and Frances M. Smith; m. Diane R. Cramer, Dec. 4, 1959 (div. June 1994); children: Lisa B., Thomas M., Amy R.; m. Donna Thomas Kjonaas, Jan. 1995. V.p. Overland Express Inc., Indpls., 1978-82; v.p. ops. R.T.C. Transp. Inc., Forest Pk., Ga., 1982-83; with Midwest Coast Transport L.P., Sioux Falls, S.D., 1983—, sr. v.p., 1983-84; pres. Midwest Coast Transport L.P., Sioux Falls, S.D., 1984-89, prin., pres., chief exec. officer, 1989—, also bd. dirs.; pres. Willis Shaw Express, Elm Springs, Ark., 1999—. Bd. dirs. Interstate Carrier Conf., Nat. Perishable Logistics Assn. Bd. dirs. Sioux Valley Hosp., 1991-2000, United Way, Sioux Falls, 1991-2000. Office: Midwest Coast Transport LP 1600 E Benson Rd Sioux Falls SD 57104-0822 E-mail: smithm@mct-comcar.com.

SMITH, MYRON JOHN, JR., librarian, author; b. Toledo, May 3, 1944; s. Myron John and Marion Oliva (Herbert) S.; 1 son, Myron John III. Student, Coll. Steubenville, 1962; AB, Ashland Coll., 1966; MLS, Western Mich. U., 1967; MA, Shippensburg U., 1969; postgrad., U. Wis., Purdue U.; LittD, Cardinal Newman Coll., 1982. Rsch. librarian G.W. Blunt White Libr., Mystic Seaport, Conn., 1967-68; asst. librarian Western Md. Coll., Westminster, 1969-72; libr. dir. Huntington (Ind.) Pub. Libr., 1972-76; prof. history and libr. sci., dir. librs. Benedum Libr. Salem-Teikyo U.; dir., then assoc. dir. aviation program Salem (W.Va.) Coll., 1976-90; prof. history and libr. sci., libr. dir. Tusculum Coll., Greeneville, Tenn., 1990—. Mem. Am. Com. on History 2d World War, Assn. for Bibliography of History Author: American Naval Bibliography Series, 1972-74, Huntington Centennial Handbook, 1973, The Sophisticated Lady: The Battleship Indiana in World War II, 1973, World War II at Sea: A Bibliography of Sources in English, 1976, (with Robert Webber) Sea Fiction Guide, 1976, The Cloak and Dagger Bibliography, 1976, World War I in the Air, 1977, Air War Chronology 1939-45, 1977, Air War Bibliography Series, 1977—, The Mountain State Battleship: USS West Virginia, 1979, Air War Southeast Asia, 1979, The Soviet Navy, 1941-1978, 1979, The Secret Wars Series, 1980-81, The Soviet Air and Strategic Rocket Forces, 1941-1980, 1981, The Soviet Army, 1941-1980, 1981, Equestrian Studies: The Salem College Guide, 1981, The Cloak and Dagger Fiction Guide: An Annotated Guide to Spy Thrillers, 1981, (with Terry White) 3d edit., 1994, The Mountaineer Battlewagon: USS West Virginia, 1982, The Keystone Battlewagon: USS Pennsylvania, 1983, The Golden State Battlewagon: USS California, 1983, Watergate: A Bibliography, 1983 World War II: Mediterranean and European Theaters, 1984, The United States Navy and Coast Guard, 1946-1983: A Bibliography of English Language Works and 16mm Films, 1984, U.S. Television Network News: A Guide to Sources in English, 1984, Battleships and Battlecruisers, 1884-1984: A Bibliography and Chronology, 1985, Baseball: A Comprehensive Bibliography, 1986, 99th Infantry Division Bibliography, 1986, The Airline Bibliography: The Salem College Guide to Sources on Commercial Aviation, Vol. I, The United States, 1986, Vol. II, Airliners and Foreign Carriers, 1987, Passenger Airliners of the United States, 1926-86: A Pictorial Guide, 1987, rev. edit. through 1991, 1991, 3d rev. edit. through 1995, 4th revised edit., 2002, Brooklyn/Los Angeles Dodgers: A Bibliography, 1987, American Warplane Bibliography, 1989, Volunteer Battlewagon: The U.S.S. Tennessee (BB-43), 1989; editor: Sports Teams and Players Bibliography Series, 1987, Battle and Leaders Bibliography Series, 1988, 100 Years of Opportunity: A Pictorial History of Salem College, 1888-1988, 1988, Pro Football Bio-Bibliography, 1920-1988, 1989, Pearl Harbor, December 7, 1941: An Annotated Bibliography, 1991, Battles of the Coral Sea and Midway, 1942: A Bibliography, 1991, World War II at Sea, 1974-1989: A Bibliography, 1990, Professional Football: The Official Pro Football Hall of Fame Bibliography, 1993, Baseball: A Comprehensive Bibliography-1st Supplement: 1985-1991, 93, The College Football Bibliography, 1994, Glimpses of Tusculum College: A Pictorial History, 1794-1994, 1994, Baseball: A Comprehensive Bibliography-2d Supplement: 1992-1997, 1998, The Airline Encyclopedia, 1909-2000, 2002; contbr. articles to various jours. Recipient Nelson Ross award Profl. Football Rsch. Assn., 1993; 1st Am. recipient Richard Franck Gold medal Bibliothek für Zeitgeschichte, Stuttgart, Fed. Rep. Germany, 1981. Mem. ALA, U.S. Naval Inst., U.S. Mil. Inst., U.S. Air Force Found., Assn. Bibliog. of History (pres. 1981-82), Alliance of Librs. in Northeast Tenn. (pres. 1997—), Beta Phi Mu, Phi Alpha Theta. Clubs: Optimist. Office: Tusculum Coll PO Box 5005 Greeneville TN 37743-0001 Office Phone: 423-636-7320.

SMITH, NANCY ANGELYNN, federal agency administrator; b. Nashville, Mar. 28, 1950; d. Russell Monroe and Louise (Stephenson) Smith; m. Richard Christian Egan, Jan. 1, 1999. Student, Blair Acad. Music, 1966, Am. Internat. Acad. Europe, 1970; BA in Psychology with distinction, Rhodes Coll., 1972; MS with honors, U. Tenn., 1974; cert. in acctg., U. New Orleans, 1985, U. SC, 1987. Contract adminstr. State of Tex. Dept. Health and Human Svcs., Houston, 1976-78; dept. Head Coop. Edn. Program No. Va. C.C., Annandale, 1978-81; revenue agt. IRS Dept. of Treasury, Nashville, 1988-99, mgr., adminstr. IRS, 1999—. Faculty rep. Faculty Senate No. Va. C.C., Annandale, 1979—81; comm. rep. IRS, 2002—. Contbr. articles to profl. jours. Vol. Voter Registration program, Denver, 1981—84, Adopt-a-Sch., Nashville, 1993—97, Tenn. State Guard; disaster relief coord. Ky. and Tenn., 1998—99, Red Cross Inst., 1976—78, VITA, 1990—95; vol. Congresswoman Pat Shroeder, Denver, 1981—84, Al Gore for Senate, Nashville, 1987—88, Federica Pena for Mayor, Denver, 1981—; bd. dirs. No. Va. C.C., Annandale, 1978—81. Mem.: DAR, Advancement Individual Minorities, Profl. Mgrs. Assn., Cert. Fraud Examiners Assn., Gamma Beta Phi, Alpha Omicron Pi (chmn. bd. dirs. Colo. chpt.), Omicron Nu (hon.), Phi Kappa Pi (hon.). Avocations: painting, skeet shooting, camping, historical battlefields, collecting edged weapons.

SMITH, NANCY HOHENDORF, retired sales and marketing executive; b. Detroit, Jan. 30, 1943; d. Donald Gerald and Lucille Marie (Kopp) Hohendorf; m. Richard Harold Smith, Aug. 21, 1978 (div. Jan. 1984). BA, U. Detroit, 1965; MA, Wayne State U., 1969. Customer rep. Xerox Corp., Detroit, 1965-67, mktg. rep. Univ. Microfilms subs. Ann Arbor, Mich., 1967-73, mktg. coord., 1973-74, mgr. dir. mktg., 1975-76, mgr. mktg., 1976-77, major account mktg. exec., 1978-79, New Haven, 1979-80, account exec. State of N.Y. N.Y.C., 1981, N.Y. region mgr. customer support Greenwich, Conn., 1982, N.Y. region sales ops. mgr., 1982, State of Ohio account exec. Columbus, 1983, new bus. sales mgr. Dayton, Ohio, 1983, major accounts sales mgr., 1984, info. systems sales and support mgr., quality specialist Detroit, 1985-87, new product launch mgr., ops. quality mgr., 1988, dist. mktg. mgr., 1989-92, major accounts sales mgr., 1992—; graphics arts industry sales mgr., 1998—; ret. Reg. graphic arts industry cons. mgr., 1999. Named to Outstanding Young Women of Am., 1968, Outstanding Bus. Woman, Dayton C. of C., 1984, Women's Inner Circle of Achievement, 1990. Mem. NAFE, Am. Mgmt. Assn., Women's Econ. Club Detroit, Detroit Inst. Arts Founders' Soc., Detroit Hist. Soc., Detroit Hist. Soc. Republican. Roman Catholic. Avocations: interior decorating, reading, music, art. Home: 6462 West Oaks Dr West Bloomfield MI 48324-3269

SMITH, NANCY L. information technology executive; BS in Mgmt. and Orgnl. Behavior, U. San Francisco. Western regional sales mgr., nat. sales mgr. Electronic Arts, Redwood City, Calif., 1984, v.p. sales, 1988—93, sr. v.p. N.Am. sales and distbn., 1993—96, exec. v.p. N.Am. sales, 1996—98, exec. v.p., gen. mgr. N.AM. pub., 1998—. Office: Electronic Arts Inc 209 Redwood Shores Pkwy Redwood City CA 94065-1175*

SMITH, NANCY WOOLVERTON, journalist, real estate agent, appraiser, antiques broker; b. San Antonio, July 31, 1947; d. Tillman Louis and Enid Maxine (Woolverton) Brown; 1 dau., Christina Elizabeth Woolverton Jones; m. William F. Pry II, Mar. 7, 1998 (div. July 31, 2003). Student, Ecole Nouvelle de la Suisse, Romande, Lausanne, Switzerland, 1962, Vanderbilt U., 1964; BA, So. Meth. U., 1968, postgrad., 1969-70. Cert. S.E. Paralegal Inst., Ancien Regime Christie's (London), antiques and residential contents. Tchr. spl. edn. Hot Springs Sch. Dist. (Ark.), 1970-72; reporter, soc. editor Dallas Morning News, 1974-82; soc./celebrity columnist Dallas Times Herald, 1982-91; owner, pub. High Society, Society Fax; bus .editor DFW Cmty. Newspapers divsn. Lionheart Newspapers Inc., Plano, Tex., 1999—; co-founder Decorative Arts Soc. Dallas, For Worth. Realtor, Ebby Halliday Realtors; stringer Washington Post, 1978; owner Nancy Smith Pub. Rels. Contbg. editor Ultra mag., Houston, 1981-82, Tex. Woman mag., Dallas, 1979-80, Profl. Woman mag., Dallas, 1979-80; mem. bd. advisors Ultra Mag., 1985—; columnist North Dallas People; writer D Homes; appeared on TV series Jocelyn's Weekend, Sta. KDFI-TV, 1985. Bd. dirs. TACA arts support orgn., Dallas, 1980—, asst. chmn. custom auction, 1978-83; judge Miss Tex. USA Contest, 1984; bd. dirs. Am. Parkinson Disease Assn. (Dallas chpt.), mem. adv. bd. Cattle Baron's Ball Com., Dallas Symphony Debutante presentations; mem. bd. dirs. Dallas Opera Women's Bd., Northwood Inst. Women's Bd., Dallas Symphony League; mem. Friends of Winston Churchill Meml. and libr., Dallas Theatre Ctr. Women's Guild, Childrens' Med. Ctr. Aux.; mem. women's com. Dallas Theatre Ctr.; hon. mem. Crystal Charity Ball Com.; mem. Cmty. Coun. Greater Dallas Cmty. Awareness Goals Com. Impact '88, 1985—; com. mem. Dallas Arboretum, Preservation Dallas; co-chmn. Multiple Sclerosis San Simeon Gala, 1988; celebrity co-chmn. Greer Garson Gala of Hope 1990-91; gala chmn. Greer Garson Gala of Hope for Am. Parkinson's Disease Assn., 1991-93; chmn. gala benefit Northwood U., 1994; co-chmn. star-studded stomp Mar. Dimes, 1994; mem. Femmes du Monde spl. activities com., 1999 luncheon com., com. Dallas Coun. World Affairs; bd. dirs. Dallas Ballet's Lone Star Adagio. Mem.: DAR, Internat. Soc. Appraisers (accredited; antiques and residential contents cert.), Dallas Press Club, Nat. Press Club, Soc. Profl. Journalists (v.p. coms. 1978—79), Decorative Arts Soc. Dallas/Ft. Worth (CEO, appraiser, co-founder), French Heritage Soc., Lancaster Hist. Soc., Dallas Mus. Art League, Daus. of Republic of Tex. (registrar 1972), Dallas So. Meml. Assn., Dallas County Heritage Soc. (bd. dirs.), Dallas Opera Guild, City of Plano Sister Cities Com., Flagler Mus., Bent Tree Country Club, Dallas Knife and Fork Club, S'Amuser, Kermis Club, Coterie Club, Thalia Club, Rondo/Carrousel Club, The 500 Club (Dallas), Argyle Club (sec. 1983—84), Pub. Affairs Luncheon Club, Plano Rotary Club, Trippers Club, Tower Club. Home: 5727 Covehaven Dr Dallas TX 75252-4934 Office Phone: 214-625-1162. E-mail: nancywoolvertonsmith@comcast.net., nancysmithpry@aol.com.

SMITH, NEAL EDWARD, congressman; b. Hedrick, Iowa, Mar. 23, 1920; s. James N. and Margaret M. (Walling) S.; m. Beatrix Havens, Mar. 23, 1946; children— Douglas, Sharon. Student, U. Mo., 1945-46, Syracuse U., 1946-47; JD, Drake U., 1950. Bar: Iowa 1950. Farmer, Iowa, 1937—; sole practice, 1950-58; atty. 50 sch. bds. in Iowa, 1951-58; asst. county atty. Polk County, Iowa, 1951; mem. 86th-103rd Congresses from 4th Dist., 1959—. Chmn. Polk County Bd. Social Welfare, 1954-56; pres. Young Democratic Clubs Am., 1953-55. Served with AUS, World War II. Decorated Air medal with 4 oak leaf clusters, Purple Heart, nine battle stars. Mem. Am. Bar Assn., Farm Bur., Farmers Union, DAV. Clubs: Masons. Home: Plaza Box 90 300 Walnut Des Moines IA 50309 Office: Davis Brown Koehn Shors The Financial Ctr 666 Walnut St Ste 2500 Des Moines IA 50309-3904

SMITH, NEIL, professional football player; b. New Orleans, Apr. 10, 1966; Student, U. Nebr. Defensive end Kansas City Chiefs, 1988—96, Denver Broncos, 1997—. Player Pro Bowl, 1991—93. Named defensive lineman, The Sporting News All-Am. team, 1987. Office: Denver Broncos 13655 Broncos Pkwy Englewood CO 80112-4150

SMITH, NEWMAN DONALD, retired financial executive; b. Chesterville, Ont., Can., Dec. 26, 1936; s. Clarke Harold and Ethelwyn Irene (Cross) S.; chartered acct., 1961; certified mgmt. acct.; 1966; chartered Inst. of Secretaries, 1967; m. Mary Elizabeth Murdoch, June 27, 1964; children: Clarke Murdoch, Brian Newman. With Coopers & Lybrand Inc., Ottawa, Ont., 1955-62; sec.-treas. Deloro Smelting & Refining Co. Ltd., Ottawa, 1963-69, M.J. O'Brien Ltd., Ottawa, 1963-69; exec. sec. Andres Wines Ltd. and subs., Winona, Ont., 1969-94, CFO, 1980-94, sr. exec. v.p. ops., 1978-94, ret.; dir. Les Vins Andres du Quebec Ltee., Peller Wines of Calif., Watleys Ltd., Superior Wines Ltd., Andres Wines (B.C.) Ltd., Andres Wines (Alta.) Ltd., Andres Wines Atlantic Ltd.; bd. dirs., chmn. Strewn Estate Winery. Fellow Chartered Inst. Secs.; mem. Fin. Execs. Inst., Chartered Accts., Hamilton Golf and Country Club, Hamilton Club. Home: 463 Ontario St Ancaster ON Canada L9G 3E1 Office Phone: 905-468-1229.

SMITH, NICK, congressman, farmer; b. Addison, Mich., Nov. 5, 1934; s. LeGrand John and Blanche (Nichols) S.; m. Bonnalyn Belle Atwood, Jan. 1, 1960; children: Julianna, Bradley, Elizabeth, Stacia. BA, Mich. State U., 1957; MS, U. Del., 1959. Radio & TV farm editor Sta. WDEL, Wilmington, Del., 1957-59; radio editor Sta. KSWD, Wichita Falls, Tex., 1959-60; capt. intelligence USAF, Tex., 1959-61; mem. twp. bd. Somerset Twp., Addison, 1962-68; asst. dep. adminstr. USDA, Washington, 1972-74; state rep. Mich. Ho. of Reps., Lansing, 1978-82; state senator Mich. State Senate, Lansing, 1982-92; mem. U.S. Congress from 7th Mich. dist, 1993—, mem. agr., sci., and internat. rels. coms. Chmn. Mich. Senate Agrl. Com., 1982-92, Mich. Senate Corrections Appropriation Com., 1984-90, Mich. Senate Mil. Affairs Com., 1984-90, Mich.Senate Fin. Com., 1990-92 Del. Am. Assembly on World Population & Hunger, Washington, 1973; nat. del. on U.S.-Soviet Cooperation and Trade, 1991; former trustee Somerset Congl. Ch. Capt. USAF, 1959-61. Fellow Kellogg Found., 1965; named Hon. FFA State Star Farmer, 1987, SCF Conservator of Yr. Hillsdale County, 1988. Mem. Mich. Farm Bur. (bd. dirs.), Jackson C. of C., Mich. State U. Alumni Club, Masons. Republican. Office: US House of Reps 2305 Rayburn House Office Bldg Washington DC 20515-2207 also: 110 First St Ste A Jackson MI 49201

SMITH, NORMAN OBED, physical chemist, educator; b. Winnipeg, Man., Can., Jan. 23, 1914; came to U.S., 1950, naturalized, 1958; s. Ernest and Ruth (Kilpatrick) S.; m. Anna Marie O'Connor, July 1, 1944; children: Richard Obed, Graham Michael, Stephen Housley. B.Sc., U. Man., 1935, M.Sc., 1936; PhD, NYU, 1939. Teaching fellow NYU, 1936-39; mem. faculty dept. chemistry U. Man., Winnipeg, 1939-50, asst. prof., 1946-49, assoc. prof., 1949-50, Fordham U., N.Y.C., 1950-65, prof. chemistry, 1965-84, prof. emeritus, 1984—, chmn. dept., 1974-78. Sr. phys. chemist Arthur D. Little, Inc., Cambridge, Mass., 1957; indsl. cons. Author: (with others) The Phase Rule and Its Applications, 1951, Chemical Thermodynamics, A Problems Approach, 1967, Elementary Statistical Thermodynamics, A Problems Approach, 1982; contbr. to: Ency. Brit, 1974. Fellow Chem. Inst. Can.; mem. Am. Chem. Soc., Asso. Can. Coll. Organists, Am. Guild Organists (dir. chpt. 1964-66, 79-82, 91-92), Sigma Xi, Phi Lambda Upsilon. Home: 811 E Central Rd Apt 112 Arlington Heights IL 60005-3293

SMITH, NORMAN RAYMOND, academic administrator; b. Toronto, Ont., Can., Oct. 24, 1946; s. William Raymond and Jeanne (Malin) S.; m. Susan Robinson, Dec. 26, 1981; 1 child, Caroline Robinson. BS, Drexel U., 1969, MBA, 1971; EdD, Harvard U., 1984; HLD (hon.) (hon.), Phila. U., 2001, Wagner Coll., 2002. Assoc. dean students Drexel U., Phila., 1971-73; v.p., dean of students, professor Phila. Univ., 1973-78; asst. dean Harvard Grad. Sch. Edn., Cambridge, Mass., 1978-80, John F. Kennedy Sch. Govt., Harvard U., Cambridge, 1980-84; exec. v.p. Moore Coll. Art, Phila., 1984-87; pres., prof. Wagner Coll., S.I., NY, 1988—2002, pres. emeritus, 2002—; pres., prof. Richmond, The Am. Internat. U. London, 2002—. Dir. Dime Bancorp; assoc. Harvard U. Philosophy of Edn. Rsch. Ctr., Cambridge, 1987—. Author: Selecting the Right College, 6th edit., 2000. Chair mayor's cabinet transition search City of Boston, 1983-84; trustee N.Y. Coun. of Ind. Colls. and Univs., 1994-97. Lt. U.S. Army, 1969-73. Recipient U. medal Drexel U., 1993, Pres.'s medal NYU, 1994. Mem. Ind. Coll. Fund N.Y. (sec.-treas.), Harvard Club of N.Y.C., Richmond County Country Club. Office: Richmond U Queens Rd Richmond-upon-Thames TW10 6JP England Home: 26 Kensington Gate London W8 5NA England Office Phone: 020-8332-8246.

SMITH, NUMA LAMAR, JR., lawyer; b. Rock Hill, S.C., Nov. 22, 1915; s. Numa Lamar and Grace (Hanes) S.; m. Mary Catherine Gray, Mar. 24, 1941; children: Patricia Gray (dec.), Elizabeth Hanes, Lamar Douglas. AB, Furman U., 1938; LL.B. with distinction, Duke U., 1941. Bar: N.Y. 1942, D.C. 1946. Assoc. firm White & Case, N.Y.C., 1941-42, Miller & Chevalier, Washington, 1946-49, partner, 1949-83, counsel, 1983—; bd. visitors, 1973-83. Sr. fellow Duke U. Law Sch., 1979-80 Assoc. editor: Duke Law Jour, 1940-41. Served with U.S. Army, 1942-46; with Judge Adv. Gen. Corps 1944-46. Recipient Gen. Excellence award Furman U., 1938 Fellow Am. Bar Found.; mem. ABA, D.C. Bar Assn., Am. Law Inst., Duke Law Alumni Assn. (pres. 1967-69), Order of Coif, Met. Club (Washington), Burning Tree Club (Bethesda, Md.), Washington Golf Club (Arlington, Va.), The Club at Pelican Bay, Sigma Alpha Epsilon. Baptist. Home: 7515 Pelican Bay Blvd Naples FL 34108-6520

SMITH, O. BRUTON, automotive company executive; Chmn., CEO Sonic Automotive, Inc., Charlotte, NC, Speedway Motor Sports, Inc., Charlotte; owner operator Town and Country Ford and various other pvt. bus., Charlotte, NC. Office: Sonic Automotive Inc 6415 Idlewild Rd Ste 109 Charlotte NC 28212

SMITH, ORIN C. food products executive; MBA, Harvard U., 1967; BA in Fin., Econ., Acctg. and Statis., U. Wash., 1965. With Touche Ross & Co., 1969—77, 1980—85, State of Wash. Office Mgmt. and Budget, 1977—80, 1985—87, No. Air Freight and Danzas Corp., 1987—90; from v.p., CFO to pres., COO Starbucks, Seattle, 1990—2000, pres., CEO, 2000—. Avocations: golf, skiing, reading. Office: Starbucks PO Box 34067 Seattle WA 98124-1067

SMITH, ORIN ROBERT, chemical company executive; b. Newark, Aug. 13, 1935; s. Sydney R. and Gladys Emmett (DeGroff) S.; m. Stephanie M. Bennett-Smith; children: Lindsay, Robin; 1 stepchild, Brendan. BA in Econometrics, Brown U., 1957; MBA in Mgmt., Seton Hall U., 1964; PhD in Econs. (hon.), Centenary Coll., 1991; LLD (hon.), Monmouth Coll., 1994. Various sales and mktg. mgmt. positions Allied Chem. Corp., Morristown, N.J., 1959-69; dir. sales and mktg. Richardson-Merrell Co., Phillipsburg, N.J., 1969-72; with M&T Chems., Greenwich, Conn., 1972-77, pres., 1975-77; with Engelhard Minerals & Chems. Corp., Menlo Park, Edison, N.J., 1977-81, corp. sr. v.p., 1978-81, pres. div. minerals and chems., 1978-81, also bd. dirs., 1979-81, pres., dir. various U.S. subs., 1979-81; exec. v.p., pres. div. minerals and chems. Engelhard Corp., Menlo Park, Edison, 1981-84, bd. dirs., 1981—, pres., CEO, Iselin, N.J., 1984-95, chmn., CEO, 1995—; also bd. dirs. Bd. dirs. Summit Bank Co., The Summit Bancorp, Vulcan Materials Co., PE Corp., Ingersoll-Rand Corp., Engelhard Corp., Mfrs. Alliance. Trustee N.J. State C. of C., Inst. for Tech. Advancement; mem. bd. overseers N.J. Inst. Tech.; trustee Plimoth Plantation; 1st vice chmn. bd. trustees Centenary Coll.; past dir. Minorco, La. Land and Exploration Co.; past trustee Henry R. Kessler Found., Inc.; past chmn. Ind. Coll. Fund N.J.; past dir.-at-large U. Maine Pulp and Paper Found. Lt. (j.g.) USN, 1957-59. Mem. Chem. Mfrs. Assn. (past bd. dirs.), Econ. Club (N.Y.C.), Union League Club (N.Y.C.), Duxbury Yacht Club, New Bedford Yacht Club, N.Y. Yacht Club. Office: Engelhard Corp 101 Wood Ave S Iselin NJ 08830-2703

SMITH, ORVILLE AUVERNE, physiology educator; b. Nogales, Ariz., June 16, 1927; s. Orville Auverne and Bess (Gill) S.; m. Clara Jean Smith; children— Nanette, Marcella. BA in Psychology, U. Ariz., 1949; MA, Mich. State U., 1950, PhD, 1953. Instr. psychology Mich. State U., East Lansing, 1953-54; fellow U. Pa., Phila., 1954-56; trainee dept. physiology and biophysics U. Wash., Seattle, 1956-58, instr. physiology and biophysics, 1958-59, asst. prof., 1959-61, 62-63; asst. dir. Regional Primate Research Ctr., 1962-69, assoc. prof., 1963-67, prof., 1967-97; assoc. dir. Regional Primate Research Center, 1969-71, dir., 1971-88, prof. emeritus, 1997—. Contbr. articles to profl. jours. Mem. Am. Physiol. Soc., Am. Soc. Primatologists (pres. 1977-79), Internat. Congress Physiol. Scis., Am. Assn. Anatomists, AAAS, Pavlovian Soc. N.Am. (pres. 1977-78), Internat. Primatological Soc., AAUP, Neurosci. Soc. Home: 30311 201st Ct SE Kent WA 98042-5920 Office: U Wash Nat Primate Rsch Ctr PO Box 357330 Seattle WA 98195-7330

SMITH, OZZIE (OSBORNE EARL SMITH), retired professional baseball player; b. Mobile, Ala., Dec. 26, 1954; m. Denise Jackson, Nov. 1, 1980; children: Osborne Earl Jr., Dustin Cameron. Grad., Calif. State Poly. U., San Luis Obispo. Shortstop San Diego Padres Baseball Club, Nat. League, 1977—82, St. Louis Cardinals Baseball Club, Nat. League, 1982—96; baseball analyst St. Louis Cardinals Sta. KPLR, St. Louis, 1997—. Named Member of World Series Championship Team, 1982; named to All-Star Team, Nat. League, 1981—92, 1994, Sporting News, 1982, 1984—87, Baseball Hall of Fame, 2002; recipient Most Valuable Player award, Nat. League Championship Series, 1985, Golden Glove award, 1980—92, Silver Slugger award, 1987. Avocations: jazz, word puzzles, backgammon. Office: 2250 Ball Dr Saint Louis MO 63146-8602

SMITH, PAMELA HYDE, ambassador; b. Tacoma, July 1945; m. Sidney G. Smith (dec.); 2 children. BA in Art History, Wellesley Coll., 1967. Joined US Info. Agy., 1975; asst. & cultural attaché US Embassy, Bucharest, 1976—77; special asst. to USIA Dir., 1977—81; cultural asst. US Embassy, Belgrade, 1982—86; dep. chief Acad. Exch. Program USIA, 1986—91; press attaché US Embassy, Jakarta, 1991—95; dir. Office Geog. Liaison U.S. Info. Agy., 1995—97; pub. affairs officer US Embassy, London, 1997—2001; U.S. amb. to Moldova Dept. State, 2001—. Office: Dept of State Amb 7080 Chisinau Pl Washington DC 20521

SMITH, PATRICIA, state representative; b. Bklyn., June 14, 1943; two children. AS, U. S. Fla., 1974; BS, Norwich U., 1991. Former town clk. and treas. Sudbury; rep. Vt. Ho. of Reps., 1996—. Mem. Vt. Munic Clkrs. and Treas. assn. (v.p.), N.E. Assn. Town Clks., Internat. Inst. Munic Clks. Roman Catholic.

SMITH, PATRICIA ANNE, special education educator; b. West Chester, Pa., Aug. 19, 1967; d. William Richard and Carol Anne (Benn) S. BS in Spl. Edn. cum laude, West Chester U., 1989; postgrad., Immaculata Coll., 1993-98. Cert. mentally and physically handicapped tchr., Pa. Learning support tchr. Chester County Intermediate Unit, Downingtown, Pa., 1989-90, early intervention tchr., 1990-92; autistic support tchr. Coatesville (Pa.) Area Sch. Dist., 1992—, event coord. WOYC workshops, 1993-2000, event coord. WOYC ext. workshops, 1999-2000, event coord. WOYC childrens workshops, 1999-2000. Presenter ann. conf. Pa. Assn. of Resources for People with Mental Retardation, Hershey, 1994, Pa. Fedn. Coun. for Exceptional Children 2003 Conv., 44th Ann. conv. No Child Left Behind in Pa., Pa. Fedn. Coun. for Exceptional Children Ann. Conf., Grantville, 2003; co-presenter ARC, 1996, Paoli Meml. Hosp., 1997; presenter info. sessions ann. conf. Del. Valley Assn. for Edn. of Young Children, Phila., 1994, Lions, Downingtown, Pa., 1992, early childhood conf. Capital Area Assn. for Edn. of Young Children, Harrisburg, Pa., 1995, vols. Caln Athletic Assn. Challenger League, 1995-96, Chester County MH/MR Consultation and Edn. Adv. Bd. Com., 1997-2000; mentor West Chester U., 1995-98. Mem. recreation adv. bd. dirs. Assn. for Retarded Citizens, Exton, Pa., 1993-98, Daisy Girl Scout Leader, 1995-96; vol. tutor Chester County Libr. Adult Literacy Program, 1995-98, vol. monitor, Residential Living Options Home, 2001—; respite provider ARC, Kencrest, 1998—. Recipient Outstanding Svc. award Coatesville Area Parent Coun., 1994, 96, Vol. award Friendship PTA, 1993, 96, 99, Pa. Early Childhood Edn. Assn. Workshop presenter award, 1993; grantee Pa.Dept. Edn., 1993, Coatesville Area Sch. Dist., 1990, Pa. Bur. Spl. Edn., 2001, 02, CCRES, 2003. Mem.: ASCD, Coun. for Exceptional Children, Autism Soc. Am., Nat. Assn. for Edn. of Young Children, Kappa Delta Pi. Republican. Roman Catholic. Home: 501 Clover Mill Rd Exton PA 19341-2505 Office: Friendship Elem Sch 296 Reeceville Rd Coatesville PA 19320-1520 Office Phone: 610-383-3770.

SMITH, PATRICIA GRACE, government official; b. Nov. 10, 1947; d. Douglas and Wilhelmina (Griffin) Jones; m. J. Clay Smith, Jr., June 25, 1983; children: Eugene Douglas, Stager Clay, Michelle L., Michael L. BA in English, Tuskegee Inst., 1968; postgrad., Auburn U., 1969-71, Harvard U., 1974, George Washington U., 1983, Fed. Exec. Inst., 1997. Cert. exec. mgmt. tng. devel. assignments Dept. Def., 1986, U.S. Senate Commerce Com., 1987. Instr. Tuskegee Inst., Ala., 1969-71; program mgr. Curber Assocs., Washington, 1971-73; dir. placement Nat. Assn. Broadcasters, Washington, 1973-74, dir. pub. affairs, 1974-77; assoc. prodr. Group W Broadcasting, Balt., 1977, prodr., 1977-78; dir. affiliate rels. and programming Sheridan Broadcasting Network, Crystal City, Va., 1978-80; dep. dir. policy, assoc. mng. dir. pub. info./reference svc. FCC, Washington, 1992-94, acting assoc. mng. dir., pub. info. and reference svcs., 1994—. Chief of staff office assoc. adminstr. for comml. space transp. FAA, U.S. Dept. Transp., 1994-96, dep. assoc. adminstr. for comml. space transp., 1996-97, acting assoc. adminstr., 1997, assoc. adminstr., 1998—. Vice-chmn. Nat. Conf. Black Lawyers Task Force on Comms., Washington, 1975-87; trustee, mem. exec. com., nominating com., youth adv. com. Nat. Urban League, 1976-81; mem. comms. com. Cancer Coordinating Coun., 1977-84; mem. Braintrust Subcom. on Children's Programming, Congl. Black Caucus, 1976—; mem. adv. bd. Black Arts Celebration, 1978-83; mem. NAACP; mem. journalism and comms. adv. coun. Auburn U., 1976-78; mem. Washington Urban League, 1985—; bd. dirs. Black Film Rev., 1989-91; mem. D.C. Commn. on Human Rights, 1986-88, chmn., 1988-91; mem. adv. coun. NIH, 1992-96; mem. bd. advisors The Salvation Army, 1993-2000. Named Outstanding Young Woman of Yr., Washington, 1975, 78; recipient Sustained Superior Performance award FCC, Washington, 1982-95, Disting. Alumnus award Tuskegee U., 1996, C. Alfred Anderson award, 2002. Mem. Women in Comms., Inc. (mem. nat. adv. com.), Broadcasters Club (bd. dirs. 1976-77), Lambda Iota Tau. Democrat. Baptist. Avocations: writing, swimming. Home: 4010 16th St NW Washington DC 20011-7002 Office: DOT/AST 800 Independence Ave SW Rm 331 Washington DC 20591-0001 Office Phone: 202-267-7793.

SMITH, PATRICK JOHN, editor, writer; b. N.Y.C., Dec. 11, 1932; s. H. Ben and Geraldine (Wilson) S.; m. Elisabeth Munro, Nov. 27, 1964; children: Douglass Munro, Matthew Wilson. Student, Phillips Exeter, 1951; AB, Princeton U., 1955. Freelance writer and critic, 1958-70; editor, pub. The Mus. Newsletter, N.Y.C., 1970-77; pres. Music Critics Assn., Washington, 1977-81; dir. opera mus. theater program NEA, Washington, 1985-89; editor Opera News, N.Y.C., 1989-98, editor-at large, 1998—. Author: The Tenth Muse: A History of the Opera Libretto, 1970, A Year at the Met, 1983. Office: Opera News 70 Lincoln Center Plz New York NY 10023-6548

SMITH, PATTI, state representative; m. Leroy Smith; 5 children. Attended, Mt. Hood C.C. State rep., dist. 52 Oreg. House Rep., Salem, 2003—; owner Family Farm. Chair Trade and Econ. Devel. Com.; mem. Agr. and Natural Resources Com.; support enforcement officer Baker County Dist. Atty.; adminstrv. sec. Woodland Park Hosp.; staff asst. Multnomah County Charter Rev. Com. Mem.: Farm Bur., East Multnomah County Pioneer Assn., Crown Point Hist. Soc., Troutdale Hist. Soc. Republican. Office: 900 Court St NE H-487 Salem OR 97301

SMITH, PAUL FREDERICK, economist, former educator; b. Mansfield, Ohio, Dec. 21, 1919; s. Phillip Fred and Myrtle Grace (Robinson) S.; m. Margaret Alice Peacock, Oct. 30, 1942; children: Terence James, Barbara Jo Smith Moren. AB, U. Chgo., 1941; A.M., Northwestern U., 1946; PhD, Am. U., 1955. Economist bd. govs. Fed. Res. System, 1947-59; prof. fin. U. Pa., Phila., 1959-85, chmn. fin. dept., 1963-67, 72-75; vice-dean, dir. doctoral programs Wharton Sch. Bus., 1976-85. Assoc. staff mem. Nat. Bur. Econ. Research, 1960-70 Author: Consumer Credit Costs, 1949-59, 1964, Economics of Financial Institutions and Markets, 1971, Money and Financial Intermediation, 1977, Comparative Financial Systems. Served with USNR, 1941-46. Decorated Bronze Star, Purple Heart. Mem. Am. Econs. Assn., Am. Fin. Assn. Home: 1429 Dubonnet Ct Fort Myers FL 33919-2711

SMITH, PAUL LETTON, JR., geophysicist; b. Columbia, Mo., Dec. 16, 1932; s. Paul Letton and Helen Marie (Doersam) S.; m. Mary Barbara Noel; children: Patrick, Melody, Timothy, Christopher, Anne. BS in Physics, Carnegie Inst. Tech., 1955, MSEE, 1957, PhD in Elec. Engring., 1960. From instr. to asst. prof. Carnegie Inst. Tech., Pitts., 1955-63; sr. engr. Midwest Rsch. Inst., Kansas City, Mo., 1963-66; from rsch. engr. to sr. scientist and group head Inst. Atmospheric Scis., S.D. Sch. Mines and Tech., Rapid City, 1966-81; vis. prof. McGill U., Montreal, Que., Can., 1969-70; chief scientist Air Weather Svc. USAF, Scott AFB, Ill., 1974-75; dir. Inst. Atmospheric Scis., S.D. Sch. Mines and Tech., Rapid City, 1981-96, prof. emeritus, 1996—. Lectr. Tech. Svc. Corp., Silver Spring, Md., 1972-91; vis. scientist Alberta Rsch. Coun., Edmonton, Can., 1984-85; dir. S.D. Space Grant Consortium, Rapid City, 1991-96; Fulbright lectr. U. Helsinki, 1986. Contbr. over 60 articles to profl. jours. Fellow Am. Meteorol. Soc. (Editor's award 1992); mem. IEEE (life, sr.), Weather Modification Assn. (Thunderbird award 1995), Sigma Xi. Home: 2107 9th St Rapid City SD 57701-5315 Office Phone: 605-394-2291. E-mail: paul.smith@sdsmt.edu.

SMITH, PAUL TILLMAN, engineering executive, writer; b. Speedway City, Ind., Oct. 13, 1927; s. Paul Tillman and Ethel R. (Ellis) Smith; divorced; children: Bill, Paula, David. Student, Butler U., 1952, GM Inst., 1953—55. Prodn. staff Internat. Harvester, Indpls., 1949—51, RCA, Indpls., 1952—53; prodn. mgr., engr. allison divsn. GM, Indpls., 1953—60; quality control mgr. Gatos Rubber Co., Denver, 1960—69; pres. Colo. Mart Industries, Inc., Arvada, Colo., 1969—82, PDB, Inc., Denver, 1983—2003, ColoCashFlo, Inc., Denver, 2003—. Author: Divorced Men Have Feelings Too, 1989, Is Now the Time for Re-evaluation, 2004. Bd. dirs. C. of C., 1956—85. With USN, 1945—48. Republican. Achievements include patents in field. Avocations: skiing, flying, golf, racquetball, photography. Office: ColoCashFlo Inc PO Box 1809 Arvada CO 80001 Office Fax: 720-488-9835. Personal E-mail: paulsbk@msn.com.

SMITH, PAUL VERGON, JR., retired gas industry executive; b. Lima, Ohio, Apr. 25, 1921; s. Paul Vergon and Aleta Rose (Bowers) S.; m. Alta Fern Chipps, Mar. 2, 1945; children: Douglas, Marsha, Jeffrey, Alison. AB, Miami U., Oxford, Ohio, 1942; MS, U. Ill., 1943, PhD, 1945. With Exxon Research & Engring. Co., 1946-66, 72-86, mgr. pub. affairs, 1972—86, mgr. ednl. and profl. soc. relations, Florham Park, N.J., 1981-86; asst. dir. chem. research Esso Petroleum Co., Abingdon, Eng., 1966-67; dir. chem. research Esso Research S.A., Brussels, 1967-71; mem. adv. bd. Cache, Inc., Austin, Tex., 1979-86; pres. APS Assocs., Westfield, N.J., 1986-90. Bd. dirs., treas. Jets, Inc., Alexandria, Va.; dir. CENTCOM, Ltd.; mem. exec. bd. N.J. Bus./Industry/Sci. Edn. Consortium. Patentee in field; contbr. numerous articles to profl. jours., chpts. to books. Bd. dirs. United Way of Union County, N.J., 1980-86; chmn. research adv. council Miami U., 1980-84. Recipient Pres.'s award Am. Assn. Petroleum Geologists, 1955; Spl. award N.J. Sci. Tchrs. Assn., 1985. Mem. AAAS, Am. Chem. Soc. (dir. 1978-86, chmn. bd. 1984-86; Belden award 1984), Am. Soc. Engring. Edn. (dir. 1980-86, v.p. 1980-86), Country Club Naples, Phi Beta Kappa, Sigma Xi, Omicron Delta Kappa, Phi Eta Sigma, Alpha Chi Sigma, Pi Mu Epsilon, Sigma Pi Sigma, Phi Lambda Upsilon. Republican. Methodist.

SMITH, PEG L. foundation administrator; b. Ind. Tchr. Head Start, 1974—77, dir. child adult resource svcs., 1977—89, dir. child adult resource svcs. children's div., 1989—91; dir. step ahead initiative Office of Gov., 1991—95; exec. dir. Ind. Youth Inst., Indpls., 1995—98, Am. Camping Assn., Matrinsville, Ind., 1998—. Spkr. in field. Office: Am Camping Assn 5000 State Rd 67 North Martinsville IN 46151-7902

SMITH, PEGGY O'DONIEL, retired physicist; b. Lakeland, Fla., Nov. 27, 1920; d. John Arthur and Carrie Mattie (Jackson) O'Doniel; m. Fenton Frederick Smith, Oct. 11, 1943; children: James Scott, Stephen Arthur, Melody Ann, Candy Lou. Aviation Pilot Lic., Stetson U., Deland, Fla., 1941; BS in Sci. and Math., Fla. So. Coll., 1942; MA in Edn., U.S. Internat. U., San Diego, 1968. Physicist degausser U.S. Navy, Key West, Fla., 1942, physicist compass compensator Charleston, S.C., 1943, physicist magnetic signature analyst Washington, 1944; tchr. Chula Vista (Calif.) Sch. Dist., 1963-73, math specialist, 1974-77; owner Mineral Store, Chula Vista, 1977-82; ret. Leader math. workshops for girls, 1992-96. Author: Laz Goes to New Zealand; contbr. articles to profl. jours. Del. White House Conf. on Edn., 1956; sec. Chula Vista Rep. Women, 1995-97; chmn. Orphans of Italy, 1957-58. Recipient Kazanjian award, Joint Coun. Econ. Edn., Chula Vista, 1972, Fla. So. Coll. Alumni Achievement citation, 1999; Chula Vista Sch. Dist. math grantee, 1975. Mem. AAUW (v.p. 1989, 2001-03, 04—), Inner Circle, Calif. Ret. Tchrs. Assn. (v.p. 1998-2000), San Diego Gem and Mineral Soc. Avocations: golf, mineral collecting, coin collecting/numismatics, bridge, travel. Home: 87 K St Chula Vista CA 91911-1409

SMITH, PERRY MARSHALL, lawyer; b. Worcester, Mass., Apr. 28, 1958; s. Russell Howard and Frances Mary (Gullberg) S.; m. Eva Margaret Ribarits, Apr. 9, 1988. AB, Dartmouth Coll., 1980; JD, Am. U., 1984; LLM in Taxation, Boston U., 1987. Bar: N.Y. 1985, Mass. 1985, U.S. Dist. Ct. Mass. 1985, U.S. Tax Ct. 1986, U.S. Supreme Ct. 1989. Asst. counsel State Mut. Life Assurance Co., Worcester, 1984-87; atty. New Eng. Mut. Life Ins. Co., Boston, 1987-90; dir. estate and bus. planning Commonwealth Fin. Group, Waltham, Mass., 1990-97; dir. of fin. svcs. Carlin, Charron & Rosen LLP, Worcester, Mass., 1997—2000, Baystate Fin. Svcs., LLC, 2000—. Lectr. Met. Coll. Boston U., 1991—; trustee, treas. Holt-Elwell Meml. Found., Hebron, H.H., 1996—. Mem.: Am. CLU and Chartered Fin. Cons., Mass. Bar Assn. Republican. Avocations: coin collecting/numismatics, tennis, swimming, hiking. Home: 42 Beechwood Rd Wellesley MA 02482-2333 Office: Baystate Fin Svcs LLC One Exeter Plz Fl 14 Boston MA 02116 Office Phone: 617-585-4535. E-mail: psmith@baystatefinancial.com.

SMITH, PETER, chemist, educator, consultant; b. Ashton-Upon-Mersey, Cheshire, Eng., Sept. 7, 1924; came to U.S., 1951; s. Peter and Winifred Emma (Jenkins) S.; m. Hilary Joan Hewitt Roe, 1951; children: Helen Andrews Winifred, Eric Peter, Richard Harry, Gillian Carol. BA Queens' Coll., Cambridge U., 1946, MA, 1949, PhD, 1953. Jr. sci. officer Royal Aircraft Establishment, Farnborough, Hampshire, Eng., 1943-46; demonstrator chemistry dept. Leeds U., Yorkshire, England, 1950-51; postdoctoral research fellow in chemistry Harvard U., Cambridge, Mass., 1951-54; asst. prof. chemistry Purdue U., West Lafayette, Ind., 1954-59, Duke U., Durham, N.C., 1959-61, assoc. prof., 1961-70, prof., 1970-95, prof. emeritus chemistry, 1995—. Contbg. author: chem. research jours. Fulbright post-doctoral scholar Fulbright Commn., Harvard U., 1951-53 Mem. Am. Chem. Soc., Royal Soc. Chemistry, Am. Phys. Soc., Sigma Xi, Phi Lambda Upsilon, Alpha Chi Sigma Office: Duke U Dept Chemistry Paul M Gross Chem Lab PO Box 90346 Durham NC 27708-0346 Home: Apt A237 2600 Croasdaile Farm Pkwy Durham NC 27705-1336 E-mail: psmith@chem.duke.edu.

SMITH, PETER LEONARD, diversified financial services company executive; b. N.Y.C., Feb. 6, 1932; s. Purcell Leonard and Elizabeth (Wright) S.; m. Janet Andrews, May 3, 1964; children: Sarah, Andrew. BA, Yale Coll., 1955; cert. in advanced cryptology, Nat. Security Agy., 1965; MS, Southeastern U., 1977. Cashier Paine Webber, Washington, 1972-74; sr. examiner SEC, Washington, 1974-97; spl. investigator NASDR, Inc., N.Y.C., 1997-98; sr. v.p. Monument Funds Group, Inc., 1998—2001; v.p. Monument Series Fund, Inc., Bethesda, Md., 1998—2001; registered rep. Intersecurities, Inc., McLean, Va., 2001—02; sr. compliance officer FRB Nat. Bank Trust, Bethesda, Md., 2002—03; dir. compliance Amerimutual Fund Distbrs., Inc., 2003—. Served to lt. (s.g.) USNR, 1956-67. Home: 4834 Langdrum Ln Chevy Chase MD 20815-5413

SMITH, PETER WALKER, finance executive; b. Syracuse, N.Y., May 19, 1923; s. Stanley Sherwood and Elizabeth Wilkins (Young) S.; m. Lucile Elizabeth Edson, June 22, 1946; children: Andrew E., Laurie Smith-Frailey, Pamela C. (Mrs. Denison W. Schweppe, Jr.), Stanley E. B.Chem. Engring., Rensselaer Poly. Inst., 1947; MBA, Harvard U., 1948; LL.B., Cleve. Marshall Law Sch., 1955. Bar: Ohio 1955; Registered profl. engr., Ohio. Div. controller Raytheon Co., Lexington, Mass., 1958-66; v.p. finance, indsl. systems and equipment group Litton Industries Inc., Stamford, Conn., 1966-70; v.p. finance, treas. Copeland Corp., Sidney, Ohio, 1970-74; v.p. fin., treas., dir. Instrumentation Lab. Inc., Lexington, Mass., 1974-78; chief fin. officer, treas. Ionics, Inc., Watertown, Mass., 1978-80; v.p. fin., treas. Data Printer Corp., Malden, Mass., 1980-84, Orion Research Inc., Boston, 1984-87; pvt. practice cons. Concord, Mass., 1987—. Mem. fin. adv. bd., Northeastern U., Boston. Lt. AUS, 1943-46, 50-52. Mem. Fin. Execs. Inst., Am. Prodn. and Inventory Control Soc. (founding), Rensselaer Soc. Engrs., Sigma Xi, Tau Beta Pi. Home and Office: 100 Newbury Ct Concord MA 01742

SMITH, PETER WILLIAM EBBLEWHITE, electrical engineering educator, scientist, physicist; b. London, Nov. 3, 1937; m. Jacqueline Marie Mankiewicz, June 18, 1966; children: Christal, Dawn N. BSc, McGill U., Montreal, Que., Can., 1958, MSc, 1961, PhD, 1964. Profl. physicist. Mem. of staff Can. Marconi Co., Mont., 1958-59; mem. tech. staff Bell Labs., Holmdel, N.J., 1963-83; dist. mgr. Bellcore, Red Bank, N.J., 1984-88, div. mgr., 1988-92; prof. elec. and computer engring. U. Toronto, 1992—2003, prof. emeritus, 2003—; exec. dir. Ont. Laser and Lightwave Rsch. Ctr., 1992-95; dir. Nortel Inst. Telecom., 1999—2003. Editor-in-chief IEEE Press Progress in Lasers and Electro-Optics Series, 1987—92, Optics Letters, 1989—95; contbr. over 300 articles to profl. jours., chapters to books. Bd. dirs. Monmouth Arts Found., Red Bank, 1965-82. Recipient Sr. Scientist award NATO, 1979. Fellow IEEE (life, Quantum Electronics award 1986, Third Millennium medal 2000), Optical Soc. Am. (bd. dirs., chmn. bd. editors); mem. IEEE Lasers and Electro-Optics Soc. (pres. 1984). Achievements include first demonstration of waveguide gas laser, non-linear optical interface; development of hybrid bistable optical devices; 34 patents in field. Office: U Toronto Dept Elec & Computer Engring Toronto ON Canada M5S 3G4

SMITH, PETER WOLFGANG, physicist, artist; b. Rostock, Germany, May 16, 1929; U.S. citizen, 1983; s. Hans Schmidt-Isserstedt and Gertrude Calo; m. Marie Smith, Sept. 8, 1954; children: Nicholas, Lydia, Caroline. Scholar, King's Coll. Choir Sch., Cambridge, Eng., 1940-43, Felsted Sch., Essex, Eng., 1943-48; student, Cambridge Art Coll., 1950; BS with 1st honors in natural philosophy, St. Andrews (Scotland) U., 1952; postgrad., Edinburgh U., 1952-54. Sci. officer Admiralty Signal and Radar Establishment, Portsmouth, Eng., 1954-60; scientist Plessey Co., Hampshire, Eng., 1960-67; supr. Norden Systems, Norwalk, Conn., 1967-89; cons. Peter Smith, Westport, Conn., 1989—; artist Pierre Cochon, Westport, 1993—. Patentee in field; contbr. articles to profl. jours.; artist exhibiting in Wessex shows, U.K., 1956-60, various Conn. shows, 1996—. Mem. Inst. of Physics of London. Avocations: music, art history, golf. Home and Office: 7 Darbrook Rd Westport CT 06880-3611

SMITH, PHILIP A. academic administrator; b. Prince Edward Is., Can. Grad., Providence Coll., 1963; M, St. Stephen's Coll.; D in Philosophy and Religion, Drew U. Mem. philosophy dept. Providence Coll., R.I., 1981-91, pres., 1994—. Office: Providence Coll Harkins Hall 103 549 River Ave Providence RI 02918-0002

SMITH, PHILIP JOHN, industrial and systems engineering educator; b. Bradenton, Fla., July 11, 1953; s. John Fredrick and Valerie Eline (Polk) S. BA in Psychology, U. Mich., 1975, MS in Indsl. and Ops. Engring., 1976, PhD in Psychology and Indsl. Engring., 1979. Lectr. dept. indsl. engring. U. Mich., Ann Arbor, 1979-80, rsch. scientist Ctr. for Ergonomics, 1979-80; asst. prof. dept. indsl. engring. Ohio State U., Columbus, 1980-86, assoc. prof., 1986-92, prof. indsl. and sys. engring., 1992—, dir. Inst. for Ergonomics, 1998—. Cons. Ford, Dearborn, Mich., 1986—, Metron, Washington, 1998—, PPG, Columbus, Ohio, 1999-2000, Booz Allen Hamilton, 2001-02. Co-editor: Challenges in Indexing Electronic Text and Images, 1994; contbr. articles, paper to profl. publs. Mem. IEEE Sys., Man and Cybernetics, Am. Soc. for Info. Sci., Assn. Computing Machinery (spl. interest group for info. retrieval 1992-93); fellow Human Factors Soc. Avocation: dressage. Home: 7197 Calhoun Rd Ostrander OH 43061-9335 Office: Ohio State U Engring Dept 1971 Neil Ave Columbus OH 43210-1210 Business E-Mail: Smith.131@osu.edu.

SMITH, PHILIP JONES, lawyer; b. York, Pa., May 14, 1941; s. Clark S. and Margaret Ann (Jones) S.; m. Ann F. Johnson, Apr. 21, 1973; 1 child, James M. BA cum laude, Williams Coll., 1963; LLB, U. Va., 1966. Bar: Mass. 1967. Assoc. Ropes & Gray, Boston, 1967-76, ptnr., 1976—. Lectr. Boston U. Sch. of Law, Boston, 1984-98. Contbr. chpts. to books, articles to profl. jours. Bd. dirs., pres. Greater Boston Youth Symphony Orch., Boston, 1978-2000; bd. dirs., v.p. pres. Keewaydin Found., Salisbury, Vt., 1980—, pres., 2002—; bd. dirs., past treas. Project STEP, Boston, 1987-95; overseer, chair facilities com. New Eng. Conservatory, Boston, 1989-95. Fulbright scholar, U. Madrid, 1966—67. Mem.: ABA, Essex County Club, N.Y. Yacht Club, Eastern Yacht Club (sec. 1977—83, bd. dirs. 2001—), Order of Coif. Home: 35 Harbor Ave Marblehead MA 01945-3636 Office: Ropes & Gray One Internat Pl Boston MA 02110-2624 Office Phone: 617-951-7744. E-mail: Psmith@Ropesgray.com.

SMITH, PHILIP MEEK, science policy consultant, writer; b. Springfield, Ohio, May 18, 1932; s. Clarence Mitchell S. and Lois Ellen (Meek) Dudley. BS, Ohio State U., 1954, MA, 1955; DSc (hon.), NC State U., 1986. Mem. staff U.S. Nat. Com. for Internat. Geophys. Yr., NAS, 1957-58; program dir. NSF, 1958-63, dir. ops. U.S. Antarctic Rsch. program, 1964-69, dep. head divsn. polar programs, 1970-73, exec. asst. to dir. and sci. advisor to pres., 1974-76; chief gen. sci. br. Office Mgmt. and Budget Exec. Office of Pres.,

1973-74; assoc. dir. Office Sci. and Tech. Policy, Exec. Office of Pres., 1976-81; exec. officer NRC-NAS, Washington, 1981-94; ptnr. McGeary and Smith, Washington, 1995—2004; chmn. external adv. com. Nat. Computational Sci. Alliance, 1997—2001, mem., 2002—03, prin. Smith Sci. Policy and Mgmt., Santa Fe, 2004—. Bd. dirs. Aurora Flight Scis. Corp.; adv. cons. bd. U. Ala. Geophys. Inst., 1994—98; adv. bd. Sci.'s Next Wave, 1998—2002; advisor Com. for Econ. Devel., 1997; com. on sci., tech. & health aspects fgn. policy agenda U.S. NRC, 1998—2000, com. on sci. and tech. for counterism, 2001—02; chair com. orgn. & strategy Sci. Com. Antarctic Rsch., 1999—2000; co-chair adv. bd. Calif. Inst. Telecom. & Info. Tech., 2000—; mem. NRC Com. on Sci. Basis for Decision Making in Internat. Sustainable Devel. Orgns., 2002, U.S. Nat. Com. to the Internat. Polar Yr., 2003—. Author: (with others) The Frozen Future, a Prophetic Report from Antarctica, 1973; contbr. numerous articles to profl. jours. Bd. dirs. Washington Project for Arts, 1983-84, Washington Sculptors Group, 1983-84. 1st lt. U.S. Army, 1955-57. Mem. AAAS, Antarctican Soc., Cosmos Club (Washington), Am. Alpine Club (Golden, Colo.), Sigma Xi. Office: Smith Sci Policy & Mgmt 767 Acequia Madre 2 Santa Fe NM 87505-2868 Office Phone: 505-660-3878. E-mail: pmsmith@erols.com.

SMITH, PHILIP W. epidemiologist; b. Chgo., Dec. 4, 1946; s. James J. and Mary E. Smith; m. Sharon W. Smith, May 28, 1982; children: Nathan, Alexander, Matthew. BS in Chemistry, U. Wis., 1968; MD, U. Chgo., 1972. Diplomate Am. Bd. Internal Medicine with subspecialty in infectious disease. Intern U. Iowa, 1972-73, resident in internal medicine, 1973-75, fellow in infectious diseases, 1975-77; epidemiologist Clarkson Hosp., Omaha, 1977-98, chief sect. of infectious diseases U. Nebr. Med. Ctr., Omaha, 1998—. Editor: Infection Control in Long Term Care Facilities, 1984, 2d edit., 1994. Recipient Sir William Osler Tchg. award U. Nebr. Dept. Internal Medicine, 1983. Fellow ACP, Infectious Diseases Soc. of Am. Avocations: philosophy, poetry. Office: 985400 Nebraska Med Ctr Omaha NE 68198-0001

SMITH, PHILLIP J. food products executive; V.p., controller various divsn. Cullum Cos. Inc., Dallas, 1975-84; v.p., CFO Market Basket Food Stores, Tex., 1984-87; controller Stater Bros., Colton, Calif., 1987, v.p., controller, sr. v.p., CFO, 2000—. Office: Stater Bros Markets 21700 Barton Rd Colton CA 92324

SMITH, PHILLIP THURMOND, historian, educator; b. Van Nuys, Calif., Dec. 11, 1942; s. John Thomas McElroy and Eloise (Coggin) Smith; m. Ellen Laurie Walker, June 27, 1970; children: Roger Stephen, Kristen Susan. BA, U. Tex., El Paso, 1964; postgrad., Westfield Coll., U. London, 1967-68; MA, Ind. U., 1969; MPhil, Columbia U., 1975, PhD with distinction, 1976. Asst. dir. grad. admissions Columbia U., N.Y.C., 1969-70; lectr. U. Mass., Boston, summer 1976, Endicott Coll., Beverly, Mass., 1976-78; asst., assoc. prof. history St. Joseph's U., Phila., 1978-96, prof. history, 1996—, chmn. dept. history, 1988-94, 2001—04. Author: (book) Policing Victorian London, 1985, Mafeking Memories, 1996. Capt. U.S. Army, 1964—66. Fellow NEH, 1978, 1988, 1991; grantee Cooper-Woods Study, English-Speaking Union, 1979. Mem.: Phila. Conf. Modern European History, Anglo-Am. Assocs., Mid. Atlantic Conf. Brit. Studies, NE Victorial Studies Assn., N.Am. Conf. Brit. Studies, Am. Hist. Assn., Delaware Valley Amateur Astronomers, Columbia U. Club. Democrat. Avocations: classical guitar, tennis, bicycling, astronomy. Home: 1310 Delmont Ave Havertown PA 19083-2626 E-mail: psmith@sju.edu.

SMITH, PHILLIPS GUY, banker; b. Orange, N.J., Sept. 15, 1946; s. Phillips Upham and Helen Ottilie (Voderberg) S.; m. Ann Dixon Schickhaus, Dec. 29, 1973; children: Guy Dixon, William Schickhaus, Louisa Upham. B in Engring., Stevens Inst. Tech., Hoboken, N.J.; MBA, U. Pa., 1975. Comml. banking rep. The Bank of N.Y., N.Y.C., 1976-78, asst. treas., 1978-79, asst. v.p., 1979-80, v.p., 1980-85, sr. v.p., 1985-93; mng. dir. Internat. Strategy Svcs., Inc., N.Y.C., 1993-2000; prin. Sippican Group LLC, Greenwich, Conn., 2000—. Vestryman Ch. of The Heavenly Rest, N.Y.C., 1983-88, treas., 1985-87; trustee Tabor Acad., Marion, Mass., 1987—, treas., 1991—. Lt. USN, 1970-74, Vietnam. Mem. Racquet and Tennis Club, Down Town Assn., Rockaway Hunting Club, Nantucket Yacht Club. Episcopalian. Home: 9 E 94th St New York NY 10128-0611 Office: Sippican Group LLC 15 E Putnam Ave Ste 3280 Greenwich CT 06830-5424 E-mail: psmith@sippicangroup.com.

SMITH, PHYLLIS MAE, healthcare consultant, educator; b. Coeur d'Alene, Idaho, May 2, 1935; d. Elmer Lee Smith and Kathryn Alice (Newell) Wilson. Diploma, Luth. Bible Inst., Seattle, 1956, Emanuel Hosp. Sch. Nursing, Portland, Oreg., 1959, Coll. San Mateo, Calif., 1971. Staff nurse in surgery Emanuel Hosp., Portland, 1962-63; head nurse ctrl. svc. Sacred Heart Hosp., Eugene, Oreg., 1964-69; dir. ctrl. svcs. Peninsula Hosp., Burlingame, Calif., 1969-74; pres. Phyllis Smith Assocs., Inc., Lewiston, Idaho, 1975-88; sr. tech. advisor, dir. ednl. programs Parkside Material Mgmt. Svcs., Park Ridge, Ill., 1988-90; AIDS coord. Asotin County Health Dist., 1989-2000. Lectr., cons. in field in over 14 countries. Contbr. to manuals and profl. jours. Mem. NAFE, Internat. Assn. Hosp. Ctrl. Svc. Mgmt. (dir. edn. 1973-88, chmn. technician edn. and affairs com. 1978-88, John Perkins award 1977, Cheshire award 1977, Lifetime Achievement award 2003), Assn. for Advancement Med. Instrumentation. Lutheran. Avocations: fishing, walking, photography, chess, reading. Home and Office: 1415 Chestnut St Clarkston WA 99403-2429 Office Phone: 509-751-1180.

SMITH, R. GORDON, lawyer; b. Roanoke, Va., May 28, 1938; BA with highest honors, U. Va., 1960; LLB magna cum laude, Harvard U., 1964. Bar: Va. 1964. Law clk. to judge U.S. Ct. Appeals (5th cir.), 1964-65; ptnr. McGuire, Woods, Battle & Boothe, Richmond, Va., 1969—. Exec., legislation editor Harvard Law Rev., 1963-64; bd. dirs. Scott & Stringfellow Fin., Inc., Trigon Healthcare, Inc., Va. C. of C. Fellow Am. Bar Found.; mem. Va. Bar Assn. (pres. 1987-88), Am. Law Inst., Phi Beta Kappa, Omicron Delta Kappa. Office: McGuire Woods 901 E Cary St Richmond VA 23219-4057

SMITH, R. J., JR., oil company executive; b. Big Spring, Tex., Sept. 9, 1930; s. R. J. and Myrtle (O'Quinn) S.; m. Sarah Sue Holmes, Sept. 8, 1950 (div. 1962); children: Molly Smith Frank, Cassie Smith Roop; m. Sandra Ann Schroeder, Jan. 21, 1971. Student, Abilene Christian U., 1948-50, So. Meth. U., 1951-52, Goethe U., Frankfurt, Germany, 1953-55; LLD, Northwood U., 1983. Aero. engr. Chance-Vought Aircraft, Dallas, 1951-52; ind. oil operator Dallas, 1960-62; ops. chief Leland Fikes, Dallas, 1963-66; owner, operator Texon Petroleum Corp. (sold to Exxon USA 1983), Dallas, 1967-83; owner, pres. Cheyenne Petroleum Corp., Dallas, 1967—, Texan Petroleum Corp., Dallas, 1985—; pres., CEO Lehndorff Minerals, 1989—. Bd. dirs. Aztec Energy Corp., Collins Found., Dallas. Bd. dirs., then chmn. bd. dirs. Effie and Wofford Cain Found., Dallas, 1979—; chmn. bd. Friends Dallas Police; bd. dirs. U. Tex. Southwestern Med. Ctr. Fund, So. Meth. U. John Tower Ctr. Polit. Studies, Calvert Collins Found., Dallas, 2003-; chmn. bd. govs. Northwood U., Tex., trustee, West Palm Beach, Fla., Midland, Mich. and Dallas, 1968—; Tex. del. at large Rep. Nat. Conv., 1996; dir. Bob Dole for Pres. Com., Tex. Mem. Ind. Prodrs. Assn. Am., Tex. Ind. Prodrs. and Royalty Owners, Mid-Continent Prodrs. Assn., N.Mex. Ind. Prodrs. Assn., Preston Trail Golf Club, Dallas Gun Club, Crescent Club, Montaigne Club, Bent Tree Country Club (alt. Tex.), Del Mar Turf Club (Calif.). Republican. Office: Texan Petroleum Corp 2626 Cole Ave Ste 603 Dallas TX 75204-0823

SMITH, RALPH ALEXANDER, cultural and educational policy educator; b. Ellwood City, Pa., June 12, 1929; s. J. V. and B. V. Smith; m. Christiana M. Kolbe, Nov. 16, 1955. AB, Columbia Coll., 1954; MA, Columbia U., 1959, EdD, 1962. Faculty art history and arts edn. Kent (Ohio) State U., 1959-61, Wis. State U., Oshkosh, 1961-63, SUNY, New Paltz, 1963-64; faculty edn. and art edn. U. Ill., Urbana-Champaign, 1964—, prof. cultural and ednl. policy & aesthetic edn., prof. emeritus, 1996—. First Italo DeFrancesca Meml. lectr. Kutztown State U., 1974; Leon Jackman Meml. lectr., Perth, Australia, 85; Dean's lectr. Coll. Fine Arts and Comm., Brigham Young U., 1985; disting. vis. prof. Ohio State U., 1987; sr. scholar Coll. Edn., U. Ill., 1991; Dunbar lectr. Millsaps Coll., 1993; John Landrum Bryant lectr. Harvard U., 1999. Founder, editor: Jour. Aesthetic Edn., 1966—2000; editor: (book) Aesthetics and Criticism in Art Education, 1966, Aesthetic Concepts and Education, 1970, Aesthetics and Problems in Education, 1971, Regaining Educational Leadership, 1975, Cultural Literacy and Arts Education, 1991, Discipline-Based Art Education, 1989; editor: (with Alan Simpson) Aesthetics and Arts Education, 1991; editor: (with Bennett Reimer) The Arts, Education and Aesthetic Knowing, 1992; editor: (with Ronald Berman) Public Policy and the Aesthetic Interest, 1992; editor: General Knowledge and Arts Education, 1994, Excellence II: The Continuing Quest Art Education, 1995, Online Bibliography: Discipline Based Art Education, 1997, Readings in Discipline-Based Art Education: A Literature of Educational Reform, 2000; co-author: Research in the Arts and Aesthetic Education: A Directory of Investigators and Their Fields of Inquiry, 1978, Excellence in Art Education: Ideas and Initiatives, 1987, The Sense of Art: A Study in Aesthetic Education, 1989; author (with Albert William Levi): Art Education: A Critical Necessity, 1991; contbg. editor: Arts Edn. Policy Rev., 2001—. With Med. Svc. U.S. Army, 1954—57. Recipient spl. merit recognition, Coll. Edn., U. Ill., 1975, Disting. Lectr. Studies in Art Edn. award, 1991. Fellow: Nat. Art Edn. Assn. (Disting., Manuel Barkan Meml. award 1973, Nat. Educator award 2000); mem.: Ill. Art Edn. Assn. (Disting.), Coun. Policy Studies Art Edn. (1st exec. sec. 1978—82). Home: 2909 Heathwood Ct Champaign IL 61822-7659 Office: 360 Education 1310 S 6th St Champaign IL 61820-6925 Business E-Mail: ras@uiuc.edu.

SMITH, RALPH EARL, virologist; b. Yuma, Colo., May 10, 1940; s. Robert C. and Esther C. (Schwarz) S.; m. Sheila L. Kondy, Aug. 29, 1961 (div. 1986); 1 child, Andrea Denise; m. Janet M. Keller, 1988. BS, Colo. State U., 1961, PhD, U. Colo., 1968. Registered microbiologist Am. Soc. Clin. Pathologists. Fellow Duke U. Med. Ctr., Durham, N.C., 1968-70, asst. prof., 1970-74, assoc. prof., 1974-80, prof. virology, 1980-82; prof., head dept. microbiology Colo. State U., Ft. Collins, 1983-88, prof. microbiology, assoc. v.p. rsch., 1989-99, interim v.p. rsch., 1990-91, prof. microbiology, assoc. v.p. rsch., 1991-99, interim head dept. microbiology, 1999—2002, prof. microbiology, immunology and pathology, 2002—. Cons. Bellco Glass Co., Vineland, N.J., 1976-80, Proctor & Gamble Co., Cin., 1985-86, Schering Plough Corp., Bloomfield, N.J., 1987-89. Contbr. articles to profl. jours.; patentee in field. Bd. dirs. Colo. Ctr. for Environ. Mgmt., v.p. for rsch.; mem. pollution prevention adv. bd. Colo. Dept. Pub. Health and Environment; mem. Rocky Mountain U. Consortium on Environ. Restoration, Environ. Inst. Rocky Flats; asst. scoutmaster Boy Scouts Am., Durham, 1972-82, com. mem., Ft. Collins, 1986-91; mem. adminstrv. bd. 1st United Meth. Ch., Ft. Collins. Eleanor Roosevelt fellow Internat. Union Against Cancer 1978-79. Mem. AAAS, Am. Soc. Microbiology, N.Y. Acad. Scis., Am. Soc. Virology, Gamma Sigma Delta. Democrat. Methodist. Avocations: photography, hiking. Home: 2406 Creekwood Dr Fort Collins CO 80525-2034 Office: Colo State U Dept Microbiology/Immun Path Fort Collins CO 80523-0001 Office Phone: 970-491-6119. Business E-Mail: ralph.smith@colostate.edu.

SMITH, RALPH LEE, author, musician; b. Phila., Nov. 6, 1927; s. Hugh Harold and Barbara (Schatkin) S.; m. Betty H. Smith, Sept. 1954 (div. Jan. 1963); children: David Bruce, Robert Hugh; m. Mary Louise Hollowell, 1971 (div. 1977); m. Shizuko Maruyama, 1977; 1 child, Lisa Koyuki. BA, Swarthmore Coll., 1951; MEd, U. Va., 1987. Folk musician on Appalachian dulcimer; recs. include Dulcimer: Old Time and Traditional Music, 1973, Tunes of the Blue Ridge and Great Smoky Mountains, 1983, Old Time Dulcimer and Harmonica Tunes, 2003; author: The Story of the Dulcimer, 1986, Appalachian Dulcimer Traditions, 1997, Songs and Tunes of the Wilderness Road, 1999, Folk Songs of Old Kentucky, 2003. Recipient writing awards Columbia U. Grad. Sch. Journalism, U. Mo. Grad. Sch. Journalism, AMA. Home: 1662 Chimney House Rd Reston VA 20190-4302 Office Phone: 703-405-1489. E-mail: rls2@erols.com.

SMITH, RALPH WESLEY, JR., retired federal judge; b. Ghent, N.Y., July 16, 1936; s. Ralph Wesley and Kathleen S. (Callahan) S.; m. Nancy Ann Fetzer, Dec. 30, 1961 (div. 1981); children: Mark Owen, Tara Denise, Todd Kendall; m. Barbara Anne Milian, Nov. 8, 1982; stepchildren: Kim Highter, Jeffrey Highter, Eric Highter. Student, Sorbonne, U. Paris, Paris, 1954-55; BA, Yale U., 1956; LLB, Albany Law Sch., 1966. Bar: N.Y. 1966, U.S. Dist. Ct. (no. dist.) N.Y. 1966. Assoc. Hinman, Straub Law Firm, Albany, N.Y., 1966-69; chief asst. dist. atty. Albany County, N.Y., 1969-73, dist. atty., 1974; regional dir. state nursing home investigation Asst. Atty. Gen., Albany, 1975-77; dir. State Organized Crime Task Force, 1978-82; U.S. magistrate judge U.S. Dist. Ct. (no. dist.) N.Y., Albany, 1982-2001. Judge moot ct. Albany Law Sch., 1983-2001; lectr. N.Y. State Bar Assn., 1985—, Am. Inns of Ct., 1994-99. Capt. (ret.) USNR, 1957-82. Mem. Fed. Magistrate Judges Assn. (dir. 2d cir. 1992-99), Columbia County Magistrates Assn. Republican. Roman Catholic. Avocations: fishing, bicycling, skiing, sailing, camping. Home: 40 Wequasset Rd Harwich Port MA 02646

SMITH, RANDOLPH RELIHAN, plastic surgeon; b. Augusta, Ga., Aug. 13, 1944; s. Lester Vernon and Maxine (Relihan) S.; m. Becky Jo Hardy; children: Katherine, Randolph, Rebecca, Michael. BS, Clemson U., 1966, LLD (hon.), 1997; MD, Coll. Ga., 1970. Diplomate Am. Bd. Otolaryngology, Am. Bd. Plastic Surgery. Intern Bowman Gray Sch. Medicine Wake Forest U., Winston-Salem, NC, 1970-71; resident in surgery and otolaryngology Duke U., Durham, NC, 1971-75; resident in plastic and reconstructive surgery Med. Coll. Ga., 1975-77; Christine Kleinert fellow in hand surgery U. Louisville, 1977; attending physician U. Hosp., Augusta, 1977—. Asst. clin. prof. plastic surgery Med. Coll. Ga., 1978—; pres. med. staff Univ. Hosp., Augusta, mem. exec. coun. health care sys.; vol. surgeon in developing countries, 1982—; dir. Walton Way Indemnity. Contbr. articles to profl. jours. Trustee, chmn. bd. Univ. Health, Inc.; trustee Clemson U. Found.; mem. bd. visitors Clemson U.; sec. Ga. Bank Fin. Corp.; vestryman, sr. warden St. Paul's Episc. Ch.; bd. dirs. United Way, Ga. Bank and Trust Co. of Augusta, Richmond County Hosp. Authority. Maj. med. corps USAR, 1971—78. Recipient Book of Golden Deeds award, Exch. Club of Augusta, 1997, Civic Endeavor award, Richmond County Med. Soc., 1998, Jack A. Raines Humanitarian award, Med. Assn. Ga., 1999, Pride in Profession award, AMA, 2001, award for yrs. of svc. to Polish patients and edn. of Polish surgeons, City Coun. Nowy Sacz, Poland, 2001. Fellow ACS, Am. Acad. Otolaryngology; mem. Am. Soc. Plastic and Reconstructive Surgeons, Am. Soc. Aesthetic Plastic Surgery, Ga. Soc. Plastic and Reconstructive Surgeons, Southeastern Soc. Plastic and Reconstructive Surgeons, Exch. Club of Augusta (bd. dirs., pres. 2001), Augusta Symphony League, Beech Island Agrl. Club, Rotary (Paul Harris fellow 1998), Alpha Omega Alpha. Office: Univ Hosp Med Ctr 1348 Walton Way Ste 6300 Augusta GA 30901-2772 E-mail: clemsonrs50@aol.com.

SMITH, RAOUL NORMAND, computer science educator; b. West Warwick, R.I., May 15, 1938; s. Luke Joseph and Lucienne (Anchambault) S.; m. Mary Frances Hand, Nov. 12, 1966; children: Stephen Edward, Timothy Luke. AB, Brown U., 1963, AM, 1964, PhD, 1968. Instr. Northwestern U., Evanston, Ill., 1967—68, asst. prof., 1968—73, assoc. prof., 1973—80; sr. mem. of tech. staff GTE Labs., Waltham, Mass., 1981—83, prin. mem. of tech. staff, 1983; prof. Northeastern U., Boston, 1983—2000, dir. grad. schs., 1984—85, dir. rsch., 1985—86, prof. emeritus, 2000—; vis. prof. Jilin U. of Tech., Changchun, China, summer 1985; v.p. China Edn. Corp., 2000—02. Chmn. bd. dirs. Cognitive Computers, Newton, Mass., 1985-87; prin. Raoul N. Smith and Assocs., Cons. Author: Dictionary of Artificial Intelligence, 1989, The Language of Jonathan Fisher, 1985, Probabilistic Performance Models of Language, 1973; co-author: Lexical-Semantic Relations, 1980. Trustee Acton (Mass.) Hist. Soc., 1988-90, dir., 2002—; mem. AIDS action com., 1985-88. With USAF, 1957-61. Grantee NSF, 1966, 66-67, 71, Am. Philos. Soc., 1974, Am. Coun. of Learned Socs., 1974, Nat. Endowment for the Humanities, 1975, 76-79. Mem. Assn. for Computing Machinery (co-chair spl. interest group on computer and human interaction 1981-85), Union Club. Avocations: antique porcelain, silver and jewelry. Home: 206 Nagog Hill Rd Acton MA 01720-3228 E-mail: raoulS500@aol.com.

SMITH, RAYMOND EDWARD, retired health care administrator; b. Freeport, N.Y., June 17, 1932; s. Jerry Edward and Madelyn Holman (Jones) S.; m. Lena Kathryn Jernigan Hughes, Oct. 28, 1983; children: Douglas, Ronald, Kevin, Doris Jean, Raymond. BS in Edn., Temple U., 1953; MHA, Baylor U., 1966. Commd. 2d lt. U.S. Army, 1953, advanced through grades to lt. col., 1973, helicopter ambulance pilot, 1953-63; comdr. helicopter ambulance units Korea, 1955, 1961; various hosp. adminstrv. assignments, 1963-73; pers. dir. Valley Forge (Pa.) Gen. Hosp., 1966; adminstr. evacuation hosp. Vietnam, 1967; dep. insp. Walter Reed Gen. Hosp., Washington, 1970; dir. personnel divsn. Office of Army Surgeon Gen., Washington, 1971-73, ret., 1973; adminstr. Health Care Ctrs., Phila., Phila. Coll. Osteo. Medicine, 1974-76; dir. bur. hosps. Pa. Dept. Health, Harrisburg, 1976-79; contract mgr. Blue Cross of Calif., San Diego, 1979-88, Cmty. Care Network, San Diego, 1989—95; ret., 1995. Decorated Bronze Star, Legion of Merit. Mem. Am. Hosp. Assn., Am. Legion, Ret. Officers Assn., Kappa Alpha Psi, Sigma Pi Phi. Episcopalian. Home: 7630 Lake Adlon Dr San Diego CA 92119-2518

SMITH, RAYMOND LEIGH, plastic surgeon; b. Norristown, Pa., Sept. 27, 1940; s. Walter Joseph and Pauline C. (Wolfskill) S.; m. Coralynn Elder, Jan. 8, 1966; children: Susan, Elizabeth, Christine. BS, Ursinus Coll., 1962; MD, Temple U., 1966. Diplomate Nat. Bd. Med. Examiners, Am. Bd. Plastic Surgery. Active staff Reading Hosp., Pa., 1976—, chief sect. of plastic surgery, 1994-2000. Mem. ACS, Republican Majority Found., Washington Legal Found. Mem. Am. Soc. Plastic Surgeons, Robert H. Ivy Soc., Am. Assn. Hand Surgery, Northeastern Soc. Plastic Surgeons, Pa. Med. Soc., Lipoplasty Soc. N.Am., Berks County Med. Soc. Lutheran. Office: 926 Penn Ave Wyomissing PA 19610-3017

SMITH, RAYMOND LLOYD, former university president, consultant; b. Vanceboro, Maine, Jan. 25, 1917; s. Ivan and Genevieve (Gatcomb) S.; m. Beatrice Bennett, Dec. 4, 1943; children: Bennett Charles, Martin Lloyd. BS in Mining Engring. cum laude, U. Alaska, 1943; MS in Metall. Engring, U. Pa., 1951, PhD in Metall. Engring, 1953; D.Sc. (hon.), Western Mich. U.; LL.D., No. Mich. U.; D.Eng. (hon.), Mich. Technol. U., S.D. Sch. Mines and Tech. Instr. math. U. Alaska, 1946-47, asst. prof. metallurgy, 1948-49; rsch. assoc. dept. metallurgy U. Pa., 1949-53; sr. rsch. metallurgist Franklin Inst. Labs., Phila., 1953, sect. chief metallurgy, 1954-56, assoc. dir., 1957, tech. dir., 1958-59; prof., head metall. dept. Mich. Technol. U., Houghton, 1959-64, coord. rsch., 1960-64, pres., 1965-79, Am. Soc. Metals, 1979 80, Houghton (Mich.) Daily Mining Gazette, 1979-81, R. L. Smith, Inc. Am. Soc. Metals/The Metallurgical Soc. joint disting. lectr. in materials; lectr. in field. Contbr. numerous articles to metall. sci. jours.; patentee in field. With AUS, 1943—46. Recipient Distinguished Alumnus award U. Alaska, Clair M. Donovan award Mich. Tech. U., D. Robert Yarnall award U. Pa. Engring. Sch.; Outstanding Service award Air Force ROTC; Rotary Paul Harris fellow. Fellow Metall. Soc., AIME (Henry Krumb meml. lectr. 1981), Am. Soc. for Metals (hon.); mem. Scabbard and Blade, Blue Key, Tau Beta Pi, Alpha Sigma Mu (hon. lectr. 1982), Alpha Phi Omega, Phi Kappa Phi, Theta Tau. Home: PO Box 726 Green Valley AZ 85622-0726 *A sense of humor is one of the important building blocks for that firm sense of balance so necessary to meet the challenges of life. It's like the seasoning of a chef's masterpiece.*

SMITH, RAYMOND THOMAS, anthropology educator; b. Oldham, Lancashire, Eng., Jan. 12, 1925; s. Harry and Margaret (Mulchrone) S.; m. Flora Alexandrina Tong, June 30, 1954; children: Fenela, Colin, Anthony. BA, Cambridge (Eng.) U., 1950, MA, 1951, PhD, 1954. Sociol. research officer govt., Brit. Guiana, 1951-54; research fellow U. W.I., 1954-59; prof. sociology U. Ghana, 1959-62; sr. lectr. sociology, prof. anthropology U. West Indies, 1962-66; prof. anthropology U. Chgo., 1966-95, prof. emeritus, 1995—, chmn. dept. anthropology, 1975-81, 84-85, 94-95. Vis. prof. U. Calif.-Berkeley, 1957-58, McGill U., Montreal, 1964-65; mem. com. on child devel. rsch. and pub. policy NRC, 1977-80; dir. Caribbean Consortium Grad. Sch., 1985-86. Author: The Negro Family in British Guiana, 1956, British Guiana, 1962, 2d edit., 1980, Kinship and Class In The West Indies, 1988, The Matrifocal Family, 1996; co-author: Class Differences in American Kinship, 1978; editor: Kinship Ideology and Practice in Latin America, 1984; contbr. articles to profl. jours. Co-investigator urban family life project U. Chgo., 1986-90. Served with RAF, 1943-48. Guggenheim fellow, 1983-84 Fellow Am. Anthrop. Assn.; mem. Assn. Social Anthropologists. Office: Univ Chicago Dept Anthropology 1126 E 59th St Chicago IL 60637-1580 E-mail: r-smith@uchicago.edu.

SMITH, RAYMOND W. investment banking executive; b. Pitts., 1937; BS, Carnegie-Mellon U., 1959; MBA, U. Pitts., 1969. Budget dir. AT&T, 1976-77; v.p.-regulatory Bell of Pa. and Diamond State Tel., Phila., 1981-83, pres., chief exec. officer, 1983-85; vice chmn., chief fin. officer, dir. parent co. Bell Atlantic Corp., Phila., 1985-88, pres., chief oper. officer, 1988, chmn., CEO, 1989-98, Rothschild North America, Inc., N.Y.C., 1999—. Bd. dirs., founder Arlington Capital Ptnrs., 1999, U.S. Airways, CBS Corp.; mem. Bus. Roundtable, 1990—; mem. nat. adv. bd. Pvt. Sector Coun., 1990—; mem. James Madison nat. coun. Libr. of Congress, 1990—. Pub. playwright. Mem. Lincoln Ctr., Pres. Commn.-Arts and Humanities, WETA, Carnegie Corp., Carnegie Mellon, Rockham Ventures. With Signal Corps, U.S. Army, 1959-60. Office: Rothschild North Am Inc 1251 Avenue Of The Americas New York NY 10020-1104

SMITH, REBECCA BEACH, federal judge; b. 1949; BA, Coll. William and Mary, 1971; postgrad., U. Va., 1971-73; JD, Coll. William and Mary, 1979. Assoc. Wilcox & Savage, 1980-85; U.S. magistrate Ea. Dist. Va., 1985-89; dist. judge U.S. Dist. Ct. (ea. dist.) Va., Norfolk, 1989—. Exec. editor Law Review, 1978-79. Active Chrysler Mus. Norfolk, Jean Outland Chrysler Libr. Assocs., Va. Opera Assn., Friends of the Zoo, Friends of Norfolk Pub. Libr., Ch. of the Good Shepherd. John Marshall Soc. fellow; recipient Acad. Achievement and Leadership award St. George Tucker Soc.; named one of Outstanding Women of Am., 1979. Mem. ABA, Va. State Bar Assn., Fed. Bar Assn. Supreme Ct. Hist. Soc., Fourth Cir. Judicial Conf., The Harbor Club, Order of Coif., Phi Beta Kappa. Office: US Dist Ct US Courthouse 600 Granby St Ste 358 Norfolk VA 23510-1915

SMITH, REBECCA LYNN, language educator; b. Camp Springs, Md., Oct. 16, 1967; d. D. E. and Edith M. Smith. *Great-great-great grandfather William Richmond served with Gen. Lewis in the American Revolution. Great-grandfather served with Gen. Rosecrans in the American Civil War. Smith is working on tracing William's relations in Bristol, England, where William's father embarked for America in the mid 1700s.* A in Bus., San Antonio Coll., 1989; BA in English, U. Tex. San Antonio, 2000, M in English, 2003. Supr. Roy Maas' Youth Alternatives, Boerne, Tex., 1993—97. Mem.: Beth Sichma, Alpha Phi, Sigma Tau Delta. Avocations: watercolor painting, travel. Home: 12205 Wilderness Trail San Antonio TX 78233 Office: NW Vista Coll 3535 N Ellison Dr San Antonio TX 78251

SMITH, REBECCA MCCULLOCH, human relations educator; b. Greensboro, N.C., Feb. 29, 1928; d. David Martin and Virginia Pearl (Woodburn) McCulloch; m. George Clarence Smith Jr., Mar. 30, 1945; 1 child, John Randolph. BS, Woman's Coll., U. N.C., 1947, MS, 1952; PhD, U. N.C., Greensboro, 1967; postgrad., Harvard U., 1989. Tchr. pub. schs., N.C., S.C.; instr. U. N.C., Greensboro, 1958—91, asst. prof. to prof. emeritus human devel./family studies. Dir. grad. program, 1975-82; ednl. cons. depts. edn. N.C., S.C., Ind., Ont., Man.; vis. prof. N.W. La. State U., 1965, 67, U. Wash., 1970, Hood Coll., 1976, 86. Author: Teaching About Family Relationships, 1975, Klemer's Marriage and Family Relationships, 2d edit., 1975, Resources for Teaching About Family Life Education, 1976, Family Matters: Concepts in Marriage and Personal Relationships, 1982; co-author: History of the School of Human Environmental Sciences: 1892-1992, 1992, assoc. editor Jour. Applied Family and Child Studies, 1980-90; ednl. cons. Current Life Studies, 1977-84. Bd. dirs. Sch. HES Alumni, 1997-99. Named Outstanding Alumna Sch. Home Econs., 1976; recipient Sperry award for service to families N.C. Family Life Coun., 1979. Mem. Nat. Coun. Family Rels. (exec. com. 1974-76, treas. 1987-89, Osborne award 1973), U. N.C. at Greensboro Alumni Assn. (chair membership recruitment com. 1994-96). Home: 1212 Ritters Lake Rd Greensboro NC 27406-7816 Office: U NC Dept Human Devel Sch Human Environ Scis Greensboro NC 27412-0001

SMITH, REGINALD BRIAN FURNESS, retired anesthesiologist, educator; b. Warrington, Eng., Feb. 7, 1931; s. Reginald and Betty (Bell) S.; m. Margarete Groppe, July 18, 1963; children: Corinne, Malcolm. MB, BS, U. London, 1955; DTM and H, Liverpool Sch. Tropical Medicine, 1959. Intern Poole Gen. Hosp., Dorset, Eng., 1955-56, Wilson Meml. Hosp., Johnson City, N.Y., 1962-63; resident in anesthesiology Med. Coll. Va., Richmond, 1963-64, U. Pitts., 1964-65, from clin. instr. to prof., 1965-78, acting chmn. dept. anesthesiology, 1977-78; anesthesiologist in chief Presbyn. Univ. Hosp., Pitts., 1976-78; dir. anesthesiology Eye and Ear Hosp., Pitts., 1971-76; prof., chmn. dept. U. Tex. Health Sci. Ctr., San Antonio, 1978-98, anesthesiologist in chief hosps., 1978-98, clin. prof. anesthesiology, 1999—, clin. prof. rehab. medicine, 2003—, med. dir. hyperbaric medicine and woundcare unit Univ. Hosp., 1993-2000, mem. med. staff Univ. Hosp., 2003—; ret., 2000. Contbg. editor: Internat. Ophthalmology Clinics, 1973, Internat. Anesthesiology Clinics, 1983; contbr. articles to profl. jours. Served to capt. Brit. Army, 1957-59. Fellow ACP, Am. Coll. Anesthesiologists, Am. Coll. Chest Physicians; mem. AMA, Internat. Anesthesia Rsch. Soc., Am. Soc. Anesthesiologists (pres. Western Pa. 1974-75), Tex. Soc. Anesthesiologists, San Antonio Soc. Anesthesiologists (pres. 1990), Tex. Med. Assn., Bexar County Med. Soc. Home: 213 Canada Verde St San Antonio TX 78232-1104

SMITH, RICHARD A. manufacturing executive; B. U. Chgo.; MBA, Northwestern U.; JD, St. Louis U. Former asst. treas., asst. to CFO Ralston Purina; former v.p. and treas., v.p. and contr. of Payless Show Source divsn. May Dept. Stores; former v.p. fin., CFO Arvin Industries, Inc. (now Arvin Meritor, Inc.); CFO, chief adminstrn. officer Zonetrader.com, 2000—01; CFO Lennox Internat., Richardson, Tex., 2001—. Mem.: Mo. Bar, Mfrs. Alliance, Fin. Execs. Inst. Office: Lennox Internat 2140 Lake Park Blvd Richardson TX 75080

SMITH, RICHARD ALAN, neurologist, medical association administrator; Student, Brandeis U., 1958-61; grad., U. Miami, 1965. Intern in medicine Jackson Meml. Hosp., Miami, Fla., 1965-66; resident in neurology Stanford U. Hosp., Palo Alto, Calif., 1966-69; head neurology br. Navy Neuropsychiatric Rsch. Unit, San Diego, 1969-71; mem. assoc. staff microbiology Scripps Clinic and Rsch. Found., La Jolla, Calif., 1972-79, mem. assoc. staff neurology, 1972-82; dir. Ctr. Neurologic Study, San Diego, 1979—; mem. sr. staff Scripps Meml. Hosp., La Jolla, 1982—. Mem. med. adv. bd. Multiple Sclerosis Soc., San Diego; founder neurosci. network Ams. Drs., Gurnee, Ill., 1995—; pres. Coordinated Clin. Rsch. Corp., San Diego, 1996—; vis. scholar neurosci. dept. U. Calif., San Diego, 2000—. Editor: Interferon Treatment for Neurologic Disorders, 1988, Handbook of Amyotrophic Lateral Sclerosis, 1992; contbr. articles to profl. jours. Recipient Henry Newman award San Francisco Neurologic Soc., 1968; NIH STTR grantee, 1996-97; Skaggs Clin. scholar Scripps Rsch. Inst., 1998—. Mem. AAAS, Am. Acad. Neurology (assoc.). Achievements include 6 U.S. patents; work on methodology for enhancing the systemic delivery of Dextromethorphan for the treatment of neurological and medical disorders, including emotional lability, pain, cough. and drug addiction. Office: 9850 Genesee Ave Ste 320 La Jolla CA 92037-1208 E-mail: cns@cts.com.

SMITH, RICHARD BOWEN, retired national park superintendent; b. Grandville, Mich., Mar. 8, 1938; s. William Jr. and Mary Elizabeth (Bowen) S.; m. Katherine Theresa Short, Sept. 21, 1980. BA in History, Albion Coll., 1960; MA in English, Mich. State U., 1967. Tchr. Grand Rapids (Mich.) Jr. H.S., 1960-66; vol. Peace Corps, Asuncion, Paraguay, 1968-70; ranger Nat. Pk. Svc., Yosemite, Calif., 1971-76, ranger. instr. Grand Canyon, Ariz., 1976-78, ranger, legis. specialist Washington, 1978-80, asst. supt. Everglades, Fla., 1980-83, assoc. regional dir. ops. Phila., 1984-86, supt. Carlsbad Caverns, N.Mex., 1986-88, assoc. regional dir. ops. Santa Fe, 1988-89; assoc. regional dir. resources mgmt. Nat. Park Service, Santa Fe, 1990-94; cons. on protected area mgmt. in L.Am., 1994—; temp. supt. Yellowstone Nat. Pk., 1994—; owner R & K Internat., 1994—2000; assoc. Orgnl. Quality Assocs.,, 2000—. Pres. Assn. Nat. Park Rangers, 1977-78; coord. Congress of Internat. Ranger Fedn., San Jose, Costa Rica, 1997, v.p., 1998-2000, pres., 2000-03. Bd. dirs. Yellowstone Assn., 1995-97, Ptnrs. in Parks, 1998-2000. Recipient Meritorious Svc. award Dept. Interior, 1992. Mem. Assn. Nat. Park Rangers (chmn. internat. com. 1997-2000), George Wright Soc. (bd. dirs. 1998—). Home: 2 Roadrunner Trl Placitas NM 87043-9424 E-mail: rsmith0921@aol.com.

SMITH, RICHARD CHARLES, not-for-profit administrator, educator; b. St. Paul, July 30, 1947; s. Arthur George Smith, Edna Alma Smith; m. Joan Rita Oxendine. BA, Calif. State U., San Bernardino, 1976; MBA, U. Calif., Riverside, 1981. Dir. mktg. SCW and Assoc., Riverside, Calif., 1981—84; dir. mktg. and ops. Thomas and Assoc., Riverside, 1984—85; v.p. br. adminstrn. First Fed. Savings and Loan, Ridgecrest, Calif., 1985—90; gen. mgr. KLOA Radio, Ridgecrest, 1990—92; dir. mktg. Ridgecrest Auto Ctr., Ridgecrest, 1992—94; exec. dir. Partnership to Preserve Indep. Living for Srs. and Persons with Disabilities, Riverside, 1994—. Mem. Riverside County Integrated Home and Cmty. Based Long Term Care Task Force, Riverside, 1998—, Riverside County Disability Adv. Com., Calif., 2000—, Riverside County C.A.R.E. Team, 2001—. Prodr.: (ednl. videos) Health Education Program Series, 2002; contbr. articles to profl. jours. E5 Army, 1966—69, Vietnam. Office: Partnership for Independent Living 6296 Rivercrest Dr Ste K Riverside CA Office Phone: 909-697-4697. Personal E-mail: rsmith@vitalco.net. Business E-Mail: rsmith@vitalco.net.

SMITH, RICHARD EMERSON (DICK SMITH), make-up artist; b. Larchmont, N.Y., June 26, 1922; s. Richard Roy and Coral (Brown) S.; m. Jocelyn De Rosa, Jan. 10, 1949; children: Douglas Todd, David Emerson. BA, Yale U., 1944. Pioneer dir. first TV make-up dept. NBC-TV, N.Y.C., 1945-59; make-up dir. David Susskind Prodns., N.Y.C., 1959-61; freelance make-up artist, cons., 1961—. Lectr. Yoyogi Animation Sch., Tokyo, 1992—, Polytek Devel. seminar, 1996; key spkr. Internat. Make-up and Effects Trade Show, 1997-99; featured make-up expert in Movie Magic tv documentaries, Monster Effects, 1994, Aging Effects, 1995; lectr. on spl. make-up effects. Credits include Requiem for a Heavyweight, 1962, The World of Henry Orient, 1963, Mark Twain, Tonight!, 1967 (Emmy award 1967), Midnight Cowboy, 1968, Little Big Man, 1969, The Godfather, 1971, The Exorcist, 1973, The Godfather, Part II, 1974, The Sunshine Boys, 1975, Taxi Driver, 1975, Altered States, 1979, Scanners, 1980, Ghost Story, 1981, The Hunger, 1982, Amadeus, 1983 (U.S. Acad. award 1984, Brit. Acad. award 1985), Starman, 1984, Poltergeist III, 1987, Everybody's All-American, 1988, Sweet Home (Japanese film), 1988, Dad, 1989, Death Becomes Her, 1991, Forever Young, 1992; author: The Advanced Professional Make-Up Course, 1985, The Basic 3-D Make-up Course, 2002; permanent exhbn. of make-up work from Little Big Man, The Exorcist, Amadeus, others, at N.Y. Mus. of the Moving Image, 1992—; columnist Makeup Artist Mag., 1997—. Honored on his 50th ann. in make-up by Am. Film Inst., Visionary Cinema, Cinefex mag., 1995. Home and Office: 27 Wilford Ave Branford CT 06405-3822 Office Phone: 203-488-8111. E-mail: pros355@aol.com.

SMITH, RICHARD ERNEST, retired insurance company executive; b. Adrian, Mich., Oct. 29, 1935; s. Albert Forrest and Thelma (Brock) S.; m. Joanne Piplow, Oct. 11, 1955; children: Kathryn, Albert, Sharon, Richard, Heidi. Student, Spring Arbor Coll., 1955. CLU. Mgr. White Hardware, Adrian, 1950-59; dist. mgr. Met. Life, Adrian and Lafayette, Ind., 1959-75; dir. regional Ohio Nat. Life, Cin., 1975-78; agy. v.p. Provident Life, Bismarck, N.D., 1978-86, pres., 1986-90. Bd. dirs. Provident Life Ins. Co. Commr. City of Adrian, 1966-71; trustee Medctr. One, Bismarck, 1986—, Bismarck State Coll. Found., 1987-91; bd. dirs., v. chmn. Mackinac Straits Hosp., St. Ignace, Mich., 1995—, Bismarck Devel. Assn., 1987-91, Greater Adrian Devel. Assn., 1966-70. Mem.: Apple Creek Country (Bismarck), Elks. Republican. Avocation: travel. Home: N5072 Epoufette Bay Rd Naubinway MI 49762-9722

SMITH, RICHARD HOWARD, banker; b. Tulare, Calif., Aug. 27, 1927; s. Howard Charles and Sue Elizabeth (Cheyne) S.; B.A., Principia Coll, 1958; LL.B., LaSalle U., 1975; postgrad. Sch. Banking U. Wash., 1970-72; m. Patricia Ann Howery, Mar. 12, 1950 (dec. Sept. 2001); children: Jeffrey Howard, Holly Lee, Gregory Scott, Deborah Elaine; m. Charlene Burruel, Mar. 27, 2004. Prin., Aurora Elementary Sch., Tulare, 1951-53; prin. Desert Sun Sch., Idyllwild, Calif., 1953-55; trust adminstr. trainee Bank of Am., San Diego, 1955-58, asst. trust officer, Ventura, Redlands, Riverside and L.A., 1958-65; asst. trust officer Security Pacific Bank, Fresno, Calif., 1965-68; trust officer, 1968-72, v.p., mgr., 1972-88, Pasadena, 1988-94; v.p. Bank of Am., L.A., 1994-95; ret., 1995; pres. Fiduciary Svcs., Fresno, 1995—; instr. San Bernardino Valley Coll., 1962-, Fresno City Coll., 1977-. With USN, 1945-46. Home: 3222 W Dovewood Ln Fresno CA 93711-2125 Office: Smith Fiduciary Svc 163 7081 N Marks Ave #104 Fresno CA 93711-0232 Office Phone: 559-432-6573.

SMITH, RICHARD JACKSON, elementary school educator; b. Mt. Airy, N.C., Feb. 17, 1947; s. Robert Wayne and Ruth (Jackson) S.; m. Sue Monday, Sept. 10, 1971 (dec. Nov. 21, 1981); 1 child, Richard Jackson Jr. BA, U. N.C., 1972; MA, Appalachian State U., 1975; EdD, U. N.C., 1994. Elem. tchr. Surry County Schs., Dobson, NC, 1967-96, Title I parent coord., 1992-96, K-5 instnl. specialist, 1996—2003; project coord. Reading Is Fundamental, 1996-2000. Part-time instr. grad. equivalency diploma/adult basic edn. and effective tchr. tng. classes Surry C.C., Dobson, 1988-92, tchr. literacy class, 1999-2000; adj. faculty Lees-McRae Coll., 2003—; cons. Eckerd Family Youth Alternatives, Inc., 1994-96. Local and dist. chmn., state treas. N.C. Polit. Action Com. for Edn., Raleigh, 1976-81; state exec. com. N.C. Dem. Party, Raleigh, 1981-83; trustee, deacon First Bapt. Ch. of Pilot Mountain, 1988—, Sunday sch. dir. 1991—, mem. nominating com., 1991—, sec. bd. deacons 1990-91, vice chmn. 1996-97, chmn. 1997-99; trustee Charles M. Stone Meml. Libr., 1997-2000, vice chmn., 1998-99, chmn., 1999-2000; chaplain Pilot Mountain Camp, 2000—; bd. dirs. Surry County chpt. ARC, chair nominating com., 2000—, vcie chair, 2003—. Mem. ASCD, NEA (congressional lobbying 1976-80), Internat. Reading Assn. (local unit chair 1986-90), N.C. Assn. Educators (local, dist. pres. 1979-81, local, dist., state chmn. legis. commn. 1980-81), Gideon Internat., Pilot Mountain Jaycees (life, charter, pres. 1979-80, Officer of Yr. 1978, 79), Geneal. Soc. Rockingham & Stokes Counties, Stokes County Hist. Soc., SCV (Stokes County camp 1994—), Masons (32 degree, Scottish Rite, amb. 1990—, lodge master 1990, edn. chmn. 1986—, scholarship chmn. 1986—, Cert. of Meritorious Svc. 1988, adv. bd. Masonic Home for Children at Oxford 2001—, dist. dep. grand master Grand Lodge of N.C. 2001—). Home: PO Box 127 517 E Main St Pilot Mountain NC 27041-8519 Office: Surry County Schs PO Box 364 Dobson NC 27017-0364 E-mail: drrichardsmith@yahoo.com., SmithR@SurryCountyk12.nc.us.

SMITH, RICHARD JAMES, retired music educator; b. Baton Rouge, La., Nov. 28, 1950; s. Jimmie P. and Agnes Mae Smith; m. Dewanna Ann Davis, July 3, 1992 (div. Apr. 30, 2003); m. Lenora Faye McMillon, Mar. 3, 1981 (div. Feb. 28, 1988); m. Elissa Sisk Parks, Oct. 14, 2003; 1 child, James. MusB Edn., La. State U., 1972, MusM Edn., 1977, PhD, 1986. Cert. tchr. La. State Dept. Edn., 1972. Band dir. Northside H.S., Atlanta, 1972—73, Pointe Coupee Ctrl. H.S., LaBarre, La., 1991—94, Glen Oaks H.S., Baton Rouge, 1994—95, Claiborne Acad., Haynesville, La., 1995—97, Jonesboro-Hodge H.S., Jonesboro, La., 1997—98; piano instr. Recreation and Parks Commn., Baton Rouge, 1998—99; band dir. East Iberville H.S., St. Gabriel, La., 1999—2000; piano instr. Recreation and Parks Commn., Baton Rouge, 2000—; band dir. Redemptorist H.S., Baton Rouge, 1973—74, East Beauregard H.S., DeRidder, La., 1974—77, Hammond H.S., Hammond, La., 1977—78, Silliman Inst., La., 1978—81, Mansfield H.S., Mansfield, La., 1981—83; dir. band and choir Breaux Bridge H.S., Breaux Bridge, La., 1984—85; band dir. Raynaud Mid. Sch., Lake Charles, La., 1985—86, Tallulah H.S., Tallulah, La., 1988—91. Composer: (music) Marche Triumphe, 1974, Hall of Justice Concert March, 1986, In God We Trust Concert March, 1988, The Blue and Gold Concert March, 1988, River City Grand March, 1989, Freedom and Unity Concert March, 1989, Morning Star Concert March, 1990, Symphonic March No. 1, 1990, Bayou-Fest Concert March, 1990, Symphonic March No. 2, 1991, The Golden Eagle Concert March, 2002, March of the Trojans, 1975, Adagio for Unaccompanied Flute, 1975, Serenade for Unaccompanied Flute, 1975, Sonata for Unaccompanied Flute, 1975, Soliloquy for Unaccompanied Flute, 1997, Symphonic Essay for Band, 1973, In Memoriam, 1976, Elegy, 1980, Capriccio Jubilante, 1982, A Memorial Tribute, 1996, Memories of Friendship, Love, and Thanks, 1997, The Noble Knights Concert March, 1976, Go, Trojans, 1974, East Beauregard High School Alma Mater, 1974, Fight On!, 1978, Silliman Institute Alma Mater, 1978, Pointe Coupee Central High School Alma Mater, 1991, Claiborne Academy Alma Mater, 1995, A Touch of Tenderness, 1999, Requiem Mass in D Minor, 1977; author: (dissertation) Theoretical Analyses and Practical Applications to the Rehearsal and Performance of Selected Wind-Band Compositions by W. Francis McBeth, 1986, musician; composer: (music) The Silver Star Concert March, 1980; author: (newspaper article) Director Says Children Deserve Music Education, Importance of Music Education Stressed, Musical Education Important, (unpublished report) Theoretical Introductions in Selected American Tune-Books from 1761 to 1794: A Study of Clefs, Voice Parts, and Instructions to Singing, The Origins and Early Development of the Sixteenth-Century Italian Ensemble Canzona, The Administration of the High School Marching Band, Recent Researches in Motor Learning: Implications for Music Teaching, (state music magazine article) W. Francis McBeth - Composer, Conductor, Teacher, and Musician; composer: (music) Freedom Express Concert March, 1982, Marche Jubilante, 1982, Marche Royale, 1984, Marche Symphonique, 1985, Hail to Liberty Concert March, 1986. Mem. Baton Rouge Concert Band, Baton Rouge, La., 1977—81, Lafayette Concert Band, Lafayette, La., 1984—85, Lake Charles Cmty. Band, Lake Charles, La., 1986—88, North La. Cmty. Band, Monroe, La., 1989—91, Baton Rouge Concert Band, Baton Rouge, La., 2001—02. Recipient Mem. of All-American Coll. TV Band - La. State U. Marching Band, Chevrolet Corp., 1970, Superior Rating at Dist. Band Festival - Tallulah H.S. Band, La. Music Educators Assn., 1991, Superior Rating at Dist. Choir Festival - Breaux Bridge H.S. Choir, 1985, First Pl. in Mansfield Christmas Parade - Mansfield H.S. Band, Mansfield, LA, Chamber of Commerce, 1981. Mem.: NEA (life), U.S. Achievement Acad. (nat. adv. bd. 1983—2002), La. Bandmasters Assn., La. Music Educators Assn., Music Educators Nat. Conf., La. Educators Assn. (life), Pi Kappa Lambda, Kappa Kappa Psi (life Outstanding pledge 1969). Avocations: travel, reading, performing music, building 3-d puzzles, playing miniature golf. Home: 10515 Tallowwood Ave Baker LA 70714 Office: Recreation and Parks Commission 3140 N Sherwood Forest Dr Baton Rouge LA 70814 Office Fax: None. Personal E-mail: rjsmith4@bellsouth.net. E-mail: none.

SMITH, RICHARD JAY, anthropologist, orthodontist, educator; b. Aug. 10, 1948; s. Benjamn and Miriam Smith; m. Linda Sharon Harris, Aug. 22, 1970; children: Jason Andrew, Owen Harris, Hilary Rachele. BA, CUNY, 1969; MS in Anatomy, DMD, Tufts U., 1973; PhD in Anthropology, Yale U., 1980. Asst. clin. prof. orthodontics U. Conn., Farmington, 1976—79; asst. prof. U. Md., Balt., 1979—81, assoc. prof., 1981—84; prof. orthodontics, biomed. sci., chmn. dept. orthodontics, adj. prof. anthropology Washington U., St. Louis, 1984—91, assoc. dean, 1987—89, dean Sch. Dental Medicine, 1989—91, cons. orthodontics Cleft Palate and Craniofacial Anomalies Team, 1984—91, prof. anthropology, 1991—2001, chmn. dept. anthropology, 1993—, Ralph E. Morrow disting. univ. prof., 2001—, dir. program in applied statistics, 2002—. Vis. assoc. prof. cell biology Sch. Medicine Johns Hopkins U., Balt., 1980—84; orthodontic cons. St. Louis VA Med. Ctr., 1986—91; mem. staff Barnes Hosp., 1986—91, St. Louis Children's Hosp., 1985—91. Editor-in-chief: Jour. Balt. Coll. Dental Surgery, 1981—84, contbr.: numerous articles in orthodontics, anthropology, comparative biology to profl. jours. Am. Fund for Dental Health dental tchr. tng. fellow, 1977—78, postdoctoral fellow, NIH, 1978—79. Fellow: Am. Coll. Dentists, Internat. Coll. Dentists; mem.: ADA, Internat. Primatological Soc., Am. Assn. Phys. Anthropologists, Am. Assn. Orthodontists, Alumni Assn. Student Clinicians (bd. govs. 1984—90, pres. 1988—89, Alan J. Davis award 1983). Home: 816 S Bemiston Ave Saint Louis MO 63105-2602 Office: Washington U Dept Anthropology One Brookings Dr Saint Louis MO 63130 E-mail: rjsmith@wustl.edu.

SMITH, RICHARD MILLS, editor-in-chief; b. Detroit, Jan. 12, 1946; s. William Steele Smith and Janet (Mills) Morrison; m. Lee Ann Vanderstoep (div.); children: Scott William, Anna Mills; m. Soon-Young Yoon, Oct. 20, 1978; 1 child, Song-Mee. BA summa cum laude, Albion Coll., 1968; postgrad., Columbia U., 1968—69, MS, 1970; LLD (hon.), Albion Coll., 1993. Reporter Associated Press, NY, 1969; assoc. editor foreign dept. Newsweek, NY, 1970—73, gen. editor nat. affairs dept., 1973—74, editor Asian region, bur. chief Hong Kong, 1974—77; mng. editor Newsweek Internat., NY, 1977—81; asst. mng. editor Newsweek, NYC, 1982, exec. editor, 1983, editor in chief, 1984—, pres., 1991—98, chmn., 1998—. Chmn. Mag. Pub. Am., 1996—97. Trustee Albion Coll; bd. dirs. Cooper-Hewitt Nat. Design Mus., Smithsonian Instn., Harvard AIDS Inst. Recipient Disting. Alumni award, Albion Coll., 1974, Henry Johnson Fisher award, Mag. Pub. of Am., 2001. Mem.: Century Assn., Coun. on Fgn. Rels., Mag. Pubs. Assn. (chmn.), Am. Soc. Mag. Editors (mem. exec. com. 1985—88), Phi Beta Kappa. Office: Newsweek Inc 251 W 57th St New York NY 10019-1802

SMITH, RICHARD THOMAS, retired electrical engineer; b. Allentown, Pa., June 15, 1925; s. Raymond Willard and Mary (Rau) S.; m. Naomi Elsie Anthony, May 26, 1956; children: Cynthia Louise, Carol Ann. BS with honors, Lehigh U., 1946, MS, 1947; PhD, Ill. Inst. Tech., 1955. Registered profl. engr., Mass., Okla., Tex., Gt. Britain. Instr., Lehigh U., Bethlehem, Pa., 1947-50; analytical and design engr. Gen. Electric Co., Schenectady, 1952-58; asst. prof. U. Tex., Austin, 1958-61; George Westinghouse prof. elec. engring. Va. Poly. Inst., Blacksburg, 1961-62; project dir. Tracor, Inc., Austin, 1962-64; sr. engr., asst. dir., dir., v.p. Southwest Research Inst., San Antonio, 1964-66; Okla. Gas and Electric prof. elec. engring. U. Okla., Norman, 1966-68; prof. elec. machinery Rensselaer Poly. Inst., Troy, N.Y., 1968-70; NSF fellow U. Colo., 1970; Alcoa&UMR Disting. prof. elec. engring. U. Mo., Rolla, 1970-73; inst. engr., dir. Nondestructive Testing Info. Analysis Center, Southwest Research Inst., San Antonio, 1973-83; cons., 1983—. Adj. prof. U. Tex., 1974-83, prof., 1983-87; cons., reviewer numerous cos. Author: Analysis of Electrical Machines, 1982; patentee in field. Recipient Excellence Fund U. Tex., 1959, DuPont Meml. prize Lehigh U., 1946 Fellow AIAA (assoc.), Instn. Elec. Engrs. (Eng.); mem. Am. Soc. Engring. Edn., I.E.E.E. (1st paper prize 1960, 63, sr.), N.Y. Acad. Scis., I.E.E.E. (numerous coms.), Internat. Electrotech. Commn. (adv. group 1971-74), Sigma Xi, Tau Beta Pi, Pi Mu Epsilon, Phi Eta Sigma, Eta Kappa Nu, Phi Kappa Phi. Office: 402 Yosemite Dr Hollywood Park TX 78232-1251 E-mail: snar@idworld.net.

SMITH, RICHARD WENDELL, lawyer; b. May 29, 1912; s. Walter Charles and Mary Frances (Goodale) Smith; m. Patricia Adelle Lahr, Apr. 8, 1947; children: Laurie Patricia, Barton Richard. AB, Nebr. Wesleyan U., 1933; JD, Harvard U., 1938. Bar: (Nebr.) 1938, (U.S. Dist. Ct. Nebr.) 1938, (U.S. Ct. Claims) 1949, (U.S. Ct. Appeals (7th and 8th Fed. cirs.)), (U.S. Supreme Ct.) 1955. Spl. agt. FBI Dept. Justice, Washington, 1942—44; ptnr. Woods and Aitken, Lincoln, Nebr.; reorgn. trustee Am. Buslines, Inc., 1954—58; lectr. constrn. law Fed. Publs., Washington, 1974—96. Contbr. articles to profl. jours. Bd. dirs. Nebr. Wesleyan U., Lincoln, 1958—74, sec., life mem.; sec. Harvard Schs. and Scholarship Com., 1948—; trustee Nebr. Art Assn., 1984—86; bd. dirs. Lincoln Symphony Orch. Assn., Lincoln Cmty. Theater, 1982—87. To lt. USNR, 1944—46. Mem.: ABA (governing com. forum on constrn. industry 1983—89), Nebr. Bar Assn., Rotary (pres. 1981—82). Republican. Office: Woods & Aitken 301 S 13th St Ste 500 Lincoln NE 68508-2578 Home: # 3 225 N 56th St Lincoln NE 68504-3519

SMITH, RICHEY, manufacturing executive; b. Akron, Ohio, Nov. 11, 1933; s. Thomas William and Martha (Richey) S.; m. Sandra Cosgrave Roe, Nov. 25, 1961; children: Mason Roe, Parker Richey. Grad. The Hotchkiss Sch.; BS, U. Va., 1956. Asst. to pres. Sun Products Corp., Barberton, Ohio, 1960-64, v.p., 1964-67, gen. mgr., dir., 1967-69, chmn., CEO, 1969-76; prin. A.T. Kearney Co., Cleve., 1977-87; chmn., CEO Richey Industries, Inc., Medina, Ohio, 1987—. Bd. dirs. Jaite Packaging, Inc. Exec. com. Gt. Trail coun. Boy Scouts Am.; chmn. capital funds dr. Summit County Planned Parenthood; trustee, found. pres. Old Trail Sch., Barberton Citizens Hosp., Medina County Arts Coun., Akron Regional Devel. Bd.; treas. Friends of Metro Park; found. trustee, vestryman St. Paul's Episcopal Ch.; corp. bd. Cleve. Mus. of Art; bd. govs. The Hotchkiss Sch. Lt. USN, 1957—60, lt. USNR, 1961—69. Mem. Ohio Commodores, Bluecoats (trustee), Navy League (pres. Akron coun. 1972-73), Young Pres. Orgn., Portage Country Club (bd. dirs.), Mayflower Club, Sawgrass Country Club (Fla.) Farmington Country Club (Charlottesville, Va.), Rotary (trustee Akron 1974-75), Yale Club (N.Y.C.), Rockwell Springs Trout Club, Chi Psi (pres.). Home: 721 Delaware Ave Akron OH 44303-1303 Office: 910 Lake Rd Medina OH 44256-2453 Office Phone: 330-725-4997 x 304. E-mail: rsmith@richeyind.com.

SMITH, ROBERT BOULWARE, III, vascular surgeon, educator; b. Atlanta, June 15, 1933; s. Robert Boulware Jr. Smith and Mary Eva (Black) Fanning; m. Florence Chance Limehouse, Aug. 22, 1953; children: Victoria Joanne Smith Harkins, Robert Boulware IV, Brian Scott. MD, Emory U., 1957. Diplomate Am. Bd. Surgery, Am. Bd. Vascular Surgery. Intern in surgery Columbia Presbyn. Hosp., N.Y.C., 1957-58, resident in surgery, 1960-65; asst. prof. surgery Emory U. Sch. Medicine, Atlanta, 1966-69, assoc. prof., 1969-77, prof., 1977—, head gen. vascular surgery, 1984-98. Chief surg. svc. VA Med. Ctr., Atlanta, 1969-88; assoc. med. dir. Emory U. Hosp., 1993-95, med. dir., 1995—. Contbr. numerous articles, book chpts. to profl. publs.; co-editor: Trauma to the Thorax and Abdomen, 1969, Medical Management of the Surgical Patient, 1982, 3d edit., 1995. Capt. M.C., U.S. Army, 1958-60. Mem. ACS, Am. Surg. Assn., So. Assn. Vascular Surgery (sec. 1986-91, pres. 1992-93), Soc. Vascular Surgery, Assn. VA Surgeons (pres. 1983-84, Disting. Svc. award 1988), Ga. Surg. Soc. (pres. 1992-93), Atlanta Vascular Soc. (pres. 1986-88), Internat. Soc. for Cardiovasc. Surg. (pres. 1996-97). Phi Beta Kappa, Alpha Omega Alpha. Republican. United Methodist. Avocations: music, travel. Home: 2701 Coldwater Canyon Dr Tucker GA 30084-2358 Office: Emory Univ Hosp B207 1364 Clifton Rd NE Atlanta GA 30322-1013 Office Phone: 404-727-8145. Business E-Mail: robert_smith@emory.edu.

SMITH, ROBERT CHARLES, political science educator, researcher; b. Benton, La., Feb. 12, 1947; s. Martin and Blanch (Tharpe) S.; m. Scottie Bess Gibson, May 6, 1952; children: Blanch, Jessica, Scottus-Charles. BA, U. Calif., Berkeley, 1970; MA, UCLA, 1972; PhD, Howard U., 1976. Asst. prof. Coll. at Purchase SUNY, 1976-80; assoc. prof. Howard U., Washington, 1980-88; prof. Prairie View (Tex.) Agrl. Mech., 1988-89, San Francisco State U., 1989—. Rsch. assoc. Columbia U., N.Y.C., 1972-73, 78-80; guest scholar Joint Ctr. Polit. Studies, Washington, 1985-86. Author: Racism in the Post Civil Rights Era, 1995, We Have No Leader: African Americans, 1996, Encyclopedia of African American Politics, 2003; co-author: Race, Class and Culture, 1992; co-editor: Urban Black Politics, 1978. Co-founder Congress of Black Faculty, Washington, 1987; founding fellow Open Mind: Cultural Diversity, 1988; co-chair Bay Area Malcum 25th Anniversary Com., 1990. Recipient Disting. PhD Alumni award, Howard U., 1998. Mem. Am. Polit. Sci. Assn., Nat. Conf. Black Polit. Scientists, Ctr. for Study Presidency, Acad. Polit. Sci. Baptist. Avocations: reading, walking. Home: 5044 Santa Rita Rd Richmond CA 94803-3236 Office: San Francisco State U 1600 Holloway Ave San Francisco CA 94132-1722 Address: 5044 Santa Rita Rd Richmond CA 94803-3236 E-mail: rcs@sfsu.edu.

SMITH, ROBERT CLINTON, former senator; b. Trenton, N.J., Mar. 30, 1941; s. Donald and Margaret (Eldridge) S.; m. Mary Jo Hutchinson, July 2, 1966; children: Jennifer L., Robert Clinton, Jason H. AA, Trenton Jr. Coll., 1963; BA, Lafayette Coll., 1965; postgrad., Long Beach State U., 1968-69. Tchr., realtor, Wolfeboro, N.H., 1970-85; chmn. Gov. Wentworth Dist. Sch. Bd., 1978-84; mem. 99th-101st Congresses from 1st N.H. dist., Washington, 1985-90, U.S. Senate from N.H., Washington, 1990—2003. Mem. armed svcs., environ. and pub. works, chmn. ethic com., chmn. and sen. judiciary com. With USN, 1962-69, Vietnam. Mem. Am. Legion, Theta Xi. Republican. Roman Catholic. Mailing: 758 Lake Wellington DR Wellington FL 33414-7968

SMITH, ROBERT EARL, space scientist; b. Indpls., Sept. 13, 1923; s. Harold Bennett and Bernice (McCaslin) S.; m. Elizabeth Lee Usak, Jan. 3, 1947 (dec. 1984); children: Stephanie Lee, Robert Michael, Cynthia Ann, Kelly Andrew; m. Lyla Lee Lewellen, July 1, 1988. BS, Fla. State U., 1959, MS, 1960, U. Mich., 1969, PhD, 1974. Enlisted U.S. Army Air Force, 1943-44; advanced through grades to maj. U.S. Air Force, 1955; airway traffic

controller Berlin, 1945; staff weather reconnaissance officer 9th Air Force, 1956; ret., 1963; project scientist Atmospheric Cloud Physics Lab.; dep. chief atmospheric scis. div. NASA/Marshall Space Flight Ctr., Ala., 1963-86; sr. scientific cons. Univs. Space Rsch. Assn., Huntsville, Ala., 1986-87; sr. computer cons. Computer Scis. Corp., Huntsville, 1987-89; chief space sci. and applications div. FWG Assocs., Inc., Huntsville, 1989-92; NASA program mgr. Physitron, Inc., Huntsville, 1992-96; sr. computer scientist Computer Scis. Corp., Huntsville, 1996—2002. Mem. AIAA, Pi Mu Epsilon, Sigma Phi Epsilon. Home: 125 Westbury Dr SW Huntsville AL 35802-1619

SMITH, ROBERT ELLIS, lawyer, journalist; b. Providence, Sept. 6, 1940; s. Ronald Bancroft and Clarice (Evans) S.; children: Marc O., David E., Benjamin E., Gregor E. BA, Harvard U., 1962; JD, Georgetown U., 1975. Bar: D.C. 1976, R.I. 1987. News reporter Detroit Free Press, 1962-65, Newsday, Garden City, N.Y., 1966-70; asst. dir. Office for Civil Rights HEW, Washington, 1970-73; pub. Privacy Jour., Washington and Providence, 1974—; pvt. practice Block Island, RI, 1978—; spl. asst. atty. gen. State of R.I., Providence, 1991-92; vice-chmn. R.I. Coastal Resources Mgmt. Coun., 1996—2002. Mem. D.C. Commn. Human Rights, 1983-85. Author: Privacy: How to Protect What's Left of It, 1979, Compliation of State and Federal Privacy Laws, 1976, 78, 81, 84, 88, 92, 97, 2002, Workrights, 1983, Celebrities and Privacy, 1985, The Law of Privacy Explained, 1993, Our Vanishing Privacy, 1993, Ben Franklin's Web Site, 2000, Block Island Trivia, 2003. Pres. Block Island Conservancy, 1990-94; arbitrator R.I. Superior Ct.; chair Harvard Crimson Grad. Bd., 1999-2002. With U.S. Army, 1963-65. Mem. ABA, R.I. Bar Assn., Harvard Club. Avocation: writing. Office: Privacy Jour PO Box 28577 Providence RI 02908-0577 also: PO Box 984 Block Island RI 02807 0984 Office Phone: 401-274-7861. E-mail: orders@privacyjournal.net.

SMITH, ROBERT EVERETT, lawyer; b. N.Y.C., Mar. 15, 1936; s. Arthur L. and Augusta (Cohen) S.; m. Emily Lucille Lehman, July 17, 1960; children: Amy, Karen, Victoria. BA, Dartmouth Coll., 1957; LLB, Harvard U., 1960. Bar: N.Y. 1960, U.S. Dist. Ct. (so. dist.) N.Y. 1962, U.S. Ct. Appeals (2d cir.) 1963, U.S. Supreme Ct. 1967, U.S. Dist. Ct. (ea. dist.) N.Y. 1969, U.S. Ct. Appeals (3d cir.) 1982, U.S. Ct. Appeals (9th cir.) 1988. Assoc. Paul, Weiss, Rifkind, Wharton & Garrison, N.Y.C., 1960-65; from assoc. to ptnr. Baar, Bennett & Fullen, N.Y.C., 1965-74; ptnr. Guggenheimer & Untermyer, N.Y.C., 1974-85, Rosenman & Colin LLP, N.Y.C., 1985-98, chmn., 1994-97, counsel, 1998—2002, KMZ Rosenman, N.Y.C., 2002—. With U.S. Army, 1961-64. Mem. ABA, N.Y. State Bar Assn., Assn. of Bar of City of N.Y., Fed. Bar Coun., N.Y. County Lawyers Assn., Internat. Bar Assn., Am. Arbitration Assn. (nat. panel arbitrators), Am. Law Inst. Office: KMZ Rosenman 575 Madison Ave Fl 26 New York NY 10022-2585 Office Phone: 212-940-8850. E-mail: robert.smith@kmzr.com.

SMITH, ROBERT F. (BOB SMITH), rancher, former congressman; b. Portland, Oreg., June 16, 1931; m. Kaye Tomlinson; children: Christopher, Matthew, Tiffany. BA in Bus. Adminstrn. and Econs., Willamette U., 1953. Mem. Oreg. Ho. of Reps., 1960-73, spkr., 1969-73; mem. Oreg. State Senate, 1973-82, leader republican caucus, 1977-83; mem. 98th-105th Congresses from 2d dist. Oreg., 1983-94; pres. Smith West Co., Portland, 1995-96, cons. Medford, Oreg., 1999—. Dir. First State Bank Oreg., Key Bank; dir. exch. bd. Farmers Ins.; dir. bd. trustee Willamette U. Named one of Harney County, Oreg.'s Leading Citizens, 1957, one of Oreg.'s Outstanding Young Men, 1961. Republican. Office: Smith West Co 843 E Main St Ste 400 Medford OR 97504-7137

SMITH, ROBERT FREEMAN, history educator; b. Little Rock, May 13, 1930; s. Robert Freeman and Emma Martha Gottlieb (Buerkle) S.; m. Alberta Vester, Feb. 1, 1951 (dec. 1985); children: Robin Ann, Robert Freeman III; m. Charlotte Ann Coleman, Sept. 9, 1985. BA, U. Ark., 1951, MA, 1952; PhD, U. Wis., Madison, 1958. Instr. U. Ark., Fayetteville, 1953; asst. prof. Tex. Luth. Coll., Seguin, 1958-62; assoc. prof. U. R.I., Kingston, 1962-66, U. Conn., Storrs, 1966-69; prof. history U. Toledo, 1969-86, disting. univ. prof., 1986—. Vis. prof. U. Wis., Madison, 1966-67. Author: The United States and Cuba: Business and Diplomacy 1917-1960, 1961 (Tex. Writers' Roundup award 1961), What Happened in Cuba: A Documentary History of U.S.-Cuban Relations, 1963, The United States and Revolutionary Nationalism in Mexico, 1916-1932, 1973 (Ohio Acad. History award 1973), The Era of Caribbean Intervention, 1890-1930, 1981, The Era of Good Neighbors, Cold Warriors, and Hairshirts, 1930-82, 1983, The Caribbean World and the United States: Mixing Rum & Coca-Cola, 1994; contbr. to numerous publs. Retired Col. 7th Hist. Detachment, Ohio Mil. Res. 1st lt. U.S. Army, 1953-55. Knapp fellow in history U. Wis., 1957; Tom L. Evans rsch. fellow Harry S. Truman Libr., Independence, Mo., 1976-77, Mexican Ministry Fgn. Rels. fellow, 1991-92. Mem. Soc. Historians of Am. Fgn. Rels., Soc. Mil. History, U.S. Naval Inst., Ohio Acad. History, So. Hist. Assn., Orgn. Am. Historians, Assn. U.S. Army, State Guard Assn. of U.S., Am. Legion, Masons, Scottish Rite, Shriners, Army Hist. Found., Inst. Land Warfare, Sons of Confederate Vets., Phi Beta Kappa, Phi Alpha Theta. Episcopalian. Avocation: photography. Home: 4110 Dunkirk Rd Toledo OH 43606-2217 Office: U Toledo Dept History Toledo OH 43606

SMITH, ROBERT HAMIL, writer, fund raiser; b. Oak Park, Ill., Nov. 8, 1927; s. Henry Garfield and Mary Ellen (Hamil) S.; m. Mary Helen Kingsley, Dec. 29, 1948; children: David H., Mark K., Steven H., Rebecca Anne. Student, U. Denver, 1946-48; LLB, 1953, JD, 1960. Dep. clk. County Ct. City and county of Denver, 1948-53; with Colo. Ins. Group, 1953-59; mgr. claims dept. R.H. Smith & Assocs., 1959-64; cons. Am. BApt. Home Mission Soc., 1964-68; assoc. dir. devel. Ill. Wesleyan U., 1968-69; asst. to chancellor U. Calif., San Diego, 1969-77; exec. dir. devel. Scripps Clinic and Rsch. Found., La Jolla, Calif., 1977-82; v.p. devel., 1982-88; pres. Cartographic Enterprises, 1981—. Owner C Books, 1981. Author: Guide to Harbors, Anchorages and Marinas So. and No. California edits., 1983, The Physician as a Fundraiser, 1984, Naval Inst. Guide to Maritime Museums in U.S./Canada, 1991, Smith's Guide to Maritime Museums U.S./Canada, 1993; pub.: Maritime Museums of North America Including Canada, 1998, Smith's Guide to Maritime Museums of North America, 3 parts, 2003, Smith's Guide to Maritime Museums of North America, publication of 6th update, 2004. Bd. dirs. Nat. Com. on Planned Giving, 1990-94; fund raising cons. deferred giving; trustee San Diego Maritime Mus., 2002—. Served with USNR, 1945. Mem. Nat. Soc. Fund Raising Execs., Internat. Yachting Fellowship of Roatrians (San Diego fleet comdr. 1979-81). Baptist. Home and Office: PO Box 176 Del Mar CA 92014-0176 E-mail: rhs2@ix.netcom.com.

SMITH, ROBERT HUGH, former engineering construction company executive; b. Wichita, Kans., Dec. 29, 1936; s. Richard Lyon and E. Eileen (O'Neal) S.; m. Melinda Louise Fitch, Sept. 26, 1959 (div. Dec. 1969); children: Robert Blake, Thomas Hugh; m. Margaret Anne Moseley, Dec. 11, 1971; 1 child, Steven Richard. BS, Kans. State U., 1959; MS, U. Kansas, 1964, PhD, 1970. Sr. process engr. FMC Corp., Lawrence, Kans., 1959-64; rsch. engr. Phillips Petroleum Co., Bartlesville, Okla., 1964-66; group leader Standard Oil of Ohio, Warrenville Heights, Ohio, 1966-67; sr. rsch. assoc., group leader Atlantic Richfield, Plano, Tex., 1970-80; regional mgr., sr. mgr., sales mgr. Fluor Daniel, Houston and Marlton, N.J., 1980-90; v.p., gen. mgr. Badger Design & Construction, Tampa, Fla., 1990-93; exec. v.p., COO Process divsn. Black & Veatch, Overland Park, 1993-2000. Patentee in the field; contbr. to profl. jours. Adv. bd. dept. chem. engring, coll. of engring. U. Kans., Lawrence, 1993—; mem. adv. bd. coll. engring. Kans. State U., 1998—. Recipient Disting. Svc. award Kans. State U., 1998; named into Engring. Hall of Fame Kans. State, Chem. and Petroleum Engring. Hall of fame, U. Kans., 2000. Fellow AIChE (chmn., vice chmn., sec. Dallas chpt. 1962—, Engr. of Yr. award Dallas chpt. 1980, exec. bd. Engr. and Cons. Contracting divsn.), Phi Lambda Upsilon, Sigma Xi. Avocations: tennis, sailing, skiing, reading.

SMITH, ROBERT J., JR., real estate executive; b. Rochester, N.Y., June 1, 1951; s. Robert and Irene (Frisbie) S.; m. Sherry L. Silberman, July 5, 1981; 1 child, Jordan. Student, Ohio U., 1969-73. CPA, Ohio. Gen. mgr. Televac, Inc., Athens, 1975—; CFO, gen. mgr. Practice Mgmt., Inc. (PMI), Cleve., 1988—. Mem. AICPA. E-mail: televac@aol.com.

SMITH, ROBERT JOHN, anthropology educator; b. Essex, Mo., June 27, 1927; s. Will Dan and Fern (Jones) S.; m. Kazuko Sasaki, Aug. 22, 1955. BA summa cum laude, U. Minn., 1949; MA, Cornell U., 1951, PhD, 1953. Engaged in cultural anthrop. field research, N.S., Can., 1950, 1951-52, 55, 57-58, 1966-67; mem. faculty Cornell U., 1953—, prof. anthropology, 1963-74, Goldwin Smith prof. anthropology, 1974-97, prof. emeritus, 1997—, chmn. dept. Asian studies, 1961-66, chmn. dept. antropology, 1967-71, 76-82, prof. emeritus, 1997—. Vis. prof. anthropology U. Ariz., 1971, U. Hawaii, 1978, Nat. Mus. Ethnology, Osaka, Japan, 1982 Author: (with Cornell) Two Japanese Villages, 1956, (with Cornell, Saito and Maeyama) Japanese and Their Descendants in Brazil, 1967; editor: (with Beardsley) Japanese Culture: Its Development and Characteristics, 1962, Social Organization and the Applications of Anthropology, 1974, Ancestor Worship in Contemporary Japan, 1974, Kurusu: The Price of Progress in a Japanese Village, 1951-75, 1978, (with Wiswell) Women of Suye Mura, 1982, Japanese Society: Tradition, Self and the Social Order, 1983, (with K. Smith) Diary of a Japanese Innkeeper's Daughter, 1984 Served with AUS, 1944-46. Tng. grantee Social Sci. Rsch. Coun., Japan, 1951-52; recipient Individual Exch. award to Japan Inst. Internat. Edn., 1957-58; Fulbright lectr. Tokyo Met. U., 1962-63; NSF rsch. grantee, 1965-67; Japan Found. grantee, 1979; awarded Order of the Rising Sun, Govt. of Japan, 1993. Fellow Assn. Asian Studies (v.p. 1987-88, pres. 1988-89), Soc. Applied Anthropology (editor jour. Human Orgn. 1961-66). Home: 107 Northview Rd Ithaca NY 14850-6039

SMITH, ROBERT L. medical research administrator; b. N.Y.C., Mar. 29, 1941; m. Carolee Smith, 1968; children: Jana, Shayna, Marni. BEE, CCNY, 1962; MSEE, NYU, 1966; PhD in Neurosci., Syracuse U., 1973. Devel. engr. Wheeler Lab., Gt. Neck, N.Y., 1962-64; lectr. elec. engring. CCNY, 1964-66; instr. elec. engring. Syracuse (N.Y.) U., 1970-74, from asst. prof. to assoc. prof. sensory rsch., 1974-85, prof. neurosci. and bioengring., 1985—, dir. Inst. Sensory Rsch., 1993—. Assoc. editor Jour. Acoustical Soc. Am., 1986-89. NIH fellow, 1979-84. Fellow Acoustical Soc. Am.; mem. Assn. Rsch. Otolaryngology, Soc. Neurosci., Sigma Xi. Achievements include research in neurophysiology and neural coding in the auditory nervous system; single unit recording from the cochlea, auditory nerve and cochlear nucleus; mathematical modeling of the results and systems analysis of the auditory system; biomedical engineering. Office: Syracuse U Inst for Sensory Rsch 621 Skytop Rd Syracuse NY 13244-0001

SMITH, ROBERT LOUIS, construction company executive; b. Parkersburg, W.Va., Apr. 19, 1922; s. Everett Clerc and Janet (Morrison) S.; m. June Irene Odbert, Oct. 25, 1948; children: Peter Clerc, Morrison James, Edna Louise. BS in Civil Engring., Lehigh U., 1944. Design engr. Chrysler Corp., 1944-46; engr. Harrison Constrn. Co., Charleston, W.Va., 1946-47; sr. engr. Creole Petroleum Co., Las Piedras, Venezuela, 1947-55; v.p. Rea Constrn. Co., Charlotte, N.C., 1955-64; exec. v.p. Warren Bros. Co., Cambridge, Mass., 1964-68, pres., 1968-79; also dir.; sr. v.p. Ashland Oil, Inc., Ky., 1974-79; pres. Robert L. Smith & Assos., Lexington, 1979—; pres., dir. Tree Farm Devel. Corp., Cambridge, 1979—. Dir. Panastalto (S.A.), Wilder Constrn. Co., Inc., J.H. Shears Sons, Inc. Fellow ASCE; mem. Nat. Asphalt Pavement Assn. (dir.), Phi Beta Kappa, Tau Beta Pi, Sigma Chi. Republican. Unitarian Universalist. Home and Office: 1010 Waltham St Apt A412 Lexington MA 02421-8065 Office Phone: 781-861-0489. E-mail: 103710.3552@compuserve.com.

SMITH, ROBERT LUTHER, management educator; b. Kutztown, Pa., Feb. 18, 1927; s. Paul Luther and Esther Florence (Schwoyer) S.; m. Canda Eure Banks, Aug. 18, 1951; children: Kimberley Smith Kidd, Valerie Smith Eudy, Alexandra. BS, U.S. Naval Acad., 1949; MSA, George Washington U., 1975, DBA, 1984. Commd. USN, 1949-72, advanced through grades to comdr.; commanding officer USS Grouper, 1962-65; engr. and repair officer U.S. Submarine Base, Groton, Conn., 1965-67; supt. of test Portsmouth Naval Shipyard, Portsmouth, N.H., 1967-70; asst. project mgr. Naval Systems Submarine Acquisition, Washington, 1970-72; project mgr. EG&G, Washington Analytical, Rockville, Md., 1972-80; pres. Interface Resources Ltd., Alexandria, Va., 1980—; lectr. George Mason U., Fairfax, Va., 1981-84; prof. Coll. of Notre Dame of Md., Balt., 1984-98. Faculty Dealer Mgmt. Inst., Columbus, Ohio, 1981—83; cons. in field of orgn. performance. Sr. warden St. Paul's Episcopal Ch., Alexandria, 1980-81; mem. Alexandria Health Svcs., 1983—. Mem.: Am. Soc. for Quality, Kena Shrine, Scottish Rite, Kiwanis Alexandria (pres. 1985—86, del. to internat. 1985), Masons, Beta Gamma Sigma. Republican. Home: 1102 Bayliss Dr Alexandria VA 22302-3506 Office Phone: 703-836-4555. Personal E-mail: doc4orgztn@aol.com.

SMITH, ROBERT MASON, academic administrator; b. Sill, Okla., May 5, 1945; s. Arnold Mason and Lillyan (Scott) Smith; m. Ramona Lynn Stukey, June 15, 1968; children: David, Angela. BA, Wichita State U., 1967; MA, Ohio U., 1968; PhD, Temple U., 1976. Debate coach Princeton (N.J.) U., 1971-73; debate coach Wichita (Kans.) State U., 1973-87; assoc. dean Coll. Liberal Arts and Scis., 1977-87; dean coll. arts and scis. U. Tenn., Martin, 1987-99; provost and vice pres. for academic affairs Slippery Rock Univ., 1999—2002, interim pres., 2002—04, pres., 2004—. Dir. Govt. Sch. for Humanities, 1996—99; spl. asst. U.S. Dept. Human Svcs., Washington, 1980—81. Mem. State Behavioral Sci. Regulatory Bd., Topeka, 1984—87; trustee Leadership Kans., Topeka, 1986—87; founder, bd. dirs. WestStar Regional Tenn. Leadership Program, 1989—99. Recipient Excellence in Tchg. award, Coun. for Advancement and Support of Edn., 1994, Crystal Apple award for Outstanding Tchg., 1995, Award for Disting. Leadership, Nat. Assn. Cmty. Leadership, 1995, Gov.'s Award for Outstanding Achievement, 1999, Preceptor award, 1999; fellow, Health Human Svc. Mem.: Tenn. Speech Comm. Assn., Tenn. Coun. Colls. Arts and Scis. (pres. 1993—94), Assn. for Comm. Adminstrn. (pres. 1988), Kans. Speech Comm. Assn. (pres. 1977, Outstanding Coll. Speech Tchr. award 1977), Rotary Club, Phi Theta Kappa, Beta Theta Pi, Phi Eta Sigma, Phi Kappa Phi. Baptist. Home: 106 Ojibwa Dr Butler PA 16001-0528 Office: Slippery Rock Univ Pres 300 Old Main Slippery Rock PA 16057 Office Phone: 724-738-2000.

SMITH, ROBERT MICHAEL, lawyer, mediator, arbitrator; b. Boston, Nov. 4, 1940; s. Sydney and Minnie (Appel) S.; m. Catherine Kersey, Apr. 14, 1981 (dec. 1983); m. Clarissa Redmond, Feb. 11, 1999 (dec. 2001). AB cum laude, Harvard Coll., 1962; diploma, Centro de Estudos de Espanol, Barcelona, 1963; MA in Internat. Affairs, Columbia U., 1964, MS in Journalism with high honors, 1965; JD, Yale U., 1975. Bar: Calif., N.Y., D.C., U.S. Supreme Ct.; barrister Inner Temple, London; solicitor Supreme Ct. of Eng. and Wales; accredited mediator Hong Kong Internat. Arbitration Ctr.; chartered arbitrator, Eng.; registered mediator Ctr. de Mediation et d'Arbitrage Paris. Intern in econ. devel. UN, Geneva, 1964; corr. Time Mag., N.Y.C., 1965-66, The N.Y. Times, Washington, 1968-72, 75-76; atty. Heller, Ehrman, White & McAuliffe, San Francisco, 1976-78; spl. asst. Office of Atty. Gen. of U.S., Washington, 1979-80; dir. Office Pub. Affairs U.S. Dept. Justice, Washington, 1979-80; mem. U.S. delegation U.S. v. Iran Internat. Ct. of Justice, The Hague, 1980; asst. U.S. atty. No. Dist. Calif., San Francisco, 1981-82; counsel, sr. counsel to sr. litigation counsel Bank of Am. NT & SA, San Francisco, 1982-86. Lectr. FBI Acad., Quantico, Va., 1980, Internat. Bankers Assn. Calif., 1994, Calif. Bankers Assn., 1994, Cmty. Bankers No. Calif., 1994, 95; judge Golden Medallion Broadcast Media awards State Bar of Calif., 1985; judge pro tem Mcpl. Ct. City and County of San Francisco, 1989—; conciliator Peninsula Conflict Resolution Ctr.; panelist World Intellectual Property Orgn., Geneva; arbitrator internat. Commercial arbitration ctrs., Vancouver, Cairo, Singapore, Kuala Lumpur, India; CPR Panel of Disting. Neutrals; mem. panel Nat. Assn. for Dispute Resolution. Author: Alternative Dispute Resolution for Financial Institutions, 1995, revised, 1996, 97, 98; bd. editors Yale Law Jour., 1974-75; editor Litigation, jour. ABA litigation sect., 1978-81; mem. editl. adv. bd. Bancroft-Whitney, 1991-94; contbr. articles to profl. jours. Bd. dirs. Neighborhood Legal Assistance Found., San Francisco, 1985-87, Nob Hill Assn., San Francisco, 1985-93; bd. dirs., fin. com. St. Francis Found., San Francisco, 1993-94. 1st lt. inf., USAR, 1965-71. Recipient UPI Award for Newswriting, 1958; Harvard Coll. scholar, 1958-62, Fulbright scholar, 1962-63; Columbia U. Internat. fellow, 1964-65. Fellow Internat. Acad. Mediators, Am. Coll. Civil Trial Mediators, Hong Kong Inst. Arbitrators, Chartered Inst. Arbitrators (London); mem. ABA (corp. counsel com. 1986-96, alternative dispute resolution sect. 1994-98), Assn. Atty. Mediators (v.p. No. Calif. chpt. 1995), State Bar of Calif. (pub. affairs com. 1982-85, litigation sect. 1990-96), Bar Assn. of San Francisco (bench-bar media com. 1985-96, alternative dispute resolution com. 1994-98), Assn. Bus. Trial Lawyers No. Calif., Assn. of Former U.S. Attys. No. Dist. Calif., Am. Arbitration Assn. (mem. comml. arbitration panel, No. Calif. adv. coun., mediator Am. Arbitration Ctr. for Mediation), Nat. Assn. Dispute Resolution, The Mediation Soc. (chmn. bd., pres.), Profl. Atty. Mediators, Cmty. Bds. of San Francisco (conciliator), French-Am. C. of C., German-Am. C. of C. West U.S., Harvard Club of San Francisco (bd. dirs. 1986-94, pres. 1992-94), Yale Club of San Francisco (bd. dirs. 1989-94), Soc. Profls. in Dispute Resolution, Columbia U. Alumni Club of No. Calif. (exec. com. 1978-92). Office: 127 Lawton St San Francisco CA 94122-3719 E-mail: rms@robertmsmith.com.

SMITH, ROBERT MYRON, investment company executive; b. Hartford, Conn., Jan. 10, 1930; s. Sterling Bishop and Harriet (Chamberlain) S.; m. Ellen Prouty, March 31, 1956 (div. 1982); m. Mary Peterson, Dec. 26, 1982; children: Catherine, Allison, Deborah, Elizabeth, Melissa. BA, Wesleyan U., Middletown, Conn., 1951; MBA, U. Pa., 1957. Underwriter Travelers Ins. Co., Hartford, 1951-56; asst. sec. Investors Mgmt. Co., Elizabeth, N.J., 1957-62; asst. v.p. Security Trust Co., Rochester, N.Y., 1962-64; exec. v.p. Keystone Custodian Funds, Inc., Boston, 1964-74; sr. v.p. Reliance Ins. Co., Phila., 1974-80; pres. Intervest Capital Mgmt., N.Y.C., 1980-81, J. Rothschild Capital Mgmt. Corp., N.Y.C., 1981-83, Ansbacher (Dublin) Asset Mgmt. Ltd., N.Y.C., 1983-95, Smith Adv. Ltd., Annapolis, MD, 1995—, also bd. dirs. Bd. dirs. Gabelli Comstock Strategy Fund, Gabelli Comstock Capital Value Fund, Rye., N.Y. Mem. fin. com. Town of Cohasset, Mass., 1973-74; treas. First Parish in Cohasset, 1969-73, trustee, Severn Sch., Severna Park, MD. Served to 1st lt. USAF, 1951-53. Mem. Inst. CFA's, Balt. Security Analysts Soc., Assn. for Investment Mgmt. and Rsch. Avocations: sailing, gardening, bridge. Home: 812 Coach Way Annapolis MD 21401-6417 E-mail: smithadvisors@compuserve.com.

SMITH, ROBERT NELSON, former government official, anesthesiologist; b. Toledo, Apr. 2, 1920; s. Robert Frederick and Amy Laura (Nelson) S.; children: Sandralyn, Sharon, Robert Nelson, Marilyn Anne, Marcia, Elizabeth. Student, U. Mich., 1938-39; BS, U.S. Mil. Acad., 1943; MS, MIT, 1945; MD, U. Nebr., 1952. Diplomate Am. Bd. Anesthesiologists. Commd. capt. USAAF, 1943, resigned, 1948; intern Toledo Hosp., Ohio, 1952-53, resident, 1954-57; anesthesiologist KFC Med. Corp., Toledo, 1954-76; asst. sec. def. for health affairs Washington, 1976-78; bd. dirs. Ohio Med. Indemnity Corp., Columbus, 1968-78. Mem. anesthetic and life support drugs adv. com. FDA, Dept. HHS, 1986-90; mem. disability adv. coun. SSA, Dept. HHS, 1986-89; mem. Ohio Pub. Health Coun., 1976—. Chmn. State Health Planning Council, 1974-76; mem. Statewide Health Coordinating Council, until 1976; gov. apptd. mem. Ohio Pub. Health Council, 1997-2002. Recipient Sec. Def. medal for outstanding pub. service, 1977 Mem. AMA (Ho. of Dels. Resolution of Commendation), Ohio Med. Assn. (pres. 1970, commendation 1977), Am. Soc. Anesthesiology, Inverness Club, Rotary, The Toledo Club. Clubs: Inverness (Toledo). Home: 3424 Gallatin Rd Toledo OH 43606-2442

SMITH, ROBERT POWELL, former ambassador, former foundation executive; b. Joplin, Mo., Mar. 5, 1929; s. Powell Augusta and Estella (Farris) S.; m. Alice Irene Rountree, Aug. 22, 1953; children: Michael Bryan, Steven Powell, Karen Louise, David Robert. BA, Tex. Christian U., 1954, MA, 1955. Fgn. svc. officer Dept. State, 1955-81; press officer Washington, 1955; vice-consul Lahore, Pakistan, 1956—58; 2d sec. Beirut, 1959-61; consul and prin. officer Enugu, Nigeria, 1962-65; officer-in-charge Ghanaian Affairs, 1966; officer-in-charge Nigerian Affairs, dep. dir. Office West African Affairs, 1967-69; dep. chief of mission, counselor of embassy Pretoria, South Africa, 1970-74; amb. to Malta, 1974-76; amb. to Ghana, 1976-79; amb. to Liberia, 1979-81. Pres. Africa Wildlife Leadership Found., 1981-85. Served with USMCR, 1946-49, 50-52. Decorated Air medal.; recipient Meritorious Honor award State Dept., 1967 Mem. Am. Fgn. Service Assn. Baptist.

SMITH, ROBERT RUTHERFORD, university dean, communication educator; b. Buffalo, Nov. 18, 1933; s. Thomas Newlands and Mary Jane (Rutherford) S.; m. Suzanne Louise Stines, June 7, 1958; children: Eric Anthony, Gwendolyn Anne. BA cum laude, U. Buffalo, 1955; MA, Ohio State U., 1956, PhD, 1963. Prof. communication, chmn. divsn. broadcasting and film Sch. Pub. Communication, Boston U., 1961-78; prof., dean. Sch. Communication and Theater Temple U., Phila., 1978-95. Author: poems Participations, 1972; criticism Beyond the Wasteland, 1980, (with G. Ingram and R. Marler) Fishing the Delaware Valley, 1997; editor TV Quar., 1971, Feedback, 1973-76; contbr. articles to profl. jours. Mem. communication com. Mass. Coun. Chs., 1971-76. Served with USAR, 1959-64. Mem. Broadcast Edn. Assn. (pres. 1984-85), Broadcast Pioneers (pres. Phila. 1985-86), Soc. Profl. Journalists (pres. 1983-85), Appalachian Mountain Club (Boston), Delmont Club (pres. 1992-94), Genesis Club, Choral Art Soc. (chmn. 1997). Home: 6 Trout Farm Ln Plympton MA 02367-1617 E-mail: suzrobs@cs.com.

SMITH, ROBERT SAMUEL, banker, former agricultural finance educator; b. Laconia, NH, June 16, 1920; s. Samuel W. and Winnifred (Page) S.; m. Mary Morgan, June 20, 1942; children: Patricia, Peggy, Morgan Scott, Sharon, Starlee. BS, Cornell U., 1942, MS, 1950, PhD, 1952. County agrl. agt. Livingston County, Mt. Morris, NY, 1942-44, Lewis County, Lowville, NY, 1944, Belknap County, Laconia, 1947-49; assoc. prof. edn. Cornell U., Ithaca, NY, 1952-54, assoc. prof. farm mgmt., 1954-58, prof. agrl. fin., 1958-77, W.T. Myers prof. agrl. fin., 1977-81; chmn. Tompkins County Trust Co., Ithaca, NY, 1978-92, chmn. emeritus, 1992—. Trustee Mut. of NY/MONY Fin. Svc., NYC, 1981—93, emeritus, 1993—99; bd. dir. Challenge Industries, Ithaca, NY; advisor Ministry of Agr., Israel, 1960—61, Agrl. Devel. Bank of Iran, Iran, 1968. Contbr. numerous articles to profl. jour. Elder First Presbyn. Ch., Ithaca, NY, 1970; bd. dir. Am. Agriculturist Found., Ithaca, 1980, East Lawn Cemetery Assn., Ithaca, 1987; bd. dir. emeritus Hospicare Found., Ithaca. 1st lt. U.S. Army, 1944—47, ETO. Recipient Tax Edn. award IRS, Buffalo, 1973, Disting. Svc. citation NY State Agrl. Soc., 1982. Mem. Country Club of Ithaca, City Club Ithaca, Phi Kappa Phi, Epsilon Sigma Phi. Republican. Avocations: golf, bridge. Home: 60 Wedgewood Dr Ithaca NY 14850-1063 Office: Tompkins County Trust Co The Commons Ithaca NY 14850

SMITH, ROBERT SHERLOCK, judge; b. N.Y.C., Aug. 31, 1944; s. Robert and Janet W. (Welt) S.; m. Dian Goldston Smith, Aug. 31, 1969; children: Benjamin Eli, Emlen Matthew, Rosemary Friedman. BA, Stanford U., 1965; LLB, Columbia U., 1968. Bar: N.Y. 1968, U.S. Dist. Ct. (so. dist.) N.Y. 1969, U.S. Dist. Ct. (ea. dist.) N.Y. 1977, U.S. Ct. Appeals (2d cir.) 1970, U.S. Ct. Appeals (4th cir.) 1986, U.S. Ct. Appeals (1st cir.) 1988, U.S. Ct. Appeals (7th cir.) 1989, U.S. Ct. Appeals (6th cir.) 1995, U.S. Ct. Appeals (D.C. and 8th cirs.) 1997, U.S. Ct. Appeals (5th cir.) 1999, U.S. Tax Ct. 1974, U.S. Supreme Ct. 1979. Assoc. Paul, Weiss, Rifkind, Wharton & Garrison, N.Y.C., 1968-76, ptnr., 1976—2003; spl. counsel Kornstein, Veisz, Wexler & Pollard, 2003—04; assoc. judge N.Y. Ct. Appeals, N.Y.C., 2004—. Vis. prof. Columbia Law Sch., N.Y.C., 1980-81, lectr. law, 1981-90. Mem. ABA, N.Y. State Bar Assn. (vice chair com. on jud. adminstrn. 2001-), Assn. Bar City N.Y. (com. fed. legis. 1981-84, com. on judiciary 1984-87, com. on bicentennial of U.S. Constitution 1988-91), Federalist Soc. N.Y. (pres. lawyers chpt. 1994-2003). Republican. Mem. Reformed Ch. Office: 71 Thomas St New York NY 10013 Office Phone: 212-815-0884. Business E-Mail: rssmith@courts.state.ny.us.

SMITH, ROBERT VICTOR, university administrator; b. Glendale, N.Y., Feb. 16, 1942; s. Robert Arthur and Marie Marlene (Florence) S. BS in Pharm. Sci., St. John's U., Jamaica, N.Y., 1963; MS in Pharm. Chemistry, U. Mich., 1964, PhD in Pharm. Chemistry, 1968. Asst. prof., then assoc. prof. U. Iowa, Iowa City, 1968-74; assoc. prof., asst. dir. U. Tex., Austin, 1974-77, area coordinator basic pharmaceutics, 1975-76, assoc. dir. Drug Dynamics Inst., 1977-78, dir. Drug Dynamics Inst., Coll. Pharmacy, 1979-85, James E. Bauerle Centennial prof. Coll. Pharmacy, 1983-85; prof., dean Coll. Pharmacy, Wash. State U., Pullman, 1985-86, vice provost for rsch., dean Grad. Sch., 1987-97; vice provost for rsch. and grad. edn., dean Grad. Sch., U. Conn., Storrs, 1997-2000; provost, vice chancellor acad. affairs U. Ark., Fayetteville, 2000—. Cons. E.R. Squibb, New Brunswick, N.J., 1979-82, Upjohn Co.,

Kalamazoo, 1982-85; external examiner U. Malaysia, Penang, 1981-82; mem. sci. adv. bd. Biodecision Labs., Pitts., 1985-86; Wash. Exposition Sci. Tech. Found., 1989-90; mem. noms. com. Coun. Grad. Schs., Washington, 1990-91, 96-97; accreditation evaluator Northwest Assn. Schs. and Colls., Seattle, 1991-97; mem. exec. com. grad. deans African-Am. Inst., N.Y., 1992-2000; bd. dirs. Coun. Grad. Schs., 1998, Grad. Record Exam, 1999-2003; exec. sec. U. Ark. 2010 Commn., 2000—; chair Southeastern Conf. Provosts Group, 2003-04. Author: Textbook of Biopharmaceutic Analysis, 1981, Graduate Research: A Guide for Students in the Sciences, 1998, Development and Management of University Research Groups, 1986, The Elements of Great Speechmaking: Adding Drama and Intrigue, 2004. Bd. dirs. Wash. Tech. Ctr., 1990-92; exec. sec. 2010 Commn. Grantee NIH, 1974-83; fellow Acad. Pharm. Scis., 1981, Am. Assn. Pharm. Scientists, 1987; recipient Disting. Alumnus award Coll. Pharmacy U. Mich., 1990, Outstanding Svc. award Wash. State U., Grad. and Profl. Student Assn., 1993, 95. Mem. Am. Assn. Colls. Pharmacy (chmn. research and grad. affairs com. 1983-84), U.S. Pharmacopeia (revision com. 1985-90), Acad. Pharm. Scis. (chmn., vice chmn. 1983-85, 90, Presdl. citation 1985), Wash. Rsch. Found. (bd. dirs. 1989-97). Unitarian Universalist. Home: 665 Samara Cir Fayetteville AR 72701-3035 Office: U Ark Adminstrn Bldg Fayetteville AR 72701 Office Phone: 479-575-5459.

SMITH, ROD, professional football player; b. May 15, 1970; postgrad in econ. & fin., postgrad in gen. bus., postgrad in mktg. & mgmt., Mo. So. State Coll. Wide receiver Denver Broncos, 1994—. Office: Denver Broncos Football Club 13655 Broncos Pky Englewood CO 80112

SMITH, RODERICK JOEL, behavioral consultant, researcher, educator; b. Ft. Worth, Nov. 15, 1946; s. Bill Joel and Vicky Marrarow Smith; m. Patricia Lee Payne, Sept. 30, 1978; children: Rachael Jena, Adam Joel. BA in Anthropology, San Francisco State U., 1972, MA in Spl. Edn., 1973. Tchr. John Swett Sch. Dist., Selby, Calif.; v.p., dir. Vallejo (Calif.)-Benicia Assn.; resource specialist, coord. spl. edn. Alpine (Calif.) Unified Sch. Dist.; behavior cons. Washoe County Schs., Reno, Smith/Peltier & Assocs., Reno. Adj. prof. Sierra Nevada Coll., Incline, Nev. Mem. Nev. State Bully Free Task Force, Carson City, 2000—; appointed Calif. Devel. Disabilities Bd. Area III, Sacramento, 1982—86. Mem.: NEA, Am. Coun. on Rural Spl. Edn., Phi Delta Kappa. Avocations: teaching, learning, improving the lives of children. Home and Office: Smith/Peltier & Assocs 861 Barber Way Gardnerville NV 89460

SMITH, RODGER FIELD, financial executive; b. Milw., Jan. 23, 1941; s. Millard Beale and Alice Catherine (Field) S.; m. Sarah Godfrey, June 19, 1964 (dec. Dec. 1999); children: Rodger F. Jr., Scott G., Reid W. BSChemE, U. Wis., 1964, MBA in Fin. with distinction, 1965. V.p. Allis Chalmers, Milw., 1966-76; mng. dir. Greenwich (Conn.) Assocs., 1976—. Trustee Harbor Funds, Toledo, 1987—; bd. dirs. Arlington Capital, London, 1992—; dean's adv. bd. U. Wis. Bus. Sch. Author articles and spkr. on investing pension funds. Fund raiser United Way, Milw., 1966-76. Mem.: Bascom Hill Soc., U. Wis. Alumni Assn. (nat. bd. dirs. 1994—2000), Wee Burn Country Club (fin. com.), Beta Gamma Sigma, Tau Beta Pi (chmn. trust adv. com. 1986—). Avocations: travel, golf, tennis, coin collecting/numismatics. Office: Greenwich Assocs Office Park Eight Greenwich CT 06831-5195 Office Phone: 203-629-1200. E-mail: rodger@greenwich.com.

SMITH, RODNEY, retired electronics executive; b. 1941; BSEE, Southampton Coll. Advanced Tech., Eng. Various positions to v.p., gen. mgr. Fairchild Semiconductor Corp., Mountain View, Calif., 1969-83; pres., CEO Altera Corp., San Jose, Calif., 1983—2000, chmn., 1983—, ret., 2003—.

SMITH, RODNEY WIKE, engineering executive; b. Havre de Grace, Md., July 29, 1944; s. Marshall Thomas and Ellen Nora (Wike) S.; m. Mary Katherine Trent, Dec. 20, 1967; children: Scott Walker, Craig Duncan. BS, Va. Poly. Inst. and State U., 1972. Registered profl. engr., Va., N.C. Project engr. Hercules Inc., Radford, Va., 1967-72; planning engr. Va. state Water Control Bd., Richmond, 1972; project mgr. Cen. Shenandoah Planning Dist. Commn., Staunton, 1972-76; v.p., br. office mgr. Patton, Harris, Rust & Assocs., Bridgewater, Va., 1976-82, prin. in charge office Buchanan, W.Va., 1980-82; sr. v.p. Copper & Smith, PC, Harrisonburg, Va., 1982-88; pres. R.W. Smith & Assocs. PC, Verona, Va., 1988-95, Va. Sports Tech., Verona, Va., 1995—, Intellectual Properties Inc., Hampton, Va., 1996—; sr. project mgr. Olver, Inc., Blacksburg, Va., 1998—2003. Contbr. articles to profl. jours.; 4 patents in field. Apptd. to Va. Resources Authority Citizens Adv. Commn., 1987-91. Named Exec. of Yr. Profl. Secs. Internat.; Copper and Smith listed among fastest growing pvt. cos. by Inc. mag., 1987. Mem. Nat. Soc. Profl. Engrs., Water Polllution Control Fedn. Republican. Lutheran. Home: 227 Lebanon Church Rd Staunton VA 24401-6405

SMITH, ROGER WINSTON, political theorist, educator; b. Birmingham, Ala., July 9, 1936; s. Buford Houston and Sarah Louise (Trucks) S.; m. Martha Christin Daniels, Jan. 16, 1960; children— Louisa, David AB magna cum laude, Harvard U., 1958, postgrad. in law, 1958-59; MA in Polit. Sci., U. Calif.-Berkeley, 1963, PhD in Polit. Sci., 1971. Teaching assoc. U. Calif.-Berkeley, 1965-66; asst. prof. govt. Coll. William and Mary, Williamsburg, Va., 1967-72, assoc. prof., 1972-80, prof, 1980-2001, prof. emeritus, 2001—. Sr. lectr. politics Glasgow (Scotland) U., 1977-78; lectr. N.E.H., 1988; cons. Nelson-Hall Pubs., Chgo.; mem. coun. Inst. Internat. Conf. on the Holocaust and Genocide, Jerusalem; film cons. Armenian Heritage Project. Co-author, editor: Guilt: Man and Society, 1971; co-author: Genocide and the Modern Age, 1987, Genocide, vol. 2, 1991, Bearing Witness to the Holocaust, 1939-89, 1987, The Coming Age of Scarcity, 1998, Pioneers of Genocide Studies, 2002, When will Genocide Ever End?, 2002, On the Edge of Scarcity, 2002; editor: Genocide, 1999; contbg. editor Internet on the Holocaust and Genocide; contbr. articles to profl. jours. Served to 1st lt. U.S. Army, 1960-62, Japan Fellow NSF, 1966, College of William and Mary, 1977 Mem. Am. Polit. Sci. Assn., Internat. Assn. Genocide Scholars (co-founder, v.p., past pres.), Human Rights Watch. Democrat. Baptist. Avocations: gardening, walking, opera. Home: 102 Lake Dr Williamsburg VA 23185-3113 Office: Coll William and Mary Dept Govt Williamsburg VA 23187

SMITH, ROLAND BLAIR, JR., university administrator; b. Washington, Mar. 21, 1946; s. Roland Blair and Annie Louise S.; m. Valerie Peyton, June 16, 1969; children: Rovelle Louise, Roland Blair III. BA, Bowie State U., 1969; MPA, Ind. U., 1976; EdD, Harvard U., 1988. Dir. upward bound Notre Dame (Ind.) U., 1973-83, 86-88, dir. Ctr. for Edn. Opportunity, 1980-83, assoc. prof., 1991-96, dir. urban inst., 1992-96; assoc. provost Rice U., Houston, 1996—. Tchg. fellow and grad. asst. Harvard U., 1983-86; exec. asst. to pres. U. Notre Dame, Notre Dame, Ind., 1988-96; 1st v.p., treas. Pvt. Industry Coun., St. Joseph Coun., Ind., 1987-91; cons. Lilly Endowment, Indpls., 1990-91; outside reviewer Nat. Ctr. Ednl. Stats, Washington, 1991-92; chmn. bd. dirs. Nat. Assn. Presidential Assts. in Higher Edn., Washington, 1993-94. Contbg. author: (ency.) African- American Education, 1996. Commr. Martin Luther King Fed. Holiday Commn., Washington, 1993-94; trustee YMCA of Michiana, St. Joseph County, Ind.; bd. dirs. NRTS Corp., City of South Bend, Ind., 1993-96, Harvard Alumni Assn. Bd., Cambridge, Mass., 1995—, LifeGift Organ Donation Ctr., 2000—; bd. visitors Bowie State U., 1998—; mem. South Bend Elkhart camp United Negro Coll. Fund. Recipient Outstanding Achievement award Bowie (Md.) State U., 1985; Named Disting. Alumnus Ind. U., South Bend, Ind., 1983, Nat. Assn. for Equal Opportunity in Higher Edn. (Bowie State U.), 1998. Mem. Am. Assn. Higher Edn. (Black caucus vice chair 1995-97, chair 1997-99, Service award 1998), Phi Delta Kappa, Kappa Alpha Psi (Achievement award 1986). Democrat. Methodist. Office: Rice U PO Box 1892 - MS #3 Houston TX 77251-1892 E-mail: rbsmith@rice.edu.

SMITH, RONALD EDWARD, ophthalmologist; b. Walkersville, Md., Oct. 7, 1942; s. Harry Otto and Marjorie Lee Smith; m. Sara Gutelius Watt, Sept. 4, 1965 (div. Oct. 1977); children: Kelly, Matt; m. Suzette Edith Le Blanc, Sept. 6, 1980. BA, Johns Hopkins U., 1964, MD, 1967. Diplomate Am. Bd. Ophthalmology. Intern Johns Hopkins Hosp., Baltimore, Md., 1967—68; resident opthalmology Johns Hopkin's Hosp., Baltimore, Md., 1968—72; asst. prof. U. So. Calif., L.A., 1975—78, assoc. prof., 1978—81, prof., 1981—95, prof., chmn. dept. ophthalmology, 1995—. Co-author: Intraocular Inflammation, 1980, Vitrectomy Techniques, 1983, Uveitis: A Clinical Approach, 1986. Lt. comdr. USPHS, 1973—78. Recipient gold medal, Internat. Uveitis Study Group, 1998, Light award, Braille Inst., 1998. Mem.: Am. Acad. Ophthalmology (pres. 1994—95, 1998—, chmn. found. 1998—99). Avocations: golf, skiing, tennis. Office: USC Dept Ophthalmology 2617 E Chapman No 301 Orange CA 92829

SMITH, RONALD EHLBERT, lawyer, educator, pastor, public speaker, writer, motivator, real estate developer; b. Atlanta, Apr. 30, 1947; s. Frank Marion and Frances Jane (Canida) S.; m. Annemarie Krumholz, Dec. 26, 1969; children: Michele, Erika, Damian. BME, Stetson U., 1970; postgrad., Hochschule Fuer Musik, Frankfurt, Fed. Republic Germany, 1971-74; Masters in German Lit., Germany & Middlebury Coll., 1975; JD, Nova U., 1981; postgrad., Gammon Sem. Sch., 2000—. Bar: Fla. 1982, U.S. Dist. Ct. (mid. dist.) Fla. 1983, U.S. Ct. Appeals (11th cir.) 1990, Ga. 1994, U.S. Dist. Ct. (no. dist.) Ga. 1994; cert. ednl. leader, Ga. Asst. state atty. 10th Jud. Cir. Ct., Bartow, Fla., 1982-85; pvt. practice Lakeland, Fla., 1985-94, Atlanta, 1994—; of counsel Mark Boychuk & Assocs., 1998—. Asst. 10th Jud. Cir. Ct., Bartow, 1981-82; instr. Broward County C.C., Ft. Lauderdale, Fla., 1976-79, 91-94, pub. and pvt. schs., Broward County, Atlanta Schs., 1998-2002, Offenbach, Germany, 1971-78; instr. Polk C.C. and Police Acad., Winter Haven, Fla., 1981-94; adj. prof. English, Ga. State U., 1996—; adj. prof. law DeKalb Coll., 1997-2002; part-time police instr. Police Acad., Forsyth, Ga., 1996—; music instr. Atlanta Pub. Schs., 1999-2002. Tchr., drama dir. Disciples I and II, United Meth. Ch., Lakeland, 1980-94, Glenn Meml. United Meth. Ch., Atlanta, 1994—, cand. to ministry, 2000—; Billy Graham counseling supr., 1994—; promoter Promise Keepers, 1995—; spkr., promoter ProNet, 1996—; min. music Scott Blvd. Bapt. Ch., Decatur, Ga., 1998, Gideon Internat., 1999-2002; cert. candidate Ordained Ministry United Meth. Ch. Freedom Bridge fellow German Acad. Exch. Svc., Mainz, 1974-75. Mem. ABA, Christian Legal Soc., Lakeland Bar Assn., Am. Immigration Lawyers Assn., Phi Delta Kappa. E-mail: smith321@bellsouth.net.

SMITH, RONALD EMORY, financial executive; b. Shelburne, NS, Can., May 26, 1950; s. Edgar Earle and Ida Mae (Porter) S.; children: Stephen, Sarah, Susan. BBA, Acadia U., Wolfville, N.S., 1971. Chartered acct., N.S. Staff acct., mgr. Clarkson Gordon (now Ernst & Young), Halifax, 1971-78, Toronto, 1978-80; prin., ptnr. Woods Gordon (now Ernst & Young), Toronto, 1980-87; CFO Maritime Tel. & Tel., Halifax, 1987-99, Emera Inc., Halifax, 2000—. Bd. dirs. Bangor (Maine) Hydro-Electric Co., Can. Pension Plan Investment Bd. Gov. Can. Unity Coun., 1994—; bd. govs. Acadia U., 1994—; chmn. Atlantic Provinces Econ. Coun., Halifax, 1993-95, Roeher Inst., 1997-2000; pres. Can. Assn. for Cmty. Living, 1989-93, chmn. Min.'s Task Force on Physician Policy Devel., N.S., 1991-93; mem. coun. fin. execs. Conf. Bd. Mem. Fin. Execs. Inst., Can. Inst. Chartered Accts., Inst. Chartered Accts. N.S., Ashburn Golf Club. Roman Catholic. Avocations: golf, hiking, travel, genealogy. Office Phone: 902-428-6573. E-mail: ron.smith@ns.sympatico.ca.

SMITH, RONALD J. computer company executive; Bachelor's, Gettysburg Coll.; Master's in Physics, PhD in Physics, U. Minn. With Intel Corp., 1978—, mgr. Logic Tech. Devel. Group, gen. mgr. programmable logic device operation and gate array operation, mgr. day-to-day ops. PCI Components div., v.p. and gen. mgr. Computing Enhancement Group, v.p. Wireless Comm. and Computing Group, 1999—2001, sr. v.p. and gen. mgr. Wireless Comm. and Computing Group, 2001—. Spkr. in field. Contbr. articles to profl. jours. Recipient Disting. Alumni award, Gettysburg Coll., 1996. Mem.: IEEE, Am. Phys. Soc. Office: 2200 Mission College Blvd Santa Clara CA 95052

SMITH, RONALD LYNN, health system executive; b. Algona, Iowa, Sept. 22, 1940; s. Russell Malcom and Helen Lucille (Gridley) S.; m. Jacqueline Sue Yarger, Dec. 23, 1962 (div. Aug. 1981); children: Sheri Rene, Gregory Mark, Brenton Alan; m. Sylvia Jo Grotjan, Dec. 31, 1982; 1 child, Russell Lynn. BS, Iowa State U., 1962; postgrad., U. S.D., 1963; MA, U. Iowa, 1965. With Harris Hosp.-Methodist, Ft. Worth, 1967-82, assoc. exec. dir., 1974-76, exec. dir., 1977-82; pres., CEO Harris Meth. Health System, Ft. Worth, 1982—; sr. exec. v.p. Tex. Health Resources, 1997-98. Mem. Premier, Inc., Nat. Com. for Quality Health Care; mem. adv. coun. Hill-Rom Co., 1991; mem. healthcare exec. adv. coun. IBM, 1991; mem. bd. Tex. Commerce Bank. Trustee Tarrant County United Way, 1977-79, campaign chmn., 1992, chmn. bd. trustees 1993, chmn. bd. dirs., 1994, area-wide svcs. chair, 1988-91, self-sufficiency task force; bd. mem. Tex. Rsch. League, 1990-95, nat. bd. visitors Tex. Christian U., 1990—; bd. visitors Tex. Wesleyan U., 1995—. Fellow Am. Coll. Hosp. Execs.; mem. Tex. Hosp. Assn. (trustee 1983-87, chmn. 1986-87), Tex. Healthcare Coun., Healthcare Leadership Coun., Dallas-Ft. Worth Hosp. Coun. (pres. 1981), Ft. Worth C. of C. (bd. dirs. 1992), Rotary. Methodist.

SMITH, RONALD S. online retail executive; BS in Math and Physics, Dalhousie U.; B Mech. Engring., The Tech. U. Nova Scotia. Former pres. Merisel, N. Am. Distbn.; pres., CEO Beyond.Com. Corp, Santa Clara, Calif., 2000—. Office: Beyond Com Corp 3200 Patrick Henry Dr Santa Clara CA 95054-1816

SMITH, RONALD THOMAS, environmental scientist; b. Palmerton, Pa., Feb. 17, 1952; s. Albert Hubert and Jeanne Alice (Kemmerle) S.; m. Jeri Lee Hammond, June 21, 1997; children: Clara Lucy, Curran Troy. BA in English, U. Notre Dame, 1974; MS in Environ. Sci., Ind. U., 1983. Chemist City of Bloomington (Ind.), 1984-91; rsch. sci. Ind. Geol. Survey, Bloomington, 1994—. Sci. advisor and activist McRae & McRae Attys., Bloomington, 1987, People Against the Incinerator, 1988-92, Thousands of People, 1983-87. Author: The Blind Eagle Blues: Power and Poison in the Heartland, 2003. Environ. activist Citizens Clearinghouse on Hazardous Waste, Arlington, Va., 1987; founder Ind. Voters Party, 1991; pro se litigant Schalk & Smith vs. Lee Thomas, U.S. Ct. Appeals (7th cir.), 1990. Notre Dame scholar, 1970-74; recipient Giraffe Award for Pub. Svc., Giraffe Soc. Am., Everett, Wash., 1992. Mem.: Nat. Coalition Against Mass Burn Incineration, Pi Alpha Alpha. Avocations: writing, music, politics, outdoors activities. Office: Ind U Ind Geol Survey 611 N Walnut Grv # S427 Bloomington IN 47405-2208

SMITH, ROWLAND JAMES, educational administrator; b. Johannesburg, S. Africa, Aug. 19, 1938; s. John James and Gladys Spencer (Coldrey) S.; m. Catherine Anne Lane, Sept. 22, 1962; children: Russell Claude, Belinda Claire. BA, U. Natal, 1959, PhD, 1967; MA, Oxford U., Eng., 1967. Lectr. English U. Witwatersrand, Johannesburg, S. Africa, 1963-67; asst. prof. Dalhousie U., Halifax, N.S., Can., 1967-70, assoc. prof. English, 1970-77, prof., 1977-88, McCulloch prof., 1988-94, chmn. English dept., 1977-83, 85-86, dir. Centre for African Studies, 1976-77, asst. dean arts and scis., 1972-74, dean arts and social scis., 1988-93, provost Coll. Arts and Scis., 1988-89, 90-91, 92-93; vis. prof., rsch. assoc. Multidisciplinary Ctr. Can. Studies, U. Rouen, 1994; prof. Wilfrid Laurier U., Waterloo, 1994—2004, v.p. acad., 1994—2004; prof. English U. Calgary, 2004—, dean humanities, 2004—. Author: Lyric and Polemic: The Literary Personality of Roy Campbell, 1972; editor: Exile and Tradition: Studies in African and Caribbean Literature, 1976, Critical Essays on Nadine Gordimer, 1990, Postcolonizing the Commonwealth: Essays in Literature and Culture, 2000. Bd. govs. Halifax Grammar Sch., 1972-74, Neptune Theatre Found., 1977-78; selection com. IODE Meml. Scholarships for N.S., 1969-71, Rhodes Scholarships N.S., 1972-74; edn. com. Victoria Gen. Hosp., 1986-90; dir. publicity and promotion N.S. Rugby Football Union, 1987-89; chair liaison com. edn. dept. N.S. U., 1990-93; book prize jury Can. Fedn. for Humanities, 1990, regional judge (Can. and the Caribbean) Commonwealth Writers Prize, 1991; chair com. on employment and ednl. equity Coun. Ont. Univs., 1996-99, chair working group on post-diploma degrees, 1999-2001; bd. dirs. Opera Ontario, 2001-04; active Coll. Univ. Consortium Coun., 2000-02; chmn. Ontario Coun. Acad. V.P., 2002-04. Recipient Transvaal Rhodes scholar, 1960; vis. fellow Dalhousie U., 1965-66, vis. scholar Ctr. Canadian Studies U. Western Sydney, Macarthur, New South Wales, 1996; Can. Council leave fellow, 1974-75, research grantee, 1977; grantee Social Scis. and Humanities Research Council of Can., 1978, internat. grantee, 1985, grantee Cultural Personalities Exchange program Assn. Canadian Studies in Australia and New Zealand, 1996, grantee Cultural Personalities Exch. Program, Assn. in Can. Studies in German Speaking Countries, 1997. Mem. Assn. Can. Univ. Tchrs. English (sec.-treas. 1968-70, profl. concern com. 1979-81), Can. Assn. for Commonwealth Lit. and Lang. Studies (exec. mem. 1989-92, pres. 1995-99), Can. Assn. Chmn. English (v.p. 1981-82, pres. 1982-83, exec. mem.-at-large 1985-86), Can. Fedn. Humanities (aid to scholarly publs. com. 1979-85, bd. dirs. 1992-94), MLA (div. chmn. 1984, mem.), Social Scis. and Humanities Rsch. Coun., Can. (chair rsch. grants adjudication com. 1994-96), Can. Rsch. Chairs Program (Coll. Reviewers 2000—), Internat. Coun. for Can. Studies (Can. scholarship and fellowship selection com. 2003—), Can. Fedn. for the Humanities and Social Scis. (aid to scholarly publs. com. 2004—). Office: Office Dean Humanities Univ Calgary Calgary AB Canada T2N 1N4 E-mail: rowsmith@ucalgary.ca.

SMITH, ROY PHILIP, judge; b. L.I., NY, Dec. 29, 1933; s. Philip Aloysius and Virginia (Collins) S.; m. Elizabeth Helen Wink, Jan. 23, 1965; children: Matthew P., Jean E. BA, St. Joseph's Coll., Yonkers, N.Y., 1956; JD, Fordham U., 1965. Bar: N.Y. Asst. reg. counsel FAA, N.Y.C., 1966-79; adminstrv. law judge U.S. Dept. Labor, Washington, 1979-83; adminstrv. appeals judge Benefits Rev. Bd., Washington, 1983—, chmn., chief adminstrv. appeals judge, 1988-90. Adj. prof. aviation law Dowling Coll., Oakdale, N.Y., 1972-79; adj. prof. transp. law Adelphi U., Garden City, N.Y., 1975-79; vis. prof. Georgetown U. Law Sch., 1989—. With U.S. Army, 1957-59. Mem.: Fed. Adminstrv. Law Judges Conf. (treas. 1983—84, exec. com. 1982—83), Assn. Bar of City of N.Y. (sec.-treas. aeronautics com. 1978—79), Georgetown U. Libr. Assocs., Friendly Sons of St. Patrick, Edgemoor Club. Avocation: tennis. Home: 6700 Pawtucket Rd Bethesda MD 20817-4836 Office: Benefits Rev Bd 200 Constitution Ave NW Washington DC 20210-0001 Business E-Mail: smith-roy@dol.gov.

SMITH, RUBY LUCILLE, retired librarian; b. Nobob, Ky., Sept. 19, 1917; d. James Ira and Myrtie Olive (Crabtree) Jones; m. Kenneth Cornelius Smith, Dec. 25, 1946; children: Kenneth Cornelius, Corma Ann. AB, Western Ky. State Tchrs. Coll., 1943, MA, 1966. Tchr. rural schs., Barren County, Ky., 1941-42; tchr. secondary sch. English, libr. Temple Hill Consol. Sch., Glasgow, Ky., 1943-47, 49-51, 53-56, sch. libr., 1956-83. Sec. Barren County Cancer Soc., 1968—70, Barren County Fair Bd., 1969—70; leader 4-H Club, 1957—72; coord. tax-aide program AARP, 1985—88, dist. dir., 1988—2000, local chpt. v.p., 1996—98, pres., 1999—2000, instr. 55 Alive Mature Driving, 1993—; sec. Oak Grove Bapt. Ch., 1979—; coun. mem. Barren County; bd. dirs. Barren County Hist. Found., Inc., 1997—; trustee Mary Wood Weldon Meml. Libr., 1964—, Barren County Pub. Libr. Bd., 1969—2001; sec. Barren County Pub. Libr., 1969—2001; trustee Barren County Hist. Found., 1996—. Mem. NEA (life), Ky. Edn. Assn., Ky. Sch. Media Assn. (sec. 1970-71), 3d Dist. Libr. Assn. (pres. 1944, 66), Barren County Edn. Assn. (pres. 1960-62, treas. 1979-80), 3d Dist. Ret. Tchrs. Assn. (pres. 1991-92), Ky. Ret. Tchrs. Assn. (v.p. 1992-93, pres.-elect 1993-94, pres. 1994-95), Glasgow-Barren County Ret. Tchrs. Assn. (pres. 1984-86, 96-98, sec. 1989, treas. 1990), Ky. Libr. Trustee Assn. (bd. dirs. 1985-98, pres. 1986-88, 93-95, dir. Barren River region 1985-97), Barren County Rep. Women's Club, Monroe Assn. Woman's Missionary Union (dir. 1968-72, 79-83, sec. 1985-98), Monroe Assn. Bapts. (libr. dir. 1972-88), Ky. Libr. Assn., South Ctrl. Hist. Soc. (v.p. 1997-98, pres. 1998-2000), DAR (chaplain Edmund Rogers chpt. 1998—), Delta Kappa Gamma (pres. Delta chpt. 1996-98).

SMITH, RUSSELL BRYAN, lawyer; b. Ft. Worth, Nov. 1, 1936; s. Russell Bryan Sr. and Marie Antoinette (Hornick) S.; children: Robert B., Donna Sue. BBA, So. Meth. U., 1959, JD, 1962. Bar: Tex. 1962, U.S. Dist. Ct. (no., ea., we. and so. dists.) Tex., U.S. Ct. Appeals (5th cir.) 1962, U.S. Ct. Appeals (8th cir.) 1981, U.S. Ct. Appeals (11th cir.) 1982, U.S. Supreme Ct. 1967, U.S. Ct. Claims 1987, U.S. Ct. Appeals (fed. and D.C. cirs.). Assoc. Woodruff and Hill, Dallas, 1959-65; ptnr. Woodruff, Hill Kendall and Smith, Dallas, 1965-75; with Smith & Smith, L.L.P., Dallas, 1975—. Concession chmn. Byron Nelson Golf Classic, 1975-2001; mem. Dallas Assembly, 1973-87, Dallas Big Bros., 1967—; bd. trustees Dallas Hist. Soc., 1978-87, Dallas 40, 1967—; bd. dirs. Dallas Police Athletic Assn., 1979-86, Dallas Urban League, 1978-86, Dallas Zool. Soc., 1980—, Greater Dallas Planning Coun., 1978-92; bd. dirs., gen. counsel, vice chmn. bd. dirs. State Fair Tex., 1972—; adv. coun. St. Paul Hosp., 1974-88; mem. Dallas City Coun., 1971-75, dep. mayor pro tem, 1973-75; bd. dirs. Greater Dallas Sesquicentennial Commn., 1982-87. With USNR, 1955-62. Recipient Disting. Svc. award Dallas Jaycees, 1976, award Tex. Jaycees, 1972; named Outstanding Man in Dallas, 1975, Cy Johnston Spirit award, 1998; named Ky. col. Fellow Coll. State Bar (charter); mem. ABA, Tex. Bar Assn., Am. Bd. Trial Advs., Internat. Assn. Gaming Attys., Nat. Assn. Amusement Ride Safety Ofcls., Dallas Bar Assn., Dallas Estate Coun., Am. Judicature Soc., Dallas Bar Found., Bar Assn. Fifth Fed. Cir. (charter), U.S. Claims Ct. Bar Assn., Sports Lawyers Assn., Internat. Amusement and Leisure Def. Assn., Outdoor Amusement Bus. ASsn., Internat. Assn. Amusement Parks and Attractions, Internat. Assn. Fairs and Expns., Internat. Profl. Rodeo Assn., Salesmanship of Dallas Club (life), All Sports Assn. (pres. 1977), Dallas Athletic Club, Woodvale Fishing Club, Rock Creek Barbecue Club (life), Phi Alpha Delta. Methodist. Avocations: fishing, boating, travel, hunting. Office: Two Turtle Creek Village 3838Oak Lan Ave Ste 1222 Dallas TX 75219 E-mail: attorneys@smith-firm.com.

SMITH, RUSSELL FRANCIS, transportation executive; b. Washington, Mar. 26, 1944; s. Raymond Francis and Elma Gloria (Daugherty) S. Student East Carolina U., 1964, N.C. State U., 1964-65; BS with honors, U. Md.-Coll. Park, 1969, MBA, 1975. Exec. asst. mgr. Hotel Corp. Am. Internat. Inn and Mayflower Hotel, Washington, 1966-68; sr. venture capital cons. Initiative Investing Corp., Washington, 1968-69; pres., gen. mgr. Associated Trades Corp., Washington, 1970-74; cons. in fin., Greenbelt, Md., 1974-76; mng. cons. Bradford Nat. Corp., Washington, 1976-79; v.p. OAO Corp., Washington, 1979-81; ptnr. for fin. evaluation and ops. analysis Blake, Brunell, Lehmann & Co., Washington, 1981-86; v.p. mgmt. services adminstrn. United Airlines Svcs. Corp., Lakewood, Colo., 1986-91, cons. Venture Fund of Washington, 1991—. Chmn. com. on wildlife Prince George Humane Soc., Hyattsville, Md., 1968-71, Soc. for Prevention Cruelty to Animals, Hyattsville. 1971-75. Served with U.S. Army, 1963-66. Decorated Silver Star medal, Bronze Star medal with V device, Purple Heart. Mem. Am. Fin. Assn., Ops. Research Soc. Am., Am. Acctg. Assn., N.Am. Soc. Corp. Planners, Internat. Assn. Math. Modeling, Assn. MBA Execs. (registered investment advisor), Beta Gamma Sigma, Beta Alpha Psi. Libertarian.

SMITH, RUSSELL JACK, former intelligence official; b. Jackson, Mich., July 4, 1913; s. Lee C. and Georgia L. (Weed) S.; m. Rosemary Thomson, Sept. 5, 1938; children: Stephen M., Scott T., Christopher G. AB, Miami U., Oxford, Ohio, 1937; PhD, Cornell U., 1941. Asst. instr. English Cornell U., 1937-41; instr. English Williams Coll., 1941-45; with OSS, 1945; asst. prof. English Wells Coll., 1946-47; with CIA, 1947-74, mem. bd. nat. estimates, 1957-62, dir. current intelligence, 1962-66, dep. dir. for intelligence, 1966-71; spl. asst. U.S. Embassy, New Delhi, 1971-74; rsch. cons., 1975—. Assigned Nat. War Coll., 1951-52, U.S. rep. Brit. Joint Intelligence Com., Far East, Singapore, 1954-56. Author: John Dryden, A Study in Controversy, 1941, The Unknown CIA: My Three Decades with the Agency, 1989, The Little Red House that Jack Built, 2002, (novels) The Secret War, 1986, The Singapore Chance, 1991, Lodestone, 1993, Whirligig, 1994, Always Afternoon, 1997, Time's Prism, 2000, Downriver, 2001, The Listener, 2002. Recipient Nat. Civil Svc. League award, 1971, Disting. Intelligence medal CIA, 1974. Mem. Phi Beta Kappa, Phi Delta Theta, Omicron Delta Kappa. Home: 1138 Bellview Rd Mc Lean VA 22102-1104

SMITH, RUSSELL WESLEY, management and computer applications consultant, organizational development trainer; b. Penn Yan, N.Y., Jan. 23, 1947; s. Wesley Sanford and Gladys Klothe Smith; m. Janice Larzelere, June 16, 1984; stepchildren: Gerald Allen, Christopher Michael. AAS, SUNY, 1973; BS cum laude, N.H. Coll., 1976; BS in Computer Sci., SUNY, Rochester, 1993. Cert. prodn. and inventory control mgr., cert. Novell adminstr. Evaluator SUNY Empire State Coll., Rochester, 1992-94; cons. Naus & Newlyn, Inc., Paoli, Pa., 1977-78, C. Todd, Inc., Haddonfield, N.J., 1978-79; assoc. Resource Assocs., Inc., Newmarket, N.H., 1979-84; pres.

Smith Klothe Assocs., Warsaw, N.Y., 1983-95; processing supt. Champion Products, Inc., Perry, N.Y., 1988-91; prin. Watkins Concepts Co., Lusby, Md., 1991-95; mgr. functional tech. Oracle Corp., Redwood City, Calif., 1995—. Cons. Resource Mgmt. Group, Boston, 1984-85, Bus. Planning Group, Westport, Conn., 1985-88, project mgr. Robert Bell & Co., Balt., 1976-77. With Signal Corps, U.S. Army, 1966-68. Home: 3308 Forest Gale Dr Forest Grove OR 97116-1074 Office: 1000 SW Broadway Ste 1200 Portland OR 97205-3064

SMITH, RUTH HODGES, city clerk; b. Roanoke, Va., Jan. 15, 1931; d. James Elpherson and Ruth Elizabeth (Morgan) Hodges; m. Leon Menaclus Smith, June 18, 1978 (dec.); children: Dorothy Ruth Smith Swift, Marvis Frances Smith Mills. Student, Potomac State Coll., 1949-51. Cert. mcpl. clk. Va. Legal sec. Commonwealth Atty., Woodstock, Va., 1952-54; adminstrv. asst. Nelson Oil Corp., Mt. Jackson, Va., 1954-56; exec. sec., office mgr. Tidewater Va. Devel. Co., Norfolk, Va., 1956-72; from corp. sec. to purchasing agt. Nepratex Industries, Virginia Beach, Va., 1972-77; realtor, life agt. Real Estate/Ins., 1977—; city clk. City of Virginia Beach, 1978—. Sec.-treas. Hospice Virginia Beach, 1981-86; liaison, coord. Mayor's Sister City Commn., 1993—; mem. IIMC Acad. Advanced Edn., 1984-87, 87— (Quill award 1991); founder Z House shelter for battered spouses. Mem. Internat. Mcpl. Clks. (bd. dirs. 1986-89, chair internat. com. 1989-91, chair year 2000 planning com. 1998—), Va. Mcpl. Clks. Assn. (pres. 1982-84, master mcpl. clk. 2000—, treas. 2002), Lifelong Acad. Advanced Edn., 1996—. Club: Pilot (officer 1960-72). Lodges: Zonta Internat. (dir. 1983-90), Order Eastern Star (worthy grand matron grand chpt. Va. 1993-94, worthy matron Westminster chpt. #99 2000), Daus. of Nile, Shriners. Avocations: crafts, bicycling, skating, travel. Home: 1153 Belvoir Ln Virginia Beach VA 23464-6766 Office: City of Virginia Beach Room 281 City Hall Virginia Beach VA 23456

SMITH, RYAN ARTHUR HAROLD, mental health services professional, writer; b. Port Jervis, N.Y., Aug. 27, 1977; s. Craig Steven and Isabel Hodges Smith; m. Michelle Leigh Boff, Dec. 21, 2002; 1 stepchild, Darby Autumn Shae McCaslin 1 child, Connor Riley. BA in Psychology, Pa. State U., 2001; MA in Psychology, Suffield U., 2003. Processing and cognitive enhancement tng., cert. applied behavioral analysis (level 3), discrete trial instrn. (level 3); protective immobilization/passive restraint. Data analyst Ctr. Applied Behavioral Scis. Pa. State U., University Park, 2000; processing and cognitive enhancement trainer/counselor Harmonic Progressions, State College, Pa., 2001; therapeutic support staff New Hope of Pa., Inc., Wyoming, 2002, adminstrv. case mgr., 2002—03; intensive case mgr. Allegheny Children's Initiative, Pitts., 2003—04; family-based mental health sr. clinician, 2004—. Therapeutic support staff Western Psychiat. Inst. and Clinic, Pitts., 2003—; cons. in field. Petition co-organizer Allegheny County Green Party, Pitts., 2003—; mem. Soka Gakkai Internat., Pa., 2002—03. Mem.: APA (assoc.), Psi Chi (life; philanthropy com. 2000—01). Buddhist. Avocations: neurotheology, evolutionary psychology, religious study, writing/poetry, yoga/meditation. Office: Allegheny Children's Initiative 2304 Jane St Pittsburgh PA 15203 Office Phone: 412-390-3825. Personal E-mail: ras229@adelphia.net. E-mail: rsmith@citizencare.org.

SMITH, SALLYE WRYE, librarian; b. Birmingham, Ala., Nov. 11, 1923; d. William Florin and Margaret (Howard) Wrye; m. Stuart Werner Smith, Sept. 20, 1947 (dec. June 1981); children: Carol Ann, Susan Patricia, Michael Christopher, Julie Lynn, Lori Kathleen. BA, U. Ala., 1945; MA, U. Denver, 1969. Psychometrician U.S. Army, Deshon Gen. Hosp., Butler, Pa., 1945-46, U.S. Vet. Adminstrn. Vocat. Guidance, U. Ala., Tuscaloosa, 1946; clin. psychologist U.S. Army, Walter Reed Gen. Hosp., Washington, 1946-47, U.S. Army, Fitzsimons Gen. Hosp., Denver, 1948, U.S. Vets. Adminstrn., Ft. Logan, Colo., 1948-50; head sci.-engring. libr. U. Denver, Colo., 1969-72; instr., reference libr. Penrose Libr., U. Denver, 1972-80, asst. prof., reference libr., 1980-90, interim dir., 1990-92, asst. prof. emerita, 1992—. Vis. prof. U. Denver Grad. Sch. Libr. Info. Mgmt., 1975-77, 83; info. broker Colo. Rschrs., Denver, 1979—; cons., presenter The Indsl. Info. Workshop Inst. de Investigaciones Tecnologicas, Bogota, Colombia, 1979, LIPI-DRI-PDIN workshop on R&D mgmt., Jakarta, Indonesia, 1982; mem. BRS User Adv. Bd., Latham, N.Y., 1983-86. Indexer: Statistical Abstract of Colorado 1976-77, 1977. Recipient Cert. of Recognition, Sigma Xi, U. Denver chpt., 1983. Mem. ALA, Am. Soc. Indexers, Spl. Libr. Assn., Colo. Assn. Librs., Phi Beta Kappa, Beta Phi Mu. Office: Colo Researchers PO Box 22779 Denver CO 80222-0779

SMITH, SAM, columnist, author; b. Bklyn., Jan. 24, 1948; s. Leon and Betty (Pritzker) S.; m. Kathleen Ellen Rood, Jan. 24, 1976; children: Connor, Hannah-Li. BBA in Acctg., Pace U., N.Y.C., 1970; MA in Journalism, Ball State U., Muncie, Ind., 1974. Acct. Arthur Young & Co., N.Y.C., 1970-72; reporter Ft. Wayne (Ind.) News Sentinal, Ft. Wayne, 1973-76, States News Svc., Washington, 1976-79; press sec. U.S. Senator Lowell Weicker Jr., 1979; writer/reporter Chgo. Tribune, 1979-90, columnist, 1991—. Commentator ESPN Radio. Author: The Jordan Rules, 1991, Second Coming, 1995; contbg. writer (magazine) ESPN Mag.; contbr. articles ESPN Mag., ESPN Radio. With USAR, 1970-76. Named Ball State U. Journalism Alumnus of Yr.; named to Ball State U. Journalism Hall of Fame, 2002; recipient Journalism awards, AP, UPI, Sigma Delta Chi, Sports Local Emmy award, WGN-TV. Mem.: Basketball Writers Assn. (pres. 1998—). Office: Chicago Tribune 435 N Michigan Ave Chicago IL 60611-4066

SMITH, SAM CORRY, retired foundation executive, consultant; b. Enid, Okla., July 3, 1922; s. Chester Hubbert and Nelle Kate (Corry) S.; m. Dorothy Jean Bank, Sept. 21, 1945; children: Linda Jean, Nancy Kay, Susan Diane. Student, Phillips U., 1940-43; BS in Chemistry, U. Okla., 1947, MS in Chemistry, 1948; PhD in Biochemistry, U. Wis., 1951. Asst. and assoc. prof. Med. Sch. U. Okla. Med. Sch., Oklahoma City, 1951-55; assoc. dir. grants Research Corp., N.Y.C., 1957-65, dir., 1965-68, v.p. grants, 1968-75; exec. dir. M.J. Murdock Charitable Trust, Vancouver, Wash., 1975-88. Foundation cons., 1988—; pres. Pacific Northwest Grantmakers Forum, 1983-84. Contbr. sci. articles to profl. jours. Trustee Nutrition Found., Washington, 1976-84, Internat. Life Scis. Inst., Washington, 1984-86; bd. councilors U. So. Calif. Med. Sch., L.A., 1977-82; mem. adv. com. Coll. Natural Scis. Colo. State U., 1977-80; pres. Cardiopulmonary Rehab. Programs Oreg., 1990-91; bd. dirs. Clark Coll. Found., 1992-98. Named Boss of Yr., Am. Bus. Women's Assn., 1982, Bus. Assoc. of Yr., 1983. Fellow AAAS; mem. Am. Chem. Soc. Avocations: tennis, photography, gardening. Home: 5204 Dubois Dr Vancouver WA 98661-6617 *Personal philosophy: "There is no limit to what a man can do or where he can go if he doesn't mind who gets the credit." Author unknown.*

SMITH, SAMUEL HOWARD, academic administrator, plant pathologist; b. Salinas, Calif., Feb. 4, 1940; s. Adrian Reed and Elsa (Jacop) Smith; m. Patricia Ann Walter, July 8, 1960; children: Samuel, Linda Kjelgaard. BS in Plant Pathology, U. Calif., Berkeley, 1961, PhD in Plant Pathology, 1964; D (hon.), Nihon U., Tokyo, 1989, Far Eastern State U., Vladivostok, Russia, 1997. NATO fellow Glasshouse Crops Research Inst., Sussex, England, 1964-65; asst. prof. plant pathology U. Calif., Berkeley, 1965-69; assoc. prof. Pa. State U., University Park, 1969—74, prof., 1974—85, head dept. plant pathology, 1976—81, dean Coll. Agr., dir. Pa. Agrl. Expt. Sta. and Coop. Extension Service, 1981—85; pres. Wash. State U., Pullman, 1985—2000, pres. emeritus, 2000—. Bd. dirs. Blethen Corp., 1994—, Met. Mortgage & Securities, 2000—, Nat. Assn. State Univs. & Land-Grant Colls., 1994—, chair, bd. dirs., 1999—2000, exec. dir., W.K. Kellogg Found., Food & Soc. Project, 2000—, mem. Audit & Fin. Com., 1999—2000, chair, Coun. Pres.', 1998—99, exec. dir., Com. Food & Soc., 2000—, mem. Ad-Hoc Com. Fed. Support Agrl. Sci., Ext., & Edn., 1998—2000, mem. Commn. Info. Tech., 1994—2000, chair, Commn. Info. Tech., 1994—96, mem. Pres.' Policy Bd. Info. Tech., 1997—2000, mem. Kellogg Commn. Twenty-First Century State & Land-Grant Univs., 1995—2000; chair, exec. com. NCAA, 1997—99, Div. I bd. dirs., 1997—99, mem. Pres.' Commn., 1994—97, chair, Pres.' Commn., 1996—97, div. I chair, Pres.' Commn., 1995; bd. dirs. The Tech. Alliance, 1996—2000, Assn. Western Univs., 1993—2000; mem. adv. com. Wash. Sch. Employees Credit Union, 1993—95, Battelle Pacific N.W. Lab., 1993—2000; mem. Wash. Coun. Internat. Trade; chair of pres.' and chancellors Pacific-10 Conf. CEOs, 1993—94; bd. dirs. Norman Borlaug U., 2000—02, Seattle Times, 1998—; pres., bd. dirs. Talaris Rsch. Inst., 2000—; bd. trustees Western Gov.'s U., 1997—, spl. adv. to pres., 2000—, chair, pres. adv. coun., 1996—, exec. com., 1997—, chair, acad. policy com., 1997—, mem., nominating com., 1997—. Bd. trustees Pilchuck Glass Sch., 2001—, Wash. State Hist. Soc., 2000—. Mem.: Am. Phytopath Soc., Pi Kappa Alpha (hon.).

SMITH, SARAH JANE (SALLY SMITH), mayor; b. Pekin, Ill., Jan. 23, 1945; d. Claude P. and Jane (Prettyman) S.; B.S. in Music Edn., U. Ill.; postgrad. U. Alaska. Tchr. jr. high sch. Los Angels City Schs., 1968-69; adminstrv. asst. Office of Gov. of Alaska, 1971-74; project field rep Alaska Dept. Community and Regional Affairs, 1974-76; expeditor H.W. Blackstock, Inc., 1979-82; mem. Alaska Ho. of Reps. from 20th Dist., 1977-83, majority whip, 1977-79, mem. fin. com., 1979-81, chmn. rules chmn., 1981; exec. dir. Fairbanks Pvt. Industry Council, 1983-84; dir. div. pub. services Alaska Dept. Revenue, 1984—; mayor City and Borough of Juneau, 2000—. Dir. choir Juneau Meth. and Presbyn. chs., 1972-74, 86—, Fairbanks Presbyn. Ch., 1974-75; historian Fairbanks Drama Assn., 1974-76; adv. bd. Assn. Children with Learning Disabilities, 1978-80; commr. Fairbanks Historic Preservation Commn., 1982-84; bd. dirs. Friends of U. Alaska Mus., 1983-84. Named Outstanding Freshman Legislator, 1976. Mem. Fairbanks Assn. Arts. Democrat. Club: PEO.

SMITH, SCOTT CLYBOURN, media company executive; b. Evanston, Ill., Sept. 13, 1950; s. E. Sawyer and Jerolanne (Jones) S.; m. Martha Reilly, June 22, 1974; children: Carolyn Baldwin, Thomas Clybourn. BA, Yale U., 1973; M.Mgmt., Northwestern U., 1976. With Northern Trust Co., Chgo., 1973-77, Tribune Co., Chgo., 1977—93, sr. v.p., chief fin. officer, 1989 91, sr. v.p. for devel., 1991-93; pres., CEO, pub. Sun Sentinel Co., Ft. Lauderdale, Fla., 1993-97; pres., pub., CEO Chgo. Tribune Co., 1997—. Episcopalian. Office: Chgo Tribune Co 435 N Michigan Ave Chicago IL 60611-4066

SMITH, SELMA MOIDEL, lawyer, composer; b. Warren, Ohio, Apr. 3, 1919; d. Louis and Mary (Oyer) Moidel; 1 child, Mark Lee. Student, UCLA, 1936-39, U. So. Calif. Law School, 1939-41; JD, Pacific Coast U., 1942. Bar: Calif. 1943, U.S. Dist. Ct. 1943, U.S. Supreme Ct. 1958. Gen. practice law; mem. firm Moidel, Moidel, Moidel & Smith, 1943—. Field dir. civilian adv. com. WAC, 1943—45; charter mem. nat. bd. Med. Coll. Pa. (formerly Woman's Med. Coll. Pa.), 1953—, mem. exec. bd., 1976—80, pres., 1980—82, chmn. past pres. com., 1990—92, spkr., honoree 50th anniversary gala, 2003. Author: A Century of Achievement: The National Association of Women Lawyers, 1998, The First Women Members of the ABA, 1999; composer: Espressivo-Four Piano Pieces (orchestral premiere, 1987, performance Nat. Mus. Women in the Arts, 1989), numerous works. Decorated La Orden del Merito Juan Pablo Duarte (Dominican Republic), 1956. Fellow: Am. Bar Found. (life); mem.: ASCAP, ABA (jr. bar conf. 1946-52, activities com. 1948-49), Calif. Supreme Ct. Hist. Soc. (bd. dirs. 2001—), ABA Sr. Lawyers Divsn. (vice-chair editl. bd. Experience mag. 1997-99, chair arts com. 1998-99, chair editl. bd. Experience Mag. 1999-2001, exec. coun. 1999—, Experience mag. adv. bd. 2001-, nominating com. 2003—04, co-chair newsletter 2003—, Dist. Svc. award 2003—), Assn. Learning in Retirement Orgns. in West (pres. 1993-94, exec. com. 1994-95, Disting. Svc. award 1995), Plato Soc. UCLA (discussion leader UCLA Constitution Bicentennial Project 1985-87, moderator UCLA extension lecture series 1990, Toga editor 1990-93, sec. 1991-92, chmn. colloquium com. 1992-93, Exceptional Leadership award 1994), Euterpe Opera Club (chair auditions 1972, chair awards 1973-75, v.p. 1974-75), Docents LA Philharm. (press and pub. rels. 1972-75, cons. coord. 1973-75, v.p. 1973-83, chair Latin Am. Cmty. Rels., Recognition and Honor award, 1978), Calif. Fedn. Music Clubs (chair Am. music 1971-75, conv. chair 1972), Nat. Fedn. Music Clubs (vice-chair Western region 1973-78), Nat. Assn. Composers USA (dir. 1974-79, luncheon chair 1975), Calif. Pres. Coun. (1st v.p.), LA Bus. Women's Coun. (pres. 1952), Calif. Bus. Women's Coun. (dir. 1951), Coun. Bar Assns. LA County (charter sec. 1950), So. Calif. Women Lawyers Assn. (pres. 1947, 1948), Inter-Am. Bar Assn., League of Ams. (dir.), Nat. Assn. Women Lawyers (regional dir. western states, Hawaii 1949-51, jud. adminstrn. com. 1960, nat. chair world peace through law com. 1966-67, liaison to ABA Sr. Lawyers Divsn. 1996—, chair bd. elections 1997-98, centennial com. 1997-99, chair com. unauthorized practice of law, social commn. UN, Lifetime Svc. award 1999), LA Lawyers Club (pub. defenders com. 1951), LA Bar Assn. (servicemen's legal aid com. 1944-45, psychopathic ct. com. 1948-53, Outstanding Svc. award 1993), State Bar Calif. (conf. com. on unauthorized practice of medicine 1964, Disting. Svc. award 1993), Women Lawyers Assn. LA (hon life 1998; chair Law Day com. 1966, subject of oral hist. project 1986, 2001), Iota Tau Tau Legal Scholastic Soc. (dean LA 1947, supreme treas. 1959-62, 1st prize 1942). Home: 5272 Lindley Ave Encino CA 91316-3518

SMITH, SERAFINA GANGEMI, artist, drug counselor; b. Phila., Sept. 1, 1919; d. Guiseppe I. and Maria Josephine (Meo) Gangemi; widowed, 1988; children: FRancisco Sidney, Guiseppe Scott, Maria Leslie. AA, U. Hawaii Windward Coll., Kaneohe, 1982; BA, U. Hawaii West Oahu, Pearl City, 1985; BA profl. studies, U. Hawaii, 1997. Cert. guardian ad litem for judiciary State of Hawaii. Ind. art instr., Forrest Heights, Md., 1963-67; stable mgr. Camp Smith Marine Base, Aiea, Hawaii, 1973-74; counselor Rehab. Hosp. of Pacific, Honolulu, 1979; counselor, cons. Hina Mauka Alcohol Rehab. Ctr., Kaneohe, 1980-82. State del. Al-Anon, Honolulu, 1982-84; bd. dirs. Pacific Inst. Chem. Dependency, Honolulu, 1983—; speaker on alcholism and family systems, 1981—; mgr. art gallery Hawaii Maritime Ctr., 1992—; studied with Guido del Corso, Verona, Italy, 1956-60, Lester Cook, Nat. Gallery, Washington, 1963-67, Dr. Chan, Oriental Inst. of Art, Washington, 1964-65, J. Woodward, Washington, 1965-66, Renzetti, Phila. Acad. of Arts, 1966-67, Douglas Walton, La. Tech., 1988—. Exhibited in group shows at Hawaii Watercolor Soc. Exhbn., 1992 (Bank of Hawaii award), 91 (Cresent Bd. award), Water Color Encounter, La. Tech. U., 1990 (Best in Show-Proffecial Judging award); one-women show Hawaii Maritime Mus., 1992; author: My Sicilian Family's Favorate Recipes, 2003. Vol. Hospice Hawaii, Honolulu, 1981-83, Suicide Crisis and Prevention Hotline, Honolulu, 1986-90, Hawaii Maritime Ctr., Honolulu, 1988—. Mem. AAUW (bd. dir. Hawaii unit 1986-87), Assn. for Christian Character Develop., team sponsor, Nat. Italian-Am. Found. (coun. mem.), Hawaii Joint Police Assn., U. Hawaii West Oahu Alumni Assn., Assn. Hawaii Artists (publicity chair 1990—), Hawaii Watercolor Soc., Nat. Mus. Women in Arts. Democrat. Roman Catholic. Avocations: cooking, designing clothes, travel.

SMITH, SHARMAN BRIDGES, state librarian; b. Lambert, Miss. BS, Miss. U. for Women, Columbus, 1972; MLS, George Peabody Coll., Nashville, 1975. Head libr. Clinton (Miss.) Pub. Libr., 1972-74; asst. dir. Lincoln-Lawrence-Franklin Regional Libr., Brookhaven, Miss., 1975-77, dir., 1977-78; info. svcs. mgr. Miss. Libr. Commn., Jackson, 1978-87, asst. dir. libr. ops., 1987-89, dir. libr. svcs. div., 1989-92; state libr. State Libr. Iowa, Des Moines, 1992—2001; exec. dir. Miss. Libr. Commn., Jackson, Miss., 2001—. Recipient Iowa Computer Using Educators Friend of Edn. award, 1995, Iowa Libr. Assn. Mem. of Yr. award, 1996. Office: Miss Libr Commn 1221 Ellis Ave Jackson MS 39209

SMITH, SHARRON WILLIAMS, chemistry professor; b. Ashland, Ky., Apr. 3, 1941; d. James Archie and May (Waggoner) Williams; m. William Owen Smith, Jr., Aug. 16, 1964; children: Leslie Dyan, Kevin Andrew. BA, Transylvania U., 1963; PhD, U. Ky., 1975. Chemist Proctor & Gamble, Cin., 1963-64, NIH, Bethesda, Md., 1974-75; tchr. sci. Lexington (Ky.) Pub. Schs., Bethesda, Md., 1964-67; asst. prof. chemistry Hood Coll., Frederick, Md., 1975-81, assoc. prof., 1981-87, prof., 1987—, chair dept. chemistry and physics, 1982-86, 95-99, acting dean grad. sch., 1989-91, Whitaker prof. chemistry, 1993—. NDEA fellow, 1967-70, Beneficial-Hodson faculty fellow Hood Coll., 1984, 92; grantee Hood Coll. Bd. Assocs., 1981, 85, 91, NSF, 1986, 2001. Mem. AAAS, Am. Chem. Soc. (E. Emmet Reid award 2001), Mid.-Atlantic Assn. Liberal Arts and Chemistry Tchrs. (pres. 1984-85). Democrat. Office: Hood Coll Dept Chemistry Frederick MD 21701 Office Phone: 301-696-3675. E-mail: ssmith@hood.edu.

SMITH, SHAUNTE RENEE, secondary school educator, poet; b. Wolfeboro, N.H., Aug. 24, 1971; d. Katheryn Smith Hazel and Joseph Smith, Constance Louise Smith and Kermit C. Brooks, W. Rogers Hazel (Stepfather) BA in English, Paine Coll., 1995; MEd Ednl. Leadership, Cambridge Coll., 2003. Cert. tchr. State Ga. Profl. Stds. Commn., 1998, ednl. leadership State Ga. Profl. Stds. Commn., 2003. Educator Dekalb County Sch. Sys., Decatur, Ga., 1998—. Coord. Murphey Candler Elem. Title One After-School Tutorial Program, Lithonia, Ga., 2003—. Author: (book of poems) A Creative Entrance into the Human Soul. Mem. Christian Meth. Episcopal Young Adult Fellowship, Covington, Ga., 1998—2003. Lettie P. Whitehead scholar, Paine Coll., 1991—95, Laymen Scholarship, Augusta Christian Ministrial Alliance, 1994. Mem.: Delta Sigma Theta (life; pres. 1993—95). Home: 2557 Hillvale Circle Lithonia GA 30058 Office: Dekalb County BOE/Murphey Candler Elem 6775 S Goddard Road Lithonia GA 30038 Personal E-mail: shaunter_smith@yahoo.com.

SMITH, SHEILA MARIE, lawyer; b. Chgo. d. Donald Thomas and Catherine Ellen (Mariga) Morrison; m. Melvin Smith, Nov. 11, 1989. BSEE, Purdue U., 1981; JD, U. Cin., 1995. Bar: Ohio 1995, U.S. Dist. Ct. (so. dist.) Ohio 1996, U.S. Ct. Appeals (6th cir.) 1996, U.S. Supreme Ct., 1999. Mfg. engr., 1981-92; assoc. Freking & Betz, Cin., 1995-99, ptnr., 2000—. Spkr. in field. Named to Order of Coif U. Cin., 1995. Mem. ABA, Am. Trial Lawyers Assn., Nat. Employment Lawyers Assn., Ohio Employment Lawyers Assn., Cin. Employment Lawyers Assn., Ohio Bar Assn., Cin. Bar Assn. Avocations: golf, travel, cooking. Home: 3345 Legendary Trails Dr Cincinnati OH 45245-3074 Office: Freking & Betz 215 E 9th St Fl 5 Cincinnati OH 45202-2139 E-mail: ssmith@frekingandbetz.com.

SMITH, SHERWOOD HUBBARD, JR., retired electric utilities executive; b. Jacksonville, Fla., Sept. 1, 1934; s. Sherwood Hubbard and Catherine Gertrude (Milliken) S.; m. Eva Hackney Hargrave, July 20, 1957; children: Marlin Hamilton Dohlman, Cameron Hargrave Callaway, Eva Hackney Davis. AB, U. N.C., 1956, JD, 1960; D civil laws, St. Augustine's Coll., 1988; LDD, Campbell U., 1990; HHD, Francis Marion Coll., 1990. Bar: N.C. 1960. Assoc. Lassiter, Moore & Van Allen, Charlotte, 1960-62; ptnr. Joyner & Howison, Raleigh, 1962-65; assoc. gen. counsel Carolina Power & Light Co., Raleigh, 1965-70, sr. v.p., gen. counsel, 1971-74, exec. v.p., 1974-76, pres., 1976-92, CEO, 1979-96, chmn. bd., 1980-99, chmn. emeritus, 1999—. Dir. No. Tel Network, Northwestern Mut. Life Inst. Co. Trustee Z Smith Reynolds Found., 1978-96, Nat. Humanities Ctr., 1990-93; bd. dirs. N.C. Citizens for Bus. and Industry, chmn., 1985-86; bd. dirs. Rsch. Triangle Found. of N.C., N.C. Inst. Medicine; mem. bd. govs. Ctr. for Creative Leadership; mem., chmn. Triangle Univs. Ctr. Advanced Studies, 1986—; mem. Kenan Inst. Pvt. Enterprise; former chmn. bd. trustees, chmn. Rex Hosp; gov. Boys and Girls Clubs of Am. Recipient Nat. Humanitarian award Am. Lung Assn., 1993, Outstanding Leadership award in Mgmt. scis. Am. Soc. Mech. Engrs., 1983, A.E. Finley Disting. Svc. award Greater Raleigh C. of C., 1985, Disting. Citizenship award N.C. Citizens Bus. and Industry, 1997; named to N.C. Bus. Hall of Fame, 1999. Mem.: Greater Raleigh C. of C. (pres. 1979), Phi Beta Kappa. Home: 408 Drummond Dr Raleigh NC 27609-7006 Office: Carolina Power & Light Co PO Box 1551 One Hanover Square Bldg Raleigh NC 27602-1551

SMITH, SHERWOOD PAUL, plastic surgeon; b. Sault St. Marie, Ont., Can., May 25, 1941; came to U.S., 1972; s. Irwin and Sophie Edith (Freeman) S.; m. Judith Ann Gebhard, Jan. 24, 1966; 1 child, Stephen Barclay. MD, U. Toronto, 1965; MSc, McGill U., 1969. Diplomate Am. Bd. Plastic Surgery. Plastic surgeon Olympia (Wash.) Plastic Surgeons Inc. PS, 1972—. Vol. plastic surgeon Gen. Hosp. Columbo, Sri Lanka, 1985—. Fellow ACS, Royal Coll. Physicians and Surgeons of Can.; mem. Olympia Yacht Club, South Sound Sailing Soc. Avocations: sailing, bicycling, hiking, mountain climbing. Office: Olympia Plastic Surg Inc PS PO Box 12569 Olympia WA 98508-2569

SMITH, SHIRLEY, artist; b. Wichita, Kans., Apr. 17, 1929; d. Harold Marvin and Blanche Carrie (Alexander) S. BFA, Kans. State U., 1951; postgrad., Provincetown (Mass.) Workshop, 1962-66. One-woman shows include 55 Mercer St. Gallery, N.Y.C., 1973, Wichita Art Mus., Kanas, 1978, Stamford Mus. and Nature Ctr., Conn., 1987, Aaron Gallery, Washington, 1987, 1988, Joan Hodgell Gallery, Sarasota, Fla., 1987, Marianna Kistler Beach Mus. 38 Yr. Retrospective, Kans. State U., 1999—2000, John Jay Gallery, N.Y.C., 2000, Represented in permanent collections Whitney Mus. Am. Art, Phoenix Art Mus., The Aldrich Mus. Contemporary Art, Ridgefield, Conn., Ulrich Mus., Wichita State U., Kans. State U., Everson Mus., Syracuse, N.Y., U. Calif. Berkeley Art Mus., Marianna Kistler Beach Mus., Kans. State U., Manhattan, Telfair Mus. of Art, Savannah, Ga. Recipient Grumbacher Cash award for mixed media New Eng. Exhibition, Silvermine, Conn., 1967, Acad. Inst. award Am. Acad. Arts and Letters, N.Y.C., 1991, Richard Florsheim Art Funds grantee, 1998, Retrospective Opening grantee, 1999. Mem. Artist Equity. Democrat. Presbyterian. Home: 141 Wooster St New York NY 10012-3163

SMITH, SHIRLEY A. state legislator, state representative; b. 1950; 2 children. AA, Cuyahoga C.C.; BA, Cleve. (Ohio) State U. Rep. Ohio State Ho. Reps., Columbus, 1998—. Mem. banking, pensions and securities com. Ohio State Ho. Reps., mem. criminal justice com., mem. health com., mem. childrens healthcare and family svcs. subcom., mem. juvenile and family law com. Mem.: NOW, Ohio Legis. Women's Caucus, Nat. Black Caucus of State Legis., Women in Govt., Emily's List. Democrat. Office: Ohio State House Reps 77 South High Street 10th Floor Columbus OH 43215-6111

SMITH, SIBLEY JUDSON, JR., historic site administrator, educator; b. Alexandria, La., June 26, 1955; s. Sibley Judson and Eunice Lee (Raulins) S.; children: Jacob Lee, Casey Raulins. Student, N.E. La. U., 1973-76; BA in History magna cum laude, Christopher Newport Coll., 1985; MA in Am. Studies, Coll. of William and Mary, 1992. Mus. interpreter Colonial Williamsburg (Va.) Found., 1979-87; coord. of interpretation Hist. Hudson Valley, Inc., Tarrytown, N.Y., 1987-88; historic site mgr. Philipse Manor Hall State Hist. Site, Yonkers, N.Y., 1988-91; exec. dir. Hist. Allaire (N.J.) Village, Inc., 1991-97; dir. edn. Vietnam Era Ednl. Ctr., N.J. Vietnam Vets. Meml. N.J. Dept. Mil. and Vet. Affairs, Holmdel, 1997—. Mem. Alpha Chi, Alpha Psi Omega. Avocations: gardening, theater, movies, mus. Office: Vietnam Era Ednl Ctr 1 Memorial Ln PO Box 648 Holmdel NJ 07733-0648 Office Phone: 732-335-0033. E-mail: sjsmith@njvvmf.org.

SMITH, SIDNEY L. advertising executive; Chmn. Westwayne Inc., Atlanta. Office: Westwayne Inc 1100 Peachtree St NE Ste 1800 Atlanta GA 30309-4502

SMITH, SIDNEY OSLIN, JR., lawyer; b. Gainesville, Ga., Dec. 30, 1923; s. Sidney Oslin and Isabelle Caroline (Charters) S.; m. Patricia Irwin Horkan, Aug. 4, 1944 (dec. Oct. 19, 2001); children— Charters Smith Wilson, Ellen Smith Andersen, Sidney Oslin III. AB cum laude, Harvard Coll., 1947; LL.B. summa cum laude, U. Ga., 1949. Bar: Ga. 1948. Ptnr. Telford, Wayne & Smith, Gainesville, Ga., 1949-62; asst. solicitor Superior Cts., Northeastern Jud. Cir. Ga., 1951-61, judge, 1962-65, U.S. Dist. Ct. (no. dist.) Ga., 1965-68, chief judge, 1968-74; ptnr. Alston, Miller & Gaines, Atlanta, 1974-82, Alston & Bird, Atlanta, 1982-94, of counsel, 1994—. Chmn. Gainesville Bd. Edn., 1959-62; trustee Brenau Coll., Gainesville, 1974—, chmn., 1976-84; mem. state bd. regents Univ. System of Ga., 1980-87, chmn., 1984-85. Served to capt. U.S. Army, 1943-46, ETO. Fellow ABA, Am. Coll. Trial Lawyers; mem. Am. Law Inst., Am. Judicature Soc., Commerce Club, Chattahoochee Club, Phi Beta Kappa, Phi Kappa Phi, Phi Delta Phi, Phi Delta Theta. Democrat. Episcopalian. Home: 3206 Club Pointe Way Gainesville GA 30506-1638 Office: Alston & Bird 1 Atlantic Ctr Atlanta GA 30309-3400 E-mail: smit977@bellsouth.net.

SMITH, SIDNEY RUFUS, JR., linguist, educator; b. Greensboro, N.C., Sept. 18, 1931; s. Sidney Rufus and Page (Johnston) S.; m. Vera Pautzsch, Apr. 19, 1969 (div. 1975); children: Stephanie Alice, Eric Brian. BA, Duke U., 1953; PhD, U. N.C., 1965. Asst. prof. U. Conn., Storrs, 1965-66, U. N.C., Chapel Hill, 1966-71, assoc. prof., 1971-79, prof., 1979—, chmn. Germanic

langs., 1979-89, 94-97, chmn. linguistics, 1981-84, prof. emeritus, 1997—. Author numerous articles for profl. publs. Local troop leader Girl Scouts U.S.A. Served to sgt. AUS, 1953-56. Recipient Stephen Freeman award N.E. Conf. Teaching Langs., 1969, cert. of merit Goethe Inst., 1997. Mem.: Am. Assn. Tchrs. German, Soc. Advancement Scandinavian Study. Democrat. Office: U NC Dept Germanic Langs Chapel Hill NC 27599-0001 Business E-Mail: srsmith@email.unc.edu. E-mail: srsmith@mindspring.com.

SMITH, SIDONIE, literature educator; Student, U. Sheffield, Eng., 1965; BA, MA, U. Mich., 1966; PhD, Case Western Res. U., 1971. Tchg. asst. Case Western Res. U., 1968—70; instr. Cuyahoga C.C., 1969—71; asst. dean Coll. Continuing Edn. Roosevelt U., 1971—72; asst. prof. U. Ariz., 1973—78, assoc. prof., 1978—83; assoc. prof. Eng. and women's studies Binghamton U., 1983—89, prof. Eng., comparative lit., and women's studies, 1989—96; prof. women's studies and Eng. U. Mich., Ann Arbor, 1996—. Program officer instl. grants edn. divsn. NEA, Washington, 1981—82; assoc. dean acad. affairs, arts and sci. and Harpur Coll. SUNY, Binghamton, assoc. dean adminstrn., arts and sci., and Harpur Coll., acting dean arts and sci. and Harpur Coll., interim dean arts and sci. and Harpur Coll.; dir. grad. studies dept. Eng. Binghamton U., NY, 1991—93; dir. women's studies U. Mich., Ann Arbor, 1996—. Author: Where I'm Bound: Patterns of Slavery and Freedom in Black American Autobiography, 1974, A Poetics of Women's Autobiography: Marginality and the Fictions of Self-Representation, 1987, Subjectivity, Identity, and the Body: Women's Autobiographical Practices in the Twentieth Century., 1993; co-editor: De/Colonizing the Subject: Gender and the Politics of Women's Autobiography, 1992, Getting a Life: Everyday Uses of Autobiography, 1996, Writing New Identities: Gender, Nation, and Immigration in Contemporary Europe, 1997, Indigenous Australian Voices: A Reader, 1998, Women, Autobiography, Theory: A Reader, 1998; contbr. articles to profl. jours. Fellow Canterbury fellow, 1993; grantee Ford grant, 1971, Travel grant, U. Ariz. Found., 1978; scholar Sr. Fulbight scholar, 1994. Mem.: Comparative Lit. Assn., Soc. Study of Narrative Lit., Midwest Modern Lang. Assn., Modern Lang. Assn. Am. (exec. coun. 2000—, exec. bd. divsn. life writing 1989—94, exec. bd. divsn. women's studies lit. 1994—99). Office: Univ Mich 234 West Hall Ann Arbor MI 48109-1092 E-mail: sidsmith@umich.edu.

SMITH, SIMEON CHRISTIE, III, lawyer, judge; b. Alexandria, La., Feb. 4, 1941; s. Simeon Christie II and Margaret Ford (Ferguson) S.; m. Shirley Mae Pearce, Jan. 28, 1967; children: Simeon Christie IV, E. Pearce Smith. BA, La. State U., 1964; JD, Loyola U., New Orleans, 1967. Bar: La. 1967, U.S. Dist. Ct. (we. dist.) La. 1972, U.S. Ct. Appeals (5th cir.) 1972, U.S. Dist. Ct. (mid. dist.) La. 1973, U.S. Dist. Ct. (ea. dist.) La. 1976, U.S. Supreme Ct. 1976, U.S. Ct. Appeals (11th cir.) 1981. Assoc. Wood & Jackson, Leesville, La., 1967-69; ptnr. Jackson Smith, Leesville, 1969-75; sr. ptnr. Smith, Ford & Clark, Leesville, 1975-95, The Smith Law Firm, L.L.P., Leesville, 1996—. Ward judge, Leesville, 1978—. Mem. ATLA, Am. Judicature Soc., La. Trial Lawyers Assn. (mem. bd. govs. 1976-90), La. State Bar Assn. (mem. ho. of dels. 1975-79), 30th Jud. Dist. Bar Assn. (pres. 1974-76). Democrat. Methodist. Office: PO Drawer 1528 300 Courthouse St Leesville LA 71496-1528

SMITH, SPENCER BAILEY, engineering and business educator; b. Ottawa, Ont., Can., Jan. 31, 1927; s. Sidney B. and Etta (Bailey) S.; m. Mildred E. Spidell, Dec. 31, 1954 B in Engring., McGill U., 1949; MS, Columbia U., 1950, DSc in Engring., 1958. Adminstrv. engr. Mergenthaler Linotype Co., N.Y.C., 1953-58; ops. research mgr. Raytheon Co., Newton, Mass., 1958-61; ops research mgr. Montgomery Ward & Co., Chgo., 1961-66; assoc. prof., then prof. Ill. Inst. Tech., 1966-96, prof. emeritus, 1996—, chmn. dept. indsl. and systems engring., 1971-77, dir. Stuart Sch. Office of Research, 1977-82. Tchr. TV courses Nat. Tech. U. Author: Computer-Based Production and Inventory Control, 1989; contbr. articles to profl. jours.; patentee on order quantity calculator, 1964. Vol. cons. on sch. redistricting Elem. Sch. Dist., Evanston, Ill., 1972-74 Research grantee Harris Trust and Savs. Bank, 1968-70, Ill. Law Enforcement Commn., 1972-74, U.S. Army C.E., 1981, Am. Prodn. and Inventory Control Soc., 1980 Mem. INFORMS, Inst. Indsl. Engrs., ASME, Am. Prodn. and Inventory Control Soc. Clubs: University (Chgo.). Presbyterian. Home: 2530 Lawndale Ave Evanston IL 60201-1158 E-mail: montrosemillennium@comcast.net.

SMITH, STAN VLADIMIR, economist, financial service company executive; b. Rhinelander, Wis., Nov. 16, 1946; s. Valy Zdenek and Sylvia Smith; children: Cara, David. BS in Ops. Research, Cornell U., 1968; MBA, U. Chgo., 1972, PhD in Econs., 1997. Diplomate Am. Bd. Disability Analysts. Lectr. U. Chgo., 1973; economist bd. govs. Fed. Res. System, Washington, 1973-74; staff economist First Nat. Bank of Chgo., 1974; assoc. December Group, Chgo., 1974-77; founding pres. Seaquest Internat., Chgo., 1977-85; mgr., ptnr. Ibbotson Assocs., Chgo., 1981-85; pres. Corp. Fin. Group, Ltd., Chgo., 1985—. Expert econ. witness in field; adj. prof. DePaul U. Coll. Law, Chgo., 1990. Author: Economic/Hedonic Damages, 1990; founding editor Stocks, Bonds, Bills and Inflation yearbook, 1983-2001; bd. editors Jour. Forensic Economics, 1990-2001; also contbr. articles in field. Founder, exec. dir. Inst. for Value of Life, 1996. Fellow Allied Chem., 1967, John McMullen Trust, 1969; grantee Ford Found., 1972, U.S. Fed. Res., 1973. Fellow: Am. Coll. Forensic Examiners (bd. cert. 1996—); mem.: Soc. Litig. Economists (bd. govs. 1999—), Acad. Econ. and Fin. Experts, Am. Bd. Forensic Examiners, Nat. Future Assn. (arbitrator), Am. Arbitration Assn. (arbitrator 1994—96), Nat. Acad. Econ. Arbitrators (founder 1989—), Nat. Assn. Forensic Econs. (v.p. 2000—03), Am. Fin. Assn., Am. Econ. Assn., Alpha Delta Phi. Office: Corp Fin Group Ste 600 1165 N Clark St Chicago IL 60610-7861 Office Phone: 312-943-1551. E-mail: stan@CFG-Economics.coM.

SMITH, STANDISH HARSHAW, not-for-profit developer; b. Germantown, Pa., Dec. 28, 1931; s. Standish Oscar and Kathryn Jeanette (Harshaw) Smith; m. Joan H. Lallou, Dec. 29, 1956; children: Hamilton, Robertson. BA, Kenyon Coll., 1956; postgrad., State U. Iowa, 1956-58, Villanova U., 1959-61, U. Pa., 1963, Temple U., 1967. Rsch. analyst Rowland and Lo., Haddonfield, N.J., 1961, Franklin Inst., Phila., 1961-63, RCA Svc. Co., Moorestown, N.J., 1963-64, Fed. Aviation Agy., Pomona, N.J., 1964-66, Gen. Elec., Phila., 1966-70; founder, treas. Aqua Systems, Inc., Villanova, Pa., 1970-72; founder, owner Auto. Bus., Phila., 1970-84; ret., 1984-91; founder Heirs, Inc., Villanova, 1991-92. Human factors engr. Burroughs Corp., Paoli, Pa., 1959—61; lectr. Burroughs Night Sch., Paoli, 1960; founder Heirs, Inc., Villanova, Pa. Inventor Marine pipelaying sys., 1973; contbr. articles to profl. jours. Mem.: Merion Cricket Club, Mayflower Soc. Avocation: piano. Office: 1744 Cedar Ln Villanova PA 19085-2018 Office Phone: 610-527-6260. E-mail: stancedar@comcast.net.

SMITH, STANFORD SIDNEY, former state treasurer; b. Denver, Oct. 20, 1923; s. Frank Jay and Lelah (Beamer) S.; m. Harriet Holdrege, Feb. 7, 1947; children: Monta Smith Ramirez, Franklin Stanley. Student, Calif. Inst. Tech., 1941-42, Stanford U., 1942-43; BS, U.S. Naval Acad., 1946. Pres. Vebar Livestock Co., Thermopolis, Wyo., 1961—; mem. Wyo. Senate, 1974-76; pres. Wyo. Wool GrowersAssn., 1976-78; mem. Wyo. Ho. of Reps., Cheyenne, 1978-82; treas. State Wyo., Cheyenne, 1983-99; ret., 1999. Dir. Coun. of State Govts., 1990-92; v.p. Wyo. Wool Growers, dir., 1976-82. County commr. Hot Springs County, Wyo, 1966-74. Lt. USN, 1943-54. Decorated Bronze Star Mem. Nat. Assn. State Treas. (pres. 1990-91). Republican. Methodist. Home: 10023 W Palmer Dr Sun City AZ 85351-3918

SMITH, STANLEY BERTRAM, clinical pathologist, allergist, immunologist, anatomic pathologist; b. Phila., 1929; MD, Washington U., St. Louis, 1956. Diplomate Am. Bd. Clin. Pathology, Am. Bd. Allergy and Immunology, Am. Bd. Anatomic Pathology. Intern Barnes Hosp., St. Louis, 1956—57; resident in pathology Jackson Meml. Hosp., 1957—62; fellow in immunology Sch. Medicine Yale U., New Haven, 1963—65; pathologist Miami (Fla.) Children's Hosp., 1966—. Mem. AAAS, AMA, Internat. Acad. Pathology, Am. Soc. Clin. Pathology, Coll. Am. Pathologists, Am. Soc. Hematology. Office: Miami Children's Hosp 3100 SW 62nd Ave Miami FL 33155-3009 E-mail: Stanley.Smith@mch.com.

SMITH, STANTON KINNIE, JR., lawyer; b. Rockford, Ill., Feb. 14, 1931; s. Stanton Kinnie Smith and Elizabeth (Brown) Stanton; m. Mary Beth Sanders, July 11, 1953; children: Stanton E., Kathryn A., Dana. BA, Yale U., 1953; JD, U. Wis., 1956. Bar: Ill. 1956, Mich. 1976. Ptnr. Sidley & Austin Law, Chgo., 1964—75; vice chmn., gen. counsel Am. Natural Resources Co., Detroit, 1975—87; sr. v.p. The Coastal Corp., Houston, 1985—87; vice chmn., gen. counsel CMS Energy Corp., Jackson, Mich., 1987—88, pres., 1988—92, vice chmn., 1992—96, vice chmn., bd. dirs., 2002—04; sr. spl. counsel Skadden, Arps, Slate, Meagher & Flom, N.Y.C., 1996—2002. Bd. dirs. Clarcor Corp., Mich. Natural Corp., Mich. Nat. Bank. Trustee Founders Soc., Detroit Inst. Arts, Rockford Coll.; devel. bd. mem. Yale U.; trustee Mich. Opera Theatre; bd. advisors U. Wis. Law Sch., Mich. State U., Pub. Utility Inst. Mem.: ABA, Chgo. Bar Assn., Mich. Bar Assn. Office: CMS Energy Corp Legal Dept One Energy Plaza Jackson MI 49201*

SMITH, STEPHEN ALLEN, mathematician, educator; s. William Francis and Gertrude Elizabeth Smith; m. Karen Ann Jensen, Apr. 27, 2002; children: Gregory, Daniel. BS in Math., U. Cin., 1965; MS in Math., Stevens Inst. Tech., 1967; PhD in Engring.-Econ. Sys., Stanford U., 1972. Rsch. scientist Xerox Rsch. Ctr., Palo Alto, Calif., 1972—82; J.C. Penney prof. Leavey Sch. Bus. Santa Clara U., Calif., 1982—. Prin. Pricing Strategy Assocs., Berkeley, Calif., 1984—95; adv. bd. Spotlight Solutions, Inc., Cin., 1998—2003, StoreSight Sys., Palo Alto, 2000—. Author: New Service Opportunities for Electric Utilities, 1993; mem. editl. bd.: Ops. Rsch. Jour., 1984—2000, Inst. Indsl. Engring., 1997—; contbr. articles to profl. jours. Recipient award for best pub. paper, Jour. Retailing, 1991. Mem.: Inst. Ops. Rsch. and Mgmt. Sci. (chmn. bus. applications 1986—90, sr. editor Mfg. and Svc. Ops. Mgmt. Jour. 2002—). Office: Santa Clara Univ Dept OMIS 500 El Camino Real Santa Clara CA 95053 E-mail: ssmith@scu.edu.

SMITH, STEPHEN AUSTIN, communications educator; b. Fayetteville, Ark., May 15, 1949; s. Austin Clell and Margaret (King) S.; m. Lindsley Farrar Armstrong, Aug. 6, 1994; children: Caleb Jefferson, Margaret Cecilia. BA in Comm., U. Ark., 1972, MA in Comm., 1974; PhD in Comm. Studies, Northwestern U., 1983. Chief staff Atty. Gen. Ark., Little Rock, 1977-78; exec. asst. Gov. Ark., Little Rock, 1979-80; prof. comm. U. Ark., Fayetteville, 1982—. Author: Myth, Media and the Southern Mind, 1985; author, editor: Clinton on Stump, State, and Stage, 1994. State legislator Ark. Ho. of Reps., Little Rock, 1971-75; v.p. Ark. Constl. Conv., Little Rock, 1979-80. Recipient Madison prize So. States Comm. Assn., 1991. Fellow Am. Comms. Assn.; mem. Speech Comm. Assn. (chair, vice-chair Commn. on Freedom of Expression 1987—, Golden Anniversary Monograph award 1992, Haiman award 1989, Wichelns award 1978). Democrat. Unitarian Universalist. Office: U Ark Dept Comm 417 Kimpel Hall Fayetteville AR 72701 E-mail: Libertas@uark.edu.

SMITH, STEPHEN F. food service executive; b. El Dorado, Ark. m. Jan Smith; 6 children. Student, South Ark. U. Mgr. Sysco Corp., Jackson, Minn., 1980—81, v.p. wholesale co. El Paso, Tex., 1981—83, pres., CEO Atlanta, 1983—87, Little Rock, 1987—95, Orlando, 1995—2002, sr. v.p. food svc. ops. Ocoee, Fla., 2002—. Office: Sysco Corp 200 W Story Rd Ocoee FL 34761-0130

SMITH, STEPHEN GRANT, communications executive; b. N.Y.C., Mar. 6, 1949; s. John J. and Nora O.S.; m. Sarah Rowbotham Bedell, May 22, 1982; children: R. Kirk Bedell, Elisabeth DeCou Bedell, David Branson Smith. Student, Deerfield Acad.; BA, U. Pa., 1971. City Hall reporter Daily Hampshire Gazette, Northampton, Mass., 1971-73; spl. assignment reporter Albany Times-Union, 1973-74; dep. regional editor Phila. Inquirer, 1974-76; asst. met. editor Boston Globe, 1976-78; sr. editor Horizon Mag., 1978; staff writer Time Mag., 1978-80, sr. editor, 1980-82, Nation editor, 1982-85, acting asst. mng. editor, 1985-86; exec. editor Newsweek Mag., 1986-91; Washington news editor Knight-Ridder newspapers, 1991-94; founding editor Civilization Mag., Washington, 1994-96; editor Nat. Jour., 1996-98, U.S. News and World Report, 1998-2001; exec. v.p. Winner & Assocs., 2001—02; v.p., dir. comm. Brookings Instn., 2003—. Mem. Bd. Overseers U. Pa., 2001—. Mem. Coun. on Fgn. Rels., World Affairs Coun. Washington, U. Pa. Alumni Soc. (exec. com. 1994-2000), Fourth Estate Golf Soc., Nat. Press Club, Brook Club, Century Club, Met. Club, Chevy Chase Club, Beefsteak Club, White's Club, Overseas Press Club, Sakonnet Golf Club, Penn Club, Royal St. George's Golf Club. Office: Brookings Instn 1775 Massachusetts Ave Washington DC 20036-2188 E-mail: sgrasmith@aol.com.

SMITH, STEPHEN JAMES, lawyer, director; b. Milw., Feb. 16, 1949; s. James Milon and Helen Kathryn Smith; m. Jerilyn Sue Jenson, Feb. 6, 1971; children: Justin Paul, Lindsay Jeane, Erika Helen. BA magna cum laude, Luther Coll., 1971; JD cum laude, Northwestern U., 1976. Bar: Wis. 1976. Auditor Arthur Andersen & Co., Chgo., 1971-73; ptnr. Hostak, Henzi & Bichler, Ltd. (formerly Thompson & Coates), Racine, Wis., 1976—. Reporter taxation sect. Wis. State Bar; mem. adv. bd. and steering com. Sustainable Racine, Inc., 1997-99. Bd. dirs. Goodwill Industries S.E. Wis., Racine, 1980-83, Goodwill Industries Milw., 1983-2002, Racine Area United Way, 1982-88, Taylor Home, 1985-91, 1997-2001, pres., 1998-2000; bd. dirs. Racine Cmty. Found., 1991-99, pres., 1997-99; founder The Family Vision Experience, 2002. Mem. ABA, Wis. State Bar. Lutheran. Office: Hostak Henzl & Bichler SC 840 Lake Ave Racine WI 53403-1566 Office Phone: 262-632-7541. E-mail: ssmith@hhb.com.

SMITH, STEPHEN L. computer company executive; BSEE, Rice U. Design engr. Hewlett-Packard, Cupertino, Calif.; device physicist static RAM tech. devel. Intel Corp., 1979, state RAM design mgr., EEPROM design mgr., design mgr. i386 SX and i386 SL processors, asst. gen. mgr. Mobile Computing Group, engring. mgr. Pentium Processor div., gen. mgr. Pentium Processor div., 1995—97, v.p. and dir. Intel Pentium 4 Processor task force, v.p. and dir. desktop platform ops., 1997—. Patentee in field. Office: 2200 Mission College Blvd Santa Clara CA 95052

SMITH, STEPHEN MARK, lawyer; b. Newport News, Va., July 1, 1948; s. Joseph and Marian (Sturman) S.; m. Dawn Lee Williams, Dec. 10, 1978; children: Ryan David, Miles Stephen. BA in Psychology, William & Mary, 1971, JD, 1974. Bar: Va. 1974, N.Y. 1975, D.C. 1975, U.S. Supreme Ct., U.S. Ct. Appeals (2d, D.C., 4th cirs.). Lawyer Rothblatt, Rothblatt, et al., N.Y.C., 1974-76, Joseph Smith Ltd., Hampton, Va., 1976-99; founding mem. Brain Injury Law Ctr. P.C. Bd. dirs. Enrenfried Techs. Mem. com. Va. Beach Dems., 1990—; bd. dirs., coord. Va. state Trial Lawyers Pub. Justice. Included in Best Lawyers in Am., 1997—. Mem. ATLA, Am. Bd. Trial Lawyers (diplomate), Am. Bd. Trial Advocates, Va. Trial Lawyers Assn. (bd. dirs. 1978—), Brain Injury Assn. Va. (bd. dirs. 1997—). Avocations: fishing, reading, boating, jogging, golf. Office: Brain Injury Law Center 2100 Kecoughtan Rd Hampton VA 23661 Home: PO Box 829 Virginia Beach VA 23451-0829

SMITH, STEPHEN MARK, music educator; b. Columbia, Mo., Feb. 23, 1954; s. Elmer Lee and Josephine Ann Smith; m. Pamela Layne Snella, July 30, 1978; 1 child, Christopher Stephen. A of Music, Morton Coll., 1974; BS in Music Edn., U. Ill., 1977; M of Spl. Edn., U. North Fla., 1995, postgrad., 2001—02. Cert. tchr. Fla. Dept. Edn., 1988. Commd. ensign USN, 1978, advanced through grades to lt., ret., 1988; music resource tchr. special edn. Duval County Sch. Dist. Music Dept., Jacksonville, Fla., 1988—. Presenter in field. Cubmaster Boy Scouts of Am., Jacksonville, 1988—90, scoutmaster, 1992—93, merit badge counselor, 1994—2002. Decorated Sea Svc. Ribbon, Sea Svc. Ribbon First Star, Navy Expeditionary Medal, Pistol Marksman Ribbon, Rifle Marksman Ribbon, Navy Achievement Medal; named Arts Educator of Yr., Cultural Coun., Jacksonville, 1997, Feature Article Educator Teaches in the Key of Success, The Times Union Newspaper, Jacksonville, 1998; recipient cert. of Appreciation, Future Educators Am., 1998; grantee, U.S. Dept. Edn., 1995, 1996, Duval Pub. Edn. Found., Jacksonville, 1996, 1996, Duval Pub. Edn. Found., 1996, U.S. Dept. Edn., 1997, The Cultural Coun. Greater Jacksonville, 1997, U.S. Dept. Edn., 1998, Duval County Pub. Found., 1998, U.S. Dept. Edn., 1999, Duval Pub. Edn. Found., 1999, The Cultural Coun. of Greater Jacksonville, 1999, Jacksonville Elec. Authority and The Alliance for World Class Edn., 2000, The Alliance for World Class Edn., 2000. Mem.: Fla. Elem. Music Educators Assn. (state dist. rep. 1990—91), Fla. Music Educators Assn., The Am. Legion, Pi Lambda Theta, Delta Sigma Pi. Democrat-Npl. Roman Catholic. Avocations: guitar, sailing, camping, computer gaming, flying. Office: Duval County Sch Bd Music Dept 1701 Prudential Dr Jacksonville FL 32207

SMITH, STEPHEN RANDOLPH, aerospace executive; b. Des Moines, Apr. 17, 1928; s. Norvin Ellis and Helen (Heberling) S.; m. Margaret Anne Graves, Dec. 20, 1950; children: Stephen Randolph Jr., Susan Canning, Sara Kutler, Anne Barrette, Julia Carroll. BSME, Stanford U., 1951, MSME, 1952; MBA Advanced Mgmt. Program, Harvard U., 1974. Registered profl. engr., Calif. Sr. analyst, preliminary design engr. Northrop & Garrett Corps., L.A. and Hawthorne, Calif., 1952-55; propulsion lead design engr. Northrop Corp., Hawthorne, 1955-59, engring. rep. ea. dist. Washington, 1959-60, T-38/F-5/F-5X program mgr. Hawthorne, 1960-75, v.p. Iran ops. Tehran, 1975-78, v.p. advanced stealth projects Hawthorne, 1978-83, v.p. engring. and advanced devel., 1983-86, v.p., program mgr. F-20/YF-23A, 1986-88, corp. v.p., gen. mgr. aircraft divsn., 1988-92; cons. tech. mgmt. Palos Verdes, Calif., 1992—. Bd. mem. Quarterdeck Ptnrs., Inc., L.A. and Washington, 1992—; NASA Advanced Aeronautics Com., 1984-86; invited lectr. aircraft design USAF Acad., 1983. Author, designer, patentee in field. Bd. dirs. Boy Scouts Am., L.A. coun., 1986—, explorer exec. com., 1943—; pres. Penn Srs., Palos Verdes, Calif., 1996; trustee Western Mus. Flight; jr. warden St. Francis Ch. Sgt. U.S. Army, 1946-48. Recipient Disting. Civilian Svc. medal for Tacit Blue, U.S. Dept. Def., Washington, 1983. Fellow AIAA (chmn. L.A. sect. 1985-86, adv. bd. 1988—, Spl. Citation 1994), Inst. Advancement Engring.; mem. Soc. Automotive Engrs. (chmn. aerotech. 1986-87, honors 1987), Sierra Club, Trailfinders Conservation Coun. (life, coun. chief 1940), Redondo Beach Yacht Club (charter), King Harbor Yacht Club (charter). Republican. Episcopalian. Avocations: competitive sailing, tennis, backpacking, skiing, running. Home and Office: 2249 Via Guadalana Palos Verdes Estates CA 90274

SMITH, STEPHEN ROSS, endocrinologist; b. Iowa City, Mar. 5, 1938; s. Wendell Ross and Ruth Anne (Frudenfeld) S.; m. Elaine Cashman Frazier, July 4, 1964 (div. Dec. 1990); children: Julia Helene, Stuart Ross; m. Regina Alilada Clarito, Dec. 26, 1990; 1 child, Alexander Ross. AB, Princeton U., 1959; MD, Harvard U., 1963. Instr. medicine Johns Hopkins U. Sch. Medicine, Balt., 1970-72, asst. prof. medicine, 1972-73, 82—; chief endocrinology Kern County Hosp., Bakersfield, Calif., 1973-76; assoc. prof. medicine Tex. Tech. U. Sch. Medicine, El Paso, 1977-80; chief medicine Thomason Gen. Hosp., El Paso, 1977-80, Bon Secours Hosp., Balt., 1980-83, Security Forces Hosp., Riyadh, Saudi Arabia, 1984-88; pvt. practice Balt., 1988—; med. dir. Nat. Clin. Rsch. Ctrs., Bethesda, Md., 1988-93. Pres. med. staff Univ. Specialty Hosp., Balt., 1996—; rsch. assoc. Johns Hopkins Ctr. Med. Rsch. and Tng., Calcutta, India, 1970—72; bd. dirs. El Paso Diabetes Assn., 1978—80; cons. Liberty Med. Ctr. Diabetes Mgmt. Ctr., Balt., 1991—98, pharm. industry, 1993—. Contbr. articles to profl. jours. Capt. USAF, 1965-67. Fellow ACP; mem. Am. Diabetes Assn., Am. Fedn. Clin. Rsch., Princeton Club Md., Hampton Swim Club, Bodie Island Beach Club (pres. 2002—, bd. dirs. 2000—). Republican. Avocations: swimming, travel, history. Office: 8709 Harford Rd Baltimore MD 21234-4607 Office Phone: 410-882-4741.

SMITH, STEVEN DELANO, professional basketball player; b. Highland Park, Mich., Mar. 31, 1969; Student, Mich. State U. Guard Miami Heat, 1991-94, Atlanta Hawks, 1994-99, Portland Trailblazers, 1999—. Named Sporting News All-Am. First Team, 1990, 91, NBA All-Rookie Team, 1992, Dream Team II, 1994. Office: San Antonio Spurs 1 SBC Ctr San Antonio TX 78219-3604

SMITH, STEVEN J. communications company executive; b. Milw., Apr. 10, 1950; married; 2 children. BA in Communication Arts, U. Wis., 1972; Cert. Advanced Mgmt. Program, Harvard U., 1995. Advt. salesperson Sta. WTMJ-AM, subs. Jour. Comm., Milw., 1976; gen. mgr. Sta. WKTI-FM, Milw., 1980-83; v.p., gen. mgr. WTMJ-AM and WKTI-FM, subs. Jour. Comm., Milw., 1983-85, KTNV-TV, ABC-TV affiliate, Las Vegas, 1985; pres. Jour. Broadcast Group Inc. subs. Jour. Comm., 1987-92, Jour. Comm., 1992—, COO, 1996—, CEO, chmn., 1998—. Trustee Faye McBeath Found., Med. Coll. of Wis., Boys and Girls Club of Greater Milw.; bd. dirs. YMCA of Greater Milw., United Performing ArtsFund, Milw. Met. Assn. of Commerce; co-chair Safe & Sound, Milw.; past chmn. bd. dirs. Am. Heart Assn. of Wis. Mem. Wis. Broadcasters Assn. (past bd. dirs.), Milw. Area Radio Stas. (past pres.).

SMITH, STEVEN LEE, judge; b. San Antonio, Apr. 19, 1952; s. Bill Lee and Maxine Rose (Williams) S.; m. Rebecca Ann Brimmer, Aug. 5, 1978; children: William Christopher, Laura Charlotte. B in Music Edn. magna cum laude, Abilene Christian U., 1974; JD, U. Tex., 1977. Bar: Tex. 1977. U.S. Dist. Ct. (so. dist.) Tex. 1979, U.S. Dist. Ct. (we. dist.) Tex. 1980; cert. civil trial lawyer, Tex. Bd. Legal Specialization. Assoc. Dillon & Giesenschlag, Bryan, Tex., 1977-80, ptnr., 1980-84, Dillon, Lewis, Elmore & Smith, Bryan, 1985-88, Hoelscher, Lipsey, Elmore and Smith, College Station, Tex., 1988-94; asst. mcpl. judge City of College Station, 1988-91, presiding mcpl. judge, 1992-95; judge Brazos County Ct. at Law # 1, Bryan, 1995-98, 361st Dist. Ct., Bryan, 1999—. Past chair Nat. Conf. Spl. Ct. Judges. Chmn. Brazos Valley chpt. March of Dimes, 1983-84; Leadership Brazos Devel. Program, Bryan/Coll. Sta. C. of C., 1984-85; pres. Meml. Student Ctr. Opera and Performing Arts Soc., College Station, 1985-86; trustee Abilene Christian U., 2001—. Recipient Charles Plum Disting. Svc. award Tex. A&M U., 1986. Mem. U. Tex. Law Sch. Alumni Assn. (dist. dir. 1986-89), U. Tex. Ex-Students Assn. Exec. Coun. (club rep. 1987-88), Optimists (pres. 1982-83). Mem. Ch. Of Christ. Avocations: golf, flying. Home: 3840 Cedar Ridge Dr College Station TX 77845-6275 Office: 361st Dist Ct 300 E 26th St Ste 305 Bryan TX 77803-5361 Office Phone: 979-361-4380. E-mail: ssmith@co.brazos.tx.us.

SMITH, STEVEN RAY, law educator; b. Spirit Lake, Iowa, July 8, 1946; s. Byrnard L. and Dorothy V. (Fischbeck) S.; m. Lera Baker, June 15, 1975. BA, Buena Vista Coll., 1968; JD, U. Iowa, 1971, MA, 1971. Bar: Iowa 1971, Ky. 1987, Ohio 1992. From asst. to assoc. dean Sch. Law U. Louisville, 1974-81, acting dean, 1974-75, 76, prof. law, 1971-88, assoc. in medicine Med. Sch., 1983-88; dep. dir/ Assn. Am. Law Schs., 1987-88; dean, prof. law Cleve. State U., 1988-96; pres., dean and prof. Calif. Western Sch. of Law, 1996—. Author: Law, Behavior and Mental Health: Policy and Practice, 1987; contbr. chpts. to books, articles to profl. jours. Trustee U. Louisville, 1980-82, SCRIBES, 1993—; bd. dirs. San Diego Mediation Ctr., 2003—, pres. Ky. Congress of Senate Faculty Leaders, 1982-84; bd. trustees Am. Bd. Profl. Psychology, 1994-2001; bd. dirs. Nat. Register of Health Svc. Providers in Psychology, 2002—, San Diego Vol. Lawyers Program, 1998—, San Diego Mediation Ctr., 2003—; sec., bd. dirs. Assn. for Accreditation of Human Rsch. Protection Programs, 2001—. Recipient Grawemeyer award Innovative Teaching. Metrovesity Consortium, 1983. Fellow Ohio State Bar Found., ABA (stds. rev. com. 1991-95, govt. rels. com. 1993-95, joint commn. ABA/Assn. Am. Law Schs. financing of legal edn. 1993-94, 97-98, coun. sect. legal edn. and admission to the bar 1997—, vice chair sect. on legal edn. and admission to the bar 2003—); mem. APA (pub. mem. ethics com.), Am. Econs. Assn., Assn. Am. Law Schs. (chmn. librs. com., dep. dir. 1987-88, mem. accreditation com. 1993-96, chair accreditation com. 1994-96), Ohio State Bar Assn. (coun. of dels. 1992-96), Order of Coif, City Club of Cleve. (pres. 1994-95). Office: Calif Western Sch Law Office of Pres 225 Cedar St San Diego CA 92101-3046

SMITH, STEVEN W. judge; b. Tex. m. Susan Smith; children: Emily, Allison. BBA in Fin., U. Tex., Arlington, 1983; JD with honors, U. Tex., 1986. Judge Tex. State Supreme Ct., Austin, 2002—. Office: Tex Supreme Ct PO Box 12248 Austin TX 78711

SMITH, S(TEWART) GREGORY, ophthalmologist, inventor, product developer, consultant, author; b. Wyandotte, Mich., Jan. 24, 1953; s. Stewart Gene and Veronica (Latta) S. BA in Econs. with distinction, U. Mich., 1974; MD, Wayne State U., 1978. Diplomate Am. Bd. Ophthalmology, Nat. Bd.

Med. Examiners. Intern, Sacred Heart Med. Ctr., Spokane, Wash.,1978; resident in ophthalmology U. Minn., Mpls., 1979-82, fellow cornea and anterior segment surgery, 1982-83; practice medicine specializing in cornea and anterior segment surgery, and ophthalmology Wilmington, Del., 1983—; clin. prof. ophthalmology U. Pa., Hershey Med. Ctr., 1984—; clin. asst. prof. Thomas Jefferson U.; attending surgeon Wills Eye Hosp., Phila., 1995—; mem. sr. faculty 3M Vision Care Dept., Mpls., 1984-90, rsch. cons., 1984, lectr., 1983—, cons. Am. Cyanamid Opthalmic Divsn., 1990-94, Am. Home Product, 1995—; lectr. in field, Korea, Hong Kong, Thailand, Malaysia, Phillipines, France, Spain, Ireland, Portugal, Holland, Denmark, England, Sweden; cons. Am. Home Products, 1995—, cons. Alcon, 1999—; Author: Complications ofIntraocular Lenses and Their Management, 1988, Can You Really See Perfectly Again Without Glasses?, 1996; co-author: Vision Without Glasses, 1990, Sight for Life, 1990; contbr. articles to Fly Fisherman Mag. and other profl. publs. Patentee investigational devices and pharmaceutical, tilt control for automotive vehicles. Recipient award for Best Sci. Poster, Contact Lens Assn. of Ophthalmologists, 1980; Best Film award Internat. Congress of Cataract Surgeons, 1985; Grand Prize Am. Soc. Cataract and Refractive Surgeons Film Festival, 1986. Fellow Am. Intraocular Implant Soc., Castroviejo Soc. (Best Paper award 1984), AMA, Eye Bank Assn. Am., Am. Soc. Cataract and Refractive Surgery Internat. Soc. Refractive Surgery, Am. Acad. Ophthalmology (Honor award 1996), Assn. for Rsch. and Vision in Ophthalmology, Internat. Intraocular Implant Club, Wills Eye Hosp. Alumni Soc., European Soc. Cataract & Refracture Soc. Avocations: fly fishing, hunting, saxophone, tennis, skiing. Home: Nine Gates Rd Yorklyn DE 19736 Office: 1100 N Grant Ave Wilmington DE 19805 2671 Office Phone: 302-655-3388.

SMITH, STUART LYON, psychiatrist, corporate executive; b. Montreal, Que., Can., May 7, 1938; s. Moe Samuel and Nettie (Krainer) S.; m. Patricia Ann Springate, Jan. 2, 1964; children: Tanya, Craig. BSc, McGill U., 1958, MD, CM, 1962, diploma in psychiatry, 1967; LLD (hon.), Mt. Allison U., 1992, Royal Rds. U., 2000. Intern. Montreal Gen. Hosp., 1962-63, resident in psychiatry, 1963-67; from asst. prof. to assoc. prof. medicine McMaster U., Hamilton, Ont., Can., 1967-75; leader Ont. Liberal Party Ont. Legislature, 1976-82, leader of the opposition, 1977-82; chmn. Sci. Coun. Can., Ottawa, 1982-87; pres. RockCliffe Rsch. and Tech., Inc., 1987—, Philip Utilities Mgmt. Corp., Toronto, Ont., 1994-97. Chmn. com. inquiry Can. U. Edn., 1989—91; chmn. Ensyn Tech. Inc., 1990—; sr. adv. ICF Cons., 2002; chmn. Nat. Round Table on Environment and Economy, Ottawa, 1995—2002; chmn. bd. dirs. Humber Coll., 2002—04, Esna Tech., Inc., 2004—. Decorated knight Nat. Order of Merit (France); McLaughlin travel fellow, 1964-65. Fellow Royal Coll. Physicians and Surgeons of Can. Personal E-mail: smithstuart@rogers.com.

SMITH, STUART SEABORNE, writer, government official, union official; b. N.Y.C., Jan. 27, 1930; s. Purcell Leonard and Elizabeth (Wright) S.; m. Birte Moeller Jacobsen, Apr. 27, 1956 (div. 1972); children: Stuart Seaborne, Bjarne Moeller; m. Editha Maria Fuchs, Jan. 3, 1973; children: Cornelia Gerda, Melanie Carla. Grad., Lawrenceville (N.J.) Sch., 1948; student, Princeton U., 1948—51, U. Heidelberg, Germany, 1953—54, U. Madrid, 1954—55, U. Copenhagen, 1955—56. Reporter Balt. Sun, 1957-65, fgn. corr. chief Bonn (Germany) bur., 1965-69, corr. Washington Bur., 1969-70; with ABA, 1970-71, Dept. Justice, Washington, 1971—; exec. dir. Capitol Employees Organizing Group, 1979—; pub. Balt. Banner, 1965. Served with AUS, 1951-53. Recipient Spl. award for meritorious svc. Washington-Balt. Newspaper Guild, 1965, Meritorious Svc. award Dept. Justice, 1985, 87, Sustained Superior Performance award Dept. Justice, 1992, 93. Mem. Am. Fedn. State, County and Mcpl. Employees (pres. coun. 26 1977-80, 87-95, chief steward Local 2830 1975-80, 81-82, pres. 1982—, Meritorious Svc. award Local 2830, 1980). Home: 10522 Tyler Ter Potomac MD 20854-4059 Office: Office Of Justice Programs Washington DC 20531-0001 Office Phone: 202-307-0784. Personal E-mail: stuart.smith20@verizon.net. Business E-Mail: stu@ojp.usdoj.gov. *I believe in honor and democracy and social justice. I further believe that for the most part we are the ignorant slaves of political and philosophical superstitions, but in the end the truth shall set us free.*

SMITH, SUE FRANCES, newspaper editor; b. Lockhart, Tex., July 4, 1940; d. Monroe John Baylor and Myrtle (Krause) Mueck; m. Michael Vogtel Smith, Apr. 20, 1963 (div. July 1977); 1 child, Jordan Meredith; m. Kirkland Gideon Smith, Apr. 17, 1999. B of Journalism, U. Tex., 1962. Feature writer, photographer Corpus Christi Caller Times, 1962-64; feature writer, editor Chgo. Tribune, 1964-76; features editor Dallas Times Herald, 1976-82; sales assoc. Bumpas Assocs., Dallas, 1982-83; asst. mng. editor for features Denver Post, 1983-84, assoc. editor, 1984-91; asst. mng. editor in charge of Sunday paper Dallas Morning News, 1991-94, asst. mng. editor Lifestyles, 1994-96, dep. mng. editor Lifestyles, 1996—2001, dep. mng. editor recruiting/devel., 2001—. Active Coun. Pres., 1993; juror Pulitzer Prize, 2002-03. Mem. Am. Assn. Sunday and Feature Editors (pres. 1993), Newspaper Features Coun. (pres. 2002), Tex. Associated Press Mng. Editors (pres. 1999-2000), Delta Gamma. Home: 6241 Park Meadow Ln Plano TX 75093-8863 Office: 508 Young St Dallas TX 75202-4893 E-mail: ssmith@dallasnews.com.

SMITH, SUSAN ELIZABETH, guidance director; b. Phila., Mar. 24, 1950; d. E. Burke Hogue and Janet Coffin Hogue Ebert; m. J. Russell Smith, June 17, 1972 (div. June 1989); 1 child, Drew Russell. BS in Elem. Edn., E. Stroudsburg Coll., 1972; MEd in Counseling, U. Okla., 1974, postgrad., 1976-77, Trenton State Coll., 1989-90; EdM in Devel. Disabilities, Rutgers U., 1992, postgrad., 1994—. Cert. elem. tchr., N.C.; cert. elem. tchr., early childhood edn. tchr., guidance and counseling, Okla.; cert. elem. tchr., guidance and counseling, tchr. of handicapped, psychology tchr., supr. instrn., dir. student pers. svcs., N.J. Elem. tchr. Morton Elem. Sch. Onslow County Schs., Jacksonville, N.C., 1971-72; instr. U. Isfahan, Iran, 1974-76; guidance counselor Moore (Okla.) Pub. Schs., 1976-77; counselor Johnstone Tng. Ctr. N.J. Divsn. Devel. Disabilities, Bordentown, 1988-90; spl. edn. tchr. Willingboro (N.J.) Schs., 1990-91; guidance counselor Haledon (N.J.) Pub. Schs., 1991-92; spl. edn. adj. tchr. Gateway Sch., Carteret, N.J., 1991-93; guidance counselor Bloomfield (N.J.) Pub. Schs., 1992-94; dir. guidance Somerville (N.J.) Pub. Schs., 1994-95. Adj. prof. in spl. edn. Essex County (N.J.) Coll., 1994; guidance Ft. Lee (N.J.) Schs., 1995-2001; guidance dir. Bogota Schs., N.J., 2001-02, Closter Schs., Closter, N.J., 2002—; cons., seminar and workshop presenter on behavior mgmt., parenting skills, and behavior modification techniques; cons. N.J. Fragile X Assn. Author: Motivational Awards for ESL Students, 1993, Parent Contracts to Improve School Behaviors, 1996; contbr. articles to profl. jours. Leader Boy Scouts Am., Oklahoma City, 1983-87, com. chmn., Redmond, Wash., 1987-88. Recipient Rsch. award ERIC/CAPS, 1992, Svc. award N.J. Fragile X Assn., 1993. Mem. ACA, Am. Sch. Counselor Assn. (grantee 1992), N.J. Counseling Assn., N.J. Sch. Counseling Assn., Assn. for Multicultural Counseling and Devel., AAUW, Assn. for Counselor Edn. and Supervision, N.J. Assn. for Counselor Edn. and Supervision, N.J. Prins. and Suprs. Assn., Nat. Assn. Coll. Admissions Counselors (grantee 1995), Alpha Omicron Pi. Episcopalian. Home: 916 Lincoln Pl Teaneck NJ 07666-2572

SMITH, SUZANNE M. federal agency administrator; BA, Pa. State U.; MD, Med. Coll. Pa.; MPH, Emory U., 1991; MPA, Harvard U. With CDC, Atlanta, 1983—97, chief, Health Care and Aging Studies br., Divsn. Adult and Cmty. Health, 1997—2003, acting dir., pub. health practice program office, 2003—. Office: CDC 1600 Clifton Rd Atlanta GA 30333*

SMITH, TAD RANDOLPH, lawyer; b. El Paso, Tex., July 20, 1928; s. Eugene Rufus and Dorothy (Derrick) S.; m. JoAnn Wilson, Aug. 24, 1949; children: Laura Borsch, Derrick, Cameron Ann Compton. LLB, U. Tex., 1951, BBA, 1952. Bar: Tex. 1951. Assoc. firm Kemp, Smith Duncan & Hammond P.C., El Paso, Tex., 1951-52, ptnr., 1952-81, CEO, 1975—98, shareholder, 1981—99; of counsel Kemp Smith, LLP, El Paso, 1999—. Active United Way of El Paso; chmn. El Paso County Reps., 1958-61, Tex. Rep. State Exec. Com., 1961-62; alt. del. Rep. Nat. Conv., 1952, 62, del. 1964, dir. El Paso Elec. Co., 1961-90, State Nat. Bank of El Paso, 1969-90, The Leavell Co., 1970-94; trustee Robert E. and Evelyn McKee Found., 1970-90, Property Trust of Am., 1971-91; mem. devel. bd. U. Tex., El Paso, 1973-81, v.p., 1975, chmn. 1976; dinner treas. Nat. Jewish Hosp. and Rsch. Ctr., 1977, chmn. 1978, presenter of honoree, 1985; bd. dirs. NCCJ 1965-76, chmn. 1965-78; bd. dirs. Southwestern Children's Home, El Paso, 1959-78; trustee Hervey Found., 1990-99, Lydia Patterson Inst., 1994-99. Named Outstanding Young Man, El Paso Jaycees; named to Bd. of Fellows, U. Tex., El Paso, 1997—2001; recipient Humanitarian award, El Paso chpt. NCCJ, 1983. Fellow Am. Bar Found., Tex. Bar Found.; mem. ABA, Tex. Bar Assn., El Paso Bar Assn. (pres. 1971-72), El Paso C. of C. (dir. 1979-82), Sigma Chi. Republican. Methodist. Home: PO Box 831 Alto NM 88312 Office: Kemp Smith LLP Wells Fargo Plz 221 N Kansas St Ste 1700 El Paso TX 79901

SMITH, TEFFT WELDON, lawyer; b. Evanston, Ill., Nov. 18, 1946; s. Edward W. and Margery T. (Weldon) S.; m. Nancy Jo Smith, Feb. 25, 1967; children: Lara Andrea, Tefft Weldon II. BA, Brown U., 1968; JD, U. Chgo., 1971. Bar: Ill. 1971, D.C. 2000, U.S. Supreme Ct. 1977. Sr. litigation ptnr. Kirkland & Ellis LLP, Chgo., 1971—, ptnr.-in-charge competition and antitrust practice group. Mem. adv. bd. Bur. Nat. Affairs Antitrust and Trade Regulation Reporter; instr. trial advocacy. Contbr. numerous articles on trial practice and antitrust issues to law jours. Mem. ABA (litigation sect., antitrust law sect.), Econ. Club, Univ. Club, Mid-Am. Club, Sea Pines Country Club (Hilton Head, S.C.). Avocations: squash, ferraris, sculpture. Office: Kirkland & Ellis 200 E Randolph St Fl 54 Chicago IL 60601-6636 also: 655 15th St NW Washington DC 20005-5701 Home: 700 New Hampshire Ave NW Washington DC 20037

SMITH, THELMA TINA HARRIETTE, gallery owner, artist; b. Folkston, Ga., May 5, 1938; d. Harry Charles and Malinda Estelle (Kennison) Causey; m. Billy Wayne Smith, July 23, 1955; children: Sherry Yvonne, Susan Marie, Dennis Wayne, Chris Michael. Student, U. Tex., Arlington, 1968-70; studies with various art instrs. Gen. office worker Superior Ins. Corp., Dallas, 1956-57, Zanes-Ewalt Warehouse, Dallas, 1957-67; bookkeeper Atlas Match Co., Arlington, 1967-68; sr. acct. Automated Refrigerated Air Conditioner Mfg. Corp., Arlington, 1968-70; acct. Conn. Gen. Life Ins. Corp., Dallas, 1972-74; freelance artist Denton, Tex., 1974—; gallery owner, custom framer Tina Smith Studio-Gallery, Mabank, Tex., 1983—. Painting in pub. and pvt. collections in numerous states including N.Y., Fla., Ga. and N.D.; editor Cedar Creek Art Soc. Yearbook, 1983—. Treas. Cedar Creek Art Soc., 1987-88, 89—; mem. com. to establish state endorsed Arts Coun. for Cedar Creek Lake Area, Gun Barrel City, Tex. Recipient numerous watercolor and pastel awards Henderson County Art League, Cedar Creek Art Soc., Cmty. Svc. award Mayor Wilson Tippit, Gun Barrel City, Tex., 1986. Mem. Southwestern Watercolor Soc. (Dallas), Soc. Outdoor Painters, Pastel Soc. of the S.W. (Dallas), Cedar Creek Art Soc. (Gun Barrel City)(v.p. 1983-86, treas.), Profl. Picture Framers Assn. Baptist. Avocations: water activities, gardening. Studio: Tina Smith Studio-Gallery 251 Shady Shores Dr Mabank TX 75156-

SMITH, THOMAS A. lawyer, investment company executive; b. Springfield, Ill., Dec. 14, 1956; BA, Wabash Coll., 1978; JD, St. Louis U., 1983, MBA, 1984. Bar: Ill. 1984, Mo. 1985, N.Y. 1990; lic. series 7 Nat. Assn. Securities Dealers, series 24 Nat. Assn. Securities Dealers. Enforcement atty. Ill. Securities Dept., 1984—85; staff atty. divsn. investment mgmt. U.S. SEC, 1986—89; sr. assoc. Wilkie Farr & Gallaghar, 1989—91; asst. gen. counsel Dreyfus Corp., 1991—93, N.Y. Life Ins. Co., N.Y.C., 1994—96, assoc. gen. counsel, 1996—97, v.p., assoc. gen. counsel, 1997—99; exec. v.p., gen. counsel Van Kampen Investments, Inc., 1999—2001; mng. dir., gen. counsel U.S. investment mgmt. Morgan Stanley, N.Y.C., 2001—. Co-author: (book) Regulation of Investment Companies. Office: Morgan Stanley Law Dept 1221 Ave of the Americas 5th Fl New York NY 10020

SMITH, THOMAS CLAIR, retired manufacturing company executive; b. Indiana, Pa., Mar. 14, 1925; s. William Bryan and Edna Louise (Thomas) S.; m. Marilyn Louise Globisch, May 29, 1948; children: Claudia Lynn Smith Holtry, Craig Randall. BSME, Pa. State U., 1946; A, Alexander Hamilton Bus. Inst., 1949. Registered profl. engr., Pa., N.J., Del. Structural test engr. Chance Vought Aircraft Co., Bridgeport, Conn., 1946-48; test engr. Fed. Mogul Bearings Co., Lancaster, Pa., 1949-51; fuse engr. to mgr. materials Hamilton Watch Co. (name now Hamilton Tech.), Lancaster, Pa., 1952-70; plant mgr. Woodstream Corp., Lititz, Pa., 1970-79, v.p. mktg., 1980—87, ret., 1987. Faculty, coach Lacrosse Franklin and Marshall Coll., Lancaster, 1950-53. Pub. Smith, Bryan, Allison & Morris Geneal. Chart, 1989; author and pub. of 1600 person geneal. chart in Libr. of Congress, 1989; patentee electric watch, 1957, swivel snap, 1975; author Penna Law 110 of 1992 and Pa. Law 22 of 1994/saving ancestral cemeteries. Pres. bd. dirs. Lancaster County Mental Health Assn., 1952-60, Lancaster County Cmty. Svc. Ctr., 1968-78; pres., bd. dirs. Am. Cancer Soc., 1970-72, bd. dirs., 1965-97, life bd. dirs., 1998—; bd. dirs. Hearing Conservation Assn., Lancaster, 1955-60, ARC, Lancaster, 1967-86, United Way, Lancaster, 1968-72, Ephrata (Pa.) Area Rehab. Ctr., 1986—, Grave Concern, Inc., 1994—; pres. Ephrata (Pa.) Area Rehab. Found., 1997—; mem. All-Am. Lacrosse Team, 1945, Heritage Ctr. Lancaster, 1980—, Ind. County Hist. Soc., 1984—, Greene County Hist. Soc., Waynesburg, Pa., 1985—, Selective Svc. Bd., 1992—; trustee Lancaster County Hist. Soc., 1992-98, mem., 1983—; judge elections, Lancaster County, 1994-2001. Named Boss of Yr., Am. Bus. Women's Assn., 1978, Vol. of Yr., Am. Cancer Soc., 1998, Tennis Family of Yr. Pa. N.J., Del., 1970; named to Lancaster County Tennis Hall of Fame, 2001; recipient Outstanding Svc. award, Mental Health Assn. Lancaster, 1961, Edward D. Eshelman award as Humanitarian of Yr., Am. Cancer Soc., 1991. Mem. Order of Crown of Charlemagne in U.S.A. (life), Pa. State U. Alumni Club (life), Pa. Sons of Revolution (bd. dirs., sec. 1990—), Phi Delta Theta (pres. Pa. State U. chpt. 1945), Wheatland Tennis Club (v.p. 1990-94, pres. 1995-96). Clubs: Lancaster Country (chmn. tennis com. 1960-75). Republican. Presbyterian. Avocations: genealogy, tennis, skiing. Home: 1420 Quarry Ln Lancaster PA 17603-2426 *You only go through this life on earth once. Don't waste that time. Put it to use in helping to make the earth a better place.*

SMITH, THOMAS EUGENE, investment company executive, financial consultant; b. Brown's Summit, NC, Aug. 23, 1930; s. Howard Cleveland and Annie May (Warren) S.; m. Joan Cretcher Hopkins, Sept. 22, 1948; 1 dau., Vicki Joan. Student, George Washington U., 1948-50, Am. U., 1950-55 (intermittently). Pres., dir. T. Eugene Smith, Inc. investment co. and real estate and fin. cons. co., Falls Church, Va., 1950—; pres. The Potomac Corp., Falls Church, Va., 1960-74; pres., dir. Nat. Bank of Fairfax, Va., 1975-81, dir.; exec. v.p. First & Mchts. Nat. Bank, Richmond, Va., 1981-83; chmn., dir. Decisions and Designs, Inc., McLean, Va., 1983-86; ptnr. Braddock-Ravensworth Ltd. Partnership, 1964—; sec., dir. Port Royal, Inc., 1965—; ptnr. Lee Graham Shopping Ctr., 1969—; chmn., pres., dir. Am. Mobile Home Towns, Inc., holding co., 1969-85; dir., pres. Topsail, Inc., 1983-89; ptnr. Potomac Greens Assn., 1986—. Bd. dirs. Growth Fund of Washington, Am. Funds Tax Exempt Series I, Washington Mut. Investors, M.G. Thalheimer Realty Advisors, Inc.; chmn., bd. dirs. River Capital Corp., Alexandria, Va., 1986-89, J. Webb, Inc., 1986—; acting dir., mgmt. com. Alexandria 20/20, 1988-91, acting dir., 1988-89; pres., dir. Pender Marina Holdings, Inc., 1988—, Pender Land Holdings, Inc., 1990—; adv. bd. CSX Realty, 1992-2003. Bd. dirs. Wolftrap Found., Washington, 1974-84; trustee Sta. WETA-TV, 1978-86; mem. Nat. Capital Planning Commn., Washington, 1980-83, vice chmn., 1981-83; mem. Va. Hwys. and Transp. Commn., Richmond, 1982-86; trustee Ch. Schs., Diocese of Va., 1983-88; mem. Va. Gov.'s Coun. Econ. Advisors, 1985-94, Met. Washington Airports Authority, 1986-94; chmn. Fairfax County Transp. Commn. for the Future, 1988-89; dir. Air and Space Heritage Coun., 1987-90. Mem.: Nat. Assn. Small Bus. Investment Cos. (treas. and bd. dirs. 1962—66), Met. Club (Washington). Democrat. Episcopalian. Home: 666 Tintagel Ln Mc Lean VA 22101-1835 Office Phone: 703-243-2041.

SMITH, THOMAS GORDON, architect; b. Oakland, Calif., Apr. 23, 1948; s. Sheldon Wagers and Margaret (Prendergast) S.; m. Marika Wilson, Dec. 19, 1970; children— Alan, Stuart, Demetra, Andrew, Philip, Duncan. A.B., U. Calif.-Berkeley, 1970, M.Arch., 1975. Lic. architect, Calif. Prin. Thomas Gordon Smith, Architect, Chgo., 1980—; instr. archtl. history Coll. of Marin, Kentfield, Calif., 1976-77; guest instr. archtl. design So. Calif. Inst. Architecture, Santa Monica, 1983; guest lectr., seminar leader Kunstegeschichtlieches Institut der Philipps Universitat, Marburg, W.Ger., 1983; guest tchr. U. Ill., Chgo., UCLA, 1984; assoc. prof. U. Ill., Chgo.; chmn. Sch. Architecture U. Notre Dame, Ind., 1989-98. Exhibited art in shows at Santa Barbara Mus. Art, 1977, Cooper-Hewitt Mus., Chgo. Art Inst., 1980, Louisiana Mus. Modern Art, Copenhagen, 1981, Venice Biennale, 1980, Smith Coll. Mus. Art, 1981, La Jolla Mus. Modern Art, Calif., 1982, Deutsches Architekturmuseum, Frankfurt, W.Ger., 1984; revision of Modern IBM Gallery, N.Y., 1987; author: Classical Architecture: Rule and Invention, 1987, Vitruvias on Architecture, 2003. Bd. dirs. Soc. Cath. Liturgy. U. Calif. grad. fellow, 1974, John K. Branner fellow, 1975, Rome Prize fellow, 1979; grantee Graham Found. Advanced Study in Fine Arts, 1984, 87, Am. Philos. Soc., 1987. Mem. AIA (Grad. fellow 1973), Soc. Archtl. Historians. Home: 1903 Dorwood Dr South Bend IN 46617-1818 Office: 2025 Edison Rd South Bend IN 46637 E-mail: archtgs@aol.com.

SMITH, THOMAS HUNTER, ophthalmologist, ophthalmic plastic and orbital surgeon; b. Silver Creek, Miss., Aug. 10, 1939; s. Hunter and Wincil (Barr) S.; m. Michele Ann Campbell, Feb. 27, 1982; 1 child, Thomas Hunter IV. BA, U. So. Miss., 1961; MD, Tulane U., 1967; BA in Latin Am. Studies, Tex. Christian U., 1987, MA in History, 1995, PhD in L.Am. History, 1999. Diplomate Am. Bd. Ophthalmology (bd. examiners 1983-90). Intern Charity Hosp., New Orleans, 1967-68; resident in ophthalmology Tulane U., New Orleans, 1968-71; dir., sec. bd. dirs. Ophthalmology Assocs., Ft. Worth, 1971-99; adj. prof. history of medicine and L.Am. history Tex. Christian U., Ft. Worth, 2000—01; adj. instr. history of medicine and pub. health, L.Am. history Tulane U., 2001—03. Clin. prof. Tex. Tech U. Med. Sch., Lubbock, 1979-99; guest lectr., invited speaker numerous schs., confs., symposia throughout N.Am., Ctrl. Am., South Am., Europe and India; hon. mem. ophthalmology dept. Santa Casa de São Paulo Med. Sch. Contbr. articles to profl. jours. Cons. ophthalmologist Helen Keller Internat.; deacon South Hills Christian Ch.; mem. Rocky Mountain Coun. Latin Am. Studies. Recipient Tex. Chpt. award Am. Assn. Workers for the Blind, 1978, Recognition award Lions Club Sight & Tissue Found., Cen. Am., 1977-79; named to Alumni Hall of Fame U. So. Miss., 1989. Fellow ACS, Am. Acad. Ophthalmology (bd. counsellors 1995-98), Am. Acad. Facial Plastic and Reconstructive Surgery; mem. Tex. Med. Assn. (com. socio-econs.), Pan-Am. Assn. Ophthalmology (adminstr. 1988-93, bd. dirs. 1993-99), Internat. Cos. Cryosurgery, Royal Soc. Medicine (affiliate), Tex. Soc. Ophthalmology and Otolaryngology, Peruvian Ophthalmol. Soc. (hon.), Santa Casa De São Paulo (hon. assoc.), Tex. Ophthalmol. Assn. (past mem. exec. coun., treas.), Tex. Med. Assn., Tarrant County Med. Soc., Byron Smith Ex Fellows Assn., Tarrant County Multiple Sclerosis Soc. (past pres.), Tarrant County Assn. for Blind, Tulane Med. Alumni Assn. (bd. dirs.), S.Am. Explorers Club, Colonial Country Club, Petroleum Club Ft. Worth, Sigma Xi, Omicron Delta Kappa. Mem. Christian Ch. (Disciples Of Christ). Avocations: hunting, fishing, flying, world travel.

SMITH, THOMAS J. surgeon, educator; BA cum laude, Amherst Coll., 1967; MD, Tufts U. Sch. Medicine, 1971. Diplomate Am. Bd. Surgery, Nat. Bd. Med. Examiners. Intern, resident in surgery Tufts New Eng. Med. Ctr., Boston, 1971-73, chief resident in surgery, 1975-78; clin. assoc. surgery br. Nat. Cancer Inst., Bethesda, Md., 1978-80; from asst. prof. to assoc. prof. surgery Tufts U. Sch. Medicine, 1980-94; assoc. prof. U. South Fla., 1994; asst. prof. clin. surgery Columbia U., N.Y.C., 1995—. Clin. prof. surgery U. Medicine and Dentistry N.J. Med. Sch., 1997—. Editl. bd. Internat. Jour. Cancer Rsch. & Treatment, Oncology; contbr. articles, abstracts to profl. jours. Mem. Am. Coll. Physician Execs., Am. Soc. Clin. Oncology, Soc. Surg. Oncology (edn. com. 1988—), Am. Cancer Soc. (Sword of Hope award com.). Office: Everett Clinic 3901 Hoyt Ave Everett WA 98201 Office Phone: 425-339-5442. Business E-Mail: tsmith@everettclinic.com.

SMITH, THOMAS KENT, retired radiologist, viticulturist; b. Bowling Green, Ohio, Aug. 21, 1934; s. Robert O. and Roslyn Smith; m. Jaleh Saidi, Feb. 1, 1974; children: Jeffrey, Todd, Mark, Blake, Tyler. BS with high honors, U. Cin., 1957; MD, Case Western Res. U., 1961. Intern Nat. Naval Med. Ctr., Bethesda, Md., 1961-62; resident in radiology VA Med. Ctr., Long Beach, Calif., 1965-69; fellow in radiologic pathology Armed Forces Inst. Pathology, Washington, 1968; dir. radiology Harriman Jones Med. Group, Long Beach, 1969-88; fellow in MRI/CT U. Calif., San Francisco, 1988-89; dir. MRI Orange County MRI, Fountain Valley, Calif., 1989-90; chmn. dept. diagnostic imaging Kaiser Permanente Med. Ctr., Honolulu, 1990-2000, dir. MRI, 1994-2000; ret. Mem. adv. bd. Hawaii Permanente Med. Group, Honolulu, 1990—2000; assoc. clin. prof. radiology U. Hawaii, Honolulu, 1990—2000; asst. clin. prof. U. Calif., Irvine, Calif., 1970—88, clin. instr., San Francisco, 1988—89, asst. clin. prof., 1989—97; cons. in radiologic devel. Kaiser Permanente Internat., 1996—98; owner Rubaiyat Vineyard, Sonoma County, Calif. Lt. Med. Corps, Nuc. Submarine Svcs. USN, 1961—65. Fellow Am. Coll. Radiology; mem. Hawaii Radiol. Soc. (pres. 1992-93), Radiol. Soc. N.Am., Internat. Soc. Magnetic Resonance in Medicine, Margulis Soc., Alpha Omega Alpha, Sonoma County Grape Growers Assn., Sonoma Valley Vintners and Growers Alliance, Rhone Rangers,. Avocations: fishing, travel, viticulture. Home: Rubaiyat Vineyard 5409 Sonoma Mountain Rd Santa Rosa CA 95404-8884 Fax: 707-544-4117. Office Phone: 707-525-1441. E-mail: rubaiyatvineyard@aol.com.

SMITH, THOMAS RAMSAUR, JR., lawyer; b. Feb. 12, 1938; AB, Princeton U., 1960; LLB, U. Va., 1963. Assoc. Sidley Austin Brown & Wood LLP, N.Y.C., 1963-71, ptnr., 1971-96, ptnr, 2003—, mng. ptnr., 1996—2003. Office: Sidley Austin Brown & Wood 787 7th Ave New York NY 10019 Office Phone: 212-839-5535. Business E-Mail: tsmith@sidley.com.

SMITH, THOMAS RAYMOND, III, software engineer; b. Phila., Dec. 6, 1946; s. Thomas Raymond and Naomi (Hart) S.; m. Marguerite Anne LeMoyne de Martigny, Sept. 6, 1969; children: Michelle Renée, Heather Anne, Thomas Raymond IV. Student, MIT, 1964-68. Sr. analyst Dabcovich and Co., Lexington, Mass., 1969—71; sr. analyst, prin. Multi-Logic Corp., Burlington, Mass., 1970—73; cons. engr. Digital Equipment Corp. (now Hewlett-Packard Co.), Palo Alto, Calif., 1974—. Co-editor: IEEE Dictionary, 1993; author, co-editor numerous stds. books for Internat. Electrotech. Commn. and IEEE, 1984-93. Mem.: IEEE (chmn. various stds. coms. 1980—). Home: 36 Toppans Ln Newburyport MA 01950-3843 Office: Hewlett-Packard Co ZK01-3/H42 110 Spit Brook Rd Nashua NH 03062-2711 Business E-Mail: smith@alum.mit.edu.

SMITH, THOMAS WILLIAM, neuropathologist; b. Columbus, Ohio, Sept. 22, 1946; BS, Ohio State U., 1968; MD, Cornell U., 1972. Diplomate Am. Bd. Pathology. Resident in pathology N.Y. Hosp., N.Y.C., 1972-73; resident in neuropathology Peter Bent Brigham Hosp., Boston, 1973-76, resident in pathology, 1977-78; resident in radiology Mass. Gen. Hosp., Boston, 1976-77; staff pathologist, prof. pathology and neurology U. Mass. Med. Sch., Worcester, 1978—, dir. neuropathology and diagnostic electron microscopy, —. Contbr. over 112 articles to profl. jours., chpts. to books. Mem. Am. Assn. Neuropathologists, Am. Acad. Neurology, Soc. of Exptl. Neuropathology, Internat. Acad. Pathology. Office: Univ of Massachusetts Med Sch Dept Pathology 55 Lake Ave N Worcester MA 01655-0002 E-mail: smitht@ummhc.org.

SMITH, THOMAS WINSTON, Business E-Mail: twsmith@calcot.com.

SMITH, TOM, playwright, theater arts educator; b. Rochelle, Ill., May 17, 1969; s. Janet Anne and Ronald K Smith. BA in Theater Arts, Whitman Coll., 1991; MFA in Directing and Acting, U. Mo., 1994. Author (director, playwright) various plays. Recipient various playwriting awards. Home: 1303 Monte Vista #8 Las Cruces NM 88001 Office: NMSU Theatre Arts PO Box 30001; MSC 3072 Las Cruces NM 88003-8001 Personal E-mail: kirbysr@hotmail.com. Business E-Mail: tomsmith@nmsu.edu.

SMITH, TOM W. surveyor, researcher; s. George Robert and Judy Anne Smith; m. Barbara Anne Pressler, June 28, 1969; children: Robert John, Mark William, Kimberly Anne. BA, Pa. State U., 1971, MA, 1972; PhD, U. Chgo., 1979. Gen. social survey dir. Nat. Opinion Rsch. Ctr., U. Chgo., 1980—. Contbr. articles to profl. jours. Mem.: World Assn. for Pub. Opinion Rsch.

(standards chair 2000—04), Am. Assn. for Pub. Opinion Rsch. (assoc. conf. chair 2003—). Office: Nat Opinion Rsch Ctr 1155 E 60th St Chicago IL 60637 Office Phone: 773-256-6288. Business E-Mail: smitht@norc.uchicago.edu.

SMITH, TOOTIE, state representative; m. Nate Smith; 1 child. AS, Mt. Hood C.C.; BS cum laude, Concordia Coll. State rep., dist. 28 Oreg. House Rep., Salem, 2001—03, state rep., dist. 18, 2003—; mng. ptnr. Rural Resources, Inc., Meadowbrook Hill Farm; libr. asst. Molalla Elem. Sch. Mem. com. Agr. and Forestry; vice chair Student Achievement and Sch. Accountability; mem. sub com. Ways and Means Edn. Office: 900 Court St NE H-290 Salem OR 97301

SMITH, TRINA, academic administrator; b. Rogersville, Ala., Sept. 18, 1971; d. Will Buford and Margaret Cannon Smith. BS, Athens State U., 1993; MS, U. Ala., Huntsville, 2000; M of Accountancy, U. Ala., 2001. Cert. Notary Pub. Br. ops. supr. Union Planters Bank, Athens, Ala., 1994—2000; acct. Calhoun Coll., Decatur, Ala., 2000—. Dir. Habitat for Humanity, Athens, 1994—2000; mem. adv. bd. Dogwood Festival Com., Athens, 1999. Vol. Jr. Achievement, Decatur, Ala., 1997—2000, Care Assurance Sys. for Aging and Homebound, Athens, 1995—99, Found. of Aging, Athens, 1999—2002. Recipient Outstanding Support award, Habitat for Humanity, 1996. Mem.: NAFE, NAACP, Am. Inst. of Cert. Pub. Accts., Nat. Assn. Black Accts., Am. Acctg. Assn., Am. Soc. Women Accts., Nat. Notary Assn., Inst. Mgmt. Accts. Baptist. Avocations: gardening, photography, collecting antiques, investments, outdoor activities. Home: 13708 Dart Cir Athens AL 35611 Office: Calhoun Cmty Coll Hwy 31 S Decatur AL 35609

SMITH, TROY ALVIN, aerospace research engineer; b. Sylvatus, Va., July 4, 1922; s. Wade Hampton and Augusta Mabel (Lindsey) S.; m. Grace Marie Peacock, Nov. 24, 1990. BCE, U. Va., 1948; MS in Engring., U. Mich., 1952, PhD, 1970. Registered profl. engr., Va., Ala. Structural engr. U.S. Army C.E., Norfolk, Va., Wilmington, N.C., Washington, 1948-59; chief structural engr. Brown Engring. Co., Inc., Huntsville, Ala., 1959-60; structural rsch. engr. U.S. Army Missile Command, Redstone Arsenal, Ala., 1960-63, aerospace engr., 1963-80, aerospace rsch. engr., 1980-96; engr. emeritus U.S. Army Aviation and Missile Command, Redstone Arsenal, Ala., 1996—. Contbr. articles AIAA Jour., Jour. Sound and Vibration, 14 major U.S. Army tech. reports on analysis of shells and other structures. With USNR, 1942-46, PTO. Fellow Dept. Army, 1969. Mem. N.Y. Acad. Scis., Assn. U.S. Army, Elks, Sigma Xi. Achievements include research on procedures for analysis of structures. Home: 2202 Yorkshire SE Decatur AL 35601-3470

SMITH, TURNER TALIAFERRO, JR., lawyer; b. Washington, Dec. 16, 1940; s. Turner Taliaferro and Lois (Fisk) S.; m. Christine H. Perdue; children: Turner T., III, John Webb Tyler. BA magna cum laude, Princeton U., 1962; LLB cum laude, Harvard U., 1968. Bar: Va. 1968, D.C. 1977. Ptnr. Hunton & Williams, Richmond, Va., 1975—; tchr. environ. law Washington and Lee U., 1978, Coll. William and Mary, 1979, 80, tchr. internat. environ. law, Geo. Mason Law Sch., 2004. Mem. ABA (chmn. standing com. environ. law 1983, 84, 85, chmn. corp., banking and bus. law sect. com. on environ. controls 1973-80), Va. Bar Assn. Office: Hunton & Williams 1900 K St NW 12 Fl Washington DC 20001 Office Phone: 202-955-1692. Business E-Mail: tsmith@hunton.com.

SMITH, V. KERRY, economics professor; b. Jersey City, Mar. 11, 1945; s. Vincent C. and Dorothy E. (Linehan) S.; m. Pauline Anne Taylor, May 10, 1969; children: Timothy, Shelley. AB, Rutgers U., 1966, PhD, 1970. Asst. prof., then assoc. prof. Bowling Green State U., Ohio, 1969-72; rsch. assoc. Resources for Future, Washington, 1971-73; assoc. prof. SUNY, Binghamton, 1973-75, prof., 1975-78; sr. fellow Resources for Future, Washington, 1976-79; prof. U. N.C., Chapel Hill, 1979-83; Centennial prof. Vanderbilt U., Nashville, 1983-87; Univ. Disting. prof. N.C. State U., 1987-94, univ. disting. prof., dir. Ctr. Environ. and Resource Econ. Policy, 1999—; Arts and Scis. prof. environ. econs. Duke U., 1994-99. Adviser energy div. Oak Ridge Nat. Lab., 1978-80, U. N.C. Inst. Environ. Studies, 1980-83; mem. panel NSF, 1981-83, sci. adv. bd. EPA. Author: Monte Carlo Methods, 1973, Technical Change, Relative Prices and Environmental Resource Evaluation, 1974, The costs of Congestion: An Econometric Analysis of Wilderness Recreation, 1976, Structure and Properties of a Wilderness Travel Simulator: An Application to the Spanish Peaks Area, 1976, The Economic Consequences of Air Pollution, 1976, Scarcity and Growth Reconsidered, 1979, (with others) Explorations in Natural Resource Economics, 1982, (with others) Environmental Policy Under Reagan's executive Order, 1984, (with W.H. Desvousges) Measuring Water Quality Benefits, 1986, (with others) Environmental Resources and Applied Welfare Economics, 1988, (with R.J. Kopp) Valuing Natural Assets: The Economics of Natural Resource Damage Assessment, Resources for the Future, 1993, Estimating Economic Values for Nature, 1996, (with others) The Smoking Puzzle: Information, Perception and Choices, 2003; editor Advances in Applied Micro Econs. series; contbr. numerous articles to profl. jours. Guggenheim fellow, 1976; grantee Resources for Future, 1970, 73, 74, 86, Fed. Energy Adminstrn. 1975, N.Y. Sea Grant Inst., 1975, Ford Found., 1976, NSF, 1977, 79, 83, Electric Power Rsch. Inst., 1978, Nat. Oceanic and Atmospheric Adminstrn., 1980, Sloan Found., 1981, 86, EPA, 1983-88, N.C. Sea Grant Program, 1987-93. Russell Sage Found., 1989-91; recipient Frederick V. Waugh medal Am. Agrl. Econ. Assn., 1992. Fellow Am. Agrl. and Econ. Assn.; mem. Am. Econ. Assn., Am. Statis. Assn., Econometric Soc., So. Econ. Assn. (exec. com. 1981-83, 1st v.p. 1987, pres. elect 1988, pres. 1989), Assn. Environ. and Resource Economists (bd. dirs. 1975-79, v.p. 1979-80, chmn. com. 1982-83, pres. 1985-86, Disting. Svc. award 1989). Business E-Mail: kerry.smith@ncsu.edu.

SMITH, VALENE SMITH, anthropologist, educator; b. Spokane, Wash., Feb. 14, 1926; d. Ernest Frank and Lucy (Blachly) S.; m. Edwin Chesteen Golay, June 7, 1970 (dec. June 1980); m. Stanley George McIntyre, Nov. 26, 1983 (dec. Oct. 2000). BA in Geography, U. Calif., 1946, MA in Geography, 1950; PhD in Anthropology, U. Utah, 1966. Cert. travel counselor. Prof. earth sci. L.A. City Coll., 1947-67; prof. anthropology Calif. State U., Chico, 1967—. Cons. World Tourism Orgn., Madrid, 1987. Editor: Hosts and Guests: The Anthrop. 1989, Tourism Alternatives: Potentials and Problems in the Development of Tourism, 1992, Hosts and Guests Revisited, 2001. Mem. Soroptimist Internat., Chico, 1968—; founding pres. Chico Mus. Assn., 1978. Named Fulbright prof., Peshawar, Pakistan, 1953—54; recipient Athena award, U.S. C. of C., 1988. Mem. Internat. Acad. for Study Tourism, Cert. Travel Counselors, Am. Anthrop. Assn., AAUW, Canyon Oaks Country Club, Soroptimists. Republican. Avocations: travel, aviation, photography. Office: U Calif Dept Anthropology Chico CA 95929-0004 Business E-Mail: vsmith@csuchico.edu.

SMITH, VAN P. holding company executive; b. Oneida, N.Y., Sept. 8, 1928; m. Margaret Ann Kennedy, Nov. 19, 1960; children: Lynn Ann Smith Walters, Mark Charles, Paul Gregory, Susan Colleen Smith Newell, Victor Patrick. AB in Pub. Adminstrn. and Econs., Colgate U., 1950; JD, Georgetown U., 1955; LLD (hon.), Ball State U., 1980; D of Bus. (hon.), Vincennes U., 1985; LLD (hon.), Ind. State U., 1986; LLD (hon.), Colgate U. Bar: D.C., Ind. Assoc. Warner, Clark & Warner, Muncie, Ind., 1955-56; co-founder, dir. Ontario Corp. of Muncie, 1956-63, sec. then v.p. sales, 1956-63, pres., CEO, 1963-97, also chmn. bd., 1978—. Chmn. bd. Ontario Corp. Found., all in Muncie, and other subs. Ontario Corp.; chmn. bd. Hoosier Motor Club, Indpls.; ptnr. Smittie's Men's Store, Village Developers, all in Muncie. Rep. mem. Ind. Ho. of Reps., 1960-62; del. Ind. and Nat. Rep. Conv.; pres. Muncie Police & Fire Commn., 1963-66; mem. parochial sch. bd. St. Mary's Sch., Muncie, 1968-70; mem. Ind. Employment Security Bd., 1969-71, Ind. Commn. Higher Edn., 1971-93, Nat. Adv. Council SBA, 1982-87, Gov.'s Fiscal Policy Adv. Council, 1982-87, Ind. Labor & Mgmt. Council, 1983-90, Ind. Econ. Devel. Council, 1985-90, Presdl. Observation Team Phillipine Nat. election, 1986, Presdl. Trade Mission to several Far Eastern countries, 1984; bd. dirs. Bus.-Industry Polit. Action Com., 1984-98; trustee Colgate U., 1985-96, chmn. emeritus; trustee La Lumiere Sch., 1983-87, Acad. for Community Leadership, 1975—; bd. dirs. Muncie Symphony Assn., 1980-88, pres. 1986-87; pres. Del. County United Way, 1969-70; bd. dirs. Newman Found. Ind., 1969-90, Religious Heritage Am. 1986-88; active St. Mary's Cath. Parish, Muncie; mem. Diocese of Lafayette Bishop's Com. 100, 1969-80, pres. 1969-70; bd. regents Cath. U. Am., Washington, 1986-90, trustee 1993-2003, vice chmn. bd., 2001-03; trustee Interlochen (Mich.) Ctr. for Arts, 1991—, vice chmn., 2001. Served 1st lt. USAF, 1951-53. Named one of Outstanding Young Men of Am., Jaycees, 1960; recipient Bus. and Layman award, Religious Heritage Am., 1984, Ind. Cath. Layman award, Faith, Family & Football of Ind., Inc. 1985, Civic Service award, Ind. Assn. Cities and Towns, 1985; invested Knight Comdr. of Equestrian Order of Holy Sepulchre of Jerusalem, 1986. Mem. ABA, Ind. Bar Assn., Ind. Mfrs. Assn. (chmn. 1978-80, bd. dirs. 1978—), Forging Industry Assn. (pres. 1976-77), Alliance of Metalworking Industries (chmn. 1978-80), U.S. C. of C. (chmn. numerous coms., active panels and councils 1977—), Ind. State C. of C. (exec. com. 1982—), Rotary (past pres.), Elks, K.C., Meridian Hills Country Club, Theta Chi (pres. Iota chpt. 1950), Delta Theta Phi, Beta Gamma Sigma (hon.), Delta Sigma Pi (hon.). Clubs: Columbia, Skyline (Indpls.); Ind. Soc. of Chgo. Office: 123 E Adams St Muncie IN 47305-2402

SMITH, VERNON G. education educator, state representative; b. Gary, Ind. BS, Ind. U., 1966, MS, 1969, EdD, 1978; postgrad., Ind.U.-Purdue U., 1986-90. Tchr. Gary Pub. Schs. Systems, 1966-71, resource tchr., 1971-72; asst. prin. Ivanhoe Sch., Gary, 1972-78; prin. Nobel Sch., Gary, 1978-85, Williams Sch., Gary, 1985-92; part-time counselor edn. div. Ind. U. N.W., Gary, 1967-69, adj. lectr., 1987-92, assoc. prof., 1992—; mem. Ind. Ho. of Reps., Indpls., 1990—. Columnist Gary Crusader, 1969-71; speaker Devel. Tng. Inst., 1986—. Author: (with D. McClam) Building Bridges Instead of Walls—History of I.U. Dons, Inc., 1979; also articles. Mem. Gary City Coun., 1972-90; precinct committeeman Gary Dem. Com., 1972-92; founder, chmn. Gary City-wide Festival Com.; bd. dirs. N.W. Ind. Urban League; founder, pres. I.U. Dons, Inc.; past pres. Gary Cmty. Mental Health Bd.; v.p. Gary Common Coun., 1982, 85-87, pres., 1976, 83-84, 88; past mem. bd. dirs. Little League World series; founder, past sponsor Youth Ensuring Solidarity, Young Citizens' League; chmn. Ind. Commn. on Status of Black Males, 1992—; mem. Gov.'s Commn. for Drug-Free Ind., 1990—. Recipient citation in edn. Gary NAACP, 1970, Good Govt. award Gary Jaycees, 1977, Outstanding Svc. award Gary Young Dems., 1979, Businessman of Yr. award Gary Downtown Mchts., 1979, Bd. Dirs. Svcs. award Gary Cmty. Health Ctr., 1982, G.O.I.C. Dr. Leon H. Sullivan award, 1982, Gary Jaycees Youth award, 1983, Info Newspaper Outstanding Citizen of N.W. Ind. and Info. Newspaper's Outstanding Educator award, 1984, Post Tribune Blaine Marz Tap award, 1984, Gary Cmty. Sch. Corp. Speech Dept. Recognition award, 1984, Gary Cmty. Mental Health Ctr.'s 10th Yr. Svc. award, 1985, Roosevelt H.S. Exemplary Svc. award, 1985, Gary Crusader 25th Anniversary award, 1986, Purdue U. Ednl. Opportunity Programs Black History Svc. award, 1986, Educator Par Excellence award Williams Sch., 1987, Black Woman Hall of Fame Found. Success award, 1987, Black Women Hall of Fame Bethune-Tubman-Truth award, 1987, Our Lady of Perpetual Help Ch. Hon. Mem. award, 1987, Gary Educator of Christ Adminstr. Leadership award, 1988, NBC-LEO Appreciation award, 1988, Gary Cmty. Schs. Presenters award, 1991, Mr. G.'s Svc. award, 1991, Appreciation award Ind. Assn. Chiefs Police, 1992, Meth. Hosp., 1992, Bros. Keeper, 1992, Svc. award Ind. Assn. Elem. and Mid. Sch. Prins., 1992, N.W. Ind. Black Expo's Sen. Carolyn Mosby Above and Beyond award, 1995, In the Bethune Tradition award Nat. Coun. Negro Women, 1996, Citizen Yr. award NASW (Ind. chpt.), 1997, 98, Appreciation award Ind. chpt., 1997, Presenters award, Gary Cmty. Sch. Corp. Parent Involvement Program, 1996, Appreciation award, Pitman Square Sch., 1997, 98, 99, Alumni Appreciation award, Froebel High Sch., 1997, 98, 2002, Svc. award, Ind. League Municipal Clerks and Treas., 1998, Facet Excellence in Tchg. award, 1998, Brothers Keeper Appreciation award, 1999, Appreciation award, Lake County Assn. for the Retarded, 1999, New Hope award, 1999, New Hope Men's Day award, 2000; featured cover story Big Brothers Big Sisters Am. Newsletter for Diversity, 2000, Appreciation award, Hoosier Boys Town, 2000, Appreciation award, Gary Reading Coun., 2000, Outstanding Commitment award, Nat. Assn. Social Workers Region I, 2000, Svc. award, Ivanhoe Sch., 2002, Drum Major award, Gary Frontiers, 2002, Majestic Star award, 2002, Appreciation award, City of Lake Station, 2002, New Hope African Am.- Frederic Douglas award, 2003. Mem.: NAACP (life Ovington award 1999), No. Ind. Assn. Black Sch. Educators (founder), Ind. Assn. Sch. Prins., Ind. U. N.W. Alumni Assn. (life Disting. Educator award 1992), Phi Delta Kappa (25 Yr. award (N.W. Ind. chpt.) 1996), Omega Psi Phi (life Omega Man Yr. award 1974, Citizen Yr. award 10th dist. 1989, appreciation award Omicron Rho chpt. 1991, Citizen Yr. award (Alpha Kappa Kappa chpt.) 2003, Man Yr. award (Alpha Kappa Kappa chpt.) 2003). Baptist. Home: PO Box M622 Gary IN 46401-0622 Office: Ind U NW 3400 Broadway # 339 Gary IN 46408-1101 Office Phone: 219-980-7120.

SMITH, VERNON LOMAX, economist, researcher; b. Wichita, Kans., Jan. 1, 1927; s. Vernon Chessman and Lula Belle (Lomax) S.; m. Candace C. Allen, Mar. 13, 2002. BSEE, Calif. Inst. Tech., 1949; MA in Econs., U. Kans., 1952; PhD in Econs., Harvard U., 1955; D of Mgmt. (hon.), Purdue U., 1990. Asst. prof. econs. Purdue U., West Lafayette, Ind., 1955-58, assoc. prof., 1958-61, prof., 1961-65, Krannert prof., 1965-67; prof. Brown U., Providence, 1967-68, U. Mass., Amherst, 1968-75, U. Ariz., Tucson, 1975—2001, Regents' prof., 1988—2001; prof. econs. & law George Mason U., 2001—. Contbr. articles to profl. jours. Fellow Ctr. for Advanced Study in Behavioral Scis., Stanford, Calif., 1972-73; Sherman Fairchild Disting. Scholar Calif. Inst. Tech., Pasadena, 1973-74; adj. scholar CATO Inst., Washington, 1983—; recipient Nobel prize in econs., 2002. Fellow AAAS, Am. Acad. Arts and Scis., Econometric Soc., Am. Econ. Assn. (Disting. fellow); mem. NAS, Pvt. Enterprise Edn. Assn. (Adam Smith award). Office: George Mason U Interdisc Ctr for Econ Sci 4400 University Blvd MSN 1B2 Fairfax VA 22030

SMITH, VERONICA LATTA, real estate corporation officer; b. Wyandotte, Mich., Jan. 13, 1925; d. Jan August and Helena (Hulak) Latta; m. Stewart Gene Smith, Apr. 12, 1952; children: Stewart Gregory, Patrick Allen, Paul Donald, Alison Veronica Hurley, Alisa Margaret Lyons, Glenn Laurence. BA in Sociology, postgrad., U. Mich., 1948. Tchr. Coral Gables (Fla.) Pub. Sch. Sys., 1949—50; COO Latta Ins. Agy, Wyandotte, 1950—62; treas. L & S Devel. Co., Grosse Ile, Mich., 1963—84; v.p. Regency Devel., Riverview, Mich., 1984—. Active U. Mich. Bd. Regents, 1985-92, regent emeritus, 1993—; mem. Martha Cook Bd. Govs., U. Mich., pres., 1976-78; del. Rep. County Conv., Grand Rapids, Mich., 1985, 87, 89, 91, 92, 94, 96, Lansing, Mich., 1996, Detroit, 1986, 88, 90, 92, 97; mem. pres. adv. com. Campaign for Mich., 1992-97, mem. campaign steering com., 1992-97. Mem. Mich. Lawyers Aux. (treas. 1975, chmn. 1976, 77, 78, 79), Nat. Assn. Ins. Women (cert.), Faculty Women's Club U. Mich. (hon.), Radrick Farms Golf Club (Ann Arbor), Pres.'s Club U. Mich., Investment Club (pres. 1976, sec. 1974-75, treas. 1975-76), Alpha Kappa Delta. Home: 22225 Balmoral Dr Grosse Ile MI 48138-1403

SMITH, VIN, sports editor, business owner, novelist; b. Whittier, Calif., May 19, 1944; s. M. Clifford and Anna Eugenia (Hill) S.; m. Marthea Karen Callaham, May 15, 1969 (div. 1979); children: Jayare Smith, Eric Smith; m. Ginger Hammon, Oct. 20, 1984; children: Amy Michelle, Stacey Erin, Kellie Rae. Student, Columbia Sch. Broadcasting, San Francisco, 1967; AA, Cuesta Coll., 1974; grad., Am. Sch. of Piano Tuning, 1978. Sales mgr. Sta. KTAT, Frederick, Okla., 1967-69; announcer KOCY, Oklahoma City, 1969; owner Melmart Markets, San Luis Obispo, Calif., 1971-73, Am. Direct Sales, Grover City, Calif., 1973-79; instr. piano Valley View Acad., Arroyo Grande, Calif., 1977-78, Long Piano Co., San Luis Obispo, 1977-79, piano technician, 1978-79; owner Chocolate Piano, Yreka, Calif., 1979—; instr. piano Makah Indian Tribe, Neah Bay, Wash., 1981-82; sports editor New Words Digest, Bakersfield, Calif., 1988—. Cons., stress evaluator seminar Yreka Stress Therapy Clinic, 1986-87; founder Vinco Distbrs. (formerly Vinco Enhancement Sys.), 1998; chair piano dept. Bogus Sch., 1999—, internat. relationship counselor Ask Me com., 2000-03, askdrpiano.com., 2000. Author: (novel) Neon Streets, 2002, Lincoln Park, 2003, Ride the High Waves, 2003; sports columnist New Words Digest, 1987-91; guest columnist Siskiyou Daily News, 1991-94; nat publicist chamber music concerts So. Oreg. State Coll., 1993—; host (TV Show) Vin and Friend, 2003—; contbr. articles to profl. jours. Chmn. heart fund Tillman County Okla., 1968; pub. co-chmn. Siskiyou County No-Prop 174, 1994; campaign worker Ken Jourdan for sheriff, Yreka, 1986; publicity dir. Gene Breceda for supr., 1993-94. Recipient Cert. of Appreciation, Siskiyou County, 1988, Achievement award, 1988, Golden Poet award World of Poetry, 1989, Living Treasure award Siskiyou County, 2003. Mem. Nat. Writers Club (chmn. student com. Yreka chpt. 1988), Author's Guild, Inc., Author's League of Am., Mystery Writers Am., Soc. Children's Book Writers, Jr. C. of C. (sgt.-at-arms Frederick chpt. 1967-69), Kiwanis, Moose. Avocations: horse shoe pitching, photography, reading. Home: 710 Knapp St Yreka CA 96097-2343 Office: Chocolate Piano Svcs PO Box 447 Yreka CA 96097-0447 E-mail: drpiano@earthlink.net.

SMITH, VINCENT C. information technology executive; married; 2 children. Bachelor, U. Del. Sales mgr. Oracle Corp., 1987—92; co-founder, v.p. Worldwide Sales and Mktg., Patrol Software N.Am., 1992—94; dir. open systems BMC Software, 1994; dir. Quest Software, Irvine, Calif., 1995—, CEO, 1997—, chmn. bd., 1998—. Dir. Emergent Info. Techs., Inc. Office: Quest Software 8001 Irvine Center Dr Irvine CA 92618

SMITH, VINCENT MILTON, lawyer, designer, Feng Shui lecturer, consultant, writer; b. Barbourville, Ky., Nov. 21, 1940; s. Virgil Milton and Louis (McGalliard) Smith; children: Jessica Todd, Duncan. BA, Harvard U., 1962; LLB, Yale U., 1965. Bar: N.Y. 1966. Assoc. Breed, Abbott & Morgan, N.Y.C., 1965-70, Debevoise & Plimpton, N.Y.C., 1970-75, ptnr., 1975-95; CEO Lang, Winslow & Smith Co., Chatham, N.J., 1995-98; owner The VMS Feng Shui Design Co., 1998—, Panergetics, LLC, 2002. Mem. adv. bd. Chgo. Title Ins. Co., N.Y.C., 1979—2002; vis. Feng Shui prof. Berea (Ky.) Coll., 1999, Williams Coll., Williamstown, Mass., 2001—02; Feng Shui lectr. N.Y. Open Ctr., 1999—; co-founder, chmn. bd. Keen Co., 2000—. Trustee Chatham Players, N.J., 1967-77, 87-91, Summit Friends Meeting, Chatham, 1973-99, N.J. Shakespeare Festival, Madison, 1975-80, Playwrights Theatre N.J., 1989-91. Mem.: Harvard, N.Y. Athletic. Mem. Soc. Of Friends. Office: Debevoise & Plimpton 875 3rd Ave Fl 23 New York NY 10022-6225 E-mail: vmsdesign@aol.com.

SMITH, VIRGIL BAKER, retired electrical engineer; b. Bastrop, La., Oct. 13, 1916; s. George and Virginia (Mallette) Smith; m. Phyllis Patterson, Nov. 10, 1945; children: Nancy E., Patricia A., Randall T. BSEE, La. State U., Baton Rouge, 1935-39. Supr., elec. engr. USN, Washington, 1941-77, ret., 1977; sr. elec. engr. George G. Sharp Inc., Arlington, Va., 1981-82, Sys. & Applied Sci. Corp., Arlington, 1982-85, Designers & Planners, Arlington, 1985-91; ret., 1991. Contbr. articles to profl. jours. Com. chmn. Indian Guides Boy Scouts Am., Four Corners, Md., 1949; trustee elem. sch., Four Corners, 1950. Recipient Superior Civilian Svc. award, USN, 1978, Spl. Achievement award, 1975.

SMITH, VME EDOM (VERNA MAE EDOM SMITH), sociology educator, freelance writer, photographer; b. Marshfield, Wis., June 19, 1929; d. Clifton Cedric and Vilia Clarissa (Patefield) Edom; children: Teri Smith Freas, Anthony Thomas. AB in Sociology, U. Mo., 1951; MA in Sociology, George Washington, 1965; PhD in Human Devel., U. Md., 1981. Tchr. Alcohol Safety Action Program Fairfax County, Va., 1973-75; instr. sociology No. Va. C.C., Manassas, 1975-77, asst. prof., 1977-81, assoc. prof., 1981-84, prof., 1984-94, prof. emerita, 1995, coord. coop. edn., 1983-89, Chancellor's Commonwealth prof., 1991-93; adj. faculty Tidewater C.C., 1996—; freelance writer, editor and photographer, 1965—; dir. Clifton C. Edom Truth With a Camera (photography workshops), 1994—. Asst. prodr. history of photography program Sta. WETA-TV, Washington, 1965; rsch. and prodn. asst., photographer, publs. editor No. Va. Ednl. TV, Sta. WNVT, 1970—71; cons. migrant divsn. Md. Dept. Edn., Balt., 1977; rschr. photographer Roundabout presch. high sch. series Am. Values Sta. WNVT, 1970—71; documentary photographer Portsmouth (Va.) Redevel. and Housing Authority, 1998—2000. Author, photographer: Middleburg and Nearby, 1986; co-author: Small Town America, 1993; contbr. photography to various works including Visual Impact in Print (Hurley and McDougall), 1971, Looking Forward to a Career in Education (Moses), 1976, Child Growth and Development (Terry, Sorrentino and Flatter), 1979, Photojournalism (Edom), 1976, 80, Migrant Child Welfare, 1977, (Cavenaugh), Caring for Children, 1973 (5 publs. by L.B. Murphy), Dept. Health, Edn. and Welfare, Nat. Geog., 1961, Head Start Newsletter, 1973-74, Women in Photojournalism, Nat. Press Photographers Assn., Nat. Fedn. Press Women, Photographic Soc. Am., Va. Found. for Humanities and Pub. Policy exhibits. Mem. ednl. adv. com. Head Start, Warrenton, Va. Recipient Emmy, Ohio State Children's Programming award; Fulbright-Hays rsch. grantee, 1993, Va. Found. for Humanities and Pub. Policy grantee, 1997-99. Mem. Va. Assn. Coop. Edn. (com. mem.). Democrat. E-mail: vme@macs.net.

SMITH, W. PRESTON, publishing executive, educator, real estate broker; b. Little Rock, Oct. 30, 1938; s. Arthur W. and Syble M. Smith; children: Cynthia Ann Smith Jones, Carey R. BS, Little Rock U., 1959; postgrad., Henderson State U., Arkadelphia, Ark., 1968-69, Ark. State U., 1969, Texarkana Coll., 1981-82, U. Ark., Pine Bluff, 1983, Tulane U., Miss. County C.C., 1985; MEd, U. Ark., 1984. Cert. sch. adminstr., social studies tchr., Laubach reading instr. Tchr. math. and social studies 4th St. Jr. H.S., North Little Rock, 1959-61; owner Walker Enterprises, Hot Springs Village, Ark., 1964—; tchr. Malvern (Ark.) Pub. Schs., 1967-68, Prattsville (Ark.) H.S., 1968-69, Poyen (Ark.) H.S., 1969-70, Horatio (Ark.) H.S., 1981-82, Bingham Rd. Acad., Little Rock, 1982-83, Luxora (Ark.) H.S., 1985, Stanton Rd. Sch., Little Rock, 1986; tchr., prin. Dept. Correction Sch. Dist., Ark., 1989-95; ret., 1995. Mem. sci. textbook selection com., Prattsville H.S., 1968-69; mem. math. stds. com. Ark. Coun. Tchrs. Math., Little Rock, 1983; lectr. Zero Down seminars on creative real estate financing; owner Silver Dollar Press Inc. Author, pub.: Jokebook of the Century, 1989; author: Jokebook of the Century, vol. II, 1990, vol. III, 1991, How To Start Your Own Business, 1992, Forms For Business, vol. I and II, 1995, Consumers Should Know, vols. I-IV, 1996, vols. V-IX, 1997, How to Adjust and Repair Your Sewing Machine, Jokebook of the Century, Vol 4, Color A Laugh! Create a Colorful Comic, 2003, vol. I-II, The Spirit Tales of Silver Wolf and His People, 2003, The Adventures of Jake Hardy and His Friends, Vol. 1, 2004. Past pres., song leader Sunday Sch. class; former mem. Ch. choir. Mem. AARP (past pres. England, Ark. chpt., chpt. specialist), Ark. Assn. Ednl. Adminstrn. (assoc.), Ark. Ret. Tchr. Assn. (state membership chmn. 1998-2001), Lonoke County Ret. Tchr. Assn. (pres. 1997-2000). Lodges: Order of DeMolay (master councillor). Avocations: candlemaking, refinishing furniture, tape recording classical music. Home and Office: Po Box 8394 Hot Springs Village AR 71910-8394

SMITH, W. STUART, strategic planning director; b. Binghamton, N.Y., May 2, 1943; married. B, Washington & Lee U., 1965; M, Mich. State U., 1967, Va. Commonwealth U., 1974. Adminstrv. resident MUSC Med. Ctr., Charleston, S.C., 1973-74, asst. dir., 1974-79, assoc. dir., 1979-83, dir. ops., 1983-87, dir. mktg., 1987-92, exec. dir., 1993-94, dir. strategic planning, 1994—, interim v.p. clin. ops., 1997-98, CEO, 1997-98, v.p. clin. ops., 1999—, exec. dir., 1999—. Mem. S.C. Hosp. Assn. (bd. dirs.). Office: Med U SC 171 Ashley Ave Charleston SC 29425-0100

SMITH, WALTER JOHN, lawyer; b. Omaha, Apr. 19, 1948; s. Walter H. and Margaret A. (Ortman) S.; m. Mary Lou Dreves, June 20, 1970; children: Benjamin, Michael, Jeffrey. JD, Creighton U., 1972; LLM, Harvard U., 1975. Bar: Nebr. 1972, Tex. 1975. Law clk. to Judge E.A. Tamm U.S. Ct. Appeals (D.C. cir.), 1972-73; mem. Monen, Seidler, McGill, Festerson & Koley, Omaha, 1973-74; mem., then sr. ptnr. Baker & Botts, Houston, 1975—. Bd. dirs. Reprogenesis, Cambridge, Mass. Mem. Houston Club. Office: Baker & Botts 3000 One Shell Plz 1200 Smith St Ste 1200 Houston TX 77002-4592

SMITH, WALTON NAPIER, lawyer; b. Macon, Georgia, Feb. 26, 1942; s. Robert Monroe and Marion Rose (Napier) S.; m. Susan Rush (Baum), Oct. 10, 1970; children: Rush Hendley, Berkeley Bosman. BA, Dartmouth Coll., 1964; JD, Harvard U., 1967. Bar: Ga., 1966; D.C., 1972; Ill., 1978; U.S. Supreme Ct., 1971. Counsel Nat. R.R. Passenger Corp., Washington, 1971-75; assoc. Lord, Bissell, and Brook, Washington and Chgo., 1975-79, ptnr. Chgo. and Atlanta, 1980—2004. Sec. Brit. Am. Bus. Group. Mem. bd. America's Watershed Land Keeper. Capt. JAGC U.S. Army, 1964—71. Decorated

Bronze Star, Army Commendation Medal. Mem. ABA, State Bar Ga., Nat. Assn. R.R. Trial Counsel. Democrat. Episcopalian. Office: The Proscenium 1170 Peachtree St Ste 1900 Atlanta GA 30309 E-mail: wsmith@lordbissell.com.

SMITH, WARREN ALLEN, writer; b. Minburn, Iowa, Oct. 27, 1921; s. Harry Clark and Ruth Marion (Miles) S. BA, U. No. Iowa, 1948; MA, Columbia U., 1949. Chmn. dept. Eng. Bentley Sch., N.Y.C., 1949-54, New Canaan (Conn.) H.S., 1954-86; founder, pres., chmn. bd. Variety Sound Corp., N.Y.C., 1961-90; pres. Afro-Carib Records, 1971-90, Talent Mgmt., 1982-90, AAA Rec. Studio, 1985-90; founder, pres. Variety Rec. Studio, 1961-96. Instr. Columbia U., 1961-62. Author: Who's Who in Hell, 2000, Celebrities in Hell, 2002; book rev. editor: The Humanist, 1953—58; editor: (jour.) Taking Stock, 1967—93, Pique, 1990—93, Van Rijn's Pad, 1991, Janestreeter, 1997—98; contbr. book revs. Libr. Jour.; editl. assoc.: Free Inquiry, 1992—2000, columnist: G & L Humanist, 1996—, syndicated columnist: Manhattan Scene in W.I. newspapers; syndicated columnist Humanist Potpourri in Free Inquiry, 1994—98; drama critic: Brontë Newsletter, 1995—2000, book reviewer: New Humanist, 1997—2000, CD prodr.: Manuel Salazar: Costa Rica's Forgotten Tenor, writer: The Villager, 2002—. Pres. Taursa Fund, 1971-73; bd. dirs. Jane Street Corp. Treas. Secular Humanist Soc. N.Y., 1988-93; sec. Jane St. Corp., 1995-97, 98-99; with Jane Street Authors, 2000—; with ACT UP, Hume Soc.; founding mem. Voltaire Soc. Am. With AUS, 1942-46; signer Humanist Manifesto II, 1973, Humanist Manifesto, 2000, Humanist Manifesto III, 2003. Recipient Leavey award Freedoms Found. at Valley Forge, 1985. Mem.: ASCAP, N.Y. Soc. Ethical Culture, Bertrand Rusell Soc. (bd. dirs. 1973—, v.p. 1977—80), Brit. Humanist Assn., Conn. Edn. Assn., Rationalist Press Assn., Am. Unitarian Assn., Internat. Press Inst., N.Y. Skeptics Soc. (bd. dirs. 1990—94), Asociación Iberoamericana Ético Humanista (hon.), Stonewall Vets. Orgn. (treas. 1998—99), Omaha Beach Vets. Assn., Mensa, Mensa Investment Club (chmn. 1967—2001), Humanist Book Club (pres. 1957—62). Avocation: teratology. Home and Office: 31 Jane St Apt 10 D New York NY 10014-1980 E-mail: wasm@mac.com.

SMITH, WARREN JAMES, optical scientist, consultant, lecturer, author; b. Rochester, N.Y., Aug. 17, 1922; s. Warren Abrams and Jessie Madelyn (Forshay) S.; m. Mary Helen Geddes, May 18, 1944 (dec. 1999); children: David Whitney, Barbara Jamie; m. Dung My Luong, Dec. 24, 2000. BS, U. Rochester, 1944; postgrad., U. Calif., Santa Barbara, 1960. Physicist Clinton Engr. Works, Tenn. Eastman Co., Oak Ridge, 1944-46; chief optical engr. Simpson Optical Mfg. Co., Chgo., 1946-59; mgr. optical sect. Raytheon Corp., Santa Barbara, 1959-62; v.p. R & D, Infrared Industries, Santa Barbara, 1962-87; chief scientist Kaiser Electro-Optics, Inc., Carlsbad, Calif., 1987—. Lectr. U. Wis., Madison, 1972—, Genesee Computer Ctr., Rochester, 1982—93, U. Rochester, 1988—92, Sinclair Optics, 1994—2000; cons. in field; expert witness. Author: Modern Optical Engineering, 1966, 3d edit., 2000, Modern Lens Design, 1992, 2nd edit., 2004, Practical Optical System Layout, 1997; editor McGraw-Hill series Optical and Electro-Optical Engineering; also articles. Fellow: Optical Soc. Am. (nat. pres. 1980, organizer, chmn. tech. confs., Fraunhofer medal 2001), Internat. Soc. Optical Engring. (life; nat. pres. 1983, organizer, chmn. tech. confs., Gold medal 1985, Dirs. award 1992), Sigma Chi. Avocations: tennis, sailing. Home: 1165 Countrywood Ln Vista CA 92081-5334 Office: Kaiser Electro Optics Inc 2752 Loker Ave W Carlsbad CA 92008-6603 Office Phone: 760-438-9255 x 234. E-mail: wsmith@keo.com.

SMITH, WAYNE ALAN, state legislator, financial executive; b. Wilmington, Del., Aug. 23, 1962; s. Wayne Sylvanus and Carlene (List) S.; m. Lisa Kay Schmidinger, Feb. 9, 1991. BS, U. Del., 1984; M in Govt. Adminstrn., MA, U. Pa., 1988. Supr. Beneficial Nat. Bank, USA, Wilmington, Del., 1984-86; asst. v.p. Newbold's/Am. Capital Group, Phila., 1988-89; investment banker Janney Montgomery Scott, Inc., Phila., 1989-91; CFO George & Lynch, Inc., New Castle, Del., 1991—, also bd. dirs.; mem. Del. Ho. of Reps., Dover, 1990, 92—, chmn. revenue and fin. com., 1990—. Lectr. govt. U. Pa., Phila., 1989-91. Republican. Methodist. Avocations: reading, history buff.

SMITH, WAYNE CALVIN, chemical engineer, consultant; b. Beaver, Okla., Mar. 19, 1935; s. Dean C. and Loraine S.; m. Suellyn Joyce Canon, Aug. 18, 1984. BS, Okla. U., 1958, MSChemE, 1964; PhDChemE, Colo. U., 1974. Registered profl. engr., Tex., Okla., Colo.; cert. emergency response specialist. Process engr. Shell Oil Co., Deer Park, Tex., 1958-59; sr. devel. engr. Monsanto, Pensacola, Fla., 1965-66; project leader Phillips Petroleum Co., Bartlesville, Okla., 1967-69; acting chief process control EPA Nat. Enforcement Investigations Ctr., Denver, 1971-78; firm wide mgr. pollution control Dames & Moore, Golden, Colo., 1978-81; regional mgr. Hittman Assocs., Englewood, Colo., 1981-82; pres. Encon Environs Control Svcs., Golden, Colo., 1982-83; chief hazardous waste mgmt. Woodword-Clyde Cons., Englewood, 1983-84; exec. cons. Kellogg Corp., Littleton, Colo., 1984-86; program mgr. Radian Corp., Austin, Tex., 1986-93; prin. engr., program mgr. Tetra Tech, Inc., Oklahoma City, 1993—2003; project mgr. FPM Group Ltd., Midwest City, Okla., 2003—04. Contbr. over 30 articles to profl. jours. Capt. USMC, 1959-62. Scholar Magnolia Petroleum Co., 1956-58; fellow Phillips Petroleum Co., 1962-64, Marathon Oil Co., 1966-67, Gulf Oil Co., 1969-71. Mem. AIChE, Am. Arbitration Assn., The Greens Country Club, Sigma Xi. Baptist. Avocations: golf, woodworking. E-mail: wcssjs@sbcglobal.net.

SMITH, WAYNE RICHARD, lawyer; b. Petoskey, Mich., Apr. 30, 1934; s. Wayne Anson and Frances Lynetta (Cooper) S.; m. Carrie J. Swanson, June 13, 1959; children: Stephen, Douglas (dec.), Rebecca. AB, U. Mich., 1956, JD, 1959. Bar: Mich. 1959. Asst. atty. gen. State of Mich., 1960-62; pros. atty. Emmet County (Mich.), 1963-68; dist. judge 90th Jud. Dist., Mich., 1969-72; city atty. City of Petoskey, 1976-98. Trustee North Central Mich. Coll., 1981-98, chmn., 1992-97; trustee/chmn. N. Ctrl. Mich. Coll. Found., 1999—; mem. No. Mich. Community Mental Health Bd., 1972-92, chmn., 1979-81. Mem. Emmet-Charlevoix Bar Assn. (pres. 1967), State Bar Mich., Mich. State Bar Found. Presbyterian. Home and Office: 365 E Main St PO Box 4677 Harbor Springs MI 49740-4677

SMITH, WAYNE THOMAS, healthcare company executive; b. Jan. 29, 1946; BS, Auburn Univ, 1968, MS, 1969; M in hosp. adminstrn., Trinity U.; postgrad., King's Fund Coll. Hosp. Adminstrn. With Trinity Univ, 1971-73, Humana Inc, Louisville, 1973-96, v.p. ctrl. hosp. region, 1978-80, sr. v.p., 1980-85, exec. v.p., 1985-86, pres., COO group health divsn., 1986-96, also bd. dirs.; exec. v.p. Humana Health Care Ops., Louisville, 1991-96; ret. Humana Inc., 1996; pres., CEO, Cmty. Health Sys., Brentwood, Tenn., 1996—, chmn. bd., 2001—. Exec. v.p. health plan ops., bd. dirs. Humana Health Plan, Inc., Louisville; pres. Humana Health Ins. Nev., Inc., Humana Health Plan Fla., Inc., Humana Health Plan Ohio, Inc., Humana Health Chgo. Ins. Co., Humana Kansas City, Inc.; pres., COO Humana Health Plan Tex., Prime Health Mgmt. Svcs.; pres., bd. dirs. HMPK, Inc.; bd. dirs. Praxair, Inc.; chmn. bd. Fedn. Am.'s Hosps. Bd. dirs. Gov.'s Scholars Program, Ky., Actors Theatre of Louisville, Ky. Ctr. for the Arts, The Louisville Orchestra; bd. overseers U. Louisville; mem. exec. com. Greater Louisville Fund for the Arts; past chair bd. dirs. Louisville Collegiate Sch. With U.S. Army, 1969-73, capt., 1973. Mem. Group Health Assn. Am. (bd. dirs.), Health Ins. Assn. Am. (bd. dirs.). Office: Community Health Systems 155 Franklin Rd Ste 400 Brentwood TN 37027-4646

SMITH, WENDY HAIMES, federal agency administrator; b. Tex. m. Jay L. Smith. BA in Econs., U. Mich.; postgrad., Ohio State U., Am. U., Washington Studio Sch., Aspen Inst., Wye, Md., 1997. Cert. real estate agt. Office mgr. Haimes Travel Agy., Ohio, 1972-73; mgmt. intern US Dept. Commerce, 1973-75, country specialist for Korea, 1973, spl. asst. to dep. asst. sec. for internat. commerce, 1973-74, project officer, maj. projects divsn., 1974-75, project mgr. indsl. sys., maj. projects divsn., 1975-77, country specialist for Brazil, 1978, project mgr., hydrocarbons and chem. process plants, maj. export projects divsn., 1977-79, exec. asst. to dep. asst. sec. of commerce for export devel. and staff dir. Pres. Export Coun., 1979-81, dir. Pres. Export Coun., 1981-92, acting dir. Office Planning and Coordination, 1988-89, dir. adv. coms. and pvt. sector programs Internat. Trade Adminstrn., 1992-97; dir. Trade Info. Ctr., Wash., DC, 1997—, acting dir. office of export promotion, 1999, 2000-01; acting dir. Office Expert Assistance and Bus. Outreach, 2003—. Author, editor US Trade in Transition: Maintaining the Gains, 1988, co-author, editor The Export Imperative, 1980, Coping with the Dynamics of World Trade in the 1980s, 1984; Exhibited in group shows at Courtyard Gallery, Brian Logan Artspace, Artists Mus., Washington, Designer's Art Gallery, Bethesda, Md., one-woman shows include Courtyard Gallery, Washington, 2001. Active Art League, Smithsonian Instn., Washington Opera Guild; bd. dir. Washington Studio Sch; one man show Courtyard Gallery, 2001.

SMITH, WENDY HOPE, lawyer; b. N.Y.C., Jan. 19, 1957; d. Morton and Doris Smith. AB, Smith Coll., 1978; JD, Boston U., 1981. Bar: N.J. 1981, U.S. Dist. Ct. 1981, U.S. Ct. Appeals (3d cir.), Supreme Ct. U.S. Law sec. to judge Superior Ct. N.J., Bergen County, 1981-82; assoc. firm Sellar, Richardson, Stuart & Chisholm, Roseland, N.J., 1982-89, ptnr., 1989-97, Sellar Richardson, P.C., 1997-2000, Marshall, Dennehey, Warner, Coleman & Goggin, Roseland, N.J., 2000—. Mem. adv. com. Inst. CLE, 1983-91. Mem. ABA, N.J. Bar Assn., Bergen County Bar Assn., Essex County Bar Assn., Mensa, Smith Coll. Alumnae Assn. (fund rep. 1978-83). Home: 401 Hancock Ct Edgewater NJ 07020-1627 Office: Marshall Dennehey Warner Coleman & Goggin 425 Eagle Rock Ave Ste 302 Roseland NJ 07068 Office Phone: 973-618-4100.

SMITH, WENDY L. foundation executive; b. Chgo., Sept. 12, 1950; d. John Arthur and Dolores Mae (Webb) Rothenberger; m. Alan Richard Smith; children: Angela Fuhs, Erica Smith. Ed., Oakton C.C., Des Plaines, Ill., 1986, Mundelein Coll., 1990. Purchasing clk. AIT Industries, Skokie, Ill., 1975-76; purchasing agt. MCC Powers, Skokie, 1976-78; office mgr. Spartan Engring., Skokie, 1978-80, Brunswick Corp., Skokie, 1980—; successively sr. sec., coord. indsl. rels., dir. Brunswick Found., Lake Forest, Ill., 1982-89, pres., 1989—. Asst. sec. Brunswick Pub. Charitable Found., Lake Forest, 1989—; mem. adv. com. Found. for Ind. Higher Edn., Stamford, Conn., 1989—, Coun. Better Bus. Burs., Arlington, Va., 1988-90; bd. dirs. Associated Colls. of Ill., 1991—; bd. dirs., mem. trustees com., mem. compensation and benefits com. Donors Forum of Chgo., 1988-93. Bd. dirs. INROADS/Chgo., Inc., 1994—; mem. steering com. Dist. 57 Edn. Found., Mt. Prospect, Ill., 1996—. Recipient Pvt. Sector Initiative Commendation, U.S. Pres., 1987-89. Mem. Donors Forum Chgo. (treas. 1988-91, bd. dirs., mem. exec. com., chairperson audit and fin. com., mem. trustees com. 1992—), Coun. on Founds., Ind. Sector Suburban Contbns. Network (chairperson 1987-89), Women in Philanthropy Corp. Founds. (mem. cmty. rels. com. 1985-87), Chgo. Women in Philanthropy. Avocations: antique restoration, pleasure reading, bowling, golf.

SMITH, WILBUR LAZAR, radiologist, educator; b. Warwick, N.Y., Oct. 11, 1943; s. Wilbur and Betty (Norris) S.; m. Rebecca Rowlands, June 19, 1965; children: Jason, Daniel, Joanna, Noah, Ethan, Jacob. BA, SUNY, Buffalo, 1965, MD, 1969. Diplomate Am. Bd. Radiology, Am. Bd. Pediat., Am. Bd. Pediatric Radiology. Intern, then resident Buffalo Children's Hosp., 1969-71; resident in pediatric radiology Cin. Gen. and Children's Hosp., 1971-74; asst. prof. pediatrics and radiology Ind. U., Indpls., 1975-78, assoc. prof., 1978-80, acting dir. pediatric radiology, 1979-80; assoc. prof. U. Iowa, Iowa City, 1980-82, prof., 1982—, dir. med. edn. in radiology, 1980-86, vice chmn. dept. radiology, 1986-94, interim head, 1994-96, dir. pediatric radiology, 1980-92; chmn. dept. radiology Henry Ford Health Sys., Detroit, 1998-99; prof. radiology Wayne State U., Detroit, 2000—, chmn. dept. radiology, 2002—; staff radiologist Mich. Children's Hosp., Detroit, 2000—. Vice chmn. radiology for academics Wayne State U., 2001, radiology residency dir., 01, prof., chmn. dept. radiology, 2002—. Assoc. editor Gastrointestinal Imaging in Pediatrics, Acad. Radiology, 1992—, Radiology 101; exec. assoc. editor Acad. Radiology, 1997-2000, assoc. editor, 2000—; contbr. articles to profl. jours. Mem. equity adv. com. Iowa City Sch. Bd., 1983-87. Served with USAR, 1969-77. Fellow Am. Acad. Pediatrics, Am. Coll. Radiology; mem. AMA, Radiol. Soc. N.Am., Iowa Radiol. Soc. (pres. 1987-88), Assn. Univ. Radiologists (pres. 1995-96), Soc. Pediat. Radiology (treas. 1995-98, rep. coun. Acad. Socs. of AAMC 1996-2002). Mem. Soc. Of Friends. Avocation: photography. Home: 10124 Lasalle Blvd Huntington Woods MI 48070-1162 Office: Detroit Receiving Hosp Dept Radiology (3L8) 4201 St Antoine Detroit MI 48201 Office Phone: 313-745-4443. Business E-Mail: wlsmith@med.wayne.edu.

SMITH, WILBURN JACKSON, JR., retired bank executive; b. Charlotte, N.C., June 13, 1921; s. Wilburn Jackson and Banna (Oswalt) S.; m. Terry Mosteller, Jan. 4, 1944; children: Kenneth M., M. Scott (dec.), Wilburn Jackson III, Curtis Todd. BS in Acctg., U. N.C., 1943; postgrad. in comml. banking, Rutgers U. Sch. Banking, 1953, postgrad. in investment banking, 1956. With First Union Nat. Bank, Charlotte, 1946-74, exec. v.p., 1960-67, 1st exec. v.p., 1967-74; pres., mng. trustee Cameron-Brown Investment Group, Raleigh, N.C., 1974-78; chmn. loan policy com. N.C. Nat. Bank, Charlotte, 1979-88. Cons. in field. Served with USN, 1943-46. Recipient Citizenship award Charlotte Civitan, 1972. Mem. Robert Morris Assocs., Myers Park Country Club (Charlotte). Baptist. Home: WJS Finan Svcs Inc c/o Wilburn Jackson Smith Jr 2222 Selwyn Ave #404 Charlotte NC 28207-2779

SMITH, WILL, actor, rap artist; b. Phila., Sept. 25, 1968; s. Caroline and Willard Smith; m. Sheree Smith, 1992 (div. 1995); 1 child, Willard III; m. Jada Pinkett Smith, 1997; children: Jaden Christopher Syre, Willow Camille Reign. Albums (as The Fresh Prince with DJ Jazzy Jeff): And in this Corner..., 1989, Homebase, 1991, Rock the House, 1987, He's the DJ, I'm the Rapper, 1988, Code Red, 1993, Big Willie Style, 1997, Willennium, 1999, Maximum Will Smith, 2000, Born to Reign, 2002, Greatest Hits, 2002; (singles) Just One of Those Days, 1987, Girls Ain't Nothing But Trouble, 1988, Brank New Funk, 1988, A Nightmare on My Street, 1988, Jazzy's Groove, 1989, I Think I Can Beat Mike Tyson, 1989, The Things That U Do, 1991, Summertime, 1991, Ring My Bell, 1991, I'm Looking for the One (To Be With Me), 1993, Boom! Shake the Room, 1993; TV series: The Fresh Prince of Bel-Air, 1990-96, (also exec. prodr. 1994-96), Happily Ever After: Fairy Tales for Every Child (voice only), 1995; TV series (exec. prod. only) All of Us, 2003, The Seat Filler, 2004.; TV appearances: Blossom, 1991, All of Us, 2003; Movies: Where the Day Takes You, 1992, Made in America, 1993, Six Degrees of Separation, 1993, Bad Boys, 1995, Independence Day, 1996 (Blockbuster Entertainment award Favorite Actor Sci-Fi), Men In Black, 1997 (MTV Movie awards Best Fight, Best Movie Song, ASCAP award Most Performed Songs for Motion Picture, Blockbuster Entertainment award Favorite Actor Sci-Fi), Welcome to Hollywood, 1998, Enemy of the State, 1998, Wild Wild West, 1999, The Legend of Bagger Vance, 2000, Ali, 2001, Men in Black II, 2002, Bad Boys II, 2003, I, Robot, 2004 (also exec. prod.), Shark Tale (voice only), 2004; exec. prodr. only, Showtime, 2002. Recipient ShoWest Conv. awards Actor of Yr., 1999, Spl. Internat. Box Office Achievement award 1997. Office: Creative Artists Agy c/o Ken Stovicz 9830 Wilshire Blvd Beverly Hills CA 90212-1804*

SMITH, WILLARD GRANT, psychologist; b. Sidney, NY, June 29, 1934; s. Frank Charles and Myrtle Belle (Empet) S.; m. Ruth Ann Dissly, Sept. 14, 1957; children: Deborah Sue Henri, Cynthia Lynn Koster, Andrea Kay Richards, John Charles. BS, U. Md., 1976; MS, U. Utah, 1978, PhD, 1981. Diplomate Am. Bd. Forensic Examiners, Am. Bd. Psychol. Specialities, Am. Bd. Disability Analysts; lic. psychologist Utah, cert. sch. psychologist nat. . Tchg. asst. dept. ednl. psychology U. Utah; rsch. asst. U. Utah Med. Ctr., 1976-78; rsch. cons. Utah Dept. Edn., 1977; program evaluator Salt Lake City Sch. Dist.; program evaluator, auditor Utah State Bd. Edn., 1978; sch. psychologist Jordan Sch. Dist., Sandy, Utah, 1978-82, tchr., 1979-80; exec. dir. Utah Ind. Living Ctr., Salt Lake City, 1982-83; spl. edn. cons. Southeastern Edn. Svc. Ctr., Utah, 1983-85; sch. psychologist Jordan Sch. Dist., Sandy, Utah, 1985-96; assoc. psychologist Don W. McBride & Assocs., Bountiful, Utah, 1989-91; pvt. practice Sandy, Utah, 1991—. Master sgt. USAF, 1953-76. Decorated Air Force Commendation medal with 2 clusters. Fellow Am. Coll. Forensic Examiners (life); mem. APA, Nat. Assn. Sch. Psychologists, Air Force Assn., Air Force Sgts. Assn., Ret. Enlisted Assn., Am. Legion, VFW, Phi Kappa Phi, Alpha Sigma Lambda. Home: 8955 Quail Hollow Dr Sandy UT 84093-1903 Office Phone: 801-942-5356.

SMITH, WILLIAM CHARLES, lawyer; b. Batavia, N.Y., June 9, 1930; s. William F. and Verna B. (Busmire) S.; m. Lucia P. Pierce, July 10, 1954; children: William Charles, Leonard P., Victoria J. BA, U. Buffalo, 1952; LLB, Harvard U., 1955. Bar: Maine 1955, D.C. 1962, Fla. 1995, U.S. Dist. Ct. Maine, 1956, U.S. Tax Ct. 1960, U.S. Ct. Appeals (1st cir.) 1977, U.S. Ct. Claims 1985, U.S. Supreme Ct. 1960. Assoc., Portland, Maine, 1955-57; ptnr. Hutchinson, Pierce, Atwood & Allen, Portland, 1957-59; counsel Office Tax Legis. Counsel, U.S. Treasury Dept., Washington, 1959-61; ptnr. Pierce, Atwood, Scribner, Allen, Smith and Lancaster, Portland, 1961-96, of counsel, 1996—. Exec. com. Fed. Tax Inst., New Eng. Vice chmn. budget com. United Community Services, 1966-68, chmn., 1968-70, nat. budget and consultation com., 1969-71; bd. dirs. Portland Goodwill, Inc., 1967-69, United Way, Inc., 1968-74, 75-80, Portland Widow's Wood Soc., 1962—; trustee Portland Regional Opportunity Program, 1967-68, Freyburg Acad., 1976-96, Found. Blood Research, 1979-85. Mem. ABA, Maine Bar Assn., D.C. Bar, Fla. Bar, Cumberland County Bar Assn., Am. Law Inst., Am. Coll. Trust and Estate Counsel, Am. Coll. Tax Counsel, Portland Country Club, Mid-Ocean Club (Bermuda), Meadows Country Club (Fla.), Cumerland Club (Maine). Republican. Unitarian Universalist. Home: 392 Spring St Portland ME 04102-3642 Office: Pierce Atwood One Monument Sq Portland ME 04101-1110 E-mail: wsmith@pierceatwood.com.

SMITH, WILLIAM CLARKE, clergyman; b. Bend, Oreg., Jan. 22, 1926; s. Jay Harvey Smith and Amelia Grace (Starr) Poor; m. Veta Maxine Davidson; children: Carolyn Jean Aldama, Virginia Ann Bennett, Barbara Lynn Logan, Rebecca Ruth Sickler, Donald Allen, Patricia Bea Bingham, Dwight David. AB cum laude, Ouachita Bapt. U., 1949; postgrad., Golden Gate Bapt. Theol. Sem., 1951-53. Ordained to ministry So. Bapt. Ch., 1948. Pastor Owensville Bapt. Ch., Ark., 1949-50, Grace Bapt. Ch., Corning, Calif., 1951; assoc. pastor 1st So. Bapt. Ch., Richmond, Calif., 1951-53; pastor Montalvin Bapt. Ch., San Pablo, Calif., 1953-60, 1st So. Bapt. Ch., Clovis, Calif., 1961-85, Hillside Bapt. Ch., La Puente, Calif., 1985, Trinity Bapt. Ch., Modesto, Calif., 1986-89; ret., 1989. Mem. exec. bd. So. Bapt. Conv. Calif., 1981-85, cons. stewardship dept., 1976-99, parliamentarian, 1964, 69, 74, 78; pres. Calif. So. Bapt. Ministers Conf., 1979—, Clovis Ministerial Fellowship, 1963-65, 67-70, 75-77; mem. So. Bapt. Bd. Child Care, 1964-67, chmn., 1966, 67; moderator Mid-Valley So. Bapt. Assn., 1965-66, clk., 1969-78, 89-2000; moderator Fresno Bapt. Assn., 1962-64. Chmn. fin. com. Clovis Civic Improvement Bond Com., Calif., 1976; chmn. religion com. Clovis Bicentennial Com., 1975-76; active Clovis Parks Adv. Com., 1977-78. With U.S. Army, 1944-46. Republican. Home: 2644 Crescent Ave Clovis CA 93612-4404

SMITH, WILLIAM DOUGLAS, lawyer; b. Spartanburg, S.C., Apr. 3, 1958; s. Milton Alfred and Suzanne (Earnhardt) S.; m. Alison Evans Smith; children: Cameron McIver, Anna Douglas. BA, Wofford Coll., 1980; JD, U. S.C., 1983. Bar: S.C. 1983, U.S. Dist. Ct. S.C., U.S. Ct. Appeals S.C. Assoc. Johnson, Smith Firm, Spartanburg, S.C., 1983-86, ptnr., 1986—. Mem. S.C. Ho. of Reps., 1992—, spkr. pro tempore, 2000—. Mem. S.C. Bar Assn., Spartanburg County Bar Assn., S.C. Golf Assn. (bd. dirs. 1995). Republican. Presbyterian. Avocation: golf. Home: 19 Springdale Ln Spartanburg SC 29302-3410 Office: Johnson Smith 220 N Church St Spartanburg SC 29306-5104

SMITH, WILLIAM EDWARD, sales executive, telecommunications executive; b. Port Washington, N.Y., Mar. 24, 1940; s. William Edward and Elizabeth Ann (Willis) S.; m. Kathleen Ann Guy, Nov. 4, 1972 (div. June 1979). AAS, Broome Tech. C.C., Binghamton, N.Y., 1960. Various sales mgmt. positions Contel, Sherburne, N.Y., 1973-84; br. sales mgr. NYNEX (BISC), Syracuse, 1984-94; region sales mgr. ACC Local Svc., Syracuse, 1994-95; sr. acct. mgr. Nortel Networks, Richardson, Tex., 1995-98; region mgr. Triton Network Sys., Orlando, Fla., 1998-2001; prin. assoc. W.E. Smith Assoc., Sherburne, 2001—. Founding mem. Tri Valley Aviation Assn., Norwich, N.Y., 1974-78; committeeman Rep. County Com., Sherburne, 1976-80; pres. Sherburne Rotary Club, 1981-82, Upper Chenango Valley Assn., 1983-85. Splst. 4 U.S. Army, 1963-65. Republican. Roman Catholic. Avocations: woodworking, flying, clay shooting, golf. Home: 168 Webb Rd Sherburne NY 13460-3732 E-mail: williame@citilink.com.

SMITH, WILLIAM FRENCH, II, safety engineer, special projects administrator; b. Bay City, Tex., Nov. 30, 1941; s. William and Willie Mae (Perry) S.; m. Sylvia Knight, Feb. 4, 1977; children: William III, Maurice. BS, Tuskegee U., 1964; postgrad., Washington U., 1968—70. Equipment engr. Boeing Co., Huntsville, Ala., 1964-67; plant design engr. McDonnell Douglas Corp., St. Louis, 1967-69; project engr. St. Louis County Govt., 1969-72; divsn. engr. E.I. duPont de Nemours & Co., Inc., Wilmington, Del., 1972-74, Victoria, Tex., 1972-74; engring. mgr. Westinghouse Corp., Millburn, NJ, 1974-76; bldg. safety engr. Denver Pub. Schs., 1976—, project adminstr., 1977—, energy conservationist, 1978—; pres. Smith Environ. Consulting, Denver, Las Vegas, Nev. Dir. hazardous materials Tuskegee U., Denver, 1985—88, environ. safety dir., 1988—; reservist Fed. Emergency Mgmt. Agy.; pres. Smith Environ. Consulting. Bd. dirs. Denver Opportunities Industrialization Ctr., 1979-80, Nat. Commn. on Future of Regis Coll.; mem. Mayor's Citizens Adv. Com. on Energy, 1980—, City of Lakewood Sr. Citizens Adv. Coun., Lakewood Bd. Appeals, Lakewood Code Enforcement Com.; past bd. dirs. Colo. Alliance Environ. Edn., Colo. Emergency Planning Commn.; past v.p. The Rocky Mountain Poison and Drug Ctr. Served with USNR, 1979—. Recipient Pres.'s Nat. award for energy conservation, 1980. Mem. Am. Soc. Safety Engrs., Colo. Assn. Sch. Energy Coords., Am. Assn. Blacks in Energy, Denver Pub. Schs. Black Adminstrs. and Suprs. Assn. (treas.), Colo. Environ. Health Assn., Nat. Asbestos Coun., Colo. Hazardous Waste Mgmt. Soc., Colo. Hazardous Materials Assn. (past treas.), Denver Emergency Planning Commn., Civil Air Patrol, Colo. Renewable Energy Soc., Colo. Energy Network, Nat. Assn. Minority Contractors, Environ. Consulting (pres.), Internat. Hazardous Materials Assn., Tuskegee U. Alumni Assn. Republican. Home: 102 S Balsam St Lakewood CO 80226-1344 Office: Denver Public Schs 2800 West 7th Ave Denver CO 80204-4117 Office Phone: 303-233-3335. E-mail: wmfrenchsmith1@aol.com.

SMITH, WILLIAM G. transportation executive; Chmn., pres., CEO Smithway Motor Xpress Corp., Ft. Dodge, Iowa, 1993—. Office: Smithway Motor Xpress Corp 2031 Quail Ave Fort Dodge IA 50501-8511 Fax: 515-576-8794.

SMITH, WILLIAM HENRY PRESTON, freelance/self-employed writer, editor, former telecommunications industry executive; b. Pleasanton, Tex., Sept. 8, 1924; s. Sidney Newton and Willie Gertrude (Cloyd) S.; m. Frances Dixon, July 1, 1950; children: Juliet, Dixon, David. B.J., U. Tex., 1949. Reporter Dallas Morning News, 1949-52; advt. asst. Dallas Power & Light Co., 1952-55; dir. pub. relations Greater Boston C. of C., 1955-58; with New Eng. Telephone and Telegraph Co., Boston, 1958-86, asst. v.p., 1966-75, corp. sec., 1975-83, dir. pub. relations, 1983-86; free-lance writer Dover, Mass., 1986—. Editor: Bus. Ethics Resource Newsletter. Bd. dirs., v.p. Mass. Soc. for Prevention Cruelty to Children; bd. dirs. Bus. Ethics Found., Urban Dynamics Adv. Coun.; mem. support policies com. United Way Mass; bd. advisors to pres. Andover Newton Theol. Sch. With paratroopers U.S. Army, 1943-46. Decorated Purple Heart, U.S. Army, Bronze Star, U.S. Army. Mem. Am. Soc. Corp. Secs., Friars, Dedham Country and Polo Club, Down Town Club, Wellesley Coll. Club, Sigma Delta Chi, Delta Kappa Epsilon. Republican. Home and Office: 3236 Wingfield Lake Rd Williamsburg VA 23185-7519

SMITH, WILLIAM HUGH, SR., retired audit manager, consultant; b. Peoria, Ill., Feb. 12, 1920; s. Hugh N. and Catherine Litta (Obrien) S.; m. Betty Lou Uth Smith, June 4, 1941; children: Beverly Ann Clark, William H. Smith Jr., Millie Judkins, Hugh N. Smith, Patrick James Smith. BSBA with honors, U. Dayton. Cert. Fraud Examiner; cert. Fin. Mgr. Mgr. Hugh H. Smith CPA, Chgo., 1946—66; resident mgr. CPA Firms, Chgo., 1966—76; v.p., auditor United Am. Bank, Chgo., 1976—79; audit mgr. City of Anaheim, Calif., 1979—96. Charter Life mem. Rep. Presdl. Task Force, Washington, 1982-. Capt. US Army, 1941-46. Mem. Inst. Internal Auditors (bd. govs. Orange County chpt., internat. com. on govt. affairs), Cert. Fraud Examiners. Republican. Roman Catholic. Home: 24001 Muirland Blvd sp 309 Lake Forest CA 92630-4813

SMITH, WILLIAM HULSE, forestry and environmental studies educator; b. Trenton, N.J., May 9, 1939; s. Philip Andrews and Marion (Hulse) S.; m. Judith Chapin Pease, July 6, 1963 (div. 1982); children— Scott William, Philip Chapin; m. Deborah Banks Coit, June 17, 1983; 1 child, Tyler Banks. BS, Rutgers U., 1961, PhD, 1965; M.F., Yale U., 1963. Asst. prof. forestry Rutgers U., 1965-66; asst. prof. Yale U., 1966-72, assoc. prof., 1972-75, prof., 1975—, dean, 1981-83, 98-99, Clifton R. Musser prof. forest biology, 1985—, dean, 1998-99; emeritus, 2001; sr. ecologist NESCAUM, 2001—; dir. Yale Sch. Forestry & Environ. Svcs., 2002—03. Mem. sci. adv. bd. U.S. EPA, 1990—; adj. faculty So. N.H. U., 2003—, Plymouth (N.H.) State U., 2004—. Author: Tree Pathology, 1970, Air Pollution and Forest Ecosystems, 1981, 2d edit., 1990. Mem. Conn. Siting Coun., 1985—2001. NSF grantee, U.S. Dept. Agr. Forest Service grantee. Mem. Soc. Am. Foresters, Am. Phytopath. Soc., Ecol. Soc. Am. Home: PO Box 585 Center Harbor NH 03226-0585 E-mail: whulsesmith@aol.com.

SMITH, WILLIAM JAY, author; b. Winnfield, La., Apr. 22, 1918; s. Jay and Georgia (Campster) S.; m. Barbara Howes, Oct. 1, 1947 (div. June 1965); children: David Emerson, Gregory Jay; m. Sonja Haussmann, Sept. 3, 1966. Student, Institut de Touraine, Tours, France, 1938; BA, Washington U., St. Louis, 1939, MA, 1941; postgrad., Columbia U., 1946-47; postgrad. Rhodes scholar, Oxford U., 1947-48; postgrad., U. Florence, Italy, 1948-50; Litt.D., New Eng. Coll., 1973. Asst. in French Washington U., 1939-41; instr. English and French Columbia U., 1946-47; lectr. English Williams Coll., 1951, poet in residence, lectr. English, 1959-64, 66-67; Ford Found. fellow Arena Stage, Washington, 1964-65; writer in residence Hollins Coll., 1965-66, prof. English, 1967, 70-80, prof. emeritus, 1980. Poet laureate Libr. of Congress, Washington, 1968-70, hon. cons. in Am. letters, 1970-76; vis. prof., acting chmn., writing divsn. Sch. Arts, Columbia U., 1973, 74-75; mem. staff Salzburg (Austria) Seminar, 1975; mem. jury Nat. Book award, 1962, 70, 75, Neustadt Internat. prize for lit., 1978, Com. of Pegasus Prize for Lit., 1979-98; poet in residence Cathedral St. John the Divine, N.Y., 1985-88. Author: Poems, 1947, Celebration at Dark, 1950, Laughing Time, 1955, Poems, 1947-57, Boy Blue's Book of Beasts, 1957, Puptents and Pebbles: A Nonsense ABC, 1959, Typewriter Town, 1960, The Spectra Hoax, 1961, What Did I See, 1962, Ho for a Hat, 1964, (with Louise Bogan) The Golden Journey; Poems for Young People, 1965, The Tin Can and Other Poems, 1966, If I Had a Boat, 1966, Poems from France, 1967, Mr. Smith and Other Nonsense, 1968, New and Selected Poems, 1970, The Streaks of the Tulip, selected criticism, 1972, Poems from Italy, 1973, Venice in the Fog, 1975, The Telephone, 1977, Laughing Time, 1980, The Traveler's Tree, New and Selected Poems, 1980, Army Brat, a Memoir, 1980, A Green Place: Modern Poems, 1982, Plain Talk: Epigrams, Epitaphs, Satires, Nonsense, Occasional Concrete and Quotidian Poems, 1988, Ho for a Hat (rev.), 1989, Collected Poems 1939-1989, 1990, Laughing Time: Collected Nonsense, 1990, Birds and Beasts, 1990, Big and Little, 1992 (with Carol Ra) Behind the King's Kitchen: A Roster of Rhyming Riddles, 1992, The Cyclist, 1995 (with Carol Ra) The Sun is Up: A Child's Year of Poems, 1996, The World Below the Window: Poems 1937-1997, 1998, Here is My Heart: Love Poems, 1999, The Cherokee Lottery: A Sequence of Poems, 2000, Around My Room, 2000, The Spectra Hoax (paperback reissue), 2000, The World Below the Window: Poems, 1937-1997, 2002, The Girl in the Glass: Love Poems, 2002; translator: (with Emanuel Brasil) Brazilian Poetry 1950-80, 1984, (with Ingvar Schousboe) The Pact: My Friendship with Isak Dinesen by Thorkild Bjørnvig, 1983, (with J.S. Holmes) Dutch Interior: Post-War Poetry of the Netherlands and Flanders, 1984, Scirocco by Romualdo Romano, 1951; Poems of a Multimillionaire by Valery Larbaud, 1955, Selected Writings of Jules Laforgue, 1956, Children of the Forest by Elsa Beskow, 1969, Two Plays by Charles Bertin: Christopher Columbus and Don Juan, 1970, The Pirate Book by Lennart Hellsing, 1972, (with Leif Sjöberg) Agadir by Artur Lundkvist, 1979, Moral Tales of Jules Laforgue, 1985, Collected Translations: Italian, French, Spanish, Portuguese, 1985, (with Dana Gioia) Poems from Italy, 1985, (with Leif Sjöberg) Wild Bouquet: Nature Poems by Harry Martinson, 1985, (with Sonja Haussmann Smith) The Madman and the Medusa by Tchicaya U Tam'Si, 1989, Songs of Childhood by Federico Garcia Lorca, 1994, Berlin: The City and the Court, 1995, (with Leif Sjöberg) The Forest of Childhood: Poems from Sweden, 1996, Gyula Illyés: Selected Poems, 1999; editor: Herrick, 1962, Light Verse and Satires by Witter Bynner, 1978, (with F.D. Reeve) An Arrow in the Wall: Selected Poetry and Prose by Andrei Voznesensky, 1986 (one of 16 Best Books of 1986, N.Y. Times), Life Sentence: Selected Poems of Nina Cassian, 1990. Mem. Vt. Ho. of Reps., 1960-62. Served to lt. USNR, 1941-45. Recipient Alumni citation Washington U., 1963; prize Poetry mag., 1945, 64; Henry Bellamann Major award, 1970; Russell Loines award Nat. Inst. Arts and Letters, 1972; Gold medal Labor Hungary 1978; Golden Rose award New Eng. Poetry Club, 1979, médaille de vermeil French Acad., 1991, Pro Cultura Hungarica medal, Hungary, 1993; Nat. Endowment for Arts fellow, 1972, 95; NEH fellow, 1975, 89; Ingram Merrill fellow, 1982; Camargo Found. fellow, 1986, René Vásquez Díaz prize Swedish Acad., 1997. Mem. Am. Acad. Arts and Letters (v.p. for literature 1986-89), Am. Assn. Rhodes Scholars, Acad. Am. Poets, Authors Guild, P.E.N. Clubs: Century. Home: 63 Luther Shaw Rd Cummington MA 01026-9787 also: 52-56 rue d'Alleray 75015 Paris France

SMITH, WILLIAM RANDOLPH (RANDY SMITH), health care management executive; b. Spartanburg, SC, July 23, 1948; s. Jesse Edward and Helen (Knox) S.; m. Donna Marie HAwthorne, July 18, 1970; children: Kirstin Leigh, Andrea Marie. BA, Furman U., 1970; MHA, Duke U., 1972. Exec. dir. Riverside Hosp., Wilmington, Del., 1974-79; assoc. exec. dir. Brookwood Med. Ctr., Brimingham, Ala., 1979-81, exec. dir., 1983-85; v.p. ops. Am. Med. Internat., Atlanta, 1981-89, interim CFO Beverly Hills, Calif., 1989—90, chief adminstrv. officer Dallas, 1990, exec. v.p. ops., 1990-95; exec. v.p. Tenet Health Corp, Dallas, 1995—2003, pres. Western divsn., 2003. Bd. dirs. EPIC Healthcare Group, Dallas, 1989-92. Bd. dirs. Ala. Symphony Assn., Birmingham, 1985, State of Ala. Ballet, Birmingham, 1983-85, Esoterix, Inc., 1997—. Lt. U.S. Army, 1972-74. Mem. Fedn. Am. Health Systems (bd. dirs. 1989-99, pres. 1993, chmn. 1994). Episcopalian. Avocations: skiing, tennis, automobiles. Office: Tenet Healthcare Inc 14001 Dallas Pkwy Ste 200 Dallas TX 75240-4346

SMITH, WILLIAM RAY, retired biophysicist, retired engineer; b. Lyman, Okla., June 26, 1925; s. Harry Wait and Daisy Belle (Hull) S. BA, Bethany Nazarene Coll., 1948; MA, Wichita State U., 1950; PhD, UCLA, 1967. Engr. Beech Aircraft Corp., Wichita, Kans., 1951-53; sr. group engr. McDonnell Aircraft Corp., St. Louis, 1953-60; sr. engr. Lockheed Aircraft Corp., Burbank, Calif., 1961-63; sr. engr. scientist McDonnell Douglas Corp., Long Beach, Calif., 1966-71; tech. staff Rockwell Internat., L.A., 1973-86, CDI Corp.-West, Costa Mesa, Calif., 1986-88; sr. engr. scientist McDonnell Douglas Aircraft Corp., Long Beach, 1988—93; ret., 1993. Tchr. math. Pasadena Nazarene Coll. (now Point Loma Nazarene Coll., San Diego), 1960-62, Glendale Coll., Calif., 1972; asst. prof. math. Mt. St. Mary's Coll., L.A., 1972-73; math. cons. L.A. Union Rescue Mission Bank of Am. Learning Ctr., 1995—, Wayfarer's Ministry 1997—, Heart of L.A. Youth, 2001--. Vol. Heart of LA Youth; Deacon Presbyn. Ch. Recipient Recognition cert., NASA, 1982. Mem. Town Hall Calif., Yosemite Assocs., UCLA Faculty Club, Sigma Xi, Pi Mu Epsilon. Republican. Avocations: sailing, photography, teaching sunday school first grade. Home: 2405 Roscomare Rd Los Angeles CA 90077-1839 Business E-Mail: billsmit@lafn.org.

SMITH, WILLIAM RAYMOND, farmer, horse breeder; b. Bowling Green, Ky., June 5, 1932; s. William Raymond and Rose Velta (Biggerstaff) Smith; m. Robin Sommers, July 12, 1954 (div. July 1977); children: Dana Leslie Henning, Lauren Reneé Imgrund; m. Lee Ann McClathchey, Dec. 31, 1944 (div. May 2003). BA in Liberal Arts, U. Chgo., 1953, MA in English, 1959, PhD in History of Culture, 1961. Lic. thoroughbred trainer. Asst. prof. English Pa. State U., Univ. Park, 1961-63, Haverford (Pa.) Coll., 1963-66, Scripps Coll., Claremont, Calif., 1966-67, exec. officer literature divsn., 1966-67; chmn. integrative studies Shimer Coll., Mt. Carroll, Ill., 1967-70; asst. prof. humanities Reed Coll., Portland, 1970-71; prof. history and philosophy U. Pitts., Johnstown, Pa., 1971-98, acad. dean, 1971-72; ret., 1998. Fulbright prof. Am. studies U. Utrecht, Netherlands, 1969—70. Author: History as Argument, 1966, The Rhetoric of American Politics, 1969; co-author: The Colonial Legacy, 1971, Nineteenth Century Literary Criticism, 1986. With U.S. Army, 1955—57. Fellow, Union Rsch. Higher Edn., 1968. Avocation: fox hunting rider. Home: Loghouse Farm 445 Mt Zion Rd Dillsburg PA 17019 E-mail: loghousefarm@aol.com.

SMITH, WILLIAM REECE, JR., lawyer; b. Athens, Tenn., Sept. 19, 1925; s. William Reece and Gladys (Moody) S. BS, U. S.C., 1946; JD, U. Fla., 1949; Rhodes scholar, Oxford U., 1949-52; LL.D., U. So. Fla., 1973, Rollins Coll., 1980, U. Fla., 1980, U. S.C., 1981, Stetson U., 1985; D.C.L., Central Meth. Coll., 1980, New Eng. Coll., 1980; D.H.L., Calif. West Sch. Law, 1981; DBA, Tampa (Fla.) Coll., 1991; LHD, U. So. Fla., 1990. Bar: Fla. 1949. Mem. firm Carlton, Fields, Ward, Emmanuel, Smith and Cutler, Tampa, 1953—, now chmn.; emeritus, interim pres. U. So. Fla., 1976-77; city atty. Tampa, 1963-72. Asst. prof. law U. Fla., 1952-53; adj. prof. law Stetson U., 1954-59, 91—; past pres. Am. Bar Endowment, Fla. Legal Svcs., Inc. Past pres. Tampa Philharmonic Assn., Fla. Gulf Coast Symphony, Inc.; sec. Fla. Rhodes Scholar Selection Com., 1969-94. Midshipman and ensign USNR, 1943—46. Named Outstanding Young Man of Tampa, 1961; recipient Good Govt. award Fla. Jr. C. of C., 1965, Disting. Am. award Tampa Chpt. Nat. Football Found., 1977, Humanitarian award B'nai B'rith Found., 1977, Pres.'s award Fla. Assn. Retarded Citizens, 1978, Von Briesen award Nat. Legal Aid and Defender Assn., 1980, Brotherhood award NCCJ, 1980, Herbert Harley award Am. Judicature Soc., 1983, Citizen of Yr. award Civitan Club, 1986, Algernon Sydney Sullivan award, U. S.C., 1987, Pub. Svc. award Stetson U. Coll. Law, 1990, C.H.I.E.F. award Fla. Ind. Colls. and Univs., 1990, Professionalism award Am. Inns of Ct., 2002. Fellow Am. Coll. Trial Lawyers, Internat. Acad. Trial Lawyers, Am. Bar Found. (past pres.), Fla. Bar Found. (past pres.); mem. ABA (chmn. jr. bar conf. 1960-61, life, ho. dels., sec. 1967-71, pres. 1980-81, Gold medal 1989, Pro Bono Publico award 1994), Internat. Soc. Barristers, Am. Law Inst. (mem. coun.), Internat. Bar Assn. (past pres.), Inter-Am. Bar Assn. (mem. exec. coun. 1972-77), Fla. Bar Assn. (pres. 1972-73), Hillsborough County Bar Assn. (pres. 1963), Nat. Conf. Bar Pres. (pres. 1978-79), Greater Tampa C. of C. (pres. 1986-87). Methodist. Home: PO Box 3239 Tampa FL 33601-3239 Office: Carlton Fields Ward Emmanuel Smith & Cutler 1 Harbour Pl 777 S Harbour Island Blvd Tampa FL 33602-5729 Office Phone: 813-223-7000. Business E-Mail: rsmith@carltonfields.com.

SMITH, WILLIAM ROBERT, utility company executive; b. Mt. Clemens, Mich., Nov. 11, 1916; s. Robert L. and Elsie (Chamberlain) S.; m. Sandra Martha Philips; children from previous marriage: William R. (dec.), Laura A. (dec.). BS, Detroit Inst. Tech., 1947; postgrad., Detroit Coll. Law, U. Mich. Grad. Sch. Bus. Adminstrn. Registered profl. engr., Mich., Ohio. Indsl. engr. Detroit Edison Co., 1934-60; mgr. econ. devel. East Ohio Gas Co., Cleve., 1960-80; mgr. nat. accounts Consol. Natural Gas Co., Cleve., 1980-85; dir. mktg. Edison Polymer Innovation Corp., 1985-88; exec. dir. Western Res. Econ. Devel. Coun., 1988-97; pres. T.S.T. Corp.; ret. Bd. dirs. Animal Protective League and Humane Soc. Served with USAAF, 1942-45. Fellow Am. Indsl. Devel. Coun.; mem. Indsl. Devel. Rsch. Coun., Assn. Ohio Commodores, Delta Theta Tau. Presbyterian. Home: 99 Gillette St Painesville OH 44077-2931

SMITH, WILLIAM S., JR., education association administrator; BS in Chemistry, Tex. A&M U., 1970, PhD in Chemistry, 1974. Postdoctoral rschr. U. Calif., Irvine; program mgr. FAA; graduate rsch. Tex. A&M U., 1971—74; phys. scientist FAA, U.S. Dept. Transp., 1977—85; sci. advisor subcom. on space, com. on sci., space and tech. U.S. Ho. of Reps., 1985—88, staff dir. subcom., 1988—94, dep. Dem. chief of staff, 1994—98; v.p. for programs Assn. Univs. for Rsch. in Astronomy, Inc., Washington, 1998—2000, interim pres., 1999—2000, pres., 2000—. Recipient Exceptional Svc. award, NASA, Sci. and Tech. Fellowship award, Dept. Commerce, 1984. Office: AURA Inc Ste 350 1200 New York Ave NW Washington DC 20005

SMITH, WOOLLCOTT, statistician, educator; b. Balt., June 9, 1941; s. Henry Clay and Nancy Woollcott S.; m. Leah Johnson, Feb. 3, 1968; children: Amelia, Keston. BS, Mich. State U., 1962, MS, 1964; PhD, Johns Hopkins U., 1969. Asst. prof. U. N.C., Chapel Hill, 1969-72; sr. statis. Woods Hole (Mass.) Oceanographic Instn., 1972-81; prof. Temple U., Phila., 1981—, dir. Data Analysis Lab., 1982—89, chmn. stats. dept., 2001—04. Sr. rsch. fellow Woods Hole Oceanographic Instn., 1996-98. Author: (book) The Cartoon Guide to Statistics, 1993; editor: (book) Ecological Diversity in Theory and Practice, 1979. Mem. Am. Statis. Assn. (pres. Phila. chpt. 1988-89). Office: Stats Dept/Temple Univ N Broad & Cecil D Moore Philadelphia PA 19122

SMITH, YEARDLEY, actress; b. Paris, July 3, 1964; Voice of Lisa Simpson, Maggie Simpson and others The Simpsons, 1989—. Actor: (films) Heaven Help Us, 1985, The Legend of Billie Jean, 1985, Maximum Overdrive, 1986, Three O'Clock High, 1987, Listen to Me, 1989, Zwei Frauen, 1989, City Slickers, 1989, Toys, 1992, Jingle All the Way, 1996, Just Write, 1997, As Good As It Gets, 1997, (voice only) We're Back! A Dinosaur's Story, 1993,: (TV films) Mom's On Strike, 1984, Tickets, Please, 1988; (TV series) Brothers, 1984, The Tracey Ullman Show, 1987—89, Herman's Head, 1991, Dharma & Greg, 1997—99, 2001—02, (TV guest appearance) Tales from the Darkside, 1986, Mama's Family, 1986, Mathnet, 1987, Sydney, 1990, Likely Suspects, 1992, Hey Hey, It's Sunday, 1994, Empty Nest, 1994, Smart Guy, 1997, Teen Angel, 1997, Sports Night, 1998, Nash Bridges, 1999, Becker, 2003, (theatre) More, 2004. Office: Ste 725E 9100 Wilshire Blvd Beverly Hills CA 90212-3441*

SMITH, YVONNE SMART, advertising executive; b. Asheville, N.C. BFA, Auburn U. Asst. art dir. Mademoiselle mag., N.Y.C.; art dir. Cargill, Wilson & Acree Advt. divsn. Doyle Dane Bernbach; v.p., assoc. creative dir., exec. art dir. Chiat/Day Advt., L.A., sr. v.p., assoc. creative dir. Venice, Calif., Venice, N.Y.C., London, mng. ptnr., creative dir. L.A.; prin. Yvonne Smith, Inc. Guest lectr. UCLA, Art Ctr. Coll. Design, L.A., U. So. Calif., L.A., Art Dirs. Club, Paris; co-chair Internat. Clio Awards, 1999. Subject profl. articles. Recipient One Show awards, N.Y. Art Dirs. Club, Andy awards, Belding awards, award, Art Dirs. Club, Steven Kelly awards, Clio awards, Emmy award, 1998, Silver and Bronze Lions, Cannes Film Festival, 1998. Office: 21344 Rambla Vista Malibu CA 90265-5348

SMITH, ZACHARY ALDEN, political science and public administration educator; b. Stanford, Calif., Aug. 8, 1953; s. Alden Wallace and Lelia (Anderson) S. BA, Calif. State U., Fullerton, 1975; MA, U. Calif., Santa Barbara, 1979, PhD, 1984. Adj. lectr. polit. sci. U. Calif., Santa Barbara, 1981-82; asst. prof., dir. Ctr. for Island and Ocean Resources Mgmt. U. Hawaii, Hilo, 1982-87, assoc. prof., 1987-89, No. Ariz. U., Flagstaff, 1989-93, prof., 1993—2001, regents prof., 2001—. Author: Groundwater and the Future of the Southwest, 1984, Groundwater Policy in the Southwest, 1985, Groundwater in the West, 1989, The Environmental Policy Paradox, 4th edit., 2004, Hawaii State and Local Government, 1992, Politics and Public Policy in Arizona, 1993, 4th edit., 2004, Environmental Politics and Policy in the West, 1993, Groundwater Management in the West, 1999, Hawaii Politics and Government, 2000, The National Environmental Policy Act: Promise Unfilled, 2001, Fresh Water Issues, 2003, Ocean Politics and Policy, 2003. Active campaign for various state propositions, 1970, 74, 76; elected to Orange County (Calif.) Dem. Cen. Com., 1976-78; councilman City of Flagstaff, 1996-98. Rsch. grantee U. Calif., Los Alamos (N.Mex.) Sci. Lab., Water Resources Ctr., Davis, Calif., U.S. Dept. HUD. Mem. ASPA, Am. Water Resources Assn., Am. Polit. Sci. Assn., Southwestern Social Sci. Assn., Western Polit. Sci. Assn., Western Social Scis. Assn. (exec. coun. 1995-99). Office: No Ariz U Dept Polit Sci PO Box 15036 Flagstaff AZ 86011-0001

SMITH, ZADIE, writer; b. London, Eng., 1975; Grad. in English, Cambridge U.; postgrad., Harvard U. Author: (novels) White Teeth, 2000, The Autograph Man, 2002. Office: 1745 Broadway #B1 New York NY 10019-4305*

SMITH, ZANNIE O. retired career officer; b. Columbia, S.C., Mar. 27, 1943; BA in History, U. Tampa; M in Bus. Mgmt., Webster U., St. Louis. Enlisted 82d airborne divsn. U.S. Army, 1962, commd. 2d lt., advanced through grades to maj. gen.; chief of staff U.S. Army Res. Command, Atlanta, 1995; asst. divsn. comdr. ops. 10th Mountain Divsn. and Ft. Drum, 1997; dep. comdg. gen., chief of staff I Corps and Ft. Lewis, 1998—2003; ret., 2003. Decorated Def. Superior Meritorious Svc. award, Legion of Merit with 5 oak leaf clusters, Def. Meritorious Svc. medal, Meritorious Svc. medal with 4 oak leaf clusters, Army Commendation medal with 2 oak leaf clusters, Armed Forces Expeditionary medal, four Vietnam Svc. medals, Good Conduct medal, Bronze Star medal with V and 2 oak leaf clusters, Air medal with oak leaf cluster; recipient Combat Infantryman's badge, Ranger Tab, Air Assault badge.*

SMITH, SR. JACKIE WAYNE, minister; b. Killeen, Tex., Sept. 28, 1956; s. Jackie Melvin and Carolyn May Smith(Stepmother), Elsie Marie and Gene Cartwright(Stepfather); m. Susan Elizabeth Battaglia, Aug. 29, 1975; children: Jackie Wayne Smith Jr., Suzanne Yates Jill, Jeffery Smith Alan, Carolyn Mishelle Smith. AAS in Mgmt., Thomas Nelson C.C., 2000; BS in Facility Engring., Trinity Coll. and U., Sioux Falls, S.D., 2001. Cert. plant maintenance mgr., Assn. for Facilities Engring., 2000; correctional chaplain Ch. of God Chaplain's Commn., 2003, ordained min. Ch. of God, 2004. Master electrician County of York, Va., 1989—95; chaplain Southeastern Correctional Ministry, Newport News, Va., 1991—2003; mgr. of bldg. maintenance York County Sch. Divsn., Va., 1995—2001; dir. of ops. Rappahanock Westminster Canterbury, Lancaster, Va., 2001—02; sr. chaplain Southeastern Correctional Ministry, Hampton, Va., 2003—. Bd. dirs. Southeastern Correctional Ministry, Hampton, Va., 2000—03. With USAF, 1974—76. Named to, Hall of Christian Excellence, 2000; recipient Layman's Award for Christian Excellence, 2000. Republican. Pentacostal. Avocations: preaching, travel. Home: 6523 Belroi Rd Gloucester VA 23061 Office: Southeastern Correctional Ministry 40 Kings Way Hampton VA 23669 Personal E-mail: srchapjack@rivnet.net.

SMITH-COX, ELIZABETH SHELTON, art educator; b. Washington, Feb. 12, 1924; d. Benjamin Warren and Sarah Priscilla (Harrell) Shelton; m. John Edwin Smith, Aug. 16, 1947 (dec. July 1992); children: Shelley Hobson, Dale Henslee, John Edwin Jr.; m. Headley Morris Cox Jr., Dec. 30, 1994. BA in Art, Meredith Coll., 1946; MEd in Supervision and Adminstrn., Clemson U., 1974. Youth dir. St. John's Bapt. Ch., Charlotte, N.C., 1946-47; art tchr. Raleigh (N.C.) Pub. Schs., 1947-49, East Mecklenberg H.S., Charlotte, 1968-69, D. W. Daniel H.S., Central, S.C., 1970-86; art instr. U. S.C., Columbia, 1966-68; adj. prof. Clemson (S.C.) U., 1991-93; artist-in-residence edn. program S.C. Arts Commn., Columbia, 1991-2001. Exhibited in numerous one and two person shows and in group exhibits; solo show at Meredith Coll. Rotunda Gallery, Raleigh, 2002; invitational alumnae exhibit Meredith Coll., 2000; exhibited in 2-person show Pickens County (S.C.) Mus., 2000; featured artist F. Hanson Discovery Ctr., Clemson, 2003. Vol. worker, editor newsletter Pickens County Habitat for Humanity, Clemson, 1981—; vol. art tchr. St. Andrew's Elem. Sch., Columbia, 1962-68; vol. Habitat for Humanity Mission to Honduras, summers 1996—; trustee Friends of Lee Gallery, Clemson U., 2003-2004. Recipient Svc. to Mankind award Clemson Sertoma Club, 1997, Disting. Alumni award Meredith Coll., 1996; named S.C. Tchr. of Yr., S.C. Dept. Edn. and Ency. Britannica, 1976, Citizen of Yr., Clemson Rotary Club, 1979; Ann. Student Scholarship named Liz Smith-Cox Student Scholarship, 2003. Mem. S.C. Art Edn. Assn. (pres. 1978, Lifetime Svc. award 1990, Lifetime Achievement in Art Edn. award 1995, Liz Smith-Cox scholar 2003), Nat. Art Edn. Assn. (ret. art educator affiliate, pres. 1994-97, Disting. Svc. award 1995, Electronic Gallery 1999, 2000, 01, 02, 03, Ret. Art Educator of Yr. award 2000, Elizabeth's O'Neil Verner S.C. Gov.'s award for individual in Arts Edn. 2003), Nat. Art Edn. Found. (trustee 1996-2002, S.C. Watercolor Soc. (Mem. with Excellence 1993), Upstate Visual Artists (Best in Show award). Baptist. Avocations: travel, reading, writing, music. Home: 1604 Six Mile Hwy Central SC 29630-9483 E-mail: lizhmcox@innova.net.

SMITHEE, JOHN TRUE, lawyer, state legislator; b. Amarillo, Tex., Sept. 7, 1951; s. John J. and Mildred B. (True) S.; m. Becky Collins, Aug. 18, 1979; children: Jennifer, Rebecca, John True. BBA, West Tex. State U., Canyon, 1973; JD, Tex. Tech U., 1976. Bar: Tex. 1976, U.S. Supreme Ct., 1983. Atty. Templeton, Smithee, Hayes, Heinrich & Russell, Amarillo, Tex., 1976—; mem. Tex. Ho. of Reps., Austin, 1985—, chmn. ins. com., 1993—. Mem. State Bar Tex., Amarillo Bar Assn. Republican. Home: 2808 Parker St Amarillo TX 79109-3546 Office: Templeton Smithee Hayes Fields Young & Heinrich PO Box 15010 Amarillo TX 79105-5010

SMITH-EPSTEIN, MARY KATHLEEN, dancer; b. Austin, Tex., Sept. 12, 1940; d. Walter Bentley Jr. and Kathleen Beatrice (Lancaster) Smith; m. Witaly Osins, June 6, 1967 (div. 1975); m. Howard Irwin Epstein, June 20, 1987. Grad. high sch., Dallas. Demi soloist Am. Festival Ballet, European Tour, 1961; prin. dancer HET Nat. Ballet, Amsterdam, Holland, 1962-67; guest artist Berliner Ballet, Berlin, 1964, Ballet De L'Atlantique, Nantes, France, 1967-68, Cologne, Fed. Republic Germany, 1968-70, Ballet Spectacular, Miami, Fla., 1973-74; prin. dancer Opernhaus, Hannover, Fed. Republic Germany, 1968-70, Musiktheater, Gelsenkirchen, Fed. Republic Germany, 1968-71, Ballet Van Vlaanderen, Antwerp, Belgium, 1971-73, Ballet De Wallonie, Charleroi, Belgium, 1973-74, Irish Nat. Ballet, Cork, Ireland, 1975-85, Chgo. Ballet, 1977-78, Ballet Met., Columbus, Ohio, 1978-79; founder, co-dir. Conservatory Classical Dance, Eugene, Oreg., 1989—. Founder N.W. Chamber Ballet, 1988—; artistic dir. 8 Dance Ensemble; guest tchr. Imperial Eleven Ballet, 2000-01, Internat. Ballet Sch., 2000. Choreographer: (ballet) Opus 1, 1978, For Him From Her, 1982, The Catalyst, 1983 (Bursary Irish Arts Council award 1985), Pas De Deux, 1985 (Bursary Irish Arts Council 1985), Logic of the Heart, 1988, Masquerade Suite, 1988, Tango, 1999, Nocturne, 1998, Pro-Fun-Ditties, 1997, No One Knew, 1997; choreographer Ballet N.W., Performing Ensemble Conservatory Classical Dance, 1989—. Treas. Neighborhood Watch, Vida, Oreg., 1988-89, bd. mem. (sec. to pres.) of Lane Arts Coun., 1993-96; dir. bldg. fund, pres. bd. dirs. Kaygu Dakshang Chuling, 1995—. Alexandra Danilova scholar, Dallas, 1958. Buddhist. E-mail: hepsteinor@earthlink.net.

SMITHER, HOWARD ELBERT, musicologist, educator; b. Pittsburg, Kans., Nov. 15, 1925; s. Elbert S. and Ethel (Schwab) S.; m. Doris J. Arvin (div. 1976); children: Thomas A., Jesse N. Woodsmith; m. Ann M. Woodward. AB magna cum laude, spl. honors in music, Hamline U., 1950; MA in musicology, Cornell U., 1952; postgrad., U. Munich, 1953-54; PhD in musicology, Cornell U., 1960. Instr. Oberlin Coll. and Conservatory of Music, Oberlin, Ohio, 1955-57, asst. prof., 1957-60, U. Kans., Lawrence, 1960-63; assoc. prof. Tulane U., New Orleans, 1963-68, U. N.C., Chapel Hill, 1968-71, prof., 1971-79, dir. grad. studies in music, 1977-79, 83-84, 86-88, James Gordon Hanes prof. humanities in music, 1979-92, James Gordon Hanes prof. emeritus humanities in music, 1992—; John Bird prof. of music U. Wales, Cardiff, 1993-95. Lectr., chmn. panels regional, nat. and internat. meetings, confs., symposiums, 1964-90. Author: A History of the Oratorio, Vol. 1, The Oratorio in the Baroque Era: Italy, Vienna, Paris, 1977 (transl. Italian), Vol. 2, The Oratorio in the Baroque Era: Protestant Germany and England, 1977 (Deems Taylor award ASCAP 1978), Vol. 3 The Oratorio in the Classical Era, 1987, Vol. 4, Oratorio in the 19th and 20th Centuries, 2000; editor Oratorios of the Italian Baroque, 1983—, The Italian Oratorio 1650-1800, Vols. 1-3, 6, 8, 11-13, 16, 18-20, 24-25, 27, 1986-87; Oratorios of the Italian Baroque, 1983—; editor, translator poems in Alfred Einstein's The Italian Madrigal, 1971; music rev. editor Notes, 1967-69; mem. editorial bd. Detroit Monographs in Musicology, 1971-87; chmn. editorial bd. Early Musical Masterworks: Editions and Commentaries, 1978-83; mem. editorial bd. Videodisc Music Series, NEH, 1982-86; contbr. articles to profl. jours. Fellow Cornell U., 1953-54, NEH, Italy, 1972-73, England, 1979-80, Guggenheim, 1984-85; Fulbright sr. rsch. grant in Italy, 1965-66, sr. Fulbright lectr. Moscow State Conservatory, 1990. Mem. Am. Mus. Soc. (chmn. S.E. chpt. 1969-71, mem. coun. 1969-71, 75-77, bd. dirs. 1977-79, pres. 1980-82, del. to Am. Coun. Learned Socs. 1984-88, to Internat. Congress Strasbourg 1982), Music Libr. Assn. (bd. dirs. 1968-70), Soc. for Am. Music, Internat. Assn. Jazz Educators, Internat. Trumpet Guild. Avocations: hiking, jazz trumpet performance.

SMITHERAM, MARGARET ETHERIDGE, health facility administrator, director; b. Atlanta, Jan. 5, 1938; d. Philip Fitzgerald and Mary Catharine (Dwyer) E.; m. Roy Charles McCracken, May 5, 1975; m. William Bertram Smitheram, Aug. 17, 1985. BA, Emory U., 1960; M in Health Adminstrn.,

Washington U., St. Louis, 1973. Registered record administr., 1960-71; spl. asst. to dir. VA Med. Ctr., Roseburg, Oreg., 1973-74; hosp. administrn, specialist VA Central Office, Washington, 1974-75; asst. dir. trainee VA Med. Ctr., Phila., 1976, assoc. dir. Hampton, Va., 1976--80, Buffalo, N.Y., 1980-81; presdl. exchange exec. Kimberly Clark Corp., Neenah, Wis., 1981-82, Roswell, Ga., 1981-82; dir. VA Med. Ctr., Grand Island, Nebr., 1982-94; interim dir. Grand Island-Hall County Health Dept., 1996-97; instr. Cerritos Coll., 1969-70. Bd. dirs. Project 2M Coordinating Coun., Inc., Grand Island, 1985-87, Hall County Leadership Unlimited, Inc., 1990. Bd. dirs. Grand Island Area United Way, 1987-90 (pres. 1989), Grand Island Concert Assn, 1987-92, Ctrl. Nebr. Goodwill Industries, Inc., 1987-93 (pres. 1991-92). Fellow Am. Coll. Healthcare Execs. (life); mem. rev. bd. State of Nebr. Foster Care, Am. Hosp. Assn., Fed. Exec. Assn. (pres. Grand Island chpt. 1987), Nebr. Hosp. Assn., Grand Island C. of C. (bd. dirs. 1988-92, legis. affairs com 1984-85, priorities com. 1984-85, govtl. affairs com. 1984-88, nominating com. 1991-92, 94-95, audit com. 1992-93, pres. club 1993-94), Rotary Internat. Club #1485 (v.p. 1998-2000, pres. 2000-2001, District 5630 Group Study Exchange Team Leader to South Korea District 3710, 1999, Paul Harris fellow). Home: 221 Trail of the Flowers Georgetown TX 78628 E-mail: montuma@juno.com.

SMITHEY, DONALD LEON, airport authority director; b. St. Louis, Aug. 31, 1940; children: Kelly, Jill. Student, St. Ambrose Coll., 1962; BS in Bus. Mgmt., So. Ill. U., 1966; postgrad., U. Mo., St. Louis, 1973-74. Asst. ops. dispatcher Ozark Airlines, 1971-72; transp. analyst Olin Corp., 1972-78, cost acct., 1978-80; commr. St. Louis Regional Airport Authority, 1971-80, chmn., 1974-80, airport dir., 1980-83; asst. dir. Cedar Rapids Mcpl. Airport, 1983-85; dir. adminstrn. Omaha Airport Authority, 1985-87, dep. exec. dir., 1987-89, exec. dir., 1989—. With USN Air Res. 1963-66, USN, 1966-68. Mem. Am. Assn. Airport Execs. (Great Lakes chpt.), Airports Coun. Internat., Iowa Airport Exec. Assn. (past pres.), Ill. Pub. Airports Assn. (past v.p.), Exptl. Aircraft Assn., Omaha Rotary Club, Masonic Lodge (Bethalto, Ill.), Tangier Shrine (Omaha), Quiet Birdmen Assn., Silver Wings Fraternity. Office: Omaha Airport Authority 4501 Abbott Dr Omaha NE 68110-2698

SMITH-HILLIKER, RENÉE ANNE, administrative assistant, writer; b. Pitts., Nov. 9, 1963; d. Charles Guy Smith and Carolyn Marie Cunningham-Smith; m. Arthur Hughes Hilliker, July 23, 1988; children: Laurel Victoria, Alexander James. BA in Journalism and Comm., Point Park U., 1986. Program dir. Boys and Girls Club, Summerside, Canada; head librn. Grand Centre (Alta.) Dist. Libr., Canada, U. Pitts.; exec. asst. PNC Bank, Westinghouse. Officer United Boys and Girls Brigade, Pitts. Avocations: painting, writing, hiking, cooking, adventure travel.

SMITHIES, OLIVER, geneticist, educator; b. Halifax, Eng., June 23, 1925;, naturalized; PhD in Biochemistry, Oxford U., Eng., 1951. Postdoctoral fellow phys. chemistry U. Wis., Madison, 1951—53, from asst. prof. to prof. genetics and med. genetics, 1960—63, Leon J. Cole prof., 1971—80, Hilldale prof., 1980—88; rsch. asst., assoc. Connaught Med. Rsch. Lab., Toronto, Canada, 1953—60; Excellence prof. dept. pathology and lab. medicine U. N.C., Chapel Hill, 1988—. Mem. nat. adv. med. sci. coun. NIH, 1985. Contbr. articles to profl. jours. Recipient William Allen Meml. award, Am. Soc. Human Genetics, 1964, Karl Landsteiner Meml. award, Am. Assn. Blood Banks, 1984, Internat. award, Gairdner Found., 1990, 1993, State of N.C. award, 1994, Alfred P. Sloan Jr. prize, 1994, Hypertension Rsch. award, CIBA, 1996, Cardiovasc./Metabolic Disease Rsch. award, Bristol-Meyers Squibb, 1997, Rsch. Achievement award, AHA, 1998, Albert Lasker award for Med. Rsch., 2001, Max Gardner award, 2002, Wolf prize in medicine, 2003; scholar Markle, 1961. Fellow: AAAS; mem.: Inst. Medicine, 2004, Genetics Soc. Am. (v.p. 1974, pres. 1975), Am. Acad. Arts & Sci., NAS. Achievements include research in on targetted modification of specific genes in living animals. Office: Univ N C Dept Pathology & Lab Med Chapel Hill NC 27599-0001

SMITH-JONES, MARY EMILY, elementary school physical education educator; b. Ducktown, Tenn., Jan. 9, 1949; d. Oscar Clinton and Mary Myrtice (Hayes) S. Student, Kennesaw (Ga.) Jr. Coll., 1967-69; BS in Edn., Ga. So. Coll., 1971; MEd, Delta State U., 1974; EdS, West Ga. Coll., 1991. Cert. tchr., Ga. Tchr. phys. edn. East Hall High Sch., Gainesville, Ga., 1971-73, Morrow (Ga.) Elem. Sch., 1974—. Mem. com. to write phys. edn. curriculum for grades kindergarten through 4 State of Ga.; mem. com. to write elem. phys. edn. curriculum Clayton County, Ga. Mem. AAHPERD (mem. conv. hospitality com. 1991), Ga. Assn. Health, Phys. Edn., Recreation and Dance (exhibits chairperson 1992, 93). Home: 180 Falling Waters Dr Jonesboro GA 30236-5485 Office: Morrow Elem Sch 6115 Reynolds Rd Morrow GA 30260-1151

SMITH-MOONEY, MARILYN PATRICIA, city government official, management consultant and facilitator; b. Jamaica, NY, July 5, 1942; d. Raymond Lionel and Katherine Marie (Doepp) Cowan; m."Jack" (John) J. Mooney, Sept. 1, 2002; 1 child, Paul William Hibner. Student various aviation schs., St. Joseph's Coll., N.Y. cert. in Leadership and Human Resources Devel., Goldratt Inst., Conn., JONAH cert. Inst. Elected Ofcls., Advanced Inst. for Elected Ofcls., Leadership Charlotte Class of 97-98, Local Govt. Leadership Fla., Class IV-99. Exec. sec. to chief design Wiedersum Assoc., Arch. and Engr., Valley Stream, NY, 1960-61; office mgr., arch. apprentice, interior designer Keith I. Hibner, Arch., Hicksville, Garden City, NY, 1961-73; owner, pres. Hibner Atelier, Ltd., Garden City, 1968-75; interior design and gen. constrn. Garden City, 1968-76; office mgr., tech. planning, manual writer for county dept. structure & operation Ward Assoc./Planning Assoc., Arch. and Engr., Bohemia, NY, 1975-76; chief pilot, flight/ground aviation instr. Islip Aviation Ltd., NY, 1974-77; exec. asst. to pres. Arkay Packaging Corp., Hauppauge, NY, 1977-86; in-house constrn. mgr., 1980-82; adminstrn. and human resources mgr. Arkay Packaging Corp., Hauppauge, NY, 1986-89, dir. corp. devel., 1989, dir. materials mgmt., 1989-90. Cert. assoc. Goldratt Inst. for LI/Metro NY area, 1990-92; owner Concepts for Constructive Change, Educators and Facilitators for Continuous Improvement, Lake Grove, NY, 1990-92; ind. aviation flight/ground instr. airplane and instrument, 1977—; safety counselor FAA, 1974-92, FAA Ea. region counselors coord., 1985-86; mem. city charter rev. com. City Punta Gorda, Fla., 1996; mem. city coun. City of Punta Gorda, Fla., 1996—, vice mayor, 1998-99, 2000-01, first woman mayor, 2001-02, 2002-03; selected "top 100" west influential in Charlotte County by "Charlotte SUN", 2002, 2003; past bd. dir., officer Aviation Coun. LI; founder Seminar on Air Travel for Everyone (S.A.F.E.), 1975, Fly-C-Cure/We Air Condition People, 1979; city coun. appointee to S.W. Fla. Regional Planning Coun., 1999—, Charlotte County tourist devel. coun., 1998—, Charlotte County Assembly, 1998, 2001, Punta Gorda Historic Mural Soc., past mem. bd. dir.; county appointee Enterprise Charlotte Econ. Devel. team. Author articles, seminar syllabus. Past mem. nat. panel Consumer Arbitrators, Nat. Consumer Arbitration Program, Better Bus. Bur.; lic. comml. pilot, flight and ground instr.; chmn. bd. Charlotte Skatepark, Inc.; past Bd. mem., past officer Punta Gorda Elks Lodge 2606. Past chmn. ninety-nines L.I. chpt., founding internat. chmn. safety edn., Amelia Earhart Bronze medal 1975, Old Punta Gorda, Inc.; mem. various cmty. non-profit org., (past mem. bd. dir.). Home: 654 Andros Ct Punta Gorda FL 33950-5809

SMITH-SANDERS, CAROL ANN, music therapist, psychologist; b. Montgomery County, Tenn., Apr. 19, 1951; d. Carl and Ruth (Gettinger) S. BME in Music Therapy, U. Kans., 1974; MA in Clin. Psychology, Mid. Tenn. State U., 1977; EdS in Human Svc. Mgmt., Vanderbilt U., 1979; EdD in Ednl. Adminstrn., Auburn U., 1997. Gen. therapeutic recreation specialist VA Med. Ctr., Murfreesboro, Tenn., 1973-79, music therapist Marion, Ind., 1979, chief recreation therapy service Tucson, 1979-84, chief recreation therapy Northport, N.Y., 1984-87, health systems specialist Dir.'s Office Cleve., 1987-88, adminstrv. asst. to assoc. dir., 1988-91, adminstrv. asst. to chief of staff Tuskegee, Ala., 1991-97; sr. health sys. specialist, med. dir. clin. programs Ctrl. Ala. Vets. Health Care sys., 1997—. Adj. instr. Mid. Tenn. State U., part-time 1978—; guest speaker, 1975—; facilitator AchieveGlobal. Contbr. articles to profl. jours. Mem. Am. Psychol. Assn. (assoc.), Nat. Assn. Music Therapy (cert.), NAFE, Phi Kappa Phi. Home: 1003 Wallace Ave Opelika AL 36801-6958 Office Phone: 334-725-3080. E-mail: carol.sanders@med.va.gov.

SMITHSON, CHARLES WAYNE, economist, consultant; b. Dallas, Sept. 29, 1946; s. Charles Winston and LaVerne (Putman) S.; m. Cynthia Ann Thomas, May 18, 1973; children: Nathan Thomas, Charles Matthew. BA in Econs., U. Tex., Arlington, 1969, MA, 1973; PhD, Tulane U., 1976. Instr. econs. U. New Orleans, 1975-76; asst. prof. Tex. A&M U., College Station, 1976-82, assoc. prof., 1983-85; sr. economist FTC, CPSC, 1982-83; v.p. Chase Manhattan Bank, N.Y.C., 1985-87, mng. dir. risk mgmt. rsch., 1990—94, sr. v.p., 1994—95; AT&T resident mgmt. fellow Simon Grad. Sch. Bus. U. Rochester, NY, 1987; prof. fin, dir. PhD program U. North Tex., Denton, 1987-88; v.p. product devel., risk mgmt. products Continental Bank, Chgo., 1988-89, mng. dir. rsch., product devel. global trading, distbn., 1989-90; mng. dir. sch. fin. products CIBC World Markets, N.Y.C., 1995—99; mng. ptnr. Rutter Assocs., N.Y.C., 1999—. Mem. working group Group of 30 Derivatives Project. Author: (with others) The Economics of Mineral Extraction, 1980, (with S.C. Maurice) Managerial Economics, 1981, (with S.C. Maurice) The Doomsday Myth: 10,000 Years of Economic Crisis, 1984, (with others) Managing Financial Risk, 1990, 94, 98, (edited collection with C.W.Smith) Handbook of Financial Engineering, 1990, Credit Protfolio Management, 2003; assoc. editor Financial Management; author (with others) of numerous monographs; adv. bd. Jour. Applied Corp. Fin.; contbr. articles to profl. jours. and other publs. 1st lt. USAF, 1969—73. Mem. Fin. Mgmt. Assn., Am. Econ. Assn., Internat. Assn. Fin. Engrs. (bd. dirs.). Avocations: fishing, golf, sailing, snorkeling. Home: 190 Shelter Ln Jupiter FL 33469 Office: 60 E 42ND St RM 2816 New York NY 10165-2822

SMITHSON, LOWELL LEE, lawyer; b. Kansas City, Mo., Apr. 29, 1930; s. Spurgeon Lee and Lena Louise (Ruddy) S.; m. Rosemary Carol Leitz, Jan. 30, 1960 (div. Sept. 1985); m. Phyllis Galley Westover, June 8, 1986; children: Carol Maria Louise, Katherine Frances Lee. AB in Polit. Sci., U. Mo., 1952, JD, 1954. Bar: Mo. 1954, U.S. Dist. Ct. (we. dist.) Mo. 1955, U.S. Supreme Ct. 1986. Ptnr. Smithson & Smithson, Kansas City, 1956-59; assoc. Spencer, Fane, Britt & Browne, Kansas City, 1959-64, ptnr., 1964—. Adj. prof. law U. Mo., Kansas City, 1982. Pres. Kansas City Mental Health Assn., 1963-65; mem. bd. pres. All Souls Unitarian Ch. Kansas City, 1965-67; chmn. com. select dean for law sch. U. Mo., 1983. Btry. Comdr. U.S. Army, 1954-56, Korea. Mem. Kansas City Bar Assn., Lawyers Assn. Kansas City, Assn. Trial Lawyers Am., Western Mo. Def. Lawyers Assn., Fed. Energy Bar Assn., Phi Beta Kappa, Phi Delta Phi. Democrat. Unitarian Ch. Avocations: skiing, reading, painting, swimming, canoeing. Home: 1215 W 65th St Kansas City MO 64113-1803 Office: Spencer Fane Britt & Browne 1000 Walnut 1400 Commerce Bank Bldg Kansas City MO 64106-2140 Office Phone: 816-474-8100. E-mail: lsmithson@spencerfane.com.

SMITH-THOMPSON, PATRICIA ANN, public relations consultant, educator; b. Chgo., June 7, 1933; d. Clarence Richard and Ruth Margaret (Jacobson) Nowack; m. Tyler Thompson, Aug. 2, 1992; children from previous marriage: Deborah, Kurt, Nancy, Janna, Gail, Lori. Student, Cornell U., 1951—52; BA, Centenary Coll., Hackettstown, N.J., 1983. Prodn. asst. Your Hit Parade Batten, Barton, Durstine & Osborne, 1953-54; pvt. practice polit. cons., 1954-66; legal sec., asst. Atty. John C. Cushman, 1966-68; field dep. L.A. County Assessor Office, 1968-69; pub. info. officer L.A. County Probation Dept., 1969-73; dir. consumer rels. Fireman's Fund, San Francisco, 1973-76; spl. projects officer L.A. County Transp. Commn., 1977-78; tchr. Calif. State U., Dominguez Hills, 1979-86. Editor, writer Jet Propulsion Lab., 1979—80; pub. info. dir. L.A. Bd. Pub. Works, 1980—82; pub. info. cons. City of Pasadena, Calif., 1982—84, pub. rels. cons., 1983—90; cmty. affairs cons. Worldport L.A., 1990—92; tchr. Kern County Schs., 2002—. Contbr. articles to profl. jours. Active First United Meth. Ch. Commn. Missions and Social Concerns, 1983—89; bd. dirs. Depot, 1983—87; mem. devel. com. Pasadena Guidance Clinics, 1984—85; pres. Cultural Arts Assn., Bear Valley Springs, 1999—2000, Calif. Press Women, Bay Area, 1975. Recipient Pro award, L.A. Publicity Club, 1978, Outstanding Achievement award, Soc. Consumer Affairs Profls. Bus., 1976, Disting. Alumni award, Centenary Coll., 1992. Mem.: Nat. Assn. Mental Health Info. Officers (3 regional awards 1986), Calif. Press Women (pres. Bay area 1975—76, award 1974, 1978, 1983, 1984, 1985, Cmty. Rels. 1st pl. winner 1986, 1987, 1988, 1989), Nat. Press Women (Calif. chpt. pres. 1975—76, Pub. Rels. award 1986), Pub. Rels. Soc. Am. (accredited mem., consumer program award 1977, 2 awards 1984, Joseph Roos Cmty. Svc. award 1985). Republican. Home and Office: 24145 Jacaranda Dr Tehachapi CA 93561-8309 Office Phone: 661-821-3804.

SMITS, EDWARD JOHN, museum consultant; b. Freeport, NY, Dec. 11, 1933; s. Karl M. and Jennie (Spring) S.; m. Ruth K. Hall; children: E. John, Robert K., Theodore R. BA, Hofstra U., 1955; MA, NYU, NY, 1959. Curator Nassau County Hist. Mus., East Meadow, NY, 1956-70; dir. mus. svc. Div. Mus. Svc. Nassau County, Syosset, NY, 1971-92. Nassau County historian, 1985—; planning coord. Mus. at Mitchel Ctr., 1994-2001; chmn. Nassau County Centennial Com.; CEO, Museums at Mitchel Cradle of Aviation, 2002-. Author: Long Island Landmarks, 1970, Creation of Nassau County, 1959, Nassau, Suburbia USA, 1974. Trustee Friends for L.I.'s Heritage, Nassau County Hist. Soc.; trustee, past pres. Levittown Libr. Bd. 1st lt. U.S. Army, 1955-56. Fulbright grantee, 1965; recipient Nassau County disting. svc. award, 1970, alumni disting. svc. award Hofstra U., 1970, H. Sherwood Historic Preservation on L.I. award Soc. for the Preservation of L.I. Antiquities, 1975. Mem. Am. Assn. Mus. Avocations: book collecting, antique toys, golf. Home: 14 Wavy Ln Wantagh NY 11793-1202

SMITS, HELEN LIDA, physician, medical administrator, educator; b. Long Beach, Calif., Dec. 3, 1936; d. Theodore Richard Smits and Anna Mary Wells; m. Roger LeCompte, Aug. 28, 1976; 1 child, Theodore. BA with honors, Swarthmore Coll., 1958; MA, Yale U., 1961, MD cum laude, 1967. Intern, asst. resident Hosp. U. Pa., 1967-68; fellow Beth Israel Hosp., Boston, 1969-70; chief resident Hosp. U. Pa., 1970-71; chief med. clinic U. Pa., 1971-75; assoc. adminstr. for patient care svcs. U. Pa. Hosp., 1975-77; v.p. med. affairs Community Health Plan Georgetown U., Washington, 1977; dir. health standards and quality bur. Health Care Financing Adminstrn., HHS, Washington, 1977-80; sr. rsch. assoc. The Urban Inst., Washington, 1980-81; assoc. prof. Yale U. Med. Sch., New Haven, 1981-85; assoc. v.p. for health affairs U. Conn. Health Ctr., Farmington, 1985-87; prof. community medicine U. Conn. Sch. Medicine, Farmington, 1985-93; hosp. dir. John Dempsey Hosp., Farmington, 1987-93; dep. administr. Health Care Financing Adminstrn., Washington, 1993-96; pres., chmn. Health Right, Inc., Meriden, Conn., 1996-99; vis. prof. Robert F. Wagner Grad. Sch. Pub. Svc., NYU, 1999—2001. Commr. Joint Com. on Accreditation Hosps., Chgo., 1989-93, chair, 1991-92; mem., co-chair strategic framework bd. Nat. Forum on Health Care Quality Measurement and Reporting, 2000—01; Fulbright lectr. faculty medicine Eduardo Mondlane U., Maputo, Mozambique, 2003-. Contbr. numerous articles to profl. jours. Bd. dirs. The Ivoryton Playhouse Fedn., Inc., 1990-92, The Connecticut River Mus., 1990-93, Hartford Stage, 1990-93; mem. Dem. Town Com., Essex, Conn., 1982-89. Recipient Superior Svc. award HHS, Washington, 1982; Royal Soc. Medicine Found. fellow, London, 1973; Fulbright scholar, 1959-60. Mem. ACP (master, regent 1984-90), Inst. Medicine, Nat. Acad. Scis., Phi Beta Kappa, Alpha Omega Alpha. Episcopalian. Avocations: sailing, cooking, gardening. Office: 4 Washington Sq N Rm 23 New York NY 10003-6671

SMITS, JIMMY, actor; b. N.Y.C., July 9, 1955; two children. Master's degree, Cornell Univ., 1982. Appearances include Off-Broadway prodns., tours with regional theatres; (TV series) Miami Vice, 1984, L.A. Law, 1986-91 (Outstanding Actor in Dramatics Series Emmy award 1990), NYPD Blue, 1994-99; (TV movies) Rockabye, 1986, The Highwayman, 1987, Glitz, 1988, The Broken Cord, 1991, Stephen King's The Tommyknockers, 1992; (films) Running Scared, 1986, The Believers, 1987, Old Gringo, 1988, Vital Signs, 1989, Fires Within, 1989, Switch, 1990, Gross Misconduct, 1992, The Cisco Kid, 1993, Solomon & Sheba, 1994, My Family, 1994, Marshal Law, 1995, Murder in Mind, 1996, Lesser Prophets, 1997, Bless the Child, 2000, The Million Dollar Hotel, 2000, Price of Glory, 2000, Star Wars: Episode II - Attack of the Clones, 2002, Angel, 2003. Avocations: football, basketball, softball, reading. Office: care Sherman Mgmt 1516 S Beverly Dr Apt 304 Los Angeles CA 90035-3059

SMITS, RIK, retired professional basketball player; b. The Netherlands, Aug. 23, 1966; m. Candice Smits; children: Jasmine, Derrik. Grad., Marist Coll., 1988. Center Ind. Pacers, 1988—2000. Named to, NBA All-Rookie First Team, 1998. Avocations: Roadrunner cartoon memorabilia, rebuilding old cars.

SMITS, RONALD FRANCIS, English educator, poet; b. Bayonne, NJ, Dec. 22, 1943; s. Edwin Joseph and Florence Ann Smits; m. Bonnie Lee Brown, June 10, 1970 (div. Mar. 1976); 1 child, Ronald Thomas. AB, Rutgers U., 1966; MS, Ind. State U., 1969; PhD, Ball State U., 1978. Instr. English, Kaskaskia Coll., Centralia, Ill., 1969-74; instr. Ball State U., Muncie, Ind., 1976-78; asst. prof. English, Indiana U. Pa., 1979-92, assoc. prof., 1992-96, prof., 1996—. Contbr. poems to jours. 1st lt. U.S. Army, 1966-68, Vietnam. Doctoral fellow Ball State U., 1974-78; Disting. Faculty Award, Creativ Arts, Indiana U. Pa, 1993; recipient Outstanding Faculty award English Assn. of Pa. State U., 2002. Avocations: walking, nature hikes, walks through city neighborhoods, nature study, reading. Home: PO Box 466 Ford City PA 16226 0466 Office: Ind U of Pa Armstrong County Campus Kittanning PA 16201 Office Phone: 724-543-1078.

SMITTLE, NELSON DEAN, military analyst, artist; b. Peebles, Ohio, Sept. 19, 1934; s. Nelson John and Alma Katherine (Green) S.; m. Claire Wiggins, May 5, 1973. BS, BFA, U. Cin., 1962, MA, 1971. Commd. 2d lt. U.S. Army, 1962; staff officer U.S. Army Photo Agy. Pentagon, Washington, 1966; detachment comdr. tactical comms. Republic South Vietnam, 1967-68; commn. transferred to USAF, 1970; instr. art U. Cin., 1972; comdr. 907th communications squadron Rickenbacker AFB, Ohio, 1972; dir. ops. fixed communications Air Combat Command Langley AFB, Va., 1982; dir. info. systems AWACS, 1984-85; dep. chief of staff standard systems Air Material Command, 1985; comdr. engring. installation divsn. Tinker AFB, Okla., 1988; commd. col., ret. USAF, Cin., 1988, 91, ret., 1991; pres. Falcon Techs., Cin., 1991-98; tchr. Princeton City Sch. Dist., Cin., 1992-94; pres. Thumbs Up Aerospace Art, Cin., 1998—; instr. art history Cin. State Tech. & Cmty. Coll., 2000—; mil. analyst 700 WLW AM Radio, Cin., 2001—, WCPO TV, 2003—, WXIX TV, 2001—; lectr. Thumbs Up Am., Ams. at War, 2001—. Asst. prof., adj. faculty drawing and painting U.C. Clermont Coll., 2002—; lectr. USAF Mus., Ams. at War, 2002—; cons. Air War Coll., Air Univ., Maxwell AFB, Ala., 1987—, Def. Systems Mgmt. Coll., Ft. Belvoir, Va., 1988—; faculty Cin. Acad. Leadership U. Cin. Coll. Law, 2003—. Author: Army Visual Presentation, 1966 (medal 1966), Famous Moments in Aerospace History, 1997; exhibited in group shows Mus. of Flight, Seattle, 1997, Midland (Mich.) Arts Ctr., 1997, Wichita Ctr Arts, 1998, Ralice Studio, Cin., 1998, Master Works Exhibit, Cin., 1999, Cin. Mus. Ctr., 1998, Mus. Aviation, Warner Robbins, Ga., 1999, Pub. Libr. Cin., Hamilton County, Ohio, 1999, Cin. Art Club, 2001, Kathy McCoy Design Studio, Batavia, Ohio, 2004; author cover art Jour of League of World War I Aviation Historians, Jour. WWI Aviation Historians, 1999 Mem. Batavia (Ohio) City Coun., 1972; pres. Ohio Buckeye Wing Assn., Columbus, 1973; mem. Air Force Policy Coun., Washington, 1978; congl. campaign mgr., 1993; bd. dirs. Cin. Art Club, 1995-96. Decorated Commendation medal; recipient Meritorious Svc. medal Dept. Def., 1986, 91. Mem.: VFW, DAV, Mil. Officers Assn. Am. (dir. pub. affairs Cin. chpt.), Am. Soc. Aviation Artists, Res. Officers Assn., Air Force Assn., Aircraft Owners and Pilots Assn., 82d Airborne Assn. Avocations: freelance writer, walking, science fiction, lecturer, military analyst. Home and Office: Thumbs Up America 198 Palisades Pointe Cincinnati OH 45238-5653 Office Phone: 513-922-6018.

SMOAK, EVAN L. lawyer; b. Columbia, S.C., Jan. 30, 1967; s. Lewis E. and Phyllis Anderson. BAS cum laude, U. S.C., 1989; JD, U. Va., 1992. Bar: Conn. 1992, N.Y. 1993, U.S. Dist. Ct. (so. and ea. dists.) N.Y. 1993, U.S. Ct. Appeals (2d cir.) 2000. Actor S.C. Ednl. Television, Columbia, 1977-86; atty. Werner & Kennedy, N.Y.C., 1992-97; assoc., ptnr. Barger & Wolen, N.Y.C., 1997—. Art auction co-chair Empire State Pride Agenda, N.Y.C., 1996-98, devel. com., 1999—, bd. dirs., 2000—, N100 fundraiser co-chair, 2001-02, exec. com. 2002—, bd. counsel, 2002-04; vice-chair fall dinner fundraiser, 2002, co-chair, 2003—. Recipient Thomas Moore Craig award U. S.C., 1988; Carolina scholar, 1985-89, Nat. Merit scholar, 1985-89. Mem. ABA, Assn. Bar of City of N.Y., Phi Beta Kappa, Omicron Delta Kappa. Democrat. Home: 445 W 23d St New York NY 10011 Office: Barger & Wolen LLP 10 E 40th St 40th Fl New York NY 10016 Office Phone: 212-557-2800.

SMOAK, JEFF C., JR., music educator; b. Savannah, Ga., May 8, 1962; m. Cheryl D. Judy, July 9, 1988; 1 child, Cameron. BA in Music Edn., Charleston (S.C.) So. U., 1984; MA in Ch. Music, DMA, So. Bapt. Theol. Sem., 1991. Adj. prof. of music So. Bapt. Theol. Sem., Louisville, 1991—94; prof. and music dept. chmn. Cumberland Coll., Williamsburg, Ky., 1994—. Min. music Main St. Bapt. Ch., Williamsburg, Ky., 2003—. Min. of music Greenland Bapt. Ch., Corbin, Ky., 1994—2003. Mem.: Music Educators Nat. Conf., Am. Choral Dirs. Assn., Nat. Assn. of Tchrs. of Singing. Office: Cumberland College Music Department 7525 College Station Drive Williamsburg KY 40769 E-mail: jsmoak@cumberlandcollege.edu.

SMOAK, LEWIS TYSON, lawyer; b. Orangeburg, S.C., Feb. 11, 1944; s. William B. and Louise (Dempsey) S.; m. Elizabeth Adams Babb, July 16, 1969; children— Katherine, Blair, Tyson. B.A., Furman U., 1966; J.D., U. S.C., 1969. Bar: S.C. 1969, D.C. 1982. Founder, Ogletree, Deakins, Nash, Smoak and Stewart, Greenville, S.C., 1969— . Fellow Coll. Labor and Employment Lawyers; mem. ABA, Greenville County Bar Assn., S.C. Bar Assn., D.C. Bar Assn., Poinsett Club, Greenville Country Club, Wade Hampton Golf Club (Cashiers, N.C.), Doonbeg (Ireland) Golf Club. Office: 300 N Main St Greenville SC 29601

SMOAK, RANDOLPH DUNCAN, JR., surgeon; b. Bamberg, S.C., May 5, 1933; MD, Med. Coll. S.C., 1959. Diplomate Am. Bd. Surgery. Intern Grady Meml. Hosp., Atlanta, 1959-60; resident surgery Med. U. S.C.-Teaching Hosps., 1962-65, resident, tchg. fellow, 1965-66; fellow surgery MD Anderson Cancer Ctr., Houston, 1966-67; surg. staff Orangeburg (S.C.) Calhoun Regional Hosp., 1967-87, emeritus staff, 1987; clin. prof. surgery Med. U. S.C., Charleston, 1987—, U.S.C. Sch. Medicine, Columbia, 86—. Fellow ACS; mem. AMA (pres. 2000-01), So. Med. Assn., Soc. Head and Neck Surgeons, So. Soc. Clin. Surgeons, Soc. Clin. Oncology. Office: 275 Mason Rd Orangeburg SC 29118-8201 Business E-Mail: smoak@ama-assn.org.

SMOCK, DONALD JOE, governmental liaison, political consultant; b. Ponca City, Okla., Sept. 24, 1964; s. Joe Clellan and Ruth Esther Smock. BA in Polit. Sci., U. Ctrl. Okla., 1991, MA in Urban Affairs, 1993. Rschr. The Nigh Inst. State Govt., Edmond, 1993-94. U. Ctrl. Okla. del. to Ctr. Study of Pres. Symposium, Washington, 1993; govt. liaison Elizey Electric Motor Co., 1994-96; govt. affairs dir. Oklahoma City Met. Assn. Realtors, 1997—. Charter founder Ronald Reagan Rep. Ctr., 1989; del. State of Okla. Rep. Presdl. Task Force, 1996; mem. Rep. Presdl. Trust, 1996. Recipient Okla. Rep. Blue Key award, 1984, Presdl. Commn., 1992, Merit cert. Rep. Nat. Com., 1990; named to Ronald Reagon Rep. Ctr. Presdl. Commemorative Honor Roll, 1991; by order of President George Bush flag dedicated in name Rotunda of U.S. Capitol, 1990. Mem. Tau Kappa Epsilon (Delta Nu colony inductee, chpt. advisor 1990-92, Fraternity for Life inductee, David Crain Leadership award 1986, Ed Howell Leadership award 1988-89, Red Carnation Ball dedicated in name 1989-90, 94, Top Alumnus 1990-91), Pi Sigma Alpha. Republican. Mem. Ch. of Christ. Home: PO Box 6323 Edmond OK 73083-6323

SMOCK, RAYMOND WILLIAM, historian; b. Jeffersonville, Ind., Feb. 8, 1941; s. Richard and Lottie (Paciorek) S.; m. Phyllis Lee Chadwick, Feb. 12, 1961 BA, Roosevelt U., Chgo., 1966; PhD, U. Md., College Park, 1974. Rsch. asst. Md. Constl. Conv., Annapolis, 1967-68; lectr. in history U. Md., College Park, 1968-72; co-editor The Booker T. Washington Papers, 14 vols., 1972-83; pres. Instructional Resources Corp., Lanham, Md., 1976-83, Rsch. Materials Corp., College Park, 1982-83, dir., 1982-85; historian, dir. Office for Bicentennial, U.S. Ho. of Reps., Washington, 1983-89, Office of Historian, U.S. Ho. of Reps., Washington, 1989-95. Mem. editl. advisors Md. Historian, College Park, 1971—95; exec. dir. Robert C. Byrd Ctr. for Legis. Studies, Shepherd

Coll., Shepherdstown, W.Va., 2002—. Author: A Talent for Detail: The Photographs of Miss Frances Benjamin Johnston 1889-1910, 1974; co-editor: A Guide to Manuscripts in the Presidential Libraries, 1985, Masters of the House, 1998; editor: Booker T. Washington in Perspective: The Essays of Louis R. Harlan, 1988; author, editor: Landmark Documents on the U.S. Congress, 1998. Ford Found. fellow, 1970; recipient Philip M. Hamer award Soc. Am. Archivists, 1979 Mem. Nat. Coun. Pub. History, Assn. for Documentary Editing (pres. 1983-84), Orgn. Am. Historians, So. Hist. Assn., Soc. History in Fed. Govt. (v.p./pres.-elect 2000— Avocations: photography, astronomy. E-mail: RaySmock@aol.com.

SMOCK, TIMOTHY ROBERT, lawyer; b. Richmond, Ind., June 24, 1951; s. Robert Martin and Thelma Elizabeth (Cozad) S.; m. Martha Carolene Middleton, Apr. 4, 1992; children: Andrew Zoller, Alison Pierce. BA, Wittenberg U., 1973; JD cum laude, Ind. U., 1977. Bar: Ind. 1977, Ariz. 1979, U.S. Dist. Ct. (so. dist.) Ind. 1977, U.S. Dist. Ct. Ariz. 1979, U.S. Ct. Apeals (7th cir.) 1977, U.S. Ct. Appeals (9th cir.) 1979. Jud. clk. Ct. of Appeals of Ind., Indpls., 1977-79; assoc. Lewis and Roca, Phoenix, 1979-82; assoc./shareholder Gallagher & Kennedy, Phoenix, 1982-89; ptnr. Scult, French, Zwillinger & Smock, Phoenix, 1989-94, Smock and Weinberger, Phoenix, 1994-99, Richards and Smock, Phoenix, 1999—. Judge, pro tempore Maricopa County Superior Ct., Phoenix, 1989—; faculty, State Bar Course on Professionalism, Ariz. Supreme Ct./State Bar, Phoenix, 1992—; speaker, Continuing Legal Edn., Maricopa County and Ariz. State Bar, 1988—. Mem. ABA, Ariz. Bar Assn., Maricopa Bar Assn., Def. Rsch. Inst. Office: Richards and Smock 1202 E Missouri Ave Ste 150 Phoenix AZ 85014-2900 Office Phone: 602-277-8449. E-mail: Timothy.Smock@azbar.org.

SMOKE, RICHARD EDWIN, lawyer, investment advisor; b. Detroit, Sept. 16, 1945; s. Bruno Donald and Else Marie (Reinvaldt) S. BA, Kalamazoo (Mich.) Coll., 1967; JD, Wayne State U., 1970. Bar: Mich. 1970, Calif. 1975, U.S. Supreme Ct. 1980. Gen. counsel Grosse Ile (Mich.) Bridge Co., 1975-78, pres., 1980-83, v.p., 1983—88; gen. counsel Campbell-Ewald Co., Warren, Mich., 1978-80; pvt. practice law, investment adviser Grand Rapids, Mich., 1985—2002. Dir. Kent County Cmty. Mental Health, 1996; adj. faculty Davenport Coll., 1993-95; trustee Grand Rapids Charter Twp., 1991-96; commr. County of Kent, 1996-2002. Bd. dirs. World Affairs Coun. Western Mich., Grand Rapids, 1988-93, pres., 1991-92; mem. exec. com. Kent County Rep. Party, Grand Rapids, 1989-92, 1995-2002; trustee Kalamazoo Coll., 1970-79. London-Sloan fellow, 1983. Mem.: Univ. Club of San Francisco, State Bar Calif., State Bar Mich. Home: 835 Pine Street #16 San Francisco CA 94108 Office Phone: 415-397-1403. E-mail: RESMOKE@CS.COM.

SMOKER, ROY ELLIS, retired military officer; b. Richmond, Ind., Dec. 7, 1943; s. Vernon Willard and Emma May (Creager) S.; m. Linda Carol Kensinger, Sept. 7, 1969; children: Cheryl Lynn, Deborah June; m. JoAnn Bratcher, May, 2001. BA in Econs. and Math., Blackburn Coll., 1965; MA in Econs., U. N.D., 1967; PhD, U. Mo., 1984. Commd. 2d lt. USAF, 1971, advanced through grades to col., 1992, chief rsch. integration Office Productivity and Rsch., 1980-82, sr. mil. estate program analyst Office Sec. Def., 1982-84, sr. logistics analyst, 1984-85, dep. dir., dir. program control Milstar Joint Program Office, 1985-89, chief econ. analysis asst. sec. USAF for fin. mgmt., 1989-90, chief space and strategic def., 1990-91; dir. bus. ops. Titan Sys. Program Office, 1991-93; comptroller Arnold (Tenn.) Engring. Devel. Ctr., 1993-95, Air Force Devel. TestCtr., 1995-97, Air Force Space and Missile System Ctr., 1997-2000; dir. program mgmt. MCR Fed., Inc., 2001—. Bd. dirs. Aerospace Fed. Credit Union, 1998-2000; fin. advisor Alzheimer's Assn., Tullahoma, Tenn., 1993-95; chmn. bd. trustees 1st United Meth. Ch., Huntington Beach, Calif., 1987-89. Decorated Joint Svc. Achievement medals, Air Orgnl. Excellence award, and numerous others. Mem. Mo. U. Alumni Assn., Air Force Assn., Soc. Cost Estimating and Analysis, Am. Soc. Mil. Comptrollers (pres. L.A. chpt. 1998), Franklin County C. of C. (bd. dirs. 1993-95). Office Phone: 310-640-0005.

SMOKER, WENDY RUE KARTINOS, neuroradiologist, consultant, educator; b. Evanston, Ill., Feb. 28, 1948; d. Nicholas John and Marjorie (Smith) Kartinos; 1 child, Andrew Jason Smoker. BS, U. Iowa, 1971, MS, 1972, MD, 1977. Diplomate Am. Bd. Radiology, cert. added qualification in neuroradiology Am. Bd. Radiology. Asst. prof. radiology U. Iowa Hosps., Iowa City, 1982-86; assoc. prof. radiology U. Utah, Salt Lake City, 1986-90, acting dir. neuroradiology, 1989-90; prof. radiology Med. Coll. of Va., Richmond, 1990—2001, dir. neuroradiology, 1990-2000, prof. neurosurgery, 1997—2001, prof. otolaryngology, 1998—2001; prof. radiology U. Iowa Hosps., Iowa City, 2002—, dir. neuroradiology, 2002—. Contbr. chpts. to books; dep. editor Radiology, 1997-01; mem. editl. adv. bd. Am. Jour. Neuroradiology, 1989-97, The Radiologist, 1993-96, Stroke, 1996-97. Fellow: Am. Coll. Radiology; mem.: Am. Roentgen Ray Soc. (Silver medal 1992, Gold medal 1993), Radiol. Soc. N.Am. (program com. 1992—97), Am. Soc. Neuroradiology (sec. 1996—98), Am. Assn. Women Radiologists (treas. 1993—99, v.p. 2002—03), Am. Soc. Head and Neck Radiology (pres. 1998—99, 1st past pres. 1999—2000, councilor 1999—). Avocations: scuba diving, river rafting, jazz singing. Office: U Iowa Hosps Dept Radiology 200 Hawkins Dr 0436 JCP Iowa City IA 52242- E-mail: wendy-smoker@uiowa.edu.

SMOKVINA, GLORIA JACQUELINE, nursing educator; b. East Chicago, Ind., July 29, 1937; Diploma in nursing, St. Margaret Hosp. Sch. Nursing, 1959; BSN, DePaul U., 1964; MSN, Ind. U., 1966; PhD in Nursing, Wayne State U., 1977. RN, Ind. Staff and charge nurse surgical units St. Catherine Hosp., East Chgo., Ind., 1959-61, charge nurse surgical units, 1962-64; asst. head nurse ICU El Camino Hosp., Mountain View, Calif., 1961-62; instr. nursing South Chgo. Community Hosp., Chgo., 1964-65; asst. prof. med.-surgical nursing U. Evansville, Ind., 1966-70; assoc. prof. nursing Purdue U. Calumet, Hammond, Ind., 1970-80, prof. nursing, 1980—, acting head dept. nursing, 1986-87, head dept. nursing, 1987—, head sch. nursing, 1996—, dean schs. of profl. programs, 1996—2002, dean Sch. of Nursing, 2002—. Bd. dir. Health East Chgo. Cmty. Bd., St. Catherine Hosp.; cons. ICU St. Catherine Hosp., 1971, 74, 77, 79, 81, staff nurse, 71, 74, 77, 79, 81; cons. Vis. Nurses Assn., 1979, 80, Klapper, Issac & Parish Law Firm, Indpls., 1995; mem. adv. com. Vis. Nurse Assn. of NW Ind., 1977—; mem. Statewide Task Force on Nursing in Ind., 1987—; mem. Health E. Chgo. Task Force, 1996—; peer reviewer Coll. Nursing Valparaiso U., Ind., 1989; mem. gov. bd. St. Margaret Mercy Healthcare Ctrs. Inc., 1992—, chair quality svcs. com., 1992—, v.p., 1998—2001; mem. gov. bd. Sisters of St. Francis Regional Bd.; expert witness in several cases. Contbr. chpt. to Normal Aging: Dimensions of Wellness, 1986, Medical-Surgical Nursing, 1981; contbr. articles to profl. jours.; numerous rsch. projects. Mem. planning com. Lake County Health Fair, 1975, 77, nursing chair, 1978-80; chmn. nominations com. Ind. League for Nursing, 1995—; mem. adv. bd. Horizon Career Coll., Merriville, Ind., 1994—; mem. adv. com. Community Ctr. Devel. Corp., Hammond, 1993—, Three City Empowerment Zone E. Chgo., Gary and Hammond, 1994-95, grad. edn. Ind. U. Purdue U., 1981-85, Westhaysen Med. Edn. Trust Com. Calument Nat. Bank, Hammond, 1987—; mem. panel Healthy E. Chgo., 1994-96; mem. Community Health Assn., 1979-84; v.p. Am. Heart Assn. N.W. Ind. affiliate, 1984-87, mem. edn. com. 1982-87; bd. dirs. Our Lady of Mercy Hosp., Dyer, Ind., 1989-92, Health Adv., 1979-82; bd. dirs. Am. Heart Assn. Ind. affiliate, 1981-87, chair community programs, 1982-87; bd. dirs. Lakeshore Health Care System, 1988-89, quality assurance com. Grantee HHS, 1983-85, 84, 85-88, 90—, Helene Fuld Health Trust, 1989, 92, 93-94, Pub. Health Svc., 1989-90, 1990-91, Meth. Hosp., 1993-98; recipient Meritorious Svc. award Am. Cancer Soc. of N.W. Ind., 1979, Lake Area United Way, 1979, Cert. of Recognition Am. Heart Assn., 1983-84, Med. and Sci. Disting. Program award, 1985, Franciscan Award, Svc. Recogn. St. Margaret Mercy Healthcare Ctr., 2002. Mem. AACN, N.W. Ind. Orgn. Nurse Execs., Nurse Exec. Resource Group (U. Chgo.), Nat. League for Nursing, Ind. Deans and Dirs. of AD, BS and Higher Degree Programs, Nurse Exec. Forum, Wayne State Alumni Assn., St. Margaret Alumni Assn. (v.p. program com., chmn. scholarship com.), Ind. U. Alumni Assn., Mu Omega (chpt. commitment award 1994, chair fin. com. 1991—), Sigma Theta Tau (hon.). Office: Purdue U Calumet 2200 169th St Hammond IN 46323-2068 E-mail: smokvina@calumet.purdue.edu.

SMOLANSKY, BETTIE MORETZ, sociology educator; b. Columbia, S.C., June 1940; d. Walter Jennings Sr. and Opal (Ledford) Moretz; m. Oles M. Smolansky, Dec. 29, 1966; children: Alexandra Smolansky Zentmeyer, Nicholas Jennings. AB in Sociology, Lenoir-Rhyne Coll., 1962; MA in Sociology, Duke U., 1964; PhD in Sociology, Pa. State U., 1984. Instr. sociology Moravian Coll., Bethlehem, Pa., 1964-68, asst. prof., 1968-82, asst. dean, 1980-82, assoc. prof., 1982-88, prof., 1988—, chair dept. sociology, 1991-97, interim dean faculty, 1998-99, dean acad. affairs, 2000—01. Trustee Moravian Coll., 1977-81, 91-95, NEH visitor core curriculum workshop, 1985, sec. presdl. search com., 1996-97; mem. curriculum evaluation conf. Bklyn. Coll., 1988. Co-author: The USSR and Iraq, 1991 (AAAS Marshall Schulman prize 1992), The Lost Equilibrium, 2001. Bd. dirs. Northampton County Area on Aging, Bethlehem, 1984-90, 2003—; vice chair United Way Allocations Panel, Bethlehem, 1984-90; chair YWCA Commn. on Status of Women, Bethlehem, 1992-94; bd. dirs. YWCA of Bethlehem, 1993-97, 98-2002, 1st v.p., 1998-2000, pres., 2001-02. Recipient NDEA fellow, 1962-64, Disting. Alumnus award Lenoir-Rhyne Coll., 1995. Mem. Am. Sociol. Assn., Ea. Sociol. Assn., Lehigh Valley Assn. Acad. Women (pres. 1988-89, Woman of Yr. 1995-96), ODK (advisor 1987-90), AKD (advisor 1991—). Home: 3665 Walt Whitman Ln Bethlehem PA 18017-1553 Office: Moravian Coll Dept Sociology 1200 Main St Bethlehem PA 18018-6614 Fax: 610-861-3980. Office Phone: 610-861-1317. E-mail: mebms01@moravian.edu.

SMOLANSKY, OLES M. humanities educator; b. Ukraine, USSR, May 2, 1930; came to U.S. 1950; s. Mykola S. and Irene (Plinto) S.; m. Bettie Moretz, Dec. 29, 1966; children: Alexandra, Nicholas. BA, NYU, 1953; MA, Columbia U., 1955, PhD, 1959. Instr. UCLA, 1960-62; asst. prof. Lehigh U., Bethlehem, Pa., 1963-66, assoc. prof., 1966-70, prof., 1970-85, univ. prof., 1985—. Author: The Soviet Union and the Arab East Under Khrushchev, 1974, The USSR and Iraq: The Soviet Quest for Influence, 1991; co-editor: Russia and America: From Rivalry to Reconciliation, 1993, Regional Power Rivalries in the New Eurasia: Russia, Turkey, and Iran, 1995, The Lost Equilibrium: International Relations in the Post-Soviet Era, 2001; contbr. articles to profl. jours. Recipient joint fellowship, Rockefeller Found. and Ford Found., N.Y.C., 1962-63, sr. rsch. joint fellowship, Rsch. Inst. on Communist Affairs and Mid. East Inst., Columbia U., N.Y.C., 1972-73, rsch. fellowship, Ford Found., N.Y.C., 1980-81. Mem. Internat. Studies Assn., Am. Assn. for Advancement of Slavic Studies (Marshall Shulman award 1992), Mid. East Studies Assn., Mid. East Inst. Democrat. Greek-Orthodox. Avocations: music, sports. Home: 3665 Walt Whitman Ln Bethlehem PA 18017-1553 Office: Lehigh U Dept Internat Rels Bethlehem PA 18015 Office Phone: 610-758-3388. Business E-Mail: oms0@lehigh.edu.

SMOLEK, ROCHELLE THÉRÈSE, interior designer; b. Stamford, Conn., Jan. 31, 1948; d. Joseph Peter and Gladys Therese Bruno; m. Howard Thomas Uhal, Oct. 19, 1972 (div. July 1995); 1 child, Geoffrey Thomas; m. Frank D. Smolek, Jr., Aug. 30, 1995; stepchildren: Jason David, Kevin Kent. Designer Celange, Inc., N.Y.C., 1976-79, Len Coleman Designs, Charleston, S.C., 1980-83; cons. Rochelle T. Uhal Interiors, Cleve., 1983-86; owner Heritage Interiors, Ledyard, Conn., 1988-94; designer Jane Mabry Interior Design, Alpharetta, Ga., 1994-95; owner Fine Room Design, Inc., Roswell, Ga., 1995—. Chair 1999 Magnolia Ball, Bullock Hall, Roswell, 1999; chair Encore ASA Atlanta Symphony Assoc., 1996, asst. membership chair, 1998-99, showhouse opening night party, 1996, 97, chmn. Ensemble unit, 2001-, designer for decoration show house, 2000, 01. Mem. Am. Soc. Interior Design, Interior Design Soc. Republican. Roman Catholic. Avocation: travel.

SMOLENSKI, LISABETH ANN, family practice physician; b. Pitts., Oct. 1, 1950; d. Anthony Edward and Betty Jean (Gross) S.; m. William Ward Daniels, May 24, 1980; 1 child, Kathryn Elizabeth. BA, Carlow Coll., 1972; MD, Hahnemann U., 1982. Diplomate Am. Bd. Family Practice. Resident in family practice West Jersey Health Sys., Voorhees, N.J., 1982-85; pvt. practice, Somerville, Tenn., 1985-90, Memphis, 1990—2003; with Spectrum Pain Clinics, Franklin-Nashville, Tenn., 2003—. Sec. exec. com. med. staff Meth. Hosp. Somerville, 1988-90. Fellow Am. Acad. Family Physicians. Republican. Avocation: reading. Office: Spectrum Pain Clinics 324 Cool Springs Blvd Franklin TN 37067 Office Phone: 615-794-5009.

SMOLENSKY, EUGENE, economics professor; b. Bklyn., Mar. 4, 1932; s. Abraham and Jennie (Miller) S.; m. Natalie Joan Rabinowitz, Aug. 16, 1952; children: Paul, Beth. BA, Bklyn. Coll., 1952; MA, Am. U., 1956; PhD, U. Pa., 1961. Prof. econs. U. Wis., Madison, 1968-88, chmn. dept., 1978-80, 86-88; dir. Inst. for Research on Poverty, U. Wis., 1980-83; dean Grad. Sch. Pub. Policy, U. Calif., Berkeley, 1988-97, prof. pub. policy, 1997—. Author: Public Expenditures, Taxation and the Distribution of Income: The U.S., 1950, 61, 70, 77. Mem. Nat. Acad. Pub. Adminstrn., 1994; mem. com. on child devel. rsch. and pub. policy NAS, Washington, 1982-87, mem. com. on status of women in labor market, 1985-87. With USN, 1952-56. Mem. Am. Econs. Assn. Democrat. Jewish. Avocation: collecting old master etchings and lithographs. Home: 669 Woodmont Ave Berkeley CA 94708-1233 Office: U Calif Dept Pub Policy 2607 Hearst Ave Berkeley CA 94720-7305 Office Phone: 510-253-3979. Business E-Mail: geno@socrates.berkeley.edu.

SMOLLER, BRUCE MELVYN, psychiatrist; b. Chgo., Sept. 19, 1944; s. Norman and Beatrice Betty (Janows) Smoller; m. Cosette Nieporent, Aug. 20, 1967; children: Jamie, Lauren. AB, Cornell U., 1965; MD, Tulane U., 1969. Diplomate Am. Bd. Psychiatry and Neurology. Intern Maimonides Med. Ctr., N.Y.C., 1969-70; resident in orthopedic surgery Einstein Med. Ctr., N.Y.C., 1970-73; resident in psychiatry Cornell Med. Ctr., N.Y.C., 1973-76; pvt. practice in psychiatry with emphasis on clin. and rsch. aspects of pain Bethesda, Md., 1976—; chmn. dept. psychiatry Holy Cross Hosp., Silver Spring, Md., 1980-83; assoc. clin. prof. psychiatry George Washington U., 1977-91, clin. prof. psychiatry, 1991—. Cons. NIH, 1979—2001. Co-author: Pain Control: The Bethesda Program; editor: Md. Medicine, The State Med. Jour. With Med. Corps USAR, 1970—78. Mem.: Med. and Chirurgical Faculty of Md., Montgomery County Med. Soc. (pres.). Office: 5530 Wisconsin Ave Bethesda MD 20815-4404 Office Phone: 301-951-4466. E-mail: bsmoller@radix.net.

SMOLOWITZ, IRA EPHRAIM, finance educator, academic dean; b. Bklyn., May 16, 1941; s. Sam and Pearl (Pargament) S.; m. Judith Mary Marsala, Sept. 2, 1973; children: Peter Craig, Tara Joan. BA, CUNY Bklyn. Coll., 1963; MBA, Baruch Coll., N.Y.C., 1965; PhD, Rensselaer Poly. Inst., 1984. Asst. prof., then assoc. prof. fin. Siena Coll., Albany, N.Y., 1977-87; prof. fin., dean Sch. Bus. Adminstrn., dir. MBA program Am. Internat. Coll., Springfield, Mass., 1988—93, dean bus. bus. rsch. & program devel., 1993—. Contbr. articles to profl. jours. V.p. edn., bd. dirs. Bnai Jacob synagogue, Springfield, 1988-93. Recipient Spl. award SBA/Greater Springfield C. of C., 1990, Dean's Leadership award Acad. Bus. Adminstrn., 1993. Mem. Fin. Execs. Inst. (treas. Springfield chpt. 1989-90, sec. 1990-91, v.p. 1991-92, pres. 1992-93), Am. Prodn. and Inventory Control Soc., Western Mass. Internat. Trade Assn., Greater Springfield C. of C., New Eng. Colls. Bus. Adminstrn. Office: Am Internat Coll 1000 State St Springfield MA 01109-3151 Office Phone: 413-245-3369. E-mail: ismolowitz@acad.aic.edu. *Don't confuse lack of opportunity with failure to seize the opportunity.*

SMOLTZ, JOHN ANDREW, professional baseball player; b. Warren, Mich., May 15, 1967; With Detroit Tigers, 1985—87; pitcher Atlanta Braves, 1987—. Named Nat. League Pitcher of the Yr., Sporting News, 1996; named to All-Star Game, Nat. League, 1989, 1992, 1993, 1996, 2002, 2003; recipient Cy Young award, Baseball Writers' Assn. Am., 1996. Achievements include leading in strikeouts in Nat. League, 1992. Office: Atlanta Braves Turner Field PO Box 4064 Atlanta GA 30302-4064

SMOLYANSKY, JULIE, consumer products company executive; d. Michael and Ludmila Smolyansky. BA, U. Ill., 1996. Dir. sales and mktg. Lifeway Foods Inc., Morton Grove, Ill., 1997—2002, pres., 2002—, CEO, 2002—, CFO, 2002—, treas., 2002—, dir. Avocation: running. Office: Lifeway Foods Inc 6431 West Oakton Ave Morton Grove IL 60053*

SMOOK, MALCOLM ANDREW, chemist, chemical company executive; b. Seattle, Aug. 22, 1924; s. Joseph Murray and Bonnie (Hanson) S.; m. Mary Louise Nominee, Dec. 19, 1945; children— Frances Lynn Fenton, Valerie Dale Martin. BS, U. Calif., Berkeley, 1945; PhD in Organic Chemistry, Ohio State U., 1949. With E. I. duPont de Nemours & Co., Wilmington, Del., 1949—, research supr., 1952-53, div. head, 1953-57, asst. lab. dir., 1957-60, lab. dir., 1960-63, asst. research dir., 1963-75, gen. lab. dir., 1975-80, mgr. patents and regulatory affairs, 1980-84; cons. Malcolm A. Smook, Inc., 1985—. Mem. adv. com. NASA, 1971-76 Contbr. articles to profl. jours.; holder 9 patents. Served to lt. (j.g.) USN, 1943-46. Socony Vacuum fellow, 1948-49 Mem. Am. Chem. Soc., Sigma Xi. Home and Office: 59 Rockford Rd Wilmington DE 19806-1003 Personal E-mail: mal.smook@verizon.net.

SMOOT, BURGESS HOWARD, federal official; b. Washington, Mar. 28, 1947; s. James Elias and Frances Galdinia (Hawkins) S.; m. Ann Louise Gordon, Aug. 9, 1982; children: Frederick Hawkins, Chanel Gordon, Ervine Gholston, Shemerrian. Cook Freedmans Hosp., Washington, 1968-70; mail & file clk. Asst. Chief of Staff Intelligence, Washington, 1970-74; adminstrv. asst. logistics Office Joint Chiefs of Staff, Pentagon, Washington, 1974-77, adminstrv. asst. policy & plans, 1977-80. Author: (poetry) Lost in the Beginning. Capt. Neighborhood Watch Group, Fort Washington, Md., 1995-97; presdl. election official, 2000—, primary election judge for Md., 2002, primary and gen. presdl. election judge, 2004; judge for Md. gov., 2002; pres. Sunday Schs. 12yrs. through adult Capital Ward, 2002—. With U.S. Army, 1965-68, Civil Air Patrol, 1964-65. Decorated Army Commendation medal, Combat Infantry badge, Good Conduct medal, Nat. Def. medal, Vietnam Svc. medal, Vietnam Campaign ribbon. Mem. Disabled Am. Vets. (comdr., svc. officer, sgt. at arms, hon. guard), Masons. Democrat. Mem. Lds Ch. Avocations: baseball, football, wrestling, bowling, pool. Home: 10103 Kathleen Dr Fort Washington MD 20744-2530

SMOOT, DAVID PAUL, finance company executive; b. Guthrie, Okla., Jan. 9, 1947; s. Jerry Edward and Katherine Ann (Doyle) S.; m. Marie Kathleen Stokes, Aug. 6, 1971; children: Aimee, Melissa. Student, Cumberland Coll., 1965—67, Glassboro State Coll., 1967, U. Cin., 1968—69. Regional mgr. Dennison Mfg., Chgo., 1969-77, Wordstream, Chgo., 1978-79; dist. mgr. AM Jacquard, San Francisco, 1979-82; co-founder, v.p. sales Phaser Systems Pub. Co., San Francisco, 1980-82; dir. ctrl. ops. Digital Rsch., Schaumburg, Ill., 1982-85; founder, chmn. bd., CEO Software Funding Internat., Deerfield, Ill., 1985-89, Software Funding Internat. (acquired by The Meridian Group), Deerfield, Ill., 1989; pres. Meridian Software Funding, 1989-92, Am. Indian Svcs. Inc., 1992-95; pres., founder Airborne Remote Mapping, 1995-98, Am. Indian Fin. Svcs. LLC, 1998—; founder, CEO Native Am. Water, LLC, 2002—. Mem. Native Vision program Johns Hopkins U. Hosp., NFL Players Assn. and Nick Lowery Found. Bd. of Consult Little City Home for Retarded, Palatine, Ill., 1986; founder, CEO Pro Players Classic Golf Invitational to Benefit Indigenous Youth, 1999—. Served with U.S. Army, 1969-75. Mem. Assn. Data Processing Sevcs. Orgns., Software Pubs. Assn., Syntopicaon XII, IBM PC User's Group (spkr.). Avocations: basketball, sailing, camping, fishing, tennis. Home: 6831 E Sunset Sky Cir Scottsdale AZ 85262-7161 Office: Native Am Water LLC 11 Sundial Cir Ste 19 PO Box 3800 Carefree AZ 85377 Business E-Mail: dsmoot@natawa.com.

SMOOT, LEON DOUGLAS, chemical engineering educator, former dean; b. Provo, Utah, July 26, 1934; s. Douglas Parley and Jennie (Hallam) S.; m. Marian Bird, Sept. 7, 1953; children: Analee, LaCinda, Michelle, Melinda Lee. BS, Brigham Young U., 1956, B in Engring. Sci., 1957; MS, U. Wash., 1958, PhD, 1960. Registered profl. engr., Utah. Engr. Boeing Corp., Seattle, 1956; teaching and research asst. Brigham Young U., 1954-57; engr. Phillips Petroleum Corp., Arco, Idaho, 1957; engr., cons. Hercules Powder Co., Bacchus, Utah, 1961-63; asst. prof. Brigham Young U., 1960-63; engr. Lockheed Propulsion, Redlands, Calif., 1963-67; vis. asst. prof. Calif. Inst. Tech., 1966-67; assoc. prof. to prof. Brigham Young U., 1967—2003, prof. emeritus, 2003—, chmn. dept. chem. engring., 1970-77, dean Coll. Engring. and Tech., 1977-94, dean emeritus, 1994—. Expert witness on combustion and explosions; founding dir. Advanced Combustion Engring. Research Ctr. (NSF), 1986-97; cons. Hercules, Thiokol, Lockheed, Teledyne, Atlantic Research Corp., Raytheon, Redd and Redd, Billings Energy, Ford, Bacon & Davis, Jaycor, Intel Com Radiation Tech., Phys. Dynamics, Nat. Soc. Propellants and Explosives, France, DFVLR, West Germany, Martin Marietta, Honeywell, Phillips Petroleum Co., Exxon, Nat. Bur. Standards, Eyring Research Inst., Systems, Sci. and Software., Los Alamos Nat. Lab., others. Author 5 books on coal combustion; contbr. over 200 articles and tech. jours. Mem. AIChE, ASME, Nat. Fire Protection Assn., Am. Soc. Engring. Edn., Combustion Inst., Rsch. Soc. Am., Sigma Xi, Tau Beta Pi, Phi Lambda Epsilon. Republican. Mem. Lds Ch. Office: Brigham Young U Chem Engring Dept 435 T CTB Provo UT 84602

SMOOT, OLIVER REED, JR., lawyer, trade association administrator; b. San Antonio, Aug. 24, 1940; s. Oliver Reed and Angie Frances (Watters) Smoot; m. Sandra Lee Curry, July 25, 1964; children: Stephen Reed, Sheryl Anne. BS, MIT, 1962; JD, Georgetown U., 1966. Bar: DC 1966, Va. 1967. Computer sys. mgr. Inst. Def. Analyses, Arlington, Va., 1962-69; from program mgr., v.p., to exec. v.p. and treas. Info. Tech. Industry Coun. (formerly Computer & Bus Equipment Mfrs. Assn.), Washington, 1969-2000; v.p. extrnal vol. stds. rels. Info Tech Industry Coun., Washington, 2000—. Author (with others): (book) Computers and the Law, 3d edit., 1981; chpt. editor: book Toward a Law of Global Communications Networks, 2001. Pres. Internat. Orgn. Standardization, 2003—; chmn. Am. Nat. Stds. Inst., 2001—02, 2003—. Mem.: ABA (chmn. sci. and tech. sect. 1989—90), Assn. Computing Machinery, Computer Law Assn. (pres. 1990—91). Methodist. Avocations: alpine skiing, gardening. Office: Info Tech Industry Coun 1250 I St NW Ste 200 Washington DC 20005-3922

SMOOT, RAYMOND D., JR., academic administrator; b. Lynchburg, Va., Jan. 21, 1947; s. Raymond Dillard and Gladys Masencup Smoot; m. Jean Newlon Smoot; children: Amanda, Ben. BA, Va. Tech., Blacksburg, 1969; M Edn., Va. Tech., 1971; PhD, Ohio State U., Columbus, 1976. Dir. Carilion Health Sys., Roanoke, Va., 1997—, New River Valley Med. Ctr., 2002—; v.p. adminstrn., treas. Va. Tech., Blacksburg. Bd. dirs. First Nat. Bank, Christiansburg; chmn. bd. Va. Tech. Corp. Rsch., 1995--; chmn. investment com. Va. Retirement Sys. Mem. Sanitation Authority, Blacksburg, 1993--; bd. dirs. Roanoke C. of C., 1995—, Warm Hearth Retirement Ctr., 1988—, Smithfield/Preston Found., 1996—, Va. Coll. Osteo. Medicine, 2002—; commr. Hotel Roanoke Conf. Ctr., 1993—. Staff Sgt. US Army, 1969-75. Episcopalian. Office: Va Tech 312 Burruss Hall 0142 Blacksburg VA 24061

SMORAL, VINCENT J. electrical engineer; b. Syracuse, N.Y., May 13, 1946; s. Anthony Vincent and Stephanie (Koutin) S.; m. Theresa W. Gut, Aug. 5, 1967; children: Jennifer, Laura, Anne. BSEE, Syracuse U., 1967. Jr. engr. Fed. Sys. Div. IBM, Owego, NY, 1967-68, adv. engr. logic design, 1968-80, sr. engr./sys., 1980-90, sr. engr./program mgr., 1990-93; sr. engr. Lockheed Martin Fed. Sys. Co., Owego, 1994—2000; program mgr. Eastman Kodak C&GS, Rochester, 2000—. Designer 688 Class Sonar, An/UYS-1 Signal Processor, AWACS Computer, 3838 Array Processor, 1968-80; mgr. AN/UYK-43 Computer, AWACS Computer, Rugged Processor, F117 Processor, 1980-93; patentee in field. Fellow AIAA (assoc.; mem. nat. computer systems tech. com. 1990-95); mem. IEEE, KC. Democrat. Roman Catholic. Avocations: swimming, sailing, fishing, skiing. Home: 12 Founders Grn Pittsford NY 14534-2165 Office: Eastman Kodak Co Commerical & Govt Sys 1447 Paul St Rochester NY 14653-7214 Office Phone: 585-726-5401. E-mail: vsmoral@rochester.rr.com.

SMOTHERS, ANN ELIZABETH, museum director; b. Chgo., Dec. 20, 1946; With adminstn. Mercy Hosp., Iowa City, 1982-85; asst. dir. Old Capital Mus., Iowa City, 1985-95, dir., 1995—. Recipient Hon. Achievement for Women award YWCA, 1996. Mem. Altrusa. Office: Old Capitol Mus Univ Iowa 24 Old Capitol Iowa City IA 52242 E-mail: ann.smothers@niowa.edu.

SMOTHERS, JIMMY, editor, sportswriter; b. Geraldine, Ala., Jan. 4, 1933; s. John Ezra and Lois Olga (Taylor) S.; m. Mary Kay Brock, July 7, 1954; 1 child Jim Jr. Student, Jacksonville State U., 1951—54. Sports editor Gadsden (Ala.) Times, 1960—. Contbr. articles to popular mags. With USNG, 1952-65. Recipient Helms award, more than 70 AP awards including Sweepstake award for writing, 1996, Lifetime Achievement award All-Am. Football Found., 1997, Jacksonville State Hall of Fame, Ala. Sports Writer of Yr. award, 1999, Media of Yr. award Ala. Jr. Coll., 2001; nominated for Pulitzer prizes, 1963; inductee Etowah County (Ala.), Ala. Sport Writers Halls of Fame, 1997, DeKalb County (Ala.) Sports Hall of Fame, 1998, Ala. H.S. Hall of Fame, 2001. Mem. Ala. Sports Writers Assn. (sec.-treas. 1971—), Baseball Writers Assn., Coll. Football Writers Assn., Jacksonville State U. Alumni Assn. (past. Alumnus of Yr.). Avocations: fishing, studying civil war. Office: Gadsden Times PO Box 188 Gadsden AL 35902-0188

SMOTRICH, DAVID ISADORE, architect; b. Norwich, Conn., Oct. 6, 1933; s. Max Z. and Ida (Babinsky) S.; m. Bernice D. Strachman, Mar. 25, 1956; children— Ross Lawrence, Maura Faye, Hannah. AB, Harvard Coll., 1955, MArch, 1960. Master planning team, Town of Arad, State of Israel, 1961-62; assoc. Platt Assocs., N.Y.C., 1963-65; gen. ptnr. Smotrich & Platt, N.Y.C., 1965-74, Smotrich Platt & Buttrick, N.Y.C., 1975-76, Smotrich & Platt, N.Y.C., 1976-85, David Smotrich & Ptnrs., N.Y.C., 1985—. Cons. to Jerusalem Master Plan Office, Israel Ministry of Housing, 1967. Planning bd. Town of New Castle, N.Y., 1974-81; exec. bd. Road Rev. League, Bedford, N.Y., 1966-70. With AUS, 1955-57. Recipient Bard award, 1969, 85, Archtl. Record award, 1971, 73-75, 78, Design award HUD, 1980. Mem. AIA (Nat. Honor award 1969, N.Y. State Honor awards 1984, 94, Cmty. Design awards 1991, 93, AIA Coll. of Fellows 1993), Assn. Engrs. and Archs. in Israel, Phi Beta Kappa, Harvard Club (N.Y.C.). Home: 7 Mayberry Close Chappaqua NY 10514-1113 Office: David Smotrich & Ptnrs 443 Park Ave S New York NY 10016-7322 Office Phone: 212-889-4045. E-mail: ds@dsmotricharch.com.

SMOTZER, THOMAS DAVID, mathematician; b. Cleve., Ohio, Sept. 24, 1966; s. David Michael and Waltraut Ann Smotzer; m. Cynthia Anderson, July 6, 1991; children: Madeline Anne, Zachary Thomas, Jacob Edwin. B, Baldwin Wallace Coll., 1988; D, Ind. U., 1995. Assoc. prof. Youngstown State U., Youngstown, Ohio, 1995—. Contbr. articles to profl. jours. Grantee, NSF, 1999—. Mem.: Math. Assn. Am. Avocations: piano, reading. Office: Youngstown State U One University Plz Youngstown OH 44555 E-mail: tsmotzer@math.ysu.edu.

SMOUSE, H(ERVEY) RUSSELL, lawyer; b. Oakland, Calif., Aug. 13, 1932; s. Hervey Reed and Vernie (Rush) Smouse; m. Creta M. Staley, June 15, 1955; children: Kristin Anne, Randall Forsyth, Gregory Russell. AB, Princeton U., 1955; LLB, U. Md., 1958. Bar: Md. 58, U.S. Tax. Ct. 79, U.S. Ct. Appeals (4th cir.) 60, U.S. Supreme Ct. 74. Atty. Atty. Gen.'s Honors Program, Dept. Justice, Washington, 1958—60; asst. U.S. atty. Dist. Md., 1960—62; assoc. Pierson and Pierson, Balt., 1962—64; atty. B.&O. R.R., Balt., 1964—66; mem. Pierson and Pierson, 1966—69, Clapp, Somerville, Black & Honemann, Balt., 1969—74; pvt. practice Law Offices H. Russell Smouse, 1974—81; mem. Melnicove, Kaufman, Weiner & Smouse, P.A., Balt., 1981—89, chmn. litigation, 1985—89; mem. Whiteford, Taylor & Preston, Balt., 1989—93, chmn. litigation dept., 1989—93; head gen. litigation Law Offices Peter G. Angelos, 1993—; gen. counsel Balt. Orioles, 1993—. Permanent mem. jud. conf. U.S. Ct. Appeals (4th cir.); vice chmn. Legal Aid Bur. Balt. City, 1972—73. Fellow: Am. Coll. Trial Lawyers; mem.: ATLA, ABA, Nat. Assn. R.R. Trial Counsel (exec. com., v.p. ea. region 1986—92), Bar Assn. Balt. City (chmn. grievance com. 1969—70, chmn. judiciary com. and nominating com. 1980, mem. exec. com. 1969—70, 1980, chmn. exec. com. lawyers' com. for ind. judiciary 1989—96), Md. State Bar Assn. (gov. 1981—83), Am. Law Inst. Republican. Presbyterian. Office Phone: 410-649-2000.

SMUCKER, RICHARD K. food company executive; m. Emily Delp; 1 child. Grad., Miami U., Ohio; MBA, Wharton Sch. Bus., U. Penn. Pres. The J.M. Smucker Co., 1987—, co-CEO, 2001—. Bd. dirs. The J.M. Smucker Co., Wm. Wrigley Jr., Co., Internat. Multifoods, The Sherwin-Williams Co., Internat. Foodservice Mfr. Assoc.; bd. trustees Cleveland Orchestra, Culinary Inst. Am. Office: 1 Strawberry Ln Orrville OH 44667-1241*

SMUCKER, TIMOTHY P. food company executive; m. Jennifer Coddington; 3 children. BS Economics, Coll. of Wooster, 1967; MBA Mktg., Wharton Sch. Bus., U Penn, 1969. Chmn. The J.M. Smucker Co., 1984—, co-CEO, 2001—. Bd. dirs. The J.M. Smucker Co., Huntington BancShares, Inc., Dreyer's Grand Ice Cream, Inc., Grocery Mfr. Am., Inc.; bd. trustees Coll. of Wooster; mem. steering com. Heartland Edn. Community. Office: 1 Strawberry Ln Orrville OH 44667-1241*

SMUCKLER, RALPH HERBERT, dean, political scientist, educator; b. Milw., Apr. 10, 1926; s. Robert H. and Celia (Berliand) Smuckler; m. Lillian Zembrosky, July 6, 1946; children: Gary, Sandra, Harold. BA, U. Wis., 1948, MA, 1949, PhD, 1952. Mem. faculty Mich. State U., East Lansing, 1951-93, prof. polit. sci., 1963-93, dean internat. studies and programs, 1968-90, asst. to pres., 1987-91, emeritus prof., dean, 1993—. Mem. tech. assistance team in Saigon Mich. State U., 1955—56, chief advisor tech. assistance team in Saigon, 1958—59; v.p. Edn. and World Affairs, N.Y.C., 1963—64; rep. Ford Found., Pakistan, 1967—69; dir. U.S. Internat. Sci. and Tech. Coop. Planning Office, Washington, 1978—79; mem. rsch. adv. com. AID, 1972—82, chmn., 1973—82, dep. asst. adminstr., 1991—92. Author (with Leroy Ferguson): Politics in the Press, 1953; author: (with George Belknap) Leadership and Participation in Urban Political Affairs, 1956; author: (with R. Berg) New Challenges New Opportunities: U.S. Cooperation for International Growth and Development in the 1990s, 1988; author: A University Turns to the World, 2002; contbr. articles to profl. jours. Mem. adv. com. Kellog Found. Nat. Fellowship Program, 1980—84; mem. bd. sci. and tech. for internat. devel. Nat. Acad. Sci., 1982—88, chmn., 1984—88; v.p. Mich. UN Assn., 1972—76; State of Mich. chmn. UN Day, 1960; bd. dirs. Midwest Univs. Consortium Internat. Activities, 1965—67, 1969—90; trustee Inst. Internat. Edn., 1974—91. With inf. AUS, 1944—46. Decorated Bronze Star; recipient Disting. Citizen award, Steuben Jr. H.S., Milw., 1965, John Gilbert Winant Humanitarian award, Marine City, Mich., 1976, Outstanding Faculty award, Phi Beta Delta Internat., 1990. Mem.: Nat. Assn. Fgn. Student Affairs (governing bd. 1986, M. Houlihan award 1990), Nat. Assn. State Univs and Land-Grant Colls. (chmn. internat. acad. affairs com. 1986—90), Assn. Internat. Edn. Adminstrs. (pres. 1986—87), Soc. Internat. Devel., Am. Polit. Sci. Assn., Mich. State U. Club, Phi Kappa Phi (named Disting. Mem. 1990). Jewish. Home: 4201 Cathedral Ave NW Apt 814W Washington DC 20016-4965 E-mail: ralphhs@aol.com.

SMUIN, MICHAEL, choreographer, director, dancer; b. Missoula, Mont., Oct. 13, 1938; m. Paula Tracy; 1 child, Shane. Studied with Christensen Bros.; studied, San Francisco Ballet Sch.; DFA, U. Mont., 1984. Dancer U. Utah Ballet, Salt Lake City, 1955-57; dancer, choreographer, dir. San Francisco Ballet, 1957-62, 73-85; dancer Am. Ballet Theatre, N.Y. State Theatre, N.Y.C., 1967; prin. dancer, choreographer Am. Ballet Theatre, 1969-73, resident choreographer, 1992—; founder, dir. Smuin Ballets/SF, 1994—. Worked as free-lance dancer with wife Paula Tracy, ind. choreographer; co-chmn. dance adv. panel Nat. Endowment for the Arts, Washington; mem. U.S. dance study team, People's Republic of China, 1983. Dir., musical stager, choreographer: (with Donald McKayle) Sophisticated Ladies, 1981 (Tony award nomination best direction of musical 1981, Outer Critics Circle award 1981); dir., choreographer: Chaplin, 1983, Shogun, 1990; choreographer: Anything Goes, 1987 (Tony award best choreography 1988, Drama Desk award best choreography 1988), Pulcinella Variations, Private Lives, 1991; staged dance works for Leslie Caron, Mikhail Baryshnikov, Rudolf Nureyev with Am. Ballet Theatre/Paris Opera Ballet, 1986; prodr. for San Francisco Ballet: Cinderella, Romeo and Juliet, The Tempest, A Song for Dead Warriors; dir.: Faustus in Hell, Peter and the Wolf, Very Merrily, Verdi, To The Beatles, Revisited, 2001, Stabat Mater, 2001; choreographer: (films) Rumble Fish, 1983, The Cotton Club, 1984, Fletch Lives, 1989, Bram Stoker's Dracula, 1992, So I Married an Axe Murderer, 1993, Angie, 1994, The Fantasticks, 1995; tech. adviser: (film) The Golden Child, 1986, Star Wars Trilogy, 1997; choreographer: (TV) The Tempest, 1981 (Emmy award nomination outstanding achievement in choreography, 1981), A Song for Dead Warriors, 1984 (Emmy award outstanding achievement in choreography 1984), Cinderella, 1985, Romeo and Juliet; dir. Suites by Smuin, Nutcracker on Ice; (TV spls.) Jinx, 1985, Voice/Dance: Bobby McFerrin and the Tandy Beal Dance Company, 1987; choreographer: (TV episode) Corridos! Tales of Passion and Revolution, 1987; creator: (TV show) The Omo, 1987; dir., choreographer: (TV spl.) Linda Ronstadt's Canciones de Mi Padre, 1989, Aid and Comfort. Recipient Dance Magazine award, 1983. Office: Smuin Ballets/SF 1314 34th Ave San Francisco CA 94122-1309

SMULKSTYS, INGA, operations and management executive; b. Ind., July 1961; BA in Pub. Policy, U. Chgo.; MPA, Ind. U. Neighborhood specialist Cmty. Devel. and Planning, City of Ft. Wayne, Ind., 1986, housing program mgr., 1987-88; adminstr. asst. to Rep. Jill Long, Ind., 1989-95; exec. asst. to under sec. for rural devel., Jill Long Thompson Dept. Agr., Washington, 1995-96, dep. under sec. for ops. and mgmt. rural devel., 1996—. Office: Dept Agr Rural Devel Ops and Mgmgt 1400 Independence Ave SW Washington DC 20250-0003

SMUNT, MARSHA LYNN HAEFLINGER, financial executive; b. Chgo., July 9, 1955; m. Timothy Lawrence Smunt, Aug. 17, 1974. BS in Acctg., Purdue U., 1976; MBA in Finance and Investments, Ind. U., 1980. CPA, cert. mgmt. acct., fin. mgmt.; CFA level I. Auditor Deloitte & Touche, St. Louis, 1977-78; analyst corp. diversification McDonnell Douglas Corp., St. Louis, 1979; sr. fin. analyst Cummins Engine Co., Columbus, Ind., 1980-81, capital investments mgr., 1981-82; corp. capital analysis mgr. Gen. Dynamics Corp., St. Louis, 1982-84, corp. mgr. fin. planning, 1984-87; sr. capital investments Anheuser-Busch Cos., Inc., St. Louis, 1987-88, mgr. treasury ops., 1988-91, exec. asst. to treas., 1991-92, mgr. investor rels., 1992-94; dir. fin. planning and forecasting R.J. Reynolds Internat. Inc., Winston-Salem, N.C., 1995-96; sr. v.p. corp. analysis Wachovia Corp., Winston-Salem, 1997-99, sr. v.p. investor rels., 1999—. Mentor, career symposium spkr. MBA program Wake Forest U., 1995-96; bd. dirs. Sawtooth Ctr. for Visual Art; with Jr. League, Habitat for Humanity. Mem. AICPA, Inst. Mgmt. Accts. (treas., bd. dirs. Piedmont-Winston-Salem chpt.), Profl. Women of Winston-Salem (pres. 1999-2000, bd. dirs.), Nat. Investor Rels. Inst. (pres. St. Louis chpt. 1993-94), Beta Gamma Sigma. Home: 1061 W Kent Rd Winston Salem NC 27104-1131

SMUTNY, JOAN FRANKLIN, academic director, educator; b. Chgo. d. Eugene and Mabel (Lind) Franklin; m. Herbert Paul Smutny; 1 child, Cheryl Anne. BS, MA, Northwestern U. Tchr. New Trier H.S., Winnetka, Ill.; mem. faculty, founder, dir. Nat. H.S. Inst. Northwestern U. Sch. Edn., Chgo.; faculty, founder, dir. h.s. workshop critical thinking/edn. Nat. Coll. Edn., Evanston, Ill., exec. dir. h.s. workshops, 1970-75; founder, dir. Woman Power Through Edn. Seminar, 1969-74; dir. Right to Read Seminar in critical reading, 1973-74; dir. seminar gifted h.s. students, 1973; dir. gifted programs for 6th, 7th, 8th graders Evanston pub. schs., 1978-79; dir. gifted programs 1st-8th grade Glenview (Ill.) pub. schs., 1979—. Dir. gifted programs Nat.-Louis U., Evanston, 1980-82, dir. Ctr. for Gifted, 1982—; dir. Bright and Talented Project, 1986—, North Shore Country Day Sch., Winnetka, 1982—; dir. Job Creation Project, 1980-82; dir. New Dimensions for Women, 1973; dir. Thinking for Action in Career Edn. Program 1976-79; dir. TACE, dir. Humanities Program for Verbally Precocious Youth, 1978-79; co-dir., instr. seminars in critical thinking Ill. Family Svc., 1972-75; writer ednl. filmstrips in lang. arts and lit. Soc. Visual Edn., 1970-74; spkrs. bur. Coun. Fgn. Rels., 1968-69; adv. com. edn. professions devel. act U.S. Office Edn., 1969—; state team for gifted, Ill. Office Edn., Office of Gifted, Springfield, Ill., 1977; writer, cons. Radiant Ednl. Corp., 1969-71; cons. ALA, 1969-71, workshop leader and spkr. gifted edn., 1971—; coord. career edn. Nat. Coll.Edn., 1976-78, dir. Project 1987—, dir. Summer Wonders, 1986—, Creative Children's Acad., bd. dirs., Worlds of Wisdom and Wonder, 1978—; dir. Future Tchrs. Am. Seminar in Coll. and Career, 1970-72; cons. rsch. & devel. Ill. Dept. Vocat. Edn., 1973—; evaluation cons. DAVTE, IOE, Springfield, Ill., 1977, mem. Leadership Tng. Inst. Gifted, U.S. Office Edn., 1973-74; dir. workshops for h.s. students; cons., spkr. in field; dir. Gifted Young Writers and Young Writers confs., 1978, 79; dir. Project '92 The White House Conf. on Children and Youth; mem. adv. bd. Educating Able Learners, 1991—; chmn. bd. dirs. Barbereux Sch., Evanston, 1992—; asst. editor, editl. bd. Understanding our Gifted, 1994—. Author: (with others) Job Creation: Creative Materials, Activities and Strategies for the Classroom, 1982, A Thoughful Overview of Gifted Education, 1990, Your Gifted Child—How to Recognize and Develop the Special Talents in Your Child from Birth to Age Seven, 1987, paperback, 1991, Education of the Gifted: Programs and Perspectives, 1990, Teaching Gifted Young Children in the Regular Classroom, 1997, Gifted Girls, 1998, Stand Up For Your Gifted Child, 2001, Gifted Education: Promising Practices, 2003, Differentiated Instruction, 2003, Differentiating For the Young Child, 2004; editor: The Young Gifted Child: Potential and Promise: An Anthology, 1998, Underserved Gifted Populations, 2003; contbg. editor Roper Rev., 1994—; asst. editor Understanding Our Gifted, 1995—; editor, contbr. Maturity in Teching; writer ednl. filmstrips The Brothers Grimm, How the West Was Won, Mutiny on the Bounty, Dr. Zhivago, Space Odyssey 2001, Christmas Around the World; editor IAGC Jour. for Gifted, 1994—; adv. bd. Gifted Edn. Press Quar., 1995—; contbr. editor numerous books in field; contbr. articles to profl. jours. including Chgo. Parent Mag.; reviewer programs for Gifted and Talented, U.S. Office Edn., 1976-78; editor Creativity Series Ablex, 1998—. Mem. AAUP, Nat. Assn. Gifted Child (nat. membership chmn. 1991—, co-chmn. schs. and programs, co-editor newsletter early childhood divsn.), Nat. Soc. Arts & Letters (nat. bd., 1st and 3d v.p. Evanston chpt. 1990-92), Mortar Bd., Outstanding Educators of Am. 1974, Pi Lambda Theta, Phi Delta Kappa (v.p. Evanston chpt. rsch. chmn. 1990-92). Home: 633 Forest Ave Wilmette IL 60091-1713 *Commitment to education is defined as contribution. We who are privileged to work in education know that the focus is the educant-the learner. Gifted education is particularly vital in that it discerns the needs of bright, talented children who have an immense amount to contribute to our country and our world. Gifted children are our country's most neglected resource--and most needed. It is my privilege to work in this area, to work with children, parents and teachers. The community of mankind is needed to support the talent and growth of the gifted. Then we are really contributing to the educant.*

SMYNTEK, JOHN EUGENE, JR., editor; b. Buffalo, Aug. 24, 1950; BA, U. Detroit, 1972. Asst. instr. Mich. State U., East Lansing, 1981; features editor Free Press, Detroit, 1985-92; dir. online svcs. and dir. libr. Free Press Plus, Detroit, 1992-95, spl. features and syndicate editor, 1995—; asst. instr. U. Detroit Mercy, 2000—01. Vis. fellow in journalism Duke U., 1988; profl. student publs. advisor U. Detroit Mercy, 1992—94; bd. visitors Wayne State U. Coll. Fine, Performing and Comm. Arts, 2001—. Recipient Fine Arts Reporting award, Detroit Press Club, 1985. Roman Catholic. Office: Detroit Free Press 600 W Fort St Detroit MI 48226-2706 Office Phone: 313-222-5169. E-mail: smyntek@freepress.com.

SMYRE, CALVIN, political organization executive, state legislator; b. May 17, 1948; div.; 1 child. BS in Bus. Adminstrn., Fort Valley State U. Mem. Ga. Ho. of Reps. Dist. 92, Atlanta, 1974—92, asst. adminstrn. floor leader, 1983; mem. Dem. Nat. Com., 1984, adminstrn. floor leader; mem. Ga. Ho. Reps. Dist. 136, 1993—. Chmn. univ. sys. Ga. com.; mem. appropriations com., rules com.; banker; exec. v.p. corp. affairs Synovus Fin. Corp.; chmn. rules com., Ga. Dem. Party, 2001—; mem. appropriations com., ethics com., higher edn. com., spl. rules com. Nat. sec. Nat. Black Caucus State Legislators; bd. trustees Med. Coll. Ga. Found., Morehouse Sch. Med., Jack D. Hughston Found.; chmn. bd. trustees Fort Valley State U. Found.; former nat. pres. Fort Valley State U. Nat. Alumni Assn.; bd. advisors Atlanta U. Sch. Social Work. With U.S. Army. Democrat. Office: Georgia House of Representives 415 State Capitol Atlanta GA 30334 also: Georgia Democratic Party 1100 Spring Street, Suite 710 Atlanta GA 30309

SMYRNIOS, NICHOLAS A. physician, educator; b. Saugus, Mass., Sept. 2, 1959; s. Philip Nicholas and Mary Eunice Smyrnios; m. Roxanne Kim, Sept. 2, 1995; children: Alexandra Kim, Philip Nicholas. BS, Tufts U., 1981; MD, Albany Med. Coll., 1985. Diplomate in internal medicine, pulmonary diseases and critical care medicine Am. Bd. Internal Medicine. Asst. prof. medicine U. Mass. Med. Sch., Worcester, 1991-98, assoc. prof. medicine, 1998—, dir. fellowship in critical care medicine, 1996—; dir. med. ICU, U. Mass. Meml. Med. Ctr., Worcester, 1992—. Spkr. in field. Editor: Review of Intensive Care Medicine, 1999; contbr. articles to profl. jours. Vol., St. Spyridon Cathedral, Worcester, 1996—. Will Rogers Pulmonary fellow, 1988-90. Fellow Am. Coll. Chest Physicians (gov. for Mass. 1999—), Fellow Am. Coll. Physicians; mem. AMA, Am. Thoracic Soc., Soc. Critical Care Medicine. Greek Orthodox. Avocations: music, sports. Office: U Mass Meml Healthcare Pulmonary Divsn 55 Lake Ave N Worcester MA 01655-0002

SMYTH, CRAIG HUGH, fine arts educator; b. N.Y.C., July 28, 1915; s. George Hugh and Lucy Salome (Humeston) S.; m. Barbara Linforth, June 24, 1941; children: Alexandra, Edward Linforth (Ned). BA, Princeton U., 1938, MFA, 1941, PhD, 1956; MA (hon.), Harvard U., 1975. Sr. mus. aid, rsch. asst. Nat. Gallery Art, Washington, 1941-42; officer-in-charge, dir. Cen. Art Collecting Point, Munich, 1945-46; lectr. Frick Collection, N.Y.C., 1946-50; asst. prof. Inst. Fine Arts NYU, 1950-53, assoc. prof. Inst. Fine Arts, 1953-57, prof. Inst. Fine Arts, 1957-73, acting dir. Inst. Fine Arts, acting head dept. fine arts Grad. Sch. Arts and Scis., 1951-53, dir. inst., head dept. fine arts Grad. Sch., 1953-73; prof. fine arts Harvard U., 1973-85, prof. emeritus, 1985—; Samuel Kress prof. Ctr. for Advanced Study in Visual Arts Nat. Gallery Art, Washington, 1987-88; dir. Villa I Tatti Harvard U. Ctr. Italian Renaissance Studies, Florence, 1973-85. Art historian in residence Am. Acad. in Rome, 1959-60; mem. U.S. Nat. Com. History Art, 1955-85; alt. U.S. mem. Comité Internat. d'Histoire de l'Art, 1970-83, U.S. mem., 1983-85; chmn. adv. com. J. Paul Getty Rsch. Inst. History of Art and Humanities, 1982-99; mem. architect selection com. J. Paul Getty Trust, 1983-84; mem. organizing com., keynote speaker 400th Anniversary of Uffizi Gallery, 1981-82; vis. scholar Inst. Advanced Study, Princeton, N.J., 1971, mem., 1978, visitor, 1983, 85-86; vis. scholar Bibliotheca Hertziana, Max Planck Soc., Rome, 1972, 73; mem. vis. com. dept. art and archaeology Princeton U., 1956-73, 85-89; mem. adv. com. Villa I Tatti, 1985-92; trustee Hyde Collection, Glens Falls, N.Y., 1985-87, The Burlington mag., 1987—; mem. commn. Ednl. & Cultural Exch. between Italy and U.S., 1979-83. Author: Mannerism and Maniera, 1963, rev. edit. with introduction by E. Cropper, 1992, Bronzino as Draughtsman, 1971, Michelangelo Architetto (with H.M. Millon), 1988, English edit., 1988, Repatriation of Art from the Collecting Point in Munich After World War II, 1988; editor: Michelangelo Drawings (Nat. Gallery of Art), 1992; editor (with Peter M. Lukehart), contbr.: The Early Years of Art History in the United States, 1993; founding chmn. (periodical) I Tatti Studies: Essays in the Renaissance, 1984-85; contbr. to profl. jours. Hon. trustee Met. Mus. Art, N.Y.C., 1968—; trustee Inst. Fine Arts, NYU, 1973—; mem. mayor's com. Piazza Della Signoria, Florence, 1975-78. Lt. USNR, 1942-46. Decorated Chevalier Legion of Honor France, U.S. Army Commendation medal, Netherlands Medal for Svc. to the State; sr. Fulbright Rsch. fellow, 1949-50, honored by establishment of CHS professorship, Inst. of Fine Arts NYU, 1999. Mem. Am. Acad. Arts and Scis., Am. Philos. Soc., Coll. Art Assn. Am. (bd. dirs. 1953-57, sec. 1956), Accademia Fiorentina delle Arti del Disegno (academician, assoc.), Accademia di San Luca (hon. 1995), Harvard Club (N.Y.C.), Century Assn. (N.Y.C.), Phi Beta Kappa. Address: PO Box 539 Cresskill NJ 07626-0039

SMYTH, DAVID, writer, editor; b. Buenos Aires, Feb. 7, 1929; came to U.S. 1962, naturalized 1970; s. Currell Hutchinson and Jessie Rodger (Dodds) S.; m. Elli Helene Dusterhoft, Nov. 9, 1968; 1 child, Clifford Dieter. BA, Cambridge (Eng.) U., 1951, MA, 1967. Tech. writer, copywriter, 1953-55; movie promotion writer, 1956; owner Ace Translation Agy., Buenos Aires, 1957-58; sec. Found. Econ. Edn., 1959; cables editor Buenos Aires Herald, 1960; lexicographer Simon & Schuster English-Spanish Dictionary, 1961; Latin Am. desk editor UPI, N.Y.C., 1962-63, AP, N.Y.C., 1963-73, world svcs. fin. editor, 1973-96; freelance writer, translator, editor, 1997—. Author: You Can Survive Any Financial Disaster, 1977, Worldly Wise Investor, 1988; co-author: The Speculator's Handbook, 1974, Unusual Investments That Could Make You Rich, 1978, No Cost/Low Cost Investing, 1987. Served with Argentine Army, 1952. Mem. N.Y. Fin. Writers Assn. Home: 8 Beechwood Ave Metuchen NJ 08840-2107 E-mail: Currell@aol.com.

SMYTH, DONALD MORGAN, chemical educator, researcher; b. Bangor, Maine, Mar. 20, 1930; s. John Robert and Selma (Eubanks) S.; m. Elisabeth Luce, Aug. 1, 1951; children: Carolyn, Joanne. BS in Chemistry, U. Maine, 1951; PhD in Inorganic Chemistry, MIT, 1954. Sr. chemist Sprague Electric Co., North Adams, Mass., 1954-58, sect. head, 1958-61, dept. head, 1961-71; assoc. prof. Lehigh U., Bethlehem, Pa., 1971-73, prof., 1973-95, dir. Materials Rsch. Ctr., 1971-92, Paul B. Reinhold prof. materials sci., engring. and chemistry, 1988-95; emeritus, 1995—. Mem. various coms. Lehigh U., 1973-95; mem. materials rsch. adv. com. NSF, 1984-88, chmn., 1985-86, co-chair ad-hoc com. to brief dir., 1986; mem. coun. materials sci. Dept. Energy, 1986-90; presenter in field. Contbr. articles to profl. jours. Recipient Libsch Rsch. award Lehigh U., 1990, Buessem award Dielectrics Rsch. Ctr., Pa. State U., 1991; grantee in field. Fellow Am. Inst. Chemists, Am. Ceramic Soc. (com. edn. electronics divsn. 1974-78, chmn. Lehigh Valley sect. 1978-79, counselor 1982-00, assoc. editor jour. 1988-92, best paper award 1987, 95, Kraner award Lehigh Valley sect. 1990, Sosman lectr. 1996); mem. Am. Chem. Soc., Nat. Acad. Engring., Materials Rsch. Soc., Electrochem. Soc. (various coms., sec. dielectrics and insulation divsn. 1967-69, vice chmn. 1969-70, chmn. 1970-71, rsch. award battery divsn. 1960). Achievements include patents (with others) for Solid-State Battery Cell with Complex Organic Electrolyte Material, Capacitor with Dielectric Film Having Phosphorous-Containing Component Therein, Solid Barrier Electrolyte Incorporating Additive, others; research in defect chemistry and electrical properties of complex oxides. Home: 3429 Mountainview Cir Bethlehem PA 18017-1807 Office: Lehigh U Materials Rsch Ctr 5 E Packer Ave Bethlehem PA 18015-3102 Office Phone: 610-758-3852. Business E-Mail: dms4@lehigh.edu.

SMYTH, GLEN MILLER, management consultant; b. Abingdon, Va., July 26, 1929; s. Glen Miller and Kathleen (Dunn) S.; m. Cynthia Olson, Aug. 25, 1954 (div. 1967); children: Catherine Ellen, Glen Miller, III, Cynthia Allison; m. Lilian Castel Edgar, Oct. 31, 1968; children: Stephanie Castel, Kimberley Forsyth, Lindsay Dunn. BA, Yale U., 1951; MS in Psychology, Rutgers U., 1958. Mktg. rep. Wheeling Stamping Co., N.Y.C., 1953-56; personnel dir. Celanese Internat., N.Y.C., 1958-71; mgr. orgn. and Manpower Internat. and Can. group Gen. Electric Co., N.Y.C., 1971-73; sr. v.p. human resources Northwest Bancorp., Mpls., 1973-82; sr. v.p. Calif. Fed. Savs., L.A., 1983-85; v.p. Career Transition Group, L.A., 1985-87; pres. Fuchs, Cuthrell & Co., Inc., L.A., 1987-93, Fuchs & Co., L.A., 1993-94; pres., CEO Smyth, Fuchs & Co., Inc., L.A., 1995-99; v.p. Spherion, 1998—. Leader seminars. Co-author: International Career Pathing, 1971; Contbr. articles to profl. jours. Served with AUS, 1951-53. Mem. Am. Psychol. Assn., Nat. Fgn. Trade Coun. (founder, past chmn. human resources, orgn. com. 1966—), Human Resources Planning Soc., Employment Mgmt. Assn., Jonathan Club, Yale Club of N.Y., North Ranch Country Club, Phi Gamma Delta. Home: 1115 Westcreek Ln Westlake Village CA 91362-5467

SMYTH, JOEL DOUGLAS, newspaper executive; b. Renovo, Pa., Nov. 8, 1941; s. Bernard John and Eva Mae (Stone) S.; m. Madonna Robertson, Nov. 29, 1959; children: Deborah Sue, Susan Kelly, Michael Robertson, Patricia Ann, Rebecca Lee, Jennifer Neilia. Student, Lycoming Coll., 1959. Reporter Del. State News, Dover, 1960-62, news editor, 1962-65, mng. editor, 1965-70, editor, pres., 1970-78; editor Del. Sunday News, 1964-65; pres. Ind. Newspapers, Inc., Dover, 1970-89, chmn., CEO, 1989—. Founding pres. Valley Citizen's League, 1987-90. Recipient writing awards. Mem. AP Mng. Editors Assn. (dir.), Am. Soc. Newspaper Editors, Young Pres.'s Orgn., Sigma Delta Chi. Home: 39833 N 100th St Scottsdale AZ 85262-2975 Office: Independent Newspaper Inc PO Box 70001 Dover DE 19903 Home: 39833 N 100th St Scottsdale AZ 85262-2975

SMYTH, JOSEPH PATRICK, retired naval officer, physician; b. Norwalk, Conn., Mar. 2, 1933; s. Patrick and Helen (Heffernan) S.; m. Ursula Marie (Kirwin), Dec. 28, 1960; children: Donna, Jennifer, Joseph. BA, Fairfield U.,

1960; MD, Creighton U., 1964. Diplomate Am. Bd. Med. Examiners. Commd. ensign USN, 1963, advanced through grades to rear adm., 1988; intern Phila. Naval Hosp., 1964-65, internal medicine resident, 1965-68, staff physician, 1968-69; internist, chief of medicine U.S. Naval Hosp., DaNang, Vietnam, 1969-70, Orlando, Fla., 1970-76, chief of medicine, exec. officer Yokosuka, Japan, 1976-80, exec. officer Oakland, Calif., 1980-82, comdg. officer, 1984-86, Okinawa, Japan, 1982—84, Naval Med. Command European Region, London, 1986-90; dep. dir. for med. readiness The Joint Staff, Pentagon, Washington, 1990-92; retired US Navy, 1992; med. dir. Volusia County (Fla.) Dept. of Corrections, 1994—. Instr. medicine Jefferson Med. Coll., 1966-69; preceptor USN Physician Asst. Program, Orlando, 1971-76; inst. mgmt. course Navy Med. Dept., Washington, 1986; Joint Staff med. coord. for entire Gulf War build-up reporting to JCS chmn. Gen. Colin Powell Operation Desert Shield/Storm, Saudi Arabia, 1990-91. Physician Orange County, Fla. Alcohol Ctr., Orlando, 1974-76. Decorated Def. Superior Svc. medal, Legion of Merit, Meritorious Svc. medals with 2 oak leaf clusters, Navy Commendation medal with combat V. Mem. AMA, Assn. Mil. Surgeons of U.S., Am. Acad. Med. Adminstrs. (Levandowski award 1991), Fla. Med. Assn., Am. Acad. Physician Execs., Orange County Med. Soc. Republican. Roman Catholic. Home: 400 Sweetwater Blvd S Longwood FL 32779-3422 Office Phone: 386-254-1547.

SMYTH, JOSEPH PHILIP, travel industry executive; b. N.Y.C., Aug. 16, 1939; s. Joseph P. and Virginia S. (Gibbs) S.; m. Janet Hughes; 1 child, Philip. BA, Hamilton U., 1961; MBA, Harvard U., 1967; student, Naval Intelligence Sch., 1961-62. Dir. planning N.E. Airlines, Boston, 1967-70; acct. supr. Wells, Rich, Greene, N.Y.C., 1970-72; sr. v.p. mktg. Inter-Continental, N.Y.C., 1972-86, Hilton Hotels, Beverly Hills, Calif., 1986-88; head of ops. Cunard, N.Y.C., 1988-94; sr. v.p. fleet ops. Holland Am., Seattle, 1994; chmn Gibbs Bros., Huntsville, Tx., 1995—. Bd. mem. First Nat. Bank Huntsville, Tex. Lt. USN, 1961-65, ETO. Mem. Harvard Club. Avocation: running. Home: 1088 Park Ave New York NY 10128-1132 Office: Gibbs Bros PO Box 711 Huntsville TX 77342-0711

SMYTH, JOSEPH VINCENT, manufacturing executive; b. Belfast, Ireland, July 18, 1919; s. Joseph Leo and Margaret M. (Murray) S.; m. Marie E. Cripe, Mar. 22, 1941; children: Kevin W., Brian J., Ellen M., Vincent P. BS cum laude, U. Notre Dame, 1941. With Arnolt Corp., Warsaw, Ind., 1946-63, exec. v.p., gen. mgr., until 1963; pres., gen. mgr. Hills-McCanna Co., Carpentersville, Ill., 1963-72; pres. Lunkenheimer Co., Cin., 1972-79; v.p. Condec Flow Control Group, Chgo., 1979-82; cons., 1982—. Mem.: K.C. Address: 7656 Spring Bay Cove Orlando FL 32819-7208

SMYTH, NICHOLAS PATRICK DILLON, surgeon; b. Dublin, Apr. 1, 1924; arrived in U.S., 1951; s. Patrick Joseph and Nano Elizabeth (Dillon) S.; m. Elizabeth Stavely Long; children: Sheila, Brian, Nicholas, Augustine, Patrick. BSc, Univ. Coll. Dublin, 1946, MSc, 1948, MB, BChir, 1949; MS, U. Mich., 1954. Diplomate Am. Bd. Surgery, Am. Bd. Thoracic Surgery. Intern Mater Misericordiae Hosp., Dublin, 1949-50, Norfolk and Norwich Hosp., England, 1950-51; resident in gen. surgery Henry Ford Hosp., Detroit, 1951-55; resident in thoracic surgery George Washington U. Hosp., Washington, 1957-59; pvt. practice Washington, 1959-86; clin. prof. surgery emeritus George Washington U. Sch. Medicine, Washington. Mem. staff Washington Hosp. Ctr., George Washington U. Med. Ctr. Contbr. articles to profl. jours.; patentee in field. Capt. M.C., U.S. Army, 1955-57. Fellow: ACS, Am. Coll. Cardiology; mem.: N.Am. Soc. Pacing and Electrophysiology, So. Thoracic Surg. Assn., Soc. Thoracic Surgery, Am. Assn. Thoracic Surgery. Republican. Roman Catholic. Avocation: writing.

SMYTH, PAUL BURTON, lawyer; b. Phila., Aug. 15, 1949; s. Benjamin Burton and Florence Elizabeth (Tomlinson) S.; m. Denise Elaine Freeland, May 31, 1975. BA, Trinity Coll., 1971; JD, Boston Coll., 1974. Bar: Conn. 1974, D.C. 1975, U.S. Dist. Ct. D.C., 1980, U.S. Supreme Ct., 1985. With Dept. Interior, 1974—. Atty. Office of Hearings and Appeals, Arlington, Va., 1974—76, acting dir., 1993—94, dep. assoc. solicitor for land and water uses, 1995—; atty. Office of Solicitor, Washington, 1976—82, asst. solicitor for land use and realty, 1982—87, dep. assoc. solicitor for energy and resources, 1987—95; lectr. environ. law George Washington U. Law Sch., Washington, 1997—2001. Editor: Federal Reclamation and Related Laws Annotated, Reclamation Reform Act Compilation, 1982—88; contbr. articles to legal pubs. Bd. dirs. EcoVoce, 1998—; trustee Rocky Mtn. Mineral Law Found., 1999—2001. Mem. ABA (coun. 1991-94, budget officer 1994-98, sec. natural resources, energy and environ. law, exec. editor Nat. Resources and the Environ. 1989-91). Office: Office of Solicitor Dept Interior 18th And C Sts NW Washington DC 20240-0001 Office Phone: 202-208-4506. E-mail: paulb.smyth@verizon.net.

SMYTH, RICH, publishing executive; Pub. So. Living, 2003, v.p., 2000, advt. dir., 1998—2000, nat. sales mgr., 1996—98, hired, 1988—96. Office: Southern Living PO Box 523 2100 Lakeshore Drive Birmingham AL 35209 also: Southern Living 20th Floor 1271 Avenues of the Americas New York NY 10020-1391

SMYTH, RUSSELL P. food products executive; B in acctg., MBA, Northern Ill. U. Various positions in the fin. arena McDonald's Corp., 1984—97; v.p. Latin Am. Group, 1996—99; sr. v.p., internat. relationship ptnr. for Southeast and Ctrl. Asia, 1999—2001; pres. McDonald's Ptnr. Brands, 2001—03, McDonald's Europe, 2003—. Mem.: Ill. CPA Soc., Fed. Inst. of Cert. Pub. Accountants. Office: McDonald's Corp McDonald's Plaza Oak Brook IL 60523

SMYTH, THEODORE HILTON, real estate developer; b. New London, Conn., Apr. 3, 1915; s. Joseph H. and Ida Mae (Towson) S.; m. Elizabeth Norton McBride, Apr. 2, 1949; children: Elizabeth Towson, Theodore Hilton Jr. BA, Bard Coll., 1937, PhD, 1973; D of Bus. Adminstrn. (hon.), Hillsdale Coll., 1997. Shoe buyer Melville Shoe Corp., 1937-40; commercial aviator Am. Overseas Airlines, N.Y., 1946-50; investment counselor Lakeside Co., Seattle, 1950-52; real estate developer Hawaii, 1952—; ltd. ptnr. Conversion Project, Atlanta, 1980. Pres. Santa Barbara (Calif.) Symphony, 1960-62, dir., 1958-68; dir. United Way, Santa Barbara, 1970-74, Calif. Tech. Assocs., Pasadena, 1980-85; chmn. Info Genesis, Santa Barbara, 1985—; former trustee Bard Coll.; mem. bd. vistors and govs. St. John's Coll., 1990-96. Lt. Comdr. USNR, 1940-45. Republican. Avocations: tennis umpiring, swimming, tennis. Home: 4234 Cresta Ave Santa Barbara CA 93110-2410

SMYTHE, CHEVES MCCORD, internist, geriatrician, educator, dean; b. May 25, 1924; Student, Yale Coll., 1942—43; MD cum laude, Harvard, 1947. Diplomate Am. Bd. Internal Medicine, Am. Bd. Geriatrics. Intern, asst. resident Harvard Med. Svc., Boston City Hosp., 1947—49, chief resident, 1954—55; resident chest svc. Bellevue, 1949—50; rsch. fellow Presbyn. Hosp., N.Y.C., 1950—52; assoc. medicine Med. Coll. S.C. Sch. Medicine, 1956—58, asst. prof. medicine, 1958—60, assoc. prof. medicine, 1960—66, dean, 1963—65; attending physician Wesley Meml., Cook County North Side VA Hosps., Chgo., 1967—70; with Aga Khan U. Hosp., Karachi, Pakistan, 1990—91; dean faculty health scis., prof. medicine Aga Khan U., Karachi, Pakistan, 1982—85, prof., chmn. dept. medicine, 1990—91; chief Med. Svcs. at LBJ Hosp., Houston, 1991—95; prof. divsn. gen. medicine dept. internal medicine U. Tex. Med. Sch., Houston, 1970—, dean, 1970—75, dean pro tem, 1995—96. Assoc. med. dir. Hermann Hosp., 1996—. Bd. dirs. Assn. Am. Assoc. Med. Colls., Office: U Tex Med Sch 6431 Fannin St 1-108 Houston TX 77030-1501

SMYTHE, WILLIAM RODMAN, physicist, researcher; b. Los Angeles, Jan. 6, 1930; s. William Ralph and Helen (Keith) S.; m. Carol Richardson, Nov. 27, 1954 (dec. Dec. 1987); children: Stephanie, Deborah, William Richardson, Reed Terry; m. Judith Brean Travers, Jan. 1, 1989. BS, Calif. Inst. Tech., 1951, MS, 1952, PhD, 1957. Engr. Gen. Electric Microwave Lab., Palo Alto, Calif., 1956-57; asst. prof. U. Colo., 1958-63, assoc. prof., 1963-67, prof., 1967-95, chmn. nuclear physics lab., 1967-69, 81-83, 90-92, prof. emeritus, 1995—. Group leader Rocky Mountain Rescue Group, 1967-68. Mem. Am. Phys. Soc. Clubs: Colorado Mountain (Boulder). Achievements include inventing negative ion cyclotron, fractional turn cyclotron. Home: 2106 Knollwood Dr Boulder CO 80302-4706 E-mail: Rod.Smythe@colorado.edu.

SNADER, JACK ROSS, publishing company executive; b. Athens, Ohio, Feb. 25, 1938; s. Daniel Webster and Mae Estella (Miller) S.; m. Sharon Perschnick, Apr. 4, 1959; children: Susan Mae, Brian Ross. BS, U. Ill., 1959. Cert. mgmt. cons. With mktg. Richardson-Merrell, Cin., 1959-65, Xerox Corp., N.Y.C., 1965-67, Sieber & McIntyre, Chgo., 1967-69; pres. Systema Corp., Northbrook, Ill., 1969—. Author Systematic Selling, 1987, The Sales Relationship, 1988. Mem. ASTD, Inst. Mgmt. Cons. Office: Systema Corporation Ste 240 633 Skokie Blvd Northbrook IL 60062-2824 E-mail: jrsnader@systema.com.

SNAIR, ROGER CLIFFORD, writer, comedian; b. Bklyn., Nov. 20, 1955; s. William and Caryle Dianne Snair; m. Bernice Undercuffler, Sept. 19, 1987. BS, Am. U., 1977. Statis. analyst Opinion Rsch., Wilmington, Del., 1984; rsch. interviewer Comm. Concepts, Wilmington, 1984; copywriter Mister Write, Newark, 1985—90, 1990—96; census enumerator U.S. Census Bur., Cherry Hill, NJ, 1990; distbr. nostalgia items Roger's Retroland, Newark, 1996—. Author: (novels) Spice and Steam, 1990, The Lost Science of Rocketry, 2001. Bd. worker Camden County (N.J.) Bd. Elections, 1998—. Republican. Methodist. Avocation: jogging. Home: 239 Grant Ave Mount Ephraim NJ 08059 Office: Roger's Retroland PO Box 1101 Newark DE 19715

SNAPP, ELIZABETH, librarian, educator; b. Lubbock, Tex., Mar. 31, 1937; d. William James and Louise (Lanham) Mitchell; m. Henry Franklin Snapp, June 1, 1956 (div. Dec. 2001). BA magna cum laude, North Tex. State U., Denton, 1968, MLS, 1969, MA, 1977. Asst. to archivist Archive of New Orleans Jazz Tulane U., 1960-63; catalog libr. Tex. Woman's U., Denton, 1969-71, head acquisitions dept., 1971-74, coord. readers svcs., 1974-77, asst. to dean Grad. Sch., 1977-79, instr. libr. sci., 1977-88, acting Univ. libr., 1979-82, dir. librs., 1982—2002, dir. librs. emeritus, 2002—, univ. historian, 1995—2002; adj. prof. dept. history and govt. Tex. Woman's U., Denton, 2002—; rsch. assoc. Tex. Woman's U. Libr., Denton, 2002—. Chair-elect Tex. Coun. State U. Librs., 1988—90, chmn., 1990—92; adv. com. on libr. formula Coord. Bd. Tex. Coll. and Univ. Sys., 1981—92; Libr. Sys. Act adv. bd. Tex. State Libr. and Archives Commn., 1999—2002; del. OCLC Nat. Users Coun., 1985—87, by-laws com., 1985—86, com. on less-than-full-svcs. networks, 1986—87; trustee AMIGOS Libr. Svcs., 1994—2000, sec. bd. trustees, 1996—97, vice-chmn. bd. trustees, 1997—99, chair bd. trustees, 1999—2000; project dir. NEH consultancy grant on devel. core curriculum for women's studies, 1981—82; chmn. Blue Ribbon com. 1986 Gov.'s Commn. for Women to select 150 outstanding women in Tex. History; project dir. math./sci. anthology project Tex. Found. Women's Resources; co-sponsor Irish Lecture Series, Denton, 1968, 70, 73, 78. Co-editor: Read All About Her! Texas Women's History: A Working Bibliography, 1995; contbr. articles to profl. jours. Trustee, treas. Adult Day Care of North Tex., 2002—04, v.p., 2004—; sec. Denton County Dem. Caucus, 1970. Recipient Ann. Pioneer award, Tex. Woman's U., 1986, Women's Studies Vision award, 1998. Mem.: AAUW (legis. br. chmn. 1973—74, br. v.p. 1975—76, br. pres. 1979—80, state historian 1986—88, treas. 1998—99), ALA (stds. com. 1983—85), AAUP, Tex. Assn. Coll. Tchrs. (pres. Tex. Woman's U. chpt. 1976—77), So. Conf. Brit. Studies, Women's Collecting Group (chmn. ad hoc com. 1984—86), Tex. Hist. Commn. (judge for Farenbach History prize 1990—93), Tex. Libr. Assn. (program com. 1978, Dist. VII chmn. 1985—86, archives and oral history com. 1990—92, co-chair conf. program com. 1994, Tall Texan selection com. 1995—96, treas. exec. bd. 1996—99, Centennial com. 2000—02), AAUW Ednl. Found. (rsch. and awards panel 1990—94), Alliance Higher Edn. (chair coun. libr. dirs. 1993—95), Rotary Internat. (sec. local chpt. 1999—2002), Soroptomist Internat. (pres. Denton chpt. 1986—88), Women's Shakespeare Club (pres. 1967—69), Pi Delta Phi, Alpha Lambda Sigma (pres. 1970—71), Alpha Chi, Beta Phi Mu (pres. chpt. 1976 1978, sec. nat. adv. assembly 1978—79, pres. 1979—80, nat. dir. 1981—83). Methodist. Home: 2513 Coffey Dr Denton TX 76207-0002 Office: TWU Sta PO Box 424093 Denton TX 76204-4093 E-mail: Snappe@charter.net. *The idealistic dreams of youth can be translated into making a difference in the work place and in your personal life if you develop a big picture that includes the ideas of individuals of diversity and if you give life your full attention, enthusiasm and courage and give a few your steadfast friendship.*

SNAPP, HARRY FRANKLIN, historian, educator; b. Bryan, Tex., Oct. 15, 1930; s. H.F. and Ethel (Manning) Snapp; m. Elizabeth Mitchell, June 1, 1956 (div. Dec. 20, 2001). BA, Baylor U., 1952, MA, 1953; PhD, Tulane U., 1963. Instr. U. Coll. Tulane U., 1960—62; asst. prof. history Wofford Coll., 1963—64, U. North Tex. (formerly North Tex. State U.), Denton, 1964—69, assoc. prof., 1969—94; dir. Tex. Rsch. Ctr. Biog. Study of Women, Denton, 1995—; pres., dir. Read All About Her Tex. Women's Biographic Ctr., Inc., 1995—. Editor: Brit. Studies Mercury, 1970—84, Tex. Acad., 1973—76; co-editor: Read All About Her! Texas Women's History: A Working Bibliography, 1995, enlarged edit., 1997; author (with others): West Texas Historical Assn. Year Book, 1994, 1996; contbr. articles to profl. jours. Mem. Bridwell Assocs. of So. Meth. U., Friends of Southwestern Art, Am. Com. Irish Studies; mem. adv. com. on acad. freedom and tenure policy, coord. bd. Tex. Coll. and Univ. System. Recipient North Tex. State U. Faculty Rsch. award, 1966, 1967. Mem.: AAUP (pres. North Tex. chpt. 1968—69, pres. Southwestern regional conf. 1971—72, pres. Tex. conf. 1974—76, nat. coun. 1976—86), Butler Soc. (Ireland), Northamptonshire Record Soc., Libr. History Round Table, Libr. Rsch. Round Table, Hist. Assn. (London), Tex. State Hist. Assn., Panhandle-Plains Hist. Soc., West Tex. Hist. Assn. (bd. dirs. 1997—), Am. Hist. Assn., So. Conf. Brit. Studies (sec.-treas. 1969—84), Tulane U. Alumni Assn., Lambda Chi Alpha, Alpha Chi. Methodist. Home: 1904 N Lake Trl Denton TX 76201-0602 Office: Read All About Her Tex Women's Biographic Ctr Inc PO Box 424053 Denton TX 76204-4053

SNAPPER, ERNST, mathematics professor; researcher; b. The Netherlands, Dec. 2, 1913; came to U.S., 1938, naturalized, 1942; s. Isidore and Henrietta (Van Buuren) S.; m. Ethel Lillian Klein, June 1941; children: John William, James Robert. MA, Princeton U., 1939, PhD, 1941; MA (hon.), Dartmouth Coll., 1964. Instr. Princeton, 1941-45, vis. asso. prof., 1949-50, vis. prof., 1954-55; asst. prof. U. So. Calif., 1945-48, asso. prof., 1948-53, prof., 1953-55; NSF post-doctoral fellow Harvard, 1953-54; Andrew Jackson Buckingham prof. math. Miami U., Oxford, Ohio, 1955-58; prof. math. Ind. U., 1958-63, Dartmouth, 1963—, Benjamin Pierce Cheney prof. math., 1971—79. Mem. Am. Math. Soc., Math. Assn. Am. (pres. Ind. sect. 1962-63, Carl B. Allendoerfer award 1980), Assn. Princeton Grad. Alumni (governing bd.), Soc. for Preservation Bridges of Konigsburg, Phi Beta Kappa (hon.), Pi Mu Epsilon (hon.). Home: PO Box 67 Norwich VT 05055-0067 Office Phone: 603-646-3075.

SNARE, CARL LAWRENCE, JR., retired accountant, financial planner; b. Oct. 25, 1936; s. Carl Lawrence and Lillian Marie (Luoma) Snare. BBA, Northwestern U., 1968; postgrad., San Francisco State U., 1976-77, Roosevelt U.; BS, SUNY, 1995. CPA Calif.; CFP Calif. Asst. sec., controller Bache Halsey Stuart & Shields Inc. (now Prudential Securities), Chgo., 1968-73; controller Innisfree Corp. div. Hyatt Corp., Burlingame, Calif., 1973-76; cash mgr. Portland (Oreg.) GE, 1976-79; chief fin. officer, controller Vistar Fin. Inc., Marina del Rey, Calif., 1979-82; pres. Snare Properties Co., Long Beach, Calif., 1984-96, Snare Fin. Svcs. Corp., Rialto, Calif., 1985-89, Carl Snare & Assocs., Long Beach; v.p., treas. Carson Estate Co., Rancho Dominguez, Calif., 1988-96; pres., CEO Glenshire Homes, Inc., Phoenix, 1996-98; pres., ceo Glenshire Tech., Boulder, Colo., 1997-99; acct., fin. planner Calif.; ret. Mem.: AICPA, Founder Cash Mgmt. Assn.

SNAREY, JOHN ROBERT, psychologist, researcher, medical educator; b. 1948; s. John Herbert and Esther Snarey; m. Carol Dunn Snarey, 1970; children: Johnny, Elizabeth. BS, Geneva Coll., 1969; MA, Wheaton (Ill.) Coll., 1973; EdD, Harvard U., 1982. Postdoctoral rsch. fellow dept. psychiatry Harvard U., Cambridge, Mass., 1982-84; assoc. rsch. psychologist Wellesley Coll., 1984-85; assoc. prof. human devel. and edn. Northwestern U., Evanston, Ill., 1985-87; prof. human devel. and ethics Sch. Theology and dept. psychology Emory U., Atlanta, 1987—. Mem. senate Emory U., Atlanta, 2001—, pres., 2003—04. Author: How Fathers Care for the Next Generation, 1993; mem. editl. bd. Harvard Ednl. Rev., 1979—81, Jour. Psychology and Theology, 1986—90, Jour. Moral Edn., 1998—, Am. Ednl. Rsch. Jour., 2001—, mem. editl. adv. bd. Lawrence Erlbaum Assocs., 1988—90; editor: Conflict and Continuity: A History of Ideas on Social Equality and Human Development, 1981, Race-ing Moral Formation, 2004; contbr. articles to profl. jours. Recipient Exemplary Dissertation award, Nat. Coun. Social Studies, 1982, Outstanding Human Devel. Rsch. award, Am. Ednl. Rsch., 1988, James D. Moran Book award, Assn. Family and Consumer Sci., 1994, Marie C. Keel, Excellence in Mentoring award, 2003. Mem.: APA, Nat. Coun. Family Rels., Soc. Rsch. Child Devel., Assn. Moral Edn. (exec. bd. 1986—, treas. 2001—04, pres. 2004—, program chair 1997, Kuhmerker Dissertation award 1983), Am. Ednl. Rsch. Assn. (divsn. E exec. bd. 1990—2000, moral devel. and edn. spl. interest group co-chair 1994—96, sec. divsn. E 1997—99). Office: Emory U Bishops Hall 66 Atlanta GA 30322-0001 Office Phone: 404-727-4185. Business E-Mail: jsnarey@emory.edu.

SNEAD, GEORGE MURRELL, JR., army officer, scientist, consultant; b. San Diego, Nov. 6, 1922; s. George Murrell and Helen (Olsen) S.; m. Kathleen Hill Dawson, Apr. 26, 1947; children: George Murrell III, James M., William M., John P., Edward W. BS, Va. Mil. Inst., 1943; MS, U. Ill., 1948; PhD, U. Va., 1953. Commd. 2d lt. U.S. Army, 1943, advanced through grades to brig. gen., 1969; with Central Germany campaign 805th Signal Co., Europe, 1945-46; Aleutian sector comdr. Alaska Communication System, 1948-50; sta. at Electronic Warfare Center, 1953-56; student U.S. Army Command and Gen. Staff Coll., 1956-57; signal adviser MAAG, 1957-58; signal officer Dept. Army, 1958-60; acting dir. research ballistic missile def. Advanced Research Projects Agy., 1960; with U.S. Army Satellite Communications Agy., 1960-63; student Nat. War Coll., 1963-64; div. signal officer 24th Inf. Div., 1964-65; comdg. officer 7th Signal Group, 1965; dir. Communication /ADP Lab., 1966-68; exec. asst. chief of staff Communications Electronics, Dept. Army, 1968; dir. army research Dept. Army, 1968-71; dep. comdr. Army Strategic Communications Command, 1971-73; prin. scientist Gen. Research Corp., 1973-82; pres. Nat. Sci. Ctr. Found., Burke, Va., 1982-84. Chmn. bd. Am. Fed. Savs. & Loan Assn., Lynchburg, Va., 1985-86; sci./bus. cons., 1986—. Active Boy Scouts Am., 1958-68; bd. dirs. Ctrl. Youth Summer Activities, Ft. Monmouth, 1960-63, Arthritis Found., Washington, 1981-84, Lynchburg Symphony, 1990-95; pres. Acad. Music Theatre, Lynchburg, 1985-95; trustee, vice chmn. bd. dirs. Westminster-Canterbury, Lynchburg, 1991-99; trustee Sci. Mus. Va., 1995—; elder Presbyn. Ch., 1986—. Decorated D.S.M., Legion of Merit with two oak leaf clusters, Bronze Star, Air medal, Army Commendation medal with 4 oak leaf clusters. Mem. Assn. U.S. Army, Armed Forces Communications and Electronics Assn. (sec. Washington chpt. 1968-69), Sigma Xi, Kappa Alpha. Office: PO Box 3306 Lynchburg VA 24503-0306

SNEAD, JAMES ARRINGTON, architect; b. Richmond, Va., June 24, 1950; s. John Elwood and Anna Ruth (Reiche) S. BA, U. N.C., 1972; MArch, Va. Tech. U., 1978. Assoc. CS&D Architects, Balt., 1980-84; v.p., pres. Ziger Hoopes & Snead, Balt., 1984-93; pres. Ziger/Snead Architects, Balt., 1994—. Trustee Gilman Sch., Balt., 1990—, treas., 1998—; mem. adv. bd. Md. Inst. Sch. Continuing Studies, Balt., 1991—, chmn., 1998—. Mem. AIA. Democrat. Presbyterian. Avocations: golf, travel, sailing, skiing. Office: Ziger/Snead Architects 1006 Morton St Baltimore MD 21201-5411

SNEAD, RICHARD THOMAS, restaurant company executive; b. Washington, Apr. 19, 1951; s. Walter Thomas and Ruth Claire (Reeves) S.; m. Marilyn Wolke; children: Richard Adam, Eric Thomas. BS in Engring., U. Tenn., 1973. Project mgr. First Fla. Bldg. Corp., Miami, 1974-78; constrn. mgr. Burger King Corp., San Francisco, 1978-79; nat. constrn. dir. Miami, 1979-81; dir. devel. Boston, 1981-84; regional v.p. Detroit, 1984-86; sr. v.p. devel. Miami, 1986-87; exec. v.p. devel., eastern div. mgr. (including responsibility for minority affairs), 1987-88; pres. Burger King Internat. Div., 1988-89; mng. dir. Burger King U.K., 1989-92, Lenscrafters div. of U.S. Shoe, U.K., 1992-93; sr. v.p. Lenscrafters U.S.A., Cin., 1993-94, pres. Sight & Save div. and new bus. devel. Internat. div., 1994-96; sr. v.p. ops. and retail devel. Casual Corner Group, Inc., Enfield, Conn., 1996-97; exec. v.p. internat. Friday's Hospitality Worldwide, Dallas, 1997—. COO internat., 1998—; pres., CEO Restaurants Worldwide, 2002—. Republican. Avocations: running, golf, skiing, motorcycling. Office: Friday's Hospitality Worldwide 7450 Lyndon B Johnson Fwy Dallas TX 75251-1413

SNEAD, THOMAS G. healthcare executive; b. Halifax County, Va. Grad., Va. Commonwealth U. With KPMG, 1976; mgr. subsidiary fin. Trigon Healthcare Inc., 1985, CFO, pres., COO, 1997—, CEO, 1999—. Office: Trigon Healthcare 2015 Staples Mill Rd Richmond VA 23230 also: PO Box 27401 Richmond VA 23279

SNEDAKER, CATHERINE RAUPAGH (KIT SNEDAKER), editor; d. Paul and Charity (Primmer) Raupagh; m. William Brooks; children: Eleanor, Peter William; m. 2d Weldon Snedaker. BA, Duke U. Promotion mgr. Sta. WINR-TV and WNBF-TV, Binghamton, N.Y.; TV editor, feature writer Binghamton Sun, 1960-68; mem. staff, food editor, restaurant critic L.A. Herald Examiner, 1978-80, food and travel editor. Author: The Great Convertibles; editor: The Food Package; guest editor: Mademoiselle mag., 1942; contbr. numerous articles on food and travel to nat. mags. and newspapers. Recipient 3 awards L.A. Press Club, VISTA award, 1979. Democrat. Home: 140 San Vicente Blvd Apt A Santa Monica CA 90402-1533

SNEDDEN, JAMES DOUGLAS, retired health service management consultant; b. Toronto, Ont., Can., Mar. 4, 1925; s. David Morrison and Sarah Hayton (Monteith) S.; m. Elizabeth Ann McCauley, Dec. 20, 1953. BComm, U. Toronto, 1948; CA, Inst. Chartered Accts. Ont., 1951; FCA, Ont., 1978. With Hosp. for Sick Children, Toronto, 1952-86, asst. dir., 1961-67, adminstr., 1967-70, chief exec. officer, 1970-86; nat. dir. health and social service cons. Peat, Marwick & Ptnrs., 1986-87; pres. J. Douglas Snedden and Assocs., 1987-97. Bd. dirs. Mallinckrodt Can., Cyberfluor Can. Hon. dir. Woodgreen Community Centre, Toronto, 1963-65, v.p., 1965-67, pres., 1967-69, hon. mem. bd. dirs., 1973—; past bd. dirs. Hosp. Coun. Met. Toronto; mem. Bd. Trade Met. Toronto, 1965-97; bd. dirs. United Way Met. Toronto, 1986-89; bd. dirs. Wedgewood at Bonita Bay, Bonita Springs, 1990-94, pres., 1992-94. Served with RCAF, 1943-45. Decorated Can. Centennial medal. Fellow Can. Coll. Health Svc. Execs. (founding mem. 1970, bd. dirs. 1972-83, treas. 1978-81, chmn. 1981-82, past chmn. 1982-83), Inst. Chartered Accts. Ont. (life), Acad. of Medicine, Toronto; mem. Am. Coll. Healthcare Execs. Clubs: University, Bd. of Trade. Presbyterian. E-mail: jdsnedden@juno.com.

SNEDEKER, JAMES PETER, music educator; b. Princeton, N.J., Apr. 24, 1959; s. Richard Stockton and Mary Ellen Snedeker. BA, Bucknell U., 1981; MusM, U. Mass., 1999. Cert. Music Edn. Mass., 1999. Tchr. instrumental music Shutesbury Elem. Sch., Shutesbury, Mass., 2000—; editor Northfield Mt. Hermman Sch., Mass., 2003—. Pvt. music tchr. Red Barn Music Studio, Amherst, Mass., 2000—; musician Jim Rice Quintet, Worcester, Mass.; freelance musician. Composer: (swing tune) Bagel Toasted; author: (record review) Brilliant Corners for the International Association of Jazz Record Collectors Journal (1984), (advertisement for aloe wrap body wraps) Have You Ever Seen a Fat Mummy? (1987) (cited in Art Direction Mag., 1988), (advertisement for trumpet history video) Watch 600 Years of Trumpet in 30 Minutes (2001); composer: (jazz tune) Majority, (percussion music) A Short Walk with Bill (1998); contbr. articles to profl. jours. Recipient Editor's Choice Award for Photography, Internat. Libr. of Photography, 1998. Mem.: Nat. Assn. Music Edn. Achievements include invention of The Chesterhorn-a device that allows trumpet players with paralyzed/arthritic fingers to depress valves with no effort; Running: Finished in top 7% of the 1985 New York City Marathon; Weight Lifting: Finished in top 6% of entrants for the 2001 International Body for Life competition. Avocations: running and weight lifting, drawing/painting, lindy hop dancing, woodworking, astronomy. Home: 248 Amherst Rd #E8 Sunderland MA 01375 Office: Smith College Northampton MA 01063 Personal E-mail: jpsned@hotmail.com.

SNEDEKER, JOHN HAGGNER, university president; b. Plainfield, N.J., May 30, 1925; s. Alfred H. and Anna Marie (Ward) S.; m. Noreen I. Davey, Dec. 30, 1950; children— John D., Philip A., Patrick W. BS cum laude, MA, N.Y. U., 1951; Ed.D., Ind. U., 1959. Dir. lab. human devel. U. Mont., 1952-56; cons. psychologist research Purdue U., 1955; assoc. prof., dir. bur. research Ball State U., 1956-61; prof. higher edn., research asso. Ind. U., 1958; prof., dean Western Wash. State U., Bellingham, 1961-62; pres. Western N.Mex. U., Silver City, 1962—. Mem. exec. bd. Internat. Coun. Spl. Edn., 1952-56; Rocky Mountain regional rep. APA, 1953-56; mem. Gov. Wash. Com. Licensing Tchr. Edn., 1961, Wash. State Legislature Rsch. Tech. Com., 1961. Author or co-author rating scales, attitude and opinion measurement devices; contbr. jours. Bd. dirs. Nat. Sci. Fair; trustee N.Mex. Health Found. Served with U.S. Army, 1943-48. Fellow AAAS; mem. Midwest Psychol. Assn., Inter-Am. Soc. Psychology, Am. Ednl. Research Assn., Holland Soc. N.Y. Address: 2200 Pinon St Silver City NM 88061-7735

SNEED, JAMES LYNDE, lawyer; b. Tulsa, June 24, 1938; s. Earl and Cornelia (Lynde) S.; m. Jane Barnes, Sept. 5, 1959; children: David, Elizabeth, Thomas. AB cum laude, Harvard U., 1960; JD, U. Okla., 1963. Bar: Okla. 1963, U.S. Dist. Ct. (no. dist.) Okla. 1963. Ptnr. Conner, Winters, Randolph & Ballaine, Tulsa, 1962-70; chmn., pres., ptnr. Sneed, Lang, Adams & Barnett, Tulsa, 1970-86; pvt. practice Tulsa, 1986—. Bd. dirs. Grand River Dam Authority, 1974-79; trustee Hillcrest Med. Ctr., Tulsa, 1974-92, Okla. Nature Conservancy, 2000—; active Salvation Army Bd., 1995—. Fellow Am. Bar Found., Okla. Bar Found. (pres. 1982—, chmn. 1985); mem. ABA, Okla. Bar Assn., Okla. Bar Assn., Tulsa County Bar Assn., Am. Judicature Soc., Summit Club, Tulsa Tennis Club (pres. 1978-81), Order of Coif, Phi Delta Phi. Democrat. Presbyterian. Home: 1618 E 30th Pl Tulsa OK 74114-5308 Office: 309 Philtower 427 S Boston Ave Tulsa OK 74103-4141 E-mail: jlsneedlaw@sbcglobal.net.

SNEED, JIMMY, chef, restaurant owner; married; 3 children. Studied with Guenther Seeger; student with Jean-Louis Palladin, Le Cordon Bleu. Exec. chef Windows on Urbana Creek; chef with Jeff Buben The Four Seasons; sous-chef Capital Hill Club, 1980; chef, owner The Frog and the Redneck, Richmond, Va., 1993—. Translator to Am. students Le Cordon Bleu cooking sch. Appearance America's Greatest Chef. Named 1 of Am.'s finest chefs, Esquire mag., 2000. Office: 1423 E Cary St Richmond VA 23219

SNEED, JOSEPH TYREE, III, federal judge; b. Calvert, Tex., July 21, 1920; s. Harold Marvin and Cara (Weber) Sneed; m. Madelon Juergens, Mar. 15, 1944 (dec. Dec. 1998); children: Clara Hall, Cara Carleton, Joseph Tyree IV. BBA, Southwestern U., 1941; LLB, U. Tex., Austin, 1947; SJD, Harvard, 1958. Bar: Tex. 1948. From instr. bus. law to prof. U. Tex., Austin, 1947—57, asst. dean, 1949—50; counsel Graves, Dougherty & Greenhill, Austin, 1954—56; prof. law Cornell U., 1957—62; prof. Stanford Law Sch., 1962—71; dean, prof. of law Duke Law Sch., 1971—73; dep. atty. gen. U.S. Justice Dept., 1973; judge U.S. Ct. Appeals (9th cir.), San Francisco, 1973—87, sr. judge, 1987—. Author: The Configurations of Gross Income, 1967, Footprints on the Rocks of the Mountain, 1997; contbr. articles to profl. jours. With USAF, 1942—46. Mem.: ABA, NY Bar Assn., Fed. Bar Assn., Assn. of Am. Law Schs., Am. Jud. Soc., Am. Law Inst. (cons. estate and gift tax project 1960—69), State Bar Tex., Order of Coif. Office: US Ct Appeals PO Box 193939 San Francisco CA 94119-3939 also: US Ct Appeals 9th Cir 95 Seventh St San Francisco CA 94103-1526

SNEED, MARIE ELEANOR WILKEY, retired secondary school educator; b. Dahlgren, Ill., June 12, 1915; d. Charles N. and Hazel (Miller) Wilkey; m. John Sneed, Jr., Sept. 18, 1937; children: Suzanne (Mrs. Geoffrey B. Newton), John Corwin. Student, U. Ill., 1933-35; BS, Northwestern U., 1937; postgrad., Wayne State U., 1954-60, U. Mich., 1967. Tchr. English, drama, creative writing Berkley (Mich.) Sch. Dist., 1952-76. Mem. Mich. Statewide Tchr. Edn. Preparation, 1968-72, regional sec., 1969-70; mem. Pleasant Ridge Arts Coun., 1982—; mem. Pleasant Ridge Parks and Recreation Commn., 1982-88, sr. citizen cons., 1989—; chmn. Student Tchr. Planning Com. Berkley, 1971-72. Mem. NEA, Mich. Edn. Assn., Berkley Edn. Assn. (pres. 1961-62, 82-87), Oakland Tchr. Edn. Coun. (exec. bd. 1973-76), Farm Bur. Ill., Founder's Soc., Phi Alpha Chi, Pi Lambda Theta, Alpha Delta Kappa, Alpha Omicron Pi. Clubs: Pleasant Ridge Woman's (pres. 1980-83), Royal Oak Rep. Woman's, Nomad's. Home: 21 Norwich Rd Pleasant Ridge MI 48069-1027 also: Miller Heritage Farm LLC Dahlgren IL 62828

SNEED, MICHAEL (MICHELE SNEED), columnist; b. Mandan, N.D., Nov. 16, 1943; d. Richard Edward and June Marie (Ritchey) S.; m. William J. Griffin, Sept. 16, 1978; 1 child, Patrick BS, Wayne State U., 1965. Tchr. Barrington High Sch., Ill., 1965-66; legis. asst. Congressman Ray Clevenger, 1966-67; reporter City News Bur., Chgo., 1967-69, Chgo. Tribune, 1969-86, columnist, 1981-86; pres. sec. Mayor Jane Byrne, Chgo., 1979; gossip columnist Chgo. Sun-Times, 1986—. Co-editor Chgo. Journalism Rev., 1971-72 Vice pres. No. Mich. U. chpt. Young Democrats, 1962 Mem.: Women's Athletic. Roman Catholic. Avocation: gardening. Office: Chgo Sun-Times Inc 401 N Wabash Ave Chicago IL 60611-5642

SNEED, PAULA ANN, food products executive; b. Everett, Mass., Nov. 10, 1947; d. Thomas Edwin and F. Mary (Turner) S.; m. Lawrence Paul Bass, Sept. 2, 1978; children: Courtney Jameson. BA, Simmons Coll., 1969; MBA, Harvard U., 1977; D Bus. Adminstrn. (hon.), Johnson & Wales U., 1991. Ednl. supr., femal coord. Outreach Program for Problem Drinkers, 1969-71; dir. plans, program devel. and evaluations Ecumenical Ctr. in Roxbury, Mass., 1971-72; program coord. Boston Sickle Cell Ctr., 1972-75; asst. product mgr. Gen. Food Corp., White Plains, N.Y., 1977-79, assoc. product mgr., 1979-80; product mgr. Gen. Foods Corp., White Plains, N.Y., 1980-82, sr. product mgr., 1982-83, product group mgr., 1983-86, category mgr., 1986-87, v.p. consumer affairs, 1986-90, pres. food svc. div., sr. v.p., 1990-95; sr. v.p. mktg. svcs. Kraft Foods N.Am., 1995—. Mem. bd. dirs. Hercules Inc. Bd. dirs. Crispus Attucks Scholarship Fund, Ridgewood, N.J., 1982—, bd. dirs. Westchester/Fairfield Inroads. Recipient Benevolent Heart award Graham-Windham, 1987, Black Achiever award Harlem YWCA, 1982, MBA of Yr. Harvard Bus. Sch., 1987, Benevolent Heart award Graham Windham Soc., 1987; named MBA of Yr. Harvard Bus. Sch. Black Alumni Orgn., 1987; named one of 100 Top Black Women in Corp. Am. Ebony Mag., 1990, 91, 21 Most Influential African Ams. in Corp. Am., 1991, 97 (ONe of 40 Most Influential, 1993), Breakthrough 50 Exec. Female Mag., 50 Most Powerful Women Mgrs., 1994, 25 Most Influential Mothers Working Mother Mag., 1998; inducted Acad. Women Achievers N.Y. YWCA, 1990. Mem. AAUW, Exec. Leadership Coun., adv. coun. to dean Howard U. Bus. Sch., Nat. Assn. Negro Bus. and Profl. Women, Coalition of 100 Black Women, Soc. Consumer Affairs Profls., Women's Forum. Office: Kraft Foods Inc Three Lakes Dr Northfield IL 60093-2753 Home: 1755 Paddock Ln Lake Forest IL 60045-3675

SNEED, RAPHAEL CORCORAN, physiatrist, pediatrician; b. Selma, Ala., 1942; MD, U. Ala., 1968. Diplomate Am. Bd. Pediat., Am. Bd. Phys. Medicine and Rehab. Intern U. Ala. Hosp. Clinic, Birmingham, 1968-69, resident in pediat., 1969-71, resident in phys. medicine and rehab., 1981-83, fellow in phys. medicine and rehab., 1983-84; with Children's Rehab. Ctr. Miss. Med. Ctr., Jackson. Mem. Am. Acad. Pediat., Am. Acad. Phys. Medicine and Rehab. Office: U Miss Med Ctr Children's Rehab Ctr 2500 N State St Jackson MS 39216-4505

SNEED, RICHARD DURWOOD, JR., lawyer; b. New Orleans, May 31, 1946; m. Martha Sue Trimble, Mar. 29, 1968; children: Laurie, Kellie. BA in Econs., U. South Fla., 1968; JD, Stetson U., 1971. Bar: Fla. 1971, U.S. Dist. Ct. (so. dist.) Fla. 1972, U.S. Tax Ct. 1975, U.S. ct. Appeals (5th cir.) 1975, U.S. Supreme Ct. 1975, U.S. Ct. Appeals (11th cir.) 1981, U.S. Dist. Ct. (mid. dist.) Fla. 1990. Assoc. Fee, Parker & Neil, Ft. Pierce, Fla., 1971-73; shareholder Sneed & Messer, P.A., Ft. Pierce, 1973-89; pvt. practice Richard D. Sneed, Jr., P.A., Ft. Pierce, 1989—99. Commr. Ft. Pierce Housing Authority, Ft. Pierce, 1989—; bd. dirs. Learn To Read, Inc.; vice chancellor to Bishop Ctrl. Diocese Fla. Mem.: ATLA, ABA, Ft. Pierce Bar Assn., Fla. Bar (standing com. unlicensed practice law 1986—, probate litigation com., probate law com., cert. real estate lawyer), Exch. Club (pres. Ft. Pierce 1980), Phi Alpha Delta. Episcopalian. Avocations: show horses, flying, vintage sports car racing. Office: Mardi Exec Ctr 1905 25th St S Ste 20604 Fort Pierce FL 34947

SNEED, RONALD ERNEST, engineering educator emeritus; b. Oxford, NC, Nov. 23, 1936; s. Henry Ernest and Jewel Leigh (Hughes) S.; m. Shelba Jean Walters, June 8, 1958; children: Kathy Geneva Grosvenor, Jennie Leigh Berrier. BS in Agrl. Engring., N.C. State U., 1959, PhD in Biol. and Agrl. Engring., 1971. Registered profl. engr., N.C.; cert. irrigation designer, contractor, landscape irrigation auditor, and irrigation specialist. Sales trainee John Deere Co., 1959-60; ext. specialist N.C. State U., 1960-62, ext. instr., 1962-69, 70, ext. asst. prof., 1971-75, ext. assoc. prof., 1971-80, prof., 1980-92, prof. emeritus, 1993—; project engr. Agri-Waste Tech., Inc., 1993-2000, Irrigation Consulting, Inc., 1995—; project engr. Divsn. Soil and Water N.C. Dept. Environ. and Nat. Resources, 1997-99. Cons. Lexington (N.C.) Swine Breeders, 1973, 1st Colony Farms, Creswell, N.C., 1977-78, Greek Tobacco Co. Uruguay, 1973-84, Internat. Potato Ctr., Lima, Peru, 1981-85, Philip Morris Tobacco Co., Richmond, Va., 1992-94, Johnston County Dept. Pub. Utilities, 2000-01, Town of Cary, 1999-2000, Merial Select Inc., 1999-2003, Earth-Tec, 1999-2003, Hobbs, Upchurch & Assocs., P.A., 2001-02, Craven County Com. of 100, Ltd., 1995, Murphy Family Farms, 1997-2000, Larry Eason Farms, 1998, Panoramic Farm, Inc., 1997-99, Latham's Nursery, Inc., 1998—, numerous others. Maj. gen. U.S. Army, 1960-95, ret. Recipient Outstanding Paper award So. region Am. Soc. Hort. Sci., 1986, 91; Ronald E. Sneed Irrigation Soc., Inc. scholarship established in his honor, 1991. Fellow Am. Soc. Agrl. Engrs. (ednl. aids competition Blue Ribbon 1963-64, 68, 78-79, 85, 89, 91-92, Gunlogson Countryside Engring. award 1992, Outstanding Paper award 1984), The Irrigation Assn. (life tech. mem., Man of Yr. 1981), N.C. Irrigation Soc., Inc. (Oustanding Contbn. to Irrigation award 1973, former tech. advisor), Soil and Water Conservation Soc., N.C. Land Improvement Contractors Assn. (former tech. advisor), Carolinas Irrigation Assn. (hon.), Res. Officers Assn. (life), Civitan (Civitan of Yr. 1998). Democrat. Baptist. Office: 3405 Malibu Dr Raleigh NC 27607-6505 E-mail: rsneed@intrex.net.

SNEED, THOMAS K. oil industry executive; b. Dayton, Ohio; B in Computer and Info. Sci., Ohio State U. Computer applications programmer Marathon Oil Corp., Findlay, Ohio, 1981—84, data base mgmt., 1984—92, supr., corp. sys. and programming, 1992—97, mgr. info. tech. svcs., 1997—98; mgr. computer svcs. Speedway SuperAmerica, LLC, Enon, 1998—2000, v.p. info. tech. svcs., 2000—02; mgr. info. tech. svcs. Marathon Ashland Petroleum, LLC, Findlay, 2002—03; chief info. officer Marathon Oil Corp., Houston, 2003—. Office: Marathon Oil Corp Corp Headquarters 5555 San Felipe Rd Houston TX 77056-2723

SNEERINGER, STEPHEN GEDDES, lawyer; b. Lancaster, Ohio, Mar. 27, 1949; s. Stanley Carlylle and Mary Eleanor (Fry) S.; m. Kristine Karen Serfling, Oct. 6, 1974; children: Mary Rhonda, Robyn Kathleen. BA magna cum laude, Denison U., 1971; JD, Washington U., 1974. Bar: Mo. 1974. Sr. v.p. A.G. Edwards & Sons Inc., St. Louis, 1974—. Arbitrator N.Y. Stock Exch., NASD Dispute Resolution, Nat. Futures Assn., Am. Arbitration Assn. Editor: Urban Law Ann., 1973-74; bd. editors Securities Arbitration Commentator. Am. Jurisprudence scholar, 1974. Mem. ABA (dispute resolution sect., arbitration com.), Mo. Bar Assn., Securities Industries Assn. (arbitration com.), Futures Industries Assn., Nat. Assn. Securities Dealers (mem. nat. arbitration and mediation com. 1992-94, 2001-03), Securities Industry Conf. on Arbitration. Office: AG Edwards & Sons Inc 1 N Jefferson Ave Saint Louis MO 63103-2205

SNEIDER, JOYCE PAPPACHRISTOU, dietitian, educator; b. Springfield, Mass., May 15, 1932; d. Hector and Henrietta (Hemerling) Flores; m. Stanley Sneider; children: Dianne, Donna, Paul Jr., Gary. AA, Nassau Community Coll., 1970; BA in Math., Sci. and Home Econs. with honors, Queens Coll., 1973; MA, MS in dietetics/nutrition, NYU, 1976; postgrad., Nova U., 1989—. Cert. tchr., N.Y.C., N.Y., tchr. home econs., health edn., sci., Fla.; lic. dietitian, nutritionist Fla. Tchr. Roslyn High Sch., Elmont Meml. High Sch.; dietitian L.I. (N.Y.) Jewish Hosp.; dietician St. Mary's Hosp.; instr. nutrition Cath. Med. Ctr. Nursing, 1974-76; chief dietician Jamaica (N.Y.) Hosp., 1976-80; tchr. Broward Coutny (Fla.) Bd. Educators, 1981—2000; pvt. practice, 2000—. Adj. prof. Nassau Community Coll., Fla. Internat. U., 1980-81. Contbr. articles to profl. jours. Mem. Am. Dietetics Assn., Am. Home Econs. Assn. (cert.), Fla. Dietetics Assn., Fla. Assn. Computer Educators, Fla. Correctional Edn. Assn., Fla. Assn. Alternative Educators, Phi Beta Kappa, Kappa Delta Pi. E-mail: Joysta@earthlink.net.

SNEIDER, ROBERT M. petroleum exploration engineer; PhD in Geology and Mining Engring., U. Wis. With Shell Oil, Shell Devel.; ptnr. Sneider and Meckel Assocs., Inc., 1974-81; pres. Robert M. Sneider Exploration, Inc., Houston, 1981—. Disting. lectr. in field. Mem.: MAE, Soc. Petroleum Engrs., Petroleum Exploration Soc. Australia, Am. Assn. Petroleum Geologists. Office: Sneider Exploration 2203 Twin Oaks Blvd Kemah TX 77565

SNELL, ALMA HOGAN, artist; b. Crow Agency, Mont., Jan. 10, 1923; d. George Washington and Helen (Goes Ahead) Hogan; m. William Frederick Snell, Sept. 20, 1947; children: Ted, Faith Lynn, Pearl Jean, William Frederick, Jr. Student, Flandreau High Sch., S.D., Mont. Advisor Mus. Am. Indian Art, Washington, 1997-98; presenter in field. Author; Grandmothers Grand Child, 1999, Taste of Heritage, 2003. Ethnobotanis Taste of Heritage, Yellowtail, Mont., 2001; v.p. Pretty Shield Found., Billings, Mont., 2000-2001. Recipient Mont. Plaque of Honor Mont. Indian Edn. Assn., 1989, Folk and Traditional Art Apprenticeship award Mont. Arts Coun., 2000-2001, Key to City of Indpls. award Mayor of Indpls. Avocations: writing, cooking, beading, field work, reading. Home: PO Box 7548 Yellowtail MT 59035 Office: 2906 2nd Ave N Billings MT 59101-2026

SNELL, BRUCE M., JR., retired judge; b. Ida Grove, Iowa, Aug. 18, 1929; s. Bruce M. and Donna (Potter) Snell; m. Anne Snell, Feb. 4, 1956; children: Rebecca, Brad. AB, Grinnell Coll., 1951; JD, U. Iowa, 1956. Bar: Iowa 1956, N.Y. 1958. Law clk. to presiding judge U.S. Dist. Ct. (no. dist.) Iowa, 1956-57; asst. atty. gen., 1961-65; judge Iowa Ct. Appeals, 1976-87; justice Iowa Supreme Ct., Des Moines, 1987—2001; ret., 2001. Comments editor: Iowa Law Rev. Mem.: ABA, Am. Judicature Soc., Iowa State Bar Assn., Order Coif. Methodist. Home: PO Box 192 Ida Grove IA 51445-0192

SNELL, CHARLES MURRELL, physicist, astrophysicist; b. Johnson City, Tenn., Aug. 19, 1946; s. Murrell Watkins and Ruth Snell. BS, Vanderbilt Univ., 1967; MS, Univ. Ariz., 1969. Physicist U.S. Army Corps. Engrs., Livermore, Calif., 1971-73, Lawrence Livermore Lab., Livermore, 1973-78, Los Alamos (N.M.) Nat. Lab., 1978—. Contbr. over 100 articles to profl. publs.; patentee in field. With U.S. Army, 1969-71. Mem. Phi Beta Kappa. Avocations: astronomy, hiking, walking. Office: Los Alamos Nat Lab Los Alamos NM 87545-0001 E-mail: cms@lanl.gov.

SNELL, ESMOND EMERSON, biochemist; b. Salt Lake City, Sept. 22, 1914; s. Heber Cyrus and Hedwig Emma (Ludwig) S.; m. Mary Caroline Terrill, Mar. 15, 1941; children: Esmond Emerson (dec.), Richard T., Allan G., Margaret Ann. BA, Brigham Young U., 1935; MA, U. Wis., 1936, PhD, 1938, D.Sc. (hon.), 1982. Rsch. assoc. chemistry U. Tex., 1939-41, asst. prof. chemistry, 1941-43, assoc. prof., 1943-45, prof. chemistry, 1951-56; assoc. prof. biochemistry U. Wis., 1945-47, prof., 1947-53, on leave 1951-53; prof. biochemistry U. Calif., 1956-76, chmn. dept., 1956-62; prof. microbiology and chemistry U. Tex., Austin, 1976-90, Ashbel Smith prof., 1981-90, prof. emeritus, 1990—, chmn. dept. microbiology, 1976-80. Guggenheim Meml. Found. fellow U. Cambridge, 1954-55, Max-Planck Institut für Zellchemie, München, 1962-63, U. Wash., Seattle, Rockefeller U., N.Y.C., Hebrew U., Jerusalem, 1969; Walker-Ames prof. biochemistry U. Wash., Seattle, spring 1953. Author numerous research articles in sci. jours.; Editor: Volume III Biochemical Preparations, 1963-64, Chemical and Biological Aspects of Pyridoxal Catalysis, 1963, Pyridoxal Catalysis, Enzymes and Model Systems, 1968; Mem. editorial bd. Jour. Am. Chem. Soc., 1948-58, Jour. Biol. Chemistry, 1949-59, Biochemistry, 1961-70, Biochem. and Biophys. Research Communication, 1970-85, Biofactors, 1988-91; editor: Ann. Rev. Biochemistry, 1969-83. Recipient U.S. Sr. Scientist award Alexander von Humboldt Found., 1977 Fellow AAAS, Am. Inst. Nutrition (Meade-Johnson B-Complex award 1946, Osborne-Mendel award 1951); mem. Nat. Acad. Scis., Am. Acad. Arts and Scis., Japanese Biochem. Soc. (hon.), Am. Chem. Soc. (chmn. div. biol. chemistry 1954, Kenneth A. Spencer award 1974, Nebr. Lectureship award 1983), Am. Soc. Biol. Chemists (pres. 1961-62, William Rose award 1985), Soc. Am. Bacteriologists (Eli Lilly award in bacteriology and immunology 1945), Am. Acad. Microbiology. E-mail: eesnell@yahoo.com.

SNELL, JAMES BLAINE, music educator; b. Lodi, Ohio, Feb. 16, 1957; s. John Edwin and Clara Sauder Snell; m. Nancy Eileen Hudson, June 12, 1982; children: Jacob, Daniel, Alex. MusB in Edn., Wittenberg U., 1979; MusM in Music Edn., Akron U., 1987. Dir. choirs Buckeye Local Schs., Valley City, Ohio, 1979—82, Barberton City Schs., Ohio, 1982—83; chair dept. music Orange City Schs., Pepper Pike, Ohio, 1984—. Founder/dir. Wittenberg U. Jazz Choir, Springfield, Ohio, 1978—79; chancel choir dir. Lodi United Meth. Ch., Ohio, 1982—83; dir. music Garfield Meml. United Meth. Ch., Pepper Pike, Ohio, 1986—. Singer: (performance) Carnegie Hall Centennial Honors Choir. Guest performance Rotary, Kiwanis, Lions, Am. Cancer Soc., Mar. of Dimes, Salvation Army, Red Cross, Sight Ctr., Crippled Children's, Fred WaringsSoc., food banks, sr. centers, churches and synogogues, Ohio, 1984—2004. Recipient Tchr. of Month award, NewsChannel Five, 2002. Mem.: Am. Choral Dirs. Assn., Music Educators Nat. Conf. Avocations: music, travel, golf, skiing, reading. Home: 110 Silver Springs Tr Chagrin Falls OH 44022 Office: Orange City Schs 32000 Chagrin Blvd Pepper Pike OH 44124

SNELL, LINDA S. physician, medical educator; b. Salford, Eng., Apr. 24, 1952; BA, U. Alta., 1971, MD, 1975; MHPE, U. Ill., Chgo., 1997. Sr. physician Royal Victoria Hosp., Montreal, 1990—; assoc. dean continuing med. edn. McGill U., Montreal, 1994-2000, dir. divsn. gen. internal medicine, 1994—. Fellow ACP, Royal Coll. Physicians Can.; mem. Can. Soc. Internal Medicine (pres. 1994-96). Office: Divsn Gen Internal Medicine 687 Pine Ave W Rm A 4-21 Montreal QC Canada E-mail: snell@med.mcgill.ca.

SNELL, NED COLWELL, financial planner; b. Cowley, Wyo., May 16, 1944; s. Jay Hatton and Freda Hope (Colwell) S.; m. Barbara Anne Frandsen, Apr. 24, 1969; children: Taylor Anthony, Trevor Cameron. BA, U. Utah, 1969; CLU, Am. Coll., 1983, ChFC, 1985. English tchr. Granite Sch. Dist., Salt Lake City, 1969-71; ins. agt. Prudential Ins. Co., Salt Lake City, 1971-76; pres. Snell Fin. Corp., Salt Lake City, 1976—. Co-author: By the Throat, Selected Poems, 2001; editor: Utah Sings, Vol. 8, 2004—05; co-editor: Nine One One, Poetry Anthology. Bd. dirs. Utah chpt. Arthritis Found., Salt Lake City, 1980-82, pres. 1982-83; missionary Mormon Ch. 1963-66; chmn. voting dist. 2604 Rep. Nominating Convs., 1986, 90. Recipient Golden Key Soc. Devel. award, 1990; named Poet Laureate/Jessee Poet, Poets at Work, 2000. Mem. NALU (Nat. Sales Achievement award 1971-89, Nat. Quality award), Am. Soc. CLU and ChFC (bd. dirs. Utah chpt. 1990-93, treas. 1993-94, v.p. 1994-96, pres. 1996-97, com. chmn. Grant Taggart symposium 1996—), Million Dollar Round Table (knight 1988—), Salt Lake Assn. Life Underwriters (bd. dirs. 1974-76, 80-82), Utah State Poetry Soc. (pres. elect, 2003-2005), Nat Fedn. of State Poetry Socs. (vice chancellor, 2004-2005). Republican. Avocations: creative writing, fly tying, fishing, basketball, tennis. Office: 1800 S West Temple Ste 416 Salt Lake City UT 84115-5854 Home: 1963 S 1200 E Apt 712 Salt Lake City UT 84105-3529 Office Phone: 801-466-3200. E-mail: sbsenior@aol.com.

SNELL, PATRICIA POLDERVAART, librarian, consultant; b. Santa Fe, Apr. 11, 1943; d. Arie and Edna Beryl (Kerchmar) Poldervaart; m. Charles Eliot Snell, June 7, 1966. BA in Edn., U. N.M., 1965; MSLS, U. So. Calif., 1966. Asst. edn. libr. U. So. Calif., L.A., 1966—68; med. libr. Bedford (Mass.) VA Hosp., 1968—69; asst. law libr. U. Miami, Coral Gables, Fla., 1970—71; acquistions libr. U. N.Mex. Law Sch. Libr., Albuquerque, 1971—72; order libr. Los Angeles County Law Libr., 1972—76, cataloguer, 1976—90; libr. Parks Coll., Albuquerque, 1990—92; records technician Technadyne Engring. Cons. to Sandia Nat. Labs., 1992—93; libr. Tireman Learning Materials Ctr. U. N.Mex., Albuquerque, 1993—96, instr. libr. sci. program Coll. Edn., 1991—; rsch. technician City of Albuquerque, 1996—. Ch. libr. Beverly Hills Presbyn. Ch., 1974-90, ch. choir libr., 1976-90. Southwestern Library Assn. scholar 1965. Mem.: ALA, N.Mex. Libr. Assn., Pi Lambda Theta. Avocations: travel, reading. Office: Law Libr BCMDC 5800 Shelly Rd SW Albuquerque NM 87151 E-mail: psnell@mercury.berno.gov.

SNELL, RICHARD, holding company executive; b. Phoenix, Nov. 26, 1930; s. Frank L. and Elizabeth (Berlin) S.; m. Alice Cosette Wiley, Aug. 1, 1954. BA, Stanford U., 1952, JD, 1954. Bar: Ariz. Ptnr. firm Snell & Wilmer, Phoenix, 1956-81; pres., chmn., chief exec. officer Ramada Inc., Phoenix, 1981-89; chmn., chief exec. officer Aztar Corp., 1989-90, chmn., bd. dirs., 1990-92; chmn. bd. dirs. Pinnacle West Capital Corp., Phoenix, 1990—2001; chmn. Ariz. Pub. Svc., 1990—2001; bd. dirs. Pinnacle West Capital Corp., Phoenix. Adv. bd. Bank One Ariz. NA; bd. dirs. Aztar Corp., Ctrl. Newspapers Inc.; bd. dirs., chmn. Ariz. Pub. Svc. Co. Trustee Am. Grad. Sch. Internat. Mgmt., Phoenix; past pres. YMCA Met. Phoenix and Valley of Sun. With U.S. Army, 1954-56. Mem. ABA, Ariz. Bar Assn., Paradise Valley Country Club, Phoenix Country Club. Republican. Lutheran. Office: Pinnacle West Capital Corp 400 N 5th St Phoenix AZ 85004 also: Pinnacle West PO Box 53999 Phoenix AZ 85072-3999

SNELL, RICHARD A. equipment manufacturing company executive; b. 1942; BA, Union Coll., Albany, N.Y.; MBA, U. Pa. Brand mgmt. position Procter & Gamble, Cin.; various sr. positions, including v.p. maktg. Smith-Kline Beecham; exev. v.p. Quaker State Corp., until 1986; various positions Tenneco, Inc., 1987-96, in charge automotive retail bus., sr. v.p., head Walker Mfg. divsn., until 1993, pres., CEO Tenneco Automotive, 1993-96; chmn., CEO, pres. Fed.-Mogul Corp., Southfield, Mich., 1996—. Bd. dirs. Schneider Nat. Nat. bd. dirs. Big Bros. Am.; bd. dirs. United Way Cmty. Svcs. Mem. Equipment Mfrs. Assn. (past chmn.). Office: Fed-Mogul Corp 26555 Northwestern Hwy Southfield MI 48034-2199

SNELL, RICHARD SAXON, anatomist; b. Richmond, Surrey, Eng., May 3, 1925; came to U.S., 1963; s. Claude Saxon and Daisy Lilian S.; m. Maureen Cashin, June 4, 1949; children: Georgina Sara, Nicola Ann, Melanie Jane, Richard Robin, Charles Edward. MB, BS, Kings Coll., U. London, 1949, PhD, 1955, MD, 1961. House surgeon Sir Cecil P.G. Wakeley, Kings Coll. Hosp. and Belgrave Hosp. for Children, London, 1948-49; lectr. anatomy Kings Coll., U. London, 1949-59, U. Durham, Eng., 1959-63; asst. prof. anatomy and medicine Yale U., 1963-65, assoc. prof., 1965-67, vis. prof. anatomy, 1969; prof., chmn. dept. anatomy N.J. Coll. Medicine and Dentistry, Jersey City, 1967-69; vis. prof. anatomy Harvard U., 1970, 71, 80, 86; prof. anatomy Coll. Medicine, U. Ariz., Tucson, 1970; prof., chmn. dept. anatomy George Washington U. Med. Ctr., Washington, 1972-88, prof. emeritus, 1988—. Author: Clinical Embryology for Medical Students, 1972, 3d edit., 1983, Clinical Anatomy for Medical Students, 1973, 6th edit., 2000, Clinical Anatomy, 7th edit., 2003, Atlas of Normal Radiographic Anatomy, 1976, Atlas of Clinical Anatomy, 1978, Gross Anatomy Dissector, 1978, Clinical Neuroanatomy for Medical Students, 1980, 5th edit., 2001, Student's Aid to Gross Anatomy, 1986, Clinical Anatomy for Anesthesiologists, 1988, Clinical Anatomy of the Eye, 1989, 2d edit., 1997, Gross Anatomy: A Review with Questions and Explanations, 1990, Neuroanatomy: A Review with questions and Explanations, 1992, Clinical Anatomy for Emergency Medicine, 1993, Clinical Neuroanatomy: An Illustrated Review with Questions and Explanations, 3d edit., 2001, Clinical Anatomy: An Illustrated Review with Questions and Explanations, 4th edit., 2003; contbr. articles to med. jours. Med. Research Council grantee, 1959; NIH grantee, 1963-65 Mem. Anat. Soc. Gt. Britain, Am. Soc. Anatomists, Alpha Omega Alpha. Home: 518 Boston Post Rd Madison CT 06443-2930

SNELLING, BARBARA W. retired state legislator; b. Fall River, Mass., Mar. 22, 1928; d. Frank Taylor and Hazel (Mitchell) Weil; m. Richard Arkwright Snelling, June 14, 1947 (dec. Aug. 1991); children: Jacqueline, Mark, Diane, Andrew. AB magna cum laude, Radcliffe Coll., 1950; D of Pub. Svc. (hon.), Norwich U., 1981; LLD (hon.), Middlebury Coll., 1997; LLD (hon.), St. Michaels Coll., 2002. Pres. Snelling and Kolb, Inc., 1982-95; lt. gov. State of Vt., 1993-97; mem. Vt. Senate, Montpelier, Vt., 1997—99, 2001—02, ret., 2002. Bd. dir. U.S. Inst. Peace; mem. adv. bd. Westaff Inc. of Vt., 1997—. Trustee Radcliffe Coll., 1990-95; bd. dirs. Vt. Cmty. Found., 1986-94, Shelburne Mus., 1988-98; mem. Vt. Ednl. Partnerships, 1992—2000; v.p. for devel. and external affairs U. Vt., 1974-82; mem. Vt. State Bd. Edn., 1971-77; trustee Champlain Coll., 1971-74; mem. Vt. Alcohol and Drug Rehab. Commn., 1970-73, Shelburne Sch. Bd., 1958-73, chmn. 1965-73; mem. Vt. Edn. Adv. Coun., 1968-71, New Eng. Tchr. Edn. Adv. Com., 1968-70, Bd. of Sch. Dirs., Champlain Valley Union H.S., 1962-69, chmn. 1962-68, others; mem. New Eng. Bd. Dollars for Scholars, 1997-2002; bd. dirs. Vt. Program for Quality, 1997—2002; mem. Champlain Valley Area Health Edn. Coun., 1997—2002. Recipient Fanny G. Shaw award for Disting. Cmty. Svc., Burlington Cmty. Coun., 1972, Laymen's award Vt. Edn. Assn., 1965, Hope award MS Cmty. Champion, 1996, Philanthropy Day award Nat. Soc. Fundraising Execs., 1997, Susan B. Anthony award YWCA of Vt., 2001; named Vt. Citizen of Yr. Vt. State C. of C., 2002, Robert Skiff Cmty. Svc. award Lake Champlain C. of C., 2002, Vt. Children's Trust Found. award, 2002, Patricia S. Walton award Vt. Soc. for Pub. Adminstrn., 2002, AHEC Bi State Primary Care Assn. award, 2002, Vt. Alzheimer's Assn. award, 2002, Gold Heart, Am. Heart Assn., 2002. E-mail: ulfkiel@aol.com.

SNELLING, DIANE, state senator, artist; b. Phila., Mar. 18, 1952; BA, Radcliffe Coll., 1974; MA in Art, N.Y. U., 1994. Artist; senator State of Vt., 2002—. Lectr. arts and comm. Trinity Coll., Vt., 1994—97; bd. advisor Friends of U. Vt. Horticulture Farm, 2001—02. Mem. Hinesburg Planning Commn., 1984, Hinesburg Selectboard, 1985—91, Chittenden Affordable Housing Com., 1989—90; bd. trustees King St. Youth Ctr., 1992—95; adv. bd. Robert Hull Fleming Mus., 1994—2001. Republican. Office: 304 Piette Rd Hinesburg VT 05461

SNELLING, GEORGE ARTHUR, banker; b. St. Petersburg, Fla., June 27, 1929; s. William Henry and Eula Hall S.; m. Carolyn Shiver, Mar. 3, 1962; children— George, John S. BSBA, U. Fla., 1951. Partner Smoak, Davis, Nixon & Snelling, C.P.A.s, Jacksonville, Orlando, Fla., 1956-66; v.p. planning Barnett Banks of Fla., Jacksonville, 1966-76; exec. v.p. 1st Bancshares of Fla., Boca Raton, 1976-78; exec. v.p. Fla. Nat. Banks of Fla., Jacksonville, 1978-80; exec. v.p. corp. devel., chief fin. officer Sun Banks of Fla., Orlando, 1981-85; exec. v.p. corp. devel. SunTrust Banks, Inc., Atlanta, 1986-90; pres. Unicoy, Inc., Atlanta, 1991—. Trustee Fla. So. U. Served with USAF, 1951-55. Mem. AICPA. Democrat. Methodist. Home and Office: Unicoy Inc 2682 Varner Dr Atlanta GA 30345-1559 E-mail: gsnellingsr@msn.com.

SNELLING, ROBERT ORREN, SR., franchising and employment executive; b. Aug. 16, 1932; s. Louis Raymond and Gwendolyn Anne (Preble) S.; m. Joan E., 1951 (dec. 1979); children: Robert, Krista; m. Anne Morris, June 30, 1979; children: Rick Spragins, Leigh Crews, Linda Paulk. Student, Pa. State U., 1951-52; Dr. Lit. (hon.), Albright Coll., 1968. Profl. employment counselor Snelling & Snelling, Phila., 1952-53, gen. mgr., 1954—62, pres., 1962—96, chmn. bd. dirs., 1969—2000, CEO, 1997—2000; bus. and franchising cons., 2000—. Spkr., lectr. in field. Author: The Opportunity Explosion, 1969, Jobs—What They Are-Where They Are-What They Pay, 1985, rev. edit., 1992, The Right Job, 1987, rev. edit., 1992; contbr. articles to profl. jours. Mem. long-range planning Sarasota 2000, 1976; mem. pvt. sector employment svcs. com. Dept. Labor, 1982; mem. Com. on Skilled Employment Brokering Svcs., 1984; mem. White Ho. Com. on Small Bus., 1986; mem. adv. com. to U.S. Sec. William Brock, 1986; mem. Gov.'s Select Com. on Workforce 2000, 1988—89, chmn. govtl. regulations and benefits subcom., 1989; apptd. to Nat. Com. for Employment Policy, 1994—97; trustee Regent U., 1988—, Found. for Thought and Ethics, 1990—, Acts 29, 1998—. With U.S. Army, 1953—54. Recipient Golden Plate award, 1964, W.O. Blanchet award, Pa. Assn. Pers. Svc., 1976, Outstanding Citizen award, Assn. Pers. N.Y., 1977, award for excellence, Am. Acad. Achievement, 1964, Harold B. Nelson award, 1985. Mem. Internat. Franchise Assn., Nat. Assn. Pers. Cons., Nat. Assn. Temp. Svcs., U.S. C. of C. Republican.

SNELLINGS, ELEANOR CRAIG, retired economics educator; b. Laurinburg, NC, Nov. 3, 1926; d. Carl Brackett and Eleanor (Johnston) Craig; m. Henry L. Snellings Jr., Oct. 1, 1960 (dec. 1970); 1 child, Hill. BA, U. NC, 1947, MA, 1950; PhD, Duke U., 1959. Instr. U. Ark., Fayetteville, 1948—49, U. NC, Greensboro, 1949—56; rsch. assoc. Fed. Res. Bank of Richmond, Va., 1956—58, assoc. economist, 1959—60, economist, 1960—62; adj. faculty Va. Commonwealth U., Richmond, 1962—68, assoc. prof. econs., 1968—92; econ. dir. South River Assn., Greensboro, 1974—77. Grantee, So. Fellowships Fund, 1954, So. Bus. Adminstrn. Assn., 1981—82. Home: Apt 833 1600 Westbrook Ave Richmond VA 23227-3322

SNELSON, KENNETH DUANE, sculptor; b. Pendleton, Oreg., June 29, 1927; s. John Tavner and Mildred F. (Unger) S.; m. Katherine Eve Kaufmann, May 2, 1972; 1 child, Andrea Nicole. Numerous. Student, U. Oreg., 1946-47, Black Mountain Coll., 1948-49, Chgo. Inst. Design, 1950-51, Academie Montmartre, Paris, 1951-52; D of Arts and Humane Letters (honoris causa), Rensselaer Poly. Inst., 1985. Subject of articles in art publs.; one-man shows U.S. and Germany, Holland, including Portrait of an Atom, Balt., 1979-80, De Cordova and Dana Mus. and Park, Lincoln, Mass., 1984, Zabriskie Gallery, 1984, Yoh Art Gallery, Osaka, Japan, 1991, Contemporary Sculpture Ctr., Tokyo, 1995, Maxwell Davidson Gallery, N.Y.C., 1994, Marlborough Gallery, N.Y.C., 1999; major retrospective, Hirshhorn Mus. and Sculpture Garden of Smithsonian Instn., 1981, Albright-Knox Art Gallery, Buffalo, 1981, N.Y. Acad. Scis., 1989; group shows include Mus. Modern Art, N.Y.C., 1967, Whitney Mus., N.Y.C., 1966, 69, 70, Albright Knox Gallery, 1968, Prospect '68, Dusseldorf, Germany, 1968, Salon International de Galeries Pilotes, Lausanne, Switzerland, 1970, Sammlun Etzold, Kolnischer Kunstverein, Cologne, Germany, 1970, Expo '70, Osaka, Japan, 1970, Fondation Maeght, St. Paul de Vence, France, 1970, Art Inst. Chgo., 1972; represented in permanent collections including, Mus. Modern Art, Whitney Mus. Am. Art, cities of Hannover and Hamburg, Germany, Rijksmuseum Kroller Muller, Otterlo, Holland, Rijksmuseum, Amsterdam, Holland, Japan Iron, Steel Fedn., Osaka, City of Balt., Hirshhorn Mus., Milw. Art Center, City of Buffalo, Mus. Modern Art, Shiga, Japan; author: Full Circle: Panoramas of Paris, Venice, Rome, Siena and Kyoto, 1990; patentee discontinuous compression structures, model for atomic forms. Served with USNR, 1945-46. DAAD fellow Berlin Kunstlerprogram, 1976; recipient AIA Artist's medal, 1981, Art award Am. Inst. Arts and Letters, 1987, Prix Ars Electronica Siemens AG for Computer Graphics, Linz, Austria, 1989, Lifetime Achievement award Internat. Sculpture Ctr., 1999, Elizabeth N. Watrous prize for sculpture Nat. Acad. Design, 2002. Mem. Am. Acad. Arts and Letters. E-mail: k_snelson@mindspring.com. *My art is concerned with nature in its most fundamental aspect, the patterns of physical forces in space.*

SNETSINGER, KENNETH GEORGE, retired mineralogist; b. San Francisco, Feb. 21, 1939; s. Ercell Aneas Snetsinger and Coral Binning; m. Judith Cady Briggs Etheridge, Feb. 17, 1977. BS, Stanford U., 1961, MS, 1962, PhD, 1966. Rsch. asst. U.S. Geol. Survey, Menlo Park, Calif., 1958—62; instr. Stanford U., Palo Alto, Calif., 1963—66; postdoctoral rsch. assoc. NASA/Ames Rsch. Ctr., Moffett Field, Calif., 1966—69, rsch. scientist, 1969—93. Chmn. Source Evaluation Bd. NASA/Ames Rsch. Ctr., 1990—93, NASA Assoc., 1993—2000. Contbr. articles to profl. jours. Postdoctoral rsch. assoc., NAS, 1966—69. Mem.: N.Y. Acad. Scis., Am. Geophys. Union, Sigma Xi (grantee 1964). Achievements include discovery of several new minerals; mineralogical studies of returned lunar samples; mineralogical analysis of atmospheric aerosols collected at high altitudes. Home: PO Box 62 Sunol CA 94586

SNIBBE, PATRICIA MISCALL, advertising executive; b. Hackensack, N.J., June 1, 1932; d. Jack and Margaret Lois (Drake) Miscall; m. Richard Wilson Snibbe, Sept. 8, 1962; stepchildren: John Robinson, Paul Clor. BFA, R.I. Sch. Design, 1954; postgrad., New Sch. for Social Rsch., 1975-80, U. London, 1989. Art dir., film prodr. Peckham Prodns., N.Y.C., 1960-64; dir. art, ptnr. Stallman and Snibbe, N.Y.C., 1964-66; dir. art Shevlo Advt., N.Y.C., 1966-72, Bernard Hodes Advt., N.Y.C., 1972-77; owner, creative dir. Archtl. Film Libr., N.Y.C., 1978-88, creative dir., 1980—; pres. Crommelin and Bliss, Parfumier, N.Y.C., 1988—. Author and artist: Feminist Funnies, 181—; author: (with Richard W. Snibbe) The New Modernist in World Architecture, 1999. Recipient Golden Cir. award Affiliated Advt. Agys. Internat., 1975-77, Creativity award of distinction, 1978. Mem. NOW (bd. dirs. N.Y.C. 1983-84), Graphic Artists Guild (steering com. Cartoonists Guild divsn. 1984-85), NATAS, Archeol. Inst. Am. Avocation: abstract modern painting. Office: 3 Baltimore St 1 Providence RI 02909-5603

SNIDER, BARRY B. organic chemist; b. Chgo., Jan. 13, 1950; s. Gordon L. and Ruth C. (Tobias) S.; m. Katalin Boros, July 12, 1975; 1 child, Emily L. BS in Chemistry, U. Mich., 1970; PhD, Harvard U., 1973. Postdoctoral fellow Columbia U., N.Y.C., 1973-75; asst. prof. Princeton (N.J.) U., 1975-81; assoc. prof. Brandeis U., Waltham, Mass., 1981-85, prof., 1985—, chmn. dept. chemistry, 1992-95, Breskin prof. organic chemistry, 1998—. Recipient scholar award Dreyfus Found., 1982; Sloan Found. fellow, 1979; Japan Soc. for Promotion of Sci. fellow, 1999. Mem. Am. Chem. Soc. (Arthur C. Cope scholar 1995), Royal Soc. Chemistry. Office: Brandeis U Dept Chemistry Waltham MA 02454 E-mail: snider@brandeis.edu.

SNIDER, DAVID ANDREW, theater educator, theater director, actor; s. Marlin Lester and Brenda Kay Snider; m. Alexandria Anne Dery, Sept. 29, 2001. BA in English Lit. and Russian Lang., Dickinson Coll., 1993; MFA, NYU Tisch Sch. Arts, 1999. Resident actor Jean Cocteau Repertory, N.Y.C., 1994—95; exec. asst. FCB Advt., 1995—96; grad. asst. NYU Tisch Sch. Arts, 1996—99; Robert Moss resident dir. Playwrights Horizons, 2000—01; artistic dir. lab co. Hangar Theatre, Ithaca, 2001—01; sch. programs mgr. and dir. camp Shakespeare The Shakespeare Theatre, Washington, 2001—. Peer reviewer U.S. Dept. Edn., Washington, 2003; mem. bd. advisors Nat. Overture for Edn. and the Arts, 2003—; dir. H St. Playhouse, 2003; mem. Shakespeare lab NY Shakespeare Festival, N.Y.C., 1995—. Dir.: (performance) Sinking Up; actor: Ambition Facing West, Suicide Weather, Love's Labours Lost, The Revenger's Tragedy, Julius Caesar, The Merry Wives of Windsor, The Marriage Proposal, Uncle Vanya, Awake and Sing!, Many Colors Make the Thunder-King, The Changeling; dir.: Love's Lost Hour, Home, and The Ice Wolf (Drama League Directing fellow, 2001); performance, Lobby Hero (Robert Moss Resident Dir. award, 2001); actor: (performance) New York University Graduate Acting Program (fellow, 1996), The Cherry Orchard, The Country Wife, Hamlet (Michael Tuch Acting fellow, 1994), Macbeth, Twelfth Night, The Importance of Being Earnest, Ah, Wilderness!. Fellow, NYU, 1996—99. Mem.: Alpha Lambda Delta, Phi Beta Kappa. Independent. Avocations: mountain climbing, running, weightlifting, writing, travel. Office: The Shakespeare Theatre 516 8th St SE Washington DC 20003

SNIDER, EDWARD MALCOLM, professional hockey club executive; b. Washington, Jan. 6, 1933; s. Sol C. and Lillian (Bonas) Snider; children: Craig Alan, Jay Thomas, Lindy Lou, Tina Suzanne, Sarena Lynn, Samuel Everett. BS, U. Md., 1955. CPA Md. Maj. stockholder, exec. v.p. Edge Ltd., Washington, 1957—63; v.p. Phila. Eagles Football Club, 1964—67; owner Phila. Flyers Hockey Club, 1967—; chmn. bd. Spectrum Arena, Phila., 1967—; bd. govs. NHL, 1967—. Established Spectacor (now Comcast-Spectacor), chmn. bd., 1996; adv. bd. Sol C. Snider Entrepreneurial Ctr. U Pa.; bd. overseers Wharton Sch. U. Pa.; bd. dirs. Inst. for Cancer and Blood Diseases Hahnemann U., Simon Weisenthal Ctr.; bd. trustees Inst. for Objectivist Studies. Office: Phila Flyers Phila 76ers First Union Center, 3601 S Broad St Philadelphia PA 19148-5250

SNIDER, GEORGE RUNYON, JR., franchising company executive; b. Huntington, W.Va., Jan. 25, 1941; s. George R. and Marjorie Steuart S.; m. Nora C. Jacobs, Aug. 26, 1988; children: George R. III, Jeremy W. BA, Yale U., 1962. Assoc. dir. pub. affairs Procter & Gamble Co., Cin., 1972-76; dir. pub. rels. BF Goodrich Co., Akron, Ohio, 1977-82; dir. mktg. BF Goodrich Chem. Group, Cleve., 1982-88; dir. mktg. and comms. Walter & Haverfield, Cleve., 1988-92; pres., CEO SRA Internat., Inc., Akron, 1992—. Trustee Old Trail Sch., Bath, Ohio, 1982-88, trustee emeritus, 1989—. Named one of 100 Most Influential People in Recruiting Industry, Recruiter Mag., 2002. Mem.: Soc. Cin., Nat. Assn. Pers. Svcs. (dir., chmn. govt. affairs com. 1997—2000, chmn. pub. rels. 2000—01), Mory's Assn. (New Haven), The Club at Key Ctr. (Cleve.). Office: SRA Internat Inc 3737 Embassy Pkwy Ste 200 Akron OH 44333-8369

SNIDER, JAMES RHODES, radiologist; b. Pawnee, Okla., May 16, 1931; s. John Henry and Gladys Opal (Rhodes) S.; B.S., U. Okla., 1953, M.D., 1956; m. Lynadell Vivion, Dec. 27, 1954; children— Jon, Jan. Intern, Edward Meyer Meml. Hosp., Buffalo, 1956-57; resident radiology U. Okla. Med. Center, 1959-62; radiologist Holt-Krock Clinic and Sparks Regional Med. Center, Ft. Smith, Ark., 1962-66, dir. Fairfield Community Land Co., Little Rock, 1968-87, Fairfield Communities, Inc., 1968-87. Mem. Ark. Bd. Pub. Welfare, 1969-71. Bd. dirs. U. Okla. Assn., 1967-70, U. Okla. Alumni Devel. Fund, 1970-74; bd. visitors U. Okla. Served to lt. comdr. USNR, 1957-62. Mem. Am. Coll. Radiology, Radiol. Soc. N.Am., Am. Roentgen Ray Soc., AMA, Phi Beta Kappa, Beta Theta Pi, Alpha Epsilon Delta. Asso. editor Computerized Tomography, 1976-88. Home: 5814 Cliff Dr Fort Smith AR 72903-3845 Office: 1500 Dodson Ave Fort Smith AR 72901-5128

SNIDER, L. BRITT, government executive; b. Rocky Mount, N.C., Jan. 12, 1945; s. Arnold Holmes and Kate Mills (Suiter) S.; m. Virginia Lansford, Aug. 24, 1974; 1 child, Britt Arnold. BA, Davidson (N.C.) Coll., 1966; JD, U. Va., 1969. Counsel judiciary subcom. on constl. rights U.S. Senate, Washington, 1971-75, counsel select com. on intelligence, 1975-76; ptnr. Ketner & Snider, Salisbury, N.C., 1976-77; counsel govt. ops. subcom. on govt. info. U.S. Ho. Reps., Washington, 1977; asst. dep. undersec. counterintelligence and security Dept. Def., Washington, 1977-87; minority counsel U.S. Senate Intelligence Com., Washington, 1987-89, gen. counsel, 1989-95, staff dir. commn. on roles and capabilities of U.S. Intelligence Cmty., 1995-96; sr. fellow Ctr. for Study of Intelligence, 1996-97; spl. counsel to dir. CIA, 1997-98, inspector gen., 1998-2001. Staff dir. Commn. to Rev. Security Practices and Procedures Dept. Def., Washington, 1985. Served to capt. U.S. Army, 1969-71, Vietnam. Mem. Va. Bar Assn., D.C. Bar Assn. Democrat. Episcopalian. Avocations: golf, jogging, reading.

SNIDER, LAWRENCE K. lawyer; b. Detroit, Dec. 28, 1938; s. Ben and Ida (Hertz) S.; m. Maxine Bobman, Aug. 12, 1962; children: Stephanie, Suzanne. BA, U. Mich., 1960, JD, 1963. Bar: Mich. 1964, Ill. 1991. Ptnr. Jaffe, Snider, Raitt & Heuer, Detroit, 1968-91, Mayer, Brown & Platt, Chgo., 1991—. Mem. Nat. Bankruptcy Conf., Am. Coll. Bankruptcy, 1991—. Contbr. articles to profl. jours. Mem. Mich. Coun. for the Arts, 1990-91. Avocations: photography, collections. Office: Mayer Brown & Platt 190 S La Salle St Ste 3100 Chicago IL 60603-3441

SNIDER, MARIE ANNA, syndicated columnist; b. Croghan, N.Y., Aug. 9, 1927; d. Nicholas and Dorothy (Moser) Gingerich; m. Howard Mervin, Nov. 27, 1954; children: Vada Marie, Conrad Howard. BS, Goshen Coll., 1949; M in Religious Edn., Mennonite Bibl. Sem., 1957; MS, Kans. State U., 1980. High sch. tchr. Rockway Collegiate, Kitchener, Ont., Can., 1949-53; freelance writer, 1953-54; pub. rels. Goshen Coll., Ind., 1955-57; free-lance writer, homemaker, 1957-67; info. editor Prairie View, Inc., Newton, Kans., 1967-76, dir., pub. info. & edn., 1976-85, dir. communications, 1985-91; freelance writer, columnist North Newton, 1991—; syndicated columnist "This Side of 60", 1992—. Bd. dirs. Health Systems Agy. of S.E. Kans., 1981-86, v.p., 1986-87; workshop presenter Nat. Coun. of Community Mental Health Ctrs., Atlanta, 1980, N.Y., 1982, 89, Miami, 1987. Editor: Media and Terrorism--The Psychological Impact, 1976; columnist: This Side of 60. Pres. City Council, N Newton, 1977-79, pres. 1980. Recipient 1st Pl. MacEachern award Assn. of Hosp. Pub. Rels., 1981, 1st Pl. Media award Nat. Coun. Community Mental Health Ctrs., 1977, 84, runner-up Pub. Rels. award Nat. Assn. Pvt. Psychiat. Hosps., 1980. Mem. Nat. Soc. Newspaper Columnists. Democrat. Avocations: research on role of women in american comics (speaker and media interviews on this topic), empowerment in aging. Home and Office: PO Box 332 North Newton KS 67117-0332 Office Phone: 316-283-2309. E-mail: thisside60@aol.com.

SNIDER, ROBERT F. chemistry educator, researcher; b. Calgary, Alta., Can., Nov. 22, 1931; s. Edward C. and Agnes S. (Klaeson) S.; children: Wendy A., Timothy J., Terry E., Geoffrey Y, Eric A. M. Burrough. BS, U. Alta., 1953; PhD, U. Wis., 1958. Postdoctoral fellow NRC Can., Ottawa, 1958; instr. II U. B.C., Vancouver, Canada, 1958-60, asst. prof., 1960-65, assoc. prof., 1965-69, prof., 1969-96, prof. emeritus, 1997—. Vis. rsch. prof. U. Leiden, Netherlands, 1973—74. Recipient Gov. Gen. Gold medal U. Alta., 1953; U. Wis. WARF unassigned fellow, 1953-55; Izaac Walton Killam Meml. fellowship, 1985-86. Fellow Chem. Inst. Can., Royal Soc. Can.; mem. Am. Phys. Soc. Home: 3952 W 29th St Vancouver BC Canada V6S 1T9 Office: U BC 2036 Main Mall Vancouver BC Canada V6T 1Z1 E-mail: snider@chem.ubc.ca.

SNIDER, ROBERT LARRY, management consultant; b. Muskogee, Okla., Aug. 10, 1932; s. George Robert and Kathryn (Smiser) S.; m. Gerlene Rose Tipton, Nov. 26, 1953; children: Melody Kathryn Porter, Rebecca Lee. BS in Indsl. Engring., U. Houston, 1955, postgrad., 1956, Pomona Coll., 1960. Cert. mgmt. cons. Instr. U. Houston Coll. Engring., 1955-56; sr. indsl. engr. Sheffield Steel Corp., Houston, 1955-59, Kaiser Steel Co., Fontana, Calif., 1959-60; cons. Arthur Young & Co., L.A., 1960-61; mgmt. analyst Iranian Oil Exploration & Producing Co., Masjidi-Suliman, Iran, 1961-62; cons., 1962-65; v.p. operating methods divsn. Booz, Allen & Hamilton, Inc., Dallas, 1965-69, mgr., 1969—; prin., gen. cons. practice Peat Marwick Mitchell, CPAs, Houston, 1969-71; exec. v.p. mfg. Sterling Electronics Corp., Houston, 1971-72, COO, pres., 1972-77; CEO, pres. Rapoca Energy Corp., Cin., 1977-79; mng. ptnr., cons. Coopers & Lybrand, Southwest, Houston, 1979-81; mng. dir. S.W. region Korn Ferry Internat., Houston, 1981-86; ptnr.-in-charge Houston Mgmt. Cons. Practice, 1986-91; ptnr. cons. Southwest Enterprise Coopers & Lybrand, Houston, 1991-92, ptnr. S.W. Mfg. Cons. Process Improvement Group, 1992-93, internat. cons. ptnr., 1993-95; mng. ptnr. RLS Profl. Svcs. LLC, 1995—; chmn., dir. L&G Snacks, 1997-2000. Chmn. L&G Snacks. Trustee Gene Cragg Caring Forever Found., 1997—99; past chmn. bd. mem. found. bd. and adminstrv. bd. Chapel Wood Meth.Ch.; former mem. adminstrv. bd. Memorial Dr. Meth. Ch., Houston, 1997—99; sr. trustee 1st Christian Ch. Conroe Remainder Trust, 2002—; chmn. adminstrv. bd. 1st United Meth. Ch., Willis, Tex., 2001—02; deacon, steward 1st Christian Ch., Conroe, Tex., 2003—; past bd. dirs. Houston Jr. Achievement, exec. com.; ret. exec. com. Houston Grand Opera, bd. dirs.; sr. trustee Tipton-Snider Minister Edn. Fund., 1999—. With C.E. AUS, 1956. Recipient Outstandng Mil. Engr. award Soc. Mil Engrs., 1955; named Disting. Alumni, Cullen Coll. Engring., U. Houston, 1991. Mem.: U. Houston Alumni Assn. (life; exec. com. 1985—94, pres. and chmn. bd. 1990—93, past bd. dirs.), Phi Kappa Phi, Phi Theta Kappa. Home and Office: 9387 Escondido Dr Willis TX 77318-6621

SNIDER, STACEY, film company executive; b. Phila., Penn., Apr. 29, 1961; m. Gary Jones; children: Katie, Natalie. BA, U. of Penn., 1982; JD, U. of Calif. at Los Angeles, Sch. of Law, 1985. Dir. of development Guber-Peters Entertainment Co., 1986—90, exec. v.p., 1990—92; pres. prodn. TriStar Pictures, 1992-96; co-pres. prodn. Universal Pictures, Universal City, Calif., 1996-98, head prodn., 1998, pres. prodn., 1998—99, co-chmn., 1999, chmn., 1999—. Bd. dirs. Am. Film Inst. Bd. dirs. Spl. Olympics of So. Calif.; bd. trustees Art Ctr. Coll. of Design, Pasadena, Calif. Recipient Dorothy and Sherrill C. Corwin Human Rels. Award, Am. Jewish Com., 2003. Office: Universal Pictures 100 Universal City Plz Universal City CA 91608-1002*

SNIDER, TIMOTHY R. mining executive; BS in Chemistry and Geology, No. Ariz. U., 1979; grad. advanced mgmt. program, U. Pa., 1996. Pres. Phelps Dodge Morenci Inc., Morenci, Ariz.; pres., COO Phelps Dodge Mining Co., 1998—; sr. v.p. Phelps Dodge Corp., 1998, pres., COO, 2003—; joined Phelps Dogde, Bisbee, Ariz., 1970. Office: Phelps Dodge Corp One North Central Ave Phoenix AZ 85004*

SNIFFEN, FRANCES P. artist; d. Esther Wade; m. Richard Sniffen; children: William, Kevin, Jeffrey, John, Caroline. BFA, Corcoran Coll. Art and Design, 1996. Resident artist Arlington Arts Ctr., Arlington, Va., 2001—, tchr. art summer workshop; studio Millennium Art Ctr., Washington, 2003. Mem. women's com. Nat. Mus. Women in Arts, Washington, 2001—. Author (with Caroline Sniffen): Coloring Shadows, 1994 (Dorothy Tabak Meml. award NAWA, 2002); exhibitions include Artscape 97, Balt., Md., 1997, WPA Space, Washington, 1998, Bristol (RI) Art Mus., 2001, The DCCA, Wilmington, Del., 2002, Russian Embassy Cultural Ctr., Washington, 2002, Attleboro (Mass.) Mus., 2002, IASG, 2002, Tsinghua U., Bejing, China, Gallery K, Washington, 2002, Biennale Internazionale Dell'Arte Contemporanea Citta di Firenze, 2003, one-woman shows include Gallery K, Wash., 2003, mentioned in critical review by John Blee, Art Critics Rev., Georgetowner Newspaper, 2003. Mem. gala com. Imperial Collections, State Hermitage Mus. for Nat. Mus. Women in the Arts, Washington, 2003; vol. White House, Washington, 1992—93; mem. art com., event chmn. Hospitality Info. Svc. Meridian House Internat., Washington, 1986—; mem. women's com., event chair Nat. Symphony Orch. Kennedy Ctr., Washington, 1986—; women's bd. exec. vol. Georgetown U. Hosp., Washington, 1988—2002. Mem.: Nat. Assn. Women Artists, Inc. (juried membership, N.Y.C.). Avocations: creative writing, music, sports, politics, nutrition.

SNIFFEN, MICHAEL JOSEPH, hospital administrator; b. Ossining, N.Y., June 16, 1949; s. John Francis and Mary Agnes (Madden) S.; m. Anne Marie Gillick; children: Kevin, Kristina. BS, Fordham U., 1971; MBA in Hosp. Adminstrn., Baruch Coll., 1977. Dir. of fin. planning Westchester div. N.Y. Hosp., White Plains, N.Y., 1971-74, assoc. dir. N.Y.C., 1974-80, sr. assoc. dir., assoc. dean Cornell Med. Ctr., 1980-87; pres., CEO Overlook Hosp., Summit, NJ, 1987-96; exec. v.p., COO Atlantic Health Sys., Florham Park, NJ, 1996—2000; prs., CEO BSCPC, Hoboken, NJ, 2001—. Exec. dir. Cornell Health Policy Program, N.Y.C., 1984-87; adminstr. program Commonwealth Fund, N.Y.C., 1978-81; adv. bd. Robert Wood Johnson Found.-Teaching Nursing Home Program, Princeton, N.J., 1980-86. Vol. March of Dimes, Tarrytown, N.Y., 1984-88; bd. dirs. St. Columbans Sch., Peekskill, N.Y., 1981-84; mem. various svc. clubs, Westchester County, N.Y., 1976-91. Fellow Am. Coll. Healthcare Execs.; mem. Hosp. Fin. Mgmt. Assn. (advanced mem.), Echo Lake Country Club (Westfield, N.J.), Baltusrol Country Club (Springfield, N.J.). Roman Catholic. Avocations: golf, college basketball. Office: BSCPC 308 Willow Ave Hoboken NJ 07030 Home: 340 1/2 Garden St Hoboken NJ 07030

SNIPES, WESLEY, actor, film producer; b. Orlando, Fla., July 31, 1962; m. April Snipes, 1984 (div. 1990); 1 child, Jelani Asar; 1 child, Isnet. Grad., SUNY, Purchase, 1980, D (hon.) in Humanities and Fine Arts. Appeared in Broadway plays Boys of Winter, Execution of Justice, Death and King's Horsemen; (films) Streets of Gold, 1986, Vietnam War Story (ACE award for best actor 1989), Mo'Better Blues, 1989, Major League, 1989, King of New York, 1990, New Jack City, 1991 (NAACP Image award for outstanding actor), Jungle Fever, 1991, The Waterdance, 1992, White Men Can't Jump, 1992, Passenger 57, 1992, Rising Sun, 1993, Demolition Man, 1993, Boiling Point, 1993, Sugar Hill, 1994, Drop Zone, 1994, To Wong Foo, Thanks for Everything, Julie Newmar, 1995, The Money Train, 1995, The Fan, 1996, Murder at 1600, 1997, U.S. Marshals, 1998, One Night Stand, 1998 (Venice Film Festival Volpi Cup award for best actor), Play it to the Bone, 1999, Liberty Stands, 2002, Zigzag, 2002; actor, prodr., martial arts choreographer Blade, 1998; actor, prodr. Blade II, 2002, Blade: Trinity, 2004; actor, exec. prodr. Art of War, 2000, Undisputed, 2002; prodr. The Big Hit, 1998, Down in the Delta, 1998, Dr. Ben, 2001; (TV) H.E.L.P., 1990, The Real Malcolm X, 1992, America's Dream, 1996 (NAACP Image award for best actor in a TV movie/series); actor, prodr. (TV) Future Sport, 1998; actor, exec. prodr.

Disappearing Acts, 2000; TV guest appearances include The Bernie Mac Show, 2001. Address: 301 N Canon Dr Ste 228 Beverly Hills CA 90210 also: Nadashinghа Fan Club PO Box 490 New York NY 10014*

SNITKOFF, GAIL GOODMAN, immunologist, educator; d. Alvin and Muriel Goodman; m. Louis Steven Snitkoff, June 12, 1976; children: Joshua, Benjamin. PhD, N.Y. State Downstate Med. Ctr., Bklyn., 1974—79. Instr. Union Coll., Schenectady, NY, 1984—86; rsch. asst. prof. Albany Med. Ctr., NY, 1986—91; asst. prof. Albany Coll. Pharmacy, NY, 1991—96, assoc. prof., 1996—. Contbr. articles to profl. jours. Mem. Planned Parenthood, 1980—2004; pres. Schenectady Hadassah, NY, 2003—; mem. NARAL, 1990—2004; mem., bd. trustees Congregation Gates of Heaven, Schenectady, NY, 1986—92; pres. Schenectady Area Midrasha, NY, 1995—. Fellow, NSF, 1979—80, NIH, 1980—82; grantee, 1987—90. Mem.: AAAS (assoc.), N.Y. Acad. Sci. (assoc.), Sigma Xi (assoc.), Am. Assn. Microbiology (assoc.), N.Y.C. Ballet Guild (assoc.), Glass Art Soc. (assoc.), Saratoga Performing Arts Ctr. (life). Jewish. Achievements include patents for Immunogenic Composites Capable of Selectively Inducing Antibody Production, Pharmaceutical Compositions Employing the Same Method of Selectively Inducing Antibody Production. Avocations: performing arts, contemporary crafts, knitting, reading, travel. Home: 2154 Lynnwood Dr Niskayuna NY 12309 Office: Albany Coll Pharmacy 106 New Scotland Ave Albany NY 12208 Office Phone: 518-445-7227. E-mail: snitkofg@acp.edu.

SNITZER, ELIAS, physicist; b. Lynn, Mass., Feb. 27, 1925; s. Isaac and Jenny (Sussman) Snitzer; m. Shirley Ann Wood, Nov. 22, 1950; children: Sandra, Barbara, Peter, Helen, Louis. BSEE, Tufts U., 1946; MS in Physics, U. Chgo., 1950, PhD, 1953. Rsch. physicist Honeywell Corp., Phila., 1954-56; assoc. prof. Lowell Technol. Inst., Mass., 1956-58; dir. rsch. Am. Optical Co., Southbridge, Mass., 1959-76; mgr. applied physics United Technologies Rsch., East Hartford, Conn., 1977-84; mgr. fiber optics Polaroid, Cambridge, Mass., 1984-88; prof. Rutgers U., 1989-97, prof. emeritus, 1997—. Contbr. articles to profl. jours. With USN, 1943—46. Fellow: Am. Phys. Soc., Ceramic Soc., Optical Soc. Am. (John Tyndall award 1994); mem.: IEEE (George Morey award 1971, Quantum Electronics award 1979, Charles Townes award 1991, Otto Schott award 1999, Opto-Electronic Rank prize 2000, LEOS Millenium award 2001), NAE. Democrat. Jewish. Achievements include invention of glass laser; fiber laser amplifier. Home and Office: 78 Ivy Rd Wellesley MA 02481 Office Phone: 781-431-2605. Personal E-mail: esnitzer@optonline.net.

SNIVELY, STEPHEN WAYNE, lawyer; b. Danville, Ill., Apr. 27, 1949; s. Roberts Eyster and Margaret Louise Snively; m. Heather Lea Patten, Mar. 19, 1988; children: Toby, Ben, Madeline, Taylor. BA, U. Ill., 1971, JD, 1975. Bar: Ill. 1975, Fla. 1980. Assoc. Kavanagh, Scully, Sudow, White & Frederick, Peoria, Ill., 1975-80, Maguire, Voorhis & Wells, P.A., Orlando, Fla., 1980—; merged with Holland & Knight LLP, Orlando, 1998—. Seminar speaker, 1987. Contbr. articles to profl. jours. Bd. dirs. Found. for Orange County Pub. Schs., Orlando, 1987-96, officer, 1987-96, pres., 1993-94, chmn., 1994-96; bd. dirs. Found. for Hospice of Ctrl. Fla., Inc., 1995-96; treas., bd. dirs. HCF Found., Inc., 1996—, pres., 1998—. Mem. ABA (retail leasing com.), Fla. Bar (liaison to land surveyor com. 1982—), Orange County Bar Assn., Internat. Coun. Shopping Ctrs., Fla. C. of C. (Leadership Fla. 1991-92), Fla. Zool. Soc. (sec., bd. dirs. 1991-96), Tiger Bay Club, Phi Beta Kappa. Republican. Presbyterian. Avocations: running, writing, computers, photography. Office: Holland & Knight LLP 200 S Orange Ave Ste 2600 Orlando FL 32801-3453 E-mail: ssnively@hklaw.com.

SNODDY, CHRIS RAYMOND, athletic trainer; b. Nashville, Nov. 19, 1959; s. Raymond Thomas and Farris (Duke) S. BS, David Lipscomb Coll., 1981; MA, Appalachian State U., 1987. Lic. athletic trainer. Real estate salesperson McKinney & Co., Nashville, 1980-89; head athletic trainer David Lipscomb U., Nashville, 1981-91; sr. athletic trainer Ctr. Sports Medicine, Bapt. Hosp., Nashville, 1993—; coord. sports medicine Bapt. Hosp., Nashville, 1997—99, mgr., 1999—2001, dir., 2001—03; head athletic trainer Skyline Med. Ctr., 2003—. Dir. sports medicine Pinnacle Rehab., Nashville, 1991-92; cons. sports medicine David Lipscomb H.S., Nashville, 1982-91; adj. faculty Free Will Bapt. Bible Coll., Nashville; cons. Lipscomb U. Sports Medicine. Editor: Where to Go Camping Guide, 1980; contbr. articles to Flying Eagle mag. Recipient Mayor's medallion City of Nashville, 1986, Silver Beaver award Boy Scouts Am., 1995, named Eagle Scout, 1976, Clin. Athletic Trainer of Yr., 1992, 2003. Mem. Nat. Athletic Trainers Assn., Tenn. Athletic Trainers Soc. Mem. Ch. of Christ. Lodges: Civitan (bd. dirs. Nashville 1986-87, pres. 1990), Wa-Hi-Nasa (lodge advisor 1995—), Order of Arrow (assoc. advisor Tenn. and Ky. chpts. 1984-87, Founder's award 1976). Avocation: skiing. Home: 315 Bowwood Dr Nashville TN 37217-2301

SNODDY, JAMES ERNEST, education educator; b. Perrysville, Ind., Oct. 6, 1932; s. James Elmer and Edna May (Hayworth) S.; m. Alice Joanne Crowder, Aug. 15, 1954; children: Ryan Anthony, Elise Suzanne. BS, Ind. State U., 1954; MEd, U. Ill., 1961, EdD, 1967. Tchr. Danville (Ill.) Pub. Schs., 1954-57, prin., 1961-64; instr. U. Ill., Champaign, 1965-67; prof. edn. Mich. State U., East Lansing, 1967-72, 78-96, chmn. dept. elem. and spl. edn., 1972-78, ret., 1996, prof. emeritus, 1997—; dir. Program CORK, 1978-82. With U.S. Army, 1955-57. Mem. Am. Assn. for Adult and Continuing Edn., Commn. of Profs. of Adult and Continuing Edn. Methodist. Home: 1926 Creek Lndg Haslett MI 48840-8704 Office: Mich State U 419 Erickson Hall East Lansing MI 48824-1034 E-mail: jsnoddy@pilot.msu.edu.

SNODGRASS, JONATHAN WAYNE, music educator, pastor; b. Huntsville, Ala., June 7, 1967; s. Horace Nathaniel and Margie Alice Snodgrass; m. Lisa Salange Sullivan, Dec. 19, 1998; 1 child, Kennady Alese. BS, Ala. A & M U., 1991. Music educator Decatur City Schs., Ala., 1992—95, Huntsville City Schs., 1997—. Mentor Fellowship of Christian Leaders, Decatur, Ala., 1992—95. Youth pastoral ministry First Seventh Day Adventist Ch., Huntsville, 2001. Recipient Mid. Sch. Tchr. of the Yr., Huntsville Bd. of PTAs, 2000. Mem.: Music Educators Nat. Conf. (assoc.). Home: 156 Winter Ridge Dr Madison AL 35757 Office: Acad Sci& Foreign Lang 3221 Mastin Lake Road Huntsville AL 35810 Personal E-mail: jwgrass357@aol.com. E-mail: jsnodgrass@hsv.k12.al.us.

SNODGRASS, LOUISE VIRGINIA, state legislator, dental assistant; b. Balt., June 28, 1942; d. Peter Francis and Mary Frances (Gelwicks) Kramer; m. Franklin P. Snodgrass III, Sept. 9, 1962; children: Anne, Mark. Cert. dental asst., U. Md., Balt. Lic. dental asst. Dental asst., 1966—; mem. Md. Ho. of Dels. from Dist. 3, 1995—. Mem. Commerce and Govt. Matters Subcom. Md. Ho. of Dels., mem. Subcom. on Procurement, Unfunded Mandates Task Force. Elected liaison Md. State Bd. Dental Examiners; mem. Frederick County (Md.) Ctrl. Com., 1986-94, past vice chair, past sec., 1986-90; bd. dirs. Md. Mayors Assn., 1991-94, hon. mem., 1994; past pres. Frederick County Coun. Govt., 1991, 92, 93; liaison to transp. svcs. adv. com. Md. Mcpl. League, 1990-94, chmn. state conv., 1991, legis. mem., 1991-94, appointed to subcom. on annexation, 1992, legis. chmn., 1993-94, past pres., v.p., sec.-treas. Frederick chpt.; Mayor Middletown, Md., 1986-94; active J. Elmer Harp Med. Ctr., Inc. Assn., Frederick Meml. Hosp. Aux., Frederick County Rep. Men's Club; life mem. Middletown Hist. Soc. Named Outstanding Legislator of Yr., Md. Mcpl. League, 1995, cert. appreciation, 1996. Mem. Md. Dental Assts. Assn. (past pres.), Am. Dental Assts. Assn. (trustee). Office: Md Ho of Dels House Office Bldg Rm 324 Annapolis MD 21401

SNODGRASS, LYNN, small business owner, former state legislator; married; children: Jenne, Megan. BS in Elem. Edn., Oreg. State U., 1973; degree, Portland State U., 1975. Owner Drake's 7 Dees Nursery & Landscape Co., Oreg.; mem. Oreg. Ho. of Reps., 1995—2000; dep. majority leader, 1995-97; majority leader, 1997—2000; speaker of the house Oregon House of Reps, Salem, 1998—2000. Mem. Damascus (Oreg.) Sch. Dist. Budget Com., 1985-88, Damascus Sch. Bd., 1991-94; mem. Oreg. Ho. of Reps. Human Resources and Edn. Com. (Edn. sub-com.), 1995-97, Labor Com., 1995-97, Commerce Com. (Bus. sub-com.), 1995-97, Children and Families Com., 1995-97, Emergency Bd. Com. (Edn. sub-com.), 1995-97, Interim Edn. Com., 1995-97, Legis. Administrn. Com., 1995—, Rules and Election Com., 1997—. Mem., past pres. Mt. Hood Med. Ctr. Found.; bd. dirs. Specialized Housing, Inc., Metro Home Builder; mem. Good Shepherd Cmty. Ch.; tchr. Jr. Achievement; classroom vol. Avocations: racquetball, reading, singing, camping, cooking. Fax: 503-986-1347.

SNOEYINK, VERNON L. civil engineer, educator; BS in Civil Engring., U. Mich., 1964, MS in Sanitary Engring., 1966, PhD in Water Resource Engring., 1968. Asst. prof. sanitary engring. U. Ill., Urbana, 1969-73, from assoc. prof. to prof. environ. engring., 1973—, Ivan Racheff Prof. Environ. Engring. Dir. Water Campus NSF Sci. and Tech. Ctr. Mem. NAE. Office: U Ill Dept Civil Engring Newmark Civil Engring Lab 205 N Mathews Ave Urbana IL 61801

SNOOK, PAUL, real estate company executive; b. Swindon, Wilt, Eng., Dec. 31, 1949; arrived in U.S., 1979; s. Eric Arthur and Eira Glynis Snook; m. June Chambers, Apr. 17, 1971 (div. Sept. 1977); m. Elizabeth Keefe, June 25, 1979 (div. Jan. 2003); children: Sarah, Erica. Student, Northamton (Eng.) Coll. Exec. property mgr. Zaremba Mgmt. Svcs. Inc., Cleve., 1979-85, dir. mktg. ops., 1985-88; sr. v.p. Riverview Mgmt. Co., Akron, Ohio, 1988-96; pres. Strategic Property Mgmt., Cleve., 1999—, Paul Snook & Assocs., Cleve. Contbr.: Professional Apartment Rental Techniques, 1999. Recipient Cmty. Improvement award City of Mayfield Heights, 1986. Mem. No. Ohio Apt. Assn. (trustee 1985—, Mgr. of Yr. 1994, Pres. award 1987, 88, 89, 90), Inst. of Real Estate Mgmt. (Pres. award 1987, 88, 89, 90, cert. property mgr.), Cleve. Area Bd. of Realtors. Avocation: sailing.

SNOOK, QUINTON, construction company executive; b. Atlanta, July 15, 1925; s. John Wilson and Charlotte Louise (Clayson) S.; m. Louis Mullen, Jan. 19, 1947; children: Louis Ann Snook Matteson, Quinton A., Edward M., Clayson S., Charlotte T. Student, U. Idaho, 1949-51. Rancher, Lemhi Valley, Idaho, 1942—; owner, mgr. Snook Constrn., Salmon, Idaho, 1952—; owner Snook Trucking, Salmon, Idaho, 1967—, Lemhi Posts and Poles, Salmon, Idaho, 1980—. Construction company executive; b. Atlanta, July 15, 1925; s. John Wilson and Charlotte Louise (Clayson) S.; student U. Idaho, 1949-51; m. Lois Mullen, Jan. 19, 1947; children: Lois Ann Snook Matteson, Quinton A., Edward M., Clayson S., Charlotte T. Rancher, Lemhi Valley, Idaho, 1942—; owner, mgr. Snook Constrn., Salmon, Idaho, 1952—, owner Snook Trucking, 1967—, Lemhi Posts and Poles, 1980—. Mem. Lemhi County Commn., Dist. 2, 1980-93. Named to Idaho Agrl. Hall of Fame, 1996. Mem. Am. Quarter Horse Assn., Farm Bur., Nat. Rifleman's Assn., Idaho Assn. Commrs. and Clerks (sec. 1986, v.p. 1987, pres. 1988), Am. Hereford Assn., Idaho Cattlemen's Assn., Elks. Republican. Episcopalian. Active Lemhi County Commn., Dist. 2, 1980-93. Named to Idaho Agrl. Hall of Fame, 1996. Mem. Am. Quarter Horse Assn., Farm Bur., Nat. Riflemans Assn., Idaho Assn. Commrs. and Clerks (sec. 1986, v.p 1987, pres. 1988), Am. Hereford Assn., Idaho Cattlemens Assn., Elks. Republican. Episcopalian. Home: 9 Quinton Ln Salmon ID 83467

SNOOK, STOVER HOFFMAN, social sciences educator, researcher; b. Ventnor, NJ, July 28, 1932; s. Stover Garfield and Leah Jane (Hoffman) Snook; m. Marie Melanie Rohrer, June 26, 1954; children: John Stover, Suzanne Marie, Linda Jeanne. BA, Hartwick Coll., 1954; MA, Fordham U., 1960; PhD, Tufts U., 1969. Lic. psychologist Mass., 1973, bd. cert. profl. ergonomist 1993. Staff psychologist Dunlap & Assoc., Stamford, Conn., 1956—62; asst. v.p. Liberty Mut. Ins. Co., Hopkinton, Mass., 1962—97; lectr. Harvard Sch. Pub. Health, Boston, 1974—. Com. on human factors Nat. Rsch. Coun., Wash., DC, 1984—87; adv. panel on rsch. Am. Phys. Therapy Assn., Alexandria, Va., 1996—99; cumulative trauma com. Am. Nat. Standards Inst., Chgo., 1990—97. Contbr. articles to profl. jours., chapters to books. Recipient Festschrift, Ergonomics, 1999, Kraft Innovation award, Human Factors and Ergonomics Soc., 1997, Extension award, McKenzie Inst. Internat., 2001. Fellow: Am. Psychological Soc. (fellow), Ergonomics Soc. (fellow, Ann. Lectr. 1978), Human Factors and Ergonomics Soc. (fellow, Tech. Group award 1992). Democrat. Unitarian. Achievements include development of psychophysical guidelines for manual handling tasks; guidelines for reducing low back pain and disability; incidence and cost data for industrial low back disorders. Avocations: travel, astronomy, history, music. Home: 10472 S E Amberjack Ct Hobe Sound FL 33455

SNORTLAND, HOWARD JEROME, education financial consultant; b. Sharon, N.D., June 22, 1912; s. Thomas and Aline (Vig) S.; m. Anna Adeline Anderson, Sept. 1, 1940; children— Jan Signe, Kristi Jo, Howard Jay. BA, U. N.D., 1937, MS, 1958. Cashier N.D. Workmen's Compensation Bur., 1937-42, N.D. State Treas.'s Office, 1945-48; with N.D. Dept. Pub. Instrn., Bismarck, 1948-81, supt. pub. instrn., 1977-81; edn. fin. cons., 1981—. Pres. State Econ. Coun., 1978; nat. pres. Com. Ednl. Data Systems, 1965-67 Chmn. Burleigh ARC, 1963-67, bd. dirs., 1946—, vice chmn., 1964—; bd. dirs. Burleigh County Tb Assn., 1950—; stated clk. United Presbyterian Ch., 1942—; pres. N.D. United Christian Campus Fellowship, 1964-67, N.D. Westminster Found., 1963-70; mem. N.D. Synod Coun., 1970—; chmn. United Way Fund, 1983. Served with USAAF, 1942-45. Recipient Summit Conf. award for outstanding pub. svc., 1976. Mem. NEA, N.D. Edn. Assn., N.D. Sch. Bus. Ofcls., N.D. Assn. Adminstrs., Nat. Assn. Adminstrs., N.D. Assn. Ret. Employees (pres. 1987—), Am. Assn. Ret. Persons (vice chmn. N.D. legis. com. 1992-94, chmn. 1994—), Kiwanis, Phi Beta Kappa, Phi Delta Kappa (dir. emeritus).

SNOUFFER, NANCY KENDALL, English and reading educator; b. Long Branch, N.J., Aug. 22, 1941; d. Percival Wallace and Ruby Mae (Braswell) Kendall; m. Eugene Joseph Snouffer, Aug. 27, 1966; 1 child, Kendall Ann. BA in English, Gettysburg (Pa.) Coll., 1962; MA in English and Journalism, U. N.C., 1964; MS in Edn. and Reading, Western Ill. U., 1974; postgrad., U. Mo., 1976-78. Instr. English U. N.C., Wilmington, 1963-65, Shaw U., Raleigh, N.C., 1965-66; from instr. to asst. prof. English Wright Coll. and Chgo. City Colls., 1967-74; from instr. to asst. prof. reading Western Ill. U., Macomb, 1974-81; prof. comm., lang. and reading Del Mar Coll., Corpus Christi, Tex., 1982—, reading coord., 2001—. Mem. adv. bd. Tex. A&M U., Corpus Christi, 1993—; cons. in field. Author: College Reading Power, 5th edit., 1976-82; assoc. editor jour. Epistle, 1980-83, mem. editoral bd., 1983-85; contbr. articles to profl. jours. Master Tchr. Del Mar, 1986. Grantee Western Ill. U., 1974-81, Del Mar Coll., 1982—, NISSOD Tchg. Excellence award, 1993, Coll. Acad. Support Program Tex. State level Lifetime Achievement award. Mem. Tex. Assn. Developmental Educators, Tex. Coll. Reading Learning Assn. (chair So. membership 1994—, state sec. 1995-97, pres.-elect 1997-98, pres. 1998-99, past pres. 1999-2000, Lifetime Achievement award 2002), Nat. Assn. Devel. Educators (co-chair nat. com., profl. liaison), Internat. Reading Assn., Corpus Christi Literacy Coun. (bd. dirs. 1986—, sec. 1988-93, vice-chair 1991-92, v.p.-elect 2000-01, chair 2001—), Harbor Playhouse (bd. dirs. 1988, 91-93, chair 2001-03), Alliance Francaise. Republican. Episcopalian. Avocations: tennis, travel, reading. Home: 4206 Acushnet Dr Corpus Christi TX 78413-2004 Office: Del Mar Coll 101 Baldwin Blvd Corpus Christi TX 78404-3805

SNOW, CHARLES, lawyer; b. Bklyn., May 3, 1932; s. Irving S. and Bessie S.; m. Deanna Friedman, Jan. 15, 1961; children: Lisa C., Amy M. BA, U. Vt., 1954; LLB, Bklyn. Law Sch., 1959. Bar: N.Y. 1959, U.S. Dist. Ct. (ea. and so. dists.) N.Y. 1961, U.S. Ct. Appeals (2d cir.) 1961, U.S. Supreme Ct. 1965. Dep. asst. atty. gen. N.Y. Dept. Law, N.Y.C., 1959—60; asst. U.S. atty. U.S. Dist. Ct. (ea. dist.) N.Y., Bklyn., 1960—61; asst. regional adminstr. SEC, N.Y.C., 1961—68; ptnr. Wofsey Certilman Haft Snow & Becker, PC, N.Y.C., 1968—77, Snow Becker Krauss, P.C., N.Y.C., 1977—. Gen. counsel Securities Traders' Assn. N.Y. Chmn. Harrison (N.Y.) Planning Bd., 1977-88; mem. New Castle Planning Bd., 1991-97. Mem. N.Y. State Bar Assn. (mem. bus. sect., com. on securities regulation), Securities Traders Assn. N.Y. (hon.). Republican. Jewish. Office: 605 3rd Ave New York NY 10158-0180 Office Phone: 212-455-0300. E-mail: csnow@sbklaw.com.

SNOW, CUBBEDGE, JR., lawyer; b. Macon, Ga., May 20, 1929; AB, Emory U., 1951; JD magna cum laude, Mercer U., 1952. Bar: Ga. 1952. Ptnr. Martin, Snow, LLP, Macon. Col. JAGC, USAFR, 1952-89. Fellow Am. Coll. Trial Lawyers, Am. Bar Found. (state chmn. 1988-92), Fedn. Ins. and Corp. Counsel, Ga. Def. Lawyers Assn., Am. Prepaid Legal Svcs. Inst. (bd. dirs. 1983-89); mem. ABA (ho. of dels. 1984—, chmn. prepaid legal svcs. com. 1986-88, bd. govs. 1993-96), Macon Bar Assn. (pres. 1967), State Bar Ga. (pres. 1974-75), Am. Judicature Soc. (bd. dirs. 1978-82, Herbert Harley award 1986), Phi Beta Kappa, Phi Alpha Delta, Omicron Delta Kappa. Office: Martin Snow LLP 240 3rd St PO Box 1606 Macon GA 31202-1606

SNOW, EDWIN FAWCETT, management consultant; s. Edwin James and Suzanne Fawcett Snow; m. Mary Anna Siemion, June 28, 1986; m. Cynthia Suzanne Ramsey, June 24, 1961 (div. Dec. 5, 1983); children: John Edwin, Cynthia Currie Nickell. BS in Mech. Engring., U. of Ill., 1959; MBA and MS in Indsl. Engring., Carnegie Mellon U., 1964. EIT Ill., registered profl. engr., Ky. Detail and sr. draftsman Internat. Harvester, East Moline, Ill., 1955—56; lab. technician Am. Air Filter, Moline, Ill., 1957; layout draftsman Internat. Harvester, East Moline, 1958; staff asst., sales engr. Westinghouse Electric Corp., Pitts., 1959—64; sr. assoc. rsch. dir. Batton Barton Durstine & Osborne, N.Y.C., 1964—68; asst. to the pres., mgr. Andre Debrie divsn. Applied Devices Corp., N.Y.C., 1968—71; mgr. mktg. and govt. projects USC Inc., Pitts., 1971—72; mgr. mktg. comm. rsch. GE, Louisville, 1972—78; dir. mktg. rsch. Glenmore Distilleries Co., Louisville, 1978—83; mgmt. cons., exec. supr. George S. May Internat. Co., Park Ridge, Ill., 1984; dir., survey rsch. and analysis Urban Studies Ctr., U. of Louisville, 1984—85; mktg. and sales dir. Nemeth Engring., Crestwood, Ky., 1988—2002; owner, mktg. and mgmt. cons. EF Snow and Assocs., Crestwood, 1985—. Mktg. dir. EVA, Goshen, Ky., 2000—; adj. prof. mktg. decision making Ind. U. S.E., New Albany, 1983—84; adj. prof. mktg. mgmt. Carnegie Mellon U. Grad. Sch. Indsl. Adminstrn., Pitts., 1967. Co-author: (cost benefit model) Brookings Institute Press, (chpt.) Applications of Management Science in Marketing, Models of Buyer Behavior. Scoutmaster Boy Scouts of Am., Louisville, 1977—79. 1st lt. U. S. Army Corps of Engrs., 1959—62. Recipient Harvard Book award, Moline H.S., 1959, Herman Nelson Meml. scholarship, U. of Ill., Coll. of Engring., 1957. Master: Masons (Compass #223); mem.: ASME, Inst. for Ops. Rsch. and Mgmt. Sci., U. of Ill. Alumni Assn., Plantation Swim Club (pres., chmn. bd. 1976—78), Tau Beta Phi, Pi Tau Sigma, Phi Eta Sigma, Delta Phi (pres. Tau chpt. 1956—58). Republican. Episcopalian. Achievements include development of Measuring effectiveness of advertising - applications of the DEMON model; NEWS - New Product Early Warning System; Mixed Goal Programming for Non-linear Budgetary Decisions; patents for Leak Detection System for a Nuclear Reactor; Sampling Slide Valve (nuclear reactor; Remote Controlled Highwall Mining System (coal); Remote Controlled Mining System (coal). Avocations: sailing, tennis, gardening, computers, photography. Home: 2213 W Highway 22 Crestwood KY 40014 Personal E-mail: nedsnow@bellsouth.net.

SNOW, GEORGE BARTLETT, city official, accountant; b. Feb. 23, 1943; s. Frank Batchelder and Corinne Althea (Fuller) Snow; m. Tuula Anita Kahila, Feb. 6, 1965; children: Frank Edwin II, James Hooper. BS in Acctg., Babson Coll., 1964. Acct. Morgan & Morgan, Boston, 1965—70; town acct. Town of Marblehead, Mass., 1970—, data processing coord., 1986—, fin. dir., 1994—. Treas., bd. dirs. Employees Fed. Credit Union, Marblehead, 1979—; mem. com. to rewrite Uniform Mcpl. Acctg. Sys. Manual, 1983—94; acctg. tchr. Mass. Mcpl. Auditors and Accts. Assn., Amherst, 1981—. Clk. Town of Marblehead Bd. Selectmen, 1970—75; mem. Marblehead Retirement Bd., 1970—; trustee Abbot Fund, Town of Marblehead, 1970—90; mem., clk. sch. bldg. com. Town of Marblehead, 1971—72; mem. Marblehead Harbor Study Com., 1997—98. Mem.: Sugarloaf Condo. Pres.' Assn. (pres. 1995—2001), Sugarloaf Phase VII Condo. Assn. (pres. 1988—), Govtl. Fin. Officers Assn., Mass. Govtl. Fin. Officers Assn. (v.p. 1986—87, pres. 1987—88), Mass. Mcpl. Auditors and Accts. Assn. (pres. 1981—82, chmn. legis. com. 1983—88), North Shore Auditors and Accts. Assn. (pres. 1981—82), Onamor Hills Neighborhood Assn. (treas. 1988—94), Pleon Yacht Club (dir. 1979—82), Boston Yacht Club (treas. 1974—78). Home: 242 W Shore Dr Marblehead MA 01945-1324 Office: Town of Marblehead Mary A Alley Bldg 7 Widger Rd Marblehead MA 01945 E-mail: snowb@town.marblehead.ma.us.

SNOW, JAMES BYRON, JR., otolaryngologist, research administrator, educator; b. Oklahoma City, Mar. 12, 1932; s. James B. and Charlotte Louise (Andersen) S.; m. Sallie Lee Ricker, July 16, 1954; children: James B., John Andrew, Sallie Lee Louise. BS, U. Okla., 1953; MD cum laude, Harvard U., 1956; MA (hon.), U. Pa., 1973. Diplomate Am. Bd. Otolaryngology (dir. 1972-90). Intern Johns Hopkins Hosp., Balt., 1956-57; resident Mass. Eye and Ear Infirmary, Boston, 1957-60; prof., head dept. otorhinolaryngology Sch. Medicine U. Okla., Oklahoma City, 1962-72; prof., chmn. dept. otorhinolaryngology and human communication U. Pa., 1972-90; dir. Nat. Inst. on Deafness and Other Comm. Disorders, NIH, Bethesda, Md., 1990-97. Mem. nat. adv. coun. neurol. and communicative disorders and stroke NIH, 1972-76, 82-86; chmn. Nat. Com. Rsch. Neurol. and Communicative Disorders, 1979-80. Editor: Am. Jour. Otolaryngology, 1979-83; Contbr. articles to sci. and profl. jours. Officer, M.C., U.S. Army, 1960-62. Recipient Regents award for superior tchg. U. Okla., 1970, Golden award Internat. Fedn. Otorhinolaryngological Socs., 1989, Disting. Achievement award Deafness Rsch. Found., 1993, Presdl. Meritorious Exec. Rank award, 1994; named to Soc. Scholars Johns Hopkins U., 1991. Fellow Japan Broncho-Esophagological Soc. (hon.), Am. Laryngological Assn. (hon.); mem. ACS (regent 1982-90), AMA (coun. on sci. affairs 1975-86), Soc. Univ. Otolaryngologists (pres. 1975), Am. Acad. Otolaryngology-Head and Neck Surgery, Assn. Acad. Depts. Otolaryngology (pres. 1981-82), Am. Laryngol., Rhinol. and Otol. Soc., Am. Otol. Soc. (merit award 2003), Am. Laryngol. Assn. (editor 1983-89, pres. 1990-91), Am. Broncho-Esophagol. Assn. (editor trans. 1973-77, pres. 1979), Collegium Otorhinolaryngologicum (pres. 2000-02), Phi Beta Kappa, Alpha Omega Alpha. Home: 33506 Tuckahoe River Rd Easton MD 21601-6752 E-mail: jsnow@crosslink.net.

SNOW, JOEL ALAN, research director; b. Brockton, Mass., Apr. 1, 1937; s. George H. Jr. and Mary W. (Sproul) S.; m. Laetitia Harrer, June 29, 1957 (div. 1983); children: Jonathan E., Nicholas H.; m. Barbara Kashian, Feb. 7, 1992; stepchildren: James, Alexander. BS in Physics, U. N.C., 1958; MA in Physics, Washington U., St. Louis, 1963, PhD in Physics, 1967. Fellow Ctr. Advanced Study U. Ill., Champaign, 1967-68; program dir. for theoretical physics NSF, Washington, 1968-70, head office of interdisciplinary rsch., 1969-71, dep. asst. dir. for sci. and tech., rsch. applications, 1971-74, dir. office of planning and resources mgmt., 1974-76, dir. div. of policy rsch. and analysis, 1976; sr. policy analyst, office of sci. and tech. policy Exec. Office of the Pres., Washington, 1976-77; assoc. dir. for rsch. policy U.S. Dept. Energy, Washington, 1977-81, dir. sci. and tech. affairs, 1981-88; assoc. v.p. for rsch. Argonne Nat. Lab., U. Chgo., 1988-92; dir. Inst. for Phys. Rsch. and Tech. Iowa State U., Ames, 1993-98, prof. elec. and computer engring., 1993—, prof. polit. sci., 1998-2000, exec. assoc. dir. Internat. Inst. Theoret./Applied Physics, 1998—. Rsch. assoc. dept. physics U. Ill., Urbana, 1967-68; instr. physics and electronics U.S. Navy Nulcear Power Sch., New London, Conn., 1958-61; sci. tech. organizer Pres.'s Coun. on Superconductivity, 1987, NSF program rsch. applied to nat. needs, 1971, designer, mgr., founder NSF program interdisciplinary rsch. relevant to problems of society, 1969. Contbr. over 130 articles to mags. and profl. jours. Lt. (j.g.) USN, 1958-61. Recipient Meritorious Svc. award NSF, 1972, Meritorious award William A. Jump Found., 1973, Arthur S. Fleming award Downtown Jaycees, 1974; NSF postdoctoral fellow Ctr. for Advanced Study U. Ill., 1967-68; NSF fellow, 1963-65. Fellow AAAS, Am. Phys. Soc.; mem. IEEE, Am. Chem. Soc., Am. Nuc. Soc., World Future Soc., Sigma Xi, Phi Beta Kappa, Phi Kappa Phi. Achievements include pioneering devel. of federal programs in environment, solar and geothermal energy and energy conservation, sustainable development; fed. programs in technology transfer to industry; developed collaborations between univ., govt. and industry; fostering internat. collaboration in sci., engring. and edn. E-mail: jasnow@iastate.edu.

SNOW, JOHN WILLIAM, secretary of treasury; b. Toledo, Aug. 2, 1939; s. William Dean and Catharine (Howard) S.; m. Fredrica Wheeler, June 11, 1964 (div. 1973); children: Bradley, Ian; m. Carolyn Kalk, Aug. 31, 1973; 1 child, Christopher BA, Kenyon Coll./U. Toledo, 1962; PhD, U. Va., 1965; LLB, George Washington U., 1967. Asst. prof. econs. U. Md., College Park,

1965-67; assoc. Wheeler & Wheeler, Washington, 1967-72; asst. gen. counsel Dept. Transp., Washington, 1972-73, dep. asst. sec. for policy, plans and internat. affairs, 1973-74, asst. sec. for govtl. affairs, 1974-75, dep. under sec., 1975-76; adminstr. Nat. Hwy. Traffic Safety Adminstrn., Washington, 1976-77; v.p. govt. affairs Chessie System Inc., Washington, 1977-80; sr. v.p. corp. services CSX Corp., Richmond, Va., 1980-84, exec. v.p., 1984-85; pres., CEO Chessie System R.R.s, Balt., 1985-86, CSX Rail Transport, Jacksonville, Fla., 1986-87, CSX Transp., Jacksonville, Va., 1987-88; pres., COO CSX Corp., Richmond, Va., 1988-89, pres., CEO, 1989-91, chmn., pres., CEO, 1991—2003, also bd. dirs.; sec. U.S. Dept. Treasury, Washington, 2003—. Adj. prof. law George Washington U., 1972-75; vis. prof. econs. U. Va., Charlottesville, spring 1977; vis. fellow Am. Enterprises Inst., Washington, spring 1977. Mem. Va. State Bar. Clubs: Chevy Chase, Metropolitan (Washington); Country of Va. (Richmond). Episcopalian. Office: US Dept Treasury Office Sec 1500 Pennsylvania Ave Washington DC 20220*

SNOW, KARL NELSON, JR., public management educator, university administrator, former state senator; b. St. George, Utah, July 1, 1930; s. Karl Nelson and Wanda (McGregor) S.; m. Donna Jean Dain, Jan. 29, 1960; children: Karl Nelson, III, Melissa, Daniel D., Jeanmarie, Elisabeth, Howard H. BS, Brigham Young U., Provo, Utah, 1956; MA, U. Minn., 1958; MPA, U. So. Calif., 1965, DPA, 1972. Budget examiner Minn. Dept. Adminstrn., 1956-59; staff asst., instr. Sch. Pub. Adminstrn. U. So. Calif., 1959-62; mem. faculty Brigham Young U., Provo, Utah, 1962-96, dir. Inst. Govt., 1969-79, prof. pub. mgmt., 1979—, asst. exec. v.p., 1987-91; state legis. fiscal analyst, 1966-70; mem. Utah Senate from 16th Dist., 1972-85, majority leader, 1981-85. Chmn. Utah State House Fellowship Commn., 1973-79, Utah Constl. Revision Commn., 1977-89; bd. dirs. Legis. Leaders Found., 1981-85; chmn. bd. trustees Utah Tech. Fin. Corp., 1983-94; pres., trustee Utah Tech. Equity Found., 1994-96; chmn. Conf. of State Sponsored Seed and Venture Funds, 1993-96; internat. affairs rep. LDS Ch., N.Y.C., 1997-2000. Bd. editors Public Adminstrn. Rev, 1969-70, State and Local Govt. Rev, 1977-83; contbr. articles to profl. jours. Missionary Mormon Ch., 1950-52, mem. stake high coun., 1975-85, 93-97, bishop, 1985-90, dir. ch. internat. affairs, N.Y.C., 1997-2000; mem. Warren Burger Prison Task Force, 1983-87; bd. dirs. Utah Innovation Found., 1984-88. Adminstrv. fellow State of Minn., U. Minn., 1956-57; Univ. fellow U. So. Calif., 1959-61. Mem. Am. Soc. Pub. Adminstrn. (chpt. pres. 1968-69), dir. nat. council (1969-72), Sons Utah Pioneers. Home: 1847 N Oak Ln Provo UT 84604-2140

SNOW, MARINA SEXTON, writer; b. Boston, Apr. 9, 1937; d. Charles Ernest Snow and Katherine Alice Townsend; m. Richard DeVere Horton, 1958 (div. 1968); children: Heather Kertchem, James Horton; m. Charles A. Washburn, 1978 (div. 1979). BA, U. Iowa, 1958; MA in Speech Pathology, N.Mex. State U., 1967; MA in Librarianship, San Jose State U., 1976; MA in Theatre Arts, Calif. State U., Sacramento, 1979. Cert. clin. competence Am. Speech and Hearing Assn. Tchr. ESL Inst. Colombo-Americano, Cali, Colombia, 1958-59; tchr. Las Cruces (N.Mex.) Pub. Schs., 1964-66; speech therapist Sutter County Schs., Yuba City, Calif., 1967-72; reference libr. Calif. State U., Sacramento, 1976-95. Author: (novels) The Walking Wounded, 2001 (Best First Novel of 2001-2002 award Bay Area Ind. Pub. Assn., 2001), Look No Further, 2004, (plays) Apricot Coffee, Alkali Flat, (short stories) The Black Iris, 1999; contbr. articles to profl. jours. Pres. Alkali Flat Neighborhood Assn., Sacramento, 1987—94. Mem.: Calif. Writer's Club, Sacramento Old City Assn. Avocations: theater, historic preservation, gardening.

SNOW, MARLON O. trucking executive, state agency administrator; m. Ann; children. Gen. mgr. spl. commodities Milne Truck Lines, Phoenix, LA, 1970-81; gen. mgr. spl. commodities, sales Motor Cargo, Salt Lake City, 1981-82; owner MST Trucking, Inc., Salt Lake City, 1982—. V.p. Utah Motor Carriers for State of Utah, 1997-98; bd. dirs. Zions Bank. Mem. State Bd. Edn., 1994-97, chair, 1995-97; trustee Utah Valley State Coll., 1998; mem. Ho. of Reps., Utah, 1999-2001; bd. regents Bd. Higher Edn. State of Utah, 2001—; bd. dirs. Children's Justice Ctr., State of Utah, 2002-, Riverside Country Club; mem. bd. I.H.C. Hosp. Utah County. Mem. Utah Valley State Coll. Found. (bd. dirs. 1991—), Alpine Sch. Dist. Found. (bd. dirs. 1990-94). Office: 1247 E 430 N Orem UT 84097-5400

SNOW, MICHAEL D. health facility administrator; BS in Acctg., U. Alabama; MBA, Troy State U. CEO Doctor's Hosp., Metairie, La.; v.p., oper. Gulf Coast Divsn., 1995—96; pres. Gulf Coast Divsn., HCA, 1996—2004; COO HealthSouth Corp., Birmingham, Ala., 2004—. Chmn. bd. trustees Tex. Hosp. Assn., 2002—03. Tex. Governor's Spl. Com. on Medicaid Reform; Am. Hosp. Assn. Reg. Policy Bd. Mem.: Am. Heart Assn. (chmn., Houston Chpt.). Office: HealthSouth One HealthSouth Pkwy Birmingham AL 35243

SNOW, REBECCA, lawyer; b. Boulder City, Nev., Dec. 7, 1960; BA summa cum laude, Brigham Young U., 1983; JD cum laude, Harvard U., 1986. Bar: Nev. 1986, D.C. 1987. Legis. aide U.S. Dept. Interior Office Legis. Counsel, Washington, 1982, 83; ptnr. Covington & Burling, Washington, 1994—. Co-author: Superfund Law and Procedure, 1992. Office: Covington & Burling PO Box 7566 1201 Pennsylvania Ave NW Washington DC 20044-7566

SNOW, ROBERT ANTHONY, journalist; b. Berea, Ky., June 1, 1955; s. James Allen and Betty Jo (Threlkeld) S.; m. Jill Ellen Walker, Sept. 26, 1987; children: Kendall Elizabeth, Robert Walker, Kristin Anna. BA, Davidson Coll., 1977; postgrad. in Philosophy and Econs., U. Chgo., 1978-79. Editl. writer The Greensboro (N.C.) Record, 1979-81, The Virginian Pilot, Norfolk, 1981-82; editl. page editor The Daily Press, Newport News, Va., 1982-84; dep. editl. page editor The Detroit News, 1984-87, columnist, 1993—; editl. page editor The Washington Times, 1987-91; dep. asst. to pres. comm., dir. speechwriting The White House, Washington, 1991-92, dep. asst. for media affairs to Pres., 1992-93; columnist USA Today, Arlington, 1993—; syndicated columnist Creators Syndicate, 1993-2001. Substitute host Rush Limbaugh Radio Program, 1994—; polit. analyst Good Morning America, 1995; host Fox News Sunday, 1996—. Active Leadership Washington. Mem. Coun. Fgn. Rels. Avocations: sports, music, travel, writing. Office: Fox News Sunday 400 N Capitol St NW Ste 550 Washington DC 20001-1502

SNOW, SUE, principal; Math. tchr. Carrollton (Ga.) Jr. High Sch.; curriculum dir. Rockdale County Pub. Schs., Conyers, Ga.; prin. Conyers Mid. Sch. Named Ga. State Math. Tchr. of Yr., 1992.

SNOW, THEODORE PECK, astrophysics educator; b. Seattle, Jan. 30, 1947; s. Theodore P. and Louise (Wertz) S.; m. Constance M. Snow, Aug. 23, 1969; children: McGregor A., Tyler M., Reilly A. BA, Yale U., 1969; MS, U. Wash., 1970, PhD, 1973. Mem. rsch. staff Princeton (N.J.) U., 1973-77; prof. U. Colo., Boulder, 1977—, dir. Ctr. for Astrophysics and Space Astronomy, 1986-96, dir. Fiske Planetarium, 2000—. Mem. instrument devel. teams for far Ultraviolet Spectroscopic Explorer, 1999—, Cosmic Origins Spectrograph to be installed in Hubble Space Telescope. Author: (textbook) The Dynamic Universe, 1983, 4th edit., 1991, Essentials of the Dynamic Universe 4th edit., 1993 (textbook excellence award Text and Academic Authors Assn. 1994), Physics, 1986, Universe: Origins and Evolution, 1997; contbr. over 200 articles to profl. jours. Fellow Royal Astron. Soc.; mem. Am. Astron. Soc., Astron. Soc. Pacific, Sigma Xi. Achievements include discovery, through observations in ultraviolet visible, and infrared wavelengths, and through laboratory measurement of chemical reactions, of several important processes involving interstellar gas and dust, and their roles in star formation and late stages of stellar evolution. Office: U Colo Ctr Astrophysics Space Astronomy Campus Box 389 Boulder CO 80309-0389 Office Phone: 303-492-7669. Business E-Mail: tsnow@casa.colorado.edu.

SNOW, TOWER CHARLES, JR., lawyer; b. Boston, Oct. 28, 1947; s. Tower Charles and Margaret (Harper) S. BA in English magna cum laude, Dartmouth Coll., 1969; JD, U. Calif., Berkeley, 1973. Bar: Calif. 1973, U.S. Dist. Ct. (no. dist.) Calif. 1973, U.S. Ct. Appeals (9th cir.) 1973, U.S. Supreme Ct. 1976, U.S. Dist. Ct. (ea. dist.) Calif. 1979, U.S. Ct. Appeals (fed. cir.) 1980, U.S. Ct. Claims 1980, U.S. Ct. Appeals (2d cir.) 1987, N.Y. 1988, U.S. Dist. Ct. (ea. and so. dists.) N.Y. 1988, U.S. Dist. Ct. (ctrl. dist.) Calif. 1989, U.S. Dist. Ct. (no. dist.) Tex. 1995, U.S. Dist. Ct. (so. dist.) Calif. 1996, U.S. Dist. Ct. Ariz. 1996. Ptnr., chmn. litigation dept. Orrick, Herrington & Sutcliffe, San Francisco, 1973-89; ptnr. Shearman & Sterling, San Francisco, 1989-94; ptnr., chmn. securities litigation group, mem. policy com. Brobeck, Phleger & Harrison, LLP, San Francisco, 1995-97; chmn., CEO Brobeck, Phleger & Harrison, San Francisco, 1998—2001; ptnr., mem. Americas Mgmt. Group, Clifford Chance LLP, 2002—. Arbitrator Nat. Assn. Securities Dealers, Am. Stock Exch., N.Y. Stock Exch., Pacific Coast Stock Exch., Superior Ct. City and County San Francisco, Am. Arbitration Assn.; lectr. in field. Author numerous law handbooks and articles to prof. jours. Mem. San Francisco Mus. Soc., San Francisco Symphony, San Francisco Ballet, San Francisco Opera, Am. Conservatory Theatre. Named Best Lawyer in the U.S. in his Field, Corp. Bd. Member Mag., 2001; named one of 100 Most Influential Lawyers in Am., Nat. Law Jour., 2000, 100 Most Influential Lawyers in Calif., Calif. Law and Bus., 2000, 2002, 100 Most Influential Lawyers in World, Lawyer Mag. (U.K.), 2002; Rufus Choate Scholar. Mem. ABA (chmn. subcom. pub. offering litig. 1984-88, co-chair task force on securities arbitration 1988-89, vice chair securities litig. com. 1986-88), Continuing Edn. Bar (bus. law inst. planning com. 1986), Securities Industry Assn., Nat. Inst. Trial Advocacy, San Francisco Bar Assn. (pres. securities litig. sect. 1995). Democrat. Avocations: travel, skiing, running, scuba diving, films. Home: 177 Ridge Dr Napa CA 94558-9777 Office Phone: 415-778-4702. Business E-Mail: tower.snow@cliffordchance.com.

SNOWBARGER, VINCE, former congressman; b. Kankakee, Ill., Sept. 16, 1949; s. Willis Edward and Wahnona Ruth (Horger) S.; m. Carolyn Ruth McMahon, Mar. 25, 1972; children: Jeffrey Edward, Matthew David. BA in History, So. Nazarene U., 1971; MA in Polit. Sci., U. Ill., 1974; JD, U. Kans., 1977. Bar: Kans. 1977, U.S. Dist. Ct. Kans. 1977, Mo. 1987. Instr. Mid-Am. Nazarene Coll., Olathe, Kans., 1973—76; ptnr. Haskin, Hinkle, Slater & Snowbarger, 1977—84, Dietrich, Davis, Dicus et al, 1984—88, Armstrong, Teasdale, Schafly & Davis, Overland Park, 1989—92, Holbrook, Heaven & Fay, P.C., Merriam, 1992—94, Snowbarger & Veatch LLP, Olathe, 1994—96; mem. 105th Congress from 3rd Kans. dist., 1997—99; exec. dir. Kans. Assn. Am. Educators, 2000—01; asst. exec. dir. for legis. affairs Pension Benefit Guaranty Corp., Washington, 2002—. Mem. Kans. Legislature, Topeka, 1985-96; majority leader Ho. of Reps., 1993-96; mem. Olathe Planning Commn., 1982-84, Leadership Olathe; divsn. chmn. United Way, Olathe, 1985-88, chmn. citizen rev. com., 1991-95. Mem. Olathe Area C. of C. (bd. dirs. 1984). Republican. Nazarene. Avocation: politics. Office: 1200 K St NW Washington DC 20005-4026 Home: 12676 Lace Falls Loop Bristow VA 20136-1295 Office Phone: 202-326-4010. E-mail: snowbarger.vince@pbge.gov.

SNOWDEN, BERNICE RIVES, former construction company executive; b. Houston, Mar. 21, 1923; d. Charles Samuel and Annie Pearl (Rorex) Rives; m. Walter G. Snowden; 1 child. Grad., Smalley Comml. Coll., 1941; student, U. Houston, 1965. With Houston Pipe Line Co., 1944-45; clk.-typist Charles G. Heyne & Co., Inc., Houston, 1951-53, payroll asst., 1953-56, sec. to pres., also office mgr., 1956-62, sec. to pres., also controller, 1962-70, sec.-treas., 1970-77, CFO, also dir. Mem. Women in Constrn., Nat. Assn. Women in Constrn. (past pres.), San Leon C. of C., Lord and Ladies Dance Club. Methodist. Home: 6611 Kury Ln Houston TX 77008-5101

SNOWDEN, DAVID L. protective services official; BA, Calif. State U., Fullerton. Chief of police, Beverly Hills, Calif. Recipient Am.'s Star award U.S. Marshal's Office, Sherman Block Law Enforcement Profl. of Yr. award Calif. Peace Officers Assn., 2003. Mem. Calif. Police Chiefs Assn. (past pres.), Orange County Chiefs and Sheriffs Assn. (past pres.), L.A. County Chiefs Assn. (past pres.). Office: 464 N Rexford Dr Beverly Hills CA 90210

SNOWDEN, LAWRENCE FONTAINE, retired aircraft company executive, retired marine corps general officer; b. Charlottesville, Va., Apr. 14, 1921; s. Lawrence Fontaine Snoddy and Beatrice M. (Huffman) S.; m. Martha Roselyn Ham, Nov. 17, 1942; children: John Stephen, Brian Fontaine. Student, Stetson U., 1938-39; BS, U. Va., 1942; MA, Northwestern U., 1950; postgrad., Harvard U., 1968; grad., Indsl. Coll. Armed Forces, 1967. Commd. 2d lt. USMC, 1942, advanced through grades to lt. gen., 1975; comdr. 7th Marine Regt., Vietnam, 1966; ops. officer III Marine Amphibious Force, Vietnam, 1967; asst. dir. personnel Hdqrs. Marine Corps, Washington, 1968-69, dir. systems support group, 1969-70; dir. Marine Corps Devel. Ctr., Quantico, Va., 1970-72; chief of staff U.S. Forces, Japan, 1972-75; U.S. chmn. UN Bd., Japan, 1973-75; chief of staff Hdqrs. U.S. Marine Corps, 1977-79; ret., 1979; v.p. Far East Internat. Service Co. Hughes Aircraft Co., 1979-86, group v.p. Internat. Ground Systems Group, 1986-88; pres. Snowden Internat. Assocs., Tallahassee, Fla., 1988—. Recipient Silver Beaver award Boy Scouts Am., Disting. Eagle Scout award; decorated Disting. Svc. medals (2), Legion of Merit (5), Army Commendation medal, Navy Commendation medal, Purple Heart (2), Cross of Gallantry (3) Vietnam, Second Order of Sacred Treasure Japan). Mem. Marine Corps League, U.S. Navy League, Am. C. of C. in Japan, Am.-Japan Soc., Marine Corps Assn., Econ. Club Fla., Sigma Nu. Clubs: Tokyo.

SNOWDEN, RUTH O'DELL GILLESPIE, artist; b. Gary, W.Va., Apr. 16, 1926; d. Haynes Thornton and Blanche Beaula (Boling) Gillespie; m. Eugene Louis Snowden, Dec. 21, 1946; children: Wanda Snowden Ballard, Eugene III, Ronald, Marian Snowden Warren, Jeffry. RN, Natharith Coll., 1946; student Sch. Art, Transylvania U., 1983-84, U. Ky., 1985-89. RN. Painter, publicity chmn. Artists's Attic Inc., Lexington, Ky., 1988-89. Exhibited in group shows at U. Ky. Art Mus., Lexington, 1988, 5th Internat. Juried Exhibition Pastels, Nyack, N.Y., 1988, Small Paintings Nat., Ky. Highlands Mus., Ashland, 1988, The Appalachian Cen., U. Ky., 1988, Ft. Wayne (Ind.) Mus. Art, 1986, John Howard Sanden Nat. Artists Seminar, Washington, Nat. Artists' Seminar, Chgo., Huntington (W.Va.) Galleries, Nat. Nursing Art Exhibit, Meth. Med. Cen., Peoria, Ill., Chautauqua Art Assn. Galleries, N.Y., 1990, Central Bank gallery, Chatauqua, 1990, Pastel & Chisel Acad. Fine Arts, 1990, Opera House Gallery, 1990, Sacramento Fine Arts Ctr., 1990, Ariel Gallery, Soho, N.Y., 1990, 91, Sumi-e Soc. Am., Inc., 1993, Watercolor Soc. Ala., 1994; represented in the Director of American Portrait Artists, Am. Portrait Soc., Huntington Harbour, Calif.; numerous local and nat. shows; in pvt. collections. Recipient Assn. Alliance award Am. Frame Co., 1993, Elizabeth Morris Genious award, 2002, Winsor Newton Merchandising award Summie Soc. Am., 2002. Mem. Oil Pastel Assn., Winchester Art Guild, Lexington Art League, Ky. Watercolor Assn. (Bluegrass regional dir. 1988, 89, 90, 91, 92), Ky. Guild Artists and Craftsmen, Inc., Northwest Pastel Soc., Degas Pastel Soc., Pen & Brush Soc. (Perfect Proportion award). Avocations: golf, bowling. Home: 2800 Old Boonesboro Rd Winchester KY 40391-8805 Office: Artists Attic Inc Victorian Square 401 W Main St Lexington KY 40507-1640

SNOWE, OLYMPIA J. senator; b. Augusta, Maine, Feb. 21, 1947; d. George John and Georgia G. Bouchles; m. John McKernan. BA, U. Maine, 1969; LLD (hon.), U. Maine, Machias, 1982, U. Maine, Orono, 1981, Nasson Coll., 1981, Bowdoin Coll., 1982, Colby Coll., 1985; LHD (hon.), Thomas Coll., 1987; LLD (hon.), Suffolk U., 1994; DSc (hon.), Maine Maritime Acad., 1995; LLD (hon.), Colby Coll., 1996, U. New England, 1996; hon. degree, John F. Kennedy Sch. Govt. Harvard U., 1997; LLD (hon.), Bates Coll., 1998. Businesswoman; mem. Maine Ho. of Reps., 1973-76, Maine Senate, 1976-78, 96th-103d Congresses from 2d Maine Dist., 1979-94, mem. budget com., foreign affairs com., com. on aging, 1979-94; co-chair Congl. Caucus for Women's Issues, 1983-94; U.S. senator from Maine, 1995—. Mem. Senate com. armed svcs., 1997-2001, chair, seapower subcom., Senate com. on commerce, sci. and transp., 1995—, chair, oceans and fisheries subcom., Senate Budget com., 1995—, Senate com. small business, 1995—, Senate com. Fgn. Rels., 1995-97; counsel to asst. majority leader, 1997—, House Budget com., 1991-95, House Fgn. Affairs com., 1979-95, House Aging com. 1979-95, Congl. Caucus on Women's Issues 1979-84, co-chair 1983-95; dep. Repub. Whip, 1984-95; dep. Whip, 1996-97; corporator Mechanics Savs. Bank. Recipient Homeric award for adv. of human rights Chian Fedn., 1999, award for "Excelling in Standing up for Choice" Women's Campaign Fund, 1999, Spirit of Enterprise award U.S. Chamber of Commerce, 1997, 99, Woman of Yr. award Glamour Mag., 1998, David and Sherry Huber award for leadership on family planning, women's health issues, Family Planning Assn. of ME, 1998, Golden Bulldog award Watchdogs of the Treasury, Inc., Wash., 1994, 96, 98, Guardian of Small Business award Nat. Fedn. Indep. Bus., Wash., 1994, 96, 98, Responsible Choices award Planned Parenthood of Am., 1998, Spl. honor Nat. Assn. Devel. Orgns., 1998, Disting. Pub. Svc. award Am. Legion, Wash., 1998, Neil W. Allen award Greater Portland Chamber of Commerce, 1997, Legis. award for outstanding svc. to schs. and pub. librs., White Ho. Conf. on Libr. and Info. Svcs. Task Force, Wash., 1997, Pub. Leadership award, Nat. Breast Cancer Coalition, 1997, Magnificent Seven award Bus. & Profl. Women/USA, Wash., 1997, Deborah Morton award Westbrook Coll., Portland, ME, 1997, Golden Gavel award U.S. Senate Leadership, Wash., 1996, Nat. Osteoporosis Assn. award for leadership, Wash., 1996, award for leadership U.S. Distance Learning Assn., Crystal City, Va., 1996, award for leadership United Hellenic Am. Cong., 1995, William H. Natcher Disting. Svc. award Com. for Edn. Funding, 1995, Pub. Svc. award Am. Coll. Obstetricians and Gynecologists, 1995, Nat. Security Leadership award Am. Security Coun., Wash., 1994, Thomas Jefferson award Nat. Am. Wholesale Grocers Assn./Internat. Foodsvc. Distbrs. Assn., 1994, Grace Caucus award Citizens Against Govt. Waste, 1994, Sound Dollar award Free Cong. Found., 1994, Appreciation award Agrl. Stblzn. and Conservation Com. Somerset County chpt., Lifetime Achievement award Am. Hellenic Inst., 1994, Golden Heart award Assn. for Children for Enforcement of Support, ME chpt., 1993, Am. Social Health Assn. award on behalf of women's health issues, 1993, Medal of St. Andrew presented by His All Holiness Dimitrios Ecumenical Patriarch of Constantinople, Wash., 1990, Congrl. Waste Watchers award Coalition to Reform the Davis-Bacon Act, 1990; named to "CQ 50" Congrl. Quarterly Mag., Wash., 1999, Maine Women's Hall of Fame, 1999, Washingtonian Mag. 100 Most Powerful Women, 1997, All Maine Women Honor Soc. U. Maine, 1996, Deficit Reduction Honor Roll Concord Coalition, 1994, Honor Roll for dairy farmer support Associated Milk Prodrs., 1993; named Taxpayer's Hero for preventing govt. waste Citizens Against Govt. Waste, 1997, No Nonsense Am. Women, No Nonsense Coun. on Women's Issues, 1995, Congresswoman of Yr. Nat. Assn. for Transp. Alternatives, 1986; honored by Nat. Coalition for Osteoporosis and Related Bone Diseases, 1999, Edn. and Libr. Networks Coalition, 1997, Am. Assn. Univ. Pres., 1996, Pub. Policy Com. for Hellenic-Am. Women, 1995, Nat. Vietnam Vet. Coalition, 1994. Mem.: Philoptochos Soc. Republican. Greek Orthodox. Office: US Senate 154 Russell Senate Bldg Washington DC 20510-1903 E-mail: olympia@snowe.senate.gov.

SNOW-SMITH, JOANNE INLOES, art history educator; b. Balt. d. Henry Williams and Elsie Orrick (Bagley) Snow; m. Robert Porter Smith (dec.); children: Joanne Tyndale Darby, Henry Webster Smith, III (dec.), Constance Elizabeth Bagley, Cynthia Porter Bloom, Robert Porter Smith, Jr.; m. Robert Edward Willstadter. BA, Goucher Coll.; MA, U. Ariz., 1968; PhD, UCLA, 1976. Prof. Italian Renaissance art history U. Wash., Seattle, 1981—. Program dir. of art history U. Wash. Rome Ctr. in Palazzo Pio, Rome, 1998, 2000, 2002. Author: (book) The Salvator Mundi of Leonardo da Vinci, 1982 (Internat. award 1983), The Primavera of Sandro Botticelli: A Neoplatonic Interpretaion, 1993; contbr. numerous articles to profl. jours. Recipient Rsch. Professorship to study in Oxford and London, U. Wash. Grad. Sch., 1986. Mem. Nat. Soc. Colonial Dames of Am., Renaissance Soc. of Am., Leonardo Soc./U. London, Coll. Art Assn., Seattle Art Mus., Met. Mus. Art, Ashmolean Mus. (Oxford, Eng.). Home: 1414 Shenandoah Dr E Seattle WA 98112-3730 Office: Univ Wash PO Box 353440 Seattle WA 98195-3440 E-mail: jsnowsmi@u.washington.edu.

SNYDER, ALAN CARHART, financial services executive; b. N.Y.C., May 25, 1946; s. John I. and Elfrida (Bendix) S.; m. Mary Burgoyne, Feb. 9, 1974. BS, BA, Georgetown U., 1968; MBA, Harvard U., 1973. Cons. Reynolds Securities, N.Y.C., 1972-73; exec. v.p. Dean Witter Reynolds, N.Y.C., 1975-85; sole proprietor Shinnecock Ptnrs., N.Y.C., 1985-89, mng. ptnr., 1989—; pres., chief oper. officer, bd. dirs. First Exec. Corp., L.A., 1990-91; COO, Exec. Life Ins. Co., L.A., 1991-93; CEO, Aurora Nat. Life Assurance Co., LA, 1993-94, cons. L.A., 1994-95; mng. ptnr. Shinnecock Group L.L.C., L.A., 1994—; chmn., CEO, pres. Answer Fin. Inc., L.A., 1997—. Baker scholar Harvard Bus. Sch., 1973.

SNYDER, ALLEGRA FULLER, dance educator; b. Chgo., Aug. 28, 1927; d. R. Buckminster and Anne (Hewlett) Fuller; m. Robert Snyder, June 30, 1951 (div. Apr. 1975, remarried Sept. 1980); children: Alexandra, Jaime. BA in Dance, Bennington Coll., 1951; MA in Dance, UCLA, 1967. Asst. to curator, dance archives Mus. Modern Art, N.Y.C., 1945-47; dancer Ballet Soc. of N.Y.C. Ballet Co., 1945-47; mem. office and prodn. staff Internat. Film Found., N.Y.C., 1950-52; editor, dance films Film News mag., N.Y.C., 1966-72; lectr. dance and film adv., dept. dance UCLA, 1967-73, chmn. dept. dance, 1974-80, 90-91, acting chair, spring 1985, chair of faculty Sch. of the Arts, 1989-91, prof. dance and dance ethnology, 1973-91, prof. emeritus, 1991—; pres. Buckminster Fuller Inst., Santa Barbara, Calif., chairwoman bd. dirs., 1984—. Vis. lectr. Calif. Inst. Arts, Valencia, 1972; co-dir. dance and TV workshop Am. Dance Festival, Conn. Coll., New London, 1973; dir. NEH summer seminar for coll. tchrs. Asian Performing Arts, 1978, 81; coord. Ethnic Arts Intercoll. Interdisciplinary Program, 1974-73, acting chmn., 1986; vis. prof. performance studies NYU, 1982-83; hon. vis. prof. U. Surrey, Guildford, Eng., 1983-84; cons. Thyodia Found., Salt Lake City, 1973-74; mem. dance adv. panel Nat. Endowment Arts, 1968-72, Calif. Arts Commn., 1974-91; mem. adv. screening com. Coun. Internat. Exch. of Scholars, 1979-82; mem. various panels NEH, 1979-85; core cons. for Dancing, Sta. WNET-TV, 1988—. Dir. film Baroque Dance 1625-1725, in 1977; co-dir. film Gods of Bali, 1952; dir. and wrote film Bayanihan, 1962 (named Best Folkloric Documentary at Bilboa Film Festival, winner Golden Eagle award); asst. dir. and asst. editor film The Bennington Story, 1952; created films Gestures of Sand, 1968, Reflections on Choreography, 1973, When the Fire Dances Between Two Poles, 1982; created film, video loop and text Celebration: A World of Art and Ritual, 1982-83; supr. post-prodn. film Erick Hawkins, 1964, in 1973. Also contbr. articles to profl. jours. and mags. Adv. com. Pacific Asia Mus., 1980-84, Festival of the Mask, Craft and Folk Art Mus., 1979-84; adv. panel Los Angeles Dance Currents II, Mus. Ctr. Dance Assn., 1974-75; bd. dirs. Council Grove Sch. III, Compton, Calif., 1976-81; apptd. mem. Adv. Dance Com., Pasadena (Calif.) Art Mus., 1970-71, Los Angeles Festival of Performing Arts com., Studio Watts, 1970; mem. Technology and Cultural Transformation com., UNESCO, 1977. Fulbright research fellow, 1983-84; grantee Nat. Endowment Arts, 1981, Nat. Endowment Humanities, 1977, 79, 81, UCLA, 1968, 77, 80, 82, 85; recipient Amer. Dance Guild Award for Outstanding Achievement in Dance, 1992. Mem. Am. Dance Therapy Assn., Congress on Rsch. in Dance (bd. dirs. 1970-76, chmn. 1975-77, nat. conf. chmn. 1972), Coun. Dance Adminstrs., Am. Dance Guild (chmn. com. awards 1972), Soc. for Ethnomusicology, Am. Anthrop. Assn., Am. Folklore Soc., Soc. Anthropology of Visual Comm., Soc. Humanistic Anthropology, Calif. Dance Educators Assn. (conf. chmn. 1972), L.A. Area Dance Alliance (adv. bd. 1978-84, selection com. Dance Kaleidoscope project 1979-81), Fulbright Alumni Assn. Home: 15313 Whitfield Ave Pacific Palisades CA 90272-2548 Office: Buckminster Fuller Inst 111 N Main St Sebastopol CA 95472-3448

SNYDER, ANDREA, performing arts association administrator; BS, The Am. U.; MA in Arts Mgmt., NYU. Asst. to dir. Dance Notation Bureau; assoc. adminstr. Cunningham Dance Found.; adminstr. of arts dance dept. NYU Tisch Sch.; booking agent Sheldon Soffer Mgmt.; exec. dir. Laura Dean Dancers & Musicians; asst. dir. Nat. Endowment for Arts Dance Program, 1987—93; dir. Nat. Initiative to Preserve Am.'s Dance, 1993—2000; pres., exec. dir. Dance/USA, Washington, 2000—. Adj. prof. The Am. U. Office: Dance USA 1156 15th St NW Washington DC 20005

SNYDER, ANTHONY EDWARD, communications executive; b. Cleve., Jan. 30, 1970; s. Edward Eugene and Henrietta Snyder; m. Sara Frischkorn, May 28, 1994; children: Emma Irene, Truman Henry, Frank Herbert. BA, Bowling Green State U., Ohio, 1988—92. Staff writer Buckeye Pub. - The Morning Jour., Lisbon, Ohio, 1993—93; comm. coord. & assoc. editor of publications Slovene Nat. Benefit Soc., Imperial, Pa., 1993—97; vice pres. and dir. fraternal & comm. Join Hands Day/Nat. Fraternal Congress of Am.,

Naperville, Ill. Pres. Suburban Chicagoland Chpt. - Pub. Rels. Soc. of Am., 2004, Bowling Green State U. Chicagoland Alumni Assn., 2003—04. Named to Honor Roll, Assn. Advance Am., 1997, 1998, 1999, 2000, 2001, 2002, 2003, 2004; recipient award of Excellence, 1998, Spark Plug award (Most Active Mem.), Greater O'Hare Chpt. - Pub. Rels. Soc. of Am., 1998, ADDY, Am. Advt. Awards - Regional Competition, 2000, Ky. Col., Gov. of Ky., 2001, Chgo. Skyline award, Pub. Rels. Soc. of Am. (Chgo. and Greater O'Hare Chapters), 2001, Spectra award of Excellence, Internat. Assn. of Bus. Communicators' Chgo., 2001, APEX award for Publ. Excellence, Comm. Concepts, 2001, 2002, 2003, Trumpet award (Silver in 2001 and Gold in 2002), Publicity Club of Chgo., 2001, 2002, 2002 Olympic Torch Bearer, U.S. Olympic Com., 2002, Toys for Tots Commdr.'s award, USMC, 2002, award of Merit, Internat. Assn. of Bus. Communicators/Chgo., 2002, Communicator awards, 2002, Excellence in Assn. Publs. award, Assn. Trends, 2002, 2003, 2004, award of Excellence, The Dalton Pen Comm. Awards Program, 2002, award of Merit, The Dalton Pen Comm. Award Program, 2003, Top 100 Publicity Materials of 2003, League of Am. Comm. Profls., 2003, Golden Web award, Inernat. Assn. of Web Masters and Designers, 2003-2004. Mem.: Assn. Forum of Chicagoland, Slovene Nat. Benefit Soc., Lambda Chi Alpha (life). Presbyn. Avocations: reading, writing. Home: 2201 Waynesburg Street Naperville IL 60565 Office: Join Hands Day 1240 Iroquois Ave Suite 301 Naperville IL 60563 Personal E-mail: anthonysnyder@hotmail.com.

SNYDER, ARLEN DEAN, actor; b. Rice, Kans., Mar. 5, 1933; s. Glenn Arlen and Sylvia Thelma (Guiot) S.; m. Angela Thornton, Jan. 7, 1970 (div. July 1976); m. Joanne Elizabeth Burke, May 8, 1983; 1 child, Kimble Burke. BA in Theater, U. Tulsa, 1957; MA in Theater, U. Iowa, 1959. Facilities designer Diamond Clr. Theatre, Durango, Colo., 1961, ptnr., mgr., actor, 1961—63. Instr. dept. cinema Hunter Coll., NYC, 1975-76. Dir.: (plays) Under Milkwood, 1974, Miss Pete, 1975; appeared in motion pictures including Yanks, 1978, Heartbreak Ridge, 1986, Bird, 1987, Internal Affairs, 1989, Marked For Death, 1990, Mommy's Day, 1996, The Overlookers, 2003, Lobster Farm, 2004; recurring roles (TV series) Dallas, TV 101, Eisenhower & Lutz, Designing Women; guest appearances (TV series) Hart to Hart, M*A*S*H, Murder She Wrote, Benson, Dynasty, Private Benjamin, St. Elsewhere, Quantum Leap, Trial By Jury, others; appeared in theatrical plays including The Candy Apple, 1970, Trial of the Catonsville Nine, 1972, Big Broadcast on E. 53rd, 1973, One World at a Time, 1973, The Poison Tree, 1974, 75, Streamers, 1976, The Trip Back Down, 1977, Curse of the Starving Class, 1978, Better Living, 1989, Mr Rickey Calls A Meeting, 1992, Madalyn Murray O'Hair in Exile, 2003; starred in TV series including Secret Storm, 1966-68, As The World Turns, 1968-69, Dear Detective, 1979, The Texas Rangers/Pilot, 1981, Trauma Center, 1983, One Life to Live, 1984, Macgruder and Loud/Pilot, 1984; actor (TV films) Young Love, First Love, 1979, Attica, 1979, Red Flag, 1980, RFK, 1981, Bus Stop, 1982, Night Partners, 1983, North & South Book II, 1986, The Oliver North Story, 1989, Frog Girl, 1989, Terror in Copper Valley, 1989, The Beach Boys' Story, 1990, Willing To Kill: The Texas Cheerleader Story, 1992, Cora Unashamed, PBS, 1999; recs. for Iowa's Books for the Blind and Handicapped. Bd. dirs. San Fernando Valley (Calif.) Arts Coun., 1987-88, mem. bd. advisors, 1989-90, pres., 1991. With US Army, 1953-55. Named Leading Male Performer, LA Weekly, Matrix Theatre, 1989. Mem. AFTRA, SAG (bd. dirs. 1991), Actors' Equity Assn., Players' Club (bd. dirs. 1974-76), Theta Alpha Phi. Green Party. Avocations: anti-establishment commentary, set design, political history, farming, cabinet making. Office: 4580 Broadway Ste 4F New York NY 10040-2114 Office Phone: 212-304-3934. E-mail: arlen@snarlin.com.

SNYDER, ARNOLD LEE, JR., retired air force officer, research director; b. Washington, Oct. 12, 1937; s. Arnold Lee and Frances May (Humbert) S; m. Patricia Dorine Ward, July 6, 1963; children: Heinrick Jason, Sonya Doreen, Ross Nansen. BCE, George Washington U., 1960; MS, U. Colo., 1966; PhD, U. Alaska, 1972. Commd. 2d lt. USAF, 1960; advanced through grades to col., 1981; chief space environ. support sys. devel. sect. Air Force Global Weather Central, Offutt AFB, Nebr., 1972-76; chief ionospheric dynamics br. Geophysics Lab., Hanscom AFB, Mass., 1976-80; test dir. CONUS OTH-B radar system, Columbia Falls AFB, Maine, 1980-81, program dir. Hanscom AFB, 1981-85; dir. Office of Tech. Support, 1985-87; tech. dir. U. Lowell Ctr. Atmospheric Rsch., 1987-89; with The Mitre Corp., 1989-96; pvt. practice, 1996—. Adj. prof. U. Lowell, 1987-89. Contbr. articles to sci. jours. Recipient Legion of Merit, Meritorious Svc. medal with one oak leaf cluster, Commendation medal USAF, R&D award, 1981; Def. Value Engring. award, 1984; Henry Harding scholar, 1955-56. Mem. Am. Geophys. Union, Am. Meteorol. Soc., Air Force Assn., Sigma Xi. Home and Office: 22 Blake Rd Orrington ME 04474-3637

SNYDER, ARTHUR, publishing executive; b. Valley Stream, NY, Feb. 6, 1925; s. Arthur and Kathryn (Staubitzer) Snyder; m. Betty Lain Harper, July 8, 1950; children: Susan, Arthur, Betsy, Jack, Heidi, Bonnie. B in Metall. Engring., Cornell U., 1950, MBA, 1952. Mfg. engr. Norton Co., Worcester, Mass., 1952-56, chief acct., 1956-58, asst. contr., 1958-59, mgr. data processing, 1959-61, contr., 1961-65; exec. v.p. A.M. Best Co., Oldwick, NJ, 1965-67, pres., 1968—, chmn., 1971—. Author: (book) Principles of Inventory Control and Managing Capital Expenditures. 1st lt. AUS, 1942—45. Decorated Battlefield Commn., Bronze Star with oak leaf cluster, Purple Heart. Mem.: U.S. Srs. Golf Assn., Cornell Soc. Engrs., Fin. Execs. Inst., Loch Lomond Golf Club (Scotland), Lyford Cay Club (Nassau, Bahamas), Baltusrol Golf Club (Springfield, NJ). Presbyterian. Home: Lloyd Rd Bernardsville NJ 07924-1710 Office: A M Best Company Inc Ambest Rd Oldwick NJ 08858 Office Phone: 908-439-3316. Business E-Mail: snydera2@ambest.com.

SNYDER, BARBARA K. pediatrician, educator; MD, George Washington U., 1979. Diplomate in pediatrics and adolescent medicine Am. Bd. Pediatrics. Intern Children's Nat. Med. Ctr., Washington, 1979—80, resident in pediatrics, 1980—82; fellow in adolescent medicine U. Rochester (N.Y.) Sch. Medicine, 1986—88; chief divsn. adolescent medicine, dept. pediatrics Robert Wood Johnson Med. Sch., New Brunswick, NJ, 1990—, assoc. prof., 1994—, dir. eating disorders program, adolescent medicine program, 1990—. Office: U Medicine and Dentistry NJ-Robert Wood Johnson Med Sch Dept Pediats New Brunswick NJ 08903-0019 Office Phone: 732-235-7896.

SNYDER, BARBARA ROOK, academic administrator; BA, Ohio State U., 1976; JD, U. Chgo. Law clk. for Judge Luther M. Swygert U.S. Ct. Appeals for the Seventh Cir.; with Sidley & Austin, Chgo.; joined law faculty Case Western Res. U., 1983, Ohio State U., Columbus, 1988, assoc. dean for acad. affairs, 2000—01, vice provost for acad. policy and human resources, 2001—04, interim provost, 2002—04, exec. v.p., provost, 2004—, Joanne W. Murphy/Class of 1965 professorship Moritz Coll. Law. Office: Ohio State U Office Acad Affairs 203 Bricker Hall 190 N Oval Mall Columbus OH 43210*

SNYDER, BROCK ROBERT, lawyer; b. Topeka, Sept. 18, 1935; s. Ralph and Helen (Fritze) S.; m. Carol Lee Cunningham, June 5, 1957 (div. Nov. 1976); children: Lori, Holli, Staci; m. Sheryl Anita Clarke, Apr. 1, 1985 (div. Apr. 1997); children: Brock Robert II, Samantha. BS, U. Kans., 1957; JD, Washburn U., 1964. Bar: Kans. 1964. Ptnr. Eidson, Lewis, Porter & Haynes, Topeka, 1964-82; sole practice Topeka, 1982—. Lectr. on sch. discipline and due process, 1975-80; pres. Kans. Legal Services, Topeka, 1977-80. Served to capt. USMC, 1957-61. Fellow Kans. Bar Assn. (chmn. legal assts. com. 1983-84); mem. ABA, Kans. Trial Lawyers Assn. (bd. govs.), Topeka Bar Assn., Topeka Legal Aid Soc. (pres. 1976-78). Republican. Lutheran. Avocation: scuba. Office: 1401 SW Topeka Blvd Topeka KS 66612-1818 Office Phone: 913-232-1700. E-mail: brsnyder@inlandnet.net.

SNYDER, CAROLYN ANN, education educator, librarian; b. Elgin, Nebr., Nov. 5, 1942; d. Ralph and Florence Wagner. Student, Nebr. Wesleyan U., 1960—61; BS cum laude, Kearney State Coll., 1964; MS in Librarianship, U. Denver, 1965. Asst. libr. sci. and tech. U. Nebr., Lincoln, 1965-67, asst. pub. svc. libr., 1967-68, 70-73; pers. libr. Ind. U. Librs., Bloomington, 1973-76, acting dean of univ. librs., 1980, 88-89, assoc. dean for pub. svcs., 1977-88, 89-91, interim devel. officer, 1989-91; adminstrv. army libr. Spl. Svcs. Agy., Europe, 1968-70; dean libr. affairs So. Ill. U., Carbondale, 1991-2000, prof., dir. found. rels., 2000—. Team leader Midwest Univs. Consortium for Internat. Activities-World Bank IX project to develop libr. sys. and implement automation U. Indonesia, Jakarta, 1984-86; libr. devel. cons. Inst. Tech. MARA/Midwest Univs. Consortium for Internat. Activities Program in Malaysia, 1985; ofcl. rep. EDUCAUSE, 1996-2000; mem. working group on scholarly comm. Nat. Commn. on Librs. and Info. Sci., 1998-2000. Editor Library and Other Academic Support Services for Distance Learning, 1997; contbr. chpt. to book and articles to profl. jours. Active Humane Assn. Jackson County, 1991—, Carbondale Pub. Libr. Friends, 1991—. Morris Libr. Friends, 1991-. Cooperative Rsch. grant Coun. on Libr. Resources, Washington, 1984. Mem. ALA (councilor 1985-89, Bogle Internat. Travel award 1988, H.W. Wilson Libr. Staff devel. grant 1981), Libr. Adminstrn./Mgmt. Assn. (pres. 1981-82), Com. on Instnl. Coop./Resource Sharing (chair 1987-91), Coalition for Networked Info. (So. Ill. U. at Carbondale rep. 1991-2000), Coun. Dirs. State Univ. Librs. in Ill. (chair 1992-93, 99-2000), Coun. on Libr. and Info. Resources Digital Leadership Inst. Steering Com. (Assn. Rsch. Librs. rep. 1998-2000), Ill. Assn. Coll. and Rsch. Librs. (chair Ill. Bd. Higher Edn. liaison com. 1993-94), Ill. Network (bd. dirs.), Ind. Libr. Assn. (chair coll./univ. divsn. 1982-83), U.S. Grant Assn. (bd. dirs. 1992—), Ill. Libr. Computer Sys. Orgn. (policy coun. 1992-95, 96-2000), Nat. Assn. State Univs. and Land Grant Colls. (commn. on info. tech. and its distance learning and libr. bds. 1994-96), NetIllinois (bd. dirs. 1994-96), OCLC Users Coun. (elected rep. 1995-98), Big 12 Plus Libr. Consortium (chair 1997-98), Nat. Commn. on Librs. and Info. Sci. Working Group on Scholarly Comm., Assn. Rsch. Libr. (vis. program officer 2000-01). Avocations: antiques, theater, movies, reading. Office: So Ill U Ctrl Devel Carbondale IL 62901-6632 Office Phone: 618-453-1447.

SNYDER, CHARLES AUBREY, lawyer; b. Bastrop, La., June 19, 1941; s. David and Shirley Blossom (Haas) S.; m. Sharon Rae Veta, Aug. 29, 1963; children: David Veta, Shelby Haas, Claire Frances. BBA, Tulane U., 1963; JD, La. State U., 1966. Bar: La. 1966. Assoc. firm. Milling Benson Woodward, LLP and predecessors, New Orleans, 1966-69, ptnr., 1969—. Bd. dirs. Delta Petroleum Co., Terre aux Boeufs Land Corp., Kemper and Leila Williams Found., v.p., 2004-. Bd. dirs. New Orleans Speech and Hearing Ctr., pres., 1978-80; bd. dirs. City Pk. Commn., 1991-98, pres., 1995, dir. emeritus, 1999-2004; bd. dirs. New Orleans Mus. Art, 1996-2002, 2004-, v.p., 1998-99, sec., 1999-2000. Fellow Am. Bar Found., La. Bar Found.; mem. ABA, La. Bar Assn. (chmn. sect. on corp. and bus. law 1982-83), New Orleans Bar Assn., Am. Law Inst., La. Law Inst. (coun. 2000-, coms. on mineral code and revision of partnership law, property law), Plimsoll Club, Bienville Club, Beta Gamma Sigma. Home: 74724 River Rd Covington LA 70435-2222 Office: Milling Benson Woodward LLP 909 Poydras St Ste 2300 New Orleans LA 70112-1010 E-mail: csnyder@millinglaw.com.

SNYDER, CHARLES ROYCE, sociologist, educator; b. Haverford, Pa., Dec. 28, 1924; BA, Yale U., 1945W, MA, 1949, PhD, 1954. Mem. staff Ctr. Alcohol Studies Yale U., 1950-60, asst. prof. sociology, 1956-60; prof. sociology So. Ill. U., Carbondale, 1960-85, chmn. dept., 1964-75, 81-85, prof. emeritus, 1985—. Vis. prof. human genetics Sackler Sch. Medicine, Tel Aviv U., 1980; cons. behavioral scis. tng. com. Nat. Inst. Gen. Med. Scis., NIH, 1962-64; mem. planning com., chmn. program 28th Internat. Congress Alcohol and Alcoholism, 1964. Author: Alcohol and the Jews, 1958; editor: (with D.J. Pittman) Society, Culture and Drinking Patterns, 1962; editorial bd. Quar. Jour. Studies on Alcohol, 1957-83; assoc. editor Sociol. Quar., 1960-63. Mem. theol. commn. United Ch. of Christ, 1964-71; bd. dirs. Ill. Stewardship Alliance, 1990-95. With USNR, WWII. Fellow Am. Sociol. Assn.; mem. Soc. Study Social Problems (v.p. 1963-64, rep. to council Am. Sociol. Assn. 1964-66), Midwest Sociol. Soc. (bd. dirs. 1970-71), AAUP. Home: Apt 1606 8680 E Alameda Ave Denver CO 80247

SNYDER, CLAIR A. state legislator; b. Boston, Oct. 6, 1924; divorced; 2 children. BS, N.H. Coll., Portsmouth, 1978; postgrad., U. N.H., Durham. Formerly acct. and bus. mgr.; now mem. N.H. Ho. of Reps. Bd. dirs. N.H. Sch. Bd. Assn., 1987—; trustee various trust funds; chmn. N.H. Sch. Bd. Ins. Trust, 1993-94. Mem. Bus. and Profl. Women. Office: NH House of Reps State Capitol Concord NH 03301

SNYDER, DANIEL, professional sports team executive, communications executive; b. Nov. 23, 1964; m. Tanya Snyder. Founder, chmn., CEO Snyder Communications, Inc. (sold to Havas), 1985—2000; chmn. bd., owner Washington Redskins, 1999—. Bd. dirs. McLeod USA, Ventiv Health; mem., broadcast com. and ventures com. NFL. Bd. dirs. Ctr. for Missing and Exploited Children, Parents in Charge; exec. leadership cabinet Martin Luther King, Jr. Nat. Meml. Found. Project; bd. dirs. Wash. Children's Nat. Med. Ctr.; founder Wash. Redskins Leadership Coun. Mem.: Wash. Bd. Trade, Bus. Executives for Nat. Security. Office: c/o Washington Redskins 21300 Redskin Park Rd Ashburn VA 20147*

SNYDER, DAVID RICHARD, lawyer; b. Kalamazoo, Mich., Oct. 9, 1949; s. Richard E. and Margaret L. (Vanderplough) S.; m. Phyllis Alford, Aug. l4, l97l; children: Jason Richard, Carrie Lynn. BA with high honors, Mich. State U., l97l; JD with distinction, Cornell U., l974. Bar: Calif. l974. Assoc. Jenkins & Perry, San Diego, 1974-77, ptnr., 1978-83, Aylward, Kintz & Stiska, San Diego, 1983-86, Luce, Forward, Hamilton & Scripps, San Diego, 1986-93, Pillsbury Madison & Sutro LLP, San Diego, 1993—; mng. bd. Pillsbury Winthrop LLP, San Diego, 1999—, exec. vice chmn., 2004—. V.p., dir. San Diego Venture Group, 1989-91; adj. prof. Calif. Western Sch. Law, San Diego, 1982-84; lectr. Calif. Continuing Edn. of Bar, 1983—. Co-author: Drafting Legal Instruments, l982; editor Cornell Law Rev., 1973-74. Bd. dirs. Boys Club Chula Vista, Calif., 1979-83; pres. Corpus Christi Parish Coun., Bonita, Calif., 1988-90; trustee Children's Hosp. Found., San Diego, 1988—, chmn., 1990-92. Mem.: ABA (fed. securities law com. 1987—, chmn. subcom. on ann. rev. fed. securities regulation, dir. corp. dirs. forum), Corp. Dirs. Forum (bd. dirs. 2001—), San Diego County Bar Assn., State Bar Calif., Am. Electronics Assn. (bd. dirs., mem. exec. com. San Diego chpt. 1991—93), Order of Coif, Phi Beta Kappa. Republican. Roman Catholic. Office: Pillsbury Winthrop 101 W Broadway Ste 1800 San Diego CA 92101-8298

SNYDER, DONALD BENJAMIN, biology professor; b. N. Manchester, Ind., Oct. 6, 1935; s. Benjamin Franklin and Eva Katherine (Speicher) S.; m. Wilma Frankie Simpson, Aug. 8, 1965; children: Douglas, Jonn. BS, Manchester Coll., Ind., 1957; MS, Ohio State U., 1959, PhD, 1963; postgrad., U. Puerto Rico, 1966. Cert. wildlife biologist. From grad. asst. in zoology to rsch. fellow in wildlife Ohio State U., 1957-63; biology instr. Houghton (N.Y.) Coll., 1963; asst. prof. biology So. (S.C.) Wesleyan U., 1963-64, Geneva Coll., Beaver Falls, Pa., 1964-69; prof. biology Edinboro (Pa.) U., 1969-96, Pymatuning Lab. of Ecology U. Pitts., Pitts., 1982, 88, 89. Bird records com. Presque Isle Audubon Soc., Erie, Pa., 1975—; vol. for wildlife Pa. Game Commn., Harrisburg, 1990-96; ornithol. tech. com. Pa. Biol. Survey, Harrisburg, 1991—. Contbr. numerous articles to profl. jours. Committeeman Boy Scouts Am., Laketon, Ind., 1965-70; elder Christian & Missionary Alliance Ch., Erie, 1987-90, 98—; trustee Purple Martin Conservation Assn., Edinboro, Pa., 1988—. Equipment grantee Atomic Energy Commn., Oak Ridge, Tenn., 1966; recipient Meritorious Svc. award Edinboro U. Pa., 1974. Mem. Wildlife Soc., Assn. Field Ornithologists, Commonwealth of Pa. Univ. Biologists, Beta Beta Beta. Avocations: hiking, biking, canoeing. Home: 13190 Cambridge Rd Edinboro PA 16412-2837 E-mail: dbswfs@lycos.com.

SNYDER, DONALD EDWARD, corporate executive; b. Rochester, N.Y., Nov. 10, 1928; s. Benjamin Orman and Arlien Henrietta (Wing) S.; m. Dorothy Edna Stanke, Oct. 16, 1954; children— Donald Edward, Anne Arlien Snyder Marone, Barbara Lynn Snyder Mitchell, Richard John Snyder. AB, Cornell U., 1950, JD, 1952; postgrad., Ind. U., 1962. Bar: N.Y. 1953. Pvt. practice law, 1953-56; with Eastman Savs. and Loan Assn., 1956-68, pres., 1970-75, chmn. bd., 1979-88; asst. to treas. Eastman Kodak Co., Rochester, 1968-70, gen. credit mgr., 1975-77, with Comptroller's div., 1977-78, asst. treas., 1978-79, treas., 1979-88; chmn. Eastman Kodak Credit Corp., 1985-88; chief exec. officer, chmn. bd., pres. Corp. Officers and Dirs. Assurance Ltd., Hamilton, Bermuda, 1990-93. Bd. dirs. Greater Rochester chpt. Epilepsy Found. Am., 1979-85, Allendale Mut. Ins. Co., 1983-92; bd. dirs. Luth. Ch.-Mo. Synod, 1983-95; vice chmn. bd., chmn. fin. com., mem., chmn. audit com., 1989-95; bd. dirs., mem. exec. com. ACE Ltd., 1985-90, EXEL Ltd., 1985-90, CODA Ltd., 1986-93; mem. investment rev. com. United Way of Greater Rochester, 1979-2000; trustee Seneca Zool. Soc., 1983-90. With USNR, 1946-48. Mem. N.Y. State Bar Assn., Monroe County Bar Assn., Rochester C. of C. (trustee 1980-86), Cornell Club (Rochester), Phi Kappa Tau (nat. fin. advisor, mem. nat. coun. 1988-95, treas., mem. exec. com. Phi Kappa Tau Found. 1991-2002). Home and Office: 14 Hidden Springs Dr Pittsford NY 14534-2897 also: 2700 N AIA Ste 705 Fort Pierce FL 34949

SNYDER, DONALD IVANDALE, music educator, musician; b. Fort Wayne, Ind., Jan. 5, 1956; s. Ivandale Everett and Helen Rachael Pauling Snyder. BS, U. Indpls., 1978; MusM, U. Houston, 1985. Certified Teacher Ind. Dept. of Pub. Instrn., 1978, Tex. Edn. Dept., 1981, SUNY-Dept. of Edn., 1987, NJ. Dept. of Edn., 1992. Music specialist Humble Ind. Sch. Dist., Tex., 1981—87, Greenburgh Ctrl. Sch. Dist. 7, Hartsdale, NY; vocal/gen. music specialist NYC Bd. of Edn., Brooklyn, 1990—97; music specialist Orange Twp. Bd. of Edn., NY, 1997—98; music specialist/guest lectr. Garfield Bd. of Edn., NJ, 1998—2003; music specialist/cons. East Brunswick Pub. Schs., 2004—. Music edn. cons. Beech Grove City Schs., Ind., 1986—; alumni guest lectr. U. of Indpls., 2000; guest lectr. Concordia Coll. of NY, Bronxville, 2000; conf. presenter NY State Sch. Music Assn., 2001, NJ Music Educators Assn., 2001, Ind. Music Educators Assn., Muncie, 2001; profl. choral musician Episcopal Ch. of Epiphany, New York, NY, 2003—; conf. presenter Music Educators Nat. Conf., Reston, Va., 2003—. Dir. of tour guide services St. Michael's Ch., New York, NY, 1996, dir. of aids outreach, 2001, parish coun. mem., 2002; mem. com. for certification and admission of new parishes Episcopal Diocese of NY, 2003; sales chair Kodaly Music Educators Orgn. of NY, 2000—04; sec. designate Diocesan Episcopal AIDS Com., New York, NY, 2000. Mem.: Am. Orff-Schulwerk Assn., Am. Orgn. of Kodaly Educators, Am. Choral Directors Assn., Music Educators Nat. Conf. (assoc.). Liberal. Episcopal. Avocations: cooking, theater, art, bycling. Home: 461 Central Park West New York NY 10025-3848 Office Phone: 732-613-5815. Personal E-mail: dsnydermus@aol.com.

SNYDER, EDWARD ADAMS, dean, economics professor; b. Danville, Pa., July 3, 1953; s. Harry Coolidge and Fay (Adams) S.; m. Kimberly Marie Snyder; children: Alison Marie, Jeffrey Adams, Kevin James. Ba in Econs. and Govt., Colby Coll., 1975; M of Pub. Policy, U. Chgo., 1978, PhD in Econs., 1984. Staff economist Antitrust div. U.S. Dept. Justice, Washington, 1978—82; asst. prof. bus. econs. and pub. policy Sch. Bus. Adminstrn. U. Mich., Ann Arbor, 1982—90, assoc. prof. Sch. Bus. Adminstrn., 1990-94, prof. Sch. Bus. Adminstrn., 1994-98, chair bus. econ. and pub. policy, Sch. Bus. Adminstrn., 1992—95; dean Darden Bus. Sch. U. Va., Charlottesville, 1998—2001; dean U. Chgo. Grad. Sch. Bus., 2001—, prof., 2001—02, George Pratt Shultz prof., 2002—. Rsch. fellow Office for Study of Pub. and Pvt. Instns., U. Mich.; cons. Antitrust div. U.S. Dept. Justice, Chgo., 1982-85, Fed. Home Loan Bank Bd., Washington, 1989; antitrust expert, 1985—; John M. Olin vis. assoc. prof. U. Chgo., 1991-92; dir. William Davidson Inst. Mich. Bus. Sch., 1992-95. Author: Crisis Resolution in the Thrift Industry, 1989; contbr. articles to econ. jours. and law revs., 1985-98. Avocations: foreign policy, sports, sailing. Office: U Chgo Grad Sch of Bus 5807 S Woodlawn Ave Chicago IL 60637 Office Phone: 773-702-1680. E-mail: tsnyder@chicagogsb.edu.

SNYDER, ESTHER, food service executive; m. Harry (dec.); children: Guy, Rich. Founder, pres. In-N-Out Burger, Baldwin Park, Calif., 1948—. Office: In-N-Out Burger 13502 Hamburger Ln Baldwin Park CA 91706-5885

SNYDER, FRANCINE, psychotherapist, registered nurse, writer; b. Balt., Mar. 13, 1947; d. Jack and Naomi (Rapoport) S. AA, C.C. Balt., 1968; BA in Psychology, Antioch Coll. W, 1973; MA in MFCC, Azusa Pacific Coll., 1975; PhD in Clin. and Ednl. Psychology, Internat. Coll., 1981. RN, Hawaii; lic. marriage, family, and child counselor diplomate in psychotherapy counselor, Calif.; instr., Calif.; counselor, Calif.; credentialed cmty. coll. counselor, Calif., cmty. coll. instr. health, phys. care svcs., related techs., nursing and psychology; doctoral addictions counselor, cert. addiction specialist, cognitive behavioral therapist; endorsed domestic violence counselor 1, 2 & 3 Nat. Bd. Cognitive Behavioral Therapists. Staff and relief nurse Midway Hosp., L.A., 1972-77; counselor So. Calif. Counseling Ctr., L.A., 1972-77; counselor, exec. bd. mem., steering com. mem. Healing Ctr. for the Whole Person, Northridge, Calif., 1974-75; counselor The Family Home, North Hollywood, Calif., 1976; pvt. practice Beverly Hills, Calif., 1975-86; asst. had nurse St. Johns Mental Health Ctr., Santa Monica, Calif., 1977-79; counselor Calif. Family Study Ctr., Burbank, 1979-80; pvt. practice Kauai, Hawaii, 1986—; clin. dir., therapist Kauai YWCA Sex Abuse Treatment Program, Hawaii, 1989-90; clin. cons. Iniki Ohana Project, Kapaa, Hawaii, 1993. Student nurse Johns Hopkins Hosp., Balt., 1965-68; head and relief nurse, team leader, 1966-70; nurse Nix Meml. Hosp., San Antonio, Tex., 1970; staff nurse, team leader Cmty. Hosp, Chandler, Ariz.; cons. Slim Bionics Med. Group, L.A., 1974-75; instr. Pierce Coll., Woodland Hills, Calif., 1977, Saint Johns Med. Ctr., Santa Monica, Calif., 1977-79, Maple Ctr., Beverly Hills, Calif., 1979-80. Speaker in field. Mem. Am. Anorexia Nervosa/Bulimia Assn., Inc., Am. Mental Affiliates for Israel (exec. bd., head of allocations com.), Am. Assn. Marriage and Family Therapists (clin.), Internat. Platform Assn., Calif. Assn. Marriage and Family Therapists (clin.), Assn. for Humanistic Psychology, Children's Coalition for TV, Ctr. for the Healing Arts, Alliance for Survival, UCLA Alumni Assn.; cons. Help Anorexia, Inc., Performance Design Syss. Office: InnerVisions Change Tech PO Box 1303 Hanalei HI 96714-1303

SNYDER, FRANKLIN FARISON, hydrologic engineering consultant; b. Holgate, Ohio, Nov. 11, 1910; s. Samuel Lewis and Nettie May (Farison) S.; m. Mary Elizabeth Bruton, Oct. 1, 1938; children: Marilyn Kay Snyder Lutz, Carol Lamb Snyder Garnett, Gregory Lewis(dec.). Student, U. Toledo, 1928-30; B.C.E., Ohio State U., 1932, C.E., 1942; postgrad., Dept. Agr. Grad. Sch., 1940-42, 62. Registered profl. engr., Ohio. Hydraulic engr. U.S. Geol. Survey, Washington, 1934-35; hydraulic engr. TVA, Knoxville, 1936-37, Pa. Dept. Forests and Waters, Harrisburg, 1938-39, U.S. Weather Bur., Pitts. and Washington, 1940-42, Office Chief Engrs., Washington, 1942-66; ptnr. Nunn, Snyder & Assocs., Fairfax, Va., 1972-78. Hydrologic engring. cons., McLean, Va., Can., Mex., Sudan, Greece, Bangladesh, Pakistan, Colombia, Jamaica, 1954-90; mem. Internat. St. Lawrence River Bd. Control., 1961-74, U.S. Nat. Com. for Internat. Hydrol. Decade, 1964-67, mem. commn. for Hydrology, World Meteorol. Orgn., 1960-72. Contbr. articles to profl. publs. Supr. Citizens Assn. Security Patrol, Chesterbrook Woods, McLean, 1978-94. Recipient exceptional civilian service award War Dept., 1946, Outstanding Civil Engring. Alumnus award Ohio State U. Civil Engring. Alumni Assn., 1989, Disting. Alumnus award Ohio State U., 1990; named to Gallery of Disting. Civilian Employees, C.E., 1983 Fellow ASCE (Cross medal); mem. Am. Geophys. Union, Am. Meteorol. Soc., Nat. Acad. Engring., Cosmos Club Washington, Sigma Xi, Tau Beta Pi. Republican. Presbyterian. Avocations: genealogy, golf, travel. Home: 1128 Astoria Ln Peachtree City GA 30269 Personal E-mail: fsny007@aol.com.

SNYDER, GEORGE EDWARD, lawyer; b. Battle Creek, Mich., Feb. 7, 1934; s. Leon R. and Edith (Dullabahn) S.; m. Mary Jane Belt, July 27, 1957 (div. Sept. 23, 1982); children: Sara Lynn, Elizabeth Jane; m. Claudia Gage Brooks, Feb. 25, 1984 BS, Mich. State U., 1957; JD, U. Mich., 1960. Bar: Mich. 1961, U.S. Dist. Ct. (we. and ea. dists.) Mich. 1961. With Gen. Electric Co., 1957-58; asso. firm Miller, Johnson, Snell & Commisky, Grand Rapids, 1960-62, Goodenough & Buesser, Detroit, 1962-66; partner firm Buesser, Buesser, Snyder & Blank, Detroit and Bloomfield Hills, 1966-85, Meyer, Kirk, Snyder & Lynch PLLC, Bloomfield Hills, 1985—. Chmn. bd. dirs. Bill Knapps Mich., Inc., 1998-2000. Chmn. E. Mich. Environ. Action Council, 1974-78; pub. mem. inland lakes and streams rev. com. Mich. Dept. Natural Resources, 1975-76. Served as 2d lt. AUS, 1957. Fellow Am. Acad. Matrimonial Lawyers (pres. Mich. chpt. 1991-92), Am. Coll. Family Trial Lawyers, Am. Bar Found., Internat. Acad. Matrimonial Lawyers, Mich. Bar Found; mem. ABA, Am. Judicature Soc., Am. Arbitration Assn. (panel arbitrators), State Bar Mich. (chmn. family law com. 1968-72, mem. rep. assembly 1972-78, chmn. rules and calendar com. 1977-78, mem. family law sect. coun. 1973-76, environ. law sect. coun. 1980-85, prepaid legal svcs. com. 1973-82, com. on judicial selection 1974, com. on specialization 1976-82), Detroit Bar

Assn. (chmn. family law com. 1966-68), Oakland County Bar Assn., Delta Upsilon (chmn. trustees, alumni chpt. dep. 1965-70), Tau Beta Pi, Pi Tau Sigma, Phi Eta Sigma. Clubs: Detroit Athletic, Birmingham (Mich.) Athletic. Episcopalian. Home: 32965 Outland Trl Bingham Farms MI 48025-2555 Office: Meyer Kirk Snyder & Lynch PLLC Ste 100 100 W Long Lake Rd Bloomfield Hills MI 48304-2773 Business E-Mail: gsnyder@meyerkirk.com.

SNYDER, GLENN HERALD, political science educator, writer; b. Superior, Wis., Oct. 8, 1924; s. Herald Arthur and Alma Pauline (Hillestad) S.; m. Otty Verhoogh, Jan. 21, 1951; children: Abigail, Jared, Adam. BS, U. Oreg., 1948; MA, Columbia U., 1953, PhD, 1956. Reporter Wall St. Jour., N.Y.C., 1949-51; tchg. fellow Wesleyan U., Middletown, Conn., 1953-55; rsch. assoc., lectr. Columbia U., N.Y.C., 1955-58; rsch. assoc. Princeton (N.J.) U., 1958-60; from asst. to assoc. prof. Univ. Denver, 1960-62; vis. assoc. prof. U. Calif., Berkeley, 1962-1964; from assoc. prof. to prof. SUNY, Buffalo, 1964-84; prof. U. N.C., Chapel Hill, 1984-1991, prof. emeritus, 1991—. Chmn. bd. Ctr. for Internat. Conflict Studies, Buffalo, 1965-82. Author: Deterrence and Defense, 1961, Stockpiling Strategic Materials, 1967, Alliance Politics, 1997; co-author: Strategy, Politics, and Defense Budgets, 1962, Conflict Among Nations, 1977. 2d lt. U.S. Army, 1943-45. Grantee NSF, 1969-76; fellow The Wilson Ctr., 1981-82, Guggenheim Found., 1990-91. Mem. Am. Polit. Sci. Assn., Triangle Inst. Security Studies. Avocations: music (piano), golf. Home: 750 Weaver Dairy Rd Apt 163 Chapel Hill NC 27514-1482 Business E-Mail: gsnyder1@email.unc.edu.

SNYDER, GRAYDON F. religion educator; b. Peru, Ind., Apr. 30, 1930; s. Clayton Fisher and Irene Elizabeth (Fisher) S.; m. Lois Hannah Horning, June 13, 1953; children: Jonathan Edvard, Anna Christine, Stephen Daniel. BA, Manchester Coll., North Manchester, Ind., 1951; MDiv, Bethany Theol. Sem., Chgo., 1954; ThD, Princeton Theol. Sem., 1961. Asst. prof. Bibl. studies Bethany Theol. Sem., Chgo., 1959-65, prof. Oak Brook, Ill., 1965-79, dean, 1975-86, Wieand prof. N.T. studies, 1979-86; acad. dean, prof. N.T. Chgo. Theol. Sem., 1986-90, prof. N.T., 1990-96, adj. prof. N.T., 1996-99. Mem. accrediting commn. Assn. Theol. Schs., 1976-82. Author: Ante Pacem, 1985, First Corinthians, 1992, Health and Medicine in the Anabaptist Tradition, 1995, Inculturation of the Jesus Tradition, 1999, Irish Jesus, Roman Jesus, 2002, Ante Pacem, rev. edit., 2003; mem. editl. bd. Bibl. Rsch., 1965-95, Brethren Life and Thought, 1962-94. Mem. Bd. Edn. # 88, Elmhurst, Ill., 1970-73; chmn. bd. trustees Bethany Hosp., Chgo., 1979-92; del. governing bd. Nat. Coun. Chs., 1986-91. Fellow Westar Inst.; mem. Soc. Bibl. Lit., Chgo. Soc. Bibl. Rsch. (pres. 1969), Studiorum Novi Testamenti Societas. Mem. Ch. of The Brethren. Avocation: early christian art. Home: 5475 S Ridgewood Ct Chicago IL 60615-5314 E-mail: graydonsny@aol.com.

SNYDER, HELEN DIANE, state senator; Project/event mgr.; Rep. senator dist. 15 N.Mex. State Senate. Mem. corps. and transp., Indian and cultural affairs coms. N.Mex. State Senate. Office: NMex State Senate State Capitol Mail Rm Dept Santa Fe NM 87503 Home: 7006 Elna Ct NE Albuquerque NM 87110-1408 E-mail: senate@state.nm.us.

SNYDER, HERB, state legislator; b. Winchester, Va., Sept. 7, 1953; m. Stephanie Shaffer; children: Jason, Rod, Terra, Mariah, Herb II, Joseph. BS, Shepherd Coll. Mem. W.Va. Senate, Charleston, 1997—. Mem. banking and ins. com., energy com., industry and mining com., health and human resources com., govt. orgn. com., judiciary com., natural resources com. Chmn. Jefferson County Solid Waste Authority, 1991-96; mem. Jefferson County Commn., 1991-96. Mem. Farm Bur., Ruritans. Democrat. Methodist. Office: WVa Senate 1900 Kanawha Blvd E Rm 221W Charleston WV 25305-0009 also: PO Box 400 Great Cacapon WV 25422-0400

SNYDER, JACK L. international relations educator; Past dir. Inst. War & Peace Studies Columbia U., past chmn. dept. polit. scis., 1997-2000, prof., 1982—. Office: Columbia Univ Dept of Polit Scis 420 W 118th St New York NY 10027-7213

SNYDER, JAMES P. audio and digital television engineer, videographer, editor; Student, George Washington U., 1982-84; cert. AM broadcast tech., No. Va. Community Coll., 1986; BA in Comm. and Visual Media, Am. U., 1993; BA in CLEG, 1993. Prodn. asst. Sta. WIPB-TV, Muncie, Ind., 1980-84; prodn./engring. asst., bd. operator Sta. WBST-FM, Muncie, 1982-83; chief engr. Sta. WRGW, Washington, 1982-84; technician George Washington U., Marvin Ctr., Washington, 1982-87; engring. asst. Sta. WPFW-FM, Washington, 1984-85; ops. dir. Stas. WAMU/WVAU-FM, Washington, 1985-86; founder, dir. Sta. WRGW Radio/TV, Washington, 1984-87; mng. dir. Sta. WRGW-AM-FM, Washington, 1986-87; news/tech. dir. Sta. WVAU-AM/FM, Washington, 1990; adminstrv. asst. Sullivan & Cromwell, Washington, 1985-92; libr. asst. Paul, Weiss, Rifkind, Wharton & Garrison, Washington, 1989; asst. to the acad. counselor Sch. Communication, Am. U., Washington, 1990-91, sr. asst. to the acad. counselor, 1991; technician, projectionist CAS Media Ctr., 1989-96; chief engr. Am. TV & WVAU Radio, 1990-98; ops. coord. internat. program sales Discovery Channel Inc., 1994; engr. and HDTV editor Advanced Television Test Ctr., 1995-96; engr. Fox News Washington Bureau, 1996-98; ops. dir. Unity Motion High Definition System, 1998; Digital TV engring. specialist, studio course lectr. Harris/PBS DTV Express, 1998-99; cons. Digital TV, 1995—; Digital TV engring. specialist, studio course lectr. PBS DTV Strat. Svs. Group, 2000—02; sr. video engr. Intelsat, Ltd., 2003—. Freelance engr., TV/HDTV prodn. specialist, ops. specialist, videographer, editor, 1991—; founding mem. Am. U. CATV/Fiber Optic Systems Com., 1991; engring. cons. digital and high definition TV David Sarnoff Rsch. Ctr., Model HDTV Sta. WHD TV Inc., PBS Adv. TV Field Test Project, Turner Engring., Unity Motion HDTV Satellite Svc., PBS Digital TV Strategies Svcs. Group, Advanced TV Tech. Ctr., FedNet-Fed. Network, Inc., ABC Radio Network, Caribiner Internat, News Corp., 1995—; freelance engr. Reuters Television, 1996—; digital TV cons., 1995—. Audio-visual dir. Planned Parenthood of East-Cen. Ind., Muncie, 1982-83; George Washington U. coord. D.C. Spl. Olympics Superdance, 1984-85; bd. dirs. Vol. Clearinghouse of D.C. Student Network, Rosslyn, Va., 1985. Recipient Cert. Appreciation Planned Parenthood of East-Cen. Ind., 1982, Cert. Appreciation D.C. Spl. Olympics, 1984, Cert. Appreciation Ea. Ind. Community Television, 1980. Mem. IEEE, Soc. Motion Picture and TV Engrs., Soc. Broadcast Engrs., Audio Engring. Soc., Wash. Exec. Broadcast Engrs., Soc. Cable TV Engrs. Avocations: historical research, educational advancement, collecting stamps and coins, bicycling, electronics. Office: 606 N Imboden St Ste 302 WWA Alexandria VA 22304

SNYDER, JEAN MACLEAN, lawyer; b. Chgo., Jan. 26, 1942; d. Norman Fitzroy and Jessie (Burns) Maclean; m. Joel Martin Snyder, Sept. 4, 1964; children: Jacob Samuel, Noah Scot. BA, U. Chgo., 1963, JD, 1979. Bar: Ill. 1979, U.S. Dist. Ct. (no. dist.) Ill. 1979, U.S. Ct. Appeals (7th cir.) 1981. Ptnr. D'Ancona & Pflaum, Chgo., 1979-92; prin. Law Office of Jean Maclean Snyder, Chgo., 1993-97, 2004—; trial counsel The MacArthur Justice Ctr. U. Chgo. Law Sch., 1997—2004, of counsel, 2004—. Contbr. articles to profl. jours. Mem.: Lawyers for the Creative Arts (bd. dirs. 1995—97), ACLU of Ill. (bd. dirs. 1996—99), ABA (mem. coun. on litigation sect. 1989—92, editor-in-chief Litigation mag. 1987—88, co-chair First Amendment and media litigation com. 1995—96, co-chair sect. litigation task force on gender, racial and ethnic bias 1998—2001, standing com. on strategic comms. 1996—2001). Office Phone: 773-285-5100. Business E-Mail: jean_snyder@law.uchicago.edu.

SNYDER, JED C. foreign affairs specialist; b. Phila., Mar. 24, 1955; s. David and Lynn S. BA, Colby Coll., 1976; MA, U. Chgo., 1978, postgrad., 1978—79. Rsch. asst. U. Chgo., 1979; asst. rschr. Pan Heuristics divsn. R & D Assocs., Marina del Rey, Calif., 1979-80, assoc. rschr., asst. divsn. mgr., 1980-81, cons., 1982-83, Sci. Applications, Inc., 1979-81, Rand Corp., Santa Monica, Calif., 1979-81, Los Alamos (N.Mex.) Nat. Lab., 1984; sr. spl. asst. to dir. Bur. of Politico-Mil. Affairs, Dept. State, Washington, 1981-82; rsch. assoc. Internat. Security Studies Program, Woodrow Wilson Internat. Ctr. for Scholars, Smithsonian Instn., Washington, 1982-84; dep. dir. nat. security studies Hudson Inst., 1984-87; sr. rsch. fellow Nat. Strategy Info. Ctr., 1988-90; mgr. internat. strategic planing MPRI, Inc., 1997-2000; sr. nat. security advisor Dyncorp, 2001—02; sr. analyst CNA Corp., 2002—; cons. Strategic Planning and Internat. Affairs, Washington, 2002—. Cons. Rand Corp., 1983—88; founder, chmn. Washington Strategy Seminar, 1984—90, pres., corp. dir., 1984—93; appointee v.p. Bush's Adv. Task Force on Mid-East, 1987—88; cons. Office of Sec. of Def., 1988—92; apptd. supervisory rsch. prof., sr. fellow and team leader Inst. for Nat. Strategic Studies Nat. Def. U., 1992—97. Contbr. articles on U.S. fgn. policy and mil. def. to profl. publs. Trustee Kents Hill (Maine) Sch., 1987-92. Guest scholar Sch. Advanced Internat. Studies, Johns Hopkins U., 1982-83; fellow U. Chgo., 1979, Inter-Univ. Seminar on Armed Forces and Soc., 1980, MacArthur Sr., 1985-86, Herman Kahn, 1985-86, Smith Richardson, 1987-88, John M. Olin, 1987-88; selected as a Young Am. Leader, Am. Coun. on Fed. Republic of Germany, 1984. Mem. Internat. Inst. for Strategic Studies, Royal United Svcs. Inst., U.S. Naval Inst., Fgn. Policy Rsch. Inst., Coun. on Fgn. Rels. Office: Strategic Planning and Internat Affairs 1718 M St NW 197 Washington DC 20036-4504 Office Phone: 703-824-2225. E-mail: snyder7@attglobal.net.

SNYDER, JOEL BENNETT, engineering executive, educator; b. N.Y.C., Feb. 4, 1936; s. Sol and Anne (Bernstein) S.; m. Harriet Brenda Polinsky, Aug. 11, 1957; children: Eileen Schneyman, Jeffrey, Sharon Jones. BEE, Poly. Inst. Bklyn., 1956, MSEE, 1964. Registered profl. engr., N.Y.; chartered engr., U.K. Mathematician and programmer IBM, N.Y.C., 1956-58; engr. Airborne Instruments Lab., Melville, N.Y., 1958-60; sr. project engr. Harman Kardon, Plainview, N.Y., 1960-63; ptnr. Snyder Assocs., Plainview, N.Y., 1963—. Sr. industry prof. Poly. U., Bklyn., 1984-99; spkr. in field; bd. dirs. Motiontronics for Sci., N.Y.C., 1990—, Multimedia for Sports, N.Y.C., 1995—, Internet Golf Multimedia, N.Y.C., United Engring. Found., N.Y.C., 2002—, Homeland Security Industries Assn., 2003–. Editor: Data Systems Engineering Magazine, 1970; patentee video play counting techniques, 1986; contbr. numerous articles to profl. jours. Recipient George Gronner award Mid-Island Y, Plainview, N.Y., 1987, Achievement award Engrs. Joint Coun., 1998. Mem. IEEE (citation of honor, 1979, Centennial medal, 1984, Gruenwal award, 1994, Millennium medal 2000, Larry K. Wilson Transnat. award 1999, pres. elect 2000, pres. 2001, v.p. prof. activities 1995-96, region 1 dir. 1992-93), Alumni Assn. Poly. U., Bklyn. (dedicated alumnus award 1989, disting. alumnus award, 2002, life. dir.). Office: Snyder Assocs 58 Diamond Dr Plainview NY 11803-2120 Office Phone: 516-349-1555. E-mail: jbsnyder@snyderassoc.com., j.snyder@ieee.org.

SNYDER, JOHN EDWARD, JR., education educator; b. Ft. Meade, Md., Aug. 20, 1963; s. John Edward and Wanda June Snyder; m. Jennifer Lynn Yauch, Jan. 30, 1999. BA, Ft. Lewis Coll., Durango, Colo., 1988; MA, U. N.Mex., 1991, PhD, 1999. Asst. prof. Pacific U., Forest Grove, Oreg., 1998—99; asst. prof., math. and computer info. sys. Sul Ross State U., Alpine, Tex., 1999—2003, assoc. prof., chmn. dept. computer sci. and math., 2003—. Home: 505 N 3d St Alpine TX 79830-3603 Office: Sul Ross State U Box C-18 Alpine TX 79831

SNYDER, JOHN GORVERS, lawyer; b. Boston, June 20, 1960; s. Philip Francis and Sylvia (Gorvers) S.; m. Hinda Mala Simon, July 8, 1984; children: Monica Paige, Kimberly Blaine. BA, Johns Hopkins U., 1982; JD, Cornell U., 1987. Bar: Mass. 1988, U.S. Dist. Ct. Mass. 1989. Assoc. banking law, bus. law and corp. law dept. Craig and Macauley P.C., Boston, 1987—94, ptnr. banking law, bus. law and corp. law dept., 1995—2000; sr. v.p. and gen. coun. Simon Cos., LP, Braintree, Mass., 2000—. Lectr. New England Coll. Fin., 1994-2000. Active Combined Jewish Philanthropies, Boston, 1991—, Anti-Defamation League, Boston, 1993-94, Buckingham, Browne & Nichols Sch. Annual Fund, 1999-. Mem. Mass. Bar Assn., Boston Bar Assn., Phillips Exeter Acad. Alumni Assn., Phi Alpha Delta Internat., Omicron Delta Kappa (Johns Hopkins U. chpt., pres. 1981-82), Delta Upsilon (Johns Hopkins U. chpt.). Avocations: golf, tennis. Home: 7 Laurus Ln Newton Center MA 02459-3138 Address: The Simon Cos LP Attn: John G Snyder SVP 639 Granite St Braintree MA 02184-2605

SNYDER, JOHN JACOB, researcher; b. Harrisburg, Pa., USA, Sept. 21, 1946; s. John Jacob and Evelyn R. (Gutshall) Snyder. BA., Dickinson Coll., 1968; MA., U. of Deleware, 1976. Hist. rsch. Loise Steinman Von Hess Found., Columbia, Pa., 1975—78; cons. arch. hist. Hist. Preservation Trust of Lancaster County, 1978—83, rsch. cons., 1983—. Bd. mem. James Buchanan Found., Lancaster, Pa., 1976—92, Heritage Ctr. Museum, Lancaster, Pa., 1988—97. Co-author: Clocks of Lancaster County, Clocks of Berks County; contbr. articles to jour. Pres. Rock Ford Found., Lancaster, Pa., 1992—94, chmn. Acquisitions com., 1994—. Mem.: Hist. Soc. York County, Hist. Soc. Perry County, Hist. Soc. Lancaster County, Hist. Soc. Chester County, Hist. Soc. Berks County. Republican. Lutheran. Home and Office: PO Box 40 1938 Water St Washington Bord PA 17582

SNYDER, JOHN MICHAEL, lobbyist, public relations director; b. Kingston, N.Y., Dec. 18, 1939; s. John Ignace and Agatha (Flick) S.; m. Ling-Ling Woo, Jan. 1, 1996. BA, Georgetown U., 1961, MA, 1968. Legis. sec. U.S. Ho. of Reps., Washington, 1964-65; assoc. editor The Am. Rifleman, Washington, 1966-74; chief lobbyist, dir. publs. and pub. affairs Citizens Com. for Right to Keep and Bear Arms, Washington, 1975—; mgr. Telum Assoc. LLC, 2003—. Author: (book) Gun Saint, 2003—; editor: (newsletter) Point Blank, 1974—; editor: (Capitol Hill editor) Gun Week, 1986—. Active Arlington County Rep. Com., 1994-2002. Recipient Grand Knighthood award Order of Michael the Archangel, 1988, Cicero award Nat. Assn. Federally Licensed Firearms Dealers, 1996. Mem. Am. Fedn. Police (nat. v.p. pub. rels. 1989—), Nat. Assn. Chiefs of Police (v.p. pub. affairs 1995—, v.p. Washington Liaison 2000—), Second Amendment Found. (treas. 1986—), St. Gabriel Possenti Soc. Inc. (pres. 1989—), Sr. Power Campaign Com. (treas. 2001-), Coun. for Am. (dir.), The Asia Soc., Internat. Platform Assn., Kiwanis Internat., Coun. for Am. (bd. dirs.), Nat. Press Club, Capitol Hill Club. Republican. Roman Catholic. Avocations: swimming, bicycling, reading, movies, theater. Home: PO Box 2844 Arlington VA 22202 Office: Citizens Com Right to Keep and Bear Arms 1090 Vermont Ave NW Ste 800 Washington DC 20005-4961 E-mail: gundean@aol.com., john0849@aol.com.

SNYDER, JOSEPH JOHN, editor, historian, author, lecturer, consultant; b. Aug. 27, 1946; s. Joseph John and Amy Josephine (Hamilton) S.; m. Sally Hale Walker, July 4, 1973; children: Lauren Elizabeth, Brian Joseph Seth. BA in Anthropology, George Washington U., 1968; MA in Anthropology, U. N.Mex., 1973. With U.S. CSC, Washington, 1974-77; editor, writer U.S. Nat. Pk. Svc., Harpers Ferry, W.Va., 1977-81; cons. editor Early Man mag., Evanston, Ill., 1978-83; spl. project editor Sea Power Mag., 1986-87, cons. editor, 1987—, Jour. Archaeoastronomy, 1987—. Freelance writer, 1978—; pres. Sta. at Shepherdstown Inc., 1992-2000; pres., chmn. bd. dirs., Atlantic & Pacific High Speed Railway, Inc., 1993—; lectr. Maya archaeology Norwegian-Caribbean Lines, Miami, Fla., 1982; cons. in field. Author: Kenneth Westcott James Transport Menu Collection, 1998, A.D. 2025: Transportation in America, 1995, Musings from a New Manse, 1999, The Phaistos Disc, A Commentary, 1999, Fragments of My Fleece, 2000, 1859: Turning Point of the Modern Era, 2001; editor: The Only Fight the Cops Could Not Stop, 1998; book rev. assoc. editor: Athena Rev., 1999—; contbr. articles to popular mags. Pres. Tourism Found., Inc., 1996—99, Duffield Sta., Inc., 2003—; chmn. pks. com. Neighborhood Planning Adv. Group Croydon Pk., Rockville, Md., 1980—81; bd. dir. Agrl. R&D Orgn., 1985—; v.p. bd. dir. Hagerstown (Md.) Roundhouse Mus., 1989—91, Hagerstown-Washington County Conv. and Visitors Bur., 1993—96, sec., 1993—96. With U.S. Army, 1969—71, Vietnam. Decorated Bronze Star. Mem.: Nat. Ry. History Soc., Nat. Geog. Soc. (cons. 1987—), Am. Com. to Advance Study of Petroglyphs and Pictographs (editor), Hakluyt Soc., Coun. Md. Archaeology, Internat. Assn. Torch Clubs, James Rumsey Torch Club (pres. 1997—99, 2003—), Navy League of U.S. (pres. Frederick-Hagerstown coun. 1993—). Democrat. Home: 106 Ashley Dr Shepherdstown WV 25443-9767 Office Phone: 304-876-3208. Personal E-mail: sws2@earthlink.net.

SNYDER, KATHLEEN THERESA, state agency administrator; b. Balt., Oct. 8, 1951; children: Jay, Matt, Carrie. BS, U. Md., 1973; MS, Am. U., 1978. Info. specialist Prince George's Pub. Sch., 1981—84, exec. v.p. adv. coun., 1984—87; exec. v.p. Prince George's Md. Chamber, 1987—92; pres., CEO Alexandria (Va.) Chamber, 1992—99, Md. C. of C., 1999—. V.p. Va. Assn. C. of C., 1996—99; bd. mem. Am. C. of C. Execs., 2000—01; pres. Mo. Assn. Ch. Execs., 2003. Mem. Scholarship Fund Alexandria, 1994—99; founding bd. First Night Alexandria, 1994—99; chair employers adv. com. Alexandria Works, 1996—99. Named Chamber Exec. of Yr., Va. Assn. Chamber Execs., 1996, Bus. Woman of Yr., Alexandria Commn. on Women, 1996, Cert. Chamber Exec., Am. C. of C. Execs., 2000, Md. Top 100 Women, 2001, 2003; recipient Brotherhood/Sisterhood award, Nat. Conf. Christians and Jews Prince George's chpt., 1992. Office: Md C of C Ste 100 60 West St Annapolis MD 21401

SNYDER, L. MICHAEL, hospital administrator; b. May 10, 1935; BA, Brown U., 1957; MD, Chgo. Med. Sch., 1962. Dir. hematology-blood bank St. Vincent Hosp., Worcester, Mass., 1968-86, chair dept. lab. medicine, 1986-91; chair dept. hosp. labs. U. Mass. Med. Ctr., Worcester, 1991-98, U. Mass. Meml. Health Care, Worcester, 1998—. Contbr. numerous articles and abstracts to profl. publs. and confs., including New Eng. Jour. of Medicine, Biochimica et Biophysica Acta, Brit. Jour. Haematology, Am. Soc. Hematology meetings, Internat. Soc. Exptl. Hematology meetings. Office: U Mass Meml Med Ctr 365 Plantation St Ste 200 Worcester MA 01605 Business E-Mail: snyderm@ummhc.org.

SNYDER, LEE DANIEL, historian, educator; b. Waterbury, Conn., June 4, 1933; s. Clermont Jennings and Ethel Bentley Snyder; m. Anna Hopkins Givens, June 3, 1961; children: Rebecca Claire, Timothy Clermont. BA, Williams Coll., 1951—55; MDiv, Union Theol. Sem., N.Y.C., 1959—61; PhD, Harvard U., 1955—66. Ordained elder United Meth. Ch., 1961. Asst. prof. Ithaca Coll., NY, 1963—64, Ohio Wesleyan U., Delaware, Ohio, 1964—69; prof. history New Coll. of Fla., Sarasota, 1969—2003, prof. emeritus, 2004—. Elder N.Y. Conf. United Meth. Ch., N.Y.C., 1961—98; dir., medieval/renaissance studies New Coll. of Fla., Sarasota, 1982—2004. Author: (scholarly monograph) Macro-History, A Theoretical Approach to Comparative World History; contbr. articles to scholarly jours. Danforth Grad. fellow, 1955-63, Fulbright grantee, Mainz, Germany, 1956-57, NEH Summer Seminars and Insts. scholar, Nat. Humanities Found., 1978, '81.'85, '89, '91, '94. Fellow: Internat. Soc. for Comparative Study of Civilizations; mem.: Am. Soc. Ch. History, Medieval Acad. Am. Home: 941-46th St Sarasota FL 34234 Office Phone: 941-355-4513. E-mail: lsnyder@ncf.edu., lldsnyder@aol.com.

SNYDER, LEWIS EMIL, astrophysicist, educator; b. Ft. Wayne, Ind., Nov. 26, 1939; s. Herman Lewis and Bernice (McKee) S.; m. Doris Jean Selma Lautner, June 16, 1962; children: Herman Emil, Catherine Jean. BS, Ind. State U., 1961; MA, So. Ill. U., 1964; PhD, Mich. State U., 1967. Research assoc. Nat. Radio Astronomy Obs., Charlottesville., Va., 1967-69; prof. astronomy dept. U. Va., Charlottesville, 1969-73, 74-75; vis. fellow Joint Inst. for Lab. Astrophysics, U. Colo., Boulder, 1973-74; prof. astronomy dept. U. Ill., Urbana, 1975—, chair astronomy dept., 2002—. Co-editor: Molecules in the Galactic Environment, 1973; contbr. articles to sci. jours. NASA-Am. Soc. Engring. Edn. summer fellow, 1972, 73; Alexander von Humboldt Found. sr. U.S. scientist award, 1983-84. Mem. AAAS, Astron. Soc. Pacific, Am. Phys. Soc., Am. Astron. Soc., Internat. Astron. Union, Union Radio Scientifique Internationale, Alexander von Humboldt Assn. Am. Lutheran. Office: U Ill 1002 W Green St Urbana IL 61801-3074

SNYDER, LIZA, actress; b. Northampton, Mass., Mar. 20, 1968; Appeared in T.V. movie Race Against Time: The Search for Sarah, 1996; T.V. series Sirens, 1993, Jesse, 1998-2000, Yes, Dear, 2000-; T.V. guest appearance Chgo. Hope, 1996; Film appearance in Pay it Forward, 2001. Office: William Morris Agency One William Morris Pl Beverly Hills CA 90212

SNYDER, MARION GENE, lawyer, former congressman; b. Louisville, Jan. 26, 1928; s. M. G. and Lois (Berg) S.; 1 son, Mark; m. Patricia C. Robertson, Apr. 10, 1973; 3 step-children. LLB cum laude, Jefferson Sch. Law, Louisville, 1950; JD, U. Louisville, 1969. Bar: Ky. bar 1950, D.C. bar 1970. Practiced law, Louisville, 1950-76; ret.; farmer, 1957-80; city atty., 1953-57; magistrate 1st dist. Jefferson County, 1957-61; real estate broker, 1949—; mem. 88th Congress from 3d Ky. Dist., 1963-65, 90th-99th congresses from 4th Ky. Dist., 1967-87, ret., 1987; sole practice, 1987-91. V.p. Ky. Magistrates and Commrs., 1958. Vice pres. Jeffersontown Civic Center, 1953-54; pres. Lincoln Republican Club Ky., 1960-61, 1st Magisterial Dist. Rep. Club, 1955-57. Mem. Ky. Bar Assn., Ky. Farm Bur., Ky. Real Estate Brokers, Lions, Optimists (prs. Jeffersontown club 1957-58), Jesters, Shriners, Masons. Home: 383 Juli Fe Dr Naples FL 34110-1123

SNYDER, MARK JEFFREY, financial consultant, actuary; b. Bklyn., May 16, 1947; s. Milton A. and June (Freed) S.; m. Gloria Carol Beskin, May 31, 1969; children: Chad Alan, Heather Lynn. B of Engring. Sci., SUNY, Stony Brook, 1969. CLU; chartered fin. cons.; registered fin. planner. Ins. agt. Mass. Mut. Life Ins., Holbrook, N.Y., 1971-79; dist. mgr. Guardian Life Ins. Co., Port Jefferson, N.Y., 1979-81; v.p. pensions Exec. Planners, Ronkonkoma, N.Y., 1981-84; pres. CAS Adv. Services, Inc., Patchogue, N.Y., 1984-93; mng. exec. Integrated Resources Equity Corp., Patchogue, 1986-89, Royal Alliance Assocs., Inc., Patchogue, 1990—; pres. Snyder Fin. Svcs., Patchogue, 1986-91, Snyder Kresh Pension Svcs. Inc., Patchogue, 1989-97, Snyder Kresh Fin. Svcs., Inc., Medford, N.Y., 1990-98, Mark J. Snyder Fin. Svcs., Medford, 1998—. Speaker in field. Moderator, host Moneywise, Brookhaven Cable TV, Port Jefferson Sta., N.Y., 1987-88; host. WLIM Radio program; contbr. articles to profl. jours. Mem. South Setauket (N.Y.) Civic Assn., 1972—, Three Village Dem. Club, Setauket, 1984—; bd. dirs., pres. Suffolk Estate Planning Coun., 1991-92; chmn. planned giving com. Suffolk County coun. Boy Scouts Am., 1985-87, 93—, mem. exec. bd. 1985—, v.p. 94—, mem. trust com., 1989-98, chmn. Boy Scouts Am. endowment devel. trust com., 1985-87, 93—; v.p. Suffolk County Coun.; pres. SUNY at Stony Brook Alumni Assn., 2000—. Named one of top 300 fin. planners in the country, Worth mag., 1998, top 250, 1999, 2001; named to Rsch. Mag. Advisor Hall of Fame; recipient top 250, Worth mag., 2002. Mem. Soc. Fin. Svcs. Profls.Registered Fin. Planners L.I. (bd. dirs., pres. 1986-87), Pension Forum L.I. (bd. dirs., chmn. pub. rels. 1986-88), Rotary Internat., KP. Democrat. Jewish. Avocations: racquetball, swimming. Office: Royal Alliance Assocs Inc 1731 N Ocean Ave Medford NY 11763-2649

SNYDER, MARK STEVEN, theater educator; b. Fort Waayne, Ind., Jan. 14, 1950; s. Dudley Eugene and Norma Jean Snyder; children: Christopher Steven, Sarah Jane. PhD, U. of Mo., Columbus, 1997—99; MFA, Fla. Atlantic U., Boca Raton, 1999—2001; MA Theatre, Miami U., 1995—97; BA Theatre, Purdue Univ., Fort Wayne, Ind., 1990—95; BA English, Ind. U., Fort Wayne, Ind., 1989—95. Cert. Acting HB Studios, 1969, Stella Adler Studio, NY, 1971, Grotowski Workshop, NY, 1999, Suzuki Acting Northwestern U., Ill, 2000. Owner & master tchr. Actors Studio Boca, Boca Raton, 2001—; prof. of theatre Palm Beach CC, 1999—2003, New World Sch. of the Arts, Miami, 1998—2003, Broward CC, Davie, Fla., 1999—2002; dir. & master acting tchr. Tom Arnold Acting Workshop, Ottumwa, Iowa, 1998—; instr. U. of Mo., Columbia, 1998—2001; dir. and instr. Miami U., Oxford, Ohio, 1995—98. Author: (non-fiction) Directing The Glass Menagerie: A Metatheatrical Approach; dir.: (stage play) Gertrude Sterin and A Companion, Six Characters in Search of an Author, (choreographer) (stage musical) CHESS, COMPANY, Cabaret, Les Miserables, (stage play) A Winters Tale, The Blue Room, (choreographer) (stage musical) Man of LaMancha (Mabry Best Play, 2002), (stage play) The Balcony (Best of the Best: Miami Festival, 2002); author: (non-fiction) Tennessee Williams in Key West; dir.: (stage play) Stop Kiss, (choreographer) (stage musical) Forever Plaid, (stage play) Vieux Carre (Best Rediscovered Play. Wiliams Festival, 2003), (choreographer) (stage musical) Jeckyl and Hyde, (stage play) Translations (Eugene Turner Award, 2003), La Turista, Beirut (Critics Choice: South Fla., 1999), Tenness See Williams One Acts (Best Dir. Summer Shorts. Captiva, Fla., 1999), (choreopgrapher) (stage musical) Fiddler On the Roof, (choreographer) The Fantastiks; author: (non-fiction) The Musical in American Theatre History; dir.: (stage play) The Birthday Party, Clothes for a Summer Hotel, The Glass Menagerie (Best Play of Season, 1997), Dutchman, Endgame, Moon for the Misbegotten, All In The Timing; actor: As You Like It, Mamas Hung You In The Closet. . . ., (stage

musical) HAIR; dir.: (stage play) Small Craft Warnings; actor: Wonderful Tennessee, Prometheus Bound, The Imaginary Invalid, A Nightingale Sang in Berkely Square, (stage musical) West Side Story, Gypsy, (stage play) Merry Wives of Windsor, Piaf, Our Town; author (play adaptation). (stage play) Six Characters In Search of an Author; dir.(choreographer): (stage musical) The Rocky Horror Picture Show, (stage play) Sweet Bird of Youth, Wozeck, (choreographer) (stage musical) Stop the World I Want to Get Off, (stage play) Suddenly Last Summer. New theatre devel. Boca Fine Arts, 2000—02; membership com. ACLU; diversity in tchg. So. Poverty Law Ctr.; activist writer Amnesty Internat.; com. mem. Dem. Nat. Party; mem. Sierra Club, Greenpeace, World Wildlife Fund. Recipient Summa Cum Laude, Miami U., 1998, Prof. of the Yr., New World Sch. of the Arts, 2000, Asst. Prof. of the Yr., Palm Beach CC, 2001, 2002; fellow Moscow Art Theatre Fellowship, Nat. Endowment for the Arts, 2001. Mem.: Speech Comm. Assn., The Ibsen Soc., Actors Equity, Soc. of Stage Directors and Choreographers (assoc.), Am. Theatre in Higher Edn. (assoc.), Theatre Comm. Group, NY Drama Club. Democrat-Npl. Achievements include research in Tennessee Williams Undiscovered Plays; nationally recognized scholar on playwright Tennessee Williams. Avocations: sailing, book collecting, film, swimming, gourmet cooking. Office: Actors Studio Boca 154 NW 16th Street Boca Raton FL 33432 E-mail: actorstudioboca@aol.com.

SNYDER, NATHAN, entrepreneur; b. Hartford, Conn., Oct. 7, 1934; s. Saul and Betsy (Wand) S.; m. Geraldine Wolff, Dec. 27, 1964; children: Hannah Abigail, Alexander Lowell Wolff. AB, Harvard U., 1956; LLB, Columbia U., 1963; postgrad. in bus., NYU, 1967-68. Bar: N.Y. 1963. Assoc. Paul, Weiss, Rifkind, Wharton & Garrison, N.Y.C., 1963-66, v.p., sec. Randolph Computer Corp., Greenwich, Conn., 1966-69, exec. v.p., gen. counsel, bd. dirs., 1969-73; exec. v.p., chief operating officer BanCal Tri-State Corp. (holding co. Bank of Calif.), San Francisco, 1974-76; v.p. acquisitions CBS Inc., N.Y.C., 1976-87; pres. VS & A Communications Ptnrs., N.Y.C., 1987-89, The Snyder Co., New Canaan, Conn., 1989—. Lectr. of mgmt. Golden Gate U., San Francisco, 1974-76, Annenberg Sch. Comms., Phila., 1982-87; bd. dirs. First Eagle Funds, N.Y.C. Editor: Columbia Law Rev., 1962-63. Vol. legal services Office Econ. Opportunity, 1963; bd. dir. S.W. Regional Planning Agy. Served to lt. USNR, 1956-60. Harlan Fiske Stone scholar, 1964-65 Mem. Harvard Club (N.Y.C.), Harvard Club (v.p. Fairfield County).

SNYDER, PATRICIA DI BENEDETTO, theater director and administrator; BA in English and Speech Edn., SUNY, Albany, 1967; MA in Theater Arts, Syracuse U., 1967; PhD in Arts and Humanities, NYU, 1991; DPub. Svc. (hon.), Sage Colls. Tchr. English, speech and drama West Genesee Sr. High Sch., Camillus, N.Y., 1962-64; tchr. English and drama, chair humanities teaching team Chestnut Hill Mid. Sch., Liverpool, N.Y., 1964-66; grad. asst. Syracuse (N.Y.) U., 1966-67; instr. dept. theatre SUNY, Albany, 1967-74, spl. asst. to chancellor, adj. assoc. prof. dept. theatre, 1974-75, founder, producing dir. Empire State Youth Theatre Inst., 1975-92; exec. dir. Gov. Nelson A. Rockefeller Empire State Plz. Performing Arts Ctr. Corp., 1982-89; producing dir., CEO N.Y. State Theatre Inst. Corp., 1992—. Cons. Spanish and Portuguese Mins., Madrid and Lisbon, 1968, U.S. Office Edn. 1979, Spanish Min. Culture, 1982, Time Warner, Inc., 1991; mem. edn. bd. Saratoga Performing Arts Ctr., 1973; apptd. arts and humanities planning com. N.Y. State Edn. Dept., 1975; mem. arts task force on arts in edn. NEH, 1977; apptd. N.Y. State Edn. Commr.'s Adv. Coun., 1978; panelist U.S. Children;s Lit. Assn., 1978; del. UNESCO Conf., Sibenek, Yugoslavia, 1979; lectr. Syracuse U., 1988; mem. acad. coun. Richard Porter Leach Fund for Arts, 1989; adj. prof. theatre Russell Sage Coll., 1992.; lectr. and presenter in field. Prodr. (stage prodns.) The Wizard of Oz, 1977, Lancashire Lad, 1980, Sleeping Beauty, 1981, 83, 90, Handy Dandy, 1985, Rag Dolly, 1986, Aladdin, 1987, Hizzoner!, 1988, 89, Beauty and the Beast, 1991, Slow Dance on the Killing Ground, 1993 (Best dir. theatre N.E. Metroland for '94); exec. prodr. (CD) Atlantic Theatre, A Tale of Cinderella, 1995; stage and video dir. A Tale of Cinderella, 1995; contbr. articles to profl. jours. Guest fellow Hungaraian Theatre Inst., 1970, USSR Min. Culture, 1970, 84; recipient Mayor's medal City of Milan, Italy, 1977, Spl. Recognition award John F. Kennedy Ctr. for Performing Arts, 1978, 81, Recognition award NATAS, 1986, Albany League Arts award, 1986, Spl. Recognition award N.Y. State Theatre Edn Assn., 1993, silver award Worldfest, 1996, cert. merit Chgo. Internat. Film Festival, 1996. Mem. Am. Theatre Assn. (commn. on theatre devel. 1976, Spl. Recognition citation 1973, 74, Jennie Heiden award 1985), Children's Theatre Assn. Am. (Zeta Phi Eta award 1972), League Am. Theatres and Prodrs., Soc. State Dirs. and Choreographers, Assn. Internat. du Theatre pour l'Enfants et al Jeunesse (del. 1968, 70, 74, 78, 79 congresses, exec. com. 1969, fundraiser 1972 conf., editor ofcl. report 1973, chair U.S. ctr. 1977), N.Y. Women in Film and TV, N.Y. League Profl. Theatre Women, U. Albany Alumni Assn. (Disting. Alumni award 1987), Cosmopolitan Club, Phi Delta Kappa. Home: 722 N Broadway Saratoga Springs NY 12866-1621 Office: NY State Theatre Inst PO Box 28 Troy NY 12181-0028

SNYDER, PETER M. medical educator, medical researcher; BA in Biology summa cum laude, Luther Coll., 1984; MD, U. Iowa, 1989. Diplomate Am. Bd. Internal Medicine, Am. Bd. Cardiovasc. Disease. Resident in internal medicine U. Tex., Dallas, 1989—92; fellow in cardiovasc. diseases Dept. Internal Medicine U. Iowa Hosp. & Clinics, Iowa City, 1992—96, asst. prof. Dept. Internal Medicine, 1996—2000, assoc. prof. internal medicine and physiology and biophysics, 2000—. Contbr. articles to profl. jours. Recipient Clinician Scientist award, 1996, Katz Basic Sci. award, 1998; fellow Student Rsch., U. Iowa, 1985, Student, Am. Heart Assn., 1987—88. Mem.: ACP, Alpha Omega Alpha. Achievements include research in sodium channel structure and function. Office: U Iowa Coll of Medicine Dept Internal Medicine 200 Hawkins Dr Iowa City IA 52242-1009

SNYDER, RICHARD GERALD, research scientist, administrator, educator, consultant; b. Northampton, Mass., Feb. 14, 1928; s. Grant B. and Ruth (Putnam) S.; m. Phoebe Jones, March 2, 1949; children: Dorinda, Sherrill, Paul, Jeff, Jon, David. Student, Amherst Coll., 1946-48; BA, U. Ariz., 1956, MA, 1957, PhD, 1959. Diplomate Am. Bd. Forensic Anthropology. Tchg. asst. dept. anthropology U. Ariz., Tucson, 1957-58, assoc. rsch. engr. Applied Rsch. Lab., Coll. Engring., 1958-60, mem. staff Ariz. Transp. and Traffic Inst., 1959-60, assoc. prof. sys. engring., 1960; chief phys. anthropology Civil Aeromed. Rsch. Inst. FAA, Oklahoma City, 1960-66, rsch. pilot, 1962-66, acting chief Protection and Survival Labs., 1963-66; mgr. biomechanics dept. Office Automotive Safety Rsch. Ford Motor Co., Dearborn, Mich., 1966-68, prin. rsch. scientist, 1968; assoc. prof. anthropology U. Mich., Ann Arbor, 1968-73, prof., 1973-85; rsch. scientist Hwy. Safety Rsch. Inst. U. Mich. Trans. Rsch. Inst., Ann Arbor, 1968—85; head biomed. dept. U. Mich., Ann Arbor, 1969-84, dir. NASA Ctr. of Excellence in Man-Vehicle Syss., 1984-85, prof. emeritus, 1985—, rsch. scientist emeritus, 1989—, named chair, R.G. Snyder disting. prof. indsl. and ops. engring, 2004—; pres. Biodynamics Internat., Tucson, 1986—. Pres., bd. dirs. George Snively Rsch. Found., 1992-98; assoc. prof. sys. engring. U. Ariz., 1960; adj. assoc. prof. U. Okla., 1963; rsch. assoc. Zoller Lab., U. Chgo., 1964-65, rsch. assoc. dept. anthropology, 1965-67; assoc. prof. Mich. State U., East Lansing, 1967-68; cons. USAF Aerospace Med. Rsch. Labs., Nat. Acad. Scis., U.S. Dept. Transp., adv. com. Office Naval Rsch. Dept. Navy, numerous others. Assoc. editor Jour. of Comm., 1961-63; cons. editor Jour. Biomechanics, 1967-81;mem. editl. bd. Product Safety News, 1973—; adv. bd. Aviation Space and Environ. Medicine, 1980-91, 94—; mem. editl. rev. bd. Stapp Car Crash Jour., 2001-03; contbr. chpts. to books and numerous articles to profl. jours. Judge Internat. Sci. Fair, Detroit, 1968; mem. coun. Explorer Scouts, Ann Arbor, 1968-70; dir. Am. Bd. Forensic Anthropology, 1978-84, 85-91; dir. Snell Meml. Found., 1990—; bd. dirs. N.Mex. Rsch. Inst., 1996-2000. 1st lt. USAF, 1949-54, Korea. Decorated Disting. Flying Cross, 3 Air medals; recipient Met. Life award Nat. Safety Coun., 1970, Admiral Luis de Flores Flight Safety award Flight Safety Found., 1981; named to Safety and Health Hall of Fame Internat., 1993, Ariz. Aviation Hall of Fame, 1998. Fellow AAAS, Aerospace Med. Assn. (Harry G. Moseley award 1975, Profl. Excellence award 1978, John Paul Stapp award in aerospace biomechanics 1994), Royal Anthrop. Inst., Am. Anthrop. Assn., Am. Acad. Forensic Scis. (T. Dale Stewart award 1992), Soc. Automotive Engrs. (Arch T. Colwell Merit award 1973, Aerospace Congress award 1982, Tech. Contbns. to Air Transport Safety), Explorers Club; mem. AIAA (assoc. fellow), Ariz.-Nev. Acad. Sci., Internat. Soc. Aircraft Safety Investigators, Aerospace Physiologists Soc., Sigma Xi, Beta Beta Beta. Republican. Congregationalist. Avocations: aviation, aerospace medicine, forensic anthropology. Home: 3720 N Silver Dr Tucson AZ 85749-9709 Office: Biodynamics Internat Tucson AZ 85749

SNYDER, ROBERT JOHN, lawyer; b. Phila., June 2, 1952; s. Robert John and Lilja (Anderson) S. BA cum laude, St. John's U., 1974; JD, U. N.D., 1977. Bar: N.D. 1977, Minn. 1977, U.S. Dist. Ct. N.D. 1977, U.S. Ct. Appeals (8th cir.) 1982, U.S. Supreme Ct. 1982. Ptnr. Coles & Snyder, Chartered, Bismarck, ND, 1977—89, Wheeler, Wolf, Bismarck, ND, 1989—93, Snyder Coles Lawyers, Bismarck, ND, 1993—99, Snyder Law Office, Bismarck, ND, 1999—. Judge, Bismarck Teen Ct., 1999—; alt. bd. dirs. Legal Aid N.D., Bismarck, 1982-84. Vol. Bismarck United Way, 1979; active talking book S.D. State Program for Handicapped, Pierre, 1983-84. Named one of Outstanding Young Men of Am., 1979. Mem. ABA, Assn. Trial Lawyers A., N.D. Bar Assn. (com. revision o pattern jury instrns. 1981, revision code of profl. responsibility 1983-87), Internat. Platform Assn., Mensa, Intertel. Bismarck Jaycees (outstanding officer 1979, Outstanding Young Bismarcker 1985), Apple Creek Country Club, Elks, Ky. Cols., Porsche Club Am., St. Legal Motorcycle Club. Office: Snyder Law Office PO Box 1321 Bismarck ND 58502-1321 E-mail: snyhunt@btinet.com.

SNYDER, ROBERT LYMAN, materials scientist, educator; b. Plattsburgh, N.Y., June 5, 1941; s. George Michael and Dorothy (Lyman) M.; m. Sheila Nolan, Sept. 1, 1963; children: Robert N., Kristina M. BA, Marist Coll., 1963; PhD, Fordham U., 1968. Postdoctoral fellow NIH U. Pitts., 1968; NRC fellow NASA Elec. Rsch. Ctr., Cambridge, Mass., 1969; asst. prof. ceramic sci. Alfred (N.Y.) U., 1970-77, assoc. prof., 1977-83, prof., 1983-96, dir. Inst. Ceramic Superconductivity, 1987-96; prof., chmn. dept. materials sci. and engring. Ohio State U., Columbus, 1996—2002; prof., chmn. Sch. Materials Scis. and Engring. Ga. Inst. Tech., Atlanta, 2003—. Vis. prof. Lawrence Livermore (Calif.) Lab., 1977, 78, U.S. Nat. Bur. Stds., Gaithersburg, Md., 1980, 81, Siemens AG Ctrl. Rsch. Labs., Munich, 1983, 91; invited prof. U. Rennes, France, 1995. Author: Introduction to X-Ray Powder Diffractometry, 1996; author, editor 8 books; contbr. chpts. to books and over 220 articles to profl. jours. Deputy mayor Village of Alfred, 1973-77; pres. Alfred Vol. Fire Co., 1979-88. Recipient Chancellor's award SUNY, 1980, numerous research grants; named Faculty Exch. scholar SUNY, 1978-96. Fellow Am. Ceramic Soc. (Outstanding Educator award 1999), Am. Soc. Metals, Internat. Ctr. Diffraction Data; mem. TMS (Leadership award 2002), NAS (U.S. nat. com. on crystallography 1991-95, Codata 2001—), Nat. Inst. Ceramic Engrs., Am. Crystallography Assn. (chmn. applied crystallography div. 1988-92), Materials Rsch. Soc., Ceramic Ednl. Coun., Internat. Ctr. Diffraction Data (bd. dirs. 1986-92, elected chmn. bd. dirs. 1996-2000), Internat. X-ray Analysis Soc. (pres. 2000-2001), Edward Orton Jr. Ceramic Found. (bd. dirs. 1996—), Alfred and Allegany County Fire Assn., Sigma Xi, Phi Kappa Phi. Democrat. Achievements include numerous patents for practical superconductors. Office: Ga Inst Tech Sch Materials Sci and Engring Atlanta GA 30332-0245 Home: 195 14th St NE Ste 1 Atlanta GA 30309-2682 Office Phone: 404-894-2888.

SNYDER, ROGER ALAN, physician, neurologist; b. Phila., Apr. 8, 1939; s. Harry Z. and Ida Snyder; m. Margaret Zemel, June 23, 1962 (div. Apr. 1996); children: Richard Owen, Karen Dana. AB, Harvard Coll., 1961; MD, U. Pa., 1965. Diplomate Am. Bd. Psychiatry and Neurology. Intern, med. resident U. Rochester, 1965-67; rsch. assoc. NIH, 1967-70; neurology resident U. Pa., 1970-73; fellow Mass Eye and Ear Infirmary, 1972; clin. instr. Georgetown U. Med. Ctr., Washington, 1974-76, clin. asst. prof., 1976—. Bd. dirs. N.Va. chpt. Am. Heart Assn., 1979-83. Fellow Am. Acad. Neurology; mem. Harvard Alumni Assn. (dir. 1990-93), Harvard Club (Washington, pres. 1986-88). Avocations: sailing, tennis. Office: 8316 Arlington Blvd Ste 602 Fairfax VA 22031-5216

SNYDER, SID, state legislator, retail executive; b. Kelso, Wash., July 30, 1926; m. Bette Kennedy, 1951; children: Sid Jr., Karen, Sally. Student, Lower Columbia C.C. Grocer, owner, operator Sid's Supermarket, Seaview, 1953—; mem. Wash. Senate, Dist. 19, Olympia, 1990—; dep. sec. senate Wash. Senate, Olympia, 1988, sec. senate, 1969-88, asst. chief clk., 1957-69; Dem. majority leader; mem. agr. and rural econ. devel. com.; mem. natural resources com.; mem. parks and recreation com.; mem. rules com.; mem. ways and means com.; mem. econ. and rev. forest coun.; mem. oral history adv. bd. Chmn. bd. dirs. Bank of the Pacific; ptnr. Westwind Manor Long Beach; bd. dirs. Columbia Bank. Hon. bd. dirs. Ilwaco Heritage Mus.; bd. dirs. Long Beach Peninsula Info. Ctr., Wash. State Hist. Soc., Columbia River Maritime Mus. With USAR, WWII. Democrat. Office: 311 Legislative Bldg Olympia WA 98504-0001

SNYDER, SOLOMON HALBERT, psychiatrist, pharmacologist; b. Washington, Dec. 26, 1938; s. Samuel Simon and Patricia (Yakerson) S.; m. Elaine Borko, June 10, 1962; children: Judith Rhea, Deborah Lynn. MD cum laude, Georgetown U., 1962, DSc (hon.), 1986, Northwestern U., 1981; PhD (hon.), Ben Gurion U., 1990; DSc (hon.), Technion Inst., 2002, Mt. Sinai Med. Sch., 2004. Intern Kaiser Found. Hosp., San Francisco, 1962-63; rsch. assoc. NIMH, Bethesda, Md., 1963-65; resident psychiatry Johns Hopkins Hosp., Balt., 1965-68; assoc. prof. psychiatry and pharmacology Johns Hopkins Med. Sch., 1968-70, prof., 1970-77, disting. svc. prof. psychiatry and pharmacology, 1977-80, disting. svc. prof. neurosci., psychiatry, and pharmacology, 1980—, dir. dept. neurosci., 1980—. Wellcome disting. prof. U. Wash., 1999; lectr. in field. Author: Uses of Marijuana, 1971, Madness and the Brain, 1973, Opiate Receptor Mechanisms, 1975, The Troubled Mind, 1976, Biologic Aspects of Mental Disorder, 1980, Drugs and the Brain, 1986, Brainstorming, 1989; editor Perspectives in Neuropharmacology, 1971, Frontiers in Catecholamine Research, 1973, Handbook of Psychopharmacology, 1974; contbr. articles to profl. jours. Served with USPHS, 1963-65. Recipient Outstanding Scientist award, Md. Acad. Scis., 1969, John Jacob Abel award, Am. Pharmacology Soc., 1970, A.E. Bennett award, Soc. Biol. Psychiatry, 1970, Gaddum award, Brit. Pharm. Soc., 1974, F.O. Schmitt award in neuroscis., MIT, 1974, Rennebohm award, U. Wis., 1976, Stanley Dean award, Am. Coll. Psychiatrists, 1978, Lasker award, 1978, Wolf prize, 1983, Dickson prize, 1983, Sci. Achievement award, AMA, 1985, Ciba-Giegy-Drew award, 1985, Strecker prize, 1986, Edward Sachar Meml. award, Columbia U., 1986, Sense of Smell award, Fragrance Rsch. Found., 1987, J. Allyn Taylor prize, 1990, Pasarow Found. award, 1991, Bower award, Achievement Sci. Franklin Inst., 1991, Joseph Priestley prize, Dickinson Coll., 1992, Baxter award, Am. Assn. Med. Colls., 1995, Bristol-Myers-Squibb Neurosci. prize, 1996, City of Medicine award, 2000, Gerard prize, Soc. Neurosci., 2000, Salmon medal, 2001, Lieber prize, NARSAD, 2001, Disting. lectr., U. Tex., Houston, 2002, Presdl. lectr., Sloan-Kettering Cancer Inst., N.Y., 2002, Goldman-Rakie prize, NARSAD, 2003. Fellow: Am. Philos. Soc., Am. Acad. Arts and Scis., Am. Psychiat. Assn. (Hofheimer award 1972, Disting. Svc. award 1989, Judd Marnor award 2000), Am. Coll. Neuropsychopharmacology (Daniel Efron award 1974); mem.: Inst. Medicine, Am. Pharmacology Soc., Am. Soc. Biol. Chemists, Soc. for Neurosci. (pres. 1979—80, Presdl. lectr. 2000, History of Neurosci. lectr. 2001), Nat. Acad. Scis. (Sarnat prize in mental health 2001). Home: 3801 Canterbury Rd Unit 1102 Baltimore MD 21218-2379 Office: Johns Hopkins U Med Sch Dept Neurosciences 725 N Wolfe St Baltimore MD 21205-2105 Office Phone: 410-955-3024.

SNYDER, SUSAN LEACH, science educator, writer; b. Columbus, Ohio, Nov. 25, 1946; d. Russell and Helen Marie (Sharpe) Leach; m. James Floyd Snyder, June 18, 1988. BS in comprehensive sci. edn., Miami U., 1968; MS in entomology, U. Hawaii, 1970. Gen. and health sci. tchr. Columbus Pub. Schs., 1971-73; life, earth & physical sci. tchr. Upper Arlington (Ohio) Schs., 1975—2000. Author: The Ocean Environment, 1992, 96; co-author: Focus on Earth Science, 1987, 89, Merrill Earth Science, 1993, 95. Glencoe Earth Science, 1997, 99, 2002, The Air Around Us, 2002, The Changing Surface of Earth, 2002, The Water Planet, 2002; mem. author team: Science Interactions, 1993, 95, 98, Science Voyages, 2000, 2001, Glencoe Science, 2002, 2003, Integrated Science, 2003; contbr. articles to profl. jours. Trustee N.Am. Astrophys. Obs., Delaware, Ohio, 1983-97; pres. Consortium of Aquatic and Marine Educators Ohio, 1983-84; sec. Ohio chpt. Nat. Tchrs. of Yr., 1993-95; docent, vol. Conservancy of S.W. Fla. Mus. Natural History, 2000—. Named Outstanding Earth Sci. Tchr. of State of Ohio and East Cen Sect. Nat. Assn. Geology Tchrs., 1983, Ohio Tchr. of Yr. Ohio State Dept. Edn., 1987, Finalist Nat. Tchr. of Yr. Coun. of Chief State Sch. Officers, 1987; Pres. award for Excellence in Sci. and Math Teaching Nat. Sci. Tchrs. Assn., 1992, Outstanding Tchr. award Geological Soc. Am., 1992. Mem. Nat. Sci. Tchrs. Assn. (Exemplary Earth Sci. Teaching Team 1983, 84, 85, conf. workshop presenter 1985), Nat. Marine Educators Assn. (Nat. Outstanding Marine Sci. Tchr. 1984-85, bd. mem. 1984, hist. com. chair, 2000—, conf. workshop presenter 1983, 84, 86, 92), Great Lakes Educators of Aquatic and Marine Scis. Avocation: photography. Home: 1361 Marlyn Dr Columbus OH 43220-3973

SNYDER, TERESA ANN, medical/surgical nurse; b. Evansville, Ind., Mar. 4, 1946; d. Stephen Michael and Fredricka Otilia (Memmer) Kurtz; m. James Howard Snyder, June 12, 1976; children: Katrina Michelle, Jacqueline Sue. Diploma, Lakewood (Ohio) Sch. Practical Nursing, 1965; BSN, U. Akron, 1989. Emergency room nurse Parma (Ohio) Community Hosp.; cardiac nurse Cleve. Clinic Found.; neuro-sci. and med.-surg. nurse Akron (Ohio) City Hosp. Acting mem., corr. sec., pres. Summa Nursing Senate, Summa Health Care, Akron City Hosp. V.p. Chatham Vol. Fire and Rescue Assn. Mem. Acad. Med. Surg. Nurses (bd. dirs. N.E. chpt.), N.E. Ohio chpt. Acad. Med. Surg. Nursing (gen. bd. mem., exec. bd. dirs., pres. elect 2001-2002, pres. 2002—), Nat. Acad. of Med. Surg. Nurses (regional dir.-elect 2002—), Sigma Theta Tau. Home: 10145 Shaw Rd Spencer OH 44275-9306

SNYDER, THOMAS J. automotive company executive; With Delco Remy divsn. of GM Corp., 1962 94, product mgr. heavy duty systems, pres., CEO, dir. Delco Remy Internat., Inc., Anderson, Ind., 1994—. Bd. dirs. St. John's Health Systems. Office: Delco Remy Internat Inc 2902 Enterprise Dr Anderson IN 46013

SNYDER, VIC, congressman, physician; b. Medford, Oreg., Sept. 27, 1947; m. Betsy Singleton. BA in Chemistry, Willamette U., 1975; MD, U. Oreg. Health Scis. Ctr., 1979; JD, U. Ark., Little Rock, 1988. Resident family practice U. Ark. Med. Scis., 1979-82; physician family practice Ark., 1982—; mem. Ark. State Senate, 1991-96, U.S. Ho. Reps. from 2d Ark. dist., 1997—; mem. armed svc. com., veterans affairs com. Med. missions to Cambodian regufee camps, Thailand, El Salvadoran regufee camps, Honduras, mission hosp., Sierra Leone, Africa, Ethiopian refugee camp, Sudan. With USMC, 1967-69. Democrat. Methodist. Office: 1330 Longworth House Office Bl Washington DC 20515-0402 also: 3118 Fed Bldg 700 W Capitol Ave Little Rock AR 72201-3225 E-mail: snyder.congress@mail.house.gov.

SNYDER, WALLACE S. advertising association executive, lawyer; m. Jean Magnuson; 2 children. BA, JD, U. Iowa. Bar: D.C. From trial atty. to assoc. dir. Fed. Trade Commn., assoc. dir.; from sr. v.p. to pres., CEO Am. Advt. Fedn., Washington, 1985—92, pres., 1992—, CEO, 1992—, gen. counsel, 1989—. Bd. dir. The Ad Coun., The Am. Advt. Fedn. Found., The Advt. Edn. Found., Nat. Advt. Rev. Coun. With U.S. Army. Mem.: ABA, Fed. Bar Assn. Office: American Advertising Federation 1101 Vermont Ave NW Washington DC 20005-6306

SNYDER, WILLARD BREIDENTHAL, lawyer; b. Kansas City, Kans., Dec. 18, 1940; s. N.E. and Ruth (Breidenthal) S.; m. Lieselotte Dieringer, Nov. 10, 1970 (dec. Nov. 1975); 1 child, Rolf; m. T.J. Sewall, May 17, 1996. BA, U. Kans., 1962, JD, 1965; postgrad., Hague Acad. Internat. Law, The Netherlands, 1965-66, U. Dijon, France, 1966; grad., Command and Gen. Staff Coll., Ft. Leavenworth, Kans., 1977. Bar: Kans. 1965, Mo. 1986, U.S. Tax Ct. 1977, U.S. Ct. Mil. Appeals 1981, U.S. Dist. Ct. Kans. 1965, U.S. Supreme Ct. 1977. Atty., Kansas City, 1970-80, 85—; trust officer, corp. trust officer Security Nat. Bank., Kansas City, 1980-83, corp. sec., 1983-85; pres. Real Estate Corp. Inc., Leawood, Kans., 1984—; adv. dir. United Mo. Bank, 1985-90. Bd. dirs. Blue Ridge Bank, mem. trust com. Bank Holding Co., 1991—; German Consul (H) for Kans., Western Mo., 1972—. Active Platte Woods (Mo.) City Coun., 1983-84; bd. govs., pres. Liberty Meml. Assn.; past pres. MacJannett Found., Talloires, France; chmn. Breidenthal-Snyder Found.; nominating and exec. com. Hoover Pres. Libr.; bd. dirs., dir. Unicorn Theatre, 1998-2004, KCKs Cmty. Found.; trustee St. Mary Coll., 1998-2001; bd. regents Rockhurst U.; bd. dirs. Wy. Co. Kans. Cmty. Found., Kansas City Metro Crime Com; trustee Navy SEAL Mus., Ft. Pierce, Fla.; vol. Kansas City Cmty. Kitchen. Col. inf., ret. USAR & KARNG. Decorated Bundesverdienst Kreuz Ikl Bundeswehr Kreuz (silver), Bundeswehr Kreuz (gold)(Germany); Legion of Merit; KARNG medal of excellence; named to Hon. Order Ky. Cols.; recipient Golden Honour badge German Vet. Orgn., Bavaria, 1988, Mil. Order of WW award; named to OCS Hall of Fame. Mem. Mo. Bar Assn., Kansas City Bar Assn., Kansas City Hosp. Attys., Mil. Order of World Wars (chpt. comdr. 1983-84, regional comdr. 1987-91, Patrick Henry award), Nat. Eagle Scout Assn. Avocations: scuba, hunting, notgeld collections, cartridge collection. Office: 8014 State Line Rd Ste 203 Shawnee Mission KS 66208-3712 Personal E-mail: wbs11@mindspring.com.

SNYDER, WILLIAM BURTON, insurance company executive; b. Clarksburg, W.Va., July 9, 1929; s. William Burton and Mary Catherine (Cornwell) Snyder; m. Georgie Gaye, Oct. 27, 1951 (dec.); children: William Burton, Melissa Ann. BBA in Acctg. cum laude, Tex. Tech U., 1955. With Travelers Ins. Co., 1955-77, v.p., 1970-77; with Govt. Employees Ins. Co., Washington, 1977-93; chmn., pres., CEO GEICO Corp., 1985-93; gen. ptnr. Merastar Ptnr. LLP, 1993—2004; chmn. bd. dirs. Auto Body Am., Inc., 2004—. Bd. dirs. Doctor's Preferred, Inc.; mem. adv. bd. Riggs Nat. Bank. Dir. Nat. Capital Area coun. Boy Scouts Am. Capt. USAF, 1950—53. Decorated Air medal. Mem.: Nat. Assn. Ind. Insurers (hon.; past chmn.), Kenwood Country Club (Bethesda, Md.). Republican. Baptist.

SNYDER, WILLIAM T. university chancellor; Chancellor, now chancellor emeritus U. Tenn., Knoxville, Tenn., 1992—. Office: Univ of Tenn Office of Chancellor 533 Andy Holt Tower Knoxville TN 37996-0001

SNYDER, WILLIAM W. corporate financial executive; m. Valerie Snyder; 2 children. BSBA, M in Accountancy, U. Mo. CPA. With pub. acctg. Deloitte & Touche; v.p., controller, v.p. leasing and adminstrn. promoted to sr. v.p., chief info. officer Fleet Svs.; corp. contr. Enterprise Rent-A-Car, 1984—89, asst. v.p., 1989, v.p., v.p. fleet adminstrn., 1994, v.p. info. sys., 1995, sr. v.p., chief info. officer, 1998, sr. v.p., 2002—03, CFO, 2002—, exec. v.p., 2003—. Office: Enterprise Rent-A-Car 600 Corporate Park Dr Saint Louis MO 63105*

SNYDERMAN, NANCY, surgeon, medical journalist; m. Doug Snyderman; 3 children. PhD in medicine, U. Nebr. Med. Sch. Cert. otolaryngology U. Pitts., UMDA. Resident in pediatrics and ear, nose, and throat surgery U. Pitts.; dir. head and neck surgery U. Ark. Med. Scis., 1983—87; surgical practice Calif. Pacific Med. Ctr., San Francisco, 1988—; med. corr. Good Morning Am., 1987—2003, 20/20, 1987—2003, ABC News, 1987—2003; v.p. med. affairs corp. staff Johnson & Johnson, 2003—. Contbr. to med. jour.; author: Dr. Nancy Snyderman's Guide to Good Health for Women Over Forty, Necessary Journeys, Girl in the Mirror: Raising Adolescent Daughters. Mem.: Am. Acad. of Otolaryngology Head and Neck Surgery (bd. dirs.). Achievements include reporting on med. topics affecting both men and women; traveled and reported extensively from Eastern and Western Europe, Saudi Arabia during Persian Gulf War, Russia, Somalia, Kosovo, Pakistan, and Afghanistan. Office: Calif Pacific Med Ctr 2100 Webster St #320 San Francisco CA 94115 Office Phone: 415-923-3319. Office Fax: 415-600-7890.

SNYDERMAN, RALPH, medical educator, physician; b. Bklyn., Mar. 13, 1940; 1 child, Theodore Benjamin. BS, Washington Coll., Chestertown, Md., 1961; MD magna cum laude, SUNY, Bklyn., 1965, DSc (hon.) Health Sci. Ctr., 1996. Diplomate Am. Bd. Internal Medicine, Am. Bd. Allergy and Immunology. Intern Duke U. Hosp., Durham, 1965-66, med. resident, 1966-67; public health officer NIH, 1967-72; Howard Hughes med. investigator, asst. prof. medicine and immunology Duke U. Hosp., Durham, N.C., 1972-74, assoc. prof., 1974-77, chief divsn. rheumatology and immunology, 1975-87, prof. medicine and immunology, 1980-87, Frederic M. Hanes prof.

medicine and immunology, 1984-87, adj. prof. medicine, 1987-89; surgeon USPHS, NIH, Bethesda, Md., 1967-69; sr. staff fellow Nat. Inst. Dental Rsch., NIH, Bethesda, Md., 1969-70, sr. investigator immunology sect. lab. microbiology and immunology, 1970-72; chief divsn. rheumatology Durham VA Hosp., Bethesda, Md., 1972-75; v.p. med. rsch. and devel. Genentech, Inc., South San Francisco, Calif., 1987-88, sr. v.p. med. rsch. and devel., 1988-89; chancellor for health affairs, dean Sch. Medicine Duke U., Durham, NC, 1989—2004, James B. Duke prof. medicine, 1989—2004; pres., CEO Duke U. Health Sys., Durham, 1998—2004. Howard Hughes med. investigator, Durham, 1972-77; dir. Lab Immune Effector Function, Howard Hughes Med. Inst., Durham, 1977-87; adj. prof. medicine U. Calif., San Francisco, 1987-89. Editor: Contemporary Topics in Immunobiology, 1979, Inflammation: Basic Concepts and Clinical Correlates, 1988, 2nd edit., 1992, Medical Clinics of North America, 1997, Journ. Integrated Med., 1997, Proceedings of Amer. Physician, 1997; contbr. articles to profl. jours. Recipient McLaughlin award, 1978, Alexander von Humboldt award Fed. Republic Germany, 1985, award for lifetime achievements in inflammation rsch. Ciba-Geigy Morris Ziff, 1992, Bonazinga award Soc. for Leukocyte Biology, 1993, Disting. Alumni Achievement award SUNY Bklyn., 1995, Disting. Alumni achievement award Washington Coll., 1995, Disting. Alumni citation, 1996, Lifetime Achievement award Arthritis Found., Eastern Reg., 1997, Lifetime Achievement award Argentine Nat. Acad. Medicine, 1998, others. Mem.: NAS, Am. Acad. Arts and Scis., Soc. for Med. Adminstrs., Assn. Am. Med. Colls. (chair task force on clin. rsch. 1998, chmn. coun. deans 1999—2000, chmn. 2001—02), Am. Coll. Rheumatology, Assn. Acad. Health Ctrs., Am. Soc. for Biochemistry and Molecular Biology, Assn. Am. Physicians, Am. Fedn. Clin. Rsch., Soc. for Leukocyte Biology, Am. Assn. Cancer Rsch., Am. Acad. Allergy, Am. Soc. Clin. Investigation, Am. Assn. Immunologists, Assn. Am. Physicians (pres. 2003—04), Inst. Medicine, Sigma Xi.

SNYDERS, DIRK JOHAN, electrophysiologist, biophysicist, educator; b. Wilrijk, Antwerpen, Belgium, July 18, 1955; came to U.S., 1984; s. Godlief Stefaan and Mariette L. (Dieu) S. BS in Med. Sci., U. Antwerp, Belgium, 1976, MD with great honor, 1980. Lic. physician, cert. cardiologist, Belgium. Resident then fellow in internal medicine and cardiology Univ. Hosp. Antwerp, 1980-84; postdoctoral fellow U. Calif., San Francisco, 1984-85; instr. medicine Vanderbilt U., Nashville, 1986-87, asst. prof., 1987-95, assoc. prof. medicine and pharmacology, 1995—. With V.I.B. dept. biophysics and pharmacology Antwerp U., 1998—2003; prof. biochemistry U. Antwerp, 1998—, vice-chair dept. biochemistry, 1999—2001, chair dept. biomed. scis., 2001—, prof. biomed. scis., 2001—, vice chair rsch. coun., 2004—. Co-author: The Heart and the Cardiovascular System, 1991; mem. editorial bd. Circulation Rsch.; reviewer Jour. Gen. Physiology, Cardiovascular Rsch., Jour. Molecular and Cellular Cardiology, Molecular Pharmacology, European Jour. Pharmacology, Biophys. Jour., Jour. Biol. Chemistry; contbr. articles to profl. jours. Lt. Med. Svc., Belgian Army, 1987-88, Germany. Recipient Specia award Specia NV., Belgium, 1980; hon. fellow Belgian Am. Ednl. Found., NATO rsch. fellow, 1984, med. rsch. fellow Alta. Heritage Found., 1984; rsch. grantee NIH, Am. Heart Assn. Fellow Am. Heart Assn. (basic sci. coun.); mem. AAAS, Biophys. Soc., Soc. Gen. Physiologists, European Working Group (cardiac cellular electropmysiology bd. mem.) Achievements include research on mechanism of action of "specific bradycardiac agents", use-dependent unblocking and voltage clamp validation of modulated receptor theory (cardiac sodium channels and antiarrhythmic agents), electrophysiology and pharmacology of cloned channels molecular localisation of antiarrhythmic drug binding sites, cardiac potassium channels (including human), molecular ion channel structure-function relationships, molecular basis of congenital excitability disorders. Office: Antwerp U Dept Biomed Scis Universiteitsplein 1 T4 2160 Antwerp Belgium Address: Fazantenlaan 6 Antwerp B2610 Belgium Office Phone: 011-32-3-820-2335. E-mail: dirk.snyders@ua.ac.be.

SNYDMAN, DAVID RICHARD, infectious diseases specialist, educator; b. Phila., Sept. 23, 1946; m. Diane Canter, June 26, 1971; children: Laura Kate, Alexander Julian. BA, Williams Coll., 1968; MD, U. Pa., 1972. Diplomate Am Bd. Infectious Disease, Am. Bd. Internal Medicine. Intern New Eng. Med. Ctr., Boston, 1972-73, resident in medicine, 1973-74; asst. prof. Sch. Medicine Tufts U., Boston, 1979-84, assoc. prof., 1984-90, prof. medicine and pathology, 1990—; hosp. epidemiologist New Eng. Med. Ctr., Boston, 1979-89, 1998—, dir. clin. microbiology, 1987-98, chief divsn. infectious diseases, 1998—. Epidemic intelligence svc. officer CDC, Atlanta, 1974—76. Assoc. editor: Yearbook of Infectious Diseases, 1986-98, Yearbook of Medicine, 2003—; contbr. to 12 books; contbr. over 200 articles to profl. jours. Lt. comdr. USPHS, 1974-76. Grantee NIH, 1982-93; recipient U. Pa. A.O.J. Kelly prize, 1972, Tufts U. Sch. Medicine Zucker prize, 1998. Fellow Infectious Disease Soc. (Bristol fellow 1978-79, Ken Kaplan Clinician award Mass. chpt., 2003); mem. ACP (Tchng. and Rsch. scholar 1979-82), Soc. Hosp. Epidemiologists, Am. Soc. Transplant Physicians, Mass. Infectious Diseases Soc. (Ken Kaplan clinician 2003). Achievements include first description of Lyme arthritis; rsch. in hosp. infections, intravenous catheter-associated infections, transplant-related infectious diseases, antibiotic resistance, sepsis, cytomegalovirus prevention; developer of cytomegalovirus immune globulin. Office: New Eng Med Ctr 750 Washington St Boston MA 02111-1526 Office Phone: 617-636-5788. E-mail: DSnydman@tufts-nemc.org.

SO, EDWARD Y. computer company executive; b. Hong Kong, 1953; BSEE, U. Hawaii, 1975; MSEE, Princeton U., 1976, MA, 1977, PhD, 1979. From process engr. Livermore tech. devel. to asst. dir. Calif. tech. and mfg. Intel Corp., 1979—98, v.p., dir. Calif. tech. and mfg., 1998—. Office: Intel Corp 2200 Mission Coll Blvd Santa Clara CA 95052

SO, YUEN T. neurologist, educator; s. Wing Yee So and Yuk Wa Chan; m. Susan E. So, June 16, 1979; children: Andrew, Cynthia. BS, Northwestern U., 1974; PhD, Rockefeller U., 1979; MD, Yale U., 1983. Diplomate Am. Bd. Psychiatry and Neurology. Asst. prof. neurology U. Calif., San Francisco, 1989—94; assoc. prof. neurology Oreg. Health Scis. U., Portland, 1994—99; dir. neurology clinic Stanford U. Med. Ctr., Calif., 1999—; dir. neurology residency program Stanford U., Calif. Author over 80 chpts. and other pubs.; contbr. chapters to books. Named Outstanding Tchr., U. of Calif., San Francisco, 1993, Oreg. Health Scis. U., 1998, Stanford U., 1999. Fellow: Am. Assn. Electrodiagnostic Medicine; mem.: Am. Acad. Neurology, Am. Neurol. Assn. (hon.). Office: Stanford U Dept Neurology Stanford U Med Ctr #5235 Stanford CA 94305-5235

SOAPES, THOMAS F. archivist; b. Independence, Mo., Nov. 11, 1945; s. Lloyd Munday and Cleo A. Soapes; m. Emily Jane Williams, Sept. 6, 1980. BS in Edn., U. Mo., Columbia, 1967, MA, 1969, PhD, 1973. Archivist for planning and program Office of Presdl. Librs., Nat. Archives, Washington, 1978—89; chair archives divsn. Nat. Air and Space Mus., Smithsonian Instn., Washington, 1990—. Dir. Eleanor Roosevelt oral history project Franklin D. Roosevelt Libr., Hyde Park, NY, 1977—78; archivist, oral historian Dwight D. Eisenhower Libr., Abilene, Kans., 1973—77. 1st lt. U.S. Army, 1971—72, Vietnam. Mem.: Mid-Atlantic Regional Archives Conf., Orgn. of Am. Historians. Office: Nat Air and Space Mus Smithsonian Instn MRC 322 Washington DC 20560

SOARES, CARL LIONEL, quality assurance professional, metrologist; b. New Bedford, Mass., Sept. 14, 1944; s. Lionel Francis and Sarah Vincent (Flor) Soares; m. Jean Rosalee Bettencourt, Nov. 11, 1965 (div. Oct. 1974); children: Kevin Carl, Keith Christopher, Kenneth Craig. Student in Indsl. Tech., Fitchburg State Coll., 1980—. Quality assurance specialist Cornell-Dubilier Electronics, Inc., New Bedford, Mass., 1965-66; computer controlled test equipment technician Raytheon Co., Waltham, Quincy, North Dighton, Mass., 1966-79, quality control supt. Waltham, 1982-85, metrologist, dept. quality dir., 1979-96; pres., treas., mgr. S.&O. Cleaning Corp. d/b/a The MAIDS, New Bedford, 1995—. Chmn. bd. dirs. New Bedford Coun. Substance Abuse; rec. sec. New Bedford First Night Com.; clk. Southeastern Network; bd. dirs., mem. first night com., events chmn. Buttonwood Park Zool. Soc.; mem. Friends of Dartmouth Librs.; choir mem. St. James Ch. With USN, 1963—65. Mem.: Am. Legion. Roman Catholic. Avocations: gardening, bicycling, records and cds, computers, music. Home: 205 Maple St New Bedford MA 02740-3513 Office Phone: 508-984-0013. Personal E-mail: maidsnb@aol.com.

SOARES, JOSEPH ARLIE, sociologist, educator; s. Kenneth Anthony Soares and Elizabeth Jane Wharton; m. Felicitas Meta Maria Opwis, May 14, 2000; 1 child, Axel Leon Opwis Soares. BA, Rutgers U., Newark, 1981; MA, Harvard U., 1985, PhD, 1991. Lectr. Harvard U., Cambridge, Mass., 1991—93; asst. prof. Yale U., New Haven, 1993—99, assoc. prof., 1999—2003, Wake Forest U., Winston-Salem, NC, 2003—. Dir. of undergrad. studies Yale U., 1999—2002; cons. Brain Res., Inc., N.Y.C., 2003, Oxford U., Oxford, 2002, Dist. Atty.'s Office, Houston, 1994; grants panel reviewer U.S. Dept. Edn., Washington, 2001. Author: (academic book) Decline of Privilege (Outstanding Book of the Yr. from the Culture Sect. of the Am. Sociol. Assn., 2000), (book reviews) Am. Jour. Sociology, Contemporary Sociology, (internet web site) Social Life of American Cities; contbr. articles to profl. jours. Leadership coun. So. Poverty Law Ctr., Montgomery, Ala., 2001—04; organizer of conv. session Am. Sociol. Assn., Washington, 2003—04; minority mentor Yale U., 1992—99. Recipient De Lancey K. Jay Prize for Best Dissertation, Harvard U., 1991, Harvard-Danforth Cert. of Distinction in Tchg., 1985, Name included on Wall of Tolerance, Rose Parks and So. Poverty Law Ctr., 2001; fellow Jacob Javits fellow, U.S. Dept. of Edn., 1987—90, Krupp fellow, Ctr. for European Studies, Harvard U., 1986—87; scholar Buttenweiser scholar, Harvard U., 1983, War Meml. scholar, Rutgers U., 1981. Mem.: AAUP, Am. Sociol. Assn. (Best book 2000), Phi Beta Kappa. Avocations: billards, swimming, salsa dancing. Home: 7620 Penland Drive Clemmons NC 27012 Office: Wake Forest University PO Box 7808 Reynolda Sta Winston Salem NC 27109 Office Phone: 336-758-4986. Home Fax: 336-758-1988. Office Fax: 336-758-1988. Personal E-mail: soaresja@wfu.edu. E-mail: soaresja@wfu.edu.

SOAVE, ANTHONY, manufacturing executive; Pres., CEO Soave Enterprises, Detroit. Office: Soave Enterprises 3400 E Lafayette St Detroit MI 48207-4962

SOAVE, ROSEMARY, internist; b. N.Y.C., Jan. 23, 1949; BS, Fordham U., 1970; MD, Cornell Med. Coll., 1976. Diplomate Am. Bd. Internal Medicine, Subspecialty Bd. in Infectious Diseases. Intern, resident N.Y. Hosp., N.Y.C., 1976-79; chief med. resident Meml.-Sloan Kettering Cancer Ctr., N.Y.C., 1979-80; fellow infectious diseases N.Y. Hosp., N.Y.C., 1980-82, asst. prof. medicine, 1982-89, assoc. prof. medicine and pub. health, 1989—. Spkr. in field; mem. Nat. Insts. Allergy and Infectious Diseases-AIDS and Related Diseases Study Sect. Contbr. numerous articles to profl. jours., chpts. to books, reviews and abstracts to profl. jours. Recipient Mary Putnam Jacobi fellowship for rsch., 1981-82, Leopold Schepp Rsch. fellowship, 1983-84, Nat. Found. for Infectious Diseases Young Investigator Matching Grant award, 1984-85; NIH grantee, 1986-89, 83-86, 87-90, 99-00. Fellow ACP, Infectious Diseases Soc. Am.; mem. AAAS, Am. Fedn. Med. Rsch., N.Y. Acad. Scis., Am. Soc. for Microbiology, Harvey Soc., Sigma Xi. Office: NY Presbyn Hosp Weill Cornell Med Ctr Box 125 1300 York Ave New York NY 10021-4805

SOBCZAK, JUDY MARIE, clinical psychologist; b. Detroit, Dec. 28, 1949; d. Thaddeus Joseph and Bernice Agnes (Sowinski) Gorski; m. John Nicholas Sobczak, Aug. 17, 1974. BE cum laude, U. Toledo, 1971, PhD, 1987; postgrad., Ea. Mich. U., 1980—82. Lic. psychologist. Tchr. Ottawa (Ohio)-Glandorf Schs., 1971-73; prin., tchr. St. Mary Sch., Assumption, Ohio, 1973-77; tchr. Our Lady of Perpetual Help Sch., Toledo, 1978-79; staff psychologist Outer Dr. Hosp., Lincoln Park, Mich., 1987-90; psychologist Adult/Youth Devel. Svcs., Farmington, Mich., 1991-95, Davis Counseling Ctr., Farmington Hills, Mich., 1996—2002; with Northwestern Cmty. Svcs. (now Lifespan Clin. Svcs.), Livonia, Mich., 1996-2000, Orchard Hills Psychiat. Ctr., Plymouth, Mich., 1996-98; psychologist in pvt. practice, 2002—. Adj. asst. prof. Madonna U., Livonia, 1987-94. Eucharistic min. St. Anthony Cath. Ch., Belleville, Mich., 1991—, parish coun. 1993-96; Cath. Svc. Appeal co-chmn., 1993-96; sec. bd. dirs. Children Are Precious Respite Care Ctr., 1995; mem. Detroit Symphony Orch. Auction Com., 2003. Fellow Mich. Women Psychologists (charter, newsletter editor 1987-92, treas 1989-93, Plaque of Appreciation 1992-96, sec. 1993-97, pres.-elect 1997-98, pres. 1998-99, past pres. 1999-2000, cons. editor 1993-99); mem. APA, Mich. Psychol. Assn., Phi Kappa Phi. Home: 41498 Mckinley St Belleville MI 48111-3439 Office: 28175 Haggerty Rd Novi MI 48377 Office Phone: 248-994-7690.

SOBEHART, HELEN C, academic administrator, educator; b. Pitts., Pa., Mar. 5, 1948; d. Leonard Arthur Zaremski and Helen Olga Baric; m. Joseph A Sobehart, Jan. 25, 1969; children: Michael J, Anthony J. BA, Slippery Rock U., 1971; MS, Duquesne U., 1976; DA, Carnegie Mellon U., 1986. Learning disabilities tchr. North Hills Sch. Dist., Pitts., 1973—77; coord. of pers. devel. Alleghen Intermediate Unit, Pittsburgh, Pa., 1977—80, Inst. Support Sys. of Pa., Gibsonia, Pa., 1980—88; dir. Spl. Edn. Consortium, Greenville, Pa., 1988—90; acting. supr. Fox Chapel Area Sch. Dist., Pitts., RI, 1990—97; assoc. dir. Lab. for Student Success, Phila., 1997—98; dir. lead instr. and IDPEL Duquesne U., Phila., 1998—. Bd. mem. Edni. Policy and Issues Ctr., Pitts., 1999—, Pa. Assn. Sch. Adminstrn. Women's Caucus, Pitts., 2000—, Pa. Leadership and Devel. Ctr., Harrisburg, Pa., 2000—. Guest editor Internat. Monograph on Leadership, 2000—04; editor: Am. Assn. Sch. Adminstrn. Women's Conf., Pa. Assn. Sch. Adminstrn. Women's Caucus. Ch. lector, eucharistic min. Epiphany Ch., Pitts.; bd. v.p. Bradley Ctr. for Children and Youth, Pitts.; homeless bd. Homeless Children and Families Fund, Pitts. Recipient Goldstar award, Pitts. Coun. on Pub. Edn., 2002. Mem.: Am. Edn. Rsch. Assn., Pa. Assn. Sch. Administrators, Am. Assn. Sch. Administrators. Avocations: walking, gardening, travel, classical music. Office: Duquesne University School of Education Leadership Inst 600 Forbes Ave, 730 Fisher Hall Pittsburgh PA 15282 Business E-Mail: sobehart@duq.edu.

SOBEL, ALAN, electrical engineer, physicist; b. N.Y.C., Feb. 23, 1928; s. Edward P. and Rose (Naftalison) S.; m. Marjorie Loebel, June 15, 1952; children: Leslie Ann, Edward Robert. BSEE, Columbia U., 1947, MSEE, 1949; PhD in Physics, Poly. Inst. Bklyn., 1964. Lic. Profl. Engr., N.Y. and Ill. Asst. chief engr. The Electronic Workshop, N.Y.C., 1950-51; head, functional engr. Fairchild Controls Corp., 1951-56; project engr. Skiatron Electronics and TV Corp., 1956-57; sr. rsch. engr. Zenith Radio Corp., Glenview, Ill., 1964-78; v.p. Lucitron inc., Northbrook, Ill., 1978-87, pres., 1987; pvt. practice cons. Evanston, Ill., 1988—; v.p. Machine Vision and Control Internat. Inc., 1994—2003, LightWave Technologies Corp., 2000—. Asst., instr. Poly. Inst. Bklyn.,1957-64; mem. program coms. SID Internat. Symposium, Internat. Display Rsch. Conf., 1970—. Inventor: 14 patents on various display and electron devices; author 55 papers on electronics, physics, electronic displays, etc.; editor Jour. Soc. Info. Display, 1991—99; adv. editor Info. Display Mag., 1991-2003; assoc. editor: IEEE Trans. on Electron Devices, N.Y., 1970-77. Mem. Democratic Party of Evanston. NSF fellow, 1959, 60. Fellow Soc. Info. Display (Lewis and Beatrice Winner award 2002); mem. IEEE (sr., life), SPIE, Am. Phys. Soc., Sigma Xi. Democrat. Home and Office: 633 Michigan Ave Evanston IL 60202-2552 Business E-Mail: as1285@columbia.edu.

SOBEL, BURTON ELIAS, physician, educator; b. N.Y.C., Oct. 21, 1937; s. Lawrence J. and Ruth (Schoen) Sobel; m. Susan Konheim, June 19, 1958; children: Jonathan, Elizabeth. AB, Cornell U., 1958; MD magna cum laude, Harvard U., 1962. Intern Peter Bent Brigham Hosp., Boston, 1962-63, resident, 1963-64, 66-67; clin. asso., cardiology br. NIH, Bethesda, Md., 1964-66, 67-68; asst. prof. medicine U. Calif. at San Diego, La Jolla, 1968-71; asso. prof. medicine, dir. myocardial infarction research unit, dir. coronary care, 1971-73; asso. prof. medicine Barnes Hosp.-Washington U., St. Louis, 1973-75; adj. prof. chemistry Washington U., St. Louis, 1979-94; prof. medicine Barnes Hosp.-Washington U., 1975—, dir. cardiovascular div., 1973—, program dir. specialized ctr. rsch. ischemic heart disease, 1975-89, program dir. specialized ctr. rsch. in coronary and vascular diseases, 1990-94, program dir. principles in cardiovascular rsch., 1975-94; chmn. and E.L. Amidon prof. medicine, prof. biochemistry U. Vt., Burlington, 1994—; physician-in-chief Med. Ctr. Hosp. Vt., Burlington, 1994—; physician-in-chief Fletcher Allen Health Care, Burlington, 1995—; dir. Cardiovasc. Ctr., Fletcher Allen Health Care the U. Vt., Burlington, 2003—. Program dir. Collaborative Clin. Trial Therapy to Protect Ischemic Myocardium Washington U., 1977, prin. investigator Specialized Ctr. of Rsch. in Ischemic Heart Disease, 1975—95, program dir. Principles in Cardiovasc. Rsch., 1975—95, program dir. Nat. Rsch. and Demonstration Ctr. in Ischemic Heart Disease, 1985—95; prin. investigator BARI, II, NIH Fibrinalysis and Coagulation Core U. Vt., 2000; chmn. cardio renal drugs U.S. Pharmacopeial Conv., 1990—; bd. dirs. Scios Corp., Corvas Corp., Ariad Corp., Bristol Myers Squibb Corp., Fletcher Allen Health Care; scientific adv. bd. CV Therapeutics, Inc.; sci. adv. bd. Epix Med., Inc., New River Pharm., Inc. Assoc. med. editor: Heart Bull, 1971—72; editor: Clin. Cardiology, 1971—74; mem. circulation bd. Clin. Guides to Med. Mgmt., 1971—; editor: Clin. Guides to Med. Mgmt., 1996—, Circulation, 1983—88; cons. editor Circulation; mem. editl. bd.: Circulation Rsch., 1974—, Annals Internal Medicine, 1976—, Am. Jour. Cardiology, 1976—, Cardiology Digest, 1976—77, Jour. Clin. Investigation, 1977—, Jour. Continuing Edn. Cardiology, 1978—, Am. Jour. Physiology: Heart and Circulatory Physiology, 1978—, Cardiology in jElderly, 1991—, Current Med. Lit., —, Churchill Livingstone edtl. adv. bd.: Internat. Seminars Cardiovascular Medicine, 1978—, Cardiology in Rev., 1992—; mem. editl. bd. Internat. Jour. Cardiology, Fibrinolysis, 1986; assoc. editor: Internat. Jour. Cardiology, Fibrinolysis, 1990—, mem. editl. bd.: Current Opinion in Cardiology, —; editor, 1989—; mem. editl. bd. Can. Jour. Cardiology, 1995—, Arteriosclerosis, Thrombosis, and Vascular Biology, 1996—, Clin. Therapeutics, 1996, Clin. Insights in Diabetes, 1999, Heart Disease, 2000, Diabetes Treatment Today, 2000, Am. Jour. Geriatric Cardiology, 2000, Diabetes Care, 2002—, Current Diabetes Revs., 2004—; editor: Coronary Artery Disease, 1989—. Served to lt. comdr. USPHS, 1964—68. Recipient Career Rsch. Devel. award, USPHS, 1972, Internat. Recognition award, Heart Rsch. Found., 1981, Disting. Achievement award, Am. Heart Assn. Sci. Couns., 1984, award, Robert J. and Claire Posatow Found., 1988, Va. Heart Ctr., 1991, Drake award, Maine Heart Assn., 1992. Master: ACP, ASIM; fellow: AAAS (councilor 1997—), Am. Coll Angiology, Am. Coll. Cardiology (Disting. Scientist award 1987), Royal Soc. Medicine, Am. Heart Assn. (coun. on basic cardiovasc. scis., clin. coun., circulation and arteriosclerosis, thrombosis and vascular biology, James B. Herrick award 1992, Spl. Recognition award coun. on arteriosclerosis, thrombosis and vascular biology 1999), Molecular Medicine Soc.; mem.: Internat. Soc. Applied Cardiovasc. Biology, Soc. Exptl. Biology and Medicine (councilor 1998—, pres. bd. govs. 2002—), Assn. Profs. Cardiology (pres.-elect 1992), Internat. Soc. Fibrinolysis and Thrombolysic (councilor), Western Soc. Clin. Rsch., Cardiac Muscle Soc., Am. Physiol. Soc., Assn. Am. Physicians, Am. Soc. Clin. Investigation (councilor, instnl. rep. 1997—), Assn. Univ. Cardiologists, Am. Fedn. Clin. Rsch. (councilor), Alpha Omega Alpha. Home: 171 Lost Cove Rd Colchester VT 05446-7473 Office: Fletcher Allen-MCHV Campus Fletcher 311 Burlington VT 05401 E-mail: burt.sobel@vtmednet.org.

SOBEL, HOWARD BERNARD, osteopath, educator; b. N.Y.C., May 15, 1929; s. Martin and Ella (Sternberg) S.; m. Ann Louise Silverbush, June 16, 1957 (dec. May 1978); children— Nancy Sobel Schumer, Janet Sobel Medow, Robert; m. Irene S. Miller, June 8, 1980; stepchildren— Avner Saferstein, Daniel Saferstein, Naomi Saferstein AB, Syracuse U., 1951; D.O., Kansas City Coll. Osteopathy and Surgery, 1955. Intern Zieger Osteo. Hosp., Detroit, 1955-56; gen. practice osteo. medicine Redford Twp., Mich., 1956-74, Livonia, Mich., 1974—. Chief of staff Botsford Gen. Hosp., Farmington, Mich., 1978; mem. faculty Mich. State U. Coll. Osteo. Medicine, 1969—, clin. assoc. prof. family practice, 1973—; mem. exec. and med. adv. coms. United Health Orgn. Mich.; mem. Venereal Disease Action Com., Mich.; apptd. to asst. impaired osteo. physicians Mich., 1983 Mem. Am. Osteo. Assn. (ho. of dels. 1981—), Mich. Assn. Osteo. Physicians and Surgeons (ho. of dels.), Am. Coll. Osteo. Rheumatologists, Coll. Am. Osteo. Gen. Practitioners, Osteo. Gen. Practice Mich., Wayne County Osteo. Assn. (pres.) Jewish. Home: 6222 Northfield Rd West Bloomfield MI 48322-2431 Office: 28275 5 Mile Rd Livonia MI 48154-3944

SOBEL, HOWARD D. dermatologist; b. 1950; MD, Albert Einstein Coll. of Medicine, Bronx, NY, 1973. Cert. in Dermatologic and Cosmetic Surgery. Residency in dermatology and dermatologic surgery Emory U. Sch. Medicine, Atlanta; clin. attending physician in dermatology and dermatologic surgery Lenox Hill Hosp., Beth Israel Hosp., and Cabrini Med. Ctr.; dir. Skin and Spa Cosmetic Surgery Ctr., NY. Editor-in-chief Internat. Jour. of Cosmetic Surgery and Aesthetic Dermatology, appeared on numerous television and radio programs (including: Sally Jesse Raphael Show, Home Show, Good Day NY, CNBC, MSNBC, New York 1, and Channels 2, 4, 5, and 7 News programs). Mem.: Am. Soc. Laser Surgery, Am. Soc. Hair Restoration Surgery, Am. Soc. Liposuction Surgery, Am. Acad. Dermatological Surgery, Am. Acad. Cosmetic Surgery, Am. Acad. Dermatology. Achievements include helping to pioneer the union of dermaology with cosmetic surgery; the first surgeon in 1986 to perform liposuction using the tumescent solution purely under local anesthesia; founder and chmn. of HDS Labs, the manufacturer if DDF (Doctor's Dermatologic Formula). Avocations: skiing, tennis. Office: Skin and Spa Cosmetic Surgery Ctr 960A Park Ave New York NY 10028 Office Phone: 212-288-0060.*

SOBEL, JOEL KENNETH, economist; s. Robert and Flora Rosenbaum Sobel; m. Kathryn A. Woolard; 1 child, Benjamin. BS, U. Mich., 1974; PhD, U. of Calif., 1978. Prof. U. Calif., La Jolla, Calif., 1978—. Office: U Calif San Diego Dept Econs 0508 La Jolla CA 92093

SOBEL, MARK ESAR, pathologist, researcher; b. N.Y.C., Apr. 14, 1949; s. Abraham David and Selma Etta (Spitzer) S. BA, Brandeis U., 1970; MD, Mt. Sinai Sch. Medicine, N.Y.C., 1975; PhD in Biomed. Scis., CUNY, 1975. Diplomate Nat. Bd. Med. Examiners. Med. intern, clin. fellow in pediatrics Children's Hosp. Med. Ctr./Harvard U. Med. Sch., Boston, 1975-76; rsch. assoc. NIH, Bethesda, Md., 1976-79, 80-83; sr. investigator Nat. Cancer Inst., Bethesda, 1983-92, chief molecular pathology sect., 1992-2001; sr. exec. dir. Am. Soc. Investigative Pathology, Bethesda, 2001—. Vis. scientist Max Planck Inst. for Biochemistry, Martinsried bei Munchen, Germany, 1979-80; dir. Concepts in Molecular Biology course Am. Soc. Investigative Pathology, Rockville, Md., 1987-99. Contbr. more than 100 articles to profl. jours.; patentee in field. Capt. USPHS, 1975-2001. Recipient Commendation medal USPHS, 1989, other awards. Mem. Am. Soc. for Biochemistry and Molecular Biology, Am. Soc. Investigative Pathology (councilor 1995-97, vice pres.-elect 1997-98, v.p. 1998-99, pres. 1999-2000), Assn. for Molecular Pathology (sec.-treas. 1995-97, pres.-elect 1998, pres. 1999), Assn. Accreditation Human Rsch. Protections Programs (bd. dirs. 2001—), Phi Beta Kappa, Alpha Omega Alpha, Sigma Xi. Jewish. Avocations: classical music, english history (plantagenet and tudor periods). Office: Am Soc Investigative Pathology 9650 Rockville Pike Bethesda MD 20814-3993 Business E-Mail: mesobel@asip.org.

SOBELL, NINA R. artist; b. Patchogue, N.Y., May 4, 1947; d. Jack and Helen Ruth (Rosenberg) S.; m. Christopher Rogers Shearer, Sept. 8, 1982 (div. Mar. 1987); 1 child, Jacqueline Corianne. BFA, Temple U., 1969; MFA, Cornell U., 1971. Cert. educator N.Y. Vis. artist Calif. Inst. of the Arts, Valencia, 1975, Sch. of Architecture, London, 1976; vis. lectr. dept. art Reading (Eng.) U., 1976-77; vis. lectr. dept. design & sculpture UCLA, 1979, assoc. prof. electronic imagery, 1984-85; artist-in-residence interactive telecomm. program NYU, N.Y.C., 1991-92, artist-in-residence Ctr. Digital Multimedia, 1994—; instr. video prodn. Sch. Visual Arts, N.Y.C., 1992-93; dir. tech. integration Aux. Svc. High Schs., N.Y.C. Bd. Edn., 1994—. Artist-lectr. Documenta VII, Kassel, Germany, 1977; juror U.S. Film and Video Festival, L.A., 1984; juror media arts divsn. N.Y. State Coun. on the Arts, N.Y.C., 1994; artist-presenter Siggraph, New Orleans, 1996; resident Banff Ctr. for the Arts, 1998-99. Prin. works include installation Interactive Brainwave Drawings, 1974—, interactive installation Videophone Relay, 1977-79; artist/dir. HIV-INFO Interactive Call-In TV Show, Manhattan Pub.-Access Cable, 1992, ParkBench Pub-Access Web Kiosks, 1994—; curriculum designer Online Art Network for At-Risk Youth, N.Y.C. Bd. Edn., 1996; represented in permanent collection Mus. Modern Art, N.Y.C., Whitney Mus. Art Whitney Web Site. Installation/Lecture grantee Found. Art Resources, 1981; Installation grantee

N.Y. State Coun. Arts, 1981. Mem. Art and Sci. Collaborations, Inc., Coll. Art Assn., Assn. Ind. Video and Filmmakers, United Fedn. of Tchrs. Democrat. Jewish. Avocations: swimming, cooking, biking, birdwatching, skating. Home: 128 E Broadway # 506 New York NY 10002-6373 Office: NYU Ctr Digital Multimedia 719 Broadway Fl 12 New York NY 10003-6860

SOBELLE, RICHARD E. lawyer; b. Cleve., Mar. 18, 1935; BA, Stanford U., 1956, JD, 1960; LLM, U. So. Calif., 1967. Bar: Calif. 1961, U.S. Supreme Ct. 1969. Exec. Tracinda Corp. Mem. ABA (mem. corp., banking and bus. law sect. 1969-95), State Bar Calif. (del. to conf. state bar dels. 1965-77, mem. exec. com. bus. law sect. 1977-78), L.A. County Bar Assn. (mem. exec. coun., jr. barristers 1965-68, mem. exec. com. bus. and corps. sect. 1973-75). Office: Tracinda Corp 150 S Rodeo Dr Ste 250 Beverly Hills CA 90212-2417 Office Phone: 310-271-0638.

SOBER, DEBRA EVONNE, environmental services administrator; b. Oklahoma City, May 20, 1953; d. Donald E. and Zona E. (Taylor) Tillman; m. Gary L. Sober, May 24, 1980; children: Kara, Jeffrey, Kimberly, Riley Nicole. BS, Columbia Pacific U. Lic. water and wastewater operator; registered X-ray lab. technician; notary pub. Chmn. bd. PACE Corp., Austin, 1986—; gen. mgr. Envir-O-Spec, Inc., Austin, 1972-95; owner, pres. Environ. Tng., Inc., 1980—. Cons. B40-Gon PX-109, 1990—. Author numerous textbooks on water and wastewater treatment and operation. Founder ann. Just Fishin Show, Austin, 1989; bd. dirs. Austin Women's Soccer League, 1991-93; bd. dirs., founder Austin Amateur Soccer Assn., 1991; women's commr. Tex. State Soccer Assn. South, 1994-99, v.p., 1999— (Mem. Soccer Hall of Fame 1999); nat. cup commr. United States Soccer Fedn./U.S. Amateur Soccer Assn., Region III, 1996—. Mem. Nat. Environ. Tng. Assn., Tex. Water Utilities Assn. (chmn. pub. rels. 1981-85, safety chmn. 1987-88), Okla. Water and Pollution Control Assn., Am. Water Works Assn., Water Pollution Control Fedn., Am. Bus. Women's Assn., N.W. Adult Athletic Assn. (founder and dir. 1986), N.W. Austin Women's Basketball Assn. (founder and pres. 1986), N.W. Austin Women's Soccer Assn. (founder and pres. 1986), Beta Sigma Phi. Baptist. Office: PO Box 200815 Austin TX 78720-0815 Home: 3080 S Lakeshore Drive Saint Joseph MI 49085

SOBER, SIDNEY, retired diplomat, educator; b. N.Y.C., Nov. 12, 1919; s. Isaac and Mary (Krug) S.; m. Elizabeth Holmes Sober, Apr. 2, 1947; children: Stephen, Elizabeth (dec.). BA magna cum laude, CCNY, 1939; MA, George Washington U., 1964. Fgn. svc. officer Dept. of State, Tananarive, Prague, Reykjavik, Ankara, Bombay, 1947-63; econ. affairs South Asia, dir. regional affairs Bur. Near Ea. and So. Asian Affairs, Dept. of State, Washington, 1964-69; staff dir. Interdepartmental Regional Group for Near East and So. Asia, 1967-69; min. counselor, dep. chief of mission Am. Embassy, Islamabad, Pakistan, 1969-73, chargé d'affaires, 1972-73; sr. dep. asst. sec. state N.E. & S. Asia, frequently acting asst. sec. state Dept. of State, 1974-78; chair South Asia Seminar Fgn. Svc. Inst., Dept. of State, Washington, 1982-96. Vis. prof., adj. prof. Am. U., Washington, 1978-87; cons. Sisco Assocs., Washington, 1984-93; fgn. affairs officer Dept. of State, Washington, 1981—. Past pres. Sumner Village Cmty. Assn. Lt. (j.g.) USNR, 1944-46. Mem. Am. Fgn. Svc. Assn., Diplomatic and Consular Officers Ret., Asia Soc., Mid. East Inst., Phi Beta Kappa. Home: 10450 Lottsford Rd #5111 Mitchellville MD 20721-3302

SOBERON, PRESENTACION ZABLAN, state bar administrator; b. Cabambangan, Bacolor, Pampanga, Philippines, Feb. 23, 1935; came to U.S., 1977; naturalized, 1984; d. Pioquinto Yalung and Lourdes (David) Zablan; m. Damaso Reyes Soberon, Apr. 2, 1961; children: Shirley, Sherman, Sidney, Sedwin. Office mgmt., stenography, typing cert., East Cen. Colls., Philippies, 1953; profl. sec. diploma, Internat. Corr. Schs., 1971; A in Mgmt. Supervision, Skyline and Diablo Coll., 1979, LaSalle Ext. U., 1980-82; AA, cert. in Mgmt. and Supervision, Diablo Valley Coll. With U.S. Fed. Svc. Naval Base, Subic Bay, Philippines, 22 yrs, clerical, stenography and secretarial postitions, 1955-73, adminstrv. asst., 1973-77; secretarial positions Mt. Zion Hosp. and Med. Ctr., San Francisco, 1977, City Hall, Oakland, Calif., 1978; with State Bar Calif., San Francisco, 1978-79; secretarial positions gen. counsel divsn. and state bar ct. divsn., adminstrv. asst. fin. and ops. divsn., 1979-81; office mgr. sects. and coms. dept., profl. and pub. svcs., 1981-83; appointment adminstr. office of bar rels., 1983-86; adminstr. state bar sects. bus. law sect., estate planning, trust and probate law sect., labor and employment law sect., office of bar rels., 1986-89; adminstr. antitrust and trade regulation law sect., labor and employment law sect., workers' compensation sect., edn. and meeting svcs., 1989-96; adminstr. criminal law sect., 1996—; labor and law employment law sect., 1996—; internat. law sect., 1996—; workers' compensation sect., 1996—; edn. and meeting svcs., 1996-98; ret., 1998. Disc jockey, announcer Radio Sta. DZYZ, DZOR and DWHL, Philippines, 1966-77. Organizer Neighborhood Alert Program, South Catamaran Circle, Pittsburg, Calif., 1979-80. Recipient 13 commendation certs. and outstanding pers. monetary awards U.S. Fed. Svc., 1964-77, 20 Yr. U.S. Fed. Svc. cert., 1975, Nat. 1st prize award Nat. Inner Wheel Clubs Philippines, 1975, Kaiser Vol. Svc. Mem.: NAFE, Am. Soc. Assn. Execs., Our Lady Queen of the World Ch. Filipino Assn. (lectr., min.), SRF Tigers No. Calif., Castillejos Assn. No. Calif., N.Y.C. Ulongapo-Subic Bay Assn. Am. (Pitts. rep. 1982—87, bus. mgr. 1988—89, 1997—, bus. mgr. Ulo Ng Apo Assn. Am. 2003—04, pub. rels. officer 1993—94). Roman Catholic. Home: 207 South Catamaran Circle Pittsburg CA 94565-3613 Office: State Bar of Calif 180 Howard St San Francisco CA 94105-1639

SOBERON KURI, ALEJANDRO, performing company executive; Founder, chmn., CEO Corporacion Interamerica de Entretenimiento, Mexico City, 1990—. Office: CIE Corporativo Paseo de las Palmas No 1005 Col Lomas de Chapultepec 11 Mexico City Mexico

SOBEY, DAVID FRANK, food company executive; b. Stellarton, N.S., Can., Mar. 22, 1931; s. Frank Hoyse and Irene (MacDonald) S.; m. Faye B. Naugle, June 2, 1953; children: Paul David, Janis Irene Hames. D of Commerce (hon.), St. Mary's U., 1991. With Sobeys Inc., Stellarton, 1949—, store mgr., dir. merchandising and advt., v.p., exec. v.p., pres., dep. chmn., chief exec. officer, dir., 1981-85, chmn., 1985—2001, chmn. emeritus, 2001—. Mem. Order of Can., 1996; bd. dirs. Empire Co. Ltd., Sobeys Inc., Sobey Leased Properties Ltd., Crombie Properties Ltd., Sobeys Land Holdings Ltd.; chmn. The Sobey Found., Frank H. Sobey Fund for Excellence in Bus. Studies. Bd. dirs. The Sobey Art Found., Boy Scouts Can., Atlantic Salmon Fedn. Mem.: Abercrombie Golf Club, City Club (New Glasgow), Halifax Club. Office: Sobeys Inc 115 King St Stellarton NS Canada B0K 1S0

SOBEY, DONALD CREIGHTON RAE, real estate developer; b. New Glasgow, N.S., Can., Oct. 23, 1934; s. Frank Hoyse and Irene (MacDonald) S.; m. Elizabeth H. Purvis; children: Robert George Creighton, Irene Elizabeth, Kent Richard. B of Commerce, Queen's U.; LLD (hon.), Dalhousie U., 1989. Dir. Alliance Atlantis Corp., 1989—; pres. Empire Co. Ltd., 1969, chmn., 1985—; also bd. dirs. Bd. dirs. Crombie Properties Ltd., Toronto-Dominion Bank, Sobeys Inc., Trader Classified Media NV, bd. suprs.; bd. dirs. World Wildlife Found., Highliner Foods, Stora Enso Port Hawksbury. Gov. Olympic Trust Can.; patron 1986 World Congress on Edn. and Tech.; mem. Conf. Bd. Can.; found. chmn. Camp Hill Med. Ctr.; mem. Club de Rels. d'Affaires Can.-France; chair bd. dirs. Nat. Gallery Can.; bd. govs. Can. Unity Coun. Mem. Internat. Assn. for Students Econs. and Commerce. Avocations: skiing, tennis, music, art, travel. Office: Empire Co Ltd 115 King ST Stellarton NS Canada B0K 1S0

SOBEY, EDWIN J. C. museum director, oceanographer, consultant; b. Apr. 7, 1948; s. Edwin J. and Helen (Chapin) S.; m. Barbara Lee, May 9, 1970; children: Ted Wooddall, Andrew Chapin. BS, U. Richmond, 1969; MS, Oreg. State U., 1974, PhD, 1977. Rsch. scientist Sci. Applications, Inc., Boulder, Colo., 1977-79, divsn. mgr., 1979-81; exec. dir. Sci. Mus., West Palm Beach, Fla., 1981-88, Mus. Sci. and History, Jacksonville, Fla., 1988, Nat. Invention Ctr., Akron, Ohio, 1989-92, Fresno (Calif.) Met. Mus., 1993-95; ednl. cons., 1995—. Exec. dir. A.C. Gilbert's Discovery Village, Salem, Oreg., 1997-99; pres. Northwest Invention Ctr., 1999—; founder Nat. Toy Hall of Fame, 1998; instr. mus. mgmt. U. Wash., 1998-2001. Author: Complete Circuit Training Guide, 1980, Strength Training Book, 1981, (with others) Aerobic Weight Training Book, 1982, The Whole Backpacker's Catalog, 1988, Increasing Your Audience, 1989, Inventing Stuff, 1995, Wrapper Rockets and Trombone Straws-Science at Every Meal, 1996, Car Smarts, 1997, Just Plane Smart, 1998, Young Inventors at Work, 1999, How to Enter and Win an Invention Contest, 1999, Fantastic Flying Fun with Science, 2000, Wacky Water Fun with Science, 2000, Inventing Toys: Kids Having Fun Learning Science, 2001, How to Build Your Own Prize-Winning Robot, 2002; mem. editl. adv. bd. Invent Mag., 1989-92; exec. prodr.: (TV show) Idea Factory, Sta. KFSN-30, Fresno, 1995-97; co-host: (ednl. TV show) Blow the Roof Off, 1992. Alumni v.p. Leadership Palm Beach County; expdn. leader Expdn. Tng. Inst., S.E. Alaska, 1980; mem. U.S. Antarctic Rsch. Program, 1974; founder, bd. dirs. Visually Impaired Sports Program, Boulder, 1978-81; fitness instr. YMCA Boulder, 1977-81; convener 1st Nat. Conf. Sports for the Blind, 1979; bd. dirs. Leadership Palm Beach; vice chmn. County Com. on Artificial Reefs; treas. Leadership Akron Alumni Assn., 1990-91, class pres. Leadership Akron; v.p. Ohio Mus. Assn., 1991-92, pres., 1992-93; bd. dirs. Fla. Mus. Assn., 1988-89; mem. adv. bd. Marine Sci. Inst., 1990—. Lt. USN, 1970-73. Fellow Explorers Club (chair Pacific Midwest chpt. 2002—); mem. Marine Tech. Soc. (sect. chmn. 1982-84), Coral Reef Soc. (chpt. pres. 1982-87), Nat. Inventive Thinking Assn. (bd. dirs. 1989—). Home: 2420 178th Ave NE Redmond WA 98052-5820 E-mail: sobey@verizon.net.

SOBIESKI, JAROSLAW, aerospace engineer; b. Wilno, Poland, Mar. 11, 1934; came to U.S., 1966; naturalized, 1971. s. Stanislaw and Sabina Sobieszczanski; m. Wanda Dlugosz, Dec. 31, 1958; children: Margaret Ann, Ian Patrick. BS aeros., Tech. U. Warsaw, 1955, MS aeros., 1957, DEng, 1964. Cons. Polish Aircraft Industries, Warsaw, 1957-64; asst. and adj. prof. Tech. U. Warsaw, Warsaw, 1955-64; rsch. assoc. Tech. U. Norway, Trondheim, 1964-66; assoc. prof. St. Louis U., 1966-71; aerospace engr. NASA Langley Rsch. Ctr., Hampton, Va., 1971-89, head rsch. office, 1979-93, chief scientist, 1993-94, multidisciplinary rsch. coord., 1994—2001, mgr. Computational AeroScis. team, 1996—2001, sr. rsch. scientist, 2001—. Mem. faculty George Washington U., 1972—, U. Va., 1992-99; pres. and cons. engr. Tech. Analysis Optimization, Inc. Hampton, Va., 1982—. Co-editor: Structural Optimization jour., 1989—; contbr. articles to profl. jours. Recipient Wright Bros. medal, SAE, 2000. Fellow AIAA (mem. tech. com., Nat. Multidisciplinary Design Optimization award 1996); mem. International Soc. for Structural and Multidisciplinary Optimization (founding mem. exec. bd. 1992—2003). Home: 518 Elizabeth Lake Dr Hampton VA 23669-1724 Office: NASA Langley Rsch Ctr MS 240 Hampton VA 23681-0001 Office Phone: 757-864-2799.

SOBIN, LESLIE HOWARD, pathologist, educator; b. N.Y.C., Feb. 10, 1934; s. Martin L. and Kitty N. Sobin; m. Margareta E.D. Ahlstrom, Dec. 21, 1962; 1 child, Annika D. BS, Union Coll., 1955; MD, SUNY, N.Y.C., 1959. Diplomate Am. Bd. Pathology. Instr. pathology Cornell U. Med. Coll., N.Y.C., 1962-65, asst. prof. pathology, 1965; WHO visiting prof. pathology Univ. Kabul, Afghanistan, 1965-68; assoc. prof. pathology Cornell U. Med. Coll., 1968-70; pathologist WHO, Geneva, 1970-81; prof. pathology Uniformed Svcs. Univ. Health Scis., Bethesda, Md., 1984—; head WHO collaborating ctr. tumor classification Armed Forces Inst. Pathology, Washington, 1983—99, dir. sci. publs., 1987—, chief gastrointestinal pathology, 1991—, co-chmn. dept. hepatic/gastrointestinal pathology, 2004—. Adj. prof. pathology Cornell U. Med. Coll., 1980-2001, Georgetown U. Med. Coll., 1992—; expert, panel on cancer WHO, Geneva, 1981—. Author: Pathology Primer in Verse, 1978, 91, Tales of the Ampulla of Vater, 1994, The Last Examination: The Prosecutor's Guide to the Autopsy—In Verse, 1996; editor: International Histological Classification of Tumors, 1970-2002; co-editor: WHO Classification of Tumors, 2000—, TNM Classification of Tumors, 1987, 97, 2002, Prognostic Factors in Cancer, 1995, 2001; adv. editor (oncology) International Dictionary of Medicine and Biology, Churchill's Medical Dictionary. Recipient Sr. Exec. Svc. award Dept. of Army, 1990, Meritorious Presdl. Rank award, 1991. Fellow Royal Coll. Pathologists; mem. Internat. Acad. Pathology (sec. 1982-88).

SOBKOWICZ, HANNA MARIA, neurology researcher; b. Warsaw, Jan. 1, 1931; came to U.S., 1963; d. Stanislaw and Jadwiga (Ignaczak) S.; m. Jerzy E. Rose, Mar. 12, 1972. BA, Girls State Lyceum, Gilwice, Poland, 1949; M.D, Med. Acad., Warsaw, 1954, PhD, 1962. Intern. 1st Internal Med. Clinic Med. Acad., Warsaw, 1954-55; resident 1st Internal Med. Clinic, Med. Acad., Warsaw, 1955-59, Neurol. Clinic, Med. Acad., 1959, jr. asst., 1959-61, sr. asst., 1961-63; research fellow neurology Mt. Sinai Hosp., N.Y.C., 1963-65; Nat. Multiple Sclerosis Soc. fellow Columbia U., N.Y.C., 1965-66; asst. prof. neurology U. Wis., Madison, 1966-72, assoc. prof., 1972-79, prof., 1979—. Contbr. articles to profl. jours. NIH research grantee, 1968— Mem. Internat. Brain Rsch. Orgn., Assn. Rsch. in Otolaryngology, Soc. Neurosci., Internat. Soc. Devel. Neurosci. (editorial bd. 1984—), Electron Microscopy Soc. Am. Office: U Wis Dept Neurology 1300 University Ave Madison WI 53706-1510 Office Phone: 608-262-7332. Business E-Mail: hmsobkow@facstaff.wisc.edu.

SOBLE, MARK RICHARD, lawyer; b. San Francisco, Dec. 25, 1964; life ptnr. Leslye Soble, Nov. 2000. BA with deptl. honors, Stanford U., 1985; JD, U. Mich., 1988. Bar: Calif. 1988, U.S. Dist. Ct. (cen. dist.) Calif. 1988, U.S. Dist. Ct. (ea. dist.) Calif. 1990, U.S. Dist. Ct. (no. and so. dists.) Calif. 2003. Law clk. to chief judge U.S. Dist. Ct. for S.D., Pierre, 1988-89; assoc. Lewis, D'Amato, Brisbois & Bisgaard, L.A., 1989-90; counsel enforcement div. Fair Polit. Practices Commn., Sacramento, 1990-96, sr. counsel, 1996—2001; dep. atty. gen. civil div. Office of Calif. Atty. Gen., 2001—. Note editor U. Mich. Jour. Law Reform, 1987-88. Raymond K. Dykema scholar U. Mich. 1987. Mem. State Bar Calif., Sacramento County Bar Assn. (mng. editor Docket 1997, mem.-at-large bar coun. 1998-00).

SOBOL, ELISE SCHWARCZ, music educator; b. Chgo., June 12, 1951; d. Morton and Harriet Jacobsohn Schwarcz; m. Lawrence Paul Sobol, Aug. 21, 1977 (div. Sept. 1989); children: Marlon I., Aaron L. AA, Simon's Rock of Bard Coll., 1971; student, Mannes Coll. Music, 1971—73, Juillard Sch. Music, 1973—74; BA, New Sch. for Social Rsch., 1985; MA, Columbia U., 1987. Staff auditorium events, concerts, lectures Met. Mus. Art, 1972-73; sec. to pres. Harry Beall Mgmt. Inc., N.Y.C., 1973-76; sales rep. M.L. Falcone Pub. Rels., N.Y.C., 1976-77; asst. to pres. Jacques Leiser Artist Mgmt., N.Y.C., 1977-78; artist rep. Elise Sobol Mgmt. Inc., South Huntington, N.Y., 1978-82; tchr. music Nassau Boces Elem., 1988—; dir. L.I. Music Workshop, 1992—. Adj. prof. NYU Steinhardt Sch. Edn., 2000—; advisor arts and humanities Internat. Biog. Ctr., Cambridge, England; guest lectr. NYU, 1999, Hofstra, 2000; adj. faculty C.W. Post Coll. L.I. U., 2000; instr. SUNY, Farmingdale, 1993—98; music tchr. The Roslyn Middle Sch., 1987—88; dir. Early Musical Devel. Program for Children at Calling All Kids, South Huntington, 1981—86; tchr. young and adult piano students, 1968; piano adj. educator N.Y. State, 1993—. Musician: (piano concerts) Chamber Music series at U.S. Mil. Acad., N.Y./N.J. met. area concerts, Disting. Artists series, 2002—03, Met. Area Concerts, 2003, Am. Assn. Univ. Women Commentary and Concerts, 2003; author: An Attitude and Approach for Teaching Music to Special Learners, 2001; musician: (commentary and concert) A Gentlewoman's Pursuit, AAUW, 2003. Active Nassau Boces Elem. Program PTA, cultural arts coord., 1988—. Recipient Award of Honor, L.I. Very Spl. Arts Festival, 1993, Spl. Citation N.Y. State Assembly Ames Elem. Program, 1998, Spl. Recognition Nassau Music Educators Assn., 1999, 1st prize Dr. Martin Luther King Jr. Performing Arts Competition for Exceptional Students Nassau County, 1999, 2000, 01, Internat. Peace Prize, United Cultural Convention, May 2002, Town of Oyster Bay citation, 2002; nominated N.Y. Senate Women of Distinction Program, 2003; named Internat. Musician of Yr., 2004. Mem. NAFE, ASCD, AAUW, N.Y. State Sch. Music Assn. (chair music for spl. learners 1993—), Amnesty Internat., Music Educators Nat. Conf., Music Tchrs. Nat. Assn., Nassau Music Educators Assn., Nat. Mus. for Women, Met. Mus. of Art. Home: 21 Saxon St Melville NY 11747

SOBOL, HAROLD, retired dean, manufacturing executive, consultant; b. Bklyn., June 21, 1930; s. Stanley and Minnie S.; m. Marion Gross, Dec. 29, 1957; children— Diane, Neil, Jessica, Martin. BSE.E., CUNY, 1952; MSE.E., U. Mich., 1956, PhD, 1960. Research asst. Willow Run Labs. U. Mich., 1952-55, research assoc., 1956-59; staff mem. IBM Research, Yorktown Heights, N.Y., 1960-62; with RCA Labs., Princeton, N.J., 1962-73, staff engr., 1970-72, head communication tech., 1972-73; sr. mem. tech. staff Collins Radio Rockwell-Internat., Dallas, 1973-74; dir. product devel. Collins Transmission Systems div., 1974-85; dir. engring. Rockwell Telecommunications, 1985-86, v.p. engring., 1986-88, ret., 1988; prof. elec. engring., assoc. dean U. Tex., Arlington, 1988-93. Author: Advances in Microwaves Volume 8, 1974; contbr. in field. Cubmaster Tex.-Okla. council Boy Scouts Am., Dallas, 1978-80. Sperry fellow, 1955-56 Fellow IEEE (pres. microwave theory and techniques soc. 1979); mem. Am. Phys. Soc., Nat. Mgmt. Assn., Sigma Xi, Tau Beta Pi, Eta Kappa Nu. Office: U Tex PO Box 19019 Arlington TX 76019-0001

SOBOL, LAWRENCE RAYMOND, lawyer; b. Kansas City, Mo., May 8, 1950; s. Haskell and Mary (Press) S.; m. Maureen Patricia O'Connell, May 29, 1976; children: David, Kevin. BBA, U. Tex., 1972; JD, U. Mo., 1975. Bar: Mo. 1975, U.S. Dist. Ct. (ea. dist.) Mo. 1975. Gen. counsel, gen. ptnr. Edward D. Jones & Co., Maryland Heights, Mo., 1975—. Allied mem. N.Y.C. Stock Exchange, 1977—; sec. Lake Communications Corp., Conroe, Tex., 1984-86, LHC Inc., EDJ Holding Co. Inc., Unison Capital Corp., 1990—, Cornerstone Mortgage Investment Group, 1987-92; sec., bd. dirs. Cornerstone Mortgage Inc., St. Louis, 1986; v.p., bd. dirs. Tempus Corp., St. Louis, 1984—. Omar Robinson Meml. scholar U. Mo., 1974-75. Mem. ABA (securities law com. 1982—), Met. St. Louis Bar Assn. (securities law sect.), Nat. Assn. Securities Dealers (dist. bus. com., registered prin. officer, nat. arbitration com. 1991—), Securities Industry Assn. (fed. regulation securities com. 1987-88), Persimmon Woods Country Club, Lake Las Vegas South Shore Country Club, Phi Eta Sigma. Avocations: tennis, golf. Office: Edward D Jones & Co 12555 Manchester Rd Saint Louis MO 63131-3729

SOBOL, ROBERT E. medical company executive; BA in Philosophy, Boston U.; MD, Chgo. Med. Sch. Diplomate Am. Bd. Internal Medicine with subspecialty in med. oncology. Resident U. So. Calif. Med. Ctr., U. Calif., San Diego; founder GeneSys Therapeutics; founder, v.p. IDEC Pharms. Corp.; dir. clin. sci. Sidney Kimmel Cancer Ctr., San Diego; exec. v.p., COO GenStar Therapeutics, San Diego, 1996—, pres., 1996—2000, CEO, dir., 1998—. Achievements include development of of clinical applications of immuno therapy and gene therapy for the treatment of cancer; research in in gene therapy protocols for treatment of colon carcinoma; treatment of brain tumor patient with cytokine gene therapy. Office: Ste 200 6555 Nancy Ridge Dr San Diego CA 92121-3221

SOBOLEV, ALEXANDRE ANDREEVICH, physicist; b. Ramenskoye, Russia, June 18, 1952; s. Andrew Puzirev and Anna (Soboleva) Terekhova; m. Yaroslava Stepanovna Schumliakovskaya, Nov. 5, 1975 (div. 1980); 1 child, Yegor; m. Tatiana Arkadievna Silitch, Dec. 19, 1992; 1 child, Maria. MSc, Moscow Inst. Engring. Physics, 1978, PhD, 1990. Rschr. Inst. Physics & Power Engring., Obninsk, Russia. Dep. Obninsk City Coun., 1989-93. Jr. sgr. Soviet Army, 1971-73. Mem.: Obninsk Phys. Soc., Moscow Phys. Soc. Mem. Orthodox Ch. E-mail: sobolev9@videotron.ca.

SOBOLEWSKI, JOHN STEPHEN, computer scientist, consultant; b. Krakow, Poland, July 14, 1939; came to U.S., 1966; s. Jan Zygmund and Stefania (Zwolinska) S.; m. Helen Skipper, Dec. 17, 1965 (div. July 1969); m. Carole Straith, Apr. 6, 1974; children: Anne-Marie, Elisa, Martin. BE, U. Adelaide, Adelaide, South Australia, 1962, ME, 1966; PhD in Computer Sci., Wash. State U., 1971. Sci. officer Weapons Research Establishment, Salisbury, South Australia, 1964-66; asst. prof. computer sci. Wash. State U., Pullman, 1966-73; dir. research, assoc. prof. U. Wash., Seattle, 1973-80, dir. computer svcs., 1980-88; assoc. v.p. computing U. N.Mex., Albuquerque, 1988—. Cons. govt. and industry, Seattle, 1973—; mem. bd. trustees Fisher Found., Seattle, 1984—. Author: Computers for the Dental Office, 1986; contbr. articles to profl. jours. Served as engr. with Royal Australian Army, 1957-60. Australian govt. scholar, 1954-60, Elec. Res. Bd. scholar CSIRO, Melbourne, Australia, 1961-64. Mem. IEEE, Computer Soc. Roman Catholic. Avocation: mineral collecting. Home: 18422 57th Ave NE Kenmore WA 98028 Personal E-mail: mwminerals@hotmail.com. Business E-Mail: jssob@unm.edu.

SOBOLEWSKI, TIMOTHY RICHARD, marketing executive; b. Buffalo, May 29, 1951; s. Richard Theodore and Gertrude Marie (Chudzik) S.; m. Melissa R. Thorburn, Apr. 13, 1985; 1 child, Richard; m. Deborah L. Leone, Nov. 9, 2002. AB, Columbia U., 1972. Regional mgr. Universal Communicatons, Roanoke, Va., 1977—80; ptnr. Systems Planning Assocs., Braintree, Mass., 1980—81; v.p. Telecon, Inc., Boston, 1981—83; sr. mktg. cons. Telelogic, Inc., Cambridge, Mass., 1983—84; dist. mgr. Republic Telcom, Braintree, 1985; founder, pres., gen. mgr. Operaworld, Inc., Boston, 1985—89; v.p. Homisco, Inc., Melrose, Mass., 1989—95; dir. sales & mktg. DINE Sys., Amherst, NY, 1995—97; pres. One Call Software, Amherst, 1998—99; registered rep. AXA Advs., Williamsville, NY, 1999—2000, New Eng. Fin., Williamsville, 2000—03, MONY Group, Williamsville, 2003—04, Quick & Reilly, Buffalo, 2004—. Cons. Opera Con Brio, Brookline, Mass., 1986-92. Mem. Puritan Club (Braintree). Democrat. Roman Catholic. Office: Quick & Reilly 20 Fountain Plz Buffalo NY 14202

SOBRE, JUDITH BERG, education educator; b. Bklyn., Apr. 28, 1941; d. Sidney and Ruth (Aronson) Berg; m. Josep Miquel Sobre, Sept. 9, 1969 (div. Aug. 1975); 1 child, Miriam Shoshana. BA, NYU, 1962; MA, Harvard U., 1964, PhD, 1969. Asst. prof. art history U. Oreg., Eugene, 1968—74; assoc. prof. U. Tex., San Antonio, 1974—84, prof. art history, 1984—. Author: Behind the Altar Table, 1989 (Am. Soc. for Hispanic Art History Studies award, 1990), Bartolome de Cardenas El Bermejo, 1997, San Antonio on Parade, 2003. Recipient TR Fehrenbach award, Tex. Hist. Commn., 2003; Fullbright scholar, Madrid, 1966—67, Com. Conjunto fellow, 1983—84, Rsch. grantee, U. Tex., 2000. Mem.: Am. Culture Assn., Am. Soc. for Hispanic Art History Studies, Coll. Art Assn. Jewish. Avocations: hiking, skiing, cooking. Office: Dept Art and Art History U Tex at San Antonio 6900 N Loop 1604 West San Antonio TX 78249-0642 Office Phone: 210-458-4367. E-mail: jsobre@satx.rr.com.

SOBRERO, KATE (KATHRYN MICHELE SOBRERO), professional soccer player; b. Pontiac, Mich., Aug. 23, 1976; BA in Bus., U. Notre Dame, 1997. Mem. U.S. Nat. Women's Soccer Team, 1995—2001; profl. soccer player Boston Breakers (WUSA), 2001—03. Mem. U.S. Under-20 Nat. Team, 1993—. Named Defensive Most Valuable Player, NCAA Final Four, 1995. Achievements include on cover of Soccer Am. mag., 1995; member Notre Dame NCAA National Championship Team, 1995; member U.S. World Cup Championship Team, 1999; member U.S. Olympic Silver Medal Team, 2000. Office: US Soccer Fedn 1801-1811 S Prairie Ave Chicago IL 60616

SOBUS, KERSTIN MARYLOUISE, physician, physical therapist; b. Washington, June 16, 1960; d. Earl Francis and Dolores Jane (Gill) G.; m. Paul John Jr., March 10, 1990; children: Darlene Marie, Julieann Marie. BS in Phys. Therapy summa cum laude, U. N.D., 1981, MD, 1987. Clinic instr. pediatric physical therapy U.N.D. Sch. Medicine, Grand Forks, 1981-83; pediat. phys. theraist child evaluation-treatment program Med. Rehab. Ctr., Grand Forks, 1981-83, med. dir. program, 1997—; asst. prof. dept. pediatrics, asst. prof. dept. physical medicine and rehab. U. Ark. for Med. Scis., Little Rock, 1992-96; resident in internal medicine Sinai Hosp. Balt., 1987-88; resident in phys. medicine and rehab. Johns Hopkins program Sinai Hosp., Balt., 1988-91; pediatric rehab. clin. and rsch. fellow Alfred I. DuPont Inst., Wilmington, Del., 1991-92; pediatric pysiatrist Altru Health System, Grand Forks, 1997—. Contbr. articles to med. jours. Mem. Am. Acad. Cerebral Palsy and Devel. Medicine, Alpha Omega Alpha Honor Soc. Office: Altru Health Sys PO Box 6002 1300 S Columbia Rd Grand Forks ND 58201-4012 Home: 7451 S 25th St Grand Forks ND 58201

SOCHACKI, ANDRZEJ, mechanical engineer, researcher, tourism educator; b. Warsaw, July 26, 1948; came to U.S., 1973; s. Jerzy and Halina (Błażejczyk) S.; married. MS, Warsaw U., 1969; AAS, Maricopa Tech. Coll., Phoenix, 1983; postgrad., Ariz. State U., 1985. Sr. mech. engr. Roger Bus.

Products div. Rogers Corp., Mesa, Ariz., 1986-87; sr. mech. design engr. Parker Aerospace Co., Phoenix, 1987-88; sr. project engr. Micro-Rel Inc., Tempe, Ariz., 1988-90; cons., project engr., pres., owner Design & Fabricating Co., Phoenix, 1985-96; founder, pres., chmn. The Vagabond Ctr., Phoenix, 1992; tool engr. Boeing Co., Mesa, Ariz., 1996-98; tchr., lectr. traveling Tourism and Hotels Mgmt. Coll., Warsaw, 1998—. Contbr. edni. articles to publs. Recipient award Medtronic Corp., Phoenix, 1989. Mem. Soc. Mfg. Engrs. (sr.). Roman Catholic. Avocations: piano, research, 6 times travel around the world by car, plane, sailboat, train, and twice by motorcycle. Home and Office: The Vagabond Ctr 3715 E Taylor St Phoenix AZ 85008-6316 E-mail: asochacki@yahoo.com.

SOCHEN, JUNE, history professor; b. Chgo., Nov. 26, 1937; d. Sam and Ruth (Finkelstein) S. BA, U. Chgo., 1958; MA, Northwestern U., 1960, PhD, 1967. Project editor Chgo. Superior and Talented Student Project, 1959-60; high sch. tchr. English and history North Shore Country Day Sch., Winnetka, Ill., 1961-64; instr. history Northeastern Ill. U., 1964-67, asst. prof., 1967-69, assoc. prof., 1969-72, prof., 1972—. Author: The New Woman, 1971, Movers and Shakers, 1973, Herstory: A Woman's View of American History, 1975, 2d edit., 1981, Consecrate Every Day: The Public Lives of Jewish American Women, 1981, Enduring Values: Women in Popular Culture, 1987, Cafeteria America: New Identities in Contemporary Life, 1988, Mae West: She Who Laughs Lasts, 1992, From Mae to Madonna: Women Entertainers in 20th Century America, 1999; editor: The New Feminism in 20th Century America, 1972, Women's Comic Visions, 1991; contbr. articles to profl. jours. Nat. Endowment for Humanities grantee, 1971-72 Office: Northeastern Ill U 5500 N Saint Louis Ave Chicago IL 60625-4679 Office Phone: 773-442-5607. E-mail: j-sochen@neiu.edu.

SOCHYNSKY, YAROSLAV, lawyer, arbitrator, mediator; b. Feb. 5, 1946; BA in English, Colgate U., 1967; JD, Georgetown U., 1970. Bar: Calif., N.Y. Assoc. White & Case, N.Y.C., 1970-71; law clerk to Hon. William T. Sweigert U.S. Dist. Ct. (no. dist.) Calif., 1971-73; assoc. Landels, Ripley & Diamond LLP, San Francisco, 1973-76; sr. ptnr. Landels, Ripley & Diamond, San Francisco, 1976-2000; mediator Am. Arbitration Assn., San Francisco, 2000—. Lectr. Calif. Continuing Edn. Bar, 1985, Equity Asset Mgr.'s Assn., 1987, Calif. Dept. Real Estate, 1986-89). Originator, co-author California ADR Practice Guide, 1992; co-author Real Property Practice and Litigation, 1990; case and notes editor, mem. editorial bd. Georgetown Law Jour.; contbr. articles and monographs to profl. jours. Fellow, Coll. Comml. Arbitrators. Fellow Chartered Inst. Arbitrators (London); mem. ABA (mem. exec. coun. sect. on real property, probate and trust, lectr. 1988, 89, 91), Am. Arbitration Assn. (cert. mediator, mem. pres.' panel of mediators, large and compley case panel, internat. panel, real property valuation panel, No. Calif. adv. coun., lectr. 1990, speaker various panels, No. Calif. Outstanding Mediator award 1991), San Francisco Bar Assn. Office: Am Arbitration Assn 225 Bush St Fl 18 San Francisco CA 94104-4211 E-mail: yarko@aol.com.

SOCOL, MICHAEL LEE, obstetrician, gynecologist, educator; b. Chgo., Oct. 3, 1949; s. Joseph and Bernice (Bofman) S.; m. Donna Kaner, Dec. 17, 1972. BS, U. Ill., 1970; MD, U. Ill., Chgo., 1974. Diplomate Am. Bd. Ob-Gyn., Am. Bd. Maternal-Fetal Medicine. Resident obstetrics and gynecology U. Ill. Hosp., Chgo., 1974-77; clin. rsch. fellow dept. obstetrics and gynecology L.A. County-U. So. Calif. Med. Ctr., 1977-79; assoc. attending physician Northwestern Meml. Hosp., Chgo., 1980-86, attending physician dept. ob-gyn., 1986—; co-dir. Northwestern Perinatal Ctr., Chgo., 1987—; head maternal-fetal medicine, chief obstetrics Northwestern U. Med. Sch., Chgo., 1987—, dir. maternal-fetal medicine fellowship program, 1987-99, asst. prof. obstetrics and gynecology, 1979-84, assoc. prof., 1984-92, prof., 1992—. Vice chmn. dept. ob-gyn Northwestern Meml. Hosp., Chgo., 1992—. Author: (with others) Clinical Obstetrics and Gynecology, 1982, 1984, Diagnostic Ultrasound Applied to Obstetrics and Gynecology, 1987, Principles and Practice of Medical Therapy in Pregnancy, 1992; peer reviewer Am. Jour. Obstetrics and Gynecology, 1980—, Obstetrics and Gynecology, 1984—; contbr. numerous articles to profl. jours. Fellow Am. Coll. Ob-Gyn., Soc. Maternal-Fetal Medicine, Soc. for Gynecol. Investigation, Am. Gynecol. and Obstet. Soc.; mem. Assn. Profs. Gynecology and Obstetrics. Avocation: marathon running. Office: 333 E Superior St Ste 410 Chicago IL 60611-3015

SOCOL, SHELDON ELEAZER, university official; b. N.Y.C., July 10, 1936; s. Irving and Helen (Tuchman) S.; m. Genia Ruth Prager, Dec. 26, 1959; children: Jeffrey, Steven, Sharon, Robyn, Leslie, Steven Warren. BA, Yeshiva U., 1958; JD, NYU, 1963. From asst. bursar to dir. student fins. Yeshiva U., N.Y.C., 1958-70, sec., 1970—, chief fiscal officer, 1971-72, v.p. bus. affairs, 1972—. Mem. N.Y. State Adv. Coun. on Fin. Assistance to Coll. Students, 1969-76; asst. dir. Tng. Inst. for Fin. Aid Officers, Hunter, Coll., CUNY, 1970-71; mem. presdl. adv. com. Temple U., 1986; mem. regents adv. task force N.Y.C. Regional Plan for Higher Edn., 1971-73; bd. dirs. N.Y. Structural Biology Ctr., 2000; spkr. in field. Pres. Minyon Park Estates, Inc. Mem. NEA, Nat. Assn. Coll. and Univ. Attys., Met. N.Y.C. Fin. Aid Adminstrs. Assn., Ea. Assn. Student Fin. Aid Officers, Am. Mgmt. Assn., Am. Assn. for Higher Edn., Nat. Assn. Coll. and Univ. Bus. Officers, Soc. Coll. and Univ. Planning, Mid. States Assn. Colls. (evaluation team Commn. on Higher Edn., U. Medicine and Dentistry N.J., 1985, Upstate Health Sci. Ctr. 1986, Carnegie-Mellon U. 1988, Albany Med. Ctr. 1989). Office: Yeshiva U 500 W 185th St New York NY 10033-3299 E-mail: dses@ymail.yu.edu.

SOCOLOW, ARTHUR ABRAHAM, geologist; b. Bronx, N.Y., Mar. 23, 1921; s. Samuel and Yetta (Solomon) S.; m. Edith S. Blumenthal, Apr. 10, 1949; children: Carl, Roy. Jeff. BS, Rutgers U., 1942; MA, Columbia U., 1947, PhD, 1955. Reg. profl. geologist, Commonwealth Pa. Photogrammetrist, U.S. Army Air Corps, 1942-46; with Eagle Picher de Mexico, 1947; instr. geology So. Methodist U., 1948-50; dir. geology field camp Colo., 1948-50; asst. prof. Boston U., 1950-55; geologist Def. Minerals Exploration Authority, Alaska, 1952; assoc. prof. U. Mass., 1955-57; econ. geologist Pa. Geol. Survey, 1957-61, dir., state geologist, 1961-86; cons. geologist Gloucester, Mass., 1986—; prof. environ. geology Salem (Mass.) State Coll., 1993-98; dir. New Eng. Govs. Conf. Project on Aggregate Resources New Eng., 1990-97. Mem. Outer Continental Shelf Policy Com., 1974-88, Pa. rep., 1978-88; lectr. mineral conservation Pa. State U., 1959-75; mem. earth sci. source materials NSF, 1959; chmn. ann. field conf. Pa. Geologists, 1961-86; past mem. U.S. Nat. Com. on Tunnelling Tech.; mem. com. on N.Y. State low level waste program Nat. Acad. Sci.; past mem. gov.'s adv. com. Nat. Coun. on Environ. Quality; past chmn. Pa. Water Resources Coordinating Com.; geol. advisor Boston Mus. Sci., 1955-57. Former editor Pa. Geol. Bull.; mem. editorial bd. Northeastern Geol. Jour.; contbr. over 100 publs. and papers on environ. and econ. geology to profl. jours. Served with USAAF, 1942-46. Fellow Geol. Soc. Am. (sec.-treas. N.E. sect., past nat. councilor), Mineral Soc. Am., AAAS (past pres. geography-geology sect.), Soc. Econ. Geologists; mem. AAUP, Am. Geol. Inst., Nat. Assn. Geology Tchrs. (past regional pres., Ralph Digman award for contbns. to geologic edn. 1980), Am. Meteoritical Soc., Assn. Am. State Geologists (past pres., editor, compiler State Geological Surveys-A History 1988), Am. Geophys. Union, Am. Commn. Stratigraphic Nomenclature (past chmn.), Gloucester Conservation Commn. (chmn.), Fgn. Policy Assn. (past chpt. pres.), Sigma Xi. Clubs: Internat. Torch (past pres. chpt.). Home and Office: 26 Salt Island Rd Gloucester MA 01930-1945 Office Phone: 978-283-7490. E-mail: docsoc@earthlink.net. *I have great respect for the individualism of man in the midst of a society and a world where there is an unavoidable interrelationship and interdependence of man upon man, and of man upon his environment. While we strive to maintain our individualism, we must share our common resources and our common aspirations. This is the challenge that makes our lives worth living.*

SODAL, INGVAR EDMUND, electrical engineer, scientist; b. Hemne, Norway, Feb. 12, 1934; came to U.S., 1962; s. Ingebrigt L. and Johanna Sodal; m. Sally Rollins; 1 child, Silje M. Degree in elec. engring., Trondheim Tech. Coll., Norway, 1959; BSEE, U. Colo., 1964. Engr. Fjeldseth Engring., Trondheim, 1959-61; rsch. engr. U. Norway, Trondheim, 1961-62, U. Colo. Med. Ctr., Denver, 1964-66, rsch. assoc., 1966-75, instr., lectr., 1975-79; vis. rsch. assoc. dept. engring. U. Colo., Boulder, 1974-75, lectr., 1975-76; asst. prof., div. head. Ohio State U., Columbus, 1979-82, mem. grad. faculty, 1982; pres., chief exec. officer Masstron, Inc., Boulder, Colo., 1983-87; chief scientist Paradygm, Boulder, 1987-89; pres. Pacemark, Inc., Boulder, 1989-90, Med. Physics Colo., Inc., 1991—. Contbr. articles to profl. jours., chpts. to books; holder 6 patents in field. Instr. and/or program coord. in Scandinavian folklore and folk dancing for numerous groups and instns. throughout U.S., Can., and Norway, 1959—. Grantee, NIH, others. Mem. Village Arts Coalition, Sons of Norway. Office: 1550 Moss Rock Pl Boulder CO 80304-1543 E-mail: sodaling@norsk.us., ingvarsodal@netscape.net.

SODANO, SALVATORE F. stock exchange executive; BA in Acctg. and Econ., Hofstra U., 1977, M in Fin. and Investments, 1983. V.p., group head Bankers Trust Co., 1983-90; mgmt. price Waterhouse, Morgan Guaranty Internat. Fin. Corp.; v.p., dep. controller to sr. v.p., chief mgr. Am. Divsn. Westpac, 1983-90; vice-chmn., COO, dep. COO, exec. v.p. NASD, 1990-00; chmn., CEO Am. Stock Exchange, New York, 1999—. Mem. bd. trustees Hofstra U., bus. adv. bd. Merrill Lynch Ctr. for Study Internat. Fin. Svcs.; bd. dirs. Securities Ind. Automation Corp., 1999-2002; pres. Securities Dealers Ins. Co., Ltd. Mem. Econ. Club (N.Y., recipient Ellis Island Medal Honor). Office: American Stock Exchange 86 Trinity Pl New York NY 10006*

SODEMAN, NANCY ELIZABETH, retired literature educator; b. Duluth, Minn., Jan. 23, 1931; d. Skafte Ruthford and Arba Agnes Whiting; m. Walter John Sodeman, July 25, 1952 (dec.); children: Catherine S. Bilodeau, Barbara S. Coombs. BA, Coll. St. Scholastica; postgrad., Northwestern U., So. Meth. U., U. Minn.; MA, PhD, Ga. State U. H.S. english tchr., Minn., 1952—54; speech and drama tchr. various pub. schs., 1954—57; bus. English tchr. bus. coll., 1954—57; writing and lit. tchr. Dekalb Coll., 1967—72, Atlanta Bapt. Coll., 1967—72, Ga. State U., 1967—72; mgr. radio sta. for the blind NTRB, 1980—81; comm. and market rsch. cons., 1981—83; facilitator Nat. Franchise Mktg. Svcs., 1983—84; tchr. English dept. Collin County C.C. Author: Support for the Survivor (Ethel Ward McLemore award, 1994); contbr. articles to mags. and newspapers. Vol. tutor, tchrs. aide elem. pub. sch., Richardson, Tex.; vol. Mil. Officer Assn.; Tex. rep. Vets. Widows Internat. Network; docent Women's Mus., Dallas, 2000—03; pres. Ret. Officers Women's Club; adjunct Ret. Officers Assn.; v.p. Outreach for Widowed Persons Svc.; N.Am. coord. Thomas More/John Fisher Congress, London, 1984—85; vol. chaplain Dallas County Jails; counselor Fed. Prison, Seagoville; rep. Am.-Scandinavian Student Exch.; cultural dir. VASA; treas. Ret. Officers' Wives Club, 1989—90; bd. dirs. Transition Svc. Ctr., Inc. Home: 419 Valley Cove Richardson TX 75080

SODEN, JOHN P. publishing executive; b. Yakima, Wash., Aug. 25, 1942; BA, U. Wash., 1964. Paperback buyer Univ. Bookstore, Seattle, 1964-66; lib. svcs. coord. Am. News Co., 1966-68; trade sales rep. Little Brown & Co., L.A., 1968-70; sales mgr. U. Wash. Press, Seattle, 1971-76, mktg. mgr., 1977-90, assoc. dir., gen. mgr., 1991-96, dir., 1996—. Bd. dirs. Wash. Ctr. for the Book. Recipient Nancy Pryor Blakenship award Wash. State Gov.'s Writers Awards, 1995. Mem. Pacific N.W. Booksellers Assn. (v.p. 1975-78, bd. dirs.). Office: U Wash Press PO Box 50096 Seattle WA 98145-5096

SODEN, RICHARD ALLAN, lawyer; b. Feb. 16, 1945; s. Hamilton David and Clara Elaine (Seale) S.; m. Marcia LaMonte Mitchell, June 7, 1969; children: Matthew Hamilton, Mark Mitchell. AB, Hamilton Coll., 1967; JD, Boston U., 1970. Bar: Mass. 1970. Law clk. to judge U.S. Ct. Appeals (6th cir.), 1970-71; assoc. firm Goodwin, Procter & Hoar LLP, Boston, 1971-79, ptnr., 1979—. Instr. Law Sch. Boston Coll., Chestnut Hill, Mass., 1973-74. Mem. South End Project Area Com.; hon. dir. United South End Settlements, pres., 1977-79; chmn. Boston Mcpl. Rsch. Bur., 1996-97, pres., 1997-99; pres. Boston Minuteman coun. Boy Scouts Am.; trustee Judge Baker Children's Ctr., chmn., 1994-96, pres., 1992-94; trustee New Eng. Aquarium, Boston U., 1995-2001; bd. visitors Boston U. Goldman Sch. Grad. Dentistry; mem. bd. overseers WGBH; mem. Mass. Minority Bus. Devel. Commn.; mem. Adv. Task Force on Securities Regulation; mem. Adv. Com. on Legal Edn.; steering com. Lawyers Com. for Civil Rights under Law, chmn., 1992-94. Mem. ABA (chmn. standing com. on bar svcs. and activities, Commn. on Lawyer Assistance Programs Adv. Coun. on Diversity 1998-2000), Nat. Bar Assn., Mass. Bar Assn. (past vice chmn. bus. law coun. 1990-91), Boston Bar Assn. (pres. 1994-95), Mass. Black Lawyers Assn. (pres. 1980-81). Home: 42 Gray St Boston MA 02116-6210 Office: Goodwin Procter LLP Exchange Pl Boston MA 02109-2803

SODERBERG, BO S. marketing executive; b. Avesta, Sweden, Mar. 22, 1939; came to U.S., 1979; s. John Sigfrid and Elisabet A. (Bjorkvall) S.; m. Kerstin Linnea Nordling; children: Monica, Mikael, Bogge, Margareta. BS in Engring., TGO, Orebro, Sweden, 1960; MBA, Fla. Inst. Tech., 1985. Mng. dir. Scandinavian Computer Systems, Stockholm, 1967-69; pres. Bror Andersson AB (BRA), Stockholm, 1969-78; exec. dir. Cap Gemini Sogeti, Paris, 1978-80, Cap Gemini Inc., Washington, 1980-82; pres. DMA Marketing Inc., Palm Bay, Fla., 1982-86, Prisma Am. Inc., Vero Beach, Fla., 1986-87, also bd. dirs.; pres. Scandinavian USA Bus. Ctr., Inc., Clearwater, Fla., 1988-92, DMA Mktg. Inc., St. Petersburg, Fla., 1993-98, Atlanta, 1998—. Seminar instr. Swedish Computer Soc., Stockholm, 1970-78; instr., lectr. Swedish Soc. for Info. Processing, Stockholm, 1972-78; lectr. Fla. Outdoor Advt. Assn.,Orlando, Fla., 1986-87. Served as specialist Sweden Air Force, 1960-61. Home: 3375 Spring Hill Pkwy # 1034 Smyrna GA 30080 Office: 3525 Piedmont RD NE STE 7-300 Atlanta GA 30305-1330

SODERBERG, DALE LEROY, English language educator, drama director, producer; b. Warren, Pa., Apr. 24, 1929; s. Leroy Wilbur and Olive Hazel (Conboy) S.; m. Marjorie Ann Hamm, Aug. 19, 1951; children: David J., Valli K., W. Mark, Lisa T., Kathi L. BA, Gettysburg Coll., 1951; BD, Luth. Theol. Sem., Gettysburg, Pa., 1954. Cert. secondary English tchr., N.Y., 1968; ordained mins. Luth. Ch., 1954. Pastor Grace Luth. Ch., Clarion, Pa., 1954-57; mission developer, 1st pastor Our Saviour's Luth. Ch., Horseheads, N.Y., 1957-60; dir. Ecclesia Tours (Luth. Fgn. Tours), Horseheads and North Syracuse, N.Y., 1958-67; mgr. Soderberg Travel Svc., Corning, N.Y., 1960-62; pastor St. John's Luth. Ch., Syracuse, N.Y., 1962-66; guest chapel preacher Wittenberg U., Ohio, 1966; tchr. English Ft. Myers (Fla.) High Sch., 1967-68; tchr. English, dir. drama Hamilton (N.Y.) Cen. Sch., 1968-92; retired, 1992; sermon and story writer Ecclesia Svcs., Hamilton, 1984-96. Lay preacher Upstate N.Y. Synod Evang. Luth. Ch. Am., Syracuse, 1968—; advisor student tchrs.at Hamilton Cen. Sch. for Colgate U., Hamilton, 1975-92; clk. Hamilton Stores, Yellowstone Nat. Park, summer 1948, 93. Author: (novels) Pawns, 1980, The Amsterdam Connection, 1999, A Time for Choosing, 2001, Mr. Protestant, 2002, The Winds of Change, 2003, The Manipulators, 2004. Dir. tours to Europe, Holy Land and Luth. mission fields in Brit. Guiana, East and West Africa, and India; bd. dirs. Luth. Homes Found., 1993-96; vol. missionary religious edn. tchr. U. of Papua New Guinea, Goroka, spring 1996; mem. Global Missions Team, Upstate N.Y. Synod Evang. Luth. Ch. Am., Syracuse, 1999—; organizer and dir. Bishop's tour to Zimbabwe, 2001. Mem. N.Y. State United Tchrs., Hamilton Tchrs. Assn., N.Y. State Ret. Tchrs. Assn. Republican. Avocations: travel, photography, home video, creative writing, Hemingway specialization. Home: 1907 Preston Hill Rd Hamilton NY 13346-9522

SODERBERG, LEIF G. electronics company executive; BA, Harvard Coll.; MS in Mgmt., MIT. Various positions ending with ptnr. McKinsey & Co., Cleveland and Scandinavia, 1978-93; head bus. strategy Land Mobile Products Sector, Network Svcs. Bus. Motorola Inc., 1993-94, v.p., gen. mgr. Network Svcs. and Bus. Strategies Group, 1994—98, sr. v.p. Systems Solutions Group, 1998—2000, sr. v.p., gen. mgr., strategy, business development and industry relations, 2000—02, sr. v.p., dir., Motorola's global strategy and corporate development organization, 2002—. Mem. Clearnet's Nominating Com. Office: Motorola 1301 E Algonquin Rd Schaumburg IL 60196-1078

SODERBORG, MARTIN TODD, elementary school educator; b. Logan, Utah, June 3, 1966; s. William Lund Soderborg, Jr. and Margaret Ann Soderborg; m. Gretchen Adele Soderborg, Sept. 8, 1990; children: Kaleigh Ann, Taylor Celeste, Payton Todd(dec.), Sadie Adele. B in Elem. Edn., Utah State U., 1992; M in Secondary Edn., So. Utah U., 1998. Cert. Supervision and Adminstrv. Tchr. 5th grade Lincoln County Sch. Dist., Pioche, Nev., 1992—93, tchr. 6th grade, 1993—94, tchr. 7th and 8th grade social studies Panaca, Nev., 1994—. Basketball coach Lincoln County H.S., Panaca, 1992—98, track coach, 1993—, H.S. radio club advisor, 1997—. Scoutmaster Boy Scouts Am., Panaca, 1993—97, scouting coord., 1997—2002, varsity coach, 2003—. Mem.: ASCD, Lincoln County Edn. Assn. (sec. 1992—95, v.p. 1995—). Republican. Mem. Lds Ch. Avocations: basketball, tennis, drawing, bicycling. Home: PO Box 432 Panaca NV 89042 Office: Meadow Valley Middle Sch PO Box 567 Panaca NV 89042

SODERLIND, STERLING EUGENE, newspaper industry consultant; b. Rapelje, Mont., Sept. 6, 1926; s. William John and Florence (Longbotham) S.; m. Helen Boyce, Apr. 9, 1955; children: Steven (dec.), Sarah, Lori. BA, U. Mont., 1950; Rhodes Scholar, Oxford U., Eng., 1950-52. Reporter Mpls. Tribune, 1952-55; reporter Wall St. Jour., Chgo., 1955-56, Southeastern bur. chief Jacksonville, Fla., 1956-57, mem. page one editing staff N.Y.C., 1957-65, asst. mng. editor, 1966-70, mng. editor, 1970; econs. editor Dow Jones & Co., Inc., N.Y.C., 1970-77, asst. to pres., 1975-77, v.p., 1977-91; newspaper industry cons., 1992—. Served with USNR, 1944-46. Congregationalist. Home: 58 Wellington Ave Short Hills NJ 07078-3308

SODERQUIST, LARRY DEAN, law educator, lawyer, consultant, writer; b. Ypsilanti, Mich., July 20, 1944; s. Hugo E. and Emma A. (Johansen) S.; m. Ann Mangelsdorf, June 15, 1968; children: Hans, Lars. BS, Ea. Mich. U., 1966; JD, Harvard U., 1969; DMin, Trinity Sem., 1998. Bar: N.Y. 1971, Tenn. 1981. Assoc. Milbank, Tweed, Hadley & McCloy, N.Y.C., 1971—76; assoc. prof. law U. Notre Dame, South Bend, Ind., 1976—80, prof., 1980—81; vis. prof. law Vanderbilt U. Law Sch., Nashville, 1980—81, prof., 1981—. Dir. corp. and securities law inst. 1993—; of counsel Baker, Donelson, Bearman, Caldwell & Berkowitz, P.C.; spl. master U.S. Dist. Ct. (no. dist.) Ohio, 1977; vis. prof. law Harvard U. Law Sch., Cambridge, Mass., 1999. Author: Corporations, 1979, 5th edit., 2001, Understanding the Securities Laws, 4th edit., 2003, Securities Law, 1998, 2d edit., 2004, Securities Regulation, 5th edit., 2003, Corporate Law and Practice, 2d edit., 1999, Law of Federal Estate and Gift Taxation: Code Commentary, 1978, Analysis, 1980, Investor's Rights Handbook, 1993; (novels) The Labcoat, 1998, The Iraqi Provocation, 2003; contbr. articles to profl. jours. Capt. U.S. Army, 1969-71. Decorated Army Commendation medal. Mem. ABA, Am. Law Inst. Home: 2000 Grand Ave Ste 801 Nashville TN 37212 Office: Vanderbilt U Sch Law 131 21st Ave S Nashville TN 37203-1120 Office Phone: 615-322-2607. Business E-Mail: larry.soderquist@vanderbilt.edu.

SODERQUIST, RONALD BRUCE, minister, ministry consultant; b. Pine City, Minn., Mar. 16, 1943; s. Russell Eugene and Abigail Mae (Berger) S.; m. Carol Lynn Peterson, Aug. 20, 1966; children: Peter Gustav, Ingrid Ann-Marie, Anna Kristine. BA, Northwestern Coll., 1965; MA, U. Wis., 1967; DMin, Bethel Theol. Sem., 1993. Ordained min. So. Bapt. Conv., 1988. Acad. dean Kings Inst. Coll., Koronodal, Cotabato, The Philippines, 1967-69; asst. prof. English Trinity Coll., Deerfield, Ill., 1969-70; student ministry staff Campus Crusade for Christ, L.A., Mpls., Madison, 1970-77, regional dir. midwest, 1977-80, internat. rep. in Sweden, 1980-84; spl. rep. Christian Embassy, Washington, 1984-87, dir. mil. ministry, 1987-98; adj. prof. MS in Orgnl. Leadership Program Geneva Coll., 1998; min., cons. Campus Crusade's U.S. Ministry, 1999—2001; city dir. Priority Assocs., Mpls., 2001—. Recipient Disting. Alumnus award, Northwestern Coll. St. Paul, 1999. Avocations: travel, photography, reading. Home: 5371 S Park Dr Savage MN 55378 Office Phone: 612-730-7037. E-mail: ron@servantleadership.com.

SODERSTROM, EDWARD JONATHAN, academic administrator, consultant; b. Grand Rapids, Mich., Nov. 17, 1954; s. Edward Carl and Anne Josephine Soderstrom; m. Gail Louise DeWitt, June 25, 1977; children: Rachelle Louise, Kari Anne, Luke Edward. AB, Hope Coll., 1972—76; PhD, Northwestern U., 1976—80. Rsch. staff Oak Ridge Nat. Lab., Tenn., 1980—84; dir., tech. commercialization Martin Marietta Energy Systems, Inc., Oak Ridge, 1984—94; dir., program devel. Lockheed Martin Energy Rsch. Corp., Oak Ridge, 1994—96; mng. dir., office of coop. rsch. Yale U. Bd. dirs. L2 Diagnostics LLC, New Haven, PhytoCeutica, Inc., New Haven, Agilix Corp., New Haven, Icionic Therapeutice, Nat. Tech. Transfer Ctr., Wheeling, W.Va., Applied Spine Tech., Inc., New Haven. Author: Social Impact Assessment, Impacts of Hazardous Tech., refereed jour. articles, book chapters. Pres., dir. Aid to Distressed Families of Appalachian Counties, Oak Ridge, Tenn., 1986—92; dir. United Way Anderson County, Oak Ridge, 1992—96, Enterprise Ctr. of New Haven, 1999—2003, Kern United Meth. Ch., Oak Ridge, 1988—92; elder Christ Chapel of the Christian & Missionary Alliance, Madison, Conn., 2000—04. Recipient Phi Beta Kappa, Phi Beta Kappa, 1976, Award for Excellence in Tech. Transfer, Fed. Lab. Consortium, 1986, Elm/Ivy Award, Cmty. Found. of Greater New Haven, 1999, named 87th Daily Point of Light by Pres. George H. W. Bush; fellow Pre-doctoral Fellow, NIMH, 1976 - 1979, Post-doctoral Fellow, NSF, 1980; grantee Pres. Scholar, Hope Coll., Sigma Chi Rsch. award. Mem.: Assn. of Fed. Tech. Transfer Executives (pres. 1993—93), Licensing Exec. Soc., Assn. of U. Tech. Managers (v.p. pub. policy 2003—04), Omicron Kappa Epsilon (pledge master 1976—76). Republican. Mem. Christian Ch. Avocations: golf, hunting, backpacking, hiking, bicycling. Home: 115 Opening Hill Rd Madison CT 06443-1922 Office: Yale U Office of Coop Rsch 433 Temple St New Haven CT 06511 Office Phone: 203-436-8096. Business E-Mail: jon.soderstrom@yale.edu.

SODERVICK, BRUCE WERNER, sculptor, art educator; b. Chgo., Feb. 28, 1939; s. Werner and Bertha Amelia (Lott) S.; m. Judith Zerbe, May 29, 1980. BS, Ind. U., 1962; MFA, So. Ill. U., 1967. Asst. prof. Ohio U., Chillicothi, 1967-71; prof. Rochester (N.Y.) Inst. Tech., 1971—. Artist residency Bemis Found., Omaha, 1985-86; vis. artist Ill. State U., Normal, 1987, Oxbow Art Inst. Chgo., 1991, Artpark, Lewiston, N.Y., 1994; co-dir. Sodervick Studios, Sodus, N.Y., 1977—; artist selection panel Regional N.Y. State Arts Coun., Lyons, 1993-94; moderator creative symposium SUNY, Oswego, 1993. One-man exhibits include SUNY, Oswego, 1992, Coffey Gallery, Rochester, 1994; group exhibts include Kittrell/Riffkind Gallery, Dallas, 1993, John Elder Gallery, N.Y.C.; featured artis Berkshire Ctr. Contemprary Glass, West Stockbridge, Mass., Waterside Gallery, West Stockbridge, Mass., Sculpture Installation Pedvale Open Air Art Mus., Sabile, Latvia, 2000; guest artist Hodgell Gallery, Sarasota, Fla., 1995. Coord. hist. ch. resorations, Episc. Diocese, Rochester, 1992-93; cons. hist. preservation, planning bd. chmn. Village of Sodus, 1992-94. Recipient Sculpture Installation award Rochester Arts Selection Com., 1986, First prize Sculpture Everson Mus., 1990; grantee S.C. Arts Commn., 1987. Mem. AAUP, ABYC, USSA, Coll. Arts Assn. Am., Glass Arts Soc., Sodus Bay Hist. Soc., Wayne County Coun. Arts. Achievements include research in glass casting with copper laden bronze, cast glass into cast iron, photo-emulsions into cold glass surfaces. Home: 27 E Main St Sodus NY 14551-1042 Office: Rochester Inst Tech Coll Imaging Arts & Scis/Sch Art 73 Lomb Memorial Dr Bldg 07A Rochester NY 14623-5603 E-mail: bwsodervick@hotmail.com.

SODHANI, ARVIND, computer company executive; Bachelor's, Master's, U. London; MBA, U. Mich., 1978. Asst. treas. Intel Europe Intel Corp., 1981—84, asst. treas., 1984—88, treas., 1988—90, v.p. and treas., 1990—. Office: 2200 Mission College Blvd Santa Clara CA 95052

SODINI, PETER J. food service executive; b. Jan. 26, 1941; With Fazio's div. of Fisher Foods Inc., 1976-78, Boys Markets Inc., L.A., 1978-1990, Buttrey Food & Drug Co., Great Falls, Mo., 1990-91; pres., EEO, Purity Supreme, North Billerica, Mass., 1991-98; CEO, Pantry, Sanford, N.C., 1998—. Office: Pantry PO Box 1410 Sanford NC 27331-1410

SODOLSKI, JOHN, retired association administrator; b. Menasha, Wis., Apr. 11, 1931; s. L.V. and L.W. (Pinkowski) S.; m. C.J. Eppard BS, U. Wis., 1953. Vice pres. Electronic Industries Assn., Washington, 1961-83; pres. U.S. Telephone Assn., Washington, 1983-93; ret., 1993. Served to 1st lt. USMC, 1955 Home: PO Box 1014 Middleburg VA 20118-1014

SODROSKI, JOSEPH G. medical educator; b. Coaldale, Pa. BS, Allentown Coll., 1976; MD, Jefferson Med. Coll., 1980. Intern in medicine New Eng. Deaconess Hosp., Boston, 1980—81; rsch. fellow in microbiology Dana-Farber Cancer Inst., Sch. Pub. Health Harvard U., Boston, 1981—84, from instr. to assoc. prof. div. human retrovirology Dana-Farber Cancer Inst., 1984—96, prof. div. human retrovirology Dana-Farber Cancer Inst., 1996—97, from instr. assoc. prof. dept. pathology Med. Sch., 1984—96, prof. dept. pathology Med. Sch., 1996—, assoc. prof. dept. cancer biology Sch. Pub. Health, 1992—96, prof. dept. cancer biology Sch. Pub. Health, 1996—97, prof. dept. cancer immunology and AIDS Dana-Farber Cancer Inst., 1997—, prof. dept. immunology and infectious diseases Sch. Pub. Health, 1997—. Chief div. human retrovirology Dana-Farber Cancer Inst. Harvard U., Boston, 1993—97; dir. Ctr. AIDS rsch. Dana-Farbert Inst. Beth Israel Deaconess Med. Ctr./Children's Hosp., Boston, 1994—; mem. sci. adv. bd. Ariel Project for prevention on HIV transmission from mother to infant, 1992—; mem. various coms. confs. in field; mem. external sci. adv. com. div. infectious diseases Mass. Gen. Hosp., 2000; mem. various coms. NIH; mem. sci. adv. bd. Aaron Diamond AIDS Rsch. Ctr. City N.Y., 1989—; mem. sci. adv. bd. Ctr. Human Retrovirology Thomas Jefferson U., 1995. Editor: Jour. Virology, 1993—98; editor: (assoc. editor) AIDS Scis., 1995—; reviewing editor AIDS, 1987—90, Jour. AIDS, 1988— (Howard Temin award for basic sci., 1993), AIDS Rsch. and Human Retroviruses, 1990—, Virology, 1991—, Jour. Virology, 1998—. Recipient Scholar award, Leukemia Soc. Am., 1986, Stohlman Meml. Scholar award, 1991, David Gottlieb Meml. Lectureship, U. Ill., 1993, Best of What's New award, Popular Sci. mag., 1998; fellow, Am. Found. AIDS Rsch., 1986; grantee, NIH, 1986—2002, Dept. Army, 1987—90, Am. Found. AIDS Rsch., 1987—88, postdoctoral fellow, NIH, 1981, Damon Runyon-Walter Winchell fellow, Damon Runyon-Walter Winchell Found., 1982, Spl. fellow, Leukemia Soc. Am., 1985. Mem.: AAAS, Clin. Immunology Soc., Am. Soc. Virology, Am. Soc. Microbiology, Delta Epsilon Sigma, Alpha Omega Alpha, Sigma Xi. Office: Dept Immunology and Infectious Diseases Dana-Farber Cancer Inst 44 Binney St Jimmy Fund Bldg Rm 824 Boston MA 02115

SODT, PETER CHRISTIAN, pediatrician, cardiologist; b. Exeter, N.H., Oct. 19, 1948; s. William George and Rita Anne Sodt; m. Kaye Dianne Sodt, May 8, 1971. MD, Northwestern U., 1980. Cert. Am. Bd. of Pediat., 1988. Pediatric cardiologist Luth. Gen. Hosp., Park Ridge, Ill., 1986—94, Midwest Children's Heart Specialists, Hoffman Estates, 1995—; attending cardiologist Children's Meml. Hosp., Chgo., 2002—. Fellow: Am. Acad. Pediat., Am. Coll. Cardiology. Office: Midwest Children's Heart Specialists 1575 N Barrington Rd #430 Hoffman Estates IL 60194 Office Phone: 847-884-1212. E-mail: drsodt@doctor.com.

SODUMS, DZINTARS, writer; b. Riga, Latvia, May 13, 1922; arrived in US, 1963; s. Andrejs and Ella Brastins Sodums; m. Skaidrite Kronbergs, Feb. 23, 1946 (dec. May 1999); children: Andris, Marcis. Student, Lynn C.C., 1975-80. Translator: Ulysses, 1960, 93, Narziss und Goldmund, 1951, 2002, Waste Land, 1990, Four Quartets, 1999. Mem. Latvian Writers Assn. in Exile. Democrat.

SOEDERSTROM, ELISABETH ANNA, opera singer; b. Stockholm, May 7, 1927; d. Emanuel Albert and Anna (Palasova) S.; m. Sverker Olow, Mar. 29, 1950; children: Malcolm, Peter, Jens. Student, Opera Sch., Stockholm; also pupil of Andrejewa Skilondz. Appearances include Stockholm Opera, 1950, Salzburg Festival, 1955, Glyndebourne Opera, 1957, 59, 61, 63, 64, Met. Opera, 1959, 60, 62, 63, 83, 86-87, 99; sang three leading roles in Rosencavalier within one year, 1959; toured USSR, 1966; others roles include Fiordiligi in Cosi Fan Tutte, Susanna and Countess in Figaro, Countess in Capriccio, Countess in Queen of Spades; radio, TV and concert appearances in U.S. and Europe; artistic dir., Drottningholm Ct. Theatre, 1993-97; author: I Min Tonart, 1978, Sjung ut, Elisabeth!, 1986. Decorated Order of Vasa, Sweden, 1997, Stelle Della Solidarieta Dell'Italia; recipient King Olav's reward, Norway, prize for best acting Royal Swedish Acad., 1965, Literis et Artibus award, 1969; named comdr. Most Disting. Order Brit. Empire, CBE, comdr. des Arts et des Lettres, Singer of the Ct., Sweden, prof. Swedish Govt.; recipient Ingmar Bergman award, 1988. Mem. Royal Acad. Music Gt. Britain (hon.). Office: Drottningholms Theatre Mus Box 15417 S-10465 Stockholm Sweden

SOEJIMA, DAISUKE, international trade engineer, economist; b. Tokyo, Jan. 17, 1959; s. Aritoshi and Hiroko Soejima; m. Kiyomi Soejima, Sept. 26, 1987; children: Sayuri, Taiga, Chiaki. BS in Econs., Tokyo U., 1983; MBA, Georgetown U., 1991. Assoc. cons., mgr. coord. Mitsubishi Corp., Tokyo, 1991-95; mgr. Mitsubishi Internat. Corp., Washington, 1995-97, mgr. project and planning N.Y.C., 1997-98, mgr. chem. groups M&A divestitures, 1998-2001; dir. E-Commerce Devel., 1999—2004, unit mgr. investment and devel., 2001—04; pres., CEO Mitsubishi Food Ingredientc, Inc., N.Y.C., 2004—. Sr. rschr. Japan Inst. for Econ. Rsch., Tokyo, 1981—83; founding assoc. Inst. Strategic Leadership, Japan. Grad. adv. bd. Georgetown U. Mem.: Asian Chem. Mgmt. and Rsch. Assn., Cornell Club, Met. Club, Alpha Mu Alpha, Beta Gamma Sigma. Home: 71 Hoyt St Darien CT 06820-3116 Office: Mitsubishi Internat Corp 520 Madison Ave New York NY 10022-4213 E-mail: daisuke.soejima@mitsubishicorp.com.

SOENEN, MICHAEL J. flower company executive; BA, Kalamazoo Coll., 1992. Mem. staff Salomon Brothers Inc., 1993-96; assoc. Perry Corp., 1996; dir. sales promotion FTD Inc., 1997-98, v.p. mktg., 1998; pres., CEO, dir. FTD.Com, Inc., Downers Grove, Ill., 1999—. Office: FTD Com Inc 3113 Woodcreek Dr Downers Grove IL 60515-5412

SOERING, JENS, writer; b. Bangkok, Aug. 1, 1966; s. Klaus and Anne-Claire Soering. Author: The Way of the Prisoner, 2003, An Expensive Way to Make Bad People Worse, 2004; contbr. articles to profl. jours. Roman Catholic. Home: c/o Lantern Books One Union Sq W Ste 201 New York NY 10003-3303

SOETEBER, ELLEN, journalist, editor; b. East St. Louis, Ill., June 14, 1950; d. Lyle Potter and Norma Elizabeth (Osborn) S.; m. Richard M. Martins, Mar. 16, 1974. BJ, Northwestern U., 1972. Edn. writer, copy editor Chgo. Today, 1972-74; reporter Chgo. Tribune, 1974-76, asst. met. editor, 1976-84, assoc. met. editor, 1984-86, TV and media editor, 1986, met. editor, 1987-89, assoc. mng. editor for met. news, 1989-91, dep. editor editorial page, 1991-94; mng. editor South Fla. Sun-Sentinel, Ft. Lauderdale, 1994-2001; editor St. Louis Post-Dispatch, 2001—. Fellow journalism U. Mich., Ann Arbor, 1986-87. Named to Hall of Achievement, Medill Sch. of Journalism, 2003. Office: The St Louis Post-Dispatch 900 N Tucker Blvd Saint Louis MO 63101 Office Phone: 314-340-8181. Business E-Mail: esoeteber@post-dispatch.com.

SOFAER, ABRAHAM DAVID, lawyer, educator, judge, consultant; b. Bombay, May 6, 1938; arrived in U.S., 1948, naturalized, 1959; m. Marian Bea Scheuer, Oct. 23, 1977; children: Daniel E., Michael J., Helen R., Joseph S., Aaron R., Raphael J. BA in History magna cum laude, Yeshiva Coll., 1962; LLB cum laude, NYU, 1965. Bar: N.Y. 1965, D.C. 1988. Law clk. to Hon. J. Skelly Wright U.S. Ct. Appeals (D.C. cir.), Washington, 1965-66; law clk. to Hon. William J. Brennan Jr. U.S. Supreme Ct., Washington, 1966-67; asst. U.S. atty. U.S. Dist Ct. (so. dist.) N.Y., N.Y.C., 1967-69; prof. law Columbia U., N.Y.C., 1969-79; judge U.S. Dist. Ct. (so. dist.) N.Y., 1979-85; legal advisor U.S. Dept. State, Washington, 1985-90; ptnr. Hughes Hubbard & Reed, Washington, 1991-94; George P. Shultz disting. scholar, sr. fellow Hoover Instn., Stanford U., 1994—. Hearing officer N.Y. Dept. Environ. Conservation, 1975-76. Author: War, Foreign Affairs and Constitutional Power: The Origins, 1976; contbr. articles to legal, polit., fgn. jours.; editor-in-chief: NYU Law Rev, 1964-65. Served with USAF, 1956-59. Root-Tilden scholar NYU, 1965. Mem. ABA, Fed. Bar Assn., N.Y.C. Bar Assn., N.Y. Bar Assn., Am. Law Inst. Jewish. Office: Stanford Univ The Hoover Instn Stanford CA 94305-6010 Fax: 650-723-2103. Office Phone: 650-725-3763. E-mail: sofaer@hoover.stanford.edu.

SOFFAR, WILLIAM DOUGLAS, lawyer; b. Houston, Sept. 8, 1944; s. Benjamin and Esther Goldy (Garfinkel) S.; m. Nancy Elise Axelrod, Mar. 29, 1969 (div. Sept. 1989), m. Gail Shinbaum, Jan. 16, 2000; children: Pamela Beth, Stephanie Michelle, Jill Denise. BA, U. Houston, 1966, JD, 1969. Bar: Tex. 1969, U.S. Dist. Ct. (so. dist.) Tex. 1970, U.S. Ct. Appeals (5th cir.) 1974, U.S. Supreme Ct. 1974; cert. mediator in civil law and family law. Atty. examiner U.S. Interstate Commerce Commn., Washington, 1969-70; atty. Law Office of Adolph Uzick, Houston, 1970-72, Walsh & Soffar, Houston, 1972-73; lawyer, sole practice Law Offices of William D. Soffar, Houston, 1973-74; ptnr. Soffar & Levit, Houston, 1974—. Family law and civil mediator, basic mediation and family mediation trainer Atty.-Mediator's Inst. Bd. dirs. Miller Theater Adv. Coun., Houston, 1985-90, Zina Garrison Found., Houston, 1989-91. Mem. Houston Bar Assn. (bd. dirs., family law sect. mem. 1989-90), Jewish Cmty. Ctr. (health club com. 1971—), Jewish Family Svc. (bd. dirs. 1970-71), Phi Delta Phi. Jewish. Avocations: travel, reading, raquetball. Office: 6575 West Loop S Ste 630 Bellaire TX 77401-3604

SOFIA, R. D. pharmacologist; b. Ellwood City, Pa., Oct. 8, 1942; BS, Geneva Coll., 1964; MS, Fairleigh-Dickenson U., 1969; PhD in Pharmacology, U. Pitts., 1971. Rsch. biologist Lederle Labs., N.Y., 1964-67; rsch. assoc. pharmacology Union Carbide Corp., 1967-69; sr. pharmacologist Pharmakon Labs., Pa., 1969, sr. rsch. pharmacologist, 1971-73, dir. dept. Pharmacology and Toxicology, 1973-76, v.p. biology rsch., 1976-80, v.p. R&D, 1980-82; v.p. pre-clin. and clin. rsch. Wallace Labs., Cranbury, 1982—. Cons. Pharmakon Labs., 1969-71. Mem. Am. Soc. Pharmacology and Experimental Therapeutics, Soc. Toxicology, SOc. Neuroscience, Internat. Soc. Study Pain, Am. Rheumatism Assn. Achievements include research in pharmacology and toxicology of various constituents of marijuana, development of new drugs for cardiovascular pulmonary and central nervous system diseases and pain relief. Office: Carter Wallace Pharmaceutical 265 Davidson Ste 300 Somerset NJ 08873-4120

SOFIA, SABATINO, astronomy educator; b. Episcopia, Italy, May 14, 1939; came to U.S., 1961; married, 1963; 2 children. BS, Yale U., 1963, MS, 1965, PhD in Astrophysics, 1966. Rsch. assoc. astrophysics Goddard Inst. Space Studies NASA, N.Y.C., 1966-67; from assoc. prof. to prof. astronomy U. South Fla., Tampa, 1967-73; vis. fellow Joint Inst. Lab. Astrophysics, Boulder, Colo., 1973-74; sr. rsch. assoc. U. Rochester, N.Y., 1974-75; adj. prof. astronomy U. Fla., 1975-78; staff scientist NASA, 1975-77; sr. rsch. assoc. solar physics Nat. Acad. Sci., Nat. Rsch. Coun., 1977-79; space scientist Goddard Space Flight Ctr., Greenbelt, Md., 1979-85; mem. space and earth sci. adv. com. NASA, 1985-88; prof. astronomy Yale U., New Haven, 1985—, chmn. astronomy dept., 1993-99. Mem. Am. Astron. Soc., Internat. Astron. Union, Am. Geophys. Union. Office: Yale U Dept Astronomy PO Box 208101 260 Whitney Ave New Haven CT 06520-8101 E-mail: sofia@astro.yale.edu.

SOFTIC, TANJA, artist; BFA, U. Sarajevo, Bosnia and Herzegovina, 1988; MFA, Old Dominion U./Norfolk State, 1992; student bookbinding, letterpress, Ctr. Book Arts, N.Y.C., 1993; student hand papermaking, Dieu Donne Paper Mill, N.Y.C., 1993. Printer Kathy Caraccio Printmaking Workshop, N.Y.C., 1991; adj. instr. Norfolk (Va.) State U., 1991—92; asst. prof. art Rollins Coll., 1992—2000; assoc. prof. art Richmond (Va.) U., 2000—. Asst. to gallery dir. Old Dominion U. Gallery, Norfolk, 1991—92; juror various exhbns., 1993—94; instr. workshops on printmaking history and techniques for docents Ctr. Fla. Art Mus., 1992—95; presenter in field. One-woman shows include various mus., Dubrovnik, Yugoslavia, 1989, Stanley Gallery, Norfolk, 1990, Collegium Artisticum, Sarajevo, 1991, Peninsula Fine Arts Ctr., Newport News, Va., 1992, Cornell Fine Arts Mus., Rollins Coll., Winter Park, Fla., 1994, Wyndy Moorehead Fine Arts, New Orleans, 1994, Coker Coll. Art Gallery, Hartsville, S.C., 1995, Kendall Gallery of Miami-Dade C.C., Miami, Fla., 1996, Allen R. Hite Art Inst., U. Louisville, 1996, Catherine J. Smith Gallery, Appalachian State U., Boone, N.C., 1997, exhibited in group shows at City Hall Gallery, Orlando, Fla., 1994 (Purchase award), Jacksonville (Fla.) C.C. Gallery, 1995 (hon. mention), U. Wis. at Parkside Gallery, Kenosha, 1995, Niagara C.C. Art Gallery, Buffalo, 1995, Catherine D. Smith Gallery, Appalachian State U., Boone, 1995, Kanagawa Prefectural Gallery, Japan, 1995, Paul Mesaros Gallery, W.Va. U., Morgantown, 1996, Hokkaido Mus. Modern Art, Sapporo, Japan, 1996, others, Represented in permanent collections. Recipient Best Debut prize, XV Biennial of Watercolor of Yugoslavia, 1989, Purchase award, Valencia Small Works, 1994, Orlando Biennial, 1994; fellow Grad. fellow, Old Dominion U. Coll. Arts and Letters, 1989; grantee Visual Artist grantee, Southeastern Coll. Art Conf., 1994; scholar Charles Sibley Grad. scholar, 1990—91, Artist scholar, Acad. Arts and Scis. of Bosnia and Herzegovina, 1990—91. E-mail: tsoftic@richmond.edu.

SOFTNESS, DONALD GABRIEL, marketing and manufacturing executive; b. Bklyn. s. Burt H. and Ida (Kaiser) S.; m. Sydell Meyerson; children: Michael, Anita May, Beth. AB, NYU, 1949, MBA, 1959; L.H.D., St. John's U., 1979. Chmn. Softness Group, Inc., N.Y.C., 1960-79; pres. Softness Groupe, N.Y.C., 1979—, SecureVue, Inc., N.Y.C., 1984—. V.p., maj. prin. Radio Stas. WVJ-AM-FM, Newark and N.Y.C.; mem. faculty Advt. Week seminars Advt. Age; prodr., promoter Bklyn. Rollathon (skating marathon). Co-author: Cardiologists' Guide to Health and Fitness Through Exercise, 1979; contbr. articles to bus. and trade jours. Patentee in mech. field. Served with USN. Mem. Public Relations Soc. Am., Internat. Radio TV Soc., Am. Coll. Sports Medicine Clubs: N.Y. Yacht. Home and Office: 28 Trues Dr West Islip NY 11795-5139 Office: SecureVue Inc 251 E 51st St New York NY 10022-6534 Office Phone: 212-752-5960.

SOGG, WILTON SHERMAN, lawyer; b. Cleve., May 28, 1935; s. Paul P. and Julia (Cahn) S.; m. Saralee Frances Krow, Aug. 12, 1962 (div. July 1975); 1 child, Stephanie; m. Linda Rocker Lehman, Dec. 22, 1979 (div. Dec. 1990); m. Nancy Rosenfield Walsh, June 2, 1991. AB, Dartmouth Coll., 1956; JD, Harvard U., 1959; postgrad., London Grad. Sch. Bus. Studies, 1974-76. Bar: (Ohio) 1960, (Fla) 1970, (U.S. Tax Ct.) 1961, (U.S. Supreme Ct.) 1969. Assoc. Gottfried, Ginsberg, Guren & Merritt, 1960-63, ptnr., 1963-70, Guren, Merritt, Feibel, Sogg & Cohen, Cleve., 1970-84; of counsel Hahn, Loeser, Freedheim, Dean and Wellman, Cleve., 1984-85; ptnr. Hahn Loeser & Parks LLP, Cleve., 1986-2000; of counsel McCarthy, Lebit, Crystal & Liffman Co., Cleve., 2001—. Trustee, pres. Cleve. Jewish News; adj. prof. Cleve. State U. Law Sch., 1960—; lectr. Harvard U. Law Sch., 1978-80. Author: (with Howard M. Rossen) new and rev. vols. of Smith's Review Legal Gems series, 1969—; editor: Harvard Law Rev.; contbr. articles to profl. jours. Trustee Jewish Cmty. Fedn. of Cleve., 1966-72; bd. overseers Cleveland Marshall Coll. Law, Cleve. State U., 1969—, vis. com. Coll. Bus. Adminstrn., 1996-2001, 2003-; mem. U.S. and State of Ohio Holocaust commns. Fulbright fellow U. London, 1959-60. Mem. Ohio Bar Assn., Fla. Bar Assn., Germany Philatelic Soc., Audubon Soc. (bd. dirs., v.p. Ohio chpt. 2003—), Oakwood Club, Union Club, Chagrin Valley Hunt, Club Phi Beta Kappa. Home: PO Box 278 Gates Mills OH 44040-0278 Office: McCarthy Lebit Crystal & Liffman 1800 Midland Bldg 101 W Prospect Ave Cleveland OH 44115-1088 Office Phone: 216-696-1422. Business E-Mail: wss@mccarthylebit.com.

SOHAILI, MONIRA, special education educator, writer; b. Pune, India, Nov. 4, 1933; d. Ispandiar and Keshvar Yaganegi; m. Shahpur Sohaili, Oct. 15, 1953 (dec. Dec. 2000). BA in Edn., Northeastern Ill. U., 1981, MA, 1982. Cert. behavioral therapy Behavioral Therapy Tng. Ctr., L.A., 1996. Tchr. Parramalta Marist H.S., Australia, 1970—71; guide Bahai House of Worship, Chgo., 1973—83; ESL instr. Cuban/Hatian Refugee Program, Chgo., 1983—84, Chgo. Bd. Edn., 1984—87; ESL and Eng. instr. Santa Monica (Calif.) City Coll., 1987—89; ESL, Eng. and reading tchr. Le Conte Mid. Sch., L.A., 1989—96; head dept. Ctr. Mid. Sch., 1994—96, spl. edn. tchr., 1996—, dept. head, 1996—2000; tchr. spl. edn. J. Burroughs Mid. Sch., L.A., 2000—. Storyteller in field, 2002—. Author: (children's book) Monira's Fables, 2000, From Earth and Beyond, 2003. Coord. childproof medicine vials donation, Papua New Guinea, 1995—97. Recipient Cert. of Achievement, L.A. USD Lang. Acquisition, 1993, I Made a Difference award, L.A. Dept. Edn., 1995. Mem.: NEA (reading and writing program 1990—), Calif. Tchrs. Assn. (assisted in program 1990—). Avocations: reading, writing, travel, swimming. Office: John Burroughs HS 600 McCadden Pl Los Angeles CA 90005 Address: PO Box 95 Santa Monica CA 90406 0095 Home: 840 23rd St Santa Monica CA 90403-2102

SOHAYDA, D. PAUL, music educator; s. David George Sohayda and Wendy Marie Rodgers; m. Carlie Elizabeth Donnelly, Oct. 12, 2002. B in music edn., Youngstown State U., 1994—99. Assoc. dir. Warren Jr. Mil. Band, Youngstown, Ohio, 1997—; dir. of bands Mathews Local Schs., Vienna, Ohio, 1999—2004, Liberty County H.S., Hinesville, Ga., 2004—. Mem.: Music Educators Nat. Conf., Ohio Edn. Assn., Ohio Music Edn. Assn.

SOHL, JOYCE DARLENE, religious organization administrator; b. Aurora, Ill., Dec. 15, 1935; m. Lowell Sohl (dec.); children: John, Stephen. BA, Westmar Coll., 1957; MA, U. Nebr., 1959; MBA, Fordham U., 1984. Math. tchr. Irving Jr. H.S., Lincoln, Nebr., 1959-61, Lincoln H.S., 1961-64; assoc. treas. gen. bd. global ministries women's divsn. United Meth. Ch., 1976-90, dep. gen. sec. gen. bd. global ministries women's divsn., 1991—. Author: (book) Managing Our Money, Workbook on Women and Finance; (videos) Giving: A Gift of God's Grace, 1988, Called to Mission, 1994, Managing Our Money, 1990, Count Me In, 1994; columnist: monthly column Responsively Yours, in Response, 1991—; also articles in ch. publs. and program materials for program book of Women's Soc. of World Svc. and United Meth. Women. Past mem. bd. trustees, treas. Meml. United Meth. Ch., White Plains, current lay del. to ann. conf., mem. pastor/parish rels. com., adminstrv. bd., substitute organist; bd. dirs. Scarritt-Bennett Ctr.; trustee Bennett Coll., Greensboro, N.C. Mem. NAFE, Am. Mgmt. Assn. Office: Gen Bd Global Ministries United Meth Ch 475 Riverside Dr Rm 1504 New York NY 10115-0122

SOHLMAN, MICHAEL, foundation administrator; b. Stockholm, 1944; s. Rolf R. and Zinaida (Yarotskaya) S. BA, U. Uppsala, Sweden, 1964, postgrad. in econs. and polit. sci., 1968, U. Stockholm, 1968. Asst. sec. to Commn. Environ. Problems, 1969; with Ministry of Industry, 1972-74; with internat. divsn. Ministry of Fin., 1974-76, with budget dept., 1976, head of planning econ. dept., 1982-84, dir. of budget, 1985-87; fin. counsellor, permanent Swedish del. OECD, 1977-80; with rsch. dept. Social-Dem. Parliamentary Group, 1981 82; under-sec. of state Ministry of Agriculture, 1987-89; under-sec. of state for fgn. affairs Ministry for Fgn. Affairs, 1989-91; exec. dir. Nobel Found., Stockholm, 1992—. Chmn. bd. dirs. Royal Dramatic Theatre, Stockholm, 1993-96; chmn. bd. dirs. Post Pension Fund; bd. dirs. Axel Johnson Internat. Mem. Royal Swedish Acad. Scis., Acad. of Engring. Scis. Office: Nobel Foundation PO Box 5232 102 45 Stockholm Sweden

SOHMER, BERNARD, mathematics educator, administrator; b. N.Y.C., July 16, 1929; s. Sol and Florence (Schonfeld) S.; m. Margot Rosette, July 27, 1952; children: Emily Sohmer Tai, Olivia Sohmer Rosenbaum. BA, NYU, 1949, MS, 1951, PhD, 1958. Lectr. CCNY, N.Y.C., 1952-57, faculty, 1958—, prof. math., 1969—, dean students, 1969-72. Asst. prof. NYU, 1957-58; trustee PSC-CUNY Welfare Fund, 1982-97; v.p. student affairs CCNY, N.Y.C., 1972-75, chmn. faculty senate, 1977-79, 85-91, 2002—03, ombudsman, 1991-98, 2002-03, chmn. liberal arts and sci. faculty coun., 1979-85, pres. Hillel, 1988-2001. Sec. Univ. Faculty Senate, CUNY, 1992-94, vice chair, 1994-98, chair, 1998-2002, ex-officio bd. trustees, 1998-2002. Mem. AAAS, AAUP (pres. CCNY chpt. 1966-67, sec. 1977-78), Am. Math. Soc., Math. Assn. Am. (pres. elect N.Y. Met. sect. 1989-90, pres. 1992-93, past pres. 1993-94, gov. 1996-98), Profl. Staff Congress (chair CCNY chpt. 1993-96, exec. coun. 1997-2000). Home: 3345 92nd St Jackson Heights NY 11372-1851 also: 176 E 77th St New York NY 10021 Office: The City College 139th St Convent Ave New York NY 10031-5150 E-mail: bescc@cunyvm.alby.edu.

SOHN, CATHERINE ANGELL, pharmaceutical executive, pharmacist; b. San Francisco, Mar. 21, 1953; d. Vincent Herbert and Margaret Ann Ware Angell; m. John Edwin Sohn, Aug. 10, 1974; children: Karen Elizabeth, Jennifer Michele. Ed., U. Calif., Davis; PharmD, U. Calif., San Francisco, 1977. Registered pharmacist, Calif., Pa. Pharmacist Kaiser Permanente, San Francisco, 1977-78; asst. prof. pharmacy Phila. Coll. Pharmacy and Sci., 1978-82; mgr. med. affairs Smith Kline & French, Phila., 1982-86; assoc. dir. bus. devel. pharm. divsn. Smith Kline Beecham, Phila., 1986-88, product dir., 1988-93, v.p. worldwide strategic product devel., 1994-97; v.p. worldwide bus. devel. Glaxo Smith Kline Consumer Healthcare, Phila., 1998—. Lectr. St. Andrew the Apostle, Gibbsboro, NJ, 1989—; adv. bd. Healthcare Bus. Women's Assn., N.Y.C., NY, 1996—; bd. overseers U. Calif. Sch. Pharmacy, San Francisco, 1997—; health adv. bd. Johns Hopkins U. Sch. Pub. Health, Balt., 1998—. Author: (with others) Applied Clinical Therapeutics, 1980, Handbook of Non-Prescription Drugs, 1980, rev. edit., 1982; contbr. chpts. to profl. pubs. Mem. Am. Pharm. Assn., Calif. Pharmacists Assn., Consumer Healthcare Products Assn. (chmn. internat. affairs com. 1998—, bd. dirs. 1999—), Licensing Exec. Soc., Rho Chi. Roman Catholic. Avocations: family activities, swimming, bicycling. Office: GlaxoSmithKline FP1370 200 N 16th St Philadelphia PA 19102-1282

SOHN, CHANG WOOK, energy systems researcher, educator; b. Seoul, Republic of Korea, Jan. 10, 1947; parents Kye Taek and Young Bo (Koh) S.; m. Chung Hae Han Sohn, Aug. 24, 1974; children: Douglas Jemin, Sammy Sungmin. BS in Engring., Seoul Nat. U., 1969; MS in Mech. Engring., Tex. Tech. U., 1975; PhD in Mech. Engring., U. Ill., 1980. Registered profl. engr., Ill. 1st lt. Korean Army, 1969-71; tchr. KyungGi H.S., Seoul, 1971-72; rsch. asst. Tex. Tech. U., Lubbock, 1973-74, U. Ill., Urbana, 1974-79, rsch. assoc., 1979-80; rsch. engr. U.S. Army Engring. R & D Ctr., Champaign, Ill., 1980-84, acting. team leader, 1992, prin. investigator, 1984—, project leader, 1995—2000. Adj. assoc. prof. U. Ill., Urbana, 1992-97; vis. rsch. fellow Korea Inst. Energy Rsch., 1995-96. Contbr. articles on fluid mechanics, heat transfer to profl. jours, ASHRAE transactions. Recipient Tech. Transfer award U.S. Army Corps of Engrs., Washington, 1991, Spl. Act award U.S. Army Yuma (Ariz.) Proving Ground, 1988; Korea Inst. Energy Rsch. fellow, 1995-96; Achievement Medal for Civilian Svc, Dept. Army. Mem. ASME (K-19 com. 1993-2000), ASHRAE (com. chair Cool Storage Design Guide 1992, air conditioning rsch. ctr. industry adv. bd. mem. 1991-96). Home: 2910 Robeson Park Dr Champaign IL 61822-7609 Office: US Army ERDC-CERL PO Box 9005 Champaign IL 61826-9005 E-mail: c-sohn@cecer.army.mil.

SOHN, HONG YONG, chemical engineer, educator, metallurgical engineer, educator; b. Kaesung, Kyunggi-Do, Republic of Korea, Aug. 21, 1941; arrived in U.S., 1966; s. Chong Ku and Soon Deuk (Woo) Sohn; m. Victoria Bee Tuan Ngo, Jan. 8, 1971; children: Berkeley Jihoon, Edward Jihyun. BSChemE, Seoul (Republic of Korea) Nat. U., 1962; MSChemE, U. N.B., Can., 1966; PhD in Chem. Engring., U. Calif., Berkeley, 1970. Engr. Cheil Sugar Co., Busan, Republic of Korea, 1962-64; rsch. assoc. SUNY, Buffalo, 1971-73; rsch. engr. DuPont Co., Wilmington, Del., 1973-74; prof. metall. engring., adj. prof. chem. engring. U. Utah, Salt Lake City, 1974—. Cons. Lawrence Livermore Nat. Lab., 1976—, Cabot Corp., 1984—, DuPont Co., 1987—, Utah Power and Light Co., 1987—, H. C. Starck, 1997—. Co-author: (book) Gas-Solid Reactions, 1976; co-editor: Rate Processes of Extractive Metallurgy, 1979, Extractive Metallurgy of Refractory Metals, 1980, Advances in Sulfide Smelting, 2 vols., 1983, Recycle and Secondary Recovery of Metals, 1985, Gas-Solid Reactions in Pyrometallurgy, 1986, Flash Reaction Processes, 1988, Metallurgical Processes for the Year 2000 and Beyond, 1988, Metallurgical Processes for the Early Twenty-First Century, 2 vols., 1994, Proceeding of the Julian Szekely Memorial Symposium on Materials Processing, 1997, Value-Addition Metallurgy, 1998, Sulfide Smelting, 2002, Metallurgical and Materials Processing: Principles and Technologies, 3 vols., 2003; contbr. articles to profl. jours. Recipient Fulbright Disting. lectr., 1983; Camille and Henry Dreyfus Found. Tchr. scholar, 1977, Japan Soc. Promotion Sci. fellow, 1990. Mem.: AIChE, AIME (James Douglas Gold medal 2001), Korean Inst. Chem. Engrs. (Fellow award 1998), Korean Acad. Sci. and Tech., Minerals, Metals and Materials Soc. (past dir., Extractive Metallurgy Lectr. award 1990, champion H. Mathewson Gold medal award 1993, Extraction and Processing Sci. award 1990, 1994, 1999). Achievements include patents for process for treating sulfide-bearing ores, continuous solvent extraction with bottom gas injection. Office: U Utah 135 S 1460 E Rm 412 Salt Lake City UT 84112-0114 Office Phone: 801-581-5491. Business E-Mail: hysohn@mines.utah.edu. *For-*

tunate are those who earn a living by doing what they would rather be doing even if they do not have to do it to earn a living. Material wealth accumulated by doing what one does not enjoy doing is not worth the effort.

SOHN, JEANNE, librarian; b. Milton, Pa. d. Robert Wilson and Juliette Lightner (Hedenberg) Gift; m. Steven Neil Sohn, Nov. 23, 1962. BA, Temple U., 1966; MSLS, Drexel U., 1971. Lit. bibliographer Temple U., Phila., 1971-75, chief of collection devel., 1975-81; asst. dean for collection devel. U. N.Mex., Albuquerque, 1981-86, assoc. dean for libr. svcs., 1986-89; dir. libr. svcs. Cen. Conn. State U., New Britain, 1989—. Cons. New Eng. Assn. Schs. and Colls., Winchester, Mass., 1991—. Mem. editorial bd. Collection Mgmt., 1984—; contbr. articles to profl. jours. Mem. Gov.'s Blue Ribbon Commn. on the Future of Libraries, 1994-96. Mem. ALA, New Eng. Libr. Assn., Conn. Libr. Assn., Assn. Coll. and Rsch. Librs., Beta Phi Mu. Home: 1820 Boulevard West Hartford CT 06107-2815 Office: Cen Conn State Univ Elihu Burritt Libr New Britain CT 06050

SOHN, LOUIS BRUNO, lawyer, educator; b. Lwów, Poland, Mar. 1, 1914; came to U.S., 1939, naturalized, 1943; s. Joseph and Fryderyka (Hescheles) S.; m. Elizabeth Mayo. LLM, Diplomatic ScM, John Casimir U., 1935; LLM, Harvard U., 1940, SJD, 1958; LLD (hon.), Free U. Brussels (Flemish sect.), 1990, George Washington U., 2000. Asst. to Judge M. O. Hudson, 1941-48; John Harvey Gregory teaching fellow Harvard Law Sch., 1946-47, lectr. law, 1947-51, asst. prof. law, 1951-53, John Harvey Gregory lectr. in world orgn., 1951-81, prof. law, 1953-61, Bemis prof. internat. law, 1961-81; Woodruff prof. internat. law U. Ga., 1981-91; vis. Congl. prof. George Washignton U. Law Sch., 1991-92; Disting. rsch. prof. and dir. rsch. and studies Internat. Rule of Law Ctr., George Washington U. Law Sch., 1992—. Disting. fellow Jennings Randolph program U.S. Inst. Peace, 1991-92; cons. U.S. ACDA, 1960-70, Office Internat. Security Affairs, Dept. Def., 1963-70; rsch. asst. joint project for internat. law of future ABA and Can. Bar Assn., 1943-44; asst. to del. Permanent Ct. Internat. Justice, San Francisco Conf. UN, 1945; exec. sec. legal subcom. on atomic energy Carnegie Endowment for Internat. Peace, 1946; asst. reporter on progressive devel. internat. law Am. and Canadian bar assns., 1947-48; cons. UN secretariat, 1948, 69, legal officer, 1950-51; counselor internat. law Dept. State, 1970-71, cons., 1982—; U.S. counsel Internat. Ct. Justice, 1971, 84; U.S. del. to UN Law of Sea Conf., 1974-82; U.S. del. head Athens Conf. on Settlement Internat. Disputes, 1984. Author: Cases on World Law, 1950, Cases on United Nations Law, 1956, 2d edit., 1967, (with G. Clark) World Peace Through World Law, 1958, 3d edit., 1966, Basic Documents of African Regional Organizations, 4 vols, 1971-72, (with T. Buergenthal) International Protection of Human Rights, 1973, (with K. Gustafson) The Law of the Sea in a Nutshell, 1984, International Organization and Integration: student edit. 1986, (with T. Buergenthal) The Movement of Persons Across Borders, 1992, Rights in Conflict: The United Nations v. South Africa, 1994; also articles on internat. legal subjects; editor devel. internat. law: Am. Bar Assn. Jour, 1947-50; editorial bd.: Am. Jour. Internat. Law, 1958— . Recipient World Peace Hero award World Federalists of Can., 1974, Grenville Clark award, 1984, William A. Owens award for creative rsch. in social and behavioral scis. U. Ga., 1985, Harry Leroy Jones award Washington Fgn. Law Soc., 1993, Internat. Human Rights award UN Assn. Nat. Capital Area, 1997. Mem. ABA (hon., co-rapporteur joint working group with Can. Bar Assn. on peaceful settlement of disputes 1976—, vice chmn. internat. law and practice sect. 1983-91, chmn. 1992-93, mem. coun. 1993-97, councillor 1997—, Leonard J. Theberge award 1992), Am. Soc. Internat. Law (mem. exec. coun. 1954-57, v.p. 1965-66, hon. v.p. 1980-87, 90—, pres. 1988-90, Manley O. Hudson medal 1996), World Parliament Assn. (legal advisor 1954-64), Internat. Law Assn. (v.p. Am. br.), Am. Law Inst. (assoc. reporter Fgn. Rels. Law 1978-87), Inst. Internat. Law (Geneva) (reporter on consensus in internat. law 1997-99), Fedn. Am. Scientists (vice chmn. 1963, mem. coun. 1964-65, 68-69), Commn. Study Orgn. Peace (chmn. 1986-98). Home: 801 15th St S Apt 1504 Arlington VA 22202-5023 Office: George Washington U Law Sch 720 20th St NW Washington DC 20052-0001

SOHN, RAYNA MAYER, medical analyst, researcher, legal analyst; b. Chgo., Jan. 14, 1938; d. Jacob DeCosta and Dorothy Mayer; widowed; children: Andrew, Douglas; m. Herbert Sohn (div. 1969); children: Marc, Tracy, Dana Teitler. BA with honors, UCLA, 1958. Pres. Vista Del Mar, L.A.; asst. to sr. v.p. Calif. Fed. Savings, L.A.; medical-legal analyst John D. Hayes & Assocs., Chgo. Translator laws SDL, Dominican Republic. Coord. campaign Sen. Arthur Berman; former lobbyist disabled, Chgo. and Washington. Mem. Phi Beta Kappa, Alpha Epsilon. Democrat. Jewish.

SOHN, YOUNG K. information technology executive; BSEE, U. Pa.; MBA, MIT. Co-founder Tektra Corp., Switzerland; product engr. Hewlett Packard; product mktg. mgr. microprocessor group Intel Corp., bus. unit mgr. PC chipset bus., mktg. and sales exec. dir. worldwide channel mktg.; pres. Ent. and Pers. Storage Group Quantum Corp., 1992; pres., mng. dir. Quantum Asia-Pacific; pres., CEO Oak Tech., Inc., Sunnyvale, Calif. Bd. dirs. PLX Tech., Earjam.com, Brainwave.com, Watab Ptnrs. Mem.: Asian Am. Mfg. Assn. (bd. dirs.), Young Pres. Orgn. Office: Oak Technology Inc 1390 Kifer Rd Sunnyvale CA 94086-5305

SOIFER, AVIAM, law educator, dean; b. Worcester, Mass., Mar. 18, 1948; married; 2 children. BA cum laude, Yale U., 1969, MA in Urban Studies, JD, Yale U., 1972. Bar: Conn. 1974, U.S. Dist. Ct. Conn. 1974, U.S. Supreme Ct. 1994. Law clk. to Judge Jon O. Newman U.S. Dist. Ct. Conn., 1972-73; asst. prof. U. Conn. Sch. Law, 1976-77, assoc. prof., 1977-78, prof., 1978-80, Boston U. Sch. Law, 1980-93, 98—; dean Boston Coll. Law Sch., 1993-98. Vis. prof. Boston U. Sch. Law, 1979-80. Author: Law the the Company We Keep, 1995; contbr. numerous articles to profl. jours. Vice chair Supreme Jud. Ct. Mass. Task Force on Jud. Edn., 1996-2001; mem. steering com. 1st Cir. Task Force on Gender, Race and Ethnicity, 1995-99; trustee New Eng. Med. Ctr., 1997—, Cambridge Health Alliance, 2002-. Recipient Disting. Sr. Rsch. award Boston Coll., 2001-02; named Disting. Scholar Legal Studies Inst., U. Wis., 2001-; Harvard Program in Law and Humanities fellow, 1976-77; Kellog Nat. fellow, 1981-84. Mem. ABA (commn. on coll. and univ. legal studies 1996-2000. Office: Boston Coll Law Sch 885 Centre St Newton Center MA 02459-1148

SOIFER, JED JOSHUA, mathematics and science educator; b. Bklyn., Mar. 11, 1941; s. David and Fanny (Birdee) Soifer; m. Barbara Jean Temme, July 12, 1992; children: Michael, Bridget. BS, Monmouth U., 1964; MA in Tchg., Fairleigh Dickinson U., 1966. Tchr. Hawaii pub. schs., Maui; prof. math. and physics Atlantic C.C., Mays Landing, NJ. With U.S. Army, 1959—60. Mem.: Math. Assn. Am. Avocations: photography, kayaking, hiking, computers.

SOJKA, GARY ALLAN, biologist, educator, academic administrator; b. Cedar Rapids, Iowa, July 15, 1940; s. Marvin F. and Ruth Ann (Waddington) Sojka Green; m. Sandra Kay Smith, Aug 5, 1962; children: Lisa Kay, Dirk Allan. BS, Coe Coll., 1962; MS, Purdue U., 1965, PhD, 1967, DSc (hon.), 2002; DL (hon.), Lycoming Coll., 1995. Rsch. assoc. Ind. U., Bloomington, 1967-69, asst. prof., 1969-73, assoc. prof., 1973-79, prof., 1979-84, assoc. chmn. biology, 1977-79, chmn. biology, 1979-81, dean arts and scis., 1981-84; pres. Bucknell U., Lewisburg, Pa., 1984-95, prof. biology, 1984—. Mem. higher edn. commn. Mid. States Assn. Colls. and Schs., 1992-96, chmn. task force on instnl. effectiveness, 1999-2000; chmn. tax policy subcom. Nat. Assn. Ind. Colls. and Univs., 1991-93; mem. study group on internat. edn. Am. Coun. Edn., 1992-94. Mem. So. Ind. Health Sys. Agy., Bedford; vice chair Am. Livestock Conxervancy, 2003—; chmn. bd. dirs. Stone Belt Coun. Ret. Citizens, Bloomington, 1977—78; mem. nominating com. Ind. Assn. Ret. Citizens, Indpls., 1979; bd. dirs. Geisinger Med. Found., Danville, Pa., 1985—97, 2003—, mem. regional bd., 1997—2003; chmn. Pa. Assn. Ind. Colls. and Univs., 1989—90; mem. pres.'s commn. NCAA, 1993—95; mem. planning adv. com. Snyder County, Pa., 1996—98, mem. planning commn., 2001—; bd. dirs. Bethesda Found., Lewisburg, 1996—98; trustee, bd. dirs. Am. Livestock Conxervancy, 2001—, vice chair, 2003—; dir. WITF Public Broadcasting, Harrisburg, bd. trustees, 2003—; gov. Inst. European Studies, 0989—1994, Citizen for the Future of Pa., 1999—. Recipient Ind. U. Sr. Class Tchg. award, 1975, Frederick B. Lieber award, 1977, Coe Coll. Alumni award of merit, 1982, Gary A. Sojka award Bucknell U., 1992, Cmty. Leadership award Susquehanna Valley Boy Scouts, 1994, Sheepskin award for Disting. Svc. to Higher Edn. Pa. Assn. Colls. and Univs., 2000, ECAC Appreciation award, Bucknell U., 2003, Adam Smith award Econ. Pa., 2003, Disting. Svc. medal Reading (Pa.) Ind. Day Coms., 2004; named to Coe Coll. Athletic Hall of Fame, 1988; Gary A. Sojka Pavillion named in his honor, 2003. Mem.: AAAS, Pa. Assn. Coll. and Univs. (interim pres. 1997—98, exec. com., Sheepskin award 1999, Sheepskin award 2000), Phila. Soc. Promotion of Agriculture, Am. Coun. Edn. (study group on internat. edn. 1992—94), Nat. Assn. Independent Colls. and Univs. (subcom. chmn. 1991—93), Am. Soc. Biol. Chemists, Am. Acad. Microbiology, Am. Soc. Microbiology, Omicron Delta Kappa, Sigma Nu, Sigma Xi. Baptist. Office: Bucknell U Dept Biology Lewisburg PA 17837

SOKAL, ROBERT REUVEN, biology professor, writer; b. Vienna, Jan. 13, 1926; came to U.S., 1947, naturalized 1958; s. Siegfried and Klara (Rattner) S.; m. Julie Chen-Chu Yang, Aug. 12, 1948; children: David Jonathan, Hannah Judith. BS in Biology, St. John's U., Shanghai, Republic of China, 1947; PhD in Zoology, U. Chgo., 1952; DSc (hon.), U. Crete (Greece), 1990. From instr. to prof. U. Kans., Lawrence, 1951-69; prof., then leading prof., Disting. prof. SUNY, Stony Brook, 1969-95, dept. chmn., 1980-83, vice provost for rsch. and grad. studies, 1981-82, disting. prof. emeritus, 1995. Fulbright vis. prof. Hebrew/Tel Aviv U., Israel, 1963-64, U. Vienna, Austria, 1977, 78, 84; vis. prof. Inst. Adv. Studies, Oeiras, Portugal, 1971-80; vis. disting. prof. U. Mich., 1975-76; vis. prof. Coll. de France, Paris, 1989. Author: Principles of Numerical Taxonomy, 1963, Biometry, 1969, 3d rev. edit., 1995, Statistical Tables, 1969, 3rd rev. edit. 1995, Introduction to Biostatistics, 1973, 2d rev. edit., 1987, Numerical Taxonomy, 1973; editor Am. Naturalist, 1969-74. Recipient Charles Darwin Lifetime Achievement award in phys. anthropology, 2004; Career investigator NIH, 1964-69; sr. fellow NSF, 1959-60, NATO fellow, 1974, Guggenheim fellow, 1975-76, 84; Ctr. Advanced Study in Behavioral Sci. fellow, 1992-93. Fellow AAAS, Am. Acad. Arts and Scis.; mem. Soc. Study Evolution (pres. 1977), Am. Soc. Naturalists (hon. mem., pres. 1984), The Classification Soc. (pres. 1969-71), Internat. Fedn. Classification Socs. (pres. 1988-89), Nat. Acad. Scis., Linnean Soc. London (fgn.), Soc. Systematic Zoology (hon.), Natural History Mus. (Paris, corr. mem.), B'nai Brith Lodge (pres. 1966). Democrat. Jewish.

SOKOL, DAVID L. energy services provider company executive; b. Omaha, Nebr., 1956; married; children: D.J.(dec.), Kelly. BSCE, U. Nebr., Omaha, 1978; hon. doctoral degree, Bellevue (Nebr.) U. With Citicorp, Henningson, Durham and Richardson, Inc.; pres., CEO, bd. dirs. Ogden Projects, Inc.; pres., CEO Peter Kiewit Energy Company, 1991; chmn., CEO MidAm. Energy Holdings Co. (succesor to CalEnergy Co., Inc.), Des Moines, 1991—, pres., from 1991. Co-chmn. for Campaign Nebr., U. Nebr. Found., dir.; mem. Met. Omaha Conv., Sports and Entertainment Authority; bd. dirs. Creighton U., Coll. World Series Omaha, Inc., Omaha Airport Authority, Strategic Command Consultation Co., Joslyn Art Mus., River City Roundup and Rodeo, Nebr. Easter Seal Soc., Mt. Michael Abbey H.S., Archdiocese of Omaha, Girls, Inc., Mid-Am. coun. Boy Scouts Am., Muscular Sclerosis Soc.-Midlands Chpt., United Way Midlands, Edison Electric Inst., Creighton U.; bd. govs. Knights of Ak-Sar-Ben; leadership adv. bd. bd. dir. NCAA; adv. com. arts JFK Ctr.; chmn. Met. Entertainment and Convention Authority Named CEO of Yr., Fin. Times Energy, 2000; recipient Individual Achievement award, Energy Daily, 2001. Mem. Del. Assn. Profl. Engrs., Neb. Soc. Profl. Engrs.; life mem. Horatio Alger Assn. Avocations: hockey, hunting, fishing, running, horseback riding. Office: MidAm Energy Holdings Co 666 Grand Ave PO Box 657 Des Moines IA 50303-0657*

SOKOL, JAN D. lawyer; b. N.Y., May 27, 1952; BS magna cum laude, Rutgers U., 1974; JD Northwestern Sch. of Law, Lewis and Clark Coll., 1977. Bar: Oreg. 1978, U.S. Dist. Ct. (dist. Oreg.), U.S. Ct. Appeals (9th cir.) 1981, U.S. Claims Ct. 1982, U.S. Supreme Ct. 1982. Law clerk to Hon. George A. Juba U.S. Dist. Ct. (dist. Oreg.), 1978-79, law clerk to Hon. Gus J. Solomon, 1979-80, law clerk to Hon. James A. Redden, 1980; mng. mem. Stewart, Sokol & Gray, 1994. Case note and comment editor Environmental Law, 1976-77. Mem. ABA (mem. forum com. on the construction industry, fidelity and surety, forest resources com.), Multnomah County.

SOKOL, ROBERT JAMES, obstetrician, gynecologist, educator; b. Rochester, N.Y., Nov. 18, 1941; s. Eli and Mildred (Levine) S.; m. Roberta Sue Kahn, July 26, 1964; children: Melissa Anne, Eric Russell, Andrew Ian. BA in Philosophy with highest distinction, U. Rochester, 1963, MD with honors, 1966. Diplomate Am. Bd. Ob-gyn. (assoc. examiner 1984-86), Sub-Bd. Maternal-Fetal Medicine. Intern Barnes Hosp., Washington U., St. Louis, 1966-67, resident in ob-gyn., 1967-70, asst. in ob-gyn., 1966-70, rsch. asst., 1967-68, instr. clin. ob-gyn., 1970; Buswell fellow in maternal fetal medicine Strong Meml. Hosp.-U. Rochester, 1972-73; fellow in maternal-fetal medicine Cleve. Met. Gen. Hosp.-Case Western Res. U., 1974-75, assoc. obstetrician and gynecologist, 1973-83, asst. prof. ob-gyn., 1973-77; asst. program dir. Perinatal Clin. Rsch. Ctr., 1973-78, co-program dir., 1978-82, program dir., 1982-83, acting dir. obstetrics, 1974-75, co-dir., 1977-83, assoc. prof., 1977-81, prof., 1981-83, assoc. dir. dept. ob-gyn., 1981-83; prof. ob-gyn. Wayne State U., Detroit, 1983-2000, dist. prof. ob-gyn., 2000—, chmn. dept. ob-gyn., 1983-89, mem. grad. faculty dept. physiology, 1984—, interim dean Med. Sch., 1988-89, dean, 1989-99, pres. Fund for Med. Rsch. and Edn., 1988—99; chief ob-gyn. Hutzel Hosp., Detroit, 1983-89; interim chmn. med. bd. Detroit Med. Ctr., 1988-89, chmn. med. bd., 1989-99, sr. v.p. med. affairs, 1992-99, trustee, 1990-99; past pres. med. staff Cuyahoga County Hosps.; mem. profl. adv. bd. Educated Childbirth Inc., 1976-80; dir. C.S. Mott Ctr. for Human Growth and Devel., 1983-89, 99—. Sr. Ob cons. Symposia Medicus; cons. Grant Planning Task Force Robert Wood Johnson Found., Nat. Inst. Child Health and Human Devel., Nat. Inst. Alcohol Abuse and Alcoholism, Ctr. for Disease Control, NIH, Health Resources and Svcs. Adminstrn., Nat. Clearinghouse for Alcohol Info., Am. Psychol. Assn.; mem. alcohol psychosocial rsch. rev. com. Nat. Inst. Alcohol Abuse and Alcoholism, 1982-86; mem. ob-gyn. adv. panel U.S. Pharmacopial Conv., 1985-90, adv. com. on policy Am. Jour. Ob-gyn., 1999-, internat. adv. bd. Karmanos Cancer Inst., Detroit, Mich., 2002-; mem. clin. rsch. task force Assn. Am. Med. Colls., 1998-2000; mem. WSU Faculty Devel. Coun., 2003—. Mem. internat. editl. bd. Israel Jour. Obstetrics and Gynecology; reviewer med. jours.; mem. editl. bd. Jour. Perinatal Medicine; editor-in-chief Interactions: Programs in Clinical Decision-Making, 1987-90; rschr. computer applications in perinatal medicine, alcohol-related birth defects, perinatal risk and neurobehavioral devel.; contbr. chpts. to books and articles to profl. jours. Mem. Pres.'s leadership coun. U. Rochester, 1976—80, permanent trustee, 1986—; mem. exec. com. bd. trustees Oakland Health Edn. Program (OHEP), 1987—2000, permanent trustee, 2000—; vice chmn. bd. Am. U. of the Caribbean, 2004—; bd. dirs. Grand Theatre, London, Canada, 2002—, vice chair, 2004—. Maj. M.C. USAF, 1970—72. Recipient 15 sci. rsch. awards, 1986—. Mem.: APHA, ACOG (chmn. steering com. drug and alcohol abuse contract 1986—87, rep. ctr. for disease control & prevention task force 2000—, editor-in-chief ACOG Update 2001—), NAS (Inst. of Medicine, com. to study fetal alcohol syndrome 1994—96), AMA, Soc. Maternal-Fetal Medicine Found. (bd. chmn. 2003—), Wayne State U. Acad. Scholars, Soc. Physicians Reproductive Choice and Health, World Assn. Perinatal Medicine, Internat. Soc. Computers in Obstetrics, Neonatology, Gynecology (v.p. 1987—89, pres. 1989—92), Soc. for Neuroscis. (Mich. chpt.), Am. Med. Soc. on Alcoholism and Other Drug Dependencies, Am. Gynecol. and Obstet. Soc., Neurobehavioral Teratology Soc., Soc. Perinatal Obstetricians (pres.-elect 1987—88, pres. 1988—89, v.p., Achievement award 1995), Rsch. Soc. Alcoholism, Ctrl. Assn. Obstetricians-Gynecologists (pres.-elect 1997—99, pres. 1999—2000), Detroit Acad. Medicine (pres.-elect 1999—2001, pres. 2001—02), Wayne County Med. Soc., Mich. Med. Soc., Royal Soc. Medicine, Assn. Profs. Ob-gyn., Perinatal Rsch. Soc., Soc. Gynecologic Investigation, Am. Med. Informatics Assn., Chgo. Gynecol. Soc. (hon.), Detroit Physiol. Soc. (hon.), Alpha Omega Alpha, Sigma Xi, Phi Beta Kappa. Republican. Jewish. Home: 7921 Danbury Dr West Bloomfield MI 48322-3581 Office: Wayne State U CS Mott Ctr for Human Growth and Devel Detroit MI 48201 Office Phone: 313-577-1337. Business E-Mail: rsokol@moose.med.wayne.edu. *The drive for academic accomplishment was instilled early in childhood in a home environment which placed value on a multiplicity of interests in science and the arts. My parents taught me what to do. In retrospect, exposure to strong role models-professors of philosophy, pathology, psychiatry and obstetrics-gynecology-takes on increased importance-these individuals showed me how to do it. My family continues to support me in seeking and meeting new challenges. The opportunity to develop and transmit new knowledge sustains a high level of activity. I enjoy what I do.*

SOKOLOFF, AUDREY L. lawyer; b. Providence, R.I., 1966; AB, Dartmouth Coll., 1987; JD, U. Calif., LA, 1990. Bar: Calif. 1990, N.Y. 1999. Atty. Skadden, Arps, Slate, Meagher & Flom LLP, New York, 1999—. Office: Skadden Arps Slate Meagher & Flom LLP Four Times Sq New York NY 10036

SOKOLOFF, LEON, pathology educator; b. Bklyn., May 9, 1919; s. Barnet and Ray (Cohen) Sokoloff; m. Barbara Snow, June 1950 (dec. 1960); children: Michael D., Naomi B. Sokoloff Berry; m. Beverly Beinfeld Trachtenberg, July 18, 1971. BA, NYU, 1938, MD, 1944; postgrad., Columbia U., 1938—39. Diplomate Am. Bd. Pathology. Resident Bellevue Hosp., N.Y.C., 1948—52; chief sect. on rheumatic diseases Lab. Exptl. Pathology, NIH, Bethesda, Md., 1953—73; prof. pathology SUNY, Stony Brook, 1973—91, emeritus, 1991—. Vis. prof. Royal Soc. Medicine, England, 1985. Author: Biology of Degenerative Joint Disease, 1969; editor: The Joints and Synovial Tissue, 1978; contbr. articles to profl. jours. Served to capt. USPHS, 1953—73. Recipient J. van Breemen medal, Dutch Rheumatism Assn., 1967, Disting. Alumnus award, NYU, 1975; grantee, NIH, 1973—87. Master: Am. Coll. Rheumatology; mem.: Am. Soc. Investigative Pathology, Am. Coll. Vet. Pathologists (hon.). Jewish. Avocation: medical history. Office: SUNY Dept Pathology Health Sci Ctr Stony Brook NY 11794-8691 E-mail: leobevsok@aol.com.

SOKOLOFF, LOUIS, physiologist, neuroscientist; b. Phila., Oct. 14, 1921; married; 2 children. BA, U. Pa., 1943, MD, 1946; Dr. (hon.), Philipps U. Marburg, Germany, 1990; MD (hon.), U. Rome, 1992; ScD (hon.), Georgetown U., 1992, Mich. State U., 1993, U. Pa., 1997. Intern Phila. Gen. Hosp., 1946-47; rsch. fellow in physiology U. Pa. Grad. Sch. Medicine, 1949-51, instr., then assoc., 1951-56; assoc. chief, then chief sect. cerebral metabolism NIMH, Bethesda, Md., 1953-68, chief lab. cerebral metabolism, 1968—. Chief editor Jour. Neurochemistry, 1974-78. Served to capt. M.C. U.S. Army, 1947-49. Recipient F.O. Schmitt medal in neurosci., 1980, Albert Lasker clin. med. research award, 1981, Karl Spencer Lashley award Am. Philos. Soc., 1987, Disting. Grad. award U. Pa., 1987, Nat. Acad. Scis. award in Neurosci., 1988, Georg Charles de Hevesy Nuclear Medicine Pioneer award Soc. Nuclear Medicine, 1988, Mihara Cerebrovascular Disorder Rsch. Promotion award, 1988. Mem. NAS, Inst. Medicine (sr.), Am. Physiol. Soc., Assn. Rsch. Nervous and Mental Diseases, Am. Biophys. Soc., Am. Acad. Neurology, Am. Neurol. Assn., Am. Soc. Biol. Chemists, Am. Soc. Neurochemistry. Achievements include development of methods for measurement of cerebral blood flow and metabolism in animals and man. Office: NIMH/NIH Bldg 36 Rm 1A07 9000 Rockville Pike Bethesda MD 20892-4030 Office Phone: 301-496-1371.

SOKOLOV, IGOR, physicist, researcher; arrived in Can., 1994,arrived in US, 2000; s. Yurij M. Sokolov and Larissa P. Sokolova; m. Elena A. Yuplova, Apr. 22, 1994; children: Maksim I., Nina A. MS, St. Petersburg State U., Russia, 1984; PhD, D.I. Mendeleev Metrology Inst., St. Petersburg, Russia, 1994. Post doc. fellow St. Petersburg Inst. for Tech., St. Petersburg, Russia, 1991—94; rsch. assoc. U. Toronto, Canada, 1994—2000; asst. prof. Clarkson U., Potsdam, NY, 2000—. Cons. Procter and Gamble, 2003—; guest lectr. Ministry of Edn., Sci., Sports and Culture Govt. of Japan, 1993, 96, 98; guest lectr. German Sci. Found., 1987. Author over 70 papers in sci. jours. Recipient Best Young Rschr. of Yr., D.I.Mendeleev Metrology Inst., 1985, 1986, 1987; fellow E.L. Ginzton Internat. award, Stanford U., 1992-1994; grantee, Soros Found., 1993-1994. Mem.: Am. Vacuum Soc., Am. Chem. Soc., Am. Phys. Soc. Achievements include patents for electro-separation. Office: Clarkson U 8 Clarkson Ave Potsdam NY 13699-5820

SOKOLOV, RICHARD SAUL, real estate company executive; b. Phila., Dec. 7, 1949; s. Morris and Estelle Rita (Steinberg) S.; m. Susan Barbara Saltzman, Aug. 13, 1972; children: Lisa, Anne, Kate. BA, Pa. State U., 1971; JD, Georgetown U., 1974. Assoc. Weinberg & Green, Balt., 1974-80, ptnr., 1980-82; v.p., gen. counsel The Edward J. DeBartolo Corp., Youngstown, Ohio, 1982-86, sr. v.p. devel., gen. coun., 1986-94; pres., CEO DeBartolo Realty Corp., Youngstown, Ohio, 1994-96; pres., COO Simon DeBartolo Group, Indpls., 1996-98; pres, COO Simon Property Group, Indpls., 1998—. Mem. investment com. Jewish Fedn., Youngstown, 1992—; trustee U. Wis.-Madison Ctr. for Urban Land Econs. Rsch., Youngstown/Mahoning Valley United Way. Alumni fellow Pa. State U., 2000. Mem. Internat. Coun. Shopping Ctrs. (trustee 1994—, chmn. 1998-99), Urban Land Inst. (assoc.). Office: Simon Property Group 115 W Washington St Ste 1465 Indianapolis IN 46204-3464

SOKOLOW, LLOYD BRUCE, lawyer, psychotherapist; b. N.Y.C., Nov. 3, 1949; s. Edwin Jay and Harriet (Corman) S.; m. Christina Carol Smolinski, Jan. 27, 1979; children: Joshua, Jessica. BA, U. Buffalo, 1971, MS, 1974, JD, 1978, PhD, 1979. Bar: U.S. Dist. Ct. (we. dist.) N.Y. 1979, Conn. 1985, U.S. Dist. Ct. Conn. 1986. Rsch. scientist Rsch. Inst. on Alcoholism, Buffalo, 1976—80; legal cons. N.Y. Gov.'s Task Force on Drinking and Driving, Albany, 1979—82; pvt. practice Schenectady, NY, 1986—2000; counsel, exec. dir. Conifer Park, Scotia, NY, 1981—83; counsel, dir. substance abuse svcs. Inst. of Living, Hartford, Conn., 1984—86; founder, exec. dir. Lifestart Health Svcs., 1986—2000; prin. Lloyd Sokolow & Assocs., Schenectady, 2000—. Atty. Town of Knox, NY, 1980—92; cons., 2000—. Bd. dirs. Schenectady Community Svc. Bd., 1982—89; pres. Schenectady Cmty. Svc. Bd., 1989; mem. Surrogate Decision Making Commn., 1990—2001, N.Y. Commn. on Quality of Care; dir. addictions State of Md., 1988—89; counsel Apogee, Inc., 1996—98. Regent scholar NY State, 1967; Univ. fellow U. Buffalo, 1973, Baldy Law fellow, 1979. Mem.: APA. Office: 2183 Grand Blvd Niskayuna NY 12309-5843 E-mail: lpilotus@yahoo.com.

SOKOLSKY, ROBERT LAWRENCE, journalist, entertainment writer; b. Boston, May 18, 1928; s. Henry and Lillian (Gorodetzky) S.; m. Sally-Ann Moss, Aug. 11, 1955; 1 son, Andrew E. AB, Syracuse (N.Y.) U., 1950. Reporter Springfield (Mass.) Union, 1950; asst. dir. pub. info. ARC, Syracuse, 1952-54; entertainment editor Syracuse Herald-Jour., 1954-61, Buffalo Courier Express, 1961-72, Phila. Bull., 1972-82; entertainment writer Riverside (Calif.) Press-Enterprise, 1983-2000; syndicated TV columnist Ottaway News Svc., 1988-96, Scripps Howard, 1996-2000; freelance writer, radio commentator pub. radio, 2000—; columnist San Bernardino Sun, 2001—; entertainment editor Inland Empire News Radio, 2001—. Radio show host; freelance writer; guest lectr. Contbr. columns in newspapers, 2001, articles to profl. jours. Bd. dirs. Brush Hollow Civic Assn., Evesham Twp., N.J. Served with U.S. Army, 1950-52. Recipient Sigma Delta Chi award for feature writing, 1950, award for entertainment coverage Twin Counties Press Club, 1984, 87, Lifetime Achievement award Inland Theatre League, 2001. Mem. Am. Newspaper Guild (Page One award for opinion writing), Syracuse Press Club, Greater Buffalo Press Assn., TV Critics Assn., Soc. Profl. Journalists (Excellence in Journalism award 1989, 93), Pen and Pencil Club of Phila., Variety Club. Republican. Jewish. Home and Office: 3080 Saratoga St Riverside CA 92503-5435 E-mail: rsokolsky@charter.net.

SOLA, AUGUSTO, pediatrician, educator; m. Marta Rogido; children: Mariana, Carolina, Augusto Jr., Ignacio. BS (Bilingual), Belgrano Day Sch., Buenos Aires, Argentina, 1967; MD, Buenos Aires Nat. U. Sch. of Medicine, Argentina, 1973. Dir. neonatal clin. services U. of Calif., San Francisco, 1991—97, prof. pediat., 1995—97; dir. divsn. of neonatology Cedars-Sinai Med. Ctr., LA, 1997—2001; prof. pediat. U. of Calif., LA, 1997—2001; dir. divsn. of neonatal-perinatal medicine Emory U. Sch. of Medicine, Atlanta, 2001, co-director, devel. progress clinic, 2001—, prof. pediat. and obstetric-s,gynecology (tenured), Goddard scholar, 2001—. Prof. pediat., dir. neonatology U. Buenos Aires, 1985—91; dir. neonatal fellowship program Cedars-Sinai Med. Ctr., LA, 1998—2001; cons. Am. Assn. of World Health, 1998—.

Author: (book) Cuidados Intensivos Neonatales-Fisiopatologia y Terapeutica, Cuidados Especiales del Feto y Recien Nacido, Fisipatologia y Terapeutica, (manuscript) Jour. of Pediats. Nominee Ten Outstanding Young Profl. of the World, Internat. Jr. Chamber, 1989; recipient E.H. Christopherson award on Internat. Child Health, Am. Acad. of Pediat., 1999. Fellow: Am. Acad. of Pediat.; mem.: AAAS, Am. Acad. of Pediat. Sect. on Internat. Child Health, Soc. of Pediatric Rsch. Office: Emory Univ 2040 Ridgewood Dr Atlanta GA 30322 E-mail: asola2@emory.edu.

SOLA, JURE, electronics executive; BSEE, San Jose State U., 1972. Various mgmt. positions Lika Corp., Stockton, Calif., 1972-80; various mgmt positions Sanmina Corp. and predecessor, 1980—, now pres. & chmn., 1991—2001; co-chmn. Sanmina-SCI, 1999—2002, CEO, 2001—, chmn., 2002—. Office: Sanmina Corp 2700 N 1st St San Jose CA 95134-2015

SOLA, VICTORIA M. announcer, writer; b. Englewood, N.J., Nov. 11, 1952; d. Salvador Felix and Hedda Blanc (Westhead) Solá; 1 child, Frank Salvador Solá Grillo. Student, Fairleigh Dickinson U., N.J., 1970—72. Radio host, prodr. jazz WFDU-FM Radio, Teaneck, NJ, 1981—83, jazz dir., 1982—86, radio host, prodr. Latin, 1983—, Latin music dir., 1983—; contbr. editor Descarga Catalog, N.Y.C., 1996—2002; columnist Latin London Mag., 1999, Latin Beat Mag., Gardena, Calif., 1998—. Latin jazz planning com. adv. Smithsonian Inst. Traveling Exhbn. Svc., Washington, 1999—2002, narrator, 2002. Coord. ann. on-air fundraiser for Latin music programming WFDU-FM, Teaneck, NJ, 1983—; participant on-air drive for blood donors Bergen Cmty. Regional Blood Ctrs., Paramus, NJ, 1986. Mem.: Internat. Latin Music Hall of Fame (adv. com. 1999—, Spl. Recognition award 2001). Democrat. Avocations: reading, photography, drawing, writing. Office: WFDU-FM 1000 River Rd Teaneck NJ 07666 Office Phone: 201-692-2806 10. Office Fax: 201-692-2807. E-mail: vickisola1@aol.com.

SOLAN, STUART MILEY, physician; b. Washington, Aug. 20, 1951; s. George Miley and Marjorie Ann (Sonneman) S.; m. Carol Jean Cummins, Oct. 14, 1952; children: Christopher Miley, Melissa Ann. BA, W.Va. U., 1973; MD, Med. Coll. Va., 1977. Diplomate Am. Bd. Family Practice. Intern, then resident Riverside Hosp., Newport News, Va., 1977-80; pvt. practice Commonwealth Primary Care, Richmond, Va., 1980—; asst. clin. prof. family practice Med. Coll. Va., Richmond, 1982-2000, assoc. clin. prof. family practice, 2000—. Pres. med. staff St. Lukes Hosp., Richmond, 1986-87, trustee, 1986-87; question writer Am. Bd. Family Practice, 1989-93. Deacon, elder Third Presbyn. Ch., Richmond, 1987—. Fellow Am. Acad. Family Physicians; mem. Va. Acad. Family Physicians (v.p. 1991-92, pres. 1993-94, Va. Family Dr. of Yr. 1991-92), Richmond Acad. Medicine. Avocations: hunting, fishing, pocket billiards, civil war history. Home: 9001 Chapaqua Ct Richmond VA 23229-7745 Office: Commonwealth Primary Care 10431 Patterson Ave Richmond VA 23233-5101 Office Phone: 804-741-6200.

SOLANO, CARL ANTHONY, lawyer; b. Mar. 26, 1951; s. Nick D. and Catherine A. (Occhiato) S.; m. Nancy M. Solano, 1989; children: Melanie A., Carla Nicole. BS magna cum laude, U. Scranton, 1973; JD cum laude, Villanova U., 1976. Bar: Pa. 1976, U.S. Dist. Ct. (ea. dist.) Pa. 1978, U.S. Ct. Appeals (3d cir.) 1980, U.S. Ct. Appeals (5th cir.) 1981, U.S. Supreme Ct. 1982, U.S. Ct. Appeals (9th cir.) 1986, U.S. Dist. Ct. (mid. dist.) Pa. 1988, U.S. Ct. Appeals (6th cir.) 1988, U.S. Ct. Appeals (fed. cir.) 1989, U.S. Ct. Appeals (6th cir.) 1988, U.S. Ct. Appeals (7th cir.) 1996. Law clk. Hon. Alfred L. Luongo U.S. Dist. Ct. (ea. dist.) Pa., Phila., 1976—78; assoc. Schnader, Harrison, Segal & Lewis, Phila., 1978—84, ptnr., 1985—. Adj. prof. Villanova U. Sch. Law, 1999—2001. Mem.: ABA, Justinian Soc., St. Thomas More Soc., Phila. Bar Assn. (chair bar news media com. 2003), Pa. Bar Assn. (statutory law com. 1980—95), Am. Law Inst., Order of Coif, Pi Gamma Mu. Roman Catholic. Home: 5 Barrister Ct Haverford PA 19041-1137 Office: Schnader Harrison Segal & Lewis LLP 1600 Market St Ste 3600 Philadelphia PA 19103-7287 Office Phone: 215-751-2202. E-mail: CSolano@Schnader.com.

SOLANO, HENRY L. lawyer; m. Janine Solano; children: Mateo, Amalia, Guadalupe. BS in Mech. Engring., U. Denver; JD, U. Colo.; LLD (hon.), U. Denver. Asst. atty. gen. Human Resources divsn. Colo. Dept. Law, 1977-82; asst. U.S. atty. Dist. Colo., 1982-87; U.S. atty. for Colo. U.S. Dept. Justice, Denver, 1994-98; solicitor U.S. Dept. Labor, Washington, 1998-2001; ptnr. LeBoeuf, Lamb, Greene & MacRae L.L.P., Denver, 2001—. Exec. dir. Colo. Dept. Instns., 1987-91, Colo. Dept. Regulatory Agys., 1987; acting exec. dir. Colo. Dept. Corrections, 1989-90; chair Cabinet Coun. on Families and Children, 1990-91; mem. adv. com. U.S. Atty. Gen., 1994-95; lectr. Kennedy Sch. Govt. Bd. dirs. Nat. Latino Children's Inst., Mex.Am. Legal Def. Edn. Fund, Denver Housing Authority, Denver Women's Commn., Colo. Dept. Social Svcs., Colo. Transit Constrn. Authority, Regional Transit Dist. Office: 136 S Main St Ste 1000 Salt Lake City UT 84101-1685

SOLANO, JULIO RAFAEL, priest, educator; b. Barranquilla, Atlantico, Colombia, Sept. 12, 1946; came to U.S., 1971; s. Domingo Rafael Solano and Christine Balderrama. Degree in acctg., Centro Intensificacion Comml., Bogota, Colombia, 1970; BA, St. John Vianney Coll. Sem., Miami, Fla., 1989; MDiv, St. Vincent de Paul Regl. Sem., Boynton Beach, Fla., 1993. Transitional deacon St. Louis Cath. Ch., Miami, 1992—93; asst. pastor St. Elizabeth Cath. Ch., Pompano Beach, Fla., St. Patrick Cath. Ch., Miami Beach, Fla., 1996—98; parochial vicar St. Coleman Cath. Ch., Pompano Beach, 1998—99, St. Elizabeth of Hungary Cath. Ch., Pompano Beach, 1999—2001, St. Vincent Cath. Ch., Margate, Fla., 2001—02; pastor Our Lady Queen of Heaven Cath. Ch., North Lauderdale, Fla., 2002—. Tchr. La Salle H.S., Miami, 1996-98; asst. chaplain Serra Club Internat. Pompano Beach, 1994-95. Mem. KC, Assn. Sacerdotes Hispanos. Democrat. Roman Catholic. Avocations: travel, reading, writing, stamps, coins. Office Phone: 954-971-5400.

SOLAR, RICHARD LEON, banker; b. Boston, Aug. 15, 1939; s. Hervey L. and Mildred (Beckerman) Solar; m. Stephanie Bennett; children: Andrew, Lisa. BA, Harvard U., 1961; MBA, Columbia U., 1963. Asst. v.p. Bankers Trust Co., N.Y.C., 1963—71, sr. v.p., mng. dir., 1976—96; treas. Val D'Or Inds., N.Y.C., 1971—74, Diamondhead Corp., Mountainside, NJ, 1975—76; sr. v.p., dir. Gerber Childrens Wear Inc., N.Y.C., 1996—2002; dir. Marvel Enterprises, 2002—. Mem.: Wyantenuck Country Club (Great Barrington, Mass.). E-mail: solar4922@aol.com.

SOLARO, ROSS JOHN, physiologist, biophysicist; b. Wadsworth, Ohio, Jan. 9, 1942; s. Ross and Lena (Chuppa) S.; m. Kathleen Marie Cole, Sept. 18, 1965; children: Christopher, Elizabeth. BS, U. Cin., 1965; PhD, U. Pitts., 1971. Asst. prof. Med. Coll. Va., Richmond, 1973-77; assoc. prof. pharmacology and physiology U. Cin., 1977-81, prof. pharmacology and cell biophysics, 1981-85, prof. physiology, 1981-88; prof. physiology, head U. Ill., Chgo., 1988—, disting. univ. prof., 1998—. Sec. gen. Internat. Soc. Heart Rsch., 1989-93, sec./treas., 1995-98, pres., 1999, assoc. chair dept. physiology; chmn. exptl. cardiovasc. study sect. NIH, 1990-92; vice-chmn. physiology U. Cin., 1987-88. Editor: Protein Phosphorylation in Heart Muscle, 1986; contbr. articles to profl. jours. including Nature, Jour. Biol. Chemistry, Circulation Rsch. Chmn. rsch. coun. Am. Heart Assn., Met. Chgo., 1990-92. Grantee NIH, 1977—, Fogarty fellow, 1986; Brit. Am. Heart fellow Am. Heart Assn., 1974-75; Sr. Internat. fellow U. Coll. London, 1987. Mem. Am. Physiol. Soc. (chmn. subgroup), Am. Soc. Pharm. Exptl. Therapeutics, Biophys. Soc. (chmn. subgroup 1983-84). Office: U Ill at Chgo MC901 Physiology & Biophysics 835 S Wolcott Ave Chicago IL 60612-7340

SOLBERG, JAMES JOSEPH, industrial engineering educator; b. Toledo, May 27, 1942; s. Archie Norman and Margaret Jean (Olsen) S.; m. Elizabeth Alice Snow, May 28, 1966; children: Kirsten Kari, Margaret Elizabeth. BA, Harvard U., 1964; MA, MS, U. Mich., 1967, PhD, 1969. Asst. prof. U. Toledo, 1969-71; assoc. prof. Purdue U., West Lafayette, Ind., 1971-81, prof., 1981—, dir. engring. rsch. ctr., 1986—. Author: Operations Research, 1976 (Book of the Yr. 1977); contbr. over 100 articles to profl. jours. Mem. NAE, Inst. Indsl. Engrs. (Disting. Rsch. award 1982), Soc. Mfg. Engrs., AAAS. Achievements include invention of CAN-Q which is a method for predicting performance of manufacturing systems used by hundreds of companies. Office: Purdue U Sch Industrial Engineering West Lafayette IN 47907-1287

SOLBERG, LARRY D. retail executive; Sr. v.p. fin. CVS Corp., Woonsocket, RI, 1996—, controller CVS Pharmacy, Inc., 1996—2000, controller, 2000—. Home: CVS Corporation Corporate HQs One CVS Dr Woonsocket RI 02895

SOLBERG, MARY ANN, federal agency administrator; Grad., Western Mich. U. Dep. dir. Office Nat. Drug Control Policy Exec. Office of Pres., Washington, 2001—; exec. dir. Coalition of Health Comtys., Troy (Mich.) Cmty. Coalition for Prevention of Drug and Alcohol Abuse; various positions Troy Adult and Cmty. Edn., 1977—91. Mem. adv. com. to develop a nat. prevention sys. Nat. Ctr. for Substance Abuse Prevention; mem. adv. com. Nat. Ad Coun.'s Cmty. Anti-Drug Campaign; mem. Pres.'s Commn. on Drug-Free Cmtys., 1998, co-chairperson. Office: Exec Office of Pres Office Nat Drug Control Policy 750 17th St NW Washington DC 20503

SOLBERG, WINTON UDELL, history educator; b. Aberdeen, S.D., Jan. 11, 1922; s. Ole Alexander and Bertha Georgia (Tschappat) S.; m. Ruth Constance Walton, Nov. 8, 1952; children— Gail Elizabeth, Andrew Walton, Kristin Ruth. AB magna cum laude, U. S.D., 1943, LHD (hon.), 1987; student, Biarritz (France) Am. U., 1946; A.M., Harvard, 1947, PhD, 1954. Instr., then asst. prof. social scis. U.S. Mil. Acad., 1951-54; instr., then asst. prof. history Yale U., 1954-58; fellow Pierson Coll., 1955-58, Morse fellow, 1958; James Wallace prof. history Macalester Coll., 1958-62, vis. prof. U. Ill., 1961-62, assoc. prof. history, 1962, prof., 1967—, chmn. dept. history, 1970-72. Research fellow Ctr. Study History of Liberty in Am., Harvard U., 1962-63; summer research scholar Henry E. Huntington Library, San Marino, Calif., 1959; dir. Coe Found. Am. Studies Inst., summers 1960-62; lectr., cons. Army War Coll., 1959-62; lectr. U.S. Command and Gen. Staff Sch., 1963-64; Fulbright lectr. Johns Hopkins U. Bologna, 1967-68, Moscow (USSR) State U., 1978, U. Calcutta India, 1993; vis. prof. Konan U., Kobe, Japan, 1981; USIA Lectr., Korea and Malaysia, 1985, Korea, 1992. Author: The Federal Convention and the Formation of the Union of the American States, 1958, The Constitutional Convention and the Formation of the Union, 1990, The University of Illinois, 1867-1894, An Intellectual and Cultural History, 1968, Redeem the Time: The Puritan Sabbath in Early America, 1977, History of American Thought and Culture, 1983, Cotton Mather, The Christian Philosopher, 1994, The University of Illinois, 1894-1904: The Shaping of the University, 2000; also articles. Mem. Ill. Humanities Council, 1973-75; sec. Council on Study of Religion, 1981-85. Served to maj. inf. AUS, 1943-46, 51-54; lt. col. U.S. Army Res. Recipient Faculty Achievement award Burlington No. Found., 1986, Disting. Teaching award U. Ill. Coll. Liberal Arts and Scis., 1988; NEH sr. fellow, 1974-75; NSF research grantee, 1981-82 Mem. Am. Hist. Assn., So. Hist. Assn., Orgn. Am. Historians, Am. Studies Assn. (pres. Mid-Am. 1985-86), Am. Soc. Ch. History (pres. 1985-86), AAUP (chpt. pres. 1965-66, mem. council 1969-72, 1st v.p. 1974-76), Phi Beta Kappa. Episcopalian. Home: 8 Lake Park Rd Champaign IL 61822-7101 Office: U Ill History Dept Urbana IL 61801 Office Phone: 217-244-2078. Business E-Mail: wsolberg@uiuc.edu.

SOLBRIG, INGEBORG HILDEGARD, literature educator, writer; b. Weissenfels, Germany, July 31, 1923; arrived in U.S., 1961, naturalized, 1966; d. Reinhold J. and Hildegard M. A. (Ferchland) Solbrig. Grad. in chemistry, U. Halle, Germany, 1948; BA summa cum laude, San Francisco State U., 1964; postgrad., U. Calif., Berkeley, 1964-65; MA, Stanford U., 1966, PhD in Humanities and German, 1969. Asst. prof. U. R.I., 1969-70, U. Tenn., Chattanooga, 1970-72, U. Ky., Lexington, 1972-75; assoc. prof. German U. Iowa, 1975-81, prof., 1981-93, prof. emerita, 1993—. Domestic and abroad lectr. Author: Hammer-Purgstall und Goethe, 1973, Modulationen von Gold und Licht in Goethes Kunstmärchen, 1997, Momentaufnahmem, 2000, J.G. Herder: Echo of the Cultural Philospher's Ideas in Early African-American Intellectual Writing, 2000, Maria Sibylla Merian..., 2001; main editor: Rilke Heute, Beziehungen und Wirkungen, 1975; editor (and translator): Reinhard Goering: Seeschlacht/Seabattle, 1977; editor: Orient-Rezeption, 1996, Orient-Rezeption, Fischer Lexikon Literatur, 1996; mem. editl. bd.: Kairoer Germanistische Studien, vol. 9 & 10, 1998; contbr. articles to profl. jours., chpts. to books; editor: Orient-Rezeption, Fischer Lexikon Literatur, 2000. Mem. Iowa Gov.'s Com. 300th Anniversary German-Am. Rels. 1683-1983, 1983. Named Ky. Col., 1975; recipient Hammer-Purgstall Gold medal, Austria, 1974; fellow, Stanford U., 1965—66, 1968—69, Austrian Ministry Edn., 1968—69; Delta Phi Alpha Deutsche Ehrenverbindung, U. Ky., 1973, Old Gold fellow, Iowa, 1977, Am. Coun. Learned Socs. grantee, German Acad. Exch. Svc. grantee, 1980, Sr. Faculty Rsch. fellow in humanities, 1983, NEH grantee, 1985, May Brodbeck fellow in humanities, 1989, numerous summer faculty rsch. grants. Mem.: MLA (life), Soc. for History Alchemy and Chemistry, Internat. Herder Soc. (founding mem.), Goethe Soc. N.Am., Inc., Can. Soc. 18th Century Studies, Am. Soc. 18th Century Studies, Deutsche Schiller Gesellschaft, Goethe Gesellschaft, Internat. Vereinigung fur Germanische Sprach und Lit. Wiss., Egyptian Soc. Lit. Criticism (hon.). Avocations: horseback riding, photography, writing, travel, theology. Home: 1126 Pine St Iowa City IA 52240-5711 Personal E-mail: isolbrig@blue.weeg.uiowa.edu. *The circumstances of my life took me to many places and cultures. Despite the discord and problems plaguing many parts of this planet, let us not forget that it's the home of the human family, our home. Always remember: Life is, by definition, change.*

SOLDAN, ANGELIKA, philosopher, political scientist, educator; b. Hennigsdorf, Germany, Feb. 10, 1953; d. Hans and Erika Potempa; m. Wolfgang Karl Soldan, May 8, 1987; 1 child, Anja Soldan. MA in Philosophy, Humboldt U., 1975, PhD, 1990, Martin Luther U., Halle-Wittenberg, Germany, 1982. Assoc. prof. philosophy, polit. ethics Humboldt U., Berlin, 1989-91; adj. prof. philosophy, ethics, govt. U. Tex., Brownsville, 1991-98, lectr. social issues and philosophy, 1999—2000, asst. prof., 2000—. Sr. lectr. U. Wis. Eau Claire, 1998-99. Contbr. articles to profl. jours. Supporter Sch. Tchr. Exch. Program USA-Germany, 1991—; co-founder Gesellschaft für Solidarische Entwicklungszusammenarbeit, 1990. Mem. Am. Philos. Assn., Internat. Fromm Soc. Office: U Tex Brownsville 80 Fort Brown St Brownsville TX 78520-4956 Office Phone: 956-544-8260. Business E-Mail: asoldan@utb.edu.

SOLDNER, PAUL EDMUND, artist, ceramist, educator; b. Summerfield, Ill. s. Grover and Beulah (Geiger) S.; m. Virginia I. Geiger, June 15, 1947; 1 child, Stephanie. BA, Bluffton Coll., 1946; MA, U. Colo., 1954; MFA, L.A. County Art Inst., 1956; DFA (hon.), Westminster Coll., 1992. Tchr. art Medina (Ohio) County Schs., 1946-47; supr. art, asst. county supr. Wayne County Schs., Wooster, Ohio, 1951-54; tchr. adult edn. Wooster Coll., 1952-54; vis. asst. prof. ceramics Scripps Coll., 1957-66, prof., 1970-91, prof. emeritus, 1991—. Prof. Claremont (Calif.) Grad. Sch., 1957-66, prof., 1970-92; prof. U. Colo., Boulder, 1966-67, U. Iowa, Iowa City, 1967-68; pres. Soldner Pottery Equipment, Inc., Aspen, Colo., 1956-77; mem. steering com. Internat. Sch. Ceramics, Rome, 1965-77; advisor Vols. for Internat. Assistance, Balt., 1966-75; craftsman, trustee Am. Craft Coun., N.Y.C., 1970-74, trustee emeritus, 1976-77; dir. U.S. sect. World Craft Coun., 1970-74; dir. Anderson Ranch Ctr. for Hand Art Sch., 1974-76; speaker 6th Internat. Ceramics Symposium Syracuse, 1989; participant Internat. Russian Artists Exchange Program, Riga, Latvia, 1989; cons. in field. Author: Kilns and Their Construction, 1965, Raku, 1964, Paul Soldner, A Retrospective View, 1991; contbr. articles to profl. jours.; subject of 5 films; 156 one-man shows including Cantini Mus. Modern Art, Marseille, France, 1981, Thomas Segal Gallery, Boston, 1982, Elements Gallery, N.Y., 1983, Louis Newman Gallery, L.A., 1985, Susan Cummins Gallery, Mill Valley, Calif., 1989, Great Am. Gallery, Atlanta, 1986, Patricia Moore Gallery, Aspen Colo., 1987, Coleg Prifysgol Cymru, Aberystwyth, Wales, 1987, Joan Hodgell Gallery, Sarasota, Fla., 1988, Esther Saks Gallery, Chgo., 1986, 88, El Camino Gallery Art, Toraance, Calif., 1987, San Antonio Art Ctr., San Angelo, Tex., 1988, traveling exhibit, 12 U.S. mus., 1992—, Besson Gallerie, London, 1996, Bernard Palissy Mus., France, 1996; 335 group shows including Nelson-Atkins Mus., Kansas City, Mo., 1983, Los Angeles Mcpl. Art Gallery, 1984, 27th Ceramic Nat. Exhibition, Everson Mus. Art, Syracuse, N.Y., 1986, Victoria & Albert Mus., London, 1986, Chicago Internat. New Art Forms Exposition, 1986, Hanover Gallery, Syracuse, N.Y., 1987, L.A. County Mus. of Art, 1987, Crain/Wolov Gallery, Tulsa, 1987, Contem Crafts Gallery, Portland, Oreg., 1988, Oakland (Calif.) Art Mus., 1988, Munson Gallery, Santa Fe, 1988, Japanese Influence on Am. Ceramics, Everson Mus., Syracuse, N.Y., 1989, traveling retrospective, 1991-93; hon. vis. artist Shigaraki Ceramic Cultural Park, Japan, 1994; works in permanent collections, Nat. Mus. Modern Art, Kyoto, Japan, Victoria and Albert Mus., London, Smithsonian Instn., Washington, Los Angeles County Mus. Art, Oakland Art Mus., Everson Mus. Art, Syracuse Australian Nat. Gallery, Taipei Fine Arts Mus.; curator Mirror Images Exhibit, Craft Alliance Gallery, St. Louis, 1989. Served with U.S. Army, 1941-46. Decorated Purple Heart; grantee NEA, 1991, Louis Comfort Tiffany Found., 1966, 72, Nat. Endowment for Arts, 1976, Colo. Gov.'s award for the Arts & Humanities, 1975; voted one of Top Twelve Potters World-Wide, Ceramics Monthly mag., 1981; Scripps Coll. Faculty Recognition award, 1985; named Hon. Mem. Coun., Nat. Coun. on Edn. for Ceramic Arts, 1989. Fellow Collegium of Craftsmen of the U.S.; mem. Internat. Acad. Ceramics, Nat. Coun. on Edn. for Ceramic Arts. Achievements include being the originator of Am. Raku philosophy and techniques in ceramics. Home: PO Box 90 Aspen CO 81612-0090

SOLE, MICHAEL JOSEPH, cardiologist; b. Timmins, Ont., Can., Mar. 5, 1940; s. Fred and Lillian Sole; m. Susan Karen Samuels, May 26, 1964; children: David Frederick, Leslie Meredith. BSc, U. Toronto, Ont., Can., 1962, MD, 1966. Cert. Coll. Physicians and Surgeons Ont.; diplomate Am. Bd. Internal Medicine. Rotating intern, jr. asst. resident, sr. asst. resident in internal medicine Toronto Gen. Hosp., 1966-69; cardiology fellow Cardiovasc. Rsch. Inst., U. Calif., San Francisco, 1969-71; cardiology fellow Peter Bent Brigham Hosp., Boston, 1971-73, jr. assoc. medicine, 1973-74; rsch. assoc. MIT, Cambridge, 1973-74; instr. medicine Harvard Med. Sch., 1973-74; from asst. to assoc. prof. medicine U. Toronto, 1974-83, prof. medicine and physiology, 1983—, mem. staff inst. med. sci., 1978—, dir. cardiology rsch., 1987-89, dir. centre cardiovasc. rsch., 1989-99, Searle chair cardiovasc. rsch., 1998—; staff cardiologist Toronto Hosp., 1974-89, dir. non-invasive cardiology, 1974-79, dir. cardiology rsch., 1979-89, dir. divsn. cardiology, 1989-98, dir. cardiovasc. program, 1992—97, dir. Peter Munk Cardiac Ctr., 1992—97. Vis. prof. Harvard U., 1975, NIH, Bethesda, Md., 1981, U. B.C., 1982, 91, 92, Capital Med. Sch. and Beijing Hosp., 1985, U. Tokyo, 1992, others; mem. Can. Govt. Task Force Diagnostic Ultrasound, 1976-78; vice-chmn. econs. com. dept. medicine Toronto Gen. Hosp., 1977, chmn., 1978, 79, chmn. emeritus, 1980, mem. various coms., 1981-98, chmn. cardiology rsch. com., 1988-89, mem. cardiovasc. collaborative practice group, 1989-92; rsch. assoc. Ont. Heart Found., 1979-89; assoc. rsch. inst. pediat. Hosp. Sick Children, Toronto, 1979—; mem. med. staff Mt. Sinai Hosp., Toronto, 1979—; mem. adv. bd. Merck Pharms., 1983—, Boots Pharms., 1992-93; mem. Health Rsch. and Devel. Coun., Province of Ont., 1983-86, mem. exec. com., 1984-86; Levesque lectr. Montreal Heart Inst., 1984; mem. cardiovasc. panel Med. Rsch. Coun. Can., 1985-87; mem. heart and blood vessel rsch. adv. com. Toronto Hosp., 1986-89; chmn. cardiovasc. rsch. adv. com. faculty medicine U. Toronto, 1986-87, mem. various coms., 1987—, chmn. rsch. com. dept. medicine, 1987-88, mem. rsch. adv. bd., 1989-97, chair life scis. com., 1990-92, chair decanal promotions com. faculty medicine, 1992-94; mem. exec. com. Centre Cardiovasc. Rsch., 1998-99, chmn. sci. com., 1989-99, mem. exec. com. cardiovasc. clin. rsch. lab., 1992-99, chmn. rsch. com., 1992-99; Pfizer vis. fellow Clin. Rsch. Inst., Montreal, 1988; mem. sr. adv. com. Toronto Western Hosp., 1989-90; Katz vis. prof. U. Chgo., 1989; mem. provincial working group cardiovasc. svcs. Ministry of Health, 1990-91, mem. ctrl. east region cardiovasc. patient care mgmt. group, 1990-91; mem. trial devel. com. diabetes atherosclerosis intervention study WHO and Fournier Pharms., 1991-93, mem. trial exec. com., 1993-2000; mem. Joint Med. Rsch. Coun. Can./Pharm. Mfrs. Assn. Can. Adv. Com. Sci., 1993; mem. organizing coms. various sci. meetings; presenter in field. Mem. editl. bd. Can. Jour. Cardiology, 1988—, Index and Revs. Congestive Heart Failure, 1988-90, Hypertension Can., 1988-90, European Jour. Pharmacology, 1992-96, Cardiosci., 1993, Jour. Heart Failure, 1994—, Circulation, 1996—, Jour. Molecular Medicine, 1996—, Jour. Molecular Cell Cardiology, 1999-2001; mem. internat. editl. bd. Cardiology Digest, 1992—; contbr. chpts. to books and articles to profl. jours.; patentee in field. Recipient Robert Beamish Leadership award, Inst. CV Sci., U. Man., 2001; fellow Ivan Smith Rsch. fellow, U. Toronto, 1964, Hunter fellow, Ont. Heart Found., 1973; grantee Grantee, Heart & Stroke Found. Ont., 1969—, Med. Rsch. Coun. Can., 1982—92, 1994—97; scholar Walter Watkins scholar, U. Toronto, 1962. Fellow Am. Coll. Cardiology (abstract reviewer 1989, 91), Royal Coll. Physicians and Surgeons; mem. Am. Soc. Clin. Investigation, Assn. Am. Physicians, Am. Heart Assn. (fellow couns. clin. cardiology, hypertension, circulation and basic sci., mem. exec., basic sci. coun. 1986-89, mem. Katz prize selection com. 1988-90), Can. Soc. Clin. Investigation, Can. Cardiovasc. Soc. (mem. young investigators award panel 1982-84, mem. student presentation award com. 1988-90, mem. nat. task force cardiovascular sci. 1992-93, Ann. Rsch. award 1975, Rsch. Achievement award 1989), Heart and Stroke Found. Can. (mem. sci. rev. bd. 1976-79, vice-chmn. 1980-83, chmn. hypertension and cardiovasc. pharmacology panel 1982-83, chmn. molecular biology, biochemistry, pathology panel 1989-90), Can. Med. Assn. (mem. coun. 1982-87), Am. Fedn. Clin. Rsch., Ont. Med. Assn. (alt. del. Toronto Gen. Hosp. bd. 1988-90), Heart and Stroke Found. Ont. (mem. med. rsch. com. 1978-81, bd. dirs. 1986-92, 96—, mem. fin. com. 1986-90, 96-97, mem. corp. rels. com. 1990-92, mem. rsch. policy com. 1991-93, 96-97, chmn. 1997-99, mem. exec. com. 1997-99, nomination com. 1997-99, chmn. 50th anniversary com., mem. audit com., Disting. Rsch. prof. 1989-96, Murray Robertson Meml. lectr. 1989), Internat. Soc. Heart Rsch. (exec. Am. sect. 1979-88, lectr. Latin Am. sect. 1995), Banting Rsch. Found. (hon. sec.-treas. 1979-81), Gairdner Found. (mem. rev. panel 1979-94), Heart Failure Soc. Am. (publs. com. 2000-03, nominating com. 2001-04), Alpha Omega Alpha. Office: Toronto Gen Hosp Eaton N 13-212 200 Elizabeth St Toronto ON Canada M5G 2C4 Office Phone: 416-340-3471. E-mail: michael.sole@uhn.on.ca.

SOLECKI, R. STEFAN, anthropologist, educator; b. Bklyn., Oct. 15, 1917; s. Kazimierz John and Mary (Tarnawski) S.; m. Rose Muriel Lilien, June 24, 1955; children— John Irwin, William Duncan. B.Sc., City Coll. N.Y., 1941; MA, Columbia, 1950, PhD in Anthropology, 1958. Archaeologist Smithsonian Instn., 1948-54; archaeol. asst. anthropology Columbia U., N.Y.C., 1954-55, mem. faculty, 1959-88, prof. anthropology, 1965-88, prof. emeritus, 1989—, chmn. dept., 1975-78; adj. prof. dept. anthropology Tex. A&M Univ., College Station, 1989—; assoc. curator old world U.S. Nat. Mus., 1957-59. Archael. expdns. to Alaska, 1949, 61, Iraq, 1950-51, 53, 56-57 (field dir.), 60, 78, Sudanese Nubia, 1961, Turkey, 1963, Syria, 1963, 64, 65, 88, 89, Iran, 1968, Lebanon, 1969-73, France, 1975, Ea., Midwestern and Western U.S.; collaborator in archaeology Smithsonian Instn., 1953; cons. UNESCO, 1959. Served with AUS, 1943-45. Fulbright scholar, Iraq, 1952-53; William Bayard Cutting travelling fellow Columbia, 1956-57; Fulbright-Hays faculty research awardee Syria, 1980-81; Fulbright fellow, Iraq, 1988-89. Fellow Am. Anthrop. Assn., Arctic Inst. Am., N.Y. Acad. Scis. (chmn. anthropology sect. 1977-79); mem. N.Y. Archaeol. Assn. (pres. 1960-62), N.Y. Oriental Club (pres. 1965), Profl. Archeologists of N.Y.C. (pres. 1980-81), Soc. Archaeology, Am. Schs. Oriental Research (assoc. trustee 1969-71), Prehistoric Soc., Deutsches Archaeologisches Inst., Soc. Préhistorique Français, Archaeol. Inst. Am. (exec. com. 1968-70), Assn. Field Archaeology (pres. 1972-74). Home: 86 Park Pl South Orange NJ 07079-2303 Office: Columbia U Dept Anthropology New York NY 10027

SOLEIMANI, MASSOUD, internist, rheumatologist; b. Rasht, Iran, Jan. 5, 1955; MD, U. del Salvador, Buenos Aires, 1991. Diplomate Am. Bd. Internal Medicine and Rheumatology. Intern Meml. Med. Ctr., Savannah, Ga., 1992-93; resident Providence Hosp., Southfield, Mich., 1993-95; fellow Wayne State U.-Hutzel Hosp., Detroit, 1995-98; with Health Care Ptnrs., Pasadena, Calif. Office: Healthcare Ptnrs Med Group 450 E Huntington Dr Arcadia CA 91001

SOLENDER, ROBERT LAWRENCE, real estate executive, retired newspaper executive; b. Rochester, N.Y., Sept. 1, 1923; s. Samuel S. and Catherine (Goldsmith) S.; m. Ellen Van Raalte Karelsen, Nov. 25, 1948; children:

Elizabeth, Jefferson, Katherine. BA, Oberlin Coll., 1943. Asst. to pres. Craven & Hedrick, Inc., N.Y.C., 1946-49; with Dallas Times Herald, 1949-75, v.p., advt. dir., 1964-69, v.p., gen. mgr., 1969—71, v.p. sales, 1971—75; dir. NorthPark Nat. Bank, 1973—93; prin. Robert L. Solender & Assocs., Dallas, 1975—; mng. ptnr. The Devonshire Co., Dallas, 1978-95. Interim chmn., CEO, AccuBanc Mortgage Corp., 1992. Pres. Dallas Child Guidance Clinic, 1956, Dallas Assn. Mental Health, 1958, Hope Cottage Children's Bur., 1973—; bd. dirs. Dallas Theatre Center, Child Care Assn. Met. Dallas, Friends of the Dallas Pub. Libr.; trustee Southwestern Med. Found.; mem. adv. council Communities Found. of Tex.; assoc. Dallas Mus. Art; bd. dirs., mem. exec. com. Dallas County United Way, 1973. Served to lt. USNR, 1944-46, PTO. Mem.: Masons. Home: 9131 Devonshire Dr Dallas TX 75209-2411

SOLER, ESTA, foundation administrator; Founder, pres. Family Violence Prevention Fund, 1980—. Cons. and adv. Dept. Justice, U.S. Dept. Health and Human Svcs., CDC, others; bd. dirs. The Ctr. on Fathers, Families and Pub. Policy. Co-author: Ending Domestic Violence: Changing Public Perceptions/Halting the Epidemic, 1997. Bd. dirs. Blue Shield Calif. Found., Bay Area United Way Safe Cmtys. Cabinet. Recipient Koret Israel Prize, 1989, Public Health Heroes award, U. Calif., 1998; fellow, Kellogg Found. Nat. Leadership, 1990. Office: 383 Rhode Island St Ste 304 San Francisco CA 94103-5133

SOLES, ADA LEIGH, former state legislator, government advisor; b. Jacksonville, Fla., May 19, 1937; d. Albert Thomas and Dorothy (Winter) Wall; m. James Ralph Soles, 1959; children: Nancy Beth, Catherine. BA, Fla. State U., 1959. Mem. New Castle County Libr. Adv. Bd., 1975-80, 95—, chmn., 1975-77; chmn. Del. State Libr. Adv. Bd., 1975-78; mem. Del. State Ho. Reps., 1980-92; sr. advisor Gov. of Del., 1993-94; mem. U. Del. Libr. Assocs. Bd., 1995—; adminstrv. asst. U. Del. Commn. on Status of Women, 1976-77; acad. advisor U. Del. Coll. Arts and Scis., 1977-92. Mem. LWV (state pres. 1978-80), Phi Beta Kappa, Phi Kappa Phi, Mortar Bd., Alpha Chi Omega. Episcopalian.

SOLES, WILLIAM ROGER, insurance company executive, director; b. Whiteville, N.C., Sept. 16, 1920; s. John William and Margaret (Watts) S.; m. Majelle Marrene Morris, Sept. 22, 1956 (dec. 1993); children: William Roger, Majelle Janette. BS in Commerce, U. N.C., 1947, postgrad., 1956; LLD, Campbell U., 1981; DHL, High Point U., 1996. With Jefferson Standard Life Ins. Co., Greensboro, N.C., 1947—, v.p., mgr. securities dept., 1962-64, asst. to pres., 1964-66, exec. v.p., mgr. securities dept., 1966, pres., also dir., 1967-86; chmn., pres., chief exec. officer Jefferson-Pilot Life Ins. Co.; retired, 1993; chmn., pres. Jefferson-Pilot Corp., retired, 1993. Trustee, past chmn. High Point U.; past chmn. Wesley Long Community Hosp.; trustee, past chmn. Ind. Coll. Fund N.C.; past pres. Bus. Found. of N.C.; bd. dirs., past chmn. N.C. Ins. Edn. Found. Served with USAAF, 1941-45. Mem. N.C. Citizens for Bus. and Industry (past chmn.), Am. Council Life Ins. (past chmn., dir.), Beta Gamma Sigma. Clubs: Greensboro Country. Home: 604 Kimberly Dr Greensboro NC 27408-4914 Office: Jefferson-Pilot Corp PO Box 21008 Greensboro NC 27420-1008

SOLET, MAXWELL DAVID, lawyer; b. Washington, May 15, 1948; s. Leo and Pearl (Rose) S.; m. Joanne Marie Tolksdorf, Sept. 27, 1970; children: David Marc, Paul Jacob. AB, Harvard U., 1970, JD, 1974. Bar: Mass. 1974, U.S. Tax Ct. 1976, U.S. Ct. Claims 1976, U.S. Supreme Ct. 1976. Assoc. Gaston Snow & Ely Bartlett, Boston, 1974-79, Mintz, Levin, Cohn, Ferris, Glovsky & Popeo, P.C., Boston, 1979-82, ptnr., 1982—. Mem.: ABA, Nat. Assn. Bond Lawyers (mem. steering com. bond atty.'s workshop 1992—95), Boston Bar Assn. (chmn. tax sect. 1987—89, mem. multidisciplinary practice task force 2000—01, mem. audit com. 2003—), Mass. Bar Assn., Cambridge Hist. Soc. (bd. mem. 1999—2000, sec. 2001—). Home: 15 Berkeley St Cambridge MA 02138-3409 Office: Mintz Levin Cohn Ferris Glovsky & Popeo PC One Financial Ctr Boston MA 02111 Office Phone: 617-348-1739. E-mail: msolet@mintz.com.

SOLEY, DAVID BENJAMIN, composer; arrived in U.S., 1979; s. Alfred T. Soley and Gladys S. Beckford. MusB, Calif. State U., Northridge, 1987; D in Musical Arts, Stanford U., 1993. Asst. prof. music Stanford (Calif.) U., 1995—99, Rice U., Houston, 1999—2001; composer N.Y.C., 2001—. Composer: (songs) Camaïeu, 1997, tondo (...unreceding on), 2002, Laberinto IV, 2004. With U.S. Army, 1980—83. Recipient award to student composers, Broadcast Music, Inc., 1986, 1987, Bearns prize, Columbia U., 1987; Guggenheim fellow, John Simon Guggenheim Meml. Found., 1993. Office: Church St Station PO Box 3360 New York NY 10008

SOLEY, ROBERT LAWRENCE, plastic surgeon; b. N.Y.C., Feb. 26, 1935; s. Max and Saide (Leader) S.; m. Judy Wasserman, June 16, 1963; children: John, Jill. BS, Yale U., 1956; MD, NYU, 1959. Diplomate Am. Bd. Surgery, Am. Bd. PLastic Surgery. Intern Bellevue Hosp., N.Y.C., 1959-60; resident in gen. surgery Mt. Sinai Hosp., N.Y.C., 1960-65; resident in plastic surgery Hosp. U. Pa., Phila., 1967-69; practice medicine specializing in plastic surgery White Plains, N.Y., 1969—. Mem. staff, mem. med. bd. White Plains Hosp., 1985—88, chief sect. plastic surgery, 1988—94. Contbr. articles to profl. jours. Capt. M.C., USAF, 1965-67. Grantee USPHS, 1968-69. Fellow ACS; mem. Am. Soc. Plastic Reconstructive Surgery, Am. Soc. Aesthetic Surgery, N.Y. State Med. Soc. (mem. ho. of dels.), Westchester County Med. Soc. (pres. 1996-97, bd. dirs. 1988—), Rotary (bd. dirs. White Plains chpt. 1982-85). Home: 30 Griffin Ave Scarsdale NY 10583-7661 Office: 170 Maple Ave White Plains NY 10601-4710 Office Phone: 914-997-9600. E-mail: bob@soley.com.

SOLGANIK, MARVIN, real estate executive; b. Chgo., Nov. 7, 1930; s. Harry and Dora (Fastoff) S.; m. Judith Rosenberg, Sept. 11, 1960; children: Randall, Janet, Robert. BBA, Case Western Res. U., 1952. Real estate broker, Cleve., 1950-65, Herbert Laronge Inc., Cleve., 1965-68; sr. v.p. real estate Revco D.S., Inc., Twinsburgh, Ohio, 1968—, corp. dir., 1974—. Adj. prof. Ohio No. U.; guest lectr. Cleve. State U., Case Western Res. U. Sch. Law, Cuyahoga C.C., Ohio No. U., Cleve. Real Estate Bd., CASE Sch. Law. Vol. jewish Welfare Fund, Shaker heights, Ohio; chmn. capital and budget coms. Jewish Fedn.; chmn. Agnon Sch. Bdlg. Com.; bd. dirs. Bellfair-J.C.B.-Home for Emotionally Disturbed Children, Visconsi Cos, Cleve. Inst. Music. Recipient Appreciation award Am. Soc. Real Estate Appraisers, Akron-Cleve. chpt., 1971 Mem. Nat. Assn. Corp. Real Estate Officers, Internat. Council Shopping Ctrs. Office: D S Revco 22925 Holmwood Rd Shaker Heights OH 44122-3005

SOLIDUM, JAMES, finance and insurance executive; b. Honolulu, Mar. 12, 1925; s. Narciso and Sergia (Yabo) S.; m Vickie Mayo, Aug. 14, 1954; children: Arlin James, Nathan Francis, Tobi John, Kamomi Teresa. Student, U. Hawaii, 1949-50; BA, U. Oreg., 1953. CLU. Promotional salesman Tongg Pub. Co., 1953—54; editor Fil-Am. Tribune, 1954—55; master planning technician Fed. Civil Svc., 1955—57; publs. editor Hawaii Sugar Planters Assn., 1957; field agt. Grand Pacific Life Ins. Co., 1957—59, home office asst., 1959—60, supr., 1960—62, asst. v.p., 1962—64; propr. J. Solidum & Assoc., Honolulu, 1964—; pres. Fin. Devel. Inst., 1967—. Contbg. writer Paradise of Pacific Mag., 1957-58, Hawaii Agrl. Mag., 1957-58; gen. ptnr. R.Z. Limited Partnership, 1981—; v.p. Grand Pacific Life Ins. Co., 1983-90; bd. dirs. Hawaii Econ. Devel. Corp., 1982-89; mem. adv. com. Honolulu dist. SBA, 1971-77; bd. advisors Philippine Consulate of Hawaii, 1959. Pres. Keolu Elem. PTA, 1960-62; mem. satisfaction com. Hawaii Visitors Bur., 1963-66; chmn. budget and rev. panel IV, Aloha United Way, 1966-72, bd. dir., 1971-77, 82-88, chmn. bd., 1984; mem. mgmt. svcs. com., 1977, mem. cen. com., 1977-82, chmn. budget and allocations com., 1982-84; chmn. Kamehameha Dist. fin. com. Aloha coun. Boy Scouts Am., 1966; vice chmn. Businessmen's Cancer Crusade, 1965; chmn. Operation Bayanihan, Hawaii Immigration Task Force, 1970; participant Oahu Housing Workshop, State of Hawaii, Hawaii chpt. HUD, 1970; mem. task force on housing and transp. Alternative Econ. Futures for Hawaii, 1973; chmn. Bicentennial Filipiniana, 1976; campaign chmn. State Rep. Rudolph Pacarro, 1964-68; mem. exec. com. Campaign for Reelection U.S. Senator Hiram L. Fong, 1970, Gov. William Quinn for U.S. Senate, 1976; Rep. candidate for Hawaii Ho. of Reps., 1972; mem. Rep. Citizens Task Force on Housing, 1973; trustee St. Louis Alumni Found., 1970—, Kuakini Med. Ctr., 1984-86, Palama Settlement, 1975-82, v.p., 1976, treas., 1980-82; bd. mgrs. Windward YMCA, 1964-67; bd. advisers St. Louis H.S., 1963-64; bd. gov. Goodwill Industries, 1964; bd. dir. Children's Ctr., Inc., 1975-77, Hawaii Multi-Cultural Arts Ctr., 1977-81, treas., 1979; fin. chmn. St. Stephen's Parish Coun., 1974—; bd. dir. St. Louis Fine Arts Ctr., 1985-88; mem. steering com. Conf. Filipino Voter Registrars, 1962. With U.S. Army, 1945-47. Recipient Man of Yr. award Filipino C. of C., 1965, cert. of merit Aloha United Way, 1971, Wisdom mag. honor award, 1974, Outstanding Alumnus honor medal St. Louis High Sch., 1976, Island Treasure award Cath. Ch. Hawaii, 2003. Mem. Hawaii State C. of C. (bd. dir. 1964-67, chmn. legis. com. 1966-67, v.p. 1970, chmn. election judges 1971, mem. ad hoc com. bus.-youth rels. 1970—, Filipino C. of C. (past pres. 1965, com. chmn.), Am. Soc. CLU, Honolulu Assn. Life Underwriters (bd. dir. 1963-66, del. nat. conv. 1967, chmn. life underwriters tng. coun. 1962-67), Hawaii Estate Planning Coun., Hawaii Plantation Indsl. Editors Assn. (sec.-treas. 1957), St. Louis Alumni Assn. (bd. dir., chmn. fin. 1969-75, pres. 1976, treas. 1977—), Phi Kappa Sigma. Republican. Roman Catholic. Home: 2622 Waolani Ave Honolulu HI 96817-1362 Office: 225 Queen St Apt 12-a Honolulu HI 96813-4603

SOLIMAN, KARAM FARAH ATTIA, pharmacy educator; b. Cairo, Oct. 15, 1944; came to the U.S., 1968; s. Farah Attia and Elaine (Kellini) S.; m. Samia Gorgy Sidhom, Aug. 2, 1973; children: John, Gina, Mark, Mary. BS, Cairo U., 1964; MS, U. Ga., 1971, PhD, 1972. Asst. prof. Sch. Vet. Medicine Tuskegee (Ala.) U., 1972-75; assoc. prof. Fla. A&M U.-Coll. Pharmacy, Tallahassee, 1975-79, prof., 1979—, chmn. divsn. basic pharm. sci., 1981—, asst. dean, 1993—, disting. prof., 1997—. Author: (with others) Practical Clinical Pharmacy, 1977, Chronopharmacology and Chronotherapeutics, 1981; contbr. articles to profl. jours. Rsch. grantee NIH. Mem. Am. Assn. Coll. Pharmacy, Am. Soc. Pharmacology and Exptl. Therapeutics, Am. Physiol. Soc., Neurosci. Soc., Endocrine Soc. Democrat. Avocations: reading, gardening. Home: 5358 Pembridge Pl Tallahassee FL 32309-6800 Office: Coll Pharmacy Fla A&M Univ Tallahassee FL 32307 Fax: 850-599-3667. E-mail: ksoliman@famu.edu.

SOLIMAN, SAM, gas, oil and chemical industry executive, investment company executive; BS in chemical engring., Texas A&M Univ., 1984. Assoc. McKinsey & Co., 1993—95; CFO Koch Industries, 2000—02; pres. Koch Investment Group, 2001—. Lt. USN, 1984—89. Office: Koch Industries 20 E Greenway Plaza Houston TX 77046 E-mail: solimans@kochind.com.

SOLINGER, JANET W. museum executive; b. Cin., Dec. 20, 1921; d. Fred and Dorothy G. (Gross) Weiland; widowed; children: Dorothy, Regina, Martha. BA, U. Cin., 1943; MA, NYU, 1973; DFA (hon.), Corcoran Coll. of Art, 1998. Asst. to pres. Hebrew Union Coll., Cin., 1957-60; adminstr. Jewish Mus., N.Y.C., 1961-65; exec. dir. Finch Coll., N.Y.C., 1965-66; dir. pub. info. and spl. events NYU, 1966-72; dir. Smithsonian resident assoc. program Smithsonian Instn., Washington, 1972-93; v.p. Corcoran Gall. of Art, Washington, 1994—. Lectr. in field. Author: Museums and Universities: New Paths for Continuing Education, 1990, Marketing the Arts, 1992; contbr. articles to profl. jours. Named Washingtonian of Yr., Washingtonian mag., 1984; recipient decorations, Belgium, 1980, The Netherlands, 1981, Germany, 1982, Gold medal, Smithsonian Inst., 1990, Wash. Woman of the Millenium award, Art Table, 2000; Fulbright Fellow, New Zealand, 1992. Mem. AIA (hon.), Washington Archtl. Found. (bd. dirs. 1996-2001), Art Table (bd. dirs. 1994-2000), Faberge Found. (bd. dirs. 1991—), Cosmos Club, Kenwood Golf and Country Club. Democrat. Jewish. Avocations: golf, bridge, reading, travel. Home: 2801 New Mexico Ave NW Washington DC 20007-3921 Office: Corcoran Gall of Art 500 17th St NW Washington DC 20006-4804 Office Phone: 202-639-1771. E-mail: jsolinger@corcoran.org.

SOLIS, CARLOS, lawyer; b. Managua, Nicaragua, May 15, 1945; came to U.S., 1952; s. Carlos and Luisa (Serrano) S. BA, U. San Francisco, 1967, JD, 1969. Bar: Calif. 1970, U.S. Dist. Ct. (cen. and no. dists.) Calif. 1970, U.S. Ct. Appeals (9th cir.) 1970, U.S. Dist. Ct. (ea. dist.) Calif. 1972, U.S. Dist. Ct. (so. dist.) Calif. 1973, U.S. Supreme Ct. 1973. Assoc. Kindel & Anderson, L.A., 1976, ptnr., 1976—96, Heller Ehrman White & McAuliffe LLP, 1996—. Exec. legal counsel, bd. dirs. internat. student ctr. UCLA, 1976-86, exec. v.p., 1981-86; instr. atty. asst. program UCLA, 1977-79; bd. advisors Los Angeles Internat. Trade Devel. Corp., 1981-87. Assoc. editor U. San Francisco Law Rev., 1968-69; contbr. articles to profl. jours. Bd. dirs. ARC, L.A., 1978-93, 95—, chmn. audit com., 1985-88, bd. advisors, 1993—; bd. dirs. March of Dimes, L.A., 1982-87, L.A. Pub. Theater Found., 1978-81, Young Musicians Found., 1979-80, Boys and Girls Club East L.A., 1986-89; bd. dirs. Am. Diabetes Assn., L.A., 1986-93, chmn., 1989-91, bd. dirs. Calif., 1988-93, chmn., 1992-93, mem. nat. minority initiative task force, 1986-92, bd. dirs. Nat., 1993-95; vice chmn. bd. L.A. United Way, 1982-83, bd. dirs., 1980—, corp. bd. dirs., 1982-96, treas., 1989-93; pres. L.A. Open Golf Found., 1979-80. Recipient Alumni award U. San Francisco, 1969, Province award Phi Delta Phi, 1969. Mem. Los Angeles Jr. Chamber (pres., chmn. bd. dirs. 1980-81, Most Improved com. award 1975, Dir. of Yr. award 1977, Outstanding Bus. Leader award 1980), Assocs. Los Angeles C. of C., Los Angeles Area C. of C. (bd. dirs. 1979-80), U. San Francisco Alumni Assn. (pres. San Gabriel Valley chpt. 1976-80), Latin Am. Ctr. Assocs. (pres. 1980-82, bd. advisors 1980-88), Alpha Sigmu Nu, Phi Delta Phi. Home: 201 La Vereda Rd Pasadena CA 91105-1227 Office: Heller Ehrman White & McAuliffe LLP 601 S Figueroa St 40th FL Los Angeles CA 90017-5758 Business E-Mail: csolis@hewm.com.

SOLIS, HILDA LUCIA, congresswoman, educational administrator; b. Los Angeles, Oct. 20, 1957; d. Raul and Juana (Sequiera) S.; m. Sam H. Sayyad, June 26, 1982. BA in Polit. Sci., Calif. State Poly U., 1979; MA in Pub. Adminstrn., U. So. Calif., 1981. Interpreter Immigration and Naturalization Service, Los Angeles, 1977-79; editor in chief Office Hispanic Affairs, The White House, Washington, 1980-81; mgmt. analyst Office Mgmt. and Budget, Washington, 1981-82; field rep. Office Assemblyman Art Torres, L.A., 1982; dir. Calif. Student Opportunity and Access, Whittier, 1982—; rep. 57th assembly dist. Calif. State Assembly, Sacramento, 1992-94; mem. Calif. Senate from 24th dist., 1994-2000, U.S. Congress from Calif. 32nd dist., Washington, 2001—; mem. resources com., energy & commerce com., former mem. edn. and workforce com. Cons. South Coast Consortium, L.A., 1986—; mem. South Coast Ednl. Opportunity Pers. Consortium. Bd. dirs. Calif. Commn. on Status of Women, 1993—; corr. pres. Friendly El Monte (Calif.) Dem. Club, 1986—; mem. credentials com. Calif. Dem. Com., 1987-88; trustee Rio Hondo C.C., 1985-92. Recipient Meritorious Svc. award Dept. Def., 1981, Young Careerist award El Monte Bus. and Profl. Women, 1987; fellow Nat. Edn. Inst., Kellogg Found., 1984-85. Mem. Western Assn. Ednl. Opportunity Pers. (sec. bd. dirs. 1986—), Comision Feminil de Los Angeles (bd. dirs. 1983-84, edn. chmn.), Women of Moose. Democrat. Roman Catholic. Home: 5250 La Madera Ave El Monte CA 91732-1236 Office: 1725 Longworth House Office Bldg Washington DC 20515*

SOLKOFF, JEROME IRA, lawyer, consultant, lecturer; b. Rochester, N.Y., Feb. 15, 1939; s. Samuel and Dorothy (Krovetz) S.; m. Doreen Hurwitz, Aug. 11, 1963; children: Scott Michael, Anne Lynn. BS Sch. Indsl. Rels. and Labor Rels., Cornell U., 1961; JD, U. Buffalo, 1964. Bar: N.Y. 1965, Fla. 1974, U.S. Dist. Ct. (we. dist.) N.Y. 1965; cert. specialist Elder Law, Elder Law Found., The Fla. Bar. Assoc. Nusbaum, Tarricone, Weltman, Bilgore & Silver, Rochester, N.Y., 1964-66, Mousaw, Vigdor, Reeves, Heilbronner & Kroll, Rochester, 1966-70; sr. mcpl. atty. Urban Renewal Agy., Rochester, 1970-73; sole practice Rochester, 1970-73; chief legal counsel Arlen Realty Mgmt., Inc., Miami, Fla., 1973-75; assoc. Britton, Cohen, Kaufman, Benson & Schantz, Miami, 1975-76; chief legal counsel First Mortgage Investors, Miami Beach, Fla., 1976-79; ptnr. Cassel & Cassel, P.A., Miami, 1979-82; sole practice Deerfield Beach, Fla., 1982—. Lectr. on fgn. investment practices in U.S., Eng., 1981-88, Montreal, Que., Can., 1981, estate planning, 1982—, medicaid law and elder law, 1988—. Author: Fundamentals of Foreign Investing in American Real Estate and Businesses, 1981, Checklist of N.Y. Mortgage Foreclosure Procedures, 1970, History of Municipal Employee Unions, 1964, Practice Guide for Florida Elder Law, 1996, and yearly supplements. Bd. dirs. Broward Homebound Program, 1990—, pres. 1998-99; bd. dirs. Jewish Cmty. Ctrs. of South Broward, Fla., 1979-90, NE Alzheimers Daycare Ctr., Inc., 1990-92; mem. exec. bd. dirs. Broward Alzheimers Assn., 1995—; co-chair Fla. Alzheimers Pub. Policy steering com., 1999-2001. Named Advocate of Yr., Broward County Legal Aid Assn., 2003. Mem. ABA (mem. sects. real property, trust and probate law), Fla. Bar Assn. (sects. real property, trust and probate law, vice-chmn. com. on the elderly 1987-91, lectr. estate planning for the aging and disabled 1989—, founder, chmn. elder law sect. 1994-95, elder law sect., chmn. ethics com. 1998-2000), Nat. Acad. Elder Law Attys., Elder Law Attys.

SOLL, BRUCE A. retail executive; Degree in Econs. and Polit. Sci., Claremont McKenna Coll., 1979; degree in Law, So. Calif. Law Sch., 1982. Bar: Calif. Former counsel US Sec. Commerce; sr. v.p., counsle Ltd. Brands, Columbus, Ohio, 1991—. Mem. Ohio Bicentennial Commn.; bd. dirs. Columbus Symphony Orch., Ohio State U. Wexner Ctr. Found. Office: Ltd Brands Three Ltd Pkwy Columbus OH 43230

SOLL, HERBERT D. lawyer; b. 1936; BS, U. Denver, 1958, LLB, 1960. Dir. Peace Corps, Rio de Janeiro, 1967—70; chief pub. defender Alaska, 1971—75; trust territory pub. defender, 1975—79; dir. criminal prosecution, 1986—90; dir. Peace Corps, Sao Tome, 1990—93; judge Superior Ct., 1979—86; atty. gen. No. Mariana Islands, Saipan, 2000—. Office: Office Atty Gen PO Box 10007 Adminstrn Bldg Saipan MP 96950 E-mail: acsoll@gtepacifica.net.

SOLLENDER, JOEL DAVID, management consultant, finance company executive; b. NYC, Nov. 11, 1924; s. Samuel and Flora (Blumenthal) S.; m. Dorothy Leaf, Aug. 6, 1958; children: Jeffrey D., Jonathan L. BS, N.Y. U., 1946. C.P.A., N.Y. Staff auditor Ernst & Young, N.Y.C., 1946-50; with United Mchts. & Mfrs., Inc., N.Y.C., 1950-86, corp. contr., 1977—, sr. v.p., 1980—, chief acctg. officer, 1976—, also bd. dirs.; assoc. dir. N.Y. Hist. Soc., N.Y.C.; mem. adv. coun. to Office of Charities Registration Dept. State, N.Y. State, 1988-89; v.p. fin. Piedmont Industries, N.Y.C., 1989-90; exec. v.p., CFO Earthworm Inc., 1990—92; fin. mgmt. cons.; sr. cons. Internat. Exec. Svc. Corps Agy. for Internat. Devel., Kazakstan, 1996—. Adv. coun. San Diego State U., 1997—; audit com. San Diego Mus. Art, 1997-2002, 04—; fin. com. Globe Theater, 2003. Served with U.S. Army, World War II. Decorated Combat Infantry Badge, Purple Heart with cluster, Prisoner of War medal, Bronze Star. Mem. AICPA, N.Y. State Soc. CPAs (chief fin. officer com.), Am. Inst. Corp. Contrs., Rancho Bernardo (Calif.) Men's Club, Bailiwick Club (Greenwich, Conn.), Greenhaven Yacht Club (Rye).

SOLLMAN, GEORGE HENRY, venture capitalist; b. Michigan City, Ind., Nov. 2, 1941; s. Henry Charles and Margaret Elisabeth (Gockel) S.; m. Maureen Tosh, July 12, 1968; children: Jennifer, Erich. Spl. student, MIT, 1965—66; BSEE, Northwestern U., 1964; MSEE, Northeastern U., 1967. Engring. dir. Honeywell Info. Systems, Waltham, Mass., 1964—73; product line mgr. Control Data, Hawthorne, Calif., 1973—76; v.p., gen. mgr. Shugart/Xerox, Sunnyvale, 1976—84; spl. ptnr. Sand Hill Venture Group, Menlo Park, 1984; pres., CEO Centigram Corp., San Jose, 1985—97, AtMotion Inc. (now OpenWave Corp.), Redwood City, Calif., 1997—2000, Arabesque Investments LLC, Atherton, Calif., 2000—; chmn. First Virtual Corp., Redwood Shores, Calif., 2004—, Corticon Techs., San Mateo, Calif., 2000—. Bd. dirs. T-Ventures, Venture Capital arm of Deutsche Telecom, Bonn, Germany, 2001-; chmn. nat. bd. dirs. Am. Elec. Assn.; presdl. nomination Semicondr. Tech. Coun.; co-chmn. Alexis d'Toqueville Soc.; mem. adv. coun. Joint Venture Silicon Valley; chmn. adv. bd. Leavey Sch. Bus., Santa Clara U., 2000-. Patentee in field. Co-chmn. United Way of Santa Clara County; mem. steering com. George Lucas Ednl. Found., Marin County. Home: 242 Polhemus Ave Atherton CA 94027-5439 Office: Arabesque Investments LLC 242 Polhemus Ave Atherton CA 94027-5439 E-mail: george_sollman@hotmail.com.

SOLLORS, WERNER, English language, literature and American studies educator; PhD, Freie U., Berlin, 1975. Wissenschaftlicher asst., asst. prof. John F. Kennedy Inst. Freie U., Berlin; from asst. to assoc. prof. English and Comparative Lit. Columbia U.; Henry B. and Anne M. Cabot Prof. English Lit., prof. Afro-Am. studies Harvard U., Cambridge, Mass. Author: Amiri Baraka/LeRoi Joines: The Quest for a Populist Modernism, 1978, Beyond Ethnicity: Consent and Descent in American Culture, Neither Black Nor White Yet Both: Thematic Explorations of Interracial Literature, 1997; contbr. chapters to books Das amerikanische Drama der Gegenwart, 1976, The Harvard Encyclopedia of American Ethnic Groups, 1980, Reconstructing American Literary History, 1986, 1986, Columbia Literary History of the United States, 1988, 1988, Critical Terms for Literary Study, 1990, 1990, Looking Inward, Looking Outward: From the 1920s through the 1940s, 1990, 1990, Nationale und kulturelle Identitat: Studien zur Entwicklung des kollektiven Bewusstseins in der Neuzeit, 1991, Immigrants in Two Democracies: French and American Experience, 1992, Intersecting Boundaries: The Theatre of Adrienne Kennedy, 1992, Il razzismo e le sue storie, 1992, Swedes in America: Intercultural and Interethnic Perspectives on Contemporary Research, 1993, Multiculturalism and the Canon of American Culture, 1993, Configurations de l'ethnicite aux Etats-Unis, 1993, History & Memory in African-American Culture, 1994, Thematics: New Approaches, 1995, Thematics Reconsidered: Essays in Honor of Horst Jr. Daemmrich, 1995, Performances in American Literature and Culture, 1995, New Essays on Henry Roth's Call It Sleep, 1996, Families, 1996, Cultural Difference and the Literary Text, 1996, Beyond Pluralism, 1998, The Sally Hemings-Thomas Jefferson Relationship, 1999, Columbia Companion to 20th Century American Short Fiction, 2001, Dream-Fluted Cane: Essays on Jean Toomes and the Harlem Renaissance, 2001, Not English Only: Redefining "American" in American Studies, 2001, American Studies and Peace, 2001, Mixed-Race Literature, 2001; editor: A Bibliographic Guide to Afro-American Studies, 1972, A Bibliographic Guide to Afro-American Studies Supplement I, 1974; co-editor: Bibliographie amerikanistischer Veröffentlichungen in der DDR bis, 1968, 1976, Varieties of Black Experience at Harvard, 1986, The Invention of Ethnicity, 1989, The Life Stories of Undistinguished Americans as Told by Themselves, 1990, 1999, The Return of Thematic Criticism, 1993, Cane, 1993, Blacks at Harvard: A Documentary History of African-American Experience at Harvard and Radcliffe, 1993, The Black Columbiad: Defining Moments in African-American Literature and Culture, 1994, Theories of Ethnicity: A Classical Reader, 1996, The Promised Land, 1997, Multilingual America: Transnationalism, Ethnicity and the Languages of American Literature, 1998, The Multilingual Anthology of American Literature, 2000, The Norton Critical Edition of Olaudah Equiano, 2000, Interracialism: Black-White Intermarriage in American History, Literature and Law, 2000, The Adrienne Kennedy Reader, 2001, German? American? Literature?: New Directions in German-American Studies, 2002, Interracial Literature: An Anthology of Black-White Contacts in the Old World and the New, 2004; contbr. articles to profl. jours. Recipient Constance Rourke prize Am. Studies Assn., 1990; John Simon Guggenheim Meml. fellow, Andrew W. Mellon faculty fellow Harvard U., Walter Channing Cabot fellow Harvard U., 1997-98; NEH fellow, 1999-00. Fellow: Am. Acad. of Arts and Scis. Office: Harvard U Barker Center 12 Quincy St Cambridge MA 02138-3804

SOLLOWAY, C. ROBERT, retired forest products company executive; b. Vancouver, B.C., Can., May 19, 1935; s. Harold Eugene and Elva Merle (McAllister) S.; m. Ila Noreen Kelly. B in Commerce, U. B.C., 1959, LLB, 1960. Bar: Can., 1961. Asst. to exec v.p., asst. to pres. West Coast Transmission Co. Ltd., Vancouver, 1962-68; corp. counsel, asst. sec. Weldwood of Can. Ltd., Vancouver, 1968-73, gen. counsel, sec., 1973-75, v.p., gen. counsel, sec., 1975-2000. Mem. Law Soc. B.C., Can. Bar Assn., Vancouver Bar Assn. Clubs: Vancouver; Vancouver Lawn Tennis and Badminton. Anglican.

SOLMAN, JOSEPH, artist; b. Vitebsk, Russia, Jan. 25, 1909; came to U.S. 1912; s. Nathan and Rose (Peskin) S.; m. Ruth Romanofsky (dec. July 1999); children: Paul, Ronni,. Nat. Acad. of Design, 1927-30. Nat. Academician 1967. Easel painter WPA, N.Y.C., 1935-41; pvt. art instr. N.Y.C., 1951-66; art instr. CUNY, N.Y.C., 1967-75; artist N.Y.C., 1935—. Exhibitions: Retrospective at Phillips Mem. Mus., Washington, 1949, Retrospective at Wichita

(Kansas) Mus. of Art, 1984; author: books, Joseph Solman, Crown Publishers, 1966, Monotypes of Joseph Solman, Da Capo Press, 1977, Joseph Solman, Da Capo Press, 1995; artist: several paintings. Recipient of several awards for paintings and portraits including the Nat. Inst. of Arts & Letters, 1961, and 8 prizes from the Nat. Acad. of Design Annuals, 1967-89. Mem. Nat. Acad. of Design (treas. 1979-85), Fedn. of Modern Painters & Sculptors (exec. bd. 1968-89); fellow (life) Art Student League.

SOLMER, RICHARD, surgeon; b. South Bend, Ind., Feb. 11, 1947; MD, U. Mich., 1972. Diplomate Am. Bd. Plastic Surgery. Surgical intern Hosp. of the U. Pa., Phila., 1972-73; gen. surgical resident Calif. Hosp. Med. Ctr., L.A., 1976-80; plastic surgery resident Allentown (Pa.) Affiliated Hosp., 1980-82; pvt. practice Huntington Beach, and Newport Beach, Calif., 1982—. Fellow Am. Coll. Surgeons; mem. Am. Soc. Plastic Surgeons. Office: 307 Placentia Ave Ste 208 Newport Beach CA 92663-3308

SOLMSSEN, PETER, retired academic administrator; b. Berlin, Nov. 1, 1931; m. Kathleen Mailliard, Dec. 2001. AB, Harvard U., 1952; JD, U. Pa., 1959. Atty. Ballard, Spahr, Andrews & Ingersoll, Phila., 1959-60; with U.S. Fgn. Service, 1961; vice consul Singapore, 1962-63; asst. to under sec. of state, 1963-65; 2d sec., 1965-67; Cultural attache U.S. Dept. State, Sao Paulo, Brazil, 1967-70; adviser on arts Washington, 1974-80; dep. ambassador at large for cultural affairs, 1981-83; pres. Phila. Coll. Art, 1983-87, U. of the Arts, Phila., 1987-2000. One-man photography exhbns. include: Mus. Art, Sao Paulo. Author and illustrator. Mem.: Philadelphia; Century Assn.

SOLNIT, REBECCA, writer, art critic; Author: Secret Exhibition: Six California Artists of the Cold War Era, 1994, Savage Dreams: A Journey into the Landscape Wars of the American West, 1995, A Book of Migrations: Some Passages in Ireland, 1998, Wanderlust: A History of Walking, 2001, As Eve Said to the Serpent: On Landscape, Gender and Art, 2001, Hollow City: The Siege of San Francisco and the Crisis of American Urbanism, 2002, Motion Studies: Time, Space and Eadweard Muybridge, 2003, River of Shadows, 2003 (Nat. Book Critics Circle award, 2004). Grantee Guggenheim Fellowship, NEA Fellowship. Office: c/o Bloomsbury USA 175 5th Ave New York NY 10010

SOLO, ROBERT ALEXANDER, economist, educator; b. Phila., Aug. 2, 1916; s. Louis C. and Rebecca (Muchnick) S.; m. Roselyn Starr; 1 dau., Tova Maria. BS, Harvard U., 1938; MA, Am. U., 1941; PhD, Cornell U., 1953. Economist fed. and war agys., 1939-41; author, script chief Sta. WCAU-TV, Phila., 1949-50; mem. faculty Rutgers U., New Brunswick, N.J., 1953-55, McGill U., Montreal, Que., Can., 1955-56, CCNY, 1956-58; sr. research economist Princeton U., 1965-66; prof. dept. econs. Mich. State U., East Lansing, 1966-87, prof. emeritus, 1987—; dir. Inst. Internat. Bus. and Devel. Studies, 1966-68. Mem. faculty Johns Hopkins U., Balt., summer 1953, U. Mich., Ann Arbor, summer 1958; lectr. L'Ecole Practique des Hautes Etudes, Sorbonne, Paris, 1964-65; research Institut Recherch Economique et Planification, lectr. U. Grenoble, France, 1972-73; prof. associe U. Paris IV, Dauphine, 1971, 73; cons. NASA, 1965-67, OECD, 1963-65, Commonwealth of P.R., 1959-61, U.S. Dept. Justice, 1994-96; project chmn. Study on Info. Tech., Nat. Conf. Bd., 1969-72; project dir. Nat. Planning Assn., Washington, 1961-63; U.S. del. Yugoslavian Conf. on Transfer of Tech., Belgrade, 1974; mem. Alan T. Waterman award Com., 1976-77; expert witness Dept. Justice, Washington, L.A., 1995-97. Author: Economics and the Public Interest, 1955, Synthetic Rubber: A Case Study in Technological Development under Public Direction, 1959 (reprinted as Across the High Technology Threshold 1980), Economic Organizations and Social Systems, 1967 (reissued 2001), (with Everett Rogers) Inducing Technological Change for Economic Growth and Development, 1973, The Political Authority and the Market System, 1974, Organizing Science for Technology Transfer in Economic Development, 1975, The Positive State, 1981, (with Charles Anderson) Value Judgement and Income Distribution, 1981, Opportunity Knocks: American Economic Policy after Gorbachev, 1991, The Philosophy of Science and Economics, 1991, The Super Power and the Serb, 1998, The Song of Songs: The Harvard Version, 1998, also other books in field; contbr. chpts. to books, articles to profl. jours. Fulbright fellow, 1972-73 Mem. Council European Studies (steering com., exec. com., chmn. research com. 1974-77). Home: 4609 Chippewa Dr Okemos MI 48864-2009 E-mail: solo@pilot.msu.edu.

SOLOMON, ANDREW WALLACE, author; b. NYC, Oct. 30, 1963; s. Howard and Carolyn Ruth (Bower) S. BA in English magna cum laude, Yale U., 1985; BA, MA in English, Jesus Coll., Cambridge U., Cambridge, Eng., 1987. Editl. intern Met. Mus. Art, NYC, 1981, editl. asst., 1982, asst. editor, 1983, editor, 1986; intern dept. old master paintings Sotheby's NY, 1984; galleries corr., contbg. editor Harpers and Queen, London, 1987-91; contbg. editor HG, 1991-93; contbg. writer The NY Times Mag., 1993—2000. Author: The Irony Tower: Soviet Artists in a Time of Glasnost, 1991, A Stone Boat, 1994, The Noonday Demon: An Atlas of Depression, 2001 (Nat. Book award, finalist Pulitzer Prize); contbr. articles to profl. jours. Bd. dirs. World Monuments Fund, Outward Bound, Hurricane Island Sch., Alliance for the Arts, The American Coun. for Cultural Policy, The Victoria and Albert Mus., The Alex Fund, Depression Ctr. of U. Mich., The Worcester (Mass.) Found. Jesus Coll. Travel grantee, Cambridge U., 1986; Yale Conservation Project fellow for travel, 1985; Brit.-Am. Project fellow; Bogliasco fellow, 1998; recipient Nat. Book award Books for a Better Life, 2001, New Visions award QPB, Ken award Nat. Alliance for Mentally Ill., Charles T. Ruby Loss award, 2002, Silvano Arieti award, 2002, Didi Hirsch Cmty. Svc. award, 2002, Lambda award ALA. Mem. Groucho Club, Oxford & Cambridge Club, Chelsea Arts Club, Century Assn., Nat. Arts Club, Coun. on Fgn. Rels., Conservators Coun. of NY Pub. Libr. Democrat.

SOLOMON, ARTHUR CHARLES, pharmacist; b. Gary, Ind., May 30, 1947; s. Laurence A. and Dorothy B. (Klippel) S.; m. Janet Evelyn Irak, Aug. 23, 1969; children: Thomas, Michael, Mark, Jill. BS in Pharmacy, Purdue U., 1970, MS in Clin. Pharmacy, 1972; PharmD. Registered pharmacist; cert. nuclear pharmacist. Clin. prof. pharmacy U. Tex., Austin, 1972-75; v.p. Nuclear Pharmacy, Inc., Atlanta, 1975-83; exec. v.p., COO Diagnostek, Inc., Albuquerque, 1983-95; pres. Health Care Svcs., Inc., 1990-95; exec. v.p., COO Value Rx, Albuquerque, 1995-96; pres. Solomon and Assocs., Albuquerque, 1996-97; pres., CEO, dir. SP Pharms. LLC, Albuquerque, 1997—2001; sr. v.p. Cardinal Health, Albuquerque, 2001—. Adj. prof. U. N.Mex., 1992—. Contbr. articles to profl. jours. Named Disting. Alumnus Purdue U., 1998. Fellow Am. Soc. Cons. Pharmacists, Parental Drug Assn.; mem. Am. Pharm. Assn., Am. Assn. Pharm. Scis., Am. Soc. Hosp. Pharmacy, Nat. Assn. Retail Druggists, Nat. Coun. Prescription Drug Programs, Am. Managed Care Pharmacy Assn. (pres., dir.), Rho Chi, Pi Kappa Phi. Republican. Roman Catholic. Avocations: golf, woodworking, gardening. Home: 1504 Catron Ave SE Albuquerque NM 87123-4218 Office: Cardinal Health 4401 Alexander Blvd NE Albuquerque NM 87107 Business E-Mail: art.solomon@cardinal.com.

SOLOMON, ARTHUR KASKEL, biophysics educator; b. Pitts., Nov. 26, 1912; (married); 2 children. AB, Princeton U., 1934; MA, Harvard U., 1935, PhD in Phys. Chemistry, 1937; PhD in Physics, Cambridge U., Eng., 1947, Sc.D., 1964. Research assoc. in physics and chemistry Harvard, 1939-41; officer Brit. Ministry Supply, 1941-43; mem. staff Radiation Lab., Mass. Inst. Tech., 1945; asst. prof. phys. chemistry Med. Sch., Harvard, 1946-57, asso. prof. biophysics, 1957-68, prof., 1968-82, prof. emeritus, 1982—; assoc. in biophysics Peter Bent Brigham Hosp., Boston, 1950-72; dir. Read's Inc., Balt., 1946-77, pres., 1961-77. Mem. U.S. Nat. Com. for Pure and Applied Biophysics, 1965-72, U.S. Nat. Com. for Biology, 1966-71; mem. U.S. Nat. Com. for UNESCO, 1969-74, mem. U.S. del. to gen. assembly, Nairobi, 1976; mem. vis. com. biology dept. Brookhaven Nat. Lab., 1961-65; mem. NRC com. on radiology, 1957-59, com. on growth, 1954-57; sec. Gen. Internat. Union for Pure and Applied Biophysics, 1961-72; mem. NIH radiation study sect., 1960-63, biophys. sci. tng. com., 1963-68, chmn., 1966-68; mem. U.S. del. Gen. Assembly of UNESCO, Paris, 1978; mem. adv. panel on sci., tech. and society UNESCO, 1981-84; mem. bd. internat. orgns. and programs Nat. Acad. Scis., 1973-80, chmn., 1977-79; mem. Commn. on Internat. Relations, 1977-79; mem. exec. com. Internat. Council Sci. Unions, 1966-72; U.S. del. 17th, 18th Gen. Assemblies of Internat. Council Sci. Unions, Athens, 1978, Amsterdam, 1980; chmn. disting. fellowship com. Internat. Council Sci. Unions-UNESCO, 1980-85; chmn. Harvard com. on higher degrees in biophysics, 1959-80; chmn. Harvard Med. Sch. Oral History Com.; chmn. Harvard Council on the Arts, 1973-76 Mem. editorial bds.: Quarterly Revs. of Biophysics, 1972-74, Journal Gen. Physiology, 1958-90. Trustee Inst. Contemporary Art, Boston, 1946-76, pres., 1965-71; bd. overseers Boston Mus. Fine Arts, 1978-84; mem. collectors com. Nat. Gallery Art, Washington, 1985-88. Decorated Order Andres Bello Venezuela). Fellow AAAS, Am. Acad. Arts and Scis.; mem. Am. Chem. Soc., Am. Physiol. Soc., Biophysics Soc., Soc. Gen. Physiology. Clubs: Cosmos (Washington); St. Botolph (Boston); Harvard (N.Y.C. and Boston). Home: 27 Craigie St Cambridge MA 02138-3457

SOLOMON, BARRY JASON, healthcare administrator; b. Boston, May 16, 1934; s. Samuel and Ethel (Fleishman) Solomon; m. C. Priscilla Fugate, June 29, 1958; children: R. Stephen, Jon, Julie Ellen. BS in Biology and Chemistry, Tufts U., 1955; MBA in Health Care Adminstrn., Xavier U., Cin., 1960; MPH in Health Care Adminstrn., U. N.C., 1989. Chief med. record adminstr. USPHS Hosp., Lexington, Ky., 1956-59; asst. dir. Union Meml. Hosp., Balt., 1960-61; asst. adminstr. James Lawrence Kernan Hosp., Balt., 1961-67; asst. to dean, lectr. health edn. and med. care sects. Yale U. Sch. Medicine, New Haven, 1967-70; dir. health svcs., clin. asst. prof. pharmacy adminstrn. U. R.I., Kingston, 1970-76; assoc. dir. for adminstrn. USPHS Hosp., Norfolk, Va., 1976-81; dir., COO, sr. fellow in social medicine Montefiore Hosp., Bronx, N.Y., 1981-84; assoc. v.p. for med. affairs, mem. exec. coun. of Med. Sch. U. South Fla., Tampa, 1984-89; assoc. prof., acting chmn. dept. comprehensive medicine U. So. Fla., Tampa, 1984-89, assoc. prof. Coll. Pub. Health, 1984-89; cons. in health adminstrn., Columbia, Md., 1989-93; v.p. for acad. affairs North Broward Hosp. Dist., Ft. Lauderdale, Fla., 1993-96; chmn. bd. dirs. Sr. Benefit Ctrs. Am., Inc., 1998-2000. 1st v.p. bd. trustees and CEO Count and Countess de Hoernle Alzheimer's Pavillion, 2000—; pres., bd. dirs. Villa D'Este Condominium, Inc., 1999—2001; bd. dirs. Vis. Nurse Corp., 1987—90; bd. dirs., mem. exec. and nominating coms. Vis. Nurse Assn. Tampa Bay, 1987—90; mem. planning com. bd. trustees Hillsborough County Hosp. Authority, 1986—88; mem. profl. affairs com. bd. trustees H. Lee Moffitt Cancer Ctr. and Rsch. Inst., 1986—88; mem. affiliation com. S.W. Fla. Blood Bank, 1988—89; instr. hosp. adminstrn. Xavier U., 1960; course asst., instr. Am. Med. Record Assn., 1962—72; instr. Howard U. Coll. Continuing Edn., Washington, 1993; cons. St. Elizabeth Hosp., Covington, Ky., 1959, City Hosp. Ctr. Elmhurst, 1965, Hall-Brooke Hosp., Westport, Conn., 1968—69, Conn. Mental Health Ctr., New Haven, 1969—70, South County Hosp., Wakefield, RI, 1970—76, Centurion Hosp., Tampa, 1989, Primary Care Svcs., Tampa, 1991, Holland & Knight, Tampa, 1991, NCC Internat., Colchester, England, 1991, F. W. Assocs., Tampa, 1989—92, Decking Design, Norfolk, 1986—93, SMinc., Columbia, 1993, Internat. Flooring & Protective Coatings, Inc., Norfolk, 1993—; sr. cons. Meisel Assocs., Inc., N.Y.C., 1983—. Contbr. articles to profl. jours. Mem. Nat. Com. Religion and Health, 1982—84; mem., vice chmn. Chariho Sch. Bd., Richmond, RI, 1974—76; mem. Broward Econ. Devel. Coun., Inc.; trustee Montefiore-Mosholu Cmty. Ctr., 1981—84. Lt. USPHS, 1956—59, capt. USPHS, 1976—81. Recipient citation, Suncoast chp. Am. Heart Assn., 1988. Fellow: Am. Coll. Healthcare Execs.; mem.: APHA. Avocation: tennis. Home: 2863 Via Venezia Deerfield Beach FL 33442-8633

SOLOMON, BILLY K. army officer; b. Oakwood/Fairfield, Tex., Nov. 16, 1944; BS in Agr. Edn., Prairie View A&M Coll.; MA in Contracting and Acquisition Mgmt., Fla. Inst. Tech.; student, Armed Forces STaff Coll., Logistics Exec. Devel. Course, Indsl. Coll. Armed Forces, DoD CAPSTONE Worldwide Tng. Program for Gen. Officers. Commd. 2d lt. U.S. Army, 1966, advanced through grades to lt. gen.; chief of staff U.S. Army Materiel Command, to 1997; dir. logistics and security assistance U.S. Army Ctrl. Command, MacDill AFB, Fla., 1997-99; commdg. gen. Combined Support Command, Fort Lee, Va., 1999—2002; ret. Decorated Def. DSM with oak leaf cluster, DSM, Legion of Merit with 2 oak leaf clusters, Bronze Star with oak leaf cluster, Def. Superior Svc. medal, Meritorious Svc. medal with three oak leaf clusters, Army Commendation medal with 1 oak leaf cluster, Army Achievement medal, Armed Forces Res. medal, others*

SOLOMON, CAREN GROSSBARD, internist; b. N.Y.C., Feb. 20, 1963; MD, Harvard U., 1988. Resident Brigham and Women's Hosp., Boston, 1988-90, fellow in endocrinology, 1990-93, assoc. physician, 1993—. Asst. prof. medicine Harvard Med. Sch., 1998—. Mem.: AMA, Endocrine Soc., Mass. Med. Soc., Am. Diabetes Assn. Office: Brigham Womens Hosp Div Womens Health 45 Francis St # St5 Boston MA 02115-6105

SOLOMON, CONNIE SCOTT, chief of staff; d. Arthur M. and Christine A. Scott; m. Maurice Cochran Solomon (div.); children: Allison Lee, Curtis Scott. BS in Edn., U. Kans., Lawrence, 1962; MS, U. Kans., 1967. Tchr. Kans. City (Kans.) Pub. Sch., tchr, spl. edn.; dir. Teen Age Mother's Sch., Kans. City, Kans.; dir. Hosp. sch. U. Kans. Med. Sch.; dir. vol. El Paso County Dist. Attorney, Colo.; field dir. U.S. Senator William Armstrong, Colo. Springs, U.S. Senator Hank Brown, Colo. Springs, 1984—93; dist. dir. and chief of staff U.S. Congressman Joel Hefley, Wasington and Colo. Springs, 1993—; sec. of state candidate Colo., 1994. Bd. mem. Workout, Jr. League; mem. Mental Health Bd.; mem. AUSA bd. U.S. Army; bd. mem. Fine Arts Ctr. Mem. Rep. Exec. Com., Colo. Mem.: Denver Social Register, Garden of Gods Club. Republican. Meth. Avocations: reading, exercise, painting, travel.

SOLOMON, DANIEL, architectural firm executive; MA emeritus prof. of arch.(hon.), Univ. of Calif., Berkeley; BA arch., Columbia Univ., Stanford Univ. Dir. Solomon ETC, San Francisco, 1967; prof. arch. (emeritus) Univ. of Calif., Berkely, Calif., 1966—2000. Author: (book) ReBuilding, 1992, Global City Blues, 2003. Named list of 100 foremost arch., Arch. Digest, 1991, 1995. Achievements include co-founder of the Congress for New Urbanism. Office: Solomon ETC 1328 Mission St, 4th Fl San Francisco CA 94103

SOLOMON, DAVID HARRIS, geriatrician, educator; b. Cambridge, Mass., Mar. 7, 1923; s. Frank and Rose (Roud) Solomon; m. Ronda L. Markson, June 23, 1946; children: Patti Jean Sinaiko, Nancy Ellen. AB, Brown U., 1944; MD, Harvard U., 1946. Intern Peter Bent Brigham Hosp., Boston, 1946—47, resident, 1947—48, 1950—51; fellow endocrinology New Eng. Center Hosp., Boston, 1951—52; faculty UCLA Sch. Medicine, 1952—, prof. medicine, 1966—93, vice chmn. dept. medicine, 1968—71, chmn. dept., 1971—81, assoc. dir. geriatrics, 1982—89; dir. UCLA Ctr. on Aging, 1991—96; prof. emeritus UCLA, 1993—. Chief med. svc. Harbor Gen. Hosp., Torrance, Calif., 1966—71; cons. Wadsworth VA Hosp., L.A., 1952—93, Sepulveda VA Hosp., 1971—93; cons. metabolism tng. com. USPHS, 1960—64, endocrinology study sect., 1970—73; cons. RAND Corp., 1997—. Editor: Jour. Am. Geriatric Soc., 1988—93; contbr. numerous articles to profl. jours. Recipient Ollie Randall award, Nat. Coun. on the Aging, 2004. Master: ACP (John Phillips Meml. award 2002); mem.: AAAS, UCLA Med. Alumni Assn. (Extraordinary Merit award 2002), Gerontol. Soc. Am. (Freeman award 1997), Am. Geriatrics Soc. (bd. dir. 1985—93, Milo Leavitt award 1992, Disting. Svc. award 1993, Edward Henderson award 1999), Am. Fedn. Aging Rsch. (Irving S. Wright award 1990), Western Assn. Physicians (councillor 1972—75, pres. 1983—84), Inst. Medicine Nat. Acad. Sci., Am. Thyroid Assn. (pres. 1973—74, Disting. Svc. award 1986), Endocrine Soc. (Robert H. Williams award 1989), We. Soc. Clin. Rsch. (councillor 1963—65, Mayo Soley award 1986), Am. Soc. Clin. Investigation, Assn. Am. Physicians, Assn. Profs. of Medicine (pres. 1980—81), Alpha Omega Alpha, Sigma Xi, Phi Beta Kappa. Home: 2103 Ridge Dr Los Angeles CA 90049-1153 Office Phone: 310-471-5256. Personal E-mail: dsolomon1@earthlink.net.

SOLOMON, DIANE HURST, neurologist; b. Albuquerque, Jan. 28, 1956; d. E. Henry and Jonel Tinson Hurst; m. Dale Edward Solomon, Jan. 20, 1979; children: Stuart, Scott, Spencer. BA in Psychology, Biology, U. Tex., 1978; MA in Clin. Psychology, Corpus Christi State U., 1980; MD, U. Tex., Health Sci. Ctr., San Antonio, 1986. Diplomate Am. Bd. Psychiatry and Neurology. Resident neurology U. Tex. Health Sci. Ctr. San Antonio, 1987-91, chief resident neurology, 1990-91, fellow geriatrics, 1991-92, clin. instr., 1991-93, asst. prof., 1993—, clin. assoc. prof. dept. medicine, 1998—; dir. neurology S. Tex. Vets. Health Care Sys., Kerrville, 1997—. Co-author: Behavioral Neurology of Movement Disorders, 1995, Surgical Management of Cerebrovascular Disease, 1995, Textbook of Neuroanesthesia and Neurological Dysfunction, 1997; contbg. author: Clinical Anesthesia Practice, 2000. Mem. med. and sci. com. Am. Heart Assn., Austin, 1996—2001, liaison stroke coun. Tex. affiliate, 1996—2001; co-chmn. Stroke Awareness Task Force, San Antonio, 1996—2001; chmn. pub. awareness com. Tex. Coalition Cardiovascular Disease and Stroke, Austin, 1999—2000; mem. Tex. Dept. Health Cardiovascular Disease and Stroke Coun., 2000—03, vice chmn., 2001—03; Stephen's minister Univ. United Meth. Ch., 2002—; mem. exec. com. TMA Stroke Project, Austin, 1995—2003, chmn., 1999—2003, mem. cardiovascular disease com., 1999—; bd. dirs. Am. Heart Assn., 1997—, affiliate bd. mem., 2001—, nominating com., 2002, pres. San Antonio divsn., 2002—03. Named Disting. Alumnus Corpus Christi State U., 1983, Outstanding Young Women Am., 1984, Paul V. Ledbetter Physician Vol. of the Yr. award Tex. affiliate Am. Heart Assn., 1998, Stroke Vol. of Yr., 2000. Fellow: Am. Heart Assn. (Outstanding Achievement award 2001, Disting. Svc. award San Antonio divsn. 2001), Stroke Coun.; mem.: Bexar County Med. Assn., Tex. Med. Assn., Tex. Neurol. Soc., Am. Fedn. Clin. Rsch., Am. Acad. Neurology (mem. profl. and pub. info. com.). Methodist. Avocations: poetry, playing the harp, skiing, camping, swimming. Office: U Tex Health Sci Ctr San Antonio Dept Medicine, Neurology 7703 Floyd Curl Dr San Antonio TX 78284-6200 E-mail: solomondd@cs.com.

SOLOMON, DOROTHY JEANNE ALLRED, writer, communications executive; b. Salt Lake City, June 24, 1949; d. Rulon Clark and Mabel (Finlayson) Allred; m. Bruce Craig Solomon, Jan. 8, 1968; children: Denise, Layla, Jeffrey, Laurie. BA in Lit., Theater and Speech, U. Utah, 1971, MA in Lit. and Creative Writing, 1981. Cert. secondary edn. educator, Utah. Storyteller, libr. Salt Lake City Libr., 1971; tchr. Salt Lake Sch. Dist., 1971-74; instr. U. Utah/Columbia Coll., Salt Lake City, 1974-80; writer-in-residence Utah Arts Coun., Salt Lake City, 1980-93; human devel. trainer Lifespring, San Rafael, Calif., 1983-87; media specialist Rivendell Psychiat. Hosps., West Jordan, Utah, 1987-90; curriculum writer Positive Action Pub., Twin Falls, Idaho, 1990-96; co-founder, v.p. Rising Star Comm. and Team Resource Assocs., Salt Lake City, 1994—. Bd. dirs. Rising Star Comm. Author: In My Father's House, 1984 (1st prize Biography, 1981, Pub. prize 1982), Inside Out: Creative Writing, 1989, Of Predators, Prey and Other Kin, 1996 (1st prize Non-fiction 1996); contbr. stories to anthologies Stories That Shape Us, What There Is, The Best of Writers at Work, A New Genesis, Great and Peculiar Beauty, In Our Lovely Deseret, Mormon Fictions, 1998, Predators, Prey, and Other Kinfolk: Growing Up in Polygamy, 2003 (WILLA award 2004); screenwriter: In My Father's House, 1986-87. Bd. dirs. The Children's Ctr., Salt Lake City, 1982-85, Writers at Work, Park City, Utah, 1986-89, Lifespring Found., San Rafael, Calif., 1985-89; mem. curriculum com. Salt Lake Sch. Dist., 1971-74; coord. (with Bruce Solomon) lit. arts Utah Arts Festival "Performing Word", Salt Lake City, 1982; vol. Big Sisters, Salt Lake City, 1970-71; coord. cmty. edn. Rivendell Conf., West Jordan, Utah, 1987-89. Recipient Disting. Journalism 1st prize Am. Acad. Pediat., San Francisco, 1979, 1st prize feature writing Sigma Delta Chi, Salt Lake City, 1979, 1st prize essay Utah Original Writing Contest, Salt Lake City, 1995, 1st prize Biography, 1981, 96, award of excellence Gov.'s Media Awards, Utah, 1990, Utah State Pub. prize, 1982. Mem. Associated Writing Programs, Acad. Am. Poets, Sierra Club, Amnesty Internat. Mem. Lds Ch. Avocations: golf, reading, movies, environmental protection, child/family advocacy projects. Home: 6521 Snowview Dr Park City UT 84098-6167 Office Phone: 801-975-1000. E-mail: emeralddor@aol.com.

SOLOMON, ELINOR HARRIS, economics professor; b. Boston, Feb. 26, 1923; d. Ralph and Linna Harris; m. Richard A. Solomon, Mar. 30, 1957; children: Joan S. Griffin, Robert H., Thomas H. AB, Mt. Holyoke Coll., 1944; MA, Radcliffe U., 1945; PhD, Harvard U., 1948. Jr. economist Fed. Res. Bank Boston, 1945-48; economist Fed. Res. Bd. Govs., Washington, 1949-56; internat. economist U.S. State Dept., Washington, 1957-58; professorial lectr. Am. U., Washington, 1964-66; sr. economist antitrust div. U.S. Dept. Justice, Washington, 1966-82; prof. econs. George Washington U., Washington, 1982—. Econ. cons., Washington, 1982—; expert witness antitrust, fin. networks, electronic funds transfer cases, Washington, 1988—. Author: Virtual Money, 1997; author, editor: Electronic Funds Transfers and Payments, 1987, Electronic Money Flows, 1991; contbr. articles on econs., banking and law to profl. jours. Mem. Am. Econs. Assn., Nat. Economists Club (bd. govs. 1997-2000), The Cosmos Club (chair Digital Age series 1999-2001, chmn. Frontiers of Sci. 2001-2004, chmn. program com. 2004—). Home: 6805 Delaware St Chevy Chase MD 20815-4164 Office: George Washington U Dept Econ Washington DC 20052-0001

SOLOMON, GAIL ELLEN, physician; b. Bklyn., May 26, 1938; d. Samuel and Estelle (Suffin) S.; m. Harvey Hecht, Oct. 28, 1962; children: Daniel, Jonathan, Elizabeth. AB, Smith Coll., 1958; MD, Albert Einstein Coll. Medicine, 1962. Diplomate Am. Bd. Pediats., Am. Bd. Psychiatry and Neurology (assoc. examiner), Am. Bd. Electroencephalography, Am. Bd. Electroencephalography and Neurophysiology, Am. Bd. Clin. Neurophysiology. Intern in pediat. Bronx Mcpl. Hosp. Ctr., 1962-63, resident in pediat., 1963-64, N.Y. Hosp.-Cornell U. Med. Coll., N.Y.C., 1964-65; NIH vis. fellow in neurology and child neurology Columbia-Presbyn. Med. Ctr., N.Y.C., 1965-68, NIH vis. fellow in clin. neurophysiology and electroenceph.; instr. neurology Columbia U. Coll. of Physicians and Surgeons, N.Y.C., 1968-69; instr. in neurology and pediat. Cornell U. Med. Coll., 1969-70, asst. prof. neurology and pediat., 1970-76; asst. attending in neurology and pediat. N.Y. Hosp., N.Y.C., 1969-76, dir. electroencephalography, 1969—; assoc. prof. clin. neurology and pediat. Cornell U. Med. Coll., 1976—, assoc. prof. clin. neurology in psychiatry, 1983; assoc. attending in neurology and pediat. N.Y. Hosp., 1976—, assoc. attending neurologist in psychiatry, 1983—. Mem. joint com. for stroke facilities NIH; mem. FDA Peripheral and CNS Adv. Com., 1979-83, chmn., 1983, cons., 1983-84; mem. med. audit com. N.Y. Hosp., mem. utilization rev. com.; mem. profl. adv. bd. N.Y. State Epilepsy Assn.; adj. attending physician in neurology Meml.-Sloan Kettering Cancer Ctr., 1982-93; assoc. attending pediatrician Hosp. Spl. Surgery, 1987—; neurology cons. Blythedale Children's Hosp., Valhalla, N.Y., 1991—, Meml.-Sloan Kettering Cancer Ctr., 1993—. Author: (with F. Plum) Clinical Management of Seizures: A Guide for the Physician, 1976, (with Plum and Kutt) 2d edit., 1983; editor: (with Kaufman and Pfeffer) Child and Adolescent Neurology for Psychiatrists, 1992, Neurologic Disorders: Developmental and Behavioral Sequelae, 1999; contbr. articles to profl. jours., chpts. to med. books. Fellow Am. Acad. Neurology, Am. Acad. Pediats., Am. Electroencephalographic Soc. mem. AMA (Physician's Recognition award in Continuing Med. Edn.), N.Y. State Med. Soc., N.Y. County Med. Soc., Am. Med. Women's Assn., Am. Epilepsy Soc., Am. Acad. Clin. Neurophysiology, Eastern EEG Soc., Am. Med. EEG Assn., Child Neurology Soc., Internat. Child Neurology Assn., Tristate Child Neurology Soc., Assn. for Rsch. in Nervous and Mental Diseases, N.Y. Acad. Sci. Avocations: art museums, reading literature, french language, travel. Office: NY Presbyn Hosp Cornell U Med Coll 525 E 68th St New York NY 10021-4870

SOLOMON, HENRY, university dean; b. Bronx, N.Y., Nov. 28, 1926; s. Max and Tillie (Gilerowitz) S.; m. Jacqueline Mona Cohen, May 31, 1953; 1 son, Michael Robert. BA, Bklyn. Coll., 1949; MA, NYU, 1950, PhD, 1960. Rsch. assoc., then sr. staff investigator and dep. prin. investigator Logistics Rsch. Project George Washington U., 1950—66, prof. econs., chmn. dept., 1962—74, 1991—96, dean Grad. Sch. Arts and Scis., 1974—90, prof. and dean emeritus, 1996—. Dep. asst. adminstr. econs., acting asst. adminstr. planning, research and analysis SBA, 1966-67; cons. in field. Assoc. editor: Naval Research Logistics Quar., 1957-90 . Served with U.S. Army, 1945-46. Recipient Founder's Day award N.Y. U., 1960 Mem.: Am. Econ. Assn. Home: # 603 5450 Whitley Park Terr Bethesda MD 20814 Office: George Washington Univ Funger 507 Washington DC 20052-0001: E-mail: henry20814@aol.com.

SOLOMON, HILDA PEARL, wholesale executive; b. Conway, S.C., Dec. 15, 1948; d. Ezel and Dorothy (Gottlieb) S. BFA, U. S.C., 1968. Buyer Solomon Bros. Dept. Store, Conway, 1969-73; coutourier sales Julius Lewis, Memphis, 1973-75; buyer Helen of Memphis, 1975-78, George M. Muse Clothing Co., Atlanta, 1978-83; sales rep. Whiting & Davis Co. Inc.,

Plainville, Mass., 1983-84, exec. sales mgr. southeast dist., 1984-92; owner Solomon, Atlanta, 1992—. Sec. bd. dirs. Bur. Wholesale Accessory Reps., Atlanta, 1983-87, Accessories On 6 Atlanta Apparel Mart, 1986-87; dir. trade shows, key accounts, export mgr., 1994-98; nat. key account mgr. Westminster, Inc., 1999-2000; dir. sales Decorative Expressions, Inc., Atlanta, 2000—. Prin. works include Posh Petals, Atlanta, 1986—. Mem. Atlanta Hist. Soc., Young Careers High Mus. Art. Jewish. Avocations: design, travel, writing. Home: 2917 Hamilton Sq Decatur GA 30033-1140

SOLOMON, HOWARD, pharmaceutical company executive; b. Aug. 12, 1927; s. David and Faye (Gussow) S.; m. Carolyn Ruth Bower, Dec. 17, 1961; children: Andrew Wallace, David Frederick; m. Sarah Durie Billinghost, Aug. 27, 2003. BSS, CCNY, 1949; LLB, Yale U., 1952. Bar: N.Y. 1952. Atty. Moses & Singer, N.Y.C., 1952-55, Kay Scholer, Fierman Hays & Handler, N.Y.C., 1956-60; pres. Hildred Mgmt. Corp., N.Y.C., 1967-83; dir. Forest Labs., Inc., N.Y.C., 1964—. Chmn., CEO Forest Labs., Inc., 1998—; dir. Pharmax Ltd., Bexley, Kent., U.K., 1979—; trustee Cold Spring Harbor Labs., N.Y.-Presbyn. Hosp. Bd. dirs. Met. Opera; bd. dirs. Lincoln Ctr. for Performing Arts. Mem. N.Y. State Bar Assn., Yale Club, Harmonie Club of N.Y. Office: Forest Labs Inc 909 3rd Ave New York NY 10022-4731

SOLOMON, JACK AVRUM, JR., lawyer, automotive distributor, art dealer; b. Omaha, Oct. 25, 1928; s. John A. and Matilda (Bienstok) S.; m. Josephine J. Kleiman, June 1948 (div. Mar. 1971); children: Debra, Alisa, Michael, Rena; m. Carolyn Summers, Dec. 1973. BS, U. Nebr., 1950, LL.B. cum laude, 1952; LL.M. (Cook fellow), U. Mich., 1953. Bar: Nebr. 1950, Ill. 1951. Practice law, Chgo., 1950—; with firm Stiefel, Greenberg, Burns, Baldridge & Solomon, 1953-66, ptnr., 1958-66, Solomon, Rosenfeld, Elliot & Stiefel, and predecessor, 1966—, sr. ptnr., 1966—. Dir. Amco Industries, Inc., Chgo., 1968—, chmn. bd., 1968-69, sec., gen. counsel, 1969—; sec., dir. Mogen David Wine Corp., Chgo., 1964-71; chmn. bd., dir. Arts and Leisure Corp., 1969-76; pres., chmn. bd., dir. Circle Fine Art Corp., 1968-94; chmn. bd. S2 Art Group, Ltd., 1996—, Re Society, 1997—, Art of the Movies.com, 1999—; pres. The Las Vegas Art Dist., 2002--. Mem. Ill., Nebr. bar assns.; mem. Fine Art Pubs. Assn. (pres. 1982—); Mem. Order of Coif. Jewish (pres. temple 1959-61). Club: Nat. Arts (N.Y.C.). Home: 2870 Augusta Las Vegas NV 89109 Office: 1 E Charleston Las Vegas NV 89104 Office Phone: 702-868-7880. E-mail: jsolomon@s2art.com.

SOLOMON, JACK D. investment banker; b. Detroit, Mich., July 27, 1930; s. Alexander C. and Anita Ruth Solomon; m. Karla Marie Frantzve, Mar. 26, 2002; children: Jacqueline Cheryl Tal, David Neal, Gregg Harvey, Diana Ruth Rothstein, Moriah Chloé Dee. AA, L.A. City Coll., 1954; BA, L.A. State Coll., 1956, Calif. State Univ., 1958. V.p. JSH Electronics Corp., 1954—60; dir. Harwit Internat. Corp., 1954—60; pres. Fed. Electronics, 1960—66; pres., chmn. Advanced Patent Tech. Corp., 1968—84; pres. Gaming and Tech. Corp., 1976—83, APT Games Inc., 1978—80; co-found., dir. Am. Bank of Commerce, 1978—83; found., chmn. New Age Corp., 1980—94; pres. Genesis investment Corp., 1986—. Dir. Houston Fearless Corp., 1962—65, Western Transistor Corp., 1962—68; chmn. of the bd. dirs. Western Fed. Fin. Corp., 1964—66; dir. Fed. Land and Devel. Corp., 1964—90, Fed. Rsch. and Devel., 1965—83; chmn. of the bd. Advanced Patent tech., 1967—83. Nat. dir. Equal Opportunities Found., 1963—66; sponsor Nat. Hosp. Denever, Colo.; co-founder Israeli Armored Corps Mus.; patron Orr Chadash Orphanage Israel; vice chmn. Calif. Dem. Coun., 1966—70; candidate Calif. State. Sen., 1966; dir. United Jewish Fedn., 1965—67; mem. com. L.A. C. of C.; mem. World Affairs Coun.; mem. of pres. cabinet Am. Israel pub. Affairs Com.; mem. Las Vegas C. of C.; dir. Utah Shakespeareon Festival, 1999—2000. Sgt. USAF, 1948—52, serv. on the Berlin Airlift in Germany. Decorated Medal for Humane Action USAF; recipient Man of the Yr., Southern Calif., 1963, Marshall Medal for Outstanding Social Svc., 1964, Carson White award, 1964, Disting. Svc. award, L.A. Affairs Com., 1966, Disting. Citizen award, City of Montreal, 1966, Meritorious award, Dem. Party, 1966, Ken. Col., 1970, Wall of Honor, Hebrew Univ. of Jerusalem, 1976, Israeli State Med., 1990, Pres. Medal, Suleiman Demirel Pres. of Turkey, 1992. Mem.: Am. Air Mus. in Britian (found. mem.), Armed Forces Commn. and Electronics Assn., Nat. Aeronautics Assn., Internat. Assn. of Bus. and Profl. (hon.), B'nai B'rith, Pres. Club Utah Valley State Coll., Pres. Club Brigham Young Univ., Pres. Club World Jewish Congress (life), 32nd Degree Mason, Scottish Rite (life). Achievements include funded and restored the ancient Zion's Gate and Plaza in Jerusalem; constructed the Colo. Belle Hotel and Casino one of the first of its kind in Laughlin, Nev. Avocation: art.

SOLOMON, JOHN DAVIS, aviation executive; b. Kingfisher, Okla., Oct. 22, 1936; s. Edward Dempsey and Mary Blanche (Smith) S.; m. Mildred Oraline Brammer, July 16, 1968 (div. Mar. 1984); children: Jennifer Leigh, Jason Lewis; m. Sheila Mary McLeod, Nov. 23, 1985. BA, Okla. State U., 1958. Asst. mgr. airport City of Oklahoma City Dept. Aviation, 1963-66, City of Tulsa Airport Authority, 1966-70; dir. aviation City of Oklahoma City., 1970-77, Clark County Dept. Aviation, Las Vegas, Nev., 1977-86; dir. environ. planning Landrum & Brown, Aviation Planners, Cin., 1986-88; dep. dir. aviation City of Houston Airport System, 1988-90; dir. aviation City of Kansas City, Mo., 1990-96; asst. dir. aviation City of Phoenix, 1997—. Editor Airport Mgmt. Jour., 1975; contbr. articles to aviation jours. Mem. Am. Assn. Airport Execs. (bd. dirs., ex-officio, accredited 1965, pres. 1979, Pres.'s award 1975, Disting. Svc. award 1991), Airports Coun. Internat. (bd. dirs. 1985-86), Kappa Sigma. Avocations: art, music, collecting military miniatures. Office: Dept Aviation Sky Harbor Airport 3400 E Sky Harbor Blvd Phoenix AZ 85034-4403

SOLOMON, LEWIS DAVID, law educator; b. N.Y.C., Aug. 25, 1941; s. Milton A. and Ruth (Lewis) S.; m. Janet Stern, Mar. 28, 1971; 1 son, Michael Stern. BA, Cornell U., 1963; JD, Yale U., 1966. Bar: N.Y. 1969. Law clk. U.S. Dist. Ct., Wilmington, Del., 1966-67; assoc. Colton, Weissberg, Hartnick & Yamin, N.Y.C., 1968-73; assoc. prof. law U. Mo.-Kansas City Law Sch., 1973-77; prof. law George Washington U. Nat. Law Ctr., Washington, 1977—. Author: Federal Income Taxation: Problems and Materials, 1979; Trusts and Estates: A Basic Course: Problems, Planning and Policy, 1981; Corporations: Law and Policy, Materials and Problems, 1982, Corporate Acquisitions, Mergers and Divestitures, 1983, Tax Planning Strategies, 1985, Taxation of Investments, 1987, 2nd edit., 1994, Problems Cases and Materials on Federal Income Taxation, 1987, Corporations: Law and Policy, Materials and Problems, 4th rev. edit. 1998, Federal Taxation of Estates, Trusts and Gifts: Cases, Problems and Materials, 2d edit., 1998, Trusts and Estates: Cases, Problems and Materials, 1989, Corporations: Explanations and Examples, 1990, Corporate Finance and Governance, revised edit., 1996, Business Workout Strategies: Tax and Legal Aspects, 1992, Asset Protection Strategies: Tax and Legal Aspects, 1993, Business Contracts: Forms and Tax Analysis, 2nd. edit., 1994, Estate Planning: Complete Guide and Workbook, 1994, Law of Estates, Trusts and Gifts, 1996, Asset Protection Strategies: Tax and Legal Aspects, 2d edit., 2001, The Individual Tax Base, 2002, Valuation A Closely Held Business: Legal and Tax Aspects, 1998, Estate and Gift Tax Handbook, 1998. Carnegie Endowment for Internat. Peace grantee, 1976. Mem. ABA, Phi Beta Kappa. Home: 5600 Wisconsin Ave Apt 1107 Chevy Chase MD 20815 Office: George Washington U Law Sch 2000 H 720 20th St NW Washington DC 20052

SOLOMON, LIBERTINA, pharmacist, educator; b. Botosani, Romania, Feb. 5, 1926; d. Harry and Betty Segal; m. Monel Solomon, June 12, 1948; children: Silyiu, Aniela. PhD in Biology, U. Bucharest, 1970. Registered pharmacist. Asst. prof. U. Al. L. Cuza, Iasi, Romania, 1949—59, assoc. prof., 1959—72, prof., 1972—89, rschr., 1959—89, chief dept. animal biology, 1975—80; pharmacist, asst. Bronx Lebanon Hosp., N.Y.C., 1990—. Mem. Com. of According Drs. Degree, Romania, 1975—89. Contbr. more than 80 articles and rsch. papers to profl. jours., chapters to books. Mem.: N.Y. Acad. Sci. Achievements include discovery of 16 new species of gamasida (Acari) and over 160 new species of Romanian fauna; soil and parasitic gamasides. Avocation: travel. Home: 729 W 186 St Apt 2E New York NY 10033

SOLOMON, MARILYN KAY, educator, consultant; b. Marshall, Mo., Oct. 16, 1947; d. John W. and Della M. (Dille) S. BS, Ctrl. Mo. State U., 1969; MS, Ind. U., 1974. Cert. in early childhood and nursery sch. edn., Mo., Ind. Tchr. Indpls. Pub. Schs., 1969—74; dir. Singer Learning Ctrs., Indpls., 1974—78; v.p. ECLC Learning Ctrs., Inc., Indpls., 1978—95; pres., CEO, owner Early Learning Ctrs., Inc., Indpls., 1995—; owner, pres., CEO Solomon Antique Restoration, Inc., Indpls., 1996—, The Shoppes at Guilford Junction, 2002—; pres., CEO Woodford Group, 1995—. Mem. OJT tng. task force Dept. Labor, Washington; mem. nat. task force for parenting edn. HEW, Washington; cons. to numerous corps. on corp. child care; built 29 child care ctrs. for corps., hosps. and govt. Co-author curricula. Founding bd. dirs. Mid City Pioneer, Indpls., 1977; mem. adv. bd. Enterprise Zone Small Bus. Incubator, Indpls., 1995-2002; founding bd. dirs. Family Support Ctr., Indpls., 1983, pres. bd. dirs., 1985-87; founding mem., co-chair Voices for Children, 1996—; mem. White Rivers Gardens State Park, Indpls. Mus. Art, 500 FEstival Assn. Recipient Outstanding Leadership award Ind. Conf. on Social Concerns, 1975, 76, 77, Children's Mus. Edn. award, 1974; named to Outstanding Young Women of Am., 1984. Mem. Indpls. Mus. Art, Ind. Lic. Child Care Assn. (v.p. 1992, pres. 1974, 75), State of Ind. Quality and Tng. Coun. (chair 1992), Step Ahead-Marion County (rep. for child care 1992—, co-chair educare com. 1999—), Ind. Alliance for Better Child Care (bd. dirs. 1992, adv. bd. 1990-95), Pub. Broadcasting (tng. com. 1992-99, child devel. tng. com. 1996-99), Order Ea. Star, Indpls. Zool. Soc. (charter). Office: Early Learning Ctrs Inc 1315 S Sherman Dr Indianapolis IN 46203-2210 E-mail: earlylearn@iquest.net.

SOLOMON, MARK RAYMOND, lawyer, educator; b. Pitts., Aug. 23, 1945; s. Louis Isadore and Fern Rhea (Josselson) S. BA, Ohio State U., 1967; MEd, Cleve. State U., 1971; JD with hons., George Washington U., 1973; LLM in Taxation, Georgetown U., 1976. Bar: Ohio, Mich., U.S. Dist. Ct. (ea. dist.) Mich., U.S. Ct. Appeals (6th cir.), U.S. Tax Ct., U.S. Ct. Fed. Claims. Tax law specialist corp. tax br. Nat. Office of IRS, 1973—75; assoc. Butzel, Long, Gust, Klein & Van Zile, Detroit, 1976—78; dir., v.p. Shatzman & Solomon, P.C., Southfield, Mich., 1978—81; prof., chmn. tax/bus. law dept., dir. MS in Taxation Program Walsh Coll., Troy, Mich., 1981—; of counsel in tax matters Meyer, Kirk, Snyder & Lynch, PLLC, Bloomfield Hills, Mich., 1981—. Adj. prof. law U. Detroit, 1977-81. Editor: Cases and Materials on Consolidated Tax Returns, 1978, Cases and Materials on the Application of Legal Principles and Authorities to Federal Tax Law, 1990. Mem. Mich. Bar Assn., Phi Eta Sigma. Avocation: bridge (life master). Home: 2109 Golfview Dr Apt 102 Troy MI 48084-3926 Office: Meyer Kirk Snyder & Lynch PLLC 100 W Long Lake Rd Ste 100 Bloomfield Hills MI 48304-2773 also: Walsh Coll 3838 Livernois Rd Troy MI 48083-5066 Office Phone: 248-647-5111. E-mail: msolomon@walshcollege.edu.

SOLOMON, MAYNARD ELLIOTT, music historian, former recording company executive; b. N.Y.C., Jan. 5, 1930; s. Benjamin and Dora (Levine) S.; m. Eva Georgiana Tevan, Jan. 22, 1951; children: Mark Jonathan, Nina Stephanie, Maury David. BA, Bklyn. Coll., 1950; postgrad., Columbia U., 1950-51. Co-founder, co-owner Vanguard Rec. Soc., Inc., N.Y.C., 1950-86; faculty grad. div. CUNY, 1979-81. Vis. prof. SUNY Stony Brook, 1988, Columbia U., N.Y.C., 1990, Harvard U., Cambridge, Mass., 1992, Yale U., New Haven, 1994-95; scholarly advisor Beethoven Archive, Bonn, 1997—; faculty grad. divsn. Juilliard Sch., 1998—. Author: Marxism and Art, 1973, Beethoven, 1977 (translated into German, French, Spanish, Portuguese, Japanese, Italian, Bulgarian), Myth, Creativity and Psychoanalysis, 1978, Beethoven's Tagebuch, 1982, Beethoven's Tagebuch, German translation, 1990, Italian translation, 1992, Japanese translation, 2001, Beethoven Essays, 1988, Italian translation, 1998; Mozart: A Life, 1995 (translated into Swedish, Italian, Japanese), Late Beethoven, 2003; editor: Joan Baez Songbook, 1964; contbg. editor: Beethoven Forum, Am. Imago; mem. editl. bd. Beethovenhaus edit. Beethoven's Letters; editor: Memories of Beethoven, 1992; prodr. over 100 folk music albums; contbr. articles to profl. jours. Recipient Deems Taylor award ASCAP, 1978, 89, 96, Disting. Vis. award U. Toronto, 1996. Mem. PEN, Am. Musicol. Soc. (bd. dirs. 1984-86, Otto Kinkeldey award 1989, hon. mem. 1999), Authors Guild, N.Y. Inst. for Humanities, Phi Beta Kappa. Home: 1 W 72nd St New York NY 10023-3486

SOLOMON, NEAL EDWARD, management consultant, executive recruiter, social theorist, entrepreneur, author; b. San Diego, Mar. 9, 1960; s. Donald Jay and Roberta Yvonne (Recht) S. BA in Philosophy, Reed Coll., Portland, Oreg., 1981; AM in Philosophy, U. Chgo, 1982. Founder Calif. Legal Search, 1983—; chmn., CEO Geodesic Dynamics, 2000—; founder Catalyst Learning Strategies, 2002. Author: A Turning Point in World History?, 1992, High Performance Venture Characteristics, 1992, Dilemmas of Democracy (3 vols.: A Critique of Liberalism, A Critique of Political Ideology, and The Limits of Social Theory), 1992, The Problem of Modernity, 1993, Theoretical Foundations of Dynamic Macroeconomics, 1993, The Evolution of Philosophy, 1995, Legal Management Theory, 2d edit., 1997, Transformation of the Corporate Law Firm, 1998, others. Democrat. Achievements include inventions regarding electronic commerce and intelligent systems. Address: 388 Market St Ste 500 San Francisco CA 94111-5313 E-mail: ulysses@well.com.

SOLOMON, NORMAN, author, columnist; b. Washington, July 7, 1951; s. Morris Jacobson and Miriam (Abramowitz) S.; m. Cheryl D. Higgins, May 31, 1996. Freelance journalist, 1974—; syndicated columnist Creators Syndicate, LA, 1992—; exec. dir. Inst. for Pub. Accuracy, Washington, 1997—. Pub. spkr. and lectr., 1977—; assoc. Fairness and Accuracy In Reporting, NYC, 1989—. Author: The Power of Babble, 1992, False Hope: The Politics of Illusion in the Clinton Era, 1994, The Trouble with Dilbert: How Corporate Culture Gets the Last Laugh, 1997, The Habits of Highly Deceptive Media: Decoding Spin and Lies in Mainstream News, 1999 (George Orwell award for disting. contbn. to honesty and clarity in pub. lang.); co-author: Adventures in Medialand, 1993 (Hugh M. Hefner 1st Amendment award), Wizards of Media Oz, 1997, Target Iraq: What the News Media Didn't Tell You, 2003. E-mail: mediabeat@igc.org.

SOLOMON, PAUL ROBERT, neuropsychologist, educator; b. Bklyn., Aug. 27, 1948; s. Maynard and Norma Harris (Ruben) S.; m. Suellen Zablow, Aug. 16, 1970; children: Todd, Jessica. BA in Psychology, SUNY, New Paltz, 1970, MA in Psychology, 1972; PhD in Psychology, U. Mass., 1972. Diplomate Am. Coll. Forensic Examiners; lic. psychologist, Mass. Prof. psychology and neurosci. Williams Coll, Williamstown, Mass., 1976—, neurosci. program chmn., 1990-95; dir. memory disorders clinic S.W. Vt. Med. Ctr., Bennington, 1990—; pres. Clin. Neurosci. Rsch. Assocs., 1997—. Bd. dirs. No. Berkshire Mental Health Assn., North Adams, Mass. Author: Scientific Writings, 1985, Memory, 1989, Psychology 4th edit., 1993; contbr. articles to profl. jours. Bd. dirs. W. Mass. Alzheimers Assn., 1992—. Recipient Distinguished Teaching award U. Mass., Amherst, 1975; Rsch. grantee EPA, NIH, NSF, 1978—; Rsch. fellowships NIH, 1979, NSF, 1980. Fellow APA, AAAS, Am. Psychol. Soc.; mem. Soc. for Neuroscience. Home: 130 Forest Rd Williamstown MA 01267-2029 Office: Williams Coll Dept Psychology Williamstown MA 01262

SOLOMON, PHYLLIS LINDA, social work educator, researcher; b. Hartford, Conn., Dec. 6, 1945; d. Louis Calvin and Annabell Lee (Nitzberg) S. BA in Sociology, Russell Sage Coll., 1968; MA in Sociology, Case Western Res. U., 1970, PhD in Social Welfare, 1978. Lic. social worker, Pa. Rsch. assoc. Inst. Urban Studies Cleve. State U., 1970-71; program evaluator Cleve. State Hosp., 1971-74; project dir. Ohio Mental Health and Mental Retardation Rsch. Ctr., Cleve., 1974-75; rsch. assoc. Psychiat. Rsch. Found. of Cleve., 1975; project dir. Ohio Mental Health and Mental Retardation Rsch. Ctr., 1977-78; rsch. assoc. dir. rsch. and mental health planning Fedn. for Cmty. Planning, 1978-88; prof. dept. mental health scis., dir. sect. mental health svcs. and systems rsch. Hahnemann U., Phila., 1988-94; prof. Sch. Social Work U. Pa., Phila., 1994—. Secondary appointment Prof. Social Work in Psychiatry U. Pa. Sch. Medicine, 1994—; adj. prof. dept. psychiatry Allegheny U., 1994-97. Author: (with others) Community Services to Discharged Psychiatric Patients, 1984; co-editor: New Developments in Psychiatric Rehabilitation, 1990, Psychiatric Rehabilitation in Practice, 1993; editl. adv. bd. Community Mental Health Jour., 1988—; editl. bd. Jour. Rsch. in Social Work, 1997-2000, Social Work Forum, 1997—, Health and Social Work, 1998-2000, Psychiat. Rehab. Jour., 1999—, Mental Health Svcs. Rsch. Jour., 2001—, Brief Treatment and Crisis Intervention, 2001—, Social Work, 2003—; contbr. articles to profl. jours. Trustee Cleve. Rape Crisis Ctr., 1981-84, CIT Mental Health Svcs., Cleve., 1985-88; mem. citizen's adv. bd. Sagamore Hills (Ohio) Children's Psychiat. Hosp., 1984-88; bd. dirs. Plan of Pa., 2004—, pres., 2004—. Named Evaluator of the Yr., Ohio Program Evaluators Group, 1987; recipient Ann. award Cuyahoga County Cmty. Mental Health Bd., 1988, Armin Loeb award Internat. Assn. Psychosocial Rehab. Svcs., 1999, Outstanding Non-Psychiatrist award Am. Assn. Cmty. Psychiatrists, 2002. Mem. NASW, Internat. Assn. Psychosocial Rehab. Svcs., Soc. for Social Work and Rsch. (1st place award for pub. article 1997). Jewish. Home: 104 Woodside Rd Apt A108 Haverford PA 19041-1831 Office: U Pa Sch Social Work 3701 Locust Walk Philadelphia PA 19104-6214

SOLOMON, RANDALL LEE, lawyer; b. Dayton, Ohio, June 8, 1948; BA summa cum laude, Wright State U., 1970; JD, Case Western Res. U., 1973. Bar: Ohio 1973, U.S. Dist. Ct. (no. dist.) Ohio 1973, U.S. Ct. Appeals (6th cir.) 1973, U.S. Ct. Appeals (fed. cir.) 1988, U.S. Supreme Ct. 2002. Ptnr. Baker & Hostetler, Cleve. Speaker in field. Fellow Am. Coll. Trial Lawyers; mem. ABA (mem. litigation, tort and ins. practice sects.), Ohio State Bar Assn., Cleve. Bar Assn. (chair litigation sect. 1991-92), Nat. Inst. Trial Advocacy (mem. nat. session 1978), Def. Rsch. Inst., Anthony J. Celebrezze Inn. of Ct. (master). Office: Baker & Hostetler LLP 3200 Nat City Ctr 1900 E 9th St Ste 3200 Cleveland OH 44114-3475 E-mail: rsolomon@bakerlaw.com.

SOLOMON, RICHARD HARVEY, political scientist; b. Phila., June 19, 1937; s. Bertram Harvey and Ellen (Harris) S.; m. Anne G. Keatley, Dec. 16, 1991. Student, Harvard U., 1959-63, Yale U., 1961, 63-64; SB, MIT, 1960, PhD, 1966. Tech. photographer, lab. worker Photon, Inc., Cambridge, Mass., 1957; rschr. Polaroid Corp., 1959-61; rsch. assoc. Ctr. for Chinese Studies U. Mich., Ann Arbor, Mich., 1966-71, from asst prof. to prof. polit. sci., 1966-71; staff mem. NSC, Washington, 1971-76; head. polit. sci dept. The Rand Corp., Santa Monica, Calif., 1976-86, program dir. Internat. Security Policy Research, 1977-83; mem. Pres.' Commn. on Fgn. Lang. and Internat. Studies Washington, 1978-80; mem. Chief of Naval Ops. exec. panel, 1983—; dir. policy planning staff Dept. of State, Washington, 1986-89, asst. sec. of state for East Asian and Pacific affairs, 1989-92; U.S. ambassador to Philippines, 1992-93; pres. U.S. Inst. of Peace, Washington, 1993—. Author: Mao's Revolution and the Chinese Political Culture, 1999, Chinese Political Negotiating Behavior, 1999, Exiting Indochina, 2000; contbr. articles to profl. jours. Office: US Inst of Peace 1200 17th St NW Ste 200 Washington DC 20036-3011 Business E-Mail: msullivan@usip.org.

SOLOMON, RISA GREENBERG, clinical social worker, child and family therapist, former entertainment industry executive; b. N.Y.C., June 22, 1948; d. Nathan and Frances (Guttman) Greenberg; m. Philip Howard Solomon, June 21, 1970 (dec. 1994); children: Elycia Beth, Cynthia Gayle. BA, NYU, 1969, MA, 1970, MSSW, 1996. Asst. editor Redbook Mag., N.Y.C., 1969-70; assoc. editor Greenwood Press, Westport, Conn., 1970-71; mng. editor Dushkin Pub., Guilford, Conn., 1971-72; freelance editor Yale U. Press, New Haven, 1972-75; v.p. ops. Videoland, Inc., Dallas, 1980-82; v.p. Video Software Dealers Assn., Cherry Hill, N.J. and Dallas, 1981-83; pres. Videodome Enterprises, Dallas, 1983-94; clin. social worker, child and family therapist pvt. practice, Dallas, 1994—. Cons. Home Rec. Rights Coalition, Washington, 1983—84; spkr. in field of child and adolescent therapy. Bd. dirs. Congregation Anshai Emet, Dallas, 1985-86. Mem. Video Software Dealers Assn. (founder, dir. 1981-82). Democrat. Jewish. Avocations: water and snow skiing, world travel, tennis, scuba diving. Office: 17103 Preston Rd Ste 100 Dallas TX 75248 Office Phone: 972-248-7248. E-mail: rgs8961@msn.com.

SOLOMON, ROBERT, economist; b. N.Y.C., May 2, 1921; s. Sol and Betty (Brownstone) S.; m. Fern Rice, Sept. 11, 1946 (dec. 2001); children: Carol Ann, Barbara Betty, Anne Eleanor. BA, U. Mich., 1942; MA, Harvard U., 1947, PhD, 1952. With Fed. Res. Bd., 1947-76, assoc. adviser research div., 1963-65, adviser research div., 1965, adviser to bd. govs., 1965-76, dir. div. internat. fin., 1966-72; sr. fellow Brookings Instn., Washington, 1976-80, guest scholar, 1980—. Pres. RS Assos., pub. Internat. Econ. Letter, 1981—; vice chmn. deps. of com. of 20 IMF, 1972-74; adj. prof. Am. U., 1962-67; sr. staff economist Coun. Econ. Advisers, 1963-64. Author: The International Monetary System, 1945-81, 1982, Partners in Prosperity, 1991, Money on the Move, 1999, The Transformation of the World Economy, 1999; contbr. articles to profl. jours. 1st lt. USAAF, 1942—45. Decorated D.F.C., Air medal; named Officier Legion of Honor France; recipient Rockefeller Pub. Service award, 1971. Mem. Am. Econ. Assn., Coun. on Fgn. Relations. Clubs: Cosmos (Washington). Home and Office: 8502 W Howell Rd Bethesda MD 20817-6827 E-mail: Rsolo52178@aol.com.

SOLOMON, ROBERT CHARLES, philosopher, educator; b. Detroit, Sept. 14, 1942; s. Charles M. and Vita (Petrosky) S. BA, U. Pa., 1963; MA, U. Mich., 1965, PhD, 1967. Teaching fellow U. Mich., Ann Arbor, 1965-66; lectr. Princeton (N.J.) U., 1966-67, 67-68; asst. prof. U. Pitts., 1969-71, CUNY, 1971-72; assoc. prof. philosophy U. Tex., Austin, 1972-77, prof., 1977—, Quincy Lee Centennial prof., 1986-97, disting. tchg. prof., 1997—. Vis. prof. U. Pa., UCLA, U. Auckland, N.Z., La Trobe U., Melbourne, Australia, U. B.C.; chmn. Phi Beta Kappa Emerson Award Com.; cons. in field. Author: From Rationalism to Existentialism, 1972, The Passions, 1976, Introducing Philosophy: Problems and Perspectives, 1977, History and Human Nature: A Philosophical Review of European History and Culture, 1750-1850, 1979, Love: Emotion, Myth and Metaphor, 1981, In the Spirit of Hegel, 1983, (with C. Calhoun) What Is an Emotion?, 1984, It's a Good Business, 1985, (with Kristine Hanson) Above the Bottom Line, 1983, From Hegel to Existentialism, 1987, Continental Philosophy After 1750, 1988, About Love, 1988, A Passion for Justice, 1990, Ethics: A Briefer Introduction, 1991, Ethics and Excellence, 1992, Entertaining Ideas, 1992, (with J. Solomon) Up the University, 1993, (with Kathleen Higgins) A Short History of Philosophy, 1996, A Passion for Wisdom, 1997, A Better Way to Think About Business, 1999, The Joy of Philosophy, 1999, (with Kathleen Higgins) What Nietzsche Really Said, 2000, (with Fernando Flores) Building Trust, 2000, Spirituality for the Skeptic, 2002, Not Passions Slave, 2003, Living with Nietzsche, 2003; editor: Phenomenology and Existentialism, 1972, Nietzsche, 1973, Existentialism, 1974, (with Kathleen Higgins) Reading Nietzsche, 1988, From Africa to Zen, 1993, The Age of German Idealism, 1993, (with Mark A. Murphy) What Is Justice?, 1990, Wicked Pleasures: Meditations on the Seven Deadly Sins, 1999, What is an Emotion, 2003, Thinking about Feeling, 2004; contbr. articles to profl. jours. Recipient Outstanding Tchr. award Standard Oil Co., 1973, Pres.' Teaching Excellence award, 1985, 96., Chad Oliver Honors Tchg. award, 1998; named to Acad. Disting. Tchrs., 1997. Mem. Am. Philos. Assn., N.Am. Nietzsche Soc., Internat. Soc. Rsch. on Emotions (pres.), Soc. for Bus. Ethics, Acad. Disting. Tchrs.

SOLOMON, ROBERT DOUGLAS, pathology educator; b. Delavan, Wis., Aug. 28, 1917; s. Lewis Jacob and Sara (Ludgin) S.; m. Helen Fisher, Apr. 4, 1943; children: Susan, Wendy, James, William. Student, MIT, 1934—36; BS in Biochemistry, U. Chgo., 1938; MD, Johns Hopkins U., 1942. Intern John's Hopkins Hosp., 1942-43; resident in pathology Michael Reese Hosp., 1947-49; lectr. U. Ill., Chgo., 1947-50, fellow NIH pathology, 1949-50; asst. prof. U. Md., Balt., 1955-60; assoc. prof. U. So. Calif., L.A., 1960-70; chief of staff City of Hope Nat. Med. Ctr., 1966-67; prof. U. Mo., Kansas City, 1977-78, SUNY, Syracuse, 1968-78; chief of staff The Hosp., Sidney, NY, 1985-86; adj. prof. biology U. N.C., Wilmington, 1989—. Cons. VA Hosp., Balt., 1955-60, Med. Svc. Lab., Wilmington, 1989-93; active in field of bariatrics, 1997—. Co-author: Progress in Gerontological Research, 1967; contbr. papers and profl. jours. and rsch. in biochemistry, revascular of heart, carcinogenesis, cancer chemotherapy, atherogenesis, discovery of reversibility of atherosclerosis, chemistry of urochrome pigments. V.p. Rotary, Duarte, Calif., 1967; v.p. and pres. Force for an Informed Electorate. Capt. Med. Corps, AUS, 1943-46, PTO. Grantee NIH, Fleischmann Found., Am. Heart Assn., Nat. Cancer Inst., 1958-70. Fellow ACP (pres. Md. chpt.), Western Geriat. Soc. (founding); mem. Coll. Am. Pathologists (past pres. Md. chpt.), Am. Soc. Clin. Pathologists, Assn. Clin. Scientists, Am. Chem. Soc., Royal Soc. Medicine (London),

Phi Beta Kappa, Sigma Xi. Achievements include development of fiber-optic arterial catheter for visualization and making movies of aortic endothelium in vivo. Home: 7715 Blue Heron Dr W Wilmington NC 28411-6303 Personal E-mail: RdSolomon@aol.com.

SOLOMON, ROBERT H. lawyer; b. Bklyn., Aug. 23, 1958; s. Murray and Mildred (Teger) S.; m. Felicia Irene Smith, June 30, 1985; children: Zachary, Alexander. BS in Econ cum laude, U. Pa., 1979; JD, Duke U., 1982. Bar: N.Y. 1983, U.S. Supreme Ct., U.S. Ct. Internat. Trade, U.S. Dist. Ct. (ea. & so. dists.) N.Y. Assoc. LeBeouf Lamb Leiby & MacRae, N.Y.C., 1982-84, Wofsey Certilman Haft et al, N.Y.C., 1984-87, Zimmer Victor Schwartz et al, N.Y.C., 1987-89; prin. Robert H. Solomon P.C., Long Beach, 1989—. Arbitrator N.Y. Dist. Ct., Hempstead, 1989—, ct. examiner, Nassau County, NY. Trustee Long Beach Bdn. Edn., 1995; bd. dirs. Long Beach Med. Ctr., 2002; pres. Lido Home Civic Assn. David Siegal scholar Duke U., 1980-82, Regents scholar, 1980. Mem. ABA, N.Y. State Bar Assn., Bar Assn. of N.Y.C., Nassau County Bar Assn., Long Beach Lawyers Assn. (pres. 1995-2000), Wharton Club. Avocation: tennis. Office: 24 E Park Ave Long Beach NY 11561-3504 E-mail: Pennduke@aol.com.

SOLOMON, RUSSELL M. retail products executive; b. 1925; CEO MTS; chmn. bd. Tower Records, West Sacramento, Calif. Office: Tower Records PO Box 919001 West Sacramento CA 95691-9001

SOLOMON, SAMUEL, biochemistry educator, administrator; b. Brest Litovsk, Poland, Dec. 5, 1925; s. Nathan and Rachel (Greenberg) S.; m. Sheila R. Horn, Aug. 11, 1953 (div. 1974); children: David Horn, Peter Horn, Jonathan Simon; m. Augusta M. Vineberg, July 12, 1974. BS with honors, McGill U., 1947, MS, 1951, PhD in Biochemistry, 1953. Rsch. asst. Columbia U., 1953-55, assoc. in biochemistry, 1958-59, asst. prof., 1959-60; assoc. prof. biochemistry and exptl. medicine McGill U., 1960-66, prof., 1967-95, prof. emeritus, 1995—, prof. ob-gyn., 1976-95; dir. endocrine lab. Royal Victoria Hosp., Montreal, Que., 1965-95, dir. research inst., 1982-85; affilate dept. pharmacology U. Sherbrooke, 1995—. Mem. endocrinology and metabolism grants com. Med. Rsch. Coun. Can., 1967-71, regional dir. for Que., 1993-95; vis. prof. endocrinology U. Vt., 1964; cons. in field; Joseph Price orator, 1982, Am. OB-GYN Soc.; mem. steering com. Pharm. Mfg. Assn. Med. Rsch. Coun. Can. Partnership, 1993—; Med. Rsch. Coun. Can. dir. for McGill U., 1993-95. Co-editor: Chemical and Biological Aspects of Steroid Conugation, 1970; mem. editl. bd. Endocrinology, 1962; assoc. editor Can. Jour. Biochemistry, 1967-71, Jour. Med. Primatology, 1971; contbr. articles to profl. jours. Mem. bd. govs. McGill U., 1975-78; mem. steering com. European Study Group on Steroid Hormones, 1974-99, chmn. steering com., 1983-99, chmn. program com., 1990-91; mem. Dubin Commn. on Inquiry Drugs in Athletes, 1988-90. Decorated officer Order of Can. 1997; recipient McLaughlin medal Royal Soc. Can., 1989, Michel Sarrazin prize, 1997. Fellow Chem. Inst. Can., Am. Ob-Gyn. Soc. (hon.), Perinatal Rsch. Soc. Am. (pres. 1976), Soc. Gynecol. Investigation (program chmn. 1980), Endocrine Soc. (publ. com. 1986-89). Home: 239 Kensington Ave 804 Montreal QC Canada H3Z 2H1 Office: Royal Victoria Hosp M315 687 Pine Ave W Montreal QC Canada H3A 1A1

SOLOMON, SEAN CARL, geophysicist, lab administrator; b. L.A., Oct. 24, 1945; BS geophysics, Calif. Inst. Tech., 1966; PhD geophysics, MIT, 1971. From asst. prof. to prof. geophysics MIT, Cambridge, 1972-92; dir. dept. terrestrial magnetism Carnegie Instn. Washington, 1992—. Vis. scientist Lunar Sci. Inst., 1975, Lawrence Livermore Nat. Lab., 1978, Jet Propulsion Lab., 1990—91; guest investigator Woods Hole Oceanographic Inst., 1979—92; vis. faculty Inst. Geophysics and Planetary Physics, dept. earth and space scis. UCLA, 1982—83; Roland and Jane Blumberg vis. prof. planetary scis. U. Tex., Austin, 1988; vis. assoc. divsn. geol. and planetary scis. Calif. Inst. Tech., 1990—91; mem. various groups, teams, coms. NASA, 1974—; earthquake hazards reduction program peer rev. panel U.S. Geol. Survey, 1975, 85; lunar and planetary sci. coun. Univs. Space Rsch. Assn., 1978—80, 1991—93; tech. rev. panel, geophysics rev. panel Dept. Def., 1981—86; chmn. steering com. space sci. working group Assn. Am. Univs., 1987—89; rev. panelist NSF, 1986, 88, 95, 96, 2001, 03; chmn. standing com. global seismic network Inc. Rsch. Instns. Seismology, 1988—90; participant numerous oceanographic expeditions, 1967—88. Editor (assoc. editor): Proceedings of the Lunar and Planetary Sci. Conf., 1976, 1978, Jour. Geophys. Rsch., 1976—78, Physics of the Earth and Planetary Interiors, 1977, Eos Transactions of Am. Geophys. Union, 1979—81, Geophys. Rsch. Letters, 1986—88; editor: Tectonophysics, 1981; mem. editl. bd.: Physics and Chemistry of Earth, 1981—85, Astrobiology, 2001—, Earth and Planetary Sci. Letters, 2001—, mem. editl. com.: Ann. Rev. Earth and Planetary Scis., 1993—97; contbr. articles to profl. jours. Recipient Arthur L. Day prize, NAS, 1999; fellow Grad., NSF, 1966—68, Postdoctoral, 1971—72, Fannie and John Hertz Found., 1968—71, Alfred P. Sloan Rsch., 1977—81, John Simon Guggenheim Meml., 1982—83. Fellow: AAAS, Geol. Soc. Am. (G.K. Gilbert award 1999), Am. Geophys. Union (pres. elect and pres. 1994—98, pres. planetology sect. 1984—88, chmn. geophys. monograph bd. 1983—84, numerous coms.), Am. Acad. Arts and Scis.; mem.: NAS, Seismol. Soc. Am., Am. Astron. Soc. (divsn. planetary scis.), Tau Beta Pi. Office: Carnegie Instn Dept Terrestrial Magnetism 5241 Broad Branch Rd NW Washington DC 20015-1305 E-mail: scs@dtm.ciw.edu.

SOLOMON, SOLOMON SIDNEY, endocrinologist, pharmacologist, scientist; b. N.Y.C., Dec. 2, 1936; s. Nathan and Irene (Oransky) S.; m. Linda M. Shaw, June 17, 1962 (div. 1980); children: Joan Geller, Rebecca Karen. AB in Chemistry, Harvard U., 1958; MD, U. Rochester, 1962. Intern in internal medicine New Eng. Med. Ctr., Tufts U., Boston, 1963; resident in internal medicine Boston City Hosp., 1964, 65; fellow in endocrinology and metabolism U. Wash. Sch. Medicine, Seattle, 1965-67; teaching fellow Tufts U. and Boston City Hosp., Boston, 1964-65; asst. prof., assoc. prof. then prof. medicine U. Tenn. Sch. Medicine, Memphis, 1969—, assoc. dean for rsch., 1983-98, prof. pharmacology, 1986—; chief endocrinology and metabolism VA Med. Ctr., Memphis, 1971—. Cons. in field; mem. merit rev. bd. VA Rsch. Svc., Washington, 1978—81, Washington, 1999—2002. Coeditor: The Lab in Clinical Diagnosis, l98l; contbr. numerous articles and abstracts to profl. jours. Capt. MC, USAF, 1967-69. Harvard Coll. scholar, 1954-58; Whipple scholar, 1959-62; VA and NIH grantee, 1965—. recipient career and devel. award VA Ctrl. Office Rsch. Svc., 1969-71, 1st place for excellence in clin. rsch. Memphis Area Health Industry Couns., 1994. Fellow Am. Coll. Endocrinology; mem. Am. Diabetes Assn. (pres. Tenn. chpt. 1975-76, rsch. com., chmn. metabolism sect. 1982), So. Soc. Clin. Investigation (chmn. metabolism sect. 1975, 88, nominating com. 1989), Endocrine Soc., Am. Fedn. for Clin. Rsch. (counselor south sect. 1976-79), Am. Soc. Clin. Investigation, Cen. Soc. for Clin. Rsch., Am. Soc. Pharmacology and Exptl. Therapy, Fedn. Am. Soc. Exptl. Biology. Jewish. Avocations: antique furniture, history, music, tennis, running. Home: 5196 Longmeadow Dr Memphis TN 38134-4316 Office: VA Med Ctr 1030 Jefferson Ave Memphis TN 38104-2127 Office Phone: 901-577-7274. E-mail: ssolomon@utmem.edu. *At the risk of being mundane, my philosophy in life has always been to get involved...my motto is "I came to play, not to watch."*.

SOLOMON, STEPHEN L. lawyer; b. N.Y.C., Aug. 15, 1942; s. Sam and Ruth (Goldblum) S.; m. Regina Fisher, Aug. 14, 1969; children: Todd, Lisa. AB, Columbia Coll., 1964; LLB, NYU, 1967. Bar: N.Y. 1967, U.S. Dist. Ct. (so. and ea. dists.) 1969, U.S. Ct. Customs 1970, U.S. Supreme Ct. 1975. Assoc. Burns, Jackson, Summit, N.Y.C., 1969-74; ptnr. Miller, Singer, Michaelson & Raives, N.Y.C., 1974-79; ptnr., pres. Jarblum, Solomon & Fornari, PC, N.Y.C., 1979-97; ptnr. Rubin Baum LLP, N.Y.C., 1997—2002, Sonnenschein Nath & Rosenthal, N.Y.C., 2002—. Contbr. articles to profl. jours. Active Com. on Philanthropic Orgns., N.Y.C., 1980-83; bd. dirs. Emanu-El Midtown YM/YWHA, N.Y.C., 1979-85, Columbia Coll. Alumni Assn. Mem. Assn. Bar City of N.Y. Democrat. Home: 40 Fifth Ave New York NY 10011-8843 Office: Sonnenschein Nath & Rosenthal LLP 1221 Ave of Americas New York NY 10020

SOLOMON, SUSAN, chemist, scientist; b. Chicago, Ill., Jan. 19, 1956; d. Leonard Marvin and Alice (Rutman) Solomon; m. Barry Lane Sidwell, Sept. 20, 1988. BS in Chemistry, Ill. Inst. Tech., 1977; MS in Chemistry, U. Calif., Berkeley, 1979, PhD in Chemistry, 1981; D (hon.), Tulane U., Williams Coll., SUNY at Stony Brook, Ill. Inst. Tech., U. Colo. Sr. scientist aeronomy lab. NOAA, Boulder, Colo., 1981—88, program leader middle atmosphere group aeronomy lab., 1988—. Adj. faculty U. Colo., 1982—; head project sci. Nat. Ozone Expdn., McMurdo Station, Antarctica, 1986, McMurdo Station, Antarctica, 87; co-chair Intergovernmental Panel on Climate Change. Co-author: Aeronomy of the Middle Atmosphere, 1984; contbr. articles to sci. jours. Named Solomon Glacier and Solomon Saddle in honor of leadership in Antarctic rsch., 1994; recipient Gold medal, U.S. Dept. Commerce, 1989, Scientist of the Yr. award, 1992, Nat. Medal of Sci., 2000, Arthur S. Flemming awrd, Common Wealth award, Common Wealth Trust, Ozone award, UN Environ. Programme. Fellow: Am. Geophys. Union (J.B. McElwane award 1985), Am. Meteorol. Soc. (Henry G. Houghton award, Carl-Gustaf Rossby award 2000), Royal Meteorol. Soc.; mem.: European Acad. Scis. (foreign assoc.), French Acad. Scis. (foreign assoc.), US Nat. Acad. Scis., Am. Acad. Arts and Scis., NAS. Avocations: creative writing, crafts, scuba diving. Office Phone: 303-497-3483. Business E-Mail: ssolomon@al.noaa.gov.*

SOLOMON, WILLIAM TARVER, general construction company executive; b. Dallas, Aug. 11, 1942; s. Marion Bryant and Margaret (Moore) S.; m. Gay Ferguson, Feb. 15, 1964; children— William Tarver Jr., Meredith M. BSCE, So. Meth. U., 1965; MBA, Harvard U., 1967. With Austin Industries, Inc., Dallas, 1967—, chmn., pres., CEO, 1970—; chmn. Austin Comml., Inc., Dallas, Brit. Am. Ins. Co., Dallas; chmn., CEO Austin Industries, Inc., Dallas, now chmn. Bd. dirs. A.H. Belo Corp., Nat. Bank Tex. Past chmn. Dallas Citizens Coun. and Greater Dallas C. of C.; bd. dirs. Baylor U. Med. Ctr. Found., Dallas Mus. Art; trustee Southwestern Med. Found., So. Meth. U. Recipient citation of honor Dallas chpt. AIA, 1985, Humanitarian award NCCJ, Dallas, 1982, Champion of Free Enterprise award Associated Builders and Contractors, 1985, Outstanding Alumni award Southern Meth. U., 1988; inductee Tex. Bus. Hall of Fame, 1996. Mem. ASCE, Young Pres.'s Orgn. (past chmn. Dallas chpt.), Dallas Assembly, Salesmanship Club Dallas, Dallas C. of C. (bd. dirs.). Republican. United Methodist Home: 3830 Windsor Ln Dallas TX 75205-1743

SOLOMON-ARNOLD, IRENE LENA, language educator; d. Silas Solomon and Stella Luke-Solomon; children: Cathrine Stella Arnold-Webster, Earnest Roscoe Arnold Jr., Victoria Faye Arnold. AAS, U. of Alaska, Fairbanks, 1990—94; diploma Native Lang. instr., Yukon Native Lang. Ctr., 2002. Youth counselor United Crow Band, Tok, Alaska, 1987—90; native lang. instr./educator Alaska Gateway Sch. Dist., Yukon Coll., Tok, 1990—95; mgr. Tanana Chiefs Conf., Berta Moses Patient Hostel, Fairbanks, Alaska, 1995—2000; instr. Tanacross lang. U. Alaska, Fairbanks, 2000—. Translator (writer): (tanacross athabascan language) Computer Booklets (Native Lang. Educator of the Yr., 1995); author: Tanacross Athabascan Phrases and Conversations. Participant/organizer native cultural events, Alaska, 1980—. Democrat. Episcopalian. Avocations: alaska native arts and crafts, attend cultural events, travel, read, being a grandmother. E-mail: fnila@uaf.edu.

SOLOMONS, GUS, JR., (GUSTAVE MARTINEZ), choreographer, dancer, writer; b. Boston; s. Gustave Martinez and Olivia Mae. Student, Boston Conservatory of Music, 1956-59; BArch, MIT, 1961; postgrad., Martha Graham Sch., N.Y.C., 1961-66. Dance soloist Martha Graham Co., N.Y.C., 1964-65, Donald McKayle Co., 1961-64, Merce Cunningham Co., N.Y.C., 1965-68; artistic dir. The Solomons Dance Co., N.Y.C., 1972—; dean, artistic dir. Calif. Inst. of the Arts, Valencia, 1976-78. Vis. artist-in-residence U. Calif., Santa Cruz, Calif. State U., Long Beach, others; dance panelist Nat. Endowment Arts; various other other state art couns., 1983—; assoc. prof. dance numerous colls., univs., including UCLA, Un. Nev.-Las Vegas, Tex. Christian U., York, Simon Fraser, NYU; mem. faculty Tisch Sch. of Arts, 1994—; USIA cons. to Nat. Dance Co., Tanzania, East Africa, 1988, Argentina, 1994. Appearances on TV networks, Sta. WGBH-TV, Boston; choreographr for various univs. and dance cos.; writer dance criticism for Village Voice, Dance Mag., others. Grantee Nat. Endowment for Arts, 1983—, N.Y. State Coun. on the Arts, 1972—; fellow Nat. Endowment for Arts, 1978-80; recipient Master Tchr. award NYU/Tisch, 1996, Bessie award, 2000, Robert A. Muh award for disting. MIT artist/alumnus, 2001, Balasaraswat/Beineke Disting. Tchg. award, 2004. Studio: 889 Broadway New York NY 10003-1212 E-mail: gus.solomonsjr@nyu.edu. *The content of a good dance is the truth about its maker. Performing it is a confession to the audience. The dancer places himself in the position of ultimate vulnerability each time he performs; it is at once cleansing, fulfilling, and courageous.*

SOLOMONS, MARK ELLIOTT, lawyer, art dealer, entrepreneur; b. Buffalo, Mar. 4, 1946; s. Alvin and Trude (Salant) Solomons; m. Jill E Kent, Aug. 20, 1978. BA, U. Rochester, 1967; JD, U. Pa., 1970; LLM, George Washington U., 1973. Staff atty. U.S. Dept. Labor, Washington, 1970-73, counsel coal miners benefits, 1973-77, legis. counsel, 1977-80; prin. Kilcullen Wilson & Kilcullen, Washington, 1980-86; ptnr. Arter and Hadden, Washington, 1986-2001, mem. exec. com., 1989-98; shareholder Greenberg Traurig, Washington, 2001—. Guest lectr law and hist SUNY, Stony Brook, 1970—76, Univ Mich, 1977—78, Hobart Col, 1972—76; prin Coun for Excellence in Govt, 1991—; co-owner Frogeye Co; chmn Atlantic Threadworks, 1998—2001; del Atlantic Treaty Asn Gen Assembly, 2000—. Contbr. articles to profl jours. Trustee China Found, 1997—, chair, nominating com., 1997—. Master: Am Inn of Ct (counselor 1996—97); mem.: ABA (chair workers compensation and employers liability comt 1987—88, sr. vice chair 1988—, vice chair appellate advocacy comt), NY Bar Asn, DC Bar Asn, Fed Bar Asn (chair regulatory reform comt 1988—89). Republican. Office: Greenberg Traurig LLP 800 Connecticut Ave NW Washington DC 20006 E-mail: solomonsm@gtlaw.com.

SOLOMONSON, KATHERINE, architecture educator; PhD in History of Art, Stanford U. Prof. Stanford U.; co-dir. study of cultural landscape of East Palo Alto, Calif.; assoc. prof., dept. co-head U. Minn., Coll. Arch. and Landscape Arch., Mpls. Mem. nat. register nominations com. Minn. State Rev. Bd.; mem. bd. bldgs. of U.S. Soc. Archtl. Historians; mem. com. on the press U. Minn. Press. Author: The Chicago Tribune Tower Competition: Skyscraper Design and Cultural Change in the 1920s, 2001. Recipient Ralph Rapson award for disting. tchg., Roy Jones award for outstanding rsch. Office: Univ Minn CALA 145F Rapson Hall 89 Church St SE Minneapolis MN 55455*

SOLON, LEONARD R(AYMOND), retired physicist, educator, consultant; b. White Plains, N.Y., Sept. 11, 1925; s. Morris and Rebecca (Bobrov) S.; m. Charlotte Rothman, June 30, 1946; children: Miriam Solon Weintraub, Matthew Benjamin, Emily Solon Bader. BA, Hamilton Coll., 1947; MSc, Rutgers U., 1949; PhD, NYU, 1960. Cert. Am. Bd. Health Physics. Physicist Nuc. Devel. Assocs., Inc., White Plains, 1950-52; asst. chief, then chief radiation br. AEC, N.Y.C., 1952-60; dir. applied nuc. tech. Tech. Rsch. Group, Inc., Syosset, N.Y., 1960-62; cons. Burns & Roe, N.Y.C., 1962-64, Servo Corp. Am., Hicksville, N.Y., 1962-64; mgr. R&D Del Electronics Corp., Mt. Vernon, N.Y., 1964-67; founder, exec. v.p., tech. dir. Hadron, Inc., Yonkers, N.Y., 1967-75; dir. bur. radiation control N.Y.C. Dept. Health, 1975-91; ret., 1991. Lectr., then adj. assoc. prof. N.Y.U. Inst. Environ. Medicine, 1955-93; environ. & radiol. health cons.; prof. health physics U.S. Mcht. Marine Acad., 1963. Contbr.: Dictionary of American Biography, 1995, The Scribner Encyclopedia of American Lives, vol. 1, 2, 3, 4, 5, 1998-2002; contbr. articles to profl. jours. Served with inf. U.S. Army, 1944-46, ETO. Decorated Combat Inf. badge, Bronze Star. Mem. AAAS, Am. Nuc. Soc., Health Physics Soc., Am. Phys. Soc., N.Y. Acad. Scis., Conf. Radiation Control Program Dirs., Radiol. and Med. Physics Soc. N.Y., Phi Beta Kappa, Sigma Xi. Achievements include co-patentee for laser photocauterizer used in treatment of detached retina; powering lasers using nuclear sources. Home and Office: 185 Valencia H Delray Beach FL 33446 Office Phone: 631-673-1134. E-mail: crsolon@aol.com.

SOLOV, ZACHARY, choreographer, ballet artist; b. Phila., Feb. 15, 1923; s. Carl Nathan and Sima (Silnutzer) S. Student, Littlefield Ballet Sch., 1937-40, U. of the Dance, 1947. Appeared with, Am. Jubilee, N.Y. World's Fair, 1940, tour with, Littlefield Ballet, 1941, Am. Ballet, S.A., 1941; with, Dance Players, summer quarters, New Hope, Pa., 1942, The Lady Comes Across, N.Y. City, 1942, Ballet Theatre, London, 1946; choreographer ballet master, Met. Opera, N.Y. City. Served as staff sgt. A.A.C., 1943-46. Recipient Capezio Dance award, 1952. Office: 200 W 58th St New York NY 10019-1432

SOLOVE, DANIEL JUSTIN, law educator; s. Leslie Jo and Richard S. Solove. JD, Yale Law Sch., 1997; AB, Wash. U., St. Louis, MO, 1994. Bar: Pa. 1998, D.C. 1998. Assoc. prof. of law Seton Hall Law Sch., Newark, 2000—04, George Wash. U. Law Sch., Washington, 2004. Adv. bd. Electronic Privacy Info. Ctr., Washington, 2004—; bd. of governors Law and Humanities Inst., New York, NY, 2002—; exec. com. AALS Defamation and Privacy Sect., Washington, 2004—. Author: (book) The Digital Person: Tech. and Privacy in the Info. Age; co-author (Marc Rotenberg): Info. Privacy Law; contbr. articles to prof. jours. Recipient Phi Beta Kappa, Phi Beta Kappa, 1993. Office: George Wash Univ Law School 2000 H Street NW Washington DC 20052 Office Phone: 202-994-9514. Business E-Mail: dsolove@law.gwu.edu.

SOLOVY, JEROLD SHERWIN, lawyer; b. Chgo., Apr. 10, 1930; s. David and Ida (Wilensky) S.; m. Kathleen Hart; children: Stephen, Jonathan. BA, U. Mich., 1952; LLB, Harvard U., 1955. Bar: Ill. 1955. Assoc. Jenner & Block, Chgo., 1955-63, ptnr., 1963—, chmn., 1991—. Chmn. Spl. Commn. on Adminstrn. Justice in Cook County, 1984-91, Ill. Supreme Ct. Spl. Commn. on Adminstrn. of Justice, 1992-93, Criminal Justice Project of Cook County, 1987-91. Mem. Cook County Jud. Adv. Council, Chgo., 1975-77, 82-89, chmn., 1989-91; trustee U.S. Supreme Ct. Hist. Soc., 1993—. Fellow Am. Coll. Trial Lawyers; mem. ABA, Chgo. Bar Assn., Ill. State Bar. Assn., Am. Law Inst. Clubs: Standard, Lake Shore Country (Chgo.). Office: Jenner & Block 1 E IBM Plz Ste 4400 Chicago IL 60611-5698 E-mail: jsolovy@jenner.com.

SOLOW, ROBERT MERTON, economist, educator; b. Bklyn., Aug. 23, 1924; s. Milton Henry and Hannah Gertrude (Sarney) Solow; m. Barbara Lewis, Aug. 19, 1945; children: John Lewis, Andrew Robert, Katherine. BA, Harvard U., 1947, MA, 1949, PhD, 1951, DLitt (hon.), 1992; LLD (hon.), U. Chgo., 1967, Brown U., 1972, U. Warwick, 1976, Tulane U., 1983, Dartmouth Coll., 1990, Rensselaer Poly. Inst., 2003; DLitt (hon.), Williams Coll., 1974, Lehigh U., 1977, Wesleyan U., 1982, Boston Coll., 1986, Harvard U., 1992, Colgate U., 1990; DSc (hon.), U. Paris, 1975, U. Geneva, 1982, Bryant Coll., 1988; D of Social Sci. (hon.), Yale U., 1976, U. Mass., Boston, 1989; D Social Sci. (hon.), U. Helsinki, 1990, SUNY, Albany, 1991, U. Glasgow, 1992, Rutgers U., 1994; D (hon.), U. Chile, 1992; Conservatoire, Nat. des Arts et Mètiers, Paris, 1994; D in Engring., Colo. Sch. Mines, 1996; postgrad, U. Buenos Aires, 1999; D in Lit. Humanities, NYU, 2000. Mem. faculty MIT, 1949—95, prof. econs., 1958—95, inst. prof., 1973—95, prof. emeritus, 1995—; W. Edwards Deming prof. NYU, 1996—97. Sr. economist Coun. Econ. Advisers, 1961—62, cons., 1962—68, RAND Corp., 1952—64; Marshall lectr., fellow commononer Peterhouse Cambridge (Eng.) U., 1963—64; Eastman vis. prof. Oxford U., 1968—69; overseas fellow Churchill Coll., Cambridge; sr. fellow Soc. Fellows, Harvard U., 1975—89; bd. dirs. Boston Fed. Res. Bank, 1975—80, chmn., 1979—80; active President's Commn. on Income Maintenance, 1968—70, President's Com. on Tech., Automation and Econ. Progress, 1964—65, Carnegie Commn. Sci., Tech. and Govts., 1988—93, Nat. Sci. Bd., 1994—2000; found. fellow Russell Sage Found., 2001—. Author (with R. Dortman, P. Samuelson): Linear Programming and Economic Analysis, 1958; author: Capital Theory and the Rate of Return, 1963, The Sources of Unemployment in the United States, 1964, Growth Theory, 1970, Price Expectations and the Behavior of the Price Level, 1970; author: (with M. Dertouzos, R. Lester) Made in America, 1989; author: The Labor Market as a Social Institution, 1990; author: (with F. Hahn) A Critical Essay on Modern Macroeconomic Theory, 1995; author: Learning from "Learning by Doing", 1997; author: (with J. Taylor) Inflation, Unemployment and Monetary Policy, 1998; author: Monopolistic Competition and Macroeconomic Theory, 1998, Work and Welfare, 1998; editor (with Alan Krueger): The Roaring Nineties, 2002. Bd. dirs., mem. exec. com. Nat. Bur. Econ. Rsch.; trustee Inst. for Advanced Study, Princeton U., 1972—78, Woods Hole Oceanographic Inst., 1988—, Alfred P. Sloan Found., 1992—, Resources for the Future, 1994—2003, Urban Inst., 1994—, German Marshall Fund of U.S., 1994—2002, Ctr. Advanced Study Behavioral Scis., 1982—95, chmn., 1987—95. With U.S. Army, 1942—45. Decorated Bronze Star U.S. Army; recipient David A. Wells prize, Harvard U., 1951, Seidman award in polit. economy, 1983, Nobel prize in Econs., 1987, Nat. Medal of Sci., 2000; fellow, Ctr. Advanced Study Behavioral Scis., 1957—58, Russell Sage Found., 2000—. Fellow: Am. Acad. Arts and Scis., Brit. Acad. (corr.); mem.: NAS (coun. 1977—80, 1995), AAAS (v.p. 1970), Internat. Econ. Assn. (pres. 1999—2002), Econometric Soc. (pres. 1964, exec. com.), Am. Econ. Soc. (exec. com. 1964—66, v.p. 1968, pres. 1979, John Bates Clark medal 1961), Royal Irish Acad. (hon.), Order Pour le Merite (Germany), Acad. dei Lincei, Am. Philos. Soc. Home: 528 Lewis Wharf Boston MA 02110-3920 Office: MIT Dept Econs Cambridge MA 02139

SOLOWAY, ALBERT HERMAN, medicinal chemist; b. Worcester, Mass., May 29, 1925; s. Bernard and Mollie (Raphaelson) S.; m. Barbara Berkowicz, Nov. 29, 1953; children: Madeleine Rae, Paul Daniel, Renee Ellen. Student, U.S. Naval Acad., 1945-46; BS, Worcester Poly. Inst., 1948; PhD, U. Rochester, 1951. Postdoctoral fellow Nat. Cancer Inst. at Sloan-Kettering Inst., N.Y.C., 1951-53; research chemist Eastman Kodak Co., Rochester, N.Y., 1953-56; asst. chemist Mass. Gen. Hosp., Boston, 1956-61, asso. chemist, 1961-73; asso. prof. med. chemistry Northeastern U., Boston, 1966-68, prof. medicinal chemistry, chmn. dept., 1968-71, prof. medicinal chemistry and chemistry, chmn. dept. medicinal chemistry and pharmacology, 1971-74; dean Coll. Pharmacy and Allied Health Professions, 1975-77; dean Coll. Pharmacy Ohio State U., Columbus, 1977-88, prof. medicinal chemistry, 1977-98, Kimberly prof. pharmacy, 1997-2000, dean, prof. emeritus, 1998—. Author rsch. in medicinal chemistry, boron neutron capture therapy of cancer. Recipient Disting. Achievements in Boron Sci. award, Boron USA, 1994. Fellow AAAS, Acad. Pharm. Soc.; mem. AHS, Am. Chem. Soc., Am. Assn. Coll. Pharmacy, Am. Assn. Cancer Rsch., Torch Club Columbus (pres. 2004—). Office: Ohio State U 500 W 12th Ave Columbus OH 43210-1214 Business E-Mail: soloway.1@osu.edu.

SOLOWAY, DANIEL MARK, lawyer; b. Buffalo, Jan. 21, 1959; s. Sol Murray and Shirley (Prashker) S.; m. Natalie Ann-Marie Chin, June 10, 1989; children: Rachael Ann, Rebecca Leigh. BA cum laude, SUNY, Buffalo, 1982; JD with honors, Fla. State U., 1985. Bar: Fla. 1985, U.S. Dist. Ct. (no. dist.) Fla. 1985, (mid. dist.) Fla. 1995, (so. dist.) Ala. 1986, U.S. Ct. Appeals (11th cir.) 1985, U.S. Supreme Ct. 1989; bd. cert. in civil trial law, Fla.; cert. Nat. Bd. Trial Advocacy, 1998, civil ct. mediator, 2000. Law clk. Circuit Judge, Tallahassee, 1983-84, Douglass, Davey, Cooper & Coppins, Tallahassee, 1984-85; ptnr. McKenzie & Soloway, Pensacola, Fla., 1985-98; pvt. practice Daniel M. Soloway, P.A., Pensacola, 1998—. Author: Criminal Justice: An Analysis Toward Reform, 1981; contbr. articles to profl. jours.; editor Escambia-Santa Rosa Bar Assn. newsletter, 1989-90, Dry Shoes, Fla. Bar Jour., 1992. Profl. adv. bd. N.W. Fla. Epilepsy Soc., Pensacola, 1989—; speaker on AIDS, State of Fla. Dept. HRS, 1988—; active Escambia County Human Rels. Commn., 1996-98. Recipient Pro Bono Svc. award Escambia-Santa Rosa Bar, 1989-90, Pro Bono Svc. Pres.'s award Fla. Bar, 1990. Mem. Million Dollar Advocates Forum (diplomat), ABA, Assn. Trial Lawyers Am., Escambia-Santa Rosa Bar Assn. (editor newsletter 1989-90), Acad. Fla. Trial Lawyers (speaker 1993—), Nat. Orgn. Social Security Claimants Reps. Democrat. Jewish. Avocation: writing. Office: 901 Scenic Hwy Pensacola FL 32503-6866

SOLOWAY, RICHARD LEWIS, electronic manufacturing company executive; b. Long Branch, NJ, Feb. 27, 1946; Studied, N.Y. Inst. Tech., Old Westbury. V.p. Nat. Alarm Products Co., Farmingdale, NY, 1970—72; co-founder Napco Security Sys. Inc., Amityville, NY, 1972, v.p., 1972—81, sec., treas., 1975—, chmn. bd., 1981—. Named Entrepreneur of Yr. in Mfg., Ernst & Young, 2001. Office: NAPCO Security Sys Inc 333 Bayview Ave Amityville NY 11701-2800 Office Phone: 631-842-9400 x120.

SOLSO, THEODORE M. manufacturing executive; m. Denny; 3 children. BA, DePauw U., 1969; MBA, Harvard U., 1971. Asst. to v.p. personnel Cummins Engine Co., Inc., Columbus, Ind., 1971, exec. dir. personnel, 1977-80, v.p. spl. engine markets, 1984-86, v.p. mktg., 1986-88, v.p., gen. mgr. engine bus., 1988-92, exec. v.p. opers., 1992-95, COO, 1994-00, pres., 1995-00, chmn., CEO, 1999—; dir. adminstrn. CAEMI Cummins., Brazil; v.p., mng. dir. Holset Engring. Co., Ltd. (Cummins' U.K. subs.), 1980-84. Bd. dirs. Ashland, Inc., Cyprus Amax Minerals, Inc. Bd. trustees DePauw U.; bd. advisors U. Mich. Sch. Bus.; past bd. dirs. Heritage Fund Bartholomew County, Ind.; chmn. campaign Bartholomew County United Way; bd. dirs. Otter Creek Golf Course, Columbus, Ind. Mem. Mfrs. Alliance (bd. trustees). Office: Cummins Engine Co Inc 500 Jackson St Columbus OH 43206-1353

SOLTANIAN-ZADEH, HAMID, research scientist, educator; arrived in U.S., 1987; s. Mirza-Ahmad Soltanian-Zadeh and Fatemeh Rismanian; m. Nahid Raee-Ezabadi, June 22, 1971; children: Sepeedah, Somayyeh, Sameeraa. PhD, U. of Mich., 1992. Sr. staff scientist Henry Ford Health Sys., Detroit, 1988—. PhD advisor U. of Mich., Ann Arbor, 1997—2001, Wayne State U., Detroit, 1998—. Conf. presenter (Hon. Mention award, 1999, 2000, 2002, 2003); contbr. articles to profl. jours. Named Outstanding Rschr., Dept. of Justice, 1993; rsch. grantee, NIH, 1993—99, NSF, 2000—03. Mem.: IEEE, Internat. Soc. for Optical Engring., Internat. Soc. of Magnetic Resonance in Medicine. Achievements include research in Medical Image Analysis Algorithms and Software. Office: Henry Ford Health Sys 1 Ford Pl 2F Detroit MI 48202 E-mail: hamids@rad.hfh.edu.

SOLTERO-HARRINGTON, LUIS RUBÉN, retired surgeon, educator; b. San Juan, P.R., Sept. 4, 1925; s. Augusto Rafael Soltero and Anna Lila Harrington; m. Alice Joyce Carpenter, Apr. 24, 1958; children: Luis Ruben, Kathleen Ann, Susan Joyce, Robert Richard, Sharon Theresa. BS in Agr., U. P.R., Rio Piedras, 1945; BM, MD, Northwestern U., Chgo., 1949. Diplomate Am. Bd. Surgery, Nat. Be. Med. Examiners, P.R. Rd. Med. Examiners. Intern Michael Reese Hosp., Chgo., 1949-50; resident in gen. surgery Aguadilla (P.R.) Dist. Hosp., 1950-51; resident in gen. surgery, instr. Baylor U. Coll. Medicine and Affiliated Hosps., Houston, 1954-59; resident in gen. surgery Jefferson Davis, VA and M.D. Anderson Hosps., Houston, 1954-57; resident in pediatric, thoracic and cardiovasc. surgery St. Luke's-Tex. Children's Hosp., Houston, 1957-59; asst. prof. surgery U. P.R. Sch. Medicine, 1960-64, assoc. clin. prof., 1972-73, assoc. clin prof., 1973—, in charge devel. heart surgery program, 1960-64, dir. surgery residency tng. program, 1961-64; pvt. practice, San Juan, PR, 1959—2003. Prof. surgery U. del Caribe Sch. Medicine, Cayey, P.R., 1981—; cons. in cardiovasc. and thoracic surgery Med. Examing Bd. P.R., San Juan, 1989; chief thoracic and cardiovasc. surgery Tchrs. Hosp., San Juan, from 1959; dir. surgery residency tng. program Univ. Hosp., Rio Piedras, from 1961; cons. in thoracic and cardiovasc. surgery San Juan City Hosp., 1962—, cons. in surgery, 1964—; cons. in surgery Presbyn. Hosp., 1972—, Mimiya's Hosp., 1987—; cons. in thoracic and cardiovasc. surgery Indsl. Hosp., San Juan, 1975—, Hosp. Met., 1982—, Clinic Fernández García, 1983—; chief surgery Ruiz Arnau Hosp., Bayamon, P.R., 1978—; asst. dir. ICU, Hosp. del Maestro, 1987—; bd. dirs. Rsch. Found. Cardiovasc. Surgery Tex., 1984—, Am. Cancer Soc., 1974; mem. Nat. Adv. Cun. Mended Hearts, Inc., 1969. Author: (textbook) The Management of the Acutely Ill Patient, 2002; contbr. articles to med. jours.; patentee partial occlusion vascular clamp to be used in small blood vessels; inventor respirator for infants based on electronic equipment. Capt., M.C., USAF, 1953-54. Recipient award for outstanding work in cardiovasc. surgery Lions Club, Hato Rey, 1961. Fellow Am. Acad. Pediat., Am. Coll. Legal Medicine (assoc.); mem. AMA (physician recognition award 1986); mem. Denton A. Cooley Cardiovasc. Surg. Soc., Michael E. De Bakey Internat. Cardiovasc. Soc., Pan Am. Med. Assn. (coun. pediatric surgery), P.R. Soc. Cardiology, Am. Heart Assn., P.R. Hear Assn., Phi Chi. Avocations: travel, horticulture, bridge.

SOLTES, JOANN MARGARET, retired music educator, realtor; b. Sewickley, Pa., Nov. 11, 1942; d. Mary Ann Soltes. BS in Music Edn., Duquesne U., 1964; MA, Mich. State U., 1977; student, Goethe Institut, Germany, 1992, Big Bend Coll., 1992. Music tchr. grades K-12 Ctr. Twp. Schs., Monaca, Pa., 1964—69; facilitator of masters program Nat.-Louis U., Heidelberg, Germany, 1995—99; music tchr., classroom tchr. Dept. Def. Dependent Schools Overseas, Okinawa, Turkey, Germany, Japan, 1969—99; realtor Coldwell Banker, Monaca, Pa., 1999—; substitute tchr. Facilitator The Study of Teaching Study Groups, Schweinufirt, Germany, 1992—95; presenter in field, Germany and Japan, 1992, Germany and Japan, 85. Mem. sch. advisory coun. Schweinfurt Am. Sch., Germany, 1995—96, mem. fine arts com., 1987—, chair grade level com., 1990—91, mem. sch. improvement com., 1989—90; vol. Adult Literacy Action, Beaver, Pa., 1999—2002; Ch. organist. Mem.: AAUW, Assn. for Supervision and Curriculum Devel., Beaver Falls Bus. and Career Women's Club (program chmn.), Beaver County Assn. Realtors, Nat. Assn. Realtors, Pa. Assn. Realtors, Community Concert Patron Board, Outlook Club, Phi Delta Kappa. Roman Catholic. Avocations: reading, cooking, bridge, singing, theatrical performance, church organist. Office: Coldwell Banker 3468 Brodhead Rd Monaca PA 15061

SOLTYS, FLORENCE GRAY, social worker; d. Olsie Glenn Gray and Addie Rebecca Hill; m. John Joseph Soltys; children: Jacqueline, Rebecca. BS, U. TN, 1958; RD, Mass. Gen. Hosp., 1959; MSW, U. NC, 1984. Clin. dietitian Mass. Gen. Hosp., Boston, 1960—63; dir. social work & bereavement Triangle Hospice, Chapel Hill, NC, 1985—87; assoc. clin. prof. U. NC Sch. Medicine, Chapel Hill, 1998—; assoc. clin. prof. and chair aging U. NC Sch. Social Work, Chapel Hill, 1998—; adj. assoc. prof. U. NC Sch. Nursing, Chapel Hill, 1998—. Chair Chapel Hill Parks and Recreation, 1981—87, Orange County Aging Bd., Chapel Hill, 1992—, Master Aging plan for Orange County, Chapel Hill, 2000—. Editor (author): American Society on Aging; author: (documentary) An Unlikely Friendship. Bd. Intervention Reminiscing Soc., Wis., 1995; leadership coun. Am. Soc. on Aging, San Francisco, 1993; bd. chair Dept. on Aging, Chapel Hill, 2000; vice chair Carol Woods Retirement, Chapel Hill. Named Trustee of Yr., Am. Assn. Homes and Svcs. to Aging, 2003; recipient Disting. Tchg., U. NC at Chapel Hill, 2001, Trustee Yr., Non-Profit Homes State NC, 2001, Leadership in Aging, Duke U., 2002, Sharon W. Wilder award, Long Term Care Assistance Advocacy, 2003. Fellow: N.C. Inst. Aging (assoc.); mem.: NASW (assoc.; bd. mem. 1986—91), N.C. Commn. on Aging, Am. Soc. Aging (assoc.; leadership coun. 1993—2003). Office: Sch Social Work 301 Pittsboro St CB# 3550 Chapel Hill NC 27599-3550 E-mail: fgsoltys@email.unc.edu.

SOLTYS, STEPHEN ROBERT, mathematician, educator; b. Sellersville, Pa., May 10, 1965; s. Paul Peter and Ellen Joan Soltys; m. Delma Jean High, Feb. 10, 1965; children: Alec Robert, Erinn Brittany, Adam Paul, Emily Brooke. BA in Math., Messiah Coll., Grantham, PA, 1987; EdM in Math. Edn., Millersville U., PA, 1993; EdD in Math. Edn., Temple U., Philadelphia, PA, 2000—. Secondary Mathematics Education Pa., 1987. Math. educator Manheim Ctrl. H.S., Manheim, PA, Pa., 1987—. Mem.: Math. Assn. of Am., Ctrl. Pa. Math. Assn., Nat. Coun. of Teachers of Math., Phi Delta Kappa. Brethren/Mennonite. Avocations: mathematics, sports, weightlifting. Home: 64 Brookfield Dr Ephrata PA 17522 Office: Manheim Ctrl Sch Dist 400 Adele Ave Manheim PA 17545 E-mail: soltyss@mcsd.k12.pa.us.

SOLTZ, JUDITH E. insurance company executive, lawyer; BA, Barnard Coll., 1968; JD cum laude, Boston Coll., 1971; LLM in Taxation, NYU, 1978. Tax atty. Conn. Gen. Corp., 1973—85; asst. gen. counsel Cigna Corp., 1985—90, v.p. taxes, 1990—98, sr. v.p., assoc. gen. counsel, 1998—2001, exec. v.p., gen. counsel, 2001—. Mem. exec. com. CPR Inst. Dispute Resolution; past mem. adv. coun. Hartford Inst. Ins. Taxation; past chair tax com. Am. Ins. Assn. Trustee Acad. Natural Scis. Phila. Mem.: ABA (tax and bus. law sects.). Office: Cigna Corp 1 Liberty Pl Philadelphia PA 19192-1552

SOLUM, JOHN HENRY, flutist, educator, author; b. New Richmond, Wis., May 11, 1935; s. Irwin M. and Helen L. (Anderson) S.; m. Millicent Kemp Hunt, July 30, 1960; children: Eric, Andrew. AB, Princeton U., 1957. Concert flutist, 1957—; tchr. Ind. U., Bloomington, 1973, Vassar Coll., Poughkeepsie, N.Y., 1969-71, 77—, Oberlin (Ohio) Conservatory, 1976. Dir. Bath (Eng.) Summer Sch. Baroque Music, 1979-89; artistic dir. Conn. Early Music Festival, New London, 1982-99; pres. N.Y. Flute Club, 1983-86; mem. music adv. panel NEA, 1990-93; arts adv. panel N.H. Arts Coun., 1995-98. Composer Cadenzas for Mozart's Flute Concertos, 1964; editor flute music; music critic for Notes, Pro Musica, The Consort; author: The Early Flute, 1992; contbg. author: New Grove Dictionary of Musical Instruments, New Grove Dictionary of Music and Musicians; contbr. articles to Mus. Am., Flutist Quar., Hist. Performance Mag., Woodwind World, Traversieres, Revue de la Société Liégeoise de Musicologie; flutist throughout N.Am., 1957—, Europe, 1962—, Asia, 1969—, S.Am., 1978—, Russia, 1983—; rec. artist Albany, Arabesque, Boston Skyline, Brunswick, Cambridge, Chesky, Columbia, CRI, Decca Gold Label, EMI, Epiphany, Innova, MCA Westminster, MSR, Philips, RCA, Seraphim, Smithsonian, Vanguard, others. Chmn. Hanoverian Found., 2000—. Recipient Phila. Orch. Youth Contest award, 1957. Mem. Nat. Flute Assn. (treas. 1989-94, Disting. Svc. award 1998), Dolmetsch Found. (bd. dirs.), Galpin Soc., Am. Musical Instrument Soc., Century Assn. (N.Y.). Home: 10 Bobwhite Dr Westport CT 06880-1001

SOLYMOSY, EDMOND SIGMOND ALBERT, international marketing executive, retired army officer; b. Budapest, Pest, Hungary, Sept. 3, 1937; came to U.S., 1949; s. Sigmond Ladislas and Gabrielle (Lindelof) S.; m. Mary Ellen Via, Sept. 9, 1961; children: Edmond S.A. Jr., Stephan G., Philip A. BSME, Tex. A&M U., 1960, BBA, 1961, MBA, 1970; postgrad., Mich. U., 1985, Harvard U., 1991. Commd. 2d lt. U.S. Army, 1961, advanced through grades to gen., 1985; student Nat. Def. U., Washington, 1980-81; comdr. 1st Air Def. Arty. Brigade, Ft. Bliss, Tex., 1981-83; chief of staff U.S. Army Air Def. Ctr., Ft. Bliss, 1983; dir. Human Resources Directorate, Hdqrs. Dept. Army, Washington, 1983-85; dep. comdr. U.S. Army Community and Family Support Ctr., Alexandria, Va., 1985-86; chief of staff U.S. Army I Corps, Ft. Lewis, Wash., 1986-88; chief exec. U.S. Office of Def. Coop., Athens, Greece, 1988-91; ret., 1991; pres. Global Project Mgmt., Houston, 1991—, Am. Southwest Properties Inc., 1993-95, Prime Daniel Asset Mgmt. Corp., 1997-2001; sr. ptnr. Solymosy Investment Assocs., 2000—; owner Bar-O-S Farms. Advisor Sec. of Army Panel, Washington, 1983-86, Hellenic-Am. C. of C., Athens, 1988-91; bd. dirs. Am. Ikarus Inc., Maxoil Inc., So. Nat. Bank Tex.; hon. consul Republic of Hungary; chmn. Houston Com. on Fgn. Rels. Author: Continental Economic Alliances, 1981. Sponsor Spl. Olympics, Ft. Lewis, 1986; advisor Mil. Mus., Ft. Lewis, 1986-88; regional v.p. Mediterranean coun. Boy Scouts Am., Athens, 1988-91; mem. devel. com. Tex. A&M U., College Station, 1991, advisor Ctr. for Internat. Bus.; mem. bd. advisors Mosher Inst. for Internat. Policy Studies; mem. Mil. Com., Houston.; bd. dirs. Tex. A&M U. Rsch. Found. Decorated D.S.M., Def. D.S.M., Combat Infantryman's Badge, Airborne Parachutist's Badge, Army Ranger, Legion of Merit (3); recipient U.S. and Vietnamese awards for heroism, Greek Disting. Svc. award, 1991. Mem. Assn. U.S. Army (Svc. to Soldiers award 1985), VFW, Armed Forces YMCA (chmn. com. 1982, Nat. Vol. of Yr. award 1983), Am. Quarter Horse Assn., Am. Palomine Horse Breeders Assn., Internat. Propeller Club (Greece advisor 1989), Kiwanis Club Houston, Hungarian Knights Hospitaller of Order of St. John. Republican. Lutheran. Avocations: sports, jogging, sailing, fishing, hunting. Home: 10150 Dogwood Tr College Station TX 77845-6740 Office: Global Project Mgmt PO Box 27253 Houston TX 77227-7253 E-mail: essglobal@aol.com.

SOLZHENITSYN, ALEKSANDR ISAYEVICH, writer; b. Kislovodsk, Russia, Dec. 11, 1918; imprisoned under Joseph Stalin for critical comments, 1945-53; exiled to Soviet Cen. Asia, 1953; freed from exile, 1956; expelled from USSR, 1974; arrived back in Russia, 1994; m. Natalya Reshetovskaya, 1940 (div.), remarried, 1956 (div.); m. Natalia Svetlova, 1970; children: Yermolai, Ignat, Stephan. Corr. student in philology, Moscow Inst. History, Philosophy and Lit., 1939-41; degree in math. and physics, U. Rostov, 1941; LittD, Harvard U., 1978. Author: Odin den' Ivana Denisovicha, 1962 (pub. as One Day in the Life of Ivan Denisovich, 1963), Dlia pol'zy dela, 1963 (pub. as For the Good of the Cause, 1964), Sluchai na stantsii Krechetovka/Matrenin dvor, 1963 (pub. as We Never Make Mistakes, 1963), Etudy i krokhotnye rasskazy, 1964 (pub. as Stories and Prose Poems, 1971, as Prose Poems, 1971, as Matryona's House and Other Stories, 1975), V kruge pervom, 1968 (pub. as The First Circle, 1968; Prix du Meilleur Livre Etranger France 1969), Rakovyi korpus, 1968 (pub. as Cancer Ward, 1968; Prix du Meilleur Livre Etranger France 1969), Le Droits de l'écrivain, 1969, Sobranie sochinenii (6 vols.), 1969-70, Six Etudes, 1971, Avgust chetyrnadtsatogo, 1971 (pub. as August 1914, 1972), Nobelevskaia lektsiia po literature, 1972 (pub. as Nobel Lecture, 1972, as One Word of Truth, 1972), Arkhipelag Gulag (3 vols.), 1973-76 (pub. as The Gulag Archipelago, 1974-78), Prusskie nochi: poema napisannaia v lagere v 1950, 1974 (pub. as Prussian Nights, 1977), Iz-pod glyb, 1974 (pub. as From Under the Rubble, 1975), Mir i nasilie, 1974, Pis'mo vozhdiam Sovetskogo soiuza, 1974 (pub. as Letter to the Soviet Leaders, 1974), A Pictorial Autobiography, 1974, Solzhenitsyn, the Voice of Freedom, 1975, Bodalsia telenok s dubom, 1975 (pub. as The Oak and the Calf, 1980), Lenin v Tsiurikhe, 1975 (pub. as Lenin in Zurich, 1976), Detente: Prospects for democracy and Dictatorship, 1975, America, We Beg You to Interfere, 1975, Amerikanskie rechi, 1975, Warning to the Western World, 1976, A World Split Apart, 1978, Alexander Solzhenitsyn Speaks to the West, 1978, Sobranie sochinenii, 1978, The Mortal Danger, 1980, East and West, 1980, Issledovaniia noveishei russkoi istorii, 1980, Publitsistika: stat'i i rechi, 1981, Krasnoe koleso: povestvovan'e v otmerennykh srokakh Uzel I: Avgust chetyrnadtsatogo, 1983 (pub. as The Red Wheel: A Narrative in Discrete Periods of Time, 1989), Krasnoe koleso: povestvovan'e v otmerennykh srokakh Uzel II: Oktiabr'shestnadtsatogo, 1984, Krasnoe koleso: povestvovan'e v otmerennykh srokakh Uzel III: Mart semnadtsatogo, 1986, Rasskazy, 1990, Kak nam obustroit' Rossiiu, 1990, Krasnoe koleso: povestvovan'e v otmerennykh srokakh Uzel IV: Aprel'semnadtsatogo, 1991, Rebuilding Russia: Toward Some Formulations, 1991, Les Invisibles, 1992, Nashi pliuralisty: otryvok iz vtorogo toma "Ocherkov literaturnoi zhizni", 1992, The Russian Question At the End of the Twentieth Century, 1995; (plays) Olen' i shalashovka, 1968 (pub. The Love-Girl and the Innocent, 1969), Svecha na vetru, 1968 (pub. Candle in the Wind, 1973), Pir podebitelei, 1981 (pub. as Victory Celebrations, 1983), Plenniki, 1981 (pub. as Prisoners, 1983), P'esy i kinostsenarii, 1981; editor: Russkii slovar' iazykovogo rasshireniia, 1990. Arty. officer Russian Army, World War II. Recipient Lenin prize nomination, 1964, Nobel prize for lit., 1970, Freedoms Found. award Stanford U., 1976, Templeton Found. prize, 1983. Mem. Am. Acad. Arts and Scis., Hoover Inst. War, Revolution and Peace (hon.), Russian Acad. of Scis. (field of lang.). Address: Ul Tverskaya 12 kv 169 125 990 Moscow Russia

SOMACH, S. DENNIS, communications executive; b. Allentown, Pa. s. Lawrence and Lillian Rose Somach. BA in English, Art, Moravian Coll., 1975. Announcer Sta. WSAN, Allentown, 1971-75, program dir., 1975; announcer, music dir. Sta. WYSP-FM, Phila., 1975-81; producer Evening/PM Mag., Phila., 1980-82; producer, pres. Denny Somach Prodns., Havertown, Pa., 1979—. Pres. Cinema Records, Phila., 1986—; pres., founder Musicom Internat., 1992—; pres., founder Music Art LLC, 1997—. Prodr.: (radio shows) Psychedelic Psnack, 1985—, Ticket to Ride, 1985—, Legends of Rock, 1985—, Don Kirshner's History of Rock 'n' Roll, 1990, The Rock of the Century, 1999, The Classics, 1999—, (TV shows) Hot Spots, USA Network, 1982-84, Rock 'n' Roll Show CBS-TV, 1983, John Debella Show, 1990; exec. prodr.: (albums) Dave Mason, 1987, Patrick Moraz, 1987, Johnny Winter, 1988, Eric Johnson, 1990, Barbara Mandrell, 1994, Alan Parsons, 1998; author: Ticket to Ride, 1989, Meet the Beatles...Again, 1996. Recipient Grammy award for best rock instrumental Eric Johnson's Cliffs of Dover, 1992. Avocations: travel, magic, collecting records. Office: 812 W Darby Rd Havertown PA 19083-4607

SOMASEGAR, SIVARAMA KICHENANE, information technology executive; b. 1965; m. Akila Somasegar; children: Sahana, Archana. BSEE, Anna U., India; MS in Computer Engring., La. State U. From software design engr. to v.p. Microsoft, Redmond, Wash., 1989, v.p. windows engring. solutions & svc. group. Office: One Microsoft Way Redmond WA 98052-6399

SOMASUNDARAN, PONISSERIL, surface and colloid engineer, applied science educator; b. Pazhookara, Kerala, India, June 28, 1939; arrived in U.S., 1961; s. Kumara Moolayil and Lakshmikutty (Amma) Pillai; m. Usha N., May 25, 1966; 1 child, Tamara. BS, Kerala U., Trivandrum, India, 1958; BE, Indian Inst. Sci., Bangalore, 1961; MS, U. Calif., Berkeley, 1962, PhD, 1964. Rsch. engr. U. Calif., 1964, Internat. Minerals & Chem. Corp., Skokie, Ill., 1965-67; rsch. chemist R.J. Reynolds Industries, Inc., Winston-Salem, NC, 1967-70; assoc. prof. Columbia U., N.Y.C., 1970-78, prof. mineral engring., 1978-83, La Von Duddleson Krumb prof., 1983-97; dir. NSF Industry U. Coop. Rsch. Ctr. in Novel Surfactants, 1998—; hon. prof. Wuhan Inst. Chem. Tech., 2001—. Chmn. Henry Krumb Sch. Chem. Engring., Materials Sci. and Mining Engring., Columbia U., 1988—97; dir. Langmuir Ctr. for Colloids and Interfaces Columbia U., 1987—; cons. numerous agys., cos., including NIH, B.F. Goodrich, NSF, 1974, Alcan, 1981, UNESCO, 1982, Sohio, 1984—85, IBM, 1984, Am. Cyanamid, Duracell, 1988—89, DuPont, 1989, Canmet, 1990—93, Unilever, 1991—, Engelhard, 1991—94, UOP, Alcoa, 1991—92, Allied Signal, GAF, 1999—2000, INCO, Arch.Chem.; mem. panel NRC; chmn. numerous iannternat. symposia and NSF workshops; mem. adv. panel Bur. Mines Generic Ctr., 1983—91; keynote and plenary lectr. internat. meetings; hon. prof. Ctrl. South U. Tech., China; Brahm Prakash prof. metallurgy and material sci. Indian Inst. Sci., Bangalore, 1990; hon. rsch. advisor Beijing Gen. Rsch. Inst., 1991—; Henry Krumb lectr. AIME, 1988. Editor: (books) Fine Particles Processing, 1980; hon. editor-in-chief Colloids and Surfaces, 1980—, Ency. of Colloids and Interfaces, —; contbr. articles to profl. jours.; editor-in-chief: Encyclopedia of Colloid and Surface Chemistry. Pres. Keralasamajam of Greater N.Y., N.Y.C., 1974-75; bd. dirs. Fedn. Indian Assocs., N.Y.C., 1974-95, Vols. in Svc. to Edn. in India, Hartford, Conn., 1974—; mem. planning bd. Village of Piermont, N.Y., 1995-2000, mem. zoning bd. appeals, 2000—, mem. citizens adv. com., 2000—. Recipient Disting. Achievement in Engring. award, AINA, 1980, Antoine M. Gaudin award Soc. Mining Engrs.-AIME, 1983, Achievements in Applied Sci. award 2d World Malayalam Conf., 1985, Robert H. Richards award, AIME, 1986, Arthur F. Taggart award Soc. Mining Engrs.-AIME, 1987, honor award Assn. Indian in Am., 1988, VHP award of Excellence, Ellis Island medal of Honor, 1990, Commendations citation State of N.J. Senate, 1991; named Mill Man of Distinction, Soc. Mining Engrs.-AIME, 1983, Disting. Alumnus award Indian Inst. Sci., Bangalore, 1989, Outstanding Contbns. and Achievement award Cultural Festival India, 1991, Recognition award SIAA, 1992, Asian-Am. Heritage award Asian Am. Higher Edn. Coun., 1994. Fellow Russian Acad. Nat. Scis. (fgn.), Chinese Acad. Engring. (fgn.) Indian Nat. Acad. Engring., Instn. Mining and Metallurgy (U.K.); mem. AICE, NAE, Soc. Mining Engrs. (bd. dirs. 1982-85, Disting. mem. award, also others), Engring. Found. (chmn. bd. 1993-95, chmn. conf. com. 1985-88, bd. exec. com. 1985-88, bd. dirs. 1991—, Frank Aplan award 1992), Am. Chem. Soc., N.Y. Acad. Scis., Russian Acad. Natural Scis. (fgn.), Internat. Assn. Colloid and Surface Scientists (councillor 1989-92), Indian Material Rsch. Soc. (hon.), Chinese Acad. Engring., Sigma Xi. Achievements include patents for in field. Office Phone: 212-854-2926. E-mail: psomasunda@aol.com.

SOMBERG, JOHN CHARIN, cardiologist, medicine and pharmacology educator; b. N.Y.C., Oct. 8, 1948; AB, NYU, 1970; MD, N.Y. Med. Coll., 1974. Diplomate Nat. Bd. Med. Examiners. Intern Met. Hosp. Ctr., N.Y.C., 1974-75, med. jr. resident, 1975-76; chief med. resident N.Y. Med. Coll., 1976-77; fellow cardiovascular medicine Peter Bent Brigham Hosp., Harvard Med. Sch., Boston, 1977-79, instr. medicine, 1979-80; asst. prof. medicine and pharmacology Albert Einstein Coll. Medicine, Bronx, N.Y., 1985-88; chief cardiology sect. VA Med. Ctr., North Chicago, Ill., 1988-89; assoc. prof., chief divsn. clin. pharmacology Chgo. Med. Sch., North Chgo., 1988-89, prof. medicine and pharmacology, chief divsns. cardiology and clin. pharmacology, 1989—98; prof. medicine and pharmacology, chief divsn. clin. pharmacology, dir. Rush Analytical Laboratories Rush U., Chicago, Ill., 1998—. Founder and pres. Academic Pharmaceuticals, Lake Bluff, Ill. Editor Jour. Clin. Pharmacology, 1985-1994; editor-in-cheif Am. Jour. Therapeutics, 1994—; mem. editorial bd. Am. Jour. Cardiology; contbr. articles, revs., abstracts to profl. publs., chpts. to books. Fellow Am. Coll. Clin. Pharmacology (reagent 1986-1994); mem. Am. Heart Assn. (mem. bd. govs. Chgo. chpt.), Am. Fedn. Clin. Rsch., Fedn. for Advancement of Sci. and Exptl. Biology. Home: PO Box 869 Lake Forest IL 60045-0869

SOMBROTTO, VINCENT R. postal union executive; b. N.Y.C., June 15, 1923; s. Raymond and Agnes (McCormick) S.; Feb. 23, 1957; children: Gloria, Vincent, Lisa, Leslie, Jacqueline, Stephen, Mara. Grad. high sch. Letter carrier, N.Y.C., 1947-71; br. pres. Nat. Assn. Letter Carriers, N.Y.C., 1971-79, pres. Washington, 1979—. Dir. Fund For Assuring An Ind. Retirement; v.p., mem. exec. council AFL-CIO; bd. dirs. Ctr. Nat. Policy; chmn. Employee Thrift Adv. Council of Fed. Retirement Thrift Investment Bd. Bd. adv. Sidney Harmon Program on Tech. Pub. Policy and Human Devel., Harvard U.; adv. com. Nat. Assembly Vol. Health and Social Welfare Orgns.; nat. v.p. Muscular Dystrophy Assn.; mem. adv. council Am. Diabetes Assn.; mem. President's Commn. Employment of Handicapped. Served with AUS, 1943-45. Mem. Fed. Adv. Council Occupational Safety and Health, Postal Telephone and Telegraphy Internat. (mem. exec. council) Office: Nat Assn Letter Carriers 100 Indiana Ave NW Ste 709 Washington DC 20001-2196

SOMER-GREIF, PENNY LYNN, lawyer; b. New Hyde Park, NY, Mar. 30, 1970; d. Stanley Jerome and Janice Somer; m. Brian Scott Greif. BS, SUNY, Binghamton, 1992; JD, Am. U., 1995. Bar: N.J. 1996, N.Y. 1996, D.C. 2000. Atty.-advisor U.S. SEC, Washington, 1995-2000; assoc. Arnold & Porter, Washington, 2000—. Avocations: reading, exercise. Office: 555 Twelfth NW Washington DC 20004-1206 Office Phone: 202-942-6402.

SOMERHALDER, JOHN W., II, gas industry executive; Sr. v.p. El Paso Corp., Houston, 1992—96, pres. El Paso Energy Resources Co., 1996, exec. v.p. pipeline group, pres. pipeline group, 2001—. Pres. Tenn. Gas Pipeline, 1996—2000, chmn. bd. dirs., 2000—, So. Natural Gas, 2000—, El Paso Natural Gas, 2000—; chmn. Interstate Natural Gas Assn. Am. Found., 2001. Office: El Paso Corp PO Box 2511 1001 Louisianna St Houston TX 77002

SOMERMAN, MARTHA J. dean, dental educator; m. Norm Schiff. DDS, NYU, 1975; PhD, U. Rochester, 1980. Diplomate Am. Acad. Periodontology. Asst. prof., periodontics and pharmacology Balt. Coll. Dental Surgery, 1984—87, assoc. prof., pharmacology, 1987—91; William K. and Mary Anne Najjar prof., dept. periodontics, prevention and periodontics U. Mich. Sch. Dentistry, 1991—2002, chair dept. periodontics, prevention and geriatrics, 1991—2001, assoc. dean rsch., 2001—02; assoc. prof., pharmacology U. Mich. Med. Sch., 1991—95, prof., pharmacology, 1995—2002; dean U. Wash. Sch. Dentistry, 2002—. Contbr. articles to profl. jours. Fellow: AAAS; mem.: Am. Assn. Dental Rsch. (past pres.). Office: RMD 322 Box 356365 Seattle WA 98195*

SOMERS, ANNE RAMSAY, retired medical educator; b. Memphis, Sept. 9, 1913; d. Henry Ashton and Amanda Vick (Woolfolk) Somers; m. Herman Miles Somers, Aug. 31, 1946; children: Sara Ramsay, Margaret Ramsay. BA, Vassar Coll., 1935; postgrad., U. N.C., 1939—40; DSc (hon.), Med. Coll. Wis., 1975. Ednl. dir. Internat. Ladies Garment Workers Union, 1937—42; labor economist U.S. Dept. Labor, 1943—46; rsch. assoc. Haverford Coll., 1957—63; rsch. assoc. indsl. rels. sect. Princeton U., 1964—84; prof. U. Medicine and Dentistry of N.J.-R. Wood Johnson Med. Sch. (formerly Rutgers Med. Sch.), 1971—84, adj. prof., 1984—2002. Adj. prof. geriat. medicine U. Pa. Sch. Medicine, 1990—2002; mem. Nat. Bd. Med. Examiners, 1983—86; cons. in health econs., health edn., geriats., gerontology, realted areas. Author: Hospital Regulation: The Dilemma of Public Policy, 1969, Health Care in Transition: Directions for the Future, 1971; author: (with H.M. Somers) Workmen's Compensation: The Prevention, Rehabilitation and Financing of Occupational Disability, 1954; author: Medicare and the Hospitals, 1967, Doctors, Patients and Health Insurance, 1961, Health and Health Care: Policies in Perspective, 1971; author: (with N.L. Spears) The Continuing Care Retirement Community: A Significant Option for Long Care?, 1992; editor (with D.R. Fabian): he Geriatric Imperative: An Introduction to Gerontology and Clinical Geriatrics, 1981. Mem. bd. visitors Duke U. Med. Ctr., 1972—77, U. Tex. Health Scis. Ctr., Houston, 1982—86. Named to Health Care Hall of Fame, 1993; recipient Elizur Wright award, Am. Risk and Ins. Assn., 1962.

Fellow: Coll. Physicians Phila. (hon.), Am. Coll. Hosp. Adminstrs. (hon.); mem.: Nat. Acad. Social Ins., Inst. Medicine of NAS, Soc. Tchrs. of Family Medicine (hon.). Home: Pennswood Village # C-202 Newtown PA 18940-2401

SOMERS, CLIFFORD LOUIS, lawyer; b. Portland, Maine, Dec. 27, 1940; s. Norman Louis and Adeline Wilhemina (Witzke) Somers; m. Jennie Sierra Somers; children from previous marriage: Alan Mark, Penelope Lee. BA, U. Fla., Gainsville, 1965, JD, 1967. Bar: Fla 1967, US Ct Mil Appeals 1968, US Dist Ct (mid dist) Fla 1972, cert.: (civil trial lawyer), (mediator). Ptnr. Burton, Somers & Reynolds, Tampa, 1975-77, Miller, McKendree & Somers, Tampa, 1977-85, McKendree & Somers, Tampa, 1985-89, Somers and Morgan, Tampa, 1989-91, Somers and Assocs., Tampa, 1991-99, Barr, Murman, Tonelli, Slother & Sleet, Tampa, 1999—. Instr law Univ Fla, Gainesville, 1967; secy, treas Chester H Ferguson-Morris S White Inn, Am Inns Ct, 1987—89, pres-elect, 1989—90, pres, 1990—91. Contbr. articles to profl jours. With U.S. Army, 1961—64, Vietnam, capt JAG U.S. Army, 1968—72, mil judge JAG U.S. Army, 1971—72. Mem.: Am Bd Trial Attys (vpres Tampa chpt 1990—91), Def Research Inst (chmn 2d dist area west coast 1985—95), Fla Bar Asn (chmn procedure rules comt 1991—92), Brandon Vets Post and Park, Am Legion (comdr Post 278 1975). Avocations: writing, aerobics, weightlifting. Home: 17920 Gulf Blvd #1903 Redington Shores FL 33708 Office: Barr Murman Tonelli Slother & Sleet Ste 1700 201 E Kennedy Blvd Tampa FL 33602-5829 E-mail: csomers@barrmurman.com.

SOMERS, DANIEL E. telecommunications industry executive; b. Detroit; m. Mary Jane Somers; five children. BS in Fin., Stonehill Coll. Investment banker and fin. analyst, CFO Imasco Ltd., Montreal, Can., Hardee's Restaurant subsidiary Imasco Ltd., Rocky Mount, N.C.; pres. Radio Atlantic Holdings Ltd., Nova Scotia; exec. v.p., CFO Bell Can. Internat., Inc., 1992-95; creator Cable & Wireless Comm., U.K.; chmn., CEO Bell Cablemedia, plc, London; sr. exec. v.p., CFO AT&T; pres., CEO AT&T Broadband, Englewood, Colo., 1999—. Bd. dirs. BCE Cable Ltd., BCI Internat. Holdings Ltd., Bell Cablemedia, plc, Videotron Holdings Ltd. Office: AT&T Broadband 188 Inverness Dr W Englewood CO 80112

SOMERS, JOHN ARTHUR, insurance company executive; b. Cin., Feb. 24, 1944; s. Arthur Edward and Margaret Mary (Netschke) S.; m. Ann-Christin Ahlander, Dec. 28, 1968; children: Monica Ann, Christina Elizabeth, Mark Edward BS in Econs., Villanova U., 1966; postgrad., Sch. Law, U. Conn., 1966-67; MBA in Fin., U. Conn., 1972. Asst. town mgr. Town of Newington, Conn., 1970-72; v.p. Prudential Ins. Co. Am., Newark, 1972-81; sr. v.p. Tchrs. Ins. & Annuity Assn., N.Y.C., 1981—, exec. v.p., 1996—. Bd. dirs. Cmty. Preservation Corp., Guardian Life. Roman Catholic. Office: Tchrs Ins & Annuity Assn Am 730 3rd Ave New York NY 10017-3206

SOMERS, K(ARL) BRENT, consumer products company executive; b. Logan, Utah, Aug. 4, 1948; s. W. Karl and Beth (Johnson) S.; m. Kathryn Lenhart, Aug. 8, 1978; children: Anne Marie, Mary Margaret, Andrew, Robert, Maren. BS, Utah State U., 1972; MBA, Brigham Young U., 1975. Fin. analyst U.S. Shoe Corp., Cin., 1975-80, dir. corp. fin. planning, 1979-83, asst. treas., 1983-85; v.p. fin. Cin. Shoe Co., Cin., 1985-86; treas, Precision Lenscrafters, Cin., 1986-87, dir. fin. and acctg., 1987, chief fin. officer/v.p. fin. and acctg., 1987-90; chief fin. officer/v.p. fin. U.S. Shoe Corp., Cin., 1990—; sr. exec. v.p., CFO KeyCorp, Cleve. Office: Key Corporation 127 Public Sq Cleveland OH 44114-1306

SOMERS, LOUIS ROBERT, retired food company executive; b. Pontiac, Mich., Aug. 8, 1926; s. Jay G. and Maggie (Gee) S.; m. Rynda Horinga, July 28, 1950; children: Linda, Laurie. BS, Mich. State U., 1950. With Kellogg Co., Battle Creek, Mich., 1955-88; controller Kellogg Internat., 1967-70, 72-75; fin. dir. Kellogg Gt. Brit. Ltd., 1970-72; v.p. fin., treas. Kellogg Co., 1975-85, sr. v.p. fin., 1985-88. Trustee Alma Coll., 1982—2001; bd. govs. ARC, 1985—92, chmn. audit com.; bd. dirs. Mich. State U. Devel. Fund, 1983—88.

SOMERS, SALLY WEST, librarian; b. Duncan, Okla., July 6, 1939; d. Mahlon Clifford and Lorene (Shore) West; m. Dale Andrew Somers, Oct. 15, 1961 (dec. Mar. 1972); children: Jennifer, Stephen Andrew. BA, Trinity U., 1961; postgrad., East Tex. State U., 1966; MLS, Emory U., 1975; postgrad., Ga. State U., 1976. Adminstrv. asst., bookkeeper Ga. State U. Libr., Atlanta, 1972-74; head serials receiving U. Ga. Librs., Athens, 1976-79, head acquistions dept.; asst. univ. libr. tech. svcs. Tulane U., New Orleans, 1989-99; asst. dir. tech. svcs. Fla. State U., Tallahassee, 2000—. Co-editor: Practical Issues in Collection Development, 1995; author book article; contbr. articles to profl. jours. Scholar Ga. Libr. Assn., 1974, Emory U., 1974. Mem. ALA (com. chair serials sect., 1990, 1994-95), Assn. for Libr. Collections and Tech. Svcs. Avocations: walking, reading. Office: Tulane Univ Libr 7001 Freret St New Orleans LA 70118-5549

SOMERS, SUSAN EILEEN, business educator; b. Quincy, Mass., Mar. 28, 1951; d. Donald William and Flora (Andrews) S. BS, Northeastern U., Boston, 1984; MBA, Utah State U., 1985. Adminstr. Stone & Webster Engrs., Boston, 1973-83; prof. Quincy (Mass.) Coll., 1986—. Cons. Quincy 2000, 1995-96, Sml. Bus. Mgmt. Ctr., Logan, Utah, 1985-86. Mem. Internat. Pers. Mgmt. Assn., Phi Delta Kappa, Sigma Epsilon Rho. Avocations: reading, travel, crafts. Office: Quincy College 34 Coddington St Quincy MA 02169 E-mail: ssomers@quincycollege.edu.

SOMERS, SUZANNE MARIE, actress, writer, singer; b. San Bruno, Calif., Oct. 16, 1946; d. Frank and Marion Mahoney; m. Greg Somers (div.); 1 child; m. Alan Hamel, 1977. Student, Lone Mountain Sch., San Francisco Coll. for Women; studies with Charles Conrad. Owner, founder Suzanne Somers Collection. Actress: (films) American Graffiti, 1973, Billy Jack Goes to Washington, 1977, Yesterday's Hero, 1979, Nothing Personal, 1980, Rusty: A Dog's Tale, 1997; (TV films) Sky Heist, 1975, It Happened at Lakewood Manor, 1977, Happily Ever After, 1978, Zuma Beach, 1978, Goodbye Charlie, 1985, Totally Minnie, 1988, Rich Men, Single Women, 1990, Seduced by Evil, 1994, Devil's Food, 1996, Love-Struck, 1997, No Laughing Matter, 1998, The Darklings, 1999; (TV series) Anniversary Game, 1969, High Rollers, 1974, Three's Company, 1977-81, She's the Sheriff, 1987-89, Step by Step, 1991—98; (TV mini-series) Hollywood Wives, 1985; actress, co-exec. prodr.: (films) Exclusive, 1992; host: (TV series) The Suzanne Somers Show, 1994, VH1's 8-Track Flashback, 1995, Candid Camera (co-host), 1997-2000; performer Las Vegas (Nev.) Hilton, MGM Grand, Las Vegas, Sands Hotel, Atlantic City, USO, various TV commls.; author: Touch Me Again, 1973, Keeping Secrets (autobiography), 1988, Suzanne Somers' Eat Great, Lose Weight, 1997, After the Fall: How I Picked Myself Up, Dusted Myself Off and Started All Over Again (autobiography), 1998, Suzanne Somers' Get Skinny on Fabulous Food, 1999, Suzanne Somers 365 Ways to Change Your Life, 1999, Eat, Cheat, and Melt the Fat Away, 2001, The Sexy Years: Discover the Hormone Connection, 2004. Recipient Humanitarian award, Nat. Council on Alcoholism, 1992, President's award, Nat. Assoc. of American Drug Counselors.*

SOMERS, VIREND KRISTEN, physician, researcher; b. Durban, Natal, South Africa; came to the U.S., 1986; MB, BChir cum laude, U. Natal, Durban, 1980; PhD, Oxford (Eng.) U., 1986. Diplomate Am. Bd. Internal Medicine subspecialty cardiology, fellow Am. Coll. of Cardiology. Intern U. Natal, Durban, 1981, resident, 1982; Nuffield scholar Oxford U., 1983-86; resident medicine U. Iowa, Iowa City, 1988-91, fellow cardiology, 1991-93, faculty cardiology, 1993-99; prof. medicine Mayo Clinic, Rochester, Minn., 2000—; clin. investigator Mayo Found., 2002—. Cons. Am. Soc. Hypertension, 1999. Mem. editl. bd. Circulation, 1998—, Jour. Hypertension, 1998—, Sleep, 2002—; cons. editor Am. Jour. Physiology-Regulatory and Integrative, 2001—. Recipient Demuth Young Investigator prize Internat. Soc. Hypertension, 1988, 94, Malherbe Disting. Alumnus award U. Natal, 1998, Young Scholar award Am. Soc. Hypertension, 2000; Nuffield Dominion scholar Oxford U., 1983-86. Fellow Am. Coll. Cardiology, High Blood Pressure Coun., Coun. on Circulation; mem. Am. Soc. Clin. Investigation, Am. Heart Assn. (established investigator, Cournand Comroe award 1993), Assn. Univ. Cardiologists. Office: Mayo Clinic 200 1st St SW Rochester MN 55905-0002

SOMERSET, HAROLD RICHARD, retail executive; b. Woodbury, Conn., Sept. 25, 1935; s. Harold Kitchener and Margaret Mary (Roche) S.; m. Marjory Deborah Ghiselin, June 22, 1957 (dec. Jan. 1984); children: Timothy Craig, Paul Alexander; m. Jean MacAlpine DesMarais, Jan. 2, 1985; stepchildren: Cheryl Lyn DesMarais, James Fenelon DesMarais. BS, U.S. Naval Acad., 1957; B.C.E., Rensselaer Poly. Inst., Troy, N.Y., 1959; LL.B., Harvard U., 1967. Bar: Mass. 1967, Hawaii 1973. Commd. ensign U.S. Navy, 1957, advanced through grades to lt., 1961; service in U.S. and Hawaii; resigned, 1964; with firm Goodwin, Procter & Hoar, Boston, 1967-72; corp. counsel Alexander & Baldwin, Inc., Honolulu, 1972-74, v.p., gen. counsel, 1974-78, group v.p.-sugar, 1978-79, exec. v.p.-agr., 1979-84; with Calif. & Hawaiian Sugar Co., San Francisco, 1984-93, exec. v.p., chief operating officer, 1984-88, pres., chief exec. officer, 1988-93, bus. cons., 1994—2002; pres., CEO Longs Drug Stores Corp., 2002. Bd. dirs. Longs Drug Stores Corp., Brown and Caldwell. Mem. adv. bd. San Francisco Nat. Maritime Mus. Home: 19 Donald Dr Orinda CA 94563-3646

SOMERSON, PAUL, editor-in-chief; Former v.p., editor-in-chief P.C. Computing, San Francisco; v.p., ed. dir. Ziff Davis Develop. Group, 2000—. Office: Ziff Davis Publishing 11766 Wilshire Blvd Los Angeles CA 90025

SOMERVILLE, ANDREA LYNN, music educator, musician; b. Rochester, N.Y., Feb. 11, 1964; d. Richard Thomas and Jaqueline Jean Somerville. BMusEd, Potsdam State, N.Y., 1987; MMusEd, Bowling Green State, Ohio, 1991. Registered Susuki Assn. of Am., SAS cert. of Adminstrn. U. Rochester. Tchr. music (orch.) Brockport Pub. Schs., NY, 1987—89, Greece Ctrl. Sch. Dist., Rochester, 1991—. Violin tchr. Pk. Ave. Suzuki Ctr., Rochester, NY, 1991—; violinist Rochester Area Musicals, 1991—, Angelicus String Quartet, 2001—; tchr. summer string camps, N.Y. and Ohio. Mem.: Music Educators Nat. Assn. Avocations: mentor tchr., travel, gardening, reading.

SOMERVILLE, ATWELL WILSON, JR., medical editor, director; b. Charlottesville, Va., Nov. 24, 1949; s. Atwell Wilson and Anne Carter Somerville. AB in English, U. N.C., 1972, PhD in English, 1992; MA in English, U. Va., 1977. Editor in life scis. Bd. of Editors in the Life Scis., Inc.; instr. Warren Wilson Coll., Ashville, N.C., 1974-76, dir. pub. info., 1982-83, dir. admissions, 1983-87; instr. Va. Episcopal Sch., Lynchburg, 1978-80; comms. coord. So. Highland Handicraft Guild, Asheville, 1980-82; instr. U. N.C.-Chapel Hill, 1988-92, U. N.C.-Greensboro, 1988-92; med. editor dept. anesthesiology Wake Forest U. Sch. Medicine, Winston-Salem, NC, 1992—2003; rsch. adminstrv. coord., Dept. Pub. Health Sci. Wake Forest U. Sch. Med., Winston-Salem, NC, 2003—. Editl. cons. Regional Anesthesia and Pain Medicine jour., 1996-98; asst. book rev. sect. Anesthesiology jour., Phila., 1997. Author: The Tuesday Club of Annapolis (1745-1756) as Cultural Performance, 1996, A History of the Department of Anesthesiology: 1942-1997, The Wake Forest University School of Medicine, 1998; editor: Appalachia/America: The Proceedings of the 1980 Appalachian Studies Conference, 1981; mem. editl. bd. Anesthesia Patient Safety Newsletter, 2001-; contbr. articles to profl. publs. Coach Optimist Soccer Program, Winston-Salem, 1995—2000; mem. chorale Wake Forest Univ., 2000—. Morehead scholar, 1968-72; Mason fellow, 1976-77; recipient (2) 1st Pl. award Coun. for Advancement and Support of Edn., 1987. Mem.: Soc. Scholarly Publishing, The Am. Assn. for History Medicine, Soc. Early Americanists, N.C. Soc. Anesthesiologists, Am. Med. Writers Assn., Am. Soc. Anesthesiologists, Coun. Sci. Editors, Phi Beta Kappa. Office: Wake Forest U Sch Medicine Dept Pub Health Sci 2000 West First Street Piedmont Plaza II Winston Salem NC 27104 Business E-Mail: wsomerv@wfubmc.edu.

SOMERVILLE, RICHARD CHAPIN JAMES, atmospheric scientist, educator; b. Washington, May 30, 1941; s. James William and Mollie (Dorf) S.; m. Sylvia Francisca Bal, Sept. 17, 1965; children: Anatol Leon, Alexander Chapin. BS in Meteorology, Pa. State U., 1961; PhD in Meteorology, NYU, 1966. Postdoctoral fellow Nat. Ctr. Atmospheric Rsch., Boulder, Colo., 1966-67; rsch. assoc. geophysical fluid dynamics lab. NOAA, Princeton, N.J., 1967-69; rsch. scientist Courant Inst. Math. Scis., N.Y.C., 1969-71; meteorologist Goddard inst. space studies NASA, N.Y.C., 1971-74; adj. prof. Columbia U., NYU, 1971-74; head numerical weather prediction sect. Nat. Ctr. Atmospheric Rsch., Boulder, 1974-79; prof. meteorology Scripps Inst. Oceanography, U. Calif.-San Diego, La Jolla, 1979—. Author: The Forgiving Air: Understanding Environmental Change, 1996. Fellow: AAAS, Am. Meteorol. Soc.; mem.: Am. Geophys. Union. Office: U Calif San Diego Scripps Inst Oceanography 9500 Gilman Dr Dept 0224 La Jolla CA 92093-0224

SOMERVILLE, WALTER RALEIGH, JR., government official; b. Macon, N.C., Feb. 17, 1930; s. Walter Raleigh and Bettie Lou (Hunt) S.; m. Jean Renwick Nava, Sept. 12, 1975; 1 child, Thomasine A. Walker-Adams, 1 stepchild, Pamela Nava-Whitter. BA in Bus. Adminstrn., U. Md., 1970. cert. sr. exec. edn. program Fed. Exec. Inst., 1975; diploma program sr. mgr.s in govt. John F. Kennedy Sch. Govt., Harvard U., 1992. Personnel staffing specialist FAA, Washington, 1962-65; personnel mgmt. specialist OEO, Washington, 1965-67, Office Sec. Transp., Washington, 1967-70; chief civilian equal opportunity div. USCG Transp. Dept., Washington, 1970-83, dir. civil rights, 1983-96, asst. commandant civil rights, 1996—. Trainee Fed. Exec. Devel. Program, 1975-76. Chmn. fin. com. Christ United Meth. Ch., Washington, 1976-85, chmn. adminstrv. coun., 1985-86; mem. human rels. edn. bd. Dept. Def., 1983-85; mem. Dept. Def. Equal Oportunity Coun.; chmn. placement and counseling com. for industry cluster Paul Quinn Coll.; bd. trustees USCG Acad., 1994—. Served in USAF, 1951-60. Recipient Outstanding Performance award, 1981, 82, 83, Proclamation award City Coun. New Orleans, 1987, Key to City of Franklin, Ky., 1992, Sr. Exec. Svc. Cash Performance award, 1993, 2000, Outstanding Contbns. to Higher Edn. Spl. award Nat. Assn. Equal Opportunity in Higher Edn., 1995, nat. role model innovator award Minority Access, Inc., 2000; named to Nat. Assn. Equal Opportunityin Higher Edn. Registry of Disting. Individuals, 1995. Mem. Am. Mgmt. Assn., NAACP (diamond life membership, Roy Wilkins meritorious svc. award, 1987, Benjamin L. Hooks disting. svc. award, 1993), Sr. Execs. Assn., Washington Urban League (life), U. Md. Alumni Assn. (century club), Nat. Urban League (charter mem. Pres.'s Club, mem. black exec. exch. program, vis. prof. historically black colls. and univs.). Home: 1228 4th St SW Washington DC 20024-2302 Office: 2100 2nd St SW Washington DC 20593-0002

SOMES, JOAN MARIE, emergency nurse; b. St. Paul, Aug. 17, 1952; d. Richard and Jane (Blaiser) Friesen; m. Michael Somes, Nov. 15, 1975. BA in Nursing, Coll. of St. Catherine, St. Paul, 1974; paramedic cert., Inver Hills C.C., Inver Grove Heights, Minn., 1976; MSN, U. Minn., 1989; PhD in Health Adminstrn., Columbia So. U., Orange Beach, Ala., 2002. RN, Minn.; cert. emergency nurse; nat. registered EMT-paramedic; cert. ACLS instr., PALS instr.; cert. TNCC instr.; cert. CATN instr., ENPC instr.; cert. ACLS-EP instr. Paramedic A.L.F. Ambulance, Apple Valley, Minn., 1987-97; charge nurse emergency dept. Divine Redeemer Hosp., South St. Paul, Minn., 1974-94; staff nurse emergency dept. St. Joseph's Hosp., St. Paul, 1994—, emergency dept. educator/staff nurse, 1999—. Instr. numerous local cmty. colls., hosps. and ambulance svcs.; item writer CEN exam., 1994-96, 96-98; edn. specialist Regions Emergency Med. Svcs., 1994—; spkr. in field; co-chair Cornerstones Emergency Nursing Conf., 2000. Author nursing home study courses; consulting editor Man. of Emergency Dept. and Urgent Care Instrns., 2001--; contbr. articles to profl. jour. Grantee Glaxo Pharm. Co., 1989, Health East Found. 1991, 94, 97, 98, recipient Mary Piner award Minn. Emergency Nurses Assn. State Coun. 1994-98. Mem.: Vision Coun. for Profl. Devel., Nat. Emergency Nurses Assn. (chair geriatric com. 2003, mem. exam item writer com. 2003—), Emergency Nurses Assn. (chair state trauma com. 1994—95, sec. treas. Minn. state coun. 1994—95, sec. 1996—98, sec. treas. Minn. state coun. 1997—98, 1999—2000, pres. Greater Twin Cities chpt. 2001—02, state coun. rep. 2001—03, dir./state coun. liaison Greater Twin Cities chpt.).

SOMIT, ALBERT, political educator; b. Chgo., Oct. 25, 1919; s. Samuel and Mary (Rosenblum) S.; m. Leyla D. Shapiro, Aug. 31, 1947; children: Scott H., Jed L. AB, U. Chgo., 1941, PhD, 1947. Prof. polit. philosophy N.Y. U., 1945-65; chmn. dept. polit. sci. State U. N.Y. at Buffalo, 1966-69, exec. v.p., 1970-80; acting pres. SUNY, Buffalo, 1976-77; pres. So. Ill. U., Carbondale, 1980-87, disting. service prof., 1987—. Fellow Netherlands Inst. Advanced Study, 1978-79; Nimitz prof. polit. philosophy U.S. Naval War Coll., 1961-62 Author: (with Joseph Tanenhaus) The Development of American Political Science: From Burgess to Behavioralism, 1967, expanded edit., 1982, (with Tanenhaus) American Political Science: A Profile of A Discipline, 1964, Political Science and the Study of the Future, 1974, Biology and Politics: Recent Explorations, 1976, (with others) The Literature of Biopolitics 1963-1977, 1978, 1980, 1983, 1986, Biopolitics and Mainstream Political Science A Master Bibliography, 1990, (with Wildenmann) Hierarchy and Democracy, 1991, (with Peterson) The Dynamics of Evolution, 1992, (with Wildenmann) The Victorious Incumbent: A Threat to Democracy?, 1994, (with Peterson) The Political Behavior of Older Americans, 1994, Research in Biopolitics: Human Nature and Politics, 1995, Birth Order and Political Behavior, 1996, Recent Explorations in Biology and Politics, 1997, Darwinism, Dominance, and Democracy: The Biological Basis of Authoritarianism, 1997. Served with AUS, 1950-52. Address: 4971 Cindy Ave Carlsbad CA 92008

SOMJEN, GEORGE GUSTAV, physiologist; b. Budapest, Hungary, May 2, 1929; came to U.S., 1962; s. Laszlo and Margit (Ranschburg) S.; m. Eva Herman, 1952 (dec. 1974); children: Monika, Maria, Georgette, Evelyn; m. Amalia Deutsch, 1976. Grad., U. Amsterdam Med. Faculty, 1956; MD, U. N.Z., 1962. Research asst. Pharmaco-therapeutic Lab., U. Amsterdam, 1953-56; lectr., sr. lectr. dept. physiology U. Otago, Dunedin, N.Z., 1956-62; prof. physiology Duke U., Durham, N.C., 1963-2000; prof. emeritus, 2000—. Cons. Nat. Inst. Environ. Health Scis., 1971-75. Author: Sensory Coding in the Mammalian Nervous System, 1972, Neurophysiology: The Essentials, 1983; editor: Neurophysiology Studied in Man, 1972, Mechanisms of Cerebral Hypoxia and Stroke, 1988, Ions in the Brain, 2004. Recipient research grants NIH, 1964-2000. Mem. Am. Physiol. Soc., Soc. Neurosci., Internat. Union Physiol. Sci. (mem. com. edn. 1986-93, chmn., 199397), Internat. Pathophysiol. Soc. (mem. com. edn.), Collegium Europaeum Jenense (corr.) Hungarian Physiol. Soc. (hon.). Office: Duke U Dept Cell Biology Div Physiology PO Box 3011 Durham NC 27710-0001 Office Phone: 919-681-8404. Business E-Mail: g.somjen@cellbio.duke.edu.

SOMMARUGA, CORNELIO, humanitarian services organization administrator, diplomat; b. Rome, Dec. 29, 1932; s. Carlo and Anna Maria (Valagussa) S.; m. Ornella Marzorati; 6 children. LLD, U. Zurich, Switzerland, 1957; D of Polit. Affairs (hon.), U. Fribourg, Switzerland, 1985; D in Internat. Rels. (hon.), U. Minho, Portugal, 1989; D of Medicine (hon.), U. Bologna, Italy, 1991; D in Law (hon.), U. Nice, Sophia-Antipolis, France, 1992, Seoul Nat. U., Republic of Korea, 1992; PhD in Law (hon.), Geneva U., 1997; LHD (hon.), Webster U., 1998. Various diplomatic positions Swiss Confedn.'s Svc., 1960-73; dep. sec. gen. European Free Trade Assn., Geneva, 1973-75; minister plenipotentiary Dept. Pub. Economy, Berne, Switzerland, 1976-77, amb. plenipotentiary, 1977-80, del. Swiss Govt. for Trade Agreements, 1980-83, state sec. external econ. affairs, 1984-86; pres. Internat. Com. Red Cross, Geneva, 1987-99, Assn. Initiatives of Change Internat., Caux, Switzerland, 2002—. Pres. Geneva Internat. Ctr. for Humanitarian Demining, 2000—; chmn. bd. Karl PopperFound., Zug, 2000—. Recipient Presdl. award Tel-Aviv U., 1995, North-South prize Coun. of Europe, 2001, Dr. Jean Mayer Global Citizenship award Tufts U., 2003. Home: 16 chemin Crets-de-Champel CF-1206 Geneva Switzerland Office: GICHD BP 1300 CH-1211 Geneva Switzerland E-mail: c.sommaruga@gichd.ch.

SOMMER, ALFRED, ophthalmologist, medical educator, researcher; b. N.Y.C., Oct. 2, 1942; s. Joseph and Natalie Sommer; m. Jill Abramson Sommer, Sept. 1, 1963; children: Charles Andrew, Marni Jane. BS summa cum laude, Union Coll., 1963; MD, Harvard U., 1967; MHS in Epidemiology, Johns Hopkins U., 1973. Diplomate Am. Bd. Ophthalmology, Nat. Bd. Med. Examiners. Tchg. fellow in medicine Harvard U. Med. Sch., Boston, 1968—69; dir. Nutritional Blindness Prevention Rsch. Program, Bandung, Indonesia, 1976—79; vis. fellow Inst. Ophthalmology U. London, 1979—80; founding dir., Dana Ctr. for Preventive Ophthalmology Johns Hopkins Med. Insts., Balt., 1980—90; assoc. prof. Johns Hopkins U., Balt., 1981—85, prof. ophthalmology, epidemiology and internat. health, 1985—, dean Johns Hopkins Sch. Hygiene and Pub. Health, 1990—. Vis. prof. ophthalmology U. Padjadjaran, Indonesia, 1976—79; cons., advisor Helen Keller Internat., N.Y.C., 1973—; cons., chmn. com. NIH, Bethesda, Md., 1981—; bd. dirs. Internat. Agy. for the Prevention of Blindness, Geneva; cons., com. mem. NAS, Washington, 1989; chmn. program adv. group on blindness prevention WHO, Geneva, 1989—90, com. mem., 1978—90, expert com., 1990—; chmn. steering com. Internat. Vitamin A Cons. Group, Washington, 1975—; pres. Internat. Fedn. of Tissue Banks; chmn. sci. adv. bd. Edna McConnell Clark Found.; mem. Internat. Coun. Ophthalmology; dir. Becton Dickenson Corp., 1998—, Acad. Ednl. Devel., T. Rowe Price Group, 2003—, Internat. Trachoma Initiative Found. of NIH, 2004—; lectr. in field; chair expect cmty. health global governance initiative World Econ. Forum; dir. Lasker Found., 2004—. Author: Epidemiology and Statistics for the Ophthalmologist, 1980, Nutritional Blindness: Xerophthalmia and Keratomalacia, 1982, Vitamin A Deficiency: Health, Survival and Vision, 1995, Detection and Control of Vitamin A Deficiency and Xerophthalmia, 1978, 1982, 1995; chmn. bd. overseers Am. Jours. Epidemiology and Epidemiologic Revs., 1990—, also bd. dirs., —; contbr. articles to profl. jours. Recipient Charles A. Dana Found. award for Pioneering Achievement in Health, 1988, Disting. Svc. award for Contbn. to Vision Care, APHA, 1988, E.V. McCollum Internat. Lectureship in Nutrition, Am. Inst. Nutrition, 1988, Second Ann. Am. Coll. Advancement in Medicine Achievement award in Preventative Medicine, 1990, Disting. Contbn. to World Ophthalmology award, Internat. Fedn. Ophthal. Socs., 1990, Smadel award, Infectious Diseases Soc. Am., 1990, Doyne Meml. award, Oxford, 1995, Albert Lasker award Clin. Rsch., 1997, Helmut Horten Rsch. award, 1997, Gold medal, Singapore Ophthalmology Soc., 1997, Duke Elder Gold medal, Internat. Coun. Ophthalmology, 1998, Prince Mahidol award for contbns. to pub. health, 1998, Bristol-Meyers Nutrition Rsch. award, 2001, Danone Internat. award in nutrition rsch., 2001, Warren Alpert Found. prize, Harvard Med. Sch., 2003, Howe medal, Am. Opthal. Soc., 2003. Mem.: NAS, Acad. Ophthalmology Internat., Internat. Coun. Ophthalmology, Chgo. Ophthal. Soc. (Gifford Meml. award 1997), Pa. Coll. Physicians (de Schweinitz award 1996), Assn. Schs. of Pub. Health (pres.), Internat. Assn. to Prevent Blindness (bd. dirs. 1978—), Nat. Soc. to Prevent Blindness (bd. dirs. 1989), Am. Acad. Ophthalmology (chmn. pub. health com. 1982—88, chmn. Quality of Care/Clin. Guidelines 1986—90, Hon. award 1986, Sr. Hon. award 1997, blindness prevention award 1998, Jackson Meml. lectr. award 1999), Inst. Medicine of NAS (Food and Nutrition bd.). Achievements include first to detail and publish epidemiologic approach disaster assessment; nutritional indices predict subsequent mortality in children, surveillance and containment is effective intervention strategy for controlling smallpox; vitamin A deficiency increases childhood mortality and vitamin A supplementation decreases childhood mortality; nerve fiber layer is valuable diagnostic and prognostic sign of early glaucoma; routine preventive services cost-effective in eye disease; clinical guideline development and importance of outcome assessment; research in epidemiologic and public health approaches to ophthalmology, blindness prevention, and improved health and survival. Office: Johns Hopkins U Bloomberg Sch Pub Health 615 N Wolfe St Rm 1041 Baltimore MD 21205-2103 Fax: 410-955-0121. E-mail: asommer@jhsph.edu.

SOMMER, ANNEMARIE, pediatrician; b. Königsberg, Prussia, Federal Republic Germany, Jan. 1, 1932; came to U.S., 1955; d. Heinrich Otto and Maria Magdalena (Kruppa) S. BA, Wittenberg U., Springfield, Ohio, 1960; MD, Ohio State U., 1964. Diplomate Am. Bd. Pediat., Am. Bd. Med. Genetics. Intern Grant Hosp., Columbus, Ohio, 1964-65; resident in pediat. Children's Hosp., Columbus, 1965-67; NIH fellow in med. genetics, 1968-70; from asst. prof. pediatrics to assoc. prof. Coll. Medicine Ohio State U., Columbus, 1975-97, prof., 1997-99, chief genetics div., 1984-98. Mem. adv. bd. Heinzerling Found., Columbus, 1980—; bd. dirs. Regional Genetics Ctr., Columbus. Contbr. articles to profl. jours. Com. mem. Ohio Prevention MR/DD

Coalition, Columbus, 1987; bd. dirs. Franklin County Bd. Health, Columbus, 1985—. Fellow Am. Acad. Pediatrics, Am. Bd. Med. Genetics, Am. Coll. Med. Genetics (founder); mem. Ctrl. Ohio Pediatric Soc., Midwest Soc. for Pediatric Research, Dublin (Ohio) Hist. Soc. Lutheran. Home: 4700 Brand Rd Dublin OH 43017-9530 Office: Ohio State Coll Medicine Sect Human and Molecular Genetics 700 Childrens Dr Columbus OH 43205-2664

SOMMER, HOWARD ELLSWORTH, textile executive; b. Kansas City, Mo., May 1, 1918; s. Frederick H. and Edna O. (Olsen) S.; m. Sarah Scott McElevey, June 20, 1942; children: Scott E., Paul F. BA magna cum laude, Dartmouth Coll., 1940, degree in engring. (hon.), 1997; MBA, Harvard U., 1942. Cert. mgmt. cons. With Wolf & Co. CPAs, Chgo., 1946-76, chmn. mng. group, 1960-76; dir. Jockey Internat., Kenosha, Wis., 1959—, sr. v.p., chmn. audit com., 1979-89. Author: Procedural Routine for a Business Audit, 1947; also articles. Counsellor, Chgo. chpt. Boy Scouts Am.; vestryman, warden Episcopalian ch. Lt. col. AUS, 1942-46. Decorated Bronze Star; Croix de Guerre with palms; Medaille de la Reconnaissance (France) Mem. ASME, Assn. Cons. Mgmt. Engrs. (cert. of Award 1956, v.p. 1970-72), Inst. Mgmt. Cons. (cert. mgmt. cons., past dir.), Univ. Club (pres., dir. Chgo. chpt. 1959-61), Indian Hill Club, Harvard Bus. Sch. Club (dir. Chgo. chpt. 1958-59), North Shore Cotillion Club, Dartmouth Club, Halter Wildlife Club, Masons (32 degree), Shriners, Phi Beta Kappa, Chi Phi.

SOMMER, JAMES KOCH, lawyer; b. Crawfordsville, Ind., June 5, 1932; s. Edwin John and Sophia Kurth (Koch) Sommer; m. Michael Jean Stewart, Feb. 23, 1963; children: John Stewart, Whitney Suzanne. BA, Yale U., 1954; LLB, Harvard U., 1959. Bar: Ind. 1959, U.S. Supreme Ct. 1970. Assoc. Barnes, Hickam, Pantzer & Boyd, Indpls., 1959—62; founding ptnr. and dir. Sommer Barnard (and certain predecessor firms), Indpls., 1962—2003, of counsel, 2003—. Chmn. Indpls. Regulatory Study Commn., 1992—93. Fellow: Indpls. Bar Found. (Disting.); mem.: ABA, Bar Assn. Seventh Fed. Ct., Ind. Bar Assn. Home: 105 Curacao Ln Bonita Springs FL 34134 Office: Sommer Barnard One Indiana Sq Ste 3500 Indianapolis IN 46240 Office Phone: 317-713-3500.

SOMMER, ROBERT GEORGE, public relations executive; b. N.Y.C., Feb. 6, 1959; s. Ernest Lorge and Donna Anne (Lapin) S.; m. Marjorie Ann Glaser, Oct. 20, 1985; children: Alexander David, William Ernest. BA, Columbia U., 1983; MA, Rutgers U., 1984. Policy analyst EPA, Washington, 1984-85; profl. staff, speechwriter energy and commerce com. U.S. Ho. of Reps., Washington, 1985-87; exec. v.p. MWW/Strategic Communications, East Rutherford, N.J., 1987—. Bd. dirs. Ridgewood Savings Bank of N.J. Contbr. editls. to N.Y. Times. Commr. Environ. Commn. Village of Ridgewood, N.J., 1989—, N.J. Pub. BroadcastingAuthority, 1990-94; chmn. Ridgewood Dem. Com., 1989-93, Eagleton Inst. of Politics Found., 1993-96, Rutgers Univ.; trustee Cmty. Resource Coun., 1990, Gov. Elect Environ. Task Force, Trenton, N.J., Dem. Nat. Com., Washington, 1992—, N.J. Network Found., 1994—; del. Dem. Nat. Conv. 1992; vice chair N.J. Network, Newark, 1992-94; bd. mem. Boy Scouts Am., 1994—, Pub. Affairs Coun., Washington, 1998—; bd. govs. Ramaso Coll., Mahwah, N.J., 1997—. Mem. Pub. Rels. Soc. Am., Nat. Assn. Profl. Environ. Communicators, N.J. Assn. Environ. Commissioners, Trenton, (adv. bd.) 1990—. Jewish. Home: 211 Sunset Ave Ridgewood NJ 07450-2420

SOMMER, WARREN K. anesthesiologist, educator; MD, SUNY, 1965. Diplomate Am. Bd. Anesthesiology. Intern Newark Beth Israel Hosp., 1965—66, resident in anesthesiology, 1966—68; physician dept. anesthesia Robert Wood Johnson U. Hosp., New Brunswick, NJ. Office: Robert Wood Johnson U Hosp One Robert Wood Johnson Pl New Brunswick NJ 08901-1977

SOMMERFELD, JUDE THOMAS, chemical engineer, educator; b. Cin., Ohio, Feb. 4, 1936; s. Henry Anthony and Hilda Catherine (Diffley) S.; m. Rosemary Sniatkowski, May 17, 1958 (div. 1983); children: Loretta, Margaret, Maria, Joanna; m. Elizabeth Ryder, Apr. 18, 1992. B in Chem. Engring., U. Detroit, 1958; MS in Engring., U. Mich., 1960, PhD, 1963. Registered profl. engr., Ga. Sys. engr. Monsanto Co., St. Louis, 1963-66; dir. process engring. BASF-Wyandotte Corp., Mich., 1966-70; assoc. prof. Ga. Inst. Tech., Atlanta, 1970-75, prof., 1975—2002, cons., 2002—. Contbr. numerous articles to profl. jours. Fellow AIChE. Roman Catholic. Avocations: tennis, guitar, classical music, whitewater rafting. Home: 103Falls Dr Westminster SC 29693 Office: Dept Chem Engring Ga Tech U Atlanta GA 30332-0100 Office Phone: 404-894-2873. E-mail: jude.sommerfeld@che.gatech.edu.

SOMMERFELD, MARIANNA, retired social worker, writer; b. Frankfurt, Germany, Jan. 25, 1920; d. Martin and Helene (Schott) S. BA, Smith Coll., 1940; MA, Radcliffe Coll., 1946; MSW, Simmons Coll., 1957. Lic. ind. social worker. Tchr. Latin, German, English Burnham Sch. Girls, Northampton, Mass., 1940-43; German translator Yale Inst. Human Rels., New Haven, 1943-44; tchr. Northfield (Mass.) Sch. Girls, 1944-45; psychiat. social worker McLean Hosp., Belmont, Mass., 1957-59, Gaebler Children's Unit/Met. State Hosp., Waltham, Mass., 1959-62, Boston U./Boston City Hosp., 1962-67, New Eng. Med. Ctr., Boston, 1967-71; pvt. practice Cambridge, Mass., 1962-68; supr. clin. social work Erich Lindemann Mental Health Ctr., Boston, 1971-90; writer, 1976—. Author: Marianna Sommerfeld: Diary of a Single Woman, 1991. Vol. Cambridge Sch., 1993. Mem. NOW, AFL-CIO, Planned Parenthood, Nat. Writers Union, Women's Nat. Book Assn., PEN New Eng. (assoc.).

SOMMERFELDT, JOHN ROBERT, historian, educator; b. Detroit, Feb. 4, 1933; s. Melvin John and Virginia Zita (Gruenheck) S.; m. Patricia Natalie Levinske, Aug. 25, 1956; children: Ann, James, John, Elizabeth. AB, U. Mich., 1954, AM, 1956, PhD, 1960. Instr. history Stanford U., 1958-59; from instr. to prof. Western Mich. U., 1959-78; prof. history U. Dallas, 1978—, chmn. dept. history, 1984-87, univ. pres., 1978-80. Dir. Medieval Inst., Western Mich. U., 1961-76; exec. dir. Inst. Cistercian Studies, 1973-78; dir. Center Contemplative Studies, 1976-78; pres. Cistercian Publs., 1973-79, chmn. bd., 1976-79 Author: The Spiritual Teachings of Bernard of Clairvaux, 1991, Bernard of Clairvaux On the Life of the Mind, 2004, Bernard of Clairvaux On the Spirituality of Relationship, 2004; editor: Studies in Medieval Culture, 12 vols., 1964-78, Studies in Medieval Cistercian History, II, 1977, Cistercian Ideals and Reality, 1978, Simplicity and Ordinariness, 1980, The Chimaera of His Age: Studies in Bernard of Clairvaux, 1980, Abba: Guides to Wholeness and Holiness, East and West, 1981, Erudition at God's Service, 1987, Bernardus Magister, 1992, Studiosorum Speculum, 1993, Studies in the Theology of St. Thomas Aquinas, 1995. Fulbright scholar, 1954-55; Univ. fellow U. Mich., 1956-57. Mem. Medieval Acad. Am., Am. Hist. Assn., Am. Catholic Hist. Assn., Am. Soc. Ch. History, Phi Beta Kappa, Phi Eta Sigma, Phi Kappa Phi. Republican. Roman Catholic. Home: 2809 Warren Cir Irving TX 75062-8938 Office: U Dallas Dept History Irving TX 75062-4736 Office Phone: 972-721-5370. E-mail: jrsommer@udallas.edu.

SOMMERFELT, SOREN CHRISTIAN, foreign affairs, international trade consultant, former Norwegian diplomat, lawyer; b. Oslo, May 9, 1916; s. Soren Christian and Sigrid (Nicolaysen) Sommerfelt; m. Frances Bull, June 27, 1947 (dec. May 12, 2002); 1 child, Cathrine. LLD, Oslo U., 1940. Joined Norwegian Fgn. Svc., 1941; pvt. sec. to fgn. minister, UN sec. gen. Trygve Lie, 1941-44; assigned to UN Secretariat, 1946, Divsn. Refugees' and Displaced Persons, 1st sec. Norwegian Embassy, Copenhagen, 1948-50; counselor Norwegian del. to NATO, 1950-52; dep. head. econ. dept. Norwegian Ministry Fgn. Affairs, 1953-56, head, 1956-60; amb., head Norwegian del. to European Free Trade Assn., Gen. Agreement on Tariffs and Trade (GATT), and UN European Office, 1960-68; chmn. GATT Contracting Parties, 1968; amb. to Fed. Republic Germany, 1968—73; amb. to U.S.A., 1973—79; amb. to Italy, 1979—81; head Norwegian del. negotiating entry into European Communities, 1970-72; counsel Arent, Fox, Kintner, Plotkin & Kahn, Washington, 1982-84; ptnr. cons. firm Washington Resources, Inc., 1984-91; sr. ptnr. Sommerfelt Assocs., Washington, 1992—. Decorated comdr. Order St. Olav, Norway, grand cross Order of Merit, Fed. Republic Germany, grand cross Order of Merit, Italy, comdr. with star Order of North Star, Sweden, comdr. Order of Leopold II, Belgium, knight Order of Falcon, Iceland, knight Order of Dannebrog, Denmark. Mem. Metropolitan Club (Washington), Chevy Chase Club (Md.), Norske Selskab Club (Oslo). Home: PO Box 1183 Middleburg VA 20118-1183 Office: Sommerfelt Assocs 1250 24th St NW Washington DC 20037-1124

SOMMERLAD, ROBERT EDWARD, environmental research engineer; b. Jersey City, Aug. 27, 1937; s. Herman Francis and Helen Rita (Joyce) S.; m. Margaret Doreen Breen, Sept. 9, 1961; children: Sharon K., Michael E., Ellen J. BSME, N.J. Inst. Tech., 1960, MSME, 1963, postgrad., 1965. Devel. engr., rsch. assoc. Foster Wheeler Energy Corp., Livingston, NJ, 1960-71, head air pollution control sect., 1971-74; v.p. contract ops. Foster Wheeler Devel. Corp., Livingston, 1974-84; pres. Enviresponse Inc., Livingston, 1985-86; dir. bus. devel. Energy and Environ. Rsch. Corp., Edison, NJ, 1987-88; cons., 1988-89; dir. environ. bus. devel. Midwest Rsch. Inst., Falls Church, Va., 1989-90; mgr. combustion tech. Rsch.-Cottrell Cos., 1990-92, cons., 1992-93; mktg. dir. PSI Powerserve, Andover, Mass., 1993-94, cons., program mgr., 1994-95; cons. Gas Rsch. Inst., Chgo., 1995-98, GE Energy and Environ. Rsch. Corp., Gurnee, Ill., 1998—2003; pvt. cons., 2003—; cons. Coll. Lake County, Grays Lake, Ill., 2004—. Mem. coal combustion and applications working group U.S. Dept. Energy U. San Diego, 1981-84. Patentee in field. V.p. Cranford (N.J.) Cmty. Pools Parents Assn., 1975-77, 86-87, pres., 1977-79, 84-89; chmn. N.J. Swimming and Diving Conf., Cranford, 1986-89; v.p. Stonebrook Crossings Homeowners Assn., Gurnee, 1998-2000, pres., 2000—; com. for family aquatic ctr. Gurnee Park Dist., 1996-2002; mem. dept. pub. works com. Village of Gurnee, 2002—; mem. St. Paul the Apostle Choir, 2000-, Parish Pastoral Coun., 2003-. Recipient Outstanding Achievement award Westfield YMCA, 1975. Fellow ASME (mem. rsch. com. indsl. and mcpl. waste 1971—, vice chmn. 1972-74, sec. 1987-91, mem. environ. affairs com. 1982-92, mem. dioxin com. 1985-92, mem. bd. performance test codes 1986-97, chmn. boiler-calorimeter com. 1986-89, numerous com. and conf. chairmanships); mem. Air and Waste Mgmt. Assn. (mem. AE-1 com. on particulate and associated acid gases, sec. 1991-94, vice chair 1996), Watchung Amateur Ski Club (mem. exec. bd. 1986-87) (Mountainside, N.J.). Roman Catholic. Home: 1368 Knottingham Dr Gurnee IL 60031-5632 Office Phone: 847-856-1390.

SOMMERS, GEORGE R. lawyer; b. N.Y.C., Jan. 27, 1955; BA, U. So. Fla., 1975; JD, NYU, 1987. Bar: N.J. 1987, U.S. Dist. Ct. N.J. 1987, N.Y. 1988, U.S. Dist. Ct. (all dists.) N.Y. 1988, U.S. Ct. Appeals (3d cir.) 1988, U.S. Ct. Appeals (2d cir.) 1989, U.S. Supreme Ct. 1992. Assoc. Sullivan & Cromwell, N.Y.C., 1987-90; pvt. practice lawyer N.Y.C., 1990—. Pres. Bill of Rights Found., N.Y.C., 1994—. *George Sommers has a diverse litigation practice, ranging from tax law to personal inquiry to civil rights. He was lead counsel in several high profile class actions. His successes in civil rights actions are the subject of numerous law review notes and commentary including ones in the "Harvard Law Review," and the basis for several moot court competitions including one at the Yale Law School. See, e.g., Loper v. New York City Police Dept., 999 F.2d 699 (2d Cir. 1993).* Seidler scholar NYU Sch. Law, N.Y.C., 1985. Mem. Hoboken Bar Assn. (pres. 1994). Jewish. Avocations: sailing, chess. Office: 51 Newark St Hoboken NJ 07030-4548 Office Phone: 212-709-8389., 201-656-6575.

SOMMERS, ROBERT THOMAS, editor, publisher, author; b. Balt., Aug. 6, 1926; s. Thomas Michael and Pearl Florence (Glendenning) S.; m. Helen Louise Ray, Oct. 19, 1952; children— Thomas Michael II, Patricia Ray. BS, U. Md., College Park, 1950. Reporter Evening Sun, Balt., 1950-62; reporter Evening Star, Washington, 1962-66; editor U.S. Golf Assn. Jour., N.Y.C., 1966-72, Far Hills, N.J., 1972-92. Author: The Oxford Book of Golf Anecdotes, 1995, 2d edit., 2004, The U.S. Open: Golf's Ultimate Challenge, 1987, 2nd edit., 1996, Bobby Jones in Chapman's Library of Golf, 1992; co-author: Great Shots, 1989; contbr. articles to profl. jours. Served with U.S. Coast Guard, 1944-46, PTO. Mem. Golf Writers Assn. Am., Assn. Golf Writers Gt. Britain, Authors Guild, Plainfield (N.J.) Country Club, Ballybunion Golf Club (Ireland), Kingston Heath Golf Club (Australia), Royal and Ancient Golf Club of St. Andrews (Scotland), The Legacy Golf and Tennis Club (Fla.). Republican. Episcopalian. Avocations: reading, golf, music. Home and Office: 8083 Spendthrift Ln Port Saint Lucie FL 34986-3122 E-mail: r.sommers@worldnet.att.net.

SOMMERS, STEPHEN, film director, scriptwriter, film producer; b. Indianapolis, IN; Motion picture dir., writer, prodr. Writer, dir. Catch Me If You Can, 1989, The Adventures of Huck and Finn, 1993, The Jungle Book, 1994, Deep Rising, 1998, The Mummy, 1999; The Mummy Returns, 2001; writer, prodr. Tom and Huck, 1995, The Scorpion King, 2002; writer, prodr., dir., Van Helsing, 2004; prodr. T.V. movie Oliver Twist, 1997; dir. Terror Eyes, 1989; writer Gunmen, 1994. Office: c/o Jim Wiatt William Morris Agy 151 El Camino Dr Beverly Hills CA 90212*

SOMMERS, WILLIAM PAUL, management consultant, research and development institute executive, think-tank executive; b. Detroit, July 22, 1933; s. William August and Mary Elizabeth (Baietto) S.; m. Josephine A. Sommers; children: William F., Clare M., John C. Hughes, Joanna M. Weems, Russell L. Hughes. BSE (scholar), U. Mich., 1955, MSE, 1956, PhD (Riggs fellow, Texaco fellow, Univ. fellow), 1961. Rsch. assoc. U. Mich. Inst. Sci. and Tech., Ann Arbor, 1958-61; chief chem. propulsion space and missile sys. Martin Marietta Corp., Balt., 1956-58, 61-63; v.p. Booz, Allen & Hamilton, Inc., Bethesda, Md., 1963-70, pres. Tech. Mgmt. Group, 1973-79, sr. v.p., 1979-92; exec. v.p. Iameter, Inc., San Mateo, Calif., 1992-94; pres., CEO SRI Internat., Menlo Park, Calif., 1994-98, ret., 1998. Bd. dirs. Deutsche Scudder Fin. Svcs., Evergreen Solar, Inc., Pressure Sys., Inc., Gukenheimer Enterprises, Zassi Med., H2 Gen. Contbr. articles to profl. jours., also chpt. in book. Pres. Washington chpt. U. Mich. Alumni Club, 1970-71; v.p. Wildwood manor Citizens Assn., 1968-70; chief Adventure Guide program YMCA, 1971-72; bd. visitors Coll. Engring. U. Calif., Davis; mem. nat. adv. bd. Coll. Engring. U. Mich.; mem. conf. bd. Internat. Coun. on Innovation and Tech. Mem.: Met. Club (D.C.), Ponte Vedra Inn and Country Club, Wianno Yacht Club, Marsh Landing Country Club, Willow Bend Country Club, Pi Tau Sigma, Tau Beta Pi, Sigma Xi. Republican. Roman Catholic. E-mail: williamp.sommers@comcast.net.

SOMMESE, ANDREW JOHN, mathematics professor; b. N.Y.C., May 3, 1948; s. Joseph Anthony and Frances (Lia) S.; m. Rebecca Rooze DeBoer, June 7, 1971; children: Rachel, Ruth. BA in Math., Fordham U., 1969; PhD in Math., Princeton U., 1973. Gibbs instr. Yale U., New Haven, 1973-75; asst. prof. Cornell U., Ithaca, N.Y., 1975-79; assoc. prof. U. Notre Dame, Ind., 1979-83, prof. of math., 1983—, chair dept. math., 1988-92, Vincent J. Duncan and Annamarie Micus Duncan chair math., 1994—. Mem. Inst. for Advanced Study, Princeton, N.J., 1975-76; guest prof. U. Bonn, Germany, 1978-79; guest rschr. Max Planck Inst. for Math., Bonn, 1992-93; cons. GM Rsch., Warren, Mich., 1986-97. Editor: Manuscripta Mathematica jour., 1986-93, Advances in Geometry, 2000;mem. editl. bd. Milan Jour. Math., 2002; contbr. articles to profl. publs. Recipient Rsch. award for Sr. U.S. Scientists Alexander Von Humboldt found., 1993; A.P. Sloan Found. rsch. fellow, 1979. Mem. Am. Math. Soc., Soc. for Indsl. and Applied Math., Phi Beta Kappa. Office: U Notre Dame Dept Math Notre Dame IN 46556 E-mail: sommese@nd.edu.

SOMOGYI, JENNIE, dancer; b. Easton, Pa. Studied with Madame Nina Youshkevitch; student, Sch. Am. Ballet. Apprentice N.Y.C. Ballet, 1993—94, mem. corps de ballet, 1994—98, soloist, 1998—2000, prin., 2000—. Dancer (ballets) The Nutcracker, Allegro Brillante, Apollo, Tschaikovskys Pas De Deux, Glass Pieces, The Sleeping Beauty, Swan Lake, Quartet for Strings, Appalachia Waltz, Urban Dances, Swerve Poems, Polyphonia. Recipient Mae L. Wien award, The Princess Grace Found. award, Martin E. Segal award. Office: NYC Ballet NY State Theatre 20 Lincoln Ctr Plz New York NY 10023-6913

SOMSEN, HENRY NORTHROP, retired lawyer; b. New Ulm, Minn., Aug. 12, 1909; s. Henry N. and Meta (Koch) S.; m. Anne Elizabeth Duncan, Sept. 12, 1936 (dec.); children: Pennell Anne, Stephen Duncan. BA, U. Minn., 1932, JD, 1934. Bar: Minn. 1934. Practice law, New Ulm, 1934-85; ptnr. Somsen, Dempsey, Johnson & Somsen, 1934-40, Somen Dempsey & Somsen, 1940-46, Somsen & Somsen, 1946-55; sole practice, 1955-64; ptnr. Somsen & Dempsey, 1965-71, Somsen Dempsey & Schade, 1971-85, of counsel, 1985—. Bd. editors U. Minn. Law Rev., 1932-33. Trustee Minn. State Parks Found., 1967-77; bd. dirs. Minn. Council State Parks, 1956—, pres., 1974-75; bd. dirs., pres. New Ulm Community Concert Assn., 1947-85; bd. dirs. Union Hosp., New Ulm, 1959-77, Highland Homes, Inc., 1970-79, New Ulm Meml. Found., 1958-79; bd. dirs. New Ulm Industries Inc., 1952-85, pres., 1968-77; bd. dirs. New Ulm Industries Found., Inc., 1953-85, pres., 1968-77, bd. dirs. 1953-83, chmn., 1958-83 Farmers and Mchts. Bank, New Ulm, Minn.; bd. dirs. Klossner State Bank, Minn., 1947-84, State Bond and Mortgage Co., 1950-80, Am. Artstoone Co., 1955-84, others; mem. City Charter Commns., 1940, 51, 66, pres., 1966. Served from pvt. to capt. JAG, AUS, 1943-46. Mem. ABA, Minn. Bar Assn., Am. Judicature Soc., Am. Arbitration Assn. (panel of arbitrators 1967-85), Mpls. Club, Masons, Rotary, Shriners, Psi Upsilon, Phi Delta Phi. Episcopalian. Home: 211 2d St NW Apt 1907 Rochester MN 55901-3101

SONDE, THEODORE IRWIN, lawyer; b. N.Y.C., Jan. 7, 1940; s. Martin and Anne (Greenbaum) S.; m. Susan Kolisch, Sept. 10, 1964; children: Andrea Martine, David Ian. BA, CCNY, 1961; LLB, NYU, 1964; LLM, Georgetown U., 1967. Bar: N.Y. 1964, D.C. 1978, U.S. Supreme Ct. With SEC, Washington, 1964-80, asst. gen. counsel Office Gen. Counsel, 1970-74, assoc. dir. divsn. enforcement, 1974-80; dir. Office Enforcement, FERC, Washington, 1980-81; mem. firm Cole, Corette & Abrutynn, 1982-90, Dechert, Price & Rhodes, 1990—2002, Crowell & Moring, Washington, 2002—. Adj. prof. Georgetown U. Law Sch. 1977-95, George Washington U. Nat. Law Ctr., 1976-82. Contbr. articles to law jours. Office: Crowell & Moring 1001 Pennsylvania Ave NW Washington DC 20004 E-mail: tsonde@crowell.com.

SONDEL, PAUL MARK, pediatric oncologist, educator; b. Milw., Aug. 14, 1950; s. Robert F. and Audrey J. (Dworkus) S.; m. Sherie Ann Katz, Jan. 1, 1973; children: Jesse Adam, Beth Leah, Elana Rose, Jodi Zipporah. BS with honors, U. Wis., 1971, PhD in Genetics, 1975; MD magna cum laude, Harvard Med. Sch., Boston, 1977. Diplomate Nat. Bd. Med. Examiners, Am. Bd. Pediatrics; lic. physician, Wis. Postdoctoral rsch. fellow Harvard Med. Sch., Boston, 1975-77; intern in pediatrics U. Minn. Hosp., Mpls., 1977-78; resident in pediatris U. Wis. Hosp. and Clinics, Madison, 1978-80; asst. prof. pediatrics, human oncology and genetics U. Wis., Madison, 1980-84, assoc. prof., 1984-86, prof. pediatrics, human oncology and genetics, 1987—, head divsn. pediatric hematology/oncology, program leader, 1990—; assoc. dir. U Wisc. Cancer Ctr., 1996-99. Sub-fellow pediat. oncology; Midwest Children's Cancer Ctr., Milw., 1980; vis. scientist dept. cell biology Weizmann Inst. Sci., Rehovot, Israel, 1987, 2000; chmn. immunology com. Children's Cancer Group 1990-2001; cancer ctr. rev. com. Nat. Cancer Inst., 1997-2000. Sr. editor Clin. Cancer Rsch., 1996-99; mem. editl. bd. Jour. Immunology, 1985-87, Jour. Nat. Cancer Inst., 1987—, Jour. Biol. Response Modifiers, 1990—, BLOOD, 1992—, Natural Immunity, 1992—; contbr. articles to Jour. Exptl. Medicine, Jour. Immunology, Cellular Immunology, Immunol. Revs., Med. Pediatric Oncology, Wis. State Med. Jour., Jour. Biol. Response Modifiers, Jour. Pediatrics, Jour. Clin. Oncology, Jour. Clin. Investigation, and others. State of Wis. Regents scholar, 1968; J.A. and G.L. Hartford Found. fellow, 1981-84. Mem. Am. Assn. Immunologists, Am. Assn. Clin. Histocompatibility Typing, Am. Fedn. Clin. Rsch., Am. Soc. Pediatric Hematology/Oncology, Am. Assn. Cancer Rsch., Am. Soc. Transplant Physicians, Am. Soc. Clin. Oncology, Am. Acad. Pediatrics, Leukemia Soc. Am. (bd. dirs. Wis. chpt. 1987-90 Achievements include patent for Typing Leukocyte Antigens; research on clinical and immunological effects of human recombinant Interleukin-2 and monoclonal antibodies. Home: 1114 Winston Dr Madison WI 53711-3161 Office: U Wis K4/448 Clin Sci Ctr 600 Highland Ave Madison WI 53792-3284 Office Phone: 608-263-9069. Business E-Mail: pmsondel@facstaff.wisc.edu.

SONDERBY, SUSAN PIERSON, federal judge; b. Chicago, May 15, 1947; d. George W. and Shirley L. (Eckstrom) Pierson; m. James A. De Witt, June 14, 1975 (dec. 1978); m. Peter R. Sonderby, Apr. 7, 1990. AA, Joliet Jr. Coll., Joliet, Ill., 1967; BA, U. Ill., 1969; JD, John Marshall Law Sch., 1973. Bar: Ill., 1973; U.S. Dist. Ct. (cen. and so. dists.) Ill., 1978,; U.S. Dist. Ct. (no. dist.) Ill., 1984; U.S. Ct. Appeals (7th Cir.), 1984. Assoc. O'Brien, Garrison, Berard, Kusta, and De Witt, Joliet, Ill., 1973-75, ptnr., 1975-77; asst. atty. gen. consumer protection div., litig. sect. Office of the Atty. Gen., Chgo., 1977-78, asst. atty. gen., chief consumer protection divsn. Springfield, Ill., 1978-83; U.S. trustee (no. dist.) Ill. Chgo., 1983-86; judge U.S. Bankruptcy Ct. (no. dist.) Ill., Chgo., 1986—, chief fed. bankruptcy judge, 1998—2002. Mem. law faculty Fed. Jud. Tng. Ctr., Ill., Practicing Law Inst., Ill., U.S. Dept. Justice, Ill., Nat. Bankruptcy Inst., Ill., Ill. Continuing Edn.; spl. asst. atty. gen., Ill., 1972—78; adj. faculty De Paul U. Coll. Law, Chgo., 1986; past mem. U.S. Trustee adv. com., Ill.; consumer adv. coun. Fed. Res. Bd., Ill.; past sec. of State Fraudulent I.D. com. Dept. of Ins. Task Force on Improper Claims Practices, Ill.; former chair pers. rev. bd., mem. task force race and gender bias, U.S. Dist. Ct.; jud. conf. planning com. 7th Cir. Jud. Conf.; former mem. Civil Justice Reform Act Adv. Com.; mem. Adminstrv. Office of the U.S. Cts. Bankruptcy Judges Adv. Group; former mem. Ct. Security com.; mem. Adminstrv. Office of the U.S. Cts. Budget and Fin. Coun. Contbr. articles to profl. jour. Mem. Fourth Presbyn. Ch., Art Inst. Chgo.; past mem. Westminster Presbyn. Ch., Chgo. Coun. of Fgn. Rels.; past bd. dirs. Land of Lincoln Coun. Girl Scouts U.S.; past mem. individual guarantors com. Goodman Theatre, Chgo.; past chair clubs and orgns. Sangamon County United Way Capital campaign; past bd. dirs., chair house rules com. and legal subcom. Lake Point Tower; past mem. Family Svc. Ctr., Aid to Retarded Citizens, Henson Robinson Zoo. Named Young Career Woman, Bus. and Profl. Women, One of Ten Outstanding Bankruptcy Judges, Turnarounds and Workouts, 2002; recipient Spl. Achievement Award, Dept. Justice, 1984, Disting. Svc. Alumni Award, Joliet Jr. Coll., 1987, Disting. Alumni Award, John Marshall Law Sch., 1988, Dir. Award, Exec. Office U.S. Trustee, Leadership Award, Internat. Orgn. Women Exec., Outstanding Svc. to Bench, Am. Bankruptcy Inst., 1990. Master: Abraham Lincoln Marovitz Inn of Ct. (former pres., membership com.); fellow: Am. Coll. Bankruptcy (circuit admissions com.); mem.: ATLA, Comml. Law League Am. (former exec. coun. mem., bankruptcy and insolvency sect., coord. with nat. conf. bankruptcy judges com.), Nat. Conf. Bankruptcy Judges (co-chair ednl. program com. conf. 2001, liaison with bankruptcy rev. commn. com.), Bar Assn. (7th cir.) (former treas., judicial conf. planning com.), Am. Bankruptcy Inst. (bd. dirs. Chgo. chpt.), Fed. Bar Assn., Chgo. Archtl. Found., John Marshall Law Sch. Alumni Assn. (bd. dirs.), Nordic Law Club (past legis. com.), Lawyers Club Chgo. (hon.). Avocations: travel, flying, interior decorating. Office: US Bankruptcy Ct 219 S Dearborn St Ste 638 Chicago IL 60604-1702

SONDEREGGER, THEO BROWN, psychology educator; b. Birmingham, Ala., May 31, 1925; d. Ernest T. and Vera M. (Sillox) Brown; children: Richard Paul, Diane Carol, Douglas Robert. BS, Fla. State U., 1946; MA in Chemistry, U. Nebr., 1948; MA in Exptl. Psychology, 1960; PhD in Clin. Psychology, U. Nebr., 1965. Lic. psychologist, Nebr., Calif; clin. lic., cert. Nebr. Asst. prof. U. Nebr. Med. Ctr., Omaha, 1965-71, Nebr. Wesleyan U., Lincoln, 1965-68, U. Nebr., Lincoln, 1968-71, assoc. prof., 1971-76, prof., 1976-94; ret., 1994; prof. emeritus, 1995—. Vol. assoc. prof. U. Nebr. Med. Ctr., 1972-77, courtesy prof. med. psychology, 1977-95. Editor: Nebr. Symposium on Motivation, 1974, 84, 91, Problems of Perinatal Drug Dependence: Research and Clinical Implications, 1986, Neurobehavioral Toxicology and Teratology vol. 8, 1988-89, Problems of Perinatal Drug Dependence, 1979, 82, 84, Feminist Therapy Interchange, 1988-89, 91, Perinatal Substance Abuse: Research and Clinical Implications, 1992, Agendas for Aging, 1994-97. Mem. grant rev. coms. Nat. Inst. Drug Abuse, 1983-84, 85, 91-94. Tribute to Women award Lincoln YMCA, 1985, named Outstanding Rsch. Scientist Nebr. Chpt. Sigma Xi, 1991, Outstanding Contbn. to Status of Women, U N-L Chancellors Commn. on Status of Women, 1994, Pound Howard Disting. Career Achievement award, 1996. Fellow: AAAS, Am. Psychol. Soc., Am. Psychol. Assn.; mem.: Region V Adv. Coun. on Drugs, Fetal Alcohol (bd. dir. child guidance ctr. 1997—2002, bd. dir. UN-L emeriti assoc. 1999—2001), Soc. Neuroscis., Nebr. Psychol. Assn. (pres. 1972), Internat. Soc. Psychoneuroendocrinology,

Internat. Soc. Devel. Psychobiology, Midwestern Psychol. Assn., Advanced Feminist Therapy Inst., Altrusa YWCA, Sigma Xi (pres. 1986), Phi Beta Kappa (sec. Nebr. chpt. 1974). Avocations: painting, photography.

SONDERS, ELIZABETH ANN, diversified financial services company executive; BA in Econs. and Polit. Sci., U. Del., 1986; MBA in Fin., Fordham U., 1990. Mng. dir., mem. mgmt. com. Avatar Assocs.; mng. dir., mem. investment policy com. U.S. Trust divsn. Charles Schwab, 1999—2002; sr. mng. dir., chief investment strategist Charles Schwab & Co., N.Y.C., 2002—. Named to, Crain's N.Y. Bus. "40 under 40", 2004. Office: Charles Schwab 1211 Avenue of the Americas New York NY 10036*

SONDERS, LAWRENCE J. obstetrician, gynecologist; s. Max S. and Lily Sonders; m. Susan Lipnitzky, Apr. 2, 1935; children: Mark S., Jane L. BA, Bklyn. Coll., 1952. Cert. physician N.Y., 1956. Attending physician dept. ob-gyn. White Plains Hosp., NY, 1962—. Dir. dept. ob-gyn. White Plains Hosp. Med. Ctr., 1970—77. Capt. Med. Corps U.S. Army, 1961—63. Mem.: Soc. Advancement Humanistic Studies Medicine (bd. dirs. 2002—), Phi Beta Kappa. Avocations: ship model making, photography, skiing, travel, scuba diving.

SONDHEIM, STEPHEN JOSHUA, composer, lyricist; b. NYC, Mar. 22, 1930; s. Herbert and Janet (Fox) Sondheim. BA, Williams Coll., 1950. Composer, lyricist. Vis. prof. comtemporary theatre Oxford U., England. Lyricist West Side Story, 1957 (Tony award), Gypsy, 1959, Do I Hear a Waltz?, 1965, music and lyrics A Funny Thing Happened on the Way to the Forum, 1962, Anyone Can Whistle, 1964, Evening Primrose, 1966, Company, 1970 (Tony award, 1971), Follies, 1971 (Tony award, 1972), A Little Night Music, 1973 (Tony award, 1973), The Frogs, 1974, Pacific Overtures, 1976, Sweeney Todd, 1979 (Tony award, 1979), Merrily We Roll Along, 1981, Sunday in the Park with George, 1984 (Pulitzer prize, 1985), Into the Woods, 1987 (Tony award, 1988), Assassins, 1991, Passion, 1994 (Tony award, 1994), Bounce, 2003, (incidental music) Girls of Summer, 1956, Invitation to a March, 1961, Twigs, 1971, additional lyrics Candide, 1973, (anthologies) Side by Side by Sondheim, 1976, Marry Me a Little, 1981, You're Gonna Love Tomorrow, 1983, Putting It Together, 1993, (film scores) Stavisky, 1974, Reds, 1981; composer: songs for film Dick Tracy, 1990 (Acad. award); co-author: (films) The Last of Sheila, 1973, Birdcage, 1996, Getting Away with Murder, 1996. Recipient Creative Arts medal, Brandeis U., 1982, Grammy awards, 1970, 1973, 1975, 1979, 1984, 1988, Kennedy Ctr. Honor for Lifetime Achievement, 1993, Nat. medal of arts, NEA, 1997, Praemium Imperiale, 2000. Mem.: Am. Acad. and Inst. Arts and Letters.

SONDIK, EDWARD J. health science administrator; BEE, MEE, U. Conn.; PhD in Elec. Engring., Stanford U. Faculty dept. engring econ. sys. Stanford U.; acting dir. Nat. Cancer Inst., acting dept. dir., dept. dir. divsn. cancer prevention and control, assoc. dir. surveillance program; dir. Nat. Ctr. Health Stats., Ctrs. Disease Control Prevention, Hyattsville, Md., 1996—. Sr. adv. health stats. Sec. Health Human Svcs. Office: Dept Health Human Svcs Nat Ctr Health Stats Presidential Bldg 6525 Belcrest Rd Rm 1140 Hyattsville MD 20782-2003*

SONE, HIRO, chef, restaurant owner, writer; b. Ichihasama, Japan; m. Lissa Doumani. Grad., Ecole Technique Hoteliere Tsuji, Osaka, Japan. From dishwasher to sous chef Italian restaurant, Tokyo; from mem. staff to head chef Spago, L.A., former sous chef Tokyo; co-owner, chef Terra, St. Helena, Calif., 1988—. Author (with Lissa Doumani): Terra, Cooking from the Heart of the Napa Valley, 2001. Nominee Am. Express Best Chef, Calif., James Beard Found., 2001; recipient James Beard Best Chef Calif. award, 2003. Office: Terra 1345 Railroad Ave Saint Helena CA 94574

SONEGO, IAN G. assistant attorney general; b. Louisville, May 27, 1954; s. Angelo and Zella Mae (Causey) S. BA in Polit. Sci. with high honors, U. Louisville, 1976, JD, 1979. Bar: Ky. 1979, U.S. Dist Ct. (ea. dist.) Ky. 1980, U.S. Dist. Ct. (we. dist.) Ky. 1989, U.S. Ct. Appeals (6th cir.) 1989, U.S. Supreme Ct. 1990. Asst. atty. Office Commonwealth's Atty. Pike County, Pikeville, Ky., 1980, sr. asst. atty., 1988-89; assoc. John Paul Runyon Law Firm, Pikeville, 1981-87; asst. atty. gen. Office Atty. Gen., Frankfort, Ky., 1989—. Lectr. criminal law Ky. Bar Assn., Jenny Wiley Park, 1981, Ky. Prosecutors Confs., 1989, 93; mem. Atty. Gen.'s task force child sexual abuse, 1992-94, Nat. Conf. on Domestic Violence, 1996. Contbg. editor Ky. Prosecuter Newsletter, 1991—. Recipient Kesslman award, U. Louisville, 1975, Bd. trustee award, 1979, Outstanding Prosecutor award, Ky. Atty., Award Outstanding Advocacy, Assn. Govt. Attys. in Capital Litigation, 2001. Mem.: Ky. Commonwealth's Attys. Assn. (hon.; lectr. 1987, 90, chmn. com. ethics 1984—86, bd. dirs. 1983—85, Spl. award 1987). Office: Office Atty Gen Criminal Appellate Divsn 1024 Capital Center Dr Frankfort KY 40601-8204 E-mail: isonego@law.state.ky.us.

SONENBERG, JACK, artist; b. Toronto, Ont., Can., Dec. 28, 1925; s. Solomon and Leah (Saltzman) S.; m. Phoebe Helman, June 7, 1949; 1 dau., Maya. Student, N.Y. U., 1949; B.F.A., Washington U., 1951. Mem. faculty dept. art Queens Coll., 1970-72, Bklyn. Coll., 1972, Bklyn. Coll. (Sch. of Visual Arts), 1962-73; mem. faculty Pratt Inst., Bklyn., 1968—; chmn. painting and drawing dept. Pratt Inst. Bklyn., 1973—. One-man shows, Byron Gallery, N.Y.C., 1965, 68, Hampton Inst., 1968, U. No. Iowa, 1969, Grand Rapids (Mich.) Art Mus., 1968, Flint Inst. Arts, 1972, Fischbach Gallery, N.Y.C., 1973, 55 Mercer Gallery, N.Y.C., 1980, group shows include, Whitney Mus., 1967, 73, Mus. Modern Art, 1974, Art Inst. Chgo., 1975, Pratt Inst., Bklyn., 1980, Rutgers U., N.J., 1980, Nat. Gallery, Washington, 1980, Moscow Artists Union, 1989; group shows include Painting Self-Evident, Piccolo Spolete, 1992; represented in permanent collections, Guggenheim Mus., Whitney Mus., Washington U., Met. Mus., Bradley U., Nat. Gallery Can., W.Va. U. Ford Found. grantee, 1966; Guggenheim Found. grantee, 1973, N.Y. State CAPS, 1973-76, Nat. Endowment Arts grantee (sculpture), 1984-85, N.Y. Found. for the Arts grantee (painting) 1989. Office: Pratt Inst Sch Art and Design Brooklyn NY 11205

SONENSHEIN, ABRAHAM LINCOLN, microbiology educator; b. Paterson, N.J., Jan. 13, 1944; s. Israel Louis and Celia (Rabinowitz) S.; m. Gail Entner, Jan. 28, 1967; children: Dina Miriam, Adam Israel. AB, Princeton U., 1965; PhD, MIT, 1970. Postdoctoral fellow U. Paris, Orsay, France, 1970-72; asst. prof. Tufts U., Boston, 1972-78, assoc. prof., 1978-82; prof. microbiology Tufts U. Sch. Medicine, Boston, 1982—. Vis. prof. U. Paris, 1998. Rsch. grantee NIH, 1972—; fellow Am. Cancer Soc., 1970-72. Mem. AAAS, Am. Soc. for Microbiology, Am. Acad. Microbiology, Fedn. Am. Scientists, Sigma Xi. Office: Tufts U Dept Molecular & Microbiol 136 Harrison Ave Dept & Boston MA 02111-1800*

SONFIELD, ROBERT LEON, JR., lawyer; b. Houston, Oct. 28, 1931; s. Robert Leon and Dorothy Harriett (Huber) S.; 1 dau., Sheree. BA, U. Houston, 1956, LLB, JD, 1959; PhD (hon.), U. Eastern Fla., 1962; LLD (hon.), London Inst. Applied Rsch., 1973; cert. fed. taxation, NYU, 1973; cert. securities regulation, Harvard U., 1983. Bar: Tex. 1959, U.S. Supreme Ct. 1959, U.S. Dist. Ct. Tex. 1960, U.S. Tax Ct. 1960, U.S. Ct. Appeals 1960, U.S. Ct. Claims 1974. Mng. dir. Sonfield & Sonfield, Houston, 1959—. Mem. nat. adv. coun. Nat. Fedn. Ind. Bus. Author: Corporate Financing by Sale of Securities to the Public, 1969, Mergers and Acquisitions, 1970, Student Rights, 1971, The Limited Partnership as a Vehicle for Real Estate Investment, 1971, Integration of Partnership Offerings, 1974, The Grantor Trust Rules After The Tax Reform Act of 1986, Incentive Equity Program, Corporate Name Protection Along With Name Registration, A Guide to SEC Corporate Filing, Organizational Professionals' Residual Litigation and Investment Strategy, Comparing California, Delaware and Nevada: Corporate Laws in Light of California Corporations Code Section 2115 and Offering of Unregistered Securities Only to Accredited Investors, Disclosure Policies, Practices and Procedures For Public Companies, Regulation of Franchises, How to Become a Publicly Held Company Via the Registered Ditribution of a Percentage of Your Company's Stock to Shareholders, numerous others. Recipient St. John Garwood award, 1957, Frio-Finnegan Outstanding Alumnus award, 1970-71, citation for outstanding contbn. to legal profession, 1971. Mem. Am. Tax Lawyers Assn. (pres.), Lawyers Soc. Houson, Am. Judicature Soc., ABA, Tex. Bar Assn. (dist. com. on admission to state bar, chmn. clients security fund com.), Houston Bar Assn. (com. chmn. coun., tax sect.), Tex. Equal Access to Justice Found., Houston Bar Found., Real Estate Securities and Syndication Inst., Huguenot Soc. of London, Order Stars and Bars, SAR, Sons Confederate Vets., Mil. Order World Wars, Mil. and Hospitaller Order St. Lazarus of Jerusalem, Knightly Assn. St. George the Martyr, Smithsonian Assocs., Houston Heritage Soc., Houston Mus. Fine Arts, Newcomen Soc. N.Am., Phi Delta Phi, Delta Sigma Phi, Met. Club (N.Y.C.), Argyle Club (San Antonio), Houston Club, Houstonian Club. Office: Sonfield & Sonfield 770 S Post Oak Ln Houston TX 77056-6665 Office Phone: 713-877-8333. E-mail: robert@sonfeld.com.

SONG, CHUNSHAN, chemist, chemical engineer, educator; b. Shijiazhuang, Hebei, China, Feb. 11, 1961; came to U.S., 1989; s. Jingsheng Song and Fengxian He; m. Lu Sun, Jan. 10, 1985; children: Lucy J., James J. BS in Chem. Engring., Dalian (China) U. Tech., 1982; diploma in Japanese, N.E. Shifan U., Changchun, China, 1983; MS in Applied Chemistry, Osaka (Japan) U., 1986, PhD in Applied Chemistry, 1989. Postdoc. rsch. assoc. Osaka Gas Co., 1989; rsch. assoc. Pa. State U., University Park, 1989-94, asst. prof. fuel sci., 1994-97, assoc. prof., 1997—2003, assoc. dir. lab. hydrocarbon process chemistry, 1995-98, dir. applied catalysis in energy lab., 1998—2003, prof., 2003—, dir. clean fuels and catalysis program, 2003—. Editor: Catalytic Conversion of Polycyclic Aromatic Hydrocarbons, 1996, Advances in Catalysis and Processes for Heavy Oil Conversion, 1998, Shape-Selective Catalysis, 1999, Catalysis in Fuel Processing and Environmental Protection, 1999, Chemistry of Diesel Fuels, 2000, CO2 Conversion and Utilization, 2002, Environmental Challenges and Greenhouse Gas Control for Fossil Fuel Utilization in the 21st Century, 2002, Fuel Processing for Fuel Cells, 2002; contbr. articles to Catalysis Today, Energy Fuels, Catalysis Letters, Fuel, Fuel Processing Tech., Ind. Engring. Chem. Rsch., Applied Catalysis, Studies in Surface Sci. and Catalysis, Chemtech. Agy. Recipient Outstanding Svc. award, Internat. Pitts. Coal Conf., 2001; fellow Agy. Ind. Sci. Tech. fellow, Japan, 1995, NEDO, Japan, 1998. Mem.: Am. Chem. Soc. (co-chair several symposia 1995—, program com. petroleum chemistry divsn. 1996—, exec. com. 1997—, chmn. website com. 1997—2000, chmn. program for fuel chem. divsn., exec. com. of fuel chem. divsn. 2000—, chair-elect 2003), AIChE, AAAS. Achievements include development of concept for designing sulfur-resistant noble-metal catalysts, tri-reforming process concept for production of synthesis gas using waste flue gas; discovery of new method for preparing highly active molybdenum sulfide catalysts by using water and Mo precursor; established several new shape-selective catalytic reactions of polycyclic hydrocarons, including ring-shift isomerization, conformational isomerization, shape-selective alkylation, and shape-selective hydrogenation; established the features and reaction pathways of thermal degradation and stabilization of coal-derived and petroleum-derived aviation jet fuels in pyrolytic regime; established a new desulfurization process concept of selective adsorption for removing sulfur (SARS). Office: Pa State U Energy and Geo-Environ Engring Dept Fuel Sci Program 206 Hosler Bldg University Park PA 16802-5001 E-mail: csong@psu.edu.

SONG, JOSEPH, pathologist, educator; b. Pyong Yang, Korea, May 11, 1927; s. Ha Ju and Hwa Soon (Koh) S.; m. Kumsan Ryu, Apr. 12, 1958; children: Patricia, Michael, Jeff. MD, Seoul (Korea) U. Sch. Medicine, 1950; MS in Pathology, U. Tenn., Memphis, 1956; MD, U. Ark. Med. Sch., Little Rock, 1965. Diplomate Am. Bd. Pathology. Pathologist in charge State Cancer Detection Survey, Providence, 1956-59; assoc. pathologist Providence Lying-In Hosp., 1959-61; assoc. prof. pathology U. Ark. Med. Ctr., Little Rock, 1961-64; dir. lab. Mercy Hosp., Des Moines, Iowa, 1965-92, cancer rschr., 1993-95; clin. prof. pathology Creighton U. Sch. Medicine, Omaha, Nebr., 1968-95; med. dir. Corning Clin. Labs., Des Moines, 1995-97; ret. Cons. EPA, Washington, 1975-85; pres. med. staff Mercy Hosp., Des Moines, 1981 Author: (book) The Human Uterus, 1964, Pathology of Sickle Cell Anemia, 1971 (award 1975), Beyond the Horizon, 1995. Elder Winsdor Presbyn. Ch., Des Moines, 1964; com. mem. Aldersgate Meth. Ch., Des Moines, 1995. Major Med. Corps, 1950-52, Korea. Recipient Martin Luther King Med. Achievement award, So. Christian Leadership Conf., Statesmanship award Am. Assn. Med. Adminstrs., Las Vegas, Nev., 1987. Fellow Am. Coll. of Physicians, Coll. of Am. Pathologists, Am. Soc. of Clin. Pathology, Am. Assn. for Cancer Rsch. Methodist. Avocation: classical music. Home: 2345 Park Ave Des Moines IA 50321-1505

SONG, PING, research scientist, educator; BS in agronomy, Jiangsu Agrl. Coll., China, 1990; MS in plant physiology and biochemistry, 1993; PhD in plant biology, Nanjing Agrl. U., 2000. Tchr. Yangzhou Univ., 1993—, jr. lectr. in plant physiology and biochemistry, 1993—96, instr. of plant physiology and biochemistry, 1996—2001, assoc. prof. of plant physiology and biochemistry, 2001—; postdoctoral rsch. assoc. U. Tenn., 2002—. Contbr. articles to profl. jours., chapters to books. Recipient Jiangsu Agrl. scholarship, 1987—90, Postgrad scholarship, Yangzhou Univ., 1991, Disting. Young Scientific and Tech. Worker, Yangzhou City, 1999—2002. Mem.: Chinese Soc. of Agronomy, Chinese Soc. of Plant Physiology, Chinese Soc. of Biochemistry and Molecular Biology, Am. Assn. for Cancer Rsch. Achievements include research in apoptotic pathways related to oncogene induced cellular transformation; studies of subcellular and biochemical events involved in inducing cells to growth inhibition related to homeostasis or dormancy; perception of plants to osmotic stress signals and its relation to abscisic acid biosynthesis; mechanisms of methyl jasmonate inducing the opening of rice florets; photosynthesis and photoinhibition. Office: Dept of Pathobiology Coll of Vet Medicine, U Tenn G108, 3500 Sutherland Ave Knoxville TN 37919 Office Phone: 865-974-5837.

SONG, XUEDONG, chemist; b. Luiyang, Hunan Province, China, Nov. 14, 1966; arrived in U.S., 1992; m. Xin Chen; children: Jerry children: Anna. BS, Fudan U., Shanghai, China, 1988; PhD, U. Rochester, 1996. Tech. staff mem. Los Alamos (N.Mex.) Nat. Lab., 1997—2001; sr. rsch. scientist Kimberly Clark Co., Roswell, Ga., 2001—. Achievements include research in biomimic membrane; molecular aggregation; invention of biosensors; patents for biosensors; patents pending for medical diagnostics.

SONG, YONGYI, librarian; b. Shanghai, Dec. 15, 1949; arrived in U.S., 1989; s. Changrui Song and Meiqing Jia; m. Xiaohua Helen Yao, Jan. 1, 1980; 1 child, Xiao. BA, Inst. Shanghai Edn., 1985; MA, U. Colo., 1992; MLS, Ind. U., 1995. Instr. comparative lit. Pa. State U., State College, 1992—93; Chinese bibliographer U. Pitts., 1995—97; sr. libr. East Asian studies/langs. and area studies Dickinson Coll., Carlisle, Pa., 1997—. Author: The Cultural Revolution: A Bibliography, 1966-1996, 1998, The Cultural Revolution and Heterodox Thoughts, 2001; chief editor The Chinese Cultural Revolution Database, 2002. Recipient 21st Century Nat. Libr. award, Syracuse U. Sch. Info. Studies, NY, 2004; grantee, Chan's Journalism and Culture Found., NYC, 2000; scholar, Pa. Libr. Assn., 2001. Office: Dickinson Coll Libr High St and College St Carlisle PA 17013 Office Phone: 717-245-1867. Business E-Mail: songy@dickinson.edu.

SONNECKEN, EDWIN HERBERT, management consultant; b. New Haven, July 22, 1916; s. Ewald and Pauline (Halfmann) S.; m. Elizabeth Gregory, June 3, 1939; children: William H., Richard G., Paul D. BS, Northwestern U., 1938; MBA, 1940. With Montgomery Ward & Co., Chgo., 1940-42; price adminstr. OPA, Chgo., 1943; mgr. sales B.F. Goodrich Co., Akron, Ohio, 1943-53; dir. planning Ford Motor Co., Dearborn, Mich., 1953-57; pres. Market Planning Corp., N.Y.C., 1957-61; from dir. corp. planning and research to v.p. corp. bus. planning Goodyear Tire & Rubber Co., 1961-80; chmn. Mktg. Sci. Inst., Cambridge, Mass., 1980-84, also trustee, chmn. research policy com.; mgmt. cons., Akron, 1985—. Pres. Akron (Ohio) chpt. Am. Mktg. Assn., 1950, v.p. Detroit chpt., 1955, nat. v.p., dir., 1957, nat. pres., 1964-65, mem. global mktg. coun., 1986—. Pres. YMCA, Akron, 1978; chmn. trustees First Congl. Ch., Akron, 1985, chmn. endowment trust, 1987—. Served with AUS, 1945-46. Mem. Am. Statis. Assn., Am. Assn. Pub. Opinion Research, Nat. Assn. Bus. Economists, Am. Mktg. Assn., Internat. Mktg. Fedn. (pres.), European Soc. for Opinion and Market Research, Beta Gamma Sigma, Portage Country (Akron). Avocation: golf. Home and Office: Apt 333 100 Brookmont Rd Akron OH 44333-3094

SONNEDECKER, GLENN ALLEN, pharmaceutical historian, pharmaceutical educator; b. Creston, Ohio, Dec. 11, 1917; s. Ira Elmer and Leta (Linter) S.; m. Cleo Bell, Apr. 3, 1943; 1 child, Stuart Bruce. BS, Ohio State U., 1942; MS, U Wis., 1950, PhD, 1952; Dr. Sci. honoris causa, Ohio State U., 1964, Phila. Coll. Pharmacy and Sci., 1989; PharmD honoris causa, Mass. Coll. Pharmacy, 1974. Lic. pharmacist. Mem. editorial staff Sci. Service, Washington, 1942-43; editor Jour. Am. Pharm. Assn. (practical pharmacy edit.), Washington, 1943-48; asst. prof. U. Wis., 1952-56, asso. prof., 1956-60, prof., 1960-81, Edward Kremers prof., 1981-86; sec. Am. Inst. History of Pharmacy, 1949-57, dir., 1957-73, 81-85, hon. dir. life, chmn. bd., 1988-89; editor-in-chief RPh, 1978-80. Sec., bd. dirs. Friends of Hist. Pharmacy, 1945-49; chmn. Joint Com. on Pharmacy Coll. Librs., 1960-61; U.S. del. Internat. Pharm. Fedn., 1953, 55, 62; U.S. rep. to Mid. East Pharm. Congress, Beirut, 1956; sec. sect. history of pharmacy and biochemistry Pan-Am. Congress Pharmacy and Biochemistry, 1957. Co-author books; contbr. to pharm. and hist. publs. Recipient Edward Kremers award (for writings), 1964, Nat. award Rho Chi, 1967, Schelenz plaquette Internat. Soc. for History of Pharmacy, 1971, Remington honor medal Am. Pharm. Assn., 1972, Urdang medal, 1976, Folch Andreu prize, Spain, 1985, Profile award Am. Found. Pharm. Edn., 1994; Am. Found. fellow, 1948-52, Guggenheim fellow, 1955, Fulbright Rsch. scholar, Germany, 1955-56. Mem. Am. Pharm. Assn. (life mem.; sec. sect. history of pharmacy 1949 50, vice chmn. 1950-51, chmn. 1951-52, rsch. assoc. 1964-65, chmn. joint task force with Acad. Pharm Scis. 1985, hon. chmn. bd. trustees 1985), Internat. Acad. History Pharmacy (1st v.p. 1970-81, pres. 1983-91, hon. pres. 1991—), Am. Assn. History of Medicine (exec. coun. 1966-69), Internat. Gesellschaft fur Geschichte der Pharmazie (exec. bd. 1965-89), hon. mem. socs. for history of pharmacy of Italy, Benelux, pan-Arab, Spain; mem. Sigma Xi, Rho Chi (mem. nat. exec. coun. 1957-59), Phi Delta Chi. Unitarian Universalist. Home: 2030 Chadbourne Ave Madison WI 53726-4047

SONNEMAN, EVE, artist; b. Chgo., 1946; d. Eric O. and Edith S. BFA, U. Ill., 1967; MFA, U. N.Mex., 1969. One-woman shows include Castelli Gallery, N.Y.C., 1976, 78, 80, 82, 84-86, Tex. Gallery, Houston, 1976, 78, 80, 82, 85, Galerie Farideh Cadot, Paris, 1978, 80, 83, François Lambert Gallery, Milan, Italy, 1980, 87, Mpls. Inst. Arts, 1980, La Noveau Musèe, Lyon, France, 1980, Musèe de Toulon, France, 1983, Centre Georges Pompidou, Paris, 1984, Circus Gallery, L.A., 1989, 97, Jones Troyer Fitzpatrick, Washington, 1989, Zabriskie Gallery, N.Y., 1990, Gloria Luria Gallery, Miami, 1990, Grand Central Terminal, N.Y.C., 1991, Charles Cowles Gallery, 1992, Sidney Janis Gallery, N.Y.C., 1996, La Geode Mus., Paris, 1996, Cirrus Gallery, 1997, Bruce Silverstein Gallery, N.Y., 2002, Jadite Gallery, N.Y., 2002, 03, 04, Galeria Turchi, Sienna, Italy, 2002; author: America's Cottage Gardens, 1990, Where Birds Live, 1992; co-author: How To Touch What, 2000; photographs subject of book Real Time, 1976. Grantee Nat. Endowment Arts, 1971, 78, Polaroid Corp., 1978; Cartier fellowship, France, 1989. Address: 446 W 47th St Apt 5C New York NY 10036-2381 Office Phone: 212-582-9375. E-mail: evesonneman@earthlink.net.

SONNEMANN, HARRY, electrical engineer, consultant; b. Munich, Sept. 3, 1924; came to U.S., 1938, naturalized, 1944; s. Leopold and Emmy (Markus) S.; m. Shirley E. Battles, Nov. 25, 1949; children: Carol Jean, Joyce Elaine, Patricia Ann. BS, Poly. Inst. Bklyn., 1954. Research electroence-phalography, 1944-47; asst. to dir. electronics dept. AEC contract, Columbia U., 1947-50; supr. electronics shop Columbia Hudson Labs., 1951-53, head electronics dept., 1954-59; asst. dir. Project Artemis, 1959-64, Project Artemis (Hudson labs.), 1961-64; asst. dir. field engring. Advanced Research Projects Agy., Nuclear Test Detection Office, 1964-67; acting dep. dir. Nuclear Test Detection Office, 1967-68; spl. asst. in electronics to asst. sec. navy for research and devel. Navy Dept., 1968-76, spl. asst. to asst. sec. navy for research and devel., 1976-77; asst. to chief engr. NASA, 1977-78, dep. chief engr., 1978-84, asst. chief engr., 1984-86, cons., 1986—; pres. SBC Assocs., McLean, Va., 1988-95. Chmn. Dept. Def. Tactical Satellite Exec. Steering Group, 1968-69, chmn. Dept. Def. nav. satellite exec. steering group, 1969-70, 72-73 Treas. Art League. No. Va., 1967-68; pres. Rotonda Condominium Unit Owners Assn., 1982-84, 97-98, 99-2000. Mem.: Washington Figure Skating (dir. 1968-73, treas. 1969-72), Ice Club of Washington (pres. 1974-76). Home and Office: 7452 Spring Village Dr # 434 Springfield VA 22150-4951 E-mail: HSSBC@aol.com.

SONNENBERG, FRANK A. internist; MD, UCLA, 1980. Diplomate Am. Bd. Internal Medicine. Intern UCLA, 1980—81, resident in internal medicine, 1981—83; fellow in clin. decision making New Eng. Med. Ctr., Boston, 1984—86; physician divsn. gen. internal medicine Robert Wood Johnson U. Med. Group, New Brunswick, NJ, 1990—; assoc. dir. clin. informatics Informatics Inst. of UMDNJ, 2003—. Office: Robert Wood Johnson Univ Med Group Clinical Acad Bldg 125 Paterson St Ste 5100A New Brunswick NJ 08901-1977

SONNENBERG, HARDY, data processing company research and development executive, engineer; b. Schoensee, Fed. Republic Germany, Apr. 12, 1939; s. Gustav and Wanda (Neumann) S.; m. Doris Linda Adam, June 20, 1964; children: Kevin, Denise. BS, U. Alta., 1962; MS, Stanford U., 1964, PhD, 1967. Registered profl. engr., Ont. Advanced devel. engr. GTE Sylvania, Mountain View, Calif., 1966-68, engring. specialist, 1968-70, sect. mgr., 1970-73; dir. rsch. Optical Diodes Inc., Palo Alto, Calif., 1973-74; mem. rsch. staff Xerox Rsch. Centre Can., Mississauga, Ont., 1975-78, area mgr., 1978-80, lab. mgr., 1980-86, mgr. rsch. ops., 1986-87, mgr. tech. and engring. systems, 1987-94, v.p. rsch. and tech., 1994-96; pres. Calixo Cons., Freelton, Ont., 1997—. Chmn. indsl. adv. coun. McMaster U., Hamilton, Ont., 1990-93, active, 1987-94. Contbr. articles to profl. jours.; patentee in field. Chmn. bd. dirs. local ch., Hamilton, Ont., 1983-85, 89-93, 98-2002; pres. Sheridan Park Assn., Mississauga, 1988-89; chmn. Conf. Bd. Can. Rsch. Mgrs. Forum, 1991-93. Recipient cert. of recognition for invention NASA, 1973, 74, Achievement award Xerox Corp., 1981, Charles E. Ives Engring. award, 1983. Mem.: IEEE (sr.), Assn. Profl. Engrs. Ont., Am. Phys. Soc., sigma Xi. Avocations: outdoor activities, singing, church participation. Home and Office: 900 Hwy 97 Box 126 Freelton ON Canada L0R 1K0

SONNENFELD, BARRY, director, cinematographer; b. New York, NY, Apr. 1, 1953; Cinematographer (films) Blood Simple, 1984, Compromising Positions, 1985, Three O'Clock High, 1987, Raising Arizona, 1987, Throw Momma from the Train, 1987, Big, 1988, When Harry Met Sally..., 1989, Miller's Crossing, 1990, Misery, 1990, (TV movies) Out of Step, 1984 (Emmy award best cinematography 1984), Double Take, 1985, Welcome Home, Bobby, 1986, Classified Love, 1986; dir. (films) The Addams Family (uncredited cameo appearance), 1991, Addams Family Values (also actor), 1993, Get Shorty, 1995, Men In Black, 1997, Maximum Bob (TV, also exec. prodr.), 1998, Wild Wild West, 1999 (also prodr.), Chippendales, 2000; dir., co-prodr.: For Love or Money, 1993; prodr.: Out of Sight, 1998 (exec.), Fantasy Island (TV, exec.), 1998, Secret Agent Man, 2000, The Crew, 3000. Office: Creative Artists Agy c/o Fred Specktor 9830 Wilshire Blvd Beverly Hills CA 90212 also: United Talent Agency 9560 Wilshire Blvd Fl 5 Beverly Hills CA 90212-2401

SONNENFELD, DAVID ALLAN, sociologist; s. Joseph Sonnenfeld and Valerie Christine Wilmot; m. Kathleen Elizabeth McGrath, Jan. 26, 2001; m. Cynthia Jo Solem, Jan. 2, 1981 (div. June 25, 1997); children: Raphael Andrew, Joshua Emile, Nathan Isaac. BA, U. Oreg., 1973; MA in Sociology, U. Calif., Santa Cruz, 1991, PhD in Sociology, 1996. Vis. rsch. fellow Ctr. for Resource and Environ. Studies, Australian Nat. U., Canberra, 1993—94; asst. prof. sociology Wash. State U., 1996—2003, assoc. prof. cmty. and rural sociology, 2003—, affiliated faculty Asia program, 1996—. Vis. rsch. fellow Social Rsch. Inst. Chulalongkorn U., Bangkok, 1996—2002; S.V. Ciriacy-Wantrup vis. scholar U. Calif., Berkeley, Calif., 1998—2000; guest prof., WIMEK fellow environ. policy group Wageningen U., Netherlands, 2003—04, rsch. fellow environ. policy group, Netherlands, 2004—. Editor: Ecological Modernisation Around the World, 2000, Symposium on Global-

ization, Governance, and the Environment, American Behavioral Scientist, 2002. Recipient Fulbright Dissertation Rsch. award, Fulbright Fgn. Scholarship Bd. (Australia), 1993—94; Switzer Environ. fellow, Switzer Found., 1995—96, Dissertation Rsch. fellow, Inst. on Global Conflict and Cooperation, U. Calif., 1993—94, 1994—95. Mem.: Assn. for Asian Studies, Internat. Sociol. Assn. (rsch. com.on environment and soc.), Am. Sociol. Assn. (sect. on the polit. economy of the world-system, sect. on environment and tech.). Office: Washington State Univ 2710 University Dr Richland WA 99354

SONNENFELD, JOSEPH, geographer, researcher; b. N.Y.C., Sept. 1, 1929; s. Isaac and Miriam (Goldhirsh) S.; m. Valerie Wilmot, Sept. 1952 (div. Aug. 1968); children: David Allan, Michael Jacob, William Edward; m. Liana Bisiani, June 19, 1982; children: Kristin Selina Cruz, Sondra Nell Robbins. BS, Oreg. State Coll., 1952; PhD, Johns Hopkins U., 1957. Instr. U. Del., Newark, 1955-57, asst. prof., 1957-62, assoc. prof., 1962-68; prof. Tex. A&M U., College Station, 1968-93, prof. emeritus, 1993—, asst. dean for acad. affairs, 1975-79. Contbr. articles to profl. jours. Wenner-Gren Found. for Anthropol. Rsch. fellow, 1954; Rsch. grantee Arctic Inst. N.Am., 1954, 63, Office of Naval Rsch., 1954, 63, Tex. A&M U., 1970, NSF, 1991. Mem. AAAS, Am. Psychol. Soc., Assn. Am. Geographers, Behavioral and Brain Scis. (assoc.), Current Anthropology (assoc.), Internat. Arctic Social Sci. Assn., Sigma Xi. Home: 302 W 11th St Port Angeles WA 98362-7605

SONNENFELD, MARC JAY, lawyer; b. Bryn Mawr, Pa., Sept. 16, 1946; s. Burton David and Rochelle (Galant) S. BA, Swarthmore Coll., 1968; JD, Harvard U., 1971. Bar: Pa. 1971, Mass. 1971, D.C. 1977, Fla. 1978, U.S. Supreme Ct. 1976. Lectr. Wellesley (Mass.) Coll., 1971-72; law clk. to chief judge U.S. Dist. Ct. (ea. dist.) Pa., Phila., 1972-73; assoc. Ewing & Cohen, Phila., 1973-74, Morgan, Lewis & Bockius, Phila., 1974-78, ptnr., 1978—. Dem. committeeman, Phila., 1980-84; chmn. Pa. Lawyers for Dem. Victory, 1988; bd. mgrs. Swarthmore Coll., 1989—, gen. chmn. ann. fund, 1985-87; trustee Am. Inns of Ct. Found.; mem. bd. mgrs. Swarthmore Coll. Fellow Am. Coll. Trial Lawyers; mem. ABA, Pa. Bar Assn., Phila. Bar Assn. (exec. com. young lawyers sect. 1976-79, appellate cts. com., fed. cts. com., state civil jud. procedures com., nominating com., chmn. city policy com., chmn. profl. responsibility com. 1985, co-chmn. legis. liaison com. 1987-91, bus. banking and corp. law sect., vice chmn. bd. govs. 1986, chmn. 1987, chmn. ann. meeting 1991, asst. treas. 1996, co-chair commerce cost task force 1996-97), Harvard Law Sch. Assn. of Phila. (pres.1987-88), Swarthmore Coll. Annual Fund (bd. mgrs.). Jewish. Avocations: reading, sailing. Office: Morgan Lewis & Bockius 1701 Market St Philadelphia PA 19103-2921 Home: 234 Cuylers Ln Haverford PA 19041

SONNENFELDT, HELMUT, former government official, educator, consultant, author; b. Berlin, Sept. 13, 1926; came to U.S., 1944, naturalized, 1945; s. Walter H. and Gertrud (Liebenthal) S.; m. Marjorie Hecht, Oct. 4, 1953; children— Babette Sonnenfeldt Lubben, Walter H., Stewart H. AB, Johns Hopkins, 1950, MA, 1951. With Dept. State, Washington, 1952-77; formerly dir. Office Rsch. and Analysis for USSR and Eastern Europe, 1965-69; lectr. Sch. Advanced Internat. Studies, Johns Hopkins U., 1958-69, vis. scholar, 1977-78; guest scholar Brookings Instn., Washington, 1978—. Sr. mem. Nat. Security Coun., 1969-74; counselor Dept. State, 1974-77. Former gov. UN Assn. of U.S.; dir. Atlantic Coun. of U.S., World Affairs Coun. Washington; trustee Johns Hopkins U. With AUS, 1945-46. Mem. Coun. on Fgn. Rels. N.Y., Pi Delta Epsilon. Home: 5600 Wisconsin Ave Apt 1505 Chevy Chase MD 20815-4412 Office: Brookings Instn 1775 Massachusetts Ave NW Washington DC 20036-2103 Office Phone: 202-797-6028. Business E-Mail: hsonnenfeldt@brookings.edu.

SONNENSCHEIN, ADAM, lawyer; b. N.Y.C., Oct. 15, 1938; s. Harry D. and Sybil (Reinus) S.; m. Phyllis Cokin, Oct. 25, 1968; children: Andrew, Michael. BA, Amherst Coll., 1960; LLB, Columbia U., 1965. Bar: N.Y. 1965, Mass. 1970. Assoc. Berlack, Israels & Liberman, N.Y.C., 1965—70; ptnr. Sprague Assocs., Boston, 1970—72, Walter & Sonnenschein, Boston, 1972—78, Hausserman, Davison & Shattuck, Boston, 1978—83, Foley Hoag LLP, Boston, 1983—. Mem. ABA, Mass. Bar Assn., Boston Bar Assn., Assn. of Bar of City of N.Y. Office: Foley Hoag LLP 155 Seaport Blvd Boston MA 02210-2600

SONNENSCHEIN, DAVID, music educator, composer; b. Hamburg, Germany, Nov. 2, 1928; s. Abraham and Elsa Sonnenschein; m. Tamar Gronemann, June 23, 1957; children: Iris, Nurit, Orna. Mus D, Boston U., 1976; MusM, New Eng. Conservatory, Boston, 1968. Dir. Tiberias Conservatory, Tiberias, Israel, 1962—66; music tchr. Reali Sch., Haifa, Israel, 1962—66; instr. Emmanuel Coll., Boston; assoc. prof. music Northeastern U., Boston, chair dept. music, 1993—99. Condr. Chamber Orch., Hamburg, Germany, 1959—62, Hamburg, 1959—61; guest condr. Hamburg Symphony Orch., Hamburg, Germany, 1959—61; condr. Haifa Chamber Choir, Haifa, Israel, 1962—63; assoc. condr. Haifa Symphony Orch., Haifa, Israel; condr. Melrose Symphony Orch., Melrose, Mass., Polymnia Choral Soc., Melrose, Mass., 1971—81; guest condr. Boston Pops Orch., Boston, 1974—79; condr. Northeastern U. Symphony Orch., Boston, 1972—88, Concert Arts Orch., Boston, 1973—84. Author: (music courseware) The Anatomy of Music. Recipient Innovative Excellence in Learning, Tchg. and Tech., Ninth Internat. Conf. on Coll. Tchg., Learning and Tech., 1998; fellow, Brandeis U., 1968—70, Lady Davis, Haifa Technion, 1980—81; scholar, New Eng. Conservatory, 1966—68. Achievements include first to Developer of Music Courseware and Learning Modules for Distance Learning. Avocations: sailing, hiking, cross country skiing. Home: 169 Bonad Rd Chestnut Hill MA 02467 Office: Northeastern University Huntington Ave 373 Ryder Hall Boston MA

SONNENSCHEIN, HUGO FREUND, academic administrator, writer, economist, educator; b. N.Y.C., Nov. 14, 1940; s. Leo William and Lillian Silver Sonnenschein; m. Elizabeth Gunn, Aug. 26, 1962; children: Leah, Amy, Rachel. AB, U. Rochester, 1961; MS, Purdue U., 1963, PhD, 1964, PhD (hon.), 1996; PhD (hon.), Tel Aviv U., 1993; D (hon.), U. Autonoma Barcelona, Spain, 1994; PhD (hon.), Lake Forest Coll., 1995, North Ctrl. Coll., 2001, U. Chgo., 2002. Faculty dept. econs. U. Minn., 1964—70, prof., 1968—70; prof. econs. U. Mass., Amherst, 1970—73, Northwestern U., 1973—76, Princeton (N.J.) U., 1976—87, Class of 1926 prof., 1987—88, provost, 1991—93; dean, Thomas S. Gates prof. U. Pa. Sch. Arts & Scis., Phila., 1988—91; pres. U. Chgo., 1993—2000, Hutchinson disting. prof., pres. emeritus, 2000—. Vis. prof. U. Andes, Columbia, 1965, Tel Aviv U., 1972, Hebrew U., 1973, U. Paris, 1978, U. Aix-en-Provence, France, 1978, Stanford U., 1984—85; bd. dirs. Van Kampen Mutual Funds. Editor: Econometrica, 1977—84; mem. editl. bd.: Jour. Econ. Theory, 1972—75, Jour. Math. Econs., 1974—, SIAM Jour., 1976—80; contbr. articles to profl. jours. Trustee U. Rochester, 1992—, U. Chgo., 1993—. Fellow, Social Sci. Rsch. Coun., 1967—68, NSF, 1970—, Ford Found., 1970—71, Guggenheim Found., 1976—77. Fellow: Econometric Soc. (pres. 1988—89), Am. Acad. Arts and Scis.; mem.: NAS, Am. Philos. Soc.

SONNENSCHEIN, RALPH ROBERT, physiologist; b. Chgo., Aug. 14, 1923; s. Robert and Flora (Kieferstein) S.; m. Patricia W. Niddrie, June 21, 1952; children— David, Lisa, Ann. Student, Swarthmore Coll., 1940—42, U. Chgo., 1942—43; BS, Northwestern U., 1943, BM, MS, Northwestern U., 1946, MD, 1947; PhD, U. Ill., 1950. Research asst. in physiology Northwestern U. Med. Sch., 1944-46; intern Michael Reese Hosp., Chgo., 1946-47; successively research fellow clin. sci., research asst. psychiatry, research asso. psychiatry U. Ill. Med. Sch., Chgo., 1947-51; mem. faculty U. Calif. Med. Sch., Los Angeles, 1951-88, prof. physiology, 1962-88, prof. emeritus, 1988—; liaison scientist Office Naval Research, London, 1971-72. Author papers on pain, innervation of skin, peripheral circulation. Served with AUS, 1943-46. Spl. research fellow USPHS, 1957-58; fellow Swedish Med. Research Council, 1964-65; grantee USAF; grantee Office Naval Research; grantee NIH; grantee NSF. Mem. Am. Physiol. Soc., Microcirculatory Soc., Soc. Exptl. Biology and Medicine, AAAS, Hungarian Physiol. Soc. (hon.). Home: 18212 Kingsport Dr Malibu CA 90265-5636 Office: U Calif Sch Medicine Dept Physiology Los Angeles CA 90095-1751

SONNIER, JOSEPH A. lab administrator, physician; MD, La. State U. Sch. Medicine, 1979. Cert. in Anatomic and Clin. Pathology 1983. Mng. dir. Unipath Ltd.; regional mng. dir., southwest region AmeriPath, pres., 2003—. Office: AmeriPath Inc 7289 Garden Rd Ste 200 Riviera Beach FL 33404*

SONNIER, PATRICIA BENNETT, business management educator; b. Park River, N.D., Mar. 25, 1935; d. Benjamin Beekman Bennett and Alice Catherine (Peerboom) Bennett Brenckinridge; m. William McGregor Castellini (dec.); m. Cecil Sherwood Sonnier; children: Bruce Bennett Wells (Nabil Subhani), Barbara Lea Ragland. AA, Allan Handcock Coll., Santa Maria, Calif., 1964; BS magna cum laude, U. Great Falls, 1966; MS, U. N.D., 1967, PhD, 1971. Fiscal acct. USIA, Washington, 1954-56; pub. acct. Bremerton, Wash., 1956; statistician USN, Bremerton, Wash., 1957-59; med. svcs. accounts officer USAF, Vandenberg AFB, Calif., 1962-64; instr. bus. adminstrn. Western New Eng. U., 1967—69; vis. prof. econs. Chapman Coll., 1970; vis. prof. U. So. Calif. Sys., Griffith AFB, N.Y., 1971-72; assoc. prof., dir. adminstrv. mgmt. program Va. State U., 1973-74; assoc. prof. bus. adminstrn. Oreg. State U., Corvallis, 1974-81, prof. mgmt., 1982-90, emeritus prof. mgmt., 1990—, univ. curriculum coord., 1984-86, dir. adminstrv. mgmt. program, 1974-81, pres. Faculty Senate, 1981. Mem. Interinstl. Faculty Senate, 1986-90, pres., 1989-90; exec. dir. Bus. Enterprise Ctr., 1990-92, Enterprise Ctr. L.A., Inc., 1992-95; commr. Lafayette Econ. Devel. Authority, 1994-2000, treas., 1995-96, vice chmn., 1996-97, chmn., 1997-98, past chmn., 1998-99, sec., 1999-00, chmn. bldg. com., 1999-00; cons. process tech. devel. Digital Equipment Corp., 1982. Pres., chmn. bd. dirs. Adminstrv. Orgnl. Svcs., Inc., Corvallis, 1976-83, Dynamic Achievement, Inc., 1983-92; bd. dirs. Oreg. State U. Bookstores, Inc., 1987-90, Internat. Trade Devel. Group, 1992-97; cons. Oregonians in Action, 1990-91, sec., 1999, 2000; cert. adminstrv. mng. pres. TYEE Mobil Home Park, Inc., 1987-92; del. N.Mex. State Rep. Conv., 2002. Fellow Assn. Bus. Comm. (internat. bd. 1980-86, v.p. Northwest 1981, 2nd v.p. 1982-83, 1st v.p. 1983-84, pres. 1984-85); mem. Am. Bus. Women's Assn. (chpt. v.p. 1979, pres. 1980, named Top Businesswoman in Nation 1980, Bus. Assoc. Yr. 1986), Assn. Info. Sys. Profls. (chpt. v.p. 1977, chpt. pres. 1978-81), Adminstrv. Mgmt. Soc., AAUP (chpt. sec. 1973, chpt. bd. dirs. 1982, 84-89, pres. Oreg. conf. 1983-85, pres. chpt. 1985-86), Am. Vocat. Assn. (nominating com. 1976), Associated Oreg. Faculties, Nat. Bus. Edn. Assn., Better Bus. Bur. (sec. 1994, 99, treas. 1995, vice-chair 1996, chmn. 1997, past chair 1998, chmn. nominating com. 1999, blue ribbon edn. com. 1999-2000, chmn. pub. rels.), Nat. Assn. Tchr. Edn. for Bus. Office Edn. (pres. 1976-77, chmn. pub. rels. com. 1978-81), La. Bus. Incubation Assn. (sec.-treas. 1993-95), Corvallis Area C. of C. (v.p. chamber devel. 1987-88, pres. 1988-89, chmn. bd. 1989-90, Pres.' award 1986), Boys and Girls Club of Corvallis (pres. 1991-92), Sigma Kappa, Rotary Corvallis (bd. dirs. 1990-92, dir. voc. svcs. 1991-92, pres.-elect 1992), Rotary Lafayette (bd. dirs. 1993—, cmty. svc. dir. 1993-94, treas. 1995-96, sec. 1996-97, v.p. 1997-98, pres. 1998-99, Dist. 6200 award 2000), Alherns for Gov. Com., Acadiana Rep. Women (first v.p. 1997, 98, pres. 1998-2000, asst. state CAP chmn. 1999-2000, gen. chmn. La. Fedn. Rep. Women's Clubs State Conv. 1997, Leadership La. 1998), Albuquerque Federated Rep. Women (hospitality chmn. 2003), Rotary of Albuquerque del Norte (silent auction chmn. 2001-02, dep. dir. internat. svc. com. 2002, dep. dir. permanent fund dist. 5520, asst. gov. 2003-04, chmn. internat. svcs. dist. 5220, 2003-04, chmn. Rotary Local Yellow Pages 2002, award Dist. 6200, 2000). Office Phone: 505-298-1245. Personal E-mail: PatriciaSonnier@aol.com.

SONNONSTINE, TERRY JAMES, research executive specialty chemicals company; b. Lake Charles, La., Nov. 16, 1947; s. Nowland and Rena (Dronet) S.; m. Catherine M. Price, Aug. 9, 1969; children: Max, Seth, Kyle. Student, Davidson Coll., 1965-67; BS, McNeese State U., 1969; PhD, Tulane U., 1974. Tech. dir. 3M, St. Paul, 1982-88; dir. Software and Electronics Resource Ctr. 3M, St. Paul, 1988-90; exec. dir. Sumitomo 3M, Tokyo, 1990-94; bus. devel. dir. 3M, St. Paul, 1994-96, tech. dir. visual systems divsn., 1997—. Contbr. articles to profl. jours. Bd. dirs. Am. Sch. in Japan, Chofu, 1992-94. Roman Catholic. Avocations: acoustic guitar, fishing, computers. Home: 4218 Lakeway Blvd Austin TX 78734-5000 Office: 3M Austin Center 6801 River Place Blvd Austin TX 78726-9000

SONNTAG, BERNARD H. retired agrologist, public service executive; b. Goodsoil, Sask., Can., June 27, 1940; s. Henry R. and Annie (Heesing) S.; m. Mary L. Ortman, Aug. 10, 1963; children: Calvin, Galen, Courtney Anne. BSA, Sask. U., Saskatoon, 1962, MSc, 1965; PhD, Purdue U., 1971. Economist Agriculture Can., Saskatoon, 1962-66; cons. D.W. Carr & Assoc., Ottawa, Ont., Can., 1966-68; economist Agriculture Can., Lethbridge, Alta., 1968-79, Saskatoon, 1979-80, dir. rsch. sta. Brandon, Man., 1980-86, Swiftcurrent, Sask., 1986-89, Lethbridge, 1989-95; dir. gen. Prairie Farm Rehab. Adminstrn., Regina, Sask., Can., 1996-01; pres. Sonntag Agrl. Svcs., Saskatoon, Sask., Can., 2001—. Pres. Man. Inst. Agrologists, Brandon, 1984. Recipient Leadership award Bell Can., 1993; named Disting. Agrologist, Alta. Inst. Agrologists, 1995. Fellow Agrl. Inst. Can.; mem. Rotary. Roman Catholic. Home: Sonntag Agrl Svcs 318 Collinsster Rd Saskatoon SK Canada S7N 4K7 Office: Sonntag Agrl Svcs 1800 Hamilton St Regina SK Canada S4P 4L2

SONS, RAYMOND WILLIAM, journalist; b. Harvey, Ill., Aug. 25, 1926; s. William Henry and Gladys Lydia (Steinko) S.; m. Bettina Dieckmann; children: David, Pamela Sons Clarke, Ronald. BA, U. Mich., 1950. Reporter, mng. editor Murphysboro (Ill.) Daily Ind. edit. So. Illinoisan newspaper, 1950-52; assoc. news editor Middletown (Ohio) Jour., 1952-53; reporter, asst. city editor, sportswriter, sports editor Chgo. Daily News, 1953-78; sports editor, columnist Chgo. Sun-Times, 1978-92. Served with USAAF, 1945-46. Recipient Best Sports Story in Ill. award U.P.I., 1970, Marshall Field award for outstanding editorial contbn. to Chgo. Daily News, 1972; Best Sports Column award AP Sports Editor, 1979, Best Sports Column award Ill. AP, 1987, Chgo. Journalism Hall of Fame, 1996. Roman Catholic. Home: 4100 Torrington Ct Fort Collins CO 80525-3419

SONSINI, LARRY W. lawyer; b. Rome, N.Y., Feb. 5, 1941; AB, U. Calif., Berkeley, 1963; LLB, U. Calif., 1966. Bar: Calif. 1966. Ptnr. Wilson, Sonsini, Goodrich & Rosati, Palo Alto; prof. securities regulation Boalt Hall Sch. law U. Calif., Berkeley, 1984—. Mem. exec. com. Securities Re Mem. ABA (com. on fed. regulation securities, subcom. on registration statements), Am. Law Inst. Office: Wilson Sonsini Goodrich & Rosati 650 Page Mill Rd Palo Alto CA 94304-1050

SONSTEBY, CHARLES M. food service executive; Exec. v.p., CFO Brinker Internat., Dallas. Office: 6820 LBJ Fwy Dallas TX 75240

SONTAG, ED W. federal agency administrator; BA in Spl. Edn., MA in Elementary Sch. Adminstrn. and Supervision, SUNY; PhD in Spl. Edn. Adminstrn., Syracuse U. Resident scholar for Wisc. Gov. Tommy G. Thompson; deputy asst. sec. U.S. Dept. Interior, 1989—92; prof. U. Wisc. - Stevens Point Sch. Edn., 1992—99; senior-level positions Ill. State Bd. Edn., U.S. Dept. Edn., Ind. U., Wisc. and N.Y. pub. sch. sys.; dep. chief of staff, mgmt. & ops. U.S. Dept. Health and Human Svcs., 2001, asst. sec. adminstrn. and mgmt., 2001—. Recipient U. Wisc.-Steven Point Vice Chancellor Merit award, Dept. Interior Disting. Safety award. Office: US Dept Health and Human Svcs 200 Independence Ave SW Rm 309 Washington DC 20201*

SONTAG, FREDERICK EARL, philosophy educator; b. Long Beach, Calif., Oct. 2, 1924; s. M. Burnett and Cornelia (Nicholson) S.; m. Carol Furth, June 10, 1950; children: Grant Furth, Anne Burnett Karch. BA with great distinction, Stanford U., 1949; MA, Yale U., 1951, PhD, 1952; LLD (hon.), Coll. Idaho, 1971. Instr. Yale U., 1951-52; asst. prof. philosophy Pomona Coll., Claremont, Calif., 1952-55, assoc. prof., 1955-60, prof., 1970—, Robert C. Denison prof. philosophy, 1972—, chmn. dept. philosophy, 1960-67, 76-77, 1980-84; chmn. coord. com. in philosophy Claremont Grad. Sch. and Univ. Ctr., 1962-65. Vis. prof. Union theol. Sem., N.Y.c., 1959-60, Collegio de Sant' Anselmo, Rome, 1966-67, U. Copenhagen, fall 1972; theologian-in-residence Am. Ch. in Paris, fall 1973; fulbright regional vis. prof., India, East Asia, Pacific areas, 1977-78; mem. nat. adv. coun. Kent Fellowship Program of Danforth Found., 1963-66. Author numerous books, the most recent being; Love Beyond Pain: Mysticism Within christianity, 1977, Sun Myung Moon and the Unification Church, 1977, also German, Japanese and Korean transl.; (with John K. Roth) God and America's Future, 1977, What Can God Do?, 1979, A Kierkegaard Handbook, 1979, The Elements of Philosophy, 1984, (with John K. Roth) The Questions of Philosophy, 1988, Emotion, 1989, The Return of the Gods, 1989, Willgenstein and the Mystical, 1995, Uncertain Truth, 1995, The Descent of Women, 1997, The Acts of the Trinity, 1997, Truth and Imagination, 1998, 2001: A Spiritual Odyssey, 2001, The Mysterious Presence, 2002. Pres. bd. dirs. Claremont Family Svc., 1960-64; trustee The Coro Found., L.A. and San Francisco, 1967-71; bd. dirs., chmn. ways and means com. Pilgrim Place, Claremont, 1970-77. With AUS, 1943-46. Vis. scholar Ctr. for Study Japanese Religions, Kyoto, Japan, spring 1974; vis. fellow East-West Ctr., Honolulu, summer 1974; Wig Disting. prof. award, 1970, 76. Mem. Am. Philos. Assn., Metaphys. Soc. Am. Soc. on Religion in Higher Edn. (Kent fellow 1950-52), Am. Acad. Religion, Phi Beta Kappa. Congregationalist. Office: Pomona Coll 551 N College Ave Claremont CA 91711-4410

SONTAG, JAMES MITCHELL, cancer researcher; b. Denver, Dec. 8, 1939; s. Samuel Henry and Rose Hazel (Silverman) S.; m. Elizabeth Crockett Tunis; children: Ariella, Eythan. BS, Lamar State Coll. Tech., Beaumont, Tex.; MS, U. Ill., 1967; PhD, Weizmann Inst. Sci., Rehovot, Israel, 1971; MPH, Harvard U., 1982. Postdoctoral fellow Damon Runyon Meml. Fund Cancer Rsch., 1971-72; guest worker Nat. Cancer Inst., NIH, Bethesda, Md., 1972-73, staff fellow, 1973-74, exptl. oncologist, 1973-76, mgr. carcinogen bioassay program, 1973-76, asst. to divsn. dir. cancer cause and prevention, 1976-80; exec. sec. Clearinghouse on Environ. Carcinogens, 1976-80, asst. dir. for interagy. affairs Office of Dir., 1980-82, spl. asst. epidemiology and biostatistics program, 1982-96; chief office divsn. ops. & analysis divsn. cancer epidemiology and genetics Nat. Cancer Inst., 1996-99; ind. contractor working with grassroots artisans on e-commerce projects, 1999—. Author, editor in field. Served with AUS, 1956-59. Beaumont LWV scholar, 1963-65 Mem. Beta Beta Beta.

SONTAG, PETER MICHAEL, travel management company executive; b. Vienna, Apr. 25, 1943; came to U.S., 1960; s. Otto Schiedeck and Maria Katharina (Schmidt) Cigalle; children: Alicia Alexandra, Julie Katherine. Diploma in hotel mgmt., Schule fuer Gastgewerbe, Vienna, 1960; BS magna cum laude, West Liberty State Coll., 1969, LLD, 1991; MBA, Columbia U., 1971. Steel worker Weirton (W.Va.) Steel Co., 1965-69; fin. analyst Citicorp, N.Y.C., 1970-71; ops. staff exec. ITT, N.Y.C., 1971-73; asst. v.p. Sun Life Ins. Co. Am., Balt., 1974-75; exec. v.p. Travel Guide, Inc., Balt., 1975-76; pres. Travelwhirl, Inc., Balt., 1976-78; founder Gelco Travel Services, Mpls., 1978-83; chmn., chief exec. officer Sontag, Annis & Assocs., Washington, 1983-86, US Travel Systems, Inc., Washington, 1986-95; CEO Fast Lane Travel Inc., Washington, 1995-97, Crown Mktg. Group, Clearwater, Fla., 1997-98; chmn. Travel Industries Colo. Inc., 1999; pres., CEO 800 Travel Systems, Inc., 1999—, also bd. mem. Pub. Travel Bus. Mgr., 1983-86; speaker in field, 1983—. With Austrian Air Force, 1963-64. Named one of Twenty Five Most Influential Execs. in Travel Industry Travel Bus. News, 1985, 87, 88, 89; named Delta Sigma Pi scholar. Mem. Alpha Phi Sigma, Delta Mu Delta (charter), Lakewood Country Club. Republican. Avocations: skiing, sailing, photography, collecting antique cars. Office: THOR Inc 382 S Arthur Ave Louisville CO 80027-3010

SONTAG, SUSAN, writer; b. N.Y.C., Jan. 16, 1933; m. Philip Rieff, 1950 (div. 1958); 1 son, David. BA, U. Chgo., 1951; MA in English, Harvard U., 1954, MA in Philosophy, 1955. Instr. English U. Conn., Storrs, 1953-54; editor Commentary, N.Y.C., 1959; lectr. philosophy City Coll., N.Y.C., 1959-60, Sarah Lawrence Coll., Bronxville, 1959-60; instr. dept. religion Columbia U., N.Y.C., 1960-64. Writer in residence Rutgers U., 1964-65. Author: (novels) The Benefactor, 1963, Death Kit, 1967, The Volcano Lover: A Romance, 1992, In America (Nat. Book award 2000), Where the Stress Falls, 2001, Regarding the Pain of Others, 2003; (plays) Alice in Bed: A Play in Eight Scenes, 1993; (stories) I, Etcetera, 1978, The Way We Live Now, 1991; (essays) Against Interpretation, 1966 (Mat. Book award nomination 1966), Styles of Radical Will, 1969, Trip to Hanoi, 1969, On Photography, 1977 (Nat. Book Critics Circle award for criticism 1978), Illness as Metaphor, 1978, Under the Sign of Saturn, 1980, AIDS and Its Metaphors, 1989; (anthology) A Susan Sontag Reader, 1982; screenwriter, dir.: (films) Duet for Cannibals, 1969, Brother Carl, 1971; dir.: (films) Promised Lands, 1974, Unguided Tour, 1983; editor, author of introduction: Antonin Artaud: Selected Writings, 1976, A Roland Barthes Reader, 1982, Danilo Kis's Homo Poeticus: Essays & Interviews, 1995. Guggenheim fellow, 1966, 75, Rockefeller Found. fellow, 1965, 74, MacArthur fellow, 1990-95; recipient George Polk Meml. award, 1966, 2002, Ingram Merrill Found. award in lit. in field of Am. Letters, 1976, Creative Arts award Brandeis U., 1976, Malaparte prize, 1992, Peace Prize, German Bookseller Assoc., 2003; named Officier de l'Ordre des Arts et des Lettres, France, 1984. Mem. Am. Acad. Arts and Scis. (elected 1993), Am. Acad. Arts and Letters (Arts and Letters award 1976), PEN (pres. Am. Ctr. 1987-89). Office: Farrar, Straus & Giroux 19 Union Square West New York NY 10003

SOO, TECK MUN, neurosurgeon; b. Kuala Lumbpur, Malaysia, May 16, 1962; arrived in US, 1999; s. Wah and Ngan (Chin) Soo; m. Doris Wah-Lung Tong; children: Alexandra, Christopher. MB, BChir, Trininty Coll., Dublin, Ireland, 1987; MA, Trininty Coll., 1992. Diplomate Am. Bd. Neurosurgeons. Lectr. neurosurgery U. Toronto, Canada, 1998—99; neurosurgeon Providence Hosp., Southfield, Mich., 1999—. Hutchison scholar, Trinity Coll., Dublin, 1981. Fellow: Royal Coll. Surgeons (Hong Kong), Royal Coll. Can. Surgeons, Royal Coll. Surgeons (Edinburgh); mem.: ACS. Avocation: fishing. Office: Ste 601 22250 Providence Dr Southfield MI 48075 Office Phone: 248-569-7745.

SOOD, ASHISH, marketing professional; b. Delhi, India, Jan. 14, 1968; s. Raman Kumar and Rita Raman Sood; m. Amita Dang, Oct. 18, 1994; children: Aditya, Nitish. Diploma in application programming, Computer Point Acad., Delhi, India, 1994; MBA in Mgmt. Tech., Nanyang Technol. U., Singapore, 2000; postgrad., U. So. Calif., 2001—. Area sales mgr. north zone Crompton Greaves Ltd., Delhi, 1989—95; mktg. mgr. Megahertz Infosys Pte Ltd., Delhi, 1995—97; product quality mgr. ops. Philips Electronics Singapore Pte Ltd., 1997—2000. Recipient Cert. of Merit, DPS, Delhi, 1984; vis. scholar Nat. scholar, All India SSE, 1983; Merit scholar, EEWT, Faridabad, 1983—85. Mem.: Instn. Engineers India (assoc.; assoc.), Singapore Productivity and Standards Bd. (assoc.; assessor 2001), BVQI Regional Inst. Environ. Tech. (assoc. Environ. Mgmt. Sys. ISO 14000 Lead Assessor 1998). Office: Univ So Calif Acctg Bldg 306E Los Angeles CA 90089-0443 E-mail: ashish.sood@marshall.usc.edu.

SOO HOO, GUY W. internist, educator; b. Winslow, Ariz., Aug. 11, 1955; m. Stella Gee, Apr. 22, 1989; children: Melissa A. Soohoo, Stephanie M. Soohoo, Alexander M. Soohoo. BS, George Wash. U., 1973—77; MD, U. N.Mex Sch. Medicine, 1977—81; MPH, U. Calif., LA Sch. Pub. Health, 1984—85. Internal Medicine Am. Bd. Internal Medicine, 1984, Pulmonary Diseases Am. Bd. Internal Medicine, 1988, Critical Care Am. Bd. Internal Medicine, 1989, cert. Am. Bd. Internal Medicine, 1999. Dir., med. icu VA Greater LA Healthcare Sys., Los Angeles, Calif., 1989—. Assoc. clin. prof. medicine U. Calif., LA Sch. Medicine, 1997—. Mem., ex-chairman Am. Lung Assn. LA County, 1997—98; mem. Am. Lung Assn. Calif., Oakland, 1996—. Recipient Tchr. Yr., West LA VAMC; Internal Medicine, 1997, 1998, 2002, 2003, Phi Beta Kappa, George Wash. U., 1977. Mem.: ACP, Soc. Critical Care Medicine, Am. Coll. Chest Physicians, Am. Thoracic Soc. Achievements include research in Lack of efficacy of aerosolized pentamidine in the treatment of Pneumocystis carinii pneumonia and use of non-invasive ventilation in hypercapnic respiratory failure. Office: West Los Angeles VAMC 11301 Wilshire Blvd Los Angeles CA 90073

SOOKIK, BONNIE W. air transportation executive; b. NJ; B in psychology, George Wash. U.; MS in admin., Calif. State U.; grad., Advanced Mgmt. Inst. Claremont Grad. Sch. Mgmt. Douglas Aircraft; oper. McDonnell Douglas Space Sys.; quality assurance and leadership Boeing Space and Comm.; v.p.

of people Boeing Space and Comm. Unit, 2001; pres. Shared Svcs. Group, Bellevue, Wash., 2002; sr. v.p. Boeing Co., Office Internal Governance, Chgo., 2003—. Office: Boeing Co 100 N Riverside Chicago IL 60606

SOON, BOON YI, engineer; b. Singapore, Oct. 18, 1971; s. Ren Joo Soon and Yoke Lan Lee. MS in Electro-Optics, U. Dayton, 1997, MS in Applied Math., 2000, PhD in Electro-Optics, 2002. Rsch. engr. U. Dayton Electro-Optics Program, Dayton, Ohio, 1996—2002. Contbr. articles to profl. jours. Charles Buckley scholar, 1993-95, Dayton Area Grad. Studies Inst. scholar, 1998-2002. Mem. Tau Beta Pi, Eta Kappa Nu, Phi Kappa Phi, Pi Mu Epsilon, Golden Key. Avocations: running, surfing the net, movies. Office: U Dayton Electro-Optics Program Dayton OH 45469-0245 E-mail: boonyi@yahoo.com.

SOONG, TSU-TEH, engineering science educator; b. Honan, China, Feb. 10, 1934; s. Tung and Yu-Hsieh (Lee) S.; m. Dorothy Yen-Ling Tsai, June 5, 1959; children— Karen, Stephen, Susan. BS, U. Dayton, 1955; postgrad., U. Ill., 1955-56; MS, Purdue U., 1958, PhD, 1962. Instr. engring. sci. Purdue U., 1958-62; sr. research engr. Jet Propulsion Lab., Pasadena, Calif., 1962-63; asst. prof. engring. sci. SUNY, Buffalo, 1963—66, asso. prof., 1966—68, prof., 1968—. Part-time lectr. engring. UCLA, 1962-63; part-time rsch. mathematician Cornell Aero. Lab., Buffalo, 1964-67, prin. rsch. mathematician, 1967-70 NSF Sci. Faculty fellow Tech. U. Delft, Netherlands, 1966-67; Humboldt Sr. Scientist, U. Hanover, Fed. Republic of Germany, 1987-88. Fellow ASCE (Norman medal 1999, Newmark medal 2002); mem. NSPE, Earthquake Engring. Rsch. Inst., Sgma Xi, Tau Beta Pi. Achievements include research in stochastic processes and structural control in engring. Home: 249 Wellingwood Dr East Amherst NY 14051-1750 Business E-Mail: tsoong@eng.buffalo.edu.

SOON-SHIONG, PATRICK, pharmaceutical executive; MSc, U. Brit. Columbia; MD, U. Witwatersrand. CEO, chmn. bd. VivoRx, Inc., 1994—98; pres., CFO, dir. Am. BioScience, Inc., 1994—; CEO, chmn. bd. Am. Pharm. Partners, Inc., Schaumburg, Ill., 1996—, pres., 2001—. Fellow: ACS, Royal Coll. Physicians and Surgeons Can. Achievements include patents in field. Office: American Pharmaceutical Ptnrs Inc Woodfield Exec Ctr 1101 PerimeterDr 300 Schaumburg IL 60173*

SOORIYAARACHCHI, GAMINI SARATHCHANDRA, oncologist, hematologist, educator, researcher; b. Kosgama, Sri Lanka; m. Chandrika Senerath; children: Jasmine, Marcus. MBBS with honors, U. Ceylon, Colombo, Sri Lanka, 1970; diploma in child health, Conjoint Bd. Examiners, London, 1975; diploma in obstetrics, Royal Coll. Ob-Gyn Gt. Britain, 1975. Diplomate Am. Bd. Internal Medicine, Am. Bd. Geriatric Medicine, Am. Bd. Med. Oncology, Am. Bd. Hematology; mem. exam. Royal Coll. Physicians, 1974. Intern U. Ceylon Tchg. Hosps., 1970-71; sr. house officer Guildford (Eng.) Hosps., 1971-73; registrar St. Helens (Eng.) Hosp., 1974-75; sr. house officer Royal Marsden Hosp. and Inst. Cancer Rsch., Sutton, Eng., 1973-74; fellow in med. oncology and hematology U. Wis. Comprehensive Cancer Ctr., Madison, 1975-77; cons. med. oncologist and hematologist Rockford (Ill.) Clinic and Rockford Meml. Hosp., 1977-83, Oncology Hematology West and Alegent Bergan Mercy Cancer Ctr., Omaha, 1983—; med. dir. Alegent Bergan Mercy Cancer Ctr., Omaha, 1984—; co-dir. bone marrow transplantation program Oncology Hematology West and Alegent Bergan Mercy Med. Ctr., Omaha, 1993—. Asst. clin. prof. medicine U. Ill. Sch. Medicine, Rockford, 1977—83; bd. dirs. Cancer Biotherapy Rsch. Group, Franklin, Tenn., 1993—; mem. at-large med. exec. com. Alegent Bergan Mercy Med. Ctr., 2002—03, pres.-elect & vice chmn., 2003—; bd. dirs. Missouri Valley Cancer Consortium, Omaha, 1994—, pres., 1999—2001; assoc. clin. prof. medicine Creighton U. Sch. Medicine, Omaha, 1984—96, clin. prof., 1996—; chmn. prof. edn. Am. Cancer Soc., 1986, Nebr. divsn., 87; bd. dirs. Douglas and Sarpy Counties, Neb., 86, Nebr. divsn., 87; med. dir., founding mem. No. Ill. Hospice Assn., Rockford, 1980—83; mem. novel therapeutics com., audit com., ethnic diversity com. N. Ctrl. Cancer Treatment Group, Mayo Clin., Rochester, Minn. Contbg. author: Cancer Genetics in Women, 1987; contbr. over 50 articles and astracts to med. jours., including Jour. Clin. Oncology, Blood, Archives Surgery, Jour. Immunotherapy, Cancer Investigation, Annals Pharmacotherapy, Jour. Am. Acad. Dermatology, Jour. Clin. Pathology. Fellow ACP, Royal Coll. Physicians (London), Soc. for Biol. Therapy; mem. AMA, Royal Coll. Surgeons (Eng.), Am. Soc. Clin. Oncology, Am. Soc. Hematology, Am. Soc. for Blood and Marrow Transplantation, Nebr. Med. Assn. Office: Alegent Health Bergan Mercy Cancer Ctr 7710 Mercy Rd Ste 122 Omaha NE 68124-2346

SOOUDI, MATTHEW M. retired surgeon; b. Iran, Oct. 24, 1934; came to U.S., 1962; s. Yahya and Iran (Nicknejad) S.; m. Joyce J. Sooudi, Oct. 2, 1965; 2 children. MD, U. Iran, 1962. Diplomate Am. Bd. Surgery, Am. Bd. Colon and Rectal Surgery, Internat. Bd. Proctology. Intern. Bon Secours Hosp., Grosse Pointe, Mich., 1962-63; resident Grace Hosp., Detroit, 1963-67, Ferguson Clinic, Grand Rapids, Mich., 1967-68; pvt. practice St. Elizabeth Hosp., Tex., Beaumont (Tex.) Med. Hosp., Bapt. Hosp., Tex.; ret., 1996. Fellow ACS, Am. Soc. Colon and Rectal Surgeons, Internat. Assn. Proctologists; mem. AMA, Am. Assn. Phys. Surgeons, So. Med. Assn., Tex. Med. Assn., Tex. Soc. Colon and Rectal Surgeons. Address: 980 Thomas Rd Beaumont TX 77706-4621

SOOY, WILLIAM RAY, information technology executive; b. Jan. 12, 1951; s. Edward Leinau and Alice Elizabeth (Franklin) S.; m. Jean Marie Sooy, Sept. 17, 1976; children: Jennifer, Karen, Diana, Julia. BSEE, U. Miami, 1973, MS, 1977. Registered profl. engr., Fla. Engr. Fla. Power and Light, Miami, 1973-80, prin. engr. nuc. instrumentation and control, power sys. controls, sys. protection designer, 1981-97; tech. rsch. cons., designer internet svcs., mgr. sys. ops. Energy Mktg. and Trading, Fla. Power and Light, 1998-2000; sr. fin. analyst Energy Mktg. and Trading, 2000—02; sr. engr. Progress Energy, Lake Mary, Fla., 2002—03; sr. dir. info. tech. Garden of Life, West Palm Beach, Fla., 2004—. Engr. Harris Corp., Melbourne, Fla., 1980-81; adj. prof. elec. engring. Palm Beach C.C., 2000—. Mem.: IEEE (sr.), MENSA. Home: 12735 Ellison Wilson Rd North Palm Beach FL 33408-2113 E-mail: wrsooy@hotmail.com.

SOPANEN, JERI RAINER, photography director; b. Helsinki, Finland, Aug. 14, 1929; came to U.S., 1950; s. Rainer and Helvi Raakel (Salminen) S.; m. Carolyn Maier, 1952 (div. 1956); 1 child, Erik; m. Eileen A. Humeston, 1961 (div. 1980); ptnr. Christine Huneke, 1975 (separated 1991); children: Anya Maarit, Mark; m. Marja Roth, 2000. MusB, Lawrence Coll., 1952; BA, U. So. Calif., 1956. Ind. dir. photography Sopanen Films, Inc., N.Y.C., 1966—. Dir. photography: (films) My Dinner With Andre, 1982, The Gig, 1986, The Luckiest Man in the World, 1989; (documentaries) The Brain, 1986, The Ring of Truth, 1987, The Mind (Emmy award 1989); dir. photography Nova programs, 1991—, Gardens of the World with Audrey Hepburn, 1993. With U.S. Army, 1952-54. Mem. Dirs. Guild Am., Internat. Assn. Theatrical Stage Employees. Democrat. Avocation: cross country skiing. Home and Office: 100 W 89th St Apt 8D New York NY 10024-1936 Office Phone: 212-799-0679. E-mail: jrsopanen@aol.com.

SOPER, JAMES HERBERT, botanist, curator; b. Hamilton, Ont., Can., Apr. 9, 1916; s. Herbert Armitage and Anna Eliza Gertrude (Cooper) S.; m. Jean Elizabeth Morgan, Aug. 17, 1946; children: Nancy Elizabeth, Mary Florence, Daphne Evans, Ian Morgan. BA, McMaster U., 1938, MA, 1939; PhD (Harris fellow, Austin fellow), Harvard U., 1943. Mem. faculty U. Toronto, 1946-67, curator, 1946-67, prof. botany, 1966-67; chief botanist Can. Mus. Nature, Ottawa, Ont., 1967-81, curator emeritus, 1981—, rsch. assoc., 1993-95. Author: Mt. Revelstoke National Park Wildflowers, 1976, Shrubs of Ontario, 1982; contbr. articles to profl. jours. Served with RCAF, 1943-45. Recipient Royal Jubilee medal, 1978 Mem. Royal Canadian Inst. (life) (pres. 1962-63), Canadian Bot. Assn. (pres. 1982-83), Ottawa Field Naturalists Club, Fedn. Ont. Naturalists (hon.).

SOPER, JOHN TUNNICLIFF, obstetrician-gynecologist, educator; b. Iowa City, Mar. 15, 1952; MD, U. Iowa, 1978. Cert. in ob-gyn. Intern U. Utah Med. Ctr., Salt Lake City, 1978-82, resident in ob-gyn., 1978-82; fellow in gynecol. oncology Duke U., Durham, 1982-85; attending physician Duke U. Med. Ctr., Durham, 1982—, Rex Hosp., Raleigh, N.C., 1995—, Womens Hosp., Greensboro, N.C., 1995—, Wesley Long Hosp., Greensboro, 1995—; asst. prof. Duke U., 1982-83, 83-89, assoc. prof., 1989-93, prof., 1995—. Mem. ACOG, Am. Soc. Clin. Oncology, Soc. Gynecol. Oncologists, Mid-Atlantic Gynecologic Oncology Soc. Office: Duke U Med Ctr PO Box 3079 Durham NC 27715-3079

SOPER, NATHANIEL JOLAS, surgeon; b. Iowa City, July 10, 1955; MD, U. Iowa Coll. Medicine, 1980. Diplomate Am. Bd. Surgery. Resident in gen. surgery U. Utah Hosps., Salt Lake City, 1980—86, fellow in digestive disease, 1986—88; staff surgeon Barnes Hosp., St. Louis, 1988—2003, Jewish Hosp., St. Louis, 1988—2003, VA Med. Ctr., St. Louis, 1988—2003, St. Louis Regional Med. Ctr., 1988—2003; vice chair clin. affairs, dir. minimally invasive surgery, dept. surgery Northwestern U., Chgo., 2003—. Prof. surgery Washington U., St. Louis. Mem. Assn. Acad. Surger, Am. Surg. Assn., Am. Coll. Surgeons, Internat. Soc. Digestive Surgery (pres.), Soc. Univ. Surgeons, St. Louis Surg. Soc. (past pres.), Soc. Am. Gastrointestinal Endoscopic Surgeons (past pres.), Southern Surg. Assn., Soc. for Surgery of the Alimentary Tract. Office: Vice-chair Clinical Affairs Northwestern U Dept Surgery 201 E Huron St Galter 10-105 Chicago IL 60611 Office Phone: 312-695-1419.

SOPHER, AVIVA BRACHA, physician; b. Bklyn., Oct. 8, 1969; d. Jerry and Sharon Harriet Hartstein; m. Jonathan Elliot Sopher, Sept. 6, 1993; children: Ehud Roë, Ittai Benjamin, Matan Julian. BA, Barnard Coll., 1991; MD, NYU, 1995; MS, Columbia U., 1999. Resident Greenwich (Conn.) Hosp., 1995—96, Jacobi Med. Ctr., Bronx, NY, 2003—; rsch. fellow Columbia U., N.Y.C., 1999—2003. Co-author: Body Composition, 2004. Mem.: AMA, Am. Acad. Pediat. Avocations: travel, languages, exercise. Personal E-mail: avivasopher@yahoo.com.

SOPHER, VICKI ELAINE, museum curator; b. Streator, Ill., May 22, 1943; d. Donald Bird and Thelma Elsie (Saxton) Watson; m. Terry Ray Sr., Jan. 20, 1962 (div. Aug. 1982); 1 child, Terry Ray Jr. AA, No. Va. Community Coll., 1973; BA, Am. U., 1976; MS, Bank State Coll. Edn., 1986. Adminstrv. asst. Decatur & Wilson House, Washington, 1977-81; asst. dir. Decatur House/Nat. Trust for Hist. Preservation, Washington, 1981-84, dir., 1984-95; exec. dir. Hammond-Harwood House Assn., Annapolis, Md., 1996-98, Getty Mus. Mgmt. Inst., 1998—; curator Nat. Am. Red Cross, Washington, 1999—. Cons.; founder, pres. Historic House Mus. Met. Washington. Mem. Am. Assn. Museums, Mid-Atlantic Assn. Museums, Am. Assn. for State and Local History, Victorian Soc. Am. (bd. dirs.). Home: 2621 12th St S Arlington VA 22204-4819 Office: Am Red Cross 1730 E St NW Washington DC 20006-5300 E-mail: sopherv@juno.com.

SOPKIN, GEORGE, cellist, music educator; b. Chgo., Apr. 3, 1914; s. Isador and Esther (Sopkin) S.; m. Thelma Friedman, July 5, 1936; children— Monica, Paula; m. Carol Borchard Durham, Aug. 30, 1956; children— Edwin, Anthony. Student with, Daniel Saidenberg, Am. Conservatory Music, 1930-32; with, Emmanuel Feurermann, Chgo., Mus. Coll., 1932-34; D.Mus. (hon.), Northland Coll., 1977. Assoc. prof. music U. Wis., 1940-42, artist-in-residence, 1963-79, prof., 1967-77, Disting. prof., 1977-85; prof. Carnegie Mellon U., 1985—, formed trio concert tour of Europe, 1985. Staff ABC, Chgo., 1946-52; artist-in-residence Northwestern U., 1952-55, U. Wisconsin-Milw., Cleve. Inst.; founder New Eng. Piano Quartette, 1980 Mem., Kansas City (Mo.) Philharmonic Orch., 1933-34, Chgo. Symphony Orch., 1934-40, Pro Arte String Quartet, 1940-42, founder, 1946, since mem., Fine Arts Quartet, Chgo., soloist, Kansas City (Mo.) Philharmonic Orch., Chgo. Symphony Orch., Ill. Symphony Orch., Milw. Chamber Orch., Saidenberg Symphonette, frequent TV appearances; artist of film for, Ency. Brit. films, Nat. Ednl. TV films; recording artist for, Mercury, Decca, Concert-disc, Everest, numerous tours, Europe. Bd. dirs. Contemporary Concerts, Inc., Chgo. Served with USAAF, 1943-45. Mem. Lincoln Acad. Address: PO Box 134 Surry ME 04684-0134

SOPKO, ANDREW S.J. musician, educator; b. Steubenville, Ohio, Aug. 23, 1928; s. Andrew Stephen Sopko and Anna Isaysky Sopko; m. Leigh Guy, Oct. 1989 (div. Dec. 1990); children: Michelle Marie, Michael, Christopher. Student, Phila. (Pa.) Conservatory Music, 1947—48, Dalcroze Sch. Music, 1948—49; MusB, Cleve. (Ohio) Inst. Music, 1955; student, Humboldt State U., 1956—57, U. So. Calif., 1958—59; cert. in Clin. and Ednl. Hypnosis, Hypnosis Motivation Inst., LA, Calif., 1971; MA, Pacific Western U., 1981, PhD, 1982. Instr. Fla. Atlantic U., Boca Raton, Fla., 1977—78, Miami-Dade (Fla.) C.C., 1979—80, Clark County C.C., Las Vegas, 1981—82; vis. choral dir. McCullough HS, The Woodlands, Tex., 1985; music dir. Orch. Tng. Program St. Vincent de Paul Sch., Houston, 1985—86; interim pianist and voice coach UCLA, 1986—87; interim music theatre dir. Calif. State U., LA, 1987; dance music dir. New Orleans (La.) Ctr. Creative Arts, 1987—88; music dir. Oklahoma Riverside Acad., La Place, La., 1989; music instr. East Ctrl. HS, Hurley, Miss., 1990—91; instr. Ala. Sch. Math. and Sci., Mobile, Ala., 1991—93; part time musi and choral instr. Little Flower Sch., Mobile, 1993—94; instr. C.C. So. Nev., Las Vegas, 1995—96, Clark County C.C., Las Vegas, 1995—96. Adj. instr. C.C. So. Nev., Las Vegas, 1975—76, 1981—83, 1995—96, Ala. Sch. Math. and Sci., Mobile, Ala., 1988—89; instr. music Dance Dept. New Orleans (La.) Ctr. Creative Arts, 1987—88; founder, dir. Kaleidoscope Chamber Pops Orch., Las Vegas and Gulf Coast, 1981—94; pianist, condr. Clark County Libr. Dist., Las Vegas, 1981—83; guest condr. numerous prodns. Author: A Spectrum of Music Theory, 1981, Dynamics of Musical Isometrics, 1985; composer: (songs) Sonatina Rhapsody, 1950, Abandonment, 1981, over 80 others. Scholar, Dalcroze Sch. Music, 1948—49, David Diamond, 1948—49, Arthur Loesser and Cleve. (Ohio) Inst. Music, 1951—54. Mem.: Am. Soc. Composers, Authors, and Pub., Music Tchrs. Nat. Assn., Music Educators Nat. Conf., Musicians Union, La. Composer's Guild. Avocations: travel, clinical hypnosis, reading. Home: PO Box 42813 Las Vegas NV 89116

SOPPELSA, JOHN JOSEPH, decal manufacturing company executive; b. Cleve., Apr. 23, 1948; s. Anthony Joseph and Elizabeth Ann (McCarthy) S.; m. Nikki Lynn Stevens, Sept. 7, 1968. Student, Cleve. State U., 1966-68, Baldwin-Wallace Coll., Berea, Ohio, 1985. Sales rep. Manning Studios, Inc., Cleve., 1967-70, Pitney-Bowes, Inc., Stamford, Conn., 1970-72, Wampole Chem., Stamford, 1972-75; pres. Sun Art Decals Inc., Cleve., 1975—. Office: Sun Art Decals Inc 885 W Bagley Rd Berea OH 44017-2903

SORA, SEBASTIAN ANTONY, business machines manufacturing executive, educator; b. N.Y.C., June 29, 1943; s. Joseph Louis and Angelina Maria (Maletta) S.; m. Janet Lee Dietz, Apr. 11, 1970 (dec. July 1972); 1 child, Joseph Walter; m. Mary Frances Elizabeth Boscketti, Oct. 12, 1974; children: Joseph Walter, Sebastian Nicholas, Frances Ann, Jenny Concetta. BS, Bklyn. Coll., 1964; MBA, Iona Coll., 1974, PMC, 1976; DPS, Pace U., 1989. Math. modeller Assoc. Univs. Inc., 1964-66; with U.S. Coast and Geodetic Survey, Washington, 1967-70; mgr. programming IBM, Yorktown, N.Y., 1966-67, 70-75, programmer, modeller, 1970-72, mgr. program system and design Fishkill, N.Y., 1971-77, analyst on market models Harrison, N.Y., 1977-81, sr. programmer Boeblingen, Fed. Republic Germany, 1981-82, mgr. rsch. staff 1st Josephson system Yorktown, 1982-84, program dir. Systems Rsch. Inst. N.Y.C., 1984-87; mgr. edn. program World Trade Corp. IBM, North Tarrytown, N.Y., 1989-90; mgr. promotional-artificial intelligence systems IBM, White Plains, N.Y., 1990—; assoc. prof. MIS Montclair State Coll., Upper Montclair, N.J., 1992-95; pres. Bus. Edn. Systems Tech., 1992-95. Assoc. prof. info. sci. Pace U., White Plains, N.Y., 1977-96; asst. prof. telecomm. Iona Coll., New Rochelle, N.Y., 1986; asst. prof. mgmt. Manhattan Coll., Bronx, N.Y., 1988; cons. AID, Washington, 1989; vis. prof. L.I. U., 1997; assoc. prof. computer sci. Marymount Coll., Tarrytown, 1999, mgmt. and info sys. Adelphi U., 2002—; spkr. in field. Editor Jour. Value Based Mgmt., 1987—, Jour. Cross Cultural Mgmt., Jour. of Am. Mgmt., 1994-99; pub. Paradegon Shifts in Edn: Paradise Lost or Regained, U. Press of Am., Info. Sys. Ethics, Northeast Decision Sci. Inst., 2004; contbr. articles to profl. jours.; patentee fluxless solder. Mem. IEEE (technol. leadership com. 1986—, info. policy com. 1986-95), Data Processing Mgmt. Assn., Assn. Computing Machinery. Roman Catholic. Home and Office: Internat Bus Edn Sys Techs 1 Christie Ct Somers NY 10589-2430 E-mail: sora@us.ibm.com., sailor@attglobal.net.

SORBELLO, JOSEPH CHARLES, retired lawyer; b. Redlands, Calif., Apr. 8, 1925; s. Salvatore and Maria (Gallotto) S.; m. Sharon Broome, June 3, 1945, Margaret Pillsbury, June 10, 1969 (dec. June 1995); m. Marguerite Geftakys, Apr. 23, 1997. BS in Pharmacy, Wash. State U., 1951; JD, Lincoln U., 1975. Bar: Calif. 1975; lic. pharmacist Calif., Wash. Owner Community Pharmacy, Edgemont, Calif., 1955-60; pharmacist Owens Pharmacy, Bishop, Calif., 1961-69; supervising insp. Calif. State Bd. Pharmacy, San Francisco, L.A., 1969-87; pvt. practice Westminster, Calif., 1987-95; ret., 1996. Lectr. in pharmacy law U. So. Calif., L.A., 1984, 85, 86. Bd. dirs. Moreno Valley Sch. Dist., Sunny Mead, Calif. Staff sgt. USMC, 1942-46, PTO. Mem. Masons, Nu Beta Epsilon, Rho Chi. Democrat. Avocation: amateur radio. Home: 3942 S Mission Rd Fallbrook CA 92028-9455

SORBER, CHARLES ARTHUR, academic administrator; b. Kingston, Pa., Sept. 12, 1939; s. Merritt Walter and Marjory (Roachford) S.; m. Linda Ellen Babcock, Feb. 20, 1972; children: Kimberly Ann, Kingsley Charles. BS in Sanitary Engring., Pa. State U., 1961, MS in Sanitary Engring., 1966; PhD, U. Tex., 1971. Sanitary engr. U.S. Army, France and Fed. Republic Germany, 1961-65; chief gen. engring. br. U.S. Army Environ Hygiene Agy., Edgewood Arsenal, Md., 1966-69; comdr. U.S. Army Med. Environ. Rsch. Unit, Edgewood Arsenal, Md., 1971-73; dir. environ. quality divsn. U.S. Army Med. Bioengring. R&D Lab., Frederick, Md., 1973-75; asst. dean coll. scis. and math. U. Tex., San Antonio, 1976-77, acting dir. divsn. earth & phys. scis., 1977-80, dir. Ctr. Applied Rsch. & Tech., 1976-80, assoc. dean coll. engring. Austin, 1980-86, L.B. (Preach) Meaders prof., 1985; dean sch. engring. U. Pitts., 1986-93; pres. U. Tex.-Permian Basin, Odessa, 1993-2001; prof. U. Tex., Austin, 2001—; interim vice chancellor for spl. engring. programs U. Tex. Sys., 2002—03; interim pres. U. Tex., Arlington, 2003—04, spl. engring. advisor. Bd. dirs., adv. coun., cons. various cos. and agys. Author, co-author more than 140 papers, book chpts., reports on land application of wastewater and sludges, water and wastewater reuse, water and wastewater disinfection and higher edn. Recipient Disting. Alumnus award Wilkes Coll., 1987, Disting. Grad. award Coll. of Engring., U. Tex., Austin, 1994, Outstanding Engring. Alumnus award Pa. State U., 1994; John A. Focht teach fellow U. Tex.-Austin, 1982. Fellow: ASCE; mem.: NSPE, Coun. Pub. Univ. Presidents and Chancellors (exec. com. Tex. 1994—95, sec.-treas. 1999—2001), Am. Water Works Assn., Am. Soc. Engring. Edn., Water Environ. Fedn. (com. chmn. 1983—85, 1986—89, 1993—96, bd. control 1988—94, v.p. 1990—91, pres.-elect 1991—92, pres. 1992—93, Svc. award 1985, 1989, 1990, 1996), Am. Acad. Environ. Engrs. (trustee 1994—97, 2002—, diplomate, Gordon Maskew Fair award 1993), The U. Tex. Club. Office: U Tex Sys OHH 201 Austin TX 78701 Office Phone: 512-322-3776.

SORBY, DONALD LLOYD, university dean; b. Fremont, Nebr., Aug. 12, 1933; s. Lloyd A. and Orpha M. (Simmons) S.; m. Jacquelyn J. Burchard, Nov. 7, 1959; children: Thomas, Sharon. BS in Pharmacy, U. Nebr., 1955; MS, U. Wash., 1958, PhD, 1960. Dir. pharm. services U. Calif., San Francisco, 1970-72; chmn. dept. pharmacy practice Sch. Pharmacy, U. Wash., Seattle, 1972-74; dean Sch. of Pharmacy, U. Mo., Kansas City, 1974-84, Sch. of Pharmacy, U. Pacific, Stockton, Calif., 1984-95, dean emeritus, 1995—; dir. Longs Drug Stores, 1995—. Contbr. articles to profl. jours. Named Disting. Alumnus, U. Nebr. Coll. Pharmacy, 2000. Mem. Am. Pharm. Assn. (Linwood F. Tice award 1995), Am. Assn. Colls. of Pharmacy (pres. 1980-81), Calif. Pharm. Assn., Calif. Soc. Health-Sys. Pharmacists, Sigma Xi, Phi Kappa Phi, Rho Chi. Home: 4362 Yacht Harbor Dr Stockton CA 95204-1126 Office: U Pacific Sch Pharmacy Stockton CA 95211-0001 Personal E-mail: dsorby@att.net.

SOREL, EDWARD, artist; b. N.Y.C., Mar. 26, 1929; s. Morris and Rebecca (Kleinberg) Schwartz; m. Nancy Caldwell, May 29, 1965; children: Jenny, Katherine; children by previous marriage: Madeline, Leo. Diploma, Cooper Union, 1951; DFA (hon.), Art Inst. Boston, 1998. Co-founder Pushpin Studio, 1953; free-lance artist, 1956—; syndicated Sorel's News Service, 1969-70, King Features. Author, illustrator: Making the World Safe for Hypocrisy, 1972; exhibited in Pushpin Studio retrospective at the Louvre, 1970, other European galleries, 1970-71; exhibited one-man show, Graham Galleries, N.Y.C., 1973, 78, Galerie Bartsch & Chariau, Munich, 1986, Retrospective Exhibition Cooper Union, 1987, Susan Conway Galleries, Washington, 1992, Soc. Illustrators Am. Mus. Illustration, N.Y.C., 1993, Davis and Langdale Galleries, N.Y.C., 1994, 97, Nat. Portrait Gallery, Washington, 1999; illustrator: Pablo Paints a Picture, 1961, Gwendolyn the Miracle Hen, 1963 (N.Y. Herald Tribune Book award for illustration 1962), What's Good for a Five-Year-Old, 1969, The Duck in the Gun, 1969, Word People, 1970, Magical Storybook, 1972, Superpen, 1978, The Zillionaire's Daughter, 1990, First Encounters, 1994, Unauthorized Portraits, 1997, Johnny on the Spot, 1998, The Saturday Kid, 2000; contbr. to The Nation, The New Yorker, American Heritage and The Atlantic mags. Recipient awards Soc. Illustrators, Art Dirs. Club N.Y.; Augustus St. Gauden's medal Cooper Union; George Polk award for satiric drawing, 1981; Page One award Newspaper Guild of N.Y. for best editorial cartoon (magazines), 1988, Hamilton King award Soc. Illustrators, 1990, John Singleton Copley medal Smithsonian Instn., 1999, Art Dirs. Hall of Fame, 2001, Karikaturpreis Deutschen Anwaltschaft 2002.

SORELL, KITTY JULIA, public relations executive; b. Vienna, Apr. 20, 1937; came to U.S. 1938; d. Bruno Alexander and Ilse (Fischl) Singerman. BA, Syracuse U., 1959. Lic. realtor Real Estate Bd. N.Y. Spl. events coord. Gimbel's, N.Y.C., 1966—69; pub. rels./account exec. Hamra Assocs., N.Y.C., 1969—71; spl. events/pub. rels. dir. Stern Bros., Paramus, NJ, 1972; pub. rels. account exec. Zachary & Front, N.Y.C., 1972—76; dir. pub. rels. RSM&K Advt., N.Y.C., 1976—77; owner Kitty Sorell Pub. Rels., N.Y.C., 1977—; realtor, v.p., assoc. broker Corcoran Group, N.Y.C., 1994—. Reporter Wisdom's Child, 1981-84, The Villager, 1986-88; lectr. in field. Contbg. editor Mktg. Maker mag., 1976. Fundraiser WNET-TV, N.Y.C., 1974-75; vol. pub. rels. Sheridan Sq. Triangle Assn., N.Y.C., 1984-89; pres. bd. dirs. Apt. House Coop., 1991—; bd. dirs. Greenwich Village Alliance, 1994—; mem. Greenwich Village Soc. for Hist. Preservation, 1999—. Mem. Am. Soc. Profl. and Exec. Women, Publicity Club. Democrat. Jewish. Avocations: books, theater. Office: Kitty Sorell Pub Rels 250 W 57th St New York NY 10107 Office Phone: 212-539-4968. E-mail: kjs@corcoran.com.

SORELLE, RUTH DOYLE, medical writer, journalist; b. Port Arthur, Tex., Oct. 9, 1948; d. Richard Thomas and Ruth Elaine (Droddy) D.; m. Paul Charles SoRelle, Apr. 10, 1970; children: Danielle Amanda, Richard Paul. BJ, U. Tex., 1971; MPH, U. Tex., Houston, 1988. Reporter Port Arthur News, summer 1968, 69, Univ. and Info. Svc., Austin, Tex., 1970-71; med. editor U. Tex. MD Anderson Hosp., Houston, 1973-74; editor Resources Devel. Corp., Houston, 1974-76; med. editor Baylor Coll. Medicine, Houston, 1977-78; copy editor Houston Chronicle, Houston, 1978-79, med. writer, 1979-99; sr. dir. for spl. projects Baylor Coll., 1999—, editor 2 online newsletters. Instr. U. Houston, 1986, 87, 89; editor websites. Leader Presbyn. Youth Fellowship, Houston, 1989. Recipient John P. McGovern award Am. Med. Writers Assn., Community Svc. award Tex. Assoc. Press, 1993, Katie award Dallas Press Club, 1992, 93, Anson Jones award Tex. Med. Assn., 1981, 83, 85, 86, 88, 90, 92, 95, 96, 98, Francis C. Moore award Harris County Med. Assn., 1984-98, Silver Star Tex. award Tex. Hosp. Assn., 1984, 86, 89, 92, Tex. Pub. Health Assn. award, 1981, 89, 90, 91, 94, Houston Area Health Care Coalition's Health Policy Leadership award, 1990, Paul Ellis award Am. Heart Assn., 1988, 95, Nat. Multiple Sclerosis Soc. award for med. writing, 1998, Inernat. Health Reporting award Pan Am Health Orgn., 1998, others. Mem. Am. Med. Writer's Assn. (bd. dirs. southwest chpt. 1994-95), Press Club of Houston (Deadline Coverage award 1984, Investigative Series award 1990, Mag. Feature award 1994). E-mail: dsorelle@bcm.tmc.edu.

SOREN, DAVID, archaeologist, educator, writer; b. Phila., Oct. 7, 1946; s. Harry Friedman and Erma Elizabeth (Salamon) Soren; m. Noelle Louise Schattyn, Dec. 22, 1967. BA, Dartmouth Coll., 1968; MA, Harvard U., 1972, PhD, 1973. Cert. Rome Classics Ctr. Curator of coins Fogg Art Mus.,

Cambridge, Mass., 1972; asst. prof. U. Mo., Columbia, 1972-76, assoc. prof., dept. head, 1976-81; prof. U. Ariz., Tucson, 1982-97, Regents prof., 1997—, dept. head, 1984-89. Guest curator Am. Mus. Natural History, N.Y.C., 1983—90, lectr, 1993—; creator, dir. Kourion Excavations, Cyprus, 1982—89, Portugal, 1983—84, Am. Excavations, Lugnano, Italy, 1988—93; pot cons., field dir. Tunisa Excavations, Chgo. Oriental Inst./Smithsonian Instn., 1973—78; dir. excavations Chianciano, Terme, Italy, 1995—; dir. Orvieto (Italy) Inst. Classical Studies, 2002—; resident in classical archaeology Am. Acad., Rome, 2002. Author: (book) Unreal Reality, 1978, Rise and Fall of Fantasy Film, 1980, Carthage, 1990, Carthage, French edit., 1994, Vera-Ellen: The Magic and the Mystery, 1999, 2d edit., 2003, Excavation of a Roman Villa, 1999, Kourion: Search for a Lost Roman City, 1988, Corpus des Mosaiques de Tunisie, 1972, Corpus des Mosaiques de Tunisie, 3d rev. edit., 1986, Carthage: A Mosaic of Ancient Tunisia, 1987; editor: Excavations at Kourion I, 1987; contbg. editor: Archaeology Mag.; prodr.: (films) Carthage: A Mirage of Antiquity, 1987; creator, guest curator (internt traveling exhbn.) Carhtage: A Mosaic of Ancient Tunisia, 1987—92; editor, founder: Roscius, 1993—95; creative cons. (TV miniseries) Lost Civilizations, 1994; contbr. articles to profl. jours.; prodr.: (documentaries) BBC-TV documentary Malaria and the Fall of Rome, 2002; author: Vera-Ellen: The Magic and the Mystery; 2d edit., 2003. Named Outstanding Am. Under 40, Esquire Mag., 1985, hon. Italian citizen, Lugnano, Italy, 1989; recipient Cine Golden Eagle, 1980, Angenieux Film award, Indsl. Photography Mag., 1980, Oustanding Am. Under 40 award, C. Johns Hopkins-Britain's Royal Inst. Internat. Affairs, 1985; grantee, NEH, 1979, 1987, Fulbright, Lisbon, 1983. Fellow: Brit. Royal Inst. Internat. Affairs; mem.: Luso-Am. Commn. (citation 1983—84), Archaeol. Inst. Tucson (pres. 1983—86), Am. Sch. Oriental Rsch. (dept. rep. 1981—85), Nat. Geog. Soc. (project dir. 1983—84). Office: U Ariz Dept Classics 371 Mlb Tucson AZ 85721-0001 Office Phone: 520-621-1689. Business E-Mail: soren@u.arizona.edu.

SORENSEN, ALLAN CHRESTEN, service company executive; b. Edson, Alta., Can., Apr. 27, 1938; came to U.S., 1962, naturalized, 1965; s. Henry and Vivien A. Sorensen; children: Scott, Jody. BS in Pharmacy, Drake U., 1961. Salesman Hoffman LaRoche Pharm. Co., Kitchener, Ont., Can., 1961-62; salesman Personnel Pool of Am., Inc., Chgo., 1962-63, sales mgr., 1963-67, dir., pres., 1967-89, chief exec. officer, 1978-91, chmn. interim svcs., 1989-97; vice chmn., co-founder Interim Healthcare Inc., Ft. Lauderdale, 1997—2004, CEO, 2004—; dir. Republic Svcs., Inc., Ft. Lauderdale, 1998—. Mem. Am. Staffing Assn. (past pres., bd. dirs.), Am. Assn. for Homecare (past chmn., bd. dirs.), Broward Workshop. Republican. Home: 333 Sunset Dr #708 Fort Lauderdale FL 33301 Office: Interim Healthcare Inc 1601 Sawgrass Corporate Pkwy Sunrise FL 33323-2827

SORENSEN, ANDREW AARON, university president; b. Pitts., July 20, 1938; s. Albert Aaron and Margaret (Lindquist) S.; m. Donna Ingemie, Aug. 4, 1968; children: Aaron Ashley, Benjamin Samuel. BA, U. Ill., 1959; BDiv, Yale U., 1962, MPh, 1970, PhD, 1971; MPH, U. Mich., 1966. Asst. prof. Cornell U., Ithaca, N.Y., 1971-73, U. Rochester, N.Y., 1973-76, assoc. prof., 1976-83; prof., dean U. Mass., Amherst, 1983-86, Johns Hopkins U., Balt., 1986-90, exec. dir. AIDS Inst.; provost, v.p. acad. affairs U. Fla., Gainesville, 1990-96; pres. U. Ala., Tuscaloosa, 1996—2002, U. SC, Columbia, 2002—. Chmn. administrv. bd. Whitney Marine Biol. Lab., 1990—96; chmn. editl. bd. Univ. Press. Fla., 1990—96; vis. fellow U. Cambridge, 1979—80; past pres. So. U. Conf. Author 7 books; contbr. over 100 articles to profl. jours. Vice chmn. bd. dirs. Chautauqua Instn., 1996-98. U.S. Dept. Edn. fellow Lincoln U., 1966-67, NSF fellow Harvard U., 1975-76. Mem.: So. Univ. Conf. (past pres.), Univ. Rsch. Assn. (trustee), Southeastern Univs. Rsch. Assn. (past chmn. coun. presidents). Presbyterian. Home and Office: President's House U S Carolina Columbia SC 29208 Office Phone: 803-777-2931. Business E-Mail: sorensen@gwm.sc.edu.

SORENSEN, CARL EDWARD, company executive; b. San Diego, Sept. 21, 1964; s. Carl Edward and Bonnie Jean Sorensen; m. Cynthia Ann Sorensen, June 5, 1987; 1 child, Carl Edward. B Bus. Mgmt., St. Leo Coll., Norfolk, Va., 1995; M Bus. Fin. and Acctg., Mont. State U., Bozeman, 1998. Commd. USN, 1983, advanced through grades to comdr., 1998; owner, pres., CEO Sorensen Enterprises Inc., Virginia Beach, Va., 1998—. Adv. bd. chmn. Rural Bus. Enhancement, Virginia Beach; chmn. Pennys From Heaven, Sunbury, S.C. Mem. DAV, WW II Meml. Fund, Elks. Republican. Methodist. Avocations: buying small companies, improving and selling them, antique collecting. Home and Office: Sorenson Enterprises 5049 Hunt Club Chase Suffolk VA 23435-3203

SØRENSEN, ERIK, international company executive; b. Randers, Denmark, July 19, 1944; s. Christen and Erna Sørensen; m. Brigitte Berg; children: Anne Marie, Thomas, Anne Louise, Anne Mette, Anne Sophie. MS in Chemistry, Tech. U. Denmark, 1968; MBA in Internat. Fin., Cph Sch. Econs., 1971. Sr. economist Novo Industri A/S, Bagsvaerd, Denmark, 1970-71, mgr. econs. and planning, 1972-74, v.p. sales and mktg., 1974-80, pres. bioindsl. group, 1980-88; pres. Health Care Grp Novo Nordisk A/S, Denmark, 1988-1995; pres., CEO Christian Hansen Group, Denmark, 1995—. Bd. dirs., chmn. ISS A/S. Lt. Danish Army, 1968-70. Office: Chr Hansen Group Bøge Allé 10 2970 Hoersholm Denmark

SORENSEN, GILLIAN MARTIN, United Nations official; b. Columbus, Ohio, Mar. 4, 1941; d. John Butlin and Helen (Hickam) Martin; m. Theodore C. Sorensen, June 28, 1969; 1 child, Juliet. BA, Smith Coll., 1963. Commr. N.Y.C. Commn. for UN and Consular Corps, 1978-90; pres. Nat. Conf., 1990-93; undersec gen., spl. advisor for pub. policy UN, N.Y.C., 1993-97, UN asst. sec. gen. for external rels., 1997—2003; sr. advisor UN Found., N.Y.C., 2003—. Del. Dem. Nat. Conv., 1976, 84, 88. Mem.: Acad. Coun. on the UN, Women's Forum, Coun. on Fgn. Rels. Democrat. Office: UN Found 801 Second Ave Ste 404 New York NY 10017 Office Phone: 212-697-3315.

SORENSEN, JEAN, artist; b. San Diego, Nov. 18, 1920; d. William James and Hallie (Moran) Hart; m. Ralph James Sorensen, Sept. 1, 1939; children: Ellen Marie Pacchetti, Ann Christine Coons, James Christian. Student, San Jose State U., 1938-39, U. Calif., Santa Cruz, 1972—. Tchr. watercolor workshop DeAnza State Coll., Cupertino, Calif., 1984, Santa Clara Valley Watercolor Soc., Yosemite Nat. Park, 1984; tchr. botany Stanford U., 1985; ptnr. View Points Art Gallery, Los Altos, Calif., 1972-92; pres. View Prints Art Gallery, Los Altos, Calif., 1988-90. Exhibitor at Palazzo Veccico, Florence, Italy, 1972, Soc. Western Arts, DeYoung Mus., San Francisco, 1970-75; guest exhibiter biennial Kofu Watercolor Exhibit, Japan, 1983; commd. painting City of Syktyvhear, Russia, 1990, Tait Mus. Art, Los Gatos, Calif., 1997, Rose Shensen Gallery, Triton Mus., Santa Clara, Calif., 2001. Vol. docent Mid-Peninsula Regional Park Open Space Dist., San Mateo and Santa Clara counties, Calif., 1977-91. Mem. Nat. Assn. Women Artists, Soc. Western Artists, Allied Artists West (pres. 1990-92), Santa Clara Valley Watercolor Soc., Monterey County Watercolor Soc., Calif. Native Plant Soc. Avocations: genealogy, botany.

SORENSEN, JOHN NOBLE, retired mechanical and nuclear engineer; b. Mpls., Jan. 2, 1934; s. Alfred Noble and Helen Viola (Baker) S.; m. Joan Elizabeth Reiche, Sept. 15, 1954; children: Laura Elizabeth, Nancy Helen, Karen Lynn. BSME, U. N.D., 1955; MSME, U. Pitts., 1958. Cert. engr. Sr. engr. Westinghouse Electric, Pitts., 1955-67; v.p., gen. mgr. NUS Corp., Rockville, Md., 1967-86; v.p., dir. Grove Engring., Inc., Rockville, 1986-93; tech. asst. to commr. NRC, Washington, 1993-97, sr. fellow adv. com. on reactor safeguards, 1997—2001, sr. fellow adv. com. on nuclear waste, 1997—2001, spl. asst. spent fuel project office, 2002—03, retired, 2003. Mem. ASME, NSPE, Am. Nuclear Soc., Sigma Xi. Home: 629 Crocus Dr Rockville MD 20850-2046 Office: Nuclear Regulatory Commn 11545 Rockville Pike Rockville MD 20852-2747 Personal E-mail: jsoren5605@aol.com.

SORENSEN, LEIF BOGE, physician, retired educator; b. Odense, Denmark, Mar. 25, 1928; came to U.S., 1955, naturalized, 1963; s. Henry V. and Mary (Nielsen) S.; m. Janice D. Nolan; 1 child, Heidi. BS, Odense Katedralskole, 1946; MD, U. Copenhagen, Denmark, 1953, PhD in Biochemistry, 1960. Intern Copenhagen County Hosp., Hellerup, Denmark, 1954; resident Copenhagen Municipal Hosp., 1955, U. Chgo. Hosp., 1957-60; faculty, scientist U. Chgo. and Franklin McLean Meml. Research Inst., 1956—; prof. medicine U. Chgo., 1970—2002; attending physician dept. medicine, assoc. chmn. dept. Pritzker Sch. Medicine, U. Chgo., 1976-99. Interim chmn. dept. medicine U. Chgo., 1997-98; cons. FDA, 1972—. Mem. editl. bd. Jour. Lab. and Clin. Medicine, 1964-70, Arthritis and Rheumatism, 1965-72; Contbr. articles to profl. jours. With M.C. Danish Army, 1951. Fulbright scholar, 1955; Ill. Arthritis Found. grantee, 1970-72; NIH Fogarty Internat. Center sr. fellow, 1980 Mem. AAAS, Am. Rheumatism Soc., Am. Soc. Clin. Investigation, Central Soc. Clin. Research, N.Y. Acad. Scis., Danish Med. Assn., Ill. Acad. Gen. Practice., Am. Geriatrics Soc., Gerontologic Soc. Am., Am. Fedn. Aging Research Home: 1700 E 56th St Apt 2801 Chicago IL 60637-5093 E-mail: leif@medicine.bsd.uchicago.edu.

SORENSEN, LINDA, lawyer; b. Eureka, Calif., Mar. 3, 1945; BS, U. Wis., 1967; JD, U. Calif., 1976. Bar: Calif. 1976, U.S. Dist. Ct. (no. dist.) Calif. 1976, U.S. Ct. Appeals (9th cir.) 1976, U.S. Dist. Ct. (ea. dist.) Calif. 1977. Assoc., ptnr. Rothschild, Phelan & Mortali, San Francisco, 1976-88; dir. Howard, Rice, Nemerovski, Canady, Falk & Rabkin, San Francisco, 1988-95; shareholder Feldman, Waldman & Kline, P.C., San Francisco, 1997-99; pvt. practice Berkeley, Calif., 1999—; of counsel Stromsheim & Assoc., 2001—. Mem. ABA (mem. subcom. on avoiding powers, bus. bankruptcy com. 1983-95), Bar Assn. of San Francisco (chmn. comml. law and bankruptcy sect. 1984, editor fed. cts. com., no. dist. Calif. digest 1979-82). Office: PO Box 7997 Berkeley CA 94707-7997 Fax: 510 845 1785. E-mail: lindasorensen@earthlink.net.

SORENSEN, POUL HENRIK BREDAHL, physician, research scientist, pathologist; b. Copenhagen, Oct. 11, 1956; s. Paul Bredahl and Inger Sorensen, Alex Eisenberg; 1 child, Derek Lee. BS, U. B.C., Can., 1980, MD, 1984, PhD, 1988. Cert. Anatomic Pathology Royal Coll. of Physicians and Surgeons of Can., 1991. Postdoctoral fellowship U. of Minn., Mnpls., 1991—92, U. of So. Calif., LA, 1992—93; clin. asst. prof. U. of Brit. Columbia, Vancouver, Canada, 1993—96, clin. assoc. prof., 1996—98, assoc. prof., 1998—. Dir. molecular pathology lab. Children's and Women's Health Ctr. of Brit. Columbia, Vancouver, Canada, 1993—; chair and dir., johal program pediat. oncology basic and translational rsch. Depts. of Pathology and Pediat., U. of Brit. Columbia, Vancouver, Canada, 1999—; chair, biopathology and translational rsch. com. Children's Oncology Group, Bethesda, Md., 2002—. Recipient Lotte-Strauss award, Soc. for Pediat. Pathology, 1994, Young Investigator award, 1996, Children's Oncology Group, 1999, Translational Rsch. award, 2003; Centennial Fellowship, Med. Rsch. Coun. of Can., 1991—93. Mem.: Soc. for Pediat. Pathology (rsch. com. mem. 1993—), Children's Oncology Group (soft tissue sarcoma com. 1996—2003, chair, biopathology and translational rsch. com. 2002—). Achievements include research in Identification of series of genetic changes thought to underlie malignant transformation in specific subtypes of childhood cancer; Discovery of first known chromosomal translocation leading to a genetic alteration as a primary event in human breast cancer (human secretory breast carcinoma); application of signal transduction analysis for the identification of potential therapeutic targets in childhood cancer; development of series of molecular genetic tools used world-wide for diagnosis of specific subtypes of childhood cancers. Office: Univ of Brit Columbia Rm 3082 950 W 28th Ave Vancouver BC Canada V5Z4H4 Office Phone: 604-875-2936. Home Fax: 604-875-3417; Office Fax: 604-875-3417. Personal E-mail: psor@interchange.ubc.ca. E-mail: psor@interchange.ubc.ca.

SORENSEN, RAYMOND ANDREW, physics educator; b. Pitts., Feb. 27, 1931; s. Andrew J. and Dora (Thuesen) S.; m. Audrey Nickols, Apr. 2, 1953; 1 dau., Lisa Kirsten. BS, Carnegie Inst. Tech., 1953, MS, 1955, PhD, 1958. Mem. faculty Columbia, 1959-61; asst. prof. Carnegie-Mellon U., Pitts., 1961-65, assoc. prof., 1965-68, prof. physics, 1968—, chmn. dept., 1980-89. NSF sr. postdoctoral fellow, 1965-66 Fellow AAAS, Am. Phys. Soc. Home: 3621 Hilton Way Shingle Springs CA 95682

SORENSEN, SHAWN RICHARD, secondary school educator; b. American Fork, Utah, Aug. 8, 1968; s. Richard James Sorensen, Jr.; m. Colette Littlefield Sorensen, Aug. 31, 1991; children: Sabrina Marie, Ashley Deawn, Halen Shawn. Student, Dixie Coll., 1986—88; BS in Theatre/Comm., Weber State U., 1995; MA in Theatre/Comm., Wichita State U., 2000. Tchr. Rigby (Idaho) High, Idaho, 1995—98; grad. asst. Wichita (Kans.) State U., 1998—2000; tchr. North Branch (Mich.) H.S., 2000—. Auditorium coord., drawing club advisor, dir. North Branch H.S., 2000—. Mem.: Mich. Edn. Assn. Office: North Branch Area Schs PO Box 3620 North Branch MI 48461

SORENSEN, SHEILA, state legislator; b. Chgo., Sept. 20, 1947; d. Martin Thomas Moloney and Elizabeth (Koehr) Paulus; m. Wayne B. Slaughter, May, 1969 (div. 1976); 1 child, Wayne Benjamin III; m. Dean E. Sorensen, Feb. 14, 1977; (stepchildren) Michael, Debbie, Kevin, Dean C. BS, Loretto Heights Coll., Denver, 1965; postgrad. pediatric nurse practicioner, U. Colo., Denver, 1969-70. Pediatric nurse practicioner Pub. Health Dept., Denver, 1970-71, Boise, Idaho, 1971-72, Boise (Idaho) Pediatric Group, 1972-74, Pediatric Assocs., Boise, 1974-77; mem. Idaho Ho. Reps., 1987-92, Idaho Senate, Dist. 13, Boise, 1992—; chair senate health and welfare com. Idaho Senate, 1992-94, chair senate majority caucus, 1994-96, vice chair state affairs com., 1996-98, chair state affairs, 1998—. State chair Am. Legis. Exchange Coun. Precinct committeeman Ada County Rep. Ctrl. Com., Boise, 1982-86, dist. vice chair, 1985-88; polit. chair Idaho Med. Assn. Aux., 1984-87, Ada County Med. Assocs., 1986-87; bd. dirs. Family Practice Residency Program, 1992-94, Univ./Cmty. Health Sci. Assn., Bishop Kelly Found., 1993—99; chair Senate Majority Caucus, 1995-96, chair state affairs com., 1999—; mem. adv. com. on health care edn. and workforce devel. State Bd. Edn., mem. adv. bd. Drug Free Idaho., Boise State U. Master of Health Sci. Recipient AMA Nathan Davis award for Outstanding State Legislator, 1994. Mem. Nat. Conf. State Legislators, Nat. Orgn. Women Legislators (state chair), Am. Legis. Exch. Coun. (Legis of Yr. award 1999). Roman Catholic. Office Phone: 208-870-8081. Personal E-mail: sheila.sorensen@hawaii.rr.com.

SORENSON, ARNE M. hotel executive; b. Tokyo; BA, Luther Coll., 1980; JD, U. Minn., 1983. Law clk. to Hon. Ellsworth Van Graafeiland U.S. Ct. Appeals (2d cir.), 1983—84; assoc. attorney Latham & Watkins, Washington, 1984—90; ptnr. Latham & Watkins, Washington, 1990—96; sr. v.p. bus. devel. Marriott Internat. Inc., Washington, 1996-98, exec. v.p., CFO, 1998—, pres., continental European lodging, 2003—. Office: Marriott Internat Inc 1 Marriott Dr Washington DC 20058-0001

SORENSON, GEORGIA LYNN JONES, political scientist, educator; b. Abilene, Tex., Aug. 23, 1947; d. Wyly King and Olive M. (Sorenson) Jones; 1 child, Suzanna Simmonds Strasburg. BA, Am. U., 1974; MA, Hood Coll., 1976; PhD, U. Md., 1992. Social scientist Nat. Inst. Edn., Washington, 1978-79, U.S. Commn. Civil Rights, Washington, 1976-79; sr. policy analyst The White House, Washington, 1979-80; founder, sr. scholar James MacGregor Burns Acad. Leadership U. Md., College Park, 1980—. Adv. mem. W.K. Kellogg Found. Nat Fellows, Battle Creek, Mich., 1996-99. Co-author: (with James MacGregor Burns) Dead-Center: Clinton-Gore Leadership and the Perils of Moderation, 1999; editor: (with George Goethals and James MacGregor Burns) Encyclopeida of Leadership, 2004; contbr. articles to profl. jours. Chair Md. Women's Polit. Caucus, 1991-94; mem. White House Productivity Coun., Washington, 1979; mem. V.P. Youth Employment Task Force, 1979-80. Mem. Am. Polit. Sci. Assn., Internat. Soc. Polit. Psychologists, A.K. Rice Inst. Office: James MacGregor Burns Acad Leadership Univ Md College Park MD 20742-0001 Office Phone: 301-405-6100. Business E-Mail: gsorenson@academy.umd.edu.

SORENSON, JAMES ROGER, public health educator; b. Yakima, Wash., Feb. 9, 1943; s. Paul Olaf and Helen Leona (Anderson) S.; m. Nancy Ellen O'Neal, May 24, 1968;1 child, Peter Matthew. BA in Sociology, U. Wash., 1965, MA in Sociology, 1966; PhD in Sociology, Cornell U., 1970. Asst. prof. Princeton (N.J.) U., 1969-74; assoc. prof. Boston U. Sch. of Medicine, 1974-84, Boston U. Sch. of Pub. Health, 1979-84; prof. Boston Univ. Schs. of Medicine and Pub. Health, 1984-85; prof. Sch. Pub. Health U. N.C., Chapel Hill, 1985—. Cons. NIMH (Changing Role of Women Com.), 1971, Rutgers U. Ednl. Decision Making Project, 1970-74, Nat. Inst. Child Health and Human Devel., 1977-79, Nat. Heart, Lung and Blood Inst., Sickle Cell Br., 1977-80, 1991-92, Boston Comprehensive Sickle Cell Ctr., 1979-85, Nat. Ctr. for Human Genome Rsch., 1990-91; com. mem. Ea. Sociol. Soc. Papers Com., 1970-73, Genetics Core Group, Inst. for Soc., Ethics and the Life Scis., 1971-76, NYU com. on Med. and Ethical Issues in Treating Spina Bifida, 1973-74, Nat. Found. March of Dimes Clin. Rsch. (Human) adv. com. 1974-75; sci. assoc. Boston City Hosp., 1975-85, N.E. Group on Med. Edn., 1976-77; also many coms. at U. N.C. including Dean's Cabinet Sch. of Pub. Health, 1985—; dir. and chair steering com. Sch. of Pub. Health Promotion/Disease Prevention Program, 1986-89; adv. bd. Injury Prevention Rsch. Ctr., many others. Author: (with others) In Sickness and in Health: Social Dimensions of Medical Care, 1981, Reproductive Pasts, Reproductive Futures: Genetic Counseling and Its Effectiveness, 1981; also numerous articles to profl. jours. and chpts. to books; reviewer Am. Jour. Med. Genetics, Am. Jour. Preventive Medicine, Am. Jour. Pub. Health, Archives of Pathology and Laboratory Medicine, Human Relations, Jour. of Health and Social Behavior, Jour. Am. Geriatrics Soc., Milbank Meml. Fund Quarterly, New Eng. Jour. of Medicine, Patient Edn. and Counseling, Prenatal Diagnosis, Sci., Tech. and Human Values, Social Sci. and Medicine; exec. editor: Health Edn. Rsch., 1996—. Mem. adv. coun. Com. to Combat Huntington's Disease, Mass. chpt., 1979-85, edn. and comty. adv. bd. Am. Heart Assn., N.C. affiliate, 1986-89. Named fellow NIMH, Cornell U., 1967-69, Inst. of Soc., Ethics and Life Scis; named Falk lectr. Ea. Sociol. Soc., 1975-76; recipient Disting. Alumnus award Yakima Valley Coll., 1985; grantee; Mass. Dept. Pub. Health, Nat. Found., March of Dimes, NIDA, Nat. Cancer Inst. and others (19 grants in all). Mem. Am. Pub. Health Assn., Soc. Profl. Health Educators, N.C. Soc. Profl. Health Educators, Coun. on Health Edn. in Higher Edn., N.C. Pub. Health Assn., Phi Beta Kappa, Delta Omega. Avocations: music, theater. Home: 21 Wysteria Way Chapel Hill NC 27514-1637 Office: U NC Sch Pub Health 326 Rosenau Hall 7400 Chapel Hill NC 27599-0001

SORENSON, KATHERINE ANN, elementary school educator; b. Hastings, Minn., Aug. 30, 1947; d. Fredrick William Nearing and Marguerite Lucille Keene-Nearing; m. Michael Alfred Sorenson; children: Brock, Scott. BS in Edn., Black Hills State Coll., 1972; MA in Early Childhood Edn., U. Colo., Denver, 1995. Profl. tchr. lic. Colo., cert. reading recover tchr. Tchr. Maternity Mary Cath. Sch., St. Paul, 1967—68, St. Andrew's Cath. Sch., St. Paul, 1968—70, Hill City Pub. Sch., 1972—73, Groton Pub. Sch., 1973—75; substitute tchr. Billings Pub. Sch., 1975—76; tchr. Livingston Pub. Sch., 1977—85; asst. dir. childcare Children's Creative Encounters, Littleton, Colo., 1986—87; tchr. Cherry Creek Sch. Dist., Eastridge Elem., Aurora, Colo., 1987—96, 1996—, creator immerson program for mobile at risk students, edn. cons., 2004—. Co-author: Blue Ribbon Application, 1998 (Blue Ribbon School, 1999), Reading Recovery Longitudinal Analysis, National Association for Year Round Education Application. Pack leader Boy Scouts Am., Parker, 1988—94, bd. dirs., 1988—94; mem. Cherry Creek Schs. North Area Task Force, Aurora, 2001—; Sunday sch. tchr. St. Mary's Cath. Ch., Livingston, 1978—84, religious edn. coord., 1981—82; Sunday sch. tchr. Ave Maria Cath. Ch., Parker, 1992—94; mem. team fundraising Parker Baseball, 1989—92; sec. Moorhead Foster Parent Assn., 1976—77. Recipient Dewitt Wallace Libr. Power award, Dewitt Wallace Found., 1997, Exemplary Reading Program award, Colo. Coun. Internat. Reading, 1998-1999, Tchr. of the Yr. award, Cherry Creek Sch.-Eastridge Elem., 2003. Mem.: Cherry Creek Edn. Assn., Reading Recovery Assn., Colo. Coun. Internat. Reading Assn. Avocations: reading, sewing, travel, south west history, baseball. Home: 11182 Cambridge Ct Parker CO 80138 Office: Eastridge Elem Sch 11777 E Wesley Ave Aurora CO 80014

SORENSON, KATY, county commissioner; married; 2 children. BS, U. Wis., 1977, MSW, 1980. Exec. dir. Calif. Women Lawyers Bar Assn.; legis. aide Ill. State Senator Dawn Clark Netsch; commr. dist. 8 Metro Dade County Commn., Fla., 1994—. Apptd. mem. Gov.'s Commn. to Study Bldg. Codes; apptd. chair Fla. Assn. Counties' Select Com. on Telecomms. Chair Citizens' Coalition for Pub. Schs.; pres. Women's Emergency Network, Palmetto Elem. Sch. PTA; legis. chairperson Dade County Coun. PTA; fundraiser EMILY's List; active F.C. Martin Elem. Sch. PTA, Palmetto Mid. Sch. PTA. Mem. AAUW, Nat. PTA (life). Office: Office County Commr 111 NW 1st St Fl 2 Miami FL 33128-1902

SORENSON, LIANE BETH MCDOWELL, women's affairs director, state legislator; b. Chgo., Aug. 13, 1947; d. Harold Davidson McDowell and Frances Elanor (Williams) Daisey Van Kleeck; m. Boyd Wayne Sorenson, June 30, 1973; children: Nathan, Matthew, Dana. BS in Edn., U. Del., 1969, M in Counseling with honors, 1986. Tchr. Avon Grove Sch. Dist., West Grove, Pa., 1969-70, Alexis I. duPont Sch. Dist., Wilmington, Del., 1970-73, Barrington (Ill.) Sch. Dist., 1973-75; counseling intern Medill Intensive Learning Ctr.-Christina Sch. Dist., Newark, Del., 1985; counselor Family Violence Shelter CHILD, Inc., Wilmington, 1985, 86-87, dir. parent edn. programs, 1987-88; dir. Office Women's Affairs, exec. dir. Commn. on Status of Women U. Del., Newark, 1988—; mem. Dist. 6 Del. Senate, Dover, 1992—, minority whip. Chair Del. Ho. Edn. Com., 1992—, Adv. Bd. Del. Breast Cancer Coalition, 1998—; commr. Edn. Commn. State Del.; mem. tng. com. Nat. Conf. State Legislatures; mem. Bd. Women's Network Nat. Conf. State Legislatures; mem. joint sunset com. Del. Legislature, Del. House of Reps., 1992-94, Del. Senate, 1994—, Del. Legis. Joint Fin. Com. Del. Legis., 1994—, Coun. State Govts. Toll Fellowship. Presenter papers various meetings & confs. Pres. bd. dirs. Nursing Mothers, Inc., 1980-81; trustee Hockessin Montessori Sch., 1982-84, enrollment chair, 1982-83; trustee Hockessin Pub. Libr., 1982-84, pres. bd., 1982-84; bd. dirs. Del. Coalition for Children, 1986-88; bd. dirs. Children's Bur. Del., 1984-87, sec., 1985-87; pres. Jr. League Wilmington, 1986-87, rsch. coun. v.p., 1985-86; bd. dirs. YWCA New Castle County, 1989-91; pres. Del. Women's Agenda, 1986-88; vice-chair Women's Leadership Ctr., 1992—; mem. Del. Work Family Coalition; bd. dirs. Del. divsn. Am. Cancer Soc., 1993—. Grantee Del. Dept. Svcs. to Children, Youth and Their Families, 1987-88, 1988, State of Del. Gen. Assembly, 1992; recipient Disting. Legis. Svc. award Del. State Bar Assn., 1997, Del Tufo award Delaware Humanities Forum, 1999. Mem.: Hockessin Hist. Soc. (bd. mem. 2000—), Del. Family Law Commn., Del. Alliance for Arts in Edn., Del. Greenway and Trails Coun., Am. Assn. for Higher Edn. (chair women's caucus 1991—92, program chair women's caucus 1990—91, pre-conf. workshop coord. women's caucus 1990 Ann. Conf.), Rotary (charter mem. Hackessin Pike Creek club 1994—). Republican. Methodist. Avocations: camping, hiking. Office: State of Delaware Legislative Hall Rm 210 PO Box 1401 Dover DE 19903-1401

SORENSON, OLAV, sociologist, finance educator; b. Columbus, Ohio, Sept. 11, 1969; s. John D. and Ruth Sather Sorenson; m. Constanca Medeiros Esteves, May 18, 2002. AB, Harvard U., 1991; MA, PhD, Stanford U., 1997. Asst. prof. strategy U. Chgo., 1997—99; asst. prof. policy UCLA, 1999—2003, assoc. prof. policy, 2003—. Prin. Sorenson Cons., L.A., 1997—; mem. sci. adv. bd. IntegriGen, Novato, Calif. Editor: (annual volume) Advances in Strategic Management: Geography and Strategy; contbr. articles to profl. jours. Grantee, NSF, 2001—03; Century III Leader scholar, NASSP and Shell Oil, 1997, Nat. Merit scholar, Gustavus Adolphus Coll., 1987—88, Luth. Brotherhood scholar, Luth. Brotherhood, 1987—91. Mem.: Am. Economics Assn., Acad. Mgmt., Am. Sociol. Assn. Avocations: tennis, volleyball. Office: UCLA Anderson Sch 110 Westward Blvd Box 951481 Los Angeles CA 90095-1481 E-mail: osorenso@anderson.ucla.edu.

SORENSON, PERRY, resort facility executive; m. Sally Slagle; children: Eric, Karin, Bjorn. MBA with honors, U. Utah. Dist. dir. Holiday Inns, Hawaii, 1980-83, regional v.p., 1983-86; v.p., chief operating officer Embassy Suites, Inc., 1986-88; chief operating officer Outrigger Hotels and Resorts, 1988—. Avocations: reading, running, tennis. Office: Outrigger Hotels & Resorts 2375 Kuhio Ave Honolulu HI 96815-2992

SORENSON, ROGER A. international relations consultant; b. Salina, Utah, May 4, 1928; s. Elmo S. Sorenson and Nellie Jensen; m. Shirley Rae Sorenson, Sept. 15, 1930; children: Erik Roger, David E., Karl W., Laurie. BA, Brigham Young U., 1955, MA, 1958; postgrad., Johns Hopkins U., 1965-66. Internat. economist Dept. State, Washington, 1966-69, mem. policy planning staff, 1975-77; deputy chief of mission U.S. Embassy, Dublin, Ireland, 1969-74; minister U.S. Mission, Geneva, 1977-79; permanent rep. UN Agys., Rome, 1979-82; dir. N.Am. office Food and Agr. Orgn. UN, Washington, 1983-90; internat. rels. cons. Sorenson Consulting Co., Chevy Chase, Md., 1991—. Head of U.S. delegation to renegotiation of Nice Agreement, State Dept. Geneva, 1977; signatory Nice Treaty, 1977. Recipient Meritorious Svc. award Dept. State, Washington, 1966, Superior Honor award Dept. State, Washington, 1969, 74, 80. Mem. DACOR House. Achievements include patents in field. Avocations: music, literature. Home: 806 Northpoint Dr Salt Lake City UT 84103-3346 Personal E-mail: rogera@xmission.com.

SORENSON, SCOTT K. manufacturing executive; BSc, U. Utah; MBA, Harvard U. V.p. Hillenbrand Industries Inc., Batesville, Ind., 2001—, CFO, 2001—. Office: Hillenbrand Industries Inc 700 State Rte 46 E Batesville IN 47006-8835*

SORENSTAM, ANNIKA, professional golfer; b. Stockholm, Oct. 9, 1970; m. David Esch. Student, U. Ariz. With Women's Profl. Golf European Tour, 1992—, LPGA, 1993—, Swedish Nat. Team, 1987-92, Solheim Cup Team, 1994, 96, 98. Recipient Vare Trophy award, 1998, Espy Awards for Best Female Golfer, ESPN, 1996, 1998, 1999, 2002-2004; named Rolex Player of Yr., 1995, 97, 98, 2000-2003 Achievements in Tournaments won include: Australian Ladies Open, 1994, U.S. Women's Open, 1995, 96, Ladies Masters, 1995, 2000, 2002, LPGA Championship, 1997, 2002-2004, Women's British Open, 2003, first woman since 1945 to appear in a PGA Tour event, 2003, inducted into World Golf Hall of Fame, 2003, 51 career LPGA Tour victories. Office: LPGA 100 International Golf Dr Daytona Beach FL 32124-1092*

SOREY, THOMAS LESTER, JR., architect, educator; b. Wichita Falls, Tex., Jan. 26, 1927; s. Thomas Lester and Katherine (Peak) S.; m. Carolyn Drake, Dec. 24, 1959 (div. 1973); 1 child, Drake. Student, U. Okla., 1944—47; BArch, Okla. State U., 1952; MArch, Harvard U., 1954. Registered arch., Okla. Designer McKim Mead & White, Archs., NYC, summer 1954; ptnr. Sorey Hill & Sorey Archs., Oklahoma City, 1958-70; pvt. practice Oklahoma City, 1971-95; vis. prof. architecture U. Okla., Norman, 1972-74, prof. architecture, 1975-90, prof. emeritus architecture, sculptor, 1991—. Work included in books: Oklahoma Landmarks, 1967, Houses Architects Design for Themselves, 1974, Architecture in Oklahoma: Landmark and Vernacular, 1978, Affordable Houses Designed by Architects, 1979, Oklahoma Homes Past and Present, 1980; sculptor in one-man and group exhbns. Oklahoma City, Norman, Tulsa, 1977—. Mem. prof. adv. com. Okla. State U. Sch. Architecture, Stillwater, 1967-69, Neighborhood Alliance, Inc., Oklahoma City, 1971-73; founding dir. Contemporary Arts Found., Oklahoma City, 1965-67; dir. Sunbeam Family Svcs., Oklahoma City, 1967-75; trustee Oklahoma City Art Mus., 1968-77, v.p., 1975; mem. Citizens League of Ctrl. Okla., Interfaith Alliance. With U.S. Army, 1954-56. Recipient Award of Excellence for House Design, Archtl. Record, 1968, Assocs. Disting. Lectr. award U. Okla., 1984-86. Mem. AIA (pres. Oklahoma City sect. 1965, bd. dirs. Okla. chpt. 1968-69, 75-77), Men's Dinner Club. Democrat. Avocations: photography, travel, reading non-fiction, racket sports. Home and Office: 3801 Ives Way Norman OK 73072-4009

SORG, DAVID JOSEPH, materials physicist; b. St. Marys, Pa, May 30, 1947; s. Leonard George and Rita Mary Sorg; m. Ann Carol Friedl, July 29, 1978; children: David Jude, Joseph Mark. BS in physics, Fordham U., 1969. Grad. rsch. asst. Pa. State U., State Coll., 1971—75; materials physicist Keystone Carbon Co., St. Marys, Pa., 1976—95, Thermometrics Inc., St. Marys, 1995—2001, GE Thermometrics, 2001—. Instr. physics Pa. State U. DuBois, 1998—. Sunday sch. tchr. St. Marys Ch., 1976—94, 2000—01; rep. Elk Mgmt. Com., Pa Game Commn., 1980—98. With U.S. Army, 1969—71, Korea. Recipient assoc. of tech. honor, Bowthorpe PLC., 1998. Mem.: Am. Assn. of Physics Tchrs. Republican. Roman Catholic. Achievements include patents for yttrium chromia - chromia themistor; method of making wafer based sensors and wafer chip sensors. Avocations: reading, exptl. hort., hist. studies. Office: GE Thermometrics 967 Wind Fall Rd Saint Marys PA 15857

SORGE, JOSEPH ANTHONY, molecular biologist; b. Newark, Mar. 23, 1954; s. Joseph S. and Margaret (Ticken) S.; m. Maryanne Kinchla, July 2, 1984. BS in Biology, BS in Chemistry, MIT, 1975; MD cum laude, Harvard U., Boston, 1979. Intern Brown U., Providence, 1979-80; post-doctoral fellow Cold Spring Harbor (N.Y.) Lab., 1980-82; asst. mem. Scripps Clinic and Research Inst., La Jolla, Calif., 1983—, staff physician, 1985—. Sci. dir. Stratagene, San Diego, 1984-86, chief exec. officer, 1985—. Contbr. articles on molecular biology to profl. jours. Recipient Research Service award NIH, 1981-83, Research Investigator award NIH, 1983-91, Jr. Faculty award Am. Cancer Soc., 1985-86, Pew Scholars award, Pew Meml. Trust, 1985-89. Mem. AAAS, Am. Soc. Microbiology. Avocations: skiing, surfing. Office: Stratagene Holding Corporation 11011 N Torrey Pines Rd La Jolla CA 92037

SORGE, KAREN LEE, commercial printing company executive, consultant; b. Warwick, N.Y., May 27, 1958; d. Wesley Thomas and Margaret Anne (Storms) Kervatt; m. David W. Farquhar, July 16, 1982 (div. Feb. 1990); 1 child: Lauren Nicole; m. Thomas E. Sorge, May 16, 1997; children: Natalie MaKalen Sorge, Ryan Thomas. AS, Roger Williams Coll., 1978, BS cum laude, 1980. Office mgr. Price-Rite Printing Co., Dover, N.J., summer 1975-76; cons. SBA, Bristol, R.I., 1978-80; account exec. P.M. Press Inc., Dallas, 1980-90, sales trainer, 1984-85; v.p. KDF Bus. Forms Inc., Dallas, 1984-90; account exec. Jarvis Press, Dallas, 1990—; pres. Print Trends, Dallas, 1990—. Printer Tex. Aux. Charity Auction Orgn., Dallas, 1985, Cystic Fibrosis, Dallas, 1989—93, Life Enhancement Assn. Programs Found., 1992—, Dallas Soc. Visual Comm., 1992, AIDS Resources Com., Dallas chpt. Cerebral Palsy, 1994, Lloyd-Paxton AIDS Benefit, 1994, Feast for the Eyes Gala-Benefit to Prevent Blindness, 2001, Genesis Women's Shelter, 2002, others. Recipient award Clampitt Paper Co., Dallas., 1982, P.M. Press Inc., 1983-89, Mead Paper Co., 1985-89, Feast for the Eyes Gala, 2001, Gold award Adrian Advt., 2004. Mem. Printing Industry in Am. (recipient Judges Favorite award 1992, Best of Show Hon. Mention award 1994, gold award Best of Tex. 1996), Internat. Assn. Bus. Communicators, Nat. Bus. Forms Assn. Republican. Baptist. Avocation: piano. Home: 2600 Raintree Dr Southlake TX 76092-5536 Office Phone: 817-424-5252.

SORGEN, ELIZABETH ANN, retired educator; b. Ft. Wayne, Ind., Aug. 21, 1931; d. Lee E. and Miriam N. (Bixler) Waller; m. Don DuWayne Sorgen, Mar. 8, 1952; children: Kevin D., Karen Lee Sorgen Hoeppner, Keith Alan. BS in Edn., Ind. U., 1953; MS in Edn., St. Francis Coll., Ft. Wayne, 1967. Tchr., bldg. rep. and math. book adoption rep. East Allen County Schs., Monroeville, Ind., 1953-94, ret., 1994. Founder nursery sch., choir mem. St. Marks Luth. Ch., Monroeville, 1960—; vol. Sci. Ctrl.; pres. Heritage Homemakers, 1990-2000; substitute tchr. Recipient Golden Apple award East Allen County Schs., 1976, Monroeville Tchr. of Yr. award, 1993. Mem.: AAUW, Ft. Wayne Ret. Tchrs. Assn. Avocations: square and line dancing, camping, gardening. Home: 25214 Lincoln Hwy E Monroeville IN 46773-9710

SORGI, MERCEDES PRIETO, psychologist; b. Havana, Cuba, Sept. 8, 1953; came to the U.S., 1961; d. Roberto Isaac and Dora Natalia (Fernandez) Prieto; m. John David Sorgi, Sept. 2, 1978; children: James, John, Roberto. BA in Psychology, Vanderbilt U., 1974; MA in Spl. Edn., George Peabody Coll., 1976; EdS in Spl. Edn., U. Miami, 1978; PhD in Sch. Psychology, Kent State U., 1994—. Cert. sch. psychologist, Ohio. Lead tchr. Mailman Ctr. for Child Devel., Miami, Fla., 1976, parent tng. coord., 1976-78; owner, buyer, salesperson The Land of Make Believe Shop, Hudson, Ohio, 1979-87; pre-sch. owner Mother's Day Out, Hudson, 1984-87; Open Doors program dir. Hattie Larlham Found., Mantau, Ohio, 1986-91, dir. cmty. alternatives, 1988-92; pvt. cons. N.E. Ohio Agys., 1992-93; sch. psychology intern Orange (Ohio) Sch. Dist., 1996-97; sch. psychologist Seton Elem. Sch., Hudson, 1997-98; tchg. fellow Kent State U., 1997-99; bilingual sch. psychologist Cleve. City Schs., 1998—. Bd. mem., chair various coms. Summit County Assn. for Retarded Citizens, Akron, Ohio, 1980—; mem. adv. bd. Pre-Sch. Parents Assn., Hudson, 1982-85, Chem. Abuse Reduction Through Edn., Hudson, 1983-85; founding mem., chair Hattie Larlham League Hudson, 1985—. Mem. Rep. Women's League, Hudson, 1983-94; coun. mem. St. Mary Parish Coun., Hudson, 1985-88. Mem. APA, Nat. Assn. Sch. Psychologists, Ohio Assn. Sch. Psychologists, Cleve. Assn. for Sch. Psychologists, Support Spl. Edn. in Hudson (founder), Grad. Orgn. Sch. Pscyhology Studies (founder, chair). Roman Catholic. Avocations: gardening, horses, antiques. Home: 333 Aurora St Hudson OH 44236-2917

SORIANO, ALFONSO GUILLEARD, professional baseball player; b. San Pedro De Macoris, Dominican Republic, Jan. 1, 1978; Profl. baseball player N.Y. Yankees, 1999—2004, Texas Rangers, 2004—. Named All-Star Game MVP, 2004; named to Am. League All-Star Game, 2002—04. Achievements include led Am. League in Hits (209), Runs 128, and Stolen Bases (41), 2002. Office: c/o Texas Rangers 100 Ballpark Way Arlington TX 76011*

SORIANO, NANCY MERNIT, editor-in-chief; married; 1 child. Degree in Art History, Bard Coll. Former editor Good Food; former contbg. editor Cosmopolitan, Food & Wine, Brides; joined Country Living, 1982, assoc. decorating editor, home bldg. and arch. editor, exec. editor, 1995—98, editor-in-chief, 1998—. Founder Country Living Restoration Mag., 1996. Design editor (book series) American Country Design, Time Life Books, editor spl. interest publ. Country Living Dream Homes; co-author: (books) Country Living Decorating Style: The New Look of Country, 1999, Country Living Decorating with Baskets: Accents for Every Room, 2000, Country Living Decorating with Candles, 2000, Country Living Handmade Christmas: Decorating Your Tree and Home, 2001, Country Living Handmade Halloween, 2002, Stylish Renovations: Design Ideas for Old and New Houses, 2002. Office: Heart Mags 224 W 57th St Fl 7 New York NY 10019-3212*

SORKIN, AARON, scriptwriter; b. June 9, 1961; Prodr.: (TV series) Sports Nights, 1998; prodr., writer, creator: TV series The West Wing, 1999, writer: screenplays A Few Good Men, 1992, Malice, 1993; writer: (films) The American President, 1995. Office: Endeavor Talent Agy # 1000 9701 Wilshire Blvd Beverly Hills CA 90212

SORKIN, ADAM J. English educator; b. N.Y.C., Aug. 9, 1943; s. Samson Z. and Anna Sorkin; m. Nancy Rosen, June 28, 1964; children: Rachel, Erica. AB with distinction, Cornell U., 1964, MA, 1965; PhD, U. N.C., 1972. Instr. dept. English U. Ill., Chgo., 1965-66, U. N.C., Chapel Hill, 1970-71; instr. lit. faculty arts and humanities Stockton State Coll., Pomona, N.J., 1971-73; asst. prof. English divsn. lang. arts Bluefield (W.Va.) State Coll., 1974-78; disting. prof. English Pa. State Delaware County, Media, 1978—. Adj. instr. dept. lit. and lang. Drexel U., Phila., 1973; adj. instr. dept. English C.C. Phila., 1973. Editor: Politics and the Muse: Studies in the Politics of Recent American Literature, 1989, Conversations with Joseph Heller, 1993; contbg. editor Poetry N.Y., 1999-02, advisory editor, Absinthe: New European Literature, 2002—; contbr. numerous articles to profl. jours.; translator numerous books and poetry. Finalist Weidenfeld prize for translation, Oxford, 1997, 2000; recipient Grant, Witter Bynner Found., 2002—03, Moldova Grant, Soros Found., Fulbright Rsch. award in creative writing, U. Bucharest, 1990, Translation prize, Crossing Boundaries, 1997, Kenneth Raxroth Meml. Translation prize, 1999, prize, Writers' Union of Moldova, 2003; Fulbright lectr., Romania, 1980—81, Internat. RSch. Exchg. Bd. fellow, 1991, Translation grant, Arts Coun. England, 1997, 2000, Eric Mathieu King Fund grant, Am. Poets, 1999. Mem. Am. Literary Translators Assn. (bd. dirs., sec. 1999-01), Acad. Am. Poets. Home: 54 Princeton Rd Havertown PA 19083-3622 Office: Pa State Delaware County 25 Yearsley Mill Rd Media PA 19063-5522 Office Phone: 610-892-1444. E-mail: ajs2@psu.edu.

SORKIN, IRA LEE, lawyer; b. N.Y.C., May 30, 1943; s. Nathan and Rosalie (Cohen) S.; m. Ellen M. Sorkin, Aug. 24, 1969; children: Roger David, Peter Neil. BA, Tulane U., 1965; JD, George Washington U., 1968. Trial atty. SEC, N.Y.C., 1968-71, adminstr., 1984-86; asst. U.S. atty. U.S. Atty.'s Office (so. dist.) N.Y., 1971-76, dep. chief, criminal divsn., 1976; ptnr. Squadron Ellenoff Plesent & Lehrer, N.Y.C., 1977-84, Squadron Ellenoff Plesent & Sheinfeld, N.Y.C., 1986—95, Squadron, Ellenoff, Plesent & Sheinfeld LLP, N.Y.C., 1997—2002; chief legal officer Nomura Securities Internat. Inc., N.Y.C., 1995-97; ptnr. Carter, Ledyard & Milburn LLP, N.Y.C., 2002—. Lectr. Nat. Inst. Trial Advocacy, N.Y.C., 1981-91, Securities Industry Assn. Contbr. articles to profl. jours. Tutor inner city students N.Y.C. Sch. Sys., 1996-97. Mem. ABA, N.Y. Coun. Def. Lawyers, Assn. of the Bar for the City of N.Y. Avocations: golf, reading, skiing. Office: Carter Ledyard & Milburn LLP 2 Wall St New York NY 10005 E-mail: sorkin@clm.com.*

SORKIN, LAURENCE TRUMAN, lawyer; b. Bklyn., Oct. 20, 1942; s. Sidney and Lilly (Kowensky) S.; m. Joan Carol Ross, June 25, 1972; children: Andrew Ross, Suzanne Ross. AB summa cum laude, Brown U., 1964; LLB, Yale U., 1967; LLM, London Sch. Econs./Polit. Sci., 1968. Law clk. to Judge J. Joseph Smith U.S. Ct. Appeals (2d cir.), 1968-69; assoc. Cahill Gordon & Reindel, N.Y.C., 1969-75, ptnr., 1975—. Vis. lectr. Yale U., 1972, 73; lectr. various profl. orgns.; rsch. asst. to Lester and Bindman for book Race and Law in Great Britain, 1972. Contbr. to State Antitrust Law (Lifland), 1984; author: (with Lifland, Sorkin and Van Cise) Understanding the Antitrust Laws, 1986. Bd. dirs. Legal Aid Soc., N.Y.C., 1988-94, N.Y. Lawyers for Pub. Interest, 1990-93. Fulbright scholar, 1967-68. Mem. ABA (antitrust law sect. 1978—), N.Y. State Bar Assn. (antitrust sect., chmn. com. on legislation 1978-79, sect. sec. 1979-80, chmn. com. on mergers 1987-89, chmn. Clayton Act com. 1989-94, exec. com. 1989-94, comml. and fed. litigation sect. chmn. com. antitrust 1996-98), Assn. Bar City N.Y. (com. trade regulation 1974-77, 95-98, com. on electric funds transfer 1979-80), Yale Law Sch. Assn. (exec. com. 2000—), Phi Beta Kappa. Office: Cahill Gordon & Reindel 80 Pine St Fl 17 New York NY 10005-1702 Office Phone: 212-701-3209. E-mail: lsorkin@cahill.com.

SORLEY, LEWIS, writer; b. West Point, N.Y., Aug. 3, 1934; s. Merrow Egerton Sorley and Louise MaBelle Barnes; m. Virginia Mezey Sorley, Nov. 21, 1970; 1 child from previous marriage, Kathleen Stone; stepchildren: Douglas Becker, Timothy Becker, Susan Becker Pelkey. BS, U.S. Mil. Acad., 1956; MA, U. Pa., 1963; MPA, Pa. State U., 1973; PhD, Johns Hopkins U., 1979; Grad., U.S. Army War Coll., 1973. Intelligence officer CIA, Washington, 1976-83; writer Potomac, Md., 1983—. Exec. dir. Assn. Mil. Colls. and Schs. of U.S., Potomac, 1998—; bd. dirs. Army Hist. Found., Arlington, Va. Author: (books) Arms Transfers Under Nixon: A Policy Analysis, 1983, Thunderbolt: General Creighton Abrams and the Army of His Times, 1992, Honorable Warrior: General Harold K. Johnson and the Ethics of Command, 1998 (recipient Army Hist. Found.'s Disting. Book award 1998), A Better War: The Unexamined Victories and Final Tragedy of America's Last Years in Vietnam, 1999 (nominated for Pulitzer prize), Vietnam Chronicles, 2004. Lt. col. U.S. Army, 1956-76. Recipient Peterson prize Year's Best Scholarly Article on Am. Mil. History, Ea. Parks and Monuments Assn., 1991, George Washington Honor medal Freedoms Found., Valley Forge, Pa., 1966, Gold medallion, Order of St. George U.S. Armor Assn., 1999, others; decorated Legion of Merit (2 oak leaf clusters), Meritorious Svc. medal, Air medal (2 oak leaf clusters) Army Commendation medal. Mem.: Army Hist. Found. (dir. 2000—, sec. bd.dirs. 2001—), Soc. Mil. History, Assn. of Grads./U.S. Mil. Acad. (trustee 1983—89), Soc. Cin (bd. dirs. 1980—86), Nat. Eagle Scout Assn., Army Navy Club.

SOROKIN, ETHEL SILVER, lawyer; b. Hartford, Conn., 1928; d. Jacob M. and Jennie (Klein) Silver; m. Milton Sorokin, June 25, 1950; children: Rachel B., Sharon L., Leo T. BA, Vassar Coll., 1950; LLB with honors, U. Conn., 1953. Bar: Conn. 1953, U.S. Dist. Ct. Conn. 1955, U.S. Ct. Appeals (2d cir.), U.S. Supreme Ct. 1960. Assoc. Levine & Katz, Hartford, Conn., 1953-56; ptnr. Sorokin & Sorokin, Hartford, Conn., 1956-89, Sorokin, Gross & Hyde PC, Hartford, Conn., 1989-93, of counsel, 1994—2001. Lectr. law., advisor law rev. U. Conn., 1955-58, 61-66; sec. Conn. Jud. Rev. Coun., 1978-92; spkr. in field. Editor-in-chief U. Conn. Law Rev., 1953; mem. editl. bd. Conn. Bar Jour., 1951-56; contbr. articles to profl. jours. Trustee U. Conn. Law Found., Hartford, 1976-92, pres., 1978-79; dir. treas. Ctr. for First Amendment Rights, Inc., 1993-96, pres., 1996-2004. Recipient Dean C. Avery award, The Day of New London, 1997, Disting. Svc. award, U. Conn. Sch. Law, 1989, Pub.'s award for enhancement of first amendment and media, Ct. Law Tribune, 2004. Mem. ABA (media law com., 1st amendment com.), Conn. Bar Assn. (family law sect., chmn. legis. com. 1984-87, chmn. UMPA study com. 1986, media-law com. 1992—, Media Law award 1996). Office: Ctr for 1st Amendment Rights Inc 90 Statehouse Sq Hartford CT 06103-3708 E-mail: esorokin@pullcom.com., ethel@cfarfreedon.org.

SOROKIN, PETER PITIRIMOVICH, physicist, researcher; b. Boston, July 10, 1931; s. Pitirim Alexandrovich and Elena Petrovna (Baratynskaya) S.; m. Anita J. Schell, Oct. 1, 1977; children: Elena P., Paul P. AB, Harvard U., 1952, MS, 1953, PhD, 1958. Staff physicist IBM Watson Rsch. Ctr., Yorktown Heights, N.Y., 1957-68, fellow, 1968—. Contbr. articles in quantum electronics and astrophysics to profl. jours.; patentee laser devices. Recipient Michelson medal Franklin Soc., 1974; R.W. Wood award Optical Soc. Am., 1978; Harvey prize, 1984; IBM fellow, 1968—; APS Schawlow prize, 1991. Mem. Nat. Acad. Sci. (Comstock award 1983), Am. Acad. Sci., N.Y. Acad. Sci. Home: 5 Ashwood Rd South Salem NY 10590-1601 Office: IBM T J Watson Rsch Ctr PO Box 218 Yorktown Heights NY 10598-0218 E-mail: sorokin@us.ibm.com.

SOROS, GEORGE, fund management executive; b. Budapest, Hungary, Aug. 12, 1930; came to U.S., 1956; s. Tivadar and Elisabeth (Szucs) S.; m. Annaliese Witschak, Sept. 17, 1960 (div. June 1983); children: Robert, Andrea, Jonathan; m. Susan Weber, June 19, 1983; children: Alexander, Gregory. BS, London Sch. Econs., 1952; LLD (hon.), New Sch. for Social Rsch., 1990; D. Civil Law, U. Oxford, Eng., 1990; LHD (hon.), Yale U., 1991. Arbitrage trader F.M. Mayer, N.Y.C., 1956-59; analyst Wertheim & Co., N.Y.C., 1959-63; v.p. Arnhold and S. Bleichroeder, N.Y.C., 1963-73; sole proprietor Soros Fund Mgmt., N.Y.C., 1973—; chmn. Soros Fund Mgmt., LLC, N.Y.C., 1996—. Author: The Alchemy of Finance, 1987, 2nd edit., 1994, Opening the Soviet System, 1990, Underwriting Democracy, 1991, Soros on Soros: Staying Ahead of the Curve, 1995, The Crisis of Global Capitalism: Open Society Endangered, 1998, Open Society: Reforming Global Capitalism, 2000, George Soros on Globalization, 2002, The Bubble of America Supremacy: Correcting the Misuse of American Power, 2004. Mem. Coun. on Fgn. Rels., N.Y.C., 1988—, Royal Inst. Internat. Affairs, London, 1990—, Bretton Woods Com., Washington, 1989; mem. exec. com. Helsinki Watch, N.Y.C., 1982—; mem. com. Americas Watch, N.Y.C., 1982—; chmn., founding pres. Ctrl. European U., Budapest, 1991; chmn. Open Soc. Fund, 1981, Open Soc. Inst., 1993, founds. in Albania, Belarus, Bosnia and Herzegovina, Bulgaria, Croatia, Czech Republic, Estonia, Georgia, Hungary, Kazakhstan, Kyrgyzstan, Latvia, Lithuania, Macedonia, Moldova, Poland, Romania, Russia, Slovakia, Slovenia, South Africa, Rroma, Ukraine, Yugoslavia. Recipient honor Lawyers Co. for Human Rights, N.Y.C., 1990. Avocations: tennis, skiing, chess, backgammon. Office: Soros Fund Mgmt 888 7th Ave Ste 3300 New York NY 10106-0001*

SOROS, SUSAN WEBER, educational administrator; b. Bklyn., Apr. 15, 1955; d. Murray and Iris (Horowitz) Weber; m. George Soros, June 19, 1983; children: Alexander George, Gregory James. BA, Barnard Coll., N.Y.C., 1977; MA, Parsons Sch. Design, N.Y.C., 1990; PhD, Royal Coll. Art, London, 1998. Asst. dir. New York: The State of Art Exhbn., Albany, 1977; assoc. prodr. The Big Picture (film), 1978, In Search of Rothko (film), 1979; dir. Philip Colleck of London, Ltd., N.Y.C., 1988-91; exec. dir. The Open Soc. Fund, Inc., N.Y.C., 1985-91; pub. Source: Notes in the History of Art, N.Y.C., 1980—; founder, dir. The Bard Grad. Ctr. for Studies in Decorative Arts, N.Y.C., 1991—. Author: The Secular Furniture of E.W. Godwin, 1999, Rediscovering H.W. Batley (1846-1932), British Aesthetic Movement Artist and Designer, 1999, (exhbn. catalog) E.W. Godwin: Aesthetic Movement Architect and Designer, 1999, Trustee Am. Fedn. of the Arts, N.Y.C., 1995-98, the Bklyn. Mus., 1992—, Bard Coll., Annandale, N.Y., 1991—; mem. vis. com. European sculpture and decorative arts Mus. of Fine Art, 1994—, Watson Libr., 1995—, Met. Mus. Art, Thomas J. Watson Libr. Recipient Woman of Achievement award Women in Fin. Devel., 1996, Bard medal for outstanding svc. Bard Coll., 1995, Award for Achievements in Art Edn., AWED, 1993, Gold Medal award Nat. Arts Club, 1997, Spirit of the City award Cathedral Ch. of St. John the Divine, 1999, George Wittenborn Meml. Book award, 2000, Henry-Russel Hitchcock award N.Y. Met. chpt. Victoria Soc. in Am., 2000, Philip C. Johnson award Soc. Archtl. Historians, 2000; named Woman of Achievement, Barnard Coll. Mem. Am. Assn. Mus. (applied art com. 1992—), Furniture History Soc., Internat. Coun. Mus. Office: The Bard Grad Ctr for Studies in Decorative Arts 18 W 86th St New York NY 10024-3602

SOROSKY, JERI RUTH, academic administrator; b. Chgo. d. Hans S. and Florence J. (Hurwitz) Pakula; m. Gene E. Sorosky; children: Cindi, Dana, Lesli. BA, Roosevelt U., Chgo., 1952; MEd, Fla. Atlantic U., Boca Raton, 1967; EdS, Nova Southeastern U., Ft. Lauderdale, Fla., 1972; EdD, MS, Nova Southeastern U., 1981. Cert. adminstr., supr., media specialist, gifted and elem. educator, Fla. Chairperson Elem. Highland Oaks, North Miami Beach, Fla., 1967-75; mem. faculty gifted program Highland Oaks Gifted Ctr., North Miami Beach, 1975-85; chairperson gifted program Miami (Fla.) Dade C.C., 1985-2000; site adminstr. grad. tchr. edn. program Nova. Southeastern U., Ft. Lauderdale, 1992—. Adj. prof. Nova Southeastern U., Ft. Lauderdale, 1979-87, adv. doctoral practicums, 1985-2000, cluster coord., 1987—, admissions com. doctoral programs Tech. & Distance Edn. and Child & Youth Studies, 1996—; chairperson gifted edn. Dade County Schs., Miami, 1990-93; mem. com. State Gifted Task Force, Tallahassee, 1992; presenter in field. Author: GEM Major Module in Gifted Education, 1981, Ideas Unlimited, 1985, Guide for Elementary Educators, 1995, Technology in the Curriculum, 1998; editor: Readings: Gifted Education, 1991, Early Childhood Education, 1982. Project chairperson Kids in Distress, Ft. Lauderdale, 1989. Named Woman of Yr. Bus. Profl. Women, 1985. Mem. Fla. Assn. Gifted (charter, v.p. 1975-97), Nova Southeastern U. Alumni (bd. dirs. 1981-97), AAUW, Phi Delta Kappa (chairperson newsletter 1985-97). Avocations: dance, technology. Office: Nova Southeastern U 1750 NE 167th St North Miami Beach FL 33162-3017

SORRELL, DAVID G. state agency administrator; BA in Finance, U. Alabama, 1973; grad. degree, U. Wis., 1985. With Bank of N.C., Jacksonville, 1973—74; various positions Ga. Dept. Banking & Finance, 1974—97, sr. dep. commr. banking, 1997—2002, acting commr. banking, 2002—03, commr. banking, 2003—. Mem.: Ga. Bankers Assn., Nat. Assn. State Credit Union Suprs. (govt. rels. com.), Conf. State Bank Suprs. (bd. dirs., tech. com.). Office: 2990 Brandywine Rd Ste 200 Atlanta GA 30341-5565*

SORRELL, MICHAEL E. consulting company executive, hospitality executive; b. Pasadena, Calif., Mar. 31, 1945; s. James Hendrick Sorrell and Marie Vivian Bristow. AA, Normandale C.C.; BA, Concordia Coll. Pres., CEO, owner Daggers/La. Inc., Metairie, 1987-89, Mesa Cons. Svcs./MN/Inc., Mpls., 1989-94, Mesa Cons. Svcs., Inc., Las Vegas, 1994—; pres., CEO, majority ptnr. W&S Hospitality Group, Inc., 1999—; ptnr., dir. Sr. Owl Inc., 1999—; chmn., CEO Bristow-Norwich Internat. Corp., 2000—. With USN, 1963-69, 74-89. Mem. VFW, Nat. Assn. Small Bus., Nat. Lic. Beverage Assn., Inst. Mgmt. Cons., Soc. Human Resources Mgmt., Soc. Hospitality Cons., Am. Legion, Fleet Res. Assn., Navy League U.S., U.S. Naval Inst., Amateur Athletic Union of U.S., Marine Meml. Club, Victory Svcs. Club. Roman Catholic. Avocations: golf, hiking, tennis. Office: Bristow-Norwich Internat Corp 3888 W Sahara Ave Ste 33 Las Vegas NV 89102-0505 Office Phone: 702-364-0989. E-mail: MesaConsultant@aol.com., BristowNorwich1@aol.com.

SORRELL, ROZLYN, singer, recording artist, actress, educator, entrepreneur; b. Bklyn. d. Nathaniel Otis and Cupid Viola (Logan) S. BA in Theatre, CUNY, 1976, MS in Edn., 1985. Cert. tchr., Calif., NY. Tchr. LA Unified Sch. Dist., 1997, Sylvan Learning Ctr., LA, 1998, Westmark Sch., Encino, Calif., 2000, Achievement Sch., Raleigh, NC, 2002; mem. Albert McNeil Jubilee

Singers, LA, 1994—2000. Voice tchr., LA, 1992—; bus. cons., LA, 1989—. Actress various TV programs, comml.s., stage prodn. and films, 1986—; soloist Temple of Music and Art, Tucson, 1990, El San Juan (PR) Hotel, 1985, Hour of Power, Glory of Christmas, Glory of Easter, Garden Grove, Calif., 1994—, Miyazaki Civic Culture Hall, Japan, 1996, Anaheim Pond, Calif., 1997, Honolulu Symphony, 1998, Hollywood Bowl, Calif., 1998, Gospel Recording Artist, 2000, Spiritual Awakening, WRAL-TV, N.C., 2004, Pops in the Park, Regency Theatre, Cary, NC, 2004, African Am. Cultural Ctr., Raleigh, NC, 2004. Mem. AFTRA, SAG, Actors Equity Assn. Avocations: dance, walking, working out, theater. Office Phone: 866-686-0713. Business E-Mail: sorrell@bww.com.

SORRELL, WILLIAM H. state attorney general; b. Burlington, Vt., Mar. 9, 1947; s. Marshal Thomas and Esther Sorrell; children: McKenzie, Thomas. AB, U. Notre Dame, 1970; JD, Cornell U., 1974. Dep. state's atty. Chittenden County State of Vt., 1975—77, state's atty. Chittenden County, 1977—78, 1989—92; ptnr. McNeil, Murray & Sorrell, 1978—89, sec. adminstrn., 1992—97; atty. gen. State of Vt., 1997—. Bd. dir. Am. Legacy Found. Pres. United Cerebral Palsy Vt.; sec. Vt. Coalition Handicapped; bd. dirs. Winooski Valley Pk. Dist., Am. Legacy Found. Mem.: Nat. Assn. Attys. Gen. (pres.). Democrat. Office: Office Atty Gen 109 State St Montpelier VT 05609-0001 Office Phone: 802-828-3171. Business E-Mail: bsorrell@atg.state.vt.us.

SORRELS, CARRIE L. federal agency administrator; BA in Polit. Sci., Tex. Tech U., 1983; MPA, Tex. Tech. U., 1985. Presdl. mgmt. intern Office Space Sci. and Applications NASA, Washington, 1985, program analyst, 1989—93, dir. policy and bus. mgmt. divsn. Office Space Scis., 1993—. Pub. svc. fellow, 1983. Office: NASA Hdqrs Mail Code S 300 E St SW Washington DC 20546

SORRENTINO, CHARLENE H. federal judge; b. 1942; BA, U. Fla., 1963; JD cum laude, U. Miami, 1967. Law clk. to Judge Charles Fulton U.s. Dist. Ct., 1967-71; asst. fed. pub. defender Miami, 1971-75; magistrate judge U.S. Dist. Ct. (so. dist.) Fla., Miami, 1975—. Mem. Fla. Bar Assn. Office: 132 US Courthouse 300 NE 1st Ave Miami FL 33132-2126

SORRENTINO, GILBERT, English language educator, novelist, poet; b. Bklyn., Apr. 27, 1929; s. August E. and Ann Marie (Davis) S.; m. Victoria Ortiz; children: Jesse, Delia, Christopher. Student, Bklyn. Coll., 1950—51, student, 1954—55. In various positions, 1947-70; including reins. clk. Fidelity and Casualty Co., N.Y.C., 1947-48; freight checker Ace Assembly Agy., N.Y.C., 1954-56; packer Bennett Bros. Inc., N.Y.C., 1956-57; messenger Am. Houses, Inc., N.Y.C., 1948-49; shipping-room supr. Thermo-fax Sales, Inc., Queens, N.Y., 1957-60; editor Grove Press, N.Y., 1965-70; tchr. Columbia U., 1966, Aspen Writers Workshop, 1967, Sarah Lawrence Coll., 1972, The New Sch. for Social Rsch., 1976—; NEH chairperson in lit. U. Scranton, 1979; prof. English Stanford U., Calif., 1982—99, prof. emeritus, 1999—. Editorial cons. Contemporary Lit., 1989-97. Author: The Darkness Surrounds Us, 1960, Black and White, 1964, The Sky Changes, 1966, The Perfect Fiction, 1968, Steelwork, 1970, Imaginative Qualities of Actual Things, 1971, Corrosive Sublimate, 1971, Splendide-Hotel, 1972, Flawless Play Restored, 1974, A Dozen Oranges, 1976, White Sail, 1977, Sulpiciae Elegidia/Elegiacs of Sulpicia, 1977, The Orangery, 1978, Mulligan Stew, 1979, Aberration of Starlight, 1980, Selected Poems, 1958-80, 1981, Crystal Vision, 1981, Blue Pastoral, 1983, Something Said: Essays, 1984, Odd Number, 1985, Rose Theatre, 1987, Misterioso, 1989, Under the Shadow, 1991, Red the Fiend, 1995, Pack of Lies: A Trilogy, 1997, Gold Fools, 2001, Little Casino, 2002, The Moon in Its Flight, 2004. With U.S. Army, 1951—53. Recipient Samuel Fels award in fiction Coord. Coun. Lit. Mags., 1974, John Dos Passos prize, 1981, Am. Acad. and Inst. Arts and Letters award in lit., 1985, Lannan Lit. award for fiction, 1992; John Simon Guggenheim Meml. fellow, 1973-74, 87-88; grantee Creative Artists Pub. Svc. Program, 1974-75, Nat. Endowment for Arts, 1974-75, 78-79, 83-84. Mem. PEN Am. Ctr.

SORRIN, MARY LOUISE, artist; b. Woodward, Okla., Mar. 9, 1946; d. Harland Ralph and Mary Elizabeth McCurdy; m. Bruce Michael Sorrin, Oct. 31, 1969; children: Aimee Lynn, Sean David, Keri Leigh. Diploma in nursing, St. John's Hosp., 1967; AA, Ulster County C.C., 1979. Exhbns. include Women Creating-A Celebration of Cape Cod Women, 1996-98, Leo Diehl Exhbn., 1996-98, Midwest Pastel Soc. Nat., 1996, Cape Cod Art Assn., 1997, 99 (1st pl. 1999), Newport Art Mus., 1998, Northwest Pastel Soc., 1998, Creative Arts Ctr., 1998, Internat. Assn. Pastel Soc., 1999, Northern Colo. Artist Assn., 1999, La Fond Galleries, 1999, Conn. Pastel Soc. (Bd. Dirs. award 2000), Pastel Soc. West Coast, Hudson Valley Art Assn., Pastel Soc. No. Fla., Pastel Painters Soc. Cape Cod, Pastel Soc. Southwest (Merit award), Pastel Soc. (Mountain High award 2001). Pres. chpt. Vietnam Veterans Am., 1985; treas. West Hurley (N.Y.) Libr. Assn. 1st lt. Army Nurse Corps, 1967-69. Mem. Pastel Painters Soc. Cape Cod (treas. 1994-98), Pastel Soc. West Coast, Pastel Soc. Southwest, Pastel Soc. Conn. Democrat. Roman Catholic. Avocations: reading, movies, gardening. Home: 2721 N Meridian Pl Oklahoma City OK 73127-1917 E-mail: mlousorr@swbell.net.

SORSBY, JAMES LARRY, home building company executive; b. Houston, May 31, 1955; s. J.B. Jr. and Viola (Lueckemeyer) S.; m. Terry Prince, July 28, 1984; children: Carson Drew, Cameron Brent. BBA, Stephen F. Austin State U., 1977. Loan officer 1st Mortgage Co. Tex., Houston, 1977-82; pres. The MortgageBanque, Inc., Houston, 1982-88; sr. v.p., treas. Hovnanian Enterprises, Inc., Red Bank, N.J., 1988-2000, CFO, treas., 2000—. Bd. dirs. Am. S.W. Fin. Corp., Phoenix. Office: Hovnanian Enterprises Inc 10 Highway 35 PO Box 500 Red Bank NJ 07701

SORSCHER, MARVIN LOEB, religious studies educator, rabbi; b. Bklyn., Apr. 29, 1924; s. Abraham and Miriam (Cohen) S.; m. Sylvia London, Feb. 7, 1954; children: Esther S. Rister, Abraham M., Sroya S. BA, Yeshiva Coll., 1946; MA, Hunter Coll., 1950; MHL, Yeshiva U., 1950, MS, 1958, DHL, 1968. Cert. sch. adminstr. and supr., N.Y.; cert. guidance counselor, N.Y. Pres. Yeshiva Haichel Ha Torah, Bklyn., 1969—; guidance counselor John D. Wells Jr. H.S., Bklyn., 1970-74, Franklin D. Roosevelt H.S., Bklyn., 1975-89; chmn. fgn. lang. dept. Washington Irving Evening H.S., Bklyn., 1973-80; rabbi Beth Aaron Synagogue, Bklyn., 1990—; chmn. Hebrew regents testing com. N.Y. State Edn. Dept., 1976—; instr. Yeshiva Tores Emes H.S., Bklyn., 1997—. Mem. edn. adv. bd. Yeshiva Gedolah Acad., Bklyn., 1990—; exam. scorer (in Hebrew and Yiddish) oral and written tchr. cert. lics. Nat. Evaluations Systems, N.Y.; translator Hebrew and Yiddish langs. N.Y.C. Bd. Edn., Hard of Hearing-Visually Impaired Bur., 1997—. Author: Havah Nasocheach, Part I, 1969, Part 2, 1972; Manual of Tape Scripts, 1970, Lashon V'Dibbur, 1971, The Laws of Shabbos Erev Pesach, 1974, Blessings and Prayers for the Sabbath Holidays and Special Occasions, 1974, Hakshaiv Va Anai, 1976, I Can Learn Hebrew, 1986. Recipient 1st prize (trip to Israel) Torah Quiz Contest, Jewish Press, 1989. Mem. Am. Assn. Tchrs. Hebrew (pres. 1970—), Assn. Orthodox Jewish Tchrs. (life mem.; former v.p., mem. exec. bd. 1972—). Home: 1375 57th St Brooklyn NY 11219-4637 Office: Beth Aaron Synagogue 2261 Bragg St Brooklyn NY 11229-5401

SORSTOKKE, SUSAN EILEEN, systems engineer; b. Seattle, May 2, 1955; d. Harold William and Carrol Jean (Russ) Sorstokke. BS in Systems Engring., U. Ariz., 1976; MBA, U. Wash., Richland, 1983. Warehouse team mgr. Procter and Gamble Paper Products, Modesto, Calif., 1976-78; quality assurance engr. Westinghouse Hanford Co., Richland, Wash., 1978-80, supr. engring. document ctr., 1980-81; mgr. data control and adminstrn. Westinghouse Electric Corp., Madison, Pa., 1981-82, mgr. data control and records mgmt., 1982-84; prin. engr. Westinghouse Elevator Co., Morristown, N.J., 1984-87, region adminstrn. mgr. Arleta, Calif., 1987-90; ops. rsch. analyst Am. Honda Motor Co. Inc., Torrance, Calif., 1990-95; project leader parts sys. Am. Honda Motor Co., Inc., Torrance, Calif., 1995-96, mgr. parts systems and part number adminstrn., 1996-97, mgr. parts systems, 1997-2000, mgr. supply chain mgmt., 2000—02, mgr. process control and regulatory issues, 2002—. Adj. prof. U. LaVerne, Calif., 1991—92; pres. Fussy Cuts Inc., Torrance, Calif., 2000—. Advisor Jr. Achievement, 1982—83; literacy tutor Westmoreland Literacy Coun., 1983—84; host parent EF Found., Saugus, Calif., 1987—88, Am. Edn. Connection, Saugus, 1988—89, 1991; instr. Excell, L.A., 1991—92; mem. Calif. Acad. Math. and Sci., 1996—97. Mem.: Am. Inst. Indsl. Engrs., Soc. Women Engrs., Optomists Charities Inc. (bd. dirs. Acton, Calif. 1991—94). Republican. Methodist. Home: 2567 Plaza Del Amo Unit 205 Torrance CA 90503-8962 Office: Am Honda Motor Co Inc Dept Parts 100 5C 3B 1919 Torrance Blvd Torrance CA 90501-2722

SORTE, JOHN FOLLETT, investment firm executive; b. Boston, June 30, 1947; s. Martin Eugene and Elizabeth Foster (Bradley) S.; m. Colleen Sarah Costello, July 28, 1979; children: Bradley Follett, Laura Elizabeth, Kathryn Clare. BAChemE, Rice U., 1969, M in Chem. Engring., 1970; MBA, Harvard U., 1972. Assoc. Shearson Hammill & Co., Inc., N.Y.C., 1972-74; v.p. Shearson Hayden Stone, Inc., N.Y.C., 1974-79; 1st v.p. Shearson Loeb Rhoades, Inc., N.Y.C., 1979-80, Drexel Burnham Lambert, Inc., N.Y.C., 1980-82, mng. dir., 1982-88, exec. v.p., 1989-90, pres., CEO, dir., 1990-92; pres., CEO New Street Capital Corp., N.Y.C., 1992-94; pres. New Street Advisors L.P., N.Y.C., 1994—2001; pres., CEO, dir. Morgan Joseph & Co. Inc., N.Y.C., 2001—. Chmn. N.Y. Media Group, Inc., 1995-2001; bd. dirs. Vail Resorts, Inc., WestPoint Stevens, Inc. Office: Morgan Joseph & Co Inc 600 Fifth Ave 19th Fl New York NY 10020-2302 E-mail: jsorte@morganjoseph.com.

SORTER, BRUCE WILBUR, federal program administrator, educator, consultant; b. Willoughby, Ohio, Sept. 1, 1931; s. Wilbur David and Margaret Louise (Palmer) S.; m. Martha Ann Weirich, Sept. 2,1960 (div. 1967); 1 child, David Robert. BA, U. Md., 1967; MCP, Howard U., 1969; PhD, U. Md., 1972. Cert. community developer. Commd. USAFR, 1967, advanced through grades to lt. col., 1964; sr. planner, cons. Md. Nat. Capital Park and Planning Com., 1968-71; instr. psychology, sociology Howard and P.G. C.C., Columbia and Largo, Md., 1971-72; cmty. resource devel. dept. Md. Coop. Extension Svc., U. Md., College Park, Md., 1972-92; coord. rural info. ctr. Md. Coop. Ext. Svc., U. Md., College Park, 1989-92; affiliate prof. U. Md., 1985-92, ret., 1996. Ext. advisor USDA Internat. Programs, Washington, 1991-96; co-author, co-dir. Dept. Edn. Coun. Effectiveness Tng. Program, 1979-81; author First County Energy Conservation Plan, Prince George's County, 1978-85. Author, co-author 12 books; contbr. articles to profl. publs., chpts. to books. Developer, dir. teamwork tng. programs U.S. Dept. Edn., U.S. Dept. Agriculture, Brazil, Poland, Nat. Grange, 1972-92; cons. Fed. Power Commn. U.S., 1973-75, State Dept. Natural Resources, Md., 1978-79, Dept. Edn., Brazil, 1981-82, Nat. Grange, 1987, Edn. Ext. Svcs., Poland, 1991-92. Urban Planning fellow Howard U., 1968, Human Devel. fellow U. Md., 1970; recipient Meritorious Svc. award Dept. Def., 1983, Disting. Community Svc. award Md. Community Resource Devel. Assn., 1983, Citation for Outstanding Svc., Ptnrs. of Am., 1983, Excellence in Ednl. Programs award Am. Express, 1984, Project of Yr. award Am. Psychol. Assn., 1976, Award of Yr. Am. Vol. Assn., 1976, Achievement award Nat. Assn. of Counties, 1980. Mem. Internat. Cmty. Devel. Soc. (bd. dirs., Achievement award for outstanding contbn. to cmty. devel. 1985, Disting. Svc. award 1990), Md. Cmty. Resource Devel. Assn. (sec.-treas. 1979, pres. 1980, 88-89). Republican. Methodist. Avocations: volunteer work, tennis, sailing, skiing. *Decide where you want to go. Ask yourself, is it worth the cost? If the answer is yes, then go with determination for time is in short supply.*

SORTER, GEORGE HANS, accounting and law educator, consultant; b. Vienna, Dec. 2, 1927; came to U.S., 1938; s. Alfred and Hertha (Kohn) S.; m. Dorienne Lachman, Aug. 18, 1966; children: David, Ivan, Adrienne. Ph.B., U. Chgo., 1953, MBA, 1955, PhD, 1963. C.P.A., N.Y. Instr. U. Chgo., 1955-58, asst. prof., 1959-63, assoc. prof., 1963-65, prof., 1966-74; Vincent C. Ross prof. acctg., prof. of law NYU, N.Y.C., 1974—. Arthur Young prof. U. Kans., 1969; Coopers & Lybrand prof. Tuck Sch. Dartmouth Coll., 1982; bd. dirs. NYU Credit Union, 1982-85; dir. Greater N.Y. Savs. Bank, N.Y.C., 1983-97; audit com. City of N.Y., 1985-94. Author: Accounting Theory, 1963, Accounting Thoughts of W.W. Werntz, Boundaries of Accounting Universe, 1978, Relevant Financial Statements, 1978, Financial Accounting: An Events and Cash Flow Approach, 1990, The Mix-Max Co., 1990. Mem. Ill. Sch. Bd. Dist. 233, Flossmoor, 1970-74; bd. dirs. Sch. Emotionally Disturbed Children, Chgo., 1960-74, Renaissance Soc., 1956-74, Found. Acctg. Edn., N.Y.C., 1975-79. Erskine fellow U. Canterbury, 1979 Mem. Am. Acctg. Assn. (v.p 1980-81 Outstanding Acctg. Educator), N.Y. State Soc. C.P.A.s (dir. 1980-82), Am. Inst. C.P.A.s, Fin. Acctg. Standard Adv. Com. Home: 375 S End Ave Apt 15E New York NY 10280 Office: NYU Tisch Hall 40 W 4th St New York NY 10012-1106

SORTLAND, PAUL ALLAN, lawyer; b. Powers Lake, ND, July 30, 1953; s. Allan Berdette and Eunice Elizabeth (Nystuen) S.; m. Carolyn Faye Anderson, June 23, 1979; children: Joseph Paul, Martha Marie, Nicholas John, Benjamin David. BA, St. Olaf Coll., 1975; JD, U. Minn., 1978. Bar: Minn. 1978, N.D. 1981, U.S. Dist. Ct. Minn. 1979, U.S. Dist. Ct. N.D. 1980, U.S. Ct. Appeals (8th cir.) 1987, U.S. Supreme Ct. 1991. Assoc. Alderson & Ondov, Austin, Minn., 1978-80, Qualley, Larson & Jones, Fargo, N.D., 1980-83; ptnr. Holand, Lochow & Sortland, Fargo, 1983-85; pres. Sortland Law Office, Fargo, 1985-88; ptnr. Messerli & Kramer, Mpls., 1988-92; Sortland Law Office, Mpls., 1993—. Adj. prof. bus. law Moorhead State U., 1987. Mem. ATLA, ND Bar Assn., Minn. Bar Assn. (cert. civil trial specialist), Kiwanis, Million Dollar Advocates Forum, Upper Lake Minnetonka Yacht Club, Gamma Eta Gamma. Lutheran. Home: 120 Quebec Ave S Minneapolis MN 55426-1509 E-mail: sortland@sortland.com.

SORTUN, ANA, food service executive; b. Seattle; Fluency degree, L'Ecole Francais; grand diplome, La Varenne Ecole de Cuisine, Paris; diploma in Wine Studies, L'Academie du Vin. Pastry asst. and rounds cook with chef Tom Douglas Café Sport, Seattle; exec. chef Aigo Bistro, Concord, Mass., 1990; co-opener with Moncef Medeb 8 Holyoke, Cambridge, Mass.; exec. chef Casablanca, Cambridge; chef, owner Oleana, Cambridge, 2001—. Nominee Best New Restaurant, James Beard, 2002, Best Chef, Northeast, 2003, 2004; named Best New Chef, Boston Mag., Rising Star in the city's restaurant cmty., Esquire Mag. Avocation: travel. Office: Oleana 134 Hampshire St Cambridge MA 02139 Office Phone: 617-661-0505. E-mail: oleanarestaurant@earthlink.net.

SORTWELL, CHRISTOPHER T. food products executive; MBA, U. Chgo. With McKinsey & Co.; dir. corp. planning and devel. Stroh Brewery Co., 1985, v.p. corp. planning and devel., CFO, sr. v.p., 1990-96, CFO, exec. v.p., 1996—; exec. v.p., CFO, sec. Aurora Foods Inc., St. Louis, 2000—. Office: Aurora Foods Inc 11432 Lackland Rd Saint Louis MO 63146

SORVINO, MIRA, actress; b. Tenafly, N.J., Sept. 28, 1967; d. Paul S. m. Christopher Backus, June 11, 2004. AB, Harvard U., 1990. Appeared in films including Amongst Friends, 1993, The Second Greatest Story Ever Told, 1994, Quiz Show, 1994, Barcelona, 1994, Tarantella, 1996, Sweet Nothing, 1996, Mighty Aphrodite, 1995 (Oscar for Best Supporting Actress), The Dutch Master, 1994, Blue in the Face, 1995, Beautiful Girls, 1996, (TV) Parallel Lives, 1994, The Buccaneers, 1995, Norma Jean and Marilyn, 1996, Jake's Women, 1996, Romy and Michele's High School Reunion, 1997, The Replacement Killers, 1998, Mimic, 1997, Free Money, 1998, Summer of Sam, 1999, At First Sight, 1999, Joan of Arc: The Virgin Warrior, 2000, The Great Gatsby, 2000, prodr. Famous, 2000, Triumph of Love, 2001, The Grey Zone, 2001, Wise Girls, 2002, Semana Santa, 2002, Between Strangers, 2002, Gods and Generals, 2003 (TV); assoc. prodr. Amongst Friends, 1993. Office: The William Morris Agy 151 El Camino Dr Beverly Hills CA 90212

SORVINO, PAUL, actor; b. N.Y.C., 1939; Attended, Am. Musical and Dramatic Acad. Artistic dir. Am. Stage Co., Teaneck, NJ 1986-90. N.Y.C. stage debut in Bajour, 1964; actor in (plays) including The Baker's Wife, Mating Dance, Skyscraper, That Championship Season, King Lear, An American Millionaire, For My Last Number, We'll Get By, Philemon, (films) The Gambler, 1970, Where's Poppa, 1970, Panic in Needle Park, 1971, Cry Uncle, Made for Each Other, 1971, The Day of the Dolphin, 1973, A Touch of Class, 1973, I Will, I Will ... For Now, 1976, Oh God!, 1977, The Brink's Job, 1978, Shoot It, Black, Shoot It, Blue, Slow Dancing in the Big City, 1978, The Bloodbrothers, 1979, Lost and Found, 1979, Cruising, 1980, Reds, 1981, That Championship Season, 1982, I, The Jury, 1982, Off the Wall, Turk 1982, A Fine Mess, 1985, The Stuff, 1986, Vasectomy, 1986, Dick Tracy, 1990, Goodfellas, 1990, The Rocketeer, 1991, The Firm, 1993, Nixon, 1995, Romeo and Juliet, 1996, Love Is All There Is, 1996, Escape Clause, 1996, Dog Watch, 1996, Love is All There Is, 1996, Romeo and Juliet, 1996, Men with Guns, 1997, Money Talks, 1997, American Perfekt, 1997, Most Wanted, 1997, Bulworth, 1998, Knock Off, 1998, Ringside, 1999, That Championship Season, 1999, Prince of Central Park, 1999, Harlem Aria, 1999, Goodnight Joseph Parker, 1999, Dead Broke, 1999, Amati Girls, 2000, Family Man, 2000, Longshot, 2000, Perfume, 2001, See Spot Run, 2001, Plan B, 2001, Witches to the North, 2001, Rhode Island Blue, 2001, Irishman: The Legend of Danny Greene, 2001, Ciao America, 2002, Hey Arnold! (voice), 2002, The Cooler, 2003, Mambo Italiano, 2002, Goodnight, Joseph Parker, 2004; (TV miniseries) Seventh Avenue, 1977, (TV movies) Tell Me Where it Hurts, 1974, It Couldn't Happen to a Nicer Guy, 1974, Dummy, 1979, A Question of Honor, 1982, Chiefs, 1983, My Mother's Secret Life, 1984, With Intent to Kill, 1984, Surviving, 1985, Betrayed by Innocence, 1986, Don't Touch My Daughter, 1991, Perry Mason: The Case of the Wicked Wives, 1993, Parallel Lives, 1994, The Art of the Cigar (host), 1996, Joe Torre: Curveballs Along the Way, 1997, That Championship Season, 1999, The Thin Blue Lie, 2000, Mafia Doctor, 2003; (TV series) We'll Get By, 1975, Bert D'Angelo/Superstar, 1976, The Oldest Rookie, 1987, Law and Order, 1991-92, Star Trek: The Next Generation (guest appearance), 1994, That's Life, 2000-02. Office: Gersh Agy c/o Larry Taube 232 N Canon Dr Beverly Hills CA 90210-5302*

SOSA, ERNEST, philosopher, educator; b. Cardenas, Cuba, June 17, 1940; s. Ernesto and Maria (Garriga) S.; m. Sara Mercedes, Dec. 21, 1961; children: E. David, Adrian J. BA, U. Miami, 1961; MA, U. Pitts., 1962, PhD, 1964. Instr. U. Western Ontario, London, Ontario, Can., 1963-64, U. Pitts., 1964; postdoctoral fellow Brown U., Providence, 1964-66; asst. prof. U. Western Ontario, London, Ontario, 1966-67; asst. prof. to full prof. Brown U., Providence, 1967-74, chmn. of philosophy, 1970-76, full prof., 1974—, Romeo Elton prof., 1981—. Vis. prof. U. Miami, 1970, Nat. U. Mexico, 1979, 80, 81, Harvard U., Cambridge, Mass., 1982, U. Salamanca, 1995, 98, Oxford U., 1997; disting. vis. prof. Rutgers U., 1998—; John Locke lectr. Oxford U, 2004; co-chair program com. 20th World Congress of Philosophy, 1998. Author: Knowledge in Perspective, 1991; gen. editor book series, Cambridge Univ. Press, 1990—2002, Blackwell Publishers, 1991—; editor Philosophy and Phenomenol. Rsch.; co-editor: Nous; contbr. numerous articles to profl. jours. Grantee NSF, 1970-72, Exxon Ednl. Found., 1980-82; recipient Sr. fellowship NEH, 1988-89. Mem. Am. Acad. Arts and Scis., Am. Philos. Assn. (sec.-treas. 1974-82, chair internat. coop. com. 1984-89, ea. divsn. rep. 1995—, pres. ea. divsn. 2004-, v.p. ea. divsn. 2003-04), Am. Coun. Learned Socs./Soviet Acad. Commn., Internat. Fedn. Philos. Soc. (steering com. 1988-98, v.p. 1988-93), Institut Internat. de Philosophie (exec. com. 1993-96). Avocations: running, travel. Office: Brown U Dept Philosophy Providence RI 02912-0001

SOSA, KENA, primary school educator, writer; b. San Antonio, Tex., Feb. 19, 1978; d. Mark Rolen and Theresa Lynn Mayfield; m. Jose L. Sosa, Nov. 29, 2002. BA in Eng., Our Lady of the Lake U., San Antonio, TX, 2000. Cert. tchr. Pre-K -6, Bilingual and ESL Tex., 2002. Kindergarten tchr. Dallas Ind. Sch. Dist., 2001—. Author: The Kangaruins, 2001; contbr. articles to prof. jours. Vis. scholar Ezra Jack Keats Meml. fellow, U. Minn., Kerlan Collection, 2003. Mem.: Japan Am. Soc. Office: Lorenzo DeZavala Elementary 3214 N Winnetka Dallas TX 75212 Personal E-mail: kenamayfieldsosa@yahoo.com.

SOSA, SAMUEL (SAMMY SOSA), professional baseball player; b. San Pedro de Macoris, Dominican Republic, Nov. 12, 1968; With Tex. Rangers, 1989; outfield Chgo. Cubs, 1992—. Selected to N.L All-Star Team, 1995, 98-2002, 2004; led Nat. League in runs, 1998, 2001-2002; led Nat. League in home runs, 2000, 2002; led Nat. League in RBI's 1998, 2001; record for new major league baseball record for homeruns in a single month (21), 1998; single season club record of 35 homeruns at Wrigley Field, 1998; winner Roberto Clemente award for outstanding svc. to cmty. Major League Baseball, 1998. Achievements include hit 500th career home run, April 4, 2003. Office: Chgo Cubs 1060 W Addison St Chicago IL 60613-4383*

SOSKEL, NORMAN TERRY, physician; b. Sept. 1, 1948; s. Fred and Ruth (Chapel) S.; m. Judith Anne Barrie, Apr. 9, 1980; children: Daniel Aaron, Shira Anne. BA, U. Va., 1970, MD, 1974. Cert. piano tchr. St. Louis Inst. Music. Intern Hosp. of St. Raphael-Yale U., New Haven, 1974-75; resident in internal medicine Salem (Va.) VA Hosp.-U. Va., 1975-77; pulmonary fellow U. Utah, Salt Lake City, 1977-80, instr. medicine, 1980-82, asst. prof. medicine, 1982-84, U. Tenn., Memphis, 1984-89, assoc. prof. medicine, 1989-92; pvt. practice pulmonary and critical care medicine, 1992—. Adj. instr. pathology U. Utah, Salt Lake City, 1980-83; assoc. chief pulmonary sect. VA Med. Ctr., Memphis, 1989-92; dir. pulmonary medicine Eastwood Hosp., Memphis, 1992-95; clin. assoc. prof. dept. medicine pulmonary divsn. U. Tenn., 1992—; founder, med. dir., chmn. bd. Sarcoidosis Ctr., Memphis, 2000; cons. in field. Contbr. articles to profl. jours. Recipient Paderewski medal Nat. Guild Piano Tchrs., 1967, Pulmonary Acad. award Nat. Heart-Lung-Blood Inst., 1980-84, Career Devel. and Merits awards VA, 1984-87; Am. Lung Assn. fellow; Utah Heart Assn. grantee. Fellow ACP, Am. Coll. Chest Physicians (interstitial lung disease steering com., Govs. Cmty. Svc. award 2000); mem. AAAS, Am. Lung Assn., Am. Thoracic Soc. (respiratory cell and molecular biology sect.), World Assn., Sarcoidosis and Other Granulamatous Disorders, Sarcoidosis Rsch. Inst. (bd. dirs.), N.Am. Assn. Sarcoidosis and Other Granulomatous Disorders, Nat. Speleol. Soc., Western Connective Tissue Soc., So. Connective Tissue Soc., N.Y. Acad. Sci., Sigma Chi. Achievements include research in T cell antigen receptor expression in sarcoidosis and other diffuse infiltrative lung diseases, connective tissue metabolism and damage in the lung especially the role of elastin and its destruction and synthesis in emphysema. Office: 6005 Park Ave Ste 501 Memphis TN 38119-5215 Office Phone: 901-761-5877. Business E-Mail: soskelnt@sarcoidcenter.com.

SOSMAN, MARTHA B. state supreme court justice; b. Boston, Mass., Oct. 20, 1950; BA Middlebury Coll, JD U. Mich. Assoc. Foley, Hoag & Eliot, Boston, 1979—84; with U.S. Atty.'s Office, Boston, 1984—89; founding ptnr. Kern, Sosman, Hagerty, Roach & Carpenter, Boston, 1989—93; apptd. judge Superior Ct., Concord, Mass., 1993; assoc. justice Mass. Supreme Jud. Ct., 2000—. Office: Supreme Judicial Ct Judges 1 Beacon St #3 Boston MA 02108-3107

SOSNICK, FAY MAXINE, retired educator, volunteer; b. N.Y.C., June 25, 1914; d. Philip and Gussie (Cohen) Shapiro; m. Max Sosnick, Dec. 25, 1937 (dec. Sept. 1989); children: Renee Beth Bain, Janet Ruth Hughes. BA in Chemistry, Math. and Sci., Hunter Coll., 1934; MEd in Math., Fairleigh Dickinson U., 1964; AAS in Philosophy, Brookdale C.C., N.J., 1984. Auditor U.S. Fin. Office, 1943-46; acctg., analyst and payroll staff Quindar Electronics, NJ, 1965—68; exec. Inglemoor Nursing Homes, 1969-74. Creator, organizer Home Owners Assn., The Guardian-Newspaper Pub. Condo. Assn., 1973-76; creator, liaison Self-Help Groups in Arthritis, Fitness, Svcs. to Hosp., Freehold Boro Hosp., 1974—, ombudsmen's team; vol. govtl. svc. Sr. Health Ins. N.J. State, 1976-80; with Brookdale C.C. Alumni Assn., N.J., 1983-87; mem. juvenile conf. com. Superior Ct. Chancery Divsn., N.J., 1985-89; creator patient support group St. Peters U. Hosp., Circle of Friends, Cmty. Sr. Ctr.; resident, program chmn. Sr. Homes, Temple. Recipient Svc. award, Bikun Choleem. Avocations: study of voice, choir, sing alongs, retreats, music appreciation groups. Achievements include creator of ombudsmen's team for redress of grievances plans to create a community at own residence; working with governor and legislative bodies to create a community of residents of senior living facilities.

SOSNOVSKY, GEORGE, chemist, educator; b. St. Petersburg, Russia, Dec. 12, 1920; PhD, U. Innsbruck, 1948, PhD (hon.). Rschr. CSIRO and ICI, Australia, 1949—56; postdoctoral rsch. assoc. U. Chgo., 1956—59; assoc. prof. IIT, Chgo., 1963—66; spl. sr. rsch. fellow of Pub. Health Svcs., U. Coll., London, 1967—68, U. Tubingen, 1967—68; from prof. to prof. emeritus, adj. prof. dept. chemistry U. Wis., Milw., 1967—. Fellow Royal Soc. of Chemistry, London, 2002. Author: Free Radical Reactions in Preparative Organic Chem-

istry, 1964; co-founding editor: Synthesis, Internat. Jour. Methods in Synthetic Organic Chemistry; editor, 1969—85; contbr. over 174 articles to profl. jours. Regional dir. Nat. Found. for Cancer Rsch., 1980—85. Fellow: Royal Soc. Chemistry. Office: U Wis-Milw Dept Chemistry Milwaukee WI 53201

SOSNOWSKI, V. SUSAN, state legislator; b. Warwick, R.I., Dec. 20, 1955; m. Michael Sosnowski; children: Ronald, Deborah, Stephen, Michael Jr. Grad., Ocean State Bus. Inst. Co-owner Sosnowski Farm, West Kingston, R.I., 1986—; mem. R.I. Senate, Dist. 6, Providence, 1996—. Vice chair fin. com. R.I. State Senate, spl. legis. com., joint environ. and energy com., dep. majority leader, chair conservation com.; lobbyist R.I. Nurserymen's Assn., 1995, 96; mem. Gov.'s Adv. Coun. On Environ., 1997. Mem. bd. dirs. Farm Family Ins. Co., 1993-95; mem. R.I. Audubon Soc., Richmond Grange, Save the Bay; mem. Clean Water Fin. Agy.; mem. South Kingstown Planning Bd., 1993-96, South Kingstown Dem. Town Com., 1997-99. Mem. R.I. Nursery and Landscape Assn., N.E. Organic Farming Assn., South Kingstown Farmer's Market Assn., Rotary. Office: RI State Senate Ste House Providence RI 02903 E-mail: sen-sosnowski@rilin.state.ri.us.

SOSOKA, JOHN RICHARD, consulting firm executive, engineer; b. LA, Nov. 30, 1929; s. John and Mary (Kovach) S.; m. Audrey T. Trezona, Apr. 26, 1952; children: John Richard Jr., Cathie Ann, Karen Elizabeth. BS in Gen. Engring., UCLA, 1952; MBA, Calif. State U., 1975. Registered mech., elec., fire protection, metallurgy, control systems and civil engr., Calif. Project engr. Stathem Instrument, L.A., 1954-55; staff engr. Aerojet Gen., Azusa, Calif., 1955-60; tech. dir. Unitek Corp., Monrovia, Calif., 1960-65; staff engr. TRW Systems, Redondo Beach, Calif., 1965-69; engr. mgr. Allen-Jones Electronics, Gardena, Calif., 1969-70; sect. head City of Long Beach, Calif., 1970-79; pres. Sosoka & Assocs., Los Alamitos, Calif., 1979-90; exec. v.p. Sparvan, Inc., Long Beach, Calif., 1990-91; pres., CEO P2S Engring., Inc., Long Beach, Calif., 1991—. Fellow ASHRAE (dir. and regional chair 1990-93, Disting. Svc. award 1988), Inst. Advancement Engring., L.A. Coun. Engrs. and Scientists (Disting. Engr. award); mem. Assn. Energy Engrs. (v.p. 1980-81, Energy Engr. of Yr. award 1985). Republican. Episcopalian. Achievements include patent in Welding. Home: 848 Roxanne Ave Long Beach CA 90815-5013 Office: P2S Engineering Inc 5000 E Spring St Ste 800 Long Beach CA 90815-5218 Office Phone: 562-497-2999. Business E-Mail: john.sosoka@p2seng.com.

SOSS, DANIEL LEE, social work educator; b. Spokane, Wash., May 30, 1931; s. Walter Lee and Ethelyn F. (Daniel) S.; m. Dorine C., June 17, 1955; children: Nancy Lee, Mark Daniel, Shari Lee, Michael Wayne. BA, Ea. Wash. U., 1955; MSW, U. Wash., 1963. Asst. prof. emeritus Wash. State U., Pullman; adminstr. juvenile ct. Whitman County Superior Ct., Colfax, Wash.; pub. health adminstr. Thurston-Mason Health Dist., Olympia, Wash. Dir. social svcs. Nursing Home and Retirement Ctr. Mem. Nat. Eagle Scout Assn. Home: HC 1 Box 394-C Naples ID 83847-9722

SOSTARICH, MARK EDWARD, lawyer; b. Milw., Apr. 10, 1953; s. Edward Michael and Sophia (Hibler) S.; m. Karen Sue Baranek, June 12, 1976; children: Samantha Nicole, Alex Edward. BA with distinction, U. Wis., 1975, JD cum laude, 1978. Bar: Wis. 1978, U.S. Dist. Ct. (ea. and we. dists.) Wis. 1978, U.S. Ct. Appeals (7th cir.) 1988, U.S. Trademark Trial and Appeal Bd. 2004. Assoc. Godfrey & Kahn, Milw., 1978-84, ptnr., 1984-96, Petrie & Stocking SC, Milw., 1997—2004; pvt. practice South Milw., 2004—. Editor-in-chief U. Wis. Law Rev., 1978, mem., 1977. Mem. bd. visitors U. Wis., Madison, 1983—88; commr. South Milw. (Wis.) Housing Authority, 1985—86; mem. South Milw. Fire and Police Commn., 1986—92, sec., 1987—91, pres., 1991—92; mem. Wis. Elections Bd., 1987—95, vice chmn., 1990, chmn., 1991; mem. Dem. Nat. Com., 1993, 1995—97; chmn. Dem. Party of Wis., 1995—97; mem. platform and resolutions com. Wis. Dem. Party, 1984—86, 1st vice chmn., 1993, chmn., 1986—2000; mem. Assn. State Dem. Chairs, 1995—97; chmn. Milw. County Dem. Party, 1986—97, v.p., 2001, pres., 2001—04; mem., usher, HS Sunday sch. tchr., chmn. organ fundraising com. Trinity Luth. Ch., South Milw.; mem. bd. dir. Arthritis Found. of Wis. Mem. ABA, Wis. Bar Assn., Milw. Bar Assn., Seventh Cir. Ct. Appeals Bar Assn. Avocations: state and local politics, photography, collecting contemporary art. Home: 1785 Tamarack St South Milwaukee WI 53172-1048 Office: Law Offices Mark E Sostarich 6 South Church St Elkhorn WI 53121 Office Phone: 262-723-5041. Personal E-mail: msostarich@wi.rr.com.

SOSTILIO, ROBERT FRANCIS, office equipment marketing consultant; b. Boston, Nov. 17, 1942; s. Natale J. and Louise Sostilio; m. Gail Marie McGuinness, Apr. 17, 1966. Student, U. Maine, 1960-61, Broward Jr. Coll., Ft. Lauderdale, 1967-70, Miami-Dade Jr. Coll., 1979. Product assurance engr. Saxon Copystatics, Miami, Fla., 1970-77; internat. svc. mgr. Saxon Export Corp., Miami, 1977-80; nat. svc. mgr. Cybernet Internat., Warren, N.J., 1980-81; mgr. nat. copier svc. Monroe Systems for Bus., Morris Plains, N.J., 1981-82; nat. OEM mgr. Panasonic Indsl. Co., Secaucus, N.J., 1982-86; assoc. dir. copier rsch. Dataquest, San Jose, Calif., 1987-90; mgr. product program Ricoh Corp., West Caldwell, N.J., 1986-87, dir. copier mktg., 1990-94, dir. strategic planning, 1994-96; group svc. dir. converging digital peripherals Cap Ventures, 1996—2000; pres., CEO Sostilio and Assocs. Internat. Inc., Ocala, Fla., 2002—. Editor: (newsletter) Multifunctionality, 1987, Color Copiers, 1989. Block capt. Meadow Ridge Civic Assn., Basking Ridge, NJ, 1985—87; sgt.-at-arms UNICO Nat., San Jose, 1990. With USN, 1964—67. Roman Catholic. Avocations: woodworking, home remodeling, dog training, travel, cooking. Office: Sostilio & Assocs Internat PO Box 830190 Ocala FL 34483 E-mail: sostilio@flash.net.

SOSVILLE, DICK, sales and marketing executive; V.p. sales and mktg. The Dow Chem. Co., Midland, Mich., v.p. engring. plastics, 1997—. Office: The Dow Chem Co 2030 Dow Ctr Midland MI 48674-0001

SOTAK, JOHN JOSEPH, priest, educator; b. Evergreen Pk., Ill., July 2, 1951; s. John Joseph Sotak and Elizabeth Ann Wyrobek. BA, DePaul Univ., Chgo., 1984; MDiv, Cath. Theol. Union, Chgo., 1990. Sports copy editor Des Moines Register, Des Moines, 1969—83; tchr. Providence Cath. H.S., New Lenox, Ill., 1990—94; tchr., chaplain Bishop McNamara H.S., Kankakee, Ill., 1994—2000, Cascia Hall Prep. Sch., Tulsa, Okla., 2000—. Softball coach Bishop McNamara H.S., Kankakee, Ill., 1994—2000, Cascia Hall Prep. Sch., Tulsa, Okla., 2000—. Mem.: Order of St. Augustine, Orgn. of Am. Hist., Nat. Fastpitch Coaches Assn. Roman Cath. Avocations: gardening, fishing, history. Home: 2520 So Yorktown Ave Tulsa OK 74114-2809 Office: Cascia Hall Prep Sch 2520 So Yorktown Ave Tulsa OK 74114-2809 Office Phone: 918-746-2629.

SOTELINO, GABINO, chef; b. Vigo, Spain; Mem. staff Hotel Ritz, Madrid, Plaza Athanee, Paris, Koons Hotel, Switzerland, Hilton Internat. Hotels, Montreal Expo., Madison Hotel, Washington; exec. chef Capitol Hill Restaurants, Washington, Le Perrouquet, Chgo.; head chef The Pump Room, Chgo., 1980; owner, chef Ambria, Chgo., 1980—, Un Grande Cafe, Chgo., 1981—, Cafe Ba-Ba-Reeba!, Chgo., 1985—, Mon Ami, Chgo., 1998—. Named Chef of Yr., Chefs of Am., 1990; recipient Perrier-Jouet Chef of Midwest award, James Beard Found., 1997, Medalla Merito Nacional os Fpain, 1990, Academie Culinaire de France. Mem.: Euro-Toque Inc. (pres. U.S. chpt.), Grand Master Chefs Assn. (nat. chmn.), Commanderie des Corden Bleus de France. Office: Ambria 2300 N Lincoln Park W Chicago IL 60614

SOTER, GEORGE NICHOLAS, advertising executive; b. Chgo., May 16, 1924; s. Nicholas A. and Emily (Damascus) S.; m. Effie Hartocollis, Feb. 7, 1949; children: Nicholas, Thomas, Peter. Student, U. Chgo., 1947-51. Writer McCann-Erickson, Chgo., 1951-53; with Needham, Louis & Brorby, Chgo., 1954-62, v.p., creative dir. N.Y.C., 1958-62; v.p., assoc. creative dir. Lennen & Newell Inc., N.Y.C., 1962-67; v.p., co-dir. creative svcs., mgmt. supr. Kenyon & Eckhardt Inc., N.Y.C., 1968-73; exec. v.p., creative dir. Pampuzac-Soter Assocs. Inc., N.Y.C., 1974-76; sr. writer Marsteller Inc., N.Y.C., 1980-82; v.p., creative Lord, Geller, Federico, Einstein, Inc., N.Y.C., 1982-87; sr. v.p., creative dir. Great Scott Advt. Co. Inc., N.Y.C., 1987-93; dir. Soter Advt. & Mktg. Consulting Svcs., N.Y.C., 1993—; copy editor Am. Mgmt. Assn., N.Y.C., 1995—. Founder, pres. Greek Island Ltd., N.Y.C., 1963—86; dir. Interpub. Product Devel. Workshop, N.Y.C., 1967. With U.S. Army, 1943-47, ETO. Home and Office: 468 Riverside Dr # 71 New York NY 10027 Office Phone: 212-930-8030.

SOTER, STEVEN, research scientist; BSc in Astronomy, UCLA, 1965; PhD in Astronomy, Cornell U., 1971. Rsch. asst. radio astronomy project Aerospace Corp., El Segundo, Calif., 1964—66; rsch. asst. Ctr. for Radiophysics and Space Rsch., Ithaca, NY, 1966—71, rsch. assoc., 1973—79, sr. rsch. assoc., 1980—87; fellow Miller Inst. for Basic Rsch. in Sci., Berkeley, Calif., 1971—73; asst. to dir. Smithsonian Instn. Nat. Air and Space Mus., 1988—97; rsch. scientist dept. astrophysics Am. Mus. Natural History, N.Y.C., 1997—. Co-dir. Helike Project, Greece, 1988—. Co-writer, head rsch. (TV series) Cosmos, 1977—80. Office: Am Mus Natural History Dept Astrophysics Central Park West at 81st St New York NY 10024

SOTIR, MARK, automotive rental executive; B in Econs., Amherst Coll.; MBA, Harvard U. Group mktg. mgr. Coca-Cola Co.; sr. v.p. worldwide mktg. Budget Rent-A-Car Corp., 1997-98, pres., 1999-2000; v.p. ops. and reservations Budget Group, Inc., Daytona Beach, Fla., 1998-99, pres. worldwide reservation svcs., 1999-2000, pres. N.Am. vehicle rental ops., pres., COO, 2000—. Office: Budget Group Inc 4225 Naporville Rd Lisle IL 60532

SOTIRHOS, MICHAEL, ambassador; b. N.Y.C., Nov. 12, 1928; m. Estelle Manos; 2 children BBA, CCNY, 1950. Ptnr. Ariston Sales Co., Ltd., 1948, founder, chmn., 1958—; chmn. bd. Ariston Interior Designers, Inc., 1973-83; U.S. amb. to Jamaica, 1985-89; U.S. amb. to Greece, 1989-93. Bd. dirs. Alexander S. Onassis Found.; cons. various internat. shipping ad pharm. firms. Former mem. Nat. Vol. Service Adv. Council; former chmn. Internat. Ops. Com., Peace Corps; mem. nat. adv. council SBA, 1976; former chmn. Nat. Republican Heritage Groups Council Decorated comdr. Order of Distinction (Jamaica); recipient Man of Yr. award Nat. Rep. Heritage Groups Coun. Republican.

SOTO, JOCK, dancer; b. Gallup, N.M., 1965; Student, Phoenix Sch. Nallet, Sch. Am. Ballet. Mem. corps de ballet N.Y.C. Ballet, 1981-84, soloist, 1984-85, prin. dancer, 1985—. Appeared in The Magic Flute, 1981, Bagaku, The Nutcracker, Mozartiana, Rubies, Symphony in C, The Four Temperaments, Western Symphony, Stravinsky Violin Concerto, Symphony in Three Movements, Cortege Hongrois, Liebeslieder Walzer, A Midsummer Night's Dream, Brahms/Handel, Glass Pieces, Moves, The Four Seasons, In The Night, Opus 19/The Dreamer, I'm Old Fashioned, Delibes Divertissement, A Schubertiad, Concerto for Two Solo Pianos, Celebration, Allegro Brillante, A Schubert Sonata, X-Ray; N.Y.C. Ballet's Balanchine Celebration, 1993. Recipient Dance Mag. award, 2003. Office: NYC Ballet NY State Theater 20 Lincoln Center Plz New York NY 10023-6913

SOTO, NELL, state senator; b. Pomona, Calif., June 18, 1926; children: Philip, Robert, Michael, Patrick, Anna, Tom. Grad., Pomona High Sch., 1944; student, Mt. San Antonio Jr. Coll., 1946—49, UCLA. Govt. affairs rep. Equal Opportunity Agy., 1971—73; commr. status of women L.A. County, 1972—74; pers. dir. Rest Haven Hosp., 1973—76; govt. affairs rep. Health Sys. Agy., 1976—80; commr. cmty. life commn. City of Pomona, 1979—83, mem. city coun., 1987—98; govt. affairs rep. Rapid Transit Dist., 1984—94; mem., dist. 61 Calif. State Assembly, 1998—2000; mem., dist. 32 Calif. State Senate, 2000—. Mem. Air Quality Mgmt. Dist., 1993—99, Vets. Affairs Com., Transp. Com., Local Govt. Com., Ins. Com., Govtl. Orgn. Com.; chair Pub. Employment and Retirement Com. Mem. PTA St. Joseph Sch. and Giano Sch., Nogales H.S., Nogales, Calif., 1955—78. Democrat. Roman Catholic. Mailing: State Capitol Rm 4074 Sacramento CA 95814 Office: 822 N Euclid Ave Ontario CA 91762 Office Phone: 916-445-6868.

SOTO, PATRICIA MCFARLANE, elementary school educator; b. Oak Park, Ill., Aug. 21, 1948; m. Alex Soto. BA, Fla. State U., 1970; MSc in Edn., Fla. Internat. U., 1991. Nat. bd. cert. tchr. 1996. Tchr., sci. dept. chair George Washington Carver Middle Sch., Coconut Grove, Fla., 1984—. Named Outstanding Health Educator, Ednl. Devel. Corp. Mem.: Nat. Sci. Tchrs. Assn. (Optical Data Corps. Videodisc Tech. award 1992), Nat. Bd. for Profl. Tchg. Stds. (bd. mem.). Office: Carver Middle Sch 4901 Lincoln Dr Coconut Grove FL 33133-5699

SOTO, RAMONA, training specialist; b. East Chicago, Ind., Apr. 14, 1963; d. Robert Rudy and Antonia (Perez) S. Student, Purdue U., 1982-86, U. Ill., Chgo., 1990, DePaul U., 1992-95. Salesperson The Gap, Inc., Ind., 1979-84, asst. mgr., 1984-88, tng. mgr., 1988-90; tng. specialist Montgomery Ward & Co., Ill., 1990-93; temp. worker The Richard Michael Group, Chgo., 1993, Resort Travel Corp, Oakbrook Terrace, Ill., 1993; ind. tng. cons. Chgo., 1994—. Tutor Cabrini Green Tutoring Program, Chgo., 1991-98, tutor tng. mgr., 1991-94, tutor preparing an attitude for learning, leadership and success, 1991-94, jr. asst. advisor and coord., 1995-96. Mem. ASTD. Avocations: exercise, reading, volunteering, cooking, biking. Home: 1130 W Morse Ave Chicago IL 60626-3507

SOTO-FERNANDEZ, LILIANA, education educator; b. Banes, Oriente, Cuba, Apr. 25, 1954; came to U.S., 1970; d. Juan Antonio and Laudelina Soto; m. Vicente Antonio Fernandez, Aug. 20, 1977. BA magna cum laude, Bklyn. Coll., 1976; MPhil, CUNY, 1986, PhD, 1994. Fellow CUNY, 1994, asst. prof., 1997—. Adj. asst. prof. Bklyn. Coll., 1985-97, St. John's U., Staten Island, N.Y., 1989-97, Wagner Coll., Staten Island, 1996; ednl. cons. St. John Neumann, Staten Island, 2000—. Author: La Autobiografia Ficticia en Miguel de Unamuno, Garmen Martin Gaite y Sereprún, 1996, Grolier, 2000; editor: Voices, 1995 RCIA tchr., edn. cons. St. John Neumann, Staten Island, 2000—. Mem. AATSP (newsletter editor, exec. bd. dirs. 2000—), MLA, Latino Civic Assn. (exec. bd. dirs. 2001), Fgn. Lang. Soc. (co-faculty adv. 1997—), Sigma Delta Pi, Sigma Delta Mu (hon.), Circulo de Cultura Panamericano. Roman Catholic. Home: 23 Koenig Ln Freehold NJ 07728-2806

SOTOMAYOR, SONIA, federal judge; b. N.Y.C., June 25, 1954; d. Sonia and Celina (Baez) Sotomayor; m. Kevin Edward Noonan, Aug. 14, 1976 (div. 1983). BA summa cum laude, Princeton U., 1976; JD, Yale U., 1979; LLD honoris causa (hon.), 1999, JD (hon.) honoris causa, 2001. Bar: N.Y. 1980, U.S. Dist. Ct. (ea. and so. dists.) N.Y. 1984. Asst. dist. atty. Office of Dist. Atty. County of N.Y., N.Y.C., 1979—84; assoc., ptnr. Pavia & Harcourt, N.Y.C., 1984—92; fed. judge U.S. Dist. Ct. (so. dist.) N.Y., N.Y.C., 1992—98; cir. judge U.S. Ct. Appeals (2d Cir.), N.Y.C., 1998—. Adj. prof. NYU Sch. Law, 1998; lectr. law Columbia Law Sch., 1999. Editor: Yale U. Law Rev., 1979. Mem. State Adv. Panel on Inter-Group Rels., N.Y.C., 1990—92, 1990—91; bd. dirs. P.R. Legal Def. and Edn. Fund, N.Y.C., 1980—92, State of N.Y. Mortgage Agy., N.Y.C., 1987—92, N.Y.C. Campaign Fin. Bd., 1988—92. Mem.: ABA, Assn. Hispanic Judges, Am. Philos. Soc., NY Women's Bar Assn., P.R. Bar Assn., Hispanic Bar Assn., Phi Beta Kappa. Office: US Courthouse 410 US Corthouse 40 Centre St New York NY 10007-1502

SOTOMORA-VON AHN, RICARDO FEDERICO, pediatrician, educator; b. Guatemala City, Guatemala, Oct. 22, 1947; s. Ricardo and Evelyn (von Ahn) S.; m. Eileen Marie Holcomb, May 9, 1990; m. Victoria Monzon, Nov. 26, 1971; children: Marisol, Clarisa, Ricardo III, Charlotte Marie. MD, San Carlos U., 1972; MS in Physiology, U. Minn., 1978. Diplomate Am. Bd. Pediats., Am. Bd. Pediat. Cardiology, Am. Bd. Neonatology-Perinatal Medicine. Rotating intern Gen. Hosp., Guatemala, 1971-72; pediat. intern U. Ark., 1972-73, resident, 1973-75; fellow in pediat. cardiology U. Minn., 1975-78; rsch. assoc. in cardiovasc. pathology United Hosps., St. Paul, 1976; fellow in neonatal-perinatal medicine St. Paul's Children's Hosp., 1977-78, U. Ark., 1981-82; instr. pediats. U. Minn., 1978-79; pediat. cardiologist, unit cardiovasc. surg. Roosevelt Hosp., Guatemala City, 1979-81; asst. prof. pediats. cardiology and neonatology U. Ark., Little Rock, 1981-83; pvt. practice Little Rock, 1983—. Fellow: Am. Coll. Angiology, Am. Coll. Chest Physicians, Am. Coll. Cardiology, Am. Acad. Pediat.; mem.: AAAS, ABA, Soc. Critical Care Medicine, So. Soc. Pediat. Rsch., Ctrl. Ark. Pediat. Soc., Guatemala Coll. Physicians and Surgeons, Soc. Pediat. Echocardiology, Am. Heart Assn., N.Y. Acad. Scis., Ark. Med. Soc., Soc. Genealogists London, Guatemala Acad. Genealogy, Heraldry and Hist. Studies (corr.), The Country Club of Little Rock, The Little Rock Club, Little Rock Country Club. Home: 25 River Ridge Cir Little Rock AR 72227-1523 Office: Ste 820 Medical Towers II Little Rock AR 72205 E-mail: rfsotomora@aol.com.

SOUD, GINGER, city councilwoman; m. A.C. Soud Jr.; children: Jeff, John, Adrian. City councilwoman-at-large Jacksonville (Fla.) City Coun., 1994—, chmn. Pub. Health and Safety Com., mem. Land Use and Zoning Com., mem. Telecomm. Com., v.p., 1998-99, pres., 1999—. Real estate broker Mem. Nat. Assn. Realtors, Fla. Assn. Realtors, Jacksonville Assn. Realtors, Jacksonville Women's Network. Republican. Office: 117 W Duval St Ste 425 Jacksonville FL 32202-5712

SOUDER, MARK EDWARD, congressman; b. Ft. Wayne, Ind., July 18, 1950; s. Edward Getz and Irma (Fahling) S.; m. Diane Kay Zimmer, July 28; children: Brooke Diane, Nathan Elias, Zachary. BS, Ind. U., Ft. Wayne, 1972; MBA, U. Notre Dame, 1974. Mgmt. trainee Crossroads Furniture Co., Houston, 1974; mktg. mgr. Gabberts Furniture & Studio, Mpls., 1974-76; mktg. mgr., exec. v.p. Souder's Furniture & Studio, Grabill, Ind., 1976-80, pres., 1981-84; econ. devel. liaison for U.S. Rep. Dan Coats, from 1983; mem. U.S. Congress from Ind. 3rd Dist. (formerly 4th), 1995—, Ho. Select Com. on Homeland Security. Mem. edn. and workforce com., govt. reform and oversight com., small bus. com., natural resources com. Publicity chmn. Grabill County Fair, 1977—; advisor Dan Coats for Congress Com., 1980 81; mem. Ind. Area Devel. Coun.; mem. bus. alumni adv. com. Ind. U.-Ft. Wayne. Mem. Midwest Home Furnishings Assn. (dir. 1976-84, past treas., exec. v.p.), Ft. Wayne, Grabill C. of C., Allen County Hist. Soc., Alumni Assn. Ind. U. at Ft. Wayne (dir., past pres.), Alumni Assn. U. Notre Dame. Republican. Mem. Apostolic Christian Ch. Home: 13733 Ridgeview Ct Grabill IN 46741 Office: US House Reps 1227 Longworth House Office Building Washington DC 20515-1404

SOUDERS, JEAN SWEDELL, artist, educator; b. Braham, Minn., July 13, 1922; d. John Almond and Frances Johanna (Alm) Swedell; m. Robert Livingston Souders, Sep. 22, 1945 (dec. 1985). BA, Duluth (Minn.) State Coll., 1944; postgrad., Minn. Sch. of Art, 1944, Walker Sch. of Art, 1948; MA, U. Iowa, 1955, MFA, 1956. Instr. art St. Olaf Coll., Northfield, Minn., 1947-50; instr. craft U. Minn., 1951; prof. art history painting Calif. State U., Chico, Calif., 1957-74, prof. art history, 1959-60, faculty gen. studies, 1971-73. Exhbn. Creative Art Ctr., 1975, Des Moines Art Ctr., Crocker Mus. of Art, Chico State U. and Chico Art Gallery, 1994, and various others; paintings in over 200 collections. Mem.: Women Artists Assn. San Francisco, Mus. of Women in the Arts, Nat. Archives (work and exhibit records). Lutheran. Avocations: photography, hiking, backpacking, classical music.

SOUHAM, GÉRARD, communications executive; b. Paris, May 30, 1928; s. Lucien and Mary-Françoise (Husson) S.; m. Eliane Meyrat, June 23, 1951; children: Glenn (dec.), Yan, Philip. Diploma, Am. Community Sch., Paris, 1948; cert., Ecole Commerciale de Paris. Chargé de mission State Dept., Europe, 1950-52; pub. info. officer Allied Air Forces NATO, Fontainebleau, 1953-55; chmn. bd., chief exec. officer J. Walter Thompson, Paris, 1955-75, v.p. N.Y.C., 1970-75; prin. S3C Gerard Souham Group Communication Cos., Paris and Lausanne, Switzerland, 1975—, SC3 Gerard Souham Group Communication Cos., N.Y.C., 1979—. Bd. dirs. Am. Overseas Meml., I.T. Fin., AVON, France, Mattel-France, S3C Souham Group, Milan; chmn. bd. Turner Prodn. Europe, 1994—98, IT Fin. Corp.; vice chmn. bd. Avon. Author: Général Souham Comte de l'Empire, 1964, Impressions sur..., 1970, Souham, 1989, Sur les Champs de Bataille de la Révolution et de l'Empire, 1990. Mem. pvt. sector internat. and pub. rels. coms. USIA, 1985; mem. world bd. govs. USO, Washington, 1984, chmn. fundraising com., 1989—, pres., Paris, 1995, bd. dirs. 2000—. Decorated officer Legion of Honor (France); officer Order of Leopold, knight Belgian Crown (Belgium). Mem. Internat. Advt. Assn. (v.p. pub. svc., bd. dirs.), Internat. Inst. Strategic Studies London, France, USA (bd. dirs.), Am. Overseas Meml. Assn. (bd. dirs. 1988—), USAF Assn. (life), HM Guards Polo (Windsor, Eng.) (life), Polo de Bagatelle (Paris), N.Y. Athletic, Yacht of Monaco. Roman Catholic. Avocation: collecting fine bindings. Office: Souham Group Comm 500 5th Ave New York NY 10110-0002

SOUKUP, BETTY A. state legislator; b. Clarksburg, W.Va. m. Robert Soukup; 3 children. AS in Bus. Mgmt., BA in Comms. Arts. Mem. Iowa Senate from 15th dist., Des Moines, 1998—; mem. agr. com., mem. appropriations com.; mem. small bus., econs. devel. and tourism com. Iowa Senate, Des Moines, mem. ways and means com. Democrat. Office: State Capitol 9th And Grand Ave Des Moines IA 50319-0001 E-mail: betty_soukup@legis.state.ia.us.

SOUL, VERONIKA, filmmaker, animator; b. Balt., Md., Oct. 23, 1944; d. Anna and James Soul. BA, St. John's Coll., 1962—66. Animator, dir., designer Nat. Film Bd. of Can., Montreal, 1974—91; ind. film maker, 1972—. Dir.: (films) A Said Poem (screened at Film Forum, N.Y.C., 1979), Tales from the Vienna Woods (nominee Experimental category, Canadian Film Awards, 1975, Dallas Internat. Film Festival, Director's Choice, 1978), (video) Ghost Story (in Libr. of Congress video collection; premiere at Mus. of Modern Art, NYC, PBS premiere, New TV series, 1993), (films) Unknown Soldiers (Toronto Internat. Film Festival, Hon. Mention, Shorts, 1991, screened at Mus. of Modern Art, N.Y.C., 1993; Film Forum,N.Y.C., 1992., 1991), End Game in Paris (Yorkton Film Festival, Best Direction, Best Editing, Best Sound Editing, 1982), N.J. Nights (Melbourne Film Festival, Spl. Commendation, 1981), Interview (Melbourne Internat. Film Festival, Grand Prix, 1980; Varna Film Festival, 1st prize, 1980, Montreal World Film Festival, Prix Du Jury, 1979., 1980), How the Hell Are You?, (video) The Law is in the Seed (in video exhibit at Mus. of Modern Art, N.Y.C., 1993; part of Emmy-awarded Poetry Spots series, WNYC-TV, 1991., 1993). Recipient Listed in Le Dictionnaire du cinema quebecois, 1991; fellow NYFA Fellowship in Film, N.Y. Found. for the Arts, 1991, U.S.-Japan Artists Exch. Fellowship, U.S.-Japan Friendship Commn., 1992, Sr. Fulbright Rsch. Fellowship, Fulbright (CIES), 1996-1997; grantee Can. Coun. film prodn. grant, The Can. Coun. for the Arts, 1973, 1979, 1983, NEA film prodn. grant, Nat. Endowment for the Arts, 1989, NYSCA film prodn. grant, N.Y. State Coun. on the Arts, 1990, Soros Open Ctr. video prodn. grant, Soros Documentary Fund, 1998-99.

SOULE, GEORGE ALAN, literature educator, writer; b. Fargo, ND, Mar. 3, 1930; s. George Alan and Ruth Georgia (Knudsen) S.; m. Carolyn Richards, Nov. 24, 1961; 1 child, Katherine. BA, Carleton Coll., 1951; postgrad., Corpus Christi Coll., Cambridge (Eng.) U., 1952-53; MA, Yale U., 1956, PhD, 1960. Instr. English lit. Oberlin (Ohio) Coll., 1958-60; asst. prof. U. Wis., Madison, 1960-62; from asst. prof. to prof. Carleton Coll., Northfield, Minn., 1962-95, prof. emeritus, 1995—, chair English dept., 1980—83; tchr. Cannon Valley Elder Collegium, 1998—, vice chair, 2003—, also bd. dirs. Cons. Ednl. Testing Svc., Princeton, NJ, 1967-84, 94-97; lectr. Wordsworth Winter Sch., Grasmere, UK, 2003-. Author: Four British Women Novelists: An Annotated and Critical Secondary Bibliography, 1998; editor: Theatre of the Mind, 1974; contbr. articles to profl. jours. Mem. libr. bd. City of Northfield, 1997-2000; bd. dirs. Northfield Area Found., 2001-02. With U.S. Army, 1954-55. Internat. fellow Rotary, 1952-53, Sterling pre-doctoral fellow Yale U., 1957-58. Mem.: Anthony Powell Soc., The Iris Murdoch Soc., Friends of Dove Cottge, Boswell Soc. of Auchinleck, Johnson Soc. of Lichfield, Mayflower Soc., Oxford and Cambridge Club, Rotary, Phi Beta Kappa. Episcopalian. Avocations: cooking, travel, Jeopardy (Champion Sr. Tournament 1990). Home: 313 Nevada St Northfield MN 55057-2346 Office: Carleton Coll 1 N College St Northfield MN 55057-4001 Fax: 507-645-5099. E-mail: gsoule@charter.net.

SOULE, ROBERT D. safety and health educator, administrator; b. DeTour Village, Mich., July 8, 1941; s. Harold M. and Mildred M. (Abear) S.; m. Mary Ann Kretzschmar, June 13, 1964; children: Dawn Marie, Robert John, Rebecca Ann. BS, Mich. State U., 1963; MS in Chem. Engring., Purdue U., 1965; EdD in Higher Edn. Adminstrn., U. Pitts., 1993. Cert. safety profl. cert in indsl. hygiene; registered profl. engr., Mich., Ind., Tex. Calif. Environ. health engr. Dow Chem. Co., Midland, Mich., 1965-69, sr. indsl. hygienist

Freeport, Tex., 1969-70; v.p. Clayton Environ. Cons., Southfield, Mich., 1970-77; prof. safety and health Indiana U. of Pa., 1977—, assoc. dean health & human svcs., 1999-2000. Cons. in pvt. practice, Indiana, Pa., 1977—. Contbr. chpts. to books; mem. editorial bd. Am. Indsl. Hygiene Assn. Jour., 1979-85, Occupational Hazards, 1992-98, Professional Safety, 1998—. Fellow Am. Indsl. Hygiene Assn.; mem. Am. Conf. Govtl. Indsl. Hygienists, Am. Soc. Safety Engrs. (profl.), Am. Acad. Indsl. Hygiene (sec.-treas.). Office: Indiana U Pa Safety Scis Dept 123 Johnson Indiana PA 15705-1087 Office Phone: 724-357-3270. Business E-Mail: bobsoule@iup.edu.

SOULEN, ROBERT JOHN, physicist; b. Phoenixville, Pa., July 16, 1940; s. Robert John and Barbara Soulen; m. Rosemarie Soulen; children: Stephanie Harrington, Heidi Clarke. BA, Rutgers U., New Brunswick, N.J., 1962, PhD, 1966. Rsch. physicist Nat. Inst. of Stds. and Tech., Gaithersberg, Md., 1966—86, Naval Rsch. Lab, Washington, 1986—. Recipient Gold medal, U.S. Dept Commerce, Keithley award, Am. Phys. Soc. Fellow: Am. Phys. Soc. Office: Naval Rsch Lab 4555 Overlook Ave Washington DC 20032 E-mail: soulen@anvil.nrl.navy.mil.

SOULTOUKIS, DONNA ZOCCOLA, library director; b. Princeton, NJ, July 28, 1949; d. Peter Joseph and Josephine (Taraschi) Zoccola; m. Dimitrios Athanasios Soultoukis, July 26, 1980. AB, Georgian Ct. Coll., Lakewood, N.J., 1971; MS, Drexel U., 1976; Cert., Italian U. for Foreigners, Perugia, 1974. Libr. asst. Geology Libr. Princeton U., 1971-73; libr. Friends Hosp., Phila., 1976-86, dir. libr. svcs., 1986-98; head libr. Temple U., Sch. Podiatric, 1998-99; ref. libr. MCP/Hahnemann U., Phila., 1999-2000; sr. info. scientist Bristol-Myers Squibb Pharm. Rsch. Inst., Hopewell, N.J., 2000; libr. Our Lady of Lourdes Sch. Nursing, Camden, NJ, 2001—. Cons. Lower Bucks Hosp., Bristol, Pa., 1991-95. Vol. outreach program Old St. Joseph's Ch., Phila., 1992-95, sanctuary min., 1993—, pastoral coun., 1995-98, 2001–, outreach program, bd. dirs., 1997-2001, bd. ministers 1999-2001. Mem. Med. Libr. Assn. (chair mental librs. divsn. 1991-93, chair tech. com. 1996—), Spl. Librs. Assn. (Phila. chpt. bd. dirs. 1985-88, pres. 1982-84, chmn. long-range planning 1993, mem. adv. bd. 1995-2001, sec. solo divsn. 2000-01, devel. com. 2003-). Avocations: travel, cooking. Home: 290 Cinnabar Ln Yardley PA 19067-5717 Office Phone: 856-782-2105.

SOUNEY, PAUL FREDERICK, pharmacist; b. Bristol, Conn., Mar. 29, 1947; s. Frederick Raymond and Julia Yvonne (Weeks) S.; m. Billie Lorraine Petersen, Apr. 7, 1972; children: Jared Paul, Jeremy Christian. BS, Northeastern U., 1971, MS, 1984. Drug info. pharmacist Hartford (Conn.) Hosp., 1971-77; pharmacy supervisor Boston Hosp. for Women, 1977-81; clin. rsch. pharmacist Channing Labs./Harvard Med. Sch., Boston, 1981-92; med. info. scientist Astra Merck Inc., Providence, 1992-97; field sci. ptnr. N.E. Customer Ctr. Astra Pharms., L.P., Providence, 1997-99; med. mktg. scientific leader AstraZeneca Pharms., Wayne, Pa., 1999-2000, group dir. med. mktg., 2000, nat. sci. dir. GI, 2000—03, sr. dir. med. affairs, 0200—2004. Dir. drug info. Brigham and Women's Hosp., Boston, 1981-90, dir. clin. pharmacy, 1985-92, Principles Scientific Commercialization LLC, 2004-; cons. in field. Editor: Comprehensive Pharmacy Review, 5th edit., 2003; contbr. articles to profl. jours.; editl. adv. panelist Internat. Pharm. Abstracts, Pharmacy Practice News, Am. Jour. Gastroenterology. Treas. men's club First Congl. Ch., 1993-2000; vol. Mansfield (Mass.) Animal Shelter, 1990-94. Mem. Am. Coll. Clin. Pharmacy, Am. Soc. Health Sys. Pharmacists, Am. Pharmaceutical Assn., Acad. Managed Case Pharmacy, New Eng. Coun. Hosp. Pharmacists, Northeastern Univ. Alumnae Assn. Office: Scientific Commercialization LLC 2 Clover Ln Kennett Square PA 19348-1555 E-mail: paul.souney@astrazeneca.com.

SOURDIFF, GERALD, retired insurance company executive; CFO Luth. Bros., Mpls., 60 2001. Office: Luth Bros 625 4th Ave S Minneapolis MN 55415-1624

SOURIAL, ALFY SAIF, surgeon; b. Tanta, Egypt, Jan. 10, 1928; s. Saif and Erada Atiah (El-Sanady) S.; m. Elizabeth Ann Siebert, 1960; children: Edward S., Wynn Heather; m. Shirley Ann Maniscalco, Oct. 7, 1971; children: Dean Michael, Jill Soraya. MD, Cairo U., 1950. Diplomate Am. Bd. Surgery. Intern Doctors Hosp., Cleve., 1955-56, resident in surgery, 1956-57, Huron Rd. Hosp., Cleve., 1957-60; fellow in surgery Case Western Res. U., Cleve., 1960-61; surgeon Valley Hosp., Pomona, Calif., 1962-72; pvt practice Thousand Oaks, Calif., 1970-93; active staff Los Robles Hosp., Thousand Oaks, 1968-92, hon. staff, 1992—. Author: Beyond Mathematics, A Standard Physical Particle and the Unified Field of Energy; patentee in field. Lt. col. USAF, 1982-87. Fellow ACS; mem. AMA. Office Phone: 909-338-0880. E-mail: Asourial@aol.com.

SOURIAN, PETER, writer, English educator; b. Boston, Apr. 7, 1933; s. Zareh Missak and Zabelle (Bayentz) S.; m. Eve Jeanne Pocquet, Sept. 25, 1971; children: Mark, Delphine. BA, Harvard U., 1955. Lectr. ext. divsn. NYU, N.Y.C., 1963-65; instr. English Bard Coll., Annandale-on-Hudson, N.Y., 1965-66, asst. prof., 1966-68, assoc. prof., 1968-75, prof., 1975—, dept. chmn., 1984-86, 90-94. Faculty New Sch. Social Rsch., NYC, 1975-2000; TV critic Nation mag., NYC, 1975-81; mem. Anahit Prize Com., 1988—; nat. adv. panel George Polk Awards Com., 1979-92. Author: Miri, 1957, The Best and Worst of Times, 1961, The Gate, 1965, (essays and criticism) At The French Embassy in Sofia, 1992; mem. editl. bd. Ararat Quar., 1975—; contbr. articles to popular mags, profl. jours. Bd. dirs. Armenian Ctr. Columbia U., N.Y.C., 1988-97; mem. Clemente Course Humanities Adv. Bd., 1999—. With U.S. Army, 1957-59. Recipient Bardian award Bard Coll. Alumni, 2000; Lilly Endowment grant, 1976, Kellogg Found. grant, 1977. Mem. MLA, PEN, Nat. Book Critics Circle, Century Assn. Home: 30 E 70th St New York NY 10021-4942 Office: Bard Coll Annandale on Hudson Annandale On Hudson NY 12504 Office Phone: 845-758-6822.

SOURKES, THEODORE LIONEL, biochemistry educator; b. Montreal, Que., Can., Feb. 21, 1919; s. Irving and Fannie (Golt) S.; m. Shena Rosenblatt, Jan. 17, 1943; children: Barbara, Myra. B.Sc., McGill U., 1939, M.Sc. magna cum laude, 1946; PhD, Cornell U., 1948; D.U. honoris causa, U. Ottawa, Can., 1990. Asst. prof. pharmacology Georgetown U. Med. Sch., 1948-50; research asso. dept. enzyme chemistry Merck Inst. Therapeutic Research, Rahway, N.J., 1950-53; sr. research biochemist Allan Meml. Inst., Montreal, 1953-65; dir. lab. neurochemistry Allan Meml. Inst. Psychiatry, 1965—; mem. faculty McGill U., Montreal, 1954—, prof. biochemistry, 1965—, prof. psychiatry, assoc. dean of medicine for research Faculty Medicine, 1972-75; prof. pharmacology, 1990—; emeritus, 1991. Mem. Que. Med. Research Council, 1971-77; sr. fellow Parkinson's Disease Found., N.Y.C., 1963-66; assoc. mem. McGill Ctr. for Medicine, Ethics and Law, 1991. Author: Biochemistry of Mental Disease, 1962, Nobel Prize Winners in Medicine and Physiology, 1901-1965, 1967; sect. editor Internat. Jour. of the History of Neuroscis., 1996—. Decorated Officer Order of Canada; laureate of the Wilder Penfield Prix du Que. for Biomed. Sci., 1998. Fellow Royal Soc. Can.; mem. Canadian Biochem. Soc., Pharmacol. Soc. Can., Canadian Coll. Neuropsychopharmacology (Heinz Lehmann award 1982, medal 1990), Am. Soc. Biol. Chemists, Am. Soc. Pharmacology and Exptl. Therapeutics, Am. Soc. Neurochemistry, Internat. Soc. History of Neuroscis. (medal 2001), Internat. Soc. Neurochemistry, Internat. Brain Research Orgn., Venezuelan Order Andrés Bello, Wilder Penfield Prix du Québec, Sigma Xi. Achievements include research and publs. on drugs for treatment high blood pressure; 1st basic research on methyldopa; elucidation of role of dopamine and other monamines in nervous system; first trials of L-dopa in Parkinson's disease, biochemistry of mental depression, pathways of stress in the nervous system, imaging serotonin in brain, history of biochemistry. Home: 3033 Sherbrooke St W # 303 Montreal QC Canada H3Z 1A3 Office: McGill U 1033 Pine Ave W Montreal QC Canada H3A 1A1 E-mail: theodore.sourkes@mcgill.ca.

SOURS, JAMES KINGSLEY, association executive, former college president; b. Corydon, Iowa, Sept. 16, 1925; s. James N. and Virginia (Kantor) S.; m. Alice Hyde, July 11, 1947; children— James W., Mary Jan, David Bryan. Student, Phillips U., 1943; BA, U. Wichita, 1949; MPA, Harvard U., 1951, PhD, 1954. Adminstrv. aid City Mgr.'s Office, Wichita, 1947-49; mem. faculty Wichita State U., 1951-65; prof. polit. sci., head dept., 1958-62; dean Fairmount Coll. Arts and Scis., 1962-65; chmn. Fairmount Coll. Arts and Scis. (Center Urban Studies), 1957-63; pres. So. Oreg. State Coll., Ashland, 1969-79; ednl. cons. Dankook U., Seoul, 1979-80, dir. Inst. Asian Studies and Cultures, 1990-97; ednl. cons. Korean Ministry Edn., 1979-80. Exec. v.p. Am. Coll. Testing Program, Iowa City, 1965—68; hon. Fulbright (Dept. of State and U. Iowa), vis. prof. polit. sci. U. Istanbul, Turkey, 1968—69; vis. prof. Dankook U., Seoul, Republic of Korea, 1976, 1979—80; dir. devel. Oreg. Shakespearean Festival Assn., 1980—85; v.p., bd. dirs. Dankook U. Am., 1990—97; bd. dirs. Rogue Valley Manor Found.; pres. bd. dirs. Internat. Wildlife Recovery Ctr., Eagle Point, Oreg., 1999—; chmn. bd. dirs. Aletheia Psycho-Phys. Found., 1988—96; mem. Jackson County Strategic Planning Adv. Com., 1999—2000. Author: series Some Observations on the Management of Large Cities, 1957; also numerous articles. V.p. NCAA, 1959-64; founding pres. Urban League Wichita, 1953-56; pres. PTA Fairmount Elem. Sch., 1959-60; chmn. Wichita City Commn. Human Rels., 1962; trustee Carpenter Found., 1983-87, v.p., 1984-87; chmn. Sedgwick County, Kans. chpt. ARC, 1964, Jackson County, Oreg. chpt., 1973-75; bd. dirs. So. Oreg. Hist. Soc., 1987-89; mem. Oreg. Am. Revolution Bicentennial Commn., 1972-76; chmn. com. nursing edn. Wesley Med. Ctr., Wichita, 1962-64. Served with USNR, 1943-46. Adminstn. fellow Harvard U., 1949-51. Democrat. Home: 3100 Payne Rd Medford OR 97504-9407

SOUSA, RONALD WAYNE, foreign language educator; b. Santa Cruz, Calif., Aug. 14, 1943; s. Daniel and Ulala Kathryn (Snyder) S.; m. Joyce Ann Burton, Mar. 16, 1968; children: Jonathan David, Benjamin Joseph. BA, U. Calif., Berkeley, 1966, MA, 1968, PhD, 1973. Asst. prof. Portuguese and Latin Am. studies U. Tex., Austin, 1971—74; asst. prof. Spanish and Portuguese U. Minn., Mpls., 1974—76, assoc. prof. Spanish and Portuguese, 1976—82, prof. Spanish, Portugese and comparative lit., 1982-93; prof. Portuguese, Spanish and comparative lit. U. Ill., Urbana, 1994—, head dept. Spanish, Italian and Portuguese, 1994—2000, interim head, 2004—. Vis. prof. of Portuguese U. Calif., Berkeley, 1977; program chmn. dept. comparative lit. U. Minn., 1983-87, 90-92, chmn. dept. cultural studies and comparative lit., 1992-93. Author: The Rediscoverers, 1981, Voz autoritaria y experiencia fascista: José Saramago, 2003; co-author: Reading the Harper, 1996, The Humanities in Dispute, 1998; editor-translator: Control of the Imaginary, 1988, Yes, Comrade, 1993; translator: The Passion According to G.H., 1988; translator: Yes Comrade, 1993, This Little Lusitanian House, 2003; Memoirs of a Militia Sergeant, 1999; co-translator, The Murmuring Coast, 1995; contbr. articles to various publs. and mags. Office: U Ill Spanish Italian Portuguese 4080 FLB/707 S Matthews Urbana IL 61801

SOUTAS-LITTLE, ROBERT WILLIAM, mechanical engineer, educator; b. Oklahoma City, Feb. 25, 1933; s. Harry Glenn and Mary Evelyn (Miller) Little; m. Patricia Soutas, Sept. 3, 1982; children: Deborah, Catherine, Colleen, Jennifer, Karen. BS in Mech. Engring, Duke U., 1955; MS, U. Wis., 1959, PhD, 1962. Design engr. Allis Chalmers Mfg. Co., Milw., 1955-57; instr. mech. engring. Marquette U., 1957-59; instr. U. Wis., Madison, 1959-62, asst. prof., 1962-63, Okla. State U., 1963-65; prof. Mich. State U., 1965—2001, chmn. dept. mech. engring., 1972-77, chmn. dept. biomechanics, 1977-90; dir. biomechanics evaluation lab., 1989—; prof. emeritus Mich. State U., Lansing, 2001—. Cons. A. C. Electronics Co., Ford Motor Co., CBS Research Lab., B. F. Goodrich Co.; lectr. AID, India, 1965 Author: Elasticity, 1973, Engineering Mechanics: Statics, 1999, Engineering Mechanics: Dynamics, 1999; contbr. articles to profl. jours. Vice pres. Okemos (Mich.) Sch. Bd., 1967-72; mem. Meridian Twp. (Mich.) Charter Commn., 1969-70, Meridian Twp. Zoning Bd. Appeals, 1969-71. Recipient award for excellence in instrn. engring. students Western Electric Co., 1970-71, Disting. Faculty award, 1996; NSF grantee, 1964-69, 79, NIH grantee, 1973-75, 79—. Fellow ASME; mem. Soc. Engring. Sci., Am. Soc. Biomechanics, Internat. Soc. Biomechanics, N.Am. Soc. Clin. Gait and Movement Analysis, Sigma Xi, Pi Tau Sigma, Ta Beta Pi. Home: 187 S Highland Dr Leland MI 49654-1143 Office: PO Box 1143 Leland MI 49654-1143 Business E-Mail: soutas@egr.msu.edu.

SOUTER, DAVID HACKETT, United States Supreme Court justice; b. Melrose, Mass., Sept. 17, 1939; s. Joseph Alexander and Helen Adams (Hackett) Souter. BA, Harvard U., 1961, LLB, 1966; Rhodes scholar, Oxford U., 1961—63, MA, 1989. Bar: N.H. 1967. Assoc. Orr & Reno, Concord, 1966—68; asst. atty. gen. N.H., 1968—71; dep. atty. gen., 1971—76; atty. gen., 1976—78; assoc. justice Superior Ct. N.H., 1978—83, N.H. Supreme Ct., 1983—90; judge U.S. Ct. Appeals (1st cir.), NH, 1990; assoc. justice U.S. Supreme Ct., Washington, 1990—. Trustee Concord Hosp., 1973—85, pres. bd. trustees, 1978—84; bd. overseers Dartmouth Med. Sch., 1981—87. Mem.: N.H. Bar Assn., N.H. Hist. Soc. (v.p. 1980—85, trustee 1976—85), Phi Beta Kappa. Republican. Episcopalian.

SOUTH, STEPHEN A. academic administrator; Pres. South Coll., Knoxville, Tenn., 1989—. Office: South Coll Office of the President 720 N 5th Ave Knoxville TN 37917-6721

SOUTHARD, ATHALIE ANNE, retired elementary school educator; b. Old Town, Maine, June 25, 1938; d. Wendall Earl and Harriet Eleanor Mosher; m. John Allen Southard, Sept. 3, 1959; children: Jeffrey Allen, Julie Anne Southard Haight. BME, U. Mary Hardin-Baylor, Belton, Tex., 1960. Elem. music tchr. Killeen Ind. Sch. Dist., Tex., 1960—63, 1975—78, 1981—98; pvt. piano tchr., 1960—78, 1981—2004. Asst. line dance tchr. 55 and Up, Harker Heights, Tex., 2000—04; nursing home entertainer. Mem.: Nat.Music Tchrs. Assn. (cert.), Ctrl. Tex. Music Tchrs. Assn. (pres. 2001—04), Tex. Music Tchrs. Assn. (state coord. student composition competition 2001—04), Music Tchrs. Nat. Assn. (state coord. student composition competition 2001—04), Ctrl. Tex. Fedn. Music Club, Nat. Guild of Piano Tchrs. Avocations: reading, line dancing, sewing, piano.

SOUTHARD, PAUL RAYMOND, financial executive; b. Albany, N.Y., May 15, 1948; s. Harold G. and Frances L. (Shaylor) S. BS, Rochester Inst. Tech., 1970. CPA, N.Y. Staff acct. Haskins & Sells, CPA's, Rochester, N.Y., 1969-70; sr. acct. Maurice F. Sammons & Co., CPAs, Rochester, 1970-73; fin. mgr. Radionics, Inc., Webster, N.Y., 1973-82, contr., 1982-87, Kitchen Concepts, Co., Fairport, N.Y., 1987-88, Spectra Svcs., Inc., Rochester, 1989-93, Rochester Lino & Carpet, 1993-94, Arena Products Inc., 1994-95, Overland Constrn., Inc., 1996-2000, ICS Telecom, Inc., Rochester, 2000, Ancoma, Inc., 2004—. Mem. N.Y. State Soc. CPAs. Home: 1096 Everwild Vw Webster NY 14580-8740

SOUTHARD, WILLIAM G. lawyer; b. Toledo, Ohio, May 6, 1953; s. James Theodore and Dorothy (Fergusson) S.; m. Martha Donelan, Aug. 14, 1976. BA, Williams Coll., 1975; JD, Columbia U., 1978. Bar: Ill. 1978, U.S. Dist. Ct. Ill. 1979, Mass. 1981, U.S. Dist. Ct. Mass. 1981, U.S. Ct. Appeals (1st cir.) 1985. Assoc. Schiff Hardin & Waite, Chgo., 1978-81, Bingham, Dana & Gould LLP, Boston, 1981-85, ptnr., 1985—, dep. chmn. litig., 1994-2000, chmn. litig., 2000—02, dep. chair litigation, 2002—. Assoc. editor Columbia Jour. Transnat. Law, 1978; contbr. articles to profl. jours. Mem. ABA, ASTM, Boston Bar Assn. Office: Bingham McCutchen LLP 150 Federal St Fl 15 Boston MA 02110-1745 E-mail: southawg@bingham.com.

SOUTHBY, RICHARD MCKELLAR FAIRFAX, health services educator, consultant; b. Melbourne, Victoria, Australia, Feb. 3, 1940; arrived in U.S., 1979, naturalized, 1985; s. Robert and Marie Heywood (Whyte) Southby; m. Janet Sue Rexrode, June 9, 1979. B.Com., U. Melbourne, 1965; M.P.A. Cornell U., 1967; PhD, Monash U., Clayton, Victoria, Australia, 1973. Rsch. asst. Inst. Applied Econ. Research U. Melbourne, 1965; Sloan scholar in hosp. and med. care adminstrn. Cornell U., Ithaca, NY, 1965—67; tchg. fellow Monash U., 1967—70, sr. tchg. fellow dept. social and preventive medicine Faculty of Medicine, 1970, lectr. in social and preventive medicine, 1971—75, sr. lectr., 1975—78; commr. Australian Hosps. and Health Services Commn., Canberra, 1975; dir. pub. health services research and tchg. Sch. Pub. Health and Tropical Medicine U. Sydney, Australia, 1978—79; assoc. dean health svcs. and Friesen prof. internat. health and health policy and prof. health care scis. The George Washington U. Med. Ctr., Washington, 1979—2001, dean, Ross prof. internat. health, sch. pub. health and health svcs., 2001—03, exec. dean, disting. prof. global health, 2003—. Adj. prof. dept. preventive medicine and biometrics Sch. Medicine Uniformed Services U. Health Scis. Dept. Def., Bethesda, Md., 1979—; dir. Interagy.-Inst. for Fed. Health Care Execs., 1984—; cons. in hosp. adminstrn. Walter Reed Army Med. Ctr., Washington, 1983—. Author (with E. Chesterman): Australia: Health Facts, 1979; editor (with others): Health Care Technology Under Financial Constraints, 1987, Health Care Law and Ethics, 1989, AIDS and Long Term Care: A New Dimension, 1989. Fellow: Royal Soc. Medicine (U.K.), Australian Coll. Health Svc. Execs., Am. Coll. Legal Medicine (hon.); mem.: APHA, Assn. Mil. Surgeons U.S, Internat. Epidemiol. Assn., Cosmos Club (Washington), Wallaby Club. Anglican. Avocations: tennis, gardening, hiking. Office: George Washington U Med Ctr Washington DC 20037 Office Phone: 202-416-0429.

SOUTHERLAND, DERRICK THEODORE, microbiologist; b. Temple Hills, Md. s. Theodore and Vernetta S. BS, N.C. AT&T State U., 1994; MS, Howard U., 1997. Rsch. scientist Lab Support, Rockville, Md., 1997-99; claims examiner U.S. Dept. Labor, Washington, 1999—. Mem. Am. Soc. Microbiology, Am. Inst. Biol. Scis., N.C. AT&T State U. Alumni Assn. Avocations: reading, swimming, photography, classic automobiles. Home: 4304 19th Ave Temple Hills MD 20748-5620 Office: 800 N Capitol St NW Rm 800 Washington DC 20211 E-mail: dsoutherland@hotmail.com.

SOUTHERLAND, S. DUANE, manufacturing executive; b. Durham, N.C., Apr. 24, 1949; s. Sydney Duane and Beatrice Marie (Carver) S.; m. Linda F. Lewis, Jan. 5, 1974, 1 child, S. Duane III. BSE, Duke U., 1971, MS in Engring., 1973, MBA, 1974. Ops. analyst Cooper Group Div. Cooper Industries, Apex, N.C., 1974-78, planning analyst Houston, 1978-81, dir. fin. Cooper Electronics Div. Nashua, N.H., 1981-83, gen. mgr. Conn. ops. Kirsch Div. Beacon Falls, Conn., 1983-87, pres. Kirsch Div. Sturgis, Mich., 1987-94; pres., CEO Conso Products Co., Union, S.C., 1995-98; pres., CEO, dir. Equality Specialties, Inc., N.Y.C., 1999—2001; pres., CEO Conso Products, Union, SC, 2002—. Republican. Baptist.

SOUTHERN, HUGH, retired performing arts manager; b. Newcastle-on-Tyne, Eng., Mar. 20, 1932; came to U.S., 1955; s. Norman and Phyllis Margaret (Hiller) S.; m. Jane Rosemary Llewellyn, Dec. 18, 1954 (div.); children: Hilary, William Norman; m. Kathy Ayers Dwyer, Dec. 10, 1988; 1 child, Jaime Andres. BA, King's Coll., Cambridge, Eng., 1956. Assoc. account exec. Fuller & Smith & Ross, N.Y.C., 1956-58; treas. Westport Country Playhouse (Conn.) 1958; adminstrv. mgr. Theatre Guild-Am. Theatre Soc., N.Y.C., 1959-62; asst. dir. Repertory Theatre, Lincoln Ctr., N.Y.C., 1962-65; gen. mgr. Nat. Repertory Theatre, N.Y.C., 1965-67; mgmt. assoc. San Francisco Opera, 1967-68; exec. dir. Theatre Devel. Fund, N.Y.C., 1968-82; dep. chmn. programs Nat. Endowment for Arts, Washington, 1982-89, acting chmn., 1989; gen. mgr. Met. Opera Assn. Inc., N.Y.C., 1989-90; dir. Va. Festival of Am. Film, Charlottesville, Va., 1995-96. Acting dir. performing arts program N.Y. State Council on Arts, N.Y.C., 1974-75, acting exec. dir., 1976; dir. New Dramatists, N.Y.C., 1978-82, Film Forum, N.Y.C., 1978-82; trustee Actor's Fund Am., N.Y.C., 1978-85 Trustee Manhattan Country Sch., N.Y.C., 1970-82, chmn., 1971-74; mem. Mayor's Com. on Cultural Policy, N.Y.C., 1974-75. Home: 3406 18th St N Arlington VA 22207 E-mail: hsouth2@aol.com.

SOUTHERN, LARRY GILMER, explosive safety specialist; b. Mt. Airy, NC, Feb. 10, 1959; s. Ed Southern and Gladys Viola Woodruff Payne; m. Donna Hartley Turner, Feb. 14, 1981 (div. Apr. 1986); 1 child, Victor Ross; m. Robin Michele Spicer, Dec. 26, 1996. Explosive Ordnance Disposal Technician, Naval Sch., Indian Head, Md., 1978. Foreman, tank cleaning Caldwell Indsl. Svcs., Lenoir, NC, 1983-84; dir. ops., indsl. svc. Petroleum Mgmt. Inc., Davie, Fla., 1984-85, Integrated Resource Recovery, Davie, 1985-87, dir. safety and hazardous ops., 1988-89; project mgr. HAZMAT response Four Seasons Environ., Greensboro, NC, 1987-88, spl. ops. safety coord., 1993-95; ordnance mechanic Johnson Controls World Svcs., Inc., Cocoa Beach, Fla., 1989-93; safety specialist HASP Inc., Knoxville, Tenn., 1996-97; safety mgr. Molten Metal Tech. Inc., Oak Ridge, 1997-98; health and safety specialist EET Corp., Knoxville, Tenn., 1998-2000, WESK EM LLC, Knoxville, 2000-01; field materials and skills technician Boeing Co., 2001—. Served with USAF, 1978-. Mem. Internat. Assn. Bomb Technicians and Investigators (assoc.), Am. Soc. Safety Engrs. (assoc.). E-mail: sout6631@bellsouth.net.

SOUTHERN, NANCY C. utilities executive; Co-chmn., CEO ATCO Ltd. and Can. Utilities, Calgary, Canada, 2000—02, pres., CEO, 2003—, also bd. dirs. Exec. v.p. Spruce Meadows; bd. dirs. Shell Can. Ltd., Akita Drilling Ltd., Sentgraf Enterprises Ltd. Former mem. Can. Equestrian Team. Office: ATCO Ltd 1500/1600 909 11th Ave SW Calgary AB Canada T2R 1N6

SOUTHERN, ROBERT ALLEN, lawyer; b. Independence, Mo., July 17, 1930; s. James Allen and Josephine (Ragland) S.; m. Cynthia Agnes Drews, May 17, 1952; children: David D., William A., James M., Kathryn S. O'Brien. BS in Polit. Sci., Northwestern U., 1952, LL.B., 1954. Bar: Ill. 1955. Assoc. Mayer, Brown & Platt (now Mayer, Brown, Rowe & Maw), Chgo., 1954-64, ptnr., 1965-96, mng. ptnr., 1978-91, L.A., 1991-96; CEO So. Assocs., Grayslake, Ill., 1997—, Chapel Hill, NC. Editor in chief Northwestern U. Law Rev., 1953-54. Trustee, v.p., gen. counsel LaRabida Children's Hosp. and Rsch. Ctr., Chgo., 1974-89; trustee Kenilworth (Ill.) Union Ch., 1980-88; pres. Joseph Sears Sch. Bd., 1977-79; trustee Rush U. Med. Ctr., 1983-91, life trustee, 1991—; bd. dirs. Boys and Girls Clubs Chgo., 1986-91; governing mem. Orchestral Assn. Chgo., 1988-93. With U.S. Army, 1955-57. Mem. Chgo. Bar Assn., Lawyers Club Chgo., Order of Coif, Govs. Club (Chapel Hill, N.C.), Chgo. Club. Office: 96200 Carteret Chapel Hill NC 27517-8324 E-mail: rsouthern2@earthlink.net.

SOUTHERN, RONALD D. diversified corporation executive; b. Calgary, Alta., Can., July 25, 1930; s. Samuel Donald and Alexandra (Cuthill) S.; m. Margaret Visser, July 30, 1954; children: Nancy, Linda. BSc, U. Alta., Edmonton, 1953; LLD (hon.), U. Calgary, 1976, U. Alberta, 1991. Chmn., CEO ATCO Ltd. and Can. Utilities Ltd., Calgary, 1994—99, chmn., 2003—; chmn., CEO ATCO Ltd., Calgary, 1994-99, Can. Utilities Ltd., Calgary, 1994-99, co-chmn., CEO, 1999—2002; chmn. ATCO Ltd and Can. Utilities, Calgary, 2003—. Chmn., bd. dirs. Akita Drilling Ltd.; bd. dirs. Sentgraf Enterprises Ltd., ATCO Ltd., Can. Utilities Ltd.; co-chmn., CEO Spruce Meadows, 1999—; chmn. Spruce Meadows Round Table. Decorated Order of Can., comdr. Brit. Empire; recipient Disting. Entrepreneur award U. Man. Faculty Mgmt., 1990; inducted into Can. Bus. Hall, 1995; named Businessman of Yr. U. Alta., 1986, CEO of the Yr. Fin. Post, 1996. Mem. Ranchmen's Club. Calgary Golf and Country Club. Office: ATCO Ltd & Can Utilities 1600 909-11 Ave SW Calgary AB Canada T2R IN6 Office Phone: 292-7550.

SOUTHGATE, MARIE THERESE, physician, editor; b. Detroit, Apr. 27, 1928; d. Clair and Josephine Marie (Hoefeyzers) S. BS, Coll. St. Francis, 1948, LLD (hon.), 1974; MD, Marquette U., 1960. Duplomate Nat. Bd. Med. Examiners. Rsch. editor Ill. Inst. Tech. Rsch. Inst., Chgo., 1951-55; intern St. Mary's Hosp., San Francisco, 1960-61; sr. editor Jour. of AMA, Chgo., 1962-75, dep. editor, 1975-88, sr. contbg. editor, 1988—. Mem. editorial bd. Forum, from 1978; mem. ad hoc com. on biol. scis. Ill. Bd. Huigher Edn., 1969-70; mem. ad hoc com. on lay deacons Archdiocese Chgo., 1973; trustee Coll. St. Francis, from 1978. Editor-in-chief Marquette Med. Rev., 1959-60. Mem. AMA, AAAS, Am. Med. Women's Assn. (v.p Chgo. chpt. 1967-68, mem. continuing med. edn. com. from 1978), Coun. Biology Editors. Office: JAMA 515 N State St Chicago IL 60610-4325

SOUTHGATE, RICHARD W. lawyer, director; b. Chgo., May 6, 1929; m. Anna Fisher Hart, Aug. 25, 1951; children— Richard W., Sarah B., Rebecca W. C., John P. AB cum laude, Harvard U., 1951, LL.B. cum laude, 1954. Bar: Mass. 1954. Assoc. Covington & Burling, Washington, 1956-58; assoc., then ptnr., chmn. policy com. Ropes & Gray, Boston, 1958-94; vol. atty. Greater Boston Legal Svcs., 1995—. Mem. Mass. Commn. on Anti-Takeover Laws; adj. prof. Northeastern U. Sch. Law, Boston, 1996-97. Author: (with Donald W. Glazer) Massachusetts Corporation Law and Practice, 1991. Moderator,

Town of Manchester, Mass., 1976-94. Served as sgt. U.S. Army, 1954-56 Mem. Boston Bar Assn., ABA, Mass. Bar Assn. Clubs: Essex County, Somerset; Harvard (Boston). Home: 22 School St Manchester MA 01944-1336 Office: Greater Boston Legal Svcs 197 Friend St Boston MA 02114-1802

SOUTHWELL, DONALD G. insurance company executive; From head Life and Health Ins. Group to pres., COO Unitrin, Inc., Chgo., 1996—2002, pres., 2002—, COO, 2002—, bd. dir. Office: Unitrin Inc 1 E Walker Dr Chicago IL 60601*

SOUTHWELL, KRISTINA LYNN, archivist, librarian; d. Tom T. and Arvetta J. Southwell. BA in English, U. of Okla., 1992, M of Libr. and Info. Studies, 1994. Asst. archivist for rsch. and pub. svcs. Archives of the Episcopal Ch., Austin, Tex., 1995—96; project archivist Cherokee Nation Papers Project U. Okla., Norman, 1994—95, asst. prof. of bibliography Western History Collections, 1999—; curator John and Mary Nichols Collections U. Okla./, Norman, 2001—. Pres. Okla. Conservation Congress, Oklahoma City, 2004—. Compiler: Guide to Manuscripts in the Western History Collections of the University of Oklahoma; compiler Guide to Photographs in the Western History Collections of the University of Oklahoma; author: (guide) The Walter Stanley Campbell Collection: Inventory and Index; editor: Cherokee Nation Papers Inventory and Index; contbr. articles to profl. jours. Mem.: ALA, Okla. Conservation Congress, Soc. of Am. Archivists, Soc. of S.W. Archivists. Office: U Okla Librs Western History Collections 630 Parrington Oval Rm 452 Norman OK 73019 E-mail: klsouthwell@ou.edu.

SOUTHWICK, CHARLES HENRY, zoologist, educator; b. Wooster, Ohio, Aug. 28, 1928; s. Arthur F. and Faye (Motz) S.; m. Heather Milne Beck, July 12, 1952; children: Steven, Karen. BA, Coll. Wooster, 1949; MS, U. Wis., 1951, PhD, 1953. NIH fellow, 1951-53; asst. prof. biology Hamilton Coll., 1953-54; NSF fellow Oxford (Eng.) U., 1954-55; faculty Ohio U., 1955-61; assoc. prof. pathobiology Johns Hopkins Sch. Hygiene and Pub. Health, Balt., 1961-68, prof., 1968-79; assoc. dir. Johns Hopkins Internat. Ctr. for Med. Rsch. and Tng., Calcutta, India, 1964-65; chmn. dept. environ., population and organismic biology U. Colo., Boulder, 1979-82, prof. biology, 1979—, prof. emeritus, 1993—. Rschr. and author publs. on animal social behavior and population dynamics, influences animal social behavior on demographic characteristic mammal populations, primate ecology and behavior, estuarine ecology and environ. quality; mem. primate adv. com. Nat. Acad. Sci.-NRC, 1963-75, com. primate conservation, 1974-75; mem. Gov.'s Sci. Adv. Com. State of Md., 1975-78; mem. com. on rsch. and exploration Nat. Geog. Soc., 1979-2000; mem. adv. bd. Caribbean Primate Rsch. Ctr., 1987-99, Wis. Primate Rsch. Ctr., 1990-98; mem. Integrated Conservation Rsch., 1989-2002. Editor, author: Primate Social Behavior, 1963, Animal Aggression, 1970, Nonhuman Primates in Biomedical Research, 1975, Ecology and the Quality of Our Environment, 1976, Global Ecology, 1985; Ecology and Behavior of Food-Enhanced Primate Groups, 1988; author: Global Ecology in Human Perspective, 1996. Recipient Fulbright Rsch. award India, 1959-60, Tchg. Excellence award U. Colo., 1993. Fellow AAAS, Acad. Zoology, Animal Behavior Soc.; mem. Am. Soc. Zoologists, Ecol. Soc. Am., Am. Soc. Mammalogists, Am. Soc. Primatology (Disting. Primatologist award 1994), Internat. Primatology Soc., Am. Inst. Biol. Scis. Business E-Mail: charles.southwick@colorado.edu.

SOUTHWICK, PAUL, retired public relations executive; b. West Newton, Mass., Mar. 27, 1920; s. Alfred and Pauline (Winkler) S.; m. Susan Barbara Heider, Feb. 24, 1947; children: Thomas Paul, Peter Alfred, Linda Susan. AB in Econs. cum laude, Harvard Coll., 1943. Coor. AP, Concord, N.H., 1947-49; UP UPI, Washington, 1949-57; mem. profl. staff govt. info. subcom. U.S. Ho. Reps., 1957-59; legis. asst., adminstrv. asst. U.S. Senator Long of Hawaii, 1959-62; dep. adminstr. charge accelerated pub. works program Area Redevel. Adminstrn., 1962-63; spl. asst. The White House, 1963-65; spl. asst. for congl. rels. Office of U.S. Sec. Commerce, 1965-67; v.p. Newmyer Assocs., Inc., Washington, 1967-87; ind. cons., 1987-93; ret., 1993. With USNR, 1941-45, PTO. Mem. Nat. Press Club (Washington). Democrat. Presbyterian. Home: 4012 Underwood St Bethesda MD 20815-5028

SOUTHWORTH, JAMIE MACINTYRE, retired education educator; b. Ironton, Ohio, Oct. 16, 1931; d. Gaylord and Lydia Marcum (Adkins) MacIntyre; m. Horton C. Southworth; children: Jaye, Brad, Alexandra, Sueann, Janet, Jim. BS, Ball State U., 1952, MA, 1961; EdD, U. Pitts., 1981; attended, Oxford (Eng.) U., 1997. Cert. adminstr. and tchr., reading specialist, Pa. Instr. Mich. State U., East Lansing, 1964-67; instr., coord. U. Minn., Mpls., 1967-71; rsch. assoc. Pitts. Pub. Schs., 1971-80; assoc. prof. California U., Pitts., 1988, prof. edn., 1993—, state grants educator, 1990-95, dir. leadership tng. proposal, 1996-00; ret., 2000. Chancellor state adv. com., California U. rep., 1994—, faculty profl. devel. com. state rep., 1991-99; invited participant Oxford (Eng.) U. Leadership Studies, 1995, 97; cons. TITL project Duquesne U.; CEO Learning Tree Corp., 1975-2000; presenter, rsch. conf. 2000, Waikato U., New Zealand, rsch. young childrens conf. 2000-02, San Diego; chair-IRA, internat. conf. nat. Fulbright scholars, San Francisco, 2002. Contbr. articles to profl. jours. Recipient Seal of St. Peter's Coll., Oxford, 1997; U.S. Office of Edn. title III & IVC grantee; grantee Pa. Vocat. Tech. State, 1990-91, 93, Bibliotherapy Project California Univ. Pa., 1992, Pa. State, 1993, Pa. Campus Compac, 1993. Mem. Am. Assn. Colls. Tchr. Edn., NEA Young Children, Kappa Delta Pi (counselor), Phi Delta Kappa.

SOUTHWORTH, LINDA JEAN, artist, critic, educator, poet; b. Milw., May 11, 1951; d. William Dixon and Violet Elsie (Kuehn) S.; m. David Joseph Roger, Nov. 16, 1985 (div. July 1989). BFA, St. John's U., Queens, N.Y., 1974; MFA, Pratt Inst., Bklyn., 1978. Pvt. practice self-employed, N.Y.C., 1974—; art critic Resident Publs., N.Y.C., 1993-95. Adj. prof. art history St. Francis Coll., Bklyn., 1985-94; artist-in-residence Our Saviour's Atonement Luth. Ch., N.Y.C., 1993-95. One-woman shows include Galimaufry, Croton-on-Hudson, N.Y., 1977, Kristen Richard Gallery, N.Y.C., 1982, Gallery 84, 1990, The Bernhardt Collection, Washington, 1991, Netherland Club, N.Y.C., 1992, Chuck Levitan Gallery, Soho, 1996, Seventh and Second Photo Gallery, 1998, Pen & Brush Solo Award Show, 2001, N.Y.C. Pub. Libr., 2002, exhibited in group shows at Union St. Graphics, San Francisco, 1974, Nuance Gallery, Tampa, 1987, 1988, Illustrators Ann. Drawing Show, N.Y.C., 1989—90, Salmagundi Club, 1991, 1992, Henry Howells Gallery, 1992—93, Mus. Gallery, 1994, Cavalier Gallery, Greenwich, Conn., 1995, CaribGallery, N.Y.C., 1996, N.Y. State Mus., 1997, Knickerbocker Gallery, 1999, Maison Royale, New Orleans, La., 2002, Christmas Card/UNICEF, 1992, Represented in permanent collections Peltz,Walker & Dubinsky, Valois of Am., one-woman shows include New York City Pub. Libr., 2002. Recipient first prize award annual watercolor exhibit, Pen and Brush, 2000. Mem. Pen and Brush, Poetry Soc. Am. Mem. Collegiate Ch. Avocations: ballroom dancing, old inns and architecture. Home: 106 Cabrini Blvd Apt 5D New York NY 10033-3422 E-mail: linda@lindasouthworth.com.

SOUTHWORTH, ROD BRAND, retired computer science educator; b. Binghampton, NY, Aug. 24, 1941; s. William Tanner Southworth and Ruth Evelyn (Brabham) Woods; m. Patrice Marie Gapon, Jan. 10, 1978 (div.); children: Suzi Lynn, Judi Leigh, Megan Marie, Robin Ashley. BS in Bus., U. Ariz., 1965; MS in Mgmt. Sci. and Info Systems, Colo. State U., 1978. Mktg. rep. IBM, Denver, 1966-69; system analyst Colo. State U., Fort Collins, 1969-73, grad. tchg. asst., 1978-79; project mgr. Systems and Computer Tech., Portland, Oreg., 1973-75, asst. dir. Fairbanks, Alaska, 1975-77; instr. computer info. systems Laramie County C.C., Cheyenne, Wyo., 1979-99; now semi-ret. Author: (software) PC-DOS/MS-DOS Simplified, 1st edit. 1988, 3rd edit. 1992, DOS Complete and Simplified, 1990, DOS Essentials, 1991, DOS 5 Simplified, 1992, DOS 6.2 Simplified, 1994. Mem. Civil Air Patrol, Cheyenne, 1991. Mem. Data Processing Mgmt. Assn. (assoc. level model curriculum 1984-85), Assn. Computing Machinery (assoc. level computer info. processing model curriculum 1991-92), Am. Contract Bridge League. Avocations: bridge, water-skiing, fishing, stamp collecting/philately, tennis. Home: 1929 Cheyenne Pl Cheyenne WY 82001 Office: Laramie County Comm Coll 1400 E College Dr Cheyenne WY 82007-3204 E-mail: southwor@Lccc.cc.wy.us.edu.

SOUTHWORTH, WILLIAM DIXON, retired education educator; b. Union City, Tenn., Dec. 28, 1918; s. Thomas and Gertrude (Dyer) S.; m. Violet Kuehn, July 22, 1944; children: Geoffrey Scott, Linda Jean. PhB, Marquette U., 1948, MEd, 1950; PhD, NYU, 1961. Tchr., coach La Follette Sch., Milwaukee County, Wis., 1948-51; teaching dist. prin. Grand View Sch., Milwaukee County, 1951-56; supervising dist. prin. Maple Dale Sch., Milwaukee County, 1956-58; bldg. prin. Main St. Sch., Port Washington, N.Y., 1958-65; asst. supt. for elem. edn. Huntington (N.Y.) pub. schs., 1965-67; assoc. prof., acting head dept. adminstrn. and supervision St. John's U., Jamaica, N.Y., 1967, chmn. dept., 1968-73, prof., 1968-84. Parliamentarian for 35 internat., nat. regional orgns., expert witness, pub. moderator, and workshop leader. Author: Care and Nurture of the Doctoral Candidate, 1968, 74, Q The Story of Captain Quimby Scott, U.S. Navy WWII, 1997, The Art of Successful Meetings, 1997, Murder on the Flagship, 1998, Corpsman!, 1998, Murder Impossible, 2002, The Wonderful World of Words: How to Build and Retain a Superior Vocabulary, 2002, The Sensual Sailor, 2003, Murders in Old Main, 2004; contbr. over 270 articles to ednl. jours., condominium and parliamentary publs. Served with USN, 1938—44. Lutheran. Home: Apt 608 7100 Sunshine Skyway Ln S Saint Petersburg FL 33711-4926 Office Phone: 727-864-1952. E-mail: vibilfid1@juno.com., wsouthworth@earthlink.net. *In the conflicting demands of self and society, one must strike a balance by retaining the uniqueness of one's individuality while serving the society that nurtured that uniqueness. It is in the balance thus struck that the complete person evolves self-esteeming, and socially involved.*

SOUTHWORTH, WILLIAM WALTER, lawyer, title insurance company executive; b. Cleve., Feb. 23, 1942; s. William A. and Ruth (Able) S.; m. Gaye B. Flanagan, June 15, 1968; children: Julie K., William J. AB, Rutgers U., 1964; JD, Boston U., 1967. Bar: Mass. 1967, U.S. Dist. Ct. Mass. 1972. Assoc. Keith, Reed and Wheatley, Brockton, Mass., 1972-74; title atty. Lawyers Title Ins. Corp., Boston, 1974-78; v.p., mgr., counsel Title USA Ins. Corp. N.Y., Boston, 1978-89; v.p. Security Title & Guaranty Co., 1989-93; asst. v.p. Fidelity Nat. Title Ins. Co. N.Y., 1993—. Contbg. author Crocker's Notes on Common Forms, 1995, Crocker's Notes on Common Forms Supplement, 1997, Crocker's Notes on Common Forms 8th edit., 2000, Crocker's Notes on Common Forms Supplement, 2000. Chmn. Heart Sunday, Am. Heart Assn., Brockton, 1975; bd. dirs. Brockton Symphony Orch., 1976-79; trustee, treas. Prelude Concert Series, Scituate, Mass., 1984. Capt. AUS, 1968-72. Mem. Boston Bar Assn. (co-chmn. real estate legis. com. 1996-2003, chair 2000), Mass. Conveyancers Assn., New Eng. Land Title Assn. (pres. 1983-84), Scituate Tennis Club. Home: 31 Lotus Ave Scituate MA 02066-2638 Office: Fidelity Nat Title Ins Co N Y 133 Federal St Boston MA 02110-1703 E-mail: wsouthworth@fnf.com.

SOUTTER, THOMAS DOUGLAS, retired lawyer; b. N.Y.C., Nov. 1, 1934; s. Thomas G. and Hildreth H. (Callanan) S.; m. Virginia Hovenden; children: Alexander D., Christopher A., Hadley H. BA, U. Va., 1955, LL.B., 1962; postgrad., Advanced Mgmt. Program, Harvard U., 1980. Bar: N.Y. 1962, R.I. 1969. Atty. Breed, Abbott & Morgan, N.Y.C., 1962-68; with Textron Inc., Providence, 1968-95, gen. counsel, 1970-95, v.p., 1971-80, sr. v.p., 1980-85, exec. v.p., gen. counsel, 1985-95; cons., 1995-97. Mem. adv. bd. Internat. and Comparative Law Ctr., 1975-95; mem. Assn. Gen. Counsel; bd. dirs. Avco Fin. Svcs., Inc., 1985-95, Paul Revere Corp. 1993-95; trustee New England Legal Found. Nat. chmn. ann. giving campaign U. Va. Law Sch., 1992-94, mem. exec. com. campaign, 1995-2000; former trustee Providence Preservation Soc., Providence Performing Arts Ctr.; mem. U. Va. Arts and Scis. Alumni Coun.; mem. Narragansett coun. Boy Scouts Am. Lt. USNR, 1955-59. Mem. ABA, N.Y. State Bar Assn., R.I. Bar Assn., Internat. Bar Assn. Office: 2 White Birch Ln Barrington RI 02806-4932 E-mail: tdsout@aol.com.

SOUVEROFF, VERNON WILLIAM, JR., business executive; b. L.A., Aug. 12, 1934; s. Vernon William Sr. and Aileen (Young) S.; m. Aileen Patricia Robinson; children: Gail Kathleen, Michael William, Kirk Laron. BS in E.E., Stanford U., 1957; postgrad., Ohio State U., 1958-59. With Litton Industries, Beverly Hills, Calif., 1960-75; with ITT Corp., N.Y.C., 1975-87; prin. Bus. Acquisitions and Investments, 1988—; corp. v.p. ITT Corp., N.Y.C., 1983-84, sr. v.p., 1984-87; pres. ITT Gilfillan, 1979-83; group exec. ITT Def. Space Group, 1983-84; CEO ITT Telecom and Electronics N.Am., 1984-86; pres., chief exec. officer ITT Def. Tech. Corp., 1986-87. Mem. U.S. Def. Policy Adv. Com. on Trade, Washington, 1984-88; bd. advisors, investor Venture Resources, Venture Capital, 1988-92; bd. dirs. Elanix, Inc., Formida Holdings Ltd., Australia; chmn. bd. dirs. Formida Software Corp., San Jose, Calif. Author books on def. downsizing. Served as officer USAF, 1957-60 Recipient Exec. Salute award Los Angeles C. of C., 1981. Mem. IEEE (life), Nat. Contracts Mgmt. Assn., Electronics Industries Assn., Am. Def. Preparedness Assn. (former dir.), Nat. Security Indsl. Assn., Air Force Assn., Navy League, Assn. U.S. Army, Alamo Town Assn. (bd. mem.), S.R. Valley YMCA (chmn.). Presbyterian.

SOUZA, DIANE D, corporate financial executive; BS in acctg. with high honors, U. Mass.; AS in dental hygiene, Forsyth Sch. at Northeastern U. CPA. Dir. northeast ins. Price Waterhouse; sr. mgr. Deloitte Haskins & Sells; asst. v.p. Aetna Inc., 1994—96; v.p., CFO Large Case Pensions divsn. of Aetna Inc., 1996—98; v.p., dir. of internal audit Aetna Inc., 1998—2001, v.p., nat. customer ops., 2001—. Mem.: Conn. Soc. of CPA's (mem. ins. com.), Am. Inst. Cert. Pub. Accountants. Office: Aetna Inc 151 Farmington Ave Hartford CT 06156

SOUZA, GILVAN CASTRO, operations and management educator; b. Goiania, Brazil; BS in Aero. Engring., Tech. Inst. Aeronautics, Sao Jose dos Campos, Brazil, 1990; MBA, Clemson U., 1995; PhD, U. of N.C., 2000. Product devel. engr. Volkswagen, Sao Paulo, Brazil, 1991—94; asst. prof. U. of Md., Coll. Pk., Md., 2000—. Contbr. articles to profl. jours. Recipient Outstanding Grad. Student Rsch. award, Kenan Inst., U. of NC, 1998, Summer Rsch. award, U. of Md., 2001; scholar, Technol. Inst. of Aeronautics, Brazil, 1986—90. Mem.: Decision Sciences Inst., Prodn. and Ops. Mgmt. Soc., Inst. for Ops. Rsch. and Mgmt. Sci. Office: University of Maryland Smith School of Business College Park MD 20742

SOUZA, LAWRENCE M. health facility administrator; AB in Bacteriology, U. Calif., Berkeley, 1975; PhD in Molecular Biology, UCLA, 1980. With Amgen, Thousand Oaks, Calif., 1981—, v.p. molecular and cellular biology, dir. exploratory programs, sr. v.p. rsch., 1997—. Adj. prof. dept. microbiology and immunology UCLA. Office: Amgen Inc One Amgen Center Dr Mailstop 27-5-A Thousand Oaks CA 91320-1789

SOUZDALTSEV, IGOR NIKOLAYEVICH, economist; b. Krasnousolsky, Bashkiria, Russia, Nov. 30, 1962; came to U.S., 1995; s. Vladimir Egorovich Baev and Tamara Georgievna Souzdaltseva; m. Elena Alfredovna Ratner, June 22, 1985; 1 child, Svyatoslav. BA in History, Krasnodar (Russia) State U., 1985. Social scis. tchr. H.S., Krasnodar, 1985-90; market analyst E.V.A. Co., Krasnodar, 1990-95, Marlin Trading Co., Inc., Ballston Spa, N.Y., 1995-97, Coriander LLC, Ft. Lee, N.J., 1997-2000; chmn. Inst. Natiology, LLC, N.Y.C., N.Y., 2000—. Author: Natiology: Social Science for the Third Millennium, 1999. Mem. AAAS, Am. Polit. Sci. Assn., Fin. Markets Assn., Assn. Study of Nationalities, N.Y. Acad. Scis. Fax: 212-208 3095. E-mail: igor.souzdaltsev@natiology.com.

SOVENYHAZY, GABOR FERENC, surgeon; b. Budapest, Hungary, Apr. 7, 1947; MD, SUNY, 1975. Diplomate Am. Bd. of Colon and Rectal Surgeons. Intern Maimonides Med. Ctr., Bklyn., 1974-75, resident in gen. surgery, 1976-79; resident in colon and rectal surgery Grant Hosp., Columbus, 1979-80; pvt. practice, 1980—; hosp. appt. Spartanburg Gen. Hosp., S.C.; asst. prof. colon and rectal surgery U. S.C. Fellow ACS, Am. Soc. Colorectal Surgery, Piedmont Colorectal Assn., Am. Soc. Gastrointestinal Endoscopy, Am. Soc. Colon and Rectal Surgeons. Office: 11 Doctors Park Dr Ste 210 Spartanburg SC 29307-1008

SOVERN, MICHAEL IRA, law educator; b. N.Y.C., Dec. 1, 1931; s. Julius and Lillian (Arnstein) S.; m. Lenore Goodman, Feb. 21, 1952 (div. Apr. 1963); children: Jeffrey Austin, Elizabeth Ann, Douglas Todd; m. Eleanor Leen, Aug. 25, 1963 (div. Feb. 1974); 1 child, Julie Danielle; m. Joan Wit, Mar. 9, 1974 (dec. Sept. 1993); m. Patricia Walsh, Nov. 12, 1995. AB summa cum laude, Columbia U., 1953, LLB (James Ordronaux prize), 1955, LLD (hon.), 1980; PhD (hon.), Tel Aviv U., 1982; LLD (hon.), U. So. Calif., 1989. Bar: N.Y. 1956, U.S. Supreme Ct. 1976. Asst. prof., then assoc. prof. law U. Minn. Law Sch., 1955-58; mem. faculty Columbia Law Sch., 1957—, prof. law, 1960—, Chancellor Kent prof., 1977—, dean Law Sch., 1970-79; chmn. exec. com. faculty Columbia U., 1968-69, provost, exec. v.p., 1979-80, univ. pres., 1980-93, pres. emeritus, 1993. Rsch. dir. Legal Restraints on Racial Discrimination in Employment, Twentieth Century Fund, 1962-66; spl. counsel to gov. N.J., 1974-77; cons. Time Mag., 1965-80; mem. panel of arbitrators N.J. Bd. Mediation, Fed. Mediation and Conciliation Svc.; bd. dirs. Sequa, Asian Cultural Coun., Shubert Orgn., Comcast Corp., Sta. WNET-TV, NAACP Legal Def. Fund, 1976-97, Freedom Forum Newseum; chmn. N.Y.C. Charter Revision Commn., 1982-83; co-chmn. 2d Cir. Commn. on Reduction of Burdens and Costs in Civil Litigation, 1977 80; chmn. Commn. on Integrity in Govt., 1986; pres. Italian Acad. Advanced Studies in Am., 1991-93, Shubert Found., 1996—; chmn. Japan Soc., 1993—2004, hon. chmn., 2004—; chmn. Am. Acad. Rome, 1993—, Sotheby's, 2000—; chmn. nat. adv. coun. Freedom Forum Media Studies Ctr., 1993-2001. Author: Legal Restraints on Racial Discrimination in Employment, 1966, Law and Poverty, 1969, Of Boundless Domains, 1994; host Sta. WNET-TV series Leading Questions. Mem. Pulitzer Prize Bd., 1980-93, chmn. pro tem, 1986-87; trustee Kaiser Family Found., 1994-2002, Presdl. Legal Expense Trust, 1994-98; chmn. Sotheby's, 2000 Decorated commendatore Order of Merit (Italy), Order of the Rising Sun, Gold and Silver Star (Japan); recipient Alexander Hamilton medal Columbia Coll., 1993, Citizens Union Civic Leadership award, 1993, Town Hall Friend of the Arts award, 2001. Fellow Am. Acad. Arts and Scis.; mem. ABA, Coun. Fgn. Rels., Assn. Bar City N.Y., Am. Philos. Soc., Am. Arbitration Assn. (panel arbitrators), Am. Law Inst., Econ. Club, Nat. Acad. Arbitrators. Office: Columbia U Sch Law 435 W 116th St New York NY 10027-7297 Office Phone: 212-854-7848.

SOVEY, WILLIAM PIERRE, manufacturing executive; b. Helen, Ga., Aug. 26, 1933; s. Louis Terrell and Kathryn Bell (White) S.; m. Kathryne Owen Doyle, Dec. 28, 1958; children: Margaret Elizabeth, John Todd. BSI.E., Ga. Inst. Tech., 1955; grad., Advanced Mgmt. Program, Harvard U., 1976. Gen. mgr. automotive div. Atwood Vacuum Machine Co., Rockford, Ill., 1963-68; v.p. internat. A.G. Spalding & Bros., Inc., Chicopee, Mass., 1968-71; pres. Ben Hogan Co. div. AMF Inc., Ft. Worth, 1971-77, corp. v.p., group exec. indsl. products group Stamford, Conn., 1977-79, pres., chief operating officer, dir. White Plains, N.Y., 1982-85; pres., chief operating officer Newell Rubbermaid Inc., Freeport, Ill., 1986-92, CEO, 1992-97, 2000—, also bd. dirs. Served with USN, 1955-58. Home: PO Box 31102 Sea Island GA 31561-1102 Office: Newell Rubbermaid 29 E Stephenson St Freeport IL 61032

SOVIERO, JOSEPH C. chemical company executive; b. 1938; BS, Polytech. Inst. Bklyn., 1960; MS, NYU, 1965. With Union Carbide Corp., Danbury, Conn., 1965—, corporate v.p., 1990—. Office: 39 Old Ridgebury Rd Danbury CT 06810-5103

SOVIK, EDWARD ANDERS, architect, consultant; b. Honan, China, June 9, 1918; s. Edward Anderson and Anna (Tenwick) S.; m. Genevieve Elaine Hendrickson, June 29, 1946 (dec.); m. Anne Running, Mar. 25, 2001; children: Rolf, Martin, Peter. BA, St. Olaf Coll., 1939; student, Art Students League N.Y., 1939-40, Luther Theol. Sem., 1940-42; MArch, Yale U., 1949; DFA (hon.), Concordia Coll., 1981. Ret. chmn. SMSQ, Architects and predecessors, Northfield, Minn.; prof. art emeritus St. Olaf Coll., Northfield. Lectr. on ch. design at various confs., schs., univs.; participant, planner, del. numerous domestic and fgn. confs. on religion and architecture; mem., officer various profl., religious and pub. bds. and commns. Author: Architecture for Worship; Contbr. numerous articles to mags., anthologies.; works include chs., coll. and univ. bldgs., instns. With USMC, 1942-45; maj. Res. Decorated D.F.C., Purple Heart, Air medals; recipient Diekmann award, N.Am. Acad. Liturgy, 2003. Fellow AIA; mem. AIA Minn. (pres. 1977, Gold medal 1981), Phi Beta Kappa. Democrat. Lutheran. Home: 711 Summit Ave Northfield MN 55057-1568 E-mail: sovik@rconnect.com.

SØVIK, NILS, education educator; b. Os in Hordaland, Norway, June 18, 1928; s. Bertin and Nilsina (Lekven) S.; m. Gerd Margrethe Sørhuus; children: Edmund, Øyvind. MA, U. Oslo, 1960, PhD, 1972. Asst. prof. U. Trondheim, Norway, 1963-67; rsch. scholarship U. Wis., Madison, 1968-70; assoc. prof. U. Trondheim, 1971-77, dir. rsch. social sci., 1977-80, prof. edn., 1981. Author: Developmental Cybernetics of Handwriting and Motor Coordination, 1975. Mem. Royal Norwegian Soc. Scis. and Letters (leader humanities 1988-89, sec. gen. 1990-96). Avocation: music. Home: Tyholtveien 16 N-7052 Trondheim Norway Office: Dept Edn NTNU N-7491 Trondheim Norway E-mail: nils.sovik@svt.ntnu.no.

SOVOCOOL, MARY ANNE ELIZABETH CRANSTON, secondary school educator; b. Oct. 22, 1931; d. Ray Leeo and Elizabeth Marceline (Carroll) Cranston; m. Wilbur John Sovocool, June 17, 1951 (div. 1975); children: Robert Cranston, Sharon Louise Sovocool Harris, John Ray, Wayne Lewis, Patricia Elaine, Daniel Arnold, Charles Paul, Kathleen Elizabeth Sovocool Del Plato, Kenneth Brian. BS, Cornell U., 1952; postgrad., SUNY, Brockport, 1968—75. Sci. tchr. Churchville Chili Ctrl. Sch., 1967—71; tchr. spcl. edn. Monroe Orleans #2 Bd. Coop. Ednl. Svcs., Spencerport, NY, 1972—81; sci. tchr. Churchville-Chili Ctrl. Sch., Churchville, NY, 1972—81, tchr. spl. edn., 1981—94, Monroe-Orleans # 2 Bd. Coop. Edn., Spencerport, NY, 1981—94, Churchville-Chili Cen. Sch.; home tutoring LeRoy Ctrl. Sch., 1994—. Curriculum adv. com. Churchville-Chili Schs.; tchr., developer awareness program Churchville-Chili Ctrl. Sch., interdisciplinary programs; presenter in field, 1992. Mem. rules com. LeRoy Vol. Ambulance, 1980—; elder, deacon, trustee 1st Presbyn. Ch., LeRoy, NY, 1970—. Mem.: NEA, Genessee County Cornell U. Alumni Admissions Ambs. Network, Chruchville-Chili Edn. Assn. (exec. coun.), N.Y. Edn. Assn., Cornell Club (bd. dirs. fedn. Cornell Clubs, past pres. Genesee-Orleans, past pres. Cornell Women's Club Batavia), Cornell Women's Club Batavia, Women of the Moose (LeRoy chpt.), Order Ea. Star (chpt. matron 1996, 2001). Avocations: reading, sewing, painting, poetry. Home: 29 Wolcott St Le Roy NY 14482-1446

SOWA, ARTUR, mathematician, researcher; b. Poland, Oct. 27, 1965; came to U.S., 1992; s. Witold and Lucyna Sowa; m. Jolanta Sowa, Aug. 15, 1987; children: Izaak, Oliver. MS in Math., Warsaw U., 1990; PhD in Math., CUNY, 1995. Postdoctoral asst. CUNY, N.Y.C., 1995-97; postdoctoral rsch. assoc. Yale U., New Haven, 1997-2000, lectr., 2000; scientist Pegasus Imaging Corp., Tampa, Fla., 2000—02; online instr. U. Phoenix, 2003. Contbr. articles to profl. jours. Recipient 1st prize, The Marcinkiewicz Competition, Poland, 1990, Rsch. Associateship award, NRC, 2001. Mem.: IEEE, Math. Assn. Am. Avocations: philosophy, hiking, music. Achievements include rsch. in mesoscopic description of correlated systems of electrons and the mesoscopic mechanics. Home: 109 Snow Crest Trl Durham NC 27707-6102 E-mail: ArturSowa@mesoscopia.com.

SOWA, FRANK XAVIER, entrepreneur, futurist, educator, speaker; b. Akron, Ohio, Aug. 9, 1957; s. William Walter and Olga Susan (DeMay) S. BA in English and Chemistry, Muskingum Coll., 1979. Reporter Dix Publs., Cambridge, Ohio, 1976-78; editor Messenger Newspapers, Akron, 1978-79; mgr. corp. communications Davy McKee Corp., Cleve., 1979-81; mgr. market communications Roadway Package System, Pitts., 1984-85; owner, chief exec. officer Xavier Communications, Pitts., 1982-87, The Xavier Group, Ltd., Pitts., 1986—89, CEO, pres., 1990—, Seed.Net Computer Online Incubator, Pitts., 1994—98. Cons. CC. Allegeny County, Pitts., 1986-88, instr., 1987, LaRoche Coll., Pitts., 1982-83, U. Aron, 1982, U. Pitts. Gov.'s Internat. Studies, 1988-91; chmn. Pitts. Quality and Productivity Exposion, 1991, 7th Ann. Pitts. Quality Conf., 1991; chmn. econ. devel. com. SMC Bus. Couns., 1993-95; bd. dirs. OMEGA Fed. Credit Union, 1994-98; tech. solutions cons.

Ednl. Tech. Assocs., N.Y.C., 1998-2000; bd. dirs. Three Rivers Ednl. Tech. Conf.; presenter in field. Author: Pittsburgh Reinvented, 1985, National Quality Standards (ISO 9000) for Training and Instruction, (software) Chronometics Modeller, 1987; editor Pitts. Trends Newsletter, 1984-89; columnist Boardwatch Mag., 1994-98; contbr. articles to profl. jours. Chmn. N.H. Civic-Cultural Ctr., Pitts., 1987-88; adv. coun. Smaller Mfrs. Coun., 1987-93; sec., bd. dirs. Imaginarium Children's Theatre, Pitts., 1985; active World Affairs Coun., 1987-92, UN's 21st Century Studies, 1986-89, Pa. High-Tech. Coun., Greater Pitts. Reg. Econ. Revitalization Initative, 1994-95; nat. transport policy adv. unit Dept. Transp.; campaign mem. Muskingum Leadership Coun., 1994. Recipient Brownfield Pub. Svc., Pa. Jaycees, 1987. Mem. NSPE, Am. Soc. Quality Control (bd. dirs. Pitts. sect. 1990-95), Def. Preparedness Assn. (bd. dirs. Pa. 1991-95), Pitts. Inst. for the Future (pres., chmn. 1988-90), Assn. Online Profls. (founding mem.), World Future Soc., Am. Entrepreneurs Soc., Congl. Inst. for Future, Western Pa. Conservancy, Gov.'s Scanning Bd., Soc. Internat. Bus. Economists, Inst. Internat. Mgmt. Cons., Econs. Club.

SOWALD, BEATRICE KRONICK, lawyer; b. Amsterdam, N.Y., May 29, 1927; d. Maurice and Rose (Gray) Kronick; widowed; children: Malcolm, Debra, Heather. BA, Ohio State U., 1948, JD, 1966. Bar: Ohio 1966, U.S. Supreme Ct. 1987, U.S. Dist. Ct. (so. dist.) Ohio, 1970. Supr. Legal Aid Soc., Columbus, Ohio, 1967-80; ptnr. Sowald & Sowald, Columbus, 1980-84; judge Franklin County Ct. of Common Pleas, Columbus, 1984, Franklin County Mcpl. Ct., Columbus, 1985; ptnr. Sowald, Sowald & Clouse, Columbus, 1986—. Mem. Ohio Bd. of Bar Examiners, Columbus, 1996-99. Editor: Ohio Domestic Relations Law, 1996, 2002. Trustee Legal Aid Soc., Columbus, 1989-97. Mem. Ohio State Bar Assn. (coun. of delegates 1983—, Ohio Bar medal award, 2004), Columbus Bar Assn. (Professionalism award 1993), Franklin County Trial Lawyers. Home: 125 Eastmoor Blvd Columbus OH 43209-2017 Office: Sowald Sowald & Clouse 400 S 5th St Ste 101 Columbus OH 43215-5430 Office Phone: 614-464-1877.

SOWARDS, STEVEN WESLEY, librarian; BA, Stanford U., Palo Alto, Calif., 1973; PhD, Ind.U., Bloomington, 1981; MLS, Ind. U., Bloomington, 1986. Reference libr. Hanover Coll., Ind., 1986—88; humanities libr. Swarthmore Coll., Pa., 1988—96; head libr., social scis. and humanities reference Mich. State U., East Lansing, 1996—98, head libr., main libr. reference, 1998—. Mem.: ALA, Mich. Libr. Assn., Sierra Club (life). Office: Mich State Univ Librs 100 Library East Lansing MI 48824

SOWDER, ERIC D. retail executive; BBA, Va. Commonwealth U. With Lowe's Cos., Inc., 1984—, various pos., including merchandising v.p. for lawn and garden plumbing categories, and v.p. logistics, sr. v.p. logistics, 2002—. Office: Lowes Cos Inc 1605 Curtis Bridge Rd Wilkesboro NC 28697

SOWDER, FRED ALLEN, foundation administrator, alphabet specialist; b. Cin., July 17, 1940; s. William Franklin and Lucille (Estes) S.; m. Sandra Ann Siegman, July 15, 1961 (div. Sept. 1963); 1 child, William. Student, Cin. Sch. Ct. Reporting, 1975; diploma Self-Health Insts., Sch. of Med. Masso-Therapy, 1985; diploma, Cin. Sch. Hypnosis, 1989. Founder World Union Universal Alphabet, Cin., 1981—, Internat. Assn. Sch. Massage, Cin., 1988—. Inventor of hundreds of published and unpublished alphabets and writing systems, including light wave, color and musical tone systems and tactile systems for the blind; author: Sowder Shorthand, 1980, Universal Alphabet: What and Why, 1981, Your Intimacy Quotient: The Symptoms, Causes & Consequences of Intimacy Deprivation, 1996; contbr. numerous articles to mags. State dir. Soc. Separationists, Cin., 1967-70; bd. dirs. ACLU of Ohio, ACLU Found., 1984-89, sec., Cin. chpt., 1984-89. Mem. AAAS, Amnesty Internat., Ohio Com. to Abolish Capital Punishment, No. Ky. Right to Life, Urban Appalachian Coun. Home: PO Box 252 Cincinnati OH 45201-0252 Office: World Union Universal Alphabet PO Box 252 Cincinnati OH 45201-0252

SOWDER, KATHLEEN ADAMS, marketing executive; b. Person county, N.C., Feb. 9, 1951; d. George W. and Mary W. (Woody) Adams; m. Angelo R. LoMascolo, Apr. 11, 1980 (div.); 1 child, Mary Jennifer. BS, Radford Coll., 1976; MBA, Va. Poly. Inst., 1977. Bd. cert. in security mgmt. Cert. Protection Profl. Asst. product mgr. GTE Sylvania, Waltham, Mass., 1978—79, product mgr. video products, 1979—80; comml. mktg. mgr. Am. Dist. Telegraph, N.Y.C., 1980—87; v.p. mktg. ESL, Hingham, Mass., 1987—91; exec. v.p. Falcon Detection Techs., Inc., Plymouth, Mass., 1991—94; gen. mgr. Westec Bus. Security, Irvine, Calif., 1995—2000; CEO Nova Security Sys., Fullerton, Calif., 2000—. Mem.: Am. Soc. Indsl. Security (past chair standing com. on phys. security), Am. Mktg. Assn. Republican. Office: Nova Security Systems 819 Pueblo Fullerton CA 92835 Home: 10473 La Sombra Ave Fountain Valley CA 92708-5210 E-mail: ksowder@novasecuritysystems.com.

SOWDER, ROBERT ROBERTSON, architect; b. Kansas City, Kans., Dec. 29, 1928; s. James Robert and Agnes (Robertson) S.; m. Joan Goddard, July 26, 1954; 1 dau., Lisa Robertson Lee. BA, U. Wash., 1953; B.Arch., U. Va., 1958; grad. diploma in Architecture, Ecole Des Beaux Arts, Fontainebleau, France, 1952. Designer Architects Collaborative, Boston, 1958-59, Peirce & Pierce (architects), Boston, 1959-63; asso. Fred. Bassetti & Co. (architects), Seattle, 1963-67; partner Naramore, Bain, Brady & Johanson (architects), Seattle, 1967-81; pres. NBBJ Internat., 1976-81; architect TRA, Seattle, 1981-83; v.p. Daniel, Mann, Johnson & Mendenhall, San Francisco, 1983-93; prin. RRS Consulting, 1993—. Archtl. design critic Boston Archtl. Ctr., 1961-62. Important works include Ridgeway III Dormitories, Bellingham, Wash. (Dept. Housing and Urban Devel. Honor award), Seattle Rapid Transit (HUD Excellence award), Safeco Ins. Co. Home Office Complex, Seattle, King County Stadium, Balt. Conv. Ctr., Oreg. Conv. Ctr., San Francisco (Moscone) Conv. Ctr. Expansion, Honolulu Conv. Ctr., Wilmington (Del.) Conv. Ctr. Mem. Redmond (Wash.) Design Rev. Bd., 1996-2000. Served with CIC U.S. Army, 1954-56. Recipient Premier Prix D'Architecture Ecole Des Beaux Arts, Fontainebleau, 1951, 52, Prix D'Remondet Fontainebleau, 1952 Mem. AIA (emeritus), Internat. Assn. Assembly Mgrs., Seattle Tennis Club, Seattle Rainier Club, Scarab, Sigma Chi. Episcopalian. Home and Office: 17032 NE 135th Ct Redmond WA 98052-1715

SOWELL, DEBRA ANN OLSON, mathematician, educator, academic administrator; b. Aberdeen, S.D., Dec. 13, 1948; d. Stanley John and Margaret Jane Olson; m. Russell Wayne Sowell; 1 child, Elizabeth Jane Whitehead. BA, U. S.D., 1971; MA in Tchg., U. Nebr., 1975; PhD, Okla. State U., 1996. Math. tchr. Monroe Pub. Schs., Key West, Fla., 1971—73; instr., ext. divsn. U. Nebr., Lincoln, 1974; prof. math. Oral Roberts U., Tulsa, 1976—, chair dept. math., 1995—99, assoc. dean sch. arts and sciences, 1996—96, dean instrn., 1997—. Adj. instr. math. Tulsa U., 1976. Author: Statistics: An Intuitive Approach, 4th Edition, Introductory Statistics for Business and Economics, (study guide) Study Guide for Statistics: An Intuitive Approach, 4th Edition. Named to Hall of Fame, Okla. State Sci. and Engring. Fair, 1998; fellow Maude Hammond Fling fellow, U. Nebr.; grantee Summer Math. Acad., Okla. State Regents Higher Edn., Leadership Devel. Inst., Coun. Christian Colls. and Univs. Mem.: Okla. State Sci. and Engring. Fair (Hall of Fame 1998), Pi Mu Epsilon, Phi Kappa Phi, Phi Beta Kappa, Kappa Mu Epsilon (rec. sec.). Home: 714 North Butternut Ct Broken Arrow OK 74012 Office: Oral Roberts U 7777 South Lewis Ave Tulsa OK 74171 Business E-Mail: dsowell@oru.edu.

SOWELL, LAVEN, retired music educator; b. Wewoka, Okla., Jan. 9, 1933; s. Vestal Laven and Viola Jane Sowell. MusB, U. Okla., 1955; MA, Columbia U., 1964; postgrad., Manhattan Sch. Music, 1956—57, Conservatoire de Musique de Fontainebleu, France, 1966; studied with Clark Snell, Martial Singher, Joseph Benton, John Brownlee, Samuel Margolis, Nadia Boulanger. Choral condr. Edison H.S., Tulsa, 1961—70; chorus master Tulsa Opera, 1962—94; dir. music 1st Presbyn. Ch., Tulsa, 1969—85; prof. music U. Tulsa, 1970—91. Vocal adjudicator various mus. orgns.; tchr. pvt. voice lessons. Co-author: Tulsa Opera Chronicles, 1992; author: My Music Notebook, 2000. Bd. dirs. Tulsa Opera. Recipient Gov.'s Arts award, State of Okla., 1991. Mem.: Tulsa Accredited Music Teacher's Assn., Okla. Music Teacher's Assn. Democrat. Presbyterian. Avocations: travel, reading, opera. Home: 3800 W 71st Apt 2312 Tulsa OK 74132-2153

SOWELL, R. DOUGLAS, medical association administrator, podiatrist; m. Linda Sowell; 1 child, Jennifer. BS in Psychology, U. Okla., 1971; DPM, Ill. Coll. Pediat. Medicine, 1978. Diplomate Am. Bd. Podiatric Surgery. Resident Thorek Hosp. and Med. Ctr.; podiatrist St. Anthony Hosp., Hillcrest Hosp. and Med. Ctr., Edmond Regional Med. Ctr., Deaconess and Bapt. Hosps., Oklahoma City. Fellow: Am. Coll. Podiatric Med. Rev., Am. Coll. Podiatric Physicians, Am. Coll. Foot and Ankle Surgeons; mem.: Am. Podiatric Med. Assn. (trustee, pres.). Office: Am Pediat Med Assn 9312 Old Georgetown Rd Bethesda MD 20814

SOWER, MILENE A. nursing educator; b. LaCrosse, Wis., Oct. 14, 1939; d. Miles Marcus and Dorethea Rose (Cox) Morrison; children: Karlene A. Mrosko, Paula B. Utley. BSN, Coll. St. Scholastica, Duluth, Minn., 1961; MA, U. Iowa, 1972, PhD, 1980. Dir. nursing edn. Moline (Ill.) Pub. Hosp. Sch. Nursing; dir. nursing adminstrn. grad. prog. U. S.C., Columbia; dean nursing Coastal Carolina Coll., Conway, S.C.; exec. sec. N.Y. State Bd. for Nursing, N.Y. State Edn. Dept., Albany; ret., 2001. Contbr. articles to profl. jours. Mem. Am. Nurses Assn., Am. Bus. Women's Assn. Home: 1960 Bell Rd Crossville TN 38571-7476

SOWERS, AMELIA BARNET, speech and language pathologist; b. Houston, Mar. 13, 1952; d. Albert Glenn and Helen June (Meador) Barnet; m. George Vernon Sowers Jr., Aug. 23, 1975; children: George Vernon III, Adam Glenn. BA, U. Houston, 1975, MA, 1993. Lic. and cert. speech-lang. pathologist, Tex. Speech-lang. pathologist Aldine Ind. Sch. Dist., Houston, 1976-78, Tomball (Tex.) Ind. Sch. Dist., 1978-83, Conroe (Tex.) Ind. Sch. Dist., 1984-96; pvt. practice, 1996—. Mem. Crighton Players; organizer Crighton Kids, Crighton Players Performing Arts Sch. for Youth; apptd. to City of Conroe Commn. on Arts & Culture; pres. Crighton Theatre Found. 1999-2001; clin. supr. Grad. Sch., Tex. Women's U. 1997-98. Mem. NEA, Am. Speech, Lang. and Hearing Assn., Tex. Speech and Hearing Assn., Tex. Tchrs. Assn., Houston Assn. Comm. Disorders, Montgomery County Performing Arts Soc. (com.), Conroe Svc. League (v.p. 2004-2005). Methodist. Avocations: reading, crafts, dance, community theatre. Home and Office: 25 Village Hill Dr Conroe TX 77304-3525

SOWERS, JODI LOUISE, music educator; d. Edward Eugene and Margaret Rose Sowers; m. Gregory Paul Smith, July 10, 1999; children: Alyssa Rose Smith, Nathan Paul Smith. BA, U. Indpls., 1996; Master of Music, Butler U., 1998. Tchr. flute U. Indpls., 2000—; tchr. flute and music history Ind. U. Purdue U. Indpls., 2000—. Mem.: Indpls. Musician's Union. Avocations: music, scrapbooks, gardening, running, theater. Home: 4238 Tarragon Ter Indianapolis IN 46237

SOWERS, WESLEY HOYT, lawyer, management consultant; b. Whiting, Ind., Aug. 26, 1905; s. Samuel Walter and Bertha E. (Spurrier) S.; m. Gladys Krueger, Jan. 21, 1929; children: Penny (Mrs. David Buxton), Wesley Hoyt Jr. BS, Purdue U., 1926, MS, 1927; JD, DePaul U., 1941; grad., Advanced Mgmt. Program, Harvard, 1960. Bar: Ill. 1940; registered patent atty. and practitioner ICC. Chemist Shell Oil Co., East Chicago, Ind., 1927-29; sales engr. Nat. Lead Co., St. Louis, 1929-31; lab. supr. patent atty. Pure Oil Co., Chgo., 1932-42; v.p. Bay Chem. Co., New Orleans, 1942-50, Frontier Chem. Co., Wichita, Kans., 1950-57; pres. Frontier Chem. div. Vulcan Materials Co., 1957-65; exec. v.p., dir. Vulcan Materials Co., Birmingham, 1958-65; mgmt. counsel, 1965—. Mem. health professions vis. com. Wichita State U. Patentee in field Past chmn. Met. Planning Commn., Wichita and Sedgwick County, 1958; commr. Kans. Econ. Devel. Bd.; chmn. Kansas Com. for Constitutional Revision, Sedgwick County U.S. Savs. Bonds Sales; past chmn. Kans. Radio Free Europe; past mem. adv. com. Kans. Geol. Survey; mem. Kans. Senate, 1970-81; former mem. engring. adv. council Sch. Engring. and Architecture, Kans. State U.; regent, trustee Wichita State U., HCA/Wesley Med. Ctr., Wichita; bd. dirs. Health Systems Agy. of Southeast Kans., Bd. of Health Sedgwick County, Inst. Logopedics, Quivira council Boy Scouts Am., YMCA, Health Systems Agy. S.E. Kans.; past trustee Midwest Research Inst.; mem. adv. bd. Kans. U. Bus. Sch.; vis. com. Coll. Health Profession, Wichita State U.; chmn. Kans. Health Care Providers Malpractice Commn.; mem. Kans. Health Care Costs Commn., Kans. Health Coordinating Council, Wichita/Sedgwick County Bd. Health; mem. gov.'s adv. commn. Kans. Dept. Health and Environment. Mem. AAAS, Kans. C. of C. (past pres., past dir.), Wichita C. of C. (past pres. 1959, past dir., Uncommon Citizen award 1988), Kans. Assn. Commerce and Industry (past pres., dir.), Am. Chem. Soc., AAAS, Smithsonian Assocs., Soc. Chem. Industry, Ill. Bar Assn., Wichita Bar Assn., Phi Delta Theta. Lodges: Rotary. Home and Office: 600 W Arapaho Rd Apt 1034 Richardson TX 75080

SOWERS, WILLIAM ARMAND, civil engineer; b. Willis, Va., Apr. 23, 1923; s. Harry Cline and Effie Vivian (Slusher) S.; m. Gale Johnson, May 20, 1978; children: Jane Dixon, Jean Marie. Student, Roanoke Coll., 1940-42; BCE, Va. Poly. Inst., 1947, BS in Archtl. Engring., 1948. Registered profl. engr., Va. Assoc. Brown, Wells & Meagher, Roanoke, Va., 1948-50; ptnr. R.L. Brown and Assocs., Roanoke, 1950-53, Sowers, Knowles & Rodes, Roanoke, 1953-59, Sowers, Rodes & Whitescarver, Roanoke, 1959-84, Sowers & Assocs., Roanoke, 1984-94; DJG Sowers, Mann Sowers-Mann, Roanoke, 1994-96; ptnr. McKinney, Sowers-Mann, 1996-97, McKinney & Co., 1997-98, ret., 1998. Trustee ACEC Health Life Ins., St. Louis, 1975-83; commr. city planning City of Roanoke, 1976-92. Mem. Am. Cons. Engrs. (nat. pres. 1970-72), Cons. Engrs. Coun. Va. (svc. award 1972), Va. Soc. Profl. Engrs. (Svc. to Profession award 1972), Illuminating Engring. Soc., Shenandoah Club, Masons. E-mail: gbpiedmont@aol.com.

SOWMAN, HAROLD GENE, ceramic engineer, researcher; b. Murphysboro, Ill., July 21, 1923; s. Harold Thomas and Thelma (Crombar) S.; m. Gladys May Wright, Dec. 8, 1945; children— Letitia Ann, Daniel Patrick BS in Ceramic Engring., U. Ill., 1948, MS in Ceramic Engring., 1949, PhD in Ceramic Engring., 1951. Assoc. ceramist Titanium Alloy, Niagara Falls, N.Y., 1951-52; research assoc. Knolls Atomic Power Lab., Gen. Electric Co., Schenectady, 1952-57; various supervisory and mgmt. positions in nuclear materials research and devel. 3M Co., St. Paul, 1957-65, research specialist, 1965-67, sr. research specialist, 1967-70, corp. scientist, 1970-87. Friedberg Meml. lectr. Nat. Inst. Ceramic Engrs., 1988. Author articles, govt. reports on research and devel. of ceramic and nuclear materials; patentee in field Served to 2d lt. AUS, 1943-46 Recipient Hon. Alumni award for disting. service in engring. U. Ill. Coll. Engring., 1983 Fellow Am. Ceramic Soc. (John Jeppson medal 1985, Samuel Geijsbeek award 1989); mem. Nat. Acad. Engring., Acad. of Ceramics, 3M Carlton Soc., Tau Beta Pi (chpt. Eminent Engr. award 1983). Home: 4770 Aston Gardens Way Unit 304 Naples FL 34109

SOX, HAROLD CARLETON, JR., physician, educator, editor; b. Palo Alto, Calif., Aug. 18, 1939; s. Harold Carleton and Mary (Griffiths) Sox; m. Carol Helen Hill, Aug. 26, 1962; children: Colin Montgomery, Lara Katherine. BS, Stanford U., 1961; MD cum laude, Harvard U., 1966. Diplomate Am. Bd. Internal Medicine. Intern and resident Mass. Gen. Hosp., Boston, 1966—68; clin. assoc. Nat. Cancer Inst., Bethesda, Md., 1968—70; instr. Dartmouth Med. Sch., Hanover, NH, 1970—73; asst. prof. medicine to prof. clin. medicine Stanford U. Sch. Medicine, Calif., 1973—88; Joseph Huber prof., chmn. dept. medicine Dartmouth Med. Sch., 1988—2001; editor Annals of Internal Medicine ACP, Phila., 2001—. Pretest writing com. Am. Bd. Internal Medicine, 1992—94; panel mem. Nat. Bd. Med. Examiners, Physician Assts. Nat. Certifying Exam., 1973—76; chair com. on priority-setting for health tech. assessment Inst. Medicine, 1990—91, U.S. preventive svcs. task force chair, 1990—95, mem., 1998—2001; chair Inst. Medicine com. on HIV and U.S. blood supply, 1994—95; chair task force to revise internal medicine residency curriculum Federated Coun. Internal Medicine, 1993—97; chair Inst. Medicine Com. Health Effects Persian Gulf War Svc., 1998—2000; mem. nat. adv. com. Generalist Physician Scholars program Robert Wood Johnson Found., 1992—; physician Leaders Nat. Drug Policy, 1997—; founding chair exec. com. Medicare Coverage Adv. Com., 1999—2003; mem. report rev. com. NRC, 2000—. Author: Medical Decision Making, 1988; editor: Common Diagnostic Tests, 1987, Common Diagnostic Tests, 2d edit., 1990; mem. editl. bd.: Med. Decision Making, 1980—87, Jour. Gen. Internal Medicine, 1985—87, New Eng. Jour. Medicine, 1990—97, cons. assoc. editor: Am. Jour. Medicine, 1988—95, assoc. editor: Sci. Am. Medicine, 1995—2001; contbr. chapters to books, articles to profl. jours. Master: ACP (clin. efficacy assessment subcom. 1985—92, bd. regents 1991—2000, chmn. ednl. policy com. 1994—97, pres. 1998—99); fellow: AAAS, Royal Australasian Coll. Physicians (hon.); mem.: Inst. Medicine Nat. Acads., Assn. Am. Physicians, Soc. for Med. Decision Making (trustee 1980—83, pres. 1983—84, 4th Career Achievement award 1998), Soc. for Gen. Internal Medicine (coun. 1980—83, Robert J. Glaser Career Achievement award 2000), Alpha Omega Alpha. Home: 232 Philip Pl Philadelphia PA 19106 Office: Am Coll Physicians 190 N Independence Mall W Philadelphia PA 19106-1572 Office Phone: 215-351-2620. Personal E-mail: hsox@mail.acponline.org.

SOYARS, M. DOUGLAS, academic administrator, music educator; b. Danville, Va., Sept. 1, 1934; s. Clyde Edward and Garnet Raine Soyars; m. Julia Reid Yancey, Dec. 30, 1956; children: Julia Ashworth Soyars-Berman, Katie Ingram Cumberland. MusB in Music Edn., James Madison U., 1956; MusM in Performance - Woodwinds, U. Mich., 1964, PhD, 1967. Musician Starlighters, Harrisonburg, Va., 1952—56; chmn. music dept. Heidelberg Dependent Schs., Germany, 1960—62; instr. Adrian Coll., Mich., 1963—65; lectr. music edn. Syracuse U., NY, 1967—69, dir. bands, 1969—71, dean sch. music, 1971—80, asst. dean Coll. Visual and Performing Arts, 1971—80, chmn. music industry, 1983—. Founding dir. U.S. Army in Europe Soldiers Chorus, 1959; music dir. N.Y. State Spl. Olympics, Syracuse, 1971; cons. to design Master of music N.Y. state Crane Sch. Music, Potsdam, 1974; cons. Coll. Exam Bd., N.Y.C., 1975—76. Arranger: choral music, arranger: marching band music, composer small ensemble, concert band and orch. music; contbr. articles to profl. jours. Apptd. mem. Fayetteville Historic Commn., NY, 1994—98. With U.S. Army, 1956—60. Named a Soyars award for most outstanding music industry student, Sefnor Sch. Music, 2003; recipient Ville de Bruxelles medal, Mayor of Brussels, 1970, Macy's Roley award, Macy's Thanksgiving Parade Com., N.Y.C., 1972, Disting. Prof. award, Syracuse U. Coll. of Visual and Performing Arts, 2000; fellow, U. Mich., Ann Arbor, 1965—67; grantee, Verizon Found., 2003. Mem.: Music and Entertainment Industry Educators Assn. Avocations: painting, soccer, fishing, home restoration. Home: 114 E Genesee St Fayetteville NY 13066 Office: Syracuse U 119D Crouse Coll Syracuse NY 13244 Office Phone: 315-443-1216. E-mail: mdsoyars@syr.edu.

SOYER, DAVID, cellist, music educator; b. Phila., Feb. 24, 1923; s. Samson and Esther (Faggin) Soyer; m. Janet Putnam, June 23, 1957; children: Daniel, Jeffrey. Student pub. schs., N.Y.C.; DFA (hon.), U. South Fla., 1976, SUNY, 1983. Prof. cello Curtis Inst. Music, 1967; prof. music U. Md.; prof. Manhattan Sch. Music Boston U. Musician (cellist): Bach Aria Group, 1948—49, Guilet Quartet, 1949—51, New Music Quartet, 1954—55, Guarneri String Quartet, 1964— (5 Grammy awards for Guarneri Quartet recs.). With USNR, 1942—46. Mem.: Century Assn. Jewish. Home: 6 W 77th St New York NY 10024-5125 Office: Herbert Barrett Mgmt care H Beall Mgmt 1776 Broadway Ste 1610 New York NY 10019-2083

SOYFER, VALERY NIKOLAYEVICH, geneticist, biophysicist; b. Gorky, RSFSR, USSR, Oct. 16, 1936; came to U.S., 1988; s. Nikolay Ilya Soyfer and Anna A. Kuznetsova; m. Nina I. Yakovleva, Aug. 12, 1961; children: Marina, Vladimir. BS in Agronomy, Timiryazev Agrl. Acad., Moscow, 1957; MS in Biophysics, Lomonosov State U., Moscow, 1961; PhD in Molecular Genetics, Kurchatov Inst. Atomic Energy, Moscow, 1964; D Phys. and Math. Scis., Moscow, 1994. Head Group Inst. Gen. Genetics, Moscow, 1966-70; dir. Lab. Molecular Genetics, Moscow, 1970-79; sci. dir. USSR Inst. Applied Molecular Biology and Genetics, Moscow, 1974-76; pres. Moscow Ind. U., 1985-88; disting. prof. Ohio State U., Columbus, 1988-90; Robinson prof. George Mason U., Fairfax, Va., 1990-93, disting. prof. molecular genetics, 1993—. Sci. sec. Coun. on Molecular Biology and Genetics, Moscow, 1972-80; mem. USSR Govtl. Coun. on Molecular Biology and Molecular Genetics, 1974-80; invited lectr. Halle-Wittenburg U., German Democratic Republic, 1975; prin. investigator USSR State Com. on Sci., 1972, 74, 78, NIH, 1990, Dept. of Energy, 1992, Open Soc. Inst., 1995-98. Author: Molecular Mechanisms of Mutagenesis, 1969, History of Molecular Genetics, 1970, Molekulare Mechanismen der Mutagenese und Reparatur, 1976, Power and Science, History of the Crushing of Soviet Genetics, 1989, Lysenko and the Tragedy of Soviet Science, 1994, Triple Helical Nuclec Acids, 1995; contbr. more than 200 articles on molecular genetics, biophysics and history of sci. to Nature, Science Mutation Rsch., Nucleic Acids Rsch., others. Chmn. bd. Friends of St. Petersburg Ind. U., N.Y., 1990—; pres. USSR Amnesty Internat. Group, Moscow, 1983-88. Recipient Gregor Mendel gold medals of Czech Nat. Acad. Scis. and Czech Soc. History Scis., 1995, 96, N. Vavilov silver medal, Russian Acad. Natural Scis., 2002. Mem. USSR Soc. Geneticists and Breeders (founding), Gt. Britain Genetical Soc., USSR Biochem. and Microbiol. Soc., Internat. Soc. for History, Philosophy and Social Studies of Biology (charter), European Culture Club (charter), Internat. Sci. Fedn. (bd. dirs. 1992-95, chmn. bd. Internat. Soros Sci. Edn. program), Nat. Acad. Scis. Ukraine, Russian Acad. Natural Sci., Am. Soc. of Biochemistry and Molecular Biology, others. Achievements include discovery of DNA Repair in higher plants; establishment of correlation between structural damages in DNA and mitagenesis rate in higher plants; co-development of the method of photofootprinting of DNA triplexes, the role of environmental contamination in mutagenesis of organisms. Office: George Mason U Ste 3024 D King Hall Fairfax VA 22030

SOYINKA, WOLE, writer; b. Abeokuta, Nigeria, July 13, 1934; s. S. Ayo and Eniola S. Soyinka. Student, U. Ibadan, U. Leeds, Eng. Play reader Royal Ct. Theater, London; Woodruff prof. arts and African Am. studies Emory U., Atlanta, 1995—2003; prof. Internat. Inst. Letters, U. Nev. Rsch. fellow in drama U. Ibadan, 1960-61; lectr. in English U. Ife, 1962-63, research prof. dramatic lit., 1972, prof. comparative lit., head dept. dramatic arts, 1977-85; Goldwin Smith prof. Africana studies and theatre arts Cornell U., 198890; artistic dir. Orisun Theater, 1960; chmn. Internat. Theatre Orgn., UNESCO; pres. Internat. Parliament of Writers, 1998-2001. Author: (plays) The Lion and the Jewel, 1959, The Swamp Dwellers, 1959, A Dance of the Forests, 1960, The Trials of Brother Jero, 1961, The Strong Breed, 1962, The Road, 1964, Kongi's Harvest, 1965, Madmen and Specialists, 1961, Before the Blackout, 1971, Jero's Metamorphosis, 1974, Camwood on the Leaves, 1973, The Bacchae of Euripides, 1974, Death and the King's Horseman, 1975, Opera Wonyosi, 1978, A Play of Giants, 1984, From Zia With Love, 1994, Beatification of An Area Boy, 1998, King Baabu, 2001; (novels) The Interpreters, 1964, The Forest of a Thousand Demons, Season of Anomy, 1973; (non-fiction) The Man Died, 1972, Aké: The Years of Childhood, 1982, Isarà: A Voyage Around Essay, 1989, IBADAN: The Penkelemes Years, 1994, The Open Sore of a Continent, A Personal Narrative of the Nigerian Crisis, 1996; (essays) The Burden of Memory, The Muse of Forgiveness, 1999; (poetry) Idanre and Other Poems, 1967, Poems of Black Africa, 1975, Ogun Abibiman, 1977, A Shuttle in the Crypt, 1972, Mandela's Earth and Other Poems, 1988, Outsiders, 1999, Samarkand and Other Markets I Have Known, 2002; (film) Blues for a Prodigal, 1985; (radio play) A Scourge of Hyacinths, 1993; (essay collection) Art, Dialogue and Outrage, 1992. Recipient Prisoner of Conscience prize Amnesty Internat., Jock Campbell-New Statesman Lit. award, 1959, John Whiting Drama prize, 1966, Dakar Negro Arts Festival award, 1966, Nobel Prize in Literature, 1986, Leopold Sedar Senghor award, 1986, Enrico Mattei award for humanities, 1986; Rockefeller Found. grantee, 1969; named Comdr. French Legion of Honor, 1989, Comdr. Fed. Republic Nigeria, 1986, Comdr. of Order of Italian Republic, 1990; Churchill Coll. fellow, 1970-71. Mem.: AAAL., Fellow African Acad. Scis. Office: Essay Found PO Box 935 Abeokuta Ogun State Nigeria

SOYSTER, MARGARET BLAIR, lawyer; b. Washington, Aug. 5, 1951; d. Peter and Eliza (Shumaker) S. AB magna cum laude, Smith Coll., 1973; JD, U. Va., 1976. Bar: N.Y. 1977, U.S. Dist. Ct. (so. and ea. dists.) N.Y. 1977, U.S. Ct. Appeals (2nd cir.) 1979, U.S. Supreme Ct. 1981, U.S. Ct. Appeals (4th cir.) 1982, U.S. ct. Appeals (11th cir.) 1987, U.S. Ct. Appeals (7th cir.) 1991, U.S. Ct. Appeals (3d cir.) 1992. Assoc. Rogers & Wells, N.Y.C., 1976-84, ptnr., 1984-99, Clifford Chance U.S. LLP, N.Y.C., 2000—. Mem. ABA, Assn. of Bar of City of N.Y., Nat. Assn. Coll. and Univ. Attys., Phi Beta Kappa. Office: Clifford Chance US LLP 31 W 52nd St New York NY 10019

SOZANSKY, MICHAEL WILLIAM, JR., lawyer; b. Charleroi, Pa., June 17, 1949; s. Michael William and Mildred Marie (Buchta) S.; m. Deborah Ann Conti, June 15, 1985; children: Sarah Elizabeth, Alexander Michael. BA, Duquesne U., 1971; JD, Temple U., 1980. Bar: Pa. 1980, N.J. 1982, U.S. Dist. Ct. N.J. 1982, U.S. Tax Ct. 1989, U.S. Ct. Appeals (3d cir.) 1989, U.S. Supreme Ct. 1989, U.S. Dist. Ct. (ea. dist.) Pa. 1991. Legal aide N.J. Civil Svc. Commn., Trenton, 1976-80; law clk. to presiding justice N.J. Tax Ct., Trenton, 1980-81; dep. atty. gen. State of N.J., Trenton, 1981-84; assoc. Schaff, Mahon, Motiuk, Gladstone & Conley, Flemington, N.J., 1985-87; pres. Ligorano & Sozansky, P.C., Flemington, 1987—98, Archer & Greiner, P.C., 1998—2001, Norris, McLaughlin & Marcus, P.A., 2001—04, Conley & Sozanky, 2004—. Cons. N.J. Dept. Pers., Trenton, 1989-91. Mem. Hunterdon County Facilities Com., 1989-96; pres. Hunterdon County Edn. Found., 1993-2002. Mem. ATLA, ABA, N.J. Bar Assn. (trustee 2003-), Hunterdon County Bar Assn. (pres. 1998-99), Assn. Trial Lawyers N.J. Republican. Roman Catholic. Avocation: computer science. Office: Conley and Sozansky LLC 119 Main St PO Box 662 Flemington NJ 08822-0662

SPACE, THEODORE MAXWELL, lawyer; b. Binghamton, NY, Apr. 3, 1938; s. Maxwell Evans and Dorothy Marie (Boone) S.; m. Susan Shultz, Aug. 18, 1962 (div. Apr. 1979); children: William Schuyler, Susanna; m. Martha Collins, Apr. 6, 1991. AB, Harvard U., 1960; LLB, Yale U., 1966. Bar: Conn., 1966, U.S. Dist. Ct. Conn. 1966, U.S. Supreme Ct. 1970, U.S. Tax Ct. 1989, U.S. Ct. Appeals (2nd cir.) 1967, U.S. Ct. Appeals (6th cir.) 1992, U.S. Ct. Appeals (11th cir.) 1994, U.S. Dist. Ct. (ea. dist.) Mich. 1997. Assoc. Shipman & Goodwin LLP, Hartford, Conn., 1966-71, ptnr., 1971—, mng. ptnr., 1984-87, adminstv. ptnr., 1988-91. Mem. Bloomfield (Conn.) Bd. Edn., 1973-85, chmn., 1975-85, treas. Citizens Scholarship Found., Bloomfield, 1971-73, bd. dirs., 1973-91; mem. Bloomfield Human Rels. Commn., 1973-75; mem. Bloomfield Town Dem. Com., 1976-83; corporator Hartford Pub. Libr., 1976—; trustee Conn. Hist. Soc., 1997—2003, mem. libr. com., 1990—, chair, 1993-2000; chmn. fin. com., coun. mem. Unitarian Soc. Hartford, 1988-91; dir. Old State House Assn., 2003. Lt. (j.g.) USN, 1960-63. Mem. ABA, Conn. Bar Assn. (mem. exec. com. adminstrv. law sect. 1980—), Hartford County Bar Assn., Am. Law Inst., Am. Health Lawyers Assn., Conn. Health Lawyers Assn., Swift's Inn, Hartford Club. Democrat. Unitarian Universalist. Avocations: reading, classical music. Home: 59 Prospect St Bloomfield CT 06002-3038 Office: Shipman & Goodwin LLP One American Row Hartford CT 06103-2833

SPACEK, SISSY (MARY ELIZABETH SPACEK), actress; b. Quitman, Tex., Dec. 25, 1949; d. Edwin S. and Virginia S.; m. Jack Fisk, 1974; children: Schuyler Elizabeth, Virginia Madison. Student, Lee Strasberg Theatrical Inst. Motion picture appearances include Prime Cut, 1972, Badlands, 1974, Carrie, 1976 (Acad. award nomination for best actress 1976), Three Women, 1977 (Best Supporting Actress 1977), Welcome to L.A., 1977, Heartbeat, 1980, Coal Miner's Daughter, 1980 (Acad. award best actress 1980, Golden Globe best actress 1980, Brit. Acad. award nomination best actress 1980, L.A. Film Critics for best actress 1980, Nat. Soc. Film Critics best actress 1980), Raggedy Man (Golden Globe nomination best actress 1981), 1981, Missing, 1982 (Acad. award nomination best actress, Golden Globe nomination best actress 1982, Brit. Acad. award nomination best actress 1982), The River, 1984 (Acad. award nomination best actress), Marie, 1985, 'Night Mother, 1986, Crimes of the Heart, 1986 (Acad. award nomination best actress, Golden Globe best actress 1986), Violets Are Blue, 1986, JFK, 1991, The Long Walk Home, 1990, Hard Promises, 1992, Trading Mom, 1994, The Grass Harp, 1995, Affliction, 1997, Blast From the Past, 1998, Songs in Ordinary Time, 2000, In the Bedroom, 2001 (Best Actress in Drama Golden Globe 2001, Am. Film Inst. award, Ind. Spirit award, Broadcast Critics award, Chgo. Film Critics award, Fla. Film Critics award, Golden Satellite award, Sundance Film Festival award, Southeastern Film award, N.Y. Film Critics award, L.A. Film Critics award 2001), Midwives, 2001, (TV movie) Last Call, 2002 (nominee Outstanding Supporting Actress in Miniseries or Movie Emmy award) Tuck Everlasting, 2002, Home at the End of the World, 2004; TV movie appearances include Straight Story, 1999, In the Bedroom, 2001 (Acad. award nomination best actress 2001, Brit. Acad. award nomination best actress 2001, Brit. Film Critics Choice award best actress 2001, Sundance Film Festival Spl. prize 2001, Golden Globe best actress 2001, Ind. Spirit award best felmale lead 2001, AFI, Actress of Yr. 2001, L.A. Film Critics best actress 2001, N.Y. Film Critics best actress 2001, SAG nomination best actress 2001, nominee Best Actress Acad. award 2001), The Migrants, 1973, Katherine, 1975, Verna: USO Girl, 1978, A Private Matter, 1992, A Place for Annie, 1994, The Good Old Boys, 1995, Streets of Laredo, 1995, If These Walls Could Talk, 1996, Midwives (SAG nomination best actress 2001), 2001, Beyond the Call (Emmy nomination best actress 2002), 2002; guest host TV show Saturday Night Live, 1977; appeared in episode TV show The Waltons. Office: care Creative Artists Agy LLC c/o Steve Tellez 9830 Wilshire Blvd Beverly Hills CA 90212-1804*

SPACEY, KEVIN, actor; b. South Orange, N.J., July 26, 1959; Student, Juilliard Sch., 1979-81. Artistic dir. Old Vic Theatre, London, 2003—. Stage appearances include Henry IV, part I, 1981, Barbarians, 1982, Hurlyburly, 1985, Long Days Journey into Night, 1986, National Anthems, 1988, Lost in Yonkers, 1991 (Tony award for Best Featured Actor, 1991, Drama Desk award, 1991), Playland, 1993, The Iceman Cometh, 1997 (Tony award Best Male Performance/Drama 1999); TV appearances include (series) Wiseguy, 1987-88, (films) The Murder of Mary Phagan, 1988, Will You Remember Me, 1990, Fall From Grace, 1990, Darrow, 1991; films include Heartburn, 1986, Working Girl, 1988, Rocket Gibraltar, 1988, Dad, 1989, See No Evil, Hear No Evil, 1989, A Show of Force, 1990, Henry and June, 1990, Glengarry Glen Ross, 1991, Consenting Adults, 1992, The Ref, 1994, Outbreak, 1995, Swimming With Sharks, 1995, The Usual Suspects, 1995 (Acad. award for best supporting actor 1996), Seven, 1995, A Time to Kill, 1996, Looking for Richard, 1996, Midnight in the Garden of Good and Evil, 1997, L.A. Confidential, 1997, Hurlyburly, 1998, The Negotiator, 1998, A Bug's Life (voice), 1998, American Beauty, 1999 (Best Actor Oscar)., Pay it Forward, 2000, K-Pax, 2001, The Shipping News. 2001, The Life of David Gale, 2003 also: William Morris Agy 151 S El Camino Dr Beverly Hills CA 90212-2704 Office: Altman Greenfield & Salvaje 200 Park Ave S Fl 8 New York NY 10003-1503

SPACH, JULE CHRISTIAN, church executive; b. Winston-Salem, N.C., Dec. 21, 1923; s. Jule Christian and Margaret Stockton (Coyner) S.; m. Nancy Clendenin, Sept. 18, 1948; children: Nancy Lynn Lane, Margaret Cuningham, Ann Thomerson, Cecelia Welborn, Robert Spach. Student, Va. Mil. Inst., 1942-43; BSChemE, Ga. Inst. Tech., 1949; postgrad., Union Theol. Sem., Richmond, Va., 1951-52, Duke U., 1955-56; MA in Ednl. Adminstrn., U. N.C., Greensboro, 1976; LHD (hon.), Stillman Coll., Tuscaloosa, Ala., 1977; LittD (hon.), Belhaven Coll., Jackson, Miss., 1977; LLD, King Coll., Bristol, Tenn., 1977. Salesman Mengle Corp. subs. Internat. Container Corp., Winston-Salem, 1950-52; from prof. scis., athletic dir. to pres. Quinze de Novembro Coll., Garanhuns, Pernanbuco, Brazil, 1952-64; edn. dir. Cruzada ABC-Recife, Pernanbuco, 1965-70, pres., 1969-70; exec. sec. Parliamentary Christian Leadership, Brasilia, Fed. Dist., Brazil, 1970-73; exec. dir. Presbyn. Mission in Brazil, Campinas, Sao Paulo, 1973-75; moderator Gen. Assembly of Presbyn. Ch. in U.S., Atlanta, 1976-77; exec. dir. Triad United Meth. Home, Inc., Winston-Salem, 1977—. Dir. First Home Fed. Savs. and Loan Author: (biography) Every Road Leads Home, 1997. Bd. dirs. Instituto Gammon, Presbyn. Ch. U.S., Forsyth County Coun. on Aging Forsyth County Sr. Svcs. Forsyth County, Covenent Fellowship of Presbyns., William Black Lodge, Synod of N.C., Presbyn. Ch. U.S.A.; bd. visitors Lee's McRae Coll., Montreat Anderson Coll.; mem. cabinet United Way, 1987; chmn. Winston-Salem Forsyth County Coun. on Svcs. to Homeless; chmn. bd. dirs. Sr. Svcs., Inc., Winston-Salem, Missionary Family Counseling Svc. With USAAF, 1943-45, prisoner of war, Poland. Decorated Purple Heart; recipient Jefferson award, 1991; named Hon. Citizen of Brazil. Mem. Sertoma Club (3 Svc. awards), Lions, Rotary. Republican. Home: Arbor Acres 1244 Arbor Rd Apt 197 Winston Salem NC 27104-1199 Office: 1240 Arbor Rd Winston Salem NC 27104-1106 E-mail: jspach1@triad.rr.com. *The Christian faith teaches us that the greatest of all gifts is love. This gift comes from God, and it is ours through the presence of His spirit dwelling in us. This love gives man peace within and with his fellow man.*

SPACH, MADISON STOCKTON, cardiologist, educator; b. Winston-Salem, N.C., Nov. 10, 1926; s. Jule Christian and Margaret (Stockton) S.; m. Cecilia Goodson, June 25, 1949; children: Madison Jr., Joyce, Susan, David. AB, Duke U., 1950, MD, 1954. Diplomate Am. Bd. Pediatrics, Am. Bd. Pediatric Cardiology. Intern and resident dept. pediatrics Duke U., Durham, N.C., 1954-57, resident, 1955-56, fellow cardiology, 1956-57; prof. pediatrics Duke U. Sch. Medicine, Durham, N.C., 1968—, James B. Duke prof. pediatrics, 1977, prof. physiology, 1978-88, chief pediatric cardiology, 1986-91, prof. cell biology, 1988—. Pres. Soc. for Pediatric Rsch., 1974; chmn. SubBoard of Pediatric Cardiology, 1975-77, Nat. Heart, Lung, Blood Inst. Manpower Com., 1982-85. Author more than 200 published papers on cardiovascular rsch.; mem. editl. bd. Circulation, 1981-91. With USN, 1944-46, PTO. Recipient Disting. Scientist award N.Am. Soc. Pacing and Electrophysiology, 1997, Life Time Achievement award Duke U., 2000. Fellow Am. Coll. Cardiology, Am. Inst. for Med. and Biomed. Engring.; mem. N.Y. Acad. Scis., Internat. Soc. for Heart Rsch. (Am. sect.), Am. Physiol. Soc., Phi Beta Kappa, Alpha Omega Alpha. Democrat. Presbyterian. Office: Duke U Med Ctr PO Box 3475 Durham NC 27710-0001

SPACKMAN, THOMAS JAMES, radiologist; b. Oak Park, Ill., Apr. 24, 1937; s. Thomas Frederick and Louise Mary (Kaiser) Spackman; m. Donna S. Stewart, June 25, 1960; children: Kirsten, Thomas James, Victoria. BA, DePauw U., 1959; MD, Western Res. U., 1964; diploma in bus. studies, London Sch. Econs., 1987. Intern, then resident in internal medicine Yale-New Haven Med. Ctr., 1964-66, resident in diagnostic radiology, 1966-68, fellow clin. rsch. tng. unit, 1968-69; instr., then asst. prof. radiology Yale U. Med. Sch., New Haven, 1969-74; assoc. prof. U. Pa. Med. Sch., 1974-78; prof. radiology U. Conn. Med. Sch., Farmington, 1978—, head dept., 1978-90; dir. radiology St. Francis Hosp. and Med. Ctr., Hartford, Conn., 1992-93; pres. Elscint, Inc., Hackensack, NJ, 1993-97; sr. v.p. Elscint, Ltd., Haifa, Israel, 1993-97; pres. Spackman Assocs., Vero Beach, Fla., 1997—; chmn. Xicon Technologies LLC, Vero Beach, 1997-98; v.p. physician affairs Quorum Health Resources, 2000—02, Cambio Health Solutions LLC, 2000—; chmn. Navix Diagnostix, Inc., 2002—. Mem. Conn. Med. Exam. Bd., 1980—86; bd. dirs. Elscint, Inc. Mem. editl. adv. bd. Diagnostic Imaging, 1989—92; contbr. articles to profl. jours., chapters to books. Fellow: Am. Coll. Radiology; mem.: AMA, Radiol. Soc. N.J., Soc. Pediatric Radiology, Assn. Univ. Radiolgoists. E-mail: tspackman@cambiohealth.com.

SPACKS, PATRICIA MEYER, English educator; b. San Francisco, Nov. 17, 1929; d. Norman B. and Lillian (Talcott) Meyer; 1 child, Judith Elizabeth Spacks. BA, Rollins Coll., Winter Park, Fla., 1949, DHL, 1976; MA, Yale U., 1950; PhD, U. Calif., Berkeley, 1955. Instr. English Ind. U., Bloomington, 1954-56; instr. humanities U. Fla., Gainesville, 1958-59; from instr. to prof. Wellesley Coll., Mass., 1959-79; prof. English Yale U., New Haven, 1979-89, chmn. dept., 1985-88; Edgar F. Shannon prof. English U. Va., 1989—, chmn. dept., 1991-97. Author: The Poetry of Vision, 1967, The Female Imagination, 1975, Imagining a Self, 1976, The Adolescent Idea, 1982, Gossip, 1985, Desire and Truth, 1990, Boredom: The Literary History of a State of Mind, 1995. Fellow Guggenheim Found., 1969-70, NEH, 1974, Am. Council Learned Socs., 1978-79, Nat. Humanities Ctr., 1982-83, 89. Mem. MLA (2nd v.p. 1992, 1st v.p. 1993, pres. 1994, mem. adv. com. 1976-80, mem. exec. coun. 1986-89), Am. Acad. Arts and Scis., Am. Coun. Learned Socs. (mem. bd. trustees 1992—, vice chair 1994-97, chair 1997—), Am. Philos. Soc. Office: U Va Dept English PO Box 400121 219 Bryan Hall Charlottesville VA 22904-4121 Home: 502 Pebble Hill Ct Charlottesville VA 22903-7873

SPADA, DOMINICK, pharmacist; b. Bklyn., Oct. 21, 1969; s. Vito and Maria A. (Palazzo) S. BS in Pharmacy, L.I. U., 1992; MA in Health Adminstrn. Registered pharmacist, N.Y.; cert. orthotic fitter. Staff pharmacist Cobble Court Pharmacy, Bklyn., 1992-94; dir. pharmacy, corp. bus. officer Ocean Breeze Infusion Care, S.I., 2000—; dir. pharmacy svcs. NYU Hosp., N.Y.C., 1998-2000; dir. pharmacy/supervising pharmacist Ocean Breeze Infusion Care, S.I., 1994-98, CEO, 2002—; cons. pharmacist, 1999—. Bd. dirs. Cmty. Bd. #3, Staten Island, 1996-97, 99—; mem. Rocco Laurie Patrolmen's Scholarship Fund, Staten Island, 1995—. Named Drug Topics Pharmacist of Yr., Homecare divsn., 2001; recipient Anderson gold medal, L.I. U. Schwartz Coll. Pharmacy, 1992, PSSNY, Innovative Pharmacist award, 2002. Mem. Nat. Assn. Retail Druggists, Am. Pharm. Assn., Pharm. Soc. State of N.Y. (Innovative Pharmacist award 2002), Am. Soc. Health Sys. Pharmacists, Nat. Hospice Orgn. Roman Catholic. Avocations: travel, computers, career-oriented activities, fishing. Home: 193 Connecticut St Staten Island NY 10307-1521 Office: Ocean Breeze Infusion Care 27 Brienna Ct Staten Island NY 10309 Office Phone: 718-987-4114.

SPADA, JAMES, author, photographer, publisher; b. S.I., N.Y., Jan. 23, 1950; s. Joseph Vincent and Mary Ruberto S. Student, Wagner Coll., 1968-71, Calif. State U., 1979-80. Pres. Spada Publs., L.A.; pub. Barbra Quar., L.A., 1980-83. Author: Barbra: The First Decade—The Films and Career of Barbra Streisand, 1974, The Films of Robert Redford, 1977, The Spada Report, 1979, Streisand—The Woman and the Legend, 1981, Monroe—Her Life in Pictures, 1982, Judy and Liza, 1983, Hepburn: Her Life in Pictures, 1984, The Divine Bette Midler, 1984, Fonda: Her Life in Pictures, 1985, Shirley and Warren, 1985, Grace: The Secret Lives of a Princess, 1987, Peter Lawford: The Man Who Kept the Secrets, 1991, More Than A Woman: An Intimate Biography of Bette Davis, 1993, Streisand: Her Life, 1995, Jackie: Her Life in Pictures, 2000; photographer: Black & White Men, 2000, Ronald Reagan: His Life in Pictures, 2001, John and Caroline: Their Lives in Pictures, 2001, Julia: Her Life, 2004; book packager The 1984 Marilyn Monroe Pin-Up Calendar, 1983, The Telephone Book, 1984, Elizabeth Taylor: A Biography in Photographs, 1984, Bette Davis: A Biography in Photographs, 1985, Natalie Wood: A Biography in Photographs, 1986; one-man photography shows at Against the Grain Gallery, Cape Cod, 1998, Gallery One, Boston, 2000, Radiant Light Gallery, Portland, Maine, 2001. Democrat.

SPADE, DAVID, actor; b. Birmingham, Mich., July 22, 1964; Actor on TV's Saturday Night Live, Just Shoot Me, 1997-2003; appeared in films: Police Academy 4: Citizen on Patrol, 1987, Coneheads, 1993, PCU, 1994, Tommy Boy, 1995, Black Sheep, 1996, A Very Brady Sequel, 1996, Eight Heads in a Duffel Bag, 1997, Senseless, 1998, The Rugrats Movie (voice), 1998, Lost & Found (also writer, exec. prodr.), 1999, Little Nicky, 2000, The Emperor's New Groove (voice), 2000, Joe Dirt, 2001, Dickie Roberts: Former Child Star, 2003; actor, writer, exec. prodr. David Spade: Take the Hit (TV), 1998; exec. prodr. Jerome, 1999; appeared on TV shows The Facts of Life, ALF, The Larry Sanders Show, The Dennis Miller Show, Beavis and Butt-head (voice), The Daily Show, BioRhythm. Office: Endeavor Talent Agy 9701 Wilshire Blvd Fl 10 Beverly Hills CA 90212-2010*

SPADE, KATE (KATHERINE NOEL SPADE), apparel designer; b. Kansas City, Mo., 1962; m. Andy Spade, 1994. BA in journalism and broadcasting, Arizona State U., 1985. From asst. to accessories editor Mademoiselle mag., 1985—92; co-founder, designer Kate Spade Inc., N.Y.C., 1993—; designer Kate Spade paper and social stationary, 1998—, Kate Spade shoe collection, 1999—, Kate Spade glasses, 2001, Kate Spade beauty, 2002—; co-founder Jack Spade, 1999—, Kate Spade Home, 2002—. Designer (uniforms) Song Airlines (subs. Delta Airlines), 2004. Recipient Perry Ellis award, New Fashion Talent, Coun. Fashion Designers of Am., 1996, Accessory Designer of the Year, 1998, FiFi award for Bath & Body Star of the Year, U.S. Fragrance Found., 2003, FiFi award for Best Fragrance in Ltd. Distribution, U.K. Fragrance Found., 2003. Achievements include stores opening in N.Y.C. in 1996, Boston and LA in 1998, and Chicago and San Francisco in 2000. Office: Kate Spade Inc 48 W 25th St New York NY 10010*

SPADE-SHENKER, GEORGE LAWRENCE (GEORGE SHENKER), scientist; b. Sioux City, Iowa, Dec. 14, 1945; s. Walter Charles and LaVancha May (Green) S.; m. Carol Margaret Deaton, Mar. 14, 1966 (div. June 1985); children: Aaron Michael, Margaret. Mem. earthquake study group for China, U.S. Citizen Amb. Programs, 1989. Contbr. articles to profl. jours. Mem. AAAS, Internat. Soc. Philos. Enquiry, Am. Math. Soc., Math. Assn. Am., N.Y. Acad. Scis., Mensa. Avocations: poetry, painting, music. Home and Office: PO Box 2260 Columbia Falls MT 59912-2260

SPADORA, HOPE GEORGEANNE, real estate company executive; b. Long Branch, N.J., May 13, 1965; d. Joseph Vincent and Gladys Beatrice (Clayton) S.; life ptnr. Rebecca Elise DeAnda; 1 child, Clayton Vincent Spadora. Cert. in Mktg. Comm., San Jose State U., 1988; AA in Biology with hons., Cabrillo Coll., Aptos, Calif., 1991; BA in Sociology with hons., U. Calif., Santa Cruz, 1993; M in Corp. Real Estate, Inst. Corp. Real Estate, 1998. Lic. real estate broker, Calif. Fin. analyst Lam Rsch., Fremont, Calif., 1993-94, portfolio mgr., 1994-96; v.p. internat. svcs. Cawley Internat., San Jose, Calif., 1996-97; v.p. real estate facilities Sybase Corp., Emeryville, Calif., 1997—. Bd. dirs. Emeryville (Calif.) Industries Assn., 1997-98. Mem. editl. bd. Jour. of Corporate Real Estate. Mem. Human Rights Campaign, San Francisco, 1997, The Commonwealth Club of Calif., San Francisco, 1998, Calif. Elected Womens Assn. for Edn. and Rsch., Sacramento, 1998; bd. dirs. Emeryville Cmty. Action Program. Mem. Internat. Assn. Corp. Real Estate Executives, Nat. Assn. Corp. Real Estate Execs., Bldg. Owners and Mgrs. Assn. Democrat. Avocations: golf, fishing, sailing, boating. Office: Sybase 6475 Christie Ave Emeryville CA 94608-1010

SPAEDER, ROGER CAMPBELL, lawyer; b. Cleve., Dec. 20, 1943; s. Fred N. and Luceil (Campbell) S.; m. Frances DeSales Sutherland, Sept. 7, 1968; chidlren: Michael, Matthew. BS, Bowling Green U., 1965; JD with honors, George Washington U., 1970. Bar: D.C. 1971, U.S. Dist. Ct. D.C. 1971, U.S. Ct. Appeals (D.C. cir.) 1971, U.S. Ct. Claims 1979, U.S. Dist. Ct. Md. 1984, U.S. Ct. Appeals (2d and 4th cirs.) 1985, U.S. Supreme Ct. 1976. Asst. U.S. atty. D.C., Washington, 1971-76; ptnr. Zuckerman Spaeder LLP, Washington, 1976—. Faculty Atty. Gen. Advocacy Inst., 1974-76, Nat. Inst. Trial Adv., 1978-79; adj. faculty Georgetown U. Law Ctr., 1979-80, Am. U. Ctr. Adminstrn. Justice, 1976-79; lectr. D.C. Bar Continuing Legal Edn. Programs, 1980-90; Cardozo Prize judge Yale Law Sch., 1992; master Edward Bennett Williams Inn of Ct., 1996—; mem. D.C. Cir. Jud. Conf., 1991. Contbr. articles to profl. jours. and chpts. to books. Recipient Spl. Achievement award Dept. Justice, 1971. Mem. ATLA, ABA (co-chair com. on complex crimes litigation 1989-92, divsn. co-dir. sect. litigation 1992-94), Bar Assn. D.C. (lectr. Criminal Practice Inst. 1977-80), D.C. Bar (com. criminal jury instrns. 1972, divsn. cts. lawyers, adminstrn. of justice 1976-78; adv. com. continuing legal edn. 1986), Def. Rsch. Inst., Assn. Plaintiffs' Trial Attys., Nat. Assn. Criminal Def. Lawyers, Omicron Delta Kappa. Home: 7624 Georgetown Pike Mc Lean VA 22102-1412 Office: Zuckerman Spaeder LLP 1201 Connecticut Ave NW Fl 12 Washington DC 20036-2605 Office Phone: 202-778-1800.

SPAEPEN, FRANS AUGUST, applied physics researcher, educator; b. Mechelen, Belgium, Oct. 29, 1948; arrived in U.S., 1971; s. Jozef F. M. and Ursula (Roppe) Spaepen; m. Moniek Steemans, Aug. 21, 1973; children: Geertrui M., Elizabet U., Hendrik J. L. Burgerlijk Metaalkundig Ingenieur, U. Leuven, Belgium, 1971; PhD, Harvard U., 1975. IBM postdoctoral fellow Harvard U., Cambridge, Mass., 1975-77, asst. prof. applied physics, 1977-81, assoc. prof., 1981-83, Gordon McKay prof. applied physics, 1983—2002, Franklin prof. applied physics, 2002—, dir. Materials Rsch. Lab., 1990—98, dir. Rowland Inst., 2002—. Vis. prof. U. Leuven, 1984, Deutsches Zentrum für Luft-und Raumfahrt-Köln, 2000, Forschungszentrum Jülich, 2001; chmn. Gordon Conf. on Phys. Metallurgy, 1988; NRC com. on solid state scis., 1990—93; NRC com. on condensed matter and materials physics, 1996—98; Krengel lectr. Technion, Israel, 1994; mem. summer rsch. group Los Alamos Nat. Lab., 1986—99; mem. sci. and tech. steering com. Brookhaven Nat. Lab.; chmn. scientific adv. bd. Netherlands Inst. for Metals Rsch. Co-editor: (series) Solid State Physics; mem. editl. bd. Jour. Applied Physics, Applied Physics Letters, 1990—93, 1999—2001, Applied Physics Revs., 1991—97, Phys. Rev., 1994—99, Jour. Non-Crystalline Solids, 1990—94; editor (prin. editor): Jour. Materials Rsch., 2001—; contbr. articles to profl. jours., chpts. to books. Recipient Best Paper award, Acta Metallurgica, 1994, Humboldt award, 1999, R.F. Mehl award, TMS Inst. Metals, 2002. Fellow: AIME-The Metall. Soc., Am. Phys. Soc. (chmn. divsn. materials physics 1992); mem.: Max Planck Soc. (external mem.), Vlaamse Academie voor Wetenschappen en Kunsten (fgn.), Orde van den Prince, Vlaamse Ingenieurs Vereniging, Materials Rsch. Soc. (councillor 1986—88, co-chmn. fall meeting Boston 1990, councillor 1990—92, chmn. program com. 1993—2000, Woody award 1998), Am. Soc. Metals (lectr.). Office: Harvard U Div Engring and Applied Scis 29 Oxford St Cambridge MA 02138-2901 Business E-Mail: spaepen@deas.harvard.edu.

SPAETH, EDMUND BENJAMIN, JR., retired lawyer, retired law educator, former judge; b. Washington, June 10, 1920; s. Edmund B. and Lena (Link) S. AB magna cum laude, Harvard U., 1942, LLB, 1948. Bar: Pa. 1949. Judge Ct. of Common Pleas, Phila., 1964-73, Superior Ct of Pa., 1973-86, pres. judge, 1983-86; of counsel Pepper Hamilton LLP, Phila., 1986—2002. Adj. prof. U. Pa. Law Sch., 1976-97; chair Pennsylvanians for Modern Cts., 1987-2000. Fellow Am. Bar Found. (life); mem. Am. Law Inst. (life), Am. Judicature soc., Order of Coif, Phi Beta Kappa. Home: Cathedral Village Apt L-206 600 E Cathedral Rd Philadelphia PA 19128-1933

SPAETH, GEORGE LINK, physician, ophthalmology educator, writer, educator; b. Phila., Mar. 3, 1932; s. Edmund Benjamin and Lena Marie (Link) S.; m. Ann Ward, May 17, 1955; children: Kristin Lea Crowley, George Link Jr., Eric Edmund. BA magna cum laude, Yale U., 1954; MD cum laude, Harvard U., 1959; postgrad., U. Mich., 1960, U. Pa., 1961. Resident surgeon Wills Eye Hosp., Phila., 1961-63, attending surgeon, 1970—, dir. glaucoma svc., 1968—; clin. fellow NIH, Bethesda, Md., 1963-65; instr. U. Pa., Phila., 1965-68; pvt. practice Phila., 1965-68; prof. ophthalmology Temple U. Med. Sch., Phila., 1968-75, Jefferson Med. Coll., Phila., 1975—, Louis Esposito glaucoma rsch. prof., 2000—. Ophthalmologist Chestnut Hill Hosp., Phila., 1975—; attending surgeon, Graduate Hosp.; cons., Bryn Mawr Hosp., Wills Eye Hosp., Hosp. Jefferson Med. Coll. Author: 18 books in ophthalmology, surgery, and med. ethics, 1970—; contbr. over 500 articles to profl. jours.; editor Ophthalmic Surgery jour., 1985-96; editl. editor Ophthalmic Surgery and Lasers; mem. editl. bd. Jour., Ocular Surgery News, Glaucoma Abstracts; manuscript reviewer, New Eng. Jour. Medicine, Med. Letter Drugs and Therapy, others; patentee differometer, tonometer tip cover. Pres. Chestnut Hill Cmty. Assn., Phila., 1970-72; founder, CEO Internat. Soc. Spaeth Fellows, 1975—; trustee, founder, pres. E.B. Spaeth and Glaucoma Svcs. Found., 1978—, Profls. for Nuclear Army Control, 1985-88; tustee, treas. Thomas Skelton Harrison Found., Inc., 1984—; interviewer Yale Alumni Schs. Com., Phila., 1965—; Yale Class coun., 1968—, Yale Assn. Alumni Reps., 1996-2002; trustee Recording for the Blind and Dyslexia, 1996-2002, Internat. Arts-Medicine Assn., Pa. Ballet, 2002—, Bach Festival of Phila., 2002—, Squirrel Island Chapel, Maine; curriculum com. Jefferson Med. Coll., 1987-90; institutional review bd. Jefferson Med. Coll., 1990-95; pres. Phila. Glaucoma Inst., 1997—. Lt. comdr. USPHS, 1963-68. Recipient Pub. Svc. medal Chestnut Hill Coll., 1972, Sir Stuart Duke Elder Glaucoma award Internat. Glaucoma Soc., 1986, Newberg award Lawyers Alliance for World Security, 1995, Derrick Vail award Internat. Soc. Prevention of Blindness, 1996, Trantas award Greek Ophthalmol. Soc., 2000, Frominopolous prize Greek Glaucoma Soc., 2003, 2nd Pl. large flower and vegetable garden Pa. Horticultural Soc., 2003-; NIH grantee, 1968—; presented 32 named lectrs., 1970—. Fellow Am. Acad. Ophthalmology (chmn. ethics com. San Francisco 1987-95, coun. 1980-93, vice chmn. residency rev. com. Chgo. 1982-88, Sr. honor award 1988, life time achievement award 1999), Am. Assn. Rsch. in Vision and Ophthalmology, Royal Coll. Ophthalmologist, United Kingdom, Danish Ophthalmological Soc., Ind. Soc. of Ophthalmology; mem. Am. Glaucoma Soc. (pres. 1983-85), Coll. Physicians Phila. (sec. 1976-84), Phila. County Med. Soc., Pa. Acad. Ophthalmology (pres. coun.), German Ophthalmological Congress, Physicians for Social Responsibility (pres. emeritus Phila. chpt.), ACS (bd. govs., chmn. adv. coun. for ophthalmology), Phila. Club, Phila. Cricket Club, Phi Beta Kappa, Alpha Omega Alpha. Democrat. Episcopalian. Avocations: composing music, piano, sports, photography, gardening. Office: Wills Eye Hosp 11th Fl 840 Walnut St Philadelphia PA 19107-5109 Office Phone: 215-825-9020.

SPAETH, KARL HENRY, retired chemical company executive, lawyer; b. Phila., Mar. 12, 1929; s. Edmund Benjamin and Lena Marie (Link) S.; m. Ann Dashiell Wieland, Sept. 14, 1963; children: Karl Henry, Edmund Alexander, Christopher Philip. AB, Haverford Coll., 1951; postgrad., Oxford U., 1955; JD, Harvard U., 1958. Bar: Pa. 1959, U.S. Ct. (ea. dist.) Pa. 1959, U.S. Ct.

Appeals (3d cir.) 1959. Assoc. MacCoy, Evans & Lewis, Phila., 1959-62; counsel for fgn. ops. Scott Paper Co., Phila., 1962-69; v.p., ops. sec. Quaker Chem. Corp., Conshohocken, Pa., 1969-95, ret. v.p., 1995, ret. corp. sec., 1998. Bd. dirs. Greater Phila. Devel. Corp., 1991-98; bd. dirs., sec.-treas. Edmund B. Spaeth Clin. Rsch. Found., 1982—; chmn. bd. dirs. Pa. Chem. Industry Coun., 1984-86. Chmn. bd. trustees Quaker Chem. Found., 1982-2003; bd. overseers Univ. Mus., U. Pa., Phila., 1983-89, 90-96; bd. dirs. Opera Co. Phila., 1988-2003; bd. dirs. Chestnut Hill Acad., Phila., 1976-83, pres. 1979-83; mem. Whitemarsh Twp. Bd. Suprs. Pa., 1969-75, chmn., 1972-74; mem. Com. of Seventy, Phila., 1984-96. Comdr. USNR, 1952-55, ret. Mem. Pa. Bar Assn. (chmn. sect. on internat. and comparative law 1980-92), Phila. Com. on Fgn. Rels. (exec. com., sec. 1984-94, chmn. 2001—), Phila. Club, Phila. Athenaeum, Libr. Co. of Phila., Phila. Cricket Club, Oxford Union Club, Univ. Barge (sec. 1988-94), Mil. Order Fgn. Wars (registrar 1989-91, vice commdr. 1991-93). Republican. Anglican. Home: 2129 Harts Ln Conshohocken PA 19428-2416 E-mail: khspaeth@comcast.net.

SPAETH, NICHOLAS JOHN, lawyer, former state attorney general; b. Mahnomen, Minn., Jan. 27, 1950; AB, Stanford U., 1972, JD, 1977; BA, Oxford U., Eng., 1974. Bar: Minn. 1979, U.S. Dist. Ct. (Minn.) 1979, U.S. Ct. Appeals (8th cir.) 1979, N.D. 1980, U.S. Dist. Ct. (N.D.) 1980, U.S. Supreme Ct. 1984. Law clk. U.S. Ct. Appeals (8th cir.), Fargo, N.D., 1977-78; law clk. to Justice Byron White U.S. Supreme Ct., Washington, 1978-79; pvt. practice, 1979-84; atty. gen. State of N.D., Bismarck, 1984-93; ptnr. Dorsey & Whitney, Fargo, 1993-99, Oppenheimer, Wolff & Donnelly, Mpls., Calif., 1999, Cooley Godward, Palo Alto, Calif., 1999—. Adj. prof. law U. Minn., 1980-83. Rhodes scholar, 1972-74. Democrat. Roman Catholic. Office: 5200 Metcalf Ave Overland Park KS 66202-1265 E-mail: nicholas.spaeth@ercgroup.com.

SPAGNOLETTI, ROBERT J. state attorney general; BS, Lafayette Coll.; JD, Georgetown Univ. Bar: NJ, NY, Washington, DC. Litig. assoc. Mayor Day Caldwell & Keaton, Houston, Skadden, Arps, Salte, Meagher & Flom, NY & DC; Chief of Domestic Violence Unit Office of U.S. Atty., Washington, DC, 1995, Chief of Sex Offence and Domestic Violence Sec., 1998—2003; Attn. Gen. Washington, DC, 2003—. Prof. law Georgetown Univ. Law Ctr. Recipient Young Lawyer of Year award, Bar Assn. of DC, 1997, Sullivan Award, Asst. US Atty. Assn., 2002. Office: Office of the Attorney General 1350 Pennsylvania Avenue NW Washington DC 20004

SPAGNOLO, MARK F. telecommunications industry executive; BS, Newark Coll. Engring. With Data Sys.; pres., CEO UUNET; CEO Broadwing Comms., Austin, Tex., 2001—; pres., CEO SiteSmith, Metromedia Fiber Network, 2001; prin., owner The Spagnolo Group, LP, 2002—. Office: Broadwing Communications LLC 1122 Capital of Texas Hwy S Austin TX 78746-6426*

SPAGNOLO, SAMUEL VINCENT, internist, pulmonary specialist, educator; b. Pitts., Sept. 3, 1939; s. Vincent Anthony and Mary Grace (Culotta) S.; children: Samuel, Brad, Gregg; m. Dorcas R. Hardy, Sept. 29, 1996. BA, Washington & Jefferson Coll., 1961; MD, Temple U., 1965. Diplomate Am. Bd. Internal Medicine, Bd. Pulmonary Disease, lic. physician Fla., Calif., Md., D.C., Va., Ariz., Pa., Mass. Sr. resident in medicine VA Med. Ctr., Boston, 1969-70, chief resident in medicine, 1970-71; Harvard Clin. and Rsch. fellow in pulmonary diseases Mass. Gen. Hosp., Boston, 1971-72; asst. chief med. svc. VA Med. Ctr., Washington, 1972-75, acting chief med. svc., 1975-76, chief pulmonary disease sect., 1976-94, chief of staff, 1998-99, dir. respiratory care & sr. attending in pulmonary diseases, 1999—; instr. in medicine Boston U. Sch. of Medicine, Tufts U. Sch. Medicine, Boston, 1970-71; clin. and rsch. fellow in pulmonary diseases Harvard U. Sch. of Medicine, Mass. Gen. Hosp., Boston, 1971-72; attending physician George Washington U. Med. Ctr., 1972—; clin. asst. prof. medicine Georgetown U., Washington, 1975-77; asst. prof. medicine George Washington U. Sch. of Medicine and Health Scis., Washington, 1972-75, assoc. prof., 1975-81, prof. medicine, 1981—, dir. divsn. pulmonary diseases and allergy, 1978-93; assoc. chmn. dept. medicine George Washington U. Med. Ctr., Washington, 1986-89. Cons. in pulmonary diseases The Washington Hosp. Ctr., Washington, D.C., 1977—, Will Rogers Inst., White Plains, N.Y., 1980—, U.S. Dept. Labor, Washington, 1980—, Walter Reed Army Med. Ctr., Washington, 1987; rep. Am. Coll. Chest Physicians to Am. Registry Pathology, Washington, 1981-92; numerous radio tv appearances on Health Oriented Programs; invited lectr. in U.S., Russia, Jordan; chmn., mem. many coms. George Washington U. Sch. of Medicine, George Washington Med. Ctr., VA Med. Ctr., Washington; med. chest cons. in attempted assasination of former Pres. Regan. Author: Clinical Assessment of Patients with Pulmonary Disease, 1986; co-author: (with A.E. Medinger) Handbook of Pulmonary Emergencies, 1986, Handbook of Pulmonary Drug Therapy, 1993, (with Witorsch, P.) Air Pollution and Lung Disease in Adults, 1994; mem. editl. bd. CHEST, 2002—; contbr. numerous articles to profl. jours. including Med. Clin. N.Am., Chest, So. Med. Jour., Am. Jour. Cardiology, Jour. Am. Med. Assn., Clin. Rsch., Am. Rev. Respiratory Disease, Am. Lung Assn. Bull., Clin. Notes on Respiratory Diseases, Jour. Nuclear Medicine, Drug Therapy; presenter abstracts at profl. meetings. Pres., chmn. Found. Vets. Health Care, 1998—. Lt. cmmdr. U.S. Pub. Health Svc., 1966-68; founder, chmn. bd. Found. Vets. Health Care, 1998—. Decorated Cavaliere in Order of Merit, Republic of Italy, 1983; nominated for Golden Apple award by med. students Geo. Washington Sch. of Medicine, Phila., 1977; recipient cert. appreciation D.C. Lung Assn., 1983. Fellow ACP (coun. critical care 1983-85), Am. Coll. Chest Physicians (gov. D.C., coun. of govs. 1989-96); mem. Am. Thoracic Soc. (exec. com. D.C. chpt. 1978, 85, 89, mem. adv. com. Tb control, 1978-84, pres. D.C. chpt. 1981-83), Nat. Assn. VA Physicians (sec. 1987-89, v.p. 1989-91, pres. 1992-98), Internat. Lung Found. (pres. 1991—). Achievements include first major review of patient outcome during early history of intensive care units; an analysis of mechanisms of hypoxemia in patients with chronic liver disease; first report of Pneumocystis Carinii Pneumonitis in patients with lung cancer; first prospective evaluation of short course therapy reported in U.S. using Isoniazid and Rifampin; first American report using laser through fiberoptic bronchoscope to treat lung cancer; first report to evaluate continuous intravenous morphine to control pain in cancer patients; description of a simple technique to measure the total lung volume non-invasively using the routing chest x-ray. Office: Geo Washington U 5-403A 2150 Pennsylvania Ave NW Washington DC 20037-3201 Office Phone: 202-741-2237.

SPAGNUOLO, MARIO, physician; b. Naples, Italy, Apr. 14, 1930; s. Vincent Spagnuolo and Ronca Julia; m. Kathryn Birchall, July 10, 1962; children: Mario, Sandra, Peter, Eugene, JoAnne, Matthew, Stephanie, Riley. MD, U. Naples (Italy), 1954. Diplomate Am. Bd. Internal Medicine. Instr. in medicine NYU Med. Sch., N.Y.C., 1961—65; clin. asst. in medicine NYU Med. Svc. Bellevue Hosp., N.Y.C., 1961—65; clin. dir. Irvington House, N.Y.C., 1962—71; asst. attending in medicine NYU Hosp., N.Y.C., 1963—74, NYU Med. Ctr., Med. Svc. Bellevue Hosp., N.Y.C., 1966—75; dir. Bellevue Juvenile Rheumatoid Arthritis Clinic, N.Y.C., 1968—78; assoc. attending in medicine Knickerbocker Hosp. and Columbus Hosp., N.Y.C., 1968—72; sr. attending St. John's Hosp., 1980; dir. medicine St. John's Riverside Hosp., Yonkers, NY, 1988—92, mem. med. bd., 1982—, vice chief of staff, 1992—, dir. performance improvment com., 1992—, chief of staff, 1997—99, trustee, 1997—. Mem. adv. med. bd. Assoc. Cardiac League N.Y., 1965—73; pres. We. Westchester Network, Inc. PHO, 1994—98; bd. dirs. Westchester Health Svcs. Network MSO; cons. St. Joseph's Hosp., Yonkers, NY, 1982—; mem. quality assurance7 com. N.Y. State PRO, 1984—, mem. sanction com., 1990—. Contbr. articles to profl. jours. Named Man of the Yr., Italian Assn. Hosps., 2000. Avocation: painting. Office: 944 N Broadway Ste 201 Yonkers NY 10701

SPAHN, JAMES FRANCIS, marketing professional; b. Dubuque, Iowa, Oct. 4, 1957; s. Ervin Henry and Denise Marie (Shuhert) S.; m. Beverly Joan Burns, Oct. 22, 1983. Grad., Brown Inst. Tech., 1977. Lic. real estate commn.; cert. mktg. dir. Mktg. dir., cert. shopping ctr. mgr. The Cafaro Co., Dubuque, 1979-80; mktg. dir. The Herring Marathon Group, Dallas, 1980-83, Dusco Property Mgmt., Inc., Lancaster, Pa., 1983-87, Jim Wilson and Assocs., Montgomery, Ala., 1987—. Co-author: Operating Shopping Centers, 1984. Mem. Cen. Bus. Dist. Revitalization Task Force, Savannah, Ga., 1984-86, Transit Task Force, Savannah, 1985-86; bd. dirs. Conv. and Vis. Bur., Savannah, 1986-87. Recipient Addy awards Dubuque Advt. Club, 1980. Mem. Internat. Coun. Shopping Ctrs. (Maxi award 1982, Maxi finalist 1987, 89, 90, 94, 2002, 03), Savannah Advt. Club (bd. dirs. 1984-87), Birmingham Advt. Club (Addy awards 1983-87, 89). Roman Catholic. Avocations: camping, bicycling. Home: 7375 Thomas Hall Dr Trussville AL 35173-1851 Office: Jim Wilson & Assocs Inc 3000-400 Riverchase Galleria Birmingham AL 35244-2315

SPAHR, CLINTON S., JR., retired elementary education educator; b. Bayshore, N.Y., Feb. 3, 1942; s. Clinton Smith and Averil Witona (Courier) S. BS, Hofstra U., 1967, MA, 1972. Tchr. Brentwood (N.Y.) Pub. Schs., 1966-97. Mem. Am. Philatelic Soc., Brentwood Tchrs. Assn., Internat. Soc. World Stamp Collectors. Avocations: collecting stamps, tapes, cds, books. Home: 62 Clarendon Rd Lake Ronkonkoma NY 11779

SPAHR, ELIZABETH, environmental services administrator; b. Warren, Ohio, Nov. 12, 1930; d. Sullivan and Elizabeth (St. Clair) Spahr; children: Gretchen, Carolyn. BS, Case Western Res. U., 1952, MS, 1954, PhD, 1957, MBA, 1973. Sr. rsch. scientist NASA, Cleve., 1956-71; mgr. internat. ops., mgr. spl. projects The Std. Oil Co., Cleve., 1973-86; v.p. strategic planning Ameritrust Corp., Cleve., 1987-92; dir. fin. & adminstrn. AAUW, Washington, 1993-98; CEO Technol. Exec. Inst., 1998—2002; pres. AcromaTech Group, Inc., 1999—2002; assoc. dir. U. Md. Ctr. for Environ. Scis. Horn Point Lab., Cambridge, 2002—. Dir. supply emergency team Internat. Energy Agy., Paris, 1984-86; chair fed. women's program Fed. Exec. Bd., Cleve., 1969-71. Trustee Case Western Res. U., Cleve., 1988-92, chair ann. fund, 1989-93; pres. bd. dirs. Cuyahoga City Hosp. Found., Cleve., 1983-85. Grantee USPHS, 1952-56. Mem. Women in Tech., Arlington C. of C., Strategic Alliance Va. Employers, Strategic Alliance Md. Employers. Office: Univ Md Ctr Environ Sci Horn Point Lab PO Box 775 Cambridge MD 21613-0775 Home: PO Box 352 Trappe MD 21673-0352 E-mail: espahr@hpl.umces.edu.

SPAHR, FREDERICK THOMAS, association executive; b. South Bend, Apr. 27, 1939; s. Ervin Leonard and Elizabeth Mary (Layden) S.; m. Patricia Margaret McGraw, Aug. 6, 1966; children— Susan, John, Kathryn, Joseph. BA, Ind. U., Bloomington, 1961; M.Ed., Boston U., 1963; PhD, U. So. Calif., 1968. Asst. prof. Pa. State U., 1968-70; dep. exec. sec. Am. Speech Lang. Hearing Assn., Rockville, Md., 1971-79, exec. dir., 1980—. Treas. Nat. Com. for Rsch. in Neurol. and Communication Disorders, 1983-89. Fellow Am. Speech-Lang.-Hearing Assn, Honors Nat. Student Speech, Lang. and Hearing Assn. Am. Soc. Assn. Execs. (Key award 1987, bd. dirs. 1995-98), Greater Washington Soc. Assn. Execs. (chmn. bd. dirs.), Washington Assn. Rsch. Found. (chmn. bd. trustees), Assn. Coun. of Montgomery Co. (Md.,pres.), World Future Soc., Phi Delta Kappa. Office: Am Speech-Language-Hearing Assn 10801 Rockville Pike Rockville MD 20852-3226

SPAID, GREGORY P. academic administrator, art educator; b. Mishawaka, Ind. m. Susan R. Spaid. BA in Art, Kenyon Coll., 1969; MFA, Ind. U., 1976. Mem. faculty Berea (Ky.) Coll., 1976—79; prof. art Kenyon Coll., Gambier, Ohio, 1979—, chair art dept., 1984—88, assoc. provost, 1999—2002, acting provost, 2002—03, provost, 2003—. Tchr. summer programs Kenyon Coll., Gambier, Ohio, Santa Fe, Bozeman, Mont., Nantucket Island Sch. Design Art. Photography published in books, The Man Who Created Paradise, 2001, On Nantucket, 2002, Represented in permanent collections Mus. Modern Art, N.Y.C., J. Paul Getty Mus., L.A., Santa Barbara (Calif.) Mus. Art, Smithsonian Instn., Nat. Mus. Am. Art, Washington, Dayton (Ohio) Art Inst., Chase Manhattan Bank, N.Y.C. Fellow Photo Educators fellow, Eastman Kodak, 1993; Individual Artist's fellow, Ohio Arts Coun., 1984, 1986, 1995, 2000, Fulbright Rsch. fellow, Italy, 1987, Profl. Devel. Assistance grantee, Ohio Arts Coun., 1990, Artist Project grantee, 1995. Office: Ransom Hall 21 Kenyon College Gambier OH 43022-9623*

SPAIN, FREDERICK WILLIAM, retired secondary school educator, writer; b. Detroit, Jan. 21, 1933; s. Frederick Carl and Leona Marie Spain; m. Elizabeth Jane LaBonte, May 5, 1959 (div. Apr. 20, 1979); children: Raymond Frederick, Susan Mary Spain Klein; m. Gloria Jean Roehm, May 26, 1979; stepchildren: Karl Allen Walz, Vicki Lynn Walz Spain-Brookshear. BA in English, Alma Coll., 1956. Cert. tchr. Mich. English tchr. Alpena (Mich.) Pub. Schs., 1962—75, Waterford (Mich.) Lady of Lakes H.S., 1979—83, St. Clement H.S., Center Line, Mich., 1986—89; sci. tchr. St. Benedict Elem. Sch., Pontiac, Mich., 1978—79; English tchr., athletic coach Aquinas H.S., Augusta, Ga., 1983—86; driver edn. tchr. Brandon H.S., Ortonville, Mich., 1986—2001; ret., 2001. Pres. Bestway Driving Sch., Clarkeston, Mich., 1989—99. Author: (children's book) Missy the Mutt, Maynerd the Australian Cockatiel, 1998, Missy Surprise Birthday Party, 1989, The Adventures of Randy Raccoon, 1999; contbr. poetry to lit. publs. (Editor's Choice award Disting. Poets Am., 93, Editor's Choice award Best Poems of 1996, 96). Pres. Cath. Sch. Bd., Alpena, 1968—70; bd. dirs. Mich. Driver and Safety Edn., Lansing, 1995—97. With U.S. Army, 1956—58. Mem.: Audubon Soc. Avocations: fishing, horse racing. Home: 7864 S 1 1/2 Rd Wellston MI 49689 Office: Roehm Pubs 7864 S 1-1/2 Rd Wellston MI 49689 E-mail: roehm-pub@ispwest.com.

SPAIN, JAMES DORRIS, JR., biochemist, educator; b. Washington, Feb. 3, 1929; s. James Dorris and Frances (Pitkin) S.; m. Patricia Mann, Oct. 3, 1952; children: James Williamson, Caryn Ann, Mary Alisa. Student, Tulane U., 1947-48; BS, Mich. Technol. U., 1951; MS, Med. Coll. Va., 1953; PhD, Stanford, 1956. Research fellow biochemistry U. Tex.-M.D. Anderson Hosp. and Tumor Inst., 1955-56; assoc. prof. dept. chemistry Mich. Technol. U., Houghton, 1956-62, head dept. biol. scis., 1962-68, prof. biochemistry, 1962-84, prof. emeritus, 1985—. Dir. Ctr. for Instrnl. Computing, Ea. Mich. U., Ypsilanti, 1984-85; vis. prof. Clemson U., S.C., 1985-94; pres. Electronic Homework Sys., Inc., 1994—; cons. Computer Applications in Biology and Chemistry; dir. SUMIT Courseware Devel. Project, 1979-82. Author: Some Computer Programs for Biology, 1970, Biological Simulation Techniques, 1972, Lake Superior Basin Bibliography, 1976, BASIC Computer Models in Biology, 1978, Basic Microcomputer Models in Biology, 1982, Developing Chemical Skills with Computerized Instruction, 1990, Computer Simulation in Biology: A Basic Introduction, 1992, Chemi-Skill-Bildr Electronic Homework System, 1994, ChemSkill Builder for Windows, 1997, ChemSkill Foundations, 1998, Chem Skill Builder/2000, 1999, GOB-ChemSkills, 2002; contbr. articles to profl. jours. Chmn. adv. council St. Josephs Hosp. Sch. Nursing, 1967; Trustee, pres. Portage Twp. Sch. Bd., 1968-76; trustee Copper Country Intermediate Sch. Dist., 1975-78. Recipient Faculty Research award Mich. Technol. U., 1965 Mem. Am. Chem. Soc. (past sect. v.p., chmn.), Rotary, Sigma Xi, Phi Lambda Upsilon. Clubs: Miscowaubik (gov. 1971-74, 79-82), Boscobel Country. Episcopalian. Home: 42498 Lakeshore Dr Chassell MI 49916-9006 Office Phone: 801-836-3949. Personal E-mail: jspain.chemskil@prodigy.net.

SPAIN, JAMES WILLIAM, political scientist, writer, investor; b. Chgo., July 22, 1926; s. Patrick Joseph and Mary Ellen (Forristal) S.; m. Edith Burke James, Feb. 21, 1951; children: Patrick, Sikandra, Stephen, William. MA, U. Chgo., 1949; PhD, Columbia U., 1959. Cons. sec. army, 1949—50; with U.S. Fgn. Svc., 1951—53; rschr., lectr. Columbia, 1955—62; mem. policy planning coun. State Dept., 1963—64; dir. Office Rsch. and Analysis for Near East and South Asia, 1964—66; country dir. Pakistan and Afghanistan, 1966—69; charge d'affaires Am. Embassy, Rawapindi, 1969; consul gen. Istanbul, Turkey, 1970-72; minister Am. embassy, Ankara, 1972-74; diplomat-in-residence, vis. prof. history and govt. Fla. State U., Tallahassee, 1974-75; amb. to Tanzania Dar es Salaam, 1975-79; amb., dep. permanent rep. UN, N.Y.C., 1979; amb. to Turkey, Ankara, 1980-81; amb. to Sri Lanka, Colombo, 1985-89; fgn. affairs fellow Carnegie Endowment for Internat. Peace and Rand Corp., Washington, 1982-84; guest resident investor Colombo, Sri Lanka, 1991—. Chmn. Lanka Infrastructure Ltd.; bd. dirs. Hawk Mountain Fed. Express, Ltd.; adj. prof. polit. sci. Am. U., Washington, 1965-67. Author: The Way of the Pathans, 1962, The Pathan Borderland, 1963, American Diplomacy in Turkey, 1984, Pathans of the Latter Day, 1995, Innocents of the Latter Day, 1997, In Those Days: A Diplomat Remembers, 1998, Holding Out in the Eternal City, 2000, The Emperor's Medallion, 2000, The Devils' Mountain, 2000, Digging the Desert, 2000, The Tribsmen's Treasure, 2000, The Monks' Secret, 2000, The Islands' Quota, 2000, Holy Ireland, 2001, Out Beyond, 2002, Innocents, 2002, To Boil a Stew, 2002. Pres. bd. trustees Joseph Frazer Meml. Hosp. With U.S. Army, 1946-47. Fellow Ford Found., 1953-55; recipient Presdl. Exec. award, 1983, Wilbur I. Carr award for Disting. Diplomacy, 1989. Mem. Coun. Fgn. Rels., Washington Inst. Fgn. Affairs, Assn. Diplomatic Studies and Tng., Cosmos Club. Home: Galle Face Ct II # 42 Colombo 3 Sri Lanka Office Phone: 94-11-243-7179. E-mail: jwspain@sltnet.lk.

SPAIN, RICHARD COLBY, lawyer; b. Evanston, Ill., Nov. 17, 1950; s. Richard Francis and Anne Louise (Brinckerhoff) S.; m. Nancy Lynn Mavec, Aug. 3, 1974; children: Catherine Day, Sarah Colby. BA cum laude, Lawrence U., 1972; JD, Case Western Reserve U., 1975; LLM in taxation, John Marshall Law Sch., 1985. Bar: Ohio 1975, Ill. 1982, U.S. Dist. Ct. (no. dist.) Ohio 1977, U.S. Dist. Ct. (no. dist.) Ill. 1982, Mass. 1996. Ptnr. Spain & Spain, Cleve., 1975-82, Whitted & Spain, PC, Chgo., 1985-89, Spain, Spain & Varnet PC, Chgo., Northborough, Mass., 1989—; assoc. Canel Whitted & Whitted, Chgo., 1982-85. Dir., sec. Stone Perforating Co., Chgo., 1988—, Chgo. EDM, Inc., Chgo., Wheeling, Ill., 1994—. Contbr. articles to profl. jours. Treas. ARC Ill., 1993-2003; dir. Chgo. Youth Symphony Orch., 1983-2002. Mem.: Carlton Club (Chgo.), Chikaming Country Club (dir. 1992—94). Home: 1320 N State Pkwy Chicago IL 60610-2118 Office: Spain Spain & Varnet PC 33 N Dearborn St Ste 2220 Chicago IL 60602-3118 E-mail: rspain@spainspainvarnet.com.

SPAIN, SHERYL SCARBROUGH, school counselor, educator; b. Columbus, Ohio, Feb. 13, 1944; d. Ernest James and Martha Adams Scarbrough; m. C. Michael Spain, Aug. 6, 1965; children: Christopher Charles, Todd Michael. BS, Ga. State U., 1970, MS, 1987. Cert. sch. counselor K-12 Ga. Instr. Winsalem Jr. Coll., Winston Salem, NC, 1975—78; instr., dept. head Herzing Inst., Birmingham, Ala., 1981—84; tchr. Cobb County Schs., Marietta, Ga., 1984—87, sch. counselor, 1987—2004. Workshop presenter, coord. Bells Ferry Elem., Marietta, 1992—, coord. sheriff's awards Cobb County Sheriff, 1995—; mem. crisis response team Cobb County Schs., Marietta, 2000—. Mem. Citizen's Adv. Counsel, Marietta, 1993—95. Presbyterian. Avocations: reading, tennis, travel. Home: 2492 St James Dr Southport NC 28461

SPAIN, THOMAS B. retired state supreme court justice; Justice Ky. Supreme Ct, Frankfort, 1991-95; ret., 1995; of counsel Whitfield & Cox P.S.C. Office: Whitfield & Cox PSC 29 E Center St Madisonville KY 42431-2037 Office Phone: 270-821-0656.

SPAINHOWER, JAMES IVAN, retired college president; b. Stanberry, Mo., Aug. 3, 1928; s. Elmer Enoch and Stella Irene (Cox) S.; m. Joanne Steanson, June 10, 1950; children: Janet Dovell, James Jeffrey. BA, Phillips U., Enid, Okla., 1950, LLD (hon.), 1967; BD, Lexington (Ky.) Theol. Sem., 1953; MA in Polit. Sci., U. Mo., Columbia, 1967, PhD, 1971, U. Ark., 1954; diploma, U. Pacific Sch. Religion, Berkeley, Calif., 1958; DPA (hon.), Culver-Stockton Coll., 1973; LL.D. (hon.), Maryville Coll., St. Louis, 1976; Litt.D. (hon.), Kirksville (Mo.) Coll. Osteo. Medicine, 1977; D.H.L. (hon.), Mo. Valley Coll., 1984; LLD (hon.), Eureka Coll., 1989, Lynchburg Coll., 1993. Ordained to ministry Christian Ch. (Disciples of Christ), 1950; pastor chs. in Ark. and Mo., 1953-70; mem. Mo. Ho. of Reps. from, Saline County, 1963-70; pres. Asso. Med. Schs. Mo., Jefferson City, 1970-72; part-time prof. polit. sci. Lincoln U., Jefferson City, 1970-72; treas. State of Mo., 1973-80; pres. Sch. of Ozarks, Point Lookout, Mo., 1981-82, Lindenwood Coll., St. Charles, Mo., 1983-89; pres. divsn. higher edn. Christian Ch. (Disciples of Christ), 1989-93. Author: Pulpit, Pew and Politics, 1979. Chmn. Mo. del. Dem. Nat. Conv., 1976; elected mem. Acad. Squires, 1981; 1st chmn. Mo. Children's Trust Fund, 1984-86. Recipient Mental Health award Mo. Mental Health Assn., 1967, Meritorious Service award St. Louis Globe Dem., 1968, Harry S. Truman award Saline County Young Democrats, 1970, citation of merit Alumni Assn. U. Mo., 1975; named Mo. Lay Educator of Year Mo. chpt. Phi Delta Kappa, 1968 Home and Office: 8067 Old White River Rd Rogers AR 72756-7662 E-mail: spainy@cox-internet.com.

SPAKE, KLUANE, minister, writer; b. Sarasota, Fla., Jan. 24; d. H. Austin and M. June Simonds; m. Rodell A Spake; children: Shawn Miller, Rod, David; 1 child, Dyanna. PhD, N.D., Vision Christian U., Romana, Calif., 1991. Pastor Jubilee, Dededo, 1984—99, traveling spkr. and author Atlanta, 1999—. Lectr. in field; internat. dir. Vision Internat. U. Author: From Enmity to Equality, 1999, Understanding Headship, 1999, (children's book) "Angel's Friends", 2001, Finding Wisdom, 2000, Whole & Holy, 1999. Mem. governing bd. sr. citizens Govt.of Guam, Agana, 1995—97. Mem.: Internat. Coalition Apostles, Nat. Christian Coun. Assoc., Internat. Convent of Faith Ministers, Faith Christian Fellowship. Personal E-mail: spake@mindspring.com.

SPAKE, NED BERNARR, energy company executive; b. Montpelier, Ohio, Sept. 18, 1933; s. Lewis W. and Gertrude E. (Foley) S.; m. Marilyn Rae Faulk, July 14, 1956; children: Julie Ann Spake Scott, Cynthia Ann Spake Lovern B. Indsl. Engring., U. Fla., Gainesville, 1957; MBA, Rollins Coll., Winter Park, Fla., 1967. Mgr. Fla. Power Corp., Winter Park, Fla., 1962-72, dir. St. Petersburg, Fla., 1972-76, asst. v.p., 1976-78, v.p., 1978-83, Fla. Progress Corp., St. Petersburg, 1983-86; pres., CEO, dir. Progress Technologies Corp., St. Petersburg, Fla., 1985-89; pres., CEO, chmn. bd. Advanced Separation Technologies, Inc., St. Petersburg, Fla., 1985-89; pres., CEO Rein Energy Corp., Alachua, Fla., 1989-92, The Nouveau Group Inc., Winter Park, Fla., 1992—, also bd. dirs. Patentee in field Mem. adv. coun. Engring. Sch. U. Fla., Gainesville, 1978-95; bd. dirs. U. Fla. Rsch. Found., Inc., 1986-94; dir. GelTech, Inc., 1986-87. Recipient Disting. Svc. award Coll. Engring. U. Fla., 1988. Lutheran. Home and Office: Apt 5B 633 N Park Ave Winter Park FL 32789-3237 Office Phone: 407-539-0106.

SPALDING, ANDREW FREEMAN, lawyer; b. Toledo, Ohio, June 24, 1951; s. Dean and Shirley Louise (Maitland) S.; m. Adele Taylor, May 17, 1980; children: Amy Louise, Adam Freeman, Audrey Wade, Abigail Maitland. BA, U. Calif., Berkeley, 1973; JD, So. Meth. U., 1977. Bar: Tex. 1977, U.S. Dist. Ct. (so., ea. and we. dists.) Tex. 1978, U.S. Ct. Appeals (5th cir.) 1978; bd. cert. civil trial law, personal injury trial law. Assoc. Bracewell & Patterson, LLP, Houston, 1977-84, ptnr., 1985—. Notes and comments editor So. Meth. U. Law Jour., Dallas, 1976-77. Fellow Tex Bar Found., Houston Bar Found.; mem. State Bar Tex., Houston Bar Assn., Tex. Assn. Def. Counsel, Def. Rsch. Inst., Knights Momus, Krewe Maximilian, Pan Tex. Assembly, Houston Country Club. Office: Bracewell & Patterson 2900 S Tower Pennzoil Pla 711 Louisiana St Ste 2900 Houston TX 77002-2781 Office Phone: 713-221-1220. E-mail: Andrew.Spalding@bracepatt.com.

SPALDING, CATHERINE, lawyer; b. Lebanon, Ky. d. Hugh C. and Bernadette (Hill) S. BS in Biology, Spalding U., Louisville, 1970; JD, U. Louisville, 1983. Bar: Ky., U.S. Ct. Appeals (6th cir.), Ct. Vets. Appeals, Fed. Dist. Ct. Pvt. practice law, Louisville, 1983—; asst. county atty. Jefferson County, 1993—2000, family ct. atty., guardian ad litem, 2000—. Editor newsletter Ky. Bar Assn. Family Law Sect.; editor book supplement: Kentucky Family Law, 1990. Past bd. dirs. LWV, Portland Mus. Louisville. Mem. ABA, Ky. Bar Assn. (chair family law sect. 1990-91, newsletter editor 2003—, spkr., moderator seminars), Louisville Bar Assn. (chair social security sect. 1992-93), AAUW (past bd. dirs.), DAR (past bd. dirs.) Optimist Club (past bd. dirs.), LWV (past bd. dirs.). Avocation: skiing. Home: 1917 Trevilian Way Louisville KY 40205-2139 Office: Ste 3 325 W Ormsby Ave Louisville KY 40203-2907 Office Fax: 502-634-4488.

SPALDING, HELEN H. library director; BA in English, U. Iowa, 1972, MA in Libr. Sci., 1974; MPA, U. Mo., Kansas City, 1985. Serials records libr. Iowa State U. Librs., Iowa, 1974—76, serials cataloger, 1976—79; head tech. svcs. U. Mo. Kansas City Librs., 1979—85; assoc. dir. librs. U. Mo., Kansas City, 1985—. Coun. Libr. Resources Acad. Libr. mgmt. intern Northwestern U., 1983—84; spkr. in field. Mem.: Assn. Coll. and Rsch. Librs. (pres. 2002—03). Office: Univ Mo Kansas City 5100 Rockhill Rd Kansas City MO 64110-2499

SPALDING, JAMES STUART, retired telecommunications company executive; b. Edinburgh, Scotland, Nov. 23, 1934; arrived in Can., 1957, permanent resident, 1962; Student, Edinburgh U., 1951-52, Glasgow U., 1953. Gen. mgr., dir. United Corps. Ltd., Montreal, Que., Can., 1970-72; from pension fund mgr. to exec. v.p. fin. BCE, Inc., Montreal, 1972-90. Mem. Inst. Chartered Accts. Scotland, Order Chartered Accounts Que., Fin. Execs. Inst. Can. (past chmn.), Montreal Soc. Fin. Analysts (past pres.). Home: 126 King St E Brockville ON Canada K6V 1B9 E-mail: stuart231134@aol.com.

SPALTY, EDWARD ROBERT, lawyer; b. New Haven, Oct. 1, 1946; s. Kermit and Elinor Turgeon; m. Suzy Clune; children: Thomas John, Kathleen Tess. AB, Emory U., 1968; JD, Columbia U., 1973. Bar: Mo. 1975, Nebr. 1997, Kans. 1998, Colo. 2003, U.S. Dist. Ct. (we. dist.) Mo. 1975, U.S. Ct. Claims 1977, U.S. Ct. Appeals (8th cir.) 1984, U.S. Ct. Appeals (10th cir.) 1999, U.S. Supreme Ct. 1994, U.S. Dist. Ct. (ea. dist.) Wis. 2004. Assoc. Webster & Sheffield, N.Y.C., 1973-74; mng. ptnr. Armstrong Teasdale LLP, Kansas City, Mo., 1991-2001, ptnr., 1980—. Contbr. articles to profl jours. Chmn. bd. dirs. Mo. Easter Seals, 1990—92; founding mem. Heartland Franchise Assn.; bd. dirs., sec., vice chmn. Nat. Easter Seal Soc. With U.S. Army, 1968—70. Mem.: ABA (litigation sect, franchising forum comt), Intern. Rels. Coun. Kansas City, Def. Rsch. Inst., Mo. Orgn. Def. Attys., Lawyers Assn. Kansas City, Kansas City Met. Bar Assn. (chmn antitrust and franchise law comt, co-chair 14th and 16h ann Nat Franchise Law Inst), Mo. Bar Assn. (civil rules and procedures comt), Lex Mundi (regional vice chair N.Am. dispute resolution), German-Am C. of C. (v.p. Kansas City chpt), Nat. Golf Club Kansas City (founder), Phi Delta, Pi Sigma Alpha, Sigma Nu. Home: 13703 NW 73rd St Parkville MO 64152-1120 Office: Armstrong Teasdale LLP 2345 Grand Blvd Ste 2000 Kansas City MO 64108-2617 Office Phone: 816-221-3420. Business E-Mail: espalty@armstrongteasdale.com.

SPALVINS, JANIS GUNARS, steamship company executive; b. Riga, Latvia, May 26, 1936; arrived in Australia, 1949; s. Peter Spalvins and Hilda (Dritmanis) Blumentals; m. Cecily Westall Rymill, Dec. 16, 1961; children: John Rymill and Richard Rymill. B in Econ. Group sec., dir. Camelec Group of Cos., South Australia, 1955-73; asst. gen. mgr. The Adelaide Steamship Co. Ltd., South Australia, 1973-77, chief gen. mgr., dir., 1977-81, mng. dir., 1981-90; dir., chief exec. David Jones Ltd., Australia, 1980, 1988—91; dir. Macmahon Holdings, Ltd., 1987—92; chmn., dir. Galufo Pty. Ltd., 1991—. Fellow Australian Inst. Mgmt., Inst. Dirs., Chartered Inst. Secs., Chartered Practicing Accts., Cruising Yacht of SA, Mt. Osmond Golf Club. Avocations: sailing, tennis, snow and water skiing. Home: 2 Brookside Rd Springfield SA 5061 Australia

SPANBOCK, MAURICE SAMUEL, lawyer; b. N.Y.C., Jan. 6, 1924; s. Benjamin and Belle (Ward) S.; m. Marion Rita Heyman, Nov. 21, 1954; children: Jonathan H., Betsy W. BA, Columbia U., N.Y.C., 1944; LLB, Harvard U., 1950. Bar: N.Y. 1950. Assoc. Goldstone and Wolff, N.Y.C., 1950-52; ptnr. Carro and Spanbock (name changed to Carro, Spanbock, Kaster et al), N.Y.C., 1952-94; of counsel Kleinberg Kaplan Wolff & Cohen, N.Y.C., 1994—. Trustee Carnegie Coun. on Ethics and Internat. Affairs, N.Y.C., 1980-86, 93-2000, hon. trustee, 2002--, chmn. bd., 1987-92; hon. pres. Lincoln Square Synagogue, N.Y.C.; sec. Ohr Torah Stone Instns. Israel. Cpl. AUS, 1943-46, ETO. Mem. ABA (chmn. com. on taxation, patent, trademark and copyright law sect. 1979-81), Assn. of Bar of City of N.Y. (com. on copyright 1965-67, art law com. 1977-80, 86-88), Fed. Bar Coun., Nat. Panel Arbitrators, Am. Abitration Assn., Practising Law Inst. (panel on copyrights, 1979). Jewish. Home: 88 Central Park W New York NY 10023-5209 Office: Kleinberg Kaplan Wolff & Cohen 551 5th Ave Fl 18 New York NY 10176-1800

SPANDORFER, MERLE SUE, artist, educator, author; b. Balt., Sept. 4, 1934; d. Simon Louis and Bernice P. (Jacobson) S.; m. Lester M. Spandorfer, June 17, 1956; children: Cathy, John. Student, Syracuse U., 1952-54; BS, U. Md., 1956. Mem. faculty Cheltenham (Pa.) Sch. Fine Arts, 1969—; instr. printmaking Tyler Sch. Art Temple U., Phila., 1980-84; faculty Pratt Graphics Ctr., N.Y.C., 1985-86. One woman shows include Richard Feigen Gallery, N.Y.C., 1970, U. Pa., 1974, Phila. Coll. Textiles and Sci., 1977, Ericson Gallery, N.Y.C., 1978, 79, R.I. Sch. Design, 1980, Syracuse U., 1981, Marian Locks Gallery, Phila., 1973, 78, 82, Temple U., 1984, Tyler Sch. Art, 1985, University City Sci. Ctr., 1987, Gov.'s Residence, 1988, Wenninger Graphics Gallery, Provinceton, Mass., 1989, Widener U. Art Mus., 1995, Gloucester County Coll., 1996, Mangel Gallery, 1992, 97, 2000, 03, Cabrini Coll., 1999; group shows Bklyn. Mus. Art, 1973, San Francisco Mus. Art, 1973, Balt. Mus. Art, 1970, 71, 74, Phila. Mus. Art, 1972, 77, Fundacio Joan Miro, Barcelona, Spain, 1977, Del. Mus. Art, Wilmington, 1978, Carlsberg Glyptotek Mus., Copenhagen, 1980, Moore Coll. Art, Phila., 1982, Tyler Sch. Art, 1983, William Penn Meml. Mus., Harrisburg, Pa., 1984, Ariz. State U., 1985, Tiajin Fine Arts Coll., China, 1986, Beaver Coll., Phila., 1988, The Port of History Mus., Phils., 1987, Sichuan Fine Arts Inst., Chong Qing, China, 1988, Glynn Vivian Mus., Swansea, Wales, 1989, Phila. Mus. Art, 1990, Fgn. Mus., Riga, Latvia, 1995, Woodmere Art Mus., Phila., 1996, Am. Coll., 1997, Cheltenham Ctr. for the Arts, Phila., 1997, Rowan Coll., 1997, Villanova U., 1998, U. Pa., 1999, U. of the Arts, 2001, others; represented in permanent collections Met. Mus. Art, N.Y.C., Whitney Mus. Am. Art, N.Y.C., Mus. Modern Art, N.Y.C., The Israel Mus., Balt. Mus. (gov.'s prize and purchase award 1970), Phila. Mus. Art (purchase award 1977), Toyoh Bijutsu Gakko, Tokyo, Library of Congress, Temple U.; commd. works represented in U. Pa. Inst. Comtemporary Art, 1991; co-author: Making Art Safely, 1993. Recipient award Balt. Mus. Art/Md. Inst. Art, 1971, Govs. prize and Purchase award Balt. Mus. Art, 1970, Outstanding Art Educators award Pa. Art Edn. Assn., 1982, Purchase award Berman Mus., 1995, Artist Equity award, 1996; grantee Pa. Coun. Arts, 1989. Mem. Am. Color Print Soc., Pa. Art Edn. Assn. Jewish. Office: 307 E Gowen Ave Philadelphia PA 19119-1023 E-mail: lesspand@home.com.

SPANEL, HARRIET, state legislator; b. Audubon, Iowa, Jan. 15, 1939; 3 children. BS in Math., Iowa State U., 1961. Mem. Wash. Ho. of Reps., 1987-93, Wash. Senate, Dist. 40, Olympia, 1993—. Office: Wash Senate PO Box 40440 Olympia WA 98504-0440

SPANFELLER, JAMES JOHN, JR., publishing executive; b. Phila., Aug. 25, 1956; s. James John Sr. and Patricia Ann (Durkin) S. BA, Union Coll., Schenectady, N.Y., 1979. Assoc. pub. Soho News, N.Y.C., 1979-81; dir. Alan Western Communications, N.Y.C., 1981-83; pub. Newsweek on Campus, N.Y.C., 1983-86; nat. sales mgr. Newsweek, N.Y.C., 1986—, sales dir., 1987-89; assoc. pub., sr. v.p. Playboy Mag., 1989-93; pub. Inc. mag., 1993—96, Ziff-Davis Yahoo! Internet Life, 1996—98; v.p. Yahoo! Internet Life, 1998-2000, 1998—2000; pres., CEO Forbes.com, 2001—. Mem. mktg. com. Mag. Pub. Assoc.; bd. dirs. Am. Bus. Media, 2004—. Author: The Fantastic Airplane, 1979. Mem.: N.Y. Athletic. Office: Forbes.com 24 W 23rd St 11th Fl New York NY 10010 Office Phone: 212-366-8999. Office Fax: 212-366-8801.

SPANGLER, ARNOLD EUGENE, investment banker; b. Ft. Dodge, Iowa, Aug. 1, 1948; s. Kermit Charles and Cora (Buroos) Spangler; m. Penelope Angell, Nov. 8, 1980; children: Christopher Paul, Allison Elizabeth. BS, Iowa State U., 1970; MBA, Harvard U., 1972. Assoc. Hornblower & Weeks-Hemphill, Noyes, N.Y.C., 1972-74; product officer Citibank, N.Y.C., 1974-76, Lazard Freres & Co. LLC, N.Y.C., 1976—89, gen. ptnr., 1983-89; mng. dir. mergers and acquisitions Paine Webber Inc. (UBS), N.Y.C., 1989-91; sr. advisor Bentley Assocs., L.P., N.Y.C., 1992-93; mng. dir. Mancuso & Co., N.Y.C., 1993—. Bd. dirs. Wayn-Tex. Inc., Waynesboro, Va. Home: 1165 Park Ave New York NY 10128-1210 Office Phone: 212-344-1866.

SPANGLER, ARTHUR STEPHENSON, JR., psychologist; b. Boston, June 20, 1949; s. Arthur Stephenson and Barbara Louise (Fellows) Spangler; m. Deborah A. Kauders, Nov. 27, 1971; children: Heather Anita, Rebecca Haley. BS, Hobart Coll., 1971; MEd, Boston Coll., 1974; ScD, Boston U., 1985. Diplomate Am. Acad. Pain Mgmt.; lic. psychologist, Mass., clin. social worker, Mass.; bd. cert. rehab. counselor, Mass. Mass. counselor Met. State Hosp., Waltham, 1971-73; rehab. counselor J.T. Berry Rehab. Ctr., North Reading, Mass., 1974-75; program coord. Shore Collaborative, Medford, Mass., 1975-76; dir. instl. sch. programs South Shore Collaborative, North Weymouth, Mass., 1976-79; dir. mental retardation program South Shore Mental Health Ctr., Quincy, Mass., 1979-85; coord. outpatient clinic Boston Pain Ctr., Spaulding Rehab. Hosp., 1985-86; v.p., dir. behavioral medicine svcs. Mass. Bay Counseling, Quincy, 1985—; dir. indsl. disability mgmt. svcs., psychologist chronic pain program Miriam Hosp., Providence, 1987-88; psychologist John Graham Headache Ctr. Faulkner Hosp., Boston, 1992-94. Adj. prof. Sargent Coll., Boston U., 1990—99. Vol. counselor Multi-Svc. Ctr., Newton, Mass., 1973-75; bd. dirs. Newton-Wellesley-Weston-Needham Cmty. Mental Health and Mental Retardation Ctr., Newton, 1976-80, pres. 1979-80; mem. Boston Symphony Assn. Vols. Recipient award Nat. Assn. Retarded Citizens, 1974. Mem.: ACA, APA (assoc.), New Eng. Pain Assn., Soc. Behavioral Medicine, Internat. Assn. for Study of Pain, Assn. for Study of Pain. Episcopalian. Home: 151 Tremont St # 11P Boston MA 02111-1110 Office: 36 Weston Ave Quincy MA 02170-1833

SPANGLER, CLEMMIE DIXON, JR., construction company executive; b. Charlotte, N.C., Apr. 5, 1932; s. Clemmie Dixon and Veva C. (Yelton) S.; m. Meredith Jane Riggs, June 25, 1960; children: Anna Wildy, Abigail Riggs. BS, U. N.C., 1954; MBA, Harvard U., 1956; LHD (hon.), Queens Coll., 1985; LLD (hon.), Davidson Coll., 1986, Furman U., 1993; LLD U. N. Carolina (hon.), 2003. Pres. C.D. Spangler Constrn. Co., Charlotte, 1958-86, Golden Eagle Industries, Inc., 1968-86; chmn. bd. Bank of N.C., Raleigh, 1973-82; dir. NCNB Corp., 1983-86; chmn. N.C. Bd. Edn., 1982-86; pres. U. N.C., Chapel Hill, 1986-97; CEO, chmn. C.D. Spangler Constrn. Co., Charlotte, 1997—. Bd. dirs. BellSouth Corp., Atlanta; chmn. bd. dirs. Nat. Gypsum Co., Charlotte. Past deacon Myers Park Bapt. Ch., vice-chmn. Charlotte-Mecklenburg Bd. Edn., Charlotte, 1972-76; past trustee Charlotte Symphony Orch., Crozer Theol. Sem.; past chmn. Charlotte adv. bd. Salvation Army; past bd. dirs. YMCA, Equitable Life Assurance Soc., Jefferson-Pilot Corp.; pres. bd. trustees Mint Mus. Art; bd. dirs. Union Theol. Sem., 1985-90, Assocs. Harvard Bus. Sch.; pres. bd. overseers Harvard Coll., 2003. With U.S. Army, 1956-58. Recipient Liberty Bell award Mecklenburg County Bar Assn., 1985, Alumni Achievement award Harvard Bus. Sch., 1988. Mem. Assn. Am. Univs., Bus. Higher Edn. Forum, Harvard Club (N.Y.C.), Univ. Club (N.Y.C.), Quail Hollow Country Club (Charlotte). Office: CD Spangler Constrn Co Office of Chmn Box 36007 Charlotte NC 28236-6007

SPANGLER, DAVID SHERIDAN, composer, director, creative arts educator, writer; b. Belleville, Kans., June 3, 1948; s. Robert Richard Spangler and Marjorie Claire (Forman) Barrett; m. Cynthia Adler (div. 1981); m. Martha Helen Obrecht; children: Marjorie Anne, Catherine Helen, Isadora Maxine, Sheridan Rose. BFA, Carnegie-Mellon U., 1970. Instr. jazz U. Pitts., 1971-72; pres. Spangler Prodns., Inc., Ft. Lauderdale, Fla., 1974—; music dir., producer AC & R Advt., Inc., N.Y.C., 1975-77; assoc. music dir. Grey Advt., Inc., N.Y.C., 1977-79; producer, writer MZH & F Music Prodns., Inc., N.Y.C., 1980-85; founder, dir. Lovewell Inst. for the Creative Arts, Ft. Lauderdale, Kans., 1987—; artistic dir. The Drama Ctr., Deerfield Beach, Fla., 1992. Conducted seminars in creative edn., 1990-00. Composer, lyricist: (film) So Fine, 1981, (TV series, records, videos) Romper Room, 1982—; composer (Broadway show) Elizabeth 1, 1974, Nefertiti, 1977, Chgo. 2004; soloist (original live tour) Bernstein's Mass, 1974; co-writer, dir. Dancing Animals, 1988, Children of the Sun, 1989; dir. The Cover of Life, 1992. On-site evaluator, panelist Fla. Dept. State divsn. Cultural Affairs - Theatre & Arts Instns., 1998-00; bd. dirs. Miami City Ballet, 2000; v.p. Theatre League S. Fla.; program adminstr./artistic dir. of interdisciplinary arts master's program Nova-Southeastern Univ., 2004—. Recipient Merit award Awards for Creative Excellence in Communications, 1971, Big Apple Radio award N.Y. Market Radio Broadcasters Assn., 1983. Mem. Nat. Acad. Rec. Arts and Scis., Dramatist Guild. Clubs: N.Y. Athletic (N.Y.C.). Libertarian. Home and Office: 1600 NE 18th Ave Fort Lauderdale FL 33305-3446 Office Phone: 954-262-8363.

SPANGLER, DENNIS LEE, physician; b. Akron, Ohio, Nov. 8, 1947; s. Wesley Daniel and Florence Adele (Smith) S.; m. July 7, 1972; children: Mathew Brian, Adam Christopher. BS, U. Akron, 1969; MD, Ohio State Med. Sch., 1973. Diplomate Am. Bd. Pediatrics, Am. Bd. Allergy and Immunology. Intern U. Fla. Med. Sch., Gainesville, 1973-74, resident, 1974-75, fellow allergy and clin. immunology, 1975-77; pvt. practice Atlanta Allergy Clinic, P.A., 1977—; chief med. officer Atlanta Allergy and Asthma Clinic, 1995—. Dir. chronic lung clinic Ga. Bur. Crippled Children, 1984-97; asst. clin. prof. pediatrics Med. Coll. of Ga., 1980-2001; vice chair divsn. of allergy Children's Healthcare of Atlanta, 2000—. Past pres., bd. dirs. midwest branch Ga. Lung Assn., Atlanta, 1981-82, med. adv. com., 1978—; pres. Fla. Pediatric Alumni Assn., Gainesville, 1985-86. Fellow Am. Acad. Pediatrics, Am. Acad. Allergy and Immunology, Am. Coll. Allergy, Asthma and Immunology (therapeutics com. 1983-88, chmn. drug and anaplylaxis com. 1988—, chmn. com. 1987—, bd. regents 1996-99), Am. Assn. Cert. Allergists (bd. govs. 1988—, bd. sec. 1997, v.p. 1998, pres. elect 1999, pres. 2000)); mem. Am. Thoracic Soc., Ga. Med. Assn., Cobb County Med. Soc., Southeastern Allergy Assn., Cherokee Country Club. Roman Catholic. Avocations: scuba diving, creating stain glass windows. Office: Atlanta Allergy Asthma Clinic 1965 N Park Pl Atlanta GA 30339-2012

SPANGLER, DOROTHY BENITA, artist; b. St. Louis, Mar. 9, 1928; d. Fred and Della (Baker) Reynolds; m. Charles B. Spangler, Feb. 26, 1926; children: Charles Jr., Cathy D. Student, Coll. San Mateo, 1946-48, Henery Henche Sch. Art, Cape Cod, Mass., 1968. Pvt. practice window decorator, Mt. View and Los Altos, Calif. Exhbns. include Winblad Gallery, San Francisco, 1965-68, So. Pacific Gold Spike Centennial, San Francisco and Japan, 1967, Provence Town Charles Hawthorne Mus., 1968, Gallery DeTours, San Francisco and Carmel, Calif., 1968-86, Lawrence Ross Gallery, Beverly Hills and Palm Dessert, Calif., 1986-89, Gage Galleries, Newport Beach and Irvine, Calif., 1989-91, Union Square Galleries, San Francisco, 1991-2000, Christopher Clark Galleries, San Francisco, 2001, Windsor Fine Art, New Orleans, 2002, Hospic Mask Project, 2002; represented in permanent collections Monterey Inst. Internat. Studies, San Francisco Hist. Soc. Bd. mem., historian Los Altos Art Club. Recipient 1st place Santa Clara Valley Hist. Landmarks, 1963, 2nd place oil award Cupertino Fine Arts Exhibit, 1964, Best of Show award West Valley Hist. Soc. Art Show, 1967, 1st annual prize Provincetown Art Assn., 1983; guest of hon. Acad. Jacques Boitiat, Barbizon, France, 1992. Mem. Musée de la Grenovillere-Croissy sur Seine, Nat. Mus. Women in the Arts. Avocations: travel, family, reading, gardening, crafts. Home: 1285 Portland Ave Los Altos CA 94024

SPANGLER, EDRA MILDRED, clinical psychologist; b. Webbville, Ky., Sept. 6, 1941; d. Chester A. and Laura B. (Webb) Sawyer; m. Robert Noel Spangler, Sept. 6, 1959; children: Robert Mark Spangler, Kendra Lynn Lovett. AS in Bus. Adminstrn., Franklin U., 1975; BA in Social Psychology, Park Coll., 1979; MA in Mgmt. and Supervision, Ctrl. Mich. U., 1980; D in Psychology, Wright State U., 1989. Lic. psychologist Ohio, Fla.; diplomate clin. hypnotherapy; diplomate Am. Bd. Psychol. Specialties in Med. Psychology, Forensic Clin. Psychology and Neuropsychology. With adminstrn., mgmt., fin. and computer sys. design various pvt. and govt. orgns., 1958-85; psychology assoc. Stonegate Psychol. Assocs., Columbus, Ohio, 1989-91; dir. pain & stress program The Rehab. Ctr., Columbus, 1991-94; pvt. practice, 1991—; mem. med. staff Riverside Meth. Hosps., Columbus, 1992—, health psychologist, 1993-95, Mind/Body Med. Inst., 1993-95; mem. med. staff Grady Meml. Hosp., Delaware, Ohio, 1997—. Fellow Biofeedback Cert. Inst. of Am.; mem. Am. Pain Soc., Am. Coll. Forensic Examiners, Ohio Psychol. Assn., Fla. Psychol. Assn., Assn. Applied Psychophysiology and Biofeedback. Avocations: reading, travel, hiking, family, research in mind/body. Office: Wedgewood Behavioral Health 4141 N Hampton Dr Powell OH 43065-7550

SPANGLER, MARY, college president; BA, Chestnut Hill Coll.; MA in English, UCLA, DEdn, 1994. Prof. English L.A. Valley Coll., assoc. dean of admissions, dean of student svcs., v.p. acad. affairs, pres., 1997—. Adj. faculty Sch. of Edn. Nat. U.; presenter in field. Co-author four textbooks; contbr. articles to profl. jours. Mem. exec. edn. coun. U. Phoenix; adv. com. edn. svcs. C.C. League of Calif.; state chancellor Calif. C.C.; adv. com. Calif. Acad. Partnership Program. Mem. Hollywood C. of C. (bd. dirs.), Am. Assn. for Higher Edn., Nat. Coun. for Rsch. and Planning, Assn. for Rsch. on Nonprofit Orgns. and Vol. Action, Assn. of Calif. C.C. Adminstrs., Pi Lambda Theta. Office: Los Angeles City Coll 855 N Vermont Ave Los Angeles CA 90029-3516

SPANGLER, NITA REIFSCHNEIDER, volunteer; b. Ukiah, Calif., Apr. 17, 1923; d. John Charles and Olga Augusta (Wuertz) Reifschneider; m. Raymond Luper Spangler, Sept. 22, 1946 (dec.); children: Jon Martin, Mary Raymond, Thor Raymond. BA, Univ. Nev., 1944. News reporter Redwood (Calif.) City Tribune, 1944-46, Country Almanac, Woodside, Calif., 1969-77. Mem. bd. dirs. San Mateo (Calif.) County Hist. Assn., 1961-68, pres., 1964-66; founder, 1st pres. Portolá Expedition Bicentennial Found., 1966-70; chmn. San Mateo County Scenic Rds. Com., 1967-76; mem. San Mateo County Hist. Resource Adv.; mem. commn. San Mateo County Parks and Recreation, 1983-97, past chmn.; cons. hwy. aesthetics Cal Trans., 1981-83; mem. sch. coms. Recipient Commendation, County Bd. Suprs., 1968, 1977, 92. Mem. Sierra Club, Western History Assn., Mormon History Assn., Nev. State Hist. Soc. (life), San Mateo County Hist. Assn. (life), Resolution of Thanks 1968, 76, 94), Friends Redwood City, Kappa Alpha Theta. Democrat. Episcopalian. Avocation: historic preservation. Home: 970 Edgewood Rd Redwood City CA 94062-1818

SPANGLER, RONALD LEROY, retired television executive, aircraft executive, automobile collector; b. York, Pa., Mar. 5, 1937; s. Ivan L. and Sevilla (Senft) S.; m. Svetlana Gavrilova; children: Kathleen, Ronald Jr., Beth Anne, Pavel. Student, U. Miami (Fla.), 1955-59. Radio announcer Sta. WSBA, York, 1955-59; TV prodr. Sta. WBAL-TV, Balt. and NBC TV, 1958-65; pres., chmn. bd. LewRon Television, N.Y.C., Hollywood, Calif., 1965-78, Spanair Inc.; distbr. Rockwell bus. aircraft, 1975-85. Owner Prancing Horse Farm; collector, dealer, racer vintage and modern Ferrari automobiles; racer numerous courses including LeMans, Daytona, Sebring; Ferrari cons. (PBS show) Motorweek; cons. Bentley Motor Cars, Pininfarina S.P.A. Mem. Video Tape Producers Assn. N.Y.C., Rolls Royce Owners Club, Ferrari Clubs Am. and Italia, Mercedes Benz Club Am., Porsche Club Am. Home: Prancing Horse Farm 3710 Ady Rd Street MD 21154-1432 Office Phone: 410-452-5500. Personal E-mail: PHFarmFerrari@aol.com.

SPANGLER, STANLEY EUGENE, international relations educator; b. Billings, Mont., Apr. 7, 1929; s. John Harold Spangler and Winifred Watt; m. Addie Belle Moore, Sept. 21, 1968; children: John Wayland Spangler, Julia Watt Spangler Garlatz. BA, U. Mont., 1952; MA, Columbia U., 1958; PhD, U. N.C., 1978. Program officer Asia Found., San Francisco, 1960-65; assoc. regional dir. Fgn. Policy Assn., Atlanta, 1965-69; dir. Office Pub. and Internat. Affairs U. N.C. Extension Divsn., Chapel Hill, 1969-73; exec. dir. World Affairs Coun. Boston, 1973-81; internat. program advisor Fletcher Sch. Law and Diplomacy, Medford, Mass., 1983-84; sr. fellow Air Univ. USAF, 1984-89; Sec. of Navy sr. fellow U.S. Naval War Coll., Newport, R.I., 1989-92, sr. fellow, prof. strategy, 1993—. Prof. govt. and fgn. affairs Bentley Coll., Waltham, Mass., 1995—; commr. U.S. Nat. Commn. for UNESCO, Washington, 1976-81; pres. Nat. Coun. World Affairs Orgns., Washington, 1977-80; mem. editl. adv. bd. Fgn. Policy Assn., N.Y.C., 1975-78; exec. mem. Nat. Def. Exec. Res., Washington, 1980-97. Author: Force and Accommodation in World Politics, 1991; contbr. articles to profl. jours. Dir. Curtis-Saval Internat. Ctr., Boston, 1976-81; mem. exec. com., bd. dirs. Ala. World Affairs Coun., Montgomery, 1986-89; bd. dirs. Ctr. for Internat. Visitors, Boston, 1978-81; mem. African studies adv. com. Boston U., 1978-80. Capt. USAF, 1954-56. Johns Hopkins U. fellow, 1952-53; Columbia U. scholar, 1957-58. Mem. AAUP, Am. Polit. Sci. Assn., Boston Com. on Fgn. Rels., Phi Beta Delta. Democrat. Methodist. Avocations: hiking, writing, travel, reading. Home: 17 Kings Way Scituate MA 02066-2609 E-mail: s.spangler@comcast.net.

SPANIER, GRAHAM BASIL, university president; b. Capetown, South Africa, July 18, 1948; s. Fred and Rosadele (Lurie) Spanier; m. Sandra Kay Whipple, Sept. 11, 1971; children: Brian Lockwood, Hadley Alison. BS, Iowa State U., 1969, MS, 1971; PhD, Northwestern U., 1973. Assoc. dean, prof. in charge Pa. State U., University Park, 1973—82, pres., 1995—; vice-provost, prof. SUNY, Stony Brook, 1982—86; provost, v.p. for acad. affairs Oreg. State U., 1986—91; chancellor U. Nebr., Lincoln, 1991—95. Chmn. Presdl. Adv. Group on Info. Tech., 1997—99, Kellogg Commn. on Future of State and Land-Grant Univs., 1997—2000; bd. dirs. Univ. Corp. for Advanced Internet Devel., U.S. Dept. Edn. Commn. on Opportunity in Athletics, 2002—03; host TV and radio programs, 1973—2003; bd. dirs. Citizens Bank of Pa.; vice-chmn. Worldwide U. Network, 2003—. Founding editor: Jour. Family Issues. Del. White House Conf. on Families, Washington, 1980; Pres., chmn. bd. dirs. Christian Children's Fund, Richmond, Va., 1985—94; bd. dirs. Nat. 4H Coun., 1997—2000. Named Outstanding Young Alumnus, Iowa State U., 1982; Woodrow Wilson fellow, 1972. Mem.: Assn. Am. Univs. (com. intellectual property 1997—), Acad. Health Ctrs. (commn. on future of acad. health ctrs. 1996—98), Am. Assn. State Colls. and Univs. (joint commn. on accountability report 1993—95), Nat. Collegiate Athletic Assn. (pres. commn. 1995—97, bd. dirs., exec. com. 1997—2001, divsn. I bd. dirs., chmn. 1998—2001), Am. Coun. on Edn. (commn. on women 1992—95), Nat. Assn. State Univs. and Land Grant Colls. (exec. com. coun. on acad. affairs 1990—91, bd. pres. commn. on info. technologies 1993—99, chmn. 1996—99, bd. dirs. 1997—, chmn. coun. of pres. 1999—2000, bd. chair 2002), Am. Assn. Family and Consumer Scis. (Moran award 1972), Am. Sociol. Assn. (family sect. chmn. 1983—84), Population Assn. Am., Nat. Coun. Family Rels. (pres. 1987—88, Outstanding Grad. Student award 1972), Am. Assn. for Marriage and Family Therapy, Worldwide Univs. Network (vice chair 2003—). Democrat. Avocations: aviation, magic, athletics, public broadcasting. Office: Pa State Univ Office of Pres 201 Old Main University Park PA 16802-1503

SPANIOLO, JAMES D. academic administrator; b. 1946; m. Sally Spaniolo; children: Jamie, Sarah. BA in Polit. Sci., Mich. State U., 1968; MPA, JD, U. Mich., 1975. Asst. to pres. Mich. State U., 1970—72; atty. Paul & Thompson, Miami, Fla., 1975—77; staff counsel The Miami Herald, 1977—78, gen. counsel, 1979—83, gen. exec., 1983—85; assoc. gen. counsel Am. Newspaper Pubs. Assn., Washington, 1978—79; v.p. human resources, asst. to pub. Detroit Free Press, 1985—89; v.p., chief program officer John S. and James L. Knight Found., 1986—96; dean Coll. Comm. Arts and Scis. Mich. State U., 1996—2004; pres. U. Tex., Arlington, 2004—. Mem. journalism adv. bd. John S. and James L. Knight Found.; mem. accrediting com. Accrediting Coun. on Edn. and Journalism and Mass Comm. Mem. nat. bd. dirs. Mich. State U. Alumni Assn. Office: U Tex PO Box 19088 Arlington TX 76019-0088*

SPANN, GEORGE WILLIAM, management consultant; b. Cuthbert, Ga., July 21, 1946; s. Glinn Linwood and Mary Grace (Hiller) S.; m. Laura Jeanne Nason, June 10, 1967; children: Tanya Lynne, Stephen William. BS in Physics with honors, Ga. Inst. Tech., 1968, MS, 1970, MS in Indsl. Mgmt., 1973. Engr. Martin Marietta Corp., Orlando, Fla., 1968-70; rsch. scientist Engring. Exptl. Sta., Ga. Inst. Tech., 1970-75; v.p., dir. Metrics, Inc., mgmt. and engring. cons., Atlanta, 1973-78, pres., dir., 1978—; v.p., dir. Exec. Data Sys., Inc., 1981—. Mem. Ga. Energy Policy Coun., Ga. Metrication Coun., NASA applications survey group for Landsat follow-on; mem. com. on practical applications of remote sensing from space Space Applications Bd. NRC; market rsch. cons. NOAA, NASA, pvt. cos. Author papers, reports to profl. publs. Regents scholar, 1964. Mem. Am. Soc. Photogrammetry, Urban and Regional Info. Sys. Assn., Atlanta Jaycees, Tau Beta Pi, Phi Kappa Phi, Sigma Pi Sigma. Home: 3475 Clubland Dr Marietta GA 30068-2509 Office: Bldg 14 1640 Powers Ferry Rd SE Marietta GA 30067-5491

SPANN, LAWRENCE HENRY (CHIP SPANN), physician associate; b. Buffalo, Jan. 23, 1951; s. Lawrence Henry and Mildred Mary (Dotterweich) S.; m. Elizabeth Robinson, Oct. 4, 1996. BA in English, U. Miami, Coral Gables, Fla., 1974; BS in Health Scis., Duke Univ., 1982; MS in Health Scis., Duke U., 1992; PhD, Union Inst. and Univ., 2003. Cert. exercise program dir. Am. Coll. Sports Medicine, physician asst. Nat. Commn. Cert. Physician Assts. Physician assoc. coagulation svcs. Duke U. Med. Ctr., Durham, NC,

1996—2000, sr. physician assoc., 1982-88, 96-00; sr. physician assoc., program dir. Heart Disease Reversal Clinic, Durham, 1993-96; program dir. St. Francis Hosp., Greenville, S.C., 1988-91; exec. dir. Preventive Med. Rsch. Inst., Sausalito, Calif., 1991-93; dir. LAMP (Lit., Arts and Medicine Program) Sutter Med. Ctr., Sacramento, 2001—. Co-author: (chpt.) Interventional Cardiology, 1994; contbr. articles to profl. jours.; compiler, editor Poet Healer: Contemporary Poems for Health and Healing, 2004. Fellow Am. Assn. Cardiovasc. Pulmonary Rehab., Am. Acad. Physician Asst.; mem. Am. Heart Assn. Avocations: poetry, writing, creative expression. Office: 2522 E St Sacramento CA 95816 E-mail: lifebard@aol.com.

SPANNER, ROBERT ALAN, lawyer; b. Cleve., Mar. 27, 1948; s. Bernard L. and Gertrude (Wolkov) Shimberg. B.A., Stanford U., 1970, J.D., 1973. Bar: Calif. 1974, Ill. 1974, U.S. Dist. Ct. (no. dist.) Ill. 1974, (no. dist.) Calif. 1977; U.S. Ct. Appeals (7th cir.) 1974, (9th cir.) 1978. Law clk. Alaska Supreme Ct., Juneau, 1973-74; assoc. Jenner & Block, Chgo., 1974-77, Severson, Werson, Berke & Melchior, San Francisco, 1977-83; prin. Beckford, Spanner & Kelley, Palo Alto, Calif., 1983—; pub. mem. instl. biosafety com. U. Calif.-San Francisco, 1977-81. Author: Who Owns Innovation+19, 1984; also articles in computer and bus. jours. Adv. Criminal Justice Adv. Com., San Francisco, 1981-83, Adv. Com. to 9th Circuit on Anti-Trust Pattern Jury Instrns., 1982; bd. advisors Gorilla Found., 1981— . Mem. Am. Electronics Assn. (lawyers com.). Office: Beckford Spanner & Kelley Two Embarcadero 2200 Geng Rd Palo Alto CA 94303

SPANNHAKE, ERNST WILLIAM, medical educator, academic administrator; PhD, U. Md., 1975. Prof. physiology Johns Hopkins U., Balt., assoc. chair dept. environ. health scis. Office: Johns Hopkins U Dept Environ Health Scis 615 N Wolfe St Baltimore MD 21205-2103

SPANNINGER, BETH ANNE, lawyer; b. Bucks County, Pa., July 3, 1950; d. Feryl Louis and Nancy Elizabeth (Hendricks) S. AB magna cum laude, Muhlenberg Coll., 1972; MA, MEd, Lehigh U., 1975; JD, Temple U., 1979. Bar: Pa. 1979. Asst. dist. atty. Phila. Dist. Atty.'s Office, 1979-81; assoc. Bolger, Picker, Hankin & Tannenbaum, Phila., 1981-86, ptnr., 1986-88; sr. counsel SmithKline Beecham Corp., Phila., 1988-96; v.p., assoc. gen. counsel Glaxosmithkline, Phila., 1996—. Mem. ABA, Pa. Bar Assn., Phila. Bar Assn. (law com. 1992—), Phi Beta Kappa. Avocations: literature, jogging, theater, piano. E-mail: beth.a.spanninger@gsk.com.

SPANO, ROBERT, conductor; b. Conneaut, Ohio, May 7, 1961; Grad., Oberlin Conservatory Music; student, Curtis Inst. Music. Asst. condr. Boston Symphony Orch., 1990-93; faculty Oberlin (Ohio) Conservatory of Music, 1989—; music dir. Bklyn. Philharm. Orch., 1996—; musical dir. Atlanta Symphony Orch., Atlanta, Ga., 2000—. Faculty mem. Tanglewood Music Ctr., head conducting fellowship program, 1998—; guest condr. Boston Symphony Orch., Chgo. Symphony Orch., Cleve. Orch., L.A. Philharm., Nat. Symphony Orch., Phila. Orch., Royal Opera Covent Gardens, Welsh Nat. Opera, Orch. Filharmonica della Scala, City of Birmingham Symphony. Office: Atlanta Symphony Orch 1293 Peachtree St NE Ste 300 Atlanta GA 30309-3552

SPANOS, ALEXANDER GUS, construction company owner, professional sports team owner; b. Stockton, Calif., Sept. 28, 1923; m. Faye Spanos; children: Dean, Dea Spanos Berberian, Alexis Spanos Ruhl, Michael. LLD (hon.), U. Pacific, 1984. Chmn. bd. dirs. A.G. Spanos Constrn. Inc., Stockton, Calif., 1960—; chmn. bd. dirs. A.G. Spanos Mgmt. Inc., Stockton, Calif., 1967—, A.G. Spanos Enterprises Inc., Stockton, Calif., 1971—, A.G. Spanos Devel. Inc., Stockton, Calif., 1973—, A.G. Spanos Realty Inc., Stockton, Calif., 1978—, A.G.S. Fin. Corp., Stockton, Calif., 1980—, A.G. Spanos Securities Corp., Stockton, Calif., 1981—, San Diego Chargers, 1984—. Former trustee Children's Hosp., San Francisco, San Francisco Fine Arts Mus.; trustee Eisenhower Med. Ctr., Rancho Mirage, Calif.; hon. regent U. Pacific, Stockton, 1972-82; gov. USO, Washington, 1982—; former gov. Ronald Reagan Presdl. Found.; chmn. U.S. chpt. U.S. Greece bus. coun. Served with USAF, 1942-46. Recipient Albert Gallatin award Zurich-Am. Ins. Co., 1973, Horatio Alger award Horatio Alger Found., 1982, medal of Honor Statue of Liberty-Ellis Islan Found., 1982. Mem. Am. Hellenic Ednl. Progressive Assn., Calif. C. of C. (bd. dirs. 1980-85). Republican. Greek Orthodox. Avocation: golf. Office: San Diego Chargers Qualcomm Stadium PO Box 609609 San Diego CA 92160-9609 also: A G Spanos Cos Ste 1A 1341 West Robinhood Dr Stockton CA 95207 E-mail: agspr@agspanos.com.

SPANOS, DEAN A. professional sports team executive; b. Stockton, Calif., May 26, 1950; s. Alex G. Spanos; m. Susan Spanos; children: Alexander Gus, John Dean. BBA, U. Pacific, 1972. Pres., vice-chmn. San Diego Chargers, 1984—; pres. Spanos corp. entities; vice-chmn. AGS Fin. Corp. 1969. Co-winning team in Sr.'s Reunion Tournament, Dallas, 1985. Past bd. regents U. Pacific. Named co-winner, Bing Crosby Nat. Pro-Am. Golf Tournament, 1985, winner, Bob Hope Chrysler Classic, 1990, 1991, AT&T Nat. Pro-Am. Golf Tournament, 1990; recipient Most Valuable Amateur trophy. Avocation: golf. Office: San Diego Chargers 4020 Murphy Canyon Rd San Diego CA 92123-4407

SPANOS, POL DIMITRIOS, engineering educator; b. Messini, Peloponnesus, Greece, Feb. 27, 1950; came to U.S., 1973; s. Dimitrios Constandin Spanos and Aicaterine Polychronis Bonaros; children: Demetri, Eudokia. Diploma in mech. engring., Nat. Tech. U., Athens, 1973; MSCE, Calif. Inst. Tech., 1974, PhD in Applied Mechanics, 1976. Registered profl. engr., Tex., Greece. Rsch. asst. Calif. Inst. Tech., Pasadena, 1973-76, rsch. fellow, 1976-77; from asst. prof. to assoc. prof. U. Tex.-Austin, 1981-84, P.D. Henderson assoc. prof. engring., 1983-84; prof. mech. engring. and civil engring. Rice U., Houston, 1984-88, L.B. Ryon endowed chair in engring., 1988—. Cons. on analytical and numerical applications of theory of dynamics and vibrations, worldwide. Author: Random Vibrations, Probabilistic Offshore Mechanics, Probabilistic Methods in Civil Engineering, Random Vibration and Statistical Linearization, Dynamic Analysis of Non-Linear Structures by the Method of Statistical Quadratization, Stochastic Finite Elements: A Spectral Approach, Computational Stochastic Mechanics, Probabilistic Structural Mechanics: Advances in Structural Reliability Methods, Random Vibrations: A Broad Perspective; contbr. to profl. jour. issues devoted to dynamics and vibrations; mem. editl. bd. 8 jours.; editor-in chief or co-editor 2 primary jours. on mechanics. Recipient European award of sci. N.V. Phillipps Co., Eindhoven, Netherlands, 1969, Presdl. Young Investigator award in earthquake engring. NSF, 1984-89, Cert. merit McDonnell Douglas Astronautics Co., Houston, 1987, G.R. Brown award for superior tchg. Rice U., 1995, 96, Newmark medal for lifetime contbns. to dynamics and vibrations ASCE, 1999; named hon. citizen, Messini, Greece, 2002; inducted into The Acad. of Athens, Greece, 2003. Fellow ASCE, AAM, ASME (participant tech. confs. and coms., Pi Tau Sigma Gold medal 1982, W.L. Huber Civil Engring. Rsch. prize 1989, G.L. Larson Meml. award 1991, Alfred M. Freudenthal medal 1992, Humboldt Rsch. award 1995, Disting. Lectr. 1997—, Newmark medal 1999, Theodore Von Karman medal 2003); mem. Am. Acad. Mechanics, Earthquake Engring. Rsch. Inst., Internat. Assn. for Structural Safety and Reliability (rsch. prize in the area of stochastic dynamics 1997), Hellenic Profl. Soc. (sponsor scholarship com.), A. von Humboldt Assn. Am. (life). Office: Rice U Dept Mech Engring MS 321 PO Box 1892 Houston TX 77251-1892 Fax: (713) 348-5191. E-mail: spanos@rice.edu.

SPANOVICH, MILAN, retired civil engineer; b. Steubenville, Ohio, Feb. 19, 1929; s. Stanley and Katherine (Komazec) S.; m. Sylvia J. Tomko, Apr. 16, 1971. BS Civil Engring, Carnegie-Mellon U., 1956, MS Civil Engring., 1957. Registered profl. engr., Pa., Ohio, Va., W.Va., Mich., Ky., N.J. Instr. Carnegie-Mellon U., 1957-60; charter assoc., v.p. E. D'Appolonia Assocs., 1957-61; mem. civil engring. staff U. N.Mex., 1961-63; founder, sr. cons. Engring. Mechs., Inc., Pitts., 1963-96. Contbr. articles on soil mechs. to tech. jours.; patentee found. systems. Bd. dirs. Carnegie Mellon U. Andrew Carnegie Soc. Recipient Pitts. Young Civil Engr. of Yr. award, 1969 Fellow ASCE (Pitts. Civl Engr. of the Yr. 1987, chmn. numerous coms.), Am. Cons. Engrs. Council; mem. Cons. Engrs. Council Greater Pitts. (pres. 1972-74), Engring. Soc. Western Pa. (dir. 1972, 77-83), Nat. Soc. Profl. Engrs., Pa. Soc. Profl. Engrs. (pres. Pitts. chpt. 1971, Hornfeck award Pitts. chpt. 1979, state dir. 1976-79, Disting. Service award Pitts. chpt. 1985, Pa. Engr. of the Yr. 1988, Profl. Devel. award 1989, Outstanding Svc. award Pitts. chpt. 1993), ASTM (chmn. task com. on relative density of granular soils 1959-63), Am. Concrete Inst., Hwy. Research Bd., Internat. Soc. Soil Mechs. and Found. Engring., Pitts. Geol. Soc., Am. Arbitration Assn., Profl. Engrs. in Pvt. Practice (chmn. 1970-71), Pitts. Builders Exchange, Soc. Explosives Engrs., Am. Soc. Hwy. Engrs., Carnegie-Mellon U. Alumni Assn. (mem. planning com.), Chi Epsilon Nat. Civil Engring. Honor Soc.

SPANSKY, ROBERT ALAN, retired computer systems analyst; b. Hamtramck, Mich., July 29, 1942; s. Harry Joseph and Alicia Eileen (Kossak) S. BS, U. Detroit, 1964, MBA, 1967. Asst. br. mgr. Nat. Bank Detroit, 1965-67, sr. asst. br. mgr., 1969-71; computer programmer Ford Motor Co., Dearborn, Mich., 1972-76, sys. analyst, project leader, 1976-99; ret., 1999. Active in food delivery to elderly Focus Hope, Detroit, 1990—2001; chmn. 75th anniversary reunion dinner dance St. Matthew Parish, 2002. Sgt. U.S. Army, 1967—69, Vietnam. Recipient 25-Yr. Svc. award Alpha Kappa Psi/Ford Motor Co., 1987, 97; decorated Commendation medal. Mem. Assn. MBAs, Elks, Alpha Kappa Psi (chmn. Detroit centennial celebration 2004, Disting. Svc. award 1967, 83, 91). Roman Catholic. Avocations: coin collecting/numismatics, stamp collecting/philately, landscaping. Home: 5574 Haverhill St Detroit MI 48224-3245 Personal E-mail: rspansky@msn.com.

SPANTON, WILLIAM FLOYD, ins. co. exec., lawyer; b. Cleve., Aug. 1, 1918; s. William Timothy and Ethel Osty (Schramm) S.; m. Margaret M. Schleyer, Aug. 19, 1943. B.A., Yale U., 1939, LL.B., 1942. Bar: N.Y. 1946, Del. 1953, Minn. 1965. Assoc. Root, Ballantine, Harlan, Busby & Palmer, N.Y.C., 1946-48; house counsel Gen. Baking Co., N.Y.C., 1948-51; asst. counsel and sec. Continental Am. Life Ins. Co., Wilmington, Del., 1953-65; gen. counsel and sr. v.p., sec. Northwestern Nat. Life Ins. Co., Mpls., 1965-83; ret., 1983; legal cons. Mut. Service Ins., St. Paul, 1983— . Served to col. USAAF, 1941-45, 50-52. Mem. ABA, N.Y. State Bar Assn., Minn. Bar Assn., Del. Bar Assn., Assn. Life Ins. Counsel, Minn. Life and Health Ins. Guaranty Assn., Ins. Fedn. Minn. Republican. Episcopalian. Lodge: Masons. Home: 2242 Prince Ln Naples FL 34112-5345

SPARACINO, PHILIP WILLIAM, psychotherapist, consultant; s. Philip Napoli and Tina Sparacino. BA in English, Adelphi U., 1975; MA in Drama and Theatre, Queens Coll., 1984. Cert. critical incident stress mgmt.-advanced CISM II Internat. Critical Incident Stress Found. English tchr. Locust Valley (N.Y.) H.S., 1980—81; adj. instr. acting Adelphi U., Garden City, NY, 1981—82; pvt. tchr. acting Garden City, 1982—85; dir. Sara's Ctr., Great Neck, NY, 1985—89; tchr., tutor Creative Tutoring, Inc., Plainview, NY, 1989—97; clin. practitioner drama therapy Family Svc. League, Huntington, NY, 1997—. Lectr. speaking poetry Dowling Coll., Oakdale, NY, 1994, Oakdale, 95, Oakdale, 97; cons. drama therapy United Cerebral Palsy Suffolk, Hauppauge, NY, 2002—. Author poetry. Avocations: bodybuilding, antique weapons. Home: 5 Hemlock Ave Huntington NY 11743

SPARBERG, MARSHALL STUART, gastroenterologist, educator; b. Chgo., May 20, 1936; s. Max Shane and Mildred Rose (Haffron) S.; m. Eve Gaymont Enda, Mar. 15, 1987. BA, Northwestern U., 1957, MD, 1960. Intern Evanston Hosp., Ill., 1960-61; resident in internal medicine Barnes Hosp., St. Louis, 1961-63; fellow U. Chgo., 1963-65; practice medicine specializing in gastroenterolgy Chgo., 1967—; asst. prof. medicine Northwestern U., 1967-72, assoc. prof., 1972-80, prof. medicine, 1980—; instr. Wash. U., St. Louis, 1961-63, U. Chgo., 1963-65. Author: Ileostomy Care, 1969, Primer of Clinical Diagnosis, 1972, Ulcerative Colitis, 1978, Inflammatory Bowel Disease, 1982; contbr. numerous articles to profl. jours. Pres. Fine Arts Music Found., 1974-76, Crohn's Disease and Colitis Found. of Am., pres. Ill. chpt., 1994-97; bd. dirs. Lyric Opera Guild, 1974-94, Chamber Music Soc. North Shore Chgo., 1984—; physician to Chgo. Symphony Orch., 1981-97. With USAF, 1965-67. Named Outstanding Tchr. Northwestern U. Med. Sch., 1972 Mem. AMA, ACP, Am. Gastroent. Assn., Am. Coll. Gastroent. (bd. govs.), Chgo. Med. Soc., Chgo. Soc. Internal Medicine, Chgo. Soc. Gastroenterology (pres.), Chgo. Soc. Gastrointestinal Endoscopy (pres.) Office: 676 N Saint Clair St Ste 1525 Chicago IL 60611-2862 Office Phone: 312-944-7080.

SPARER, MALCOLM MARTIN, rabbi; b. N.Y.C. m. Erna Reichl (dec. Sept. 1990); children: Ruth, Arthur (dec.), Jennifer, Shoshana. AB, M in Hebrew Lit., Yeshiva U.; MA in Sociology, CCNY; cert. in pastoral counseling, Des Moines Coll. Osteopathic Medicine; PhD in Sociology, NYU. Ordained rabbi, 1953. Pres. Menorah Inst., San Francisco, 1981—; exec. dir. Rabbinical Coun. Calif., L.A., 1957-66; chaplain U. Pa.; adminstr. Tchr's. Coll. of West Coast, Torah U. (now Yeshiva U.), 1957-66; rabbi Beth El Jacob, Des Moines, 1966-69, Chevra Thilim, San Francisco, 1969-72. Pres. No. Calif. Bd. Rabbis, 1977-96, pres. emeritus, 1996—; sr. lectr. San Francisco C.C.; liason Union of Orthodox Jewish Congregations Am., 1957-66, moderator radio series Lest We Forget, 1962, moderator TV spls. Sta. KNXT, L.A., 1964-65, Des Moines, 1967-69; instr. dept. philosophy Drake U., 1966-69; pres. San Francisco dist. Zionist Orgn. Am., 1969-82, also bd. dirs.; chmn., mem. nat. bd. San Francisco Bay Area Zionist Fedn., 1971-84; co-chmn. Jerusalem Fair, 25th Ann. State of Israel, 1973; chmn. Commn. on Soviet Jewry, Jewish Cmty. Rels. Coun., 1974-81; cons. internat. leaders, founder Menorah Inst.; cons. Commn. on Christian-Jewish and Moslem Rels. to European Parliament Nations; cons. in field; writer, lectr. colls., ch. groups on Judaica and world affairs; chmn. dept. world affairs/internat. politics C.C. San Francisco; former chaplain Letterman Army VA Hosp., San Francisco Presidio; co-founder Black and Jewish Clergy; mem. San Francisco Coun. Chs., bd. dirs. food bank program, United Jewish Appeal, chmn. rabbinic cabinet of western region; invited mem. del. bishops and ch. leaders various denominations conducting meml. svc. at Dachau on 50th ann. Reich's Kristallnacht, Fed. Republic Germany, 1988. Hon. chmn. Mayor's Commn. on Holocaust Meml., San Francisco; mem. Mayor's Task Force for Homeless; co-chmn. Gov.'s Family Task Force, San Francisco. With USN, WWII, Korean War, chaplain USAF. Annual Jerusalem Lectr. Series named in his honor, 1998. Address: PO Box 15055 San Francisco CA 94115-0055

SPARGO, BENJAMIN H. educator, renal pathologist; b. Six Mile Run, Pa., Aug. 11, 1919; s. Benjamin H. and Lillian (Rankin) S.; m. Barbara Scollard, Mar. 12, 1942; children— Janet, Patricia. BS in Biol. Scis, U. Chgo., 1948, MS in Pathology, MD with honors, U. Chgo., 1952. Intern Univ. Hosp., Ann Arbor, Mich., 1953-54; resident pathology U. Chgo. Med. Sch., 1954-55, mem. faculty, 1954—, prof. renal pathology, 1964-95; prof. pathology emeritus, 1995—; assoc. chmn. dept., 1974-80. Cons. Armed Forces Inst. Pathology, 1975-79, Midwest Regional Organ Bank of Ill., 1989-94. Served with USAAF, 1941-46. Recipient Rsch. Career award Nat. Heart Inst., 1964-99, Disting. Svc. award Kidney Found. Ill., 1991, Disting. Lifetime Achievement award Renal Pathology Soc., 1996. Mem.: US-Can. Acad. Pathology (chmn. edn. com. 1975—77). Home: 5550 S South Shore Dr Chicago IL 60637-5051

SPARGO, CAROLYN MARIE, language educator, music educator; b. Mpls., Minn., June 14, 1957; d. Ragnar Johnson and Kathlyn Emma Bradford Johnson; m. Lawrence Edward Spargo, Oct. 3, 1981; children: Antonio Lorenzo, Annika Lena, Thomas Ragnar. B.A. in Music Edn., Augsburg Coll., 1980, MA in Leadership, 2004. Nat. Guild Piano Teachers, Tex., 1975, cert. Minn. State Bd. Edn., 1980, Music Teachers Nat. Assn., Ohio, 1980, Minn. Music Teachers Assn., 1980, cert. music tchr. Wis. State Bd. Edn., 1999. Pvt. piano tchr. Spargo Music Studio, Mpls., 1975—; preschool music Minn., 1976—; missionary, 1996—98; Swedish lang. tchr., 1999—; pub. sch. tchr. Amery Schs., Wis., 1999—2002; swedish lang. tchr. Wis. Indianhead Tech. Coll., Amery, Wis., 2000—; choir dir. Home Schoolers and Cmty. Edn., Minn., 2002—. Mentor Lilly Grant Alumni Mentorship Program, Augsburg Coll., 2003—. Advancement chmn. Boy Scouts of Am., Amery, Wis., 1999—2003, crew advisor, 2001—, com. chair, 2003—. Recipient Concordia Lang. Villages 5 Yr. Citation of Excellence Award, Concordia Coll., 1999 - 2003, Scouter Tng. Award, Boy Scouts of Am., 2002. Mem.: Minn. Music Teachers Forum (assoc.; newsletter editor 1990—93), Augsburg Parent Adv. Bd. (assoc.; represent student commuters 2002—), ASI Spelmanslag Swedish fiddle (assoc.), Am. Swedish Inst. (assoc.; Spelmanslag youth fiddle scholarship com. 2004—07, Svea club pres. 2004—), SWEA Internat. (assoc.), Svenska Klubben (assoc.; pres. 2002—03), Vasa Order of Am. (assoc.; vice chmn. 2001—03, 25 Yrs. 2001—, 30 Yrs.). Mem. Christian Ch. Avocations: swedish folk fiddling, travel, ice skating, swimming, golf. Home: 3225 McKnight Rd Chaska MN 55318 Personal E-mail: spargo@usfamily.net.

SPARKMAN, STEVEN LEONARD, lawyer; b. Sarasota, Fla., May 30, 1947; s. Simeon Clarence and Ursula (Wahlstrom) S.; m. Terry Jeanne Gibbs, Aug. 23, 1969; children: Joanna Jeanne, Kevin Leonard. BA, Fla. State U., 1969, JD, 1972. Bar: Fla. 1972, U.S. Dist. Ct. (mid. dist.) Fla. 1974, U.S. Ct. Appeals (5th cir.) 1975. Legal rsch. asst. Office Gen. Counsel, Fla. Dept. Revenue, Tallahassee, 1971; legis. intern com. on cmty. affairs Fla. Ho. of Reps., Tallahassee, 1971-72; jud. rsch. aide Fla. 2d Dist. Ct. Appeals, Lakeland, 1972-73; asst. county atty. Hillsborough County, Tampa, Fla., 1973-75; assoc. Carlton, Fields, Ward, Emmanuel, Smith & Cutler, P.A., Tampa, 1975-80, sr. atty., 1980-2001; pvt. practice Plant City, Fla., 2001—. Mem. bd. visitors Fla. State U. Coll. Law, 1994-2000. Trustee Fla. Bapt. Children's Homes, Inc., 2004—; deacon 1st Bapt. Ch., Plant City, 1980—; sec., bd. dirs. Bapt. Towers Plant City, Inc., 1981—84; bd. dirs. Tampa Kiwanis Found., 1997—2000. 1st lt. USAFR, 1973. Mem.: ABA, Plant City Bar Assn. (sec. treas 2003—), Fla. Bar Assn. (exec. coun. local govt. law sect. 1978—79), Kiwanis (Plant City, bd. dirs. 2003—). Democrat. Office: Steven L Sparkman PA 212 N Collins St Ste 1 Plant City FL 33563 Office Phone: 813-759-1444. E-mail: sls@sparklaw.com.

SPARKS, BENNETT SHER, military officer; b. Pitts., Oct. 10, 1925; s. Julius and Anna K. Sparks; m. Elizabeth Regina Sparks, May 8, 1943; children: Bennett Sher Jr., James Robert, Richard T.(dec.), John N., Julieann, Donna Beth(dec.). Diploma, Navy War Coll., 1973, Army War Coll., 1988, Armed Forces Staff Coll., 1978, Nat. War Coll., 1978; PhD in Philosophy (hon.), Sampson U., Oxford, Eng., 1986. Lic. aircraft pilot. Commd. ensign USCG, 1957, advanced through grades to rear admiral, 1985, reserve inspector 11th Coast Guard Dist., sr. res. officer Pacific Area, sr. res. officer Atlantic Area N.Y.C., comdr. Navy's No. Calif. Maritime Def. Zone San Francisco; comdr. Navy's Maritime Def. Zone USCG, sector 6, Charleston, S.C.; ret. USCG, 1993; nat. dep. exec. dir. Res. Officers assn. U.S., Washington, 1987-91, dir. adminstrn. and dir. fin. Res. Officers assn., 1987-91. Civilian aviator Geodetic Survey, Alaska; bd. dirs. Bank of Hollywood; chief U.S. Delegation to CIOR, NATO Hdqrs., Belgium, 1985-86; internat. sec.-gen. Inter-Allied Confedn. of Res. Officers, Brussels, 1992-94. Chmn. bd. trustees ROA/US, Washington; mem. Calif. Vets. Bd., 1995—, chmn., 1998—99; bd. dirs. Sonoma County (Calif.) Area Agy. of Aged, 2002—; bd. dirs. Calif. North Bay chpt. Alzheimer's Assn., 2002—. Decorated Legion of Merit, Coast Guad Commendation medals (2), Coast Guard Achievement medal, Humanitarian Svc. medal, Arctic Svc. medal, Coast Guard Combat Air Crew Wings, others; recipient Navy Disting. Pub. Svc. medal Sec. of Navy, 1983, Coast Guard Disting. Pub. Svc. medal Comdt. of Coast Guard, 1983, 93. Mem. Res. Officers Assn. U.S. (pres. 1982-83). Home: 573 Pistachio Pl Windsor CA 95492-8168

SPARKS, BILLY SCHLEY, lawyer; b. Marshall, Mo., Mar. 1, 1923; s. John and Clarinda (Schley) S.; m. Dorothy O. Stone, May 14, 1946; children: Stephen Stone, Susan Lee Sparks Raben Taylor, John David. AB, Harvard U., 1945, LLB, 1949. Bar: Mo. 1949. Ptnr. Langworthy, Matz & Linde, Kansas City, Mo., 1949-62, Linde, Thomason, Fairchild, Langworthy, Kohn & Van Dyke, Kansas City, 1962-91; ret., 1991. Mem. Mission (Kans.) Planning Coun., 1954-63; treas. Johnson County (Kans.) Dem. Ctrl. Com., 1958-64; candidate for rep. 10th Dist., Kans., 1956, 3d Dist., 1962; mem. Dist. 100 Sch. Bd., 1964-68, pres., 1967-69; mem. Dist. 512 Sch. Bd., 1969-73, pres., 1971-72; del. Dem. Nat. Conv., 1964;; mem. Kans. Civil Svc. Commn., 1975-90. Lt. USAAF, 1944-46. Mem. ABA, Mo. Bar Assn., Kansas City Bar Assn., Law Assn. Kansas City, Harvard Law Sch. Assn. Mo. (past dir.), Nat. Assn. Sch. Bds. (mem. legis. com. 1968-73), St. Andrews Soc., Harvard Club (v.p. 1953-54), The Kansas City (Mo.) Club, Milburn Golf and Country Club, Am. Legion, Kansas City C. of C. (legis. com. 1956-82), Mem. Christian Ch. Home and Office: 8517 W 90th Ter Shawnee Mission KS 66212-3053

SPARKS, CHARLES EDWARD, pathologist, educator; b. Peoria, Ill., July 29, 1940; s. William Joseph and Meredith (Pleasants) S.; m. Janet Lindsay Dehoff, Aug. 18, 1977; children: William, Debra, Robert. BS in Biology, MIT, 1963; MD, Thomas Jefferson U., 1968. Diplomate Am. Bd. Pathology, Am. Bd. Clin. Chemistry. Rsch. asst. Mass. Gen. Hosp., Boston, 1963; intern NY Hosp., Cornell Naval Hosp., St. Albans, 1968-69; resident in clin. pathology Hosp. of U. Pa., 1972-75; fellow in cardiopulmonary medicine U. Pa., Phila., 1975-76, asst. instr., 1972-75; fellow in biochemistry Med. Coll. Pa., Phila., 1976-77, instr., 1976-77, asst. to assoc. prof. biochemistry and physiology, 1977-82; assoc. prof. pathology U. Rochester (NY), 1982-88, prof. pathology, 1988—. Advisor med. scientist tng. program U. Rochester, 1984-92; attending pathologist, dir. clin. chemistry unit Strong Meml. Hosp., 1982—, chair rsc. adv. com., assoc. chair pathology, 1994—, dir. grad. studies in Integrative Biomed. Scis., 1998—. Contbr. articles to profl. jours.; patentee in field. Chairperson Endocrinology VA Merit Rev. Study Sect., 2000—. Lt. comdr. USN, 1969—72. Postdoctoral fellow NIH, 1975-77. Mem. AAAS, Am. Diabetes Assn. (co-chmn. nat. symposium meeting 1988), Acad. Clin. Lab. Physicians and Scientists, Am. Heart Assn. (fellow coun. on arteriosclerosis, mem. nominating com.). Office: Dept Pathology U Rochester 601 Elmwood Ave Rochester NY 14642-0001

SPARKS, DALE BOYD, allergist, health facility administrator; b. Springfield, Mo., July 14, 1929; s. Roscoe R. and Ruby V. (Boyd) S.; children: Susan L., Laura A., Lisa M., Jennifer G.; m. Leeanna M. Molccyk Priboy, Apr. 21, 2001. AB, BS, Southwest Mo. State U., 1951; BS in Medicine, U. Mo., 1953; MD, St. Louis U., 1955. Diplomate Am. Bd. Allergy and Immunology. Intern Kansas City (Mo.) Gen. Hosp. U. Med. Ctr., 1955-56; resident U. Mo. Hosp., 1958-60; fellow in allergy and immunology Northwestern U., 1960-61; mem. cons. staff Parkview Cmty. Hosp., 1961—; mem. med. staff Riverside County Regional Med. Ctr., 1961-2000, dir. respiratory therapy, 1968-85, dir. respiratory therapy and diagnostic svcs., 1965—, chmn. dept. medicine, 1978-98, chief med. staff, 1990-98; acting dir., health officer Riverside Pub. Health Dept., 1991-93. Clin. prof. medicine Loma Linda U. Mem. editl. bd. Immunology and Allergy in Practice, 1980—. Lt. USNR. Fellow ACP (coun. subsplty. socs. 1988—), Am. Coll. Allergy and Immunology (disting., bd. regents 1989-93, pres. 1990-91, chmn. fin. com./treas. 1990-93, recert. com.), Coll. Allergy, Asthma and Immunology; mem. AMA, Am. Lung Assn. (bd. dirs. 1990-95), Am. Heart Assn. (bd. dirs. 1964-70, pres. 1966), Joint Coun. Am. Allergy and Immunology (bd. dirs. 1985-90), Calif. Med. Assn., Calif. Soc. Allergy, Inland Soc. Internal Medicine, Riverside County Med. Assn. (bd. councilors 1980-99, del. CMA 1988-99), Riverside County Found. Med. Care (exec. com., past pres.). Home and Office: 29368 Big Range Rd Canyon Lake CA 92587 Personal E-mail: dsparksmd@aol.com.

SPARKS, DAVID STANLEY, university administrator; b. Phila., Dec. 8, 1922; s. Richard Frederick and Grace Dorothy (Tuttle) S.; m. Phyllis Ann Bate, June 12, 1949; children: Robert F., E. Anne. AB, Grinnell (Iowa) Coll., 1944; MA, U. Chgo., 1945, PhD, 1951. Instr., asst. prof., asso. prof. U. Md., College Park, 1947-65, prof. history, 1965—, assoc. dean grad. studies and research, 1967-70, dean, 1970-77, acting vice chancellor for acad. affairs, 1976-77, acting v.p. grad. studies and research, 1978-79, v.p. grad. studies and research, 1979-87, acting v.p. for acad. affairs, 1982-83, v.p. acad. affairs, grad. studies and research, 1987-88, vice chancellor for acad. affairs, 1988-91, vice chancellor emeritus, 1991. Vis. professorial lectr. dept. history Johns Hopkins, 1965; mem., chair Grad. Record Examinations Bd., 1979-85. Co-editor, author: American Civilization: A History of the United States, 1960, The Making of American Democracy, Readings and Documents, 2 vols, 1962; Editor: Inside Lincoln's Army: The Diary of General Marsena Rudolph Patrick, 1964. Recipient research awards Am. Philos. Soc., 1958, Social Sci. Research Council, 1957 Mem. Am., So. hist. assns., Orgn. Am. Historians, Am. Assn. U. Profs. (pres. U. Md. chpt.), Nat. Acad. Univ. Research Adminstrs., Phi Kappa Phi. Clubs: Cosmos (Washington). Home: 10500 Rockville Pike Apt 1309 Rockville MD 20852-3350

SPARKS, DON BERTRAND, retired geophysicist; b. Somerville, Tex., Oct. 4, 1930; s. Bunyan F. and Daisy B. Sparks; m. Wanda F. Kinsala, July 30, 1952 (div. Mar. 1990); m. Lou Kimball Sparks, Mar. 15, 1991; children: Neva Dione, Don B. Jr. BA in Math. & Physics, Tex. A&M U., 1951; grad., Air War Coll., 1978. Geophysicist various oil cos., Tex.; commd. 2d lt. USAF, 1952, advanced through grades to lt. col.; sr. flight test engr. B-58 plane Convair, Ft. Worth; ops. mgr. space flight ops. facility, data sys. engr. mariner 2/venus, data sys. engr. mariner/mars Calif. Tech./NASA, Pasadena, Calif., 1961—80, ret., 1990, USAF, 1980. Advisor AF Civil Air Patrol, Pasadena, 1970—80. Avocation: fishing. Address: PO Box 291958 Kerrville TX 78029

SPARKS, DONALD EUGENE, interscholastic activities association executive; b. St. Louis, May 26, 1933; s. Lloyd Garland and Elsie Wilma (Finn) S.; m. Gloria Helle, Sept. 22, 1951; children: Robert, Michael, Donna Lyn. BS in Edn., Truman State Univ., 1956, MA, 1959, postgrad., 1962-63. Cert. tchr. and principal, Mo. High sch. coach, athletic dir. The Parkway Sch. Dist., Chesterfield, Mo., 1959-77; assoc. dir. Mo. High Sch. Activity Assn., Columbia, 1977-81; asst. dir. Nat. Fedn. State High Sch. Assns., Kansas City, Mo., 1981-98, retired, 1998. Recipient spl. Nat. Athletic Dir.'s and Nat. Coach and Nat. Ofcl. citations Nat. Fedn. State High Sch. Assns., 1972; named to Truman State U. Athletics Hall of Fame, 1996, Greater St. Louis Athletics Hall of Fame, 1978. Mem. Nat. Interathletic Adminstrs. Assn. (Disting. Service award 1979). Home: 20 Whispering Sands Dr Sarasota FL 34242-1665 Office: Nat High Sch Athletics Hall of Fame 2000 PO Box 690 Indianapolis IN 46206-0690

SPARKS, JACK NORMAN, college dean; b. Lebanon, Ind., Dec. 3, 1928; s. Oakley and Geraldine Ruth (Edrington) S.; m. Esther Lois Bowen, Apr. 11, 1953; children: Stephen Michael, Robert Norman, Ruth Ann, Jonathan Russell. BS, Purdue U., 1950; MA, U. Iowa, 1951, PhD, 1960. Tchr. math. Leyden Community High Sch., Franklin Park, Ill., 1954-58; rsch. asst. U. Iowa, Iowa City, 1958-60; assoc. prof. applied stats., dir. bur. of rsch. U. No. Colo., Greeley, 1960-65; assoc. prof. ednl. psychology Pa. State U., State Coll., 1965-68; dir. corr. Campus Crusade for Christ, San Bernardino, Calif., 1968-69; dir. Christian World Liberation Front, Berkeley, Calif., 1969-75; pastor, ch. overseer New Covenant Apostolic Order, Berkeley, 1975-77; dean St. Athanasius Acad. Orthodox Theology, Santa Barbara, Calif., 1977-87, St. Athanasius Coll., Santa Barbara, 1987-93, St. Athanasius Acad. of Orthodox Theology, Elk Grove, Calif., 1996—. Cons. Measurement Rsch. Ctr., Iowa City, 1959-60, Western States Small Schs. Project, Greeley, 1962-65, Colo. Coun. on Edn. Rsch., Denver, 1963-65; project dir. Orthodox Study Bible Old Testament Project, 1998—. Author: Letters to Street Christians, 1971, The Mind Benders, 1977, 79, The Resurrection Letters, 1978, The Preaching of the Apostles, 1987, Victory in the Unseen Warfare, 1993; editor: Apostolic Fathers, 1978, 88; gen. editor: The Orthodox Study Bible, 1993, Virtue in the Unseen Warfare, 1995, Prayer in the Unseen Warfare, 1996, Christ Is Our Holiness, 1996, The Coming of the Prince, 1997, Tradition in the Early Church, 1997, The Letters of St. Ignatius, 1998, Faith and Godlines, 1999, Pentecost: A Homily of St. John Chrysostom, 2000, No Graven Image, 2000, The Valley of the Shadow of Death, 2000, Death, Fear of Death, Hope of Resurrection, 2000, Kindling the Fire Within, 2000, How Can Jesus Be Both God and Man, 2001, The Annunciation, 2001, The Bride of Christ, 2001, The Boundless Beauty, 2001, Walking Through the Night, 2001, Out of the Depths, 2002, Redemption and Reconciliation, 2002, A Family Baptized, 2003, Zeal and Patience, 2003. Trustee Rock Mont Coll., Denver, 1962-77, Thomas Nelson Co., Nashville, 1977-78. 1st lt. U.S. Army, 1952-54. Mem. Am. Sci. Affiliation, Assn. Orthodox Theologians, Conf. on Faith and History, Phi Delta Kappa (pres. Epsilon chpt. 1959-60). Republican. Orthodox Christian. Home: 8758 Williamson Dr Elk Grove CA 95624-1829 Office: St Athanasius Acad Orthodox Theology 10519 E Stockton Blvd Ste 170 Elk Grove CA 95624-9704 E-mail: frjack@saaot.edu.

SPARKS, JANET LINDSAY DEHOFF, pathology educator; b. Lawrence, Mass., Sept. 13, 1950; d. Ronald Lee and Barbara Isabelle (Platt) DeHoff; m. Charles Edward Sparks, Aug. 18, 1977; 1 child, Robert. BA in Biology, BS in Med. Tech., U. Pa., 1972, PhD in Pathology, 1980. Cert. med. technologist Am. Soc. Clin. Pathologists. Instr. clin. chemistry U. Pa., Phila., 1974-76; fellow Wistar Inst. Anatomy and Biology, Phila., 1975-80; postdoctoral fellow U. Rochester (N.Y.), 1983-85, scientist, 1985-94, asst. prof. pathology and lab. medicine, 1994-96, assoc. prof. pathology and lab. medicine, 1996—. Cons. NIH, Indpls., 1994-96. Contbr. numerous articles to profl. jours.; patentee in field. Nat. NIDDK RO1 grantee, 1995—. Fellow Coun. on Arteriosclerosis Thrombosis and Vascular Biology; mem. AAAS, Am. Soc. Clin. Pathologists, Am. Diabetes Assn., Am. Heart Assn. (coun. on arteriosclerosis, coun. on clin. cardiology), N.Y. Lipid Club, N.Y. Acad. Scis. Office: U Rochester Dept Pathology 601 Elmwood Ave # 626 Rochester NY 14642-0001 E-mail: janet_sparks@ume.rochester.edu.

SPARKS, JOHN EDWARD, lawyer; b. Rochester, Ind., July 3, 1930; s. Russell Leo and Pauline Anna (Whittenberger) S.; m. Margaret Joan Snyder, Sept. 4, 1954; children: Thomas Edward, William Russell, Kathryn Chapman McCarthy. AB, Ind. U., 1952; LL.B., U. Calif., Berkeley, 1957; postgrad., London Sch. Econs., 1957-58. Bar: Calif. 1958, U.S. Supreme Ct., 1968. Assoc. Brobeck, Phleger & Harrison, San Francisco, 1958-66, ptnr., 1967-95, of counsel, 1996—2003. Adj. prof. law U. San Francisco, 1967-69; pres. Legal Aid Soc. San Francisco, 1978-79, dir., 1971-81. Editor U. Calif. Law Rev., 1956-57. Served to 1st lt. Q.M.C. U.S. Army, 1952-54, Korea. Recipient Wheeler Oak Meritorious award U. Calif., Berkeley, 1986. Fellow Am. Bar Found., Am. Coll. Trial Lawyers; mem. State Bar Calif., Bar Assn. San Francisco (bd. dirs. 1974-75), ABA, Am. Judicature Soc., Boalt Hall Alumni Assn. (pres. 1983-84), Pacific Union Club (San Francisco), Democrat. Office: 111 Southampton Ave Berkeley CA 94707 E-mail: jsparks458@aol.com.

SPARKS, KENNETH R. association executive; b. Mar. 26, 1934; BS, Syracuse U., 1956, MS, 1961, PhD, 1964; JD, George Washington U., 1967. Dir. rsch. Voice of Am. USIA, Washington, 1964-67; dep. dir. pub. affairs U.S. Office Econ. Opportunity, Washington, 1967-68, dir., 1968-69; pres. U.S. Cultural and Trade Ctr. Commn., Washington, 1988—90; dep. dir. Fed. City Coun., Washington, 1970-72, exec. v.p., 1972—2004; dir. Fed. Res. Bank of Richmond, 2004. Mem. Econ. Club of Wash. (sec. 1985—). Office: 1156 15th St NW Ste 600 Washington DC 20005-2431 Office Phone: 202-223-4560. E-mail: krsparks@aol.com.

SPARKS, LINDSAY, information technology executive; Mainframe sys. programmer, 1980; from leader enterprise customer unit to corp. v.p. Microsoft, Redmond, Wash., 1992, corp. v.p. Office: One Microsoft Way Redmond WA 98052-6399

SPARKS, MILDRED THOMAS, state agency administrator, educator; b. Montgomery, Ala., Oct. 2, 1942; d. Leon and Annie Lee (Johnson) Thomas; m. John H. Sparks, Aug. 29, 1964; children: Melanie J. Bosak, Jennifer L. David-Gerhartz, Regina F. BS, Ala. State U., 1964; MS, Pepperdine U., 1978; postgrad., Claremont Coll., Calif. State U., Boston Coll. Cert. reading specialist, contract mgmt., U. Phoenix, U. Wyo. Tchr. Dayton (Ohio) Schs., 1964-66, Oxon Hill (Md.) Schs., 1966-70; technician Reading Lab. Grambling (La.) State U., 1972; reading lab. aide Calif. City (Calif.) Schs., 1975; reading instr. Cerro Coso So. Outreach, Edwards AFB, Calif., 1976-78; substitute tchr. San Bernardino City Schs., 1979, Aquinas H.S., San Bernardino, 1978-79; reading lab. tchr. San Bernardino H.S., 1979; instr. reading lab. San Bernardino Valley Coll., 1980-81, assoc. prof. reading, dept. head, 1981-86; contract adminstr. Hercules Missile Ordinance and Space Group, Magna, Utah, 1986, Alliant Techsys. (formerly Hercules Missile Ordinance and Space Group), 1987-97; dir. Office of Black Affairs State of Utah, 1997—2000; instr. Salt Lake CC, Salt Lake City, 2003—, pres., Diversity Coun. Tchg. Cir. - Courage Teach, 2003—. Mem. gen. edn. com., pres.'s diversity coun., Salt Lake CC. Mem. Black Adv. Coun., Office of Black Affairs, AARP (mem. Utah bd., safety program instr.); presenter workshops, cmty. events; troop vol. Girl Scouts U.S.; vol. The March of Dimes, Am. Heart Assn., Visitation of the Elderly Homebound, Am. Cancer Soc. and Marriage and Family Workshop for Teens, Cath. Cmty. Svcs.; civil rights movement participant Ala. Bus Boycott; mem. minority health adv. bd. Utah Health Dept.; mem. Cath. Women League, Black Caths. Utah, Salt Lake City, African Am. Task Force, Gov.'s Initiative on Family Today, Anti-Discrimination Com.; planning com. United Way Greater Salt Lake, vol.; past pres. Salt Lake Diocesan Pastoral Coun., vol.; mem. Americorp Legacy program, Salt Lake County, Utah State Bd. Aging and Adult Svcs. Mem. Calif Tchrs. Assn., Nat. Coun. Tchrs. English, Assn. Supervision and Curriculum Devel., Western Coll. Reading Assn., Bus. and Profl. Women's Club, Link's, Jack and Jill of Am. Inc., Delta Kappa Gamma, Alpha Kappa Alpha. Roman Catholic (Norton lav lector). Avocations: reading, writing, gardening, cross country skiing. Home: 3790 Becky Cir Salt Lake City UT 84109-3302 Office: Salt Lake CC Coll Devel Edn 4600 S Redwood Rd Salt Lake City UT 84123 E-mail: msparks@dced.state.ut.us.

SPARKS, NICHOLAS, writer; b. Omaha, Dec. 31, 1965; s. Patrick Michael and Jill Emma Marie (Thoene) Sparks; m. Catherine Sparks, 1989; children: Miles, Ryan, Landon, Lexie, Savannah. Grad. with high honors, U. Notre Dame, 1988. Author: (novels) The Notebook, 1996, Message In a Bottle, 1998, A Walk To Remember, 1999, The Rescue, 2000, A Bend in the Road, 2001, Nights in Rodanthe, 2002, The Guardian, 2003, The Wedding, 2003, Three Weeks With My Brother, 2004. Office: c/o Author Mail Warner Books 1271 Avenue of the Americas New York NY 10020

SPARKS, ROBERT DEAN, medical administrator, gastroenterologist; b. Newton, Iowa, May 6, 1932; s. Albert John and Josephine Emma (Kleinendorst) S.; children: Steven Robert, Ann Louise, John James. BA, U. Iowa, 1955, MD, 1957; D of Humanitarian Svc. (hon.), Creighton U., 1978. Diplomate Am. Bd. Internal Medicine. Intern Charity Hosp. of La., New Orleans, 1957-58, resident in internal medicine, 1958-59, asst. in medicine, 1958-59; fellow in gen. medicine and gastroenterology Tulane U. Sch. Medicine, 1959-62, instr. medicine, 1959-63, asst. prof., 1963-64, assoc. prof., 1964-68, prof., 1968-72, asst. dean, 1964-67, assoc. dean, acting dean, 1967-68, vice dean, 1968-69, dean, 1969-72, chief sect. gastroenterology, 1968-72; chancellor Med. Ctr. U. Nebr., 1972-76, prof. medicine, 1972-76; v.p. U. Nebr. System, 1972-76; health program dir. W.K. Kellogg Found., Battle Creek, Mich., 1976-81, v.p. programming, 1981-82, sr. v.p., 1982, pres., chief programming officer, 1982-86, pres., 1982-88, trustee, 1988, pres. emeritus, cons., 1988-92; pres., CEO, Calif. Med. Assn. Found., Sacramento, 1995-98, sr. assoc., 1998—. Cons. U. Tenn. Health Sci. Ctr., 1988-90, Boston U. Health Policy Inst., 1989-90; bd. dirs., mem. sci., compensation and trust rev. coms. Syntex Corp., Palo Alto, Calif., 1987-91, v.p. product safety and compliance, 1991-93; mem. overseers com. to visit Harvard U. Med. and Dental Schs., 1984-90; mem. vis. com. U. Miami Sch. Medicine, 1982-86; assoc. med. dir. for addiction treatment svcs., dir. for edn. and rsch., Battle Creek Adventist Hosp., 1990-91; v.p. Howe-Lewis Internat Inc., Menlo Park, N.Y., 1993-94, cons., 1994-95. Mem. editl. bd. Alcoholism Treatment Quar., 1985--; contbr. articles to profl. jours. Bd. dirs. Nat. Coun. on Alcoholism and Drug Dependence, N.Y.C., 1982-93, treas., 1986-88, chmn., 1989-90, past chmn., 1991-92; bd. dirs. Battle Creek Symphony Orch., 1981-88, Lakeview Sch. Dist., Battle Creek, 1979-83, 88-91; trustee Monsour Med. Found., Jeannette, Pa., 1976-90, interim pres. 1989, chmn. bd., pres., 1989-90; mem. President's Adv. Bd. on Pvt. Sector Initiatives, Washington, 1986-89; chmn. bd. dirs. Bard Coll. Health Policy and Practice Inst., 1988-96, Consumer Health Info. Rsch. Inst., 1990-95, Chelsea-Arbor Treatment Ctr., 1990-91; bd. dirs. Calhoun County Bd. Health, 1988-91, chmn., 1989-91; mem., bd. dirs. Mental Health and Addictions Found. Mich., Battle Creek, 1991-93. Recipient Harvard Dental award Harvard U. Sch. Dental Medicine, 1992, Disting. Alumni award for achievement U. Iowa Coll. Medicine, 1998, annual Robert D. Sparks Cmty. Health Leadership Achievement award CMA Found., 2000. Fellow ACP; mem. AMA, Nat. Acad. Scis. Inst. Medicine (com. study of treatment and rehab. svcs. for alcoholism and alcohol abuse, bd. mental health and behavioral medicine), Coun. Mich. Founds. (trustee 1986-88), Assn. Am. Med. Colls. (disting. svc. mem. 1975—), Phi Eta Sigma, Alpha Omega Alpha. Republican. Methodist. Avocations: tennis, bridge, reading, travel. Home and Office: 5004 Gresham Dr El Dorado Hills CA 95762-7703 E-mail: rdsparksmd1@earthlink.net.

SPARKS, ROBERT RONOLD, JR., lawyer; b. Bklyn., Dec. 4, 1946; s. Robert Ronold Sr. and Marjorie Anne (Boehm) S. BA, Va. Mil. Inst., 1969; JD, U. Va., 1972. Bar: U.S. Dist. Ct. (D.C. cir.) 1979, U.S. Dist. Ct. (ea. dist.) Va. 1979, U.S. Ct. Appeals (2d cir.) 1986, U.S. Ct. Appeals (D.C. cir.) 1975, Va. 1972, U.S. Ct. Appeals (4th cir.) 1982, U.S. Ct. Mil. Appeals 1976, U.S. Tax Ct. 1978, U.S. Supreme Ct. 1981, U.S. Dist. Ct. Md. 1993. From assoc. to ptnr. Sedam & Herge, McLean, Va., 1977-85; ptnr. Herge, Sparks & Christopher, McLean, 1985—. Mem. bd. Regents James Monroe Law Office Mus. and Meml. Library, Fredericksburg, Va., 1983-86. Mem. Fairfax County Redevel. and Housing Authority, Fairfax, 1981-82; commr. Fairfax County Indsl. Devel. Authority, 1980-81, Fairfax County Planning Commn., 1983-89. Lt. USNR, 1972-77, Philippines. Mem. Va. Bar Assn., D.C. Bar Assn., Rotary (treas., bd. dirs. 1978-80). Roman Catholic. Home: 6448 Spring Ter Falls Church VA 22042-3141 Office: Herge Sparks Christopher 6862 Elm St Ste 360 Mc Lean VA 22101-3867

SPARKS, ROBERT WILLIAM, retired publishing executive; b. Seattle, Dec. 30, 1925; s. James Donald and Gladys (Simmons) S. Student, U. Wash., 1947-50; BA, U. Hawaii, 1954, MA, 1965. Editor, various pubs., 1947-64; mng. editor U. Hawaii Press, 1964-66, dir., 1967-87. Cons. East-West Ctr., Jour. Hawaiian History, Japanese and Chinese book pubs., 1987-92; advisor New World Press, Beijing, 1986; mem. adv. bd. to pres. Kamehameha Schs. Author: Seattle, Sitka, San Francisco, 1955, Letters From an Island, 1962, New Endings, 1989, Riding Backwards, 2002; contbr. articles to internat. pub. jours. Served with AUS, 1944-46, PTO. Recipient McInerny editorship, 1953; Pacific House citation Pacific and Asian Affairs Council, 1974 Mem. Assn. Am. Univ. Presses, Assn. Am. Publishers, Internat. Assn. Scholarly Publishers, Soc. for Scholarly Pub., Hawaiian Hist. Soc., Hawaii Found. History and Humanities, Honolulu Acad. Arts, Bishop Mus. Assn. Home: 66 Queen St PH4102 Honolulu HI 96813-4449

SPARKS, SAM, federal judge; b. 1939; BA, U. Tex., 1961, LLB, 1963. Aide Rep. Homer Thornberry, 1963; law clk. to Hon. Homer Thornberry U.S. Dist. Ct. (we. dist.) Tex., 1963-65; assoc. to ptnr., shareholder Hardie, Grambling, Sims & Galatzan (and successor firms), El Paso, Tex., 1965-91; dist. judge U.S. Dist. Ct. (we. dist.) Tex., 1991—. Fellow Am. Coll. Trial Lawyers, Tex. Bar Found. (life); mem. Am. Bd. Trial Advocates (advocate), State Bar Tex. Office: US Dist Ct Judge 200 W 8th St Ste 100 Austin TX 78701-2333

SPARKS, THOMAS E., JR., lawyer; b. Little Rock, Jan. 11, 1942; children: Thomas Gunnar, Erik Richard, Andrew Pal. BS, Washington and Lee U., 1963; JD, U. Ark., 1968; LLM, Harvard U., 1970. Bar: Ark. 1968, Calif. 1970. Assoc. Pillsbury Madison & Sutro, San Francisco, 1970-76; ptnr. Pillsbury, Madison & Sutro, San Francisco, 1977-84, Baker & McKenzie, San Francisco, 1984-87, Pillsbury Madison & Sutro, San Francisco, 1987-2000, Pillsbury Winthrop, San Francisco, 2001—. Trustee Grace Cathedral, San Francisco. 1st lt. U.S. Army, 1965. Mem. ABA, Calif. Bar Assn., Olympic Club (San Francisco), Calif. Tennis Club (pres. 2000). Office: Pillsbury Winthrop 50 Fremont St San Francisco CA 94105-2230

SPARKS, WILLIAM SHERAL, retired seminary librarian; b. Alden Bridge, La., Oct. 30, 1924; s. Fred DeWitt and Truda (Bradford) S.; m. Joy Eleanor Young, Aug. 8, 1947; 1 child, David Frederick. AB, Phillips U., 1946; MDiv, Christian Theol. Sem., 1949; ThM, Iliff Sch. of Theology, 1955, ThD, 1957; MA, U. Denver, 1962. Pastor chs., 1950-60; asst. libr. Kans. Wesleyan U., Salina, 1962-66; dir. libr. and info. svcs. St. Paul Sch. of Theology, Kansas City, Mo., 1966-93, ret., 1993. Horowitz Found. fellow Hebrew Union Coll.-Jewish Inst. of Religion, 1949-52. Mem. Am. Theol. Libr. Assn.

SPARLIN, JENNIFER ROBIN, communications educator, writer; b. Wichita, Kans., June 13, 1971; d. Randall Morris and Pamela Bell Sparlin; m. Derek Michael Richardson, Jan. 6, 1996. BFA in Theatre Arts, Friends U., 1993; MA in Comm. and Theatre/Drama, Wichita State U., 1999. Dance instr. Machi's Sch. Dance, Wichita, 1990—96; children's ministry intern Friendswood (Tex.) Friends Ch., 1993; drama instr. Christian Ctr. Acad., Wichita, Kans., 1993—94; writing ctr. tutor Wichita State U., 1996—98, grad. tchg. asst., 1998—99; adj. instr. speech and theatre Cowley County C.C., Arkansas City, 1999—2001; adj. instr. speech Butler C.C., El Dorado, Kans., 1999—; lectr. comm. Newman U., Wichita, 2000—01. Author: (novel) A Sword for Mary, 2002; actor(asst. dir.): A Midsummer Night's Dream, 1991, The Patient, 2000, The Imaginary Invalid, 2001, (singer, dancer): Once Upon a Mattress, 1993, (singer, dancer, dance captain): Oklahoma!, 2001,: The Celebration, 1990, Lepers, 1990, You Can't Take it With You, 1990, The Tempest, 1991, Painting Churches, 1992, The Visitors from Forest Hill, 1992, Hamlet, 1992, The Importance of Being Ernest, 1996, Blythe Spirit, 1997, The Bowling Ball, 1997, Good Sam, 1999, Harvey, 2001; dancer The Nutcracker, 1975—79, 1990—91, Ragman, 1990; dir.: Where Have All the Lightning Bugs Gone?, 1992; playwright Patroness, 1998, Pretty Girl, 1998, Overtime, 1998, The Way of the Wabbits, 1998, The Secret of the Old House, 1999, Meeting, 2001, American Angels, 2003; choreographer Godspell, 1994. Recipient Fourth pl. in short story writing, Accelerated Christian Edn. Internat. Student Conv., 1986. Mem.: Elliott Soc., Wichita State U. Alumni Assn., Soc. Children's Book Writers and Illustrators (assoc.). Presbyterian. Avocations: writing, dance, theater, cooking, travel. E-mail: jsparlin@butlercc.edu.

SPARLING, MARY LEE, biology professor; b. Ft. Wayne, Ind., May 20, 1934; d. George Hewson and Velmah Evelyn (McClain) S.; m. Albert Alcide Barber, Sept. 1, 1956 (div. Jan. 1975); children: Bonnie Lee Barber, Bradley Paul Barber. BS, U. Miami, Coral Gables, Fla., 1955; MA, Duke U., 1958; PhD, UCLA, 1962. Lectr. UCLA, 1962-63; asst. prof. Calif. State U., Northridge, 1966-72, assoc. prof., 1972-76, prof., 1976—. Statewide acad. senator Calif. State U., 1996-98. Contbr. articles to profl. jours. NSF grantee Calif. State U., Northridge, 1971-72, 81-83, 89, NIH grantee Calif. State U., Northridge, 1987-89. Mem. AAUP (pres. 1981-82), Am. Soc. Cell Biology, Soc. for Devel. Biology, Am. Soc. Zoologists, Sigma Xi (bd. dirs. Research Triangle, N.C. 1974-91). Avocations: tennis, gardening, travel. Home: 3662 Stoner Ave Los Angeles CA 90066-2839 Office: Calif State U Biology Dept Northridge CA 91330-0001

SPARROW, HERBERT GEORGE, III, lawyer, educator; b. Ft. Bragg, N.C., May 26, 1936; s. Herbert George and Virginia (Monroe) S.; m. Nancy Woodruff, Mar. 4, 1962; children: Amy Winslow, Edward Harrison, Herbert G. IV, Alison Kidder. AB cum laude, Princeton U., 1958; JD, U. Mich., 1961. Bar: Mich. 1961, Calif. 1964, D.C. 1979, U.S. Ct. Claims 1982, U.S. Tax Ct. 1983, U.S. Ct. Mil. Appeals 1962, U.S. Supreme Ct. 1976. Assoc. Dickinson Wright PLLC, Detroit, 1965-70, ptnr., 1970—. Adj. prof. Detroit Coll. Law, Mich. State U., 1977-99. Author numerous articles environ. law.; speaker in field. Bd. dirs. Family Life Edn. Coun., Grosse Pointe, Mich., 1982-88, Adult Well-Being Svcs., Inc., Detroit, 1995-2001; cons. Adult Well-Being Svcs. Inc., 2001—. Capt. JAGC, U.S. Army, 1962-65. Mem. ABA, Mich. Bar Assn. (rep. assembly 1979-85, environ. law sect. coun. 1985-91), Calif. Bar Assn., D.C. Bar Assn., Detroit Bar Assn., Am. Arbitration Assn. (panel arbitrators 1975—), Mich. State Bar Found. (fellow 1989—), Environment Law Inst. (assoc.), Phi Delta Phi (pres. Kent Inn Assn., Ann Arbor 1985-97). Office: Dickinson Wright PLLC 500 Woodward Ave Ste 4000 Detroit MI 48226-3416

SPARTZ, ALICE ANNE LENORE, retired retail executive; b. NYC, May 14, 1925; d. John Francis and Alice Philomena (Murray) Rattenbury; m. George Eugene Spartz, Oct. 29, 1949; children: Mary Elizabeth, James, Barbara, Anne, Thomas, William, Michael, John, Matthew, Clare, Robert, Richard. Student, Wright Coll., 1945-47, No. Ill. U., 1950; AA, Triton Coll., 1987. Svc. rep. Ill. Bell Tel., Chgo., 1945-46; stewardess United Airlines, Denver, 1947-49; ret. mgr. Family Life League Resale Shop, Oak Park, Ill., 1987-95; retired, 1995. Mem. Cicero Cmty. Coun., Ill., 1967—69, Pk. Dist. Oak Pk. Com., 1973—74; active Ill. Right to Life Com., Chgo., 1971—2002, Com. Pro-Life Cath., Chgo., 1992—; pres., bd. trustees Trailwood Village Bd., Kingwood, Tex., 2003; bd. dirs. Direct Energy Techs., A Solar Co., Tex.; mem. St. Martha's Roman Cath. Ch.; former bd. dir. Ill. Pro-Life Coalition, Family Life League; vol. canteen worker ARC, Chgo., 1942—45. Mem.: Trailwood Village Cmty. Assn. (trustee 2004). Republican. Roman Catholic. Avocations: travel, sewing, reading, swimming, pro-life activist. Office: 2026 Seven Oaks Dr Kingwood TX 77339

SPATAFORE, ANTHONY R. financial executive; b. Bklyn., Nov. 15, 1952; s. Anthony C. and Mercedes (Santiago) S; m. Deborah Spatafore. Student, Bklyn. Coll.; Cert. Fin. Planning, Adelphi U., 1982. Registered fin. planner; registered investment advisor, SEC. Agt. Paul Revere Ins. Co., N.Y.C., 1974-76; ins. cons. M.O.N.Y., N.Y.C., 1976-79; fin. planner Home Life Ins. Co., N.Y.C., 1979-82; pres., fin. planner ARS Fin. Svcs., Inc., Valley Stream, N.Y., 1982—. Contbr. articles to profl. jours. Mem. Internat. Assn. Registered Fin. Planners (bd. govs. 1987-89), Internat. Assn. Fin. Planning, Inst. Cert. Fin. Planners (local bd. dirs. 1987—, pres. L.I. Soc.), Nat. Assn. Securities Dealers. Republican. Roman Catholic. Avocation: tennis. Office: Jericho Atrium 500 N Broadway Jericho NY 11753

SPATARO, JANIE DEMPSEY WATTS, writer; b. Chattanooga, May 17, 1951; d. Ray Dean and Anne America (Dempsey) Watts; m. Stephen Anthony Spataro, June 18, 1977; children: Anthony Dempsey, Stephen Jackson. BS in Journalism, U. Calif., Berkeley, 1974; MA in Broadcast Journalism, U. So. Calif., 1982. Writer, editor McGiffin Newspapers, South Gate, Calif., 1976; news bur. mgr. Loyola Marymount U., Westchester, Calif., 1976; asst. dir. pub. relations Hawthorne Cmty. Hosp., Calif., 1977—78; pub. rels. cons. Security Pacific Bank, L.A., 1978—82; writer Cable Card, Inc., Marina del Rey, Calif., 1983, Reality Prodns., Huntington Beach, Calif., 1983—86; pres. Write Path, Inc., 1997—. Writer, pridr., editor (TV documentary) Who's Minding the Children?, 1983, screenwriter, Monkey Doll, Fireworks, Oatmania, Soft Shoes, Hard World; author: (novel) Moon Over Taylor's Ridge. Office: 100 Wilshire Blvd Ste 200 Santa Monica CA 90401-1111 Office Phone: 310-917-4557.

SPATT, ARTHUR DONALD, federal judge; b. 1925; Student, Ohio State U., 1943-44, 46-47; LLB cum laude, Bklyn. Law Sch., 1949. Assoc. Davidson & Davidson, N.Y.C., 1949, Lane, Winard, Robinson & Schorr, N.Y.C., 1950, Alfred S. Julien, N.Y.C., 1950-52, Florea & Florea, N.Y.C., 1953; pvt. practice N.Y.C., 1953-67, Spatt & Bauman, N.Y.C., 1967-78; justice 10th judicial cir. N.Y. State Supreme Ct., 1979-82; adminstrv. judge Nassau County, 1982-86; assoc. justice appellate div. Second Judicial Dept., 1986-89; dist. judge U.S. Dist. Ct. (ea. dist.) N.Y., Bklyn., 1989-90, Uniondale, N.Y., 1990-2000, Central Islip, N.Y., 2000—. Book review editor Bklyn. Law Review, 1948—49. Active Jewish War Vets. With USN, 1944—46. Mem. ABA, Assn. Supreme Ct. Justices State of N.Y., Bar Assn. Nassau County, Jewish Lawyers Assn. Nassau County, Long Beach Lawyers Assn. Office: Long Island Courthouse 1024 Federal Plaza Central Islip NY 11722-4445

SPATT, HARTLEY STEVEN, humanities educator; b. Bklyn., Nov. 21, 1947; s. Milton E. and Blanche S. (Bakstansky) S.; m. Wendy Doroshkin, June 13, 1971; children: Martin, Samantha. BA summa cum laude, Colgate U., 1970; MA, NYU, 1971, Johns Hopkins U., 1973, PhD, 1975. Asst. prof. Towson State U., Balt., 1974-76, SUNY Maritime Coll., Bronx, 1976-81, assoc. prof., 1981-87, prof., 1987—, Disting. Tchg. prof., 2004—, assoc. v.p. for acad. affairs, 1999—2002. Writer, editor A.L. Fierst, Greatneck, N.Y., 1977-80, Reference Works, 1993-2001; bus. mgr. Victorian Studies Bull., N.Y.C., 1983—; writer Chernow Editl. Svcs., N.Y.C., 1985-90. Contbr. articles to Victorian Poetry, Walt Whitman Rev., other profl. jours. NEH fellow, 1979, 82, 86, 2004. Mem. MLA, N.E. Victorian Studies Assn. (chair nominations 1985—), William Morris Soc. U.S. (sec.-treas. 1984—), Phi Beta Kappa. Republican. Jewish. Office: Maritime Coll Suny Bronx NY 10465 E-mail: hspatt@sunymaritime.edu.

SPATT, ROBERT EDWARD, lawyer; b. Bklyn., Mar. 26, 1956; s. Milton E. and Blanche S. (Bakstansky) S.; m. Lisa B. Malkin, Aug. 11, 1979; 1 child, Mark Eric. AB, Brown U., 1977; JD magna cum laude, U. Mich., 1980. Bar: N.Y. 1981. Assoc. Simpson Thacher & Bartlett, N.Y.C., 1980-87, ptnr.,

1987—. Mem. ABA, N.Y. State Bar Assn., City of N.Y. Bar Assn., Order of Coif. Avocations: photography, boating, reading. Office: Simpson Thacher & Bartlett 425 Lexington Ave New York NY 10017-3954 E-mail: RSpatt@stblaw.com.

SPATZ, KENNETH CHRIS(TOPHER), JR., statistics educator; b. Tyler, Tex., Mar. 25, 1940; s. Kenneth Christopher and Mary E. (Harton) S.; m. Thea Siria, May 31, 1961; children: Mark C., Kenneth S., Elizabeth A. BA, Hendrix Coll., 1962; PhD, Tulane U., 1966. Asst. prof. U. of the South, Sewanee, Tenn., 1966-69; assoc. prof. U. Ark., Monticello, 1971-73; prof. Hendrix Coll., Conway, Ark., 1973—2003. Author: Basic Statistics: Tales of Distributions, 1st edit., 1976, 7th edit., 2001. Fellow U. Calif., Berkeley, 1969-71. Office: Hendrix Coll Dept Psychology Conway AR 72032 Home: 615 Davis St Conway AR 72034 E-mail: Spatz@hendrix.edu.

SPAULDING, DAN, public relations executive; BA, MA, U. Mich. Commd. USN; aide, pub. affairs officer to comdr. Tng. Command U.S. Pacific Fleet, San Diego, 1969-72; news anchor/prodr./reporter Staf. WFRV-TV, Green Bay, Wis., Sta. WEYI-TV, Flint-Saginaw, Mich.; mem. faculty U. Wis., Green Bay; news dir. Sta. KOMU-TV, Columbia, Mo., Sta. WOTV-TV 8; with Seyferth & Assocs., Inc., Grand Rapids, Mich., 1989-94, exec. v.p., 1994—. Active West Mich. Environ. Action Com. Mem. Pub. Rels. Soc. Am. (accredited). Office: Seyferth Spaulding Tennyson 40 Monroe Center NW, Suite 202 Grand Rapids MI 49503-3003

SPAULDING, FRANK HENRY, librarian; b. Danielson, Conn., July 12, 1932; s. Jacob Lindhurst and Frances (Upham) S.; m. Eugenia Jenewicz, May 25, 1963; children— Geoffrey Michael, Jennifer Anne. AB, Brown U., 1957; MSLS, Case Western Res. U., 1961. Supr. info. ctr. Colgate-Palmolive Co., Piscataway, N.J., 1961-65; group supr. library tech. processes Bell Labs., Holmdel, N.J., 1965-70, head library ops., 1970-84; mgr. library services AT&T Bell Labs., Holmdel, 1985-87, mgr. mktg. library network, 1984-86; library/info. cons., 1987—. Pres. Sp. Libraries. Assn. 1986-87; treas. Am. Soc. for Info. Sci., 1983-86; pres. Documentation Abstracts, N.Y.C., 1983-85; dir. Universal Serials and Book Exchange, Washington, 1984-85, Palinet, Phila., 1978-81. Compiler: Managing the Electronic Library, 1983; author: Today's Information Specialist-Tomorrow's Knowledge Counselor in 2006, International Information: International Librarianship; creator: Task Force on the Value of the Information Professional, 1987. Mem. Buten Mus. Wedgwood. Served to lt. USN, 1957-60. Mem. ALA (com. on accreditation 1989-93), Spl. Librs. Assn. (del. to Internat. Fedn. Libr. Assn. and Inst. 1987-89), Am. Soc. Info. Sci. and Tech. E-mail: frankspaulding@msn.com.

SPAULDING, MAR, retired special education educator, therapist; b. Bellevue, Ky., Oct. 16, 1933; d. Mickey and Blanche Harris; m. Stan Lee Spaulding; children: Karla, Julie Underwood, Lisa Williams, Gregory. MA, Ea. Mich. U., 1978; BS, George Mason U., 1973. Cert. educator Emotionally/Neurologically Impaired, Pre-primary Impaired 1978. Head tchr. in nursery sch., Ann Arbor, Mich., 1973—75; intern Ypsilanti State Mental Instn., Mich., 1975—76; tchr. emotionally impaired and pre-primary impaired Monroe County Intermediate Dist., Monroe, Mich., 1978—93. Leader of groups of parents of handicapped children Monroe County Intermediate Sch. Dist., Monroe, Mich., 1978—93, mem. of grant com., 1980—96, tester on child find com., 1979—85. Author: (children's educational book) Kate Lynn's Fantastic Dream, 1999 (Spl. Edn. Tchr. of the Yr. in Monroe County, Mich., 1995), (companion book) Activities to use with Kate Lynn's Fantastic Dream. Includes cognitive, speech and language, fine motor, gross motor and behavioral, emotional skill areas for teachers and parents., 1999. Story lady Head Start, Baker Devel. Ctr., Punta Gorda, Fla., 1996—2002; tutor Continuing Edn. Ctr. and Even Start, Port Charlotte and Punta Gorda, 1996—2003; membership involvement chairperson Peace River Power Squadron, Punta Gorda, 1996—2003; pub. spkr. topics concerning early childhood edn. Early Childhood Edn. Assn. of SW Fla., Punta Gorda, 1999—2003. Recipient Writer's Award, US Power Squadrons, 2001. Mem.: AAUW (Ft. Myers, Fla. chpt.), U.S. Sail and Power Squadrons, Thomas Paine Nat. Hist. Soc., Nat. Honor Soc., Phi Kappa Phi. Liberal. Avocation: travel, sailing (lived on 41 foot sailboat from 1993 to 1996),writing children's stories, swimming, biking, reading, playing the piano, attending concerts and plays, hiking. Home: 1536 Islamorada Blvd Punta Gorda FL 33955 Personal E-mail: marstan@nut-n-but.net.

SPAULDING, WALLACE HOLMES, retired federal agency professional; b. Oakland, Calif., Sept. 3, 1928; s. Wallace Holmes and May Gibbons (Alves) S.; m. Dorothy Anne Wollon, Jan. 30, 1960; children: James Wallace, Anne Catherine Bridger. AB, U. Calif., Berkeley, 1950; MA, Johns Hopkins U., 1951; PhD, U. Pa., 1969. Rschr. CIA, McLean, Va., 1952-91; ret., 1991. Author: Is the Comintern Coming Back?, 1998; contbr. chpts. to books and articles to profl. jours. V.p. Fellowship of Concerned Churchmen, L.A.; pres. Found. for Christian Theology, Washington; Am. regional sec. Soc. of Mary, McLean. Col. (ret.) USAR, 1950—81. Decorated Meritorious Svc. medal U.S. Army; Fulbright scholar, The Philippines, 1951-52. Mem. Phi Beta Kappa, Alpha Delta Phi, Pan Xenia. Avocations: hiking, bicycling, domestic and foreign travel. Home: 1206 Buchanan St Mc Lean VA 22101-2943 E-mail: whsdws@erols.com.

SPAWN, KEVIN LEWIS, education educator; b. Oneida, NY, Oct. 31, 1962; s. Alan Elsworth and M. S. Spawn; m. Nyla Darlene Spawn, Nov. 29, 1986; 1 child, Adam Alan James. BA, Gordon Coll., 1992; MA, Gordon-Conwell Theol. Sem., 1994; PhD, Oxford U., 1999. Lectr. Gordon Coll., Wenham, Mass., 1993—94, Randolph-Macon Coll., Reading, England, 1996, Oxford U., England, 1996—98; lector Oxford Ctr. for Hebrew, 1996—98; prof. of bible and theology Simpson U., 1998—. Author: (book) As It Is Written and Other Citation Formulae in OT, 2002; contbr. articles. E-4 USAF, 1980—84. Recipient Pusey Ellerton Hebrew award, Oriental Inst. Oxford U., 1996, Segal award, 1996, Overseas Rsch. award, Oxford U. and Chancellors of UK, 1995—97. Mem.: Evang. Theol. Soc., Soc. of Pentecostal Studies, Soc. of Bibl. Lit. Avocation: bicycling. Office: Simpson U 2211 College View Dr Redding CA 96003

SPEAKES, LARRY MELVIN, public relations executive, writer; b. Cleveland, Miss., Sept. 13, 1939; s. Harry Earl and Ethlyn Frances (Fincher) Speakes; m. Aleta Merkel, Oct. 5, 2001; children from previous marriage: Sondra LaNell, Barry Scott, Jeremy Stephen. Student, U. Miss., 1957-61; Litt. D. (hon.), Ind. Central U., 1982, BA in Journalism, 2001. News editor Oxford (Miss.) Eagle, 1961-62; news editor Bolivar Comml., Cleveland, 1962-63, mng. editor, 1965-66; dep. dir. Bolivar County Civil Def., 1963-65; gen. mgr. Progress Pubs., Leland, Miss., 1966-68; editor Leland Progress, Hollandale Herald, Bolivar County Democrat, Sunflower County News; press sec. U.S. Senator J.O. Eastland of Miss., 1968-74; staff asst. Exec. Office of Pres., Mar.-May 1974; press asst. to spl. counsel to Pres., May-Aug. 1974; asst. White House press sec., 1974-76, asst. press sec. to Pres., 1976-77; press sec. to Gerald R. Ford, 1977; v.p. Hill & Knowlton, Inc., internat. pub. relations and pub. affairs counsel, Washington, 1977-81; prin. dep. press sec. and asst. to Pres. of U.S., Washington, 1981-87; sr. v.p. Merrill Lynch & Co., Inc., N.Y.C., 1987-88; v.p. comm. No. Telecom Ltd., Washington and Toronto, Ont., Can., 1991-93; sr. v.p. corp. rels. U.S. Postal Svc., Washington, 1994-98, sr. advisor to postmaster gen., 1998—, mgr. of advt., 2001—. Corp. comm. cons., lectr. on press and politics, 1988-91. Author: Speaking Out: The Reagan Presidency From Inside the White House; contbr. Crisis Repsponse: Inside Stories on Managing Image Under Siege. Recipient Presdl. Citizens medal, 1987, Gen. Excellence award Miss. Press Assn., 1988, Disting. Journalism Alumni award U. Miss., 1981, Hall of Fame, 1985, Silver Em. Miss. Scholastic Press Assn., 1988, Spl. Achievement award Nat. Assn. Govt. Communicators, 1983, Silver Anvil award Pub. Rels. Soc. Am., 1988, NY Addy Gold TV comml. award; named to Top 100 PR Profls. of Century, PR Week mag., 1999, Pub. Rels. Hall of Fame, D.C. chpt. PRSA, 1999. Mem. Arthur Page Soc. (trustee), Pub. Rels. Seminar, Sigma Delta Chi, Kappa Sigma (Man of Yr. 1982), Lambda Sigma, Omicron Delta Kappa. Methodist.

SPEAR, ALLAN HENRY, former state senator, historian, educator; b. Michigan City, Ind., June 24, 1937; s. Irving S. and Esther (Lieber) S. BA, Oberlin Coll., 1958, LLD (hon.), 1997; MA, Yale U., 1960, PhD, 1965. Lectr. history U. Minn., Mpls., 1964-65, asst. prof., 1965-67, assoc. prof., 1967-2000; mem. Minn. State Senate, St. Paul, 1973-2000, chmn. jud. com., 1983-93; chmn. crime prevention com., 1993-2000; pres. Minn. State Senate, 1993—2000; vice-chair Minn. Campaign Fin. and Pub. Disclosure Bd., 2001—03. Vis. prof. Carleton Coll., Northfield, Minn., 1970, Stanford U., Palo Alto, Calif., 1970. Author: Black Chicago, 1967. Mem. Internat. Network Gay and Lesbian Ofcls. Avocations: cooking, travel, reading, classical music. Home: 2429 Colfax Ave S Minneapolis MN 55405-2942

SPEAR, CHRIS, federal agency administrator; b. Auburn, Nebr. m. Michelle Spear; 2 children. B Polit. Sci., U. Wyo. Staff mem. Sen. Alan Simpson, Wyo., 1993; staff dir. Sen. Subcom. Employment, Safety and Tng.; legis. dir. Sen. Tim Hutchinson, Ark.; asst. sec. policy U.S. Dept. Labor, Washington, 2001—. Office: US Dept LAbor Policy 200 Constitution Ave NW Washington DC 20210

SPEAR, HARVEY M. lawyer; b. Providence, May 24, 1922; s. Alfred and Esther S.; m. Ruth Abramson, June 27, 1965; children: Jessica, Elizabeth Anne. AB, Brown U., 1942; LL.B., Harvard, 1948; MA, George Washington U., 1949, LL.M., 1952, S.JD, 1955. Bar: Mass. 1948, D.C. 1948, N.Y. 1954, U.S. Supreme Ct. 1954; CPA, Md. Asst. U.S. atty. D.C., 1945; legal asst. to chmn., asst. to vice chmn. SEC, 1948—50; spl. asst. to atty. gen. Dept. Justice, 1951—54; pvt. practice law N.Y.C. and Washington, 1956—; counsel Cadwalader Wickersham & Taft, N.Y.C., 1996—. Contbr. articles to profl. jours. Mem.: ABA, Assn. of Bar of City of NY. Home: 765 Park Ave New York NY 10021-4254 Office: 100 Maiden Ln New York NY 10038-4818 Home: 78 Hither Ln East Hampton NY 11937

SPEAR, LAURINDA HOPE, architect; BFA, Brown U., 1972; MArch, Columbia U., 1975. Registered architect, Fla., N.Y.; cert. Nat. Coun. Archtl. Registration. Founding prin. Arquitectonica (ARQ), Miami, Fla. Lectr. in field. Prin. works include Pink Ho., Miami, Fla., 1978, The Palace, Miami, 1982 (Honor award Miami chpt. AIA 1982), The Atlantis, Miami, 1982 (Miami chpt. AIA award 1983), The Imperial, Miami, 1983, Casa los Andes (Record Hos. award Archtl. Record 1986), North Dade Justice Ctr., Miami, 1987 (Honor award Miami chpt. AIA 1989), Rio, Atlanta, 1988 (Honor award Miami chpt. AIA 1989), Banco de Credito del Peru, Lima, 1988 (Honor award Miami chpt. AIA 1989), The Ctr. Innovative Tech., Herndon, Va., 1988 (Honor award Va. chpt. AIA 1989, Honor award Miami chpt. 1990, Merit award Fairfax, Va., County Exceptional Design Awards Program 1990), Sawgrass Mills (Merit award Miami chpt. AIA 1990, Honor award Fla. chpt. 1991), Miracle Ctr. (Honor award Miami chpt. AIA 1989), Internat. Swimming Hall of Fame, Ft. Lauderdale, Fla., 1991, Banque de Luxembourg, 1993, Disney All-Star Resorts, Orlando, Fla., 1994, U.S. Embassy, Lima, 1994, USCG Family Housing, Bayamon, P.R., 1994, Altamira Ctr., Caracas, Venezuela, 1994, Festival Walk, Hong Kong, 1998, Miami Fed. Courthouse, Am. Airlines Arena, Miami, 1999, Philips Arena, Atlanta, 1999, Miami Internat. Airport D-E-F Wrap. Mem. beaux arts support group Lowe Art Mus., Miami; bd. dirs. Miami Youth Mus. Recipient Design Awards citation Progressive Architecture, 1975, 80, Rome Prize in Architecture, 1978, Award of Excellence, Atlanta Urban Design Commn., 1989; inductee Interior Design Hall of Fame, 1999. Fellow AIA (Silver medal for design 1998); mem. Internat. Womens Forum. Office: Arquitectonica 550 Brickell Ave Ste 200 Miami FL 33131-2517

SPEAR, PAUL STANLEY, psychology educator, musician; b. Minot, Nd, July 26, 1941; s. Paul Edwin and Anna Louise (Meier) S.; life ptnr. Michael Eugene Rowe; children: Kimiko Victoria Bostwick, Paul Armstrong. BA in Psychology, Taylor U., Upland, Ind., 1963; MA in Psychology, U. Wyo., Laramie, 1965; PhD in Psychology, U. Denver, 1968. Instr. U. Denver, 1966—67; asst. prof. psychology San Diego State U., 1968—70; prof. psychology Calif. State U., Chico, 1970—, chair psychology, 1998—. Mem. and author CSU-SUNY-CUNY Joint Com., Long Beach, Calif. and N.Y.C., 1993—98. Contbr. articles. Organist St. John's Episcopal Ch., Chico, 1972—2003; chmn. bd. dirs. Chico Symphony Orch., 1978—84. Mem.: APA, Western Psychol. Assn., Soc. Rsch. in Child Devel. Democrat. Episcopalian. Avocations: swimming, travel, piano, bridge. Home: 5 Sir Aaron Ct Chico CA 95928 Office: Calif State U 1st and Normal Chico CA 95929-0234 Office Phone: 530-898-5147. Business E-Mail: pspear@csuchico.edu.

SPEAR, PETER D. academic administrator; BA, Rutgers U., 1966; PhD in Physiol. Psychology, Yale U., 1970. Postdoctoral fellow dept. neurology Stanford (Calif.) U. Sch. Medicine, 1970—72; asst. prof. psychology Kans. State U., 1972; mem. faculty dept. psychology U. Wis., Madison, 1976—78, prof., 1981, chair dept. psychology, 1990—94, assoc. dean social scis. Office Letters and Sci., 1994—96, provost, vice chancellor for acad. affairs, 2001—; dean Coll. Arts and Scis. U. Colo., Boulder, 1996—2001. Co-author: Psychology: Perspectives on Behavior. Office: Univ Wis Madison 150 Bascom Hall 500 Lincoln Dr Madison WI 53706*

SPEAR, RICHARD EDMUND, art history educator; b. Michigan City, Ind., Feb. 3, 1940; s. Irving S. and Esther Marion (Lieber) S.; m. Athena Tacha, June 11, 1965. BA, U. Chgo., 1961; MFA, Princeton U., 1963, PhD, 1965. Mem. faculty Oberlin (Ohio) Coll., 1964-2000, prof. art history, 1975-83, Mildred Jay prof. art history, 1983-2000; dir. Allen Meml. Art Mus., 1972-83; vis. disting. prof. U. Md., College Park, 1998—. Harn Eminent Scholar prof. U. Fla., 1997-98; disting. vis. prof. George Washington U., Washington, 1983-84; trustee Intermuseum Conservation Assn., 1972-83, pres., 1975-77. Author: Caravaggio and His Followers, 1971, 75, Renaissance and Baroque Paintings from the Sciarra and Fiano Collections, 1972, Domenichino, 1982, Domenichino, 1581-1641, 1996, The Divine Guido, 1997, From Caravaggio to Artemisia, 2002; editor-in-chief Art Bull., 1985-88; contbr. articles to profl. jours. Regional exec. bd. ACLU, 1974-76. Recipient Premio Daria Borghese Gold medal, 1972; Fulbright scholar Italy, 1966-67; Am. Coun. Learned Socs. fellow, 1971-72; NEH fellow, 1980-81, sr. fellow Ctr. Advanced Study in Visual Arts Nat. Gallery Art, 1983-84, Guggenheim fellow, 1987-88; Nat. Humanities Ctr. fellow, 1992-93, Rockefeller Found./Bellagio Ctr. fellow, 1996, Bogliasco Found./Liguria Study Ctr. fellow, 2003. Mem. Coll. Art Assn. Am. Democrat. Home: 3721 Huntington St NW Washington DC 20015-1817 Office: U Md Dept Art History & Archeol College Park MD 20742-0001 Office Phone: 202-362-2347.

SPEAR, SCOTT LAWRENCE, plastic surgeon; b. Chgo., Aug. 25, 1948; s. Louis and Esther S.; m. Cynthia Staley Spear; children: ALexandra, Geri, Louis. BA (hon.), U. Mich., Ann Arbor, 1968; MD, U. Chgo., 1972. Cert. Mass., 1986, Calif., 1992, Fla., 1990, Washington, 1981—, Md., 1982—, Va., 1982—. Intern Beth Israel Hosp., Boston, 1972-73; jr. residency San Francisco Gen. Hosp., 1973-74, Beth Israel Hosp., Boston, 1974-75, sr. residency, 1976-78; plastic surgery residency U. Miami, 1978-80; asst. prof. plastic surgery U. Fla., Gainesville, 1980-81, Georgetown U. Sch. Medicine, Washington, 1981-86, assoc. prof. plastic surgery, 1988-90, prof. plastic surgery, 1990—. Dir. Nat. Capitol Tng. program, Washington, 1992—, Divsn. of Plastic and Reconstructive Surgery, Georgetown U. Sch. Medicine, Washington, 1992—; vis. prof. U., Tex., 1982, U. Fla., 1982, 84, 85, 86, 87, Nat. Naval Med. Ctr., 1983, 85. Contbr. articles to profl. jours. Mem. ACS, Med. Soc. of D.C., Plastic Surgery Ednl. Found., Am. Cleft Palata Assn., Nat. Capital Soc. of Plastic Surgeons, Am. Soc. of Maxillofacial Surgeons, Am. Soc. of Plastic and Reconstructive Surgeons, Northeastern Soc. of Plastic and Reconstructive Surgeons, Am. Assn. Plastic Surgeons, Am. Soc. for Aesthetic Plastic Surgery. Office: Georgetown U Med Ctr 3800 Reservoir Rd NW Washington DC 20007-2113 Office Phone: 202-444-8751. E-mail: spears@gunet.georgetown.edu.

SPEARING, ANTHONY COLIN, English literature educator; b. London, Jan. 31, 1936; came to U.S., 1987; s. Frederick and Gertrude (Calnin) S. MA, Cambridge U., Eng., 1960. W.M. Tapp rsch. fellow Gonville-Caius Coll. Cambridge U., 1959-60, asst. lectr. in English, 1960-64, official fellow Queens' Coll., 1960-87, life fellow, 1987—, dir. studies in English, 1967-85, lectr. in English, 1964-85, reader in medieval English lit., 1985-87; vis. prof. English U. Va., Charlottesville, 1979-80, 84, prof. English, 1987-89, Kenan prof. English, 1989—. William Matthews lectr. Birkbeck Coll., London, 1983—84; invited lectr. numerous colls. and univs. Eng., Europe, Can., U.S.; Lansdowne vis. fellow U. Victoria, 1993; Benjamin Meaker vis. prof. U. Bristol, 2003. Author: Criticism and Medieval Poetry, 1964, rev. edit., 1972; (with Maurice Hussey and James Winny) An Introduction to Chaucer, 1965; The Gawain-Poet: A Critical Study, 1970, Chaucer: Troilus and Criseyde, 1976, Medieval Dream-Poetry, 1976, Medieval to Renaissance in English Poetry, 1985, Readings in Medieval Poetry, 1987, The Medieval Poet as Voyeur, 1993; editor: The Pardoner's Prologue and Tale (Chaucer), 1965, rev. edit., 1994, The Knight's Tale (Chaucer), 1966, rev. edit., 1995, The Franklin's Prologue and Tale (Chaucer), 1966, rev. edit., 1994; co-editor: (with Elizabeth Spearing) Shakespeare: The Tempest, 1971, Poetry of the Age of Chaucer, 1974, The Reeve's Prologue and Tale (Chaucer), 1979, Julian of Norwich: Revelations of Divine Love, 1998; translator: The Cloud of Unknowing and Other Works, 2001; contbr. numerous articles to profl. jours. Mem. Medieval Acad. Am., Internat. Assn. U. Profs. English, New Chaucer Soc. (trustee 1986-90). Office: Univ Va Dept English 219 Bryan Hall PO Box 400121 Charlottesville VA 22904-4121 E-mail: acs4j@virginia.edu.

SPEARMAN, DAVID HAGOOD, veterinarian; b. Greenville, S.C., Nov. 16, 1932; s. David Ralph and Elizabeth (Hagood) S.; m. Patsy Lee cordle, Dec. 18, 1954; children: Kathleen Elizabeth, David Hagood. Student, Clemson Coll., 1950-52, BS, 1975; DVM, U. Ga., 1956. With Cleveland Park Animal Hosp., Greenville, 1956-57; individual practice vet. medicine Easley, S.C., 1957—, Powdersville, S.C., 1957-96. Mem. S.C. State Bd. Vet. Examiners, 1981-87, chmn., 1987; advisor Pickins County Planning and Devel. Bd., 1972—; pres. Northside Parent-Tchr. Orgn., 1965-67; mem. adv. bd. vet. technicians program Tri-County Tech., 1975-76; mem. admissions com. Vet. Coll., U. Ga., 1975; mem. adv. com. pre-Vet Club, Clemson U.; chmn. Easley Zoning Bd., 1980-83; mem. S.C. Bd. Vet. Examiners, 1982-89, chmn., 1987. Mem. AVMA (alt. del. 1992-95, S.C. del. 1996-99), Blue Ridge Vet. Med. Assn. (founder, pres., sec.), S.C. Assn. Veterinarians (pres. 1974-75, publicity chmn. 1975—, chmn. animal health technician com., Veterinarianof Yr. 1985), Am. Animal Hosp. Assn. (assoc.), S.C. Wildlife, Pickens County Horse, Cattle and Fair Assn. (pres.), Jr. C. of C. (past officer, Key Man award 1959), Trout Unltd. (state dir.), Pickens County Foxhunters Assn., Clemson U. Tiger Lettermen Assn., Easley Boosters Club, Easley C. of C., World Wildlife Fund, Nat. Wildlife Fedn., Audubon Soc., Nature Conservancy, Internat. Platform Assn., Pickens County Hist. Soc., Lions (pres., internat. del. 1971, 73), Pendleton Farmers Soc., Eastatoee Valley Cmty. Club, Commerce Club, Cliffs at Glassy, Alpha Psi, Alpha Zeta. Presbyterian (deacon, elder, youth leader 1972-74, chmn. orgn. com. 1973-75, 83-85, pulpit com., chmn. nursery bldg. com., stewardship com.). Avocations: photography, fly fishing, bridge. Home: Burdine Springs PO Box 327 Easley SC 29641-0327 Office: 6714 Calhoun Memorial Hwy Easley SC 29640-3672

SPEARMAN, MORRIS LEROY, aeronautics and aerospace researcher; BS in Aeronautical Engring., Auburn U., 1943. Instr. aeronautical engring. Auburn U., 1943-44; aero. rsch. engr. NACA/NASA, Hampton, Va., 1944-58, sect. head stability & control, 1958-62, br. head supersonic aerodynamics, 1962-74, chief scientist mil. & fgn. tech., 1974-79, sr. tech. specialist aero. sys., 1979—. Fellow AIAA (Aerodynamics award 1998); mem. Air Force Assn., Air and Space-Smithsonian, Va. Acad. Sci., Auburn Alumni Engring. Coun. Achievements include first low-speed wind-tunnel tests of swept wings in the U.S., some of the first tests at transonic speeds in the U.S. by means of the transonic-bump technique, including a configuration which became the Bell X-1 experimental research airplane, leading to exploration of supersonic flight phenomena; work lead to design features to overcome problems of stability and control of supersonic flight; responsible for the first supersonic tests for research programs including the variable wing sweep concept for multi-mission aircraft, canard-type aircraft and missiles, supersonic transport concepts, and lifting-body reentry concepts; current research on advanced concepts for new, large subsonic transports; involvement in the development of research airplanes, tactical fighter airplanes, light-weight-fighter airplanes, various missiles, reentry vehicles and supersonic transport and high-speed civil transport airplanes. Office: NASA Langley Rsch Ctr Mail Stop 248 6 W Taylor St Hampton VA 23681-2102 Office Phone: 757-864-5226. Business E-Mail: m.l.spearman@larc.nasa.gov.

SPEARMAN, PATSY CORDLE, real estate broker; b. Richmond, Va., Aug. 23, 1934; d. Lee Pierce and Kathleen Jeanette (Munn) Cordle; m. David Hagood Spearman, Dec. 18, 1954; children: Kathleen Elizabeth, David Hagood. AA, Coll. William and Mary, 1952; student, U. Ga., 1953-54; grad., Realtors Inst., 1979; BS (hon.), Oglala Lakota Coll., Kyle, S.D., 2002. Copywriter Cabell Eanes Advt. Agy., Richmond, 1952; clk. athletic dept. U. Ga., Athens, 1954-55, sec. Coll. Agr., 1955-56; real estate saleswoman Merrill Lynch/C. Dan Joyner & Co., Inc. (now The Prudential), Greenville, S.C., 1978—. Past pres. Women of Ch.; Presbyn. Ch. Sunday sch. tchr. and youth leader. Recipient numerous awards for obtaining eye bank donors Lions Club and S.C. Eye Bank, Listing Agt. of Yr., 1985-87, 89, 90-93, Sales Agt. of Yr., 1987, 90, 91, 92. Mem. Nat. Assn. Realtors (cert. residential specialist), Real Estate Securities and Syndication Inst., S.C. Assn. Realtors, Greenville Bd. Realtors, Pickens County Bd. Realtors (chmn. cmty. svcs. com., edn. com., membership com. chmn.), Women's Coun. Realtors, Million Dollar Club (life, charter, Greenville and Pickens County), Am. Vet. M.A. Aux. (S.C. del. 1992-98, 2003, alt. del. 1999, del. 2003), S.C. Vet. Aux. (treas. 1988-92), Internat. Platform Soc., Inst. Noetic Scis., Smithsonian Assocs., Nat. Wildlife Fedn. (life), World Wildlife Fedn., Wilderness Soc., Sierra Club, Greenpeace, S.C. Wildlife Assn., Audubon Soc., Cousteau Soc., Smithsonian Inst., Better Homes (Easley) Club, Commerce Club Greenville (life), Greenville Little Theater, Eastatoee Valley Assn., Easley Foothills Theatre, Warehouse Theater, Nature Conservancy, Edisto Hist., Cliffs at Glassy Country Club. Home: 505 Asbury Cir Easley SC 29640-1343 Office: PO Box 327 Easley SC 29641-0327

SPEARS, ALEXANDER WHITE, III, tobacco company executive; b. Grindstone, Pa., Sept. 29, 1932; s. Alexander White and Eva Marie (Elliott) S.; m. Shirley Pierce; 1 child, Craig Stewart. BS, Allegheny Coll., Meadville, Pa., 1953; PhD, SUNY, 1960. Research asso., then research fellow SUNY, Buffalo, 1956-58; instr. Millard Fillmore Coll., Buffalo, 1958-59; with Lorillard Corp., Greensboro, N.C., 1959-2000, v.p. R & D, 1971-74, sr. v.p. ops. and rsch., 1975-79, exec. v.p. ops. and rsch., 1979-91, vice chmn., COO, 1991-95, chmn., CEO, 1995-99; chmn. Lorillard Tobacco Co., Greensboro, 1999-2000, also bd. dirs. Asst. prof. Guilford Coll., 1961-65, mem. bd. assocs., 1990, 91, trustee, 1995—. Patentee in field; past editor: Tobacco Sci. Jour. Chmn. Coun. on Edn., 1974, mem. exec. com., 1987; chmn. model sch. task force Greensboro Bd. Edn. and Greensboro C. of C., 1975; mem. N.C. Humanities Coun., 1978-81, Piedmont Triad Airport Authority, 1993-99, treas., 1995-97, vice chmn., 1997-99; bd. dirs. United Way of Greensboro, 1980-85, 97—, chmn., 2000, chmn. campaign cabinet, 1999; bd. dirs. N.C. Bus. Com. on Edn., 1983-84, Greensboro Devel. Corp., 1985—, pres., 1992-94, exec. commn., 1987—; chmn. Greensboro Area United Negro Coll. Fund, 1982, N.C. AT&T St. U., Focus on Excellence campaign, 1984-86, Greensboro Pub. Sch. Fund, 1987; capital campaign chmn. Greensboro Area Girl Scouts U.S., 1987; bd. dirs. N.C. A&T U. Found., 1985-93, trustee, 1990—, sec., 1995-97, vice chmn., 1997-99, chmn., 2000—; bd. dirs. Greensboro NCCJ, 1990-92, chmn. ann. dinner, 1991, N.C. Citizens for Bus. and Industry, 1984-88, YMCA, 1989-96, chmn., 1993-95; chmn. Hayes-Taylor Capital Campaign, 1990; bd. dirs. Ctr. Indoor Air Rsch., 1988-99, chmn., 1991-95, Coun. for Tobacco Rsch., 1990-99; mem. U.S. Tech. Study Group Cigarette Safety Act of 1984, U.S. Study CPSC Tech. Adv. Group Cigarette Safety Act. of 1990; adv. bd. U. N.C., Greensboro, 1988-94; chmn. fundraiser campaign Greensboro Hist. Mus., 1988-89, trustee, 1989—; mem. Forward Guilford II Exec. Com., 1998—; chmn. bd. visitors Greensboro Coll., 1990-94; mem. Greensboro Cmty. Initiative, 1996—; mem. adv. coun. N.C. Ctr. for Nonprofits, 1999—. Recipient Disting. Achievement award in tobacco sci. Philip Morris, 1970, Nat. Brotherhood award NCCJ, 1999, Citation award N.C. Piedmont Triad region, 1999; named to Jr. Achievement Bus. Leaders Hall of Fame, 1994, and YMCA Hall of Fame, 1994, hon. life mem. YMCA, 1996—. Mem. AAAS, Am. Chem. Soc., Soc. Applied Spectroscopy, Am. Mgmt. Assn., N.Y.

Acad. Scis., Am. Judicature Soc. (hon.), Internat. Coop. Ctr. Sci. Rsch. Relative to Tobacco (sci. com. 1972), Greensboro C. of C. (bd. dirs. 1974-75, 86-87, 96-99, chmn. 1997, Nathaniel Greene award 1975, hon. chmn. 1994 Kmart Greater Greensboro Open). Presbyterian. Office: Lorillard Tobacco Co 714 Green Valley Rd Greensboro NC 27408-7018 also: PO Box 10529 Greensboro NC 27404-0529

SPEARS, BRITNEY, singer; b. McComb, Miss., Dec. 2, 1981; d. Jamie and Lynne Spears; m. Jason Alexander, Jan. 2, 2004 (annulled); m. Kevin Federline, Sept. 18, 2004; 2 stepchildren. Singer: (albums) Baby One More Time, 1999, Oops! I Did It Again, 2000 (Billboard Album artist of the Year, 2000), Britney, 2001, In the Zone, 2003; actor(voice): (TV films) Hooves of Fire, 1999, Legends of the Lost Tribe, 2002, : (films) Longshot, 2000, Crossroads, 2002; composer: (songs) (for film Drive Me Crazy) You Drive Me Crazy, 1999, (for film Pokémon the First Movie: Mewtwo Strikes Back) Soda Pop, 1999, (for film On The Line) Let Me Be, 2001, (for film Jimmy Neutron: Boy Genius) Intimidated, 2001, (for film Austin Powers in Goldmember) Boys, 2002. Britney Spears Found. Recipient Female Artist of the Year, Billboard, 1999, New Artist of the Year, 1999, Best New Artist, Am. Music Awards, 2000. Mailing: Jive Records 137 W 25th St New York NY 10001-7216

SPEARS, DAVID D. trading commission executive; m. Pam Spears; 2 children. BS in Agrl. Econs., Kans. State U., 1979. Various positions to asst. v.p. Wichita Bank for Coops., 1979-89; legis. asst. Senator Robert Dole, Washington, 1989-92, state dir. Wichita, 1992-96; commr. Commodity Futures Trading Commn., Washington, 1996 . Office: US Commodity Futures Trading Commn Three Lafayette Ctr 1155 21st St NW Washington DC 20036-3308

SPEARS, DIANA FAYE, computer scientist; b. N.Y.C., Aug. 17, 1952; d. Stanley R. and Vivian E. Sadin. BA, U. N.Mex., 1974; MA, U. Md., 1986, PhD, 1990. Programmer/analyst Goddard/NASA, Greenbelt, Md., 1978-80; computer scientist Nat. Bur. Stds., Gaithersburg, Md., 1980-86, Naval Rsch. Lab., Washington, 1986-2001; prof. U. Wyo., Laramie, 2001—. Assoc. editor jour. in field. Mem. AAAI, Assn. Women in Sci., Women in Sci. and Engring., Am. Math. Soc., Sigma Xi. Avocations: art, skiing, hiking, biking. Office: Dept Computer Sci U Wyo Laramie WY 82071-3682 E-mail: dspears@cs.uwyo.edu.

SPEARS, DIANE SHIELDS, artist, retired art academy administrator; b. Seattle, May 21, 1942; d. Richard Keene McKinney and Dorothy Jean (Shields) Thacker; m. Howard Truman Spears, Sept. 3, 1977; 1 child, Truman Eugene. BA in Art, English, Edn., Trinity U., 1964; MA in Christian Counseling, San Antonio Theol. Sem., 1986, D of Christian Edn., 1988. Cert. tchr. secondary edn., elem. edn., ednl. supervision, Tex. Instr. ESL Dliel-Geb (Def. Lang. Inst.), San Antonio, 1973-74, Ceta/Ace Bexar County Sch. Bd., San Antonio, 1975-78; tchr. elem. edn., art, music New Covenant Faith Acad., San Antonio, 1983-89; instr. ESL Jewish Family Svc., San Antonio, 1991; tchr. elem. art Edgewood Ind. Sch. Dist., San Antonio, 1992-93, dist. art specialist, 1993-95, fine arts coord., 1995—99, dir. visual arts, 2002—04; tchr. 4th-7th grade reading, lang. arts, art tchr. Pipe Creek Christian Sch., Tex., 2004—, admistrv. asst. reading program, art tchr., 2004—. Owner, operator Art for Kings, San Antonio, 1985—2004, Spears Art Studio, Inco., 2004—. Illustrator teacher-created materials-lit. activities for young children, 1989-90; author: (art curriculum) Art for Kings, 1987; editor: (art curriculum) Edgewood Ind. Sch. Dist. Elem. Art Curriculum, 1993; exhibited in group shows at Charles and Emma Frye Mus., Seattle, 1966, 68, Centro Cultural Aztlan Galerie Expression, 1998 (Best of Show 1998). Dir. intercessory prayer New Covenant Fellowship, San Antonio, 1980-90. Recipient awards for painting and graphics, San Antonio, 1996-98. Mem.: San Antonio Art Edn. Assn. (1st pl. 1995), Tex. Art Edn. Assn. (1st pl. graphics divsn. 1995), Nat. Mus. for Women in Arts (charter). Republican. Avocations: water-skiing, motorcycle riding, sewing, writing. Home: 264 Mountain Dr Lakehills TX 78063-6725 E-mail: shieldsandspears@earthlink.net.

SPEARS, DONALD EDWARD, management consultant; b. Bay City, Mich., May 31, 1945; s. James Edward and Eula Fay (Sappington) Spears; children: Carlos Robert, Kevin M. Keller, Alex E. BA, Coll. of the Ozarks, Pt. Lookout, Mo., 1967; MPA, The Am. U., 1975. Sr. assoc. Mgmt. Sys. Internat., Washington, 1981—; v.p./co-founder Resolution Dynamics, Inc., 1988—. Adj. prof. The Am. U., Washington, 1990—94. Pres. bd. trustees Wash. Ethical Soc., Wash., DC, 1997—99. With U.S. Army, 1967—69. Democrat. Avocations: art, sculpting, naturalist.

SPEARS, GEORGANN WIMBISH, marketing executive; b. Ft. Worth, Apr. 21, 1946; d. George Vardeman and Lela Ellon (Clifton) Wimbish. BA in Govt. and History, Tex. Christian U., 1969. Cert. secondary govt. and history tchr., Tex. V.p., gen. mgr., feature editor, contbg. writer Sports Today Mag., Arlington, Tex., 1982-83; editor corp. newsletter, contbg. writer Amason Internat. Mktg., Dallas, 1983-85; supply mgr., customer svc. rep., dir. Am. Photocopy, Arlington, 1985-92; v.p., dir. Mineral Wells (Tex.) Clay Products, Inc., 1993-96; v.p. mktg., vice chmn. bd. dirs. Educators Industries, Inc., Ft. Worth, 1996—, chmn. bd. dirs., 1995—; v.p., vice chmn., bd. dirs. Superior Properties, Inc., 1995—. Active Jewel Charity Ball, Ft. Worth, 1979—, Rep. Party of Tex., Austin, 1983—, PETA, 1992—; vol. ICU and CCU Arlington Meml. Hosp., 1983-86; vol. John Peter Smith Hosp., 1980-82. Mem. U. North Tex. Athletics (trustee 1994—), People for Ethical Treatment of Animals, Barnaby Club, Jr. Women's Club Ft. Worth (sec.-treas. 1979-80, v.p. 1980-81, pres. 1981, bd. dirs. 1981-82). Republican. Episcopalian. Avocations: creative writing, decorating, horseback riding. Office: Educators Industries Inc 1909 Rockbrook Dr Arlington TX 76006-6615

SPEARS, JAE, state legislator; b. Latonia, Ky. d. James and Sylvia (Fox) Marshall; m. Lawrence E. Spears; children: Katherine Spears Cooper, Marsha Spears-Duncan, Lawrence M., James W. Student, U. Ky. Reporter Cin. Post, Cin. Enquirer newspapers; rschr. Stas. WLW-WSAI, Cin.; tchr. Jiya Gakuen Sch., Japan; lectr. U.S. Mil. installations East Anglia, Eng.; del. State of W.Va., Charleston, 1974-80; mem. W.Va. Senate, Charleston, 1980-1993. Mem. vis. com. W.Va. Extension and Continuing Edn., Morgantown, 1993-2000, W.Va. U. Sch. Medicine, 1992—; with state sen., 1980-93; apptd. to Jud. Hearing Bd., 1993-2000. Chmn. adv bd. Sta. WNPB, 1992-94; congl. liaison Am. Pub. TV Stas. and Sta. WNPB-TV, 1992-97; mem. coun. W.Va. Autism Task Force, Huntington, 1981-90; mem. W.Va. exec. bd. Literacy Vols. Am., 1986-90, 94—, pres., 1990-92; mem. Gov.'s State Literacy Coun., 1991-97; bd. dirs. Found. Ind. Colls. W.Va., 1986—; mem. regional adv. com. W.Va. Gov.'s Task Force for Children, Youth and Family, 1989; mem. USS W.Va. Commn., 1989; mem. exec. com. W.Va. Employer Support Group for Guard and Res., 1989, mem. steering com., 1990-92. Decorated Purple Heart (hon.); recipient Susan B. Anthony award NOW, 1982, edn. award Profl. Educators Assn. W.Va., 1986, ann. award W.Va. Assn. Ret. Sch. Employees, 1985, Meritorious Svc. award W.Va. State Vets. Commn., 1984, Vets. Employment and Tng. Svc. award U.S. Dept. Labor, 1984, award W.Va. Vets. Coun., 1984; named Admiral in N.C. Navy, Gov. of N.C., 1982, hon. Brigadier Gen. W.Va. N.G., 1984, One of 11 Women Pioneers of W.Va. Legislature, W.Va. U. Inst. for Pub. Affairs, 1997. Mem. DAR, VFW (aux.), Bus. and Profl. Women (Woman of Yr. award 1978), Nat. League Am. Pen Women (Pen Woman of Yr. 1984), Nat. Order Women Legislators, Am. Legion (aux.), Delta Kappa Gamma, Alpha Xi Delta. Democrat. Home and Office: PO Box 98 Shinnston WV 26431

SPEARS, JAMES GRADY, small business owner; b. Port Arthur, Tex., July 20, 1941; s. John Grady and Dorothy Nell (Haney) S. Grad. high sch., Port Arthur. Adminstr. Child Health & Devel. Studies, Oakland, Calif., 1962-69; sales mgr. Sunshine Biscuits Inc., Houston, 1969-75; owner, pres. S.W. Tookie Inc./Tookie's Restaurant, Seabrook, Tex., 1975—. Mem. Greater Houston Conv. and Visitors Bur., Clear Lake Conv. Visitors Bur. With USN, 1959-62. Mem. Tex. Restaurant Assn., Houston Restaurant Assn., Seabrook Assn., Old Seabrook Assn. Republican. Roman Catholic. Avocations: collectibles, fine art, antiques, listening to records, self improvement. Home: 16310 Hickory Knoll Dr Houston TX 77059-5311 Office: SW Tookie Inc/Tookie's Restaurant 1202 Bayport Blvd Seabrook TX 77586-3406

SPEARS, LOUISE ELIZABETH, minister, secondary school educator; b. Liberty, Miss., Feb. 2, 1945; d. Willie and Alice Gray Spears; 1 child, Guy Alice. BSc, Alcorn State U., 1966; MSc, Ind. U., 1969; PhD, U. N. Colo., 1975; MDiv, Garrett-Evang. Theol. Sem., 1983. Cert. African Meth. Episcopal Ch., 90; Tchr. Ga. Tchr. Hazlehurst H.S., Hazlehurst, Miss., 1967—68; tchg. asst. Ind. U., Bloomington, Ind., 1968—70; tchr. Ala. State U., Montgomery, Ala., 1970—72, Ky. State U., Frankfort, Ky., 1972—73, Jackson State U., Jackson, Miss., 1975—81; pastor United Meth. Ch., Keosauqua, Iowa, 1983—85, Detroit, 1985—88; tchr. Clarke County Sch. Dist., Athens, Ga., 1998—; pastor African Meth. Episcopal Ch., various, Ga., 2000—. Realtor Ga. Real Estate, Atlanta, 1989—92; academic adminstr. Emmanuel Bible Coll., Macon, Ga., 1992—93; substitute tchr. Atlanta Pub. Sch., Atlanta, 1994—98; co-chmn. Augusta Ga. Conf., Augusta, Ga., 2001, mem. stewardship commn.; fin. coord. Reach Out and Touch Club, Inc., 2002—03; mem. Athens-Clarke County Commn. on Disability, 2003; mem. career and tech. edn. exec. adv. bd. Athens-Clarke County Commn. on Disability; mem. career and tech. edn. adv. bd. Tech. Prep Awareness, 2003, mem. sub-com., 03. Co-author: National Poetry Book, 1995; featured cover story: Zebra Mag., 2001. Bd. dir. Reach Out & Touch Club, Inc., Athens, 2001—. Recipient Cmty. Svc. award, Reach Out & Touch Club, Inc., 2000. Mem.: NEA, Nat. Assn. Social Studies, Reach Out and Touch Club (fin. coord.). Democrat. African Meth. Episcopal. Avocations: reading, travel, writing, listening, helping. Home: 200 Crane Drive 18 Bogart GA 30622 Office: Alternative Education Program 440 Dearing Extension Athens GA 30606

SPEARS, MARIAN CADDY, dietetics and institutional management educator; b. East Liverpool, Ohio, Jan. 12, 1921; d. Frederick Louis and Marie Caddy Spears-Ralston; m. Sholto M. Spears, May 29, 1959; m. Joseph D. Ralston, May 29, 1998. BS, Case Western Res. U., 1942, MS, 1947; PhD, U. Mo., 1971. Chief dietitian Bellefaire Children's Home, Cleve., 1942-53; head dietitian Drs. Hosp., Cleve., 1953-57; assoc. dir. dietetics Barnes Hosp., St. Louis, 1957-59; asst. prof. U. Ark., Fayetteville, 1959-68; assoc. prof. U. Mo., Columbia, 1971-75; prof., head dept. hotel, restaurant, instn. mgmt. and dietetics Kans. State U., Manhattan, 1975-89. Cons. dietitian small hosps. and nursing homes; cons. dietetic edn. Author: Foodservice Organizations Textbook, 4th edit., 2000, Foodservice Procurement Textbook, 1st edit., 1998, 99; contbr. articles to profl. jours. Recipient Kans. State U. Advancement award, 1997. Mem. Am. Dietetic Assn. (Copher award 1989), Am. Sch. Foodsvc. Assn., Food Systems Mgmt. Edn. Coun., Soc. Advancement of Foodsvc. Rsch., Nat. Restaurant Assn., Coun. Hotel, Restaurant, Inst. Mgmt. Edn., Manhattan C. of C., Sigma Xi, Gamma Sigma Delta, Omicron Nu, Phi Kappa Phi. Office: Kans State U 105 Justin Hall Manhattan KS 66506-1400 Home: 2025 Meadowlark Rd Manhattan KS 66502-4558

SPEARS, ROBERT FIELDS, lawyer; b. Tulsa, Aug. 1, 1943; s. James Ward and Berneice (Fields) S.; m. Jacquelyn Castle, May 10, 1961; children: Jeff, Sally. BBA, Tex. Tech. U., 1965; JD, U. Tex., 1968. Bar: Tex. 1968. Assoc. Rain, Harrell, Emery, Young & Doke, Dallas, 1968-73, ptnr., 1974-87, Locke Purnell Rain Harrell, Dallas, 1987-91; gen. counsel Fin. Industries Corp., Austin, Tex., 1991-96; gen. counsel, sec. Lone Star Techn. Inc., Dallas, 1996—. Pres. Sr. Citizens of Greater Dallas, 1988. Mem. ABA, Tex. Bar Assn., Dallas Bar Assn., Dallas Country Club, Phi Delta Phi. Republican. Baptist. Avocation: tennis. Office: Lone Star Technologies Inc PO Box 803546 Dallas TX 75380-3546

SPEARS, RONALD DEAN, judge; b. Michigan City, Ind., July 30, 1951; s. Lonnie and Frances Ellen (Benad) Spears; m. Annette Jean Greffe, Dec. 22, 1973; 1 child, Donald Dean. BA, U. Ill., 1974; JD, So. Ill. U., 1977. Bar: Ill. 1977, U.S. Dist. Ct. (ctrl. and so. dists.) Ill. 1977, U.S. Ct. Appeals (7th cir.) 1977, U.S. Supreme Ct. 1983. Law clk. U.S. Dist. Ct., Springfield, Ill., 1977-79; ptnr. Miley, Meyer, Austin, Spears & Romano, P.C., Taylorville, Ill., 1979—93; judge Ill. Cir. Ct., 4th Jud. Cir., Taylorville, 1993—. Atty. City of Taylorville. Col. JAGC, Ill. Army N.G. Mem.: ABA, Lincoln-Douglas Am. Inn of Ct., Christian County Bar Assn. (pres. 1987), Ill. State Bar Assn. (bd. govs. 1997—2002), Toastmasters (pres. 1988), So. Ill. U. Law Sch. Alumni Assn. (pres. 1984), Optimists (pres. 1986, lt. gov. 1986—87). Home: 3501 Lake Dr Taylorville IL 62568-8930 Office: Ill Cir Ct 4th Jud Cir Rm 316 Christian County Courthouse Taylorville IL 62568-2245 E-mail: jspears@chipsnet.com.

SPEARS, SALLY, lawyer; b. San Antonio, Aug. 29, 1938; d. Adrian Anthony and Elizabeth (Wylie) S.; m. Tor Hultgreen, July 15, 1961 (div. Jan. 1983); children: Dagny Elizabeth, Sara Kirsten, Kara Spears. BA, U. Tex., 1960, LLB, 1965. Bar: Tex. 1961, Ill. 1971. Practice law, Stamford, Conn., 1966-67, Chgo., 1970-71, Northbrook, Ill., 1972-73, Toronto, Ont., Can., 1973-81; assoc. firm Cummings & Lockwood, Stamford, 1966-67, Kirkland & Ellis, Chgo., 1970-71; sr. atty. Allstate Ins. Co., Northbrook, Ill., 1971-73; gen. counsel, sec. Reed Paper Ltd., Reed Ltd., Toronto, 1973-78, Denison Mines Ltd., Toronto, 1978-81; pvt. practice law San Antonio, 1981—. Apptd. by Sec. of Def. to serve on Def. Adv. Com., Women in the Svcs., 1997-99. Author: Call Sign Revlon: The Life and Death of Navy Fighter Pilot Kara Hultgreen, 1998. Mem. Tex. Bar Assn., San Antonio Bar Assn., Bankruptcy Bar Assn., Bexar County Women's Bar Assn., San Antonio County Club, The Club at Sonterra. Home: 433 Evans Ave San Antonio TX 78209-3725 Office: Ste 106 8151 Broadway San Antonio TX 78209-1938 Office Phone: 210-826-7020. Personal E-mail: sespears@swbell.net.

SPEAS, BRUCE ORBURN, theater educator; s. Orburn Lee Speas. BA, U. Richmond; MFA, Va. Commonwealth U.; MA, Bowling Green U. Mng. dir. Raft Theatre, N.Y.C., 1981—89; instr. Longwood U., Farmville, Va., 1996—99; asst. prof. U. Tenn., Knoxville, 2000—; resident dir. Clarence Brown Theatre, Knoxville, Tenn., 2000—. Author: (theatrical play) Stitch & Yubie (Dramalogue Award, Outstanding Writing, 1990), Goodbye Henry (Barn Playwright Festival, NJ, 1988), Summer Storm (NY and LA Prodn.). Mem. panel Knoxville Arts Coun. Mem.: Southeastern Theatre Conf. (assoc.), Theatre Comm. Group (assoc.), Alpha Psi Omega, Pi Kappa Phi. Office: U Tenn 206 McClung Tower Knoxville TN 37996

SPEAS, CHARLES STUART, human resources consultant, entrepreneur; b. Phila., Jan. 1, 1944; s. Austin LeRoy and Peggy Elaine (Drake) S.; m. Julie Ellen Royce, Apr. 10, 1965; children: Eric S. Speas, Robert Austin Speas. Student, Tri-State Coll., U. Notre Dame, Purdue U. Lic. agt. in life, accident and health ins., Ind. Sr. scheduling coord. Excel Industries, Elkhart, Ind., 1966-73; corp. dir. pers. EFP Corp., Elkhart, 1973-97; pvt. practice, 1997-98; founder Speas Enterprises, Inc., Hickory, NC, 1998—; human resources adv. Magellan Group, Hickory, NC, 2002—04. Cons. various Elkhart, Hickory, Goshen area bus., 1980—. Contbr. articles profl. jours. Participant Soviet/Am. Conf. on Trade and Econ. Cooperation, Kremlin, 1991. With USAF, 1962-66. Mem. Ind. Pers. Assn., Goshen Indsl. Club (recipient cert. of appreciation 1990), Soc. for Human Resources Mgmt., Elkhart C. of C. (task force on healthcare availability/cost). Republican. Avocations: woodworking, fishing, gardening, golf. Home: 5724 Rocky Mountain Rd Granite Falls NC 28630

SPECHT, ALICE WILSON, university libraries dean; b. Caracas, Venezuela, Apr. 3, 1948; (parents Am. citizens); d. Ned and Helen (Lockwood) Wilson; m. Joe W. Specht, Dec. 30, 1972; 1 child, Mary Helen. BA, U. Pacific, 1969; MLS, Emory U., 1970; MBA, Hardin-Simmons U., 1983. Libr. social scis. North Tex. State U., Denton, 1971-73; reference libr. Lubbock (Tex.) City and County Libr., 1974-75; system coord. Big Country Libr. System, Abilene, 1975-79; assoc. dir. Hardin-Simmons U., 1981-88, dir. univ. librs., 1988—. Apptd. Mayor's Task Force Libr. Svcs., 1995-96. Author bibliog. instrn. aids, 1981-90; editor; The College Man, For Pilots Eyes Only. Mem. mayor's task force Abilene Pub. Libr., 1995—96; mem. Libr. Sci. Art. Bd. for Tex. Recipient Boss of Yr., Am. Bus. Women's Assn., 1994. Mem.: ALA, Abilene Libr. Consortium (chair adminstrv. coun. 1990, coord. nat. conf. 1991, chair adminstrv. coun. 1993, coord. nat. conf. 1993, chair adminstrv. coun. 1998, 2002, coord. nat. conf. 2002), Tex. Libr. Assn. (chair com. 1978—84, sec.-treas. coll. and univ. librs. divsn. 1993—94, legis. com. 1994—), Texshare Ednl. Working Group (chair 1999, 2002, libr. systems act adv. bd. mem. 2001—), Rotary (chair com. 1989—90). Home: 918 Grand Ave Abilene TX 79605-3233 Office: Hardin-Simmons U PO Box 16195 2341 Hickory St Abilene TX 79698-6195 Business E-Mail: aspecht@hsutx.edu.

SPECHT, CHRISTIAN EDWARD, writer; b. Shirley, Mass., June 11, 1962; s. Christian Leroy and Rita Eileen Specht. BA, Western Ill. U., Macomb, 1981—85. Adminstrv. spec. US Army, Ft. Lewis/Johnston Atoll, 1987—90; data controller United Engineers & Constructors, Johnston Atoll, 1990—93; sales rep. Madison Newspapers Inc., Wis., 1994—98; customer svc. Elan Fin. Services, Milw., 1999—2001; writer self-employed, Milw., 2002—. Author: (novels) The Yoop, 2002, Bridge To Nowhere, 2002, The Wild Land, 2004. SP41990 U.S. Army, Johnston Atoll. Lutheran. Avocation: fishing.

SPECHT, DENNIS, company executive; Former CFO, COO, Svcs. Group Am., Seattle; now dynamicsoft, Inc., East Hanover, N.J. Office: Dynamicsoft Inc 600 Lanidex Plz Parsippany NJ 07054-2711 Fax: (206) 933-5247.

SPECHT, GORDON DEAN, retired petroleum executive; b. Garner, Iowa, June 3, 1927; s. Reuben William and Gladys (Leonard) S.; m. Cora Alice Emmert, May 24, 1952; children: Mary Ellen, Grant. BS in Chem. Engring., Iowa State U., 1950, MS in Chem. Engring., 1951; SM in Chem. Engring., MIT, 1954. Engr. Exxon Corp. Bayway Refinery, Linden, N.J., 1951-59, systemn services div. mgr., 1960-61, engring. services div. mgr., 1962-63, chem. coordination div. mgr., 1964; mgr. systems dept. Exxon Corp.-Exxon Chem. Co., N.Y.C., 1965-70; sr. advisor communications and computer scis. dept. Exxon Corp., Florham Park, N.J., 1971-76, assoc. cons., 1977-85; retired, 1986. Asst. scoutmaster Boy Scouts Am., Westfield, N.J., 1986—; sr. qualified observer Sperry Obs., Cranford, N.J., 1986—; celestial navigation instr. U.S. Power Squadrons, 1990—. With U.S. Army, 1945-46, 1st lt. C.E., 1952-53, Korea. Decorated Bronze Star. Mem. Am. Inst. Chem. Engrs., Amateur Astronomers, Inc., No. N.J. Sail and Power Squadron, MIT Club of No. N.J., MIT Club of Princeton, Nat. Eagle Scout Assn., Tau Beta Pi, Phi Lambda Upsilon, Phi Kappa Phi, Tau Kappa Epsilon. Republican. Methodist. Achievements include patents in field. Avocations: astronomy, sailing, canoeing, swimming, bicycling. Home: 5930 Encina Rd Goleta CA 93117

SPECIALE, RICHARD, investment company executive; b. N.Y.C., Aug. 16, 1945; BSBA, Georgetown U., 1967; MBA, NYU, 1976. Sr. acct. Price Waterhouse & Co., N.Y.C., 1969-74; mng. dir. J.P. Morgan and Co. Inc., N.Y.C., 1974-99; mng. prin. Aequitas, LLC, N.Y.C., 1998—. Bd. dirs. instnl. owners divsn. Real Estate Bd. N.Y., 1984—, chmn., 1991-98, mem. bd. govs., 1988-90, 92—, exec. com. 1997—; bd. dirs. Downtown-Lower Manhattan Assn., Inc., N.Y.C., Grand Ctrl. Partnership Inc.; mem. adv. bd. Real Estate Inst., NYU, 1984—; dir. Realty Found. of N.Y., 1994—. Bd. dirs. Children's Arts and Scis. Workshops, N.Y.C., 1978-84; trustee Dance Theatre Found., N.Y.C., 1984—, Alvin Ailey Am. Dance Theatre, N.Y.C., 1984—; mem. real estate and constrn. coun. Lincoln Ctr., 1985—. Mem. AICPA, N.Y. State Soc. CPAs, Industrial Devel. Rsch. Coun. Office: Aequitas LLC 600 Madison Ave New York NY 10022-1615 Fax: 212-371-1078. E-mail: rspeciale@aequitas.net.

SPECK, EUGENE LEWIS, internist; b. Boston, Dec. 17, 1936; s. Robert A. and Anne (Rosenberg) S.; m. Rachel Shoshana; children: Michael Robert, Keren Sara. AB, Brandeis U., Waltham, Mass., 1958; MS, U. Mass., 1961; PhD, George Washington U., 1966, MD, 1969. Diplomate Am. Bd. Internal Medicine with subspecialty in infectious diseases. Intern N.Y. Hosp.-Cornell, 1969-70; rsch. assoc. NIH, Bethesda, Md., 1970-72; resident Barnes Hosp.-Washington U., 1972-73; instr. medicine Washington U., St. Louis, 1972-73; fellow Strong Meml. Hosp.-U. Rochester, 1973-75; instr. medicine U. Rochester, N.Y., 1973-75, asst. prof. medicine, 1975-80, U. Nev., Las Vegas, 1980-85, assoc. prof., 1985-95, prof. medicine, 1995—; dir./co-dir. infectious disease unit U. Med. Ctr. of So. Nev., Las Vegas, 1980—; ptnr. Infectious Diseases Consultants, 1983—. Cons. Clark County Health Dept., Las Vegas, 1980—, U. Med. Ctr. So. Nev., Las Vegas, 1980—, Sunrise Hosp., Las Vegas, 1980—, Valley Hosp., Las Vegas, 1980—. Contbr. articles to profl. jours., chpts. to books. Recipient Disting. Physician award, State of Nev., 2002. Fellow ACP; mem. Am. Soc. Microbiology, Infectious Disease Soc. Am., Alpha Omega Alpha. Avocations: tennis, skiing, racquetball. Home: 2228 Chatsworth Ct Henderson NV 89074-5309 Office: Infectious Diseases Cons 3006 S Maryland Pkwy Ste 780 Las Vegas NV 89109-2292 Office Phone: 702-737-0740.

SPECK, LAWRENCE W. architect, educator; b. Houston, Apr. 22, 1949; s. H.K. and Esther (Elliot) S.; m. Cynthia Alexander, Jan. 2, 1971 (div. 1988); children: Sloan Garret, Harrison Alexander; m. Amanda Mayhew Dealey, Oct. 3, 1992. BS in Mgmt., BS in Art and Design, MIT, 1971, MArch, 1972. Registered architect, Mass., Tex. Instr. MIT, Boston, 1972-75; asst. prof. U. Tex., Austin, 1975-79, assoc. prof., 1979-84, prof., 1984—; dean U. Tex. Sch. Arch., Austin, 1993—; prin. Lawrence W. Speck Assocs., Austin, 1975—. Dir. Ctr. Study Am. Architecture U. Tex., Austin; adj. curator architecture Dallas Mus. Art, 1985-87. Editor: Architecture for the Emerging American City, 1985; author: Landmarks of Texas Architecture, 1986; co-editor: New Regionalism, 1987. Bd. dirs. Buell Ctr. Columbia U., N.Y.C., 1985-87. Fulbright Sr. scholar Council for Internat. Exchange Scholars, 1978. Fellow AIA (5 design awards Austin chpt. 1984-87); mem. Tex. Soc. of Architects (3 design awards 1986), Soc. Arch. Historians, Sigma Chi. Avocations: athletics, children's literature. Office: 606 West Ave Austin TX 78701-2725

SPECK, SAMUEL WALLACE, JR., state official; b. Canton, Ohio, Jan. 31, 1937; s. Samuel Wallace Sr. and Lois Ione (Schneider) S.; m. Sharon Jane Anderson, Jan. 20, 1962; children: Samuel Wallace III, Derek Charles. BA, Muskingum Coll., 1959; postgrad., U. Zimbabwe, Harare, 1961; MA, Harvard U., 1963, PhD, 1968. Prof. polit. sci. Muskingum Coll., New Concord, Ohio, 1964-83, asst. to pres., 1986-87, exec. v.p., 1987, acting pres., 1987-88, pres., 1988-99; assoc. dir. Fed. Emergency Mgmt. Agy., 1983-86; mem. Ohio Ho. of Reps., 1971-76; state senator from Ohio 20th Dist., 1977-83; dir. Dept. Natural Resources, mem. Gov's. cabinet State of Ohio, 1999—. Bd. dirs. Camco Fin. Corp., Cambridge, Ohio, Advantage Savs. Bank; pres. Eastern Ohio Devel. Alliance, 1990-92; Fund for Improvement of Postsecondary Edn., 1990-92, chmn. 1991. Contbr. numerous articles on African and Am. govt. and pub. policy. Bd. dirs. Ohio Tuition Trust Authority, 1991-93, Internat. Ctr. for Preservation Wild Animals, Lake Erie Commn., 1999—; bd. dirs., chmn. Ohio Water Resources Coun., 1999—; mem. Great Lakes Commn., 1999—, chmn., 2002—; mem. Ohio Power Siting Bd., 1999—; mem. Ohio Pub. Works Commn., 2003—. Recipient Outstanding Legislator award VFW/DAV/Am. Legion, Conservation Achievement award State of Ohio, Disting. Svc. award, Nat. Gov. Conf., 2004, Conservation Leadership award, Ohio Nature Conservancy. Mem. Assn. Ind. Colls. and Univs. of Ohio (chmn. 1992-94). Republican. Home: 240 Greenbriar Ct Worthington OH 43085-3055 Office: Dir OH Dept of Natural Resources 1930 Belcher Dr # D-3 Columbus OH 43224-1392

SPECK, WILLIAM T. former physician, health facility administrator; BS, Rutgers U.; MD, Wake Forest U. Sch. Medicine, 1968. Resident Columbia U., N.Y.C., fellow, with dept. pediat. and microbiology; with dept. pediat. Case Western Reserve U., Cleve., prof., chmn., dir., dept. pediat.; CEO Rainbow Babies and Children's Hosp., Cleve., 1982—92; pres., CEO Presbyn. Hosp. in City of N.Y./Columbia-Presbyn. Med. Ctr., 1992—99; interim dir., CEO Marine Biol. Lab., Woods Hole, Mass., 2000—. Office: Marine Biol Lab 7 MBL St Woods Hole MA 02543

SPECTER, ARLEN, senator; b. Wichita, Kans., Feb. 12, 1930; s. Harry and Lillie (Shanin) S.; m. Joan L. Levy, June 14, 1953; children: Shanin, Stephen. Student, U. Okla., 1947-48; BA Internat. Rels., U. Pa., 1951; LL.B., Yale U., 1956. Asst. counsel Warren Commn., Washington, 1964; magisterial investigator Commn. of Pa., 1965; asst. dist. atty. City of Phila., 1959-63, dist. atty., 1966-74; ptnr. Dechert Price & Rhoads, Phila., 1956-66, 74-80; U.S. senator from Pa., 1981—. Lectr. law Temple U., 1972-75, U. Pa., 1968-72; chmn. Appropriations Subcom. on Labor, Health and Human Svcs. and Edn. and Related Agys., Subcom. on Agr., Rural Deve. and Related Agys., Subcom. on

Transp., Subcom. on Def., Subcom. on Fgn. Opers., Jud. Subcom. on Antitrusts, Bus. Rights, and Competition, Subcom. on Immigration, Subcom. on Terrorism, Tech. and Govt. Info., Govtl. Affairs Subcom. on Internat. Security, Proliferation and Fed. Svcs., Permanent Subcom. on Investigations, Subcom. on Oversight of Govt. Mgmt., Restructuring and D.C. Bd. editors Law Jour.; contbr. articles to profl. jours. 1st Lieutenant, U.S. Air Force, 1951-53. Recipient Youth Svcs. award B'nai B'rith, 1966; recipient Sons of Italy award, 1968, Community Humanitarian award Bapt. Ch., 1969, man of Yr. award, Temple Beth Ami, 1971, N.E. Cath. High Sch. Outstanding Achievement award, 1973. Mem. Phi Beta Kappa. Republican. Jewish. Office: US Senate 711 Senate Hart Bldg Washington DC 20510-0001

SPECTER, RICHARD BRUCE, lawyer; b. Phila., Sept. 6, 1952; s. Jacob E. and Marilyn B. (Kron) S.; m. Jill Ossenfort, May 30, 1981; children: Lauren Elizabeth, Lindsey Anne, Allison Lee. BA cum laude, Washington U., St. Louis, 1974; JD, George Washington U., 1977. Bar: Mo. 1977, U.S. Dist. Ct. (ea. and we. dists.) Mo. 1977, U.S. Ct. Appeals (8th cir.) 1977, Ill. 1978, Pa. 1978, U.S. Dist. Ct. (ea. dist.) Ill. 1979, U.S. Ct. Appeals (7th cir.) 1979, Calif. 1984, U.S. Dist. Ct. (cen. dist.) Calif. 1985, U.S. Ct. Appeals (9th cir.) 1986, U.S. Dist. Ct. (so. dist.) Calif. 1987, U.S. Dist. Ct. (no. dist.) Calif. 1988, U.S. Supreme Ct. 1999. Assoc. Coburn, Croft, Shepherd, Herzog & Putzell, St. Louis, 1977-79; ptnr. Herzog, Kral, Burroughs & Specter, St. Louis, 1979-82; exec. v.p. Uniqey Internat., Santa Ana, Calif., 1982-84; pvt. practice law L.A. and Irvine, Calif., 1984-87; ptnr. Corbett, Steelman, & Specter, Irvine, 1987—. Instr. Nat. Law Ctr. George Washington U. 1975. Mem. ABA, Ill. Bar Assn., Mo. Bar Assn., Pa. Bar Assn., Calif. Bar Assn. Jewish. Home: 37 Bull Run Irvine CA 92620-2510 Office: 18200 Von Karman Ave Ste 200 Irvine CA 92612-1086 E-mail: rspecter@corbsteel.com.

SPECTOR, DANIEL EARL, historian, educator; b. Pensacola, Fla., Dec. 19, 1942; s. Joseph and Dorothy Margaret (Givens) S.; m. Esta Gelda Rappaport, Aug. 9, 1964; children: Warren Leigh, Susan Artemis (dec.). BA, George Washington U., 1963; postgrad., U. Fla., 1963-64; MA, U. Tex., 1972, PhD, 1975. Adj. instr. Jacksonville (Ala.) State U., 1975-77; chief skill qualification test br. U.S. Army Mil. Police Sch., Ft. McClellan, Ala., 1975-80; supr. edn. specialist U.S. Army Chem. Sch., Ft. McClellan, 1980-82; chief U.S. Army Chem. Sch. Standardization & Analysis Div., Ft. McClellan, 1982-84; dep. dir. U.S. Army Chem. Sch. Directorate of Tng. & Doctrine, Ft. McClellan, 1984-88; adj. prof. U. Ala., Birmingham, 1986—2001; chem. corps historian U.S. Army Chem. Sch., Ft. McClellan, 1988-94; adj. prof. Troy State U., Ft. Benning, Ga., 2003—. Accreditation coord. U.S. Army Chem. Sch., Ft. McClellan, 1984-90; accreditation team chief So. Assn. Colls. and Schs., Atlanta, 1985-90; U.S. Army rep. EURO-NATO nuc., biol. and chem. workgroups, 1984-90. Author: Chemical School Annual Historical Reviews, 1988-90. Mem. Jacksonville Kiwanis, 1981-92. Alumni scholar George Washington U., 1959-63; NDEA fellow U. Fla., 1963-64, NDFL fellow U. Tex. 1972-73. Mem. Middle Eastern Studies Assn., Middle East Inst., Am. Hist. Assn., Soc. Mil. History, Ala. Assn. Historians, MENSA, Temple Beth-El, Scottish Rite, Hiram Lodge, Ala. Master Gardener, Legion of Honor, Chapel of Four Chaplains, Phi Alpha Theta. Democrat. Jewish. Avocations: gardening, fishing, pistol shooting. Home: 1317 7th Ave NE Jacksonville AL 36265-1174 Office Phone: 256-435-4798. Personal E-mail: drspector@cableone.net.

SPECTOR, DAVID M. lawyer; b. Rock Island, Ill., Dec. 20, 1946; s. Louis and Ruth (Vinikour) S.; m. Laraine Fingold, Jan. 15, 1972; children: Rachel, Laurence. BA, Northwestern U., 1968; JD magna cum laude, U. Mich., 1971. Bar: Ill. 1971, U.S. Dist. Ct. (no. dist.) Ill. 1971, U.S. Ct. Appeals (7th cir.) 1977, U.S. Ct. Appeals (4th cir.) 1984, U.S. Dist. Ct. (cen. dist.) Ill. 1984, U.S. Supreme Ct. 1999, N.Y. 2002, U.S. Ct. Appeals (2d cir.) 2002. Clk. Ill. Supreme Ct., Chgo., 1971-72; ptnr., assoc. Isham, Lincoln & Beale, Chgo., 1972-87; ptnr. Mayer, Brown & Platt, Chgo., 1987-97, Hopkins & Sutter, Chgo., 1997-2001, Schiff, Hardin LLP, Chgo., 2001—. Chmn. ABA Nat. Inst. on Ins. Co. Insolvency, Boston, 1986; co-chmn. ABA Nat. Inst. on Internat. Reins.: Collections and Insolvency, NY, 1988; chmn. ABA Nat. Inst. on Life Ins. Co. Insolvency, Chgo., 1993; spkr. in field. Editor: Law and Practice of Insurance Company Insolvency, 1986, Law and Practice of Life Insurer Insolvency, 1993; co-editor: Law and Practice of International Reinsurance Collections and Insolvency, 1988; contbr. articles to profl. jour. Mem. ABA (chair Nat. Inst. on Life Insurer Insolvency 1993), Chgo. Bar Assn., Lawyer's Club of Chgo. Office: Schiff Hardin LLP 6600 Sears Tower Chicago IL 60606 Home: 1418 Lake Shore Dr Chicago IL 60611 E-mail: dspector@schiffhardin.com.

SPECTOR, ELEANOR RUTH, corporation executive; b. N.Y.C., Dec. 2, 1943; d. Sidney and Helen Lebost; m. Mel Alan Spector, Dec. 10, 1966; children: Nancy, Kenneth. BA, Barnard Coll., 1964; postgrad. sch. pub. adminstrn., George Washington U., 1965-67; postgrad sch. edn., Nazareth Coll., 1974. Indsl. investigator N.Y. State Dept. Labor, White Plains, 1964-65; mgmt. intern Navy Dept., Washington, 1965, contract negotiator, 1965-68, contract specialist, 1975-78, contracting officer/br. head, 1978-82, dir. div. cost estimating, 1982-84; dep. asst. sec. def. for procurement Washington, 1984-91; dir. Def. Procurement, Washington, 1991-2000; v.p. contracts Lockheed Martin Corp., Bethesda, Md., 2000—. Advisor Nat. Contract Mgmt. Assn., 1984— Recipient Def. Meritorious Civilian Svc. medal, 1986, 93, 96, Meritorious Svc. Presdl. award, 1989, 94, Disting. Civilian Svc. Presdl. award, 1990, 97, Def. Disting. Civilian Svc. medal, 1991, 94, 2000, Nat. Pub. Svc. award, 1998, Sec. Def. award for Excellence, 1997. Office: Lockheed Martin Corp MP 110 6801 Rockledge Dr Bethesda MD 20817-1877

SPECTOR, GERSHON JERRY, otolaryngologist, educator, researcher; b. Rovno, Poland, Oct. 20, 1937; came to U.S., 1949; naturalized, 1956; m. Patsy Carol Tanenbaum, Aug. 28, 1965. BA, Johns Hopkins U., 1960; MD cum laude, U. Md., 1964. Intern Beth Israel Hosp., Boston, 1964-65; resident in surgery Sinai Hosp., Balt., 1965-66; resident in otolaryngology Mass. Eye and Ear Infirmary, Boston, 1966-69, Peter Bent Brigham Hosp., Boston, 1968-69; teaching fellow in otolaryngology Harvard U. Med. Sch., Boston, 1968-69; assoc. physician Ill. Crippled Children's Svc., Carbondale, 1971; mem. faculty Washington U. Med. Sch., St. Louis, 1971—, assoc. prof. otolaryngology, 1974-76, prof., 1976—; chief dept. otolaryngology St. Louis County Hosp., 1971-77. Mem. staff Washington U. Med. Ctr., Barnes Hosp.; dir. temporal bone bank, 1971-81; guest examiner Am. Bd. Otolaryngology, 1975-77; rsch. cons. neurosci. group, G.D. Searle Pharm. Corp. Mem. editl. bd. Laryngoscope, 1978, editor-in-chief, 1984-94; contbr. articles to med. jours. With U.S. Army, 1969-71. Hancock scholar, 1962. Fellow ACS; mem. AAAS, AMA, Am. Acad. Ophthalmology and Otolaryngology (Honor award 1979), St. Louis Med. Soc., St. Louis County Med. Soc., Am. Coun. Otolaryngology, St. Louis Ear, Nose and Throat Club (pres. 1986), So. Med. Assn., Deafness Rsch. Found., Pan. Am. Assn. Otorhinolaryngology and Broncho Esophagology, Am. Soc. Head and Neck Surgery, Soc. Univ. Otolaryngologists, Am. Laryngol., Rhinol. and Otol. Soc. (Edmund Prince Fowler award 1974), Am. Soc. Cell Biology, Electron Microscopy Soc., N.Y. Acad. Scis., Am. Assn. Anatomists, Am. Acad. Facial Plastic and Reconstructive Surgery, Am. Neuro-Otology Soc., Gesellschaft fur Neurootologie und Aequilibrimoetrie A.V., Barany Soc., Am. Radium Soc., Assn. Acad. Surgery, Am. Fedn. Clin. Oncologic Socs., Am Otol. Soc., Acoustical Soc. Am., Soc. for Neurosci., Internat. Skull Base Soc. (founding), Brazilian Skull Base Soc. (hon.), Centurion Club, Alpha Omega Alpha, Psi Chi. Home: 7365 Westmoreland Dr Saint Louis MO 63130-4241 Office: Washington U Med Sch Saint Louis MO 63110 Office Phone: 314-362-7252. Business E-Mail: spectorg@ent.wustl.edu.

SPECTOR, MARTIN WOLF, lawyer, business executive; b. Phila., 1938; BA, Pa. State U., 1959; JD, U. Pa., 1962. Bar: Pa. 1962. Judge U.S. Dist. Ct., until 1967; asst. gen. counsel ARA Services, Phila., assoc. gen. counsel, 1969-76, v.p., 1976-83, gen. counsel, 1983—, formerly sr. v.p.; exec. v.p. ARAMARK, Phila., 1985—. Served to lt. USN, 1953-56. Office: ARAMARK 1101 Market St Ste 45 Philadelphia PA 19107-2988

SPECTOR, MELBOURNE LOUIS, retired foreign service officer; b. Pueblo, Colo., May 7, 1918; s. Joseph E. and Dora (Bernstein) S.; m. Louise Vincent, Nov. 23, 1948; 1 son, Stephen David. BA with honors, U. N.Mex., 1941. Intern U.S. Bur. Indian Affairs, 1941, Nat. Inst. Pub. Affairs, 1941; personnel asst. Office Emergency Mgmt., 1941-42; chief classification div. War Relocation Authority, 1942-43, Hdqrs. USAAF, 1943-45; employment officer UNRRA, 1945-46; pvt. employment, 1946-47; personnel officer Dept. State, 1947-49; detail Econ. Coop. Adminstrn., 1948; dep. dir. personnel Econ. Coop. Adminstrn., Marshall Plan, Paris, 1949-51; dep. dir., acting dir. personnel Econ. Coop. Adminstrn., Mut. Security Adminstrn., FOA, 1951-54; asst., dep. dir. Mission to Mexico, ICA, 1954-57, acting dir., 1957-59; chief C. Am., Mex. and Caribbean div. ICA, 1959-61; dir. Office Personnel Mgmt., AID, 1961-62; exec. dir. Bur. Inter-Am. Affairs, Dept. State, 1962-64; commd. consul gen., sec., 1964; counselor for adminstrv. affairs Am. embassy, New Delhi, India, 1964-66; seminarian Sr. Seminar Fgn. Policy, Dept. State, 1966-67; exec. dir. U.S.-Mex. Commn. for Border Devel. and Friendship, 1967-69, Am. Revolution Bicentennial Commn., 1969-71; mem. mgmt., policy and coordination staffs Dept. State, 1971-73; ret., 1973; cons., 1973—. Mem. Fgn. Svc. Grievance Bd., 1976-77; advisor Peace Corps Dir., 1979-80; exec. dir. Am. Consortium for Internat. Pub. Adminstrn., 1980-84, 93-94, dir. Marshall Plan Oral History Project, 1987-97. Mem. Cosmos Club, Am. Soc. Pub. Adminstrn., Pi Kappa Alpha, Phi Kappa Phi. Home: 6414 Bannockburn Dr Bethesda MD 20817-5430

SPECTOR, MICHAEL JOSEPH, agribusiness executive; b. N.Y.C., Feb. 13, 1947; s. Martin Wilson and Dorothy (Miller) S.; m. Margaret Dickson, Sept. 14, 1977. BS in Chemistry, Washington and Lee U., 1968. Rsch. chemist Am. Viscose, Phila., 1968-69; pres. MJS Entertainment Corp., Miami, Fla., 1970-84; also MJS Internat., Inc.; ptnr. Old Town Key West Devel. Ltd., Fla., 1977—2002; vice dean Consular Corp of P.R., 2003—, dean, 2004. Pres. MJS Entertainment of Can., Inc., Toronto, Canada, Margo Farms, MJS Prodns., Inc., N.Y.C.; chmn., CEO Margo Caribe, Inc., Dorado, PR, 1981—, bd. dir.; pres. Costa Del Norte Devel., Inc., Dorado, 1998—; bd. dir. Goodwill Industries So. Fla., v.p. fin., 1980; bd. dir. Plz. Bank of Miami; hon. Consul Belgium in P.R., U.S. V.I., 2000, Turks & Caicos Islands, West Indies; dir. Consular Corp. of P.R., 2002, vice-dean, 2003—04. Internat. judge The Floralies Exhbn., Gent, Belgium, 2000; knight Sociedad Heraldica Espanola, 2003—. With AUS, 1969-70. Robert E. Lee rsch. grantee Washington and Lee U., 1967-68; named Agri-bus. Exec. of Yr., Govt. of P.R., 1999. Mem. Nat. Assn. Record Merchandisers (dir. Nova divsn., chmn. one-stop distbn. com. 1982-83), Country Music Assn., Dorado Beach Golf and Tennis Club, Bankers Club P.R., Ocean Reef Club (Key Largo, Fla.), Grove Isle Club (Coconut Grove, Fla.). Achievements include patent for synthetic stretching process. Home: Call Box 1370 Dorado PR 00646-1370 Business E-Mail: mspector@margocaribe.com.

SPECTOR, PHIL, record company executive; b. Bronx, N.Y., Dec. 25, 1940; m. Veronica Bennett, 1968 (div. 1974); children: Gary Phillip and Louis Phillip (twins), Donte Phillip, Nicole and Phillip (twins). Student, UCLA. Producer with Atlantic Records, 1960-61; founder Philles Records, 1962; now pres. Warner-Spector Records, Inc.; also Mother Bertha Music. Mem. mus. group: Teddy Bears, 1958-59; producer records for Gene Pitney, Ike and Tina Turner, Ben E. King, the Beatles, Righteous Bros., Checkmates, Crystals, Ronettes, John Lennon, George Harrison, The Ramones, Yoko Ono, others; producer album A Concert for Bangladesh (Grammy award); composer songs including You've Lost That Lovin' Feelin' (7 million performances; named most performed song in U.S. broadcasting history 1997), others; appeared in films Tami, Easy Rider; prod., TV documentary film A Giant Stands 5 Ft. 7 In.; prod. film That Was Rock. Named to Rock and Roll Hall of Fame, 1989; named Country Music Song of Yr. Songwriter and Pub. for To Know Him Is To Love Him, 1989; recipient lifetime achievement award U. Calif., Berkeley, 1994, Phila. award Phila. Music Alliance, 1994 (includes star on Phila.'s Walk of Fame), Trustees award (Grammy) NARAS, 2000; inducted into Songwriters Hall of Fame, 1996. Office: c/o Warner-Spector Records Inc 686 S Arroyo Pky Pasadena CA 91105-3233 E-mail: phillesrecords@earthlink.net.

SPECTOR, PHILLIP LOUIS, lawyer; b. L.A., July 15, 1950; s. Everett L. Spector and Rebecca (Horn) Newman; m. Carole Sue Lebbin, May 11, 1980; children: Adam, David. Student, U. Birmingham, Eng., 1970-71; BA with highest honors, U. Calif., Santa Barbara, 1972; M in Pub. Policy, JD magna cum laude, Harvard U., 1976. Bar: Calif. 1976, D.C. 1978, U.S. Ct. Appeals (D.C. cir.) 1983, U.S. Supreme Ct. 1983, U.S. Dist. Ct. D.C. 1985. Law clk. U.S. Ct. Appeals (2d cir.), Brattleboro, Vt., 1976-77; law clk. to U.S. Supreme Ct., Washington, 1977-78; assoc. asst. to Pres. U.S., Washington, 1978-80; assoc. Verner, Liipfert, Bernhard & McPherson, Washington, 1980-83; ptnr. Goldberg & Spector, Washington, 1983-92, Paul, Weiss, Rifkind, Wharton & Garrison, Washington, 1992—, mng. ptnr. Washington office, 2001—. Cons. U.S. exec. br. Close-Up Found., Alexandria, Va., 1980—. Co-author: Communications Law and Practice, 1995, Communications and Technology Alliances: Business and Legal Issues, 1996; contbr. articles to profl. jours. Mem. Coun. on Fgn. Rels., N.Y.C., 1980-85; moot ct. judge Nat. Assn. Attys. Gen., Washington, 1987—; adviser Dem. caucus U.S. Ho. Reps., Washington, 1981-83; speechwriter, podium prodr. Dem. Nat. Convs., N.Y.C., 1980, Phila., 1982, San Francisco, 1984, Atlanta, 1988, N.Y.C., 1992, Chgo., 1996, L.A., 2000, Boston, 2004. Recipient Disting. Achievement in Pub. Svc. Medal U. Calif., Santa Barbara, 1981, Close-Up Found. awards Via Satellite Mag., Vol. Recognition award Nat. Assn. Attys. Gen., 1993; named Leading Satellite Specialist in Washington, European Counsel, 2000. Mem. ABA (former chair internat. comm. law com.), Fed. Comms. Bar Assn., Bethesda Country Club, Addison Res. Country Club, Wintergreen Club, Phi Beta Kappa. Jewish. Office: Paul Weiss Rifkind Wharton & Garrison 1615 L St NW Ste 1300 Washington DC 20036-5694 Office Phone: 202-223-7340. E-mail: pspector@paulweiss.com.

SPECTOR, ROBERT DONALD, language professional, educator; b. N.Y.C., Sept. 21, 1922; s. Morris and Helen (Spiegel) S.; m. Eleanor Helen Luskin, Aug. 19, 1945; children: Stephen Brett, Eric Charles. BA, L.I. U., 1948, DHL, 1994; MA, NYU, 1949; PhD, Columbia U., 1962. Instr. L.I. U., Bklyn., 1948-59, asst. prof., 1959-62, assoc. prof., 1962-65, prof. English, 1965-94, chmn. senate, 1966-67, 69-70, chmn. dept., 1970-75, dir. humanities and comm. arts, 1975-84, coord. div. of humanities and div. of comms. and performing arts, 1990—, dir. humanities, 1984-90, prof. emeritus, 1993—. Editor, cons. Johnson Reprint Corp., 1967-84 Author: English Literary Periodicals, 1966, Tobias George Smollett, 1968, updated edit., 1989, Pär Lagerkvist, 1973, Arthur Murphy, 1979, Tobias Smollett: A Reference Guide, 1980, The English Gothic, 1983, Backgrounds to Restoration and Eighteenth-Century English Literature, 1989, Political Controversy, 1992, Smollett's Women, 1994, Samuel Johnson and the Essay, 1997, Love Poems & Others, 1998, Mélanje a Deux, 1999, Nature's Bounty in Brooklyn, 2000, Poems of Love and Laughter, 2003, New Poems, 2003; editor: Essays on the Eighteenth Century Novel, 1965, Great British Short Novels, 1970, 9 other vols. English and Am. lit., revs. and articles, poetry, fiction. Trustee L.I. U., 1969-70; chmn. George Polk Award Com., 1977—. Served with USCGR, 1942-46. Recipient L.I. U. Trustee award for scholarly achievement, 1978, Tristram Walker Metcalfe Alumnus of Year, 1981; Swedish Govt. travel and research grantee, 1966; fellow Huntington Library, 1974; fellow Folger Library, 1975; fellow Newberry Library, 1976 Mem. MLA, Am.-Scandinavian Found. (publs. com. 1962-84), P.E.N., Acad. Am. Poets. Home: 1761 E 26th St Brooklyn NY 11229-2405 Office Phone: 718-488-1115.

SPECTOR, RONALD H. historian, educator; b. Pitts., Jan. 17, 1943; s. David D Spector and Ethel Barsky; m. Dianne B. Frank, Sept. 27, 1970; children: Daniel A, Jonathan A. AB, Johns Hopkins U., Balt., 1964; MA, Yale U., New Haven, 1966; PhD, Yale U., 1967. Asst. pro. history La. State U., Baton Rouge, 1969—71; historian U.S. Army Ctr of Mil. History, Washington, 1971—84; prof. of history U. of Ala., Tuscaloosa, 1984—90; prof of history and internat. rels. Elliott Sch. of Internat. Affairs, George Wash. U., Washington, 1990—, dir. security policy studies, 1990—96. Disting. vis. prof. Keio U., Tokyo, 2000—01; chmn., dept of history George Wash. U., Washington, 1997—2000; vis. prof. of strategy Nat. War Coll., Washington, 1995—96; Fulbright sr. lectr. Haifa U., Haifa, Israel, 1993—94; dir. of naval history and curator Navy Dept. Dept. of Def., Washington, 1986—89; Fulbright sr. lectr. Jamia Millia Islamia, New Delhi, 1977—78; cons. in field. Author: (history) At War At Sea: Sailors and Naval Combat In the Twentieth Century (Soc. For Mil. Hist. Disting. Book Award; Wash. Post Best Books, 2001), After Tet: The Bloodiest Year In Vietnam, Eagle Against The Sun:The American War With Japan (Theodore And Franklin Roosevelt Prize In Naval History;NEW YORK TIMES Notable Books Of 1984, 1985), Advice And Support: The Early Years Of the U.S. Army In Vietnam (New Republic Best Books Of 1984, 1984). Cons. Smithsonian Inst. Nat. Mus. Am. Hist. Lt. col. USMCR, 1967—97. Decorated Navy Acheivement Medal with V device USMC. Mem.: Dept. of Army Hist. Adv. Com., Am. Com. On the History Of the Second World War (bd. of directors 1992—2002), Soc. for Mil. History (v.p. 1989—91). Avocation: stamp collecting/philately. Office: George Washington U Dept of History Washington DC 22052 Office Phone: 202-994-6425. Personal E-mail: spector@gwu.edu. E-mail: spector@gwu.edu.

SPECTOR, ROSE, state supreme court justice; BA, Columbia U.; JD, St. Mary's Sch. Law, 1965. Judge County Ct. at Law 5, 1975-80, 131st Dist. Ct., 1981-92; justice Tex. Supreme Ct., 1993-98; atty. Bickerstaff, Heath, Pollan, Kever & McDaniel, L.L.P., Austin, Tex., 1998—. Office: Bickerstaff Heath et al 1700 Frost Bank Plz 816 Congress Ave Ste 1700 Austin TX 78701-2643

SPECTOR, SHELLY, company executive; MS, Syracuse U. Pres., creative dir. Spector & Assocs., 1991—. Recipient Creative All Star Nat. award, 1998. Office: 636 Morris Tpke Short Hills NJ 07078-2608

SPECTOR, WARREN J. investment banker; m. Margaret Whitton. Grad., Duke U. Exec. v.p., head fixed income group The Bear Stearns Companies, Inc., N.Y.C., 1997—; pres., co-COO The Bear Stearns Companies, N.Y.C., 2001—. Vol. Gift of Life Bone Marrow Registry; chmn., Wall Street div. United Jewish Appeal; bd. dirs. New York Shakespeare Festival. Named a Forty Under Forty, Crain's NY Business, 1996. Office: The Bear Stearns Companies Inc 245 Park Ave New York NY 10167-0002*

SPEECE, RICHARD EUGENE, civil engineer, educator; b. Marion, Ohio, Aug. 23, 1933; s. Irvin Ward S. and Desta May (Speece); m. Jean Margaret Edscorn, Nov. 15, 1969; children: Eric Jordan, Lincoln Dana. BCE, Fenn. Coll., 1956; M of Engring., Yale U., 1958; PhD, MIT, 1961. Assoc. prof. civil engring. U. Ill., Urbana, 1961-65; prof. N.Mex. State U., 1965-70, U. Tex., Austin, 1970-74; Betz chair prof. environ. engring. Drexel U., Phila., 1974-88; Centennial prof. Vanderbilt U., Nashville, 1988—. Vis. scholar Cambridge (Eng.) U., 1994; cons. to govt., industry. Contbr. articles to profl. jours.; patentee in field. Recipient hon. mention for best paper Trans. Am. Fisheries Soc., 1973 Mem. Assn. Environ. Engring. Profs. (Disting. Faculty award 1970, disting. lectr. 1978, trustee 1981-83, Engring. Sci. award 1982), ASCE (J. James Cross medal 1983), Am. Soc. Microbiologists, Water Environ. Fedn. (Harrison Prescott Eddy medal 1966), U.S. ANC (Founder's award 1991), Internat. Assn. on Water Pollution Rsch. and Control. Office: Vanderbilt U Dept Civil Engring Nashville TN 37235

SPEED, CYNTHIA AGNES, retired mathematics educator; d. Carter Coleman and Lillian Jeannette Speed. BA, Calif. State U., Sacramento, 1962; MA, Stanford U., 1967. C.C. Supr. credential Calif., 1980, C.C. Instr. credential Calif., 1973, gen. secondary tchg. credential Calif., 1963. Tchg. asst. in ednl. stats. U. of Calif., Berkeley, Calif., 1963; math. instr. Hiram W. Johnson Sr. H.S., Sacramento, 1963—67, John F. Kennedy Sr. H.S., Sacramento, 1967—69; math. lectr. Calif. State U., Sacramento, 1969—69, Calif. Poly. State U., San Luis Obispo, Calif., 1969—71; math. instr. Santa Rosa Jr. Coll., Calif., 1973—73; math. instr. and dept. chair Mendocino Coll., Ukiah, Calif., 1973—2003; ret., 2003. Exec. com. mem. Tech. in the Redwoods Conf., Ukiah, Calif., 1988—89; course descriptors com. mem. Calif. Articulation Number Sys., Sacramento, 1986—88; chairperson, creator, and organizer Math. Contest for Jr. and Sr. H.S. Students in Mendocino and Lake Counties, Ukiah, Calif., 1975—79. Author: (computer program) Technology in the Redwoods Computer Contest Prize Winners, Lake View Water Co. Billing Program, Black Bart Trail Rd. Assn. Dues Assessment Program. V.p. and mem. Lake View Mut. Water Co., Redwood Valley, Calif., 1977—; treas. and mem. Black Bart Trail Rd. Assn., Redwood Valley, Calif., 1977—. Mem.: AAUW, NEA, Calif. Teachers Assn., Nat. Coun. of Teachers of Math., Calif. Math. Coun., Math. Assn. of Am., Calif. Math. Coun., Cmty. Colls. (mem. at large), Calif. State U. Sacramento Alumni Assn., Stanford Alumni Assn., Delta Kappa Gamma. Roman Catholic. Avocations: piano, swimming, golf, dance, travel. Home: 4949 Black Bart Trail Redwood Valley CA 95470 Office: 1232 43d St Sacramento CA 95819 Personal E-mail: sac67449@saclink.csus.edu.

SPEED, LESLIE BOKEE, lawyer; b. Balt., Jan. 19, 1949; d. William George and Jean Alice (LaVine) Speed. BA, U. Colo., 1972; JD, U. Denver, 1977. Bar: Colo. 1978, Md. 1999. Assoc. Holland and Hart, Denver, 1978-84, ptnr., 1984-93; dir., shareholder Parcel Mauro P.C., Denver, 1993-98; ptnr. Gallagher, Evelius & Jones, Balt., 1998—. Author: Corporate Powers, 1990; gen. editor U. Denver Law Rev., 1977. Bd. dirs. Denver Broncos Charities Fund, 1993-98, Colo. Lawyers Health Program, 1994-98, Bryn Mawr Sch. Alumnae Assn., 1999-2000; mem., sec. Colo. state adv. com. to U.S. Commn. on Civil Rights, Denver, 1974-77; sec. Denver Broncos Youth Found., 1984-98. Mem. ABA, Colo. Bar Assn. (co-chmn. gaming, entertainment and sports law com. 1994-95), Denver Bar Assn., Md. State Bar Assn. Balt., Sports Lawyers Assn. (bd. dirs. 1988-2002), Order of St. Ives. Democrat. Episcopalian. Home: 2901 Boston St Apt 608 Baltimore MD 21224-4891 Office: Gallagher Evelius & Jones 218 N Charles St Ste 400 Baltimore MD 21201-4033

SPEED, SHANNON ELEANORA, anthropologist, educator; b. L.A., Feb. 10, 1964; d. William James and Iris Ann Speed; m. Miguel Angel de los Santos, Aug. 5, 2001; 1 child, Camila de los Santos Speed. PhD, U. Calif., Davis, 2001. Vis. scholar Helen Kellogg Inst. Internat. Studies, Notre Dame, Ind., 2002—03; asst. prof. anthropology U. Tex., Austin, 2001—. Author: (jour. article) Human Rights Quar., Cultural Dynamics, Polit. and Legal Anthropology Rev., (chpt. in edited vol.) Women of Chiapas, (book chpt.) Human Rights in the Maya Region. Advisor Chiapas Cmty. Human Rights Defenders' Network, San Cristobal de Las Casas, Mexico, 1999—. Recipient Minority Dissertation award, Am. Anthrop. Assn., 2000; fellow Dissertation Rsch. Fellowship on Peace and Security in a Changing World, MacArthur Found. / Social Sci. Rsch. Coun., 1998—2000, Dissertation Fellowship, Ford Found., 2000—01, Vis. Scholar Fellowship, Ctr. for U.S.-Mexican Studies, U. Calif. San Diego, 2000—01, Helen Kellogg Inst. of Internat. Studies, U. Notre Dame, 2002. Mem.: Latin Am. Studies Assn., Am. Anthropological Assn. Office: Univ Tex at Austin Dept of Anthropology EPS 1104 Austin TX 78723 Office Phone: 512-232-5386. Home Fax: 512-471-6585. Personal E-mail: sspeed@mail.utexas.edu. E-mail: sspeed@mail.utexas.edu.

SPEER, DAVID BLAKENEY, industrial executive; b. Sault Ste. Marie, Ont., Apr. 6, 1951; s. Richard Norwood and Mary (Davis) S.; m. Barbara Ann Brugenhemre, June 22, 1974; children: Blake, Sarah. BS in Indsl. Engring., Iowa State U., 1973; MBA, Northwestern U., 1977. Sales engr. Precision Paper, Wheeling, Ind., 1976-78, sales mgr., 1976-78; regional sales mgr. ITW Buildex, Itasca, Ill., 1978-81, nat. sales mktg. mgr., 1981-84, v.p., gen. mgr., 1984-92, ITW Paslode, Lincolnshire, Ill., 1992; group v.p., constrn. products Illinois Tool Works Inc. (ITW), 1994—95, exec. v.p. global construction products bus., 1995—2004, exec. v.p. finishing systems bus., 1997—2004, exec. v.p. global Wilsonart laminate bus. unit, 2003—04, pres., 2004—. Bd. dirs. Rockwell Automation, Inc. Advisory bd. Northwestern U. Master of Mgmt. and Mfg. program. Mem. Am. Mgmt. Assn., Am. Mktg. Assn., Am. Soc. Indsl. Engrs., Midwest Indsl. Mfg. Assn. Office: Ill Tool Works Inc 3600 W Lake Ave Glenview IL 60025-5811*

SPEER, JACK ATKESON, publisher; b. Wichita, Kans., July 3, 1941; s. Jack Shelley and Shannon C. Speer; m. Judith Ann Fuller, Aug. 5,1967; children: Martin Fuller, Elizabeth Speer Goodwin. BS in Indsl. Adminstrn., Kansas. State U., 1966, ML, 1967; postgrad., U. Mo., 1967, U. So. Calif., 1969; IBM Pres.'s Class, Harvard U., 1980. Mem. advt., editorial, mech. staffs Wichita Eagle-Beacon, 1954-64; editorial asst. Emporia (Kans.) Gazette,

1964-65; supr. libr. data processing Kans. State U., Emporia, 1965-67, mgr. data processing ctr. Manhattan, 1967-69; mgr. systems and programming John Wiley Inc.-Becker & Hayes Inc., Bethesda, Md., 1969-72; dir. libr. info. systems Informatics Inc. Info. Systems Group, Rockville, Md., 1972-77; v.p. ops. Arcata Real Estate Data Inc., Miami, Fla., 1977-79; mgr. electronic info. systems Arcata Publs. Group, Norwalk, Conn., 1979-83; v.p. mktg./sales, data imaging group The William Byrd Press, Richmond, Va., 1983-84; sr. v.p. ops. NewsBank Inc., New Canaan, Conn., 1984-85; pres., pub. Buckmaster Pub., Mineral, Va., 1986—. Mem. faculty Cath. U. Am. Libr. Sch., Kans. State U. Libr. Sch.; customer adv. coun. U.S. Postal Svc., 1996—. Author: Amateur Radio Call Directory, 1982—, Buckmaster's Ann. Stockholder Reports, 1986—, Front-Page-News (CD-ROM and Internet), 1989, HamCall (CD-ROM and Internet), 1988—; compiler Libraries and Automation: A Bibliography, 1967, The Living Bible Concordance, 1972. Trustee Jefferson-Madison Regional Libr., 1990-91; commr. Louisa County Planning Commn.; pres. Louisa County Libr. Found. Mem. ALA, NRA, Am. Radio Relay League, Nat. Info. Standards Orgn. (CD-ROM com), D.C. Libr. Assn. (pres.), Rotary, Sigma Tau Gamma. Office: Buckmaster Pub 6196 Jefferson Hwy Mineral VA 23117-3425 E-mail: speerj@buck.com.

SPEER, JOHN GORDON, metallurgist, educator, materials scientist, educator; b. Bethlehem, Pa., July 24, 1958; s. Robert John and Joyce P. Speer; m. Julia Victorovna Chebakova, Feb. 15, 2003; children: Kaitlyn children: Gabriella Macy. BS, Lehigh U., 1980; PhD, U. Oxford, Eng., 1983. Rsch. engr. Bethlehem Steel Corp., 1983—89, rsch. supr., 1989—97; prof. Colo. Sch. Mines, Golden, 1997—. Contbr. articles to profl. jours. Recipient Elbert S. Gary Gold medal, Am. Iron and Steel Inst., 1994, Luiz Dumont Villares, Associacao Brasileira de Metallurgia e Materiais, 2001, William Spraragen award, 2004. Fellow: ASM Internat. (Marcus A. Grossman award 1989); mem.: Am. Welding Soc. (William Sprarageh Meml. award 2004, William Spraragen Meml. award 2004), Soc. Automotive Engrs., Iron and Steel Soc. (ISS Professorship 1999), Am. Platform Tennis Assn., Deer Creek Golf Club, Vincent's Club, Phi Eta Sigma, Tau Beta Pi, Sigma Xi. Christian Evangelical. Achievements include patents for new steel products and processes. Office: Colorado School Mines Dept Metallurgical and Materials Engrg Golden CO 80401

SPEER, KEVIN PAUL, surgeon; b. Evansville, Ind., June 8, 1959; m. Marcy Carlson Carlson, Mar. 24, 1984; children: Kira Carlson, Casey Carlson. MD, Johns Hopkins U., 1985. Lic. physician N.C., 1992. Assoc. prof. orthopedics Duke U. Med. Ctr., Durham, NC, 1992—2000; pvt. practice Southeastern Orthopedics, Raleigh, NC, 2000—. Fellow, Am. Orthop. Assn., 1992. Fellow: AAOS. Office: Southeastern Orthopedics 3404 Wake Forest Rd Ste 201 Raleigh NC 27609 E-mail: kspeer@nc.rr.com.

SPEER, NANCY GIROUARD, health care administrator; b. Mankato, Minn., Sept. 14, 1941; d. Jared and Katherine (Schmitt) How; m. Robert L. Girouard, Aug. 29, 1964 (dec. Mar. 1983); children: Robert James Girouard, Mark Jared Girouard; m. David J. Speer, Dec. 21, 1985 (dec. Aug. 1999). BA, Wellesley Coll., 1963; MA in Tchg., Wesleyan U., 1965; cert. mgmt., Smith Coll., 1985. Tchr. secondary sch. Bunnell H.S., Stratford, Conn., 1964-65; tchr., class advisor Lincoln Sch., Providence, 1965-69; substitute tchr. Mankato, 1972-74; pub. info. dir. City of Mankato, 1974-78; univ. editor, dir. pub. affairs forum Mankato State U., 1978-79; comms. mgr. Humphrey Inst., U. Minn., Mpls., 1980-83, dir. external rels., 1983-87, dir. devel. and external rels., 1987-95; dir. devel. Breck Sch., Mpls., 1996-2000; v.p. Abbott Northwestern Hosp., Mpls., 2000—02, Planned Parenthood of Minn. and S.D., 2002—. Steering com. Minn. Meeting, Mpls., 1990-96. Contbr. articles to mag. and periodicals; photographer for publ. and newspapers. Bd. dirs. Minn. Newspaper Found., St. Paul, 1985-91, chair, 1990-91, bd. dirs., vice-chair Cabrini House, Mpls., 1993-97; bd. dirs., sec. Minn. Ctr. for Book Arts, Mpls., 1990-97; bd. dirs. Minn. Landmark Ctr., St. Paul, 1994-2000; dir. Minn. Women's Campaign Fund, Mpls., 1994-2000, co-pres. bd., 1997; vice chair, bd. dirs. Loft Lit. Ctr., 2000—; vice-chair Met. Airport Commn., 1999-2003; trustee Lake Forest Acad. Bush Leader fellow, 1985-87. Avocations: literature, nature, books.

SPEER, RICHARD JOHN, security consultant; b. Oxnard, Calif., Aug. 21, 1958; s. Richard McCord Speer and Betty Jean Wilson. Grad. H.S., Las Vegas, Nev. Enlisted U.S. Army, 1976, advanced through grades to sgt. first class, infantryman 82nd Airborne Divsn., 1976-81, infantry squad leader, 1981-87, infantry squad leader 4th Infantry Divsn. Ft. Carson, Colo., 1987-88, heavy weapons specialist Spl. Forces Ft. Bragg, 1988-94, project mgr. spl. projects, 1995-98, ret., 1998; ops. support mgr., nuclear security cons. Securitas Security Svcs., NJ, 1998—. Life mem. Rep. Nat. Com., Washington, 1994—. Decorated Army Commendation medal 3rd award U.S. Army, 1984, Meritorious Svcs. medals U.S. Army, 1991, 96, 98. Mem. Heritage Found., N.Am. Hunting Club (life). Avocation: amateur philatelist.

SPEERS, ROLAND ROOT, II, lawyer; b. Jacksonville, Fla., Oct. 8, 1933; s. Roland Root and Alice (Calkins) S.; m. Florence Briscoe, Dec. 18, 1954; children: Kirsten, Guy, Gina Marie. BA cum laude, UCLA, 1955, JD, 1958. Bar: Calif. 1958, D.C. 1978. Dep. commr. corps. Calif. Dept. Corps., Los Angeles, 1958-59; sec., gen. counsel Suburban Cos., Pomona, Calif., 1959-64; sec. Amcord, Inc., Los Angeles, 1964-66, asst. to pres., 1968, v.p. corp. devel., 1969, v.p., gen. counsel, 1970, sr. v.p., 1971, exec. v.p., 1972-75, pres., 1975-94; ptnr. Speers, Dana, Teal Balfour & MacDonald, Costa Mesa, Calif., 1977-97. Dir. Logicon, Inc., Torrance, Calif., Twelve Eleven Press, Newport Beach, Calif. Co-author: The Malloy Chronicles: The Hidden Empire, 2003, The Malloy Chronicles: The Rheingold List, 2004. Trustee Pitzer Coll., Pomona, 1975-80; bd. councillors Center Pub. Affairs U. So. Calif., 1976-81; bd. dirs. Newport Harbor Art Mus., 1977-82; sr. warden St. James Episcopal Ch., 1993. Mem. D.C. Bar Assn., State Bar Assn. Calif., UCLA Alumni Assn., UCLA Law Sch. Alumni Assn., Phi Alpha Delta. Clubs: Big Canyon Country (Newport Beach).

SPEERSTRA, KAREN M. former publishing executive; b. Toledo, Ohio, July 25, 1940; BA, U. Wis., 1962. Dir. music & art acquisition William C. Brown Pub., Debuke, Ill., 1981-87; tech. pub. dir. Focal Press Digitals Press Newnes & Butterworth Heinemann, Woburn, Mass., 1991-00, ret., 2000—.

SPEERT, ARNOLD, academic administrator, chemistry educator; b. Bronx, N.Y., June 19, 1945; s. David Jack and Dorothy Bernice (Feldman) S.; m. Myrna Goldstein, June 11, 1967; children: Alan Michael, Debra Beth. BS, CCNY, 1966; PhD, Princeton U., 1971. Asst. to dean grad. and rsch. program William Paterson Coll., Wayne, N.J., 1970-71, from asst. to assoc. prof. chemistry, 1970-80, prof., 1980-85, asst. to. v.p. acad. affairs, 1971-78, assoc. dean acad. affairs, 1978-79, v.p. acad. affairs, 1979-85; pres. William Paterson U., Wayne, N.J., 1985—. Bd. dirs. State Farm Indemnity Co. Trustee Barnert Hosp., Paterson, 1986—, chmn. bd. trustees, 1998—; trustee Jewish Fedn. North Jersey, Wayne, 1986-96, YM & YWHA No. N.J., Wayne, 1988—, Respiratory Health Assn., 1990-93; bd. dirs. William Paterson Univ. Found., 1985—. Mem. Am. Assn. State Colls. and Univs. (bd. dirs. 1993-95), Tri-County C. of C. (bd. dirs. 1986-94), N.J. State Bd. Examiners, N.J. Pres.'s Coun. (chair 1996—). Home: 48 Brandon Ave Wayne NJ 07470-6032 Office: William Paterson Univ 300 Pompton Rd Wayne NJ 07470-2152

SPEESE, MARK E. rental company executive; Student, We. Mich. U. Regional mgr. Thorn Americas, 1979—86; from v.p. N.J. Ops. to chmn., CEO Rent A Center, Plano, Tex., 1986—2001; chmn. Rent A Ctr., 2001—, CEO, 2001—. Bd. dirs. Rent A Ctr. Office: Rent A Center 5700 Tennyson Pkwy Plano TX 75024*

SPEICHER, CARL EUGENE, pathologist; b. Carbondale, Pa., Mar. 21, 1933; s. William Joseph and Elizabeth Marcella (Connolly) S.; m. Mary Louise Walsh, June 21, 1958; children: Carl E. Jr., Gregory, Erik. BS in Biology, King's Coll., 1954; MD, U. Pa., 1958; student, Sch. of Aerospace Medicine, Brooks AFB, Tex., 1969. Diplomate Am. Bd. Pathology. Intern U. Pa. Hosp., Phila., 1958-59, resident, 1959-63; chief lab. svcs. USAF Hosp., London, Eng., 1963-66, USAF Med. Ctr. Wright Patterson, Dayton, Ohio, 1966-70; dir. clin. labs. and chmn. dept. pathology Wilford Hall USAF Med. Ctr., San Antonio, 1971-77; prof. dept. pathology Ohio State U., Columbus, 1977—2000, vice chair dept. pathology, 1992—2000, prof. emeritus dept. pathology, 2000—; dir. clin. svcs. Ohio State U. Med. Ctr., Columbus, 1977—2000; dir. clin. lab. Stoneridge Med. Ctr., Ohio State U., 2000—. Co-author: Choosing Effective Laboratory Tests, 1983; author: (book) The Right Test, 1990, 3d edit., 1998. Col. USAF, 1956-77. Decorated Legion of Merit; fellow in med. chemistry SUNY, Syracuse, 1970-71. Mem. AMA, Ohio Soc. Pathologists, Ctrl. Ohio Soc. Pathologists, Am. Assn. for Clin. Chemistry, Assn. Clin. Scientists, Coll. Am. Pathologists, Am. Soc. Clin. Pathologists, Alpha Omega Alpha. Office: Ohio State U Med Ctr 410 W 10th Ave Columbus OH 43210-1228

SPEIDEL, DAVID HAROLD, geology educator; b. Pottsville, Pa., Aug. 10, 1938; s. Harold O. and Edith M. (Rosser) S.; m. Margaret Helen Liebrecht, Sept. 8, 1962. BS, Franklin and Marshall Coll., Lancaster, Pa., 1960; PhD, Pa. State U., 1964. Rsch. assoc. Pa. State U., 1964-66; asst. prof. to prof. dept. geology Queens Coll., CUNY, Flushing, 1966—2003, chmn. dept., 1980-88, dean faculty sci., 1970-79, chmn. faculty senate, 1992-96, provost, sr. v.p. acad. affairs, 1998-2000, emeritus, 2003, ret., 2003. Maj. projects sect. head, earth scis. NSF, 1988-89; vis. scholar Sr. Specialists div. Congl. Rsch. Svc., Washington, 1977-78 Author: (with A.F. Agnew) Natural Geochemistry of Our Environment; editor (with L. Ruedisili and A.F. Agnew) Perspectives on Water: Uses and Abuses; contbr. articles to profl. jours. Fellow Geol. Soc. Am.; mem. AAAS, Am. Ceramic Soc., Am. Geophys. Union, Am. Inst. Profl. Geologists, Nat. Hazards Soc., Sigma Xi. Office: Queens Coll Sch Earth & Environ Scis Flushing NY 11367 E-mail: david_speidel@qc.edu.

SPEIDEL, JOHN JOSEPH, public health physician, educator; b. Iowa City, Iowa, Sept. 17, 1937; s. Thomas Dennis and Edna (Warweg) Speidel; m. Melissa Jane Webster, Oct. 7, 2001; 1 child from previous marriage, Sabrina Brett. AB cum laude, Harvard U., 1959, MD, 1963, MPH, 1965. Diplomate Nat. Bd. Med. Examiners, Am. Bd. Preventive Medicine. Intern St. Luke's Hosp., N.Y.C., 1963-64; resident N.Y.C. Dept. Health, 1965-67, dep. dir. maternal and infant care project, 1966-67; chief rsch. divsn. Office Population, AID, Dept. of State, Washington, 1969-76, assoc. dir., 1977, dep. dir., acting dir. office, 1978-83; v.p. Population Action Internat. (formerly Population Crisis Com.), 1983-87, pres., 1987-95; program officer population Hewlett Found., 1995—2001, program dir. population, 2002—03; adj. prof. Ctr. Reproductive Health Rsch. and Policy U. Calif., San Francisco, 2003—. Lectr. population and family planning Georgetown U., 1973—75. Editor (with others): (book) Female Sterilization, 1971, Hysteroscopic Sterilization, 1974, Intrauterine Devices, 1974, Control of Male Fertility, 1975, Advances in Female Sterilization Technology, 1976, Risks, Benefits and Controversies in Fertility Control, 1978, Reversal of Sterilization, 1978, Pregnancy Termination, 1979, Vaginal Contraception, 1979; contbr. articles to profl. jours. Served to maj. U.S. Army, 1967—69. Recipient Meritorious Unit citiation, Office of Population, 1969—71, Arthur S. Flemming award, Washington Downtown Jaycees, 1972. Mem.: Population Assn. Am., Am. Pub. Health Assn. (Carl S. Shultz award 1982). Office: U Calif San Francisco CRHRP Dept Ob Gyn 3333 California St Ste 335 San Francisco CA 94118 Business E-Mail: speidelj@obgyn.ucsf.edu.

SPEIER, JOHN LEO, JR., retired chemist; b. Chgo., Sept. 29, 1918; s. John L. and Mary Jane (Dickman) S.; m. A. Louise Kimmel, Oct. 21, 1944; children: Susan, Genevieve, Dorothy, Margaret, John L. III, Thomas J. B.Sc., St. Benedict's Coll., 1941; M.Sc., U. Fla., 1943; PhD, U. Pitts., 1947. Naval Stores research fellow U. Fla., 1941-43; research fellow Mellon Inst., Pitts., 1943, sr. fellow, 1947-56; mgr. organic research Dow Corning Corp., Midland, Mich., 1956-69, scientist in corp. research, 1969-75, sr. scientist in corp. research, 1975-93; retired, 1994. Contbr. numerous articles to profl. jours., 1950—; holder 100 patents prodn. organosilicon compounds and allied products. Named Indsl. Research and Devel. Scientist of Yr. Indsl. Research/Devel. mag., 1978 Mem. AAAS, Am. Chem. Soc. (Frederick Stanley Kipping award 1990), Sigma Xi.

SPEIGHTS, MICHAEL DAVID, newsletter editor; b. Owensboro, Ky., May 12, 1951; s. Marion Thomas and Joy Lee (Griffin) S.; m. Claire Elaine Macdonald, Aug. 1, 1998. BA with honors, Northeastern U., 1973. Researcher, reporter Congl. Quar., Washington, 1974-77; staff asst. Senator Richard Schweiker, Washington, 1977; anchor, reporter Sta. WILM, Wilmington, Del., 1979-80; reporter, producer Sta. WUHY-FM, Phila., 1980-81, Sta. WABE-FM, Atlanta, 1982-83; editor Padres' Trail, St. Michaels, Ariz., 1984-88; campaign assoc. Ketchum, Inc., Pitts., 1988-89; editor Report on Literacy Programs Bus. Pubs., Inc., Silver Spring, Md., 1989—2003, editor Am. Marketplace and U.S. Census Report, 1989-96, editor Report on Edn. of the Disadvantaged, 1997-2000; editor HazMat Transport News, 2000—, Drug Detection Report, 2003—. Freelance reporter, producer Nat. Pub. Radio, 1980-83. Past assoc. editor Francisco; contr. articles to profl. jours. Vol. Navajo Nation Spl. Olympics, St. Michaels, 1986, Franciscan Covenant Program, Ft. Defiance, Ariz., 1984-85. Roman Catholic. Avocations: reading, travel, auto racing. Home: 5805 Edson Ln Apt T2 Rockville MD 20852-2922 Office: Bus Pubs Inc 8737 Colesville Rd Ste 1100 Silver Spring MD 20910-3958

SPEIR, WILLIAM ARTHUR, JR., critical care physician; b. Macon, Ga., July 18, 1939; s. William Arthur Speir and Esther Marie Garland; m. Mary Hazelton Lehmann, June 8, 1963; 1 child, Mary-Butler S. Mathieson. BS in Chemistry, U. Ga., 1961; MD, Med. Coll. Ga., 1965. Asst. prof. pulmonary medicine Med. Coll. Ga., Augusta, 1971-75, assoc. prof. pulmonary medicine, 1975-80, prof. medicine pulmonary/critical care medicine, 1980-2000, prof. emeritus medicine, 2000—, med. dir. med. ICU, 1977-79, 91-00, chief sect. pulmonary diseases, 1979-92; clin. prof. medicine Mercer U. Sch. Medicine, Macon, Ga., 2000—. Contbr. over 170 articles, abstracts to profl. jours., 4 chpts. to books. Bd. dirs. Augusta Opera Assn., 1973-80. Lt. comdr., surgeon USPHS, 1966-68. Recipient Pulmonary Acad. award Nat. Heart, Lung and Blood Inst., 1974-79, Order of St. Obscurus award RTH Laennec Assn., 1983; named Col., Hon. Order Ky. Cols., 1980—. Fellow Am. Coll. Chest Physicians (gov. for Ga. 1998-2002, bylaws com. 1993-99, steering com. sect. on respiratory pathophysiology 1984-86, com. undergrad. med. edn. 1976-79, pres. So. chpt. 1980-81, 93-94, Disting. Faculty award 1991), Am. Coll. Critical Care Medicine; mem. Am. Thoracic Soc. (edn. com. 1977-81, councilor-at-large 1980, Disting. Educator award 1972), So. Med. Assn. (chmn. sec. chest diseases 1980-81, 93-94, Paul A. Turner Meml. Lectr. award 1983, 86), Soc. Critical Care Medicine (mem. grad. med. fellowship com. 2004—), Phi Rho Sigma Med. Soc. Episcopalian. Avocations: painting, writing, cooking, music, gardening. Personal E-mail: bandmspeir@comcast.net.

SPEIRS, DEREK JAMES, diversified corporation financial executive; b. Montreal, Que., Can., Dec. 21, 1933; s. James B. and Marie C. (Hunt) S.; m. Carol Alice Cumming, Dec. 8, 1967 (div. Feb. 1989); children: Lara Marie, Gregory Ross, Scott Lawrence Gordon. B. Commerce with honors in Econs., McGill U., 1954, MBA, 1959. Chartered acct., Can., chartered corp. sec. Devel. dir. fine papers, corp. acctg. dir. Domtar, Inc., Montreal, 1970-72, dir. corp. devel., 1976-78, v.p. fin., corp. devel., 1978-89, sr. v.p. fin. and corp. devel., 1989-91; v.p., sec. fin. Consoltex, Montreal, 1972-76, bus. cons., 1991—; pres. Speirs Fin. Inc., Speirs Cons. Inc., Speirs Capital Inc. Mem. Can. Inst. Chartered Accts., Fin. Execs. Inst., C.D. Howe Inst., Lac Marois Country Club, St. James Club, Montreal Amateur Athletic Assn. Avocations: travel, skiing. Home: 365 Stanstead Ave Mont-Royal Montreal QC Canada H3R 1X5 Office: Ste 1100 2 Pl Alexis Nihon Montreal QC Canada H3Z 3C1 E-mail: speirsco@netcom.ca.

SPEIRS, GREG, artist; Art dir. Grooves Mag., N.Y.C., 1977—79, Changes, Inc., 1980—85. Artwork, Panther Dream Ski for K-2 Corp, 1992, Original Lithuanian Olympic Basketball Jerseys, Am. Eagle Artwork U.S. Olympic Team Bobsleds, 2002, prin. works include for Prince Albert of Monaco Monaco Monk. Named to Soc. Illustrators, N.Y., N.Y., 1975, 1976. Achievements include created first 'Extreme Sports' licensed property character, Scully. Owner: 'Scully' and 'Skullman' trademarks; artist's 'Scully' character is enshrined in Basketball Hall of Fame, Springfield, Mass. on Dec 07, 1993; trademarked slam dunking skeleton' image, Skullman, first seen on Lithuanian Olympic Tie Dye, Basketball Jerseys. Office: No Rules Graphics and Slammin Sports Box #125 Yonkers NY 10710 Office Phone: 800-362-1886. Personal E-mail: skully77@cloud9.net. E-mail: skully77@cloud9.net.

SPEIZER, FRANK E. physician, researcher; BA, Stanford U., 1957, MD, 1960. Prof. environ. sci. Harvard Sch. Pub. Health; Edward H. Kass prof. medicine Harvard Med. Sch., mem. environ. epidemiology program dept. environ. health, co-dir. Channing Lab. dept. medicine; sr. physician Brigham & Women's Hosp. Prin. investigator Nurses Health Study, Brigham and Women's Hosp., Harvard Med. Sch. Contbr. articles to profl. jours. Recipient Charles S. Mott prize, 2001. Mem.: Inst. Medicine. Achievements include research in the natural history of respiratory diseases, environmental risks for chronic diseases including risks for cancer and cardiorespiratory diseases. Office: Channing Lab 181 Longwood Ave Boston MA 02115 Business E-Mail: frank.speizer@channing.harvard.edu.

SPEJEWSKI, EUGENE HENRY, physicist, researcher; b. East Chicago, Ind., Sept. 15, 1938; s. Henry Louis and Carrie Jane (Fuss) S.; m. Norma Beverly Seekins, June 8, 1963; children: Maria Suzanne, Beverly Anne, Andrew John, Jeannette Michelle. BS, U. Notre Dame, 1960; PhD, Ind. U., 1966. Research assoc. Ind. U., Bloomington, 1965-67, Princeton U., 1967-69, instr., 1969-71; asst. prof. Oberlin Coll., Ohio, 1971-72; dir. UNISOR, Oak Ridge Assoc. Univs., 1972-85, mgr. SDS program, 1985-86, chmn. spl. projects div., 1986-89; v.p., dir. tng. and mgmt. systems div. Oak Ridge Inst. for Sci. and Edn., 1989-95, v.p., assoc. dir. for edn. and tng. group, 1995-98; cons. Oak Ridge Nat. Lab., 1999—. Vis. prof. physics U. Tenn., Knoxville, 1981-84, adj. prof.; mem., chmn. HHIRF Users Exec. Com., Oak Ridge Nat. Lab., 1982-84; referee U.S. Dept. Energy, various profl. jours. Co-editor: Future Directions in Studies of Nuclei Far from Stability, 1980; contbr. articles to profl. jours. Referee U.S. Soccer Fedn.; bd. dirs. Oak Ridge Community Playhouse, 1985-88, 95—. Mem. AAAS, Am. Phys. Soc., Am. Mgmt. Assn., Oak Ridge Sertoma Club (sec., treas., pres., chair bd. dirs.), Sigma Xi. E-mail: gene@mail.phy.ornl.gov.

SPELFOGEL, EVAN J. lawyer, educator; b. Boston, Jan. 28, 1936; s. Morris R. and Helen S. (Steinberg) S.; m. Beverly Kolenberg; children: Scott, Douglas, Karen. AB, Harvard U., 1956; JD, Columbia U., 1959. Bar: Mass. 1959, N.Y. 1964, U.S. Supreme Ct. 1969. Atty. Office of Solicitor, U.S. Dept. Labor, Washington, Boston, 1959-60, NLRB, Boston, N.Y.C., 1960-64; assoc. Simpson, Thacher & Bartlett, N.Y.C., 1964-69, Dewey, Ballantine, N.Y.C., 1969-77; ptnr. Fellner, Rovins & Gallay, N.Y.C., 1977-80, Summit, Rovins & Feldesman, N.Y.C., 1981-91, Epstein Becker and Green, P.C., N.Y.C., 1991—. Adj. prof. law Baruch Coll., CCNY. Bd. editors Developing Labor Law: The Board, The Courts and the National Labor Relations Act, also co-editor-in-chief Supplements; bd. sr. editors Employee Benefits Law; contbr. articles to profl. jours. Fellow Coll. Labor and Employment Lawyers; mem. ABA (sect. on labor and employment law, exec. com. 1978-86, co-editor sect. newsletter 1976-92, editl. bd. The Labor Lawyer 1986—, mem. ho. dels. 1987-90, sect. dispute resolution 1992—), FBA (coun. on labor law), N.Y. State Bar Assn. (chmn. labor and employment law sect. 1977-78, exec. com. 1975—, ho. dels. 1978-79, com. on profl. discipline 1987-90), Assn. of Bar of City of N.Y. (labor com. 1968-71, 87-90, employee benefits com. 1992-96), Indsl. Resl. Rsch. Assn. (sec. N.Y. chpt. 1999-2000, pres. 2000-01), Am. Arbitration Assn. (nat. panel labor arbitrators), Harvard Varsity Club, Phi Alpha Delta. Home: 17 Parkside Dr Great Neck NY 11021-1042 Office: Epstein Becker & Green, PC 250 Park Ave New York NY 10177-0001 Office Phone: 212-351-4539. E-mail: espelfogel@ebglaw.com.

SPELFOGEL, SCOTT DAVID, lawyer; b. Boston, Nov. 27, 1960; s. Evan. J. and Beverly (Kolenberg) S. BS, Boston U., 1982; JD, Syracuse U., 1985; LLM, Boston U., 1990. Bar: Mass. 1985, N.Y. 1986, U.S. Dist. Ct. (no. dist.) N.Y. 1986, U.S. Dist. Ct. Mass. 1987; lic. real estate broker, Mass., 1987. Assoc. Jeffrey M. McCrone, P.C., Syracuse, N.Y., 1985-87, Tatarian Law Offices, Boston, 1987-88; asst. gen. counsel The Berkshire Group, Boston, 1988-90, v.p., asst. gen. counsel, 1990-96, v.p., gen. counsel, 1996, sr. v.p., gen. counsel, 1997—. Mem. ABA, Am. Corp. Counsel Assn., Boston Bar Assn., N.Y. Bar Assn., Mass. Bar Assn. Home: 27 Sentry Hill Rd Sharon MA 02067-1521 Office: The Berkshire Group 1 Beacon St Ste 1500 Boston MA 02108-3116 Office Phone: 617-574-8385. E-mail: scott.spelfogel@berkshire-group.com.

SPELKE, ELIZABETH SHILIN, psychology educator; b. N.Y.C., May 28, 1949; d. Alan Shilin and Ruth (Simon) Spelke; m. Elliott M. Blass, Oct. 23, 1988; children: Mae Bridget, Joseph Alan. BA, Radcliffe/Harvard U., 1971; PhD, Cornell U., 1978; Dr. honoris causa, Umeå (Sweden) U., 1993, U. Paris, 1999. From asst. prof. to assoc. prof. U. Pa., Phila., 1977-86; prof. Cornell U., Ithaca, N.Y., 1986-96, MIT, Cambridge, Mass., 1996—2001, Harvard U., Cambridge, 2001—. Recipient Disting. Sci. Contbn. award APA; named of of Am.'s Best in Sci. and Medicine, Time mag., 2001; Fulbright Sr. Rsch. awardee, 1984-85; Guggenheim fellow, 1988-89, Cattell fellow, 1992-93. Fellow AAAS, Am. Psychol. Soc. (William James fellow), Soc. Exptl. Psychologists; mem. NAS, Cognitive Neurosci. Soc., Psychonomic Soc., Am. Acad. Arts and Scis. Achievements include research on early development of perception by human infants; research on development of reasoning about objects, space, and number by children. E-mail: spelke@wjh.harvard.edu.

SPELLACY, WILLIAM NELSON, obstetrician, educator, gynecologist, educator; b. St. Paul, May 10, 1934; s. Jack F. and Elmyra L. (Nelson) Spellacy; m. Lynn Larsen; children: Kathleen Ann, Kimberly Joan, William Nelson. BA, U. Minn., 1955, BS, 1956, MD, 1959. Diplomate subsplty. cert. in maternal and fetal medicine Am. Bd. Ob-Gyn. Intern Hennepin County Gen. Hosp., Mpls., 1959—60; resident U. Minn., Mpls., 1960—63; practice medicine specializing in ob-gyn. Mpls., 1963—67, Miami, Fla., 1967—73, Gainesville, Fla., 1973—79, Chgo., 1979—88; prof., head dept. U. Ill. Coll. Medicine, Chgo., 1979—88; prof., chmn. dept. U. So. Fla. Coll. Medicine, Tampa, 1988—. Prof. dept. ob-gyn. U. Miami, 1967—73; prof., chmn. dept. U. Fla., 1973—79. Contbr. articles to med. jours. Mem.: ACOG, AMA, Inst. Medicine, Ill. Med. Soc., Soc. Perinatal Obstetricians, Ctrl. Assn. Obstetrics and Gynecology, South Atlantic Soc. Obstetrics and Gynecology, Perinatal Rsch. Soc., Am. Diabetes Assn., Assn. Profs. Gynecology and Obstetrics, Am. Fertility Soc., Endocrine Soc., Am. Assn. Obstetricians and Gynecologists, Soc. Gynecol. Investigation, Am. Gynecol. and Obstet. Soc., Am. Gynecol. Soc., Rotary. Episcopalian. Home: 845 Seddon Cove Way Tampa FL 33602-5704 Office: U South Fla Coll Medicine Dept OBGYN 4 Columbia Dr Ste 514 Tampa FL 33606-3589

SPELLER, KERSTIN G. RINTA, psychologist; b. Washington, Nov. 18, 1949; d. Eugene and Saga (Lindberg) Rinta; Thomas Hughes Speller, Sept. 4, 1971; five children. AB, Ohio U., 1971, MS, 1972; PhD, SUNY, Buffalo, 1983. Cert. sch. psychologist. Sch. psychologist Iroquois Ctrl. Schs., Elma, N.Y., 1974-78; cons. psychologist Amherst, N.Y., 1979-84; program dir. Child's Play Preschool Program, Amherst, 1986-95; sch. psychologist Holland (N.Y.) Schs., 1995—2004. Project dir. ISO-9001 GEMCOR, Buffalo, 1993-2004, corp. dir. human rels., 1998-2002. Bd. dirs. Heritage Ctrs. (Assn. Retarded Children), Erie County, N.Y., 1983-2000, govt. affairs com. chair, 1995-2000. Mem. Nat. Assn. Sch. Psychologists, USTA (ea. mgmt. bd., regional v.p. western region 1996-2003, nat. awards com. 1999-2002), Country Club Buffalo, Buffalo Tennis and Squash Club, East Aurora Pony Club, Village Glen Tennis and Fitness Club. Home: 5 Preston Beach Rd Marblehead MA 01945-2005

SPELLER, ROBERT ERNEST BLAKEFIELD, publishing executive; b. Chgo., Jan. 19, 1908; s. John Ernest and Florence (Larson) S.; m. Flora Maxine Elliott Watkins (dec. May 1997); children: Robert Ernest Blakefield, Jon Patterson. Student, Columbia U., 1929. Mng. editor Fgn. Press Svc., 1930-31; pres. Mohawk Press, 1931-32, Robert Speller Pub. Corp., 1934-52, Record Concerts Corp., 1940-53, Robert Speller & Sons, Pubs., inc., 1955—, Norellyn Press, Inc., 1960-83, Transglobal News Svc., Inc., 1960—. Corresp.

Raleigh News & Observer, 1949-53; pub. Hough's Ency. Am. Woods, 1957—, mng. editor 1964-75; chmn. bd., pres., chief exec. officer Nat. Resources Publs., Inc., 1968-84; pres., dir. Transglobal Resources Devel. Corp., 1983—; owner, operator, prodr. Concert Theatre, N.Y.C., 1939-43, mgr. Otto Klemperer, Leon Barzin, Margaret Speaks, others; pub. East Europe Mag., 1970-; sec., dir. Encoder Research & Devel. Corp., 1971—, Pecos Internat., Inc., 1974-77; v.p., dir. Pecos Western Corp. of Del., 1973-83; dir. Gen. Research Corp., Fashion Form Mfg. Corp. Mem. founding bd. USO Trustee Philippa Schuyler Meml. Found. With Signal Corps U.S. Army, 1944—45. Mem. Gourmet Soc. (founder), Am. Legion, Local 38 Musicians Assn. AFL, Westchester Country Club, Lions Club, Sierra Club, Columbia U. Club (N.Y.C.), Delta Chi. Episcopalian. Office: 115 E 9th St New York NY 10003-5414 Office Phone: 212-473-0333.

SPELLER, ROBERT ERNEST BLAKEFIELD, JR., choreographer; b. NYC, Feb. 5, 1936; s. Robert E.B. and Flora Maxine Elliott (Watkins) S. Student, Duke U., 1954-56, NYU, 1958-59, New Sch. for Social Rsch., 1967-68. V.p. Robert Speller & Sons, Publishers, N.Y.C., 1963—; coordinator models New School Soc. Rsch., Parsons, N.Y.C., 1972-2001; instr. Baruch Col., N.Y.C., 1980-83. English lang. sec. Prince Felix Youssoupoff, Paris, 1961—63. Choreographer many shows including Toulouse, 1981, The Ritz, 1983, Let's Misbehave, 1985-86; dir. I Died Yesterday, 1983; translator: The Mime (by Jean Dorcy), 1961. Mem. SAG, AFTRA, Actors' Equity Assn. (councillor, 1967-73), Am. Guild Variety Artists, Soc. Stage Dirs. and Choreographers N.Y., N.Y. Geneal. and Biog. Soc. Episcopal. Office: Robert Speller and Sons 115 E 9th St New York NY 10003-5414 Office Phone: 212-473-0333.

SPELLERBERG, ELINOR M. riding instructor; b. Seymour, Ind., Feb. 27, 1927; d. Ellis Leroy and Edna (Linke) Hawk; m. Thomas Richard Spellerberg, May 10, 1947; children: Eric (dec.), Scott, Janet, Jeffrey, Lance. Student, Ohio State U., 1945-47. Horse breeder and trainer, Tiffin, Ohio, 1960-99; dressage instr., 1980-2001; judge dressage horses Am. Horse Show Assn., Lexington, Ky., 1982-2001; ret, 2002—. Head instr. Riding for Handicapped, Tiffin; mem. U.S. Equestrian Team, 1990-2001. Author, illustrator: The Test, 1995, (workbook) 4-H Dressage, 1990. Mem. exec. com. Elder Coll. Terra C.C., Fremont, Ohio, 1995-2001; mem. sch. bd. Mohawk H.S., Sycamore, Ohio, 1962-71; leader Seneca County 4-H, Tiffin, 1969-90; established Hope on Horseback, Tiffin, 1975-90, 1st 4-H Handicapped Riding Club and Program, Ohio, State 4-H Horse com.; sec. 4-H English divsn. Ohio State Fair; bd. dirs. Freedom Trails Therapeutic Riding Program, 2002-03. Named Woman of Yr., VFW, Tiffin, 1991, hon. chpt. farmer Future Farmers Am.; recipient Svc. award Kiwanis Club, Tiffin, 1990. Republican. Avocation: painting. Home: 1379 W Township Rd 58 Tiffin OH 44883

SPELLER-BROWN, BARBARA JEAN, pediatric nurse practitioner; b. Windsor, N.C., Feb. 8, 1958; d. Thomas Franklin and Esther Lee (Bond) Speller; m. Samuel Brown Jr., Nov. 16, 1985; children: Samuel, Shaun, Shea, Shanele, Samara. BSN, Howard U., 1981; MSN, U. Utah, 1993. Cert. PNP. Charge nurse Rosebud (S.D.) Indian Health Facility, 1981-82, Carl Albert Indian Health Facility, 1982-83; asst. head nurse Pitt County Meml. Hosp., Greenville, N.C., 1984-85; staff nurse St. Bernardine's Hosp., San Bernardino, Calif., 1986, San Bernardino Cmty. Hosp., 1986-87; staff nurse/charge nurse Gorgas Army Hosp., Panama, 1987-90; charge nurse Humana Hosp. Davis North, Layton, Utah, 1990-93; staff nurse Primary Children's Med. Ctr., Salt Lake City, 1990-93; clin. preceptor, PNP Cmty. Health Care Inc., Capital Heights, Md., 1994-95; faculty PNP Our Kids Ctr. Vanderbilt U. Med. Ctr., Nashville, 1995-2000; CPNP pediat. Walter Reed Army Med. Ctr., 2001, Army Med. Ctr., 2001—02; pediat. nurse practitioner hematology/oncology Children's Nat. Med. Ctr., 2002—. Mem. Gospel choir The Word of God Bapt. Ch.; scholarship chairperson Watchcare. 1st lt. USPHS, 1981—83. Named Outstanding Young Woman Am. Delta Sigma Theta. Mem. ANA, Nat. Assn. PNPs, Sigma Theta Tau, Phi Kappa Phi. Home: 11020 Lake Victoria Ln Bowie MD 20720 E-mail: workingmom04@aol.com.

SPELLING, AARON, film and television producer, writer, actor; b. Dallas, Apr. 22, 1923; s. David and Pearl (Wall) Spelling; m. Carole Gene Marer, Nov. 23, 1968; children: Victoria Davey, Randall Gene. Student, Sorbonne, U. Paris, France, 1945-46; BA, So. Meth. U., 1950. Actor Thomas-Spelling Prodn., LA, 1953-69; screenwriter Zane Grey Series, LA, 1972-76; prodr. Zane Grey Theater, LA, 1977-86, The Dick Powell Show, LA, 1986—; co-owner with Danny Thomas Thomas-Spelling Prodn., LA, 1969-72; co-pres. Spelling-Goldberg Prodn., LA, 1972-76; pres. Aaron Spelling Prodn., Inc., LA, 1977-86, chmn., CEO, 1986—. Author (producer or exec. prodr.): (numerous TV plays and movies over 58 TV series) including The Mod Squad, The Rookies, Family, Nightingales, Dynasty, The Colbys, Love Boat, Hotel, Beverly Hills 90210, Charlie's Angels, Fantasy Is., Starsky and Hutch, T.J. Hooker, Matt Houston, Hart to Hart, Melrose Pl., 7th Heaven, Savannah, Sunset Beach, Pacific Palisades, Charmed, Titans; also 130 TV movies for ABC, CBS, NBC including After Jimmy, And the Band Played On; prodr.(or exec. prodr.): (films, theatrical) including Mr. Mom, Night Mother, Surrender, Loose Cannons, Cross My Heart, Soapdish, The Mod Squad; author: Aaron Spelling-A Prime Time Life, 1996. Bd. dirs. Am. Film Inst. Served with USAF, 1942—45. Decorated Decorated Bronze Star medal, Purple Heart with oak leaf cluster; named Man of Yr., Publicists Guild Am., 1971, Man of Yr. B'nai B'rith, Beverly Hills chpt., 1972, 1985, NAACP Humanitarian of Yr., 1983, Man of Yr. Scopus award, Am. Friends of Hebrew U., 1993; named to TV Acad.'s Hall of Fame; recipient Eugene O'Neill awards, 1947, 1948, NAACP Image awards, 1970, 1971, 1973, 1975, Winston Churchil medal of Wisdom, 1988, Lifetime Achievement award, People's Choice Awards, 1996, Courage to Dream award, Fulfillment Fund, 1996, GLADD award, 1st prodr. honored by Mus. of Broadcasting, honored for contbns. to victims' rights by City of Las Vegas. Mem.: Acad. Motion Picture Arts and Scis., Writers and Dirs., The Caucus of Prodrs., Prodrs. Guild Am., Writers Guild Am. (award 1962), Hollywood TV Acad. Arts and Scis., Hollywood Radio and TV Soc., Big Brothers of Am., Friars. Democrat. Jewish. Office: Spelling Television Inc 5700 Wilshire Blvd Fl 5 Los Angeles CA 90036-3659

SPELLINGS, MARGARET LAMONTAGNE, assistant to US President on domestic policy; b. Houston, 1958; married. BA, U. Houston. Worked for Tex. Gov. William P. Clements, mem. of Tex. House Rep.; assoc. exec. dir. Tex. Assn. Sch. Bds.; polit. dir. Gov. George W. Bush gubernatorial campaign, Tex., 1994; sr. adv. to Gov. George W. Bush, Tex., 1994—2000; asst. to Pres. George W. Bush for domestic policy, 2001—. Host online interactive forum Ask the White House. Named one of 100 Most Powerful Women in Wash., Washingtonian mag., 2001. Office: Asst to Pres for Domestic Policy Exec Office Bldg Rm 464 Washington DC 20502

SPELLMAN, DOUGLAS TOBY, advertising executive; b. Bronx, NY, May 12, 1942; s. Sydney M. and Leah B.S.; m. Ronni I. Epstein, Jan. 16, 1966 (div. Mar. 1985); children: Laurel Nicole, Daren Scott; m. Michelle Ward, Dec. 31, 1986; 1 child, Dallas Ward Spellman. Media buyer Doyle, Dane, Bernbach, Inc., NYC, 1964-66; various postions, 1966-72; media supr. Ogilvy & Mather, Inc., LA, 1972-73; media dir. Vitt Media Internat., Inc., LA, 1973-74; v.p., dir. West Coast ops. Ind. Media Svcs., Inc., LA, 1974-75; owner Douglas T. Spellman, Inc., LA, 1975-77, pres., chmn. bd., 1977-82; pres., COO Douglas T. Spellman Co. div. Ad Mktg., Inc., 1982-85; pres., CEO, chmn. bd. Spellbound Prodns. and Spellman Media divs. Spellbound Comms, 1984-86; gen. ptnr. Faso & Spellman, 1984-86; COO, pres. Yacht Mgmt. Internat., Ltd., 1984-86; v.p. media Snyder, Longino Advt. div. Snyder Advt., 1986-91; advt./media cons., 1986-90; gen. ptnr. Nucleus Nuance, LA, 1987-88, Conv. Photos Unltd., Hawaii, 1988-89; v.p. mktg. Pacific Med. Products, Inc., LA, 1990-91. Media dir. Kennedy-Wilson Inc., LA, 1991-94; dir. media and advt. svcs. Goddard & Claussen/First Tuesday, LA, 1994-97; v.p. advt. and mktg. Cosmetic Tech. Internat., Inc., LA, 1997-98; mng. dir. Med. Mktg. and Advt., LA, 1998-99; dir. media svcs., Publicis Dialog-FusionDM, San Francisco, 1999-2000; mgr. media, promotions and direct mktg. Pleasant Holidays, LLC, LA, 2001—; guest lectr. Sch. Bus. UCLA, 1964-69. Served with USAR N.G., 1964-69. Mem. Aircraft Owner and Pilots Assn., NRA, Calif. Pistol and Rifle Assn., Rolls royce Owners, Mercedes Benz Am., Aston Martin Owners, Phi Zeta Kappa, Phi Omega Epsilon. E-mail: spellman.doug@att.net.

SPELLMAN, MITCHELL WRIGHT, surgeon, academic administrator, educator; b. Alexandria, La., Dec. 1, 1919; s. Frank Jackson and Altonette Beulah (Mitchell) S.; m. Billie Rita Rhodes, June 27, 1947 (dec.); children: Frank A., Michael A. (dec.), Mitchell A., Maria S. Weaver, Melva A., Mark A., Manly A. (dec.), Rita S. Parks; m. Adrienne Foster Williams, Feb. 14, 2001 (dec. Dec. 2001). AB magna cum laude, Dillard U., 1940, LLD (hon.), 1983; MD, Howard U., 1944; PhD in Surgery, U. Minn., Mpls., 1955; DSc (hon.), Georgetown U., 1974, U. Fla., 1977. Intern Cleve. Met. Gen. Hosp., 1944-45, asst. resident in surgery, 1945-46, Howard U. and Freedmen's Hosp., Washington, 1946-47, chief resident in thoracic surgery, 1947-48, tchg. asst. in physiology, 1948-49, chief resident in surgery, 1949-50, tchg. asst. in surgery, 1950-51; asst. prof. surgery Howard U., 1954-56, assoc. prof., 1956-60, prof., 1960-68; dir. Howard surgery svc. at DC Gen. Hosp., 1961-68; fellow in surgery U. Minn., 1951-54; sr. resident in surgery U. Minn. Med. Sch. and Hosp., 1951—54; dean Charles R. Drew Postgrad. Med. Sch., LA, 1969-77, prof. surgery, 1969-78; asst. dean, prof. surgery Sch. Medicine, UCLA, 1969-78; clin. prof. surgery Sch. Med., U. So. Calif., 1969-78; dean for med. svcs., prof. surgery Harvard Med. Sch., Boston, 1978-90, dean emeritus for med. svcs., 1990—, dean emeritus for internat. projects, 1990—, prof. surgery emeritus, 1990—; dir. internat. exch. programs Harvard Med. Internat., 1995—; exec. v.p. Harvard Med. Ctr., 1978-90. Fellow Ctr. for Advanced Study in Behavioral Scis.; vis. prof. Stanford U., 1975-76; bd. dirs. Kaiser Found. Hosps., Kaiser Found. Health Plan, 1971-89; mem. DC Bd. Examiners in Medicine and Osteopathy, 1955-68; mem. Nat. Rev. Com. for Regional Med. Programs, 1968-70; spl. med. adv. group, nat. surg. cons. VA, 1969-73; mem. Commn. for Study Accreditation of Selected Health Ednl. Programs, 1970-72; chmn. adv. com. br. med. devices Nat. Heart and Lung Inst., 1972; Am. health del. to visit People's Republic of China, 1973; hon. dir. State Mut. Cos., 1990—; mem. com. mandatory retirement in higher edn. NAS/NRC, 1989-91; panel on internat. programs Nat. Libr. Medicine, 1996-97; adv. bd. faculty medicine and health scis. United Arab Emirates U., 2004—. Mem. editl. bd.: Jour. Medicine and Philosophy, 1977-90; contbr. articles on cardiovasc. physiology and surgery, measurement of blood volume, and radiation biology to profl. jours. Past bd. dirs. Sun Valley Forum on Nat. Health; mem. ethics adv. bd. HEW, 1977-81; bd. dirs. Harvard Cmty. Health Plan, 1979-84; former trustee Occidental Coll.; former bd. overseers com. to visit univ. health svc. Harvard, bd. overseers Harvard Cmty. Health Plan, 1984-95; former regent Georgetown U., bd. dirs., 1986-92; former vis. com. U. Mass. Med. Ctr.; mem. bd. visitors UCLA Sch. Medicine; mem. corp. MIT; adv. bd. PEW Scholars Program in Biomed. Scis., 1984-86; bd. dirs. Med. Edn. for South African Blacks, 1985—; adv. bd. United Arab Emirates U. Faculty of Medicine and Health Scis., 2004-. Recipient Disting. Alumnus award Dillard U., 1963, Disting. Postgrad. Achievement award Howard U., 1974, Outstanding Achievement award U. Minn., 1979, Surg. Alumnus of Yr. award U. Minn., 1991, Disting. Support citation Charles R. Drew U. of Medicine, 2002; named U. Minn. Dept. Surgery Alumnus of Yr., 1991; Markle scholar in med. scis., 1954-59; Commonwealth Fund fellow, U. Minn., Mpls., 1955. Mem. AMA, AAAS, AAUP, ACS, Nat. Med. Assn. (William A. Sinkler Surgery award 1968), Soc. Univ. Surgeons, Am. Coll. Cardiology, Am. Surg. Assn., Inst. Medicine of NAS (chmn. program com. 1977-79, governing coun. 1978-80), Nat. Acad. Practice in Medicine, Am. Assn. Sovereign Mil. Order of Malta (Knights and Dames of Malta), Soc. Black Acad. Surgeons, MIT Corp. (life mem. emeritus), Cosmos Club. Roman Catholic. Office: Harvard Med Internat 1135 Tremont St Ste 900 Boston MA 02120 Office Phone: 617-535-6400.

SPELLMAN, THOMAS JOSEPH, JR., lawyer; b. Glen Cove, N.Y., Nov. 11, 1938; s. Thomas J. and Martha H. (Erwin) S.; m. Margaret Mary Barth, June 23, 1962; children: Thomas Joseph, Kevin M., Maura N. BS, Fordham U., 1960, JD, 1965. Bar: N.Y. 1966, U.S. Dist. Ct. (so. and ea. dist.) N.Y. 1968, U.S. Ct. Appeals (2nd cir.) 1980, U.S. Supreme Ct. 1981. Staff atty. Allstate Ins. Co., N.Y.C., 1966-69; trial atty. Hartford Ins. Co., Hauppauge, N.Y., 1969-71; ptnr. Wheller & Spellman, Farmingville, N.Y., 1971-76, Devitt, Spellman, Barrett, Callahan & Kenney, LLP, Smithtown, N.Y., 1976—. Mem. grievance com. 10th Jud. Dist., Westbury, N.Y., 1984-92. Trustee Acad. St. Joseph, Brentwood, N.Y., 2000-04; bd. govs. St. Catherine of Sienna Med. Ctr., Smithtown, NY, 2002--. Capt. USAR, 1960-68. Fellow: N.Y. Bar Found., Am. Bar Found.; mem.: N.Y. Bar State Bar Assn. (ho. of dels. 1989—, nominating com. 1992—93, v.p. 1996—98), Suffolk County Bar Assn. (bd. dirs., sec.-treas. v.p. 1982—, pres. 1992—93), Swordfish Club. Westhampton Beach, N.Y. (bd. dirs., sec. 2000—01). Home: 8 Highwoods Ct Saint James NY 11780-9610 Office: Devitt Spellman et al 50 Route 111 Ste 314 Smithtown NY 11787-3700

SPELLMIRE, GEORGE W. lawyer; b. Oak Park, Ill., June 10, 1948; Student, Brown U.; BA, Ohio State U., 1970; JD, De Paul U., 1974. Bar: Ill. 1974, U.S. Dist. Ct. (no. dist.) Ill. 1974, U.S. Tax Ct. 1984, U.S. Ct. Appeals (7th cir.) 1984, U.S. Supreme Ct. 1994. Ptnr. Hinshaw & Culbertson, Chgo., 1982-98, D'Ancona & Pflaum, Chgo., 1998—2003, Spellmire & Sommer, Chgo., 2003—. Author: Attorney Malpractice: Prevention and Defense, 1988, supplemental edit., 1990; co-author: Accounting, Auditing and Financial Malpractice, 1998, supplemental edit., 2000, Accountants' Legal Liability Guide, 1990, Illinois Handbook on Legal Malpractice, 1982, Associates Primer for the Prevention of Malpractice, 1987. Mem. ABA, Am. Coll. Trial Lawyers, Soc. Trial Lawyers, Fed. Trial Bar, Internat. Assn. Def. Counsel (legal malpractice com., def. counsel practice mgmt. com.), Ill. State Bar Assn. Office: 77 W Wacker Dr Ste 4800 Chicago IL 60601-1664 Office Phone: 312-606-8721. E-mail: gws@spellmireSommer.com.

SPELMAN, LUCY H. zoological park administrator; b. Bridgeport, Conn. BS in Biology, Brown U., 1985; DVM, U. Calif., Davis, 1990. Intern in small animal medicine and cardiology Dr. S. Ettinger and Assocs., L.A., 1990—91; resident in zool. medicine NC State Coll. Vet. Medicine/NC State Zool. Park, Asheboro, 1991—94; assoc. vet. med. officer Nat. Zool. Pk., Washington, 1995—99, sr. vet. med. officer, 1999—2000, dir., 2000—. Vet. advisor giant panda species survival plan Am. Zoo and Aquarium Assn., 1998—. Editor: Jour. Zoo and Wildlife Medicine, 1994—. Mem.: Am. Coll. Zool. Medicine (mem. exam. com. 1995—). Office: Nat Zool Park 3001 Connecticut Ave NW Washington DC 20008

SPELTS, RICHARD JOHN, lawyer; b. Yuma, Colo., July 29, 1939; s. Richard Clark and Barbara Eve (Pletcher) S.; children: Melinda, Meghan, Richard John Jr.; m. Gayle Merves, Nov. 14, 1992. BS cum laude, U. Colo., 1961, JD, 1964. Bar: Colo. 1964, U.S. Dist. Ct. Colo. 1964, U.S. Supreme Ct. 1968, U.S. Ct. Appeals (10th cir.) 1970, U.S. Dist. Ct. (ea. dist.) Mich. 1986. With Ford Motor Internat., Cologne, Germany, 1964-65; legis. counsel to U.S. Senator, 89th and 90th Congresses, 1967-68; minority counsel U.S. Senate Subcom., 90th and 91st Congresses, 1968-70; asst. U.S. atty., 1st asst. U.S. atty. Fed. Dist. of Colo., 1970-77; pvt. practice Denver, 1977-89; risk mgr. sheriff's dept. Jefferson County, Golden, Colo., 1990-91. Selected for Leadership Denver, 1977; recipient cert. for outstanding contbns. in drug law enforcement U.S. Drug Enforcement Adminstrn., 1977, spl. commendation for criminal prosecution U.S. Dept. Justice, 1973, spl. commendation for civil prosecution U.S. Dept. Justice, 1976. Mem. Fed. Bar Assn. (chmn. govt. torts seminar 1980), Colo. Bar Assn. (bd. govs. 1976-78), Denver Bar Assn., Colo. Trial Lawyers Assn., Denver Law Club, Order of Coif. Republican. Methodist. Home and Office: 9671 Brook Hill Ct Lone Tree CO 80124-5431

SPENA, RONDA GALE, music educator; b. Lakeland, Fla., Dec. 27, 1962; d. James Donald and B. Arneta Ferguson; m. Marten L. Spena, July 19, 1986; children: Andrew Conner, Adam Pearce, Aimee Kathrine. MusB in Ch. Music, Stetson U., 1984; MusM in Vocal Performance, Southwestern Bapt. Theol. Sem., 1986. Cert. Profl. Educator Assn. of Christian Schools Internat., 2003. Adj. voice instr. Lake City C.C., Fla., 1990—91; pvt. voice, piano instr. Wellington, Fla., 1991—94; music tchr. Village Christian Acad., Fayetteville, NC, 1998—. Instr. voice Meth. Coll., Fayetteville, 1999—2003. Singer: (soloist) Messiah. Mem. Chaminade Music Club, Fayetteville, 1996—98; pianist Village Bapt. Ch., Fayetteville, 1996—, soloist, 1994—; dir. women's missionary union First Bapt. Ch., Lake City, 1989—90. Mem.: Music Educator's Nat. Conv. Conservative. Office: Village Christian Academy 908 S McPherson Church Rd Fayetteville NC 28303 Office Phone: 910-483-0720.

SPENCE, ANDREW, artist, painter; b. Bryn Mawr, Pa., Oct. 4, 1947; s. Thomas and Elizabeth Spence; m. Mary Stewart Stoll, June 24, 1977. BFA, Temple U., 1969; MFA, U. Calif., Santa Barbara, 1971. One-man shows include TransAvant Garde Gallery, Austin, Tex., 1989, Barbara Krakow Gallery, Boston, 1989, Barbara Toll Fine Arts, N.Y.C., 1982-83, 85, 87-88, 90, Compass Rose Gallery, Chgo., 1990, James Corcoran Gallery, L.A., 1990, Max. Protetch Gallery, N.Y.C., 1992-93, Barbara Scott Gallery, Miami, 1993, 96, Worcester (Mass.) Art Mus., 1991, Morris Healy Gallery, N.Y.C., 1996, Art Resources Transfer, N.Y.C., 2000, Edward Thorp Gallery, N.Y.C., 2001, 2002; exhibited in group shows including Corcoran Gallery of Art, Washington, 1987, Hirshhorn Mus. and Sculpture Garden, Smithsonian Instn., Washington, 1989, Whitney Mus. Am. Art, N.Y., 1989, 91-92, Met. Mus. Art, N.Y.C., 1993, Am. Acad. Arts and Letters, N.Y.C., 1994, Wall Street Rising, N.Y.C., 2002; represented in permanent collections including Balt. Mus. Art, Carnegie Mus. Art, Pitts., Cleve. Mus. Art, Cin. Art Mus., Hirshhorn Mus. and Sculpture Garden, Laguna Gloria Art Mus., Met. Mus. Art, N.Y.C., San Diego Mus. Contemporary Art, Walker Art Ctr., Whitney Mus. Am. Art, N.Y.C. Painting grantee Nat. Endowment for Arts, 1987; Guggenheim fellow, 1994.

SPENCE, A(NDREW) MICHAEL, dean, finance educator; b. Montclair, N.J., 1943; BA in Philosophy summa cum laude, Princeton U., 1966; BA, MA in Maths., Oxford U., 1968; PhD in Econs. with honors, Harvard U., 1972. Asst. prof. polit. econ. Kennedy Sch. Govt. Harvard U., Cambridge, Mass., 1971-75, hon. rsch. fellow, 1975—76, vis. prof. econs. dept., 1976-77, prof. econs., 1977-83, prof. bus. adminstrn., 1979-83, George Gund prof. econs. and bus. adminstrn., 1983-86, chmn. bus. econs. PhD program, 1981-83, chmn. econs. dept., 1983-84, dean Faculty Arts and Scis., 1984-90; assoc. prof. dept. econs. Stanford U., Calif., 1973-75, Philip H. Knight Prof., dean Grad. Sch. Bus., 1990-99, Philip H. Knight Prof. Emeritus, prof. mgmt., 1999—; ptnr. Oak Hill Venture Ptnrs. and Oak Hill Capital Ptnrs., Menlo Park, Calif., 1999—. Bd. dirs. Gen. Mills, Inc., Nike, Inc., Exult Inc., Siebel Syss. Inc., Blue Martini Software, Torstar Corp., ITI Edn.; mem. econs. adv. panel NSF, 1977-79; chmn. Nat. Rsch. Coun. Bd. on Sci., Tech. and Econ., Policy, 1990-97. Author: Market Signaling: Informational Transfer in Hiring and Related Processes, 1974; Co-author: Industrial Organization in an Open Economy, 1980, Competitive Structure in Investment Banking, 1983; past mem. editl. bd. Am. Econs. Rev., Bell. Jour. Econs., Jour. Econ. Theory and Pub. Policy; contbr. over 50 articles to profl. jours. Mem. econs. adv. com. Sloan Found., 1979—. Recipient J.K. Galbraith prize for excellence in tchg., 1978, Nobel prize in econ. scis., 2001; Danforth fellow, 1966, Rhodes scholar, 1966. Fellow Am. Acad. Arts & Scis., 1983-, Econometric Soc.; mem. Am. Econ. Assn. (John Bates Clark medal 1981). Office: Stanford U Grad Sch Bus Bldg 350 Memorial Way Stanford CA 94305-5015*

SPENCE, BARBARA E. publishing company executive; b. Bryn Mawr, Pa., July 8, 1921; d. Geoffrey Strange and Mary (Harrington) Earnshaw; m. Kenneth M. Spence Jr., June 29, 1944; children: Kenneth M. III, Christopher E., Hilary B. Grad. high sch. Movie, radio editor Parade Mag., N.Y.C., 1941-45; with Merchandising Group, N.Y.C., 1946-47; exec. dir. Greenfield Hill Congl. Ch., Fairfield, Conn., 1958-74, dir. religious edn., 1968-74; assoc. Ten Eyck-Emerich Antiques, 1974-76; personnel dir. William Morrow & Co., Inc., N.Y.C., 1976-91; ret., 1991. Chmn. pub. relations, bd. dirs. ARC, 1951-56, Family Service Soc., Fairfield, 1956-57, 61-63; chmn. pub. relations Citizens for Eisenhower, 1952, Fairfield Teens Players, 1968-71; bd. dirs. Fairfield Teens, Inc., 1965-70, Planned Parenthood of Greater Bridgeport, 1969-75, chmn. pub. affairs, 1971-72, chmn. personnel, 1972-73, chpt. vice chmn., 1973-75; pres. steering com. Am. Playwrights Festival Theatre, Inc., Fairfield, 1969-70, v.p., bd. dirs., 1971—; bd. govs. Unquowa Sch., Fairfield, 1963-69; bd. dirs. Fairfield U. Playhouse, 1971-73, Downtown Cabaret Theatre, Bridgeport, 1975-76; bd. missions Southport Congl. Ch., 1998. Mem. AAP (compensation survey com.), Fairfield Women's Exch. (bd. dirs. 1993). Home: 101 Twin Brooks Ln Fairfield CT 06430-2834

SPENCE, DONALD POND, psychologist, psychoanalyst; b. N.Y.C., Feb. 8, 1926; s. Ralph Beckett and Rita (Pond) S.; m. Mary Newbold Cross, June 2, 1951; children: Keith, Sarah, Laura, Katherine. AB, Harvard U., 1949; PhD, Columbia U., 1955. Lic. psychologist, N.J., N.J. From rsch. asst. to prof. psychology NYU, 1954-74; prof. psychiatry Robert Wood Johnson Med. Sch., Piscataway, N.J., 1974-95; ret., 1995. Vis. prof. psychology Stanford (Calif.) U., 1971-72, Princeton (N.J.) U., 1975-95, Louvain-le-Neuve, Belgium, 1980, William Alanson White Inst., N.Y.C., 1992; mem. personality and cognition rsch. rev. com. NIMH, 1969-73. Author: Narrative Truth and Historical Truth, 1982, The Freudian Metaphor, 1987, The Rhetorical Voice of Psychoanalysis, 1994; mem. editl. bd. Psychoanalysis and Contemporary Thought, Psychol. Inquiry, Theory and Psychology; contbr. articles to profl. jours. With U.S. Army, 1944-46, ETO. Recipient rsch. scientist award NIMH, 1968-74; decorated 2 battle stars. Fellow APA (pres. theoretical and philos. divsn. 1992-93), Am. Psychoanalytic Assn., N.Y. Acad. Sci., Sigma Xi. Democrat. Home: 9 Haslet Ave Princeton NJ 08540-4913 E-mail: dpshaslet@aol.com.

SPENCE, GERALD LEONARD, lawyer, writer; b. Laramie, Wyo., Jan. 8, 1929; s. Gerald M. and Esther Sophie (Pfleeger) S.; m. Anna Wilson, June 20, 1947; children: Kip, Kerry, Kent, Katy; m. LaNelle Hampton Peterson, Nov. 18, 1969. BSL, U. Wyo., 1949, LLB, 1952, LLD (hon.), 1990. Bar: Wyo. 1952, U.S. Ct. Claims 1952, U.S. Supreme Ct. 1982. Sole practice, Riverton, Wyo., 1952-54; county and pros. atty. Fremont County, Wyo., 1954-62; ptnr. various law firms, Riverton and Casper, Wyo., 1962-78; sr. ptnr. Spence, Moriarity & Schuster, Jackson, Wyo., 1978—2002, Spence, Moriarity & Shockey, 2002—03, Spence Law Firm, 2004—. Lectr. legal orgns. and law schs. Author: (with others) Gunning for Justice, 1982, Of Murder and Madness, 1983, Trial by Fire, 1986, With Justice for None, 1989, From Freedom to Slavery, 1993, How To Argue and Win Every Time, 1995, The Making of a Country Lawyer, 1996, O.J.: The Last Word, 1997, Give Me Liberty, 1998, A Boy's Summer, 2000, Gerry Spence's Wyoming: The Landscapes, 2000, Half Moon and Empty Stars, 2001, Seven Simple Steps to Personal Freedom, 2001, The Smoking Gun, 2003. Mem. ABA, Wyo. Bar Assn., Wyo. Trial Lawyers Assn., Assn. Trial Lawyers Am., Nat. Assn. Criminal Def. Lawyers Office: The Spence Law Firm LLC PO Box 548 Jackson WY 83001-0548 Office Phone: 307-733-7290.

SPENCE, JAMES ROBERT, JR., television sports executive, educator; b. Bronxville, N.Y., Dec. 20, 1936; s. James Robert and Mary Jeffery (Grant) S.; m. Betsy Jo Viener, June 16, 1992. BA, Dartmouth Coll., 1958. Prodn. asst. ABC Sports, Inc. (known as Sports Programs, Inc. through 1966), N.Y.C., 1960-63; asst. to exec. producer ABC's Wide World of Sports, 1963-66, coordinating prodr., 1966-70; v.p. program planning ABC Sports, Inc., 1970-78, sr. v.p., 1978-86; pres. Sports Television Internat. Inc., N.Y.C., 1986—. Adj. assoc. prof. broadcasting NYU Sch. Continuing and Profl. Studies, N.Y.C., 1999—2001; vis. instr. Coll. William and Mary, Williamsburg, Va., 2004. Author: Up Close and Personal - The Inside Story of Network Television Sports, 1988. Served with U.S. Army, 1958-60. Mem.: Westchester Country (Rye, N.Y.). Office: Sports TV Internat Inc PO Box 6242 New York NY 10150-6242

SPENCE, JANET BLAKE CONLEY (MRS. ALEXANDER PYOTT SPENCE), civic worker; b. Upper Montclair, N.J., Aug. 17, 1915; d. Walter Abbott and Ethel Maud (Blake) Conley; m. Alexander Pyott Spence, June 10, 1939; children: Janet Spence Kerr, Robert Moray, Richard Taylor. Student, Vassar Coll., 1933-35; cert., Katharine Gibbs Sch., 1936. Active various community drives; chmn. Darien (Conn.) Assembly, 1955-56; sec., chmn. Wilton Jr. Assembly, 1961-63; subscription chmn. Candlelight Concerts Wilton, Conn., 1963-65; rec. sec. Pub. Health Nursing Assn. Wilton Bd., 1964-67; corr., rec. sec. Royle Sch. Bd., Darien, 1952-55; fund raiser Vassar Class of 1937; mem. Washington Valley Community Assn.; mem. N.J. Symphony Orch. League, treas. Morris County br. 1978-83, corr. sec. 1982-83, pres. 1985-89, acting pres. 1989—, state coun. mem. 1985-89, acting pres. Morris br. 1989-90; docent Macculloch Hall Historica Mus., Morristown, N.J., 1992—. Mem. Vassar Alumni Assn., Dobbs Alumni Assn., Jersey Hills Vassar Club Morristown (ann. fund raiser), Woman's Club (sec. 2003—), Wilton Garden Club (life), Washington Valley Cmty. Assn. (life corr. sec. 1977-82, pres. 1982-84, v.p. 1984-85, co-pres. 1985-86, chmn. membership com.

1987-89, archives com. 1988—, treas. 1990—), Washington Valley Home Econs. Club, Del. Ref. Club (charter mem.). Mem. United Ch. Of Christ. Home: Apt 5D 1212 Foulk Rd Wilmington DE 19803-2752 Address: 8 Evergreen Ave Kennebunk ME 04043

SPENCE, MICHAEL ALLAN, lawyer; b. Green Bay, Wis., Mar. 15, 1956; s. William Allan and Lorraine (Samuels) S. BS magna cum laude, U. Wis., Green Bay, 1980; JD, William Mitchell Coll. of Law, St. Paul., 1984. Bar: Wash. 1985. Assoc. Law office of Thomas A. Durkin, Chgo., 1984-85; govtl. affairs dir. Snohomish & County Bd. of Realtors, Everett, Wash., 1985-87; govtl. affiars dir. Seattle-King County Assn. of Realtors, Seattle, 1987—; also legal counsel, 1988—. Mem. ABA, Wash. State Bar Assn. (mem. Environmental and Land Use Com. 1985—). Avocations: sailing, skiing. Office: Seattle-King County Assn of Realtors 12015 115th Ave NE Ste 295 Kirkland WA 98034-6925

SPENCE, NANCY JOAN, state representative; b. Denver, Dec. 12, 1936; m. Peter Spence; 4 children. Attended, Colo. State U. State rep. dist. 39 Colo. Ho. of Reps., Denver, 1998—, mem. joint com. on edn., joint com. on legis. ethics, and transp. and energy com. Mem. Interstate Migrant Edn. Coun., Cherry Creek Schs. Bd. Edn., Colo., 1980—93. Named Woman of Yr., Villager Newspapers, 1991, Legislator of Yr., Colo. Assn. Cmty. Centered Bds., 2001, Bus. Legislator of Yr., Colo. Assn. Commerce and Industry, 2000, Legislator of Yr., Am. Heart Assn., 1999; recipient Guardian of Small Bus. award, Nat. Fedn. Ind. Bus., 2002, Pres.'s award, U. Colo. Sch. Dentistry, Alumni Legis. Recognition award, U. Colo., 2001. Republican. Roman Catholic. Office: State Capitol Denver CO 80203

SPENCE, PAUL HERBERT, librarian; b. Geraldine, Ala., Dec. 25, 1923; s. John Clardy and Leila (Carrell) S.; m. Ruth Schmidt, May 9, 1954 (dec. Aug. 2003); children— John Carrell, Peter Schmidt, Robert McCollough AB, Emory U., 1948, MA, 1956; PhD, U. Ill., 1969. Asst. reference librarian Emory U., Atlanta, 1950-53; periodical reference librarian Air U., Maxwell AFB, 1953-56; dir. library Air Force Inst. of Tech., Wright-Patterson AFB, Ohio, 1957-58; asst. dir. social studies U. Notre Dame, South Bend, Ind., 1959-60, U. Nebr., Lincoln, 1960-63; history and polit. sci. librarian U. Ill., Urbana, 1963-66; assoc. dir. libraries U. Ga., Athens, 1966-70, dir. libraries U. Ala., Birmingham, 1970-84, collection devel. librarian, 1985-89, prof. emeritus, 1989—, libr. cons., 1990—. Bd. dirs. Southeastern Library Network, Atlanta, 1973-75. Served with U.S. Army, 1943-46, ETO Mem. ALA (council mem. 1976-78), Ala. Library Assn. (treas. 1975-76), Southeastern Library Assn. (pres. 1980-82) Democrat. Presbyterian. Home: 614 Warwick Rd Birmingham AL 35209-4426 Office: U Ala at Birmingham 172 Sterne Libr Birmingham AL 35294-0001 E-mail: pspence@beowulf.mhsl.uab.edu.

SPENCE, RICHARD DEE, retired rail transportation executive; b. Tucumcari, N.Mex., Apr. 7, 1925; s. Andrew Doke and Myrtle Hannah (Roach) S.; m. Mary Ames Kellogg, July 24, 1976; children: Mary B., Ames T., Richard T.; children from previous marriage: Diana, Richard N. BS, UCLA, 1949; grad., Transp. Mgmt. Program, Stanford U., 1956, Sr. Execs. Program, MIT, 1962. With So. Pacific Transp. Co., San Francisco, 1946-75, asst. v.p. ops., 1967-69, v.p. ops., 1969-75; pres., chief oper. officer Consol. Rail Corp., Phila., 1975-78; pres. L&N R.R. Co., Louisville, 1978-80; exec. v.p. ops. Family Lines Rail System, 1980-84; cons. in field, 1984-90; dir., prin. Skippingdale Paper Products, England, 1986-97. With USN, 1943-46. Mem. Ponte Vedra Club, Sawgrass Club, Bohemian Club, Golf House Club of Elie (Scotland), Phi Kappa Sigma. Republican. Episcopalian. Home and Office: 339 Ponte Vedra Blvd Ponte Vedra Beach FL 32082-1813

SPENCE, ROBERT DEAN, physics educator; b. Bergen, N.Y., Sept. 12, 1917; s. La Vergne Robert and Jennie (Waterman) S.; m. Helen Holbrook, June 14, 1942; children— John, Elizabeth, Janet, Barbara. BS, Cornell U., 1939; MS, Mich. State U., 1942; PhD, Yale, 1948. Asst. prof. physics Mich. State U., East Lansing, 1947-49, assoc. prof., 1949-52, prof., 1952-86, emeritus, 1986—. Vis. prof. U. Bristol, Eng., 1955-56, Technische Hogesch., Eindhoven, Netherlands, 1964, Rijks universiteit, Leiden, Netherlands, 1970-71 Recipient Distinguished Faculty award Mich. State U., 1963; Guggenheim fellow, 1955-56 Mem. Nat. Soc. Profl. Engrs., Sigma Xi, Phi Kappa Phi. Research and publs. on math. physics, chem. physics, magnetism. Home: 1849 Ann St East Lansing MI 48823-3707

SPENCE, ROBERT LEROY, publishing executive; b. Carlisle, Pa., Sept. 13, 1931; s. Leroy Oliver and Esther Helen (Lau) S.; m. Barbara Amelia Hunter, Sept. 1, 1954 (div. Sept. 1978); children— Robert Roy, Bonnie Leigh; m. 2d, Maryanne Elizabeth Yacono, Jan. 10, 1979 BA, Dickinson Coll., 1953; postgrad, Temple U., 1955-57, Rutgers U., 1956, 59-60, U. Pa., 1960. Cert. tchr., N.J. Chmn. dept. math. Haddon Heights High Sch., N.J., 1954-62; sr. editor Silver Burdett Co., Morristown, N.J., 1962-64; editor-in-chief Harcourt Brace Jovanovich, Inc., N.Y.C., 1964-81; v.p. pub. Harper & Row Publishers, Inc., N.Y.C., 1981-85, Scribner Ednl. Pubs. div. Macmillan, Inc., N.Y.C., 1985; pres. R&M Spence, Inc., Sparta, N.J., 1985—. Author textbook series: Growth in Mathematics, 1978, Excel in Mathematics, 1989-90, Mathematics Plus: Multicultural Projects, 1993; editor: Financial Planning for The Baby Boomer Client, 2000, 2d edit., 2004, Money Forever, 2002. Mem. Assn. Am. Pubs. (mem. exec. com. 1981-84), Nat. Council Tchrs. Math., Internat. Reading Assn., Am. Numismatic Assn. Avocations: rare coin collecting, coin newsletter author and publisher, artist, writer. Home and Office: 37 Heather Ln Sparta NJ 07871-3538 E-mail: rlsmys@tellurian.net.

SPENCE, ROY MILAM, JR., advertising executive; BA in Govt., U. Tex., 1971. Founder, pres. GSD&M Advt., Austin, Tex., 1971—. Office: GSD&M Advertising 828 W 6th St Austin TX 78703-5420

SPENCE, SANDRA, retired professional society administrator; b. McKeesport, Pa., Mar. 25, 1941; d. Cedric Leroy and Suzanne (Haudenshield) S. BA, Allegheny Coll., 1963; MA, Rutgers U., 1964. With Pa. State Govt., Harrisburg, 1964-68, Appalachian Regional Commn., Washington, 1968-75; legis. rep. Nat. Assn. Counties, Washington, 1975-77; fed. rep. Calif. Dept. Transp., Washington, 1977-78; dir. congl. affairs Amtrak, Washington, 1978-81, corp. sec., 1981-83; dir. computer svcs. Nat. R.R. Passenger Corp., Washington, 1983-84; co-owner Parkhurst-Spence Inc., 1985; owner The Spence Group, 1986-90; v.p. Bostrom Corp., Washington, 1990-92; exec. dir. Soc. Glass and Ceramic Decorators, 1992-2000. Chmn. legis. com. Womens Transp. Seminar, 1977-79, dir., 1982-83, v.p., 1983-84, chmn. edn. com., 1982-83; com. on edn. and tng. Transp. Rsch. Bd., 1982-85; mng. ptnr. Cambio Capital Club, 1996. Contbr. articles to profl. jours. Commnr. DC Commn. for Women, 1983—88, sec., 1983—88; pres. Found. for Work of Laity, 2001—; del. Ward III Dem. Com., 1982—90, 1st vice chmn., 1987—88; bd. dir. DC Habitat for Humanity, 1998—2002, chmn. devel. com., 1998—2000, sec., 2000—01; corr. sec. Sussex County (Del.) Habitat for Humanity, 2003—. Fellow Eagleton Inst. Politics, 1963-64; recipient Achievement award Transp. Seminar, 1982, 83 Mem. Greater Washington Soc. Assn. Execs. (vice-chair law and legis. com. 1989-90, chmn. 1990-91, chmn. scholarship com. 1992-93, bd. dirs. 1993-96, Rising Star award 1989, Chmn.'s award for Govt. Rels. 1991), Am. Soc. Assn. Execs. (mgmt. cert. 1987), Phi Beta Kappa. Home: 18471 Seashell Blvd Lewes DE 19958 Personal E-mail: sandy_s@juno.com.

SPENCE, SARAH, comparatist educator; b. N.Y.C., Aug. 14, 1954; d. Donald Pond and Mary Newbold Spence; m. James Harvey Spence McGregor, Oct. 1, 1946; 1 child, Edward Isham Spence McGregor. BA, Brown U., 1976; MA, Columbia U., PhD, 1981. Asst. prof. comparative lit. Calif. State U., Long Beach, 1982—87; assoc. prof. comparative lit. U. Ga., Athens, 1987—94, assoc. prof. classics, 1994—96, prof. classics, 1996—. Author: Rhetorics of Reason and Desire, Texts and the Self in the Twelfth Century; editor: The French Chansons of Charles d'Orleans; translator; editor: Poets and Critics Read Vergil; translator (editor-in-chief): Literary Imagination, 1999—. Fellow Mrs. Giles Whiting Dissertation fellow, 1979—80, NEH, 1981—82, Harvard U., 1984—85, Bunting fellow, Radcliffe Coll., 1992—93; grantee Mellon fellow. Mem.: MLA, Societe Guilhem IX, Assn. Lit. Scholars and Critics, Am. Philol Assn. Office: U Ga Dept of Classics 221 Park Hall Athens GA 30602

SPENCE, SIQUE (MARY STEWART SPENCE), art dealer; b. Balt., Aug. 16, 1946; d. Joseph Adolphus and Nell Orum (Jones) Stoll; m. Ronald A. Kuchta, Nov. 2, 1969 (div. 1975); m. Andrew R. Spence, June 24, 1977. Dir. Galeria del Sol/Fairtree Fine Crafts Inst., Santa Barbara, Calif., 1970-75; asst. to dir. Arco Ctr. for the Visual Arts, L.A., 1975-77; registrar Droll/Kolbert Gallery, N.Y.C., 1977-78; gallery asst. Nancy Hoffman Gallery, N.Y.C., 1978-81, dir., 1981—. Office: Nancy Hoffman Gallery 429 W Broadway New York NY 10012-3799 Fax: 212-334-5078.

SPENCE, TERRY R. state legislator; b. Wilmington, Del., Nov. 30, 1941; m. Nancy Spence; children: Terry Jr., Mark, Greg, Laura. AS, Goldey Beacom Coll.; BBA, Wilmington Coll. Mem. Dist. 18 Del. Ho. of Reps., spkr. of house, 1987—, ethics and adminstrv. coms., legis. coun.; acct. exec. Brooks Courier Svc. Co., Wilmington, Del. Hon. mem. Wilmington Manor Vol. Fire Co. Recipient Disting. Legis. award MADD, 1987, Disting. Legis. Svc. award Del. Bar Assn., 1986. Mem. NRA, Del. Assn. Retarded Citizens, Del. Assn. Blind Athletes, Lions. Home: 26 Freeport Rd New Castle DE 19720-3019 Office: PO Box 1401 Dover DE 19903-1401 E-mail: tspence@legis.state.de.us.

SPENCER, C. STANLEY, insurance company executive; b. Canton, Pa., Sept. 24, 1940; s. Clarence N. and Maude E. (Phipps) S.; m. Carol M. Vest, Aug. 23, 1962; children: Greg, Mike. BS in Agrl. Engring., Pa. State U., 1961. Regional sales mgr. W.T. Grant Co., N.Y.C., 1966-76; engr. Hoover Well Service, Zion, Ill., 1976-80, Nielson Iron Works, Racine, Wis., 1980-82; spl. agent Prudential Ins. Co., Racine, 1982-84, div. mgr., from 1984; v.p. legal dept. Am. Family Mut. Ins. Co., Madison, Wis. Recipient 1st Place Barbershop Chorus award, Racine, 1984, Kenosha, 1985, Manitowoc, 1986, 1st Place Barbershop Quartet award, Kenosha, Wis., 1986. Mem. Life Underwriters Assn. (v.p. 1985-86), Soc. for the Preservation and Encouragement of Barber Shop Quartet Singing in Am. (pres. Racine 1984-85). Clubs: Toastmasters (1st Place 1985). Republican. Home: 6234 Larchmont Dr Racine WI 53406-5120 Office: American Family Mutual Insurance Company 6000 American Pkwy Madison WI 53783-0001

SPENCER, CAROLE A. medical association administrator, medical educator; BSc in Applied Biochemistry, Bath U. Tech., Bath, Somerset, Eng., 1969; PhD, Glasgow U., Scotland, 1972. Lic. clin. chemist med. technologist Calif., 1985. Lectr. in biochemistry Glasgow U., Scotland, 1972—73; asst. prof. rsch. medicine U. So. Calif., L.A., 1980—88, assoc. prof. rsch. medicine, 1988—94, prof. rsch. medicine, 1995—, dir. Endocrine Svcs. Lab., 1980—, GCRC Core Lab. dir. Clin. Rsch. Ctr., 1977—, GCRC Core Low Level Ligand Detection lab. dir., 1993—. Biochemist dept. pathol. biochemistry Glasgow Royal Infirmary, 1973—77; lectr. in field; cons. in field. Editl. bd. Jour. Clin. endocrinology and Metabolism, 1984—88, Am. Assn. Clin. Chemistry Jours., 1996—, Hormone and Metabolic Rsch., 1996—, reviewer Annals of Internal Medicine, —, Clin. Chemistry, —, Gerontology, —, Hormone and Metabolic Rsch., —, Jour. of Clin. Endocrinology and Metabolism, —, Jour. of Clin. Investigation, —, Jour. of Endocrinol. Investigation, —; contbr. articles to profl. jours. Mem.: European Thyroid Assn., Assn. Clin. Biochemists U.K., Endocrine Soc., Clin. Ligand Assay Soc. (Disting. Scientist award 1998), Am. Thyroid Assn. (pub. health com. 1991—, pres., exec. coun. 1995—), Am. Fedn. Clin. Rsch., Am. Assn. Clin. endocrinologists, Am. Assn. Clin. Chemists (Outstanding Spkr. award 1992, 1997), Cross-Town Endocrine Club. Achievements include research in includes thyroid physiology and pathology; thyroglobulin and thyroid cancer; thyroid hormone metabolism; immunoassay techniques. Office: U Southern Calif EDM111 9560 Los Angeles CA 90089

SPENCER, CAROLINE, retired library director; BA, AMLS, U. Mich. Past pres. Hawaii Libr. Assn. Office: HI State Public Lib 478 S King St Honolulu HI 96813-2901

SPENCER, DAVID ANTHONY, geologist, researcher; b. London, Nov. 7, 1963; s. Henry William George and Veronica Clair (Bonanno) S. BSc in Geology with honors, U. Exeter, Eng., 1986; Diploma, MSc in Structural Geology, U. London, 1988; Dr Natural Sci., Swiss Fed. Inst. Tech., Zurich, 1993. Chartered geologist, European geologist. Ins. claims broker Winchester Bowring Ltd., London, 1982-83; platinum exploration geologist Eastern Bushveld Complex, South Africa, 1986-87; rsch. fellow Swiss Fed. Inst. Tech., Zürich, 1988-89, rsch. and tchr. asst., 1989-92, vis. ETH rsch. fellow, 1992-93, vis. rsch. fellow, 1993-94, rsch. fellow in tectonics Zurich, 1994-97; vis. lectr. U. of the Punjab, Lahore, Pakistan, 1995; vis. scientist Tokyo Inst. Tech., Zurich, 1996; rsch. asst. prof., lectr. in structural geology U. Maine, Orono, 1997-98; geologist Saga Petroleum ASA, Norway, 1998—99; project mgr. numerous rsch. projects; founder Spencer Structural Cons., 2000; sr. reservoir geologist Roxar Software Solutions, 2003—. Vis. scientist U. Beijing, 1986; vis. prof. U. of the Punjab, Lahore, 1997—; Himalayan regional coordinating com. Internat. Lithosphere Program, 1992-96, com. tectonic map of Himalaya, 1995; organizer confs. in field; founder, moderator, coord. HimNet, 1994-96; presenter, cons., lectr. in field. Contbr. numerous articles to profl. jours.; European regional editor Himalayan Notes, 1994-97; reviewer numerous internat. jours. in field; assoc. editor The Professional Geologist. Found. gov. Raine's Found. Sch., 2002—; trustee The Raine's Found., 2002—. Sir John Cass Found. scholar, 1987-88, travel award, 1988; recipient travel award Swiss Geol. Soc., 1991, 93, Huber-Kudlich Found., 1992, Swiss Acad. Natural Scis., 1992, Pub. award Staub Fund, 1992, Educational Tng. award Saga Petroleum ASA; rsch. fellow Swiss Nat. Sci. Found., 1994-97; recipient Duke of Edinburgh Gold award, 1987. Fellow Geol. Soc., Royal Geog. Soc., Royal Soc. Arts, Am. Geog. Soc., Geol. Assn. of Can.; mem. AAAS, Inst. Petroleum, Royal Instn. of Gt. Britain, Royal Scottish Geog. Soc. (profl. assoc.), Order of Internat. Fellowship, Internat. Assn. Structural/Tectonic Geologists, Mineral. Soc., European Assn. Geoscientists and Engrs., Soc. for Sedimentary Geology, Geosci. Info. Soc., Computer Oriented Geol. Soc., European Union Geoscis., Am. Geophys. Union, Assn. Geoscientists for Internat. Devel., Geol. Soc Am., Geol. Soc. Switzerland, Geol. Soc. Pakistan, Geol. Soc. Punjab, Geol. Soc. Nepal, Swiss Mineral. and Petrological Soc., Soc. for Mining, Metallurgy and Exploration, Geochem. Soc., Am. Chem. Soc., Petroleum Exploration Soc. of Gt. Britain, Am. Assn. Petroleum Geologists, Nat. Geog. Soc., Assn. Am. Geographers, Can. Assn. Geographers, Brit. Assn. for Advancement of Sci., Sci. Exploration Soc., N.Y. Acad. Scis., Nat. Earth Sci. Tchrs. Assn., Nat. Assn. Geosci. Tchrs., Assn. for Sci. Edn., Himalayan Found., Himalayan Club, Himalayan Explorers Club, Nepal Studies Assn., Internat. Assn. for Ladakh Studies, Integrated Mountain Rsch. Soc., Internat. Mountain Soc., Brit. Mountaineering Coun., Sigma Xi. Avocations: mountain climbing, guitar, long distance walking, sports.

SPENCER, DAVID JAMES, lawyer; b. Altadena, Calif., June 23, 1943; s. Dorcy James and Dorothy Estelle (Pingry) S.; m. Donna Rae Blair, Aug. 22, 1965; children: Daniel, Matthew. BA, Rocky Mountain Coll., 1965; JD, Yale U., 1968. Bar: Minn. 1968, U.S. Dist. Ct. Minn. 1968, U.S. Ct. Appeals (8th cir.) 1970. Mem. firm Briggs and Morgan, P.A., Mpls. and St. Paul, 1968—2003. Bd. dirs. RS Eden, Inc. Contbg. author 10 William Mitchell Law Rev., 1984; contbr. articles to profl. jours. Trustee Rocky Mountain Coll., Billings, Mont., 1980-01; bd. dirs. River Valley Arts Coun., 1996-01, Stillwater Area Arts Ctr. Alliance, 1998-01, Homeward Bound, Inc., 1999—; pres., bd. dirs. St. Croix Friends of Arts, Stillwater, Minn., 1981-84; bd. dirs. Valley Chamber Chorale, Stillwater, 1989-92; v.p. Minn. Jaycees, St. Paul, 1974; elder Presbyn. Ch. Recipient Silver Key St. Paul Jaycees, 1974; Disting. Svc. award Rocky Mountain Coll., 1981, Outstanding Svc. award, 1988, Disting. Achievement award, 1992. Fellow Am. Coll. Real Estate Lawyers; mem. ABA, Minn. Bar Assn., Ramsey County Bar Assn., Stillwater Country Club, Stillwater Sunrise Rotary Club (bd. dirs. 1997-99). Presbyterian. Avocations: trout fishing, golf, singing. Home: 10135 Waterfront Dr Woodbury MN 55129 E-mail: dspencer36@earthlink.net.

SPENCER, DAWN JOYCE, librarian, educator; b. St. Louis, Nov. 7, 1938; d. Leslie Sylvan II and Iris Nunn (Burdick) S. AB, Syracuse U., 1964, MA, 1967, MA, 1995. Cert. secondary education educator, N.Y., Calif. Exec. sec. to permanent observer Rep. Korea to UN UN, N.Y.C., 1964-65; secondary level social studies tchr. Bd. Edn., Utica, N.Y., 1966-69; mgr. apt. complex Oakland, Calif., 1969-75; lectr. Fukushima (Japan) U., Fukushima Med. Coll., Sakura no Seibo Women's Coll., Kennedy Internat. Coll., 1975-94; dir. Bowerston (Ohio) Pub. Libr., 1996—. English fluency instr. to migrant workers N.Y. Dept. Edn., Clinton, summers 1967-68; sr. lectr. Fukushima Women's Coll., 1982-94. Pres. Syracuse-in-Asia, 1962-64; advisor U.S. Mil. Svc. Recruitment, Utica, N.Y., 1966-69; active ASPCA, HSUS, APL, Oakland, 1969-75, Fukushima Organic Farm Cooperative, 1982-94, Japan Animal Welfare Soc., Tokyo, 1993-94, African Wildlife Found., Am. Rivers, Best Friends Animal Sanctuary, Ctr. Marine Conservation, Defenders of Wildlife, numerous others. Mem. AARP, ASPCA, Bowerston Women's Club, Am. Legal Def. Fund, Greenpeace, Nat. Audubon Soc., African Wildlife Found., World Wildlife Fund, others. Democrat. Avocations: animal welfare, snow and water skiing, jazz, computers. Office: Bowerston Pub Libr 200 Main St Bowerston OH 44695 Fax: 740-269-8503. E-mail: djspence@tusco.net., spenceda@oplin.lib.oh.us.

SPENCER, DENNIS DEE, medical educator, director; b. Bedford, Iowa, Apr. 1, 1945; s. George and Wilma Spencer; m. Susan S. Spencer; children: Andrea, Joanna; children: Christopher, Kathleen. Grad., Grinnell Coll.; MD, Wash. U., St. Louis, 1971. Intern Barnes Hosp., St. Louis, 1971—72; resident in neurological surgery Yale-New Haven Hosp., 1972—76, assoc. neurosurgeon, 1977—80, attending neurosurgeon, 1980—87; prof. neurosurgery Yale U. Sch. Medicine, 1985—, chief neurosurgery, Nixdorff-German Prof., 1987—97, chmn. dept. neurosurgery, Harvey and Kate Cushing Prof., 1997—, dir. epilepsy program, acting dean, 2003—04. Mem.: Am. Epilepsy Soc. (bd. dirs., Milken Family Found. Clin. Investigator Award 1999), Am. Bd. Neurol. Surgeons, Am. Assn. Neurol. Surgeons, Soc. Neurol. Surgeons. Achievements include pioneer in sterotaxic cellular replacement therapy for patients with parkinson's desease. Office: Yale Neurosurgery Yale Physicians Bldg 3rd Fl 800 Howard Ave New Haven CT 06519*

SPENCER, DONALD SPURGEON, historian, academic administrator; b. Anderson, Ind., Jan. 29, 1945; s. Thomas E. and Josephine (Litz) S.; m. Pamela Sue Roberts, June 19, 1965; 1 child, Jennifer Wynne. BA, Ill. Coll., 1967; PhD, U. Va., 1973. Asst. prof. history Westminster Coll., Fulton, Mo., 1973-76, Ohio U., Athens, 1976-77; from asst., assoc. to full prof., assoc. dean, asst. provost U. Mont., Missoula, 1977-90; provost SUNY, Geneseo, 1990-93; pres. Western Ill. U., Macomb, 1994—. Author: Louis Kossuth and Young America, 1978, The Carter Implosion: Jimmy Carter and the Amateur Style of Diplomacy,1989; contbr. articles to jours. in field. With U.S. Army, 1968-71, Korea. Woodrow Wilson Found. fellow, 1968; Danforth Found. univ. teaching fellow, 1971. Mem. Phi Beta Kappa. Congregationalist. Office: W Ill Univ Office of the President Sherman Hall Macomb IL 61455 Home: 124 Links Of Leith Williamsburg VA 23188-7461

SPENCER, DOUGLAS LLOYD, chemist, manufacturing executive; b. Berkeley, Calif., July 19, 1952; s. Alma Glenn and Anna Lea (Lloyd) S.; m. Connie Jeanette Whitesel, Aug. 23, 1974; children: Jeanette Dawn, Jared Douglas, Jilissa Annette, Janine Marie, Janelle Renee, Jeffrey Brian. AA, Diablo Valley Coll., 1971; BS, Brigham Young U., 1974. Lab instr., chemistry dept. Brigham Young U., 1973-74; rsch. chemist Dow Chem. Western divsn., Pittsburg, Calif., 1975-80; pres. Sunset Distbg., Inc., Brentwood, Calif., 1980-82, Maier & Assocs., Inc., Brentwood, Calif., 1982-83, Doug Spencer & Assocs., Placerville, Calif., 1983-94; buyer, major wholesale merchandise distbr. Bacar, Inc., San Jose, Calif., 1995-97; life agt. Beneficial Life, Sacramento, 1997—2000; sales mgr. Fortel Traffic Inc., Hollister, Calif., 2001—02; agt. MSI Ins., Morgan Hill, Calif., 2002—. Mem. Brentwood Planning Commn., 1980-81; missionary, dist. zone leader Ea. States Mission, 1971-73; active Boy Scouts of Am. Rossmoor residents scholar, 1969-71, Brigham Young U. scholar, 1973-74. Republican. Mem. Lds Ch. Avocations: camping, fishing, gardening. Home: 2010 Clearview Dr Hollister CA 95023-6239 Office Phone: 408-779-7488. E-mail: sixjs@hollinet.com.

SPENCER, EDGAR WINSTON, geology educator; b. Monticello, Ark., May 27, 1931; s. Terrel Ford and Allie Belle (Shelton) S.; m. Elizabeth Penn Humphries, Nov. 26, 1958; children: Elizabeth Shawn, Kristen Shannon. Student, Vanderbilt U., 1949—50; BS, Washington and Lee U., 1953; PhD, Columbia U., 1957. Lectr. Hunter Coll., 1954-57; mem. faculty Washington and Lee U., 1957—, prof. geology, head dept., 1962-95, Ruth Parmly prof. Pres. Rockbridge Area Conservation Coun., 1978-79, co-pres. 1992-98; NSF sci. faculty fellow, New Zealand and Australia; dir. grant for humanities and pub. policy on land use planning Va. Found., 1975; dir. grant Petroleum Rsch. Fund, 1981-82; leader field trip Ctrl. Appalachian Mts. Internat. Geol. Congress, 1989. Author: Basic Concepts of Physical Geology, 1962, Basic Concepts of Historical Geology, 1962, Geology: A Survey of Earth Science, 1965, Introduction to the Structure of the Earth, 1969, 3d edit., 1988, The Dynamics of the Earth, 1972, Physical Geology, 1983, Geologic Maps, 1993, 2nd edit., 2000, Earth Science-Understanding Environmental Systems, 2003. Recipient Va. Outstanding Faculty award Va. Coun. of Higher Edn., 1990. Fellow Geol. Soc. Am., AAAS; mem. Am. Assn. Petroleum Geologists (dir. field seminar on fold and thrust belts 1987, 88-91), Am. Inst. Profl. Geologists, Am. Geophys. Union, Nat. Assn. Geology Tchrs., Yellowstone-Bighorn Rsch. Assn., Phi Beta Kappa (hon.), Omicron Delta Kappa (hon.), Sigma Xi. Home: PO Box 1055 Lexington VA 24450-1055

SPENCER, ELIZABETH, author; b. Carrollton, Miss., 1921; d. James Luther and Mary James (McCain) S.; m. John Arthur Blackwood Rusher, Sept. 29, 1956. BA, Belhaven Coll., 1942; MA, Vanderbilt U., 1943; LittD (hon.), Southwestern U. at Memphis, 1968; LLD (hon.), Concordia U. at Montreal, 1988; LittD (hon.), U. of the South, 1992; DLitt (hon.), U. N.C., Chapel Hill, 1998, Belhaven Coll., 1999. Instr. N.W. Miss. Jr. Coll., 1943-44, Ward-Belmont, Nashville, 1944-45; reporter The Nashville Tennessean, 1945-46; instr. U. Miss., Oxford, 1948-51, 52-53. Vis. prof. Concordia U., Montreal, Que., Can., 1976-81, adj. prof., 1981-86; vis. prof. U. N.C., Chapel Hill, 1986-92. Author: Fire in the Morning, 1948, This Crooked Way, 1952, The Voice at the Back Door, 1956, The Light in the Piazza, 1960, Knights and Dragons, 1965, No Place for an Angel, 1967, Ship Island and Other Stories, 1968, The Snare, 1972, The Stories of Elizabeth Spencer, 1981, Marilee, 1981, The Salt Line, 1984, Jack of Diamonds and Other Stories, 1988, (play) For Lease or Sale, 1989, On the Gulf, 1991, The Night Travellers, 1991, (memoir) Landscapes of the Heart, 1998, The Southern Woman, 2001; contbr. short stories to mags. and anthologies. Named to N.C. Hall of Fame, 2002; recipient Women's Dem. Com. award, 1949, recognition award, Nat. Inst. Arts and Letters, 1952, Richard and Hinda Rosenthal Found. award, Am. Acad. Arts and Letters, 1957, Fortner award for lit., 1998, Award of Merit medal for the short story, 1983, 1st McGraw-Hill Fiction award, 1960, Henry Bellamann award for creative writing, 1968, Salem award for lit., 1992, Dos Passos award for fiction, 1992, N.C. Gov.'s award for lit., 1994, Corrington award for lit., 1997, Richard Wright award for lit., 1997, award for non-fiction, Miss. Libr. Assn., 1999, Brooks medal, Fellowship of So. Writers, 2001, Thomas Wolfe award for lit., 2002, William Faulkner award for lit. excellence, 2002; fellow, Guggenheim Found., 1953; Kenyon Rev. fellow in fiction, 1957, Bryn Mawr Coll. Donnelly fellow, 1962, Nat. Endowment for Arts grantee in lit., 1983, Sr. Arts Award grantee, Nat. Endowment for the Arts, 1988. Mem. Am. Acad. Arts and Letters, Fellowship of So. Writers (charter; vice chancellor 1993-97). Home: 402 Longleaf Dr Chapel Hill NC 27517-3042 E-mail: elizabeth0222@earthlink.net.

SPENCER, FRANK COLE, medical educator; b. Haskell, Tex., 1925; MD, Vanderbilt U., 1947. Intern Johns Hopkins U., Balt., 1947-48, fellow in surgery, 1947-48, asst. resident in surgery, 1953-54; resident in surgery Johns Hopkins Sch. Medicine, Balt., 1954-55; surgeon, outpatient dept. Johns Hopkins Hosp., 1955; resident in surgery Wadsworth VA Ctr. Hosp., 1949-50; fellow cardiovascular surgery USPHS, Los Angeles, 1951; asst. prof. surgery Johns Hopkins U., 1955-59, assoc. prof., 1959-61; prof. surgery U. Ky.; chmn. dept. surgery, George David Steward prof. surgery NYU, until 1998, now prof.

surgery sch. medicine and dir. patient safety. Served to lt. M.C., USN, 1951-53. John and Mary R. Markle scholar in med. sci. Johns Hopkins U., 1956. Office: NYU Sch Medicine Dept Surgery 550 1st Ave New York NY 10016

SPENCER, FREDERICK GILMAN, former newspaper editor; b. Phila., Dec. 8, 1925; s. F. Gilman and Elizabeth (Hetherington) S.; m. Isabel Brannon, July 3, 1965; 1 child, Isabel; children by previous marriage: Amy, Elizabeth Blair, F. Gilman, Jonathan. Student pub. and pvt. schs.; LHD (hon.), U. Colo., 1994. Copyboy Phila. Inquirer, 1947-49; photographer-reporter Chester (Pa.) Times, 1949, 1952-59; photographer, sports editor Mt. Holly (NJ) Herald, 1949-52; mng. editor Main Line Times, Ardmore, Pa., 1959-63; asst. city editor Phila. Bull., 1963-64; editorial spokesman Sta. WCAU-TV, Phila., 1964-67; editor The Trentonian, Trenton, N.J., 1967-75, Phila. Daily News, 1975-84, NY Daily News, N.Y.C., 1984-89; editor-in-chief Denver Post, 1989-93, columnist, 1993-96. With USNR, 1943-46. Recipient Pulitzer Prize for editorial writing, 1974, George Polk Career Award, 2003. Mem. Am. Soc. Newspapers Editors, Sigma Delta Chi.*

SPENCER, GEORGE HENRY, lawyer; b. Vienna; s. Frank Henry and Lillian (Godin) S.; m. Joan Betty Spencer, Sept. 16, 1956 (dec.); children: Lucy, Margaret, Robert, Nancy; m. Mollie Cole Sabol, Oct. 31, 1987; stepchildren: Jeanne, Marta. BE, Yale U., 1948; JD, Cornell U., 1952. Bar: D.C., N.Y. Examiner U.S. Patent Office, 1952-54; sole practice N.Y.C., Washington, 1954-62; ptnr. Spencer & Frank, Washington, 1962-98, Venable, LLP, Attys. at Law, Washington, 1998—2003; counsel Fitch, Even, Tabin & Flannery, Washington, 2003—. Master of bench Prettyman-Leventhal Am. Inn of Ct.; lectr. World Trade Inst. Served to capt. JAGC, U.S. Army, 1956-62. Mem. ABA, Am. Patent Law Assn., Lawyer-Pilots Bar Assn., Am. Arbitration Assn. (panel of arbitrators), Cosmos Club (Washington). Avocations: aviation, music, German and French language studies, poetry. Home: 1102 Flor Ln Mc Lean VA 22102-1737 Office: Fitch Even Tabin & Flannery 1801 K St NW Ste 401L Washington DC 20006-1201 Office Phone: 202-419-7000. Business E-Mail: ghspencer@fitcheven.com. E-mail: specole@aol.com.

SPENCER, HARRISON CLARK, JR., public health administrator, educator; b. Balt., Sept. 22, 1944; s. Harrison Clark, Sr. and Dorothy Margaret (Stokes) Spencer; m. Christine Michel Spencer, Apr. 30, 1977; children: Harrison Clark III, Peter Michel. BA, Haverford Coll., Pa., 1965; MD, Johns Hopkins U., Balt., 1969; MPH, U. Calif., Berkeley, 1972; DTM&H, U. London, 1972. Cert. Calif., 1969. Rsch. med. officer Ctrl. Am. Rsch. U., San Salvador, El Salvador, 1975—77; med. officer CDC, Atlanta, 1977—79, chief, parasitic diseases, 1987—90; sr. lectr., dir. malaria rsch. U. Nairobi Med. Sch., Kenya Med. Rsch. Ctr., 1979—84; sr. med. officer WHO, Geneva, 1984—87; dean Tulane Sch. Pub. Health & Tropical Medicine, New Orleans, 1991—96, London Sch. Hygiene & Tropical Medicine, 1996—2000; pres., CEO Assn. Schools of Pub. Health, Washington, 2000—. Mem. U.K. Gen. Med. Coun., London, 1996—2000. 0.6 USPHS, 1970—91. Recipient Commendation Medal, USPHS, 1984, 1991, Outstanding Svc. Medal, 1989. Fellow: U.K. Acad. Med. Scis., Am. Coll. Preventive Medicine, Am. Coll. Physicians; mem.: Inst. Medicine, 2004. Episcopalian. Home: 2718 N St NW Washington DC 20007 Office: Assn Schs of Pub Health 1101 15th St NW Ste 910 Washington DC 20005 Business E-Mail: hspencer@asph.org.

SPENCER, HARRY IRVING, JR., retired bank executive; b. Worcester, Mass., Feb. 3, 1925; s. Harry Irving and Bertha (Johnson) S.; m. Violet Virginia Bergquist, Sept. 16, 1950; children— Nancy Elaine, Harry Irving III, Carol Helen. BA, Clark U., 1950. With Worcester County Nat. Bank, 1950-82, asst. treas., 1954-58, cashier, 1958-82, v.p., 1966-69, sr. v.p., 1969-77, exec. v.p., cashier, 1977-82, clk., dir., 1980-82; exec. v.p., cashier, sec. Shawmut Worcester County Bank, N.A., 1982-88, also bd. dirs. Sec., treas., dir. Nobility Hill Realty Corp.; dir. Worcester Capital Corp., Wornat Leasing Corp. Bd. dirs. Worcester Taxpayers Assn. Methodist (trustee). Clubs: Kiwanis; Economic (Worcester, Mass.), Plaza (Worcester, Mass.). Home: 79 Birchwood Dr Holden MA 01520-1939 Office: 446 Main St Worcester MA 01608-2359

SPENCER, HERBERT HARRY, structural engineering researcher, computer analyst; b. Vienna, Jan. 2, 1928; came to U.S., 1953; s. Ingenieur Oskar and Bronia (Steinberger) Schnabel; m. Margot Goldrei (div.); m. Sara Slomka, July 24, 1992. *Paternal grandparents Eduard and Klara (Stein) Schnabel left Prag in 1885 for Vienna and lived at Obere Viaduktgasse 10; 1 son (Oskar) and 3 daughters (Grete,Isabella, Irma); lifelong printer with imperial government, subsequently voluntary administrator for Vienna Jewish community; personal presentation of distinguished citizen Golden Wedding commemoration from Vienna burgomaster 1935; home expropriated by Austrian Nazis, 1940; Klara killed by Austrian Nazis in Vienna, 1941; Eduard killed en route to Theresienstadt concentration camp, 1942. Maternal grandparents Leopold and Ida (Sandberg) Steinberger lived alternately at Vienna and Trzebinia, Galicia; Leopold killed by Nazis in Lemberg; Ida killed in concentration camp.* BSc, U. London, 1948, PhD, 1976; MS, Poly. Inst. Bklyn., 1955. Jr. engr. asst. Tarmac Ltd., Coventry, England, 1944-45, George Wimpey & Co., Coventry, 1945-46, Kershaw & Kaufman, London, 1946-48; engr. William Halcrow & Ptnrs., London, 1948-49, Hydraulic Dept., Nazareth, Israel, 1949-50, Quibuts Eyn Hashofet, Galilee, Israel, 1950-51, Rendel Palmer & Tritton, London, 1951-53; rsch. asst. Poly. Inst. Bklyn., 1953-55; instr. Yale U., New Haven, 1955-56; rsch. asst., lectr. Columbia U., N.Y.C., 1956-59; asst. prof. San Diego (Calif.) State Coll., 1959-61; rsch. assoc. Caltech, Pasedena, Calif., 1961-62; asst. prof. U. So. Calif., L.A., 1961-65; sr. scientist Ford Instrument Co., Sperry Gyro, L.I.C., NY, 1965-66, Tech. Rsch. Group, Melville, N.Y., 1966-67; engr. cons. Spencer Rsch., N.Y.C. and London, 1967-77; sr. lectr. Hatfield (Eng.) Poly., 1970-77; vis. assoc. prof. U. Pitts., 1976-77; assoc. prof. La. State U., Baton Rouge, 1977-79; vis. rsch. cons. Columbia U., N.Y.C., 1979; asst. prof. Rutgers U., New Brunswick, N.J., 1979-82. Pres. Spencer Sci. Computing, New Brunswick, 1982—; vis. prof. Aero Lab., Technion, Haifa, Israel, 1988, Rutgers U., Piscataway, N.J., 1998—. Contbr. articles to rsch. publs. Mem. ASCE, ASME, Israeli Soc. Engrs. and Architects, Gesellschaft für Angewandte Mathematik und Mechanik, Structural Rsch. Coun., Mensa, Intertel. Home: 10-8M Landing Ln New Brunswick NJ 08901-1070 Office: Spencer Sci Comp PO Box 4191 Highland Park NJ 08904-4191 Office Phone: 732-246-0499. E-mail: hspencer@rci.rutgers.edu.

SPENCER, JAMEEL HAASAN, marketing professional; b. Newark, N.J. s. Margaret Jackson; m. Cheryl Fox; children: Jamani, Nia. BA in Polit. Sci. and Mktg., Rutgers U., 1990. With Shaquille O'Neal's TWISM clothing label; nat. sales dir. Vibe and Blaze Mag., 1998—99; co-founder, nat. music and entertainment dir. Vanguarde Media, 1999—2000; chief mktg. officer Bad Boy Worldwide Entertainment Group, 2000—; pres. Blue Flame Mktg. and Advt., N.Y.C., 2000—. Named to, Crain's NY Bus. "40 under 40", 2004. Office: Blue Flame Mktg and Advt 16th Fl 1440 Broadway New York NY 10018*

SPENCER, JAMES A. automotive executive; b. Chgo., Ill. BBA, Hanover Coll., 1975; MBA, Ball State U., 1982. Exec. v.p. Daewoo-HMS Industries, Taegu, 1989—91; customer dir. Chevrolet-Pontiac-GM of Can., 1991—92; plant mgr. Delphi Saginaw Steering Systems, Athens, Ala., 1992—96, dir. sales, mktg., ventures, and planning, 1996—2000; pres. Delphi Asia-Pacific, Tokyo, 2000; pres. Delphi Packard electrical systems Delphi Corp., Warren, Ohio, 2000—, v.p., 2000—. Exec. champion Delphi Operations, Mexico. Office: Delphi Packard Electronic Systems PO Box 431 408 Dana St Warren OH 44486 also: Delphi Corp World Headquarters 5725 Delphi Dr Troy MI 48098-2815

SPENCER, JAMES H. social sciences educator, consultant; b. N.Y.C., Dec. 29, 1967; s. James H. and Dao Nguyen Spencer. BA, Amherst (Mass.)Coll., 1990; MEM, Yale U., New Haven, 1995; PhD, U. Calif., LA, 2002. Program coord. US NGO Forum on VietNam, Cambodia and Laos, NYC, 1991—93; rsch. assoc. Nautilus Inst., Berkeley, 1995—96; program assoc. Ford Found., NYC, 1996—2000; rsch. assoc. U. Calif., LA, 1998—2002; asst. prof. U. Hawaii at Manoa, Honolulu, 2002—. Cons. Orbis Internat., NYC, 1999—, Ford Found., NYC, 1996—; rsch. assoc. U. Calif., LA, 2002—03. Contbr. articles to profl. jours. Fellow Environ. Leadership Program, Boston, 1990—. Thomas J. Watson Fellow, Watson Found., 1990—91. Office: U Hawaii at Manoa 2424 Maile Way Honolulu HI 96822

SPENCER, JANE RENE, music educator; b. Sedalia, Mo., May 30, 1964; d. James Richard and Mary Jane Craig; m. John Parker Spencer Jr., July 18, 1992; children: Patricia Leanne, Olivia Nicole, Mary. MusB in edn., SW Bapt. U., 1982—86; MusM in edn., SW Mo. State U., 1987—98. Orff Level I SW Mo. State U., Mo., 1998, Kodaly Level I Ctrl. Mo. State U., Mo., 2003. H.s. band and choral dir. Morgan County R-II Schools, Stover, Mo., 1986—87, Miller R-II Schools, Miller, Mo., 1987—96; elem. music instr. Mt. Vernon R-5 Schools, Mt. Vernon, Mo., 1996—. Oake nat. adv. bd. Kodaly of the Ozarks, Mt. Vernon, Mo., 2003—. Project leader Farm and Home Boosters 4-H Club, Miller, Mo., 2003—03; initiated start of parochial sch. Round Grove Bapt. Ch., Miller, Mo., 1998—2003, children's ch. dir., 1995—2002, worship band leader, 1997—2003; organized food alllergy awareness week info. for sw mo. Ozarks Food Allergy Support Group, Springfield, Mo., 2000—03. Recipient KODE-TV Outstanding Edn. Program, 2004; CMKE scholarship, Ctrl. Mo. Kodaly Educators, 2003. Mem.: Midwest Kodaly Music Educators Assn., Orgn. of AM. Kodaly Educators, Mo. Music Educators Assn. (assoc.; dist. sec./treas. 1988—92), Kodaly of the Ozarks (OAKE) (assoc.; pres. 2003—), Orgn. of Am. Orff Educators (assoc.; social chairperson 2002—04), Music Educators Nat. Conf. (assoc.), Mo. State Teachers Assn. (assoc.). Conservative-R. Bapt. Avocations: reading, swimming, walking. Home: 9204 Lawrence 2040 Miller MO 65707

SPENCER, JEAN, food products executive; b. Bklyn., Oct. 26, 1946; d. Frederic R. and Lucy Anne Spencer. BBA cum laude, Adelphi U., 1973, MBA, 1989; MS in Human Nutrition, U. Bridgeport, 1998. Notary public, 1986—. Exec. adminstrv. mgmt. Underwriters Labs., Inc., Melville, NY, 1966—2003, ret., 2003; pres., CEO All Natural Health Corp., Seaford, NY, 1990—2002; ret. Vol., life mem. Nat. Ski Patrol, Colo. Recipient NASTAR, Bronze medal, Silver medal. Mem. Am. Coll. Nutrition, Am. Soc. Quality Control, Nat. Nutritional Foods Assn., Nat. Ctr. for Homeopathy. Avocations: skiing, bicycle riding, physical fitness, opera, theater. Office: All Natural Health Inc 3830 Sunrise Hwy Seaford NY 11783-2634

SPENCER, JOHN HEDLEY, biochemistry educator; b. Stapleford, Eng., Apr. 10, 1933; emigrated to Can., 1956; s. Thomas and Eva (Johnson) S.; m. Magdeliene Vera Kulin, Sept. 16, 1958; children: Robin Anne, David Thomas, Mark Stewart. BSc, U. St. Andrews, Scotland, 1955, BSc with honors, 1956; student, Montreal Cancer Rsch. Soc., 1956-59; PhD, McGill U., 1960. Damon Runyon Meml. Fund postdoctoral fellow Columbia U., N.Y.C., 1959-61; mem. faculty McGill U., Montreal, 1961-78, assoc. prof. biochemistry, 1966-71, prof., 1971-78; prof. biochemistry Queen's U., Kingston, Ont., 1978-98, head biochemistry, 1978-90, prof. emeritus, 1998—. Vis. scientist NICHHD/NIH, Bethesda, Md., 1987-88; vis. prof. U. Montreal, 1992-93. Author: The Physics and Chemistry of DNA and RNA, 1972; co-editor: Planet Earth: Problems and Prospects, 1995. Recipient Ayerst award Can. Biochem. Soc., 1972 Fellow Royal Soc. Can.; mem. AAAS, Can. Biochem. Soc. (treas. 1966-69, pres. 1979-80), Can. Fedn. Biol. Socs. (pres. 1981-82), Canadians for Health Rsch. (bd. dirs. 2001—), Biochem. Soc., Am. Soc. Biochemistry and Molecular Biology, Royal Soc. Can., Sigma Xi. Home: 36 Kenwoods Cir Kingston ON Canada K7K 6Y1 E-mail: spencerj@post.queensu.ca.

SPENCER, KATHELEN V. insurance company executive; m. Tracy Spencer; 3 children. BA in Polit. Sci., Emory U.; JD, U. Ga., 1982. Bar: Tex., Ga. Lawyer pvt. practice, Columbus, Ga., 1983-85; assoc. counsel AFLAC, Columbus, Ga., 1985-87, dep. counsel, 1987-89, v.p., dir. pub. rels., 1989-92, sr. v.p., dep. counsel, dir. corp. comm., 1992—. Bd. dirs. Columbus Bank and Trust Co.; mem. AFLAC Donations Com., dir. shareholder svcs. dept. Trustee Brookstone Sch., Columbus Coll. Found., Pastoral Inst., Columbus Mus; mem. adv. bd. Emory U. Sch. of Pub. Health; past pres. Jr. League Columbus; alumna Leadership Ga. Office: AFLAC Inc 1932 Wynnton Rd Columbus GA 31999-0002

SPENCER, LARA, television personality, journalist; married, 2000; 1 child. BA in Journalism, Pa. State U. Reporter WDEF-TV, Chattanooga, News 12, L.I., NY, WABC, NY Eyewitness News, 1995—2001; contbr. ABC News' Good Morning Am., 1999—2001, corr., 2001—04; host PBS' Antiques Roadshow, WGBH-PBS, 2004—; co-host with Pat O'Brien Paramount TV The Insider, 2004—. Office: Antiques Roadshow-WGBH 125 Western Ave Allston MA 02134*

SPENCER, LARRY, member of parliament; Student, Met. Jr. Coll., Draughn's Bus. Coll.; diploma in Theology, So. Baptist Coll. Pastor Brown's Chapel Bapt. Ch., Paragould, Ark., 1970—74, Discovery Bapt. Ch., Regina, 1974—83, Covenant Bapt. Ch., Regina, 1983—87, Bapt. Union of We. Can., Swift Current, 1990—91, Discovery Bapt. Ch., 1991—2000; mem. House of Commons, Regina, Canada, critic human resources develop Can. family issues. Can. Alliance Caucus. Office: House of Commons Regina-Lumsden-Lake Ctr 6244 Rochdale Blvd Regina SK S4X 4K8 Canada E-mail: spencer.l@parl.gc.ca.

SPENCER, LONABELLE (KAPPIE SPENCER), political agency administrator, lobbyist; b. Owatonna, Minn., Aug. 3, 1925; d. Reuben Alvin and Florence Elizabeth (Wells) Kaplan; m. Mark Rodney Spencer, Sept. 14, 1947 (dec. May 1986); children: Gregory Mark, Gary Alan, Carol Ann (Spencer) Glumac, Dane Kaplan. BA, Grinnell Coll., 1947. State bd. legis. chair Am. Assn. Univ. Women, Iowa, 1978-82, nat. legis. com., 1980-83, nat. bd. legis. chair, 1982-83, nat. legis. and program coms., 1985-89, nat. bd. dir. for women's issues, 1985-89; founder, dir. Nat. Gender Balance Project, Sarasota, Fla., 1988—; bd. dirs., nat. steering com. Nat. Women's Political Caucus, Washington, 1992-97. Lobbyist, cmty. activist state legis. and congress, Fla. Iowa, Washington, 1974—; pub. policy cons. women's orgns., nationwide, 1978—; rep. Fla. women's pol. caucus ERA summit, Washington, 1992—. Author: (pub. policy manuals) Don't Leave It All to the Experts, 1981, Take An Unratified State to Launch, 1981, I Think We Need a Woman...It's a Man's World Unless Women Vote, 1983, Woman Power: It's a Capitol Idea, 1995, Gender Balance Project-USA: Politics and Decision Making, 1995, Whose Money Is It Anyway: Wills and Trusts for Women, 1999; exhibitor, presenter in field. U.S. rep. World Assn. Girl Guides Girl Scouts U.S., Acapulco, Mex., 1965, bd. dirs. Moingona Coun. Girl Scouts U.S., 1965-75; Rep. candidate Iowa senate, Des Moines, 1976; del., workshop presenter Internat. Fedn. Univ. Women, Netherlands, New Zealand, Finland, Sweden, 1983, 86, 89, workshop presenter U.S./China Joint Conf. on Women's Issues, Beijing, China, 1995, Nongovernmental Orgn. Forum, Huairou, China, 1995; trustee Grinnell (Iowa) Coll., 1993—; Iowa del. to Nat. Women's Conf., 1977; founder Fla. Women's Consortium, 1989; mem. People to People Internat.; tour leader Mission in Understanding to Cuba, 2001. Recipient Girl Scout awards Moingona Girl Scout Coun., Des Moines, 1969, 73, 78, Christine Wilson medal for Equality and Justice, Iowa Women's Hall of Fame, Des Moines, 1990; named gift honoree Am. Assn. Univ. Women, Des Moines and Sarasota, Fla. branches, Iowa and Vt. divsns., 1980, 82, 87, 92; named in National Women's Hall of Fame Book of Lives and Legacies, 2002. Mem. AAUW (leader corps, various coms. 1975—), UN Fund for Women (UNIFEM), Nat. Assn. Commns. for Women, Vet. Feminists of Am. (Medal of Honor 2000), Women in Senate and House WISH-LIST (founder 1992. Republican. Avocation: travel. Home: 3735 Beneva Oaks Way Sarasota FL 34238-2524

SPENCER, MARGARET GILLIAM, lawyer; b. Spokane, Wash., Aug. 30, 1951; d. Jackson Earl and Margaret Kathleen (Hindley) Gilliam; m. John Bernard Spencer, Feb. 21, 1993. BA in Sociology, U. Mont., 1974, MA in Sociology, 1978, JD, 1982. Bar: Mont. 1982, Colo. 1982. Assoc. Holland & Hart, Denver, 1982-84, Roath & Brega, P.C., Denver, 1984-88, shareholder, dir., 1988-89; spl. counsel Brega & Winters, P.C., Denver, 1989; corp. counsel CH2M Hill, Inc., Denver, 1989—. Democrat. Episcopalian. Avocations: skiing, scuba diving. Office: CH2M Hill Inc 9191 S Jamaica St Englewood CO 80112

SPENCER, MARK BENNER, education educator; b. Fort Worth, Tex., Jan. 13, 1954; s. Robert Benner and Mildred Sue Spencer. BA in history, North Tex. State U., Denton, TX, 1977—81; MA in European history, North Tex. State U., 1982—84; MA in english, Ohio State U., 1984—88; PhD in medieval history, U. of Ky., 1991—95; AM in latin, U. of Ill., 1996—98; PhD in comparative lit., U. of Ark., 1998—2001. Instr. of liberal arts Warren County C.C., Washington, NJ, 1989—91; asst. prof. of english and humanities Southeastern Okla. State U., 2001—. Author: (book) Thomas Basin (1412-1490): The History of Charles VII and Louis XI. Mem.: MLA, Am. Hist. Assn., Medieval Acad. of Am. Home: 408 N 3d Ave Durant OK 74701 Office: Southeastern Oklahoma State University Box 4121 Durant OK 74701 Office Phone: 580-745-2921. E-mail: mspencer@sosu.edu.

SPENCER, MARY HELEN, interior designer; b. Paris, Tex., Oct. 21, 1950; d. Otha Cleo and Billie Ermine (Abernathy) S. Student, East Tex. State U., 1969-72. Interior designer William Hammon & Assoc., Dallas, 1973-75; sales rep. Seymour Mirrow Co., Dallas, 1975-76; prin. Mary Spencer Co., Dallas, 1976—. Cons. design dept. East Tex. State U., Commerce. Fund raiser Am. Paralysis Assn., Dallas, 1979, Wadley Whoppee, Dallas, 1986, Easter Seals Soc., Dallas, 1987. Mem. Inst. Bus. Designers, Assn. Women Entreprenuers. Republican. Methodist. Avocations: sailing, reading, planning. Home: 6943 Wildgrove Ave Dallas TX 75214-3837 Office: The Spencer Co 2713 Mckinney Ave Dallas TX 75204-2563

SPENCER, MARY MILLER, civic worker; b. Comanche, Tex., May 25, 1924; d. Aaron Gaynor and Alma (Grissom) Miller; 1 child, Mara Lynn. BS, U. North Tex., 1943. Cafeteria dir. Mercedes (Tex.) Pub. Schs., 1943-46; home economist coord. All-Orange Dessert Contest Fla. Citrus Commn., Lakeland, 1959-62, 64; tchr. purchasing sch. lunch dept. Fla. Dept. Edn., 1960. Clothing judge Polk County (Fla.) Youth Fair, 1951-68, Polk County Federated Women's Clubs, 1964-66; pres. Dixieland Elem. Sch. PTA, 1955-57, Polk County Coun. PTA's, 1958-60; chmn. pub. edn. com. Polk County unit Am. Cancer Soc., 1959-60, bd. dirs., 1962-70; charter mem., bd. dirs. Lakeland YMCA, 1962-72; sec. Greater Lakeland Cmty. Nursing Coun., 1965-72; trustee, vice-chmn. Polk County Eye Clinic, Inc., 1962-64, pres., 1964-82; bd. dirs. Polk County Scholarship and Loan Fund, 1962-70; mem. exec. com. West Polk County (Fla.) Cmty. Welfare Coun., 1960-62, 65-68; mem. budget and audit com. Greater Lakeland United Fund, 1960-62, bd. dirs., 1967-70, residential chmn. fund drive, 1968; mem. adv. bd. Polk County Juvenile and Domestic Rels. Ct., 1960-69; sec. bd. dirs. Fla. West Coast Ednl. TV, 1960-81; mem. Polk County Home Econs. Adv. Com., 1965-71; mem. exec. com. Suncoast Health Coun., 1968-71; worker children's svcs. divsn. family svcs. Dept. Health and Rehab. Svcs., State of Fla., 1969-70, social worker, 1970-72, 74-82, social worker Overpayment Fraud Recoupment unit, 1977-81, with other pers. svcs., 1981-82, supr. Overpayment Fraud Recoupment unit, 1982-83, pub. assistance specialist IV, 1984-89; bd. dirs. Lake Region United Way, Winter Haven, 1976-81; mem. Polk County Cmty. Svcs. Coun., 1978-88; with other pers. svcs. Emergency Fin. Assistance Housing Program, 1990-96. Mem. AAUW (pres. Lakeland br. 1960-61), Nat. Welfare Fraud Assn., Fla. Congress Parents and Tchrs. (hon. life, pres. dist. 7 1961-63, chmn. pub. rels. 1962-66), Fla. Health and Welfare Coun., Fla. Health and Social Svc. Coun., Polk County Mental Health Assn., U. North Tex. Alumni Assn., Order Ea. Star. Democrat. Methodist. Home and Office: PO Box 2161 Lakeland FL 33806-2161

SPENCER, MELVIN JOE, health facility administrator, lawyer; b. Buffalo Center, Iowa, Jan. 2, 1923; s. Kenos W. and Jennie (Michaelson) S.; m. Dena Joyce Butterfield, Mar. 1, 1952; children: Dennis Norman, Gregory Melvin, Shelly Lynn Spencer Goodnight. AB, U. Mich., 1948, JD, 1950. Bar: Iowa 1950, Mo. 1950, Okla. 1961. Practiced in, Kansas City, Mo., 1950-61, Oklahoma City, 1961—; assoc., then ptnr. Watson, Ess, Marshall & Enggas, 1950-61; ptnr. Miller & Spencer (and predecessor firm), 1961-75, of counsel, 1975-80; adminstr. Deaconess Hosp., 1975-92, cons., 1992-93. Dir. Union Bank & Trust Co., Oklahoma City, 1977-88, 89-96, adv. dir., 1996-99; dir., sec. Hosp. Casualty Co., 1977-92; dir., treas. VHA of Okla., Inc., 1986-92. Assoc. editor Mich. Law Rev., 1949-50. Mcpl. judge City of Roeland Park, Kans., 1952, mem. city coun., 1954; area Rep. precinct chmn., 1968-69; del. Rep. State Conv., 1968, 96; bd. dirs. Deaconess Hosp., Oklahoma City, Christian Counseling Ctr., 1973-75; trustee Okla. Hosp. Assn., 1978-84, chmn. bd. trustees, 1983, trustee Okla. Co. Med. Soc. Found., 2002—; trustee, vice chmn. bd. dirs. Ctrl. Coll., McPherson, Kans., 1972-86; trustee Okla. Ambulance Trust, 1984-87; mem. adv. bd. Okla. State U. Tech. Inst., 1980-92; bd. dirs. Emergency Med. Svcs. Ctrl. Okla., 1975-78, FMC Ministries, Inc.; mem. const. coun. Free Meth. Ch. World Fellowship, 1975-95; chmn. Free Meth. Found., 1988-99; gen. counsel Free Meth. Ch. N.Am., 1969-95, mem. bd. adminstrn., 1969-99, sec., 1985-95, mem. investment com., 1976-88, chmn. investment com., 1986-88. Capt. USAAF, 1943-46. Named Layman of Yr., Free Meth. Ch. N.Am., 1984; recipient W. Cleveland Rodgers Disting. Svc. award Okla. Hosp. Assn., 1985; fellow Cen. Coll. Acad. of Achievers, 1990. Mem. Okla. Bar Assn., Oklahoma County Bar Assn., Men's Dinner Club, Order of Coif, Phi Beta Kappa, Phi Kappa Phi. Home: 5910 N Shawnee Ave Oklahoma City OK 73112-1627

SPENCER, REX LEROY, retired secondary school educator; b. Kendallville, Ind., Jan. 29, 1944; s. Richard Donald and Mildred Francis (Fourman) Spencer; m. Diana Carole Land, Nov. 21, 1981; children: Katie Jo, Emily Paige. BS, Defiance Coll., 1966; MA, Ball State U., 1970. Cert. tchr. Ohio. Tchr. Ansonia (Ohio) HS, 1966-80, 1986—2003, Ansonia Mid. Sch., 1982-86; ret., 2003. Instr. Edison CC, Piqua, Ohio, 1983—88, Defiance (Ohio) Coll., 1989—92. Named Outstanding Am. History Tchr., Darke County DAR, 1992. Mem.: NEA, Am. Registry Outstanding Professionals, Ohio Coun. Social Studies, Nat. Coun. Social Studies, Ansonia Edn. Assn. (pres. 1976—77, treas. 1991—98), Ohio Edn. Assn., Defiance Coll. Alumni Assn. (bd. dirs. 1976—79, v.p. 1979—80, pres. 1980—82). Methodist. Avocations: golf, bicycling, walking, antique collecting, singing with gospel quartet.

SPENCER, RICHARD HENRY, lawyer; b. Kansas City, Mo., Nov. 29, 1926; s. Byron Spencer and Helen Elizabeth (McCune) Hockaday; m. Barbara G. Rau, Aug. 2, 1952 (div. 1955); 1 chlid, Christina G. Cuevas; m. Katherine Graham, Dec. 28, 1957; children: Elisabeth M., Katherine S. Rivard. BS in Engring., Princeton U., 1949; LLB, U. Mo., 1952. Bar: Mo. 1952, U.S. Dist. Ct (we. dist.) Mo. 1955. Assoc. Spencer, Fane, Britt & Browne, Kansas City, 1952-59, ptnr., 1959-94; ret. ptnr., 1995—. Co-author: Fiduciary Duties, Rights and Responsibilities of Directors, 1985. Sec., bd. dirs. Met. Performing Arts Fund, Kansas City, 1984—; trustee Barstow Sch., Kansas City, 2002--. Mem. ABA, Mo. Bar Assn., Kansas City Club (pres. 1974), Kansas City Country Club (pres. 1986). Episcopalian. Avocations: hunting, golf, travel. Home: 77 Le Mans Ct Shawnee Mission KS 66208-5230 Office: Spencer Fane Britt & Browne 1400 Commerce Bank Bldg 1000 Walnut St Kansas City MO 64106-2140

SPENCER, RICHARD PAUL, biochemist, educator, physician; b. N.Y.C., June 7, 1929; s. David E. and Frances (Fried) S.; m. Gwendolyn Enid Williams, Apr. 7, 1956; children: Carolyn Roberts, Jennifer Holt, Priscilla James. AB, Dartmouth Coll., 1951; MD, U. So. Calif., 1954; MA (NSF fellow, Helen Hay Whitney fellow), Harvard U., 1958, PhD, 1961. Intern Beth Israel Hosp., Boston, 1954-55; practice medicine specializing in nuclear medicine; mem. faculty biophysics U. Buffalo, 1961-63; chief radioisotope service VA Hosp., Buffalo, 1961-63; asso. prof. nuclear medicine Yale Sch. Medicine, 1963-68, prof., 1968-74; prof., chmn. dept. nuclear medicine U. Conn. Health Center, 1974-97, prof., vice chmn. Dept. Diagnostic Imaging, 1997—2000, residency dir. nuclear medicine, 2000—. Author: The Intestinal Tract, 1960, (with others) Biophysical Principles, 1965, Radionuclide Studies of the Spleen, 1975, Clinical Focus on Nuclear Medicine, 1977, Handbook of Nuclear Medicine, 1977, Therapy in Nuclear Medicine, 1978, Radiopharmaceuticals: Structure-Activity Relationships, 1981, Interventional Nuclear Medicine, 1984, New Procedures In Nuclear Medicine, 1988; contbr. (with others) articles to profl. jours. Mem. Am. Physiol. Soc., AAAS, Soc. Nuclear Medicine, Biophys. Soc. Achievements include co-discovery of functional

asplenia; developed first complete description of relationship of food intake to reproductive success and to longevity in a species. Office: U Conn Health Ctr Farmington CT 06030-2804 E-mail: rspencer@adp.uchc.edu.

SPENCER, RICHARD THOMAS, III, healthcare industry executive, b. Oak Park, Ill., Mar. 18, 1936; s. Richard Thomas Spencer Jr. and Lois Anne (Pollock) Spencer; m. Andrea B. Schlickeiser, June 26, 9196; 1 child, Richard Thomas IV. BA, U. Mich., 1959; postgrad., U. Pa., 1976, Stanford U., 1984, Clemson U., 1985. Mktg. group Mobil Oil Co., Detroit, 1962; internat. trade specialist U.S. Dept. Commerce, Detroit, 1963—64; account exec. J. Walter Thompson Co., Detroit, 1965—66; sales mgr. Sarns Inc., Ann Arbor, Mich., 1967—69; v.p. mktg. Cordis Dow Corp., Miami, Fla., 1970—81; pres. mktg. divsn. Cordis Corp., Miami, 1982—87; pres., CEO Uni-Med Internat. Corp., Miami, 1988—2000; exec. v.p., COO, bd. dirs. World Med. Mfg. Corp., Sunrise, Fla., 1995—2000. Bd. dirs. Viacor Corp., Wilmington, Mass., Bioheart, Inc., Weston, Fla., Hyperion, Inc., Miami; cons. in field. Contbr. articles to profl. jours. With CIC U.S. Army, 1959—61. Republican. Avocations: skiing, golf, running, stereo equipment, geopolits. Home: 3641 N 47th Ave Hollywood FL 33021-2211 Home and Office: 811 E Hill Rd North Troy VT 05859 Office Phone: 954-558-3689.

SPENCER, ROGER FELIX, psychiatrist, psychoanalyst, medical educator; b. Apr. 19, 1934; came to U.S., 1941; s. Eugene S. Spitzer and Santa Spencer; m. Barbara Ann Houser, Aug. 18, 1958; children: Geoffrey, Jennifer, Rebecca. BS, Yale Coll., 1956; MD, Harvard Med. Sch., 1959. Diplomate Am. Bd. Psychiatry. Intern N.C. Meml. Hosp., Chapel Hill, 1959-60, resident in psychiatry, 1960-63; instr. U. N.C. Sch. Medicine, Chapel Hill, 1963-66, asst. prof., 1966-69, assoc. prof., 1969-76, prof., 1976—. Dir. of liaison and cons., U. N.C., 1967-77, dir. out patient psychiatry, 1977-95. Contbr. more than 25 articles and short stories to profl. jours. and lit. mags. Recipient Career Tchr. award NIMH, 1965-67. Fellow Am. Psychiat. Assn. (life), Am. Psychoanalytic Assn.; mem. N.C. Psychoanalytic Soc. (past pres.), N.C. Neuropsychiat. Assn. (past pres.). Office: UNC Hosps Dept Psychiatry CB 7160 Chapel Hill NC 27599-7160 Office Phone: 919-966-5772. Business E-Mail: roger_spencer@med.unc.edu.

SPENCER, SAMUEL REID, JR., education consultant, former college president; b. Rock Hill, S.C., 1919; m. Ava Clark; 1948; children: Samuel Reid, Ellen Spencer Henschen, Ava Clayton, Frank. AB summa cum laude, Davidson Coll., 1940, LLD (hon.), 1964; MA, Harvard U., 1947, PhD, 1951; LHD (hon.), Oglethorpe U., 1977, Queens Coll., 1983, Bridgewater Coll., 1986, Marymount U., 1988, Hollins Coll., 1991, Mary Baldwin Coll., 1992; LittD (hon.), Washington and Lee U., 1991. With Vick Chem. Co., N.Y.C., 1940; research asst. to Grenville Clark, Dublin, N.H., 1947-48; asst. to pres. Davidson Coll., 1951-54, dean of students, asso. prof. history, 1954, dean of students, prof. history, 1955-57; pres. Mary Baldwin Coll., 1957-68, Davidson (N.C.) Coll., 1968-83, pres. emeritus, 1983—; pres. Va. Found. for Ind. Colls., Richmond, 1983-88; sr. cons. Acad. Search Consultation Svc., 1989—2000; interim pres. Hollins Coll., 1990-91. Dir. Piedmont Bank & Trust Co.; Fulbright lectr. U. Munich, 1965-66; mem. Bd. Fgn. Scholarships, 1980-83, chmn., 1982-83; bd. dirs. Assn. Am. Colls., 1976-83, chmn. assn., 1981-82; pres. So. Univ. Conf., 1979-80; mem. commn. govtl. relations Am. Council Edn., 1973-76. Author: Decision for War, 1917, 1953, Booker T. Washington and the Negro's Place in American Life, 1955, (with J. Garry Clifford) The First Peacetime Draft, 1986. Bd. dirs. Grenville Clark Fund, Dartmouth Coll., 1973—, Charlotte-Mecklenburg chpt. Urban League, 1979-83, 2000—; trustee Agnes Scott Coll., 1975-91, Mary Baldwin Coll., 1996—; trustee Union Theol. Sem., Richmond, Va., 1985-94, chmn., 1988-94. Maj. AUS, 1940-45. Austin fellow Harvard, 1947-48; Rosenwald fellow, 1948-49; Kent fellow Nat. Council on Religion in Higher Edn., 1949-51 Mem. Fulbright Assn. (bd. dirs. 1989-92), Phi Beta Kappa, Omicron Delta Kappa. Presbyterian (bd. Christian edn.). Address: PO Box 1117 Davidson NC 28036-1117 Personal E-mail: samrs2@aol.com.

SPENCER, SHIRLEY ANN, secondary school educator, speech educator, literature educator; b. Dayton, Ohio, Mar. 8, 1953; d. Omar and Bertha King (Spencer) Whitaker; m. Donald Eugene Lebkisher, Nov. 27, 1977 (div. Nov. 1986); children: Laura Ann, Lindsey Marie; m. William Daniel Burkhalter, Dec. 12, 1987 (div. Aug. 2000). BS in English, Speech & Theatre Edn., Wright State U., 1976; MA in Interpersonal Comm., Ctrl. Mich. U., 1977; Ednl. Specialist in English, Ga. So. U., 1993. Cert. tchg. in Eng., speech and theatre Ga. Tchr. speech Ctrl. Mich. U., Mt. Pleasant, Mich., 1976-77; tchr. ESL and speech Ctrl. Tex. Coll., Killeen, 1978; tchr. speech European divsn. U. Md., Heidelberg, Germany, 1979-81; tchr. Baker H.S., Columbus, Ga., 1982-83, Brookstone, Columbus, Ga., 1983-84; tchr. speech Columbus (Ga.) Coll., 1986; tchr. English Shaw H.S., 1985-86, Jonesboro (Ga.) H.S., 1986-89; tchr. speech, English and theater Glynn Acad. H.S., Brunswick, Ga., 1989—. Instr. for workshops Communications Unltd., Columbus, 1985. Co-author: (textbook) Tools for the Speaker, 1985; contbr. articles to profl. jours. Recipient Teaching assistantship Ctrl. Mich. U., 1976-77; named Tchr. of Yr., Glynn Acad. H.S., 1994-95. Mem. Nat. Coun. Tchr. English, Ednl. Theater Assn., Ga. Theatre Conf. (sec. 2000-2003), Internat. Thespian Soc. Sponsor. Methodist. Avocations: play directing, the Glynn Academy Players, dance. Office: Glynn Acad H S 1001 Mansfield St Brunswick GA 31520-7349

SPENCER, THOMAS MELVIN, III, soft drink company executive; b. Richmond, Va., Feb. 16, 1949; s. Thos Melvin Jr. and Frances (Lawson) S.; m. Leslie Graham Murray, Sept. 14, 1984. AB, U. N.C., 1972. With fountain sales dept. Coca-Cola U.S.A., Atlanta, 1973-80; with Russell Pierce and Assocs., Richmond, Va., 1980-81; mgr. fountain sales div. Allegheny Pepsi, Richmond, Va., 1982; corp. mktg. equipment mgr. Pepsi Bottling Ventures, LLC, Raleigh, N.C., 1983—. Mem. Nat. Soft Drink Assn. Democrat. Presbyterian. Home: 1115 Lakeside Dr NW Wilson NC 27896-2015 Office: Pepsi Bottling Ventures LLC 1800 Pepsi Way Garner NC 27529-7231

SPENCER, WALTER JESSE, accountant, consultant; b. Hamlet, N.C., Feb. 25, 1921; s. Walter Jordan and Willie Brigman Spencer; m. Evelyn Baldwin, Aug. 29, 1925; children: Walter Jesse Jr., John Baldwin. BS in Commerce, U. N.C., 1948. CPA, N.C. Staff acct. G.C. Lundin & Co., CPA, Laurinburg, N.C., 1948-51; ptnr. Lundin & Spencer, CPA, Rockingham, N.C., 1951-62, W. Jesse Spencer & Co., CPA, Rockingham, 1962-75, Dixon, Odom & Co., PLLC, High Point, N.C., 1975-86; pvt. practice Rockingham, 1986—. Dir. adv. First Bank, Troy, N.C., 2004-. Bd. pres. Richmond C.C. Found., Hamlet, N.C., 1985-2002, First Bank, Troy, 2004—; pres. N.C. Bapt. Found., Cary, 1997-98, Found. for Richmond County, Rockingham, 1998—. With USNR, 1942-46, PTO. Named Citizen of Yr., Richmond C.C. Found., Hamlet, 1991. Mem.: AICPA, N.C. Assn. CPA's (bd. dirs. 1984), Rotary Club Rockingham (pres. 1988—89, Paul Harris fellow 1989). Democrat. Baptist. Avocations: travel, reading, golf. Home and Office: 720 Scotland Ave Rockingham NC 28379-3149

SPENCER, WILLIAM COURTNEY, foundation executive, international business executive; b. Uniontown, Pa., Sept. 15, 1919; m. Evelyn Van Cleve Bailey, Aug. 6, 1942; children: Courtney Lloyd, Henry Bailey, Edward Ashley. AB, Drew U., 1941; AM, Columbia U., 1946, EdD, 1952. Tchr. Scarsdale (N.Y.) Pub. Schs., 1946-49; dir. Univ. Sch. Columbia, 1949-52; prof. edn. and adminstrn. U. Del., 1952-55; prof., dir. grad. program tchr. edn. NYU, 1955-59, prof. higher edn. and internat. affairs, 1960-61; prof. adminstrn. U. Chile, Santiago, 1959-60; dir. Interam. affairs Inst. Internat. Edn. and asst. sec. gen. Coun. Higher Edn. in Am. Republics, 1961-65; assoc. dean Grad. Sch. Bus. Columbia U., 1965-67, sr. asst. to pres., 1967-69; pres. Western Coll., Oxford, Ohio, 1969-74, The Lindenwood Colls., 1974-79; v.p. Trans Internat. Mgmt. Corp., 1979-88; spl. adviser Fund for Higher Edn., 1979-82, pres., 1982-86; spl. asst. to pres. Internat. Exec. Svc. Corps, Stamford, Conn., 1988; dir. internat. devel. svcs. Nippon Manpower Ltd, Tokyo, 1988-91; pres. Trans Internat Exec. Svcs., 1988—. Cons. UNESCO Latin Am. major project in edn., Chile, 1959-60, project edn. and econ. planning, India, 1962; cons. Am. Coun. Edn., 1960-61; del. Pan-Am Assembly on Population, 1965; mem. standing com. on internat. edn. Coll. Entrance Exam. Bd., 1972-74; cons. Am. Med. Internat. Inc., 1980, McGraw Hill Internat. Book Co., 1981, AID, Indonesia, 1982, Thermo-Electron Corp., China, 1984, Internat. Exec. Svc. Corps, Jamaica, 1989, Costa Rica, 1991, 93, Hungary, 1991. Author: Education and World Responsibility, 1965, also articles; editor: Art and the University, 1964, University and National Development, 1965, Agriculture and the University, 1965. Bd. dirs. Internat. Sch. Svc., 1963-69, chmn., 1967-69, mem. Mo. master planning com. Coordinating Bd. Higher Edn., 1975-79; pres. Ind. Colls. and Univs. of Mo., 1977-79; bd. dirs. St. Louis Coun. on World Affairs, 1977-79; mem. scholarship bd. Timken Co. Ednl. Fund, 1971-76; bd. dirs. Internat. Inst. Energy Conservation, 1984-89, Conn. River Mus., 1988-2002. Lt. comdr. USNR, 1942-46. Decorated Purple Heart; commendation medals from Royal Navy, U.S. Navy. Mem. Coun. Fgn. Relations, N.Y. Yacht Club, Essex (Conn.) Yacht Club, North Cove Yacht Club. Home: 7214 Spring Village Dr 406 Springfield VA 22150

SPENCER, WILLIAM DAVID, music educator; b. Huntsville, Ala., Sept. 27, 1952; s. Morris Lee and Ruth Sammons Spencer; m. Carol Hosey; children: Kimberly Daye Bellis, Noel Andrew, Ethan Alexander. BS, Auburn U., Ala., 1974; MusM, U. So. Miss., 1976; PhD, U. North Tex., 1996. Brass instr. William Carey Coll., Hattiesburg, Miss., 1976—77; band dir. Clayton Co. Schs., Morrow, Ga., 1978—80, Huntsville(Ala.) HS, 1980—; jazz instr. U. Ala., Huntsville, 1982—84. Dist. chmn. Ala. Bandmasters Assn., Huntsville, Ala. Recipient Citation of Excellence, Nat. Band Assn., 1986, 1999, 2004; fellow, U. North Tex., 1989—90. Mem.: Pi Kappa Lambda, Phi Beta Mu. Home: 117 Noble Dr SE Huntsville AL 35802-1609 Office: Huntsville HS 2304 Billie Watkins Ave Huntsville AL 35801 Office Phone: 256-533-1793. Home Fax: 256-428-8051; Office Fax: 256-428-8051. Personal E-mail: wspence2@bellsouth.net. E-mail: dspencer@hsv.k12.al.us.

SPENCER, WILLIAM EDWIN, telephone company executive, engineer; b. Mar. 22, 1926; s. Erwin Blanc and Edith Marie (Peterson) S.; m. Ferne Arlene Nieder, Nov. 14, 1952; children: Elizabeth Ann, Gary William, James Richard, Catherine Sue. Student, U. Kansas City, 1942; AS, Kansas City Jr. Coll., 1945; BSEE, U. Mo., 1948; postgrad., Iowa State U., 1969. Registered profl. engr., Kans. With Southwestern Bell Telephone Co., Kansas City, Mo., 1948-50, Topeka, 1952-61, sr. engr., 1966-69, equipment maintenance engr., 1967-76, bell engrng. ops. mgr., 1976-79, dist. mgr., 1979—86. Mem. tech. staff Bell Telephone Labs., N.Y.C., 1961-62, Holmdel, N.J., 1962-66; pres., owner W.E. Spencer Co.; mem. U.S. Senatorial Club, 1985—. Patentee in field. Mem. Rep. Presdl. Task Force, 1984—; supervising judge Shawnee County Election Commn.; trustee, bd. dirs. Brookwood Covenant Ch., also pres. Joy Sr. Group. With AUS, 1950-52. Recipient Best Kans. Idea award Southwestern Bell Telephone Co., 1972, cert. of appreciation Kans. Miss Teen Pageant, 1984, Rep. Presdl. League of Merit, 1992—. Mem. IEEE, NSPE, Kans. Engrng. Soc., Topeka Engrs. Club (pres.), Telephone Pioneers Assn. (life mem., rep., Sunflower and Heartland chpt., Topeka life mem., coun. pres. and club pres.), Nat. Geog. Soc., Kans. Hist. Soc., Am. Assn. Ret. Persons, U. Mo.-Columbia Alumni Assn., Nat. Travel Club, Topeka Geog. Soc., Active Prime Timer (historian). Republican. Home: 3201 SW Macvicar Ct Topeka KS 66611-1800 Office: 220 SE 6th Ave Topeka KS 66603-3507 Personal E-mail: wespenc@attglobal.net.

SPENCER, WILLIAMETTA, composer, retired music educator; d. Samuel Joseph Spencer and Viva Jewell; m. Rosario Salvatore Rizzo, Sept. 7, 1957 (dec.). BA, Whittier (Calif.) Coll.; MusM, U. So. Calif., PhD, 1974. Fulbright scholar Ecole Normale de Musique, Paris, 1955—56; prof. music Rio Hondo Coll., Whittier; vis. prof. music, composer in residence Whittier Coll. Musician: (composition) At The Round Earth's Imagined Corners. Mem.: Mu Phi Epsilon. Home: 12129 Beverly Blvd #3D Whittier CA 90601 Home Fax: 562-499-1419. Personal E-mail: wspencer815@cs.com.

SPENGLER, DAN MICHAEL, orthopedic surgery educator, researcher, surgeon; b. Defiance, Ohio, Feb. 25, 1941; s. Harold A. and Wilhelmina Spengler; m. Cynthia Niswonger; children: Christina, Craig. BS, Baldwin-Wallace Coll., 1962; MD, U. Mich., 1966. Diplomate Am. Bd. Orthopaedic Surgery (bd. dirs. 1988-97). Rotating intern King County Hosp., Seattle, 1966-67; resident in orthopedics U. Mich., Ann Arbor, 1970-73; asst. prof. U. Wash., Seattle, 1974-78, assoc. prof., 1978-83. Author: Low Back Pain, 1982. Bd. dirs. Musculoskeletal Transplant Found.; bd. trustees Jour. of Bone and Joint Surgery, 2004—. Fellow: Am. Acad. Orthopaedic Surgeons; mem.: ACS, Internat. Soc. for Study of Lumbar Pain, Assn. Bone and Joint Surgeons, Am. Bd. Orthopaedic Surgeons (pres. 1993—94), Am. Orthopaedic Assn. (pres. 2003—04), U. Nashville Club. Avocations: flying, golf, running, skiing. Office: Vanderbilt U Dept Orthopedic Rehab 1161 21st Ave S #D4219MCN Nashville TN 37232-2550 Business E-Mail: dan.m.spengler@vanderbilt.edu.

SPENGLER, PAUL ALBERT, grants and foundation administrator; b. Buffalo, Feb. 18, 1947; s. Albert Henry and Hazel Mae Spengler; m. Cheryl Ann Spengler, June 22, 1985; stepchildren: Jennifer Ann MacFarlane, Mara Elizabeth Sroczyk. BS, SUNY, Buffalo, 1969, MA, 1973; PhD, U. Del., 1977. Dep. commr. Erie County Dept. Youth Svcs., Buffalo, 1984-87; dir. cmty. svcs. Salvation Army, Buffalo, 1988-93; dir. grants Niagara County C.C., Sanborn, N.Y., 1993-99; dir. found. giving Roswell Pk. Cancer Inst., Buffalo, 2000—. Cons. Edn. Devel. Ctr., Newton, Mass., 1978, Erie C.C., Buffalo, 1999-00, Genesee C.C., Batavia, N.Y., 1999, Adirondack C.C., Queensbury, N.Y., 1999; adj. instr. D'Youville Coll., Buffalo, 1988-90. Author: Yankee Swedish and Italian Acculturization and Economic Mobility in Jamestown New York from 1860 to 1920, 1980; contbr. articles to profl. jours. Sec. standing com. Episcopal Diocese Western N.Y., Buffalo, 1998-2002; vestryman Episcopal Ch. Good Shepherd, Buffalo, 1998—2001, 04-05; mem. adj. gis. commn. homelessness Erie County Legis., Buffalo, 1991-93. N.Y. State Regents scholar, 1965-69; Andelot fellow U. Del., 1973-74, 75-76, 76-77. Democrat. Avocations: reading, gardening, classical music. Home: 26 Groveland St Buffalo NY 14214-1012 Office: Roswell Pk Alliance Elm And Carlton Sts Buffalo NY 14267-0001

SPENSER, IAN DANIEL, chemist educator; b. Vienna, June 17, 1924; m. Anita Fuchs, Sept. 5, 1951; children: Helen Ruth, Paul Andrew. B.Sc. with honors, U. Birmingham (Eng.), 1948; PhD in Biochemistry, U. London, 1952, D.Sc. in Organic and Biochemistry, 1969. Demonstrator in biochemistry King's Coll., U. London, 1948-52, asst. lectr. in biochemistry Med. Coll. St. Bartholomew's Hosp., 1952-54, lectr., 1954-57; postdoctoral fellow div. pure chemistry NRC Can., Ottawa, Ont., 1953-54; asst. prof. biochemistry McMaster U., Hamilton, Ont., Can., 1957-59, assoc.prof., 1959-64, prof., 1964-68, prof. chemistry, 1968-89, prof. emeritus, 1989—; Akademischer Gast Laboratorium für Organische Chemie/Eidgenössische Technische Hochschule, Zürich, Switzerland, 1971, 89; vis. prof. Inst. Organic Chemistry, Tech. U. Denmark, Lyngby, 1977, Inst. Organische Chemie/Univ. Karlsruhe, Fed. Republic Germany, 1981, Institut für Pharmazeutische Biologie, Universität Bonn, Federal Republic of Germany, 1989. Research in biosynthesis of alkaloids, biosynthesis of vitamin Bl and vitamin B6. Recipient Sr. Scientist award NATO, 1980; recipient Can.-Japan Exchange award, 1982-83, Univ. Club of Hamilton award, 1990. Fellow Royal Soc. Can., Chem. Inst. Can. (John Labatt Ltd. award 1982-83), Royal Soc. Chemistry (U.K.); mem. Biochem. Soc., Am. Soc. Biochemistry Molecular Biol., Am. Soc. Pharmacognosy, Phytochem. Soc. N. Am. Office: McMaster U Dept Chemistry Hamilton ON Canada L8S 4M1 E-mail: spenser@mcmaster.ca.

SPERA, DOMINIC GREGORIO, music educator, writer; b. Kenosha, Wis., Apr. 18, 1932; s. Costanzo and Anita Spera; m. Patty Jean Graber, Jan. 22, 1956; children: Gregory Allen, Mark Christopher. MusB in Edn., MusB in Trumpet, Ind. U., 1967, MusM in Edn., 1968. Bandsman U.S. Army, Fort Sheridan, Ill., 1953—56; profl. musician N.Y.C., 1957—67; dir. of instrumental music U. Jr. and Sr. HS, Bloomington, Ind., 1967—68; prof. of music U. of Wis., Eau Claire, Wis., 1968—77; prof. of music Sch. Music Ind. U., Bloomington, 1977—97, prof. emeritus Sch. Music, 1997—. Profl. trumpet player various TV shows, N.Y.C., 1958—66, Radio City, N.Y.C., 1958—66, City and Roxy Theaters, Bands of Lionel Hampton, Charlie Barnet, Benny Goodman, Tito Puente, Tommy Dorsey Bands, N.Y.C., 1958—66; profl. trumpet player with Burt Bacharach, Johnny Mathis, Henry Mancini, Andy Williams, Frank Sinatra, International Locations, 1966—92. Composer: (songs) Over 100 Pub. Compositions; author: Take the Lead; trumpet soloist and composer (albums) Yamaha Trumpet Series; author: Blues and the Basics, Making the Changes, Stretching Out; trumpet soloist, composer, producer (albums) Make a Joyful Noise, Chops Don't Fail Me Now; trumpet soloist, composer, producer: albums Dominic Spera Big Band. Dir. Eau Claire (Wis.) Jazz Festival, 1968—77; founder, dir. U. Alta. Summer Jazz Camp-, Edmonton, Canada, 1979—2002; founder, dir. Bloomington (Ind.) Jazz Festival, 1981—2002. Pvt. first class U.S. Army, 1953—56. Recipient awards, 19 US States, Can., and Australia, 1968—2002, Outstanding Svc. award, Internat. Assn. of Jazz Educators, 1974, 1982; grantee, NEA, 1976. Mem.: Internat. Trumpet Guild (life), Internat. Assn. of Jazz Educators (life), Music Educators Nat. Conf. (life). Achievements include first to first published jazz composition utilizing the 12 tone system of composition introduction and allegro for jazz ensemble and percussion, 1972; first published theme and variations for jazz ensemble, 1977. Avocations: painting, travel. Home and Office: 2293 Winding Brook Ct Bloomington IN 47401

SPERAKIS, NICHOLAS GEORGE, artist; b. N.Y.C., June 8, 1943; s. George and Cathren (Cokatas) S.; m. Yolanda de Carmen Mesa, Feb. 1, 1983. Student, Pratt Inst., 1960, NAD, 1960-61, Art Students League N.Y., Pratt Graphic Art Center, 1961-63. Instr. Sumitt (N.J.) Art Center, 1971, New Sch. Social Research, N.Y.C., 1972—, Fashion Inst. Tech., N.Y.C., 1977—. Exhibited one-man shows at Paul Kessler Gallery, 1963, 64, Provincetown, Mass., Hinckley and Brohel Art Gallery, Washington, 1964, N.Y.C., 1965, Mari Galleries, Woodstock, N.Y., 1966, 67, 68, Larchmont, N.Y., 1967, Eric Schindler Galleries, 1965, Richmond (Va.) Art Gallery, N.Y. U. Student Loeb Center, 1969, L.I. U., 1971, Pratt Inst., 1971, Bienville Gallery, New Orleans, 1972, 74, Pace U., N.Y.C., 1972, Lerner-Heller Gallery, N.Y.C., 1975, 76, Daedal Gallery, Balt., 1976, Reading Mus. Art, (Pa.), 1977, Bklyn. Mus., 1977, Washington Irving Gallery, N.Y.C., 1982, Museo Universitario Del Chopo, Mexico City, 1984, Forum Gallery, N.Y.C., Mus. Contemporary Art, Bogota, The Atler Gallery, Munich, 1989, Galerieverein Blankenese, Hamburg, Fed. Republic Germany, 1988, Galeria Sextante, Bogota, 1989, La Francia, Centro de Arte, Medellin, Colombia, 1989, various woodcut exhbns., Alexander S. Onassis Ctr. N.Y.U., 1995, Claudia Carr Gallery, N.Y.C., 1997-98, The Old Print Shop, N.Y.C., 1998, Stephen Gang Gallery, N.Y.C., 2000, Andrew Edlin Fine Arts, N.Y.C., 2003, others; exhibited group shows, Mercy Hurst Coll., Erie, Pa., 1963, 64, Bklyn. Mus., 1964, 77, Jewish Mus., 1964, Chrysler Mus., 1964, 65, Assoc. Am. Artists Galleries, N.Y.C., 1965, Norfolk (Va.) Mus. Arts Scis., 1965, Long Beach (Calif.) Coll., 1969, Am. Acad. and Nat. Inst. Arts and Letters, 1969, 75, Mid West Mus-Am-Art, 1981, numerous others, print exhbns., France, Italy, Spain, other European Countries, Far East, 1970-71, Lerner-Heller Gallery, 1973, 76, Amherst Coll., 1974, Worcester (Mass.) Mus. Fine Art, 1977, Reading (Pa.) Mus. Art, 1977, Galeria El Museo Santate de Bogota, Colombia, 1992, Mus. Modern Art, Rio de Janeiro, Brazil, 1992, travel Ams., Europe, 1992, Rhino Horn, N.Y.C., 1994, WhiteHall, N.Y.C., 1993, 94, Barnard/Biderman Fine Art, N.Y.C., 1994, 10th Ann. Art Miami 2000, 2000, Siron Studios, N.Y.C., 2001; represented in permanent collections Bklyn. Mus., Walter P. Chrysler Mus., Norfolk, Va., Norfolk Mus. Arts and Scis., N.Y.C. Public Library, Phila. Mus. Fine Arts, Worcester Mus. Fine Art, Flint (Mich.) Art Inst., Mus. Modern Art, N.Y.C., U. Conn., Storrs, Amherst Coll., Okla. Fine Arts Center Mus., Am. Acad. and Nat. Inst. Arts and Letters, Detroit Inst. Fine Art, Corcoran Gallery of Art, Midwest Mus. Am. Art, Exeter Acad., Conn., Mus. Modern Art, N.Y.C., print collections Nat. Mus. Am. Art Smithsonian Instn., DeHunter Mus. Art, Chattanooga, Libr. of Congress, Washington, High Mus. Art, Atlanta, Free Libr., Phila., Kunst Mus., Fine Arts Mus. Bern Switzerland, Australian Nat. Gallery, Canberra, Snite Mus. Art, U. Notre Dame, Ind., Bibliotheque Royale Albert/ER, Bruxelles, Belgium, Museo Rayo, Roldanillo, Colombia, Stedelijk Mus., Amsterdam, The Netherlands, Hirshhorn Mus., Washington, Mus. Modern Art Santa Fe de Bogota, Nordjyllands Kunstmus., Aalborg, Denmark, Banco Bozano Simonsen, Rio de Janeiro, Mus. Modern Art, Bogota, Rose Art Mus. Brandeis U., Conn.; organized (with others), Rhino Horn artist group, N.Y.C., 1970. Recipient First Prize Purchase award Mercy Hurst Coll., 1964; Lawrence and Hinda Rosenthal award Am. Acad. and Nat. Inst. Arts and Letters, 1969; Guggenheim graphics fellow, 1970; McDowell Colony summer residency, 1976 Mem. Soc. Am. Graphic Artists. Address: 245 W 29th St Fl 12A New York NY 10001-5208 *Art doesn't bring out the voters for candidates X or Z. Art brings forth an experience and enters the knowledge of the viewer, so it helps the individual consider new channels and modes of behavior. One of the reasons there is so much censorship of art is due to the power art has to transform people at the roots not into some action but in a more generalized manner in terms of understanding institutions and traditions for what they really are. I think art changes emotions more than it changes specific ideas.*

SPERATI, CARLETON ANGELO, retired industrial scientist; b. Fergus Falls, Minn., Sept. 1, 1918; s. Carsten Emmanuel S. and Martha Eline Johnson; m. Eloise Morris, June 1, 1941; children: Charles Robert, William Eller, Solveig Sperati Korte. AB, Luther Coll., Decorah. Iowa, 1934—38; MA in Chemistry, U. Ill., Urbana, 1939, PhD in Organic Chemistry, 1941. Lab. asst. Union Oil Calif., San Pedro, Calif., 1940; rsch. chemist E. I. DuPont de Nemours, Inc., Arlington, 1941—50; supr. E. I. DuPont de Nemours & Co, Wilmington, Del., 1952—55; sr. supr. E. I. DuPont de Nemours & Co, 1955—60, rsch. assoc., 1960—69; rsch. fellow E. I. DuPont de Nemours & Co., Parkersburg, W.Va.; cons. E. I. DuPont de Nemours & Co, 1979—98; C. Paul Stocker prof. of engring. (first appointee to the position) Ohio U., Athens, Ohio, 1979—81, Stocker adj. prof. of chem. engring., 1981—. Cmn. U.S.A. tech. adv. group tech. com. 37 on terminology Internat. Orgn. Standardization, Geneva, 1989—98; presenter in field. Contbr. articles to profl. jours. Fellow: ASTM Internat. (Frank W. Reinhart award in terminology 1991, Award of Merit 1998); mem.: Am. Chem. Soc. (life Best Paper of Yr. 1986). Lutheran. Achievements include patents in field. Avocations: music, travel, reading, white water canoeing, skiing. Home: 23 Mustang Acres Parkersburg WV 26104-8040 Office Phone: 304-485-2374. Personal E-mail: pka00099@alpha.wvup.wvnet.edu.

SPERBER, DANIEL, physicist; b. Vienna, May 8, 1930; came to U.S., 1955, naturalized, 1967; s. Emanuel and Nelly (Lieberman) S.; m. Ora Yuval, Nov. 29, 1963; 1 son, Ron Emanuel. M.Sc., Hebrew U., 1954; PhD, Princeton U., 1960. Tng. and rsch. asst. Israel Inst. Tech., Haifa, 1954-55, Princeton U., 1955-60; sr. scientist, rsch. adviser Ill. Inst. Tech. Rsch. Inst., Chgo., 1960-67; assoc. prof. physics Ill. Inst. Tech., 1964-67, Rensselaer Poly. Inst., Troy, N.Y., 1967-72, prof., 1972—. Nordita prof. Niels Bohr Inst., Copenhagen, 1973-74, NATO research fellow, vis., prof., 1974-77; vis. prof. G.S.I., Darmstadt, Fed. Republic Germany, 1983; sr. Fulbright research scholar, Saha Inst. Nuclear Physics, Calcutta, India, 1987-88. Contbr. over 100 sci. papers to profl. jours. Served to capt. Israeli Army, 1948-51. Fellow Am. Phys. Soc.; mem. Israel Phys. Soc., N.Y. Acad. Scis., Sigma Xi. Jewish. Home: 1 Taylor Ln Troy NY 12180-7162 Office: Rensselaer Poly Inst 110 8th St Dept Physics Troy NY 12180-3522 E-mail: sperbd@rpi.edu. *My goals are to further an understanding of nature by basic research in nuclear theory and to introduce a new generation to this research.*

SPERBER, MARILYN JANICE, special education educator; b. N.Y.C., Feb. 24, 1947; d. Max Schuman and Doris (Behr) Schuman Friedman; m. Mark Victor Sperber, Mar. 24, 1968; children: Dustin Cory, Jonathan Kyle. BS in Edn., SUNY, New Paltz, 1968, MS in Spl. Edn., 1976; postgrad., Fordham U., 1989-90. Cert. elem. tchr., K-12 spl. edn. tchr., N.Y. Elem. tchr. Mamaroneck (N.Y.) Ctrl. Sch., 1968-69, N.Y.C. Pub. Schs., 1969-70; edn. therapist Astor Day Treatment Ctr., Poughkeepsie, N.Y., 1976-80; spl. educator The Children's Annex, Kingston, N.Y., 1980-84; instr. Jr. Coll. of Albany, N.Y., 1984-87; spl. educator R.C.G. BOCES, Castleton, N.Y., 1984-87; asst. prof. Sullivan County C.C., Loch Sheldrake, N.Y., 1987-95; spl. educator resource rm. Benjamin Cosor Elem. Sch., Fallsburg, N.Y., 1987—. Author: Why Am I Doing This?, 1998. Grantee Fallsburg Ctrl. Schs., 1991, Hudson Valley Portfolio Project, 1993-96. Mem. Fallsburg Tchrs. Assn. (asst. treas. 1990—), Sullivan Reading Coun., N.Y. State Reading Coun., Phi Delta Kappa. Avocations: bicycling, walking, aquasize, skiing. Home: 96 Edwards Rd Monticello NY 12701-3420 Office: Benjamin Cosor Elem Sch Brickman Rd Fallsburg NY 12733

SPERBER, MARTIN, pharmaceutical company executive, pharmacist; b. N.Y.C., Aug. 6, 1931; s. David and Gertrude (Besen) S.; m. Ellen Claire Marx, June 7, 1953; children— Steven Jay, Susan Barbara Parnes. BS, Columbia U., N.Y.C., 1952. Registered pharmacist. Pharmacist, dir. sales and mktg. Henry Schein, Inc., N.Y.C., 1953-65, v.p., 1965-80, pres., COO Melville, N.Y., 1980-89, vice chmn., 1989-93, also bd. dirs.; pres., COO Schein Pharm., Inc., Florham Park, N.J., 1985-89, chmn., chief exec. officer, 1989—, chmn., CEO, pres., also bd. dirs.; chmn., CEO Danbury Pharm. Inc. (owned by Schein Pharm., Inc.), Carmel, N.Y., 1989—, also bd. dirs.; chmn., CEO Schein Pharm. Inc., Phoenix, 1989—; also bd. dirs. Steris Labs., Inc. (owned by Schein Pharm., Inc.), Phoenix. Mem. coun. of overseers Arnold and Marie Schwartz Coll. Pharmacy, L.I. U.; bd. dirs. Am. Found. for Pharm. Edn. Mem. Am. Pharm. Assn. Office: Watson Pharma Inc PO Box 1953 Morristown NJ 07962-1953

SPERDUTO, MICHAEL A. corporate financial executive; From sr. acct. to v.p., CFO Engelhard, Iselin, NJ, 1983—2001, v.p., 2001—, CFO, 2001—. Office: Engelhard 101 Wood Ave PO Box 770 Iselin NJ 08830-0770

SPERELAKIS, NICHOLAS, SR., physiology and biophysics educator, researcher; b. Joliet, Ill., Mar. 3, 1930; s. James and Aristea (Kayaidakis) S.; m. Dolores Martinis, Jan. 28, 1960; children: Nicholas Jr., Mark (dec.), Christine, Sophia, Thomas, Anthony. BS in Chemistry, U. Ill., 1951, MS in Physiology, 1955, PhD in Physiology, 1957. Tchg. asst. U. Ill., Urbana, 1954-57; instr. Case Western Res. U., Cleve., 1957-59, asst. prof., 1959-66, assoc. prof., 1966; prof. U. Va., Charlottesville, 1966-83; Joseph Eichberg prof. physiology Coll. Medicine U. Cin., 1983-96, chmn. dept., 1983-93, Eichberg prof. emeritus, 1996—. Cons. NPS Pharm., Inc., Salt Lake City, 1988-95, Carter Wallace, Inc. Cranbury, N.J., 1988-91; vis. prof. U. St. Andrews, Scotland, 1972-73, U. San Luis Potosi, Mex., 1986, U. Athens, Greece, 1994; Rosenblueth prof. Centro de Investigacion y Avanzades, Mex., 1972; mem. sci. adv. com. several internat. meetings, editl. bds. numerous sci. jours. Co-editor: Handbook of Physiology: Heart, 1979; editor: Physiology and Pathophysiology of the Heart, 1984, 2d edit., 1988, 3rd edit., 1994, 4th edit., 2000, Calcium Antagonists: Mechanisms of Action on Cardiac Muscle and Vascular Smooth Muscle, 1984, Cell Interactions and Gap Junctions, vols. I and II, 1989, Frontiers in Smooth Muscle Research, 1990, Ion Channels in Vascular Smooth Muscle and Endothelial Cells, 1991, Essentials of Physiology, 1993, 2d edit., 1996, Cell Physiology Source Book, 1995 (Outstanding Acad. Book, Choice Am. Libr. Assn. 1996, 98), 3d edit., 2001, Electrogenesis of Biopotentials, 1995; assoc. editor Circulation Rsch., 1970-75, 75-80, Molecular Cellular Cardiology; regional editor Current Drug Targets, 2000-02; contbr. more than 500 articles to profl. jours. Lectr. Project Hope, Peru, 1962. Sgt. USMC, 1951-53, Res., 1953-59. Recipient Disting. Alumnus award Rockdale (Ill.) Pub. Schs., 1958, Rsch. Excellence award Am. Heart Assn. Ohio, 1995, Visionary award Am. Heart Assn., S.W. Ohio, 1996; U. Cin. Grad. fellow, 1989; NIH grantee, 1959-99. Mem. IEEE, Engring. in Medicine and Biology, Am. Physiol. Soc. (chair steering com. sect. 1981-82), Biophys. Soc. (coun. 1990-93), Am. Soc. Pharmacology and Exptl. Therapeutics, Internat. Soc. Heart Rsch. (coun. 1980-89, 92-98), Am. Hellenic Ednl. Progressive Assn. (pres. Charlottesville chpt. 1980-82), Ohio Physiol. Soc. (pres. 1990-91), Phi Kappa Phi. Independent. Greek Orthodox. Avocations: ancient Greek coins, stamp collecting/philately. Office: U Cin Coll Medicine 231 Bethesda Ave Cincinnati OH 45229-2827

SPERGEL, IRVING ABRAHAM, social worker, researcher; b. N.Y.C., Jan. 17, 1924; s. Julius and Frieda Mann Spergel; m. Bertha Jampel Spergel, June 27, 1949 (dec. Nov. 1989); children: Barry Alexander, Mark Jonathan, Daniel Jeremy; m. Annot Mary McGiffin, Oct. 5, 1996. BSS, CCNY, 1946; MA, Columbia U., 1948, PhD in Social Work, 1960; MSW, U. Ill., 1952. Program asst. YM-YWHA, Wilmington, Del., 1948—49; gang worker, supr. N.Y.C., 1950, 1952; ct. rep. Youth Bd., N.Y.C., 1954, 1958, 1960; dir. Neighbors United St. Club project Lenox Hill Neighborhood House, NY, 1954—57; from asst. to assoc. prof. U. Chgo., 1960—66, prof., 1967—92, George Herbert Jones prof., 1993—2002, George Herbert Jones prof. emeritus, 2002—. UN youth adv. Hong Kong Govt., 1970—71; external examiner social work Chung Chi Coll., 1978—97; cons. Hong Kong Coun. Social Svc., 1978—97; cons., rschr. in field. Author: Racketville, Slumtown, Haulberg, 1964, Street Gang Work, 1966, Community Problem Solving, 1969, The Youth Gang Problem: A Community Approach, 1995. Mem. Ill. Gov.'s Commn. on Gangs, 1995—96, Nat. Youth Gang Adv. Com., Boys and Girls Clubs Am., 1989—91; mem. acad. adv. com. Ill. Criminal Justice Info. Authority, 1989—. With U.S. Army, 1943—46, ETO. Grantee, Ford Found., 1960, NIMH, 1960—61, U.S. Dept. Justice, 1987—2003. Jewish. Office: U Chgo Sch Social Svc Adminstrn 969 E 60th St Chicago IL 60637 Office Phone: 773-702-1134.

SPERLIK, ROBERT VAL, JR., music educator, musician; b. Oak Park, Ill., Dec. 15, 1959; s. Robert Val and Dorothy J. Sperlik. BS in Music Edn., U. of Ill., Champaign-Urbana, 1982; MA in Music Performance, DePaul U., Chgo., 1986. Cert. Tchr. Ill., 1982. Dir. of percussion J. S. Morton HS, Berwyn-Cicero, Ill., 1983—96; dir. of percussion Morton Coll., Cicero, Ill., 1984—2000; band dir. Sch. Dist. 100, Berwyn, Ill., 1987—. Percussion cons. Shorewood H.S. Band, Shorewood, 1999—; founder-director Take-Ten Percussion Ensemble, Berwyn, Ill., 1996—; prin. percussionist Lake Shore Symphony, Chgo.; jazz band dir. Dist. 100 Heritage Mid. Sch., Berwyn, Ill., 1999—; prin. percussionist Classical Symphony Orch., Chgo., 1985—2001, Lincolnwood Chamber Orch., Lincolnwood, Ill., Salt Creek Ballet Co., Chgo., Chgo. Symphonic Wind Ensemble, Ill.; theatre percussionist Cir. Theatre, Forest Park, Ill.; percussionist Chgo. Chamber Orch., Beijing Opera Orch., Kumamato Youth Symphony, Festival Marimba Orch. Musician: (percussion soloist) The World of Percussion, 1995, (marimba soloist) DePonte Concertino for Marimba, 2002. Recipient Ill. State Scholarship, State of Ill., 1984 through 1986, First Pl. Percussion Ensemble, Ill. H.S. Music Assn., 1983 through 1996, Divsn. 1 State Band Contest, Ill. Grade Sch. Music Assn., 1989, 1993, 1997, 1999, Dist. 100 Honor Band Day, City of Berwyn, 1997. Mem.: NEA, Chgo. Fedn. of Musicians, Percussive Arts Soc., Music Educators Nat. Conf., Ill. Edn. Assn. Episcopalian. Avocations: performing, bicycling, reading, sports, travel.

SPERLING, ALLAN GEORGE, lawyer; b. NYC, Dec. 10, 1942; s. Saul and Gertrude (Lober) Sperling; m. Susan Kelz, 1965 (div. 2001); children: Matthew Laurence, Stuart Kelz, Jane Kendra; m. Ferne Goldberg, 2001. Bar: N.Y. 1969, U.S. Ct. Appeals (2d cir.) 1975. Law clk. to presiding justice U.S. Dist Ct., New Haven, 1967-68; assoc. Cleary, Gottlieb, Steen & Hamilton, N.Y.C., 1968-75, ptnr., 1976—. Editor Yale Law Jour. Bd. dirs. Vol. Lawyers for the Arts, 1998—, Merce Cunningham Dance Found., NYC, 1985-98, 2000—, chmn. bd., 1992-98; chmn. bd. Rye (NY) Arts Ctr. Inc., 1985-88, bd. dirs., 1990-94; bd. dirs. Friends of the Neuberger Mus. Art, Purchase, NY, 1989-2004, chmn. bd., 1997-2000. Mem.: N.Y. State Bar Assn., Phi Beta Kappa, Order of the Coif. Home: 2 Fifth Ave New York NY 10011 Office: Cleary Gottlieb Steen & Hamilton 1 Liberty Plz Fl 43 New York NY 10006-1470 Office Phone: 212-225-2000. Business E-Mail: asperling@cgsh.com.

SPERLING, DANIEL, engineering educator, transportation studies director; b. Albany, NY, Mar. 27, 1951; s. Benjamin and Carolyn Scheinzeit Sperling; m. Patricia Margaret Alice Davis, June 28, 1981; 1 child, Rhiannon Elizabeth Davis. BA, Cornell U., N.Y., 1973; PhD, U. of Calif., Berkley, 1982. City planner Peace Corps, Tegucigalpa, Honduras, 1973—75; environ. scientist EPA, San Francisco, 1976—77; prof. U. of Calif., Davis. Founding chmn. transport rsch. bd. Alternative Transp. Fuels Com., 1989—96. Author: New Transportation Fuels, 1988, Future Drive, 1995; co-author: Road Ecology, 2003; mem. editl. bd.: Transp. Rsch. D. Environment. Testimony U.S. Congress Hearing on Energy Policy, Washington, 1991; testimony, partnership for new generation vehicle U. S. Congress, Washington, 1996; testimony, freedom car U.S. Congress, Washington, 2002. Recipient Disting. Pub. Svc. award, U. of Calif. Davis, 1996, Clean Air, Am. Lung Assn., 1997, Sci. Leadership and Tech. Excellence award, Coalition for Clean Air, 2002. Mem.: Nat. Acad. of Sci. (com. on sustainable transp. 1995—97, com. on transp. in China 2001—02, com. on hydrogen prodn. and use 2002—03). Office: Inst of Transp Studies U of California Davis Davis CA 95616

SPERLING, GEORGE, cognitive scientist, educator; s. Otto and Melitta Sperling BS in Math., U. Mich., 1955; MA in Psychology, Columbia U., 1956; PhD in Psychology, Harvard U., 1959. Rsch. asst. in biophysics Brookhaven Nat. Labs., Upton, N.Y., summer 1955; rsch. asst. in psychology Harvard U., Cambridge, Mass., 1957-59; mem. tech. rsch. staff Acoustical and Behavioral Rsch. Ctr., AT&T Bell Labs., Murray Hill, N.J., 1958-86; prof. psychology and neural sci. NYU, N.Y.C., 1970-92; disting. prof. cognitive scis., neurobiology and behavior U. Calif., Irvine, 1992—. Instr. psychology Washington Sq. Coll., NYU, 1962-63; vis. assoc. prof. psychology Duke U., spring 1964; adj. assoc. prof. psychology Columbia U., 1964-65; acting assoc. prof. psychology UCLA, 1967-68; hon. rsch. assoc. Univ. Coll., U. London, 1969-70; vis. prof. psychology U. Western Australia, Perth, 1972, U. Wash., Seattle, 1977; vis. scholar Stanford (Calif.) U., 1984; mem. sci. adv. bd. USAF, 1988-92. Recipient Meritorious Civilian Svc. medal USAF, 1993; Gomberg scholar U. Mich., 1953-54; Guggenheim fellow, 1969-70, APS fellow. Fellow: APA (Disting. Sci. Contbn. award 1988), AAAS, Am. Psychol. Soc. (William James fellow), Optical Soc. Am. (Tillyer award 2002), Am. Acad. Arts and Sci.; mem.: NAS, Soc. Math. Psychology (chmn. 1983—84, exec. bd. 1979—85), Soc. Exptl. Psychologists (Warren medal 1996), Psychonomic Soc., Soc. Computers in Psychology (steering com. 1974—78), Eastern Psychol. Assn. (bd. dirs. 1982—85), Ann. Interdisciplinary Conf. (founder, organizer 1975—), Assn. Rsch. in Vision and Ophthalmology, Sigma Xi, Phi Beta Kappa. Office: U Calif SS Plz A Dept Cognitive Scis Irvine CA 92697-5100 E-mail: sperling@uci.edu.

SPERLING, GODFREY, JR., journalist; b. Long Beach, Calif., Sept. 25, 1915; s. Godfrey and Ida (Bailey) Sperling; m. Betty Louise Feldmann, June 22, 1942; children: Mary McAuliffe, John Godfrey. BS, U. Ill., 1937; JD, U. Okla., 1940. Bar: Ill. 1940. Pvt. practice, Urbana, Ill.; reporter Champaign-Urbana News-Gazette, 1940-41; mem. staff Christian Sci. Monitor, 1946—, Midwest bur. chief, 1957-62, N.Y. bur. chief, 1962-65, news mgr., asst. chief Washington bur., 1965-73, nat. polit. corr., 1970-83, chief Washington Bur., 1973-83, sr. Washington columnist, 1984—, cons. to pub., 2002—. Lectr. nat. affairs, 1955—; Woodrow Wilson vis. fellow, 1976—. Served to maj. USAF, 1941—46, col. USAF, Res. Recipient Alumni Achievement award, U. Ill., 1987, Spl. citation, Nat. Press Found. for unique contbns. to Am. journalism, 1994; Godfrey Sperling Jr. Christian Sci. Monitor Jour. fellow, U. Ill., 2003. Mem.: Navy Officers Club, Overseas Writers Club (Washington), Nat. Press Club (Washington), White House Press Corr. Assn., Congl. Press Corr. Assn., Mass. Bar Assn., Ill. Bar Assn., Okla. Bar Assn., Sperling Breakfast Group (host 1966—), Cosmos Club (Washington), Gridiron Club Washington (pres. 1991), Sigma Delta Chi. Christian Scientist. Home: 8101 Connecticut Ave Apt N500 Chevy Chase MD 20815-2827 Office: Christian Science Monitor 910 16th St NW Washington DC 20006-2903 Office Phone: 202-785-4400.

SPERLING, IRENE R. publishing executive; Asst. mktg. coord. seminars and trade shows Security World Publ., 1979—80; asst. show mgr. Cahners Expn. Group Kitchen and Bath and Office Product Shows, 1980—83, co-pub., 1983—86, v.p. sales and mktg., 1986—2000, publ., 2000—; publisher Tradeshow Week, LA, 2000—02; v.p. spl. projects and internat. sales Trade Show Exec. Mag., 2003—. Office: Trade Show Exec 21250 Hawthorne Blvd Ste 500 Torrance CA 90503 E-mail: isperling@tsweek.com.

SPERLING, JOY HARMON, lawyer; b. Bklyn., Mar. 25, 1961; d. Aaron and Lenore Harmon; m. Norman Jay Sperling, July 1, 1984; 1 child, Daniel Steven. BA cum laude, Rutgers U., 1983, JD, 1986. Bar: N.J. 1986, U.S. Dist. Ct N.J. 1986, U.S. Ct. Appeals (3d cir.) 1995, U.S. Dist. Ct. (so. dist.) N.Y. 1998. Clk. to Hon W.P. Diana, Assignment and Chancery Judge Superior Ct. of N.J., Somerville, N.J., 1986-87; assoc. Pitney, Hardin, Kipp & Szuch, Morristown, N.J., 1987-95, ptnr., 1996—. Mem. ABA, N.J. State Bar Assn., Phi Beta Kappa. Home: 11 Argonne Farm Dr Bridgewater NJ 08807-1480 Office: Pitney Hardin Kipp & Szuch PO Box 1945 Morristown NJ 07962-1945 E-mail: jsperling@pitneyhardin.com.

SPERLING, SCOTT EDWARD, software consultant, Bible expositor; b. Tucson, Jan. 11, 1961; s. Fritz Eric and Ruth Ann S.; m. Moon Hee, March 16, 1985; children: Scott Edward, Charlotte Moon. BSc in Applied Physics, Calif. Inst. Tech., Pasadena, 1983; BSc in Info. Computer Sci., U. Calif., Irvine, 1985. Software engr. Interstate Electronics, Anaheim, Calif., 1985-87, Hughes Aircraft, Fullerton, Calif., 1987-88, software cons. Azusa, Calif., 1991-92; software engr. Librascope Corp., Glendale, Calif., 1988-91; software cons. Litton Guidance & Control Sys., Woodland Hills, Calif., 1993—; prin., owner Scripture Studies Inc., SSper Inc., Foothill Ranch, Calif., 1994—, 1997—. Author, editor Scripture Studies, 1994—. Avocations: music, literature. Home and Office: 20010 Via Natalie Yorba Linda CA 92887-3152 E-mail: ssper@aol.com.

SPERLING, SHELDON J. prosecutor; BA Northeastern State Coll., JD U. Tulsa. Pvt. practice, Tulsa, 1979—82; asst. dist. atty. Okla. Dist. Atty.'s Office, 1983—85; asst. U.S. atty. Ea. Dist. Okla. U.S. Dept. Justice, 1985—89, 1st asst. U.S. atty., criminal chief, 1989—2000, U.S. atty., 2000—. Office: 1200 W Okmulgee St Muskogee OK 74401

SPERO, BARRY MELVIN, health facility administrator; b. Richmond, Va., July 13, 1937; s. Stanley Leo and Jean (Marmorstein) Spero; m. Merle Burns, May 29, 1960; children: Amy, Robin, Melissa. BA, U. Richmond, 1959; MHA, Med. Coll. Va., 1961. Asst. adminstr. Bapt. Hosp., Nashville, 1963-66, adminstrv. dir., 1966-68; v.p., dir. hosp. adminstrn. Hosp. Affiliates, Inc., Nashville, 1968-71; exec. dir. Bon Secours Hosp., Grosse Pointe, Mich., 1971-77; pres. The Mt. Sinai Med. Ctr., Cleve., 1977-85; pres., pres. NeWell Health Care System Newton-Wellesley Hosp., 1985-90; pres. Maimonides Med. Ctr., Bklyn., 1990-95; pres., CEO Masonicare, Wallingford, Conn., 1995—. Mem. pers. practice com. Combined Jewish Philantropies; chmn. United Way West Suburban Hosp. divsn.; regional bd. mem. Bay Bank Middlesex; mem. Perpetual Benevolent Fund Com., Blue Print 2000, Commonwealth Mass.; bd. dirs. Premier Health Alliance, chmn., 1981—84; bd. dirs. Premier Preferred Care, Healthfirst; trustee Villa Maria Nursing Ctr./Bon Secours Hosp., 1974—94, chmn., bd. dirs., 1988—94; bd. dirs. Conn. Assn. Not-for-Profit Providers for the Aging, League Vol. Hosps. and Homes, 1991—95, chmn.-elect, 1992—95; mem. State of Ohio Gov.'s Commn. on Health Care Cost, 1984—85; various coms. Coun. Tchg. Hosps., 1992—95; treas. Vol. Hosps. Am., Mass., 1986—90; chmn. hosp. adv. com. Blue Cross N.E. Ohio, 1983—85; trustee Med. Instrumentation Sys., 1978—84; bd. dirs. Am. Assn. Homes and Svcs. for the Aging, 1998—; adv. bd. Gateway Cmty. Coll. Fellow: Am. Coll. Healthcare Execs.; mem.: Greater New Haven C. of C. (bd. dirs.), Ohio Hosp. Assn. (bd. trustees 1981—85, exec. coun.), Mass. Hosp. Assn. (com. on health sys. 1986—90, bd. trustees 1987—90, com. on Medicare payment for outpatient svcs. 1989—90), Met. Boston Hosp. Coun. (chmn. 1988—90), New Eng. Healthcare Assembly (Blue Ribbon com. 1985—90), Greater Cleve. Hosp. Assn. (bd. trustees 1981—85, exec. coun.), Greater N.Y. Hosp. Assn. (bd. govs. 1992—94), Am. Assn. Homes Svcs. Aging (bd. dirs. 1997—), Conn. Hosp. Assn. (bd. dirs. 1997—2000), Coun. Tchg. Hosps. (various coms. 1992—94), Am. Hosp. Assn. (com. on Medicare payment for outpatient svcs. 1989—90). Jewish. Avocation: Avocations: golf, tennis, scuba diving. Office: Masonicare PO Box 70 Wallingford CT 06492-7001 Office Phone: 203-679-5000. E-mail: bspero@masonicare.org.

SPERO, JOAN EDELMAN, foundation president; b. Davenport, Iowa, Oct. 2, 1944; d. Samuel and Sylvia (Halpern) Edelman; m. C. Michael Spero, Nov. 9, 1969; children: Jason, Benjamin. Student, L'Inst. d'Etudes Politiques, Paris, 1964-65; BA in Internat. Rels. with honors, U. Wis., 1966; MA, Columbia U., 1968, PhD, 1973; LLD (hon.), Amherst Coll., 1997. Asst. prof. Columbia U., N.Y.C., 1973-79; amb. of U.S. to UN Econ. and Social Coun., N.Y.C., 1980-81; v.p. Am. Express Co., N.Y.C., 1981-83, sr. v.p. internat. corp. affairs, 1983-89; treas., sr. v.p., 1989-91; exec. v.p. corp. affairs and communications Am. Express Co., 1991-93; under sec. for econ., bus. and agrl. affairs Dept. of State, Washington, 1993-97; pres. Doris Duke Charitable Found., N.Y.C., 1997—. Vis. scholar Fed. Res. Bank N.Y., 1976—77; bd. dirs. IBM Corp., 1st Data Corp., Delta Air Lines Inc. Author: The Politics of International Economic Relations, 6th edit., 2003, The Failure of the Franklin National Bank, 1980; contbr. articles to profl. jours. Trustee Wis. Alumni Rsch. Found., 1997—, Columbia U., 1998; trustee emeritus Amherst Coll.; mem. Coun. Am. Ambs. Named to Acad. Women Achievers, YWCA, 1983; named Fin. Woman of Yr., Fin. Women's Assn., 1990; recipient George Washington U. Disting. Statesperson award, 1994; Woodrow Wilson fellow. Mem. Am. Acad. Diplomacy, Coun. on Fgn. Rels. (bd. dirs.), Am. Philos. Soc., Phi Beta Kappa. Democrat. Jewish. Avocations: writing, swimming. Office: Doris Duke Charitable Found 650 5th Ave 19th Fl New York NY 10019-6108 Office Phone: 212-974-7000.

SPERO, JOSEPH J. secondary school educator; b. Buffalo, Nov. 21, 1968; s. John J and Gloria J Spero; m. Cathleen J Spero, Dec. 31, 1998; 1 child, Mara C. BA, Canisius Coll., Buffalo, NY, 1986—91; EdM, U. Buffalo, 1994—98. Secondary cert. NYS Edn. Dept, 1993, permanent cert. NY, 1998. English tchr. Bishop Timon-St. Jude HS, Buffalo, 1993—95; English and social studies tchr. Lockport City Sch. Dist., Lockport, NY, 1995—. Bldg. rep. Lockport Ednl. Assn., Lockport, NY, 2003—. Exec. bd. mem. Western NY Writing Project, Buffalo, 2003. Fellow, Western NY Writing Project, 1997, 2003. Office: Lockport High Sch 250 Lincoln Avenue Lockport NY 14094 Office Phone: 716-478-4450.

SPERO, KEITH ERWIN, lawyer, educator; b. Cleve., Aug. 21, 1933; s. Milton D. and Yetta (Silverstein) S.; m. Carol Kohn, July 4, 1957 (div. 1974); children: Alana, Scott, Susan; m. Karen Weaver, Dec. 28, 1975. BA, Western Res. U., 1954, LLB, 1956. Bar: Ohio 1956. Assoc. Sindell, Sindell & Bourne, Cleve., 1956-57, Sindell, Sindell, Bourne, Markus, Cleve., 1960-64; ptnr. Sindell, Sindell, Bourne, Markus, Stern & Spero, Cleve., 1964-74, Spero & Rosenfield, Cleve., 1974-76, Spero, Rosenfeld & Bourne, LPA, Cleve., 1977-79, Spero & Rosenfield Co. LPA, 1979—. Tchr. bus. law U. Md. overseas div., Eng., 1958-59; lectr. Case-Western Res. U., 1965-69; instr.; nat. panel arbitrators Am. Arbitration Assn. Author: The Spero Divorce Folio, 1966, Hospital Libaiblity for Acts of Professional Negligence, 1979. Trustee Western Res. Hist. Soc., 1984—2000, exec. com., 1992—2000; v.p., chmn. libr. display and collections com. Western Res. Hist. Soc, 1992—95, chmn. history mus. com., 1995—99; commodore Dugway Creek Yacht Club, 1985—87; bd. dirs. Vail Valley Inst., 2000—. 1st lt. JAG USAF, 1957—60, capt. Res. USAF, 1960—70. Fellow Am. Acad. Matrimonial Lawyers; mem. ABA, Ohio Bar Assn., Cleve. Bar Assn., Cuyahoga County Bar Assn., Ohio Acad. Trial Lawyers (pres. 1970-71), Assn. Trial Lawyers Am. (state committeeman 1971-75, bd. govs. 1975-79, sec. family law litigation sect. 1975-76, vice-chmn. 1976-77, chmn. 1977-79), Am. Bd. Trial Advs., Order of Coif, Masons, Sonnenalp Golf Club (Edwards, Colo.), Phi Beta Kappa, Zeta Beta Tau, Tau Epsilon Rho. Jewish. (trustee, v.p. congregation 1972-78). Office: 440 Leader Bldg E 6th and Superior Cleveland OH 44114-1214 E-mail: keith@vail.net.

SPERO, MORTON BERTRAM, retired lawyer; b. N.Y.C., Dec. 6, 1920; s. Adolph and Julia (Strasburger) S.; m. Louise Thacker, May 1, 1943; children: Donald S., Carol S. Flynn. BA, U. Va., 1942, LLB, 1946. Bar: Va. 1946, U.S. Supreme Ct. 1961. Mem. legal staff NLRB, Washington, 1946-48; pvt. practice Petersburg, Va., 1948—70, 1985—2001; sr. ptnr. Spero & Levinson, Petersburg, 1970-75, Spero & Diehl, Petersburg, 1975-85; ret., 2001. Chmn. The Community Bank, Petersburg, 1976-79, dir., 1976-91. Chmn. United Fund Drive, 1960, bd. dirs., 1999—; pres. Dist. IV Petersburg Coun. Social Welfare, Southside Sheltered Workshop, 1965, pres. Congregation B'rith Achim, 1973; bd. dirs. World Fund, 1999-2001. Lt. USNR, 1943-45. Recipient Outstanding Mem. award Petersburg chpt. B'nai B'rith, 1966; Svc. to Law Enforcement award Petersburg Police Dept., 1965. Fellow Am. Acad. Matrimonial Lawyers; mem. Va. Bar Assn., Petersburg Bar Assn. (pres. 1981-82), Va. State Bar (coun. 1981-84, chmn. criminal law sect. 1972, chmn. family law sect. 1979, bd. dirs. litigation sect. 1983-86, Lifetime Achievement award for family law sect. 1995), Va. Trial Lawyers Assn. (v.p. 1972), Civitan Club (hon.), Rotary, Elks (exalted ruler 1968). Democrat. Jewish. Home: 9706 Bunker Ct Petersburg VA 23805-9125

SPERO, NORA MANCINI, realtor, writer; d. Anthony Joseph and Shirley Sheer Mancini; m. Richard Anthony Spero, July 13, 1996. Student, Mt. Holyoke Coll., 1967—68, Bradford Coll., 1968—70; AA, Merrimack Coll., 1976. Lic. realtor N.H. Bd. Realtors. Buyer cosmetics Birch Super Drug, Chelmsford, Mass., 1975—80; sales trainer N.Eng. area Pantene Divsn. Hoffman-LaRoche, Nutley, NJ, 1978—81; dir. sch. Finishing Touch Modeling Sch. N.Eng, Lowell, Mass. and Nashua, N.H., 1980—89; dir. agy. Bianca Model Agy., Boston, 1981—90; dir. pub. Finelle Cosmetics Co., Lawrence, 1989—95; realtor Linda Roberts Realty Assn., Salem and Windham, NH, 1994—. Owner Design Write Co., Salem, NH, 1980—90. Author: How to Look Like a Million Without Spending It, 1980, (novels) About-Face-An Artist's Eye Mystery, 2003. Mentor Sch. to Jobs Program, Salem H.S., 1996—. Mem.: Granite State Bd. Realtors, Mensa, VFW. Avocations: reading, writing, public speaking, motivating others. Office: Linda Roberts Realty Assoc 1 Manor Pkwy Salem NH 03079

SPERO, RAND KEVIN, management consultant; b. Youngstown, Ohio, Apr. 10, 1955; s. Leslie Wayne and Elaine Carol Spero; m. Barbara Ann Hall, May 1, 1992; children: Emma, Daniel. BA in Psychology cum laude, Vassar Coll., 1977; MBA in Mktg., UCLA, 1980; EdM in Orgnl. Behavior, Harvard U., 1985. Staff Sen. Howard Metzenbaum, Washington, 1977; instr. Close Up Found., Washington, 1978; lectr. Northeastern Grad. Sch. Mgmt., Boston, 1987, 89, 90; corporate mktg. dir. Continental Cablevision, Boston, 1980-84; pres. Spero Assocs., Lexington, Mass., 1984—. Dir. WMXS, Brockton, Mass., 1987-88. Producer, host Career Crossroads (Cable TV) 1990-91; contbr. articles to profl. jours. Trustee Mass. Eye and Ear Infirmary, Boston, 1996—. Avocations: bicycling, swimming, guitar. Office: Spero Assocs 11 Heritage Dr Lexington MA 02420-1104

SPERRIN, GRAHAM FREDERICK, marketing professional; b. London, Eng., Aug. 22, 1956; s. Frank Reginold and Joyce Ivy Sperrin; m. Kim Julie Hollox; children: Luke, Justin. Degree in Elec. & Electronic Engring., Thames Poly., London, 1979. Sr. design engr. Marconi Comm., Chelmsford, 1979—83; prin. design engr. Electro Optic Develop., Basildon, 1983—86; European product mktg. mgr. Anritsu Co., Luton, 1987—98, mktg. mgr. Richardson, Tex., 1998—. Contbr. articles to profl. jours. Mem.: IEEE, Inst. Elec. Engineers (chartered engr. 1980), Inst. Mgmt. (assoc.). Office: Anritsu Co 1155 E Collins Blvd Richardson TX 75081

SPERRY, LEN THOMAS, psychiatrist and preventive medicine educator; b. Milw., Dec. 1, 1943; s. Leonard V. and Wanda R. (Sadowski) S.; m. Patricia L. Garcia, June 11, 1977; children: Tracey, Christen, L. Timothy, Steven, Jonathon. BA, St. Mary's U. Minn., Winona, Minn., 1966; PhD, Northwestern U., 1970; MD, U. Cen. Technol. Studies, Dominican Republic, 1981. Diplomate Am. Bd. Profl. Psychology, Am. Bd. Psychiatry and Neurology, Am. Bd. Preventive Medicine. Asst. prof. Marquette U., Milw., 1971-74; assoc. prof. U. Wis., Milw., 1974-75, U.S. Internat. U., San Diego, 1976-78; resident in psychiatry and preventive medicine Med. Coll. Wis., Milw., 1982-85; fellow in behavioral medicine U. Wis. Med. Sch., Milw., 1984-85; assoc. prof. psychiatry, preventive medicine Med. Coll. Wis., Milw., 1986-92, prof., 1992-2000, prof. cmty. and family medicine, 1998-2000, vice chair dept. psychiatry, 1997-2000, clin. prof. psychiatry, 2000—; prof. health adminstrn., prof. psychology Barry U., Miami Shores, Fla., 2000—02, dir. doctoral program in counseling, 2003; prof., dir. doctoral program in counseling Fla. Atlantic U., 2002—. Author: Learning Performance and Individual Differences, 1972, Contract Counseling, 1974, You Can Make It Happen: Self-Actualization and Organization, 1977, Together Experience, 1978, Aderian Counseling and Psychotherapy, 1987, Psychiatric Case Formulations, 1992, Psychopathology and Psychotherapy, 1993, 2d edit., 1996, Psychiatric Consultation in the Workplace, 1993, Handbook of Diagnosis and Treatment of DSM-IV Personality Disorders, 1995, Psychopharmacology and Psychotherapy, 1995, Treatment Outcomes in Psychotherapy and Psychiatric Interventions, 1996, Aging in the 21st Century, 1996, Family Therapy: Ensuring Treatment Efficacy, 1997, The Disordered Couple, 1997, The Intimate Couple, 1998, Brief Therapy Strategies with Individuals and Couples, 2000, Ministry and Community, 2000, Integrative and Biopsychosocial Therapies, 2000, Spirituality in Clinical Practice, 2001, Transforming Self and Community,

2002, Effective Leader, 2002, Becoming an Effective Therapist, 2003, Becoming an Effective Health Care Manager, 2003, Sec, Priestly Ministry and the Church, 2003, Couple and Family Assessment, 2004, Executive Coaching, 2004; contbr. articles to profl. jours. Bd. dirs. Am. Coun. on Sci. and Health, Nat. Acad. for Certified Family Therapists, St. Camillus Health Ctr., 1996-2000; cons. dir. Staff Devel. Am. Appraisal Assn., Milw., 1972-76. Northwestern U. fellow, 1969, Med. Coll. Wis. grantee, 1981. Fellow APA (Harry Levinson award 1998), Am. Psychiat. Assn. (chair com. on psychiatry in workplace 1993—), Am. Coll. Preventive Medicine, Am. Coll. Psychiatrists, Am. Bd. Profl. Psychology, Am. Bd. Psychiatry and Neurology, Acad. Orgnl. and Occupational Psychiatry (v.p. 1993-96, Alan McLean lifetime achievement award 2000), Group for Advancement of Psychiatry, Coalition for Family Diagnosis. Avocations: reading, racquet sports, music. Office: Barry Univ 11300 NE Second Ave Miami Shores FL 33161-6695 E-mail: lsperry@mail.barry.edu.

SPERRY, MARTIN JAY, lawyer; b. Troy, N.Y., May 15, 1947; s. Raymond Leon and Selma (Jenkins) S.; m. Faith S. Sperry; children: Jana, Douglas, Jill. BSBA, U. Fla., 1969, JD, 1971. Bar: Fla. 1972, U.S. Dist. Ct. (mid. dist.) Fla. 1972, U.S. Dist. Ct. (so. dist.) Fla. 1974, U.S. Supreme Ct. 1976, N.Y. 1983. Sr. law clk. to chief judge U.S. Dist. Ct. (mid. dist.) Fla., Orlando, 1972-74; ptnr. Carey, Dwyer, Cole, Selwood & Bernard, Ft. Lauderdale, Fla., 1974-78, Krathen & Sperry, Ft. Lauderdale, Fla., 1978-84, Selwood & Sperry, Ft. Lauderdale, Fla., 1984-85, Sperry, Shapiro & Kashi, Ft. Lauderdale, Fla., 1985—. Mem. Fourth Dist. Ct. Appeals Judicial Nominating Commn., 1996-2000. Contbg. author: Casebook of Florida Constitutional Law, 1971. Served as capt. U.S. Army Reserves, 1969-77. Mem. Acad. Fla. Trial Lawyers (diplomate), Assn. Trial Lawyers Am. (sustaining), N.Y. State Bar Assn., Fla. Bar Assn. (bd. cert. civil trial lawyer), Fed. Bar Assn., Nat. Bd. Trial Advs. (cert. civil trial adv.), Am. Bd. Trial Advocates, Am. Inns of Ct. Lodges: B'nai B'rith. Democrat. Jewish. Avocations: sports, travel. Office: 1776 N Pine Island Rd Ste 324 Plantation FL 33322 Office Phone: 954-423-6553. E-mail: msperry@ssklawgroup.com.

SPERZEL, GEORGE E., JR., former personal care industry executive; b. 1951; BS in Bus. Adminstrn./Mgmt., U. Louisville, 1977. With General Electric Co., 1977-93; v.p., CFO Andrew Jergens Co., Cin., 1993-2000, Kao Am. Inc., Wilmington, Del., 1995-2000; svp and CFO Alliant Exchange, Inc., 2000—. Office: Alliant Food Service 9933 Woods Dr Skokie IL 60077-1057

SPETH, CAMILLE, engineer; b. Midvale, Utah, Aug. 24, 1956; d. Gerald L. and Dora (Goff) S. Grad. high sch., Indpls. Systems coord. Allied Fidelity, Indpls., 1984-85; bus. analyst EDS/MIC, Detroit, 1985-91; local area network adminstr. EDS/GMAC, Detroit, 1991-97; network engr. Elec. Data Systems, Corydon, Ind., 1997—. Author: (manuals) V4 Users Guide, 1985, Genealogy Training Manual, 1990, Network Users Guide, 1992, Site Administration Manual, 1997. Leader Ch. Young Women Camp, 1975-85, coach sports program, 1975-85. Mem. NAFE, Ind. High Sch. Athletic Assn. (high sch. sports referee 1976—), Netware Users Internat. Avocations: music, golf, woodworking. Home and Office: 1970 Lears Ln NE Corydon IN 47112-7657 E-mail: camispeth@earthlink.net.

SPETH, GERALD LENNUS, education and business consultant; b. Logan, Utah, July 14, 1934; s. Fredrick William and Elizabeth LaVern (Nuttall) S.; m. Dora Goff, Aug. 11, 1955; children: Camille, Michael Gerald, Mark Alan, Janell, Doreen. BS, Utah State U., 1956; MBA, Ind. U., 1969; EdD, Ball State U., 1988. Auditor Ernst & Ernst, Salt Lake City, 1956, 58-59; officer 1st and 2d lt. U.S. Army, 1956-58, officer capt. to col., 1959-82; controller Columbia Club, Indpls., 1982-83; sr. v.p. Allied Fidelity Corp., Indpls., 1983-85; adj. faculty Ind. Cen. U., Indpls., 1982-85; prof., dir. grad. bus. progs. U. Indpls., 1985-2001. Cons. in field. Counselor in stake presidency, bishop, area welfare dir., mission pres., high councilor LDS Ch., 1965—. Decorated Legion of Merit, Bronze Star medal. Mem. Am. Soc. Mil. Comptrollers, U.S. Govt. Accts. Assn., Beta Gamma Sigma, Sigma Iota Epsilon, Alpha Kappa Psi, Kappa Delta Psi, Delta Mu Delta. Home: 8337 Goldfinch Cir Indianapolis IN 46256-1629 Office: U Indpls 1400 E Hanna Ave Indianapolis IN 46227-3630 Business E-Mail: speth@uindy.edu.

SPETH, JAMES GUSTAVE, dean, environmental studies educator, lawyer; b. Orangeburg, S.C., Mar. 4, 1942; s. James Gustave and Amelia St. Clair (Albergotti) S.; m. Caroline Cameron Council, July 3, 1965; children: Catherine Council, James Gustave, Charles Council. BA summa cum laude, Yale U., 1964, LLB, 1969; MLitt, Oxford U., 1966; LLD (hon.), Clark U., 1995; MSE (hon.), Coll. of the Atlantic, 2001. Bar: D.C. 1969. Law clk. to Justice Hugo L. Black U.S. Supreme Ct., 1969-70; sr. staff atty. Natural Resources Def. Council, Washington, 1970-77; mem. Council Environ. Quality, Washington, 1977-79, chmn., 1979-81; prof. law Georgetown U. Law Ctr., Washington, 1981-82; pres. World Resources Inst., Washington, 1982-93; adminstr. UN Devel. Program, N.Y.C., 1993-99; dean, prof. Yale Sch. Forestry and Environ. Studies Yale U., 1999—. Founded World Resources Inst.; organized Western Hemisphere Dialogue environ. and devel., 1990; chaired U.S. Task Force internat. devel. and environ. security. Contbr. articles to profl. jours.; speaker in field. Bd. dirs. World Resources Inst., Nat. Resources Def. Coun., Woods Hole Rsch. Ctr., Keystone Ctr., Leadership award 1994. Recipient Resources Def. award Nat. Wildlife Fedn., 1976, Barbara Swain award of honor Nat. Resources Coun. Am., 1992, Environ. Law Inst. Lifetime Achievement award, 1999, Blue Planet prize, 2002; named to Global 500 Honor Role UN Environ. Program, 1988; Rhodes scholar, 1964-66. Mem. Coun. on Fgn. Rels. (N.Y.C.). Episcopalian. Home: 88 Mulberry Farms Rd Guilford CT 06437-3215 E-mail: gus.speth@yale.edu.

SPETRINO, RUSSELL JOHN, retired utility company executive, lawyer; b. Cleve., Apr. 22, 1926; s. John Anthony and Madeline Spetrino; m. Marilyn Folk, July 17, 1954 (dec.); children: Michael J., Ellen A. Spetrino Raines; m. Mildred Pilkton, June 26, 1993. BS, Ohio State U., 1950; LL.B., Western Res. U., 1954. Bar: Ohio 1954. Asst. atty. gen., Ohio, 1954-57; atty.-examiner Public Utilities Commn. of Ohio, Columbus, 1957-59; atty. Ohio Edison Co., Akron, 1959-69, sr. atty., 1970-73, gen. counsel, 1973-78, v.p., gen. counsel, 1978-87, exec. v.p., gen. counsel, 1987-89, ret., 1989. Served with inf. U.S. Army, 1944-46. Mem. Portage Country Club. Republican. Home: 6075 Pelican Bay Blvd 104 Naples FL 34108-8170 E-mail: rspetrino@aol.com. *The importance of— and the strength that can be derived from— simple intellectual honesty never ceases to amaze me. It is so much easier to deal successfully with others when every effort is made to understand their views, and your own views are based upon thoughtful, honest conviction.*

SPEVACK, MARVIN, English educator; b. N.Y.C., Dec. 17, 1927; s. Nathan and Miriam (Propper) S.; m. Helga Husmann, May 28, 1962; 1 child, Edmund Daniel. BA, CCNY, 1948; MA, Harvard U., 1950, PhD, 1953. Instr. English CCNY, 1955-61; asst. prof. City Coll. N.Y., 1961-63; prof. English, U. Muenster, Germany, 1963-89, dir. English seminar, 1964-89, dir. Inst. Erasmianum, 1974-89; Fulbright lectr. U. Münster, Germany, 1961-62. Vis. prof. U. Munich, 1962-63, NYU, summer 1966, Harvard U., summer 1973, U. N.Mex., 1985-86, Bowling Green State U., fall 1989; fellow Folger Shakespeare Libr., 1970, 98; hon. rsch. fellow Univ. Coll., London, 1980-81, 94—; vis. fellow Wolfson Coll., Cambridge (Eng.) U., 1984; scholar-in-residence Ctr. for Renaissance and Baroque Studies, U. Md., spring 1989; vis. rsch. fellow Inst. for Advanced Studies in Humanities, U. Edinburgh, Scotland, 1991. Author: Harvard Concordance to Shakespeare, 1973, A Complete and Systematic Concordance to the Works of Shakespeare, 9 vols., 1968-80, Robert Burton, Philosophaster, 1984, Shakespeare: The second, Third, and Fourth Folios, 1985, New Cambridge Julius Caesar, 1988, Shakespeare-Text, Language and Criticism: Essays in Honor of Marvin Spevack, 1988, New Variorum Antony and Cleopatra, 1990, A Shakespeare Thesaurus, 1993, James Orchard Halliwell- Phillipps: A Classified Bibliography, 1997, A Victorian Chronicle: The Diary of Henrietta Halliwell-Phillipps, 1999, James Orchard Halliwell-Phillipps: The Life and Works of the Shakespearean Scholar and Bookman, 2001, Isaac D'Israeli on Books: Pre-Victorian Essays on the History of Literature, 2004; also articles and editions. Served with AUS, 1953-55. Guggenheim fellow, 1973-74, Andrew W. Mellon Found. fellow Huntington Libr., 1992, Ctr. for Book fellow Brit. Libr., London, 1994-95. Mem. MLA, Internat. Assn. Univ. Profs. English, Internat. Shakespeare Assn., The Bibliog. Soc., Deutsche Shakespeare Gesellschaft W., Shakespeare Assn., Soc. Textual Scholarship, Harvard Club (N.Y.C.), Harvard of Rhein-Ruhr Club (Germany), Phi Beta Kappa. Home: 14 Potstiege 48161 Münster Germany Office: 12-20 Johannisstrasse 48143 Münster Germany

SPEYER, JAMES L. oncologist; b. Flushing, NY, July 26, 1948; MD, Johns Hopkins U., 1974. Cert. Internal Medicine 1977, Hematology 1978, Med. Oncology 1979. Intern NY Presbyn. Hosp., N.Y.C., 1974—75, resident in medicine, 1975—76, resident in hematology, 1976—77; fellow Nat. Cancer Inst., Bethesda, Md., 1977—79; assoc. dir. clin. affairs NYU Cancer Inst., N.Y.C., 1998—, assoc. dir. clin. and hosp. ops., 2003—; prof. clin. medicine NYU, N.Y.C., 1980—, prof. medicine, 2002—. Office: NYU Cancer Inst 530 1st Ave New York NY 10016-6402 Business E-Mail: james.speyer@med.nyu.edu.

SPEYER, JERRY I. real estate company executive; b. 1941; BA, Columbia Coll., 1962; MBA, Columbia U., 1964. Sr. v.p., dir. Tishman Realty & Construction Co., Inc., co-founder, pres., CEO Tishman Speyer Properties, N.Y.C., 1978—. Chmn. emeritus Columbia U., Real Estate Board of NY; bd. mem. Federal Reserve Bank of NY, YankeeNets, Rand Corp., Carnegie Hall, Real Estate Roundtable, Urban Land Inst.; mem. Council on Foreign Relations, Economic Club of NY. Vice chmn. Museum of Modern Art, NY Presbyterian Hospital; co-chair NYC Partnership. Office: Tishman Speyer Properties 520 Madison Ave New York NY 10022 Office Phone: 212-715-0300.*

SPEZIALE, JOHN ALBERT, lawyer; b. Winsted, Conn., Nov. 21, 1922; s. Louis and Mary (Avampato) S.; m. Mary Kocsis, Aug. 12, 1944; children: John Albert, Marcia Jean. BA in Econs., Duke U., 1943, JD, 1947. Bar: Conn. 1948. Clk. Judiciary Com. of Conn. Gen. Assembly, 1949; judge Mcpl. Ct., Torrington, Conn., 1949-51; dir. CD, 1951-52; fed. atty. OPS, 1951-52; mem. Conn. State Jud. Council, 1955-59; sr. partner firm Speziale, Mettling, Lefebre & Burns, Torrington, 1958-61; city atty. Torrington, 1957-59; treas. State of Conn., 1959—61; judge Conn. Ct. Common Pleas, 1961-65, Conn. Superior Ct., 1965-77; presiding judge Conn. Superior Ct. (Appellate div.), 1975-77, chief judge, 1975-77, mem. exec. com., 1975-84, chmn. exec. com., 1977-81; justice Conn. Supreme Ct., 1977-81, chief ct. adminstr., 1978-81, chief justice, 1981-84; sr. ptnr. Cummings & Lockwood, Hartford, 1984-92; of counsel Hartford, 1992—2003, Stamford, Conn., 2003—. Atty. trial referee Conn., 1986—; mem. exec. com. Nat. Conf. State Trial Judges, 1970-74; faculty advisor grad. session Nat. Coll. State Judiciary, U. Nev., 1973; mem. Conn. Jud. Rev. Coun., 1975-77; co-chmn. planning commn. criminal adminstrn. Conn. Justice Commn., 1975-78; mem. Conn. Commn. on Adult Probation, 1976-77, Adv. Coun. on Ct. Unification, 1976-78, Conn. Bd. Pardons, 1977-78; mem. exec. com. Nat. Bd. Trial Advocacy, 1983-88, dir. 1988—; mem. mediation com. Ctr. Pub. Resources, 1985—; chmn. State-Fed. Rels. Com. Conf. of Chief Justices, 1983-84; chmn. adv. bd. Use of Vol. Lawyers to Supplement Jud. Resources, Nat. Inst. Justice and Nat. Ctr. for State Ctrs., 1983-87; mem. lawyers com. Nat. Ctr. for State Cts., 1985-88; chmn. subcom. jud. decisions Nat. Assn. Ins. Commrs. Adv. Coun. Environ. Liability Ins., 1985-87; mem. Panel of Trial and Appellate Judges, Asbestos Claims Facility, 1986—; arbitrator Ins. Arbitration Forums, Inc., 1986—, others. Trustee Conn. Jr. Republic, 1975-83; bd. dirs. Newington Children's Hosp. 1983-86, corporator 1983—; chmn. awards com. Freedoms Found. at Valley Forge, 1982, trustee Nat. Council, 1986—; fellow Pvt. Adjudication Found. Duke U. Sch. Law, 1986—. Lt. (j.g.) USNR, 1942-46, PTO. Recipient Conn. Trial Lawyers Jud. award, 1977; 1st Unico Nat. Disting. Key award, 1977; Citizen of Yr. award Elks, 1982; Alva P. Loiselle lifetime achievement award, 1984; Disting. Service award Nat. Ctr. for State Cts., 1985; Significant Practical Achievement award Ctr. for Pub. Resources Legal Program, 1985; Conn. Law Rev. award, 1985. Fellow Am. Bar Found. (life), Conn. Bar Found. (charter life fellow, chmn. James W. Cooper fellows 1994-97, John A. Speziale Symposia named in his honor); mem. ABA (vice chmn. 1984-86, com. on stds. jud. adminstrn. jud. adminstrn. divsn.), Inst. Jud. Adminstrn., Am. Judicature Soc. (dir. 1978-82), Conn. Bar Assn. (com. on alternative dispute resolution 1985-87, com. on liaison with state cts. 1986-92), Hartford Bar Assn., Litchfield County Bar Assn., Supreme Ct. Hist. Soc., Am. Arbitration Assn. (comml. panel arbitrators 1987-2001, panelist large complex case program 1993-2001), Am. Fedn. Musicians (life), Sons of Italy of Am., Conn. State Srs. Golf Assn., Inc., Litchfield County Univ. Club, Torrington Country Club, Unico Club (life), Bear Lakes Country Club (Fla.), K.C., Phi Beta Kappa. Roman Catholic. Home: 278 Windtree St Torrington CT 06790-7904 Office: Cummings & Lockwood 107 Elm St Stamford CT 06902 Office Phone: 203-351-4202. Personal E-mail: judgespeziale@aol.com.

SPHIRE, RAYMOND DANIEL, anesthesiologist, educator; b. Detroit, Feb. 12, 1927; s. Samuel Raymond and Nora Mae (Allen) S.; m. Joan Lois Baker, Sept. 5, 1953; children— Suzanne M., Raymond Daniel, Catherine J. BS, U. Detroit, 1948; MD, Loyola U., Chgo., 1952. Diplomate Am. Bd. Anesthesiology. Intern Grace Hosp., Detroit, 1952-53; resident Harvard Anesthesia Lab.-Mass. Gen. Hosp., 1953-55; attending anesthesiologist Grace Hosp., Detroit, 1955-72, dir. dept. inhalation therapy, 1968-70; sr. attending anesthesiologist, dir. dept., dir. dept. respiratory therapy Detroit-Macomb Hosps. Assn., 1970—, trustee, 1978—, chief of staff, 1980—. Clin. asst. prof. Wayne State U. Sch. Medicine, 1967—; clin. prof. respiratory therapy Macomb Community Coll., Mount Clemens, Mich., 1971—; examiner Am. Registry Respiratory Therapists, 1972—; insp. Joint Rev. Com. Respiratory Therapy Edn., 1972— Co-author: Operative Neurosurgery, 1970, First Aid Guide for the Small Business or Industry, 1978 With AUS, 1944-45; 1st lt. M.C., USAF, 1952 Fellow Am. Coll. Anesthesiologists, Am. Coll. Chest Physicians; mem. AMA, Am. Soc. Anesthesiologists, Wayne County Soc. Anesthesiologists (pres. 1967-69), Am. Assn. Respiratory Therapists, Soc. Critical Care Medicine, Country Club of Detroit, Grosse Pointe Club, Cumberland Club (Portland, Maine), Severance Lodge. Roman Catholic. Home: 19874 Westchester Dr Clinton Township MI 48038-6417 Office: 119 Kercheval Ave Grosse Pointe MI 48236-3696

SPICER, HAROLD OTIS, retired English language educator, communications educator; b. Gosport, Ind., Dec. 10, 1921; s. Otis R. and Hattie Grace (Wampler) S.; m. Hilda Jane Templeton, June 12, 1946 (dec. Nov. 1994); children: Sherry Lynne (dec. May 1987), Sylvia Jean, Stephen Michael, Zachary Ian. BA, DePauw U., 1947, MA, 1949; PhD, Ind. U., 1962. Instr. English DePauw U., Greencastle, Ind., 1947-49, asst. prof. English, 1957-63; from instr. to prof. English We. Ill. U., Macomb, 1949-57; adj. prof. English Ind. U., Indpls., 1960-63; assoc. prof. to prof. English Ind. State U., Terre Haute, 1963-85; ret., 1985. Sec. Main Street, Greencastle, 1993-95. Author: Covered Bridges of Putnam County, 1989, Organizational Handbook for Council on Aging, 1989 (Ameritech Tchr. Vol. award 1989), James Whitcomb Riley: Hoosier Poet, 1993; co-author: DePauw: Pictorial History, 1987; editor Ten O'Clock News, a museum newsletter, 2003—; author, narrator, interviewer 20th Century Golden Memories, 2001-02. Pres. Ret. Tchrs. Putnam County, Greencastle, 1988-90, Putnam County Coun. on Aging, 1990-96 (Man of Yr. award 1994); bd. dirs. Heritage Preservation Soc., Greencastle, 1993—, Putnam County Found., 1995-2002, sec., 2000-2003; pres. West Ctrl. Ind. Area Agy. on Aging, 2000. Recipient Danforth Tchr. grant, 1959, Man of Yr. award Area 7 Agy. on Aging West Ctrl. Ind. Econ. Devel. Dist., Terre Haute, 1994; named Older Hoosier of Yr. Ind. Gov.'s Conf., Indpls., 1994, RSVP Vol. of Yr., 1995, Ameritech Vol. Tchr. of Yr., 1989, Martin H. Miller Vol. of Yr. award Ind. Family and Social Svcs. Adminstrn., 1999, Outstanding Leadership award in area/agy. on aging Ind. Assn. Area Agys. on Aging, 2000. Life mem. VFW; mem. Am. Legion, Am. Assn. Retired Persons (pres. Putnam County chpt. 1995-96, 99—2002), Greencastle C. of C. (Putnam County Citizen of Yr. 1996, bd. dirs. 1995-99), West Ctrl. Ind. Civil War Roundtable (v.p. 1998-2000), Kiwanis Club Greencastle. Avocations: music, writing, travel. Home: 706 Highwood Ave Greencastle IN 46135-1420 E-mail: halos@ccrtc.com.

SPICER, HOLT VANDERCOOK, retired speech and theater educator; b. Pasadena, Calif., Feb. 1, 1928; s. John Lovely and Dorothy Eleanor (Clause) S.; m. Marion Arel Gibson, Aug. 16, 1952; children: Mary Ellen, Susan Leah, Laura Alice, John Millard. BA, U. Redlands, 1952, MA, 1957; PhD, U. Okla., 1964. From instr. speech and theatre to prof. S.W. Mo. State Coll., 1952-93, emeritus prof., 1993—, head dept. speech and theatre, 1967-71, dean Sch. Arts and Humanities, 1971-85. Chmn. Dist. 4 Nat. Debate Tournament Com., 1955, 58, 64, 68 Vestryman Episcopalian Ch., 1981—85, 1998—2001; bd. dirs. Springfield (Mo.) Cmty. Ctr., 1981—. Named Debate Coach of Decade U.S. Air Force Acad., 1965, Holt V. Spicer Debate Forum, 1988; recipient Alumni Achievement award in Speech and Debate U. Redlands, 1991, Alumni award of appreciation S.W. Mo. State U., 1996; team won CEDA Nat. Debate championship, 1992. Mem.: AAUP, Am. Forensic Assn., Speech Communication Assn. Episcopalian. Home: 2232 E Langston St Springfield MO 65804-2646 E-mail: holtspicer9@mchsi.com.

SPICER, MICHAEL E. lab administrator; BS in Acctg., U. Va.; MBA, Harvard U. CPA. Fin. and acctg. White River Corp., The Chinet Co., Kraft Gen. Foods, Deloitte & Touche; v.p., fin. Orchid BioScis., Inc., Princeton, NJ, 2001, v.p., fin., CFO. Office: Orchid BioScis Inc 4390 US Rte 1 Princeton NJ 08540*

SPICER, RONALD L. financial services educator; b. Louisville, Jan. 21, 1949; s. Robert Joseph and Ann (Stafford) S.; m. Joan E. Vining, Dec. 20, 1969 (div. June 1988); children: Jennifer Joan Spicer McMullen, Ronald Geoffrey; m. JoAnn F. Snyder, Feb. 18, 1989; 1 child, Veronica Michelle. BS in Psychology and Sociology, Carroll Coll., 1971; MA in Orgn. Mgmt., U. Phoenix, 1997; MBA in Bus., Regis U., 1999; postgrad., Capella U., 2000—. CPCU, CLU, CHFC, ARM. V.p. sales Alexander & Alexander, Atlanta, 1982-88; exec. v.p. Powell and Co., Atlanta, 1988-89; v.p. sales Corroon and Black, Balt., 1989-90; broker, owner Profl. Ins. Brokers, York, Pa., 1990-93; sr. account exec. Hilb, Rogal and Hamilton, Denver, 1993-95; ins. program coord. Pikes Peak C.C., Colorado Springs, 1995-97; pres., CEO Peak Profl. Svcs., Inc., Colorado Springs, 1997—, owner, 1997—. Adv. com. Ins. Inst. of Am., Malvern, Pa., 1995—; mem. next generation com., Life and Health Ins. Edn. Assn., N.Y.C., 1996-97. Author: (book) Colorado P&C PreLicense Course, 1998, Colorado Life and Health Pre-License Course, 1999; contbr. articles to profl. jours. Mem. Soc. CPCU (Pikes Peak chpt. pres. 1998-99, pres. 1999-2000), Soc. Fin. Svc. Profls. (Pikes Peak chpt. pres. 2000-01), Optimist (pres. Uptown Club 1979-81), Masons. Republican. Episcopal. Lutheran. Avocations: skiing, camping, scuba diving. Office: Peak Profl Svcs Inc 953 Bayfield Way Colorado Springs CO 80906 E-mail: ronspicer3@aol.com.

SPICER, SUSAN, food service executive; Apprentice to Chef Daniel Bonnot Louis XVI Restaurant, New Orleans, 1979; chef under Chef Ronald Durand Hotel Sofitel, Paris, 1982; owner, chef de cuisine Savoir Faire bistro, New Orleans, 1982; cons. chef to Marc Haeberlin of l'Auberge de l'Ill Meridien Hotel, New Orleans, 1985—86; owner, chef Bistro at Maison deVille, New Orleans, 1986—90; ptnr., chef Bayona, New Orleans, 1990—. Guest chef James Beard Ho., Cunard's Sea Goddess, Oriental Hotel, Bangkok. Recipient James Beard award, Best Chef, Southeast Region, 1993, Mondavi Culinary Excellence award, 1995, Ivy award, Restaurant and Instn. mag., 1996, 5 Beans award, New Orleans Times Picayune, 1996. Office: Bayona 430 Dauphine St New Orleans LA 70112

SPICKNALL, JOAN, music educator; b. Arlington, Va., Feb. 13, 1942; d. Joseph Richard and Rhoda Louise (Beran) Singer; m. Marvin Herbert Spitz, Dec. 12, 1992; children from previus marriage: Lisa Sharon Spicknall Fruth, Richard Mark Spicknall. B of Mus, Peabody Conservatory, 1962, MusM, 1963; D of Musical Arts, U.Md., 1974. Grad. asst. U. Md., College Park, 1966-69; asst. prof. St. Mary of the Woods (Ind.) Coll., 1971-83; instr. piano pvt. practice, Columbia, Md., 1983-88; instr. Essex C.C., Balt., 1983-84, Loyola Coll., Balt., 1983-84, Howard C.C., Columbia, 1983-86; pres., dir. Suzuki Music Sch. Md., Inc., Columbia, 1988—. Adj. prof. Rose-Hulman Inst. Tech., Terre Haute, Ind., 1973-83; piano tchr. Howard County Schs., 1986—; guest faculty, lectr. nat. and internat. music convs., 1991-. Pianist (new 2 CD album): The Piano Music of Aaron Copland, 2004; contbr. articles to profl. articles, newspapers, jours., and mags. Mem. MTNA, SAA, Inc., ISA, AAUW, SAGWA, MENC, CMS, People to People Amb. Programs, Music Educator's Dels., Mu Phi Epsilon, Delta Kappa Gamma. Home: 10659 Green Mt Cir Columbia MD 21044 Office: Suzuki Music Sch Md Inc PO Box 1284 Columbia MD 21044-0284 E-mail: director@suzukimusicschool.com.

SPIEGEL, ALLEN, federal agency administrator, internist; MD cum laude, Harvard Med. Sch., 1971. Intern and resident in internal medicine Mass. Gen. Hosp., Boston; mem. Nat. Inst. Diabetes and Digestive and Kidney Disease's Endocrinology Rsch. Tng. Program; sr. investigator Metabolic Diseases Branch; scientific dir., clinical physiology Nat. Inst. Diabetes and Digestive and Kidney Disease, 1974—79, branch chief, Lab. of Immunoregulation, 1980—; chief of molecular pathophysiology section Metabolic Diseases Branch, 1985—88; dir. Nat. Inst. Diabetes and Digestive and Kidney Diseases, 1984—. Recipient Jacobaeus prize, Novo Nordisk Insulin Found., 1990, Komrower Meml. Lecture award, Soc. for the Study of Inborn Errors of Metabolism, 1996, Edwin B. Astwood Lecture award, Endocrine Soc., 1998. Office: Nat Inst of Diabetes and Digestive and Kidney Diseases 31 Center Dr Rm 9A04 Bethesda MD 20892*

SPIEGEL, DAVID, psychiatrist; b. N.Y.C., Dec. 11, 1945; s. Herbert Spiegel and Natalie Shainess; m. Helen Margaret Blau, July 25, 1976; children: Daniel, Julia. BA, Yale Coll., 1967; MD, Harvard Med. Sch., 1971. Lic. psychiatrist Calif., Mass., N.Y.; diplomate Am. Bd. Med. Examiners, Am. Bd. Psychiatry and Neurology. Resident Mass. Mental Health Ctr. and Cambridge Hosp., 1971-74; resident tutor, premedical advisor Winthrop House Harvard Coll., Cambridge, Mass., 1972-74; clin. instr. Stanford (Calif.) U. Sch. Med., 1974-75; staff psychiatrist San Mateo (Calif.) County Mental Health Program, 1974-75; from acting asst. prof. to prof. psychiatry/behavioral scis. Stanford U. Sch. Med., 1975-94, Jack, Lulu and Sam Willson prof., 2002—. Chief brief treatment inpatient unit Palo Alto Vets. Adminstrn. Med. Ctr., Calif., 1975-76; dir. social psychiatry cmty. svcs. Palo Alto Vets. Adminstrn., 1976-80; dir. psychiatry clinic Stanford U. Med. Ctr., 1980-89, assoc. dir. psychiat inpatient therapeutic cmty. 1981-83, assoc. chair psychiatry, med. dir. Ctr. for Integrative Medicine, 1997—; med. dir. Stanford U. Clinic, 1986-87; assoc. rsch. psychiatrist U. Calif., San Francisco, 1986-91; dir. Ctr. on Stress and Health Stanford U. Med. Ctr., 2001—. Editor: Progress in Psychiatry Series, 1984—, mem. editl. bd., 1986-89; med. co-editor: Internat. Jour. Clin. Exptl. Hypnosis, 1988-95; assoc. editor: Am. Jour. Clin. Hypnosis, 1985—, Am. Jour. Psychiatry, 1991-95, The Breast, 1994—; consulting editor: Health Psychology, 1990-91; mem. editl. bd.: Jour. of Psychosocial Oncology, 1983—, Jour. Traumatic Stress, 1986-90, Dissociation, 1988—, Psycho Oncology, 1991, Consciousness and Cognition, 1991—, Health Psychology, 1992, Columbia U. Sch. Pub. Health Newsletter, 1994—. Mem. data processing policy com. Dept. Mental Health, Mass., 1972-73, bd. dirs. No. Calif. Burn Coun., 1976-84; pub. mem. Chief Justice's Spl. Com. to Study Appellate Practices in First Appellate Dist., 1977-81. Recipient Treya Killam Wilber award Cancer Support Cmty, 1993, Pierre Janet Writing award Internat. Soc. for Study Dissociation, 1994, Edward A. Strecker, M.D. award The Inst. of Pa. Hosp. and Jefferson Med. Coll., 1995; 8th Annual Chrysalis Gala honoree CHEMOcare, 1993. Fellow Am. Coll. Psychiatry, Am. Psychiat. Assn. (Marmor award, 2004), Am. Soc. Clin. Hypnosis, Am. Psychiat. Assn., Assn. for Clin. Psychosocial Rsch., Soc. Behavioral Medicine, Soc. for Clin. and Exptl. Hypnosis (pres. 1995-97, Schneck Strecker award 1996); mem. Urgent Action Network, Amnesty Internat, Am. Coll. Psychiatrists (pres. elect 2003-04). Office: Stanford U Sch Med 401 Quarry Rd Stanford CA 94305-5718

SPIEGEL, ELWYN, advertising agency executive, creative director; b. N.Y.C., Apr. 26, 1926; s. Morris and Rose Ann (Nemetzky) S.; m. Doris Kay, Apr. 25, 1954 (dec.); children: Elizabeth Ann Simendinger, Susan Gail Ambrose, Laura Faith Ciecierski. BSEE, N.C. State U., 1945; BS in Econs., Columbia U., 1950. Pres. Ad Infinitum, Inc., Hackensack, N.J., 1954-63; exec. v.p. Alden Advt. Agy., N.Y.C., 1964-81; pres. Spiegel/Labatt-Simon, Inc., N.Y.C., 1981-88, Compris, Inc., N.Y.C., 1989-96, Elwyn Spiegel & Ptnrs., N.Y.C., 1996—. Cons. in field. Creative dir. TV commls. including Colorforms, 1976 (Clio award, 1976), creative dir. (mag.) Russell Fabrics, 1981; author: Get a New Life, The Jackknife Gypsies. Judge, Clio Awards, N.Y.C., 1975. Recipient Silver award, Neographics 1977, Addy (4), Am. Advt. Fedn.,

1977-80, Desi (8), Graphics Design USA, 1981-82, Clio (3), Clio Adv. Bd., 1981. Mem. Nat. Trust for Hist. Preservation, Kiwanis (pres. 1954-55), Alpha Delta Sigma. Avocations: photography, music, sports cars, literature, writing. Office: Elwyn Spiegel & Ptnrs 325 E 41st St New York NY 10017-5955

SPIEGEL, EVELYN SCLUFER, biology professor; b. Phila., Mar. 20, 1924; d. George and Helen (Laurantos) Sclufer; m. Melvin Spiegel, Apr. 16, 1955; children: Judith Ellen, Rebecca Ann. BA, Temple U., 1947; MA, Bryn Mawr Coll., 1951; PhD, U. Pa., 1954. Asst. program dir. for regulatory biology NSF, Washington, 1954-55; instr. in biology Colby Coll., Waterville, Maine, 1955-59; rsch. assoc. Dartmouth Coll., Hanover, N.H., 1961-74, rsch. assoc. prof. biology, 1974-78, rsch. prof. biology, 1978-91; rsch. prof. biology emerita, 1991—. Vis. scholar Calif. Inst. Tech., Pasadena, 1964-65, U. Calif.-San Diego, La Jolla, 1970, Nat. Inst. for Med. Rsch., Mill Hill, Eng., 1971, NIH, Washington, 1975-76, U. Basel (Switzerland) Biocenter, 1979, 80, 81, 82, 85. Contbr. numerous articles to profl. jours., chpts. to books and book reviews. Mem. Soc. for Devel. Biology, Marine Biol. Lab. Corp. (trustee 1981-86, 88-92). Office: Dartmouth Coll Dept Biol Scis Hanover NH 03755

SPIEGEL, HERBERT, psychiatrist, educator; b. McKeesport, Pa., June 29, 1914; s. Samuel and Lena (Mendlowitz) S.; m. Natalie Shainess, Apr. 24, 1944 (div. Apr. 1965); children: David, Ann; m. Marcia Greenleaf, Jan. 29, 1989. BS, U. Md., 1936, MD, 1939. Diplomate Am. Bd. Psychiatry. Intern St. Francis Hosp., Pitts., 1939-40; resident in psychiatry St. Elizabeth's Hosp., Washington, 1940-42; practice medicine specializing in psychiatry N.Y.C., 1946—; attending psychiatrist Columbia-Presbyn. Hosp., N.Y.C., 1960—; faculty psychiatry Columbia U. Coll. Physicians and Surgeons, 1960—. Adj. prof. psychology John Jay Coll. Criminal Justice, CUNY, 1983-; mem. faculty Sch. Mil. Neuropsychiatry, Mason Gen. Hosp., Brentwood, N.Y., 1944-46. Author: (with A. Kardiner) War Stress and Neurotic Illness, 1947, (with D. Spiegel) Trance and Treatment: Clinical Uses of Hypnosis, 1978, 2d edit., 2004; subject of book: (by Donald S. Connery) The Inner Source: Exploring Hypnosis with Herbert Spiegel, M.D.; mem. edit. bd.: Preventive Medicine, 1972; Contbr. articles to profl. jours. Profl. advisory com. Am. Health Found.; pub. edn. com., smoking and health com. N.Y.C. div. Am. Cancer Soc.; adv. com. Nat. Aid to Visually Handicapped. Served with M.C. AUS, 1942-46. Decorated Purple Heart. Fellow Am. Psychiat. Assn., Am. Coll. Psychiatrists, Am. Soc. Clin. Hypnosis, Am. Acad. Psychoanalysis, Internat. Soc. Clin. and Exptl. Hypnosis, William A. White Psychoanalytic Soc., N.Y. Acad. Medicine, N.Y. Acad. Scis.; mem. Am. Orthopsychiat. Assn., Am. Psychosomatic Soc., AAAS, AMA, N.Y. County Med. Soc. Office: 19 E 88th St New York NY 10128-0557

SPIEGEL, JAYSON LESLIE, lawyer, organization executive; b. N.Y.C., Mar. 1, 1959; s. Jack and Frieda Rhoda (Michaelson) S.; m. Deborah Marie Scott, Nov. 1, 1986; children: Kyle Reid, Alicia Jean. AB, Georgetown U., 1980; JD, U. Va., 1983; postgrad., USMC Command and Staff Coll., 1991, Army Comd. & Gen. Staff Coll., 1996. Bar: Md. 1984, D.C. 1985, U.S. Ct. Appeals (D.C. cir.) 1986, U.S. Ct. Mil. Appeals 1987, U.S. Ct. Appeals (4th cir.) 1987, U.S. Supreme Ct. 1988, U.S. Ct. Claims 1990. Law clk. to assoc. judge Md. Ct. Appeals, Balt., 1983-84; assoc. Jordan, Coyne, Savits & Lopata, Washington, 1985-91, ptnr., 1991-94; dep. asst. sec. U.S. Army, 1994-99, acting asst. sec., 1997-98; exec. dir. Res. Officers Assn., 1999—2003; sr. nat. def. counsel Ball Janik, LLP, 2003—. Lectr. law and transfusion medicine NIH, 1989, 91-94. Contbr. articles to profl. jours. Mem. recreation adv. bd. Montgomery County, Md., 1989-93. With USAR, 1981—, Desert Shield/Desert Storm, 1990-91. Mem. ABA (young lawyers mem. com. on law and nat. security, vice chair internat. criminal law com. 1991-94), D.C. Bar Assn. (founder, chmn. com. on law and nat. security 1987-94, Com. Chmn. of Yr. 1988, 91), Md. Bar Assn., Mil. Coalition (bd. dirs. 1999—), Nat. Def. Indsl. Assn., Conf. of Def. Assn. (Can.), Res. Officers Assn. (life), U.S. C. of C. (com. of 100 assn. execs.), Army and Navy Club. Avocations: running, tennis. Business E-Mail: jspiegel@dc.bjllp.com.

SPIEGEL, JERROLD BRUCE, lawyer; b. N.Y.C., Apr. 11, 1949; s. Seymour S. and Estelle (Minsky) S.; m. Helene Susan Cohen, Mar. 3, 1972; children: Dana Sean, Amy Barrett, Evan Tyler. BS, Queens Coll., 1970; JD cum laude, NYU, 1973. Bar: N.Y. 1974. Assoc. Austrian, Lance & Stewart, N.Y.C., 1973-75, Gordon Hurwitz Butowsky Baker Weitzen & Shalov, N.Y.C., 1975-79; ptnr. Shapiro Spiegel Garfunkel & Driggin, N.Y.C., 1979-86, Frankfurt Kurnit Klein & Selz P.C., N.Y.C., 1986—. Editor Ann. Survey Am. Law, 1972-73, Mem. ABA (corp. law sect.), Order of the Coif, Omicron Delta Epsilon. Office: Frankfurt Kurnit Klein & Selz PC 488 Madison Ave Fl 9 New York NY 10022-5754 E-mail: jbspiegel@aol.com.

SPIEGEL, JOHN WILLIAM, banker; b. Indpls., Mar. 14, 1941; s. William Sordon and Elizabeth (Hall) S.; children: W. Robert, John F., Bradley H. BA, Wabash Coll., 1963; MBA, Emory U., 1965; postgrad., Nova Southeastern U., 1993—99. Rsch. assoc. IMEDE (Mgmt. Inst.), Lausanne, Switzerland, 1965-66; mgmt. trainee Trust Co. Bank, Atlanta, 1966-67, bond portfolio mgr., 1967-72; data processing mgr. Trust Co. Ga., Atlanta, 1972-78, treas., 1978-85; vice chmn., CFO SunTrust Banks Inc., Atlanta, 1985—. Mem. exec. com. CFO divsn. ABA, 1987-90, chair, 1989-90; former instr. Morehouse Coll. and Banking Schs.; bd. dirs. Bentley Pharms., Colonial Properties. Mem. exec. com., bd. dirs. Alliance Theatre, Atlanta, 1985—92, pres., 1989—91; bd. dirs. High Mus. Art, Atlanta, 1985—, chmn., 1997—98; founding pres. Young Audiences Atlanta, Inc., 1982—84, mem. adv. bd., 1985—; pres. bd. vis. Grady Meml. Hosp., 1983—90; v.p. exec. bd. Atlanta Area coun. Boy Scouts Am., 1983—92, treas., 1989—91, mem. adv. bd., 1992; mem. adv. coun. Ga. State U. Sch. Accountacy, 1981—85, chmn. curriculum subcom., 1983—84; mem. exec. com., trustee Morehouse Sch. Medicine, 1984—93, chmn. fin. com., 1987—90, chmn., 1990—92; mem. Leadership Atlanta, 1976—, trustee, 1990—94; trustee, mem. exec. com. Robert W. Woodruff Arts Ctr., Inc., 1976—2001, treas., 1976—83, chmn. fin. com., 1984—89, 1993—97, chmn., 1998—2001; chmn. fin. com., bd. dirs. Schenck Sch., 1986—88; exec. vice chmn. bd. trustees Holy Innocents Episcopal Sch., 1976—79, bd. dirs., treas., 1987—90; bd. dirs. Atlanta Opera, 1986—98, United Way Met. Atlanta, 1994—98, Rock Tenn. Co., 1989—, Sallie Mae, 1993—97, Suburban Lodges Am., Inc., 1999—2002; mem. bd. visitors Emory U., 1991—95; trustee ESR Children's Health Care System, Inc., 1997—, bd. dirs., 1999—; trustee Wabash Coll., 1997—99; mem. dean's adv. coun. Goizueta Bus. Sch., Emory U., 1994—; bd. dirs., chmn. fin. com. Am. Cardiovasc. Rsch. Inst., 2002—03; bd. dirs. and mem. exec. com. Atlanta Coll. Art, 2003—. Mem. Bank Adminstrn. Inst. (bd. dirs. 1987-92, 99-, rsch. oversight com. 1992-98, treas. 1999, chmn. 2000-03). Home: 3745 Randall Mill Rd NW Atlanta GA 30327-2747 Office: SunTrust Banks Inc 303 Peachtree St NE Atlanta GA 30308-3201

SPIEGEL, LAWRENCE HOWARD, advertising executive; b. NYC, Oct. 9, 1942; s. Melvin Arthur and Rose (Black) S.; m. Christy Mansfield; children from previous marriage: Robert, David. BA, NYU, 1963. Print buyer William Esty Co., N.Y.C., 1964-65, broadcast buyer, 1965-66; media planner Batten, Barton, Durstine & Osborn, Inc., N.Y.C., 1966-67, media supr., 1967-68, assoc. media dir., 1969-72, v.p., 1972-74; media group head Jack Tinker & Ptnrs., N.Y.C., 1968-69; v.p. Tracy-Locke, Dallas, 1974-80, sr. v.p., 1980-84, exec. v.p., 1984-89; prin. The Richards Group, Dallas, 1989—. Pres. Tex. Coun. Advt., 1991-97, Leading Agy. Network, 1997—; dir. Dream Fund, 1999—. Guest editor Mktg. and Media Decision mag., June 1982. Mem. Dallas Cable Bd., 1983-86; chmn. mktg. com. U. Tex., Dallas, 1984-89; pres. Cable Access Dallas, Inc., 1985-86; trustee Dallas Symphony Assn., 1978—; bd. dirs. Equest Inc., 1991-92, DREAM Fund, 1999—. Mem. Assn. Broadcasting Execs. Tex. (pres. 1975-76), Am. Women in Radio and TV, Inc. (bd. dirs. 1992-93). Republican. Avocations: skiing, sailing. Office: The Richards Group 8750 N Central Expy Ste 1200 Dallas TX 75231-6436 Office Phone: 214-891-5843.

SPIEGEL, LINDA F. lawyer; b. Bronx, NY, Mar. 13, 1953; d. Rubin E. and Edna (Zucker) S.; m. Paul Duboff, June 12, 1983; 1 child, Joshua Michael. AB, Barnard Coll., Columbia U., 1974; JD, Boston U., 1978. Bar: N.J. 1978, U.S. Dist. Ct. N.J. 1978, N.Y. 1980, U.S. Dist. Ct. (so. and ea. dists.) N.Y. 1980, U.S. Supreme Ct. 1982. Tax editor Prentice Hall, Englewood, N.J., 1978; pvt. practice, Hackensack, N.J., 1978-83, 88—; assoc. Friedman, Carney & Wilson, Newark, 1983-84; pvt. practice New Milford, N.J., 1984-85; assoc. LaFianza and Strull, Hackensack, 1985-87, ptnr., 1987-88. Instr. Inst. Legal Asst. and Paralegal Tng., Mahwah, NJ, 1978-81; chair Bergen County Youth Svcs. Commn., 2003-04. Spkr. Boy Scouts Am., Bergen, N.J., 1980; atty.-acct. divsn. United Jewish Cmty., River Edge, N.J., 1978—; trustee Women's Am. Orgn. Rehab. through Tng., 1987-88; chmn. Jean Robertson Women Lawyers Scholarship Found., Inc., 1987-94. Mem. ABA, Am. Arbitration Assn. (comml. and constrn. arbitator 1989—), N.J. Women Lawyers Assn., N.J. State Bar Assn., Bergen County Bar Assn. (trustee 1989-94, editor-in-chief Bergen Barrister 1991-94), Women Lawyers in Bergen County (pres. 1987-89, editor-in-chief newsletter 2003—), B'nai Brith. Democrat. Avocations: theater, tennis, swimming, square and country dancing. Office: 79 Main St Ste 1 Hackensack NJ 07601-7126 Office Phone: 201-489-1001. E-mail: lfsesq@aol.com. *Notable cases include: A.L. vs. P.A., 213 N.J. Super 391, 1986, cert. den 107, J.J. 110, 1987.*

SPIEGEL, MARILYN HARRIET, real estate executive; b. Bklyn., Apr. 3, 1935; d. Harry and Sadie (Oscher) Unger; m. Murray Spiegel, June 12, 1954; children: Eric Lawrence, Dana Cheryl Mann, Jay Barry. Grad. high sch., Bklyn. Exec. sec. S & W Paper Co., N.Y.C., 1954-58; salesperson Red Carpet Realtors, Los Alamitos, Calif., 1974-75, Coll. Park Realtors, Garden Grove, Calif., 1975-79; owner, broker S & S Properties, Los Alamitos, 1979—. Named Realtor of Yr., 1989. Mem. Calif. Assn. Realtors (bd. dirs. 1984—), West Orange County Bd. Realtors (bd. dirs. 1984—, 1st v.p. 1987, pres. 1988), Million Dollar Sales Club, Long Beach C. of C., Seal Beach C. of C., Orange County C. of C., Summit Orgn., Toastmasters (pres. founders group Garden Grove, 1990). Home: 1371 Oakmont Rd Apt 150D Seal Beach CA 90740-3732 Office: S & S Properties 3502 Katella Ave Ste 208 Los Alamitos CA 90720-3130

SPIEGEL, MELVIN, retired biology educator; b. N.Y.C., Dec. 10, 1925; s. Philip Edward and Sadie (Friedman) S.; m. Evelyn Sclufer, Apr. 16, 1955; children: Judith Ellen, Rebecca Ann. BS, U. Ill., 1948; PhD, U. Rochester, 1952; MA (hon.), Dartmouth Coll., 1967. Research fellow U. Rochester, 1952-53, Calif. Inst. Tech., 1953-55, 64-65; asst. prof. Colby Coll., 1955-59; mem. faculty Dartmouth Coll., Hanover, N.H., 1959—, prof. biology, 1966-93; prof. emeritus Dartmouth Coll, Hanover, N.H.; chmn. dept. biol. scis. Dartmouth Coll., Hanover, N.H., 1972-74. Summer investigator Marine Biol. Lab., Woods Hole, Mass., 1954—; sr. rsch. biologist U. Calif.-San Diego, 1970-71; vis. prof. biochemistry Nat. Inst. Med. Rsch., Mill Hill, London, 1971; vis. prof. Biocenter, U. Basel, 1979-82, 85; Wilson Meml. lectr. U. N.C., 1975; program dir. developmental biology NSF, 1975-76; mem. cell biology study sect. NIH, 1966-70 Editl. bd.: Biol. Bull., 1966-70, 71-75, Cell Differentiation, 1979-88; contbr. articles to profl. jours. Trustee Marine Biol. Lab. Corp.; mem. exec. com., trustee Marine Biol. Lab., 1976-80. Fellow AAAS; mem. Am. Soc. Cell Biology, Am. Soc. Devel. Biology, Internat. Soc. Devel. Biologists (sec.-treas. 1977-81, bd. dirs. 1981-85). Home: 15 Barrymore Rd Hanover NH 03755-2401 Office Phone: 603-646-2324. E-mail: melvin.spiegel@dartmouth.edu.

SPIEGEL, PHYLLIS, public relations consultant, journalist; b. Bronx, N.Y. d. Bernard and Lillian (Horowitz) Finkelberg; m. Stanley Spiegel, Sept. 20, 1959 (div. 1981); children: Mark, Adam. BA, NYU. Feature writer various newspapers, pubs., 1960's-70's; dir. pub. rels. Mort Barish Assocs., Princeton, N.J., 1975-80; account exec. pub. rels. Keyes Martin, Springfield, N.J., 1980-84; pres. Phyllis Spiegel Assocs., Plainsboro, N.J., 1984—. Pub. rels. dir., founder Red Oak Coop. Nursery Sch., Middletown, N.J., 1960's, Matawan (N.J.) Student Enrichment Program, 1960s-70s; pub. rels. cons., event organizer New Philharm. of N.J., Morristown, 1991-93; mem. Child Placement Rev. Bd. of Family Ct., Mercer County, N.J., 1994-98. Recipient Commendation from Gov. N.J. for U. Med. and Dentistry of N.J. campaign, 1983, Commendation for N.J. Pharm. Assn. campaign Pub. Rels. News Assn., 1979. Mem. Soc. for Humanistic Judaism (bd. dirs. 1983-85). Avocations: film and theatre, classical music, reading, travel, walks. Office: Phyllis Spiegel Assocs PO Box 243 Plainsboro NJ 08536-0243

SPIEGEL, S. ARTHUR, federal judge; b. Cin., Oct. 24, 1920; s. Arthur Major and Hazel (Wise) S.; m. Louise Wachman, Oct. 31, 1945; children: Thomas, Arthur Major II, Andrew, Roger Daniel. BA, U. Cin., 1942, postgrad., 1949; LLB, Harvard U., 1948. Assoc. Kasfir & Chalfie, Cin., 1948-52; assoc. Benedict, Bartlett & Shepard, Cin., 1952-53, Gould & Gould, Cin., 1953-54; ptnr. Gould & Spiegel, Cin., 1954-59; assoc. Cohen, Baron, Druffel & Hogan, Cin., 1960; ptnr. Cohen, Todd, Kite & Spiegel, Cin., 1961-80; judge U.S. Dist Ct. Ohio, Cin., 1980—; sr. status, 1995—. Served to capt. USMC, 1942-46. Mem. ABA, FBA, Ohio Bar Assn., Cin. Bar Assn., Cin. Lawyers Club. Democrat. Jewish. Office: US Dist Ct 838 US Courthouse 5th Walnut St Cincinnati OH 45202

SPIEGEL, SIEGMUND, architect; b. Gera, Germany, Nov. 13, 1919; came to U.S., 1938, naturalized, 1941. s. Jakob and Sara (Precker) S.; m. Ruth Josias, Apr. 13, 1945; children: Sandra Renee, Deborah Joan. Student, Colll. City N.Y., 1939-40, Columbia U., 1945-50; DHL (hon.), Hofstra U., 1993. Registered arch., N.Y., N.J., Mass., Md., Va., Pa., Conn., Ga., Vt., Tenn., N.H., Fla.; lic. profl. planner, N.J. Draftsman Mayer & Whittlesey, Archs., N.Y.C., 1941-47, office mgr., 1947-55; pvt. practice arch. East Meadow, N.Y., 1956—. Author: The Spiegel Plan; contbr. articles to Progressive Arch.; prin. works include Syosset (N.Y.) Hosp., 1962, Reliance Fed. Savs. and Loan Assn. Bank, Queens, N.Y., 1961, Louden Hall Psychiat. Hosp., 1963, Human Resources Sch., Albertson, N.Y., 1964, Nassau Ctr. for Emotionally Disturbed Children, 1968, Harbor Club Apt., Babylon, N.Y., 1968, Reliance Fed. Bank, Albertson, 1967, North Isle Club and Apt. Cmty., Coram, N.Y., 1972, County Fed. Savs. & Loan Assn., Commack, N.Y., 1972, Birchwood Glen Apt. Cmty., Holtsville, N.Y., 1972, Bayside Fed. Savs. & Loan Bank Plaza, Patchogue, N.Y., 1973, L.E. Woodward Sch. for Emotionally Disturbed Children, Freeport, N.Y., 1974, Birchwood Sagamore Hills, Blue Ridge and Bretton Woods Condominium Cmtys., Coram, N.Y., 1975, Maple Arms Condos, Westbury, N.Y., 1982, Dept. Pub. Works, Freeport, N.Y., Nuc. Molecular Resonance Bldg., 1983. Served with AUS, 1941-45, ETO. Decorated Purple Heart, Bronze Star, Croix de Guerre with palme (Belgium); recipient grand prize for instnl. bldgs. (for Syosset Hosp.), L.I. Assn., 1963, grand prize Human Resources Sch., 1966, grand prize Stony Brook Profl. Bldg., 1966, Beautification award, Town Hempstead, N.Y., 1969, Archi award for Harbour Club Apts., L.I. Assn., 1970, for Birchwood Blue Ridge Condominiums, 1974, Dr. Martin Luther King Jr. award Nassau County, 1986, Louise E. Yavner award N.Y. State Bd. Regents, 1992; fellow Acad. Mktg. Sci., L.I. U., 1971. Mem. AIA, N.Y. State Assn. Archs., East Meadow C. of C. (pres. 1966), Kiwanis Club. Home: Carlton Terr 6-D 10245 Collins Ave Bal Harbour FL 33154-1407

SPIEGELBERG, EMMA JO, business education educator, academic administrator; b. Mt. View, Wyo., Nov. 22, 1936; d. Joseph Clyde and Dorcas (Reese) Hatch; m. James Walter Spiegelberg, June 22, 1957; children: William L., Emory Walter, Joseph John. BA with honors, U. Wyo., 1958, MEd, 1985; EdD, Boston U., 1990. Tchr. bus. edn. Laramie (Wyo.) H.S., 1960-61, 65-93, adminstr., 1993-97; prin. McCormick Jr. H.S., Cheyenne, Wyo., 1997—2002; exec. dir. Wyo. Assn. Secondary Sch. Prins., 2001—. Author: Branigan's Accounting Simulation, 1986, London & Co. II, 1993; co-author: Glencoe Computerized Accounting, 1993, 2d edit., 1995, Microcomputer Accounting: Daceasy, 1994, Microcomputer Accounting: Peachtree, 1994, 3d edit., 2000, Microcomputer Accounting: Accpac, 1994, Computerized Accounting with Peachtree, 1995, 2000, 02. Mem. United Ch. of Christ; bd. dirs. Cathedral Home for Children, Laramie, 1967-70, 72—, pres., 1985-88, Laramie Plains Mus., 1970-79. Named Wyo. Bus. Tchr. of Yr., 1982, Wyo. Asst. Prin. of Yr., 1997. Mem.: NASSP, NEA, Wyo. Assn. Secondary Sch. Prins. (sec., treas. 1997—2001), Albany County Edn. Assn. (sec. 1970—71), Wyo. Edn. Assn., Wyo. Bus. Edn. Assn. (pres. 1979—80), Internat. Soc. Bus. Edn., Mt. Plains Bus. Edn. Assn. (Wyo. rep. to bd. dirs. 1982—85, pres. 1987—88, Sec. Tchr. of Yr. 1991, Leadership award 1992), Nat. Bus. Edn. Assn. (bd. dirs. 1987—88, 1991—96, Sec. Tchr. of Yr. 1991), Wyo. Vocat. Assn. (exec. bd. 1978—80, pres. 1981—82, exec. sec. 1986—89, Outstanding Contbns. to Vocat. Edn. award 1983, Tchr. of Yr. 1985), Am. Vocat. Assn. (policy com. region V 1984—87, region V Tchr. of Yr. 1986), U. Wyo. Alumni Assn. (bd. dirs. 1985—90, pres. 1988—89), Laramie C. of C. (bd. dirs. 1985—88), Zonta Internat. (Laramie) (v.p. 2002—03, pres. 2003—), Delta Pi Epsilon, Pi Lambda Theta, Chi Omega, Alpha Delta Kappa (state pres. 1978—82), Phi Delta Kappa, Kappa Delta Pi. Home: 3301 Grays Gable Rd Laramie WY 82072-5031 Office Phone: 307-745-5468.

SPIEGELBERG, HANS LEONHARD, medical educator; b. Basel, Switzerland, Jan. 8, 1933; came to U.S., 1961; s. Hans G. S.; m. Elizabeth von der Crone, May 19, 1962; children: Franzi, Daniel, Markus. MD, U. Basel, Basel, 1958. Med. diplomate, Switzerland. Intern and resident in pediatric allergy and immunology Dept. of Medicine, U. of Basel, Switzerland; intern and resident in allergy and immunology NYU, N.Y.C., 1961-63; with Scripps Rsch. Inst., La Jolla, Calif., 1963-90; prof. U. Calif., San Diego, 1990—, now prof. emeritus. Cons. VA Med. Ctr., L.A., 1966-90. Editor (jour.) Seminars in Immunopathology, 1988—. Home: 2234 Paseo Dorado La Jolla CA 92037-3208 Office: U Calif San Diego 9500 Gilman Dr La Jolla CA 92093-5004

SPIEGELBERG, HARRY LESTER, retired paper products company executive; b. New London, Wis., Apr. 24, 1936; s. Harry Henry and Gladys Louise (Kalt) S.; m. Bonnie Faye Ludden, Jan. 23, 1960; children: Susan Faye Spiegelberg Schuldes, Sharon Louise Spiegelberg Kozlowski, Stephen Harry, Scott Charles. BSChemE, U. Wis., 1959; MS, Inst. Paper Chemistry, Appleton, Wis., 1963, PhD, 1966; MBA, U. Chgo., 1980. Teaching asst. U. Wis. Coll. Engring., Madison, 1957-59; engr. Kimberly-Clark Corp., Neenah, Wis., 1959-61, rsch. scientist, 1965-68, mgr. new concepts, 1968-73, dir. R & D, 1973-84, v.p. consumer tissue rsch., 1985-92, v.p. tech. and patent strategy, 1992-93, v.p. tech. transfer, 1993-96, ret., 1996. Mem., past chmn. vis. com. dept. chem. engring. U. Wis., 1985—, mem., past chmn. indsl. liaison coun. Coll. Engring., 1987-93; founder, vice chmn. Paper Industry Internat. Hall of Fame; past pres. Ctr. Project Inc.; paper industry bus. columnist, 1999—. Contbr. chpt. to book; patentee in nonwovens and tissue fields. Capt. C.E. USAR, 1959-67. Recipient Disting. Svc. citation U. Wis., 1986. Congregationalist. Avocations: bicycling, backpacking, kayaking, antique farm equipment. Home: 3624 S Barker Ln Appleton WI 54915-7038 E-mail: hspiegel@athenet.net.

SPIEGELMAN, ART, author, cartoonist; b. Stockholm, Feb. 15, 1948; s. Wladek and Andzia (Zylberberg) S.; m. Francoise Mouly, July 12, 1977; children: Nadja, Dashiell. Student, Harpur Coll. (now SUNY), Binghamton, N.Y. Creative cons., artist, designer, editor, writer Topps Chewing Gum, Inc., Bklyn., 1966-88; editor Douglas Comix, 1972; contbg. editor Arcade, the Comics Revue, 1975-76; founding editor Raw, 1980—; artist, contbg. editor New Yorker, 1992—2003. Instr. San Francisco Acad. Art, 1974-75, N.Y. Sch. Visual Arts, 1979-87. Author, illustrator: The Complete Mr. Infinity, 1970, The Viper Vicar of Vice, Villainy, and Vickedness, 1972, Ace Hole, Midge Detective, 1974, The Language of Comics, 1974, Breakdowns: From Maus to Now: An Anthology of Strips, 1977, Work and Turn, 1979, Every Day Has Its Dog, 1979, Two-Fisted Painters Action Adventure, 1980, Maus: A Survivor's Tale, 1986 (Joel M. Cavior award for Jewish Writing 1986, Nat. Book Critics Cir. nomination 1986, Pulitzer prize 1992), Maus, Part Two, 1992 (Nat. Book Critics Cir. nomination 1992, Pulitzer prize 1992), Open Me...I'm a Dog!, 1997; (with J.M. March) The Wild Party, 1994; (with F. Mouly) Read Yourself Raw, 1987, In the Shadow of No Towers, 2001; contbr. The Apex Treasury of Underground Comics, 1974; compiling editor (with B. Schneider) Whole Grains: A Book of Quotations, 1972; exhbns. include N.Y. Cultural Ctr., Inst. Contemporary Art, London, Seibu Gallery, Tokyo, Mus. Modern Art, N.Y.C., 1991, Galerie St. Etienne, N.Y.C., 1992, Ft. Lauderdale Mus. Art, 1993; creator Wacky Packages, Garbage Pail Kids and other novelties; contbr. to numerous underground comics. Recipient Playboy Editorial award for best comic strip, 1982, Yellow Kid award for best comic strip author, 1982, Regional Design award Print mag., 1983, 84, 85, Inkpot award San Diego Comics Conv., 1987, Stripschappening award for best fgn. comics album, 1987, Alpha Art award Angoulerne, France, 1993. Office: c/o The Steven Barclay Agency 321 Pleasant St Petaluma CA 94952-2648

SPIELBERG, STEPHEN PAUL, dean, educator; b. 1945; m. Laurel A. Spielbery. AB, Princeton U., 1966; PhD in pharmacology, U. Chgo., 1971; MD, U. Chgo. Pritzker Sch. Medicine, 1973. Pediat. resident Children's Hosp. Med. Ctr., Boston, 1974—75; instr. to asst. prof. pediat. & pharmacology Johns Hopkins U. Sch. Medicine, 1971—81; assoc. prof. to prof. pediat. & pharmacology U. Toronto, 1981—92, dir. Ctr. for Drug Safety Rsch., 1988—92; sr. scientist rsch. inst. Hosp. for Sick Children, Toronto, established & headed div. pediat. clin. pharmacology and toxicology, 1987—92; exec. dir. exploratory biochemical toxicology and clin. and regulatory develop. Merck Labs., 1992—97; v.p. pediat. drug develop. Johnson & Johnson Pharm. Rsch. & Develop., Titusville, NJ, 1997—2003, established dept. of pediat. drug develop.; v.p. health affairs Dartmouth Coll., 2003—; dean & prof. pediat. and pharmacology and taxicology Dartmouth Med. Sch., 2003—. Adj. prof. pediat., medicine and pharmacology Thomas Jefferson U.; adj. prof. pediat. Robert Wood Johnson Med. Sch.; mem. adv. bd. PediaLink; mem. Fed. Adv. Com., Nat. Children's Study, Nat. Inst. of Child Health and Human Develop.; chair Pediat. Task Force, Pharm. Rsch. and Mfr. of Am.; bd. dirs. Found. for NIH; mem. panel on ethics and pediat. clin. trials Inst. Medicine; mem. pediat. adv. subcom. FDA; mem. sci. adv. bd. Elizabeth Glaser Pediat. Rsch. Network. Recipient Rawls-Palmer Award, Am. Soc. for Clin. Pharmacology and Therapeutics, 1992, Werner Kalow Award for Pharmacogenetics and Drug Safety, 1995, William B. Abrams Award and Lectureship, FDA & Am. Soc. for Clin. Pharmacology and Therapeutics, 2001, Exceptional Service Award, Pharm. Rsch. and Mfr. of Am., 2003. Fellow: Nat. Inst. of Child Health and Human Develop. Office: Dartmouth Med Sch 1 Rope Ferry Rd Hanover NH 03755

SPIELBERG, STEVEN, motion picture director, producer; b. Cin., Dec. 18, 1946; m. Amy Irving, Nov. 27, 1985 (div. 1989); 2 children: Max Samuel, Sasha; m. Kate Capshaw Oct. 12, 1991; 5 children. BA, Calif. State U., Long Beach; D of creative arts (hon.), Brandeis U., 1986; DHL (hon.), Yale U., 2002. Founder Amblin Entertainment (Universal Studios), Dreamworks SKG (with Jeffrey Katzenberg and David Geffen); dir. (films): The Sugarland Express, 1974, Jaws, 1975, Close Encounters of the Third Kind, 1977 (also co-writer), Raiders of the Lost Ark, 1981, Indiana Jones and the Temple of Doom, 1984, Indiana Jones and the Last Crusade, 1989, Hook, 1991, Jurassic Park, 1993, Minority Report, 2002; dir., prodr. (films): E.T. The Extra-Terrestrial, 1982, Twilight Zone: The Movie, 1983, The Color Purple, 1985, Empire of the Sun, 1987, Always, 1989, Schindler's List, 1993 (Golden Globe award Best Drama & Best Dir., Best Picture & Best Dir. Acad. awards, Bundesverdienstkreuz mit Stern, Fed. Rep. of Germany's highest hon., 1998), Saving Private Ryan, 1998 (Golden Globe award for Best Dir., 1999, Best Director Academy award, 1998, nominee Best Picture Academy award, 1999, disting. pub. svc. award, U.S. Navy's highest civilian hon., 1999), Artificial Intelligence, 2001 (also writer), Catch Me If You Can, 2002, The Terminal, 2004; prodr. (films): Poltergeist, 1982 (also co-writer), An American Tail: Fievel Goes West, 1991; exec. prodr. (films): I Wanna Hold Your Hand, 1978, Used Cars, 1980, Continental Divide, 1981, Gremlins, 1984, The Goonies, 1985, Back to the Future, 1985, Young Sherlock Holmes, 1985, The Money Pit, 1986, An American Tail, 1986, Innerspace, 1987, *batteries not included, 1987, Who Framed Roger Rabbit?, 1988, The Land Before Time, 1988, Dad, 1989, Back to the Future Part II, 1989, Joe Verses the Volcano, 1990, Back to the Future Part III, 1990, Gremlins 2: The New Batch, 1990, Arachnophobia, 1990, Cape Fear, 1991, We're Back!: A Dinosaur's Story, 1993, The Flintstones, 1994, The Little Rascals, 1994, Balto, 1995, Casper, 1995, Men in Black, 1996, Twister, 1996, The Lost World, 1997, Amistad, 1997, Deep Impact, 1998, The Mask of Zorro, 1998, The Last Days, 1998, Holocaust Szemei (Eyes of the Holocaust), 2000, Jurassic Park III, 2001, Shrek, 2001, Price for Peace, 2001, Men in Black II, 2002; actor (films): The Blues Brothers, 1980; dir. (TV movies) Night Gallery, 1969, Duel, 1971, Something Evil, 1972, Savage, 1973; exec. prodr. (TV series) including: Steven Spielberg's Amazing Stories, 1985-87, Tiny Toon Adventures, 1990-92, Family Dog, 1993, Animaniacs, 1993-98, SeaQuest DSV, 1993-95, Steven Spielberg Presents Toonsylvania, 1998, Pinky, Elmyra & the Brain, 1998; exec. prodr. (TV movies): The Unfinished Journey, 1999, Semper Fi, 2000, Shooting War,

2000, We Stand Alone Together, 2001, (TV mini-series) Band of Brothers, 2001, (Emmy award for outstanding mini-series, 2002) Taken, 2002 (Emmy award outstanding mini-series, 2003). Recipient Man of Yr. award Hasty Pudding Theater, Harvard U., 1983, Outstanding Directorial Achievement award for feature films Dirs. Guild Am., 1985, Film award Brit. Acad. Film and TV Arts, 1986, Irving Thalberg Mem. award Acad. Motion Picture Arts and Scis., 1987, Golden Lion award for career achievement Venice Film Festival, 1993, Life Achievement award Am. Film Inst., 1995, named Entertainment Weekly's Most Powerful Person in Entertainment, 1997, Lifetime Achievement award, Dir. Guild Am., 2000. Fellow Brit. Acad. Film and TV Arts. Achievements include winning film contest with 40-minute war movie, Escape to Nowhere, at age 13; made film Firelight at age 16, and made 5 films while in coll.; became TV dir. at Universal Pictures at age 20. Office: Creative Artists Agy 9830 Wilshire Blvd Beverly Hills CA 90212-1804

SPIELBERGER, CHARLES DONALD, psychology educator, behaviorial medicine, clinical and health psychologist; b. Atlanta, Mar. 28, 1927; s. A.R. and Eleanor (Wachman) S.; m. Carol Lee, June 4, 1971. BS, Ga. Tech., 1949; BA, U. Iowa, 1951, MA, 1953, PhD, 1954. Asst. prof. med. psychology Duke U., Durham, N.C., 1955-58, from asst. prof. to assoc. prof. psychology, 1955-63; prof. psychology Vanderbilt U., Nashville, 1963-66; tng. specialist in psychology NIMH, Bethesda, Md., 1965-67; prof. psychology, dir. clin. training program Fla. State U., Tallahassee, 1967-72; prof. psychology U. South Fla., Tampa, 1972—85, dir. clin. tng., 1972—78, disting. univ. rsch. prof., 1985—. Fellow Netherlands Inst. for Advanced Study, Wassenaar, 1979-80, 85-86; cons. FAA, NIMH, VA, USAF, others. Author: Anxiety and Behavior, 1966, Understanding Stress and Anxiety, 1979, Anxiety in Sports, 1989, Test Anxiety: Theory, Assessment and Treatment, 1995; editor: Stress and Anxiety Series, 1975; editor: (gen.) Centennial Psychology Series, 1979—; editor: (in-chief) Encyclopedia of Applied Psychology, 2004—. Named Disting. scholar U. South Fla., 1973, Disting. Sci. Contbr., Fla. Psychol. Assn., 1977, 88, Outstanding Faculty Rschr., U. South Fla., 1985. Fellow APA (pres. 1991-92, nat. treas. 1987-90, coun. v.p. 1994-99, 2001-, pres. divsn. clin. psychology 1989, pres. divsn. cmty. psychol. 1975-76, pres. divsn. internat. psychol., 2002, Disting. Sci. Contbr. to Cmty. Psychology 1982, Disting. Sci. and Prof. Contbr. Clin. Psychology 1989, Disting. Contbr. Edn. Psychology 1992, Disting. Contbr. Profl. Practice 1993, APA/APF Gold Medal Disting. Contbr., 2003, pres. divsn. media psychol., 2005); mem. Southeastern Psychol. Assn. (pres. 1975-76), Soc. for Personality Assessment (pres. 1986-89, Disting. Sci. Contbr. 1990), Nat. Coun. Sci. Soc. Presidents (chair 1996-2000), Internat. Stress Mgmt. Assn. (pres. 1992-2000), Internat. Coun. Psychologists (pres. 1986-87), Internat. Assn. Applied Psychology (pres. 1998-2002), Psi Chi (nat. pres. 1980-83). Home: 11313 Carrollwood Dr Tampa FL 33618-3703 Office: U South Fla Dept Psychology Tampa FL 33620 Office Phone: 813-974-2342.

SPIELER, HELMUTH, physicist; b. Irvington, NJ, Aug. 25, 1945; m. Sigrid Spieler. Dipl. Phys., Tech. U. Munich, Germany, 1971, Dr. rer. nat., 1974. Staff scientist Tech. U. Munich, 1973—75, GSI - Gesellschaft fuer Schwerionenforschung, Darmstadt, Germany, 1975—82, Lawrence Berkeley Nat. Lab., Calif., 1982—87, sr. staff scientist, 1987—. Proposal and project reviewer U.S. Dept. of Energy; manuscript reviewer IEEE Trans. Nuc. Sci., Nuc. Instruments and Methods. Mem.: IEEE, Am. Phys. Soc. Achievements include development of instrumentation for experimental particle physics and cosmology. Office: Lawrence Berkeley Nat Lab 1 Cyclotron Rd MS 50B6222 Berkeley CA 94720 E-mail: hgspieler@lbl.gov.

SPIELMAN, ANDREW IAN, biochemist; b. Tirgu Mures, Romania, June 23, 1950; arrived in Can., 1982; s. Joseph and Rachel S.; m. Kathy Szabó, Dec. 15, 1977; 1 child, Robert-Dan. DMD, U. Medicine and Pharmacy, Tirgu Mures, 1974; cert. specialist in oral surgery, Technion, Haifa, Israel, 1982; MSc, U. Toronto (Can.), 1985, PhD in Oral Biology and Biochemistry, 1988. Asst. mem. Monell Chem. Senses Ctr., Phila., 1988-89; clin. assoc. U. Pa. Sch. Dental Medicine, Phila., 1989-92; affiliate mem. Monell Chem. Senses Ctr., Phila., 1989—; prof. and former chair dept. basic sci. and craniofacial biology NYU Coll. Dentistry, N.Y.C., 1996, assoc. dir. rsch., 1992-00, head biol. sci., medicine and surgery divsn., 1999—2001, assoc. dean acad. affairs, 2001—. Presenter in field. Author: (with others) Encyclopedia of Human Biology, 1991; editor: Experimental Cell Biology of Taste and Olfaction, 1995; contbr. articles to Brain Rsch., Chem. Senses, Jour. Dental Rsch., Archives Oral Biology, Experientia, Physiology and Behavior, Am. Jour. Physiology, Jour. Chem. Ecology, Jour. Neurophysiology, Critical Rev. in Oral Medicine and Biology, Jour. of Biol. Chemistry, Biochemistry, Nature (Neurosci.), also procs. V.p., bd. dirs. Trimethylaminuria Found., 2001—. Republican fellow Univ. of Medicine and Pharmacy, Tirgu-Mures, 1972, U. Toronto Open fellow, 1983, Med. Rsch. fellow Med. Rsch. Coun. can., 1983-88. Mem. AAAS, Internat. Assn. for Dental Rsch., N.Y. Acad. Sci., Assn. for Chemoreception Scis., Am. Assn. Oral Biologists (bd. dirs. 1996-99, pres.-elect 1999-2000, pres. 2000), Sigma Xi. Jewish. Achievements include research on the molecular basis of bitter taste mechanisms; on the interaction of saliva and taste; on identification of sweat-odor binding proteins in human axillary secretion. Office: NYU Coll of Dentistry 345 E 24th St New York NY 10010-4020

SPIELMAN, BARBARA HELEN NEW, retired editor; b. Canton, Ohio, June 28, 1929; d. Arthur Daniel and Helen Barbara (Rickenmann) New; m. David Vernon Spielman, Nov. 24, 1956; children: Daniel Bruce, Linda Barbara. BS in English and History Edn. cum laude, Miami U., Oxford, Ohio, 1951. Cert. tchr. Ohio, Tex. Tchr. Canton Pub. Schs., 1951-53; vets. aide U. Tex., Austin, 1954-57; copy editor, mng. editor U. Tex. Press, Austin, 1964-91; ret., 1991. Editl. cons. Amon Carter Mus., Ft. Worth, 1970—, Ctr. Mex. Am. Studies, Austin, 1980, Jack S. Blanton Mus. Art (formerly Archer M. Huntington Art Gallery), Austin, 1975—; mem. search com. for dir. U. Tex. Press, Austin, 1991. Editl. cons. Chicago Manual of Style, 13th edit., 1975. Officer PTA, Austin, 1964—73; troop leader Girl Scouts U.S., Austin, 1970—73; editl. cons. 64 Beds Project Homeless and Hungry, Austin, 1989—. Mem.: Seton Med. Ctr. Aux., Althenoi, Smithsonian Instn., Nat. Geog. Soc., Phi Beta Kappa, Sigma Sigma Sigma, Kappa Delta Pi. Democrat. Presbyterian. Avocations: reading, gardening, piano, painting, drawing. Home: 3301 Perry Ln Austin TX 78731-5330

SPIELMAN, JOSEPH D. automotive executive; b. New York, Feb. 9, 1945; BS in Mech. Engring., GMI, 1968. Supr. body shop GM, Fisher body plant, Flint, Mich., 1975—79, prodn. mgr., 1979—80, mgr., 1980—84; dir. mfg. engring. GM Can. Group, 1984—88, mfg. mgr., 1988—91; v.p., gen. mgr. GM Rear Drive Auto Divsn., 1991—92, GM Midsize Car Divsn., 1992—94, GM Metal Fabricating Divsn., 1994—2003; gen. mgr. vechicle mfg. GM, 2003—. Pres. The Hundred Club of Flint, Inc.; exec. Kettering U. Named to Nat. Corvette Mus. Hall of Fame, 2001, Engr. Soc. of Detroit Coll. Fellows, 2001. Mem.: Soc. Automotive Engrs., Nat. Soc. Profl. Engrs. Office: GM Corp PO Box 300 300 Renaissance Ctr Detroit MI 48265-3000

SPIELVOGEL, CARL, former ambassador, international business and marketing executive; b. N.Y.C., Dec. 27, 1928; s. Joseph and Sadie (Tellerman) S.; m. Barbaralee Diamonstein, Oct. 27, 1981; children: David, Rachel, Paul. BBA, CUNY, 1956, LLD (hon.), 1984. Reporter, columnist N.Y. Times, 1950-60; with McCann-Erickson, Inc., Interpublic Group of Cos., Inc., N.Y.C., 1960-74, vice chmn., chmn. exec. com., dir., 1974-80; chmn., chief exec. officer Backer & Spielvogel, Inc., 1980-87; chief exec. officer, chmn. bd. dirs. Backer Spielvogel Bates Worldwide, Inc., N.Y.C., 1987-94; chmn., CEO, United Auto Group, Inc., 1994—97; U.S. amb. to the Slovak Rep. U.S. Dept. State, Bratislava, 2000—01. Dir. Manhattan Industries, Franklin Corp.; bd. dirs. Hasbro, Inc., 1984- Chmn. Com. in Pub. Interest, 1975-79, Tri-State United Way, 1984; pres. bd. trustees Baruch Coll. Fund, 1979; mem. Bus. Com. Arts; bd. dirs., mem. exec. com. Mt. Sinai Hosp., N.Y.C.; bd. dirs. N.Y. Coun. Humanities, N.Y. Philharm., 1987—, Asia Soc., 1989—; trustee Lincoln Ctr. for Performing Arts, 1987—; chmn. Mayor's Com. for Pub.-Pvt. Partnerships; mem. exec. com. Bus. Mktg. Corp., N.Y.C.; chmn. com. div. WNET-Pub. Broadcasting; trustee, mem. exec. com., chmn. bus. com. Met. Mus. Art; mem. internat. adv. bd. bus. coun. UN; bd. govs. U.S. Govt. Broadcasting, 1995-2000. Recipient Human Relations award Anti-Defamation League, 1972, Achievement award Sch. Bus. Alumni, CCNY, 1972, Citizens Union award, 1980, Disting. Alumni award for Outstanding Career Accomplishment Baruch Coll., 1990; named Marketer of Yr. N.Y. chpt. Am. Mktg. Assn., 1982, Outstanding Exec. Crain's N.Y. Bus., 1987. Mem. Mcpl. Art Soc.

SPIELVOGEL, SIDNEY MEYER, investment banker; b. N.Y.C., July 14, 1925; s. Hyman and Rae (Mandel) S.; m. Beverly Anne Gold, Dec. 18, 1960; 1 son, Peter James. BSS., CCNY, 1944; A.M., Harvard U., 1946, MBA, 1949. Economist Treasury Dept., Washington, 1946-47; assoc. dept. mgr. Alexander's Dept. Stores, 1949-53; asst. to mdse. mgr., dept. mgr. Bloomingdale's Dept. Store, 1953-56; with Prudential-Bache Securities Inc., 1956-88, 1st v.p., 1971-75, sr. v.p., 1975-85, mng. dir., 1986-88. Dir. MoneyMart Assets Inc., 1976-96, pres., 1981-87; lectr. Hunter Coll., N.Y.C., 1963-68, The New Sch., 1993-96. Bd. dirs. Emanu-el Midtown YM-YWHA, N.Y.C., 1975-91; mem. Harvard Grad. Soc. Coun., 1983-88, 89-92, 94—, chmn., 1985-87. Mem. Phi Beta Kappa. Clubs: Harvard (N.Y.C.), Harvard Bus. Sch. (N.Y.C.), World Trade Center (N.Y.C.). Home: 245 E 19th St New York NY 10003-2639 Office: Corp Capital Cons Inc 230 Park Ave Rm 1000 New York NY 10169-0999

SPIERER, ROBERT, family practice physician; b. S.I., N.Y., June 26, 1945; s. Efram and Regina (Stern) Spierer; m. Marilyn J Borak, July 7, 1968; children: Sharon, Henry, Eric. BA, Columbia U., 1967; MD, Albert Einstein Coll. Medicine, 1971. Diplomate in internal medicine and geriatric medicine Am Bd. Internal Medicine, Am. Bd. Pediatrics, Am. Bd. Family Medicine, Am. Bd. Emergency Medicine. Intern Montefiore Med. Ctr., Bronx, NY, 1971-72, resident in pediatrics, 1972-73, 1975-76; resident in internal medicine U. Medicine and Dentistry of N.J., Newark, 1976-77; physician Edison (N.J.) Med. Group, 1977-98, Monroe Medical Group, 1999—. With USPHS, 1973—75. Office: Monroe Med Group 369 Applegarth Rd Monroe Township NJ 08831-3732 Office Phone: 609-395-1900.

SPIERKEL, GREGORY M. information technology executive; b. 1957; BA, Carleton U., Ottawa, Can.; MBA, Georgetown U., Wash., DC; attended, Advanced Manufacturing Program at INSEAD, Fontainbleau, France. Mng. dir. Mitel Telecom, United Kingdom, 1986—89; gen. mgr. Mitel Far East Ltd., Hong Kong, 1989—90; pres., CEO, N. Am. Mitel Inc., Reston, Va., 1992—96, v.p., global sales and marketing, 1996—97; sr. v.p., pres. Ingram Micro Inc., Santa Ana, Calif., 1997—99; pres. Ingram Micro Asia-Pacific, 1997—99; exec. v.p. Ingram Micro Inc., 1999—; pres. Ingram Micro Europe, 1999—; officer Ingram Micro Inc., 1997—. Office: Ingram Micro Inc 1600 E St Andrew Pl Santa Ana CA 92705-4931 Office Phone: 714-566-1000. Office Fax: 714-566-7900.

SPIERS, RONALD IAN, diplomat; b. Orange, N.J., July 9, 1925; s. Thomas Hoskins and Blanca (De Ponthier) S.; m. Patience Baker, June 11, 1949; children: Deborah Wood, Peter, Martha, Sarah. BA, Dartmouth Coll., 1948; M in Pub. Affairs, Princeton U., 1950. With AEC, 1950-54; officer-in-charge disarmament and arms control Dept. State, Washington, 1955-61, dir. NATO affairs, 1962-66; polit. counselor Am. Embassy, London, 1966-69; asst. sec. for Politico-Mil. Affairs U.S. Dept. State, 1969-73; amb. to Bahamas, Am. Embassy, Nassau, 1973-74, dep. chief of mission London, 1974-77; U.S. permanent rep. to CENTO Coun., 1977-79; amb. to Turkey, Am. Embassy, Ankara, 1977-80; asst. sec. for intelligence and rsch., mem. U.S. Intelligence Bd. U.S. Dept. State, Washington, 1980-81; amb. to Pakistan, Am. Embassy, Islamabad, 1981-83; under-sec. for mgmt. U.S. Dept. State, 1983-89; under-sec. gen. for polit. affairs UN, N.Y.C., 1989-92; internat. affairs cons. Dept. State, 1992—. Career ambassador U.S. Fgn. Svc., 1984. Served to lt. (j.g.) USN, 1943-46, PTO. Woodrow Wilson fellow Princeton U., 1948. Fellow Nat. Acad. of Pub. Adminstrn.; mem. Am. Fgn. Svc. Assn., Internat. Inst. Strategic Studies, Coun. on Fgn. Rels., Am. Acad. of Diplomacy, Washington Inst. Fgn. Affairs. Home: 1320 Middletown Rd South Londonderry VT 05155-9145 E-mail: embassy@adelphia.net.

SPIES, ALLAN, telecommunications executive; m. Karen Spies; 2 children. BS in Physics, Calif. Luth. U.; M. Mgmt., Pace U. With US West, Denver, v.p. fin., contr., exec. v.p., CFO, 1997—; v.p., CFO US West Multimedia Comm., a divsn. US West Media Group, Denver; bd. dirs. InfoNow Corp., Denver, 2000—. Office: InfoNow Corp 1875 Lawrence St Ste 1100 Denver CO 80202

SPIES, DAVID EDWARD, music educator, researcher; MusB with honors in Performance with distinction, U. of Wis., 1991; Artist Diploma, Yale U., New Haven, 1994; MusM in Performance, Yale U., 1993; D. Mus. Arts in Performance, U. of North Tex., 1999. Cert. tchr. Tuba Okla. Music Teachers Assn., 2002. Tchg. asst. (applied low brass/brass area coord./modern jazz: bebop and beyond/the art of rec.) Yale U. Sch. of Music, New Haven, 1992—94; freelance musician Dallas/Ft. Worth, Tex., 1994—2002; pvt. instr. low brass Lewisville Ind. Sch. Dist., Tex., 1994—2002; tchg. fellow (tuba/euphonium studio) U. of North Tex. Coll. of Music, Denton, 1996—99; instr. of low brass Southeastern Okla. State U., Durant, 1996—2002, Northwestern State U. of La., Natchitoches, 1999—2000; freelance musician Madison, Wis., 2003—; instr. of music Marian Coll., Fond du Lac, Wis., 2003; vis. asst. prof. of music U. of Iowa, 2003—. Web mng. editor Internat. Tuba-Euphonium Assn., 2003—, new materials reviewer, 1992—; clinician Tex. Bandmasters Assn., San Antonio, 2002; adjudicator, Rich Matteson Internat. Jazz Improvisation competition Internat. Tuba-Euphonium Assn., 2001; project asst. oral history Am. Music Project, Yale U., New Haven, 1994; founding dir. Merry Tubachristmas Texoma. Musician: (recording) Reflections (Shreveport Symphony Orch.), Teaching Music Through Performance In Band-Resource Recordings, Vol. 2-Grades 2/3 (North Tex. Wind Symphony), Teaching Music Through Performance In Band-Resource Recordings, Vol. 1-Grades 2/3 (North Tex. Wind Symphony), Deja View (North Tex. Wind Symphony), Dream Catchers (North Tex. Wind Symphony), Wind Dances (North Texas Wind Symphony), Dialogues and Entertainments (North Tex. Wind Symphony), Common Sense-Emergency Music), WASBE 99 Live (North Tex. Wind Symphony), Wildflowers (North Tex. Wind Symphony), Luminaries (North Tex. Wind Symphony), Bird Songs (North Tex. Wind Symphony), Tributes (North Tex. Wind Symphony), CEMIsonics: The Threshold of Sound; Music from CEMI, Gustav Mahler: Symphony No. 9 (Yale Symphony Orchestra), The Civil War Music Collector's Edit. (First Brigade Civil War Brass Band), Making History Live Vol. 12-Concert Favorites (First Brigade Civil War Brass Band), Making History Live Vol. 11-Classics On The Battlefield (First Brigade Civil War Brass Band), Making History Live Vol. 10-Dusty Roads and Camps (First Brigade Civil War Brass Band), Sojourns (North Tex. Wind Symphony), Soundscapes (North Tex. Wind Symphony); contbr. articles to profl. jours., encys.; musician: (recording) Common Sense performer, composer collaborative. Recipient Alumni Prize, Sch. of Music, Yale U., 1993, Doctoral scholar, U. of North Tex., 1995, The Outstanding Student In Instrumental Studies award, U. of North Tex. Coll. of Music, 1998, 1999; grantee Trewartha Honors grant, U. of Wis.-Madison, 1990; scholar Stanley Knight and Frances Louise Kirchoff Tapp scholar, Sch. of Music, Yale U., 1992, Doctoral scholar, U. of North Tex., 1994. Mem.: United Serpents, The Hist. Brass Soc., Chamber Music Am., Coll. Music Soc., Nat. Assn. of Coll. Wind and Percussion Instrs., Am. Fedn. of Musicians, Internat. Tuba-Euphonium Assn., Golden Key, Tex. Music Educators Assn., Phi Eta Sigma, Phi Kappa Phi, Pi Kappa Lambda. Achievements include Performed with Ft. Worth and Shreveport symphony orch., N.Y. Woodwind quintet, Meridian Arts Ensemble and Can. Brass; performed with Kenny Wayne Shepherd, LeAnn Rimes, Roy Clark and James Taylor; performed 20 solo recitals in U.S; premiered seven original works for tuba composed for him by James Wintle, James Grant, David Drexler and Michael Basford.

SPIES, KAREN BORNEMANN, writer, education consultant; b. Renton, Wash., Sept. 5, 1949; d. William Edward and Aina Jeanette (Johnson) Bornemann; m. Allan Roy Spies, July 18, 1970; children: Karsten, Astrid. BA, Calif. Luth. U., Thousand Oaks, 1970; MEd, U. Wash., 1974. Vice prin., tchr. Lake Washington Sch. Dist., Kirkland, Wash., 1971-79; tchr. various pub. schs. NJ, 1979-82; kindergarten tchr. Mt. Park Sch., Lake Oswego, Oreg., 1982-84; writer, seminar leader, cons. Wash., 1984—87. Lectr. Arapahoe C.C., Littleton, 1988-98; ski instr. various locations, 1974—; curriculum writer Augsburg-Fortress Pubs.; lectr. in field. Author: Family Activities for the Christmas Season, 1988, Denver, 1988, Raffi: The Children's Voice, 1989, Visiting in the Global Village, Vol. I, 1990, Vol. II, 1991, Vol. III, 1992, Vol. IV, 1993, Vol. V, 1994, Everything You Need to Know About Grieving, 1990, Competitiveness, 1991, Barbara Bush, 1991, George Bush, 1991, Everything You Need to Know About Incest, 1992, Our National Holidays, 1992, Our Money, 1992, The American Family: Can It Survive?, 1993, Everything You Need to Know About Diet Fads, 1993, Our Folk Heroes, 1994, Earthquakes, 1994, Our Presidency, 1994, Isolation vs. Intervention, 1995, Buffalo Bill Cody: Western Legend, 1998, Franklin D. Roosevelt, 1999, John F. Kennedy, 1999, Heroes in Greek Mythology, 2002, The Iliad and Odyssey in Greek Mythology, 2002, Pan Am Flight 103: Terrorism over Lockerbie, 2003. Bd. Regents Calif. Luth. Univ.; organist Wooden Cross Luth. Ch., 1977—79; bd. dirs. Human Svcs. Inc. Recipient Notable Social Studies Trade Books for Young People, 2000; Title III grantee, 1974. Mem. AAUW, Soc. Children's Book Writers and Illustrators, Mensa, Profl. Ski Instrs. Am., Colo. Authors' League, Pi Lambda Theta. Republican. Lutheran. Avocations: tennis, reading, sewing, skiing, golf. E-mail: buddyspies@msn.com.

SPIESS, F. HARRY, JR., lawyer; b. Norristown, Pa., Mar. 17, 1943; s. F. Harry and Sara E. (Jenkins) S.; m. Merrily S. Brown, Aug. 22, 1964; children: Jill, Blake, Alexandra, Ryan. AB, Lafayette Coll., Easton, Pa., 1964; JD, Villanova U., 1968. Bar: Pa. 1968. Assoc. Greenwell Porter Smaltz Royal, Wayne, Pa., 1968-72, ptnr., 1972-95, Davis Bennett Barr & Spiess, Wayne, 1995—2001, Davis Bennett Spiess & Prendergast, 2002—. Mem. Radnor Twp. Meml. Day Parade Com., 1976—, pres., 1985; pres. Wayne Jaycees, 1972-73, Rotary Club of Wayne, 1976-77, bd. dirs., counsel Radnor Hist. Soc., 1993-2003; chairman mem. Hist. Assn. Tobyhanna Twp., 1996—; chmn. Constellation Dist. Boy Scouts Am., 1997-2001. Named Pa. Superlawyer, 2004; recipient Robert Morris Citizenship award, 2001, Pro Bono Pub. award, Del. County Legal Assistance, 2002. Mem. Pa. Bar Assn., Delaware County Bar Assn. (sec. 1981, chmn. golf com. 1994—, dir. 2000-2002, Pres.'s award 2002), Monroe County Bar Assn., Main Line Lawyers Forum (past pres.), Wayne Bus. Assn. (pres. 1987-89), St. Davids Golf Club (counsel, sec.-treas. 1995-2004). Avocations: golf, reading, fishing. Home: Lansdowne Ave Wayne PA 19087 Office: Davis Bennett Spiess & Prendergast PO Box 191 130 W Lancaster Wayne PA 19087 Office Phone: 610-688-6200. Business E-Mail: hspiess@davisbennett.com.

SPIESS, FRED NOEL, oceanographer, educator; b. Oakland, Calif., Dec. 25, 1919; s. Fred Henry and Elva Josephine (Monck) S.; m. Sarah Scott Whitton, July 25, 1942 (dec. Sept. 2002); children: Katherine Spiess Dallaire, Mary Elizabeth Spiess DeJong, John Morgen Frederick, Helen Spiess Shamble, Margaret Josephine Deligio-Spiess. AB, U. Calif., Berkeley, 1941, PhD, 1951; MS, Harvard U., 1946. With Marine Phys. Lab., U. Calif., San Diego, 1952—, dir., 1958-80, U. Calif. Inst. Marine Resources, 1980-88, Scripps Inst. Oceanography, La Jolla, 1964-65, prof. oceanography, 1961-90, prof. emeritus, rsch. prof., 1990—; chair U. Calif. Acad. Coun. and Assembly U. Calif. Bd. Regents, 1988-90. Mem. Naval Rsch. Adv. Commn., 1978-81; mem. com. on geodesy Nat. Acad. Scis., 1980 84, mem. ocean studies bd., 2004—, mem. Def. Sci. Bd., 1976-79; chair Acad. Senate Task Force U. Calif., Merced, 1999-2001. Capt. USNR, 1941-79. Decorated Silver Star medal, Bronze Star medal; recipient John Price Wetherill medal Franklin Inst., 1965; Compass Disting. Scientist award Marine Technol. Soc., 1971; Robert Dexter Conrad award U.S. Sec. of Navy, 1974, Navy Disting. Pub. Svc. award, 1990; Newcomb Cleveland prize AAAS, 1981 Fellow Acoustical Soc. Am. (Pioneers of Underwater Acoustics medal 1985), Am. Geophys. Union (Maurice Ewing award 1983), Marine Tech. Soc. (Lockheed award 1985); mem. Nat. Acad. Engring., Phi Beta Kappa, Sigma Xi. Home: 9450 La Jolla Shores Dr La Jolla CA 92037-1137 Office: U Calif San Diego Scripps Inst Oceanogra La Jolla CA 92093-0205 Office Phone: 858-534-1621. E-mail: fspiess@ucsd.edu.

SPIESS, GARY A. lawyer; BA, Dartmouth Coll., 1962; LLB, Harvard U., 1966. Bar: Mass. 1966. Assoc. atty. Bingham Dana & Gould, 1966-76; 1st v.p., dep. gen. counsel Bank of Boston, 1975-86, dep. gen. counsel, 1986-87, gen. counsel, cashier, 1987—. Mem. Boston Bar Assn. (past pres.) Office: care Boston Bar Assn 16 Beacon St Boston MA 02108-3707

SPIGARELLI, JAMES L. science administrator; BA in Chemistry, MS in Chemistry, PhD in Chemistry, Kans. State Coll. Various positions Midwest Rsch. Inst., Kansas City, Mo., 1961—78, v.p., 1978—91, sr. v.p., 1991—97, exec. v.p., 1997—98, COO, 1998—99, pres., CEO, 1999—. Bd. dirs. Sci. City, Kansas City Mus., KCCatalyst, Brush Creek Cmty. Ptnrs., Sci. Pioneers. R&D task force Kansas City Area Life Scis. Inst., 1999; trustee U. Mo., Kansas city, Avila Coll., Rockhurst U.; bd. dirs. Kansas City Area Life Scis. Inst., 2000. Named Tech. Leader of Yr., Silicon Prairie Tech. Assn., 2000; recipient Meritorious Achievement award, Pitts. State U. Fellow: Coll. Arts and Scis. Alumni, Kans. State U. Office: Midwest Rsch Inst 425 Volker Blvd Kansas City MO 64110-2299

SPIKE, MICHELE KAHN, lawyer; b. Paterson, N.J., Oct. 1, 1951; d. Nathan and Clara (Spinella) Kahn; m. John Thomas Spike, May 26, 1973; 1 child, Nicholas Nathan. BA summa cum laude, Conn. Coll., 1973; JD cum laude, Boston U., 1976. Bar: N.Y. 1977, U.S. Dist. Ct. (so. and ea. dists.) N.Y. 1977. Assoc. Hale, Russell & Gray, N.Y.C., 1976-82; sole practice, N.Y.C., 1982-86; with Dolgenos, Newman & Cronin, N.Y.C., 1986-89; sole practice, Florence, Italy, 1989—. Chair commn. on ministry of the baptized Convocation of Am. Episcopal Chs. in Europe, 1994-2002; bd. dirs. The Genesis Ctr., Inc., 1994—; mem. Ecumenical Commn., Florence, 2002—; bd. dirs. St. James Am. Episcopal Ch., Florence, 2002—; mem. Standing Commn. on Anglican and Internat. Peace with Justice Concerns, 2004—. Mem. Bar Assn. City N.Y., Phi Beta Kappa. Home: 152 Engle St Tenafly NJ 07670-2704 also: Piazza de Mozzi 5 50125 Florence Italy

SPILHAUS, ATHELSTAN FREDERICK, JR., oceanographer, association executive; b. Boston, May 21, 1938; s. Athelstan F. and Mary (Atkins) S.; m. Sharon Brown, June 11, 1960; children— Athelstan F. III, Ruth Emily, Mary Christina S.B. in Chem. Engring., MIT, 1959, S.M. in Geology and Geophysics, 1960, PhD in Oceanography, 1965. Cert. meeting profl. Phys. scientist U.S. Govt., Washington, 1965-67; asst. exec. dir. Am. Geophys. Union, Washington, 1967-70, exec. dir., 1970—. Bd. dirs. Renewable Natural Resources Found., Washington. Editor newspaper EOS. Chmn. Conv. Liaison Council, Washington, 1981-82. Fellow AAAS, Washington Acad. Sci., Am. Geophys. Union (hon.), Indian Geophys. Union, Geol. Soc. Am., Royal Astonomical Soc.; mem. Am. Soc. Limnology and Oceanography, Council Biology Editors, Am. Inst. Physics (mem. gov. bd. 1988—), Philos. Soc. Washington (pres. 1982-83), Geol. Soc. Can., Geol. Soc. Washington (2d v.p. 1975), Am. Soc. Assn. Execs., Assn. Am. Pubs. (div. exec. com. 1980-82, 94-97), Assn. Earth Sci. Editors (dir. 1972-78, pres. 1977), Coun. Engring. and Scientific Soc. Execs. (dir. 1976-82, pres. 1980-81), Internat. Union Geodesy Geophysics (fin. com. 1987—2003, chmn. 1999-2003), Canadian Geophys. Union, European Geophys. Soc., Cosmos Club (Washington, pres. 1992-93), Chesapeake Yacht Club (Md.). Home: 10900 Picasso Ln Rockville MD 20854-1710 Office: Am Geophys Union 2000 Florida Ave NW Washington DC 20009-1231

SPILIOTIS, JOYCE A. state legislator; State rep. Mass. House, 2003—. Mem. Mass. Dem. State Com., N. Shore Labor Coun.; counilor-at-large City of Peabody; trustee City of Peabody Libr., 1986—88. Democrat. Office: State House Rm 540 Boston MA 02133

SPILKA, KAREN, state legislator, lawyer; BS in Social Work, Cornell U.; JD, Northeastern U. Sch. Law. Mem. Mass. Ho. of Reps., Boston, 2001—. Founder Mentoring Programs for New Women Legislators and New Women Aides. Bd. dirs. Metro West Econ. Rsch. Ctr., Metro West YMCA; Ashland Sch. Com.; Ashland Fiscal Affaris Com.; bd. dirs. So. Middlesex Assn. for Retarded Citizens. Mem.: Indsl. Relations Rsch. Assn., Mass. Bar Assn., Boston Bar Assn. Democrat. Office: Rm 443 State House Boston MA 02133 Office Phone: 617-722-2460.

SPILKER, LINDA JOYCE, aerospace scientist; b. Mpls., Apr. 26, 1955; d. Arthur Elzear and Bonnie Joy (Jansen) Bies; m. John Leonard Horn, Jr., July 31, 1976 (div.); children: Jennifer, Jessica; m. Thomas Richard Spilker, 1997. BA in Physics, Calif. State U., Fullerton, 1977; MS in Physics, Calif. State U., L.A., 1983; PhD in Geophysics and Space Physics, UCLA, 1992. Rep. Voyager Infrared Radiometer and Spectrometer expt. Jet Propulsion Lab., Pasadena, Calif., 1977-90, sci. assoc. Voyager Photopolarimeter, 1984-90, sc. assoc. Voyager Infrared Radiometer and Spectrometer, 1988-90, study scientist Cassini asst., 1988-90, co-investigator Cassini Composite Infrared Spectrometer, 1990—, dep. project scientist Cassini mission, 1990—, prin. investigator planetary geology and geophysics, 1993—. Mem. planetary sci. data steering group NASA, Washington, 1991-95, adv. coun. for planetary data sys. ring node, Moffett Field, Calif., 1990—. Contbr. chpt. Van Nostrand Encyclopedia of Planetary Science, 1994; contbr. jour. articles Icarus. Pres. North San Gabriel Valley Dem. Club, Monrovia, Calif., 1992-94. Named to Hall of Fame, Placentia-Yorba Linda Unified Sch. Dist., 1998—99; recipient Exceptional Service medal, NASA, 1990, Sci. Achievement award, 1992, Disting. Alumna award, Calif. State U., 1996. Mem. AAAS, Divsn. of Planetary Sci. Democrat. Presbyterian. Avocations: hiking, astronomical observing, piano, jogging. Home: 457 Granite Ave Monrovia CA 91016-2324 Office: Jet Propulsion Lab MS 230-205 4800 Oak Grove Dr Pasadena CA 91109-8001 Business E-Mail: Linda.J.Spilker@jpl.nasa.gov.

SPILLANE, DENNIS KEVIN, lawyer; b. N.Y.C., Sept. 15, 1953; s. Denis Joseph and Mary Kate (Sullivan) S. BA magna cum laude, Manhattan Coll., 1974; JD, N.Y. Law Sch., 1978; MS in Taxation, Pace U., 1986, post-masters cert. in bus., 1992. Bar: N.Y. 1979, U.S. Dist. Ct. (ea. and so. dists.) N.Y. 1979, U.S. Tax Ct. 1986, D.C. 1988, U.S. Ct. Appeals (2d cir.) 1988, U.S. Supreme Ct. 1988, Conn. 1989. Asst. dist. atty. Borough of Bronx, N.Y.C., 1978-85; prin. atty. N.Y. State Tax Dept., N.Y.C., 1985-87; supervising atty. Office of Profl. Discipline, N.Y. State Edn. Dept., 1987—. Prof. law and taxation Pace U., 1987—. Contbr. articles to profl. jours. Mem. Conn. Bar Assn, N.Y. State Bar Assn., D.C. Bar Assn. Conservative. Roman Catholic. Office: NY State Edn Dept 475 Park Ave S Frnt 3 New York NY 10016-6901 E-mail: dspillan@mail.nysed.gov.

SPILLANE, MARY CATHERINE, television producer; b. S.I., N.Y., Nov. 30, 1956; d. Joseph Bernard and Mary Catherine (Minoque) Spillane. BA, U. Hartford, 1978. Exec. sec. CBS Evening News, N.Y.C., 1978-80, asst. to prodr., 1980; weekend prodr./E.N.G. coord. Sta. KTVI-TV, St. Louis, 1981-82, spl. projects prodr., 1982-83, asst. news dir., 1983-86; assoc. prodr. CBS News, Detroit, 1986, N.Y.C., 1986-87, sr. prodr., 1987-89, Washington, 1989-93, prodr., 1993-99, CBS Weekend News, London, 1999—. Avocations: reading, travel, cooking, gardening. Office: CBS News 68 Knightsbridge London SW1X 7LL England

SPILLANE, MICKEY (FRANK MORRISON SPILLANE), author; b. Bklyn., Mar. 9, 1918; s. John Joseph and Catherine Anne S.; m. Mary Ann Pearce, 1945 (div.); children: Kathy, Ward, Mike, Carolyn; m. Sherri Malinou, Nov. 1964 (div.); m. Jane Rodgers Johnson, Oct. 1983. Attended, Kans. State Coll. Scripter, asst. editor Funnies, Inc., in 1940's; co-founder Spillane-Fellows Prodns., Nashville, 1969. Author: (mystery-suspense novels) I, the Jury, 1947, Vengeance is Mine!, 1950, My Gun Is Quick, 1950, The Big Kill, 1951, One Lonely Night, 1951, The Long Wait, 1951, Kiss Me, Deadly, 1952, Tough Guys, 1960, The Deep, 1961, The Girl Hunters, 1962, Day of the Guns, 1964, The Snake, 1964, Bloody Sunrise, 1965, The Death Dealers, 1965, The Twisted Thing, 1966, The By-Pass Control, 1967, The Delta Factor, 1967, Body Lovers, 1967, Killer Mine, 1968, Me. Hood!, 1969, Survival: Zero, 1970, Tough Guys, 1970, The Erection Set, 1972, The Last Cop Out, 1973, The Flier, 1973, Tomorrow I Die, 1984, The Killing Man, 1989, (children's books) The Day the Sea Rolled Back, 1979 (Junior Literary Guild award 1979), The Ship That Never Was, 1982, Black Alley, 1996; screenwriter, actor: (films) The Girl Hunters, 1963; creator: (TV series) Mike Hammer, 1984-87; editor: Murder Is My Business, 1994, (with Max Collins) Vengeance is Hers, 1997, Golden Age of Marvel Comics, 1998, Private Eyes, 1998, Century of Noir, 2002; appeared in Miller Lite Beer commls. Served to capt. USAAF, World War II. Named Grand Master, Mystery Writers Am., 1995. Address: care E P Dutton Signet Publicity 375 Hudson St New York NY 10014-3658

SPILLER, EBERHARD ADOLF, physicist, researcher; b. Halbendorf, Ger., Apr. 16, 1933; came to U.S., 1968; s. Walter Richard and Ruth Elfriede Spiller; children: Michael, Bettina. Diploma, U. Frankfurt, Ger., 1960, PhD, 1964. With U. Frankfurt, 1960-68; physicist IBM Research Center, Yorktown Heights, N.Y., 1968-93; emeritus physicist IBM, 1993-97; owner Spiller X-Ray Optics, 1996—. Guest prof. Tech. U. Denmark, 1994-95, U. Ctrl. Fla., 1996; vis. scientist European Synchrotron Radiation Facility, Nat. Inst. Stds. and Tech., 1997—, Lawrence Livermore Lab., Calif., 1997—. Author: Soft X-Ray Optics, 1994. Fellow AAAS, Am. Optical Soc., Photo-Optic Instrumentation Soc.; mem. German Phys. Soc. Achievements include research in solid state physics, laser and coherence optics, nonlinear optics, thin films, soft x-rays, x-ray microscopy, lithography; inventor multilayer x-ray optics, x-ray astronomy, x-ray lithography. Office: Lawrence Livermore Nat Lab MS-L210 Livermore CA 94551 Office Phone: 925-423-4938. E-mail: spiller@llnl.gov.

SPILLERS, WILLIAM RUSSELL, civil engineering educator; b. Fresno, Calif., Aug. 4, 1934; s. William Horton and Marguerite Ester (Johnson) S.; m. Priscilla Watson, Sept. 10, 1960 (div. 1981); children: Sarah, William, Lars; m. Sandra Lynn Newsome, July 15, 1983 (div. 1995); m. Joy Bechard, Mar. 13, 2000. Student, Fresno State Coll., 1951-53; BS, U. Calif., Berkeley, 1955, MS, 1956; PhD, Columbia U., 1961. Registered profl. engr., N.Y., N.J. Structural engr. John Blume Assocs., San Francisco, 1956-57; teaching asst. Columbia U., N.Y.C., 1957-61, prof. civil engring. and engring. mechanics, 1961-76; prof. civil engring. Rensellaer Poly. Inst., Troy, N.Y., 1976-90; prof., chmn. civil and environ. engring. N.J. Inst. Tech., Newark, 1990—, disting. prof. civil and environ. engring., 1995—. Cons. Weidlinger Assoc., N.Y.C., 1957-76, Geiger Berger Assoc., N.Y.C., 1957-76, DeLeuw Oh Eocha, Manchester, Eng., 1974, Parsons Hawaii, L.A., 1983, Horst Berger Ptnrs., N.Y.C., 1980; organizer NSF workshop on design theory, Troy, N.Y., 1988. Author: Automated Structural Analysis, 1972, Iterative Structural Design, 1975, Intro Structures, 1985; (with R. Levy) Analysis of Geometrically Nonlinear Structures, 1995, 2d edit., 2003, Introduction to Structures, 2002; editor 4 books including Design Theory, 1988; contbr. over 140 articles to profl. jours. Named Educator of Yr. award, Cons. Engrs. Coun. N.J., 1998; NSF fellow, 1976, Guggenheim fellow, 1968. Mem. ASCE (numerous coms., chmn. exec. com. TCCP, 1987), Internat. Assn. Bridge & Structural Engrs. Democrat. Achievements include contribution to the development of fabric structures; initiated the science of design theory; participated in development of applications of digital computers to large structural systems. Home: 7 Oak Ave West Orange NJ 07052-2409 Office: NJ Inst Tech Dept Civil & Environ Engring Newark NJ 07102 Office Phone: 973-596-2479. E-mail: spillers@adm.ujit.edu.

SPILLETT, ROXANNE, social services administrator; 1 son, Keith. BA in Edn., SUNY; postgrad., St. Lawrence U., Hunter Coll., N.Y. Tchr., curriculum writer N.Y. State Schs., 1971-73; program specialist Girl Scouts U.S.A., 1973; dir. nat. health project Boys & Girls Clubs Am., Atlanta, 1978-79, dir. program svcs., 1979-91, asst. nat. dir. program svcs., 1991-1995, v.p. N.E. regional office, 1995, acting pres., 1995-96, pres., 1996—. Vice chair bd. dirs. Nat. Assembly of Health and Human Svc. Orgns. Office: Boys & Girls Clubs Am 1230 W Peachtree St NW Atlanta GA 30309-3404*

SPILLMAN, JANE SHADEL, curator, researcher, writer; b. Huntsville, Ala., Apr. 30, 1942; d. Marvin and Elizabeth (Russell) Shadel; m. Don Lewis Spillman, Feb. 18, 1973 (dec. Jan. 1999); children: K. Elizabeth, Samuel Shadel. AB, Vassar Coll., 1964; MA, SUNY, 1965. Rsch. asst. Corning (N.Y.) Mus. Glass, 1965-70, asst. curator, 1971-73, assoc. curator Am. glass, 1974-77, curator, 1978—, head of curatorial dept., 1994-99, dep. dir. collections, 1999—2004. Cons. The White House Curator's Office, Washington, 1987-90, other museums. Author: Complete Cut and Engraved Glass of Corning, 1979, rev. edit., 1997, Knopf Collectors Guide to Glass, Vol. 1, 1982, Vol. 2, 1983, White House Glassware, 1989, Masterpieces of American Glass, 1990, The American Cut Glass Industry: T.G. Hawkes and His Competitors, 1996, also 6 other books, numerous articles; editor The Glass Club Bull., 1999—. Mem. Am. Assn. Mus. (chairperson curators com. 1989-93), Nat. Early Am. Glass Club (bd. dirs. 1989-95), Glass Circle of London. Office: Corning Mus Glass 1 Museum Way Corning NY 14830-2253

SPILLMAN, ROBERT ARNOLD, architect; b. Bethlehem, Pa., May 21, 1931; s. Otto Henry and Ruth Meredith (Miller) S.; m. Cidney Jane Brandon, July 7, 1956; children: Catherine, Sarah, Peter. BArch, Cornell U., 1954. Registered arch., Pa., N.J. Archtl. designer Office Douglass Orr, New Haven, 1956-58; ptnr. Lovelace & Spillman, Archs., Bethlehem, 1959-70; sr. ptnr. Spillman Farmer Archs., Bethlehem, 1971-82; pres. Spillman Farmer Shoemaker Pell Whildin, P.C., Bethlehem, 1983—96, sr. prin., 1997—. Trustee Laros Found., Bethlehem, 1970—; pres. Bethlehem Libr. Bd., 1970-74, United Way Northampton and Warren Counties, 1979-81, Lehigh River Found., 1992-95; v.p. Lehigh Valley Indsl. Parks, 1985-96, pres., 1996-2001; chmn. Bethlehem Bd. Hist. Archtl. Rev., 1961-82; mem. pres.'s coun. Lehigh Valley Partnership, 2001—; bd. dirs. KidsPeace, 2003—; Olympic torchbearer, 1996. 1st lt. USAF, 1954-56. Fellow AIA (pres. Ea. Pa. chpt. 1969-70); mem. Pa. Soc. Archs. (disting. bldg. awards 1971, 76, 78, 94, 2001, 02), Soc. Coll. and Univ. Planners, Bay Head Yacht Club (N.J.) (rear commodore 1985-87, vice commodore 1999-2001, commodore 2001-03). Democrat. Episcopalian. Office: Spillman Farmer Shoemaker Pell 1 Bethlehem Plz Ste 1000 Bethlehem PA 18018-5716 Business E-Mail: rspillman@spillmanfarmer.com.

SPINA, DOUGLAS JOHN, priest, educator; b. Providence, R.I., Apr. 27, 1949; s. Angelo and Gilda (Petrucci) Spina. BA, Our Lady of Providence Sem. Coll., Warwick, R.I., 1971, Cath. U., Louvain, Belgium, 1973, MA, 1974, MA in Moral and Religious Scis., 1975, PhD, 1979. Ordained Roman Cath. priest, Diocese Providence, 1976. Instr. Italian grammar and lit. Ursiline Convent Sch., Tildonc, Belgium, 1972—75; assoc. pastor St. Clement Ch., Warwick, RI, 1976—78, St. Mary's Ch., Newport, RI, 1979—81; Catholic chaplain Roger Williams U., Bristol, RI, 1979—81; instr. religion Our Lady of Providence Prep. Sem., Providence, 1981—82; from asst. to assoc. prof. religious studies Salve Regina U., Newport, RI, 1982—87; assoc. pastor St. Joan of Arc Ch., Cumberland, RI, 1987—90; chaplain, adj. prof. Bryant Coll., Smithfield, RI, 1990—96; pastor St. Anthony's Ch., Woonsocket, RI, 1992—97; adj. prof. religious studies Calif. State U., Long Beach, Calif., 1996—97; pastor Our Lady of Grace Ch., Johnston, RI, 1997—2004; chaplain Johnston Police Dept., 1998—2004, Johnston Fire Dept., 1999—2004, KC, North Providence, RI, 2001—; chaplain RI chpt. Am. Guild Organists, 2003—; pastor St. Martha's Ch., East Providence, RI, 2004—. Mem. nat. bd. dirs. Nat. Religious Studies/Theology Honor Soc., N.Y.C., 1986—88; mem. Humanities Forum of R.I., 1986; bd. dirs. Lucy' s Hearth, Middletown, RI, 1986—87; mem. Bishop's Task Force on AIDS, Roman Cath. Diocese, Providence, 1988—89. Author: (plays) Could've Been, 1988 (First Place award R.I. Cable TV Video Prodn. Competition Ednl., Instrn. Category., 1989), (Book) Reaching Across the Table: Meditations on the Journey towards Common Ground, 2001; contbr. articles short stories, poetry to various publications. Recipient Citation, Mayor, Cranston, R.I., 1976, Citation, Key to City, Mayor of Warwick, R.I., 1978, Citation, Mayor of Woonsocket, R.I., 1992, R.I. State Senate, 2001, R.I. Gov.'s Office, 2001, Mayor, Johnston, R.I., 2001. Mem.: Coll. Theology Soc., Cath. Campus Ministry Assn., R.I. Philos. Soc., Cath. Theol. Soc. Am. Avocation: collector Victorian period. Home and Office: St Marthas Rectory 2595 Pawtucket Ave East Providence RI 02914 Office Phone: 401-434-4060. Personal E-mail: Bd0521111@aol.com.

SPINA, FRANCIS X. state supreme court judge; m. Sally O'Donnell; 2 children. BA, Amherst Coll.; JD, Boston Coll. Prosecutor, Berkshire County, Mass., 1979—83; pvt. law practice Pittsfield, Mass., 1983—93; judge Mass. Superior Ct., 1993-97, Appeals Ct., Pittsfield, 1997-99; assoc. justice Mass. Supreme Jud. Ct., Boston, 1999—. Office: Supreme Judicial Ct Judges 1 Beacon St #3 Boston MA 02108-3107

SPINALE, FRANCIS G. medical educator, research cardiologist; b. Beverly, Mass., July 14, 1956; m. Molly R. Thomas, Sept. 11, 1982. BS in Biology, Northeastern U., 1979; MS in Biometry, Med. U. S.C., 1984, PhD in Pathology, 1988, MD, 1993. Diplomate Nat. Bd. Med. Examiners. Rsch. assoc., divsn. cardiothoracic surgery Med. U. S.C., Charleston, 1985-88, asst. prof., divsn. cardiothoracic surgery, 1988-92, assoc. prof. cardiothoracic surgery and physiology, 1992—, assc. prof. pediat., 1994-96, prof. surgery, anesthesiology, physiology and pediatrics, 1996—. Adj. prof. dept. bioengring. Clemson U., 1988— Contbr. over 100 articles to profl. jours.; editl. rev. bd. Am. Jour. Physiology, Jour. Molecular and Cellular Cardiology, Circulation Rsch., Annals of Thoracic Surgery, Cardiovascular Rsch., Basic Rsch. in Cardiology, PACE, Circulation; abstract reviewer Am. Heart Assn. 66th Scientific Sessions, 1993, 94, 95; editor: (book) The Pathophysiology of Tachycardia Induced Heart Failure, 1995. Recipient Sec.'s Cmty. Health Promotion award for excellence, U.S. Dept. Health and Human Svcs., 1984, grad. rsch. scholarship award Am. Lung Assn. S.C., 1986, Young Investigators award Am. Heart Assn., 1989, 1st prize Young Investigator Award Heart Inst. for Children, Chgo., 1990, 1st Investigator award R29 NIH, Heart Lung and Blood Inst., 1991, Est. Investigator award Am. Heart Assn., 1994-99; invited spkr. various confs. Mem. AMA, Acad. Surg. Rsch., Soc. Exptl. Biology and Medicine, Internat. Soc. Heart Rsch., Am. Physiol. Soc. (fellow cardiovasc. sect. 1994), S.C. Med. Assn. Office: 96 Jonathan Lucas St PO Box 250612 Charleston SC 29425-0612

SPINDEL, ROBERT CHARLES, electrical engineering educator; b. N.Y.C., Sept. 5, 1944; s. Morris Tayson and Isabel (Glazer) S.; m. Barbara June Sullivan, June 12, 1966; children: Jennifer Susan, Miranda Ellen BSEE, Cooper Union, 1965; MS, Yale U., 1966, MPhil, 1968, PhD, 1971. Postdoctoral fellow Woods Hole Oceanographic Instn., Mass., 1971-72, asst. scientist, 1972-76, assoc. scientist, 1976-82, sr. scientist, 1982-87, chmn. dept. ocean engring., 1982-87; dir. applied physics lab. U. Wash., Seattle, 1987—. Mem. naval studies bd. NRC, 1987-99; mem. Naval Rsch. Adv. Com., 1998—. Contbr. articles to profl. jours.; patentee on underwater nav. Recipient A.B. Wood medal Brit. Inst. Acoustics, 1981, Gano Dunn medal The Cooper Union, 1989, Ocean Engr. Soc. Tech. Achievement award, 1990. Fellow IEEE (assoc. editor jour. 1982—), Acoustical Soc. Am., Marine Tech. Soc. (pres. elect 1991-93, pres. 1993-95), Oceanography Soc. (Munk award 2001). Independent. Jewish. Avocations: automobile restoration, hiking. Home: 14859 SE 51st St Bellevue WA 98006-3515 Office: U Wash Applied Physics Lab 1013 NE 40th St Seattle WA 98105-6606 E-mail: spindel@APL.Washington.edu.

SPINDEL, WILLIAM, retired chemist, consultant; b. N.Y.C., Sept. 9, 1922; s. Joseph and Esther (Goldstein) S.; m. Sara Lew, 1942 (div. 1966); children: Robert Andrew, Lawrence Marshall; m. Louise Phyllis Hoodenpyl, July 30, 1967. BA, Bklyn. Coll., 1944; MA, Columbia U., 1947, PhD, 1950. Jr. scientist Los Alamos Lab, Manhattan Dist., 1944-45; instr. Poly. Inst., Bklyn., 1949-50; assoc. prof. SUNY, 1950-54; rsch. assoc., vis. prof. Columbia U., 1954-57, vis. prof., sr. lectr., 1962-74; from assoc. prof. to prof. Rutgers U., 1957-64; prof., chmn. dept. chemistry Belfer Grad. Sch. Sci., Yeshiva U., 1964-74; exec. sec., office chemistry and chem. tech. NAS-NRC, 1974-81, also staff dir. bd. on chem. scis. and tech., prin. staff officer commn. phys. scis., math. and resources, 1982-90, sr. cons., 1990-97; ret., 1997. Vis. Am. scientist, Yugoslavia, 1971-72. Contbr. articles to profl. jours. Served with AUS, 1943-46. Recipient profl. staff award NRC, 1985, Lifetime Achievement award Bklyn. Coll., CUNY, 1999; Guggenheim fellow, 1961-62; Fulbright Research scholar, 1961-62 Fellow AAAS; mem. Am. Chem. Soc. Clubs: Cosmos. Achievements include research on separation of stable isotopes, isotope effects on chemical and biological processes; developed chemical exchange process for concentrating nitrogen-15. Home: 6503 Dearborn Dr Falls Church VA 22044-1116 E-mail: wspindel@cs.com. *Working at and for the sciences has yielded a most fulfilling professional life.*

SPINDLER, GEORGE DEARBORN, anthropologist, educator, writer, editor; b. Stevens Point, Wis., Feb. 28, 1920; s. Frank Nicholas and Winifred (Hatch) S.; m. Louise Schaubel, May 29, 1942 (dec. Feb. 1997); 1 dau., Sue Carol Spindler Coleman. BS, Central State Tchrs. Coll., Wis., 1940; MA, U. Wis., 1947; PhD, U. Calif. at Los Angeles, 1952. Tchr. sch. in, Wis., 1940-42; research asso. Stanford, 1950-51, mem. faculty, 1951—, prof. anthropology and edn., 1960-78, exec. head dept., 1963-67, 84; editor Am. Anthropologist, 1962-66. Cons. editor Holt, Rinehart & Winston, 1965-91, Harcourt, 1991-99, Wadsworth-Thomson, 2002-; vis. prof. U. Wis., 1979-85, U. Calif., Santa Barbara, 1986-91, Harvard U., 1999. Author: Menomini Acculturation, 1955, (with A. Beals and L. Spindler) Culture in Process, 1967, rev. edit., 1973, Transmission of American Culture, 1959, (with L. Spindler) Dreamers Without Power, 1971, rev. edit., 1984, Burgbach: Urbanization and Identity in a German Village, 1973, (with Louise Spindler) The American Cultural Dialogue and its Transmission, 1990; editor: Education and Anthropology, 1955, (with Louise Spindler) Case Studies in Cultural Anthropology, 1960—, Methods in Cultural Anthropology, 1965—, Case Studies in Education and Culture, 1966—, Basic Units in Anthropology, 1970; editor, contbr.: Education and Culture, 1963, Being An Anthropologist, 1970, Education and Cultural Process, 1974, rev. edit., 1987, 97, The Making of Psychological Anthropology, 1978, 2nd edit., 1994, Doing the Ethnography of Schooling, 1982, Interpretive Ethnography of Schooling at Home and Abroad, 1987, Pathways to Cultural Awareness: Cultural Therapy with Students and Teachers, 1994, Fifty Years of Anthropology and Education: A Spindler Anthology, 2000. Pres. Peninsula Sch. Bd., Menlo Park, Calif., 1954-56. Served with AUS, 1942-45. Recipient Lloyd W. Dinkelspiel award Stanford U., 1978, Disting. Svc. award Soc. Internat. Diplomacy and Third World Anthropologists, 1984, Disting. Career Contbn. award Com. on Role and Status of Minorities, Am. Edn. Rsch. Assn., Nat. Acad. Edn., 1994, Father of Ednl. Ethnography award Nat. Ednl. Ethnography Conf., 2000, George and Louise Spindler award for Excellence in Anthropology Stanford U., 2001; fellow Ctr. Advanced Study of Behavioral Scis., 1956-57; subject of Vol. 17 Psychoanalytic Study of Soc. essays, 1992. Fellow Am. Anthrop. Assn.; mem. Southwestern Anthrop. Assn. (pres. 1962-63), Coun. for Anthropology and Edn. (pres. 1982, George and Louise Spindler award for outstanding contbns. to ednl. anthropology 1987, disting. Scholar award 1998), Nat. Acad. Edn. Office: Ethnographics 1247 Alice St Davis CA 95616-2174 Office Phone: 350-753-5690. E-mail: geospinner@aol.com. *My major aims as a professional observer and interpreter of human behavior are to acquire knowledge by research and disseminate understanding to others by teaching, writing, and editing. As a person I try to keep love, work, play in balanced relationship to each other, and strive for tolerance at least, and hopefully appreciation for others who are different than myself.*

SPINDLER, GEORGE S. lawyer, retired oil industry executive; BCE, Ga. Inst. Tech., 1961; JD, DePaul U., 1966. Bar: Ill. 1966. Asst. gen. counsel, patents and licensing Amoco Corp., Chgo., 1979-81, gen. mgr. info. svcs., 1981-85, v.p. planning and adminstrn., 1985-87, assoc. gen. counsel, 1987-88, dep. gen. counsel, 1988-89, v.p., gen. counsel, 1989-92, sr. v.p., gen. counsel, 1992-95, sr. v.p. law and corporate affairs, 1995-99; ret., 1999. Office: 200 E Randolph Dr PO Box 2106C Chicago IL 60690-2106

SPINDLER, JAMES ANDREW, not-for-profit executive; b. Morgantown, W.Va., Oct. 20, 1950; s. Garold Ralph and Elizabeth (Carroll) Spindler; m. Ann Bailie Trautman; 1 child, James Andrew, Jr. AB, Harvard Coll., Cambridge, Mass., 1972; MPA, Princeton U., 1975, PhD, 1983. Bus. fellow The Brookings Instn., Washington, 1980—82; v.p. Continental Ill. Nat. Bank., Chgo., 1984—85, Fed. Res. Bank of N.Y., N.Y.C., 1985—89, sr. v.p., 1989—93; mng. dir. Fin. Svcs. Vol. Corps, N.Y.C., 1993—95, exec. dir., 1995—. Mem. Basle Com. on Banking Supervision, Switzerland, 1991—93, G10 Com. on Payment and Settlement Sys., Basle, 1991—93; prin. investigator Russia Initiative Project of the Carnegie Corp. of NY, NYC, 2000—01; regulatory coun. Dubai Fin. Svc. Authority, United Arab Emirates, 2004—. Author: The Politics of International Credit: Private Finance and Foreign Policy in Germany and Japan, 1984, (Op-Ed Pieces) International Herald Tribune, San Francisco Chronicle, and The Jakarta Post, 2001. Recipient Medal of Svc. for assistance in developing Russian fin. mkts., Ctrl. Bank of Russia and the Russian Finance Ministry, 1996. Mem.: Am. Coun. on Germany, Coun. on Fgn. Relations. Presbyterian. Avocations: classical music, travel, opera, running. Office: Financial Services Volunteer Corps 800 3d Ave 11th Fl New York NY 10022 Business E-Mail: jspindler@fsvc.org.

SPINDLER, JUDITH TARLETON, elementary school educator; b. Dayton, Tenn., Mar. 4, 1932; d. Frank Willson and Julia Elizabeth (Venable) S. BS in Edn., Longwood Coll., 1953; MA in Edn., Va. Commonwealth U., 1976. Tchr. Oceana, King's Grant Sch., Virginia Beach, Va., 1953-66, Ginter Park Elem. Sch., Richmond, Va., 1966-67, Bon Air Elem. Sch., Chesterfield County, Va., 1967-87; ret., 1987. Charter mem. Web of Hope sponsored by ARC (Humanitarian award). Recipient 86 ribbons for 1st, 2nd and 3rd pl. awards various knitting competitions, 5 Best in Show awards rosette competition, including blue ribbons State Fair Va., 1998, 6 ribbons Best in Show rosette Chesterfield County Fair, 1998, 2 Best in Show Chesterfield County Fair, 1 Best in Show State Fair of Va., 3 Blue Ribbons Chesterfield County Fair, 2000, 2 Red Ribbons, 1 White Ribbon Va. State Fair, 2000, 3 Blue Ribbons Chesterfield County Fair, 2 Red Ribbons, 1 White Ribbon 1 Blue, 5 in Va. State Fair, 2002. Mem. NEA, Va. Edn. Assn., Knitting Guild Am. (qualified tchr.), Knit Wit Guild (founding mem.). Avocation: knitting. Home: Care of Scott 10201 Navarre Ct Richmond VA 23233-5543

SPINDLER, PAUL, corporate executive, consultant; b. Chgo., May 2, 1931; s. Isaac Edward and Sophie (Stein) Spindler; m. Gail Klynn; children from previous marriage: Kevin, Makayla, Sydney, Jeffrey. BA in Journalism, Temple U., 1952. Reporter Akron Beacon Jour., Akron, Ohio, 1955-58, San Francisco Examiner, 1958-59; editor Santa Clara (Calif.) Daily Jour., 1959-63; dir. pub. affairs Litton Industries, Inc., Beverly Hills, Calif., 1963-68; dir. pub. relations Internat. Industries, Beverly Hills, 1968-70; pres. Paul Spindler & Co., L.A., 1970-75; exec. v.p. Manning Selvage & Lee, Inc., N.Y.C., 1975-85; pres. The Spindler Co., L.A., 1985-87; pres. Western div. GCI Group, L.A., 1987-91; pres. GCI Spindler, L.A., 1991-96; chmn. Bristol Retail Solutions, Inc., Newport Beach, Calif., 1996-98; pres. Paul Spindler Co., L.A., 1998—. Bd. dirs. Phoenix House Calif.; bd. visitors, Temple U. Sch. Comm. and Theatre. Cpl. U.S. Army, 1952-54. With U.S. Army, 1952—54. Mem. Mountain Gate Country Club (L.A.). Democrat. Jewish. Office: Paul Spindler Co 10351 Santa Monica Blvd Ste 310 Los Angeles CA 90025 Office Phone: 310-286-0102. Business E-Mail: paul@spindlercompany.com.

SPINELLI, ANNE CATHERINE, elementary school educator; b. Chgo., Dec. 19, 1943; d. Stanley J. and Lucy A. (Schmidt) Malaski; m. Joseph P. Spinelli Jr., May 28, 1966. BS in Edn., Ohio U., 1965; postgrad., Ashland U., 1989—. Lic. tchr. kindergarten - 8th grade. Tchr. K-3 North Olmsted (Ohio) City Schs., 1965-70, master tchr., 1970-71, kindergarten tchr., 1971-74, Cloverleaf Schs., Lodi, Ohio, 1974—99; ret., 1999. Seminar presenter sci. dept. Ednl. Rsch. Coun. Am., Cleve., 1969-74, State of Ohio Supr. Assn., Columbus, 1986, Great Lakes Internat. Reading Assn., Chgo., 1993; panelist Ohio Coun. Elem. Sch. Sci. Conv., Akron, 1969; speaker Nat. Sci. Tchrs. Assn. Great Lakes Conf., Cleve., 1971, State of Ohio Proficiency Conf., Cleve., 1996, 97, 98, 2000. Co-author: North Olmsted Schools Motor Perception Book for Kindergarten, 1970, Kindergarten Home Activities Book, 1991—2002. Mem. Zoning Commn., Westfield Twp., Medina County, Ohio, 1978-90; area coord. Cancer Soc., Medina County, 1983, 85, 89, 98; mem. Zoning Bd. Appeals, Westfield Twp Medina County, Ohio, 1996-99. Jennings scholar Jennings Found., N.E. Ohio, 1987-88; named Outstanding Educator/Acad. Subjects Mid East Ohio/Spl. Edn. Regional Resouce Ctr., 1994, Medina County (Ohio) Tchr. of the Year, 1995; finalist Tchr. of Yr. for Ohio, 1996. Mem. ASCD, NEA, Ohio Edn. Assn., No. Ohio Edn. Assn., N.E. Ohio Edn. Assn., Cloverleaf Edn. Assn. (bldg. reps. 1985-99), Internat. Reading Assn., Lizotte Reading Coun., Elem., Kindergarten, Nursery Sch. Educators. Avocations: travel, gardening. Office: Westfield Elem Sch 9055 S LeRoy Rd Westfield Center OH 44251

SPINELLI, JERRY, writer; b. Norristown, Pa., Feb. 1, 1941; s. Louis Anthony and Lorna Mae (Bigler) S.; m. Eileen Mesi; children: Kevin, Barbara, Lana, Jeffrey, Molly, Sean, Benjamin. BA, Gettysburg (Pa.) Coll., 1963; MA, Johns Hopkins U., 1964. Editor Chilton Co., Radnor, Pa., 1966-89. Author: Space Station Seventh Grade, 1982, Who Put That Hair in My Toothbrush?, 1984, Night of the Whale, 1985, Jason and Marceline, 1986, Dump Days,

1988, Maniac Magee, 1990 (Newbery medal 1991, Boston Globe/Horn Book award 1991), Bathwater Gang, 1990, There's a Girl in My Hammerlock, 1991, Dump Days, 1991, Fourth Grade Rats, 1991, Bathwater Gang Get Down to Business, 1992, Do the Funky Pickle, 1992, Report to the Principal's Office!, 1992, Who Ran My Underwear Up the Flagpole?, 1992, Picklemania, 1993, Crash, 1996, Blue Ribbon Blues, 1997, Wringer, 1997 (Newbery honor award 1997), The Libaray Card, 1997, Knots in My Yo-Yo String: The Autobiography of a Kid, 1998, Stargirl, 2000, Loser, 2002, Milkweed, 2003. Avocations: tennis, reading, country music, travel.

SPINETTA, JEAN-CYRIL, airline executive; b. Paris, Oct. 4, 1943; s. Adrien Spinetta and Antoinette Brignoli; m. Nicole Ricquebourg, Nov. 22, 1969; children: Eric, Isabelle, Cécile, Adrien. Student, Paris Law Sch.; diploma, Inst. Internat. Politics, Paris; graduate, Ecole Nationale d'Administration. Assoc. tchr., 1961-69; ctrl. adminstrv. attache, 1969-70; nat. adminstr. Paris Higher Edn. Secondary Schs., 1970-72; bur. chief dept. investments and planing Nat. Edn. Ministry, 1972-76; spl. prosecutor State Coun. Govt., 1976-78; sec. gen. French Govt., 1978-81; info. svc. chief Prime Min. of France, 1981-83; dir. colls. Ministry Nat. Edn., 1983-84; cabinet dir. Min. Labour, Employment and Profl. Devel., 1984-86; inspector gen Nat. Edn. Adminstrn., 1986-88; cabinet dir. Min. Social Affairs and Employment, Min. Overseas Transport, 1988-90; pres., dir. gen. Air Internat., 1990-93; indsl. advisor Presidency of the Republic, 1994-95; adminstr. to 1st mission pub. svc. relevant to govt., 1995; CEO Air France, 1997—. Elected pres. Assn. of European Airlines, 2001—. Decorated officer Legion of Honor, officer Nat. Order of Merit (France). Avocations: tennis, skiing. Office: Air France 125 W 55th St New York NY 10019-5369 also: 45 Rue de Paris 95747 Roissy France Office Phone: 33 1 41567800.

SPINNATO, JOSEPH ANTHONY, II, obstetrician; b. Ketchikan, Alaska, May 10, 1949; s. Joseph Anthony and Ann S.; m. Diane Dusak, Apr. 26, 1969; children: Joseph Anthony III, Mark Andrew, Julie Anne. BS, U. Dayton, 1970; MD, U. Louisville, 1974. Diplomate Am. Bd. Obstetricians and Gynecologists. Resident on ob/gyn U. Louisville, 1974-77; asst. prof. ob/gyn Sch. Medicine Tex. Tech U., Lubbock, 1979-82; nutrition intern Montreal (Can.) Diet Dispensary, 1980; fellow in maternal-fetal medicine U. Tenn. Ctr. for Health Scis., Memphis, 1982-84, clin. instr. dept. ob/gyn, 1982-84; assoc. prof. divsn. maternal-fetal medicine dept. ob/gyn Coll. Medicine U. South Ala., 1984-88; dir., prof. divsn. maternal-fetal medicine dept. ob/gyn. Sch. Medicine/U. Louisville, 1988-99; prof., vice chair dept. ob/gyn. U. Cin., 2000—. Mem. ob/gyn staff Lubbock Gen. Hosp., 1979-82, City of Memphis Hosps., 1982-84, U. South Ala. Med. Ctr., Mobile, 1984-88, Norton Hosp., Louisville, 1988-99, U. Louisville Hosp., 1988-99; mem. birth defects adv. com., human resources dept. Commonwealth of Ky., 1992; dir. maternal transport Norton Hosp., 1988-93, dir. women's reproductive testing ctr., 1988-96; dir. improved pregnancy outcome project U. Louisville, 1988-93, 96-99; dir. Fetal Rev. Bd., 1990-92; dir. perinatology Christ Hosp. Cin.; presenter, lectr., rschr. in field. Spl. reviewer jours. in field; contbr. articles, abstracts to profl. publs. Dir. teenage parent program Emerson Sch., Louisville, 1988-92, 96-99. Lt. comdr. Med. Corps USN, 1977-79. Nutrition intern March of Dimes, 1980; grantee Smith Kline French Labs., 1986, NIH, 1986, NKC Cmty. Trust Fund, 1988, 95-96, WHAS Crusade for Children, 1989-90, 92, 98, Ky. Human Resources Dept., 1990, 93-94; recipient Outstanding Tchr. award, 1991, 93, APGO Excellence in Tchg. award U. Louisville, 1994. Mem. Am. Coll. Obstetricians and Gynecologists, Assn. Profs. of Gynecology and Obstetrics (Excellence in Tchg. award 1994), Soc. Perinatal Obstetricians, Soc. for Maternal-Fetal Medicine, Nat. Perinatal Assn., Jefferson County Med. Soc., Louisville Obgyn Soc., Am. Inst. Ultrasound in Medicine. Avocations: tennis, golf, music, basketball. Office: U Cin PO Box 670526 Cincinnati OH 45267-0526 E-mail: spinnaja@ucmail.uc.edu.

SPINNER, GARY FREDERICK, physician assistant, healthcare administrator; b. Newark, Nov. 8, 1949; s. Harry Spinner and Adele (Spinner) Armm; m. Janet Crocker, July 14, 1974; children: Jacob Adam, Anna Ruth. BA, Rutgers U., 1972; cert. physician asst., Yale Sch. Medicine, 1983; MPH, U. Conn., 1993. Social worker Cath. Social Svcs., Syracuse, N.Y., 1974-78; paramedic, co-dir. Plenty Ambulance Svc., Bronx, N.Y., 1978-81; physician asst. Alex Isgnt, MD, Newtown, Conn., 1983-84; physician asst., adminstr. managed care Hill Health Corp., New Haven, 1984—, COO. Corp. dir. Columbus House, New Haven, 1987—, 1st v.p.; chair Homeless Healthcare Network, New Haven, 1988-95; co-chair Conn. Dept. Social Svcs. Statewide Adv. Coun., Hartford, 1993-96; bd. dirs. Cmty. Health Network, Meridan, chair quality mgmt. and improvement com., 1995—; faculty Yale U. Sch. Medicine; presenter and lectr. in field. Chair New Haven (Conn.) Commn. on Homelessness. Recipient Humanitarian Svc. award Jack W. Cole Soc., 1986, Disting. Alumni award Yale Sch. of Medicine, 1998. Fellow Am. Acad. Physician Assts. (Outstanding Physician Asst. award 1990), Conn. Acad. Physician Assts.; mem. APHA. Avocations: travel, rock climbing, mountain climbing. Office: Hill Health Corp 400 Columbus Ave New Haven CT 06519-1233 E-mail: gary.spinner@aya.yale.edu., gspinner@hillhealthcenter.com.

SPINNER, LEE LOUIS, accountant; b. Hillsboro, Ill., Nov. 9, 1948; s. John Louis and Clara Mae (Brown) Spinner; m. Rosemary T. Dean, Mar. 2, 2002. BS in Acctg., U. Ill., 1971, MAS in Acctg., 1972; MS in Taxation, DePaul U., 1983. CPA, Ill. Sr. tax acct. Ernst & Young, Chgo., 1972-78; dir. tax returns and audits Sunbeam Corp., Chgo., 1978-82; dir. tax compliance Sara Lee Corp., Chgo., 1982-83; mgr. tax compliance AM Internat., Inc., Chgo., 1983-85; mgr. taxes Household Mfg., Inc., Prospect Heights, Ill., 1985-89; mgr. internat. taxes Pittway Corp., Chgo., 1990-2000; dir. taxes Methode Electronics, Inc., Harwood Heights, Ill., 2000—. Instr. tax tng. program Ernst & Young, 1975-78; tax advisor Sta. WIND, Call Your Acct., Chgo., 1977-78. Sec. Grant Park Accts. Softball League, Chgo., 1976-77. Mem. AICPA, Ill. CPA Soc., U. Ill. Alumni Assn. (bd. assoc., audit com. 1997—), Top Social Athletic Club, Moose, KC. Democrat. Roman Catholic. Home: 435 W Wilshire Dr Palatine IL 60067-4788

SPINOTTI, DANTE, cinematographer; b. Tolmezzo, Italy, Aug. 22, 1943; Cinematographer Mirsch Agy., L.A. Cinematographer: (films) Sotto, Sotto, 1984, The Berlin Affair, 1985, Manhunter, 1986, Choke Canyon, 1986, Crimes of the Heart, 1986, From the Hip, 1987, Illegally Yours, 1987, Beaches, 1988, Mamba, 1988, The Legend of the Holy Drinker, The Comfort of Strangers, 1989, Torrents of Spring, 1989, Hudson Hawk, 1990, True Colors, 1991, Frankie and Johnny, 1992, The Last of the Mohicans, 1992 (BAFTA winner), Blink, 1993, The Quick and the Dead, 1994, Nell, 1994, Heat, 1995, The Star Maker, 1995, (with Andrey Barkowyak) The Mirror Has Two Faces, 1995, L.A. Confidential, 1996, Goodbye Lover, 1997, The Other Sister, 1998, The Insider, 1999, Wonder Boys, 2000. Office: The Mirisch Agy Ste 700 101100 Santa Monica Blvd Los Angeles CA 90067

SPINRAD, HYRON, astronomer; b. N.Y.C., Feb. 17, 1934; s. Emanuel B. and Ida (Silverman) S.; m. Bette L. Abrams, Aug. 17, 1958; children—Michael, Robert, Tracy. AB, U. Calif. at Berkeley, 1955, MA, 1959, PhD (Lick Obs. fellow), 1961. Studied galaxies U. Calif. at Berkeley, 1960-61; planetary atmospheres work Jet Propulsion Lab., Pasadena, Calif., 1961-63; investigation atmospheres of coolest stars U. Calif. at Berkeley, 1964-70. Mem. Am. Astron. Soc., Astron. Soc. Pacific. Achievements include spl. research water vapor on Mars, molecular hydrogen on Jupiter, Saturn, Uranus and Neptune, temperature measurements on Venus atmosphere, spectra of galaxies and near-infrared observations, 71-72, location of faint radio galaxies, redshifts of galaxies, galaxy evolution and cosmology, 1973, spectroscopic observations of volatile gases in comets. Home: 7 Ketelsen Ct Moraga CA 94556-1814 Office: U Calif Dept Astronomy Berkeley CA 94720-0001

SPINRAD, ROBERT JOSEPH, computer scientist; b. N.Y.C., Mar. 20, 1932; s. Sidney and Isabel (Reiff) S.; m. Verna Winderman, June 27, 1954; children: Susan Irene, Paul Reiff. BS, Columbia U., 1953, MS (Bridgham fellow), 1954; PhD (Whitney fellow), MIT, 1963. Registered profl. engr., N.Y. Project engr. Bulova Research & Devel. Lab., N.Y.C., 1953-55; sr. scientist Brookhaven Nat. Lab., Upton, N.Y., 1955-68; v.p. Sci. Data Systems, Santa Monica, Calif., 1968-69; v.p. programming Xerox Corp., El Segundo, Calif., 1969-71, dir. info. scis., 1971-76, v.p. systems devel., 1976-78, v.p. research, 1978-83, dir. systems tech., 1983-87, dir. corp. tech., 1987-92, v.p. tech. analysis and devel., 1992-94, v.p. technology strategy, 1994-98; cons. in field, Palo Alto, Calif., 1998—. Contbr. articles to profl. jours. Mem. Nat. Acad. Engring., Calif. Coun. on Sci. and Tech., Sigma Xi, Tau Beta Pi. Achievements include patents in field. E-mail: robert@spinrad.com.

SPIOTTA, RAYMOND HERMAN, editor; b. Bklyn., Feb. 24, 1927; s. Michael Joseph and Olga Elizabeth (Schmidt) S.; m. Maria Theresa Attanasio, Apr. 17, 1949; children: Robert, Michael, Ronald, Mark, Sandra. B.M.E., Pratt Inst., 1953. Mfg. engr. Arma div. Am. Bosch Arma Corp., Garden City, N.Y., 1948-53; mng. editor Machinery mag., N.Y.C., 1953-65; editor Machine and Tool Blue Book, Wheaton, Ill., 1965-89; editorial dir. Machine and Tool Blue Book & Mfg. Systems, Carol Stream, Ill., 1989-90; cons. editor Cutting Tool Engring., Northbrook, Ill., 1992-95; acquisitions editor Hanser Gardner Publs., Cin., 1995-97, ret., 1997. Contbr. to Am. Peoples Ency. Yearbook; contbr. articles to profl. jours. Mem. DuPage County (Ill.) area council Boy Scouts Am., 1966-73. Served with AC USNR, 1944-48. Mem. Numerical Control Soc. of AIM-Tech., Soc. Am. Value Engrs., Soc. Mfg. Engrs., Am. Inst. Indsl. Engrs., Robotics Internat., Computer and Automated Sys. Assn. Roman Catholic. Home and Office: 1484 Aberdeen Ct Naperville IL 60564-9796 E-mail: r-mspiotta@mindspring.com.

SPIOTTO, JAMES ERNEST, lawyer; b. Chgo., Nov. 25, 1946; s. Michael Angelo and Vinnetta Catherine (Henninger) S.; m. Ann Elizabeth Humphreys, Dec. 23, 1972; children: Michael Thomas, Mary Catherine, Joan Elizabeth, Kathryn Ann. AB, St. Mary's of the Lake, 1968; JD, U. Chgo., 1972. Bar: Ill. 1972, U.S. Dist. Ct. (no. dist.) Ill. 1973, U.S. Ct. Appeals (3rd and 7th cir.) 1974, U.S. Supreme Ct. 1978, U.S. Ct. Appeals (9th cir.) 1984, U.S. Dist. Ct. (so. dist.) Calif. 1984. Exclusionary rule study-project dir. Law Enforcement Assistance Agy. Grant, Chgo., 1972; law clk. to presiding justice U.S. Dist. Ct., Chgo., 1972-74; assoc. Chapman and Cutler, Chgo., 1974-80, ptnr., 1980—. Chmn. program on defaulted bonds and bankruptcy Practising Law Inst., 1982—, chmn program on troubled debt financing, 1987— Author: Defaulted Securities, 1990; contbr. numerous articles to profl. jours. With USAR, 1969-75. Mem. Assn. Bond Lawyers, Soc. Mcpl. Analysts, Law Club of City of Chgo., Union League, Econs. Club Chgo. Roman Catholic. Office: Chapman and Cutler 111 W Monroe St Ste 1700 Chicago IL 60603-4006

SPIRA, MELVIN, plastic surgeon; b. Chgo., July 3, 1925; s. Samuel and Jessie (Tivin) S.; m. Rita Silver, Nov. 27, 1952; children— Mary Ann, Joel Bennett, Pamela Beth Student, Wright Jr. Coll, Chgo., 1942-43, Franklin and Marshall Coll., Lancaster, Pa., 1943-44; DDS, Northwestern U., 1947, MSD, 1951; MD, Med. Coll. of Ga., 1956. Diplomate Am. Bd. Plastic Surgery (chmn. 1984-85). Intern Duke U. Hosp., Durham, N.C., 1956-57, jr. asst. resident, 1958-59, asst. resident, 1959-60; resident Jefferson Davis Hosp, Houston, 1960-61, asst. in surgery and plastic surgery; sr. attending physician Ben Taub Gen. Hosp, Houston, attending physician, Tex. Children's Hosp., Houston, St. Lukes Episcopal Hosp., Houston; prof. Baylor Coll. Medicine, Houston, past head divsn. plastic surgery. Past chmn. Am. Bd. Plastic Surgery. Served with USN, 1943-45, 48-50 Fellow ACS; mem. Houston Surg. Soc., Am. Soc. Maxillofacial Surgeons (pres. 1974-75), Am. Soc. Plastic and Reconstructive Surgeons, Harris County Med. Soc., Plastic Surgery Research Council, So. Med. Assn., Tex. Med. Assn., Am. Trauma Soc., G.V. Black Soc., Internat. Soc. for Burn Injuries, Am. Burn Assn., Am. Cleft Palate Assn., Am. Assn. Plastic Surgeons (pres. 1992-93), Acad. Plastic Surgery Forum, Internat. Soc. Reconstructive Microsurgery, Tex. Surg. Soc., Michael E. DeBakey Internat. Cardiovascular Soc., Baron Hardy Soc., Am. Soc. for Aesthetic Plastic Surgery, Alpha Omega Alpha, Sigma Xi Avocations: skiing, photography, painting, tennis, golf. Office: Baylor Coll Medicine Div Plastic Surgery 6560 Fannin St Ste 800 Houston TX 77030-2725

SPIRA, PATRICIA GOODSITT, association executive; b. Milw. d. Lawrence Manfred and Ruth Pauline (Miller) Goodsitt; m. Marvin Alfred Spira, July 12, 1952; children: David, James, Ann, Ellen. BA in History, U. Wis., Milw., 1967. Dir. group sales Swan Theatre and Supper Club, Milw., 1962-63; mgr. box office Performing Arts Ctr., Milw., 1969-80; dir. devel. St. Louis Conservatory and Schs., 1980-81; pres. The Internat. Ticketing Assn., N.Y.C., 1981—2002; ret., 2002. Tchr. Creative Dramatics, Milw., 1962-66; adv. coun. Town Hall, N.Y.C., 1989—; bd. dirs. Theatre and Dance Co., N.Y.C., 1986-89. Bd. dirs. Milw. Chamber Music Soc., 1974-80, Soc. Preservation of Profl. Touring Entertainment History, 1998; chair bd. dirs. Great Am. Children's Theatre, 1977-80, bd. dirs. Sledgehammer Theatre, 2003—. Mem. Am. Soc. Assn. Execs. (cert.). Avocations: reading, travel, theater. Home: 645 Front St unit 607 San Diego CA 92101 E-mail: pspira@cox.net.

SPIRA, ROBERT ALAN, securities company executive; b. Chgo., Feb. 13, 1932; s. Leo and Tena Dolores (Sarnat) Spira; m. Nancy Ann Netzle (dec.); children: Leslie Gayle, James Mitchel; m. Barbara Lader (dec.). BA, Roosevelt U., Chgo., 1953. V.p. Walston & Co., Chgo., 1955-70; head new bus. Cowen & Co., N.Y.C., 1970-72; mem. instnl. sales staff Edwards & Hanly, N.Y.C., 1975-77; pres. Haas Securities Corp., N.Y.C., 1977-87; former pres., dir. Haas Devel. Corp., N.Y.C.; mem. Wall St. Planning Group, N.Y.C., 1976—. Past mem. Boston Stock Exch. (listing com.); chmn. bd. dirs. KIMG; chmn., CEO Berkeley Securities, 1988-90, Chapman, Spira & Carson, 1990—; bd. dirs. E-Data Corp.; pres., dir. Austin Davenport Assocs., Carlyle & Christie Capital Corp., Ulysses Capital Corp., Whitney, Sterling & Webster Corp., Am. Asian Enterprises, Inc., Peabody Sherman Capital Group, Inc., F.X. Knox & Co., Internat. Trading & Fin. Agy., Inc.; commentator ABC-TV fin. news, 1967-70; chmn. Russian Am. Cons. Group, Tran Eurasian Cons. Co., Inc., Advanced Techs. and Software N.Y. Trans Eurasian Materials and Testing Co., Inc.; advisor UN; lectr. Thunderbird Internat. Bus. Sch. Author: Diamonds are Forever, Almost, Ready or Not, Here Come the Banks; contbr. numerous articles on historic and econ. Bd. dirs. Boys Brotherhood Rep., Honest Ballot Assn., Rhumbline Advisers, Luscombe Aircraft Corp.; dir., chmn. KIMG Inc.; mem. Congl. Adv. Bd., Am. Security Coun., NTL Adv. Bd. With Green Berets U.S. Army, 1953-54. Mem. Nat. Option and Futures Soc., Nat. Assn. Securities Dealers (disting. bus. conduct com., arbitration panel and Wall St. planning group), Am. Commodities Exch. (listing com.), N.Y. Futures Exch., N.Y. Stock Exch., Am. Stock Exch. (allied mem., arbitration panel), Fin. Analysts and Money Mgrs. Assn., World Trade Ctrs. Assn., Am. Numismatic Assn., Am. Philatelic Soc., Nat. Options Soc. Pacific Cmty. Inst. (adv.), U.S. Senatorial Club, Big Apple Triathalon Club, Profl. Assn. Scuba Divers, NY Stock Exch. Club. Achievements include numerous patents on advanced financial and technological subjects. Home and Office: Chapman Spira & Carson 110 Wall ST 15th Fl New York NY 10005 Office Phone: 212-425-6100. E-mail: bobspira@chapmanspira.com.

SPIRES, ROBERT CECIL, foreign language educator; b. Missouri Valley, Iowa, Dec. 1, 1936; s. Roy C. and Ellen M. (Epperson) S.; m. Roberta A. Hyde, Feb. 2, 1963; children: Jeffrey R., Leslie Ann. BA, U. Iowa, 1959, MA, 1963, PhD, 1968. Asst. prof. Ohio U., Athens, 1967-69; asst. prof. dept. Spanish and Portuguese U. Kans., Lawrence, 1969-72, assoc. prof., 1972-78, prof., 1978—, chmn. dept., 1983-92. Author: La novela española, 1978, Beyond the Metafictional Mode, 1984, Transparent Simulacra, 1988, Post-Totalitarian Spanish Fiction, 1996; contbg. editor SigloXX/20th Century; editl. bd. Jour. of Interdisciplinary Literary Studies, 1993—, Ind. Jour. of Hispanic Lit., 1992—. Served with U.S. Army, 1959-61. NEH fellow, 1981-82, U.S.-Spain Joint Com. fellow, 1985-86, Hall Ctr. for Humanities fellow, 1992, Program Cultural Coop. fellow, 1993. Mem. Revista de Estudios Hispánicos (editorial bd. 1985—), Anales de Literatura Contemporánea (editorial bd. 1981—), Letras Peninsulares (editorial bd. 1987—), MLA (del. assembly 1989-91), MLA 20th Century Spain (exec. com. 1983-89), 20th Century Spanish Assn. Am. (v.p. 1989-92). Home: 2420 Orchard Ln Lawrence KS 66049-2710 Office: U Kans Dept Spanish & Portuguese Lawrence KS 66045-0001 Office Phone: 785-864-3851. E-mail: rspires@ku.edu.

SPIRN, MICHELE SOBEL, communications professional, writer; b. Newark, Jan. 26, 1943; d. Jack and Sylvia (Cohen) Sobel; m. Steven Frederick Spirn, Jan. 27, 1968; 1 child, Joshua. BA, Syracuse U., 1965; MFA, The New Sch., 1999. Creative dir. Planned Communications Svcs., N.Y.C., 1966-72, EDL Prodns., N.Y.C., 1972-73; free-lance writer Bklyn., 1973-83; dir. pub. rels. Nat. Coun. Jewish Women, N.Y.C., 1983-90, dir. communications, 1990-95; freelance writer Bklyn., 1995—. Adj. lectr. CUNY, Bklyn., 1977—81; instr. The New Sch., N.Y.C., 1999—, NYU, 2002—. Author: The Fast Shoes, 1985, The Boy Who Liked Green, 1985, The Know-Nothings, 1995; co-author: A Man Can Be..., 1981, A Know-Nothing Birthday, 1997, Birth Celebrations, 1998, New Year Celebrations, 1998; co-author: The Nutcracker, 1998, A Know-Nothing Halloween, 2000, The Know-Nothings Talk Turkey, 2000, The Bridges in London, 2000, All Washed Up, 2000, Racing To The Light, 2000, Wait Til The Midnight Hour, 2000, Jackie Joyner-Kersee, 2000, The Bridges in Paris, 2000, Race to the Sea, 2001, A Twist in Time, 2001, I Am the Turkey, 2004, The Bridges in Edinburgh, 2004, Cold-Blooded Creatures, 2004, Arachnids, 2004; editor, columnist Children's Entertainment Rev. mag., N.Y.C., 1982; columnist The Phoenix newspaper, Bklyn., 1983. Pres. Tenth St. Block Assn., Bklyn., 1989-91; vol. Model Media Program, Bklyn., 1985—. Recipient Silver medal for pub. svc. film N.Y. Internat. Film and TV Festival, 1972. Mem.: Authors Guild, Soc. Children's Book Writers and Illustrators, Mystery Writers Am. Avocations: reading, gardening. E-mail: michelesteve21@hotmail.com.

SPIRO, HERBERT JOHN, political scientist, politician, educator, ambassador; b. Hamburg, Germany, Sept. 7, 1924; came to U.S., 1938, naturalized, 1944; s. Albert John and Marianne (Stiefel) S.; m. Elizabeth Anna Petersen, June 7, 1958 (div.); children: Peter John, Alexander Charles Stiefel; m. Marion Ballin, July 22, 1985. Student, San Antonio Jr. Coll., 1942-43; AB summa cum laude, Harvard U., 1949, MA, 1950, PhD, 1953; MA (hon.), U. Pa., 1971. Adminstrv. asst. U.S. War Dept., Vienna, 1945-46; mem. faculty Harvard U., Cambridge, Mass., 1950-61, asst. prof., 1957-61; assoc. prof. polit. sci. Amherst (Mass.) Coll., 1961-65; prof. polit. sci. U. Pa., Phila., 1965-73; mem. policy planning staff Dept. State, Washington, 1970-75; ambassador to Cameroon, 1975-77; amb. to Equatorial Guinea, 1975-76; fellow Woodrow Wilson Internat. Ctr. for Scholars, Smithsonian Instn., Washington, 1978; vis. prof. polit. sci. Def. Intelligence Sch., Washington, 1979-80; univ. prof. polit. sci. John F. Kennedy Inst. for N.Am. Studies, Free U. Berlin, 1980-89. Fulbright sr. rsch. prof. U. Coll. Rhodesia and Nyasaland, 1959-60; cons. Brit. Commn. to Rev. Constn., Fedn. Rhodesia and Nyasaland, 1960, Japanese Commn. on Revision Constn., 1962; vis. assoc. prof. U. Chgo., 1961, Stanford (Calif.) U., 1963; chmn. Asian and African Studies program, Amherst-Smith-Mt. Holyoke Colls., U. Mass., 1964-65; vis. prof. internat. affairs Woodrow Wilson Sch., Princeton (NJ) U., 1966; adv. coun. polit. sci. Haverford Coll., 1966-71; affiliated with Nuffield Coll., Oxford (Eng.) U., 1967-68; resident scholar Rockefeller Found. Study Ctr., Bellagio, Italy, 1968, 78; vis. prof. govt., guest scholar Ctr. for Internat. Affairs, Harvard U., 1983; vis. scholar U. Tex., Austin, 1984-89; life mem. Brit. studies faculty seminar U. Tex., Austin, 1983—; rschr. Lyndon Baines Johnson Presdl. Libr., 1985-86; fellow Aspen (Colo.) Inst. Humanistic Studies, 1986; adj. prof. govt. U. Tex., Austin, 1989-91; participant internat scholarly and diplomatic confs.; founder Brackenridge H.S.-Wilhelm Gymnasium Exchange; lectr. in field. Author: Politics of German Codetermination, 1958, (with others) Patterns of Government, 1958, 2d edit., 1962, Government by Constitution, 1959, Politics in Africa, 1962, 2d edit., 1975, Five African States, 1963, World Politics: The Global System, 1966, (with others) Authority, Nomos I, 1958, Responsibility, Nomos III, 1960, Privacy Nomos XIII, 1971, Why Federations Fail, 1968, Responsibility in Government, 1969, The Dialectic of Representation 1619-1969, 1969, Politics as the Master Science: From Plato to Mao, 1970 (with others), Theory and Politics, 1971 (with others), Between Sovereignty and Integration, 1974, A New Foreign Policy Consensus?, 1979, (with others) The Legacy of the Constitution, 1987, (with others) Anti-Americanism, 1988; editor, contbr.: (with others) Africa: The Primacy of Politics, 1966, Patterns of African Development, 1967, 'Privatization' of U.S. Foreign Relations, 1995; contbr.: World Book Ency., Ency. Britannica, Intern. Ency. of the Social Scis.; host Spiro's Conversations, Austin Community TV, 1992-97, San Antonio Time-Warner Access TV channel 20, 1999—; contbr. articles to profl. jours. Del. Tex. State Rep. Conv., 1990-92; precinct chmn. Travis County; Rep. cand. for Tex. Ho. of Reps., 1991, U.S. House of Reps., 1992, 94, U.S. Senate, 1993. Decorated Bronze Star medal with oak leaf cluster, Purple Heart; grand officer Legion of Valor Cameroon, 1977; recipient Detur prize Harvard Coll., 1948, Bowdoin prize, 1952; John Harvard scholar, 1949-51, Holzer scholar, 1949-51; Guggenheim fellow, 1959-60, Social Sci. Research Council faculty fellow, 1962, 67-68, Rockefeller Found. fellow, 1958, Sheldon travelling fellow Harvard U., also Fulbright fellow, 1953-54; Moody grantee Lyndon Baines Johnson Found., 1985. Fellow Assn. for Diplomatic Studies; mem. African Studies Assn., Am. Polit. Sci. Assn. (coun. 1968-70, chmn. election com. 1969), Internat. Polit. Sci. Assn., Am. Soc. Polit. and Legal Philosophy, Coun. Fgn. Rels., Coun. Am. Ambs., Am. Fgn. Svc. Assn., Mil. Order Purple Heart, San Antonio World Affairs Coun., Harvard Alumni Assn. (apptd. regional dir. Tex. 1994-97), San Antonio Coll. Alumni Assn. (dir. 1999—, Disting. Former Student award 2000), Wissenschaftliche Gesellschaft Berlin, Signet Soc., Harvard U. Faculty Club, Harvard Club (N.Y.C.), Harvard Club Berlin (pres. 1985-89), Harvard Club Austin (pres. 1990-92), Harvard Club San Antonio, Phi Beta Kappa. Republican. Address: Apt 713 1 Towers Park Ln San Antonio TX 78209-6423 Personal E-mail: h.spiro@globalsbc.net.

SPIRO, MELFORD ELLIOT, anthropology educator; b. Cleve., Apr. 26, 1920; s. Wilbert I. and Sophie (Goodman) Spiro; m. Audrey Goldman, May 27, 1950; children: Michael, Jonathan. BA, U. Minn., 1941; PhD, Northwestern U., 1950. Mem. faculty Washington U., St. Louis, 1948—52, U. Conn., 1952—57, U. Wash., 1957—64; prof. anthropology U. Chgo., 1964—68; prof., chmn. dept. anthropology U. Calif., San Diego, 1968—99, prof. emeritus, 1999—. Author (with E.G. Burrows): An Atoll Culture, 1953; author: Kibbutz: Venture in Utopia, 1955, Children of Kibbutz, 1958, Burmese Supernaturalism, 1967, Buddhism and Society: A Great Tradition and Its Burmese Vicissitudes, 1971, Kinship and Marriage in Burma, 1977, Gender and Culture: Kibbutz Women Revisited, 1979, Culture and Human Nature, 1993, Oedipus in the Trobriands, 1982, Anthropological Other or Burmese Brother: Studies in Cultural Analysis, 1992, Gender Ideology and Psychological Reality, 1997; editor: Context and Meaning in Culture Anthropology, 1965. Bd. dirs. Social Sci. Rsch. Coun., 1960—62. Fellow: NAS, Am. Acad. Arts and Scis.; mem.: AAAS, Soc. for Psychol. Anthropology (pres. 1979—80), Am. Ethnol. Soc. (pres. 1967—68), Am. Anthrop. Assn. Home: 2500 Torrey Pines Rd La Jolla CA 92037-3400 Office: U Calif-San Diego 9500 Gilman Dr La Jolla CA 92093-0532 Business E-Mail: mspiro@ucsd.edu.

SPIRO, ROBERT HARRY, JR., foundation and business executive, educator; b. Asheville, N.C., Dec. 5, 1920; s. Robert Harry and Eoline Peterson (Shaw) S.; m. Terrie C. Gay, May 17, 1980; children by previous marriage: Robert Timothy, Elizabeth Susan, James Monroe. BS, Wheaton (Ill.) Coll., 1941; postgrad. Navy Supply Sch., Harvard U., 1943; postgrad., U. N.C., 1945-46; PhD, U. Edinburgh, Scotland, 1950; student, Union Theol. Sem., summers 1951-53; postdoctoral, Duke U., summer 1956; ScD (hon.), Fla. Inst. Tech. Assoc. prof. King Coll., Bristol, Tenn., 1946-50; prof. history Miss. Coll., 1950-57; pres. Blue Ridge Assembly, Black Mountain, N.C., 1957-60; dean Coll. Liberal Arts Mercer U., prof. history, 1960-64; pres. Jacksonville U., Fla., 1964-79; under sec. of Army, 1980-81; cons. to bus., 1981-84, 86-99; nat. exec. dir. Res. Officers Assn. U.S., 1984-86; chmn. RHS Imprinted Products Inc., 1988-99; past bd. mgrs. Voyager Variable Annuity of Fla., 1972-79. V.p. Am. Security Coun. Found., 1991—99, chmn., 2002—; pres. Nat. Security Caucus Found., 1997—2002; past pres. Fla. Assn. Colls. and Univs.; mem., past chmn. Ind. Colls. and Univs., 1964—79, chmn, 1967; sec.-treas. Assn. Urban Univs., 1968—76; past mem. Fla.-Columbia Ptnrs.; gen. chmn. Jacksonville Sesquicentennial Commn., 1970—72; mem. N.C. Tricentennial Commn., 1959—65; past mem. adv. coun. Robert A. Taft Inst. Govt., Inst. Internat. Edn. Editor (with D.F. Winkler and J.C. Reilly Jr.) Destroyer Squadron Two From Leyte Gulf Through Okinawa, 2002; contbr. articles to profl. publs. and encys. Trustee Southwestern Bapt. Theol. Sem., 1968—78; chmn. bd. Bapt. Coll. and Sem., Washington, 1989—2001. Ensign to lt. USNR, 1941—45, ret. rear adm. USNR, 1978. Decorated Palmes Academique (France); recipient Disting. Civilian Svc. award, Dept. of Army, 1981, Disting. Alumnus award, Navy Supply Corps Sch., 2000. Mem. Navy League U.S. (former pres. Jacksonville coun.), Naval Res. Assn. (nat. adv. coun.), Res. Officers Assn. U.S. Naval Inst., Ret. Officers Assn., Am. Legion,

Kiwanis (pres. Clinton, Miss. 1956-57; pres. Georgetown, D.C. Club 1991-92), Army-Navy Country Club (Arlington, Va.), Phi Delta Kappa, Alpha Kappa Psi, Phi Alpha Theta, Phi Kappa Phi. Home: 105 Follin Ln SE Vienna VA 22180-4957 *Esse Quam Videre "To Be Rather than to Seem" is an eloquent apothegm I learned in high school Latin classes. For me it has been a demanding goal for daily living, a worthy aspiration for each task in life and a challenging vision of what I wish and ought to be.*

SPIRTOS, MARIA, magazine publisher; BS, U. So. Calif., 1988; postgrad., UCLA, 1997. CPA, Calif. Mem. audit staff Ernst & Young, LLP, 1988-93; dir. fin. and adminstrn. Winsford Corp., 1993-96, v.p., CFO, 1996—; pres. Am. Collegiate Network, Inc., pub. U, The Nat. Coll. Mag., 1997—. Office: 1800 Century Park E Ste 820 Los Angeles CA 90067-1511

SPISAK, JOHN FRANCIS, environmental company executive; b. Cleve., Mar. 27, 1950; s. Ernest Lawrence and Adele Marie (Chipko) S.; m. Barbara Ann Heisman, June 10, 1972; children: John Stefan, Theresa Rose. BS in Chemistry, BS in Biology with honors, Purdue U., 1972. Rsch. engr. Anaconda Minerals, Tucson, 1972-79; chief metallurgist Fed. Am. Uranium, Riverton, Wyo., 1979-80; v.p. ops. Anschutz Mining Corp., Denver, 1980-87; chmn. bd. dirs. Warrenton Refining (subs. of Anschutz Corp.), Denver, 1987-89; dir., owner BE&K/Terranext, Inc., Denver, 1989—; pres. Continental Supply, Woodland, Calif., 2003—. Mem. Western States-U.S. Senate Coalition for Superfund Reform; CEO, Am. Purificaion Corp., Newport Beach, Calif., 1998-02, pres. Prosonic Corp., Marietta, Ohio, 2002-03. Contbr. articles to profl. publs.; patentee sequential flotation of sulfide ores. Named One of Fifty Colo. Top Bus. Leaders, Colo. Assn. Commerce and Industry. Mem. AIME, Soc. Mining, Metallurgy and Exploration, Nat. Assn. Environ. Mgrs. (co-founder, bd. dirs. Washington chpt., co-chmn. govt. liaison and advocacy com.), Denver Petroleum Club, Elks. Republican. Roman Catholic. Avocations: classical piano, bicycling, model railroads. Home: 9384 Oakbrush Way Lone Tree CO 80124-3070 Office: Continental Supply Co Woodland CA 95776 E-mail: tnxtceo@aol.com.

SPITLER, KENNETH F. wholesale distribution executive; b. 1949; B.A. in Philosophy, Univ. of Tulsa, 1971. With Sysco Corp, 1986—, exec. v.p., 1986—92, pres. Detroit, 1992—95, pres., CEO Houston, 1995—2000, sr. v.p. operations, northeast region, 2000—02, exec. v.p., redistribution and northeast region, 2002—03, exec. v.p. foodservice operations, 2003—. Office: Sysco Corp 1395 Enclave Pkwy Houston TX 77077

SPITZ, BARBARA SALOMON, artist; b. Chgo., Jan. 8, 1926; d. Fred B. and Sadie (Lorch) Salomon; m. Lawrence S. Spitz, Mar. 19, 1949; children—Thomas R., Linda J., Joanne L. AB, Brown U., 1947; student, Art Inst. Chgo., 1942-43, R.I. Sch. Design, 1945. One-woman exhbns. include Benjamin Galleries, Chgo., 1971, 73, Kunsthaus Buhler, Stuttgart, Germany, 1973, Van Straaten Gallery, Chgo., 1976, 80, Elca London Studio, Montreal, Que., Can., 1977, Loyola U. Chgo., 1988, Schneider, Bluhm, Loeb gallery, Chgo., 1993, Newport Beach Pub. Lib., 2002, The Ctr. Gallery, 1994; group exhibitions include Am. Acad. Arts and Letters, Library of Congress traveling print exhbn., Tokyo Cen. Mus. Arts, Nat. Acad. Design, NYC, Pratt Graphic Ctr., Honolulu Acad. Arts, Wadsworth Atheneum, Nat. Aperture, 1986—, Laguna Art Mus., others; represented in permanent collections Phila. Mus. Art, DeCordova Mus., Okla. Art Ctr., Milw. Art Ctr., Los Angeles County Mus. Art, Art Inst. Chgo., Portland Mus. Art, Wadsworth Atheneum, med. arts program UCLA, Block Mus./Northwestern U., Smart Mus./U. Chgo. Vice-chmn. Chgo. area Brown U. Bicentennial Drive; treas. Hearing and Speech Rehab. Ctr., Michael Reese Hosp., 1960; fine arts patron bd. Newport Harbor Art Mus. Mem. Print Club Phila., Boston Printmakers, Arts Club of Chgo., Soc. Am. Graphic Artists. Address: 1106 Somerset Ln Newport Beach CA 92660-5629 E-mail: bsslss@adelphia.net.

SPITZ, MARK, Olympic athlete; b. Modesto, Calif., Feb. 10, 1950; m. Suzy Weiner; 2 children. BS, Ind. U, 1972. Mem. U.S. swimming team Olympic Games, 1968, 72, guest TV swimming commentator. Former owner Beverly Hills Real Estate Co. Author: (novels) The Mark Spitz complete book of swimming, 1976, Seven Golds: Mark Spitz Own Story, 1987. Inducted as Honor Swimmer to Internat. Swimming Hall of Fame, 1977; Sullivan award for top athlete in any sport AAU, 1971; named World Swimmer of Yr., 1969, 1971, 1972. won total of 9 Olympic Gold medals, 4x100m freestyle, 4x200m freestyle, 1968, 1972, 100m freestyle, 200m freestyle, 100m butterfly, 200m butterfly, 4x100m medley, 1972; only Olympian in history to win 7 Gold medals (all World Records) in a single Olympics, Munich Olympic Games, 1972, Silver Medal, 100m butterfly, Bronze Medal, 100m freestyle, Mexico City Olympic Games, 1968, 5 Gold medals Pan-Am. Games, 1967, held 32 world records, 1967-1972; 4 times Champion NCAA, 1969-72.*

SPITZ, SEYMOUR JAMES, JR., retired fragrance company executive; b. Milw., Nov. 17, 1921; s. Seymour James and Marie (Spinette) S.; m. Elizabeth Taylor Parks, Feb. 7, 1948 (div. Aug. 1967); children: William Taylor, Elizabeth Seymour, Anne Bellin; m. Ellen C. Flynn, July 25, 1969; 1 dau., Ellen Christina. SB, MIT, 1943. With Newport Industries div. Heyden Newport Chem. Corp., Pensacola, Fla., 1946-65; asst. chief engr., 1955-57; asst. v.p., 1957-58; v.p. Newport Industries div. Heyden Newport Chem. Corp., 1959-60, exec. v.p., 1960-61, pres., 1961-65; v.p. parent co. Heyden Newport Chem. Corp., 1962-65, became group v.p., 1965; exec. v.p. Heyden Newport Chem. Corp. (renamed Tenneco Chems., Inc.), 1966; pres. Tenneco Chems., Inc., 1967-69; sr. v.p. parent co. Tenneco Inc.; pres. and dir. Internat. Flavors & Fragrances Inc., N.Y.C., 1970-85. Mem. MIT Corp. Devel. Com., 1977-86; trustee Spence Sch., 1982-88, Savannah (Ga.) Symphony, 1990-95, 98, Telfair Mus. Art, Savannah, 1993-96; MBA adv. bd. Ga. Southern U., 1998—. USN ENS-LCDR, 1943-46. Mem. Univ. Club (N.Y.C.), Larchmont Yacht Club (N.Y., trustee 1986-89), Landings Club, Oglethorpe Club (Savannah, bd. dirs. 1995-99). Home: 6 Brandenberry Rd Savannah GA 31411-2201

SPITZBERG, IRVING JOSEPH, JR., lawyer; b. Little Rock, Feb. 9, 1942; s. Irving Joseph and Marie Bettye (Seeman) S.; m. Roberta Frances Alprin, Aug. 21, 1966 (div. 1988); children: Edward Storm, David Adam; m. Virginia V. Thorndike, Dec. 24, 1988. BA, Columbia U., 1964; B.Phil., Oxford U., 1966; JD, Yale U., 1969. Bar: Calif. 1969, D.C. 1985, Va. 1995. Asst. prof. Pitzer Coll., Claremont, Calif., 1969-71; fellow Inst. Current World Affairs, N.Y.C., 1971-74; vis. lectr. Brown U., Providence, 1973; assoc prof. SUNY, Buffalo, 1974-80, dean of coll., 1974-78; gen. sec. AAUP, Washington, 1980-84; exec. dir. Coun. for Liberal Learning of Assn. Am. Colls., Washington, 1985-89; pres. The Knowledge Co., Fairfax, Va., 1985-2001; ptnr. Spitzberg & Drew, Washington, 1990-92; of counsel Spirer & Goldberg, Washington, 1993—; pvt. practice, 1993—. Coord. Alvan Ikoku Coll., Nigeria, 1979-80; cons. Bd. Adult Edn., Kenya, 1973-74, Philander Smith Coll., Little Rock, 1978-80; co-dir. nat. study on campus life for Carnegie Found. for Advancement Teaching, 1989-90. Author and editor: Exchange of Expertise, 1978, Universities and the New International Order, 1979, Universities and the International Exchange of Knowledge, 1980; author: Campus Programs on Leadership, 1986, Racial Politics in Little Rock, 1987; co-author: (with Berdahl and Moodie), Quality and Access in Higher Education, 1991, (with Virginia Thorndike) Creating Community on College Campuses, 1992; polit. columnist Prince William Times, 2001-02. Founder Coalition for Ednl. Excellence, Western N.Y., 1978-80, Advocates for the Rural Crescent, Va., 1999-2002, Coun. Liberal Learning; founding mem. Alliance for Leadership Devel., Washington, 1985; counsel GASP, Pomona, Calif., 1969-71; Dem. Committeeman, Erie County, N.Y., 1978-80; founding pres. Internat. Found. for St. Catherine's Coll., Oxford, 1986-91; v.p. Sparks-Gleedon Cmty. Coun., 2004—. Nat. winner Westinghouse Sci. Talent Search, 1960; Kellett scholar Trustees of Columbia U., 1964-66. Mem. Am. Immigration Lawyers Assn., Nat. Acad. Elder Law Attys., Washington Ethical Soc. (adj. leader 2002—), Ethical Culture Soc., Columbia Club, Yale Club (Washington), Rotary Internat. Jewish. Avocations: kids, the internet. Office Phone: 410-357-5984. Personal E-mail: ijs@aol.com.

SPITZE, GLENYS SMITH, retired educator; b. Rozel, Kans., May 20, 1919; d. Harry H. and Mary Louisa (Mishler) Smith; m. LeRoy A. Spitze, Dec. 31, 1942 (dec. Nov. 1995); children: Randall LeRoy, Kevin Lance, Kimett Alvin, Terril Christian, Shawn Smith; 1 fosterchild, Theo Ritz-Spitze. Cert. tchg., U. Kans., 1939; AA, San Jose (Calif.) City Coll., 1963; BA in Psychology, San Jose State U., 1965, MA in Child Devel., 1968. Cert. tchr., counselor, Calif. Elem. sch. tchr. Topeka County Schs., Richland, Kans., 1939-40, Kinsley (Kans.) Pub. Schs., 1940-42; presch. substitute tchr. AAUW Kindergarten, Newark, Ohio, 1945—46; presch. tchr. Meth. Ch. Facility, Campbell, Calif., 1956-58; guest lectr. Govt. Sch. Social Work, Colombo, Sri Lanka, 1965-66; instr. man-woman relationship San Jose State Free U., 1966-67; child devel. lab. psychol. examiner Child Labs San Jose State U., 1967-68; pvt. informal practice tchr., counselor, cons. San Jose, Kailua, Hawaii. Vocal music dir. grades 1-3 Southside Sch., 1940-41; 6th dist. Calif. Congress Parent-Tchrs. Social Welfare dir., officer 6th dist. com. Calif. Coun. on Crime and Delinquency, San Jose, 1956-62; mem. kindergarten com. AAUW, Newark, Ohio, 1945-46; coord. Sangha Symposium, Asian Philosophy Club, San Jose State U., 1964-65; lectr. in field. Contbr. articles, poems to profl. publs. Hon. del. Gov. Brown's Conf. on Prevention of Juvenile Delinquency, Sacramento, 1963; co-organizer Post Polio Support Group, Kailua-Kona, HI, 2000. Mem. Psi Chi. Avocations: writing, reading, swimming, snorkeling, anthropology and archeology travel. Home: 78-6800 Alii Dr KKSRC 5-103 Kailua Kona HI 96740-4421 Home (Summer): 311 E Bowman Woodland Park CO 80863 also: PO Gen Delivery Woodland Park CO 80863 E-mail: GMGlenys@webtv.net.

SPITZER, ADRIAN, pediatrician, educator; b. Bucharest, Rumania, Dec. 21, 1927; came to U.S., 1963, naturalized, 1968; s. Osias and Sophia S. S.; m. Carole Zelter, Oct. 31, 1951; 1 son, Vlad. BS, Matei Basarab Lyceum, Bucharest, 1946; MD, Med. Sch. Bucharest, 1952. Diplomate: Am. Bd. Pediatrics. Intern White Plains (N.Y.) Hosp., 1964; resident Hosp. Med. Coll. Pa., 1965-66; postdoctoral fellow pediatric nephrology Albert Einstein Coll. Medicine, 1966-67; postdoctoral fellow in renal physiology Cornell U. Med. Sch., 1967-68; practice medicine specializing in pediatric nephrology Bronx, N.Y., 1968—; asst. prof. pediatrics Albert Einstein Coll. Medicine, 1968-72, assoc. prof., 1972-76, prof., 1976—, dir. div. nephrology, 1973-99; mem. staff Bronx Mcpl. Hosp. Ctr., Hosp. Albert Einstein Coll. Medicine/Montefore Med. Ctr.; mem. Medicine B Study sect.-NIH, 1976-80. Prof. C. Donders rotating chmn. U. Utrecht, The Netherlands, 1990-91; Christiansen vis. fellow St. Catherine's Coll.; vis. fellow dept. biochemistry Oxford U., 1981-82; coord. Internat. Study Kidney Disease in Children; chmn. organizing com. 1st-7th Internat. Workshop on Devel. Renal Physiology, 1980-98, pres., 2001; mem. renal adv. com. N.Y.C. Dept. Health; sci. adv. bd. rsch. and grant com. Nat. Kidney Found., 1982; chmn. pediatric nephrology bd. Am. Bd. Pediat., 1982-83. Mem. editorial bd.: Pediatric Nephrology, Seminars in Nephrology; assoc. editor: Pediatric Renal Disease, 1979, 2d edit., 1992; editor: The Kidney Development, 1982. NIH spl fellow, 1967; John E. Fogarty Sr. Internat. fellow, 1981-82; grantee NIH, N.Y. State Health Research Council, Nat. Kidney Found.; recipient Bela Schick medal for extraordinary achievements in acad. and clin. pediatrics; The Scientific Advancement award of the Internat. Pediatr. Nephrol. Assoc. Mem.: Intersoc. Coun. for Kidney and Urinary Tract Rsch. (sec.-treas. 1984—89), Am. Pediat. Soc., Am. Acad. Pediat., Soc. Pediatric Rsch., Am. Physiol. Soc., Am. Fedn. Clin. Rsch., Am. Soc. Pediatric Nephrology (coun. 1977—80, pres. 1981—82), Am. Soc. Nephrology (com. on govtl. rels. 1999—2001), Internat. Pediatric Nephrology Assn. (hon. Sci. Advancement award), Salt and Water Club. Office: Albert Einstein Coll Medicine Montefiore Med Ctr 111 E 210th St Bronx NY 10467-2401 Office Phone: 718-655-1120. E-mail: spitzer@aecom.yu.edu.

SPITZER, ALAN, automotive executive; Student, Baldwin Wallce Coll. Gen. mgr. Dodge dealership Spitzer Mgmt. Inc., Ohio, dealer, operator, CEO Elyria, Ohio, 1990—, also chmn. bd. dirs. Mem. nat. dealer coun. Ford Motor Co., Chrysler Corp.; mem. Key Bank USA Dealer Adv. Bd. Office: Spitzer Mgmt Inc 150 E Bridge St Elyria OH 44035-5219

SPITZER, CARY REDFORD, avionics consultant, electrical engineer; b. New Hope, Va., July 31, 1937; s. Clyde Burke and Marion Jeanette (Redford) S.; m. Carrie Laura Ruth Logan, June 18, 1960; 1 child, Stiegel Logan. BSEE, Va. Poly. Inst. & State U., 1959; MS in Engring. Mgmt., George Washington U., 1970. Rsch. engr., engring. mgr. Langley Rsch Ctr., NASA, Hampton, Va., 1962-94; founder, pres. AvioniCon, Inc., 1993—. Lectr. UCLA, 1989—, George Washington U., 1994. Author: Viking Orbiter Views of Mars, 1981, Digital Avionics Systems, 1987, 2d edit., 1993, Avionics Handbook, 2000; contbr. articles to sci. publs. 1st lt. USAF, 1959-62. Recipient Volare award Airline Avionics Inst., 1988; named Va. Peninsula Engr. of Yr., 1993; recipient Digital Avionics award Am. Inst. of Aeronautics and Astronautics, 1994 Fellow: IEEE (Centennial medal 1984, Millennium medal 2000), AIAA (assoc.); mem.: Aerospace and Electronic Systems Soc. of IEEE (pres. 1973—74, editor-in-chief Trans. 1996—99, chmn. IEEE-USA aerospace policy com. 1997—2000), Exch. Club (pres. Williamsburg 1985). Methodist. Avocations: kite flying, car mechanics. Home and Office: 3409 Foxridge Rd Williamsburg VA 23188-2499

SPITZER, CRAIG M. information technology executive; BA in Econ., U. Pittsburgh. Sales assoc. NYNEX's Bus. Info. Sys. Grp.; investment banker Bear Stearns; sr. acct. exec. CoreTech; CEO Alliance Cons., 1994—. Recipient Entrepreneur of Yr., Ernst & Young, 2000, INC 500, INC Mag., 2000.

SPITZER, ELIOT LAURENCE, state attorney general; b. Bronx, June 12, 1959; m. Silda Spitzer, Oct. 17, 1987; 3 children. Grad., Princeton U., 1981; JD, Harvard U., 1984. Clk. U.S. Judge Robert W. Sweet, 1984—85; assoc. Paul, Weiss, Rifkind, Wharton & Garrison, 1985—86, Skadden Arps Slate Meagher & Flom, 1992—94; ptnr. Constantine & Ptnrs., N.Y.C., 1994—98; asst. dist. atty. State of N.Y., Manhattan, 1986—92, chief, Labor Racketeering unit, 1991—92, atty. gen. Albany, 1999—. Analyst, commentator on nat. news programs including NBC's Today Show, CNN's Burden of Proof, CNBC, Court TV; pro bono counsel N.Y. State Commn. for the Study of Youth Crime and Violence, 1993—94. Editor: Harvard Law Rev.; contbr. articles in leading newspapers and legal jours. Founder Ctr. for Cmty. Interest; trustee Montifiore Med. Ctr. Democrat. Office: Dept of Law The Capitol, 2nd Fl Albany NY 12224*

SPITZER, JOHN BRUMBACK, lawyer; b. Toledo, Mar. 6, 1918; s. Lyman and Blanche (Brumback) S.; m. Lucy Ohlinger, May 10, 1941 (dec. Oct. 13, 1971); children: John B., Molly (Mrs. Edmund Frost), Lyman, Adelbert L.; m. Vondah D. Thornbury, July 3, 1972 (dec. Nov. 2001); stepchildren: Vondah, Barbara, James R. Thornbury. Grad., Phillips Andover Acad., 1935; BA, Yale U., 1939, LLB, 1947. Bar: Ohio 1947. Law clk. to U.S. Supreme Ct. Justice Stanley Reed, 1947-48; ptnr. Marshall, Melhorn, Cole, Hummer & Spitzer, Toledo, 1955-86, Hummer & Spitzer, Toledo, 1986-89; with Hummer Legal Svcs. Corp., 1990—2002; ptnr. Spitzer and Hummer, 2002—. Pres. Spitzer Paper Box Co., 1955-63; v.p. Spitzer Bldg. Co., 1960-91, pres. 1992—. Pres. Toledo Symphony Orch., 1956-58, v.p., sec., 1958-86, trustee, 1986—. Maj. AUS, World War II. Mem.: Belmont Country Club. Congregationalist. Home: 29620 Gleneagles Rd Perrysburg OH 43551-3530 Office Phone: 419-255-1440. Personal E-mail: cmhall@sbcglobal.net.

SPITZER, MATTHEW LAURENCE, law educator, dean; b. L.A., June 23, 1952; s. William George and Jeanette Dorothy S.; m. Jean Fuksman, July 8, 1973; 1 child, Amanda Elizabeth. BA in Math., UCLA, 1973; JD, U. So. Calif., 1977; PhD in Social Scis., Calif. Inst. Tech., 1979. Assoc. Nossaman, Guthner, Knox & Elliott, L.A., 1977—79; asst. prof. Northwestern U., Chgo., 1979—81; William T. Dalessi prof. law U. So. Calif., L.A., 1987—2000, assoc. prof., 1981—84, prof., 1984—, dir. law and rational choice programs, 1990—2000, dir. Comms. Law and Policy Ctr., 1998—2000, dean, Carl Mason Franklin prof. law, 2000—; prof. law and social scis. Calif. Inst. Tech., Pasadena, 1992—2000. Vis. prof. law U. Chgo., 1996, Stanford (Calif.) U., 1997; mem. organizing com. Telecoms. Policy Rsch. Conf., Washington, 1991-94. Author: Seven Dirty Words and Six Other Stories, 1986; co-author: (with T. Hazlett) Public Policy Toward Cable Television, 1997. Recipient (shared with Elizabeth Hoffman) Ronald H. Coase prize U. Chgo., 1986. Mem.: Am. Law and Econs. Assn. (bd. dirs. 1997—2000). Avocations: paperweight collecting, audiophile. Office: U So Calif Law Sch Los Angeles CA 90089-0071

SPITZER, MATTHEW LAWRENCE, retired retail store executive; b. Pitts., June 20, 1929; s. Martin and Ruth G. S.; children: Mark, Edward, Eric, Joseph. Student, U. Buffalo, 1948-50. Lic. airline transport pilot. Product line mgr. Gen. Dynamics, Rochester, N.Y., 1962-67; dir. contracts Friden divsn. Singer, San Leandro, Calif., 1968-69; asst. v.p. Talcott Computer Leasing, San Francisco, 1970-71; pres. Spitzer Music Mgmt. Co., Hayward, Calif., 1972-95, Spitzer Helicopter Leasing Co., Hayward. Chmn. bd. Leo's Audio and Music Techs., Oakland, Calif. Mem. Masons, Mensa. Office Phone: 510-728-7727.

SPITZER, MORTON EDWARD, management consultant; b. N.Y.C., Jan. 3, 1937; s. Henry Lawrence and Martha (Michel) S.; m. Nancy Dinetz, Oct. 10, 1965; children: Matthew, Douglas. BA, Bklyn. Coll., 1957; MS, N.C. State U., 1959; PhD, N.Y. U., 1964. Dir./mgr. planning and analysis The Prudential Ins. Co. Am., Newark, 1964-74, v.p. S.W. ops. Houston, 1975-79, v.p. ordinary agys. Newark, 1979-87, pres. North Ctrl. ops. Mpls., 1988, sr. v.p. dist. agys. Newark, 1989, Woodland Hills, Calif., 1990-91; COO Liberty Life Assurance Co. Boston, Dover, NH, 1992—2002, ret., 2002. Bd. dirs. Liberty Life Assurance Co., Boston, Liberty Assignment Co., Liberty Life Distbrs. LLC, Liberty Life Securities LLC, BARCO Lto, Barbados, Limra Internat., N.Am. Life and Health of N.Y.; bd. govs. ACLI Forum 500; bd. dirs. N. Am. Co., NY, N.Am. Life and Health Ins. Co. N.Y. Co-author: The Law and Personnel Testing, 1971. Bd. dirs. Nat. Soc. to Prevent Blindness, N.J., 1986-89, nat. bd. dirs., Chgo., 1989. Mem. APA, Am. Psychol. Soc., Ea. Psychol. Assn., Sigma Xi. Avocations: tennis, art. Home: 449 E Deering Rd Deering NH 03244 E-mail: morts@optonline.net.

SPITZER, ROBERT J. academic administrator; BBA, Gonzaga U.; MPhil, St. Louis U.; STB, Gregorian U., Rome; ThM, Weston Sch. Theology, Cambridge, Mass.; PhD in Philosophy, Cath. U. of Am. Tchr. Georgetown U., 1984-90, Seattle U., 1978-80, 90-98; pres. Gonzaga U., 1998—. Co-founder U. Faculty for Life; founder, adv. Life Principles. Office: Gonzaga U 502 E Boone Ave Spokane WA 99258-0001

SPITZER, T. QUINN, management consultant company executive; married; 5 children. Grad., U. Va.; postgrad., U. Ga. Group mgr. N.Am. ops. Kepner-Tregoe, Princeton, N.J., 1978-90, chmn., CEO, 1990--99; pres. McHugh Cons., Pennington, N.J., 1999—. Dep. dir. Ariz. Dept. Corrections, 1983; cons. in field. TV and radio appearances include CNN, NPR, CNBC, Can. Broadcasting Corp.; spkr. in field. Mem. Young Presidents' Orgn., nat. Alliance Bus. (bd. dirs.). Office: McHugh Cons 2490 Pennington Rd Pennington NJ 08534-5225

SPITZER, TODD, state official; m. Jamie Spitzer; 1 child, Justin. BA, UCLA; MA in Pub. Policy, U. Calif., Berkeley; JD, U. Calif., Hastings. Tchr. English Roosevelt H.S., East Los Angeles, Calif.; res. police officer Hollenbeck divsn. L.A. Police Dept.; dep. dist. atty. Orange County Dist. Atty.'s Office, 1990—92; state assembly mem. Dist. 71 Calif. State Assembly, 2002—. Mem. judiciary com.; mem. pub. employees, retirement and social security com.; mem. pub. safety com.; mem. transp. com.; mem. water, pks. and wildlife com.; mem. VA com.; chair San Joaquin Hills Transp. Corridor Agy., 1999, 2000; dir. Foothill/Ea. Transp. Corridor Agy.; chair Orange County Transp. Authority. Trustee Brea-Olinda Unified Sch. Dist., 1992—96; mem. Orange County Bd. Suprs., 1996—2002; chair Orange County Fire Authority, 1999—2000; dir. Child Abuse Prevention Coun.; mem. Libr. Adv. Bd., Local Redevel. Authority, St. Joseph Med. Ctr. Adv. Coun. Republican. Mailing: Rm 2111 PO Box 942849 Sacramento CA 95814 Office: Ste 102 1940 N Tustin St Orange CA 92865

SPITZER, VLAD GERARD, lawyer; b. Bucharest, Romania, Mar. 3, 1956; came to U.S., 1963; s. Adrian and Carole Spitzer; m. Denise J. Borenstein, July 9, 1989; 1 child, Max Oliver. BA with honors, NYU, 1978; JD, Yeshiva U., 1981. Bar: N.Y. 1988, Conn. 1995, U.S. Dist. Ct. (so. and ea. dists.) N.Y. 1988, U.S. Dist. Ct. Conn. 1996, U.S. Ct. Appeals (2d cir.) 1994, U.S. Supreme Ct. 1995. Asst. dist. atty. Dist. Atty.'s Office of King's County, Bklyn., 1981-83; ptnr. Goldbergh & Spitzer LLC, N.Y.C., 1988-95, Stamford, Conn., 1995—2002, Spitzer & Brey LLC, Westport, Conn., 2002—. Adv. bd. Nat. Employee Rights Inst., Cin., 1997—; founding mem. Conn. Employee Rights Inst., Stamford, Conn., 1997; coop. atty. ACLU, N.Y. Civil Liberties Union; judge Wagner Nat. Lab. and Employment Law Moot Ct., N.Y. Law Sch., 1996-98. Belkin scholar, 1981. Mem. ATLA (labor and employment sect. 1996—), Assn. of the Bar of the City of N.Y., Nat. Employment Lawyers Assn., Conn. Bar Assn. (labor and employment sect. 1996—, employee benefits com. 1996—), Nat. Employee Rights Inst., Stamford-Norwalk Regional Bar Assn., Stamford Rotary Club. Office: Spitzer & Brey LLC 239 Main St Westport CT 06880

SPITZER, WALTER OSWALD, epidemiologist, educator; b. Asuncion, Paraguay, Feb. 19, 1937; Canadian citizen; MD, U. Toronto, 1962; MHA, U. Mich., 1966; MPH, Yale U., 1970. Gen. dir. Internat. Christian Med. Soc., 1966-69; asst. prof. clin. epidemiology McMaster U., Hamilton, Ont., Can., 1969-73, assoc. prof., 1973-75; prof. epidemiology McGill U., Montreal, 1975-95, prof. medicine, 1983-95, Strathcona prof. and chmn. dept. epidemiology and biostats., 1984-93, prof. emeritus, 1996—; pres. Methods in Epidemiology, Inc., 1997—; clin. prof. medicine Stanford U., 1996—. Cons. PanAm. Health Orgn., Washington, 1975, 77, Aga Khan Found., Geneva, 1983-84. Editor Jour. Clin. Epidemiology, 1981-95; contbr. articles to biomed. jours. Named Nat. Health Scientist of Can., 1981 Fellow Royal Coll. Physicians and Surgeons Can., Am. Coll. Epidemiology, Faculty of Pharm. Medicine of the Royal Colls. of Phys. of the U.K.; mem. Inst. Medicine of Nat. Acad. Scis. (U.S.). Avocations: music, sailing, photography.

SPITZLI, DONALD HAWKES, JR., lawyer; b. Newark, Mar. 19, 1934; s. Donald Hawkes and Beatrice (Banister) S.; children: Donald Hawkes III, Peter Gilbert, Seth Armstrong. AB, Dartmouth Coll., 1956; LL.B., U. Va., 1963. Bar: Va. 1963. Assoc. Willcox, Savage, Lawrence, Dickson & Spindle, Norfolk, Va., 1964-67, 68-70, ptnr., 1971-77; atty. Eastman Kodak Co., Rochester, N.Y., 1967-68; pres. Marine Hydraulics Internat., Inc., Chesapeake, Va., 1978-80; sole practice Virginia Beach, Va., 1980—. Owner Chieftain Motor Inn, Hanover, N.H., 1980-87. Comdr. USNR, 1956-70. Episcopalian. Office: 4460 Corporation Ln Ste 180 Virginia Beach VA 23462 Office Phone: 757-499-1191. Personal E-mail: airbuzzard24@aol.com.

SPITZNAGEL, JOHN KEITH, microbiologist, immunologist, physician; b. Peoria, Ill., Apr. 11, 1923; s. Elmer Florian and Anna S. (Kolb) S.; m. Anne Moulton Sirch, Feb. 2, 1947; children: John, Jean, Margaret, Elizabeth, Paul. BA, Columbia U., 1943, MD, 1946. Diplomate Nat. Bd. Med. Examiners, Am. Bd. Internal Medicine. Intern Johns Hopkins Hosp., Balt., 1946-47; resident in internal medicine Barnes Hosp., St. Louis, 1949-51; vis. investigator Rockefeller Inst., N.Y.C., 1952-53, Nat. Inst. Med. Research, London, 1967-68; mem. faculty U. N.C., Chapel Hill, 1957-79, prof. microbiology and infectious diseases, prof. medicine, 1957-79; cons. N.C. Meml. Hosp., Chapel Hill, 1974-79; ad hoc adviser NIH, 1971—; prof. microbiology and immunology, chmn. dept. Emory U., Atlanta, 1979-93, prof. emeritus microbiology and immunology, 1993—, assoc. dean rsch., 1997-98; attending physician, vol. and co-founder Good Samaritan Health and Wellness Ctr., Jasper, Ga., 2002—, chmn. exec. bd., CEO, 2004—. Mem. study sect. bacteriology and mycology NIH, 1975-79, 85-89, chmn., 1977-79. Editor: Infection and Immunity, 1970-80, Jour. Immunology, 1973-80, Jour. Reticuloendothelial Soc, 1973-80. Served with M.C. AUS, 1947-57. Recipient Research Career Devel. award USPHS, 1957-67, Disting. Service award Sch. Medicine U. N.C., Chapel Hill, 1987; USPHS postdoctoral fellow, 1968; USPHS and AEC grantee; lectureship named in his honor, Spitznagel Lectureship on Host Antimicrobial Def., Emory U., 1998. Fellow ACP, Infectious Disease Soc.; mem. AAAS (life), Am. Soc. Microbiology (div. group councilor 1977-79),

Am. Assn. Immunologists, Reticuloendothelial Soc. (pres. 1982), Infectious Disease Soc., So. Soc. Clin. Rsch., Assn. Am. Med. Sch. Microbiology and Immunology Chmn. (pres. 1990-91), Sigma Xi. Achievements include research on cell biology of human neutrophil polymorphonuclear leukocytes, and oxygen ind. mechanisms of antimicrobial phagocytoses; first to demonstrate cationic antimicrobial proteins of polymorphonuclear leukocytes granules; co-discoverer of a cationic protein of polymorph granules with antimicrobial action and a powerful attractant for mononuclear phagocytes. Home: 95 Starcross Ln # 20804 Jasper GA 30143-7883 Office: 1510 Clifton Rd NE Atlanta GA 30322-4218 E-mail: spitzna@mac.com.

SPIVACK, GLORIA JEAN, music educator; b. Boston, June 6, 1928; d. Samuel Richmond and Rose Hart; m. Herbert Leonard Spivack, Jan. 27, 1951; children: Elaine Edelle Katz, Robert Evan. MusB, Boston U., 1949, post grad., 1950; at, Ecole Normale de Musique, Paris, 1993, Lyon Conservatory, Lyon, France, 1994, Hochschule fur Musik, Graz, Austria, 1996. Cert. RI Music Tchrs. Assoc., 1972, Music Tchrs Nat. Assoc., 1972, Emeritus Music Tchrs. Nat. Assoc., 1996. Adj. prof. of piano Cmty. Coll. of RI, 1981—83; pvt. piano instr. East Greewich, RI, 1974—. Pres. RI Music Tchrs. Assn., 1976—78, Schubert Club, Providence, 1979—80, treas., 1981—84. Avocations: gardening, cooking, travel. Home and Office: 80 Birchwood Way East Greenwich RI 02818

SPIVAK, ALVIN A. retired public relations executive; b. Phila., Nov. 30, 1927; s. Herman and Bella (Haimovitz) S.; m. Martha Barry, Dec. 21, 1964; 1 dau., Denise. BS, Temple U., 1949. With I.N.S., 1949-58, Senate reporter, also mem. gen. staff, 1951-58; with U.P.I., 1958-67, White House reporter, 1960-67; pub. affairs dir. Nat. Adv. Commn. on Civil Disorders, 1967-68, Democratic Nat. Com., 1968-70; corp. pub. affairs dir. Gen. Dynamics Corp., 1970-94, ret., 1994. Served with USAAF, 1946-47. Mem. Mil. Order of Carabao, Nat. Press Club, Beta Gamma Sigma. Home: 5726 W 1st Sq SW Vero Beach FL 32968-2256

SPIVAK, JOAN CAROL, healthcare communications specialist; b. Phila., May 12, 1950; d. Jack and Evelyn Lee (Copelman) S.; m. John D. Goldman, May 17, 1980; children: Jesse, Marcus. AB, Barnard Coll., 1972; M of Health Scis., Johns Hopkins U., 1980. Freelance writer, N.Y.C., 1980-84; project dir. Impact Med. Communication, N.Y.C., 1984-87; exec. v.p., gen. mgr. health and sci. strategies Edelman Worldwide, N.Y.C., 1987—2002; pres. Prime Medica, Inc., 2002—. Co-author: (pamphlet) Lead: New Perspectives on an Old Problem, 1978; contbr. The Book of Health, 1981, articles to profl. jours. Bd. dirs. May O'Donnell Dance Co., N.Y.C., 1983-85, Chamber Ballet U.S.A., N.Y.C., 1985-87, Nat. Child Labor Commn., 1991-2000, Cases, 1995-2001. Mem. N.Y. Acad. Sci. Democrat. Jewish. Avocations: pottery, boating. Office Phone: 212-921-1250. E-mail: joan.spivak@prime-medica.com.

SPIVAK, MAURICE SIDNEY, chief project management, consultant; b. Milford, Mass., Jan. 5, 1926; s. Phillip None and Esther Sarah Spivak; m. Annette Charlotte Mann; children: Michelle Melinger, Myra Runge, Jonah. BS, The Citadel, Charleston, S.C., 1950; MS, W. Va. U., Mogantown, 1955; PhD (hon.), U.of Berkley, Southhill, Mich. Registered Profl. Engr., Wis., 1976. Biochemical asst. Mass. Gen. Hosp., Boston, 1950—53; Biochemist Worcester Found., Shrewsbury, Mass., 1955—56; chem. engr. U.S.Army, Springfield, Mass., 1956—67; project engr. U.S.Army Arsenal, Edgewood, Md., 1967—73; chief project mgmt. engring. U.S. Army Corps of Engrs., Norfolk, Va., 1973—86. Cons. U.S. Army Corps of Engrs., Norfolk, Va., 1986—99. Author: (Engineering Papers) Published in Govt. and Jour.Biolog. Chemistry, 1960 (Numerous awards, 1977). Direct commr. USNR; First V.P. B'rith Sholom, Norfolk, Va. Pvt. First Class U.S. Army, 1944—46, European Theater. Decorated Bronze Star Medal US Army, Combat Infantry badge; recipient Several Civilian Awards, Springfield Armory, 1956-1966, Numerous Awards, Edgewood Arsenal, 1967-1973, US Army Corps of Engineers, 1973-1986; fellow, Worcester Found., 1955, W. Va. U., 1955. Mem.: ASCE. Home: 821 Jennings St Virginia Beach VA 23464 Personal E-mail: MSpivak650@aol.com.

SPIVAK, STUART, retail executive; CFO Red Apple Group, N.Y.C., until 2000. Office: Gristedes Foods Inc 823 11th Ave New York NY 10019-3557

SPIVEY, BROADUS AUTRY, lawyer; b. Lakeview, Tex., Oct. 7, 1936; s. Claude Clifton and Mary Edidth (Stafford) S.; m. Ruth Ann King, Aug. 1, 1956; children: Danny C., Marci M. Diploma, Clarendon Jr. Coll., 1956; BA in Govt., U. Tex., 1960, JD, 1962. Bar: Tex. 1962, U.S. Dist. Ct. (no., so., we. and ea. dists.) Tex., U.S. Ct. Appeals (5th cir.) 1971, U.S. Ct. Claims (11th cir.) 1979, U.S. Supreme Ct. 1973, UTE Indian Tribal Ct. 1997; cert. in personal injury trial law Tex. Bd. Legal Specialization. Asst. county atty. Lubbock County, Lubbock, Tex., 1962-64; ptnr. West, Spivey & Brackett, Lubbock, 1964-65; assoc. Huff & Bowers, Lubbock, 1965-70; sole practitioner Lubbock, 1970-71; ptnr. Gibbins & Spivey, Austin, Tex., 1971-76; sr. ptnr. Spivey & Ainsworth and predecessor firms, Austin, 1976—. Author: The Trial of Contested Paternity Cases, 1977; co-author: Texas Pattern Jury Charges, vol. 3, 1982; contbr. articles to profl. jours. Fellow Internat. Soc. Barristers, Internat. Acad. Trial Lawyers (pres. 2002-03, bd. dirs. 1993—, editor law rev. The Advocate), Am. Coll. Trial Lawyers; mem. Travis County Bar Assn., Capital Area Trial Lawyers Assn. (pres. 1977-79), State Bar Tex. (pres. 2001-2002, chmn. tort and compensation sect. 1976-77, Supreme Ct. adv. com. 1984-90, pres. 2001-), Fed. Bar Assn., Tex. Bar Found., Am. Bd. Trial Advocates, Lawyer Pilots Bar Assn., Tex. Trial Lawyers Assn. (pres. 1981-82), Assn. Trial Lawyers Am. (cert., bd. govs. 1982-85), Trial Lawyers Pub. Justice (bd. dirs. 1982-93, treas. 1989-90), Delta Theta Phi (Outstanding Alumnus award, 1973, 1978). Democrat. Methodist. Avocations: skiing, piloting, reading, woodworking. Office: Spivey & Ainsworth 48 East Ave Austin TX 78701-4317

SPIVEY, BRUCE E. ophthalmologist, integrated healthcare delivery systems management executive; b. Cedar Rapids, Iowa, Aug. 29, 1934; s. William Loranzy and Grace Loretta (Barber) S.; children: Lisa, Eric; m. Patti Amanda Birge, Dec. 20, 1987. BA, Coe Coll., 1956; MD, U. Iowa, 1959, MS, 1964; MEd, U. Ill., 1969; DSc (hon.), Coe Coll., 1978. Diplomate Am. Bd. Ophthalmology (fellow, bd. dirs. 1975-83, chmn. oral exam 1976-81). Asst. prof. U. Iowa Coll. Medicine, Iowa City, 1966, assoc. prof., 1968-71; dean Sch. Med. Scis. U. Pacific, San Francisco, 1971-76; prof., chmn. dept. ophthalmology Pacific Med. Ctr. (now Calif. Pacific Med. Ctr.), San Francisco, 1971-87, pres., CEO, dir., 1976-91; exec. v.p., CEO Am. Acad. Ophthalmology, San Francisco, 1977—93; pres., CEO Calif. Healthcare System, Bay area, 1986-92; CEO Northwestern Healthcare Network, Chgo., 1992-97, Columbia Cornell Care, N.Y.C., 1997-2000, Columbia Cornell Network Physicians, N.Y.C., 1998-2000. Bd. dirs. Reliance Group Holdings Inc., Chgo.; trustee, bd. dirs., sec. bd. MedEx, Balt., 1999—; v.p. Am. Bd. Med. Spltys., 1978—80, pres., 1980—82, Coun. Med. Splty. Socs., 2000—02, dep. exec. v.p., 2002—; sec.-gen. Internat. Coun. Ophthalmology, 1994—; chmn. bd. dirs. Vol. Hosps. of Am.-No. Calif., 1985—87, nat. bd. dirs., 1991—96; nat. adv. coun. NEI/NIH, 1987—92; spl. med. adv. group Dept. Vets Affairs, 1987—93; trustee, bd. dirs., sec. bd. Ophthal. Mut. Ins. Co., 1988—; trustee, sec. bd. Phoenix Alliance, Inc., Mpls., 1993—99, PrimeSight, San Francisco, 1996—99; bd. dirs., chmn. MedBiquitous, Balt., 2001—. Contbr. over 115 articles to profl. jours.; inventor instruments for eye surgery. Bd. dirs. Pacific Vision Found., San Francisco, 1978—, U.S.-China Edn. Inst., 1979—; trustee Coe Coll., 1985—, Found. AAO, 1981—. Served to capt. U.S. Army, 1964-66. Decorated Bronze Star; recipient Emile Javal Gold medal Internat. Contact Lens Council, San Francisco, 1982, Gradle medal Pan-Am. Assn. Ophthalmol., Disting. Alumni award U. Iowa, 2003, others. Fellow ACS, Am. Acad. Ophthalmology (Disting. Svc. award 1972, Sr. Honor award 1986, Guest of Honor 1996, Lifetime Achievement award, 2002); mem. AMA, Am. Ophthal. Soc. (Howe medal 1993, bd. dirs. 1986-91, pres. 1994-95), Academia Ophthal. Internat. (Bernardo Streiff Gold medal 2002), Soc. Med. Adminstrs. (pres. 1999-2001), Internat. Congress Ophthalmology (sec.-gen. 1978-82), Internat. Coun. Ophthalmology (sec.-gen. 1994—, trustee 1986—), Pacific-Union Club. (San Francisco), Chevy Chase Club (Washington), Knickerbocker Club (N.Y.), Cosmos Club (Washington). Presbyterian. Office: 945 Green St San Francisco CA 94133 Business E-Mail: bruce@spivey.org.

SPIVEY, TED RAY, English educator; b. Fort Pierce, Fla., July 1, 1927; s. Theodore Roosevelt and Etty Pearl (Sumner) S.; m. Julia Brannon Douglass, June 30, 1962; children— Mary Leta, John Andrew. AB, Emory U., 1949; MA, U. Minn., 1951, PhD, 1954. Reporter Greenville Reporter, S.C., 1949-50; instr. Emory U., Atlanta, 1954-56; mem. faculty Ga. State U., Atlanta, 1956-89, assoc. prof. English, 1960-64, prof., 1964-89, Regents' prof., 1984-89, emeritus, 1989—. Author: (with Kenneth M. England) A Manual of Style, 1960, The Renewed Quest, 1969, The Coming of the New Man, 1971, The Journey Beyond Tragedy, 1980, Revival: Southern Writers in the Modern City, 1986, The Writer as Shaman: The Pilgrimages of Conrad Aiken and Walker Percy, 1986, To Die in Atlanta: Poems of the Civil War and After, 1987, Beyond Modernism: Toward a New Myth Criticism, 1988, A City Observed: Poems of the New Age, 1988, (with Arthur Waterman) Conrad Aiken: A Priest of Consciousness, 1989, Flannery O'Connor: The Woman, The Thinker, the Visionary, 1995, Airport: America Rediscovered, 1997, Time's Stop in Savannah: Conrad Aiken's Inner Journey, 1997, Bridges of Light: Four Poets of the Golden Isles, 2001. Served with USN, 1945-46. Urban Life Center grantee, 1977-80 Mem. So. Atlantic MLA, Brittany Club. Democrat. Episcopalian. Home: 104 Plemmons Dr Saint Simons GA 31522 9767

SPIVEY, TERRENCE, performing company executive, educator, actor, theater director, playwright; s. Lillian Marie Cole and Terry Vincent Cooper; life ptnr. Shari Reed; children: Cinque Terrell, Malikah Johnson. BA in Theatre, Prairie View (Tex.) A&M U., 1984. Theatre lectr. Touro Coll., N.Y.C., 2001—03; founding artistic dir. Powerful Long Ladder Ensemble Co., N.Y.C., 2001—; guest dir. Blackgirl Ensemble, N.Y.C., 2002—03; artistic dir. Karamu Performing Arts Theatre, Cleve., 2003—. Mem. adv. bd., playwright cons. Black Writers Alliance, 1999—2001, entertainment coord. Black Writers Reunion and Conf. Gold Pen Awards, 1999—2000, Dallas, 2000—01; Beyond the Screen commentator 3 Black Chicks Film Rev., 2000—; moderator Theatre Yahoo Groups website, 2000. Actor: West New York, other films; (plays) James Baldwin's Blues for Mister Charlie (finalist Ira Aldridge competition), The Fruits of Miss Morning, Clifford Odets's Waiting for Lefty, (music video) Anita Baker's No One In The World, (workshop stage reading) String Bean; dir.: (plays) Ntozake Shange's For Colored Girls Who Have Considered Suicide When the Rainbow is Enuf, Carlyle Brown's The Little Tommy Parker Celebrated Colored Minstrel Show, (one-man show) A Journey To Soul's Awareness; playwright: Smokestack Lightnin' (finalist Theodore Ward prize for African Am. playwriting, 1998). Avocations: weightlifting, running, basketball. Office: Karamu Performing Arts Theatre 2355 E 89th St Cleveland OH 44106 Personal E-mail: tsplywrght@aol.com.

SPIWAK, LAWRENCE J. legal association administrator; married; 1 child. BA with hons, George Washington U., 1986; JD, 1989. Bar: N.Y., Mass., D.C., U.S. Ct. Appeals (D.C. cir.). Sr. atty. Fed. Energy Regulatory Commn., 1992—94; sr. atty. Competition Divsn. Office Gen. Counsel FCC, 1994—98; pres. Phoenix Ctr. Advanced Legal and Econ. Pub. Policy Studies, Washington, 1998—. Spkr. in field; vis. prof. law U. Toulouse, France. Contbr. articles to profl. jours. Office: Phoenix Ctr Advanced Legal and Econ Public Policy Studies 5335 Wisconsin Ave NW Ste 440 Washington DC 20015-2034*

SPLANE, RICHARD BEVERLEY, social work educator; b. Calgary, Alta., Can., Sept. 25, 1916; s. Alfred William and Clara Jane (Allyn) S.; m. Verna Marie Huffman, Feb. 22, 1971. BA, McMaster U., 1940, LLD (hon.), 1990; cert. social sci. and adminstrn., London Sch. Econs., 1947; MA, U. Toronto, 1948, MSW, 1951, PhD, 1961; LLD (hon.), Wilfrid Laurier U., 1988, U. B.C., Can., 1996. Exec. dir. Children's Aid Soc., Cornwall, Ont., Can., 1948-50; with Health and Welfare Can., Ottawa, 1952-72, exec. asst. to dep. minister nat. welfare, 1959-60, dir. unemployment assistance, 1960-62, dir. gen. welfare assistance and services, 1960-70, asst. dep. minister social allowances and services, 1970-72; vis. prof. U. Alta., Edmonton, 1972-73; prof. social policy Sch. Social Work, U. B.C., Vancouver, 1973—. Cons. Govt. Can., Govt. Alta., UNICEF. Author: The Development of Social Welfare in Ontario, 1965; (with Verna Huffman Splane) Chief Nursing Officers in National Ministries of Health, 1994, 75 Years of Community Service to Canada: Canadian Council on Social Development, 1920-1995, George Davidson Social Policy and Public Policy Exemplar. Served with RCAF, 1942-45. Recipient Centennial medal Govt. Can., 1967, Charles E. Hendry award U. Toronto, 1981, Commemorative medal for 125th anniversary of Confedn. of Can., 1992, Disting. Svc. award Internat. Coun. on Social Welfare, 1996, Queen's Golden Jubilee medal, 2002. Mem. Can. Assn. Social Workers (Outstanding Nat. Svc. award 1985, Touzel award 2002, Queens Golden medal 2002), Can. Inst. Pub. Adminstrn., Can. Hist. Assn., Can. Coun. on Social Devel. (Lifetime Achievement award 1995), Internat. Assn. Schs. Social Work, Internat. Confs. Social Devel., World Federalists of Can., UN Assns. Assn. of Can. (bd. dirs. Vancouver br.), Vancouver Club, Order of Can. Mem. United Ch. Can.

SPLETE, ALLEN PETERJOHN, association executive, educator; b. Carthage, NY, June 24, 1938; s. Howard Henry and Minnie Bertha (Peterjohn) S.; m. Marilyn Lois Detweiler, June 18, 1966; children: Heidi, Michael. BA, St. Lawrence U., 1960; MA with distinction, Colgate U., 1962; PhD, Syracuse U., 1968; LHD, Campbellsville Coll., 1990; LLD, Davis and Elkins Coll., 1990; LHD, Mt. Union Coll., 1992, St. Thomas Aquinas Coll., 1992, U. Indpls., 1994, Juniata Coll., 1994, Hastings Coll., 1994; EdD, Marywood Coll., 1995; LHD, Holy Family Coll., 1996, Wesley Coll., 1996, Bluffton Coll., 2003. Adminstrv. asst. to v.p. acad. affairs Syracuse (NY) U., 1965-68, assoc. dean, exec. asst. to provost, 1968-70; v.p. for acad. planning St. Lawrence U., Canton, NY, 1970-82; pres. Westminster Coll., New Wilmington, Pa., 1982-85; exec. v.p. Coun. Ind. Colls., Washington, 1985-86, pres., 1986-2000, pres. emeritus, 2000—. Dir. Nat. Prepaid Tuition Plan, 1988-91; cons. York Coll., Pa., 1974; mem. planning and rsch. com. N.Y. State Com. on Ind. Colls. and Univs., 1975-82; statewide higher edn. adv. com. N.Y. State Senate Com. on Higher Edn., 1979-82; nat. adv. bd. Flaming Rainbow U., 1989-96; mem. adv. bd. Assn. Gov. Bds. Presdl. Search Consultation Svc., 1987-94, Academic Search Consultation Svc., 1989—, mem. Harvard Sem. for new pres. adv. bd., 1990—; bd. dirs. Tchr. Edn. Accreditation Coun., 1998—, chair, 2001—; oversight and rev. com. leadership and orgnl. devel. program United Negro Coll. Fund, 1991-96, SCT adv. coun., 1996-2001; adv. bd. Eric Nat., 1996-2003, Boyer Ctr. for Advanced Studies, 1998—; UAW/Ford U. Help Steering Com., 1997-2001; bd. dirs. Project Pericles, 1999-, CIC Pres. Consulting Svc., 2003-. Co-author: Frederic Remington-Selected Letters, 1988, A Good Place To Work: Sourcebook for the Academic Workplace, 1991; editor: (with others) Confs. on Adirondack Park, 1972-82, Can.-Am. Relations, 1974-75, Presidential Essays — Success Stories, 2000; contbr. articles to profl. jours. Chmn. planning bd. Village of Canton, 1974-81; elder Neelsville Presbyn. Ch., 1986-89; trustee Adirondack Conservancy, Wilsboro, N.Y., 1980-82; trustee Millikin U., 2000—; mem. adv. bd. Sage Scholars, 2000—. Served to 1st lt. U.S. Army, 1960-62. Recipient Alumni citation, St. Lawrence U., 1987, Algernon Sydney Sullivan award, 1997, CIC Acad. Leadership award, 2000, Henry D. Paley award, Nat. Assn. Ind. Colls. and Univs., 2001, Partnership award, Assn. Presbyn. Colls. and Univs., 2000; grantee, John Ben Snow Found., 1981. Mem. Pa. Assn. Colls and Univs. (govt. rels. com. 1983-85), Mid. States Assn. (team chmn. com. on higher edn. 1976-78, 81), Assn. Am. Colls. (project rev. cons. 1981-82), Soc. Educators and Scholars (bd. editors), Assn. Am. Colls. (pres. adv. com. 1977-78, reviewer Quill project 1978-79), St. Lawrence County Hist. Assn. (pres. 1977-82), Frederic Remington Mus. Assn., Beta Theta Pi (v.p. 1980-83). Republican. Home: 10821 Longmeadow Dr Damascus MD 20872-2240 Office: Coun Ind Colls 1 Dupont Cir NW Ste 320 Washington DC 20036-1137 E-mail: splete@earthlink.net.

SPLICHAL, CHRISTINE, restaurant owner; m. Joachim Splichal. BBA, Ecole Superieure de Commerce, Poitiers, France, 1982; MBA, Am. Grad. Sch. Internat. Mgmt., Phoenix, 1983. Formerly with Pershing Sq. Mgmt. Assn., L.A.; co-owner Patina Restaurant, L.A., 1989—, Pinot Bistro, Cafe Pinot, Pinot Hollywood. Recipient Hollywood Woman of Distinction award, L.A. Coun. Mem. Jackie Goldberg and U.S. Senator Barbara Boxer, 1996.

SPLICHAL, JOACHIM, chef, restaurant owner; b. Spaichingen, Germany; Chef La Bonne Auberge, Antibes, L'Oasis, La Napoule; sous chef Chantecler Restaurant, Nice, France; exec. chef Regency Club, L.A., 1981, Seventh St. Bistro, L.A.; owner Max Au Triangle, L.A., 1984; chef, founder Patina Restaurant, L.A., 1989—; owner Catal Restaurant, Uva Bar, Naples Ristorante e Pizzeria, Nick and Stef's Steakhouse; founder, chef The Patina Group, L.A. Author: (book) Spuds, Truffles and Wild Gnocchi. Named Best California Chef, James Beard Found., 1991, 1995, Treasure of L.A., L.A. Mayor Richard Riordan and Ctrl. City Assn., 1996, Restaurateur of the Yr., Calif. Restaurant Writers Assn., 1997, So. Calif. Restaurant Writers, 1999, Legendary Chef, Bon Appetit mag., 2002. Office: The Patina Group 400 S Hope St Los Angeles CA 90071 Office Phone: 213-239-2520.

SPLIETHOFF, WILLIAM LUDWIG, chemical company executive; b. Matamoras, Pa., Apr. 8, 1926; s. Oscar and Louisa (Rummel) S.; m. Dorothy Coffman, June 11, 1949; children: Christina Spliethoff Hansen, Karen Spliethoff Walker, William Mark; m. Marjorie Ann Johnson, Nov. 15, 1971. BS in Chemistry, Pa. State U., 1946, MS, 1948; PhD in Organic Chemistry, Mich. State U., 1953. Rsch. chemist E.I. duPont de Nemours & Co., Wilmington, Del., 1952-60; dir. market rsch. chem. divsn. Gen. Mills, Inc., Kankakee, Ill., 1960-62, mgr. comml. devel., 1962-67; asst. mng. dir. Polymer Corp., Sydney, Australia, 1967-69; v.p. Gen. Mills Chems., Inc., Mpls., 1969-77; exec. v.p. Henkel Corp., Mpls., 1977-86; mgmt. cons. Chanhassen, Minn., 1986—99, Naples, Fla., 1999—. Bd. dirs. Princess Soft Toys, Inc.; sr. v.p. Henkel of Am., N.Y.C., 1981-86; chmn. Habib-Gen., Ltd., Karachi, Pakistan, 1970-79, Nutralgum, S.P.A., Milan, 1972-85, Henkel Ireland Ltd., Cork, 1975-86; v.p. Chem-Plast, S.P.A., Milan, 1977-86, Poliamidas de Venezuela, S.A., Caracas, 1975-86, Gemisa, S.A. de C.V., Mexico City, 1979-86. Mem. bd. edn., Kankakee, 1964-67. Mem. Am. Chem. Soc., Chem. Market Rsch. Assn., Comml. Devel. Assn. (honor award 1982), Sigma Xi, Phi Lambda Upsilon. E-mail: wspliethoff@comcast.net.

SPLINTER, MICHAEL R. corporate financial executive; BEE, Univ. of Wis., Madison, Wis., 1972, MEE, 1974. Gen. mgr., exec. v.p. Intel Corp., Santa Clara, Calif., 1984—96; v.p. and asst. Gen. mgr. Tech. and Mfg. Group, Intel Corp., Santa Clara, Calif., 1996—98, v.p. and Gen. mgr., 1998—99, sr. v.p. and Gen. mgr., 1999—2001, exec. v.p. and Gen. mgr., 2001, exec. v.p. and dir., Sales and Mktg. group, 2001—03; pres. and Chief Exec. Officer Applied Materials, Inc., Santa Clara, Calif., 2003. Mem.: Applied Materials (mem. Bd. of Dir. 2003). Office: Applied Materials Inc 3050 Bowers Ave Santa Clara CA 95054

SPLINTER, WILLIAM ELDON, agricultural engineering educator; b. North Platte, Nebr., Nov. 24, 1925; s. William John and Minnie (Calhoun) Splinter; m. Eleanor Love Peterson, Jan. 10, 1952 (dec. Jan. 1999); children: Kathryn Love, William John, Karen Ann, Robert Marvin; m. Elizabeth Butters Calhoun, Feb. 9, 2002. BS in Agrl. Engring., U. Nebr., 1950; MS in Agrl. Engring., Mich. State U., 1951, PhD in Agrl. Engring., 1955. Instr. agrl. engring. Mich. State U., East Lansing, 1953-54; assoc. prof. biology and agrl. engring. N.C. State U., Raleigh, 1954-60, prof. biology and agrl. engring., 1960-68; from prof., chmn. dept. agrl. engring. to interim dean U. Nebr., Lincoln, 1968—2001, interim dean Coll. of Engring. and Tech., 2001—02; interim dir. Nebr. State Mus., 2002—. Cons. engr.; mem. exec. bd. Am. Assn. Engring. Socs.; hon. prof. Shengyang (People's Republic of China) Agrl. U. Contbr. articles to tech. jours.; patentee in field. Vol. dir. L.F. Larsen Tractor Mus. Served with USNR, 1946-51. Recipient Massey Ferguson gold medal, 1978, John Deere gold medal, 1995, Kiwanis award for disting. svc., 1994; named to Nebr. Hall of Agrl. Achievement; named Disting. Alumni, U. Nebr.-Lincoln, 2000. Recipient George Howard-Loiuse Pound award, 2001. Fellow AAAS, NSPE, Am. Soc. Agrl. Engrs. (pres., adminstrv. council, found. pres., Presdl. citation 1999); mem. Nat. Acad. Engring., Soc. Automotive Engrs., Am. Soc. Engring. Edn., Sigma Xi, Sigma Tau, Sigma Pi Sigma, Pi Mu Epsilon, Gamma Sigma Delta, Phi Kappa Phi, Beta Sigma Psi. Home: 4801 Bridle Ln Lincoln NE 68516-3436 Office: U Nebr Lincoln PO Box 830833 Lincoln NE 68583-0833 E-mail: wsplinter1@unl.edu.

SPLITT, DAVID ALAN, lawyer, writer; b. Ripon, Wis., Nov. 28, 1945; s. Orville Sylvester and Joyce Eileen (Anson) S.; m. Martha Ann Corson, Mar. 19, 1966; children: Amy Emmeline, Sarah Daisy. BA in English, Va. Poly. Inst. and State U., 1966; JD, Am. U., 1971. Bar: D.C. 1971, U.S. Supreme Ct. 1981. Tchr. Bowie (Md.) H.S., 1966-68; freelance journalist and photographer Washington, 1968-70; ptnr. Christensen, Splitt & King, Washington, 1971-74; gen. counsel D.C. Bd. Edn., 1974-79; dir. documents, 1979—82; of counsel Stein, Miller, Brodsky & Beerman, Washington, 1983-84; pvt. practice Washington, 1985—2000; sr. v.p., sr. corp. counsel Affiliated Computer Svc., Inc., 2001—. Gen. counsel D.C. Sch. Law, 1988-96, adj. prof. law, 1995-97, U. D.C., 1991-96; spl. asst. city adminstr. for fin. mgmt. systems, dir. city computer ctr., Washington, 1980-81. Dir., vice chmn. Choral Arts Soc. of Washington, 1974-84, chmn., 1984-85; dir., v.p. Traditional Music Documentation Project, Washington. Author: Post-Conviction Relief for Federal Prisoners, 1973, The Resolution of Detainers for Federal and State Prisoners, 1971; editor: Inquiry and Analysis, 1977-79, Becoming a Better Board Member, 1982, D.C. Rulemaking Handbook and Publications Style Manual, 1983, D.C. Procurement Regulations, 1987, A Guide to Procurement Law in the District, 1998; columnist: The Exec. Educator, 1978-96, eSch. News Law and Ethics, 1997—; editor, The Corporate Counselor, 2001-; editor, Policy Bytes, 2002-. Recipient Outstanding Svc. awards D.C. Govt., 1976, 78, 79, Mayor's Disting. Pub. Svc. award, 1983. Mem. ABA, Inter-Am. Bar Assn., Computer Law Assn., Aircraft Owners and Pilots Assn., Exptl. Aircraft Assn., Lawyer-Pilots Bar Assn., Am. Radio League, (licensee amateur extra class), Indian Spring Country Club. Republican. Home: 6111 Utah Ave NW Washington DC 20015-2461

SPLITTSTOESSER, WALTER EMIL, plant physiologist; b. Claremont, Minn., Aug. 27, 1937; s. Waldemar Theodore and Opal Mae (Young) S.; m. Shirley Anne O'Connor, July 2, 1960; children: Pamela, Sheryl, Riley. BS with distinction (univ. fellow), U. Minn., 1958; MS, S.D. State U., 1960; PhD, Purdue U., 1963. Plant breeder U. Minn., 1956-58; weed scientist S.D. State U., 1958-60; plant physiologist Purdue U., 1960-63, Shell Oil Co., Modesto, Calif., 1963-64; biochemist U. Calif., Davis, 1964-65; mem. faculty U. Ill., Urbana, 1965-97, prof. plant physiology, 1974-97, head vegetable crops div., 1972-82. Vis. prof., biotechnologist Univ. Coll., Dublin, Ireland, 1987; vis. prof. Univ. Coll., London, 1972, La Trobe U., Melbourne, Australia, 1995; biologist Parkland Coll., Champaign, Ill., 1974; vis. rsch. assoc. Rothamsted Exptl. Sta., Herpenden, England, 1980; disting. vis. prof. Nagoya (Japan) U., 1982. Author: Vegetable Growing Handbook, 1979, 3d edit., 1990; contbr. articles to profl. jours.; rev. editor: Analytical Biochemistry, 1969-78, NSF, 1978-79; others. Recipient J.H. Gourley award Am. Fruit Grower-Am. Soc. Hort. Sci., 1974, Outstanding Grad. Educator award, 1990; NIH fellow, 1964-65. Fellow Am. Soc. Hort. Sci. (rev. editor jour. 1969-98), Japanese Soc. Promotion of Sci.; mem. Am. Soc. Hort. Sci., Plant Growth Reg. Soc. Am., Sigma Xi (pres. 1990-91), Alpha Zeta, Gamma Sigma Delta, Delta Theta Sigma, Phi Kappa Phi. Home: 2006 Cureton Dr Urbana IL 61801-6226 Business E-Mail: splittst@uiuc.edu.

SPODAK, MICHAEL KENNETH, forensic psychiatrist; b. Bklyn., Nov. 5, 1944; s. Harry and Betty (Rahn) S.; children: Lisa Beth, Brett David. BS, Union Coll., 1966; MD, SUNY-Syracuse, 1970. Diplomate: Nat. Bd. Med. Examiners, Am. Bd. Neurology and Psychiatry. Intern Mary Imogene Bassett Hosp., Cooperstown, N.Y., 1970-71; resident John Hopkins Hosp., Balt., 1974-77; practice medicine specializing in civil and criminal forensic psychiatry Towson, Md., 1977—; chief dept. psychiatry Balt. County Gen. Hosp., Randallstown, 1978-85; mem. staff Clifton T. Perkins Hosp. Ctr., Jessup, Md., 1977-92; clin. asst. prof. psychiatry U. Md. Hosp., Balt., 1983-97; psychiat. cons. Bur. Disability Ins., Social Security Adminstrn., Workmen's compensation Commn., Balt., 1981—; dir. community forensic services Mental Hygiene Adminstrn., Md., 1982-92; faculty Nat. Jud. Coll., 1988—. Mem. Md. Task Force on Somatic Therapies Contbr. numerous articles on forensic psychiatry to profl. jours., chpt. to book. Served with M.C. USN, 1972-74. Mem. Am. Acad. Psychiatry and Law, Am. Psychiat. Assn., Md. Psychiat. Soc. (chmn. peer rev. com. 2001), Md. Med. Soc. (chmn. occupational health com. 1983-90), Baltimore County Med. Soc. Office: 26 W Pennsylvania Ave Towson MD 21204-5001 Office Phone: 410-337-0343. E-mail: mkspodak@yahoo.com.

SPODEK, BERNARD, early childhood educator; b. Bklyn., Sept. 17, 1931; s. David and Esther (Lebenbaum) S.; m. Prudence Debb, June 21, 1957; children: Esther Yin-ling, Jonathan Chou. BA, Bklyn. Coll., 1952; MA, Columbia U., 1955, EdD, 1962. Cert. early childhood edn. tchr., N.Y. Tchr. Beth Hayeled Sch., N.Y.C., 1952-56, N.Y. City Pub. Schs., Bklyn., 1956-57, Early Childhood Ctr., Bklyn. Coll., 1957-60; asst. prof. elem. edn. U. Wis.-Milw., 1961-65; assoc. prof. early childhood edn. U. Ill., Champaign, 1965-68, prof. dept. curriculum and instrn., 1968-97, dir. dept. grad. programs, 1986-87, chair dept., 1987-89, dir. hons. program, Coll. Edn., 1984-86, mem. faculty Bur. Ednl. Rsch., 1981-85, prof. emeritus, 1997—; adv. prof. Hong Kong Inst. of Edn., 1999-2001. Dir. insts. Nat. Def. Edn. Act, 1965-67, dir. experienced tchr. fellowship program, 1967-69, co-dir. program for tchr. trainers in early childhood edn., 1969-74; vis. prof. Western Wash. State U., 1974, U. Wis., Madison, 1980, Kobe Shinwa Women's U., Japan; vis. scholar Sch. Early Childhood Studies, Brisbane (Australia) Coll. Advanced Edn., Delissa Inst. Early Childhood Studies, S. Australia Coll. Advanced Edn., 1985, Beijing Normal U., Nanjing Normal U., East China Normal U., Shangai, People's Republic China, 1986; rsch. fellow Kobe U., Japan, 1996; adj. prof. Queensland (Australia) U. Tech., 2000. Author or co-author 38 books including: (with others) A Black Studies Curriculum for Early Childhood Eduication, 1972, 2d edit., 1976, Teaching in the Early Years, 1972, 3d edit., 1985, Early Childhood Education, 1973, Studies in Open Education, 1975 (Japanese trans.), Early Childhood Education: Issues and Perspectives, 1977, (with Nir-Janiv and Steg) International Perspectives on Early Childhood Education, 1982 (Hebrew trans.), with Saracho and Lee (Mainstreaming Young Children, 1984, (with Saracho and Davis) Foundations of Early Childhood Education, 1987, 2d edit. (Japanese trans.), 1991, (with Saracho) Right from the Start, 1994 (Chinese and Korean translations), Dealing with Individual Differences in the Early Childhood Classroom, 1994; editor: Handbook of Research in Early Childhood Education, 1982, Today's Kindergarten, 1986, (with Saracho and Peters) Professionalism and the Early Childhood Practitioner, 1988, (with Saracho) Early Childhood Teacher Education, 1990, Issues in Early Childhood Curriculum, 1991, Educationally Appropriate Kindergarten Practices, 1991, Issues in Childcare, 1992, Handbook of Research on the Education of Young Children (Portuguese transls.), 1993, (with Saracho), Language and Literacy in Early Childhood Education, 1993; (with Safford and Saracho) Early Childhood Special Education, 1994; (with Garcia, McLaughlin & Saracho) Meeting the Challenge of Cultural and Linguistic Diversity, 1995, (with Saracho) Issues in Early Childhood Educational Evaluation and Assessment, 1996, (with Saracho) Multiple Perspectives on Play in Early Childhood Education, 1998, (with Saracho and Pellegrini) Issues in Early Childhood Educational Research, 1998, (with Saracho) Contemporary Perspectives in Early Childhood Curriculum, 2002, (with Saracho) Contemporary Perspectives in Early Childhood Education, 2002, (with Saracho) Contemporary Perspectives on Play in Early Childhood Education, 2003, (with Saracho) Studying Teachers in Early Childhood Settings, 2003, (with Saracho) Contemporary Perspectives on Language Policy and Literacy Instruction, 2004; series editor Yearbook in Early Childhood Education, early childhood edn. publs., 1990-2000; series co-editor: Contemporary Perspectives in Early Childhood Education, 2002—; guest editor Studies in Ednl. Evaluation, 1982, Early Education and Child Development, 1995; also contbr. chpts to books, articles to profl. jours. Mem. Am. Ednl. Rsch. Assn. (chair early childhood and child devel. spl. interest group 1983-84, publs. com. 1984-86), Nat. Assn. Edn. Young Children (sec. 1965-68, bd. govs. 1968-72, pres. 1976-78, editorial adv. bd. 1972-76, book rev. editor, 1972-74, cons. editor, 1985-87 Young Children jour., mem. tchr. edn. commn. 1981-88, chair commn. on appropriate edn. 4-5 yr. old children, 1984-85, cons. editor Early Childhood Rsch. Quar. 1987-90), Nat. Soc. for Study of Edn. (1972 yearbook com.), Pacific Early Childhood Edn. Rsch. Assn. (pres. 2000—). Office: U Ill Dept Curriculum & Instrn 1310 S 6th St Champaign IL 61820-6925 Business E-Mail: b-spodek@uiuc.edu.

SPOEHEL, RONALD ROSS, information technology executive; b. L.A., Oct. 28, 1957; s. Edwin Henry and Geraldine Jean (Hoskins) S.; m. Deborah Elizabeth Bell, Jan. 29, 1994; children: Elizabeth Schuyler, James Henry. BS in Econ., U. Pa., 1979, MS in Engring., MBA, U. Pa., 1980. V.p. Bank Am., San Francisco, N.Y.C., L.A., 1980-85, Lehman Bros., N.Y.C., 1985-90; sr. v.p., chief fin. officer ICF Kaiser Internat., Washington, 1990-94; v.p. corp. devel. Harris Corp, Melbourne, Fla., 1994-2000; CEO Optinel Sys., Inc., Columbia, Md., 2000—02; chmn. Alpine Ptnrs., Washington, 2002—03; exec. v.p. Man Tech Internat., Fairfax, Va., 2003—, CFO, 2003—. Mem.: Metro Club (Washington). Home: 1210 Windrock Dr Mc Lean VA 22102-2220

SPOERI, RANDALL KEITH, healthcare company executive; b. Cleve., June 12, 1946; s. Theodore Warren and Marion (Barrick) S.; m. Kathleen Loma Bryden Hayes, Aug. 31, 1968 (div. Mar. 1981); 1 child, Jennifer Anne; m. Deborah Jean Hammett, June 20, 1981 (div. Nov. 1998); 1 child, Jason Randall; m. Laura Joan Lenhardt, Apr. 24, 1999. BS, Calif. Polytech. State U., 1968; MS, Tex. A&M U., 1970, PhD, 1976. Math. statistician U.S. Bur. of the Census, Suitland, Md., 1976-80; assoc. prof. U.S. Naval Acad., Annapolis, 1980-83; assoc. exec. dir. Am. Statis. Assn., Alexandria, Va., 1983-88; sr. corp. statistician Humana, Inc., Louisville, Ky., 1988-92; chief program coord. info. branch Health Care Fin. Adminstrn., Balt., 1993; asst. v.p. Nat. Com. for Quality Assurance, Washington, 1994-95; adminstrv. v.p. health care analysis NYLCare Health Plans, Inc., N.Y.C., 1995-98; v.p. med. and quality informatics HIP Health Plans, N.Y.C., 1998—. Author: Quantitative Methods In Quality Management, 1991; contbr. articles to profl. jours. Mem. adv. com. Health Care Fin. Adminstrn., Balt., 1990-92, bur. dir. citation, 1993, adv. bd. Juran Inst., Wilton, Conn., 1995-98. 1st lt. U.S. Army, 1970-72. Recipient Svc. award Am. Statis. Assoc., Alexandria, 1994. Fellow AAAS, Am. Soc. for Quality (health care divsn. chair 1995-96); mem. Am. Statis Assn., Inst. Indsl. Engring., Inst. for Ops. Rsch. and the Mgmt. Scis., Am. Med. Informatics Assn., Acad. for Health Svcs. Rsch. and Health Policy. Avocations: sports, music. Home: 148 Top Of The World Way Green Brook NJ 08812-1839

SPOFFORD, SALLY (SALLY HYSLOP), artist; b. N.Y.C., Aug. 20, 1929; d. George Hall and Esther (McNaull) Hyslop; m. Gavin Spofford, Mar. 11, 1950 (dec. Jan. 1976); children: Lizabeth Spofford Smith, Leslie Spofford Russell. Student, The China Inst., N.Y.C., 1949, The Art Students League, 1950; BA with high honors, Swarthmore Coll., 1952. Instr. Somerset Art Assn., Peapack, N.J., 1978-95, Hunterdon Mus. Art, Clinton, N.J., 1985—; adv. bd., lectr. Apollo Muses, Inc., Gladstone, N.J.; trustee Artshowcase, Inc. One-woman shows include Riverside Studio, Pottersville, N.J., 1985, Morris Mus., Morristown, N.J. 1989, Schering-Plough Gallery, Madison, N.J., 1989, Phoenix Gallery, N.Y.C., 1990, Robin Hutchins Gallery, Maplewood, N.J., 1992, Berlex Labs. Corp. Office, Wayne, N.J., 1992, Hunterdon Mus. Art, Clinton, 1993, 2003, Newark Acad., Livingston, N.J., 1997, Simon Gallery, Morristown, 2004; exhibited in group shows at Hickory (N.C.) Mus., 1983, Purdue U., 1983, Monmouth (N.J.), 1984, Nabisco Brands Gallery, East Hanover, N.J., 1985, 89, Hunterdon Mus. Art, 1988, 93, 99, Schering-Plough Gallery, Madison, 1988, Morris Mus., Morristown, 1989, Montclair (N.J.) State U., 1995, Williams Gallery, Princeton, N.J., 1997, Monmouth Mus., Lincroft, N.J., 1998, Newark Acad., Livingston, 2000; represented in permanent collections N.J. State Mus., Trenton, Newark Mus., Morris Mus., Morristown. Painting residency fellow Vt. Studio Ctr., 1992. Mem. Assoc. Artists N.J. (pres. 1985-87), N.J. Watercolor Soc., Federated Art Assns. of N.J. (panel mem. 1985, demonstrator 1991). Home: PO Box 443 Bernardsville NJ 07924-0443

SPOHN, WILLIAM GIDEON, JR., mathematician, retired musician; b. Lancaster, Pa., Mar. 8, 1923; s. William Gideon and Inza Mae (Huber) S.; m. Alice Liane Bailey, Sept. 13, 1946 (div.); children: Susan Jeannine Grochowina (dec.), William Gideon III (dec.), Peter Jonathan, Kathleen Anne Precht, Mary Louise; m. Evelyn Walsh Moreland, June 15, 1963 (div. Oct. 1978); m. Claire Louise Burgstahler, Dec. 19, 1987 (div. Sept. 1999). BA, St. Johns Coll., 1947; MA, U. Calif., Berkeley, 1950; PhD, U. Pa., 1962. Instr. math. Temple U., Phila., 1952-54, U. Del., Newark, 1954-56; mathematician Aberdeen Proving Ground, Md., 1954-55; instr. math. Bowling Green (Ohio) State U., 1956-59; mathematician, sr. staff Johns Hopkins U. Applied Physics Lab., Laurel, Md., 1959-84; singer, prodr. Spohn Music Co., Columbia, Md., 1981-99, ret., 1999—. Contbr. articles to profl. jours. Served to lt. USNR, 1943-46, PTO. Johns Hopkins U. Applied Physics Lab. fellow, 1966-67. Mem. Math. Assn. Am. Home: 982A Tonia Ct Eldersburg MD 21784-4913

SPOKANE, ROBERT BRUCE, biophysical chemist; b. Cleve., Aug. 5, 1952; s. Herbert Norman and Marjorie Ellen (Firsten) S.; m. Linda Carol Wright, June 20, 1976; children: Lea, Hannah, Tara. BS in Chemistry, Ohio U., 1975; MS in Biophys. Chemistry, U. Colo., 1978, PhD in Biophys. Chemistry, 1981. Cert. full cave diver. Tchg. asst. dept. chemistry U. Colo., Boulder, 1975-77, rsch. asst. dept. chemistry, 1977-81; staff scientist Procter & Gamble Co., Cin., 1981-84; rsch. scientist dept. neurophysiology Children's Hosp., Cin., 1984-90; sr. scientist, product mgr. YSI Co., Yellow Springs, Ohio, 1990—. Cons. Synthetic Blood Internat., Yellow Springs, 1992. Contbr. articles to profl. jours. Rescuer, treas. Boulder Emergency Squad, 1980; rescue diver Kitty Hawk Scuba, Dayton, Ohio, 1992. Recipient Merck Index award Ohio U., 1975. Mem. Am. Chem. Soc., N.Y. Acad. Sci., Am. Physiol. Soc., Nat. Speleological Soc. (cave diving sect.), Sigma Xi. Achievements include research in implantable glucose sensors; oxygen tonometer for peritoneal oxygen measurements; interferant removal system for biosensors for methanol, ethanol, glutamate, and glutamine, optical carbon dioxide sensor, water chemistry in submerged caves. Home: 1715 Garry Dr Bellbrook OH 45305-1362 Office: YSI Co 1725 Brannum Ln Yellow Springs OH 45387-1107 Office Phone: 937-767-7241. Business E-Mail: rspokane@ysi.com.

SPOLAN, HARMON SAMUEL, lawyer; b. Phila., Dec. 12, 1935; s. Jay and Edythe (Greenberg) S.; m. Betty Jane Evnitz, Mar. 30, 1958; children: Michael, Suzanne. AB, Temple U., 1957, LLB, 1959; postgrad., Oxford U., 1966. Bar: Pa. 1960. Ptnr. Ravetz & Shuchman, Phila., 1960-68, Blair & Co., N.Y.C., 1968-72; v.p. Butcher & Singer, Phila., 1972-74; pres. Capital First Corp., Phila., 1974-75, State Nat. Bank, Rockville, Md., 1975-78, Jefferson Bank, Phila., 1978-99; pres., bd. dirs. JeffBanks, Inc., Phila., 1986-99; sr. mem. Cozen O'Connor, Phila., 1999—. Lectr. law U. Pa., Phila., 1964-68. Author: Federal Aids to Financing, 1970; contbr. articles to profl. jours. Former chmn. bd. Huntingdon Hosp., Willow Grove, Pa., 1982—89; bd. dirs. YMHA, Phila., 1978—95, Anti-Defamation League, 1982. Named Man of Yr., Nat. Assn. Women Bus. Owners, 1978, Disting. Alumnus, Central H.S., 1975. Mem. ABA, Phila. Bar Assn. Democrat. Jewish. Office: 1900 Market St Philadelphia PA 19103-3527 Business E-Mail: hspolan@cozen.com.

SPONG, CATHERINE YVONNE, obstetrician, gynecologist, researcher; d. Edward David and Valerie Ann Spong; m. Barry Steven Gruver, Aug. 22, 1992; 1 child, Juliana Rose Gruver. MD, U. of Mo.Kans., 1985—91. Diplomate FACOG Am. Bd. Obstetrics and Gynecology, 2000, cert. Maternal Fetal Medicine Am. Bd. of Obstetrics and Gynecology, 2002. Vis. scientist Lab. Devel. Neurobiology NICHD, NIH, 1998—; chief unit on perinatal and devel. neurobiology NIMD, NIH, 2004; maternal-fetal medicine specialist, assoc. prof. Georgetown U. Med. Ctr., 1998—; chief, pregnancy, perinatology br. Nat. Inst. of Child Health and Human Devel., NIH, Bethesda, 2000—; assoc. editor Obstetrics & Gynecology, Bethesda, DC, 2001—. Sr. examiner Malcolm Baldrige Nat. Quality Award, Gaithersberg, Md., 2001—. Author sci. articles in various profl. jours. Recipient Young Investigator Award, European Neuropeptide Soc., 2000, Young Investigator Award for Excellence in Neuropeptide Rsch., Winter Neuropeptide Com., 2000, Nat. Academic Team of Coll. Students, USA Today, 1990; grantee Rsch. Fellowship, Alpha Omega Alpha, 1989-1991. Fellow: Am. Coll. of Obstetricians and Gynecologists (jr. fellow dist. chmn. 1994—95); mem.: Soc. of Maternal Fetal Medicine (Best Sci. Presentation at Nat. Meeting 1996, 2000—04), Soc. for Neuroscience, Perinatal Rsch. Soc., Soc. for Gynecologic Investigation. Achievements include patents pending for Prevention of fetal alcohol syndrome and neuronal cell death with ADNF polypeptides; Orally active peptides that prevent cell injury and death; Novel peptides enhance performance in spatial learning; Neurotrophic components of the ADNF I Complex; research in Prevention of alcohol-induced damage including fetal death, growth restriction and learning impairment in a model of fetal alcohol syndrome. Office: PPB, CDBPM, NICHD, NIH 6100 Executive Blvd Rm 4B03 MSC 7510 Bethesda MD 20892 Office Phone: 301-496-5575. E-mail: spongc@exchange.nih.gov.

SPONG, DOUGLAS K. public relations executive; B in English, Iowa State U. With Colle & McVoy, sr. v.p., mng. dir., also bd. dirs.; mng. ptnr. Carmichael Lynch Spong, 1990—. Office: Carmichael Lynch Spong Pub Rels 800 Hennepin Ave Minneapolis MN 55403-1817

SPONG, JOHN SHELBY, retired bishop; b. Charlotte, N.C., June 16, 1931; s. John Shelby and Doolie Boyce (Griffith) S.; m. Joan Lydia Ketner, Sept. 5, 1952 (dec. 1988); children: Ellen Elizabeth, Mary Katharine, Jaquelin Ketner; m. Christine Mary Bridger, Jan. 1, 1990. AB, U. N.C., 1952; M.Div., Va. Theol. Sem., 1955; D.D., St. Paul's Coll., 1976, Va. Theol. Sem., 1977; DHL (hon.), Muhlenburg Coll., 1998, Holmes Inst. Chgo., 2003. Ordained to ministry Episcopal Ch., 1955, bishop, 1976; rector St. Joseph's Ch., Durham, N.C., 1955-57, Calvary Ch., Tarboro, N.C., 1957-65, St. John's Ch., Lynchburg, Va., 1965-69, St. Paul's Ch., Richmond, Va., 1969-76; bishop Diocese of Newark, 1976-2000; ret., 2000. Mem. governing body Nat. Episc. Ch., 1973-76; vis. lectr., Harvard U. Divinity Sch., 2000, U. Pacific, Stockton, Calif., 2003. Author: Honest Prayer, 1973, This Hebrew Lord, 1974, Dialogue--In Search of Jewish-Christian Understanding, 1975, Christpower, 1976, The Living Commandments, 1977, The Easter Moment, 1980, Into the Whirlwind: The Future of the Church, 1983, Beyond Moralism, 1986, Survival and Consciousness, 1987, Living in Sin? A Bishop Rethinks Human Sexuality, 1988, Rescuing the Bible from Fundamentalism--A Biship Rethinks the Meaning of Scripture, 1991, Born of a Woman, 1992, Resurrection: Myth or Reality?, 1994, Liberating the Gospels, Reading the Bible with Jewish Eyes, 1996, Why Christianity Must Change or Die, 1998, Here I Stand: My Struggle for a Christianity of Integrity, Love and Equality, 2000, A New Christianity for a New World, 2001; columnist Beliefnet.com, 2000—02; columnist: Agormedia.com, 2002—. Elected Quartercentury Scholar Emmanuel Coll., Cambridge, Eng., 1992, named Humanist of Yr., 1999, William Belden Noble lectr. Harvard U., 2000. Mem.: Rotary. Episcopalian. Home: 24 Puddingstone Rd Morris Plains NJ 07950-1114

SPONSLER, GEORGE CURTIS, III, research administrator, lawyer; b. Collingswood, NJ, Dec. 2, 1927; s. George Curtis and Mary Grace (Hollinberger) S.; m. Bridget Ruth Butcher, Sept. 3, 1955; children: Freda Grace, Naomi Margaret Bride, Curtis Alexander. BS in Engring. Physics, Princeton U., 1949, MA, 1951, PhD, 1952; JD, George Washington U., 1981. Bar: Md. 1981, D.C. 1982, U.S. Ct. Appeals (4th cir.) 1982, U.S. Ct. Appeals (fed. cir.) 1984. U.S. Supreme Ct. 1986. With Lincoln Lab., MIT, 1952-56; liaison officer Office Naval Research, London, 1956-58, head spl. projects br. Washington, 1958-59; sr. scientist Hoffman Sci. Center, Santa Barbara, Calif., 1959-60; chief sci., dir. tech. analysis and ops. research U.S. Navy Bur. Ships, 1960-63; dir. advanced planning, fed. systems div. IBM, 1963-66, dir. center exploratory studies, 1966-68; exec. sec. div. engring. Nat. Acad. Sci.-NRC, 1968-70; pres. Law Math. and Tech. Inc., 1970—2002. On leave, Congl. fellow U.S. Senate, Washington, 1987-88; mem. adv. com. to Office Emergency Planning, Nat. Acad. Sci., 1967-72, chmn. subcom. automation, 1966-68, mem. joint adv. com. on electromagnetic pulse, 1970-74; cons. Exec. Office of Pres., 1971-73 Contbr.: Tech. Innovation, Harper Ency. of Sci.; author articles in field. Fellow AAAS (electorate nominating com. 1980-83, chmn.-elect sect. X, 1983-84, chmn. 1984-85, mem. coun. 1985-86), Am. Physics Soc.; mem. IEEE (life, sr., chmn. subcom. on privacy of communications and info. policy com. 1982-85, aerospace R&D policy com. 1990-92), Phi Beta Kappa, Sigma Xi. Democrat. Episcopalian. E-mail: sponsler@worldnet.att.net.

SPONZILLI, EDWARD GEORGE, lawyer; b. Newark, Mar. 30, 1948; s. Edward James and Dorothy Maria (Murillo) Sponzilli. BA in History with high honors, Rutgers U., 1971, JD, 1975; summer diploma, Cath. Inst. of Paris, 1971; MA, Columbia U., 1972. Bar: NJ 75, U.S. Dist. Ct. NJ 75, U.S. Ct. Appeals (3d cir.) 76, U.S. Supreme Ct. 79, DC 79, NY 81. Law clk. to judge U.S. Dist. Ct. NJ, Newark, 1975—77; assoc. Pitney, Hardin & Kipp, Morristown, NJ, 1975—81, Dunn, Pashman, Sponzilli, Swick & Finnerty (formerly Cummins, Dunn & Pashman), Hackensack, NJ, 1982—, ptnr., 1984—95, Norris, McLaughlin & Marcus, Pa., 1995—. Co-adj. prof. Rutgers U., New Brunswick, NJ, 1980—81, New Brunswick, 1994, New Brunswick, 98, mcpl. pros., 1981—, mem. Jessup Internat. Law Moot Ct. Team, 1975, coach Mock Trial Team, 1994—97; counsel Judo of NJ Inc., Cranford, 1983—; judge law sch. moot ct. competition Seton Hall, 1977—79, 1981, 81, 86; cert. civil trial atty. NJ Supreme Ct., 1997—; mem. faculty Nat. Inst. Trial Advocacy, 1995—; faculty N.J. Atty. Gens. Trial Advocacy Inst., 2002—. Contbr. articles to profl. jours. Active Rutgers U. Found., 1987—. Recipient Hancy Higgenson Dorr award, Rutgers U., 1971, Disting. Svc. award, Animals Need You-Kindness Corp., NJ, 1981, Client Protection award, NJ Supreme Ct. Fund for Client Protection, 1999; Henry Rutgers scholar. Master: Am. Inns of Ct (pres. 2000—01); mem.: ATLA, ABA (trial practice com. of litigation sect.), N.J. State Ct. Mediation (fed. arbitrator), Nat. Assn. Coll. and Univ. Attys., N.J. Def. Assn., Def. Rsch. Inst., Middlesex County Bar Assn., Essex County Bar Assn., Bergen County Bar Assn., Trial Attys. NJ (trustee 1987—), NJ Trial Lawyers Assn., Assn. Fed. Bar NJ, Fed. Bar Assn., NJ State Bar Assn. (higher edn. com.), Columbia Grad. Faculties Alumni Assn., Civil War History Assn., So. Hist. Assn., Am. Hist. Assn., Orgn. Am. Historians, Rutgers U. Law Sch. Alumni Assn. (nominating com. 1982, program dir. 1982, treas. 1991—92, sec. 1992—93, v.p. 1993—94, pres. 1994—95, exec. counsel, alumni fedn. rep.), Scarlet R Round Table Alumni Assn., Phi Alpha Delta, Kappa Sigma (sec. 1978—79, alumnus advisor 1978—99, v.p. 1979—82, pres. 1982—86, dist. grand master 1986—2000, pres. 1994—, chmn. nat. legal commn. 1995—97, trustee Gamma Upsilon chpt.), Phi Beta Kappa. Home: 37 Brookside Ave Caldwell NJ 07006-5603 Office: Norris McLaughlin & Marcus PA 721 Rt 202-206 PO Box 1018 Somerville NJ 08876-1018 Office Phone: 908-722-0700 166. Business E-Mail: egsponzilli@nmmlaw.com.

SPOOLSTRA, LINDA CAROL, minister, educator, religious organization administrator; b. Hillsdale, Mich., July 11, 1947; d. Jay Carroll and Carol Elsa (Linstrom) Lehmann; m. Gerald William Spoolstra, Feb. 17, 1973. BA, Bethel Coll., 1969; MA, Fla. State U., 1970; M of Div., McCormick Theol. Sem., Chgo., 1978; DD (hon.), Cen Bapt. Theol. Sem., Kansas City, Kans., 1988. Ordained Am. Bapt. Clergywoman. Tchr. Dade County Pub. Schs., Miami, Fla., 1970-71; ins. claims adjustor Safeco Ins. Co., Chgo., 1971-72; dir. of community outreach and edn. N. Shore Bapt. Ch., Chgo., 1972-78, assoc. pastor, 1978; pastor First Bapt. Ch., Swansea, Mass., 1978-84; exec. dir. commn. on the ministry Am. Bapt. Chs. U.S.A., Valley Forge, Pa., 1984-90; exec. minister Am. Bapt. Chs. Mass., Dedham, 1990—. Mem. Nat. Coun. Chs. Profl. Ch. Leadership, N.Y.C., 1984-90; mem. commn. on pastoral leadership Bapt. World Alliance, McLean, Va., 1986-90; mem. gen. bd. Nat. Coun. Chs. of Christ, 1990-96. Trustee Andover-Newton Theol. Sch., 1990—. Avocations: sailing, tennis, travel, classical music. Office: Am Bapt Chs Mass 20 Milton St Dedham MA 02026-2915

SPOON, ALAN GARY, venture capital company executive; b. Detroit, June 4, 1951; s. Harry and Mildred (Rudman) S.; m. Terri Alper, June 3, 1975; children: Ryan, Leigh, Randi. BS, MS, MIT, 1973; JD, Harvard U., 1976. Cons. The Boston Cons. Group, 1976-79, mgr., 1979-81, v.p., 1981, The Washington Post Co., 1982-84; v.p., contr. Washington Post, 1985-86, v.p. mktg., 1986-87; v.p. fin., CFO The Washington Post Co., 1987-89; pres. Newsweek mag., 1989-91; COO The Washington Post Co., 1991-2000, pres., 1993-2000; mng. gen. ptnr. Polaris Venture Ptnrs., Waltham, Mass., 2000—. Dir. Info. Industry Assn., Washington, 1982-83, 88-89; bd. dirs. Danaher Corp. Washington, Interactive Corp., N.Y.C.; regent Smithsonian Instn., Washington; mem. corp. MIT. Bd. dirs. Norwood Sch., 1989-93, chmn., 1993-95; bd. dirs. Smithsonian Nat. Mus. Natural History, Washington, 1994-99; trustee WETA-Pub. Broadcasting, 1986-92. Recipient award for scholarship and athletics Ea. Coll. Athletic Conf. and MIT, 1973. Office: Polaris Venture Partners 1000 Winter St Ste 3350 Waltham MA 02451-1476

SPOONER, FRANK CLYFFURDE, economic history educator; b. Cleveland, Australia, Mar. 5, 1924; s. Harry Gordon Morrison and Ethel Beatrice (Walden) S. BA, U. Cambridge, Eng., 1947, MA, 1949, PhD, 1953, LittD, 1985. Commonwealth Fund fellow U. Chgo., NYU, Columbia U., Harvard U., 1955-57, U. Paris, 1957-63; lectr. advanced studies U. Oxford, Eng., 1958-59; vis. lectr. econs. Harvard U., Cambridge, Mass., 1961-62; Irving Fisher rsch. prof. econs. Yale U., New Haven, 1962-63; mem. faculty U. Durham, Eng., 1963—, dir. Inst. European Studies, 1969-76, prof. econ. history, 1966-85, prof. emeritus, 1985—. Author: The International Economy and Monetary Movements in France, 1493-1680, 1956, English lang. edit., 1972, The International Economy and Monetary Movements in France, 1493-1725, 1972, Risks at Sea, 1983. Sub-lt. Royal Navy, 1943-46, ETO. Recipient Prix Limantour Acad. Scis. Morales et Politiques, 1957; Leverhulme Fund fellow, 1976-78, 85-86. Fellow Royal Hist. Soc., Royal Numismatic Soc., Soc. Antiquaries London; mem. Econ. History Soc., Econ. History Assn., Vereniging Economisch-Historisch Archief, Royal Econ. Soc., Am. Econ. Assn., Cliometric Soc., Assn. Marc Bloch, Hakluyt Soc., Soc. Francaise Numismatique, Mark Twain Soc., Friends Nat. Librs., United Oxford and Cambridge U. Club. Home: 31 Chatsworth Ave Bromley Kent BR1 5DP England Office: U Durham Dept Econs 23-26 Old Elvet Durham DH1 3HY England

SPOONER, JOHN D. financial planner, writer; b. Boston, July 25, 1937; s. Herbert M. and Helen F. Spooner; m. Susan Farnsworth, June 15, 1966; children: Scott Fabyan, Nicholas Monroe, Amanda Davis. AB, Harvard U., Cambridge, Mass., 1959. Dir. investments Smith Barney, Boston, 1961—. Chmn. dirs. coun. Shearson, N.Y.C., 1978, Smith, Barney, N.Y.C., 1994—95. Contbr. articles to Atlantic Mag., Playboy, Town & Country. Bd. dirs. Boys and Girls Club, Boston, 1953—. Mass. Cystic Fibrosis Found., 1980—, Mass. Cultural Coun., 1993—; vis. com. Harvard Coll., Cambridge, 1997—. Sgt Med. Corps U.S. Army, 1960—65. Recipient Literary Lights award, Boston Pub. Libr., 1993. Mem.: Harvard Club (Boston), St. Boltoph Club, The Country Club, Belmont Country Club. Achievements include co-founder and trustee The Curious George Found. Avocations: golf, painting, squash. Home: 101 Chestnut St Boston MA 02108 Office: Smith Barney Inc Boston MA 02109 E-mail: spoonersmtpeople@compus.nc.com.

SPOONER, RUSSELL EDWARD, retired printing company executive; b. Attleboro, Mass., Dec. 9, 1924; s. Howard Edward and Gladys Winifred (Schofield) Spooner; m. Maida Lenore Tillson, June 21, 1951 (div. 1970); children: Russell Edward, Lorelei Rae; m. Bessie Margaret Snowman, June 27, 1980. Grad. HS, Attleboro, Mass. Owner, mgr. Enterprise Press, Attleboro, 1947—78; pres., sec. Enterprise Press, Inc., Attleboro, 1978—86; ret., 1986. Cons. King Printing Co., Providence, 1986—88. Columnist Rehoboth Reporter, 1994—;, author numerous poems, short stories. Bd. dirs. Friends of Boyden Refuge, Taunton, Mass., 1999—, Animal Awareness, Inc., Norton, Mass., 2000—. Staff sgt. U.S. Army, 1943—45, ETO. Recipient Poet's Rev. award, 1994, Armadillo Poetry Press award, 1998. Mem.: Friends of Blanding Libr. (life), Am. Legion (life). Avocations: woodworking, gardening. Home: 5 Lorson Ln Rehoboth MA 02769

SPOOR, JAMES EDWARD, human resources executive, entrepreneur; b. Rockford, Ill., Feb. 19, 1936; s. Frank Kendall and Genevieve Eileen (Johnson) S.; m. Nancy E. Carlson, Sept. 8, 1962; children: Sybll K., Kendall P., Andrea K., Marcie K. BS in Psychology, U. Ill., 1958. Pers. mgr. Nat. Sugar Refining Co., N.Y.C., 1960-64; Pepsico, Inc., N.Y.C., Auburn, N.Y., 1964-67; mgr. internat. pers. Control Data Corp., Mpls., 1967-75; v.p. pers. and employee rels. Vetco, Inc., Ventura, Calif., 1975-79; v.p. employee rels. Hamilton Bros. Oil Co., Denver, 1979-84; pres., founder, CEO Spectrum Human Resource Systems Corp., Denver, 1984—. Cons., author, spkr. on human resources and entrepreneurism. Mem. adv. bd. Salvation Army, 1978-79; chmn. Spl. Commn. for Ventura County Bd. Suprs., 1978; mem. task force on human resources Colo. Sch. Mines, 1983; state chair Coun. Growing Cos., 1991-92, nat. pres., 1992-94; bd. dirs. Breckenridge Outdoor Edn. Ctr., 1994-98, chmn., 1996-98. Mem. Internat. Human Resources Info. Mgmt. Assn. (nat. bd. dirs. 1997—), Alpha Chi Rho ednl. found. (trustee 2003-).

SPOOR, WILLIAM HOWARD, food company executive; b. Pueblo, Colo., Jan. 16, 1923; s. Charles Hinchman and Doris Field (Slaughter) S.; m. Janet Spain, Sept. 23, 1950; children: Melanie G., Cynthia F., William Lincoln. BA, Dartmouth Coll., 1949; postgrad., Denver U., 1949, Stanford U., 1965. Asst.

sales mgr. N.Y. Export divsn. Pillsbury Co., 1949-53; mgr. N.Y. office Pillsbury Co., 1953-62, v.p. export divsn., 1962-68, v.p., gen. mgr. internat. ops., 1968-73, CEO, 1973-85, also bd. dirs., chmn. exec. com., 1987, pres., CEO, 1988, past chmn. bd. dirs. Bd. dirs. Coleman Co. Mem. regional export expansion coun. Dept. Commerce, 1966-74; bd. dirs. exec. Coun. Fgn. Diplomats, 1976-78; mem. bd. visitors Nelson A. Rockefeller Ctr., Dartmouth Coll., 1992-95; Minn. Orchestral Assn., United Negro Coll. Fund, 1973-75; chmn. Capitol City Renaissance Task Force, 1985; trustee Mpls. Found., 1985-92; mem. sr. campaign cabinet Carlson Com. U. Minn., 1985; mem. corps. rels. com. Nature Conservancy, 1985; mem. Nat. Cambodia Crisis Com., pres. pvt. sector Dept. Transp. task force, 1982, pres. pvt. sector survey on cost control, 1983; chmn. YWCA Tribute to Womwn in Internat. Industry. 2d lt. inf. U.S. Army, 1943-46. Recipient Golden Plate award, Am. Acad. Achievement, Disting. Bus. Leadership award, St. Cloud State U., Miss. Valley World Trade award, Outstanding Achievement award, Dartmouth Coll., Horatio Alger award, 1986, Medal of Merit, U.S. Savs. Bond Program; honored with William H. Spoor Dialogues on Leadership, Dartmouth Coll., honored Fair Player Minn. Women's Polit. Caucus, 1989. Mem. Grocery Mfrs. Am. (treas. 1973 84), Nat. Fgn. Trade Coun., Minn. Hist. Soc. (mem. exec. com. 1983, bd. dirs.), Minn. Bus. Partnership, River Club N.Y.C., Woodhill Country Club, Lafayette Club (Wayzata, Minn.), Mpls. Club (bd. govs. 1985, pres. 1986), Gulf Stream Bath and Tennis Club, Delray Beach Yacht Club, Gulf Stream Golf Club, Old Baldy Club (Saratoga, Wyo.), Alta Club (Salt Lake City), Phi Beta Kappa. Home: 622 Ferndale Rd W Wayzata MN 55391-9628 Office: 4900 IDS Ctr Minneapolis MN 55402 Office Phone: 612 330 4621.

SPORE, KEITH KENT, newspaper executive; b. Milw., May 29, 1942; s. G. Keith and Evelyn A. (Morgan) S.; divorced; children: Bradley, Julie, Justine; m. Kathy Stokebrand. BS in Journalism, U. Wis., Milw., 1967. City editor Milw. Sentinel, 1977-81; asst. mng. editor/news Milw. Jour. Sentinel, 1981-89, mng. editor, 1989-91, editor, 1991-95, editl. page editor, 1995, pres., 1995—, pub., 1996—. Author: (novels) The Hell Masters, 1977, Death of a Scavenger, 1980. With U.S. Army, 1961-64. Recipient Freedom of Info. award Soc. Profl. Journalists, 1995; named Mass Comms. Alumnus of Yr., U. Wis.-Milw., 1994. Mem. Greater Milw. Com. Office: Milw Jour Sentinel PO Box 661 Milwaukee WI 53201-0661 E-mail: kspore@onwis.com.

SPORLEDER, THOMAS LYNN, economist, researcher; b. Perrysburg, Ohio, Apr. 2, 1942; s. John Loren Sporleder, Ruth Cordelia Westrick; m. Marjorie Jean Stout; children: Thomas James, Candace Lynn. BS, Ohio State U., 1964, MS, 1965, PhD, 1968. Mgr. Agrl. Grading Sta. Campbell Soup Co., Napoleon, Ohio, 1961—64; prof. agrl. econs. Tex. A&M U., College Station, 1968—89; prof. agribusiness, income enhancement endowed chair Ohio State U., Columbus, 1989—. Vis. scholar USDA, Washington, 1974—75; rsch. economist Office Tech. Assessment, U.S. Congress, Washington, 1976—77; bd. dirs. Internat. Food and Agribusiness Mgmt. Assn., Washington, Ctr. for Innovative Food Tech., Toledo, Heartland Agdeavor Assn., Columbus. Contbr. articles to profl. jours. Mem.: Am. Agrl. Econs. Assn. (pres. agribus. econs. and mgmt. sect. 2002—03). Roman Catholic. Home: 4518 Elderberry Ct Upper Arlington OH 43220-3020 Office: Ohio State Univ 2120 Fyffe Rd Columbus OH 43210-1066 Personal E-mail: sporleder.1@osu.edu. Business E-Mail: sporleder.1@osu.edu.

SPORN, AARON ADOLPH, physician, educator; b. N.Y.C., Nov. 5, 1953; s. Herbert and Eunice (Aron) S. BS, SUNY, Stony Brook, 1974; MD, Columbia U., 1978. Diplomate Am. Bd. Orthopaedic Surgery. Intern. gen. surgery Roosevelt Hosp., N.Y.C., 1978-79, resident gen. surgery, 1979-80; resident, chief resident in orthopaedic surgery NYU and Bellevue Hosp., N.Y.C., 1980-83; fellow Midwest Inst. for Orthopaedics, Cin., 1983-84; v.p. medical affairs Inst. for Medicine in Sports, Trenton, N.J., 1984-85; clin. sr. instr. Hahnemann U. Med. Sch., Phila., 1986—; 1991clin. instr. Rutgers U. Med. Sch., New Brunswick, NJ, 1986—91; chief, dept. orthopaedic surgery Robert Wood Johnson U. Hosp. at Hamilton, 1994—, vice chmn., dept. surgery, 1993-95, chmn. dept. surgery, 1995—98. Vis. clin. fellow Columbia U., N.Y.C., 1978-80, teaching asst. NYU, N.Y.C., 1982-83; com. mem. Arthroscopy Bd. N.Am. Exam Com., 1989-90; cons. N.J. State Police, Trenton, 1987-92; fundraising com. orthopaedics wing Hamilton Hosp., Trenton, 1989. Contbr. articles to profl. jours. Ind. Rsch. Project grantee NIMH, 1975, 88. Fellow Am. Acad. Orthopaedic Surgery, Arthroscopy Bd. N.Am.; mem. Phi Beta Kappa. Avocations: photography, history, music. Office: Med Arts Bldg 8 Quakerbridge Plz Hamilton NJ 08619-1255

SPORN, KALMAN CHAIM, banker; b. Far Rockaway, N.Y., May 17, 1971; s. Rabbi Joseph Yochanan and Esther Perl Sporn. Student, Yeshiva U., N.Y. and Israel, 1989—92; BA, CUNY, 1994. Assoc. dir. of govt. rels. HIAS - Hebrew Immigrant Aid Soc., N.Y.C., 1993—94; liaison to congressman Charles Schumer, U.S. Ho. of Reps., Washington, 1993—94; asst. mng. dir. Helmsley -Spear Ltd., N.Y.C., 1994—96; pvt. banker Investec Bank (UK) Ltd., London, 1996—98; fin. advisor CIBC Oppenheimer, N.Y.C., 1999—2000; v.p. corp. fin. Global Supply Net.com, N.Y.C., 2000—03. Cons. Crescent Capital Ptnrs., Amman, Jordan, 2000—01. Rep. party candidate N.Y. State Assembly 69th Dist., N.Y.C., 2002—02; meeting with Pope John Paul II, Internat. Coun. of Christians and Jews, Vatican City, 1993—93. Recipient Young Bus. Leadership award, Sanz Med. Ctr. Laniado Hosp., 2001. Republican. Jewish. Avocations: contemporary art, dance, Holocaust studies, piano, travel. Home: Ste 302 210 W 70th St New York NY 10023 Personal E-mail: kalman@kalmansporn.com.

SPORN, MICHAEL BENJAMIN, cancer researcher; b. N.Y.C., Feb. 15, 1933; married; 2 children. MD, U. Rochester, 1959. Intern U. Rochester Sch. Medicine, 1959-60; mem. staff lab. neurochemistry Nat. Inst. Neurol. Diseases and Blindness, 1960-64; mem. staff Nat. Cancer Inst., Bethesda, Md., 1964-70, head lung cancer unit, 1970-73, chief lung cancer br., 1973-78, chief lab. chemoprevention, 1978-95; prof. pharmacology Dartmouth Med. Sch., Hanover, N.H., 1995—. Recipient Am. Cancer Soc. Medal of Honor, 1994. Mem. Am. Assn. Cancer Rsch. (B.F. Cain Meml. award 1991), Am. Soc. Biol. Chemistry. Achievements include research in nucleic acids and cancer, vitamin A and related compounds, carcinogenesis studies, retinoids and cancer prevention, peptide gr owth factors and transforming growth factor-beta. Office: Dept Pharmacology Dartmouth Med Sch Hanover NH 03755-3835

SPOSITO, GARRISON, soil scientist, educator, reseacher; b. L.A., Calif., July 29, 1939; s. Albert Cono (Stepfather) and Geraldine Virginia (Hanks) Sposito, Jesus Gabriel Navarro; m. Mary Elizabeth Campbell, July 10, 1976; m. Volney Susan Douglas, Nov. 22, 1960 (div. Jan. 1, 1976); children: Douglas Albert, Geraldine Harriet Bangle, Frank Andreas, Jennifer Virginia Hanks, Sara Marie Campbell, Cristina Elizabeth Terry. Student, U. Calif., Berkeley, 1957—58; PhD, U. Calif., 1965; BS, U. Ariz., 1961, MS, 1963. Prof. Sonoma State U., Rohnert Park, Calif., 1965—74, U. Calif., Riverside, 1974—88, Berkeley, 1988—. Dir. Kearney Found. Soil Sci., Berkeley, 1996—2001. Author: (textbook) An Introduction to Quantum Physics, 1970, An Introduction to Classical Dynamics, 1976, Scale Dependence and Scale Invariance in Hydrology, 1998, (monograph) The Thermodynamics of Soil Solutions, 1981, The Surface Chemistry of Soils, 1984, The Chemistry of Soils, 1989, Chemical Equilibria and Kinetics in Soils, 1994, The Environmental Chemistry of Aluminum, 1996, Hydrologic Processes from Catchment to Continental Scales, 1997, The Surface Chemistry of Natural Particles, 2004. Sr. Fulbright fellow, Fulbright Commn., 1973, Heinemann Sr. fellow, NATO, 1981, John Simon Guggenheim Found., 1984—85, Vis. Fellow, St. Cross Coll., U. Oxford, 1984. Fellow: Soil Sci. Soc. Am. (Rsch. award 1982), Am. Soc. Agronomy, European Assn. Geochemistry, Am. Geophys. Union (Rsch. award Hydrology sect. 1990, Horton medal 2004), Geochem. Soc.; mem.: Acad. Agr. France, Assn. Environ. Engieering and Sci. Profs. (Outstanding Paper award 1999), Internat. Humic Substances Soc., Clay Minerals Soc., Am. Chem. Soc., Gamma Sigma Delta, Sigma Pi Sigma, Soc. Sigma Xi. Roman Catholic. Avocations: painting, reading, collecting books & art, drawing. Office: Univ Calif Hilgard Hall MC 3110 Berkeley CA 94720-3110 Office Phone: 510-643-8297. E-mail: gsposito@nature.berkeley.edu.

SPOTNITZ, ALAN JEFFREY, cardiothoracic surgeon; b. N.Y.C., May 31, 1944; s. Hyman and Miriam (Berkman) S. BA, Harvard U., 1966; MD, Columbia U., 1970. Intern gen. surgery Beth Israel Hosp., Boston, 1970-71; rsch. fellow Columbia U., N.Y.C., 1973-74, resident gen. surgery Beth Israel Hosp., Boston, 1971-75; thoracic resident thoracic surgery Presbyn., N.Y.C., 1978-79; assoc. prof. clin. surgery Robert Wood Johnson Med. Sch., New Brunswick, NJ, 1982—87, chief sect. cardiac surgery, 1988—2001. Dir. surg. clerkship program Robert Wood Johnson Med. Sch., New Brunswick, 1982—, assoc. dir. thoracic surgery residency program U. Medicine and Dentistry N.J., 1991-2001. Author: (with others) Homograft Valve Durability: Host or Donor Influence, Heart Vessels, 1990; contbr. articles to profl. jours. Maj. USAF, 1975—77. Office: Robert Wood Johnson Med Sch 125 Paterson St New Brunswick NJ 08901 Office Phone: 908-235-7805. Business E-Mail: spotnitz@umdnj.edu.

SPOTTISWOODE, ROGER, film director, film producer; b. London, Eng., Jan. 5, 1945; Film editor TV commls. and documentaries; editor: (pictures) Straw Dogs, 1971, The Getaway, Pat Garrett and Billy the Kid, 1973, The Gambler, 1974, Hard Times, 1975; assoc. prodr.: Who'll Stop the Rain?; exec. prodr.: Baby: Secret of the Lost Legend; dir. (films) Terror Train, 1980, The Pursuit of D.B. Cooper, 1982, Under Fire, 1983, The Best of Times, 1986, The Last Innocent Man, 1987, Shoot to Kill, 1988, Turner & Hooch, 1989, Air America, 1990, Stop! Or My Mom will Shoot, 1992, Tomorrow Never Dies, 1997, The 6th Day, 2000, (TV) The Renegades, 1982, The Last Innocent Man, 1987, Third Degree Burn, 1989, Time Flies When You're Alive, 1989, And the Band Played On, 1993, Mesmer, 1994, Hiroshima, 1995, Prince Street, 1997, Noreiga: God's Favourite, 2000, The Matthew Shepard Story, 2002. Office: c/o William Morris Agency care Robert Stien 151 S El Camino Dr Beverly Hills CA 90212-2775

SPRADLEY, LOLA, state representative; b. Colo., June 28, 1946; married; 1 child. BA, BS, Regis Coll. Republican. Methodist. Office: State Capitol # 246 200 E Colfax Ave Denver CO 30386

SPRADLING, ROBERT LEDFORD, music educator, conductor; b. Knoxville, Tenn., Apr. 28, 1946; s. Stewart Ledford and Bonny Kate Spradling; m. Diana June Roland, July 9, 1966; 1 child, Scott Richard. PhD of Music Edn., Fla. State U., 1980, MusM Edn., 1969, MusB Edn., 1968. Dir. of bands, prof. of music We. Mich. U., Kalamazoo, 1993—; dir. bands, assoc. prof. music Syracuse U., Syracuse, NY, 1980—93; dir. bands Coconut Creek H.S., Coconut Creek, Fla., 1971—78, Deerfield Beach Jr. H.S., Deerfield Beach, Fla., 1969—71; asst. dir. bands James Rickards Jr.-Sr. H.S., Tallahassee, 1968—69. Co-founder, bd. mem. NY State Band Dirs. Assn., 1981—92; bd. dirs. Fla. Bandmasters Assn., 1975—77. Contbr. composition analysis Teaching Music through Performance in Band, articles to profl. jours. Ch. moderator First Bapt. Ch., Syracuse, NY, 1985—93; chair staff parish rels. com. Chapel Hill United Meth. Ch., Portage, Mich., 1999—2004. Recipient Stanbury Award, Am. Sch. Band Dirs. Assn., 1975, A. Frank Martin Award, Kappa Kappa Psi, 1992. Mem.: Music Educators Nat. Conf., Coll. Band Dirs. Nat. Assn. (ea. divsn. pres. 1993—94, nat. coord. for state chairs 1985—95), World Assn. for Symphonic Bands and Ensembles (life), Kappa Kappa Psi (A. Frank Martin award 1992), Phi Mu Alpha. Achievements include research in Conductor-Ensemble Behavior and Interaction; Students' attitudes regarding post-high school band participation; Discrimination between intonation and tone quality errors among musical instruments; National/International appearances as Guest Conductor for Professional and Amateur Bands; National/International appearances as Guest Clinician/Lecturer. Avocations: sailing, golf, sports cars, travel, reading. Office: Western Michigan University 1903 West Michigan Kalamazoo MI 49008 E-mail: spradling@wmich.edu.

SPRAFKIN, ROBERT PETER, psychologist, educator; b. N.Y.C., Dec. 18, 1940; s. Benjamin R. and Dora M. (Berman) S.; m. Barbara Marcus, July 19, 1964; children: Jeffrey P., Neal R., Noah M. AB, Dartmouth Coll., 1962; MA, Columbia U., 1964; PhD, Ohio State U., 1968. Lic. psychologist, N.Y. Asst. prof. psychology Syracuse (N.Y.) U., 1968-71, adj. assoc. prof., 1973-88, adj. prof., 1989—; chief day treatment ctr. VA Med. Ctr., Syracuse, 1971-95, dir. psychology tng. program, 1983-2001. Clin. assoc. prof. dept. psychiatry SUNY Health Sci. Ctr., Syracuse, 1973—95; cons. psychologist Assn. for Retarded Citizens, 1993—; clin. prof. dept. psychiatry SUNY Upstate Med. U., 1995—; chief Behavioral Medicine Sect. Psychology Svc., 1994—2001, acting chief psychology svc., 1994—97, sr. psychologist, 1997—2001; cons. psychologist Enabled, United Cerebral Palsy, 2001—. Co-author: Skilltraining for Community Living, 1976, Skillstreaming the Adolescent, 1980, Social Skills for Mental Health, 1993. Mem. Onondaga County Legis. Coun. on Disabled, Syracuse, 1982-94; mem. cmty. svcs. bd. County Dept. Mental Health, 1987-97. Mem. APA, Assn. Advancement of Behavior Therapy, Soc. Behavioral Medicine, Cen. N.Y. Psychol. Assn. (pres.), Dartmouth Club (pres.). Office: 300 Burnet Ave Syracuse NY 13203

SPRAGG, GREGG, retail executive; Student, N.C. State U. Exec. v.p. mktg. and ops. Finast Foods Stores, Cleve.; exec. v.p. ops. Bi Lo Supermarkets, Greenville, SC; regional v.p. ops. Sam's Club div. Wal Mart Stores, Inc., 1998—2001, exec. v.p. ops. Sam's Club div., 2001—. Office: Wal-Mart Stores Inc 608 SW Eighth St Bentonville AR 72716-6297

SPRAGGINS, JOHNNIE DAVID, social studies educator; b. Opelika, Ala., Oct. 13, 1954; s. John David and Alma Jean McCormick Spraggins; 1 child, Jada Ruth. BA, Auburn U., 1978, MA, 1988, U. Mich., 1993, PhD, 1995. Rsch. assoc. Auburn U., 1981-90; tchr. Madonna U., U. Mich.-Ann Arbor, 1990-96; prof. Randolph-Macon Coll., Ashland, Va., 1999—2001; asst. prof. Our Lady of the Lake U., San Antonio, 2001—. Advisor Woman's Studies Coun., Randolph-Macon Coll., 1999—; vis. asst. prof. SUNY, Geneseo; vis. asst. prof. Asian divsn. U. Md., Sagamihara-shi, Japan; tchr. Kitasato U., Sagamihara-shi, Kanagawa-ken, 1996-98. Contbr. articles to profl. jours. Mem. Ctr. for Rsch. on Social Orgn., Am. Sociological Assn., Soc. Applied Sociology. Democrat. Buddhist. Avocations: gardening, travel. Office: 411 SW 24th St San Antonio TX 78207 E-mail: spraj@lake.ollusa.edu.

SPRAGUE, AMARIS JEANNE, real estate broker; b. Jackson, Mich., Feb. 18, 1935; d. Leslie Markham and Blanche Lorraine (Basnaw) Reed; m. John M. Vetterling, Oct. 1985; children by previous marriage, Anthony John, James Stuart. Student, Mich. State U., 1952-53; BS, Colo. State U., 1965. Cert. real estate broker. Real estate sales Seibel and Benedict Realty, Ft. Collins, Colo., 1968-69; salesman Realty Brokers Exch., Ft. Collins, 1969-72; broker, pres. Sprague and Assocs., Inc., Realtors, Ft. Collins, 1972-80; broker assoc. Van Schaack & Co., Ft. Collins, 1980-86; broker, ptnr. The Group, Inc., 1986—. Dir. Univ. Nat. Bank. Mem. bus. adv. council Colo. State U., 1976-84, chmn. 1979-80, mem. adv. council Coll. of Engring., 1981. Named Honor Alumni, Colo. State U., 1983. Mem. Nat. Assn. Realtors, Colo. Assn. Realtors, Ft. Collins Bd. Realtors, Ft. Collins C. of C. (bd. dirs. 1978-84, pres. 1982-83). Republican. Episcopalian. Home: PO Box 475 Fort Collins CO 80522-0475 Office: 401 W Mulberry St Fort Collins CO 80521-2839

SPRAGUE, ANN LOUISE, space scientist; b. Bellfonte, Pa., Feb. 25, 1946; d. David Carpenter and Opal (Wheat) S.; m. Donald M. Hunten, 1995. BA in Geology, Syracuse U., 1969; MA, Boston U., 1980; PhD, U. Ariz., 1990. Sci. tchr. Selinsgrove Mid. Sch., 1970-79; space scientist Lunar and Planetary Lab. U. Ariz., Tucson, 1990—. Mem. Com. Lunar and Planetary Exploration (COMPLEX) NRC, 2000—. Contbg. author: Caloris Basin: An Enhanced Source for Potassium in Mercury's Atmosphere, 1990, Sulfur at Mercury, Elemental at the Poles and Sulfides in the Regolith, 1995, Water Brought In to Jupiter's Atmosphere by Fragments R and W of Comet SL-9, 1996, Distribution and Abundance of Sodium in Mercury's Atmosphere, 1985-1988, 1997, Exploring Mercury: The Iron Planet, 2003; editl. bd. ICARUS. Mem. AAAS, Internat. Astron. Union, Am. Astron. Soc. (com. divsn. planetary scis.), Am. Geophys. Union. Office: U Ariz Lunar & Planetary Lab Tucson AZ 85721-0001 Office Phone: 520-621-2282. E-mail: sprague@lpl.arizona.edn.

SPRAGUE, BILLY MICHAEL, aerospace transportation executive; b. Wichita Falls, Tex., Nov. 22, 1953; s. Billy Meryl Sprague and Virginia Maxine Vines; m. Stella Renee Schaefer, Aug. 15, 1987; children: Patricia Noel children: Billy Michael Jr., Jonathan Christian, Elizabeth Kathryn. B in Phys. Sci., BS in Physics/Engring., U. Calif., Irvine, 1979; AAS in Phys. Sci., Ft. Steilacoom, 1975. Cert. Sys. Engring. Mgmt., Martin Marietta Aerospace, Colo., 1985, Engring. Mgmt. and Supervision, Martin Marietta Aerospace, Colo., 1986. Rocket propulsion engring. R&D Boeing, Martin Marietta, Gen. Dynamics, Rockwell, Thiokol, United Technologies, 1976—95; sr. prin. scientist McDonnell Douglas Aerospace, Huntington Beach, Calif., 1995—97; mgr., advanced systems lab. Intel Corp., San Diego, 1997—99; v.p., engring. Truax Engring., Inc., Vista, Calif., 1999—2001; pres. and chief scientist Am. Astronautics Corp., Lake Tahoe, Nev., 2001—. Lectr., sys. engring. and mgmt. Maj. Aerospace Companies, 1985—95. Fellow, Emily Peasley, 1975—76. Mem.: AIAA, Phi Theta Kappa. Republican. Protestant. Achievements include development of reusable liquid propellant launch vehicle for commercial space tourism. Office: American Astronautics Corporation 276 Kinsbury Sq Ste 104 Lake Tahoe NV 89449 E-mail: bmsprague@cox.net.

SPRAGUE, CHARLES CAMERON, medical foundation president; b. Dallas, Nov. 14, 1916; s. George Able and Minna (Schwartz) Sprague; m. Margaret Frederica Dickson, Sept. 7, 1943; 1 child, Cynthia Cameron; m. Alayne W. Nelson, June 12, 1992. BBA, BS, DSc, So. Meth. U.; MD, U. Tex. Med. Branch, Galveston, 1943; DSc (hon.), U. Dallas, 1983, Tulane U., 1991. Diplomate Am. Bd. Internal Medicine. Intern U.S. Naval Med. Center, Bethesda, Md., 1943—44; resident Charity Hosp., New Orleans, 1947—48, Tulane U. Med. Sch., 1948—50; Commonwealth research fellow in hematology Washington U. Sch. Medicine, St. Louis, also Oxford (Eng.) U., 1950—52; mem. faculty Med. Sch. Tulane U., 1952—67, prof. medicine, 1959—67; dean Med. Sch. Tulane U. (Sch. Medicine), 1963—67; prof., dean U. Tex. Southwestern Med. Sch., Dallas, 1967—72; pres. U. Tex. Health Sci. Center, Dallas, 1972—86, SW Med. Found., 1987—88, chmn. bd., CEO, 1988—95; pres. emeritus U. Tex. SW Med. Ctr., 1988—95; chmn. emeritus SW Med. Found., 1995—. Mem. Nat. Adv. Coun., 1966—70; mem. adv. coun. to dir. NIH, 1973—; chmn. Gov.'s Task Force Health Manpower, 1981; mem. Gov.'s Med. Edn. Mgmt. Effectiveness Com.; chmn. allied health adv. com., coordinating bd. Tex. Coll. And Univ. Sys.; mem. coordinating bd. Tex. Higher Edn., 1989—95, vice chmn., 1990—96; mem. adv. com. Ctr. Sci. and Soc. U. Tex., Dallas, 1991—. With USNR, 1943—47. Recipient Ashbel Smith Disting. Alumnus award, U. Tex. Med. Br., 1967, Disting. Alumnus award, So. Meth. U., 1965, Sports Illustrated Silver Anniversary award, 1963. Mem.: Assn. Acad. Health Ctrs. (bd. dirs. 1982—, chmn. bd. 1985—86), Am. Soc. Hematology (pres. 1966), Assn. Am. Med. Colls. (chmn. coun. deans 1970, chmn. exec. coun. and assembly 1972—73). Office: Southwestern Medical Found Ste 150 2305 Cedar Springs Rd Dallas TX 75201-7805

SPRAGUE, EDWARD AUCHINCLOSS, retired association executive, economist; b. N.Y.C., Oct. 9, 1932; s. Irvin Auchincloss and Maude Browning (Fisher) S.; m. Patricia Ivy Cannon, Apr. 27, 1957; children: James Edward, Elizabeth Mary, Jennifer Ann. BA, Princeton U., 1954; MA, NYU, 1961. Rsch. analyst N.J. State C. of C., Newark, 1957-59; assoc. economist F.W. Dodge Corp., N.Y.C., 1959-62; economist Lehman Bros., N.Y.C., 1962-67; v.p. Nat. Assn. Mfrs., N.Y.C. and Washington, 1967-77; dir. tax policy The Tax Found., Washington, 1977-82, sr. v.p., 1985-89; exec. dir. Tax Exec. Inst., 1982-85; v.p., exec. dir. The Tax Coun., 1979-82, 86-91, cons., 1991-92, Employers Coun. on Flexible Compensation, Washington, 1992-93; ret., 1993. Editor: Building Business, 1961-62; jour. The Tax Executive, 1983-85. With U.S. Army, 1955-57. Mem. Nat. Tax Assn. Republican. Home: 2850 Prism Ct Lusby MD 20657

SPRAGUE, JACK, race car driver; m. Rhonda Sprague. Race car driver Hendrick Motorsports, Harrisburg, NC. Named Champion Craftsman Truck Series, NASCAR, 1997, 1999, 2001, Champion Busch Series, 2002. Achievements include all-time leading money winner Busch Series, 2001. Avocation: motorcycling. Office: Hendrick Motorsports 4400 Papa Joe Hendrick Blvd Charlotte NC 28262-5703

SPRAGUE, JO ANN, state legislator; b. Nashville, Nov. 3, 1931; m. Warren G. Sprague; 6 children. BA, U. Mass., 1980. Mem. Mass. Ho. of Reps., Boston, 1992-98, mem. capital budget com., 1990-92; mem. Mass. Senate, 1998—. Mem. Walpole Prison Adv. Com., 1970-92, Rep. Town Meeting, 1979—. Bd. trustees Walpole Scholar Found., 1990-92; bd. advisors NE Sinai Hosp., 1999—. 2d lt. U.S. Army, 1950-53. Mem. Walpole Vis. Nurses Assn. (bd. dirs. 1989-92), Walpole LVW, Norfolk Am. Legion (Post No. 335). Republican. Home: 305 Elm St Walpole MA 02081-1903 Office: Room 206 State House Boston MA 02133 E-mail: jsprague@senate.state.ma.us.

SPRAGUE, JOHN LOUIS, management consultant; b. Boston, 1930; s. Robert Chapman and Florence Antoinette (van Zelm) S.; m. Mary-Jane Whitney, June 19, 1952; children: John Louis, William Whitney, Catherine van Zelm, David Hyatt. AB, Princeton, 1952; PhD, Stanford, 1959. With Sprague Electric Co., North Adams, Mass., 1959-87, co-dir. engring. labs., sr. v.p. engring., 1964-65, v.p. research and devel., 1965-66, sr. v.p. semi-condr. div., 1967-76, pres., 1976-87, chief exec. officer, 1981-87; pres. John L. Sprague Assocs. Inc., 1988—2003; self-employed, 2003—. Bd. dirs. MRA Labs., Inc., Calif. Micro Devices. Chmn. Williamstown United Fund-ARC Campaign, 1961; trustee Pine Cobble Sch., 1978, Middlesex Sch., 1994-96. Lt. (j.g.) USNR, 1952-55. Mem. IEEE, Electrochem. Soc., Am. Chem. Soc., Sci. Research Soc. Am., Confrerie des Chevaliers du Tastevin, Confrerie de la Chaine des Rotisseurs, Princeton Club (N.Y.C.), Sigma Xi, Phi Lambda Upsilon. Home: 175 Bee Hill Rd Williamstown MA 01267-2703 Office Phone: 413-743-9454. E-mail: beehilljon@aol.com.

SPRAGUE, MARY GABRIELLE, lawyer; b. Phila., Oct. 7, 1957; AB summa cum laude, Harvard U., 1979; JD, Yale U., 1983. Bar: Colo. 1984, D.C. 1992. Law clk. to Hon. Jim R. Carrigan U.S. Dist. Ct. Colo., 1984-85; law clk. to Hon. Byron R. White U.S. Supreme Ct., Washington, 1986-87; ptnr. Arnold & Porter, Washington. Mem. Phi Beta Kappa. Office: Arnold & Porter 555 12th St NW Washington DC 20004-1206

SPRAGUE, PETER JULIAN, software company executive, lecturer; b. Detroit, Apr. 29, 1939; s. Julian K. and Helene (Coughlin) S.; m. Tjasa Krofta, Dec. 19, 1959; children: Carl, Steven, Kevin, Michael. Student, Yale U., 1961, MIT, 1961, Columbia U., 1962-66. Chmn. Wave Sys., Inc.; bd. dirs. Enlighten Software Inc. Bd. dirs. vwink.com, Inc. Trustee Strang Clinic. Mem. Yale Club. Office: Wave Systems Corp 1 Penn Plz Ste 2420 New York NY 10119

SPRAGUE, ROBERT L. retired psychologist; b. Clinton, Ill., Oct. 6, 1930; s. Ryburn and Thelma Mae Sprague; m. Bonnie Briggs, Apr. 25, 1991; children: Lori Ellen Scribner, Lisa Jo Elliott. AB, Anderson Coll., 1955; MA, PhD, Ind. U., 1960. Psychologist Muscatatuck State Sch., Butlerville, Ind., 1960—63; asst. prof. No. Ill. U., DeKalb, 1963—64; asst. prof., assoc. prof., prof. U. Ill., Champaign, 1964—2000, prof. emeritus, 2000—. Contbr. articles to profl. jours. Mem. and pres. Mahomet-Seymor Sch. Bd., Ill., 1973—83. Recipient Sci. Rsch. award, Calif. Legislature, 1985; grantee Hyperactivity in Children, NIMH, 1968—75, Use of Psychotropic Drugs, 1979—85, Assessing Tardive Dyskinesia, 1985—88, Mentoring and Sci. Values, NSF, 1993—96. Fellow: Am. Psychol. Assn.; mem.: AAAS (assoc. Sci. Freedom and Responsibility Rsch. award 1989). Avocation: photography. Home: 1306 Old Farm Rd Champaign IL 61821-5940 Office: University of Illinois 906 South Goodwin Urbana IL 61801

SPRAGUE, WILLIAM WALLACE, JR., retired food company executive; b. Savannah, Ga., Nov. 11, 1926; s. William Wallace and Mary (Crowther) S.; m. Elizabeth Louise Carr, Oct. 3, 1953; children: Courtney, Lauren Duane, William Wallace III, Elizabeth Louise BSME, Yale U., 1950. With Savannah Foods & Industries, Inc., 1952-94, ret., 1994, sec., 1961-62, v.p., 1962-72, pres., chief exec. officer, 1972-92, chmn. bd. dirs., CEO, 1993-94, also bd. dirs., 1999, chmn. emeritus, 1998—. Bd. dirs., pres. Adeline Sugar Factory Co., Ltd., Savannah, Coastal Mgmt. Corp., Savannah. Trustee Savannah Bus.

Group; chmn. emeritus Youth Futures Authority, Savannah. With USN, 1945-46. Named Sugar Man of Yr. and recipient Dyer Meml. award B.W. Dyer & Co., 1985; named Industrialist of Yr. Internat. Mgmt. Coun., 1988. Mem. World Sugar Rsch. Orgn. (chmn. 1982-85), The Sugar Assn. (bd. dirs.),Carolina Plantation Soc., St. Andrews Soc., Oglethorpe Club, Century Club (Savannah). Office: Sprague Enterprises PO Box 1313 Savannah GA 31402-1313

SPRANG, MILTON LEROY, obstetrician, gynecologist, educator; b. Chgo., Jan. 15, 1944; s. Eugene and Carmella (Bruno) S.; m. Sandra Lee Karabelas, July 16, 1966; children: David, Christina, Michael. Student, St. Mary's Coll., 1962-65; MD, Loyola U., 1969. Diplomate Am. Bd. Ob-gyn; Nat. Bd. Med. Examiners; CME accreditation. Intern St. Francis Hosp., Evanston, Ill., 1969-70, resident, 1972-75, sr. attending physician, 1985—; assoc. attending phsycian Evanston Hosp., 1975-79, attending physician, 1980-84, sr. attending physician, 1985—, v.p. med. staff, 1990-91, pres.-elect, 1991-92, pres., 1992-93; also bd. dirs., 1991-94; sec. exec. com. Evanston Hosp., 1993-94; chmn. ob-gyn Cook County Grad. Sch. Medicine, Chgo., 1983-91. Instr. Northwestern U. Med. Sch., Chgo., 1975-78, asst. prof., 1984-95, assoc. prof., 1995-2004, prof., 2004—; pres. Northwestern Healthcare Network Physician Leadership, 1994; lectr. acad. and civic groups OB-Gyn. Nat. Ctr. Advanced Med. Edn., 1991—; bd. dirs. Ill. Found. Med. Rev.; bd. trustees Ill. State Ins. Svcs., 1992—, chair, 1998-2000, chair rates and reserves, 2002—; bd. govs. Ill. State Med. Inter-Inst. Exch., 1987-92. Editor: Profl. Staff News, 1992-93; chmn. editorial bd. Jour. Chgo. Medicine, 1986-91; contbr. articles to profl. jours. Bd. dirs. Am. Cancer Sooc., chmn. profl. edn. com. North Shore unit, 1982-85; bd. dirs. Chgo. Community Info. Network, 1994-95; mem. Nat. Rep. Congrl. Com., 1981—, Ill. Med. Polit. Action Com.; bd. advisors Nat. Youth Leadership Forum on Medicine, Chgo., 1998—; trustee Midwest Ctr. Women's Healthcare, 2002—, pres., 2002—. With USN, 1970-72. Fellow: ACOG (chmn. Ill. sect. 1975—76), ACS (resolutions com. 2003—), Inst. Medicine Chgo., Am. Soc. Colposcopy and Cervical Pathology; mem.: AMA (com. to select pub. mem. 2003—, Physician Recognition award 1977, 1980, 1983), Gt. Lakes States Coalition of Dels. to AMA (chmn. 2003—), Orgn. State Med. Assn. Presidents (steering com. 2003—), Chgo. Found. Med. Care (med. care evaluation and edn. com. 1980—83, nominating com. 1980—84, practice guidelines com. 1984), Ednl. and Scientific Found. (bd. dirs. 1994—98), Chgo. Med. Soc. (adv. com. advt. stds. 1978—84, physician's rev. com. 1980—85, trustee ins. bd. 1982—, nominating com. 1985—, treas. 1986—89, chmn. fin. com. 1986—89, trustee 1986—92, sec. 1989—90, pres.-elect 1990—91, chmn. bd. trustees 1990—91, pres. 1991—92, immediate past pres. 1992—93, chmn. ethical rels. com. 1994—, counselor), Ill. Med. Soc. (del. to AMA 1987—, govt. affairs com. 1988—, chmn. reference com. 1989, chmn. fin. com. 1992—94, sec.-treas. 1994—96, chmn. bd. trustees 1996—98, chmn. bylaws com. 1998—99, pres.-elect 1999—2000, pres. 2000—01, immediate past pres. 2001—02, chmn. Ill. del. to AMA 2003—, chmn. Great Lakes states coalition to AMA 2003—04, mem. selection com. pub. mem. AMA bd. trustees 2003—), Physician Benefit Trust (chmn. fin. com. 1993—2004, chmn. 2004—). Roman Catholic. Avocations: reading, raising fish, swimming. Home: 4442 Concord Ln Skokie IL 60076-2606 Office: AGSO 1000 Central St Evanston IL 60201-1777 Office Phone: 847-869-3300.

SPRATT, JOHN MCKEE, JR., congressman, lawyer; b. Charlotte, N.C., Nov. 1, 1942; s. John McKee and Jane Love (Bratton) S.; m. Jane Stacy, May 31, 1968; children: Susan Elizabeth, Sarah Stacy, Catherine Bratton. AB, Davidson Coll., 1964; MA, Corpus Christi Coll., Oxford U., 1966; LL.B., Yale U., 1969. Ops. analyst Office of Asst. Sec. of Def., 1969-71; ptnr. Spratt, McKeown & Spratt, York, S.C., 1971-82; pres. Spratt Ins. Agy., Ft. Mill, 1973-82, Bank of Ft. Mill, S.C., 1973-82; mem. U.S. Congress from 5th S.C. dist., Washington, 1983—; ranking Dem. budget com., sr. mem. armed svcs. com.; former dir. Bank of York. Chmn. bd. trustees Divine Saviour Hosp., York, 1980-82; bd. dirs. Piedmont Legal Services, Inc., 1978-82; bd. visitors Davidson Coll., 1978-80; chmn. bd. visitors Winthrop Coll., 1976. Served to capt. JAGC, U.S. Army, 1969-71. Mem. S.C. Bar Assn. (ho. of dels.), ABA. Democrat. Presbyterian. Office: US Ho of Reps 1401 Longworth HOB Washington DC 20515-4005

SPRATT, JOSEPH R. (JOE SPRATT), state legislator, real estate developer; b. Hamlet, N.C., Mar. 10, 1947; s. J.R. Spratt. Student, Abraham Baldwin Agrl. Coll., 1965-67, Edison C.C., 1967-68; BS in Biol. Sci., Troy State U., 1970. Mem. Fla. Ho. of Reps., 1996—, chair natural resources com., vice chair joint legis. com. on Everglades oversight; mem. coms. on agr. and policy. Mem. S.W. Fla. Regional Planning Coun., 1989-96; mem. LaBelle City Commn., 1972-74, 77-82; mem. gov. commn. Sustainable South Fla., 1994-96, Jobs and Edn. Ptnrship. Consortium, 1995-96, Hendry County Commn., 1988-96, chmn.; chmn. Swamp Cabbage Festival; bd. dirs. Hendry-Labelle Recreation, 1990-96. Mem. Turkey Unltd. (co-chmn.), Ducks Unltd. (pres.), Jaycees (pres.), Shriners (pres.), Masons, Lions (pres.), Elks. Republican. Methodist. Avocations: fishing, hunting. Office: Fla Capitol 402 S Monroe St Tallahassee FL 32399-6526 also: 205 S Commerce Ave Ste B Sebring FL 33870-3604 also: Rm 130 Hendry County Courthouse Labelle FL 33935 E-mail: spratt.joseph@myfloridahouse.com.

SPRAY, PAUL ELLSWORTH, retired surgeon; b. Wilkinsburg, Pa., Apr. 9, 1921; s. Lester E. and Phoebe Gertrude (Hull) S.; m. Mary Louise Conover, Nov. 28, 1943; children: David C., Thomas L., Mary Lynn (Mrs. Thomas Branham). BS, U. Pitts., 1942; MD, George Washington U., 1944; MS, U. Minn., 1950. Diplomate Am. Bd. Orthop. Surgery. Intern U.S. Marine Hosp., S.I., 1944-45; resident Mayo Found., Rochester, Minn., 1945-46, 48-50; practice medicine specializing in orthop. surgery Oak Ridge, Tenn., 1950-98; ret., 1998; vol. physician Knoxville Interfaith Clinic, 1998—. Mem. active staff Oak Ridge Hosp., 1950-98, hon. staff, 98-2000, 01—, memt. staff, 2000-01; courtesy staff Harriman Hosp., Tenn., ret., 1998; vol. vis. cons. CARE Medico, Jordan, 1959, Nigeria, 1962, 65, Algeria, 1963, Afghanistan, 1970, Bangladesh, 1975, 77, 79, Peru, 1980, U. Ghana, 1982; AMA vol. physician, Vietnam, 1967, 72; vis. assoc. prof. U. Nairobi, 1973; mem. tchg. team Internat. Coll. Surgeons to Peru, 1979, 84; vis. prof. orthop. surgery U. Khartoum, 1976; hon. prof. San Luis Gonzaga U., Ica, Peru, 1979; AmDoc vol. cons. U. Biafra Tchg. Hosp., 1969; vis. prof. Mayo Clinic, 1988; sec. orthops. overseas divsn. CARE Medico, 1971-76, sec. Medico adv. bd., 1974-76, vice chmn., 1976, chmn., 1977-79, v.p. CARE, Inc., 1977-79, pub. mem. CARE bd. dirs., 1980-90, mem. bd. overseers, 1991-99; chmn. Orthops. Overseas, Inc., 1982-86, treas., 1986-88, emeritus mem., 1994; mem. U.S. organizing com. 1st Internat. Acad. Symposium on Orthops., Tianjin, China, 1983; mem. CUPP Internat. Adv. Coun., 1986-99; invited guest spkr. Japan Orthop. Assn., 1994; mem. curriculum com. Oak Ridge Inst. Continual Learning, 1999—, chmn. med. programs subcom.; bd. dirs. MMC Oak Ridge Found., 2000-, chmn., 2003-04. Mem. editl. bd. Contemporary Orthopedics, 1984-96. V.p. Anderson County Health Coun., 1975, pres., 1976—77, hon. bd. dirs.; pres. health commn. Coun. So. Mountains, 1958—65, sec., bd. dirs., 1965—66; Tenn. pres. UN Assn., 1966—67; vice-chmn. bd. Camelot Care Ctr., Tenn., 1979—82, chmn., 1982—86; hon. mem. World Orthopedic Concern, 1990; with del. to Vietnam People to People, citizen amb. to Vietnam, 1993; del. to Oak Ridge's Sister City, Obninsk, Russia, 1993; trustee Vietnam Am. Scholarship Fund, 1992—95; Rotary vol. orthopaedic surgeon Kikuyu Hosp. Rehab. Ctr. of East Africa Presbyn. Ch., 1998; bd. dirs. Meth. Hosp. Oak Ridge Found., 2000—, chmn., 2003—04. Named biographee, Mus. of Appalachia Hall of Fame; recipient Svc. to Mankind award, Serotoma, 1967, Humanitarian award, Lions Club, 1968, Freedom Citation, Sertoma, 1978, award, Amb. Goodwill Lions Club, 1979, Medico Disting. Svc. award, 1990, 1st Ann. Vocat. Svc. award, Oak Ridge Rotary, 1979, Tech. Comm. award, East Tenn. chpt. Soc. for Tech. Comm., 1983, Individual Achievement award, Meth. Med. Ctr. of Oak Ridge, 1991, Humanitarian award, Orthopaedics Overseas, 1992; fellow Melvin Jones fellow, Lions Club, 1993. Fellow ACS, Internat. Coll. Surgeons (Tenn. regent 1976-80, bd. councilors 1980-84, hon. chmn. bd. trustees 1981-83, trustee 1983-84, v.p. U.S. sect. 1982-83, mem. surg. teams com. 1983-90, Humanitarian award 1992); mem. AMA (Humanitarian Svc. award 1967, 72), Sociètè International Chirugie Orthopèdique et de Traumuatologie, So. Orthop. Assn., Western Pacific Orthop. Assn., Am. Fracture Assn., Am. Acad. Orthop. Surgeons (mem. com. on injuries 1980-86), Tenn. Med. Assn. (com. on emergency med. svcs. 1978-97), Peru Acad. Surgery (corr.), Peruvian Soc. Orthop. Surgery and Traumatology (corr.), Clin. Orthop. Soc., Mid-Am. Orthop. Soc., Rotary Club (Oak Ridge chpt., chmn. cmty. and world svc. com. 2000—, Paul Harris fellow). Home: 507 Delaware Ave Oak Ridge TN 37830-3902 Home Fax: 865-483-8657. Personal E-mail: spray507@aol.com.

SPRECHER, DAVID A. university administrator, mathematician; b. Saarbrucken, Fed. Republic Germany, Jan. 12, 1930; s. Wolfgang and Karolina (Jung) S.; children: Lorrie, Jeannie. Student, Hebrew U., 1952-54; AB, U. Bridgeport, 1958; PhD, U. Md., 1963. Instr. math. U. Md., 1961-63; asst. prof. Syracuse U., 1963-66; asso. prof. math. U. Calif.-Santa Barbara, 1966-71, prof., 1971-92, prof. emeritus, 1993—, chmn. dept., 1972-75, assoc. dean Coll. of Letters and Sci., 1975-78, dean Coll. of Letters and Sci., 1978-81, provost/dean, 1981-91. Author: Elements of Real Analysis, 1970, 2nd edit., 1987, Precalculus Mathematics, 1974, Finite Mathematics, 1976; (with P. Frank and A. Yaqub) A Brief Course in Calculus With Applications, 1971, 2nd edit., 1976; (with P. Frank) Calculus, 1975; contbr. articles to profl. jours. Served with Israeli Army, 1948-50. Mem. Am. Math. Soc., Math. Assn. Am.

SPRECHER, BARON WILLIAM GUNTHER, pianist, composer, conductor, diplomat; b. Saarbrucken, Germany, Jan. 20, 1924; arrived in US, 1952; s. Wolf and Karoline (Jung) Sprecher; m. Blossom Tag, Aug. 6, 1952. Studied piano with Prof. Wittels, Tel Aviv; studied piano with Madame Vengerova, NYC; studied composition with Paul Ben-Haim, studied conducting with Georg Singer,, Tel Aviv; hon. degree, Inst. of Vocal Arts, 1957; D in Philosophy Music (hon.), World U. Roundtable, 1988; Mus D (hon.), London Inst. Applied Rsch., 1991, DFA, HHD, London Inst. Applied Rsch., 1993; Mus D (hon.), Australian Inst. Coord. Rsch., 1991; diploma, Gran Premio Am., 1990, Paladino del Tricolore, 1990; D Musicology, Somerset U.; D Music (hon.), Atlantic Southeastern U.; Diploma, Acad. Argentina de Diplomacia; Assoc. (hon.), Inst. Affairs Internat., Paris, 1993; DD (hon.), The Christian Congregation; D rerum politicarum, LittD (hon.), U. Aeterna Lucina Vitama, 1991; DD LittD (hon.), Eng., 1994; PhD (hon.), Germany, 1994. Korrepetitor Israel Folk Opera, Tel-Aviv, 1940-43; piano soloist Israel Philharm. Orch., Tel-Aviv, 1946-48; music dir. Temple Anshe Chesed, NYC, 1966—69, Temple Sholom, Greenwich, Conn., 1976—82; pres., music dir. Bronx Philharm., NYC, 1971-83; music dir. Sta. WEVD, NYC, 1969-85; asst. pianist accompanying Lotte Lenya, Richard Tucker, Jan Peerce, Itzhak Perlman, Jan Kiepura, Ilona Massey; prof. Inst. Hautes Etudes Economiques et Sociales. Rsch. prof. Alliance Universelle Paix Connaissance, Paris, 1991; prof. Haute Ecole de Recherche, Inst. des Hautes Etudes Economiques et Sociales; mem. coun. Inst. de Documentation et D'Etudes Europeennes; dep. mem., diplomat Internat. State Parliament; dep. mem. assembly Internat. Parliament for Safety and Peace. Composer: (song book) Yinglish, piano soloist 1st performance of Gershwin's Concerto in F in Israel; composer Piano Sonata, 1945, Jerusalem Concerto for Piano and Orch., 1967, (TV spl.) Great is Thy Faith, 1970; pianist-condr. 24 record albums; mem. The First Piano Quartet (Acad. award nomination, Peabody award). Consul Sovereign State Aeterna Lucina for State and City of NY; comdr. fgn. rels. Island Du Caricom, 1995; diplomat World Jewish Congress; senator Coun. of States for Protection of Life and Human Rights, Palermo, Italy; del. at large Rep. Presdl. Task Force; active Nat. Rep. Senatorial Com., Nat. Com. to Preserve Social Security and Medicare, Ctr. for Am. Values, Sr. Coalition, Common Cause; founding sponsor Disabled Vets. Life Meml. Gold Medal Merit Soc., Washington, 2004. Decorated noble knight Noble House of Amena, knight order Knight Templars of Jerusalem, knight comdr. Lofsensis Ursinius Order, baron Order of Bohemian Crown, comdr. Order of Golden Lance (Australia), Capt. Légion de L'Aigle Mer, Baron of Montsalvat, knight Holy Grail, count San Ciriaco, comdr. fgn. rels. Island du Caricom, 1995, Sen Maison Internat. Des Intellectuels, Sen European Parliament, Internat. Parliament for Safety and Peace, diplomat World Jewish Congress, Laird-Lord of Camster, Caithness, Scotland, 1995; recipient Diplomatic medal Internat. Parliament for Safety and Peace, 1995, Gold Cross of Honour, Albert Schweitzer Soc. Austria, Albert Einstein medal, Circulo Nobiliario Caballeros U., 1992, Swan Knight (Chevalier du Cygne), Order of the Swan; named Knight of Yr., Internat. Writers and Artists Assn., 1995; recipient Medal of Merit, Rep. Presdl. Task Force, 1998, Noble Conquistador, Internat. Chivalric Order of the Knights of Justice, Music and Humanity award, 2003, Hall of Fame Music and Humanity award ABI, 2003, Disting. Leader Gold medal, 2003, Rep. Senatorial Gold medal of Freedom, 2004, others. Fellow United Writers' Assn. India; mem. ASCAP, Maison Internat. des Intellectuels, Internat. Parliament for Safety and Peace, World Parliament Confedn. of Chivalry (Grand Coun.), World Acad. Assn. of the Universe (life), Bronx Philharm. Symphony Soc., Inc. (founder, pres.), Internat. Platform Assn., Am. Fedn. Musicians, Robert Stolz Soc. Gt. Britain, World Univ. Roundtable (trustee, founder), Internat. Cultural Corr. Inst., Circulo Nobiliario de los Caballeros Universales (grandmaster U.S.), Royal Order Bohemian Crown (baron), Lègion de L'Aigle de Mer (capt.), USA United Srs. Assn. Inc. Avocations: walking, chivalry and heraldry, cats, collecting rare musical books and recordings, collecting rare medieval coins and antique coptic ethiopian crosses.

SPREITZER, ROBERT JOSEPH, biochemist, educator; BS in Biology, Cleve. State U., 1974; PhD in Biology, Case Western Res. U., 1980. Postdoctoral rsch. assoc. U. Ill., Urbana, 1980—82; postdoctoral fellow U. Geneva, 1982—84; prof. biochemistry U. Nebr., Lincoln, 1984—. Monitoring editor Plant Physiology, Rockville, Md., 1997—; cons. Maxygen, Inc., Redwood City, Calif., 2001—. Grantee, U.S. Dept. Energy, 2000, USDA, 2002. Mem.: Am. Soc. Plant Biologists, Am. Soc. Biochemistry and Molecular Biology, Am. Chem. Soc. Office: Univ Nebr N217 Beadle Ctr Lincoln NE 68588-0664 E-mail: rspreitzer1@unl.edu.

SPRENGER, GORDON M. hospital administrator; b. Albert Lea, Minn., Apr. 30, 1937; Bachelors degree, St. Olaf Coll., 1959; masters degree, U. Minn., 1961. Registrar USAF Hosp., Hamilton AFB, Calif., 1961-64; with St. Luke's Hosp., Milw., 1964-67, Northwestern Hosp., Mpls., 1967-71; exec. v.p. Abbott-Northwestern Hosp., Mpls., 1971-75, pres. ceo., 1975-88, LifeSpan, 1982-92; exec. ofcr HealthSpan, 1992-94; chief exec. ofcr Allina Health, 1994—. Prof. U. Minn., 1976—; acad. lectureship; preceptor. Mem. ACHE and AHA; Affiliated Hosp. Srvs: Past Sec. Bd mem., 1971-74; Council of Community Hosp., chair. 1980-81; Governor's Task Force on Nursing, 1981; Health Political Action Comm. of Minn., chair. 1981; Minn. Hosp. Assoc. Governmntl Relations Comm., chair. 1979, bd mem, 1978-81, exec. comm. treas., 1981; chair. elect, Minn. Hosp. Assoc., 1982; MMI Cos bd mem, currently vice chair., preceptor and faculty mem., U of Minn. Hosp. and Health Care Admin., 1982 bd of Minnehaha Acad.; disting. alumnus, St. Olaf Coll., mem. bd of regents; Voluntary Hosp. of Amer., past chair., mem. Medtronics, Inc., bd of dirs., 1991-; mem. St. Paul Cos., bd of dirs. Office: Allina Health System 5601 Smetana Dr PO Box 9310 Minneapolis MN 55440-9310 Home: 6244 Ridge Rd Chanhassen MN 55317-9438

SPREWELL, LATRELL FONTAINE, professional basketball player; b. Milw., Sept. 8, 1970; s. Latoska Fields and Pamela Sprewell; children: Aquilla, Page, Latrell II. Student, Three Rivers C.C., Poplar Bluff, Mo., 1988—90, Ala. U., 1990—92. Profl. basketball player Golden State Warriors, Oakland, Calif., 1992—98; profl. Basketball Player New York Knicks, N.Y.C., 1998—2003, Minnesota Timberwolves, 2003—. Named an NBA All-star, 1994, 1995, 1997, 2001. Avocations: music, repairing stereo equipment. Office: c/o Minn Timberwolves 600 First Ave N Minneapolis MN 55403*

SPRIESER, JUDITH A. food products company executive; BA in Linguistics, MBA in Fin., Northwestern U. CPA, Ill., 1982. Comml. banker Harris Bank, Chgo., 1974-81; dir. treasury ops. Esmark, 1981-84; asst. treas. internat. Nalco Chem. Co., 1984-87; asst. treas. corp. fin. Sara Lee Corp., 1987-90; sr. v.p., CFO Sara Lee Bakery N.Am., 1990-93, pres., CEO, 1993-94; sr. v.p., CFO Sara Lee Corp., 1994-99, CEO, Foods and Food Svc., 2000-2001; CEO Transora, Chgo., 2001—. Bd. dirs. USG Corp. Bd. dirs. Hinsdale Hosp. Found.; trustee Northwestern U. Mem. AICPA, Chgo. Network, Young Pres. Orgn., Chgo. coun. Fgn. Rels., Econ. Club, Conf. Bd. Coun. Fin. Execs. Office: Transora 10 S Riverside Plz Ste 2000 Chicago IL 60606-3801

SPRIESTERSBACH, DUANE CARYL, academic administrator, speech pathology/audiology services professional, educator; b. Pine Island, Minn., Sept. 5, 1916; s. Merle Lee and Esther Lucille (Stucky) Spriestersbach; m. Bette Rae Bartell, Aug. 31, 1946; children: Michael Lee, Ann. BEd, Winona State Tchrs. Coll., 1939; MA, U. Iowa, 1940, PhD, 1948. Asst. dir. pers. rels. Pacific Portland Cement Co., San Francisco, 1946-47; prof. speech pathology U. Iowa, Iowa City, 1948-89, prof. emeritus, 1989—, dean. Grad. Coll., v.p. ednl. devel. and rsch., 1965-89, v. pres. and dean emeritus, 1989—, acting pres., 1981-82; v.p. ops. Breakthrough, Inc., Oakdale, Iowa, 1993-94; cons., 1994—. Com. mem. Nat. Inst. Neurol. Disease and Blindess; chmn. dental tng. com. Nat. Inst. Dental Rsch., 1967—72, chmn. spl. grants rev., 1978—82; chmn. bd. dirs. Midwest Univs. Cons. Internat. Activities, Columbus, 1978—87. Author: (book) Psychosocial Aspects of Cleft Palate, 1973; author: (with others) Diagnostic Methods in Speech Pathology, 1978; co-editor: Cleft Palate and Communication, 1968, Diagnosis in Speech Language Pathology, rev. edit., 1999, The Way It Was: The University of Iowa 1964-1989, 1999. Pres. Iowa City Cmty. Theater, 1964, 1977, 1983. Served to lt. col. U.S. Army, 1941—46, ETO. Decorated Bronze Star; fellow Nat. Inst. Dental Rsch., 1971. Fellow: AAAS; mem.: Midwestern Assn. Grad. Schs. (chmn. 1979—80), Am. Cleft Palate Assn. (pres. 1961—62, disting. svc. award), Am. Speech and Hearing Assn. (pres. 1965, honor award), Assn. Grad. Schs. (pres. 1979—80), Cosmos Clug (Washington), Mortar Bd., Sigma Xi. Home: 2 Longview Knoll NE Iowa City IA 52240-9148 Office: Univ Iowa M212 Oakdale Hall Iowa City IA 52242-5000 E-mail: duane-spriestersbach@uiowa.edu.

SPRIGGS, RICHARD MOORE, ceramic engineer, research center administrator; b. Washington, Pa., May 8, 1931; s. Lucian Alexander and Kathryn (Aber) S.; m. Patricia Anne Blaney, Aug. 1, 1953; children: Carolyn Elizabeth Spriggs Muchna, Richard Moore, Alan David BS in Ceramics, Pa. State U., 1952; MS in Ceramic Engring., U. Ill., 1956, PhD, 1958. Sr. research engr. Ferro Corp., Cleve., 1958-59; sr. staff scientist, group leader, ceramics rsch. AVCO Corp., Wilmington, Mass., 1959-64; assoc. prof. metall. engring. Lehigh U., Bethlehem, Pa., 1964-67, prof. metallurgy and materials sci. and engring., 1967-80, adminstr. asst. to pres., 1970-71, asst. v.p. for adminstrn., 1971-72, v.p. for adminstrn., 1972-78, dir. phys. ceramics lab., 1964-70, assoc. dir. Materials Research Ctr., 1964-70; vis. sr. staff assoc. Nat. Materials Adv. Bd. NRC, Washington, 1979-80, sr. staff officer, staff scientist, 1980-87, staff dir. bd. on assessment of NBS programs, 1984-87; J.F. McMahon prof. ceramic engring., dir. NYS Ctr. Advanced Ceramic Tech. N.Y. State Coll. Ceramics, Alfred (N.Y.) U., 1987-97, dir. office of sponsored programs, 1988-97, prof. emeritus, 1997—. Affiliate staff scientist Pacific Northwest Lab., 1994—. Contbr. articles to profl. publs. Co-patentee in field Pres., bd. dirs. YMCA, Bethlehem, Pa., 1978-79. Served to lt. USNR, 1952-56 Fellow Armco Steel Corp., 1956-58, Am. Coun. on Edn., 1970-71; Centennial fellow Coll. Earth and Mineral Scis., Pa. State U., 1996, Alumni Achievement award, 1999, 30th Ann. SHS Medal of Honor, 1997, Disting. Engring. Alumnus awrd U. Ill., 1988. Fellow: Brit. Inst. Materials, Ceramic Soc. Japan (Centennial medal 1991), Am. Ceramic Soc. (trustee pension trust fund 1979—84, pres. 1984—85, coord. programs and meetings 1991—92, Ross Coffin Purdy award 1965, Hobard M. Kraner award Lehigh Valley sect. 1980, Orton lectr. 1988, McMahon lectr. 1988, Mueller lectr. 1996, Albert Victor Bleininger award Pitts. sect. 2000, disting. life); mem.: Serbian Acad. Scis. and Arts (fgn.), Ceramic Assn. N.Y. (sec.-treas. 1988—99), Fed. Materials Socs. (trustee 1978—84), Materials Rsch. Soc., Materials Rsch. Soc. Japan (hon.), World Acad. Ceramics (trustee 1988—96), Brit. Ceramic Soc., Ceramic Ednl. Coun., Nat. Inst. Ceramic Engrs., Internat. Inst. for Sci. of Sintering, Rotary (dir. 1982—87, pres. 1985—86). Office: Alfred U Ctr Advanced Ceramic Tech NY State College of Ceramics Alfred NY 14802 Office Phone: 607-587-8557. Personal E-mail: rmspriggs@excite.com.

SPRINCE, LEILA JOY, librarian; b. Toronto, Ont., Can., July 10, 1936; came to U.S., 1981; d. Harry and Anna Helen Caller; children: Alan Rosenthal, Joel Rosenthal; m. Arnold Joel Sprince, Feb. 16, 1982 BA, U. Toronto, 1957, B of Edn., 1962; MA, U. South Fla., 1987. Cert. tchr., Ont. Ballet dancer Volkoff Can. Ballet, Toronto, 1953-54; tchr. h.s. North York Bd. Edn., Toronto, 1958-60; libr. Broward County Libr. Sys., Plantation, Fla., 1987-88, 91-93, Margate, Fla., 1988-91, head youth svcs. Coconut Creek, Fla., 1996—2001; ret., 2001. Advisor Omnigraphics Pub., Detroit, 1993—; cons. Gale/U*X*L* Pubs., N.Y.C., 1996—; state facilitator summer programs State Libr. Fla., 1993. Contbr. articles to profl. jours. Mem. nat. children and youth membership orgns. outreach com. ALA/ALSC, 2001—. Mem. ALA (Best Books for Young Adult Cmty. spkr. 1989, 90), Fla. Libr. Assn. (spkr.), B'nai B'rith Women (fin. sec. 1983, pres. 1984, 85), Phi Kappa Phi, Beta Phi Mu. Democrat. Jewish. Avocations: music/dance, computers, travel, history. Personal E-mail: ajsprince@aol.com.

SPRING, CARL CHAFFEE, JR., medical writer; b. L.A., Nov. 17, 1936; s. Carl C. Spring, Sr. and Emilie Temple Spring; m. Alice Waters, Oct. 7, 1967. BA, Calif. State U., LA, 1960, MA, 1968. Writer, news editor, L.A., 1960—68; med. writer Audio-Digest Found., Glendale, Calif., 1968—. Melvin Jones fellow, 2002. Mem.: Am. Med. Writers Assn. (v.p. 1973—74), Lions Club (editor of bull. 1994—, program chmn. 1994—, LA Internat., pres. 2004—05), Bay Cities Shrine Club (pres. 2001—02). Republican. Episcopalian. Avocations: beach walks, swimming, travel, meteorology. Home: 3490 Wade St Los Angeles CA 90066 Office: Audio-Digest Found 1577 E Chevy Chase Dr Glendale CA 91206 Office Phone: 818-240-7500. Business E-Mail: cspring@audio-digest.org.

SPRING, KATHLEEN, writer; b. Mich. d. Edward and Mary Broilo; m. Samuel Taylor (div. 1984); 1 child, Justin; m. Paul Riethmeier (div. 1991) AD summa cum laude, Oakland C.C., 1990; BA cum laude, Wayne State U., 1993. Cert. holistic health profl. Adminstr. comm. dept. Wayne State U., Detroit, 1990-95; stringer The Daily Tribune, Royal Oak, Mich., 1992-98; writer, photographer Spring Times, Detroit, 1992-98; pub. rels. mktg., editor Fanclub Found. for Arts, Southfield, Mich., 1993-98; writer, tchr. Spring Times, Lyons, Colo., 1998—; travel cons. holistic svcs. Rocky Mt. Retreats, 1998—. Author: Small Towns, Detroits Crown, 1997, WRITERS Birthing of Creative Writing and Capturing Random Memories, 2002; dir., author, exec. prodr.: (documentaries) Sandstone Quarry History: Our Stones Gather Moss, 2001; Lyons Geology, 2002; Come Stay Awhile, 2003. Vol. PBS-Detroit, 1982-95. Named Journalist of Yr., Wayne State U., 1992; scholar numerous acad. scholarships. Mem.: Colo. Press Women (three journalism awards 2003), Denver Film Soc., Colo. Authors League, Film and Video Assn., Women in Comm., Soc. Profl. Journalists (1st v.p. 1993—98, Howard Dubin Outstanding Pro Chpt. Mem. 1996, Cir. of Excellence-Newsletter 1996). Avocations: travel, books, films, photography. Office: Spring Times PO Box 512 Lyons CO 80540-0512

SPRING, MICHAEL, editor, writer; b. N.Y.C., Oct. 14, 1941; s. Sol and Muriel (Roth) S.; m. Marjorie Hornblower Bauer, Mar. 1965 (div. 1980); children: Declan, Evan; m. Janis Abrahms, 1993. BA, Haverford Coll., Pa., 1964; MA, Columbia U., N.Y.C., 1970. Reporter Bergen Record, Hackensack, N.J., 1969-71; editor Scholastic Inc., N.Y.C., 1971-87; editorial dir. Fodor's Travel Publs., 1987-94, v.p., 1989-94; pub. Macmillan Travel, N.Y.C., 1994-99; pub. Frommer's Travel Guides John Wiley & Sons, N.Y.C., 1999—2001; pub. Wiley Travel, 2001—. Broadcaster, writer WNCN-FM, N.Y.C., 1983-84. Author: Great Weekend Escape Book, 1982, 4th rev. edit. 1990, Student's Guide to Julius Caesar, 1984; editor: American Way of Working, 1980, 50 vol. Barron's Book Notes series, 1984, Scholastic Literature Anthologies, 4 vols., 1985, 87, Great European Itineraries, 1987, Touring Europe, 1990, 3d edit. 1994; contbg. editor Conde Nast's Traveler, 1987—; travel expert CNN Travel Show, 1991-94, WCBS Radio daily travel show, 1998—. Democrat. Jewish. Home: 20 Country Rd Westport CT 06880-2525 Office: John Wiley & Sons 111 River St Hoboken NJ 07030-5774 Office Phone: 201-748-5662. Business E-Mail: mspring@wiley.com.

SPRING, TERRI, political organization executive; BA, U. Wis., 1975. 2d vice chair Dem. Party—Wis., Madison, 1994-97, state chair, 1997; legis. asst. State Senate, Madison, 1996-00; state chair Dem. Party-Wis., Madison, 2000—. Mem. Assn. State Dem. Chairs. Office: 222 State St Ste 400 Madison WI 53703-2273

SPRINGER, BYRON EUGENE, lawyer; b. June 25, 1932; s. Charles A. and Vivian E. (Kagi) Springer; m. Marion J. Peltier, June 13, 1959; children: Byron Eugene, Allison A., Carolyn J. BA, U. Kans., 1955, JD, 1960. Bar: Kans. 1960, U.S. Dist. Ct. Kans. 1960, U.S. Ct. Appeals (10th cir.) 1981. Ptnr. Springer & Springer, Lawrence, Kans., 1960—71, Barber Emerson L.C., Lawrence, 1971—. Instr. bus. law U. Kans., 1960. Mem. Kans. Ho. Reps., 1961—62. Served with U.S. Army, 1955—57. Fellow: Am. Bar Found., Kans. Bar Found. (trustee 1993—99, pres. 1997—98); mem.: ABA, Kans. Bar Assn. Office: PO Box 667 Lawrence KS 66044-0667

SPRINGER, CHARLES EDWARD, retired judge; b. Reno, Feb. 20, 1928; s. Edwin and Rose Mary Cecelia (Kelly) S.; m. Jacqueline Sirkegian, Mar. 17, 1951; 1 dau., Kelli Ann. BA, U. Nev., Reno, 1950; LLB, Georgetown U., 1953; LLM, U. Va., 1984; student Grad. Program for Am. Judges, Oriel Coll., Oxford (Eng.), 1984. Bar: Nev. 1953, U.S. Dist. Ct. Nev. 1953, D.C. 1954, U.S. Supreme Ct. 1962. Pvt. practice law, Reno, 1953-80; atty. gen. State of Nev., 1962, legis. legal adv. to gov., 1958-62; legis. bill drafter Nev. Legislature, 1955-57; mem. faculty Nat. Coll. Juvenile Justice, Reno, 1978—; juvenile master 2d Jud. Dist. Nev., 1973-80; justice Nev. Suprem Ct., Carson City, 1981—; vice-chief justice Nev. Supreme Ct., Carson City, 1987, chief justice, 1998-99, ret., 1999. Mem. Jud. Selection Commn., 1981, 98, Nev. Supreme Ct. Gender Bias Task Force, 1981—; trustee Nat. Coun. Juvenile and Family Ct. Judges, 1983—; mem. faculty McGeorge Sch. Law, U. Nev., Reno, 1982—; mem. Nev. Commn. for Women, 1991-95. With AUS, 1945-47. Recipient Outstanding Contbn. to Juvenile Justice award Nat. Coun. Juvenile and Family Ct. Judges, 1989, Midby-Byron Disting. Leadership award U. Nev., 1988. Mem. ABA, Am. Judicature Soc., Am. Trial Lawyers Assn., Phi Kappa Phi. Home: 1001 Dartmouth Dr Reno NV 89509 Office: Nev Supreme Ct Capitol Complex 201 S Carson St Carson City NV 89701-4702

SPRINGER, CHRISTINE GIBBS, management consultant, business owner, educator; b. Portland, Oreg., Nov. 23, 1947; d. Robert Lambert and Barbara (Jones) Gresham; m. Bruce Gibbs (div. 1978); m. John Lambert Springer II, 1996; 1 child, Christe. BA in English, U. Ariz., 1968; MPA in Urban Planning, Ariz. State U., 1978; PhD in Pub. Policy Adminstrn., Ind. U., 1986. Dir. tech. assistance Gov.'s Office Ariz., Phoenix, 1976-78; dir. State Local Govt. Rels., Salt River Project, Phoenix, 1978-92; prin. Red Tape Ltd. LLC, Phoenix, 1992—. Adj. prof. Ariz. State U., Phoenix, 1986—, U. Nev., Las Vegas, 2001—. Author: Boundaryless Organizations, 1992, A Guide to Effective Use of Volunteers, 1992, Word of Mouth Marketing, 1994, 7 others. Pres. Ctrl. Ariz. Homeles Shelter; pres. United Cerebral Palsy; examiner Ariz. Quality Alliance. Named one of Top 50 Women Bus. Owners in Ariz., award SBA, 1996; Alumnus of Yr. Ariz. State U., 1992. Mem. ASPA (past pres.) Westrends Coun. State Govts. (founding mem.) Am. Diabetes Assn. (bd. dirs.), Ariz. Econ. Forum (founding mem.), Health Fin. Authority, Nat. Acad. Pub. Adminstrn., Chandler C. of C. (exec. com. 1998—), Soc. Human Resource Mgmt., Coll. Healthcare Execs. Republican. Lutheran. Office: Red Tape Ltd Ste K593 4012 S Rainbow Blvd Las Vegas NV 89103 E-mail: cggs@aol.com.

SPRINGER, DAVID EDWARD, lawyer; b. Anniston, Ala., June 30, 1953; s. Donald and Theresa (Goodwyn) Springer; m. Patricia Anne Cole, Dec. 29, 1978; children: Agee Goodwyn, Chapman Lawrimore Cole. BA, Duke U., Durham, N.C., 1975; JD, Wash. Coll. Law, Am. U., Washington, D.C., 1979. Bar: D.C. 1979. Ptnr. Gardner, Carton & Douglas, Washington, 1990—92, McAuliffe, Kelly & Rafaelli, Washington, 1992—95; prin. Washington Group, Washington, 1995—99; ptnr. O'Connor & Hannan, Washington, 1999—2001, Venable LLP, Washington, 2001—. Home: 6221 29th St NW Washington DC 20015 Office: Venable LLP 575 7th St NW Washington DC 20004 Office Phone: 212-344-4400.

SPRINGER, DENIS E. former railroad executive; m. Roselyn Springer; 4 children. BSEE, U. Notre Dame; MBA, U. Chgo. With Arthur Andersen & Co., Gould, Inc., Brown, Boveri Electric Inc.; dir. fin. Santa Fe Industries, Ft. Worth, Tex., 1982-84, asst. v.p. vin., 1984-88, v.p. fin., 1988-91, v.p., treas., CFO, 1991-92, sr. v.p., CFO, 1992-95, Burlington Northern Santa Fe Corp., Ft. Worth, 1995-99; bd. dirs. Webmodal Inc., Lombard, Ill. Mem. nat. adv. bd. Chase Manhattan Bank. Bd. dirs. Jr. Achievement of chgo.; mem. Coll. of Commerce adv. coun. DePaul U., Chgo. Mem. AICPAs, Ill. Soc. CPAs, Fin. Execs. Inst. Office: Webmodal Inc Ste 3610 150 N Michigan Ave Chicago IL 60601-7569

SPRINGER, DOUGLAS HYDE, retired food company executive, lawyer; b. Englewood, N.J., Jan. 31, 1927; s. Arthur Hyde and Melicent Katherine (Messenger) S.; m. Virginia Helen Chouinard, Nov. 23, 1949; children: Susan Compton, Debora Lee. Student, Wesleyan U., 1944-45; AB, Yale U., 1947; LLB, Columbia U., 1950. Bar: N.Y. 1950. Atty. Port of N.Y. Authority, 1950-52; legal counsel Worthington Corp., Harrison, N.J., 1953-61, asst. sec., 1956-61; asst. counsel Campbell Soup Co., Camden, N.J., 1961-65, asst. sec., 1965, spl. assignments, 1966, dir. spl. studies, corp. planning, 1966-69, dir. corp. planning frozen foods, 1969-70, asst. treas., 1970-71, treas., 1971-73, v.p. fin. planning, 1973-75, v.p., controller, 1975-78, v.p., treas., 1978-88, v.p. investment mgmt., 1988-90. Trustee Meml. Health Alliance, 1981-99; trustee, treas. Virtua Health Hosp., 2000—, Meml. Hosp. Found., 1990-2002, Virtua Health Found., 2003—; mem. adv. bd. Pa. Liberty Mut. Ins. Co., 1971-88, Eastern regional adv. bd. Arkwright-Boston Mfrs. Mut. Ins. Co., 1985-90; exec. sec. Gov.'s Interstate Adv. Com., 1966; asst. to mem. Pres.'s Commn. on Postal Orgn., 1967-68; spl. asst. to chmn South Jersey Port Corp., 1969-71; mem. N.J. Econ. Devel. Council, 1972-76; mem. adv. coun. Tax Found., 1980-89. Trustee Nat. Food Processors Assn. Retirement Plan and Trust Indenture Fund, 1976-89, Perkins Ctr. for Arts, 1979-88, Ind. Coll. Fund, N.J., 1982-88; mem. exec. bd., v.p. fin. Camden County coun. Boy Scouts Am., 1978-90; mem. Y's Men's Club, Moorestown, N.J., 1990—, v.p., 1992-94, pres., 1994-95; mem. bd. Family "Y" of Burlington County, 1995—, sec. 2000—; mem. Yale Alumni Fund Bd., 1996-2002, exec. com. 1998-2002. With USNR, 1944-46. Mem. Nat. Assn. Corp. Treas. (bd. dirs. 1982-88), Phila. Treas. Club, Internat. Bus. Forum (bd. dirs. 1980-88), Phi Nu Theta, Phi Delta Phi, N.J. Soc. Pa. (pres. 1992-93, treas. 1994—). Clubs: Yale (Phila., N.Y.C.); Nassau (Princeton, N.J.), Laurel Creek (Mt. Laurel, N.J.). Home: 322 Laurel Creek Blvd Moorestown NJ 08057-3986

SPRINGER, ERIC WINSTON, lawyer; b. N.Y.C., May 17, 1929; s. Owen Winston and Maida Christina (Stewart) S.; m. Cecile Marie Kennedy, Oct. 25, 1958; children: Brian, Christina. AB, Rutgers U., 1950; LLB, NYU, 1953. Bar: N.Y. 1953, Pa. 1975, U.S. Dist. Ct. (we. dist.) Pa. 1978. Law clk. to justice N.Y. State Supreme Ct., 1955-56; research assoc. U. Pitts., 1956-58, asst. prof. law, 1958-64, assoc. prof. law, 1965-68; dir. compliance EEOC, 1967; v.p., dir. Publs. Aspen Systems Corp., Pitts., 1968-71; ptnr. Horty, Springer & Mattern, Pitts., 1971-2000, exec. v.p., 1982—, of counsel, 2000—dir. Duquesne Light Co., Pitts. Author: Group Practice and the Law, 1969. Editor Nursing and the Law, 1970; Automated Medical Records and the Law, 1971; contbg. editor monthly newsletter Action-Kit for Hosp. Law, 1973— . Bd. dirs. Presbyn. Univ. Hosp., Pitts., 1966—, Cath. Health Corp., Omaha, 1988—, Hosp. Utilization Project., Pitts., 1975-86; mem. Pitts. Commn. on Human Relations, 1963-68, chmn., 1964-68. Fellow Am. Coll. Healthcare Execs. (hon.), Am. Pub. Health Assn.; mem. ABA, Nat. Bar Assn., Allegheny County Bar Assn. (pres. 1994), Am. Acad. Hosp. Attys. (charter), Order of Coif. Democrat. Office: Of Counsel Horty Springer & Mattern PC 4614 5th Ave Pittsburgh PA 15213-3663

SPRINGER, GEORGE STEPHEN, mechanical engineering educator; b. Budapest, Hungary, Dec. 12, 1933; came to U.S., 1959; s. Joseph and Susan (Grausz) S.; m. Susan Martha Flory, Sept. 15, 1963; children: Elizabeth Anne, Mary Katherine. B in Engring., U. Sydney, Australia, 1959; M in Engring., Yale U., 1960, MSc in Engring., 1961, PhD, 1962; D (hon.), Tech. U. Budapest, 2000. Registered profl. engr., Mass. Asst. prof. mech. engring. MIT, Cambridge, 1962-67; prof. mech. engring. U. Mich., Ann Arbor, 1967-83; Paul Pigott prof. Stanford (Calif.) U., 1983—, chmn. dept. aeronautics and astronautics, 1990—2001. Author: Erosion by Liquid Impact, 1975; co-author, co-editor 12 books; contbr. over 200 articles to scholarly and profl. jours. Recipient Pub. Svc. Group Achievement award, NASA, 1988, Medal of Excellence in Composite Materials U. Del., 1999. Fellow AIAA (Engr. of Yr. 1995, Structures Structural Dynamics and Materials award 2000), ASME (Worcester Reed Warner medal 1994), Soc. Advancement Materials and Process Engring. (Delmonte award 1991); mem. Am. Phys. Soc., Soc. Automotive Engrs. (Ralph Tector award 1978), NAE, Hungarian Nat. Acad. Sci. (fgn. mem.), Am. Soc. Composites (Outstanding Rschr. award 1997). Achievements include patents in field. Office: Stanford U Dept Aeronautics & Astronautics Stanford CA 94305

SPRINGER, JEFFREY ALAN, lawyer; b. Denver, Feb. 26, 1950; s. Stanley and Sylvia (Miner) S.; m. Amy Mandel, Nov. 11 1995; children: Cydney Erin, Samantha Libby, Jackson Stanley, Harrison Louis. AB, Princeton U., 1972; JD, U. Colo., 1975. Bar: Colo. 1975, U.S. Dist. Ct. Colo. 1975, U.S. Ct. Appeals (10th cir.) 1975, U.S. Supreme Ct. 1978, U.S. Ct. Appeals (8th cir.) 1986. Assoc. Gerash & Springer, Denver, 1975-79; sole practice Denver, 1979-81; pres. Springer and Steinberg, P.C., Denver, 1981—. Mem. com. on mcpl. ct. rules Supreme Ct. Colo., 1985-86; mem. standing criminal justice act com. U.S. Dist. Ct., 1994-96. Mem. ABA, ATLA, Colo. Trial Lawyers Assn. (bd. dirs. 1988-90), Colo. Criminal Def. Bar (bd. dirs. 1985-86, 87-88, pres. 1988-89). Office: 1600 Broadway Ste 1200 Denver CO 80202-4920 Office Phone: 303-861-2800. E-mail: law@springer-and-steinberg.com.

SPRINGER, JOHN KELLEY, hospital administrator; b. Salem, Ohio, May 11, 1931; s. Wilbur Johnson and Nellie Marie (Kelley) S.; m. Jane Lee Parsons, Oct. 13, 1956; children: Kelley Lynn, Dana Lee, Susan Elizabeth, Nellie Jane. AB, Dartmouth Coll., 1953; MHA, U. Mich., 1960; LLD (hon.), Briarwood Coll., 1991. Adminstrv. resident Mary Hitchcock Meml. Hosp., Hanover, NH, 1959-60, asst. adminstr., 1960 64, assoc. adminstr., 1964-69, adminstr. for ops., 1969-71; assoc. exec. dir. Hartford (Conn.) Hosp., 1971-73, exec. dir., 1974-76, pres., 1977-87, vice chmn., CEO, 1987-89, vice chmn., 1989—92; pres., CEO Conn. Health Sys., 1986—96. Bd. dirs. Hartford Mut. Fund; pres. Combined Hosps. Alcoholism Program, Inc., 1972—75; chmn. Capital Area Health Consortium, 1987—90; lectr. Sch. Pub. Health Yale U., 1975. Deacon 1st Ch. of Christ Congl., West Hartford, 1975-79; bd. dirs. Urban League Greater Hartford, 1973-76, Hartford Sem. Found., Greater Hartford chpt. ARC, vice-chmn., 1978-80; trustee New London (N.H.) Hosp., 2003. Capt. USMC, 1953-58; col. USMCR, ret. Mem.: Lake Sunapee Vis. Nurse Assn. (bd. dirs. 2003—, trustee 2003—04), Greater Hartford C. of C. (bd. dirs. 1980—82), Am. Hosp. Assn. (coun. on fin. 1975—78, del.-at-large 1979—80, chmn. 1981—86, bd. trustees 1992—94, award of honor 1996), Conn. Hosp. Assn. (chmn. bd. trustees 1982—83), New Eng. Hosp. Assembly (pres. 1972), Am. Coll. Healthcare Execs., Lake Sunapee Yacht Club, Lake Sunapee Country Club, Twilight Club, Hartford Golf Club, Hartford Club. Home: 27 Birch Point Lane Sunapee NH 03782-2600

SPRINGER, LINDA, portfolio manager, controller; BS, Ursinus. Staff assoc. Coopers and Lybrand, 1977—79; actuary Penn Mut. Life Ins. Co., Phila., 1979—86, exec. asst. to pres., 1986—87, asst. v.p. and prod. mgr., 1987—90, v.p. and prod. mgr., 1990—92; actuary Provident Mut. Life Ins. Co., Berwyn, Pa., 1992—95, asst. v.p. and actuary, 1995—96, v.p. and contr., 1996 2000, sr. v.p. and contr., 2001—02, counselor to the dep. dir. for mgmt., office mgmt. and budget, 2002—03. Achievements include The Senatge has confirmed Linda M. Springer as Controller of the fOffice of Fed. Fin. Mgmt. in the Office of Mgmt. and Budget. Office: Eisenhower Exec Office Build 17th and Pennsylvania Aves NW Washington DC 20503

SPRINGER, MARLENE, university administrator, educator; b. Murfreesboro, Tenn., Nov. 16, 1937; d. Foster V. and Josephine Jones; children: Ann Springer, Rebecca Springer. BA in English and Bus. Adminstrn., Centre Coll., 1959; MA in Am. Lit., Ind. U., 1963, PhD in English Lit., 1969. Chair English dept. U. Mo., Kansas City, 1980-81, acting assoc. dean grad. sch., 1982; Am. Coun. of Edn. Adminstrn. fellow U. Kans., Lawrence, 1982-83; dean of grad. sch. U. Mo., Kansas City, 1983-84, assoc. vice chancellor for acad. affairs and grad. studies, 1985-89; vice chancellor for acad. affairs East Carolina U., Greenville, N.C., 1989-94; pres. CUNY Coll., Staten Island, 1994—. Author: Edith Wharton and Kate Chopin: A Reference Guide, 1976; What Manner of Woman: Essays, 1977, Thomas Hardy's Use of Allusion, 1983, Plains Woman: The Diary of Martha Farnsworth, 1986 (Choice award 1986), Ethan Frome: A Nightmare of Need, 1993. Huntington Libr. fellow, 1988. Mem.: Coun. Grad. Schs. (chair 1986—88), Assn. Tchr. Educators (chair 1992), Acad. Leadership Acad. (exec. com. 1992—94), Am. Assn. State Colls. and Univs., Am. Coun. on Edn. (profl. devel. com. 1991—, invited participant Nat. Forum 1984, bd. dirs. 2001—). Office: Coll Staten Island 2800 Victory Blvd Rm 1a-404 Staten Island NY 10314-6609

SPRINGER, MICHAEL LOUIS, federal agency administrator; b. Sarasota, Fla., Jan. 28, 1938; s. Stewart and Vergie (Fayard) S.; m. Afife Camila Chamas, Aug. 31, 1963; children: Elizabeth Karime, Michele Renee, John David. BA, George Washington U., 1964; MPA, The Am. U., 1978. With fin. mgmt. office Nat. Libr. Medicine, Bethesda, Md., 1969-71; dep. dir. mgmt. and orgn. div. EPA, Washington, 1971-73, dir. mgmt. info. and data systems div., 1973-75; sr. mgmt. assoc. mgmt. improvement and evaluation U.S. Office Mgmt. and Budget, Washington, 1977-82; dep. dir. Office Adminstrn. NRC, Washington, 1982-86; staff dir. Office Consolidation, Washington, 1987-88; dir. Office Consolidation U.S. Nuc. Regulatory Commn., Washington, 1988-94, dir. divsn. facilities and property mgmt., 1994-96, dep. dir. Office of Adminstrn., 1997-99, dir. Office Adminstrn., 1999—. Bd. dirs. Transp. Action Partnership North Bethesda and Rockville, Md., 1988-98. Mem. Citizens Adv. Com. for North Bethesda Master Plan, Montgomery County, 1990-91. Roman Catholic. Office: Nuclear Regulatory Commn Mail Stop T-7 D57 Washington DC 20555-0001

SPRINGER, PAUL DAVID, lawyer, motion picture company executive; b. N.Y.C., Apr. 27, 1942; s. William W. and Alma (Markowitz) S.; m. Mariann Frankfurt, Aug. 16, 1964; children: Robert, William. BA, U. Bridgeport, 1963; JD, Bklyn. Law Sch., 1967. Bar: N.Y. 1968, U.S. Dist. Ct. (so. and ea. dists.) N.Y. 1968, U.S. Ct. Appeals (2d cir.) 1970, U.S. Supreme Ct. 1973, Calif. 1989. Assoc. Johnson & Tannenbaum, N.Y.C., 1968—70; assoc. counsel Columbia Pictures, N.Y.C., 1970, Paramount Pictures, N.Y.C., 1970—79, v.p., theatrical distbn. counsel, 1979—85, sr. v.p., chief resident counsel East Coast, 1985—87, sr. v.p., asst. gen. counsel L.A., 1987—. Bar: N.Y. 1968, U.S. Dist. Ct. (so. and ea. dists.) N.Y. 1968, U.S. Ct. Appeals (2d cir.) 1970, U.S. Supreme Ct. 1973, Calif. 1989. Trustee West Cunningham Park Civic Assn., Fresh Meadows, N.Y., 1978—. Mem. ABA, Assn. of Bar of City of N.Y., L.A. Copyright Soc., Acad. Motion Picture Arts and Scis., Motion Picture Pioneers. Office Phone: 323-956-8408. Business E-Mail: paul_springer@paramount.com.

SPRINGER, ROBERT DALE, retired air force officer, consultant, lecturer; b. Millheim, Pa., Jan. 17, 1933; s. Simon Peter and Ruth Olive (McCool) S.; m. Bonnie Joan Brubaker, Aug. 30, 1953; children: Robert Dale Jr., Debra K. Springer Miller, Curtis A., Michele L. Becker, Tania. BA in Social Sci., George Washington U., 1964, MS in Internat. Affairs, 1969. Cert. command pilot. Commd. 2d lt. USAF; advanced through grades to lt. gen.; comdr. 435th Tactical Airlift Wing, Rhein-Main Air Base, Federal Republic Germany, 1978-80, 322d Airlift Divsn., Ramstein Air Base, Federal Republic Germany, 1980-81, Air Force Manpower and Pers. Ctr., Randolph AFB, Tex., 1982-84, 21 A.F., McGuire AFB, N.J., 1984-85; insp. gen. USAF, Washington, 1985-87; with DCS-pers. Mil. Airlift Command, Scott AFB, Ill., 1981-82, vice comdr.-in-chief, 1987-88; ret., 1988; pres. bsone, Inc., 1999—, NovaLogic Sys., 1999-2001. Media cons., lectr., 1989—; dir. Air Force Commissary Svc., San Antonio, 1982-84, Army-Air Force Exch. Svc., Dallas, 1982-84; chmn. bd. dirs. Air Force Welfare Bd., San Antonio, 1982-84; mem. adv. bd. First Bank; bd. dirs. NovaLogic, Inc. Exec. dir Air Force Meml. Found., 1992-96, pres. 1996-98, vice chmn., 1998—; trustee Aerospace Edn. Found., 1992-94, The Falcon Found., 1996—. Mem. Air Force Assn. (Presdl. Citation 1984), Airlift-Tanker Assn. (life mem., sr. v.p. 1989-94), Arnold Air Soc. (exec. dir. 1990-93, trustee 1993-2001), Ret. Officers Assn. (life), Daedalians (life), Masons (33 deg.). Lutheran. Avocations: golf, reading. Personal E-mail: bsone@nc.rr.com.

SPRINGER, SALLY PEARL, university administrator; b. Bklyn., Mar. 19, 1947; d. Nathaniel Margulies and Fanny (Schoen) S.; m. Hakon Hope; children: Erik Jacob Hope, Mollie Liv Hope. BS, Bklyn. Coll., 1967; PhD, Stanford U., 1971. Postdoctoral fellow Stanford U. Med. Sch., Calif., 1971-73; asst. prof. SUNY, Stony Brook, 1973-78, assoc. provost, 1981-85, assoc. prof., 1978-87; exec. asst. to chancellor U. Calif., Davis, 1987-92, asst. chancellor, 1982-2001, assoc. chancellor, 2001—. Author: (with others) Left Brain, Right Brain, 1981 (Am. Psychol. Found. Disting. Contbr. award 1981), 5th rev. edit., 1998, How to Succeed in College, 1982; contbr. articles to profl. jours. Mem. Internat. Neuropsychol. Soc., Psychonomic Soc. Office: Univ Calif Office Chancellor Davis CA 95616 Office Phone: 530-752-2068. Business E-Mail: spspringer@ucdavis.edu.

SPRINGFIELD, JAMES FRANCIS, retired lawyer, banker; b. Memphis, Nov. 5, 1929; s. C.L. and Mildred (White) S.; m. Shirley Burdick, June 1, 1951 (div.); children: Sidney, Susan, James Francis; m. Nancy Hardwick Ragan, Feb. 8, 1987 (dec. Jan. 1988); m. Donna Thomas Moore, Feb. 22, 1989. BA with distinction in econs., Southwestern at Memphis (now Rhodes Coll.), 1951; LLB, U. Memphis, 1960. Bar: Tenn. 1960. With Union Planters Nat. Bank, Memphis, 1951-94, exec. v.p., sr. trust officer, head trust dept., 1968-85, gen. counsel, sec. bd., 1985-94; sec. bd., exec. v.p., gen. counsel Union Planters Corp., 1985-94; ret., 1994. Mem. adv. bd. Memphis Alzheimer's Assn., 1999-2001; mem. president's coun. Rhodes Coll., Memphis, chmn., 1991-92, internat. chmn. ann. fund, 1995-96; chmn. bd. trustees So. Coll. Optometry, 1978-80; trustee Plough Found., Memphis Conf. United Meth. Ch. Found., 1978-85, U. Tenn. Med. Units Found., 1975-82, MidSouth Pub. Comm. Found., 1985-87, 98—; chmn. fin. com. Hutchinson Sch.; sec. bd. trustees Vision Edn. Found., 1977-78; bd. regents Tenn. Trust Sch., chmn., 1977; mem. pres.'s adv. coun. Lambuth Coll., 1982-85; mem. exec. bd. Chickasaw coun. Boy Scouts Am., 1983-87; bd. visitors Memphis State U. Cecil C. Humphreys Sch. Law, treas. Balmoral Civic Club, 1967-68; pres., bd. dirs. Village of Bailey Station Homeowners Assn., Inc., 2000-01; dir. Shoreline Towers Condominium Assn. Inc., 2004—. Lt. (j.g.) USNR, 1951-54. Mem. Tenn. Bar Assn. (chmn. interprofl. rels. com. 1976), Memphis and Shelby County Bar assn. (chmn. moral fitness com. 1972), Tenn. Bankers Assn. (chmn. legis.com. trust div. 1976-77, treas. 1972-73, pres. 1976-77, bd. dirs. 1976-77), Bank Adminstrn. Inst. (chmn. trust comm. 1981-82), Estate Planning Coun. Memphis (pres. 1973-74), Sigma Nu (div. comdr. 1967-68, treas., bd. dirs. House Corp. 1966-81), Omicron Delta Kappa (Rhodes Coll. chpt., pres. ODK Assocs. 2002-03). Republican. Home: 1692 Village Ridge Rd Collierville TN 38017-9793 Personal E-mail: jimmyspringfield@msn.com.

SPRINGGATE, CLARK FRANKLIN, physician, researcher; b. Champaign, Ill., Nov. 14, 1946; s. William F. and Marjorie E. (Fitch) S.; children from a previous marriage: Elizabeth, Benjamin; m. Diane Louise Rotnem, Oct. 19, 1991. AB in Biology, Boston U., 1967; PhD in Biochemistry, Boston Coll., 1972; MD, U. Miami, 1983. Diplomate Nat. Bd. Med. Examiners, Am. Bd. Pathology. Med. dir. Richardson Vicks Pharm., Shelton, Conn., 1989-91; v.p., med. dir. TSI Biomed. Rsch. Group, Medford, Mass., 1992-94. V.p. Scicor, Indpls., 1988-89; pres. Springgate Biotech, Guilford, Conn., 1991—. Biotech Regular Cons., Guilford, 1994—; designer/executor Phase I, Phase II, Phase III and Phase IV clin. trials in oncology, cardiology, rheumatology, endocrinology, infectious diseases, neurology. Contbr. articles to jours. Heart Transplant, Am. Soc. Hist. Immunogey. Bd. dirs. AIDS Protect New Haven, 1994-95; funding bd. Leap Youth Program, New Haven, 1991-92 Leukemia Soc. Am. fellow, 1972-74. Mem. AAAS, ACP Execs., Conn. State Med. Soc. Achievements include research in immune monitoring of heart transplant patients to prevent rejection and infection, diagnostic flow cytometry-oncology, gene therapy for cancer, heart disease, autoimmune disease and infectious disease. Home: 1320 Little Meadow Rd Guilford CT 06437-1659 E-mail: clarkmd@tx.netcom.com.

SPRINGSTEEN, BRUCE, singer, songwriter, guitarist; b. Freehold, N.J., Sept. 23, 1949; s. Douglas and Adele Springsteen; m. Julianne Phillips, May 13, 1985 (div. 1988); m. Patti Scialfa Springsteen; children: Evan James, Jessica Rae. Attended community coll. Performer: N.Y. and N.J. nightclubs; signed with Columbia Records, 1972, first album Greetings from Asbury Park, New Jersey, 1973, nationwide concert tours with The E-Street Band, 1974—92, albums include The Wild, The Innocent and the E-Street Shuffle, 1974, Born to Run, 1975 (Gold Record award, 1975), Darkness on the Edge of Town, 1978, The River, 1980, Nebraska, 1982, Born in the U.S.A., 1984 (Best Pop/Rock Album of Yr., Downbeat Readers Poll, 1984), Bruce Springsteen and the E-Street Band Live/1975-1985, 1986, Tunnel of Love, 1987, Chimes of Freedom, 1988, Human Touch, Lucky Town, 1992, Bruce Springsteen Greatest Hits, The Ghost of Tom Joad, 1995, Bruce Springsteen Plugged (from MTV Live), 1997, 18 Tracks (compilation with unreleased tracks), 1998, The Rising, 2002 (Grammy award best male rock vocal performance, 2003, Grammy award best rock song, 2003, Grammy award best rock album, 2003); composer: (songs) Thunder Road, Glory Days, Rosalita, Pink Cadillac, Jersey Girl, Hungry Heart, Streets of Philadelphia, 1994 (Golden Globe award for Best Original Song in a Film, 1994, Acad. award for best original song in a film, 1994, MTV Best Video from a Film award, 1994), Dead Man Walking, 1996 (Acad. award nominee for best original song in a film 1996, 1996); appears on: albums Rumble Doll with Patti Scialfa, 1993, The Wind with Warren Zevon, 2003 (Grammy award, Best Rock Performance By A Duo Or Group With Vocal for song "Disorder in the House", 2003). Recipient Grammy award for best male rock vocalist, 1984, 1987, 1994. Office: care Premier Talent Agy 3 E 54th St New York NY 10022-3108

SPRINKEL, BERYL WAYNE, economist, consultant; b. Richmond, Mo., Nov. 20, 1923; s. Clarence and Emma (Schooley) S.; m. Lory Kiefer, Aug. 29, 1993; children: Gary L., Kevin G. Student, N.W. Mo. State U., 1941-43, U. Oreg., 1943-44; BS, U. Mo., 1947; MBA, U. Chgo., 1948, PhD, 1952; LHD (hon.), DePaul U., 1975; LLD (hon.), St. Michael's Coll., 1981, U. Mo., 1985, U. Rochester, 1985, Govs. State U., 1988, U. Nebr., 1988; Doctor of Pub. Adminstrn., Marion Coll., 1988. Instr. econs. and fin. U. Mo., Columbia, 1948-49, U. Chgo., 1950-52; with Harris Trust & Savs. Bank, Chgo., 1952-81, v.p., economist, 1960-68, dir. rsch., 1963-69, sr. v.p., 1968-74, economist, 1968-81, exec. v.p., 1974-81; undersec. monetary affairs Dept. Treasury, Washington, 1981-85; chmn. Coun. Econ. Advisers, The White House, Washington, 1985-89, mem. Pres.'s Cabinet, 1987-89; pvt. cons. economist, 1989—. Cons. Fed. Res. Bd., 1955-59, Bur. of Census, 1962-70, Joint Econ. Com. U.S. Congress, 1958, 62, 67, 71, Ho. of Reps. Banking and Currency Com., 1963, Senate Banking Com., 1975; econ. adv. bd. to sec. commerce, 1967-69; bd. economists Time mag., 1968-80. Author: Money and Stock Prices, 1964, Money and Markets-A Monetarist View, 1971; co-author: Winning with Money, 1977 Pres. Homewood-Flossmoor (Ill.) Community High Sch., 1959-60. With AUS, 1943-45. Recipient Hamilton Bolton award Fin. Analysts Assn., 1968, Alexander Hamilton award U.S. Treasury, 1985, Disting. Alumnus award U. Chgo., 1986, Disting. Alumnus award U. Mo., 2000. Fellow Nat. Assn. Bus. Economists; mem. Nat. Assn. Bus. Economists, Beta Gamma Sigma. Home (Winter): 16625 Waters Edge Fort Myers FL 33908 E-mail: sprinkelec@comcast.net.

SPRINKLE, MARTHA CLARE, elementary school educator; b. Tehachapi, Calif., Oct. 17, 1944; d. William Foote and Mildred Sprinkle; BA, U. Calif., Santa Barbara, 1966; MA in Orgn. Mgmt., U. Phoenix, 2000. Cert. tchr. Calif., water aerobics instr. 1986. Tchr. Muroc Unified Sch. Dist., Edwards, Calif., 1966—71, Elk Hills Sch., Tupman, Calif., 1971—79, Tehachapi Valley Recreation and Pks., 1979—, So. Kern Unified Sch., Rosamond, Calif., 1984—2003. Planning commr. City of Tehachapi, Calif., 1984—. Home: PO Box 852 Tehachapi CA 93581

SPRINKLE, RALPH STEPHEN, podiatrist; b. Winston-Salem, N.C., Sept. 2, 1958; s. Robert Lee and Denise (Levesque) S.; m. Elizabeth Waters, Oct. 24, 1987; 1 child, Elizabeth Cathcart. BS, U. N.C., Greensboro, 1983; DPM, Dr. William Scholl Coll., Chgo., 1988. Diplomate Am. Bd. Podiatric Surgery. Pres. Georgetown (S.C.) Podiatry Group P.C., 1989—. Mem. adv. bd. Wachovia Bank, Georgetown, 1992—, Black River Dist., Georgetown, 1992-94. Fellow Am. Coll. Foot and Ankle Surgeons; mem. SAR, Sons

Confederate Vets., S.C. Podiatric Med. Assn. (treas. 1990-99), Rotary (Paul Harris fellow 1995). Episcopalian. Avocations: outdoors, hunting, fishing, church, scouting. Office: 1101 Memorial Ln Georgetown SC 29440-3311

SPRINKLE, ROBERT LEE, JR., podiatrist; b. Winston-Salem, N.C., July 13, 1932; s. Robert Lee and Elton Elizabeth Sprinkle; children: Robert III, Karen, Ralph, Richard, Roy, Randy, Drouin; m. Nancy House Dixon. Student, Salem Coll., 1952; BS, Ohio Coll. Podiatry, 1956; DPM, Pa. Coll. Podiatry, 1970. Diplomate Am. Bd. Disability Analysts, Am. Coun. Cert. Podiatric Phys. and Surgeons, Sr. Acad. Ambulatory Podiatric Surgeons. Pvt. practice, Winston-Salem, 1957—. Chmn. N.C. Bd. Podiatry Examiners, 1968-74; clin. assoc. prof. Dr. William M. School Coll. Podiatric Medicine; researcher reconstructive surgery human foot and ankle; bd. dirs. Cmty. Gen. Hosp. Found., Thomasville, N.C.; bd. dirs. Am. Coun. Cert. Podiatric Phys. and Surgeons. Chmn. Mayor's Com. on Hiring the Handicapped, 1963-64; commr. Old Hickory Coun., Boy Scouts Am., 1970-71, v.p., 1973-74, Silver Beaver award, 1969, mem. adv. bd. Old North State Coun.; pres. St. Leo's Parochial Sch. PTA, 1969-70; dir. Halfway House, 1965-66; chmn. Bishop McGuiness PTA, 1976. Recipient St. George medal Charlotte Diocese, Roman Cath. Ch., 1971; Schering grantee, 1972-74. Mem. APHA, Am. Podiatric Med. Assn. (life mem.), N.C. Podiatry Assn. (past pres., Podiatrist of Yr. 1976), Piedmont Podiatry Assn., Acad. Ambulatory Podiatric Surgeons (life mem.), Internat. Analgesia Soc., Forsyth Country Club, Colonial Country Club, Twin City Club, KC (4th degree), SAR (life; N.C. state registrar, past pres. Bethabara chpt., N.C. state pres. 2002—, mem. George Washington Found.), SCV, NRA (life), Rotary (Paul Harris fellow, dist. gov. 1976-77), St. Andrew's Soc., Sons of the Revolution (life; state chpt. sec. pres. NCSSR). Democrat. Roman Catholic. Home: 10 Mock St Thomasville NC 27360-4622 Office: ABC Family Foot and Ankle Clinic PO Box 366 17 W Main St Thomasville NC 27360-3934 also: ABC Family Foot & Ankle Clinic PO Box 5442 2057 Kerensky St Winston Salem NC 27103-3657 Office Phone: 336-472-7543. Personal E-mail: foot1@earthlink.net.

SPRINKLE, WILLIAM MELVIN, audio-acoustical engineer, engineering administrator; b. Washington, Sept. 2, 1945; s. Melvin Cline and Gladys Virginia (Miller) S.; div.; children: Timothy William, Allison Anne; m. Theresa Torregrossa Ellis, June, 2004. BS in Chemistry, Randolph-Macon Coll., 1967; M in Engring. Adminstrn., Va. Poly. Inst. & State U., 1990. Registered profl. engr., Va. Sr. cons. Sprinkle & Assocs., Kensington, Md., 1973-76; audio systems engr. Robertshaw Controls Co., Richmond, Va., 1976-80; sr. engr. TDFB-Engrs. & Archs., Richmond, 1980-85; property mgmt. officer Signet Bank, Richmond, 1985-87; asst. dir. engring. Va. Dept. Corrections, Richmond, 1987—. Mem. summer adj. faculty Eastman Sch. Music, Rochester, NY, 1974-83. Editor newsletter Richmond Area Bicycling Assn.; contbr. Time Saver Standards for Architectural Design Data, 1982. Scoutmaster Boy Scouts Am., 1970-72, unit commr., 1990-92. Named Eagle Scout Boy Scouts Am. Mem. Acoustical Soc. Am., Pres. Soc. Randolph-Macon Coll., Pi Delta Epsilon (v.p.). Methodist. Office: Dept of Corrections 6900 Atmore Dr Richmond VA 23225-5646

SPRITZER, RALPH SIMON, lawyer, educator; b. N.Y.C., Apr. 27, 1917; s. Harry and Stella (Theuman) S.; m. Lorraine Nelson, Dec. 23, 1950; children: Ronald, Pamela. BS, Columbia U., 1937, LL.B., 1940. Bar: N.Y. bar 1941, U.S. Supreme Ct. bar 1950. Atty. Office Alien Property, Dept. Justice, 1946-51; anti-trust div. Dept. Justice, 1951-54, Office Solicitor Gen., 1954-61; gen. counsel FPC, 1961-62; 1st asst. to solicitor gen. U.S., 1962-68; prof. law U. Pa., Phila., 1968-86, Ariz. State U., Tempe, 1986—; gen. counsel AAUP, 1983-84. Adj. prof. law George Wasington U., 1967; cons. Adminstrv. Conf. U.S., Ford Found., Pa. Gov.'s Justice Commn. Served with AUS, 1941-46. Recipient Superior Service award Dept. Justice, 1960; Tom C. Clark award Fed. Bar. Assn., 1968 Mem. Am. Law Inst. Home: 1024 E Gemini Dr Tempe AZ 85283-3004 Office: Ariz State Univ Coll Law Tempe AZ 85287

SPRIZZO, JOHN EMILIO, judge; b. Bklyn., Dec. 23, 1934; s. Vincent James and Esther Nancy S.; children— Ann Esther, Johna Emily, Matthew John. BA summa cum laude, St. John's U., Jamaica, N.Y., 1956; LLB summa cum laude, St. John's U., 1959. Bar: N.Y. 1960. Atty. U.S. Dept. Justice, 1959-63; asst. U.S. atty. so. dist. N.Y. Dept. Justice, N.Y.C., 1963-68, chief appellate atty., 1965-66, asst. chief criminal div., 1966-68; assoc. prof. Fordham U. Law Sch., N.Y.C., 1968-72; ptnr. Curtis, Mallet-Prevost, N.Y.C., 1972-81; dist. judge U.S. Dist. Ct. (so. dist.) N.Y., N.Y.C., 1981—. Cons. Nat. Com. for Reform of Criminal Laws, N.Y.C., 1971-72; mem. Knapp Commn., 1971-72; assoc. atty. Com. of Ct. on Judiciary, N.Y.C., 1971-72 Co-contbr. articles to profl. law revs. Mem. ABA, D.C. Bar Assn., Assn. of Bar of City of N.Y. Office: US Dist Ct US Courthouse Foley Sq New York NY 10007-1501

SPROAT, JOHN GERALD, historian, educator; b. LA, Apr. 1, 1921; s. John Gerald and Grace (Elwell) Drummond S.; m. Ruth Christensen, Mar. 18, 1967; 1 child by previous marriage, Barbara BA, San Jose State Coll., 1950; MA, U. Calif.-Berkeley, 1952, PhD, 1959. Instr. Mich. State U., 1956-57; asst. prof. Williams Coll., 1957-63; prof. Lake Forest Coll., Ill., 1963-74; prof. history U. S.C., Columbia, 1974-92, chmn. dept., 1974-83; dist. prof. emeritus, 1992—; sr. fellow Inst. for So. Studies, 1992—. Fulbright prof. Hamburg U., Fed. Republic Germany, 1961-62; vis. fellow Cambridge U., Eng., 1970; vis. prof. U. Calif., Berkeley, 1972; Fulbright prof. U. Munich, Fed. Republic Germany, 1982, Indonesia, 1993-94; Am. participant lectr. USIA, India, Pakistan, 1987; mem. S.C. Commn. Archives and History, 1974-83, chmn., 1979-83; mem. S.C. Bd. Rev. Hist. Places, 1974-86, chmn., 1978-83; del. Am. Council Learned Socs. Author: The Best Men: Liberal Reformers in the Gilded Age, 1968, 3d edit., 1972; (with others) The Shaping of America, 1972, Making Change: South Carolina Banking in the 20th Century, 1990; contbr. chpts. to books; exec. producer A Bond of Iron, S.C. ETV, 1979; gen. editor So. Classics Series. Past pres., trustee Columbia Mus. Art; pres. Historic Columbia Found., 1997-99. With USAAF, 1941-45. Grantee NEH, 1976-77, 79, 85, Shell Found., 1967, 70, 73, Lilly Endowment, 1966-67 Mem. Am. Hist. Assn., Orgn. Am. Historians, So. Hist. Assn., Summit Club. Home: 1686 Woodlake Dr Columbia SC 29206-4647 Office: U SC Inst For So Studies Columbia SC 29208-0001 Office Phone: 803-777-4477. Personal E-mail: jgsproat@sc.rr.com.

SPROAT, KEZIA VANMETER, communications executive, writer; b. Chillicothe, Ohio, Nov. 8, 1937; d. Joseph Vause and Helen Rose (Janes) Vanmeter; children: Cornelia Sisson Vanmeter, Eliza Bradford Delano. AB, Vassar Coll., 1959; MA, Ohio State U., 1963, PhD, 1975. Field dir. Miami Valley Campfire Girls, Dayton, Ohio, 1959-60; tchr. English Kingswood Sch. Cranbrook, Bloomfield Hills, Mich., 1960-61; grad. asst. Dept. English Ohio State U., Columbus, 1961-68, lectr. comparative lit., 1968-73, editor ctr. human resource rsch., 1979-85; dir. food for thought Univ. Ctr. Ministries, Columbus, 1978-79; pres. Sproat Comm., Inc., Columbus, 1985—. Editor, writer Ross Labs., Columbus, 1987-91; dir. Vanmeter Farm, Inc., Piketon, Ohio, 1993-2002; pres., founder Highbank Farm Peace Edn. Ctr., Chillicothe, 1994. Author, editor: National Longitudinal Surveys: Bibliography, 1985; editor: Malnutrition: A Hidden Cost, 1993 (2 Addy awards 1994); editor 7 books; editor Peace Grows Bull., 1996—. Founder, co-chair Community Film Assn., Columbus, 1979—; publicist Peace Grows, Inc., Columbus and Akron, Ohio, 1990—; coord. South Ctrl. Ohio Preservation Soc., 1992—; pres. Vassar Coll. Class of 1959, 1999-; mem. Martin Luther King, Jr. bd. sponsors Morehouse Coll., 2002-. Recipient Florence Howe award MLA, 1975, Mayor's award for vol. svcs Mayor of Columbus, 1980, Pres. award Abbott Labs., 1988; grantee Ohio Humanities Coun., 1977, 78. Mem. Lucy Webb Hayes Heritage Ctr., Women's Poetry Workshop. Avocations: collecting art, poetry. E-mail: keziav@aol.com.

SPROGER, CHARLES EDMUND, retired lawyer; b. Chgo., Feb. 18, 1933; s. William and Minnette (Weiss) Sproger. BA (David Himmelblau scholar), Northwestern U., 1954, JD, 1957. Bar: Ill. 1957. Assoc. Ehrlich & Cohn, 1958-63, Ehrlich, Bundesen, Friedman & Ross, 1963-72; partner Ehrlich, Bundesen, Broecker & Sproger, 1972-77; pvt. practice, 1977—2000; ret., 2000. Mem. adv. com. curriculum Ill. Inst. Continuing Legal Edn., Chgo., 1976—90; v.p. Mediation Coun. of Ill., 1986-87; arbitration panelist for Cir. Ct. Cook County, 1990—. Editor: Family Lawyer, 1962-63; contbr. articles to legal publs. Mediator Pastoral Psychotherapy Inst., 1982-86. Recipient Vol. of the Yr., Coun. for Jewish Elderly, 2004. Fellow Am. Acad. Matrimonial Lawyers (bd. examiners 1972-86, chmn. Law Day U.S.A. 1975); mem. ABA, Ill. Bar Assn. (chmn. coun. family law 1970-71), Chgo. Bar Assn. (matrimonial law com. 1958-2000), Am. Arbitration Assn. (divorce mediation com. 1983-92), Decalogue Soc., U. Mich. Club Chgo. (pres. 1988-89), Phi Alpha Delta (mem. coun. Jewish elderly, Vol. of Yr. award 2004) Address: 2800 W Birchwood Ave Chicago IL 60645-1218

SPROLE, FRANK ARNOTT, retired pharmaceutical executive, lawyer; b. Bklyn., Sept. 13, 1918; s. Frank Newland and Eleanor Arnott (Greenberg) S.; m. Sarah Louise Knapp, Sept. 23, 1944; children— Wendy Sprole Bangs, Frank J., Anne Sprole Mauk, Jonathan K., Sarah Sprole Obregon. BA, Yale U., 1942; LLB, Columbia U., 1949. Bar: N.Y. 1949. Assoc. firm Winthrop Stimson, Putnam & Roberts, N.Y.C., 1949-50; atty. Bristol-Myers Co., N.Y.C., 1950-52, asst. sec., 1952-55, sec., 1955-67, v.p., 1965-73, sr. v.p., 1973-77, vice-chmn. bd., 1977-84; ret., 1984. Officer Proprietary Assn., Washington, 1978-84; dir., officer Knapp Fund, N.Y.C., 1960-93. Pres. bd. trustees Hotchkiss Sch., Lakeville, Conn., 1980-85; trustee Internat. Inst. Rural Reconstrn., N.Y.C., and Manila, 1983-87. Lt. comdr. USNR, 1942-45, PTO. Mem. Assn. of Bar of City of N.Y., Yale Club of N.Y.C., Wee Burn Country Club, Bohemian Club, John's Island Club, Riomar Country Club. Republican. Episcopalian. Home: 394 Mansfield Ave Darien CT 06820-2112

SPROSTY, JOSEPH PATRICK, producer, writer, weapons specialist; b. Cleve., Aug. 25, 1947; s. Joseph Patrick and Anna Margret (Louchka) S. Grad., Midpark H.S., Middleburgh, Ohio, 1965; student, San Diego City Coll., 1972-73. Class 2 firearms lic. Prop builder The Goulardi Show WJW-TV8, Cleve., 1962-65; sub-agent Internat. Artists Agy., San Diego and L.A., 1982-83; casting dir. Cinemode Films, 1982; operator, owner Actors Artists Agy., L.A., 1983-87; founder, prodr., dir. Magnum Prodns., 1985; founder Sprosty Prodns., 1990. Demonstrator weapons and handling of weapons, Propmaster TV Co., Van Nuys, Calif., 1992; expert witness Laser Weapon Scam, 1984; vis. lectr. firearms safety, handling, rules and regulations governing use of firearms in motion picture, TV prodn. U. So. Calif., 1996—; animal wrangler specializing in opossums. Scripwriter: (films) Vanishing Point II, The Apartment Manager, The Big House, Rambo III (optioned), Rambo IV (revised), Boneyard, Mister Ed - Talking Again, Mister Ed - Radio Talk, Brick, Life Plus One, Gun Slave, Fixation, Last Chance (renamed Terminal Virus), You're So Beautiful, Home Dead Home, Kung Fu Cop, The Fisherman, numerous others; prodr., dir. (video) Break Disc, 1985; location mgr., armorer, weapons splst.: (film) Heat from Another Sun (retitled Maladiction), 1988; armorer, 2nd asst. dir., assoc. prodr., weapons splst.: (film) Provoked, 1989; weapons splst., armorer: (film) Big City, 1990; co-prodr., animal wrangler, weapons splst.: (film) Opossum de Oro, 1996; weapons splst.: (tv shows) Jake and the Fat Man, Black's Magic, Hill Street Blues, Murder, She Wrote, On the Edge of Death, Emerald Point N.A.S., (7 episodes) America's Most Wanted, (3 episodes) FBI: The Untold Stories, prodr., numerous others, (films) Revolt, Rocky IV, Streets of Fire, Walk in the Sun, Cloak & Dagger, One Man's Poison, Killing Zoe, Desert Storm, The Movie, Live Shot, Outer Heat, Zipperhead, Four Minute Warning, The Robbery, Spirit, Texas Payback, High Adventure, The Waterfront, The Philadelphia Experiment II, Opossum de Oro, Harlem Nights, Tango & Cash, Die Hard, Provoked, Beverly Hills Cop II, Big City, prodr., weapons splst. Big Bruce's Ballistic Babes, Girls Gone Ballistic, 2004, numerous others. Spkr. Veterans Day Calif. State U., Dominguez Hills, 1993. Served with USN, 1965-67 (hon. discharge). Mem. AFTRA, SAG (charter mem. San Diego br.). Home: 337 W Maple St Glendale CA 91204-2014 Office Phone: 818-244-9214.

SPROTT, DAVID ARTHUR, statistics and psychology educator; b. Toronto, Ont., Can., May 31, 1930; s. Arthur Frederick and Dorothy (Barry) S.; m. Muriel Doris Vogel; children: Anne, Jane. BA, U. Toronto, 1952, MA, 1953, PhD, 1955. Rsch. asst. Galton Lab., London, 1955-56; biogeneticist, clin. tchr. dept. psychiatry U. Toronto, 1956-58; assoc. prof. stats. U. Waterloo, Ont., 1958-61, prof., 1961-96, disting. prof. emeritus, 1996—, prof. psychology, 1964-96, dean math., 1966-72, chmn. dept. stats., 1966-75; prof. Centro de Investigacion en Matematicas, Guanajuato, Mex., 1993—. Vis. prof. various univs. and colls. Author: Statistical Inference in Science, Springer Series in Statistics, 2000; contbr. numerous articles to profl. jours. Recipient Gold medal Statis. Soc. Can., 1988. Fellow Am. Statis. Assn., Inst. Math. Stats., Royal Soc. Can., Royal Photog. Soc.; mem. Internat. Statis. Inst., Statis. Soc. Can. (hon.). Avocations: photography, wine making. Office: U Waterloo Math Faculty Waterloo ON Canada N2L 3G1

SPROTT, RICHARD LAWRENCE, foundation administrator, researcher; b. Tampa, Fla., Aug. 9, 1940; s. Joseph Albert and Marie Marguerite (Goaper) S.; m. Margaret Ann Weidel, June 19, 1965; children: Lynn Marie, Deborah Ann. Student, Franklin and Marshall Coll., 1958—60; BA, U. N.C., 1962, MA in Psychology, 1964, PhD in Psychology, 1965. Asst. prof. Oakland U., Rochester, Mich., 1967-69; assoc. staff scientist Jackson Lab., Bar Harbor, Maine, 1969-71, staff scientist, 1971-80; health scientist adminstr. Divsn. Rsch. Resources, NIH, Bethesda, Md., 1980-81; br. chief Nat. Inst. on Aging, Bethesda, 1981-84, assoc. dir., 1984-98; exec. dir. Ellison Med. Found., Bethesda, 1998—. Editor: Hormonal Correlates of Behavior, 1975, Age, Learning Ability and Intelligence, 1980; mem. editl. bd. Exptl. Aging Rsch. Jour., 1978-; contbr. articles to profl. jours. Mem. Bar Harbor Town Coun., 1975-79, chmn., 1978-79; mem. bd. appeals Town of Bar Harbor, 1972-75, mem. warrant com., 1972-75. NIH fellow, 1965-67; NIH grantee, 1969-79; recipient Kent award Gerontologic Soc. Am., 1997. Fellow Am. Psychol. Assn., Gerontol. Soc. Am.; mem. Behavior Genetics Assn. (membership chmn. 1979). Home: 11514 Regency Dr Potomac MD 20854-3733 Office: Ellison Med Found 4710 Bethesda Ave Ste 204 Bethesda MD 20814-5226 Office Phone: 301-657-1830. E-mail: rsprott@ellisonfoundation.org.

SPROUL, JOHN ALLAN, retired public utility executive; b. Oakland, Calif., Mar. 28, 1924; s. Robert Gordon and Ida Amelia (Wittschen) S.; m. Marjorie Ann Hauck, June 20, 1945; children: John Allan, Malcolm J., Richard O., Catherine E. AB, U. Calif., Berkeley, 1947, LL.B., 1949. Bar: Calif. 1950. Atty. Pacific Gas & Electric Co., San Francisco, 1949-52, 56-62, sr. atty., 1962-70, asst. gen. counsel, 1970-71, v.p. gas supply, 1971-76, sr. v.p., 1976-77, exec. v.p., 1977-89; gen. counsel Pacific Gas Transmission Co., 1970-73, v.p., 1973-79, chmn. bd., 1979-89, also bd. dirs. Atty. Johnson & Stanton, San Francisco, 1952-56. Bd. dirs. emeritus Hastings Coll. Law. Served to 1st lt. USAAF, 1943-46. Mem. Calif. Bar Assn. (inactive), Pacific Coast Gas Assn., Pacific-Union Club, Orinda Country Club. Home: 8413 Buckingham Dr El Cerrito CA 94530-2531 Office: Pacific Gas & Electric Co Mail Code H17F PO Box 770000 San Francisco CA 94177-0001 Office Phone: 415-973-2693.

SPROUL, ROBIN, television news bureau chief; Joined ABC, 1981—, mgr. radio news; bureau chief Wash., DC ABC Radio; dep. bureau chief ABC TV Wash., 1992—93; v.p. news coverage ABC Wash., 1993—; Wash. bureau chief ABC TV News, 1993—. Named one of 100 Most Powerful Women in Wash., Washingtonian mag., 2001. Office: ABC News 1717 DeSales St NW Washington DC 20036 Office Phone: 202-222-7200. Office Fax: 202-222-7684. Business E-Mail: robin.sproul@abc.com., robin.v.sproul@abc.com.

SPROULE, MICHAEL E. insurance company executive; b. Toronto, Canada; BA, MBA, U. of Toronto. Former sr. v.p., CFO Alper Holdings USA, Inc., N.Y.C.; senior v.p. New York Life, 1999—2001, acting CFO, 2001, senior v.p., CFO, 2002—. Office: New York Life 51 Madison Ave New York NY 10010

SPROULL, LEE S. finance educator; b. Indpls., Ind. m. Robert F. Sproull; 1 child, Katherine. BA, Wellesley Coll., Mass., 1967; MAT, Wesleyan U., Middletown, Conn., 1969; PhD, Stanford U., Palo Alto, Calif., 1977. Faculty mem. Carnegie Mellon U., Pitts., 1977—90, Boston U., 1990—2000; faculty mem. and vice dean of faculty NYU Stern Sch. Bus., 2000—.

SPROULL, ROBERT FLETCHER, research and development company executive; b. Ithaca, N.Y., June 6, 1947; s. Robert L. and Mary L. Sproull; m. Lee Sonastine, June 26, 1971; 1 child, Katherine. AB in Physics, Harvard U., 1968; MS in Computer Sci., Stanford U., 1970, PhD in Computer Sci., 1977. Mem. rsch. staff Xerox Palo Alto (Calif.) Rsch. Ctr., 1972-77; asst. prof. Carnegie Mellon U., Pitts., 1977-80, assoc. prof., 1980-83; v.p. Sutherland, Sproull & Assoc., Pitts., 1980-90; v.p., fellow Sun Microsys., Burlington, Mass., 1990—. Venture ptnr. Advanced Tech. Ventures, 1981—; mem. tech. adv. coun. R. F. Donnelley & Sons, Chgo., 1981—89; mem. adv. com. NSF, Washington, 1990—97; bd. dirs. Alphatech, Inc. Co-author: (book) Principles of Interactive Computer Graphics, 1979. Mem. sci. adv. bd. USAF, 1997—99. Sr. asst. health svcs. officer USPHS, 1970—72. Fellow: Am. Acad. Arts & Scis.; mem.: Nat. Acad. Engring. Office: SUN Microsys 1 Network Dr Burlington MA 01803-2757 Office Phone: 781-442-0353. Personal E-mail: bob.sproull@sun.com.

SPROULL, ROBERT LAMB, retired university president, physicist; b. Lacon, Ill., Aug. 16, 1918; s. John Steele and Chloe Velma (Lamb) S.; m. Mary Louise Knickerbocker, June 27, 1942; children: Robert F., Nancy M. Sproull Highbarger. AB, Cornell U., 1940, PhD, 1943; LLD (hon.), Nazareth Coll., 1983; DMusic (hon.), New Eng. Conservatory, 1997. Research physicist RCA labs., 1943-46; faculty Cornell U., 1946-63, 65-68, prof. physics, 1956-63, dir. lab. atomic and solid state physics, 1959-60, dir. materials sci. center, 1960-63, v.p. for acad. affairs, 1965-68; dir. Advanced Research Projects Agy., Dept. Def., Washington, 1963-65; v.p., provost U. Rochester, N.Y., 1968-70, pres., 1970-84, pres. emeritus, 1984—. Prin. physicist Oak Ridge Nat. Lab., 1952; physicist European Rsch. Assoc., Brussels, 1958-59; lectr. NATO, 1958-59; pres. Environ. Literacy Coun., 1997-99, chmn. 1999—; past bd. dirs., John Wiley & Sons, Charles River Labs., United Technols. Corp., Xerox Corp., Bausch & Lomb; mem. sci. adv. com. GM Corp., 1971-80, chmn., 1973-80; mem. Def. Sci. Bd., 1966-70, chmn., 1968-70; mem. Naval Rsch. Adv. Com., 1974-76, Sloan Commn. Higher Edn., 1977-79, N.Y. Regents Commn. Higher Edn., 1992-93. Author: Modern Physics, 1956, A Scientist's Tools for Business, 1997; Editor: Jour. Applied Physics, 1954-57. Trustee Deep Springs Coll., 1967-75, 83-87, Cornell U., 1972-77. Ctr. for Advanced Study in Behavioral Scis. fellow, 1973; Meritorious Civilian Svc. medal Sec. of Def., 1970. Fellow Am. Acad. Arts and Scis.; mem. Telluride Assn. (pres. 1945-47), Inst. of Def. Analysis (trustee 1984-92). Home: 6 Eliot Circle Pittsford NY 14534 E-mail: lambspr@aol.com.

SPROUSE, EARLENE PENTECOST, special education educator; b. Hopewell, Va., Apr. 23, 1939; d. Earl Paige and Sophia Marlene (Chairky) Pentecost; m. David Andrew Koren, July 3, 1957 (div. Jan. 1963); children: David Andrew Jr., Elysia Marlene, Merri Paige; m. Wayne Alexender Sprouse, Sept. 2, 1964; 1 child, Michael Wayne. AS, Paul D. Camp C.C., Franklin, Va., 1973; BS in Comm. Disorders, Old Dominion U., 1975, MEd in Spl. Edn., 1977. Tchg. cert. with endorsement in speech lang. pathology, learning disabilities and emotional disturbance, Va. Speech lang. pathologist Southampton County Schs., Va., 1975-76; learning disabled tchr. itinerant Franklin (Va.) City Pub. Schs., 1976-78, emotionally disturbed/learning disabled tchr., 1978-85, speech lang. pathologist, 1986-91, ednl. diagnostician, 1992—2003, lead tchr. spl. edn., 2000—03; resource specialist TideWater Acad., 1999—; speech lang. pathologist South Hampton Co. Pub. Sch., 2003—. Project leader curriculum guide Listening and Lang. Processing Skills, 1990-91; speech/lang. pathologist Southampton County, 2003—. Mem. Career Edn. Adv. Com., Va. Dept. Edn., 1995—; mem. field-based cons. network Old Dominion U., Coll. of William and Mary, 1997—. Recipient Excellence in Edn. award C. of C., Hampton Roads, Va., 1988-89; grantee Va. Edn. Assn., Richmond, 1994—, Project UNITE Dept. Edn., Richmond, 1994—, Project Payroll, 1999-2000, DOE/VBEP Project Second Chance, 2000-01. Mem. Franklin City Edn. Assn. (pres. 1980, 91), Internat. Dyslexia Assn., Coun. for Learning Disabilities. Methodist. Avocations: fishing, music. Home: 272 Colonia Dr Surry VA 23883 E-mail: esprouse39@hotmail.com.

SPROUSE, JAMES RICHARDSON, literature educator; b. Gallatin, Tenn., Sept. 26, 1957; s. James Miller and Betty Dozier Sprouse; m. Patti Graham Sprouse, June 7, 1981; children: Paul Richardson, Erica Elizabeth. BA, Tenn. Temple U., 1980; MA, U. Miss., 1983; PhD, U. Tenn., 1989. Grad. tchg. asst. U. Miss., Oxford, 1981—83, U. Tenn., Knoxville, 1983—87; instr. Campbell U., Buies Creek, NC, 1987—90; asst. prof. North Ga. Coll., Dahlonega, 1990—94; prof. English Pensacola (Fla.) Christian Coll., 1994—. Field faculty advisor Vt. Coll., Union Inst., Montpelier, Vt., 2001—; reader advanced placement program Ednl. Testing Svc. Coll. Bd., Princeton, NJ, 2003—. Contbr. articles to profl. jours. Grantee, Ga. Humanities Coun., 1991. Mem.: Modern Lang. Soc. (Helsinki). Baptist. Avocations: reading, bicycling, classical music. Home: 9 Jazz Pl Pensacola FL 32505 E-mail: jrspro@bellsouth.net.

SPROUT, FRANCIS, artist, educator; b. Tucson, Mar. 5, 1940; m. Lucinda H. Gedeon, Feb. 10, 1987. BFA, U. Ariz., 1967; MFA, U. Calif., La Jolla, 1972; MA, UCLA, 1990. Asst. prof. U. Denver, 1972—75; assoc. prof. Met. State Coll., Denver, 1976—87; faculty assoc. Ariz. State U., Phoenix, 1987—90; adj. faculty Purchase Coll., NY, 1991—95; adj. prof. Manhattanville Coll., 1993—, Pratt Inst. Art, Bklyn., 1995—. Exhibitions include Friends of Contemporary Art Gallery, Denver, 1972, Emerging So. Calif. Artists, Meadows Mus., So. Meth. Univ., Dallas, 1972, Colo.-Nebr. Exch., Joslyn Mus., Omaha, 1973, 74th We. Ann., Denver Art Mus., Denver, 1973, Second Colo. Ann., Denver Art Mus., 1974, 22d Denver Met., Denver Art Mus., 1974, Colo. Artists at Brigham Young, Univ. Gallery, Salt Lake City, 1975, Third Colo. Ann., Denver Art Mus., 1975, 20 x 20 Colo./N.Mex. Invitational, 1975, Fifth Colo. Ann., Denver Art Museum, Denver, 1978, Remnant Transpositions, Fine Arts Ctr., Univ. Colo., Boulder, 1979, Sixth Colo. Ann., Denver Art Mus., 1980, Shaman Show (installation), Grant St. Art Ctr., Denver, 1985, Aboriginal Transpositions, Patio Gallery, Univ. No. Colo., Greeley, 1988, Animals in Art, Art Mus., Ariz. State Univ., Tempe, 1988, Tabula Rasa, Scottsdale Ctr. for the Arts, 1990, Poetic License, Staller Gallery, SUNY Stony Brook, 1990, Fantasy in Form, The Rye Arts Ctr., NY, 1995, Neuberger Millennium Box Exhibit, Neuberger Mus. of Art, 2000, Locations: Real and Imagined, The Arts Exch., White Plains, NY, 2001, Beyond the Pale, Neuberger Mus. of Art, Purchase, NY, 2002, The Drawing Show, Art Exch., White Plains, 2003, Represented in permanent collections Johnson Pub. Co., Chgo., Johns-Manville Corp., Atlanta, Atlantic Richfield Co., Denver, Art Mus., Ariz. State Univ., Tempe, Neuberger Mus. of Art, Purchase, NY. 1st lt. Army N.G., 1957—63. Fellow, Ford Found., 1972, Inst. on Africa, Hamline U., 1978, Summer Lang. Inst., UCLA, 1985. Mem.: Westchester Arts Coun., Coll. Art Assn. Home: 921 Oyster Shell Ln Vero Beach FL 32963 Personal E-mail: sproutf@optonline.net.

SPROW, FRANK BARKER, oil company executive; b. Council Bluffs, Iowa, Nov. 20, 1939; s. Dwight Barker and Lucille (Tuttle) S.; m. Ann Bledsoe, Aug. 24, 1962; children: John, Diane. BS in Chem. Engring., MIT, 1962, MS in Chem. Engring., 1963; PhD in Chem. Engring., U. Calif., Berkeley, 1965. Jr. engr. Humble Oil and Refining Co., Baytown, Tex., 1962, sr. analyst long range supply Houston, 1971-75; sr. rsch. chem. engr./Sp/Sh Esso Rsch. and Engr. Co., Baytown, 1965-71; tech. mgr. Bayway Ref. Exxon Co. U.S.A., Linden, N.J., 1975-77, ops. mgr. Bayway Ref., 1977-79; gr. mgr. petroleum programs Exxon Rsch. and Engring. Co., Florham Park, N.J., 1979-80, v.p. synthetic fuels rsch., 1980-82, v.p. tech. support Annandale, N.J., 1982-86, v.p. corp. rsch., 1986—93, v.p. petroleum & synthetic fuels rsch., 1993—95; v.p., environment & safety ExxonMobil Corp. (formerly Exxon Corp.), 1995—. Mem. governing bd. Coun. for Chem. Rsch., Washington, 1984—; bd. dirs. Exxon Edn. Found., Dallas, 1986—. Contbr. articles to jours. in field. Bd. dirs. R & D Coun. N.J., Parsippany, 1985—, N.J. Safety Coun. Newark, 1983—; campaign officer Republican Party, various elections, Mercer County, N.J. Recipient award in computing Max Planck Soc., Fed. Republic Germany, 1988. Mem. Am. Inst. Chem. Engrs., Soc. Automotive Engrs., Nassau Club (Princeton, N.J.).

SPROWL, CHARLES RIGGS, lawyer; b. Lansing, Mich., Aug. 22, 1910; s. Charles Orr and Hazel (Allen) S.; m. Virginia Lee Graham, Jan. 15, 1938; children: Charles R., Robert A., Susan G., Sandra D. AB, U. Mich., 1932, JD,

1934. Bar: Ill. 1935. Pvt. practice, 1934—; of counsel Taylor, Miller, Sprowl, Hoffnagle & Merletti, 1986—. Dir. Simmons Engring. Corp., Petersen Aluminum Corp. Mem. Bd. Edn., New Trier Twp. High Sch., 1959-65, pres. 1962-65; mem. Glencoe Zoning Bd. Appeals, 1956 76, chmn., 1966-76; mem Glencoe Plan Commn., 1962-65; bd. dirs. Glencoe Pub. Libr., 1953-65, pres. 1955-56; trustee Highland Park Hosp., 1959-69; bd. dirs. Cradle Soc., 1968-92. Fellow Am. Coll. Trial Lawyers; mem. Chgo. Bar Assn. (bd. mgrs. 1949-51), Ill. Bar Assn., ABA, Juvenile Protective Assn. (dir. 1943-53), Northwestern U. Settlement (pres. 1963-70, dir.), Soc. Trial Lawyers, Law Club (pres. 1969-70), Legal Club (pres. 1953-54), Univ. Chgo. Club, Skokie Country Club, Delta Theta Phi, Alpha Chi Rho. Presbyterian. Home: 380 Green Bay Rd Apt 2A Winnetka IL 60093-4051 Office: 33 N La Salle St Chicago IL 60602-2603

SPRUCH, GRACE MARMOR, physics educator; b. NYC, Nov. 19, 1926; d. Isadore and Mollie (Pogel) Marmor; m. Larry Spruch, Jan. 8, 1950. BA, Bklyn. Coll., 1947; MS, U. Pa., 1949; PhD, NYU, 1955. Assoc. rsch. scientist NYU, NYC, 1955-56, 58-63, 1965-67, rsch. scientist, 1968—69; instr. The Cooper Union, NYC, 1957-58; vis. assoc. prof. Rutgers U., Newark, 1964-65, assoc. prof., 1969-75, prof., 1975—. Sci. sec. Internat. Conf. Luminescence, NYC, 1961; hon. rsch. assoc. in applied sci. Harvard U., Cambridge, Mass., 1977-78; hon. assoc. Nieman Found. for Journalism, Harvard U., Cambridge, 1977-78; mem. interview team China US Physics Examination and Application Program, 1985, 86. Author: Such Agreeable Friends, 1983, Squirrels at my Window, 2000; co-author: The Ubiquitous Atom, 1974, 21 Astounding Science Quizzes, 1982, co-editor: Luminescence of Organic and Inorganic Materials, 1962; translator: (M. Françon) Holography, 1974; co-translator: (R. Jungk) The Big Machine, 1968; contbg. editor Internat. Sci. and Tech. Mag., 1955-60; referee Am. Jour. Physics, 1973—; contbr. articles to profl. jour. Recipient Lifetime Achievement award Bklyn. Coll. Alumni Assn., 2002; fellow AAUW, Oxford (Eng.) U., 1963-64, Ctr. for Energy and Environ. Studies, Princeton U., 1981, Ctr. for Tech. Studies, NJ Inst. for Tech., 1986-87; scholar NY State Regents, Bklyn. Coll., NYC, 1943-47; Humanities grantee Dept. Higher Edn., NJ, 1989-90. Mem. ACLU, Am. Phys. Soc., Phi Beta Kappa (chpt. pres. 1978-82), Sigma Xi, Sigma Pi Sigma, Pi Delta Epsilon (hon.). Avocations: listening to music, tennis, swimming, hiking, animals. Home: 14 E 8th St New York NY 10003-5917 Office: Rutgers Univ Physics Dept 101 Warren St Newark NJ 07102-1811 Office Phone: 973-353-5428. E-mail: spruch@andromeda.rutgers.edu.

SPRUDE, MARGARET, credit services company executive; b. 1946; BS in Bus., Western Ill. U., 1977, MS of Accountancy, 1982. CPA. Various fin.-exec.-level positions card divsn. including CFO Bank of Am., 1986—2000, mng. dir., CFO Household Internat. Credit Card Svcs. divsn., 2000—. Office: Household Internat Inc 1441 Schilling Pl Salinas CA 93901-4543 E-mail: masprude@household.com.

SPRUIELL, VANN, psychoanalyst, educator, editor, researcher; b. Leeds, Ala., Oct. 16, 1926; s. Vann Lindley and Zada (Morton) S.; m. Iris Taylor, Sept. 20, 1951 (div. Oct. 1966); children: Graham, Fain, Garth; m. Joyce Ellis, Feb. 11, 1967; stepchildren: Sidney Reavey, Catherine Ellis, Matson Ellis. BS, U. Ala., Tuscaloosa, 1948; MD, Harvard U., 1952. Resident Bellevue Hosp., N.Y.C., 1952-53, N.Y. Hosp., N.Y.C., 1953-55; fellow Tulane Sch. Medicine, New Orleans, 1955-57; pvt. practice New Orleans, 1957—. Vis. rschr. Anna Freud Ctr., London, 1972-73; co-pub. JOURLIT and BOOKREV; pres. and founding mem. Psychoanalytic Archives CD-ROM Texts (PACT), New Orleans, 1993—; clin. prof. psychiatry La. State U. Sch. Medicine, Tulane U. Sch. Medicine; sec. Ctr. for Advanced Studies in Psychoanalysis, 1989—. Editl. bd. Psychoanalytic Quarterly, 1973—; N.Am. editor Internat. Jour. Psychoanalysis, London, 1988-93; editor Psychoanalysis South, 1996—; mem. various other editl. bds.; contbr. articles to profl. jours. and books. Sgt. U.S. Army, 1944-46. Mem. Am. Psychoanalytic Assn. (sec. bd. on profl. stds. 1979-92), Wyvern Club. Avocations: interdisciplinary studies, sailing. Home: 215 Iona St Metairie LA 70005-4137

SPRUNG, ARNOLD, lawyer; b. N.Y.C., Apr. 18, 1926; s. David L. and Anna (Stork) S.; m. Audrey Ann Caire; children: Louise, John, Thomas, Doran, D'Wayne. AB, Darmuth Coll., 1947; JD, Columbia U., 1950. Bar: N.Y. 1950, U.S. Dist. Ct. (so. dist.) N.Y. 1950, U.S. Patent Office 1952, U.S. Dist. Ct. (we. dist.) N.Y. 1954, U.S. Ct. Appeals (2d cir.) 1958, U.S. Ct. Customs and Patent Appeals 1958, U.S. Dist. Ct. (ea. dist.) N.Y. 1962, U.S. Dist. Ct. (no. dist.) Tex. 1971, U.S. Supreme Ct. 1971, and others. Sr. ptnr. Sprung, Kramer, Schaefer & Briscoe, Westchester, N.Y., 1950—. Lt. USN, 1943-46, PTO. Mem. ABA, N.Y. Intellectual Property Assn. Avocations: skiing, wind surfing, racquetball, biking, tennis. E-mail: asprung@aol.com.

SPRUNG, DONALD WHITFIELD LOYAL, physics educator; b. Kitchener, Ont., Can., June 6, 1934; s. Lyall MacCaulay and Doreene Bishop (Price) S.; m. Hannah Sueko Nagai, Dec. 12, 1958; children: Anne Elizabeth, Carol Hanako. BA, U. Toronto, Ont., 1957; PhD, U. Birmingham, Eng., 1961, DSc, 1977. Asst lectr. U. Birmingham, Eng., 1960-61; instr. Cornell U., Ithaca, N.Y., 1961-62; rsch. staff lab. nuclear sci. MIT, 1964-65; asst. prof. McMaster U., Hamilton, Ont., 1962-66, assoc. prof., 1966-71, physics prof., 1971—, dean faculty sci., 1975-84, 89, mem. bd. govs., 1986-90, chair dept. physics and astronomy, 1991-97. Vis. prof. U. Barcelona, Spain, 1991-92, 95, McMaster Cmty. Homes Corp. (pres. 2004-). Contbr. articles to profl. jours. C.D. Howe fellow, 1969-70, Rotary Found. fellow, 1957-58. Fellow Royal Soc. Can.; mem. Can. Assn. Physicists (Herzberg medal 1972, medal for outstanding achievement 1997), Am. Phys. Soc.; mem. Inst. Physics. Avocations: bicycling, cabinet making. Office: McMaster Univ Dept Physics and Astronomy 1280 Main St W Hamilton ON Canada L8S 4M1

SPRUNGER, KEITH L. history educator; b. Berne, Ind., Mar. 16, 1935; s. Arley and Lillian (Mettler) S.; m. Aldine Mary Slagell, June 13, 1959; children: David, Mary, Philip. BA, Wheaton Coll., 1957; MA, U. Ill., 1958, PhD, 1963. Tchr. Berne (Ind.) High Sch., 1958-60; Oswald H. Wedel prof. history Bethel Coll., N. Newton, Kans., 1963—2001. Author: Dutch Puritanism, 1982, The Learned Doctor William Ames, 1972, Voices Against War, 1973, Auction Catalogue of The Library of William Ames, 1988, Trumpets From The Tower, 1994. Recipient Harbison award for gifted teaching Danforth Found., 1972; fellow Social Sci. Rsch. Coun., 1969, Am. Coun. Learned Soc. fellow, 1976, Huntington Libr. fellow, 1982, 90; grantee Am. Philos. Soc., 1983, The Netherlands Orgn. for Advancement of Pure Rsch., 1983. Mem. AAUP, Am. Hist. Assn., Am. Soc. Ch. History (coun. 1974-76), Conf. on Faith and History. Mennonite. Avocation: book collecting. Home: 2412 Clg Ave North Newton KS 67117 Office: Bethel Coll 300 N 27th St E Newton KS 67117 Office Phone: 316-283-2500. Business E-Mail: sprunger@bethelks.edu.

SPRY, DONALD FRANCIS, II, lawyer; b. Bethlehem, Pa., Nov. 17, 1947; s. Donald Francis and Carol Annette (Bolger) S.; m. Mary Frances, June 20, 1981; stepchildren: Michael Matlaga, Michelle Fehnel. BA, Moravian Coll., 1969; JD, U. Pitts., 1972. Bar: Pa. 1972, U.S. Dist. Ct. (ea. dist.) Pa. 1975. Assoc. Law Offices of Edmund P. Turtzo, Bangor, Pa., 1973-76; ptnr. Turtzo, Spry, Powlette & Sbrocchi, P.C., Bangor, 1976-83, Turtzo, Spry, Powlette, Sbrocchi & Faul, P.C., Bangor and Stroudsburg, Pa., 1983-90, Turtzo, Spry, Sbrocchi, Faul & LaBarre, P.C., Bangor and Stroudsburg, 1990-2000; mem. King, Spry, Herman, Freund & Faul, LLC, Bethlehem, Pa., 2001—. Capt. USAR 1979-80. Mem. ABA (family law sect.), Pa. Bar Assn. (family law sect. edn. law com.), Northampton County Bar Assn. (family law com.), North County Bar Assn. (pres.-elect 1989, pres. 1990), Pa. Sch. Bds. Assn., Nat Sch. Bds. Assn., ACLU, Edn. Law Assn., Pomfret Club. Republican. Methodist. Capt. USAR, 1979-80. Mem. ABA (family law sect.), Pa. Bar Assn. (family law sect. edn. law com.) Northampton County Bar Assn. (family law com.), North County Bar Assn. (pres.-elect 1989, pres. 1990), Pa. Sch. Bds. Assn., Nat. Sch. Bds. Assn., ACLU, Edn. Law Assn., Pomfret Club. Republican. Methodist. also: 930 N 9th St Stroudsburg PA 18360-1208 Office: King Spry Herman Freund & Faul LLC 1 W Broad St Bethlehem PA 18018 Office Phone: 610-332-0390. E-mail: dfs@kingspry.com.

SPUDICH, JAMES A. biology professor; b. Collinsville, Ill., Jan. 7, 1942; married, 1964; 2 children. BS, U. Ill., 1963; PhD in Biochemistry, Stanford U., 1968. Asst. prof. biochemistry U. Calif., San Francisco, 1971-74, assoc. prof., 1974-76, prof. structural biology, biochemistry and devel. biology Stanford U. Sch. Medicine, 1977—92. Editor: Annual Rev. Cell Biology, 1987-1998. Recipient Lewis S. Rosentiel award for disting. work in basic med. rsch., 1996, Repligen Corp. award, 1997. Mem. Am. Soc. Cell Biologists (pres. 1989), Nat. Acad. of Sci., 1991, Am. Acad. of Arts and Scis., 1997. Achievements include research in molecular basis of cytokinesis amoeboid movement and other forms of cell motility. Office: Stanford U Sch Medicine Dept Biochemistry Stanford Med Ctr Beckman Ctr B400 Stanford CA 94305-5307

SPUNGIN, CHARLOTTE ISABELLE, retired secondary education educator, writer; b. Providence, June 12, 1929; d. Abraham Spungin and Golde Morrison. BA, U. RI, 1951; MEd, U. Fla., 1966; EdS, Nova Southeastern U., Davie, Fla., 1981. Tchr., head dept. social sci. South Broward HS, Hollywood, Fla., 1962-90. Cons. Fla. Atlantic U., Boca Raton, 1985-90, U. Miami, Fla., 1980-90, Broward County Sch. Dist., Ft. Lauderdale, Fla., 1990-96; tchr. trainer Fla. Performance Measurement Sys.; instr. psychology and sociology Broward C.C. Co-author: (books) (with N. Tallent) Psychology: Understanding Ourselves and Others, 1977, (with H. Besner) Gay and Lesbian Students: Understanding Their Needs, 1995, Training for Professionals Who Work with Gays and Lesbians in Educational and Workplace Settings, 1997, (curriculum guides) Creativity with Bill Moyers, 1984, World of Difference, 1987, Holocaust Curriculum Guide for the State of Florida, 1990, The Holocaust Remembered, 1986, (monograph) Southeast Asian Monograph on Comparative Educational School Systems: Singapore, Malaysia and the Indonesian Islands, 1971. Cons., bd. dirs. Holocaust Documentation Ctr., North Miami, Fla., 1985-90; bd. dirs. Fla. Coun. for Social Studies, Orlando and Tallahassee, 1979-85. Recipient Spirit of Excellence award Miami Herald, 1985, Skretting award Fla. Coun. for Social Studies, Wilma Simmons Golden Svc. award, 1985, Outstanding Svc. in Mental Health award Fla. divsn. Nat. Assn. Mental Health, Woman of Yr. in Edn. award Women in Comm., 1990; Fulbright fellow, 1970, 76; scholar NSF, 1965. Mem. APA, ASCD, Nat. Coun. on Social Studies, Fla. Coun. for Social Studies, Phi Delta Kappa, Phi Alpha Theta. Democrat. Jewish. Avocations: travel, writing, reading. Office: PO Box 8833 Fort Lauderdale FL 33310 8833 E mail: spunbar@comcast.net.

SPUNT, SHEPARD ARMIN, real estate company executive, management and financial consultant; b. Cambridge, Mass., Feb. 3, 1931; s. Harry and Naomi (Drooker) S.; m. Joan Murray Fooshee, Aug. 6, 1961 (dec. June 1969); children: Erica Frieda and Andrew Murray (twins). BS, U. Pa., 1952, MBA, 1956. Owner Colonial Realty Co., Brookline, Mass., 1953—, Cambridge, 1960—; mgr. Colonial Realty LLC, 2002—. Sr. assoc. Gen. Solids Assocs., 1956—; chmn. bd. Gen. Solids Sys. Corp., 1971-74; trustee Union Capital Trust, Boston; incorporator Liberty Bank & Trust Co., Boston; dir., clk. The Computer Co., Inc., Cambridge, 1986—, treas., 1997—; author, sponsor consumer protection, election law and pub. safety legislation Mass. Gen. Ct., 1969—, pub. safety U.S. Congress, 1998. Co-author: A Business Data Processing Service for Small Business Practitioners, 1956, A Business Data Processing Service for Medical Practitioners, 1956, rev. edit., 1959; patentee in field of automation, lasers, dieelectric bonding. Chmn. Com. for Fair Urban Renewal Laws, Mass., 1965—; treas. Ten Men of Mass., 1980; pres. New Eng. Coun. Young Reps., 1964-67, 69-71; vice chmn. Young Rep. Nat. Fedn., 1967-69, dir. region I, 1964-67, 69-71; mem. Brookline Rep. Town Com., 1960—, treas., 1996—; del. Atlantic Conf. Young Polit. Leaders, Brussels, 1973; bd. dirs. Brookline Taxpayers Assn., 1964—, v.p., 1971-72, pres., 1972—; dep. sheriff Norfolk County, 1998-99. Mem. Nat. Soc. Profl. Engrs., Rental Housing Assn., Greater Boston Real Estate Bd., Navy League, Boston Athenaeum, Copley Soc. Boston, Collector's Club N.Y., Masons, Shriners. Home: 177 Reservoir Rd Chestnut Hill MA 02467-1426 Office: 21 Elmer St Cambridge MA 02138-6107

SPURCK, RICHARD FRANCIS, materials engineer; b. Schenectady, NY, Sept. 2, 1922; s. Robert M. and Gertrude Veronica Spurck; m. Greta Elizabeth Nelson, Aug. 28, 1954; 1 child, Robert M. BS in Ceramics, Pa. State U., 1943. Devel. engr. Electron Tube divsn. GE, Schenectady, 1946—53; devel. engr. Coors Porcelain Co., Golden, Colo., 1953—55, project devel. engr., 1963—74; electron tube design engr. Machlett Labs., Springdale, Conn., 1955—63; project engr. Kyocera Internat., San Diego, 1975—77; cons. RFS Assocs., Golden, 1977—81; materials engr. Martin-Marietta, Denver, 1981—89. Ceramic head Office of Mil. Govt. of Bavaria, 1945—46. Contbr. articles to profl. jours. Staff sgt. U.S. Army, 1944—46, ETO. Recipient Nepcon award, Nat. Electric Packaging and Prodn. Conf., 1966. Fellow: Am. Ceramic Soc.; mem.: IEEE, Internat. Soc. Hybrid Microelectronics, Nat. Inst. Ceramic Engrs. Achievements include patents for electron tube structure; electron tube with flexible grid connector; electroplating rack; electrical component package. Office: RFS Assocs 2001 Table Dr Golden CO 80401

SPURLOCK, JOHN, history professor; b. Riverside, Calif., May 20, 1954; s. Lawton Moses and Clara Lucille (Lowder) Spurlock; m. Rebecca Jeanette Dibble, Aug. 4, 1979 (div. Mar. 2003); children: Ruth, Esther. BA, U. Calif., Riverside, 1976, MA, 1977; PhD., Rutgers U., 1987. Asst. prof. Bloomsburg U., Bloomsburg, Pa., 1987—89; asst. editor Paper of Albert Gallatin, NYC, 1990; asst. assoc. to full prof. Seton Hill U., Greensburg, 1990—, chair, divsn. humanities, 1999—. Cons. Electronic NJ, New Brunswick, NJ, 2001—02. Author: Free Love: Marriage and Middle-Class Radicalism in America, 1825-1860, 1988; author: (with Cynthia Magistro) New and Improved: The Transormation of American Women's Emotional Culture, 1998. Coun. Luth. Ch. of Good Shepherd, Greensburg, 1997—2003. Democrat. Lutheran. Office: Seton Hill U 1 Seton Hill Dr Greensburg PA 15601 Office Phone: 724-830-1021. E-mail: spurlock@setonhill.edu.

SPURRIER, STEVE (STEVEN ORR SPURRIER), former professional football coach; b. Miami Beach, Apr. 20, 1945; m. Jerrie Spurrier. Quarterback San Francisco 49'ers, 1967-75, Tampa Bay Buccaneers, 1976; head coach Tampa Bay Bandits, USFL, 1983—85, Duke U., 1987—90, U. Fla. Gators, 1990—2002, Washington Redskins, 2002—03. Winner Heisman Trophy, U. Fla., 1966.

SPURRIER-BRIGHT, PATRICIA ANN, professional society administrator; b. El Paso, Tex., Feb. 27, 1943; d. James Ray and Lucile Gray (Lafferty) Spurrier; m. Martin Oliver Bright, Sept. 18, 1964 (div. 1967); 1 child, James R. Student, Frederick Coll., 1962-64. Planning technician Reston Va, Inc./Gulf Reston, Inc., 1966-75; adminstrv. asst. Gulf Oil, Tulsa, 1975-79; planner Conde Engring., El Paso, Tex., 1979-82; adjutant U.S. Horse Cavalry Assn., Ft. Bliss, Tex., 1983-91; exec. dir. U.S. Cavalry Assn., Ft. Riley, Kans., 1991—, sec., 1991—. Sec. U.S. Cavalry Meml. Found., Fort Riley, 1994—; trustee Spurrier Trust, El Paso, 1990—; mem. Bigheart Cemetery Found., Barnsdale, Okla., 1989—; bd. dirs. 1st Kans. Territorial Capital. Editor The Cavalry Jour., 1990—. Mem. U.S. Army Daus. Republican. Avocations: research, painting, genealogy. Home: 1517 Leavenworth St Manhattan KS 66502-4154 Office: US Cavalry Assn PO Box 2325 Fort Riley KS 66442-0325 E-mail: cavalry@flinthills.com.

SPYERS-DURAN, PETER, librarian, educator; b. Budapest, Hungary, Jan. 26, 1932; came to U.S., 1956, naturalized, 1964; s. Alfred and Maria (Almasi-Balogh) S-D; m. Jane F. Cumber, Mar. 21, 1964; children: Kimberly, Hilary, Peter. Certificate, Free U. Budapest, 1955; MA in L.S, U. Chgo., 1960; Ed.D., Nova S Ea. U., 1975. Profl. asst. libr. adminstrn. div. ALA, Chgo., 1961-62; assoc. dir. librs., assoc. prof. U. Wis., 1962-67; dir. librs., prof. Western Mich. U., 1967-70; dir. librs., prof. libr. sci. Fla. Atlantic U., 1970-76; dir. libr. Calif. State U., Long Beach, 1976-83; prof. libr. and info. sci., dir. libr. Wayne State U., Detroit, 1983-86, dean, prof. libr. and info. sci. program, 1986-95, dean and prof. emeritus, 1995—; cons. Spyers-Duran Assocs., 1995—; acting univ. libr. Nova Southeastern U., Ft. Lauderdale, Fla., 1996-97. Vis. prof. State U. N.Y. at Geneseo, summers 1969-70; cons. publs., libr. and info. scis.-related enterprises; chmn. bd. internat. confs., 1970—. Author: Moving Library Materials, 1965, Public Libraries - A Comparative Survey of Basic Fringe Benefits, 1967; editor: Approval and Gathering Plans in Academic Libraries, 1969, Advances in Understanding Approval Plans in Academic Libraries, 1970, Economics of Approval Plans in Research Libraries, 1972, Management Problems in Serials Work, 1973, Prediction of Resource Needs, 1975, Requiem for the Card Catalog: Management Issues in Automated Cataloging, 1979, Shaping Library Collections for the 1980's, 1981, Austerity Management in Academic Libraries, 1984, Financing Information Systems, 1985, Issues in Academic Libraries, 1985; mem. editorial bd. Jour. of Library Adminstration, 1989-95. Mem. Kalamazoo County Library Bd., 1969-70; Bd. dirs. United Fund. Reciient G. Flint Purdy award for outstanding contbns. Wayne State U., 1999. Mem. ALA, Mich. Libr. Assn., Internat. Fed. Libr. Assns., Assn. Info. Sci., Fla. Libr. Assn., Calif. Libr. Assn., Fla. Assn. Community Colls., Boca Raton C. of C., U. Chgo. Grad. Libr. Sch. Alumni Club (pres. 1973-75), Solinet Mich. Libr. Consortium (founder charter bd. mem. 1973—, bd. dirs. 1973-76), Detroit Area Libr. Network (pres. bd. dirs. 1985-95), Mich. Ctr. for Book (pres. 1988-89), Am. Soc. Info. Sci., Assn. Libr. and Info. Sci. Edn. Home: 7295 Maidencane Ct Largo FL 33777-4900 Office: Wayne State Univ Librs Detroit MI 48202 Business E-Mail: spyers-duran@wayne.edu., ae8249@wayne.edu.

SPYKER, HARRY A., III, music educator; b. Dayton, Ohio, Feb. 12, 1945; s. Donna M. Spyker; m. Renee' A. Arcella; 1 child, Kelsey Justine. BS in Music Edn., Ctrl. State U., 1966; MusM, Ohio State U., 1972. Band dir. Fairborn (Ohio) Pub. Schs., 1966—68, Springfield (Ohio) North H.S., 1968—72, Deerfield Beach (Fla.) H.S./Middle Sch., 1973—86, Fla. Atlantic U., Boca Raton, 1986—87, Boca Raton (Fla.) Cmty. H.S., 1986—91, Santaluces H.S., Lantana, Fla., 1991—94, Congress Cmty. Middle Sch., Boynton Beach, Fla., 1994—. Clarinet player Springfield Symphony Orch., 1967—71; All-County Honor Band clinician/condr. 1991 and 1996 Broward County Pub. Schs., Ft.Lauderdale, Fla.; All-District Honor Band condr./clinician Palm Beach County Dist. 14, West Palm Beach, Fla. Music curriculum writing team Palm Beach County Schools, West Palm Beach, 1987—89. Mem.: Fla. Music Educators Assn., Music Educators Nat. Conf., Am. Sch. Band Dirs. Assn. (nat. chmn. for marching bands 1983—85), Fla. Bandmasters Assn. (life; Fla. adjudicator for dist. band evaluations 1977—, dist. chmn., sec. 1978—82, Twenty Five Yr. award 1998). Roman Catholic. Avocations: jogging, golf, tennis, travel, reading. Home: 2036 SW 36th Ave Delray Beach FL 33445-6651

SPYKER, LEOLA EDITH, writer, educator; b. Wallace, Mich., Mar. 15, 1925; d. Oscar Eugene Anderson and Edith Ragnhild Nelson; m. George Spyker, Feb. 16, 1951 (div. June 1967); children: Marilyn Joy, John George, Thomas Oscar, Sandra Lee. AA, N. Park U., Chgo.; BA, Bob Jones U., Greenville, S.C. Cert. in Secondary Edn. Mich., Wis., Wash., Tex. Lectr., El Carmen, Mexico, 1977—80; conf. spkr. Vida Abundante, Morelia, Mexico, 1980—2003; prof. U. Michoacab, Mexico, 1982—84. Mem. Harvest Ch., 1999—2003. Avocations: painting, travel, reading. Home: PO Box 2050 2021 Harvey Dr Mcallen TX 78501 E-mail: leolas@juno.com.

SQUATRIGLIA, ROBERT WILLIAM, university dean, educator; b. Naugatuck, Conn., Nov. 23, 1937; s. P. William and Mary Elizabeth (Ogenskis) S.; m. Betty Lee Powell, Aug. 12, 1961; children: Robert Jr., Elizabeth, Katherine, Stephen. AB, Coll. of William & Mary, 1960, MA, 1965; PhD, U. S.C., 1970. Asst. dean of men Coll. of William & Mary, 1963-67; counselor, dir. VA U. S.C., Columbia, 1967-70, instr. sch. edn., 1969; dean student svcs. SUNY, Brockport, 1970-71, v.p. student affairs, 1971-72, assoc. dean students Albany, 1972-77; assoc. prof., v.p. student affairs, dean of students Coastal Carolina U., Conway, 1977—2003, prof., dean of students, v.p. student affairs emeritus, 2003, spl. cons. univ. advancement, 2003—. Bd. dirs. United Way Horry County, 1997—. Capt. U.S. Army, 1961-63. Mem. Rotary Internat. (dist. gov. 1987-88, chair task force 1995—, internat. tng. leader 1998, permanent fund nat. advisor 1999-2001, N.Am. affairs com. 1999-2000, gen. chmn. Zone 33 and 34 Inst. 2000, Disting. Svc. award 1993, Four Avenues of Svc. award 2000, Paul Harris fellow, Rotary Found. benefactor), Bequest Soc. (dir. 2001-02), Omicron Delta Kappa (province VI chater dir., bd. dirs., Meritorious Svc. award 2002). Roman Catholic. Home: 118 Wofford Rd Conway SC 29526-8815 Office: Coastal Carolina U PO Box 261954 Conway SC 29528-6054 Business E-Mail: drbob@coastal.edu.

SQUATRITO, DOMINIC J. judge; BA, Wesleyan U., 1961; JD, Yale U., 1965. Judge U.S. Dist. Ct. Conn., 1994—. Office: US Dist Court 450 Main St Fl 2 Hartford CT 06103-3010

SQUIBB, SAMUEL DEXTER, chemistry professor; b. Limestone, Tenn., June 20, 1931; s. Benjamin Bowman and Lou Pearl S.; m. JoAnn Kyker, Dec. 15, 1951; children: Sandra Lavanne, Kevin Dexter. BS, E. Tenn. State U., 1952; PhD, U. Fla., 1956. Assoc. prof., dir. chemistry Western Carolina U., Cullowhee, N.C., 1956-60; asst. prof., dir. chemistry Eckerd Coll., St. Petersburg, Fla., 1960-63, asso. prof., 1963-64; prof. chemistry U. N.C., Asheville, 1964-94, prof. emeritus, 1994—, chmn. dept., 1964-94. Vis. prof. U. NC, Chapel Hill, 1976-81, 83-87, 92-95, Clemson U., SC, 1982; cons. So. Assn. Colls. and Schs., State of W.Va. Author: Experimental Organic Chemistry, 1972, Understanding Chemistry One, 1979, rev. 1990, Two, 1981, rev. 1991, Three, 1981, rev. 1992, Four, 1981, rev. 1992, Five, 1981, rev. 1989, Six, 1984, Chemistry One, 1976, rev. 1987, Two, 1980, rev. 1990, Experimental Chemistry One, 1976, rev. 1988, Two, 1981, rev. 1991; contbr. articles to profl. jours. Mem. Grose United Meth. Ch. Disting. Tchr. award U. N.C.-Asheville, 1983; S.D. Squibb Disting. Chemistry Lectureship U. N.C., Asheville, established 1997; named to We. Carolina Fedn. Square and Round Dancing Hall of Fame, 2001; recipient Pres.'s Svc. award, Folk, Round and Square Dancing Fedn. N.C., 2001. Fellow Am. Inst. Chemists (life, nat. publs. bd. 1988-92); mem. Am. Chem. Soc. (Charles H. Stone award Carolina Piedmont sect. 1979, Disting. Chemist award Western Carolinas sect. 1993, chmn. Tampa Bay subsect. 1963, Western Carolina sect. 1981, editor Periodic News Western Carolina sect. 1980—, Disting. Chemist award 1993), NC Inst. Chemists (pres. 1977-79, sec. 1975-77, 85-91, Disting. Chemist award 1986), Skyland Twirlers Square Dance Club, Silver Spurs Advanced Square Dance Club, Jerry's Kids Advanced Square Dance Club, Skylarks Round Dance Club, Phi Beta Kap.

SQUIER, DAVID LOUIS, manufacturing executive; b. Buffalo, Oct. 30, 1945; s. Clayton L. and Ruth H. Squier; m. Sue Sampson, Aug. 12, 1967; children: Jennifer, Allison. BS in Mech. Engring., Lehigh U., 1967; MBA, Wharton Sch., U. Pa., 1971. With mfg. mgmt. program GE, various cities, 1967-70; mgr. corp. planning Howmet Corp., Greenwich, Conn., 1971-73, mgr. corp. and bus. planning Muskegon, Mich., 1973-75, plant mgr. Hampton, Va., 1976-78, gen. mgr. Wichita Falls, Tex., 1979-82, v.p. Greenwich, 1983-87, sr. v.p., 1987-89, exec. v.p., 1989-91, COO, 1991-92, pres., CEO, 1992-2000, also bd. dirs., advisor, 2000—. Mem. rev. and prioritization bd. Iacocca Inst., Bethlehem, Pa., 1990—. Office: Howmet Corp 1 Misco Dr C Whitehall MI 49461-1755

SQUIER, JACK LESLIE, sculptor, educator; b. Dixon, Ill., Feb. 27, 1927; s. Leslie Lee and Ruth (Barnes) S.; m. Jane Bugg, June 9, 1950. Student, Oberlin Coll., 1945-46; BS, Ind. U., 1950; M)F.A., Cornell U., 1952. Instr. Cornell U., 1952, asst. prof. art, 1958-61, asso. prof., 1961-65, prof., 1965—. Designer Howatt Pottery Co., N.Y.C., 1953; account exec. Jamian Advt. Co., N.Y.C., 1954-58; asst. prof. U. Calif., Berkeley, 1960; mem. Internat. Assn. Art, UNESCO, 1964-72, mem. exec. com., 1966-69, v.p., 1969-72 One-man shows include Alan Gallery, N.Y.C., 1956, 59, 62, 64, White Mus., Cornell U., 1959, 68, Instituto de Arte Contemporaneo, Lima, Peru, 1963, Landau-Alan Gallery, N.Y.C., 1966, 69, Herbert F. Johnson Mus., Cornell Univ. (retrospective of work, 1953-93); exhibited in group shows at Mus. Modern Art, N.Y.C., 1957, Whitney Mus., N.Y.C., 1952, 54, 56, 58, 62, 67, 78, Hirshhorn Mus., Washington, 1978, Mus. Fine Arts, Boston, 1958, Chgo. Art Inst., 1960, Brussel's Worlds Fair, 1956, competition, Auschwitz, Poland, 1957, Albright-Knox Mus., Buffalo, 1968, Claude Bernard Gallery, Paris, 1957, Hanover Gallery, London, 1958; represented in permanent collections Mus. Modern Art, N.Y.C., Whitney Mus. Art, Hirshhorn Mus., Instituto de Arte Contemporaneo, Everson Mus., Syracuse, N.Y., Stanford U. Mus., St. Lawrence U. Mus., SUNY at Potsdam, Ithaca Coll., Johnson Mus. at Cornell U., Houston Mus., Hamilton Coll. Mus., Hood Mus.-Dartmouth (N.H.) U., Castellani Mus.,

Niagara U., N.Y., Fogg Mus., Harvard U., Cambridge; bronze garden piece at Fogg Mus./Harvard U., Conn. Conservancy; retrospective exhbn. Herbert F. Johnson Mus. Cornell U., 1993; work pub. in various, books, mags., newspapers, slide collections, catalogs. Served with AC USN, 1945-47. Office: Cornell U Dept Art 100 Tjaden Hall Ithaca NY 14853-7301

SQUIER, RITA ANN HOLMBERG, graphic designer; b. Norwalk, Conn., Jan. 4, 1967; d. Stig H. and Julia Mildred Tjader Holmberg; m. Michael Craig Squier, May 19, 1990. BS in Visual Arts, U. Bridgeport, 1988. Art dir., web designer Squier Design, Chatham, N.Y., 1995—; graphic designer, owner Studio 46, Chatham, 1990-99. Mem. Mooresville Artist Guild, Columbia County Coun. on the Arts. Republican. Avocations: watercolor, pen and ink, gardening, acrylics, photography. Office: Squier Design 46 Payn Ave Chatham NY 12037-1427

SQUIRE, ALEXANDER, management consultant; b. Dumfrieshire, Scotland, Sept. 29, 1917; s. Frederick John and Lillian (Ferguson) S.; m. Isabelle L. Kerr, June 23, 1945; children: Jonathan, David, Deborah, Stephen, Philip, Martha, Timothy, Rebecca, Elizabeth. BS, MIT, 1939. Research metallurgist Handy and Harman, Fairfield, Conn., 1939-41; devel. metallurgist Sullivan Machinery Co., Michigan City, Ind., 1941-42; head powder metallurgy br. Watertown Arsenal Lab., Mass., 1942-45; mgr. metall. devel. Westinghouse Electric Corp., Pitts., 1945-50; project mgr. Bettis Atomic Power Lab., Pitts., 1950-62; gen. mgr. plant apparatus div. Westinghouse, 1962-69; dir. purchases and traffic Westinghouse Electric Corp., 1969-71; pres. Westinghouse Hanford Co., Richland, Wash., 1971-79; bus. cons. Richland, 1979-80; dep. mng. dir. Wash. Public Power Supply System, 1980-85, cons., 1985—. Mem. Nat. Acad. Engring., Am. Nuclear Soc., Am. Soc. Metals, AIME, Am. Def. Preparedness Assn. Address: Pittsboro Christian Village 1825 East St Pittsboro NC 27312

SQUIRE, ANNE MARGUERITE, religious leader; b. Amherstburg, Ont., Can., Oct. 17, 1920; d. Alexander Samuel and Coral Marguerite Park; m. William Robert Squire, June 24, 1943; children: Frances, Laura, Margaret. BA, Carleton U., Ottawa, 1972, BA with honors, 1974, MA, 1975; LLD (hon.), Carleton U., 1988; DD (hon.), United Theol. Coll., 1979, Queen's U., 1985. Cert. tchr., Ont. Adj. prof. Carleton U., 1975-82; sec. div. ministry personnel and edn. United Ch. Can., Toronto, 1982-85, moderator, 1986-88. Author curriculum materials, 1959—; contbr. articles to profl. jours. Mem. bd. mgmt. St. Andrew's Coll., Saskatoon, Sask., 1982, Queens Theol. Coll., Kingston, Ont., 1999-2003; founding mem. Muslim-Christian Dialogue Group. Recipient Senate medal Carleton U., 1972. Mem. Can. Research Inst. for Advancement Women, Delta Kappa Gamma (pres. 1978-79). Mem. United Ch. Can. Office: 731 Weston Dr Ottawa ON Canada K1G 1W1 E-mail: asquire@netrover.com.

SQUIRE, JAMES C. adult education educator, engineer, consultant; b. London, Eng. s. James Lewis and Marilyn Ruth Squire; m. Laura Salva; 1 child, Kevin. BS, U.S. Mil. Acad.; PhD, MIT. Math/sci. tchr. Ctrl. Jersey Christian Schools, Asbury Pk., NJ, 1992—93; grad. student/cons. MIT, 1993—2000; prof. Va. Mil. Inst., Lexington, 2000—. Officer M.I. U.S. Army, 1989—92. Decorated Bronze Star US Army. Achievements include patents for stent expansion and apposition sensing catheter; stent slip sensing method and sys. Office: Va Mil Inst 336 Nichols Hall Lexington VA 24450 Office Phone: 540-464-7548.

SQUIRE, LARRY RYAN, neuroscientist, psychologist, educator; b. Cherokee, Iowa, May 4, 1941; s. Harold Walter and Jean (Ryan) S.; children: Ryan, Luke. BA, Oberlin Coll., 1963; PhD in Psychology, MIT, 1968; postgrad., Albert Einstein Med. Coll., 1968-70. With U. Calif., San Diego, 1970—, prof., 1981—; rsch. career scientist VA Med. Ctr., San Diego, 1980—. Lectr. in field. Editor, author: Memory and Brain, 1987; co-author: Memory: From Mind to Molecules, 1999; editor Behavioral Neuroscience, 1990-95; mem. editl. adv. bd. numerous profl. jours.; contbr. articles to profl. jours., chpts. to books. Recipient Charles A. Dana Award for Pioneering Achievements in Health and Education, 1993, Disting. Sci. Contbn. award APA, Lashley prize Am. Philosophical Soc., McGovern award AAAS; William James fellow Am. Psychol. Soc. Mem. Nat. Acad. Scis., Am. Acad. Arts and Scis., Soc. Neurosci. (pres. 1994), Am. Philos. Soc., Inst. Medicine. Office: U California San Diego Dept Psychiatry La Jolla CA 92093 Business E-Mail: lsquire@ucsd.edu.

SQUIRE, LAURIE RUBIN, media consultant; b. N.Y.C., Jan. 30, 1953; d. Daniel and Ruth Thelma (Deutsch) Rubin; m. Herbert E. Squire Jr., Aug. 6, 1975; children: Amy Ruth, Julie Wynn. BA cum laude (scholar), Finch Coll., 1974; MA, NYU, 1976; postgrad., Columbia U., 1977—. Actress TV commls., 1960-65; arts editor Finch/Metro newspaper, N.Y.C., 1970-74; co-editor Finch Alumnae mag., 1971-72; intern producer Sta. WBAI-FM, N.Y.C., 1973; music prodn. coord. Ballet Theatre spl. Sta. WNET-TV, 1973; coll. bd. writer Mademoiselle mag., 1973; intern asst. pub. affairs dir. N.Y. Cultural Ctr., 1974; mdse. coord. Sta. WOR-AM, N.Y.C., 1974-76, contbg. writer Bob and Ray's Mary Backstage serial, contbr. nostalgia features Joe Franklin Show, producer Jean Shepherd Show and sydicated markets, 1975-77, producer Bernard Meltzer What's Your Problem, 1977-80; broadcast stage mgr. Texaco Met. Opera, 1976—. Dance critic Show Bus., theatre newspaper; bd. dirs. publicity and advt. L.I. Playhouse, 1982-84; press rep. Great Neck Pla., columnist, Tribune Pub., Newsday. Contbg. writer Newsday, Can. Publs. Publicity cons. Nassau County Mus. Fine Art; v.p. pub. rels. United Community Fund. Recipient commendations for Leukemia Radiothons Peabody Broadcasting citation, 1983. Home and Office: 25 Loft Dr Martinsville NJ 08876-1400

SQUIRE, WALTER CHARLES, lawyer; b. NYC, Aug. 5, 1945; s. Sidney and Helen (Friedman) S.; m. Sara Jane Abamson; children: Harrison, Russell, Zachary, Andrew. BA, Yale U., 1967; JD, Columbia U., 1971. Bar: N.Y. 1971, U.S. Dist. Ct. (so. and ea. dists.) N.Y. 1975, U.S. Ct. Appeals (2d cir.) 1974, U.S. Supreme Ct. 1977. Ptnr. Jones Hirsch Connors & Bull P.C., NYC, 1986-98, Jacobson, Mermelstein & Squire, LLP, NYC, 1998—; prin. Squire & Co., LLC, NYC, 1998—. Bd. govs. Arthritis Found. N.Y., Inc., 1993-99; bd. dirs. MedicAlert Found., N.Y., 1990-99. Mem. ABA, N.Y. State Bar Assn., Assn. of Bar of City of N.Y., Internat. Bar Assn., Licensing Execs. Soc., Chartered Inst. Arbitrators (London), Am. Arbitration Assn. (arbitrator 1975-2000, mediator 1993—), Am. Acad. Hosp. Attys., Risk Ins. Mgmt. Soc. (lectr. 1983-84), AIDA Reinsurance & Ins. Arbitration Soc. (cert.). Office: Jacobson Mermelstein et al 52 Vanderbilt Ave New York NY 10017-3808

SQUIRES, ARTHUR MORTON, chemical engineer, educator; b. Neodesha, Kans., Mar. 21, 1916; s. Charles Loren and Vera Amber (Moore) S. AB with distinction in Chemistry, U. Mo., 1938; Ph.D, Cornell U., 1947. Design engr. M.W. Kellogg Co., N.Y.C., 1942-46; asst. dir. process devel. Hydrocarbon Research, Inc., N.Y.C., 1946-51, dir. process devel., 1951-59; cons. chem. process industries N.Y.C., 1959-67; prof. chem. engring. CUNY, 1967-74, disting. prof., 1974-76, chmn. dept. chem. engring., 1970-73; Vilbrandt prof. chem. engring. Va. Poly. Inst. and State U., Blacksburg, 1976-82, disting. prof., 1978-86, disting. prof. emeritus, 1986—. Author: The Tender Ship, 1986; editor: (with D.A. Berkowitz) Power Generation and Environmental Change, 1971; contbr. articles to profl. jours.; patentee in field Mem. N.Y. Pro Musica, 1953-60 Fellow Am. Acad. Arts and Scis., AAAS; mem. ASME, NAE, AIChE (inst. lectr.), Am. Chem. Soc. (Henry H. Storch award 1973), Internat. Soc. for Human Ethology, Human Behavior and Evolution Soc., Sigma Xi, Tau Beta Pi Avocation: performing medieval and renaissance music. Home: 2710 Quincy Ct Blacksburg VA 24060-4124 Office: Va Poly Inst and State U Dept Chem Engring Blacksburg VA 24061 Business E-Mail: verasqu@vt.edu.

SQUIRES, CONNIE JO, special education educator; b. Omaha, Nebr., July 14, 1933; d. Paul Sydney Hilt, Lillian Elvera (Holstrom) Hilt; m. Daryl Jessup Squires, Sept. 2, 1955; children: Stephen, Chadwick, Scott. BEd, Whitworth Coll., 1955; MEd, Seattle Pacific U., 1978; postgrad., U. Wash., Ea. Wash. U. Cert. tchr. spl. edn. and reading Wash., sch. psychologist Wash., drug and alcohol counselor Wash. Tchr. elem. Mead Sch. Dist., Spokane, Wash., 1955—59; tchr. spl. edn. Cle Elum Sch. Dist., 1959—60; tchr. elem. Goleta Sch., Santa Barbara, Calif., 1960—62, Anacortes Sch. Dist., Anacorte, Wash., 1962—63, Bellevue Sch. Dist., Bellevue, Wash., 1963—77; sch. psychologist/ednl. specialist Spokane Sch. Dist., 1977—88; sch. psychologist West Valley Sch. Dist., Spokane, 1990—98; ret., 1998. Counselor drug and alcohol, cons. Assocs. in Counseling, Spokane, 1984—99. Bd. dirs. Friends of Little Spokane River Valley. Named Sch. Psychologist of Yr., Washington State, 1995. Mem.: Spokane Ret. Tchrs. (bd. dirs.), Nat. Assn. Sch. Psychologists, Whitworth Women's Aux. Republican. Presbyterian. Avocations: writing, gardening, computers.

SQUIRES, GREGORY DOUGLAS, sociologist, educator; b. Cleve., Mar. 23, 1949; m. Margaret Sullivan, June 7, 1975; children: Erin Michele, Ian Jerome. PhD, Mich. State U., E. Lansing, 1972—76; BS in journalism, Northwestern U., 1971; MA, Mich. State U., 1974. Prof. urban sociology U. Wis., Milw., 1984—2000; prof. race rels. George Washington U., Washington, 2000—. Rsch. analyst U.S. Commn. on Civil Rights, Chgo., 1977—84. Bd. mem. Woodstock Inst., Chgo., 1998—2004. Recipient Reinvention Award, U.S. Housing and Urban Devel., 1996. Mem.: Am. Sociol. Assn. Office: George Washington Univ 801 22nd St NW 409 Phillips Hall Washington DC 20052 Office Phone: 202-994-6894. Business E-Mail: squires@gwu.edu.

SQUIRES, JAMES RALPH, development company executive; b. Jan. 2, 1940; s. William Guilford and Ruby Alice (Whittington) S.; m. Ann Newton, Apr. 17, 1965; children: Samuel Guilford, James Drew. Student, pub. schs., Charlotte, N.C. With Squires Constrn. Co., 1959-62; pres. SBS Builders, Inc., Charlotte, 1968-70, Ralph Squires Homes, Charlotte, 1970-88, Squires & Assocs., Realtors, 1975-88. Bd. dirs., mem. exec. com. Park Meridian Bank, 1991, Dover Mortgage, First Landmark; chmn. Squires Enterprises, Inc. Mem. Charlotte Tree Commn., 1977; bd. dirs. Athletic Found. U. N.C., Charlotte, 1979-84, Providence Day Sch., 1981-84, Better Bus. Bur., 1983, MMAES Inn, 1983-87, Charlotte Symphony; pub. mem. N.C. State Bar, 1980-85; pres. Metrolina Home Owners, 1982, bd. dirs., 1983; bd. govs. Polit. Action Com. for Bldg. Industry; mem. bd. visitors Mercy Hosp., Charlotte, 1986; bd. dirs. Mercy Hosp. Found., chmn., 1993—; chmn. new bldg. fund United Cerebral Palsy; mem. exec. coun. Mecklenburg County coun. Boy Scouts Am., 1986-90; mem. exec. coun. Muscular Dystrophy Assn., Charlotte, 1987; mem. N.C. Wildlife Resources Commn., 1995-98 bd. dirs. Harris YMCA, N.C. March of Dimes, 1997. Recipient Profile award N.C. Blue Cross/Blue Shield, 1974, Albert Gallatin merit cert., 1974; named Charlotte Builder of Yr., 1977. Mem. Nat. Homebuilders Assn., N.C. Homebuilders Assn. (v.p. 1975), Charlotte Homebuilders Assn. (pres. 1974), Charlotte Bd. Realtors, Carolina Ambs., Quail Hollow Country Club, Old North State Country Club, Grandfather Golf and Country Club, Brays Island Plantation. Republican. Baptist. Home: 6830 Phillilps Place Ct Charlotte NC 28210-2715

SQUIRES, JOHN, publishing executive; b. Pocatelllo, Idaho; Degree, U. Washington. From asst. circulation dir. People Mag. to pres. Entertainment Weekly Time Inc., N.Y.C., 1989—98, pres. Entertainment Weekly, 1998—2002, exec. v.p., 2002—. Office: Time Inc 1271 Avenue of the Americas New York NY 10020-1300

SQUIRES, JOHN HENRY, judge; b. Oct. 21, 1946; married; five children. AB cum laude, U. Ill., 1968, JD, 1971. Bar: Ill. 1971, U.S. Dist. Ct. (cen. dist.) Ill. 1972, U.S. Tax Ct. 1978. Assoc. Brown, Hay & Stephens, Springfield, Ill., 1971-76, ptnr., 1977-87; judge U.S. Bankruptcy Ct. No. Dist. Ill. ea. divsn., 1988—2001, reappointed, 2002—. Trustee in bankruptcy, 1984-87; adj. prof. law John Marshall Law Sch., Chgo., 1994, DePaul U., Chgo., 1995-96; lectr. Am. Bankruptcy Inst., Sangamon County Bar Assn., Winnebago County Bar Assn., Chgo. Bar Assn., Ill. Inst. CLE, Comml. Law League Am., DuPage County (Ill.) Bar Assn. Mem. Nat. Conf. Bankruptcy Judges, Am. Bankruptcy Inst., Fed. Bar Assn., Am. Bus. Club, Union League Club Chgo. Office: US Bankruptcy Ct No Dist Ill Ea Div 219 S Dearborn St #676 Chicago IL 60604-1702 Office Phone: 312-435-7580.

SQUIRES, RICHARD FELT, research scientist; b. Sparta, Mich., Jan. 15, 1933; s. Monas Nathan and Dorothy Lois (Felt) S.; m. Else Saederup, 1 child, Iben. BS, Mich. State U., 1958; postgrad., Calif. Inst. Tech., 1958-61. Rsch. biochemist Pasadena Found. for Med. Rsch., 1961-62; chief biochemistry sect. rsch. dept. A/S Ferrosan, Soeborg, Denmark, 1963-78; neurochemistry group leader CNS Biology sect. Lederle Labs. div. Am. Cyanamid Co., Pearl River, N.Y., 1978-79; prin. rsch. scientist The Nathan S. Kline Inst. for Psychiat. Rsch., Orangeburg, N.Y., 1979-2000, ret., 2000. Contbr. over 85 articles to profl. jours.; patentee in field. Nat. Inst. Neurol. and Communication Disorders and Stroke grantee, 1981-84. Mem. Soc. Neurosci., Collegium Internat. Neuro-Psychopharmacologicum, Internat. Soc. Neurochemistry, Am. Soc. Neurochemistry, Am. Soc. Biochemistry and Molecular Biology, Am. Soc. Pharmacology and Exptl. Therapeutics. Home: 861 Laugenour Ct Woodland CA 95776-4911 Personal E-mail: else_dick@hotmail.com.

SQUIRES, WILLIAM RANDOLPH, III, lawyer; b. Providence, Sept. 6, 1947; s. William Randolph and Mary Louise (Gress) S.; m. Elisabeth Dale McAnulty, June 23, 1984; children: Shannon, William R. IV, Mayre Elisabeth, James Robert. BA in Econs., Stanford U., 1969; JD, U. Tex., 1972. Bar: Wash. 1973, U.S. Dist. Ct. (we. dist.) Wash. 1973, U.S. Dist. Ct. (ea. dist.) Wash. 1976, U.S. Ct. Appeals (9th cir.) 1976, U.S. Supreme Ct. 1976, U.S. Ct. Fed. Claims 1982. Assoc. Oles, Morrison, Rinker, Stanislaw & Ashbaugh, Seattle, 1973-78; ptnr., chmn. litig. group Davis Wright Tremaine, Seattle, 1978-97; mem. Summit Law Group, Seattle, 1997—. Fellow Am. Coll. Trial Lawyers; mem. ABA, Internat. Bar Assn., Wash. State Bar Assn., King County Bar Assn., Wash. Athletic Club, Rainier Club (Seattle). Episcopalian. Home: 5554 NE Penrith Rd Seattle WA 98105-2845 Office: Summit Law Group 315 Fifth Ave S Ste 1000 Seattle WA 98104 Office Phone: 206-676-7054. E-mail: randys@summitlaw.com.

SQUYRES, STEVEN WELDON, astronomy educator, planetary geology researcher; b. Woodbury, N.J., Jan. 9, 1956; BA, Cornell U., 1978, PhD in Geology, 1981. Assoc. NRC, Ames Rsch. Ctr., NASA, 1981—; assoc. prof. dept. astronomy Cornell U., 1985—; mem. Planetary Geol. Working Group, NASA, 1982—. Mem. AAAS, Am. Geophys. Union. Office: Cornell U 428 Space Sciences Bldg Ithaca NY 14853 E-mail: squyres@astro.cornell.edu.

SREEBNY, LEO M. oral biology and pathology educator; b. N.Y.C., Jan. 8, 1922; s. Morris and Lillie (Bogdanoff) S.; m. Mathilda H. Sternfeld, Mar. 9, 1945; children— Oren, Daniel. BA, U. Ill., 1942, D.D.S., 1945, MS, 1950, PhD, 1954; D (hon.), Semmelweis Med. U., 2001. With dept. periodontics U. Ill., 1948-57, asso. prof., 1956-57; asso. prof., chmn. dept. oral biology U. Wash., Seattle, 1957-60, prof., 1960-75; dir. U. Wash. (Center for Research Oral Biology), 1967-75; dean Sch. Dental Medicine, SUNY-Stony Brook, 1975-79, prof. dept. oral biology and pathology, 1979—. Cons. VA Hosp., Seattle, 1960—; mem. dental study sect. NIH, 1964-68, chmn., 1967-68; mem. com. on sci. policy Nat. Acad. Sci., 1973-74; mem. med. adv. coun. Internat. Conf. on Integrative Medicine, 1998-99. Author: (with Julia Meyer) Secretory Mechanisms in Salivary Glands, 1963, The Salivary System, 1987, (with I. Van der Waal) Diseases of the Salivary Glands, 1997; contbr. numerous articles to sci., biol. jours. Mem. med. adv. bd. Sjogren's Syndrome Found., 1997, bd. govs. 1998—. Served with AUS, 1942-45; with USNR, 1946-48. Recipient Internat. Assn. for Dental Research Sci. award, 1969; Silver medal for contbns. to dental sci. and art City of Paris, 1979; Salivary Research Group Award, 1987. Mem. Fedn. Dentaire Internat. (chmn. sci. assembly com. 1973—, rep. UN Conf. on Youth 1983-84), Internat. Assn. Dental Research (bd. govs. 1981), Fedn. Dentaire Internat. (list of honor 1988), Am. Assn. Dental Research, ADA. Home: 35 Gnarled Hollow Rd East Setauket NY 11733-2929 Office: SUNY Stony Brook Sch Dental Medicine Stony Brook NY 11794-0001 E-mail: lsreebny@usa.net.

SREENIVASAN, KATEPALLI RAJU, mechanical engineering educator; b. Kolar, India, Sept. 30, 1947; married 1980; 2 children. BE, Bangalore U., 1968; ME, Indian Inst. Sci., 1970, PhD in Aeronautical Engring., 1975. JRD Tata fellow Indian Inst. Sci., 1972-74, project asst., 1974-75; fellow U. Sydney, Australia, 1975, U. Newcastle, 1976-77; rsch. assoc. Johns Hopkins U., Balt., 1977-79; from asst. prof. to assoc. prof. Yale U., New Haven, 1982-85, prof. mech. engring., 1985—2002, Harold W. Cheel prof. mech. engring., 1988—2002, prof. physics, 1990—2002, prof. applied physics, 1993—2002; Disting. Univ. prof., dir. Inst. Phys. Sci. and Tech., U. Md., College Park, 2002; Abdus Salam hon. prof., dir. Internat. Ctr. for Theoretical Physics, Trieste, Italy. Vis. scientist Indian Inst. Sci., 1979, vis. prof., 1982, Calif. Inst. Tech., Pasadena, 1986, Rockefeller U., 1989, Jawaharlala Nehru Ctr. Advancement Sci. Studies, 1992, chmn. mech. engring. dept., 1987-92; vis. sci. DFVLR, Gottingen, Germany, 1983; mem. Inst. for Advanced Study, Princeton, N.J., 1995. Recipient Narayana Gold medal Indian Inst. Sci., 1975, Disting. Alumnus award, 1992; Humboldt Found. fellow, 1983, Guggenheim fellow, 1989. Fellow AAAS, ASME, Am. Phys. Soc. (Otto Laporte award 1995), AIAA (assoc.), Am. Acad. Arts and Sci., Third World Acad. Scis. (Engring. Sci. medal 2003), Conn. Acad. Arts and Scis.; mem. NAE, Am. Math. Soc., Conn. Acad. Sci. and Engring., Sigma Xi. Achievements include research in origin and dynamics of turbulence; control of turbulent flows; chaotic dynamics; fractals. Office Phone: 39-040-224-0250. E-mail: krs@ictp.trieste.it.

SRERE, BENSON M. communications company executive, consultant; b. Rock Island, Ill, Aug. 13, 1928; s. Jacob H. and Margaret (Weinstein) S.; m. Betty Ann Cerruti, June 20, 1957; children: David Benson, Anne Michele, Peter John. BA magna cum laude, U. So. Calif., 1949. Newsman U.P., Los Angeles, 1948-56; assoc. editor Good Housekeeping mag., N.Y.C., 1956-59, sr. editor, 1959-67, asst. mng. editor, dir. spl. publs. div., 1967-68, mng. editor, 1968-72, exec. editor, v.p., 1972-75, v.p., editorial dir., 1975-76; v.p., gen. mgr. King Features Syndicate, 1976-81; v.p. Hearst Metrotone News, 1976-81; exec. asst. to pres. Hearst Corp., 1981—, v.p., 1983-94. Dir. Hearst/ABC Video Svcs., Hearst/ABC Viacom Entertainment Svcs., A&E Cable Network, Lifetime Cable Network. Trustee Optometric Center of NY Found., 1978-79. Served with U.S. Army, 1950-52. Mem. Soc. Profl. Journalists, Phi Beta Kappa, Phi Kappa Phi, Phi Eta Sigma. Home: 11 Lafayette Ct Greenwich CT 06830-5324

SRINATH, LATHA, physician; b. Bangalore, India, Jan. 1, 1958; came to U.S., 1985; d. Krishna and Shamanthaka (Ananthachar) Iyengar; m. Sampath Holevanahalli Srinath, Jan. 22, 1984; children: Shilpa, Preetha. BS, Bangalore U., 1978; MB, BChir, Bangalore Med. Coll., 1984; MD, Georgetown U., 1990. Diplomate Am. Bd. Internal Medicine. Fellow in infectious diseases U. Louisville, 1992-94; pvt. practice Boynton Beach, Fla., 1994—. Staff Bethesda Meml. Hosp., Boynton Beach, 1994—, JFK Med. Ctr., Boynton Beach, 1994—; cons. HIV Adv. Bd., Fla., 1997—. Contbr. articles to profl. jours. Nat. Merit scholar, India, 1975. Mem. Am. Assn. Physicians from India, Fla. Med. Assn., Palm Beach Med. Soc. Hindu. Avocations: travel, yoga, tennis, painting, athletics. Home: 473 N Country Club Dr Lake Worth FL 33462-1003 Office: ID Cons Inc 2623 S Seacrest Blvd Boynton Beach FL 33435-7501 Office Phone: 561-735-7531. E-mail: lsrinath@idconsults.net.

SRINIVASAN, RANGASWAMY, chemical physicist; b. Madras, India, Feb. 28, 1929; came to U.S., 1953; s. K. Rangaswamy. BSc with honors, Madras U., India, 1949; PhD, U. So. Calif., 1956. Mgr., rsch. T.J. Watson Rsch. Ctr. IBM, Yorktown Heights, N.Y., 1961-90; chief exec. officer UV Tech Assocs., Ossining, N.Y., 1990—. Vis. rsch. prof. chemistry Ohio State U., Columbus, 1966-67, Wellman Lab., Mass. Gen. Hosp., Boston, 1987-89, Columbia-Presbyn. Med. Ctr., N.Y.C., 1984-90. Editor: (books) Organic Photochemical Syntheses, Vol. 1., 1972, Vol. 2, 1976; contbr. over 200 articles to profl. jours. Guggenheim fellow, 1966; recipient award for creative invention Am. Chem. Soc., 1997, Essalen award for chemistry in the pub. interest, 1997; inductee Nat. Inventors Hall of Fame, 2002. Fellow AAAS, Am. Physical Soc. (Biol. Physics prize 1998), N.Y. Acad. Scis., Am. Soc. Laser Medicine and Surgery; mem. NAE (Inventor's Hall of Fame 2002). Achievements include invention of Ablative Photodecomposition, a laser technique for removal of microscopic thickness of organic matter such as plastics (of use in microelectronics) or tissue (of use in eye surgery).*

SRINIVASAN, SEETHA, publishing company executive; b. Bangalore, Mysore, India, Dec. 27, 1943; came to U.S., 1967; d. R. and S. (Sethuraman) Ananthakrishnan; m. Asoka Srinivasan, July 14, 1967; children: Arjun, Gautam. BA, Ferguson Coll., Poona, India, 1963; MA, U. Poona, 1965, Mills Coll., Oakland, Calif., 1969; M in Journalism and Comm., U. Fla., 1979. Instr. English Tougaloo (Miss.) Coll., 1969-72, asst. prof., 1972-77; editor Univ. Press of Miss., Jackson, 1979-82, asst. dir., exec. editor, 1982-87, assoc. dir., editor-in-chief, 1987-98; dir., 1998—. Bd. dirs. Assn. Am. Univ. Presses, N.Y.C., 1989-92. Pres. Jackson Symphony Youth Orch., 1986-88, Millsoups Arts and Lectures Series; sec. Jackson Friends of Libr., 1985-89. Office: Univ Press of Miss 3825 Ridgewood Rd Jackson MS 39211-6497

SRINIVASAN, VENKATARAMAN, marketing and management educator; b. Pudukkottai, Tamil Nadu, India, June 5, 1944; came to U.S., 1968; s. Annaswamy and Jambagalakshmi Venkataraman; m. Sitalakshmi Subrahmanyam, June 30, 1972; children: Ramesh, Mahesh. B Tech., Indian Inst. Tech., Madras, India, 1966; MS, Carnegie-Mellon U., 1970, PhD, 1971. Asst. engr. Larsen & Toubro, Bombay, 1966-68; asst. prof. mgmt. and mktg. U. Rochester, N.Y., 1971-73, assoc. prof., 1973-74, Stanford (Calif.) U., 1974-76, prof., 1976-82, dir. PhD program in bus., 1982-85, Ernest C. Arbuckle prof. mktg. and mgmt. sci., 1982—2003, Adams disting. prof. mgmt., 2003—; mktg. area coord. Stanford U., 1976—78, 1988—93, 2000—03. Mem. bd. acad. trustees Mktg. Sci. Inst., 2004—; cons. in field. Mem. editl. bd. Jour. Mktg. Rsch., 1988—, Mktg. Sci., 1980—, Mgmt. Sci., 1974-91; contbr. articles to profl. jours. Mem. Am. Mktg. Assn., Inst. Ops. Rsch./Mgmt. Scis. Hindu. Avocation: classical music.

SRISKANDA, NESAN SITHAMPARAPILLAI, engineering educator, researcher; s. Kanther Veluppillai Sithamparapillai and Rubasothy Sithamaparapillai; m. Gowsi Kumarasamy; children: Shahila, Ahila. BSME, U. S.C., 1987, MS in Math., 1989, PhD in Mech. Engring., 1996. EIT S.C. State Profl. Engrs.; cert. tchr. math. Praxis. Assoc. prof. Claflin U., Orangeburg, SC, 1998. Presenter ICTCM, 2002. Recipient Tech. Integration in Tchg., The Ctr. for Excellence in Tchg., 1999 -2000. Mem.: Am. Soc. Engring. Edn. (assoc.). Peace Party. Hindu. Office: Claflin University College Ave NE Orangeburg SC 29115 Office Phone: 803-535-5073.

SRIVASTAVA, KAILASH CHANDRA, microbiologist; b. Varanasi, India, Sept. 4, 1947; came to U.S., 1969; s. Hari and Bimla (Varma) Kishore; m. Kumkum Chandra, Feb. 27, 1977; children: Mukta, Tarun K. BS, Punjab U., 1968; MS, Seton Hall U., 1971; PhD, Univ. Coll., London, 1975. Dir. lab. ops. Ivy Med. Lab., N.Y., 1975-78; assoc. prof. Dept. Food Sci. & Technology, Londrina, Brazil, 1978-80, prof. dept. food sci. and tech., 1980-84, Forest Products Lab., Madison, Wis., 1984-86, Mich. State U., East Lansing, 1986-87; vis. sr. scientist Mich. Biotech. Inst., Lansing, 1987-88, rsch. scientist, 1988—; adj. asst. prof. Mich. State U., East Lansing, 1990—. Contbr. articles to profl. jours.; co-author: (symposium volume) Internat. Yeast Symposium, Biochemical Pentose Fermenting Yeasts, 1986, Symposium on Fuels, Technology, Novel Sources For Cellulase Production, 1985. Recipient Cert. of Appreciation, USDA, 1985, Svc. award Mich. Biotechnology Inst., 1989, Edwina Mountbatten scholarship U. London, 1975, Yusuf Ali award, 1972, Brit. Coun. studentship, 1971-74. Mem. Inst. Food Technology, N.Y. Acad. Scis., Japan Soc. for Biosci., Biotechnology & Agrochemistry. Achievements include patent on alkaophilic, thermostable lipase; elucidation of styrene degradation pathway in thermophilic Bacillus; development of microbial consortia to degrade recalcitrant compounds; isolation of novel adicuric, thermostable glucose isomerase from new organism, of novel microorganisms and novel lipase, collagenase and thermostable pullulanase enzyme producing microorganisms, new collagenase from thermophilic bacillus; first to demonstrate mesosomal structures in yeasts; research on degradation of recalcitrant, xenobiotic compounds by microbes. Office: Arctech, Inc 14100 Park Meadow Dr Ste 210 Chantilly VA 20151-2217

SRIVASTAVA, RADHEY SHYAM, research scientist, researcher; b. Bahadurganj, India, June 7, 1931; s. Umeshwar Prasad and Ganesha Devi; m. Vijay Laxmi, Feb. 12, 1959; children: Suneeta, Sanjay, Sangita. BSc, Lucknow U.,

India, 1951, MSc, 1953, cert. in French, 1957, PhD, 1963. Rsch. fellow, lectr. Lucknow U., India, 1954-56, 56-57; jr. sci. officer Def. Sci. Lab., New Delhi, 1958-61, sr. sci. officer, 1961-71, prin. sci. officer, 1971-80; dep. chief sci. officer Def. Sci. Ctr., New Delhi, 1980-91; pvt. rschr., 1991—. Rsch. fellow Royal Soc. London, Imperial Coll. Sci. and Tech., 1965; vis. scientist MRL, Melbourne, Australia, 1983, Inst. Aerospace Studies, Toronto, Can., 1980, Chiba U., 1991; vis. prof. Ernst Mach Inst., Freiburg, Germany, 1995, Tohoku U., Sendai, Japan, 2000, Chiba (Japan) U., 2000, Tokyo Denki U., 2001, Aachen U., Germany, 2002; organizing com. winter sch. in physiol. fluid dynamics, 1975. Author: Turbulence (Pipe Flows), 1977, Interaction of Shock Waves, 1994; contbr. to profl. publ. Mem. gen. body Welfare Assn., New Delhi, 1985—. Grantee Def. Rsch. Can., 1980, USAF, 1980, Min. Def., New Delhi, 1983, Min. Edn. Japan, Chiba, 1991. Fellow: NAS, United Writers' Assn. India; mem.: Indian Sci. Congress, Bharat Ganita Parishad (life), Sci. Officer's Assn. Hindu. Achievements include development of Srivastava's Theory. Home and Office: A-3/260 Janakpuri New Delhi 110058 India E-mail: ssmriti@yahoo.com.

SRIVASTAVA, SHEKHAR, research scientist; s. Paras Nath and Kusum Srivastava; m. Piyali Dhar Chowdhury, Feb. 4, 2002. MSc in Biochemistry, Dr. RML Avadh U., 1996; PhD of Biochemistry, Ctrl. Drug Rsch. Inst. and Dr. RML Avadh U., 2001; diploma, Shri Inst. Computer Scis., Lucknow, 1993. Tchr. chemistry St. Johns Intermediate Coll., Gola Gokaran Nath, India, 1996—97; rsch. asst. Ctrl. Drug Rsch. Inst., Lucknow, 1997—99, sr. rsch. fellow, 1999—2001; post doctoral fellow NYU Sch. of Medicine, 2001—. Contbr. articles to profl. jours. Recipient Jr. Scientist in Pharmacology, Assn. Scientists of Indian Origin in Am., 2002; fellow Sr. Rsch. Fellowship, Coun. Sci. and Indsl. Rsch., Delhi, India, 1999. Mem.: Fedn. of Am. Societies for Exptl. Biology (hon.; bethesda, md 1912), Biophysical Soc. (hon.; bethesda 1957), Am. Heart Assn. (hon.; dallas, tx 1924). Hindu. Achievements include patents for antisichaemic compound made in Ctrl. Drug Rsch. Inst., Lucknow, India. Avocations: music, photography, sports (badminton, cricket), cooking. Home: 66-15 Thornton Place Apt 5H Forest Hills NY 11374 Office: NYU School of Medicine 560 First Avenue TCH-519 New York NY 10016 Personal E-mail: sheksri@rediffmail.com. E-mail: srivas02@med.nyu.edu.

SRIVASTAVA, VISHNU CHANDRA, agronomy educator; b. Darvhanga, India, Jan. 20, 1943; s. Kailash and Chandrawati (Devi) Prasad; m. Kiran Verma, May 17, 1970; children: Rajinish, Manish. BS, Bihar U., Muzaffarpur, India, 1963; MS, Ranchi U., India, 1966; PhD, Moscow Agrl. Acad., 1973. Nat. bd. cert. tchr. Lectr. Ranchi Agrl. Coll., India, 1967-74; asst. prof., agronomist Birsa Agrl. U., Ranchi, 1974-78, assoc. prof., sr. scientist, 1978-86, prof., chief scientist, chmn., head agronomy, 1986-99, additional dir. rsch., 1986-87, dean faculty agr., 1994—95, 1997—2003. Cons. World Bank, Winrock Internat., 1993-94; cons. in field. Contbr. over 150 articles to profl. jours. Recipient Cert. of Appreciation for rsch. achievement USDA, 1996. Mem. Indian Soc. Agronomy (life), Indian Sci. Congress, Indian Soc. Soil Sci. Avocations: painting, photography, chess. Home: H/80 Argora Housing Colony Ranchi 834002 India

SRIVATSAN, TIRUMALAI SRINIVAS, engineering educator; s. Tirumalai Raghavachari and Radha Srinivas; m. Jayashree Srivatsan, Aug. 21, 1989; children: Sitara, Santosh. PhD, Ga. Inst. Tech., 1984. Rsch. assoc. Ga. Tech. Rsch. Inst., Atlanta, 1984—85; mgr. R&D Materials Modification Inc, Falls Church, Va., 1985—87; prof. U. Akron, Ohio, 1987—. Editor: Internat. Jour. Materials and Manf. Processes; contbr. articles over 400 profl. jours.; author: 28 books in Materials Science and Engineering. Recipient Outstanding Young Alumnus, Ga. Inst. Tech., 1996. Fellow: ASME, Am. Soc. Materials.

SROKA, JOHN WALTER, trade association executive; b. Perth Amboy, N.J., July 24, 1946; s. John and Mary (Teliszewski) S.; m. Paula J. Devitt, Aug. 17, 1968; children: Amanda, Alexandra. BA in Psychology, Fairleigh Dickinson U., 1968, postgrad., 1968-69; postgrad. in law, Am. U., 1972-73. Asst. exec. dir. Associated Gen. Contractors of Am., Washington, 1973-87; exec. v.p. Nat. Assn. Sheet Metal and Air Conditioning Contractors, Chantilly, Va., 1987—. Sgt. U.S. Army, 1969-71. Mem. Am. Soc. Assn. Execs. Roman Catholic. Office: SMACNA 4201 Lafayette Center Dr Chantilly VA 20151-1219 E-mail: jsroka@smacna.org.

SSARNO, CHRISTOPHER ED, writer; b. N.Y.C., Jan. 25, 1932; s. Christopher and Florence (Shanahan) Sarno. Grad. high sch., Medford, 1950. Mem. Medford (Mass.) Police Dept., 1958-80. Contbg. author: Tank Aces: The U.S. Marine Corps in Korea, 1951, Korean Vignettes: Faces of War, 1951, The Red Dragon: Second Round, 101 Seastories, US Marines in Korea, 1952; author (sound recordings): You'll Be Soorree, R&R in Japan, 1954; contbr. articles to mil. history publs.; author: (memoir) You'll Be Soorree (published on www.koreanwar-educator.org). With Fleet Marine Force USMC, 1950—55, Korea, Japan. Named Citizen of Yr., VFW Medford, 1972; recipient Medal of Valor, New Eng. Chief of Police Assn., 1972. Mem.: USMC Tankers Assn., 1st Marine Divsn. Assn., Semper Fidelis Soc. Boston. Republican. Roman Catholic. Avocations: tennis, travel, walking, reading, gardening. Home: 12 Butler St Medford MA 02155-1856 Office Phone: 781-393-0970. E-mail: gungho_guy@lycos.com.

SSINGLETARY, ALVIN D. lawyer; b. Sept. 27, 1942; s. Alvin E. and Alice (Pastoret) Singletary; m. Judy Louise SSingletary, Dec. 3, 1983; children: Kimberly Dawn, Shane David, Kelly Diane. BA, La. State U., 1964; JD, Loyola U., New Orleans, 1969. Bar: La. 1969, U.S. Dist. Ct. (ea. dist.) La. 1972, U.S. Ct. Appeals (5th cir.) 1972, U.S. Ct. Appeals (11 cir.) 1981, U.S. Ct. Internat. Trade 1981, U.S. Ct. Customs and Patent Appeals 1982, U.S. Supreme Ct. 1978. Instr. Delgado Coll., New Orleans, 1976—77; sole practice Slidell, La., 1970—. Spl. asst. dist. atty 22d Judicial Dist. Ct., Parish of St. Tammany, La.; sec., treas. St. Tammany Pub. Trust Fin. Authority, 1978—2002. Chmn. sustaining membership enrollment Cypress dist. Boy Scouts Am., 1989—; treas. Slidell Centennial commn.; councilman-at-large City of Slidell, 1978—2002, interim mayor, 1985; mem. Dem. State Ctrl. Com., 1978—82; mem. Rep. State Ctrl. Com. Dist. 76, La., 1996—2000; del. La.Constl. Conv., 1972—73; chmn. Together We Build Program First Baptist Ch. of Slidell, La.; bd. dir. St. Tammany Coun. on Aging. Mem.: Lions, Delta Theta Phi. Baptist. Office: PO Box 1158 Slidell LA 70459-1158 Office Phone: 985-643-9800.

STAAB, DIANE D. lawyer; BA, CUNY Hunter Coll., 1977; JD, Yeshiva U., 1980. Bar: N.Y. 1981. Assoc. atty. Hall, McNicol, Hamilton & Clark, 1980-84, Patterson, Belknap, Webb & Tyler, 1984-87; corp. counsel Internat. Paper Co., 1987—95; v.p., gen. counsel, corp. ethics/environ. compliance officer Ariz. Chem., Panama City, 1996—2001; gen. counsel Internat. Paper Europe, 2001—. Mem. ABA (mem. bus. law sect. fed. ref. of securities com. 1988-2001, vice-chmn. com. on corp. & bus. legis. subcom. on corp. governance 1992-98), Assn. of the Bar of the City of N.Y. (mem. spl. com. on election law 1987-89, mem. corp. law com. 1989-92, sec. com. on corp. law dept. 1992-93). Office: Internat Paper 400 Atlantic St Stamford CT 06921 Office Phone: 32 02 774 1254.

STAAB, THOMAS EUGENE, chemist; b. Peoria, Ill., Jan. 26, 1941; s. Leo Reuben and Mary Blanche (Griffin) S.; m. Donna Marie Murnighan, May 30, 1967; children: Lynn Anne, Thomas Patrick. BS in Chemistry, St. Louis U., 1963. R&D chemist for elastomers Victor Products divsn. Dana Corp., Chgo., 1963-65, application engr. for oil seals, 1965-68, application engring. supr. for oil seals, 1968-70, chief product engr. for oil seals, 1970-72, mgr. sales and engring. Ft. Wayne, Ind., 1973-75, prodn. supr., 1975-77, materials engr. for gaskets, 1977-79, mgr. oil seal engring. Lisle, Ill., 1979-82, chief devel. engr. materials, 1982-83, prodn. area mgr., 1983-84, mgr. materials devel., 1984-86, mgr. tech. svcs., 1986-90, environ. mgr., 1990-92, sen. tech. svc. engr., 1992-96, sr. materials engr., 1996-2001, Dana Corp., Victor Reinz divsn., Lisle, Ill., 2001—. New products mgr. Dana Corp., Lisle, 2001—. Alliance chief Y Indian Guides, 1975-76; mgr., coach Little League, 1978-81. Mem. Rubbers Mfrs. Assn. (past chmn. oil seal tech. com.), Soc. Automotive Engrs. (past mem. adv. bd. of sealing com.), Am. Chem. Soc. Roman Catholic. Achievements include patent for hydrodynamic shaft seal, rotary shaft seals, antistick, non-liquid absorbing gasket, reinforced core heavy duty gasket, constrained layer damped steel baffle, screen printable foam coating for sealing and vibration isolation of cam cover baffles. Home: 1 W Superior St Apt 4802 Chicago IL 60610-8865 Office: 1945 Ohio St Lisle IL 60532-2169

STAAB, THOMAS ROBERT, consumer product company financial executive; b. Beaver Falls, Pa., Apr. 23, 1942; s. Henry Louis and Margaret Constance (Clarke) S.; m. Angela Maria Simon, Aug. 6, 1965; children: Thomas II, Jennifer, Thea. BBA, U. Pitts., 1964, MBA, 1965. CPA, Pa. Sr. audit mgr. Price Waterhouse & Co., Pitts., 1970-77; practice fellow Fin. Acctg. Standards Bd., Stamford, Conn., 1978-80; dir. corp. acctg. and taxes Fieldcrest Cannon Inc., Eden, N.C., 1981-84, asst. contr., 1985, contr., 1986-91, v.p. fin., 1992-93, CFO, 1994-97; bd. dirs., sr. v.p., CFO Lorillard Inc., Greensboro, N.C., 1998—. Served to lt. USN, 1966-70. Mem. AICPA, Pa. Inst. CPAs. Republican. Roman Catholic. Home: 3726 NC # 65 Reidsville NC 27320 Office: Lorillard Inc PO Box 10529 714 Green Valley Rd Greensboro NC 27404-0529

STAATS, DEAN ROY, retired reinsurance executive; b. Somerville, N.J., Sept. 18, 1924; s. Roy Theodore and Mabel Ellen (Rhodes) S.; m. Marilyn Ann Hockenbury, 1947 (div. 1956; 1 child, Barry Clinton; m. Marilyn Lee Truitt, Dec. 16, 1961 B.Sc., Brown U., 1946, MA, 1948. Asst. actuary N.Am. Reassurance Co., N.Y.C., 1959-67, data processing officer, 1967-69, v.p., actuary, 1969-71, sr. v.p., 1971-84, exec. v.p., 1984-86; pres., dir. NARe Life Mgmt. Co., N.Y.C., 1985-86; rep. Life Ins. Guaranty Corp, 1977-86; U.S. mgr. Can. Reassurance Co., 1984-86; cons. actuary, 1986-89. Served to lt. (j.g.), USN, 1943-46, PTO Fellow Soc. Actuaries; mem. Am. Acad. Actuaries N.Y. Jr. Actuaries Club (pres. 1960-61), Soc. Actuaries (reins. adminstrn. com. 1984-85) Clubs: Anchor and Saber (pres. 1959-60). Republican. Avocations: art collectibles; tennis; gardening; travel. Home and Office: 3 Post Run Newtown Square PA 19073-3014

STAATS, ELMER BOYD, foundation executive, former government official; b. Richfield, Kans., June 6, 1914; s. Wesley F. and Maude (Goodall) S.; m. Margaret S. Rich, Sept. 14, 1940; children: David Rich, Deborah Rich Staats Sanders, Catharine Rich Staats Taubman. AB, McPherson (Kans.) Coll., 1935, LLD (hon.), 1966; MA, U. Kans., 1936; PhD, U. Minn., 1939; D. in Pub. Service (hon.), George Washington U., 1971, D. in Adminstrn. (hon.), U. S.D., 1973; LLD (hon.), Duke U., 1975, Nova U., 1976, U. Pa., 1981, Lycoming Coll., 1982; LHD (hon.), Ohio State U., 1982. Research asst. Kans. Legis. Council, 1936; teaching asst. U. Minn., 1936-38; staff Pub. Adminstrn. Service, Chgo., 1937-38; staff mem. U.S. Bur. Budget, Exec. Office Pres., 1939-47, asst. to dir., 1947, asst. dir. charge legis. reference, 1947-49, exec. asst. dir., 1949-50, dep. dir., 1950-53, 58-66; comptroller gen. U.S. Washington, 1966-81; pres. Harry S. Truman Scholarship Found., 1981-84, chmn., 1984—. Bd. dirs. rsch. dir. Marshall Field & Co., Chgo., 1953; exec. dir. ops. coord. bd., Nat. Security Coun., 1953-58; professorial lectr. pub. adminstrn. George Washington U., 1944-49; mem. bd. visitors Nat. Def. U., 1981-90; mem. vis. com. John F. Kennedy Sch. Govt., Harvard U., 1974-80, Grad. Sch. Mgmt., UCLA, 1976—; mem. Com. on Pub. Policy Studies U. Chgo., 1976—; trustee Nat. Inst. Pub. Affairs, 1969-77; mem. Conf. Bd., 1966; mem. dir.'s adv. coun. Met. Life Ins. Co., 1985-94, emeritus mem., 1994—; dir. Computer Data Systems, Inc., 1981—; bd. advisors Alexander Proudfoot & Co., 1981-85; mem. pub. rev. bd. Arthur Andersen & Co., 1981-91; bd. dirs. Air Products and Chems., 1981-85, Met. Life Ins. Co., 1981-85, Nat. Intergroup Inc. (formerly Nat. Steel Corp.), 1981-86; chmn. congl. panel on social security orgn., 1983-84; mem. nat. commn. on pub. svc., 1987-90; mem. commn. to rev. honor code of West Point U.S. Mil. Acad., 1988-89; mem. Govt. Acctg. Standards Bd., 1984-90; chmn. Fed. Acctg. Standards Adv. Bd., 1991-96. Author: Personnel Standards in the Social Security Program, 1939; contbr. to: Am. Polit. Sci. Rev. Trustee Am. U., 1969-81; trustee McPherson Coll., 1969-79, mem. bd. trustees and research and policy com., com. for econ. devel., 1981—; bd. govs. Internat. Orgn. of Supreme Audit Instns., 1969-80; trustee Kerr Found., 1981—; bd. dirs. George C. Marshall Found., 1984—. Recipient Rockefeller Pub. Service award, 1961, Alumni achievement award U. Minn., 1964, Disting. Service citation U. Kans., 1966, Warner D. Stockberger Achievement award, 1973, Abraham O. Smoot Pub. Service award Brigham Young U., 1975, Person of Yr. award Washington chpt. Inst. Internal Auditors, 1975, Thurston award Inst. Internal Auditors, 1988, medal of honor Am. Inst. CPAs, 1980, Engr. of Yr. award San Fernando Valley Engrs. Council, 1980, Presdl. Citizens medal, 1981, Hubert Humphrey medal, 1981, Pub. Service Achievement award Common Cause, 1981; fed. exec. award Evaluation Research Soc., 1980; named to Acctg. Hall of Fame, 1981; fellow Brookings Instn., 1938-39. Mem. Nat. Acad. Pub. Adminstrn., Assn. Govt. Accountants, Am. Acad. Polit. and Social Sci. (dir. 1966-92), Am. Soc. Public Adminstrn. (pres. Washington 1948-49, nat. coun. 1958-65, nat. pres. 1961-62), Am. Mgmt. Assns. (gen. mgmt. coun. 1966-85, trustee 1981-85), Cosmos Club (Washington), Chevy Chase (Md.), Phi Beta Kappa, Pi Sigma Alpha, Beta Gamma Sigma, Alpha Kappa Psi. Methodist. Office: Harry S Truman Scholarship Found 712 Jackson Pl NW Washington DC 20006-4901

STAATS, HOWARD E. newspaper editor; Bur. chief AP, Louisville, 1961—. Address: 525 W Broadway Louisville KY 40202-2206

STAATS, PETER S. pain medicine physician, surgeon; b. Phoenix, May 22, 1963; s. Arthur Wilbur and Carolyn (Kaiden) S.; m. Nancy Elizabeth Staats, Oct. 26, 1991; children: Alyssa, Dylan, Rachel. BSBA, JU. Calif., Santa Barbara, 1985; MD, U. Mich., 1989. Residency in anesthesia & critical care Johns Hopkins U., Balt., 1990-92, pain medicine fellow, 1992-94, chief, divsn. pain medicine, 1994—. Assoc. prof. anesthesia and oncology, Johns Hopkins U., 1994—. Contbr. more than 50 peer-reviewed articles to profl. jours.; inventor in field of pain management. Mem. Am. Pain Soc. (bd. dirs. 2000—), Nat. Pain Found. (bd. dirs. 1999—), Am. Neuromodulation Soc., So. Pain Soc. (pres. 2000—, Distinguished Svc. award 2001). Office: Johns Hopkins U 550 N Broadway Baltimore MD 21205 E-mail: pstaats@jhmi.edu.

STAATS, THOMAS ELWYN, neuropsychologist; s. Percy Anderson and Julia (Bourmorck) S.; m. Debra R.; children: Lauren Malu, Kara Kristyn, Stacy Rhnea, Ronald Derek. BA cum laude, Emory U., 1970; MA, U. Ala., 1972, PhD, 1974; postgrad., U. Tex., Tyler, 1992. Diplomate Am. Bd. Profl. Disability Cons.; lic. psychologist. Dir., chief psychologist Caddo Parish Diagnostic Ctr., Shreveport, La., 1974-81; exec. dir. Doctors Psychol. Ctr., Shreveport, 1979-91, Comprehensive Assessments, 1991—. Cons. to Charter Forest Hosp., 1989-2000, Shreveport Impairment and Disability Evaluation Ctr., 1993—; clin. assoc. prof. psychology La. State U., Shreveport, 1977-1990; clin. assoc. prof. psychiatry La. State U. Sch. Medicine, Shreveport, 1980-92, 2003—; neuropsychol. cons. to dept. psychiatry, 1992-2002; mem. faculty Am. Acad. Disability Evaluating Physicians, 1986—, Health South Impairment Evaluation Lectr. Series, 1998—. Author: Manual for the Stress Vector Analysis Test Series, 1983, The Doctors Guide to Instant Stress Relief, 1987, Stress Management and Relaxation Training System Handbook; contbr. articles to profl. jours. and popular mags. Mem. Gov.'s Com. of 1000, La., 1979. Recipient AADEP award, 1991; Grad. Rsch. Coun. fellow, 1974. Fellow Am. Inst. Stress; mem. APA, Nat. Acad. Neuropsychology, Nat. Register of Health Svc. Providers. Episcopalian. Avocations: scuba diving, gun collecting, camping, boating, paintball competition. Home: 10816 Sunrise Pt Shreveport LA 71106-9357 Office: Comprehensive Assessments Inc 1801 Fairfield Ave Ste 300 Shreveport LA 71101-4460 Office Phone: 318-424-2354. E-mail: drtomstaats@aol.com.

STABA, EMIL JOHN, pharmacognosy and medicinal chemistry educator; b. N.Y.C., May 16, 1928; s. Frank and Marianna T. (Mack) P.; m. Joyce Elizabeth Ellert, June 19, 1954; children— Marianna, Joanna, Sarah Jane, John, Mark. BS cum laude, St. John's U., 1952; MS, Duquesne U., 1954; PhD, U. Conn., 1957. Asst. prof. U. Nebr., 1957-60, prof., chmn. dept., 1968; prof. dept. pharmacognosy U. Minn., 1968—95; interim dir. R&D Tom's of Main, Kennebunk, 1996. Pres. Plants Personified, Inc., 1995—; cons. econs. plants and plant tissue culture U.S. Army Q.M.C.; cons. on drug plants and plant tissue culture NASA; cons. N.C.I. at NIH on anti-cancer natural product prodn., 1991-92; cons. Govt. of Korea, food and pharm. industry cons. NSF-Egyptian Acad. Sci. Rsch. Tech., 1984—; internat. vis. prof. Dalhousie U., 1983; cons. on Indonesia biotech. devel. World Bank-Midwestern Univs. Consortium for Internat. Activities, 1985-90, Thailand, 1989; mem. natural products revision com. U.S. Pharmacopeia, 1980—, chair subcom. natural products, 1995-2000; mem. adv. coun. on life scis. NASA, 1984-87. Mem. editorial bd.: Jour. Plant Cell, Tissue and Organ Culture, 1980-86, plant cellular and developmental biology sect. of In Vitro, 1988— Served with USNR, 1945-46, PTO. Sr. fgn. fellow NSF, Poland, 1969; Fulbright fellow, Germany, 1970; Coun. Sci. and Indsl. Rsch.-NSF fellow, India, 1973, Pakistani Coun. Sci. and Indsl. Rsch.-NSF fellow, Pakistan, 1978; fellow U.K. Sci. Engring. Rsch. Coun., 1989. Fellow AAAS; mem. Am. Soc. Pharmacognosy (pres. 1971-72), Am. Assn. Colls. Pharmacy (chmn. tchrs. sect. 1972-73, dir. 1976-77), Tissue Culture Assn. (pres. plant sect. 1972-74), Am. Pharm. Assn. and Acad. (chmn. pharmacognosy and nat. products 1977), Soc. Econ. Botany, Am. Soc. Pharmacognosy (hon.), Am. Soc. Pharmacognosy, Plants Personified, Inc. (pres. 1995—). Home: 2840 Stinson Blvd Minneapolis MN 55418-3127 Business E-Mail: staba001@tc.umn.edu.

STABEJ, RUDOLPH JOHN, computer consultant; b. Milw., Dec. 14, 1952; s. Rudolf and Katharina (Schaab) S. BS in Acctg., U. Ill., Chgo., 1975; MBA in Fin., De Paul U., 1981, MS in Computer Sci., 1986. Gen. acct. Field Mus. Nat. History, Chgo., 1975-77, Victor Bus. Products, Chgo., 1977-80, Northrop Def. Systems, Rolling Meadows, Ill., 1981-82; programmer Fed. Reserve Bank, Chgo., 1983-84; programmer/analyst Arthur Andersen & Co., Chgo., 1984-85; cons./programmer Sycomm Systems Corp., Chgo., 1985-86; pvt. practice computer cons. Chgo., 1986—. Mem. Ind. Computer Cons. Assn., Assn. Info. Tech. Profls. Avocations: tennis, golf, stamp collecting/philately. Home: 1004 Bayshore Dr Schaumburg IL 60194-1304

STABENOW, DEBORAH ANN, senator, former congresswoman; b. Gladwin, Mich., Apr. 29, 1950; d. Robert Lee and Anna Merle (Hallmark) Greer; children: Todd Dennis, Michelle Deborah. BS magna cum laude, Mich. State U., 1972, MSW magna cum laude, 1975. With spl. svcs. Lansing (Mich.) Sch. Dist., 1972-73; county commr. Ingham County, Mason, Mich., 1975-78; state rep. State of Mich., Lansing, 1979—91, state senator, 1991—94; mem. 103rd-106th Congress from Mich. 8th dist. U.S. Ho. Reps., 1997—2001; senator State of Mich., 2001—. Founder Ingham County Women's Commn.; co-founder Council Against Domestic Assault. Recipient Service to Children award Council for Prevention of Child Abuse and Neglect, 1983, Disting. Service to Mich. Families award Mich. Council Family Relations, 1983, Outstanding Leadership award Nat. Council Community Mental Health Ctrs., 1983, Snyder-Kok award Mental Health Assn. Mich., Awareness Leader of Yr. award Awareness Communications Team Developmentally Disabled, 1984, Communicator of Yr. award Woman in Communications, 1984, Lawmaker of Yr. award Nat. Child Support Enforcement Assn., 1985, Disting. Service award Lansing Jaycees, 1985, Disting. Service in Govt. award Retarded Citizens of Mich., 1986, Boxing Glove award Nat. Com. to Preserve Social Security and Medicare, 1999, Home Health Hero Nat. Assn. for Home Care, 1999, Friend of Farm Bur. Mich. Farm Bur., 1999, Leadership award Nat. Coun. of Space Grant Dirs., 1998, Outstanding Achievement Nat. Farmers Union, 1998, Legislator of Yr. award Nat. Multiple Sclerosis Soc., 1992, Assn. for Children's Mental Health, 1991, Mich. Assn. of Vol. Adminstrs., 1989, Citizens Alliace to Uphold Spl. Edn., 1989, Recognition award State 4-H Alumni, 1991, Cmty. award Mich. Mental Health, 1988; named One of Ten Outstanding Young Ams. Jaycees, 1986. Mem. NAACP, Lansing Regional C. of C., Delta Kappa Gamma. Democrat. Office: US Senate 702 Hart Senate Office Bldg Washington DC 20510 E-mail: senator@stabenow.senate.gov.

STABER, JUDY WHITE, writer, director; b. London, Eng., Jan. 3, 1943; arrived in U.S., 1959; d. Archibald Patrick Moore and Joan White; m. Colgate Salsbury, June 10, 1964 (div. Nov. 1982); children: Abigail Salsbury Pulver, Sherrod Louise Salsbury Bailey; m. John Hermann Staber, July 13, 1991. Studied, HB Studio, N.Y.C., 1961—63. Sec., asst. Equity Libr. Theatre, N.Y.C., 1961—63; rschr. Dept. Mental Health, Berkshire County, Mass., 1974—75; journalist Berkshire Courier, Great Barrington, Mass., 1976—79; mktg. dir. Shakespeare & Co., Lenox, Mass., 1979—85; publicist Berkshire County, Mass., 1985—92; cultural tourism dir. Mass. Cultural Alliance & Tourism, Boston, 1987—88; exec. dir. Spencertown Acad. Arts Ctr., NY, 1996—. Pub. rels. cons. Williamstown Conservation Lab., Mass., 1988—92, Berkshire Mus., Pittsfield, Mass., 1987—93. Writer, prodr. (TV series) Grovers Corner, Hanukkahat, 1990—92 (Emmy nom., 1992), (plays) Pantomimes, 2000—03. Democrat. Episcopalian. Avocations: gardening, reading, cooking.

STABILE, BRUCE EDWARD, surgeon; b. Monterey Park, California, Apr. 14, 1944; s. Edward Emilio and Angela (Cramandozzi) S.; m. Caroline Graston, Sept. 18, 1967; children: Jessica, Drew. BA, UCLA, 1966; MD, U. Calif., San Francisco, 1970. Diplomate Am. Bd. Surgery. From assoc. prof. to prof. vice chmn. dept. surgery Sch. Medicine U. Calif., San Diego, 1985—93, from asst. prof. to assoc. prof. Sch. Medicine, 1977-85, vice chmn. dept. surgery Sch. Medicine, 1993—. Chmn. dept. surgery Harbor UCLA Med. Ctr., Torrance, 1993—, acting med. dir., 1997-98; interim assoc. dean UCLA Sch. Medicine, 1997-98; med. expert Med. Bd. Calif., 1980—; bd. dirs. Am. Bd. Surgery, 1998-2004. Mem. editl. bd.: Jour. Surg. Rsch., 1993—97, Archives of Surgery, 1991—2004. Fellow ACS (gov. 2001-), Am. Surg. Assn.; mem. Soc. Univ. Surgeons, Assn. Acad. Surgery, Am. Gastroenterol. Assn., San Diego Soc. Gen. Surgeons (pres. 1992-93), L.A. Surg. Soc. (pres. 2000-01). Office: Harbor U Calif at L A Med Ctr 1000 W Carson St Torrance CA 90502-2004 Office Phone: 310-222-2701.

STABLEFORD, KAREN P. library and information scientist; d. George H. Paulsen and Ruth E. Kaiser; m. William K. Stableford. Dir. devel. programming James Blackstone Meml. Libr., Branford, Conn., 1999—. Mem.: Conn. Coun. on Planned Giving, Assn. Fundraising Profls.

STABLEIN, LAWRENCE A. retail executive; MBA, DePaul U. Sr. v.p. mktg. and formats Am. Stores Properties, Inc., Salt Lake City, 1995—97; sr. v.p. mktg. Jewel-Osco, 1997—2000; exec. v.p. mktg. & mdse. Albertson's, Inc., Boise, 2000—. Office: Albertsons Inc 250 Parkcenter Blvd Boise ID 83726

STABLER, LEWIS VASTINE, JR., lawyer; b. Greenville, Ala., Nov. 5, 1936; s. Lewis Vastine and Dorothy Daisy Stabler; m. Monteray Scott, Sept. 5, 1958; children: Dorothy Monteray Scott, Andrew Vastine, Monteray Scott Smith, Margaret Langston. BA, Vanderbilt U., 1958; JD with distinction, U. Mich., 1961. Bar: Ala. 1961. Assoc. Cabaniss & Johnston, Birmingham, Ala., 1961-67; assoc. prof. law U. Ala., 1967-70; ptnr. Cabaniss, Johnston, Gardner, Dumas & O'Neal (and predecessor firms), Birmingham, 1970-91, Walston, Stabler, Wells, Anderson and Bains, Birmingham, 1991-97; pvt. practice, Birmingham, 1997—. Mem. com. of 100 Candler Sch. Theology, Emory U. Bd. editors: Mich. Law Rev, 1960-61. Fellow Am. Bar Found. (life); mem. Am. Law Inst. (life), Ala. Law Inst. (mem. coun., dir. 1968-70), ABA, Ala. Bar Assn., Birmingham Bar Assn., Am. Judicature Soc., Am. Assn. R.R. Trial Counsel, Order of Coif. Methodist (cert. lay speaker). Clubs: Country of Birmingham, Rotary. Home: 3538 Victoria Rd Birmingham AL 35223-1404 Office: PO Box 53-1161 Birmingham AL 35253-1161 Office Phone: 205-802-7290.

STABLER, SCOTT LAWRENCE, historian, educator; s. Carl L and Barbara L Stabler. Phd, Ariz. State U., 2004. Grad. instr. Ariz. State U., Tempe, Ariz., 1999—; rsch. fellow Papers of Abraham Lincoln, Springfield, Ill., 2003—03. Sunday sch. tchr. Gilbert United Meth., Gilbert, Ariz., 2003—04. Grantee Rsch. grantee, Carlisle Mil. Libr., 2003. Mem.: Orgn. of Am. Historians. Home: 77 S Monterey St Gilbert AZ 85233 Personal E-mail: stabler9@yahoo.com.

STACEY, JAMES ALLEN, retired judge; b. Norwalk, Ohio, Dec. 26, 1925; s. James Calvin and Glenna (Cleveland) S.; m. Marlyn Frederick, Aug. 21, 1948; children: James A. Jr., Libble M. Romigh, Lorrie Stacey Singler, David F., CamAllison Shenigo, Tricia Stacey Berger. Student, Bucknell U., 1943-44, Ohio Wesleyan U., 1944, 46, 47, U. N.C., 1944-45; JD, Cleveland-Marshall

Law Sch., 1951. Bar: Ohio 1952, U.S. Dist. Ct. (no. dist.) Ohio 1955. Ptnr. McGory & Stacey, Sandusky, Ohio, 1954-56; assoc. Steinemann & Zieher, Sandusky, Ohio, 1956-60; ptnr. Work, Stacey & Moyer, 1960-67; judge Sandusky Mcpl. Ct., 1967-95, ret., 1995. Mem. Ohio State Traffic Law Com., 1969-95, chmn., 1978-82. Mem. Erie-Ottawa Mental Health Bd., 1968-87; mem. Ex-Offenders for Help Bd., 1975-81; bd. dirs. Camp Fire Girls, 1956-60, L.E.A.D.S., 1984-86, Sandusky C. of C., 1984-86. Served with USNR, 1943-46. Mem. Ohio State Bar Assn., Ohio Mcpl. Judges Assn. (exec. bd. 1970-80), Am. Judicature Soc., Am. Judges Assn., Erie County Bar Assn., Amvets, Sandusky Exch. Club (bd. dirs. 1999-2004), Am. Legion, Elks, Eagles Club, Italian-Am. Beneficial Club. Republican. Presbyterian. Home: 1407 Julianne Cir Sandusky OH 44870-7032

STACEY, JAMES HENRY, writer, columnist; b. Chgo., July 26, 1935; s. John James and Mary (Hollister) S.; m. Lelia West, Feb. 4, 1956 (div. Mar. 1978); children: Nicole, Michelle; m. Carol Ann Levenson, Apr. 26, 1980. BA, Grinnell Coll., 1957; MA, San Francisco State U., 1960. Asst. editor Bus. Week, Chgo., 1966-68; lectr. Northwestern U., Evanston, Ill., 1968-71; writer, devel. officer U. Chgo., 1972-76; nat. affairs editor Am. Med. News, Chgo., 1976-83, sci. news editor, 1983-86, dir. media rels., 1986-99; freelance writer Chgo., 1999—. Author: Inside the New Temple, 1993, A Wounded Name, 2001; co-author: Severed Trust, 2001; contbr. articles to mags. Avocations: theater, travel, literature. Home: Apt 3006 260 E Chestnut St Chicago IL 60611-2464 E-mail: J.STACEY@RCN.COM.

STACEY, TRUMAN, journalist, consultant; b. Port Arthur, Tex., Dec. 8, 1916; s. James Harrison and Billie (Davis) S.; m. Dorothy Mary Piboin, May 25, 1963 (dec.); m. Norma Elaine Trahan, Feb. 2, 1980 (dec.). B in Philosophy, U. Detroit, 1946, MA, 1954. Reporter Beaumont (Tex.) Enterprise, 1937-42, Oklahoma City Daily Oklahoman, 1943-44, Detroit Free Press, 1944-45; dir. pub. rels. U. Detroit, 1945-49; reporter Washington Times Herald, 1949-50; sports editor Lake Charles (La.) Am. Press, 1950-60, editor-in-chief, 1961-82; dir. communications Diocese Lake Charles, 1982-90, pres. Coun. of Cath. Men, 1990-92. Author: Louisiana's French Heritage, 1990, The Church Visible, 2000. Mem. Calcasieu Parish (La.) Family Svc. Agy., 1979-82; coord. SW La. Citizens for Ednl. Freedom, 1968-70; bd. dirs. La. Coun. Music and Performing Arts, 1967-79, Calcasieu Citizens for Decency, 1967-69, Lake Charles Symphony Orch., 1967-69. Sgt. U.S. Army, 1942-43; mem. Mayor's Armed Forces Commn., 2003—. Decorated chevalier Order of Merit France; named to La. Sports Writers Hall of Fame, 1982, Columbian Hall of Fame, 1987; recipient Merit award, Sociedad Española de La., 1978, Silver Antelope award, Boy Scouts Am., 1979, George Washington medal of Honor, Freedom Found., 1980, Faith and Freedom award, Religious Heritage Am., Inc., 1980, Harry J. O'Haire Meml. award, Serra Internat. Found., 1987, John Donahue award, 2003, Pilgrim's Shell award, Latin Patriarch Jerusalem, 1988, Nat. Silver Merit medal, Knights of Peter Claver, 1992, Gold medal of merit, 2003, Stephen T. Victory Meml. award, La. Bar Assn, 1992, Past State Deputies award, La. K.C, 1994, Spes Mundi-O'Connell award, Internat. Cath. Com. on Scouting, 2000, Donald Millet Meml. award, S.E. La. Hist. Assn., 2001, Silver St. George emblem, Nat. Cath. Com. on Scouting, 2002, Silver medal of Merit, Sacred Mil. Constantinian Order St. George, 2002, Bishop Charles Pascal Greco Lifetime Achievement award, KC, 2004. Mem.: NCCJ (Brotherhood award 1975), La. Press Assn. (bd. dirs. 1976—79), S.W. La. Hist. Assn. (pres. 2000—02), Inst. de la Maison Royale de France, Lake Charles C. of C. (Man of Yr. 1971), Am. Soc. Newspaper Editors, AP Mng. Editors Assn., La.-Miss. AP Assn. (pres. 1962—63, Merit citation 30 Yrs. Cmty. Svc. 1980), La. Sports Writers Assn., Order St. Lazarus of Jerusalem (officer). Avocations: reading, classical music, stamp collecting/philately. Home: 1802 2nd Ave Lake Charles LA 70601-6432

STACEY, WESTON MONROE, JR., nuclear engineer, physicist, educator; b. Birmingham, Ala., July 23, 1937; s. Weston Monroe and Dorothy (Toole) S.; m. Penny Smith; children: Helen Lee, Weston Monroe III, Lucia Katherine. BS in Physics, Ga. Inst. Tech., 1959, MS in Nuc. Sci., 1963; PhD in Nuc. Engring., MIT, 1966. Nuc. engr. Knolls Atomic Power Lab., Schenectady, NY, 1962-64, 66-69; assoc. dir. applied physics divsn. and dir. fusion program Argonne Nat. Lab., Chgo., 1969-77; Callaway Regents prof. Ga. Inst. Tech., Atlanta, 1977—. Author: Modal Approximation in Reactor Physics, 1967, Space-Time Nuclear Reactor Kinetics, 1969, Variational Methods in Nuclear Reactor Physics, 1972, Fusion Plasma Analysis, 1981, Fusion, 1984, Nuclear Reactor Physics, 2001; contbr. over 230 articles to profl. jours. Recipient Cert. Appreciation Dept. Energy, 1981, 88, Disting. Assoc. award Dept. Energy, 1990, Rsch. award Sigma Xi, 1998. Fellow: Am. Nuc. Soc. (bd. dirs. 1974—77, Outstanding Achievement award 1981, 1996, Seaborg medal 2001, Wigner award 2003), Am. Phys. Soc.; mem.: AAAS, Am. Soc. Engring. Edn. Office: Ga Inst Tech Nuclear Engring Dept 0425 Atlanta GA 30332-0001 Office Phone: 404-894-3714. Business E-Mail: weston.stacey@nre.gatech.edu.

STACHEL, JOHN JAY, physicist, researcher; b. NYC, Mar. 29, 1928; s. Jacob Abraham and Bertha Z. Stachel; m. Evelyn Lenore Wassermann, Feb. 8, 1953; children: Robert, Laura, Deborah. BS, CCNY, 1956; MS, Stevens Inst. Tech., 1959, PhD, 1962. Instr. physics Lehigh U., Bethlehem, Pa., 1959-61; instr. physics U. Pitts., 1961-62, research assoc., 1962-64; asst. prof. physics Boston U., 1964-69, assoc. prof., 1969-72, prof., 1972-96; dir. Ctr. for Einstein Studies, Boston U., 1985—, prof. emeritus, 1996—. Vis. rsch. assoc. Inst. Theoretical Physics, Warsaw, 1962; vis. prof. King's Coll., U. London, 1970-71, U. Paris, 1990-91, Max Planck Inst. for History of Sci., Berlin, 1994—, Calif. Inst. Tech., 1998; vis. sr. rsch. fellow Dept. Physics, Princeton U., 1977-84; rsch. assoc. U. Calif., Berkeley, 1994. Author: Einstein from B to Z, 2002, Going Critical, 2004; editor: Selected Papers Leon Rosenfeld, 1979, Foundations of Space-Time Theories, 1977, Einstein Studies, 1989—, Collected Papers of Albert Einstein, Princeton U. Press, 1977-88, Einstein's Miraculous Year, 1998. Office: Boston U Ctr Einstein Studies 745 Commonwealth Ave Boston MA 02215-1401 Business E-Mail: stachel@bu.edu.

STACHIW, JAROSLAW (JERRY) DRAHOMYR, mechanical engineer, consultant; b. Lviv, Ukraine, May 23, 1931; arrived in U.S., 1949; s. Mathew and Frances Stachiw; m. Joan Lee Atkerson, June 5, 1955; children: Michael, Mark. BSME, Okla. State U., 1955; MS in Engring. Mechs., Pa. State U., 1961, DEd in Higher Edn., 1963. Cert. profl engr. Rsch. engr. Ordnance Rsch. Lab., State College, Pa., 1959—64, Naval Civil Engring. Lab., Port Hueneme, Calif., 1964—70; sr. engr., program mgr., staff scientist for materials Naval Undersea Ctr., Naval Command Control and Ocean Surveillance, San Diego, 1970—94; cons. Stachiw Assocs., Rockport, Tex., 1972—. Author: Acrylic Plastic Viewports, 1982, Handbook of Acrylics for Submersibles, Hyperbaric Chambers and Aquaria, 2003; contbr. articles to profl. jours. 1st lt. U.S. Army, 1957—59, Redstone Arsenal, Ala. Recipient Lauritsen Bennet award, U.S. Naval Systems Ctr., 1991. Fellow: ASME (chmn. ocean engring. divsn. 1972—73, chmn. subcom. pressure vessels for human occupancy 1972—87, hon. mem. pressure vessels for human occupancy 1987, Centennial medal 1990, Mil. Oceanographer award 1970, Pressure Tech. Codes Dedicated Svc. award 1989); mem.: Marine Tech. Soc., N.Y. Acad. Scis., Sigma Xi. Achievements include patents in field. Home and Office: 505 Copano Ridge Rd Rockport TX 78382 E-mail: j.stachiw@hydroports.com.

STACK, CHARLES RICKMAN, lawyer; b. Sept. 26, 1935; s. John Joseph and Bernadett (Rickman) S.; m. Barbara Alice Levine, Oct. 12, 1963; children: Caroline K., Kevin C., Constance K. BSBA, U. Fla., 1957. Diplomate: Nat. Bd. Trial Advocacy, cert.: Fla. Bd. Trial Certification, bar: Fla. 1960, U.S. Dist. Ct. (so. dist.) Fla. 1960, U.S. Dist. Ct. (mid. dist.) Fla., U.S. Dist. Ct. (no. dist.) Fla., U.S. Ct. Appeals (11th cir.), U.S. Supreme Ct. Fla. Assoc. Macfarlane, Ferguson, Allison & Kelly, Tampa, Fla., 1960—62; ptnr. High, Stack, Lazenby, Bender, Palahach & Lacasa, Miami, 1962—2003, sr. ptnr., 1968—2003; ptnr. High, Stack, Palahach, Cruanes & Conway, Miami, 2003—, Melbourne, Fla., 2003—. Mem., sec. U.S. Dist. Ct. Peer Rev. Commn., 1983—; instr. bus. law U. South Fla., 1960—62; instr. comml. law Am. Inst. Banking, Tampa, 1960—62. Contbr. articles to profl. jours. Mem. City of Miami Downtown Devel. Authority, 1979—82; campaign fin. chmn. Fla. Presdl. Campaign for Clinton, 1992, nat. co-chmn., 1992; trustee Nat. Dem. Party, 1993—96; Dade County campaign chmn. Reubin Askew for Gov., 1970, Steve Clark for Mayor, 1972; mem. pres.'s coun. U. Fla., Trusler Soc., Pres.'s Club; Chmn. Fla. Jud. Nominations Commn. for 11th Cir., 1970—76, chmn., 1995—96; mem. Fla. Constn. Revision Com., 1968; chmn. Fla. Corp. Income Tax Com., 1972; conf. chmn. U. Fla., Trusler Soc., Pres.'s Club, 1994. Named Dem. of Yr., Fla., 1995. Fellow: Nat Bd. Trial Advocacy; mem.: ATLA, ABA, Million Dollar Advs. Forum, Brevard County Bar Assn., Dade County Bar Assn., Com. of 100, Dade County Trial Lawyers, Tex. Trial Lawyers, Acad. Fla. Trial Lawyers, Lawyers for Pub. Justice, Leading Am. Attys., Bar Register of Pre-eminent Lawyers, Fla. Bar Assn., Am. Bd. Trial Advocacy, Univ. Club (Miami). Democrat. Episcopalian. Home and Office: 525 Strawbridge Ave Melbourne FL 32901 Office Phone: 321-725-5525.

STACK, DANIEL, lawyer, financial consultant; b. July 29, 1928; s. Charles and Gertrude (Heller) Stack; m. Jane Marcia Gordon, Apr. 18, 1953; children: Joan, Gordon. BA cum laude, Bklyn. Coll., 1949; LLB, Columbia U., 1952; LLM, Georgetown U., 1955. Bar: N.Y. 1956. Project adminstr. Am. Overseas Fin. Corp., 1957—58; asst. counsel. ABC-TV, N.Y.C., NY, 1959—60; gen. counsel IFC Securities Corp., N.Y.C., 1961—63; exec. asst. to sr. v.p. N.Y. Stock Exch., 1963—64; sec. pension com. Consol. Foods Corp., Chgo., 1967—69; v.p. legal Seaway Multi Corp. Ltd., Toronto, Canada, 1969—72; v.p. mergers and acquisitions Acklands Ltd., Toronto, 1972—74; sr. v.p., sec., counsel Greenwich Svs. Bank., N.Y.C., 1978—81; sole practice N.Y.C., 1982—85; ptnr. Brennen and Stack, N.Y.C., 1986—96; cons. venture capital, corp. fin., med. edn., health care, mining, and oil N.Y.C., 1982—. Pres. Bus. and Fin. Resources, Inc., 1982—84; adj. faculty NYU; officer and dir. various pub. cos.; bd. adv. Sch. of Bus., St. John's U.; chmn. sect. on mergers and acquisitions North Am. Soc. for Corp. Planning; lectr., guest spkr. on mergers and acquisitions Fac. of Mgmt. Studies, Univ. Toronto, 1974, SUNY, Buffalo, 1976; gen. counsel Greater N.Y. Safety Coun., 1980—. Info. officer U.S. Naval Acad., 1972—; mem. Congl. mil svc. acads. nominations com. and Civil Svc. intern selection com., 1978—. Lt. j.g. USNR, 1952—55, Capt. USNR, 1983, ret. Decorated Joint Svc. Commendation medal, Naval Order of US; scholar, N.Y. Regents, 1945—49. Mem.: N.Y. State Bar Assn., Ramapo Rep. Org. Republican. Home: 8 Linda Dr Suffern NY 10901-3004

STACK, EDWARD WILLIAM, business management and foundation executive; b. Rockville Centre, N.Y., Feb. 1, 1935; s. Edward Henry and Helen Margaret (Leitner) S.; m. Christina Carol Hunt, Aug. 19, 1967; children: Amy Alison, Kimberly Anne, Suzanne Gail. BBA, Pace U., 1956; LLD (hon.), Hartwick Coll., 1982; LHD (hon.), Pace U., 1991, L.I. U., 1994. With Clark Estates, Inc., N.Y.C., 1956-2000, pres., bd. dirs., 1990-2000. Trustee N.Y. State Hist. Assn., Cooperstown, 1975—2002, Mary Imogene Bassett Hosp., 1973—, Hartwick Coll., Oneonta, NY, N.Y. State Trooper Found.; sec. Nat. Baseball Hall of Fame and Mus., Inc., Cooperstown, 1961—77, pres., chmn., 1977—93, chmn., 1993—2000, dir., 1977—; mem. adv. bd. Salvation Army Nassau County and Greater N.Y., Ctr. for Family Life, Sunset Pk., Bklyn.; bd. dirs. Farmers' Mus., Inc., Cooperstown, The Clark Found., N.Y.C., The Scriven Found., N.Y.C., United Meth. City Soc., St. Christopher-Ottilie, Glen Cove, NY, Mental Health Assn. Nassau County. Mem. Mohican Club (Cooperstown, N.Y.). Republican. Home: 25 Waverly St Glen Head NY 11545-1004 Office: 31st Fl One Rockefeller Plaza New York NY 10020 Personal E-mail: ewstack@aol.com.

STACK, FRANK HUNTINGTON, painter, retired educator; b. Houston, Oct. 31, 1937; s. Maurice Z. and Norma Rose (Huntington) S.; m. Mildred Roberta Powell, June 12, 1959; children: Joan Elaine, Robert Huntington. BFA, U. Tex., 1959; postgrad., Sch. Art Inst. Chgo., 1960-61; MA, U. Wyo., 1963. Assoc. art editor Houston Chronicle, 1959-60; instr. U. Mo., Columbia, 1963-69, prof. art, 1969-95, Catherine P. Middlebush prof. humanities, 1995-2000, prof. emeritus, 2000—. Mem. regional adv. bd. Mo. Arts Coun., Columbia, 1979-80; mem. exec. bd. U. Mo. Art and Archaeology Mus., Columbia, 1981-84; chmn. art dept. U. Mo., Columbia, 1981-83; mem. pers. com. U. Mo. Columbia Arts and Sci. Coll., Columbia, 1976-80; vis. artist W.Va. Arts Coun. and Exxon, Shepherd Coll., Shepherdstown, W.Va., 1983. Artist, author: (cartoons) The New Adventures of Jesus, 1963-95, (book of cartoons) Dorman's Doggie, 1990; illustrator artist: (graphic novel) Our Cancer Year, 1994 (Best Graphic Novel Harvey award 1995), Naked Glory: erotic art of Frank Stack. 1997; artist traveling exhibit Watercolors by Frank Stack, 1977-79; editor: (collection of comic strips) Alley Oop, 3 vols. 1946-47, 47-48, 48-49, 1990, 93, 95 (nominated Best Reprint 1991, 94, 96); mem. dv. bd. Jour. Cartoon and Comic Art, 1984—; contbg. writer The Comics Jour., 1989—. Mem. mus. rev. bd. U. Mo., 4 campus sys., Columbia, 1989. With U.S. Army, 1960-62. Recipient Rsch. Grants, U. Mo. Rsch. Coun., Columbia, 1969, 85, 93, 98, Gov.'s Arts awards Artist of Yr. Mo. Arts Coun., St. Louis, 1986. Mem. Kans. Watercolor Soc. (awards 1992, 96), Columbia Art League (adv. bd. 1978-82), Mo. Watercolor Soc. (award 2003). Avocations: historical research, art history, newspaper comics of 1930's and 40's, collector of master prints. Home: 409 Thilly Ave Columbia MO 65203-3458 Personal E-mail: stackf@missouri.edu.

STACK, GEOFFREY LAWRENCE, real estate developer; b. Trinidad, Brit. West Indies, Sept. 16, 1943; s. Gerald Francis and V. Louise (Bell) S.; m. Victoria Hammack, 1970 (div. 1986); 1 child, Kathryn; m. Nancy J. Haarer, Apr. 19, 1987; children: Alexandra, Natalie. BA, Georgetown U., 1965; MBA, U. Pa., 1972. Dir. acquisitions J.H. Snyder Co., L.A., 1972-75; from project mgr. to exec. v.p. Richards West, Newport Beach, Calif., 1975-77; pres. Regis Homes Corp., Newport Beach, 1977-93; mng. dir. Sares-Regis Group, Irvine, Calif., 1993—. Bd. dirs. Arral & Ptnrs., Hong Kong, Calif. Housing Coun., Sacramento, Tejon Ranch Co. Chmn. bd. dirs. Nat. Multihousing Coun., 1987—; trustee Urban Land Inst. Capt. USMC, 1967—70. Decorated 2 Bronze Stars, 21 Air medals, Navy Commendation medal, Purple Heart. Mem. Young Pres. Orgn., Big Canyon Country Club, Pacific Club, Olympic Club. Democrat. Roman Catholic. Office: SARES REGIS Group 18802 Bardeen Ave Irvine CA 92612-1521 Office Phone: 949-756-5959. Business E-Mail: jstack@sares-regis.com.

STACK, GEORGE JOSEPH, philosopher, writer; b. N.Y.C. s. George Francis and Elizabeth (Sullivan) S.; m. Mary K. Di Maria, July 25, 1997; children: Diane, Christopher, stepchildren: Jena, Shelley. BA, Pace U., 1960; MA, Pa. State U., 1962, PhD, 1964. Instr. humanities Pa. State U., 1962-63; instr. philosophy L.I. U., 1963-64, asst. prof., 1964-67, SUNY, Brockport, 1967-68, asso. prof., 1968-70, prof., chmn., 1970-77, 1985—94, prof., 1994—95, prof. emeritus, 1995—, also advisor Center for Philosophic Exchange, 1970-82. Cons. Choice. Author: Berkeley's Analysis of Perception, 1970, reprinted, 1991, On Kierkegaard: Philosophical Fragments, 1976, Kierkegaard's Existential Ethics, 1977;: 2d edit., 1992, Japanese transl., 1985, Sartre's Philosophy of Social Existence, 1978, reprinted, 1992, Lange and Nietzsche, 1983, Nietzsche and Emerson, 1992; contbg. author Nietzsche and Modern German Thought, 1991, Emerson/Nietzsche, 1998, The Emerson Enigma, 2003; editl. advisor: Folia Humanistica, 1970—97; contbr. numerous articles and reviews to profl. jours. Office: PO Box 92 Grapevine TX 76099-0092

STACK, J. WILLIAM, JR., management consultant; b. Lansing, Mich., July 13, 1918; s. Joseph William and Helen (Dodge) S.; m. Wolcott Rorick, Sept. 25, 1948; children: Christopher D., Nathan S., Joseph W., David R., Peter S. BA, Yale U., 1940. With Gen. Motors Corp, 1945-57; dir. mktg. Gen. Motors Corp (AC Electronics div.), 1955-57; v.p. Kurth Malting Co., Milw., 1957-59; gen. sales mgr. Massey Ferguson, Inc., Toronto, Can., 1960-62; pres., founder Stancor Ltd., Toronto, 1963-68; pres. William Stack Assocs. Inc., N.Y.C., 1968-98. Mem. Navy and Marine Corps Acquisition Rev. Com., 1974-75. Active Rep. Town Com. Lt. comdr. USNR, 1940-45. Mem. Yale Club of N.Y.C., New Canaan Country Club. Episcopalian. Home: 3185 Meadow Ridge Redding CT 06896-3227 E-mail: MSTACK@aol.com. *Success is measured by what you give back; not what you take. To help one person, to advance one worthy cause is the mark of total achievement.*

STACK, MAURICE DANIEL, retired insurance company executive; b. N.Y.C., Dec. 15, 1917; s. Maurice E. and Margaret (Brooks) S.; m. Catherine T. O'Connor, Nov. 25, 1943; children: Mary Jane, Eileen, Peter, Clare. Student, U. Notre Dame, 1935-36; BBA, Manhattan Coll., 1939; MBA, Harvard, 1941. Investment analyst Carnegie Corp., N.Y.C., 1946-48; adminstrv. asst. Tchrs. Ins. & Annuity Assn., 1948-49; investment analyst First Nat. Bank N.Y., 1949-54; fin. sec. Atlantic Mut. Ins. Co., N.Y.C., 1954-56, v.p., 1957-60, fin. v.p., trustee, 1961-66, chmn. fin. com., 1966-83. Trustee emeritus Atlantic Mutual Ins. Co. Trustee emeritus, adviser St. Vincent's Hosp.; trustee emeritus YWCA. Maj., C.E., AUS, 1941-46. Mem. K.M. Club (N.Y.C.), Harvard Club (N.Y.C.). Home: 85 Lynbrook Ave Point Lookout NY 11569-0095

STACK, PAUL FRANCIS, lawyer; b. Chgo., July 21, 1946; s. Frank Louis and Dorothy Louise Stack; m. Nea Waterman, July 8, 1972; children: Nea Elizabeth, Sera Waterman. BS, U. Ariz., 1968; JD, Georgetown U., 1971. Bar: Ill. 1971, U.S. Ct. Claims 1975, U.S. Tax Ct. 1974, U.S. Ct. Internat. Trade 1977, U.S. Supreme Ct. 1975. Law clk. U.S. Dist. Ct., Chgo., 1971-72; asst. U.S. atty. No. Dist. Ill., Chgo., 1972-75; mng. dir. Stack & Filpi, Chgo., 1976—. Bd. dirs. Riverside (Ill.) Pub. Libr., 1977-83, Suburban Libr. Sys., Burr Ridge, Ill., 1979-82; mem. Mayor's ad hoc adv. com. on Ctrl. Libr., Chgo., Ill., 1987-88; mem. bd. edn. Twp. H.S. Dist. 208, Riverside, Ill., 1989-97; pres. Village of Riverside, Ill., 1997-2001; mem. exec. com. Chgo. Area Transp. Study, 1999-2001. Mem. Chgo. Zool. Soc. (gov. 1980—, planned giving adv. com. 1996-99), Chgo. Bar Assn., Union League Club of Chgo. (bd. dirs. 1986-89). Home: 238 N Delaplaine Rd Riverside IL 60546-2035 Office: 140 S Dearborn St Ste 411 Chicago IL 60603-5201

STACK, ROBERT TIMOTHY, health facility administrator; b. Pitts., 1952; m. Mary Stack; 3 children. BA, Bethany (W.Va.) Coll., 1952; MA, Med. Coll. Va., 1977. Asst. adminstr. Southside Hosp., Pitts., 1977-79; sr. v.p., COO Cen. Med. Ctr., Pitts., 1980-81; pres., CEO Southside Hosp., Pitts., 1981-87, Borgess Health Alliance Inc., Kalamazoo, 1987—2001, Piedmont Med. Ctr., Atlanta, 2001—03, MedQuist Inc., Marlton, NJ, 2003—. Mem.: bd. dirs., MedQuist Inc., 1997-2000, 2003-, bd., American Hosp. Assoc., 1999-2001, bd. dirs., Piedmont Med. Ctr., 1997-2000. Office: MedQuist Inc Corp Offices 5 Greentree Centre Ste 311 Marlton NJ 08053

STACK, STEPHEN S. manufacturing executive; b. DuPont, Pa., Apr. 25, 1934; s. Steve and Sophie (Baranowski) Stasenko; m. Lois Sims Agnew, May 25, 1996. *During twentieth century flu pandemic, fraternal grandfather died November, 1918, in Denver, Colo. when father was 7 years-old. Mother was orphaned at age 6, when both her parents died the very same month in Dupont, Pa. Fraternal grandmother remarried and relocated to Dupont. This created opportunity for parents to meet, marry, relocate, and give birth to Stephen. Growing up in Erie, Pa., he was an honor student, lettered athlete, scout camp leader, and Lake Erie lifeguard who rescued over 20 drowning swimmers. In college, owned and operated Seven Student Dry Cleaning Service.* BSME, Case Western Res. U., 1956; postgrad., Syracuse Univ. registered profl engr., Ill. Mech. engr. Kaiser Aluminum, Erie, PA, 1956-58; instr. Gannon Univ., Erie, PA, 1958-60, Syracuse U., NY, 1960-61; engrg. supr. A.O. Smith Corp., Erie and Los Angeles, 1961-66; gen. mgr. Am. Elec. Fusion, Chgo., 1966-67; mgr.new products Maremont Corp., Chgo., 1967-69; dir. market planning Gulf and Western Ind., Bellwood, IL, 1969-71; mgmt. and fin. cons. Stack & Assocs., Chgo., 1971-76; pres. Seamcraft, Inc., Chgo., 1976—. Mem. Ill. Legis. Small Bus. Conf., 1980, Gov.'s Small Bus. Adv. Commn., 1984-94, Ill. State House Conf. on Small Bus., 1984, 86, 99; chmn. West Cell, 1988-2000, Bridge Pers. Svcs. Corp., 1989—; vice pres. Ind. Bus. Assn. Ill., 1993-94; mem. small bus. adv. counc. Fed. Res. Bank of Chgo., 1989-91, Nat. Fedn. Ind. Bus. mem. 1980—, mem. Ill. State. Leadership Coun. 1999-, del. White House Conf. on Small Bus., 1986, Nat. Small Bus. Attitudes Rsch. Panel, 1987-, pres. Chgo. Marine Heritage Soc., 1999—, mem. Navy League of the U.S., 1991—, del. Congl. Small Bus. Summit, 1998, 2000, 02, 04; with Ill. Small Bus. Leadership Coun., 2000—. *SeamCraft is an ISO 9001 certified, industrial sewing company employing about 50 people. It was started in 1958 and produces custom sewn OEM accessories (cases, covers, bags) and components for products made by other companies. The company produces for "low-tech" products such as auto jacks, air compressors, sales kits, volting booths, A/C units, batteries, etc.; as well as "hi-tech" items like micro-computers, blood analyzers, water purifiers, lasers, radar detectors, heart monitors, and IV infusers.* Treas. Sem. Townhouse Assn., 1993-94; active Lincoln Park Conservation Assn., Sheffield Neighbors Assn.; mem. adv. coun., DePaul U. Coll. Commerce, 2000—. Recipient Am. Legion awd., 1948, Case Western Res. U. Honor key, 1956, Eagle Scout awd., 1949. Mem. Ill. Mfrs. Assn. (bd. dirs. 1986-98, vice chmn. 1995-98), Small Mfrs. Action Couns. (vice chmn. 1986-87, chmn. 1988-89), Mfrs. Polit. Action Com. (exec. com. 1987-98, vice chmn. 1993-95, chmn. 1995-98), Am. Mgmt. Assn., Pres. Assn., Blue Key, Beta Theta Pi, Theta Thau, Pi Delta Epsilon. Chgo. Yacht Club, East Bank Club, Fullerton Tennis Club (pres. 1971-79, treas. 1979-83, bd. dirs. 1983-86), Lake Shore Ski Club (v.p. 1982, 91), Lincoln Park Tennis Assn. Patentee in liquid control and metering fields. Office: 932 W Dakin St Chicago IL 60613-2922

STACKELBERG, JOHN RODERICK, history professor; b. Munich, May 8, 1935; came to U.S., 1946; s. Curt Freiherr and Ellen (Biddle) von Stackelberg; m. Steffi Heuss, Oct. 10, 1965 (div. Apr. 1983); m. Sally Winkle, Mar. 30, 1991; children: Katherine Ellen, Nicholas Olaf, Emmet Winkle. AB, Harvard U., 1956; MA, U. Vt., 1972; PhD, U. Mass., 1974. Reading instr. Baldridge Reading Svcs., Greenwich, Conn., 1957-62; lang. tchr. Hartnackschule, Berlin, 1963-67; English and social studies tchr. Lake Region Union High Sch., Orleans, Vt., 1967-70; lectr. history San Diego State U., 1974-76; asst. prof. history U. Oreg., Eugene, 1976-77, U. S.D., Vermillion, 1977-78, Gonzaga U., Spokane, Wash., 1978-81, assoc. prof. history, 1981-88, prof. history, 1988—, Powers prof. of humanities, 1997—. Author: Idealism Debased, 1981, Hitler's Germany: Origins, Interpretations, Legacies, 1999, (with Sally A. Winkle) The Nazi Germany Sourcebook: An Anthology of Texts, 2002; contbr. articles to profl. jours. Pres. Spokane chpt. UN Assn., 1986-90. With U.S. Army, 1958-60. Leadership Devel. fellow Ford Found., 1969-70. Avocations: chess, tennis. Home: 530 W 24th Ave Spokane WA 99203 Office: Gonzaga U Dept History Spokane WA 99258-0001 Office Phone: 509-747-2077. E-mail: rodstackelberg@comcast.net.

STACKHOUSE, EUNICE WONDERLY, education educator, musician; b. Kans. City, Kans., Apr. 4, 1951; d. Daniel Earl and Edna Giese Wonderly; m. Stefan Brent Stackhouse, July 2, 1979. MusB Edn., Grace Coll., Winona Lake, Ind., 1973; MusM in Piano, Ind. Univ., Bloomington, Ind., 1976; Mus D, Univ. Kans., Lawrence, Kans., 1995; piano study, Univ. Indpls., 1984—88, harpsichord study, 1986—88. Adj. instr. Univ. Indpls., 1986—88, Crown Coll., St. Bonifacius, Minn., 1988—89, Sterling Coll., Sterling, Kans., 1989—91; asst. prof. music Tabor Coll., Hillsboro, Kans., 1991—92; adj. prof. Grove City Coll., Pa., 1993—94; asst. prof. music Ind. Univ. of Pa., Ind., Pa., 1995—96; assoc. prof. music Montreat Coll., NC, 1996—. Chair fine arts dept. Montreat Coll., Montreat, NC, 2001—; piano competition adj. various, 1988—. Contbr. articles pub. to profl. jour.; editor: (piano works) Three Bagtelles; author: conf. presentations (symposium) Women in Music, 1995; musician: (songs) (solo paino recitals) various coll. Pianist numerous music orgns., 1977—; workshop presenter music orgns., 1989; musician various ch., 1977—. Mem.: Minn. Music Tchrs. Assn., Asheville Piano Assn., Coll. Music Soc., N.C. Music Tchrs. Assn. (v.p. MTNA Found. 2000—, v.p. 1996—), Pi Kappa Lambda. Republican. Presbyn. Avocations: sewing, cooking, crafts, walking. Office: Montreat Coll PO Box 1267 Montreat NC 28757

STACKHOUSE, JERRY, professional basketball player; b. Kinston, N.C., Nov. 5, 1974; Student, N.C. U., 1997. Basketball player Phila. 76ers, 1995—98, Det. Pistons, 1997—2002, Washington Wizards, 2002—04, Dallas Mavericks, 2004—. Named to NBA All-Star Game, 2000, 2001. Office: c/o Dallas Mavericks The Pavillion 2909 Taylor St Dallas TX 75226*

STACKHOUSE, MAX LYNN, religious studies educator; b. Ft. Wayne, Ind., July 29, 1935; s. C. Dale and Naomi Elizabeth (Graham) S.; m. N. Jean Hostetler, Aug. 19, 1959; children: Dale Emil, David Graham, Sara Elizabeth. BA, De Pauw U., 1957, LHD (hon.), 1995; cert., Nijenrode U., Breukelen, The Netherlands, 1958; BD, MDiv, Harvard U., 1961, PhD, 1965. Ordained to ministry United Ch. of Christ, 1961. Lectr. Harvard Divinity Sch., Cambridge, Mass., 1964-66; asst. prof. Andover-Newton (Mass.) Theol. Sch., 1966-69,

assoc. prof., 1969-73, prof., 1973-78, Herbert Gezork prof., 1978-93; Stephen Colwell prof. Princeton (N.J.) Theol. Sem., 1993—2004, Rimmer and Ruth de Vries prof. theology and pub. life, 2004—. Vis. prof. United Theol. Coll., Bangalore, India, 1973, 76, 82, 87, 2000, Pacific Theol. Coll., Suva, Fiji, 1982, Das Sprackenkonvikt, East Berlin, 1983; pres. joint doctoral program Boston Coll. and Andover Newton Theol. Sch., 1988-89, chmn. rels. and soc. dept., 1975-93; dir. Kuyper Ctr. for Pub. Theology, 1994—; pres. Berkshire Inst. Theology and Arts, 1991—. Author: Creeds, Society and Human Rights, 1984, Public Theology and Political Economy, 1987, Apologia, 1988 (Best Booklist Internat. Bull. Missiology 1988), On Moral Business, 1994, Christian Ethics in a Global Era, 1996, Covenant and Committments, 1998, God and Globalization, vol. 1, 2000, vol. 2, 2001, vol. 3, 2002; author, editor 11 books; mem. editl. bd. Jour. Religious Ethics, Christian Century; contbr. articles to profl. jours. Investigation team Am. Com. for Human Rights, Philippines, 1984; pres. James Luther Adams Found., 1987-93; exec. sec. Am. Com. for Higher Edn. in India, 1986-91; dir. Kuyper Ctr. Pub. Theology, 1998—. Rsch. grantee Ctr. for Urban Studies, Harvard U., 1965-66, Assn. Theol. Schs., 1986-87, Lilly Endowment, Indpls., 1989, 91, Pew Charitable Trusts, 1993, 98; recipient Outstanding Alumnus award DePauw U., 1988. Fellow Soc. for Sci. Study of Religion (bd. dirs. 1980-84), Soc. for Values in Higher Edn.; mem. NAACP, Amnesty Internat., Am. Theol. Assn., Soc. Christian Ethics (past pres., past exec. sec.), Stockbridge Club. Democrat. Office: Princeton Theol Sem PO Box 821 Princeton NJ 08542-0803 Office Phone: 609-497-7898.

STACKPOLE, KERRY CLIFFORD, association executive; b. Putnam, Conn., Feb. 24, 1955; s. Howard Thompson Stackpole and Shyrlee Gladys Burr; m. Miriam Weisberg, July 29, 1984. MEd, Cambridge Coll., 1983. Gen. mgr. E.J. Ardon Co., Boston, 1978-82; ops. mgr. Fotobeam/Brookside, Waltham, Mass., 1982-83; assoc. dir. Printing Industries of New Eng., Natick, Mass., 1983—, v.p., 1989-91; exec. dir. Smaller Bus. Assn. New Eng., Waltham, Mass., 1991-93; pres., CEO The Assn. for Work Process Improvement, Inc., 1993-97, Electronic Messaging Assn., 1997—2000; chmn. CEO Neoterica Ptnrs., LLP, McLean, Va., 2000—. Bd. dirs. Mass. Cert. Devel. Corp., EC Inst., Denver; mem. U.S. C. of C. Com. of 100, 2000—. Recipient HIRE Trust Fund award Graphic Arts Employers of Am., 1987, 2000. Fellow Am. Soc. Assn. Execs. (cert., mem. ann. meeting adv. com. 1996-97, mem. edn. com., 1996-99, chmn., exec. mgmt. sect. coun., 1997-98, bd. dirs., 1997-98, mem. key industries assn. com. 2000—); mem. Assocs. Advance Am. Com. (chmn. 1999-2000), New Eng. Soc. Assn. Execs. (committeeman 1983-84, membership devel. com. 1989-91, chmn. edn. com. 1991-93, bd. dirs. 1991—, treas.-sec. 1994-95, chmn.-elect 1995, chmn. bd. dirs. 1996—, immediate past chmn, 1997-98, Ralph Louis Towne award 1986). Avocations: reading, cross country skiing, ocean kayaking, jazz music buff. Office: Neoterica Ptnrs LLP PO Box 7763 Mc Lean VA 22106

STACOM, DARCY A. real estate company executive; d. Matthew and Claire Stacom; m. Chris Kraus. Degree in mktg., Lehigh U., 1980. Lic. comml. real estate agent. Capital markets intermediary Cushman & Wakefield, Inc., N.Y.C., 1980—2000; exec v.p. Cushman Wakefield, Inc., N.Y.C., 2000—02; exec v.p. and ptnr. investment properties institutional group CB Richard Ellis, 2002—. Bd. dirs. Comml. Real Estate Women N.Y., mem. adv. com. Mem. adv. coun. Acad. Woman Achievers of YWCA; fundraiser United Way; mem. women's bd. Madison Sq. Boys & Girls Clubs, 1999—. Named one of Top 100 Women in Bus. in N.Y.C., Crain's N.Y. Bus. Mag. Mem.: Real Estate Bd. of N.Y. (bd. govs. 2001—). Office: CB Richard Ellis Group Inc 200 Park Ave New York NY 10166*

STACY, BILL WAYNE, academic administrator; b. Bristol, Va., July 26, 1938; s. Charles Frank and Louise Nelson (Altwater) S.; m. Sue Varnon; children: Mark, Sara, James. BSEd., S.E. Mo. State U., 1960; MS, So. Ill. U., 1965, PhD, 1968. Tchr. Malden High Sch., Mo., 1960-64; faculty Southeast Mo. State U., Cape Girardeau, 1967-89, dean Grad. Sch., 1976-79, interim pres., 1979, pres., 1980-89, Calif. State U., San Marcos, 1989-97; chancellor U. Tenn., Chattanooga, 1997—2004; headmaster Baylor Sch., Chattanooga, 2004—. Bd. dirs. River Valley Ptnrs. Bd. dirs. United Way; mem. Allied Arts Bd. Mem. Am. Assn. Higer Edn., Chattanooga C. of C. (bd. dirs.). Presbyterian. Office: Baylor Sch PO Box 1337 Chattanooga TN 37401

STACY, CURTIS ALAN, secondary school educator; b. Richlands, Va., Apr. 12, 1952; s. Virgil Ile and Leona Ruth Stacy; m. Betty Hurley, June 11, 1971; 1 child, Candice Ann Dull. BS in Chemistry, U. of Va., Wise, 1974; MA in Ednl. Adminstrn., Va. Poly. Inst. and State U., 1992. Tchr. Powell Valley H.S., Big Stone Gap, Va., 1975—78; prin./tchr. Wise County Christian Sch., Norton, Va., 1978—80; tchr. Hurley H.S., Va., 1980—2000. Bd. dirs. Buchanan Neighbors United, Grundy, Va., 2000—04, Wesley Found.-U. Va., Wise, 2002—04. Methodist. Home: 516 Vine St Lebanon VA 24266 Office: Richlands High School Tornado Alley Richlands VA Personal E-mail: curtis_stacy@earthlink.net.

STACY, DENNIS WILLIAM, architect; b. Council Bluffs, Iowa, Sept. 22, 1945; s. William L. and Mildred Glee (Carlsen) S.; m. Judy Annette Long, Dec. 28, 1968; 1 child: Stephanie. BArch, Iowa State U., 1969; postgrad., U. Nebr., 1972. Registered arch., Iowa, Tex., Colo., Mo. Designer Troy & Stalder Archs., Omaha, 1967, Archs. Assocs., Des Moines, 1968-69, Logsdon & Voelter Archs., Temple, Tex., 1970; project arch. Roger Schutte & Assocs., Omaha, 1972-73; arch., assoc. Robert H. Burgin & Assocs., Council Bluffs, 1973-75, Neil Astle & Assocs., Omaha, 1975-78; owner, prin. Dennis W. Stacy, AIA, Arch., Glenwood, Iowa, 1978-81; pres. Stacy Archs., Inc., Dallas, 1981—2001, Stacy Archtl. Studio, PLLC, 2002—. Mem. organizing com. symposiums Tex. A&M U., 1991—2004. Archtl. works include: Davies Amphitheater, 1980, Addison Nat. Bank Bldg., 1985, Villa Roma, 1988, C.U. Performing Arts Ctr., 1989, Mercedes-Benz Distbn. Ctr., 1987, Dallas Chpt. AIA Offices, 1990, Janadria Festival Arena, 1994, Physicians Consultants Clinic, 1994, Horizon Pain Mgmt. Ctr., 1995, Rheumatology Assoc. Clinic, 1996, Addison Nat. Br. Bank, 1996, Cummins Southern Plains Distbn., Fabrication and Corp. Offices Ctr., 1998, Arthur Murray Dance Studio, 2001, Tatum Residence, 2001. Mem. City of Dallas Urban Design Adv. Com., 1992-96, chmn., 1995-96; dir. Greater Dallas Planning Coun., 1997-2004; chmn. Glenwood Zoning Bd. Adjustment, 1979-81; chmn. Mills County Plant Iowa Program, 1979-81; mem. S.W. Iowa Citizen's Adv. Com., Iowa State Dept. Transp., 1977-81; regional screening chmn. Am. Field Svc. Internat./Intercultural Programs, 1974-79, Iowa-Nebr. rep., 1978-80. With U.S. Army, 1969-71. Decorated Nat. Def. Svc. medal, Vietnam Svc. medal, Vietnam Campaign medal, Army Commendation medal, Disting. Alumnus Design Achievement award Iowa State U., 1999; recipient Design Achievement award Iowa State U., 1999. Fellow AIA (chmn. nat. conv. 2000, recipient Iowa Design Honor award 1981, Dallas AIA commendation awards (2) 1990, 92, 95, 96, 97, 98, citation of honor award 1991, 92, 2001, Dallas Design awards (2) 1991, 96, 97, Tex. Design Honor award 1992, Dallas AIA Firm of Yr. award 1992, Nat. Presdl. Citation 2000, Dallas commr. design 1991, chmn. Dallas design awards 1992, pres. Dallas AIA 1996), Tex. Soc. Archs. (environ. resource com. 1994-95, chmn., Tex. arch. pub. com., 1992-98, chmn. 1997, 98), Nat. Coun. Archtl. Registration Bds., Iowa State U. Adv. Coun., 1997-2000, chmn. 1999-00, The 500 Inc. (outstanding mem. 1985), Glenwood Optimist Club (Disting. Svc. award 1982, pres. 1980-81), Masons. Home and Office: 4148 Cobblers Ln Dallas TX 75287-6725 Office Phone: 972-250-1909. Personal E-mail: dstacyarch@aol.com.

STACY, FRANCES H. federal judge; b. 1955; BA, Baylor Univ., 1977; JD, Baylor Law Sch., 1979. With U.S. Atty.'s Office (Tex. so. dist.) Criminal Divsn., 1980, Civil Rights Divsn., 1980-81, Land and Resources Divsn., 1981-87, Civil Divsn., 1987-88, Appelate Divsn., 1988-90; magistrate judge U.S. Dist. Ct. (Tex. so. dist.), 5th circuit, Houston, 1990—. Author: Federal Civil Procedure Before Trial, Lawyers Cooperative Practice Guide. Mem. Tex. Bar Found. Office: Fed Bldg 515 Rusk St Ste 7727 Houston TX 77002-2600

STACZEK, JOHN JOSEPH, academic administrator, consultant; b. Toledo, Mar. 1, 1943; s. John Louis and Marilyn Kosnikowski Staczek; m. Camille Mikulak Mikulak, June 16, 1965; children: Jason Luis, Eric Jon. AB, Ohio State U., 1965; MS, Georgetown U., 1970, PhD, 1973. Dir. applied linguistics Georgetown U., Washington, 1990—97; chmn. modern langs. Thunderbird, Glendale, Ariz., 1997—2000, v.p. for faculty, 1999—2001, dir. global svcs., 2001—. Cons. Kuwait U., 1980—92. Editor: (academic research) On Spanish, Portuguese, and Catalan Linguistics, Perspectives on Bilingualism and Bilingual Education. NSF Traineeship, Georgetown U., 1970—72, Sr. Fulbright Professorship, Nicaragua, Coun. for Internat. Ednl. Exch., 1971—72, Sr. Fulbright Professorship, Colombia, 1975, Sr. Fulbright Rsch. Professorship, Poland, 1994. Mem.: Am. Dialect Soc. Democrat. Roman Catholic. Avocations: golf, travel, hiking. Home: 36 E Paint Your Wagon Trail Phoenix AZ 85085 Office: Thunderbird Am Grad Sch Internat Mgmt 15249 N 59th Ave Glendale AZ 85306-6000 Personal E-mail: staczekj@t-bird.edu. E-mail: staczekj@t-bird.edu.

STADD, COURTNEY, federal agency administrator; With EarthWatch, Inc.; spl. asst. for space commercialization U.S. Dept. Commerce; dir. Office of Comml. Space Transp., U.S. Dept. Transp.; sr. dir. comml. space policy White House Nat. Space Coun.; founder, pres. PixSell Data Brokers Inc., Miss.; acting dep. assoc. adminstr. Office Advanced Concepts and Tech.' NASA, Washington, spl. asst. to adminstr., leader transition team, chief of staff. White House liaison. Bd. dirs. Alaska Aerospace Devel. Corp. Recipient pub. svc. award, Wash. Space Bus. Roundtable, Lloyd V. Berkner award, Am. Astron. Soc., 1994. Mem.: AIAA (sr.). Office: NASA Hdqrs Mail Code A 300 E St SW Washington DC 20546

STADDON, JOHN ERIC RAYNER, psychology, zoology, neurobiology educator; b. Grayshott, Hampshire, Eng. came to U.S., 1960; s. Leonard John and Dulce Norine (Rayner) S.; m. Lucinda Paris. BSc, Univ. Coll., London, 1960; PhD, Harvard U., 1964. Asst. prof. psychology U. Toronto, Ont., Can., 1964-67; from asst. prof. to prof. Duke U., Durham, NC, 1967-72, prof., 1972-83, J.B. Duke prof. psychology, prof. neurobiology and biology, 1983—. Author: Adaptive Behavior and Learning, 1983, The New Behaviorism, 2001, Adaptive Dynamics, 2001; editor Behavioural Processes, 1979-2001, Behavior and Philosophy, 1993-2004; mem. editl. bd. Jour. Exptl. Analysis of Behavior, 1979-82. Recipient von Humboldt prize, 1985. Fellow AAAS, N.Y. Acad. Scis., Soc. Exptl. Psychologists; mem. Phi Beta Kappa (hon.), Sigma Xi. Avocations: history, philosophy of science, public policy. Office: Duke U Dept Psychol and Brain Scis PO Box 91050 Durham NC 27708 E-mail: staddon@psych.duke.edu.

STADE, GEORGE GUSTAV, humanities educator; b. NYC, Nov. 25, 1933; s. Kurt Herman and Eva Bergit (Aronson) S.; m. Dorothy Louise Fletcher, Dec. 16, 1957; children: Bjorn, Eric, Nancy, Kirsten. BA, St. Lawrence U., 1955; MA, Columbia U., 1958, PhD, 1965. Tchr. Collegiate Sch., NYC, 1957-58; instr. Bernard Baruch Sch. Bus., NYC, 1958-59, Bklyn. Poly. Inst., 1959-60, Rutgers U.-Newark, 1960-62, Columbia U., NYC, 1962, asst. prof., 1965, assoc. prof., 1968, prof. English, 1971—. Cons. various law firms, NYC, 1960— Author: Robert Graves, 1967, Confessions of a Lady-Killer, 1979; editor: European Writers, 13 vols., Selected Letters of E.E. Cummings, 1968, Six Modern British Writers, 1974, Six Contemporary British Writers, 1976, European Writers: Selected Authors, 3 Vols., 1992, British Writers Supplement II, 1992, British Writers Supplement III, 1995, British Writers Supplement IV, 1997, consulting editl. dir. of Barnes and Noble Classics; contbr. over 100 articles and reviews, consulting edit., dir. of Barnes and Noble Classics. Mem. PEN, NY Book Critics Circle, Popular Culture Assn., MLA Home: 430 W 116th St New York NY 10027-7220 Office: Columbia U 604 Philosophy Hall New York NY 10027 Office Phone: 212-854-6410. E-mail: ggs3@columbia.edu.

STADELMAN, WILLIAM RALPH, chemical institution executive; b. Ont., Can., July 18, 1919; s. John Joseph and Lillian (Trachsell) S.; m. Jean MacLaren, Nov. 2, 1951; 1 child, Mary Laren. BASc, U. Toronto, 1941; MBA, U. Pa., 1949. Chief process engr. Can. Synthetic Rubber, Ltd., 1943-47; lectr. mktg. U. Pa., 1948-49; asst. to mgr. Pa. Salt Mfg. Co., 1950; sec.-treas. Ont. Research Found., Mississauga, 1950-64, pres., 1964-84, WRS Assocs., 1984—; dir., sr. exec. Inst. Chem. Sci. and Tech., 1985-89. Dir. Med. Tech. Investment Corp. Fellow World Acad. Art and Sci.; mem. Assn. Profl. Engrs. Ont., Innovation Mgmt. Assn. Can., Bd. Trade Met. Toronto, Club of Rome, Caledon Ski Club. Home and Office: WRS Assocs 31 Rykert Crescent Toronto ON Canada M4G 2T1 Office Phone: 416-425-4126.

STADELMANN, EDUARD JOSEPH, plant physiologist, educator, researcher; b. Graz, Austria, Sept. 24, 1920; s. Eduard Joseph and Josefa (Eigner) S.; m. Ok Young Lee, Mar. 22, 1975. BS, Bundesrealgymnasium, Graz, Austria, 1939; PhD, U. Innsbruck, Austria, 1953; Pvt. Docent, U. Freiburg, Switzerland, 1957; PhD (hon.), Agrl. U. Vienna, 1989. Sr. asst. U. Freiburg, 1962-63; rsch. assoc. U. Minn., Mpls., 1963, asst. prof., 1964-66, assoc. prof., 1966-72, prof. hort. sci., 1972-91, prof. emeritus, 1991—. Muellhaupt Scholar in Biology, Ohio State U., 1958-59; Humboldt Found. awardee, 1974-75; Fulbright award, Coun. Internat. Exchange, 1979-80, 87-88. Mem. Am. Inst. Biology, Am. Soc. Plant Physiologists, German Bot. Soc., Swiss Bot. Soc., Sigma Xi. Roman Catholic. Office: Univ Minn Dept Hort Sci 1970 Folwell Ave Saint Paul MN 55108-6007 E-mail: estadelm@tc.umn.edu.

STADLER, CRAIG ROBERT, professional golfer; b. San Diego, June 2, 1953; s. Donald Edwin and Betty M. (Adams) S.; m. Susan Barrett, Jan. 6, 1979; children: Kevin Craig, Christopher Barrett. Student, U. So. Calif. Profl. golfer PGA, Palm Beach Gardens, Fla., 1975—; winner Hope Classic, 1980, Greater Greensboro Open, 1980, Kemper Open, 1981-82, Tucson Open, 1982, Masters, 1982, World Series of Golf, 1982, 92, Canon European Masters, 1985, Dunlop Phoenix, Japan, 1987, Scandinavian Enterprise Open, 1990, Tour Championship, 1991, NEC World Series of Golf, 1992, Argentine Open, 1992, Buick Invitational Calif., 1994, Nissan Open, 1996. U.S. amateur champion, 1973; mem. (nat. teams) U.S. Walker Cup, 1975, U.S. vs. Japan, 1982, Ryder Cup, 1983, 85; mem. PGA Tour Charity Team, Nissan Open, 1999; leading money winner PGA Tour, 1982; inductee Breithard Hall of Fame, San Diego, 1996. Mem. Golf Mag. (Player of Yr. 1982) Avocations: skiing, hunting.

STADLER, DONALD ARTHUR, management engineer; b. Youngstown, Ohio, Dec. 14, 1943; s. Donald Arthur and Phyllis Helena (Lee) S.; m. Patricia McDonald, July 15, 1978; children: Jennifer, Jason. BA, Marquette U., 1966. Mgmt. analyst State of Vt., Montpelier, 1970-72; adminstr. Vt. State Dept. Health, Burlington, 1972-73; v.p. Planned Performance Co. Inc., Turnersville, N.J., 1973-79; pres. Performance Mgmt. Systems Inc., Roanoke, Va., 1979-82; chief analyst Leonhardt-Sullivan & Assocs. Inc., Tequesta, Fla., 1982-86; pres. D.A. Stadler Assocs., Inc., Roanoke, 1986-98; dir. Resource Mgmt. Corp., Boca Raton, Fla., 1997-2000, ptnr., 2001—. Mktg. cons. Planned Performance Co. Inc., Turnersville, 1984-86; performance cons. Resource Mgmt. Corp., 1995-97; novelist, 2003—. Served as sgt. U.S. Army, 1966-69. Mem. Mensa, Intertel. Clubs: Roanoke Rifle and Revolver. Roman Catholic. Avocation: competitive pistol shooter. Home and Office: 3918 St James Cir Roanoke VA 24018-2428 E-mail: dastadler@aol.com., dastadler@rmc-usa.com.

STADLER, GERALD P. transportation executive; b. 1937; married. Student, Loyola U. Sec. United Van Lines, Fenton, Mo., 1981-84, vice chmn., 1984—, also bd. dirs. Office: United Van Lines Inc 1 United Dr Fenton MO 63026-2578

STADLER, KATHERINE LOY, advertising sales executive; b. N.Y.C., Mar. 26, 1930; d. William L. and Catherine Stadler. Student, St. John's U., 1948-49, Hunter Coll., 1957-59, NYU Mgmt. Inst., 1963-69. Br. mgr. Hull Travel Service, Inc., N.Y.C., 1959-63; with Loire Imports, Inc., N.Y.C., 1963-69; dist. mgr. Sweet's divsn. McGraw-Hill Info. Sys. Co., N.Y.C., 1969-74; nat. sales mgr. Floor Covering Weekly, N.Y.C., 1974-76; account exec. Ziff-Davis Pub. Co., Hotel and Travel Index, L.A., 1976-81; founder Katherine Stadler & Assocs., 1981—83; regional mgr. Modern Salon, 1984-94; founder, CEO Bone Cancer Internat., Inc., 1999—. Mem. Nat. Cancer Inst./Consumer Advocates in Rsch. and Related Activities. Mem. Med. Mission Sisters, Roman Catholic. Ch., 1949-57; mem. Early Music Ensemble L.A., 1985-87; mem. Thousand Oaks Coun. on Aging, 2003-04. Named Sweet's Eastern Region Salesman of Yr., 1972, Salesman of Yr., Vance Pub., 1992. Mem. Nat. Assn. Profl. Saleswomen, L.A. Ad Club, Toastmasters. Home: 22 Robertson Way Newbury Park CA 91320-3939 Office Phone: 805-480-3551.

STADTER, PHILIP AUSTIN, classicist, educator; b. Cleve., Nov. 29, 1936; s. John M. and Mary Louise (Jones) S.; m. Lucia Angela Ciapponi, July 6, 1963; children: Paul, Maria, Mark. BA, Princeton U., 1958; MA, Harvard U., 1959, PhD, 1963. Instr. U. N.C., Chapel Hill, 1962-64, asst. prof., 1964-67, assoc. prof., 1967-71, prof., 1971—, chmn. dept. classics, 1976-86, prof. comparative lit., 1991—2003, Falk prof. humanities, 1991—2003, prof. emeritus, 2003—. Author: Plutarch's Historical Methods, 1965, The Public Library of Renaissance Florence, 1972, Arrian of Nicomedia, 1980, A Commentary on Plutarch's Pericles, 1989; editor: The Speeches of Thucydides, 1973, Plutarch and the Historical Tradition, 1992, Sage and Emperor, 2003. Fulbright fellow Rome, 1960-61; Guggenheim fellow Florence, Italy, 1967-68; NEH fellow, 1974-75; fellow Am. Council Learned Socs., Oxford, Eng., 1982-83 Fellow Nat. Humanities Ctr.; mem. Am. Philol. Assn. (dir. 1977-80), Am. Assn. Ancient Historians, Soc. Promotion of Hellenic Studies, Classical Assn. Middle West and South Democrat. Roman Catholic. Office: U NC Dept Classics Chapel Hill NC 27599-3145

STADTHERR, MARK A. chemical engineer, educator; B in Chem. Engring., U. Minn., 1972; PhD in Chem. Engring., U. Wis., 1976. Faculty U. Ill., Urbana-Champaign, 1976-95; chem. engring. faculty U. Notre Dame, Ind., 1996—. Presenter in field. Contbr. articles to profl. jours. Recipient Xerox award for engring. rsch., 1982, Computing in Chem. Engring. award AIChE, 1998; named GTE Emerging scholar lectr. U. Notre Dame, 1986. Achievements include research on advanced computational strategies for process engineering, application of interval analysis to chemical engineering problems, environmentally conscious process design. Office: Dept Chem Engring Univ Notre Dame Notre Dame IN 46556 Fax: 574-631-8366. E-mail: markst@nd.edu.

STADTLER, WALTER EDWARD, diplomat; b. N.Y.C., Apr. 4, 1936; s. Walter Henry and Paula (Nagl) S.; m. Maida Maria Macdonald, Mar. 4, 1937; children: Fiona, Walter Jr., Catriona. Student, Sorbonne U., Paris, 1955-56; AB, Fordham U., 1957; postgrad., Columbia U., 1957-58. With Dept. State, 1962—; vice consul Am. Consulate, Southampton, Eng., 1962-63; third sec. Am. Embassy, London, 1963-64, econ. officer, second sec. Bonn, Fed. Republic of Germany, 1966-69; personnel officer Dept. State, Washington, 1966-69; second sec. Am. Embassy, Pretoria, South Africa, 1969-72, charge' d'affaires then dep. chief of mission, 1982-85, first sec. Addis Ababa, Ethiopia, 1972-75, Stockholm, 1975-78; European affairs advisor U.S. Mission UN, N.Y.C., 1978; mem. Royal Coll. Def. Studies, London, 1979; counselor Am. Embassy, Bonn, Fed. Republic of Germany, 1980-82; mem. Sr. Seminar, Washington, 1985-86; ambassador Am. Embassy, Cotonou, Benin, 1986-90; v.p. Nat. Def. U., Ft. McNair; sr. fellow Office of the Sec. of Def., 1992—94; U.S. mem. Internat. Def. Adv. Bd. for the Baltic Republic, 1995—2000; prof. and dir., program on peacekeeping policy George Mason U., Fairfax, Va., 1995—2000; bd. chair Geodata Systems, Inc., 1999—. Bd. mem. Nat. Def. U. Found.; mem. Coop. Housing Found., Coun. on Standards for Interat. Edn. Travel. Served to capt. U.S. Army, 1958-62. Mem. Am. Fgn. Service Assn., Army and Navy Club. Roman Catholic. Avocations: music, travel, fgn. policy and polit. mil. hist. Office: 7063 Wyndale St NW Washington DC 20015-1428 Office Phone: 202-363-9894. E-mail: walter.stadtler@digicola.com.

STADTMAN, EARL REECE, biochemist, researcher; b. Carrizozo, N.Mex., Nov. 15, 1919; s. Walter William and Minnie Ethyl (Reece) Stadtman; m. Thressa Campbell, Oct. 19, 1943. BS, U. Calif., Berkeley, 1942, Ph.D, 1949. With Alcan Hwy. survey Pub. Rds. Adminstrn., 1942—43; rsch. asst. U. Calif., Berkeley, 1938—49, sr. lab. technican, 1949; AEC fellow Mass. Gen. Hosp., Boston, 1949—50; chemist lab. cellular physiology Nat. Heart Inst., 1950—58, chief enzyme sect., 1958—62, section chief lab. biochemistry, 1962—. Biochemist Max Planck Inst., Munich, Pasteur Inst., Paris, 1959—60; faculty dept. microbiology U. Md.; prof. biochemistry grad. program dept. biology Johns Hopkins U.; adv. com. Life Scis. Rsch. Office, Am. Fedn. Biol. Sci., 1974—77; chmn. dept. biochemistry Found. Advanced Edn. Scis., 1966—68; biochem. study sect. rsch. grants NIH, 1959—63; Julius Schultz Meml. vis. prof. U. Miami, 2002. Editor: Jour. Biol. Chemistry, 1960—65, Current Topics in Cellular Regulation, 1968—, Circulation Rsch., 1968—70; exec. editor: Archives Biochemistry and Biophysics, 1960—2001, Life Scis., 1973—75, Procs. NAS, 1975—81, Trends in Biochem. Rsch., 1975—78; mem. editl. bd. Biochemistry, 1969—76, 1981—. Recipient medallion, Soc. de Chemie Biologique, 1955, U. Pisa, 1966, Presdl. Rank award as Disting. Sr. Exec., 1981, Rsch. award, Am. Aging Assn., 1992, Lifetime Achievement and Mentoring award, NIH, 1998, Sci. and Humanity prize, Oxygen Club Calif., 2002, Trevor Slater award, Soc. for Free Rabical Rsch., 2002. Mem.: NAS (award in microbiology 1970), Washington Acad. Scis. (award biol. chemistry 1957, Nat. medal sci. 1979, meritorious exec. award 1980, Robert A. Welch award in chemistry 1991, Paul Glenn award in aging 1993), Am. Soc. Microbiology, Am. Acad. Arts and Scis., Am. Soc. Biol. Chemists (publs. com. 1966—70, coun. 1974—77, pres. 1983—, Merck award 1983), Am. Chem. Soc. (exec. com. biol. div 1959—64, chmn. div. 1963—64, Paul Lewis Lab. award in enzyme chemistry 1952, Hillebrand award 1969). Office: Nat Heart and Lung Inst 9000 Rockville Pike Bethesda MD 20892-0001 Office Phone: 301-496-4096. Business E-Mail: erstadtman@nih.gov.

STADTMAN, THRESSA CAMPBELL, biochemist; b. Sterling, N.Y., Feb. 12, 1920; d. Earl and Bessie (Waldron) Campbell; m. Earl Reece Stadtman, Oct. 19, 1943. BS, Cornell U., 1940, MS, 1942; PhD, U. Calif., Berkeley, 1949. Rsch. assoc. U. Calif., Berkeley, 1942-47, Harvard U. Med. Sch., Boston, 1949-50; biochemist Nat. Heart, Lung and Blood Inst. NIH, USPHS, HHS, Bethesda, Md., 1950—. Mem. Burroughs-Wellcome Fund Toxicology Adv. Commn., 1994-97; pres. Internat. Soc. Vitamins and Related BioFactors, 1998—. Editor Jour. Biol. Chemistry, Archives Biochemistry and Biophysics, Molecular and Cellular Biochemistry; editor-in-chief Bio Factors, 1991-95; contbr. articles on amino acid metabolism, methane biosynthesis, vitamin B12 biochemistry, selenium biochemistry to profl. jours. Helen Haye Whitney fellow Oxford U., Eng., 1954-55; Rockefeller Found. grantee U. Munich, 1959-60; recipient Rose award, 1987, Klaus Schwarz medal, 1988, Life Achievement Women in Sci. award L'Oreal-UNESCO, 2000, Bertrand medal and prize Assn. European Trace Elements and Metals in Biology and Medicine, Venice, 2001. Mem. NAS, Am. Soc. Microbiology, Biochem. Soc., Soc. Am. Biochemists, Am. Chem. Soc., Am. Acad. Arts and Scis., Sigma Delta Epsilon (hon.). Home: 16907 Redland Rd Derwood MD 20855-1954 Office Phone: 301-496-3002. Business E-Mail: tcstadtman@nih.gov.

STADTMAN, VERNE AUGUST, former foundation executive, editor; b. Carrizoso, N.Mex., Dec. 5, 1926; s. Walter William and Minnie Ethel (Reece) S.; m. Jackolyn Carol Byl, Aug. 26, 1949; children: Kristen Karen, Rand Theodore, Judith Dayna, Todd Alan. AB, Calif.-Berkeley, 1950. AUS, 1945-47; mng. editor Calif. Monthly, Calif. Alumni Assn., Berkeley, 1950-64; centennial editor U. Calif., Berkeley, 1964-69; assoc. dir., editor Carnegie Commn. on Higher Edn., Berkeley, 1969-73, Carnegie Council on Policy Studies in Higher Edn. Berkeley, 1973-80; v.p. gen. services Carnegie Found. for Advancement Teaching, Princeton, N.J., 1980-89. Trustee Editorial Projects Edn., Inc., 1957-91, pres., 1962-63, chmn. bd., 1980-86; guest scholar Hiroshima U., Japan, 1978 Author: California Campus, 1960, University of California, 1868-1968, 1970, Academic Adaptations, 1980; editor: (with David Riesman) Academic Transformation: Seventeen Institutions Under Pressure, 1973 (Book of Yr. award Am. Council Edn.); compiler-editor: Centennial Record of the University of California, 1967. Served with AUS, 1945-47. Recipient Alumnus Service award Calif. Alumni Assn., 1970 Mem. Am. Alumni Council (pres. 1963-64). Home: 182 Saint James Dr Sonoma CA 95476-8336

STADTMUELLER, JOSEPH PETER, federal judge; b. Oshkosh, Wis., Jan. 28, 1942; s. Joseph Francis and Irene Mary (Kilp) S.; m. Mary Ellen Brady, Sept. 5, 1970; children: Jeremy, Sarah. BS in Bus. Adminstrn., Marquette U., 1964, JD, 1967. Bar: Wis. 1967, U.S. Supreme Ct. 1980. With Kluwin, Dunphy, Hankin and McNulty, 1968-69; asst. U.S. atty. Dept. Justice, Milw.,

1969-74, 1st. asst. U.S. atty., 1974-75; with Stepke, Kossow, Trebon and Stadtmueller, Milw., 1975-76; asst. U.S. atty. Dept. Justice, 1977-78, dep. U.S. atty., 1978-81, U.S. atty., 1981-87; judge U.S. Dist. Ct. (ea. dist.) Wis., Milw., 1987—, chief judge, 1995—2002. Mem. 7th Cir. Jud. Coun., 1995—2002. Recipient Spl. Commendation award Atty. Gen. U.S., 1974, 80. Mem. ABA, State Bar Wis. (bd. govs. 1979-83, exec. com. 1982-83), Am. Law Inst., Fed. Judges Assn. (bd. dirs. 1995—, sec. 2001--). Clubs: University (Milw.). Republican. Roman Catholic. Office: 471 US Courthouse 517 E Wisconsin Ave Milwaukee WI 53202-4500

STAEHELIN, LUCAS ANDREW, cell biology educator; b. Sydney, Australia, Feb. 10, 1939; came to U.S., 1969; s. Lucas Eduard and Isobel (Malloch) S.; m. Margrit Weibel, Sept. 17, 1965; children: Daniel Thomas, Philip Roland, Marcel Felix. Dipl. Natw., Swiss Fed. Inst. Tech., Zurich, 1963, PhD in Biology, 1966. Research scientist N.Z. Dept. Sci. and Indsl. Research, 1966-69; research fellow in cell biology Harvard U., Cambridge, Mass., 1969-70; asst. prof. cell biology U. Colo., Boulder, 1970-73, assoc. prof., 1973-79, prof., 1979—. Vis. prof. U. Freiburg, 1978, Swiss Fed. Inst. Tech., 1984, 92, U. Melbourne, Australia, 1998; mem. cellular biology and physiology study sect. NIH, Bethesda, Md., 1980-84; mem. DOE panel on rsch. directions for the energy bioscis., 1988, 92; mem. NSF adv. panel for cellular orgn., 1994-96; mem. plant biology panel NASA. Editor Jour. Cell Biology, 1977-81, European Jour. Cell Biology, 1981-90, Plant Physiology, 1986-92, Plant Jour., 1991-97, Biology of the Cell, 1996-99, Planta, 2003—; editor: (with C.J. Antzen) Encyclopedia of Plant Physiology, Vol. 19, Photosynthesis III, 1986; contbr. numerous articles to sci. jours. Recipient Humboldt award Humboldt Found., 1978, Sci. Tchr. award U. Colo., 1984, Outstanding Faculty award U. Colo.-Boulder Parents Assn., 2001, Highly Cited Rschr. ISI, 2004; grantee NIH, 1971-, USDA, 1994-, NASA, 1997-; hon. sr. fellow U. Melbourne, Australia, 1998. Mem. AAAS, Am. Soc. Cell Biology, Am. Soc. Plant Physiology, German Acad. Natural Scis. Leopoldina. Home: 2855 Dover Dr Boulder CO 80305-5305 Office: Dept Molecular Cell U Colo 347 UCB Boulder CO 80309-0347 Office Phone: 303-492-8843. E-mail: staeheli@colorado.edu.

STAEHLE, ROBERT L. foundation executive; b. Rochester, NY, Apr. 22, 1955; s. Henry Carl and Isabel Montgomery S. BS in Aero. and Astronautic Engring., Purdue U., 1977. Prin. investigator Skylab Expt. ED-31 (bacteria aboard Skylab), NASA/Marshall Space Flight Center, Huntsville, Ala., 1972-74, student trainee engring., 1974-77; sci. observation analyst Caltech/Jet Propulsion Lab., Pasadena, Calif., 1977-78, engr. advanced projects group, 1978-83, mem. tech. staff system integration sect. of Space Sta., 1983-87, mem. tech. staff and space sta., user ops. team leader, 1987-88; tech. mgr. Jet Propulsion Lab., Pasadena, Calif., 1988—90, mgr. space sta. Freedom support office Pasadena ops., 1990-92, Pluto team leader, 1992-93, mgr. Pluto Express preproject, 1993-96, mgr. Ice and Fire preprojects, 1996-98, dep. mgr. outer planets/solar probe project, 1998-2000, dep. mgr. Europa Orbiter project, 2000—02, dep. mgr. X2000 Advanced Avionics project, 2002—03, prin. info. sys. and software divsn., 2003—. Prin. founder, pres. World Space Found., South Pasadena, Calif., 1979—; founding dir. So. Calif. Space Bus. Roundtable, 1987-95; bd. dirs. Altadena Foothills Conservancy, 2000—. Co-author: Project Solar Sail, New Am. Libr., 1990; contbr. articles to profl. jours. Mem. Cmty. Leaders Adv. Bd. for Irvine Scholars, Occidental Coll., L.A., 1996-97; bd. dirs. Caltech Y, 1987-93. Nat. Space Club Goddard scholar, 1977; Charles A. Lindbergh Fund grantee, 1986. Fellow Brit. Interplanetary Soc.; mem. AIAA, Tau Beta Pi, Sigma Gamma Tau. Avocations: photography, hiking, mountain biking. Office: Jet Propulsion Lab Pasadena CA 91109 Business E-Mail: robert.l.staehle@jpl.nasa.gov.

STAELIN, DAVID HUDSON, electrical engineering educator, consultant; b. Toledo, May 25, 1938; s. Carl Gustav and Margaret E. (Hudson) S.; m. Ellen Mahoney, June 16, 1962; children: Carl H., Katharine E., Paul H. SB, MIT, 1960, SM, 1961, ScD in Elec. Engring., 1965. Instr. elec. engring. MIT, Cambridge, 1965, asst. prof., 1965—69, assoc. prof., 1969—76, prof., 1976—, asst. dir. Lincoln Lab. Lexington, 1990—2001. Vis. asst. scientist Nat. Radio Astronomy Obs., Charlottesville, Va., 1968-69; cons. Jet Propulsion Lab., Pasadena, Calif., 1969, Wellesley, Mass., 1965—; dir. Environ. Rsch. and Tech., Inc., Concord, Mass., 1969-78; co-founder, chmn. PictureTel Corp., Peabody, Mass., 1984-87; mem. com. on radio frequency requirements for rsch., NAS, Washington, 1980-86, chmn. 1983-86; chmn. advanced microwave sounder working group NASA, Washington, 1981-82, mem. space applications adv. com., NASA, 1983-86; mem. adv. com. info. tech. Pres. U.S., Washington, D.C., 2003—. Co-author: Made in America, 1989, Electromagnetic Waves, 1994; contbr. articles to profl. jours. Fellow IEEE, AAAS; mem. Am. Geophys. Union, Am. Meteorl. Soc., Internat. Union for Radio Sci. Achievements include patents for grinding and polishing sheet glass, display of dynamic images, ribbon-beam cathode ray tube. Office: MIT Rm 26-341 Cambridge MA 02139

STAELIN, RICHARD, business administration educator; b. Larchmont, NY, Aug. 3, 1939; s. Richard Carl and Dorothy (Potts) S.; m. Julie Ann Fischer, Aug. 24, 1963; children: Adam, Kate. BSME, U. Mich., 1961, BS in Math., 1962, MBA, 1963, PhD, 1969. Market planner IBM, Harrison, NY, 1963-66; prof. Carnegie-Mellon U., Pitts., 1969-82; Edward and Rose Donnell prof. Duke U., Durham, NC, 1982—, assoc. dean faculty affairs, 1982-91, assoc. dean exec. edn., 2000—02, dep. dean, 2002—04; exec. dir. Teradata CRM Ctr., 2004—; mng. dir. GEMBA, 1995-97; exec. dir. Mktg. Sci. Inst., Cambridge, Mass., 1991-93. Vis. prof. Australian Grad. Sch., Kensington, 1980—81. Author: Consumer Protection Legislation and the U.S. Food Industry, 1980; mem. editl. bd. Jour. Mktg. Rsch., 1974-82, Jour. Consumer Rsch., 1976-87; area editor Mktg. Sci., 1983-88; editor-in-chief Mktg. Sci., 1995-97. Mem. Pitts. Exec. Bd.; treas. Pitts. Arts and Crafts Ctr., 1976-79; bd. dirs. Dispute Settlement Ctr., Chapel Hill, NC; bd. vis. drama dept. Duke U., 1990-96. Recipient Best Mktg. Paper award Inst. Mgmt. Sci., 1985, hon. mention, 1986, NCNB Faculty award 1990, AMA/Irwin Disting. Mktg. Educators award, 1996, O'Dell award for Best Paper JMR, 1998; HEW grantee, 1972-74, NSF grantee, 1973-79. Mem.: INFORMS, Assn. Consumer Rsch., Am. Mktg. Assn. (Converse award 2000). Office: Fuqua Sch of Bus Science Dr Rm 339 Durham NC 27706-2597 Office Phone: 919-660-7824. E-mail: rick@staelin.com.

STAFEIL, JEFF, corporate financial executive; BS in Acctg., Ind. U.; MBA, Duke U. CPA. Various positions Mobil Corp.; acct. Peterson Consulting, Ernst & Young; cons. Boz, Allen & Hamilton; v.p., corp. controller Heartland Indsl. Ptnrs.; v.p. Metaldyne, Plymouth, Mich., 2001, CFO, 2001—. Office: Metaldyne 47603 Halyard Drive Plymouth MI 48170

STAFF, JOEL V. energy executive; BA, U. Tex., Austin; MBA, Tex. A&M U., Kingsville. Various fin. and gen. mgmt. positions Baker Hughes, Inc., 1976—93; chmn., pres., CEO Nat. Oilwell, Inc., 1993—2001; chmn., CEO Reliant Resources, Inc., Houston, 2003—; also bd. dirs. Bd. dirs. Nat. Oilwell, Inc., Ensco Internat., Inc.; adv. dir. King Chapman & Broussard; devel. bd. U. Tex. Health Sci. Ctr., Houston. Adv. dir. Boys and Girls Club, Houston. Office: Reliant Energy Exec Offices PO Box 2286 Houston TX 77252-2286*

STAFFARONI, ROBERT J. lawyer; b. Sept. 19, 1952; BA, Yale U., 1973; JD, U. Pa., 1976. Bar: N.Y. 1978. Mem. Debevoise & Plimpton LLP, N.Y.C. Mem. N.Y. State Bar Assn. Office: Debevoise & Plimpton LLP 919 Third Ave 45th Fl New York NY 10022

STAFFIER, PAMELA MOORMAN, psychologist; b. Passaic, N.J., Dec. 7, 1942; d. Wynant Clair and Jeannette Frances (Rentzsch) Moorman; m. John Staffier, Jr., Apr. 5, 1975; children: M. Anthony, C. Matthew. BA, Bucknell U., 1964; MA in Psychology, Assumption Coll., Worcester, Mass., 1970, CAGS, 1977; PhD, Union Inst., 1978. Psychologist Westboro (Mass.) State Hosp., 1965; prin. psychologist, also asst. to supt., 1973-76; psychologist Moriarty Mental Health Clinic; psychiat. cons. local gen. hosp. Rsch. psychologist Wrentham (Mass.) State Sch., 1966, Cushing Hosp., Framingham, Mass., 1967; prin. psychologist, also asst. to supt. Grafton (Mass.) State Hosp., 1967-72; dir. Staffier Clinic, 1978—. Mem. Am. Psychol. Assn. (assoc.), Am. Psychol. Practitioners Assn. (founding mem.), Mass. Psychol. Assn., Nat. Register Health Svc. Providers in Psychology. Achievements include research on state hosp. closings, biochem. basis of Schizophrenia. Home: 68 Adams St Westborough MA 01581 Office: 57 E Main St Westborough MA 01581-1464 Office Phone: 508-366-0406.

STAFFIERI, VICTOR A. energy company executive; BA, Yale U., 1977; JD, Fordham U., 1980. From atty. to gen. counsel L.I. Lighting Co., Hicksville, N.Y., 1980-92; sr. v.p., gen. counsel, corp. sec. LG&E Energy Corp., Louisville, 1992, sr. v.p. pub. policy, gen. counsel, 1992-93, pres. Louisville Gas and Electric Co., 1993-97, pres. distbn. svcs. divsn., 1995-97, CFO, 1997-99, pres., COO, 1999—. Bd. trustees Bellarmine Coll., 1995—; co-chair Jefferson County-Louisville Area C. of C. Family Bus. Partnership, 1996-97; bd. dirs. Ky. Country Day, 1996—, Metro United Way, 1998—. Mem. Louisville Area C. of C. (bd. dirs. 1994-97). Office: LG&E Energy Corp Dept Corp Comm 220 W Main St Louisville KY 40202

STAFFORD, ARTHUR CHARLES, medical association administrator; b. Cleve., May 10, 1947; s. Charles Arthur and Florence Mildred (Hovey) S.; m. Patricia Anne Cz, Dec. 20, 1991. BS, Kent State U., 1977; MBA, Lake Erie Coll., 1984. Med. tech. VA, Cleve., 1977-81, supr. med. tech., 1981-97; lab. mgr. Univ. Hosps. Health System Meml. Hosp. of Geneva, Ohio, 1998-99; instr. Lake Erie Coll., Painesville, Ohio, 1980-82; mgr. customer svc. Giant Eagle Supermarket, Madison, Ohio, 2001—02; instr. Cuyahoga C.C., Cleve., 1988-91, 2003—. Pres. Kent State U. Veterans Assn., 1974, mem. Kent State U Budget Review Com., 1975. Contbr. articles to profl. jour. Mem. Am. Legion, 1974, VFW, 1973. With USN, 1968-72. Mem.: Rock and Roll Hall of Fame, Founders Club. Republican. Avocations: genealogy, computers, antiques, chess, cooking. Home: 2193 Chimney Ridge Dr Madison OH 44057-2588 E-mail: czstafford@ncweb.com.

STAFFORD, DEBBIE, state representative; widowed; 3 children; 2 stepchildren. Student, Pikes Peak Inst. Med. Tech., Nazarene Bible Coll., World Wide Coll. Auctioneering. Ordained min.; approved domestic violence counselor Colo. State rep. Colo. Ho. of Reps., Denver, state ho. dist. 40, 2000—; vice chair, health, environment, welfare and instns. com. Colo. State Senate, Denver, mem. transp. and energy com. Republican. Office: State Capitol # 320 200 E Colfax Ave Denver CO 80203

STAFFORD, DONALD GENE, chemistry professor; b. Valliant, Okla., Oct. 9, 1930; s. Otto Lewis and Rose Lavelle (Osterdock) S.; m. Jane Wright, July 5, 1951; children— Michael Royce, Robert Gene, Joel Dan. BS, U. Okla., 1957, PhD, 1969; MS, Okla. State U., 1961. Prof. sci. edn. East Cen. U., Ada, Okla., 1961-73, prof. chemistry, 1973—. Adj. prof. U. Okla., Norman, 1970—. Author: The Improvement of Science in Oklahoma (7-12), 1970, Guidelines and Successful Practices in Elementary Edn, 1970, Wings for a Dinosaur, 1972, Early Childhood Resource Book, 1972, Teaching Science in the Elementary School, 1973, 3d edit., 1979, Teaching Science in the Secondary School, 1973, Research, Teaching, and Learning with the Piaget Model, 1976, Investigations in Physical Science, 1976, The Learning Science Program K-6 (7 children's books and 7 tchr.'s guides), 1976, TOP, The Oklahoma Project, Chemistry, 1987, The Learning Cycle, 1988, The Lost City of Balee, A Novel for Young Teenagers, 2000, Don's Rhymes, A Book of Poetry, 2000. Served with AUS, 1948-53. Mem. Am. Chem. Soc., Nat. Sci. Tchrs. Assn., Okla. Sci. Tchrs. (pres. 1973-74, 78-79), Sigma Xi. Home: 2202 Fullview Dr Ada OK 74820-4436 E-mail: donjane@cableone.net.

STAFFORD, EARL W. technology executive; m. Amanda Boardley; children: Earl Jr., Jessica, Mark. B in Fin., U. Mass.; MBA, So. Ill. U. Commd. 2d lt. USAF; ret.; mgr. bus. ops. for small bus.; asst. Dept. of Def. liaison officer FAA, 1982-85; pres., CEO, Universal Sys. & Tech., Inc., Fairfax, Va., 1988—. Chmn. bd. dirs. No. Va. Urban League. Office: Universal Sys & Tech 12450 Fair Lakes Cir Fairfax VA 22033-3810

STAFFORD, FRANK P. economist, educator; b. 1962; married; 3 children. BA, Northwestern U., 1962; MBA, U. Chgo., 1964, PhD, 1968. Asst. prof. econs. U. Mich., 1966—71, assoc. prof., 1971—73, 1974—75, prof., 1978—, chmn., 1980—83. Spl. asst. for econ. affairs Office Asst. Sec. Policy, Eval. and Rsch. Dept. Labor, Washington, 1975—76, mem. small grants panel, 1978—80; vis. assoc. prof. Stanford U., 1973—74; vis. prof. U. Saarlands, Saarbruken, Germany, 1986; vis. scholar Worklife Study Ctr., Stockholm, 1988; rschr. Indsl. Inst. for Econ. and Social Rsch., Stockholm, 1979, Stockholm, 84. Editor (with F. Thomas Juster): Americans' Use of Time, 1982; bd. editors: Am. Econ. Rev., 1976—78; contbr. articles to profl. jours. Home: 3535 Daleview Dr Ann Arbor MI 48105-9686

STAFFORD, FRANK PETER, JR., economics educator, consultant; b. Chgo., Sept. 17, 1940; s. Frank Peter and Ida Gustava (Tormala) S.; m. Lilian Elisabeth Lundin, Aug. 8, 1964; children: Craig Peter, Jennifer Elisabeth, Christine Anna BA, Northwestern U., 1962; MBA, U. Chgo., 1964, PhD, 1968. Asst. prof. econs. U. Mich., 1966-71, assoc. prof., 1971-73, 74-75, prof., 1976—, chmn. dept. econs., 1980—, rsch. scientist Inst. Social Rsch., 1995—, chair budget study com., 1995—, assoc. dir. Inst. for Social Rsch., 2000—. Vis. assoc. prof. Grad. Sch. Bus.-Stanford U., 1973-74; spl. asst. for econ. affairs U.S. Dept. Labor, Washington, 1975-76; vis. prof. dept. econs. U. Saarlandes, Fed. Republic Germany, 1986; faculty rsch. assoc. Inst. Social Rsch., Ann Arbor, 1979—; vis. scholar Indsl. Inst. for Econs. and Social Rsch., Stockholm, 1979, 83, 90, Worklife Study Ctr., Stockholm, 1988, 90; Tinbergen Found. prof. U. Amsterdam, 1992, 94; panel mem. Social Sci. Rsch. Coun., N.Y.C., 1979—; rsch. assoc. Nat. Bur. Econ. Rsch., Cambridge, Mass., 1983—; prof. econs. Tinbsrgne Found. U. Amsterdam, 1992; vis. scholar U. Stockholm, 1994. Author, editor: Time Use Goods and Well Being, 1986, Studies in Labor Market Behavior: Sweden and the United States, 1981; mem. editorial bd.: Am. Econ. Rev., 1976-78; contbr. articles to profl. jours. Dir. Panel Study of Income Dynamics, 1995—. Grantee NSF, 1973, 80, 95—, NICHD, 1995—, Nat. Ins. on Aging, 1999—. Mem. Am. Econs. Assn. Home: 3535 Daleview Dr Ann Arbor MI 48105-9686 Office: U Mich Dept Econs Lorch Hall Rm 312 Ann Arbor MI 48105 Office Phone: 734-936-0323.

STAFFORD, J. FRANCIS CARDINAL, archbishop; b. Balt., July 26, 1932; s. F. Emmett and Mary Dorothy Stafford. Student, Loyola Coll., Balt., 1950—52; BA, St. Mary's Sem., Balt., 1954; STB, STL, Gregorian U., Rome, 1958; MSW, Cath. U., 1964; postgrad., Rutgers U., 1963, St. Mary's Sem. and Univ., Balt., 1973—75. Spiritual moderator Ladies of Charity Ch., Balt., 1966—76; spiritual moderator Soc. St. Vincent de Paul, Balt., 1965—76; urban vicar Archdiocese of Balt., 1966—76, monsignor, 1970, vicar gen., auxiliary bishop, 1976—82; bishop Diocese of Memphis, 1982—86; archbishop Archdiocese of Denver, 1986—96; pres. Pontifical Coun. Laity, 1996—2003; elevated to cardinal, 1998—; mem. Major Penitentiary, Apostolic Penitentiary, 2003—. Archdiocesan liaison Md. Cath. Conf., Balt., 1975—78; Oriental Orthodox/Roman Cath. cons. Nat. Cath. Conf. Bishops, 1977—85, com. on doctrine, 1978—82, chmn. ecumenical and interreligious affairs com., 1987—90; co-chmn. bilateral dialogue Roman Cath./World Meth. Coun., 1977—86; co-chmn. U.S. Roman Cath.-Luth. Dialogue, 1986—; chmn. Bishops' com. marriage and family life U.S. Cath. Conf., 1978—84; mem. gen. Synod Bishops, Vatican City, 1980. Contbr. articles to profl. jours. Trustee Good Samaritan Hosp., Balt., 1973—77, Cath. U. Am., 1990—, Blue Cross of Md., Inc., 1973—76, Balt. Urban Coalition, 1970—75; trustee, chmn. St. Thomas Theol. Sem., 1987—; bd. dirs. Assn. Cath. Charities, Balt., 1966—76, U. Md. Sch. Social Work and Planning, 1973—76. Recipient Father Kelly Alumni award, Loyola H.S., 1978, Alumni Laureate, Loyola Coll., 1979. Mem.: Oriental Orthodox Roman Cath. Consultation, World Meth. Conf. Roman Cath. Dialogue (co-chmn. 1977—86), Congregation for Doctrine of Faith, Luth. Roman Cath. Dialogue, Nat. Conf. Cath. Bishops. Office: Penitenziere Maggiore Penitenzieria Apostolica 00120 Vatican City Vatican City

STAFFORD, JAMES FRANCIS, cardinal; Ordained priest, Balt., 1957; aux. bishop, 1976; bishop Memphis, 1982—86; archibishop Denver, 1986—96; pres. Pontifical Coun. for Laity, Vatican, 1996—; elevated to Cardinal, 1998; major penitentiary Apostolic Penitentiary, Vatican City, 2003—. Office: Tribunale della Penitenzieria Apostolica Palazzo della Cancelliria 00120 Vatican City Italy E-mail: jfstafford@apostpnt.va.

STAFFORD, JOHN ROGERS, pharmaceutical and household products company executive; b. Harrisburg, Pa., Oct. 24, 1937; s. Paul Henry and Gladys Lee (Sharp) S.; m. Inge Paul, Aug. 22, 1959; children: Carolyn, Jennifer, Christina, Charlotte. AB, Dickinson Coll., 1959; LLB with distinction, George Washington U., 1962, Degree (hon.), 1994. Bar: D.C. 1962. Assoc. Steptoe & Johnson, Washington, 1962-66; gen. atty. Hoffman-LaRoche, Nutley, NJ, 1966-67, group atty., 1967-70; gen. counsel Am. Home Products Corp., NYC, 1970-74, v.p., 1972-77, sr. v.p., 1977-80, exec. v.p. Madison, NJ, 1980-81, pres., from 1981; chmn. Wyeth, 1986—2002; CEO Wyeth (pharm. and healthcare products), 1986—2001. Bd. dirs. The Chase Manhattan Corp., Honeywell Internat. Inc., Verizon Comm., J.P. Morgan Chase & Co., NYNEX Corp.; trustee Thirteen/WNET. Bd. dirs. Christopher Reeve Paralysis Found. Recipient John Bell Larner 1st Scholar award George Washington U. Law Sch., 1962, Outstanding Achievement Alumnus award, 1981 Mem.: NAM (bd. dirs.), ABA, DC Bar Assn., Baltusrol Club, Essex Fells (NJ) Country Club. Office: 5 Giralda Farms Madison NJ 07940-1021

STAFFORD, LORI, reporter; b. Birmingham, Ala. m. Jeff Stafford. Student, Auburn U., U. Ala.; MA, Northwestern U. Mem. staff TV sta., Reno, Cin., Chattanooga, Evansville, Ind.; reporter WISN, Milw. Office: WISN PO Box 402 Milwaukee WI 53201-0402

STAFFORD, REBECCA, retired academic administrator, sociologist, education consultant; b. Topeka, July 9, 1936; d. Frank C. and Anne Elizabeth (Larrick) S.; m. Willard Van Hazel. AB magna cum laude, Radcliffe Coll., 1958, MA, 1961; PhD, Harvard U., 1964. Sociology lectr., dept. social rels. Sch. Edn., Harvard U., Cambridge, Mass., 1964-70, mem. vis. com. bd. overseers, 1973-79; assoc. prof. sociology U. Nev., Reno, 1970-74, prof., 1973-80, chmn. dept. sociology, 1974-77, dean Coll. Arts and Scis., 1977-80; pres. Bemidji (Minn.) State U., 1980-82; exec. v.p., prof. sociology Colo. State U., Ft. Collins, 1982-83; pres. Chatham Coll., Pitts., 1983-91, prof. sociology, 1992-93; pres. Monmouth U., West Long Branch, NJ, 1993—2003. Cons. higher edn., 1992—, U.S. Internat. U. on Acad. Planning, 1992-94, USDA, 1992-93, Integra Bank, 1992-93, Millsaps Coll, Jackson, Miss., 1991, U. Pitts. Med. Sch., 1992-93; co-dir. acad. leadership inst. Carnegie Mellon U., 1991-93, U. Tenn., Knoxville, 1992-93; vis. scholar dept. sociology Harvard U., 1991; mem. faculty coll. mgmt. program. Carnegie Mellon U., Pitts., 1984-93; cons. adult devel. grant Harvard U. Health Svcs., Cambridge, 1979, rsch. sociologist, 1964-69; dir. ednl. enrichment project Harvard Sch. Edn., 1966-67, 69-70. Mem. editl. bd. Sociometry, 1974-77, Sociol. Focus., 1974-77; contbr. articles to profl. jours.; presenter papers at profl. confs. Trustee Monmouth Med. Ctr., 1993—, Winchester-Thurston Sch., Pitts., 1986-91, Montefiore Hosp., Pitts., 1990-93; trustee Presbyn.-Univ. Hosp., Pitts., 1984-93, exec. planning com., 1986-89, fin. com., 1989-93; pres. Pitts. Coun. Higher Edn., 1990; mem. Found. Ind. Colls. Inc. Pa., 1984-91, sec., 1986; mem. Colo. Commn. Higher Edn. Task Force on Quality, 1981; mem. adv. bd. Animal Rescue League, Pitts., 1989-93; founder Bemidji Area Women's Network, Minn., 1980-82; mem. intergovtl. planning steering com. Bemidji, 1980-82; mem. cmty. rels. com. Girl Scouts Southwestern Pa., 1983-86; mem. brotherhood dinner coun. Nat. Conf. Christians and Jews, 1985; mem. hon. centennial com. Pa. Sch. Blind Children, Pitts., 1986; mem. citizens sponsoring com. Allegheny Conf. Cmty. Devel., Pitts., 1983-91; mem. five state regional bd. First Union Nat. Bank, 1996—; bd. dirs. Pitts. Symphony, 1984-93, First Fidelity Bank, N.A., N.J., 1993-95, Integra Bank, Pitts., 1987-97, Urban League, Pitts., 1984-87, Women's Ctr., Ft. Collins, Colo., 1982-83, Coun. Colls. Arts and Scis., 1978-81; chmn. Harvard U. Grad. Sec. Coun., 1987-93. Recipient McCurdy-Rinkle prize for rsch. Eastern Psychiat. Assn., 1970; named Woman of Yr. in Edn., City of Pitts., 1986, Vectors/Pitts., 1987, Woman of Yr. in Edn., YWCA Tribute to Women, 1989, Women of Distinction award Muscular Dystrophy Assn., 1999, Women of Leadership award Monmouth County Girl Scouts Am., 1995, Woman of Achievement in Edn. award Monmouth County Adv. Commn. on Status of Women, 1994, Salute to Policymakers award Exec. Women in N.J., 1994; grantee Am. Coun. Edn. Inst. Acad. Deans, 1979, Inst. Ednl. Mgmt., Harvard U., 1984. Mem. Assn. Ind. Colls. and Univs. of N.J. (v.p. 1999—, sec. 1998-99, treas. 1994-98, pres. northeastern conf. 1995-99, bd. dirs. 1993—), Am. Coun. on Edn., Assn. Am. Colls., Soc. for Coll. and Univ. Planning (mem. instl. decision making and resource planning acad. 1994—), Ind. Coll. Fund (treas. 1995-96, bd. dirs. 1993—), Nat. Coun. Family Rels., Harvard U. Alumni Assn. (bd. dirs. 1985-87), Phi Beta Kappa, Phi Kappa Phi. Business E-Mail: Becky@monmouth.edu.

STAFFORD, ROBERT THEODORE, lawyer, former senator; b. Rutland, Vt., Aug. 8, 1913; s. Bert L. and Mable R. (Stratton) S.; m. Helen C. Kelley, Oct. 15, 1938; children— Madelyn, Susan, Barbara, Dianne. BS, Middlebury Coll., 1935, LL.D., 1960; postgrad., U. Mich., 1936; LL.B., Boston U., 1938, LL.D., 1959, Norwich U., 1960, St. Michaels Coll., 1967, U. Vt., 1970. Bar: Vt. bar 1938. City prosecutor, Rutland, 1939-42; state's atty. Rutland County, 1947-51; dep. atty. gen., 1953-54; atty. gen., 1954-56; lt. gov., 1957-58; gov., 1959-60; mem. 87th to 92d Congresses, Vt.-at-large; apptd. U.S. Senate, 1971, mem., 1972-89, chmn. com. on environment and public works, 1981-87, chmn. edn. subcom., 1981-87, ranking mem., 1987-89; ptnr. Stafford, Abiatell & Stafford, 1938-46; sr. ptnr. Stafford & LaBrake, 1946-51. Chmn. UN-U.S.A. Assn. Panel UNESCO, 1989—. Lt. comdr. USNR, 1942-46, 51-52; capt. Res. Named Disting. Scholar U. Vt., 1989, Disting. Prof. Pub. Affairs Castleton State Coll., 1989. Mem. V.F.W., Am. Legion. Clubs: Elk. Home and Office: 108 Gables Pl Rutland VT 05701-9448 Office: Castleton Coll Coolidge Libr Bldg Castleton VT 05735

STAGE, BRIAN, hotel executive; BSBA, Coll. William and Mary, 1974; grad. mgmt. exec. program, U. Minn., 1995. Mgr. Sheraton Boston Hotel and Towers, 1981; ops. mgr. Inn Am., area dir. ops. and corp. dir. sales and mktg.; v.p. sales and mktg. Inn Am. Corp.; regional v.p. ops. Radisson Hotels Worldwide, 1990-95, exec. v.p. sales and mktg., 1995-97, pres., COO, 1997-99; exec. v.p. sales, reservations and distbn. Carlson Hotels Worldwide, Mpls., 2000—. Office: Carlson Hotels and Worldwide Carlson Pky PO Box 59159 Minneapolis MN 55459-8204 E-mail: bstage@carlson.com.

STAGE, THOMAS BENTON, psychiatrist; b. Marietta, Ohio, July 23, 1926; s. John Douglas and Grace (Shawhan) S.; m. Doris Jeane Weinstock, Dec. 22, 1951; children: Samuel Ray, Amy Elizabeth, James Robert; m. Alicia Anderson Marsh, June 7, 1993. BA cum laude, Marietta Coll., 1949; MD, Ohio State U., 1952. Diplomate: Am. Bd. Psychiatry and Neurology. Intern Detroit Receiving Hosp., 1952-53; psychiat. resident, fellow Menninger Sch. Psychiatry, Topeka, 1953-56; sect. chief, chief psychiatry VA Hosp., Topeka, 1956-62, adminstr. Sheridan, Wyo., 1962-66, dir. Salem, Va., 1967-72; dep. asst. chief med. dir. for ambulatory care VA Central Office, Washington, 1972-74; dir. No. Va. Mental Health Inst., Falls Church, 1974-78; asst. commr. for mental health State of Va., Richmond, 1978-79; dir. clin. svcs. Fairfax-Falls Ch. Cmty. Svcs. Bd., Vienna, Va., 1979-82, psychiat. cons. for med. affairs, 1982-99, med. dir. Fairfax, 1999—2002, cons. quality improvements, 2002—. Instr. Menninger Sch. Psychiatry, 1958-62, U. Wyo. Sch. Nursing, 1963-66; assoc. prof. U. Va. Med. Sch., 1972-74; cons. surveyor Joint Commn. on Accreditation of Hosps., 1976-2004; cons. Crow-No. Cheyenne USPHS Hosp., 1963-66, Ala. Dept. Mental Health (Wyatt Com.), 1986-91; psychiatric cons. on accreditation Commonwealth of Va. Dept. Mental Health, Mental Retardation and Substance Abuse, 1982-2002; mem. Comprehensive Mental Health Ctr. Com., 1968-73, Gov.'s Adv. Commn. on Mental Health, 1971-74; chmn. Drug Abuse Rehab. Com., 1970-73; cons. adminstrv. psychiatry NIMH, 1975-78; chmn. steering com. Assoc. Faculties Program Community Psychiatry, Washington, 1975-77; mem. State Health Coordinating Coun., 1976-89. Contbr. articles to profl. jours. Served wtih USNR, 1944-46, PTO. Fellow Am. Psychiat. Assn. (life, disting.); mem. Am. Assn. Psychiat. Adminstrs., Washington Psychiat. Soc., Psychiat. Soc. Va., Am. Assn. Community Psychiatrists. Home: 11410 Hollow Timber Way Reston VA 20194-1906 Office: Fairfax-Falls Ch Comty Svcs Ste 800 12011 Government Center Pkwy Fairfax VA 22035-1100

STAGEBERG, ROGER V. lawyer; B of Math. with distinction, U. Minn., 1963, JD cum laude, 1966. Assoc. Mackall, Crounse & Moore, Mpls., 1966-70, ptnr., 1970-86; shareholder and officer Lommen, Nelson, Cole & Stageberg, P.A., Mpls., 1986—. Co-chmn. joint legal svcs. funding com. Minn. Supreme Ct., 1995-96. Mem. U. Minn. Law Rev. Bd. dirs. Mpls. Legal Aid Soc., 1970-2003, treas., 1973, pres., 1977, dir. of fund, 1980—, chmn. of fund, 1998-2000; chmn. bd. trustees Colonial Ch. of Edina, 1975, chmn. congregation, 1976, pres. found., 1978; officer, trustee Mpls. Found, 1983-88. Mem. Minn. State Bar Assn. (numerous offices and coms., pres. 1994), Hennepin County Bar Assn. (chmn. securities law sect. 1979, chmn. attys. referral svc. com. 1980, sec. 1980, treas. 1981, pres. 1983), Order of Coif. Office: Lommen Nelson Ste 2000 80 S 8th St Minneapolis MN 55402-2119

STAGER, DONALD K. retired construction company executive; Chmn., pres., CEO Dillingham Constrn. Holdings Inc., Pleasanton, Calif., 1982-99; with Guy F. Atkinson Co., 1952—82; ret., 1999. Recipient, Roebling award Am. Soc. of Civil Engineers, 1995, Golden Beaver award for Mgmt Beavers, Inc., 1998. Office: 957 Wapato Way Manson WA 98831-9595

STAGER, LAWRENCE E. archaeologist, educator; b. Kenton, Ohio, Jan. 5, 1943; married; 2 children. BA, Harvard U., 1965, MA, 1972, PhD in Syro-Palestinian Archeology and History, 1975. Instr. Oriental Inst., U. Chgo., 1973-74, asst. prof., 1974-75, assoc. prof. Syro-Palestinian archaeology, 1976-87; Dorot prof. archeology of Israel, Dept. Near Eastern Langs. and Civilizations and Anthropology Harvard U., Cambridge, Mass., 1986—, dir. Semite Mus. Fellow Inst. for Advanced Study, Hebrew U., 1983-84; co-dir. Am. Expdn., Idalion, Cyprus, 1972-74; dir. UNESCO Save Carthage Project, Am. Punic Archaeol. Expdn., 1975-80, Harvard Semitic Mus., 1987—, Leon Levy Expdn. to Ashkelon, Israel, 1985—; dir. Harvard Semitic Mus., Cambridge, 1987—. Author: Ashkelon Discovered, 1991, A Heap of Broken Images: Essays in Biblical Archaeology, 1998; co-author: Idalion I, Idalion II; contbr. articles to profl. jours. Mem. Am. Schs. Oriental Rsch. (editor newsletter 1975-76, assoc. trustee 1977-80, trustee 1987-90, assoc. editor bull. 1978—), Archaeol. Inst. Am. (v.p. 1986-88, trustee 1989-91), Am. Orient Soc., Soc. Bibl. Lit. Achievements include rsch. in economy, society and religion of ancient Israel; archaeology of Philistines, Canaanites and Phoenicians. Office: Harvard U Semitic Mus Dept Near Ea Langs/Civil Cambridge MA 02138-2091

STAGG, LOUIS CHARLES, English language and literature educator; b. Jan. 3, 1933; s. Louis Anatol and Gladys (Andrews) S.; m. Mary Casner, June 5, 1959; children: Robert Charles, Helen Marie. BA in English, La. Coll., 1955; MA in English, U. Ark., 1957, PhD in English, 1963. Tchg. asst. English U. Ark., 1955-59; asst. prof. William Jewell Coll., 1959-60; instr. Stephen F. Austin State U., 1960-62; asst. prof. Memphis State U. (now U. Memphis), 1962-69, assoc. prof., 1969-77, prof. English lang. and lit., 1977-98, prof. emeritus, 1998—, dir. grad. studies in English, 1985-88, dir. English Drama Players, 1968-92, dir. undergrad. advising for English, 1970-80, 88-91, chair policies and procedures com. for English, 1983-95, tenure and promotion com. for English, 1978-80, 82-86, 89-97, now cons. for 2001 program. Chmn. acad. policies com. Memphis State U. Senate, 1981-82, 88-90, 93-96, exec. com. senate, 1987-91, 93-96, parliamentarian of senate, 1987-88, 90-91, 94-96, humanities rep. budget adv. com. dean Coll. Arts and Scis., 1992-93, mem. adv. bd. Acad. Exch. Quar., 1997—, steering com., chair of schedules, originator Alliance Creative Theatre, Edn. and Rsch. series, 1986, 89-90, 92, 94, 96, 98; cons. NEH, 1975-76, 78, Ohio State U. Press, 1985-86, U. Jordan, Amman, 1985; chair policies and procedures subdivsn. Eng. dept. so. assn. colls., schs. self study, steering com. 1992-93; cons. Memphis State U. Learning Media-Ctrs. catalogue Shakespeare holdings, 1992-93, rev., 1993-95. Author: (with J. Lasley Dameron) Poe's Critical Vocabulary, 1966; author series: Index to the Figurative Language of John Webster's Tragedies, 1967, of Ben Jonson's Tragedies, 1967, of Thomas Heywood's Tragedies, 1967, of George Champman's Tragedies, 1970, of Thomas Middleton's Tragedies, 1970, of Cyril Tourneur's Tragedies, 2d edit., all 7 under title Index to the Figurative Language of the Tragedies of Shakespeare's Chief 17th Century Contemporaries, 1977, 3d edit., 1982, Index to the Figurative Language of the Tragedies of Shakespeare's Chief 18th Century Contemporaries, 1984; contbr. to Great Writers of the English Language Dramatists, 1979, 87; circulation editor Interpretations, 1976-80; contbr. articles on English and Am. drama to profl. jours., publs. on Shakespeare, other lit. publs. Mem. Memphis Oratorio Soc. Chorus, 1969-92, diction coach, 1987; mem. Memphis Symphony Chorus, 1993—, mem. symphony chorus newsletter com., 1999-2000; mem. Memphis in May Sunset Symphony Choir, 1996, Martin Luther King Tribute Concert Choir, 1995, 96, 99—, City of Memphis Faure Requiem Concert, 2001, Memphis Symphony Chorus and Orch. prodn. Rolling Requiem for 9/11/02; lay reader Episcopal Ch.; program chair Friends of Univ. Librs., 2000-02, v.p., 2002-03, pres. 2003—; mem. at large exec. com. U. Memphis Assn. Retirees, 2003-. Grantee NEH, 1967, Memphis State U., 1965, Travel grant to U.S. Libr. Congress, summer 1971. Mem. MLA (life), So. Humanities Coun. (sec.-treas. 1974-76, exec. com. 1976-83, 94-96, chmn. coun. 1993-94, chmn. sect. humanities in pluralistic soc. 1984, ad hoc com. on crisis in tchg. humanities 1977, chmn. local arrangements for convs. 1975, 94, chmn. sect. on Thomas Hardy 1996), Tenn. Philol. Assn. (pres. 1976-77, exec. com. 1977, local arrangements chmn. 1965, 69, 75, 87, chmn. Shakespeare sect. 1996), Marlowe Soc. Am. (book reviewer 1984, 86-88, 93), Am. Soc. for Theatre Rsch., Samuel Beckett Soc., Conf. on Christianity and Lit., South Cen. Conf. on Christianity and Lit. Soc. for Study of Works of Harold Pinter (life, asst. constn. revision 1988, asst. with planning 1992, treas. 1994-98, exec. com. 1994-98), Ark. Philol. Assn., Shakespeare Assn. Am. (local arrangements host com. 1985), Stratford-upon-Avon Shakespeare Festival (Eng.), Eugene O'Neill Soc., Alliance for Creative Theatre, Edn. and Rsch. (chmn. schedules com., originator of proposal 1986, 89-90, 92, 94, 96, 98, cons. residency S.E. Mo. State U. 1997), Internat. Shakespeare Assn., Am. Soc. Theatre Rsch., Internat. Soc. Theatre Rsch., Medieval and Renaissance Drama Soc., Renaissance Soc. Am., South Cen. Renaissance Conf. (chmn. nominations 1976, exec. com. 1978-80, program com. 1981-83, chmn. sect. Shakespeare 1981, 85, 95, 99, 2002, 03, 04; 16th Century lit. 1982, chmn. local arrangements 1983, symposium on humanism 1984, chmn. Shakespeare on film and the tchg. of Brit. drama 1986, chmn. music in Shakespeare's plays, 1987, chmn. sect. Thematic Approaches to Tudor/Stuart Drama 1988, chmn. sect. Medieval Influences on Renaissance drama 1993, chmn. Shakespeare's Villains: Stage and Page 1995, Adaptions of Renaissance Drama 1993, chmn. local arrangements for convention 1990, chmn. spl. session 1989, 95, Shakespeare II sect. 1996, chair Renaissance Drama Section 1999, 2001); SCRC (life), chmn. Performing Rennaissance Drama 2001, South Cen. MLA (life), assoc. editor for English, South Cen. Bull. 1982-84, nominations com. 1985-86, 95-96, book reviewer South Cen. Rev. 1983, 85-86, sec. English I.B. Renaissance, 1986, chair, 1987, sec. spl. sect. Renaissance Drama, 1988, chair Shakespeare's Tragi-comedies and tragi-comic romances, 1989, co-chair local arrangements, 1999, chair panel on renaissance drama criticism 1995, sec. renaissance drama sect. 1997, sect. chmn. 1998, mem. com. Conv., Memphis, 1999), South Atlantic MLA, South Ctrl. Coll. English Assn. (sec.-treas. 1980-81, v.p. 1981-82, pres. 1982-83, exec. com. 1983-90, co-host 1982, com. constitution revision 1989), Coll. English Assn., Internat. Patristic Medieval and Renaissance Conf. (sect. chmn. Medieval drama 1977, chair Shakespeare session 1994, chmn. Renaissance drama section 1995, chmn. 17th century Brit. lit. sect. 1996, chmn. Milton sect. 1996), Am. Theatre Assn. (chmn. sect. combining Brit. lit. and theatre in teaching of drama 1983, chmn. Shakespeare sect. 1994), Marlowe Soc. Am., Eugene O'Neill Soc., Stratford Can. Shakespeare Festival, AAUP (sec. treas. Memphis State U. chpt. 1982-86, v.p. 1986-88, pres. 1988-90), Phi Beta Kappa (pres. memphis alumni assn. 1985-88, spl. panel Soc. and New Scholarship at 37th triennial coun. 1994), Friends U. Memphis Libraries (program chair 2000-02, v.p. 2002-03, pres. 2003—), Alpha Chi. Democrat. Home: 5219 Mason Rd Memphis TN 38117-2104

STAGG, TOM, federal judge; b. Shreveport, La., Jan. 19, 1923; s. Thomas Eaton and Beulah (Meyer) S.; m. Margaret Mary O'Brien, Aug. 21, 1946; children: Julie, Margaret Mary. BA, La. State U., 1943, JD, 1949. Bar: La. 1949. With firm Hargrove, Guyton, Van Hook & Hargrove, Shreveport, 1949-53; pvt. practice law Shreveport, 1953-58; sr. ptnr. firm Stagg, Cady & Beard, Shreveport, 1958-74; judge U.S. Dist. Ct. (we. dist.) La., 1974-84, 91-92, chief judge, 1984-90, sr. judge, 1992—. Mem. Shreveport Airport Authority, 1967-73, chmn., 1970-73; chmn. Gov.'s Tidelands Adv. Council, 1969-70; del. La. Constl. Conv., 1973-74; chmn. rules com., com. on exec. dept.; mem. Gov.'s Adv. Com on Offshore Revenues, 1972-74 Active Republician party, 1950-74, del. convs., 1956, 60, 64, 68, 72; mem. Nat. Com. for La., 1964-72, mem. exec. com., 1964-68; Pres. Shreveport Jr. C. of C., 1955-56; v.p. La. Jr. C. of C., 1956-57. Served to capt., inf. AUS, 1943-46, ETO. Decorated Bronze Star, Purple Heart with oak leaf cluster, Combat Inf. badge. Mem. Am., La., Shreveport bar assns. Office: US Dist Ct 300 Fannin St Ste 4100 Shreveport LA 71101-3123 Office Phone: 318-676-3260.

STAGGERS, KERMIT LEMOYNE, II, history and political science educator, state legislator, municipal official; b. Washington, Pa., Nov. 2, 1947; s. Kermit LeMoyne and Christine Ruby (Scherich) S.; m. June Ann Wenda, Aug. 22, 1970; children: Ayn Kristen, Kyle Lee. BS, U. Idaho, 1969, MA, 1975; PhD, Claremont Grad. U., 1986. Instr. history Troy (Ala.) State U., 1975-76, U. Idaho, Moscow, 1977, Northwestern Coll., Orange City, Iowa, 1979-80, Coll. Lake County, Grayslake, Ill., 1981-82; lectr. history Chapman Coll., Orange, Calif., 1979, U. Md.-Europe, Heidelberg, Germany, 1988-89; vis. instr. history Trinity Internat. U., Deerfield, Ill., 1980; ad. instr. history Coll. St. Francis, Joliet, Ill., 1982; prof. history and polit. sci. U. Sioux Falls (S.D.), 1982—; mem. S.D. Senate, Pierre, 1995—2002, Sioux Falls City Coun., 2002—. Lectr. Diplomatic Acad. Ukrainian Fgn. Ministry and Nat. U. Kiev-Mohyla Acad., 2001; expert analyst on polit. and social issues for local radio and TV. Contbr. to profl. publs. Chair Senate Transp. Com., 1997-99. Capt. USAF, 1970-76. Recipient Guardian Small Bus. award Nat. Fedn. Ind. Bus., 1996; Malone Faculty fellow, 1993. Mem. Orgn. Am. Historians, Great Plains Polit. Sci and Pub. Affairs Assn. (pres. 2000-01), Conf. on Faith and History, Federalist Soc., Fulbright Assn., Hist. Soc., Kiwanis, Phi Alpha Theta, Phi Kappa Phi. Republican. Avocations: book collecting, travel. Home: 616 E Wiswall Pl Sioux Falls SD 57105-2030 Office: U Sioux Falls Dept History/Polit Sci 1101 W 22nd St Sioux Falls SD 57105-1699 Office Phone: 605-331-6754. Business E-Mail: kermit.staggers@usiouxfalls.edu.

STAGGERS, MARY E. minister; b. Rocky Mount, N.C., Sept. 28, 1923; d. John and Emma Jane White; m. Calvin Staggers, Jr., May 18, 1938; children: Luther, Gervis, Earlie Mae, Curtis, Herbert, Betty Joann, Yvonne. BA, Coll. New Rochelle, 1983; M in Profl. Studies, N.Y. Theol. Sem., 1985; M in Humanities, Ctr. Humanities N.Y., 1985; D of Theology of Bible, Internat. Sem. Fla., 1990; DD, Balt. Coll. Bible, 1988. Pastor Holy Redeemer Bapt. Ch., Bklyn., 1961—. Family therapist Beth Israel Hosp., N.Y.C., 1980—98; min. N.Y.C. World's Fair. Author: It's Seed Time, 1999, The Spirit Supercedes Nature, 2003. Liaison N.Y.C. Cmty. Bd. Dist. 16; v.p. Women's Nat. Evang. and Missionary Conf., 1996—2001; pres. World Conf. Gospel Explosion, 1994—, United Ladies Ministers Counsel, 1978—99; pres. Ea. N.Y. br. Women's Nat. Evang. and Missionary Conf., 1997—2001; pres. Mother's Bd. Cedar Grove Bapt. Ch., 1940—51. Mem.: N.Y.C. Clergy Conf., Ea. Bapt. Conf., So. Bapt. Conf., Nat. Bapt. Conf. Democrat. Avocations: cooking, reading, writing. Home: 133 Westervelt Ave Staten Island NY 10301 Office: Holy Redeemer Bapt Ch 855 Saratoga Ave Brooklyn NY 11212 Office Phone: 718-816-5181.

STAGGS, BARBARA, state representative; b. Hulbert, Okla., July 18, 1940; d. Truman and Veleria (Trapp) Masterson; m. Ross Staggs; children: Rick, Matt. BA in Edn., Northeastern U., 1963; MA, U. Tulsa, 1968, EdD, 1987. Tchr., adminstr.; mem. Okla. Ho. of Reps., 1995—, chair common edn. com. Named Outstanding Adminstr., Okla. Schs. Adv. Coun., 1993, Woman of Distinction, Muskogee Soroptimist's, 1996. Democrat. Office: State Capitol 2300 N Lincoln Blvd Rm 302 Oklahoma City OK 73105

STAGGS, THOMAS, entertainment company executive; Mgr. strategic planning The Walt Disney Co., Burbank, Calif., 1990—94, v.p. planning & development, 1995—97, exec. v.p., CFO, 1998—99, senior v.p., CFO, 2000—. Office: The Walt Disney Co 500 S Buena Vista St Burbank CA 91521-0006

STAGLIANO, JAMES JOSEPH, physical science educator, scientist; b. Kenosha, Wis., Nov. 15, 1965; s. James Joseph and Hazel May (Mastin) S.; m. Susan Elizabeth Cain, May 20, 1994 (div. July 14, 2000); children: James, Mary. BS in Math., U. Wis., Kenosha, 1987; MS in Physics, PhD in Physics, Auburn U., 1994. Asst. prof. physics Jacksonville (Ala.) State U., 1994-97; rschr. dept. physics Auburn (Ala.) U., 1995, lectr. in physics, summer 1996; software engr. Enterprise (Ala.) Electronics Corp., 1997-2000; adj. prof. sci. Enterprise State Jr. Coll., 1998-2000; sr. systems analyst Enterprise Electronics Corp., 2000—02, sr. scientist, 2002—. Contbr. articles to profl. jours. Mem., bd. dirs. Ala. Family Rights Assn., Huntsville, 1998-2001; mem. Citizens for Legal Accountability and Reform in Ala., Dothan, 1999-2001; pres., bd. dirs. Coffee County CASA, Inc., Enterprise, 2000—. Mem. Am. Inst. Physics, Am. Math. Soc., N.Y. Acad. Scis. Office: Enterprise Electronics Corp 128 S Industrial Blvd Enterprise AL 36330 E-mail: james_stagliano@hotmail.com.

STAGLIANO, VITO ALEXANDER, federal agency administrator, utilities executive, writer; b. Catanzaro, Calabria, Italy, May 13, 1942; arrived in U.S., 1956; s. Filippo and Maria Stagliano; m. Julie Ann Werth, Sept. 30, 1967; children: Jason Vito, Carlos Otobed. Program analyst U.S. Office Econ. Opportunity, Washington, 1968-69; exec. dir. Palau Cmty. Devel. Agy., 1969-71; program officer U.S. Peace Corps, Ghana, 1971-73, dir., 1973-74, dir. West Africa, 1974-77; counselor Interstate Commn. on Drought Control, Ouagadougou, Bourkina Faso, 1977-79; staff asst. Sec. of Energy, Washington, 1979-81; dir. River Basins Devel. Office, Dakar, Senegal, 1981-85; dir. Office of Energy Demand Policy, U.S. Dept. Energy, Washington, 1986-89, assoc. dep. undersec. of energy, 1990-91, dep. asst. sec. energy for policy planning, 1991-93; vis. scholar Resources for Future, 1993-95; dir. Energy Security Analysis, Inc., Washington, 1996-98; v.p. Commonwealth Edison Co., Chgo., 1998-2000, Calpine Corp., 2001—. Guest lectr. Harvard U., Tufts U., Nat. Def. U., Va. Mil. Inst., École Nationale Superièure, France. Co-author: (book) Energy and National Security in the 21st Century, 1995, A Shock to the System: Restructuring America's Electricity Industry, 1996; author: A Policy of Discontent: The Making of a National Energy Strategy, 2001; contbr. articles to profl. jours. Founder Micronesia Legal Svcs. Program, 1971; mem. Gridwise Architecture Bd., Chgo. Sister Cities Internat., Chgo. Symphony Orch., Joffrey Ballet of Chgo. Recipient rank of meritorious Sr. Exec., Pres. George Bush; Ampart fellow, USIA, 1981. Mem.: U.S. Assn. for Energy Econs., Internat. Assn. Energy Econs., So. Poverty Law Ctr., Am. Poetry Soc. Avocations: Roman and medieval Moorish history, 20th century poetry. Office Phone: 847-484-7720.

STAGLIN, GAREN KENT, computer service company executive, venture capitalist; b. Lincoln, Nebr., Dec. 22, 1944; s. Ramon and Darlene (Guilliams) S.; m. Sharalyn King, June 8, 1968; children: Brandon Kent, Shannon King. BS in Engring. with honors, UCLA, 1966; MBA, Stanford U., 1968. Assoc. Carr Mgmt. Co., N.Y.C., 1971-75; v.p. Crocker Nat. Bank, San Francisco, 1975-76; dir. fin. Itel Corp., San Francisco, 1976-77, pres. ins. services divsn., 1977-79; corp. v.p., gen. mgr. ADP Automotive Svcs. Group, San Ramon, Calif., 1978-91; chmn., CEO Safelite Glass Corp., Columbus, Ohio, 1991-97, chmn., 1998-2000; owner Staglin Family Vineyard, Rutherford, Calif., 1985—; pres., CEO, eOne Global L.L.C., Napa, Calif., 2000—. Bd. dirs. Certive Corp., Specialized Bicycle Corp., First Data Corp. Bd. dirs. Peralta Hosp. Cancer Inst., 1977-78, Berkeley Reportory Theatre, 1979-85; trustee Justin Sienna H.S., Napa, Calif., 1995-2000; chmn. major gifts program East Bay region Stanford (Calif.) U., 1989-92; mem. adv. bd. Stanford Bus. Sch., 1995-2000; chmn. 75th anniversary campaign Stanford Grad. Sch. Bus., 1998-2000; capital campaign UCLA Coll. Letters Sci., 2004-; pres. bd. trustees Am. Ctr. Wine, Food and Arts, Napa, Calif., 1998—2003. Lt. USN, 1968-71. Recipient Gold Spike award, Stanford U., 2000. Mem. Stanford Assocs. (bd. govs. 1985-92), World Pres. Orgn., Internat. Inst. Soc. (bd. govs. 1985-92). Democrat. Lutheran. Home: PO Box 680 1570 Bella Oaks Ln Rutherford CA 94573 E-mail: gstaglin@eoneglobal.com.

STAHL, DAVID, orchestra and opera conductor; b. N.Y.C., Nov. 4, 1949; s. Frank L. and Edith (Cosmann) S.; m. Karen Doss Shehan, Feb. 25, 1989; children: Sonya Leonore, Byron David, Anna June. B.Mus., Queens Coll., 1972, MA, 1974; studied with, Leonard Bernstein and Seiji Ozawa, Tanglewood, 1975, Gunther Schuller, Joseph Rosenstock, Walter Susskind, Max Rudolf; LLD, Coll. of Charleston. Carnegie Hall debut with Youth Symphony Orch. of N.Y., 1973; music dir., Doctors' Orchestral Soc., N.Y.C., 1973-76, asst. condr., N.Y. Philharm., 1976, assoc. condr., Cin. Symphony Orch., 1976-79, music dir. St. Louis Philharm., 1976-81, Charleston (S.C.) Symphony Orch., 1984—; guest condr., prin. guest condr., Bavarian Staatstheater am Gartnerplatz, Munich, 1996-99, Lyric Opera of Chgo., NDR Orch., Hamburg, Germany, Staatskappelle Dresden, Dusseldorf, Bamberg, Frankfurt, Hanover, Symonig orchs., Munich Philharm., Orchestre de Lyon, France, Pitts., Atlanta, Buffalo, St. Louis, Nat., Am., N.J., Dallas, Edmonton, Louisville, Toronto Syphony, Balt., Winnipeg, Indpls. Symphony orchs., Cin. Opera, Teatro Comunale di Genoa, Spoleto Festival USA, Israel Festival, Concertgebouw, Amsterdam, Stadtheater Mannheim, Staatstheatre Darmstadt, Staatsphilharmonic Rheinlandpfalz, Festival of Two Worlds, Spoleto, Italy, N.Y.C. Opera, Wash. Opera, Lake George Opera Festival, Omaha Opera, Dayton Opera, Mich. Opera Theatre, Montreal Opera, Tulsa Opera, Hawaii Opera Theatre, Teatro Massimo di Palermo, Orchestre Colonne, Long Beach Opera, Leonard Bernstein Festival, Holland, RAI Orchestra Rome, Seoul (Dem. Republic Korea) Philharm., Orchestra del Sodre, Montevideo, Uruguay; music dir.: Broadway and internat. tour. West Side Story, Porgy and Bess, Israel Fest. Recipient Gov.'s award for Excellence in the Arts, S.C. Order of Palmetto Exxon/Arts Endowment Condr. award, 1976-79, S.C. Verner award 1996. Mem. Am. Symphony Orch. League.

STAHL, DAVID A. microbiologist, educator; BS magna cum laude, U. of Wash., Seattle, 1971; MS U. of Ill., 1975, PhD U. of Ill., 1978. Pre-doctoral fellowship U. of Ill., 1971—73; tchg. asst. U. of Ill., Sch. of Life Sciences, 1973—74; grad. studies U. of Ill., 1974—77; NIH post doctoral fellowship Nat. Jewish Hosp. and Rsch. Ctr., Denver, 1978—80, sr. rsch. assoc.; asst. prof., dept. of vet. pathobiology U. of Ill., 1984—91, assoc. prof., dept. of vet. pathobiology, 1991—94; assoc. prof., dept. of civil engring. Northwestern U., 1994—96; scientist in residence DuPont CR&D, Wilmington, Del., 1998—99; prof. Northwestern U., 1996—2001; adj. prof. U. of Wash., Sch. of Medicine, 2001—. Vis. prof. U. of Minn., 1987—89, 1992; panel mem. NASA, Mars Curation and Receiving Oversight Panel, 1997—98; mem. J. Roger Porter award com., 1998—99. Recipient Bergey award, 1999, Orton K. Stark disting. lectr., Miami U., 1998, award for rsch. excellence, SmithKline Beecham, 1992, Beckman rsch. award, U. of Ill., 1992, Norman and Helen Levine award for rsch. excellence, U. of Ill., Dept. of Vet. Pathobiology, 1991. Fellow: Am. Acad. of Microbiology. Achievements include research in microbial ecology, evolution and phylogeny of microorganisms, ribosomal RNA processing, molecular phylogeny of microorganisms, molecular approaches to microbial ecology, nucleic acid structure; ribosomal RNA processing, structure and evolution of the 23S ribosomal RNA. Office: University of Washington Office: More 302 Seattle WA 98195

STAHL, FRANK LUDWIG, civil engineer; b. Fuerth, Germany; came to U.S., 1946, naturalized, 1949; s. Leo E. and Anna (Regensburger) S.; m. Edith Cosmann, Aug. 31, 1947; children: David, Robert. BSCE, Tech. Inst. Zurich, Switzerland, 1945. With Ammann & Whitney, Cons. Engrs., N.Y.C., 1946-93, project engr., 1955-67, assoc., 1968-76, sr. assoc., 1977-81, chief engr. Transp. div., 1982-93; pvt. cons., 1994—. Expert in field. Prin. works include Verrazano-Narrows Bridge, Throgs Neck Bridge, Walt Whitman Bridge, improvements to Golden Gate Bridge, rehab. of Williamsburg Bridge, N.Y.C., Royal Gorge Bridge, Colo., Interstate-10 Deck Tunnel, Phoenix; author: Cable Corrosion in Bridges and Other Structures; co-author: Golden Gate Bridge, Report of the Chief Engineer to the Board of Directors, Vol. II; contbr. articles to profl. jours. on bridge design and constrn. Recipient Gold award The James F. Lincoln Arc Welding Found., 1986, John A. Roebling medal Internat. Bridge Conf., 1992. Fellow ASCE (Thomas Fitch Rowland prize 1967, Innovation in Civil Engring. award of mert 1983, Metro. Civil Engr. of Yr. award 1987, Roebling award 1990), ASTM (vice chmn. com. A-1 on steel, stainless steel and related alloys 1978-83, chmn. steel reinforce-subcom. 1971-82, award of merit 1982); mem. Am. Inst. Steel Constrn. (Prize Bridge award 1986), Engring. Found. (rsch. coun. on structural connections), Internat. Assn. Bridge and Structural Engring., Internat. Bridge Tunnel and Turnpike Assn. Home: 20911 28th Rd Flushing NY 11360-2412 E-mail: bridgfrank@aol.com.

STAHL, GARY EDWARD, neonatologist; b. N.Y.C., Mar. 19, 1951; s. Louis and Susan (Stein) S.; m. Deborah Susan Levy, July 1, 1973; children: Adam Louis, Eric Alexander. BS, BSEE, MIT, 1973; MD, U. Rochester, 1977. Diplomate Am. Bd. Pediat. subbd. neonatal-perinatal medicine. Pediat. resident Children's Hosp., Phila., 1977-80; neonatal fellow U. Pa., Phila., 1980-83; asst. prof. pediat. U. Pa. Sch. Medicine, Phila., 1983-90; assoc. prof. pediat. Hahnemann U. Sch. Medicine, Phila., 1991-93, U. Med. Dentistry N.J., Cambden, 1993—. Head, divsn. neonatology, vice chief dept. pediats. Children's Regional Hosp., Camden, 1993—. Contbr. articles to profl. jours. Fellow Am. Acad. Pediat.; mem. Nat. Perinatal Soc., Pa. Perinatal Soc., Phila. Perinatal Soc., Physicians for Social Responsibility, Sigma Xi. Office: Children's Regional Hosp at Cooper 1 Cooper Plz Camden NJ 08103-1461

STAHL, JACK LELAND, real estate company executive; b. Lincoln, Ill., June 28, 1934; s. Edwin R. and Edna M. (Burns) S.; m. Carol Anne Townsend, June 23, 1956; children: Cheryl, Nancy, Kellea BS in Edn., U. N.Mex., 1957. Tchr. Albuquerque Pub. Schs., 1956-59; pres. House Finders, Inc., Albuquerque, 1959-65; v.p. N.Mex. Savs. & Loan Assn., Albuquerque, 1965-67; chmn. bd. Hooten-Stahl, Inc., Albuquerque, 1967-77; mem. N.Mex. Ho. of Reps., 1969-70; pres. The Jack Stahl Co., Albuquerque, 1977—; mem. N.Mex. Senate, 1981-86; lt. gov. State of N.Mex., 1987-90. Mem. N. Mex. Ho. of Reps., 1969-70, exec. bd. Gr. S.W. Coun. Boy Scouts Am, 1982-89; bd. dirs. BBB N. Mex., 1968-82, pres. 1975-76; trustee Univ Heights. Hosp.,1980-85; vice chmn. N. Mex. Bd. Fin., 1987-90, N. Mex. Cmty. Devel. Coun., 1987-90; bd. dirs. Ctr. for Entrepreneurship and Econ. Devel., 1994-96; mem. Gov.'s Bus. Adv. Coun., 1995-97. Named Realtor of Yr., Albuquerque Bd. Realtors, 1972. Mem. Nat. Assn. Realtors, Nat. Homebuilders Assn., N.Mex. Amigos, 20-30 Club (pres. 1963-64), Rotary. Republican. Methodist. Office: 1911 Wyoming Blvd NE Albuquerque NM 87112-2865 Office Phone: 505-292-6635.

STAHL, LADDIE L. electrical engineer, manufacturing company executive; b. Terre Haute, Ind., Dec. 23, 1921; s. Edgar Allen and Martha (Llewellyn) S.; m. Thelma Mae Beasley, Dec. 11, 1942; children: Stephanie, Laddie L., Craig. BSCE, Purdue U., 1942; MS in Engring., Johns Hopkins U., 1950. With GE, 1954-90, mgr. planning and resources, electronics sci. and engring., corp. research and devel., 1974-76, mgr. electronics systems programs ops., elec. sci. and engring., 1976-84, mgr. spl. programs and project devel. operation, 1984-90; dir. tech. transfer program Data Storage Systems Ctr. Carnegie Mellon U., Pitts., 1990—. Chmn. adv. group U.S. Army Electronics Command, 1971-74; mem. U.S. Army Sci. Bd., 1978-87; cons. in field. Contbr. articles to profl. publs. Mem. alumni bd. dirs. Purdue U., 1979-82. Served with U.S. Army, 1942-54, ETO; maj. gen. Res. (ret.), 1954-77. Decorated D.S.M., Legion of Merit. Mem. AIAA (sr.), IEEE (life), Am. Def. Preparedness Assn., Army and Navy Club (Washington), Tau Beta Pi, Chi Epsilon. Home: 29 Fairway Ln Rexford NY 12148-1213 Office: Carnegie Mellon U Data Storage Sys Ctr ECE Dept 5000 Forbes Ave Pittsburgh PA 15213-3815 E-mail: laddie@netheaven.com.

STAHL, LESLEY R. news correspondent; b. Lynn, Mass., Dec. 16, 1941; d. Louis and Dorothy J. (Tishler) Stahl; m. Aaron Latham; 1 child. BA cum laude, Wheaton Coll., Norton, Mass., 1963. Asst. to speechwriter Mayor Lindsay's Office, N.Y.C., 1966—67; rschr. N.Y. Election unit CBS News, 1967—68; rschr. London-Huntley Brinkley Report, NBC News, 1969; prodr., reporter WHDH-TV, Boston, 1970—72; news corr. CBS News, Washington, 1972—, White House corr., 1979-91; moderator Face the Nation, 1983-91; co-editor, corr. CBS News, 60 Minutes, 1991—. Trustee Wheaton Coll. Named Best White House Corr., Washington Journalism Rev., 1991; named to

Broadcasting Mag. Hall of Fame, 1992; recipient Tex. Headliners award, 1973, Dennis Kauff award for lifetime achievement in journalism, Fifth Estate award, Fred Friendly First Amendment award, 1996. Office: CBS News 60 Minutes 524 W 57th St New York NY 10019-2924

STAHL, MADONNA, retired judge; b. Robinson, Ill., Sept. 26, 1928; d. Lawrence Joy and Inez Lucille (Kennedy) S.; children: Khushro Ghandhi, Rustom Ghandhi, Behram Ghandhi. BS, U. Ill., 0195; JD, Albany Law Sch., 1973. Bar: N.Y. 1974, U.S. Dist. Ct. (no. dist.) N.Y. 1974, U.S. Ct. Appeals (2nd cir.) 1975, U.S. Supreme Ct. 1978. Atty. trainee N.Y. State Dept. Commerce, Albany, 1973-74; atty. Legal Aid Soc., Albany, 1974-76; ptnr. Powers, Stahl & Somers (and predecessor firms), 1976-89; part-time judge Albany City Ct., 1984-89, full-time judge, 1990-97; ret., 1997. Mem. com. on character and fitness N.Y. State Supreme Ct. A.D. 3d Dept., Albany, 1980-86; jud. hearing officer State of N.Y., 1997-2000. Lobbyist Com. for Progressive Legislation, Schenectady, 1968-70. Mem. Women's Bar Assn. State N.Y. (Capital dist. pres. 1983-84). Democrat. Unitarian Universalist. E-mail: judge_stahl@yahoo.com.

STAHL, MARILYN BROWN, interior designer; b. Boston, Dec. 11, 1929; d. Benjamin M. and Nettie D. (Glazer) Brown; m. Alvan L. Stahl, July 1, 1951; children: Robert, Barry, Kim. BS in Art Edn., Mass. Coll. Art, 1951. Instr. painting, Newton, Mass.; freelance fabric designer, 1960-63; owner gallery, 1963-66, M.B. Stahl Interiors, Chestnut Hill, Mass., 1966—. Founder, pres. Maab Inc., mfrs. French furniture, 1979; pres. Decorators' Clearing House, Newton Upper Falls, Mass. Mem. Nat. Home Fashions League, Am. Soc. Interior Designers Industry Found., Nat. Home Fashions League Industry Found. Home: 390 Commonwealth Ave Apt 201 Boston MA 02215-2824 Office: M B Stahl Interiors 1381 Washington St West Newton MA 02465 Office Phone: 617-244-2770. E-mail: MBSinteriors@aol.com.

STAHL, NANETTE, librarian, biblicist; b. Brooklyn, N.Y., July 23, 1941; d. David and Hannah Stahl; m. William W. Hallo, Oct. 18, 1998. BA, Brooklyn Coll., Brooklyn, N.Y., 1964; MLIS, Pratt Univ., Brooklyn, N.Y., 1966; PhD, Univ. Calif., Berkeley, Calif., 1993. Judaica Bibliographer Univ. Calif., Sch. of Law, Berkeley, Calif., 1970—80; head libr. Bureau of Jewish Edn., San Francisco, 1980—89; Judaica curator Yale Univ. Libr., New Haven, 1993—. Author: Law and Liminality in the Bible, 1996; editor: (book) Sholem Asch Reconsidered, 2004. Mem.: Assn. Jewish Studies, Assn. of Jewish Libr. Office: Yale Univ Libr Box 208240 130 Wall St New Haven CT 06520

STAHL, NORMAN A. educator; b. San Francisco, Apr. 21, 1949; AA, City Coll. San Francisco, 1969; BA, San Francisco State U., 1971, MA, 1976; PhD, U. Pitts., 1983. Rsch. assoc. U. Pitts., 1980-82; asst. prof. divsn. devel. studies Ga. State U., Atlanta, 1982-87; assoc. prof. dept. curriculum & instrn. No. Ill. U., DeKalb, 1987-93, prof., chair dept. curriculum & instrn., 1994-99, chair dept. literacy edn., 1999—. Author: Teaching Developmental Reading, 2003; contbr. articles to profl. jours. Pres. DeKalb Edn. Found., 1999-2001. Recipient Disting. Rsch. award Coll. Reading & Learning Assn., 1990, N.Y. Coll. Learning Skills Assn., 1996. Mem. Coll. Reading Assn. (pres. 1991-92, treas. 1985-88), Internat. Reading Assn. (pres. history reading spl. interest group 1992-94), Am. Reading Forum (chair bd. dirs. 1996-97), Nat. Reading Conf. (historian 1998-2003, bd. dirs. 2003—). Office: No Ill U Dept Literacy Edn Dekalb IL 60115 Office Phone: 815-753-9032. E-mail: stahl@niu.edu.

STAHL, NORMAN H. judge; b. Manchester, N.H., 1931; BA, Tufts U., 1952; LLB, Harvard U., 1955. Law clk. to Hon. John V. Spalding Mass. Supreme Ct., 1955—56; assoc. Devine, Millimet, Stahl & Branch, Manchester, NH, 1956—59, ptnr., 1959—90; dist. judge U.S. Dist. Ct. (N.H. dist.), 1990—92; cir. judge U.S. Ct. Appeals (1st cir.), Concord, NH, 1992—. Del to Rep. Nat. Conv., 1988. Mem.: N.H. Bar Assn. Office: US Courthouse Ste 8730 1 Courthouse Way Boston MA 02210

STAHL, PHILIP ANTHONY, physics educator; b. Milw., July 6, 1946; s. Curtis Philip and Magdalen Mary (Polacheck) S.; m. Janice Anne Johnson, Aug. 9, 1975. BA in Astronomy, U. South Fla., 1971; MPhil in Physics, U. W.I., St. Michael, Barbados, 1984. Sci. tchr. U.S. Peace Corps, Barbados, W.I., 1971-75; head sci. dept. West St. Joseph Secondary, Barbados, 1975-77, Garrison Secondary, St. Michael, Barbados, 1977-82; asst. tutor Barbados Community Coll., St. Michael, 1982-83; lectr. physics Harrison Coll., St. Michael, 1985-91; tech. writer Nucletron Corp., Columbia, Md., 1993-96. Dir. Solar Rsch. Sect., Harry Bayley Observatory, St. Michael, 1984-91; tech. writer, cons. in field. Author: Metacosmos: Cosmic Connections and Self-Actualizing Universe, 1997, The Atheist's Handbook to Modern Materialism, 2000; contbr. articles to profl. jours. Mem. Barbados Environ. Assn., St. Michael, 1987—, Barbados Cancer Soc., St. Michael, 1986—, Barbados and Latin Am. Mus. Soc., 1988—, Mensa, 1993—. Recipient Studentship award Solar Physics Div. Am. Astron. Soc., 1984, Postgrad. Rsch. grant, 1980-84. Mem.: Dynamical Astron. divsn. of Am. Astron. Soc., Solar Physics divsn. of Am. Astron. Soc., Am. Astron. Soc., Barbados Astron. Soc. (pres. 1977—80), Am. Geophys. Union, Am. Math. Soc. Achievements include development of first astronomy syllabus used at secondary level by Caribbean Examination Coun.; discovery of basic relationship between sudden ionospheric disturbances and specific types of H-alpha flare assoc. with sunspot. Home and Office: 2720 Nogal Ct Colorado Springs CO 80917 E-mail: jpstahl@msn.com.

STAHL, RAY EMERSON, freelance writer, historian, researcher; b. Latrobe, Pa., Mar. 24, 1917; s. Curtis E. and Josephine (King) S.; m. Faith Worrell, Aug. 25, 1941; children: Ellen Josephine Carpenter, Ray Emerson Jr. AB, Bethany Coll., 1938; MDiv, Butler U., 1943; EdM, U. Pitts., 1946; postgrad., St. Vincent Coll., 1939, Pitts. Sch. Accountancy, 1939-40, U. Ky., 1955; MA, Ohio State U., 1969; LittD, Milligan Coll., 1995. Ordained to ministry Disciples of Christ Ch., 1941. Min. Brentwood Christian Ch., Pitts., 1943-46, 1st Christian Ch., Erwin, Tenn., 1946-50; exec. sec. in charge bus. adminstrn. and pub. rels. Miligan Coll.ate U., Johnson City, Tenn., 1950-68; dir. pub. rels., pub. info. East Tenn. State U., Johnson City, 1968-78. Author: How to Finance the Local Church, 1953, Six Decades of Progress, 1976, History of Tennessee-Virginia Energy Corporation, 1981, Money, Wealth, the Bible and You, 1983, Greater Johnson City, A Pictorial History, Tennessee, A Pictorial History, 1983, rev. 2nd edit., 1986, A Beacon to Health Care, 1989; contbr. articles to profl. jours. Bd. dirs. United Way, ARC, Am. Cancer Soc., Reece Mus., Tipton-Haynes Hist. Assn., Johnson City Symphony; elder Christian Ch. Mem. Pub. Rels. Soc. Am. (accredited 1974—), Coun. for Advancement of Small Colls. (chmn. pub. rels. 1957-61), East Tenn. Edn. Assn. (chmn. pub. rels. 1968-76), Johnson City C. of C. (bd. dirs., ofcl. city historian 1986-99), Washington County Tenn. Hist. Assn. (pres.), Johnson City Execs. Club (pres. 1961-62), Kiwanis (sec.-treas. 1983-84, bd. dirs., Kiwanian of Yr. 1995), Theta Phi, Kappa Tau Alpha. Republican. Home and Office: 699 Stadium Dr Boone NC 28607-5423

STAHL, STEPHEN LEE, theater director, writer, producer; b. Phila., Mar. 15, 1949; s. Myer and Fridel (Goldstein) S.; m. Cornell DeFanis, Dec. 29, 1969 (div. May 1976); 1 child, Meredith. Student, Lee Strasburg Actors Studio, 1981. Artistic dir. Studio 3 Prodns., Phila., 1979-82; artistic dir., tchr. drama Actors Ctr., Phila., 1982-85; dir. Troyvay Internat., Paris, London, 1985-87, Theatre of Living Arts, Phila., 1987—, Theatre on the Sq., San Francisco; tchr. drama Freez Frame Inc., Phila., 1987—. Dir., writer, prodr. Music Found. Awards, 1989-93; instr. Duality Playhouse, N.Y.C., 1995-96. Writer, dir. plays Porno Stars at Home, Full Bloom, 1998, Queen of Hearts, 1999—, Lady Day, 1986-87 (Bay City award 1987, Creative Drama award 1987), Philly's Beat, 1985 (citation City of Phila. 1985); dir. plays Hosanna, 1981, Coupla White Chicks, 1983, He Plays Piano, 1984, Danny and the Deep Blue Sea, 1984, Sister Mary ... etc., 1985-87, Tallulah, 1987, Psycho Beach Party, 1994, Sophie, Totie and Belle, 1994, We Love Lucy, 1994, P.S. Bette Davis, 1994, 30,000 Pigs Roamed the City, 1995-96, Judy at the Wall Inn, 1995-96, Lenny, 1995-96, The Passion, 1995-96, Skirts, 1995-96, Airborn From Deerborn, Chicago Gangstertown, Full Bloom; co-producer play Heart Strings, 1990, Jerker, 1993, Women Behind Bars, 1993, Chicago's Gangsters, 1996-97. Bd. dirs. Max Goldstein Outreach, Phila., 1979-82, Young Persons Apprenticeship Program, Phila., 1979-82. Democrat. Avocations: art, design, tennis. Home: 11 N Main St # A New Hope PA 18938-1314

STAHLECKER, BARBARA JEAN, marketing professional, consultant; b. Stamford, Conn., Jan. 22, 1958; d. Roger Francis and Lillian Ann Beauleau; m. Richard Walter Stahlecker; children: Shannon Lee Banks, Brande Lauren Beach; children: Cori, Cara. Grad., Brien McMahon H.S., Norwalk, Conn., 1975. New bus. adminstr. Mutual of Omaha Ins. Co., L.A., 1983—85; ind. ins. agt. L.A., 1985—88; mktg. coord. LifeCare Assurance Corp., Canoga Park, Calif., 1988—96; v.p., nat. mktg. dir. Centrelink Ins. & Fin. Svcs., Woodland, Calif., 1996—. Author: (Continuing Education Courses) Everything You've Always Wanted to Know about LTC - and Then Some, 1998, (Continuing Education Course) The Nuts and Bolts of Long Term Care Insurance, 2000, TQ vs. NTQ LTCi, 2001; contbr. articles to profl. jours., 2001. Recipient Million Dollar Prodr. award, UNUM/Provident, 2001. Mem.: Soc. Cert. Sr. Advisors (cert. sr. advisor), Long-Term Care Profl., Am. Assn. Long-Term Care Ins. (Top Prodr. award 2000, 2001, BRAMCO Million Dollar Club award 2002), Nat. Assn. Health Underwriters (cons. 1999—). Office: Centrelink Ins & Fin Svc 20750 Ventura Blvd #300 Woodland Hills CA 91364 Business E-Mail: barbara@centrelink.com.

STAHLMAN, MILDRED THORNTON, pediatrics and pathology educator, researcher; b. Nashville, July 31, 1922; d. James Geddes and Mildred (Thornton) Stahlman. AB, Vanderbilt U., 1943, MD, 1946; MD (hon.), U. Goteborg, Sweden, 1973, U. Nancy, France, 1982. Diplomate Am. Bd. Pediat., Am. Bd. Neonatology. Intern Boston Children's Hosp., 1947—48; resident Vanderbilt Univ. Hosp., 1948—49; fellow Royal Caroline Inst. Medicine, Sweden, 1949—50; cardiac resident La Rabida Sanitarium, Chgo., 1951; instr. pediat. Vanderbilt U., Nashville, 1951—58, instr. physiology, 1954—60, asst. prof. pediat., 1959—64, asst. prof. physiology, 1960—62, assoc. prof. pediat., 1964—70, prof., 1970—, prof. pathology, 1982—, Harvie Branscomb Disting. prof., 1984, dir. divsn. neonatology, 1961—89, now prof. pediat. and pathology. Editor: Respiratory Distress Syndromes, 1989; contbr. over 175 articles to profl. publs., chpts. to books. Recipient Apgar award, Am. Acad. Pediat., 1987; grantee NIH, 1954—. Mem.: AAAS, Inst. Medicine NAS, Royal Swedish Acad. Scis., So. Soc. Pediatric Rsch. (pres. 1961—62), Am. Physiology Soc., Soc. Pediatric Rsch., Am. Pediatric Soc. (pres. 1984, John Howland award 1996). Episcopalian. Home: 538 Beech Creek Rd S Brentwood TN 37027-3421 Office: Vanderbilt U Med Ctr A-0109 Med Ctr N 21st Ave S Nashville TN 37232-2370 E-mail: mildred.stahlman@vanderbilt.edu.

STAHR, CURTIS BRENT, photographer, art association administrator, educator; b. West Union, Iowa; s. Freman H. and Lucile M. (Schreiner) S. AA, Ellsworth Coll., 1966; BFA, Peru (Nebr.) State U., 1968. Cert. tchr., Iowa, Colo., Ariz. Art dir. Iowa Falls (Iowa) High Sch., 1968-70, Wiley (Colo.) Schs., 1971-72, Judson Sch., Scottsdale, Ariz., 1973-79; freelance graphic artist, photographer and mktg. dir., 1979-88; prof. photography, photography dir. Des Moines Area C.C., 1988—; art dir. Homestead Assn., Des Moines, 1993-98. Bd. dirs. Homestead Corp., Alpha Inst., Unoged Corp., v.p., 1999; v.p. Young Masters Photographic Art Collection, 1998—; pres. Interpretive Photography, 1999; art dir. Starland Design Band Group, 1979-86, graphic effects dept. Bischoff's, 1987-88; photographic dir. ednl. exchange trip to China. Exhibited in 16 one-man art shows, in 34 invited/juried art shows; represented in numerous pvt. collections; photographer numerous field trips including migration of Am. eagle from Alaska to Fla., all 99 Iowa County Courthouses, Yellowstone Nat. Park, Grand Teton Nat. Park, Waterton-Glacier Internat. Peace Park (U.S. and Can.), Isle Royale Nat. Park, Grand Canyon Nat. Park, Denali Nat. Park, Arctic Nat. Park & Preserve, Canyon de Chelly Nat. Monument, Rainbow Bridge Nat. Monument, Devils Tower Nat. Monument, Effigy Mounts Nat. Monument, Yosemite Nat. Park, Sequoia Nat. Park, Kings Canyon Nat. Park, Japser Nat. Park (Can.), Glacier Nat. Park (Can.), Banff (Can.) Nat. Park, Terra Nova Nat. Park (Newfoundland), Boundary Waters Canoe Area Wilderness, Quetico Provincial Park, Can., North Magnetic Pole, Can., Canyonlands (Utah), Auyuittuq Nat. Park Res., Can., Ellesmere Island Nat. Park Res, Can. Yoho Nat. Park, Can., Kootenay Nat. Park, Can., Angel Falls, Venezuela, Machu Picchu, Peru; numerous cross country trips to U.S., Can., Mex., Cen. Am., S.Am., Yukon Territory and Arctic Cir. Speaker Ariz.-Calif. Lecture Series, 1982-84; chairperson art evaluation com. State of Iowa, 1970; bd. dirs. Ariz. Arts Festival, 1974-79, Muscular Dystrophy Assn. Fund Drive, Ariz., 1982-85. Recipient 14 purchase awards. Democrat. Office: Des Moines Area CC 2006 S Ankeny Blvd Ankeny IA 50021-8995

STAIB, LAWRENCE HAMILTON, biomedical engineer; b. Phila., Dec. 23, 1960; s. John Hamilton and Mildred Oakford Staib; m. Eva Kaufman, Apr. 2, 1997; 1 child, Clare Staib-Kaufman. AB, Cornell U., 1982; MS, MPhil, Yale U., PhD, 1990. Assoc. prof. diagnostic radiology, biomed. engring., and elec. engring. Yale U., New Haven, 1997—. Reviewer NIH, Bethesda, Md., 1995—. Recipient Nat. Rsch. Svc. award, Nat. Libr. Medicine, 1990—91; grantee Biomedical Engring. Rsch. grantee, Whitaker Found., 1993—98, Nat. Inst. Bioimaging and Bioengring., 2000. Mem.: IEEE. Office: Yale U Dept of Diagnostic Radiology 333 Cedar St New Haven CT 06520-8042

STAINES, DAVID MCKENZIE, English educator; b. Toronto, Aug. 8, 1946; s. Ralph McKenzie and Mary Rita (Hayes) S. BA, U. Toronto, 1967; AM, Harvard U., 1968, PhD, 1973. Asst. prof. English Harvard U., Cambridge, Mass., 1973-78, vis. assoc. prof., summers 1980, 82; assoc. prof. English U. Ottawa, Ont., 1978-85, prof., 1985—, vice-dean faculty of Arts, 1994-95, dean faculty of arts, 1995—2003. Author: Tennyson's Camelot, 1982, Beyond the Provinces: Literary Canada at Century's End, 1995; contbr. articles and revs. Arthurian lit., medieval drama and romance to profl. jours.; editor: The Canadian Imagination, 1977, The Forty-ninth and Other Parallels, 1986, Margaret Laurence: Critical Reflections, 2001; editor Jour. Can. Poetry, 1984—; gen. editor New Can. Libr., 1988—; translator The Complete Romances of Chrétien de Troyes, 1990; co-editor Elements of Literature, 1987, 90, 2004, The Short Story in English, 1991, Northrop Frye on Canada, 2003, Marshall McLuhan's Understanding Me, 2003. Recipient Lorne Pierce medal, 1998; Ind. study fellow NEH, London, 1977-78, fellow Huntington Libr., San Marino, Calif., 1979. Mem. Medieval Acad. Am. (chmn. com. on ctrs. and regional assn. 1981-87), MLA, Internat. Arthurian Soc., Assn. Can. Univ. Tchrs. English. Roman Catholic. Avocations: theater, ballet. Home: 222 Clemow Ave Ottawa ON Canada KIS 2B6 E-mail: dstaines@uottawa.ca.

STAINES, MAVIS AVRIL, artistic director, ballet principal; b. Cowansville, Que., Can., Apr. 9, 1954; d. David Russell and Betty (Knott) S.; m. Jyrki Virsunen, Feb. 4, 1988. Student, Nat. Ballet Sch., 1968-73, 81-83. Dancer Nat. Ballet of Can., 1973-78, 1st soloist, 1975-78; dancer Dutch Nat. Ballet, 1978-81; artistic dir. Nat. Ballet Sch., Toronto, Ont., Can., 1989—. Mem. artistic staff Nat. Ballet Sch., 1982, assoc. artistic dir., 1984; juror Prix de Lausanne, Switzerland, 1993, 94, 95, guest spkr., 1997; presenter Prix de Lausanne Internat. Symposium, 1997; mem. task force on classicl ballet tng. DANCE/USA, Phila., 1994; pres. Prix de Lausanne, 1998, 99, artistic pres. designate, 2001, artistic pres., 2002; bd. dirs. Kala Nidhi Fine Arts of Can. Recipient Toronto Arts award for performing arts, 1998. Office: The Nat Ballet Sch 105 Maitland St Toronto ON Canada M4Y 1E4

STAINROOK, HARRY RICHARD, retired bank executive; b. Phila., Jan. 11, 1937; s. Millward M. and Janet (Cruickshank-Smith) S.; m. Judith Ann Swann, May 21, 1966; children: Jennifer, Eric. BA, Rutgers U., 1970. Mgr. bank ops. First Pa. Bank, Phila., 1956-61, asst. v.p. br. dept., 1964-73, v.p., mgr. London office, 1973-75, v.p. internat. dept., 1975-78, sr. v.p. comml. group, 1978-81, exec. v.p., trust and investments, 1981-85; exec. v.p. trust and investments Mfrs. and Traders Trust Co., Buffalo, 1985-97; ret., 1997. Former chmn., bd. dirs. Greater Buffalo Opera Co.; former pres. Buffalo Philharm. Orch.; pres. Acad. Vocal Arts, Phila. With U.S. Army, 1961-64. Mem. World Future Soc., English Speaking Union, Saturn Club. Lutheran. Home: 150 Columbus Ave Apt 4A New York NY 10023-5964 E-mail: hs01@email.msn.com.

STAINTON, DAVID, recreational facility executive; B in History, Princeton U.; MBA, Harvard U. Mgr. spl. projects Walt Disney Pictures and TV, Burbank, Calif., 1989—91; creative exec. on Lion King, Walt Disney Feature Animation, Burbank, Calif., 1991—95, v.p., 1995—98, sr. v.p., 1998—2000; exec. v.p. Walt Disney TV Animation, Burbank, Calif., 2000—02; pres. Walt Disney Feature Animation, Walt Disney Co., Burbank, Calif., 2002—. Office: Walt Disney Co 500 S Buena Vista St Burbank CA 91521-9722

STAIR, THOMAS OSBORNE, physician, educator; b. Richmond, Va., Jan. 10, 1950; s. Frederick Rogers Jr. and Martha (Osborne) S.; m. Lucy Caldwell, Dec. 28, 1973; children: Rebecca Caldwell, Peter Caldwell. AB, U. N.C., 1971; MD, Harvard U., 1975. Diplomate Am. Bd. Emergency Medicine (examiner 1982-88). Residency dir. emergency dept. Georgetown U. Sch. Medicine, Washington, 1979-85, asst. dir. emergency dept., 1979-89, asst. dean for continuing med. edn., 1985-89, chair dept. emergency medicine, 1989-95; prof. U. Md., Balt., 1995-98; assoc. prof. Harvard Med. Sch., 1998—; attending emergency physician Brigham and Women's Hosp., Boston, 1998—. Co-author: Common Simple Emergencies, 1985, Emergency Medicine, 1997, Minor Emergencies, 1999. Recipient Excellence in Teaching award Emergency Medicine Residents Assn., 1986. Fellow Am. Coll. Emergency Physicians; mem. Soc. Acad. Emergency Medicine, Am. Med. Informatics Assn. Home: 46 Woodcliff Rd Newton MA 02461-1825 Office: 75 Francis St Boston MA 02115-6110 Office Phone: 617-732-5640. Business E-Mail: tstair@partners.org.

STAIRS, DENIS WINFIELD, political science educator; b. Halifax, N.S., Can., Sept. 6, 1939; s. Henry Gerald and Freda (Winfield) S.; m. Valerie Downing Street, Aug. 10, 1963 (div. Dec. 1986); children: Robert Woodliffe, Christopher Winfield; m. Jennifer Smith, July 18, 1987. BA, Dalhousie U., 1961, Oxford U., 1964, MA, 1968; PhD, U. Toronto, 1969. Asst. prof. dept. polit. sci. Dalhousie U., 1966-70, assoc. prof., 1970-75, dir. Centre Fgn. Policy Studies, 1971-75, prof. polit. sci., 1975—, McCulloch prof., 1995—, chmn. dept., 1980-85, v.p. acad. and rsch., 1988-93. Bd. dirs. Atlantic Coun. Can., 1979—, Inst. Rsch. Pub. Policy; mem. coun. Social Sci. and Humanities Rsch. Coun. Can., 1981-87; mem. rsch. coun. Can. Inst. Advanced Rsch., 1986-97; bd. dirs. Orgn. for Study of Nat. History of Can., 1995-98; bd. vis. Can. Forces Coll., 2002—; mem. adv. com. Can. Def. and Fgn. Affairs Inst., 2002-. Author: The Diplomacy of Constraint: Canada, the Korean War, and the United States, 1974; editl. bd. Internat. Jour., 1997—. Rhodes scholar, 1961; J.W. Dafoe postgrad. fellow internat. studies, 1965-66; Can. Coun. leave fellow, 1972-73; Social Scis. and Humanities Rsch. Coun. Can. leave fellow, 1979-80; recipient Disting. Writing award, Marcel Cadieux, 2000, 2003. Fellow Royal Soc. Can.; mem. Can. Polit. Sci. Assn. (pres.), Can. Inst. Internat. Affairs, Internat. Studies Assn. Clubs: Royal N.S. Yacht Squadron. Office: Dalhousie U Dept Polit Sci Halifax NS Canada B3H 4H6

STAKE, JAMES B. manufacturing executive; Mng. dir., 3M Mfg. Venezuela 3M Co., mng. dir., 3M Italy and regional mng. dir., so. European region, 1996—98, mng. dir., 3M Italy, 1998—99, v.p., packaging sys. divsn., 1999—2000, v.p., indsl. tape and specialties divsn., 2000—02, v.p., indsl. tape and specialties divsn. and v.p., mktg., indsl. markets, 2002, exec. v.p., display and graphics bus., 2002—. Office: 3M Co 3M Ctr Saint Paul MN 55144

STAKER, ROBERT JACKSON, judge; b. Kermit, W.Va., Feb. 14, 1925; s. Frederick George and Nada (Frazier) S.; m. Sue Blankenship Poore, July 16, 1955; 1 child, Donald Seth; 1 stepson, John Timothy Poore. Student, Marshall U., Huntington, W.Va., W.Va. U., Morgantown, U. Ky., Lexington; LL.B, W.Va. U., 1952. Bar: W.Va. 1952. Practiced in, Williamson, 1952-68; judge Mingo County Circuit Ct., Williamson, 1969-79; U.S. dist. judge So. Dist. W.Va., Huntington, 1979-95, sr. U.S. dist. judge, 1995—. Served with USN, 1943-46. Democrat. Presbyterian. E-mail: robert_staker@wvsd.uscourts.gov.

STAKIAS, G. MICHAEL, merchant banker; b. Norfolk, Va., Feb. 2, 1950; s. George and Gloria Stakias. BA, William & Mary, 1972; JD, Thomas M. Cooley Law Sch, 1976; LLM, NYU, 1977. Bar: Mich., 1976, D.C. 1980, Pa. 1980, N.Y. 1994. Atty. U.S. SEC, Washington, 1977-80; ptnr. Blank, Rome, Comisky & McCauley, Phila., 1980-98, chmn. bus. and corp. dept., 1996-98; ptnr. Liberty Ptnrs., LP, N.Y.C., 1998—. Bd. dirs. Thomas M. Cooley Law Sch., Lansing, Mich., 1988—. Mem. ABA (bus. law sect.), Patrons Found. Office: Liberty Partners LP Floor 34 1370 Ave of the Americas New York NY 10019-4602 Business E-Mail: mstakias@libertypartners.com.

STALBERG, ZACHARY, newspaper editor; b. Phila., Apr. 6, 1947; m. Deborah Lock, Sept. 2, 1990. Degree in Polit. Sci., Temple U., 1968; diploma in Exec. Edn. Program, U. Pa., 1994. Reporter Bucks County Courier Times, Levittown, Pa., 1970-71; reporter Phila. Daily News, 1971-75, city editor, 1975-77, mng. editor, 1977-79, exec. editor, 1979-84, editor, 1984—; sr. v.p. Phila. Newspapers Inc., 1984—88, exec. v.p., 1988—. Served with U.S. Army, 1968-70 Mem. Am. Soc. Newspaper Editors Office: Philadelphia Daily News 400 N Broad St Philadelphia PA 19130-4015

STALCUP, JOE ALAN, lawyer, clergyman; b. Hooker, Okla., Feb. 13, 1931; s. Herbert I. and Ruby (Gantt) S.; m. Nancy Jo Vaughn, Sept. 3, 1950; children: Melinda, Sondra Jo, Cheri Ann. BBA cum laude, So. Methodist U., 1951, JD magna cum laude, 1959, M.Th. magna cum laude, 1978. Bar: Tex. 1959. Tchr. Dallas Ind. Sch. Dist., 1951-57; assoc. atty. firm Locke, Purnell, Boren, Laney & Neely, Dallas, 1959-66; assoc. atty., partner firm Geary, Brice & Lewis, Dallas, 1966-67; founder, sr. partner firm Stalcup, Johnson, Meyers & Miller (and predecessor firm), Dallas, 1968-75; dean Sch. Theology for the Laity, 1978—80, 1992—96, 2003—. Pres. Dallas County Young Democrats, 1952-54; Bd. dirs., mem. exec. com. N. Tex. Christian Communications Commn., 1972-78; bd. dirs., v.p. Greater Dallas Council Chs., 1972-75; bd. dirs., chmn. Christian Ch. Found., 1976-84, 86-91, Christian Bd. Publ., 1991-98. Mem. ABA, Tex. Bar Assn., Dallas Bar Assn., Am. Judicature Soc., Phi Alpha Delta. Mem. Disciples of Christ (minister). Home: 7594 Benedict Dr Dallas TX 75214-1903 Office: 6510 Abrams Rd Dallas TX 75231-7217

STALEY, DAWN MICHELLE, professional basketball player; b. Phila., May 4, 1970; d. Estelle. Grad., U. Va., 1992. Profl. basketball player Brazil, France, Italy, Spain, Richmond Rage, ABL, 1996—98, Charlotte Sting, WNBA, 1999—; head women's basketball coach Temple U., 2000—. Mem. USA Basketball Teams, 1989—. Founder Dawn Staley Found. Named USA Basketball Female Athlete of Yr., 1994, MVP, Goodwill Games, 1994, Phila. Big Five Coach of Yr., 2002, Atlantic 10 Coach of Yr., 2004; named to First Team All-ABL, 1997, WNBA All-Star Team, 2001, 2002, 2003; recipient Spectrum Award, ARC, 1998, Entrepreneurial Spirit Award, WNBA, 1999, Sportsmanship Award, 1999. Achievements include mem., US Women's Basketball Gold Medal Team, Atlanta, 1996; mem., US Women's Basketball Gold Medal Team, Sydney Olympics, 2000; mem., US Women's Basketball Team, Athens Olympics, 2004; number retired at U. Va; first women in professional basketball history to record 1,000 career assists; Olympic Flag bearer, Athens Olympic Games, 2004. Office: 100 Hive Dr Charlotte NC 28208-7707*

STALEY, HARRY CHARLES, retired literature educator, poet; b. Gloversville, NY, June 26, 1924; s. Harry Joseph and Edna Clare Staley; m. Helen Raynes, July 22, 1952; 1 child, Gregory. BA, St. John's U., NYC, 1948; MA, U. Penn., Phila., 1953, PhD, 1966. Tchr. St. George High Sch., NYC, 1950—51; Wharton editor U. Penn., Phila., 1953—54; asst. prof. Loyola Coll., Balt., 1954—56; prof. U. at Albany, NY, 1956—2002, prof. emeritus, 2002—. Author: (poetry) Lives of a Shell-Shocked Chaplain, 1995, All One Breath, 2002. With arty. U.S. Army, 1942—46, ETO. Home: 397 State St Albany NY 12210

STALEY, JOHN FREDRIC, lawyer; b. Sidney, Ohio, Sept. 26, 1943; s. Harry Virgil and Fredericka May (McMillin) S.; m. Sue Ann Bolin, June 11, 1966; children: Ian McMillin, Erik Bolin. AB in History, Fresno State Coll., 1965; postgrad., Calif. State U., Hayward, 1967-68; JD, U. Calif., San Francisco, 1972. Bar: Calif. 1972. Ptnr. Staley, Jobson & Ford, Pleasanton, Calif., 1972—. Lectr. U. Calif. Hastings Coll. Law, San Francisco, 1973-74;

founding mem. Bank of Livermore (now U.S. Bank); del. U.S.-China Joint Conf. on Law, Beijing, 1987. Mem. Livermore City Coun., 1975-82, vice mayor, 1978-82; bd. dirs. Alameda County Tng. and Employment Bd., Alameda-Contra Costa Emergency Med. Svcs. Agy., Valley Vol. Ctr. With M.I., U.S. Army, 1966-67. Fellow Am. Acad. Matrimonial Lawyers; mem. ABA, Calif. State Bar, Alameda Bar Assn., Amador Valley Bar Assn., Calif. Assn. Cert. Family Law Specialists (pres. 1988-89, Hall of Fame award 1994), Hastings Coll. Law Alumni Assn. (bd. dirs.). Office: Staley Jobson & Ford Ste 310 5775 Stoneridge Mall Rd Pleasanton CA 94588-2838

STALEY, KENNETH BERNARD, civil engineer; b. Dec. 31, 1948; s. Kinzy and Bernice Florence (Williams) S.; m. Sheila Ruth Keeys, Apr. 26, 1975; children: Tabbatha, Christina, Harrison. ThM, Villanova U., 1971, MA, 1976, DD, 1978. Registerd profl. engr.; ordained to ministry Bapt. Ch., 1978. Cost estimator Joseph A. McCollum Inc., Marlton, N.J., 1967-69; expeditor R. V. Rulon Inc., Riverton, N.J., 1971; field engr. United Engrs., Phila., 1971-72; civil engr., v.p., dir. Kinzy Staley & Sons, Inc., Phila., 1972—. Vol. Aid Sickle Cell Anemia, 1974, Mendenhall Ministries, Miss.; asst. pastor Christian Stronghold Bapt. Ch., Phila., 1978—; bd. dirs. Christian R&D, Phila., Germantown Cmty. Devel., Phila.; bd. advisors Manna Bible Inst., Phila.; trustee Ctr. Urban Theol. Studies, Conservative Bapt. Sem., Phila. Prison Sys. Mem. Nat. Soc. Profl. Engrs., Assn. Cost Engrs., Am. Arbitration Assn., Am. Ceramic Soc., Am. Concrete Inst., Phila. Engrs. Club, Alpha Phi Alpha. Democrat. Home: 1130 Lakeside Ave Philadelphia PA 19126-2308 Office: Covenant Cons Group PO Box 698 Bala Cynwyd PA 19004-0698

STALEY, LYNN, English educator; b. Madisonville, Ky., Dec. 24, 1947; d. James Mulford and Florine (Hurt) Staley. AB, U. Ky., 1969; MA, PhD, Princeton U., 1973. Grad. asst. Princeton (N.J.) U., 1971-73; instr. English Colgate U., Hamilton, N.Y., 1974-75, from asst. to assoc. prof., 1975-86, prof., 1986—. Author: The Voice of the Gawain-Poet, 1984, The Shepheardes Calendar: An Introduction, 1990, Margery Kempe's Dissenting Fictions, 1994, (with David Aers) The Powers of the Holy: Religion, Politics and Gender in Late Medieval English Culture, 1996; editor: The Book of Margery Kempe, 1996; translator: The Book of Margery Kempe, 2001, Dictionary of the Middle Ages, 2004; contbr. articles to profl. jours. NEH fellow, 2003—04, Guggenheim fellow, 2003—04. Mem. MLA, Medieval Acad. Am., Renaissance Soc. Am., New Chaucer Soc., Spenser Soc. Office: Colgate U Dept English 13 Oak Dr Dept English Hamilton NY 13346-1383 Office Phone: 315-228-7667.

STALEY, THOMAS FABIAN, language professional, academic administrator; b. Pitts., Aug. 13, 1935; s. Fabian Richard and Mary (McNulty) S.; m. Carolyn O'Brien, Sept. 3, 1960; children: Thomas Fabian, Caroline Ann, Mary Elizabeth, Timothy X. AB, BS, Regis Coll., 1957; MA, U. Tulsa, 1958; PhD, U. Pitts., 1962; D.H.L., Regis Coll. Asst. prof. English Rollins Coll., 1961-62; mem. faculty U. Tulsa, 1962-88, prof. English, 1969-88, dean Grad. Sch., 1969, dean Coll. Arts and Scis., 1981-83, provost, v.p. acad. affairs, 1983-88, McFarlin prof. modern lit., 1988; prof. English, dir. Ransom Humanities Rsch. Ctr. U. Tex., Austin, 1988—, Chancellor's Centennial prof. of the Book, 1989—92, Harry Huntt Ransom chair liberal arts, 1992—. Fulbright prof., Italy, 1966-67; Fulbright lectr., 1971; Danforth assoc., 1962-67; chmn. Internat. James Joyce Symposium; dir. Grad. Inst. Modern Letters, 1970-81. Author: James Joyce Today, 1966, James Joyce's Portrait of the Artist, 1968, Italo Svevo: Essays on His Work, 1969, (with H.J. Mooney) The Shapeless God: Essays on the Modern Novel, 1968, (with B. Benstock) Approaches to Ulysses: Ten Essays, 1970, Approaches to Joyce's Portrait: Ten Essays, Jean Rhys: A Critical Study; editor: Il Punto Su Joyce, 1973, Dorothy Richardson, Ulysses: Fifty Years, 1974, Twentieth-Century Women Novelists, 1982, British Novelists, 1890-1929, Traditionalists, Dictionary of Lit. Biography, Vols. 34, 36, 70, 77, An Annotated Critical Bibliography of James Joyce, 1989, Joyce Studies: An Annual edit., 1990—, Studies in Modern Literature Series, 1990—, Reflections on James Joyce: Stuart Gilbert's Paris Journal, 1993, Writing the Lives of Writers, 1998, James Joyce Quar., 1963-89; adv. editor Twentieth-Century Lit., 1966—, Jean Rhys Rev., 1986—; bd. dirs. Eighteenth-Century Short Title Catalogue/North America, 1990; editl. bd. Tulsa Studies in Women's Literature, Jour. Modern Lit., 1989—; contbr. articles to profl. jours. Bd. dirs. Tulsa Arts Coun., 1969-76, NCCJ, 1979—, Christopher Isherwood Found.; pres. James Joyce Found., 1968-72; chmn. bd. Undercroft Montessori Sch., 1968-70, Marquette Sch., 1969-70; bd. dirs. Cascia Hall Prep. Sch.; chmn. disting. authors com. Tulsa Libr. Trust, 1984; mem. bd. commrs. Tulsa City-County Libr., chmn., 1980-82; mem. adv. coun. Tex. Inst. for Humanities; trustee Regis U., 1992—; bd. dirs. Libr. of Am., 1994—, Harlick Trust, 1994—; mem. symposium com. Lyndon Baines Johnson Presdl. Libr., 1993—. Recipient Am. Council Learned Socs. award, 1969, 80 Mem. MLA, Internat. Assn. Univ. Profs. English, Anglo-Irish Studies Assn., Am. Com. for Irish Studies, Assn. Internat. de Bibliophilie, James Joyce Soc., Hopkins Soc., Tex. Philos. Soc. (bd. dirs. 1991—), Internat. James Joyce Found. (hon. trustee), U.S. Tennis Assn., Tulsa Tennis Club, Westwood Country Club, The Athenaeum Club (London), Grolier Club (N.Y.), Edgecomb Tennis Club (Kennebunk, Maine), Tarry House, Phi Beta Kappa. Home: 2528 Tanglewood Trl Austin TX 78703-1540 also: 4 Surf Ln Kennebunk ME 04043 Business E-Mail: TFS@mail.utexas.edu.

STALEY, WARREN R. agricultural products and diversified services company executive; b. Springfield, Ill., May 14, 1942; BS in Elec. Engring., Kans. State U., 1965; MS in Bus. Adminstrn., Cornell U., 1967. With Cargill, Inc., Mpls., 1969—, gen. mgr., European corn milling bus., 1978—82, gen. mgr., Argentine ops., 1983—87, pres. for N.Am. and Latin Am., to 1998, pres., COO, 1998—2000, CEO, 1999—, chmn., 2000—. Apptd. mem. President's Export Coun. (PEC), 2003, chmn. Cargill Found. Bd. dirs. U.S. Bancorp, Target Corp., Greater Twin Cities United Way, Minn. Pvt. Coll. Coun. Office: Cargill Inc 15407 McGinty Rd, W Wayzata MN 55391*

STALFORT, JOHN ARTHUR, lawyer; b. Balt., June 9, 1951; s. John Irving and Libby Jean (Adams) S.; m. Rebecca Higgins, Aug. 21, 1976 (div. 1984); m. Anne Cheesman, July 19, 1985. BA, U. Va., 1973, MBA, JD, 1977. Bar: Md. 1977. Assoc. Miles & Stockbridge, Balt., 1977-84, ptnr., 1984—. Author: Commercial Financing Forms-Maryland, 1986. Sec. Roland Pk. Rds. and Maintenance Corp., Balt., 1978-83. Mem. ABA, Md. State Bar Assn. (chmn. sect. bus. law 1995-96), Nat. Assn. of Bond Lawyers, Balt. Country Club, Md. Club, Talbot Country Club, Phi Beta Kappa. Republican. Presbyterian. Avocations: skiing, golf, lacrosse, running. Office: Miles & Stockbridge 10 Light St Baltimore MD 21202-1487 Office Phone: 410-385-3424. E-mail: jstalfort@milesstockbridge.com.

STALHEIM, OLE HENRY V. veterinarian, educator; b. Watertown, S.D., Sept. 23, 1917; s. Henry Ole Stalheim and Ellen Charlotte Nelson; m. Vivian Elvira Elverson, June 2, 1942; children: Alan Jerard, Julie Ann Stalheim Zoet, David Olin, Jon Christopher. DVM, Tex. A&M U., 1941; MA, U. S.D., 1960; PhD, U. Wis., 1963. Vet., Vermillion, SD, 1941—58; postdoctoral rsch. fellow NIH, Vermillion, 1958—60, Madison, Wis., 1960—63; vet. med. officer Nat. Animal Disease Ctr., USDA, Ames, Iowa, 1963—85; assoc. prof., collaborator Iowa State U., Ames, 1982—89. Lectr. in field. Author: (hist. books) The Winning of Animal Health, 1994, Veterinary Conversations, 1996, H. J. Stafseth, Notable Veterinarian; contbr. scientific papers to profl. publs. Mem. Ptnrs. for the Ams., 4-H; vol. Luth. chs. Recipient Fulbright Scholar awards (2), Coun. for Internat. Exch. of Scholars, Sudan, 1980, Coun. for Internat. Exch. of Scholars, Turkey, 1987. Mem.: AVMA (co-founder, chair publs. com. 1977—80, XII Internat. Congress prize 1986), World Vets. Against Nuclear War (co-founder, sec., pres. 1983—88), Vet. Svcs. for Luth. Missions (founder, sec. 1970—), Ames Found. (co-founder 1978—, sec., pres. 1978—), Interstate Vet. Med. Assn. (pres. 1946—), S.D. Vet. Med. Assn. (pres. 1941—), Am. Vet. History Soc., Am. Acad. for Vet. Disaster Medicine (co-founder 1984—), World Assn. for the History of Vet. Medicine, Kiwanis (officer 1941—), Rotary (officer 1941—), Lions (officer 1941—). Avocations: travel, walking, music, walnut plantations. Home: 1918 George Allen Ave Ames IA 50010

STALICK, WAYNE M. chemistry educator, law firm consultant; b. Oregon City, Oreg., Aug. 24, 1942; s. Anton and Caroline Stalick; m. Chin Huang, Sept. 8, 2001; 1 child, Jonathan. BA, U. Oreg., 1964; PhD, Northwestern U., 1969. Vis. asst. prof. San Jose (Calif.) State U., 1969-70; postdoctoral fellow, instr. Ohio State U., Columbus, 1970-72; asst. prof. chemistry George Mason U., Fairfax, Va., 1972-76, assoc. prof., 1976-87, prof., 1987—2004; chair chemistry/physics Ctrl. Mo. State U., 2004—. Vis. scientist Naval Rsch. Labs., Washington, 1988—95; patent law cons. Foley & Lardner, Washington, 1997—98; session chmn. organic chemistry divsn. Pacifichem Internat. Conf., Honolulu, 2000. Co-author: Base-Catalyzed Reactions of Hydrocarbons and Related Compounds, 1977, Organic Chemistry Laboratory Manual, 3d edit., 2002, Organic Chemistry Laboratory Manual Chemistry 315, 318, 2002; contbr. articles to sci. jours. Pres. Beech Ridge Civic Assn., Fairfax, Va., 1978—87; mem. Fairfax County Pks. Adv. Com., 1982—. Grantee, NSF, 1995—2000, Thomas F. and Kate Miller Jeffress Meml. Trust, 2000—. Mem.: Chem. Soc. Washington, Va. Acad. Sci., Internat. Soc. Heterocyclic Chemistry, Am. Chem. Soc., Vintage Triumph Register Car Club, Capital Area Triumph Owners Club. Office: Dept Chemistry/Physics WCM408 Ctrl Missouri State University Warrensburg MO 64093-5055 E-mail: wstalick@gmu.edu.

STALKER, JACQUELINE D'AOUST, academic administrator, educator; b. Penetang, Ont., Can., Oct. 16, 1933; d. Phillip and Rose (Eaton) D'Aoust; m. Robert Stalker; children: Patricia, Lynn, Roberta. Teaching cert., U. Ottawa, 1952; tchr. music, Royal Toronto Conservatory Music, 1952; teaching cert., Lakeshore Tchrs. Coll., 1958; BEd with honors, U. Manitoba, 1977, MEd, 1979; EdD, Nova U., 1985. Cert. tchr. Ont., Man., Can. Adminstr., tchr., prin. various schs., Ont. and Que., 1952-65; area commr. Girl Guides of Can., throughout Europe, 1965-69; administr., tchr. Algonquin Community Coll., Ottawa, Ont., 1970-74; tchr., program devel. Frontenac County Bd. Edn., Kingston, Ont., 1974-75; lectr., faculty advisor dept. curriculum, edn. U. Man., Can., 1977-79; lectr. U. Winnipeg, Man., Can., 1977-79; cons. colls. div. Man. Dept. Edn., 1980-81, sr. cons. programming br., 1981-84, sr. cons. post secondary, adult and continuing edn. div., 1985-88, dir. post secondary career devel. br. and adult and continuing edn. br., 1989; asst. prof. higher edn., coord. grad. program in higher edn. U. Man., 1989-92, assoc. prof., coord. grad. program in higher edn., 1992-95. Cons. lectures, seminars, workshops throughout Can. Contbr. articles to profl. jours.; mng. editor Can. Jour. of Higher Edn., 1989-93. Mem. U. Man. Senate, 1976-81, 86-89, bd. govs., 1979-82; Can. rep. Internat. Youth Conf., Garmisch, Fed. Republic of Germany, 1968; vol. Can. Cancer Soc.; mem. Assn. RN Accreditation Coun., 1980-85; chair Child Care Accreditation Com., Man., 1983-90; chair Task Force Post-Secondary Accessibility, Man., 1983; vol. United Way Planning and Allocations; provincial dir., mem. nat. bd. Can. Congress for Learning Opportunities for Women. Recipient award for enhancing the Outreach activities of the univ. U. Man., 1994. Mem. Can. Soc. Study Higher Edn., Man. Tchrs. Soc., U. Man. Alumni Assn., Women's Legal Edn. and Action Fund. Home: 3844 Northwest 9Lth Way Sunrise FL 33351

STALKER, JAMES RAGHI, meteorologist, environmental services administrator; b. Papaiahpet, Andhra Pradesh, India, Sept. 4, 1963; arrived in U.S., 1989; s. R. V. Krishna Rao and Sarojini Raghi; m. Karen Ann Caldwell, Oct. 30, 2000; 1 child, Charlotte. BSME, JNTU, Hyderabad, India, 1986; MSME, U. Ala., Huntsville, 1992, MS in Atmospheric Scis., 1995, PhD in Atmospheric Scis., 1997. Postdoctoral fellow Los Alamos (N.Mex) Nat. Lab., 1997—99, tech. staff mem., 1999—2003; pres., CEO Respr. Inc., Santa Fe, 2002—. Contbr. articles to profl. jours. Mem.: AAAS, ASME, Am. Phys. Soc., Am. Math. Soc., Am. Geophys. Union, Am. Meteorol. Soc. Avocations: travel, national parks, hiking, Karate, computers. Office: Respr Inc 5 Bisbee Ct Santa Fe NM 87508-1398 E-mail: jrstalker@respr.com.

STALL, ALAN DAVID, packaging company executive; b. Moose Jaw, Sask., Can., June 14, 1951; came to U.S., 1982; s. Joel and Evelyn (Schwartz) S.; m. Carol I. Johnston; children: Jeffrey, Jennifer, Michael, Timothy. BSME, U. Sask., 1973; MBA, Lewis U., 1986. Registered profl. engr., Ont. Devel. engr. DuPont Can., North Bay, Ont., 1973-76; project engr. Union Carbide Corp. Can., Lindsay, Ont., 1976-79, engring. mgr., 1979-82; mgr. shirring rsch. Union Carbide Corp., Chgo., 1982-85; dir. engring. tech. Viskase Corp., Chgo., 1985-90, v.p. engring., 1990-95; gen. mgr. Kuko Corp., Gross-Gerau, Germany, 1995-98; pres. Films Casings Tech. Inc., Woodridge, Ill., 1996—; gen. mgr. Alfacel Inc., Woodridge, Ill., 1998—; v.p. Teepak de Mex., 2003—. Patentee breathable plastic, shirring apparatus, sausage stuffing machine, cellulose casings, cellulose regeneration. Rotary bus. exchange fellow, London, 1982. Mem. Engring. Inst. Can., Can. Soc. Mech. Engrs., Soc. Plastics Engrs., Assn. Profl. Engrs., Ont., Am. Mensa, Can. Club Chgo. Home: 23W540 James Way Naperville IL 60540-9552 Office: FCT Inc PO Box 5415 Woodridge IL 60517-0415

STALL, WILLIAM READ, writer; b. Phila., Feb. 21, 1937; s. Sidney Joseph and Helen (Read) S.; m. Carolee Ramsey, July, 1961 (div. 1979); children: Tracy Stall Ko, Erica; m. Anne Elizabeth Baker, Dec. 8, 1979. BS, U. Wyo., 1959. Reporter Laramie (Wyo.) Boomerang, 1956-59, Associated Press, Cheyenne, Wyo., 1960-63, corres. Reno, 1963-66, bur. chief, polit. writer Sacramento, 1966-74; press sec. Edmund G. Brown Jr., Sacramento, 1975-76; staff writer, asst. met. editor, corres. L.A. Times, 1976-81, editorial writer, 1984-90, polit. writer, 1990-96, editl. writer, 1997—; bur. chief Hartford Courant, Washington, 1981-84. Sr. lectr. journalism dept. U. So. Calif., 1985-94. With U.S. Army N.C., 1960-67. Recipient Pulitzer prize for editl. writing, 2004. Mem. Am. Alpine Club (dir. 1992—98). Episcopalian. Avocations: rock climbing, mountain climbing, sailing. Office: LA Times 1121 L St Ste 200 Sacramento CA 95814-3970 E-mail: bill.stall@latimes.com.

STALLARD, HUGH R. retired telephone company executive; b. Norton, Va., Jan. 31, 1937; s. Nathaniel Winfield and Evelyn (Stewart) S.; m. Alice Cheatwood, Aug. 1, 1959; children: Craig Winston, Brian Kendrick, Mark Brian. BS, Hampden-Sydney Coll., 1959. Successively staff asst. engr., foreman svc., plant supr., foreman supr., dist. plant supr., dist. plant mgr. Chesapeake and Potomac Telephone Co. of Va., Richmond, Roanoke, Newport News, Norfolk, 1960-68, from staff supr. to div. plant mgr. Northern and Culpeper, 1969-73, from gen. engring. mgr. to gen. mgr. network engring. and provisioning, Richmond Richmond, 1977-80, asst. v.p. revenue requirements, 1980-82, asst. v.p. external affairs, 1982-85, v.p., 1985-88, pres., 1988-90, pres., chief exec. officer, 1990—; staff supr. Chesapeake and Potomac Telephone Cos., Washington, 1968-69; gen. plant mgr. Chesapeake and Potomac Telephone Co. of Washington, 1973-77; pres., CEO Bell Atlantic Va., Richmond, 1990-2000; ret. Exec. adv. bd. Jr. Achievement of Richmond, 1981; adv. bd. U. Richmond, 1982; bd. dirs. Richmond Renaissance, 1985, Va. Literacy Found., 1989; mem. Va. Bus. Coun., Richmond, 1985, corp. bd. YMCA of Greater Richmond, 1986, capital funds bd. United Way Greater Richmond, 1988—; trustee Va. Found. for Ind. Colls., 1986, Hampden-Sydney (Va.) Coll., 1987. Lt. comdr. Va. C.G., 1960—. Named Chief Exec. Officer of Yr. Minority Devel. Coun., 1989, Bus. Man of Yr. Va. Literacy Found., 1989. Mem. Va. Mfrs. Assn., Va. Telephone Assn. (bd. dirs. 1984-85). Presbyterian. Office: Bell Atlantic Va 600 E Main St Ste 1000 Richmond VA 23219-2442

STALLINGS, CHARLES HENRY, retired physicist; b. Durham, N.C., Dec. 28, 1941; s. Henry Harroll and Dorothy (Powers) S.; m. Elizabeth Bright, Sept. 4, 1965; children: Deborah, Sharon. BS, N.C. State U., 1963, MS, 1964; PhD, U. Wis., 1970. Sr. physicist Physics Internat. Co. (now Maxwell Physics Internat.), San Leandro, Calif., 1970-73, dep. dept. mgr., 1974-76, dept. mgr., 1976-79, dir. satellite x-ray test facility office, 1979-81, dir. bus. devel., 1981-83, v.p., dir. rsch. devel., v.p., gen. mgr., 1983—2001; ret., 2001. Contbr. articles to tech. jours. Mem. Gen. Plan Rev. Com., Pleasanton, Calif., 1983. Mem. Am. Phys. Soc., IEEE (mem. pulsed power sci. and tech. com. 1996—, chmn. 12th internat. pulsed power conf. 1999). Home: 1717 Courtney Ave Pleasanton CA 94588-2692

STALLINGS, FRANK, JR., realtor, director; b. Concord, NC, Aug. 21, 1954; s. Frank and Theresa Ann Stallings BS in Indsl. Engring., N.C. State U., 1976; MS in Adminstrn., George Washington U., 1979. Lic. real estate agt. Tex. Jr. indsl. engr. Naval Air Rework Facility, Norfolk, Va., 1974-75; indsl. engr. Babcock & Wilcox, Lynchburg, Va., 1977-79; sr. prin. engr. NCR Corp., Columbia, S.C., 1979-82; mgr. indsl. engring. Mars Electronics, Ltd., Reading, Eng., 1987-88; liaison between European/U.S. mfg. divsn., sr. indsl. engr. M&M/MARS, Inc., Waco, Tex., 1982-84, mgr. quality assurance, 1984-87, mgr. indsl. engring., 1988-96, inbound logistics mgr., 1996-97; mng. prin. Oracle Corp., 1998—2001, practice mgr., 2001; mgmt. cons., 2001—02; CEO North Tex. Homes, 2002—; dir. project mgmt. Fin. Risk Specialists, 2003—. Coach Heart of Tex. Soccer League, Waco, 1985-87; Sunday sch. tchr. Columbus Ave. Bapt. Ch., Waco, 1988-97, mem. Missions com., 1991-96, Bapt. Youth leader, 1990-97, mem. ch. singles coun., 1989-91; Sunday sch. tchr. First Bapt. Hartsville (S.C.) Ch., 1998-2000; exec. mem. singles coun. Waco Bapt. Assn.; counselor Royal Ambs., 1990-96; children's leader Bible Study Fellowship, 1995-97. Mem. Inst. Indsl. Engrs. (sr.), Am. Soc. Quality Control, Am. Prodn. and Inventory Control Socl., Am. Radio Relay League, Project Mgmt. Inst. (cert.), Radio Amateurs Civil Emergency Svcs., Amateur Radio Emergency Svcs., Ten-10 Internat. Amateur Radio Network, Waco Amateur TV Soc. (bd. dirs. 1995-96), Appalachian Trail Soc. (life). Republican. Avocations: camping, boating, running, bicycling, amateur radio operator. Home: PO Box 89 Argyle TX 76226-0089 Business E-Mail: frank@stallings.com.

STALLINGS, NORMAN (CHARLES NORMAN STALLINGS), lawyer; b. Tampa, Fla., Apr. 3, 1914; s. Otto Pyromus and Minnie Henderson (Mitchell) S.; m. Mary Phillips Powell, Feb. 6, 1943 (dec. 1999); children: Charles Norman, Jean Katherine (dec.), Mary Anne. AB, U. Fla., 1935; JD, Harvard U., 1938, LL.M., 1940. Bar: Mo. 1939, Fla. 1940, D.C. 1941, Ga. 1946. Asso. firm Ryland, Stinson, Mag & Thomson, Kansas City, Mo., 1938-39, Sutherland, Tuttle & Brennan, Washington, 1940-41, Atlanta, 1946-49; mem. firm Shackleford, Farrior, Stallings & Evans, Tampa, Fla., 1949-84, of counsel, 1984—2002, Gray & Robinson, 2003—. Vice chmn. Hillsborough County (Fla.) Aviation Authority, 1955-61. Served to lt. col. U.S. Army, 1941-46, ETO. Decorated Bronze Star; Croix de Guerre avec Palma, Belgium. Fellow Am. Coll. Trial Lawyers; mem. ABA, Hillsborough County Bar Assn. (past pres.), Fla. Bar (past gov.), Univ. Club (past pres.), Tampa Yacht and Country Club (past gov.), Ye Mystic Krewe of Gasparilla (past capt. and king), Phi Delta Phi, Kappa Alpha. Republican. Episcopalian. Home: 3501 Bayshore Blvd Apt 805 Tampa FL 33629 Office: PO Box 3324 Tampa FL 33601-3324

STALLINGS, RONALD DENIS, lawyer; b. Evansville, Ind., Feb. 22, 1943; s. Denis and Gertrude (Tong) S.; m. Vicki Lee Chandler, Aug. 21, 1965; children: Courtnay, Claire, Ryan. B in Indsl. Engring., Ga. Inst. Tech., 1965; LLB, U. Va., 1968. Bar: Ga. 1968. Assoc. Powell, Goldstein, Frazer & Murphy LLP, Atlanta, 1968-75, ptnr., 1976-2000, co-counsel, 2001—; sr. v.p., gen. counsel, corp. sec. Reliance Trust Co., Atlanta, 2001—. Co-author: Georgia Corporate Forms, 1988. Mem. ABA, Ga. Bar Assn., Atlanta Bar Assn., Nat. Assn. Bond Lawyers, Am. Soc. Corp. Secs., Phoenix Soc. Atlanta (trustee 1987-93). Roman Catholic. Home: 4601 Polo Ln NW Atlanta GA 30339-5345 Office: Reliance Trust Co Ste 900 3384 Peachtree Rd NE Atlanta GA 30326-1106 E-mail: rstallings@relico.com.

STALLINGS, VALERIE A. physician, state agency administrator; b. N.Y.C., Nov. 27, 1943; BS in Zoology, Duke U., 1964; MD, U. N.C., 1968, MPH, 1988. Intern, resident Pediat. Med. Coll. Va., 1968-71; physician Va. Dept. Health Bur. Crippled Children, Norfolk, 1972—75, Portsmouth (Va.) Health Dept., 1972—77; dir. Tidewater Child Devel. Clin., Norfolk, 1977-82; dep. dir. Norfolk Dept. Pub. Health, 1982-89, dir., 1989—. Office: Norfolk Dept Pub Health 830 Southampton Ave Norfolk VA 23510-1001

STALLINGS, VALERIE AILEEN, retired councilwoman, consultant; b. Chgo., Dec. 23, 1939; d. Jay Sims and Mary Elizabeth (Batson) Spire; adoptive dau. Willian Mundo Spire; m. John R. Stallings, July 14, 1961 (div. 1970); children: Dana Elizabeth, Marshall Brigg. AA, Palomar (Calif.) Coll., 1978; BA, U. Calif., San Diego, 1980. Rschr., lab. mgr. Salk Inst., La Jolla, Calif., 1970-91; mem. coun. City of San Diego, 1991-2001, ret., 2001. Sabbatical rschr. Netherlands Cancer Inst., 1981; city rep. Jack Murphy Stadium Authority, San Diego, 1991-2000; chmn. pub. facilities and recreation City of San Diego, 1992-95; chmn. fiscal policy San Diego Wastewater, 1993-94; dir. San Diego Area Wastewater Mgmt. Dist., 1993—. Contbr. articles to sci. jours. Pres. Pacific Beach Dem. Club, San Diego; mem. Pacific Beach Planning Commn., San Diego. Named Legislator of Yr., SEIU Svc. Coun., 1992. Mem. Nat. Women's Polit. Caucus, Calif. Elected Women's Assn. for Edn. and Rsch., U. Calif. Alumni Assn. (bd. dirs.). Democrat. Avocations: triathlons, jogging, leading safaris in east africa, photography. Office: Dist 6 1536 Frankfort St San Diego CA 92110

STALLINGS, VIOLA PATRICIA ELIZABETH, systems engineer, educational systems specialist, retired information technology manager; b. Norfolk, Va., Nov. 6, 1946; d. Harold Albert and Marie Blanche (Welch) S.; m. (div. Oct. 1984); 1 child, Patricia N.P. Stallings. BS in Psychology, Va. State U., 1968; MBA with distinction, U. Pa., 1975; postgrad., Temple U., 1972-74, Calif. State U., San Francisco, 1973; EdD with specialization in tech., Nova Southeastern U., Ft. Lauderdale, Fla., 1996. Cert. exec. project mgr., project mgmt. profl. Project Mgmt. Inst. Tchr., supr. Peace Corps, Liberia, West Africa, 1968-71; tchr. Day Care Ctr., disruptive h.s. students Tioga Comm. Youth Ctr., 1972-73; tchr. Phila. Sch. Dist., 1972-76; bus. cons. Phila., 1976; sr. sys. engr./sr. industry svcs. specialist, retiring project mgr. IBM/K-12 Edn. and IBM Global Industry, Mt. Laurel; retiring cert. exec. project mgr. IBM Global Svcs. Task force leader IBM Corp., 1990—91. Com. mem. AFNA, 1977—83; bd. dirs. Woodrock, 1976—83, 1987—92, Unity Ch. of Christ, 1993—95, 2000—03, v.p., 1994—95, sec., 2000—01. Recipient Outstanding Svc. awards IBM Black Workers Alliance, Washington, 1984, Recipient IBM Black Workers Svc. award, 1984. Recipient Outstanding Svcs. and Achievement, 1977-2001. Mem. AAUW, World Affairs Coun., Project Mgmt. Inst., St. Joseph's Carpenter Soc. (bd. dirs. 1999—), Women of Arts, Beta Gamma Sigma. Baptist. Avocations: reading, writing, drawing, gardening, cooking, dance, sewing.

STALLMAN, DONALD LEE, corporate executive; b. Rochester, N.Y., Feb. 20, 1930; s. William F. and Clara Elizabeth (Boulle) S.; m. Dolores Anita Putney, Nov. 8, 1958; stepchildren: Nancy, Terri, Jeff. Student, Hobart Coll., Geneva, N.Y., 1948-49, U. Rochester, 1953-54. V.p. Kolstad Assocs., Inc., Rochester, NY, 1954—2002; pres. Water Treatment Assocs., Latham, N.Y., 1975—, KB Fabrications, Latham, N.Y., 1977—. Chmn. bd. Water Treatment Assocs.; vice chmn. bd. K.B. Fabrications; adv. bd., pres. Bruner Corp., Milw., 1982-83. Designer Chock-o-Lette Spl. Aircraft Wheel Chock, 1978, Water Treatment Skid for Oil Field Applications, 1980; inventor in field. Cons. Capital Dist. Planning Commn., Albany, 1980-81. With U.S. Army, 1951-53. Decorated Bronze Star medal, Purple Hearts (2). Mem. Am. Soc. Plumbing Engrs., Quiet Birdman Soc., Sigma Chi. Republican. Roman Catholic. Avocations: flying, boating, golf. Home: 16 Hillcrest Rd Latham NY 12110-4133 also: 111 Royal Park Dr Fort Lauderdale FL 33309-5893 Office: Water Treatment Assocs PO Box 367 Latham NY 12110-0367

STALLMAN, RICHARD MATTHEW, software developer; b. N.Y.C., 1953; BA in Physics, Harvard U., 1974; PhD (hon.), Royal Inst. Tech., Stockholm, 1996, U. Glasgow, 2001. Software developer MIT, Cambridge, 1971-83. Chief GNUisance, GNU Project, 1984—; founder, pres. Free Software Found., Boston, 1985—; hon. prof. Universidad Nacional de Ingeniería de Perú, 2003. Author: Free Software, Free Society, 2002; (software) EMACS, 1975, GNU EMACS, 1984, GNU C Compiler, 1988. Bd. dirs. League Programming Freedom, 1989-95, pres., 1989-92. Recipient Grace Hopper award Assn. Computing, 1990, MacArthur prize fellowship MacArthur Found., 1990, Pioneer award Electronic Frontier Found., 1998, Yuri Rubinski Insight Found. award, 1999, Takeda prize for social/econ. betterment, 2001; elected to Nat. Acad. Engring, 2002. Mem.: Am. Acad. Arts and Scis., Nat. Acad. Engring. Avocations: balkan folk dance, balinese and javanese gamelan music, reading, eating. Office: Free Software Found 59 Temple Pl Ste 330 Boston MA 02111-1307

STALLMAN, ROBERT, concert flutist, recording artist, editor, arranger; b. Boston, June 12, 1946; s. Robert Wooster and Virginia (Blume) S.; m. Hannah Day Woods, Sept. 26, 1981. MusB, New Eng. Conservatory Music, 1968, MusM, 1971; studied with, James Pappoutsakis, Boston, Alain Marion, Gaston Crunelle, Paris, J.P. Rampal. Debut Merkin Concert Hall, N.Y.C., 1980. Tchr. New Eng. Conservatory Music, 1978—82, CUNY Queens Coll., 1980—, Nat. Conservatory of Mex., 1982, Nat. U. Mex., 1991—2001, Domaine Forget, Que., Canada, 1982—85, Académie Internationale d'Eté, Nice, France, 1985, Boston Conservatory, 1986—90, Hochschule für Musik, Mannheim, Germany, 2000; founder, artistic dir. Cambridge Chamber Players & Marblehead Music Festival, 1976—96. Musician: (solo appearances) Libr. of Congress, Carnegie Hall, Alice Tully Hall, Avery Fisher Hall, Symphony Hall, Phila. Acad. Music, Wigmore Hall, Salle Pleyel, Suntory Hall, (soloist with maj. orchs. including) Am. Symphony, Mostly Mozart Festival, Royal Philharm. Orch., No. Sinfonia, Suk Chamber Orch.; guest soloist Lincoln Ctr. Chamber Music Soc., Mendelssohn, Orion, Alexander, Muir, Martinu, St. Lawrence, string quartets, festivals in Can., Spain, Czech Republic, Holland, Finland, France, Mex., Japan, U.S.; editor: (flute music) Internat. Music Co., 1984—, G. Schirmer, 1996—; author: (publs.) Flute Workout, 1995—, The Flutist's Détaché Book, 1997—, Cadenzas to the Mozart Flute Concertos, 2001—; musician: (premiere performances include works by) E. Carter, R. Danielpour, S. Dodgson, J. Harbison, K. Husa, R. Helps, W. McKinley, (recorded for) ASV, VAI Audio, Biddulph Recs., CBS Masterworks, MHS, Centaur, CRI, New World, Northeastern, Owl, Crown (Japan), (solo recs. include) American Flute, The Lyric Flute, Gypsy Flute, The Nightingale in Love, Incantations, Bach Sonatas, Blavet Sonatas, Handel Sonatas, Schubert Sonatas, (solo recs. include Mozart sonatas) Telemann Concertos, (solo recs. include) Vivaldi Concertos, Dodgson Concerto, McKinley Concerto. Fulbright grantee, 1968-69, Arcadia Found. grantee, 1994; Koussevitsky fellow, 1970; recipient Chadwick medal, 1968, C.D. Jackson prize, Tanglewood, 1970, 1st prize USA Nat. Assn. Collegiate Artists Competition, 1971; NEA Solo Recitalist grantee, 1983. Avocations: travel, swimming, reading, French culture. Address: 1530 Locust St Philadelphia PA 19102-4415 E-mail: flute@robertstallman.com.

STALLONE, SYLVESTER ENZIO, actor, writer, director; b. N.Y.C., July 6, 1946; s. Frank and Jacquline (Labofish) S.; m. Sasha Czack, Dec. 28, 1974 (div. 1985); children: Sage, Seth; m. Brigitte Nielsen, Dec. 15, 1985 (div. 1987); m. Jennifer Flavin, May 17, 1997; children: Sophia, Sistine, Scarlet. Student, Am. Coll. of Switzerland, 1965-67, U. Miami, 1967-69. Formerly, usher, fish salesman, horse trainer, delicatessen worker, truck driver, bouncer, zoo attendant, short order cook, pizza demonstrator, phys. edn. tchr., motel supt., bookstore detective Appeared in motion pictures No Place to Hide, 1970, The Party at Kitty and Stud's, 1970, Lords of Flatbush, 1973, The Prisoner of Second Avenue, 1975, Capone, 1974, Farewell, My Lovely, 1975, Death Race 2000, 1975, Cannonball, 1976, Rocky, 1976, (Oscar for Best Picture 1976, Golden Globe award for best picture 1976, Donatello award for best actor in Europe 1976, Christopher Religious award 1976, Bell Ringer award Scholastic Mag. 1976, Nat. Theatre Owners award 1976) F.I.S.T, 1978, Paradise Alley, 1978, Rocky II, 1979, Nighthawks, 1981, Victory, 1981, Rocky III, 1982, First Blood, 1982, Rhinestone, 1984, Rambo: First Blood Part II, 1985, Rocky IV, 1985, Cobra, 1986, Over the Top, 1987, Rambo III, 1988, Lock Up, 1989, Tango and Cash, 1989, Rocky V, 1990, Oscar, 1991, Stop! Or My Mom Will Shoot, 1992, Cliffhanger, 1993, Demolition Man, 1993, The Specialist, 1994, Judge Dredd, 1995, Assassins, 1995, Firestorm, 1996, Daylight, 1996, Copland, 1997, An Alan Smithee Film: Burn Hollywood Burn, 1998, Antz (voice only), 1998, Get Carter, 2000, Driven (also prod.), 2001, D-Tox, 2002, Avenging Angelo, 2002, My Little Hollywood, 2002, Taxi 3, 2003, Shade, 2003, Spy Kids 3-D: Game Over, 2003; dir. film Paradise Alley, 1978, Rocky II, 1979, Nighthawks, 1981, Rocky III, 1982, Staying Alive (also prod.), 1983, Rocky IV, 1985; author: THe Lords of Flatbush, 1974, Rocky, 1976, F.I.S.T., 1978, Paradise Alley, 1977, The Rocky Scrapbook, 1977, Rocky II, 1979, Rocky III, 1982, First Blood, 1982, Staying Alive, 1983, Rhinestone (screenplay), 1984, Rambo: First Blood Part II, 1985, Rocky IV, 1985, Cobra, 1986, Over the Top, 1987, Rambo III, 1988, Rocky V, 1990, Cliffhanger (screenplay), 1993, Driven (screenplay), 2001; exec. prod.: Heart of a Champion: The Ray Mancini Story, 1985. Recipient Star of the Year award 1977, named Show West actor of the year 1979, Artistic Achievement award Nat. Italian Am. Found., 1991, Order of Arts and Letters, French Ministry, 1992, Caesar award for Career Achievement, 1992. Mem. Screen Actors Guild, Writers Guild, Stuntmans Assn. (hon.), Dirs. Guild. Achievements include being nominated for two Oscars (acting and writing) in same year (1976); occurred for only 3d time in history. *Once in one's life, for one mortal moment, one must make a grab for immortality; if not, one has not lived.*

STALLONE, THOMAS MICHAEL KEARNEY, clinical psychologist; b. NYC, Dec. 5, 1952; s. Vito Joseph and Mary Ellen (Kearney) S.; m. Bonnie Elizabeth Wenk, May 30, 1982; 1 child, Thomas Lucius. B of Profl. Studies, N.Y. Inst. Tech., 1987; MA, Spalding U., 1991; PsyD, Pacific U., 1994. Lic. psychologist, Wash.; cert. rational emotive therapist; diplomate and fellow Am. Coll. Forensic Examiners. Internat. banker Sumitomo Bank, Ltd., N.Y.C., 1980-82, Bank of N.Y., N.Y.C., 1982-87; pvt. practice hypnosis cons. LaGrange, Ky., and N.Y.C., 1982-90; rehab. specialist Goodwill Industries Ky., Louisville, 1989; psychol. assoc. div. mental health Ky. Corrections Cabinet, La Grange, 1989-91; teaching asst. Pacific U., Forest Grove, Oreg., 1991-93; psychotherapist Portland, Oreg., 1991-95; clin. psychologist Vancouver, Wash., 1995—; dir. Attention Disorders Clinic Vancouver, 1997—. Author: The Boke of Taliesyne, 1979, The Moral Development of Healthcare Professionals, 1989, The Effects of Psychodrama on Inmates Within a Structured Residential Behavior Modification Program, 1993, Panic Symptoms in Asthma, 1994, Rational Emotive Behavior Therapy and Subpersonalities, 1997. Cons. Hist. Arms, Ltd., N.Y.C., 1983-87, N.Y. Medieval Festival, 1984-86; dir., cons. Whitestone (N.Y.) Creative Arts Workshop, 1977, Ky. Shakespeare Festival, Louisville, 1987-88; treas., advisor 4H Exec. Coun., La Grange, 1988-91; advisor Portland Metro chpt. Children and Adults with Attention Deficit Disorder, 1998—; mem. Clark County Human Resources Rev. Com., 2000-03; mem. Clark County Mental Health Rev. Bd., 2003—; trustee Celtic Internat. Families of N.Am. Decorated Grant of Arms Chief Herald of Ireland, col. of Ky. Gov. of Ky., Created Irish Sept Chieftain of Eile O'Carroll and Clan Herald His Highness Eile O'Carroll. Mem. APA, Wash. State Psychol. Assn. (media rels. and pub. edn. com.), Internat. Soc. for Profl. Hypnosis, Ancient Order Hibernians, Mensa. Avocations: meditation, martial arts, medieval history, heraldry, spirituality. E-mail: drtms@adcov.com.

STALLWORTH, ALMA GRACE, former state legislator; Grad., Highland Park Community Coll., 1956; student, Wayne State U., 1956. Mem. Mich. Ho. of Reps., Lansing, 1970-74, 81-96; dep. dir. Hist. Dept. City of Detroit, 1975-78, job developer, 1978-79. Mem. exec. com. Nat. Conf. State Legislatures, 1986-89. Commr. Wayne County Charter, Detroit, 1978-79, Martin Luther King Commn., Detroit, 1987; chair bd. dirs. Task Force on Infant Mortality, Mich. Legislature, 1987; pres. Nat. Black Child Devel. Inst., Detroit; vol. United Negro Coll. Fund, 1987—; founder, adminstr. Black Caucus Found. of Mich., 1987—. Recipient cert. of appreciation Mich. Dept. Edn., 1986, Advs. award Mich. Health Mothers, Health Babies Coalition, 1987; named Woman Leader in Pub. Health, Mi ch. Assn. Local Pub. Health, 1987, Woman of Yr., Minority Women's Network, 1988. Mem. NAACP, Nat. Conf. State Legislators (exec. commr. 1986), Nat. Black Caucus State Legislators, (sec. women's caucus), Mich. Legis. Black Causus (chair 1987), Alpha Kappa Alpha. Clubs: Cameo, Top Ladies of Distinction. Democrat. Home: 19793 Sorrento St Detroit MI 48235-1149

STALLWORTH, CHARLES DEROTHA, JR., psychologist; b. Riderwood, Ala., July 4, 1940; s. Charles D. and Annie (Horn) S. BS, Tenn. State U., Nashville, 1963; MS, Tenn. State U., 1966; postgrad., Calif. Sch. Profl. Psychology, 1977-79, U. South Ala., 1967, Tuskegee Inst., 1968, U. Ky., 1980; PhD in Psychology, Internat. Coll., 1983; cert. in mental disability law, N.Y. Law Sch., 2001. Diplomate Am. Bd. Psychotherapy, Am. Coll. Mental Health Practitioners, Am. Coll. Cert. Forensic Counselors, Acad. Cert. Neurotherapists. Psychiat. asst. Hubbard Hsop., Nashville, 1964-66; counselor, tchr. North Ctrl. H.S., Chatom, Ala., 1966-68; tchr. Washington County H.S., 1968—70; supr. adult edn. Washington County Bd. Edn., Chatom, 1968-70; dir. counseling ctr. Albany State Coll., Ga., 1970—91; pvt. practice, 1993—. Staff assistance Auburn U., 1969; counselor Spl. Svc. program Albany State Coll., 1992-93; cons. Peace Corps, 1979-81; dep. dir. gen. Internat. Biographical Ctr., Cambridge, Eng., 2004. Contbr. articles to profl. jours. Bd. dirs. Dougherty County CODAC, Inc., Albany, 1973-77; hon. mem. Ga. Sheriff's Assn. Grantee HEW, 1970-77, U.S. Office Edn., 1972; recipient Internat. Poet of Merit award Internat. Soc. Poets, 2003, Internat. Internat. Peace prize United Cultural Consortium, 2002; named Best Poems & Poets Internat. Libr. Poetry, 2003, Outstanding Scientist of the 20th Century, 2000. Mem. APA, Am. Psychotherapy Assn., Nat. Assn. Cognitive-Behavioral Therapists, Ga. Psychol. Assn., Alpha Phi Alpha. Democrat. Baptist. Achievements include research on impact of affective domain on learning outcomes and on application of cognitive therapies as a means of controlling negative effects. Home: 805 E 4th Ave Albany GA 31705-1203 Personal E-mail: ccl679@mchsi.com.

STALNAKER, LANCE KUEBLER, lawyer; b. Tampa, Fla., Jan. 2, 1948; s. Leo Jr. and June Esther Stalnaker. BS in Journalism, U. Fla., 1970, JD, 1973. Bar: Fla. 1973, U.S. Dist. Ct. (mid. dist.) Fla. 1974, U.S. Ct. Appeals (5th cir.) 1974, U.S. Ct. Appeals (11th cir.) 1981. Ptnr. Stalnaker & Stalnaker, Tampa, 1973-75; pvt. practice Tampa, 1975-83, 91—; staff atty. Legal Aid Bur. of Hillsborough County, Tampa, 1983-85, interim exec. dir., atty., 1985-86, exec. dir., atty., 1986-90. Asst. cir. ct. commr. 13th Jud. Cir., Tampa, 1981-82. Pres. St. John's Luth. Ch., 1997-99, mem. bd. dirs., 1999—; of counsel St. John Luth. Ch. Learning Ctr., 2002—; mem. steering com. Pregnancy Care Ctr. Ministries, Tampa, 1999-2000. Capt. U.S. Army Res. to 1978. Mem. Hillsborough County Bar Assn. (family law sect.), Fla. Bar (family law sect.). Office: 1319 W Fletcher Ave Tampa FL 33612-3310

STALOFF, ARNOLD FRED, financial executive; b. Dover, N.J., Dec. 12, 1944; s. William and Ida (Greenberg) S.; m. Sharon Marcia Teplitsky, June 10, 1967; children: Kimberly, Lindsay. BBA, U. Miami, 1967. Statistician U.S. Census Bur., Washington, 1967-68; fin. analyst SEC, Washington, 1968-71; sr. v.p. Phila. Stock Exch., 1971-78; v.p. Securities Industry Automation Corp., N.Y.C., 1978-80; pres. Fin. Automation Corp., Phila., 1980-83, Phila. Bd. Trade, 1983-89; pres., CEO Commodity Exch., Inc. (COMEX), N.Y.C., 1989-90; CEO Bloom Staloff Corp., Phila., 1991—2003; pres. Staloff Green, LLC, 2003—. Bd. dirs. Lehman Bros. Fin. Products, Inc.; bd. govs. Phila. Stock Exch., 1991-97. Bd. dirs. Variety Club for Handicapped Children, Phila., 1987-92; mem. adv. bd. Phila. Internat. Airport, 1988—; mem. U. Miami Pres.'s Cir. Mem. Nat. Futures Assn. (bd. dirs. 1987-90). Avocations: fly fishing, golf, skiing. Office: 320 Amour Rd Ste 210 North Kansas City MO 64116

STALTER, RICHARD B. biology professor, researcher; b. Montvale, N.J., Jan. 16, 1942; s. Lester C. and Betty R. Stalter; divorced; 1 child, Laurie. BS, Rutgers U., 1963; MS, U. R.I., 1966; PhD, U. S.C., 1968. Asst. prof. High Point (N.C.) Coll., 1968-69, Pfeiffer Coll., Misenheimer, N.C., 1969-70; fish kill expert S.C. Pollution Control Authority, Columbia, 1970-71; prof. biology St. John's U., Jamaica, N.Y., 1971—. Cons. So. Engring. Co., Atlanta, 1972-75, Cabot Corp., Boston, 1974-75; trustee N.Y. Ocean Sci. Lab., Montauk, N.Y., 1974-82. Author: Barrier Island Botany The Southeastern United States, 1993, Man in the Environment, 1996, Barrier Island Botany, 2003; contbr. articles to profl. jours. Mem. Torrey Bot. Soc., Assn. S.E. Biologists, So. Appalachian Bot. Club, N.E. Weed Sci. Soc., Skull and Cir. Honor Soc., S.C. Acad. Sci., Sigma Xi, Phi Sigma. Republican. Episcopalian. Home: 36 Glade Ln Levittown NY 11756-3918 Office Phone: 718-990-9288.

STAM, DAVID HARRY, librarian; b. Paterson, N.J., July 11, 1935; s. Jacob and Deana B. (Bowman) S.; m. Deirdre Corcoran, May 15, 1963; children—Julian, Wendell, Kathryn. AB, Wheaton Coll., 1955; postgrad., New Coll., U. Edinburgh, 1955-56; MLS, Rutgers U., 1962; postgrad., CUNY, 1963-64; PhD, Northwestern U., 1978. Asst. editor library publs., reference librarian, manuscript cataloguer New York Pub. Library, 1959-64; librarian Marlboro (Vt.) Coll., 1964-67; head tech. services dept. Newberry Library, Chgo., 1967-71, assoc. librarian, 1969-73; librarian Milton S. Eisenhower Library, Johns Hopkins U., Balt., 1973-78; Andrew W. Mellon dir. rsch. libraries N.Y. Pub. Library, N.Y.C., 1978-86; Univ. librarian Syracuse U., 1986-98, sr. scholar, History Dept., 1998—. Trustee Gladys K. Delmas Found. Author: Wordsworthian Criticism, 1974, International Dictionary of Library Histories, 2001; co-author (with Rissa Yachnin): Turgenev in English: A Checklist of Works by and about Him, 1960; contbr. articles to profl. jours. Served with USNR, 1956-58. Brit. Acad. Overseas fellow, 1975, Brit. Libr. fellow, 1995-96. Mem.: Am. Antiquarian Soc., Am. Hist. Assn., Groller Club (N.Y.C.), Princeton Club N.Y. Office: Syracuse U History Dept Eggers Hall Syracuse NY 13244 E-mail: dhstam@syr.edu.

STAMATAKIS, CAROL MARIE, lawyer, former state legislator; b. Canton, Ohio, Apr. 27, 1960; d. Emmanuel and Catherine Lucille Stamatakis; m. Michael Shklar, Mar. 23, 1985. BA in Criminology and Criminal Justice, Ohio State U., 1982; JD, Case Western Res., 1985. Bar: N.H. 1985, U.S. Dist. Ct. N.H. 1985. Atty. Elliott, Jasper & Stamatakis, Newport, N.H., 1990-93; state rep. N.H. State Legislature, 1988-94; atty. N.H. Dept. Health and Human Svcs., Concord, 1994—. Instr. Am. Inst. Banking, Claremont, 1987-88, 91-92, 95. Asst. editor: (jours.) Health Matrix: The Jour. of Health Services Mangement, 1983-85. Treas., mem. Town of Lempster N.H. Conservation Commn., 1987—; bd. dirs. Orion House, Inc., Newport, N.H., 1987-91; town chair N.H. Dem. Party, 1987—; mem. Town of Lempster Recycling Com., 1988—, Community Task Force on Drug and alcohol Abuse, 1988. Mem. N.H. Bar Assn., Sierra Club, Upper Valley Group (former vice chair and solid waste chair). Avocations: drawing, painting. Home: PO Box 807 Newport NH 03773-0807

STAMATY, MARK ALAN, cartoonist, writer, artist; b. Bklyn., Aug. 1, 1947; s. Stanley and Clara Gee Stamaty. B.F.A., The Cooper Union, 1969. Mem. faculty Parson's Sch. Design, N.Y.C., 1977-81. Author-illustrator: (children's books) Who Needs Donuts?, 1973 (Bklyn. Art Books For Children award 1974), Small in the Saddle, 1975, Minnie Maloney & Macaroni, 1976, Where's My Hippopotamus?, 1977, Too Many Time Machines, 1999, (comic strip collections) Macdoodle St., 1981, Washingtoon, 1983; cartoonist: Macdoodle St. Village Voice newspaper, 1978-79, Carrrttoooonnn, Village Voice newspaper, 1980-81, (Washington Post and syndication) Washingtoon, 1981-94, Boox, N.Y. Times Book Review, 2001—; polit. cartoonist TIME mag., 1994-96, Doodlennium, 1996-98; contbr.: The New Yorker mag., 1992—, Slate Mag., 1996—; illustrator various publs., including: (children's book) Yellow Yellow, 1971, (Bklyn. Art Books for Children award); cartoon coverage of Milan fashion show for GQ Mag., 2000—. Recipient Purchase award N.J. State Mus., about 1969, Gold medal Soc. Illustrators, 1974 Mem. PEN Am. Ctr. Avocations: impersonating Elvis Presley; watching the world; softball; swimming.

STAMBAUGH, ARMSTRONG A., JR., restaurant and hotel executive; b. Cleve., Nov. 1, 1920; s. Armstrong Alexander and Beatrice (Snyder) S.; m. Janet Turley Marting, July 26, 1943 (div. 1958); children: Susan Reed (Mrs. Roy H. Beaton, Jr.), Sally Russell (Mrs. Michael H. Huber), Elizabeth Renshaw (Mrs. Michael C. Warr); m. Aagot Hinrichsen Cain, June 10, 1972. BA, Dartmouth Coll., 1942; Indsl. Adminstr., Harvard U., 1943, MBA, 1946. Research asst., then instr. bus. adminstrn. Harvard Grad. Sch. Bus. Adminstrn., 1946-48; with Gulf Oil Corp., 1948-66, coord. sales devel. mktg. hdqrs., 1962-63, v.p. Eastern marketing region Phila., 1963-66; exec. v.p. adminstrn. Howard Johnson Co., Inc., 1966-70, exec. v.p. and adminstrn., 1970-79, exec. v.p., asst. to pres., 1979-81, dir., 1969-81; operator, developer food and lodging facilities, 1981-98. Pres. trustees Fox Chapel Country Day Sch., Pitts., 1955-57; div. vice chmn. Boston United Fund, 1961; bd. dirs. Houston Internat. Trade and Travel Fair, 1962-63, World Affairs Coun. Phila., 1964-65; dir. Phila. C. of C., 1964, 65, 66; bd. overseers Hanover Inn, Dartmouth Coll., 1979-85, chmn., 1984-85; trustee Old Sturbridge Village, Mass., 1979-01. Served to lt. (j.g.) USNR, 1943-46. Mem. Pine Valley Golf Club (N.J.), Weston Golf Club (Mass.), Edgartown Golf Club (Mass.), Kittansett Club (Mass.), Boston Skating Club, Vineyard Haven Yacht Club (Mass.), Paradise Valley Country Club (Ariz.), Delta Tau Delta. Home and Office: 5 Blossom Ln Weston MA 02493-1103 E-mail: aastam@flash.net.

STAMBAUGH, JOHN EDGAR, oncologist, hematologist, pharmacologist, educator; b. Everrett, Pa., Apr. 30, 1940; s. John Edgar and Rhoda Irene (Becker) S.; m. Shirley Louise Fultz, June 24, 1961; 4 children. BS in Chemistry cum laude, Dickinson Coll., 1962; MD, Jefferson Med. Coll., 1966, PhD, 1968. Intern Thomas Jefferson U. Hosp., Phila., 1968-69, resident, 1968-69; oncology fellow Jefferson Med. Coll., 1970-72, instr. pharmacology, 1969-70, asst. prof., 1970-74, assoc. prof., 1974-82, prof., 1982—. Pvt. practice med. oncology, hematology and cancer pain, Woodbury, N.J.; staff physician Cooper Med. Ctr., Camden, N.J., 1972—, Underwood Meml. Hosp., Woodbury, 1972—, West Jersey Hosp., 1973—, J.F. Kennedy Hosp., 1978—, Our Lady of Lourdes Hosp., 1990—. Contbr. articles to profl. jours. Fellow: Am. Soc. Pain Mgmt., Am. Acad. Pain Mgmt., Am. Coll. Clin. Pharmacology; mem.: Am. Assn. Clin. Rsch., Am. Pain Soc., Internat. Assn. for Study of Pain, Am. Assn. for Cancer Rsch., Am. Soc. Clin. Oncology, Am. Soc. for Pharmacology and Exptl. Therapeutics, Camden County Med. Soc., Gloucester County Med. Soc., N.J. Med. Soc. (del.), Am. Soc. Clin. Pharmacology, AMA, ABA, Sigma Xi. Office: 17 W Red Bank Ave Ste 101 Woodbury NJ 08096-1630 also: 100 Carnie Blvd Voorhees NJ 08043-4512

STAMBAUGH, LARRY G. finance executive; b. Topeka, Feb. 1, 1947; s. Merle J. and Eileen M. (Denslow) S.; m. Sallie M. Underwood, Jan. 18, 1969 (div. Oct. 1981); children: Matt, Julie; m. Suzanne Van Slyke, May 14, 1982; children: Todd, Scott, Andy. BBA, Washburn U., 1969. CPA, Kans. Mgr. KPMG Peat, Marwick, Mitchell Co., Kansas City, Mo., 1969-76; co-owner Automotive Investment & Devel. Co., Olathe, Kans., 1976-82; chief fin. officer CNB Fin. Corp., Kansas City, Kans., 1983-90, ABC Labs., Columbia, Mo., 1990, pres., chief exec. officer, 1990-92; chmn., pres., CEO Maxim Pharms., San Diego, Calif., 1993—. Bd. dirs. Chromagen, Inc.; chmn. bd. dirs. Advent Enterprises. Pres., dir. Big Bros. and Sisters, Kansas City, 1986-88; bd. dirs. Internat. Forum Corp. Dirs., 1996—. Mem. AICPA, Am. Mgmt. Assn., Soc. Environ. Toxicology Edn. Found. (bd. dirs.), Nat. Assn. Corp. Dirs., Columbia C. of C., Rotary Internat. Republican. Presbyterian. Avocation: photography. Home: 18130 Old Coach Dr Poway CA 92064-6631 Office: Maxim Pharms 3099 Science Park Rd Ste 150 San Diego CA 92121-1101

STAMBAUGH, REGINALD JACK, ophthalmologist; b. West Palm Beach, Fla., Jan. 1, 1930; s. Gleason Noah and Marjorie (Hilton) S.; m. Carolyn Stroupe, Nov. 24, 1965; children— Melanie, Joette, Valerie, Reginald Giles. A.B., U. Fla., 1952; M.D., U. Miami, 1959. Diplomate Am. Bd. Ophthalmology, Nat. Bd. Med. Examiners. Intern, Grady Meml. Hosp., Atlanta, 1959-60, resident 1960-64; practice medicine specializing in ophthalmology, West Palm Beach, 1963—; chief ophthalmology Good Samaritan Hosp., West Palm Beach, 1966-74; lectr. Bascom Palmer Eye Inst., U. Miami Sch. Medicine, 1964-73; mem. med. adv. bd. Fla. Soc. for Prevention of Blindness, 1972-77, Crippled Children's Soc. Palm Beach, 1965-82; pres., chmn. bd. Ophthalmic mutual Ins. Co., 1987—. Cntbr. numerous articles, papers in field. Bd. dirs. Fla. Med. Polit. Action Com., 1975-81, Palm Beach County Hall of Fame, 1977-80, Health Planning Council, 1979-81; bd. dirs. Found. Med. Care, 1979-82, pres., 1980; mem. vestry Bethesda by the Sea Ch. Palm Beach, 1981— . Served with USAF, 1952-54. Decorated Korean Presdl. citation. Mem. AMA, Am. Acad. Ophthalmology (bd. councilors 1981—87, chmn. bd. councilors 1986-87, com. eye care for Am. people 1985-86, state affairs com. 1981-83, long range planning com. 1983-86), Fla. Soc. Ophthalmology (sec.-treas. 1975-77, pres. 1980-81), Palm Beach County Med. Soc. (pres. 1977, trustee 1977). Democrat. Episcopalian. Clubs: Sailfish of Fla. (bd. govs. 1976-78); Bath and Tennis (Palm Beach). Home: 272 Queens Ln Palm Beach FL 33480-3240 Office: 1411 N Flagler Dr Ste 7600 West Palm Beach FL 33401-3419

STAMBERG, SUSAN LEVITT, radio broadcaster; b. Newark, Sept. 7, 1938; d. Robert I. and Anne (Rosenberg) Levitt; m. Louis Collins Stamberg, Apr. 14, 1962; 1 child, Joshua Collins BA, Barnard Coll, 1959; DHL (hon.), Gettysburg Coll., 1982, Dartmouth Coll., 1984, Knox Coll., U. N.H., SUNY, Brockport. Editorial asst. Daedalus, Cambridge, Mass., 1960-62; editorial asst. The New Republic, Washington, 1962-63; host, producer, mgr., program dir. Sta. WAMU-FM, Washington, 1963-69; host All Things Considered Washington, 1971-86; host Weekend Edition Nat Pub. Radio, Washington, 1987-89; spl. corr. Nat. Pub. Radio, 1990—. Bd. dirs. AIA, Washington, 1983-85, PEN/Faulkner Fiction Award Found., 1985—. Author: Every Night at Five, 1982, The Wedding Cake in the Middle of the Road, 1992, Talk: NPR's Susan Stamberg Considers All Things, 1993. Recipient Honor award Ohio U., 1977, Edward R. Murrow award Corp. for Pub. Broadcasting, 1980; named Woman of Yr., Barnard Coll., 1984; fellow Silliman Coll. Yale U., 1984—; inducted Broadcasting Hall of Fame, 1994, Radio Hall of Fame, 1996. Avocations: sketching; piano; knitting. Office: Nat Pub Radio 635 Massachusetts Ave NW Washington DC 20001-3753

ŠTAMBUK, NIKOLA, research scientist; b. Varaždin, Croatia, Mar. 25, 1959; s. Ranko and Vjera (Mrakovčić) Š.; m. Ana Lazić, Nov. 12, 1988; 1 child, Albert. MD, Zagreb (Croatia) U., 1984, MS, 1988; PhD, Inst. Med. Rsch. Occup. Health, Zagreb, 1991. Intern Sisters of Mercy Clin. Hosp., Zagreb, 1984-85; resident Railway Health Ctr., Zagreb, 1986-88; postdoctoral fellow Mc Gill U., Montreal, Can., 1991-92; rschr. Rugjer Bošković Inst., Zagreb, 1994—. Sci. com. Internat. Conf. on Math. and Computer Modelling and Sci. Computing, Berkeley, Calif., 1993, Boston, 1995, Washington, 1997. Contbr. articles to profl. jours. Mem. Internat. Assn. for Math. and Computer Modelling, Internat. Ocular Inflammation Soc., Internat. Soc. for Thymology and Immunotherapy. Achievements include the discovery of necklace model, I Ching and horseshoe map representation of the genetic code (SCA procedure), rsch. in models of artificial barriers constrn., protein transfer and molecular recognition, computer-aided drug design, compartmental volume-pressure relationships. Home: Šubićeva 16 HR-10000 Zagreb Croatia Office: Rugjer Bošković Inst Bijenička 54 HR-10000 Zagreb Croatia Office Phone: +3851 4680 193. E-mail: stambuk@rudjer.irb.hr.

STAMELMAN, RICHARD HOWARD, French and humanities educator; b. Newark, Mar. 7, 1942; s. Louis Robert and Golda (Senzer) S.; children: Emily, Gibson, Jeremy White. BA, Hamilton Coll.; PhD, Duke U. Asst. prof. French and humanities Wesleyan U., Middletown, Conn., 1967-74, assoc. prof., 1974-79, prof., 1979-93, William R. Kenan Jr. prof. humanities, 1983-92, dean humanities, 1986-89, dir. Ctr. for the Humanities, 1976-82, dir. humanities devel., 1982-85; dir. Weston Ctr. for Fgn. Langs., Lits. and Cultures Williams Coll., Williamstown, Mass., 1992-97, prof. Romance langs., lit. studies, 1992—; chmn. dept. French and Italian U. Colo., Boulder, 1991-92. Organizer (study group) Ecrire le Livre: Autour d'Edmond Jabès, Cerisy-la-Salle, France, 1987; co-dir. Edouard Morot-Sir Summer Inst. for French Cultural Studies, Hanover, N.H., 1994. Author: The Drama of Self in Guillaume Apollinaire's Alcools, 1976, Claude Garache: Prints, 1965-85, 1985, Lost Beyond Telling: Representations of Death and Absence in Modern French Poetry, 1990; editor: Contemporary French Poetry, Studies in 20th Century Literature, 1989, Ecrire le Livre: Autour d'Edmond Jabès, 1989, Italian transl., 1991, French Poetry since the War, L'Esprit Créateur, 1992; editor, prin. translator: The Lure and the Truth of Painting, Selected Essays by Yves Bonnefoy, 1995; translator: The Grapes of Zeuxis and Other Fables by Yves Bonnefoy, 1987, Once More the Grapes of Zeuxis by Yves Bonnefoy, 1989, The Last Grapes of Zeuxis by Yves Bonnefoy, 1993, Transmorphoses by Yves Bonnefoy, 1998; mem. editorial bd. French Forum; contbr. articles to profl. jours. Recipient Chevalier dans l'ordre des Palmes Académiques award French Govt., 1993; NEH fellow, 1973, John Simon Guggenheim Meml. Found. fellow, 1999; Am. Council Learned Socs. grantee, 1983 Mem. MLA (regional del. 1987-90, mem. program com. 1996-99), Societe Francaise des Parfumeurs. Home: PO Box 1624 Norwich VT 05055 Office: Williams Coll Weston Ctr Fgn Langs Lits Culture 995 Main St Williamstown MA 01267-2615 E-mail: Richard.H.Stamelman@dartmouth.edu., rstamelm@williams.edu.

STAMELOS, ELECTRA GEORGIA, artist; b. Jersey City, May 28, 1927; d. Byron D. and Eulalia (Gerachis) Mousmoules; m. William Stamelos, Apr. 26, 1953. BFA, Wayne State U., 1970; MFA, Eastern Mich. U., 1976. Instr. Nat. Art Sch., Washington, 1945-48, YWCA, Redford, Mich., 1969-73, Ann Arbor (Mich.) Art Assn., 1977—, Birmingham-Bloomfield (Mich.) Art Ctr., 1980—; lectr. fine and applied arts U. Mich., Dearborn, 1980—, dir. art collections and exhbns., 1984-92. Exhibited in Group shows at Burpee Mus., Rockford, Ill., Springfield (Ill.) Art Mus. Watercolor USA, 1977, 80, 99, Butler Mus. Am. Art, Youngstown, Ohio, 1998, 2003, Parkland Art Gallery, Champaign, Ill., 2003; one-woman shows include Cantor-Lemberg Gallery, Birmingham, Mich., Habitat Gallery, Southfield, Mich., Slusser Gallery, Ann Arbor, Shapolsky Gallery, NYC, Mickelson Gallery, Washington, Indigo Gallery, Boca Raton, Fla., 1995-98, Quincy (Ill.) U., 2000, Gallery 100, Saratoga, N.Y., Paloma Gallery, Ann Arbor; represented in permanent collections Jesse Bessard Mus., Alpena, Mich., Battle Creek (Mich.) Art Ctr., Flint Inst. of Art, Mich., Beaumont Hosp., Renal Ctr. Commn., Birmingham, Mich., 1998; author: Georgia O'Keefe, 1976, Splash I Flowers in Watercolor, 1991, Splash II Understanding Watercolor, 1991, Watercolor Magic, 2003; contbr. articles to profl. jours. Chartered commr. Livonia (Mich.) Arts Commn., 1972; commr. Livonia Hist. Dist. Study Commn., 1973; pres. Friends of the Barn, Livonia, 1972; treas. Women's Caucus for Art, Detroit, 1980. Mem. Nat. Watercolor Soc. (Purchase Signature Honor 1976, 83, 2002), Midwest Watercolor Soc., Mich. Watercolor Soc. (pres. 1975-79), Rocky Mountain Nat. Water Media Soc., Watercolor USA Honor Soc. (treas. 1993-95, pres. 1995-98), The Art Exchange (co-founder 1971), Jaycees (v.p. Livonia chpt. 1962). Greek Orthodox. Avocations: photography, travel, swimming, stain glass designer. Home: 38131 N Vista Dr Livonia MI 48152 1067

STAMES, WILLIAM ALEXANDER, realtor, cost management executive; b. Douglas, Ariz., Mar. 26, 1917; s. Alex Basil and Teresa (Ruis) S.; m. Marguerite Winifred Nelson, June 11, 1943; 1 child, Wynn Lorain. AA, Long Beach Coll., 1941; postgrad., U. Calif., Berkeley, 1962-64; cert. mgmt. practice, Naval Offices CIC Sch., Glenview, Ill., 1955; grad., Real Estate Inst., Calif. Lic. real estate assoc.; grad. Realtors Inst. Owner Stames Beverage Co., Brawley, Calif., 1945-50; liaison engr. Lockheed Missiles & Space Co., Sunnyvale, Calif., 1958-60, sr. liaison engr., 1960, adminstr., 1960-62, staff adminstr., 1962-63, sr. liaison engr., sr. design engr., 1965-70; owner, mgr. Cost Reduction Equipment Sales & Tech., Sunnyvale, 1967-76; realtor Cornish & Carey, Palo Alto, Calif., 1988-99; real estate assoc. Coldwell Banker, Coronado, Calif., 1999—. Dir. ret. activities office Naval Amphibious Base, Coronado, Calif. Author: Polaris Electrical Subsystems Design History, 1964, Poseidon Subsystem Invention, 1971. Comdr. USNR, 1941-69, ret., World War II, Korea, Vietnam; charter mem. U.S.S. Midway Aircraft Carrier Mus. Decorated DFC, Air medal with 4 gold stars; named to Charles Lindbergh chpt. DFC Soc., San Diego, 2003. Mem. Am. Mgmt. Assn., Mountain View Real Estate Bd. (pres.), Calif. Assn. Realtors (bd. dirs.), Tailhook Assn., Commonwealth San Francisco. Ret. Officers Club (-past pres. Peninsula chpt.), Lions. Home: 1060 Coronado Ave Coronado CA 92118-2439

STAMEY, THOMAS ALEXANDER, urologist, educator; b. Rutherfordton, N.C., Apr. 26, 1928; s. Owen and Virginia (Link) S.; m. Kathryn Simmons Dec. 1, 1973; children: Fred M., Charline, Thomas A. III, Allison, Theron. BA, Vanderbilt U., 1948; MD, Johns Hopkins U., 1952. Diplomate Am. Bd. Urology. Intern, then resident Johns Hopkins Hosp., 1952-56; asst. prof. urology Johns Hopkins U. Sch. Medicine, Balt., 1958-60, assoc. prof., 1960-61; assoc. prof., chmn. divsn. urology Stanford (Calif.) U., 1961-64, assoc. prof., 1964-90, prof., 1991—, chmn. dept., 1964-95. Author: Renovascular Hypertension, 1967, Pathogenesis and Treatment of Urinary Tract Infections, 1980, Urinalysis and Urinary Sediment: A Practical Guide for the Health Science Professional, 1985; editor: Campbell's Urology, edits. 4-6, 1978-92, Monographs in Urology, 1980-99. Capt. M.C., USAF, 1956-58. Recipient Sheen award ACS, 1990, Ferdinand C. Valentine award N.Y. Acad. Medicine, 1991. Mem. Am. Urol. Assn. (Ramon Guiteras award 1995, John K. Lattimer award 2000, Eugene Fuller Triennial Prostate award 2001), Am. Surg. Assn. (sr.), Inst. Medicine of NAS. Avocations: fishing, astronomy. Office: Stanford U Med Ctr Dept Urology S 287 300 Pasteur Dr Stanford CA 94305-5118 E-mail: tstamey@stanford.edu.

STAMM, ALAN, lawyer; b. Galesburg, Ill., Nov. 22, 1931; s. Gustave Frederick and Miriam (Simon) S.; m. Shelley Lynn Ramage, Mar. 19, 1978; 1 child, Lucinda Anne. Student, Universidad Nacional de Mex., summer 1950; AB, Yale U., 1952; JD, Harvard U., 1957. Bar: Calif. 1957, U.S. Supreme Ct. 1963. Assoc. Thelen, Marrin, Johnson & Bridges, San Francisco, 1957-60; staff atty. Litton Industries Inc., Beverly Hills, Calif., 1960-66, asst. sec., 1963-66; sec., gen. counsel Internat. Rectifier Corp., L.A., 1966-69, v.p., 1968-69; v.p., gen. counsel Republic Corp., L.A., 1969-71, also bd. dirs., 1970-71; v.p., gen. counsel Sat. Rev. Industries, N.Y.C., 1971-72, Mattel Inc., Hawthorne, Calif., 1972-74, staff cons., 1974-75; of counsel Long & Levit, L.A., 1975-82, O'Donnell & Gordon, L.A., 1983-87, Hedges, Powe & Caldwell, L.A., 1988-90; pvt. practice L.A., 1990—. Judge pro tem Mcpl. Ct. L.A. Jud. Dist., 1977—; arbitrator L.A. Superior Ct. 1979—, judge pro tem L.A. Superior Ct. 1989—, arbitrator Nat. Assn. Securities Dealers, 1981—. Founding trustee Ctr. for Law in the Pub. Interest; trustee Marlborough Sch., L.A.; bd. govs. Century City Hosp., L.A.; counsel bus. and profl. com. L.A. Philharmonic; bd. dirs. Yale Alumni Fund. Lt. (j.g.) USNR, 1952-54; lt. comdr. Res.; ret. Mem. ABA, Calif. Bar Assn., L.A. Bar Assn., Am. Jewish Com., Harvard Law Sch. Assn., L.A. County Art Mus., Am. Arbitration Assn. (nat. panel arbitrators), NAACP, Sierra Club, Nat. Assn. Yale Alumni (former bd. govs.), Yale Club of So. Calif. (former dir.), Harvard Club of So. Calif., Phi Beta Kappa. Home: 422 Denslow Ave Los Angeles CA 90049-3507 Office: 1950 Pelham Ave Unit 1 Los Angeles CA 90025-5835

STAMM, CHARLES H. lawyer; BA, Princeton Univ.; JD, Yale Univ. Exec. v.p., gen. counsel Tchrs. Ins. & Annuity Assn., N.Y.C. Office: Tchrs Ins & Annuity Assn 730 3rd Ave New York NY 10017-3206

STAMM, JOHN WILLIAM RANDOLPH, dentist, educator, academic dean; b. Germany, Nov. 3, 1942;, naturalized, Can., naturalized, US; married; 2 children. DDS, U. Alta., Can., 1967; DDPH, U. Toronto, Can., 1969, MScD, 1971. Diplomate Am. Bd. Dental Pub. Health. Dental dir. Baffin region Nat. Health & Welfare, 1967; pvt. dental practice Fort Saskatchewan, 1968; rsch. asst. & biometrics Sch. Hygiene & Faculty Dentistry U. Toronto, 1968—71; asst. prof. Faculty Dentistry McGill U., 1971—74, assoc. prof., 1974—80, chmn., 1974—84, prof., 1980—84; dir. Dental Rsch. Ctr. U. N.C., 1985—89; prof. U. N.C. Sch. Dentistry, 1985, asst. dean, 1985—89, dean, 1989—. Vis. prof. U. Riyadh, Saudi Arabia, 1980; mem. expert adv. panel oral health WHO, 1984—90; mem. study sect. oral biology and medicine NIH, 1988—90; cons. Que. Min. Social Affairs, 1974—76, Alta. Health Unit Assn., 1977—79, Can. Electrolytic Zinc, 1978—82, Can. Dental Assn., 1980, Am. Fund Dental Health, 1980—83, Dental Health St. Regis Indians, N.Y. State Dept. Health, 1980. Mem. editl. bd. Jour. Dental Edn., 1980—83, Jour. Cmty. Dentistry and Oral Epidemiology, 1988—, Oral Diseases, 1994, assoc. editor Caries Rsch., 1995—; contbr. articles to profl. jours. Grantee, Ont. Dept. Health, 1969, McGill U., 1973, Que. Health Sci. Rsch. Coun., 1973, Min. Social Affairs Que., 1972—74, Nat. Inst. Dental Rsch., 1976—78, 1985, Med. Rsch. Coun., 1981—84, Nat. Health and Welfare, 1982—85, NIH, 1985—, Robert Wood Johnson Found., 1986—91. Fellow: AAAS, Japanese Soc. for Promotion of Sci., Acad. Dentistry Internat., Am. Coll. Dentists, Royal Coll. Dentists of Can. (chief examiner 1980—82), Internat. Coll. Dentists; mem.: Internat. Assn. Dental Rsch. (treas. 1997—2001), Can. Soc. Pub. Health Dentists (pres. 1979—81), Can. Dental Assn., Am. Assn. Dental Rsch., Am. Assn. Pub. Health Dentists, Am. Assn. Dental Schs., Omicron Kappa Upsilon. Office: U NC Sch Dentistry Dental Ecology Cb 7450 Chapel Hill NC 27599-7450*

STAMM, KEITH G. energy executive; BS in mech. engring., U. Mo.-Columbia; MBA in fin., Rockhurst Coll. Lic. Staff Aquila's Mo. Pub. Svc.; CEO Aquila Merchant Svcs.; chmn., CEO United Energy Ltd.; pres., COO Aquila Global Networks Group; sr. v.p., COO Aquila, Kans. City, Mo., 2002—. Former bd. mem. Alinta Ltd., Uecomm. Office: Aquila 20 W 9th St Kansas City MO 64105-1711

STAMOS, JOHN, actor; b. Orange County, Calif., Aug. 19, 1963; s. Bill and Loretta Stamos; m. Rebecca Romijn, 1998, separated, 2004. Drummer with various bands. Actor: (TV series) General Hospital (Emmy award, 2 Soapy awards), Dreams, 1984, You Again?, 1986-87, Full House, 1988-95, Thieves, 2001, (TV movies) Daughter of the Streets, 1990, Captive, 1991, The Disappearance of Christina, 1993, Fatal Vows: The Alexandra O'Hara Story, 1996, A Match Made in Heaven, 1997, Sealed with a Kiss, 1999, How to Marry a Billionaire: A Christmas Tale, 2000, Fortunate Son, 2000, The Reagans, 2003; (films) Never Too Young to Die, 1986, Born to Ride, 1991, Private Parts, 1998, The Marriage Fool, 1998, Dropping Out, 2000, My Best Friend's Wife, 2001, Party Monster, 2003, I Am Stamos, 2004. Recipient Youth in Film award. Mem. AFTRA, Child Help U.S.A. (nat. spokesperson). Office: William Morris Agy care Les Stollman 151 El Camino Dr Beverly Hills CA 90212-2775*

STAMPER, EWA SZUMOTALSKA, psychologist; b. Warsaw, Sept. 8, 1954; came to U.S., 1984; d. Tadeusz and Regina S.; m. Ryszard Zwierowicz, Dec. 30, 1980 (div. Jan. 13, 1986); m. Allen Malcolm Stamper, Oct. 23, 1992. MA in Clin. Psychology, U. Warsaw, Poland, 1978; PhD in Psychology, New Sch. U., N.Y.C., 1992. Staff therapist Marital Therapy Counseling Ctr., Warsaw, 1978—79, Ctr. for Psychotherapy and Personality Growth, Warsaw, 1978—80; sr. staff therapist Lab. for Psychoedn. Polish Psychol. Assn., Warsaw, 1981—85; postgrad. affiliate Washington Sq. Inst. for Psychotherapy, N.Y.C., 1990—92; police psychologist Honolulu Police Dept., 1993—98; pvt. practice, Honolulu, 1994—. With Tng. Ctr. for Family Therapy, Warsaw, 1976 78, Stuyvesant Poly., N.Y.C., 1988—89, North Ctrl. Bronx (N.Y.) Hosp., 1988—89, Yale Psychiat. Inst., 1989—90, Castle Med. Ctr., Kailua, Hawaii, 1993—94; co-chmn. Crystal Methampetamine Forum, Honolulu, 1996—99. Mem. APA, Am. Acad. Experts in Traumatic Stress, Hawaii Psychol. Assn. (clin. divsn. rep. 1998-99). Avocations: horseback riding, raising German shorthaired pointers and Siamese cats, gardening, fiction and poetry writing, running. Office: 1188 Bishop St Ste 1108 Honolulu HI 96813-3313 Office Phone: 808-531-1991.

STAMPER, JAMES M. retired English language educator; b. Roxana, Ky., Sept. 26, 1917; s. Marion and Amanda (Combs) S.; m. Diane C. Mahoney, Aug. 12, 1967. BS in Edn., Union Coll., 1941; MA in English, U. Ky., 1946. Subs. tchr. Ermine Elem. Sch., Dry Fork Elem. Sch., 1936-37; elem. tchr. various schs., 1937-41; h.s. Eng. tchr. Whitesburg H.S., Ky., 1941-46; instr. English U. Ky., Lexington, 1946-49, U. Md., College Park, 1949-52; instr. bus. English DePaul U., Chgo., 1952-62; English tchr., cons. in high sch. English Bd. Edn., Chgo., 1962-72; ret. Chgo. Area Schs., 1972; subst. tchr. Chgo. Area schs., 1972-82. Vis. instr. in English Jacksonville (Fla.) U. Co-author: A Handbook on Oral Reading Diagnosis, Resource Materials for Essential English in the Secondary Schools, A Syllabus in Basic English; contbr. articles to profl. jours. Scholar Knights of Columbus, Union Coll., U. Ky. Mem. AARP. Home: 4501 Concord Ln Northbrook IL 60062-7163

STAMPER, MALCOLM THEODORE, publishing company executive; b. Detroit, Apr. 4, 1925; s. Fred Theodore and Lucille (Cayce) S.; m. Marion Philbin Guinan, Feb. 25, 1946; children: Geoffrey, Kevin, Jamie, David, Mary, Anne. Student, U. Richmond, Va., 1943-44; BEE, Ga. Inst. Tech., 1946; postgrad., U. Mich., 1946-49; HHD (hon.), Seattle U., 1994. With Gen. Motors Corp., 1949-62; with Boeing Co., Seattle, 1962-90, mgr. electronics ops., v.p., gen. mgr. turbine div., 1964-66; v.p., gen. mgr. Boeing Co. (747 Airplane program), 1966-69, v.p., gen. mgr. comml. airplane group, 1969-71, corp. sr. v.p. ops., 1971-72; pres. Boeing Co., 1972-85, vice chmn., 1985-90; CEO, Storytellers Ink Pub., Seattle, 1990—, also chmn. bd. dirs. Bd. dirs. Pro-Air Inc.; trustee The Conf. Bd., 1988—. Candidate for U.S. Ho. of Reps., Detroit, 1952; trustee, chmn. Seattle Art Mus.; nat. bd. dirs. Smithsonian Assocs. With USNR, 1943-46. Named Industrialist of Year, 1967; recipient Educator's Golden Key award, 1970, Elmer A. Sperry award, 1982, AIEE award, Ga. Inst. Tech. award, Sec. Dept. Health and Human Services award, Silver Beaver award Boy Scouts Am., 1989, Literary Lions award, 1995; named to Engring. Hall of Fame. Mem. Nat. Alliance Businessmen, Phi Gamma Delta.

STAMPER, ROBERT LEWIS, ophthalmologist, educator; b. N.Y.C., July 27, 1939; m. Naomi T. Belson, June 23, 1963; children: Juliet, Marjorie, Alison. BA, Cornell U., 1961; MD, SUNY-Downstate, 1965. Diplomate Am. Bd. Ophthalmology (assoc. examiner 1976-92, bd. dirs. 1992-99). Intern Mt. Sinai Hosp., N.Y.C., 1965-66; resident in ophthalmology Washington U.-Barnes Hosp., St. Louis, 1968-71; Nat. Eye Inst.-NIH fellow dept. ophthalmology Washington U., St. Louis, 1971-72, from instr. ophthalmology to asst. prof. dept. ophthalmology, 1971-72; asst. prof. dept. ophthalmology Pacific Presbyn. Med. Ctr., San Francisco, 1972-76, assoc. prof. ophthalmology, 1976-87; chmn. dept. ophthalmology Calif. Pacific Med. Ctr. (formerly Pacific Presbyn. Med. Ctr.), San Francisco, 1987-96; vice-chmn. dept. ophthalmology U. Calif., San Francisco, 1999—2003, prof. clin. ophthalmology, dir. glaucoma, 1999—. Asst. ophthalmologist Barnes Hosp., St. Louis, 1971-72, Harkness Hosp., San Francisco, 1973-74; dir. ophthalmic photography and fluorescin angiography, dept. ophthalmology Washington U., St. Louis, 1969-72; dir. resident tng. Pacific Presbyn. Med. Ctr., 1972-89, dir. glaucoma svc., vice-chmn. dept. ophthalmology, 1974-87; chief ophthalmology svc. Highland Hosp., Oakland, Calif., 1974-76; clin. instr. ophthalmology U. Calif., San Francisco, 1974-77, prof. clin. ophthalmology, 1998—; clin. asst. prof. ophthalmology U. Calif., Berkeley, 1974-78, asst. clin. prof. ophthalmology, 1978-85; sr. rsch. assoc. Smith-Kettlewell Inst. Visual Scis., San Francisco, 1972-89; project co-dir. ophthalmic curriculum for med. students Nat. Libr. Medicine, 1973-75; commr. Joint Commn. on Allied Health Pers. in Ophthalmology, 1975-87, bd. dirs., 1978-88, sec., 1980, v.p., 1982-83, pres., 1984-85; provisional asst. chief dept. ophthalmology Mt. Zion Hosp., San Francisco, 1976-87, assoc. chief dept. ophthalmology, 1982-86; ophthalmic cons. Ft. Ord, Calif., 1976—, Oakland Naval Hosp., 1978-83; instr. Stanford (Calif.) U., 1977—; glaucoma cons. U. Calif., Davis, 1978-84; vis. lectr. dept. ophthalmology Hadassah Hebrew U. Med. Ctr., Jerusalem, 1978, Oxford (Eng.) U. Eye Hosp., 1986; ind. med. examiner State of Calif., 1979—; mem. appeals hearing panel Accreditation Coun. for Grad. Med. Edn., 1986-93, mem. residency rev. com. for ophthalmology, 1993-98; mem. provisional courtesy staff Peralta Hosp., Oakland, 1988-92; mem. ophthalmic devices adv. panel USFDA, 1989-92; presenter, lectr. in field. Co-author: Update in Glaucoma, 2004; editor Ophthalmology Clinics of North Am., 1988-2004; mem. editl. adv. com. Ophthalmology, 1982-89, mem. editl. bd., 1983-94; sr. author: Becker and Shaffer's Diagnosis and Management of the Glaucomas, 7th edit., 1999; contbr. articles to profl. jours. Chmn. bd. Agy. for Jewish Edn., Oakland, 1986-89; bd. dirs. Jewish Fedn. Greater East Bay, Oakland, 1992-94; bd. dirs. Found. for Glaucoma Rsch.; mem. glaucoma adv. com. Nat. Soc. to Prevent Blindness, 1981—; mem. Am. Diabetes Assn. Surgeon USPHS, 1966-68. Recipient Nat. Soc. for Performance and Instrn. award for self-instrnl. material in ophthalmology, 1975, Honor award Am. Acad. Ophthalmology, 1982, Sr. Honor award, 1992, Statesmanship award Joint Commn. on Allied Health Pers. in Ophthalmology, 1989, Troutman Master Tchr. in Ophthalmology award, 2000; N.Y. State Regents scholar, 1961, N.Y. State scholar in medicine, 1965; Blalock student fellow UCLA Sch. Medicine, 1961, Fight for Sight student fellow dept. ophthalmology N.Y. Hosp. and Cornell Med. Ctr., 1962, 63, 64. Fellow Am. Acad. Ophthalmology and Otolaryngology (rep. to joint commn. on allied health pers., faculty home study course sect. X, chmn. sect. VIII 1983-85, bd. councilors, editl. adv. com. Opthalmology jour. 1982-89, editl. bd. Ophthalmology jour. 1983-94, and many others), ACS; mem. AMA (Physician's Recognition award 1989), Am. Ophthalmologic Soc., Assn. for Rsch. in Vision and Ophthalmology, Calif. Med. Assn. (asst. sec. sect. ophthalmology, chmn., sci. bd. rep. adv. panel on ophthalmology, 1985-91), Nat. Soc. Prevent Blindness (mem. glaucoma adv. com. 1981—, bd. dirs. 1986—), No. Calif. Soc. Prevent Blindness, Calif. Assn. Ophthalmology, Pan Am. Ophthal. (bd. dirs. 1992—), Soc., N.Y. Acad. Scis., Las Vegas Ophthal. Soc. (hon.), Am. Glaucoma Soc. (v.p. 1997-99, pres. 1999-2000), Glaucoma Rsch. Found. (bd. dirs.). Office: Dept Opht UCSF Med Ctr 8 Koret Way San Francisco CA 94143-0730 Office Phone: 415-476-3717. Business E-Mail: stamper@itsa.ucsf.edu.

STAMPKE, STUART REH, physicist, researcher; b. Burbank, Calif., Apr. 20, 1950; BS in Physics summa cum laude, Calif. State U., Northridge, 1973; PhD in Physics, Calif. Inst. Tech., Pasadena, 1982. Rsch. fellow in physics Calif. Inst. Tech., Pasadena, 1982; rsch. assoc. Mich. State U., East Lansing, 1982-86; scientist I Superconducting Super Collider Lab., Waxahachie, Tex., 1989-94; sr. scientist Aura Sys., Inc., El Segundo, Calif., 1996—2003. From vis. asst. prof. to vis. assoc. prof. U. Notre Dame, Ind., 1986-88; mem. part-time faculty Calif. State U., Northridge, 1994-96. Contbr. articles to profl. jours. on particle physics, detectors, and accelerator physics. Mem. IEEE, Am. Phys. Soc., Internat. Solar Energy Soc., Am. Solar Energy Soc. Home: 17803 Superior St Apt 215 Northridge CA 91325-4795 E-mail: srstampke@earthlink.net.

STAMPS, DOUGLAS, mechanical engineer, educator; BS, U. of Evansville, 1979; MS, MIT, 1981; PhD, U. of Mich., 1985. Assoc. prof. U. of Evansville, Evansville, Ind., 1995—; mem. tech. staff Sandia Nat. Laboratories, Albuquerque, N.Mex., 1985—95. Contbr. articles to profl. jours. Recipient Outstanding Tchr. award, Am/ Soc. for Enring. Edn., 2004. Mem.: ASME, ASEE, Combustion Inst. Achievements include patents pending for method and device to mitigate explosions in a vacuum furnace and assistive mobility device. Office: University of Evansville/ ME Dept 1800 Lincoln Ave Evansville IN 47722

STAMPS, GEORGE MORELAND, communications consultant, facsimile pioneer; b. Kuling, Jiangxi, China, June 15, 1924; came to U.S., 1926 (parents Am. citizens); s. Drew Fletcher and Elizabeth Camilla (Belk) S.; m. Helen Leone Paty, Nov. 29, 1946, children: Margaret Evalyn, Robert Fletcher, Thomas Paty, John Belk. BS magna cum laude, Wake Forest U., 1947; MA in Physics, Columbia U., 1949; postgrad., Poly. Inst. Bklyn., 1950-52. Instr. physics and math. SUNY Maritime Coll., Bronx, 1949-51; asst. chief engr., dir. tech. sales Hogan Labs. Inc., N.Y.C., 1951-59; chief engr., asst. to pres. mktg. Telautograph Corp., L.A., 1960-62; program mgr. Magnafax Program Magnavox Co., Torrance, Calif., 1963-65, mgr indsl. mktg. Urbana, Ill., 1965-71, mgr. bus. devel., 1971-73; corp. mgr. bus. devel. Xerox Corp., Stamford, Conn., 1973-76; pres. GMS Consulting, Westport, Conn., 1976-86, Oxford, Ga., 1986—. Expert witness on facsimile-visual scis. N.Y. Supreme Ct., 1982; chmn. numerous sci. and profl. confs. Contbr. over 35 articles on facsimile and telecommunication scis. to profl. jours. and govt. coms. Patentee in field. Del. Conn. Dem. Conv., Hartford, 1980; bd. dirs. Champaign-Urbana (Ill.) Symphony Orch., 1968-72, Newton County Red Cross, 1988-94; sec. Newton County Hist. Soc., 1991-93, v.p., 1993-95, pres., 1995-96; v.p. Friends of Newton County Porter Meml. Libr., 1988-91, pres., 1991-93; pres. Newton County Facilities Bd., 1997—; chmn. Newton County Facilities Bd., 1997—; co-chair Newton County Impact Fee Adv. Com., 1999—; mem. Yellow River Stakeholders Com., 2003. Decorated Air medal with two oak leaf clusters; named Friend of Newton County Libr., 1994; named Wake Forest U. Alumnus of Yr., 1997, recipient Disting. Svc. citation for sci. and tech., 1997. Mem. IEEE, Computer Soc. of IEEE, Comm. Soc. of IEEE (officer Ft. Wayne chpt. 1972-73), Geosci. and Remote Sensing Soc. of IEEE, Electronics Industries Assn. (chmn. comm. terminals and interfaces sect. 1963-73, founder TR-29 facsimile systems and equipment engring. com. 1961), Armed Forces Comm. and Electronics Assn., Am. Phys. Soc., Kiwanis (pres. Covington club 1993-94, lt. gov. 21st divsn. 1996-97), Phi Beta Kappa, Omicron Delta Kappa. Presbyterian. Home: 1280 Lake Stone Lea Dr PO Box 1299 Oxford GA 30054-1299

STAMPS, THOMAS PATY, lawyer, consultant; b. Mineola, N.Y., May 10, 1952; s. George Moreland and Helen Leone (Paty) S.; children: Katherine Camilla, George Belk, Elizabeth Margaret, Carley Lynn, Walker Paty; m. Diana Lynn Whittaker, Dec. 11, 1993. BA, U. Ill., 1973; postgrad., Emory U., 1975-76; JD, Wake Forest U., 1979. Bar: Ga. 1979, N.C. 1979. Pers. dir. Norman Jaspan, N.Y.C., 1973-74; assoc. Macey & Zusmann, Atlanta, 1979-81; prin. Zusmann, Small, Stamps & White PC, Atlanta, 1981-85; mem. Strategic Capital Am., L.L.C., 1998—. Ptnr. Destin Enterprises, Atlanta, 1983-85. Author: Study of a Student, 1973, History of Coca-Cola, 1976; asst. editor Ga. Jour. So. Legal History, 1991-94. Atty. Vol. Lawyers for Arts, Atlanta, 1981—94, Atlanta Vol. Lawyers Found.; active High Mus. Art, 1986—, Atlanta Hist. Soc., Atlanta Bot. Gardens, Atlanta Symphony Orch., Ga. Trust Hist. Preservation, Ind.; sec. Friends of Woodrow Wilson, 1988—, chmn. dinner, 1990—; trustee Ga. Legal History Found., 1989—; pres. N. Springs H.S. Touchdown Club, 2000—01; founding dir. Sandy Springs Youth Basketball Program, 1999—2000; mem. Dem. Party Ga., Atlanta, 1983—; mem. Bench and Bar Com. State Bar Ga., 1996—; chmn. Summer Law Inst., Atlanta, 1981—85; panel mem. U.S. Bankruptcy Trustees No. Dist. Ga., 1982—92. Named to Honorable Order of Ky. Colonels; recipient Svc. award Inst. Continuing Legal Edn., Athens, Ga., 1981, 86. Fellow Ga. Bar Found.; mem. Atlanta Bar Assn. (com. chmn. 1981-85, bd. dirs. litigation sect. 2001—, mem. jud. selection com. 2001—, chmn. history com. 2001—), N.C. Bar Assn., Lawyers Club, North Springs H.S. Touchdown Club (pres. 2000-01), Phi Alpha Delta (justice, Atlanta 1982-83, emeritus 1983). Office: 7715 Jett Ferry Rd Atlanta GA 30350-5419

STAMSTA, JEAN F. artist; b. Sheboygan, Wis., Nov. 2, 1936; d. Herbert R. and Lucile Caroline (Malwitz) Nagel; m. Duane R. Stamsta, Aug. 18, 1956; children: Marc, David. BS, BA, U. Wis., 1958. Guest curator Milw. Art Mus., 1986; resident artist Leighton Artist Colony, Banff, Alta., Can., 1987. One-woman shows include Am. Craft Mus., N.Y.C., 1971, Winona (Minn.) State U., 1986, Lawrence U., Appleton, Wis., 1990, Walkers Point Ctr. Arts, Milw., 1990, U. Wis. Ctr., Sheboygan, 1998, Wis. Luth. Coll., Milw., 1999, exhibited in group shows at Cleve. Mus. Art, 1977, Milw. Art Mus., 1986, 1988, Nat. Air and Space Mus., Smithsonian Instn., Washington, 1986, Madison (Wis.) Art Ctr., 1987, 1990, Paper Press Gallery, Chgo., 1988, North Arts Ctr., Atlanta, 1990, Dairy Barn Cultural Arts Ctr., Athens, Ohio, 1991, Paper Arts Festival, Appleton, 1992, Fine Arts Mus., Budapest, Hungary, 1992, Tilburg Textile Mus., Netherlands, 1993, U. Wis. Union Gallery, 1994, Holland Area Arts Coun. Gallery, U. Mich., Ann Arbor, 1996, Charles Allis Art Mus., Milw., 1996, Bergstrom-Mahler Mus., Neenah, Wis., 1998, West Bend Mus. Art, Wis., 2000, Three Rivers Arts Festival, Pitts., 2001, U. Wis. Alumni Assn., Milw., 2002, Racine (Wis.) Art Mus., 2003. NEA craftsman fellow, 1974. Avocations: swimming, travel. Home: 9313 Center Oak Rd Hartland WI 53029 E-mail: jstamsta@aol.com.

STANALAJCZO, GREG CHARLES, computer and technology company executive; b. 1959; Degree, Oakland U. With CDI Computer Svc., Inc., Troy, Mich., 1986-95, pres., 1993-95; exec. v.p., COO, co-owner Trillium Teamologies, Inc., Royal Oak, Mich., 1996—; pres., owner Stano Enterprises, L.L.C.; owner, ptnr. Sullivan Investment Group, 3rd St. Properties; ptnr. Heritage Pewter L.L.C. Office: Trillium Teamologies Inc 219 S Main St Ste 300 Royal Oak MI 48067-2611 Office Phone: 248-584-2080. E-mail: greg_stano@compuserve.com.

STANARD, CHRISTOPHER LEON, statistician; b. Washington, 1967; B of Indsl. Engring., Ga. Tech., 1990, MS in Indsl. Engring., 1992. Process tech. engr. Michelin Tire Co., Lexington, S.C., 1992-94; statistician GE Global Rsch., Schenectady, NY, 1996—2004. Founding sec. Awareness of Career and Ednl. Opportunities Inc., Atlanta, 1992. Contbr. poetry to Drumvoice mag., 1992, 93, 96, Catch the Fire, 1998, Spirit & Flame, 1997, Dark Eros, 1997; book reviewer Technometrics. Plant sect. coord. Michelin Walk Am. March of Dimes, 1993, 94. NSF grad. minority fellow, 1990-92, 94-95. Mem. Am. Soc. Quality, Nat. Soc. Black Engrs. (tech. profls. conf. pub. rels. chair 2000, mem. region I and II Profl. Devel. Conf. com. 1998, asst. nat. publs. chair 1989-90, Alumni Extension Region I Mem.-at-Large of the Yr. 1998), Inst. Indsl. Engrs., Am. Statis. Assn. (minority affairs com. 2001-03), Tau Beta Pi.

STANBERRY, D(OSI) ELAINE, English literature educator, writer; b. Elk Park, N.C. m. Earl Stanberry; 1 child, Anita St. Lawrence. Student in Bus. Edn., Steed Coll. Tech., 1956; BS in Bus. and English, East Tenn. State U., 1961, MA in Shakespearean Lit., 1962; PhD, Tex. A&M U., 1975; postgrad., North Tex. State U., U. South Fla., NYU, Duke U., U. N.C. Prof. Manatee Jr. Coll., Bradenton, Fla., 1964-67; Disting. prof. English Dickinson State U., N.D., 1967-81; retired, 1981. Author: Poetic Heartstrings, Mountain Echoes,

Love's Perplexing Obsession Experienced by Heinrich Heine and Percy Bysshe Shelley, Poetry from the Ancients to Moderns: A Critical Anthology, Finley Forest, Chapel Hill's Tree-lined Tuck, (plays) The Big Toe, The Funeral Factory; contbr. articles, poetry to jours., mags. Recipient Editor's Choice award Nat. Libr. Poetry, 1988, 95, Distinguished Professor of English Award, Dickinson State U., 1981; included in Best Poems of 1995. Mem. Acad. Am. Poets, N.C. Writers Network, N.C. Poetry Soc. (Carl Sandburg Poetry award 1988), Poetic Page, Writers Jour., Poets and Writers, Friday-Noon Poets, Delta Kappa Gamma. Home: 1840 Crawford RD Graham NC 27253-9204

STANBRIDGE, ERIC JOHN, biology professor; b. London, May 28, 1942; came to U.S., 1965; BS, Brunel U., 1964; PhD, Stanford U., 1971. Rsch. asst. Wistar Inst., Phila., 1965—67; mem. sci. staff Nat. Inst. Med. Research, London, 1968-69; research assoc. med. microbiology Stanford (Calif.) U., 1972-73, instr. med. microbiology, 1973-75; asst. prof., dept. microbiology U. Calif., Irvine, 1975-78, assoc. prof., dept. microbiology, 1978-82, prof., dept. microbiology and molecular genetics, 1982—, disting. prof., dept. microbiology and molecular genetics, 2002—. Chmn. Gordon Conf. Cancer Biology, 1985; advisor Office of Tech. Assessment, 1986; co-organizer UCLA-Triton Bioscis. Symposium, 1986; mem. external adv. bd., U. Calif. San Francisco Comprehensive Cancer Ctr., 2000-; bd. sci. advisors, Norwegian Inst. Gene Ecology, 2002-; coll. reviewers, Can. Rsch. Chairs Program, 2003-;lectr. in the field. Editorial bd. mem. Microbiol. Revs., 1985-, In Vitro, 1987-, J. Cellular Biochemistry, 1990-, Oncology Rsch., 1992-, Geno Methods, 1993-, Cancer Rsch. Ency., 1999-, Cancer Letters, 1998-; assoc. editor Cancer Research, 1985-, J. Cellular Physiology, 1989-, Molecular and Cellular Differentation, 1992-, Cancer Sci. (Japan), 2004-; contbr. articles to profl. jours. and chpts. to books; 4 US patents in the field. Fellow Leukemia Soc., 1976-1978, Internat. Union Against Cancer, 1979, Eleanor Roosevelt Internat., 1983-84, Am. Acad. Microbiology, 1986, AAAS, 1993; recipient Research Career Devel. award, NIH, 1978-83, NIH Merit award, 1987-96, Phi Kappa Phi Biology Colloquium award, Oregon State U., 1988; named one of Outstanding Young Men of Am., Jaycees, 1979. Mem. AAAS, NY Acad. Scis., Internat. Orgn. Mycoplasmologists, Am. Soc. Microbiology, Sigma Xi, Tissue Culture Assn., Internat. Orgn. Mycolplasmologist, Am. Assn. for Cancer Rsch., Internat. Soc. for Differentiation, UICC Acad. Fellows Office: U Calif Irvine B235/B210 Med Sciences Mail Code 4025 Irvine CA 92697-4025 Office Phone: 949-824-7042., 949-824-5259. Office Fax: 949-824-8598. Business E-Mail: ejstanbr@uci.edu.

STANBRO, HEATHER ASPEN, emergency medical technician; b. Medford, Oreg., Jan. 3, 1979; d. Robert Frederick and Caroline Alice Bessey; m. Jason Alan Stanbro, Sept. 1, 2000. Student, Rouge C.C., Medford, 1997—98. Registered EMT. Med. specialist U.S. Army, Schofield Barracks, Hawaii, 1999—2002, Ft. Carson, Colo., 2002—. Decorated Purple Heart U.S. Army; recipient Good Conduct medal, 2001. Mem.: Nat. Geog. Soc., Sierra Club. Democrat. Presbyterian. Avocations: quilting, hiking, camping, fishing, writing. Office: Cco 64th FSB Fort Carson CO 80913

STANBURY, JOHN BRUTON, retired pharmacologist, educator; b. Clinton, N.C., May 15, 1915; s. Walter A. and Zula (Bruton) S.; m. Jean F. Cook, Jan. 6, 1945; children: John Bruton, Martha Jean, Sarah Katherine, David McNeill, Pamela Cook. AB, Duke U., 1935; MD, Harvard U., 1939; MD (hon.), U. Leiden (Netherlands), 1975, U. Pisa, Italy, 1994. House officer Mass. Gen. Hosp., 1940-41, asst. resident, 1946, chief med. resident, 1948, mem. med. staff, 1949—; research fellow pharmacology Harvard Med. Sch., 1947; vis. prof. medicine U. Leiden, 1955; prof. exptl. medicine MIT, Cambridge, 1966-80, emeritus, 1980—. Cons. Pan Am. Health Orgn., WHO, UNICEF, U.S. AEC. Author: Endemic Goiter: The adaptation of man to iodine deficiency, 1954, Metabolic Basis of Inherited Disease, 5th edit., 1984, The Thyroid and Its Diseases, 5th edit., 1984, Endemic Goiter, 1969, Human Development and the Thyroid, 1972, Endemic Goiter and Endemic Cretinism, 1980, Prevention and Control of Iodine Deficiency Disorders, 1987, A Constant Ferment, 1991, The Damaged Brain of Iodine Deficiency, 1994, The Inborn Errors of the Thyroid System, 1994, Iodine in Pregnancy, 1998. Served from lt. (j.g.) to comdr. USNR, 1941-45. Recipient Delmar S. Fahrney medal Franklin Inst., 1993, Prince Mahidol award, Thailand, 1994. Mem. Am. Assn. Physicians, Soc. Clin. Investigation, Am. Thyroid Assn. (pres. 1969), Am. Acad. Arts and Scis., Endocrine Soc., Endocrine Socs. Finland, Colombia, Peru, Ecuador and Argentina, Internat. Coun. for Control of Iodine Deficiency Disorders (chair emeritus, Gran Oficical le Ordenar Hipoloitio Unanue, Peru)). Democrat. Episcopalian. Home: 43 Circuit Rd Chestnut Hill MA 02467-1802 E-mail: john_stanbury@hms.harvard.edu.

STANCELL, ARNOLD FRANCIS, chemical engineering educator, retired oil industry executive; b. NYC, Nov. 16, 1936; s. Francis and Maria (Lucas) S.; m. Constance Newton, Apr. 21, 1973; 1 child, Christine. B in Chem. Engring. magna cum laude, CCNY, 1958; PhD, MIT, 1962. Registered profl. engr., NY. Rsch. scientist, rsch. mgr. Mobil Oil Corp., Edison, NJ, 1962—72, chem. planning assoc., mgr. NYC, 1973—75, v.p. chem. divsn. Macedon, NY, 1976—79, mgr. corp. planning NYC, 1980—81, regional exec. mktg. and refining London, 1982—84, planning v.p. mktg. and refining NYC, 1985—86, v.p. U.S. exploration and prodn. Fairfax, Va., 1987—88, v.p. internat. exploration and producing, 1989—93; prof. chem. engring. Ga. Inst. Tech., Atlanta, 1994—2001, endowed chair prof. chem. engring., 2001—. Vis. prof. MIT, Cambridge, 1970, 1998, adv. bd., 1976—; adv. bd. CCNY, 1990—, Carnegie Mellon U., 1999—. Contbg. author: Polymer Science and Materials, 1971; contbr. articles to Jour. Applied Polymer Sci., AIChE Symposia Series, Jour. Macromolecular Sci. Recipient Profl. Achievement award, NOBCChE, 1975, Career Achievment award CCNY, 1993, Black Engineer of Yr. award U.S. Black Engrs., 1992. Fellow AIChE (Chem. Engring. Practice award 1997); mem. NAE, Nat. Acad. Engring; fellow, AIChE, Tau Beta Pi, Phi Lambda Upsilon. Achievements include mgmt. and growth of large dollar billions scale domestic and internat. businesses in chemicals, oil and natural gas; patents for petrochemical and polymer processes and plasma processes at surfaces. Office: Ga Inst Tech 778 Atlantic Dr NW Atlanta GA 30332-0100 E-mail: arnold.stancell@che.gatech.edu.

STANCIL, IRENE MACK, family counselor; b. St. Helena Island, Sept. 29, 1938; d. Rufus and Irene (Wilson) Mack; m. Nesby Stancil, Dec. 29, 1968; 1 child, Steve Lamar. BA, Benedict Coll., 1960, CUNY, 1983; MA, New World Bible Coll., 1984; SSD, United Christian Coll., 1985; cert., Mercy Coll., 1993. Supr. City of New York; tchr. local bd. edn., S.C.; supr, case worker, counselor City of New York. Mem. Am. Ctr. for Law & Justice.

STANCILL, JAMES MCNEILL, finance educator, consultant; b. Orange, N.J., July 30, 1932; s. James Sr. and Anne Jeanne (Sauter) S.; m. Catherine Jackson, Sept. 25, 1954; children: Martha A., Mary C., Christine E. AB, George Washington U., 1954, MBA, 1957; PhD in Fin. and Econs., U. Pa., 1965. Buyer Melpar Inc., Falls Church, Va., 1954-59; instr., adminstrv. officer U. Pa., Phila., 1959-64; prof. fin. U. So. Calif., L.A., 1964—. Prin. Stancill & Assocs., Pasadena, Calif., 1964—, The McNeill Bush Co. Ltd.; chmn. S.W. Products Co., 1991—97. Author: Management of Working Capital, 1970, Entrepreneurial Finance: for New and Emerging Businesses, 2004; contbr. numerous articles to Harvard Bus. Rev., 1977—. Avocations: genealogy, sailing, travel. Office: U So Calif Marshall Sch Bus Los Angeles CA 90089-0001

STANCZAK, JULIAN, artist, educator; b. Borownica, Poland, Nov. 5, 1928; came to U.S., 1950, naturalized, 1957; s. Victor and Elizabeth (Cwynar) S.; m. Barbara M. Meerpohl, June 10, 1963; children: Danuta M., Christopher. B.F.A., Cleve. Inst. Art., 1954; M.F.A., Yale U., 1956. Tchr. Art Acad. Cin., 1957-64, Cleve. Inst. Art, 1965—. One-man shows include Dayton Art Inst., 1964, Martha Jackson Gallery, N.Y.C., 1964, 65, 68, 71, 72, 75, 77, 79, Miami U., Oxford, Ohio, 1965, Feingarten Galleries, Los Angeles, 1966, Kent State U., 1968, Dartmouth, 1968, Akron (Ohio) Art Inst., 1969, Cleve. Inst. Art, 1971, London Arts Gallery, 1971, Cin. Art Mus., 1972, 80, Corcoran Gallery Art, Washington, 1972, Canton (Ohio) Art Inst., 1974, Pollack Gallery, Toronto, 1975, Ohio State U., 1976, IMF and CARE, Washington, 1978, Butler Inst. Am. Art, Youngstown, Ohio, 1980, Nat. Mus., Warsaw, Poland, 1981, Alice Simsar Gallery, Ann Arbor, Mich., 1982, 88, New Gallery, Cleve., 1983, Charles Foley Gallery, Columbus, Ohio, 1984, 88, Walker Gallery, Chgo., 1986, Carl Solway Gallery, Cin., Jane Haslem Gallery, Washington, 1986, Standard Oil Co. Hdqrs., Cleve., 1987, Alice Simsar Gallery, Ann Arbor, Mich., Boca Raton Mus. Art, Fla., 1989, Carl Solway Gallery, Cin., Charles Foley Gallery, Columbus, Ohio, Ctr. for Contemporary Art, Cleve., 1990; one man retrospective David Anderson Gallery, Buffalo, N.Y., Dennos Mus-.,Traverse City, Mich., Butler Inst. of Am. Art., Youngstown, Ohio, 2000, /Columbus Mus. of Art, 2001, Ashville Mus. of Art, N.,C., 2001, Lowe Art Mus Univ. Miami, Fla., 2001; many others; exhibited in group shows: Mus. Modern Art, N.Y.C., 1965, Albright Knox Art Gallery, Buffalo, 1965, 68, Detroit Art Inst., 1965, Larry Alrich Mus., 1965, U. Ill., 1965, Gallery Moos, Toronto, 1965, Kranert Art Mus., Urbana, Ill., 1965, San Francisco Mus. Art, 1965, Flint (Mich.) Inst. Art, 1966, Carnegie Inst., Pitts., 1967, Japan Cultural Forum, 1967, Smithsonian Instn., Washington, 1967, 69, 85, Dept. State, Washington, 1968, Cin. Art Mus., 1968, 83, Del. Art Ctr., 1970, Seibu, Tokyo, 1971, Mansfield (Ohio) Art Ctr., 1973, Butler Art Inst., Youngstown, Ohio, 1973, Minn. Art Mus., Mpls., 1973, Akron Art Inst., 1975, Indpls. Mus. Art, 1976, Bklyn. Mus. Art, 1976, 80, Cleve. Mus. Art, 1976, 77, 83, Memphis Acad. Art, 1981, Nat. Gallery Art, 1981, 85, Hirshhorn Mus. Art, 1981, Montclair Art Mus., N.J., 1982, Art Acad. Cin., 1986, Embassies Travelling Exhbn., Madrid, 1987, Warsaw, Poland, 1991; represented in permanent collections: Nat. Mus. Am. Art, Albright Knox Art Gallery, Larry Aldrich Mus., Mus. Modern Art, Dayton Art Inst., Hirshhorn Mus., Washington, Butler Inst. Am. Art, Youngstown, Ohio, Rufino Tomajo Mus., Mex., Cleve. Art Assn., Milw. Art Inst., Canton (Ohio) Art Inst., USIA, N.Y.C., Balt. Mus. Art, San Francisco Mus. Art, Herron Mus. Art, Indpls., Okla. Art Ctr., Oklahoma City, Pa. Acad. Fine Arts, Phila., Carnegie Inst., Pitts., Cleve. Mus. Art, Cin. Art Mus., Tulsa Mus. Fine Arts, Columbus (Ohio) Art Mus., Akron Art Inst., Corcoran Art Mus., Nat. Gallery, Washington, Lowe Art Mus., Coral Gables, Fla., Contemporary Art Mus., Houston, Winnipeg Fine Arts Ctr., Man., Can., Dracket Fine Art Collection, Cin., Kalamazoo Inst. Arts, Worcester Art Mus., Phoenix Art Mus., Indpls. Mus. Art, Wasserman Devel. Corp., Cambridge, Dartmouth Coll., Hanover, N.H., Etzold Sammlung, Cologne, Fed. Republic Germany, Johnson & Johnson Fine Art Collection, Conn., Nelson Rockefeller Collection, N.Y., Chase Manhattan Bank, N.Y., Mus. Fine Arts, Los Angeles, Newport Harbor Mus., Newport Beach, Calif., N.Y. State U. at Buffalo; mus. collections include Aldrich Mus. Comtemporary Art, ridgefield, Conn., Akron Art Inst., Ohio, Asheville Mus. Art, Asheville, N.C., Albright Knox Art Gallery, Buffalo, Ball State U. Mus. Art, Muncie, Ind., Balt. Mus. Art, Boca Raton, Fla., Butler Inst. Am. Art, Youngstown, Ohio, Canton Art Inst., Ohio, Carnegie Inst., Pitts.; others; represented in permanent collections at Air Products & Chems., Alcoa, Am. greetings, Cleve., Ameritrust Bank, Cleve., David Anderson Collection, Buffalo, Am. Republic Ins. Co., Des Moines, Atlantic ridgefield Com., N.Y., The Art Collection First Nat. Bank Chgo., Balt. Gas & Electric, Balt., Bank N.Y.; others; monographs include Gene Baro Corcoran Gallery Art, Washington, Rudolf Arnheim, Harry Rand, Robert Bertholf, Poetry and Rare Book Collection, SUNY Buffalo, 20 Tectronic Images and Poetry Barbara Stanczak Clev., (color and form Vibrations of Geometrical Space) Dennos Mus. ctr. Northwestern Mich. Coll., Traverse City, Mich. Recipient 1st prize Dayton Art Inst., 1964; recipient Butler Inst. Am. Art award, 1966, Cleve. Fine Arts prize, 1970, Ohio Arts Council award, 1972, Best of Show award Internat. Platform Assn., 1973-76 Mem. Abstract Artists Am., Internat. Platform Assn. Achievements include being a pioneer in optical art. Address: 6229 Cabrini Ln Seven Hills OH 44131-2848

STANDARD, JOHN ROBERT, academic administrator; b. Madison, Wis., Mar. 19, 1978; s. Robert Charles and Marion Elizabeth Standard; m. Jeanie Jo Martin, Oct. 21, 2000. BS in Global Bus., U. of Evansville, Ind., 2000; MA in Mgmt. and Orgnl. Comm., Emerson Coll., Boston, 2003. Career services assoc. U. of Evansville, 1999—2001, area coord., 2000—01; asst. dir. of campus life Mt. St. Mary's Coll., Emmitsburg, Md., 2001; residence dir. for ops. and disciplinary affairs Emerson Coll., Boston, 2002—. Mem.: NE Assn. of Coll. and U. Housing Ofcls., Nat. Assn. of Student Pers. Adminstrs., Lambda Pi Eta, Phi Kappa Tau (domain dir. 2002—03, Boradaile Undergraduate Award 1999). Office: Emerson College 120 Boylston St Boston MA 02116 Office Phone: 617-824-8155. E-mail: john_standard@emerson.edu.

STANDARD, KENNETH G. lawyer; b. Sept. 4, 1936; AB, Harvard Coll., 1958, LLB, 1962; LLM, NYU, 1971. Former v.p. and sr. counsel products divsn. Bristol-Myers Co.; dir. Office Legal Svcs. N.Y.C. Sch. Sys., 1985—89; gen. counsel labor rels. Environ. and Benefits Plans ConEd, N.Y.C., 1989—2000; spl. counsel labor and employment practice group Morgan Lewis & Bockius LLP, 2000—04; pres. N.Y. State Bar Assn., Albany, 2004—. Named one of 100 Most Powerful Minority Bus. Leaders in N.Y., N.Y. Bus., 2003. Mem.: Harvard Club (v.p. 1997—99, pres. 1999—2002). Office: NY State Bar Assn One Elk St Albany NY 12207*

STANDIFER, MICHAEL, music educator; s. John Curtis and Rose Ellen Standifer; children: Courtney, Krystia, Michael Jr., David. BA, Bethune-Cookman U.; MusM in Edn., Ala. State U. Dir. band. Mem.: Kappa Alpha Psi.

STANDIFIRD, STEPHEN SCOTT, finance educator; b. Balt., June 23, 1965; s. Ike and Barbara Ann Standifird; m. Vivian Lee Lee, Aug. 12, 2000. BSChemE, Purdue U., 1989; MBA, Northwestern U., Evanston, Ill., 1994; PhD, U. Oreg., 1999. Asst prof. mgmt. Western Wash. U., Bellingham, 1999—2003, U. San Diego, 2003—. Mem. editl. bd. Jour. Mgmt. Inquiry, 2003—. Chair Will County chpt. Keep Am. Beautiful, Joliet, Ill., 1993—94; citizen rep. Whatcom County Solid Waste Adv. Com., Bellingham, 2000—03; v.p. bd. dirs. Brigid Collins, Bellingham, 2002—03, Crime Victims Fund, San Diego, 2004—. Mem.: Western Acad. Mgmt., Acad. Mgmt. Office: U San Diego 5998 Alcala Park San Diego CA 92110-2492 E-mail: stephen2@sandiego.edu.

STANDIFORD, NATALIE ANNE, writer; b. Balt., Nov. 20, 1961; d. John Willard Eagleston and Natalie Elizabeth Standiford; m. Robert Craig Tracy, Apr. 29, 1989. BA, Brown Univ., 1983. Clerk Shakespeare and Co. Bookstore, N.Y.C., 1983; editl. asst. Random House, N.Y.C., 1984-85, asst. editor books for young readers divsn., 1985-87; freelance writer N.Y.C., 1987—. Author: The Best Little Monkeys in the World, 1987, The Bravest Dog Ever: The True Story of Balto, 1989 (Puffin award Alaska Assn. Sch. Libr. 1992), The Headless Horseman, 1992, Brave Maddie Egg, 1995, Space Dog and Roy, 1990, Space Dog and the Pet Show, 1990, Space Dog in Trouble, 1991, Space Dog the Hero, 1991 (Fifty Books of Yr. citation Fedn. Children's Book Groups 1992), The Power #2: The Witness, 1992, The Power #4: The Diary, 1992, The Power #7: Vampire's Kiss, 1992, (picture book) Dollhouse Mouse, 1989, (as Emily James) Fifteen: Hillside Live!, 1993, Jafar's Curse, 1993, (picture book) Santa's Surprise, 1992, The Mixed-Up Witch, 1993, Astronauts are Sleeping, 1996, The Stone Giant, 2000. Reader, N.Y.C. Author Read-Aloud Program, 1992—. Mem. Soc. Children's Book Writers and Illustrators, Author's Guild, Authors League Am. Avocations: travel, movies, music, the beach.

STANDING, KIMBERLY ANNA, educational researcher; b. Hagerstown, Md., Mar. 24, 1965; d. Thomas Townsend and Ruth Annadeane (Powell) Stone; m. Christopher G. Standing, May 20, 1989; children: Iain Christopher, Leah Elizabeth. BA in Math., St. Mary's Coll., 1988; MA in Higher Edn. Adminstrn., George Washington U., 1996, postgrad. Sr. analyst Westat, Inc., Rockville, Md., 1988—. Mem. Am. Edn1. Rsch. Assn., Assn. Study Higher Edn. Home: 11545 Brundidge Ter Germantown MD 20876-5500 Office: Westat Inc RW2564 1650 Research Blvd Rockville MD 20850-3195 E-mail: KimStanding@westat.com.

STANDING BEAR, ZUGGUELGERES GALAFACH, criminologist, forensic scientist, educator; b. Boston, Jan. 10, 1941; m. Nancy Lee Karlovic, July 13, 1978 (div. Aug. 1985); m. Virginia Anne Red Hawk, Mar. 22, 1988. BS, U. Nebr., 1971; MS in Forensic Sci., George Washington U., 1974; postgrad. cert. in forensic medicine, Armed Forces Inst. Pathology, 1974; MSEd, U. So. Calif., 1976; MPA, Jacksonville State U., 1981; PhD in Criminology, Fla. State U., 1986. Diplomate Am. Bd. Forensic Examiners, Am. Bd. Forensic Medicine, chmn. 2002-03; cert. coroner, Ga., 1988-92; cert. criminal justice instr., Calif., Ga. Criminal investigator U.S. Army, 1965; dist. comdr. 7th region U.S. Army Criminal Investigation Command, Seoul, 1974-77; course mgr. U.S. Army Mil. Police Sch., Ft. McClellan, Ala., 1978-81; ret. U.S. Army, 1981; instr. Fla. State U., Tallahassee, 1981-85; asst. prof. No. Ariz. U., Flagstaff, 1985-86; program coord., prof. Valdosta (Ga.) State U., 1986-95; assoc. prof. Colo. State U., Ft. Collins, 1995—2001, U. Colo., 2001—; adminstr. The Flash and Thelma Meml. Hedgehog Rescue of N.Am., Inc., 1998—. V.p. Bearhawk Cons. Group, Ft. Collins, 1986—; chair Am. Bd. Forensic Examiners. Editor Jour. Contemporary Criminal Justice, 1992. Mem., task group coord. Com. for Sexual Assault Evidence Stds., ASTM, 1993— Com. Colo State U.; mem. leadership coun. Cmty. Policing Project, Valdosta, Ga., 1993-95; treas. and v.p. edn. and rsch. No. Colo. WOLF rescue, edn., and rsch. project, LaPorte, Colo., 1995—; mem. Nat. Am. lang. preservation com. Colo. State Univ. Decorated Bronze Star medal, Meritorious Svc. medal (with oak leaf cluster). Fellow Am. Acad. Forensic Scis. (gen. sec. 1987-88, gen. chmn. 1988-90, gen. program co-chair 1995-96, Gen. Sec. Meritorious Svc. award 1996), Am. Coll. Forensic Examiners, Internat. Assn. Forensic Nurses (disting. fellow, mem. exec. bd. dirs., cons. and permissions exec., chmn. ethics com.); mem. ASTM (co-coord. sexual assault evidence stds. task group), Am. Sociol. Assn., Acad. Polit. Sci., Am. Soc. Criminology, Acad. Criminal Justice Scis. (program com. 1996-97), So. Criminal Justice Assn., Am. Assn. of U. Profs., Harley Owners Group, Internat. Hedgehog Assn. (treas.). Haudenosaunee (Native Am.). Avocations: hedgehog and wolf behavior, traditional Native American religious counseling, motorcycling. Office: Forensic Health Sci Programs Beth-El Coll Nursing and Health Scis U Colo Colorado Springs CO 80918 Home: 514 Hopi Circle Divide CO 80814

STANDISH, JOHN SPENCER, textile manufacturing company executive; b. Albany, N.Y., Apr. 17, 1925; s. John Carver and Florence (Spencer) S.; m. Elaine Joan Ritchie, Oct. 20, 1962 (div. 1984); children: John Carver, Christine Louise; m. Patricia Hunter, Nov. 9, 1985. BS, MIT, 1945. Asst. to prodn. mgr. Forstmann Woolen Co., Passaic, NJ, 1945-52; various positions Albany Internat. Corp., 1952-72, v.p., 1972-74, exec. v.p., 1974-76, vice chmn., 1976-84, chmn., 1984-98, also bd. dirs., 1958-98, chmn. emeritus, 1998—. Bd. dirs. Albany chpt. ARC, 1966-92, chpt. chmn., 1971-74, bd. govs., Washington, 1980-86; bd. dirs. United Way Northeastern N.Y., Albany, 1980-97, pres., 1984-85; trustee Albany Med. Coll. and Ctr., 1984-93, Sienna Coll., Loudonville, N.Y., 1987-2003; chmn. U. Albany Fund, 1982-87, 89-92; pres. U. Albany Found., 1992-98. Sgt. U.S. Army, 1945-46. Mem. Ft. Orange Club, Schuyler Meadows Country Club, John's Island Club (Fla.). Republican. Episcopalian. Avocations: bridge, tennis, golf. Home: 395 Llwyd's Ln Vero Beach FL 32963

STANDISH, ROBERT C. professional sports team executive; BSBA, U. Conn. Accredited offcl. judge Am. Quarter Horse Assn. Past gen. mgr., CEO Ruidoso Downs Race Track, Ruidoso, N.Mex.; exec. dir. U.S. Equestrian Team, Gladstone, N.J., 1989—. Former gen. mgr. Sheepfields Farm, New Vernon, N.J. Sheepfields Farm, New Vernon, NJ; dir., mgr. campaigns of 18 Am. Quarter Horse Assn. and one World Champion horse; former gen. mgr. The Heritage Place, Inc., Oklahoma City. Office: US Equestrian Team Pottersville Rd Gladstone NJ 07934

STANDISH, WILLIAM LLOYD, judge; b. Pitts., Feb. 16, 1930; s. William Lloyd and Eleanor (McCargo) S.; m. Marguerite Oliver, June 12, 1963; children: Baird M., N. Graham, James H., Constance S. BA, Yale U., 1953; LLB, U. Va., 1956. Bar: Pa. 1957, U.S. Supreme Ct. 1967. Assoc. Reed, Smith, Shaw & McClay, Pitts., 1957-63; ptnr., 1963-80; judge Ct. Common Pleas Allegheny County (Pa.), 1980-87, U.S. Dist. Ct. (we. dist.) Pa., 1987—. Solicitor Edgeworth Borough Sch. Dist., 1963-66. Bd. dirs. Sewickley (Pa.) Cmty. Ctr., 1981-83, Staunton Farms Found., mem., 1984-2002, trustee, 1984-92; corporator Sewickley Cemetery, 1971-87; trustee Mary and Alexander Laughlin Children's Ctr., 1972-90, Leukemia Soc. Am., 1978-80, We. Pa. chpt., 1972-80, We. Pa. Sch. Deaf, 1983—, YMCA of Sewickley, 1996—; bd. dirs. Pitts. Theol. Sem., 2001—. Recipient Pres. award Leukemia Soc. Am., 1980. Mem. ABA, Pa. Bar Assn., Allegheny County Bar Assn., Am. Judicature Soc., Acad. Trial Lawyers Allegheny County (treas. 1977-78, bd. dirs. 1979-80), Am. Inn of Ct. (Pitts. chpt. 1993—). Office: US Dist Ct 605 US Post Office Ct House 700 Grant St Pittsburgh PA 15219-1906 Office Phone: 412-208-7430.

STANDLAND, JAMIE, director, music educator; b. Marianna, Fla., Dec. 28, 1964; s. James M. and Wendra Y. Standland; m. Carol Ellen Weatherford, Jan. 23, 1988; children: Drew, Tyler, Laura Lee. B, U. Miss., 1987, M, 1999. Asst. band dir. Marianna Mid. Sch., Fla., 1988—93, Marianna High Sch., 1993—94, dir. bands, 1994—. Mem.: Am. Sch. Band Dirs. Assn., Nat. Band Assn., Fla. Bandmasters Assn. Home: 4319 Thompson Rd Marianna FL 32448 Office: Marianna High Sch 2979 Daniels St Marianna FL 32446

STANDLEY, JOHN, drug retail company executive; Sr. v.p., CFO Food 4 Less Holdings, Fred Meyer, Inc., Portland, Oreg., 1998; exec. v.p., CFO Rite Aid Corp., Camp Hill, Pa., 1999—2002, sen. exec. v.p., chief admin. officer, 2002—, CFO, 2003—. Office: Rite Aid Corp 30 Hunter Lane Camp Hill PA 17011

STANDLEY, JOHN ROBERT, city official; b. Dallas, May 16, 1928; s. Robert Richard and Lillian Mae (Glenn) S.; m. May Pearl Jones, Sept. 16, 1946 (dec. Oct. 1998); 1 child, Vicki Renee; m. Susan Ann Miller Page, Jan. 16, 2000. BBA in Indsl. Mgmt., So. Meth. U., 1958. Regional traffic mgr. Catalog Order Plant, Sears Roebuck Co., Dallas, 1944-70, mgr. traffic svcs. S.W. ter., 1970-80; transp. specialist Tex. Shippers Assn., Dallas, 1983-88; exec. dir. Buffalo (Tex.) Housing Authority, 1989—. Gen. chmn. S.W. Shippers Adv. Bd., Dallas, 1963-65. Treas. Citizens Traffic Safety Commn., Dallas, 1965-70; arbitrator Am. Arbitration Assn., 1970-80. With U.S. Army AC, 1946-47; staff sgt. USAF, 1951-52. Mem.: Knights of the York Cross of Honor, Tex. York Rite Coll. 14, Karem Shrine, Order Ea. Star (past worthy patron), KT (Dallas Commandery past comdr., Teague Commandery past comdr.), Scottish Rite, Buffalo Masons (past master), Tannehill Masons. Mem. Ch. of Christ. Office: Buffalo Housing Authority PO Drawer L Buffalo TX 75831 Office Phone: 903-322-3654.

STANDLEY-BURT, NANCY VILMA, retired psychologist, educator; b. Chgo., Aug. 6, 1934; d. Joseph and Anna (Tichna) Pav; m. Fred L. Standley, Sept. 8, 1956 (div. Mar. 1982); m. Jesse W. Burt, Dec. 18, 1982. BS, Northwestern U., 1957; MA, MacMurray Coll., Jacksonville, Ill., 1960; PhD, Fla. State U., 1969. Cert. sch. psychologist and counselor; nat. cert. counselor; lic. psychologist, Fla. Tchr. English Niles Twp. HS, Skokie, Ill., 1957-59; counselor, psychologist Maine Twp. HS, Pk. Ridge, Ill., 1960-63; instr. English Fla. State U., Tallahassee, 1963-65, asst. prof., 1965-70; assoc. prof. Fla. A&M U., Tallahassee, 1970-75, prof., 1975—2001, dir. career devel. ctr., 1973-75, dir. tchr. edn. ctr., 1982-92; adj. prof. Ctr. for Bib. Studies, 2002; prof. emeritus Fla. A&M U., Tallahassee, 2002—. Adj. prof. Tallahassee Ctr. for Bibl. Studies, 2002. Author: (with Fred Standley) James Baldwin: A Reference Guide, 1979, Critical Essays: James Baldwin, 1984; contbr. articles to profl. jours. and monographs. Named Fla. A&M U. Educator of the Century; Danforth Found. Assoc. award, 1969, 74; Salley Eckert Stevenson scholar, 1955-57. Mem. ACA, So. Assn. Counselor Edn., Fla. Counseling Assn., Fla. Assn. Counselor Edn., Big Bend Counseling (past pres.), Leon Mental Health Assn., Assn. for Counselor Edn. and Supervision, Psi Chi. Democrat. Methodist. Home: 2466 Thornton Rd Tallahassee FL 32308-6020

STANDRING, JAMES DOUGLAS, real estate developer; b. Fresno, Calif., Dec. 2, 1951; s. James Robert Pusey and Jacquelin (Moore); children: Craig Douglas, Ryan Scott, Melinda Jean, Kevin Paul. BS, Calif. State U., Fresno, 1975. Pres. Westland Industries, Inc., Portland, Oreg., 1976—; ptnr. Aloha Land and Cattle, Inc., Portland, 1982—. Bd. dirs. Tualitin Valley Econ. Devel. Corp., Portland, 1988-95; co-founder, bd. dirs. People for Washington County Charities, Beaverton, Oreg., 1985-88; mem. Westside Econ. Alliance, 1000 Friends of Oreg.; mem. steering com. Oreg. Med. Laser Ctr., 1995—. Named Portland Metro. Builder of Yr., 1992, Oreg. Builder of Yr., 1992; named to Oreg. Housing Hall of Fame, 2000. Mem. Homebuilders Assn. Metro Portland (v.p. 1988-90, pres. 1990-91), Oreg. Bldg. Industry Assn. (v.p. 1993-96, pres. 1996-97), Nat. Assn. Homebuilders, BUILD-PAC (Oreg. trustee 1992-2002,

exec. com. 1994-2000). Republican. Episcopalian. Home: Oregon Yacht Club Slip F Portland OR 97202 Office: Westland 12670 SW 68th Ave Ste 400 Portland OR 97223-8370 Office Phone: 503-639-3104. Personal E-mail: jswestland@aol.com.

STANEART, LARRY WILLIAM, technology company marketing executive; b. Pawnee, Okla., Oct. 19, 1943; s. Arthur William and Della Lorin Staneart; m. Tracy Elaine Armand, Feb. 29, 1970 (div. Apr. 1983); children: Stacy, Marci. BS, Okla. State U., 1965. Br. mgr. Xerox Corp, Tampa, Fla., 1980-83, region sales mgr. New Orleans, 1983-86, region mgr. ea. U.S. Atlanta, 1986-93, v.p. bus. svc. Rochester, N.Y., 1993-95, v.p., gen. mgr. Miami, Fla., 1995-99, v.p. indsl. transition, 1999, v.p. mktg., 1999—. Bd. dirs. Sterling Quality Coun., Fla., 1995—; mem. coun. of 100 Fla. Internat. U., Miami, 1995—. Capt. U.S. Army, 1965-68, Korea. Mem. Miami C. of C. (trustee 1995—). Avocations: golf, tennis. Home: 3020 Paddock Rd Weston FL 33331-3605

STANECK, JOSEPH L. microbiologist, science administrator; PhD in Microbiology, U. Mass. Postdoc. rschr. Mayo Grad. Sch. Medicine; microbiologist U. Cinn.; vice pres. Lab. Operations Med. Rsch. Labs., Highland Heights, Ky. Diplomate Am. Bd. Medical Microbiology 1976. Recipient bioMerieux Vitek Sonnenwirth award 1998. Fellow Am. Acad. Microbio.; mem. Am. Soc. Microbio. Office: Med Rsch Labs 2 Tennessee Dr Highland Heights KY 41076

STANEK, ALAN EDWARD, retired music educator, performer, administrator; b. Longmont, Colo., July 3, 1939; s. Edward Thomas and Mary Rose (Hicks) Stanek; m. Janette Elizabeth Swanson, Aug. 23, 1963; children: Michael Alan, Karen Leigh. B in Music Edn., U. Colo., 1961; MusM, Eastman Sch. Music, 1965; DMusArts, U. Mich., 1974. Dir. instrumental music Ainsworth Pub. Sch., Nebr., 1961-64, Cozad Pub. Sch., Nebr., 1965-67; asst. prof. music Hastings Coll., Nebr., 1967-76; prof., chmn. music dept. Idaho State U., Pocatello, 1976-2001, ret., 2001. Contbr., editor, reviewer profl. jours. including The Clarinet, Idaho Music Notes, Nebr. Music Educator. Mem. Music Educators Nat. Conf., Idaho Music Educators Assn. (chmn. higher edn. 1978-86, 97-98, pres. 1988-90, chair state solo contest 1990-92), Internat. Clarinet Assn. (sec. 1978-84, v.p. 1986-88, pres. 1996-98, historian 2002—), Coll. Music Soc., Nat. Assn. Coll. Wind and Percussion Instrs. (chmn. Idaho 1978-88), Nat. Assn. Schs. Music (sec. N.W. region 1979-82, vis. evaluator 1990—, chair N.W. region 1991-94), Rotary (pres. Gate City chpt. 1994-95). Office: Idaho State U Dept Music PO Box 8099 Pocatello ID 83209-0001 E-mail: stanalan@isu.edu.

STANFIELD, BRENT B. federal agency administrator; BS in Biol. Scis., U. Calif., Irvine, 1973; PhD in Neurobiology, Washington U., 1978. Post-doctoral trainee Washington U., St. Louis, Salk Inst. for Biol. Studies, faculty mem. Devel. Neurobiology Lab., 1981; dir. unit on devel. neuroanatomy Lab. Neurophysiology NIMH, 1987—96, acting dep. dir. divsn. intramural rsch., dir. Office Sci. Policy and Program Planning; with Office Sci. Policy NIH, dep. dir. Ctr. for Sci. Rev., 2000—03, acting dir. Ctr. for Sci. Rsch., 2003—. Asst. adj. prof. dept. neuroscis. U. Calif. Sch. Medicine, San Diego, 1982. Office: NIH Ctr for Sci Rev 6701 Rockledge Blvd Bethesda MD 20892

STANFIELD, REBECCA, radio personality; b. Newport Beach, Calif. Grad. Broadcast Journalism and History, U. Southern Calif. Assignment editor, sr. reporter Sta. KRCR-TV, Redding, Calif.; gen. assignment reporter Cable 12 News, Brooklyn Park; freelance writer Fox TV, Mpls.; news anchor Sta. WCCO Radio. Navigator Great Am. Race. Office: WCCO 625 2nd Ave S Minneapolis MN 55402

STANFILL, DENNIS CAROTHERS, business executive; b. Centerville, Tenn., Apr. 1, 1927; s. Sam Broome and Hattie (Carothers) S.; m. Therese Olivieri, June 29, 1951; children: Francesca, Sara, Dennis Carothers. BS, U.S. Naval Acad., 1949; MA (Rhodes scholar), Oxford U., 1953; LHD (hon.), U. S.C. Corporate finance specialist Lehman Bros., N.Y.C., 1959-65; v.p. finance Times Mirror Co., Los Angeles, 1965-69; exec. v.p. 20th Century-Fox Film Corp., 1969-71, pres., 1971, chmn. bd., chief exec. officer, 1971-81; pres. Stanfill, Bowen & Co., 1981-90; chmn. bd. dirs., chief exec. officer AME, Inc., 1990-91; co-chmn., co-CEO Metro-Goldwyn-Mayer, Inc., 1992-93; sr. advisor Credit Lyonnais, 1993-95; pres. Dennis Stanfill Co., 1995—. Trustee Calif. Inst. Tech.; bd. dirs. Weingart Found., 1987-2002. Served to lt. USN, 1949-59; politico-mil. policy div. Office Chief Naval Ops., 1956-59.

STANFORD, DENNIS JOE, archaeologist, museum curator; b. Cherokee, Iowa, May 13, 1943; s. William Erle and Mary L. (Fredenburg) S.; m. Margaret Brierty, June 4, 1988; 1 dau., Brandy L. BA, U. Wyo., 1965; MA, U. N.Mex., 1967, PhD, 1972. Archeologist, curator Smithsonian Instn., Washington, 1972—, head div. archeology, 1990-92, chmn. dept anthropology, 1992—2000. V.p., dir. Taraxacum Press, 1981—; mem. adv. bd. Ctr. for the Study of the First Americans, 1985—; rsch. assoc. Denver Mus. Natural History, 1989—. Author: The Walakpa Site, Alaska, 1975; editor: (with Robert L. Humphrey) Pre-Llano Cultures of the Americas, 1979, (with George C. Frison) The Agate Basin Site, 1982, (with Jane Day) Ice Age Hunters of the Rockies, 1992; editl. adv. bd. Am. Archaeology, 1997—. Trustee Mus. of Rockies, 1994-2000. Mem. Anthrop. Soc. Washington (gov. 1974-77), Soc. Am. Archeology, Am. Quaternary Assn. Research, publs. on Paleo-Indian Studies, N.Am., S.Am., N.E. Asia, especially Western U.S., Arctic. Home: 1350 Massachusetts Ave SE Washington DC 20003-1556 Office: Smithsonian Instn Washington DC 20560-0001

STANFORD, HENRY KING, college president; b. Atlanta, Apr. 22, 1916; s. Henry King and Annie Belle (Callaway) S.; m. Laurie Ruth King, Sept. 19, 1936; children: Henry, Lowry, Rhoda, Peyton. AB, Emory U., 1936, MA, 1940, LLD, 1961; postgrad., U. Heidelberg, Germany, 1936—37; MS in Govt. Mgmt., U. Denver, 1943, LLD, 1962; PhD, NYU, 1949; DCL, Jacksonville (Fla.) U., 1963; LLD, Loyola U., New Orleans, 1968, U. Akron, Kyung Hee U., Seoul, Korea, 1968, Rollins Coll., 1977, Barry Coll., 1979; DHL, U. Tampa, 1969; DLitt, U. R.I., 1970, U. Chile, Santiago, 1980; D in Higher Edn., U. Miami, 1981; DHL, Birmingham-So. Coll., 1987. Instr. Emory U., 1937-40; asst. prof. Ga. Inst. Tech., 1940-41; instr. NYU, 1943-46; prof. pub. administrn., also dir. sch. pub. administrn. U. Denver, 1946-48; pres. Ga. Southwestern Coll., Americus, 1948-50; dir. U. Ctr. in Ga., 1950-52; asst. chancellor U. Sys. of Ga., 1952-53; pres. Ga. State Coll. for Women, Milledgeville, 1953-56; chief of party NYU-Internat. Cooperation Adminstrn. Contract, Ankara, Turkey, 1956-57; pres. Birmingham-So. Coll., 1957-62, U. Miami, Fla., 1962-81, pres. emeritus, 1981—; interim pres. U. Ga., 1986-87, pres. emeritus, 1987—. Rsch. asst. Tax Found., N.Y.C., 1943-44; staff N.A.M. com. exec., 1944-46; chmn. Fed. Res. Bank Atlanta, 1969, 72. Trustee Knight Found., 1982-97; vice chmn. Invest-in-Am., 1984-86, chmn. 1986-87; chmn. Dade County Cmty. Rels. Bd., 1969-71; bd. visitors Air U., Maxwell AFB, Ala., 1963-66; trustee Caribbean Resources Devel. Found., 1978-85, pres., 1978-83, chmn., 1983-84; chmn. Jimmy Carter Hist. Site Adv. Commn., 1990-2001. Decorated Star of Africa medal Liberia, 1971; officer Order of Merit Fed. Republic of Germany, 1972; recipient Eleanor Roosevelt-Israel Humanitarian award, 1965, Outstanding Civilian Svc. award U.S. Army, 1966, Silver Medallion Fla. Region NCCJ, 1968, Ga. Region, 1987, Disting. Svc. award Ga. Coll., 1979, hon. alumnus, 1996, C.H.I.E.F. award Ind. Colls. and Univs. Fla., 1983, Sibley award Ga. Mil. Coll., 1991, Emory medal, 1991, Adrian Dominican Ednl. Leadership award Barry U., 1991, Atlanta Boys' High Alumnus award, 1992, James Blair Humanitarian award Americus, 1993, Westmeyer award pub. svc. NYU, 1993. Mem. So. Assn. Colls. and Schs. (chmn. commn. colls. 1960-62, pres. 1972-73), Nat. Assn. Ind. Colls. and Univs. (dir. 1976-80), Assn. Caribbean Univs. and Rsch. Insts. (v.p. 1965-79), Golden Key Honor Soc. (bd. dirs. 1982-91), Internat. Assn. Univ. Pres. (exec. com. 1977-81), Delta Phi Alpha, Phi Beta Kappa, Omicron Delta Kappa, Phi Sigma Iota, Alpha Kappa Psi, Phi Mu Alpha, Phi Kappa Phi, Rotary Club (pres. Americus club 1984-85). Methodist. Office: PO Box 1065 Americus GA 31709-1065 E-mail: hksumuga@sowega.net. *The greatest literary influence on my life has been Goethe's Faust, Part I. Reading it in the original German as a college student, I was struck immediately with the demands Faust made of himself in concluding the contract with Mephistopheles: he would lose his soul if he ever chose a "bed of ease," succumbed to flattery, opted for pleasure alone, or said to any one moment, "Linger awhile; you are so nice!" In other words, whenever he ceased striving, he was lost.*

STANFORD, JANE HERRING, management consultant and educator, author; b. Lockhart, Tex., Dec. 17, 1939; d. John William and Frances Argyra (Cheatham) H. Jr.; m. Rube Valton Stanford, Sept. 17, 1966; children: (Steven) Scott, Lisa Ann. BS, Texas A&M U., Kingsville; MS in Counseling, Texas A&M U., Corpus Christi; MBA, Texas A&M U., Kingsville; PhD in Orgn. Theory and Strategic Mgmt., U. North Tex. Instr. cmty. coll., Corpus Christi, 1981—88; tchg. fellow U. North Tex., Denton, 1988-90; assoc. prof. bus. policy and internat. mgmt., pres. faculty senate Texas A&M U., Kingsville, 1990—99, full mem. grad. faculty, 1992-99, grad. rsch. advisor, MBA program, Coll. Bus., 1992-98, head, asst. v.p. acad. affairs, 1998-99, ret., 1999; mgmt. cons. Strategic Mgmt. Solutions, Inc., 1999—, pres., primary cons., 2000—; vis. assoc. prof. mgmt. Coll. of Bus., Texas A&M U., Chorpus Christi, Tex., 2003—. Chair univ. assessment, budgeting and planning com. Tex. A&M U., 1997—98, internat. lectr. strategic mgmt. within internat. context, Columbia, Argentina; workshop leader and participant in acad. issues; paper presenter internat. conf. Soc. for the Advancement Mgmt., 1998—2003; initiator corp. learning cons. Key to Success guidebooks and workshops; vis. assoc. prof. mgmt. Tex. A&M U., Corpus Christi, 2003—. Author: Building Competitiveness: U.S. Expatriate Management Strategies in Mexico, 1995; contbr. articles to profl. jours. and conf. procs. Apptd. to water resources adv. com. City of Corpus Christi, 2003—. Named Leadership Corpus Christi Class of XXX, 2001—02; fellow Sys. Chancellor's fellow in leadership in higher edn. program, Tex. A&M U., 1997. Mem.: Univ. Grad. Faculty, Soc. Advancement Mgmt., Acad. Mgmt., Inst. Mgmt. Cons., Strategic Mgmt. Soc., Delta Signa Pi, Kappa Delta Pi (life). Presbyterian. Avocations: book collecting, photography, travel. Home: 13526 Carlos Fifth Ct Corpus Christi TX 78418-6913 Office: Strategic Mgmt Solutions Inc 13526 Carlos Fifth Ct Corpus Christi TX 78418-6913 E-mail: planyourbiz@aol.com.

STANFORD, JANET LEE, physician, epidemiologist; RN, Grady Meml Hosp., Atlanta, 1974; BS, Ga. State U., 1980; MPH, Emory U., 1982; PhD, John Hopkins U., 1985. Various to asst. prof. dept. epidemiology Sch. of Pub. Health and Cmty. Medicine/U. Wash., Seattle, 1986-92; assoc. prof. Sch. Pub. Health and Cmty. Medicine U. Wash., Seattle, 1992-98, prof. epidemiology Sch. Pub. Health and Cmty. Medicine, 1999—; assoc. mem. program in epidemiology Divsn. Pub. Health Scis. Fred Hutchinson Cancer Rsch. Ctr., Seattle, 1991-96, co-investigator Cancer Surveillance System, 1993-96, co-prin. investigator Tracking Resource Ctr., 1995-96; dir. Utah State Cancer Registry/U. Utah, Salt Lake City, 1996-97; prof. Divn. Pub. Health Scis./Huntsman Cancer Inst. U. Utah, Salt Lake City, 1996-97; mem. program in epidemiology/Divsn. Pub. Health Scis. Fred Hutchinson Cancer Rsch. Ctr., Seattle, 1996—, head program in prostate cancer rsch., 1997—, affil. mem. cancer prevention rsch. program, 1999—. Rschr. and investigator in field of hormonal and environ. exposures that may alter cancer risk, and how such risks may be modified by genetic predisposition. Editor: Am. Jour. Epidemiology, 1999—, assoc. editor 1991-96; editl. bd.: Human Genome Epidemiology Network, 1999—; editl. positions: Am. Jour. Pub. Health, Annals of Epidemiology, Cancer, Cancer Causes and Control, Cancer Epidemiology, Biomarkers and Prevention, Human Molecular Genetics, others; contbr. numerous articles to profl. jours. and publs. Grantee HHS, 1982-83, NIH, 1983-85; fellowships Nat. Cancer Inst., NIH, HHS, 1985-86; recipient Preventive Oncology Acad. awards Nat. Cancer Inst., NIH, HHS, 1988-93. Mem. AHA, Soc. Epidemiologic Rsch., APHA, Assn. of Wash. State Epidemiologists, Sigma Theta Tau, others. Office: Fred Hutchinson Cancer Rsch Ctr PO Box 19024 1100 Fairview Ave N MW 814 Seattle WA 98109-1024

STANFORD, JOSEPH BARNEY, medical educator, physician; b. July 9, 1961; s. Kathleen Barnett; children: Matthew Joseph, Jesse Barnett, Hyrum Porter, Caleb Dean, Thomas Barnett. BA magna cum laude, Mankato State U., 1984; MD, U. Minn., 1988. Diplomate Am. Bd. Family Practice. Resident family and cmty. medicine U. Mo.-Columbia, 1988-91, chief resident family and cmty. medicine, 1990-91, academic fellow, clinical instr. dept. family and cmty. medicine, 1991-93; asst. prof. dept. family and preventive medicine U. Utah, Salt Lake City, 1993—. Part time staff physician Cherchez La Femme Birth Svcs. Ltd., Columbia, Mo., 1991-93; med. cons. U. Utah BirthCare HealthCare, 1994—; physician N.E. Family Health Ctr., Salt Lake Regional Med. Ctr., U. Utah Hosp., Primary Children's Med. Ctr., 1993; invited observer Pontifical Acad. Scis. Working Group on Natural Fertility Regulation, Vatican, Italy, 1994. Contbr to profl. jours. Mem. Soc. Tchrs. of Family Medicine (mem. group family centered perinatal care 1990—), Am. Acad. Family Physicians, Am. Acad. Natural Family Planning (chairperson sci. and rsch. com. 1993—), Am. Holistic Med. Assn., Am. Soc. Clinical Hypnosis, Collegium Aesculapium, North Am. Primary Care Rsch. Group, Alpha Omega Alpha, Phi Kappa Phi. Avocations: hiking, camping, reading, writing, skiing. Office: U Utah Dept Family Preventive Med 50 N Medical Dr Salt Lake City UT 84132-0001

STANFORD, JOSEPH STEPHEN, diplomat, lawyer, educator; b. Montreal, Que., Can., May 7, 1934; s. Walter Albert and Geraldine (O'Loghlin) S.; m. Agnes Mabelle Walker, Nov. 16, 1957; children: Kevin, Karen, Michael. BA, U. Montreal, 1953; LLB, U. Alta., Edmonton, Can., 1956. Bar: Alta. 1957; called to Queen's Counsel 1984. Mem. Greenan, Cooney & Stanford, Calgary, Alta., 1957-60; joined Fgn. Svc., Dept. External Affairs, Govt. of Can., 1960; amb. to Israel Tel Aviv, 1979-82; also Can. high commr. to Cyprus; asst. dep. min. for Africa and Mid. East Dept. External Affairs, Ottawa, Ont., 1983-85, asst. dep. min. for Europe, 1985-87, assoc. undersec. of state for external affairs, 1987-88; dep. solicitor gen. Govt. of Can., Ottawa, 1988-93; ret., 1994; sr fellow, conflict mgr. Canadian Center Mgmt. Devel., Ottawa, 1993-96; assoc., bd. dirs. Conflict Mgmt. Group, Cambridge, Mass., 1994—97, 2002—, chmn. bd. dirs., 1997-99. Cons. Conflict Mgmt. Group, Cambridge, Mass., 1994—97. Contbr. articles on internat. law, fgn. investment and conflict resolution to profl. jours. Roman Catholic. Avocations: wilderness canoeing, tennis, skiing. Home: 58 Amberwood Cres Ottawa ON Canada K2E 7C3 Office Phone: 613-226-1328. E-mail: stanfrdj@ca.inter.net.

STANFORD, KATHLEEN THERESA, secondary school educator; b. Belize City, Belize, Sept. 28, 1933; d. Frederick Gill and Ila Mae (Cherrington) Hyde; m. Herman Emanuel Stanford., Oct. 3, 1970 (dec. Feb., 1989). Student (summer), S. We. La. U., Lafayette, 1958; BA, Seton Hill Coll., 1962; student (summer), Xavier U., New Orleans, 1956, 68; postgrad., Southern U. and A&M Coll., 1962, 67, Adelphi U., 1988, C.W. Post, N.Y., 1988. Cert. sci. tchr., La. (life). Tchr. Mem. Sisters of Holy Family Order, various cities, U.S. & Belize, 1953-69; sci. tchr., moderator Sisters of Holy Family, Grand Coteau, La., 1967-68, Lafayette, La., 1968-70; laicized, 1970; sci. tchr., sponsor of sci. fair N.Y.C. Bd. of Edn., Bklyn., 1981—. Sci. coord. La. Sci. Acad., Lafayette, 1968-70; mem. U.F.T. /IHS sci. com., N.Y.C., 1984-85. Contbr. poetry to Poetry Mags., 1974—. Hon. mem. Pres. Clinton's 2d Term Com., Washington, 1997; sci. sponsor Ford Future Scientists of Am., 1968, Dist. Sci. Fair, Bklyn., 1984; sec. Belize Parkfest of N.Y., Inc., 1990-92 Recipient Commendation for pupils 20th Internat. Sci. Fair, 1969, poetry awards Am. Poetry Assn., 1989, 90, cert. for leadership, Dem. Nat. Com., Washington, 1997. Mem. Belize Cosmopolitan Benevolent Assn. (v.p.). Democrat. Avocations: poetry, photography, bird watching, swimming, walking, singing.

STANG, ARNOLD, actor, director, writer; b. N.Y.C., Sept. 28, 1928; s. Harold Louis and Anna (Chest) S.; m. JoAnne Taggart, Sept. 21, 1949; children: David Donald, Deborah Jane Stang-Healy. Ind. actor, dir., writer, N.Y.C., 1936—. Actor: (Broadway prodns.) Front Page, A Funny Thing Happened On the Way to the Forum, Wallflower, All in Favor, (TV shows) Bonanza, Ed Sullivan Show, McHale's Navy, Bewitched, Milton Berle Show, Jack Benny Show, Jackie Gleason Show, Top Cat, Emergency, Robert Klein Show, Playhouse 90, Frank Sinatra Spls., Bob Hope Spls., What's My Line, Bill Cosby Show, Tales From The Dark Side, numerous others, (stock theatrical prodns.) Don't Drink the Water, Death Knocks, Charley's Aunt, Finian's Rainbow, Three Men on a Horse, The Gazebo, Wish You Were Here, Pajama Game, Let 'Em Eat Cake, Anything Goes, Luv, Tobacco Road, Play It Again, Sam, Annie Get Your Gun, (starring film roles) Double for Della, Arnold the Benedict, Honorable Myrtle, The Expectant Father, Dondi, The Wonderful World of the Brothers Grimm, The Aristocats, Hello Down There, Alakazam the Great, The Man With the Golden Arm, The Cottonwood, Hercules in New York, Skidoo, My Sister Eileen, Seven Days Leave, Let's Go Steady, It's A Mad, Mad, Mad World, Dennis the Menace, numerous featured roles; rec. artist numerous albums including Winnie & Baby Pooh, Winnie the Pooh, Peter and the Wolf, Arnold Stang Meets Gus Edwards, Beezy the Sneezy Bee, The Hippy Hippo, Chester the Chimp, Further Adventures of Harry the Horse. Mem. Screen Actors Guild, Acad. Motion Picture Arts and Scis., Actors Equity Assn., AFTRA. Clubs: Players (N.Y.C.). Avocations: gardening, poetry, carpentry, social work. Office: 257 Park Ave S 9th Fl New York NY 10010

STANG, PETER JOHN, organic chemist; b. Nürnberg, Germany, Nov. 17, 1941; came to U.S., 1956; s. John Stang and Margaret Stang Pollman; m. Christine Schirmer, 1969; children: Antonia, Alexandra. BS, DePaul U., Chicago, 1963; Ph. D., U. California, Berkeley, 1966; hon. degr. Moscow State Lomonossov U., 1992, Russian Academy of Sciences, 1992. Instr. Princeton (N.J.) U., 1967-68; from asst. to assoc. prof. U. Utah, Salt Lake City, 1969-79, prof., 1979-92, Disting. prof. chemistry, 1992—. Co-author: Organic Spectroscopy, 1971; author: (with others) Vinyl Cations, 1979; editor: (with F. Diederich) Modern Acetylene Chemistry, 1995, Metal Catalyzed Cross Coupling Reactions, 1998, (with Z. Rappaport) Dicoordinated Carbocations, 1997; editor-in-chief Jour. Organic Chemsitry, 2000-01; contbr. numerous articles to sci. publs. Humboldt-Forschungspreis, 1977; JSPS Fellowship, 1985; Fulbright-Hays Sr. Scholarship, 1988. Fellow AAAS; mem. NAS, Am. Acad. Arts & Scis., Am. Chem. Soc. (assoc. editor Jour. Am. Chem. Soc. 1982-99, editor 2002—). Office: U Utah Dept Chemistry 315 S 1400 East Salt Lake City UT 84112-0850 Office Phone: 801-581-8329. E-mail: stang@chemistry.utah.edu.

STANG, ROLF KRISTIAN, vocalist, actor, educator, writer, advertising executive; b. Rockford, Ill., Sept. 19, 1939; s. Trygve Ingvald and Kirsten (Anfinsen-Kristiansen) S. BA, Augustana Coll., 1961; MA, Columbia U., 1963; performance/repertoire cert., opera div., Musikhochschule, Hamburg, Germany, 1964. Vocal soloist Christoph-Weber-Barock Ensemble, Hamburg, 1965-67; German and music faculty Coll. of White Plains, N.Y., 1968-73; sec. Internat. Percy Grainger Soc., White Plains, N.Y., 1974-79, pres., 1979—. Music critic Norway Times, NYC, 1970—; advt. exec. The Frank Vos Co AS/VP, 1973-83; lectr., recital Songs of Frederick Delius, Cambridge U., 1984—; multimedia lectr. on career of Wagnerian singer Kirsten Flagstad, 1995—; lectr. on English composer Frederick Delius, 1966—. Translator Songs of Grieg, Collected Works of Grieg, 1993; composer (for solo voice, chorus and orchestra) Backward Tracings, 1974; (for soprano/15 stringed instruments) Train Window Thoughts; (for chorus/6 instruments) Hymns in Praise of Night/Nietzschean Nocturnes; Lied/Romanse Art Song and opera rep. (Am., English, German, Norwegian, Swedish) 1968—; concert vocalist numerous states and countries, 1963—; author, actor touring with one-man play on Norwegian composer Edvard Grieg, US, Norway, Eng., 1993—; Millennium characterization of Viking-age voyager Icelander Leif Eriksson, 2000—; touring as Danish author Hans Christian Andersen, 1994—, as Askeladden telling Norwegian fairytales and singing traditional songs, 1995—. Vol. Cath. Ctr. for Deaf, N.Y.C., 1975-79, Children to the Beach prog., N.Y.C., 1978-83, Reaching Out to the Homeless, N.Y.C., 1988—. Decorated knight (Norway), St. Olav medal King Harald V of Norway, 1997; named to Scandinavian-Am. Hall of Fame, 1998; recipient Leif Eriksson citation, 2000. Mem. SAG, Am. Choral Dirs. Assn. (life), Nordmanns Forbundet/Norsemen's Fedn. (hon., life), Delius Assn. of Fla. (life), Delius Soc. of Great Britain, Sons of Norway Internat., Delius Soc. of Phila. (life), Am.-Scandinavian Soc. of N.Y., Soc. for Advancement of Scandinavian Studies (life), Edvard Grieg Soc. Great Britain (hon., life). Lutheran. Avocations: furniture making, carpentry, gardening, promoting Nordic culture and music. Home: The Monks Cell 29 W 65th St New York NY 10023-6630 E-mail: rolf_k_stang@hotmail.com.

STANGE, JAMES HENRY, architect; b. Davenport, Iowa, May 25, 1930; s. Henry Claus and Norma (Ballhorn) S.; m. Mary Suanne Peterson, Dec. 12, 1954; children: Wade Weston, Drew Dayton, Grant Owen. BArch, Iowa State U., 1954. Registered architect, Iowa, Nebr., Kans., Mo., Okla. Designer Davis & Wilson, Lincoln, Nebr., 1954-62, v.p., 1962-68; v.p., sec. Davis, Fenton, Stange, Darling, Lincoln, Nebr., 1977-92, pres., 1976—93, chmn., 1978—94. Mem. State Bd. Examiners for Engrs. and Architects, 1989-92, chmn. region V NCARB, 1991. Prin. works include Dorsey Labs., 1960, East H.S., Lincoln, 1966, Lincoln Gen. Hosp., 1967, Lincoln Airport Terminal, Sq. D Mfg. Plant, Lincoln, Bryan Meml. Hosp. (masterplans and additions), 1970, 80, 90, Bryan Ambulatory Care Ctr. Med. Office Bldg., Same Day Surgery Conf. Ctr., Parking Garage, 1993-95, Nebr. Wesleyan Theatre, Lincoln, Hasting (Nebr.) YMCA, various structures U. Nebr., Lincoln, ctr. and br. offices Am. Charter Fed. Savs. & Loan, S.E. H.S. (addition), 1984, U. Nebr. Animal Sci. Bldg., 1987, Beadle Ctr., UNL, 1991, Carriage Park Parking Garage, 1995. V.p. Nebr. Jazz Orch., 1995, 2000—, pres., 1997, Nebr. Art Assn., 1996—99; deacon 1st Presbyn. Ch., 1960, chmn. bd. trustees, 1968—90, elder, 1972—87, 1997—99, chmn. property com., 1998—2000; bd. dirs. Capitol Assn. Retarded Citizens, 1968—72, 1994—, pres., 1970; chmn. United Way Campaign, 1986, chmn. bd., 1988; chmn. endowment com. Bryan Hosp. Found., 1988—90; bd. dirs. Delta Dental, 1987—92, Downtown Lincoln Assn., 1985—94, mem. steering com., 1989; mem. mayor's com. Study Downtown Redevel., 1989, pub. bldg. commn., masterplan rev. com., 1994; pres. Lincoln Ctr. Assn., 1979. Recipient Honor award Conf. on Religious Architecture-First Plymouth Ch. Addition, 1969, also numerous state and nat. awards from archtl. orgns.; inducted into Hall of Fame, Iowa H.S. Athletic Assn., 2001. Mem. AIA (Nebr. bd. dirs. 1964-65, treas. 1965, sec. 1966, v.p. 1967, pres. Nebr. 1968, mem. com. on architecture for health 1980-94, Regional Design award 1976, 88, 96), Am. Assn. Health Planners, Interfaith Forum on Religion, Art, Architecture, Lincoln C. of C. (bd. dirs. 1982), Exec. Club (pres. 1972), Crucible Club, 12 Club, Hillcrest Country Club (pres. 1977), Lincoln U. Club (sec. 1992, bd. dirs. 1991-97, pres. 1995, 96). Avocations: travel, photography, golf. Home: 3545 Calvert St Lincoln NE 68506-5744 Office: Davis Design 211 N 14th St Lincoln NE 68508-1616

STANGE, KURT C. medical educator; MD, Albany Med. Coll., 1983; PhD, U. N.C., 1989. Diplomate Am. Bd. Family Practice, Am. Bd. Preventive Medicine. Prof. family medicine, epidemiology, biostatistics, oncology and sociology Case Western Reserve U., Cleve.; physician, tchr., rschr. dept. family medicine U. Hosps. Cleve.; assoc. dir. prevention, control and population rsch. Ireland Cancer Ctr. at U. Hosps. Cleve. and Case Western Reserve U.; dir., Family Medicine Res. Div. Case Western Reserve U., Cleve. Mem. Inst. Medicine, Rsch. Assn. Practicing Physicians. Office: Case Western Reserve U Sch Medicine Dept Family Medicine 10900 Euclid Ave Cleveland OH 44106-1712 also: Dept Family Medicine U Circle Rsch Ctr 11001 Cedar Ave Ste 306 Cleveland OH 44106-3043 Fax: 216-368-4348. E-mail: kcs@po.cwru.edu.

STANGE, MARY ZEISS, writer, educator; b. Hackensack, N.J., July 5, 1950; d. Frank A. and Agatha V. Zeiss; m. Douglas C. Stange, May 7, 1983. PhD, Syracuse U., 1982. Assoc. prof. women's studies and religion Skidmore Coll., Saratoga Springs, NY, 1990—. Dir. women's studies program Skidmore Coll., 1990—98. Author: Woman The Hunter, Gun Women: Firearms And Feminism In Contemporary America; editor: (anthology) Heart Shots: Women Write About Hunting. Vol. instr. Becoming an Outdoorswoman Workshops, 1993—2000. Avocations: hunting, hiking, gourmet cooking. Personal E-mail: stange@midrivers.com.

STANGE, TERRENCE V. education educator; b. Aberdeen, S.D., Sept. 6, 1951; m. Cheryll Lynn Stange, Aug. 30, 1975. BS, No. State U., 1975, MS, 1981; PhD, U. Okla., 1993. Instr. Redfield (S.D.) State Hosp., 1975-78; remedial tchr. Simmons Jr. H.S., Aberdeen, 1978-82; adj. prof., rsch. asst. U. Okla., Norman, 1986-93; asst. prof. Ohio State U., Lima, 1993-96, Ark. State U., Jonesboro, 1996-2000; assoc. prof. Midwestern State U., Wichita Falls, Tex., 2000—. Reading cons. Ohio Lit. Coun., Lima, 1994-95; program cons.

edn. program County Econ. Devel., Lima, 1994-96; mem. adv. coun. ednl. success program Valley View Schs., Jonesboro, 1997-2000. Contbr. articles to profl. jours. Dir., vol. tutored children Faith-based Social Outreach Reading Program, Jonesboro, 1996-2000; book buddy reading to K-4 students Nettleton Pub. Schs., Jonesboro, 1999; appt. editor newsletter Profs. of Reading Tchrs. Educators, Whitewater, Wis., 2000—. Mem. AAUP, ASCD, Internat. Reading Assn., Tchg. as a Rsch. Profession, Org. of Tchr. Educators in Reading, Mid-South Rsch. Assn., Nat. Coun. Tchrs. of English, Phi Delta Kappa, Kappa Delta Pi. Democrat. Lutheran. Avocations: rollerblading, cross country skiing, drawing, biking, reading. Office: 3410 Taft Blvd Wichita Falls TX 76308-2095 Home: PO Box 1147 Wichita Falls TX 76307-1147 E-mail: terrence.stange@nexus.mwsu.edu.

STANGEL, IVAN, biomaterials scientist, educator; b. Kosice, Czechoslovakia, Sept. 8, 1946; arrived in US, 1949; s. Louis and Hermina (Aibester) Stangel; m. Cynthia Susan Palmer, Apr. 25, 1985; 1 child, Jacob Louis. DMD, U. Pa., 1970. Resident U. Coll. Hosp. U. London, 1970—71; clin. staff Luth. Med. Ctr./Sunset Park Family Health Ctr., Bklyn., 1971—72; clin. staff Polyclinique dentaire U. Lausanne, Switzerland, 1973; instr. dept. operative dentistry Sch. Dental Medicine Tufts U., Boston, 1974; pvt. practice Burlington, Vt., 1974—77; lectr. dept. operative dentistry McGill U., Montreal, 1977—78, asst. prof. dept. clin. dentistry, 1978—80, asst. prof. sect. operative dentistry divsn. prosthodontics, 1980—82, assoc. prof., 1982—, assoc. prof., dir. biomaterials sci., 1995—; owner, acting CEO, founder, sci. dir. BioMat Scis. Inc., Rockville, Md., 1999—. Asst. dental surgeon Montreal Gen Hosp., 1978—; vis. prof. Dept Biomaterials Boston U., 1983—84; cons. in field, 1990—; Guest rschr. ADA Health Found., Gaithersburg, Md., 1992—95. Editl. bd. Operative Dentistry, editl.cons. Jour. Dental Rsch., editl. cons. Dental Materials; contbr. articles profl. jours. Fellow: Acad. Dental Materials; mem.: Order Dentists Quebec, Internat. Coll. Dentists, Assn. Dental Rsch., Dental Materials Group, Internat., Coun. Physicians and Dentists, Can. Soc. biomaterials, Am. Acad. Operative Dentistry, Adhesion Soc. Avocations: sailing, running, skiing, mountain climbing. Office: BioMat Scis Inc 9700 Great Seneca Hwy Rockville MD 20817

STANGELAND, ROGER EARL, retail chain store executive; b. Chgo., Oct. 4, 1929; s. Earl and Mae E. (Shaw) S.; m. Lilah Fisher, Dec. 27, 1951; children: Brett, Cyndi Stangeland Meili, Brad. Student, St. Johns Mil. Acad., 1943-47, Carleton Coll., 1947-48; BS, U. Ill., 1949-51. With Coast to Coast Stores, Mpls., 1960-78, pres., 1972-77; sr. v.p., exec. v.p. Household Merchandising, Chgo., 1978-84; chief exec. officer, chmn. bd. Vons Grocery Co., Los Angeles, 1984-85; past CEO The Vons Cos., Inc., Arcadia, Calif., chmn., 1986—, now chmn. emeritus. Chmn. Wauconda (Ill.) Bd. Edn., 1957-60, Hopkins (Minn.) Bd. Edn., 1968-74; bd. fellows Claremont (Calif.) U. Ctr. and Grad. Sch., 1986; bd. dirs. L.A. area Boy Scouts Am.; trustee Hugh O'Brian Youth Found.; mem. CEO bd. advisors U. So. Calif. Sch. Bus. Adminstrn.; trustee St. John's Mil. Acad; bd. visitors Peter F. Drucker Grad. Mgmt. Ctr. Mem. Am. Inst. Wine and Food (bd. dirs.), Food Mktg. Inst. (chmn. bd. dirs.), Food Employers Coun. (exec. com., bd. dirs.), Mchts. & Mfrs. Assn. (bd. dirs.), L.A. Area C. of C. (bd. dirs.), Jonathan Club (L.A.), Calif. Club. Home: 842 Oxford Rd San Marino CA 91108-1214 Office: Vons Grocery Co 618 Michillinda Ave Arcadia CA 91007-6300

STANGER, ILA, writer, editor; b. N.Y.C. d. Jack Simon and Shirley Ruth (Nadelson) S. BA, Bklyn. Coll., 1961. Feature and travel editor Harpers Bazaar, N.Y.C., 1969-75; exec. editor Travel and Leisure mag., N.Y.C., 1975-85; editor in chief Food and Wine Mag., N.Y.C., 1985-89, Travel and Leisure mag., N.Y.C., 1990-93; mng. editor More mag., N.Y.C., 1993—. Writer on arts, features and travel. Mem. Am. Soc. Mag. Editors Office: More Magazine 125 Park Ave New York NY 10017-5529 Personal E-mail: ila.stanger@meredith.com.

STANGER, NORA LYNN, educational consultant; b. Ironton, Ohio, Dec. 9, 1958; d. Emma Jean Swango; m. Keefe Colin Stanger, Mar. 20, 1982; children: Hannah Jane, Hope Jocelyn. BA, Berea Coll., 1980; MSc, Abilene Christian U., 1982. Staff psychologist Abilene State Sch., Tex., 1981—83; therapist Mid-Western Children's Home, Pleasant Plain, Ohio, 1984—87; asst. program dir. Brookside Mason, Ohio, 1987—92; psychology asst. Habilitation Services, Cin., 1993—2002; founder/dir. Higher Ground, Loveland, Ohio, 2002—. Author in residence Chatfield Coll., St. Martin, Ohio, 2004—. Author: (book) Diamonds in the Dew, 2003. Inspirational spkr. Ch. of Christ, Cin., 1984—, tchr./bible instr., 1987—; writer Appalachian Connection, Cin., 2002; Appalachian folk story teller various cmty. centers, 1991—. Mem.: Greater Cin. Coll. Access Network. Achievements include encouraging higher edn. to Appalachian culture and people of poverty. Office: Higher Ground 6123 Doe Ct Loveland OH 45140 also: Chatfield Coll 20918 St Rte 251 St Martin OH 45118 Office Phone: 513-875-3344.

STANGER, ROBERT HENRY, psychiatrist, educator; b. NYC, May 19, 1937; s. Sidney and Mary (Strassner) S.; m. Andrea Rogin, Aug. 28, 1960; children: Lee Ann, David Neal. AB, Guilford Coll., 1959; MD, Emory U., 1964. Intern in internal medicine Wake Forest U., 1964-65; resident in gen. psychiatry U. Pitts., Western Psychiat. Inst. and Clinic, 1967-70; pvt. practice gen. psychiatry Monroeville, Pa., 1970-2001; med. dir. Allegheny Valley Mental Health-Mental Retardation Ctr., New Kensington, Pa., 1970-76; dir. psychiat. svcs. Allegheny Valley Hosp., Natrona Heights, Pa., 1983-96, chmn. dept. psychiatry and behavioral medicine, 1983-96; pvt. practice Natrona Heights, 1984-97. Clin. instr. psychiatry U. Pitts. Sch. Medicine, 1970-79, clin. asst. prof., 1980-2002, asst. prof. emeritus, 2002—; cons. Westinghouse Elec. Corp., East Pitts., 1977-87; ethics com. human rsch. Allegheny Valley Hosp., 1976-97; chmn. dept. psychiatry Citizens Gen. Hosp., 1978-88. Capt. M.C., U.S. Army, 1965-67, Vietnam. Mem. AMA, Am. Psychiat. Assn. (del. 1986-88), Pa. Psychiat. Soc. (councilor 1976-79, treas. 1979-80, sec. 1980-81, v.p. 1981-82, pres.-elect 1982-83, pres. 1983-84), Pitts. Psychiat. Soc. (councilor 1974-76, sec. 1977-78, pres.-elect 1978-79, pres. 1979-80), Allegheny County Med. Soc. Home and Office: 3910 Old William Penn Hwy Pittsburgh PA 15235-4837

STANHAUS, JAMES STEVEN, lawyer; b. Evergreen Park, Ill., Oct. 22, 1945; s. Wilfrid Xavier and Mary (Komanecky) S.; m. Naomi Evelyn Miller, June 27, 1971; 1 child, Heather. AB magna cum laude, Georgetown U., 1966; JD magna cum laude, Harvard U., 1970. Bar: Ill. 1970, U.S. Dist. Ct. (no. dist.) Ill. 1970. Assoc. Mayer, Brown, Rowe & Maw LLP, Chgo., 1971-76, ptnr., 1977—. Mem. ABA, Ill. Bar Assn., Chgo. Bar Assn., Chgo. Coun. Lawyers, Chgo. Estate Planning Coun., Met. Club, Riverpark Club (Chgo.), Phi Beta Kappa. Avocations: computers, tennis, racquetball. Office: Mayer Brown Rowe & Maw LLP 190 S La Salle St Ste 3100 Chicago IL 60603-3441 Office Phone: 312-701-7135.

STANIC, INJA, music educator; b. Beograd, Yugoslav, Feb. 16, 1972; arrived in U.S., 1989; d. Petar and Georgia Stanic. BA, U Md., 1993; MA, The Am. U, 1995. Rsch. assoc. Internat. Piano Archives, College Park, Md., 1993—94; piano prof. The Holton Arms Sch., Bethesda, Md., 1995—99, The Am. U., Washington, 1995—2001, The Washington Conservatory, Bethesda, 1999—; founder, dir. Internat. Sch. Music, Bethesda. Lectr. Montgomery Coll., Rockville, Md., 1996, Columbia Inst. of Fine Arts, Falls Ch., Va., 1997; adjudicator Am. Coll. of Musicians, Rockville, Md., 2002; performances Nat. Therater, IMF, US Nucleat Regulatory Comm., Capitol Hill Arts Workshop, numerous colls. and univs. Contbr. articles to profl. jours.; performer: (cd) Memories of Yugoslavia, 1996; musician: Tengo Nostalgia De Ti, 2000. Fundraiser for Yugoslavia Balkan Express, Washington, 1996; fundraiser for Bosnia & Rwanda Women for Women, Washington, 1997; fundraiser for Ecuador Latin Am. Heritage Found., Rockville, Md., 1999. Recipient Outstanding Performance, County Exec. of Montgomery County Md., 1998, Winner, Montgomery Concerto Competition, 1991; grantee Fellowship, Am. U, 1993—95. E-mail: inja@stanic.net.

STANISLAO, JOSEPH, consulting engineer, educator; b. Manchester, Conn., Nov. 21, 1928; s. Eduardo and Rose (Zaccaro) S.; m. Bettie Chloe Carter, Sept. 6, 1960. BS, Tex. Tech. U., 1957; MS, Pa. State U., 1959; Eng.ScD, Columbia U., 1970. Registered profl. engr., Mass., Mont. Asst. engr. Naval Ordnance Research, University Park, Pa., 1958-59; asst. prof. N.C. State U., Raleigh, 1959-61; dir. research Darlington Fabrics Corp., Pawtucket, R.I., 1961-62; from asst. prof. to prof. U. R.I., Kingston, 1962-71; prof., chmn. dept. Cleve. State U., 1971-75; prof., dean N.D. State U., Fargo, 1975-94, acting v.p. agrl. affairs, 1983-85, asst. to pres., 1983—, dir. Engring. Computer Ctr., 1984—, prof. emeritus indsl. engring. and mgmt., 1994—; pres. XOX Corp., 1984-90; chmn. bd., chief exec. officer ATSCO, 1989-94, chief engr., 1993—; prof. emeritus N.D. State U., 1994. Adj. prof. Mont. State U., 1994—, dir. indsl. and mgmt. engring. program, 1996—, mfg. rsch., sponsored by Nat. Sci. Found. 1997—; v.p., co-owner, bd. dirs. D.T.&J., Inc., Fargo, N.D., 1999—, London, Eng., 1999—; v.p. engring. Roll-A-Ramp, Rolla-A-Latter, and Rolla-A-conveyor, 2000—; cons. to healthcare sys., 1999—. Contbr. chpts. to books, articles to profl. jours.; patentee pump apparatus, pump fluid housing; patents pending roll-a-ramp and roll-a-latter. Served to sgt. USMC, 1948-51. Recipient Sigma Xi award, 1968; Order of the Iron Ring award N.D. State U., 1972, Econ. Devel. award, 1991; USAF recognition award, 1979, ROTC appreciation award, 1982 Mem. Am. Inst. Indsl. Engrs. (sr.; v.p. 1964-65), ASME, Am. Soc. Engring. Edn. (campus coord. 1979-81), Acad. Indsl. Engrs. Tex. Tech U., Lions, Elks, Am. Legion, Phi Kappa Phi, Tau Beta Pi (advisor 1978-79). Roman Catholic. Home: 8 Park Plaza Dr Bozeman MT 59715-9343 Business E-Mail: jstanslo@ie.montana.edu.

STANKOWSKI, PAUL FRANCIS, professional golfer; b. Oxnard, Calif., Dec. 2, 1969; m. Regina Stankowski; 1 child, Joshua. Student, U. Tex., El Paso. Pro golfer PGA, 1991—. Winner BellSouth Classic, 1996, Casio World Open, Japan, 1996, Hawaiian Open, 1997, 98. Avocation: sports. Office: c/o PGA of Am 100 Ave of the Champions PO Box 109601 Palm Beach Gardens FL 33410-9601

STANLEY, (MALCHAN) CRAIG, school superintendent, psychologist; b. Boston, Nov. 19, 1948; s. Harry Eugene and Ruth (Shultz) S.; 1 child, Jessica. BA in Psychology, Antioch Coll., Yellow Springs, Oh., 1971; MEd, Boston State Coll., 1975; EdD, Boston Coll., 1992. Counselor Fernald Sch., Waltham, Mass., 1970-71, psychologist, 1975; tchr. Boston Pub. Schs., 1972-74; sch. psychologist EdCo, Inc., Brookline, Mass., 1975-76, Greater Lawrence Ednl. Collaborative, Lawrence, Mass., 1976-77, exec. dir., 1977—. Sec. adv. commn. Mass. Dept. Edn., 1981-84; treas. Mass. Orgn. Ednl. Collaboratives, 1988-93, pres., 1993-95. Chmn. Greater Lawrence Interagy. Task Force, 1980—83; clk. Middleton Planning Bd., 1991—96; trustee Middleton Congl. Ch., 2001—. Recipient Ednl. Excellence award, Pioneer Inst., 2003, E. Robert Stephens Rsch. award, AESA, 2003. Mem.: USCG Aux., Assn. Ednl. Svc. Agys. (exec. coun. 1997—2000), Mass. Assn. Sch. Supts., Am. Assn. Sch. Adminstrs. Home: 19 Gates Rd Middleton MA 01949-1924 Office: 480 Broadway Methuen MA 01844 E-mail: craig77@comcast.net., cstanley@glec.org.

STANLEY, CRAIG A. state legislator; b. Newark, N.J., Nov. 20, 1955; 3 children. BA in polit. sci., U. of Hartford, 1998; MPA, Baruch Coll. of Pub. Affairs, 1999. North ward chair Irvington Dem. Com.; rsch. analyst Assembly Dem. Staff, 1990—92; legis. policy analyst Dept. of Environ. Protection, 1992—93; legis. Liaison Bd. of Pub. Utilities, 1993—94; assemblyman N.J. Gen. Assembly, 1996—; aide to spkr. pro-tem, 1990. Part time prof. Essex County Coll.; sales adminstr., regional mgr. Wangtabs, Inc., 1980—85; sales exec. Urban Data Sys., 1985—88; dir. corp. programs YMWCA of Newark and Vicinity, 1995—96. Mem.: NAACP, Omega Phi Epsilon Frat., N.J. Democrat. Office: 1200 Clinton Ave Ste 140 Irvington NJ 07111

STANLEY, DUFFY B. architect, planner; b. Midland, Tex., Feb. 14, 1923; s. Benjamin M. and Mary L. (White) S.; m. Irene M. Muller, July 31, 1948; children: Sheila, Lars, Brock, Sonya, Sharon. BArch, Tex. A&M U., 1948; hon. diploma, U. Autonoma de Cd. Juarez, Mex., 1977. Registered architect, Tex., N.Mex.; cert. Nat. Coun. Archtl. Registration Bds. Draftsman, designer J.J. Black, Architect, Midland, 1948-51; job capt. Carroll & Daeuble Architects, El Paso, Tex., 1951-57; pvt. practice El Paso, 1957—. Lectr. in field. Author: Open Space in the El Paso Region, 1970. Vice chmn. Citizens Environ. Coun. of El Paso, 1972—73; chmn. GARC com. West Tex. Coun. Govts., El Paso, 1977; chmn. El Paso County Hist. Commn., 1978, Zoning Bd. of Adjustment, El Paso, 1959—70; mem. Open Space Com., El Paso, 1970—71; bd. dirs. Mission Heritage Assn. of El Paso, 1977—84. Capt. U.S. Army, 1943—46, ETO. Decorated Combat Inf. badge, Bronze Star, Silver Star; recipient Caudill awrd, Tex. Assn. Sch. Bds. and AIA Tex., 1996. Mem. AIA (chpt. pres. 1964, Design award 1995, Service to Profession award 1991), FAIA. Avocations: tennis, reading, travel, family activities. Office: 303 Texas Ave Ste 704 El Paso TX 79901-1452 Office Phone: 915-532-7342. Business E-Mail: ivolta@dzn.com.

STANLEY, EDWARD ALEXANDER, geologist, forensic scientist, technical and academic administrator; b. NYC, Apr. 7, 1929; s. Frank and Elizabeth (Wolf) S.; m. Elizabeth Ann Allison, June 7, 1958; children: Karen (dec.), Scott. BS, Rutgers U., 1954; MS, Pa. State U., 1956, PhD, 1960. Rsch. geologist Amoco Petroleum Co., Tulsa, Okla., 1960-62; prof. U. Del., 1962-64, U. Ga., 1964-77; assoc. dean rsch., chmn. geology dept. Indiana (Pa.) U., 1977-81; supr. Phillips Petroleum Co., Bartlesvill, Okla., 1981-86; dir., comdg. officer NYC Police Dept. Crime Lab., 1986—94; pvt. practice, 1994—97; assoc. Internat. Environ. Svcs., 1997—. Cons. in field. Contbr. articles to profl. jours. Served to sgt. USAF, 1947-50. Grantee NSF, 1965-68, 74, Rsch. grant Office Water Resources, 1965-68; NAS exch. prof. Soviet Union, 1968-69, 73; invited guest Moscow Police Dept. Forensic Labs., 1990; invited speaker FBI Internat. Symposium on Forensic Trace Evidence, 1991, 98; recipient Commemorative medal of the lab. Dept. Botany, Jozsef Attilla U., Szeged, Hungary, 2000, Millenium medal, 2000. Fellow AAAS, Geol. Soc. Am.; mem. Am. Assn. Petroleum Geologists, Am. Acad. Forensic Sci., Am. Soc. Crime Lab Dirs., Am. Assn. Stratigraphic Palyologists, Sigma Xi. Presbyterian. Avocations: photography, music, firearms. Home: 578 Myrtle Ct Harrisburg PA 17112-2255 Personal E-mail: eas.aquila7@verizon.net.

STANLEY, ELIOT HUNGERFORD, small business owner, writer, lawyer; b. Baton Rouge, Jan. 4, 1942; s. Allan John Stanley and Ruth Ristine Moore; m. Julia Frances Adams, Aug. 29, 1981. BA in History cum laude, Harvard U., 1963; JD, George Washington U., 1972. Legis. asst. U.S. Sen. Fred Harris, Washington, 1964—65; mem. congl. liaison staff Office of Sec. HUD, Washington, 1965—66; staff dir., adminstrv. asst. Hon. Chet Holifield, Washington, 1967—69; assoc. dir. Citizens Advocate Ctr., Washington, 1970—72; acting regional counsel U.S. Commn. Civil Rights, N.Y.C., 1973—76, legal cons. Washington, 1977—81; owner, CEO New Eng. Antigenics, Portland, Maine, 1982—2003; cons., 2003—. Mem. Gov. of Maine's Trade Mission to Brazil and Argentina, 1997; mem. seminar on def. and nat. security Brookings Inst., Washington, 1967; mem. advance staff Hubert Humphrey Campaign for Pres., 1968. Author: (short stories) River Coffee and Five Others, 1995; editor: The Jewel (by Rockwell Kent), 1990 (1st pl. graphic arts award, 91); author: Nat. Report on Police Practices, U.S. Commn. on Civil Rights, 1981. Commr. Portland Civil Svc. Commn., 2003—; speech writer Sargent Shriver Campaign for V.P. U.S., 1972. Recipient Disting. Svc. award, U.S. Commn. on Civil Rights, 1975. Mem.: Baxter Soc. Maine (founder, 1st pres.), Grolier Club NY (mem. publs. com.). Democrat. Unitarian. Avocations: lecturing, book arts, ornithology, natural history. Office: PO Box 1822 Portland ME 04104 Office Phone: 207-773-2597. E-mail: jaes15@maine.rr.com.

STANLEY, ELLEN MAY, historian, consultant; b. Dighton, Kans., Feb. 3, 1921; d. Delmar Orange and Lena May (Bobb) Durr; m. Max Neal Stanley, Nov. 5, 1939; children: Ann Y. Stanley Epps, Janet M. Stanley Horsky, Gail L. Stanley Peck, Kenneth D., Neal M., Mary E. Stanley McEniry. BA in English and Journalism, Ft. Hays (Kans.) State U., 1972, MA in History, 1984. Pvt. practice local/state historian, cons., writer local history, Dighton, 1973—; cons. genealogy, 1980—. Vice chmn. State Preservation Bd. Rev., Kans., 1980-87; area rep. Kans. State Mus. Assn., 1978-84. Author: Early Lane County History: 12,000 B.C.--A.D. 1884, 1993 (Cert. of Commendation, Am. Assn. for State and Local History, 1994), Cowboy Josh: Adventures of a Real Cowboy, 1996, Early Lane County Development, 1993, Golden Age, Great Depression and Dust Bowl, 2001 (Ferguson Kans. History Book award Kans. Author Club, 2002); contbr. articles to profl. jours. Precinct woman com. Alamota Township, Kans., 1962-86; mem. Dem. State Affirmative Action Com., 1975. Recipient hon. mention for photography Ann. Christian Arts Festival, 1974, Artist of Month award Dane G. Hansen Mus., 1975. Mem. Kans. State Hist. Soc. (pres. 1990-91), Lane County Hist. Soc. (sec. 1970-78). Methodist. Avocations: fossil hunting, walking, photography, antiques. Home: 100 N 4th Dighton KS 67839 Office: 110 E Pearl St Dighton KS 67839

STANLEY, GEORGE JOEL, social services administrator, advocate; b. Wethersfield, Vt., Sept. 1, 1947; s. George and Lucretia (Lincoln) Stanley. BA, U. Mass., 1990, MEd, 1997. Lic. real estate agt. Mass. Min., missionary Watchtower Soc., Bklyn., 1960-81; founder, dir. Carefree Living Ctrs., Springfield, Mass., 1970—, Networks, Springfield, 1980—, Cult Busters, Springfield, 1981—, Free at Last, Springfield, 1981—, Caring Cmty., Vt., N.H. and Mass., 1980—, Essential Svcs., New Eng. area, 1972—, Live Free or Die, Keene, N.H., 1997—. Owner, operator thrift shops and drop-in ctrs., 1972—; bd. dirs., founder Valley Singles, Northampton, 1985—, Paradise Coalition, Northampton, Mass., 1990—97. Author: The Patriarch and Prodigal Son, 1981; contbr. articles to profl. publs. Past guardian ad litem, conservator for homeless, indigent, disabled; candidate for Mass. Senate People's Party, Springfield, 1995; vol. Michael Dukakis for Pres., 1975—83. Mem.: APA, Artists Alliance Against Violence, Nat. Artists for Mental Health. Unitarian/Episcopalian. Avocations: naturism, spirituality, community building, anything experimental.

STANLEY, HARRIETT LARI, state legislator; b. Arlington County, Va., Mar. 30, 1950; d. E. L. and Mariana T. Stanley. AB, Coll. William and Mary, 1972; MS with honors, Boston U., 1974; MBA, Harvard U., 1982. NASD registered. Asst. to dir. Close-up Found., Washington, 1974-76; spokesman Boston Edison Co., 1976-79; asst. dir. Mass. Energy Office, Boston, 1979-80, Smith Barney, Harris Upham & Co., N.Y.C., 1983-87; v.p. Prudential-Bache Capital Funding, N.Y.C., 1987-90; mng. prin. The Hadley Group, Boston, 1990-94; mem. Mass. Ho. of Reps., Boston, 1995—, vice chmn. ways & means com., 1997-2001, chair health care com., 2001—. Mem. Town Dem. Com., Merrimac, Mass., 1989—; mem. Town Fin. Com., Merrimac, 1990, vice chmn., 1990-92, town treas., 1992-95; mem. William and Mary Soc. of Alumni, 1984-90, treas., 1986-88, exec. com., 1988—, v.p., 1989. Mem. Publicity Club Boston (bd. dirs., pres. 1979-80, Bellringer award 1978). Avocation: competitive equestrian activities. Office: Ho of Reps Beacon St Rm 130 State House Boston MA 02133

STANLEY, HARRY EUGENE, physicist, researcher; b. Norman, Okla., Mar. 28, 1941; s. Harry Eugene and Ruth S.; m. Idahlia (Dessauer), June 2, 1967 (dec. Mar. 2003); children: Jannah, Michael, Rachel. BA in Physics, Wesleyan U., 1962; postgrad., U. Cologne, Germany, 1962—63; PhD in Physics, Harvard U., 1967; PhD (hon.), Bar Ilan U., Ramat Gan, Israel, 1994, Roland Eötvös U., Budapest, Hungary, 1997, U. Liege, 2001, U. Dortmund, 2001, U. Wroclaw, 2004. NSF pre-doctoral rsch. fellow Harvard U., Mass., 1963—67; mem. staff Lincoln lab. MIT, Cambridge, 1967—68, asst. prof. physics, 1969—71, assoc. prof., 1971—73; Miller rsch. fellow U. Calif., Berkeley, 1968—69; Hermann von Helmholtz assoc. prof. health sci. and tech. Health Sci. and Tech. Program Harvard U., MIT, 1973—76; vis. prof. Osaka U., Japan, 1975; prof. physics, physiology Sch. Medicine, dir. ctr. polymer studies Boston U., 1976. Joliot-Curie vis. prof. Ecole Superieure de Physique et Chimie, Paris, 1979; vis. prof. Peking U., 1981, Seoul Nat. U., 1982; hon. prof. U. Pavia; 30th Ann. Saha Meml. Lecture, 1992; Sigma Xi nat. lectr., 2002-03; dir. NATO Advanced Study Inst., Cargese, Corisca, 1985, 88, 90, IUPAP Internat. Conf. on Thermodynamics and Statis. Mechanics, 1986, Enrico Fermi Sch., Varenna, Italy, 1996, 2003, Gordon Rsch. Conf. on Water and Aqueous Solutions, 1998, NATO advanced rsch. workshop, 1999, 2001; cons. Sandia Nat. Lab., 1983-94, Dowell Schlumberger Co., 1982-92, Elscint Co., 1983-85; nat. co-chmn. Com. of Concerned Scientists, 1974-76; Disting. prof. U. Paris, 2004. Author: Introduction to Phase Transitions and Critical Phenomena, 1971, From Newton to Mandelbrot: A Primer in Theoretical Physics, 1990, Fractal Forms, 1991, Fractal Concepts in Surface Growth, 1995, Cours de physique, 1999, Introduction to Econophysics: Correlations and Complexity in Finance, 2000; editor: Biomedical Physics and Biomaterials Science, 1972, Cooperative Phenomena Near Phase Transitions, 1973, On Growth and Form: Fractal and Non-Fractal Patterns in Physics, 1985, Statis. Physics, 1986, Random Fluctuation and Pattern Growth, 1988, Correlations and Connectivity: Geometric Aspects of Physics, Chemistry and Biology, 1990, Fractals in Science, 1994, Disordered Materials and Interfaces, 1996, Physics of Complex Systems, 1997, Statis. Mechanics in the Physical Biological and Social Sciences, 1997, Application of Statis. Mechanics to Practical Problems, 1999, Structure and Function of Biological Systems under Extreme Conditions, 2002, Statis. Physics, 2000, Statis. Mechanics: From Rigorous Results to Applications, 2000, Scaling in Disordered Systems, 2002, New Kinds of Phase Transitions, 2002; editor Physica A., 1988—. Recipient Choice award, Am. Assn. Book Pubs., 1972, Macdonald award, 1986, Venture Rsch. award, Brit. Petroleum, 1989, Mass. Prof. of Yr. award, Coun. Advancement and Support of Edn., 1992, Floyd K. Richtmyer prize, 1997, Turnbull prize, 1998, Memory Ride prize, 2001, NSF Disting. Tchr. Scholar prize, 2001, Nicholson medal, 2003, Boltzmann medal, 2004, Teresiana medal, 2004; Nat. Merit scholar, Wesleyan U., 1962, Fulbright scholar, U. Cologne, 1962—63, John Simon Guggenheim Meml. fellow, 1979—80. Fellow AAAS, NAS, Am. Phys. Soc. (chmn. New Eng. sect. 1982-83, Centennial lectr. 1999); mem. NAS (non-linear sci. panel), Hungarian Phys. Soc. (hon.), Brazilian Acad. Sci. (hon.). Home: 50 Metacomet Rd Waban MA 02468-1465 Office: Boston U Ctr for Polymer Studies Boston MA 02215 Office Phone: 617-353-2617. Business E-Mail: hes@bu.edu. *The greatest joy of my prof. life is to share in the excitement of learning something new, however minor about the workings of nature. The greatest joy of my personal life is to be able to imagine that I've done my very best to meet the needs of my family and my co-workers. The greatest obstacle to happiness is the persistent feeling that it is impossible to find that tortuous path whereby both joys may occasionally be experienced.*

STANLEY, HELEN CAMILLE, composer, musician; b. Tampa, Fla. d. Edward and Lucy Gage (Crehore) S.; widowed; 1 child, Helen Marjorie. MusB, Cin. Conservatory Music, 1951; MusM, Fla. State U., 1954; BS, Muskingum Coll., 1961. Instr. music and fine arts Jacksonville (Fla.) U., 1962-67; instr. music in communications Jones Coll., Jacksonville, 1965-66; composer, condr. St. Paul's by-the-Sea, Jacksonville Beach, Fla., 1976; composer-in-residence, pianist Fla. Contemporary Ensemble, Jacksonville, 1986; ind. composer, lectr., pianist, 1963—. Cons. Beaches Fine Arts Series, Neptune Beach, Fla., 1973—. Composer Rhapsody for Electronic Tape and Orchestra, 1972 (Composition Commn. award), Allegro, Passacaglia, Sonata for trombone and piano, various instrumental and vocal works, Evocation I for piano; orchestral works on CD include: Fanfare for Orchestra (Warsaw Nat. Philharmonic Orch. and Owensboro Symphony), 1994, Passacaglia (St. Petersburg Philharmonic), Concerto Romantico, Prague, 1997, Fanfare for Orchestra (All American Celebration by Owensboro Symphony), 1999; composer website theme music The Living Music Found.; composer Dorian Diversion in Functional Chromaticism, 2003. Mem. Soc. Mayflower Descs., 1987—. Recipient Pogner Music Composition award, Cin., 1950, C. Hugo Ensemble Composition award, Cin., 1951, Anthem Descant award St. Paul's by-the-Sea, 1980, Art Ventures Fund award, 1992, Jacksonville Cmty. Found. award, 1994; named Outstanding Achievements Classical Music, Jacksonville, 1997. Mem. ASCAP, Am. Music Ctr., Am. Keyboard Artists, Performing Arts Directory, Pi Kappa Lambda. Avocations: art, walking, dance. Home: 1768 Emory Cir S Jacksonville FL 32207-7707 Studio: Aladdin Farm 12047 Aladdin Rd Jacksonville FL 32223-3201 Office Phone: 904-268-5475. E-mail: HScomposer@aol.com.

STANLEY, HUGH MONROE, JR., lawyer; b. Ft. Lewis, Wash., Oct. 25, 1944; s. Hugh Monroe Sr. and Rita (McHugh) S.; m. Patricia Page, Aug. 17, 1968; children: Allison Michelle, Matthew Monroe, Trevor Marshall. BA magna cum laude, U. Dayton, 1966; JD, Georgetown U., 1969. Bar: Ohio 1969, U.S. Ct. Appeals (6th cir.) 1983, U.S. Supreme Ct. 1979. Assoc. Arter & Hadden, Cleve., 1969-76, ptnr., 1976—2003, chmn. litigation dept.,

1983-96; ptnr. Tucker Ellis & West LLP, 2003—. Fellow Am. Bar Found., Bar Assn. Greater Cleve., Am. Coll. Trial Lawyers, Internat. Acad. Trial Lawyers, Internat. Soc. Barristers, Nat. Assn. R.R. Trial Counsel; mem. ABA, Fed. Bar Assn., Def. Rsch. Inst., Cleve. Assn. Civil Trial Attys., Ohio Assn. Civil Trial Attys. Republican. Roman Catholic. Avocation: reading. Office: Tucker Ellis & West 1150 Huntington Bldg 925 Euclid Ave Ste 1100 Cleveland OH 44115-1475 Office Phone: 216-696-3934. E-mail: hstanley@tuckerellis.com.

STANLEY, JEAN-DANIEL, geological oceanographer; b. Metz, France, Apr. 14, 1934; came to U.S., 1941, naturalized, 1946; s. Paul Emile and Madeleine (Simon) Streisguth; m. Adrienne N. Ellis, Mar. 5, 1988; children: Marc Michel, Eric Paul, Brian Northrop, Natalie Anne, Susan N. B.Sc., Cornell U., 1956; M.Sc., Brown U., 1958; D.Sc., U. Grenoble, France, 1961. Rsch. geologist French Petroleum Inst., Paris, 1958-61; asst. to dir. U.S. Waterways Expt. Sta., Vicksburg, Miss., 1961-63; asst. prof. geology Ottawa U., Ont., Can., 1963-64; rsch. assoc. prof. Dalhousie U., Halifax, N.S., Can., 1964-66; sr. scientist, oceanographer, dir. Geoarchaeology-Global Change Program, NMNH Smithsonian Instn., Washington, 1966—; adj. prof. U. Québec, 1992—2001. Cons. to govts. Mediterranean countries; sci. expert Internat. Ct. Justice, 1981—. Editor: New Concepts of Continental Margin Sedimentation, 1969, Mediterranean Sea: A Natural Sedimentation Laboratory, 1972, Marine Sediment Transport and Environmental Management, 1976, Sedimentation in Submarine Canyons, Fans and Trenches, 1978, The Shelfbreak: A Critical Interface on Continental Margins, 1983, Geological Evolution of the Mediterranean Basin, 1985, Nile Delta, A Geological Excursion, 1997; contbr. chpts to books, articles to profl. jours. Bd. dirs. Geoarchaeology and Deltas Programs. Served to capt. C.E., U.S. Army, 1961-63. Recipient médaille Alpes Maritimes, France, 1976, F.P. Shepard medal Soc. for Sedimentary Geology, 1990, Gold Trident medal Italian Acad., 1998; named Hon. Prof., East China U., 1995; grantee in field. Fellow Geol. Soc. Am., AAAS, Geol. Soc. Belgium; mem. Internat. Assn. Sedimentologists, Am. Assn. Petroleum Geologists, Soc. Econ. Paleontologists and Mineralogists, Geol. Soc. Washington, Cosmos Club (Washington), Sigma Xi. Clubs: Cosmos (Washington). Office: Smithsonian Instn E205 Nl Mus Natural History Washington DC 20560-0001 E-mail: stanley.david@nmnh.si.edu.

STANLEY, JULIAN CECIL, JR., psychology educator; b. Macon, Ga., July 9, 1918; s. Julian Cecil and Ethel (Cheney) S.; m. Rose Roberta Sanders, Aug. 18, 1946 (dec. Nov. 1978); 1 child, Susan Roberta Willhoft; m. Barbara Sprague Kerr, Jan. 1, 1980 (dec. May 2001), m. Dorothy Lee Fahey, Oct.19, 2002. BS, Ga. So. U., 1937; EdM, Harvard U., 1946, EdD, 1950; D of Ednl. Excellence (hon.), U. North Tex., 1990; LHD (hon.), State U. of West Ga., 1997. Tchr. Fulton and West Fulton High Schs., Atlanta, 1937—42; instr. psychology Newton (Mass.) Jr. Coll., 1946—48; instr. edn. Harvard U., 1948—49; assoc. prof. ednl. psychology George Peabody Coll. Tchrs., 1949—53, assoc. prof. edn., 1953—57, prof. edn., 1957—62, prof. ednl. psychology, 1962—67, chmn. dept., 1962—63; founding dir. lab. exptl. design U. Wis., Madison, 1961—67; prof. edn. and psychology Johns Hopkins U., Balt., 1967—71, prof. psychology, 1971—99, founding dir. study mathematically precocious youth, 1971—, prof. emeritus, 1999. Mem. rsch. adv. coun. Coop. Rsch. Br., U.S. Office Edn., 1962—64, mem. com. examiners for aptitude tests Coll. Entrance Exam. Bd., 1961—65, chmn., 1965—68; mem. rsch. com. Ednl. Testing Svc., 1962—67; fellow Social Sci. Rsch. Coun. Inst. Math. for Social Scientists U. Mich., summer, 1955; postdoctoral fellow stats. U. Chgo., 1955—56; Fulbright rsch. scholar U. Louvain, Belgium, 1958—59; Fulbright lectr. New Zealand and Australia, 1974; cons. U. Western Australia, 1980; fellow Ctr. for Advanced Study in Behavioral Sci., 1965—67, vis. scholar, 1983; hon. prof. Shanghai (People's Republic of China) Tchrs. U.; disting. tchr. Commn. on Presdl. Scholars, 1987, 92; vis. prof. U. Ga., 1947, U. Hawaii, 1960, Harvard U., 1963, U. North Tex., 1990, U. NSW, 1992; mem. adv. bd. Tex. Acad. Math. and Sci., 1988—99; trustee Ctr. for Excellence in Edn., 1989—93, Advanced Acad. Ga., 1999—, Ga. Acad. Math., Engring. and Sci., 1996—2001; cons. Ctr. for Talented Youth, 1998—; lectr. Esther Katz Rosen, 2002. Author: Measurement in Today's Schools, 4th edit., 1964, (with D.T. Campbell) Experimental and Quasi-Experimental Designs for Research, 1963, 66, (with Gene V. Glass) Statistical Methods in Education and Psychology, 1970, (with K.D. and B. Hopkins) Educational and Psychological Measurement and Evaluation, 3d edit., 1990, (with K.D. Hopkins, G.H. Bracht) Perspectives in Educational and Psychological Measurement, 1972; editor: Improving Experimental Design and Statistical Analysis, 1967, Preschool Programs for the Disadvantaged, 1972, Compensatory Education for Children, Ages 2-8, 1973, (with D.P. Keating, L.H. Fox) Mathematical Talent: Discovery, Description, and Development, 1974, (with W.C. George, C.H. Solano) The Gifted and the Creative: A Fifty-Year Perspective, 1977, Educational Programs and Intellectual Prodigies, 1978, (with W.C. George, S.J. Cohn) Educating the Gifted: Acceleration and Enrichment, 1979, (with C.P. Benbow) Academic Precocity: Aspects of Its Development, 1983, (with Diane Boothe) In the Eyes of the Beholder, 2004, Critical Issues for Diversity in Gifted Education; adv. editor jours. Served with USAAC, 1942-45. Julian C. Stanley chair in ednl. psychology created U. Wis., Madison, 1995; recipient awards Mensa Ednl. Rsch. Found., 1989, 97, four awards for excellence in rsch., Lifetime Achievement award, 2000. Fellow APA (pres. divsn. ednl. psychology 1965-66, div. evaluation and measurement 1972-73, Thorndike award for disting. psychol. contbns. to edn. 1978, divsn. evaluation and measurement Lifetime Contbn. award 1997, divsn. gen. psychology George Miller award 1999), AAAS, Am. Statis. Assn., Am. Psychol. Soc. (J. McKeen Cattell award 1994) Am. Psychological Found., 2002; mem. Nat. Coun. Measurement Edn. (pres. 1963-64), Am. Ednl. Rsch. Assn. (pres. 1966-67, award for disting. contbns. to rsch. in edn. 1980), Nat. Assn. for Gifted Children (2d v.p. 1977-79, Disting. Scholar award 1982), Psychometric Soc. (past dir.), AAUP (past chpt. pres.), Tenn. Psychol. Assn. (past pres.), Nat. Acad. Edn., Phi Beta Kappa (past chpt. pres.), Phi Beta Kappa Assocs., Sigma Xi, Phi Delta Kappa. Office: CTY 2701 N Charles St Baltimore MD 21218-4351 E-mail: jstanley@jhu.edu. *I am deeply indebted for my graduate education to the G.I. Bill following World War II.*

STANLEY, KAREN FRANCINE MARY LESNIEWSKI, human resources professional; b. Amsterdam, N.Y., Oct. 10, 1948; d. Francis Raymond and Genievive Mary (Klementowski) Lesniewski; m. Mark Anthony Stanley, Nov. 11, 1972. BA, Alliance Coll., 1970; MA, The Coll. St. Rose, 1976, CAS, 1987. English tchr. Middle Country Sch., Centereach, N.Y., 1970-71; English and social studies tchr. Mt. Carmel, Gloversville, N.Y., 1971-72; English tchr. Bishop Scully H.S., Amsterdam, 1972-80, Shenendehowa Ctrl., Clifton Park, N.Y., 1980-82; English tchr., head dept. Broadalbin (N.Y.) Ctrl. Sch., 1982-86; adminstrv. intern Saratoga Springs (N.Y.) City Sch. Dist., 1986-87, dir. for human resource svcs., 1987—. Bd. dirs. N.Y. State Staff Devel. Coun., 1990-92. Mem. Am. Soc. for Human Resource Mgrs., N.Y. State Assn. Women Adminstrs., Nat. Assn. Schs., Colls. and Univs., Nat. Assn. Ednl. Negotiators, Soroptimist Internat. (sec. Saratoga County chpt. 1991-92, del. Dist. I 1992-93, 96-97, asst. treas. 1994-95, treas. 1995-96, del. 1996-98), Ednl. Adminstrn. Assn./Coll. St. Rose (bd. dirs., sec. 1986-89, pres. 1989-92). Republican. Roman Catholic. Avocations: gardening, reading, sailing, golf. Office: Saratoga Springs City Schs 5 Wells St Saratoga Springs NY 12866-1205

STANLEY, KAREN M. mental health nurse, consultant; d. Wilbur L. and Dorothy M. Stanley; children: William N. Shank, Robert R. Shank. BS, Johns Hopkins U., Balt., 1976—78; MS, U. Md., Balt., 1980—84. Cert. Adult Psychiatric/Mental Health Clinical Nurse Specialist, ANCC, 1990. Nurse mgr. Johns Hopkins Hosp., Balt., 1982—86; psychiat. consultation liaison nurse Francis Scott Key Med. Ctr., 1986—93, Johns Hopkins Geriatric Ctr., 1986—93, Med. U. SC Med. Ctr., Charleston, 1993—. Bd. dirs. Johns Hopkins Nursing Alumni Assn., Balt., 1987—93; treas. Internat. Soc. Psychiat. Consultation Liaison Nurses, Pensacola, Fla., 1998—99; bd. dirs. SC Nurses Assn., Psychiat., Mental-Health Nursing Coun., Columbia, 2001—02. Contbr. articles,, chapters to books; author: (ednl. video tape) Reducing Resident Depression. Deacon First (Scots) Presbyn. Ch., Charleston, SC, 2002—, coord. martha ministry, 2002—04. Recipient Award Excellence Advanced Practice Nursing, SC Nurses Assn., 2001, Internat. Soc. of Psychiat. Consultation Liaison Nurses Leadership award, Internat. Soc. of Psychiat. - Mental Health Nurses, 2003. Mem.: ANA, Johns Hopkins Nurses Alumni Assn., Internat. Soc. Psychiat. - Mental Health Nurses, SC Nurses Assn., Phi Kappa Phi, Sigma Theta Tau. Presbyn. Achievements include research in Nursing research project sponsored by NIH-NIA under the Academic Teaching Nursing Home Core Award; Performance Improvement Project to develop an Alcohol Withdrawal Syndrome Practice Guideline. Home: 916 Trowman La Mt. Pleasant SC 29464-3585 Office: Med U SC 169 Ashley Ave Charleston SC 29425 Business E-Mail: stanleyk@musc.edu.

STANLEY, LANETT LORRAINE, state legislator; b. Atlanta, Nov. 5, 1962; d. Archie and Ethel Francis (Dixon) S. BS, U. Tenn., 1985; postgrad., Carver Bible Coll., Atlanta, 1991—. Children's reporter Sta. WXIA-TV, Atlanta, 1979-80; model, sales clk. Rich's Dept. Store, Atlanta, 1979-83; copy clk. Knoxville (Tenn.) Jour., 1984-85; reporter Atlanta Daily World, 1986; intern Sta. WTBS-TV, Atlanta, 1986; adminstrv. aide Bd. Commrs. Fulton County, Atlanta, 1986-87; mem., sec to the caucus Ga. Ho. of Reps., Atlanta, 1987—; ind. mktg. cons., 1991—. Mem. Nat. and Ga. Legis. Black Caucus, 1987. Bd. dirs. West End Med. Ctrs., Inc., 1988—, Southside Youth Athletic Acad. Assn., 1991—. Democrat. Baptist. Avocations: public speaking, swimming, bible study, travel, modeling. Office: Ga Gen Assembly Ga State Capitol Atlanta GA 30318

STANLEY, MARGARET KING, performing arts administrator; b. San Antonio, Dec. 11, 1929; d. Creston Alexander and Margaret (Haymore) King; children: Torrey Margaret, Jean Cullen. Student, Mary Baldwin Coll., 1948-50; BA, U. Tex., Austin, 1952; MA, U. Incarnate Word, 1959. Cert. elem. tchr. Tex. Elem. tchr. San Antonio Ind. Sch. Dist., 1953-54, 55-56, Arlington County Schs., Va., 1954-55, Ft. Sam Houston Schs., San Antonio, 1955-57; art and art history tchr. St. Pius X Sch., San Antonio, 1959-60; English tchr. Trinity U., 1963-65; designer-mfr., owner CrisStan Clothes, Inc., San Antonio, 1967-73; founder, exec. dir. San Antonio Performing Arts Assn., 1976-92; founder Arts Coun. of San Antonio, 1962; founding chmn. Joffrey Workshop, San Antonio, 1979; originator, founding chairwoman Student Music Fair, San Antonio, 1963; host On Stage with Margaret Stanley Sta. KTRU-FM, San Antonio, 1983-98. Orginator (ballets) Jamboree, 1984. Mem. Met. Opera Nat. Coun., 1969—80; pres. San Antonio Symphony League, 1971—74; v.p., founder San Antonio Opera Guild, 1974—76, pres., 2002—; v.p. Arts Coun. San Antonio, 1975; bd. govs. Artists Alliance San Antonio, 1982; founder Early Music Festival, San Antonio, 1990—92; artistic advisor, dir. presentation, dir. devel. San Antonio Symphony, 1992—94; founding organizer Musica San Antonio, 1997—98; v.p. Instnl. Devel. Carver Cultural Ctr., 1998—2000; adv. bd. Hertzberg Circus Collection, San Antonio Dance Umbrella, Houston Early Music, Morgan-Scott Ballet. Named to Women's Hall of Fame, San Antonio, 1984, Disting. Alumnae, St. Mary's Hall, 1990; recipient Outstanding Tchr. award, Arlington County Sch. Dist., 1954, Emily Smith award for outstanding alumni, Mary Baldwin Coll., 1973, Today's Woman award, San Antonio Light Newspaper, 1980, Woman of the Yr. in Arts award, San Antonio Express News, 1983, Erasmus medal, Dutch Consulate, 1992, Mary Baldwin Sesquicentennial medallion, 1992, Opera Guild Founder's award, 2000; Tchg. fellow, Trinity U., San Antonio, 1964—66. Mem.: S.W. Performing Arts Presenters (chmn. 1988—97), Battle Flowers Assn., Jr. League San Antonio (Vol. Extraodinaire 2001), Women in Comm. (Headliner award 1982), Assn. Performing Arts Presenters (award for creation of Jamboree 1984), Internat. Soc. for Performing Arts (regional rep. 1982—85, bd. dirs. 1991—97). Avocations: travel, reading, cooking, music, dance.

STANLEY, MARIANNE, professional athletics coach; 1 child, Michelle. BS in Sociology, Immaculata Coll., 1976. Asst. coach women's basketball Old Dominion U., Norfolk, Va., 1976—77, head coach, 1977—87; coach women's basketball U. Pa., 1987—89, U. So. Calif., 1989—93, Stanford U., Calif., 1995—96, U. Calif., Berkeley, 1996—2000; asst. L.A. Sparks, 2000—01; asst. coach Washington Mystics, Washington, 2001—02, head coach, 2002—. Mem. coaching staff US Nat. Team, 1981—93. Named Conf. Coach of the Yr., Nat. Coach of the Yr.; named to Women's Basketball Hall of Fame, 2002. Office: Washington Mystics MCI Ctr 601 F St NW Washington DC 20004*

STANLEY, MARLYSE REED, horse breeder; b. Fairmont, Minn., Sept. 19, 1934; d. Glenn Orson and Lura Mabel (Ross) Reed; m. James Arthur Stapleton, 1956 (div. 1976); 1 child, Elisabeth Katharene; m. John David Stanley, Oct. 22, 1982. BA, U. Minn., 1957. Registered breeder Arabian horses in Spain, 1976-94. Chmn. bd. dirs. Sitting Rock Spanish Arabians, Inc., Greensboro, N.C., 1978-81, pres. Hollister, Calif., 1981-91, Stanley Ranch, Yerington, Nev., 1991—. Bd. dirs. Glenn Reed Tire Co., Fairmont, Minn. Author Arabian hunter/jumper rules Am. Horse Shows Assn.; contbr. articles to horse jours. Named Palomino Queen of Minn., 1951, Miss Fairmont, 1954, Miss Minn., 1955. Mem.: AAUW, World Arabian Horse Assn., Assn. Española de Criadores de Caballos Arabes (Spain), Am. Paint Horse Assn. (nat. bd. dirs. 1967—70), Minn. Arabian Assn. (bd. dirs. 1972—75), Internat. Arabian Assn. (Minn. and Wis. 1973—76, nat. chmn. hunter-jumper com. 1976—81, chair IAHA sport horse rules com. 1998—2001, bd. dirs. region 10), Arabian Horse Registry Am., U.S. Nat. Arabian Sport Horse Finals--Show Comm., Alpha Xi Delta. Republican. Episcopalian. Avocations: fox hunting, fishing, breeding and importing Arabian horses. Office Phone: 775-463-2232.

STANLEY, MARY ELIZABETH, judge; AB, Mt. Holyoke Coll., 1970; JD, Univ. of Va., 1973. Bar: W.Va., U.S. Dist. Ct. (so. dist.) W.Va., U.S. Ct. Appeals (4th cir.). Atty. Columbia Gas Transmission Corp., 1973-76; law clk. to Judge Dennis R. Knapp, 1976-77; asst. U.S. atty., 1977-92; magistrate judge U.S. Dist. Ct. (so. dist.) W. Va., Bluefield, W. Va., 1992-01, Charleston, W. Va., 2001—. Office: Robert C Byrd US Courthouse Rm 5408 300 Virginia St E Charleston WV 25301

STANLEY, MYRTLE BROOKS, minister, educational and religious consultant; b. Balt., May 13, 1929; d. Benjamin Franklin and Ora Estell (Robinson) Brooks; m. Theodore Freeland Stanley, June 4, 1949; children: Theodora Stanley Snyder, Benjamin Brooks, Jonathan Stephen. BS, Morgan State Coll., 1951, MS, 1972; MA in Theology, St. Mary Sem. and U., Balt., 1987; postgrad., Fordham U., 1989-91; PhD, Am. U., 2001. Tchr., curriculum coord. Balt. City Pub. Schs., 1958-83; dir. propagation of faith Archdiocese of Balt., Roman Cath. Ch., Balt., 1984-95; coord. rite of Christian initiation for adults St. Matthew Roman Cath. Ch., Balt., 1996—; instr. Ch. Leadership Inst., Archdiocese of Balt., 1999—. Author, prodr. play It's Your Own Funeral, 1980, Miracle on 22d Street, 1980. Bd. dirs. Balt. Clergy and Laity Concerned, 1984-94, Towson (Md.) Cath. H.S., 1993-95, Good Samaritan Hosp., Balt., 1994-96; coord. Internat. Sisters in Struggle, 1991—. Mem. AAUW, Religious Sisters of Mercy of the Ams. (assoc.), Phi Delta Kappa.

STANLEY, PAMELA AURELIA, state legislator; b. Mar. 13, 1956; 2 children. Student, Ga. Tech., Ga. State, Morris Brown Coll. Former clk. U.S. Postal Svc.; mem. Ga. Ho. of Reps., 1992—. Mem. game, fish & parks, ins. and state planning and cmty. affairs coms. Democrat. Baptist. Home: 706 Foundry St NW Atlanta GA 30314-4004 Office: Ga Ho of Reps 512 Legislative Office Bldg Atlanta GA 30334

STANLEY, PETER WILLIAM, former academic administrator; b. Bronxville, N.Y., Feb. 17, 1940; s. Arnold and Mildred Jeanette (Pattison) Stanley; m. Mary-Jane Cullen Cosgrove, Sept. 2, 1978; 1 child, Laura. BA magna cum laude, Harvard U., 1962, MA, 1964, PhD, 1970; LHD (hon.), Occidental Coll., 1994, Rhodes Coll., 2001. Asst. prof. history U. Ill., Chgo., 1970—72, Harvard U., 1972—78, lectr. history, 1978—79; dean of coll. Carleton Coll., Northfield, Minn., 1979—84; program officer in charge edn. and culture program Ford Found., 1984—87, dir. edn. and culture program, 1987—91; pres. Pomona Coll., Claremont, Calif., 1991—2003, pres. emeritus, 2003—. Lectr. Fgn. Service Inst., Arlington, Va., 1977—89. Author: A Nation in the Making: The Philippines and the United States, 1974; co-author: Sentimental Imperialists: The American Experience in East Asia, 1981; editor: Reappraising an Empire: New Perspectives on Philippine-American History, 1984; contbr. articles to profl. jours. Trustee The Coll. Bd., 1991—99, vice-chmn., 1993—94, chmn., 1994—96, Barnard Coll., 2000—; humanities and scis. coun. Stanford U., 1986—2002; nat. adv. coun. Nat. Fgn. Lang. Ctr., 1991—2002; bd. dirs. The James Irvine Found., 1997—, chmn., 2003—; bd. dirs. The Pacific Basin Inst., 1998—, chmn., 1998—2003; bd. dirs. The Hitachi Found., 1993—2000, Assn. Am. Colls. and Univs., 1995—2001, vice-chmn., 1998—99, chmn., 1999—2000; bd. fellows Claremont Grad. U. and Claremont U. Consortium, 1991—2003; bd. overseers Nat. Bd. Ednl. Testing and Pub. Policy, 2000—. Fellow Frank Knox Meml. fellow, Harvard U., 1962—63, Charles Warren Ctr. for Studies in Am. History fellow, 1975—76. Mem.: Coun. on Fgn. Rels., Assn. Asian Studies, Am. Hist. Assn., Phi Beta Kappa. Home: 65 Knollwood Dr Old Saybrook CT 06475 Office: Pomona Coll Pres Office Claremont CA 91711-6301

STANLEY, RICHARD HOLT, consulting engineer; b. Muscatine, Iowa, Oct. 20, 1932; s. Claude Maxwell and Elizabeth Mabel (Holthues) S.; m. Mary Jo Kennedy, Dec. 20, 1953; children: Lynne Elizabeth, Sarah Catherine, Joseph Holt. BSEE, BSME, Iowa State U., 1955; MS in Sanitary Engring., U. Iowa, 1963. Registered profl. engr., Iowa. With Stanley Cons. Inc., Muscatine, Iowa, 1955—, pres., 1971-87, chmn., 1984—, also bd. dirs. Bd. dirs. Dover Resources, Inc.; bd. dirs. HON Industries, Inc., vice-chmn., 1979—; chmn Nat. Constrn. Industry Coun., 1978, Com. Fed. Procurement Archtl.-Engring. Svcs., 1979; pres. Ea. Iowa C.C., Bettendorf, 1966-68; mem. indsl. adv. coun. Iowa State U. Coll. Engring., Ames, 1969-97, chmn., 1979-81. Contbr. articles to profl. jours. Bd. dirs. N.E.-Midwest Inst., 1989-95, treas., 1991-93, chmn., 1993-95; bd. dirs. Stanley Found., 1956—, pres., 1984—, chmn., 1995—; bd. dirs. Muscatine Health Support Found., pres., 1984—; bd. dirs. Muscatine United Way, 1969-75, Iowa State U. Meml. Union, 1968-83, U. Dubuque, Iowa, 1977-93, Inst. Social and Econ. Devel., 1992-2001, Unity Healthcare, 1999—, chmn. 1999-2002; bd. govs. Iowa State U. Achievement Found., 1982-96. Recipient Young Alumnus award Iowa State U. Alumni Assn., 1966, Disting. Svc. award Muscatine Jaycees, 1967, Profl. Achievement citation Coll. Engring., Iowa State U., 1977, Anson Marston medal Iowa State U., 1991, Harry S. Truman disting. svc. award Am. Assn. C.C., 1998; Disting. Alumni Achievement award U. Iowa Alumni Assn., 1999, award for Citizen Diplomacy, Nat. Coun. for Internat. Visitors, 2000, Hoover medal, 2001, Order of Knoll Cardinal and Gold awards Iowa State U., 2004; named Sr. Engr. of Yr., Joint Engring. Com. Quint Cities, 1973; named to Disting. Engring. Alumni Acad., U. Iowa, 1998; named to Muscatine H.S. Hall of Honor, 2000. Fellow ASCE, Am. Cons. Engrs. Coun. (pres. 1976-77, Cmty. Svc. award 1997, Disting. Award of Merit 1998), Iowa Acad. Sci.; mem. IEEE (sr.), ASME, Am. Soc. Engring. Edn., Nat. Soc. Profl. Engrs., Cons. Engrs. Coun. Iowa (pres. 1967), Iowa Engring. Soc. (pres. 1973-74, John Dunlap-Sherman Woodward award 1967, Disting. Svc. award 1980, Voice of Engr. award 1987, Herbert Hoover Centennial award 1989), Muscatine C. of C. (pres. 1972-73), C. of C. of U.S. (constrn. action coun. 1976-91), Rotary, Tau Beta Pi, Phi Kappa Phi, Pi Tau Sigma, Eta Kappa Nu. Presbyterian (elder). Home: 516 Hogan Ct Muscatine IA 52761-2740 Office: Stanley Cons Inc Stanley Bldg Muscatine IA 52761

STANLEY, RICHARD P. mathematics professor; b. N.Y.C., June 23, 1944; s. Alan and Shirley (Silver) S.; m. Doris S. Skulsky, July 4, 1971; children: Kenneth, Sharon. BS, Calif. Inst. Technology, 1966; PhD, Harvard U., 1971. Math. instr. MIT, Cambridge, Mass., 1970-71; Miller research fellow Miller Inst., Berkeley, Calif., 1971-73; asst. prof. applied math. MIT, Cambridge, 1973-75, assoc. prof. applied math., 1975-79, prof. applied math., 1979-2000, Norman Levinson prof. applied math., 2000—. Cons. in field. Author: Combinatorics and Commutative Algebra, 1983, 2d edit., 1996, Enumerative Combinatorics, Vol. 1, 1986, Vol. 2, 1999. Recipient SIAM Polya Prize Soc. Indsl. and Applied Math., Guggenheim Fellowship, Guggenheim Found., 1983-84, Steele prize for math. exposition, 2001, Rolf Schock prize in math Royal Swedish Acad. Scis., 2003. Fellow Am. Acad. Arts and Scis.; mem. Nat. Acad. Scis., Am. Math. Soc., Math. Assn. Am. Office: MIT Dept Math 2-375 77 Massachusetts Ave Cambridge MA 02139-4307 E-mail: rstan@math.mit.edu.

STANLEY, ROBERT ANTHONY, artist, educator; b. Defuniac Springs, Fla., Mar. 10, 1942; m. Jane Tumosa, May 11, 1973; children: Daiva, Thomas, Daniel. BA cum laude, U. Dayton, 1964; MS, Pratt Inst., N.Y.C., 1969. Dir. art program Upward Bound project Earlham Coll., Richmond, Ind., 1967-68; lectr. art dept. U. Dayton, Ohio, 1967-68; asst. prof. art and humanities Harrisburg (Pa.) C.C., 1969-71; prof. art Oakton Coll., Des Plaines, Ill., 1971—2002, prof. emeritus, 2002—. Mem. com. League for Humanities Study Grant, Des Plaines, 1988-89; assoc. dir. Inst. for Environ. Response, N.Y.C., 1968-70; Bd. dirs. So. Shore Art Assn., 2003; presenter League for Innovation Conf., 1994, Mid-Am. Art Conf., 1997. Author: Exploring the Film, 1968 (Maxi award 1969), (interactive multimedia) VisLang, 1994; contbr. articles to profl. jours.; shows include William Penn Mus., Harrisburg, Pa., New Horizons in Art Chgo., 1974, Internat. All on Paper, Buffalo, 1979, Zaner Gallery, Rochester, N.Y., 1983, Joy Horwich Gallery, Chgo., 1988, 95, U. Oreg., Portland, 1991, Atrium Gallery, N.Y.C., 1991, Shelter Gallery, Chgo., 1992, Matrix Gallery, Chgo., Museé d'Art Contemporain, Chamalieres, France, 1994, 97, Blank Arts Ctr., Michigan City, Ind., 1997, No. Ind. Ctr. Visual and Performing Arts, Munster, Ind., 1998, Contemporary Art Ctr., Peoria, Ill., 1999, Gov.'s Mansion, Indpls., 1998, Vichy, FR, 2000, Blank Art Ctr., M.C., Ind., 2001, Koehnline Gallery, Des Plaines, 2002, 59th Salon NIAA, Munster, 2002, Exhbn. Am. Art, Chgo., 2003, Gallery Artists, Chgo., 2003, Gallery 415, Chgo., 2003, 18th Ann. Juries Exhibit, Lubeznik Ctr. Arts, M.C., 2003; solo works include U.Fr., Hammond, Ind.,, War and Peace, Chgo. Bd. dirs. Kloempken Prairie Restoration, Des Plaines, 1987-89, Brickton Art Ctr., 1998—. Grantee OCC Ednl. Found., 1989; recipient 2d Place Paragon award for video Nat. Coun. Cmty. Rels., 1985, 1st place Gold award for graphics Art Ctr. Show, Dayton Art Inst., 1969, award of merit Internat. Works on Paper, 1979, Prix de la Ville de Vichy Chamalieres Triennial, 1997, Merit award Chesteron Ind. Regl. 2000; named Top 100, World Digotal Art, 2001. Office Phone: 847-651-1312. E-mail: rastanley@comcast.net.

STANLEY, ROBERT WARREN, association executive; b. Washington, Oct. 26, 1941; s. Herbert Homer and Ida Virginia S. BA, U. Md., 1963. Editorial asst. personnel services Washington Gas Light Co., 1963-68; asst. coordinator Project Interchange, NEA, Washington, 1968-70; advt. and promotions mgr., membership dir. Assn. Supervision and Curriculum Devel., Washington, 1970-71; exec. dir. Nat. Assn. Floor Covering Installers, Washington, 1971-74; exec. v.p. Nat. Glass Dealers Assn., Washington, 1974-82; v.p. Orgn. Mgmt. Services Internat., 1982-83; exec. dir. Nat. Assn. Dental Labs., 1983-97; v.p., sec. Robwood Interiors/Desks etc., Leesburg, Va., 1991-94; v.p. Table Works Plus, Leesburg, 1994—; pres. The Robwood Grp. cons., 1997—. Mem. nat. adv. coun. Am. Subcontractors Assn., 1974-82; bd. dirs. Glass and Metal Inst., 1974-82, Nat. Constrn. Employees Coun., 1975-82; chmn. Consumer Safety Glazing Com., 1974-75, sec.-treas., 1978-82; sec. Auto Glass Industry Com. Hwy. Safety, 1975-82; co-chmn. Constrn. Industry Nat. Legis. Conf., 1975-82; chmn. task force U.S. C. of C.-sponsored Insts. Orgn. Mgmt., 1978-79; bd. dirs., trustee advisor Am. Fund for Dental Health, 1983-95, bd. dirs. Oral Health Am., 1995-97; advisor Nat. Found. for Dentistry for Handicapped, 1988-97. Author booklets, articles in field. Served with USAR, 1965. Recipient cert. of merit Nat. Glass Dealers Assn., 1975, Spl. Leadership Achievement award Nat. Assn. Dental Labs., 1987, 88, Merit award, 1988. Mem. Am. Soc. Assn. Execs., Nat. Assn. Exposition Mgrs., Nat. Assn. Execs. Club, Greater Washington Soc. Assn. Execs., Found. for Internat. Meetings (founding mem., bd. dirs. 1972-76, exec. com. 1977-82). Clubs: Masons, Shriners. Democrat. Episcopalian. Home: PO Box 98 Basye VA 22810-0098

STANLEY, RONNIE L., JR., theology educator, college dean, clergyman; b. Washington, Aug. 26, 1961; s. Ronnie L. and Marilyn Patricia Stanley; m. Vera Frances Allen, Nov. 23, 1986; children: Ashley, Lauren, Taya, Amanda. BS, Columbia (S.C.) Internat. U., 1994; ThM, Dallas Theol. Sem., 1999. Ordained to ministry Independant Evang., 1998. Supervision specialist Alston Wilkes Soc., Columbia, 1991-93; instr. comm. Columbia Internat. U., 1992-93; urban missionary, mentor The S.T.E.P. Found., Dallas, 1994-97; dir. Ctr. for Christian Growth, Oak Cliff Bible Fellowship, Dallas, 1996-98, missions dir., 1998-99; prof. theology, acad. dean Carver Bible Coll., Atlanta, 1999—; pastor Christian edn. New Calvary Missionary Bapt. Ch., Atlanta, 1999—. Bd. dirs. Renaissance Enterprises, Dallas; mem. Ctr. for Christian Leadership Thinktank, Dallas, 1996-97. Bd. dirs. Mt. Sinai Outreach Ctr., Washington,

1986. Mem. Evang. Tchrs. Assn. (cert.). Republican. Avocations: reading, writing, skating. Home: 437 Nelson St SW Atlanta GA 30313-1333 Office: Carver Bible Coll 437 Nelson St SW Atlanta GA 30313-1333 E-mail: revstanley@hotmail.com.

STANLEY, ROSALIND MARIE CALDWELL, social welfare administrator, consultant, writer; b. Shaw Air Force Base, S.C., Dec. 3, 1957; d. Rosetta and Walter Lee Caldwell; m. Arthur Leonard Stanley, June 12, 1999; children: Victoria Renee Dominguez, Jason Luis Moreno, Arthur Lee, Nathan Miles. BA in Sociology, William Paterson U., 1981; MA in Counseling, Regent U., 1993. Dir. dept. counseling Calvary Revival Ch., Norfolk, Va., 1994—96; cons., trainer, coach Because of Grace Consulting & Tng. Svcs., Lancaster, Tex., 1997—; dir., counseling & tng. Mercy Ministries Am., Nashville, 1997—98; exec. dir. Transformation (IOP) Treatment Ctr./The Potters Ho. of Dallas, 1998—99, Bog Hope Ctr., Lancaster, Tex., 2001—. Mem. Am. Assn. Christian Counselors, Fairfax, Va., 1994—; motivational spkr. Because of Grace Consulting & Tng. Svcs., Lancaster, Tex., 1997—; instr. The Potters Inst., Dallas, 2001—; family to family class tchr. Nat. Alliance for the Mentally Ill, Dallas, 2003—. Author: (self-help) Be Wiser In The Workplace: Work Ethics for Christians, Family Life: Putting God's Plan Into Action, Stress Indication Test; composer (song writer): (praise & worship song) The Coming of the Lord. Mem. Dallas County Faith-Based Abstinence Alliance Summit, 2000—; mem. human rels. commn. City of Lancaster, Tex., 2003—; mem. human svcs. adv. coun. Tex. Dept. Human Svcs., Grand Prairie, 2003—04; marriage enrichment group facilitator/counselor The Potters Ho. of Dallas Tex., 2002—; bd. dirs. Found. for Active Relationships, Dallas, 2003—. Mem.: Black African Am. Counselors (1st vice-chairperson 2003—), Am. Assn. Christian Counselors (assoc.). Avocations: family, travel, writing, reading, the arts. Office: Because of Grace HOPE CENTER PO Box 356 Lancaster TX 75146-0356 Personal E-mail: rozbog@aol.com. E-mail: rozbog@aol.com.

STANLEY, SCOTT, JR., editor; b. Kansas City, Kans., July 11, 1938; s. Winfield Scott and Irene Mae (Flint) S.; m. Janice Johns, Aug. 30, 1959 (dec. July 1992); children: Leslie, Scott, Margaret; m. Cynthia Ward, Dec. 30, 1995; 1 child, Elizabeth. BA, Earlham Coll., 1960. Mng. editor Am. Opinion mag., Boston, 1961-85; editor Rev. of The News mag., Boston, 1965-85; editor-in-chief Conservative Digest, Washington, 1985-88, Am. Press Internat., Washington, 1987—; pres. USA Tech., 1991-92; mng. editor Nutrition and Healing, 1994-2000; dep. editor Insight on the News, Washington, 1995—. Mem. nat. bd. dirs. Young Ams. for Freedom, 1960-62; public speaker and univ. lectr., 1962— Keynote speaker Am. Party Nat. Conv., 1976; pres. Ams. Legal Def. Fund, 1977—; bd. govs. Council for Nat. Policy, 1981—; bd. dirs. Free Congress Polit. Action Com., 1985-88; pres. Scott Stanley Real Estate Trust, 1988—. Recipient award of merit Young Ams. for Freedom, Freedom award Nat. Congress for Freedom. Mem.: Nat. Press, Meganset Yacht. Episcopalian.

STANLEY, SHERRY A. lawyer; b. Buffalo, N.Y., Oct. 17, 1955; d. Arthur A. and Irene S. Stanley. BA, U. West Fla., 1975; JD, U. Fla., 1978. Bar: Fla. 1978. Assoc. Mahoney, Hadlow & Adams, Miami, Fla., 1978-80; ptnr. Steel, Hector & Davis, Miami, 1980-87, Weil, Gotshal & Manges, Miami, 1987-92; sr. counsel Barnett Banks, Inc., Miami, 1992-94; ptnr. Coll, Davidson, Carter, Smith, Salter & Barkett, P.A./Shook, Hardy Bacon, Miami, Fla., 1994—2000; dir. SEMCO Energy, Inc., 2004—; exec. v.p., gen. counsel Greenstreet Ptnrs., 2001—. Dir. Semco Energy, Inc. Mem. Fla. Bar, Order of Coif, Phi Theta Kappa. Republican. Roman Catholic. Office: 201 S Biscayne Blvd Ste 320 Miami FL 33131-4324 Office Phone: 305-858-8119. Business E-Mail: sas@greenstreetpartners.com.

STANLEY, SHIRLEY DAVIS, artist; b. Mt. Vernon, N.Y., Dec. 5, 1929; d. Walter Thompson and Elsie Viola (Lumpp) Davis; m. Charles B. Coble Jr., June 11, 1951 (div. 1968); children: Jennifer Susan Farmer, Charles B. Coble III; m. Marvin M. Stanley, Dec. 18, 1983 (dec.). BA in Home Econs. and Gen. Sci., Greensboro Coll., 1951; grad., Real Estate Inst., 1962. Tchr. Dryher H.S., Columbia, SC, 1951-52, Haw River (N.C.) Sch., 1954-56, Alexander Wilson Sch., Graham, NC, 1957-58; guest essayist for news Mebane (N.C.) Enterprise, 1955-56; pres. Shirley, Inc., Burlington, NC, 1962—2004; artist, 1956—. One woman show Art Gallery Originals, Winston-Salem, 1976, Olive Garden Gallery, 21st Century Gallery, Williamsburg, Va., numerous galleries in Fla., N.C. Bd. dirs. Girl Scouts Am. Kings Daus., Burlington, 1961, Williamsburg Libr. Found., 1997—; life mem. Rep. Inner Cir., Washington, 1990—; active Salvation Army; com. mem. York County Rep. Party, 1995; vol. disaster & blood banks ARC, 1990—; founding mem. Am. Air Force Mus.; bd. dirs. William Burg Libr. Found., 1997—. Recipient Rep. Medal of Freedom, 1994, 2002, 2003. Mem. AAUW, Am. Watercolor Soc. (assoc.), Va. Watercolor Soc., Sierra Club, Williamsburg Bibliophiles, Raleigh Tavern Soc. Colonial Williamsburg, Christopher Wren Soc., Williamsburg C. of C., Williamsburg Photography Soc., Mil. Officers Assn. (life), Army-Navy Country Club. Episcopalian. Avocations: travel, gardening, writing, dance, reading. Home: 103 Little John Rd Williamsburg VA 23185-4907 also: 1953 Shirley Dr Burlington NC 27215-4831

STANLEY, STEVEN MITCHELL, paleobiologist, educator; b. Detroit, Nov. 2, 1941; s. William Thomas and Mildred Elizabeth (Baker) S.; m. Nell Williams Gilmore, Oct. 11, 1969. AB with highest honors, Princeton U., 1963; PhD, Yale U., 1968. Asst. prof. U. Rochester, 1967-69; asst. prof. paleobiology Johns Hopkins U., 1969-71, assoc. prof., 1971-74, prof., 1974, chmn. dept. Earth and planetary Scis., 1987-88, chmn. MS program in environ. scis. and policy. Assoc. in rsch. Smithsonian Instn., 1972—; mem. bd. earth scis. NRC, 1985—, vice chmn., 1988, mem. bd. earth scis. resources, 1988-88, com. on solid earth scis., exec. and steering com., 1988, 2004—, com. on geoscis., environ, and resources, 1990-96. Author: Relation of Shell Form to Life Habits in the Bivalvia, 1970, (with D.M. Raup) Principles of Paleontology, 1971, Macroevolution: Pattern and Process, 1979, The New Evolutionary Timetable: Fossils, Genes, and the Origin of species, 1981, Earth and Life Through Time, 1986, Extinction, 1987, Exploring Earth and Life Through Time, 1992, Children of the Ice Age: How a Global Catastrophe Allowed Humans to Evolve, 1996, Earth System History, 1999; mem. editl. bd. Am. Jour. Sci., 1975—, Paleobiology, 1975-82, 88—, Evolutionary Theory, 1973—. Recipient Outstanding Paper award Jour. Paleontology, 1968, Allan C. Davis medal Md. Acad. Scis., 1973, Outstanding Tech. Paper award Washington Geol. Soc., 1986, Bownocker medal Ohio State U., 1997; Guggenheim fellow, 1981 Fellow NAS, Am. Acad. Arts and Scis., Geol. Soc. Am. (chmn. Penrose com. 1978, councilor 2002—); mem. Paleontol. Soc. (councilor 1976-77, sr. councilor 1991-93, pres. 1993-94, Charles Schuchert award 1977), Soc. for Study Evolution (councilor 1982-84), Am. Geophys. Union (pub. affairs com.), Paleontol. Rsch. Inst., Am. Geol. Inst. (mem. exec. com. 1996-99, pres. 2001—). Office: Johns Hopkins U Dept Earth Planetary Sciences Baltimore MD 21218 E-mail: stanley@jhu.edu.

STANLEY, TIM, recreational facility executive; BS in Engring., U. Wash.; degree in Internat. Bus. and Tech. Mgmt., Thunderbird U., Ariz. State U. With Intel Corp., Optima/KPMG, Innova Tech, Kimberly-Clark Corp.; v.p. info. sys. Nat. Airlines, chief info. officer; ptnr. marchFIRST, USWeb; chief info. officer Harrah's Entertainment, Las Vegas. With USAF. Named one of The Top 25 Unsung Heroes of the Internet, Interactive Week Mag. Office: Harrahs Entertainment Inc One Harrahs Ct Las Vegas NV 89119

STANLEY-CHAVIS, SANDRA ORNECIA, special education educator, consultant; b. July 6, 1950; d. McKinley and Thelma Louise Stanley. BA, Ottawa (Kans.) U., 1972; MS in Edn., U. Kans., 1975, PhD (fellow), 1980; postgrad., St. George's U. Sch. Medicine, Grenada, W.I. Dir., head tchr. Salem Bapt. Nursery Sch., Jersey City, 1972—73; spl. edn. instr. Joan Davis Sch. Spl. Edn., Kansas City, Mo., 1975—76; instnl. media/materials trainee, then rsch. asst. U. Kans. Med. Ctr., 1976—79; rsch. asst. U. Kans., Lawrence, 1979; dir., coord. tng. and observation Juniper Gardens Children's project Bur. Child Rsch., U. Kans., Kansas City, 1979—82, rsch. assoc., 1980; psychol. assoc., ednl. cons. family crisis unit Internat. Youth Orgn., 1988—93; ednl. cons. Renaissance Ctr., 1994; exec. dir. 2000 Friends, 1994; asst. prof., coord. spl. edn. Albany (Ga.) State U., 1995—2000; pres. Ednl. Expansion, Inc., 2000—. Lectr., spkr., cons. edn. and med. sci. Author: papers and manuals in field. Past mem. adv. bd. Rainbows for All God's Children; past mem. God's House of Human Svcs., Inc.; mem. adv. bd. Albany Advocacy Resource Ctr.; past chmn. edn./workforce devel. com. C. of C.; vice chmn. Albany Mid. Sch. Ga. Sch. Coun.; past bd. dirs. Victory Tabernacle Missions; adv. bd. mem. Victory Tabernacle. Recipient various awards, plaques, certs of recognition; grantee, Easter Seals, 1975; scholar, Coll. Women, Inc., 1977; Christian Cmty. Health fellow. Mem.: ASCD, Nat. Coun. for Learning Disability, Coun. of Exceptional Children, Christian Med. and Dental Soc., Leadership Albany, Inc. Home: 2301 Beattie Rd Albany GA 31721-2105 E-mail: educationalexpansion@yahoo.com.

STANN, JOHN ANTHONY, investment banker; b. San Francisco, Nov. 10, 1947; s. John Peter and Mary Jane (Erny) S.; m. Judith Darlene Knapp, Apr. 27, 1973; children: John Andrew, Theodore Joseph, Rebecca Marie. BA in Econs. and Math., U. Mo., 1969. Cost acct. Monsanto Co., St. Louis, 1971-73, acctg. supr., 1973-76, salesman Brighton, Mo., 1976-79, market mgr. St. Louis, 1979-81; mfr's. rep. Farbenfabriken, Bayer, Davos & Others, St. Louis, 1981-82; A.G. Edwards & Sons, Inc., St. Louis, 1982-2000; pres. Stann Fin., St. Louis, 2000—. Investment banking advisor to numerous pvt. cos.; Dev. Comm. of Nerinx Hall H.S., 1994-97. Fundraiser Archdiocese of St. Louis, 1981-84, 87-92, YMCA, St. Louis, 1987; chmn. fin. com. St. Clare Parish, St. Louis, 1982-84; mem. Assumption Parish Coun., 1988-90, chmn., 1989-90; youth baseball mgr. Affton Athletic Assn., St. Louis, 1985-86; coun. mem. St. Justin Parish, 2001-03, campaign chmn., 2003; bd. trustees Chaminade Coll. Prep., 2002—. Lt. USNR, 1969-71. Named Man of Yr. St. John's Men's Club, 1978. Republican. Roman Catholic. Avocations: handball, golf. Home: 9148 Fox Bridge Dr Saint Louis MO 63127-1362 Office: Stann Financial LLC PO Box 270001 Saint Louis MO 63127 E-mail: john@stannfinancial.com.

STANO, SISTER DIANA, academic administrator; AB, Ursuline Coll.; PhD, Ohio State U. Prof. edn. Ursuline Coll., Pepper Pike, Ohio, chair edn. dept., dir. grad. program in non-pub. sch. adminstrn., dir. master's degree program, dean of grad. studies, dir. of instl. rsch., pres., 1996—. Bd. trustees Coll. of New Rochelle; sec. bd. trustees Ohio Found. Ind. Coll.; cons. in field. Recipient YWCA Women of Profl. Excellence award, No. Ohio Live Rainmaker in Edn. award. Mem.: In Counsel With Women, Exec. Women's Leadership Forum. Office: Ursuline Coll 2550 Lander Rd Pepper Pike OH 44124-4398

STANSBERRY, JAMES WESLEY, air force officer; b. Grafton, W.Va., Dec. 29, 1927; s. William Adrian and Phyllis Gay (Robinson) S.; m. Audrey Mildred Heinz, May 7, 1950; children: Nora G., Amy G. Stansberry Goodhand, Lisa Porten. BS, U.S. Mil. Acad., 1949; MBA, Air Force Inst. Tech., 1956. Advanced through grades from pvt. to lt. gen. USAF; chief prodn. (Kawasaki Gifu Contract Facility), Gifu, Japan, 1956-57; dep. asst. to Sec. of Def. for atomic energy Washington, 1970-71; dep. dir. procurement policy U.S. Air Force, 1972-73; dep. chief staff contracting and mfg. (Hdqrs. Air Force Systems Command), Andrews AFB, Md., 1977-81; comdr. Electronic Systems Div. Hanscom AFB, Mass., 1981-84; pres. Stansberry Assocs. Inc., 1984—. Bd. dirs. Griffon Corp., Kidde Techs., Inc., Triton. Decorated DSM with oak leaf cluster, Legion of Merit with oak leaf cluster; named Disting. grad. Lancaster (N.Y.) H.S. Methodist. Home: 930 Gulf Shore Dr Unit 9 Destin FL 32541 E-mail: us49@aol.com. *The real secrets are enthusiasm, competence and good luck; and it helps immensely to marry a good woman. Work and persistence define us, accomodating various levels of talent and intelligence. Work and persistence prevail, buttressed by discipline and determination, and perhaps supported by a sense of humor.*

STANSBERY, DAVID HONOR, ecologist, malacologist; b. Upper Sandusky, Ohio, May 5, 1926; s. Honor Gerald and Daisy Elizabeth (Kirby) S.; m. Mary Lois Pease, June 16, 1948; children: Michael David, Mark Andrew, Kathleen Mary, Linda Carol. BS, Ohio State U., 1950, MS, 1953, PhD, 1960. Instr. Ohio State U., Columbus, 1956-62, asst. prof., 1962-66, assoc. prof., 1966-71; state curator of natural history Ohio State Mus., Columbus, 1962-72; vis. scientist Smithsonian Instn., Washington, 1973-74; sr. rsch. assoc. The Ohio State Mus., Columbus, 1972—; dir. mus. of zoology Ohio State U., Columbus, 1970-92, prof. zoology, 1971-91, curator of mollusks Mus. of Biol. Diversity, 1962-2000, prof. emeritus, 1991—, curator emeritus, 2001—. Adv. bd. Ohio Biol. Survey, 1961-72; exec. com. Ohio Acad. of Sci., 1961-69; chair collection stds. Coun. of Systematic Malacologists, 1977-81; bd. govs. The Nature Conservancy, 1979-86; rsch. adv., guest lectr. Huazhong Agrl. U., Wuhan, Hubei, China, 1992; mem. faculty Upper Cumberland Biol. Sta. Tenn. Tech. U., 1987-91; presenter in field. Assoc. editor: Ohio Jour. Sci., 1960-61, editor, 1961-64; contbr. articles to profl. jours. Bd. trustees Columbus Audubon Soc., 1969-73; bd. dirs. Am. Rivers Cons. Coun., 1973-88. Recipient Oak Leaf award Nature Conservancy, 1977, Ohio Conservation Achievement award Ohio Dept. Natural Resouces, 1974, Lifetime Achievement award Freshwater Mollusk Conservation Soc., 1999, Herbert Osborn award Ohio Biol. Survey, 1999; grantees U.S. Dept. Interior, U.S. Dept. Commerce, U.S. Army Corps of Engrs., Battelle, Am. Electric Power, and others. Fellow: AAAS, Acad. Zoology, Ohio Acad. Sci.; mem.: Am. Malacol. Union (pres. 1970—71), Sigma Xi (pres. 1974—75). Achievements include building the world's largest freshwater bivalve mollusk collection at the Ohio State University Museum of Biological Diversity. Avocations: geology, history of science, evolution of ethics, linguistics. Home: 32 Amazon Pl Columbus OH 43214-3502 Office: Mus Biol Diversity Ohio State Univ 1315 Kinnear Rd Columbus OH 43212-1157 Office Phone: 614-262-2056. Personal E-mail: mlpdhs@aol.com. Business E-Mail: stansbery.1@osu.edu.

STANSBURY, HARRY CASE, state commissioner; BS in Gen. Studies, La. State U., 1968; JD, Loyola U., New Orleans, 1971; student, Oxford (Eng.) U., 1985, Harvard U., 1988; MBA, U. New Orleans, 1998; MA, Columbia U., 2000. Bar: La., N.Y., D.C., U.S. Supreme Ct., U.S. Ct. Appeals (1st-11th cirs., D.C. cir., fed. cir.), U.S. Ct. Mil. Appeals, U.S. Ct. Fed. Claims, U.S. Ct. Internat. Trade, U.S. Tax Ct., U.S. Dist. Ct. (ea., mid. and we. dists.) La., U.S. Dist. Ct. (ea., no., so. and we. dists.) N.Y., U.S. Dist. Ct. D.C. Staff atty. La. Securities Commn., New Orleans, 1971-75, dep. commr. securities, 1975—. Mem. liaison com. fed. securities code project Am. Law Inst.-ABA, 1974-80; speaker, expert witness in field. Contbr. articles to profl. jours. Mem.: ABA (mem. subcom. derivative instruments fed. regulation securities com. 1993—, sect. bus. law, sect. internat. law and practice, sect. legal edn. and admissions to bar), Harvard Law Sch. Assn., Loyola Law Alumni Assn., La. State U. Alumni Assn., Internat. Bar Assn. (mem. issues and trading in securities com. 1991—, sect. bus. law), Fed. Bar Assn. (fin. instns. and economy sect.), New Orleans Bar Assn. (vice chair corps. and bus.law com. 1992—94, chair 1994—96), Assn. Bar City of D.C., Assn. Bar City of N.Y., D.C. Bar Assn. (corp., fin. and securities law divsn.), N.Y. State Bar Assn., La. State Bar Assn. (sect. corp. and bus. law, mem. internat. law com. 1991—92), N.Am. Securities Adminstrs. Assn. (mem. registration exemption com. 1991—94), Am. Friends Rewley House, Supreme Ct. Hist. Soc. Address: 10001 Lake Forest Blvd Ste 803 New Orleans LA 70127

STANSELL, LELAND EDWIN, JR., lawyer, mediator, educator; b. Central, SC, July 13, 1934; s. Leland Edwin and Hettie Katherine (Hollis) S.; children: James Leland, Susan. BS, Fla. So. Coll., 1957; LLB, U. Miami, Fla., 1961, JD, 1968. Bar: Fla. 1961; cert. civil mediator Fla. Supreme Ct., U.S. Dist. Ct. Fla. Assoc. Wicker & Smith, Miami, 1961-62, ptnr., 1962-75; pvt. practice, Miami, 1975-99, Leland E. Stansell, Jr., P.A., Miami, 1995—. Chmn. Appellate Jud. Nominating Com., Dade County (Fla.), 1983-87; mem. adv. com. Am. Arbitration Assn., 1975-90. Served with U.S. Army, 1957. Mem. ABA (ho. of dels. 1982-86), Fla. Bar (bd. govs. 1966-70, 70-80), Dade County Bar Assn. (dir. 1969-72, exec. com. 1974-75, pres. 1975-76), U. Miami Law Alumni Assn. (dir., officer, pres. 1968-69), Fla. Criminal Def. Attys. Assn. (treas. 1964-66), Am. Judicature Soc., Am. Bd. Trial Advs., Internat. Assn. Def. Counsel, Fla. Acad. Profl. Mediators, Fedn. Ins. Counsel, Miami Beach Rod and Reel Club (pres.), Coral Reef Yacht Club, Bankers Club, Ocean Reef Yacht Club, Delta Theta Phi (pres. Miami alumni chpt. 1966, regional dir. 1968. Office: 19 W Flagler St Miami FL 33130-4400

STANSELL, RONALD BRUCE, retired investment banker; b. Hammond, Ind., Apr. 9, 1945; s. Herman Bruce and Helen Rose Stansell; m. Kathie Van Atta, Oct. 2, 1976; children: Kelsey, Kymberlie. BA, Wittenberg U., 1967; MA, Miami U., Oxford, Ohio, 1969. Investment officer First Nat. Bank, Chgo., 1969-73; mgr. investments Chrysler Corp., Detroit, 1973; asst. v.p. A.G. Becker, Chgo., 1973-76; v.p. Blyth Eastman Dillon, Chgo., 1976-79, Dean Witter Reynolds Inc., Chgo., 1979-82, First Boston Corp., 1982-88; sr. v.p. Prudential-Bache Securities, Chgo., 1988-90; ptnr. William Blair & Co., 1991-99; pres. Oakmont of Carolina, 1999—2001. Mem. Mettawa (Ill.) Zoning Bd., 1978-80; treas. Village of Mettawa, 1977-78, trustee, 1980-91. With USMCR, 1968-74. Mem. Bond Club Chgo., Investment Analyst Soc., Fixed Income Group, Bob O'Link Golf Club, Grandfather Golf Club, Forest Creek Golf Club, Belfair Golf Club, Berkeley Hall Club, Old Chatham Club, Diamond Creek Golf Club, Univ. Club.

STANSFIELD, CLAIRE, apparel designer; b. London, Eng., Aug. 27, 1964; Co-founder C&C California, 2003—. Actor: (films) The Doors, 1991, Nervous Ticks, 1992, Best of the Best II, 1993, The Swordsman, 1993, The Favor, 1994, Drop Zone, 1994, Gladiator Cop, 1994, Sensation, 1995, Red Shoe Diaries 5: Weekend Pass, 1995, The Outpost, 1995, Darkdrive, 1996, Steel, 1997, Sweepers, 1999; (TV series) Xena The Warrior Princess, Frasier, Twin Peaks. Office: c/o Lela Tillem #705 127 E 9th St Los Angeles CA 90015

STANSKY, PETER DAVID LYMAN, historian; b. N.Y.C., Jan. 18, 1932; s. Lyman and Ruth (Macow) S. BA, Yale U., 1953, King's Coll., Cambridge (Eng.) U., 1955, MA, 1959; PhD, Harvard U., 1961; D.L. (hon.), Wittenburg U., 1984. Teaching fellow history and lit. Harvard U., 1957-61, instr., then asst. prof. history, 1961-68; assoc. prof. history Stanford U., 1968-73, prof., 1973-74, Frances and Charles Field prof., 1974—, chmn. dept. history, 1975-78, 79-82, 89-90, assoc. dean humanities and scis., 1985-88. Chmn. publs. com. Conf. Brit. Studies, 1970-78; pres. Pacific Coast Conf. Brit. Studies, 1974-76, N. Am. Conf. Brit. Studies, 1983-85; vis. fellow Wesleyan Center Humanities, Middletown, Conn., 1972, All Soul's Coll., Oxford (Eng.) U., 1979, St. Catherine's Coll., Oxford (Eng.) U., 1983 Author: Ambitions and Strategies, 1964, England Since 1867, 1973, Gladstone, 1979, William Morris, 1983, Redesigning the World, 1985, On or About December 1910, 1996, Another Book That Never Was, 1998, From William Morris to Sergeant Pepper, 1999, Sassoon: The Worlds of Philip and Sybil, 2003; co-author: Journey to the Frontier, 1966, The Unknown Orwell, 1972, Orwell: The Transformation, 1979, London's Burning, 1994. Guggenheim fellow, 1966-67, 73-74; Am. Council Learned Socs. fellow, 1978-79; NEH fellow, 1983, 98-99, Royal Hist. Soc. fellow Ctr. for Advanced Study Behavioral Scis., 1988-89 Fellow Am. Acad. Arts and Scis. (coun. 1994-98, 2002—); mem. Am. Hist. Assn. (pres. Pacific Coast br. 1988-89), Conf. on Brit. Studies, Victorian Soc., William Morris Soc., AAUP, Century Assn. Home: 375 Pinehill Rd Hillsborough CA 94010-6612 Office: Stanford U Dept History Stanford CA 94305-2024 E-mail: stansky@stanford.edu.

STANTON, ALEX, public relations executive; BA, Hobart Coll. CEO Stanton Crenshaw, N.Y.C., 1995—. Mem. Pub. Rels. Orgn. Internat., Pub. Rels. Soc. Am. Office: Stanton Crenshaw 250 Park Ave S New York NY 10003-1402

STANTON, DONALD SHELDON, academic administrator; b. Balt., June 8, 1932; s. Kenneth Gladstone and Dorothy Erma (Hetrick) S.; m. Barbara Mae Hoot, June 25, 1955; children: Dale Richard, Debra Carol, Diane Karen. AB, Western Md. Coll., 1953; Litt.D., Oglethorpe U., 1999; LLD, Western Md. Coll., 1981; MDiv magna cum laude, Wesley Theol. Sem., 1956; MA, Am. U., 1960; Ed.D., U. Va., 1965; L.H.D., Columbia Coll., 1979; Litt.D., Albion Coll., 1983. Ordained to ministry United Methodist Ch., 1956; pastor Balt. and Va. confs. United Meth. Ch., 1953-59; dir. Richmond (Va.) Area Wesley Found., 1959-63; chaplain, dean of students Greensboro Coll., 1963-65; chaplain Wofford Coll., 1965-69; dir. office coll. services United Meth. Div. Higher Edn., Nashville, 1969-75; v.p. for devel. Wesleyan Coll., 1975-78; pres. Adrian Coll., 1978-88, Oglethorpe U., Atlanta, 1988-99, pres. emeritus, 1999—. Adminstr., prof. European internat. ednl. programs, summers 1960, 69-71, 73; chmn. pres.'s assn. Mich. Intercollegiate Athletic Assn., 1986-87. Contbr. articles, revs. to profl. publs. in U.S., Japan, Argentina, chpts. to books; editor: Faculty Forum, 1972-74; bass-baritone soloist. Bd. dirs. Toledo (Ohio) Symphony, 1980-83, Lewanee County Jr. Achievement, 1980-83, Found. Ind. Higher Edn., 1996-99, Nat. Conf. for Cmty. and Justice, Atlanta Region, Atlanta Area Coun. Boy Scouts Am.; chair bd. trustees U. Ctr. Ga., 1994-96; chair So. Collegiate Athletic Conf., 1994-95. Adminstrn. bldg. at Adrian Coll. named in honor of Stanton and his wife, 1988. Mem. Am. Assn. Univ. Adminstrs. (bd. dirs. 1990-93), Ga. Assn. Colls. (pres. 1992), Soc. Wesley (Disting. Alumni Recognition award 1988), Ga. Found. for Ind. Colls. (vice chair 1992), Nat. Assn. Ind. Colls. and Univs. (past mem. pub. rels. com.), Assn. Pvt. Colls. and Univs. Ga. (treas. 1996-97), Rotary, Omicron Delta Kappa, Order of Omega, Tau Kappa Epsilon, Psi Chi, Phi Eta Sigma. Home: 312 Tillman Rd Lake Junaluska NC 28745-9779 E-mail: stantons2@earthlink.net.

STANTON, FRANK LAWRENCE, JR., graphic designer, illustrator, educator; b. St. Louis, Feb. 5, 1929; s. Frank Lawrence and Rose Margaret (Haas) S.; m. Elizabeth Ann Buehrle, Oct. 16, 1965; children: Laura Ann, Carol Beth. BFA, Washington U., St. Louis, 1955; MFA, Syracuse (N.Y.) U., 1979. Illustrator New Ctr. Studio, Detroit, 1955, The Illustrators, St. Louis, 1955-60; designer, illustrator Frank Stanton Art Studio, St. Louis, 1960-66, The Stantons' Studio, St. Louis, 1966—; prof. art St. Louis Cmty. Coll., 1966-92, prof. emeritus, 1992—. Graphic comms. adv. bd. Washington U., St. Louis, 1974—75. Illustrator: (with others) Curbstone Dragons, 1972; (cookbook) Creative Homemakers-Times/Mirror, 1973, Reading for Concepts, 1970; stained glass designer Little Sisters of the Poor, St. Louis, 1958, designer, muralist, 1971; designer, muralist Bellefontaine Habilitation Ctr., St. Louis, 1981; stained glass designer: Carmelite Convent, Springfield, Mo., 1964, 1st Presbyn. Ch., Tucumcari, N.Mex., 1964, Grace Meth. Ch., Springfield, 1980, St. Monica Ch., Creve Coeur, Mo., 1982, Our Lady of Providence, St. Louis, 1988, Calvary Cemetary Mausoleum, DeSoto, Mo., 1992, St. George Ch., St. Louis, 1995, St. Catherine Laboure Ch., St. Louis, 2000, Ch. of Incarnate Word, St. Louis, 2001, Timothy Luth., St. Louis, 2001; designer, sculptor St. Monica, St. Louis, 1982, St. Philip Neri-Cath. Ctr., U. Tulsa, 1993. With USN, 1951-53. Recipient nat. tchg. excellence award U. Tex. Study, Austin, 1989. Mem. St. Louis Art Dirs. Club (1st v.p. 1971-72, awards of excellence 1960, 61, 72). Home: 12540 Pepperwood Dr Saint Louis MO 63146-3814 E-mail: fnbstan@earthlink.net.

STANTON, GEORGE PATRICK, JR., lawyer; b. Fairmont, W.Va., Nov. 21, 1933; s. George Patrick and Wilma Roberta (Everson) S.; m. Shirley Jean Champ, Sept. 3, 1956; children: George Patrick, Edward Scott. BS in Bus. Adminstrn., Fairmont Coll., 1956; MBA in Fin., U. Dayton, 1969; JD, U. Balt., 1977. Bar: Md. 1978, U.S. Dist. Ct. Md. 1978, W.Va. 1979, U.S. Dist. Ct. (so. dist.) W.Va. 1979, U.S. Dist. Ct. (no. dist.) W.Va. 1980, U.S. Ct. Appeals (4th cir.) 1985. Auditor 1st Nat. Bank Fairmont, 1955-61; asst. cashier S.C. Nat. Bank, Columbia, 1961-64; sr. sys. analyst Chase Manhattan Bank, N.Y.C., 1964-65; asst. v.p. Winters Nat. Bank, Dayton, Ohio, 1965-69, Md. Nat. Bank, Balt., 1969-74; v.p. Equitable Trust Co., Balt., 1974-79; gen. ptnr. Stanton & Stanton Attys. at Law, Fairmont, W.Va., 1979—. Asst. pros. atty. Marion Co., W.Va., 2003—; staff sect. leader, faculty Sch. for Bank Adminstrn. U. Wis., Madison, 1978-89. Treas. Montaineer Area coun. Boy Scouts Am., Fairmont, 1982-90; pres. Three Rivers Coal Festival, Inc., Fairmont, 1984-85, pres., 1985-86, bd. dirs., 1982-86; pres. Appalachian Coal Festival, 1985-86, bd. dirs., 1985—; adv. bd. Inst. for Living, Fairmont, 1983-85; pres. Firemans' CSC, Fairmont, W.Va., 1992-96; elder Christ Cmty. Ch., 2003. Mem. W.Va. Bar Assn. (Kaufman award 1997), Marion County Bar Assn. (v.p.), Md. Bar Assn., W.Va. Trial Lawyers Assn., Marion County C. of C. (bd. dirs. 1983—), Fairmont State Coll. Alumni Assn. (bd. dirs. 1982—, pres. 1992-94, Alumnus of Yr. 2002), Fairmont Field Club, Rotary, Masons. Home: 2 W Hills Dr Fairmont WV 26554-5015 Office: Stanton & Stanton PO Box 968 WesBanco Bldg Ste 707 Fairmont WV 26555-0968 Office Phone: 304-366-1240.

STANTON, JEANNE FRANCES, retired lawyer; b. Vicksburg, Miss., Jan. 22, 1920; d. John Francis and Hazel (Mitchell) S. Student, George Washington U., 1938-39; BA, U. Cin., 1940; JD, Salmon P. Chase Coll. Law, 1954. Bar: Ohio 1954. Chief clk. Selective Svc. Bd., Cin., 1940-43; instr. USAAF Tech. Schs., Biloxi, Miss., 1943-44; with Procter & Gamble, Cin., 1945-84, legal asst., 1952-54, head advt. svcs. sect. legal divsn., trade practice dept., 1954-73, mgr. advt. svcs., legal divsn., 1973-84, ret., 1984. Team capt. Cmty. Chest Cin., 1983; mem. ann. meeting com. Archaeol. Inst. Am., 1983; trustee, asst. corr. sec., statutory agt. Friends of Bronze Age Archaeology in the Aegean area, 1987—. Mem. ABA (chmn. subcom. D of com. 307 copyright sect. 1987-88, 89, 90), Ohio Bar Assn. (chmn. uniform state laws com. 1968-70), Cin. Bar Assn. (sec. law day com. 1965-66, chmn. com. on preservation hist. documents 1968-71), Vicksburg and Warren County Hist. Soc., Cin. Hist. Soc., Intercontinental Biog. Assn., Lawyers Club Cin. (exec. com., pres. 1983). Home: 3580 Shaw Ave Apt 323 Cincinnati OH 45208-1454 *Personal philosophy: Most people are good and honest. If a person does the most honorable thing, that is its own reward.*

STANTON, JOHN JEFFREY, editor, writer, print and broadcast journalist, government programs director, analyst, professional society administrator; b. Wichita Falls, Tex., July 19, 1956; s. John Joseph Jr. and Joan (Marley) S.; m. Scylla Maria Silva, Jan. 6, 1981; 1 child, Damien Kristian. BS in Pub. Adminstrn. and Bus. Adminstrn., Nichols Coll., 1978; M in Pub. Adminstrn., U. Detroit, 1980. Rsch. asst. Am. Enterprise Inst., Washington, 1977; rep. aide R.I. Ho. of Reps., Providence, 1977-78; mng. editor Am. Politics, Washington, 1982, assoc. editor, 1983, corp. advisor, 1984, sr. editor, 1985-87; editor, govt. programs mgr. ENTEK, Alexandria, Va., 1988-90, govt. programs dir., cons. Tuckerman Group, Springfield, Va., 1991; analyst, writer Nat. Security Issues, Arlington, Va., 1991—, program dir. TeleStrategies, McLean, Va., 1991-93; Washington corr., mem. editl. bd. Tech. Transfer Jour., 1994-98; editor Tech. Transfer Newsletter; asst. to pres., info. transfer specialist Am. Def. Preparedness Assn., Arlington, 1994-97; contbg. writer Nat. Def. Mag., 1996—; adminstrn. dir. Nat. Def. Indsl. Assn., Arlington, 1997—; Washington corr. Australian Def. Mag., 1998-99; editor Voice of the Indsl. Base NDIA, 1998—2000. Creator, co-host (radio) Power Breakfast, Sta. WNTR, Washington, 1987, Am. Politics Radio, 1987; commentator WAMU-NPR, WBAL, KPFA, Am. Talk Live, NYC, Radio 101, Croatia, Radio Adelaide, KCMO, Kansas City, WNTR, WAMU, WBAC, Balt.; campaign mgr. Madsen for Congress, 8th dist., Va., 2004; polit.-mil. analyst CBS News, CNN, ABC, 2001—. Co-author: America's Nightmare, 2003; author: A Power But Not Super, 2004; contbr. articles to profl. jours., popular mags. Polit. campaign cons. to Glenn Tenney, 1992—; commr. Arlington Little League Baseball, 1993, coach 1997—; mentor Arlington County Ct. Sys., 1997; varsity football coach Wakefield H.S., Arlington, Va., 1998-2002, St. Stephen's Agnes, 2003—. Recipient Doers Honoree The Washington Times, 1988. Avocation: coaching youth sports programs. Personal E-mail: cioran123@yahoo.com.

STANTON, KATHRYN, retail bookstores/educational products and services executive; b. Nov. 29, 1954; BS in Acctg., U. Ill., 1976; MBA, U. Chgo., 1996. CPA, Ill. From auditor to mgr. Arthur Anderson, Chgo., 1976-81, mgr., 1981-86; from controller to v.p. finance, CFO Follett Corp., Chgo., River Grove, Ill., 1986 97, v.p. finance, CFO River Grove, Ill., 1997—. Bd. dirs. Mus. Sci. and Industry, Chgo. Mem. Am. Inst. CPAs, Financial Exec. Inst., Ill. CPA Soc., Chgo. Council Foreign Rels. Office: Follett Corp 2233 N West St River Grove IL 60171-1895 Fax: 708-452-9347.

STANTON, LOUIS LEE, federal judge; b. N.Y.C., Oct. 1, 1927; s. Louis Lee and Helen Parsons (La Fétra) S.; m. Berit Eleonora Rask; children: L. Lee, Susan Helen Benedict, Gordon R., Fredrik S. BA, Yale U., 1950; JD, U. Va., 1955. Assoc. Davis Polk Wardwell Sunderland & Kiendl, N.Y.C., 1955-66, Carter, Ledyard & Milburn, N.Y.C., 1966-67, ptnr., 1967-85; sr. judge U.S. Dist. Ct. (so. dist.) N.Y., N.Y.C., 1985—. Served to 1st lt. USMCR, 1950-52. Fellow Am. Coll. Trial Lawyers, N.Y. Bar Found.; mem. Va. Bar Assn. Office Phone: 212-805-0252.

STANTON, MICHAEL JOHN, newspaper editor; b. New Britain, Conn., Mar. 30, 1944; s. John Martin and Helen (McNally) S.; m. Barbara Ann Mucha, Aug. 27, 1966; 1 child, Sean AB in English, Holy Cross Coll., 1966. Reporter, editor Providence (R.I.) Jour., 1968-72; press sec. Gov. R.I., Providence, 1972-77; asst. news editor St. Louis Globe-Dem., 1977-81; news copy desk chief Detroit Free Press, 1981-83, exec. news editor, 1983-85, asst. to exec. editor, 1985-86; exec. news editor Seattle Times, 1986—. Office: The Seattle Times PO Box 70 Fairview Ave N & John St Seattle WA 98111

STANTON, M(ORRIS) DUNCAN, psychologist, researcher, dean; b. Lockport, N.Y. *Forebears came from England, Scotland, Wales, the Netherlands, France, Ireland, Germany, and Lithuania. Ancestors include a country doctor, several clergy, Canada's first female medical school graduate, a civil engineer who helped build the Panama Canal, artists, teachers, writers, an attorney, a superintendent of schools, and a registered nurse. Related to: Sir Francis Drake, President Grover Cleveland, Alexander Graham Bell, Lincoln's Secretary of War Edwin M. Stanton, and Elizabeth Cady Stanton's husband, New York anti-slavery journalist, attorney and political lecturer Henry Stanton.* BA in Psychology, Afred U., 1962; MA in Clin. Psychology, The George Washington U., 1964; PhD in Clin., Cmty. Psychology, U. of Md., 1968. Lic. psychologist State of N.Y., 1971, State of Ky., 2001, bd. cert. diplomate, clin. psychology Am. Bd. Prof. Psychology, 1972, approved supr. Am. Assn. Marriage Family Therapy, 1979, bd. cert. diplomate, family psychology Am. Bd. Prof. Psychology, 1991, cert. of proficiency in the treatment of alcohol and other psychoactive substance abuse disorders Am. Psychol. Assn., 1996. Intern Walter Reed Gen. Hosp., 1966—67; lectr. U. Md., 1969—72; asst. prof. to assoc. prof., psychology in psychiatry U. of Pa. Sch. of Medicine, 1972—83; assoc. clin. dir. Penn Psychiatry, Phila. Gen. Hosp., 1972—74; dir., addicts and families prog. Phila. Child Guidance Clinic, 1974—83; dir., family therapy tng. program Drug Dependence Treatment Ctr., Phila. VA Med. Ctr., 1974—79; faculty mem. family therapy tng. ctr. Phila. Child Guidance Clinic, 1977—83; tchg. faculty Family Inst. of Phila., 1977—83; instr. Wilmington Med. Ctr., Del., 1978—79; dir., rsch. Phila. Child Guidance Clinic, Pa., 1982—83; prof., psychiatry (psychology) U. of Rochester Sch. of Medicine and Dentistry, 1983—97; dir., div. family programs, dept. psychiatry U. of Rochester Med. Ctr., 1983—93, dir., rsch., div. family programs, dept. of psychiatry, 1993—97; dean, sch. of prof. psychology and social work, prof. Spalding U., 1997—99, v.p., academic rsch., 1999, prof. emeritus, psychology, 1999—; NIH prin. investigator The Morton Ctr., 2001—. Vis. scholar Fulbright Found., U.S. Info. Agy., Argentina, 1991; appointments or affiliations with 20 med. centers, hospitals in 11 cities, 1963—; cons. The White House Office of Drug Abuse Policy, 1977—81, U.S. Info. Agency, 1987—96; chair, mem., various rev. comm., task forces, site visit teams NIDA, NIMH, NIAAA, 1975—; mem. 16 editl. bds., including Am. Jour. Drug Alcohol Abuse, Family Process, Psychosocial Stress, 1980—; mem., bd. directors Family Process Press, N.Y.C., 1982—99; spkr., presenter invited lectrs., workshops, 26 countries. *Conducted an anonymous survey of drug use among 2,372 Army personnel in Vietnam which, via testimony before the U.S. Senate Special Subcommittee on Alcoholism and Narcotics, received considerable attention in the national media. Consultant/advisory board member to over 90 government agencies, universities, medical centers, and organizations across five continents. Published reviews of the outcome studies on both family couples therapy for drug abuse (meta-analysis, 1997), and the methods for getting reluctant substance abusers to enter treatment or self-help (2004). Author of a recent, brief, and at times humorous book on how America can cure its health care system.* Author (co-author) more than 150 sci., prof. pubs. Capt., chief psychologist U.S. Army, 1968—69, Walson Army Hosp., Ft. Dix, capt., chief psychologist U.S. Army, 1969—70, 98th Med. Detachment/8th Field Hosp. (Vietnam), capt., chief psychologist U.S. Army, 1970—71, Kimbrough Army Hosp., capt., asst. chief, dir. tng. U.S. Army, 1971—72, Walter Reed Gen. Hosp. Psychology Svc. Decorated Bronze Star Medal U.S. Army; recipient Ann. Disting. Fellow Award, Pikes Peak Mental Health Ctr., 1980, Plaque of Appreciation, Found. for Parents in Action (Argentina), 1991, Shield of Police of Salta Province (Argentina), 1991, Cert. of Appreciation for Svc. on Mayor's Drug, Alcohol Treatment Program, City of Louisville, 1998; grantee, NIH (NIDA/NIAAA), 1974—84, 1995—. Fellow: Am. Assoc. Marriage and Family Therapy (Outstanding Rsch. Contbn. in Marital and Family Therapy 1980, Cumulative Contbn. Family Therapy Rsch. award 2003), APA (Pres. Citation 2001); mem.: Intl. Family Therapy Assn., Associacion Sistemica de Buenos Aires (hon.), South African Inst. Marital, Family Therapy (hon.), Nat. Coun. Family Rels. (Award Appreciation Work on Addictions 1988), Am. Family Therapy Acad. (chair alcohol and drug interest group 1982—87, Disting. Contbn. Family Systems Rsch. 1997). Office: The Morton Center 1028 Barret Ave Louisville KY 40204

STANTON, PAMELA FREEMAN, interior designer, writer; b. Jacksonville, Tex., July 18, 1941; d. William Thomas and Ruth Ethel (Branton) Freeman; m. Karl F. Edmonds, Jr., Jan. 28, 1961 (div. 1966); m. Charles Calvin Stanton, Sept. 1, 1973; 1 child, Julie Anne. AA in Bus., Kilgore Coll., 1961. Design cons., Denver, Boston and Salem, Oreg., 1963-69; exec. sec. Alexander: Alexander of Tex. Inc., Dallas, 1967-69; interior designer Milmac Furniture, Dallas, 1969-73, Homestead House, Denver, 1973-76; case aide counselor Eliot Cmty. Mental Health Ctr., Concord, Mass., 1980-82; pres., owner Stancom Designs, Virginia Beach, Va., 1990-2000; interior designer Willis Furniture Co., 2000—. Author: I Am That I Am, 1994 (Best Book of Yr. N.Am. Bookdealers Exch., 1995). Recipient Cert. of Appreciation for vol. work Emerson Hosp., Concord, 1981; named Internat. Writer of Yr., 2003. Republican. Avocations: collecting art, travel, gardening, theatre-plays, entertaining. Home and Office: 4401 Leatherwood Dr Virginia Beach VA 23462-5704

STANTON, PATRICK MICHAEL, lawyer; b. Phila., Sept. 8, 1947; s. Edward Joseph and Helen Marie (Coghlan) S.; m. Kathleen Ann Fama, Aug. 22, 1970; children: Cheryl Marie, Susan Elizabeth. BS in History, St. Joseph's U., 1969; JD, U. Va., 1972; MBA, Fairleigh Dickinson, 1984. Bar: Ohio 1972 (inactive), N.J. 1982, U.S. Dist. Ct. (so. dist.) Ohio 1972, U.S. Dist. Ct. (ea. dist.) N.J. 1982, U.S. Dist. Ct. (so. dist.) N.Y. 1984. Assoc. Taft, Stettinius & Hollister, Cin., 1972—80; labor counsel Union Camp Corp., Wayne, NJ, 1980—83; dir. labor rels., equal employment opportunity programs W.R. Grace & Co., N.Y.C., 1983—86; of counsel Shanley & Fisher, P.C., Morristown, NJ, 1986—89, ptnr., chmn. labor and employment group, 1989—95; dir. Stanton, Hughes, Diana, Cerra, Mariani & Margello, P.C., Morristown, NJ, 1995—2003; atty. Ogletree, Deakins, Nash, Smoak & Stewart, P.C., Morristown, 2004—. Adj. prof. bus. law Fairleigh Dickinson U. 1984-92; pres. Sidney Reitman employment law Am. Inn. Ct., 1997-2001. Pres., bd. dirs. N.Y. State Adv. Coun. on Employment Law, Inc., N.Y.C., 1985-86. DuPont scholar U. Va., 1970. Mem. ABA, N.J. State Bar Assn. (exec. com. labor employment law sect. 1989—, rec. sec. 1995-97, treas. 1997-99, 2d vice chair 1999-2001, 1st vice chair 2001-2003, chair 2003—), Phi Alpha Theta, Delta Mu Delta. Roman Catholic. Home: 292 Forest Ave Glen Ridge NJ 07028-1808 Office: Ogletree Deakins Nash Smoak & Stewart PC 10 Madison Ave Ste 402 Morristown NJ 07960-7303 Fax: 973-656-1611. Office Phone: 973-656-1600. Business E-Mail: patrick.stanton@ogletreedeakins.com.

STANTON, ROBERT JAMES, JR., geologist, educator; b. L.A., June 17, 1931; s. Robert James and Audrey (Franke) S.; m. Patricia Ann Burns, Sept. 13, 1953; children— John, Carol. BS, Calif. Inst. Tech., 1953, PhD, 1960; MA, Harvard U., 1956. Research geologist Shell Devel. Co., Houston, 1959-67; mem. faculty Tex. A&M U., 1967—, prof. geology, 1972-86, Ray C. Fish prof. geology, 1986-98, head dept., 1979-83, prof. geology emeritus, 1998—. Vis. prof. U. Nuremburg-Erlangen, Germany, 1984; rsch. assoc. invertebrate paleontology Natural History Mus. L.A. County. Co-author: Paleoecology: Principles and Applications, 1981, 2d edit., 1990. Served with AUS, 1953-55. Fellow Geol. Soc. Am.; mem. Internat. Paleontol. Union, Paleontol. Soc., Paleontol. Research Inst., Soc. Econ. Paleontologists and Mineralogists (Outstanding Paper award 1970), Sigma Xi, Tau Beta Pi. Home: 2297 Valleyfield Ave Thousand Oaks CA 91360 Office: Nat Hist Mus LA County Dept Invertebrate Paleontol 900 Exposition Blvd Los Angeles CA 90007 Business E-Mail: robertstanton@adelphia.net.

STANTON, ROBERT JOHN, JR., English language educator; b. Manhattan, NY, July 7, 1942; s. Robert John Stanton and Mary McGinty; m. Felicia Lena Giancola, Nov. 15, 1959; children: Robert III, Sharon. BA, Hofstra U., 1970; MA, U. Mass., Amherst, 1972, postgrad., 1974-79. Instr. English Flagler Coll., St. Augustine, Fla., 1972-74; tchg. asst. U. Mass., Amherst, 1974-77, lectr. in Rhetoric, 1979-81; English tchr. Bishop Kenny H.S., Jacksonville, Fla., 1982-83, Duval County Pub. Schs., Jacksonville, 1984-87; asst. prof. English Jacksonville U., 1987-91, assoc. prof. English, 1992—, chmn. divsn. humanities, 1993-97. Author: Seventeen British Novelists, 1978, Gore Vidal, 1978, Truman Capote, 1980, Views From A Window: Conversations with Gore Vidal, 1980; (poems) Collected Word Paintings, 2000; co-author: Beneath Mad River Mansion, 1992, Noah's Orbella, 1994, The Devil's Rood, 1996, Dangerous Words, 2003. Mem. MLA, Nat. Assn. Tchrs. English, Fla. Assn. Depts. English (pres. 1996), Swift River Hist. Soc. Democrat. Avocations: astronomy, reading, writing, observing the universe. Home: 614 15th Ave S Jacksonville Beach FL 32250 Office: Jacksonville Univ Jacksonville FL 32211 Office Phone: 904-256-7106. Business E-Mail: bstanto@ju.edu.

STANTON, ROGER D. lawyer; b. Oct. 4, 1938; s. George W. and Helen V. (Peterson) S.; m. Judith L. Duncan, Jan. 27, 1962; children: Jeffrey B., Brady D., Todd A. AB, U. Kans., 1960, JD, 1963. Bar: Kans. 1963, U.S. Dist. Ct. Kans. 1963, U.S. Ct. Appeals (10th cir.) 1972, U.S. Supreme Ct. 1973. Assoc. Stanley, Schroeder, Weeks, Thomas & Lysaught, Kansas City, 1968-72, Weeks, Thomas & Lysaught, Kansas City, 1969-80, also bd. dirs., chmn. exec. com., 1981-82, Stinson, Mag & Fizzell, Kansas City, 1983-96, chmn. products practice group, also bd. dirs., 1993-95; ptnr. Berkowitz, Stanton, Brandt, Williams & Shaw, Prairie Village, Kans., 1997—. Chmn. bd. editors Jour. Kans. Bar Assn., 1975-83; contbr. articles to profl. jours. Active Boy Scouts Am., 1973-79; pres. YMCA Youth Football Club, 1980-82; co-chmn. Civil Justice Reform Act com. Dist. of Kans., 1991-95; bd. dirs. Kans. Appleseed Found., 2000—. Fellow: Am. Coll. Trial Lawyers (state SRSC Com. 1983—88, state chmn. 1984—86, state SRSC Com. 2001—); mem.: Earl O'Conner Inn. Ct. (bd. dirs. 1972—75), Kans. Assn. Def. Counsel (pres. 1977—78), Johnson Co. Bar Assn. (chmn. bench, bar com.), Johnson County Bar Found. (pres., trustee), Kans. Bar Assn. (Pres.'s award 1982), Def. Rsch. Inst. (state co-chmn. 1979—90, Exceptionl Performance award 1979), Am. Bd. Trial Adv. (exec. com. East Kans./West Miss. chpt. 1994—99), Internat. Assn. Def. Counsel, U. Kans. Kansas City Alumni (bd. dirs. 2001—), U. Kans. Sch. Law Alumni Assn. Office: Berkowitz Stanton Brandt Williams & Stueve 4121 W 83rd St Ste 227 Prairie Village KS 66208

STANTON, RONALD P. export company executive; b. 1928; Grad., City College of NY; Ph.D. (hon.), Yeshiva U., 1982. Chmn. Transammonia, Inc., N.Y.C., 1965—. Mem. bd. of trustees Yeshiva U., New York, 1976—, vice chmn bd. of trustees, 1992—2002, chmn. bd. of trustees, 2002—; bd. mem. Lincoln Center, New York, NY Presbyterian Hospital, New York; chmn. Ministerial Commt. Office: Transammonia Inc 350 Park Ave New York NY 10022

STANTON, VIVIAN BRENNAN (MRS. ERNEST STANTON), retired guidance counselor; b. Waterbury, Conn.; d. Francis P. and Josephine (Ryan) Brennan; B.A., Albertus Magnus Coll.; M.S., So. Conn. State Coll., 1962, 6th yr. degree, 1965; postgrad. Columbia U.; m. Ernest Stanton, May 31, 1947; children— Pamela L., Bonita F., Kim Ernest. Tchr. English, history, govt. Milford (Conn.) High Sch., 1940-48; tchr. English, history, fgn. Born Night Sch., New Haven, 1948-54, Simon Lake Sch., Milford, 1960-62; guidance counselor, psychol. examiner Jonathan Law High Sch., Milford, 1962-73, Nat. Honor Soc. adv., 1966-73, mem. Curriculum Councils, Graduation Requirement Council, Gifted Child Com., others, 1940-48, 60-73; guidance dir. Foran High Sch., Milford, 1973-79, career center coordinator, 1976-79, ret., 1979. Active various community drives; mem. exec. bd. Ridge Rd PTA, 1956-59; mem. Parent-Tchr. council Hopkins Grammer Sch., New Haven; mem. Human Relations Council, North Haven, 1967-69; vol., patient rep. surg. waiting rm. Fawcett Meml. Hosp., P.C., Sun City Ctr. Emergency Squad, Good Samaritans. Mem. Nat. Assn. Secondary Schs. and Colls. (evaluation com.; chmn. testing com.), AAUW, LWV, Conn. Personnel and Guidance Assn., Conn. Sch. Counselors Assn., Conn. Assn. Sch. Psychol. Personnel, Conn., Milford (pres. 1945-47) edn. assns. Clubs: Univ., Charlotte Harbor Yacht, Sun City Ctr. Golf and Racquet. Home: 6315 Delord St New Orleans LA 70118

STANTON, WILLIAM JOHN, JR., marketing educator, author; b. Chgo, Dec. 15, 1919; s. William John and Winifred (McGann) S.; m. Imma Mair, Sept. 14, 1978; children by previous marriage: Kathleen Louise, William John III. BS, Ill. Inst. Tech., 1940; MBA, Northwestern U., 1941, PhD, 1948; D (hon.), Cath. U. Santo Domingo, Dominican Republic, 2003. Mgmt. trainee Sears Roebuck & Co., 1940-41; instr. U. Ala., 1941-44; auditor Olan Mills Portrait Studios, Chattanooga, 1944-46; asst. prof., asso. prof. U. Wash., 1948-55; prof. U. Colo., Boulder, 1955-90; prof. emeritus, 1990—; head mktg. dept. U. Colo., 1955-71, acting dean, 1963-64; assoc. dean U. Colo. (Sch. Bus.), 1964-67. Author: Economic Aspects of Recreation in Alaska, 1953; author: (with others) Challenge of Business, 1975; author: (with R. Varaldo) Italian Edition, 2d edit., 1990; author: (with others) South African Edition, 1992; author: (with K. Miller and R. Layton) Australian Edition, 4th edit., 2000; author: (with M. Etzel and B. Walker) Marketing, 13th edit., 2003, Marketing, 13th edit., Spanish, Chinese, Portuguese, Indonesian and Korean transl., 2003; author: (with Rosann Spiro and G.A. Rich) Management of a Sales Force, 11th edit., 2003; author: (with M.S. Sommers and J.G. Barnes) Canadian Edition Fundamentals of Marketing, 11th edit., 2003, Canadian Edition Fundamentals of Marketing, 11th edit., Spanish, Portuguese, Chinese, and Russian transl.; contbr. articles to profl. jour. Mem. Am. Mktg. Assn., Mktg. Educators Assn., Beta Gamma Sigma. Roman Catholic. Home: 1445 Sierra Dr Boulder CO 80302-7846

STANTON-HICKS, MICHAEL D'ARCY, anesthesiologist, pain medicine specialist; b. Adelaide, Australia, June 3, 1931; arrived in U.S., 1972; s. Cedric Stanton-Hicks and Florence (Haggett) Perrin; m. Kristina Litsmark, Aug. 4, 1969 (div. Aug. 1984); children: Erik Michael, Leif Neal; m. Ursula Koch, Aug. 27, 1985. MB, BChir, Adelaide U., 1962; Dr. med., U. Dusseldorf, 1984. Bd. equivalent Am. Bd. Anesthesiology; diplomate Am. Bd. Pain Medicine, Interventional Pain Practice, 2002. Intern Queen Elizabeth Hosp., Adelaide, 1961-62, tutor, staff anesthesiologist, 1970-72; resident Royal Postgrad. Med. Sch., London and Lasarettet Köping, 1966-68; asst. dir. anesthesiology intensive care Södersjükhuset, Stockholm, 1968 69; instr. anesthesiology U. Wash. Med. Sch., Seattle, 1969-70, asst. prof., 1972-75; prof., chmn. dept. U. Mass. Med. Sch., Worcester, 1975-83; prof. U. Colo. Health Scis. Ctr., Denver, 1983-86, vice chmn. dept., 1983-85, acting chmn., 1985-86; prof., dir. pain clinic and rsch. Johannes Gutenberg U., Mainz, Germany, 1986-88, prof., 1986—97; dir. pain mgmt. ctr. Cleve. Clinic Found., 1988-98, vice chmn. pain mgmt. and rsch. divsn. anesthesia, 1998—; prof. Lerner Coll. Medicine, Case Western Res. U., Cleve., 2004—. Med. examiner Indsl. Commn. Ohio; mem. Ohio Pain Adv. Com., Dept. Health; mem. liaison com. med. bd. Ohio Pain Com.; advisor Am. Acad. Disability Evaluating Physicians, 2000-02;; appt. to gov.'s task force on compassionate care, Dept. of Health, Ohio; prof. Cleve. Clinic, Lerner Coll. Medicine at Case Western Res. U., 2004; bd. dirs. World Inst. of Pain. Author, editor Regional Anesthesia: Advances and Selected Topics, 1978, (with Boas) Chronic Low Back Pain, 1982; co-author: (with Raj and Nolte) Illustrated Manual of Regional Anesthesia, 1988 (Most Beautiful Book of Yr. award Frankfurt, Fed. Republic Germany Pubs. Book Conv., 1989), (with Janig and Boas) Reflex Sympathetic Dystrophy, 1989, (with Janig) Reflex Sympathetic Dystrophy: A Reappraisal, 1996; author: Pain and Sympathetic Nervous System, 1989; exec. editor Pain Practice Jour., 2001—, sect. editor Complex Regional Pain Syndrome, 2002, mem. editl. bd. Pain Physician, 2002—; author: (with Wilson and Harden) CRPS: Current Diagnosis and Therapy, 2005. Squadron leader res. Royal Australian Air Force, 1962-65. Recipient Disting. Scientist award Reflex Sympathetic Dystrophy Assn., 2002, Disting. Svc. award European Regional Anaesthesia Soc., 2003; named Top Doc Good Housekeeping Mag., 2003, Disting. Svc. award European Soc. Regional Anesthesia, 2003; named Scientist of Yr. Am. Herschel Soc., 1991-92; Australian Univs. Commn. mature age scholar, 1953-60. Fellow Royal Coll. Surgeons (faculty anesthetists), Royal Coll. Anesthetists, Am. Acad. Pain Medicine; mem. Internat. Assn. Study Pain (chmn. spl. interest group on sympathetically maintained pain 1990—), World Inst. Pain (bd. dirs. 1995—), Am. Soc. Regional Anesthesia (bd. dirs. 1979-91, pres. 1989-90, Disting. Svc. award, 1998), Assn. Anesthetists Gt. Britain and Ireland, Ohio State Med. Assn., Cleve. Acad. Medicine, Am. Acad. Med. Infrared Imaging (bd. dirs. 1991-95, pres. 1994-95, William Hobbins Rsch. award 1993), Am. Acad. Disability Evaluating Physicians (adv. com. mem. complex regional pain syndrome 2000—02), Am. Pain Soc., Am. Acad. Pain Medicine, Am. Neuromodulation Soc. (pres. 1994-98, bd. dirs. 1998—), Army-Navy-Air Force Club. Republican. Anglican. Avocations: skiing, photography, travel, flying. Home: 11405 Clearfield Lane Chardon OH 44024 Office: Cleve Clinic Found 9500 Euclid Ave Cleveland OH 44195-0001 Office Phone: 216-445-9559. E-mail: stantom@ccf.org.

STANZIONE, DANIEL C. communications company executive; b. Yonkers, N.Y. BSEE, Clemson U., 1967, MS in Envrion. Systems Engring., 1968, PhD in Elec. and Computer Engring., 1972. Former pres. Bell Labs, Network Sys. Group, 1995-99; former exec. v.p., COO Lucent Technologies, Inc., Murray Hill, N.J., chief network architect, 1999—. Bd. dirs. Quest Diagnostics, Inc., Zhone Technologies, Inc., Flavion Techs., Avaya, Inc. Contbr. articles to profl. jours. and publs.; patentee in field. Bd. overseers N.J. Inst. of Technology; chmn. engring. adv. bd. Hampton U. Fellow IEEE. Office: Lucent Technologies Inc 600 Mountain Ave New Providence NJ 07974-2008

STAPLES, DAVID M. corporate financial executive; B in Acctg., Mich. State U. Audit and bus. adv. practice Arthur Andersen LLP, 1985—96; divisional v.p., strategic planning and reporting Kmart Corp., 1996—2000; v.p. fin. Spartan Stores, Grand Rapids, Mich., 2000, exec. v.p., CRO, 2000—. Office: Spartan Stores PO Box 8700 Grand Rapids MI 49518-8700

STAPLES, DONALD EDWARD, radio, film and television educator; b. N.Y.C., Apr. 15, 1934; s. Edward Daniel and Ethlyne Babcock Staples; m. Diane Staunton, June 2, 1956 (div. July 1980); children: Douglas Arthur, Daniel Charles; m. Kristen Petersen, Nov. 26, 1982; stepchildren: Julia Lynn Smith, Susan Smith Milner. BS in Speech, Northwestern U., 1955; MA in Cinema, U. So. Calif., 1959; PhD, Northwestern U., 1967. Instr. So. Ill. U., Carbondale, 1959-63; lectr. Northwestern U., Evanston, Ill., 1963-65; asst. prof. Ohio State U., Columbus, 1965-68, assoc. prof., 1968-69; prof. NYU, N.Y.C., 1969-79, Vassar Coll., Poughkeepsie, N.Y., 1972-74, U. North Tex., Denton, 1979—. Author, editor: American Cinema, 3d edit., 1991; co-author: Film Encounter, 1973; contbr. articles, film revs. to profl. jours. Mem. Greater Denton Arts Coun., 1980—, Denton Cmty. Theatre, 1980—; bd. dirs. Nat. Mus. Comms., Irving, Tex., 1983-93; juror film festivals, 1969—; mem. adv. bd. Arts and Humanities Citation Index, Phila., 1979—. Lt. (j.g.) USN, 1955-57. Univ. scholar U. So. Calif., 1957-59, Northwestern U., 1963-65; Danforth Found. assoc., 1968-85. Mem. SAG, Soc. for Cinema Studies (pres. 1974-75), Univ. Film and Video Assn. (pres. 1975-77, life mem.), Internat. Congress of Schs. of Film and TV (v.p. 1982-86), Univ. Film and Video Found. (trustee emeritus), Dallas Corinthian Yacht Club (bd. dirs. 1995-98). Methodist. Avocations: sailing, golf. Home: 2901 Montecito Dr Denton TX 76205-8513 Office: U North Tex Dept Radio/TV/Film Denton TX 76203

STAPLES, LYLE NEWTON, lawyer; b. Radford, Va., Feb. 16, 1945; s. Lester Lyle and Velma Jean (King) S.; m. Christie Mercedes Carr, Feb. 1, 1971; children: Scott Andrew, John Randolph, Brian Matthew, Melissa Ann. BA, U. Md., 1967, JD, 1972; LLM in Taxation, Georgetown U., 1977. Bar: Md. 1973, U.S. Supreme Ct. 1978, U.S. Tax Ct. 1981, U.S. Dist. Ct. Md. 1981, U.S. Ct. Appeals (4th cir.) 1981. Tax law specialist IRS, Washington, 1972-77; assoc. Hessey & Hessey, Balt., 1978-82, Rosenstock, Burgee & Welty, Frederick, Md., 1982-84; sole practice Hampstead, Md., 1984-91; mem. firm Johnson, Parker & Hess, Westminster, Md., 1991-96; pvt. practice Westminster, 1996—. Vis. asst. prof. Towson (Md.) State U., 1981—82. Treas., bd. dirs. Literacy Coun. of Carroll County, Inc., 1993-98. Served with U.S. Army, 1968-69, Vietnam. Mem. ABA, Md. Bar Assn., Fin. Planning Assn., Carroll County C. of C. Democrat. Methodist. Home: 813 Clearview Ave Hampstead MD 21074-2325 Office: Ste 210 79 E Main St Westminster MD 21157-5026 Office Phone: 410-840-2000. E-mail: lstaples@infionline.net.

STAPLES, RICHARD FARNSWORTH, lawyer; b. Providence, Nov. 24, 1919; s. Harold E. and Margaret (Smith) S.; m. Mary Kingsbury, June 20, 1942; children: Richard Farnsworth, Jr., Benjamin T., Edward K. AB, Harvard U., 1941, LLB, 1949. Bar: R.I. 1949. Ptnr. Tillinghast, Collins & Graham, Providence, 1949-81, Hinckley, Allen & Snyder, Providence, 1981-87, of counsel, 1987—. Mem. commn. on jud. tenure and discipline, 1987-93; mem. ethics adv. panel R.I. Supreme Ct., 1995-97. Chmn. sch. com. Town of Barrington (R.I.), 1956-62, mem., 1957-62; mem. State Bd. Edn., Providence, 1964-69, chmn., 1968-69; pres. R.I. Hist. Soc., 1981-83. Served to 1st lt. U.S. Army, 1943-46. Decorated Bronze Star Mem. ABA, R.I. Bar Assn., Soc. Colonial Wars, Providence Art Club, Harvard Club. Home: 229 Medway St # 104 Providence RI 02903-5723 also: 79 Loon Lake Rd Freedom NH 03836-0298 Office Phone: 401-274-2000.

STAPLES, THORI YVETTE, former soccer player; b. Balt., Apr. 17, 1974; Student in sports mgmt., N.C. State U. Asst. women's soccer coach Va. Poly. Inst. and State U. Mem. silver medal U.S. squad1993 World Univ. Games, Buffalo; mem. 3d-place U.S. team FIFA Women's World Cup, Sweden, 1995; alt. U.S. Olympic Team, 1996; 1994 NSCAA All-Am.; 3-time All-Atlantic Coast Conf. and All-South Region selection for N.C. State U. Wolfpack. Nominee Mo. Athletic Club Nat. Player of Yr., 1994, 1995; named winner N.C. state championships in long jump, 400-meter dash, 800-meter run, ACC Rookie of Yr., 1994, 5-yr. player, Columbia (Md.) Crusaders; recipient Gold medal heptathlon, Nat. Amateur Athletic Union Jr. Olympics, 1991, 1992. Office: US Soccer Fedn 1801-1811 S Prairie Ave Chicago IL 60616

STAPLETON, BEVERLY COOPER, aerospace company executive; b. Birmingham, Ala., June 4, 1933; d. Herston MacAger and Virginia (Averyt) Cooper; m. John Parker Stapleton, Aug. 31, 1959 (div. July 1981); children: Lisa Karen, Lawrence Cooper. BBA magna cum laude, U. Miami, 1954; MA, U. Ala., 1960. Tchr. Miami Beach (Fla.) H.S., Dade County Pub. Schs., 1956-59; mem. behavior R & D program U. Ala., Tuscaloosa, 1959-61; contracts adminstr. Houghton Mifflin Co., Palo Alto, Calif., 1974-78; Calif. sales rep. Prentice-Hall Inc., San Jose, 1978; contract adminstr., cost analyst United Techs., Sunnyvale, Calif., 1978-82; mgr. contract adminstrn. Echo Sci. Corp., Mountain View, Calif., 1982; contracts mgr. Lockheed Martin Corp. Missiles & Space, Sunnyvale, 1982-98; ret., 1998. Instr. master's program in contracts and materiel mgmt. St. Mary's Coll., Moraga, Calif., 1984-85; mem. adv. bd. grad. program in contracts and acquisition mgmt. Golden Gate U., San Francisco, 1984-85; contracts mgr. Hubble Space Telescope Program, 1983-85. Fellow in polit. sci. U. Ala., 1954-55; recipient Women of Achievement award Santa Clara County Commn. on Status of Women, 1985. Fellow Nat. Contract Mgmt. Assn. (cert., pres. San Francisco area chpt. 1984-85, nat. coun. fellows 1983—, nat. exec. com. 1986-88, nat. bd. dirs. 1985-86, 97-98, nat. v.p. 1987-88), Beta Gamma Sigma, Delta Delta Delta. Democrat. Presbyterian. Home: 3728 Rhoda Dr San Jose CA 95117-3421

STAPLETON, COREY, financial planner; b. Seattle, Sept. 17, 1967; BS, U.S. Naval Acad., 1992; MA, Temple U., 1995. Commd. officer USN, 1986, advanced through grades, 1997; fin. planner Prudential Ind. Fin. Svcs., 1997—. Mem. Midland Empire Pachyderm Club, 1998—; campaign aide Bob Dole for Pres. Campaign, 1996; campaign mgr. Norm Mills, Mont. State House Dist. 19, 1998; chair Yellowstone County Young Reps., 1999-2000. Mem. Am. Legion, Billings C. of C., Rotary. Office: 2015 Eastridge Dr Billings MT 59102-7904 E-mail: stapletonct@aol.com.

STAPLETON, CRAIG ROBERTS, ambassador; m. Dorothy Walker, 1971; 2 children. Real estate exec., pres. Marsh and McLennan Real Estate Advisors, Inc., N.Y., NY, 1982—2001; U.S. amb. to Czech Republic, 2001—. Former ptnr. with George W. Bush Texas Rangers, 1989—98. Former bd. dirs. Peace Corps; trustee Brunswick Sch., Greenwich, Conn.; vis. com., other coms. Harvard Univ. Office: DOS Amb 5630 Prague Pl Washington DC 20521

STAPLETON, HARVEY JAMES, physics educator; b. Kalamazoo, Dec. 22, 1934; s. Herbert James and Viola Delia (Early) S.; m. Joan Eilleen Sylvander, June 22, 1957; children: Patricia Lynne, Susan Joan, Jeffrey Denis. BS, U. Mich., 1957; PhD, U. Calif., Berkeley, 1961. Faculty physics U. Ill., Urbana, 1961—, prof., 1969-95, prof. emeritus, 1995—, assoc. dean Grad. Coll., 1980-95, assoc. vice chancellor for rsch., 1987-95; interim dean Grad. Coll., 1992; interim vice chancellor for rsch. U. Ill., 1992. Alfred P. Sloan fellow, 1962-64 Contbr. articles to profl. jours. Fellow Am. Phys. Soc.; mem. Phi Beta Kappa, Sigma Xi, Phi Sigma Kappa, Phi Kappa Phi, Phi Eta Sigma. Roman Catholic. Home: 3806 Gulf Of Mexico Dr Unit 310 Longboat Key FL 34228-2733 E-mail: hjstapleton@earthlink.net.

STAPLETON, JAMES FRANCIS, lawyer; b. Bridgeport, Conn., June 30, 1932; s. James M. and Lucy V. (Moran) S.; m. Margaret M. Daly, July 13, 1957; children: James F., Mark T., Paul and Kathleen. BSS, Fairfield U., 1954; LLB, Boston Coll., 1957; LLM, Georgetown U., 1958. Bar: Conn. 1957, U.S. Dist. Ct. (ea. and so. dists.) N.Y. 1979, U.S. Ct. Appeals (2d cir.) 1966, U.S. Dist. Ct. Conn. 1961, Mass. 1957, U.S. Supreme Ct. 1965, U.S. Ct. Appeals (D.C. cir.) 1958. Atty., Appellate Sect., Antitrust Divsn. U.S. Dept. Justice, 1957-58; assoc., ptnr. Marsh, Day & Calhoun, Bridgeport, 1958-73; city atty. City of Bridgeport, 1971-73; legis. counsel Conn. Bankers Assn., 1971-73; judge Conn. Superior Ct., 1973-78; chmn. Criminal Justice Commn. State of Conn., 1991-95; ptnr. Day, Berry & Howard, Stamford, Conn., 1978—2002, of coun., 2003—. Active Bridgeport Bd. Edn., 1960—69. Fellow Am. Bar Found., Am. Coll. Trial Lawyers (chmn. state com. 1994-96, regent 1996-2000); mem. ABA (ho. of dels. 1984-88), Am. Bd. Trial Advocates, Conn. Bar Assn. (bd. govs., ho. of dels., v.p., pres.), Fed. Bar Coun. Found. for 2d Cir. (v.p., chmn.). Home: 225 Winton Rd Fairfield CT 06430-3858 Office: Day Berry & Howard One Canterbury Green Stamford CT 06901 Office Phone: 203-977-7300. E-mail: jfstapleton@dbh.com.

STAPLETON, JAMES HALL, statistician, educator; b. Royal Oak, Mich., Feb. 8, 1931; s. James Leo and Dorothy May (Hall) S.; m. Alicia M. Brown, Apr. 3, 1963; children: James, Lara, Sara. BA, Eastern Mich. U., 1952; MS, Purdue U., 1954, PhD, 1957. Statistician Gen. Electric Co., 1957-58; asst. prof. stats. and probability Mich. State U., East Lansing, 1958-63, assoc. prof., 1963-72, prof., 1972—, chmn. dept., 1968-75, grad. dir., 1985—. Cons. Gen. Telephone Co. of Ind.; vis. prof. U. Philippines, 1978-79 Mem. USS-Mich. Swim Com., AAU, 1976-84, chmn., 1976-78; mem. Mich. AAU Exec. Bd., 1976-81. NSF fellow, 1966-67 Mem. Inst. Math. Stats., Am. Statis. Assn. Office: Mich State U Dept Statistics East Lansing MI 48823 Office Phone: 517-355-9678. E-mail: stapleton@stt.msu.edu.

STAPLETON, JEAN, journalism educator; b. Albuquerque, June 24, 1942; d. James L. and Mary (Behrman) S.; m. John Clegg, Apr. 15, 1965 (dec. Sept. 1972); m. Richard Bright, Jan. 13, 1973 (div. 1985); children: Lynn, Paul Bright; m. William Walter Farran, Nov. 9, 1996. BA, U. N.Mex., 1964; MS in Journalism, Northwestern U., 1968. Reporter Glenview (Ill.) Announcements, 1967-68, Angeles Mesa News Advertiser, L.A., 1968-69, City News Svc., Radio News West, L.A., 1969-71; press sec. polit. campaign, 1972; instr. journalism East L.A. Coll., 1973-75, prof., dept. chair, 1975—. Author: Equal Marriage, 1975, Equal Dating, 1979. Mem. NOW (pres. L.A. chpt. 1973-74), Assn. Women in Comm., Soc. Profl. Journalists, Ninety Nines, L.A. Poets Writers Collective. Democrat. Methodist. Home: 3232 Philo St Los Angeles CA 90064-4719 Office: East LA Coll 1301 Avenida Cesar Chavez Monterey Park CA 91754-6001 Office Phone: 323-265-8875.

STAPLETON, KATHARINE HALL (KATIE STAPLETON), food broadcaster, writer; m. Benjamin Franklin Stapleton; children: Benjamin Franklin III, Craig Roberts, Katharine Hall. BA, Vassar Coll., 1941. Prodr., writer, host Cooking with Katie Sta. KOA, 1979—89. Author: Denver Delicious, 1980, 3d edit., 1983, High Notes, 1985-. Chmn. women's divsn. United Fund, 1955-56; founder, chmn. Denver Debutante Ball, 1956, 57; hon. chmn. Nat. Travelers Aid Assn., 1952-56, 93-96; commr. Denver Centennial Authority, 1958-60; trustee Washington Cathedral, regional v.p., 1967-73; trustee Colo. Women's Coll., 1975-80; sole trustee Harmes C. Fishback Found.; hon. chmn. Le Bal à Versailles, 2000, 02, 04. Decorated Chevalier de L'Etoile Noire, France; recipient People-to-People citations, 1960, 66, Beautiful Activist award, Colo.-Wyo. Restaurant Assn. award, 1981, Humanitarian of Yr. award Arthritis Found., 1995, Arts award Colo. Symphony, 1998; named Chevalier de Tastevin, 1989, Comdr., 2004, Outstanding Vol. Fundraiser, Nat. Philanthropy Day, 1995, Outstanding Alumna, Barstow Sch., 2003, Comdr., 2004. Mem. Denver Country Club. Republican. Episcopalian. Home: 8 Village Rd Cherry Hills Village CO 80113-4908

STAPLETON, MARYLYN ALECIA, diplomat; b. St. Thomas, V.I., Sept. 25, 1936; d. Lambert George and Aletha C. (Callendar) John; m. Frank Stapleton, Oct. 22, 1967 (div. Apr. 1983); 1 child, Linda E. Student, Washington Bus. Inst., 1959. Reservations agt. Caribair Airlines, St. Thomas, 1954-56; sales clk. Macy's Dept. Store, N.Y.C., 1956-57, Gift Shop, N.Y.C., 1957-63; supr. Ea. Airlines, Inc., N.Y.C. and St. Thomas, 1964-86; travel cons. Caribbean Travel Agy., St. Thomas, 1986-87; asst. commr. Dept. Licensing and Consumer Affairs, Govt. of V.I., St. Thomas, 1987-95, dep. of planning and natural resources, 1995—, small bus. tech. assistance program coord., 1995—; state exec. dir. Internat. Assn. Plumbing Mech. Officials, 1999—. Owner, pres. Stapleton Enterprises, St. Thomas, 1989—. Pub. rels. officer Nevis Benevolent Soc., St. Thomas, 1966-85; state chair Dem. party V.I., 1986—, dist. chair, 1984-86; small bus. ombudsman Clean Air Act of 1990, 1998—. Recipient Legis. Resolution V.I. Legislature, St. Thomas, 1986. Mem. Internat. Assn. Plumbing and Mech. Ofcls., Nat. Assn. of Plumbing, Heating and Cooling Contrs., St. Thomas/St. John Plumbing Assn. (pres. 1995—), St. Thomas Lioness Club (treas. 1985-86, pagent chair 1986-87, pres. 1987-88, mem. chair 1988-89, Melvin Jones fellow 1989), Lions Club of Charlotte Amalie. Democrat. Anglican. Home: 148-87 Est Annas Retreat PO Box 303739 Saint Thomas VI 00803-3739 Office: Democratic Party of Virgin Islns PO Box 3739 Saint Thomas Charlotte Amalie VI 00801

STAPLETON, MICHAEL, information technology executive; PhD, Southampton U. Rschr. Brit. Petroleum; v.p. Molecular Simulations Inc.; COO Accelrys Inc. Office: Accelrys Inc 9685 Scranton Road San Diego CA 92121-3752

STAPLETON, SHERYL WILLIAMS, state representative; b. July 30, 1957; m. Edreade Stapleton; children: David, Veronica. BEd, N.Mex. State U., 1978; MA, U. N.Mex., 1987, edn. specialist, edn. adminstrn., 1990. Sch.-to-careers coord. Albuquerque Pub. Schs.; state rep. dist. 19 N.Mex. Ho. of Reps., Santa Fe, 1995—, chair, labor and human resources com., mem. N.Mex. fin. authority oversight interim com., mem. legis. edn. study interim com., edn. com., and legis. health and human svcs. interim com. Vice chair, state chair N.Mex. Dem. Party. Democrat. Office: State Capitol Room 312A Santa Fe NM 87503

STAPLETON, WALTER KING, federal judge; b. Cuthbert, Ga., June 2, 1934; s. Theodore Newton and Elizabeth Grantland (King) Stapleton; m. Georgianna Duross Stapleton; children: Russell K., Theodore N., Teryl J. BA, Princeton, 1956; LLB, Harvard, 1959; LLM, U. Va., 1984. Bar: Del. Assoc. Morris, Nichols, Arsht & Tunnell, Wilmington, Del., 1959—65; dep. atty. gen. State of Del., 1963—64; ptnr. Morris, Nichols, Arsht & Tunnell, 1966—70; judge U.S. Dist. Ct., Wilmington, Del., 1970—85, chief judge, 1983—85; judge U.S. Ct. Appeals (3d cir.), 1985—99, sr. judge, 1999—. Mem. Jud. Conf. US, 1984—85. Bd. dirs. Am. Bapt. Chs., 1978. Mem.: ABA, Del. Bar Assn., Am. Jud. Soc. Baptist. Office: US Ct Appeals 844 N King St Wilmington DE 19801-3519

STAPP, DAN ERNEST, retired lawyer, utilities executive; b. New Orleans, July 1, 1934; s. James Frank, Jr. and Marguerite Edna (Joubert) S.; m. Barbara Allan Wilmot, June 10, 1961; children: Marguerite Wilmot (dec.), Mary Darby, Paul Wilmot (dec.), James Andrew. BBA, Loyola U., New Orleans, 1955, LL.B., 1957. Bar: La. 1957. With New Orleans Pub. Service Inc., 1958-68, asst. to v.p., 1965-68; with Entergy Svcs. (formerly MSU System Svcs. Inc.), New Orleans, 1968-92; v.p., sec., asst. treas. Entergy Svcs., 1968-80, sr. v.p., 1980-92. Sec. System Fuels, Inc., New Orleans, 1972-92, Entergy Corp. (formerly Middle South Utilities, Inc.), New Orleans, 1974-92, Systems Entergy Resources, Inc., Jackson, Miss., 1974-91, Electec, Inc., 1984-91, Entergy Ops., Inc., 1990-91, Entergy Power, Inc., 1990-92. Trustee Mercy Hosp., New Orleans, 1973-80, pres., 1975, chmn. bd. devel., 1971-72; mem. pres.'s coun. Loyola U., 1975-85, chmn., 1980-82; adv. coun. Coll. Bus. Adminstrn., 1969-70; mem. adv. bd. Asso. Cath. Charities, 1979-82; gen. chmn. United Way Greater New Orleans, 1978, trustee, 1978-84; mem. exec. bd. New Orleans Area coun. Boy Scouts Am., 1980-85, pres., 1984-85. 2d lt. AUS, 1957. Mem. ABA, La. Bar Assn., New Orleans Country Club, Pickwick Club, Blue Key (past chpt. pres.), Alpha Sigma Nu, Delta Theta Phi. Republican. Roman Catholic. Home: 401 Bellaire Dr New Orleans LA 70124-1014

STAPP, OLIVIA BREWER, opera singer; b. N.Y.C., May 31, 1940; d. Henry and Jean Brewer; m. Henry Stapp III; 1 child, Henry. BA, Wagner Coll; studied with, Marjorie Mayer Steen, Ettore Campogalliani, Rodolfo Ricci and Oren Brown; Dr. honoris causa, Wagner Coll., 1988. Artistic dir. Festival Opera, N.Y.C., 1995—, Walnut Creek, Calif., 1995—. Appeared as leading soprano in Turandot, Idomeno at La Scala, Milano; Tosca, Elektra, Macbeth, Tabarro at Met. Opera, N.Y.C.; Ernani, Macbeth, Il Tabarro at Liceo Barcelona; Macbeth, Madame Butterfly, Tosca, Aida, Fanciulla del West, Lohengrin at Deutche Oper Berlin; Vespre Siciliani at Grand Theater, Geneva; Nabucco, Attila, Macbeth at Zurich Oper; Salome at The Colon Theater, Buenos Aires; Cavalleria Rusticana, Anna Bolena, Tosca, Nabucco at San Francisco; Elektra Cavalleria Rusticana at Vienna Staatsoper; Idomeneo at Munich Staatsoper; Carmen, The Consul, Ariadne auf Naxos, Anna Bolena, Roberto Deveraux, Cavalleria Rusticana at City Opera, N.Y.C.; Lady Macbeth, Nabucco, Turandot at Hamburg Staatsoper; Fanciulla del West, Aida, Nabucco, Turandot at the Arena de Verona; Turandot at Seoul, Korea; Turandot in N.H.K. Tokyo; Norma in Winnipeg, Edmonton, Montreal and Vancouver, Can.; Lady Macbeth in Chatelet Theater, Paris, others. Recipient Puccini award Vissi d'Arte, 1991, prize City of Genoa, Italy; Fulbright scholar; Sterling Patron, Mu Phi Epsilon. Address: Festival Opera Ste B215 675 Ygnacio Valley Rd Walnut Creek CA 94596-3828

STAPRANS, ARMAND, electronics executive; b. Riga, Latvia, Feb. 28, 1931; s. Theodore and Elvira (Ulmanis) S.; m. Vija Spalvins, Sept. 25, 1955; children: Silvija, Armin, Erik. Student, Willamette U., 1949-52; BSEE, U. Calif., Berkeley, 1954, MSEE, 1955, PhDEE, 1959. Rsch. asst. dept. elec. engring. U. Calif., 1955-57; engr. microwave tube div. Varian Assocs., Palo Alto, Calif., 1957-60, engring. mgr., 1960-68, ops. mgr., 1978-78, 86-89, chief engr., 1978-86, gen. mgr. coupled cavity tube divsn., 1989-92, v.p., 1990-95; gen. mgr. microwave power tube products, 1992-95; pres. microwave power tube products divsn. Comms. and Power Inds., Palo Alto, Calif., 1995-98; mgmt. cons., 1999—. Contbr. articles to profl. jours., chpt. to book; patentee microwave tubes field. Fellow IEEE (electron device adminstrv. com. 1983-88). Home: 445 Knoll Dr Los Altos CA 94024-4732 Office: Comm & Power Inds M S B 100 Microwave Power Tube Prod Divsn PO Box 50750 Palo Alto CA 94303-0665 E-mail: AStaprans@aol.com.

STARBUCK, SUSAN, literature educator, writer; b. Summit, N.J., Feb. 7, 1945; PhD, U. Wash., 1978. Core faculty Antioch U., Seattle, 1994—. Pres., founder Women's Heritage, Seattle, 1984—88. Author: Hazelwolf: Fighting the Establishment, 2002. Avocations: photography, gardening. Office: Antioch Univ Seattle 2326 6th Ave Seattle WA 98122

STARBUCK, WILLIAM HAYNES, business management educator; b. Portland, Ind., Sept. 20, 1934; AB in Physics, Harvard Coll., 1956; MS in Indsl. Adminstrn., Carnegie Inst. Tech., 1959, PhD in Indsl. Adminstrn., 1964; PhD (hon.), U. Stockholm, 1995, U. Paris, 2004. Instr. indsl. mgmt. and econs. Purdue U., West Lafayette, Ind., 1960-64, from asst. prof. to assoc. prof. adminstrv. scis. and econs., 1964-67; prof. adminstrn. Grad. Sch. Bus. and Pub. Adminstrn. Cornell U., 1967-71, prof. sociology Coll. Arts and Scis., 1968-71; sr. rsch. fellow Internat. Inst. Mgmt., Berlin, 1971—74; Helfaer prof. bus. adminstrn. U. Wis., Milw., 1974-84; ITT prof. creative mgmt. NYU, N.Y.C., 1985—. Vis. assoc. prof. social rels. Johns Hopkins U., 1966—67; vis. prof. adminstrn. London Grad. Sch. Bus. Studies, 1970—71; chmn. Coll. on Orgn., Inst. Mgmt. Scis., 1973—74; rsch. prof. U. Wis., Milw., 1974—75; vis. prof. Norwegian Sch. Econs. and Bus. Adminstrn., Bergen, 1977—78, Stockholm Sch. Econs., U. Gothenburg, Sweden, 1977—78, U. Versailles, 1998, U. Canterbury, 1999, U. Paris IX, 1999, U. Oreg., 1999, U. Aix-Marseilles, 2000, 03, U. Oxford, 2004; dir. doctoral program Grad. Sch. Bus. Adminstrn., NYU, 1985—89; mem. rsch. adv. com. USAF Pers. Rsch. Lab., 1966—69. Mem. editl. bd. Adminstrv. Sci. Quar., 1966—68, 1982—85, Jour. Applied Social Psychology, 1970—78, Jour. Mgmt. Studies, 1978—, Scandinavian Jour. Mgmt., 1984—, Jour. Behavioral Econs./Jour. Socioecons., 1988—, Brit. Jour. Mgmt., 1989—, Acctg. Mgmt. and Info. Techs., 1989—2000, Jour. Mgmt. Inquiry, 1991—, Organization, 1993—, Asian Case Rsch. Jour., 1997—, Internat. Jour. Mgmt. Revs., 1998—, Info. and Orgn., 2001; editor: Adminstrv. Sci. Quar., 1968—71, The Programmer's Corner, ICON, 1984—85; contbr. articles to profl. jours. Fulbright Rsch. fellow U. Gothenburg, 1977-78. Fellow: APA, Soc. Indsl. Orgnl. Psychology, Brit. Acad. Mgmt., Am. Psychol. Soc., Acad. Mgmt. (bd. govs. 1991—99, v.p. 1994—97, pres. 1997—98, editl. bd. Acad. Mgmt. Rev. 1981—86); mem.: NSF (adv. panel rsch. mgmt. improvement program 1974), Coun. Internat. Exch. Scholars (adv. screening com. for Sr. Fulbright awards in bus. mgmt. 1981—83, chmn. 1983—84). Office: Stern Sch Bus 40 W 4th St New York NY 10012-1118 Home: 17 G 2 Washington Square Vlg New York NY 10012-1732 Office Phone: 212-998-0232. Business E-Mail: wstarbuc@stern.nyu.edu.

STARCHER, LARRY VICTOR, state supreme court justice; b. Rocksdale, W.Va., Sept. 25, 1942; AB cum laude, W.Va. U., 1964, JD, 1967. Bar: W.Va. 1967. Judge and chief judge W.Va. Ct. (17th jud. cir.), 1977—96; justice W.Va. Supreme Ct. Appeals, 1997—, chief justice, 2003—. Pvt. practice, Morgantown, 1976—; dir. North Ctrl. W.Va. Legal Aid Soc., 1969-76; former instr. law, pub. adminstrn., and history W.Va. U.; contract adminstr. W.Va. U., 1966-67, asst. to v.p., 1967-69. Editor W.Va. Law Rev.; contbr. articles to profl. jours. Mem. City Coun. Morgantown, 1971-72; mem. W.Va. Martin Luther King, Jr. Holiday Commn. Fellow Harvard U., summer 1978. Mem. ATLA, Am. Correctional Assn., W.Va. Jud. Assn., W.Va. State Bar, Monongalia County Bar Assn., Kanawha County Bar Assn., Conf. Chief Justices, Beta Theta Pi, Phi Delta Phi, Phi Alpha Theta, Pi Sigma Alpha. Avocations: carpentry, gardening. Office: Supreme Ct Appeals State Capitol Rm E 307 Charleston WV 25305

STARCHER-DELL'AQUILA, JUDY LYNN, special education educator; b. Cuyahoga Falls, Ohio, Sept. 20, 1956; d. James Calvin and Jane Yvonne (Hart) Starcher; m. Richard Paul Dell'Aquila, July 16, 1983; 1 child, Jessica Lynn Dell'Aquila. BS in Hearing & Speech Scis., Ohio U., 1978; MEd in Deaf Edn., U. Cin., 1980; PhD in Spl. Edn., Kent State U., 1996. Cert. supr. and tchr., Ohio. Tchr. deaf Parma (Ohio) City Schs., 1978-79, Mayfield (Ohio) City Schs., 1980-81; tchr. deaf, low incidence work study coord. Trumbull County Ednl. Svc. Ctr., Warren, Ohio, 1981-84; work study coord. Cuyahoga Ednl. Svc. Ctr., Valley View, Ohio, 1984-88; instr., student tchg. supr. Kent (Ohio) State U., 1993-95; project dir. Children's Hosp. Med. Ctr./Family Child Learning Ctr., Tallmadge, Ohio, 1995-2000; coord. spl. edn. Cleveland Heights/University Heights (Ohio) City Sch. System, 2000—. Am. Sign Lang. instr. Cuyahoga C.C., Cleve., 1993-2000; dir. adv. bd. Hearing Impaired Toddler Infant & Families Program, Tallmadge, 1995-2000; mem. County Collaborative Group, Medina, Summit counties, Ohio, 1995-2000; state trainer SKI—HI, Logan, Utah, 1997—. Mem. Coun. Exceptional Children. Grantee Job Tng. & Partnership Act, Cleve., 1982, 86-88; Univ. fellow Kent State U., 1991. Democrat. Avocations: antique collector, exercise, reading. Home: 151 E Pleasant Valley Rd Seven Hills OH 44131-5601 Office: Cleveland Hgts/Univ Hgts Bd Edn 2155 Miramar Blvd University Heights OH 44118

STARCHMAN, DALE EDWARD, medical educator; b. Wallace, Idaho, Apr. 16, 1941; s. Hubert V. and Lottie M. (Alford) S.; m. Erlinda Socrates, Dec. 13, 1969; children: Ann, Cindy, Julie, Mark. Student, Rockhurst Coll., 1959—61; BS in Physics, Pitts. (Kans.) State U., 1963; MS in Radiation Biophysics, U. Kans., 1965, PhD in Radiation Biophysics, 1968. Cert. Radiol. Physicist, Health Physicist, Med. Physicist. Chief health physicist IIT Rsch. Inst., Chgo., 1968-71; radiol. physicist Mercy Hosp. Inst. of Radiation Therapy, Chgo., 1968-71; prof., head radiation biophysics Northeast Ohio U. Coll. of Medicine, Rootstown, Ohio, 1971—; pres. Med. Physics Svcs., Inc., Canton, Ohio, 1971—. Author: (with Wayne R. Hedrick and David L. Hykes) Ultrasound Physics and Instrumentation, 3rd edit., 1995; contbr. numerous articles in profl. jours., chpts. in books, monographs. Fellow Am. Coll. Radiology; mem. Am. Assn. Physicists in Medicine (bd. mem. at large 1984-86, pres. Penn-Ohio chpt. 1975-76, rec. sec. midwest chpt. 1970, mem. edn. coun. 1980-83, chmn. Am. assn. med. dosimetrists task group 1976-78, mem. physics curriculum diagnostic residents task group 2003—, mem. numerous other coms. 1975-83), Health Physics Soc. (chmn. summer sch. sub. com. 1977-78), Radiol. Soc. N.Am. (assoc. scis. com. 1976-86, task force chmn. 1983-86, mem. 1975-86), Sigma Xi, Kappa Mu Epsilon. Achievements include research areas including selection, quality assurance and acceptance testing of diagnostic x-ray units, design of radiology facilities; effects of tissue inhomogeneities on electron therapy, radiation atrophy in bone, large field therapy swing technique, polymer dosimetry, photon spectra through thick shields, fetal effects, ultrasound, mammography. Home and Office: 5942 Easy Pace Cir NW Canton OH 44718-2216

STARCK, CHRISTIAN WALTER, jurist; b. Breslau, Germany, Jan. 9, 1937; s. Walter and Ruth (Hubrich) S.; m. Brigitte Edelmann, Aug. 31, 1965; children: Annette, Johannes, Marie-Christine. Student, U. Kiel, 1957, U. Freiburg, 1958-59; Dr. iur., U. Würzburg, 1963, Habil., 1969. Clk. Fed. Constl. Ct., 1964-67; govt. ofcl., 1968-69; lectr. U. Würzburg, 1969-71; prof. pub. law U. Göttingen, Germany, 1971—, rector, 1976-77; judge Constl. Ct. Lower Saxony, Germany, 1991—. Vis. prof. U. Paris-Sorbonne, 1987; mem. TV bd. Zweites Deutsches Fernsehen, 1978-92; pres. TV bd. ARTE, 1991-2000. Author: Der Gesetzesbegriff des Grundesetzes, 1970, Spanish edit., 1979, Das Bundesverfassungsgericht im politischen Prozess, 1976, Japanese edit., 1978, Der demokratische Verfassungsstaat, 1995, La Constitution, cadre et mesure du droit, 1994, Praxis der Verfassung auslegung, 1994, Das Bonner Grundgesetz Kommentar, 4th edit., 3 vols., 1999, 2000, 2001, Freiheit und Institutionen, 2002; editor: Studien und Materialien zur Verfassungsgerichtsbarkeit, 90 vols., 1973—; co-editor: Juristenzeitung, 1978—; contbr. over 200 articles to law jours. and festschriften, —. Fellow Inst. for Advanced Study, Berlin; mem. Internat. Assn. Constl. Law (exec. com. 1981-2004, hon. pres. 2004-), Acad. Scis. Göttingen, Assn. German Profs. Pub. Law (exec. com. 1988-89, pres. 1998-99), German Assn. Comparative Law (exec. com. 1986-), Soc. Luris Publici Europaei (pres. 2003-). Home: Schlegelweg 10 D-37075 Göttingen Germany Office: Georg August Univ Platz der Göttinger Sieben 6 D-37075 Göttingen Germany E-mail: c.starck@gwdg.de.

STARER, BRIAN DOUGLAS, lawyer; b. Utica, N.Y., 1945; BS, U.S. Merchant Marine Acad., 1967; JD, Union U., 1972. Bar: N.Y. 1972, U.S. Dist. Ct. (no., so. and ea. dists.) N.Y., U.S. Ct. Appeals (2nd, 3rd and 5th cirs.) 1973, U.S. Ct. Appeals (9th cir.) 1976, U.S. Supreme Ct. 1977, U.S. Ct. Internat. Trade 1977, U.S. Ct. Customs and Patent Appeals 1980. Mem. Haight Gardner Holland & Knight, N.Y.C.; dir., mem. mgmt. com. Holland & Knight, N.Y.C., 1997—. Mng. editor Albany Law Rev., 1971-72; contbr. articles to profl. jours. Named to, Internat. Maritime Hall of Fame, 2002. Mem. ABA, Maritime Law Assn. U.S., Internat. Bar Assn., N.Y. State Bar Assn. Office: Holland & Knight 195 Broadway Fl 24 New York NY 10007-3189 Office Phone: 212-513-3200. E-mail: brian.starer@hklaw.com.

STARFIELD, BARBARA HELEN, pediatrician, educator; b. Bklyn., Dec. 18, 1932; d. Martin and Eva (Illions) Starfield; m. Neil A. Holtzman, June 12, 1955; children: Robert, Jon, Steven, Deborah. AB, Swarthmore Coll., 1954; MD, SUNY, 1959; MPH, Johns Hopkins U., 1963. Tchg. asst. in anatomy Downstate Med. Ctr., N.Y.C., 1955—57; intern in pediat. Johns Hopkins U., 1959—60, resident, 1960—62, dir. pediatric med. care clinic, 1963—66, dir. cmty. staff comprehensive child care project, 1966—67, dir. pediatric clin. scholars program, 1971—76, prof. health policy, joint appointment in pediat.,

1975—, disting. univ. prof., 1994—. Mem. Nat. Com. Vital Stats., 1994—2002; cons. DHHS; mem. nat. adv. coun. Agy. for Health Care Policy and Rsch., 1990—94; adv. subcom. on Health Systems and Svcs. Rsch. Pan Am. Health Orgn., 1988—92, 1995—; cons. Health Care Fin. Adminstrn., 1980 . Editl. bd. Med. Care, 1977—79, Pediat., 1977—82, Internat. Jour. Health Svcs., 1978—, Med. Care Rev., 1980—84, Health Svc. Rsch., 1996—, assoc. editor Ann. Rev. Pub. Health, 1996—2001; contbr. articles to profl. jours. Recipient Dave Luckman Meml. award, 1958, HEW Career Devel. award, 1970—75, Disting. Investigator award, Assn. Health Svcs. Rsch., 1995, 1st Primary Care Achievement award, Pew Charitable Trust Fund, 1994, 1st Ann. Rsch. award, Ambulatory Pediatric Assn., 1990. Fellow: Am. Acad. Pediat.; mem.: APHA (Martha May Eliot award 1995), Internat. Soc. for Equity in Health (pres. 2000—02), Ambulatory Pediatric Assn. (pres. 1980), Internat. Epidemiologic Assn., Soc. Pediatric Rsch., Inst. Medicine of NAS (governing coun. 1981—83), Alpha Omega Alpha, Sigma Xi. Office: Johns Hopkins Sch Hygiene 624 N Broadway Baltimore MD 21205-1900

STARING, GRAYDON SHAW, lawyer; b. Deansboro, N.Y., Apr. 9, 1923; s. William Luther and Eleanor Mary (Shaw) S.; m. Joyce Lydia Allum-Poon, Sept. 1, 1949; children: Diana Hilary Agnes, Christopher Paul Norman. AB, Hamilton Coll., 1947; JD, U. Calif., Berkeley, 1951. Bar: Calif. 1952, U.S. Supreme Ct. 1958. Atty. Office Gen. Counsel, Navy Dept., San Francisco, 1952-53; atty. admiralty and shipping sect. U.S. Dept. Justice, San Francisco, 1953-60; assoc. Lillick & Charles (now Nixon Peabody), San Francisco, 1960-64, ptnr., 1965-95, of counsel, 1995—. Titulary mem. Internat. Maritime Com.; bd. dirs. Marine Exch. at San Francisco, 1984-88, pres. 1986-88; instr. pub. speaking Hamilton Coll., 1947-48; adj. prof. Hastings Coll. Law, 1996-97, Boalt Hall, U. Calif., 1999. Author: Law of Reinsurance, 1993; assoc. editor Am. Maritime Cases, 1966-92, editor, 1992—; contbr. articles to legal jours. Mem. San Francisco Lawyers Com. for Urban Affairs, 1972-90; bd. dirs. Legal Aid Soc., San Francisco, 1974-90, v.p., 1975-80, pres., 1980-82. With USN, 1943-46, comdr. USNR. Fellow Am. Bar Found., Am. Coll. Trial Lawyers; mem. ABA (chmn. maritime ins. com. 1975-76, mem. standing com. admiralty law 1976-82, 86-90, chmn. 1990, ho. dels. 1986-90), Fed. Bar Assn. (pres. San Francisco chpt. 1968), Bar Assn. San Francisco (sec. 1972, treas. 1973), Calif. Acad. Appellate Lawyers, Maritime Law Assn. U.S. (exec. com. 1977-88, v.p. 1980-84, pres. 1984-86), Brit.-Am. C. of C. (bd. dirs. 1987-2001), World Trade Club San Francisco, Tulane Admiralty Inst. (permanent adv. bd.), Assocs. Maritime Mus. Libr. (dir. 1990-2001, pres. 1992-94). Office: 2 Embarcadero Ctr Ste 2700 San Francisco CA 94111-3900 Office Phone: 415-984-8310. Personal E-mail: Starlaw@att.net. Business E-Mail: gstaring@nixonpeabody.com. *"How small, of all that human hearts endure,/That part which laws or kings can cause or cure!".*

STARK, ALBERT MAXWELL, lawyer; b. Trenton, N.J., May 3, 1939; m. Ellen Stark, Nov. 20, 1966; children: Jared, Rachel. BA, Darmouth Coll., Hanover, N.H., 1960; LLD, U. Pa., Phila., 1963. Bar: N.J. 1964. Asst. to gov. of N.J., 1964; asst. atty. City of Trenton, 1965-66; asst. prosecutor Mercer County, N.J., 1967-68. Author: Beyond the Bar - Challenges in the Life of a Lawyer, 2002; host radio programs Lawline, WHWH, 1985—95, In the Pub. Interest, WIMG, 1996. Recipient Humanitarian award Thomas A. Edison State Coll., 2000, award Trial Attys. of N.J., 2000. Mem. ABA, N.J. Bar Assn., Mercer County Bar Assn., Mercer County C. of C. (Citizen of Yr. 1994), Rotary Internat. (Fred Harris fellow 1996). Avocations: writing, tennis, skiing. Office: Stark & Stark 993 Lenox Dr Ste 301 Lawrenceville NJ 08648-2316

STARK, BRUCE GUNSTEN, artist; b. Queens, N.Y., Feb. 17, 1933; s. Richard M. and Karen (Gunsten) S.; m. Joan Patricia Lauer, Nov. 19, 1960; children: Robert, Ronald. Student, Sch. Visual Arts, N.Y.C., 1955-58. Artist, cartoonist N.Y. Daily News, N.Y.C., 1961—. One-man shows Art Inst., Pitts., 1968, U. Kutztown, Pa., 1970, N.Y. Bank for Savs., N.Y.C., 1971; group shows Nat. Art Mus. Sport, N.Y.C., 1971; represented in permanent collections Everett Dirksen Library, L.D. Johnson Library, Baseball Hall Fame, Cooperstown, N.Y., Basketball Hall Fame, Mass. Served with USN, 1952-54. Recipient Nat. Cartoonist Soc.'s Rueben Catagory awards for sports, 1966, 75, spl. features, 1968; Page One award for best sports cartoon, 1970, 73 N.Y.C., 71; 3d, 4th, 6th prizes Internat. Salon de Caricatures Montreal, 1966, 68, 69; Most Outstanding Achievement award Sch. Visual Arts, 1982 Achievements include having original cartoons requested by Pres. Nixon, Johnson; 1st color cartoon appearing on front page of N.Y. Daily News. Home: 3139 Stonewater Dr Lakeland FL 33803-2572 *My goals, ideas, principles and standards of conduct are all helpfully outlined for me by God in His holy word— the Bible. I really need no other source. Whatever success has come to me, I think, is because of this, and what God has done for me, through His Son, Jesus Christ.*

STARK, DENNIS EDWIN, bank executive, director; b. Springfield, Ill., Dec. 24, 1937; s. Edwin C. and Ida (Fentem) S. BS, Ill. Wesleyan U., 1959; Sanxay fellow practical ethics, Princeton U., 1959-60; MBA, Harvard U., 1962. Adminstrv. asst. to chmn. bd. Industrial Valley Bank, Phila., 1962-64; fin. analyst E.I. DuPont de Nemours, Wilmington, Del., 1964-65; asst. treas. Old Stone Bank, Providence, 1965-68, treas., 1968-71; sr. v.p., treas., sec. Old Stone Bank and Old Stone Corp., Providence, 1971-76; exec. v.p., chief fin. officer Old Stone Corp., Old Stone Bank, 1976-86, Dime Bank, N.Y.C., 1986-88; ptnr. Bank Mgmt. Ptnrs., N.Y.C., 1988-90; sr. v.p., CFO, corp. sec. Cen Fed Bank, Pasadena, Calif., 1990-92; exec. v.p., CFO, corp. sec. Ea. Bank, Lynn, Mass., 1992-96; ptnr. Fin. Mgmt. Ptnrs., Pawtucket, R.I., 1996-99; v.p. bus. and fin., CFO U. R.I., Kingston, 1999—2003; bank dir., exec. v.p., corp. sec. Ind. Bank, East Greenwich, RI, 2003—. Bd. dirs., chmn. fin. com. Preservation Soc. Pawtucket; mem. bd. visitors Ill. Wesleyan U., Bloomington; trustee, chmn. fin. com. Preserve R.I.; chmn. fin. com., mem. Diocesan Coun. Episcopal Diocese; mem. audit com. RISD; vestry, treas. St. Martins Episcopal Ch., Providence; dep. to gen. conv. Episcopal Ch. USA, mem. planning, budget and fin. commn.; bd. dirs. exec. com. and fin. com., chmn.strategic planning com. R.I. Philharm. Mem. Fin. Execs. Inst., Harvard Bus. Sch. Assn. of R.I., Acacia (co-founder Ill. Wesleyan U. chpt.), Providence Art Club, Hope Club, Univ. Club (R.I.), Harvard Club (N.Y.C.), Agawam Hunt, Dunes Club, Brown Faculty Club, U. R.I. Univ. Club (treas.). Republican. Episcopalian. Avocations: stamp collecting/philately, coin collecting/numismatics. Home (Summer): 41 Courtway St Narragansett RI 02882-3610 Office: Independence Bank 1370 South County Trail East Greenwich RI 02818 Office Phone: 401-471-6334. Business E-Mail: dstark@independence-bank.com. E-mail: destark@cox.net.

STARK, DIANA, public relations executive; b. N.Y.C., July 01; d. Benjamin and Sara (Zelasny) S. BA, Hunter Coll. Promotion mgr. TV Guide mag., N.Y.C., 1950-61, Show Bus. Illustrated, N.Y.C., 1961-62; broadcast specialist Young & Rubicam, N.Y.C., 1962-69; pres. Stark Comms. Inc., N.Y.C., 1969-76; pub. svc. publicity account exec. Y & R E, N.Y.C., 1976-77; pres. Stark Comms. Internat., N.Y.C., 1978—. Pub. rels. workshop leader Chgo. Econ. Devel. Corp., 1973-76; cons. to Asahi Shimbun for English Language Newsletter. 1991-92, columnist Host mag., 1960-65; writer, producer programs for women's TV shows, 1962—. Book developer Ellis Island: The First Experience With Liberty, 1991. Coord. We Have Arrived, Portraits at Ellis Island, Augustus Sherman Photographs, 1902-24. Mem. NATAS (trustee 1974-78, publicity com., chmn., chpt. gov. 1972-76, 82-86, 87-91, editor N.Y. TV Directory 1987-90). Office Fax: 212-765-3670.

STARK, EVELYN BRILL, poet, musician; b. N.Y.C., Sept. 12, 1913; d. Henry Brill and Rae Hessberg; m. Morton W. Stark, Apr. 27, 1933; 1 child, Henry. BA, Barnard Coll., 1933; artist student of Edouard Dethier, Juilliard Sch. Music, 1933-40. Bd. dirs., violinist Nat. Found. Mus. Therapy, N.Y.C., 1940-50; violinist ARC Hosp. Music Unit, N.Y.C., 1950-70, Hosp. Music Unit, Protestant Coun. Chs., N.Y.C., 1950-70; bd. dirs., violinist Music Therapy Ctr., N.Y.C., 1960-80; founder, sponsor Nora Hellen Music Friends, N.Y.C., 1970-80; ret., 1980. Author: My Search for the Infinite, 2002; mem. editl. bd. Music Jour., 1969-70; recorded tapes with original programs; author: (poetry) Never Apart, 1992, 2003; (autobiography) Life is a Poem, 1999; dramatic presentations of Life is a Poem, Hartford, Conn., 2000, Essex, Conn., 2000, Brooklyn, Conn., East Haddam, Conn., Middleton, Conn.; performer (record) All About the Violin, 1969; (CD) Journey of a Soul in Music via the Infinite Way, 2003; contbr. articles to profl. jours.; author numerous poems. Donated 3 violins (Amati, Carcassi, Gragnani) to the Met. Mus. Art, N.Y.C., 1974, 80, 97. Recipient 1st prize poetry award Altrusa Internat. Middletown, Conn., 1997-98; named Poet Laureate of Conn. Gilbert and Sullivan Soc., 1998; named to Internat. Poetry Hall of Fame, 1998. Mem. Internat. Soc. Poets. Address: 317 W Main St Chester CT 06412-1057

STARK, FORTNEY HILLMAN (PETE STARK), congressman; b. Milw., Nov. 11, 1931; s. Fortney Hillman Sr. and Dorothy M. (Mueller) S.; children: Jeffrey Peter, Beatrice Ann, Thekla Brumder, Sarah Gallun, Fortney Hillman Stark III; m. Deborah Roderick; children: Hannah Marie, Andrew Peter. BS In Engring., MIT, 1953; MBA, U. Calif. Berkeley, 1960. Teaching asst. MIT, Cambridge, 1953-54; prin. Skaife & Co., Berkeley, Calif., 1957-61; founder Beacon Savs. & Loan Assn., Antioch, Calif., 1961; pres., founder Security Nat. Bank, Walnut Creek, Calif., 1963-72; mem. U.S. Congress from 13th (formerly 9th) Calif. dist., 1973—; mem. ways and means com., formerly chmn., now ranking minority mem. health subcom.; mem.joint econ. com. Bd. dirs. ACLU, 1971, Common Cause, 1971, Starr King Sch.; del. Dem. State Cen. Com.; trustee Calif. Dem. Coun. Capt. USAF, 1955-57. Mem. Delta Kappa Epsilon. Democrat. Unitarian. Office: Ho of Reps 239 Cannon Ho Office Bldg Washington DC 20515-0001

STARK, GEORGE ROBERT, health science association administrator; b. N.Y.C., July 4, 1933; s. Jack and Florence (Israel) S.; m. Mary Susan Beck, Aug. 19, 1956; children: Robert Braden, Janna Elizabeth. BA in Chemistry, Columbia Coll., N.Y.C., 1955; PhD in Chemistry, Columbia Coll., 1959. Rsch. assoc., asst. prof. Rockefeller U., N.Y.C., 1959-63; asst. prof. dept. biochemistry Stanford (Calif.) U., 1963-66, assoc. prof., 1966-71, prof., 1971-83; sr. scientist Imperial Cancer Rsch. Fund, London, 1983-85, asst. dir. rsch., 1985-89, assoc. dir. rsch., 1989-92; chair Lerner Rsch. Inst. Cleve. Clinic Found., 1992—. Reilly lectr. Notre Dame U., 1972; mem. physiol. chemistry study sect. NIH, 1974-77, study sect. Am. Cancer Soc., 1981-83; mem. European Molecular Biology Orgn. Coun., 1990; mem. sci. com. Cancer Rsch. Campaign, 1990-92 Mem. editl. bd. Jour. Biol. Chemistry, 1970-75, Cell, 1983-88, European Molecular Biology Orgn. Jour., 1990-93; contbr. over 180 articles to profl. jours. including European Molecular Biology Orgn. Jour., Jour. Biol. Chemistry, Molecular Cellular Biology, Nature, Oncogene, Proceedings of the Nat. Acad. Scis., among others. Trustee Cleve. Playhouse, 1993—. Guggenheim fellow, 1970-71, Josiah Macy, Jr. fellow, 1977-78; Yamagiwa-Yoshida Study grantee Internat. Union Against Cancer, 1981; named H.A. Sober Meml. lectr. Am. Soc. Biol. Chemists. Fellow Royal Soc.; mem. NAS, Am. Soc. Biochemistry Molecular Biology (rep. U.S. nat. com. biochemistry 1995—), European Molecular Biology Orgn. Achievements include discoveries in enzyme chemisry, interferon signaling and mammalian genetics; contributions to methodology in protein chemistry and molecular biology. Home: 2900 W Park Blvd Shaker Heights OH 44120-1812 Office: Cleve Clinic Found 9500 Euclid Ave Cleveland OH 44195-0001

STARK, HENRY, technology educator; BSEE, CCNY, 1961; MSEE, Columbia U., 1964, D in Engring. Sci., 1968. Project engr. Bendix Corp., 1961—62; rsch. engr. Columbia U., N.Y.C., 1962—69; assoc. prof. Yale U., New Haven, 1970—77; prof. Rensselaer Poly. Inst., Troy, NY, 1977—87; prof., chmn. dept. Ill. Inst. Technology, Chgo., 1988—97; Bodine disting. prof. elec. and computer engring., 1988—. Co-author: Modern Electrical Communications: Theory and Systems, 1979, Probability, Random Processes and Estimation Theory for Engineers, 1986, Modern Electrical Communications: Analog, Digital and Optical Systems, 1988, Probability and Random Processes with Applications to Signal Processes, 2002, Vector Space Projections: A Numerical Approach to Signal and Image Processing, Neural Nets and Optics, 1998; editor: Applications of Optical Fourier Transforms, 1981, Image Recovery: Theory and Practice, 1987; co-editor: Signal Processing Methods for Audio, Images and Telecommunications, 1995; contbr. articles to profl. jours., chapters to books. Grantee, NSF. Fellow: IEEE, Optical Soc. Am. (Ester Hoffman Beller prize 2000). Office: Ill Inst Technology Dept Elec/Computer Engring 3301 S Dearborn Chicago IL 60616 E-mail: eestark@ece.iit.edu.

STARK, LARRY A. commissioner; BA in history, Ohio Wesleyan U.; JD, W.Va. U. Exec. v.p. Milton Tri-County Bank; v.p. investor rels. Key Centurion Bankshares; various positions Banc One W.Va.; commr. W.Va. Divsn. Banking, 2001—. Office: State Office Bldg #3 Charleston WV 25305-0240

STARK, MARTIN J. management consultant; b. N.Y.C., May 29, 1941; s. Nathan and Lola (Belmont) S.; m. Shigemi Matsumoto, Apr. 27, 1967; AA Glendale Coll., 1960; BA, Calif. State U., 1966; postgrad. San Fernando Valley Coll. Law, 1967-70. Systems analyst Industrial Electronic Engrs., Van Nuys, Calif., 1969-71; sales mgr., 1971-73; sales rep. Columbia Artists Mgmt., Inc., N.Y.C., 1973-78, sales mgr., 1978-79, v.p. bus. affairs, mgr. data processing, 1979-82; dir. corp. affairs Kolmar-Luth Entertainment, Inc., N.Y.C., 1982-84; pres. Oryx Corp., N.Y.C., 1984-85; exec. v.p. Asco Aerospace Products, Inc., El Segundo, Calif., 1985-87; exec. v.p. Internat. Engine Parts, Inc., Chatsworth, Calif., 1987-92; pres. Stark & Assocs., Northridge, Calif., 1985-91; owner Mail Boxes Etc., 1992—; lectr. Calif. State U., Long Beach, U. So. Calif.; cons. City of N.Y., Memory Data Software, IEPO, Inc., U. So. Calif., Thornton Sch. Music. Mem. The Classical Singer's Assn., Calabasas C. of C., Delta Upsilon. Avocations: sports cars, antiques, travel. Home: 18342 Chatham Ln Northridge CA 91326-3603 Office: 23679 Calabasas Rd Calabasas CA 91302-1502 Office Phone: 818-591-1086. E-mail: mbe1047@aol.com.

STARK, NELLIE MAY, forester, ecologist, educator; b. Norwich, Conn., Nov. 20, 1933; d. Theodore Benjamin and Dorothy Josephine (Pendleton) Beetham; m. Oscar Elder Stark, Oct. 1962 (dec.). BA, Conn. Coll., 1956; AM, Duke U., 1958, PhD, 1962. Botanist Exptl. Sta., U.S. Forest Svc., Old Strawberry, Calif., 1958-66; botanist, ecologist Desert Rsch. Inst., Reno, 1966-72; prof. forest ecology Sch. Forestry, U. Mont., Missoula, 1972-92; pvt. cons. Philomath, Oreg. Pres. Camas Analytical Lab., Inc., Missoula, 1987-92. Author: Will Your Family Survive the 21st Century, 1997, Memories of Wren, Oregon, 1998, So You Want to Build a Little Log Cabin in the Woods, 2002; contbr. articles to profl. jours. Named Disting. Dau. Norwich, Conn., 1985; recipient Conn. award Conn. Coll., 1986, 54 grants. Mem. Ecol. Soc. Am. (chair ethics com. 1974, 76), Soc. Am. Foresters (taskforce 1987-88).

STARK, NORMAN, secondary school educator; b. Bronx, N.Y., Sept. 15, 1940; s. Martin and Margaret (Neuman) S.; m. Betty Joanne Kelton, Sept. 4, 1994 (dec. May 1998); 1 child, Michelle Allison; m. Lois Marie Ricketson, Dec. 25, 2001. Student, Newark State Coll., Union, 1963-69. Creative writing tchr., acting tchr., singles forum tchr., film tchr. Plantation (Fla.) High Sch., 1988; Hoover Mid. Sch. and Palm Bay H.S., Melbourne, Fla., 1995. Editor West Palm Beach News, 1979; screenplay writer, actor. With U.S. Army, 1963—69. Avocations: reading, puzzles, movies. Home: 2732 Locksley Rd Melbourne FL 32935-2433 E-mail: norman915@msn.com.

STARK, PATRICIA ANN, psychologist; b. Ames, Iowa, Apr. 21, 1937; d. Keith C. and Mary L. (Johnston) Moore. BS, So. Ill. U., Edwardsville, 1970, MS, 1972; PhD, St. Louis U., 1976. Counselor to alcoholics Bapt. Rescue Mission, East St. Louis, Ill., 1969; rschr. alcoholics Gateway Rehab. Ctr., East St. Louis, 1972; psychologist intern Henry-Stark Counties Spl. Edn. Dist. and Galesburg State Rsch. Hosp., Ill., 1972-73; instr. Lewis and Clark C.C., Godfrey, Ill., 1973-76, asst. prof., 1976-84, assoc. prof., 1984, coord. child care svcs., 1974-84; mem. staff dept. psychiatry Meml. Hosp., St. Elizabeth's Hosp., 1979-2001; supr. various workshops in field, 1974-84. Dir. child and family svc. Collinsville Counseling Ctr., 1977-82; clin. dir., owner Empas-Complete Family Psychol. and Hypnosis Svcs., Collinsville, 1982—; cons. cmty. agys., 1974—; mem. adv. bd. Madison County Coun. on Alcoholism and Drug Dependency, 1977-80. Mem. APA, Ill. Psychol. Assn., Midwestern Psychol. Assn., Nat. Assn. Sch. Psychologists, Am. Soc. Clin. Hypnosis, Internat. Soc. Hypnosis. Office: 2802 Maryville Rd Maryville IL 62062 Office Phone: 618-345-6632.

STARK, RICHARD BOIES, surgeon, artist; b. Conrad, Iowa, Mar. 31, 1915; s. Eugene and Hazel (Carson) S.; m. Judy Thornton, Oct. 31, 1967 AB, Stanford U., 1936; postgrad., U. Heidelberg, 1936—37; MD, Cornell U., 1941. Diplomate Am. Bd. Plastic Surgery (pres. 1967-68). Intern Peter Bent Brigham Hosp., Boston, 1941-42; asst. resident surgery Childrens Hosp., Boston, 1942; plastic surgeon Northington Gen. Hosp., Ala., 1945-46, Percy Jones Gen. Hosp., Mich., 1946; postwar fellow anatomy and embryology Stanford U., 1946-47; from asst. resident to resident in head and neck surgery VA Hosp., Bronx, NY, 1947-50; asst. resident, resident surgery, plastic, head and neck and gen. surgery N.Y. Hosp., NY, 1947-50; instr. surgery Cornell U., 1950-52, asst. prof., 1952-55, assoc. prof., 1955; asst. attending surgeon N.Y. Hosp., 1950-55; asst. prof. surgery Columbia U., 1955-58, assoc. prof., 1958-73, prof. clin. surgery, 1973—; assoc. attending surgeon St. Luke's Hosp., N.Y.C., 1955-58, founding attending surgeon dept. plastic surgery, 1958—; founder dept. plastic surgery, 1955. Cons. Walter Reed Med. Ctr., 1970-77 Author: Plastic Surgery, 1962, Cleft Palate, 1968, Plastic Surgery at the New York Hospital 100 Years Ago, 1952, Aesthetic Plastic Surgery, 1980, Total Facial Reconstruction, 1985, Plastic Surgery of the Head and Neck, 1986; contbr. 51 chpts. to books, more than 210 articles to profl. jours.; assoc. editor: Plastic Reconstructive Surgery, 1977-82; founding editor: Annals Plastic Surgery, 1978-81; 25 one-person art shows, 1946—; rep. in permanent art exhibits, N.Y. Hosp., St. Lukes Hosp. Chmn. Medico Adv. Bd., 1976-77; mem., v.p. CARE Bd.; v.p. Wellborn Found., N.Y.C. Served to maj. M.C., AUS, 1943-46. Decorated Bronze Star (U.S.); Medal of Honor (2) (Vietnam); cavallero Order of San Carlos (Colombia), Dieffenbach medal (Berlin), Gold medal Nat. Inst. Social Scis. Fellow ACS; mem. Am. Assn. Plastic Surgeons, Am. Soc. Plastic and Reconstructive Surgery (pres. 1966, Spl. Achievement award), Found. Am. Soc. Plastic and Reconstructive Surgery (pres. 1961-65), Am. Surg. Assn., Soc. Univ. Surgeons, French Soc. Plastic Surgeons, Brasilian Soc. Plastic Surgeons, Colombian Soc. Plastic Surgeons, Argentina Soc. Plastic Surgeons, Brit. Assn. Plastic Surgery, Peruvian Acad. Surgeons, N.Y. Surg. Soc., N.Y. Acad. Medicine (pres. Friends Rare Book Room), Plastic and Reconstructive Surgery (sec., pres. 1966), N.Y. State Med. Soc. (pres., sec., med. history), N.Y. Regional Soc. Plastic and Reconstructive Surgery (pres. 1064-65), Halsted Soc. (pres. 1973-74), James IV Assn. Surgeons, Am. Soc. Aesthetic Plastic Surgery (pres. 1974-75), Nat. Arts Club (exhibiting mem.), Century Club (profl. artist), Artist Fellowship, Lotos Club. Home: 35 E 75th St New York NY 10021-2761

STARK, ROBERT J. lawyer; b. Middletown, N.Y., July 16, 1970; s. Jeffrey and Patricia Stark. BA, Lafayette Coll., Easton, Pa., 1992; JD, Vanderbilt U., Nashville, Tenn., 1995. Bar: N.J. 1995, N.Y. 1996, U.S. Dist. Ct. NJ. 1995, U.S. Dist. Ct. (So. Dist.) N.Y. 1996, U.S. Dist. Ct. (Ea. Dist.) N.Y. 1996. Panelist and bankruptcy confs. Contbr. articles to law jours. Recipient Jessup Internat. Moot Ct. Team, Vanderbilt U. Law Sch., 1994-1995; scholar McKnight-Black Scholarship, Lafayette Coll., 1992. Mem.: Turnaround Mgmt. Assn., Bar Assn. of City of N.Y. Office: King & Spalding LLP 1185 Avenue of the Americas New York NY 10036 E-mail: rstark@akingump.com.

STARK, ROBERT MARTIN, mathematician, civil engineer, educator; b. N.Y.C., Feb. 6, 1930; s. Alexander and Julia (Gross) S.; m. Carol LaSage, Jan. 13, 1955 (dec. Mar. 1988); children: Bradley R., Timothy D., Steven M., Candice B. AB, Johns Hopkins U., 1951; MA, U. Mich., 1952; PhD, U. Del., 1965. Rsch. scientist Bausch and Lomb, Rochester, N.Y., 1955; instr. Rochester Inst. Tech., 1956-57; asst. dean engring., asst. prof. math. Cleve. State U., 1957-62; instr. U. Del., 1962-64, asst. prof. civil and environ. engring., math. scis., 1964-68, assoc. prof., 1968-76, prof., 1976—2002, prof. emeritus, 2002—; pres., cons. applied sci. R.M. Stark & Co., Inc., 2003—. Vis. assoc. prof. MIT, 1972-73; chmn. grad. program in ops. rsch.; cons. in field. Author: (with R.L. Nicholls) Mathematical Foundations for Design: Civil Engineering Systems, 1972; (with R.H. Mayer, Jr.) Quantitative Construction Management: Uses of Linear Optimization, 1983; (with R. Engelbrecht-Wiggans and M. Shubik) Auctioning, Bidding and Contracting, 1983; (with C. Sloyer, et al) Contemporary Applied Mathematics Series, 1987, Mathagrams, 1996. Commr. Del. Heritage Commn., 1990—; bd. dirs. Generations Home Care, Inc., 1989—, Wilmington Sr. Ctr., 1994—, Meals on Wheels, Del., 1990—2003, Del. Acad. Sci., 1990—, pres., 1994—96; bd. dirs., v.p. White Clay Watershed Assn., 1992—97; mem. cmty. adv. bd. WHYY Pub. Broadcasting Corp., 2002—. Recipient Outstanding Alumnus award U. Del. Dept. Civil and Environ. Engring., 1999; grantee Office Naval Rsch., 1974-81, NSF, 1969-70, U.S. Army Rsch. Office, 1966-68. Mem. AAAS, ASCE, Nat. Coun. Tchrs. Math., Inst. Mgmt. Sci., Ops. Rsch. Soc. Am., Phila. Ops. Rsch. Soc. (pres. 1970), U. Del. Assn. Ret. Faculty (pres. 2003—). Avocations: research, publs. ops. rsch., applied probability. Home: One Fox Ln Newark DE 19711 Office Phone: 302-453-0606. Personal E-mail: rstark@udel.edu.

STARK, ROBIN CARYL, psychotherapist, consultant; b. Yonkers, N.Y., Apr. 16, 1953; d. Louis and Bernice Stark. BA in Psychology cum laude with honors, Hunter Coll., 1979; MSW, NYU, 1982. Diplomate Am. Bd. Clin. Social Work; lic. social worker, N.Y.; cert. psychoanalytic psychotherapy, psychotherapy of eating disorders, trauma tng. for mental health profls., ARC. Pvt. practice psychotherapy, N.Y.C., 1983—. Mem. adj. field faculty Grad. Sch. Social Svc. Fordham U., N.Y.C., 1986—87, Grad. Sch. Social Work, Hunter Coll., N.Y.C., 1987—88; coord. patient care svcs. Achievement and Guidance Ctrs. Am., Inc., N.Y.C., 1988—89; staff psychotherapist Ctr. for Study of Anorexia and Bulimia, 1990—94, facilitator wellness support chronic & life-challenging illness, 1993—; bd. dirs. N.Y. Met. Cmty. of Mindfulness, 1999—2000; pro bono svc. provider Project Liberty's post Sept. 11 trauma counseling program, N.Y.C., 2001—. Recipient service award Young Adult Inst., 1987; N.Y.C. Youth Bur. grantee, 1983-85. Mem. NASW, Acad. Cert. Social Workers. Office: 410 E 57th St Ste 1A New York NY 10022-3059

STARK, S. DANIEL, JR., gaming industry executive; b. Port Hueneme, Calif., Mar. 26, 1953; s. S. Daniel and Eloise Marie (Fisher) S.; m. Pauline Laube Finley, June 7, 1997; 1 child, Kaitlyn Elizabeth. BS, Calif. Poly. U., Pomona, 1981; cert. in exec. mgmt., Claremont Grad. U., 1989, MA in Mgmt., 1992. Driver-guide San Diego Wild Animal Pk./Zool. Soc. San Diego, Escondido, Calif., 1974-76; attractions host Disneyland divsn. The Walt Disney Co., Anaheim, Calif., 1976-80, mgmt. intern, 1981, supr. ops., 1981-82, area supr. ops., dept. mgr., 1982-87; mgmt. cons. S.D. Stark, Jr., Las Vegas, 1985—; dir. mktg. Ramada Express Hotel & Casino, Laughlin, Nev., 1988-89; exec. dir. San Bernardino (Calif.) Conv. and Visitors Bur., 1989-98; pres., CEO Panama City Beach Conv. & Visitors Bur., 1998-99; exec. dir. Bay County (Fla.) Tourist Devel. Coun., 1998-99; dir. mktg. Boyd Gaming Corp., Las Vegas, 1999—. Part-time instr. mgmt. and mktg. So. Calif. campus U. Phoenix, 1997-98, Nev. campus, 1999—, area chair for mktg., 2001—; cons. Hemmeter Devel. Corp., Honolulu, 1985, Calif. Authority Racing Fairs, Sacramento, 1987-88, USIA for Latvian Ministry Transp., tourism divsn., 1992, U.S. Bur. Land Mgmt., tourism mgmt. project U. Alaska Sch. Mgmt.; adj. prof. Sch. Bus. and Pub. Adminstrn., Calif. State U., San Bernardino, 1992-93. Bd. dirs. Leadership So. Calif., 1993-98, grad. pub. affairs tng., 1993; congl. appointee del. White House Conf. on Travel and Tourism, 1995; mem. regional econ. strategies consortium So. Calif. Assn. Govts., 1996-98; mem. Visit Fla. Mktg. Com., 1998-99; bd. dirs. Fla. Assn. Conv. and Visitors Burs., 1998-99, Speedway Childrens Charities Las Vegas Chpt., 1999—, treas., 2000-01, chmn., 2001-2002; v.p. Cops Helping Kids, 2002-2003, pres., 2003-04; mem. spl. events com. Las Vegas Centennial Commn.; bd. trustees Crime Stoppers of Nev., Inc., 2004—. Recipient resolution Calif. Assembly, 1989, 98, San Bernardino County Bd. Suprs., 1989, City of San Bernardino Mayor and Coun., 1989, 98, Calif. Senate, 1989, 98; selected as one of 1991 Up and Coming Young Bus. Leaders in San Bernardino County; named one of Inland Empire Bus. All Stars, 1991; recipient World Champion Trail Horse award Am. Jr. Quarter Horse Assn., 1972, Calif. Tourism award for Best Spl. Event-Rt. 66 Rendezvous, 1997. Mem. Am. Horse Shows Assn. (life), Am. Quarter Horse Assn (life), Assn. Travel Mktg. Execs., Internat. Assn. Conv. and Visitors Burs. (cert. comm., conv. mktg., tourism mktg.), Pub. Rels. Soc. Am. (bd. dirs. Calif. Inland Empire chpt. 1990-95, Polaris award 1997), Calif. and Nev. Festivals and Events Assn. (pres. 1997-98, 2002—, bd. dirs. 1994-98, 2002--), Inland Empire Tourism Coun. (bd. dirs. 1996-98, exec. com. 1996-98, treas. 1997-98), Calif. Travel Industry Assn., Tourism Assn. So. Calif. (bd.

dirs. 1990-95, vice chair 1992-95), Western Assn. Convs. and Vis. Bur. (chmn. Calif. coun. 1992-94), FarmHouse Fraternity (internat. bd. dirs. 1986-94, v.p. 1990-92, Snyder Alumni award 1984). Avocations: boating, fishing, films, equestrian competition. Office: 2950 Industrial Rd Las Vegas NV 89109-1150

STARK, SUSAN R. film critic; b. N.Y.C., July 9, 1940; d. Albert A. and Lillian H. (Landau) Rothenberg; m. Allan F. Stark, June 26, 1968 (div. 1983); children: Allana Fredericka, Paula-Rose. BA, Smith Coll., 1962; MAT., Harvard U., 1963. Film critic Detroit Free Press, 1968-79, Detroit News, 1979—. Mem. Phi Beta Kappa Office: Detroit News 615 W Lafayette Blvd Detroit MI 48226-3197

STARKE, HAROLD E., JR., lawyer; b. Richmond, Va., Aug. 1, 1944; BA, Randolph-Macon Coll., 1967; JD, U. Richmond, 1971; LLM in Taxation, NYU, 1973. Bar: Va. 1971, D.C. 1981. Mem. Troutman Sanders LLP, Richmond. Editor U. Richmond Law Rev., 1970-71. Bd. trustees Randolph-Macon Coll., 1983-85, 95-97, 99—. Fellow Am. Coll. Tax Counsel; mem. ABA (taxation sect.), Va. State Bar (chmn. taxation sect. 1985-86), D.C. Bar, Richmond Estate Planning Coun., McNeill Honor Soc., Phi Delta Phi. Office: Troutman Sanders LLP Bank of Am Center PO Box 1122 Richmond VA 23218-1122

STARKEY, RICHARD See STARR, RINGO

STARKEY, RUSSELL BRUCE, JR., energy executive; b. Lumberport, W Va, July 20, 1942; s. Russell Bruce and Dorotha Mable (Field) S.; m. Joan McClellan, May 27, 1966; children: Christine, Pamela, Joanne. BS, Miami U., Oxford, Ohio, 1964; grad. student, U. New Haven, 1972-73, N.C. State U., 1974-75, U.S. Navy Schs., 1964-66, 68. From sr. engr., nuclear generation sect. to prin. engr. Carolina Power & Light Co., Raleigh, NC, 1973—75; quality assurance supr. to supt. tech. and administrn. Brunswick Steam Electric Plant, Southport, NC, 1975—77; plant mgr. H. B. Robinson Steam Electric Plant, Hartsville, SC, 1977-83; mgr. environ. svcs. Carolina Power & Light Co., Raleigh, NC, 1984-85, mgr. nuc. safety and environ. svcs. dept., 1985-88; mgr. Brunswick Nuc. Project Dept., 1988-89, v.p., 1989-92, v.p. Nuc. Svc. Dept., 1992-93; exec. v.p. energy mgmt. divsn. Hesco, Inc., 1994; from dir. indsl. electrotech. lab. to v.p. gen. tech. mgr. Advanced Energy Corp., 1994—97; cons. US Enrichment Corp., 1997—98, tng. mgr., 1998—2001, plant gen. mgr., 2001—. With USN, 1964-73. Mem.: Am. Nuclear Soc. Home: 1227 Beresford Way Paducah KY 42001-6552 Office: Bldg C-100 PO Box 1410 Paducah KY 42002-1410

STARKMAN, GARY LEE, lawyer; b. Chgo., Sept. 2, 1946; s. Oscar and Sara (Ordman) S. AB, U. Ill., 1968; JD cum laude, Northwestern U., 1971. Bar: Ill. 1971, U.S. Dist. Ct. (no. dist.) Ill. 1972, U.S. Ct. Appeals (7th cir.) 1972, U.S. Supreme Ct. 1974, Trial Bar U.S. Dist. Ct. (no. dist.) Ill. 1982, U.S. Ct. Appeals (3d cir.) 1984, U.S. Ct. Appeals (D.C. cir.) 1984. Asst. U.S. Atty. No. Dist. Ill., 1971-75; gen. counsel, dir. rsch. Citizens for Thompson Campaign Com., 1975-77; counsel to Gov. of Ill., 1977-81; admissions com. U.S. Dist. Ct. (no. dist.) Ill., 1982-90; ptnr. Ross & Hardies, Chgo., 1990—2003, McGuire Woods LLP, Chgo., 2003—. Co-author: (textbook) Cases and Comments on Criminal Procedure, 1974, 6th edit., 2003; contbr. articles to profl. jours.; reviewer in field. Chmn. state agys. divsn. Jewish United Fund Met. Chgo., 1978-81; chmn. Ill. Racing Bd., 1991-96; bd. dirs. Internat. Assn. Racing Commn., 1992-94; cmty. adv. bd. Jr. League Chgo., 1979-83. Recipient John Marshall award for appellate litigation Atty. Gen. U.S., 1974, Nat. Svc. award Tau Epsilon Phi, 1968; named one of Ten Outstanding Young Citizens, Chgo. Jr. C. of C., 1978. Mem. ABA (litigation sect.), Chgo. Bar Assn. (constl. law com.), Decalogue Soc., Northwestern U. Law Alumni Assn. Office: McGuire Woods LLP 77 W Walker Dr Ste 4400 Chicago IL 60601-1681 Business E-Mail: gstarkman@mcguirewoods.com.

STARKMAN, HAROLD S. physician, researcher; b. NYC, Mar. 16, 1953; MD, Albert Einstein Coll. Medicine, NYC, 1973—76. Cert. Pediatric Endocrinologist Am. Bd. Pediat., 1983. Dir. BD Diabetes Ctr., Morristown, NJ, 1983; assoc. prof. clin. pediat. U. Medicine and Dentistry, Newark, 2000. Consulting Pediatric Diabetes. Bd. mem. Camp Nejeda, Stillwater, NJ, 1983. Recipient Best Dr. US, Castle/Connelly, 2003. Fellow: Am. Acad. Pediat. Office: Pediat Diabetes Ctr 100 Madison Ave Morristown NJ 07962

STARKS, CAROL ELIZABETH, retired principal; b. Elizabeth, NJ, Oct. 16, 1941; d. Arthur E. and Argetha P. (Henderson) Starks. AA, Graceland Coll., Lamoni, Iowa, 1961; BA in Elem. Edn., Mich. State U., 1963; MA in Elem. Adminstrn., San Jose State U., 1972. Cert. elem. sch. tchr. Calif., life diploma for elem. edn. Calif., specialist tchr. in reading Calif., std. svc. credential in supervision Calif., elem. sch. tchr. N.J. Tchr. grade 3 Hayes Sch., Monterey, Calif., 1963—65; tchr. grade 2 Woodruff Sch., Berkeley Heights, NJ, 1965—67; tchr. remedial reading and educationally handicapped Ord Terrace Sch., Monterey, 1967—68, asst. prin., 1975—77, prin., 1984—88; tchr. grade 3 Manzanita Sch., Monterey, 1968—73; asst. prin. La Mesa Sch., Monterey, 1973—74, tchr. grade 6, 1974—75; prin. Foothill Sch., Monterey, 1977—80, Olson Sch., Monterey, 1980—84, Highland Sch., Monterey, 1988—95, Bay View Sch., Monterey, 1995—99. Interviewed as representative of elementary principals Calif. Commn. on the Tchg. Profession, 1984—85. Mem. world ch. pubs. com. Remnant Ch. Jesus Christ of Latter Day Saints, 2001—, music dir. Blue Springs congregation, 2001—, mem. world ch. hymnbook com., 2003—. Recipient Calif. Disting. Sch. Prin.'s award, 1989, 1993, Proclamation for profl. accomplishments and 19 yrs. of svc., City of Seaside (Calif.), 1995. Mem.: AAUW (sec. independence br. 2003—), Monterey Bay Sch. Adminstr. Assn. (pres. 1997—98), Assn. Calif. Sch. Adminstr. (sec./treas. Monterey Peninsula charter 1977—78, v.p. 1978—79, pres. 1979—80, treas. region X 1979—81, pres. region X 1981—82, mem. elem. adminstrn. com. 1982—86, del. to Nat. Assn. Elem. Sch.Prins. Convention 1983—84, state facilitator Elem. Adminstrn. Acad. North 1984—85, state dir. Elem. Adminstrn. Acad. North 1985—86, invited writer for case studies for Calif. sch. leadership acad. 1985—86, state del. to rep. assembly 1986—91, Region X Blanche Montague award for Outstanding Sch. Adminstr. 1987), Delta Kappa Gamma (1st v.p. Delta Lambda chpt. Calif. 1986—88, 2nd v.p. Delta Lambda chpt.Calif. 1988—90, pres. Delta Lambda chpt.Calif. 1990—92, Calif.membership task force 1991—93, Calif.personal growth and svcs. com. 1993—95, dir. area V Calif. 1995—97, state chairperson comms. com. 1997—99, mem. scholarship com. Kansas City coun. 2000—01, pres. Phi chpt. Mo. 2000—02, state comm. com. 2001—03, treas. 2002—, chair state comm. com. 2003—, Kans. City Coun. 2000—01). Republican. Remnant Ch. Of Jesus Christ Of Latter Day Saints. Avocations: travel, reading, music, computer. Home: 3341 S Cochise Ave Independence MO 64057

STARKS, DORIS N. nursing educator, administrator; b. Conecuh County, Ala., July 30, 1937; m. Wilbert L. Starks Sr., Dec. 25, 1961; children: Wilbert L. Jr., Garrick Edward. BS in Nursing, Tuskegee U., 1958; MS in Nursing, The Cath. U. of Am., 1965; PhD, Union Grad. Sch., 1978. Lic. nurse, Md. Staff nurse VA Hosp. Ctr., Tuskegee, Ala., 1958-61, insvc. edn. instr., 1965-66; staff nurse Washington Hosp. Ctr., 1963-65; asst. prof. med./surg. nursing Tuskegee U., 1966-68; prof. Community Coll. Balt, 1968, asst. chair dept. nursing, 1980-84, chair, 1984-86, chair dept. nursing and health scis., 1986-89, dir. nursing program, 1989; asst. dean, prof. nursing div. Coppin State Coll., Balt., 1990-91, dean nursing, div. nursing, 1991-98. Item writer Nat. State Bd. Exam. Test Pool. Author bi-weekly health issues column Christian World, 1976-77. Mem. adv. coun. on vocat. edn. City of Balt. 1nd lt. US Army Nurse Corps., 1959-62. Recipient plaque and commendation Tuskegee Inst. Alumni Assn., 1983, Leadership in Nursing award Md. Found. for Nursing, 1994, Strong Blacks in Health Care award, Balt., 1995; honoree Black Nurses Assn., 1984; inducted Tuskegee U. Sch. Nursing Hall of Fame, 1992. Fellow Am. Acad. Nursing; mem. ANA, Tuskegee U. Nurses Alumni Assn. (Balt. met. area chpt.), Nat. Coalition of 100 Black Women, Alpha Kappa Alpha, Sigma Theta Tau, Chi Eta Phi. Home: 9068 Bellwart Way Columbia MD 21045-2304

STARKS, FLORENCE ELIZABETH, retired special education educator; b. Summit, N.J., Dec. 6, 1932; d. Edward and Winnie (Morris) S. BA, Morgan State U., 1956; MS in Edn., CUNY, 1962; postgrad., Fairleigh Dickinson U., 1962-63, Seton Hall U., 1963, Newark State Coll. Cert. blind and visually handicapped and social studies tchr., N.J. Tchr. adult edn. Newark Bd. of Edn.; ret., 1995; tchr. N.Y. Inst. for Edn. of the Blind. Developer first class for multiple handicapped blind children in pub. sch. system, Newark, 1960; ptnr. World Vision Internat. Mem. ASCD, AFL-CIO, AAUW, Coun. Exceptional Children, Am. Assn. U. Women, Nat. Assn. Negro Bus. and Profl. Women's Club Inc., N.J. Edn. Assn., Newark Tchrs. Assn., Newark Tchrs. Union-Am. Fedn. Tchrs., World Vision Internat. (ptnr.). Home: 4 Park Ave Summit NJ 07901-3942

STARKS, FRED WILLIAM, chemicals executive; b. Millford, Ill., Aug. 16, 1921; s. Otis Earl and Evelyn Viola Starks; m. Minnie Jane Reynolds, Sept. 4, 1946; children: David F., Steven J., Daniel J. BS, U. Ill., 1943, MS, 1947; PhD, U. Nebr., 1950. Supr. US Rubber Co., Torrance, Calif., 1943—44, DuPont, Niagara Falls, NY, 1950—57; pres. Starks Assocs., Inc., Buffalo, 1957—89, chmn., 1989—. Spl. lectr. U. Buffalo, 1959—63. Lt. (j.g.) USNR, 1944—46. Avery fellow, 1948—49, USPHS fellow, 1949—50. Mem.: Am. Inst. Chemists, NY Acad. Sci., Am. Chem. Soc., Chemists Club, Buffalo Club, Cosmos, Sigma Xi. Achievements include patents in field. Home: 742 Highland Ave Buffalo NY 14223-1645 Office: Starks Assocs Inc 1280 Niagara St Buffalo NY 14213-1592

STARKS, KELLY GEORGE, systems engineer, consultant; b. Kenosha, Wis., Dec. 22, 1956; s. George Arthur Starks and Anastasia Herr; m. Carol Jeanne Klees, Feb. 24, 1982. BSME - BSCS, U. of Wis. - Parkside, 1975—80. Software analysis engr. - crew activity planning sys. (space shuttle program) McDonnell Douglas corp., Houston, 1981—87; systems engr. - army comanche attack helicopter program Apollo for Sikorski, Bridgeport, Conn., 2001—03; systems engr. - army fcs (future combat systems) program ATSI for Gen. Dynamics Land Systems, Sterling Heights, Mich., 2003—04; systems and integration analyst, - tech. and mgmt. info. sys. (space sta. fredom program) McDonnell Douglas corp., Reston, Va., 1987—92, software analysis engr. Washington, 1992—94; nasa ossf sys. adminstrn. and user support PRC Corp., Washington, 1994—94; macintosh integration and support cons. Mac Specialists, Washington, 1995—95; afatds sr. systems engr. Hughes Def. Comm., Ft. Wayne, Ind., 1995—96; crusader sr. engr./scientist Advance Possis for United Def., Mpls., 1996—98; systems/networks - sys. engr. INS for Sprint, Overland Park, Kans., 1999—99; systems engr. - ats and fdor projects Donatech for Rockwell-Collins, Cedar Rapids, Iowa, 2000—01. Recipient Spl. Achievement award, Tri-Cor, 1993. Personal E-mail: kellyst@aol.com.

STARKS, ROBERT J. (BOB STARKS), state legislator, airline pilot, realtor; b. Tampa, Fla., Oct. 14, 1945; BABA, U. South Fla., 1967. Mem. Fla. Ho. of Reps., 1986—; chmn. fin. and taxation com., 1996-97. Mem. exec. com. Vision 2000 and Edn. Task Force, 1986-87; mem. Seminole County Rep. Exec. Com.; bd. dirs., ctrl. Fla. coord. Save Our Homes, Inc., bd. dirs. Winter Park C. of C. With USN, 1967-72. Named Outstanding Young Man, Jaycees Fla. State. Mem. C. of C. (Goldenrod, Greater Seminole County, Maitland/South Seminole), Rotary. Avocations: softball, tennis, fishing. Office: Fla Capitol 402 S Monroe St Rm 222 Tallahassee FL 32399-6526 also: 4666 Tiffany Woods Cir Oviedo FL 32765-6105 E-mail: starks.bob@leg.state.fl.us.

STARKWEATHER, FREDERICK THOMAS, retired data processing executive; b. Sioux City, Iowa, Feb. 24, 1933; s. Fred Ervin and Gertrude Faye (Madden) S.; m. Margot Glassen, Nov. 19, 1959; children: Thomas Frederick, Jerry Russell, Michael Glassen. BA in Math. and Physics, U. Nebr., Omaha, 1955. Mathematician Flight Determination Lab., White Sands Missile Range, N.Mex., 1955-56; supervisory mathematician Analysis & Computation, White Sands Missile Range, 1956-81; chief data scis. divsn. Nat. Range Ops., White Sands Missile Range, 1981—93; co-owner B and T Managed Care, LLC, 2001—; owner The Spotlight Restaurant, 2002—. Nat. coun. rep. Am. Def. Preparedness Assn., Washington, 1980-93; pres. White Sands Pioneer Group, White Sands Missile Range, 1983-86; bd. dirs. Assn. U.S. Army, Washington. Author hist. and geneal. books; contbr. book revs. and articles to newspapers and mags. Chmn. El Paso (Tex.) City Planning Commn., 1980-84; bd. dirs. El Paso County Hist. Soc., 1983-87; mem. El Paso County Hist. Commn., 1983-2000. With USAR, 1955-63. Recipient Profl. Secs. Internat. Exec. of Yr. award, 1987, Conquistador award City of El Paso, 1980; named Disting. Alumnus U. Nebr., Omaha, 1985; named to Hon. Order of St. Barbara U.S. Field Arty. Assn., 1988; cited for svcs. to mankind El Paso chpt. Sertoma, 1985. Mem. Fed. Mgrs. Assn. (bd. dirs.), Freedom Found. at Valley Forge (pres. El Paso chpt., George Washington Hon. medal 1982), El Paso C. of C. (assoc. dir. 1984-92, bd. dirs.), Toastmasters (dist. gov. 1970-71), Masons, Tau Kappa Epsilon (Hall of Fame 1986). Avocations: coin collecting/numismatics, genealogy, books, weaponry.

STARLING, CAROL KING, nursing educator; b. Anniston, Ala., May 11, 1947; d. Don Edgar King and Janice Audrey Root; m. Conley W. Starling, Sept. 3, 1983; 1 child, Keith. BSN, U. Ala., 1971, MSN, 1976; PhD in Nursing, George Mason U., 1995. RN, Kans., Mo.; registered advanced practice RN, Kans. Clin. instr. dept. nursing Columbus (Ga.) Coll., 1972-73; instr. U. Ala. Sch. Nursing, Birmingham, 1974-77; asst. prof. Ga. State U. Sch. Nursing, Atlanta, 1977-78, U. Kans. Sch. Nursing, Kansas City, 1978-83, Dillard U. Sch. Nursing, New Orleans, 1984-85, La. State U. Sch. Nursing, New Orleans, 1985-87; lectr. nursing Ga. Mason U. Sch. Nursing, Fairfax, Va., 1991-94; clin. asst. prof. U. Kans. Sch. Nursing, Kansas City, 1995—. Mem. adv. bd. Adolescent Clinic, Argentine Mid. Sch., Kansas City, Kans., 1998-2001; women's health nurse practitioner U. Kans. Med. Ctr., Ob-Gyn. Outpatient Clinic, Kansas City, 1979-83. Author: (slide tape presentation) Interviewing Pregnant Adolescents, 1978. Chairperson planning com. 25th Ann. Women's Health Symposia, Kansas City, 2000; com. mem. planning com. 24th Ann. Women's Health Symposia, Kansas City, 1999; chairperson Master's Adv. Coun., U. Kans. Sch. Nursing, Kansas City, 1999-2000. Named one of Gt. One Hundred Nurses, New Orleans Dist. Nurses Assn., 1987; Profl. Nurse traineeship U.S. Dept. Health and Human Svcs., 1991-94; recipient Jayhawker RN award for outstanding tchg., 1980, Phyllis Keeney Lawrence award for outstanding tchg. in nursing, 2000. Mem. Assn. Women's Health, Obstetrics, and Neonatal Nurses, Sigma Theta Tau (undergrad. counselor 1996-2000, rec. sec. 1981-83, v.p. 1977-78). Avocation: genealogy. Office: U Kans Sch Nursing 3901 Rainbow Blvd Kansas City KS 66160 E-mail: cstarlin@kumc.edu.

STARNER, DON EDWARD, radiographer, educator; b. Zanesville, Ohio, June 28, 1959; s. Larry and Sara Ann Starner; m. Carla Marcote, Aug. 31, 1991; 1 child, Ryan. BS, The Ohio State U., 1982. Cert. Radiographer Am. Registry of Radiologic Technologists, 1982, Quality Mgmt. Radiographer Am. Registry of Radiologic Technologists, 2002, lic. Radiologic Technologist Fla. Dept. Health, 1988. X-ray technologist The Ohio State U. Hospitals, Columbus, Ohio, 1982—88; from clin. instr. to program dir. West Boca Med. Ctr. Sch. of Radiography, Boca Raton, Fla., 1988—91, program dir., 1991—96; dir. of clin. radiography edn. Indian River CC, Ft. Pierce, Fla., 1996—. Contbr. chapters to books Web-Based Training, 2001; actor: (films) Brubaker, 1980. Mem.: AAUP, Fla. Assn. of C.C., Am. Soc. of Radiologic Technologists, Am. Registry of Radiologic Technologists. Home: 6717 NW Dorothy St Port Saint Lucie FL 34983 Office: Indian River Community College 3209 Virginia Ave Fort Pierce FL 34981

STARNES, EARL MAXWELL, urban and regional planner, architect; b. Winter Haven, Fla., Sept. 14, 1926; s. Thomas Lowe and Kathryn Maxwell (Gates) S.; m. Dorothy Jean Prather, Aug. 21, 1949; children: Tom, Will, Janet, Patricia. Student, Fla. So. Coll., 1946—48; BArch cum laude, U. Fla., 1951; MS in Urban and Regional Planning, Fla. State U., 1973, PhD, 1977. Registered arch., Fla. Assoc. Courtney Stewart, Ft. Lauderdale, Fla., 1951-52, William Bigoney, Ft. Lauderdale, 1952-53, William T. Vaughn, Ft. Lauderdale, 1953, Alfred B. Parker, Miami, Fla., 1953-55, Rufus Nims, Miami, 1955-57; ptnr. Starnes & Rentscher, Miami, 1957-63, Starnes, Rentscher & Assocs., Miami, 1963-71; dir. divsn. mass transp. Fla. Dept. Transp., Tallahassee, 1971-72; dir. divsn. state planning Fla. Dept. Adminstrn., 1972-75; engaged in rsch. and cons. svc. Tallahassee, 1975; prof., chmn. urban and regional planning Coll. Architecture U. Fla., Gainesville, 1976-88, prof. urban and regional plan coord., doctoral studies, 1989-93, prof. emeritus, 1993—. Instr. architecture U. Miami, 1953; adj. asst. prof. dept. urban and regional planning Coll. Social Scis., Fla. State U., 1971-74; mem. adv. panel B8-15, Nat. Coop. Hwy. Rsch. Program, Transp. Rsch. Bd., NRC-Nat. Acad. Scis., 1974—; mem. adv. bd. Pub. Tech., Inc., 1974—; mem. North Ctrl. Fla. Regional Planning Com., 1980-85, Fla. Substate Dist. Com., 1985-87; co-chmn. Joint Liaison Com. on Divsn. Responsibility for Urban Svcs., Dade County, Fla., 1965-71; chmn. joint policy com. U. Miami-Dade County Jackson Med. Ctr., 1966-71; chmn. Cape Fla. State Park Adv. Coun., 1966-69, Dade County Landscape Ordinance Study Com., 1967-70, South Fla. Everglades Area Planning Coun., 1969-71; vis. lectr. Calif. Poly. State U., San Luis Obispo, 1988-89; cons. Urban Planning Fla. and Caribbean. Prin. works include 1st Unitarian Ch., Miami; contbr. article on archtl. planning relationship Ency. Architecture Planning, 1987, chpt. to Growth Management, 1992, chpt. and preface (with Ivonne Audivac) to Rural Sustainability in America, 1996; contbr. chpts. to books, articles on land use and urban devel. policies, wetland protection, state planning, greenways and rural sustainability to profl. jours. Active South Dade Mental Health Soc., 1967-68, Cape Fla. Acquisition Com., 1966, Dade County Downtown Govtl. Ctr. Com., 1967-71, Miami Downtown Devel. Authority, 1970, Gov.'s Task Force on Resource Mgmt., 1971-72, Nat. Task Force on Natural Resources and Land Use Info. and Tech., 1973-74, Fla. Gov.'s Commn. on Property Rights, 1993-94; county commr. Dist. 7, Dade County, 1964-71; vice mayor, 1964, 68; mem. adv. com. Legis. Coun. Subcom. on Constrn. Industry Study, 1966-68; bd. dirs., chmn. retirement and compensation com. State Assn. County Commrs., 1968-71; mem. Alachua County Budget Study Com., 1978, Fla. Land Use Adv. Com. for Phosphate Lands, 1978-80, Suwanee River Water Mgmt. Bd., 1982-87, 91-98, chmn. 1987-88; chmn. Fla. Inst. Phosphate Rsch., 1984-87; bd. dirs. 1000 Friends of Fla, 1986-2003; active Fla. Greenway's Commn., 1991-93, Fla. Greenway Coordinating Coun., 1998-99; gov.'s adv. commn. on coastal mgmt., 1997. With USCG, 1944-46. Fellow: AIA (urban design com. 1976—80), Assn. Collegiate Schs. of Planning (bd. dirs. 1986—88), Nat. Inst. Bldg. Scis. (steering com. for rsch. 1979—80), Am. Inst. Cert. Planners, Gargoyle Soc.; mem.: Phi Kappa Phi. Democrat. Unitarian Universalist. Office: PO Box 234 Cedar Key FL 32625-0234 Personal E-mail: estarnes@inetw.net.

STARNES, WILLIAM HERBERT, JR., chemist, educator; b. Knoxville, Tenn., Dec. 2, 1934; s. William Herbert and Edna Margaret (Osborne) Starnes; m. Maria Sofia Molina, Mar. 4, 1986. BS with honors, Va. Poly. Inst., 1955; PhD, Ga. Inst. Tech., 1960. Rsch. chemist Esso Rsch. & Engring. Co., Baytown, Tex., 1960-62, sr. rsch. chemist, 1962-64, polymer additives sect. head, 1964-65, rsch. specialist, 1965-67, rsch. assoc., 1967-71; instr. and rsch. assoc. dept. chemistry U. Tex., Austin, 1971-73; mem. tech. staff AT&T Bell Labs., Murray Hill, NJ, 1973-85; prof. chemistry Poly. U., Bklyn., 1985-89, head dept. chemistry and life scis., 1985-88, assoc. dir. polymer durability ctr., 1987-89; Floyd Dewey Gottwald Sr. prof. chemistry Coll. William and Mary, Williamsburg, Va., 1989—, prof. applied sci., 1990—. Invited lectr. several fgn. countries and U.S.; ofcl. guest USSR Acad. Scis., 1990, Russian Acad. Scis., 1992; disting. vis. prof. Beijing Inst. Tech., 1996; vis. scientist Tex. Acad. Scis., 1964—67; mem. bd. doctoral thesis examiners Indian Inst. Tech., New Delhi, 1988, McGill U., Montreal, 1989, MacQuarie U., Sydney, Australia, 1991, McMaster U., Hamilton, Canada, 1994; panelist, reviewer NSF Acad. Rsch. Facilities Modernization Program, 1990; channel program mentor U. Cairo, 1994—95; mem. opinion leader panel Wall St. Jour., 1995—; charter mem. dept. chemistry adv. coun. Va. Poly. Inst. and State U., 1998—; sci. advisor European Multinational Environ. Rsch. Project on PVC in Soil and Landfills, 1995—99; cons. numerous indsl. cos., govtl. and pvt. agys.; course dir. continuing edn. Editor-in-chief: Jour. Vinyl and Additive Tech., 1998—, mem. adv. bd., bd. reviewers: Jour. Vinyl Tech., 1981—83, mem. editl. bd.: Jour. Chem. and Biochem. Kinetics, 1992—, Polymer Degradation and Stability, 1997—, Internat. Jour. Coatings Sci., 2001—; mem. editl. bd. The Chemist, 2003—; contbr. chapters to books, articles to profl. jours. Named honoree Plastics History and Artifacts Program, Plastics Pioneers Assn., 2001; recipient Profl. Progress award, Soc. Profl. Chemists and Engrs., 1968, Disting. Tech. Staff award, AT&T Bell Labs., 1982, Polymer Sci. Pioneer award, Polymer News, 1988, Honor Scroll award, N.J. Inst. Chemists, 1989, Excellence in Innovation, Hampton Roads Tech. Coun., 2004; fellow, NSF, 1958—60; grantee, 1989—, Nat. Bur. Stds. Ctr. Fire Rsch., Internat. Copper Rsch. Assn., Va. Ctr. Innovative Tech., GenCorp Found., several indsl. cos. Fellow: AAAS (Project 2061 1985—86, chmn. chemistry subpanel 1985—86, mem. panel on phys. scis. and engring. 1985—86), Soc. Plastics Engrs. (nat. publs. com. 1998—2001, thesis advisor nat. award Vinyl Plastics divsn. 1996, 1998), N.Y. Acad. Scis., Am. Inst. Chemists (life); mem.: North Am. Thermal Analysis Soc., Va. Acad. Sci., Soc. Plastics Engrs., Am. Chem. Soc. (bd. dirs. southeastern Tex. sect. 1970, spkrs. bur. divsn. polymer chemistry 1976—, mem.-at-large exec. com. Va. sect. 1995), Phi Lambda Upsilon (pres. Va. Poly. Inst. chpt. 1954—55), Sigma Xi (M. A. Ferst award Ga. Inst. Tech. chpt. 1960), Phi Kappa Phi (life). Achievements include patents in field; research in degradation, stabilization, flammability, microstructures and polymerization mechanisms of synthetic polymers, especially poly(vinyl chloride); free radical chemistry; carbon-13 nuclear magnetic resonance and organic synthesis; subspecialities include organic chemistry, polymer chemistry. Office: Coll William and Mary Dept Chemistry PO Box 8795 Williamsburg VA 23187-8795 E-mail: whstar@wm.edu.

STARR, ARNOLD, neurologist, educator; b. N.Y.C., Aug. 5, 1932; s. Harry and Augusta (Rubelman) S.; children: David, Jonathan; m. Bonnie Olsen; 1 child, Noah. AB cum laude, Kenyon Coll., 1953; MD, NYU, 1957. Diplomate Am. Bd. Psychiatry and Neurology. Med. intern Beth Israel Hosp., Boston, 1957-58; resident in neurology Boston City Hosp.; teaching fellow Harvard U., Boston, 1958-60; rsch. assoc. NIH, Bethesda, Md., 1960-62; NIH spl. fellow U. Copenhagen, 1962-63, Sechenov Inst. Physiology, Moscow, 1963, Centre de Recherge Neurophysiologique, Paris, 1964-65; asst. prof. medicine Stanford U., Palo Alto, Calif., 1964-71; assoc. prof. medicine and psychobiology U. Calif., Irvine, 1972-74, prof. neurology, psychobiology and physiology, 1974-77, prof. neurology, psychobiology and cognitive scis., 1977—, prof. psychiatry, 1983—, chief div. neurology, 1973-77, founding chmn. dept. neurology, 1977-86, dir. neurology residency program, 1973-90, neurologist Irvine Med. Ctr. Orange, 1972—. Cons. Nat. Multiple Sclerosis Soc., N.Y.C.; cons., mem. bd. sci. counselors, NIH, Bethesda, Md., 1988-92; Rosenthal vis. prof. Israel Inst. Tech., Haifa, 1982, 90; vis. prof. Tanta (Arab Republic of Egypt) U., 1985, U. London, 1986-88, U. Rome, 1986-87, U. Hangzhou, People's Republic China, 1986, U. Vienna, Austria, 1989; lectr. in field. Author: Sensory Evoked Potentials, 3 vols., 1984; contbr.: Behavioral Neurosciences, 1980; editorial reviewer various jours.; contbr. numerous articles to profl. jours., book chpts. Sr. surgeon USPHS, 1960-62. Fellow Acoustical Soc. Am.; mem. Am. Neurol. Assn., Am. Acad. Neurology (therapeutics and tech. assessment subcom. 1990), Nu Sigma Nu. Avocation: pomology.

STARR, CHARLES CHRISTOPHER, foundation executive, priest; b. Atlanta, Jan. 15, 1952; s. David Homer and Margaret Mary (Bussey) S.; m. C. Kathy Wright, Dec. 15, 1984; 1 child, Anna Katherine. BA in Philosophy, St. Mary's Coll., 1975; MDiv, St. Vincent de Paul, 1980. Ordained to ministry Roman Cath. Ch., 1980; received into ministry Episcopal Ch., 1993. Assoc. pastor Sacred Heart Ch., Atlanta, 1980-82, Immaculate Heart of Mary, Atlanta, 1983, Cathedral Christ the King, Atlanta, 1983-84; vice chancellor Archdiocese of Atlanta, 1982-84; v.p. Lehfeldt and Assocs., 1985-89; dir. devel. Winship Cancer Ctr., 1989-91; exec. dir. Henry W. Grady Found., 1992-95; assoc. rector Ch. of Atonement, Atlanta, 1993—; exec. dir. Nat. Kidney Found. of Ga., Atlanta, 1995—. Pres. Transition House, Atlanta, 1988-92. Mem. Nat. Soc. Fund Raising Execs. (cert., bd. dirs. Ga. chpt. 1992—). Home: 1726 Coventry Pl Decatur GA 30030-1005 Office: Nat Kidney Found of Ga 2951 Flowers Rd S Ste 211 Atlanta GA 30341-5533

STARR, CHAUNCEY, research institute executive; b. Newark, Apr. 14, 1912; s. Rubin and Rose (Dropkin) Starr; m. Doris Evelyn Debel, Mar. 20, 1938; children: Ross M., Ariel E. EE, Rensselaer Poly. Inst., 1932, PhD, 1935, DEng (hon.), 1964, Swiss ETH, 1980; DSci (hon.), Tulane U., 1986. Rsch. fellow physics Harvard U., 1935—37; rsch. assoc. Mass. Inst. Tech., 1938—41; rsch. physicist D.W. Taylor Model Basin, Bur. Ships, 1941—42; staff radiation lab. U. Calif., 1942—43, Tenn. Eastman Corp., Oak Ridge, 1943—46, Tenn. Eastman Corp. (Clinton Labs.), 1946; chief spl. rsch. N. Am.

Aviation, Inc., Downey, Calif., 1946—49, dir. atomic energy rsch. dept., 1949—55, v.p., 1955—66; gen. mgr. N. Am. Aviation, Inc. (Atomics Internat. divsn.), 1955—60; pres. divsn. N. Am. Aviation, Inc. (Atomics Internat. div.), 1960—66; dean engring. U. Calif. at LA, 1966—73; cons. prof. Stanford U., 1974—; pres. Electric Power Rsch. Inst., 1973—78, vice chmn., 1978—87, pres. emeritus, 1987—. Dir. Atomic Indsl. Forum. Contbr. sci. articles to profl. jours. Decorated Legion of Honor France; recipient Henry D. Smyth award, Atomic Indsl. Forum, 1983, Nat. medal of Tech., 1990. Fellow: AAAS (dir.), Am. Phys. Soc. (Pake prize), Am. Nuc. Soc. (past pres.); mem.: AIAA (sr.), Royal Swedish Acad. for Engring. Scis., Nat. Acad. Engring., Am. Power Conf., Sigma Xi, Eta Kappa Nu. Home: 95 Stern Ln Atherton CA 94027-5422 E-mail: cstarr@epri.com.

STARR, DAVID, newspaper editor, publisher; b. N.Y.C., Aug. 1, 1922; s. Aaron and Helen (Simon) S.; m. Marjorie Giffen, Aug. 3, 1943; children: Pamela, Peter. BA, Queens Coll., 1942. Reporter, rewriteman L.I. Daily Press, 1942-50; exec. editor Nassau Daily Rev. Star, 1950-53; asst. editor Newark Star-Ledger, 1954-56; asso. editor L.I. Press, 1953-54, 56-62, mng. editor, 1962-69, editor, 1969-77; sr. editor Newhouse Newspapers, 1971—; pub. Springfield Republican, 1977-99, pres., 1999—. Pres. Springfield Ctrl., Inc., 1978-88, chmn., 1989-95. Trustee Nassau C.C., SUNY, 1959-66; bd. dirs. Springfield Libr. and Mus. Assn., chmn., 1988-90; mem. Mass. Cultural Coun., 1980—; bd. dirs. Am. Arts Alliance, 1988-92, chmn., 1989-92. Mem. Am. Soc. Newspaper Editors, Am. Newspaper Pubs. Assn. Office: The Republican Co 1860 Main St Springfield MA 01103-1000 E-mail: dstarr@repub.com.

STARR, HARVEY, political scientist, educator; b. NYC, Nov. 11, 1946; s. Nathan and Betty (Brand) S.; m. Madonna Kissel, June 1, 1969 (div. Dec. 1979); m. Dianne C. Luce, July 2, 1994. BA, SUNY, Buffalo, 1967; M of Philosophy, Yale U., 1970, PhD, 1971. Acting instr. polit. sci. Yale U., New Haven, 1970—71; vis. fellow in politics Dept. Politics, U. Aberdeen, Scotland, 1971—72, 1978—79; asst. prof. polit. sci. Ind. U., Bloomington, 1972—77, assoc. prof., 1977—83, prof., 1983—89; prof. in internat. affairs U. S.C., Columbia, 1989—, chair dept. polit. sci., 1998—. Author: Henry Kissinger: Perceptions of International Politics, 1984, Anarchy, Order, and Integration, 1997; co-author: Inquiry, Logic and International Politics, 1989, World Politics: Menu for Choice, 1981, 85, 89, 92, 96, 2000, 2003, The Diffusion of War: A Study of Opportunity and Willingness, 1991, Agency, Structure and International Politics, 1997, Necessary Conditions: Theory, Methodology and Applications; mem. editl. bd. Teaching Polit. Sci., 1978-81, Comparative Polit. Studies, 1979-92, Am. Polit. Sci. Rev., 1985-89, 91-95, Internat. Studies Quar., 1985-90, Jour. Politics, 1988-97, 2000-03, Internat. Interactions, 1985-91, editor, 1991-2000; contbr. articles to profl. jours. Grantee NSF, 1982-84, 98-2001. Mem. Peace Sci. Soc. (pres. 2000-2001), Peace Sci. Soc. Midwest (pres. 1978-80), Ind. Consortium for Security Studies (dep. dir. 1980-89), Data Devel. in Internat. Rsch. (exec. coun. 1986-87, 89-92), Conflict Processes Sect., Am. Polit. Sci. Assn. (exec. coun. 1989-91, pres. 1992-95, v.p. 1995-96), So. Polit. Sci. Assn. (exec. coun. 1991-94). Office: U SC Dept Polit Sci Columbia SC 29208-0001 Business E-Mail: starr-harvey@sc.edu.

STARR, ISIDORE, law educator; b. Bklyn., Nov. 24, 1911; BA, CCNY, 1932; LLB, St. John's U., Jamaica, N.Y., 1936; MA, Columbia U., 1939; JSD, Bklyn. Law Sch., 1942; PhD, New Sch. Social Rsch., 1957. Bar: NY 1937. Tchr. various high schs., N.Y.C., 1934-61; from assoc. prof. to prof. edn. Queen's Coll., 1961-75, prof. emeritus, 1975—. Dir. Inst. on Law-Related Edn., Lincoln-Filene Ctr., Tufts U., 1963, Law Studies Inst., NYC, 1974; adv. on Our Living Bill of Rights Film Series (6 films) Ency. Brit. Ednl. Corp.; mem. Ariz. Ctr. for Law-Related Edn.; coun. on pub. legal edn. State of Wash., 2001—; cons. in field. Author: The Lost Generation of Prince Edward COunty, 1968, The Gideon Case, 1968, The Feiner Case, 1968, The Mapp Case, 1968, The Supreme Court and Contemporary Issues, 1968, Human Rights in the United States, 1969, The American Judicial System, 1972, The Idea of Liberty, 1978, Justice: Due Process of Law, 1981; co-editor Living American Documents, 1971. Bd. dirs. Phi Alpha Delta Juvenile Justice Program, 1981—. 1st lt. U.S. Army, 1943-46. John Hay fellow, 1952-53; recipient Outstanding Citizen award Philip Morris Cos., 1992. Mem. ABA (hon. chair adv. commn. on Youth Edn. for Citizenship, Isidore Starr award for Spl. Achievment in Law Studies, Leon Jaworski award 1989), Nat. Coun. Social Studies (past pres.), Washington Coun. Pub. Legal Edn., Phi Beta Kappa, Phi Alpha Delta (cert. of appreciation 1981). Address: 12501 Greenwood Ave N Apt C406 Seattle WA 98133-8000

STARR, KENNETH WINSTON, dean, lawyer; b. Vernon, Tex., July 21, 1946; s. W. D. and Vannie Maude (Trimble) Starr; m. Alice Jean Mendell, Aug. 23, 1970; children: Randall Postley, Carolyn Marie, Cynthia Anne. BA, George Washington U., 1968; MA, Brown U., 1969; JD, Duke U., 1973; LLD (hon.), Hampden Sydney Coll., Shenandoah U., Mitchell Coll. Law. Bar: Calif. 1973, D.C. 1979, Va. 1979. Law clk. to Judge David Dyer U.S. Ct. Appeals (5th cir.), Miami, Fla., 1973—74; assoc. Gibson, Dunn & Crutcher, Los Angeles, 1974—75; law clk. to Chief Justice Warren E. Burger, U.S. Supreme Ct., Washington, 1975—77; assoc., ptnr. Gibson, Dunn & Crutcher, Washington, 1977—81; counselor to atty gen. of U.S. Dept. Justice, Washington, 1981—83; judge U.S. Ct. Appeals (D.C. circuit), Washington, 1983—89; solicitor gen. Dept. Justice, Washington, 1989—93; ptnr. Kirkland & Ellis, Washington, 1993—; ind. counsel for Whitewater, 1994—99; dean Pepperdine U. Sch. of Law, 2004—. Contbr. articles to legal jours. Legal advisor CAB transition team office of pres.-elect, 1980—81, SEC transition team, 1980—81; bd. adv. Duke Law Jour. Recipient Disting. Alumni awards, George Washington U., Duke U., Atty. Gen.'s award for disting. svc., 1993, Am. Values award, U.S. Indsl. Coun. Ednl. Found., 1993. Fellow: Am. Bar Found. (jud. fellows com., jud. conf. com. on bicentennial of U.S. constn.); mem.: ABA, Va. Bar Assn., D.C. Bar Assn., Calif. Bar Assn., Supreme Ct. Hist. Soc., Inst. Jud. Adminstrn. (pres.), Am. Judicature Soc., Am. Law Inst., Phi Delta Phi (Hughes chpt. Man of Yr. 1973), Order of Coif. Office: Pepperdine U Sch of Law 24255 Pacific Coast Hwy Malibu CA 90263*

STARR, KEVIN, librarian, educator; BA, U. San Francisco, 1962; MA, Harvard U., 1965, PhD, 1969; MLS, U. Calif., Berkeley, 1974; postgrad., Ch. Div. Sch. Pacific, Berkeley, 1983-84. From asst. to assoc. prof. Am. lit. Harvard U., Cambridge, Mass., 1969-74; city libr. San Francisco, 1973-76; prin. Kevin Starr Assocs., San Francisco, 1983-85; prof. comm. arts U. San Francisco, 1981-89; prof. Sch. Planning and Devel. U. So. Calif., 1989—; state libr. Calif., 1994—. Allston Burr sr. tutor Eliot House Harvard U., Cambridge, 1970-73; cons. Beyl and Boyd, Inc., San Francisco, 1979-83; sr. cons. Hill and Knowlton USA, San Francisco, 1983-84; vis. assoc. prof. English U. Calif., Berkely, 1974, vis. lectr. polit. sci., 1976, lectr. librarianship, 1978; adj. prof. humanities San Francisco State U., 1975-76; Regent's lectr. polit. sci. U. Calif., Riverside, 1977; adj. prof. English Santa Clara (Calif.) U., 1977-78; vis. prof. history U. Calif., Davis, 1985-86; vis. scholar, media fellow Hoover Inst., 1986-88; vis. fellow Ctr. Humanistic Studies, Claremont McKenna Coll., 1987; faculty master Embassy Residential Coll., 1990-94. Sr. editor New West Mag., 1977; vatican corr. Hearst Newspapers, Rome, 1978; columnist Examiner, San Francisco, 1977-83; contbng. editor L.A. Times, 1994—; contbr. articles to profl. jours., chpts. to books. Exec. aide to mayor San Francisco, 1973; bd. trustees Am. Issues Forum, 1975-76, Calif. Hist. Soc., 1992—; co-chmn. sister city com., San Francisco and Sydney, Australia, 1981-86; advisor Jr. League San Francisco, 1982-84; canidate San Francisco Bd. Suprs., 1984; councilor Am. Antiquarian Soc., 1996—; mem. Calif. Coun. Humanities, 1996—; regent Cathedral St. Mary Assumption, San Francisco, 1996—. Lt. German Army, 1962-64. Office: Calif State Lib PO Box 942837 Sacramento CA 94237-0001

STARR, LEON, retired chemical research company executive; b. Bronx, N.Y., May 2, 1937; s. Michael and Bella (Foux) S.; m. Joan Gail Linett, June 19, 1960; children— Michael Jason, Jennifer Nicole BS, Poly. Inst., Bklyn., 1958; PhD, U. Mo., 1962. Teaching asst. U. Mo., Columbia, 1958-62; chem. rschr. Mobil Chem. Co., Edison, N.J., 1962-67; various mgmt. positions then dir. tech. Celanese Corp., N.Y.C., 1967-83, corp. v.p. tech., 1983-86; pres. Celanese Rsch. Co., N.Y.C., 1983-90; pres., corp. v.p. tech. Hoechst Celanese Corp., Chatham, N.J., 1986-90, ret., 1990; pres. Lee Starr Assocs., 1991—. Adv. bd. U. Pa. 1988-90; adv. coun. Hampton U., 1988-97; nat. adv. coun. Synthesis Coalition on Engring. Edn. 1991-96; ptnr. Internat. Think-Tank Group, 1995-97; bd. dirs Internat. Fibers Corp., 2000—. Contbr. chpt. to book; patentee in field. Chmn. conservation commn. Town of Westport, 1996-, chmn., 2001—; chmn. Land Acquisition Com., Westport, 1998—. Fellow Phillips Corp., U. Mo., 1961-62, Poly. Inst. N.Y., 1985. Mem. AAAS, Assn. Rsch. Dirs. (bd. dirs. 1995-97), Am. Chem. Soc. (corp. assoc. 1983-90, bd. govs.), Natural Sci. Assn., N.Y. Acad. Scis., Soc. Chem. Industry, Chem. Mfrs. Assn. (chmn. chem. regulations and adv. com. 1977-82), Am. Inst. Chemists, Sales and Mktd. Execs. Internat. (v.p. 1972-73), STAR Residential (bd. dirs. 1994-98), Sigma Xi. Avocations: tennis, golf, sailing, collecting antique scientific instruments. E-mail: LStarr1@prodigy.net.

STARR, MONICA, company executive; b. Chgo., Oct. 8, 1958; d. Myrtis (Saville) Harrold; 1 child, Kristopher. BS, U. Ill., 1980; PhD, St. Regis U. News dir., announcer, prodn. dir., program dir. Sta. KXOK, St. Louis, 1989-93; music rsch. dir. promotions, sales coord., announcer Sta. KMJM, St. Louis, 1989-91; announcer, programming asst. Sta. WPEG, Charlotte, N.C., 1993-94; program dir. Sta. WEJM, Chgo., 1994-96, Sta. WMXD, Detroit, 1996—2002; pres., CEO Starr Innovative Concepts, Inc., West Bloomfield, Mich., 1998—. Conf. chairperson Midwest Radio and Records Assn., 1995; cons. Multiverse Networks, L.A., 1996. Spkr. Minority Spkrs. Bur., 1997. Recipient GRIOT award Midwest Radio and Records Assn., 1996, Music Pioneer award Columbia's Music Assn., 1996; named Outstanding Young Woman of Yr., 1982, 85, 97. Mem. Nat. Black Programmers Coalition (treas., v.p., pres., nat. chpt. Spirit award 1994, FM Personality of Yr. nat. chpt. 1994, Carolina's chpt. 1994), Women in Radio, Nat. Assn. Black Female Execs. in Music and Entertainment Industry. Avocations: computers, bike riding, writing, photography. Office: Starr Innovative Concepts Inc 5123 Rock Run West Bloomfield MI 48322

STARR, PAUL ELLIOT, sociologist, writer, editor, educator; b. N.Y.C., May 12, 1949; s. Saul and Sarah Marion (Buzen) S.; m. Sandra Lurie Stein, Apr. 12, 1981 (dec.); m. Ann Baynes Coiro, June 9, 2000. BA, Columbia U., 1970; PhD, Harvard U., 1978. Jr. fellow Harvard Soc. Fellows, 1975-78; asst. prof. Harvard U., Cambridge, Mass., 1978-82, assoc. prof., 1982-85; prof. sociology Princeton (N.J.) U., 1985—; founder, co-editor The Am. Prospect. Author: The Discarded Army: Veterans After Vietnam, 1974, The Social Transformation of American Medicine, 1983 (C. Wright Mills award 1983, Pulitzer prize 1984, Bancroft award 1984), The Logic of Health-Care Reform, 1992. Guggenheim Found. fellow, 1981-82. Democrat. Office: Princeton U Dept of Sociology Wallace Hall Princeton NJ 08544-1010

STARR, RINGO (RICHARD STARKEY), musician, actor; b. Liverpool, Eng., July 7, 1940; s. Richard and Elsie (Gleave) Starkey; m. Maureen Cox, Feb. 11, 1965 (div. 1975); children: Zak, Jason, Lee; m. Barbara Bach, Apr. 27, 1981. Drummer Ed Clayton Skiffle Group, 1959; drummer & singer Rory Storm's Hurricanes, 1959—62, The Beatles, 1962—69; solo performer, 1970—. Formed Pumpkinhead Records (with Mark Hudson). Musician: (albums) (with The Beatles) Please, Please Me, 1963, With the Beatles, 1963, Meet the Beatles, 1964, Beatles for Sale, 1964, A Hard Day's Night, 1964 (Grammy award best performance by a group, 1964, Grammy award best new artists, 1964), Help!, 1965, Yesterday & Today, 1966, Rubber Soul, 1966, Revolver, 1966, Sergeant Pepper's Lonely Hearts Club Band, 1967 (Grammy award album of the yr., 1967, Grammy award best contemporary album, 1967), Magical Mystery Tour, 1967, The Beatles (The White Album), 1968, Yellow Submarine, 1968, Abbey Road, 1969, Let It Be, 1970 (Grammy award best original score, 1970), Beatles Anthology, 1995 (Grammy award best long form music video, 1996, Grammy awards best pop performance & best short form music video for Free As A Bird single, 1996); film appearances (with The Beatles) A Hard Day's Night, 1964, Help!, 1965, Yellow Submarine (voice), 1968, Let It Be (also co-exec. prodr.), 1970, TV film appearances Magical Mystery Tour (also co-prodr., co-dir.), 1967; musician: (solo albums) Sentimental Journey, 1970, Beaucoups of Blues, 1970, Ringo, 1973, Goodnight Vienna, 1974, Blast from Your Past, 1975, Ringo's Rotogravure, 1976, Ringo the Fourth, 1977, Scouse the Mouse, 1977, Bad Boy, 1978, Stop and Smell the Roses, 1981, Old Wave, 1983, Starr Struck, 1989, Time Takes Time, 1992, Vertical Man, 1998, I Wanna Be Santa Claus, 1999, Ringo Rama, 2003, (with All-Starr Band) Ringo Starr and His All-Starr Band, 1989, Ringo Starr and His All-Starr Band: Live From Montreux, 1992, Ringo Starr and His Third All-Starr Band, 1997, Ringo & His New All-Starr Band, 2002; musician: (with George Harrison, Ravi Shankar and others) (albums) The Concert For Bangla Desh, 1972 (Grammy award album of the yr., 1972); actor: (films) Candy, 1968, The Magic Christian, 1969, Commonwealth, 1970, 200 Motels, 1971, Blindman (also known as Il Cieco and Il Pistolero Cieco), 1972, That'll Be the Day, 1974, Lisztomania, 1975, Sextette, 1978, Caveman, 1981, Give My Regards to Broad Street, 1984, To the North of Katmandu, 1986; actor, prodr., dir. (films) Born to Boogie, 1972, actor, prodr. Son of Dracula, 1974; actor: (TV films) Ringo, 1978, The Cooler, 1982, Princess Daisy, 1983, Alice in Wonderland, 1985, Shining Time Station Christmas: 'Tis a Gift, 1990; (TV series) Thomas the Tank Engine & Friends (voice), 1985—91, Shining Time Station, 1990—91. Decorated Order Brit. Empire; inducted with The Beatles into Rock and Roll Hall of Fame, 1988. Office: c/o KOCH Entertainment 22 Harbor Park Dr Port Washington NY 11050

STARR, ROSS MARC, economist, educator; b. Oak Ridge, Nov. 14, 1945; s. Chauncey and Doris E. S.; m. Susan S. Strauss, July 2, 1967; children: Daniel, Diana. BS, Stanford U., 1966, PhD, 1972. Cons. Rand Corp., summers 1966, 67, Western Mgmt. Sci. Inst., Grad. Sch. Mgmt., UCLA, summers 1967, 71; Cowles Found. staff rsch. economist Yale U., New Haven, 1970, faculty, 1970-74, assoc. prof. econs., 1974, U. Calif., Davis, 1975-76, prof. econs., 1976-80, San Diego, 1980—, chmn. dept., 1987-90. Vis. lectr. London Sch. Econs., 1973-74, Peoples U. China, Beijing, 1987; vis. scholar U. Calif., Berkeley, 1978-80, vis. prof., 1997. Author: General Equilibrium Theory: An Introduction, 1997; co-editor: Essays in Honor of Kenneth J. Arrow, 1986: v.1, Social Choice and Public Decision Making, v.2, Equilibrium Analysis, v.3, Uncertainty, Information and Communication; editor: Gen. Equilibrium Models of Monetary Economies, 1989; contbr. articles to profl. jours. NDEA fellow, 1966-69, Yale jr. faculty fellow, 1973-74, Guggenheim fellow, 1978-79; NSF grant, 1979-81, 83-85. Office: U Calif San Diego Dept Econs 0508 9500 Gilman Dr La Jolla CA 92093-0508 Office Phone: 858-534-3879. Business E-Mail: rstarr@ucsd.edu.

STARR, STEVEN DAWSON, photographer; b. Albuquerque, Sept. 6, 1944; s. Richard Vernon and Carol (Harley) S.; m. Marilynne Sue Anderson, Aug. 6, 1965; 1 child, Stephen Richard. Student, Antioch Coll., 1962-63, Bethel Coll., 1963-64; BA, San Jose State Coll., 1967. Photographer San Jose Mercury-News, Calif., 1966-67; photographer, picture editor A.P., 1968-73; audiovisual producer Starr Productions, Inc., Coral Gables, Fla., 1974-85; photographer Picture Group Agy., 1986-88, Saba Press, N.Y.C., 1988—2000, Corbis, 2000—. Recipient Pulitzer prize for spot news photography, 1970, Nat. Headliners award, 1970, George Polk Meml. award, 1970, Pictures of Year hon. mention, 1970 Office: Corbis 902 Broadway 4th Fl New York NY 10010 E-mail: steve@stevestarr.com.

STARR, TERRELL, state senator; b. Clayton County, Ga., June 5, 1926; m. Celeste McKinney; children: Terry, JoAnn Kennedy. Grad., Atlanta Law Sch. Real estate broker, ins. agent; mem. Ga. Senate, Atlanta, 1968—, pres. pro tempore, 2002; chmn. fin. and pub. utilities com.; vice chmn. appropriations com.; mem. banking and fin. instns., reapportionment coms.; also health and human svcs., edn. coms. Past mem. Clayton County Commn., Clayton County Libr. Bd., Clayton County Bd. Health, Atlanta Regional Met. Planning Commn.; past trustee Forest Park Sch. Dist. Youth Ctr.; deacon, former chmn. bd. of deacons First Baptist Ch., Forest Park. With USN, 1944-46. Recipient Ga. Legis. of Yr. award Ga. Sch. Counselors Assn., Nat. Legis. of Yr. award Am. Sch. Counselors Assn., Legis. of Yr. award Ga. Parks and Recreation Assn., Disting. Svc./Citizen of Yr. award C. of C.; honores received Ga. Mcpl. Assn., Ga. Assn. Children with Learning Disabilities, Ga. Moose Assn., Ga. Assn. Home Health Agys., Elem. Sch. Prins. Assn., Ga. Assn. Edn. Leaders, Gridiron Hon. Society, Am. Acad. Pediats., Nat. Assn. Home Health Care; park named in his honor City of Forest Park; Terrell Starr Human Svcs. Ctrl named in his honor Jonesboro. Mem. Peace Officers Assn. Ga. (hon., life), Jaycees (past pres., Disting. Svc. award), Rotary, Masons, Royal Arch, Tara Club, Kiwanis (past pres.), Yaareb Temple. Democrat. Office: Rm 321 State Capitol Atlanta GA 30334 also: 541 Forest Pkwy Ste 3 Forest Park GA 30297-2147

STARRATT, PATRICIA ELIZABETH, writer, actress, composer, pianist; b. Boston, Nov. 7, 1943; d. Alfred Byron and Anna (Mazur) S. AB, Smith Coll., 1965; grad. prep. dept., Peabody Conservatory Music, 1961; postgrad., Saybrook Grad. Sch./Rsch. Ctr., San Francisco, 1999. Tchg. asst. Harvard U. Grad. Sch. Bus. Adminstrn., 1965-67; mng. dir. INS Assocs., Washington, 1967-68; adminstrv. asst. George Washington U. Hosp., 1970-71; legal asst. Morgan, Lewis & Bockius, Washington, 1971-72; profl. staff energy analyst Nat. Fuels & Energy Policy Study U.S. Senate Interior Com., 1972-74; cons., exec. asst. energy resource devel. Fed. Energy Adminstrn., Washington, 1974-75; sr. cons. energy policy Atlantic Richfield Co., 1975-76; energy cons. Alaska, 1977-78; govt. affairs assoc. Sohio Alaska Petroleum Co., Anchorage, 1978-85; legal asst. Hughes, Thorsness, Gantz, Powell and Brudin, Anchorage, 1989-90; writer, media specialist corp. affairs Alyeska Pipeline Svc. Co., 1990-95; legal asst. Hughes Thorsness Powell Huddleston & Bauman LLC, 1996-97; sr. paralegal Brit. Petroleum, 1997-98; writer, editor Inst. Circumpolar Health Studies U. Alaska, Anchorage, 1998—; exec. dir. Anchorage Cmty. Theatre, 1999—2002. Mem. econ. devel. commn. Municipality of Anchorage, 1981. Actress, asst. dir. Brattle St. Players, Boston, 1966-67, Washington Theater Club, 1967-68, Gene Frankel, Broadway, 1968-69; actress Aspen Resident Theater, Colo., 1985 86, Ranyevskya (The Cherry Orchard), Anchorage, 1994, Bonfila (SLAVS!), Frau Schmidt (The Sound of Music), Anchorage, 1995, Maria (Moonlight), Anchorage, 1997, Olga (Three Sisters), Eccentric Theatre Co., Anchorage, 1998, Mrs. Barker (The American Dream), 7th Ann. Edward Albee Theatre Conf., Valdez, Alaska, 1999, Ethel (Moon Over Buffalo), Eccentric Theatre Co., Anchorage, 1999; writer, assoc. prodr.: Then One Night I Hit Her, 1983, Stephanie (Yardsale) 9th Ann. Edward Albee Theatre Conf., Valdez, Alaska, 2001, Prudence (Landfall) Loblolly Theatre Co., Pensacola, Fla., 2002; screenwriter, prodr., actress, composer, pianist: A Call to Live, 1995, Marmee (Little Women), 1997; appeared off-Broadway in to Be Young, Gifted and Black; performed as Mary in Tennessee, Blanche in A Streetcar Named Desire, Stephanie Dickinson in Cactus Flower, Angela in Papa's Wine, Elizabeth Procter in The Crucible, Candida in Candida, Zeuss in J.B., Martha in Who's Afraid of Virginia Woolf, Amy in Dinny and the Witches, as Columbina in Servant of Two Masters, as Singer in Death of Morris Biederman, as Joan in Joan of Lorraine, as Mado in Amadee, as Mrs. Rowlands in Before Breakfast, as the girl in Hello Out There, as Angela in Bedtime Story, as Hannah in Night of the Iguana, as Lavinia in Androcles and the Lion, as Catherine in Great Catherine, as Julie in Lilliom, as First Nurse in Death of Bessie Smith, as Laura in Tea and Sympathy, as Amelia Earhart in Chamber Music; appeared at Detroit Summer Theatre in Oklahoma, Guys and Dolls, Carousel, Brigadoon, Kiss Me Kate, Finnian's Rainbow; asst. to dir. Broadway plays A Cry of Players, A Way of Life, Off-Broadway play To Be Young, Gifted and Black; screenwriter Challenge in Alaska, 1986, Martin Poll Films; asst. dir. Dustin Hoffman, 1974; contbr. articles on natural gas and Alaskan econ. and environ. to profl. jours. Bd. dirs. Anchorage Comty. Theatre, Alaska Assn. Legal Assts., 1996-98; industry rep. Alaska Eskimo Whaling Commn.; mem. Alaska New Music Forum. Mem. Actors' Equity. Episcopalian. Avocations: skiing, horseback riding, biking, hiking. Home: 6920 Sea Turtle Cir Navarre FL 32566 E-mail: starward1@yahoo.com.

STARREN, JUSTIN BRUCE, medical educator; b. San Diego, Jan. 4, 1959; s. Byron and Geneva Graves Willis Starren; m. Jeanne Rene Valente, Sept. 21, 1991; children: Genevieve Dane, Quinten Dana. AB summa cum laude, Wash. U., St. Louis, 1980, MA, MD, Wash. U., St. Louis, 1987; PhD, Columbia U., 1997. Lic. N.Y., 1996. Intern UCLA Sepulveda Med. Ctr., 1987—88; resident Columbia Presbyn. Hosp., N.Y.C., 1988—90; med. dir. PA Consulting Group, Princeton, NJ, 1990—92; assoc. rsch. scientist Columbia U., N.Y.C., 1996—98, asst. prof. med. informatics and radiology, 1998—. Nsf summer rsch. program com. Columbia U., 2000—; sci. program com. Am. Med. Informatics Symposium, 1998; faculty coun. Columbia U., 1999—. Contbr. articles to profl. jours. Recipient Hugh Wilson award for Radiology Rsch., Wash. U. Sch. Medicine, 1987, Best Electronic Poster, Symposium on Computer Applications in Med. Care, 1995, Martin Epstein award, Am. Med. Informatics Symposium, 1996, Top Ten IT Innovation award, Healthcare Informatics Mag., 2002; fellow, Nat. Libr. Medicine, 1992—95; grantee, N.Y. State Ctr. Advanced Tech., 1995—97, 1997—2000, Lifescan Corp., 2001, N.Y. State Ctr. Advanced Tech., 2002—03. Mem.: Am. Telemedicine Assn., Assn. for Computing Machines, Am. Med. Informatics Assn. (chair fin. 1998—2001), Wash. U. Ballroom Dance Club (founding pres. 1977—80), Pi Mu Epsilon. Achievements include patents pending for A Method and System for Voice Activating Web Pages. Avocations: ballroom dancing, gardening. Office: Columbia U 622 W 168th St VC-5 New York NY 10032

STARRETT, FREDERICK KENT, lawyer; b. Lincoln, Nebr., May 23, 1947; s. Clyde Frederick and Helen Virginia (Meyers) Starrett; m. Linda Lee Jensen, Jan. 19, 1969; children: Courtney, Kathryn, Scott. BA, U. Nebr., 1969; JD, Creighton U., 1976. Bar: Nebr 1976, Kans 1977, US Dist Ct Nebr 1976, US Dist Ct Kans 1977, US Ct Appeals (8th and 10th cirs) 1983, Mo 1987, US Dist Ct (we dit) Mo 1987, US Supreme Ct 1993. Pvt. practice law, Gt. Bend, Kans., 1976-77, Topeka, 1977-86; with Miller, Bash & Starrett, P.C., Kans. City, Mo., 1986-90; ptnr. Lathrop Norquist & Miller, 1990-91, Lathrop and Norquist, Overland Pk., Kans., 1991-95, Lathrop & Gage L.C., Overland Pk., Kans., 1996—. Judicial nominating commr 10th Judicial Dist, 2000—04. Lt (jg) USNR, 1969—72. Mem.: ABA, Kans. Assn. of Defense Counsel, Mo. Orgn. Def. Lawyers, Def. Rsch. Inst. (state rep. Kans. 1998—2001, bd. dirs. 2002—), Am. Bd. Trials Advs. (pres. Kans. chpt. 1997), Kans. Bar Assn. (pres. litigation sect. 1985—86), Civitan Club (pres. 1985—86, Disting. Pres. award 1985—86). Democrat. Presbyterian. Avocations: aviation, scuba diving. Office: Lathrop & Gage LC Bldg 82 10851 Mastin Blvd Ste 1000 Shawnee Mission KS 66210-1669 Office Phone: 913-451-5140. Business E-Mail: fstarrett@lathropgage.com.

STARRETT, LUCINDA, lawyer; b. Washington, June 21, 1957; BA magna cum laude, Princeton U., 1979; student, U. Nigeria, Nsukka, 1980-84; JU cum laude, U. Pa., 1984. Bar: Calif. 1986. Law clerk to Hon. Dorothy W. Nelson U.S. Ct. Appeals (9th cir), 1984-85; ptnr. Latham & Watkins, L.A., 1991—. Chief comment editor Jour. Capital Markets and Securities Regulation, 1983. Mem. bd. alternative dispute resolution Western Justice Ctr. Mem. ABA, L.A. County Bar Assn. Office: Latham & Watkins 633 W 5th St Ste 4000 Los Angeles CA 90071-2005

STARRETT, WILLIAM, dancer, artistic director; b. Indio, Calif., Oct. 18, 1959; s. George Lester and Arleen (LaDroute) S. Soloist Royal Winnipeg (Can.) Ballet, 1974-76, Eglevsky Ballet, N.Y.C., 1977; mem. Am. Ballet Theater, 1977; prin. Joffrey Ballet, N.Y.C., 1978-81; guest artist Ballet West, Salt Lake City, 1981, Atlanta Ballet, 1982, No. Ballet Theatre, Manchester, England, 1983; artistic dir. Columbia (S.C.) City Ballet, 1986—. Named Sr. Medalist Jackson (Miss.) U.S. Ballet Competition, 1979; recipient Key to City, Singapore, 1985. Mem. Leadership Columbia. Office: Columbia City Ballet PO Box 11898 Columbia SC 29211-1898

STARRFIELD, SUMNER GROSBY, astrophysics educator, researcher; b. L.A., Dec. 29, 1940; s. Harold Ernest and Eve (Grosby) S.; m. Susan Lee Hutt, Aug. 7, 1966; children: Barry, Brian, Sara. BA, U. Calif., Berkeley, 1962; MA, UCLA, 1965, PhD, 1969. From lectr. to asst. prof. Yale U., New Haven, 1967-71; rsch. scientist IBM, Yorktown Heights, N.Y., 1971-72; asst. prof. Ariz. State U., Tempe, 1972-75, assoc. prof., 1975-80, prof., 1980—2001, Regents' prof., 2002—. Vis. assoc. prof. Steward Observatory, Tucson, 1978-79; vis. staff mem. Los Alamos (N.Mex.) Nat. Lab., 1974-94. Author numerous scientific papers. Grantee Ariz. State U., 1973, NSF, 1974—, NASA, 1981—; Los Alamos summer fellow, 1974, 86; Joint Inst. Lab. Astrophysics fellow, 1985-86. Fellow Royal Astron. Soc., Am. Phys. Soc. (astrophysics divsn.); mem. Internat. Astron. Union, Am. Astron. Soc. (high

energy astrophyics div., mem. publs. bd. 1978-81, chmn. publs. bd. 2002--). Achievements include discovery of thermonuclear runaway theory of nova outburst; co-discovery of hottest known class of pulsating variable stars and the cause of their pulsations, ultraviolet studies of nova cygni, 1992; HST and CHANDRA X-ray studies of novae in outburst; theoretical studies of Supernova 1a progenitors. Office: Ariz State U Dept Physics/Astronomy PO Box 871504 Tempe AZ 85287-1504 Office Phone: 480-965-3561. Business E-Mail: starrfield@asu.edu.

STARRS, JAMES EDWARD, law and forensics educator, consultant; b. Bklyn., July 30, 1930; s. George Thomas and Mildred Agatha (Dobbins) S.; m. Barbara Alice Smyth, Sept. 6, 1954; children: Mary Alice, Monica, James, Charles, Liam, Barbara, Siobhan, Gregory. BA, LLB, St. John's U., Bklyn., 1958; LLM, NYU, 1959. Bar: N.Y. 1958, D.C. 1966, U.S. Ct. Mil. Appeals 1959, U.S. Dist. Ct. (so. and ea. dists.) N.Y. 1960. Assoc. Lawless & Lynch, N.Y.C., 1958; tchg. fellow Rutgers U., Newark, 1959-60; asst. prof. law DePaul U., Chgo., 1960-64; assoc. prof. law George Washington U., Washington, 1964-67, prof. law, 1967—, prof. forensic scis., 1975—. Cons. Nat. Commn. Reform Fed. Criminal Laws, Washington, 1968, Cellmark Diagnostics, Germantown, Md., 1987—, Time-Life Books, 1993; participant re-evaluation sci. evidence and trial of Bruno Richard Hauptmann for Lindbergh murder, 1983; participant reporting sci. re-analysis of firearms evidence in Sacco and Vanzetti trial, 1986; project dir. Alfred G. Packer Victims Exhumation Project, 1989, A Blaze of Bullets: A Sci. Investigation into the Deaths of Senator Huey Long and Dr. Carl Austin Weiss, 1991, Meriwether Lewis Exhumation Project, 1992—, Frank R. Olson Exhumation Project, 1994, Jesse W. James Exhumation Project, 1995, Samuel Washington-Harewood Excavations, 1999, The Boston Strangler Re-Investigation, 2000, The Exhumation of Carl E. Williams, Sr., 2001, The Exhumation of Samuel Swan, 2002, The Gettysburg Excavations, Pa., 2002—; Snider lectr. U. Toronto, 1999, Boston Strangler Re-Investigation, 2000, Mutter Lectr. Coll. of Physicians, Phila., 2003. Author: (with Moenssens and Inbau) Scientific Evidence in Criminal Cases, 1986; (with Moenssens, Inbau and Henderson) Scientific Evidence in Civil and Criminal Cases, 1995; editor: The Noiseless Tenor, 1982; co-editor: (review) Scientific Sleuthing, 1976—; mem. editl. bd. Jour. Forensic Sci., 1980-98, Encyclopedia of Forensic Sciences; contbr. articles to profl. jours. Sgt. U.S. Army, 1950-53, Korea. Recipient Vidocq Soc. award, 1993; Ford Found. fellow, 1963; vis. scholar in residence USMC, 1984. Fellow Am. Acad. Forensic Sci. (chmn. jurisprudence sect. 1984, 1994, 1995, bd. dirs. 1986-89, 98-2001, Jurisprudence Sect. award 1988, Disting. fellow 1996); mem. ABA, Mid-Atlantic Assn. Forensic Sci. (emeritus), Assn. Trial Lawyers Am., Internat. Soc. Forensic Sci. (chmn. jurisprudence sect. 1988), Internat. Assn. for Identification, Geol. Soc. Am. Roman Catholic. Home: 8602 Clydesdale Rd Springfield VA 22151-1301 Office: George Washington U Nat Law Ctr 720 20th St NW Washington DC 20006-4306 E-mail: jstarrs@main.nlc.gwu.edu.

STARRY, DONN ALBERT, former aerospace company executive, former army officer; b. N.Y.C., May 31, 1925; s. Don Albert and Edith (Sortor) S.; m. Leatrice Hope Gibbs, June 15, 1948; children: Michael, Paul, Melissa, Melanie. BS, U.S. Mil. Acad., 1948; MS in Internat. Affairs, George Washington U., 1966. Commd. 2d lt. U.S. Army, 1948, advanced through grades to gen., 1977; svc. in Europe; comdr. 11th armored cavalry rgt., 1969-70; assigned Dept. Army Staff, 1970-72; comdr. Armor Center and Ft. Knox, Ky., 1973-76, V Corps, Europe, 1976-77; comdr. Tng. and Doctrine Command Ft. Monroe, Va., 1977-81; comdr. in chief U.S. Readiness Command, 1981-83, ret., 1983; v.p. mission analysis and tech. affairs Ford Aerospace and Communications Corp., Detroit, 1983-84, v.p., gen. mgr. space missions group, 1984-86; exec. v.p. Ford Aerospace Corp., Arlington, Va., 1987-90; spl. asst. to pres. BDM Internat., McLean, Va., 1988-90. Chmn. bd. Maxwell Techs. Inc., San Diego, 1995-97, Universal Voltronics, Brookfield, Conn., 1998—; author, lectr., counselor to govt. and industry. Mem. Def. Sci. Bd., 1985—93, Order of Aaron and Hur, Friends of Fifth of May; mem. bd. Eisenhower Found., 1995—; emeritus chmn. bd. U.S. Cavalry Meml. Found., 1995—2003; mem. bd. Army Hist. Found., 2000—; mem. Army Sci. Bd., 2002—. Decorated Def. D.S.M., Army D.S.M. with oak leaf cluster, Silver Star, Bronze Star with V, Soldier's medal, Purple Heart, Legion of Merit with 2 oak leaf clusters, French Ordre Nationale du Merite, German Knight Commdr.'s Cross of Order of Merit with Badge and Star, Disting. Flying Cross, Air Medal with 9 oak leaf clusters; named to U.S. Army Ft. Leavenworth Command and Gen. Staff Coll. Hall of Fame, 1993; recipient Gold medal The Order of St. George. Mem.: Assn. U.S. Army, U.S. Armor Assn. Episcopalian. Office: 11401 Lilting Ln Fairfax Station VA 22039-1717 E-mail: dastarry@earthlink.net.

STARTZ, RICHARD, economist; b. White Plains, N.Y., July 19, 1952; s. Arthur and Adele (Kersh) S.; m. Shelly Joyce Lundberg, Jan. 8, 1983; children: Meredith Lundberg, Glynis Lundberg. BA, Yale U., 1974; PhD, MIT, 1978. Asst. prof. fin. U. Pa., Phila., 1978-84; assoc. prof. U. Wash., Seattle, 1984-91, prof. econs., 1991—, Castor prof. econs., 1999—, chmn. dept. econs., 1995-2000. Author: 8087/80287/80387 For the IBM PC, 1983, 85, 87, Working with 1-2-3, 1985; co-author: Macroeconomics, 1997, 9th edit., 2004. Avocations: computer programming, playing with my children. Office: Univ of Washington Dept Econs PO Box 353330 Seattle WA 98195-3330 E-mail: startz@u.washington.edu.

STARYK, STEVEN SAM, violinist, concertmaster, educator; b. Toronto, Ont., Can., Apr. 28, 1932; s. Peter and Mary Staryk; m. Ida Elisabeth Busch, May 17, 1963; 1 child, Natalie. Student, Royal Conservatory of Music, Toronto, 1942-48, Harbord Collegiate Inst., 1945-48; LittD (hon.), York U., Toronto, 1980. Soloist, concertmaster CBC-Radio Can., Toronto, 1951-55, Royal Philharmonic Orch., London, 1956-59; 1st concertmaster, tchr. Concertgebouw Orch. and Amsterdam Conservatory, 1960-63; concertmaster Chgo. Symphony Orch., 1963-67; prof. of violin Oberlin (Ohio) Coll. Conservatory, 1968-72, Acad. of Music, Vancouver, B.C., Can., 1972-75, Royal Conservatory of Music, Toronto, 1975-87; concertmaster Toronto Symphony, 1982-87; prof. of violin, chair string div. U. Wash. Sch. Music, Seattle, 1987-97, prof. emeritus, 1997—. Faculty music U. Toronto, 1980-87; vis. prof. U. Victoria, 1972, U. Ottawa, 1975, Northwestern U., 1965-66; founding mem. Quartet Can., 1975-80. Soloist, recitalist, N.Am., Europe and the Far East; recording artist on EMI-HMV, CBC, Everest, Orion, other labels; biography (by Thane Lewis) Fiddling with Life, 2000. Recipient 2 Arts awards Can. Coun., Ottawa, 1968, 75, Queen's Silver Jubilee medal Govt. of Can., Toronto, Shevchenko medal, Winnipeg, Man., Can.; biography "Fiddling with Life" by T. Lewis and S. Staryk, 2002. Home: 12068 E Bella Vista Cir Scottsdale AZ 85259-6034 Office: U Wash Sch Music Mail Stop DN-10 PO Box 353450 Seattle WA 98195-3450

STARZINGER, VINCENT EVANS, political scientist, educator; b. Des Moines, Jan. 12, 1929; s. Vincent and Genevieve (Evans) Starzinger; m. Mildred Hippee Hill, June 16, 1953; children: Page Hill, Evans. AB summa cum laude, Harvard U., 1950, LLB, 1954, PhD, 1959; AM (hon.), Dartmouth Coll., 1968. Bar: Iowa 1954. Practice with firm Bannister, Carpenter, Ahlers & Cooney, Des Moines, 1954; tchg. fellow, instr. govt. Harvard, 1957-60; mem. faculty dept. govt. Dartmouth, 1960-94, chmn. dept. govt., 1972-77, 83-85, Joel Parker prof. law polit. sci., 1976-94, prof. emeritus, 1994—. Author: Middlingness: Juste Millieu Political Theory in England and France, 1815-48, 1965, republished as The Politics of the Center, 1991; contbr. articles to profl. jours. With U.S. Army, 1955—56. Recipient award, Am. Philos. Soc.; Sheldon Traveling fellow, 1950—51, Social Sci. Rsch. Coun. fellow, 1958—59, Faculty fellow, Dartmouth U., 1963—64, Earhart Found. fellow, 1970—71. Mem.: ABA, Iowa Bar Assn., Am. Polit. Sci. Assn., Cambridge (Mass.) Boat Club, Am. Alpine Club, Phi Beta Kappa. Home: Elm St Norwich VT 05055 Office: PO Box 981 Hanover NH 03755-0981 Office Phone: 603-643-6016.

STARZL, THOMAS EARL, physician, educator; b. Le Mars, Iowa, Mar. 11, 1926; s. Roman F. and Anna Laura (Fitzgerald) S.; m. Barbara Brothers, Nov. 27, 1954 (div.); children: Timothy, Rebecca, Thomas; m. Joy D. Conger, Aug. 1, 1981. BA, Westminster Coll., 1947, DSc (hon.), 1965; MA, Northwestern U., 1950, MD, PhD, 1952; DSc (hon.), N.Y. Med. Coll., 1970, Westmar Coll., 1974, Med. Coll. Wis., 1981, Northwestern U., 1982, Bucknell U., 1985, Muhlenberg Coll., 1985, Mt. Sinai Sch. Medicine, 1988; MD (hon.), U. Louvain, Belgium, 1985, U. Genova, 1988, U. Rennes, 1988; LLD (hon.), U. Wyo., 1971; LHD (hon.), LaRoche Coll., 1988. Intern Johns Hopkins U. Hosp., Balt., 1952-53, fellow, surg., 1953-54, resident, 1955-56; mem. faculty Northwestern U. Med. Sch., Evanston, Ill., 1958-61, U. Colo. Med. Sch., Denver, 1962-80, prof. surgery, 1964-80, chmn. dept. surgery, 1972-80; prof. surgery, dir. of Transplantation Inst. U. Pitts. Sch. Med., 1981—. Mem. staff Presbyn. Hosp., Univ. Hosp., Children's Hosp. of Pitts., Pitts. VA Hosp. Author: Experience in Renal Transplantation, 1964, Experience in Hepatic Transplantation, 1969; contbr. articles to profl. jours. Recipient award Westminster Coll., 1965, Achievement award Lund U., 1965, Eppinger award Soc. Internat. de Chirurgie, 1965, Eppinger prize, Freiburg, 1970, William S. Middleton award for outstanding research in VA system, 1968, Merit award Northwestern U., 1969, Disting. Achievement award Modern Medicine, 1969, Creative Council award U. Colo., 1971, Colo. Man of Yr. award, 1967, Brookdale award AMA, 1974, David Hume Meml. award Nat. Kidney Found., 1978, Pitts. Man of Yr. award, 1981; Markle scholar, 1958. Fellow ACS (Sheen award 1982), Am. Acad. Arts and Scis.; mem. Soc. Univ. Surgeons, Soc. Vascular Surgery, Am. Surg. Assn., Transplantation Soc., Deutsche Gesellschaft für Chirurgie, numerous others. Office: Thomas E Starzl Transplant Inst Ste 729 Montefiore Hosp 3459 Fifth Ave Pittsburgh PA 15213-3403 Office Phone: 412-624-0112.

STASACK, EDWARD ARMEN, artist; b. Chgo., Oct. 1, 1929; s. Clifford Clement and Elizabeth Frances (Mallek) S.; m. Mary Louise Walters, June 20, 1953 (div. 1972); children: Caren Marie, Jennifer Elizabeth, John Armen, Michael Clifford; m. Diane Miura Hirsch, June 26, 1993; 1 stepchild, David K. Hirsch. BFA with high honors, U. Ill., Urbana, 1955, MFA, 1956. Instr. in art U. Hawaii, 1956-61, prof. art, chmn. dept. art, 1969-72, program chmn. in printmaking, 1975-83, prof. emeritus, 1988; affiliate Downtown Gallery, N.Y.C., 1960-70. Author: (with J. Halley Cox) Hawaiian Petroglyphs, 1970, (with Georgia Lee) Petroglyphs of Kaho'olawe, 1993, Ka'upulehu Petroglyphs, 1994, (with Diane Stasack) Rock Art of Hawaii Volcanoes National Park, Nine Reports, 1995-2001, (with Diane Stasack) Rock Art of Kaloko-Honokohou Nat. Hist. Park, Three Reports, (with Diane Stasack) Spirit of Place, Petroglyphs of Hawaii, 1999, (with Georgia Lee) Ka'uplehu East II Petroglyphs, 2003, (with Diane Stasack) Rock Art of Pu'uhonuao Honaunau National Park, One Report, 2004; one-man shows include Honolulu Acad. Arts, 1961, 66, 69, 76, 87, U.S. embassies Istanbul and Izmir, Turkey, 1976, Am. Cultural Ctr., Bucharest, Romania, 1976, Cleve. Inst. Art, 1976, Hilo (Hawaii) Coll. Gallery, 1976, Amfac Plaza Gallery, 1978, Ryan Gallery, 1981, Art Loft, Honolulu, 1983, Commons Gallery, U. Hawaii, 1996, Hawaii Volcano Nat. Park Art Ctr., 1996; group shows include Carnegie Inst., Pitts., 1964, Krakow (Poland) Biennial, 1966, 68, Smithsonian Instn., Washington, 1967, Mexico City Mus. Modern Art, 1968, Leicester Gallery, London, 1965, Art Mus. Manila, The Philippines, 1982, 2d Internat. Biennial Print Exhibit Republic of China, 1986, Yuma Art Ctr., 1990; represented in permanent collections Mus. Modern Art, N.Y.C., Met. Mus. Art, N.Y.C., Chgo. Art Inst., Bklyn. Mus., Honolulu Acad. Arts, Hawaii State Found. Culture and the Arts, Libr. of Congress, Phila. Mus. Art, Boston Pub. Libr. Served with U.S. Army, 1952-54. Recipient numerous prizes, including; Boston Printmakers Mems. prize, 1967; Juror's awards Honolulu Printmakers, 1957, 58, 59, 62, 63, 66, 67, 68, 74, 77, 87; Soc. Am. Graphic Artists prizes, 1956, 57, 61, 62, 63, 68, 73, 78, 79, 80, 91; Tiffany Found. fellow, 1958, 62; Rockefeller Found. grantee, 1959, Hawaii Cmty. Found. grantee. 1997-2001; MacDowell Colony fellow, 1971, 75; Hawaii State and U.S. Bicentennial Commns. fellow, 1975, grantee McInerny Found., 2003. Mem. Soc. Am. Graphic Artists, Australian Rock Art Rsch. Assn., Rock Art Assn. Hawaii (emeritus pres.), Am. Rock Art Rsch. Assn., Soc. Hawaiian Archaeology, Sharlot Hall Mus. Office: 1623 Morning Stone Dr Prescott AZ 86305-5282 Office Phone: 928-778-4248.

STASH, SUSAN MICHELE, critical care nurse; b. Inglewood, Calif., Mar. 28, 1965; d. Michael Paul and JoAnn Patricia (Margan) S. BSN, Westminster Coll., Salt Lake City, 1987. RN, Calif.; cert. med.-surg. nurse ANCC. Staff nurse gen. surg. unit St. Joseph Hosp., Orange, Calif., 1987-91; staff nurse gen. med. surg. unit Castle Med. Ctr., Kailua, Hawaii, 1992-94; staff nurse renal/pulmonary/telemetry unit Mary Washington Hosp., Fredericksburg, Va., 1994-95; intermediate med. care unit staff nurse Onslow Meml. Hosp., Jacksonville, N.C., 1995-97; staff nurse progressive care unit Swedish Med. Ctr., Englewood, Colo., 1998—; staff nurse subacute ICU Hoag Meml. Hosp. Presbyn., Newport Beach, Calif., 1999—. Mem. ANA, AACN, Am. Assn. Cert. Nurses, Sigma Theta Tau.

STASHOWER, DAVID L. advertising executive; Chmn., CEO Liggett-Stashower Inc., Cleve. Active Cleve. Play House, Cleve. Opera. Inducted into Cleve. Advt. Club Hall of Fame, 1986. Mem. Am. Assn. Advt. Agys. (nat. sec./treas., trustee pension & profit sharing plans), Advt. & Mktg. Internat. Network, Ohio Motorists Assn., Cleve. Advt. Club, Neighborhood Ctrs. Assn. Office: Liggett-Stashower Inc 1228 Euclid Ave Cleveland OH 44115-1831

STASSEN, JOHN HENRY, lawyer; b. Joliet, Ill., Mar. 22, 1943; s. John H. and Florence C. (McCarthy) S.; m. Sara A. Gaw, July 6, 1968; children: John C., David A. BS, Northwestern U., 1965, JD, Harvard U., 1968. Bar: Ill. 1968. Assoc. Kirkland & Ellis, LLP, Chgo., 1968, 73-76, ptnr. 1977—. Contbr. articles to legal jours. Mem. bd. govs. Northwestern U. Libr., chmn., 2003—; bd. dirs. Landmark Preservation Coun. Ill., chmn., 2001-03. Lt. comdr., JAGC, USNR, 1969-72. Mem. ABA (past chmn. com. on futures regulation), Ill. Bar Assn., Chgo. Bar Assn., Phila. Soc., Mid America Club. Home: 1310 N Astor St Chicago IL 60610-2114 Office: Kirkland & Ellis 200 E Randolph St Ste 5900 Chicago IL 60601-6436 Office Phone: 312-861-2238. Business E-Mail: jstassen@kirkland.com.

STASTNY, JOHN ANTON, real estate executive; b. Chgo., June 30, 1921; s. John Joseph and Bozena (Brezina) S.; m. Elizabeth Regina Ossowski, Jan. 2, 1943; children: Mary Elizabeth, John Bernard. Grad. high sch., Chgo. Owner, pres. Stastny Builders, Berwyn, Ill., 1945—; founder, pres. John A. Stastny & Co., Inc., Berwyn, 1954—, Care Ctr. Profls. Inc., Berwyn, 1961-95, Fairfax Health Care Ctr., Berwyn, Ill., 1975-95; chmn. bd. Fairview Health Care Ctr., LaGrange Park, Ill., 1983-95. Pres., adv. bd. Fed. Nat. Mortgage Assn., Washington, 1971-73; chmn. bd. Fed. Home Loan Bank, Chgo., 1972-78. Contbr. articles to profl. jours.; co-founder (tech. jour.): Compendium of Multi-Family Housing, 1965. Bd. dirs. Avery Coonley Sch., Downers Grove, Ill., 1956-60, MacNeal Meml. Hosp., Berwyn, 1978-95; founding gov. West Towns Cmty. Nursing Svc., Berwyn, 1968, Washington Sq. retirement housing, Hinsdale, Ill., 1986; elected del. Cmty. Caucus, Hinsdale, 1955. With U.S. Army, 1942-43. Named Presdl. Appointee Constrn. Industry Collective Bargaining Com., Washington, 1969-71, advisor to U.S. Del. to Econ. Commn. for Europe, U.S. State Dept., Geneva, Switzerland, 1971; named to Housing Hall of Fame, Washington, 1980. Mem. Chgo. Home Builders Assn. (life mem., bd. dirs., pres. 1964-65, Award of Merit 1961), Nat. Assn. Home Builders (life bd. dirs., pres. 1971, numerous disting. service awards 1965-78), Nat. Housing Ctr. (gov., chmn. 1974), Lambda Alpha Internat. (Key award 1964). Clubs: Edgewood Valley Country (LaGrange, Ill.). Republican. Avocations: fishing, golf. Home: 3231 Golfside Dr Naples FL 34110-7006

STASZESKY, FRANCIS MYRON, independent energy consultant; b. Wilmington, Del., Apr. 16, 1918; s. Frank J. and Ruth (Jones) S.; m. Barbara F. Kearney, May 30, 1943; children— Francis Myron, John B., Barbara J., Faith A., Paul D. BSME, MIT, 1943; MSME, Mass. Inst. Tech., 1943. Mech. engr. Union Oil Co. Calif., L.A., 1943-45; with E.I. duPont de Nemours Co., Wilmington, Del., 1946-48; joined Boston Edison Co., 1948, supervising engr. design and constrn., 1948-57, supt. engring. and constrn. dept., 1957-64, v.p., asst. to pres., 1964-67, exec. v.p., 1967-79, pres., chief operating officer, 1979-83; cons., 1983—; dir. Boston Edison Co., 1968-83. Fellow ASME (life); mem. IEEE (sr., life), Nat. Acad. Engring., Engring. Soc. New Eng. (pres. 1961-62). Address: 166 Bank St Harwich Port MA 02646-1321

STATES, DAVID JOHNSON, biomedical scientist, physician; b. Boston, July 12, 1953; m. Angel W. Lee, Sept. 1, 1979. BA, Harvard Coll., 1975; MD, PhD, Harvard U., 1983. Diplomate Am. Bd. Internal Medicine. Staff scientist Nat. Magnel Lab. MIT, Cambridge, 1983-84; resident and intern in internal medicine U. Calif., San Diego, 1984-86; staff fellow NIH, Bethesda, Md., 1986-89; sr. staff fellow Nat. Ctr. Biotechnology Info. Nat. Libr. Medicine, Bethesda, 1989-92; dir., assoc. prof. inst. biomedical computing Washington U., St. Louis, 1992—. Lt. Comdr. USPHS, 1990—. Mem. AAAS, Am. Fedn. Clin. Rsch., Intenrat. Soc. Computational Biology. Office: Washington Univ Inst Biomedical Computing Campus Boc 8036 Saint Louis MO 63110

STATHIS, NICHOLAS JOHN, lawyer; b. Calchi, Greece, Feb. 27, 1924; Republican. s. John and Sylvia (Koutsonouris) S. Student, Columbia U., 1942-43, 44-48, AB, 1946, JD, 1948. Bar: N.Y. 1949. Assoc. James Maxwell Fassett, NYC, 1948—50; asst. counsel to spl. com. to investigate organized crime in interstate commerce U.S. Senate, Washington, 1951; trial atty. Fidelity & Casualty Co., NYC, 1952; law sec. to Harold R. Medina Judge U.S. Ct. Appeals (2d cir.), NYC, 1952—54; spl. dep. atty. gen. N.Y. State Election Frauds Bur., Dept. Law, N.Y.C., 1956; assoc. Watson, Leavenworth, Kelton & Taggart, NYC, 1954—60, ptnr., 1961—81, Hopgood, Calimafde, Kalil, Blaustein & Judlowe, NYC, 1981—84, Botein, Hays & Sklar, NYC, 1984—89; of counsel White & Case, NYC, 1989—93; corp. coun., dir. intellectual property Aphton Corp., NYC, 1993—. Lectr. Practising Law Inst., N.Y.C., 1968-69. Contbr. articles to profl. jours. on trademarks. Pres., exec. dir., chmn., bd. dirs. Found. Classic Theatre and Acad., 1973—; bd. dirs. Concert Artists Guild, 1974-91, Pirandello Soc., 1976—, Bklyn. Philharm. Orch., 1986-91, Orpheon, Inc., 1986-98, Friends of Young Musicians, 1998—. With AUS, 1943-44. Mem. ABA, Assn. of Bar of City of N.Y., N.Y. State Bar Assn., Fed. Bar Coun., Am. Intellectual Property Law Assn., N.Y. Intellectual Property Law Assn. Greek Orthodox. Home: 1885 John F Kennedy Blvd Jersey City NJ 07305-2113 Office: 515 Madison Ave Ste 2511 New York NY 10022-5403

STATHOPOULOS, PETER, internist; b. Hackensack, N.J., Mar. 24, 1952; s. Anastasios and Vasiliki S.; m. Diane Menichella. MD, U. Thessaloniki, 1981. Diplomate Am. Bd. Internal Medicine. Intern St. Vincent's Med. Ctr., S.I., 1981-82, resident in internal medicine, 1982-84, attending physician, 1985—. Office: 856 Castleton Ave Staten Island NY 10310-1809

STATLER, IRVING CARL, aerospace engineer; b. Buffalo, N.Y., Nov. 23, 1923; s. Samuel William and Sarah (Strauss) S.; m. Renee Roll, Aug. 23, 1953; children: William Scott, Thomas Stuart BS in Aero. Engring., BS in Engring. Math., U. Mich., 1945; PhD, Calif. Inst. Tech., 1956. Research engr. flight research dept. Cornell Aero. Lab., Inc., Buffalo, 1946-53, prin. engr. flight research dept., 1956-57, asst. head aero-mechanics dept., 1957-63, head applied mechanics dept., 1963-70, sr. staff scientist aeroscis. div., 1970-71; research scientist U.S. Army Air Mobility Research and Devel. Lab., Moffett Field, Calif., 1971-73, dir. Aeromechanics Lab., 1973-85, dir. AGARD, 1985-88; sr. staff scientist NASA Ames Rsch. Ctr., 1988-92, chief Human Factors Rsch. Divsn., 1992—. Research scientist research analysis group Jet Propulsion Lab., Pasadena, Calif., 1953-55; chmn. flight mechanics panel adv. group aerospace research and devel. NATO, 1974-76; lectr. U. Buffalo, Millard-Fillmore Coll., Buffalo, 1957-58 Served with USAAF, 1945-46 Fellow AIAA (Internat. Cooperation in Space Sci. medal 1992), AAAS, German Aerospace Soc., Royal Aero Soc.; mem. Am. Helicopter Soc., Sigma Xi. Home: 1362 Cuernavaca Circulo Mountain View CA 94040-3571 Office: NASA Ames Rsch Ctr MS 262-7 Moffett Field CA 94035 Office Phone: 650-690-6003. E-mail: istatler@mail.arc.nasa.gov.

STATON, CECIL POPE, JR., religious and academic publisher, educator, broadcast executive; b. Greenville, S.C., Jan. 26, 1958; s. Cecil Pope and Shirley Ann (Hughes) .; m. Catherine Lynn Davidson, Aug. 23, 1986. BA, Furman U., 1980; MDiv, Southeastern Bapt. Theol. Sem., 1982, ThM, 1985; DPhil, U. Oxford, 1988. Assoc. minister Washington Ave. Bapt. Ch., Greenville, SC, 1977—79; pastor Maple Heights Bapt. Ch., Greenville, SC, 1979—80, Trinity Bapt. Ch., Arcadia, NC, 1983—85; prof. Christianity Brewton-Parker Coll., Mount Vernon, Ga., 1989—91; pub., pres. Smyth & Helwys, Macon, Ga., 1990—, bd. dirs.; pres. Sta. Broadcasting, Macon, 2003—, Stroud & Hall Pubs., Macon, 2004—. Assoc. provost, 1996-2004, pub. Mercer U. Press, Macon, 1991-2003; assoc. prof. Coll. Liberal Arts, Mercer U., 1991-2004. Author: A Sturdy American Hybrid: Associated New American Colleges, 2003; editor: Interpreting Isaiah for Preaching and Teaching, 1991, Interpreting Hosea for Preaching and Teaching, 1993, Interpreting Amos for Preaching and Teaching, 1995, Why I Am a Baptist: Preserving the Baptist Heritage for the 21st Century, 1999; contbr. articles to profl. jours. Recipient Am. scholarship Regent's Park Coll., 1986-87, G. Henton Davies Prize in Hebrew, 1985, R.T. Daniel award in Old Testament, 1983, Baggott award Furman U., 1980, Richard Furman Bapt. Heritage award Furman U., 2000. Mem. Soc. Biblical Lit., Am. Acad. Religion, Nat. Assn. Bapt. Profs. Religion, Rotary (local chpt.). Baptist. Home: 103 Plantation Oaks Dr Macon GA 31220-8757 Office: 6316 Peake Rd Macon GA 31210-3960

STATON, JOHANNA BILBO, editor, writer; d. Jean and Ruth Elliott Bilbo; m. Richard Denis Staton, Jan. 20, 1968; children: Christopher Elliott, Valerie Wing. BA, Rollins Coll., 1961; MS in Journalism, Northwestern U., 1965. Asst. editor to assoc. editor Jack and Jill Mag. Curtis Pub. Co., Phila., 1965—69; freelance copy editor, 1970—. Newsletter editor Friends of the Libr., Collingswood, NJ, 1995—. Mem.: Soc. Children's Book Writers and Illustrators. Independent. Protestant. Avocation: horseback riding.

STAUB, AUGUST WILLIAM, drama educator, theatrical producer, director; b. New Orleans, Oct. 9, 1931; s. August Harry and Laurel (Elfer) S.; m. Patricia Gebhardt, Nov. 22, 1952; 1 child, Laurel Melicent. BA, La. State U., 1952, MA, 1956, PhD, 1960. Instr., tech. dir. La. State U., 1955; instr. Ea. Mich. U., 1956-58; assoc. dir. Dunes Summer Theatre, Michigan City, Ind., summers 1957-60; asst. prof., assoc. dir. univ. theatre U. Fla., 1960-64; assoc. prof. U. New Orleans, 1964-66, prof., chmn. dept. drama and communications, 1966-76; prof., head drama dept. U. Ga., 1976-95, prof. emeritus, 1996—. Exec. producer Jekyll Island Mus. Comedy Festival, 1984-88, Highlands (N.C.) Playhouse, 1989-2000, Ga. Repertory Theatre, 1991-95; staff dir. Theatre in the Square, Marietta, Ga., 1996—; exec. sec. Theatres of La.; v.p. New Orleans Internat. Jazz Festival, 1967-69; pres. S.W. Theatre Conf., 1973-74. Author: Lysistrata, 1968, The Social Climber, 1969, A Small Bare Space, 1970, Introduction to Theatrical Arts, 1971, Creating Theatre, 1973, Varieties of Theatrical Arts, 1980, 83, 94; gen. editor: Artists and Ideas in the Theatre (Peter Lang), 1989—; assoc. editor Speech Tchr., 1966-68, So. Speech Comm. Jour., 1974-77, Quar. Jour. Speech, 1977-79. Bd. dirs. Friends Ga. Mus., Athens, Ga. Symphony, Coun. Arts for Children, New Orleans, New Orleans Ctr. Creative Arts, Athens Arts. Commn., Ga. Alliance Arts Edn. Lt. AUS, 1952-54. Recipient Creativity in Rsch. medallion U. Ga., 1987, Disting. Svc. award S.W. Theater Conf., 1985; La. State U. Found. Disting. Faculty fellow, 1970-71. Fellow Coll. of Fellows of Am. Theatre (bd. dirs. 1999-2001), Coll. of Fellows of the S.W. Theatre Assn.; mem. Am. Theatre Assn. (pres. 1985-86, bd. dirs.), Univ. and Coll. Theatre Assn. (pres. 1974-75), Nat. Assn. Schs. Theatre (pres. 1981-83), Univ. Resident Theatre Assn. (bd. dirs. 1976-79), Inst. European Theatre, Nat. Theatre Conf., Am. Soc. Theatre Rsch., Internat. Fedn. Theatre Rsch. Home: 190 Ravenwood Ct Athens GA 30605-3340 Personal E-mail: gusstaub@earthlink.net. *How good it is to be able to spend a lifetime doing what one loves to do.*

STAUB, SHALOM DAVID, cultural organization administrator; b. Bklyn., Jan. 28, 1956; s. Daniel Marvin and Miriam (Rosen) S.; m. Janet Eleanor Frankel, Sept. 2, 1979; 2 children. BA, Wesleyan U., 1977, MA, 1978; PhD, U. Pa., 1985. Dir. folklife program Pa. Heritage Affairs Commn., Harrisburg, 1982-87, exec. dir., 1987-95; pres., CEO Inst. Cultural Partnerships, Harrisburg, 1995—. Adj. prof. dept. religion Dickinson Coll., Carlisle, Pa., 1987, 2001—. Author: Yemenis in New York City, 1989, Craft and Community, 1989; editor Jewish Folklore & Ethnology Rev., 1979-91. Chair Citizens for the Arts, Pa., 2001-03, vice chair, 2004—; chmn., instr. High Sch. of Jewish Studies, Harrisburg, 1995—. Fgn. Lang./Area Studies fellow U.S. Dept. of Edn., 1980-82; recipient Ione Vargus Multicultural award Multicultural Rsch. and Tng. Inst., Temple U., 1993. Fellow: Soc. Applied Anthropology, Am.

Anthrop. Assn.; mem.: Am. Folklore Soc. (exec. sec.-treas. 1991—2000, editor newsletter 1991—2000). Office: Inst Cultural Partnerships 3211 N Front St Ste 104 Harrisburg PA 17110-1342 Office Phone: 717-238-1770. E-mail: staub@culturalpartnerships.org.

STAUB, W. ARTHUR, health care products executive; b. Detroit, Dec. 25, 1923; s. Edward Elmer and Emma Josephine (Fleury) S.; m. Alla Elizabeth Edwards, June 26, 1948; children: James Randall, Sally Ann, David Scott. BS, Dartmouth Coll., 1944; MD, Temple U., 1947. Intern Muhlenberg Hosp., Plainfield, N.J., 1947-48; resident in pediatrics Abington (Pa.) Meml. Hosp., 1950-51; practice medicine specializing in pediatrics Westfield (N.J.) Med. Group, 1948-63; assoc. med. dir. Ciba Pharm. Co., Summit, N.J., 1963-66; med. dir., v.p. life sci. div. Becton-Dickinson and Co., Rutherford, N.J., 1966-70; v.p. med. affairs C. R. Bard Co., Murray Hill, N.J., 1970-88, also bd. dirs. Bd. dirs. Crestmont Fed. Savs. and Loan Assn., Edison, N.J., Colonial Trust Nat. Bank, North Palm Beach, Fla.; cons. Children's Specialized Hosp., Westfield, 1948-88, Overlook Hosp., Summit, 1948-88. Contbr. articles to profl. jours. Deacon Presbyn. Ch., Westfield, 1959—. Ensign USNR, 1944—50, to capt. USAF, 1950—53. Fellow Am. Coll. Physician Execs.; mem. AAAS, Assn. Advancement Med. Instrumentation, Health Industry Mfrs. Assn. (chmn. med. and sci. steering com.). Clubs: Echo Lake Country (Westfield) (bd. trustees 1984-88); Lost Tree (North Palm Beach, Fla., bd. govs. 1989-94, sec. 1989-94); Skytop (Pa.). Republican. Presbyterian. Avocations: golf, physical fitness, reading, sailing, travel. Home: 3330 Devonshire Way Palm Beach Gardens FL 33418 E-mail: DoctorWAS@aol.com.

STAUBACH, ROGER THOMAS, real estate executive, former professional football player; b. Cin., Feb. 5, 1942; s. Robert Joseph and Elizabeth (Smyth) S.; m. Marianne Jeanne Hoobler, Sept. 4, 1965; children: Jennifer Anne, Michelle Elizabeth, Stephanie Marie, Jeffrey, Amy Lynn. Student, Roswell (N.Mex.) Mil. Inst., 1960-61; BS, U.S. Naval Acad., 1965. Quarterback Dallas Cowboy Football Team, 1969-79; pres. Holloway-Staubach Co. (name now Staubach Co.), 1980-92; chmn., CEO, pres. Staubach Co., Dallas, 1993—; former announcer CBS Football. Author: First Down, Lifetime to Go, 1974, Time Enough to Win, 1981. Bd. dirs. Halliburton Co., Gibson Greetings, Salvation Army; active Pres. Coun. on Phys. Fitness, 1981-83. Lt. USNR, 1965-69. Recipient Heisman Trophy, 1963; played Pro Bowl, 1971, 76, 78; inducted into Nat. Football League Hall of Fame, 1985. Mem. Fellowship of Christian Athletes. Roman Catholic. Office: Staubach Co 15601 Dallas Parkway Ste 400 Addison TX 75001*

STAUBER, MARILYN JEAN, retired secondary school educator, retired elementary school educator; b. Duluth, Minn., Feb. 5, 1938; d. Harold Milton and Dorothy Florence (Thompson) Froehlich; children: Kenneth D. and James H. Atkinson; m. Lawrence B. Stauber Sr., Jan. 11, 1991. BS in Edn., U. Minn., Duluth, 1969, MEd in Math., 1977. Cert. elem. and secondary reading tchr., remedial reading specialist, devel. reading tchr., reading cons. Sec. div. vocat. rehab. State Minn., Duluth, 1956-59; sec. Travelers Ins. Co., Duluth, 1962-66; lead tchr. Title 1 reading and math. Proctor, Minn., 1969-98; ret. Mem. choirs and Choral Soc. John Duss Music, chairperson Outreach, Forbes Meth. Ch., proctor. Mem. NEA, VFW, Internat. Reading Assn., Nat. Reading Assn., Minn. Arrowhead Reading Coun., Elem. Coun. (pres. 1983-84, 86-87), Proctor Fedn. Tchrs. (recert. com. 1980—, treas. 1981-86), Proctor Edn. Assn. (chairperson recert. com.), Am. Legion, Euclid Ea. Star, Phi Delta Kappa. Home: 6713 Grand Lake Rd Saginaw MN 55779-9782

STAUBITZ, ARTHUR FREDERICK, lawyer, healthcare products company executive; b. Omaha, Nebr., Mar. 14, 1939; s. Herbert Frederick Staubitz and Barbara Eileen (Dallas) Alderson; m. Linda Medora Miller, Aug. 18, 1962; children: Michael, Melissa, Peter. AB cum laude, Wesleyan U., Middletown, Conn., 1961; JD cum laude, U. Pa., 1964. Bar: Ill. 1964, U.S. Dist. Ct. (no. dist.) Ill. 1964, U.S. Ct. Appeals (7th cir.) 1964, Pa. 1972. Assoc. Sidley & Austin, Chgo., 1964-71; sr. internat. atty., asst. gen. counsel, dir. Japanese ops. Sperry Univac, Blue Bell, Pa., 1971-78; from asst. to assoc. to dep. gen. counsel Baxter Internat. Inc., Deerfield, Ill., 1978-85, v.p., dep. gen. counsel, 1985-90; v.p. Baxter Diagnostics, 1990-91; sr. v.p., sec., gen. counsel Amgen, Inc., Thousand Oaks, Calif., 1991-92; v.p., gen. mgr. Ventures Group Baxter World Trade Corp., Deerfield, Ill., 1992-93; v.p., sec., gen. counsel Baxter Internat. Inc., Deerfield, Ill., 1993, sr. v.p., gen. counsel, 1993-97, sr. v.p. portfolio strategy, 1997-98. Bd. dirs. Aastrom Bioscis., Inc. Mem. Planning Commn., Springfield Twp., Montgomery County, Pa., 1973-74, mem. Zoning Hearing Bd., 1974-78; bd. dirs. Twp. H.S. Dist. 113, Deerfield and Highland Park, Ill., 1983-91, pres., 1989-91; trustee Food and Drug Law Inst., 1991-92, 93-96, Carthage Coll., Kenosha, Wis., 1996—, exec. com., 1999—; bd. dirs. Music of the Baroque, 1994-2001, vice-chmn.; mem. adv. bd. UA Presents; mem. adv. bd. Ariz. Cancer Ctr. Episcopalian. Home: 6251 E Placita Aspecto Tucson AZ 85750 E-mail: staubitz@msn.com.

STAUBUS, GEORGE JOSEPH, accounting educator; b. Brunswick, Mo., Apr. 26, 1926; s. George Washington and Florence Lidwina (Pittman) S.; m. Sarah Mayer, Apr. 11, 1949; children: Lindsay, Martin, Paul, Janette. BS, U. Mo., 1947; MBA, U. Chgo., 1949, PhD, 1954. C.P.A., Ill. Instr. U. Buffalo, 1947-49, U. Chgo., 1950-52; asst. prof. then prof. acctg. U. Calif.-Berkeley, from 1952, now Michael N. Chetkovich prof. emeritus. Vis. prof. NYU, 1965, London Bus. Sch., 1966-67, U. Kans., 1969-70; Erskine lectr. U. Canterbury, New Zealand, 1972, 91. Author: A Theory of Accounting to Investors, 1961, Activity Costing and Input-Output Accounting, 1971, Making Accounting Decisions, 1977, An Accounting Concept of Revenue, 1980, Activity Costing for Decisions, 1988, Economic Influences on the Development of Accounting in Firms, 1996, The Decision-Usefulness Theory of Accounting: A Limited History, 2000. Served with USN, 1944-46. Recipient Disting. prof. Calif. Soc. C.P.A.s, 1981 Fellow Acctg. Researchers Internat. Assn. (treas. 1981-83); mem. Am. Acctg. Assn. (disting. internat. lectr. 1982), Am. Inst. C.P.A.s, Fin. Execs. Inst. Office: UC Berkeley Haas Sch Bus Berkeley CA 94720-0001

STAUDERMAN, ALBERT PHILIP, JR., media consultant; b. Englewood, N.J., Dec. 14, 1936; s. Albert Philip Stauderman and Martha Louise (Dodd) Williamson; m. Helen MacKenzie Layton, Dec. 27, 1958; children: Elizabeth, Sarah, Edward (Ted). BSc, Syracuse U., 1958. Audio-visual prodn. supr. Luth. Ch. in Am., Phila., 1960-64; TV comml. prodn. supr. Procter & Gamble, Cin., 1964-71, assoc. mgr., 1971-82; dir. advt. prodn. Richardson-Vicks, Wilton, Conn., 1982-85; chmn., CEO Bird Bonette Stauderman Inc., Westport, Conn., 1985—; co-chmn., dir. Bird Bonette Stauderman Europe Ltd., London, 1996-2000, chmn., dir., 2000—, founder Sao Paulo, Brazil, 2001—; ptnr. Stauderman/Petray, LLC, Westport, Conn., 2001—. Pres. Dikaia Found., Inc., 1995—2001. Author: TV Commercial Production Cost Trends, 1985, 2d. edit., 1986; writer, dir. various pub. svc. TV Comms., 1970-82; actor Golden Age TV programs, 1949-56. Commr. Wilton (Conn.) various land use Commns., 1988—; founding pres. Syracuse U. Newhouse Sch. Alumni Assn., 1985—87; mgmt. com. vice chmn. office for comms. Luth. Ch. in Am., NY, 1978—86; chmn. comms. unit Ohio Synod of Luth. Ch. in Am., Columbus, 1978—82; pres. congregation and coun. St. Michael's Luth. Ch., New Canaan, Conn., 1999—2001. Recipient Alumni Svc. award Syracuse U., 1981. Mem. Sprite Island Yacht Club (chmn. race com. 1993-98), Williams Club (N.Y.C.), Delta Upsilon. Republican. Avocation: sailing race management official. Office Phone: 203-454-8781.

STAUDERMAN, BRUCE FORD, writer, advertising executive; b. Jersey City, Mar. 17, 1919; s. Herbert Henry and Helen Ann (Jacobus) S.; m. Claude Outhier, Mar. 23; 1946. Student, Syracuse U., 1936-38, TV Workshop, N.Y.C., 1949-50, Sch. TV Technique, 1950. V.p. TV, radio, films Meldrum & Fewsmith, Inc. (advt. agy.), Cleve., 1954-62, exec. v.p., chmn. plans bd., exec. creative dir., 1973-79; v.p., creative dir. Ogilvy & Mather (advt. agy.), N.Y.C., 1962-69, Kenyon & Eckhardt, Inc. (advt. agy.), N.Y.C., 1979-83, Barnhart & Co. (advt. agy.), Denver, 1983-84; pres. Stauderman Advt., 1984—; v.p., creative dir. Mktg. Resources Group (advt. agy.), 1985-88. Dir. TV, Intermarco-Elvinger (advt. co.), Paris, 1969-73; TV cons. gov., Ohio, 1958; mem. coun., judge C.L.I.O. Festival, 1960—; chmn. Paris jury, 1969-73; jury mem. Internat. Advt. Film Festival, Cannes, Venice, 1976— Author: England! What the Guidebooks Don't Tell You, 2004; radio, TV program writer: House of Mystery, The Big Story, Columbia Workshop, 1946-51; writer, producer, dir., WXEL-TV, Cleve., 1951-54. Mem. men's com. Cleve. Playhouse, 1958-62; chmn. TV com. Cleve. United Fund, 1958-59. Served from pvt. to 2d lt. AUS, 1941-46; to 1st lt. N.G. Essex Troop AUS, 1948-50. Mem. Am. Assn. Advt. Agys. (TV and radio adminstrs. com. 1958 62), Am. Fedn. TV and Radio Artists, Naval Club (London). Home: 8647 Falcon Green Dr West Palm Beach FL 33412-1576 E-mail: bfswriter@aol.com.

STAUDOHAR, PAUL DAVID, economics professor, labor arbitrator; b. Duluth, Minn., Dec. 3, 1940; s. Matthew Paul Staudohar and Patricia Constance Landell. BA, U. Minn., 1962; MBA, U. So. Calif., L.A., 1966, MA, 1968, PhD, 1969. Adminstrv. officer United Calif. Bank, L.A., 1964—66; instr. econ. U. So. Calif., L.A., 1967—69; asst. prof. bus. adminstrn. Calif. State, Hayward, 1969—72, assoc. prof. bus. adminstrn., 1972, prof. bus. adminstrn., 1977—. Pres. Internat. Assn. of Sports Economists, France, 1999—2002; bd. editors Jour. of Individual Employment Rights, 1992—; co-founder Jour. of Sports Econs., bd. editors, 2000—. Author: Labor Econ. and Indsl. Rels., 1994, Playing for Dollars, 1996; author, editor: Diamond Mines: Baseball and Labor, 2000, More Sports Best Short Stories, 2004. Recipient disting. svc. award, Omicron Delta Epsilon, 1981. Mem.: Indsl. Rels. Rsch. Assn., Am. Arbitration Assn., Am. Econ. Assn., Nat. Acad. of Arbitrators, Beta Gamma Sigma (hon.). Office: Calif State U Hayward 25800 Carlos Bee Blvd Hayward CA 94542 Office Phone: 510-885-3080.

STAUFFER, ERIC P. lawyer; b. Tucson, Feb. 1, 1948; s. Robert D. and Jeanne E. (Catlin) S.; m. Jane F. Snyder, Aug. 2, 1969; children: Curtis Austen, Marcus Elias, Laura Afton. BA, New Coll. of Fla., 1969; JD, Yale U., 1972. Bar: Ariz. 1972, Maine 1974, D.C. 1979. Spl. asst. to gov., fed. state coord. State of Maine, 1973-75; Maine alt. to New England Regional Commn., 1973-75; gen. counsel Maine State Housing Auth., 1976-77; adminstrv. asst. to chmn. Dem. Nat. Com., 1977-78; mem. Preti, Flaherty, Beliveau Pachios & Haley, LLC, Portland, Maine, 1978—. Bd. dirs. Jr. Achievement Maine, Inc., 1995-98; pres. Goodwill Industries No. New Eng., 1981-82, bd. dirs., 1979-93, 99—. Mem. Am. Health Lawyers Assn., Maine State Bar Assn., Ariz. State Bar, D.C. Bar, Maine Real Estate Devel. Assn. (bd. dirs. 1991—, Pub. Svc. award 1992, Founder's award 2002). Office: Preti Flaherty Beliveau Pachios & Haley LLC PO Box 9546 One City Ctr Portland ME 04112-9546 E-mail: estauffe@preti.com.

STAUFFER, JOHN WILLIAM, cultural historian; b. Lincoln, Nebr. s. William Albert and Jean Stanley Stauffer. MALS in Humanities, Wesleyan U., 1991; MA in Am. Studies, Purdue U., 1993; PhD in Am. Studies, Yale U., 1999. Asst. prof. Harvard U., Cambridge, Mass., 1999-2001, assoc. prof., 2001—03, prof., 2003—. Spkr. in field. Author: The Black Hearts of Men, 2002 (Frederick Douglass Book prize), The Meteor of War: The John Brown Story; contbr. articles to profl. jour. Newhouse fellow in writing Yale U., 1996-97, Rsch. fellow, 1994-95, History and Am. Studies Rsch. fellow, 1996, Charlotte Newcombe fellow Woodrow Wilson Nat. Fellowship Found., 1997-98; grantee NEH, 1999; recipient Ralph Henry Gabriel prize, 1999, Jan Thaddeus Tchg. award Harvard U., 2002, Frederick Douglass Book prize, 2003, Avery Craven Prize, 2003, Lincoln Prize, finalist, 2003. Mem. Soc. for Values in Higher Edn., Orgn. of Am. Historians (presenter 1998), Am. Studies Assn. (Ralph Henry Gabriel prize 1999), Daguerreian Soc., Phi Kappa Phi. Avocations: photography, tennis, ballet, dance (jazz). Home: 13 Ware St Apt 14 Cambridge MA 02138-4010 Office: Harvard U Dept English Barker Ctr 12 Quincy St Cambridge MA 02138-3804 E-mail: stauffer@fas.harvard.edu.

STAUFFER, RONALD EUGENE, lawyer; b. Hempstead, N.Y., Jan. 22, 1949; s. Hiram Eugene and Florence Marie (Hintz) S.; m. Vicki Lynn Hartman, June 12, 1973; children: Eric Alan, Craig Aaron, Darren Adam. SB, MIT, 1970; JD magna cum laude, Harvard U., 1973. Bar: D.C. 1973, U.S. Ct. Mil. Appeals 1976, U.S. Tax Ct. 1979. Ptnr. Hogan & Hartson, Washington, 1977-87, Sonnenschein Nath & Rosenthal, Washington, 1988—. Contbr. articles to profl. publs. Capt. U.S. Army, 1970-77. Mem. ABA (chair TIPS Employee Benefits Com. 1977—), D.C. Bar Assn., Tau Beta Pi, Sigma Gamma Tau. Avocations: running, water-skiing. Home: 10207 Woodvale Pond Dr Fairfax Station VA 22039-1658 Office: Sonnenschein Nath & Rosenthal 1301 K St NW Ste 600 Washington DC 20005-3317 E-mail: rstauffer@sonnenschein.com.

STAUFFER, SCOTT WILLIAM, lawyer, accountant; b. Oshkosh, Wis., Aug. 17, 1954; s. Robert Edward and Shirley Lydia (Wrasse) S.; m. Debralee Bowland, Nov. 14, 1987. BBA in Acctg., U. Wis., 1975; JD, U. Denver, 1979. Bar: Colo. 1979; CPA, Colo. Tax acct. Arthur Andersen & Co., Denver, 1979-82; tax mgr. Gary-Williams Oil, Englewood, Colo., 1982-85; pvt. practice Aurora, Colo., 1986—. Pres. Colo. Chorale, Denver, 1984-85, 92-93. Mem. ABA, AICPA, Colo. Bar Assn. (multidisciplinary practice taskforce 2000-2002, ethics com. 1997-99, vice chair, exec. coun. solo and small firm sect. 2002-04, chair 2004—), Denver Bar Assn. (chmn. law office mgmt. com. 1993-95, chmn. intraprofl. com. 1997-2004), Colo. Soc. CPA (chmn. fed. tax com. 1994-96, bd. dirs. 2000-02), Am. Assn. Atty.-CPA., Denver Tax Assn. (chair 2003), Bethany Luth. Ch. Found. (pres. 2003—). Lutheran. Avocations: singing, golf, travel, reading, computer. Home: 8147 W Frost Pl Littleton CO 80128-4325 Office: 2851 S Parker Rd Ste 720 Aurora CO 80014-2728 E-mail: sstauffer@staufferlawcpa.com.

STAUFFER, STANLEY HOWARD, retired newspaper and broadcasting executive; b. Peabody, Kans., Sept. 11, 1920; s. Oscar S. and Ethel L. (Stone) S.; m. Suzanne R. Wallace, Feb. 16, 1945 (div. 1961); children: Peter, Clay, Charles; m. Elizabeth D. Priest, July 14, 1962 (div. 1991); children: Elizabeth, Grant; m. Madeline A. Sargent, Nov. 27, 1992. AB, U. Kans., 1942; DHL (hon.), Washburn U., 2001. Assoc. editor Topeka State Jour., 1946-47; editor, pub. Santa Maria (Calif.) Times, 1948-52; rewrite and copy editor Denver Post, 1953-54; staff mem. AP (Denver bur.), 1954-55; exec. v.p. Stauffer Publs., Inc., 1955-69; gen. mgr. Topeka Capital-Jour., 1957-69; pres. Stauffer Comm., Inc., 1969-86, chmn., 1986-92. Past pres. Topeka YMCA; past chmn. adv. bd. St. Francis Hosp.; past chmn. Met. Topeka Airport Authority; trustee William Allen White Found., Midwest Rsch. Inst., Washburn U. Endowment Assn, Bd. Visitors Menningen Found. With USAAF, 1942-45. Named Chpt. Boss of Yr. Am. Bus. Women's Assn., 1976, Outstanding Kans. Pub. Kappa Tau Alpha, 1980, Legion of Honor De Molay, Topeka Phi of Yr., 1971 Mem. Kans. Press Assn. (past pres.), Inland Daily Press Assn. (past dir.), Air Force Assn. (past pres. Topeka), Kans. U. Alumni Assn. (past dir.), Kans. C. of C. and Industry (past chmn.), Def. Orientation Conf. Assn. (dir.), Topeka Country Club (past dir.), Top of the Tower Club, La Quinta (Calif.) Country Club, Masons (32d deg.), Arab Shrine, Phi Delta Theta (past chpt. pres.), Sigma Delta chi (past chpt. pres.). Episcopalian (past sr. warden).

STAUFFER, THOMAS GEORGE, retired hotel executive; b. Akron, Ohio, Mar. 4, 1932; s. Caldwell E. and Rose C. (Ortscheidt) S.; m. Lois Campsey, June 18, 1960. BS, Case Western Res. U., 1954. Cert. hotel adminstr. Pres. Renaissance Hotels Internat. (Ams.), 1954-98; ret., 1998. Trustee Cleve. Bot. Garden. Recipient Legion of Honor, Order of DeMolay. Mem. Am. Hotel and Motel Assn., Urban Land Inst., Nat. Restaurant Assn. (dir.), Rolling Rock Club, Lakewood Country Club, Masons, Shriners, Sigma Chi (Significant Sigma Chi). Home: 19 Warwick Ln Cleveland OH 44116-2305 Office: Renaissance Hotels Internat Marriott Dr Washington DC 20058-0001 E-mail: tomgstau@aol.com.

STAUFFER, THOMAS MICHAEL, former university president; b. Harrisburg, Pa., Dec. 5, 1941; s. John Nisley and Louise Lee Stauffer; children: Amity Juliet, Courtney Amanda, Winston Thomas; 1 stepchild, Elizabeth Stinson; life partner Susan Heller. Student, Juniata Coll., 1959-61; BA cum laude, Wittenberg U., Ohio, 1963; Cert. in E. European Politics, Freie U. Berlin, 1964; MA, PhD, U. Denver, 1973; Doctorate (hon.), Jackson State U., 2002. Asst. dean coll., assoc. prof. polit. sci. Keene State Coll., 1968-72; dir. fellows in acad. adminstrn., office leadership devel. Am. Coun. on Edn., 1972-78, v.p., divsn. external rels., 1978-82; pres., prof. pub. policy U. Houston-Clear Lake, 1982—91; pres., prof. pub. policy and internat. rels. Golden Gate U., 1992—99; CEO Young Pres. Orgn. Internat., 1999—2001; exec. dir. Lincoln Ctr. for Ethics in Internat. Mgmt., prof. applied global bus. Thunderbird--The Garvin Sch. of Internat. Mgmt., 2003—; CEO Upper Mgmt. Internat., 1985—. Exec. sec. Fedn. of Assn. of the Acad. Health Care Professions, 1975—80; chmn. task force on the future of Am. Coun. on Edn., 1978; exec. dir. Bus.-Higher Edn. Forum, 1978—81, Nat. Commn. on Higher Edn. Issues, 1980—81; spl. asst. to adminstr. NASA, 1991—92; internat. mgmt. cons. Exec. editor Ednl. Record and Higher Edn. and Nat. Affairs, 1978-82; author books and monographs; contbr. articles to profl. jours. and newspapers. Chair nat. bd. Challenger Ctr. for Space Sci. Edn., 1987—89, Ctr. for Advanced Space Studies, 1990—94; chmn. com. advanced tech. Tex. Econ. Devel., 1984, Houston Com. on Econ. Diversification Planning, 1984, Houston World Trade Ctr. Task Force, 1985, East Tex. 2000 Com. on Econ. Devel., S.E. Tex. Higher Edn. Coun., 1989, Clear Lake Area Econ. Devel. Found.; v.p. Houston World Trade Assn.; co-chair Tex. Sci. and Tech. Coun., 1986; pres. St. John Hosp.; vice-chair San Francisco World Trade Assn.; chair San Francisco Consortium on Higher Edn., San Francisco Mayor's Blue Ribbon Com. on Econ. Devel.; mem. steering com. Silicon Valley Mfrs. Group; bd. dirs. San Francisco C. of C. Recipient Disting. Alumni award Grad. Sch. Internat. Studies U. Denver, 1989, Tex. Senate Resolution of Commendation, 1991, Challenger Ctr. Nat. award, 1990, ACE Fellow Anniversary award, 1990, Leadership H.S. Do the Right Thing award, 1998; Am. Coun. on Edn. fellow in acad. adminstrn., 1971, Ford Found. and Social Sci. Found. fellow, 1963-68, sr. fellow Am. Leadership Forum. Home: 1806 Green St San Francisco CA 94123-4922 Office: 15249 N 59th Ave Glendale AZ 85306 Office Phone: 214-213-1709. E-mail: tomstauffer@hotmail.com.

STAUFFER, VALERIE VILAS, civic volunteer; b. N.Y.C., Aug. 29, 1935; d. Frank Jay and Kathleen Vilas Brown; m. John Eugene Stauffer, June 5, 1956; children: Jill Stauffer Cobbs, Karen Stauffer Murphy, John Christian, Peter Eugene. BA, Wellesley Coll., 1956. V.p. Stauffer Tech., Greenwich, Conn., 1985—. Editor: (nonfiction) Quality Assurance of Food, 1988, (newsletter) Round Hill Association Newsletter, 1991-92; contbr. Greenwich Rev. mag., 1971-73. Chmn. dist. 7 Rep. Town Meeting, Greenwich, Conn., 1984—, chmn. social svcs. com., 1997; chmn. Friends of Greenwich Libr., 1997—99; trustee, exec. com., sec. bd. trustees Greenwich Libr., 1999—. Mem. Greenwich Garden Club (pres. 1999-2001). Home: 6 Pecksland Rd Greenwich CT 06831-3738 Office: Stauffer Tech 6 Pecksland Rd Greenwich CT 06831-3738 Personal E-mail: stauftek@aol.com.

STAVELY, KEITH WILLIAMS FITZGERALD, librarian; b. New Brunswick, N.J., May 13, 1942; s. Homer Eaton and Elizabeth (Williams) S.; m. Kathleen Fitzgerald, Aug. 19, 1978; 1 child, Jonathan Keith. BA, Yale U., 1964, PhD, 1969; MLS, Simmons Coll., 1980. Asst. prof. English Boston U., 1969-74, Ohio State U., 1990-91; lectr. in English Boston Coll., 1975-80; adult svcs. libr. Watertown (Mass.) Free Pub. Libr., 1979-89, br. libr., 1984-89, head adult svcs., 1989-90; reference libr. Somerville (Mass.) Pub. Libr., 1991-92; asst. adminstr. Fall River (Mass.) Pub. Libr., 1992-99, adminstr., 1999—. Author: Puritan Legacies: Paradise Lost and the New England Tradition, 1630-1890, 1987, paperback edit., 1990, The Politics of Milton's Prose Style, 1975; co-author: Family Man: What Men Feel About Their Wives, Their Children, Their Parents, and Themselves, 1978, America's Founding Food: The Story of New England Cooking, 2004; contbr. articles and revs. to profl. publs. Fellow Fulbright Found., India, 1964-65, Am. Coun. Learned Socs., 1988-89, John Simon Guggenheim Meml. Found., 1989. Mem. MLA (Prize for Ind. Scholars 1987), ALA, Mass. Libr. Assn., Phi Beta Kappa. E-mail: kstavely@sailsinc.org., kstavely@cox.net.

STAVERT, ALEXANDER BRUCE, bishop; b. Montreal, Apr. 1, 1940; s. R. Ewart and Kathleen H. (Rosamond) S.; m. Diana Greig, June 26, 1982; children: Kathleen, Rosamond, Timothy. Student, Lower Can. Coll., Montreal, 1957; BA, Bishop's U., 1961; STB, U. Toronto, Ont., Can., 1964, ThM, 1976, DD (hon.), 1986. Ordained to ministry Anglican Ch. as deacon, 1964, as priest, 1965. With Mission of Schefferville, Que., 1964-69; fellow, tutor in div. Trinity Coll., U. Toronto, 1969-70, chaplain, 1970-76; with St. Clement's Mission East, St. Paul's River, Que., 1976-81; chaplain Champlain Regional Coll., Bishop's U., 1981-84; dean, rector St. Alban's Cathedral, Prince Albert, Sask., Can., 1984-91; consecrated bishop Anglican Diocese of Que., Quebec, 1991—. Anglican. Address: Diocese of Que 31 rue des Jardins Quebec City PQ Canada G1R 4L6 Office Phone: 418-692-3858. E-mail: bishop@quebec.anglican.ca.

STAVES, SUSAN, English educator; b. N.Y.C., Oct. 5, 1942; d. Henry Tracy and Margaret (McClemon) Staves. AB, U. Chgo., 1963; MA, U. Va., 1964, PhD, 1967. Woodrow Wilson intern Bennett Coll., Greensboro, NC, 1965-66; from asst. prof. to prof. Brandeis U., Waltham, Mass., 1967-93, Paul Proswimmer prof. of Humanities, 1993—2001, dept. chair, 1986-89, 95-98, prof. emerita, 2001—. Clark prof. UCLA, 1989—90. Author: Players' Scepters: Fictions of Authority in the Restoration, 1979, Married Women's Separate Property in England, 1660-1833, 1990, Studies on Voltaire and the 18th Century, (essays) Fetter'd or Free?: Collected Essays on 18th Century Women Novelists, 1986, History, Gender, and 18th Century Literature, 1994, Woman and Political Writing, 1998, Enchanted Ground: Reimagining John Dryden, 2004, Cambridge Companion to Aphra Behn, 2004; co-author (with John Brewer): Early Modern Conceptions of Property, 1994; co-editor (with Cynthia Ricciardi): Elizabeth Griffith's Delicate Distress, 1997; contbr. articles to profl. jours. Mem. ACLU, 1967—; assoc. mem. Belmont Dem. Town Com., Belmont, Mass. Woodrow Wilson fellow, 1963—64, Woodrow Wilson Dissertation fellow, 1966—67, Harvard Liberal Arts fellow, 1980—81, John Simon Guggenheim fellow, 1981—82. Mem.: AAUP, MLA (exec. com. divsn. on late 18th century English lit. 1984—86), English Inst., Am. Soc. for 18th Century Studies (exec. bd. 1987—90). Episcopalian. Avocations: hiking, squash. Office: Brandeis U Dept English MS 023 Waltham MA 02454 Office Phone: 781-736-2161. Business E-Mail: staves@brandeis.edu.

STAVIG, MARK LUTHER, English language educator; b. Northfield, Minn., Jan. 20, 1935; s. Lawrence Melvin and Cora (Hjertaas) S.; m. Donna Mae Ring, July 3, 1957; children— Anne Ragnhild, Thomas Edward, Rolf Lawrence BA, Augustana Coll., 1956, Oxford U., 1958, MA, 1962; PhD, Princeton U., 1961. Instr. to asst. prof. English U. Wis., Madison, 1961-68; from assoc. prof. to prof. English Colo. Coll., Colorado Springs, 1968—2001; ret., 2001—. Author: John Ford and the Traditional Moral Order, 1968, The Forms of Things Unknown: Renaissance Metaphor in Romeo and Juliet and A Midsummer Night's Dream, 1995; editor: Ford, 'Tis Pity She's a Whore, 1966. Fellow Danforth Found., 1956-61, Woodrow Wilson Found., 1956-57; Fulbright scholar Oxford U., 1956-58 Mem.: Shakespeare Assn. Am. Democrat. Home: 1409 Wood Ave Colorado Springs CO 80907-7348

STAVISKY, TOBY ANN, state legislator; b. N.Y.C. m. Leonard Stavisky; 1 child, Evan. BA, Syracuse U.; Grad. Degree, Hunter Coll., Queens Coll. Social studies tchr. N.Y.C. Pub. High Schs.; dist. mgr. N.E. Queens 1980 Census; mem. N.Y. Senate from 16th Dist., Albany, 1999—, mem. aging, civil svc. and pensions, edn., ranking minority higher edn., consumer protection, transp., investigations, taxation and govt. ops. coms., 2001—. Co-chair Minority Task Force on Sch. Aid Equity; mem. legis. commn. on sci. and tech.; mem. legis. commn. skills devel. and vocat. edn. Founder North Flushing Sr. Ctr., bd. dirs.; hon. trustee Whitestone Hebrew Ctr. Democrat. Office: Rm 504 Legislative Office Bldg Albany NY 12247 also: 14436 Willets Point Blvd Flushing NY 11357-3411 E-mail: stavisky@senate.state.ny.us.

STAVITSKY, ABRAM BENJAMIN, immunologist, educator; b. Newark, May 14, 1919; s. Nathan and Ida (Novak) S.; m. Ruth Bernice Okney, Dec. 6, 1942; children: Ellen Barbara, Gail Beth. AB, U. Mich., 1939, MS, 1940; PhD, U. Minn., 1943; VMD, U. Pa., 1946. Research fellow Calif. Inst. Tech., 1946-47; faculty Case Western Res. U., 1947—, prof. microbiology, 1962—, prof. molecular biology and microbiology, 1983-89, emeritus, 1989; mem. expert com. immunochemistry WHO, 1963-83; mem. microbiology fellowship com. NIH, 1963-66; mem. microbiology test com. Nat. Bd. Med. Examiners, 1970-73; chmn. microbiology test com. Nat. Bd. Podiatry Examiners, 1978-82. Mem. editl. bd. Jour. Immunological Methods, 1979-88, Immunopharmacology, 1983-96. Vice pres. Ludlow Community Assn., 1964-

66. Fellow AAAS; mem. Am. Assn. Immunologists, Am. Soc. Microbiology, Sigma Xi. Home: 14604 Onaway Rd Cleveland OH 44120-2845 Office: 2119 Abington Rd Cleveland OH 44106-2333 Business E-Mail: abs7@case.edu.

STAVOLA, JOHN JOSEPH, retired obstetrician-gynecologist; b. Hartford, Conn., Feb. 4, 1929; MD, N.Y. Med. Coll., 1956. Diplomate Am. Bd. Ob-Gyn., 1964. Intern St. Francis Hosp., Hartford; resident in ob-gyn. Hartford Hosp., 1957-60, asst. dir. ob-gyn., 1965-90; clin. asst. prof. ob-gyn. U. Conn.; pvt. practice, 1962-96; retired, 1996. With USN, 1960-62. Recipient Disting. Svc. award Hartford Hosp., 1997. Fellow Am. Coll. of Ob-Gyn. Home: 3 Danforth Ln West Hartford CT 06110-2435 E-mail: JudSTA@msn.com.

STAVREV, KRASSIMIR K. chemist, researcher; b. Shumen, Bulgaria, Nov. 11, 1958; s. Kolio K. Stavrev and Penka P. Iovcheva; m. Galina N. Nikolova, Sept. 24, 1978 (div. Jan. 1983); 1 child, Nikolay; m. Galina I. Georgieva, Feb. 3, 1985 (div. July 2001); children: Lidia, Iordan; m. Antonia M. Smillova, May 7, 2002. PhD, Sofia U., Bulgaria, 1988. Asst. prof. Sofia U., 1988-92; postdoctoral fellow Scuola Normale Superiore, Pisa, Italy, 1992-94, U. Fla., Gainesville, 1994-97; dir. sci. support Hypercube, Inc., Gainesville, 1997-98; asst. dir. Coll. Medicine, 1998—; rschr. Quantum Theory Project, Gainesville, 1999—. Home Fax: (603) 794-2408. E-mail: krasimir@ufl.edu.

STAVRIDIS, JAMES GEORGE, military officer; b. West Palm Beach, Fla., Feb. 15, 1955; s. Paul George and Shirley Anne Stavridis; m. Laura Elizabeth Hall, May 28, 1981; children: Christina Anne, Julia Elizabeth. BS, U.S. Naval Acad., Annapolis, Md., 1972; PhD, Tufts U., 1983; MA in Law and Diplomacy, 1984. Commd. ensign USN, advanced through grades to rear adm., 1972; commdg. officer USS Barry, Norfolk, Va., 1993—96; comdr. Destroyer Squadron 21, San Diego, 1997—98, Enterprise Carrier Strike Group, Mayport, Fla., 2002—04, Cruiser Destroyer Group 12, 2004—; exec. asst. Sec. of USN, Washington, 1998—2000; dir. navy ops. group USN, Washington, 2000—02. Author: Division Officer's Guide, Watch Officer's Guide, Command at Sea; contbr. articles to profl. jours. Home: 212 Moale Ave Mayport FL 32227 Office: Commander Cruiser Destroyer Group 12 Unit 60010 Fpo AA 34099-4705 Office Phone: 904.270.5645. Personal E-mail: seapay1@cs.com. E-mail: n00@ccdg12.navy.mil.

STAVRO, STEVE A. professional hockey team executive; b. Gavro, Greece, Sept. 27, 1927; m. Sally Stavro; 4 children. Chmn. bd., chief exec. officer Toronto Maple Leafs, Ont., Can.; gov. NHL. Office: Toronto Maple Leafs 60 Carlton St Toronto ON Canada M5B 1L1

STAVROPOULOS, ROSE MARY GRANT, community activist, volunteer; b. Decatur, Ill. d. Walter Edwin and Ora Lenore (Kepler) Grant; m. Stan Stavropoulos; children: Becky Ann Stavropoulos Betian, Stephanie Diane. BS, Ea. Ill. U. Cert. elem. edn. Tchr. 2nd grade Garfield Sch., Decatur, 1666; bd. dirs. Wilmot Sch. Bd. PTA, Deerfield, Moraine Girl Scout Coun., Deerfield, also bd. dirs.; chmn. Human Rels. Commn., Deerfield; mem. sr. citizen adv. com. Deerfield Park Dist.; pres. Lake County (Ill.) LWV; chmn. Deerfield Village Caucus; pres. Caring For Others, Inc., Deerfield, Deerfield Area LWV; bd. mem., pres. Deerfield Area United Way, pres. Mem. Deerfield Village Caucus Adv. Coun. Recipient Deerfield Human Rels. Humanitarian award, 1984, Lerner Life's Citizen of Month, 1987. Mem. Deerfield Area Hist. Soc., Highland Park Hosp. Aux, Legacy at Bryant Ranch Home Assn. (bd. dirs., treas., sec.), Delta Zeta. Home: 23959 Sanctuary Pkwy Yorba Linda CA 92887

STAVROPOULOS, WILLIAM S. chemical executive; b. Bridgehampton, N.Y., May 12, 1939; m. Linda Stavropoulos; children: S. William, Angela D. BS in Pharm. Chemistry, Fordham U.; PhD in Medicinal Chemistry, U. Washington; LLD (hon.), Northwood U., 1998. Rsch. chemist in pharm. rsch. Dow Chem. Co., Midland, Mich., 1967, rsch. chemist for diagnostics product rsch., 1970, rsch. mgr. diagnostics product rsch., 1973, bus. mgr. diagnostics product rsch., 1976, bus. mgr. polyolefins, 1977, dir. mktg. plastics dept., 1979; comml. v.p. Dow Chem. Co. Latin Am., Coral Gables, Fla., 1980; pres. Dow Latin Am., 1984; comml. v.p., basics and hydrocarbons Dow Chem. Co. U.S.A., Midland, 1985-87, group v.p., 1987-90; pres. Dow U.S.A., 1990—; v.p. The Dow Chem. Co., 1990, sr. v.p., 1991, pres., COO, 1993—95, CEO, 1995—2000, chmn., 2001—, CEO, 2002—. Bd. dirs. Dow Corning Corp., The Dow Chem. Co., Marion Merrel Dow Inc., BellSouth Corp., Chem. Financial Corp., Maersk Inc., NCR; trustee, Fidelity Group of Funds; bd. Am Enterprise Inst. Public Policy Rsch.; CEO Essex Chem Corp, 1988-92. Recipient Ellis Island Medal of Honor, 1998, Man of the Year award, Hellenic Am. C. of C., 2000, Palladium Medal award, Societe de Chimie Industrielle, 2001, Annual Bus. Mgmt. award, Society of Plastic Engineers, 2003. Mem.: Society of Chem. Industry (Chem. Industry Medal award 2003). Office: Dow Chem Co 2030 Dow Ctr Midland MI 48674-0001*

STAVROULAKIS, ANTHEA MERRIE, biology professor; b. Bklyn., Nov. 9, 1959; d. Zachary Stavroulakis and Evangeline Stella Spirakis. AA, CUNY, 1978; BA, NYU, 1981, MS, 1984, PhD, 1992. Grad. rsch. asst. in biology NYU, N.Y.C., 1981-92, adj. instr., 1984-89; adj. instr. sci. Borough of Manhattan C.C.-CUNY, 1986-92; asst. prof. CUNY, 1992; adj. instr. natural sci. York Coll.-CUNY, 1989-90; prof. biol. sci. Kingsborough C.C.-CUNY, 1992—. Adj. instr. biology Suffolk County C.C., 1991-92; jr. rsch. asst. in biology Brookhaven Nat. Lab., 1991-92. Author: Laboratory Manual-General Biology II, 1996, Laboratory Manual: General Biology I, 1999; contbr. articles to profl. jours. Grantee N.Y. State Edn. Dept., 1995-96, C.C. Sci. and Tech. Equipment Fund, N.Y.C., 1995, Eelgrass Remediation in Jamaica Bay, 1996, 98-2000, Eppley Found., 1999-2000, 2000—. Mem. AAAS, Am. Soc. for Microbiology, Nat. Assn. Biology Tchrs., N.Y. Acad. Scis., Profl. and Staff Congress CUNY. Democrat. Greek Orthodox. Avocations: gourmet cooking, aviculture, gardening, travel. E-mail: astavroulakis@kbcc.cuny.edu.

STAY, BARBARA, zoologist, educator; b. Cleve., Aug. 31, 1926; d. Theron David and Florence (Finley) S. AB, Vassar Coll., 1947; MA, Radcliffe Coll., 1949, PhD, 1953. Entomologist Army Research Center, Natick, Mass., 1954-60; vis. asst. prof. Pomona Coll., 1960; asst. prof. biology U. Pa., 1961-67; asso. prof. zoology U. Iowa, Iowa City, 1967-77, prof., 1977—. Fulbright fellow to Australia, 1953; Lalor fellow Harvard U., 1960 Fellow AAAS, Entomol. Soc. Am.; mem. Soc. Comparative and Integrative Biology, Am. Inst. Biol. Scis., Am. Soc. Cell Biology, Iowa Acad. Scis., Sigma Xi. Office: U Iowa Dept Biological Scis Iowa City IA 52242

STAYIN, RANDOLPH JOHN, lawyer; b. Cin., Oct. 30, 1942; s. Jack and Viola (Tomin) S.; children: Gregory S., Todd R., Elizabeth J. BA, Dartmouth Coll., 1964; JD, U. Cin., 1967. Bar: Ohio 1967, U.S. Dist. Ct. (so. dist.) Ohio 1968, U.S. Dist. Ct. D.C. 1977, U.S. Ct. Appeals (6th cir.) 1968, U.S. Ct. Appeals (fed. cir.) 1986, U.S. Supreme Ct. 1974, U.S. Ct. Appeals (D.C. cir.) 1976, U.S. Ct. Internat. Trade, 1985. Assoc. Frost & Jacobs Cin., 1967-72; exec. asst., dir. of legislation U.S. Sen. Robert Taft, Jr., Washington, 1973-74, chief of staff, 1975-76; assoc. Taft, Stettinius & Hollister, Washington, 1977, ptnr., 1978-88, Barnes & Thornburg, Washington, 1988—. Mem. adv. coun. U.S. and FGN. Comml. Svc., U.S. Dept. Commerce. Chmn., mem. numerous coms., chmn., worker campaigns for local politicians Rep. Party state and local orgns.; mem. Citizens to Save WCET-TV, 1967-72, Fine Arts Fund, 1970-72, Cancer Soc., 1970-72; chmn. agy. rels. com. Hamilton County Mental Health and Mental Retardation Bd., 1969-71, vice chmn., 1971, chmn., 1971-72; v.p. Recreation Commn., City of Cin., 1970-72; mem. funds mgmt. com. Westwood 1st Presbyn. Ch., 1968, v.p., 1969, pres., 1970, trustee, 1970, elder, 1971-72; bd. dirs. Evans Mill Pond Owners Assn., v.p., 1986, pres., 1987; chmn. Washington Nat. Cathedral Fund Com., mem. devel. com.; co-chair 1907 Soc. Mem.: ABA (sect. on internat. law and practice, vice chmn.com.on nat. legislation 1977—79, internat. sect., anti-trust sect.), D. C. Bar Assn. (com. on internat. law), Internat. Bar Assn., Am. Soc. Assn. Execs. (legal sect., internat. sect.). Avocations: theater, tennis, skiing, travel, boating. Office: Barnes & Thornburg 750 17th St NW Ste 900 Washington DC 20006-2225 Office Phone: 202-289-1313.

STAYTON, THOMAS GEORGE, lawyer; b. Rochester, Minn., May 1, 1948; m. Barbara Joan Feck, Aug. 8, 1970; children: Ryan, Megan. BS, Miami U., Oxford, Ohio, 1970; JD, U. Mich., 1973. Bar: Ind. 1973, U.S. Dist. Ct. (so. dist.) Ind. 1973, U.S. Ct. Appeals (7th cir.) 1977. Ptnr. Baker & Daniels, Indpls., 1973—. Sustaining mem. Product Liability Adv. Coun. Recipient Sagamore of the Wabash Gov. of Ind., 1988. Mem. ABA, Ind. State Bar Assn., Indpls. Bar Assn., Indpls. Athletic Club. Office: Baker & Daniels 300 N Meridian St Ste 2700 Indianapolis IN 46204-1782 Office Phone: 317-237-1260. E-mail: tstayton@bakerd.com.

STAYTON, WILLIAM RALPH, psychologist, educator; b. Kelso, Wash., Dec. 25, 1933; s. Ralph Willard and Marguerite (Hunter) S.; m. Kathleen Boucher, Sept. 4, 1954; children: Mark, John, Cheryl, Paul. BA, U. Redlands, 1956; MDiv, Andover Newton Theol. Sem., 1960; ThD, Boston U., 1967; PhD, Inst. Advanced Study of Human Sexuality, 2002. Ordained to ministry Am. Bapt. Ch., 1959. Assoc. min. 1st Bapt. Ch. in Newton, Mass., 1956-61; min. 1st Bapt. Ch., Gloucester, Mass., 1961-68; chaplain New Eng. Bapt. Hosp., Boston, 1968-71; asst. prof. U. Pa. Sch. Medicine, Phila., 1971—78; adj. assoc. prof. U. Pa. Grad. Sch. Edn., Phila., lectr., faculty, 1982—2004; asst. prof. Jefferson Med. Coll./Thomas Jefferson U., 1978-83; marriage and family therapist Wm R. Stayton & Assocs., Ltd., P.C., Phila., 1978—. Mem. faculty La Salle U., Phila., 1983-2002; prof. and coord., human sexuality program Widener U., Chester, Pa., 1999—. Editor spl. issue Topics in Clin. Nursing, 1980; contbr. articles to profl. jours., chpts. to books. Pres. Cmty. Svcs. for Human Growth, Paoli, Pa., 1989-91, bd. dirs., 1981-97. Named Man of Yr., B'nai B'rith, Gloucester, Mass., 1968; recipient Outstanding Svc. award Community Svcs. for Human Growth, 1990, Richard J. Cross award U. Medicine and Dentistry N.J., 1997, Dean's award Sch Human Svc. Professions Widener U., 2002. Mem. APA, Am. Assn. Marriage and Family Therapists, Am. Assn. Sex Educators, Counselors and Therapists (bd. dirs. 1982-86, 88-90, chmn. dist. VI 1982-86, pres. 1996-98, Outstanding Svc. award 1978-87, 87, Disting. Svc. award 2000), Sex Info. and Edn. Coun. U.S. (pres. 1985-87, sec. 1990-92), Soc. for Sci. Study Sex (chmn. ann. meeting 1983), Pa. Assn. Marriage and Family Therapists (continuing edn. com. 1985-90), Planned Parenthood Southeastern Pa. (bd. dir. 1999-, first v.p. 2001-), Phi Kappa Phi. Democrat. Home: 81 Andover Ct Wayne PA 19087-5616 Office: 987 Old Eagle School Rd Ste 719 Wayne PA 19087-1708 Office Phone: 610-971-0700. E-mail: wmstayton@aol.com.

STEAD, EUGENE ANSON, JR., physician; b. Atlanta, Oct. 6, 1908; s. Eugene Anson and Emily (White) Stead; m. Evelyn Selby, June 15, 1940; children: Nancy White, Lucy Ellen, William Wallace. BS, Emory U., 1928, MD, 1932. Intern Peter Bent Brigham Hosp., Boston, 1932—33, surg. intern, 1934—35, assoc. medicine, 1939—42, acting physician-in-chief, 1942; rsch. fellow medicine Harvard U, 1933—34; asst. resident medicine Cin. Gen. Hosp., 1935—36, resident, 1936—37; instr. medicine U. Cin., 1935—37; resident phys. Thorndike Meml. Lab.; asst. medicine Harvard and Boston City Hosp., 1937—39; from instr. medicine to assoc. HarvardU., 1938—42; prof. medicine Emory U.; physician-in-chief Grady Hosp., Atlanta, 1942—46; dean Emory U., 1945—46; physician in chief Duke Hosp., 1947—67; prof. medicine Duke U. Sch. Medicine, 1947—78, founder physician asst. program, 1967; disting. physician VA, 1978—85. Editor: Circulation, 1973—78, N.C. Med. Jour., 1983—92; contbr. articles to profl. jours. Mem.: Am. Soc. Clin. Investigation, Assn. Am. Physicians, Am. Fedn. Clin. Rsch., N.C. Med. Soc., Phi Beta Kappa, Sigma Xi, Alpha Omega Alpha. Methodist. Home: 5113 Townsville Rd Bullock NC 27507-9438 Personal E-mail: easteadjr@gloryroad.net.

STEAD, JAMES JOSEPH, JR., securities company executive; b. Chgo., Sept. 13, 1930; s. James Joseph and Irene (Jennings) S.; m. Edith Pearson, Feb. 13, 1954; children: James, Diane, Robert, Caroline. BS, DePaul U., 1957, MBA, 1959. Asst. sec. C. F. Childs & Co., Chgo., 1957-62; exec. v.p., sec. Koenig, Keating & Stead, Inc., Chgo., 1962-66; 2d v.p., mgr. midwest mcpl. bond dept. Hayden, Stone Inc., Chgo., 1966-69; sr. v.p., nat. sales mgr. Ill. Co. Inc., 1969-70; mgr. instl. sales dept. Reynolds and Co., Chgo., 1970-72; partner Edwards & Hanly, 1972-74; v.p., instnl. sales mgr. Paine, Webber, Jackson & Curtis, 1974-76; v.p., regional instl. sales mgr. Reynolds Securities, Inc., 1976-78; sr. v.p., regional mgr. Oppenheimer & Co., Inc., 1978-88; sr. v.p., regional mgr. fixed income Tucker Anthony, 1988—; instr. Mcpl. Bond Sch., Chgo., 1967— . With AUS, 1951-53. Mem. Security Traders Assn. Chgo., Nat. Security Traders Assn., Am. Mgmt. Assn., Mcpl. Fin. Forum Washington. Clubs: Execs., Union League, Mcpl. Bond, Bond (Chgo.); Olympia Fields Country (Ill.); Wall Street (N.Y.C.). Home: 1005 Hickory Ridge Ct Frankfort IL 60423-2114 Office: 1 S Wacker Dr Chicago IL 60606-4614

STEAD, JERRE L. investment company executive; b. Maquoketa, Iowa, Jan. 8, 1943; s. H. Victor and Anna Catherine (Grindrod) S.; m. Mary Joy Kloppenburg, Dec. 26, 1961; children: Joel A., Jay A. BBA, U. Iowa, 1965; grad. advanced mgmt. program, Harvard U., 1982. Mgr. regional sales Honeywell Corp., Phila., 1971-73, dir. prodn. Mpls., 1974-75, dir. distbn., 1975-76, v.p. fin. and adminstrn., Brussels, 1979-82; v.p., gen. mgr. Honeywell-Phillips Med. Electronics, Brussels, 1981-82, Honeywell Corp., Mpls., 1982-85, v.p., group exec., 1986; pres., COO Sq. D Co., Palatine, Ill., 1987-88, pres., CEO, chmn. bd., 1989-91, also bd. dirs.; chmn., CEO Global Info. Solutions AT&T, N.Y.C., 1991-95; CEO Legent Corp., Vienna, Va., 1995-96; chmn., CEO Ingram Micro, Inc., Santa Ana, Calif., 1996-2000; chmn. Holland Am. Investment Corp., 2000—. Bd. dirs. Eljer Industries, Plano, Tex., Ameritech, Chgo., USG, Chgo., TJ Internat., Inc. Mem. Pres.' coun. Am. Lung Assn., N.Y.C., 1986—, The Wash. Ctr. Nat. Campaign Com.; bus. adv. com. N.C. A&T U.; trustee Coe Coll., Cedar Rapids, Iowa, 1987; mem. coun. on competitiveness Ill. Bus. Roundtable; bd. visitors U. Iowa, Iowa City. Mem. Nat. Elec. Mfrs. Assn. (bd. govs. 1984—), Nat. Assn. Elec. Distbrs. (edn. com.), Chgo. Com., Elec. Mfrs. Club. Republican. Methodist. Office: Holland Am Investment Corp PO Box 25125 565 Fifth Ave New York NY 10017

STEADHAM, RICHARD LYNN, magazine art director; b. Sacramento, Calif., Sept. 3, 1951; s. Lyndell Harvey and Dorothy Mae (Dennis) S.; m. Karen Jean Stoner, May 2, 1971; children: Taylor Ryan, Erin Danielle, Nathan Lynn. Book designer/staff illustrator Rev. and Herald Pub. Assn., Hagerstown, Md., 1982-87; art dir. Governing Mag./Congrl. Quarterly, Washington, 1987—. Freelance illustrator, Hagerstown, Md., 1982-88, Woodbridge, Va., 1988—. Editor and designer Art Dirs. Club Newsletter, Halfbleed, 1995. Recipient Merit award Soc. Illustrators, N.Y., 1985, Comm. Arts Illustration Ann., 1994. Mem. Art Dirs. Club of Met. Washington (v.p. publs. 1994-96, Merit award 1993, editor, designer newsletter Halfbleed 1995). Soc. Pub. Designers (Merit award 1994), Va. State Soc. (George Washington chpt.), Nat. Soc. of SAR (editor, designer newsletter The Surveyor, George Washington chpt. 1988-2000, Timen Stiddem Soc. (founding officer, editor, designer of the award-winning newsletter NGS 1998, 99, 2000). Avocations: travel, gardening, family history. Office: Gov Mag-Congrl Quarterly 1100 Connecticut Ave NW Washington DC 20036-4101 E-mail: rsteadham@governing.com.

STEAD LEE, POLLY JAE See LEE, PALI

STEADMAN, DAVID ROSSLYN AYTON, business executive, corporate director; b. Wembley, Eng., June 7, 1937; came to U.S., 1980; s. Eric and Iris Sina (Smith) S.; m. Beryl Ellen Giles, Jan. 5, 1963 (div.); children: Michael, Christopher, Timothy. B.Sc. in Engring. with honors, City U., London, 1960. Mng. dir. Cossor Electronics, Harlow, Eng., 1974-78; chmn. EMI med. Electronics, London, 1978-80; pres. Raytheon Data Systems, Norwood Mass., 1980-84, Raytheon Ventures, Lexington, 1985-87; chmn., CEO GCA Corp., Andover, Mass., 1987-88; pres. Atlantic Mgmt. Assocs., Inc., Bedford, N.H., 1988—; chmn. Brookwood Cos., Inc., 1989—, Visibility, Inc., 1996-2000, CEO, 1999-2000; chmn. Visaer, Inc., 2000—. Bd. dirs. Tech/Ops-Sevcon, Inc., Aavid Thermal Techs., Inc., Telequip Corp., Express Point Tech. Svcs., Inc. Fellow Instn. Elec. Engrs. (U.K.); mem. Inst. Mgmt. (U.K.; companion), Inst. Mech. Engrs. (U.K.). Avocations: music, sailing. Office: Atlantic Mgmt Assocs Inc PO Box 10670 Bedford NH 03110 E-mail: drsteadman@aol.com.

STEADMAN, DAVID WILTON, retired museum official, church deacon; b. Honolulu, Oct. 24, 1936; s. Alva Edgar and Martha (Cooke) S.; m. Kathleen Carroll Reilly, Aug. 1, 1964; children: Alexander Carroll, Kate Montague. BA, Harvard U., 1960, MAT., 1961; MA, U. Calif.-Berkeley, 1966; PhD, Princeton U., 1974; M Theol. Studies, Ch. Divinity Sch. of Pacific, 2002. Ordained deacon Episcopal Ch., 2004. Lectr. Frick Collection, N.Y.C., 1970-71; asst. dir., acting dir., assoc. dir. Princeton U. Art Mus., 1971-73; dir. galleries Claremont Colls., (Calif.), 1974-80; art cons. Archtl. Digest, L.A., 1974-77; rsch. curator Norton Simon Mus., Pasadena, Calif., 1977-80; dir. Chrysler Mus., Norfolk, Va., 1980-89, Toledo Mus. Art, Ohio, 1989-99; ret., 2000. Author: Graphic Art of Francisco Goya, 1975, Works on Paper 1900-1960, 1977, Abraham van Diepenbeeck, 1982. Chester Dale fellow Nat. Gallery Art, Washington, 1969-70 Episcopalian. E-mail: punto31157@aol.com.

STEADMAN, E. THOMAS, gynecologist; b. Passaic, N.J., Nov. 14, 1926; s. E. TenBroeck and Rosalie (Schieb) S.; m. Marcia Winder, June 15, 1948; children: E. TenBroeck, Tracy, Dirk, Webb, Coe. BA, Amherst Coll., 1950, MA, 1953; MD, Cornell U., 1957. Diplomate Am. Bd. Ob-Gyn. Intern St. Luke's Hosp., 1957-58; resident N.Y. Hosp., 1958-63, attending ob/gyn., 1985—. Clin. prof. Cornell U. Med. Coll., N.Y.C., 1985—. Fellow ACS, Am. Coll. Ob-Gyn.; mem. Am. Fertility Soc., N.Y. Gynecol. Soc., N.Y. Med. and Surg. Soc. (pres. 1984-85), N.Y. Obstet. Soc. (pres. 1978-79). Office: 449 E 68th St New York NY 10021-6310

STEADMAN, JOHN MARCELLUS, III, English educator; b. Spartanburg, S.C., Nov. 25, 1918; s. John Marcellus and Medora Rice (Rembert) S. AB, Emory U., 1940, MA, 1941, DHL (hon.), 1976; MA (T.W. Hunt scholar), Princeton U., 1948, PhD, 1949; DHL (hon.), St. Bonaventure U., 1998. Instr. English Ga. Inst. Tech., 1941-42; asst. prof. U. N.C., 1949-51; ind. study and rsch. in English lit., 1953-61; from rsch. assoc.to sr. rsch. assoc. Henry E. Huntington Libr., San Marino, Calif., 1962—2002; mem. faculty U. Calif., Riverside, 1966—2002, prof. English, 1967—2002, faculty rsch. lectr., 1977, prof. emeritus, 1989—. Vis. disting. prof. City U. N.Y., fall, 1974 Author numerous books including Milton and the Renaissance Hero, 1967, Milton's Epic Characters, 1968, The Myth of Asia, 1970, Disembodied Laughter: Troilus and the Apotheosis Tradition, 1972, The Lamb and The Elephant: Ideal Imitation and the Context of Renaissance Allegory, 1974, Epic and Tragic Structure in Paradise Lost, 1976, Nature into Myth: Medieval and Renaissance Moral Symbols, 1979, Milton's Biblical and Classical Imagery, 1984, The Hill and the Labyrinth: Discourse and Certitude in Milton and His Near-Contemporaries, 1984, The Wall of Paradise: Essays on Milton's Poetics, 1985, Milton and the Paradoxes of Renaissance Heroism, 1987, Redefining a Period Style: "Renaissance," "Mannerist," and "Baroque" in Literature, 1990, Ryoanji Temple and Other Poems, 1993, Moral Fiction in Milton and Spenser, 1995, Reconnaissances: Poems, 1995, Winter Harvest, A Retrospective, 1996, In Earnest or Game: A Seriocomic Medley. Verses Early or Late, 1998, Siege of Contraries: Rumors of Wars Real or Metaphorical, Stories and Sketches, 1998; co-editor latest being A Milton Ency., vols. I-IX, 1978-83; editor: latest being Huntington Libr. Quar., 1962-81; mem. numerous editl. and advisory bds.; contbr. articles to profl. jours. Served to capt. USAAF, 1942-46; capt. AUS, 1951-52. Grantee Huntington Libr., 1961-62; Procter fellow Princeton U., 1949, Guggenheim fellow, 1979. Mem. Milton Soc. Am. (pres. 1973, honored scholar 1976), So. Calif. Renaissance Conf., Phi Beta Kappa, Chi Phi, Fine Arts Club. Democrat. Home: care Atria REgency 4720 Morrison Dr Apt 220 Mobile AL 36609-3345

STEADMAN, JOHN MONTAGUE, appellate court judge; b. Honolulu, Aug. 8, 1930; s. Alva Edgar and Martha (Cooke) S.; m. Alison Storer Lunt, Apr. 8, 1961; children— Catharine N., Juliette M., Eric C. Grad., Phillips Acad., Andover, Mass., 1948; BA summa cum laude, Yale U., 1952; LLB magna cum laude, Harvard U., 1955. Bar: D.C. 1955, Calif. 1956, U.S. Supreme Ct. 1964, Hawaii 1977. Assoc. Pillsbury, Madison & Sutro, San Francisco, 1956-63; atty. Dept. Justice, 1963-64; dep. under sec. army for internat. affairs, 1964-65; spl. asst. to sec. and dep. sec. def. Dept. Def., 1965-68; gen. counsel Dept. Air Force, 1968-70; vis. prof. law U. Pa. Law Sch., 1970-72; prof. law Georgetown U. Law Ctr., Washington, 1972-85, assoc. dean, 1979-84; assoc. judge D.C. Ct. Appeals, 1985—. Instr. Lincoln Law Sch., San Francisco, 1961-62, San Francisco Law Sch., 1962-63; vis. prof. U. Mich. Sch. Law, 1976, U. Hawaii Sch. Law, 1977; of counsel firm Pillsbury, Madison & Sutro, Washington, 1979-85 Editor: Harvard Law Rev, 1953-55. Sinclair-Kennedy Traveling fellow, 1955-56 Mem. Am. Law Inst., Cosmos Club, Phi Beta Kappa, Delta Sigma Rho, Zeta Psi. Episcopalian. Home: 2960 Newark St NW Washington DC 20008-3338 Office: DC Ct Appeals 500 Indiana Ave NW Washington DC 20001-2131 E-mail: jsteadman@dcca.state.dc.us.

STEADMAN, ROBERT KEMPTON, oral and maxillofacial surgeon; b. Mpls., July 8, 1943; s. Henry Kempton and Helen S.; m. Susan E. Hoffman; children: Andrea Helene, Darcy Joanne, Richard Kempton, Michael Dean. BS, U. Wash., Seattle, 1969, DDS, 1974; MD, Grace U., 2002. Diplomate Am. Bd. Oral and Maxillofacial Surgery. Residency USAF, Elgin AFB, Fla., 1974-75; resident oral and maxillofacial surgery U. Okla., 1977-80, La. State U., Shreveport, 1980-81; pvt. practice Spokane, Wash., 1981—. Cons. Group Health Coop., 1989—; mem. adv. bd. Osteoporosis Awareness Resource, 1988— Select recruiting ptnr. U. Wash. Sch. Dentistry, 1990. Fellow Am. Acad. Cosmetic Surgery, Internat. Assn. Oral and Maxillofacial Surgery, Am. Coll. Oral and Maxillofacial Surgery, Am. Soc. Oral and Maxillofacial Surgery, Acad. Gen. Dentistry; mem. Internat. Soc. Plastic, Aesthetic and Reconstructive Surgery, Am. Acad. Cosmetic Surgery, Delta Sigma Delta (pres. 1987-88). Office: 801 W 5th Ave Ste 212 Spokane WA 99204-2800

STEADMAN, STEPHEN GEOFFREY, physicist; b. Rochester, N.Y., June 28, 1942; s. Luville T. and Elizabeth (Genung) S.; m. Brigitte M. Kreuzer, Aug. 1, 1975; children: Claudia, Mark, William. BS, U. Rochester, 1964; MS, Rutgers U., 1966, PhD, 1969. Vis. scientist Univ. Erlangen-Nürnberg, Erlangen, Germany, 1969-71; asst. Univ. Freiburg, Germany, 1971-72; sr. rsch. assoc. MIT, Cambridge, Mass., 1972-74, asst. prof., 1975-79, assoc. prof., 1979-82, sr. rsch. scientist, 1982-98, sci. adminstr. lab. nuclear sci., 2004—; guest scientist Max Planck Inst., Heidelberg, Germany, 1974-75, program mgr., 1998—2001; sr. nuc. physics advisor U.S. Dept. Energy, Washington, 2001—04; sci. adminstr. MIT, Cambridge, Mass., 2004—. Program dir. nuc. physics NSF, Arlington, Va., 1994—97; E866 co-spokesman Brookhaven Nat. Lab., Upton, NY, 1992—98. Contbr. articles to profl. jours. Watertown provincial guard, 1998—; mem. Arsenal Reuse Com., Watertown, Mass., 1992—97. Mem.: AAAS, Am. Phys. Soc. Episcopalian. Avocations: piano, tropical fish. Office: MIT Lab for Nuclear Sci RM 26-505 Cambridge MA 02139 Office Phone: 617-253-2395.

STEAMER, ROBERT JULIUS, political science educator; b. Rochester, N.Y., Oct. 14, 1920; s. William August and Lotte (Becker) S.; m. Jean Worden, Apr. 12, 1947; children: Gregg Robert, James Worden. BA in Social Sci., Bucknell U., 1947; MA in Polit. Sci., U. Va., 1952; PhD, Cornell U., 1954; postgrad. law, Oxford (Eng.) U., 1968-69. Asst. prof. Oglethorpe U., 1952-55, U. Mass., 1955-56; assoc. prof. La. State U., 1956-62; prof. polit. sci., chmn. dept. Lake Forest (Ill.) Coll., 1962-72; prof. U. Mass., Boston, 1972-88, dean Coll. II, 1974-76, vice chancellor for acad. affairs, provost, 1976-79. Vis. summer prof. Tulane U., 1958, Cornell U., 1960, UCLA, 1965; staff cons. La. sect. U.S. Commn. Civil Rights, 1961 Author: The Constitution: Cases and Comments, 1959, The Supreme Court in Crisis, 1971, The Supreme Court: Constitutional Revision and the New Strict Constructionism, 1973, Chief Justice: Leadership and the Supreme Court, 1986; sr. co-author: American Constitutional Law: Cases and Commentary, 1991; contbr. articles to profl. jours. Served with USAAF, 1942-46. Recipient Gt. Tchr. award Lake Forest Coll., 1965; Lilly Found. Research award, 1967; Major Research award Project 87, 1981; hon. research fellow U. Exeter, Eng., 1981 Mem. Am. Polit. Sci. Assn., Midwest Polit. Sci. Assn. (v.p. 1970-71), New Eng. Polit. Sci. Assn. (pres. 1979-80) Home: 439 Kilbourn Rd Rochester NY 14618-3635

STEANS, PHILLIP MICHAEL, lawyer; b. Oak Park, Ill., May 23, 1943; s. William B. and Evelyn A. (Leonetti) S.; m. Randi R. Solberg, Sept. 17, 1966; children: Erik, Joshua, Molly. BA summa cum laude, Ripon (Wis.) Coll.,

1965; JD, U. Chgo., 1968. Bar: Wis. 1968, Ill. 1968, U.S. Dist. Ct. (we. dist.) Wis. 1968. Ptnr. Solberg & Steans, Menomonie, Wis., 1968-85; mng. ptnr. Steans, Skinner, Schofield & Higley, Menomonie, 1985-91; shareholder Bakke-Norman, S.C., Menomonie, 1991-94; pres. Phillip M. Steans, S.C., Menomonie, 1994—. Dist. atty. Dunn County, Wis., Menomonie, 1969-74; asst. city atty. City of Menomonie, 1969-86; asst. family ct. commr. Dunn County, 1993. NCAA scholar, 1965. Mem. Nat. Bd. Trial Advocacy (civil and criminal sect.). Avocations: racquetball, reading. Home: E5745 708th Ave Menomonie WI 54751-5515 Office: 393 Red Cedar St Ste 6 Menomonie WI 54751-2267 Office Phone: 715-235-5550. E-mail: psteans@steanslaw.com.

STEARMAN, WILLIAM LLOYD, military association executive, author; b. Wichita, Kans., June 22, 1922; s. Lloyd Carlton and Virtle Ethyl (Trusty) S.; m. Joan Crotty, May 5, 1984. BA in History and Math., U. Calif., Berkeley, 1944; MA in Internat. Rels., U. Geneva, Switzerland, 1948, PhD in Polit. Sci., 1961. Fgn. correspondent Mutual Broadcasting Sys., Austria and Ea. Europe, 1948-50; sr. officer U.S. Fgn. Svc., Washington, 1950—78; mem. nat. sec. coun. staff The White House, Washington, 1971-76, 81-93; dep. asst., asst. dir. U.S. Arms Control and Disarmament Agy., Washington, 1976-77; adj. prof. internat. affairs Georgetown U., Washington, 1977-93; exec. dir. U.S. Naval Fire Support Assn., 1996—. Author: The Soviet Union and the Occupation of Austria, 1962; contbr. articles to profl. jours. Lt. U.S. Naval Res. WWII PTO. Mem.: Cath. Acad. Scis. (academician), Knight of the Holy Sepulchre, Izaak Walton League, Diplomatic and Consular Officers Ret. Republican. Roman Catholic. Avocations: outdoor activities, art, music, history. Home: 10416 Rockville Pike Apt 301 Bethesda MD 20852-3322

STEARNS, CLIFFORD BUNDY, congressman, business executive; b. Washington, Apr. 16, 1941; s. Clifford Robert and Emily Elizabeth (Newlin) S.; m. Joan Bette Moore, 1973; 3 children: Douglas Moore, Clifford Bundy Jr., Scott Newlin. BSEE, George Washington U., 1963. Mgr. Control Data Systems, Inc., L.A., 1967-69; sr. contract adminstr. CBS, Inc., Stamford, Conn., 1969; account exec. Kutola Advt. Agy., Greenwich, Conn., 1970-71, Images 70/Wilson Haight Welch, Inc., Greenwich, 1971-72; motel owner Hatfield, Mass., 1972-77; pres., motel mgr. Stearns House, Inc., Silver Springs, Fla., 1972—88; mem. U.S. Congress from 6th Fla. dist., 1989—, mem. vets. affairs com., mem. energy and commerce com., subcoms., commerce, trade, consumer protection coms., others. Broker Silver Springs (Fla.) Real Estate, 1981-88. Trustee, vice chmn. Monroe Regional Hosp., Ocala, Fla., 1984-89; bd. dirs. Boys Club of Ocala, 1980-84; pres. Toastmaster Club L.A., 1962. Capt. USAF, 1963-67. Mem. Am. Hotel/Motel Assn., Fla. Hotel/Motel Assn., Am. Assn. Realtors, Fla. Assn. Realtors, Marion County Motel Assn. (pres. 1979), Marion C. of C. (bd. dirs. 1987—), Kiwanis (pres. Ocala club 1984). Republican. Presbyterian. Avocations: basketball, swimming, computers. Office: US Ho of Reps 2370 Rayburn House Office Bldg Washington DC 20515-0906 also: 115 SE 25th Ave Ocala FL 34471-9179

STEARNS, ELLIOTT EDMUND, JR., retired surgeon; b. Cleve., Jan. 11, 1923; s. Elliott Edmund and Sarah (Hoyt) S.; m. Martha Hudson Small, June 26, 1945; children: Michael Elliott, Philip Hoyt, Daniel Arthur. Student, Williams Coll., 1941-43; BS, U. Calif., Berkeley, 1945; MD, U. Calif., San Francisco, 1948. Diplomate Am. Bd. Urology. Intern U.S. Pub. Health Hosp., San Francisco, 1949-50; resident Sonoma Co. Hosp., Santa Rosa, Calif., 1950-51; fellow urology Cleve. Clinic, 1952-54; chief resident urology Cin. (Ohio) Gen. Hosp., U. Cin., 1954-56; med. staff St. Mary's Hosp., Tucson, 1956-87, St. Joseph's Hosp., Tucson, 1956-87, Tucson (Ariz.) Med. Ctr., 1956-87, Pima County Hosp., Tucson, 1956-87; ret., 1987. Exec. com. mem. Pima County Med. Soc., Tucson, 1970s; chief of surgery St. Joseph's Hosp., Tucson, 1980s. Author: Catapult, 1994. Capt. USAF, 1954-56. Fellow ACS. Home: 2926 N Cascada Cir Tucson AZ 85715-3421 E-mail: mestearns@aol.com.

STEARNS, FRANK WARREN, lawyer; b. Washington, July 20, 1949; s. Robert Maynard and Ermyntrude (Vaiden) S.; m. Judith Anne Ketcheson, Sept. 7, 1974; children: Frank W. Jr., Brian S., Joe G. BA, Washington & Lee, 1971; JD with honors, George Washington U., 1974. Bar: Washington DC 1975, Va. 1980, U.S. Supreme Ct. 1980, U.S. Dist. Ct. DC 1975, U.S. Ct. Appeals (DC cir.) 1975, U.S. Ct. Appeals (4th cir.) 1985. Law clk. Superior Ct. D.C., Washington, 1974-75; asst. corp. counsel Office of the Corp. Counsel, Washington, 1975-79; asst. county atty. County Atty's Office, Fairfax County, Va., 1979-80; mng. ptnr. Wilkes Artis P.C., Fairfax, Va., 1984-2001; ptnr. Venable, McLean, Va., 2001—. Bd. dirs. No. Va. Bldg. Industry Assn., 1987-94; trustee Greater Washington Bd. Trade-P.A.C., 1987-2003; chmn. tech. adv. com. NVBIA, Loudoun, Va., 1986-90. Coun. Excellence in Govt., Washington, 1989—98; Commr. Arlington County Econ. Devel. Commn., Arlington, Va., 1987—91. Mem. Barristers, Counsellors, Fairfax C. of C. (PAC trustee 2003—). Avocations: tennis, golf. Office: Ste 300 8010 Towers Crescent Dr Vienna VA 22182 E-mail: fwstearns@venable.com.

STEARNS, NEELE EDWARD, JR., investment executive; b. Chgo., Apr. 2, 1936; s. Neele Edward Sr. and Grace (Kessler) S.; m. Bonnie Ann Evans; children: Katherine Stearns Sprenger, Kendra Stearns Drozd. BA magna cum laude, Carleton Coll., 1958; MBA with distinction, Harvard U., 1960. Audit staff Arthur Andersen Co., 1962-66, audit mgr., 1966-67; asst. gen. mgr. internat. divsn. Imperial-Eastman Corp., 1967-68; asst. treas. Allied Products Corp., 1968-69, treas., 1969-72; v.p. Henry Crown (Ill.) and Co., 1972-75, v.p., controller, 1975-79; exec. v.p., COO, Henry Crown and Co., 1979-86; pres., CEO, CC Industries, Inc., Chgo., 1986-95; chmn. exec. com. Barnes Internat., Inc., Northbrook, Ill., 1996-99; chmn. Wallace Computer Svcs., Inc., 2000, Fin. Investments Corp., Chgo., 2001—, Click Commerce, Inc., 2004—. Dir. Maytag Corp., 1989—, Wallace Computer Svcs., 1990—2003, Footstar, Inc., 2000—. Trustee Evanston Northwestern Healthcare; bd. dir. Presbyn. Homes. Mem. Comml. Club Chgo., Econ. Club Chgo., Country Club Fla., Chgo. Club, Old Elm Club, Skokie Country Club, Phi Beta Kappa. Office: Fin Investments Corp 405 N Wabash River Plz 2E Chicago IL 60611 Office Phone: 312-494-4513. Business E-Mail: nstearns@fic-sff.com.

STEARNS, PETER NATHANIEL, history professor; b. London, Mar. 3, 1936; (parents Am. citizens); s. Raymond P. and Elizabeth (Scott) S.; m. Nancy Driessel (div. 1976); children: Duncan, Deborah; m. Carol Zisowitz, Mar. 26, 1978 (div. 1999); children: Clio Elizabeth, Cordelia Raymond; m. Margaret Brindle. AB, Harvard U., 1957, MA, 1959, PhD, 1963. From instr. to assoc. prof. U. Chgo., 1962-65; prof., chmn. history dept. Rutgers U., New Brunswick, N.J., 1965-74; Heinz prof. history Carnegie Mellon U., Pitts., 1974—, chmn. dept. history, 1986-92, dean Coll. Humanities and Social Scis., 1992-2000; provost George Mason U., 2000—. Co-dir. Pitts. Ctr. for Social History, 1986-92; chmn. acad. adv. coun. N.Y.C. Coll. Bd., 1982-85; chmn. Pacesetter World History commn., Coll. Bd., 1992-95, Coll. Bd. Advanced Placement World History, 1997—; mem. adv. bd. Liberal Education, 2001—. Author: The Working Classes and the Rise of Socialism, 1971, European Society in Upheaval: Social History since 1800, 1967;: European Society in Upheaval: Social History since 1800, 1975, (3d ed.), 1991, Priest and Revolutionary: Lamennais and the Dilemma of French Catholicism, 1967, (Polish tranl.), 1967, Modern Europe, 1789—1914, 1969, Revolutionary Syndicalism and French Labor: a cause without rebels, 1971, (with Harvey Mitchell) Workers and Protest: The European Labor Movement, The Working Classes and the Rise of Socialism, 1890—1914, The European Experience since 1815, 1972, 1848: The Revolutionary Tide in Europe, 1974, (publ. in England) The Revolutions of 1848, Lives of Labor: Work in Maturing Industrial Society, 1975, (German tranl.), 1975, Old Age in European Society, 1977, Face of Europe, 1977, Paths to Authority: Toward the Formation of Middle Class Consciousness, 1978, Be A Man! Males in Modern Society, 1979, (rev. ed.), 1990, (with Linda Rosenzweig) Themes in Modern Social History, 1985, (with Carol Stearns) Anger: The Struggle for Emotional Control in America's History, 1986, World History: Patterns of Change and Continuity, 1987, (rev.ed.), 1994, (3d ed.), 1998, (4th ed.), 2001, (5th ed.), 2004, (with others) Makers of Modern Europe, 1987, (rev. ed.), 1994, (with others) Documents in World History, Vol.1: The Great Tradition and Vol. 2: The Modern Centuries, 1987, Life and Society in the West, The Modern Centuries, 1987, Expanding the Past: A Reader in Social History, 1988, Life and Society in the West, The Modern Centuries, 1988, (with C. Stearns) Emotion and Social Change, Toward a New Psychohistory, 1988, (with Andrew Barnes) Social History and Issues in Consciousness and Cognition, 1989, Jealousy: Evolution of an Emotion in American History, 1989, Interpreting the Industrial Revolution, 1991, (with Michael Adas and Stuart Schwartz) World Civilizations, 1991, (rev. ed.), 1995, 2003, Meaning Over Memory: Issues in Humanities Education, 1993, The Industrial Revolution in World History, 1993, (rev. ed.), 1998, (Swedish tranl.), American Cool: Developing a 20th Century Emotional Style, 1994, Turbulent Passage: A Global History of the 20th Century, 1994, rev. edit., 2003, (with Ron Harre) Discursive Psychology in Practice, 1995, Millenium III, Century XXI, 1996, (rev. ed.), 1998, (with Hinshaw) Encyclopedia of the Industrial Revolution, 1996, (rev. ed.), 1998, Fat History: Bodies and Beauty in the West, 1997, Fat History: Bodies and Beauty in the West, rev. edit., 2002, Schools and Students in Industrial Society: Japan and the West, 1997, History in Documents, 1998, (with Lewis) Emotional History of the U.S., 1998, World History in Documents: and Comparative Analysis in World History, 1998, Battleground of Desire: The Struggle for Self-Control in Modern America, 1999, Experiencing World History, 2000, Teaching, Learning and Knowing History, 2000, Gender in World History, 2000, Consumerism in World History, 2001, (with Brindle) Facing Up to Management Faddism, 2001, Cultures in Motion, 2001; editor: Century for Debate, 1969, The Impact of the Industrial Revolution, 1972, (with Walkowitz) Workers in the Industrial Revolution, 1974, The Other Side of Western Civilization, 1979, (rev. ed.), 1984, (4th ed.), 1991, The Rise of Modern Women, 1977, (with Michael Weber) The Spencers of Amberson Avenue: A Turn-of-the-Century Memoir, 1983, (with Van Tassel) Old Age in a Bureaucratic Society, 1986, Encyclopedia World History, 2000, Encyclopedia of European Social History, 1999; contbg. editor: History of Emotions series NYU Press, Anxious Parents: A History of Modern Childrearing in America, 2003, Thinking History, 2004; author: Western Civilization in World History, 2003; contbr. over 180 articles to prof. and popular jours. Guggenheim Found. fellow, 1973-74; NEH grantee, 1981-84, 86, 90, Rockefeller Found. grantee, 1982-83. Fellow Internat. Soc. for Rsch. on Emotion; mem. Am. Hist. Soc., World History Assn., Am. Hist. Assn. (v.p., head teaching div. 1995-98), Nat. Bd. Profl. Tchg. Standards. Democrat. Avocations: racquet sports, travel. Home: 7750 Wyckland Ct Clifton VA 20124 Office: George Mason Univ Fairfax VA 22030

STEARNS, RICHARD GAYLORE, judge; b. L.A., June 27, 1944; s. Gaylore Rhodes and Jeannetta Viola (Hofheinz) S.; m. Patricia Ann McElligott, Dec. 21, 1975. BA, Stanford U., 1968; MLitt, Oxford U., Eng., 1971; JD, Harvard U., 1976. Bar: Mass. Dep. campaign mgr. McGovern for Pres., Washington, 1970-72; spl. asst. U.S. Senate, Washington, 1972-73; asst. dist. atty. Norfolk County, Dedham, 1976-79, 80-82; del. dir. Kennedy for Pres., Washington, 1979-80; asst. U.S. atty. U.S. Dept. Justice, Boston, 1982-90; assoc. justice Superior Ct. Mass., Boston, 1990-94; U.S. dist. judge U.S. Dist. Ct. Mass., Boston, 1994—. Author: Massachusetts Criminal Law: A Prosecutor's Guide, 21st edit., 2001. Mem. jud. conf. com. on federal-state jurisdiction, mem. mass torts working group; trustee Vincent Meml. Hosp., Boston. Rhodes scholar, 1968. Mem. ABA, Mass. Bar Assn., Phi Beta Kappa. Office: US Courthouse 1 Courthouse Way Ste 7130 Boston MA 02210-3009

STEARNS, ROBERT LELAND, curator; b. L.A., Aug. 28, 1947; s. Edward Van Buren and Harriett Ann (Hauck) S.; m. Sheri Roseanne Lucas, Oct. 2, 1982 (div. 1994); children: Marissa Hauck, Caroline Lucas. Student, U. Calif., San Diego, 1965-68, BFA, 1970; student, Calif. Poly. State U., San Luis Obispo, 1968. Asst. dir. Paula Cooper Gallery, N.Y.C., 1970-72; prodn. asst. Avalanche Mag., N.Y.C., 1972; dir. Kitchen Ctr. for Video/Music, N.Y.C., 1972-77, Contemporary Arts Ctr., Cin., 1977-82; dir. performing arts Walker Art Ctr., Mpls., 1982-88; dir. Wexner Ctr. for Arts, Columbus, Ohio, 1988-92; mem. Wexner Ctr. Found., Columbus, 1990-92; dir. Stearns & Assocs./Contemporary Exhbn. Svcs., Columbus, Ohio, 1992—2000; sr. prgm. dir. Arts Midwest, Minneapolis, 1998—. Adj. prof. dept. art, assoc. dean Coll. Art, Ohio State U., Columbus, 1988-92; lectr. Sch. of the Art Inst. Chgo., 2002; cons. McKnight Found., St. Paul, 1978, Jerome Found., 1978-79; chmn. Artists TV Workshop, N.Y.C., 1976-77; bd. dirs., chmn. Minn. Dance Alliance, Mpls., 1983-88; bd. dirs. Haleakala, Inc., N.Y.C.; mem. various panels Nat. Endowment for Arts, Washington, 1977-91; mem. pub. arts policy Greater Columbus Arts Coun., 1988-90; adv. coun. Bklyn. Acad. Music, 1982-84, Houston Grand Opera, 1991-93; fundraising cons. Art for Life Columbus AIDS Task Force, 2000-; mem. Advocacy Com. Ballet Met, Columbus, 2003-. Author, editor: Robert Wilson: Theater of Images, 1980, Photography and Beyond in Japan, 1995; author: Mexico Now: Point of Departure, 1997, Robert Wilson: Scenografie e Installazioni, 1997, Illusions of Eden: Visions of the American Heartland, 2000, Aspirations: Toward a Future in the Middle East, 2001, The View from Here: Recent Pictures from Central Europe and the American Midwest, 2002; editor: Dimensions of Black, 1970; exec. editor: Breakthroughs: Avant Garde Art in Europe and America 1950-1990, 1991; author and editor numerous catalogues. Mem. gov.'s residence com. State of Ohio, 2004—. Decorated chevalier Order of Arts and Letters (France); Jerome Found. travel grantee, 1986, Japan Found. travel grantee, 1991. E-mail: arts2020@aol.com.

STEARNS, ROXANN LYNN, social worker; b. Clinton, Iowa, Apr. 5, 1959; d. Donald George Letcher and Patricia Diann Johnston; m. Robert Norman Stearns, Nov. 6, 1987; children: Gregory Kyser, Lynsi Diann. BA in social services, Mt. St. Clare, 1999—2001. Coord. - family resource ctr. Camanche Sch. Dist., Camanche, Iowa, 2001—. Home: 1507 Fourth Ave Camanche IA 52730 Office: Camanche School District 508 11th Place Camanche IA 52730 Personal E-mail: r.stearns@mchsi.com. E-mail: rstearns@camanche.k12.ia.us.

STEARNS, STEWART WARREN, charitable association executive; b. Denver, Apr. 8, 1947; s. Vinton H. and Marjorie L. (Tedro) S.; m. Marjorie L. Fuller, Jan. 25, 1969; children: Theresa Lyn, Gregory Robert. BS, Ea. N.Mex. U., 1970; MA, No. Ill. U., 1973; postgrad., SUNY, Albany, 1974—. Mng. editor Studies in Linguistics, DeKalb, Ill., 1972-73; instr. No. Ill. U., DeKalb, 1972-73; cons. AID, Guatemala, 1973-74; instr. Skidmore Coll., Saratoga Springs, N.Y., 1975; OAS fellow Guatemala, 1976-77; asst. dir. Chaves County Cmty. Action Program, Roswell, N.Mex., 1977-78; exec. dir. United Way Chaves County, Roswell, 1978-83, Levi Strauss Found., Dallas, 1983-85, Cmty. Trust Met. Tarrant County, Ft. Worth, 1985-88; pres., CEO, Cmty. Found., Sarasota County, 1989—. NDEA fellow, Dallas, 1970-71. Office Phone: 941-955-3000. Business E-Mail: sstearns@sarasota-foundation.org.

STEARNS, SUSAN A, education educator; b. Fresno, Calif. PhD, U. of Okla., 1990. Chair, communication studies Ea. Wash. U., 2002—, prof., communication studies, 2001—. Exec. sec. Ctr. for Academic Integrity, Durham, NC, 2001—04. Mem. Ctr. for Academic Integrity, Durham, NC, 2000—. Rsch. grant, Ea. Wash. U., 2002. Mem.: Internat. Communication Assn. (life), Nat. Communication Assn. (life). Office: Eastern Washington University Comm 229 Cheney WA 99004

STEARNS, SUSAN TRACEY, lighting design company executive, lawyer; b. Seattle, Oct. 28, 1957; d. Arthur Thomas and Roberta Jane (Arrowood) S.; m. Ross Alan De Alessi, Aug. 11, 1990; 1 child, Chase Arthur. AA, Stephens Coll., 1977, BA, 1979; JD, U. Wash., Seattle, 1990. Bar: Calif. 1990, U.S. Ct. Appeals (9th cir.) 1990, U.S. Dist. Ct. (no. dist.) Calif 1990, U.S. Dist. Ct. (we. dist.) Wash. 1991, Wash. 1991. TV news prodr. KOMO, Seattle, 1980-86; atty. Brobeck, Phleger & Harrison, San Francisco, 1990-92; pres. Ross De Alessi Lighting Design, Seattle, 1993—. Author periodicals in field. Alumnae Assn. Coun. Stephens Coll., Columbia, Mo., 1995—. Named Nat. Order of Barristers U. Washington, Seattle, 1990. Mem. ABA (mem. state labor and employment law subcom.), Wash. State Bar Assn. (mem. bench-bar-press com.), State Bar Calif., King County Bar Assn., Bar Assn.San Francisco, Wash. Athletic Club. Avocations: travel, dance. Office: Ross De Alessi Lighting Design 3313 W McGraw Seattle WA 98199

STEBBINS, DONALD J. car parts manufacturing company executive; V.p., treas., asst. sec. Lear Corp., Southfield, Mich., sr. v.p., CFO, treas., 1997—. Office: Lear Corp 21557 Telegraph Rd Southfield MI 48034

STEBBINS, GREGORY KELLOGG, foundation executive; b. Lafayette, Ind., Jan. 10, 1951; s. Albert Kellogg and Nancy Ruth (Osborn) S. BS in Data Processing, Calif. Poly., Pomona, 1974; MBA, U. So. Calif., 1976; EdD, Pepperdine U., 1985. Account exec. ADP, Long Beach, Calif., 1977-78; salesman Grubb & Ellis, L.A., 1978-81, v.p. Beverly Hills, Calif., 1981-83; regional mgr. Hanes Co., Beverly Hills, 1983-85; pres. Stebbins Consulting Group, Santa Monica, Calif., 1989—; bd. dirs., CFO Insight Seminars, 1994—. Mem.: APA, Sigma Xi. Avocations: flying, scuba diving, photography. Office: Stebbins Cons Group 944 Princeton Dr Marina Del Rey CA 90292

STEBBINS, HENRY BLANCHARD, lawyer; b. Hartford, Conn., June 14, 1951; s. Herbert Bellows and Katherine (Reynolds) S.; m. Alison Finney, May 30, 1976; children: Duncan Finney, Martha Reynolds, H. Benjamin. BA cum laude, U. N.H., 1973; JD, Boston U., 1976. Bar: N.H. 1976, U.S. Dist. Ct. N.H. 1976. Assoc. Sheehan, Phinney, Bass & Green, Manchester, NH, 1976—80, ptnr., 1980—97, mgmt. com., 1994—97; sr. ptnr. Stebbins Lazos & Van Der Beken, Manchester, 1997—. Trustee Manchester Boys and Girls Club, 1983-2003; chmn. Vocat. Partnership Found., 1986-91; bd. dirs. Brookside Ch. Nursery Sch., 1984-90, Leadership N.H., 1994-95; bd. dirs. United Way Greater Manchester, 1986-95, chmn., 1990-92; mem. N.H. Rep. State com., 1995-99, N.H. Rep. Fin. Com., 1995-97, N.H. legal counsel Dole for Pres. Campaign; mem. fin. com. George W. Bush Presdl. Campaign; bd. dirs., legal counsel, mem. exec. com. Manchester C. of C., 1997-2001; hon. co-chair bus. adv. coun. Rep. Nat. Com., 2002-03. Named N.H. Businessman of Yr., 2003. Mem. ABA, N.H. Bar Assn., Manchester Bar Assn. (pres. 1982-83), Assn. Bank Holding Cos. (lawyers div. 1985-93), Rissa Club. Office: 66 Hanover St Manchester NH 03101-2230 Office Phone: 603-672-3700. E-mail: hstebbins@slwlaw.com.

STEBBINS, ROBERT ALAN, sociology educator; b. Rhinelander, Wis., June 22, 1938; s. William Nelson and Dorothy May (Guy) S.; m. Karin Yvonne Olson, Jan. 11, 1964; children: Paul, Lisa, Christi. BA, Macalester Coll., 1961; MA, U. Minn., 1962, PhD, 1964. Assoc. prof. Presbyterian Coll., Clinton, S.C., 1964-65; assoc. prof.to prof. Meml. U. Nfld., St. John's, Can., 1965-73; prof. U. Tex.-Arlington, 1973-76; prof. sociology U. Calgary, Alta., Can., 1976-99, faculty prof. social scis., 2000—, dept. head, 1976-82; head dept. sociology and anthropology Meml. U. Nfld., 1968-71. Author: Commitment to Deviance, 1971, The Disorderly Classroom: Its Physical and Temporal Conditions, 1974, Teachers and Meaning, 1975, Amateurs, 1979, The Magician, 1984, Sociology: The Study of Society, 2d edit., 1990, Canadian Football: The View from the Helmet, 1987, Deviance: Tolerable Differences, 1988, The Laugh-Makers: Stand-Up Comedy as Art, Business, and Life-Style, 1990, Amateurs, Professionals and Serious Leisure, 1992; co-editor: Fieldwork Experience, 1980, The Sociology of Deviance, 1982, Experiencing Fieldwork, 1991, Career, Culture, and Social Psychology in a Variety Art, 1993, Predicaments: Moral Difficulty in Everyday Life, 1993, The Franco-Calgarians: French Language, Leisure and Linguistic Lifestyle in an Anglophone City, 1994, The Connoisseur's New Orleans, 1995, The Barbershop Singer: Inside the Social World of a Musical Hobby, 1996, Tolerable Differences: Living with Deviance, 2d edit., 1996; After Work: The Search for an Optimal Leisure Lifestyle, 1998, The Urban Francophone Volunteer: Searching for Personal Meaning and Community Growth in a Linguistic Minority, 1998, The French Enigma: Survival and Development of Canada's Francophone Societies, 2000, Exploratory Research in the Social Sciences, 2001, New Directions in the Theory and Research of Serious Leisure, 2001, The Organizational Basis of Leisure Participation: A Motivational Exploration, 2002, Francophonie et langue dans un monde diverse en évolution: contacts interlinguistiques socioculturels, 2003, Volunteering as Leisure/Leisure as Volunteering: An International Assessment, 2004, Between Work and Leisure: A Study of the Common Ground of Two Separate Worlds, 2004. Pres. St. John's Orch., 1967-68; mem. Dallas Civic Symphony, 1973-76, Orch. Soc. of Calgary, 1978-97. Can. Coun. Sabbatical Leave fellow, 1972-72, Calgary Inst. for Humanities fellow, 1987-88, Killam resident fellow, 1990; NEH summer stipend, 1976; Acad. Leisure Scis. fellow, 1996—, Royal Soc. Can. fellow, 1999—. Mem. Leisure Studies Assn., Can. Sociology and Anthropology Assn. (pres. 1988-89), Internat. Sociol. Assn., Assn. for Can. Studies, World Leisure and Recreation Assn. (bd. dirs. 1997—), Social Sci. Fed. Can. (pres. 1991-92), Can. Assn. for Leisure Studies (v.p. 1993-96). Home: 144 Edgemont Estates Dr NW Calgary AB Canada T3A 2M3 Office: U Calgary Dept Sociology 2500 University Dr NW Calgary AB Canada T2N 1N4 Office Phone: 403-220-5827. E-mail: stebbins@ucalgary.ca.

STEBLETON, MICHELLE MARIE, music educator, musician; b. Midland, Mich., Apr. 10, 1966; d. Leo Frederick and Sally Joanne (Brosman) Stebleton. MusB in Horn Performance, U. Mich., 1988, MusM in Horn Performance, 1989; diploma, European Mozart Found., Prague, Czech Republic, 1993. Third horn Ann Arbor (Mich.) Symphony, 1986-89, Saginaw (Mich.) Symphony, 1988-89; hornist Lone Star Brass Quintet, Midland, Tex., 1989-90; prin. horn Midland (Tex.)/Odessa Symphony, 1989-90; adj. prof. horn Odessa (Tex.) Coll., 1990; assoc. prof. horn Fla. State U., Tallahassee, 1990—. Clinician First Internat. Swiss Horn Workshop, 1994, Nove Straseci Internat. Interpreters Course, 1996, 2001; bd. dirs., co. pres. RM Williams Pub., Tallahassee, 1997—; chair faculty senate profl. devel. and welfare com. Fla. State U., Tallahassee, 1999—; lectr. in field. Performer Internat. Mozart Festival, 1991, Orquesta Filarmonica de la UNAM, Mexico City, 1992, Vienna Philharm. Chamber Players, Sapporo, Japan, 1994, 95, Pacific Music Festival, Sapporo, Tokyo, 1994, Sapporo, Hiroshima, Tokyo, 1995, Vienna Chamber Players, Santo Domingo, Dominican Republic, 1997, Internat. Orch. Festival Santo Domingo, 1997, 99, others; soloist (concert tour Vietnam) Fla. State U. Singers, 1999. Fin. advisor Sigma Alpha Iota, Fla. State U., Tallahassee, 1994—; performer Peace Concert, Pacific Music Festival, Hiroshima, Japan, 1995; coord. dept. fundraising United Way Big Bend, Tallahassee, 1998. Recipient second prize Am. Horn Competition-Natural Horn Divsn., 1989, second prize Am. Horn Competition-Profl. Divsn., 1994, 99, Tchg. Incentive Program award State of Fla., Fla. State U., 1996; com. on faculty rsch. support grantee Fla. State U., 1992, 97. Mem. Internat. Horn Soc. (life, co-host, lectr., bd. mem. S.E. region conf. adv. bd. 1991—, first prize solo competition 1987), Nat. Assn. Coll. Wind and Percussion Instrs., Music Educators Nat. Conf., Music Tchrs. Nat. Assn., Pi Kappa Lambda. Avocations: travel, photography, T'ai Chi teaching. Home: 2519 Prest Ct Tallahassee FL 32301-3386 Office: Fla State Univ HMU 127 Tallahassee FL 32306-1180

STEC, JOHN ZYGMUNT, real estate executive; b. Stalowawola, Poland, Jan. 21, 1925; Came to U.S.A. 1947. s. Valenty and Maria (Madej) S. m. Wanda G. Baca, Oct. 13, 1956; children: David, Maria, Monica. Student, Poland, 1941-44, Kent St. U., Oh., 1965-66, student, 1966-67. Cert. Master of Corporate Real Estate. With The Singer Co., Cleve., 1952-54, dis. mgr., 1954-60, sales supr., 1960-67, dir. real estate Detroit and Chgo., 1967-73; v.p. Fabri Center of Am., Beachwood, Ohio, 1973—; sr. v.p. real estate Fabri-Centers of Am., Inc., Beachwood, Ohio, 1987—. With U.S. Army 1950-52 With U.S. Army, 1950-52. Mem. Nat. Assoc. of Corporate Real Estate (speaker, organizer 1974-77, audit Com. 1977-79, bd. dirs. 1970-82, Outstanding Achievement award 1982). Chagrin Valley Club. Repulican. Roman Catholic. Avocations: swimming, hiking, reading. Home: 725 Sagewood Dr Chagrin Falls OH 44023-6733 Office: JoAnn Stores Inc 5555 Darrow Rd Hudson OH 44236-4011 Business E-Mail: johnstec@jo-annstores.com. *Personal philosophy: Think success and you'll be successful. Perseverence of any goal leads to achievement. Learning is knowledge. Knowledge is the most powerful key that leads to greatness and opens any door.*

STECHER, ESTA E. lawyer, investment company executive; b. Mpls., Apr. 3, 1957; BA summa cum laude, U. Minn., 1979; JD, Columbia U., 1982. Bar: N.Y. 1983. Ptnr. Sullivan & Cromwell, 1982—94; gen. counsel, mng. dir. Tax dept. Goldman, Sachs & Co., N.Y.C., 1994—2000, gen. counsel, co-head, legal dept., 2000—. Mem.: ABA, Assn. Bar City of New York, N.Y. Bar Assn. Office: Goldman Sachs and Co Legal Dept 1 New York Plz 37th Fl New York NY 10004

STECHER, KENNETH W. financial corporation executive; Sr. v.p., CFO, treas. Cin. Fin. Corp., 1999. Office: 6200 S Gilmore Rd Fairfield OH 45014-5141

STECICH, RITA LOUISE, secondary school educator; b. Chgo., Oct. 1, 1949; d. Thomas Filbert Fahey and Ada Helen Tambellini; m. John Patrick Stecich, July 1, 1972; children: Eric John, Thomas John. BA in English, U. Ill., 1971; MS in Reading, Chgo. State U., 1976. Cert. secondary edn. tchr., Ill. Tchr. English and reading Tilden H.S., Chgo., 1971-77, Evergreen Park (Ill.) Comm H.S., 1990—. Union pres. Evergreen Park Tchrs. Assn., 1998—. Bd. dirs. Local Redevel. Bd. Mt. Greenwood, Chgo., 1997-99. Named Tchr. of Yr., PTA, 1998. Mem. Nat. Tchrs. English, Ill. Reading Assn.

STECK, JODI, photojournalist; Sr. nat. photo editor Assoc. Press, NY, NY, 1999—; dir. of photography The Orange County Register; asst. chief of bur. Assoc. Press, Los Angeles, Calif.; photo editor San Francisco; dir. of photography Santa Rosa Press Dem., Calif., 1989—92; photo editor NY Times, NY, NY, 1985—86, Assoc. Press, Los Angeles, Calif.; tchr. UCLA, Calif.; news editor Mesa Tribune, Ariz.; copy editor San Francisco Chronicle, Calif. While employed at the Orange County Register, the paper was honored for best use of photos in NPPA/POY competition. Office: The Assoc Press 50 Rockefeller Plz New York NY 10020

STECK, WARREN FRANKLIN, retired chemical company executive, biochemist; b. Regina, Sask., Can., May 10, 1939; m. 1963; 2 children. B in Eng., McGill U., 1960; PhD in Organic Chemistry, U. Sask., 1964. Rsch. assoc. Rsch. Inst. Okla. U., 1963-64; asst. rsch. officer Nat. Rsch. Coun. Can., 1964-70, assoc. rsch. officer, 1970-76, sr. rsch. officer, 1976-80, asst. dir., 1980-81, assoc. dir., 1982-83, dir. Plant Biotech. Inst., 1983-90, dir. gen. Plant Biotech Inst., 1991-94; asst. pres. Fytokem Inc., Saskatoon, Sask., 1995-97, v.p. tech., 1997—99; pres. Steck & Assoc. Inc., Saskatoon, 1999—. Mem. Phytochem. Soc. N.Am., Soc. Cosmetic Chemists. Achievements include rsch. in insect sex attractants and pheromones, chem. ecology.

STECKEL, RICHARD J. radiologist, educator, academic administrator; b. Scranton, Pa., Apr. 17, 1936; s. Morris Leo and Lucille (Yellin) Steckel; m. Julie Raskin, June 16, 1960; children: Jan Marie, David Matthew. BS magna cum laude, Harvard U., 1957, MD cum laude, 1961. Diplomate Am. Bd. Radiology. Intern UCLA Hosp., 1961-62; resident in radiology Mass. Gen. Hosp., Boston, 1962-65; clin., rsch. assoc. Nat. Cancer Inst., 1965-67; faculty UCLA Med. Sch., 1967—, prof. radiol. scis. and radiation oncology, 1974—2000; chmn. dept. radiol. scis. UCLA Med. Ctr., 1994-2000, prof. emeritus, 2000—; pres. Assn. Am. Cancer Insts., 1981. Dir. Jonsson Comprehensive Cancer Ctr., 1974—94; mem. staff UCLA Med. Ctr., Cottage Hosp., Santa Barbara, Calif. Author, editor 3 books; contbr. more than 130 articles to profl. jours. Fellow: Am. Coll. Radiology; mem.: Assn. Univ. Radiologists, Am. Roentgen Ray Soc., Radiol. Soc. N.Am. Mailing: 1126 Bel Air Dr Santa Barbara CA 93105 E-mail: rsteckel2000@yahoo.com.

STECKLER, LARRY, publisher, editor, writer; b. Bklyn., Nov. 3, 1933; s. Morris and Ida (Beekman) S.; m. Catherine Coccozza, June 6, 1959 (div. June 1999); children: Gail Denise, Glenn Eric, Kerri Lynn, Adria Lauren; m. Lorraine Mary Rubsamen, Oct. 16, 1999. Student, CCNY, 1951. Assoc. editor Radio-Electronics mag., NYC, 1957-62, editor, 1967-85; pub., editor-in-chief Radio Electronics mag., NYC, 1985-92; electronics editor Popular Mechanics mag., NYC, 1962-65; assoc. editor Electronic Products mag., Garden City, NY, 1965-67; editl. dir. Merchandising 2-Way Radio mag., NYC, 1975-77; v.p., dir. Gernsback Publs., NYC, 1975-84, pres., dir., 1984—2003; pub., editl. dir. Spl. Projects mag., 1980-84, Radio-Electronics Ann., 1982-84; pub., editor-in-chief Hands-On Electronics, 1984-88, Computer Digest, 1985-90, Experimenters Handbook, 1986-96, Modern Short Stories, 1987-90, Video/Stereo Digest, 1989-91, Popular Electronics Mag., 1988-99, GIZMO, 1988-99, Hobbyists Handbook, 1989-96, Sci. Probe! mag., 1989-93, Story-Masters, 1989—2001, Electronics Shopper, 1990-99, Electronics Market Ctr., 1991-99, Electronics Now Mag., 1992-99, Radio Craft, 1993-96, Poptronix Handbook, 1996—2003; pres. Claggk, Inc., 1986—2003, Silicon Chip, 1993-94, Sci. Probe Inc., 1989-93, Poptronix Inc., 1997—; pub., editor-in-chief Poptronix online, 1997—. Mem. electronics adv. bd. Bd. Coop. Ednl. Svcs., Nassau County, NY, 1975—77; pres. Electronics Industry Hall of Fame, 1985—2001; bd. dirs. Pub. Hall of Fame, 1987—89. Author books, handbooks; pub., editor-in-chief Poptronics, 2000-03, Poptronics Shopper, 2000-03, PC Tech, 2000-03; co-editor The Shofar, 1998-2002; contbr. articles to profl. jours. Bd. dirs. Nassau County coun. Camp Fire Girls, 1971-72; 1st v.p. bd. dirs. Temple Beth Am, Las Vegas, 1998-2002 pres. 2001-02. Served with U.S. Army, 1953-56. Recipient Coop. award Nat. Alliance TV and Electronic Svcs. Assns., 1974, 75; inducted into Electronics Industry Hall of Fame, 1985; ISCET Gov's. award, 1998, FESA Pres. award, 1998. Mem.: IEEE, LA Press, Soc. Profl. Journalists, Internat. Performing Magicians (exec. dir.), Internat. Underwater Explorers Soc., Am. Mgmt. Assn., Nat. Electronics Sales and Svc. Dealers Assn. (rec. sec. NY State 1976—78, treas. 1991—94, Man of Yr. award 1975, 1985, M.L. Finneyberg Excellence award 1994), Internat. Soc. Cert. electronic Technicians (chmn. 1974—76, 1979—81, dir.-at-large 1991—93, rep. to NESDA bd. 1991—93, chmn. 1993—95, Region 9 dir. 1995—97, chmn. 1999—2001, Chmn.'s award 1985), Am. Soc. Bus. Press Editors (sr.), Radio Club Am. Home: 9072 Lawton Pine Dr Las Vegas NV 89129-7044 *Do not be afraid to try the unaccepted. Do not be afraid to do the undesirable. Do what you enjoy. . .do it well. . .and after it is done. . .never regret having done it. . .only regret what you have not yet done.*

STECKLER, PHYLLIS BETTY, publishing company executive; b. NYC; d. Irwin H. and Bertha (Fellner) Schwartzbard; m. Stuart J. Steckler; children: Randall, Sharon Steckler-Slotky. BA, Hunter Coll.; MA, NYU. Editl. dir. R.R. Bowker Co., NYC, Crowell Collier Macmillan Info. Pub. Co., NYC, Holt Rinehart & Winston Info. Systems, NYC; pres., CEO Oryx Press, Scottsdale, Ariz., 1973-76, Phoenix, 1976—2000, Zephyr Info., Phoenix, 2001—; publ. cons., 2001—. Adj. prof. mktg. scholarly publs. Grad. History dept., Ariz. State U., Tempe; mem. dean's coun. Coll. of Extended Edn., Ariz. State U., Phoenix. Past chmn. Info. Industry Assn.; past chair Ariz. Ctr. for the Book; past pres. Contemporary Forum of Phoenix Art Mus.; founding mem. Nat. Edn. Network, U.S. Dept. Edn.; past pres. Friends of the Libr., U.S.A.; mem. Ariz. Women's Forum; bd. dirs. Ariz. region Com. for the Weizmann Inst. Sci. Recipient Women Who Make a Difference award The Internat. Women's Forum, 1995, Excellence in Pub. award Ariz. Book Pub. Assn., 1997, The Pub. History Program Ariz. State U. Founding Friend award, 2000; elected to Hunter Coll. Hall of Fame. Mem.: ALA, Ariz. Libr. Assn., Univ. Club of Phoenix. Home and Office: 6446 N 28th St Phoenix AZ 85016-8946 Office Phone: 602-391-6433. E-mail: pbs.zephyr@cox.net.

STEDGE-FOWLER, JOYCE, retired clergywoman; b. Spring Valley, N.Y., Mar. 2, 1926; d. Sidney and Lila Mae (Joyce) Kearsing; m. Leland Stedge, Sept. 4, 1948 (div. Apr. 1978); children: Leland Jr., Deborah Stedge-Stroud, David, Donald, Claudia, Douglas; m. Joseph Charles Fowler, June 23, 1985. BA in Liberal Arts, U. Iowa, 1947; MDiv, Union Theol. Sem., N.Y.C., 1973. Ordained to ministry Ref. Ch. in Am., 1973; cert. elem. tchr., N.Y. Elem. tchr. Ramapo I Sch. Dist., Suffern, N.Y., 1966-68, Ramapo II Sch. Dist., Spring Valley, 1968-69; pastor Rochester Ref. Ch., Accord, N.Y., 1973-76; NIMH clin. pastoral intern in mental health St. Elizabeths Hosp., Washington, D.C., 1976-77, clin. pastoral resident in supervision and consultation, 1977-79; pastor-at-large New Castle Presbytery, Wilmington, Del., 1979-82; interim pastor Coop. Parish St. George's, Port Penn, Del. City, Pencader Presbyn. chs., 1980; interim pastor 1st and Olivet Presbyn. Ch., Wilmington, 1980, Hanover Presbyn. Ch., Wilmington, 1981, Ocean City (Md.) Presbyn. Ch., 1982; pastor Christ Presbyn. Ch., Martinsville, N.J., 1982-85; min. to elderly United Presbyn. Ch., Plainfield, N.J., 1985-91; ret., 1991. Chaplain Robert Wood Johnson Health Care Ctr., Plainfield, 1985-91; cons., clin. pastoral educator and therapist, 1975-95; mem. task force on abortion Nat. Coun. Chs., 1970-73, mem. Commn. on Women in Ministry, 1973-80, mem. women's ecumenical coordinating group, 1973-79; mem. justice for women com. Elizabeth Presbytery, 1982—, mem. social issues com., 1986-91, moderator, 1991-92, mem. gen. coun., 1990-91, mem. pers. com., 1991-95; del. to Gen. Assembly, Presbyn. Ch. (U.S.A.), 1985, 91. Former leader Rockland County coun. Girl Scouts U.S.A.; former treas., fin. chmn., bd. dirs. LWV; com. mem. Water, Sewer and Fgn. Policy Rockland County Study, 1955-73; former program chmn. Women's Assn., former adult edn. chmn. Spring Valley Ref. Ch.; former mem. coun. and edn. chmn. Ctrl. Rockland Ecumenical Witness, Spring Valley; bd. dirs. Somerset Chaplaincy to Elderly, 1985-91, Somerset Chaplaincy to Ex-Offenders, 1982-86, NAMI-Familyn, 1999—. Democrat. Achievements include becoming the 1st woman ordained in the Reformed Church in America by Rockland-Westchester Classis. Home: 10 Summit Park Rd Spring Valley NY 10977-1510

STEDINGER, JERY RUSSELL, civil and environmental engineer, researcher; b. Oakland, Calif., June 22, 1951; s. Russell Phillip and Vivian Lavina (Nelson) S.; m. Robin Lee Gray, June 30, 1973; children: Matthew, Carolyn. BA, U. Calif., Berkeley, 1972; AM, Harvard U., 1974, PhD, 1977. Math. programmer Lawrence Livermore Lab., Livermore, Calif., 1973; rsch. asst., teaching fellow Engr. and Applied Physics, Harvard U., Cambridge, Mass., 1974-77; asst. prof. Civil and Environ. Engr., Cornell U., Ithaca, N.Y, 1977-83; hydrologist U.S. Geol. Survey, Reston, Va., 1983-84; assoc. prof. Civil and Environ. Engr., Cornell U., Ithaca, N.Y., 1989-93, prof., 1989—. Cons. Pacific Electric and Gas Co., San Francisco, 1989-98, U.S. Army Corps Engrs., 1999. Author: Water Resources Systems Planning and Analysis, 1981; contbr. articles to profl. jours. Scoutmaster Troop 2, Boy Scouts Am., Ithaca, N.Y., 1988-2004. Recipient Editor's Citation for Excellence in Reviewing award Am. Geophys. Union, 1983, 90, 93; named Presdl. Young Investigator, NSF, 1984-90, CEE Prof. of Yr., Chi Epsilon, 1979-80, 99-2000. Fellow Internat. Water Acad., Am. Geophys. Union; mem. ASCE (Huber Civil Engrng. Rsch. prize 1989, Julian Hinds award 1997), Soc. for Risk Analysis. Office: Cornell U Sch Civil Environ Engring 213 Hollister Hall Ithaca NY 14853-3501

STEDMAN, R VANGORDEN, artist, art historian radio and television personality; b. N.Y., 1965; s. Richard J. and Joyce (Allen) S. Student, SUNY, New Paltz, 1990, SUNY, Purchase, 1994; BA in Art History, SUNY, Binghamton, 1996. Curatorial intern Roberson Ctr. for Arts and Scis., Binghamton, 1982-83; photography, publicity and graphic design mgr. The Switch, Endicott, N.Y., 1984; emcee The Jolt, East Aurora, N.Y., 1984; TV guest host WSKG Pub. TV, Binghamton, 1984-85; radio fine arts commentator Talk Am. Radio Network Stas. WENE, WGUL, WNFB, WVOX, Upstate N.Y., also Fla., 1986-99; studio and archive dir., mgr. estates of artists Henryk Glickenstein, Emmanuel Romano, others, St. Petersburg, Fla., 1989—. Panelist Personal FX, Fox TV Network, N.Y., 1994; curator Otto Bierhals Family Collection and Archive, Greenwich, Conn., 1991—; acting curator The Gallery at Gran Finale, St. Petersburg, 1998-99. Exhibited works in shows including Tracy St. Collective, 1985, Purchase Coll., 1995, others; author fine arts and related topics article series Antiquer's Guide, Sidney, N.Y., 1986-87; art appraisal commn. Cornell U., Ithaca, N.Y., 1996; lectr., rschr. Mem. Zodiac Group/Salvador Dali Mus., 1998-99. Office: 204 37th Ave N # 351 Saint Petersburg FL 33704-1416

STEED, JOHN DAVID, consumer products company executive; B in Mktg., Western Carolina U. Joined Lowe's Cos., Inc., 1973, v.p. merchandising fashion plumbing/elec., 1998—99, v.p. merchandising western divsn., 1999—2001, sr. v.p. and gen. mgr. bldg. products, 2001—. Office: 1605 Curtis Bridge Rd Wilkesboro NC 28697

STEED, MICHELLE ELNORA, special education educator, counselor; b. Raleigh, N.C., Sept. 23, 1967; d. Johnnie Wilbert and Ednell (Thornton) S. BA, N.C. State U., 1989, MEd, 1990. Cert. spl. edn. Tchr. Franklin County Schs., Youngsville, N.C., 1999—. N.C. State U. fellow, 1989-90, All Am. scholar N.C. State U. Democrat. Baptist. Avocations: pianist, organist. Home: 5512 Thornton Rd Raleigh NC 27616-5728

STEED, THERESA JEAN, manufacturing executive; b. Grapeland, Tex., Mar. 10, 1932; d. Robert Tresband and Alma Inez (Denson) Bobbitt; m. Jarvis Lacy Steed, July 8, 1950; children: Judy Karen, Pamela Kay, Kim Lacy. Grad., Elliott Bus. Sch., Houston, 1949; BMus. Edn., So. Coll. Fine Arts, Houston, 1956; postgrad., U. Tex., 1961, Sul Ross U., Alpine, Tex., 1962; M. of Rhymes (hon.), Duke U., 1961. Exec. sec. various cos., Houston, 1950-57; elem. sch. tchr. Rosenburg (Tex.) Ind. Sch. Dist., 1957-58; kindergarten/music edn. tchr. Sonora (Tex.) Ind. Sch. Dist., 1959-65; elem. sch. tchr. Houston Ind. Sch. Dist., 1965-67, Conroe (Tex.) Ind. Sch. Dist., 1968-70; co-founder, co-owner Steed Tile & Mfg. Co., Conroe, 1965—. Author: Audio-Visual Curriculums for Music Education: Kindergarten Through Eighth Grade, 1962. Mem. Dem. Nat. Com., Washington, 1993—, Dem. Senatorial Campaign Com., Washington, 1996, Dem. Nat. Com., 2003-04. Fellow: Internat. Biographical Ctr. (life); mem.: Am. Biographical Inst., Am.'s Nat. World War II Mus. (charter), Nat. Women's History Mus. (charter), Order Eastern Star (assoc. matron 1963), Women in Constrn. (charter, reporter 1970—75), Nat. Trust for Hist. Preservation, Pilot Club, Delta Kappa Gamma (publicity chmn. 1962—65). Methodist. Avocations: cooking, gardening, grandparenting, politicking. Home: 17595 W FM1097 Montgomery TX 77356-8471 E-mail: quechick007@yahoo.com.

STEEDMAN, DORIA LYNNE SILBERBERG, organization executive; b. L.A. d. Mendel B. and Dorothy H. (Howell) Silberberg; m. Richard Cantey Steedman, Feb. 19, 1966; 1 child, Alexandra Loren. BA summa cum laude, UCLA. Producer EUE/Screen Gems, N.Y.C., 1963-66, Jack Tinker & Ptnrs., N.Y.C., 1966-68, Telpac Mgmt., N.Y.C., 1968-72; v.p. broadcast prodn. Geer DuBois Advt., N.Y.C., 1973-78, account mgr., dir. ops., 1979-92; exec. v.p., pro bono dir. creative devel. Partnership for a Drug-Free America, N.Y.C., 1992—. Bd. dirs. Friends of the Earth. Recipient Andy award Art Dirs. Club, 1968, 71; named one of 100 Best and Brightest Women in Advt., Advt. Age mag.; named Advt. Woman of Yr., 1996. Mem. Advt. Women N.Y. (pres. 1993-95), Advt. Women N.Y. Found. (pres. 1995-97), Phi Beta Kappa. Office: Partnership for a Drug-Free Am 405 Lexington Ave New York NY 10174-0002 E-mail: doria_steedman@drugfree.org.

STEEFEL, DAVID SIMON, lawyer; b. Mpls., June 27, 1951; s. Lawrence D. Jr. and Marion (Charlson) S.; m. Mary Ann Moody, May 24, 1981; children: Emily, Daniel, Katherine. BA, Carleton Coll., 1973; JD, U. Colo., 1978. Bar: Colo. 1978, U.S. Dist. Ct. Colo. 1978, U.S. Ct. Appeals (10th cir.) 1978. Assoc. Gorsuch, Kirgis, Denver, 1978-80, Holme Roberts & Owen, Denver, 1980-84, ptnr., 1984—, litig. practice group leader, 1999—. Instr. U. Colo. Law Sch., Boulder, 1978, 91. Home: 1300 Green Oaks Dr Littleton CO 80121-1331 Office: Holme Roberts & Owen 1700 Lincoln St Ste 4100 Denver CO 80203-4541 Office Phone: 303-866-0348. Business E-Mail: david.steefel@hro.com.

STEEL, DANIELLE FERNANDE, author; b. N.Y.C., Aug. 14, 1947; d. John and Norma (Stone) Schuelein-Steel. Student, Parsons Sch. Design, 1963, NYU, 1963-67. Vice pres. pub. relations and new bus. Supergirls Ltd., N.Y.C., 1968-71; copywriter Grey Advt., San Francisco, 1973-74. Author novels Going Home, 1973, Passion's Promise, 1977, Now and Forever, 1978, The Promise, 1978, Season of Passion, 1979, Summers End, 1979, To Love Again, 1980, The Ring, 1981, Loving, 1980, Love, 1981, Remembrance, 1981, Palomino, 1981, Once in a Lifetime, 1982, Crossings, 1982, A Perfect Stranger, 1982, Thurston House, 1983, Changes, 1983, Full Circle, 1984, (non-fiction) Having A Baby, 1984, Family Album, 1985, Secrets, 1985, Wanderlust, 1986, Fine Things, 1987, Kaleidoscope, 1987, Zoya, 1988, Star, 1988, Daddy, 1989, Message from Nam, 1990, Heartbeat, 1991, No Greater Love, 1991, Jewels, 1992, Mixed Blessings, 1992, Vanished, 1993, Accident, 1994, The Gift, 1994, Wings, 1994, Lightning, 1995, Five Days in Paris, 1995, Malice, 1996, The Ghost, 1997, The Ranch, 1998, The Long Road Home, 1998, The Klone & I, 1998, Silent Honor, 1997, His Bright Light, 1998, Mirror Image, 1998, Bittersweet, 1999, Granny Dan, 1999, Irresistible Forces, 1999, The Wedding, 2000, The House on Hope Street, 2000, Journey, 2000, Lone Eagle, 2001, Leap of Faith, 2001, The Kiss, 2001, The Cottage, 2002, Sunset in St. Tropez, 2002, Answered Prayers, 2002, Dating Game, 2003, Johnny Angel, 2003, Safe Harbour, 2003, Ransom, 2004, (children's) Martha's Best Friend, Martha's New School, Martha's New Daddy, Max's New Daddy, Max and The Babysitter, Max's Daddy Goes To The Hospital; contbr. poetry to mags., including Cosmopolitan, McCall's, Ladies Home Jour., Good Housekeeping. Chevalier of the distinguished Order of Arts and Letters, France. Home: PO Box 1637 New York NY 10156-1637 Office: care Dell Publishing 1540 Broadway New York NY 10036-4039*

STEEL, DAVID WARREN, music history educator, organist, harpsichordist; b. Evanston, Ill., Sept. 20, 1947; s. Sanger Bright and Madeleine Reagan Steel; m. Anne Alexander Buesser, July 16, 1990. AB, Harvard Coll., 1968; AM, U. Mich., 1976, PhD, 1982. Assoc. prof. U. Miss., Oxford, 1980—. Editor: (music edit.) Stephen Jenks Collected Works, 1995, Daniel Belknap Collected Works, 1999. Fellow, NEH, 1987. Episcopalian. Avocations: sacred harp singing, bicycling, boating. Office: U Miss Dept Music PO Box 1848 University MS 38677

STEEL, KUNIKO JUNE, retired artist; b. San Francisco, June 3, 1929; d. Jirohei and Moriyo (Shiraishi) Nakamura; m. John Schulein-Steel, Jan. 26, 1963 (dec. May 1978). Student, U. Calif., 1948-49; diploma, Am. Acad. Art, Chgo., 1951; student, Academic Julian, Paris, 1952-53, Art Inst. Chgo., 1954-55, Art Students League, N.Y.C., 1959-62, 79-85. Exhibited in group shows at Rafilson Gallery, Chgo., 1954, Arts of N.E., Silvermine, Conn., 1966, 79, 90, 92, Modern Maturity Traveling Exhibit, 1990-92, Schoharie Exhibit, Cobleskill, N.Y., 1993-94, Mus. of Modern Art, Miami, Coral Gables, Fla., 1993, 37th Chautaqua Nat. Exhibit of Am. Art, 1994, Montclair State U., 1994, 95. Vol., crafts tchr. Hosp. for Spl. Surgery, N.Y.C., 1967-84; vol. Japanese Gallery Met. Mus., 1994; past vol. costume conservation Met. Mus., N.Y.C., 1979-94. Recipient scholarship Palo Alto Quota Club, 1948, Art Students League, 1960. Avocations: designing arts and crafts, painting.

STEEL, ROBERT K. finance company executive; BA, Duke U.; MBA, U. Chgo. Joined Goldman Sachs Group Inc., 1976, head equities divsn. Europe, 1988—94, head instnl. equities U.S., 1994—98, co-head equities divsn., 1998—2001, head equities divsn., 2001—02, vice chmn., 2002—04, adv. dir., non-exec. chmn., securities divsn., 2004—; sr. fellow, ctr. bus. and govt. John F. Kennedy Sch. Govt. at Harvard U., 2004—. Vice chmn. Duke U. Bd. Trustees; chmn. Duke U. Mgmt. Co. Mem.: NYSE (mem. various coms.), Securities Industry Assn. (bd. dirs.). Office: Goldman Sachs Group Inc 85 Broad St New York NY 10004 also: JFK Sch Govt Harvard U 79 John F Kennedy St Cambridge MA 02138

STEEL, RONALD LEWIS, writer, historian, educator; b. Morris, Ill., Mar. 25, 1931; BA magna cum laude, Northwestern U., 1953; MA, Harvard U., 1955. Vice consul US Fgn. Svc., 1957-58; editor Scholastic mag., NYC, 1959-62; sr. assoc. Carnegie Endowment for Internat. Peace, 1982-83; fellow Woodrow Wilson Internat. Ctr. Scholars, 1984-85; prof. internat. relations U. So. Calif., Los Angeles, Calif., 1986—; fellow Wissenschaftskolleg zu Berlin, Germany, 1988; French-Am. found. prof. U. Paris, France, 2001—02; Shephardson sr. fellow coun. on Fgn. Rels., 2002—03. Vis. fellow Yale U., 1971-73; vis. prof. U. Tex., 1977, 79, 80, 85, Wellesley Coll., 1978, Rutgers U., 1980, UCLA, 1981, Dartmouth Coll., 1983, Princeton U., 1984; Shapiro prof. internat. rels. George Washington U., 1995-97. Author books including: The End of Alliance: America and the Future of Europe, 1964, (with G. Kimble) Tropical Africa Today, 1966, Pax Americana, 1967, Imperialists and Other Heroes, 1971, Walter Lippmann and the American Century, 1980, Temptations of a Superpower, 1995, In Love With Night: The American Romance with Robert Kennedy, 2000; editor various publs. for H.W. Wilson Co., 1961-67; contbr. to N.Y. Rev. Books; contbg. editor New Republic. Served with U.S. Army, 1954-56. Recipient Sidney Hillman award, 1968, Washington Monthly book award, 1980, L.A. Times book award for non-fiction, 1980, Nat. Book Critics Circle award, 1981, Bancroft prize Columbia U., 1981, Am. Book award for biography, 1982; Guggenheim fellow, 1973-74; French-Am. Found. fellow Ecole des Hautes Etudes, Paris, 2001-02. Mem. Council on Fgn. Relations Office: U So Calif Sch Internat Rels Los Angeles CA 90089-0001

STEEL, SHAWN, political party official; m. Michelle Park; 2 children. M in History, JD, U. So. Calif. Atty. Shawn Steel & Assocs., Rolling Hills, Calif.; former treas. bd. dirs., former vice chmn. Calif. Rep. Party, chair, 2001—. Mem.: LA Lincoln Club. Office: 1903 W Magnolia Blvd Burbank CA 91506 also: Shawn Steel & Assocs 27520 Hawthorne Blvd Ste 270 Palos Verdes Peninsula CA 90274

STEELE, ALFRED E. assemblyman; b. Clarkton, N.C., Jan. 22, 1954; BA in Theology, Northeastern Bible Coll. Chaplain, 1996—; assemblyman N.J. Gen. Assembly, 1996—; asst. minority leader, 1998—2001; dep. spkr., 2002—. Mem. Paterson Coun., 1994—. Mem. African-Am. C. of C.; exec. bd. mem. Paterson Br. NAACP. Democrat. Office: 100 Hamilton Plz Ste 1403-05 Paterson NJ 07505 E-mail: AsmSteele@njleg.org.

STEELE, ANA MERCEDES, former government official; b. Jan. 18, 1939; d. Sydney and Mercedes (Hernandez) S.; m. John Hunter Clark, June 2, 1979. AB magna cum laude, Marywood Coll., 1958. Actress, 1959-64; sec. Nat. Endowment for Arts, Washington, 1965-67, dir. budget and rsch., 1968-75, dir. planning, 1976-78, dir. program coordination, sr. exec. svc., 1979-81, assoc. dep. chmn. programs, dir. program coordination, 1982-93, acting chmn., acting sr. dep. chmn., 1993, sr. dep. chmn., sr. exec. svc., 1993-96, dep. chmn. mgmt. and budget, sr. exec. svc., 1996-98; ret., 1998. Guest lectr. George Washington U., 1987; trustee Marywood U., 1989-96, Marywood U., 1997-98. Author, editor report: History of the National Council on the Arts and National Endowment for the Arts During the Johnson Administration, 1968; editor: Museums USA (Fed. Design Coun. award of Excellence 1975), 1974, National Endowment Arts, 1965-85: A Brief Chronology of Federal Involvement in the Arts, 1985. Former reader Rec. for the Blind, N.Y.C.; former tutor Future for Jimmy, Washington; judge Helen Hayes Awards, 2003—. Named Disting. Grad. in Field of Arts, Marywood Coll., 1976; recipient Sustained Superior Performance award Nat. Endowment for Arts, 1980, Disting. Svc. award, 1983, 84, 85, 89, 92, 96, presdl. medal Marywood U., 2000; named to Disting. Alumnae Hall of Fame, Ursuline Acad., 2001. Mem. Actors' Equity Assn., Screen Actors Guild, Delta Epsilon Sigma, Kappa Gamma Pi. Home: 2475 Virginia Ave NW Apt 604 Washington DC 20037-2639

STEELE, ANITA MARTIN (MARGARET ANNE MARTIN), law librarian, legal educator; b. Haines City, Fla., Dec. 30, 1927; d. Emmett Edward and Esther Majulia (Phifer) Martin; m. Thomas Dinsmore Steele, June 10, 1947 (div. 1969); children: Linda Frances, Roger Dinsmore, Thomas Garrick, Carolyn Ann; m. James E. Beaver, Mar. 1980. BA, Radcliffe Coll., 1948; JD, U. VA., 1971; M in Law Librarianship, U. Wash., 1972. Asst. prof. law U. Puget Sound, Tacoma, 1972—74, assoc. prof. law, 1974—79, prof. law, 1979—94, dir. law libr., 1972—94; prof. law, dir. law libr. Seattle U., Tacoma, 1994—98, prof. law emeritus, 1998—. Author: (book) Martin and Carmichael Descendants in Ga., 1811-1994, 1994; contbr. articles to profl. jours.; mem. editorial adv. bds.: various law book pubs. Treas. Congl. Campaign Orgn., Tacoma, 1978, 1980; mem. adv. bd. Clover Pk. Vocat.-Tech. Sch., Tacoma, 1980—82. Mem.: Collectors' Cir. of Art Mus. Va., Am. Soc. Internat. Law, Internat. Assn. Law Librs., Am. Assn. Law Librs. Republican. Home: 4434 Pheasant Ridge Rd Condo # 303 Roanoke VA 24014-5280 E-mail: ams145@cox.net.

STEELE, CARL LAVERN, academic administrator; b. Patoka, Ill., Aug. 22, 1934; s. Boyd Alfa and Effie Jane (Corson) S.; m. Lula Irene Saliba, June 11, 1961; children: Jeffrey Van, Gregory Michael, Douglas Alan. BEd, So. Ill. U., 1956, MEd, 1960; MLS, No. Ill. U., 1971. Tchr. Shawneetown (Ill.) Community High. Sch., 1956-57; GED instr. U.S. Army, Ft. Hood, Tex. and Ulm, Fed. Republic of Germany, 1957-59; tchr. Forrest-Strawn-Wing Unit Dist., Forrest, Ill., 1959-61, Richwoods Community High Sch., Peoria, Ill., 1961-66; asst. dir. instructional materials Sauk Valley Coll., Dixon, Ill., 1966-68; dir. Ednl. Resources Ctr., Rock Valley Coll., Rockford, Ill., 1968-93; ret., 1993. Part-time traffic safety instr. Rock Valley Coll., 1992—. Asst. World Record sec. Nat. Fresh Water Fishing Hall of Fame, Hayward, Wisc., 1977-79. Served with U.S. Army, 1957-59. Mem. ALA, Assn. Ednl. Communications and Technology, Ill. Assn. Ednl. Communications and Technology (conv. chmn. 1976), No. Ill. Media Assn. (conv. chmn.), Learning Resource Commn.

ICCCA (chmn. 1981). Democrat. Presbyterian. Avocations: fishing, travel, reading, woodworking, gardening. Home: 5758 Weymouth Dr Rockford IL 61114-5569 Personal E-mail: lsteele@steele.com.

STEELE, CHARLES GLEN, retired accountant; b. Faulkton, S.D., July 24, 1925; s. Clifford D. and Emily O. (Hanson) S.; m. Shirley June Ferguson, Nov. 9, 1947 (dec.); children: Richard Alan (dec.), Deborah Ann Steele Most (dec.). BBA, Golden Gate U., San Francisco, 1951, MBA, 1962. With Deloitte Haskins & Sells, 1951-86, partner, 1963-86, partner charge Chgo. office, 1973-76, partner charge personnel and adminstrn., 1976-78, chmn., chief exec. officer, 1978-86. Instr. evening program Golden Gate U., 1952-58. Served with USNR, 1943-48, aircraft carrier fighter pilot, 1946-48. Recipient Elijah Watts Sells Gold medal for highest grade in U.S. for C.P.A. exam., 1951 Mem. AICPA. Home and Office: 5 Stonecrest Circle Rancho Mirage CA 92270

STEELE, CHARLES RICHARD, biomedical and mechanical engineering educator; b. Royal, Iowa, Aug. 15, 1933; married, 1969; 4 children. BS, Tex. A&M U., 1956; PhD in Applied Mechanics, Stanford U., 1960; PhD (hon.), Zaporozhye State U., Ukraine, 1997. Engring. specialist aircraft structure Chance-Vought Aircraft, Dallas, 1959-60; rsch. scientist shell theory Lockheed Rsch. Lab., Palo Alto, 1960-66; assoc. prof. Stanford (Calif.) U., 1966-71, prof. applied mechanics, 1971—. Lectr. U. Calif., Berkeley, 1964-65; vis. prof. Swiss Fed. Inst. Technology, Zurich, 1971-72, U. Luleå, Sweden, 1982, Chung Kung U., Taiwan, 1985, U. Cape Town, South Africa, spring 1993, U. Trento, Italy, fall 1999; tech. dir. Shelltech Assoc. Editor-in-chief: Internat. Jour. Solids Structures, 1985—. Recipient NIH Claude Pepper award, 1988, Humboldt award, 1994; named Eminent Academician Ukrainian Acad., 1998. Fellow ASME (chmn. exec. com. applied mechanics divsn. 1983-84, Warner T. Koiter medal 1999), Am. Acad. Mechanics (pres. 1989-90); mem. AIAA, NAE, Acoustical Soc. Am. Achievements include research in asymptotic analysis in mechanics; thin shell theory; mechanics of the inner ear; noninvasive determination of bone stiffness; and morphology of plants. Office: Stanford U Divsn Mechanics & Computat Durand Bldg 355A Stanford CA 94305-4040

STEELE, CYNTHIA, literary critic, translator, educator; b. Colusa, Calif., Aug. 7, 1951; d. Ned and Lorraine (Heard) S. BA in English and Spanish, Calif. State U., Chico, 1973; MA in Spanish Lit., U. Calif., San Diego, 1979, PhD in Spanish Lit., 1980. Asst. prof. Spanish Ohio State U., Columbus, 1980-85, Columbia U., N.Y.C., 1985-86; from asst. prof. to assoc. prof. Spanish U. Wash., Seattle, 1986-96, prof. Spanish, Comparative Lit. and Internat. Studies, 1996—. Mem. joint com. Latin Am. studies Social Sci. Rsch. Coun.-Am. Coun. Learned Socs., N.Y.C., 1994-96; del. West Coast MLA, N.Y.C., 1996—; bd. dirs. Inst. de Lit. Iberoamericana, Pitts., 1996—. Translator: Underground River and Other Stories by Inés Arredondo, 1996; (with David Laur) City of Memory (José Emilio Pacheco), 1997. Advanced grantee Social Sci. Rsch. Coun., 1990-91; Royalty Rsch. grantee U. Wash. Grad. Sch., 1997—. Mem. Latin Am. Studies Assn. Democrat. Avocations: movies, travel in latin america. Office: U Wash Dept Spanish & Portuguese Seattle WA 98195-0001

STEELE, DALE F. women's healthcare company executive; Co-founder, CFO, M.W. Steele Group, 1983-89, corp. sec., treas., 1994-96; owner, mgr. Dale Fitzmorris, 1989-94; co-founder, co-CEO, As We Change, LLC, 1995-98; v.p. catalog ops. Women First HealthCare, Inc., San Diego, 1998—. Fax: 619-509-1353.

STEELE, ERNEST CLYDE, retired insurance company executive; b. Corbin, Ky., May 11, 1925; s. J. Fred and Leona (McFarland) S.; m. Cora Jones, June 17, 1944 (dec. Nov. 1988); children: Gerald R., David. P.; m. Helen LeCoultre, July 7, 1990. BS with honors, U. Ky., 1948, MS, 1950. Asst. actuary Peninsular Life Ins. Co., Jacksonville, Fla., 1950-54; actuary Pioneer Life & Casualty Co., Gadsden, Ala., 1955; v.p., actuary Guaranty Savs. Life Ins. Co., Montgomery, Ala., 1956-57; exec. v.p., actuary Am. Investment Life Ins. Co., Nashville, 1958-59; pres., actuary Appalachian Nat. Life Ins. Co., Knoxville, Tenn., 1959-67; sr. v.p., chief investment officer, ops. analyst Coastal States Life Ins. Co., Atlanta, 1968-71, exec. v.p., dir., 1971-74, pres., dir., 1974-79; pres. Occidental Life Ins. Co. of N.C., 1979-85, chmn., 1986-88; pres., dir. Peninsular Life Ins. Co., 1981-83, chmn., 1986-88; exec. v.p. investments MCM Corp., 1985-88; ret., 1988. Past pres. Ga. Assn. Life Inst. Cos., 1976-77. Mem. devel. coun. U. Ky.; past pres. Gt. Smoky Mountain Coun. Boy Scouts Am., 1965—66. Served to 2d lt. U.S. Army, 1943—45. Fellow Life Mgmt. Inst.; mem. Life Office Mgmt. Assn. (past chmn. bd.), Am. Council Life Ins. (past dir.), U. Ky. Alumni Assn. (past bd. dirs.), Am. Acad. Actuaries, Pi Mu Epsilon. Republican. Baptist. Home: 103 Newell Village Cir Seymour TN 37865-5931 E-mail: ecsteele@webtv.net. *My success in life is measured by the success of those with whom I have been associated.*

STEELE, GEORGE PEABODY, retired marine transportation executive; b. San Francisco, July 27, 1924; s. James Mortimer and Erma (Garrett) S.; m. Elizabeth Yates Fahrion, July 11, 1944 (div. May 1988); children: Jane Yates Steele Marcum, James Fahrion; m. Betty McDonnell, May 20, 1988. BS, U.S. Naval Acad., 1944. Commd. ensign USN, 1944; advanced through grades to vice adm., 1973; service aboard submarines in Pacific World War II, 1945; comdr. U.S.S. Hardhead, 1955-56, comdr. nuclear powered U.S.S. Seadragon (made 1st NW passage under ice to North Pole), 1959-61, comdr. Polaris missile sub U.S.S. Daniel Boone, 1963-66; head politico-mil. policy div. Europe/NATO br. Office Chief Naval Ops., 1966-68, comdr. Naval Forces Korea, chief Naval adv. group, Korean Navy, comdr. Naval Component UN Command, 1968-70, comdr. Anti-Submarine Warfare Group 4, 1970-72; dep. asst. chief of staff Supreme Allied Comdr. SHAPE, Europe, SHAPE, Belgium, 1972-73; comdr. U.S. 7th Fleet, 1973-75, ret., 1975; exec. v.p. Interocean Mgmt. Corp., Phila., 1976-78, pres., 1978-81, chmn., chief exec. officer, 1981-89, dir., 1989-94. Chmn. bd. trustees Fgn. Policy Rsch. Inst., 1980-89, trustee, 1989-93. Author: Seadragon, Northwest Under the Ice, 1962, (with H. Gimpel) Nuclear Submarine Skippers and What They Do, 1962, Vengeance in the Depths, 1963; contbr. articles to profl. publs. and newspapers. Decorated D.S.M., Legion of Merit with 4 gold stars, Navy Cross (Peru), Order of Rising Sun (Japan), Cloud and Banner (China), Order of Nat. Security Merit (Republic Korea); recipient John B. Diman Disting. Grad. award St. George's Sch., 1994, Lowell Thomas award for submarine Arctic exploration Explorers Club, 1997, Elisha Kent Kane Gold medal for Arctic svc., 2001. Mem. Am. Polar Soc. (hon. membership medallion 2000), U.S. Naval Inst., Univ. Club, Army-Navy Club. Episcopalian. Home: 6 Upland Rd Apt 2B Baltimore MD 21210-2258

STEELE, GLENN DANIEL, JR., oncologist, healthcare system executive; b. Balt., June 23, 1944; m. Diana; 1 child, Joshua; m. Lisa; children: Kirsten, Lara. AB magna cum laude, Harvard Coll., 1966; MD, NYU, 1970; PhD, Lund U., Sweden, 1975. Intern, then resident Med. Ctr. U. Colo., Denver, 1970-76; fellow NIH in immunology Univ. Lund, Sweden, 1973-75; asst. surgeon Sidney Farber Cancer Inst., Boston, 1976-78; cons. surgeon Boston Hosp. for Women, 1977-80; clin. assoc. surgical oncology Sidney Farber Cancer Inst., 1978-79; jr. assoc. in surgery Peter Bent Brigham Hosp., Boston, 1976-82; instr. surgery Med. Sch. Harvard, Boston, 1976-78; asst. prof. surgery Med. Sch. Harvard Coll., 1978-81; asst. physician surgical oncology Sidney Farber Cancer Inst., 1979-82; assoc. prof. surgery Med. Sch. Harvard Coll., 1981-84; surgeon Brigham & Women's Hosp., 1982-84; assoc. physician surgical oncology Dana-Farber Cancer Inst., 1982-84, physician surg. oncology, 1984-95; chmn. dept. surgery, deaconess Harvard Surg. Svc. New England Deaconess Hosp., Boston, 1985-95; William V. McDermott prof. surgery Med. Sch. Harvard Coll., 1985-95; prof. Univ. Chgo., 1995—2001, dean biological scis. divsn. and Pritzker Sch. Medicine, 1995—2001, v.p. medical affairs Pritzker Sch. Medicine, 1995—2001; pres, CEO Geisinger Health System, Danville, Pa., 2001—; chair. Am. Bd. Surgery, Phila., 1999—. Assoc. editor Jour. Clin. Oncology, 1986—, Jour. Hepatobiliary-Pancreatic Surgery, 1993—; mem. editl. bd. Annals of Surgery, Annals of Surg. Oncology, Brit. Jour. Surgery, Surgery, Surg. Oncology; contbr. numerous articles to profl. jours. Recipient NIH fellow 1973-75, Am. Cancer Soc. fellow 1972-73, 76-79, various other rsch. grants. Fellow ACS (chmn. patient care and rsch. com. commn. on cancer 1989-91, mem. bd. govs. 1991-95, chmn. commn. on cancer 1991-93, mem. exec. com. commn. on cancer 1992-93); mem. Am. Assn. Immunologists, Am. Bd. Surgery (dir. 1993-98, vice-chmn. 1998—), Ill. Surg. Soc., Am. Bd. Med. Specialties, Am. Soc. Clin. Oncology, Am. Surg. Assn., Assn. Program Dirs. in Surgery, Assn. for Surg. Edn., Internat. Fedn. Surg. Colls., Internat. Surg. Group, Soc. Surg. Oncology (treas. 1994-97, v.p. 1997, pres. 1999-2000), Inst. of Medicine of NAS, others. Office: Geisinger Health System 100 North Academy Ave Danville PA 17822

STEELE, HOWARD L. psychology educator; b. Vancouver, B.C., Can., Oct. 16, 1959; arrived in Eng., 1986. s. Arnold J. and Goldie R. (Karsh) S.; m. Miriam N. Blum, Sept. 2, 1984; children: Gabriella, Joseph, Michael. BA, U. B.C., 1981, MA, 1983, Columbia U., 1986; PhD, U. Coll., London, 1991. Lectr. U. Coll., London, 1991-99, sr. lectr., 1999—. Editor: (jour.) Attachment and Human Devel., 1999; cons. editor: Infant Mental Health Jour., 1998. Recipient Overseas Rsch. Scholar award Com. of Vice-Chancellors and Prins. of Univs. of U.K., 1986-87; Commonwealth scholar, Brit. Coun., 1987-90; rsch. grantee Econ. and Social Rsch. Coun., 1992-94, 98-99. Mem. Soc. for Rsch. in Child Devel. Office: Sub-Dept Clin Health Psy Univ Coll London/Gower St London WCIE 6BT England

STEELE, HOWARD LOUCKS, economic development consultant, author; b. Pitts., Jan. 27, 1929; s. Howard Bennington and Ruby Alberta (Loucks) S.; m. Sally E. Funk, June 6, 1952 (div. 1977); children: John F., David A., Patricia A.; m. Jane R. Cornelius, July 30, 1977 (div. 1996); 1 child, Jennifer L.; m. Elaine Haddock, Aug. 23, 1997. BS, Washington and Lee U., 1950; MS, Pa. State U., 1952; PhD, U. Ky., 1962. Sales mgr. Greenville (Pa.) Dairy Co., 1952-56; owner H.L. Steele Bulk Milk Hauling, Greenville, 1955-60; asst. prof. Clemson (S.C.) U., 1956-57, assoc. prof., 1957-64, Ohio State U., Columbus, 1964-71; with Fgn. Agrl. Svc./Internat. Coop. and Devel. U.S., Dept. Agr., Washington, 1971-97; ret.; econ. devel. cons., 1997—. Project mgr. AID, Guatemala, 1976-77, Bolivia, 1977-80, Honduras, 1980-82, Sri Lanka, 1982-84, Bur. L.Am. and Caribbean USAID, Washington, 1984-88, office of the dir. tech. assistance divsn., 1988-90, with office of dep. adminstr., 1990-97; USDA liaison officer Inter-Am. Inst. Coop. in Agr., 1993-97; instr. U. Md., College Park, 1974-76; vis. prof. U. Sao Paulo, Piracicaba, Brazil, 1964-66; ptnr. Kingwood Acres Farm, Rockwood, Pa., 1966-98. Author: Commercializacao Agricola, 1971, A 200 Year History of Some Descendents of the Pioneer James Steel of Castleblaney, Ireland and Mt. Pleasant, Pennsylvania, 1994, Your Tax Dollars at Work (I'd Rather Have Gone Business Class!), 1998, Food Soldier, 2002; contbr. articles to profl. jours. Recipient Nat. Forensic Union award; named One of Outstanding Young Men U.S., U.S. Jaycees, 1965; cert. of merit Dept. Agr., 1975, 92. Mem. Am. Agrl. Econs. Assn., Internat. Assn. Agrl. Economists, SAR, Masons, Shriners, Gamma Sigma Delta, Sigma Nu. Home: 5204 Holden St Fairfax VA 22032-3418 Office Phone: 703-978-4066. Personal E-mail: ehsteele@juno.com.

STEELE, JAMES EUGENE, retired school system administrator; b. South Norfolk, Va. s. James Edward and Blanche Eugenia (Munden) S. BS in Music Edn., Coll. William and Mary, 1961; MEd in Ednl. Adminstrn. and Supervision, Temple U., 1972; EdD in Ednl. Adminstrn., Nova U., 1976. Cert. tchr., Va. Piccoloist Va. Symphony Orch., 1951-73; dir. choral music Hampton (Va.) City Schs., 1960-65, supr. music, 1965—2003; ret., 2003. Guest flute soloist Music Tchrs. Assn., Great Britain, 1962. Dir. fine arts divsn. Hampton Assn. Arts Humanities, 1967—. Mem. NEA, Va. Edn. Assn., Hampton Edn. Assn., Va. Assn. Sch. Execs., Hampton Instrnl. Suprs. Assn., Tidewater Regional Suprs., Va. Assn. Sch. Curriculum Devel., Va. Music Suprs. Assn., Va. Music Educators Assn., Music Educators Nat. Conf., Va. Choral Dirs. Assn., Va. Band and Orch. Dirs. Assn., Va. String Tchrs. Assn. Home: 132 Fayton Ave Norfolk VA 23505-4428

STEELE, JAMES HARLAN, former public health veterinarian, educator; b. Chgo., Apr. 3, 1913; s. James Hahn and Lydia (Nordquist) S.; m. Aina Oberg, 1941 (dec. 1969); children: James Harlan, David, Michael; m. Maria-Brigitte Meyer, 1969. DVM, Mich. State Coll., 1941; MPH, Harvard U., 1942. With Ohio Dept. Health, 1942-43; with USPHS, 1943-71; advancing through grades to asst. surgeon gen. for vet. affairs and chief vet. officer; chief vet. pub. health activities Communicable Disease Center, Atlanta, 1947-71; prof. environ. health U. Tex. Sch. Pub. Health, Houston, 1971-83, prof. emeritus, 1983—. Cons. WHO, 1950—, Pan-Am. Health Orgn., 1945—, FAO, UN, 1960, German Health Svc., 1986-93; vis. prof. Tex. A&M U., 1976—, all univ. prof., 1981-82; spkr. in field. Author: (with J. Arthur Myer) Bovine Tuberculosis Control in Man and Animals, 1969, 1995; editor-in-chief CRC Zoonoses Handbooks, 1979-84, cons. editor, 1994, 8 vols. transl. into Russian and Farsi, Bacterial & Viral Zoonoses, 2 vols. rev. by Beran; mem. editl. cons. bd. APHA Control Communicable Disease, 1960-2000; contbr. articles to profl. jours. and sects. to books on food hygiene and irradiation. Recipient Carlos Finlay medal, 1952, Mich. State U. Alumni award, 1958, USPHS Order of Merit, 1963, Karl F. Meyer Gold Head Cane award, 1966, Disting. Svc. award USPHS, 1971, Mich. State U. Coll. Vet. Medicine award, 1972, hon. mem. Epidemic Intelligence Svc., 1975, James Law award Cornell U., 1983, Centennial award U. Pa., 1984, Am. Vet. Med. Assn. Internat. Vet. award, 1984, Pub. Svc. award, 1993; James H. Steele Vet. Pub. Health award World Vet. Epidemiology Soc., 1975, Disting. Svc. award Am. Vet. History Soc., 1995, James H. Steele award Ctr. for Disease Control, 1998, Disting. Alumni award Mich. State U., 2001; James H. Steele ann. lectr. established in his honor U. Tex. Health Sci. Ctr., 1993, also James H. Steele Epidemiology Professorship, 1996. Fellow APHA (emeritus, 1984; Bronfman award 1971, Centennial award 1972), Am. Coll. Epidemiology (founding fellow); mem. Conf. Pub. Health Vets. (founder), Am. Soc. Tropical Medicine (emeritus), Am. Coll. Vet. Preventive Medicine (founder, hon. diploma 1983, Pres.'s award 1994), Nat. Acad. Health Practice, World Vet. Epidemiology Soc. (founder, pres. 1971), Am. Vet. Epidemiology Soc. (pres. 1966-88), World Vet. Assn. (hon.), Philippines Vet. Med. Assn. (hon.), Peru Vet. Med. Assn. (hon.), Hellenic Vet. Soc. (Athens Greece, hon. diploma, 1977), U.S. Animal Health Assn. (life), U.S.-Mex. Pub. Health Assn. (hon., life), Mil. Surgeons Assn. (hon. life), Infectious Disease Soc. Am. (emeritus), Internat. Epidemiology Soc. (emeritus), XXI World Vet. Congress (Moscow, hon. diploma 1979), German Health Svc. (hon. diploma, 1988, Order of Merit 1993), Harvard U. Alumni Assn. (Alumni award 1998), Alpha Psi. Episcopalian. Home: 10722 Riverview Way Houston TX 77042-1121 Office: Sch Pub Healthth U Tex Houston TX 77225 *I have believed firmly throughout my career that I should share my knowledge and expertise with my fellow man, be he American or citizen of the world. Those of us who are more fortunate to be endowed with intellectual advantages have an even greater responsibility to share.*

STEELE, JOHN HYSLOP, marine scientist, oceanographic institute administrator; b. Edinburgh, Scotland, Nov. 15, 1926; s. Adam and Annie H.; m. Margaret Evelyn Travis, Mar. 2, 1956; 1 son, Hugh. B.Sc., Univ. Coll., London U., 1946, D.Sc., 1964. Marine scientist Marine Lab., Aberdeen, Scotland, 1951-66, sr. prin. sci. officer, 1966-73, dep. dir., 1973-77; dir. Woods Hole Oceanographic Instn., Mass., 1977-89, pres., 1986-91. Mem. NAS/NRC Ocean Sci. Bd., 1978-88, chmn., 1986-88; mem. rsch. and exploration com. Nat. Geog. Soc.; mem. Arctic Rsch. Commn., 1988-92; trustee U. Corp. Atmospheric Rsch., 1987-91, Bermuda Biol. Sta., R.W. Johnson Found.; del. Internat. Coun. Exploration Sea; hon. prof. U. Aberdeen. Author: The Structure of Marine Ecosystems, 1974; Contbr. articles to profl. jours. Served with Brit. Royal Air Force, 1947-49. Recipient Alexander Agassiz medal Nat. Acad. Sci., 1973 Fellow Royal Soc. London, AAAS, Royal Soc. Edinburgh, Am. Acad. Arts and Scis. Home: PO Box 25 Woods Hole MA 02543-0025 Office: Woods Hole Oceanographic Inst Woods Hole MA 02543

STEELE, KAREN DORN, journalist; b. Portland, Oreg., Oct. 27, 1943; d. Ronald Gottche and Margaret Elizabeth (Cates) Moxness; m. Charles Stuart Dorn, Oct. 30, 1965 (div. Oct. 1982); children: Trilby Constance Elizabeth Dorn, Blythe Estella Dorn; m. Richard Donald Steele, July 4, 1983. BA, Stanford U., 1965; MA, U. Calif., Berkeley, 1967. Prodr. Sta. KSPS-TV, Spokane, Wash., 1970-72, dir. news and pub. affairs, 1972-82; reporter Spokesman-Rev., Spokane, 1982-87, environ./spl. projects reporter, 1987—. Contbr. articles to sci. publs. (Olive Br. award NYU Ctr. War, Peace & The Media 1989). Bd. dirs. Women Helping Women, Spokane, 1994; trustee St. George's Sch., Spokane, 1988-92. Mid-career fellow Stanford Knight Fellowship Program, 1986-87, Arms Control fellow Ctr. for Internat. Security and Arms Control, Stanford U., 1986-87; Japan Travel grantee Japan Press Found., Tokyo, 1987, rsch. grantee John D. and Catherine T. MacArthur Found., 1992; recipient Gerald Loeb award Anderson Sch. Mgmt. UCLA, 1995, George Polk award L.I. U., 1995, William Stokes award U. Mo., 1988, Nat. Headliner award, Excellence in Legal Journalism award, Wash. State Bar Assn., 2000; inductee State Hall of Journalistic Achievement, Wash. State U., Pullman, 1995. Unitarian Universalist. Office: Spokesman Rev PO Box 2160 999 W Riverside Ave Spokane WA 99201-1098 Office Phone: 509-459-5462. E-mail: karend@spokesman.com.

STEELE, KENNETH FRANKLIN, JR., science educator; b. Statesville, NC, Jan. 16, 1944; s. Kenneth Franklin and Ruth Virginia (Wilhelm) S.; m. Sheila Kay Stumpf, Sept. 3, 1966 (dec.); children: Krista Robin, Celisa Anne. BS in Chemistry, U. N.C., 1966, PhD in Geology, 1971. Registered profl. geologist, Ark., registered hydrogeologist. From instr. to assoc. prof. geology U. Ark., Fayetteville, 1970-83, dir. Ark. Water Resources Ctr., 1988—2001, prof., 1983—. Mem. State Bd. Registration for Profl. Geologists, 1992-96, 2000—, chmn., 1996, 2002-03, vice chmn., 2001-02; cons. in field. Contbr. numerous articles to profl. jour., chpts. to books; editor: Animal Waste and the Land-Water Interface. Summer faculty fellow Oak Ridge Associated Univ., 1981, 83, 85. Mem. Assn. Ground-Water Scientists and Engr., Geol. Soc. Am. (regional bd. dir. 1980-82, 84-86), Am. Water Resources Assn. (bd. dirs. 1991-94), Ark. Ground Water Assn. (bd. dir. 1988-90, 93-95, v.p. 1991, pres. 1992), Nat. Assn. Water Inst. Dirs. (counselor 1990-93), Nat. Inst. Water Resources (bd. dir. 1998-2001). Achievements include research on the importance of rainstorms on ground and surface water chemistry, nitrate and pesticide contamination of ground water. Home: 1115 Valley View Dr Fayetteville AR 72701-1603 Office: U Ark Dept Geoscis 113 Ozark Hall U Ark Fayetteville AR 72701-4040 Office Phone: 479-575-7937. Business E-Mail: ksteele@uark.edu.

STEELE, MICHAEL, lieutenant governor; b. Oct. 19, 1958; m. Andrea Steele; children: Michael, Drew. Grad., Johns Hopkins U.; JD, Georgetown U., 1991; student, Augustinian Friars Sem. Pvt. law practice; assoc. internat. law firm Cleary, Gottlieb, Steen & Hamilton, Wash., DC, 1991—97; chmn. Republican Ctrl. Com. for Prince George's County, Md., 1994—2000; cand. Md. State Comptroller, 1998; chmn. Md. Republican Party, 2000—02; lt. gov. State of Md., 2003—. Advisor to campaigns of fellow politicians; treas., advisor Michele Dyson for Congress, 1994. Host (hour long radio program) WOLB 1010AM, Balt., Md., appeared (numerous radio and TV programs including) Politically Incorrect with Bill Maher, Metro Talk, That Show With Those Black Guys, The Joe Madison Show, Extra, Capitol Sunday, BET Tonight; contbr. columns in newspapers including The Washington Times, The Washington Post, The Baltimore Sun, The Jour. Newspapers. Bd. visitors U.S. Naval Acad., 2002; commr. Nat. Fed. Election Reform Commn.; mem. St. Mary's Cath. Ch., Landover Hills, Md. Named Md. State Republican Man of Yr., Man. of Yr., Ch. cmty., 1998. Mem.: NAACP (served blue ribbon panel on election reform, bd. dirs. hospice of nat. capital area, Prince George's County chpt.), Johns Hopkins U. (bd. trustees), Johns Hopkins Soc. Black Alumni, Term Limits Coalition (chmn. 2000), Truth iN Taxation Com. (hon. co-chmn. 1996), Republican Nat. Convention Phila., Pa. (del. 2000), Republican Nat. Convention San Diego, Calif. (alt. del. 1996), Md. State Minority Outreach Task Force (chmn. 1995—97), Md. State Republican Party Victory Campaigns, Prince George's County Md. Black Republican Coun., Republican Nat. Com. (mem. exec. com.), Knights of Columbus. Office: Office of Gov 100 State Cir Annapolis MD 21401 Business E-Mail: info@mdgop.org.

STEELE, MYRON THOMAS, state supreme court chief justice; b. Taunton, Mass., July 28, 1945; s. Myron Thetus and Coleen Amelia (Polk) Steele; m. Beverly June Heaps, Feb. 4, 1967; children: Clayton Carter, Jenness Farnham. BA, U. Va., 1967, JD, 1970. Bar: Va. 1970, Del. 1970, U.S. Dist. Ct. Del. 1970, U.S. Ct. Appeals (3d cir.) 1974. Assoc. Prickett, Ward, Burt & Sanders, Dover, Del., 1970, 1973, ptnr., 1974; dep. atty. gen. State of Del., 1971—72; v.p., dir. Prickett, Jones, Elliott, Kristol & Schnee, Dover, 1974—88; assoc. judge Superior Ct., 1988—90, res. judge, 1990—94; vice chancellor Ct. Chancery, Del., 1994—2000; justice Del. Supreme Ct., 2000—, chief justice, 2004—. Chmn. Ctrl. Del. Health Care Corp., 1990—93; mem. exec. com. Del. Democratic State Com., 1974—88; bd. dirs. Childrens Bur. Del., Del. News Coun.; chmn. Consumer Affairs Bd., 1974—88. Served to 1st. lt. U.S. Army, 1970, col. ret. Del. N.G., 1974—97. Mem.: ABA (mem. jud. liaison comml. and bus. litig. com., bus. sect.), Del-Vets, Commn. on Ct. 2000 (Del.), Kent County Bar Assn. (past pres.), Va. State Bar, Del. Bar Assn. (past v.p.), Kiwanis (past pres.), Rehoboth Beach Country Club, Wilmington Club, Masons. Episcopalian. Office: 57 The Green Dover DE 19901*

STEELE, RICHARD DONALD, researcher, linguist, physicist; b. Modesto, Calif., Jan. 12, 1943; s. Warren Nelson, Jr. and Fern Marjorie (Thompson) S.; m. Karen Moxness Dorn, July 4, 1983; children: Trilby Dorn, Blythe Dorn. BS in Physics, Stanford U., 1964; MA, Harvard U., 1966, PhD in Slavic Langs., Linguistics, 1973. Asst. prof. Cornell U., Ithaca, N.Y., 1973-74; lectr. Harvard U., Cambridge, Mass., 1974-75, MIT, Cambridge, 1975-76; asst. prof. Grinnell (Iowa) Coll., 1976-80; rsch. health scientist Rehab. Rsch. Devel. Ctr., VA Med. Ctr., Palo Alto, Calif., 1982-90; mgr. comm. products Tolfa Corp., Palo Alto, Calif., 1990-96; chief scientist LingraphiCARE Am., Oakland, Calif., 1996—. Rev. rehab. proposals NIH, Washington, 1991-94. Mem. editl. bd. Assistive Tech., 1988-91; contbr. articles to Neuropsychologia, Aphasiology, Brain Lang., Archives Phys. Med. Rehab., Stroke, others. Organizing com., official Clean Air Car Race, MIT, Calif. Inst. Tech., 1970; co-organizer aphasia spkrs. series Stanford U., 1988-89. Recipient Info. Resources Mgmt. award U.S. Govt. Interagy. com., 1987, Excellence in Tech. Transfer award Tech. Utilization Found., 1993; grantee World Rehab. Fund, 1987. Mem. IEEE, Sierra Club, Phi Beta Kappa. Democrat. Achievements include research in computer aided visual communication for aphasics, dissemination of rehabilitation technologies; 3 patents for a method of communicating using graphical elements, a method of communication using sized icons. Home: 1325 E 20th Ave Spokane WA 99203-3437 Office: LingraphiCARE Am 425 Jackson St Oakland CA 94607-4329

STEELE, ROBERT EDWIN, orthopedic surgeon; b. Kansas City, Mo., Jan. 8, 1937; s. Robert Edwin and Margaret Jane (Levens) S.; m. Emily Wells Stephens, May 9, 1964; children: Edward Stephen, Thomas McKewon, Linda Katherine. AB, U. Mo., 1959; MD cum laude, Harvard U., 1963. Diplomate Am. Bd. Orthopedic Surgery; cert. Am. Acad. Orthopedic Surgeons, Assn. Arthritic Hip and Knee Surgery. Intern Mass. Gen. Hosp., Boston, 1963-64; resident in orthopedics Harvard U., 1966-71; instr. in orthopedic surgery Harvard Med. Sch., Boston, 1971; mem. med. staff Good Samaritan Hosp., Corvallis, Oreg., 1971—. Bd. dirs. Good Samaritan Hosp., 1984-88, pres. med. staff, 1985, chmn. peer rev. com., 1994. Author: Studies on Osteonecrusis, 1979. Lt. USNR, 1964-66, Vietnam. Recipient Kappa Delta award for Outstanding Orthopedic Rsch., Am. Acad. Orthopedic Surgeons, 1978. Mem. Corvallis Orthopedic Surgeons (pres. 1990). Achievements include performance of total knee replacement. Address: 560 NW Tyler Ave Corvallis OR 97330

STEELE, RODNEY REDFEARN, judge; b. Selma, Ala., May 22, 1930; s. C. Parker and Miriam Lera (Redfearn) S.; m. Frances Marion Blair, Aug. 1, 1964; children: Marion Scott, Claudia Redfearn, Parker Blair. AB, U. Ala., 1950, MA, 1951; LLB, U. Mich., 1954. Bar: Ala. 1954, U.S. Dist. Ct. (mid. dist.) Ala. 1959, U.S. Ct. Appeals (5th cir., now 11th cir.) 1981. Law clk. Ala. Ct. Appeals, 1956-57; assoc. Knabe & Nachman, Montgomery, Ala., 1957-61; asst. U.S. atty. Dept. Justice, Montgomery, 1961-66; staff atty. So. Bell T&T Co., Atlanta, 1966-67; judge U.S. Bankruptcy Ct., Mid. dist. Ala., Montgomery, 1967—, chief judge, 1985-99; ret., 1999—. Served with U.S. Army, 1954-56, Korea. Mem. ABA, Ala. State Bar, Montgomery County Bar Assn. Democrat. Episcopalian. Home: 1227 Magnolia Curv Montgomery AL 36106-2136

STEELE, SHARI, think-tank executive; Grad., Widener U.; LLM in Advocacy, Georgetown U.; MS in Instrnl. Media, West Chester U. Legal dir. Electronic Frontier Found., San Francisco, 1992—2000, exec. dir., pres., 2000—. Spkr. in field; tchg. fellow Georgetown U. Law Ctr. Office: Electronic Frontier Found 454 Shotwell St San Francisco CA 94110-1914*

STEELE, THOMAS MCKNIGHT, law educator; b. Bartlesville, Okla., June 4, 1948; s. James Robert and Erma Blanche (McKnight) S.; m. Barbara Van Curen, Mar. 23, 1973 (div. 1985); children: James Robert, Ryan Thomas, David Christopher Joyce, Justin Daniel Joyce; m. Martha Bolling Swann, Apr. 1985 (div. 1990); m. LeAnn P. Joyce, Jan. 1995. BA in History, Okla. State U., 1969; MLS, U. Oreg., 1974; JD, U. Tex., 1977. Adminstrv. asst. Tarlton Law Libr. U. Tex., Austin, 1975-77; acting law librarian Underwood Law Libr. So. Meth. U., Dallas, 1977-78, asst. law librarian, 1978-79; assoc. prof. law, dir. Franklin Pierce Law Ctr., Concord, N.H., 1979-82; asst. prof., dir. U. Miss. Law Libr., University, 1982-85; assoc. prof., dir. Wake Forest U. Sch. Law Libr., Winston-Salem, N.C., 1985-91; dir. Profl. Ctr. Libr. Wake Forest U., Winston-Salem, NC, 1991—99, prof. law, 1991—. Cons. in field; exec. dir. SCRIBES, Am. Soc. Writers on Legal Subjects, 1988—97, bd. dirs., 2002—. Editor (newsletter) Scrivener, 1986-88; mng. editor Scribes Jour. Legal Writing, 1989-91; editor Pub. Librs. and Pub. Laws, 1986-88; compiler bibliography IDEA, 1981-83, Jour. Air Law and Commerce, 1977-81; co-author: A Law Library Move: Planning Preparation and Execution, 1994, Materials and Cases on Law Practice Management: A Learning Tool for Law Students, 2003. With U.S. Army. Mem.: Legal Mkrg. Assn., Assn. Legal Adminstrs. Democrat. Baptist. Office: Wake Forest U Sch Law PO Box 7206 Winston Salem NC 27109-7206

STEELE, WILLIAM DONALD, literature educator; b. Barnsville, Ohio, Jan. 1, 1973; s. John Lewis and Linda Sue Steele; m. Heather Marie Barker, Dec. 16, 2001. MA, Mid. Tenn. State U., Mufreesboro, Tennessee, 1996—98. Level I Coach US Track and Field Assn., 2000. Instr. of english Cascade Coll., Portland, Oreg., 1999—, head cross country coach, 1999—2003. Mem. Ind. U. of Pa. English Grad. Org. Actor: (campus play) The Diaries of Adam and Eve. Mem.: Tenn. Philological Assn., Mark Twain Cir., MLA. R-Consevative. Church Of Christ. Achievements include Faculty of the Year 1999-2000, 2000-2001. Office: Cascade Coll 9101 East Burnside Street Portland OR 97216

STEELEY, JILL EDWARDS, education educator; d. Jack Hankins Edwards and Eunice Marguerite Babcock Edwards; m. Clyde Earl Steeley, Nov. 25, 1970; children: Cheryl Jean, William Earl. BS in Elem. Edn., Okla. State U., 1971; MEd in Reading, Northeastern State U., 1985; EdD in Curriculum & Instrn., Okla. State U., 1992. Cert. elem. tchr. Okla., 1971, Mo. Dept. of Edn., 1975, reading specialist Okla. State Dept. of Edn., 1985, elem. prin. Okla. State Dept. of Edn., 1992. Tchr. elem. sch. Broken Arrow Pub. Schs., Okla., 1971—85; tchr. kindergarten Doniphan Pub. Schs., Mo., 1975—76; reading specialist Broken Arrow Pub. Schs., 1985—92; prof. elem. edn. Oral Roberts U., Tulsa, 1992—2004; with Broken Arrow Pub. Schs., 2004—. Author: (poem) Published in The Reading Teacher; contbr. articles to profl. jours. V.p., sec. Broken Arrow Hist. Soc., 1999—2004; bd. mem. Teach the Children Internat., Tulsa, 1998—2004; mem., tchr., chime choir dir. Forest Ridge Bapt. Ch. Mem.: Tulsa County Reading Coun. (various positions 1982—95), Learning Disabilities Assn. Okla. (profl. adv. bd. 2000—04), Okla. Reading Coun., Soc. Children's Book Writers and Illustrators, Assn. Childhood Educators, Nat. Coun. Tchrs. English, Internat. Reading Assn., Phi Delta Kappa. Democrat. Southern Baptist. Avocations: reading, writing, gardening. Office: Liberty Elem Sch 4300 S 209th E Ave Broken Arrow OK 74014 Office Phone: 918-259-4470.

STEELMAN, DEBORAH MACON, pharmaceutical consultant; b. Sale, Mo., Feb. 4, 1955; BA, U. Mo., 1976, JD, 1978. Asst. pub. defender, Kansas City, Mo.; campaign mgr. for re-election effort Atty. Gen. John Ashcroft; dep. dir. Mo. Dept. Natural Resources; legis. dir. to Senator John Heinza, Pa.; dir. intergovernmental affairs Environ. Protection Agy., 1983—85; dep. asst. to pres. and dir. Office Intergovernmental Affairs, 1985—; pres. Steelman Health Strategies; v.p. corp. affairs Eli Lilly and Co., 2001—03, con. govtl. affairs and health policy issues, 2003—. Apptd. by Senate Majority Leader Trent Lott, healthcare advisor to George W. Bush's 2000 campaign to Medicare Commn. Named one of 100 Most Powerful Women in Wash., Washingtonian mag., 2001.

STEELMAN, SARA GERLING, art association administrator; b. Wichita, Kans., Apr. 24, 1946; d. Paul Henry and Amy (Gessner) Gerling; m. John Henry Steelman; 1 child, Amy. BS in Zoology, U. Chgo., 1967; PhD in Behavior Genetics, Stanford U., 1976. Instr. dept. psychology No. Ill. U., DeKalb, 1974-75; instr. Fullerton (Calif.) Jr. Coll., 1976-80; postdoctoral fellow dept. psychobiology U. Calif., Irvine, 1976-80; asst. prof. dept. biology Skidmore Coll., Saratoga Springs, N.Y., 1980-83; staff writer Saratogian, Saratoga Springs, 1983-86; contbg. writer Indiana Gazette, 1987-93; elected mem. Pa. Ho. of Reps., Harrisburg, 1990—2002; adminstr. Indiana Arts Coun., Indiana, Pa., 2002—. Contbr. articles to sci. publs. Co-chair com. on women in politics Pitts. Inst. Politics, 1993—. Rsch. fellow, Nat. Inst. Aging, 1979—80. Mem.: LWV, AAUW (Notable Woman 1991), Ind. Symphony Soc. (bd. dirs.), Common Cause (state bd. dirs.). Democrat. Avocations: gardening, music, horseback riding. Office: Indiana Arts Council 637 Philadelphia Indiana PA 15701 E-mail: iacinet@upia.net.

STEELMAN, SARAH, state legislator; Mem. Mo. State Senate, 1998—, mem. civil and criminal jurisprudence com., chair commerce and environment com., mem. edn. com., vice chair judiciary com., vice chair pub. health and welfare com. Republican. Home: 11820 Springhouse Ln Rolla MO 65401 Office: 900 Pine St Rolla MO 65401 also: State Capitol Bldg Rm 433 Jefferson City MO 65101 Fax: 573-751-2745.

STEELY, MELVIN T. language educator; b. Atlanta, May 9, 1939; s. Henry Thomas and Katherine Patrick Steely; m. Judy E. Pipes, Sept. 1, 1960 (div. June 1982); children: Bonnie Lynn Vernon, Karen Elizabeth Campbell; m. Nancy Gail Kunz, Dec. 31, 1987. BA, Carson-Newman Coll., Jefferson City, Tenn., 1961; MA, Vanderbilt U., Nashville, 1963; PhD, Vanderbilt U., 1971. Asst. prof. history Lambuth Coll., Jackson, Tenn., 1963—64; prof. history State U. of West Ga., Carrollton, 1964—. Author: (book) Gentleman from Georgia, 2000. Com. mem. Boy Scouts Am., 1998—; adminstrv. aide Rep. Newt Gingrich, 6th Dist. Ga., 1979—93. Mem.: AAUP (state pres. 1979—80, lobbyist 1976—96, AKIN award 1996, Sumberg award 1998), The Hist. Soc. (regional pres. 2000—), Kiwanis (disting. mem.). Methodist. Avocations: stamp collecting/philately, politics. Home: 60 S Greenwood Dr Carrollton GA 30117 Office: State Univ of West Georgia Dept History Carrollton GA 30118

STEEN, CARLTON DUANE, private investor, retired food products executive; b. Walnut Grove, Minn., June 12, 1932; s. Conrad Wendell and Hilda (Eng) S.; m. Dorothy Corinne Sorknes, Aug. 16, 1953; children: James, Craig, Jennifer. BA in Econs. cum laude, St. Olaf Coll., 1954; MA in Indsl. Relations, U. Minn., 1957. Job analyst Exxon Corp., Roselle, N.J., 1958-59; personnel adminstr. Kraft Inc., Chgo., 1959-65, compensation mgr., 1965-69, plant mgr. Decatur, Ga., 1969-70, Champaign, Ill., 1971-74, v.p. prodn. Chgo., 1974-76; pres. Indsl. Foods div., Memphis, 1976-82, Indsl. Foods Group, 1982-87. Served to capt. USAF, 1955-57. Republican. Lutheran.

STEEN, DENNIS M. real estate company executive; BBA in Acctg., U. Houston, 1981. Registered acct., Tex. State Bd. Pub. Accountancy. Mgr. Ernst and Young; with Tex. Commerce Bancshares, First Interstate Bancorp, IKON Document Svcs.; v.p., controller Camden Property Trust, Houston, 1999—2003, sr. v.p. fin., 2003—, CFO, 2003—, sec., 2003—. Office: Camden Property Trust 3 Greenway Plaza Ste 1300 Houston TX 77046*

STEEN, JOHN THOMAS, JR., lawyer; b. San Antonio, Dec. 27, 1949; s. John Thomas and Nell (Donnell) S.; m. Ida Louise Clement, May 12, 1979; children: John T. III, Ida Louise Larkin, James Higbie Clement. AB cum laude, Princeton U., 1971; JD, U. Tex., 1974. Bar: Tex. 1974, U.S. Dist. Ct. (we. dist.) Tex. 1976, U.S. Ct. Appeals (5th cir.) 1989. Assoc. Matthews & Branscomb, San Antonio, 1977-82, ptnr. Soules, Cliffe & Reed, San Antonio, 1982-83; sr. v.p., gen. counsel, dir. Commerce Savs. Assn., San Antonio, 1983-88; pvt. practice San Antonio, 1988—. Trustee San Antonio Acad., 1976-81, 87-93, chmn. bd., 1989-91; adv. coun. San Antonio Acad., 1991—; v.p. Bexar County Easter Seal Soc., San Antonio, 1976-77; trustee, vice-chmn. San Antonio C.C. Dist., 1977-82; bd. dirs. Tex. Easter Seal Soc., Dallas, 1977-80, San Antonio Rsch. and Planning Coun., 1978-81, Cmty. Guidance Ctr., 1983-84, Accord Med. Found., 1987-92; vice-chmn. Leadership San Antonio, 1978-79; dir. Fiesta San Antonio Commn., 1982-83, 93-96, 98-2001, 2003—; commr. Bexar County, San Antonio, 1982, Tex. Commn. on Economy and Efficiency in State Govt., 1985-89; adv. bd. Freeman Coliseum, 1985-91, chmn. bd. 1990-91; pres. San Antonio Performing Arts Assn., 1984-85; trustee World Affairs Coun. San Antonio, 1982—, chmn. bd., 1984-86; trustee United Way, San Antonio, 1985-92, Tex. Cavaliers Charitable Found., 1994-97, 2003—, Austin Coll., 1996-2001; bd. dirs. Houston Livestock Show and Rodeo, 2002—; mem. adv. bd. U. Tex., San Antonio, 1987—; active Pan-Tex. Assembly, 1985-2002; commr. Tex. Alcoholic Beverage Commn., 1998—, chmn., 2002-; exec. com. Rep. Eagles, 2000—; hon. dir. San Antonio Livestock Exposition, Inc., 2003—. 1st lt. USAR. Named Chevalier Confrérie de Chevaliers du Tastevin, Sous-Commanderie de So. Tex., 1994—. Fellow San Antonio Bar Found., Tex. Bar Found. (life); mem. Tex. Bar Assn., San Antonio Acad. Alumni Assn. (pres. 1976-77), Ivy Club (Princeton, N.J.), San Antonio German Club (pres. 1982-83), Order of Alamo, Tex. Cavaliers (bd. dirs. 1989-92, 94-97, comdr. 1994-95, King Antonio LXXIV 1996-97, Kings coun. 1997—, vice chmn. 2003-2004, 2004—), San Antonio Country Club (bd. govs. 1990-93, v.p. 1992-93), Argyle Club, Conopus Club (bd. dirs. 1989-90), Princeton Club San Antonio and South Tex. (pres. 1980-81), Maclean Soc. at Princeton U., Phi Delta Phi. Republican. Home: 601 Garraty Rd San Antonio TX 78209-6148 Office: 300 Convent St Ste 2440 San Antonio TX 78205-3722 Office Phone: 210-224-7700.

STEEN, LOWELL HARRISON, retired physician; b. Kenosha, Wis., Nov. 27, 1923; s. Joseph Arthur and Camilla Marie (Henriksen) S.; m. Cheryl Ann Rectanus, Nov. 20, 1969; children: Linda C., Laura A., Lowell Harrison Jr., Heather J., Kirsten M. BS, Ind. U., 1945, MD, 1948. Intern Mercy Hosp.-Loyola U. Clinics, Chgo., 1948-49; resident in internal medicine VA Hosp., Hines, Ill., 1950-53; pvt. practice Highland, Ind., 1953—; ret., 1999. Pres., CEO Whiting Clinic, 1960-85; mem. hon. staff St. Catherine Hosp., East Chicago, Ind.; hon. staff Cmty. Hosp., Munster, Ind.; bd. commrs. Joint Commn. Accreditation of Hosps. With M.C., AUS, 1949-50, 55-56 Recipient Disting. Alumni Svc. award Ind. U., 1983 Fellow ACP; mem. AMA (trustee 1975, chmn. bd. trustees 1979-81), Ind. Med. Assn. (pres. 1970, chmn. bd. 1968-70), World Med. Assn. (dir. 1978-82, chmn. 1981-82, del. world assembly), Ind. Soc. Internal Medicine (pres. 1963), Am. Soc. Internal Medicine (Disting. Internist award 1981), Lake County Med. Soc., Ind. U. Sch. Medicine Alumni Assn. (pres. 1989-90, Disting. Alumnus award 1981). Presbyterian. Home: 8800 Parkway Dr Highland IN 46322-1520 E-mail: canadlsteen@msn.com.

STEEN, LYNN ARTHUR, mathematician, educator; b. Chgo., Jan. 1, 1941; s. Sigvart J. and Margery (Mayer) S.; m. Mary Elizabeth Frost, July 7, 1940; children: Margaret, Catherine. BA, Luther Coll., 1961; PhD, MIT, 1965; DSc (hon.), Luther Coll., 1986, Wittenberg U., 1991, Concordia Coll., Minn., 1996. Prof. math. St. Olaf Coll., Northfield, Minn., 1965—. Vis. scholar Inst. Mittag-Leffler, Djursholm, Sweden, 1970-71; writing fellow Conf. Bd. Math. Sci., Washington, 1974-75; exec. dir. Math. Sci. Edn. Bd., Washington, 1992-95. Author: Counterexamples in Topology, 1970, Everybody Counts, 1989; editor: Mathematics Today, 1978, On the Shoulders of Giants, 1990, Math. Mag., 1976-80, Why Numbers Count, 1997, Mathematics and Democracy, 2001, Achieving Quantitative Literacy, 2004; contbg. editor: Sci. News, 1976-82. NSF Sci. faculty fellow, 1970-71, Danforth Found. grad. fellow, 1961-65. Fellow AAAS (sec. math. sect. 1982-88); mem. Am. Math. Soc., Math. Assn. Am. (pres. 1985-86, Disting. Svc. award 1992), Coun. Sci. Soc. Pres. (chmn. 1989), Sigma Xi (Bd. Dirs. Spl. award 1989). Home: 716 Saint Olaf Ave Northfield MN 55057-1523 Office: St Olaf Coll Dept of Math Northfield MN 55057 E-mail: steen@stolaf.edu.

STEEN, PAUL JOSEPH, retired broadcasting executive; b. Williston, N.D., July 4, 1932; s. Ernest B. and Inez (Ingebrigtson) S.; m. Judith Smith; children— Michael M., Melanie. BA, Pacific Luth. U., 1954; MS, Syracuse U., 1957. Producer, dir. Sta. KNTV, San Jose, Calif., 1957-58, Sta. KVIE, Sacramento, 1958-60; asst. prof. telecommunications Pacific Luth. U., Tacoma, 1960-67; dir. ops. Sta. KPBS San Diego State U., 1967-74; gen. mgr., 1974-93; prof. telecommunications and film, 1974-93; dir. univ. telecommunications. Co-chmn. Office of New Tech. Initiatives. Dir. (tel. program) Troubled Waters (winner Nat. Ednl. TV award of excellence 1970). With AUS. Named Danforth Assoc. Mem. Pacific Mountain Network (bd. dirs., chmn., bd. of govs. award 1993), NATAS, Assn. Calif. Pub. TV Stas. (pres.), San Diego County Sr. Golf Assn., (pres.), Coronado Maritime Found. (dir.),Pi Kappa Delta. Home: 6068 Caminito De La Taza San Diego CA 92120-5323 Personal E-mail: psteen@mail.sdsu.edu.

STEENBURGEN, MARY, actress; b. Newport, Ark., Feb. 8, 1953; m. Malcolm McDowell, 1980 (div. 1990); children: Lilly, Charlie; m. Ted. Danson, Oct. 7, 1995. Student, Neighborhood Playhouse. Films: Goin' South, 1978, Time After Time, 1979, Melvin and Howard, 1980 (Academy award best supporting actress 1981), Ragtime, 1981, A Midsummer Night's Sex Comedy, 1982, Cross Creek, 1983, Romantic Comedy, 1983, One Magic Christmas, 1985, Dead of Winter, 1987, End of the Line, 1987 (also exec. prodr.), The Whales of August, 1987, Miss Firecracker, 1989, Parenthood, 1989, Back to the Future III, 1990, The Long Walk Home, 1990 (narrator), The Butcher's Wife, 1991, Philadelphia, 1993, What's Eating Gilbert Grape, 1993, Clifford, 1994, It Runs in the Family, 1994, Pontiac Moon, 1994, Powder, 1995, Nixon, 1995, My Family, 1995, The Grass Harp, 1995, About Sarah, 1995, Trumpet of the Swan (voice), 1999, Life as a House, 2001, I Am Sam, 2001, Sunshine State, 2002, Wish You Were Dead, 2002, Hope Springs, 2003, Casa de los babys, 2003, Elf, 2003; appeared in Showtime TV's Faerie Tale Theatre prodn. of Little Red Riding Hood and (miniseries) Tender Is the Night, 1985, Gulliver's Travels, 1996;, (miniseries) Noah's Ark, 1999, Living with the Dead, 2002; TV series: Ink, 1996, Joan of Arcadia, 2003-; TV films: The Attic: The Hiding of Anne Frank, 1988, About Sarah, 1998, Picnic, 2000, Nobody's Baby, 2001, It Must Be Love, 2004, Capital City, 2004; theater appearances include: Holiday, Old Vic, London, 1987, Candida, Broadway, 1993. Nat. spokesperson Elizabeth Glaser Pediatric AIDS Found. Office: The Gersh Agency 232 N Canon Dr Beverly Hills CA 90210*

STEENBURGH, FRANK D. consumer products company executive; b. Johnstown, NY, Jan. 23, 1943; BSME, General Motors Inst., 1966; MBA, Rensselaer Poly. Inst., 1967. Sr. v.p. bus. growth Xerox Corp., Stamford, Conn., 2003—. Bd. dirs. Nat. Tech. Inst. for Deaf Found. Recipient Power of Communicatons Award, Assn. Graphic Comm., print-on-demand award, Cygnus Bus. Media. Office: Xerox Corp 800 Long Ridge Rd Stamford CT 06904

STEENHAGEN, ROBERT LEWIS, landscape architect, consultant; b. Grand Rapids, Mich., July 11, 1922; s. Abraham and Rena (Vanden Broek) S.; m. Doris Brisentine, Aug. 2, 1952; children: Deborah, Cynthia, James. A.S., Grand Rapids Jr. Coll., 1942; BS, Mich. State U., 1949. Chief landscape design Eastern design office Nat. Park Service, Phila., 1963-66; capt. planning team Nat. Park Service, Washington, 1966-70, asst. mgr. N.E. area Design Office Denver, 1971-77, assoc. mgr., 1978-80; cons. landscape architecture Lakewood, Colo., 1980—. Served to sgt. U.S. Army, 1942-45, PTO. Recipient Meritorious Service award Nat. Park Service, 1971; recipient Performance award for Nat. Bicentennial Program, 1976 Fellow Am. Soc. Landscape Architects Home: 2473 S Carr Ct Denver CO 80227-3104

STEEN-HINDERLIE, DIANE EVELYN, social worker, musician; b. Duluth, Minn., June 13, 1947; d. Julian Sem and Evelyn Synnove (Helgaas) Steen; m. John Peter Hinderlie, June 27, 1971 (div. Sept. 1987); children: Peder Donald, Erik Steen; m. John Richard Olson, July 21, 1989. BA in Asian Studies/Social Psychology cum laude, St. Olaf Coll., 1969; MusB equivalency, U. Minn. and other instns., 1970-91; postgrad., Hamline U., 1989-91. Lic. social worker, Minn.; cert. music tchr. Music Tchrs. Nat. Assn. Social worker child care licensing Hennepin County Welfare Dept., Mpls., 1970-73; mem. clergy team exch. program Luth. World Fedn., Göppingen, Germany, 1973-77; mem. clergy team, music dir. Jubilation Singers Bethel Luth. Ch., Rochester, Minn., 1978-83; mem. clergy team, music dir. youth choir First Luth. Ch., St. Louis Park, Minn., 1983-86; adminstr. Family Child Care facility, St. Louis Park, 1986-90; faculty, tchr. Stenson Suzuki Studios and Home Studio, St. Louis Park, 1988-92; small group leader, tchr. vol. Mt. Olive Ch., Children's Hosp., Mpls., 1993, 96-98; workshop and children's ministry Augsburg Coll. Youth and Family Inst., Trinity Cong., 1998—; founding dir. Fair Pay Inst., Mpls., 1995—; trainer United for a Fair Economy, 1997—. Founder orgn. and curriculum Early Childhood Orgn. for Edn. with Singing, 1993—, co-leader German-Am. youth group exch., 1979-82; co-founder Family DayCare Cert. Program and Babygarten (B-12 edn.) classes, 1970-73; bd. dirs. Midwest Coun., Nat. Peace Inst. Found., Grinnell, Iowa, 1991; presenter in field.; mem. root causes of violence action team Initiative for Violence-Free Families, 4th Jud. Dist. Minn., 1997—. Author: (tng. manual) Mother Tongue Singing/Voice Method, 1988, (study packet) School Start Time/Teen Sleep Deprivation, 1996-97, A+=Baby Church School, 2002; rec. artist, mem. ensemble record/cassettes Nowell Sing We, 1986; performer Nordic Am. Psalmodikon Forbundet, 1997—. Vol. People of Faith Peacemakers, Feminists in Faith/ReImagining and Jewish Cmty. Rels. Coun., 1992-2003, Muslim-Christian Rels. Coun., Joint Religious Legis. Coalition, Bread for the World; founder People for Reforming Early Start Time for Teens Orgn., Mpls., 1993—; mem. steering com. Progressive Cmty. and FairVote, Minn., 1994-99; local host youth com. NAACP Conv., Mpls., 1995; vol. Common Cause, St. Paul and Washington; charter mem. U.S. Holocaust Mus., 1993. Recipient appreciation plaque Christian Boy/Girl Scouts Germany; Svc. pin Am. Luth. Ch. Women; listed in Minn. Profiles, Minn. Hist. Soc. A Tribute to Outstanding Minn. Women by Marilyn Chelstrom, 2001; named Asset Builder of Month, St. Louis Park Children First Initiative, 1997; named to Honor Roll, Mendota Mdewakanton Dakota Cmty., 1999. Mem.: MADD, Minn. Music Tchrs. Assn. (first early childhood music chair 2001—03), Assn. Pre- and Perinatal Psychology and Health, Wash. Nat. Cathedral, Early Childhood Music and Movement Assn. Minn., Soc. for Psychol. Studies of Social Issues, Interfaith Alliance Minn., Nat. Luth. Choir Acad., Suzuki Assn. Americas (study area co-organizer, editl. adviser), Internat. Suzuki Assn., Nat. Assn. Tchrs. Singing and VoiceCare Network, UN Assn., Sojourner Project, Inc., World Wildlife Fund, Ctr. for Victims of Torture, Minn. Parenting Assn., Amnesty Internat., Nat. Peace Found., Germanic-Am. Inst., Am.'s Jr. Miss. Coun., Sons of Norway (lodge trustee 1991—), Phi Beta Kappa, Am. Mensa. Green. Lutheran. Avocations: reading, political activism, concerts, travel, memory albums. Office: Fair Pay Inst PO Box 16031 Minneapolis MN 55416-0031

STEENLAND, DOUGLAS, air transportation executive; married; 2 children. Graduated, George Washington U., 1976. Sr. ptnr. Verner, Liipfert, Bernhard, McPherson and Hand, Washington; v.p., dep. gen. counsel Northwest Airlines Inc., Minn., 1991—94, sr. v.p., gen. counsel, 1994—98, exec. v.p., gen. counsel and alliances, 1998—99, exec. v.p., chief corp. officer, 1999—2001, pres., 2001—, also bd. dirs., 2001—. Office: Northwest Airlines Corp 2700 Lone Oak Pkwy Eagan MN 55121

STEENSGAARD, ANTHONY HARVEY, federal agency administrator; b. Rapid City, S.D., Mar. 21, 1963; s. Harvey Hans and Dorothy Lorraine (Hansen) S. Student, Anchorage C.C., 1983-84; BSCE, U. Alaska, 1985; AAS in Indsl. Security, C.C. Air Force, 1989; BS in Criminal Justice, Wayland U., 1989; MS in Computer Systems Engring., U. Calif., San Diego, 1996; LLD in Criminal Law, PhD in Computer Engring., U. Trinity Coll., 2000; BSc in Criminological Psychology, Ruslanc Coll., 2003. Lic. pilot, radio operator; cert. hostage negotiator FBI, FBI Nat. Acad., Va., 1987; Fed. Air Marshall Sch., FAA; cert. Instr. Am. Soc. Protection Profls., 1986—, fed. emergency mgmt. agy. level III incident comdr., security specialist, 2001—, info. security specialist, intelligence and surveillance profl., 2001—. Bookseller B. Dalton Bookseller, Rapid City, 1978—81, Anchorage, 1981—83; warehouseman Sears, Roebuck & Co., Anchorage, 1983—85; air res. technician Alaska Air N.G., Anchorage, 1985—88; agt., draftsman, engring. cons., asst. intelligence officer U.S. Border Patrol, El Centro, Calif., 1988—. Fed. counter terrorism cons., 2001—; fed. info. warfare cons., 2001—; computer cons., 1994-2000; computer criminal investigator, 1999—; CEO Totalwarfare.com webzine, 1997—; founding assoc. Amazon.com.; technical support working group, technical support officer Dept. Homeland Security, 2002—; intelligence officer U.S. Coast Guard Auxiliary, 2003—. Author: Unit Security Manager's Guide Book, 1988. Vol. Spl. Olympics, Rapid City, 1981; navigator, observer Civil Air Patrol, Anchorage, 1981; mentor Municipality Anchorage Sch. Dist., 1983—84; sr. pilot Civil Air Patrol, Rapid City, 1996, pub. affairs officer, 1996—98, aerospace edn. officer, 1998—2000, wing dir. aerospace edn., 2000—; aircraft navigator US Coast Guard Aux., 2003—; Vol. U.S. Senator George McGovern's Campaign, Rapid City, 1980, Senator Tom Daschle's Campaign, Rapid City, 1980. With USNR, 1980—81, With USMCR, 1981—85, With USAF, 1985—98. Recipient Hon. Sci. award Bausch and Lomb, 1984, commendation State of Alaska, 1987, 2d commendation, 1988, Brigadier Gen. Charles E. Yeager Aerospace Achievement award, 2000, Blanchard trophy, 1990, Afghanistan royal Oder Almara el Ala, 2003. Fellow N.Am. Acad. Arts and Sci.; mem. U.S. Cavalry Assn. (heritage mem.), HTML Writer's Guild, Am. Legion, Air Force Assn., VFW, Fraternal Order Eagles, S.D. Sheriff's Assn., Fraternal Order of Police, Virtual Geog. League, WWII Meml. Soc. (charter mem.), US Naval Inst., US Coast Guard Inst., Nat. D-Day Mus. Found., Adventurer's Club. Avocations: reading, flight simulations, aviation, history, wargaming. Office: US Border Patrol 1111 N Imperial Ave El Centro CA 92243-1795 E-mail: ahsteensgaard@juno.com.

STEENSLAND, RONALD PAUL, librarian; b. Dothan, Ala., Dec. 16, 1946; s. Maurice John and Claire Folkes S.; m. Nancy Hollister, Dec. 20, 1970; 1 child, Ronald Paul. BA, Fla. State U., 1969, MS, 1970; postgrad., Miami (Ohio) U., 1972, U. Md., 1980, U.S. Army War Coll., 1995. Dir. Davidson County Pub. Libr., Lexington, N.C., 1970-73, Hidalgo County Libr. System, McAllen, Tex., 1973-76, Los Alamos County Libr., 1976-77, Lexington (Ky.) Pub. Libr., 1977—. Chmn. John Cotton Dana Library Public Relations Awards, 1977 Treas. Hildago County chpt. ARC, 1975. Served to col. USAR, 1969-70. Recipient Service award United Way. Mem. ALA, Res. Officers Assn. (sec.-treas. chpt. 100), Assn. U.S. Army (sec. Bluegrass chpt.), U.S. Chess Fedn., Southeastern Library Assn., Ky. Library Assn., Lexington C. of C., Alpha Tau Omega. Clubs: Lafayette, Pres.'s, Lexington Chess, Rotary. Baptist. Office: Lexington Pub Libr 140 E Main St Lexington KY 40507-1318 E-mail: Ron.Steensland@insightbb.com.

STEEPLES, DOUGLAS WAYNE, retired university dean, consultant, researcher; b. Great Bend, Kans, Mar. 30, 1935; s. Marion Wayne and Dorothy Augusta (King) S.; children from previous marriage: Donald Bruce, John Douglas, Sheila Margaret; m. Christine Marie MacKinnes, Dec. 8, 1990. BA Summa Cum Laude, U. Redlands, 1957; MA, U.N.C., 1958, PhD, 1961; cert., Inst. Ednl. Mgmt., Harvard U., 1981. Asst. prof. history Cal. State U., No. Ridge, Calif., 1961—64; prof. history Earlham Coll., Richmond, Ind., 1963-80; acad. v.p. Wartburg Coll., Waverly, Iowa, 1979-80; exec. v.p. Westminster Coll., Salt Lake City, 1980-83; provost Ohio U., Delaware, Ohio, 1983-85, acting pres., winter 1984; dean Coll. Liberal and Fine Arts, U. So. Colo., Pueblo, Colo., 1985-89; v.p. for acad. affairs Aurora (Ill.) U., 1989-94; dean, prof. history Coll. Liberal Arts, Mercer U., Macon, Ga., 1994-2000, ret., 2000. Cons. higher edn. mgmt.; cons., reader advanced placement program Ednl. Testing Svc., Princeton, NJ, 1976-93; cons., evaluator North Ctrl. Assn. Sch. and Coll., Chgo., 1985-1994; mem. Accreditation Rev. Commn., 1992-94; bd. dirs. Western Ind. Coll. Fund, Salt Lake City, 1980-83; bd. dirs. Am. Conf. Acad. Deans, 1995-2000, sec.-treas., 1998-99; trustee Econ. and Bus. Hist. Soc., 1995-2000, pres., 1998-99; bd. dirs. Associated New Am. Colls., 1994-00. Editor, contbg. author: Institutional Revival: Case Histories, 1986, Successful Strategic Planning Case Studies, 1989, Mng. Change in Higher Ed., 1990, Treasure from the Painted Hills: Calico Calif., 1882-1907, 1999; (with David O. Whitten) Democracy in Desperation: The Depression in the

1890s, 1998; editor John Randolph Spears, Illustrated Sketches of Death Valley, 2000, Advocate for Am. Enterprise: William Buck Dana and the Commercial and Fin. Chronicle, 1865-1910, 2001; assoc. editor Bus. Libr. Rev., 1996-2001; occational columnist for Macon Telegraph; contbr. over 45 articles and 80 book revs. to profl. jour. Adv. bd. Pueblo Symphony Orch., 1987—89; allocations com. United Way, Richmond, 1976—79, Pueblo, 1988—89, Aurora, 1990—94; vol. in svc., spl. cons. to pres. Ho-Chunk Wis. Winnebago Nation, 2001; mem. Mayor's Commn. on Restoration of Ft. Hawkins, Macon, Ga., 1997—; pipe maj. Mercer U. Pipes and Drums; pres. Luth. Inter-parish Coun., Richmond, 1975—78; bd. dir. Soc. for Use and Preservation of Resources, Richmond, 1976—79. Scholar U. Redlands, Calif., 1953-57; Danforth fellow, 1957-61; Woodrow Wilson fellow, 1957-58; Found. for Econ. Edn. fellow in bus., 1963; Am. Philos. Soc. grantee, 1966 Mem. Am. Hist. Assn., Orgn. Am. Hist., So. Hist. Assn., Soc. for Values in Higher Edn., Sierra Club, Rotary (bd. dirs. 1983-84), Palaver Club, Phi Beta Kappa (senator united chpt. 1973-79, sec.-treas. mid-Ga. alumni assoc. 1996-2000, pres. 2003—), Omicron Delta Kappa, Phi Kappa Phi (mem. planning com. 2005 triennial coun., 2003-04). Republican. Avocations: mountain climbing, running, bagpiping. Office: 656 River North Blvd Macon GA 31211-6340 E-mail: marliesesteeples@aol.com.

STEER, REGINALD DAVID, lawyer; b. N.Y.C., July 16, 1945; s. Joseph D. and Rozica (Yusim) S.; m. Marianne Spizzy, July 22, 1983; children: Derek B., Trevor A. BA, U. Minn., 1966, JD, 1969. Bar: Minn. 1969, Calif. 1973, U.S. Dist. Ct. (no., ea. so. and ctrl. dists.) Calif., U.S. Ct. Mil. Appeals 1969, U.S. Ct. Appeals (9th cir.), U.S. Ct. Appeals (11th cir.), U.S. Supreme Ct. 1981, U.S. Ct. Internat. Trade, 1994. Assoc. Pillsbury, Madison & Sutro, San Francisco, 1973-79, ptnr., 1979 2000, Skjerven Morrill, LLP, San Francisco, 2000—03, Pillsbury Winthrop, LLP, Palo Alto, Calif., 2003—04, Akin Gump Strauss Hauer & Feld, LLP, San Francisco, 2004—. Capt. U.S. Army, 1969—73. Fellow Am. Coll. Trial Lawyers; mem. ABA (antitrust and litigation sects.), San Francisco (Calif.) Bar Assn., Lawyer's Club San Francisco. Office: Akin Gump Strauss Hauer& Felld LLP 3 Embarcadero Ctr Ste 2800 San Francisco CA 94111-4046 Office Phone: 415-765-9520. E-mail: rsteer@akingump.com.

STEERE, WILLIAM CAMPBELL, JR., pharmaceutical executive; b. Ann Arbor, Mich., June 17, 1936; s. William Campbell and Dorothy (Osborne) S.; m. Lynda Gay Powers, Jan. 29, 1957; children: William, Mark, Christopher. BS, Stanford U., 1959. Sales rep. Pfizer & Co., Modesto, Calif., 1970-72; v.p., dir. ops. Pfizer Labs, N.Y.C., 1982-84; sr. v.p., dir. ops. Pfizer Pharms., N.Y.C., 1982-84, exec. v.p., 1984-86, pres., 1986-91; pres., CEO Pfizer Inc., 1991-92, CEO, 1991—2000, chmn., 1992—2001, chmn. emeritus, 2001—. Bd. dirs. NYU Med. Ctr., Health Mgmt. Assocs. (HMA), Met Life, Dow Jones. Bd. dirs. N.Y. Bot. Garden; bd. overseers Meml. Sloan-Kettering Cancer Ctr. Mem. Bus. Coun. (bd. dirs.), Univ. Club, N.Y. Yacht Club. Avocations: sailing, skiing. Office: Pfizer Inc 235 E 42nd St New York NY 10017-5755 Office Phone: 212-573-3116. Office Fax: 212-573-2200.

STEFAN, VLADISLAV ALEXANDER, academic administrator, educator, research scientist, writer; b. Yugoslavia, Feb. 5, 1948; arrived in U.S., 1981; s. Bozhidar and Rosanda Stefan.; 1 child, Andrej. BSEE, U. Belgrade, Yugoslavia, 1972, MSc, 1975; DSc, Russian Acad. Scis., Moscow, 1978. Rsch. scientist Inst. Nuc. Scis., Belgrade, 1973-79, Russian Acad. Scis., 1977-81; assoc. prof. U. Belgrade, 1979-81; vis. prof. MIT, Cambridge, 1981-82; cons. Jaycor, Inc., San Diego, 1983—. Pres., founder Stefan U., La Jolla, Calif., 1989—. Author: Genomic Medicine Ante Portas, 2004; editor: Physics and Society, 1992, Nonlinear and Relativistic Effects in Plasmas, 1992, Research Trends in Physics, 1989—; author: Dr. Faustef, 2002. Mem. AAAS, Am. Phys. Soc., Am. Soc. Genomic Medicine (pres., founder). Achievements include invention of beat wave driven free electron laser; diamond 4C's magic box. Avocations: painting, music, rock climbing. Office: The Stefan U PO Box 2946 7596 Eads Ave La Jolla CA 92038-2946 Business E-Mail: vs@stefan-university.edu.

STEFANI, GWEN RENEE, musician; b. Orange County, Calif., Oct. 3, 1969; Student, Calif. State U., Fullerton. Musician band No Doubt. Singer: (albums) No Doubt, 1992, Tragic Kingdom, 1995, Beacon Street Collection, 1995, Collector's Orange Crate, 1997, Return of Saturn, 2000, Rock Steady, 2001 (Grammy awards: Best Pop Performance By A Duo Or Group With Vocal for song "Hey Baby", 2002, Best Pop Performance By A Duo Or Group With Vocal for song "Underneath it All", 2003), (albums) The Singles 1992-2003, 2004, (songs) "Let Me Blow Your Mind" (with Eve), 2001 (Grammy award, Best Rap/Song Collaboration, 2001), "It's My Life" (MTV Video Music award Best Group Video, 2004, MTV Video Music award Best Pop Video, 2004); actor: (voice) Malice; A Kat's Tale, 2002, (film) Zoolander, 2001, (TV guest appearances) Saturday Night Live, 1996, 2001, Mad TV, 2000, Dawson's Creek, 2002, (Voice) King of the Hill, 2001.*

STEFANICS, CHARLOTTE LOUISE, retired mental health nurse; b. Leechburg, Pa., Dec. 30, 1927; d. George J. and Mary Magadelene (Boronyak) S. Diploma Sch. Nursing, St. Elizabeth Hosp., 1948; BSN, Seton Hall U., 1968; MS, Ohio State U., 1971; EdD, U. Sarasota, 1982. Diplomate Logotherapy. Various nursing positions, 1952-69; staff nurse Med. Ctr. NYU, N.Y.C., 1969-70; pvt. practice, 1971-73; instr. Sch. Nursing Duke U., Durham, N.C., 1974-77; clin. nurse specialist VA Med. Ctr., Bay Pines, Fla., 1977-93; ret., 1993. Instr., pvt. practice Community Hosp. Springfield, Ohio; cons. in field; part-time chaplain Miami Valley Hosp., Dayton, Ohio; lectr. U. South Fla. Coll. Nursing, 1978-92. Co-author (with G. Niklas): Ministry to the Sick, 1982; co-author: (with R. Peck) Learning to Say Good-bye, 1987. Vol. community classes and workshops; vol. Habitat for Humanity Internat. Hungary, nursing exchange with Chinese Nurses Assn. Mem. Assn. Death Educators and Counselors (cert.), Assn. Christian Therapists, Nurses Orgn. Vet. Affairs. Home: 1342 Rosehaven Cir Dayton OH 45429-5744 Office Phone: 937-208-6603.

STEFANO, JOSEPH WILLIAM, film and television producer, writer; b. Phila., May 5, 1922; s. Dominic and Josephine (Vottima) S.; m. Marilyn Epstein, Dec. 5, 1953; 1 son, Andrew Dominic. Ed. pub. schs. Pres. Villa di Stefano Prodns., 1962—. Toured as song and dance man in Student Prince, 1945, Merry Widow, 1946; composer music and lyrics popular songs, night club revues, indsl. shows, others, 1946-57; author screenplays The Black Orchid, 1958, The Naked Edge, 1960, Psycho, 1960, Anna di Brooklyn, 1962, Eye of the Cat, 1969, Futz, 1970, The Kindred, 1986, Blackout, 1989, Psycho IV: The Beginning, 1990, Two Bits, 1995, Psycho, 1998; TV drama Made in Japan, 1959, movies for TV, 1970-78; prodr., author TV series The Outer Limits, 1963-64, Swamp Thing, 1990; exec. con. The Outer Limits, 1995—. Recipient Robert E. Sherwood award for Made in Japan, Fund for Republic, 1959, Edgar Allen Poe award for Psycho, Mystery Writers Am., 1960, Columbia award Federated Italo-Ams. Calif., 1964, Pres.'s award Acad. Sci.-Fiction Fantasy and Horror Films, 1987, Movieguide commendation for Two Bits, One of Ten Best Films of 1995; inducted into Cultural Hall of Fame, South Phila. H.S. Mem. ASCAP, Writers Guild Am., Dirs. Guild Am., Producers Guild Am., Acad. Motion Pictures Arts and Scis., Mystery Writers Am. Home: 10216 Cielo Dr Beverly Hills CA 90210-2035 Office Phone: 310-275-8414. *For me it has always been important to succeed first in my own eyes. This personal sense of success seems warmer and surer and more likely to maintain the spirit during those moments when worldly success dances to tunes other than my own. Goals are golden. Guidelines are lines on a street map; they show how many different ways there are to go from where to when.*

STEFANOS, ASGEDET, educational consultant; b. Asmara, Eritrea, Mar. 19, 1944; arrived in U.S.A., 1963; d. Stefanos Salassie Enco and Teblez Araya; m. Kenneth D. Schlosser, Oct. 12, 1976; 1 child, Ahwat S. Schlosser. BA, Howard U., 1971, EdM, 1975, EdD, 1989. Tchg. fellow Harvard U., Cambridge, Mass., 1975, 1978, 1981; assoc. prof. U. Mass., Boston, 1989—. Vis. prof. N.E. U., Boston, 1993—94, Smith Coll., Northhampton, Mass., 1992—93; edit. advisory bd. Jour. Post Colonial Edn., Melbourne, Australia, 1999—; edit. bd. Radical Tchrs. Jour., Cambridge, Mass., 1993—; cons. Ministry Justice, Asmara, Eritrea. Contbr. chapters to books. Mem. Scholar's Task Force Smithsonian Instn., 1994—2000; mem. African Studies Assn., 1983—. Mem.: Nat. Women Studies Assn. Independent. Home: 61 Crowninshield Rd Brookline MA 02446 Office: U Mass 100 Morrissey Blvd Boston MA 02125-3393 Office Phone: 617-287-7363. E-mail: a.stefanos@comcast.net., asgedat.stefanos@umb.edu.

STEFANSEN, PEGGY ANN, special education educator; b. Newton, Kans., Sept. 16, 1953; d. Manny E. and Marjorie M. (Covalt) Osburn; m. Todd Stefansen, June 9, 1976; 1 child, Tyler. BA, Oral Roberts U., 1975; MA, Tulsa U., 1981. Tchr. learning disabilities Prague (Okla.) Pub. Schs., Chandler (Okla.) Pub. Schs., Skiatook (Okla.) Pub. Schs.; tchr. Prague Pub. Schs. Mem.: NEA, Okla. Edn. Assn., Leanring Disabilities Assn. Home: Rte 1 Box 22A Paden OK 74860 Office: Prague Elementary NBU # 3504 Prague OK 74864-2031

STEFFA, JOHN AMON, music educator, composer; s. Robert Karl and Dorothy Grace Steffa; m. Nancy Margaret Scarborough; children: Matthew, Scott Chappell. BA Edn., U. Northern Iowa, 1969, M Music, 1978; D Musical Arts, U. Tex., 1985. Orch. tchr. Cedar Falls (Iowa) Pub. Sch. Sys., 1969—72, Charleston County Sch. Dist., Charleston, SC, 1972—77, Marshalltown (Iowa) Cmty. Sch. Dist., 1978—82, Temple (Tex.) Ind. Sch. Dist., 1985—87; music prof. Bowling Green (Ohio) State U., 1987—88, Murray State U., Murray, Ky., 1988—. Music dir. Charleston County Youth Symphony, Charleston, SC, 1973—77. Composer: Voices, 2000, (transcription for clarinet and electronics) Pines of Rome, 2001, (for percussion ensemble) Bahiana, 1990, (for piano trio) Scherzo, 1991;: A Jangada, 1991, (for piano) Tangents, 1992 (Ky. Music Teachers Assn. Commn. award, 1992), (for orchestra and electronics) Character Pieces, 1993 (Ky. Arts Coun. grant support, 1993), (for solo piano) Piano Piece, 1995, (for alto saxophone and electronics) Jazzy, 1995;: Dialogue, 1995, (for eight trombones) Slide Talk, 1997, (for clarinet and piano) Canyon Music, 2000, (for clarinet and electronics), 2001, (songs) Dance Music No. 1, 1990, (for chorus, organ, percussion and dancers) Trilogy, 1996, (for flugel horn, English horn and electronics) Songs in Tribute, 2001, (for percussion ensemble) Tom, 2002, (for 12 trumpets and electronics) Fantasy, 2002, (for flute and piano) Festival Diversion, 2003, (for orch.) Sacred Valley Festival Suite, 2003. Recipient citation, Distance Edn. Report Magna Publs., 2000; fellow Al Smith fellowship, Ky. Arts Coun., 2003; grantee Profl. Assistance grant, 1992. Mem.: Ky. Music Tchrs. Assn. (composer of yr. award 1992), Music Educators Nat. Conf., Coll. Music Soc. Office: Murray State U 524 Fine Arts Bldg Murray KY 42071 Business E-Mail: john.steffa@murraystate.edu.

STEFFAN, JUDY MAE, medical/surgical nurse; b. Beatrice, Nebr., Apr. 6, 1949; d. Wilke J. and Mary Elizabeth (Shultz) Duitsman; m. William Arthur Steffan, Apr. 22, 1967; 1 child, Rodney Alan. RN, Lincoln Gen. Hosp. Sch. Nursing, 1973. Nurse Beatrice (Nebr.) Cmty. Hosp., 1973—80, Luth. Hosp., Beatice, 1980—83; pvt. duty nurse various nursing agencies, Omaha. Bus. adviser to Frank Sinatra; polit. advisor to Sen. Ted Kennedy, 1988—96, Pres. Bill Clinton, 1992—96. Author: A Presidential Story, 1996. Mem. St. Joseph's Cath. Ch., Beatrice. Recipient Bausch and Lomb Honoary Sci. award, 1966. Democrat. Roman Catholic. Achievements include discovery of re-creation and the partitioning effect. Avocations: piano, reading. Home: 420 N 86th St Lincoln NE 68505

STEFFEN, KONRAD, geography educator; b. Zurich, Zurich, Switzerland, Jan. 2, 1952; s. Ernst S. and Maria Steffen-Kurzynski; m. Regula Dorothee Werner, Feb. 10, 1952; children: Anico, Simon. PhD, Swiss Fed. Inst. Tech., Zurich, Switzerland, 1976. Prof. geography U. Colo., Boulder, 1990—, assoc. dir. Coop. Inst. Rsch. Environ. Scis., 1997—. Editor: (albums) article in Annals of Glaciology, 1993. Master: NASA (chair adv. panel for Data Arctic Active Ctr. 1991—2000), World Meteorol. Orgn. (chair Arctic Climate Sys./Climate and Cryosphere OPP panel 1998—2003); mem.: Am. Meteorol. Soc. (assoc. editor Jour. Appl. Meteorolgy 1996—2001), Glaciol. Soc. (mem. executive bd. 1992—96). Reformed Ch. Avocations: photography, travel, mountain climbing. Office Phone: 303 492 4524. Personal E-mail: konrad.steffen@colorado.edu. Business E-Mail: konrad.steffen@colorado.edu.

STEFFEN, LLOYD HOWARD, minister, religion educator; b. Racine, Wis., Nov. 27, 1951; s. Howard C. and Ruth L. (Rode) S.; m. Emmajane S. Finney, Feb. 14, 1981; children: Nathan, Samuel, William. BA, New Coll., 1973; MA, Andover Newton Theol. Sch., 1978; MDiv, Yale U., 1978; PhD, Brown U., 1984. Ordained to ministry United Ch. of Christ, 1983. Chaplain Northland Coll., Ashland, Wis., 1983-90, assoc. prof., 1982-90, Lehigh U., Bethlehem, Pa., 1990-97, chaplain, 1990—, prof., 1997—, chair dept. religion studies, 2000—; co-dir. Mellon Global Citizenship, 2003—. Mem. theol. com. Wis. Conf. United Ch. of Christ, Madison, 1985—87; mem. div. ch. and ministry NW assn. Wis. Conf., Eau Claire, 1987—90; mem. ecumenical commn. Penn N.E. Conf., 1994—96; mem. Common Ground, Bethlehem, Pa., 1994—97, chair, 1995—97; mem. ch. & ministry com. Pa. Northeast Conf., 1997—2000; mem. ethics com. St. Luke's Hosp., Bethlehem, Pa., 1998—; mem., vice-chair, bd. dirs. Religious Coalition for Reproductive Choice; non-govtl. orgn. rep. UN; 10th Curtis Lectr. Sacred Heart Univ., 1999; Frederick C. Wood Lectr. Cornell U., 2002. Author: Self-Deception and the Common Life, 1986, Life/Choice: The Theory of Just Abortion, 1994, Abortion: A Reader, 1996, Executing Justice: The Moral Meaning of the Death Penalty, 1998, The Demonic Turn: The Power of Religion to Inspire or Restrain Violence, 2003; contbr. articles to profl. jours. Town supr. Town of La Pointe, Wis., 1984-87. Recipient 1st Pilgrim Press Church and Soc. Book award, NEH Inst. award, Harvard U., 1988, East-West Ctr., 1995; fellow, Brown U., 1982; faculty devel. grant, Northland Coll., 1986, faculty devel. grantee, 1990, Lehigh U., 1994, 1998, 2003. Mem. Soc. Christian Ethics, Am. Acad. Religion, Assocs. for Religion and Intellectual Life, Assn. for Coordination of Univ. Religious Affairs. Home: 1349 Woodland Cir Bethlehem PA 18017-1636 Office: Lehigh U Johnson Hall # 36 Bethlehem PA 18015 Office Phone: 610-758-3877. Business E-Mail: lhs1@lehigh.edu.

STEFFEN, THOMAS LEE, retired judge, lawyer; b. Tremonton, Utah, July 9, 1930; s. Conrad Richard and Jewel (McGuire) S.; m. LaVona Ericksen, Mar. 20, 1953; children— Elizabeth, Catherine, Conrad, John, Jennifer Student, U. So. Calif., 1955-56; BS, U. Utah, 1957; JD with honors, George Washington U., 1964; LLM, U. Va., 1988. Bar: Nev. 1965, U.S. Dist. Ct. Nev. 1965, U.S. Tax Ct. 1966, U.S. Ct. Appeals 1967, U.S. Supreme Ct. 1977. Contracts negotiator U.S. Bur. Naval Weapons, Washington, 1961-64; private practice Las Vegas, 1965-82; justice Supreme Ct. Nev., Carson City, 1982-94, chief justice, 1995-97, ret., 1997, chmn. code of jud. conduct study com., 1991; of counsel Hutchison & Steffen, Las Vegas, also Provo, Utah, 1997—. Vice chmn. Nev. State Jud. Edn. Coun., 1983-84; chmn. Nev. State-Fed. Jud. Coun., 1986-91, mem., 1986-93. Mem. editorial staff George Washington U. Law Rev., 1963-64; contbr. articles to legal jours. Bd. dirs. So. Nev. chpt. NCCJ, 1974-75; mem. exec. bd. Boulder Dam Area coun. Boy Scouts Am., 1979-83; bd. visitors Brigham Young U., 1985-89. Recipient merit citation Utah State U., 1983 Mem. Nev. Bar Assn. (former chmn. So. Nev. med.-legal screening panel), Nev. Trial Lawyers Assn. (former dir.) Republican. Mem. Lds Ch. Avocations: reading, spectator sports. Office: Lakes Business Park 8831 W Sahara Ave Las Vegas NV 89117-5865 also: 481 E Normandy Dr Provo UT 84604-5963 E-mail: Tlsrcjnsct@aol.com.

STEFFENS, JOHN LAUNDON, brokerage house executive; b. Cleve., July 7, 1941; m. Louise Cullen, Nov. 25, 1967; children: Drew, Julie, Wesley. B in Econs., Dartmouth Coll., 1963. Various positions Merrill Lynch, N.Y.C., 1963—, exec. v.p. U.S. pvt. client group, 1990—, vice-chmn. bd. U.S. pvt. client group, 1997—, vice chmn., chmn. U.S. pvt. client group. Office: Merrill Lynch & Co Inc World Fin Ctr N Tower 250 Vesey St Fl 32 New York NY 10080-0002

STEFFENSEN, DWIGHT A. former medical products and data processing services executive; b. Fresno, Calif., 1943; BA, Stanford U., 1965. Corp. contr. Synergex Corp. (merged with Bergen Brunswig Corp. 1985), Orange, Calif., 1969-72, chief fin. officer, v.p., 1972-80, chief oper. officer, chief fin. officer, exec. v.p., treas., 1980-83, pres., chief exec. officer, 1983-85, exec. v.p., 1985—; pres. Drug Service Inc., 1975-80; pres., coo, dir. Bergen Brunswig Corp.; chmn. & CEO Merisel, Inc., El Segundo, Calif., 1996—2000.

STEFFER, ROBERT WESLEY, clergyman; b. Spokane, Wash., June 24, 1934; s. Harold Wesley and Kathryne (Trumble) S.; m. Diane DeMoisey, Aug. 19, 1960; children: Erika Kirsten, Beauregard Gregory Robert. BA, Whitworth Coll., 1956; BD, Lexington Theol. Sem., 1959; MA, Ind. U., 1966, PhD, 1967. Ordained to ministry Christian Ch. (Disciples of Christ), 1959. Civilian dir. religious edn. U.S. Army Armor Ctr., Ft. Knox, Ky., 1960-64; assoc. regional min. Christian Ch. (Disciples of Christ), Oklahoma City, 1967-71; prof. Phillips U., Enid, Okla., 1971-76; fraternal worker div. overseas ministries Christian Ch. (Disciples of Christ), Barrow-in-Furness, Cumbria, Eng., 1976-79; Lilly vis. prof. religious edn. Christian Theol. Sem., Indpls., 1979-81; dir. edn. for mission Christian Ch. (Disciples of Christ), Indpls., 1981-87; exec. regional min. Christian Ch. (Disciples of Christ) in Can., Guelph, Ont., 1987-97; interim sr. minister Eureka (Ill.) Christian Ch., 1997-98; curator Cane Ridge Hist. Preservation Project, 1998—. Sec. Coll. Chs. of Christ in Can., Guelph, 1987-97. Editor Cane Ridge Bull., 1999—; contbr. articles to religious publs. and ency. Col., chaplain USAR ret., 1964—. Lilly Found. fellow in adult edn. Ind. U., 1964-66. Mem. Disciples of Christ Hist. Soc. (life, trustee 1990-94), Religious Edn. Assn. (bd. dirs. 1994-97), Conf. Regional Mins. and Moderators (2nd v.p.), Ch. Fin. Coun. (bd. dirs. 1995-96, exec. com. 1995), Phi Delta Kappa, Theta Phi. Democrat. Mem. Disciples Of Christ. Avocations: gardening, reading, travel, music. Office: PO Box 26 Paris KY 40362-0026 Mailing: PO Box 5226 Paris KY 40362-5226 Home: 1655 Cane Ridge Rd Bourbon County KY E-mail: canerdgmt2@aol.com.

STEFFY, JOHN RICHARD, nautical archaeologist, educator; b. Lancaster, Pa., May 1, 1924; s. Milton Grill and Zoe Minerva (Fry) S.; m. Esther Lucille Koch, Oct. 20, 1951; children: David Alan, Loren Craig. Student, Pa. Area Coll., Lancaster, 1946—47, Milw. Sch. Engring., 1947—49. Ptnr. M.G. Steffy & Sons, Denver, Pa., 1950-72; ship reconstructor Kyrenia Ship Project, Cyprus, 1972-73, Inst. Nautical Archaeology, College Station, Tex., 1973—; from lectr. to prof. anthropology Tex. A&M U., College Station, 1976-88, Sara W. and George O. Yamani prof. nautical archaeology, 1989-90, prof. emeritus, 1990—. Lectr. on ship constrn. Author: Wooden Shipbuilding and the Interpretation of Shipwrecks, 1994; co-editor: The Athlit Ram, 1991; contbr. chpts. to books and articles to profl. jours. Sec. Denver Borough Authority, Pa., 1962-72. Served with USN, 1942-45. MacArthur Found. fellow, 1985. Republican. Methodist. Office: Tex A&M U Inst Nautical Archaeology College Station TX 77845

STEFFY, MARION NANCY, state agency administrator; b. Fairport Harbor, Ohio, Sept. 23, 1937; d. Felix and Anna (Kosaber) Jackopin; 1 child, Christopher C. BA, Ohio State U., 1959; postgrad., Butler U., 1962-65, Ind. U., 1983. Exec. sec. Franklin County Mental Health Assn., Columbus, Ohio, 1959-61; caseworker Marion County Dept. Pub. Welfare, Indpls., 1961-63, supr., 1963-66, asst. chief supr., 1966-73; dir. divsn. pub. assistance Ind. Dept. Pub. Welfare, Indpls., 1973-77, asst. adminstr., 1977-85; regional adminstr. Adminstrn. Children and Families Ill. Dept. Health and Human Svcs., Chgo., 1985-98; nat. dir. Performance Intitiative, 1998—. Lectr. Ball State U., Lockyear Coll., Ind. U. Grad. Sch. Social Work; mem. Ind. Devel. Disabilities Coun., 1979-81, Ind. Cmty. Svc.s Adv. Coun., 1978-81; Ind. Child Support Adv. Coun., 1976-82, Welfare Svc. League, 1968—; chmn. rules com. Ind. Health Facilities Coun., 1974-81. Chmn. Lawrence Twp. Roundtable, 1983—. Mem. Nat. Assn. State Pub. Welfare Adminstrs., Am. Pub. Welfare Assn., Network of Women in Bus. Roman Catholic.

STEFKO, JOSEPH V. government agency administrator; married. D, SUNY, Buffalo, 2002. Sr. rsch. assoc. for govt. mgmt. Ctr. for Govtl. Rsch., Rochester, NY, 1998—2002; sr. policy analyst Buffalo Fiscal Stability Authority, 2003—. Trustee Goodwill Industries of Western N.Y., Buffalo, 2002—03. Mem.: Govt. Fin. Officers Assn., Am. Polit. Sci. Assn.

STEGALL, GARY MILES, musician, music educator; b. Rock Hill, SC, July 6, 1952; s. Linson Lee and Janet Blaney Stegall. Dr. of Musical Arts, U. of Md., College Park, 1982—90; MusM, U. of SC., Columbia, 1977—80; MusB, NC Sch. of the Arts, Winston Salem, 1973—74. Asst. prof. Coastal Carolina U., Conway, 1998—, Converse Coll. Sch. of Music, Spartanburg, SC, 1995—97. Asst. to the dir. U. of Md. Internat. Piano Festival and Competition, 1984—85. Musician (performer): (compact disc) Solo Piano Music of Joseph Jongen (Rotary Internat. Grad. Fellowship, 1983). Home: 2300 Woodward Drive Conway SC 29527 Personal E-mail: garystegall@aol.com.

STEGALL, MARK D. surgeon, medical educator; b. Lubbock, Tex., June 24, 1957; BA, Harvard Coll., 1979; postgrad., Trinity Coll., Oxford (Eng.), 1979; MD, Columbia U., 1984. Diplomate Am. Bd. Surgery. Resident in surgery Presbyn. Hosp., N.Y.C., 1984-91; post-doctoral rsch. scientist Columbia U., N.Y.C., 1987-89; fellow in transplantation U. Wis., Madison, 1991-93; asst. prof. surgery, dir. pancreas and islet transplantation U. Colo., Denver, 1993-98; dir. kidney and pancreas transplantation surgery Mayo Clinic, Rochester, Minn., 1998—, chmn. divsn. transplantation surgery, 2002—; assoc. prof. surgery Mayo Med. Sch., Rochester, 1998—. Post-Doctoral Rsch. fellow N.Y. State Diabetes Fund, 1987-88; recipient NIH-NIAID Individual Nat. Rsch. Svc. award, 1988-89, Upjohn prize N.Y. State Transplantation Soc., 1988. Mem. Am. Soc. Transplant Surgeons (Upjohn award 1989, Ortho Faculty Devel. award 1995), Soc. Univ. Surgeons, Assn. Acad. Surgery. Office: Mayo Clinic Campus Box C-318 200 1st St SW Rochester MN 55905-0002

STEGEMEIER, RICHARD JOSEPH, oil company executive; b. Alton, Ill., Apr. 1, 1928; s. George Henry and Rose Ann (Smola) S.; m. Marjorie Ann Spess, Feb. 9, 1952; children: Richard Michael, David Scott, Laura Ann, Martha Louise. BS in Petroleum Engring., U. Mo., Rolla, 1950, cert. petroleum engr. (hon.), 1981; MS in Petroleum Engring., Tex. A&M U., 1951; D of Engring. (hon.), U. Mo., Rolla, 1990; D of Philanthropy, LLD, Pepperdine U. Registered profl. engr., Calif. Various nat. and internat. mgmt. positions with Unocal Corp. (formerly Union Oil Co.), L.A., 1951—, pres. sci. and tech. div., 1979-80, sr. v.p. corp. devel., 1980-85, pres., COO, 1985-88, CEO, also chmn. bd. dirs., 1988-94, bd. dirs., 1988—. Bd. dirs. First Interstate Bancorp, Found. Health Corp., Halliburton Co., Northrop Corp., Outboard Marine Corp. Patentee in field. Bd. dirs. Calif. Econ. Devel. Corp.; bd. govs. Town Hall of Calif., The Music Ctr. of L.A. County; bd. overseers Exec. Coun. on Fgn. Diplomats, Huntington Libr.; chmn. L.A. World Affairs Coun., 1990-94; pres. World Affairs Coun. of Orange County, 1980-82; chmn. Brea (Calif.) Blue Ribbon Com., 1979-80; trustee Com. for Econ. Devel., U. So. Calif., Harvey Mudd Coll., Loyola Marymount U., U. Mo., Rolla; mem. adv. bd. Northwestern U. Kellogg Grad. Sch. of Mgmt.; bd. vis. UCLA Anderson Grad. Sch. of Mgmt., U. Mo., Rolla; mem. adv. bd. Calif. State U., Fullerton, adv. coun., Long Beach; bd. dirs. YMCA of L.A., L.A. Philharm. Assn., John Tracy Clinic; chmn. L.A. area coun. Boy Scouts of Am., Calif. C. of C. chmn., 1994; gen. campaign chmn. United Way of Greater L.A., 1990-91; trustee and immediate past pres. Hugh O'Brian Youth Found., 1993-94, L.A. Archidiocese Edn. Found. Recipient Merit award Orange County Engring. Coun., 1980, Outstanding Engr. Merit award Inst. Advancement Engring., 1981, Disting. Achievement medal Tex. A&M U., Hugh O'Brian Youth Found. Albert Schweitzer Leadership award, 1990, Human Rels. award Am. Jewish Com., 1990. Mem. AIChE (Disting. Career award So. Calif. sect. 1989), NAM (bd. dirs.), Nat. Acad. Engring., Am. Petroleum Inst. (bd. dirs., Gold medal for Achievement), Soc. Petroleum Engrs. (lectr. 1978), Nat. Petroleum Coun., 25 Yr. Club Petroleum Industry (past pres.), Calif. Bus. Roundtable, Calif. Coun. on Sci. and Tech., Calif. Club. Republican. Roman Catholic. Office: 4536 Cerro Vista Dr Anaheim CA 92807 E-mail: rjstege@sbcglobal.net.

STEGER, CHARLES WILLIAM, university administrator; b. Richmond, Va., June 16, 1947; s. Charles William and Virginia Belle (Garrett) S.; m. Janet Grey Baird, Sept. 13, 1969; children: Christopher B., David C. BArch, Va. Poly. Inst. & State U., 1970, MArch, 1971, PhD, 1978. Registered architect, Va. Project planner, architect Wiley & Wilson Inc., Lynchburg, Va., 1971-72,

mgr. urban planning dept., 1973-74; dir. Environ. Design Consortium Inc., Blacksburg, Va., 1974-85; inst. grad. urban design program Coll. Architecture and Urban Studies, Va. Poly. Inst. and State U., Blacksburg, 1974-76, chmn. grad. urban design program, 1976-81; dean Coll. Architecture and Urban Studies, Va. Poly. Inst. and State U., Blacksburg, 1981-93; acting v.p. for pub. svc. Va. Poly. Inst. and State U., Blacksburg, 1990-93, v.p. for devel. and univ. rels., 1993-99; pres. Va. Tech. U., 2000—. Bd. dirs. Va. Found. Architecture, Richmond, Innovative Tech. Authority; mem. Gov.'s Secure Va. Tech. Initiative, 2001-02; mem. Gov.'s Va. Preparedness and Security Panel, 2001-02; bd. mem. Va. Advanced Shipbuilding and Carrier Integration Ctr., 2001–. Contbr. articles to jours. in field. Bd. dirs. Hollins Coll., Roanoke, Va., 1987-96, Boswil (Switzerland) Found., 1986—, Ctr. in the Square, Roanoke, 1993-99; v.p. Va. Tech. Found., Inc., 1993-99; adv. coun. Va. Ctr. on Rural Devel., 1992—; commr. Govs. Commn. on Population Growth and Devel., Richmond, 1989-94. Fellow AIA (bd. dirs. ACSA Health Facilities Rsch. Program, Washington 1989—, ACSA Coun. on Arch. Rsch., 1987—); mem. Am. Planning Assn., Am. Inst. Cert. Planners, Commonwealth Club (Richmond, Va.), Shenandoah Club (Roanoke, Va.). Avocations: cattle farming, golf, canoeing. Office: Va Tech (0131) Pres 210 Burruss Hall Blacksburg VA 24061

STEGER, EDWARD HERMAN, chemist; b. New Orleans, Dec. 11, 1936; s. Herman Christoph and Katherine (Walther) S.; m. Amy Patricia Duvall, July 29, 1960; children: David B., Sandra E. BS, Tulane U., 1958. Analytical chemist Atlantic Rsch. Corp., Gainesville, Va., 1960-64, head control lab., 1964—. Presenter at profl. confs. Contbr. articles to Fine Particle Soc. Jour. Lt. USNR, 1958—60. Mem.: NY Acad. Scis., Am. Chem. Soc., Alpha Chi Sigma, Phi Eta Sigma, Phi Beta Kappa. Baptist. Home: 4311 Alta Vista Dr Fairfax VA 22030-5302 Office: Atlantic Rsch Corp 5945 Wellington Rd Gainesville VA 20155-1633 Office Phone: 703-754-5307.

STEGER, EVAN EVANS, III, retired lawyer; b. Indpls., Oct. 24, 1937; s. Charles Franklin and Alice (Hill) S.; m. Suzy Gillespie, July 18, 1964; children: Cynthia Anne, Emily McKee. AB, Wabash Coll., 1959; JD, Ind. U., 1962. Bar: Ind. 1962, U.S. Dist. Ct. (so. dist.) Ind. 1962, U.S. Ct. Appeals (7th cir.) 1972, U.S. Tax Ct. 1982, U.S. Supreme Ct. 1982. Assoc. Ice, Miller, Donadio and Ryan and predecessor firm Ross, McCord, Ice and Miller, Indpls., 1962-69, ptnr., 1970-96, mng. ptnr., 1996-99, ret., 2000. Fellow Am. Coll. Trial Lawyers. Democrat. Presbyterian. Office: Ice Miller Box 82001 1 American Sq Indianapolis IN 46282-0020 E-mail: essteger@comcast.net.

STEGER, JOSEPH A. university president; Formerly sr. v.p. and provost U. Cin., pres., 1984—2003, pres. emeritus, 2003—. Office: U Cin PO Box 210066 Cincinnati OH 45221-0066

STEGER, RALPH JAMES, chemist; b. Meridian, Okla., Jan. 24, 1940; s. Daniel Bose and Opal Creola (Brothers) S. BS in Chemistry and Math., Langston U., 1962. Cartographer Aeronautical Chart and Info. Ctr. ACIC USAF, St. Louis, 1962-63; lab. technician Sigma Chem. Co., St. Louis, 1963; phys. scientist U.S. Army Chem. Corps, Edgewood Arsenal, Md., 1963-65; rsch. chemist Chem. Rsch., Devel. and Engring. Ctr. SMCCR Rsch. Lab., Analytical Div., Aberdeen Proving Ground, Md., 1965-86; chemist Chem. Rsch., Devel. and Engring. Ctr. SMCCR-Detection, Detection Technology, Aberdeen Proving Ground, 1986-97. Adv. com. Garrison Gents, Balt., 1980—; ACOR monitoring govt. contracts, Balt., 1987—. Contbr. articles to profl. jours. Mem. AAAS, N.Y. Acad. Sci., Okla. Hist. Soc. Office: CBDCOM-RTE Aberdeen Proving Ground MD 21010-5423 E-mail: rjsteger@erols.com.

STEGER, WILLIAM MERRITT, federal judge; b. Dallas, Aug. 22, 1920; s. Merritt and Lottie (Reese) S.; m. Ann Hollandsworth, Feb. 14, 1948; 1 son, Merritt Reed (dec.). Student, Baylor U., 1938-41; LL.B., So. Meth. U., 1950. Bar: Tex. 1951. Pvt. practice, Longview, 1951-53; apptd. U.S. dist. atty. Eastern Dist. Tex., 1953-59; mem. firm Wilson, Miller, Spivey & Steger, Tyler, Tex., 1959-70; U.S. dist. judge Ea. Dist. Tex. U.S. Dist. Ct. (ea. dist.) Tex., Tyler, 1970—, sr. judge, 1988—. Republican candidate for gov. of Tex., 1960; for U.S. Ho. of Reps., 1962; mem. Tex. State Republican Exec. Com., 1966-69; chmn. Tex. State Republican Party, 1969-70. Pilot with ranks 2d lt. to capt. USAAF, 1942-47. Mem. State Bar Tex., Masons (32 degree, Shriner). Home: 801 Meadowcreek Dr Tyler TX 75703-3524 Office: US Courthouse PO Box 1109 Tyler TX 75710-1109

STEGMAN, MICHAEL ALLEN, city and regional planning educator; b. Bklyn., Oct. 12, 1940; s. Robert and Natalie (Ohrbach) S.; m. Nancy Weiss, Aug. 12, 1962; children— Laurie Michelle, Karen Jill BA in Polit. Sci., Bklyn. Coll., 1962; M. City Planning, U. Pa., 1964, PhD in City Planning, 1966. Asst. to assoc. prof. U. N.C., Chapel Hill, 1966-74, prof. city and regional planning, 1974—, dept. chmn., 1983—, MacRae prof. pub. policy, dir. Ctr. for Community Capitalism; asst. sec. policy, devel. & rsch. HUD, Washington, 1998—. Dep. asst. sec. research HUD, Washington, 1979-81 Author: Housing Investment in the Inner City, 1972, Dynamics of Rental Housing in New York City, 1982, Housing in New York: Study of a City, 1985, Cases in Housing Finance and Public Policy; editor: Housing and Economics: The American Dilemma, 1971 Chmn. Mayor's Task Force on Human Services, Chapel Hill, N.C., 1982; mem. Housing Policy Com. Legis. Task Force on Housing, 1981-83; mem. Govs. Commn. on Housing Options for Older Adults, N.C., 1981; chmn. Chapel Hill Housing Authority, 1973-75, Chapel Hill Redevelopment Authority, 1971-73 Mem. Am. Planning Assn., Nat. Housing and Redevel. Ofcls., Nat. Low Income Housing Coalition Office: Dept Housing & Urban Devel Policy Devel & Rsch 451 7th St SW Washington DC 20410-0002

STEGMAYER, JOSEPH HENRY, housing industry executive; b. Teaneck, N.J., Jan. 4, 1951; s. Arthur Harry and Alicia (Ward) S.; m. Delene Russell. BS in Fin., U. Louisville, 1973. Spl. projects Worthington Industries Inc., Columbus, Ohio, 1973-75, dir. investor rels., 1975-77, dir. corp. rels., 1977-80, v.p. corp. devel., 1980-82, v.p., CFO, treas., 1982-93, also bd. dirs.; pres., vice chmn. Clayton Homes, Inc., Knoxville, Tenn., 1985—98, also bd. dirs.; pres. retail & CFO Champion Enterprises, Inc., Auburn Hills, Mich., 1998-2000; chmn., CEO Centex Mfg. Housing Group, Dallas, 2000—03; chmn., pres., CEO Cavco Industries, 2003—. Editor: We've Only Scratched the Surface, 1981. Chmn. YMCA, Columbus, 1981-83; pres. Columbus Zoo, 1987-90, chmn., 1990-93; bd. dirs. Muskingum Coll., 1984-93, Knoxville Zoo, Found. of Diocese of Columbus, United Way Knoxville; fin. chmn. Ronald McDonald House, Columbus; mem. chancellor's assocs. bd. U. Tenn. Named Citizen of Yr., Columbus Jaycees, 1984; recipient Outstanding Achievement in Fin. award Phi Beta Kappa, 1984. Roman Catholic. Avocations: scuba diving, travel, investing. Office: CAVCO 1001 N Central Ave Phoenix AZ 85004

STEHLE, EDWARD RAYMOND, secondary education educator, school system administrator; b. Pitts., May 30, 1942; s. Edward August and Mary Josephine (Veverka) S.; m. Alberta McConnell; 1 child, Christian Dollison (dec.). BA, U. Pitts., 1964; MA, Columbia U., 1966, doctoral student, 1966-68. Instr. European history C.W. Post Coll., Long Island U., Greenville, N.Y., 1967-68, Middlebury (Vt.) Coll., 1968-69; history master The Lawrenceville (N.J.) Sch., Lawrenceville, N.J., 1969—, dir. day students, 1978-83, asst. dir. coll. counseling, 1983-88, chmn. history dept., 1988-94; asst. dir. The N.J. Scholars Program, Lawrenceville, 1981, dir., 1982-91, chmn. bd., 1988-96, bd. dirs., 1988—. Cons. U. Del. Sea Grant Coll., Newark, 1981-82; cons. on history of migrations Statue of Liberty-Ellis Island Found., N.Y.C., 1985-88; mem. selection com. Morris County (N.J.) Summer Opportunities for Tchrs. Program, Morristown, 1985-86; trustee Craftsbury Chamber Players, Greensboro, Vt., 1985-89; N.E.H. Coun. for Basic Edn. fellowship ind. study in the humanities, 1997. Co-author: A Guide to Programming in Basic Plus, 1975; contbr. Harper's Encyclopedia of the Modern World, 1972. Vice pres. Assoc. Mems., Ch. of Christ, Greensboro, 1974-76, pres., 1976-78. Vis. scholar Cambridge (Eng.) U., 1996. Mem. Am. Hist. Assn., Nassau Club (Princeton, N.J.), Mountainview Country Club (Greensboro, Vt.), N. Am. Conf. British Studies. Democrat. Episcopalian. Avocation: painting. Home: 2810 Main St Lawrenceville NJ 08648-1017 Office: The Lawrenceville Sch Main St Lawrenceville NJ 08620-2310 E-mail: estehle@lawrenceville.org.

STEHLIN, JOHN SEBASTIAN, JR., surgeon; b. Brownsville, Tenn., June 16, 1923; s. John Sebastian and Princess (King) S.; m. Mary Elizabeth Cleary, Sept. 19, 1950 (div. 1962); 1 child, Mary Cleary. Student, Vanderbilt U., 1941-42, Notre Dame U., 1943-44; MD, Med. Coll. Wis., 1947. Diplomate: Am. Bd. Surgery. Intern Milw. Hosp., 1947-48; resident pathology Bapt. Hosp., Memphis, 1948-49; resident surgery Milw. Hosp., 1949-52; fellow surgery Lahey Clinic, Boston, 1952-53; sr. fellow surgery U. Tex., M.D. Anderson Hosp. and Tumor Inst., Houston, 1955-56; fellow surgery Lahey Clinic, Boston, 1956; mem. surg. staff U. Tex., M.D. Anderson Hosp. and Tumor Inst., Houston, 1957-67, asst. surgeon, 1957-60, asso. surgeon, 1961-67; asst. prof. surgery U. Tex. Postgrad. Sch. Medicine, Houston, 1957-60, asso. prof., 1961-63; asso. prof. surgery U. Tex. Postgrad. Sch. Medicine (Grad. Sch. Biomed. Scis.), 1963-67; clin. asso. prof. surgery Baylor Coll. Medicine, Houston, 1967—; mem. surg. staff St. Joseph Hosp., Houston, 1967—. Hon. prof. faculty medicine U. Republic Uruguay, 1965; founder, sci. dir. Stehlin Found. Cancer Research, Houston, 1969— Contbr. over 100 articles to sci. jours. Served to capt. USAF, 1953-55. Recipient humanitarian award B'nai B'rith, 1982; named to City of Houston Hall of Fame, 1985 Fellow ACS; mem. Am. Assn. Cancer Research, AAAS, AMA, Cancer Assn. Argentina (hon.), Cancer Soc. Chile (hon.), Internat. Platform Assn., Soc. Surg. Oncology, Inc., Pan Am. Med. Assn., Soc. Dermatology Uruguay (hon.), Surg. Soc. Chile (hon.), Royal Soc. Medicine, Western Surg. Assn., Southwestern Surg. Congress, So. Med. Assn., Tex. Med. Assn., Tex. Surg. Soc., N.Y. Acad. Scis., Salem Surg. Soc. (hon.), Phoenix Surg. Soc. (hon.), Harris County Med. Soc., Houston Surg. Soc., Am. Judicature Soc. Office: 1315 Calhoun St Ste 1800 Houston TX 77002-8234

STEHMAN, FREDERICK BATES, gynecologic oncologist, educator; b. Washington, July 20, 1946; s. Vernon Andrew and Elizabeth Coats (Bates) S.; m. Helen Sellinger, July 17, 1971; children— Christine Renee, Eileen Patricia, Andrea Kathleen, Lara Michelle. A.B., U. Mich., 1968, M.D., 1972. Diplomate Am. Bd. Ob-gyn. Resident in ob-gyn. U. Kans. Med. Ctr., Kansas City, 1972-75, resident in surgery, 1975-77; fellow in gynecol. oncology UCLA, 1977-79; asst. prof., attending staff Ind. U. Med. Ctr., Indpls., 1979-83, assoc. prof., 1983-87, prof., 1987—, chief gynecol. oncology, 1984-88, interim chmn., 1992-94, chair 1994—; chief ob-gyn service Wishard Meml. Hosp., Indpls., 1987-95. Author: (with B.J. Masterson and R.P. Carter) Gynecologic Oncology for Medical Students, 1975; also articles. Nat. Cancer Inst. grantee, 1981-89. Fellow Am. Coll. Obstetricians and Gynecologists, ACS (chpt. dir. 1984-92); mem. AMA, Am. Soc. Clin. Oncology, Am. Cancer Soc., Am. Gynecology and Obstetrics Soc., Ind. Med. Assn., Assn. Profs. Gynecology and Obstetrics, Central Assn. Obstetricians and Gynecologists, Gynecol. Oncology Group, K.E. Krantz Soc., Marion County Med. Soc., Soc. Gynecol. Oncologists, Western Assn. Gynecol. Oncologists, Phi Chi. Office: Ind U Med Ctr 550 University Blvd # 2440 Indianapolis IN 46202-5149

STEHN, LORRAINE STRELNICK, physician; b. Richmond, Ind., Aug. 27, 1950; d. Daniel H. and Eleanor Gayle (Robertson) Strelnick; m. Thomas Veasey Stehn, June 16, 1973; children: Alexander Veasey, Andrew Thomas. BA, Carleton Coll., 1972; DO, Coll. Osteo. Medicine & Surg., 1976. Diplomate Am. Bd. Family Practice. Intern Pontiac (Mich.) Osteo. Hosp., 1976-77; vol. med. officer U.S. Peace Corps, Swaziland, 1977-79; resident family practice St. Mary's Hosp., Port Arthur, Tex., 1980-82; family practice osteo. medicine Aransas Pass, Tex., 1982—; med. adv. Christian Svc. Ctr., Aransas Pass, Tex., 1983—. Chief staff Coastal Bend Hosp., Aransas Pass, 1985, 90, 95, North Bay Hosp., 2003. Pres. bd. dirs. Corpus Christi (Tex.) Chorale, 1995-96; pres. Aransas Pass H.S. Band Booster, 1998-2000. Recipient Svc. award Aransas Pass Jr. High, 1984. Fellow Am. Acad. Family Practice (pres. bd. dirs. profl. counseling svcs.); mem. Tex. Med. Assn., SPAR County Med. Soc. (pres. 2001-2002). Democrat. Home: 1613 S Saunders St Aransas Pass TX 78336-3107 E-mail: stehn@cableone.net.

STEIB, JAMES TERRY, bishop; b. May 17, 1940; Ordained priest Roman Cath. Ch., 1967. Titular bishop, Fallaba, 1983; aux. bishop St. Louis, 1983; consecrated bishop, 1984; bishop Diocese of Memphis, 1993—. Address: Diocese of Memphis PO Box 341669 Memphis TN 38184-1669

STEIDER, DORIS, artist; b. Decatur, Ill., Apr. 10, 1924; d. Rudy C. and Helen (Regan) Sleeter; m. Robert E. Steider, Nov. 16, 1944 (div.); children: Kristen (Mrs. Gerald Latham), Robert S., Tim D; m. Carroll B. McCampbell, May 19, 1972. BS, Purdue U.; MA, U. N.Mex. Exhibited in more than 190 maj. juried shows including Smithsonian Instn., Washington, Gilcrease Inst., Tulsa, Army Traveling Print Shows, 1963, 64, Witte Mus. Western Art, San Antonio, Mont. State Hist. Soc. Mus., Helena, Mus. N.Mex. Biennials, N.Mex. State Fair Profl. Show, Nat. Art Shows, La Junta, Colo., 1978, 81, 83, Nebraskaland Days Invitational Art Exhbn., 1976—; exhibited in over 100 one-woman shows; represented in permanent collections Holt Rinehart and Winston, Purdue U. Galleries, Time Inc., Loewen Group British Columbia, West Tex. Mus., U. N.Mex. Art Mus., N.Mex. State Fair Collection, Albuquerque Pub. Libr., over 2600 in pvt. collections; Book (by Mary Carroll Nelson) A Vision of Silence: The Egg Tempera Landscapes of Doris Steider, 1997. Mem. Albuquerque Fine Arts Adv. Bd., 1966-72; chmn. standards com. N.Mex. Arts and Crafts Bd., 1964-70; chmn. invitational rev. bd. SW Arts and Crafts Fair, 1977-78. Doris Steider St. named in her honor Albuquerque, 1989; recipient over 85 local, regional, nat. and internat. awards, Disting. Alumni honor Purdue U., 2000. Mem.: Soc. of Layerists in Multi-Media. Home: 12905 Sunrise Trail Pl NE Albuquerque NM 87111-8194 Office Phone: 505-797-1979. Personal E-mail: steiderart@cs.com.

STEIER, JEFFREY DAVID, neurologist; b. Queens, N.Y., Mar. 21, 1952; s. Morton and Ruth Steier; m. Elizabeth Schleeter, Aug. 6, 1983; children: Nathan, Julia, Emma. BA, U. Del., 1973; MD, SUNY, Buffalo, 1978. Diplomate Am. Acad. Neurology, Am. Bd. Elective Medicine, cert. Clin. Neurophysiology. Resident U. Minn. Mayo Clinic, Mpls., 1978—84; mem. staff Scottsdale Neurol. Cons., Ariz., 1984—. Mem. nat. bd. Myasthenia Gravis, Phoenix, mem. Ariz. bd.; mem. Stroke Coun., 2000—. Mem.: Am. Clinic Neurophysiology Soc., Am. Assn. Sleep Medicine, Am. Assn. Neurology, Am. Assn. Electrodiagnostic Medicine, Am. Epilepsy Soc. Avocations: astrophotography, astronomy. Office: Scottsdale Neurological Cons 10210 N 92d St 352 Scottsdale AZ 85258

STEIER, MICHAEL EDWARD, cardiac surgeon; b. N.Y.C., Mar. 22, 1942; s. Philip (deceased) and Gertrude S.; m. Sheila Elaine Finkelstein, June 9, 1963; children: Douglas, James, Lauren. BA, Long Island U., 1964; MD, Univ. Health Scis., Chgo., 1968. Diplomate Am. Bd. Surgery, Am. Bd. Thoracic Surgery. Resident in gen. surgery St. Vincent's Hosp., N.Y.C., 1969-73; resident in thoracic surgery Mayo Clinic, Rochester, Minn., 1973-75; cardiac surgeon S.W. Fla. Regional Med. Ctr., Ft. Myers, Fla., 1975—, Lee Meml. Hosp., Ft. Myers, 1975—, Cape Coral (Fla.) Hosp., 1977—, Naples (Fla.) Cmty. Hosp., 1996—; pres. Cardiac Surg. Assocs. West Fla., Ft. Myers; ret. Chief surgery, S.W. Fla. Regional Med. Ctr., Ft. Myers, 1980-82, pres. med. staff, 1982; cons. Naples Cmty. Hosp., 1996—. Capt., USAR, 1969-78. Fellow ACS, Am. Coll. Chest Physicians, Am. Coll. Cardiology; mem. Soc. for Thoracic Surgeons, N.Y. Acad. Scis., Cardiac Surg. Assn. S.W. Fla. (pres. 1993-99), Explorers Club. Office: Cardiac Surgical Assocs SW Fla 2675 Winkler Ave Fort Myers FL 33901-9342

STEIGBIGEL, NEAL H. medical educator; b. Bklyn., N.Y., Oct. 8, 1934; s. Samuel and Lillian I. Steigbigel; children: Matthew A., Amy E. AB, Princeton U., 1956; MD, Harvard U., 1960. Lic. internal medicine Am. Bd. of Internal Medicine, infectious diseases Am. Bd. of Internal Medicine. Intern, asst. resident Harvard Med. Unit, Boston City Hosp., Boston, 1960—62, sr. resident, 1964—65; assoc. lab. chem. pharmacology Medicine Br. Nat. Cancer Inst., Bethesda, 1962—64; fellow in infectious diseases Harvard Med. Unit, Thorndike Meml. Lab., Boston City Hosp., 1965—67; asst. and assoc. in medicine Beth Israel Hosp. and Harvard Med. Sch., Boston, 1967—69; from asst. prof. to assoc. prof. of medicine Albert Einstein Coll. of Medicine, Bronx, 1969—80; founder, head divsn. of infectious diseases Montefiore Med. Ctr., Bronx, 1969—2000; dir. fellowship tng. program in infectious diseases Albert Einstein Coll. of Medicine and Montefiore Med. Ctr., Bronx, 1969—2001; prof. of medicine Albert Einstein Coll. of Medicine, Bronx, 1980—2002; prof. of medicine divsn. of infectious diseases NYU Sch. of Medicine, N.Y.C., 2002—. Attending physician Montefiore Med. Ctr., Bronx, 1969—; adv. bd. The Med. Letter, New Rochelle, NY, 1976—94, New Rochelle, 2003—, contbg. editor, 1994—2003; dir. Ctr. for Health Info. Preparedness NYU. Sch. of Medicine, N.Y.C., 2002—03; attending physician N.Y. Vets. Affairs Med. Ctr., N.Y.C., 2002—, Bellevue Hosp. Ctr., N.Y.C., 2002—, NYU. Med. Ctr., N.Y.C., 2002—; vis. prof. medicine Albert Einstein Coll. Medicine, Bronx, 2002—. Lt. comdr. USPHS, 1962—64. Recipient Milbank Meml. scholarship prize, Princeton U., 1955. Fellow: ACP, Infectious Diseases Soc. of Am.; mem.: Harvey Soc., Am. Soc. for Clin. Rsch., Am. Soc. for Microbiology, N.Y. Soc. of Infectious Diseases (pres. 1998—99), Phi Beta Kappa. Achievements include research in Activity of Antimicrobial Agents; Heterosexual transmission of AIDS; Relationship of S. bovis bacteremia and colonic neoplasms. Avocations: bicycling, sailing. Office: NY Vets Affairs Med Ctr Medl Svc-111 423 E 23 St New York NY 10010 Office Phone: 212-686-7500 4470. Personal E-mail: nhs427@earthlink.net. Business E-Mail: neal.steigbigel@med.va.gov.

STEIGBIGEL, ROY THEODORE, epidemiologist, educator, research scientist; b. Bklyn., Nov. 23, 1941; s. Samuel and Lillian I. (Parker) S.; m. Julia Ann Enterline, June 10, 1967 (div. 1983), children: Keith D., Glenn N.; m. Sidonie Ann Morrison, Oct. 15, 1985; 1 child, Andrew M. BA, Carleton Coll., 1962; MD, U. Rochester, 1966. Diplomate Am. Bd. Internal Medicine, Am. Bd. Infectious Disease. Resident U. Rochester, N.Y., 1966-68, Stanford U., Palo Alto, Calif., 1970-71, fellow, 1971-73; from asst. to assoc. prof. U. Rochester, N.Y., 1973-83; prof. SUNY, Stony Brook, 1983—. Mem. adv. bd. infectious disease U.S. Pharmacopea, Rockville, Md., 1980—; mem. adv. panels NIH, Bethesda, Md., 1985-87. Contbr. over 15 chpts. to books and over 100 articles to profl. jours. Served in USPHS, 1968-70. Fellow NIH, 1971-73, grantee, 1985—. Fellow ACP, Infectious Disease Soc. Am. Office: SUNY Stony Brook Sch Medicine Hsc T 15 080 Stony Brook NY 11794-8153 Business E-Mail: roy.steigbigel@stonybrook.edu.

STEIGER, PAUL ERNEST, newspaper editor, journalist; b. N.Y.C., Aug. 15, 1942; s. Ernest and Mary Agnes (Walsh) Steiger; m. Heidi Brine, Nov. 23, 1985 (div.); children: Isabelle Amanda, William Ernest; m. Wendy Brandes, July 22, 2001; children from previous marriage: Erika Maren, Laura Arlene. BA econ., Yale U., 1964. Staff reporter Wall Street Jour., San Francisco, 1966-68, asst. mng. editor N.Y.C., 1983-85, dep. mng. editor, 1985-92, mng. editor, 1991—, v.p., 1992—; bus. writer Los Angeles Times, 1968-71, econ. corr. Washington bur., 1971-78, bus. editor L.A., 1978-83. Mem. Pulitzer Prize Bd., 1999. Co-author: (book) The 70's Crash and How to Survive It, 1970. Recipient G.M. Loeb award, UCLA, 1971, 1974, 1978, John Hancock award, 1971, George Beveridge Editor Yr. award, Nat. Press Found., 2001, Leadership award, Am. Soc. Newspaper Editors', 2002, Gerald Loeb award for Lifetime Acheivement, John E. Anderson Sch. Mgmt., UCLA, 2002, Columbia Journalism award, Columbia U. Sch. Journalism, 2002; Poynter Fellow, Yale U., 2001—02. Office: Wall Street Journal Dow Jones & Co Inc 200 Liberty St New York NY 10281-1003*

STEIGERWALD, DOUGLAS GARDINER, economics professor; b. Torrance, Calif., June 19, 1959; s. Jack and Eileen Steigerwald; m. Julia Lowell, May 22, 1995; 1 child, Gregory. PhD, U. Calif., Berkeley, 1988. Rsch. asst., bd. govs. Fed. Res., Washington, 1981-83; prof. econs. U. Calif., Santa Barbara, 1988—. Assoc. editor Econometric Revs., 1999—. Regents jr. faculty fellowship U. Calif., 1991. Office: Econs Dept U Calif Santa Barbara CA 93105

STEIGERWALD, LOUIS JOHN, III, corporate executive; b. Syracuse, NY, Dec. 24, 1953; s. Louis John Jr. and Virginia (Irving) S.; m. Mary Rescorl, May 31, 1980; children: Amy Elizabeth, Louis John IV. BS, St. Lawrence U., 1976. Salesperson Cathedral Candle Co., Syracuse, 1976-80, v.p., 1980-2001, pres., 2001—, also bd. dirs. Account exec. United Way Ctrl. NY, Syracuse, 1982-83, sect. chmn., 1984-85; active Boy Scouts Am., 1992-2003. Mem. Nat. Ch. Goods Assn. (bd. dirs. 1990-2000, pres. 1997, 98), Nat. Candle Assn. (bd. dirs. 1989-99), Ea. Ch. Goods Guild, Onondaga Hist. Assn. (bd. dirs. 2004—). Avocations: golf, tennis, woodworking, skiing, music. Office: Cathedral Candle Co 510 Kirkpatrick St Syracuse NY 13208-2100

STEIGMAN, ANDREW L. academic dean; b. N.Y.C., Aug. 30, 1933; s. Nathan and Sarah (Levine) S.; m. Meryl Fialka, June 20, 1959; children: Daria H., Jonathan S. AB summa cum laude, Princeton U., 1954; postgrad., London Sch. Econs., 1954-55, Am. U., Washington, 1958-60. Fgn. svc. officer Dept. State, various locations, 1958-69; first sec. Dept. State, U.S. Embassy, Paris, 1969-72, polit. counselor Lagos, Nigeria, 1972-75, U.S. ambassador to Gabon Libreville, Gabon, 1975-77; dir. nat. intelligence tasking office Intelligence Community Staff, Washington, 1978-80; dep. asst. sec. for personnel Dept. State, Washington, 1981-84; asst. dean/prof. internat. relations Georgetown U., Washington, 1985—, assoc. dean, 1996. Vis. fellow Woodrow Wilson Fellowship Found., Princeton, 1987-93; mem. edn. com. Atlantic Council, Washington, 1989-98. Author: The Foreign Service of the United States, 1985. With U.S. Army, 1955-57. Wilbur Carr award, U.S. Dept. State, 1985. Mem.: Am. Fgn. Svc. Assn., Am. Hist. Assn. Office: Georgetown U Sfs Icc # 301 Washington DC 20057-0001 E-mail: steigman@georgetown.edu.

STEIL, GEORGE KENNETH, SR., lawyer; b. Darlington, Wis., Dec. 16, 1924; s. George John and Laura (Donahoe) S.; m. Mavis Elaine Andrews, May 24, 1947; children: George Kenneth, John R., MIchelle Steil Bryski, Marcelaine Steil-Zimmermann. Student, Platteville State Tchrs. Coll., 1942-43; JD, U. Wis., Madison, 1950. Bar: Wis. 1950, U.S. Tax Ct. 1971, U.S. Dist. Ct. (western dist.) Wis. 1950. Assoc. J. G. McWilliams, Janesville, 1950-53; ptnr. McWilliams and Steil, Janesville, 1954-60, Brennan, Steil, Basting & MacDougall, Janesville, 1960-72; pres. Brennan, Steil & Basting (S.C., and predecessor), Janesville, 1972—. Lectr. law U. Wis., 1974; bd. dirs. Acuity Ins. Co., Sheboygan, Wis., Acuity Bank, SSB, Tomah, Wis., chmn. 2000—; trustee, bd. dirs. Roman Cath. Diocese of Madison; mem. Wis. Supreme Ct. Bd. Atty. Profl. Responsibility, 1982-87, chmn., 1984-87; chmn. gov.'s adv. coun. jud. selection State of Wis., 1987-92; chmn. Wis. Lottery Bd., 1987-90. Bd. dirs. St. Coletta Sch. for Exceptional Children, Jefferson, Wis., 1972-76, 78-84, 86-89, chmn., 1982-83; bd. regents U. Wis., 1990-97, pres., 1992-94; bd. dirs. U. Wis. Hosp. Authority, 1996—2004, chmn., 2002-04; bd. dirs., chair U. Wis. Med. Found., 1996-99. Recipient Disting. Svc. award U. Wis. Law Alumni, 1991, Cath. Leadership awrd Diocese of Madison, 1998; named Knight of St. Gregory, Pope John Paul II, 1997. Fellow Am. Bar Found. (life), Am. Coll. Trust and Estate Counsel; mem. ABA, Jamesville Area C. of C. (pres. 1970-71), State Bar Wis. (pres. 1977-78), Wis. Bar Found. (bd. dirs. 1976-2003, Charles L. Goldberg Disting. Svc. award 1990). Roman Catholic. Home: 2818 Cambridge Ct Janesville WI 53545-2797 Office: PO Box 1148 1 E Milwaukee St Janesville WI 53545 Office Phone: 608-756-4141. Business E-Mail: gsteilsr@brennansteil.com.

STEILING, DANIEL PAUL, retired railroad conductor, writer, geographer, educator; b. San Jose, Calif., June 28, 1944; s. Paul Henry and Lois Kathryn (Barton) S.; m. Mary Ellen Scioneaux, Apr. 30, 2004. Right of way agt. Caltrans - Calif. State Dept. Transp., San Francisco, 1969-70; owner Dan's Bicycle Shop, Santa Cruz, Calif., 1970-83; soil inspector Soil Svcs. Inc., San Jose, 1983-84; sr. mfg. specialist disk products divsn. IBM, San Jose, 1984-92; R.R. condr. Amtrak, San Jose, 1993-97; ret., 1997; substitute tchr. history, geography, sci. Murrieta Valley Unified Sch. Dist., 1999—2001; instr. geography Riverside C.C., 2001—. Author: Operation and Maintenance of TRACOR Thickness Measuring Guage (Liquid Nitrogen Cooled), 1987. With USAF, 1966-68. Mem. Assn. Am. Geographers, Antique Auto Club Am., Fallbrook Vintage Car Club, Ford Falcon Club Am., Early Ford v/8 Club Am. Avocations: bicycle touring, photography, antique auto restoration. Home: 42033 Via Renate Temecula CA 92591

STEIMAN, H. ROBERT, dean, dental educator; BS, ND State U., 1964; MS, Wayne State U., 1967, PhD in physiology, 1969; DDS, U. Detroit, 1973; MS in endodontics, Ind. U., 1979. Diplomate Am. Bd. Endodontics. Chmn. dept.

physiology, dept. basic scis. U. Detroit-Mercy Sch. Dentistry, named chmn. dept. endodontics, 1980, interim dean, 2000—01, dean, 2001—. Office: 8200 W Outer Dr Box 98 Detroit MI 48219*

STEIN, ANTHONY C. medical educator, researcher; PhD, Saybrook Grad. Sch., 1976—85. Pres. and tech. dir. Safety Rsch. Associates, Inc., La Canada, Calif., 1986—; adj. assoc. prof. Kans. U. Med. Ctr., Kans. City, Kans., 1989—. Mem. Transp. Rsch. Bd. Com. on Alcohol, Other Drugs and Driving, Transp. Rsch. Bd., Com. on Bicycle Transp., Internat. Coun. on Alcohol, Drugs and Traffic Safety, SAE Intelligent Transp. Systems Com. on Human Factors and Safety, Adv. Group to the U.S. Del. to the ISO on Human Factors Standards for Intelligent Transp. Systems. Del. Arroyo Verdugo Non-motorized Transp. Commn., La Canada, Calif., 1999—2000; mem. La Can. Gen. Plan Adv. Com., La Canada, Calif., 1990—91; past chmn. La Can. Vol. Emergency Response Team, La Canada, Calif., 2001—04, chmn., 1997—2000. Recipient Arch T. Coldwell award, Soc. of Automotive Engineers, 1991; Calif. State Scholar, State of Calif., 1974, 1975. Mem.: Assn. for the Advancement of Automotive Medicine, Americal Psychol. Assn., Human Factors and Ergonomics Soc., LA Chpt.

STEIN, ARTHUR OSCAR, retired pediatrician, small business owner; b. Bklyn., Apr. 3, 1932; s. Irving I. and Sadie (Brander) S.; m. Judith Lenore Hurwitz, Aug. 27, 1955; children: Susan, Jeffrey, Benjamin. AB, Harvard U., 1953; MD, Tufts U., 1957; postgrad., U. Chgo., 1963—66; BFA, San Jose State U., 1998. Intern U. Chgo. Hosps., 1957-58, resident, 1958-59, NY Hosp. Cornell U. Med. Ctr., 1959-61; pediatrician, 1963-70, Healthguard Med. Group, San Jose, Calif., 1970 72, Permanente Med. Group, San Jose, 1972-95; ret., 1995; owner Artform Photography, 2001—. Instr. pediat. Cornell U. Med. Sch., 1960-61, U. Chgo. Sch. Medicine, 1963-66, asst. prof., 1966-70; tchg. asst. photography San Jose State U., 1995—. Author: (CD) The Sketch Class. V.p. Jewish congregation 1969-70, pres. 1972-73. Capt., M.C., AUS, 1961-63. USPHS Postdoctoral fellow, 1963-66. Fellow Am. Acad. Pediat., Santa Clara County Med. Assn., Calif. Med. Assn.; mem. Light and Shadow Camera Club (pres. San Jose 1978-80), Ctrl. Coast Counties Camera Club (v.p. 1980-81, pres. 1981-82), Santa Clara Camera Club (pres. 1991). Achievements include co-discovery (with Glyn Dawson) of genetic disease lactosylceramidosis. Home: 8656 Solera Dr San Jose CA 95135 E-mail: artform2@pacbell.net.

STEIN, BARRY EDWARD, medical educator; BA, CUNY, Queens, 1966, MA, 1969; PhD, CUNY, 1971. Prof. dept. physiology Med. Coll. Va.-Va. Commonwealth U., Richmond, 1982-94, affil. prof., 1994—; prof., chair dept. neurobiology and anatomy Wake Forest U Sch. Medicine, Winston-Salem, N.C., 1994—. Bd. trustees The Gwendolyn Hardy Williams and Oliver Williams Found., Inc., 1992—; lectr. in field. Co-author: The Merging of the Senses, 1993; contbr. chpts. to books including The Cognitive Neurosciences, 1995, 99, Electrophysiology of Vision, 1991, The Development of Intersensory Perception: Comparative Perspectives, 1994, others; co-editor: The Handbook of Multisensory Processes, 2004; mem. editl. bd. Somatosensory and Motor Rsch., Jour. Cognitive Neuroscience, The Behavioral and Brain Sciences; contbr. numerous articles to profl. pubs. including Jour. Neurophysiology, Jour. Neurosci., Sci., Jour. Comparative Neurology, others Home: 1825 Georgia Ave Winston Salem NC 27104-3101 Office: Wake Forest Sch Medicine Med Ctr Blvd Winston Salem NC 27157-0001 E-mail: bestein@wfubmc.edu.

STEIN, BENJAMIN J. television personality, writer, lawyer, economist; b. Washington, Nov. 25, 1944; s. Herbert and Mildred (Fishman) S.; m. Alexandra Denman, June 22, 1968 (div. 1974)l m. Alexandra Denman, 1977; 1 child. BA, Columbia U., 1966; LLB, Yale U., 1970. Bar: Conn. Trial lawyer FTC, Washington, 1970-72; speech writer The White House, Washington, 1973-74; columnist Wall St. Jour., NYC, 1974-76; writer, commentator, columnist LA Herald-Examiner, 1978-87; TV personality Win Ben Stein's Money Comedy Ctrl., 1996—; host Turn Ben Stein On Comedy Ctrl., 1999—2001. Fin. cons. LAACO, Inc., LA; contbg. editor Am. Spectator, 1980—; law and econs. tchr. Pepperdine, Malibu, 1992—; adj. prof. Am. U., Wash., DC, U. Calif. Santa Cruz Author: On The Brink. 1977, The View from Sunset Boulevard, 1978, DREEMZ, 1978, Moneypower, 1980, 'Ludes, 1981, Financial Passages, 1986, A License to Steal, 1992, Tommy and Me, 1999, How To Ruin Your Life; author numerous articles on leveraged buy-outs and other fin. frauds for Barrons, 1984—; syndicated columnist King Features Syndicate; regular columnist LA Mag., NY Mag., E! Online; contbr. Wash. Post, Wall St. Jour.; guest speaker on fin. Fox News Channel; co-creater: (TV series) Fernwood Tonight; actor: (films) Ferris Bueller's Day Off, 1986 (ranked as one of 50 most famous scenes in Am. films), Planes, Trains, and Automobiles, 1987, Ghostbusters II, 1989, Soapdish, 1991, Honeymoon in Vegas, 1992, My Girl, 1994, Richie Rich, 1994, (TV series) The Wonder Years, 1988; voice actor: (TV series) Animaniacs, 1993, Freakazoid, 1995, The Mask, 1995. Recipient Emmy award for Best Game Show Host, 1999. Mem. Writers Guild Am., Screen Actors' Guild, Am. Fedn. TV and Radio Actors, Yak Club NYC, Friars, LA Athletic Club, Calif. Yacht Club. Republican. Jewish. Office: 8787 Shoreham Dr West Hollywood CA 90069-2231 E-mail: benstein@aol.com.*

STEIN, BENNETT MUELLER, neurosurgeon; b. N.Y.C., Feb. 2, 1931; s. Walter Charles and Marjorie Clare (Bennett) S.; m. Doreen Holmes, May 28, 1955 (dec. 1984); children: Susan, Marjorie; m. Bonita Soontit, Sept. 19, 1987; 1 child, Bennett Charles. AB, Dartmouth Coll., 1952; MD, C.M., McGill U., Montreal, Que., Can., 1955. Diplomate: Am. Bd. Neurol. Surgery, Nat. Bd. Med. Examiners. Rotating intern U.S. Naval Hosp., St. Albans, N.Y., 1955-56; Fulbright scholar Inst. Neurology, Nat. Hosp., London, 1958-59; asst. resident in surgery Presbyn. Hosp., N.Y.C., 1959-60, asst. resident in neurosurgery, 1960-63, chief resident, 1963-64; spl. fellow neuroanatomy Nat. Inst. Neurol. Diseases and Blindness, 1964-66; asso. in neurol. Surgery Columbia U. Coll. Phys. and Surgeons, 1964-68, mem. faculty, 1968—, Byron Stookey prof. neurol. surgery, 1980-96; prof. emeritus neurol. surgery Columbia U. Coll. Physicians and Surgeons, 1996—; dir. service neurol. surgery Presbyn. Hosp., 1980-96. Prof. neurol. surgery, chmn. dept. Tufts-New Eng. Med. Center, Boston, 1971-80; dir. Am. Bd. Neurol. Surgeons, 1988—. Author articles in field; mem. editorial bds. profl. jours. Served as officer M.C. USNR, 1956-58. Fellow A.C.S.; mem. Am. Assn. Anatomists, AMA, Acad. Neurol. Surgeons, Congress Neurol. Surgeons, Am. Assn. Neurol. Surgeons, Am. Acad. Neurol. Surgeons, Soc. Neurol. Surgeons, Cajal Club, Brazilian Neurol. Soc. (corr.), N.Y. State Neurosurg. Soc., New Eng. Neurosurg. Soc., Mass. Med. Soc., Boston Surg. Soc., Boston Soc. Psychiatry and Neurology, Sigma Xi, Alpha Omega Alpha, Alpha Kappa Kappa. Lutheran.

STEIN, BERNARD ALVIN, business consultant; b. Winnipeg, Can., June 4, 1923; s. Herman Louis and Rebecca (Harris) S.; m. Dorothy Lock, Jan. 1, 1942; 1 dau., Marilynn Stein Lakein. Vice-pres. food drug div. Giant Food, Inc., Washington, 1951-69; v.p., gen. mgr. Read Drug Stores, Balt., 1969-70; pres. Scotty Stores div. Sav-A-Stop, Jacksonville, Fla., 1970-71; pres., gen. mgr. Liberal Markets, Dayton, Ohio, 1971-72; pres. Pueblo Supermarkets, San Juan, P.R., 1972-74, Hills Supermarkets, Brentwood, N.Y., 1974-75, Allied Supermarkets, Detroit, 1976-78, Chatham Supermarkets, Detroit, 1978-81; CEO Network Assocs., Chgo., 1981-92; bus. cons. Balt., 1992—; pres. Jewelery Markdowns, Inc., 2003—. Pres. Jewelry website business, 2003—. Mem. Presdl. Com. for Emergency Food Controls, 1969. Served with USAAF, 1943-45. Decorated Air medal. Home: 43 Stone Pine Ct Baltimore MD 21208-1038 Office Phone: 866-486-2597.

STEIN, BERNARD L. journalist; b. Cleve. m. Marguerite Adams; 1 child, Anna. BA in Lit., Columbia U., 1963; postgrad., U. Calif., Berkeley, 1964—66; DHL (hon.), Manhattan Coll., 1999. Editor Riverdale Press, 1978—, co-pub., 1980—. Mem. team of scholars editing Mark Twain's writing for pub. U. Calif. Press; James H. Ottaway Disting. vis. prof. SUNY, New Paltz, NY, 2002. Named Writer of the Yr., N.Y. Press Assn., 1986; recipient First Amendment award, Soc. Profl. Journalists, 1989, Pulitzer Prize for editl. writing, 1998. Office: c/o Riverdale Press 6155 Broadway Bronx NY 10471-3136 Office Phone: 718-543-6065.

STEIN, DANIEL ALAN, public interest lawyer; b. Washington, Mar. 9, 1955; s. Edward Seymour and Ann Rose Stein; m. Sharon McCloe, Oct. 18, 1986; children: Claire, Corrieanne. BA, Ind. U., 1977; JD, Cath. U. Am., 1984. Bar: D.C. 1984, U.S. Dist. Ct. D.C. 1985, U.S. Ct. Appeals (D.C. cir.) 1987, U.S. Tax Ct. 1987, Md. 2002, U.S. Dist. Ct. Md. 2003. Profl. staff mem. select com. on narcotics abuse and control U.S. Ho. of Reps., Washington, 1977-81; pvt. practice Washington, 1984-89; exec. dir. Immigration Reform Law Inst., Washington, 1986-88, Fedn. for Am. Immigration Reform, Washington, 1982—86, 1989—2004, pres., 2004—. Mem. adv. bd. Social Contract periodical, Petosky, Mich., 1990—. Mem. Capitol Hill Club, Nat. Press Club. Republican. Avocations: trombone, american history, western civilization, jazz, antique books. Office: Fedn for Am Immigration Reform 1666 Connecticut Ave NW Ste 400 Washington DC 20009-1039 Office Phone: 202-328-7004.

STEIN, DANIEL L. physicist, educator; b. N.Y.C., Aug. 19, 1953; s. Nathaniel and Ruth Stein; m. Bernadette LaPolla, June 22, 1986; children: Laura R., Emily F. BSc, Brown U., 1975; PhD, Princeton (N.J.) U., 1979. Asst. prof. of physics Princeton U., Princeton, NJ, 1981—87; from assoc. prof. of physics to prof. U. of Ariz., Tucson, 1987—93, prof. physics, 1993—, head, dept. of physics, 1995—. Cons. Inst. for Def. Analyses, Alexandria, Va., 1985—, mem. def. sci. study group, 1985—88; external faculty and sci. bd. Santa Fe (N.Mex.) Inst., 1988—; gen. mem. Aspen (Colo.) Ctr. for Physics, 1987—. Recipient Undergraduate Physics prize, Brown U., 1975, Vision 2000 award, UA Commn. on the Status of Women, 1999; fellow, Princeton U., 1978—79, Alfred P. Sloan Found., 1985—89; scholar Nat. Merit Scholar, Nat. Merit Scholarship Bd., 1971. Fellow: Am. Phys. Soc.; mem.: AAAS, N.Y. Acad. of Scis. Office: Dept of Physics University of Arizona 1118 E Fourth St Tucson AZ 85721 E-mail: dls@physics.arizona.edu.

STEIN, DAVID ERIC, physicist, defense analyst; b. Jacksonville, Fla., Jan. 13, 1950; s. Stanley Wolfe and Dorothy Jean (Lilley) S. BS with high honors (J. Hillis Miller Me, U. Fla., 1971, postgrad. (Ford Found. fellow), 1971-72, MS in Physics, 1977; grad., Air Command and Staff Coll., 1982, Naval War Coll., 1995, Air War Coll., 1996. Instr. dept. physics U. Fla., Gainesville, 1971-74, NSF rsch. asst., 1974-76; commd. 1st lt. U.S. Army, 1977, advanced through grades to lt. col., 1994; maj. USAF HQ Air Force Systems Command, Andrews AFB, Md., 1992; lt. col. Air Force Sci. adv. bd., 1994-95; project engr. advanced surveillance concepts Rome Air Devel. Ctr., 1979-81; field engr. radar systems test and evaluation Rome Air Devel. Ctr. and MIT Lincoln Lab., 1981-83; radar data and imagery analyst 6585th Test Group, Holloman AFB, N.Mex., 1983-87; elec. engr. specialist LTV Aircraft Products Group, 1987-90; fellow engr. Westinghouse Electric Corp., 1990-91; ops. rsch. analyst CSCI, 1992-94, Office of Asst. Sec. of Air Force, 1995, 96-97, Joint Staff, 1996, 98-99, Army Digitization Office, 1999-2000, CACI, 2000—03, Northrop Grumman Info. Tech., 2003—. Part-time coll. faculty, 1982-84; short course instr. radar techs. George Washington U., 1991-97; adv. assoc. editor NATO Advanced Rsch. Workshop, Bad Windsheim, Germany, 1988; cons., 1994—. Editor-in-chief Applied Computational Electromagnetics Soc. Jour., 1987-93; assoc. editor: Frontier Perspectives, 2000—; contbr. articles to profl. jours.; patentee in field. With USAF Res., 1992, 94-99. Recipient Disting. Svc. award Applied Computational Electromagnetics Soc., 1994; fellow Alpha Found.'s Inst. for Advanced Study. Fellow Alpha Found. Inst. for Advanced Study, mem. Am. Phys. Soc., Am. Assn. Physics Tchrs., World Affairs Coun., Army-Navy Club, Philos. Soc. Washington, Fla. Blue Key, Phi Beta Kappa, Sigma Pi Sigma, Omicron Delta Kappa, Phi Kappa Phi. Achievements include identification of new atmospheric refractivity effects on low-altitude radar propagation, extended quantum-mech. computational technique to electromagnetic scattering, co-pioneered new acquisition sizing methodology for next-generation fighter aircraft; co-authored section of Defense Critical Technologies Plan for the Executive Office of the President; key advisor to Air Force Requirements Oversight Council; mem. U.S. delegation to NATO Y2K integrated process team; identified non-Y2K compliant NATO command and control systems and possible impact to interconnected U.S. systems; identified systems acquisition implications of alternative geostrategic futures, asymmetric-capable adversaries, new concepts in warfare, futuristic techs; co-pioneered modeling and simulation as a technology investment planning tool for an uncertain and rapidly changing national security environment. Home: PO Box 169 Linthicum Heights MD 21090-0169

STEIN, DAVID FRED, investment executive; b. N.Y.C., May 17, 1940; s. William Howard and Phoebe Louise (Hockstader) S.; m. Susan Vail Berresford, June 17, 1963 (div. 1970); 1 child, Jeremy Vail; m. Ellen Gail Cohen, Sept. l6, 1973; children: Katharine Ellen, Nicholas David. BA, Harvard U., 1962; MBA, Harvard Grad. Sch. Bus. Adminstrn., 1965. Assoc. Bache & Co., N.Y.C., 1965-68; assoc., then gen. ptnr. Kuhn Loeb & Co., N.Y.C., 1969-77; mng. dir. Lehman Brothers Kuhn Loeb, N.Y.C., 1977-83, Shearson Lehman Am. Express, N.Y.C., 1983-86; sr. exec. v.p., dir. Am. Express Bank, N.Y.C., 1986-87; mng. dir. Shearson Lehman Hutton, N.Y.C., 1987-89; mng. dir., mem. exec. com. The Stamford Co., N.Y.C., 1989-90; mng. dir. J & W Seligman & Co., N.Y.C., 1990-96, vice chmn., 1997—; co-chmn. Seligman Henderson Co., N.Y.C., 1991-98. Bd. dirs. Griffin Land & Nurseries Inc. Trustee P.R. Traveling Theatre, N.Y.C., 1970-72, Altro Health and Rebab. Ctr., Bronx, N.Y., 1975-82, Blythedale Children's Hosp., Valhalla, N.Y., 1977-2001, hon. trustee, 2001-, Montefiore Med. Ctr., Bronx, 1990—; trustee, chmn. fin. com. Riverdale Country Sch., Bronx, 1988-2000, chmn. bd. trustees, 1997-2000; trustee Children's Aid Soc.; mem. Coun. on Fgn. Rels. With U.S. Army, 1962-63. Mem. Nat. Assn. Security Dealers (internat. com. 1970-85), Century Country Club (Purchase, N.Y.), River Club (N.Y.C.), Harvard Club (N.Y.C.), Edgartown (Mass.) Yacht Club, Mill Reef Club (Antigua, Brit. V.I.), Chappaquiddick Beach Club (Edgartown). Democrat. Avocations: reading, sailing, fishing, skiing. Home: 875 Park Ave New York NY 10021-0341 Office: J & W Seligman 100 Park Ave Fl 8 New York NY 10017-5516

STEIN, DAVID TIMOTHY, minister; b. Chillicothe, Mo., Apr. 25, 1936; s. Frederick Carl and Irene Edith (Kroggel) S.; m. Judith Ann Ritchhart, June 6, 1959; children: Laurie Beth, David Scott, Timothy Christian, Michelle Ann. BA in Humanities, Concordia Coll., St. Louis, 1958; diploma in theology, Concordia Sem., St. Louis, 1961; MA in Speech, St. Louis U., 1962, PhD in Higher Edn. Adminstrn., 1979. Ordained to ministry Luth. Ch.-Mo. Synod, 1962. Prof. Concordia U., River Forest, Ill., 1962-79, dean of students, asst. to pres., dir. pub. rels., dir. placement, 1962-79; dir. parish rels. and lay tng. Luth. Gen. Hosp., Park Ridge, Ill., 1979-85; exec. adminstr. Park Ridge Ctr. Luth. Gen. Health Care System, 1985-89; sr. pastor Evang. Luth. Ch. of the Apostles, Melrose Park, Ill., 1989-91, Evang. Ch. of the Holy Spirit, Elk Grove Village, Ill., 1991—. Trustee Luth. Film Assocs., N.Y.C., 1968-80; mem. com. on campus life Luth. Ch.-Mo. Synod, Chgo., 1979-82; assoc. Hastings Inst., 1985—; pres. Ethics Mgmt. Cons. Svc., River Forest, 1988—, DayStar.net., Inc., 1999—. Author: A Circle of Love, 1967; editor Chronical of Pastoral Care, 1980-88; producer film College With a Cause, 1964 (award San Francisco Film Festival). Co-chair coll. and sch. div. Community Chest, Oak Park/River Forest, Ill., 1964-65, coach, sponsor Little League Assn., River Forest, 1970-78; active Citizens Adv. Com., River Forest, 1975-78; bd. mgrs. Gen. PTA, River Forest, 1977-78; bd. dirs. Luth. Community Svcs. for the Aged, Arlington Heights, Ill., 1985—, United Way, Luth. Child and Family Svcs. Ill., 1996—; mem. com. on human rsch. Concordia U., River Forest, 1996—; bd. trustees United Way of Elk Grove Village, Ill., 1996—. Recipient citation N.Y. Graphic Arts Soc., 1967, Chgo. Graphic Arts Soc., 1968; Aid Assn. for Luths. fellow, 1973. Mem. Park Ridge Assocs., Oak Park/River Forest Clergy Assn., Religious Pub. Rels. Coun. Inc. (pres. Chgo. chpt., nat. gov. 1986-90, DeRose Hinkhouse award 1968-87). Office: Evang Luth Ch of the Holy Spirit 150 Lions Dr Elk Grove Village IL 60007-4200 Home: 2008 Spyglass HL Leander TX 78641-8850 E-mail: dtsteinlb@aol.com. *The most significant dilemma the religious communities and traditions face in a world of diminishing services is the allocation of resources, moral, spiritual, social, educational, economic, and their applications to the growth of artificial intelligence.*

STEIN, ELEANOR BANKOFF, judge; b. NYC, Jan. 24, 1923; d. Jacob and Sarah (Rashkin) Bankoff; m. Frank S. Stein, May 27, 1947; children: Robert B., Joan Jenkins, William M. Student, Barnard Coll., 1940-42; BS in Econs., Columbia U., 1944; LLB, NYU, 1949; grad. Ind. Jud. Coll., 1986. Bar: NY 1950, Ind. 1976, US Supreme Ct. 1980. Atty. Hillis & Button, Kokomo, Ind., 1975-76, Paul Hillis, Kokomo, 1976-78, Bayliff, Harrigan, Kokomo, 1978-80; judge Howard County Ct., Kokomo, 1981-89; ret., 1989; co-juvenile referee Howard County Juvenile Ct., 1976-78. Mem. Rep. Women's Assn. Kokomo, 1980—; bd. dir. Howard County Legal Aid Soc., 1976-80; dir. Howard County Ct. Alcohol and Drug Svcs. Program, 1982-89; bd. advisors St. Joseph Hosp., Kokomo, 1979—; bd. dirs. Kokomo Human Rels. Commn., 1967-70, Howard County Children's Ctr., 1993—. Mem. law rev. bd. NYU Law Rev., 1947-48. Mem. Am. Judicature Soc., Ind. Jud. Assn., Nat. Assn. Women Judges, ABA (apptd. Ind. del. jud. adminstrn. divsn. 1987), Ind. Bar Assn., Howard County Bar Assn., Kokomo Country Club, Altrusa Club. Jewish. Home: 3204 Tally Ho Dr Kokomo IN 46902 Personal E-mail: eleanorbstein@aol.com.

STEIN, ELLEN GAIL, executive manager; b. N.Y.C., May 19, 1951; d. Manuel W. and Bella (Skutel) Stein. BA, SUNY, Stony Brook, 1972; M of Urban Planning, Hunter Coll., 1976; cert. program execs. state/local govt., Harvard U., 1985. Sr. rsch. assoc. Nassau Suffolk (N.Y.) Regional Med. Program, 1976-77; sr. planner N.Y.C. Dept. Correction, 1977—79; group leader criminal justice Mayor's Office, Dept. Ops., NY, 1979—81, dep. asst. dir. citywide spl. projects, 1981, dir. citywide audit implementation, 1981—84; adminstr. Bur. Supplied N.Y.C. Bd. Edn., N.Y.C., NY, 1984—90; mgmt. cons. Project Provide Hope, Russia, Citizen's Budget Commn., 1990-94; pres., CEO FEDVentures Inc., 1994-99; assoc. commnr. Office of CIO N.Y.C. Dept. Tech. and Telecomm., 1999—. Mem. Nat. Assn. Purchasing Mgmt., Am. Women Econ. Devel., Ctrl. Women's Focus, Gov.'s Procurement Coun. (N.Y.), Human Svcs. Coun. (contracting com.). Home: 67 Park Ter E New York NY 10034-1445 Office: 75 Park Pl Fl 9 New York NY 10007-2146 Office Phone: 212-788-2345. Personal E-mail: egstein@hotmail.com. Business E-Mail: estein@doitt.nyc.gov.

STEIN, ELLIOT, JR., business executive; b. St. Louis, Jan. 31, 1949; s. Elliot and Mary Ann (Bleiweiss) S.; m. Pamela Sztybel, Oct. 4, 1997. BA, Claremont McKenna Coll., 1971. Assoc. Lehman Bros., N.Y.C., 1972-79; chmn. Caribbean Internat. News Corp., San Juan, P.R., 1985—; ptnr. Commonwealth Capital Ptnrs., N.Y.C., 1988—. Bd. dirs. Apollo Investment Corp., ACX Pacific, Inc., VTG Holdings, Inc., Cloud Sollutions LLC, Bargain Shop Holdings, LLC; mem. adv. bd. Investigative Group Internat., 1998—. Trustee Claremont Grad. U., 1980—, New Sch. U., 1990—; bd. councillors Annenberg Sch. Comm., U. So. Calif., 1998—. Democrat. Office: Commonwealth Capital Ptnrs 444 Madison Ave Ste 703 New York NY 10022-6903

STEIN, FRANKLIN JOSEPH, import/export company executive; b. Eau Claire, Wis., Mar. 26, 1945; s. Herbert Charles Stein and Gwenn Marie Lassek. BS in Secondary Edn., U. Wis., Eau Claire, 1968; BS in Computer Sci., Coleman Coll., 1989, MIS in Info. Systems, 1995. Cert. tchr. Wis. Biology, sci., Spanish tchr. Stanley (Wis.)-Boyd H.S., 1968-71; salesman Jerry's Hammond Organ & Piano Studios, 1971—72; dept. mgr. Day Music Co., Eau Claire, 1973—74; store mgr. Tropic Waters Pet Store, Eau Claire, 1975-76, Thearle Music Co., San Diego, 1977—82; 6th grade tchr. St. Paul's Luth. Sch., Pacific Beach, Calif., 1977-78; profl. theatre organist Organ Power Pizza Restaurants, San Diego, 1977-85; store mgr. Organ Stop Inc., San Diego, 1982—89; computer programmer analyst Health Examinetics, Rancho Bernardo, Calif., 1989-91; clin. computer systems specialist SHARP Health-Care, San Diego, 1991—97; systems programmer/clin. analyst U. Calif., San Diego, 1997—2002; counselor for severely emotionally disturbed youth New Alternatives, Inc. Comprehensive Adolescent Treatment Ctr., San Diego, 2003—04; owner Franklinson Thai Imports & Unique Finds, San Diego, 2003—. Profl. organist, 1965—. Author: Technician's Manual of Thermography, 1987; editor: Manual of Thermography, 1988. Cath. music dir./organist U.S. Marine Corps Air Sta., Miramar, Calif., 1996—; sponsor Childreach, 2000—. Recipient Silver medal Piano Performance Wis. Music Educators, 1962, 63, Cert. of Merit for Excellence in Sci. Wis. Jr. Acad. of Sci., 1963. Mem.: Am. Guild of Organists. Avocations: reading, concerts, travel. Home: 10227 Kamwood Pl San Diego CA 92126-5139 E-mail: fjstein@msn.com.

STEIN, GARY S. retired judge, lawyer; b. Newark, June 13, 1933; s. Morris J. and Mollie (Goldfarb) S.; married, July 1, 1956; children— Jill, Carrie, Michael, Terri, Jo; m. Et Tilchin, July 1, 1956 AB, Duke U., 1954, LL.B. with distinction, 1956; D.H.L. (hon.), N.J. Inst. Tech., 1985. Bar: D.C. 1956, Ohio 1957, N.Y. 1958, N.J. 1963. Research asst. U.S. Senate AntiTrust and Monopoly Subcom., Washington, 1955; assoc. Kramer, Marx, Greenlee & Backus, N.Y.C., 1956-65; sole practice Paramus, N.J., 1966-72; ptnr. Stein & Kurland, Esquires, Paramus, N.J., 1972-82; dir. Gov.'s Office of Policy and Planning, Trenton, N.J., 1982-85; assoc. justice Supreme Ct. N.J., Hackensack, 1985—2002, ret., 2002; counsel Pashman Stein, Hackensack, 2002—. Mcpl. atty., Paramus, 1967-71; counsel N.J. Election Law Revision Commn., 1970; atty. Bd. Adjustment, Teaneck, N.J., 1973-82 Mem. editorial bd. Duke Law Jour., 1954-56, assoc. editor, 1955-56. Mem. Dist. Ethics Com. for Bergen County, N.J., 1977-80, chmn. 1981. Served with U.S. Army, 1957-58, 61-62 Mem. ABA, N.J. State Bar Assn. (com. on state legislation 1973-79, chmn. 1973-76, jud. selection com. 1976-81, Constl. amendment com. 1977-79, court modernization com. 1976-79), Bergen County Bar Assn., Order of Coif. Jewish. Avocation: tennis. Office: Pashman Stein Ct Plaza South 21 Main St Hackensack NJ 07601 Office Phone: 201-488-8200.

STEIN, GEORGE HENRY, historian, educator, administrator; b. Vienna, May 18, 1934; came to U.S., 1939, naturalized, 1948; m. Dorothy Ann Lahm, Nov. 22, 1963; 1 child, Kenneth. BA with honors (State Regents scholar), Bklyn. Coll., 1959; MA in History (Regents fellow), Columbia U., 1960, PhD in History (Pres.'s fellow), 1964. Lectr. history City Coll., CUNY, 1962-63; instr. dept. history Columbia U., N.Y.C., 1963-65, asst. prof., 1965-66; assoc. prof. dept. history SUNY-Binghamton, 1966-70, prof., 1970-73, disting. teaching prof., 1973-98, emeritus, 1998—, vice chmn. grad. affairs, 1974-76, v.p. acad. affairs, 1976-87, provost, 1985-87, acting pres., 1986-87. Manuscript evaluator and cons. to numerous publishers, 1964—. Author: The Waffen SS: Hitler's Elite Guard at War, 1939-45, 1966, paperback edit., 1984 (transl. into German, 1967, French, 1967, Spanish, 1973, Portuguese, 1970, Japanese, 2002); contbr. articles on modern European history to scholarly publs.; editor: Hitler, 1968; contbr. book revs. to hist. jours. Served with USAF, 1953-57. NEH fellow, 1970-71 Mem. Am. Hist. Assn. (mem. conf. group on cen. European history, conf. group for use of psychology in history), Acad. Polit. Sci., Assn. of Contemporary Historians, Am. Assn. Higher Edn., Nat. Assn. State Univs. and Land Grant Colls. (mem. council acad. affairs 1976-87), Am. Counc. Edn. (exec. com. nat. coun. chief acad. officers 1983-85), Com. Internat. d'Histoire de la Deuxieme Guerre Mondiale, WWII Studies Assn. Home: 2300 Hemlock Ln Vestal NY 13850-2633 Office: SUNY Dept History Binghamton NY 13902-6000

STEIN, HOWARD, economics professor; b. Toronto, Ont., Can., Aug. 4, 1952; came to U.S., 1977; s. David Solomon and Beulah (Tanner) S.; m. Alisa Erika Koch, June 19, 1988; children: Joshua Walter, Daniel Nathan. BA, U. Toronto, 1975; MA, U. Ottawa, Can., 1977; PhD, U. Calif., Riverside, 1983. Lectr. Dept. Econs. U. Dar es Salaam, Tanzania, 1980-82; prof. dept. econs. Roosevelt U., Chgo., 1983—2004. Vis. scholar Ctr. Rsch. on Econ. Devel., U. Mich., Ann Arbor, 1990-91, Sch. Internat. Svc., Am. Univ., Washington, 1995, Sch. of Oriental and African Studies, U. London, 1998; vis. prof. Inst. Econ. Rsch., Hitotsubashi U., Tokyo, 1995-96, Ctr. for African Am. and African studies, Dept. Epidemiology, U. Mich., 2003—. Co-author: Supporting Ownership: Swedish Development Cooperation with Kenya, Tanzania and Uganda, 2 vols., 2003; co-editor: Tanzania and the IMF: The Dynamics of Liberalization, 1992, Deregulation and the Banking Crisis in Nigeria: A Comparative Study, 2002; editor: Asian Industrialization and Africa: Studies in Policy Alternatives to Structural Adjustments, 1995. Doctoral fellow Soc. Social Sci. and Humanities Rsch. Coun. Can., 1979; Nat. Endowment for Humanities grantee, 1985; recipient U.S. Info. Agy. Spkr. and Specialist

award, 1999, 2002. Mem. Am. Econ. Assn., African Studies Assn. Avocations: ice hockey, gardening. Home: 4002 Calgary Ct Ann Arbor MI 48108 Office: U MIch CAAS 4700 Haven Hall 505 S State St Ann Arbor MI 48109-1045

STEIN, HOWARD S. banker; b. N.Y.C., Dec. 27, 1939; s. J. Zachary and Adele (Epstein) S. BA, U. Mich., 1961; MBA, Harvard U., 1963. Mem. treas.'s staff Gen. Motors Corp., N.Y.C., 1963-69; dep. dir., dir. fiscal ops. Human Resources Adminstrn., City of N.Y., 1969-71, dep. adminstr., 1972-74, 1st dep. adminstr., 1974-78; asst. commr. Manpower and Career Devel. Agy., N.Y.C., 1971-72; dep. commr. rent and housing maintenance Housing and Devel. Adminstrn., City of N.Y., 1972; v.p. Citicorp Credit Services Inc., N.Y.C., 1979-86; sr. v.p. Citicorp Retail Services Inc., N.Y.C., 1986-87; exec. dir. Landmark Mut. Funds Group of Citibank, N.A., N.Y.C., 1987-88; v.p. br. banking sect. devel. div. Citibank NA, 1989-91, sr. credit officer worldwide securities svcs. div. Fin. Instns. Group, 1991-94; group risk mgr. Global Transaction Svcs., N.Y.C., 1995—2001, head operational risk mgmt., emerging markets and transaction svcs., 2002—03; mng. dir., head operational risk mgmt. Global Corp. and Investment Bank, 2003—. Lectr. human resources policy Nova U., Ft. Lauderdale, Fla., 1973-74; field instr. adminstrn. specialization NYU Sch. Social Work, 1976-77; mem. risk mgmt. com. Participants Trust Co., 1995-99. Past Bd. dirs., chmn. program com. Vol. Urban Cons. Group, Inc.; past chmn. bd. dirs. Nova Inst; past treas., past pres., bd. dirs. Child Study Assn. Am./Wel-Met, Inc., 1963-85; past treas., bd. dirs. Career Center for Social Services Greater N.Y., Inc.; past treas., past pres. bd. dirs. Cavalier King Charles Spaniel Club U.S.A., Inc.; past bd. dirs., past sec. Child Welfare Info. Services; treas., bd. dirs., chmn. fin. com. WNYC Radio; bd. dirs. Senate Residence Owners Inc., New Goddard-Riverside Housing Devel. Fund Co., N.Y.C. Health and Hosps., Corp., 1976, Homes for the Homeless; mem. corp. Children's Mus., Boston; bd. dirs., treas., mem. fin. com. Goddard Riverside Neighborhood Houses; trustee, chair fin. com. Pratt Inst.; past mem. Dept. Disciplinary com. Supreme Ct. State N.Y. Appellate Divsn. 1st Jud. Dept.; mem. corp. adv. com. U. Mich., Coll. Lit., Sci and the Arts; bd. dirs. The Childrens' Cause. Mem.: Risk Mgmt. Assn. (co-chmn. operational risk coun. 2002—), Inst. Internat. Fin. (mem. working group on operational risk 2001—), Harvard (N.Y.C., past mem. admissions com.). Home: 1158 5th Ave New York NY 10029-6917 Office: 250 West St New York NY 10013 E-mail: howard.s.stein@citigroup.com.

STEIN, ISAAC, investment company executive; b. N.Y.C., Oct. 26, 1946; s. Simon O. and Lee F. (Herring) S.; m. Madeline F. Johnson, Aug. 17, 1968; children: Joshua Borden, Sarah Elizabeth. BA, Colgate U., 1968; MBA, Stanford U., 1970, JD, 1972. Bar: Calif. 1972. Partner firm Heller, Ehrman, White & McAuliffe, 1972-79; v.p., sec., treas., chief fin. officer, gen. counsel Raychem Corp., Menlo Park, Calif., 1979-82, sec., gen. counsel, 1982-83; pres. Waverley Assocs., Inc., Palo Alto, 1983—. Bd. dirs. ALZA Corp. Trustee Crystal Springs Uplands Sch., 1987—, Stanford U. Hosp., 1988—. Office: 525 University Ave Palo Alto CA 94301-1903

STEIN, JAY, retail executive; 2 children. With Stein Mart, Inc., Greenville, Miss., 1966-79, pres., 1979-89, chmn., CEO Jacksonville, Fla., 1989—. Bd. dirs. Promus Hotel Corp., Nations Bank Jacksonville, Bolles Sch., Nat. Conf. Christians and Jews, Am. Heritage Life Ins. Co.; trustee, mem. exec. com. John F. Kennedy Ctr. for Performing Arts; vice chmn. bd. govs. Hebrew Union Coll.; founding mem. The Holocaust Mus., Washington. Pres. Jacksonville Symphony Orch.; past mem. Mayor's Select Com. on Ethics in City Govt.; bd. mem. Peres Ctr. for Peace, Tel Aviv. Recipient Humanitarian award Nat. Conf. Christians and Jews, 1993. Office: 1200 Riverplace Blvd Jacksonville FL 32207-9046

STEIN, JEROME LEON, economist, educator; b. Bklyn., Nov. 14, 1928; s. Meyer and Ida (Shapiro) S.; m. Hadassah Levow, Aug. 27, 1950; children: Seth, Gil, Ilana. BA summa cum laude, Bklyn. Coll., 1949; MA, Yale U., 1950, PhD, 1955; Docteur honoris causa, U. de la Méditerranée, 1997. Instr. Brown U., Providence, 1953-56, asst. prof., 1956-60, assoc. prof., 1960-62, prof., 1962-70, Eastman prof. polit. economy, 1970-94, prof. emeritus, 1994—. Vis. prof. Hebrew U., Jerusalem, 1965-66, 72-73, 78; Ford Found. rsch. prof. econs. U. Calif., Berkeley, 1979-80, Sorbonne, U. Paris, 1982, Tohoku U., Sendai, Japan, 1983, Haute Etudes Comml., France, 1987, Monash U., Melbourne U., Australia, 1989, U. Aix-en-Provence, Marseille, France, 1992, 95, 96, 97, 98, U. Munich, 1994, La Sapienza, Rome, 1994; vis. prof. applied math. Brown U., 1996—. Author: Essays in International Finance, 1962, (with G.M. Borts) Economic Growth in a Free Market, 1964, Money and Capacity Growth, 1971, Monetarism, 1976, Monetarist, Keynesian and New Classical Economics, 1982, Economics of Futures Markets, 1986, International Finance Markets, 1991, Fundamental Determinants of Exchange Rates, 1995; bd. editors Am. Econ. Rev., 1974-80; assoc. editor Jour. Fin., 1964-70. Ford Found. faculty fellow, 1961-62; Social Sci. Research Council grantee, 1965-66; Guggenheim fellow, 1972-73 Mem. Am. Econ. Assn. Home: 77 Elton St Providence RI 02906-4505 Office: Brown U 182 George St Providence RI 02912-9056 Fax: 401-863-1355. Office Phone: 401-863-2143. E-mail: Jerome_Stein@BROWN.EDU.

STEIN, JOHN C. lawyer; b. Flint, Mich., May 8, 1939; s. Joseph Aloyosius and Gertrude (Carlin) S.; m. Dorothea Ruel, Nov. 20, 1965; children: John Jr., Christian, Peter, Thea. BA, U. San Francisco, 1963; JD, U. Calif. Hastings, San Francisco, 1966; cert., Mil. Justice Sch., Newport, R.I., 1968. Bar: Calif. 1966, U.S. Dist. Ct. (no., ctrl. and so. dists.) Calif. 1969. Dep. city atty. City of San Francisco, Office of City Atty., 1969-71; with The Boccardo Law Firm, San Jose, Calif., 1971—, mng. ptnr., 1981-99. Judge pro tem San Francisco County Superior Ct., 1978—, Santa Clara County Superior Ct., 1981—; lectr. U. Santa Clara Law Sch., 1985—, Hastings Coll. of Law, U. C. San Francisco. Bd. dirs. Katherine Delmar Burke Sch. Girls, San Francisco, 1988-92, Planning Orgn. for The Richmond, San Francisco, 1985-88. Capt. USMC, 1966-69. Fellow Am. Coll. Trial Lawyers; mem. ATLA, Consumer Attys. of Calif. (Trial Lawyer of Yr. San Jose), Am. Bd. Trial Advocates. Democrat. Roman Catholic. Avocations: golf, skiing, scuba diving. Office: Boccardo Law Firm 111 W Saint John St Ste 1100 San Jose CA 95113-1107

STEIN, JOSEPH, playwright; b. N.Y.C. s. Charles and Emma S.; m. Elisa Loti, Feb. 7, 1975; children by previous marriage: Daniel, Harry, Joshua; children of present marriage: John, Jenny Lyn. BSS, CCNY, 1934; MSW, Columbia U., 1937. Psychiat. social worker, N.Y.C., 1938-45. Writer: radio shows, including Raleigh's Room, 1948-49, Henry Morgan Show, 1949-52; TV shows, including Your Show of Shows, 1952-54; Sid Caesar Show, 1954-55; playwright Plain and Fancy, 1955; Mr. Wonderful, 1957, Juno, 1959, Take Me Along, 1959, Enter Laughing, 1963, Fiddler on the Roof, 1964 (Am. Theatre Wing Tony award for best musical, 1965, N.Y. Drama Critics Circle award Best Musical 1965), Zorba, 1968 (Tony nomination), Irene, 1975, King of Hearts, 1978, Carmelina, 1979, The Baker's Wife, 1983, (Olivier award nomination London 1989), Rags, 1986 (Tony nomination); screenplays Enter Laughing, 1970; Fiddler on the Roof, 1972 (Screen Writers Guild award). Mem. Authors League, Screen Writers Guild (Edwin Forrest award for Outstanding Contbr. to Theatre, 2001), Dramatists Guild Coun. Home: 1130 Park Ave New York NY 10128-1255 E-mail: elisajoe@aol.com.

STEIN, KARL N. plastic and reconstructive surgeon; b. Phila., July 1, 1940; BA in Chemistry, Temple U., 1962, MD, 1966. Diplomate Am. Bd. Plastic Surgery. Intern U. Pa. Grad. Hosp., 1966-67; resident in surgery Abington Meml. Hosp., 1967-68, SUNY Up-State Med. Ctr., 1970-71, instr. in surgery, 1970—; resident in plastic surgery Hosp. Albert Einstein Coll. Medicine, Bronx Mcpl. Hosp. Ctr., 1971-74, asst. instr. plastic surgery and hand surgery, 1974; pvt. practice in plastic surgery, 1974—. Surgeon Sherman Oaks (Calif.) Burn Ctr., 1975—; cons. L.A. Dept. Water and Power; med. legal expert for burns and plastic surgery. Author (patent) Treatment of Tar Burns, 1980. Capt. USAF, 1969-71. Fellow Am. Coll. Surgeons; mem. AMA, Am. Soc. Plastic and Reconstructive Surgeons, Am. Burn Assn., Am. Assn. Hand Surgery, Am. Soc. Aesthetic Plastic Surgery, Calif. Soc. Plastic Surgeons, Calif. Med. Assn., L.A. County Med. Assn. Office: PO Box 220340 Newhall CA 91322-0340 E-mail: karlhsteinmd@aol.com.

STEIN, KATHY W. state representative; b. Birmingham, Ala., Jan. 31, 1955; m. Alan M. Stein; children: Hadley, Scooter, Wade. JD, Univ. of KY Coll. of Law, 1983; Grad., Va. Polytechnic and State Univ.; BA, Clinch Valley Coll. of the Univ. of Va., 1974. State Rep. House of Rep., Dist. 75, 1996—; owner Kathey W. Stein, Atty. at Law, 1997—; dir. of Domestic Violence, Violence Prosecution Fayette County Atty., 1993—97; prosecutor Fayette County Atty. Office, 1993—97; Pub. Defender Fayette County Legal Aid, Inc., 1988—93; Assoc. Atty. Marshall and Gullette, 1984—86; tchr., faculty, adv. chair, county delegate Pound HS, wise County Sch. Bd., 1976—80; instr. Clinch Valley Coll. of the Univ. of Va., 1977—80; bookkeeper Appalachian Film Workshop, "Appalshop", 1974—75. Mem. Judiciary, Criminal Justice Coun.; trustee Cmty. Action Coun., 1999—; mem. Gov. Coun. on Dom. Violence, 1997—; Vice-chair Fayette County Domes. Violence Bd., 1993—; elector-at-large Va. Electoral Coll., 1980; treas., clk. Town of Wise, 1974—75; mem. Gov. Contract Rev., Gov. Task Force on the econ. Status of Women, appropriations and Revenue, Ed., Post-Secondary and subcomm., Classified Employee compensation subcomm.; vice-chair Health & Welfare; Long-term Care (Subcommittee); mem. Families and Children (subcommittee), Gardian ad Litem Comm. of the admin. Office of the Courts, Legis. Rsch. Comm. Sr. Citizens Adv. Group, Paul Mason Hiv/AIDS Task Force Rules. mem. of: Am. Civil Liberties Union, Nat. Bd.; Am. United for the Seperation of Ch. and State; Appalachian Sch. of Law, Advisory Committee; mem, Ctrl. Ky. Coun. for Peace and Justec, 1998-present; Criminal Justice Council for the Gov. Coun. on Dom. Violence fand Sexual Abuse; Vice-chmn, Fayette County Dom. Violence Prevention Bd.;Life mem., Hadassah, 1990; mem. Kentuckians for the Commonwealth, 1998-present; mem., Ky. Fairness Alliance, 1996-present; Ky. Fairness campaighn; Kentuckians for the Commonwealth; Ky. Women's Political Causus; Chair, Mental Health Comm. of the Fayette County Dom. Violence Prevention Bd.; Milbank Memorial Fund, Reforming State Group, Steering Committee Nat. conference of State Legislators; Nat. Hon. Roll of State Legislators, Ctr. for Women's studies;Nat. Org. for Woman; Nat. Org. of Woman Legislators; chmn. emeritus, Ohavay Zion Synagogue, Social Acton comm.; Southern Conference of State Legislators. Democrat. Jewish. Office: Capitol Capitol Annex Rm 429 Frankfort KY 40601 also: Dist 364 Transylvania Pk Lexington KY 40508

STEIN, LAURA, food products executive; b. 1961; BA, Dartmouth Coll., 1983; JD, Harvard Law Sch., 1987; MA, Dartmouth Coll. Bar: Calif., 1987. Tracsactional corp. lawyer Morrison & Foerster, San Francisco; asst. gen. counsel, regulatory affairs The Clorox Co., 1992—99; sr. v.p., gen. counsel The Heinz Co., Pittsburgh, Pa., 2000—. Mem. ABA, Calif. State Bar, Assn. Am. Corp. Counsel Assn., Am. Soc. Corp. Sect. Office: H J Heinz Co 600 Grant St Ste 6000 Pittsburgh PA 15219-2857

STEIN, LAWRENCE A. lawyer; b. Balt., Mar. 18, 1965; s. Hersh and Ellen (Hart) S.; m. Diane Wells, June 23, 1991; children: Joshua A., Julie E. AB, U. Chgo., 1988; JD, No. Ill. U., 1993. Bar: Ill. 1993, U.S. Dist. Ct. (no. dist.) Ill. 1993, U.S. Ct. Appeals (7th cir.) 1993, Md. 1994, U.S. Dist. Ct. Md. 1994, U.S. Supreme Ct. 1997. Shareholder Huck, Bouma PC, Wheaton, Ill., 1993—. Advisor Prairie State Legal Svcs., Carol Stream, Ill., 1993—. Commr. Glen Ellyn (Ill.) Architecture Review Commn., 1994-97. Recipient Am. jurisprudence award for excellence in appellate advocacy Lawyers Coop., 1991. Mem.: ABA, Am. Inns Ct., Ill. State Bar Assn., DuPage County Bar Assn., Phi Delta Phi. Republican. Jewish. Home: 300 Lorraine St Glen Ellyn IL 60137-5632 Office: Huck Bouma Martin Jones & Bradshaw 1755 S Naperville Rd Ste 200 Wheaton IL 60187-8144 E-mail: lstein@huckbouma.com.

STEIN, LAWRENCE V, lawyer; AB cum laude, Columbia Coll., 1971; MA, Cornell U., 1974; JD magna cum laude, U. Pa. Law Sch., 1976. Atty. Arnold & Porter, 1976—84, ptnr., 1984—92; sr. v.p., gen. counsel, sec. Genetics Inst., 1992—97; sr. v.p., chief legal counsel Wyeth-Ayerst Global Pharmaceuticals and Genetics Inst., 1997—2001; sr. vp., dep. gen. counsel Wyeth, 2001—03, sr. v.p., gen. counsel, 2003—. Office: Wyeth 5 Giralda Farms Madison NJ 07940-0874

STEIN, MARCIA, not-for-profit executive; b. Providence, Sept. 21, 1939; d. Dr. Harry L. and Dora Ann Dimond; m. Myron Stein, June 10, 1977; m. Cohen; children: Bruce Andrew Cohen, Benjamin Cohen, Lisa Cohen. BA Econ., Wellesley Coll., Wellesley, Mass., 1957—61; M in Soviet Studies, Harvard U., 1961—62; M in Soc. Work, Adelphi Univ., 1975. Cert. M.S.W. Spl. asst. to gen. dir. Comm. Svc. Soc., New York, NY, 1974—78; Bur. chief NY City Dept. for the Aging, New York, NY, 1978—89; exec. dir. City Meals on Wheels, New York, NY, 1981—89, 1993—; assoc. exec. dir. 92 St. Y, New York, NY, 1989—93. Mailing: City Meals-on-Wheels Fl 3 355 Lexington Ave New York NY 10017-6603

STEIN, MARK RODGER, allergist; b. Phila., Apr. 24, 1943; s. Eli and Norma Stein; m. Phyllis Feinstein, Dec. 27, 1964; children: Amy Lynn, Philip Warren. BA, LaSalle Coll., Phila., 1964; MD, Jefferson Med. Coll., Phila., 1968. Diplomate Nat. Bd. Med. Examiners, Am. Bd. Internal Medicine, Am. Bd. Allergy and Immunology. Intern Abington (Pa.) Meml. Hosp., 1968-69; resident internal medicine Letterman Army Med. Ctr., San Francisco, 1972-75; fellow allergy and clin. immunology Fitzsimons Army Med. Ctr., Denver, 1975-77; pvt. practice West Palm Beach, Fla., 1979—. Asst. prof. depts. medicine and pediatrics Uniformed Svcs. U. Health Scis. Sch. Medicine, Bethesda, Md., 1978—79; clin. asst. prof. dept. internal medicine U. South Fla. Coll. Medicine, Tampa, 1979—83, Tampa, 1997—2000; clin. care cons. Clin. Ctr., NIH, Bethesda, 1978—79; mem. active staff Good Samaritan Hosp., West Palm Beach, Fla., chief svc. dept. allergy, 1990—98, chief svc. allergy, 2001—; chief dept. allergy St. Mary's Hosp., West Palm Beach, 1985—98; mem. active staff Palm Beach Gardens Med Ctr.; chief allergy svc. Intracostal Health Sys., 2000—01. Editor Gastroesophageal Reflux Disease and Airway Disease, 1999; contbr. articles to profl. jours. Trustee Am. Lung Assn., West Palm Beach, 1984-93, 95—. Fellow ACP, Am. Acad. Allergy, Asthma and Immunology, Am. Coll. Allergy, Asthma and Immunology (chmn. geriat. com. 1988-90), Am. Assn. Cert. Allergists; mem. Am. Thoracic Soc., Am. Coll. Chest Physicians, Mil. Allergists, Fla. Med. Assn., Palm Beach County Med. Assn., Asthma and Allergy Found. Am., Fla. Allergy and Immunology Soc. (pres. 1987-88), Southeastern Allergy Assn. Jewish. Avocations: tennis, golf. Office: 840 Us Highway 1 North Palm Beach FL 33408-3830 Office Phone: 561-626-2006. E-mail: latallergy@aol.com.

STEIN, MARTIN (HAP), JR., real estate company executive; m. Brooke Stein; 3 children. Bachelors Degree, Washington and Lee U.; Masters Degree, Dartmouth Coll. With Regency Ctrs. Corp., Jacksonville, Fla., 1976—, pres., CEO, 1988—, chmn., 1997—. Office: Regency Ctrs 121 W Forsyth St Jacksonville FL 32202*

STEIN, MARVIN, psychiatrist, historian; b. St. Louis, Dec. 8, 1923; s. Samuel G. and Dora (Kline) S.; m. Ann Hackman, May 5, 1950; children: Leslie, David, Lisa. BS, MD, Washington U., St. Louis, 1949; grad., Phila. Psychoanalytic Inst., 1959. Intern St. Louis City Hosp., 1949-50; asst. resident in psychiatry Barnes Hosp., St. Louis, 1950-51; fellow in psychiatry Hosp. U. Pa., 1953-55; asst. prof., then assoc. prof. psychiatry U. Pa. Med. Sch., 1956-63; prof. psychiatry Cornell U. Med. Sch., N.Y.C., 1963-66; prof., chmn. dept. psychiatry SUNY Downstate Med. Ctr., Bklyn., 1966-71; chmn. dept. psychiatry Mt. Sinai Sch. Medicine, N.Y.C., 1971-87, Esther and Joseph Klingenstein prof., 1971-94, Esther and Joseph Klingenstein prof. emeritus, 1994—. Mem. fellowships rev. panel NIMH, 1961-64, chmn. mental health extramural rsch. adv. com., 1968-71, chmn. rev. com. Mental Health Aspects of AIDS, 1988-90; mem. rsch. adv. com. VA, 1965-68, mem. rsch. svc. merit rev. bd. in behavioral sci., 1972-75; chmn. Mental Health Rsch. Career Award Com., 1963-67; chmn. bd. dirs. Founds. Fund for Rsch. in Psychiatry, 1967-70; mem. behavioral medicine study sect. NIH, 1981-83, geriatric rev. com., 1986-88. Contbr. articles on brain and behavior and immune function and history of psychiatry to med. and history jours. USPHS postdoctoral fellow, 1951-53; mental health career investigator, 1956-61; sr. fellow grantee, 1961-63. Mem. Am. Psychiat. Assn. (chmn. rsch. coun. 1981-84), N.Y. Acad. Medicine (Salmon com. 1984—), Alpha Omega Alpha. Home: 5700 Arlington Ave Bronx NY 10471-1503 Office: Mt Sinai Sch Medicine 1 Gustave L Levy Pl New York NY 10029-6500 Personal E-mail: marvin.stein@mssm.edu.

STEIN, MELVIN A. accountant; b. N.Y.C., Sept. 7, 1932; s. William H. and Lillian (Goldberg) S.; m. Barbara Blumencranz, Dec. 17, 1955 (dec.); children: Susan, Karen; m. Marie Sacco, Nov. 1, 1992. BS, N.Y. U., 1953. Pvt. practice acctg., Jericho, NY, 1961-75; pres. Stein & Stein, P.C., Hicksville, 1975-81, Stein, Stein & Feit, P.C., 1982—. Bd. dir. Stern Sch. Bus. N.Y. U., treas. bd. dir., 1991—92, v.p. bd. dir., 1995—, alumni bd. dir., mem. dean adv. coun., 2002—, pres. exec. forum, 2002—, dir. entrepreneurship conf., 2000—. Mem. AICPA, N.Y. State Soc. CPAs, N.J. Soc. CPAs, C.W. Post Tax Inst., NYU Club, Princeton Club, The Exec. Forum (pres.). Jewish. Home: 7 Ingleside Ln White Plains NY 10605-5009 Office: 1 Frederick Pl Hicksville NY 11801-4205 also: Buccaneer Mall St Thomas VI 00801 Office Phone: 516-938-2100. E-mail: cpa35@aol.com.

STEIN, M(EYER) L(EWIS), journalist, magazine editor, writer; b. Escanaba, Mich., July 30, 1920; s. Alexander and Fannie Stein; m. Romana Susan Paal, Apr. 15, 1981 (dec. Feb. 1994); children: Andrea, Jeannine; stepchildren: Adam Paal, Edith Paal. BJ, U. Mo., 1942; MA, Stanford U., 1961. Reporter, telegraph editor Daily Tribune, Royal Oak, Mich., 1946-51; reporter San Francisco Examiner, 1951-60; prof., chair dept. journalism and mass comm. NYU, 1961-74; prof., chair dept. journalism Calif. State U., Long Beach, 1974-87; west coast editor Editor & Publ. mag., Palo Alto, Calif., 1981-99. Lectr. in field. Author 17 books including: Freedom of the Press, 1970, Reporting Today, 1971, How to Write Plain English, 1974, Shaping the News, 1974, When Presidents Meet the Press, 1969, Under Fire: Story of American War Correspondents, 1995, (with Susan Paterno) Introduction to Journalism, 1998, (with Susan Paterno) Talk Straight, Listen Carefully: The Art of Interviewing, 2001; lit. cons.; contbr. over 500 articles to newspapers and mags. Sgt. U.S. Army, 1942-45, Africa, Italy. Gannett fellow, 1980. Mem. Assn. Edn. in Journalism and Mass Comm. (chmn. freedom and responsibility com. 1964), Am. Soc. Journalists and Authors. Avocation: travel. Home and Office: 10 Bella Rosa Irvine CA 92602 E-mail: mlsteinav@aol.com.

STEIN, MICHAEL A. pharmaceutical executive; CFO Marriott Internat., Inc., Washington; v.p., CFO ICOS Corp., Bothell, Wash., 2001—. Office: ICOS Corp 22021 20th Ave SE Bothell WA 98021

STEIN, MICHAEL DAVID, psychologist; b. N.Y.C., Oct. 26, 1942; s. Barnet and Estelle A. (Fidell) S.; m. Cecile L. Gross, June 12, 1967; children: Peter, Nathanael. BS, CCNY, 1963, PhD, 1974. Lic. psychologist, N.Y. Supervising psychologist The Children's Village, Dobbs Ferry, N.Y., 1974-78; dir. psychology Hall-Brooke Hosp., Westport, Conn., 1979-81; chief psychologist Elmhurst (N.Y.) Hosp. Ctr., 1981-89; chief psychologist and chief psychiatry clinic Lenox Hill Hosp., N.Y.C., 1989—2003; pvt. practice N.Y.C and Hartsdale, 1975—. Author: (with others) Therapies for Adolescents, 1982. Mem. APA, Internat. Neuropsychol. Soc., N.Y. State Psychol. Assn. Avocations: classical music, reading, bread baking. Office: 140 E Hartsdale Ave Apt 1D Hartsdale NY 10530-3337 also: 130 E 77th St # 312 New York NY 10021-1851

STEIN, MILTON MICHAEL, lawyer; b. N.Y.C., Sept. 18, 1936; s. Isidore and Sadie (Lefkowitz) S.; m. Jacqueline Martin, June 17, 1962; children: April, Alicia. AB, Columbia U., 1958, LLB, 1961. Bar: N.Y. 1962, Pa. 1971, U.S. Supreme Ct. 1971. Asst. dist. atty. N.Y. County, 1962-67; sr. counsel Nat. Commn. for Reform of Fed. Criminal Law, Washington, 1967-70; asst. dist. atty., chief of appeals City of Phila., 1970-73; asst. dir. Nat. Wire Tapping Commn., Washington, 1973-75; dir. D.C. Law Revision, Washington, 1975-77; spl. asst. HUD, Washington, 1977-79; asst. gen. counsel U.S. Commodity Futures Trading Commn., Washington, 1979-83; v.p. N.Y. Futures Exch., N.Y.C., 1983-89, N.Y. Stock Exch., N.Y.C., 1989—. Mem. ABA, N.Y. State Bar Assn., Assn. of Bar of City of N.Y. Democrat. Jewish. Home: Hudson House PO Box 286 Ardsley On Hudson NY 10503-0286 Office Phone: 212-656-6928. E-mail: mstein@nyse.com.

STEIN, MITCHELL BRIAN, physician; b. Queens, NY, Nov. 11, 1954; s. Philip and Doris (Kramer) S.; m. Barbara Ellen Pollard, Mar. 24, 1980; children: Julie, Laura. BA, Columbia Coll., 1975; MD, Albert Einstein Coll. Medicine, 1979. Diplomate Am. Bd. Internal Medicine, Am. Bd. Ophthalmology. Pvt. practice, Mt. Kisco, NY, 1987—; asst. clinical prof. Albert Einstein Coll. Medicine, Bronx, N.Y., 1994—; vol. attending physician Northern Westchester Hosp. Ctr., Mt. Kisco, N.Y., 1996—. Office: 69 S Moger Ave Mount Kisco NY 10549-2217 Office Phone: 914-666-2961. Personal E-mail: mitchS11@aol.com.

STEIN, PAUL CLINTON, financial planner; b. Mpls., Feb. 27, 1960; s. Clinton W. and Pauline Stein; m. Jann Marie Matheis, Mar. 23, 1983; children: Michelle, Andrew. BS in Math. Edn., U. Minn., 1983. Registered investment advisor, series 7 rep.; lic. life, health and variable ins. rep., CFP. Orgnl. mgr. Southwestern Co., Nashville, 1980-85; sr. acct. rep. Gt. Am. Opportunities, Nashville, 1985-90; assoc. gen. agt. Luth. Brotherhood, Balt., 1990-92; sr. advisor Swenson Anderson Assocs., Mpls., 1992—, mem. adv. bd., 1996-98. Nat. spkr. on money and fin. to various schs., colls., banks and pvt. corps, and radio, 1985--. Singer, songwriter, performer various ch. and comty. concerts, corp. banquets, 1980X. Mem. Minn. Soc. Inst. CFPs (bd. dirs. 1996-98),Nat. Com. on Planned Giving, Minn. Planned Giving Coun., Fin. Planning Assn., Investment Mgmt. Cons. Assn. Republican. Office: Swenson Anderson Financial Grp 1221 Nicollet Ave Ste 400 Minneapolis MN 55403-4499

STEIN, PAUL DAVID, cardiologist; b. Cin., Apr. 13, 1934; s. Simon and Sadie (Friedman) S.; m. Janet Louise Tucker, Aug. 14, 1966; children: Simon, Douglas, Rebecca. BS, U. Cin., 1955, MD, 1959. Intern Jewish Hosp., Cin., 1959-60, med. resident, 1961-62, Gorgas Hosp., C.Z., 1960-61; fellow in cardiology U. Cin., 1962-63, Mt. Sinai Hosp., N.Y.C., 1963-64; rsch. fellow Harvard Med. Sch., Boston, 1964-66; asst. dir. cardiac catheterization lab. Baylor U. Med. Ctr., Dallas, 1966-67; asst. prof. medicine Creighton U., Omaha, 1967-69; assoc. prof. medicine U. Okla., Oklahoma City, 1969-73; prof. rsch. medicine U. Okla. Coll. Medicine, Oklahoma City, 1973-76; dir. cardiovascular rsch. Henry Ford Hosp., Detroit, 1976-94, med. dir. cardiovascular rehab., 1994-2000; dir. rsch. St. Joseph Mercy Oakland Hosp., Pontiac, Mich., 2000—; Henry Ford prof. medicine Case Western Res. U., Cleve., 1994—2000; prof. medicine Wayne State U., Detroit, 2003—. Adj. prof. physics Oakland U., Rochester, Mich., 1985—. Author: A Physical and Physiological Basis for the Interpretation of Cardiac Ausculation: Evaluations Based Primarily on Second Sound and Ejection Murmurs, 1981, Pulmonary Embolism, 1996; contbr. articles to profl. jours. Coun. on Clin. Cardiology fellow Am. Heart Assn., 1971, Coun. on Circulation fellow, 1972. Recipient Lifetime Achievement award, Am. Heart Assn., Mich. chpt., 2002. Master Am. Coll. Chest Physicians (pres. 1993); fellow ACP (Laureate award, Mich. chpt. 2003), ASME, Am. Coll. Cardiology. Office Phone: 248-858-6772. Business E-mail: steinp@trinity-health.org.

STEIN, RICHARD ALAN, cardiologist, educator; b. NYC, Apr. 7, 1942; BA, Columbia Coll., N.Y.C., 1963; MD, NYU, 1967. Diplomate in internal medicine, cardiovascular diseases, geriatrics and sports medicine Am. Bd. Internal Medicine; lic. physician, N.Y., Conn.; lic. handler radioactive materials, N.Y.C. Intern, then resident in medicine Downstate Med. Ctr.-Kings County Hosp., Bklyn., 1967-69, cardiology fellow, 1972-74; chief resident in medicine Kings County Hosp., 1971-72, attending physician; prof. medicine, chief cardiology divsn. dept. medicine SUNY-Health Sci. Ctr., Bklyn., 1985-95; chief preventive and rehab. cardiology Lenox Hill Hosp., N.Y.C., 1995-99; attending physician SUNY Hosp., Bklyn.; chief of cardiology The Bklyn. Hosp. Ctr., 1999—2003; assoc. chair dept. medicine, chief medicine Beth Israel Hosp. - Surgery Divsn., NYC, 2003—. Mem. vis. faculty Yale-New Haven Hosp., 1982; dir. cardiology fellowship program Bklyn. VA Hosp., Brookdale Hosp., S.I. U. Hosp., 1985—95; dir. cardiac rehab. program 92d St. YM-YWHA, N.Y.C.; prof. clin. medicine Weill-Cornell Med. Ctr., 1999—. Co-editor: Complementary and Alternative Medicine in Cardiovascular Disease, 2004; mem. editl. bd. Preventive Cardiology, Jour. Cmty. Health; contbr. chpt. to: Coronary Rehabilitation for the Practicing Physician, 1979, Sports Medicine for the Primary Care Physician, 1984, Anesthesia as Co-Existing Heart Disease, 1993, (with others) Diabetic Renal-Retinal Syn-

drome, 1980; sect. editor: Heart Disease: A Jour. of Cardiovasc. Disease; contbr. articles to profl. jours. Maj. USAF, 1969-71. Recipient Acad. Career award, Preventive Cardiology Acad. award NIH, 1985-90. Fellow ACS, Am. Coll. Cardiology, Am. Coll. Chest Physicians, Am. Coll. Sports Medicine, N.Y. Cardiol. Soc. (bd. dirs.), N.Y. Acad. Medicine; mem. Am. Heart Assn. (fellow coun. on clin. cardiology), Assn. Profs. Cardiology, Am. Fedn. for Clin. Rsch., Am. Heart Assn. (Heritage affiliate, chair task force on profl. edn., grantee in aid 1979-81), Sigma Xi. Office: 170 E End Ave New York NY 10128 Office Phone: 212-870-9295. Personal E-mail: rastein@msn.com.

STEIN, ROBERT A. writer, educator; b. Duluth, Minn., Aug. 5, 1933; s. A. A. and Grace (Wichterman) Stein; m. Betty Lou Pavlik, 1955; children: Robert Jr., David K., Steven J. BS in Commerce, U. Iowa, 1956, MA in Counselor Edn., 1968, MA in Writing, 1986. Cert. tchr. Iowa, profl. counselor. Commd. 2d lt. USAF, 1956, advanced through grades to col., pilot trainee, 1957, pilot 345th Squadron Sewart AFB, Tenn., 1957—61, pilot 1602nd Wing Chateauroux AB, France, 1961—64; asst. prof. aerospace studies U. Iowa, Iowa City, 1964-66, assoc. prof., 1966-68, prof., 1975-77; dir., safety and security U. Iowa Hosps./Clinics, Iowa City, 1977-85; mem. faculty divsn. writing Kirkwood CC, Iowa City, Cedar Rapids, 1984-89; writer, tchr. Iowa City, 1985—. Writer, tchr. Iowa City/Johnson County Sr. Citizens Ctr., 1994—; sports announcer U. Iowa. Author: (novels) Apollyon: A Novel, 1985, The Chase, 1988, The Black Samaritan, 1997, 2d edit., 2000, The Vengeance Equation, 2000, hardcover edit., 2001, Death Defied (Internat. Lit. award, 1988); co-author: (screenplays) WGAW-Registered, 2001. Decorated Bronze Star. Mem.: Authors League Am., Authors Guild, Mil. Affairs Assn. (charter), Air Force Assn. (life), Nat. Iowa Varsity Club (exec. bd., pres. 2002—03, Lifetime Achievement award 1999), Nat. Iowa Lettermen's Club (past pres.), Rotary (Paul Harris fellow), Daedalians, Phi Delta Kappa. Avocations: flying, travel, reading, swimming. Home and Office: 2020 Ridgeway Dr Iowa City IA 52245-3238

STEIN, ROBERT ALAN, electronics company executive; b. Chgo., Oct. 18, 1930; s. Manfred and Mildred (Rosenfield) S.; m. Frances Roslyn Berger, Dec. 25, 1960; 1 dau., Marcia Beth. BA, U. Chgo., 1950, MBA, 1953. C.P.A., Ill. Sr. auditor Scovell, Wellington & Co., Chgo., 1955—63; supr. corp. acctg. Mack Trucks, Inc., Montvale, NJ, 1963—65; v.p. fin., treas. Lionel Corp., N.Y.C., 1965—82; pres. ITI Electronics, Inc., Fairfield, NJ, 1982—. Served with U.S. Army, 1953-55. Mem. Am. Inst. CPAs. Home: 32 Stonewall Dr Livingston NJ 07039-1822 Office: 214 Little Falls Rd Fairfield NJ 07004 E-mail: itielect@aol.com.

STEIN, ROBERT ALLEN, legal association executive, law educator; b. Mpls., Sept. 16, 1938; s. Lawrence E. and Agnes T. (Brynildson) S.; m. Sandra H. Stein; children: Linda Stein Routh, Laura Stein Conrad, Karin Stein O'Boyle. BS in Law, U. Minn., 1960, JD summa cum laude, 1961; LLD (hon.), Uppsala U., Sweden, 1993. Bar: Wis. 1961, Minn. 1967. Assoc. Foley, Sammond & Lardner, Milw., 1961-64; prof. U. Minn. Law Sch., Mpls., 1964-77; assoc. dean U. Minn., 1976-77, v.p. adminstrn. and planning, 1978-80; dean U. Minn. Law Sch., 1979-94; faculty rep. men's intercollegiate athletics U. Minn., 1981-94; of counsel Mullin, Weinberg & Daly, PA, Mpls., 1970-80, Gray, Plant, Mooty, Mooty & Bennett, Mpls., 1980-94; exec. dir., COO ABA, Chgo., 1994—. Vis. prof. UCLA, 1969-70, U. Chgo., 1975-76; commr. Uniform State Laws Commn. Minn., 1973—; v.p. Nat. Uniform Laws Com., 1991-93, exec. comm., 1991—, sec., 1997—; acad. fellow Am. Coll. Trusts and Estates Counsel, 1975—; vis. scholar Am. Bar Found., Chgo., 1975-76; trustee Gt. No. Iron Ore Properties, 1982—, Uniform Laws Found., 1992—; advisor Restatement of Law Second, Property, 1977—, Restatement of Law Trusts (Prudent Investor Rule), 1989-90, Restatement of Law Third, Trusts, 1993—; chmn. bd. dirs. Ednl. Credit Mgmt. Corp., 1993—; bd. dirs. Fiduciary Counselling Inc. Author: Stein on Probate, 1976, 3d edit., 1995, How to Study Law and Take Law Exams, 1996, Estate Planning Under the Tax Reform Act of 1976, 2d edit, 1978, In Pursuit of Excellence: A History of the University of Minnesota Law School, 1980, contbr. articles to profl. jours. Founding bd. dirs. Park Ridge Ctr., 1985-95; co-chair Gov.'s Task Force on Ctr. for Treatment of Torture Victims, 1985, bd. dirs., 1985-87. Fellow Am. Bar Found (bd. dirs. 1987-94), Am. Coll. Tax Counsel; mem. ABA (coun. sect. of legal edn. and admission to bar 1986-91, vice chairperson 1991-92, chair-elect 1992-93, chair 1993-94), Internat. Acad. Estate and Trust Law (academician), Am. Judicature Soc. (bd. dirs. 1984-88), Am. Law Inst. (coun. mem. 1987—, exec. com. 1993—), Minn. Bar Assn. (bd. govs. 1979-94, exec. coun., probate and trust law sect. 1973-77), Hennepin County Bar Assn. Home: 990 N Lake Shore Dr Apt 7A Chicago IL 60611-1342 Office: American Bar Assn 750 N Lake Shore Dr Chicago IL 60611-4497

STEIN, ROBERT BENJAMIN, biomedical researcher, physician; b. Buffalo, Oct. 28, 1950; s. Frank and Eleanor (Bankoff) S.; m. Marcia Joan Lieberman, Aug. 10, 1975 (div.); children: Rebecca Anne, Joshua David; m. Sophia Anne Rose, Dec. 29, 1989 (div.); children: Susan Claire, Stephanie Michelle; m. Faye Elizabeth Sutherland, Aug. 12, 2000. BS, Ind. U., 1972; MD, PhD, Duke U., 1979. Diplomate Am. Bd. Anatomic and Clin. Pathology. House staff Duke U. Med. Ctr., Durham, N.C., 1980-83; sr. rsch. fellow Dept Virus and Cell Biology Merck Sharp & Dohme Rsch. Labs, West Point, Pa., 1983-87, assoc. dir. molecular and cardiovascular pharmacology, 1987-89, sr. dir., head dept. pharmacology, 1989-90; v.p. rsch. Ligand Pharms., Inc., San Diego, 1990-92, v.p. rsch. and preclin. devel., 1992-93, sr. v.p., CSO, 1993-96; exec. v.p., rsch. and preclin. devel. DuPont Merck, Wilmington, Del., 1996-98; exec. v.p. rsch. and preclin. DuPont Pharms., Wilmington, 1998—. Contbr. articles to profl. jours., chpts. to books. Ins. Med. scholar, 1977-79; James B. Duke scholar, 1976-78; Lang Med. Pub. award, 1979; NIH grantee, 1974-75. Fellow Am. Soc. Clin. Pathologists, N.Y. Acad. Scis., Am. Physiol. Soc., AAAS, Sigma Xi, Phi Beta Kappa, Alpha Omega Alpha. Avocations: piano, history, literature. Office: DuPont Pharms E400-2426 PO Box 80400 Wilmington DE 19880-0400 E-mail: Robert.B.Stein@dupontpharma.com.

STEIN, ROBERT FOSTER, astrophysicist, educator; b. N.Y.C., Mar. 4, 1935; s. Arthur H. and Louise (Halpern) S.; m. Laura Cooper, Dec. 21, 1958; children: Karen, Tamara. BS, U. Chgo., 1957; PhD, Columbia U., 1966. Lectr. CCNY, N.Y.C., 1959-61; rsch. fellow Mt. Wilson and Palomar Obs., Pasadena, Calif., 1966-67, Harvard Coll. Obs., Cambridge, Mass., 1967-69; asst. prof. astrophysics Brandeis U., Waltham, Mass., 1969-76; assoc. prof. astronomy Mich. State U., East Lansing, 1976-80, prof. physics and astronomy, 1981—. Cons. Smithsonian Astrophys. Obs., Cambridge, 1969-79, NASA, Washington, 1980-82, Jet Propulsion Lab., Pasadena, 1983-88; vis. fellow Joint Inst. Lab. Astrophys., Boulder, 1973-74. Author: Stellar Evolution, 1966; contbr. numerous articles to sci. publs. Mem. Am. Astron. Soc., Internat. Astron. Union, Norwegian Acad. Sci. and Letters, Lansing Area Folklore Soc. (dance coord. 1977-87, membership coord. 1989-92, co-treas. 1992—). Avocation: square and contra dancing. Office: Dept Physics/Astronomy Mich State U East Lansing MI 48824 Business E-Mail: stein@pa.msu.edu.

STEIN, RUTH ELIZABETH KLEIN, physician; b. N.Y.C., Nov. 2, 1941; d. Theodore and Mimi (Foges) Klein; m. H. David Stein, June 9, 1963; children: Lynn Andrea Stein Melnick, Sharon Lisa, Deborah Michelle. AB, Barnard Coll., 1962; MD, Albert Einstein Coll. Medicine, 1966. Diplomate Am. Bd. Pediat. Intern, then resident Bronx Mcpl. Hosp. Ctr., 1966-68; sr. resident, fellow; instr. dept. pediats. George Washington U., Washington, 1968-70; with Albert Einstein Coll. of Medicine, Bronx, 1970-77, assoc. prof. pediats., 1977-83, prof., 1983—; vice-chmn. dept. pediats. Albert Einstein Coll., 1992—2002, dir. office of acad. affairs, dept. pediats., 1997—2002; pediatrician-in-chief, dir. pediats. Jacobi Med. Ctr. (formerly Bronx Mcpl. Hosp. Ctr.), 1992-97. Vis. prof. pub. health dept. epidemiology Yale U. Sch. Medicine, New Haven, 1986-87; scholar-in-residence United Hosp. Fund, N.Y., 1995-97; dir., prin. investigator Preventive Intervention Rsch. Ctr. for Child Health, N.Y., 1983-94, Nat. Child Health Assessment Planning Project, N.Y., Behavioral Pediatric Tng. Program, N.Y.; dir. gen. pediatrics Pediat. Divsn., N.Y., 1992-97; apptd. to Montefiore Med. Ctr., North Ctrl. Bronx Hosp., Jacobi Med. Ctr.; bd. dirs. Ctr. for Child Health Rsch. of Am. Acad. Pediatrics, mem. exec. com., 1999-2004; bd. Children, Youth and Families, co-chmn. com. on evaluation of child health, 2002-04, NRC/Inst. Medicine, 1999-. Editor: Caring for Children with Chronic Illness: Issues and Strategies, 1989, Health Care for Children: What's Right, What's Wrong, What's Next, 1997; mem. editorial bd. Jour. Behavioral and Devel. Pediatrics; contbr. articles to profl. jours. Fellow Am. Acad. Pediats.; mem. APHA, Am. Pediatric Soc., Soc. for Pediat. Rsch., Ambulatory Pediat. Assn. (bd. dirs. 1982-89, pres. 1987-88, rsch. award 1995, Ray Helfer award 1999), N.Y. Acad. Medicine (chmn. N.Y. forum on child health 2001--), Soc. for Devel. and Behavioral Pediats., Alpha Omega Alpha. Jewish. Home: 91 Larchmont Ave Larchmont NY 10538-3748 Office: Albert Einstein Coll Med Montefiore Med Ctr Dept Pediat 111 E 210 St Bronx NY 10467-2804 Business E-Mail: rstein@aecom.yu.edu.

STEIN, SOL, publisher, writer, editor in chief; b. Chgo, Ill, Oct. 13, 1926; s. Louis and Zelda (Zam) S.; m. Patricia Day, Mar. 31, 1962 (div. Oct. 1997); children: Kevin David, Jeffrey Lewelyn, Leland Dana, Robert Bruce, Andrew Charles, David Day, Elizabeth Day; m. Edith Tennenbaum Shapiro, Nov. 25, 2000. BSS, CCNY, 1948; MA, Columbia U., 1949, postgrad., 1949-51. Lectr. social studies CCNY, 1948-51; sr. editor, ideological adv. staff Voice of Am., US State Dept., 1951-53; gen. editor, originator Beacon Press Paperbacks, Boston, 1954—; mng. editor Rsch. Inst. Am., 1956—58; cons. to pres. Harcourt, Brace, Jovanovich, NYC, 1958-59; exec. v.p. The Mid-Century Book Soc., NYC, 1959-62; pres., editor in chief Stein & Day Pubs., Briarcliff Manor, NY, 1962-89; pres. The Colophon Corp., Scarborough, NY, 1983-95, The WritePro Corp., 1989—2001, The Stein Software Corp., 1993—. Lectr., playwright Columbia U., 1958-60, Dialogue for Writers, Pub., U. Calif., Irvine, 1990-93; treas. The Forensic Found., N.Y.C., 1959-62; founding mem. Playwrights Group, The Actors Studio, 1957. Author: (plays) The Illegitimist, 1953 (1st prize Dramatists Alliance), A Shadow of My Enemy, 1957, (novels) The Husband, 1969, The Magician, 1971. Living Room, 1974, The Childkeeper, 1975, Other People, 1979, The Resort, 1980, The Touch of Treason, 1985, A Deniable Man, 1989, The Best Revenge, 1991 (computer software) WritePro, The Stein Creative Writing Program, 1989—, FirstAid for Writers, 1991, FictionMaster, 1993, WritePro for Business, 1996; (non-fiction) A Feast for Lawyers, 1989, Stein on Writing, 1995, How to Grow a Novel, 1999, (with James Baldwin) Native Sons, 2004; also articles, revs. poetry. Exec. dir. Am. Com. for Cultural Freedom, 1953-56; mem. exec. com. Am. Friends of Captive Nations. Served to 1st lt. AUS, 1945-47. Fellow Yaddo Found., 1952, MacDowell Colony, 1952-56. Recipient Disting. Instr. award U. Calif. at Irvine, 1992. Mem. New Dramatists Com. (coun. mem.), Internat. Brotherhood Magicians (hon. life), Writers Guild Am. East, Authors Guild, Phi Beta Kappa. Avocations: tennis, inventing computer software programs. Office: 277 E South Broadway Tarrytown NY 10591-5322 Personal E-mail: solstein@aol.com.

STEIN, STANLEY RICHARD, lawyer, fast food company executive; b. Boston, Apr. 17, 1942; s. Frederick J. and Minnie L. (Gilette) S.; m. Ann Debra Stein, July 2, 1967; children: Jason, Jamie. BA, Boston U., 1964; JD, Boston Coll., 1967. Bar: Mass., Ohio. Supervisory atty. NLRB, 1967-72; head labor rels. dept. Schottenstein, Garel & Zox, Columbus, Ohio, 1972-74; labor rels. counsel McDonald's Corp., Oak Brook, Ill., 1974-78, v.p. labor rels., 1978-81, v.p. pers. and labor rels., 1981— . Mem. ABA.

STEIN, STEPHEN WILLIAM, lawyer; b. NYC, Apr. 12, 1937; s. Melvin S. and Cornelia (Jacobowitz) S.; m. Judith N., Jan. 22, 1966. AB, Princeton U., 1959; LLB, Columbia U., 1962; LLM, NYU, 1963. Bar: N.Y. 1962. Assoc. White & Case, N.Y.C., 1963-67; atty. advisor U.S. Agy. Internat. Devel., Washington, 1967-69, regional legal advisor Mission to India New Delhi, 1969-71, asst. gen. counsel Washington, 1971-73; assoc. ptnr. Delson & Gordon, N.Y.C., 1973-87; ptnr. Kelley Drye & Warren, N.Y.C., 1987—. Mem. U.S. exec. com. Indonesian Trade, Tourism & Investment Promotion Program, 1990-92; mem. U.S.-Indonesia Trade & Investment Adv. Com., 1989-92; vis. instr. internat. Devel. Law Inst., 1993; lectr. Internat. Law Inst., Washington, 1984, 85; spkr. in field. Mem. ABA (mem. sect. internat. law, co-chair African law com. 1999-2002), Assn. Bar of City of N.Y. (mem. com. project fin. 1997-2003, mem. com. Asian affairs 1992—, former mem. others), Am. Indonesian C. of C. (bd. dirs. 1986—, pres. 1989-96). Home: 320 Central Park W New York NY 10025-7659 Office: Kelley Drye & Warren 101 Park Ave New York NY 10178-0062 Business E-Mail: sstein@kelleydrye.com.

STEIN, T. PETER, medical educator; b. London, Apr. 27, 1941; m. Florence Stein. PhD, Cornell U., 1967. Asst. prof. U. of Pa., Phila., 1969—76, assoc. prof., 1976—84; prof. U. of Medicine and Dentistry of NJ-SOM, Stratford, NJ, 1984—. Recipient Field medal, Am. Aeronautics and Astronautics Soc., 1992, Korrs Rsch. award, Am. Osteo. Assn., 2003. Office: Room 110A Sci Ctr 2 Medical Center Drive Stratford NJ 08084 Personal E-mail: tpstein@umdnj.edu. E-mail: tpstein@umdnj.edu.

STEIN, THEODORE ANTHONY, biochemist, educator; b. St. Louis, Aug. 30, 1938; s. Leonard A. and Mathilda M. S.; m. Virginia M. Loos, 1994. BS, St. Louis U., 1960; MS, So. Ill. U., 1970; PhD, CUNY, 1987. Rsch. instr. surgery Washington U. Sch. Medicine, St. Louis, 1972-75; rsch. supr. surgery L.I. Jewish-Hillside Med. Ctr., New Hyde Park, N.Y., 1975-76, rsch. coord. surgery, 1977-93; asst. prof. surgery SUNY, Stony Brook, 1978-89, Albert Einstein Sch. Medicine, Bronx, N.Y., 1989—. Dir. rsch. and dir. vascular lab. L.I. Vascular Ctr., Roslyn, N.Y., 1994—; biostats. cons. NIH grantee, 1962; Am. Liver Found. grantee, 1984. Contbr. articles to profl. jours., chpts. to books. Mem. AAAS, N.Y. Acad. Scis., Am. Fedn. Clin. Rsch., Am. Pub. Health Assn., Am. Gastroenterol. Assn., Sigma Xi. Republican. Roman Catholic. Achievements include development of chromatographic methods to determine prostaglandin and leukotriene content in tissues using fluorescent agents to increase sensitivity, elastase activity in the aorta with disease, and active anabolites of 5-fluoracil in tumors; improvement of regulation of liver growth after surgery by diet; demonstration of diagnostic value of liver function tests, surgery on obese patients interferes with sugar metabolism and intestinal function; research in etiology of pancreatitis and pharmacological modification of pancreatic function; effect of stress on the stomach and colon; investigation of the mediators of inflammatory bowel disease, the long-term reduction of stroke after carotid endarterectomy, the benefit of composite grafts for distal limb salvage, the value of completion angiography for distal bypass, risk factors which may be related to rapid growth of abdominal aortic aneurysms, the value of axillo-axillary bypass grafts. Home: 10 Glamford Rd Port Washington NY 11050-2437 Office: LI Vascular Ctr 1050 Northern Blvd Roslyn NY 11576-1503 E-mail: tajcs10@hotmail.com.

STEIN, THOMAS HENRY, social science educator; b. Elmhurst, Ill., May 17, 1949; s. Peter Leonard and Marion Edith (Zirbel) S.; m. Alberta Piazza, July 10, 1971; 1 child, Heather. BA in Polit. Sci., Loyola U., Chgo., 1971; postgrad., Loyola U., 1972-76; MS in Edn., Pacific Western U., 1988, PhD in Edn., 1989. Cert. tchr., Ill. Budget analyst, dean global studies divsn. U.S. Dept. Def., Gt. Lakes Naval Sta., Ill., 1971—72; global studies dean, tchr. social sci., coach bowling, softball Mother Guerin High Sch., River Grove, Ill., 1972—; tchr. Highland Park (Ill.) High Sch., 1981-84. Instr. Franklin Park (Ill.) Park Dist., 1977—; tchr. Triton Coll., River Grove, 1990-91; evaluator Chgo. Met. History Fair, 1980-89; faculty adviser Scholastic, Inc., N.Y.C., 1990—; dir. Students Against Animal Cruelty, River Grove, 1991—; moderator Nat. Honor Soc., 1993—; adj. faculty St. Mary's U., 2003--. With Ill. N.G., 1971-77. Recipient Outstanding Achievement award Am. Express/Assn. Am. Geographers, 1989, Heart of the Sch. award for Peace and Justice, Archdiocese of Chgo. Fellow Acad. Polit. Sci.; mem. ASCD, Nat. Coun. Social Studies, Nat. Hist. Soc., Ctr. Study of the Presidency, Nat. Cath. Edn. Assn., Orgn. History Tchrs., Am. Polit. Sci. Assn. Democrat. Roman Catholic. Home: 3601 Emerson St Franklin Park IL 60131-1713 Office: Mother Guerin High Sch 8001 W Belmont Ave River Grove IL 60171-1096 Office Phone: 708-453-6233.

STEIN, TOMIKO, infectious disease specialist; b. New Delhi, July 27, 1966; s. George Jay and Mitsue (Tokuzawa) S. BA, Smith Coll., 1988; MD, MPH, Tulane U., 1992. Intern Baylor Coll. Medicine, Houston, 1992-93, resident in internal medicine, 1993-95; fellow in infectious diseases L.A. Co-Harbor UCLA Med. Ctr., Torrance, 1995-97, fellow in HIV, 1997-98; physician AIDS Healthcare Found., L.A., 1999—. Mem. ACP, Infectious Disease Assn. Calif. (assoc.), Infectious Disease Soc. Am. (assoc.). Office: AIDS Healthcare Found 1300 N Vermont Ave Ste 407 Los Angeles CA 90027-6005 Business E-Mail: tomikos@aidshealth.org.

STEIN, ZENA A. health facility administrator, psychiatry educator; BA in History, U. Capetown, South Africa, 1941, MA in History, 1942; MB, BChir, U. Witwatersand, Johannesburg, South Africa, 1950. Dir. epidemiology of brain disorders rsch. dept. N.Y. State Psychiat. Inst., N.Y.C., 1968—; prof. pub. health Columbia U. Sch. Pub. Health, N.Y.C., 1973—, prof. pub. health Gertrude H. Sergievsky Ctr., 1977—, assoc. dir. rsch. and acad. affairs, 1986—; co-dir. HIV Ctr. for Clin. and Behavioral Studies N.Y. State Psychiat. Inst. and Columbia U., N.Y.C., 1987—; prof. psychiatry dept. psychiatry Columbia U., N.Y.C., 1991—. Cons. WHO, UNICEF; mem. study sects. NIMH, NIEHS, NIOSH, NICHD; com. mem. NAS. Co-editor: (with M. Wright, J. Scandlyn) Women's Health and Apartheid: The Health of Women and Children and the Future of Progressive Health Care in Southern Africa, 1988, (with A. Zwi) Action on AIDS in Southern Africa: Maputo Conference on Health in Transition in Southern Africa, 1990; contbr. chpts. to books and articles to profl. jours. Grantee Fogarty Ctr., NIMH. Office: HIV Ctr NY State Psychiat Inst 722 W 168th St New York NY 10032-2603

STEINAGLE, MARTIN GENE, contractor, paralegal, poet, writer; b. Buffalo, N.Y., Aug. 27, 1951; s. Raymond George and Dorothy Jean (Martin) Steinagle. Cert.: So. Career Inst., Boca Raton, Fla. (paralegal) 1987; comml. art illustrated design Wesport, Conn., 1971, electromechanicl Tech. Advanced Tng. Ctr., Kenmore, N.Y., 1983, firearms N. Am. Sch. of Firearms, Scranton, Pa., 1982. Carpenter Barden Homes, Middleport, NY, 1974—77; grademan Lockport Excavating Inc., Lockport, NY, 1978—81; illustrator Thencan, Lockport, NY, 1985—88; owner New Day Constrn., Lockport, NY, 1988—. Author: Everyday, But Not Common Poems and Quotes, 2001, More, but NotCommon Poems and Quotes, 2004, (songs) Please, Why, 1974, Every Bus on the Street, 1974, (poem) Love is Two, 1982, You're Like a Candle, 1973. Mem.: Improved Order of Red Men, Loyal Order of Moose (treas. 1985—). Democrat. Judaic Christian. Avocations: art, reading, writing, music, computers. Home and Office: 284 Willow St Apt 24 Lockport NY 14094

STEINBACH, ALICE, journalist; b. Balt. Student, U. London. Feature writer Balt. Sun, 1981—; formerly dir. pub. info. Balt. Mus. Art. Recip. Pulitzer Prize for feature writing, 1985. Office: Balt Sun 501 N Calvert St Baltimore MD 21278-0001

STEINBACH, FALKO, musician, music educator; b. Aachen, Germany, Sept. 30, 1957; arrived in U.S., 1999; s. Hans Horst Steinbach and Marthel Gawellek; m. Eva Maria Lipton; children: Tankred, Ronja. B in Piano/Theory, Musikhochschule, Cologne, Germany, 1983, MusM, 1984, D in Piano Performance, 1986; cert. in advanced studies, Guildhall Sch. Music and Drama, London, 1987. Instr. Musikschule, Lohmar, Germany, 1987—88; Lehrauftrag U. Cologne, 1989—99; asst. prof. piano U. N.Mex., Albuquerque, 1999—. Compendium of Piano Technique, 1995;, performer more than 500 concerts in Europea, U.S. and Asia, composer of more than 80 compositions mostly for piano, 11 CD's. Deutscher Akademischer Austauschdienst grant, German Dept. State, 1986, CD grant, Endowment of the Arts NRW, 1997. Mem.: Komponistenverband-Gesellschaft für Musikalische Aufführungs-und Mechanische Verfielfältigungsrechte-Gesellschaft zur Verwertung von Leistucjngsschutz, Deutscher Ton Künstlerverband, Profl. Music Tchrs. N.Mex. (bd. dirs. 1999—), Kiwanis Club Albuquerque. Roman Catholic. Avocations: music, theater, dance. Home: 1712 Notre Dame NE Albuquerque NM 87106 Office: Univ NMex Albuquerque NM 87131-1411

STEINBACH, MEREDITH LYNN, writer, educator; b. Ames, Iowa, Mar. 18, 1949; d. Christopher Gene and Joy Janice (Johnson) Steinbach; m. Charles Ossian Hartman, May 5, 1979 (div. Dec. 1991); 1 child Zachary Steinbach Hartman. BGS, U. Iowa, 1973, MFA, 1976. Teaching fellow U. Iowa, Iowa City, 1975-76; writer in residence Antioch Coll., Yellow Springs, Ohio, 1976-77; lectr. in fiction Northwestern U., Evanston, Ill., 1977-79; vis. asst. prof. U. Washington, 1979-82; Bunting fellow Harvard-Radcliffe, Cambridge, Mass., 1982-83; asst., assoc. prof. Brown U., Providence, R.I., 1983-97, prof. English, 1997—. Author: Zara, 1982, Here Lies the Water, 1990, Reliable Light, 1990, The Birth of the World As We Know It, Or, Teiresias, 1996, In the Realm of Which There Is No Sign, 1995. Recipient Pushcart prize Best of the Small Presses, 1976, R.I. award for Excellence in Lit., R.I. Coun. on Arts, 1986-87, O'Henry award for the short story, 1990, creative writing fellow in fiction Nat. Endowment for Arts, 1978; Thomas J. Watson travel grantee Thomas J. Watson Inst. for Internat. Study, France and Greece, 1993-94. Mem.: PEN, Assoc. Writing Programs, Amnesty Internat. Office: Brown U Dept of English Box 1852 Providence RI 02912 E-mail: Meredith_Steinbach@Brown.edu.

STEINBAUM, ROBERT S. publisher, lawyer; b. Englewood, N.J., Oct. 13, 1951; s. Paul S. and Esther R. (Rosenberg) S.; m. Rosemary Konner, May 26, 1982; children: Marshall, Elliot. BA, Yale U., 1973; JD, Georgetown U., 1976. Bar: D.C. 1976, N.J. 1980, N.Y. 1982. Atty. Cole & Groner P.C., Washington, 1976-79; asst. U.S. atty. U.S. Atty.'s Office, Newark, 1979-84; atty. Scarpone & Edelson, Newark, 1984-87; publ. N.J. Law Jour., Newark, 1987—. Trustee N.J. Jewish News, Whippany, 1990-95, 96—, pres., 2002-04, Blood Ctr. N.J., East Orange, 1987-93, Leadership N.J., 1990, Leadership Newark, 1997—, United Jewish Cmtys. MetroWest, N.J., 2002—. Office: NJ Law Jour PO Box 20081 238 Mulberry St Newark NJ 07101-6081 Business E-Mail: rsteinbaum@amlaw.com.

STEINBERG, ALAN WOLFE, investment company executive; b. Bklyn., Oct. 26, 1927; s. Benjamin F. and Gertrude (Wolfe) S.; m. Suzanne Nichols, Oct. 12, 1958; children: Carol Albanese, Laura Frohman, Benjamin T. AB with honors and spl. distinction in math, Columbia U., 1947, MS, 1950. Indsl. engr. USDA, Washington, 1948-50; ops. rschr. Port of N.Y. Authority, 1950-55; prof. engring. NYU, 1956-63; pres. Am. Computing Ctrs., N.Y.C., 1962-66; v.p., dir. TBS Computer Ctrs., N.Y.C., 1967-76; mng. ptnr. Alan W. Steinberg Partnership, N.Y.C. and Coral Gables, Fla., 1974—. Contbr. articles to profl. jours. Nat. advisor automation United Jewish Appeal, N.Y.C., 1965-75; trustee Fla. Nature Conservancy, Winter Park, 1990—, treas., 1990—; bd. dirs., treas. Fla. Audubon Soc., Casselberry, 1984-95, Defenders of Wildlife, Washington, 1985-95, chmn. bd. dirs. 1995-98, treas., 2000—; 1st v.p. Tropical Audubon Soc., South Miami, 1983-93. Recipient Chmn.'s award Fla. Audubon Soc., 1989, 93; funded named scholarship Columbia Coll. Fellow Fairchild Tropical Garden; mem. Columbia Coll. Alumni Assn. (bd. dirs. 1992-93, sustaining), Phi Beta Kappa. Home: 5522 Riviera Dr Coral Gables FL 33146-2747 Office: 1501 Venera Ave Ste 205 Coral Gables FL 33146-3052 E-mail: SteinbergX@aol.com.

STEINBERG, ARTHUR IRWIN, periodontist, educator; b. Pitts., Sept. 16, 1935; s. Ben and Sylvia (Jacobs) S.; m. Barbara Fay Ehrenkranz, May 23, 1959; chldren: Shari Jill, Mindy Ruth, Michael Eli. BS in Microbiology, U. Pitts., 1957, DMD cum laude, 1963, postgrad. in radiobiology, 1957-59; diploma in periodontology-immunology, Harvard U., 1966. Asst. prof. periodontology SUNY, Buffalo, 1966-67; assoc. prof. periodontology Temple U., Phila., 1967-68, assoc. prof. grad. periodontology, 1968-70; attending periodontist Phoenixville (Pa.) Hosp., 1971—95; clin. assoc. prof. U. Pa. Sch. Dental Medicine, 1981—2002, clin. prof. of gen. restorative dentistry, 2002—. Mem. infections control com., by-laws com., religious affairs com., 1977—, credentials com., 1982—; mem. staff Suburban Gen. Hosp. Norristown, Pa., 1971-80, Phoenixville Hosp., 1968-95; asst. prof. periodontics U. Pa., 1973-82, clin. assoc. prof., 1982-2002, clin. prof. of general restorative dentistry, 2000—, admissions interviewer Sch. Dental Medicine, 2002—; lectr. continuing edn., off-campus program U. Pitts., 1973-93; Fulbright-Hays lectr. Nat. U. Ireland, Cork, 1970-71; vis. prof. Cork Dental Sch. and Hosp., 1971—; lectr. Periodontology Soc. Madrid, 1980, 5th Region Soc. Periodontology Viña Del Mar, Chile, 1985; dentist in pediatrics Charlestown (Mass.) Boys Club, 1965-66; spkr. Periodontists Conv., Chgo., 1966, N.J. Coll. Medicine and Dentistry, Conn. Dental Assn., 1967, U. Ind. Schs. Dentistry and Medicine,

Phila. Ann. Dental Sci. Session, 1969, N.J. Dental Assn., 1970, Wilmington chpt. Sigma Epsilon Delta, 1974, Lehigh Valley Dental Soc.m 1974, Inst. Medicine, Bucharest, Romania, 1976, Irish Dental Assn., 1992, other confs., and convs.; participant Project Head Start, Childrens Hosp., Boston, 1966; mem. fund-raising subcom. Harvard U. Sch. Dental Medicine, 1980—; mem. faculty U. Pitts., 1988-93; commencement spkr. U. Pa. Sch. Dental Medicine, 1988, Harcum Coll. Dental Hygiene Program, 1994-95, C.C. of Phila. Dental Hygiene Program, 2002; presenter Phila. County Dental Soc., Ann. Meeting Liberty Dental Conf., 1988, 90, Acad. Gen. Dentistry Ann. Meeting, 1988; judge divsn. medicine and healthcare Del. Valley Sci. Fair, 1997; clin. prof. gen. restorative dentistry U. Pa., 2002; admissions interviewer U. Pa. Sch. Dental Medicine, 2002—. Contbg. author: The Fulbright Experience, 1987, Dentistry and the Allergic Patient, 1973; contbr. numerous articles to profl. jours. Named to Phoenixville Hosp. Hall of Honor, 1996; USPHS fellow; reipient Dean J.L.T. Appleton Excellence in CLin. Tchg. award U. Pa., 2003. Fellow Acad. Dentistry Internat., Internat. Acad. Dental Studies, Am. Coll. Dentists, Coll. Physicians Phila., Pierre Fouchard Acad.; mem. AMA, AAUP, Harvard Dental Alumni Assn., Harvard Odontological Soc., Fulbright Assn., Nat. Fulbright Alumni Assn. (a founder 1976, v.p.fin. affairs 1976-79), Am. Acad. Periodontology (ins. com. 1969, hosp. care com. 1973-74, continuing edn. spkr. 1976 conv., 1983 conv., nominating com. chmn. Pa. region to exec. coun. 1975, nat. clin. affairs com. 1984), Am. Coll. Clin. Pharmacology, Northea. Soc. Periodontists, Acad. Stomatology Phila., Phila. Acad. Scis., Sigma Xi, Omicron Kappa Upsilon (life, pres. 2004—), Psi Omega (dep. councillor Zeta chpt. 1977-79, 2004—), Masons (32 degree Shriner), Legion Honor Chapel Four Chaplains, Rotary (dir. 1973-76, chmn. found. com., chmn. internat. svc. 1974-76), B'nai B'rith, Hadassah (assoc. mem.), Harvard of Phila., 25 Yr. Club U. Pa., Area Study (pres. 1976-77), Am. Soc. Ret. Dentists. Home and Office: 1681 Pheasant Ln Norristown PA 19403-3331 Office Phone: 610-539-7727. Business E-Mail: arthurst@pobox.upenn.edu.

STEINBERG, CHARLES ALLAN, electronics manufacturing company executive; b. Bklyn., June 7, 1934; s. Joseph and Rose (Graff) S.; m. Helen Greene, June 16, 1956; children— Ruth, Steven, Bruce. BSE.E., CCNY, 1955; MSE.E., M.I.T., 1958. Mem. tech. staff Bell Telephone Labs., Whippany, N.J., 1955; research and teaching asst. MIT, 1955-58; engring. sect. mgr. Airborne Instruments Lab. div. Eaton Corp., Deer Park, N.Y., 1958-63; exec. v.p. Ampex Corp., Redwood City, Calif., 1963-86, pres., chief exec. officer, 1986-88; pres. broadcast and profl. co. Sony Corp. Am., Montvale, N.J., 1988-99, sr. advisor San Jose, Calif., 1999—. Contbr. numerous articles on med. electronics and diagnosis, info. systems to profl. jours.; patentee computer techniques in medicine. Bd. dirs. Santa Clara County (Calif.) United Fund, 1969-71. Mem. IEEE, CCNY Alumni Assn., M.I.T. Alumni Assn., Sigma Xi, Tau Beta Pi, Eta Kappa Nu. Office: Sony Electronics 3300 Zanker Rd San Jose CA 95134-1901

STEINBERG, DANIEL, preventive medicine physician, educator; b. Windsor, Ont., Can., July 21, 1922; came to U.S., 1922; s. Maxwell Robert and Bess (Krupp) S.; m. Sara Murdock, Nov. 30, 1946 (dec. July 1986); children: Jonathan Henry, Ann Ballard, David Ethan; m. Mary Ellen Stratthaus, Aug. 11, 1991; 1 stepchild: Katrin Seifert. BS with highest distinction, Wayne State U., 1941, MD with highest distinction, 1944; PhD with distinction (fellow Am. Cancer Soc. 1950-51), Harvard U., 1951; MD (hon.), U. Gothenburg, 1991. Intern Boston City Hosp., 1944-45; physician Detroit Receiving Hosp., 1945-46; instr. physiology Boston U. Sch. Medicine, 1947-48; joined USPHS, 1951, med. dir., 1959; research staff lab. cellular physiology and metabolism Nat. Heart Inst., 1951-53, chief sect. metabolism, 1956-61, chief of lab. metabolism, 1962-68; lectr. grad. program NIH, 1955, mem. sci. adv. com. ednl. activities, 1955-61, com. chmn., 1955-60; mem. metabolism study sect. USPHS, 1959-61; chmn. heart and lung research rev. com. B Nat. Heart, Lung and Blood Inst., 1977-79; vis. scientist Carlsberg Labs., Copenhagen, 1952-53, Nat. Inst. Med. Research, London, 1960-61, Rockefeller U., 1981; pres. Lipid Research Inc., 1961-64, adv. bd., 1964-73; prof. medicine Sch. Medicine, U. Calif., San Diego, 1968—. Former editor Jour. Lipid Research; mem. editorial bd. Jour Clin. Investigation, 1969-74, Jour. Biol. Chemistry, 1980-84, Arteriosclerosis, 1980—; exec. editor Analytical Biochemistry, 1978-80; contbr. articles to profl. jours. Bd. dirs. Found. Advanced Edn. in Scis., 1959-68, pres., 1956-62, 65-67. Served to capt. M.C. AUS, World War II. Mem. Nat. Acad. Scis., AAAS, Am. Acad. Arts and Scis., Am. Heart Assn. (mem. exec. com. coun. on arteriosclerosis 1960-63, 65-73, chmn. coun. arteriosclerosis 1967-69), Fedn. Am. Scientists (exec. com. 1957-58), Am. Soc. Biol. Chemists, Am. Soc. Clin. Investigation, Assn. Am. Physicians, Am. Fedn. Clin. Rsch., Inst. Medicine, European Atherosclerosis Discussion Group, Alpha Omega Alpha. Home: 7742 Whitefield Pl La Jolla CA 92037-3810 Office: U Calif San Diego Dept Medicine 9500 Gilman Dr La Jolla CA 92093-0682 Personal E-mail: dsteinb1@san.rr.com. Business E-Mail: dsteinberg@ucsd.edu.

STEINBERG, DARRELL S. state legislator; b. San Francisco, Oct. 15, 1959; BA, UCLA, 1981; JD, U. Calif., Davis, 1984. Employee rights atty. Calif. State Employees Assn., 1985—94; adminstrv. law judge State of Calif., 1994—98; lawyer Mackenroth, Ryan, and Fong, 1996—98; city councilman City of Sacramento, 1992—98; mem., dist. 9 Calif. State Assembly, 1998—. Bd. dirs. Sacramento Employment and Tng. Agy., 1992—96, Sacramento Metro Air Quality Mgmt. Dist., 1992—96, Regional Transit, 1992—96; chair Appropriations Com.; mem. Housing and Cmty. Devel., Judiciary Com., Local Govt. Com. Mem. Jewish Cmty. Rels. Coun., 1986—; pres. bd. dirs. Capital Unite Coun., 2001—. Mem.: Calif. Bar Assn. Democrat. Jewish. Mailing: PO Box 942849 Rm 2114 Sacramento CA 94249 Office: 915 L St Ste 110 Sacramento CA 95814

STEINBERG, DAVID ISAAC, social sciences educator, consultant; b. Cambridge, Mass., Nov. 26, 1928; s. Naaman and Miriam (Goldberg) S.; m. Isabel Maxwell, 1951 (div. 1962); 1 child, Christopher; m. Ann Myongsook Lee, May 15, 1964; children: Alexander L., Eric D. BA, Dartmouth Coll., 1950; MA, Harvard U., 1955; DLitt (hon.), Sungkunkwan U., Seoul, Republic of Korea. Analyst Nat. Security Coun., Washington, 1951-53; program officer Asia Found., N.Y.C., 1956-58, asst. rep., 1958-62, 1962-63, rep., 1963-68, 1968-69; cons., sr. fgn. svc. officer AID, Washington and Bangkok (Thailand), 1969-86; ret., 1986; pres. Mansfield Ctr. for Pacific Affairs, Helena, Mont., 1986-87, Sr. Resources Internat., 1989-94; disting. prof. Korea Studies Georgetown U., Washington, 1990-94; rep. The Asia Found., Seoul, Republic of Korea, 1994-97; dir. Asian studies Sch. Fgn. Svc. Georgetown U., Washington, 1997—, Disting. prof. and dir. Asian studies, 1997—. Pvt. cons., Washington, 1987—, World Bank, 1987—, Woodrow Wilson Ctr. for Scholars of the Smithsonian Instn., Dept. of State and the Agy. for Internat. Devel., the Can. Internat. Devel. Agy., Devel. Assocs., Inc., and others; founding mem. Burma Studies Found., De Kalb, Ill., 1987. Author: Burma's Road Toward Development, 1981, Burma, 1982, The Republic of Korea Economic Transformation and Social Change, 1988, The Future of Burma, 1990, Burma: The State of Myanmar, 2001, Stone Mirror: Reflections on Contemporary Korea, 2003; co-editor Georgetown Southeast Asia Survey 2002-04. 1st lt. U.S. Army, 1953-55. Fellow Lingnan U., Canton, China, 1948, Dartmouth Coll., 1950; named Disting. Prof. of Korea Studies, Georgetown U. Mem. Assn. Asian Studies, Oriental Ceramic Soc., Asia Devel. Roundtable (chmn. 1984-86, 87—), Siam Soc., Royal Asiatic Soc. (life Korea br.), Burma Rsch. Soc. (life), Asia Soc. (cons. 1988—), Cosmos Club, Royal Bangkok (Thailand) Sports Club. Home: 6207 Goodview St Bethesda MD 20817-6101 Office: Georgetown U Sch Fgn Svc Washington DC 20057 Office Phone: 202-687-0251. E-mail: DStein620@aol.com., stienbdi@georgetown.edu.

STEINBERG, DAVID JOEL, academic administrator, historian, educator; b. N.Y.C., Apr. 5, 1937; s. Milton and Edith (Albert) S.; m. Sally Levitt (div. Dec., 1986); children: Noah, Jonah; m. Joan Diamond, Aug. 28, 1987. BA magna cum laude, Harvard U., 1959, MA, 1963, PhD, 1964; LittD, Kyung Hee U., Seoul, Korea, 1989; LLD (hon), Keimyung U., Daegu, Korea. Prof. history U. Mich., 1964-73; exec. asst. to pres. Brandeis U., Waltham, Mass., 1973-77, v.p., univ. sec., 1977-83; pres. L.I. U., Brookville, N.Y., 1985—. Testified before Com. on Fgn. Affairs, U.S. Ho. of Reps., Fgn. Affairs Com. of U.S. Senate; cons. The Ford Found., UN Fund for Population Activities. Author: Philippine Collaboration in World War II, 1967 (Univ. Press award, 1969), The Philippines: A Singular and a Plural Place, 1982, 1987, Asia in Western and World History: A Guide for Tchg., 1993; co-author: The Emergence of Modern Southeast Asia: A New History, 2004. Chmn. Commn. Ind. Colls. and Univs.; past pres. Cambridge (Mass.) Ctr. for Adult Edn., chmn. L.I. Group. English Speaking Union Exch. scholar, Malvern Coll., NDEA scholar, Fulbright Found. exch. scholar. Mem. Coun. Fgn. Rels., Assn. Asian Studies (chmn. fin. com.), Harvard Club (N.Y.C.), Century Club (N.Y.C.). Democrat. Jewish. Office: LI Univ Off Pres 700 Northern Blvd Greenvale NY 11548-1320

STEINBERG, DAVID M. securities analyst; b. Boston, June 4, 1961; s. Melvin S. and Adele H. Steinberg; m. Hilary Christine Power; children: Alexandra, Andrew, Eric. BA, Colby Coll., Waterville, Maine, 1983; MBA, Harvard Bus. Sch., Boston, 1989. Economist Data Resources, Inc., Lexington, Md., 1983—87; analyst Mehta and Isaly, NYC, 1989—91; sr. analyst and mng. dir. Volpe Brown Whelan, San Francisco, 1992—99, Deutsche Banc Alex Brown, San Francisco, 1999—. Bd. of overseers Colby Coll., 2002—. Named one of Best on the Street, Wall St. Jour., 2000, 2001. Home: 3933 Clay St San Francisco CA 94118 Office: Deutsche Bank 47th Floor 101 California St San Francisco CA 94111 Office Phone: 415-617-3296. Business E-Mail: david.m.steinberg@db.com.

STEINBERG, GREGG MARTIN, financial and management consultant, investment banker; b. Columbus, Ind., Mar. 26, 1962; s. Jerry H. and Sharla C. (Waitzman) S.; m. Stacy A. Schneider, Nov. 6, 1988; 2 children. BSBA, U. Ariz., 1982; M in Mgmt., Am. Grad. Sch. Internat. Mgmt., Glendale, Ariz., 1984. V.p. fin. Bera Hotels Ltd., Phoenix, 1984-85; gen. mgr. Les Jardains Hotel, Phoenix, 1985-87; asst. dir., sr. negotiator GVA Mergers & Acquisitions, Phoenix, 1987-88; pres. Gregg M. Steinberg Ltd., Phoenix and Chgo., 1987—; prin. Berger, Goldstein Capital Group, Inc., Chgo., 1989-91; pres. Internat. Profit Assocs., Chgo., 1992—, Integrated Bus. Analysis, Toronto, 1994—. Bd. dirs., chmn. N.W. com. Jewish Coun. for Youth Svcs., Chgo., 1989-92; bd. dirs. J.C.C., 1997—. Avocations: golf, squash. Office: Integrated Business Analysis 40 King St W Ste 4900 Toronto ON Canada M5H 4A2

STEINBERG, HARRY, pulmonologist; b. Phila., Apr. 23, 1941; s. Isadore and Eddie Steinberg; m. Nola Zirin, Aug. 23, 1960; children: Peter, Dara. BS, Albright Coll., 1962; MD, Temple U., 1966. Diplomate Am. Bd. Internal Medicine. Resident in medicine Temple U., Phila., 1966—67, L.I. Jewish Hosp., New Hyde Park, NY, 1967—72, chief pulmonary medicine & critical care medicine, 1974—2000, vice chair medicine, 2000—; fellow in pulmonary disease U. Pa., Phila., 1972—74. Contbr. chapters to books, articles to profl. jours. Maj. U.S. Army, 1970—72. Rsch. grantee, NIH, Pharm. grantee, Am. Lung Assn. Fellow: ACP; mem.: AAAS, Am. Thoracic Soc. Office: LI Jewish Hosp 27005 76th Ave New Hyde Park NY 11040 Office Phone: 718-470-7271. Office Fax: 718-470-0827. Business E-Mail: hsteinberg@lij.edu.

STEINBERG, HOWARD, chemical company executive, consultant; b. Chgo., Aug. 23, 1926; s. Leo and Hattie (Seskind) Steinberg; m. Eve Taubman, Feb. 10, 1946; children: Lisa Beth Leonard, Gary Robert, Erik Jon. BS, U. Ill., Urbana, 1946—48; PhD, UCLA, 1948—51. Rsch. chemist Aerojet Gen. Corp., Azusa, Calif., 1952—52; rsch. assoc. UCLA, 1952—53; collaborator USDA, Pasadena, Calif., 1953—54; mgr. organic rsch. U.S. Borax Rsch. Corp., Anaheim, Calif., 1954—58, asst. dir., 1958—59, assoc. dir., 1959—61, dir. chem. rsch., 1961—63, v.p., 1963—69, pres., 1969—90; v.p. US Borax and Chem. Corp., LA, 1969—90, dir., 1973—90, cons., 1990—92; dir. Ireco Chem. Co., Salt Lake City, 1970—75. Author: (book) Organoboron Chemistry; co-author (book (treatise); editor: (books) Progress in Boron Chemistry; contbr. numerous research papers; numerous US and foreign patents in field of organoboron chemistry. Mem. Sci. and Engring. Adv. Coun., Calif. State Univ., Fullerton, 1964—90; dir. Orange County Cultural Groups Found., Fullerton, Calif., 1970—71. Pre-aviation cadet Air Corp U.S. Army, 1945—45. Named to Am. Men Sci., Adv. Com. apptd. by the NAS, 1961, Leading Men in the USA, 1965; AEC Fellow, UCLA, 1950—51, AEC Postdoctoral Fellow, MIT, 1951—52. Mem.: AIME, Am. Chem. Soc., Brit. Chem. Soc., Indsl. Rsch. Inst., Soc. Chem. Industry, Phi Lambda Upsilon, Pi Mu Epsilon, Sigma Xi. Achievements include researcher and coauthor with Professor Donald J. Cram in the first two papers of his seminal work (Host-Guest chemistry) leading to his 1987 Nobel Prize in Chemistry. Avocations: woodworking, golf, fiction writing. Home and Office: 16 Corte Sevilla San Clemente CA 92673 Office Phone: 949-661-9009.

STEINBERG, HOWARD ELI, lawyer, diversified financial services company executive; b. N.Y.C., Nov. 19, 1944; s. Herman and Anne Rudel (Sinnreich) Steinberg; m. Judith Ann Schucart, Jan. 28, 1968; children: Henry Robert, Kathryn Jill. AB, U. Pa., 1965; JD, Georgetown U., 1969. Bar: N.Y. 1970, U.S. Dist. Ct. (so. and ea. dists.) N.Y. 1973, U.S. Ct. Appeals (2d cir.) 1976. Assoc. Dewey, Ballantine, Bushby, Palmer & Wood, N.Y.C., 1969-76, ptnr., 1977-83; exec. v.p., gen. counsel Reliance Group Holdings, Inc., N.Y.C., 1983-2000, exec. v.p., chief corp. ops., 2000—01; exec. v.p., gen. counsel Prudential Equity Group Inc., N.Y.C., 2001—. Chmn. N.Y. State Thruway Authority, 1996—99; dep. chmn. L.I. Power Authority, 1999—. Editor: Georgetown Law Jour., 1968—69. Bd. dirs. Puerto Rican Legal Def. and Edn. Fund, Inc., 1993—95, Sheltering Arms Childrens Svc., 1997—; bd. overseers U. Pa. Sch. Arts and Scis., 1989—2002; bd. regents Georgetown U., 1999—. Capt. JAGC USAR, 1972—74. Mem.: ABA, Securities Industry Assn. (mem. fed. regulation com. 2001—, mem. exec. com. compliance and legal divsn. 2001—), Assn. Bar City of N.Y. (mem. com. securities regulation 1984—87, mem. com. corp. law 1987—90, mem. com. fed. legis. 1990—93, chair ad hoc com. Senate Confirmation Process 1991—92), N.Y. State Bar Assn., Univ Club. Office: Prudential Equity Group Inc One New York Plaza New York NY 10292

STEINBERG, JAMES JONAH, physician, medical administrator, educator; b. Winnipeg, Man., Can., Aug. 4, 1935; s. Abraham David and Goldie (Berg) S.; m. Norma Sheila Fishman, Aug. 17, 1958; children: Deborah, Rebecca. BS in Medicine, MD, U. Man., 1959, MS in Physiology, 1962. Diplomate Am. Bd. Internal Medicine. Rsch. fellow U. Man., Winnipeg, 1961-62; sr. resident in medicine Boston City Hosp., 1962-63; fellow in metabolics VAMC Boston, 1963-64; rsch. fellow Harvard Med. Sch., Boston, 1964-67; rsch. assoc. New Eng. Deaconess Hosp., Boston, 1969-74; dir. orthopedic rsch. Robert Breck Brigham Hosp., Boston, 1974-89; chief endocrine sect. VAMC West Roxbury, Boston, 1974-89; chief med. svc. VAMC Bedford, Mass., 1989—; prof. medicine Sch. Medicine Boston U., 1989—; asst., assoc. prof. medicine Harvard Med. Sch., Boston, 1974-89. Lectr. in medicine Harvard Med. Sch., Boston, 1989—; investigator NIH, 1974-89. Med. Rsch. Coun. Can. fellow, 1961-62; Med. Found., Inc. fellow, Boston, 1967-70. Avocations: chamber music, gardening, languages. Office: VAMC Bedford 200 Springs Rd Bedford MA 01730-1114

STEINBERG, JANET DEBERRY, optometrist, educator, researcher; b. Phila., July 28, 1940; d. Bill and Florence (Kurtz) DeBerry; 1 child, J. Douglas Milner. Student, Rider Coll., 1975-77; BS, Pa. Coll. Optometry, 1978, OD, 1981. Dir. Hopewell (N.J.) Valley Eye Assocs., 1982-99; also clin. assoc. Scheie Eye Inst., U. Pa., Phila., 1985—; dir. Penn Ctr. for Low Vision Rehab. and Rsch. dept. ophthalmology U. Pa., Phila., 1984—; physician U. Pa. Health Sys., Phila., 2000—; pres. Allen Vision Sys., Phila., 1997—. Asst. adj. prof. Pa. Coll. Optometry, Phila., 1983—85; mem. N.J. Low Vision Panel, 1981—; cons. healthcare industry, 1985—. Fellow Am. Acad. Optometry; mem. Am. Optometric Assn. (Optometric Recognition award 1983-89), N.J. Optometric Assn. (sci. achievement award 1999), Assn. Rsch. in Vision and Ophthalmology, Union League Phila., Corinthian Yacht Club, Beta Beta Beta. Avocations: sailing, snorkeling, scuba, golf. Office: Ralston/Penn Ctr Rm 141 3615 Chestnut St Philadelphia PA 19104-2689 Office Phone: 215-662-2600. Business E-Mail: janet.steinberg@uphs.upenn.edu.

STEINBERG, JANET ECKSTEIN, journalist; d. Charles and Adele (Ehrenfeld) Eckstein; m. Irvin S. Silverstein, Oct. 22, 1988; children: Susan Carole Steinberg Somerstein, Jody Lynn Steinberg Lazarow. BS, U. Cin., 1964. Travel cons., 1994—; pub. Paine Webber Vantage Living website, 2000—02; guest lectr. Tri State Travel Sch., 1999—2001. Freelance writer:; guest appearance Braun & Co., Sta. WLW-TV, Sta. WMKV-TV, travel editor Am. Israelite, 1996—, Jewish News, 1996—, N.J. Jewish News, 1997—; travel editor: Miami Herald Jewish Star Times, 2002—03; travel editor S. Fla. Single Living, 1988—92, Cin. Post, 1978—86, Ky. Post, 1978—86, Cin. Enquirer, 1986—94, MetroWest Jewish News, N.J., 1996—, Jewish News-New Orleans, 1996—, L.A. Jewish Jour., 1997—; contbg. editor: Travel Agt., 1986—88, Birnbaum Travel Guides, 1988—98, The Writer, 1988, 1992, 1998, Entree, 1986—97; travel columnist Northeast Mag., 1986—88, South Fla. Single Living, 1984—92, Eastside Weekend Mag., 1994—96; contbr. articles to newspapers, mags., and books. Recipient Lowell Thomas Travel Journalism award, 1984, 1985, 1990, Henry E. Bradshaw travel journalism award, 1st pl., best of show, 1988, Buckeye Travel award, Ohio Divsn. Travl & Tourism, 1992, Cipriani Best Overall WRiter award, 1981, 13 awards, Soc. Am. Travel Writers, 1981—96, 15 awards, Midwest Travel Writers, 1981—2002. Home: 900 Adams Xing Ste 9200 Cincinnati OH 45202-1677 E-mail: jxs4travel@aol.com.

STEINBERG, JONATHAN, historian; b. New York, Mar. 8, 1934; s. Rabbi Milton and Edith (Alpert) Steinberg; m. Marion Kant; m. Jill P. Steinberg, Nov. 13, 1960 (div. Oct. 2002); children: Matthew David, Daniel Andrew, Peter James. BA, Harvard U., Cambridge, MA., 1955; MA, Cambridge U., Cambridge, Eng., 1963, PhD, 1965. Rsch. fellow Christ's Coll., Cambridge, England, 1963—66; fellow tutor, vice master Trinity Hall, Cambridge, England, 1963—99; U. lectr. Cambridge U., Cambridge, England, 1963—99; prof. of European history U. Pa., Phila., 2000—. Dir. Techne, Cambridge, England, 1988—91; mem. hist. Commn. Deutsche Bank, Frankfurt, Germany, 1997—2002. Author: Why Switzerland?, 1996, All or Nothing: Axis and the Holocaust, 1941—43. Chair Duxford Saturday Workshop, Cambridge, England, 1979—87. Recipient Hon. Mem., Cormorant Club, 1990; Sr. Sixteen, Phi Beta Kappa, Alpha Chap., 1955. Fellow: Royal Hist. Soc. Democrat. Jewish. Achievements include expert witness(war crimes trial) Commonwealth of Australia V. Beresowsky. 1992; Prin. author; Deutsche Bank's investigation into its gold transactions; The Leslie Stephen lectr. Cambridge U., Nov., 1999. Avocation: playing the oboe. Office: U Pa Dept of History 208 Coll Hall Philadelphia PA 19104-6879 Home: 123 Rochelle Ave Philadelphia PA 19128

STEINBERG, JONATHAN ROBERT, judge; b. Phila., Jan. 3, 1939; s. Sigmund Hopkins and Hortense B. (Gottlieb) S.; m. Rochelle Helene Schwarts, May 30, 1963; children: Andrew Joshua, Amy Judith. BA, Cornell U., 1960; LLB cum laude, U. Pa., 1963. Bar: D.C. 1963, U.S. Ct. Appeals (D.C. cir.) 1964. Law clk. to judge U.S. Ct. Appeals (D.C. cir.), 1963-64; atty. advisor, then dep. gen. counsel Peace Corps, Washington, 1964-69; com. on labor and pub. welfare, counsel subcom. vets. affair U.S. Senate, 1969-71, counsel subcom. on R.R. retirement, 1971-73, counsel spl. subcom. on human resources, 1972-77, chief counsel com. on vets affairs, 1977-81, minority chief counsel and staff dir. com. on vets. affairs, 1981-87, chief counsel and staff dir. com. on vets. affairs, 1987-90; judge U.S. Ct. of Appeals for Vets. Claims, 1990—. Contbr. to legal jours. Bd. dirs. Bethany West Recreation Assn., Bethany Beach, Dels., 1973-84, 86-90. Mem. ABA, D.C. Bar Assn., Order of Coif. Democrat. Jewish. Office: US Ct of Appeals for Vets Claims 625 Indiana Ave NW Ste 900 Washington DC 20004-2917

STEINBERG, LAURA, lawyer; b. Phila., Feb. 3, 1948; d. Leonard and Pearl (Zeid) S.; children: Seth, Adam, Bree. BA magna cum laude with honors, Bryn Mawr Coll., 1968; JD cum laude, Harvard U., 1972. Bar: Mass. 1972, U.S. Dist. Ct. Mass. 1972, U.S. Dist. Ct. R.I. 1974, U.S. Ct. Appeals (1st cir.) 1973, U.S. Ct. Appeals (10th and D.C. cirs.) 1986, U.S. Ct. Appeals (4th cir.) 1988, U.S. Claims Ct. 1979, U.S. Supreme Ct. 1988. Assoc. Sullivan & Worcester, Boston, 1972-79, ptnr., 1979—, mem. mgmt. com., 1988-2000, head litigation dept., 1988-99. Dir. Greater Boston Legal Svcs., 1987-90. Bd. dirs. Law Firm Resources Project, Boston, 1980-86, Lawyers Com. for Civil Rights Under Law, 1998—; pres. Peirce Extended Day Program, Inc., West Newton, Mass., 1983-86. Spl. career fellow U. Calif., Berkeley, 1968-69; Fulbright scholar, 1968. Mem. Boston Bar Assn. (vice-chmn. litigation sect. 1992-94, chmn. 1994-95). Avocations: reading, tennis. Office: Sullivan & Worcester LLP One Post Office Sq Ste 2100 Boston MA 02109-2129 Office Phone: 617-338-2800. E-mail: lsteinberg@sandw.com.

STEINBERG, LAWRENCE EDWARD, lawyer; b. Dallas, Nov. 25, 1935; s. Oscar J. and Pearl L. (Soloman) S.; children: Adam Joseph, Ilana Sara, Oliver David. BBA, U. Tex., 1958; JD, So. Meth. U., 1960. Bar: Tex. 1960. Since practiced in, Dallas; ptnr. firm Steinberg Soloman & Meer, 1971-88, Johnson & Steinberg, Dallas, 1988-93; of counsel Jenkins & Gilchrist, Dallas, 1994-98; chmn., CEO Eagle Equity, Inc., Dallas, 1991—. Active Urban Rehab. Stds. Bd., Dallas, 1975-76; adv. com. affirmative action program Dallas Ind. Sch. Dist., 1974-76; regional bd. chmn. Anti-Defamation League of B'nai Brith, 1974-77, nat. exec. com., 1977—, nat. law com., 1974-87; trustee Edna Gladney Home, 1975-92; v.p., trustee Shelton Sch., 1987-90; trustee Temple Emanu-El, 1992-94, Dallas Jewish Cmty. Found., 1990-2001; pres. U. Tex. Hillel Found., 2001-2003, mem. exec. com., 2001—; bd. dirs. Jewish Fedn. Greater Dallas, 1984-87, 91-94, Dallas Coun. on World Affairs, 1998—, Stephen Wise, Acad., 1998-2002, Dallas Holocaust Ctr., 1998—, Jewish Inst. Nat. Securities Affairs, 1999—, Am. Jewish Commn., 2003—, Dallas Furniture Found., 2003-, Dallas Furniture Bank, 2004—; regional bd. chmn. Am. Israel Pub. Affairs Com., 1997-2001, nat. exec. com., 1998—. 2d lt. U.S. Army, 1959-60. Mem. Lincoln City Club, Columbian Club, Masons, Shriners, Zeta Beta Tau, Phi Delta Phi, Beta Gamma Sigma, Pi Tau Pi (nat. pres. 1964-66). Home: 10131 Hollow Way Rd Dallas TX 75229-6634 Office: 5430 LBJ Fwy Ste 1575 Dallas TX 75240

STEINBERG, LEIGH W. sports agent; b. L.A., 1949; m. Lucy Steinberg; 3 children. BA in Polit. Sci., UCLA, 1970; JD, U. Calif., Berkeley, 1973. Founder, ptnr. Steinberg, Moorad & Dunn, 1975—99; CEO Assante Sports Mgmt. Group, 1999—2003; founder, ptnr. Steinberg, Tollner & Moon, Newport Beach, Calif., 2003—. Co-author (with Michael D'Orso): Winning with Integrity: Getting What You Want Without Selling Your Soul, 1998. Mailing: Ste 800 500 Newport Ctr Dr Newport Beach CA 92660*

STEINBERG, LEO, art historian, educator; b. Moscow, July 9, 1920; arrived in U.S., 1945; s. Isaac N. and Anna (Esselson) S. PhD, NYU Inst Fine Arts, 1960; PhD (hon.), Phila. Coll. Art, 1981, Parsons Sch. Design, 1986, Mass. Coll. Art, 1987, Bowdoin Coll., 1995. Assoc. prof. art history Hunter Coll., CUNY, N.Y.C., 1961-66, prof., 1966-75; prof. Grad. Ctr. CUNY, 1969-75; Benjamin Franklin prof. art. history U. Pa., Phila., 1975-91, prof. emeritus, 1991—. Charles Eliot Norton lectr. Harvard U., 1995-96; Mellon lectr. Nat. Gallery Art, 1981-82. Author: Other Criteria, 1972, Michelangelo's Last Paintings, 1975, Borromini's San Carlo alle Quattro Fontane, 1977, The Sexuality of Christ in Renaissance Art and in Modern Oblivion, 1983, 2d enlarged edit., 1996, Encounters with Rauschenberg, 2000, Leonardo's Incessant Last Supper, 2001. Recipient award in lit. Am. Acad. and Inst. Arts and Letters, 1983; fellow Am. Acad. Arts and Scis., 1978, Univ. Coll., London U., 1979, MacArthur Found., 1986; recipent Frank Jewett Mather award, 1956, 84; Disting. scholar 2002. Mem. Coll. Art Assn. Am. (Disting. Scholar award 2002). Home: 165 W 66th St New York NY 10023-6508

STEINBERG, LOUIS MARSHALL, dentist, researcher; b. Bklyn., Aug. 1, 1954; s. Jack and Nancy Steinberg; m. Carolyn Preska Steinberg, June 9, 1954; children: Asher, Merrill. BA, Columbia U., 1976, MS, 1984; DDS, NYU, 1980. Postdoctoral fellow Inst. Human Nutrition Columbia U., N.Y.C., 1983-86, clin. rsch. assoc. Ctr. Clin. Rsch., 1986-92; pvt. practice West New York, N.J., 1989—; clin. asst. prof. N.J. Dental Sch., Newark, 1994—. Cons. McNeil Specialty Products, New Brunswick, N.J. Contbr. articles to profl. jours. N.Y. State Regents scholar NYU, 1977-80. Mem. AAAS, Internat. Assn. Dental Rsch., Acad. Gen. Dentistry, Sigma Chi (hon.). Jewish. Avocations: gardening, aquaria. Office: 6050 Boulevard E West New York NJ 07093-3901 E-mail: drlmsteinberg.lms@verizon.net.

STEINBERG, MARTY, lawyer; b. Balt., May 13, 1945; BS cum laude in Pharmacy, U. Pitts., 1968; JD cum laude, Ohio State U., 1971. Bar: Ohio 1971, Fla. 1974; U.S. Supreme Ct. 1981; Registered Pharmacist Ohio 1968. Asst. U.S. Atty., Washington, Miami, 1972-78, atty. in charge N.Y. regional offices Washington, 1978-79; chief counsel, permanent subcommittee on investigations U.S. Senate, Washington, 1979-82; ptnr. Holland & Knight, Miami, Fla.; mng. ptnr., Fla. office Hunton & Williams, Miami, 1999—. Inst. Canisius Coll. Buffalo, N.Y. 1978-79, SUNY Buffalo 1978-79, Am. U. Washington D.C. 1980-81. Contbr. articles to profl. jours. Bd. dirs. Miami Citizens Against Crime. Recipient Am. Jurisprudence award. Mem. ABA, Fla. Bar Assn., Ohio State Bar Assn., Am. Pharm. Assn., Am. Assn. Corp. Counsel, Am. Law Inst. (chmn. civic justice adv. com.) Office: Hunton & Williams Law Firm 1111 Brickell Ave Miami FL 33131

STEINBERG, MARVIN EDWARD, orthopaedic surgeon, educator; b. New Brunswick, NJ, Aug. 31, 1933; s. David and Fannie (Karshmer) S.; m. Delores Gusky White, Nov. 22, 1956; children: David, James, Susan, Julie. BA, Princeton U., 1954; MD, U. Pa., 1958; MA (status pro tem), U. Oxford, Eng., 1964. Cert. Am. Bd. Orthop. Surgery, re-cert.; lic. Pa., NJ. Asst. prof. orthop. surgery U. Pa., Phila., 1968-73, assoc. prof., 1973-80, vice chmn., 1977-2000, prof. orthop. surgery, 1980—2002, prof. orthop. surgery in medicine, 1988—2002, interim chmn., 1994-95, prof. emeritus, 2002—. Dir. Joint Reconstrn. Ctr., Hosp. U. of Pa., Phila., 1987-97; examiner Am. Bd. Orthop. Surgeons, Chgo., 1977-97. Editor, author: The Hip and Its Disorders, 1991, Revision Total Hip Arthroplasty, 1998; guest editor, author: Seminars in Arthroplasty, 1998; guest editor: Orthop. Clinics of N.Am., 1982, (jour.) Seminars in Arthroplasty, 1991; editl. cons. Clin. Orthop. and Related Rsch., 1987; assoc. editor Jour. Bone & Joint Surgery, 1992-2000; contbr. numerous articles to jours. and textbooks. Named one of The Best Drs. in Phila, Phila. Mag., 1984, 87, 94, 96; Fulbright scholar, U. Oxford, 1963-64; fellow Arthritis Found., U. Oxford, 1963-64. Fellow ACS, Am. Acad. Orthop. Surgeons; mem. AMA, Assn. for Acad. Surgery, Ea. Orthop. Assn. (pres. 1975-76), Orthop. Rsch. Soc., Internat. Soc. for Orthop. Surgery and Traumatology (sec.-treas. 1997-2000, chmn. elect 2000-02, chmn. 2002-04), Am. Orthop. Assn., Hip Soc., Girdlestone Soc., Assn. Rsch. Circulation Osseous, Lupus Found. Jewish. Avocations: travel, sailing, boating, photography. Home: 221 Winding Way Merion Station PA 19066-1217 Office: Hosp of U of Pa 3400 Spruce St Philadelphia PA 19104-4206 Office Phone: 215-349-8695. E-mail: marvin.steinberg@uphs.upenn.edu.

STEINBERG, MEYER, chemical engineer; b. Phila., July 10, 1924; s. Jacob Louis and Freda Leah S.; m. Ruth Margot Elias, Dec. 24, 1950; children: David Martin, Jay Louis. BSChemE, Cooper Union, 1944; MSChemE, Bklyn. Poly. Inst , 1949. Registered profl. engr. N.Y. Manhattan dist., Kellex Corp., Oak Ridge, Los Alamos, 1944-46; asst. chem. engr. Deutsch & Loonam, 1947-50; chem. engr. Guggenheim Brothers, Mineola, N.Y., 1950-57; head process sci. div. Brookhaven Nat. Lab., Upton, N.Y., 1957—. Expert in fossil and nuclear energy. Author: (with Martin Hallman) Carbon Dioxide Greenhouse Gas Mitigation Technologies, 1999; contbr. articles to profl. jours. Served with AUS, 1944-46. Recipient IR-100 award, 1970; Wasson award Am. Concrete Inst., 1972, Engr. of Year award, 1985, Ind. award Guest, 1985, Greenman award, Internat. Energy Agy., London UK, IEA Greenhouse Program, 1996. Fellow Am. Nuclear Soc., Am. Inst. Chem. Engrs. (dir. L.I. sect.); mem. Am. Chem. Soc., AAAS, Am. Concrete Inst., Inst. Assos. Hydrogen Energy, Sigma Xi. Democrat. Jewish. Achievements include research on nuclear and fossil energy. Home: 15 Alderfield Ln Melville NY 11747-1724 Office: Brookhaven Nat Lab Upton NY 11973 Office Phone: 631-427-0768. E-mail: mrsteinb@optonline.net.

STEINBERG, MICHAEL, music critic, educator; b. Breslau, Germany, Oct. 4, 1928; came to U.S., 1943, naturalized, 1950; s. Siegfried and Margarethe (Cohn) S.; m. Jane Bonacker, July 26, 1953 (div. 1983); children: Peter Sebastian, Adam Gregory; m. Jorja Fleezanis, July, 1983. AB, Princeton U., 1949, M.F.A., 1951; Mus. D. (hon.), New Eng. Conservatory Music, 1966. Free-lance writer, 1952—; head history dept. Manhattan Sch. Music, N.Y.C., 1957-64; music critic Boston Globe, 1964-76; dir. publs. Boston Symphony Orch., 1976-79; artistic adviser San Francisco Symphony, 1979-89, program annotator, lectr. 1989-99; artistic adviser Minn. Orch., 1989-92; artistic dir. Minn. Sommerfest, 1990-92; program annotator, lectr. N.Y. Philharmonic, 1995-2000. Vis. music faculty Hunter Coll., 1954, U. Sask. (Can.), 1959, Smith Coll., 1964, Brandeis U., 1964-65; faculty New Eng. Conservatory Music, 1968-71, Wellesley Coll., 1971-72, Brandeis U., 1971-72, Mass. Inst. Tech., 1973; disting. vis. prof. McMaster U., Hamilton, Ont., 1982; cons. NEH, Nat. Endowment for Arts, Mass. Council of Arts and Humanities, Calif. Arts Council, Rockefeller Found.; free-lance writer, lectr. Author: The Symphony: A Listener's Guide, 1995, The Concerto: A Listener's Guide, 1998. Served with U.S. Army, 1955-57. Recipient Sang prize for criticism in arts, 1969; citation for Excellence in Criticism Am. Guild Organists, 1972 Mem. Am. Internat. musicological socs. Home: 6828 Valley View Rd Edina MN 55439-1646 E-mail: fleeberg@earthlink.net.

STEINBERG, MILTON, civilian military employee; b. Cornwall, N.Y., Apr. 3, 1941; s. Samuel Lewis Steinberg, Anna Ethel Steinberg; m. Francine Steinberg (div.); children: Daniel B., Rachel T. Rubenstein; m. Rimma Steinberg, Sept. 14, 1996; stepchildren: Marina Harary, Galina Ziegler. BA in Psychology, UCLA, 1963; MS in Adminstry. Scis., City U. London, 1968. Cert. tng.; responsibility involvement and preparation of various U.S. Dept. Vet. Affairs, N.Y. State Divsn. Vet. Affairs and Am. Legion. Sales rep. Gen. Tng. Svc., N.Y.C., 1969—70; caseworker N.Y.C., Bronx, 1970—71; state vet. counselor N.Y. State, Spring Valley, 1971—. Vol. Congressman Benjamin A. Gilman campaign, Rockland County, NY, 1991—2002; sec. B'nai Jeshurun Synagogue, Monsey, NY, 1987—. Specialist 4th class U.S. Army, 1963-65. Recipient Cert. of Honor, Town of Ramapo, N.Y., 1995, Cert. of Humanitarianism, 1993, 1995, Cert. of Appreciation, Rockland County Am. Legion, 1997, 2000. Mem.: DAV (life), Nat. Mus. Am. Jewish Mil. History, Vietnam Vets. Am., Am. Legion (county svc. officer, post svc. officer), Jewish War Vets. (state svc. officer, post svc. officer, nat. svc. officer, Cert. Appreciation 1999, 2001, Cert. Merit 1995). Republican. Jewish. Avocations: gardening, reading, photography, music. Office: NY State Divsn Vet Affairs 9-B Perlman Dr Spring Valley NY 10977 E-mail: amerivet@hotmail.com.

STEINBERG, MORTON M, lawyer; b. Chgo. Ill, Feb. 13, 1945; m. Miriam C. Bernstein, Aug. 25, 1974; children: Adam Michael, Shira Judith. AB(hon.), U. Ill., 1967; JD, Northwestern U., 1971. Bar: Ill. 1971, DC 1994, Colo. 1995, New York, 2003, US Dist. Ct. 1974, US Dist. Ct. 1971, US Dist. Ct. Colo. 1998, US Ct. Appeals (7th cir.) 1971, US Supreme Ct. 1974. Assoc. Caffarelli & Wiczer, Chgo., 1971-73, Arnstein, Gluck, Lehr, Barron & Milligan, Chgo., 1974-76, ptnr., 1977-86, Piper Rudnick, LLP and predecessor, 1986—. Speaker in field. Sr. editor Jour. Criminal Law and Criminology, Northwestern U., 1969-71. Chmn. Chgo. region Leaders Tng. Fellowship, 1962-63; bd. dir. Camp Ramah in Wis., Inc., Chgo., 1974—, sr. v.p., 1992-94, pres. 1994-2003, chairman Board of Trustees, 2003—, bd. dir.; pres. The Ramah Day Camp, Inc., Chgo., 2001-2003; bd. dir., v.p. Camp Ramah in Wis. Endowment Corp., 1993-2003, pres. 2003—; bd. dir. North Suburban Synagogue Beth-El, Highland Park, Ill, 1978—, corp. sec., 1983-87, pres. 1989-91, chmn. bd. trustees, 1991-93, trustee, 1991—; mem. Nat. Ramah Commn., Jewish Theol. Sem. Am., 1987—, v.p., 1994-2003, pres., 2003-; bd. dir. Found. Conservative Judaism in Israel, 1985-90; Midwest region bd. dir. United Synagogue of Conservative Judaism, 1989-91, 94-2003; mem. arbiter's cir. Jewish Forward Newspaper, 1997-2000; trustee Am. Jewish Hist. Soc., 1998—; charter mem. US Holocaust Meml. Mus., 1992; pro bono counsel Frank Lloyd Wright Preservation Trust, Oak Park, Ill., 1996—. Served with USAR, 1969-75. Recipient Youth Leadership award Nat. Fedn. Jewish Men's Clubs, NYC, 1963; cert. of merit US Dist. Ct. Fed. Defender Program, Chgo., 1969. Mem. ABA, Internat. Wine Law Assn., DC Bar, Std. Club, Ill. State Bar Assn., Chgo. Bar Assn. Jewish. Home: 1320 Lincoln Ave S Highland Park IL 60035-3459 Office: Piper Rudnick LLP Ste 1800 203 N La Salle St Chicago IL 60601-1225 E-mail: morton.steinberg@piperrudnick.com.

STEINBERG, ROBERT PHILIP, lawyer; b. Danville, Ill., Apr. 4, 1931; s. Frederick Philip and Beulah Iona (Olmsted) S.; m. Doris Elizabeth Blank, May 10, 1958; children: Susan Elizabeth, Mary Louise. BA, DePauw U., 1953; LLB, N.Y. U., 1956. Bar: N.Y. 1956, Pa. 1959. Assoc. Shearman & Sterling, N.Y.C., 1956, Drinker Biddle & Reath, Phila., 1958-65, ptnr., 1965-97, chmn., 1992-94, of counsel, 1997-98; ptnr. Commons & Commons LLP, Phila., 1998—. V.p. Germantown Hist. Soc., Phila., 1991-95, The Phila. Theatre Co., 1992-96; pres. E. Falls Cmty. Coun., 1997-2000. Mem. Phila. Bar Assn. (treas. 1970-72). Home: 3906 W Netherfield Rd Philadelphia PA 19129-1014 Office: Commons & Commons 2967 W School House Ln Philadelphia PA 19144-5222 Office Phone: 215-849-4400. E-mail: philip.steinberg@att.net.

STEINBERG, ROY BENNETT, television producer, director, educator; b. N.Y.C., Mar. 24, 1951; s. Seymour and Flora Joyce (Matthews) S.; m. Marlena Lustik, Sept. 8, 1984, 1 child, Alexa Catherine. BA, Tufts U., 1973; MFA, Yale U., 1978. Guest artist various univs., 1978-87; dir. Circle Repertory Co. Lab., N.Y.C., 1985-90; artistic dir. John Michael Kohler Arts Ctr., Sheboygan, Wis., 1988; prodr. Guiding Light, CBS-TV, N.Y.C., 1990-98; dir. One Life To Live, 1999; prodr., dir. Days of Our Lives, NBC; prof. Muhlenberg Coll., 1999—. Freelance drama coach, N.Y.C., 1978—; script cons. Circle Repertory Co. Lab., N.Y.C., 1985-90; casting dir. Theatre Matrix, N.Y.C., 1981-83; adv. bd. Sch. Film & TV, N.Y.C., 1995—. Actor: (play) Wings, 1979 (Tony nomination 1979), (TV sp.) The Wall, 1980, (soap opera) Another World, 1985, (film) The Man Who Envied Women, 1986; dir. (play) Private Lives, 1987, Absent Friends, 1987, Broadway Bound, 1988, The Miser, 1989, The Learned Ladies, 1989, The Marriage Fool, 1989, Othello, 1989, Children, 1996, Blithe Spirit, 1997, Intuition, 1997. Five Towns Music & Art Found. scholar, 1969, 4 Emmy nominations, 1990-93. Mem. AFTRA (nat. del. 1988), Actors Equity Assn. (dep.), Soc. Stage Dirs. and Choreographers, Dirs. Guild Am., Screen Actors Guild. Avocations: travel, cooking, movies, sports, reading. Home: 3951 Sunswept Dr Studio City CA 91604

STEINBERG, SALME ELIZABETH HARJU, academic administrator, historian; b. N.Y.C. d. Johan Edward and Jenny Lydia (Peltonen) Harju; m. Michael Stephen Steinberg, Sept. 15, 1963; children: William, Katharine Lovisa. BA, Hunter Coll., 1960; MA, CCNY, 1962; PhD, Johns Hopkins U., 1971. Lectr. history Goucher Coll., Towson, Md., 1971—72; asst. prof. history Northwestern U., Evanston, Ill., 1972—75; prof. Northeastern Ill. U., Chgo., 1975—83, chmn. dept., 1983—87, assoc. provost then acting provost, 1987—92, provost, v.p. for acad. affairs, 1992—95, pres., 1995—. Author: Reformer in the Marketplace: Edward W. Bok and The Ladies' Home Journal, 1979; contbr. articles to profl. jours. Named to, Hunter Coll. Hall of Fame, 1997; recipient 14th Ann. award Appreciation, Asian Am. Coalition Chgo., 1997; grantee, Danforth Found., 1967—68. Episcopalian. Avocations: opera, theater. Office: Northeastern Ill U Office of President 5500 N Saint Louis Ave Chicago IL 60625-4679

STEINBERG, SAUL PHILLIP, holding company executive; b. N.Y.C., Aug. 13, 1939; s. Julius and Anne (Cohen) S.; m. Barbara Herzog, May 28, 1961 (div. 1977); children: Laura, Jonothan, Nicholas; m. Laura Sconocchia, Dec. 21, 1978 (div. Dec. 1983); 1 child, Julian; m. Gayfryd McNabb, Jan. 22, 1984; children: Rayne, Holden. BS, Wharton Sch., U. Pa., 1959. Founder, chmn., chief exec. officer, dir., COO Reliance Group Holdings Inc., N.Y.C. Bd. dirs Symbol Techs. Inc. Chmn. bd. overseers Wharton Sch. U. Pa.; mem. bd. overseers Cornell U. Med. Coll., N.Y.C.; trustee Jewish Med. Ctr., N.Y.C., U. Pa., N.Y. Pub. Libr. Jewish. Home: 680 Madison Ave New York NY 10021-7246 Office: Reliance Group Holdings Inc 5 Hanover Sq New York NY 10004

STEINBERG, WARREN LINNINGTON, school principal; b. N.Y.C., Jan. 20, 1924; s. John M. and Gertrude (Vogel) S.; m. Beatrice Ruth Blass, June 29, 1947; children: Leigh William, James Robert, Donald Kenneth. Student, U. So. Calif., 1943-44; BA, UCLA, 1948, MEd, 1951, EdD, 1962. Tchr. counselor, coach Jordan H.S., Watts, L.A., 1951-57; tchr., athletic coord. Hamilton H.S., L.A., 1957-62; boys' vice prin. Univ. H.S., L.A., 1962-67, Crenshaw H.S., L.A., 1967-68; cons. Ctr. for Planned Change, L.A. City Sch., 1968-69; instr. edn. UCLA, 1965-71; boys' vice prin. LeConte Jr. H.S., L.A., 1969-71, sch. prin., 1971-77; adminstrv. cons. on integration L.A. Unified Sch. Dist., 1977-81, adminstr. student-to-student interaction program, 1981-82; cprin. Gage Jr. H.S., Huntington Park, Calif., 1982-83; prin. Fairfax H.S., L.A., 1983-90. Pres. Athletic Coords. Assn., L.A. Unified Sch. Dist., 1959-60; v.p. P-3 Enterprises, Inc., Port Washington, N.Y., 1967-77, Century City (Calif.) Enterprises, 1966-88. Contbr. articles on race rels., youth behavior to profl. jours. and newspapers. V.p. B'nai B'rith Anti-Defamation League, 1968-70; mem. adv. com. L.A. City Common. on Human Rels., 1966-71, 72-76, commr., 1976—, pres., 1978-87, also chmn. edn. com.; mem. human rels. commn. L.A. Unified Sch. Dist., 1999—, mem. citizens adv. com. for student integration, 1975-79; mem. del. assembly Cmty. Rels. Conf. So. Calif., 1975-91; chmn. So. Calif. Drug Abuse Edn. Month com., 1970; bd. dirs. DAWN, The Seedling, 1993-95, Project ECHO—Entrepreneurial Concepts, Hands-On, 1996—; mem., chmn. case conf. human rels. West L.A. Coordinating Coun. With USMCR, 1943-46. Recipient Beverly Hills B'nai B'rith Presdl. award, 1965, Pres.'s award Cmty. Rels. Conf. So. Calif., 1990, Lifetime Achievement award L.A. City Human Rels. Common., 1994, award L.A. Unified Sch. Dist. Bd. Edn., 1997, commendation L.A. City Coun., 1968, 88. Mem. Beverly-Fairfax C. of C. (bd. dirs. 1988), Lions (bd. dirs. 1960-62), Kiwanis. Home: 2737 Dunleer Pl Los Angeles CA 90064-4303

STEINBERG, WILLIAM MARK, physician; b. N.Y.C., Apr. 16, 1945; s. Louis and Florence (Weisberger) S.; m. Leah Stern, 1970; 3 children. BA, Columbia Coll., 1966; MD, NYU, 1970. Intern Kings County/Downstate, N.Y.C., 1970-71; resident in medicine Boston U., 1973-74, U. Conn., Hartford, 1974-75; fellow in gastroenterology U. Fla., Gainesville, 1976-79; asst. prof. gastroenterology George Washington U., Washington, 1979-83, assoc. prof. medicine, 1983-90, prof. gastroenterology, 1990—. Fellow ACP, Am. Coll. Gastroenterology; mem. Am. Pancreatic Assn. (pres. 1995-96), Am. Gastroent. Assn. Achievements include research in diagnosis and therapy of pancreatic disorders. Office: 106 Irving St NW Washington DC 20010-2927

STEINBERGER, JACK, physicist, researcher; b. Bad Kissingen, Germany, May 25, 1921; came to U.S., 1935; s. Ludwig Lazarus and Berta (May) S.; m. Joan Beauregard, 1943, (div. 1962); children: Joseph, Richard Ned; m. Cynthia Eva Alff; children: Julia Karen, John Paul. BS in Chemistry, U. Chgo., 1942, PhD in Physics, 1948; hon. degree, Ill. Inst. Tech., 1989, U. Glasgow, 1990, Dortmund U., 1990, Columbia U., 1990, U. Autonoma de Barcelona, Spain, 1992, U. Blaise Pascal, Clermont-Ferrand, France, 1995, U. Würzburg, 1997. Mem. Inst. for Advanced Study, Princeton, N.J., 1948-49; asst. U. Calif., Berkeley, 1949-50; prof. Columbia U., N.Y.C., 1950-68, Higgins prof.,

---

...staff mem. European Orgn. for Nuclear Research, Geneva, 1968-96... prof. physics Scuola Normale, Pisa, Italy, 1986—. Ptc. U.S. Co-recipient Nobel prize in physics, 1988; recipient Nat. Matteuzzi medal Societa Italiane delle Scienze, 1991; Scis., Academia Europea, Academia Nationale dei Lincei, Sloan Found. Mem. Am. Acad. Arts and Scis., ...CH 1213 Onex Switzerland Office: European ...CH 1211 Geneva 23 Switzerland

...THOMAS, bishop; b. L.A., July 16, 1937; ... to ministry Cath. Ch., 1963; Aux. bishop ... bishop Diocese of Fresno; dir. ... bishop Diocese of Fresno St Fresno Phone: 559-488-7400. E-mail:

...professional baseball team ... Ohio, July 4, ...pres. Kinsman ... Joan Zeig, ... chmn. bd. Am. Ship Bldg. Corp.; dir. Harold Zeig, ... prin. owner NY Yankees, Bronx, 1973—90; ...transit ... owner Bay Harbor Inn, Tampa, Fla . 1988— ... Bd. dirs. Gt. Lakes Internat. Corp., Gt. Lakes Assocs., Cin. Sheet Metal & Roofing Co., Nashville Bridge Co., Nederlander-Steinbrenner Prodns. Chmn. Olympic Overview Commn.; v.p. US Olympic Com., 1989—; mem. Cleve. Little Hoover Com., group chmn., 1966; chmn. Cleve. Urban Coalition; vice chmn. Greater Cleve. Growth Corp., Greater Cleve. Jr. Olympic Found.; founder Silver Shield Found., NYC. 1st lt. USAF, 1952—54. Named Outstanding Young Man of Yr., Ohio Jr. C. of C., 1960, Cleve. Jr. C. of C., 1960, Chief Town Crier, Cleve., 1968, Man of Yr. Cleve. Press Club, 1968. Mem.: Greater Cleve. Growth Assn. (bd. dirs.). Office: NY Yankees Yankee Stadium E 161st St & River Ave Bronx NY 10451

STEINBUCHEL, CARLA FAYE, pediatrics nurse, nursing educator; b. Wichita, Kans., Aug. 6, 1949; d. Conrad Vernon Sr. and Dolores Mae (Jacobs) Jansson; children: Carla Lara, Cara Nicole, Haley Elisabeth. BS in Nursing, Wichita State U., 1978, M of Nursing, 1985; Pediatric Nurse Practitioner, U. Ala., Birmingham, 1997. Nurse supr. Osteopathic Hosp., Wichita, 1978-85; nurse Wesley Med. Ctr., Wichita, 1982-85, Huntsville (Ala.) Hosp., 1985-86; neonatal outreach coordinator North Ala. Perinatal Outreach Ctr., Huntsville, 1986-90; clin. instr.Coll. Nursing U. Ala., Huntsville, 1990-92; pediatric and neonatal clin. nurse specialist Med. Ctr. Hosp. Huntsville, Huntsville, 1991-95; pediatric clin. nurse specialist Huntsville Hosp. Sys., 1995-98, pediatric nurse mgr., 1997-98, clin. edn. specialist, 1998-2000; dir. organizational devel. and tng., 2000—01; clin. Corp .U., 2002—03; clin. nurse III ambulatory surgery unit Crestwood Med. Ctr., 2003—. Manuscript reviewer Neonatal Network, Petaluma, Calif., 1987-88. Mem. AACN (past sec. pres.), Nat. Assn. Pediatric Nurses and Practitioners. Democrat. Methodist. Avocations: travel, reading, writing. Home: PO Box 4755 Huntsville AL 35815-4755

STEINDL, FRANK GEORGE, economist, educator; b. Chgo., Aug. 26, 1935; s. Frank and Anna (Bumeder) S.; m. Joyce Ann Becker, Aug. 26, 1961; children: David F., Andrew M., Peter E., Matthew T. BA, DePaul U., Chgo., 1957; AM, U. Ill., 1958; PhD, U. Iowa, 1963. Asst. prof. Okla. State U. Stillwater, 1962-65, assoc. prof., 1965-70, prof., 1970-89, regents prof. of econ., 1989—; Ardmore prof. bus. adminstrn., 1994—. Economist Fed. Res. Bank Cleve., 1966-67; economist, counselor budget com. U.S. Senate, Washington, 1976; vis. prof. U. Munich, 1986—; Konrad Zuse guest prof. U. Bamberg, Germany, 1991; vis. scholar London Sch. Econs. Brown U., 1993-94, U. Iowa, 2000-01. Author: Monetary Interpretations of the Gt. Depression, 1995, Understanding Econ. Recovery in the 1930s: Endogenous Propagation in the Gt. Depression, 2004; contbr. articles to profl. jour. Mem. sch. bd. St. Francis Sch., Stillwater, 1973-77; scoutmaster Boy Scouts Am., 1984-86. Named Disting. Lectr., Mid-Am. State Univs. Assn., 1981-82. Mem. Am. Econ. Assn., So. Econ. Assn. (trustee 1989-91), Midwest Econs. Assn. (v.p. 1974), Southwestern Econ. Assn. (pres. 1974). Avocations: gardening, walking, opera. Home: 2206 Tanglewood Cir Stillwater OK 74074-1713 Office: Okla State Univ Dept Econs Stillwater OK 74078-1104

STEINDLER, WALTER G, retired lawyer; b. N.Y.C., Dec. 2, 1927; s. Mortimer B. and Ray (Feingold) S.; m. Carol A. Halpin, June 28, 1969; children: Mortimer, Morty, Melissa, Amy, Ellen. BA, Queens Coll., 1950; JD, NYU, 1953. Bar: N.Y. 1953, U.S. Supreme Ct. 1965, U.S. Dist. Ct. (ea. dist.) N.Y. 1972, U.S. Dist. Ct. (so. dist.) 1974, U.S. Ct. Appeals (2d cir.) 1974. Ptnr. Borden Skidell Fleck & Steindler, Jamaica, N.Y., 1955-62; pvt. practice law Babylon, N.Y., 1962-67; town atty. Town of Babylon, 1967-69; asst. county atty. Suffolk County, N.Y., 1970-71; ptnr. Sarisohn, Carner, Steindler, Lebow, Braun & Castrovinci, Commack, N.Y., 1976-93; ret., 1993. Capt., judge adv. 2d area command N.Y. Guard, N.Y.C., 1965-70; guardian ad litem 20th Jud. Cir. Lee County, Fla., 1995-98. With U.S. Army, 1946—47. Mem. Free Sons Israel (pres. 1953), Masons. Office: 350 Veterans Memorial Hwy Commack NY 11725-4330 Office Phone: 631-543-7667.

STEINEGER, CHRIS, state legislator; b. Kansas City, Kans., Jan. 8, 1962; m. Shari Wilson. BS, Kans. State U., 1986; MS, U. Kans., 1992. Staff asst. U.S. Rep. Jim Slattery, 1987-88; stock broker, 1988-90; tax auditor Kans. Dept. Revenue, 1993-95; devel. dir. Cross-Lines Coop. Coun., 1995—; mem. Kans. State Senate, 1996—, mem. assessment and tax com., commerce com., elections and local govt. com. Bd. pres. Grinter Place Friends; bd. mem. Kaw Valley Arts and Humanities, Wyandotte County Hist. Soc.; bd. sec. Kans. Dem. Leadership Coun. Com., Inc.; treas. Southside Dem. Club; v.p. Mid-County Dem. Club. Democrat. Office: 51 S 64th St Kansas City KS 66111 also: State Capitol Rm 523-S Topeka KS 66612 E-mail: steineger@senate.state.ks.us.

STEINEGER, MARGARET LEISY, non-profit organization officer; b. Newton, Kans., Feb. 8, 1926; d. Ernest Erwin and Elva Agnes (Krehbiel) L.; m. John Francis Steineger, Dec. 2, 1949; children: John Steineger III, Cindy Blair, Melissa, Chris. B., So. Meth. U., 1947; M. in Social Work, U. Kans., 1949. County vice-chair United Way, Kansas City, Kans., 1960-61; bd., sec., treas. Wyandotte County Bar Aux., Kans., 1960-63; bd. Jr. League of Kansas City, 1962-66, County Coun. PTA, Wyandotte County, 1963-66, KCK Friends of the Arts, Kansas City, 1977-79; pres. Grinter Place Mus. Friends, Kans., 1977-78; bd. Kaw Valley Arts Coun., Kansas City, 1982-86; commr. Landmarks Commn., Kansas City, 1985-87; bd. arts with the Handicapped, Wyandotte County, 1986—. Bd. dirs. Kans. Arts Adv. Bd., Grinter Place Friends, Kans., Tri-County Tourism Coun., Kans. V.p. Kans. Legis. Wives, Topeka, 1975-76; bd. dirs. KCK Friends of the Libr., Kansas City, 1984-94, Shepherd's Ctr., 1996-2002; founder Wyandotte County Libr., 1963-64, Creative Experiences, Kansas City, 1967; commr. Kans. Arts Commn., 1965-85; mem. Kaw Valley Arts and Humanities Bd., 1988-92; mem. adv. bd. Parents as Tchrs., 1992-99; mem. Kansas City Ballet Guild. Recipient Humanities award Kans. Com. for the Humanities, 1989; named Citizen of Yr. Kansas City, Kans., 1978. Mem. Kappa Kappa Gamma (C.C. Endowment Bd. 1989—). Democrat. Methodist. Avocations: skiing, sailing, inventing. Home: 6400 Valleyview Ave Kansas City KS 66111-2013

STEINEM, GLORIA, writer, editor, lecturer, activist; b. Toledo, Mar. 25, 1934; d. Leo and Ruth (Nuneviller) S.; m. David Bale, Sept. 3, 2000. BA, Smith Coll., 1956; postgrad. (Chester Bowles Asian fellow), 1957-58; D. Human Justice, Simmons Coll., 1973, PhD (hon.). Co-dir., dir. ednl. found. Ind. Rsch. Svc., Cambridge, Mass. and N.Y.C., 1959-60; contbg. editor Glamour Mag., N.Y.C., 1962-69; co-founder, contbg. editor New York Mag., 1968-72; feminist lectr., 1969—; co-founder, editor Ms. Mag., 1971-87, columnist, 1980-87, cons. editor, 1987—. Active various civil rights and peace

campaigns including United Farmworkers, Vie
the Legal Def. of Angela Davis (treas., 197
Adlai Stevenson, Robert Kennedy, Eug
George McGovern; Co-founder, bd. dir
co-founder, convenor, mem. nat. adv
1971-; co-founder, pres. bd. dirs.
founding mem. Coalition of Lab
Choice, 1979-; mem. Internat.
USA, co-founder, chmn. Libe
Conde Nast Publications,
House Publishing, 1988-,
1957, The Beach Book
Everyday Rebellions,
Within: A Book of S
corr. NBC Today
Penney-Missouri
1972, Bill of R
Yr. McCall's
1977; indu
Nat. Pres
Choice
MS

...om ...contgb. ...s. Recipient ...ard for Journalism, ...named Woman of the ...nat. Ctr. for Scholars fellow, ...ame, 1993. Mem. NOW, AFTRA, ...uthors' Guild, Phi Beta Kappa. Office: ...NW Ste 410 Washington DC 20007 also: ...y Dr Beverly Hills CA 90212-4401*

...NAMJI KIM, social studies educator; d. Yoon Hough and ...n; m. Patrick Hugo Steinemann, Apr. 14, 1987; children: Nicolas ...s, Claire Jeewon. BA, East Carolina U., 1981. V.p. edn. programs Asia Soc., NYC, 1987—2001; dir. Asia pacific edn. program East-West Ctr., Honolulu, 2001—. Chair NYC Cultural Edn. Consortium, NYC, 1999; exec. dir. Nat. Commn. Asia in Schs., NYC, 1999—2001; adv. bd. Asian Bilingual Tech. Assistance Ctr., NYC Bd. Edn., NYC, 1998—2001. Program dir. (video curriculum) Tune in Japan: Approaching Culture Through Television (NHK Internat. award, 1995), project dir. Tune in Japan: Global Connections, Tune in Korea: Geography and Society, Tune in Korea: Legacy and Transformation, (web-based curriculum) Vietnam Challenge on the Web, exec. dir. (website) AskAsia (Cody, 1995). Program planning com. Hawaii Internat. Edn. Week, Honolulu, 2001—03; bd. dirs. NC Ctr. Internat. Understanding, Raleigh, 2002—04. Grantee, Freeman Found., 1992—2004, Japan Found. Ctr. for Global Partnership, 1993—96, NEH, 1994—96, Nat. Edn. Project award, Merrill Lynch & Co. Found., Inc., 1996, Freeman Found., 1998. Mem.: ASCD, Assn. Asian Studies, Com. Tchg. About Asia, Nat. Coun. Social Studies (tchr. edn. and profl. devel. com. 1999—2002, notable books rev. panel 1999—2002). Avocations: fiddling, languages. Office: East-West Ctr 1601 East-West Rd Honolulu HI 96848

STEINER, ALAN P. military officer, government agency administrator; Commd. USN, 1976—; advanced through grades to master missile technician; chief of boat USS Rhode Island; courier security team leader submarine re-supply ships Victoria, Marshfield and Vega; with Submarine Tng. Facility, Charleston, SC, Strategic Weapons Facility, Atlantic; master chief missile technician Naval Space Command, Dahlgren, Va., 1999—. Decorated Navy Commendation medal, Marine Corps Commendation medal with 2 gold stars, Navy and Marine Corps Achievement medal with 3 gold stars, Humanitarian Svc. medal. Office: Naval Space Command Attn: Public Affairs 5280 Fourth St Dahlgren VA 22448-5300

STEINER, DAVID MILLER, lawyer; b. Phoenix, Apr. 9, 1958; s. Paul Miller and Nan (Adamson) S. BA, Columbia U., 1980; MALD, Tufts U., 1985; JD, Cornell U., 1988; M of Internat. and Pub. Affairs, Columbia U., 1989; LLM in Taxation, NYU, 1993. Bar: N.Y. 1988. English tchr. Peace Corps, Tahoua, Niger, 1980-82; law clk. to Judge Jane Restani U.S. Ct. Internat. Trade, N.Y.C., 1989-91; law clk. to Judge Reynaldo Garza U.S. Ct. Appeals (5th cir.), Brownsville, Tex., 1991-92; assoc. Wasserman, Schneider and Babb, 1993-95; with N.Y.C. Law Dept. Office of the Corp. Counsel, 1995—2002, U.S. Dept. Justice, Washington, 2002—. Mem. ABA, N.Y. County Lawyers Assn. (com. on taxation), Univ. Club, Cornell Club, Meridian Soc., Linden Cir., Young New Yorkers for the Philharm, Young Friends of Save Venice. Avocations: ballroom dancing, backgammon, running. Home: 2298 17th St NW # 3 Washington DC 20009- Office: US Dept Justice Tax Divsn PO Box 55 Ben Franklin Sta Washington DC 20044- E-mail: sirius_001@yahoo.com.

STEINER, DAVID P. waste management executive; BS in Acctg. summa cum laude, La. State U., 1982; JD with honors, UCLA, 1986. Formerly with Gibson, Dunn & Crutcher; former ptnr. Phelps Dunbar; v.p., dep. gen. counsel Waste Mgmt., Inc., Houston, 2000—01, sr. v.p., gen. counsel, corp. sec., 2001—03, exec. v.p., CFO, 2003—04, CEO, 2004—. Mem.: ABA, Calif. Bar Assn., La. Bar Assn. Office: Waste Mgmt Inc 1001 Fannin St Ste 4000 Houston TX 77002

STEINER, DONALD FREDERICK, biochemist, physician, educator; b. Lima, Ohio, July 15, 1930; s. Willis A. and Katherine (Hoegner) S. BS in Chemistry and Zoology, U. Cin., 1952; MS in Biochemistry, MD, U. Chgo., 1956; D Med. Sci. (hon.), U. Umea, 1973, U. Ill., 1984, Technische Hochschule, Aachen, 1993, U. Uppsala, 1993, Mt. Sinai Sch. Medicine, N.Y.C., 1998. Intern King County Hosp., Seattle, 1956-57; USPHS postdoctoral research fellow, asst. medicine U. Wash. Med. Sch., 1957-60; mem. faculty med. sch. U. Chgo., 1960—, chmn. dept. biochemistry, 1973-79, A.N. Pritzker prof. biochemistry, molecular biology and medicine, 1985—, sr. investigator Howard Hughes Med. Inst., 1986—. Jacobaeus lectr., Oslo, 1970; Luft lectr., Stockholm, 1984. Co-editor: The Endocrine Pancreas, 1972, discoverer proinsulin. Recipient Gairdner award Toronto, 1971, Hans Christian Hagedorn medal Steensen Meml. Hosp., Copenhagen, 1970, Lilly award, 1969, Ernst Oppenheimer award, 1970, Diaz-Cristobal award Internat. Diabetes Fedn., 1973, Banting medal Am. Diabetes Assn., 1976, Banting medal Brit. Diabetes Assn., 1981, Passano award, 1979, Wolf prize in medicine, 1985, Frederick Conrad Koch award Endocrine Soc., 1990. Mem. AAAS, Nat. Acad. Scis., Am. Soc. Biochemists and Molecular Biologists, Am. Philos. Soc., Am. Diabetes Assn. (50th Anniversary medallion 1972), European Assn. Study Diabetes, Am. Acad. Arts and Scis., Am. Philos. Soc., Sigma Xi, Alpha Omega Alpha. Home: 2626 N Lakeview Ave Apt 2508 Chicago IL 60614-1821 Business E-Mail: dfsteine@midway.uchicago.edu.

STEINER, GEORGE (FRANCIS STEINER), author, educator; b. Paris, Apr. 23, 1929; s. Frederick George and Elsie (Franzos) S.; m. Zara Shakow, 1955; children: David Milton, Deborah Tarn. BA, U. Chgo., 1949; MA, Harvard U., 1950; PhD, Oxford U., 1955; DLitt (hon.), Trinity Coll., Dublin, 1996; LittD (hon.), Louvain U., 1980, Mount Holyoke Coll., 1983, Durham U., 1995; D honoris causa, U. Bristol, 1989; DLitt (hon.), U. Glasgow, 1990, U. Liége, 1990, U. Ulster, 1993, U. Durham, 1995, Kenyon Coll., 1996, U. Rome, 1998, U. Sorbonne, 1998, U. Salamanca, 2002. Mem. staff Economist, London, 1952-56; mem. staff Inst. Advanced Study Princeton (N.Y.) U., N.J., 1956-58, Gauss lectr., 1959-60; Massey lectr., 1974; First Lord Weidenfeld prof. Comp. Lit. Oxford U., 1994—; Charles Eliot Norton prof. poetry Harvard U., 2001—. Cons. and lectr. in field; Maurice lectr. U. London, 1984, Leslie Stephen lectr. Cambridge U., 1985, W.P. Ker lectr. U. Glasgow, 1986; lectr. Page-Barbour Lectures U. Va., 1987, Gifford lectr., 1990; vis. prof. Coll. France, 1992; First Lord Weidenfield vis. prof. comparative lit., Oxford U., 1994—. Author: Tolstoy or Dostoevsky, 1958, The Death of Tragedy, 1960, Anno Domini, 1964, Language and Silence, 1967, Extraterritorial, 1971, In Bluebeard's Castle, 1971, The Sporting Scene: White Knights in Reykjavik, 1973, After Babel, 1975 (adapted for TV as The Tongues of Men, 1977), Heidegger, 1978, On Difficulty and Other Essays, 1978, The Portage to San Cristobal of A.H., 1981, Antigones, 1984, George Steiner: A Reader, 1984, Real Presences, 1989, Proofs and Three Parables, 1992, Homer in English, 1996, No Passion Spent, 1996, The Deeps of the Sea, 1996, Errata, An Examined Life, 1997, Grammars of Creation, 2001, Lessons of the Masters, 2003; editor: The Penguin Book of Modern Verse Translation, 1966, Homer: A Collection of Critical Essays (with Robert Flagles), 1962. Decorated chevalier de la Legion d'Honneur (France); Churchill Coll. fellow, 1961—; Hon. Royal Academician (London), Commandeur dans l'Ordre des Arts et des Lettres (Paris); hon. fellow Balliol Coll., Oxford, Eng., 1995, St. Anne's Coll., ...ort Story award, 1958, ...Nat. Inst. Arts and Letters, ...an Acad., 1982, P.E.N. Internat. ...grantee P.E.N., 1983; Le Prix du ...Lifetime award for Lit., 1999, Prince of ...s, 2001, Ludwig-Börne prize, Germany, 2003; ...ademician, London. Fellow British Acad.; mem. Am. ...ls. (hon.), English Assn. (pres. 1975), German Acad. Lit. ...e: Churchill Coll Cambridge England

STEINER, HENRY JACOB, law and human rights educator; b. Mt. Vernon, N.Y., June 14, 1930; s. Meier and Bluma (Henigson) S.; m. Pamela Pomerance, Aug. 1, 1982; stepchildren: Duff, Jacoba. BA magna cum laude, Harvard U., 1951, MA, LLB magna cum laude, Harvard U., 1955. Bar: N.Y. 1956, Mass. 1963. Law clk. to Hon. John M. Harlan U.S. Supreme Ct., 1957-58; assoc. Sullivan and Cromwell, N.Y.C., 1958-62; asst. prof. sch. law Harvard U., Cambridge, Mass., 1962-65, prof., 1965—, Jeremiah Smith Jr. prof. law, 1986—. Founder, dir. Law Sch. Human Rights Program, 1984—; chair univ. com. on human rights studies Harvard U., 1994—2002; bd. dirs. U. Middle East project, 1996—99, chair bd. dirs., 2000—; vis. prof. Yale U., 1972—73, Stanford U., 1965; cons. AID, 1962—64, Ford Found., 1966—69. Co-author: (textbook) Transnational Legal Problems, 4th edit., 1994, Tort and Accident Law, 2d edit., 1989, International Human Rights in Context: Law, Politics, Morals, 2d edit., 2000; author: Moral Argument and Social Vision in the Courts, 1987, Diverse Partners: Non-Governmental Organizations in the Human Rights Movement, 1991; former devels. editor Harvard Law Rev.; contbr. articles to profl. jours. Office: Harvard U Law Sch Cambridge MA 02138 E-mail: hsteiner@law.harvard.edu.

STEINER, HENRY-YORK, English language and literature educator; b. Chgo., Mar. 12, 1932; s. Richard Morrow and Deborah (Lantz) S.; m. Margaret Gray, June 3, 1957 (div.); children: Anne Elizabeth, Edward Yagi, Riley Jane; m. Leonor Coleman Flores, Jan. 13, 1990. BA, Grinnell Coll., 1956; MA, Yale U., 1957; PhD, U. Oreg., 1963. Instr. Grinnell (Iowa) Coll., 1957-59, assoc. prof., assoc. dean faculty, 1964-68; instr. U. Oreg., Eugene, 1959-62; assoc. prof. Yankton (S.D.) Coll., 1959-62; dean undergrad. studies Ea. Wash. U., Cheney, 1968-77, prof. English, 1977—. Chmn. Wash. State Folklife Coun., Olympia, 1988-92. Editor: (autobiography) St. Peter & I, 1967, (anthology) 12 Poets, 1967; contbr. articles to profl. jours., including Internat. Edn. Chmn. Spokane (Wash.) Cmty. Action, 1971-76; bd. dirs. Expo '74, Spokane World's Fair, 1972-75; dir. 49 Degrees N. Ski Patrol, Chewelah, Wash., 1982-86, 97-2001; sect. chief Inland Empire Region Nat. Ski Patrol, Spokane, 1994-97, 01, dir. 2001--. Named Patroller of Yr., Inland Empire region Nat. Ski Patrol, 1998, Patrol Dir. of Yr., Pacific N.W. divsn., 1998; Fellow Yale U. and Ford Found., 1957. Mem. AAUP (sec. Wash. State coun. 1993-98). Avocations: skiing, sailing, gardening. Home: 2627 W Gardner Ave Spokane WA 99201 Office: Ea Wash U Dept English Cheney WA 99004

STEINER, HERBERT MAX, physics educator; b. Goeppingen, Germany, Dec. 8, 1927; came to U.S., 1939, naturalized, 1944; s. Albert and Martha (Epstein) S. BS, U. Calif., Berkeley, 1951, PhD, 1956. Physicist Lawrence Berkeley Lab., Berkeley, Calif., 1956—; mem. faculty U. Calif., Berkeley, 1958—, prof. physics, 1966-2000, prof. emeritus, 2000—, William H. McAdams prof. physics, chmn. dept., 1992-95; vis. scientist European Center Nuclear Research, 1960-61, 64, 68-69, 82-83, Max Planck Inst. Physics and Astrophysics, Munich, 1976-77; vis. prof. Japanese Soc. Promotion Sci., 1978. Vis. prof. physics U. Paris, 1989-90; vis. scientist Deutsches Electron Synchrotron Lab., 1995-96. Author articles in field. Served with AUS, 1946-47. Recipient Sr. Am. Scientist award Alexander von Humboldt Found., 1976-77; Guggenheim fellow, 1960-61 Fellow Am. Phys. Soc. Office: U Calif Berkeley Dept Physics 7300 Berkeley CA 94720-0001 Office Phone: 510-486-6805. Business E-Mail: steiner@lbl.gov.

STEINER, JANET, educational association administrator; Bachelors Degree, Blackburn Coll.; Masters Degree, D in Ednl. Leadership, So. Ill. U. Instr. Blackburn Coll.; ret.; mem. Ill. State Bd. Edn., 1999—, chairperson, 2003—. Office: Ill State Bd Edn 100 N 1st St Springfield IL 62777

STEINER, JEFFREY JOSEF, industrial manufacturing company executive; b. Vienna, Apr. 3, 1937; came to U.S., 1958; s. Beno and Paula (Bornstein) S.; m. Claude Angel, Apr. 11, 1957 (div. 1972); children: Eric, Natalia, Thierry; m. Linda Schaller, Mar. 6, 1976 (div. June 1983); children: Benjamin, Alexandra. Student textile design, U. London, 1956; student textile mfg., Bradford Inst. Tech., London, 1957; HHD (hon.), Yeshiva U., 1996. Mgmt. trainee Metals and Controls div. Tex. Instruments, Attleborough, Mass., 1958-59, mgr. internat., 1959-60, pres., 1960-66, Burlington Tapis, Paris, 1967-72; chmn., pres. Cedec S.A. Engring. Co., Paris, 1973-84; chmn., CEO Fairchild Corp., N.Y.C., 1985—, Banner Aerospace, 1993—. Bd. dirs. Copley Fund, Fall River, Mass., Comms. Intelligence Corp., Corp. Express, Inc. Trustee Montefiore Med. Ctr., N.Y.C.; bd. dirs. Israel Mus., Yeshiva U. Bus. Sch. Decorated Knight of Arts (France), knight Indsl. Merit of France, chevalier de L'Ordre des Arts et des Lettres, 1990, chevalier de L'order National du Merite (France), commandatore de la Republica (Italy); recipient mayor's medal City of Paris, 1990. Mem. City Athletic Club, Racing Club, Polo Club. Jewish. Avocations: tennis, sailing. Office: The Fairchild Corp 1750 Tysons Blvd Ste 1400 Mc Lean VA 22102 Office Phone: 212-308-6700. E-mail: jsteiner@fairchild.com.

STEINER, JOHN WILLIAM, retired biophysicist; b. Chgo., Feb. 3, 1934; s. John Deacon Steiner and Bernice Marguerite Taylor; m. Phyllis Irene Rendell, July 12, 1958; children: John Alfred, Jay William. BA in Chemistry, Boston U., 1964. Analytical chemist MIT Nuc. Reactor, Cambridge, Mass., 1965—66; rsch. biophysicist biophysics dept. Boston U. Med. Ctr., Boston, 1967—99; ret., 1999. Contbr. Handbook of Lipid Research, vol. 4, 1986. Vestryman, mem. various coms. Ch. of Our Redeemer, Lexington, Mass., 1985—. Col. USAR, 1952—86. Mem.: Employer Support of Guard/Res., Res. Officers Assn. (Mass. state pres. 1999—2000). Republican. Episcopalian. Avocations: stamp collecting/philately, coin collecting/numismatics, genealogy. Home: 22 Estabrook Rd Lexington MA 02421-7540

STEINER, PAUL ANDREW, retired insurance executive; b. Woodburn, Ind., Feb. 17, 1929; s. Eli Gerig and Emma Mae (Yaggy) Steiner; m. Ruth Edna Henry, Sept. 1, 1950; children: Mark, Nancy, Jonathan, David. AB, Taylor U., 1950. CPCU. Owner feed and grain, lumber and constrn. firms, Bluffton, Ohio, 1951-64; home office rep. Brotherhood Mut. Ins. Co., Ft. Wayne, Ind., 1964-65, dir. claims, 1966-71, v.p., treas., 1968-71, pres., 1971-94, chmn. bd., 1974-2000. Trustee emeritus Taylor U.; past chmn. Summit Christian Coll.; past pres. Ft. Wayne Rescue Mission; bd. dirs. William Taylor Found. Mem.: Soc. CPCU (past nat. ethics com., past pres. No. Ind. chpt.), Mut. Ins. Cos. Assn. Ind. (past pres.), Conf. Casualty Ins. Cos. (past pres.), DEVCO Mut. Assn. (past chmn.), Nat. Assn. Mut. Ins. Cos. (past chmn. bd., Merit award 1973), Christian Assn. Primetimers (bd. dirs.), Christian Bus. Men's Com. Ft. Wayne, Nat. Assn. Evangs. (past treas., Layman of Yr. 1977), Am. Bible Soc. (sr. trustee), Ft. Wayne Rotary Club (past pres.). Republican. Mem. Fellowship Of Evangelical Churches. Home: 1825 Florida Dr Fort Wayne IN 46805-5036

STEINER, PETER OTTO, economics educator, dean; b. N.Y.C., July 9, 1922; s. Otto Davidson and Ruth (Wurzburger) S.; m. Ruth E. Riggs, Dec. 20, 1947 (div. 1967); children: Mary Catherine, Alison Ruth, David Denison; m. Patricia F. Owen, June 2, 1968. AB, Oberlin Coll., 1943; MA, Harvard, 1949, PhD, 1950. Instr. U. Calif., Berkeley, 1949-50, asst. prof. econs., 1950-57; assoc. prof. U. Wis., Madison, 1957-59, prof., 1959-68; prof. econs. and law U. Mich., Ann Arbor, 1968-91, prof. emeritus, 1991—, chmn. dept. econs., 1971-74, dean Coll. Lit., Sci. and Arts, 1981-89. Vis. prof. U. Nairobi, Kenya, 1974—75; cons. U.S. Bur. Budget, 1961—62, Treasury Dept., 1962—63, various pvt. firms, 1952—. Author: An Introduction to the Analysis of Time Series, 1956, (with R. Dorfman) The Economic Status of the Aged, 1957, (with R.G. Lipsey) Economics, 10th edit., 1993, On the Process of Planning, 1968, Public Expenditure Budgeting, 1969, Mergers: Motives, Effects, Policies, 1975, Thursday Night Poker: Understand, Enjoy and Win, 1996; contbr. articles to profl. publs. Served to lt. USNR, 1944-46. Social Sci. Research Council Faculty Research fellow, 1956; Guggenheim fellow, 1960; Ford Faculty Research fellow, 1965 Mem. Am. Econ. Assn., Econometric Soc., AAUP (chmn. com. Z 1970-73, pres. 1976-78) Home: 502 Heritage Dr Ann Arbor MI 48105-2556 E-mail: psteiner@umich.edu.

STEINER, RICHARD C. semitic linguist, educator; b. N.Y.C., Nov. 7, 1945; s. Frederick Steiner and Pearl Weiss; m. Sara K. Rosenschein, June 1, 1969; children: Chana, Shana, Rachel. BA, Yeshiva U., 1966; student, Hebrew U., Jerusalem, 1963-64; B in Hebrew Lit., Yeshiva U., 1966; postgrad., Uppsala (Sweden) U., 1966-67; PhD, U. Pa., 1974. Asst. prof. Dropsie U., Phila., 1972-73, Touro Coll., N.Y.C., 1973-75; asst. to assoc. prof. semitic langs. and lit. Yeshiva U., Bernard Revel Grad. Sch., N.Y.C., 1975-84, prof. semitic langs. and lit., 1984—. Vis. assoc. prof. U. Chgo., 1981; Gerard Weinstock vis. prof. Jewish studies, Harvard U., 1999. Author: The Case for Fricative-Laterals in Proto-Semitic, 1977, Affricated Sade in the Semitic Languages, 1982, Stockmen from Tekoa, Sycomores from Sheba, 2003; co-author: A Quantitative Study of Sound Change in Progress, 1972; contbr. articles to profl. jours. (Bibl. Archeology Soc. award 1984); editl. bd. Hebrew Ann. Rev., 1981-87, Jour. Afroasiatic Langs., 1986-92. Fellow Inst. Advanced Studies, Jerusalem, 1983-84, 94-95, Am. Scandinavian Found., 1966-67, Humphrey Inst. Social Ecology, Beersheba, Israel, 1989; rsch. grantee NEH, 1978-81, 84-88. Fellow Am. Acad. Jewish Rsch., Am. Friends of Acad. Hebrew Lang. (pres. 1998—). Office: Yeshiva U Revel Grad Sch 500 W 185th St New York NY 10033-3299 E-mail: rsteiner@ymail.yu.edu.

STEINER, RICHARD RUSSELL, textile & apparel company executive; b. Chgo., Feb. 26, 1923; s. Frank Gardner and Ruth (Cowie); m. Colleen Kearns, Dec. 6, 1949; children: Robert C., Kevin K., Sheila M. BA, Dartmouth Coll., 1948. With Steiner Corp., Salt Lake City, 1948—, divisonal dir., v.p., 1951-59, pres., 1959-2000, chmn., 2000—. Dir. Am. Uniform Co. Served with USAAF, 1942—46. Decorated D.F.C. Mem.: Alta, Salt Lake Country, Phi Beta Kappa. Office: 505 E South Temple Salt Lake City UT 84102-1004

STEINER, ROBERT FRANK, biochemist; b. Manila, Philippines, Sept. 29, 1926; came to U.S., 1933; s. Frank and Clara Nell (Weems) S.; m. Ethel Mae Fisher, Nov. 3, 1956; children: Victoria, Laura. AB, Princeton U., 1947; PhD, Harvard U., 1950. Chemist Naval Med. Research Inst., Bethesda, Md., 1950-70, chief lab. phys. biochemistry, 1965-70; prof. chemistry U. Md., Balt., 1970—, chmn. dept. chemistry, 1974—; prof. emeritus, 1996—; dir. grad. program in biochemistry U. Md., Balt., 1985. Biophysics study sect. NIH, 1976. Author: Life Chemistry, 1968, Excited States of Proteins and Nucleic Acids, 1971, The Chemistry of Living Systems, 1981, Excited States of Biopolymers, 1983, A Pilot's Tale and Other Stories, 1998, The Decoy and Other Stories, 1999, The Student Pilot and Other Stories, 2000, The Beauty Contest and Other Stories, 2002; editor Jour. Biophys. Chemistry, 1972—, Jour. Fluorescence, 1991; contbr. over 160 articles to profl. jours. Served with AUS, 1945-47. Recipient Superior Civilian Achievement award Dept. Def., 1966; NSF rsch. grantee, 1971-77, NIH, 1973-93. Fellow Washington Acad. Sci., Japan Soc. for Promotion Sci.; mem. Am. Soc. Biol. Chemists. Clubs: Princeton (Washington). Achievements include development of fluorescence techniques for studying proteins. Home: 2609 Turf Valley Rd Ellicott City MD 21042-2021 Office: 5401 Wilkens Ave Baltimore MD 21250-1000 Office Phone: 410-465-0987. Personal E-mail: xuzw63A@aol.com.

STEINER, ROBERT LISLE, retired language consultant; b. Tehran, Iran, May 21, 1921; s. Robert Lisle and Lois (Foresman) S.; m. Margaret S. Sherrard, June 4, 1944; children: Patricia Jean, Robert Lisle III, William Sherrard, John Scott. Grad., Mercersberg (Pa.) Acad., 1938; BA, Wooster (Ohio) Coll.; MA, Columbia U., 1948. Cons. Commn. Chs. on Internat. Affairs, 1948-49; cultural attache Am. embassy, Iran, 1950-52; educationist U.S. Office Edn., 1952-54; program dir. Am. Friends of Mid. East, 1954-59; v.p. Vershire Co., Vt., 1959-62; dir. Peace Corps, Kabul, Afghanistan, 1962-66; regional dir. North Africa, Near East and South Asia, 1966-69; dir. Washington office Devel. & Resources Corp., 1969-70; dir. Ctr. for Cross-Cultural Tng. and Rsch., adviser to univ. pres. on internat. affairs U. Hawaii, Honolulu, 1971-72; dir., gen. mgr. Hawaii Pub. Broadcasting Authority, 1972-73; exec. dir. N.J. Edn. Consortium, Princeton, 1973-78; pres. InterLink Lang. Ctrs., Princeton, 1979-91, chmn., 1992—. Tchr. U. Kansas City, Mo., 1957, Bradford (Vt.) Acad., 1961; poultry cons. Mid. East Tech. U., Ankara, Turkey, 1963. Councilman, v.p. Shanks Village Assn., Orangeburg, N.Y., 1948; chmn. Kabul Sch. Bd., 1965. Served as pilot USNR, 1943-46. Mem. Princeton Mid. East Soc. (sec. 1986-88, treas. 1993-95). Democrat. Presbyterian. Home: 1898 Villa Ct Lancaster PA 17603-2386 Office: Interlink Lang Ctrs 1898 Villa Ct Lancaster PA 17603-2386

STEINER, ROGER JACOB, linguistics educator, writer, researcher; b. South Byron, Wis., Mar. 27, 1924; s. Jakob Robert and Alice Mildred (Cowles) S.; m. Ida Kathryn Posey, Aug. 7, 1954 (dec. May 1992); children: David Posey, Andrew Posey, Anthony Wright. BA cum laude, Franklin & Marshall Coll., 1945; MDiv, Union Theol. Sem., 1947; MA, U. Pa., 1958, PhD, 1963. Ordained to ministry, Meth. Ch., 1947. Clergyman United Meth. Ch., N.Y., Wis., Pa., 1945-61; lectr. U. Bordeaux, France, 1961-63; instr. dept. langs. & lit. U. Del., Newark, 1963-64, asst. prof., 1964-71, assoc. prof., 1971-80, prof., 1980-85, dept. linguistics U. Del., Newark, 1985-96, prof. emeritus, 1998—. Cons. Charles Scribner's Sons, N.Y.C., 1972-75, Larousse, N.Y.C., 1981-84, Houghton-Mifflin, Boston, 1981-84, Macmillan, 1994-99. Author: Two Centuries of Spanish and English Bilingual Lexicography (1590-1800), 1970, New College French and English Dictionary, 1972, 3d edit., 2004; editor: Simon & Schuster's International Spanish Dictionary, 2d edit., 1997, Cuyás Spanish and English Dictionary, 3d edit., 1999, New College Spanish and English Dictionary, 3d edit., 2003; contbr. articles to profl. jours., chpts. to books. Recipient fellowship Am. Philos. Soc., Phila., 1971, Lilly Found., Phila., 1979-81. Mem. MLA (founder lexicography group 1974-75, chmn. 1976, 77, 80, 85), Dictionary Soc. N.Am., Phi Beta Kappa (pres. chpt. 1975-76). Republican. Avocations: languages, photography. Office: U Del Dept Linguistics Newark DE 19716-2551 E-mail: rsteiner@udel.edu.

STEINER, STANLEY F. literature educator; b. Richardton, N.D., July 18, 1952; s. John F. and Anna Maria (Greff) Steiner; m. Katherine Radloff, July 20, 1973 (div. May 1978); 1 child, Benjamin Matthew; m. Joy Lynn Berryman, Mar. 31, 1983; children: Lea Christine, Avi John. AA, Bismarck State Coll., 1972; BA, U. Mary, Bismarck, 1974; MS, Northern State U., Aberdeen, S.D., 1976; PhD, U. Wyo., 1992. Tchr., asst. prin. Bismarck Pub. Schs., ND, 1974—78, Teton County Sch. Dist., Jackson Hole, Wyo., 1978—89; prof. Boise State U., 1992—. Author: Promoting A Global Community, Through Children's Literature, 2001; editor: Frierian Pedagogy: Praxis, and Possibilities, 2000; author: Building Bridges: Books Bring Us Together, 2002. Chair literacy dept.; adv. bd. dirs. Idaho Human Rights Commn. Mem.: NCTE, Am. Libr. Assn., Internat. Reading Assn. (Notable Books for Global Soc. award 2002—). Avocations: childrens literature specialist, woodworker, hiking, cooking. Home: 1105 Pueblo St Boise ID 83702-4152 Office: Boise State U 1910 University Dr Boise ID 83725 Office Phone: 208-426-3962. Business E-Mail: ssteine@boisestate.edu.

STEINER, STUART, college president; b. Balt., July 24, 1937; s. Louis and Lillian (Block) S.; m. Rosalie Weiner, Sept. 12, 1962; children: Lisa, Susan, David, Robyn. AA, Balt. Jr. Coll., 1957; BS, U. Md., 1959; grad. cert., Fla. State U., 1962; MSW., U. Pa., 1963; JD, U. Balt., 1967; MA, Tchrs. Coll., Columbia U., 1972; EdD, Columbia U., 1987. Caseworker, then supr. and dir. juvenile ct. services Balt. Dept. Social Services, 1960-64; dir. info. and referral ctr. Healt and Welfare Coun. Met. Balt., 1964; dir. admissions and placement Harford Jr. Coll., Bel Air, Md., 1965-67; dean of students Genesee Community Coll., Batavia, NY, 1967-68, dean of coll., 1968-75, pres., 1975—. Pres. SUNY West, acting dep. to chancellor for community colls., 1985, pres. of assn. Pres. of Pub. Community Colls., 1987-89; acting pres. Fashion Inst. Tech., N.Y.C., 1997-98; CEO Ednl. Found. Fashion Industries, 1997-98; bd. dirs. Workforce Investment Bd.; commr. Commn. of Higher Edn., Mid. States Assn., 1999—. Contbr. chpts. to art books and articles to profl. jours. Bd. dirs. St. Jerome Hosp., Genesee County Community Chest, campaign chmn.; bd. dirs. Health Sci. Agy., Western N.Y.; trustee Villa Maria Coll.; trustee, v.p.

N.Y. Chiropractic Coll.; bd. dirs. St. Jerome Hosp., Genesee Mercy Healthcare, United Meml. Med Ctr.; pres. Genesee County United Way, Community Coll. of Balt. Hall of Fame. Sigma Delta scholar U. Md., 1958-59, Heuisler scholar U. Balt. Law Sch., 1960-61, Kellogg fellow, 1971-72; recipient CEO award Assn. of C.C. Trustees (N.E. region) 1997, Mem. Pvt. Indsl. Coun. (bd. dirs. 1983-2000, workforce investment bd. 2000-02). Home: 33 Woodcrest Dr Batavia NY 14020-2721 Office: Genesee Community Coll 1 College Rd Batavia NY 14020-9703 Office Phone: 585-345-6812. E-mail: ssteiner@genesee.edu.

STEINFELD, ALLAN, sports association administrator; B, City College, NY, 1969; M in Elec. Enging and Radio Astronomy, Cornell U. 1971. Staff mem. NY Road Runners Club, NYC, 1978-92, pres., 1992— Chief referee of men's and women's marathons, 1984 LA Olympics; adviser several 1V broadcasts; race dir. Fifth Ave Mile, the Advil Mini Marathon, the Trevira Twosome, NY Games; mem. exec. com. TAF's Men's Long Distance Running Com.; tech. dir., NYC Marathon, 1981-94; race dir., 1994-; adv. bd. mem., Nat. Distance Running Hall of Fame, NY. Achievements include winner, NY Roadrunner Club 8-mile Handicap Race, 1966. Office: NY Road Runners Club 9 E 89th St New York NY 10128-0602*

STEINFELD, JEFFREY IRWIN, chemistry educator, consultant, writer; b. Bklyn., July 2, 1940; s. Paul and Ann (Ravin) S. B.Sc., MIT, 1962; PhD, Harvard U., 1965. Postdoctoral fellow U. Sheffield, Yorkshire, Eng., 1965-66; asst. prof. chemistry MIT, Cambridge, 1966-70, assoc. prof., 1970-79, prof., 1980—. Author: Molecules & Radiation, 1974; co-author: Chemical Kinetics and Dynamics, 1989, 2d edit., 1999; editor: Laser and Coherence Spectroscopy, 1977, Laser-Induced Chemical Processes, 1981; co-editor: Spectrochimica Acta, 1983-98; contbr. articles to profl. jours. Treas. Ward 2 Democratic Com Cambridge, 1972-73 NSF fellow Harvard U., Cambridge, 1962-65; NSF fellow Sheffield U., 1965 66; Alfred P. Sloan Found. research fellow MIT, 1969-71; Guggenheim fellow, 1972-73 Fellow Am. Phys. Soc.; mem. AAAS, Union Concerned Scientists, Fedn. Am. Scientists, Sigma Xi, Phi Lambda Upsilon. Jewish. Office: MIT Room 2-221 Cambridge MA 02139

STEINFELD, MANFRED, furniture manufacturing executive; b. Josbach, Germany, Apr. 29, 1924; s. Abraham and Puala (Katten) S.; m. Fern Goldman, Nov. 13, 1949; children: Michael, Paul, Jill. Student, U. Ill., 1942; BS in Commerce, Roosevelt U., 1948, LLH (hon.), 1997. Rsch. analyst State of Ill., 1948-50; v.p. Shelby Williams Industries, Inc., Chgo., 1954-63, pres., 1964-72, chmn. bd., 1973-96, chmn. exec. com., 1996—. Bd. dirs. Amalgamated Trust & Savs. Bank. Mem. adv. bd. Shc. Human Ecology, U. Tenn., 1981-87, devel. coun., 1982-87; mem. adv. bd. dept. interior design Fla. Internat. U., 1981-85; life trustee Roosevelt U., Chgo.; past pres. Roosevelt U. Bus. Sch. Alumni Coun.; hon. governing mem. Art Inst. Chgo., mem. com. 20th century decorative art; bd. dirs. Jewish Fedn. Chgo., 1986-90; gen. chmn. Jewish United Fund, 1987, 97; nat. vice chmn. United Jewish Appeal, 1989-94; chmn. bd. dirs. Jewish Fedn. Chgo., 1988—. Served to 1st lt. AUS, 1942-45, 50-52. Decorated Bronze Star, Purple Heart; named Small Bus. Man of Yr., Ctrl. REgion, 1967; established Manfred Steinfeld Hospitality Mgmt. Program at Roosevelt U., Chgo., 1988; established Fernand Manfred Steinfeld Chair Judaic Studies U. Tenn., Knoxville, 1995; recipient Horatio Alger awrad of disting. Ams., 1981, Outstanding Bus. Leader award Northwood Inst., 1983, Vol. of Yr., U, Tenn., 1996, Lifetime Achievement award Hospitality Design Mag., 1999. Mem. Horatio Alger Assn. (bd. dirs. 1986-92), Standard Club, Bryn Mawr Country Club, Bocaire Country Club (Boca Raton, Fla.), Beta Gamma Sigma. Home: 1300 N Lake Shore Dr Apt 34D Chicago IL 60610-5165 Office: Mdse Mart Rm 10-124 Chicago IL 60654

STEINFELD, PHILIP SHELDON, pediatrician; b. Bronx, Mar. 4, 1932; s. Samuel and Sarah (Frishman) S.; m. Ruth L. Hyman, Aug., 1961 (div. June 1977); children: Andrea, Melissa, David; m. Sherry Lynn Rubinroit, Jan. 15, 1978; 1 child, Sara. BS, Queens Coll., 1953; MD, U. Basle, Switzerland, 1960. Diplomate Am. Bd. Pediatrics. Rotating intern Kings County Hosp. Ctr., Bklyn., 1960-61; resident pediatrics Mt. Sinai Hosp., N.Y.C., 1961-63, jr. clin. asst. pediatrics, 1963-65, sr. clin. asst., 1965-68; attending pediatrician L.I. Jewish Hosp., 1968—, North Shore Univ. Hosp., 1970—; clin. instr. pediatrics Cornell N., N.Y.C., 1986-90, clin. asst. prof. pediatrics, 1991—. Mem. adv. bd. TEMPO, Woodmere, N.Y., 1975-92, Five Town Adolescent Ctr., Woodmere, 1975-93. Fellow Am. Acad. Pediatrics. Office: 1573 Broadway Hewlett NY 11557-1428

STEINFELD, THOMAS ALBERT, retired publisher; b. N.Y.C., June 17, 1917; s. Albert and Marjorie (Lesser) S.; m. Joan Rollinson, July 29, 1945 (dec. Nov. 1973); children: Geoffrey T., Jill R.; m. Viviane Barkey, June 20, 1977. Student, G. Phillips Exeter Acad., 1934, Harvard U., 1934—35. Salesman John Orr Products, N.Y.C., 1935-36; asst. advt. mgr. Bloomingdale's, N.Y.C., 1936-37; with Playbill mag., N.Y.C., 1937—2002, pub., 1962-65, pres., 1962-68, v.p., nat. sales dir.; ret., 2002. Served to capt. AUS, 1942-46, CBI. Mem.: Aspetuck Valley Country Club (Weston, Conn.). Home: 83 W Meadow Rd Wilton CT 06897-4722

STEINFINK, HUGO, chemical engineering educator; b. Vienna, May 22, 1924; s. Mendel and Malwina (Fiderer) S.; m. Cele Intrator, Mar. 21, 1948; children: Dan E., Susan D. BS, CCNY, 1947; MS, Columbia U., 1948; PhD, Bklyn. Poly. Inst., 1954. Rsch. chemist Shell Devel. Co., Houston, 1948-51, 53-60; T. Brockett Hudson prof. chem. engring. U. Tex., Austin, 1960-2000, prof. emeritus, 2000. Contbr. articles to profl. jours. With AUS, 1944-46. Fellow Am. Mineral Soc.; mem. AIChE, Am. Chem. Soc., Am. Crystallographic Assn. (pres.-elect 1994, pres. 1995, past pres. 1996), Materials Rsch. Soc., Phi Beta Kappa, Sigma Xi, Phi Lambda Epsilon. Home: 3811 Walnut Clay Dr Austin TX 78731-4011

STEINGASS, SUSAN R. lawyer; b. Cambridge, Mass., Dec. 18, 1941; BA in English Lit., Denison U., 1963; MA in English Lit. with honors, Northwestern U., 1965; JD with honors, U. Wis., 1976. Bar: Wis. 1976, U.S. Dist. Ct. Wis. 1976. Instr. dept. English La. State U., 1965-68; instr. State Coll., L.A., 1966-68, U. Wis., Stevens Point, 1968-72; law clk. Hon. Nathan S. Heffernan Wis. Supreme Ct., 1976-77; ptnr. Stafford, Rosenbaum, Reiser and Hansen, 1977-85; judge Dane County Cir. Ct., Wis., 1985-93; ptnr. Habush, Habush & Rottier, S.C., Madison, Wis., 1993—. Lectr. civil procedure, environ. law, evidence, trial advocacy Law Sch., U. Wis., 1981—; dir. advocacy and comm., 2003—; instr. Nat. Inst. for Trial Advocacy, 1987—, trustee, 2002—; instr. Nat. Jud. Coll., 1993—. Note and comment editor Wis. Law Rev., 1974-76; co-editor: Wisconsin Civil Procedure Before Trial, 1994, The Wisconsin Rules of Evidence: A Courtroom Handbook, 1998—. Chair Wis. Equal Justice Task Force, 1989-91. Recipient Disting. Svc. award Am. Assn. Mediators, 1991; recipient award of excellence State Bar Wis., 2000; named Wis. Trial Judge of Presdl. award of Achievement Assn., 1992. Fellow Wis. Bar Found.; mem. ATLA, ABA (ho. dels. 2000—), Am. Bar Found., Am. Law Inst., Wis. Bar Assn. (pres. 1998-99), Wis. Law Alumni Assn. (bd. dirs., pres.), Wis. Acad. Trial Lawyers, Wis. Equal Justice Fund (pres.), Dane County Bar Assn., Wis. Trust Account Found. (bd. dirs. 1999—), Order of the Coif (Marygold Melli Achievement award 2001). Home: 5 Habush Habush Davis & Rottier SC 150 E Gilman St Ste 2000 Madison WI 53703-1481 E-mail: ssteinga@habush.com.

STEINGRABER, FREDERICK GEORGE, management consultant; b. Mpls., July 7, 1938; s. Frederick F. and Evelyn (Luger) S.; m. Veronika Agnes Wagner, Aug. 9, 1974; children: Karla, Frederick. BS, Ind. U., 1960, MBA, U. Chgo., 1964. Cert. mgmt. cons. Internat. banker Harris Trust, Chgo., 1960-61; with comml. loan and credit No. Trust Co., Chgo., 1964—68; assoc. A.T. Kearney, Chgo., 1969—72, prin., 1972—, officer/ptnr., 1977—, pres., COO, 1981—82, CEO, 1983—2000, chmn. emeritus, 2000, chmn., bd. advs., 2002, also bd. dirs.; mem. adv. bd. L.L.C., 1999—. Bd. dirs. Continental AG, Maytag Corp., 1999; bd. mem. Inst. for Ill., 1986, John Hancock Fin. Trend Funds3 PLC, 2001—. Chief crusader United Way Crusade of Mercy, Chgo., 1983—90; divsn.chmn., bd. dirs.l Ill. Coalition, 1989; fin. rsch. adv. com. City of Chgo., 1989—; mem. past chmn. dean's adv. coun. U. Ind. Bus. Sch., Bloomington, 1985—; bd. dirs. Ind. U. Coun.; mem. bd. dirs. Grad. Sch. Bus. U. Chgo.; mem. Northwestern U.

STEINHARDT GUTMAN... 2, 1951; d. Max E. Steinhardt and ... 1972; children: Micah, Simeon, Shanan... MFA, SUNY, Stony Brook, 1991. Adj. assoc. ... Selden, NY, 1991—2001; adj. lectr. St. Joseph's Co... 1993—97, Adelphi U., Garden City, NY, 1995—2001, Nass... Garden City, 2000—01; adj. instr. Montgomery County C.C., Blue B... 2001—02; asst. prof. art Delaware County C.C., Media, Pa., 2002—. Mus... shop mgr The Jewish Mus., N.Y.C., 1973—77; faculty cons. The Coll. Bd., Phila., 1999— 2003, Ednl. Testing Svcs., Trenton, NJ, 1995—2003; artist-in-residence Mishkenot Sha'ananim, Jerusalem, 1994 Recipient Spl. Opportunity stipend, N.Y. State Found. on Arts, 1992—94, Grumbacher Gold medallion in painting, 1995. Home: 165 Somerset Dr Blue Bell PA 19422 Office: Delaware County C C 901 S Media Line Rd Media PA 19063 Office Phone: 610-359-5382. Business E-mail: bgutman@dccc.edu

STEINHAUER, GILLIAN, lawyer; b. Aylesbury, Bucks, Eng., Oct. 6, 1938; d. Eric Frederick and Maisie Kathleen (Yeates) Pearson; m. Bruce William Steinhauer, Jan. 2, 1960; children: Alison (Humphrey) Eric, John, Elspeth. AB cum laude, Bryn Mawr (Pa.) Coll., 1959; JD cum laude, U. Mich., 1976. Bar: Tenn. 1998, U.S. Dist. Ct. (ea. dist.) Mich. 1976, U.S. Ct. Appeals (6th cir.) 1982. From assoc. to sr. ptnr. Miller, Canfield, Paddock & Stone, Detroit, 1976-92; dir. Commonwealth of Mass. Workers' Compensation Litigation Unit, Boston, 1992—2002; atty. U.S. Postal Svc., 2002—. Chancellor Cath. Ch. St. Paul, Detroit, 1976-83, 91; pres. bd. trustees Cath. Cmty. Svcs. Inc., 1989-92; bd. dirs. Spaulding for Children, 1991-92, Davenport House, 1992-96, chair 1995-96, mem. Vestry St. Michael's Ch., Marblehead, Mass., 1994-97. Mem. Mich. State Bar Found. (life), Fed. Jud. Conf. 6th Cir. (life). Home: 4010 S Galloway Dr Memphis TN 38111-6842

STEINHAUER, SHERRI, professional golfer; b. Madison, Wis., Dec. 27, 1962; Student, U. Tex. Golfer LPGA, 1986—; winner du Maurier Classic, 1992, Sprint Championship 1999, Weetabix Women's British Open Championship, 1998, 99; mem. U.S. Solheim Cup Team, 1994, 98, 2000, Japan Airlines Big Apple Classic, 1999. Achievements include 3 LPGA career hole-in-ones. Office: c/o LPGA 100 International Golf Dr Daytona Beach FL 32124-1082

STEINHAUS, JOHN EDWARD, anesthesiologist, educator; b. Omaha, Feb. 23, 1917; s. Emil F. and Pearl (Haynie) S.: m. Mila Jean Pinkerton, Feb. 21, 1943; children: Kathryn, Carolyn, Barbara, William, Elizabeth. BA, U. Neb., 1940, MA, 1941; MD, U. Wis., 1945, PhD, 1950. Diplomate: Am. Bd. Anesthesiologists. Pvt. practice specializing in anesthesiology, Madison, Wis., 1951-58, Atlanta, 1958—; faculty U. Wis., 1951-58; mem. faculty Emory U., Atlanta, 1958—, prof. anesthesiology, 1959-87, prof. emeritus, 1987—, chmn. dept., 1959-85; chief anesthesiology service Grady Meml. Hosp., 1959-77, Emory U. Hosp., 1958-85. Author: Medical Care Divided; contbr. articles to profl. jours. Past pres. Anesthesia Found. mem. Am. Soc. Anesthesiologists (past pres., Disting. Service award 1982), So. Soc. Anesthesiologists (past pres.), AMA, AAAS, Assn. U. Anesthetists (past pres.), Anesthesiology History Assn. (past pres.), Soc. Pharm. Exptl. Therapeutics, Phi Beta Kappa, Sigma Xi, Alpha Omega Alpha. Home and Office: 836 Castle Falls Dr NE Atlanta GA 30329-4114 Personal E-mail: jsteinh@emory.edu.

STEINHAUSER, JOHN WILLIAM, retired lawyer; b. Akron, Ohio, June 25, 1924; s. John Hugo and Francis Lillian (Pearson) S.; m. Patricia E. Mooney, Dec.1, 1956; children: John, Christian, Mark, Sharon. BSBA, Ohio State U., 1949; JD, U. Mich., 1950. Bar: Mich. 1950, Colo. 1972. Atty., dir. L.Am., dir. export sales, gen mgr. Africa-Far E. Chrysler Corp., dir. Chrysler Internat., dir. Africa-Far East, 1950-71; atty. Denver, 1971—; founder, dir., pres. Pearson Energy Corp., 1977—. Founder, chmn. Sharon Energy, Ltd., Denver, 1980, also dir., 1980-97. Active Colo. Rep. Com.; sponsor Denver Symphony; pres. John and Patricia Steinhauser Found. With USNR, 1943—46. Mem. ABA, Colo. Bar Assn., Mich. Bar Assn., Soc. Internat. Law, Rocky Mountain Mineral Law Found., Cherry Hills Country Club, Royal Poinciana Golf Club, Rotary. Home: 46 Charlou Cir Englewood CO 80111-1103 E-mail: jwsteinhauser@sbcglobal.net.

STEINHOFF, RAYMOND O(AKLEY), consulting geologist; b. Hart, Mich., Apr. 22, 1925; m. Anne M. Steinhoff, 1952; 1 child, Kirk O. BS, MS, So. Meth. U., 1948; PhD in Geology, Tex. A&M, 1965. Instr. geology Tex. A&M U., Coll. Sta., Tex., 1948-51; geologist Atlantic Rich., Wichita, Kans., 1951-53, Humble Oil and Refining Co., New Orleans, 1953-57; asst. prof. geology Tulane U., New Orleans, 1957-65, assoc. prof., 1965-70, chmn. dept., 1969-70; prof. and dept. head geology Stephen F. Austin State U., Nacogdoches, Tex., 1970-78; divsn. geologist Buttes, New Orleans, 1978-79; cons. geologist Graham, New Orleans, 1979-83. Cons. Trinexco, New Orleans, 1964-69. Sgt. U.S. Army, 1944—46, WWII, 1st lt. USAF, 1952—53, Korea. Mem. Am. Assn. Petroleum Geologists (emeritus), New Orleans Geol. Soc. (emeritus), Phi Kappa Phi (emeritus). Home: 6 North H St Pensacola FL 32501-4420

STEINHORN, IRWIN HARRY, lawyer, educator, corporate executive; b. Dallas, Aug. 13, 1940; s. Raymond and Libby M. (Miller) Steinhorn; m. Deborah Kelley Steinhorn, Apr. 7, 2002; 1 child, Leslie Robin. BBA, U. Tex., 1961, LLB, 1964. Bar: Tex. 1964, U.S. Dist. Ct. (no. dist.) Tex. 1965, Okla. 1970, U.S. Dist. Ct. (we. dist.) Okla. 1972. Assoc. Oster & Kaufman, Dallas, 1964-67; ptnr. Parness, McQuire & Lewis, Dallas, 1967—. Sr. v.p., gen. counsel LSB Industries, Inc., Oklahoma City, 1970-87; v.p., gen. counsel USPCI, Inc., Oklahoma City, 1987-88; ptnr. Hastie & Steinhorn, Oklahoma City, 1988-95; mem., officer, dir. Conner & Winters, Oklahoma City, 1995—. Adj. prof. law Oklahoma City U. Sch. Law, 1979—; lectr. in field. Mem. adv. com. Okla. Securities Commn., 1986—; mem. exec. adv. bd. Oklahoma City U. Sch. Law, 2000—; bd. dirs. Okla. Venture Forum, 2000—. Served to capt. USAR, 1964-70. Mem. ABA, Tex. Bar Assn., Okla. Bar Assn. (bus. assn. sect., sec.pt.eeas. 1986-87, chmn. 1988-89), Com. to Revise Okla. Bus. Corp. Act, Rotary, Phi Alpha Delta. Republican. Jewish. Home: 224 NW 18th St Oklahoma City OK 73103 Office: Conner & Winters One Leadership Sq 211 N Robinson Ave Ste 1700 Oklahoma City OK 73102-7136 Office Phone: 405-272-5750. Business E-mail: isteinhorn@cwlaw.com.

STEINKE, GREG A, music educator, administrator, composer, oboist; b. Fremont, Mich., Sept. 2, 1942; s. Donald Ferdinand John and Ella Louise (Clute) S.; m. Karen Florence Larsen, June 5, 1971; children: Carl Asa, Kyle Alban. Mus.B, Oberlin Conservatory, 1964; MMus, Mich. State U., 1967, PhD, 1976; MFA, U. Iowa, 1971. Instr. music U. Idaho, Moscow, 1967-68, dir. Sch. Music, prof. music, 1983-86; instr. music San Diego State U., 1986-88; instr. music U. Md., College Park, 1968-72; asst. prof. music Calif. State U., Northridge, 1973-75; mem. faculty Evergreen State Coll., Olympia, Wash., 1975-79; chmn. music dept., prof. Linfield Coll., Mcminnville, Oreg., 1979-83; asst. dir. U. Ariz. Sch. Music, Tucson, 1988-91; prof. of. Sch. Music Ball State U., Muncie, Ind., 1991-96; prof., dean Coll. fine Arts Millikin U., Decatur, Ill., 1996-97; mem. faculty No. Ariz. U., Flagstaff, 1997-98; chmn. art and music dept.; assoc. dean undergrad. studies Marylhurst (Oreg.) U., 1999-2001, Joseph Naumes endowed chair music, 1999-2001, ret., 2001. Guest composer Contemporary Music Festival Western Ill. U., 1982, 90-91, Charles Ives Ctr. for Am. Music, New Milford, Conn., 1982, 91, 1st Ann.

Festival of New Music, Bowling Green State U., 1980, New Music Fest XV and Symposium for New WWQ5 Mus... Biennial Festival New Music Fla. State U., 1989, 91, 93, 96, S.W. Tex. U., 1990. Birmingham So. U., 1990, N.Am. Music Fest, 2002... 1990... participant numerous music festivals, Atlantic Ctr., for Arts Assn... positions for voice, piano, instrumental chamber orch., wind ensemble, incidental music for plays; also arrangements of music, oboe ... Com. mem. 1984 86, Green Valley Concert... City Arts Commn... numerous awards including Standards Awards panel of ASCAP, ... 1986, awards Standards ... Hon. Mention, Britten... ... Composition winner Sam Houston State U... ... Composition Series XIII, 2002, 2003, Hon. Mention, U.S.A... ... Competition Series XIII, 2002, 2003... Double ... petition fellow Tucson/Pima Arts Coun... ... Spl. Project Grant, 1990. Composers ... Music Soc... Internat. Society ... Music Ctr., Soc. Composers ...

STEINMAN... and Edith Ruth (Sh... July 1986); children: Jennif... ... Eng., 1968; AB with high distin... Harvard U., 1973. Bar: Ill. 1973... Chgo., 1973-77; asst. prof. law Chgo.-Kent Coll. Law... assoc. prof., 1982-86, prof., 1986-98, Disting. prof., 1998... 1990-91. Cons. in atty. promotions Met. Dist. Greater Chgo., 1981, 85... adv. com. on 7th cir. rules. Author: Wright & Miller et al., Federal Practice and Procedure Treatise, vols. 14B, 14C; contbr. articles to law jours. Coop. atty. ACLU Ill., Chgo., 1974, Leadership Coun. for Met. Open Cmtys., Chgo., 1975, Better Bus. Bur. Met. Chgo., 1987; apptd. bd. arbitrators Nat. Assn. Security Dealers, 1989—2000; apptd. to Ill. Gov.'s Grievance Panel, 1987; bd. dirs. Pro Bono Advocates, 1995—99. Recipient Julia Beveridge award Ill. Inst. Tech., 1996, Ralph L. Brill award Chgo. Kent Coll. Law, 1997; Norman and Edna Freehling scholar Chgo.-Kent Coll. Law, 1989-93. Mem. ABA, Am. Law Inst. (advisor Fed. Jud. Code Revision project 1996-2001, cons. group complex litig. project 1990-93, restatement of the law, third, torts, products liability 1993, transnat. rules of civil procedure 2000-03), Am. Assn. Law Schs. (exec. com. civil procedure sect. 1998-99), Soc. Am. Law Tchrs., Chgo. Coun. Lawyers, AAUW (legal advocacy network 1987-2000), Chgo.-Lincoln Am. Inn. of Ct. (master 1991), Order of Coif, Phi Beta Kappa. Democrat. Jewish. Office: Chgo Kent Coll Law 565 W Adams St Chicago IL 60661-3613

STEINMAN, LAWRENCE, neurologist, educator; BA magna cum laude, Dartmouth Coll., 1968; MD, Harvard U., 1973. Diplomate Am. Bd. Psychiatry and Neurology. Intern surgery Stanford (Calif.) U. Hosp., 1973, resident pediatrics, 1974, resident pediat. and adult neurology, 1977—80; fellow in chem. immunology Weizmann Inst. Sci., 1975—77; Aharon Katzir Katchalsky fellow, 1975—76; NIH vis. fellow, 1976—77; asst. prof. depts. neurology and pediat. Stanford U., 1980—85, assoc. prof. depts. neurology, pediat. and genetics, 1985—91, prof. neurology depts. neurology and neurol. scis., pediat., 1991—. Mem. med. and sci. adv. com. Myasthenia Gravis Found., 1980—; spl. reviewer Immunologic Scis. Study Sect. NIH, 1985, mem. immunol. scis. study sect., 1991—95; organizer Midwinter Immunology Conf., Asilomar, Calif., 1986, FASEB Autoimmunity Meeting, Vt., 1990, Nat. Multiple Sclerosis Meeting, 1991; mem. search com. dept. medicine Stanford U., 1986—87, mem. search com. magnetic resonance spectroscopy, 1987—88, mem. instnl. planning com., 1988, mem. search com. dept. pediat., 90, mem. search com. office tech. licensing, 91; mem. adv. com. on pertussis immunization Nat. Inst. Medicine, 1987—90; mem. fellowship adv. com. Nat. Multiple Sclerosis Soc., 1988—91, mem. med. adv. com., 1990—95, Muscular Dystrophy Assn., 1990—95, mem. task force on genetics, 1990—; prof. Weizmann Inst. Sci., 1995—97; founder, bd. dirs., mem. sci. adv. bd. Neurocrine Biosciences, 1992—; mem. sci. adv. bd. Roche Biosciences, 1998—; bd. dirs., mem. sci. adv. bd. Neuronyx, 2000—; founder, acting pres. Tolerion, 2001—. Transmitting editor: Internat. Immunology, 1988—2001, assoc. editor: Jour. Immunology, 1991—95. Recipient Tchr.-Investigator award, NIH, 1981—86, Senator Jacob Javits Neurosci. Investigator award, Congress U.S. and NIH, 1988—2002, Dr. Friedrich Sasse award for outstanding contbns. in immunology, Free U. Berlin, 1994; NIH fellow chem. neurobiology, 1970—71. Mem.: Clin. Immunology Soc., Am. Assn. Immunologists, Am. Neurol. Assn., Am. Acad. Neurology (S. Weir Mitchell award 1979), Phi Beta Kappa. Achievements include patents for immunotherapy of autoimmune disease; polypeptide pertussis toxin vaccine; anti-t-cell receptor determinants as autoimmune disease treatment; T cell receptor variable transcripts as disease related markers; treatment of central nervous system inflammatory disease with matrix metalloprotease inhibitors; DNA vaccination for induction of suppressive T cell response. Office: Steinman Lab Stanford Univ Beckman Ctr Rm B002 275 Campus Dr Stanford CA 94305

STEINMAN, LISA MALINOWSKI, English literature educator, writer; b. Willimantic, Conn., Apr. 8, 1950; d. Zenon Stanislaus and Shirley Belle Malinowski; m. James A. Shugrue, Apr. 1968 (div. 1980); m. James L. Shugrue, July 23, 1984. BA, Cornell U., 1971, MFA, 1973, PhD, 1976. Asst. prof. English Reed Coll., Portland, Oreg., 1976-82, assoc. prof., 1982-90, prof., 1990—, Kenan prof. English lit. and humanities, 1993—. Cons. NEH, Washington, 1984-85. Author: Lost Poems, 1976, Made in America, 1987, All That Comes to Light, 1989, A Book of Other Days, 1992, Ordinary Songs, 1996, Masters of Repetition, 1998, Carslaw's Sequences, 2003; editor: Hubbub Mag., 1983—; mem. editl. bd. Williams Rev., 1991—, Stevens Jour., 1994—; contbr. articles to profl. jours. Fellow Danforth Found., 1971-75, NEH, 1983, 96, Oreg. Arts Commn., 1983, Nat. Endowment for Arts, 1984; Rockefeller Found. scholar, 1987-88; recipient Pablo Neruda award, 1987, Oreg. Inst. Lit. Arts award, 1993. Mem. MLA, Poets and Writers, PEN (N.W. chpt., co-founder, officer 1989-93). Home: 5344 SE 38th Ave Portland OR 97202-4208 Office: Reed Coll Dept English 3203 SE Woodstock Blvd Portland OR 97202-8138 E-mail: lisa.steinman@reed.edu.

STEINMAN, RALPH M. medical educator; BSc, McGill U., 1963; MD magna cum laude, Harvard U., 1968; degree (hon.), U. Innsbruck, 1998, Vrije U., Brussels, 1999. Intern and resident Mass. Gen. Hosp.; Henry G. Kunkel prof., sr. physician Rockefeller U., N.Y.C., 1995—. Editor: Jour. Exptl. Medicine. Recipient Emil von Behring prize, 1996, Freidrich-Sasse prize, 1996, Rudolf Virchow medal, 1997, Max Planck award, 1998, Coley medal, 1998, Robert Koch prize, 1999, Gairdner Found. Internat. award, 2003. Mem.: NAS, Inst. Medicine. Achievements include elucidated the role of dendritic cells in antigen presentation. Office: Lab Cellular Physiology and Immunology Rockefeller Univ 1230 York Ave New York NY 10021

STEINMAN, STEVEN L. financial company executive; Student, Columbia U. Trading rm. mgr. Stix Freidman and Co., Gattini & Co., Traubner Bach Co. Inc., Monvest Securities; founder Trimark Securities; co-founder Roundtable Ptnrs., LLC, chmn.; CEO, founder Trimark Securities, 1986; chmn. bd. dirs. Knight Trading Group, Inc. (formerly Knight/Trimark Group), Jersey City. Office: 23d Fl 525 Washington Blvd Jersey City NJ 07310

STEINMAN, THEODORE IRVING, nephrologist, educator; b. Phila., May 16, 1938; s. Jacob and Lena (Rosenberg) S.; m. Carol Zeldon, June 9, 1964; children: Kenneth, Michael Jay. BS, Pa. State U., 1960; MD, Georgetown U., 1964. Diplomate Am. Bd. Internal Medicine, Am. Bd. Nephrology. Intern in medicine Cedars-Sinai Med. Ctr., L.A., 1964-65, jr. asst. resident in medicine, 1965-66; sr. asst. resident in medicine Beth Israel Hosp., Boston, 1966-69, asst. physician, 1971-76, assoc. physician, 1976-87, physician, 1988—; teaching fellow in medicine Harvard Med. Sch., Boston, 1968-69, instr. in medicine, 1971-74, asst. clin. prof. medicine, 1974-80, assoc. clin. prof. medicine, 1980-93, prof. medicine, 1993—; rsch. fellow in nephrology, teaching fellow in medicine and nephrology Tufts New England Med. Ctr.,

Boston, 1969-71; attending physician and cons. in nephro
VA Hosp., Boston, 1971-76; assoc. in medicine Brigham
Boston, 1981-82, physician, 1982—. Cons. in nephro
and Welfare, Bur. Health Ins., Washington, 1973-75
Stoughton, Mass., 1974-90; sr. officer in medic
Bethesda, Md., 1967-68; rsch. assoc. Nat.
1967-68; vis. prof. nephrology Tulane U., Ne
U., Detroit, 1988, U. Medicine and Dentist
Sch. of Medicine, New Brunswick, N.J.
1991; vis. prof. medicine Marshfield (W
Ctr., Allentown, Pa., 1990; manuscr
Perspectives in Hypertension and R
and Issues; contbr. articles to P
1966-67, Vietnam. NIH grantee
Med. Group Rsch. and Edn.
Rsch. Inst. grantee, 1989-93
1992-93; Marion Merrill D
Nat. Kidney Found., 198
1989. Fellow ACP
1990-92); mem. Am
Rsch., Am. Israeli
Soc. Nephrology
Am. Soc. Tran
and edn. comm
Internat. S
Internat.
Orgs

...am. Blacks, ... Svc. award ... ound. of Mass., ... ans programs com. ... dney), Am. Fedn. Clin. ... Artificial Internal Organs, Am. ... ann. program com. 1991, 92, 93), ... am com. 1983-85, chmn. patient care ... Physician Execs. (awards com. 1993-94), ... nternat. Soc. Renal Nutrition and Metabolism, ... Organs (program com. 2nd Internat. Soc. Artificial ... symposium continuing ambulatory peritoneal dialysis ... Kidney Found. of Mass. (bd. dirs. 1978—, v.p. 1980-82, pres. ...85), Nat. Kidney Found. (bd. dirs. 1993—), Intersoc. Coun. Rsch. of the Kidney and Urinary Tract (exec. coun. 1993-95), Renal Physicians Assn. (bd. dir. 1985-97, nat. v.p. 1989-91, pres. 1992-93), Renal Physicians No. New England (v.p. 1985-86, pres. 1986-88), Polycistic Kidney Rsch. Found. (bd. dirs. 1995-96, vice chair 1997, chair 1998-2000), Coun. Am. Kidney Socs. (exec. com. 1998-2000), Am. Soc. Transplantation (chair clin. practices com. 1999-2000). Office Phone: 617-667-5278. Business E-Mail: tsteinma@caregroup.harvard.edu.

STEINMANN, JOHN COLBURN, architect; b. Monroe, Wis., Oct. 24, 1941; s. John Wilbur and Irene Marie (Steil) S.; m. Susan Koslosky, Aug. 12, 1978 (div. July 1989); m. Genevieve Sim, Aug. 29, 1998. BArch, U. Ill., 1964; postgrad., Ill. Inst. Tech., 1970-71. Registered architect, Wash., Oreg., Calif., N.Mex., Ariz., Utah, Alaska, Wis., Ill. Project designer C.F. Murphy Assocs., Chgo., 1968-71, Steinmann Architects, Monticello, Wis., 1971-73; design chief, chief project architect State of Alaska, Juneau, 1973-78; project designer Mithun Assos., architects, Bellevue, Wash., 1978-80; owner, prin. John C. Steinmann Assos., Architect, Kirkland, Wash., 1980-94; supr. head facilities sect. divsn. fin. Dept. Edn. State of Alaska, Juneau, 1994-96; docs. mgr. Loschky Marquardt and Nesholm, Architects, Seattle, 1996-98; project mgr. Dept. Gen. Adminstrn. Divsn. Engring. and Archtl. Svsc., State of Wash., Olympia, 1998-99; project mgr. URS Architects, Seattle, 2000—. Bd. dirs. Storytell Internat.; lectr. Ill. Inst. Tech., 1971-72. Prin. works include Grant Park Music Bowl, Chgo., 1971, Menomonee Falls (Wis.) Med. Clinic, 1972, Hidden Valley Office Bldg., Bellevue, 1978, Kezner Office Bldg., Bellevue, 1979, The Pines at Sunriver, Oreg., 1980, also Phase II, 1984, Phase III, 1986, The Pines at Sunriver Lodge Bldg., 1986, 2d and Lenora highrise, Seattle, 1981, Bob Hope Cardiovascular Rsch. Inst. lab animal facility, Seattle, 1982, Wash. Ct., Bellevue, 1982, Anchorage Bus. Pk., 1982, Garden Townhouses, Anchorage, 1983, Vacation Internationale, Ltd. Corp. Hdqs., Bellevue, 1983, Vallarta Torres III, Puerto Vallarta, Mex., 1987, Torres Mazatlan (Mex.) II, 1988, Canterwood Townhouses, Gig Harbor Wash., 1988, Inn at Ceres (Calif.), 1989, Woodard Creek Inn, Olympia, Wash., 1989, Northgate Corp. Ctr., Seattle, 1990, Icicle Creek Hotel and Restaurant, Leavenworth, Wash., 1990, Bellingham (Wash.), Market Pl., 1990, Boeing Hot Gas Test Facility, Renton, Wash., 1991, Boeing Longacres Customer Svc. Tng. Ctr. Support Facilities, Renton, 1992, Boeing Comml. Airplane Group Hdqs., Renton, 1996, U. Wash./Cascade C.C., Bothell, 1999, Wash. State U., Pullman, Wash., Sea-Tac Airport Comm. Control Ctr., Seattle, 2000, McCarty, Internet Cafe and Residence Hall Renovation, U. Wash., Seattle, 2001, K'ima Med. Ctr. Dental Clinic, Hoopa, Calif., 2001, Sea-Tac Airport Flight Info. Mgmt. Sys., 2002; 600 Bed student housing, classroom, parking mixed use project, U. Idaho, Moscow; also pvt. residences. Served to 1st lt. C.E., USAR, 1964-66, Vietnam. Decorated Bronze Star. Mem. AIA, Am. Mgmt. Assn., Nat. Coun. Archtl. Registration Bds., U. Wash. Yacht Club, Columbia Athletic Club, Alpha Rho Chi. Republican. Roman Catholic. Address: 4316 106th Pl NE Kirkland WA 98033-7919

STEINMETZ, DAVID CURTIS, religious studies educator; b. Columbus, Ohio, June 12, 1936; s. Walter Curtis and Lucy Margaret (Binderbasen) S.; m. Virginia Ruth Verploegh, June 20, 1959; children: Claire Elise, Matthew Eliot. B.A. with highest honor, Wheaton Coll., Wheaton, IL, 1954—58; B. D. summa vum laude, Drew U., Madison, NJ, 1958—61; Th.D., Harvard U., Cambridge, MA, 1961—66; Vis. scholar, U. of Goettingen, Goettingen, Germany, 1964—65. Ordained to ministry United Meth. Ch., 1959. Asst. and assoc. prof. Lancaster Theol. Sem., Lancaster, Pa., 1966—71; kearns prof. of the history of christianity Duke U., Durham, NC. Vis. prof. Harvard U., 1977; adv. coun. Interpretation, Richmond, Va., 1979-84, 87-92. Author: Misericordia dei, 1968, Reformers in the Wings, 1971, Luther and Staupitz, 1980, Luther in Context, 1986, Calvin in Context, 1995; editor Oxford Studies in Historical Theology; mem. editorial bd. Archiv für Reformationsgeschichte, 1977-93, Duke U. Monographs in Medieval and Renaissance Studies, 1972-98, Brill Studies in Medieval and Reformation Thought, Leiden, Netherlands, 1981-99. Pres. Am. Friends of the Herzog Aug. Libr., St. Louis, Mo., 1996—2002; mem., governing bd. Meeter Ctr. for Calvin Studies, Grand Rapids, Mich., 1993—99; pub. The Labytrinth Press, Durham, NC, 1981—95. Named Scholar-Tchr. of Yr. Duke U., 1986; Rockefeller doctoral fellow Rockefeller Found., 1964-66, faculty fellow Assn. Theol. Schs., 1970, 77-78, Guggenheim fellow Guggenheim Found., 1977-78, NEH summer fellow, 1990. Mem. Medieval Acad. Am., Am. Soc. Ch. History (pres. 1985), Renaissance Soc. Am., Soc. for Reformation Rsch., Am. Friends of the Herzog August Bibliothek (founding pres.). United Methodist. Achievements include research in History of Biblical Interpretation in Reformation Europe. Office: Duke University The Divinity School Durham NC 27708-0967 Personal E-mail: dsteinmetz@nc.rr.com. E-mail: steinmtz@acpub.duke.edu.

STEINMETZ, JON DAVID, mental health executive, psychologist; b. N.Y.C., June 4, 1940; s. Lewis I. and Rose (Josefsberg) S.; m. Jane Audrey Hilton, Dec. 24, 1964; children: Jonna Lynn, Jay Daniel. BA, NYU, 1962; MA, Bradley U., 1963. Lic. psychologist, Ill. Intern in psychology Galesburg (Ill.) State Rsch. Hosp., 1963-64; staff psychologist Manteno (Ill.) State Hosp., 1964-68, program dir., 1968-70, asst. dir., 1970-72; dep. dir. Manteno Mental Health Ctr., 1972-80, Tinley Park (Ill.) Mental Health Ctr., 1980-88; dir. Chgo. Read Mental Health Ctr., 1988-91; ret., 1991. Clin. dir. Jane Addams Hull House Assn., 1992-98. Trustee Village of Park Forest, Cook and Will Counties, Ill.; officer, bd. dirs. various civic orgns., Park Forest. Home: 200 Hickory St Park Forest IL 60466-1016

STEINMETZ, JOSEPH EDWARD, neuroscience and psychology educator; b. Marine City, Mich., Jan. 6, 1955; s. James Robert and Catherine Elizabeth (Gould) S.; m. Sandra Sue Bieth, Aug. 8, 1975; children: Jacob Joseph, Adam Benjamin. BS, Cen. Mich. U., 1977, MA, 1979; PhD, Ohio U., 1983. NIMH postdoctoral fellow Stanford (Calif.) U., 1983-85, rsch. assoc., 1985-87; from asst. prof. to prof. neurosci. Ind. U., Bloomington, 1987-95, prof., chair psychology, 1995—. Cons. editor: Behavior Research Methods, Instruments and Computer Jour., 1989—, Behavior Neuroscience, 1993—; contbr. numerous articles to profl. jours. NIMH grantee, 1988; recipient Troland Rsch. award NAS, 1996. Fellow Am. Psychol. Soc. (charter, bd. dirs. 1997—); mem. Internat. Brain Rsch. Orgn., Soc. for Neurosci., Sigma Xi. Democrat. Roman Catholic. Home: 3681 Lauren Ln Bloomington IN 47404-9206 Office: Program in Neural Sci Ind U Dept Psychology Bloomington IN 47405-6801

... neurosurgeon; b. Dear- ... Steinmetz; m. Bettina Flores ... nse, Marcus Alexander. MD, Tex. ... 1994—98; BS, N.Mex State U., Las ... Medical License State Med. Bd. of Ohio, ... surgery Cleve. Clinic Found., Cleve., 1999—; ... U of N Mex, Albuquerque, 1998—99. Author: ... urosurgery; author: (book chpt.) Multiple Neurosurgery ... resident program Congress of Neurol. Surgeons, Denver, ... t.-at-arms com. San Diego, 2001—01; house staff assoc. Cleve. ... ound., Cleve., 2001—03; pres. Alpha Omega Alpha, Zeta Chpt., ... ock, Tex., 1997—98; surg. edn. com. mem. Cleve. Clinic Found., 2003—04. Recipient Alpha Omega Alpha, Tex. Tech Univ., 1997, Humanitarian of the Yr. Award, Cleve. Clinic Found., Dept. Neurosurgery, 2000, Golden Head Cane Award, Tex. Tech Sch. of Medicine, 1998, Golden Key Nat. Honor Soc., Golden Key Nat. Honor Soc., 1994; grantee, Daniel Humann Found., 2002—03; scholar So. Med. Assn. Scholarship, So. Med. Assn., 1996, Robery Flygare Scholarship, Tex. Tech Sch. of Medicine, 1996, O-Neil Endowed Scholarship, 1995, Alumni Out of State Scholarship, N.Mex State U., 1994; Larson Rsch. Grant, 2004—05, Cloward Rsch. Grant, 2002—03. Mem.: N.Am. Spine Soc., Coun. State Neurosurg. Socs. (del. 2004), Am. Assn. of Neurol. Surgeons, Congress of Neurol. Surgeons (chmn., resident program 2003, co-chmn. gen. session San Francisco 2004, editl. bd. web page 2004), Alpha Omega Alpha (pres., Zeta chpt. 1997—98). Avocations: hunting, fishing, bicycling. Home: 882 Quarry Dr Cleveland Heights OH 44121 Office: Cleve Clinic Found 9500 Euclid Ave Cleveland OH 44195

STEINMETZ, RICHARD BIRD, JR., lawyer; b. Orange, N.J., Mar. 27, 1929; s. Richard Bird and Charlotte (Quinby) S.; m. Merriam Holly Miller, June 9, 1956; children: Richard Blair, Jonathan Bird, Edward Quinby. BA, Yale U., 1950; JD, Harvard U., 1955. Bar: N.Y. 1955. Assoc. Chadbourne and Parke, N.Y.C., 1955-59; with Anaconda Co., N.Y.C., 1959-79, v.p., gen. counsel, 1971-79; v.p. Colt Industries Inc., N.Y.C., 1979-82; v.p., gen. counsel Pittston Co., Greenwich, Conn., 1982-84; exec. v.p. Case, Pomeroy and Co., N.Y.C., 1984-94. Bd. dirs. Case, Pomeroy and Co. Served to capt. USMC, 1950-52. Mem. ABA, Assn. of Gen. Counsel. Republican. Episcopalian. Home: 275C Park St New Canaan CT 06840-5739

STEINMETZ, ROBERT CHARLES, architect; b. Charleston, W.Va., Oct. 16, 1951; s. Charles and Bernadine Steinmetz; m. Deborah Susan Toselle, Dec. 29, 1974. BArch, La. State U., 1974. Architect Pound Flower & Dedyler, Columbus, Ga., 1974-75, David Allan Grinnell, Atlanta, 1975, Maxwell & Lebreton, New Orleans, 1975-77; architect, assoc. Mathes Group, New Orleans, 1977-84; architect, prin. Steinmetz & Assocs., New Orleans, 1984—; arch. and interior design value resetter of computers and software Integrated Facility Sys. Corp., New Orleans, 1991—. Mem. New Orleans Mus. Art, New Orleans Preservation Res. Ctr., Nat. Trust for Hist. Preservation. Mem. AIA (chair interiors com. 1995), La. Architecture Assn., La. Landmarks Soc., Nat. Coun. Archtl. Registration Bds. (cert.), Internat. Facility Mgmt. Assn. Office: 225 Baronne St Ste 1720 New Orleans LA 70112-1772

STEINMEYER, ROBERT JAY, lawyer; b. Aug. 10, 1921; s. William F. and Willie (Davis) Steinmeyer; m. Susie (Levicki), Dec. 23, 1948; children: William Bruce, James Jay, Sharon Sue. BS, U. Nebr., 1943; post grad., Albany Law Sch., 1947—48; LLB, George Washington U., 1949. Bar: D.C. 1950, Calif. 1958. Devel. engr. G.E. Co., Schenectady, NY, 1943—46, patent atty., 1947—53, patent counsel, 1953—57, Beckman Instruments, Inc., Fullerton, Calif., 1957—63, resident counsel, 1963—71, v.p., legal, 1971—85, dir., 1984—85; sole practice Fullerton, Calif., 1985—86; of counsel Karon, Morrison, and Savikas Ltd., Fullerton, Calif., 1986—88. Mem.: ABA, Assn. Corp. Patent Counsel (pres. 1975—76), Am. Patent Law Assn., Pi Mu Epsilon, Sigma Tau, Order of Coif. Home: 813 Morningside Dr Fullerton CA 92835

STEINMILLER, JOHN F. professional basketball team executive; b. Mt. Prospect, Ill. m. Corinne Steinmiller; children: John Henry, Mary Kate. V.p. bus. ops. Milw. Bucks, 1977—. Bd. dirs. M.W. Athletes Against Childhood Cancer Fund, Milw. Big Bros.-Big Sisters, Metro Milw. YMCA; treas. Milw. Conve. and Visitors Bur.; mem. Greater Milw. Com. Recipient Contardi Commitment award MACC Fund, 1991, Vol. of Yr. award YMCA, 1996. Office: Milw Bucks 1001 N 4th St Milwaukee WI 53203-1314 E-mail: jsteinmiller@milwaukeebucks.com.

STEINSMITH, WILLIAM, internist, research scientist; b. N.Y.C., N.Y., July 31, 1933; s. David Steinsmith and Dorothy Burtoff. BS, UCLA, 1965; MD, U. Calif., San Francisco, 1968. Lic. physician and surgeon Calif. Med. Bd., Va. Bd. Medicine. Freelance polit. journalist, 1960—; postdoctoral scholar in pharmacology and pharmacokinetics dept. pharmacology U. Calif.-San Francisco, 1969—74; pvt. practice internist San Francisco, 1970—2004; asst. chief of medicine St. Joseph's Hosp., San Francisco, 1973—76; ind. rsch. in math. biology, 1974—; med. staff internist Veterans Home of Calif., Yountville, Calif., 1989—91. Author: (polit. history/analysis) Lenin, Inter-Imperialism, and National-Colonial Revolution, 1979. Recipient Owen D. Young Prize in Internat. Rels., U. Calif.- Berkeley, 1963. Mem.: San Francisco Med. Soc./U. Calif.-San Francisco Health Care Fedn. (bd. trustees, exec. com. 1973—75). Home and Office: 108 Alexander Walker Williamsburg VA 23185 Personal E-mail: bbhaywood@aol.com.

STEINWACHS, DONALD MICHAEL, public health educator; b. Boise, Idaho, Sept. 9, 1946; s. Don Peter and Emma Bertha Steinwachs; m. Sharon Kay Carlson, Aug. 25, 1972. MS, U. Ariz., 1970; PhD, Johns Hopkins U., 1973. Asst. prof. health svcs. adminstrn. Johns Hopkins U., Balt., 1973—79, assoc. prof. health policy and mgmt., 1979—86, dir. Health Svcs. Rsch. & Devel. Ctr., 1982—, prof. health policy and mgmt., 1986—, chair health policy and mgmt., 1994—. Sec. adv. com. Dept. Vets. Affairs, Washington, 1991—92; bd. dirs. Mathematica Policy Rsch., Inc. Contbr. articles to profl. jours. Bd. dirs., pres. Found. for Health Svc. Rsch.; active Gov.'s Commn. on Health Policy Rsch. and Fin., 1988—90. Capt. U.S. Army, 1973. Grantee, NIMH, Agy. for Health Care Policy and Rsch., Robert Wood Johnson Found. Mem.: Inst. Medicine NAS, Assn. Health Svc. Rsch. (bd. dirs., pres.), Ops. Rsch. Soc. Am. Achievements include development of methods for using management information systems to examine patterns of medical care, costs, and indicators of the quality of care. Office: Johns Hopkins U Dept Health Policy/Mgmt 624 N Broadway Rm 482 Baltimore MD 21205-1900

STEITZ, JOAN ARGETSINGER, biochemistry educator; b. Mpls., Jan. 26, 1941; d. Glenn D. and Elaine (Magnusson) Argetsinger; m. Thomas A. Steitz, Aug. 20, 1966. BS, Antioch Coll., 1963; PhD, Harvard U., 1967; D.Sc. (hon.), Lawrence U., Appleton, Wis., 1982, Rochester U. Sch. Medicine, 1984, Mt. Sinai Sch. Medicine, 1989, Bates Coll., 1990; DSc (hon.), Trinity Coll., 1992, Harvard U., 1992. Postdoctoral fellow MRC Lab. Molecular Biology, Cambridge, Eng., 1967-70; asst. prof. molecular biophysics and biochemistry Yale U., New Haven, 1970-74, assoc. prof., 1974-78, prof. molecular biophysics and biochemistry, 1978—, Sterling prof. molecular biophysics and biochemistry, 1978—, chair dept. molecular biophysics and biochemistry, 1996—. Investigator Howard Hughes Med. Inst, 1986—. Recipient Young Scientist award, Passano Found., 1975, Eli Lilly award in biol. chemistry, 1976, U.S. Steel Found. award in molecular biology, 1982, Lee Hawley, Sr. award for arthritis rsch., 1984, Nat. Medal of Sci., 1986, Dickson prize for Sci., Carnegie-Mellon U., 1988, Warren Triennial prize, Mass. Gen. Hosp., 1989, Christopher Columbus Disc. award in biomed. rsch., 1992, Weizmann Women and Sci. award, 1994, City of Medicine award, 1996. Fellow: AAAS; mem.: NY Acad. of Scis. (Weizmann Women & Sci. award 1994), Am. Phil. Soc., Nat. Acad. Arts and Sci., Am. Acad. Arts and Sci. Home: 45 Prospect Hill Rd Branford CT 06405-5711 Office: HHMI at Yale Univ BCMM 136 E 295 Congress Ave New Haven CT 06519-1418

STELCK, CHARLES RICHARD, geology educator; b. Edmonton, Alta., Can., May 20, 1917; s. Robert Ferdinand and Florella Maud (Stanbury) S.; m. Frances Gertrude McDowell, Apr. 24, 1945; children: David, Brian, Leland, John (dec.). BSc, U. Alta., 1937, MSc, 1941, DSc (hon.), 2003; PhD, Stanford U., 1951. Registered profl. geologist Alta. Field geologist B.C. Dept. Mines, Victoria, Canada, 1939-41, Canol Project, Norman Wells, Canada, 1941-43, Imperial Oil Co., Calgary, 1943-49; from lectr. to prof. emeritus geology U. Alta., Edmonton, 1946—. Contbr. numerous articles principally on biostratigraphy of Cretaceous to sci. publs. Decorated officer Order of Can.; recipient Disting. Educator award Am. Assn. Petroleum Geologists, 2001, Queen's Golden Jubilee medal, 2002. Fellow Royal Soc. Can.; mem. Assn. Profl. Engrs., Geologists and Geophysicists Alta. (Centennial award 1979), Geol. Assn. Can. (Logan medal 1982), Geol. Soc. Am., Can. Soc. Petroleum Geologists (Douglas medal 1994, Stanley Slipper gold medal 2002), Order of Can. (officer 1997). Conservative. Office: U Alta Dept Earth & Atmospheric Scis Edmonton AB Canada T6G 2E3

STELLA, JOHN ANTHONY, investment company executive; b. Jessup, Pa., Feb. 3, 1938; s. John Anthony and Alda (Parri) S.; m. Aurelia M. Arre, Feb. 20, 1965; children— John C., Matthew A., Krista R. BS, U. Detroit, 1960; MBA, NYU, 1965. Bus. evaluation cons. Allied Chem. Co., N.Y.C., 1965-70; treas. Spinnerin Yarn Co., Hackensack, N.J., 1970-72, Penn-Dixie Cement Corp., N.Y.C., 1972-74; v.p. finance Halecrest Co., 1974-76; treas. Rsch.-Cottrell, 1976-84, v.p., contr./treas., 1984-88; pres. John A. Stella & Assocs., Plainfield, N.J., 1988-91; sr. v.p. Investment Support Systems, Inc., Bloomfield, N.J., 1991-95. Pres. State Tax Auditing and Rsch., Inc., Bethlehem, 1993—. Served with AUS, 1960. Office: State Tax Auditing & Rsch Inc 1775 Arden Ln Bethlehem PA 18015-5829

STELLAR, ARTHUR WAYNE, educational administrator; b. Columbus, Ohio, Apr. 12, 1947; s. Fredrick and Bonnie Jean (Clark) S. BS, Ohio U., 1969, MA, 1970, PhD, 1973. Tchr. Athens (Ohio) City Schs., 1969-71; curriculum coord., tchr. Belpre (Ohio) City Schs., 1971-72; prin. elem. schs., head tchr. learning disabilities South-Western City Schs., Grove City, Ohio, 1972-76; dir. elem. edn. Beverly (Mass.) Pub. Schs., 1976-78; coord. spl. projects and systemwide planning Montgomery County Pub. Schs., Rockville, Md., 1978-80; asst. supt. Shaker Heights (Ohio), 1980-83; supt. schs. Mercer County Pub. Schs., Princeton, W.Va., 1983-85, Oklahoma City Pub. Schs., 1985-92, Cobb County, Ga., 1992-93; dep. supt. Boston Pub. Schs., 1993-95, acting supt., 1995-96; supt. Kingston (N.Y.) Sch. Dist., 1996—2001; pres., CEO High/Scope Ednl. Rsch. Found., Ypsilanti, Mich., 2001—03; v.p., chief edn. officer Renaissance Learning, Madison, Wis., 2003—. Adj. prof. Lesley Coll., Cambridge, Mass., 1976-78; adj. faculty Harvard U., 1992-93. Author: Educational Planning for Educational Success, Effective Schools Research: Practice and Promise; editor: Effective Instructional Management; cons. editor, book rev. editor Jour. Ednl. Pub. Rels.; mem. editl. bd. Jour. Curriculum & Supervision, Reading Today's Youth; contbr. articles to profl. jours. Bd. govs. Kirkpatrick Ctr.; mem. Oklahoma City Com. Econ. Devel.; founding bd. dirs. Okla. Alliance Against Drugs, Okla. Zool. Soc. Inc.; selected for Leadership Oklahoma City, 1986; bd. dirs. Leadership Oklahoma City, ARC, Okla. Centennial Sports Inc., Rip Van Winkle Coun. BSA; mem. Okla. Acad. for State Goals, State Supt.'s Adv. Coun.; mem. clin. experiences adv. com. U. Okla. Coll. Edn.; trustee Arts Coun. Oklahoma City, Omniplex Sci. and Arts Mus., Oklahoma City Area Vocat.-Tech. Dist. 22 Found.; mem. Urban Ctr. Ednl. Adv. Bd., U.S. Dept. Edn. Urban Supt. Network, Coun. Great City Schs. Bd., Urban Edn. Clearing House Adv. com., U. Okla. Adminstrn. cert. program com., Cmty. Literacy Coun. Bd.; chmn. bd. dirs. Langston U.; chair United Way Greater Okla., Sch. Mgmt. Study Group, Okla. Reading Coun. (Okla. literacy coun. reading award 1-89), Oklahoma City PTA; bd. dirs. Oklahoma County chpt. ARC, Jr. Achievement Greater Oklahoma City Bd., Okla. State Fair Bd., Horace Mann League, 1993-2000, v.p. 2000-01, pres.-elect, 2001-02, pres. 2002-03, past pres. 2003-04; v.p. Last Frontier Coun. Bd., v.p. N.Y. State PTA, 1996-2000, Kingston chpt. Rip Van Winkle Coun.; v.p. Boy Scouts Am., 1996-2001, membership chmn., 1996-97; mem. exec. bd. Nat. Dropout Prevention Ctr. Network, 1998—, chmn., 2003—; mem. curriculum com. N.Y. State Coun. Sch. Supts., 1996-2001; bd. dirs. Friends Historic Kingston, 1996-2001, Friends Senate House, Kingston, 1996-2001. Named to Linden McKinley H.S. Acad. Hall of Fame, 2003; recipient Silver Beaver award, Boy Scouts Am., 1990, Am. award, Horace Mann League, 1995—2003; fellow, Charles Kettering Found. IDEA, 1976, 1978, 1980, NEH, Danforth Found., 1987—88. Mem. ASCD (life, exec. coun., pres.-elect 1993-94, pres. 1994-95, rev. coun. 1997-2002), Mich. ASCD, Mass. ASCD, Ohio ASCD, Okla. ASCD (Publ. award 1989), N.Y. ASCD, Internat. Soc. Ednl. Planning, Internat. Reading Assn. (mem. govt. rels. com. 2003-04), Nat. Soc. Study Edn., Nat. Planning Assn., Nat. Assn. Gifted Children (life), Nat. Assn. Educators Young Children (Mich. chpt.), Am. Assn. Sch. Adminstrn. (Mich. chpt.), Nat. Coun. Tchrs. English (life), Music Educators Nat. Conf. (life), Nat. Orgn. Legal Problems Edn., Nat. Policy Bd. Ednl. Adminstrn., Am. Assn. Sch. Adminstrs. (life, Leadership for Learning award 1991), Coll. Bd. Advanced Placement Spl. Recognition award 1991, Nat. Assn. Elem. Sch. Prins. (life), Am. Edn. Fin. Assn., Nat. Assn. Edn. Young Children (life), Nat. Sch. Pub. Rels. Assn. (Honor award 1991), Am. Mus. Natural Hist. (assoc.), World Coun. Curriculum and Instrn. (life, bd. dirs. N.Am. chpt. 1996-2000, pres. 2000-02), Coun. Basic Edn., Ohio Assn. Elem. Sch. Adminstrs., Buckeye Assn. Sch. Adminstrs., Ohio U. Coll. Edn. (disting. alumnus award 1991), Okla. Assn. Sch. Adminstrs., Mass. Assn. Sch. Adminstrs., Okla. Coalition Pub. Edn., Okla. Commn. Ednl. Leadership, Urban Area Supts. (Okla. br.), Ohio U. Alumni Assn. (nat. dir. 1975-78, pres. Ctrl. Ohio chpt. 1975-76, pres. Mass. chpt. 1976-78, life mem. trustees acad.), World Future Soc. (life) Greater Oklahoma City C. of C. (bd. dirs.), Oklahoma Heritage Assn., Heritage Hills Assn. (bd. dirs.), Victorian Soc. (New England chpt.), Nat. Eagle Scout Assn. (life), Aerospace Found. (hon. bd. dirs.), PLATO, Learning, Inc. (bd. dirs. 2000-03), Tchrs. Support Network (adv. bd. dirs. 2004—), Am. Bus. Card Club, Coca Cola Collectors Club, Internat. Club, Mgmt. Consortium (bd. advisors), Detroit Inst. Arts, Henry Ford Mus., Greenfield Village; Rotary (Boston), Fulbright Alumni Assn. (life), Tau Kappa Epsilon Alumni Assn. (regional officer Mass. 1976-78, named Alumni Nat. Hall of Fame 1986, Nat. Alumnus of Yr. 1993, Excellence in Edn. award 1993), Kappa Delta Pi (life, advisor Ctrl. Okla. chpt., nat. publs. com.), Phi Delta Kappa (life). Methodist.

STELLATO, LOUIS EUGENE, lawyer; b. 1950; BBA, U. Tex., 1972; JD, U. Pitts., 1977; LLM, Temple U., 1979. Bar: PA. 1977. With Touche Ross & Co., 1979-81; with tax dept. Sherwin-Williams Co., 1981-87; sr. corp. counsel The Sherwin-Williams Co., 1987-90, asst. secy. and corp. dir. of taxes, 1990-91, v.p., gen. counsel, sec., 1991—. Office: Sherwin Williams Co 101 Prospect Ave NW Cleveland OH 44115-1075

STELLE, ROBERT E. physician, retired educator; b. Kalamazoo, Mich., Feb. 7, 1930; s. Earl Clarkson and Norma Lillian Stelle; m. Barbara Lutz, Apr. 29, 1955; children: Amy, Mark, Nancy. BA, Kalamazoo Coll., 1955; MD, U. Mich., 1959. Diplomate Am. Bd. Family Practice (charter). Intern Toledo Hosp., 1959-60; mng. ptnr. Falls Clinic P.C., Crystal Falls, Mich., 1960-79; assoc. prof. Mich. State U., Lansing, 1974-79, U. Wis., Madison, 1979-81; prof., vice chmn. dept. U. Mo., Kansas City, 1981-82, U. Colo., Denver, 1982-85; med. dir. Hertzler Clinic, Wichita, Kans., 1985-86; cons. Locum Tenens Contractors Inc., Colorado City, Colo., 1986—99. Home and Office: PO Box 19051 7710 Charles Colorado City CO 81019

STELLMACHER, JON MICHAEL, corporate financial executive; b. Green Bay, Wis., Feb. 25, 1956; s. Leroy Frederick and Helen Mae (Koss) S.; m. Rebecca Jean Hein, Aug. 20, 1976; children: James Michael, Paul Frederick, Abigail Joy. BBA with honors, U. Wis. Underwriting clk. State Life Insur. Fund, Madison, Wis., 1977-78; actuarial student Aid Assn. for Luths., Appleton, Wis., 1978-79, actuarial asst., 1979-83, asst. actuary, 1983-85, assoc. actuary, 1985-87, 2nd v.p., actuary, 1987—97, v.p., 1997—99, sr. v.p., 1999—2002; exec. v.p. Thrivent Fin. for Luths., Appleton, 2002—. Chpt. reviewer Health Ins. Textbook, Soc. Actuaries, Schaumburg, Ill., 1984-85; chmn. actuaries sect. Health Workshop Nat. Fraternal Congress Am., 1986, 88; mem. actuarial adv. com. Wis. Health Ins. Risk Sharing Pool, Madison, 1987—92; co-chmn. workshop, spring meeting Soc. Actuaries, Schaumburg, 1989, 91. Acting pres., v.p. coun. 1st English Luth. Ch., Appleton, 1984; mission interpreter Am. Luth. Ch., Appleton area, 1985-87, Sunday Sch. tchr., 1984—, mem. stewardship com., 1981-90, mem. social concerns com. 1991—94; mem. Elderly Housing Task Force, 1990-91, Benevolence Task Force, 1994; asst. den leader Cub Scouts, Boy Scouts Am., Appleton, 1989-91;

asst. coach Appleton Soccer Club, 1990-93, Odyssey of the Mind, 1990-93; coach Appleton Park and Recreation Dept., 1990-98; vice chmn. Arthur Kremin Sch. Music and Art, 2003-04; bd. dirs. Appleton Boychoir, 1994—, pres., 1999—; bd. dirs. Appleton Med. Ctr. Found., 2000—, sec., 2001—; bd. dirs. United Way Fox Cities, 2001—, co-chair campaign com., 2000; mem. sr. adv. bd. Jr. Achievement, 2001—; bd. dirs. YMCA of the Fox Cities, 2002—, Fox Cities Performing Arts Ctr., 2003—; mem. Theda Care Quality Coun., 2003—. Fellow Soc. Actuaries; mem. Am. Acad. Actuaries. Office: Thrivent Fin for Luths 4321 N Ballard Rd Appleton WI 54919 Home: 3124 E Sandpiper Ln Appleton WI 54913-7771 Office Phone: 920-628-2002.

STELLMAN, JEANNE MAGER, public health educator; b. Bensheim, W. Ger., May 27, 1947; arrived in U.S., 1948; d. Abraham and Rosalie (Shapiro) Mager; m. Steven D. Stellman, Sept. 10, 1967; children: Andrew Benjamin, Emma Deborah. BS in Chemistry, CCNY, 1968; PhD in Phys. Chemistry, CUNY, 1972. Asst. to pres. for health and safety Oil, Chem. and Atomic Workers Internat. Union, Denver, 1972—75; chief divsn. occupl. health and toxicology Am. Health Found., N.Y.C., 1977—80; exec. dir. Women's Occupational Health Resource Ctr., N.Y.C., 1978—91; clin. assoc. prof. rsch. medicine Sch. Medicine, U. Pa., Phila., 1975—80; prof. clin. pub. health Sch. Pub. Health, Columbia U., N.Y.C., 1980—. Trainee NASA, 1968—69; adj. prof. Labor Edn. Ctr. Rutgers U., 1971—76; vis. assoc. prof. U. Medicine and Dentistry N.J., Piscataway, 1987—; cons. Am. Occupl. Health Nurses Assn., 1983—85, Port Authority N.Y. and N.J., 1983—84, IVA Office Safety and Health, 1980—82, N.Y. State Dept. Health, 1982—84, Coalition Labor Union Women, 1975—80, Nat. Union Hosp. and Health Care Workers, 1975—85; cons. to spl. master Agt. Orange Vet. Payment Program, 1987—96; mem. merit peer rev. com.-cancer control Nat. Cancer Inst., 1979—81; mem. expert panel for guidelines on pregnant working women Am. Coll. Ob-Gyn., 1978; mem. environ health task force Am. Lung Assn., 1976—80; mem. task force on preventing disease, workgroup on occupl. health U.S. Surgeon Gen.'s Office, 1979; mem. adv. com. for 14 chem. carcinogens U.S. Sec. Labor, 1972; mem. tech. rev. coms. for criteria documents on cadmium, mercury, sulfur dioxide and benzene Nat. Inst. Occupl. Safety and Health; spkr. on occupl. health hazards U.S. and Can.; methodology contr. Nat. Acad. Sci., 1998—2003; mem. expert panel on World Trade Ctr. remediation EPA, 2004. Author (with S.M. Daum): (book) Work Is Dangerous to Your Health (translated into Italian, Portuguese, French, Spanish), 1973; author: Women's Work, Women's Health: Myth and Realities (translated into Italian, French, Japanese); author: (with Mary Sue Henifin) Office Work Can Be Dangerous to Your Health, 1984; editor-in-chief: ency. Ency. Occupl. Health and Safety, 4th edit., 1991—98; contbr. govt. reports, chpts. to books, artcles to profl. jours.; contbg. editor: (jour.) Environment, 1975—76; mem. editl. bd.: jour. Women and Health, 1983—85; editor, 1985—2004. Decorated Commendation award Vietnam Vets. Am., Citation for Meritorious Svc. Am. Legion, Disting. Svc. medal; named one of 80 Women to Watch in the 80's, Ms. Mag., 1980; recipient Preventive Oncology Acad. award, Nat. Cancer Inst., 1980—85, Townsend Harris Medal, CCNY, 2003; fellow, N.Y. State Regents, 1970—72, Guggenheim Found., 1989—90; grantee, NSF, 1969—70. Mem.: AAAS, APHA (governing coun. 1981—83), Sigma Xi, Am. Indsl. Hygiene Assn., N.Y. Acad. Scis., Soc. Occupl. and Environ. Health, Am. Phys. Soc., Am. Chem. Soc. (com. chem. safety 1973—79, chmn. task force on benzene 1978—79, task force safe lab practices 1978—79). Democrat. Jewish. Office: Found for Worker Vet & Environ Health Inc 117 Saint Johns Pl Brooklyn NY 11217-3401 also: Columbia U Mailman Sch Pub Health 600 W 168th St 6th Fl New York NY 10032

STELLWAGEN, ROBERT HARWOOD, biochemistry educator; b. Joliet, Ill., Jan. 6, 1941; s. Harwood John and Alma Dorothy (Handorf) S.; m. Joanne Kovacs, June 15, 1963; children: Robert Harwood, Alise Anne. AB, Harvard U., 1963; PhD, U. Calif., Berkeley, 1968. Staff fellow NIH, Bethesda, Md., 1968-69; postdoctoral scholar U. Calif., San Francisco, 1969-70; asst. prof. biochemistry U. So. Calif., L.A., 1970-74, assoc. prof., 1974-80, prof., 1980—, chmn. dept., 1981-86, vice chmn. dept., 1993—. Vis. scientist Nat. Inst. for Med. Rsch., Mill Hill, Eng., 1979. Contbr. articles to profl. jours. Recipient Henderson prize Harvard U., 1963; NSF fellow, 1963-67; NIH grantee, 1971-84. Mem. AAAS, Sierra Club, Phi Beta Kappa. Democrat. Office: U So Calif Keck Sch Medicine 1333 San Pablo St Los Angeles CA 90089-9151 Office Phone: 323-442-1149. E-mail: stellwag@usc.edu.

STELMACH, WALTER JACK, physician, medical education administrator; b. Kansas City, Kans., Mar. 7, 1926; s. Jacob and Stella (Wanchuk) S.; m. Patricia Ann Scherrer, June 19, 1948; children: Christopher Stephen, Cheryl Anne, Jeffrey David BA, U. Mo., Kansas City, 1949; MD, Kans. U., Kansas City, 1953. Diplomate Am. Bd. Family Practice (bd. dirs. 1980-85, mem. exec. com. 1980-82, pres. 1983). Intern St. Mary's Hosp. and Children's Mercy Hosp., Kansas City, Mo., 1953-54; practice family medicine Kansas City, Mo., 1954-74; clin. prof. medicine Sch. Medicine U. Mo., Kansas City, 1974—, asst. dean, chmn. coun. on evaluation, 1974-75, chmn. dept. cmty. and family medicine Truman Med. Ctr., 1977-78; pres. med. staff Bapt. Meml. Hosp., 1967-68, chmn. sect. gen. practice, 1969-71, dir. family practice residency program, 1974-93, chmn. Residency Assistance Program project bd., 1975-80; v.p. med. affairs Bapt. Med. Ctr., 1993-96. Preceptor Sch. Medicine, U. Mo., Columbia; chmn. sect. family practice Rsch. Hosp., 1969-71; participant Ditchley Park Conf. on Devel. of Health Svcs. and Med. Care, Brit., Can., U.S., 1972; mem. Grad. Med. Edn. Nat. Adv. Com., 1976-80, chmn., 1976-78; bd. dirs. Coun. of Med. Splty. Socs., 1979-81, pres., 1980-81; chmn. Coun. for Med. Affairs, 1981 Contbr. articles to med. jours., presentations to profl. confs. Pres. Family Health Found. Am., 1980-85; trustee U. Mo., Kansas City, 1981. With USN, 1943-46 Recipient John G. Walsh award, 1981, Max Cheplove award, 1981, Alumni award U. Mo., Kansas City, 1981; W. Jack Stelmach Resident Edn. Fund established in his honor Bapt. Med. Ctr., 1996. Charter fellow Am. Acad. Family Physicians (del. 1969-74, mem. commn. on edn. 1971-76, chmn. 1974-75, 75-76, bd. dirs. 1974-77, chmn. bd. 1976-77, pres. 1978-79); mem. AMA, Mo. State Med. Assn. (del. 1964-73), Mo. Acad. Family Physicians (bd. dirs. 1966-69, pres. 1973-74), Kansas City Acad. Family Physicians (pres. 1965-66), Jackson County Med. Soc. (sec. 1960-61), S.W. Clin. Soc. (sec. 1967-68, bd. dirs. 1967-69, assoc. dir. clinics 1972-73), dir. clinics 1975), Kansas City Acad. Medicine, Kans. U. Med. Alumni (1st v.p. 1972-73), Alpha Omega Alpha. Mem. Unity Ch. Home: 5252 Sunset Dr Kansas City MO 64112-2356

STELPSTRA, WILLIAM JOHN, minister; b. Paterson, N.J., Nov. 1, 1934; s. Duke and Nellie (Stapert) S.; m. Anna Rizkovsky, Sept. 6, 1958; 1 child, Linda Mae. BA, Alma White Coll., 1957; B. of Religion, Zarephath Bible Sem., 1958. Ordained to ministry Pillar of Fire Ch., 1954. Pastor Pillar of Fire Ch., Little Falls, N.J., 1956-60; evangelist Wesleyan Meth. Ch., 1960-64; founder, dir. Bethel Children's Home, Paterson, N.J., 1964-71, Bethel Ranch Rehab. for Men, West Milford, N.J., 1971—; founder, pres. World for Christ Crusade, Inc., N.J., Fla., 1960—, dir. fgn. missions, 1980—; adminstr. Fellowship House, Bloomfield, N.J., 1979—. Bright Side Manor, Teaneck, N.J., 1978—. Mem. Ocean Grove C. of C. Republican. Wesleyan Ch. Avocations: painting with oils, swimming, boating, travel, gardening. Home: 1005 Union Valley Rd West Milford NJ 07480-1220

STELTZLEN, JANELLE HICKS, lawyer; b. Atlanta, Sept. 18, 1937; d. William Duard and Mary Evelyn (Embrey) Hicks; divorced; children: Gerald William III, Christa Diane. BS, Okla. State U., 1958; MS, Kans. State U., 1961; JD, U. Tulsa, 1981. Bar: Okla. 1981, U.S. Dist. Ct. (no., ea. and we. dists.) Okla. 1981, U.S. Tax Ct. 1982, U.S. Ct. Claims 1982, U.S. Ct. Appeals (10th cir.) 1983, U.S. Ct. Appeals (Fed. cir.) 1984, U.S. Supreme Ct. 1986; lic. real estate broker. Pvt. practice, Tulsa, 1981-97. Lectr. Coll. of DuPage, Glen Ellyn, Ill., 1976, Tulsa Jr. Coll., 1981-88; dietitian, Tulsa; res. dep. for Tulsa County Sheriff's Office; 2d dep., legal Tulsa County Clk., 1997-2000. Christian counselor 1st United Meth. Ch., Tulsa, 1986—, coord. legal counseling ministry, 1985—, lay pastor, 1987—; mem. Tulsa County Bd. Equalization and Excise Tax Bd., 1989-90; mem. Leadership Tulsa XX, 1993—; recipient of Leadership Tulsa Paragon award, 1996; bd. dirs. Sister Cities Tulsa/San Luis Potosi, 1988—, South Peoria Neighborhood Connection Found., 1991—, pres., 1995-96; active Tulsa County Tax Oversight Com., 1994—, Tulsa Home Rule Charter Com., 1994—. Recipient Okla. Sr. Olympics medal. Mem. Okla. Bar Assn., Tulsa County Bar Assn., Vol. Lawyers Assn. (bd. dirs.), Am. Dietetic Assn., Tulsa Dist. Dietetic Assn., Kiwanis Internat., Mensa, DAR, Delta Zeta. Republican. Avocations: swimming, scuba diving, jogging, bicycling, reading, painting, needlecrafts, photography. Home: 6636 S Jamestown Pl Tulsa OK 74136-2615

STELZER, GUSTAV R. retired automotive executive; b. St. Louis, June 1, 1915; s. Martin J. Stelzer and Alma Mangelsdorf; m. Lorraine Louise Sueme, Feb. 3, 1940; children: Gail Messett, John J. Stelzer. Grad. in acctg. and comml. law, Mo. Bus. Sch., St. Louis, 1929. Acct. Craig Furniture Co., St. Louis, 1930-32; sales rep. Newsom & Stelzer, St. Louis, 1933-34; various positions GM Corp., various cities, 1935-66, sr. exec. regional mgr. Chevrolet Motor Divsn. Kansas City, Mo., 1966-76; ret., 1976. Author: Free Trade and the Constitution, 1987, 89, 94, The Nightmare of Camelot, An Expose of Free Trade, 1994, The State Against Religion, The Case for Equal Protection, 2001; contbr. over 130 articles to profl. publs.; appeared numerous radio and TV talk shows. Mem. World Affairs Coun., San Diego, 1981-85, Inst. of the Ams., San Diego, 1982-86; mem. adv. coun. U. San Diego Sch. Edn., 1983-85. Avocations: golf, travel, writing. Home: 1836 163d Pl SE Mill Creek WA 98012 E-mail: gusstelzer@aol.com.

STELZER, IRWIN MARK, economist; b. N.Y.C., May 22, 1932; s. Abraham and Fanny (Dolgins) S.; m. Marian Faris Stuntz, 1981. BA cum laude, NYU, 1951, MA, 1952; PhD, Cornell U., 1954. Fin. analyst Econometric Inst., 1952; tchg. fellow Cornell U., 1953-54; instr. U. Conn., 1954-55; rschr. Twentieth Century Fund, 1953 55; economist W.J. Levy, Inc., 1955 56; sr. cons., v.p. Boni, Watkins, Jason & Co., Inc., 1956-61; rschr. Brookings Instn., 1956-57; pres. Nat. Econ. Rsch. Assocs., Inc., 1961-85, I.M. Stelzer Assocs. Inc., 1986—; dir. Energy and Environmental Ctr., Harvard U., 1987-90. Dir. econ. policy studies Am. Enterprise Inst., 1990-98; bd. dirs. Regulatory Policy Inst., Oxford U.; dir. regulatory studies Hudson Inst., 1998—; adv. coun. Electric Power Rsch. Inst.; adv. com. revision of rules of practice and procedure FERC; chmn. com. on adequate power supply FPC; bd. dirs. The Energy Adv. Group of the Keystone Ctr; mng. dir. Rothschild, Inc.; mem. trade and environment policy adv. com. U.S. Trade Rep.; assoc. mem. Nuffield Coll., Oxford U.; adv. bd. Am. Antitrust Inst.; lectr. in field. Author: Selected Antitrust Cases: Landmark Decisions, 1955, The Antitrust Laws: A Primer, 1993, 4th edit., 2001; econ. columnist The Sunday Times, London, 1986—; contbg. editor The Weekly Standard; columnist Courier Mail, Australia; contbr. articles to econs. field; mem. publ. com. The Pub. Interest. Mem. Mayor's Energy Policy Adv. Group for N.Y.C.; adv. panel Pres.'s Nat. Commn. for Rev. of Antitrust Laws and Procedures; mem. Gov.'s Adv. Panel on Telecom., bd. governing trustees Am. Ballet Theatre; bd. dirs. U.S. Nat. Com., World Energy Conf., Regulatory Policy Inst., Oxford U.; mem. Fed. Energy Regulatory Com. Task Force on Pipeline Competition. Mem. Am. Econ. Assn., Reform Club, Cosmos Club, Phi Beta Kappa. Home: PO Box 1008 Aspen CO 81612-1008 Office: 1015 18th St NW Ste 300 Washington DC 20036 Office Phone: 202-777-3000. Personal E-mail: stelzer@aol.com.

STELZER, PAUL, cardiac surgeon, educator; MD, Columbia U., 1972. Diplomate Am. Bd. Surgery, Am. Bd. Thoracic Surgery. Resident gen. surgery Roosevelt Hosp., N.Y.C., 1972-77; resident thoracic surgery N.Y. Hosp.-Cornell Med. Ctr., 1979-81; attending surgeon Beth Israel Med. Ctr., N.Y.C. Assoc. prof. surgery Albert Einstein Coll. Medicine. Office: Beth Israel Med Ctr 317 E 17th St New York NY 10003-3804 Office Phone: 212-420-2584. Office Fax: 212-420-2321. E-mail: pstelzer@bethisraelny.org.

STELZNER, PAUL BURKE, textile company executive; b. Iowa City, Iowa, Jan. 1, 1935; s. Glenn W. and Ruth (Schroder) S.; m. Martha Jane Schneeberger, Aug. 23, 1958; children: Martha Elizabeth Beuke and Barrie Jane Lubbering. BS, Muskingum Coll., 1960; postgrad., Akron U., 1961-65. Tech. dir. Buckeye Fabric Finishing Co., Coshocton, Ohio, 1963-74; sec., sales mgr. Excello Fabric Finishers Inc., Coshocton, 1966-74; gen. mgr. Mineral Fiber Mfg. Corp., Coshocton, 1974-76, dir., 1998—; v.p., gen. mgr. Kellwood Co. Recreation Group, 1976-85; v.p. Am. Recreation Products, Inc., New Haven, Mo., 1985-88; v.p., gen. mgr. John Boyle & Co., Statesville, NC, 1989-93, pres., CEO, 1993—, dir., 1999—. Pres. Coshocton County Young Rep. Club, 1960-62; mem. Coshocton County Rep. Exec. Com., 1960-62; pres. Coshocton Park Bd., 1972-76; mem. Coshocton City Planning Commn., 1972-76; chmn. indsl. div. United Fund, 1973; dist. commr. St. Louis Council Boy Scouts Am., 1977-79, pres. Gateway Amica, 1986-87; dir. Indsl. Fabrics Found., 1998-2002. Served with USN, 1953-57. Mem. ASTM, Indsl. Fabrics Assn. Internat. (dir. 1973-74, 82-88, 94-99), Am. Assn. Textile Colorists and Chemists, Soc. Plastics Engrs. (sr.). Presbyterian. Home: 210 Brierwood Rd Statesville NC 28677-5408 Office: John Boyle & Co Inc 1803 Salisbury Rd Statesville NC 28677-6219

STEM, CARL HERBERT, business educator; b. Eagleville, Tenn., Jan. 30, 1935; s. Marion Ogilvie and Sara Elizabeth (Jones) S.; m. Linda Marlene Wheeler, Dec. 28, 1963; children: Anna Elizabeth, Susan Kathleen, John Carl, David Leslie. *Great-great-great-great-grandfather Jacob Stem-of Pennsylvania Dutch ancestry-migrated from the Philadelphia region after the Revolutionary War to Granville County, N.C., where there is still a farming village named Stem. In the 1830s several sons migrated to Middle Tennessee. Great-great-grandfather John Richard Stem was a lieutenant in the 55th (McKoins) Tennessee Infantry (CSA). Great-grandfather Marion Luther Stem was the first to "leave the farm", owning general merchandise stores. Grandfather Charles R. Stem practiced country dentistry for more than 50 years. Father Marion Ogilvie Stem died at the age of 28 in 1941.* BA, Vanderbilt U., 1957; AM (Woodrow Wilson fellow, Harvard scholar), Harvard U., 1960, PhD, 1969. Internat. fin. economist, bd. govs. Fed. Res. System, Washington, 1963—70; from assoc. prof. to prof. econs. Tex. Tech. U., Lubbock, 1970—75; from assoc. prof. to prof. internat. fin. Tex. Tech U., Lubbock, 1970—2001; prof. emeritus Tex. Tech. U., Lubbock, 2001—; from chmn. fin., adminstr. grad. programs, exec. assoc. dean to dean Tex. Tech U. Coll. Bus. Adminstrn., Lubbock, 1971—97, dean emeritus, 1997—. Sr. econ. adviser Office Fgn. Direct Investments, U.S. Dept. Commerce, Washington, 1973-74; cons. U.S. Dept. Treasury, 1974-75; mem. faculty Grad. Sch. Credit and Fin. Mgmt., Lake Success, N.Y., 1974-87; adj. scholar Am. Enterprise Inst. Pub. Policy Rsch., Washington, 1974-88; treas. Mission Jour., Inc., 1969-88. Editor (with Makin and Logue) Eurocurrencies and The International Monetary System; contbr. articles to profl. jours. Trustee St. Mary Plains Hosp., Lubbock, Tex., 1987-92, chmn., 1992; v.p. Tex. Coun. of Collegiate Edn. for Bus., 1977-78, pres., 1978-79; mem. acad. adv. bd. United Arab Emirates U., Al Ain, 1996—; mem. Coun. on Podiat. Med. Edn., Washington, 1998—; bd. visitors Abilene Christian U., 1998—; elder Broadway Ch. of Christ, Lubbock, 2001-04. Capt. Security Agy. AUS, 1961-62. Fulbright scholar U. Reading, Eng., 1957-58. Fellow Phi Beta Kappa; mem. Southwestern Bus. Adminstrn. Assn. (pres. 1982-83), Nat. Assn. Bus. Economists, So. Bus. Adminstrn. Assn. (v.p. 1985-86, pres. 1986-87), Lubbock Econ. Coun. (pres. 1973), Am. Assembly Collegiate Schs. Bus. (stds. com. 1981-84, bd. dirs. 1993-96), Lubbock Club (pres. 1986-87), Omicron Delta Kappa, Phi Kappa Phi, Beta Gamma Sigma, Tau Kappa Alpha, Phi Beta Kappa. Home: 12508 W 123rd St Overland Park KS 66213 E-mail: cstem@sbcglobal.net. *Most important to me are the ever timely values of our Judeo-Christian heritage- faith in God and a deep appreciation for the inherent value of man. These values have underpinned my aspirations and sustained me through disappointments. They have generated the perseverance and continual hope so vital to me as I have worked for self-growth and to make a contribution to the institutions and people with which I have been associated in various periods of my life.*

STEMBERG, THOMAS GEORGE, retail office supply store executive; b. Newark, Jan. 18, 1949; s. Oscar Michael and Erika (Ratzer) S.; m. Dola Davis Hamilton, Sept. 24, 1988. Student, Am. Internat. Sch., Vienna, 1962-67; AB, Harvard U., 1971, MBA, 1973. With Jewel Cos., Star Market, Cambridge, Mass., 1973-82, v.p. sales and merchandising, 1982; sr. v.p. sales and merchandising First. Nat. Supermarkets, Hartford, Conn., 1982-83, pres., 1983-84, Staples, Inc., Newton, Mass., 1986-88, chmn., CEO Westborough, Mass., 1988-98, Framingham, Mass., 1999—. Baker scholar Harvard Bus. Sch., 1973; R.H. Macy fellow Harvard Bus. Sch., 1973. E-mail: tom.stemberg@staples.com.

STEMBRIDGE, ALLEN FREDERICK, management educator; b. Cape Town, South Africa, Oct. 22, 1940; s. Frederick Charles and Agnes Milne Stembridge; children: Alison Lia Willauer, Graeme Allen, Megan Lisa Delacruz. Diploma in Bus., Helderberg Coll., Somerset West, South Africa, 1968; B in Commerce, U. South Africa, 1978; MBA, Andrews U., 1981, EdD, 1983. Chair dept. bus. dept. Solusi U., Bulawayo, Zimbabwe, 1970—73, Helderberg Coll., Somerset West, 1984—87; chair mgmt. and mktg. Andrews U., Berrien Springs, Mich., 1988—99, asst. dean sch. of bus.; bus. dept. chair Adventist Internat. Inst. of Advanced Studies, Silang, Philippines, 2000—01; chair dept. bus. adminstrn. Southwestern Adventist U., Keene, Tex., 2002—. Sec. Lewis, Thompson and Anglo Am. (L.T.A., Ltd.), Bellville, South Africa, 1974—77. Mem.: Inst. Adminstrn. Commerce South Africa, Delta Mu Delta, Sigma Beta Delta, Phi Kappa Phi. Home: 1408 Hyde Park Blvd Cleburne TX 76033 Office: Southwestern Adventist Univ Hillcrest Ave Keene TX 76059 Office Phone: 817-556-4771. Personal E-mail: stem@swau.edu. E-mail: stem@swau.edu.

STEMMER, EDWARD ALAN, surgeon, educator; b. Cin., Jan. 20, 1930; s. Edward Purcell and Helen Marie (Smith) S.; m. Lois Jean Moss, May 1, 1954; children: Susan Helen, Linda Diane, Paul Frederick, Nancy Joan, Carol Jean. BA, U. Chgo., 1949, MD, 1953. Diplomate Am. Bd. Surgery, Am. Bd. Thoracic Surgery. Resident in surgery U. Chgo., 1953-60; chief resident in surgery Stanford U., Palo Alto, Calif., 1960-62, instr. surgery, 1962-64; asst. prof. surgery U. Utah, Salt Lake City, 1964-65; from asst. prof. surgery to prof. surgery U. Calif., Irvine, 1966—. Acting chmn. surgery U. Calif., Irvine, 1978-80; chief surg. svc. VA Hosp., Long Beach, Calif., 1965—. Editor: Vascular Disease in the Elderly, 1997; contbr. articles to profl. jours., chpts. to books. Capt. USAF, 1955-57, maj. USAFR, 1957-72. Grantee NIH, Am. Heart Assn., 1962-72; recipient disting. svc. award Am. Heart Assn., 1971. Mem. Am. Assn. Thoracic Surgery, Assn. VA Surgeons (pres. 1979-80, disting. svc. award 1995), Am. Surg. Assn., Am. Coll. Surgeons (pres. So. Calif. chpt. 1974-75), L.A. Surg. Soc. (pres. 1986-87), Sigma Xi. Avocations: carpentry, gardening, electronics. Home: 136 College Park Dr Seal Beach CA 90740-2527 Office: VA Med Ctr 5901 E 7th St Long Beach CA 90822-5201 E-mail: edward.stemmer@med.va.gov.

STEMMLER, EDWARD JOSEPH, physician, retired association executive, retired academic dean; b. Phila., Feb. 15, 1929; s. Edward C. and Josephine (Heitzmann) Stemmler; m. Joan C. Koster, Dec. 27, 1958; children: Elizabeth, Margaret, Edward C., Catherine, Joan. BA, La Salle Coll., Phila., 1950, ScD (hon.), 1983; MD, U. Pa., 1960; ScD (hon.), Ursinus Coll., 1977, Phila. Coll. Pharmacy and Sci., 1989; LHD (hon.), Rush U., 1986, Med. Coll. Pa., 1994; ScD (hon.), SUNY, Syracuse, 1994; ScD, Georgetown U., 1998. Diplomate Am. Bd. Internal Medicine. Intern U. Pa. Hosp., 1960—61, resident in internal medicine, 1961—63, fellow in cardiology, 1963—64, chief med. resident, 1964—65, chief med. outpatient dept., 1966—67; chief of medicine U. Pa. Med. Svc., VA Hosp., Phila., 1967—73; deans com. VA Hosp., 1974—88; instr. medicine grad. divsn. medicine U. Pa., 1964—66, NIH postdoctoral rsch. trainee, dept. physiology, grad. divsn. medicine, 1965—67, assoc. in medicine grad. divsn. medicine, 1966—67; assoc. in physiology Grad. Div. Medicine, 1967—72, from asst. prof. medicine to prof., 1967—91, Robert G. Dunlop prof., 1981—91, prof. emeritus, 1991—; assoc. dean Univ. Hosp. Sch. Medicine, 1973, assoc. dean student affairs, 1973—75, from acting dean to dean, 1974—88, dean emeritus, 1989—; exec. v.p. U. Pa. Med. Ctr., 1986—89, Assn. Am. Med. Colls., 1990—94, sr. adv. to pres., 1994—95. Nominating and ad hoc governance coms. Nat. Bd. Med. Examiners, 1985, exec. com., 1986—99, vice-chmn., 1987—89, treas., 1989—91, chmn., 1991—95; ednl. policy com. Nat. Fund for Med. Edn., 1975—77; deans com. VA Hosp., 1974—89; chmn. Pa. Deans Com., 1976—87, Mid-Ea. Regional Med. Libr. Svcs., 1978—81; adv. com. dept. medicine U. Ala., Birmingham, 1985—89; vis. com. Tufts U. Sch. Medicine, 1990—94, Med. U. S.C., 1990—99, U. Calif., Davis, 1993—. Contbr. articles to profl. jours. Trustee Dorothy Rider Pool Healthcare Trust, 1991—2000, Ursinus Coll., 1991—, Wintergreen Nature Found., 1996—2001, Saw Cmty. Found., 2000—, AHC Cmty. Found., 2002—; mem. oper. bd. U. Va. Med. Ctr., 2004—. Recipient Frederick A. Packard award, 1960, Albert Einstein Med. Ctr. staff award, 1960, Roche award, 1960, Disting. Svc. award, Nat. Bd. Med. Examiners, 1999. Master: ACP (treas., chmn. investment com. 1975—80, Laureate award Ea. Pa. region 1986, Disting. Svc. award); mem.: AMA, Am. Clin. and Climatological Soc. (pres. 1997—98), Coll. of Physicians of Phila. (bd. censors, coun. 1979—85, coun. 1990—92), Assn. Am. Med. Colls. (ad hoc external exam. rev. com. 1980—82, exec. coun., coun. of deans adminstrv. bd. 1980—85, chmn. 1983—85, nat. chmn.-elect 1985—86, chmn. assembly 1986—87), Inst. Medicine, Alpha Omega Alpha. Republican. Mem. Christian Ch. Home: RR 1 Box 676 Roseland VA 22967-9209

STEMMONS, RANDEE SMITH, lawyer; b. Springfield, Mo., July 15, 1958; d. Robert Lee and Connie (Smith) S. BA, William Woods Coll., 1980; JD, U. Mo., 1983. Bar: Mo. 1983, U.S. Dist. Ct. (we. dist.) Mo., 1983. Ptnr. Stemmons & Stemmons, Mt. Vernon, Mo., 1983—. V.p. Democratic Alliance, Springfield, 1984—; mem. adv. bd. Hospice. Recipient Profl. Responsibility award Am. Jurisprudence, 1983. Mem. ABA, Assn. Trial Lawyers Am., Mo. Assn. Trial Lawyers, 39th Judicial Cir. Bar Assn. (pres. 1984—), Student Bar Assn. (v.p. 1982-83), Mt. Vernon C. of C. (bd. dirs., v.p. 1984-87, pres. 1987), Order of the Coif, Phi Delta Phi. Democrat. Presbyterian. Home: 520 E Center St Mount Vernon MO 65712-1208 Office: 101 E Dallas St Mount Vernon MO 65712-1401

STEMPEL, GUIDO HERMANN, III, journalism educator; b. Bloomington, Ind., Aug. 13, 1928; s. Guido Hermann Jr. and Alice Margaret (Menninger) S.; m. Anne Elliott, Aug. 30, 1952; children: Ralph Warren, Carl William, Jane Louise. Student, Carnegie Tech., 1945-46; AB in Journalism, Ind. U., 1949, AM in Journalism, 1951; PhD in Mass Communication, U. Wis., 1954. Sports editor Frankfort (Ind.) Times, 1949-50; instr., asst. prof. Sch. Journalism, Pa. State U., University Park, 1955-57; from assoc. prof. to prof. Dept. Journalism, Cen. Mich. U., Mt. Pleasant, 1957-65; assoc. prof. Sch. Journalism, Ohio U., Athens, 1965-68, prof., 1968-82, Disting. prof., 1982-97, dir., 1972-79, Disting. prof. emeritus, 1997—. Rsch. cons. Ohio Newspaper Assn., Columbus, 1985—; chmn. rsch. com. Coll. Media Advisors, 1963-69, 79-84; mem. adv. bd. dept. comm. arts U. West Fla., 1987-00; survey coord. Scripps Howard News Svc., 1992—; dir. Scripps Survey Rsch. Ctr., 2002—. Co-author: The Media in the 1984 and 1988 Presidential Campaigns, 1991; assoc. editor, Newspaper Rsch. Jour., 1992-2001; co-editor Web Jour. of Mass Comm. Rsch., 1997—; editor, co-author: The Practice of Political Communication, 1994; co-editor, co-author: Research Methods in Mass Communications, 1981, 2d edit., 1989, The Media in the 1984 and 1988 Presidential Campaigns, 1991, Historical Dictionary of Political Communication in the United States, 1999, Mass Communication Research and Theory, 2003; author: Media and Politics in America, 2003; editor: Journalism Quar., 1972-89; contbr. articles to profl. jours. Mem. bd. visitors Def. Info. Sch., Ft. Meade, 1985-96. Recipient Chancellor's award, U. Wis., 1977. Mem. Assn. for Edn. in Journalism and Mass Comm. (chmn. rsch. com. 1968-71; Eleanor Blum award 1989, Trayes Tchr. of Yr. 1997, Disting. Svc. award 1999, Harold C. Nelson award 2004), Soc. Profl. Journalists, Rotary (pres. Athens unit 1984-85). Democrat. Methodist. Home: 7 Lamar Dr Athens OH 45701-3730 Office: Ohio Univ Sch of Journalism Athens OH 45701 Office Phone: 740-593-2609. Business E-mail: stempel@ohio.edu.

STEMPEL, JOHN DALLAS, international studies educator; b. Easton, Pa., July 26, 1938; s. John Emmert and Mary Roberts (Farmer) S.; m. Nancy A. Dean, Feb. 11, 1961 (div. Jan. 1990); m. Susan Hodgetts, May 18, 1991; children: Amy, Alix, Jill. AB cum laude, Princeton U., 1960; MA with distinction, U. Calif., Berkeley, 1963, PhD, 1965. Jr. officer U.S. Embassy U.S. Fgn. Svc., Conakry, Guinea, 1966, acting dep. chief mission U.S. Embassy Bujumbura, Burundi, 1966-68, watch officer State Dept. Ops. Ctr. Washington, 1968-70, staff asst. to dep. sec. state, 1968-70, Ghana desk officer, 1970-72,

polit.-econ. officer U.S. Embassy, 1972-74, from sr. internal polit. reporter to dep. chief sect. to acting polit. counselor U.S. Embassy Tehran, Iran, 1975-79; diplomat-in-residence, mem. faculty U.S. Naval Acad., Annapolis, Md., 1979-81; dir. ops. ctr. Dept. State U.S. Fgn. Svc., Washington, 1981-83, dir. Office Near East and South Asian Affairs Bur. Internat. Security Affairs Dept. Def., 1983-84; spl. asst. Persian Gulf affairs U.S. Dept. State, Washington, 1984-85; consul gen. U.S. Fgn. Svc., Madras, India, 1985-88; prof. internat. studies, assoc. dir. Patterson Sch. Diplomacy and Internat. Commerce U. Ky., Lexington, 1988-93, prof. internat. studies, dir. Patterson Sch. Diplomacy, 1993—2003, sr. prof. internat. studies Patterson Sch. Diplomacy, 2003—. Adj. prof. George Washington U., Washington, 1968-72, 80-85, Am. U., Washington, 1975; prof. Regional Coop. and Devel. Coll., Tehran, 1975-78; rsch. assoc. Mershon Ctr. Ohio State U., 1972. Author: Inside the Iranian Revolution, 1981, Faith, Diplomacy and the International System, 2000; (monograph) Theory and Practice in Foreign Affairs: Why Two Worlds Seldom Meet, 1972; contbr. articles to profl. jours. Mem. exec. coun. Episcopal Diocese of Lexington, Ky. With USN, 1960-62, lt. USNR, 1962-70. Mem. Internat. Studies Assn., N.Y. Coun. on Fgn. Rels. (mem. U.S. Dept. Commerce Export Coun. Ky.). Avocations: tennis, reading, railroads, philosophy. Office: U Ky Patterson Sch Diplomacy Patterson Tower Rm 455 Lexington KY 40506-0027 Office Phone: 859-257-4666.

STEMPEL, ROBERT C. automobile manufacturing company executive; b. 1933; BSME, Worcester Polytech Inst., 1955, PhD, 1977; MBA, Mich. State U., 1970. Sr. detailer chassis design dept. Oldsmobile div. GM, Detroit, 1958-62. Sr. designer, 1962-64, transmission design engr., 1964-69, motor engr., 1969-72, asst. chief engr., 1972-73, spl. asst. to pres., 1973-74, chief engines and components engr. Chevrolet div., 1974-75, dir. engring., 1975-78, corp. v.p. and gen. mgr. Pontiac div., 1978-80, corp. v.p. European passenger car ops., Fed. Republic Germany, 1980-82, corp. v.p., gen. mgr. Chevrolet div., 1982-84, corp. v.p., group exec. Buick-Oldsmobile-Cadillac Group, 1984-86, corp. exec. v.p. Worldwide Truck & Bus Group, Overseas Group, 1986-87, corp. pres., chief operating officer, 1987-90, chmn., chief exec. officer, 1990-92, chmn., Energy Conversion Devices, Inc., Troy, Mich. Served with U.S. Army, 1956-58. Mem. NAE.

STEMPIEN, JOSEPH JEFFREY, music educator; b. Lewistown, Pa., Aug. 13, 1952; s. Joseph Victor and Thelma Elizabeth Stempien; m. Eleanor Jane Lurwick, Nov. 22, 1975; children: Heather Lynne, Aimee Leigh. MusM in Music Edn., Ithaca Coll., N.Y., 1983. Instrumental music tchr. Penn Yan Mid. Sch., Penn Yan, NY, 1978—, Hobart & William Smith Colls., Geneva, NY, 1989—; band dir. Keuka Coll., Keuka Park, NY, 2002—; choral and band dir. Penn Yan United Meth. Ch., Penn Yan, NY, 1992—; prin. trumpet Orch. of the So. Fingers Lakes, Corning-Elmira, NY, 1982—; trumpet player So. Tier All Star Jazz Band, Finger Lakes Area, NY, 1990—; mechanic Marbles Automotive, Penn Yan, NY, 2002—. Condr. Penn Yan Area Cmty. Band, Penn Yan, NY, 1991—2004. Mem.: ITG (assoc.), NYSSMA (assoc.), MENC (assoc.), Kappa Kappa Psi (life), Phi Mu Alpha (life). Home: 519 Assembly Ave PO Box 475 Keuka Park NY 14478 Office: Penn Yan Central School District 515 Liberty St Penn Yan NY 14527 Office Phone: 315-536-3366. Personal E-mail: stempien@usadatanet.net.

STEMPLER, JACK LEON, government and aerospace company executive; b. Newark, Oct. 30, 1920; s. Morris and Ida (Friedman) S.; m. J. Adelaide Williams, Oct. 28, 1950; children: Mark N., Sandra J., Carrie B. BA, Montclair (N.J.) State U., 1943; LL.B., Cornell U., 1948. Bar: N.Y., D.C. 1949. Atty. com. uniform code mil. justice Dept. Def., 1948-49, atty. adviser legis. div., 1949-50; asst. counsel Munitions Bd., 1950-53; counsel Armed Forces Housing Agy., 1952-54, Advanced Research Projects Agy., 1958-65; asst. gen. counsel logistics Dept. Def., 1953-65, asst. to sec. def. for legislative affairs, 1965-70; gen. counsel Dept. Air Force, 1970-77; asst. to sec. of def. for legis. affairs, 1977-81; v.p. legis. affairs LTV Aerospace, Washington, 1982-92; ret., 1992. Cons. in field. Served to 1st lt. USMCR, 1942-46, PTO. Recipient Outstanding Civilian Performance award Dept. Def., 1959, Distinguished Civilian Service award, 1965, Distinguished Civilian Service award with palm, 1969, with 2d bronze palm, 1970; Exceptional Civilian Service award USAF, 1973, 75, 77; awarded Presdl. rank of Disting. Exec., 1980; recipient Disting. Public Service award Dept. Def., 1981 Mem. Fed. Bar Assn., D.C. Bar Assn., Cornell Law Sch. Assn. Home: 4701 Newcomb Pl Alexandria VA 22304-1506

STENBERG, CARL W., III, public administration educator, dean; b. Pitts., July 8, 1943; s. Carl W. and Mildred (Baggs) S.; m. Kirstin D. Thompson; children: Erik Anders, Kerry Cathryn, Kaameran Baird. BA, Allegheny Coll., 1965; MPA, SUNY, Albany, 1966, PhD, 1970. Research asst. N.Y. State Div. Budget, Albany, 1967; analyst, then sr. analyst U.S. Adv. Commn. on Intergovtl. Relations, Washington, 1968-77, asst. dir. for policy implementation, 1977-83, acting exec. dir., 1982; exec. dir. Council of State Govts., Lexington, Ky., 1983-89; prof., dir. Weldon Cooper Ctr. for Pub. Svc. U. Va., Charlottesville, 1989-95, Disting. prof. pub. svc., 1991-95; prof., dean Yale Gordon Coll. Liberal Arts U. Balt., 1995—2003; prof. Sch. Govt. U. N.C., Chapel Hill, 2003—. Mem. Am. Part Program USIA, 1987; adj. prof. George Washington U., 1971, 81, Am. U., 1972-80, 82, U. Md., 1976, U. So. Calif., 1984-87; v.p. Bureaucrat Inc., Washington, 1973-77, mng. editor, 1973-77. Feature editor Pub. Mgmt. Forum Pub. Adminstrn. Rev., 1977-83, editor U. of Va. newsletter, 1994-95; co-editor-in-chief The Regionalist, 1997-2002. Pres. Reston Home Owners' Assn., Va., 1973-74; mem. U.S. del. Ad Hoc Group on Urban Problems, OECD, 1980-82. Vivien Stewart vis. fellow Cambridge U., Eng., 1980; recipient Disting. Alumni award Polit. Sci. Dept. Rockefeller Coll., 1985. Fellow: Nat. Acad. Pub. Adminstrn. (chair bd. dirs. 2002—04); mem.: Va. Alliance for Pub. Svc. (pres. 1991—92), Am. Soc. Pub. Adminstrn. (pres. 1990—91, Marshall E. Dimock award, Louis Brownlow award, Donald Stone award). Home: 301 Madera Ln Chapel Hill NC 27517-8356 Office: U NC Sch Govt CB # 3330 Knapp Bldg Chapel Hill NC 27599-3330 E-mail: stenberg@iogmail.iog.unc.edu.

STENBERG, DONALD B. lawyer; b. David City, Nebr., Sept. 30, 1948; s. Eugene A. and Alice (Kasal) Stenberg; m. Susan K. Hoegemeyer, June 9, 1971; children: Julie A., Donald B. Jr., Joseph L., Abby E. BA, U. Nebr., 1970; MBA, JD cum laude, Harvard U., 1974. Bar: Nebr. 1974, U.S. Dist. Ct. Nebr. 1974, U.S. Ct. Appeals (fed. cir.) 1984, U.S. Ct. Claims 1989, U.S. Ct. Appeals (8th cir.) 1989, U.S. Supreme Ct. 1991. Assoc. Barlow, Watson & Johnson, Lincoln, Nebr., 1974—75; ptnr. Stenberg and Stenberg, Lincoln, 1976—78; legal counsel Gov. of Nebr., Lincoln, 1979—82; sr. prin. Erickson & Sederstrom, Lincoln, 1983—85, of counsel, 2003—; pvt. practice Lincoln, 1985—90; atty. gen. State of Nebr., Lincoln, 1991—2002. Mem.: Phi Beta Kappa. Republican. Office: Erickson & Sederstrom Regency Westpointe 10330 Regency Pkwy Dr Ste 100 Omaha NE 68114-3761 Business E-Mail: donstenberg@eslaw.com.

STENBIT, JOHN PAUL, federal agency administrator; b. Oakland, Calif., June 1, 1940; s. Paul Charles and Antoinette (Inguglia) S.; m. Albertine Heederik, Aug. 19, 1966; children: Elisabeth Francesca, Antine Elaine. BS, Calif. Inst. Tech., 1961, MS, 1962; postgrad., Stanford U., 1981. Rsch. fellow Technische Hogesch., Eindhoven, The Netherlands, 1962-63, 65-67; engr. Aerospace Corp., El Segundo, Calif., 1962-68; prin. dep. dir. Office Sec. Def., Washington, 1973-77; engr. TRW, Redondo Beach, Calif., 1968-73, 77—, engr., v.p., gen. mgr. systems integration group Fairfax, Va., 1977—, exec. v.p.; asst. secy. command, control, commun. and intel. U.S. Dept. Defense, Washington, 2001—. Mem. adv. bd. Dir. Naval Intelligence, Washington, 1982-91; mem. sci. adv. group Def. Communications Agy., Arlington, Va., 1989—; cons. Def. Sci. Bd., Washington. Chmn. Internat. Children's Festival, Fairfax, 1991-92. Recipient medal for outstanding pub. svc. Sec. Def., 1977; Fulbright fellow, The Netherlands, 1962-63, Aerospace Corp., The Netherlands, 1965-67. Mem. NAE, AIAA, Security Affairs Support Assn. (bd. dirs. 1990—), Electronic Industries Assn. (bd. dirs. 1991—), Armed Forces Communications and Electronics Assn., Va. Bus. Coun., Korean-Am. Bus. Coun., Met. Club (Washington). Republican. Office: US Dept Defense Command, Control, Commun and Intel 6000 Defense Pentagon Washington DC 20301-6000

STENCER, MARK JOSEPH, healthcare administrator, consultant; b. Pitts., Mar. 19, 1955; s. Frank C. and Ramona (Calabrese) S. BFA, Carnegie-Mellon U., 1976; BA in Liberal Arts, U. Mich., 1979; MA in Mgmt., NYU, 1982. Asst. dir. NYU Office Acad. Devel., N.Y.C., 1980-82; program dir. John B. Cummings Co., Inc., Fundraising and Pub. Rels. Cons., N.Y.C., 1982-84; assoc. dir. The Statue of Liberty, Ellis Island Found., N.Y.C., 1984-86; dir. devel. Fordham U., N.Y.C., 1986-91; exec. v.p. Cambridge U., England, 1991-94; exec. campaign dir. Cmty. Counselling Svc. Co., Inc., N.Y.C., N.J., 1995-2000; exec. sr. dir. U. Chgo., N.Y. Regional Divsn., 2000—02; chief devel. officer Sisters of Mercy Health Sys., 2002—. Named Outstanding Young Man Am., 1985, 86. Mem. Ass. Fundraising Profls., Assn. Healthcae Philanthropy, Coun. Advancement and Support of Edn., Assn. for Healthcare Philanthropy. Republican. Roman Catholic. Avocation: pianist. Home: 1735-H Boulder Springs Dr Saint Louis MO 63146

STENCHEVER, MORTON ALBERT, obstetrician, gynecologist; b. Paterson, N.J., Jan. 25, 1931; s. Harold and Lena (Suresky) Stenchever; m. Diane Bilsky, June 19, 1955 (dec. 1999); children: Michael A., Marc R., Douglas A.; m. Luba Kane, Sept. 8, 2001. AB, NYU, 1951; MD, U. Buffalo, 1956. Diplomate Am. Bd. Ob-gyn., 1965. Intern Mt. Sinai Hosp., 1956-57; resident obstetrics and gynecology Columbia-Presbyn. Med. Center, N.Y.C., 1957-60; asst. prof., Oglebey research fellow Case-Western Res. U., Cleve., 1962-66, asso. prof. dept. reproductive biology, 1967-70, dir. Tissue Culture Lab., 1965-70, coordinator Phase II Med. Sch. program, 1969-70; prof., chmn. dept. obstetrics-gynecology U. Utah Med. Sch., Salt Lake City, 1970-77; prof. ob-gyn. U. Wash. Sch. Medicine, Seattle, 1977-98; prof. emeritus, 1998—; chmn. dept. U. Wash. Sch. Medicine, Seattle, 1977-98. Chmn. test com. for ob-gyn. Nat. Bd. Med. Examiners, 1979-82; cons. in urogynecology Fedn. Internat. for Gynecology & Obstetrics, 1998—. Author: Labor: Workbook in Obstetrics, 1968, Labor: Workbook in Obstetrics, 2d edit., 1993, Human Sexual Behavior: A Workbook in Reproductive Biology, 1970, Human Cytogenics: A Workbook in Reproductive Biology, 1973, Introductory Gynecology: A Workbook in Reproductive Biology, 1974; co-author: Comprehensive Gynecology, 1987, Comprehensive Gynecology, 4th edit., 2001, Caring for the Older Woman, 1991, Health Care for the Older Woman, 1996, Office Gynecology, 1992, Office Gynecology, 2d edit., 1996, Good Health, Great Sex After 40: A Woman's Guide, 1997; sr. editor: Atlas of Gynecology, 5 vols., 1997—99, assoc. editor: Ob-Gyn., 1986—2001, Ob-Gyn. Survey; editor: Clinical Updates in Women's Health Care, 2001—, ACOG Review, 2001—; mem. editl. bd.: Western Jour. Medicine; contbr. articles to profl. jours. Served to capt. USAF, 1960-62. Fellow Am. Coll. Obstetricians and Gynecologists (com. on residency edn. 1974-80, learning resource commn. 1980-86, vice chmn. 1982-83, chmn. prolog self-assessment program 1982-86, vice chair com. health care for the underserved women 1995-97), Am. Assn. Obstetricians and Gynecologists, Am. Gynecol. Soc., Am. Soc. Ob-Gyn., Pacific Coast Ob-Gyn. Soc.; mem. AAAS, AMA, Am. Bd. Ob-Gyn. (bd. dir. 1988-, v.p. 1990-92, treas. 1992-96, chmn. 1996-98, mem. resident rev. com. 1993-97, chmn. divsn. female pelvic medicine/reconstructive surgery), Assn. Profs. Gynecology and Obstetrics (chmn. steering com. teaching methods in ob-gyn. 1970-79, v.p. 1975-76, pres. 1983-84, v.p. Found. 1986-87, pres. Found. 1987-91), Pacific N.W. Ob-Gyn. Soc., Wash. State Med. Assn., Seattle Gynec. Soc. (v.p. 1981, pres.-elect 1982, pres. 1982-83), Am. Soc. Human Genetics, Ctrl. Assn. Ob-Gyn., Soc. Gynecologic Investigation, Wash. State Obstet. Soc., Tissue Culture Assn., N.Y. Acad. Sci., Utah Ob-Gyn. Soc., Utah Med. Assn., Teratology Soc., Am. Fertility Soc. Home: 8301 SE 83rd St Mercer Island WA 98040-5644 Office: Ob-Gyn 130 Knickerson St Ste 211 Seattle WA 98109

STENDAHL, BRITA KRISTINA, humanities educator, social studies educator; b. Stockholm, Jan. 10, 1925; came to U.S., 1954; d. Johan Victor and Ingeborg (Normann) Johnsson; m. Krister Stendahl, Sept. 7, 1946; children: Johan, Anna, Dan. Cand. Theology, Uppsala (Sweden) U., 1949, can. Philosophy, 1954, PhD (hon.), 1981. Hist. and lit. tchr. Gymnasium, Uppsala, Sweden, 1949-54; hist. and lit. tchr. extension program Harvard U., Cambridge, Mass., 1956-59, hist. and lit. tchr. freshman program, 1964-74; hist. and lit. tchr. seminar program Radcliffe Coll., Cambridge, 1976-84; cultural sec. Ch. of Sweden, Stockholm, 1984-88. Mem. Govt. Coun. for Coord. and Planning of Rsch., Stockholm, 1985-88. Author: (monographs) Søren Kierkegaard, 1976, The Force of Tradition, 1984, The Education of a Self-Made Woman, Fredrika Bremer, 1801-1865, 1994, (autobiography) Sabbatical Reflections, 1978; contbr. Multicultural Writers from Antiquity to 1945, 2002; book reviewer:. Co-chair Fellowship in Israel for Arab-Jewish Youth, Boston, 1972-84, 88-95; bd. dirs. The Abraham Fund, N.Y.C., 1996— Bunting fellow, Radcliffe Coll., Cambridge, Mass., 1961-63; assoc. fellow Henry A. Murray Ctr. at Radcliffe, 1981-82; recipient Myron B. Bloy award The Assn. for Religion and Intellectual Life, 1993. Mem. Arstasallskapet for Fredika Bremer-Studier (chmn. 1985—89). Democrat. Lutheran. Avocations: walking, Tai Chi.

STENDAHL, KRISTER, retired bishop; b. Stockholm, Apr. 21, 1921; came to U.S., 1954, naturalized, 1967; s. Olof and Sigrid (Ljungquist) S.; m. Brita Johnsson, Sept. 7, 1946; children: John, Anna, Daniel. Teol. kand., U. Uppsala, Sweden, 1944, teol. lic., 1949, teol.dr., 1954; Litt. D. (hon.), Upsala Coll., 1963; D.D., St. Olaf Coll., 1971, Harvard U., 1985, St. Andrews U., 1987, Calif. Luth. U., 1995; LL.D., Susquehanna U., 1973; L.H.D. (hon.), Hebrew Union Coll./Jewish Inst. Religion, 1980, Brandeis U., 1981, Loyola U., New Orleans, 1992; Teol.Dr. (hon.), U. Helsinki, 2000. Ordained priest Ch. of Sweden, 1944. Chaplain to students Uppsala U., 1948-50, instr. O.T., N.T. exegesis, 1951-54, docent, 1954; asst. prof. N.T., 1954-56; asso. prof. Harvard U. Div. Sch., 1956-58, John H. Morison prof. N.T. studies, 1958-63, Frothingham prof. Bibl. studies, 1963-68, dean, John Lord O'Brian prof. div., 1968-79, Andrew W. Mellon prof. div., 1981-84, prof. emeritus, 1985—; pastor Luth. Ch. Am., 1968-84; Robert and Myra Kraft and Jacob Hiatt Disting. prof. Christian studies Brandeis U., 1991-93; moderator consultation on ch. and Jewish people World Council Chs., 1975-85; co-dir. Osher Ctr. for Tolerance and Pluralism Shalom Hartman Inst., 1994-98. Author: The School of St. Matthew, 1954, 2d edit., 1968, The Bible and the Role of Women, 1966, Holy Week, 1974, Paul Among Jews and Gentiles, 1976, Final Account, 1995, 2d edit., Energy for Life, 1999. Recipient Disting. Service award Assn. Theol. Schs., 1988. Fellow Am. Acad. Arts and Scis.; mem. Nathan Soederblom Soc. Business E-Mail: krister_stendahl@harvard.edu.

STENEHJEM, WAYNE KEVIN, state attorney general, lawyer; b. Mohall, N.D., Feb. 5, 1953; s. Martin Edward and Marguerite Mae (Peg) (McMaster) Stenehjem; m. Tama Lou Smith, June 16, 1978 (div. Apr. 1984); 1 child, Andrew; m. Beth D. Bakke, June 30, 1995. AA, Bismarck (N.D.) Jr. Coll., 1972; BA, U. N.D., 1974, JD, 1977. Bar: N.D. 1977. Ptnr. Kuchera & Stenehjem, Grand Forks, ND, 1977—2000; spl. asst. atty. gen. State of N.D., 1983—87, atty. gen., 2000—; mem. ND Indsl. Commn., 2001—; chair RAGA, 2001—02; mem. N.D. Ho. Reps., 1976—80, N.D. State Senate, 1980—2000, pres. pro tempore, 1998—99; bd. Univ. and Sch. Lands, 2001—. Chmn. Senate Com. on Social Svcs., 1985—86, Senate Com. on Judiciary, 1995—2000, Interim Legis. Judiciary Com., 1995—2000, Legis. Coun., 1995—2000; mem. Nat. Conf. Commrs. on Uniform State Laws, 1995—2000, Gov.'s Com. on Juvenile Justice. Bd. dirs. N.D. Spl. Olympics, 1985—89; chmn. Dist. 42 Reps., Grand Forks, 1986—88; bd. dirs. Christus Rex Luth. Ch., pres., 1985—86. Named Champion of People's Right to Know, Sigma Delta Chi, 1979, N.D. Friend of Psychology, N.D. Psychol. Assn., 1990; named one of Outstanding Young Man of N.D, Jaycees, 1985; recipient Excellence in County Govt. award, N.D. Assn. Counties, 1991, Love Without Fear award, Bismarck Abused Adult Resource Ctr., 2003. Mem.: Grand Forks County Bar Assn., N.D. State Bar Assn. (Legis. Svc. award 1995). Republican. Home: 1216 Crestview Ln Bismarck ND 58501 Office: Office of the Atty Gen State Capitol Bldg 600 E Boulevard Ave Bismarck ND 58505

STENERSON, JOHN GORDEN, lumber and building materials executive; b. Ft. Rucker, Ala., Mar. 24, 1952; s. Robet Gorden and Georgiann S.; m. Shirley Mae, Nov. 14, 1981; children: Michael David, Sarah Ann, Robert John. Studetn, Moorhead State U., 1970-71; AA, Moorhead Area Vocat. Inst., 1973. Hardware mgr. Stenerson Lumber, Moorhead, Minn., 1973-74, outside sales, 1974-75, asst. mgr. Detroit Lakes, Minn., 1975-84, hardware merchandising coord. office Moorhead, 1984-85, yard mgr., 1986-94, asst. gen. mgr. corp. office, 1994-95, gen. mgr. corp. office, 1996—. Mem. city coun. City of Moorhead, 1992—; park adv. bd. chair Moorhead Park Bd., 1997—; v.p. Moorhead Healthy Cmty. Initiative, 1995-96. Mem. Jaycees (dir., v.p. 1975-83, Wiliam Brownfield award 1977), Lions. Republican. Lutheran. Avocations: snowmobiling, ice hockey, water-skiing. Home: 1702 1st Ave N Moorhead MN 56560-2304

STENGEL, ROBERT FRANK, engineering and applied science educator; b. Orange, N.J., Sept. 1, 1938; s. Frank John and Ruth Emma (Geidel) S.; m. Margaret Robertson Ewing, Apr. 8, 1961; children: Brooke Alexandra, Christopher Ewing. SB, MIT, 1960; MS in Engring., Princeton U., 1965, MA, 1966, PhD, 1968. Aerospace technologist NASA, Wallops Island, Va., 1960-63; tech. staff group leader C.S. Draper Lab., Cambridge, Mass., 1968-73, Analytic Scis. Corp., Reading, Mass., 1973-77; assoc. prof. Princeton (N.J.) U., 1977-82, prof. engring. and applied sci., 1982—, assoc. dean engring., 1994-97. Cons. GM, Warren, Mich., 1985-94; mem. com. strategic tech. U.S. Army NRC, 1989-92; vice chmn. Congl. Aero. Adv. Com., Washington, 1986-89; mem. com. on trans-atmospheric vehicles USAF Sci. Adv. Bd., 1984-85; mem. com. on low altitude wind shear and its hazard to aviation Nat. Rsch. Coun., 1983, Navy Theater Missile Defense com. NRC, 2000-01. Author: Stochastic Optimal Control: Theory and Application, 1986, reprinted as Optimal Control and Estimation, 1994, Flight Dynamics, 2004; N.Am. editor Cambridge Aerospace Series, 1993—98; contbr. over 200 tech. papers to profl. publs.; patentee wind probing device. Lt. USAF, 1960-63. Recipient Apollo Achievement award NASA, 1969, Cert. of Commendation, MIT, 1969, Excellence in Aviation award FAA, 1997, John R. Ragazzini Edn. award, AACC, 2002. Fellow IEEE, AIAA (Mechanics and Control of Flight award 2000). Home: 329 Prospect Ave Princeton NJ 08540-5330 Office: Princeton U D202 Engineering Quadrangle Princeton NJ 08544-0001 Fax: (609) 258-6109. Office Phone: 609-258-5103. E-mail: stengel@princeton.edu.

STENGEL, RONALD FRANCIS, management consultant; b. Lock Haven, Pa., Oct. 18, 1947; s. Elmer S. and Elizabeth (Heivley) S.; m. Margaret Linda Dezack, Aug. 23, 1969. BSME, U. Pa., 1969, MBA, 1976. Mfg. engr. Control Data Corp., Valley Forge, Pa., 1969-70; mgr. mfg. svcs. Knoll Internat., East Greenville, Pa., 1970-75; ptnr. mgmt. cons. Touche Ross & Co., Phila., 1976-85; pres. RF Stengel & Co. Inc., Valley Forge, 1985—. Office Phone: 610-296-8950.

STENGER, SARAH, chef; Grad., Dumas Pere Cooking Sch.; studied with chef Pierre Orsi, Pierre Orsi restaurant, Lyons, France. From apprentice to chef The Dining Room, Ritz-Carlton hotel, Chgo., 1984—. Founder Women Chefs of Chgo. Named U.S. winner, Prix Culinaire Internat. Pierre Taittinger competition, Paris, 1991, Rising Star Chef of the Yr. in Am., James Beard Found., 1994, Best Chef of the Midwest, 1998. Office: Ritz-Carlton 106 E Pearson St Chicago IL 60611

STENHOLM, CHARLES W. congressman; b. Stamford, Tex., Oct. 26, 1938; m. Cynthia Ann Watson; children: Chris, Cary, Courtney Ann. Card., Tarleton State Jr. Coll., 1959; BS in Agrl. Edn., Tex. Tech U., 1961, MS in Agrl. Edn., 1962; LL.D. (hon.), McMurry Coll., 1983, Abilene Christian U., 1991. Farmer, Tex.; past pres. Rolling Plains Cotton Growers and Tex. Electric Coops.; mem. U.S. Congress from 17th Tex. dist., Washington, 1979—; ranking Dem. mem. agr. com.; mem. Blue Dog Dem. Coalition. Co-chmn. Congl. Leaders United for a Balanced Budget. Active Bethel Luth. Ch., Ericksdahl, Tex.; charter trustee Cotton Producer Inst.; former mem. state Dem. exec. com. Recipient Gerald W. Thomas Outstanding Agriculturalist award Tex. Tech U., 1979, Am. Farmer Degree Future Farmers Am., 1979, Disting. Alumnus award Tarleton State U., 1979, Pres. Coun. award Tex. Future Farmers Am., 1981, Disting. Alumnus award Tex. Tech U., 1987, MORE Common Sense Sound Dollar awards, 1988, 90, Guardian of Small Bus. awards, 1980-92, Watchdogs of the Treasury awards, 1980-92, Legis. award Nat. Rural Health Assn., 1991, Disting. Svc. award Tex. Soc. Biomed. Rsch., 1993, Disting. Svc. award Tex. Med. Assn., 1993, Dr. Nathan Davis award AMA, 1993, Leadership in Advocacy for Children's Health award Nat. Assn. Children's Hosps., 1996, Meritorious Health Svc. award Nat. Assn. Cmty. Health Ctrs., 1997, Golden Plow award Am. Farm Bur. Fedn., 1988, 92, 96, golden Triangle award Nat. Fermers Union, 1994, Thomas Jefferson award Food Distbn. Industry, 1994, 95, Progressive Fermer Man of Yr. award, 1993, Econ. Patriot award, 1997; named Legislator of Yr. Chem. Prodrs. and Distbrs. Assn., 1992, Man of Yr. Progressive Farmer, 1993, Cooperative Hall of Fame, 1998. Mem. Tex. State Soc. (Washington, past pres.), Tex. Breakfast Club (Washington, past pres.), Rolling Plains Cotton Growers (past pres.), Stamford C. of C. (past pres.). Democrat. Lutheran. Office: 2409 Rayburn Ho Office Bldg Washington DC 20515-4317

STENHOUSE, EVERETT RAY, clergy administrator; b. Minco, Okla., May 15, 1931; s. George E. and Jessie Loraine (Dean) S.; m. Alice Irene English, Aug. 22, 1948; children: Brenda Jones, Judy Lundberg, Stephen, Andrew. Student, U. Calif. Berkeley, U. Athens, 1969-71. Ordained to ministry Assemblies of God, 1955. Pastor Wayside Chapel, Bakersfield, Calif., 1955-59, Bethel Temple, Bakersfield, 1960-63; dist. dir. youth So. Calif. Dist. Assemblies of God, Costa Mesa, Calif., 1963-67; assoc. pastor 1st Assembly of God, San Diego, 1968-69; missionary Assemblies of God Fgn. Missions, Athens, Greece, 1969-73; pastor Bethany Ch., Alhambra, Calif., 1974-79; supt. So. Calif. Dist., Assemblies of God, Costa Mesa, 1979-85; asst. gen. supt. Gen. Coun. Assemblies of God, Springfield, Mo., 1986-94. Bd. adminstrn. Nat. Assn. Evangs., Wheaton, Ill., 1986-94, Pentecostal Fellowship of No. Am., Ont., Can., 1986-94; chmn., bd. dirs. Assemblies of God Theol. Sem., Springfield, 1991-94, Ministers Benefit Assn., Springfield, 1986-94. Contbr. articles to various mags. Mem. Assemblies Of God Ch. Home: 77696 Westbrook Ct Palm Desert CA 92211-0416

STENITZER, GEORGE IGNATIUS, corporate communications executive; b. Granite City, Ill., June 30, 1956; s. George Ignatius and Beatrice Marie (Cuenca) S.; m. Donna Dwyer, Jan. 16, 1982; children: Jody Bea, Jonathan Jacob. BA in English, Quincy Coll., 1977. Editor Alton (Ill.) Citizen, 1978-80; writer Sverdrup Corp., St. Louis, 1980-84; advt. mgr. Consol. Aluminum, St. Louis, 1984-85; mgr. advt. Southwestern Bell Telecom, St. Louis, 1985-90; corp. mgr. news rels. Southwestern Bell Corp., St. Louis, 1990-94; dir. corp. positioning Ameritech Corp., Chgo., 1994-99; v.p. corp. comm. R.R. Donnelley & Sons., Chgo., 1999-2000, Tellabs, Chgo., 2000—. Mem.: Bus. Mktg. Assn. (dir. Chgo. chpt. 2001—03, exec. v.p. 2002—03, pres. 2003—), Pub. Rels. Soc. Am. (dir. Chgo. chpt. 2000—04), Nat. Investor Rels. Inst. (dir. Chgo. chpt. 2000—01), Bus. Profl. Advt. Assn. (treas. 1985—87, v.p. profl. devel. 1987—88, pres. 1988—89, pub. The St. Louis Bus. Profl. Advt. Assn. Communicator 1989—90). Roman Catholic. E-mail: george.stenitzer@tellabs.com., geo4747@yahoo.com.

STENNETT, WILLIAM CLINTON (CLINT STENNETT), television station executive, state legislator; b. Winona, Minn., Oct. 1, 1956; s. William Jessie and Carole Lee Stennett. BA in Journalism, Idaho State U., 1979. Gen. mgr. Wood River Jour., Hailey, Idaho, 1979-85, pres., pub., 1985-87; pres. Sta. KSVT-TV, Ketchum, Idaho, Sta. KSKI-FM, Sun Valley, Idaho; mem. Idaho Ho. of Reps., Boise, 1990-94; mem., minority leader Idaho Senate, Dist. 25, Boise, 1996—. Named Legislator of Yr., Idaho Soil Conservation Dists., 1994, Idaho Wildlife Found., 1996, Idaho Assn. Recyclers, 2002, Idaho Profl. Firefighters Assn., 2002; recipient Gen. Excellence award, Idaho Newspaper Assn., 1985, 1986—87. Mem.: Idaho Broadcasters (bd. dirs.), Ketchum Sun Valley C. of C. (bd. dirs. 1990—95), Rotary. Democrat.

STENSETHER, JOHN ELDON, minister; b. Mpls., Feb. 28, 1944; s. John H. and Gertie Marie (Stensaas) S.; m. Barbara L. Erickson, Sept. 3, 1966; children: Julie Lyn, Kevin John. BA, U. Minn., 1966; postgrad., Fuller Theol. Sem., Pasadena, 1966-69; PhD, Calif. Grad. Sch. Theology, Glendale, 1970. Ordained to ministry Evang. Free Ch. Am., 1972. Sr. pastor Del Rey Hills Evang. Free Ch., Playa del Rey, Calif., 1968-72, Calvary Evang. Free Ch., Essex Fells, N.J., 1972-76, Trinity Evang. Free Ch., South Bend, Ind., 1976-80, Evang. Free Ch., Turlock, Calif., 1980—. Vis. prof. Northeastern

Bible Coll., Essex Fells, N.J., 1973-75; staley disting. Christian scholar; speaker various Colls., sems. and confs. Fellow Evang. Free Ch. of Am. Ministerial, Turlock Evang. Assn. of Ministers. Office: Evang Free Ch 1360 N Johnson Rd Turlock CA 95380-3507 Office Phone: 209-667-1100. Business E-Mail: jstensether@efcturlock.org. *The older I grow, the more I experience life, the greater is my confidence in, and reliance upon, the Sovereignty of God.*

STENSON, BRIAN T. academic administrator; b. Kingston, N.Y., Nov. 6, 1949; s. Joseph Thomas and Theresa Louise Stenson; m. Catherine Joan Kosinski, June 3, 1973; children: Ryan Michael, Erin Kathleen. BA in Polit. Sci., U. Albany, N.Y., 1971, M in Pub. Adminstrn., 1972. Various positions NY State Divsn. Budget, 1975—94, deputy dir. fiscal planning, fin. and mgmt., 1995—96; vice chancellor, fin. and bus. SUNY Sys. Adminstrn. Mem. U. Albany Athletics Bd., NY, 2001—03. With U.S. Coast Guard Res., 1971—77, Albany. Avocations: cooking, running, biking, history. Home: 33 Ruxton Rd Delmar NY 12054 Office: SUNY Sys Adminstrn Broadway SUNY Plaza Albany NY 12204 Business E-Mail: stensonb@sysadm.suny.edu.

STENSON, WILLIAM FREDERICK, gastroenterologist; b. Rome, N.Y., Dec. 2, 1945; s. Frederick Vincent and Mary Catherine (Tucker) S.; m. Janet Marie Breaugh, Dec. 28, 1968; children: Catherine, Karen, Thomas. BS, Providence Coll., 1967; MD, Washington U., 1971. Diplomate Am. Bd. Internal Medicine and Gastroenterology. Intern Barnes Hosp., St. Louis, 1971-72, resident in medicine, 1972-73, 75-76; chief gastroenterology Jewish Hosp. of St. Louis, 1981—98; assoc. prof. medicine Washington U., St. Louis, 1985-91, prof. medicine, 1991—. Co-author: Manual of Nutritional Therapeutics, 1st edit., 1983, 2d edit., 1988, 4th edit., 2002; editor: (book) Inflammatory Bowel Disease, 1991, Gastrointestinal Pharmacology, 1992. Maj. USAF, 1973-75. Office: Washington U Sch Medicine PO Box 8124 Saint Louis MO 63110

STENT, ANGELA E. political scientist, educator, director; b. London, Feb. 24, 1947; arrived in U.S., 1970; d. Ronald Walter and Gabriele Stent; m. Daniel H. Yergin, Aug. 10, 1975; children: Alexander Yergin, Rebecca Yergin. BA in Econs. and History with honors, Cambridge (Eng.) U., 1969; MSc with distinction, London Sch. Econs., 1970; AM in Soviet Studies, Harvard U., 1972, PhD in Govt., 1977. Assoc. prof. dept. govt. Georgetown U., Washington, 1983—, prof. dept. govt. and Sch. Fgn. Svc., 1998—, dir. Ctr. for Eurasian, Russian and East European Studies, 2001—. Sr. policy advisor Office Policy Planning U.S. Dept. State, Washington, 1999—2001; adv. bd. mem. U.S.-Russia Bus. Coun., Women in Internat. Security, Am. Inst. for Contemporary German Studies. Author: From Embargo to Ostpolitik, 1981, Russia and Germany Reborn, 1999; contbr. articles to profl. jours. Mem.: Coun. Fg. Rels. N.Y., Cosmos Club. Office: Ctr for Eurasian Russian and East European Studies Georgetown Univ Washington DC 20057

STENT, GUNTHER SIEGMUND, molecular biologist, educator; b. Berlin, Mar. 28, 1924; came to U.S., 1940, naturalized, 1945; s. George and Elizabeth (Karfunkelstein) S.; m. Inga Loftsdottir, Oct. 27, 1951; 1 son, Stefan Loftur. BS, U. Ill., 1945, PhD, 1948; DSc (hon.), York U., 1984. Research asst. U. Ill., 1945-48; research fellow Calif. Inst. Tech., 1948-50, U. Copenhagen, Denmark, 1950-51, Pasteur Inst., Paris, France, 1951-52; asst. research biochemist U. Calif., Berkeley, 1952-56, faculty, 1956—, prof. molecular biology, 1959-94; prof. emeritus, 1994—; prof. arts and scis. U. Calif., 1967-68, chmn. molecular biology, 1980-86, chmn. molecular and cell biology, 1987-92, dir. virus lab., 1980-86. Document analyst U.S. Field Info. Agy. Tech., 1946-47; mem. genetics panel NIH, 1959-64, NSF, 1965-68; fellow Inst. Advanced Studies, Berlin, 1985-90. Author: Papers On Bacterial Viruses, 2d edit., 1966, Molecular Biology of Bacterial Viruses, 1963, Phage and the Origin of Molecular Biology, 1966, The Coming of the Golden Age, 1969, Function and Formation of Neural Systems, 1977, Morality as a Biological Phenomenon, 1978, Paradoxes of Progress, 1978, Molecular Genetics, 2d edit., 1978, Nazis, Women and Molecular Biology, 1998, Paradoxes of Free Will, 2002; mem. editl. bd. Jour. Molecular Biology, 1965-68, Genetics, 1963-68, Zeitschrift für Vererbungslehre, 1962-68, Ann. Revs. Genetics, 1965-69, Ann. Revs. Microbiology, 1966-70, Jour. Neurosci., 1988-96; contbr. aricles to profl. jours. Merck fellow NRC, 1948-54; sr. fellow NSF, 1960-61; Guggenheim fellow, 1969-70; Fogarty Resident scholar NIH, 1990-92. Mem. NAS, Am. Acad. Arts and Scis., Soc. Neurosci., Am. Philos. Soc., Acad. Scis. and Lit. of Mainz (Germany), European Acad. Scis. and Arts, Cosmos Club. Home: 145 Purdue Ave Kensington CA 94708-1032 Office Phone: 510-642-5214. Business E-Mail: stent@berkeley.edu.

STENTIFORD, BARRY MAXFIELD, education educator, military officer; b. Worcester, Mass., Nov. 11, 1964; s. Robert Edmond Stentiford and Janet Maxfield Hall; m. Vitida Sirisinha, Aug. 6, 2000. BS, Coll. Great Falls, Mont., 1990; MA, U. Mont., 1995; PhD, U. Ala., 1998. Asst. prof. history Grambling State U., 1997—. Author: (history book) The Am. Home Guard: The State Militia in the Twentieth Century, 2002. Capt. USAR, 1985—. Mem.: Res. Officers Assn., Phi Alpha Theta. Avocations: writing, speaking Thai. Home: 510 Gray Rd Dubach LA 71235 Office: Grambling State U Grambling LA 71245 Personal E-mail: bstent2746@aol.com.

STEP, EUGENE LEE, retired pharmaceutical company executive; b. Sioux City, Iowa, Feb. 19, 1929; s. Harry and Ann (Keiser) S.; m. Hannah Scheuermann, Dec. 27, 1953; children: Steven Harry, Michael David, Jonathan Allen. BA in Econs., U. Nebr., 1951; MS in Acctg. and Fin., U. Ill., 1952. With Eli Lilly Internat. Corp., London and Paris, 1964-69, dir. Elanco Internat. Indpls., 1969-70, v.p. marketing, 1970-72, v.p. Europe, 1972; v.p. mktg. Eli Lilly and Co., Indpls., 1972-73, pres. pharm. div., 1973-86, exec. v.p., 1986—. Bd. dirs. Ceregene, Cell-Genesys, Guidant Corp. 1st lt. U.S. Army, 1953-56. Mem. Pharm. Mfrs. Assn. (bd. dirs. 1980-92, chmn. 1989-90), Internat. Pharm. Mfrs. Assn. (pres. 1991-92). Home: PO Box 8997 Rancho Santa Fe CA 92067-8997

STEPAK, ASA MARTIN, writer, linguist; b. Bklyn., Nov. 23, 1950; s. Louis and Anna (Leyter) S. BA cum laude, NYU, 1973. Author: Southern Rhapsody, 1995, Southern Heritage Potpourri, 1995, Southern Heritage Revisited: A Compendium of Behind the Scene E-mail's, 2000, Music: Primordial Birdsong, 2001, Cognitive Linguistics: Oral Metaphor Construct, Knowledge Inheritance, 2002, Fundamental Basis of Sentence Competency and Word Order, 2003.

STEPAN, FRANK QUINN, chemical company executive; b. Chgo., Oct. 24, 1937; s. Alfred Charles and Mary Louise (Quinn) S.; m. Jean Finn, Aug. 23, 1958; children: Jeanne, Frank Quinn, Todd, Jennifer, Lisa, Colleen, Alfred, Richard. AB, U. Notre Dame, 1959; MBA, U. Chgo., 1963. Salesman Indsl. Chems. div. Stepan Chem. Co., Northfield, Ill., 1961-63, mgr. internat. dept., 1964-66, v.p. corporate planning, 1967-69, v.p., gen. mgr., 1970-73, pres., 1973-84; pres., chmn., CEO Stepan Co., Northfield, Ill., 1984-99, chmn., CEO, 1999—, also bd. dirs. Bd. dirs. Am. Chemistry Coun. Mem. liberal arts coun. Notre Dame U., South Bend, Ind., 1972—; bd. dirs. Big Shoulders, Chgo. 1st lt. AUS, 1959-61. Mem. Soap and Detergent Assn. (bd. dirs., exec. com., chmn.), Ill. Bus. Roundtable (policy com., sec.), Econ. Club Chgo., Exmoor Country Club, Bob O'Link Golf Club, Everglades Club, Sailfish Club Fla. Home: 200 Linden St Winnetka IL 60093-3862 Office: Stepan Co Edens & Winnetka Rds Northfield IL 60093

STEPANEK, DANIEL P. public relations executive; BS, Marquette U.; MA in Journalism, U. Iowa; MBA in Fin., Loyola U., Chgo. Previously with Combustion Engring., Borg Warner, RJR Industries; v.p., gen. mgr. CMF&Z Pub. Rels., N.Y.C.; mng. ptnr. KCSA Pub. Rels. Worldwide, N.Y.C., 1992—. Office: KCSA Pub Rels 800 2nd Ave New York NY 10017-4709 E-mail: dstepanek@kcsa.com.

STEPANEK, JOSEPH EDWARD, industrial development consultant; b. Ellinwood, Kans., Oct. 29, 1917; s. Joseph August and Leona Mae (Wilson) S.; m. Antoinette Farnham, June 10, 1942; children: Joseph F., James B., Antoinette L., Debra L. BSChemE, U. Colo., 1939; DEng in Chem. Engring., Yale U., 1942. Registered profl. engr., Colo. Engr. Stearns-Roger Mfg., Denver, 1939-45; from asst. to assoc. prof. U. Colo., Boulder, 1945-47; from cons. to dir. UN, various countries, 1947-73; cons. internat. indsl devel., U.S.-China bus. relations Boulder, 1973—. Bd. dirs. 12 corps., 1973—. Author 3 books on indsl. devel.; contbr. 50 articles to profl. jours. Exec. dir. Boulder Tomorrow, 1965-67. Recipient Yale Engring. award Yale Engring. Assn., 1957, Norlin award U. Colo. 1978, Annual award India League of Am., 1982. Mem. AAAS. Democrat. Unitarian Universalist. Avocation: ranching. Home: 1622 High St Boulder CO 80304-4224

STEPANIAN, STEVEN ARVID, II, lawyer, financial consultant; b. Charleroi, Pa., Apr. 15, 1935; s. Steven A. and Edithmarion M. (McElligott) Stepanian; m. Pamela S. Abbey, Feb. 15, 1979. AB magna cum laude, U. Pitts., 1957; LLB, Harvard U., 1963. Bar: Pa. 1964, U.S. Supreme Ct. 1967. Assoc. Reed Smith, 1963—69, ptnr., 1970—78; pvt. practice law Pitts., 1978—; ptnr., gen. counsel Marine Magnesium Co., 1988—, U.S. Windforce, 1998—. Dir. NFL Alumni, 1982—89. Maj. USAF, 1957—60, maj. USAF, 1968—69. Mem.: ABA (chair sports law com.), Pa. Bar Assn., Nemacolin Encampment Club (Pitts.), Univ. Club, Duquesne Club (past pres.). Democrat. Roman Catholic. Home: 123 Millstone Ln Pittsburgh PA 15238-1623 Office: Gateway Towers Ste 4-G 320 Fr Duquesne Blvd Pittsburgh PA 15222-1103 Office Phone: 412-281-0555. E-mail: sastepanian@uswindforce.com.

STEPANSKI, ANTHONY FRANCIS, JR., computer software company executive; b. Jersey City, N.J., June 29, 1941; s. Anthony Francis and Gertrude Stepanski; m. Jane Ellen Schuler, Sept. 5, 1965; children— Matthew A.W., Melinda Kate BA in Physics, Clark U., 1963. Sales rep. IBM Corp., N.Y.C., 1964-68; from sales rep. to sr. v.p. AGS Computers, Inc., N.Y.C. and Mountainside, N.J., 1968-82, exec. v.p., 1982-93; pres., CEO AGS Info. Services, Inc., Mountainside, 1986-93; also bd. dirs. AGS Computers, Inc., a NYNEX Co., Mountainside, mng. dir.; pres., CEO Origin Tech., N.A. (subs. Origin/Amsterdam, Netherlands), 1994—97; pvt. investor Melmatt Ptnrs., LLP, 1998-2000; CEO, bd. mem. IZODIA, plc, London, 2001—02. Trustee Clark U., Worcester, Mass., 1987-99, Children's Specialized Hosp. Found., Mountainside, 1989-96; bd. dirs. Westchester Artificial Kidney Ctr., Valhalla, N.Y., 1982-97, Westfield Symphony Orch., N.J., 1983-96. Served with USAR, 1964-65.

STEPHAN, ALEXANDER FRIEDRICH, German language and literature educator; b. Lüdenscheid, Fed. Republic Germany, Aug. 16, 1946; arrived in US, 1968; s. Eberhard and Ingeborg (Hörnig) S.; m. Halina Konopacka, Dec. 15, 1969; 1 child, Michael. MA, U. Mich., 1969; PhD, Princeton U., 1973. Instr. German Princeton (NJ) U., 1972-73; from asst. prof. to prof. German UCLA, 1973-85; prof. German U. Fla., Gainesville, 1985-2000, chmn., 1985-93; prof. German, Ohio Eminent scholar, sr. fellow Mershon Ctr., Ohio State U., 2000—. Author: Christa Wolf, 1976, Die deutsche Exilliteratur, 1979, Christa Wolf (Forschungsbericht), 1981, Max Frisch, 1983, Anna Seghers im Exil, 1993, Im Visier des FBI, 1995, paperback edit. 1998, English transl. Communazis, 2000, Anna Seghers: Das siebte Kreuz. Welt und Wirkung eines Romans, 1997; editor: Peter Weiss: Die Ästhetik des Widerstands, 1983, 3d edit., 1990, Exil. Literatur und die Künste, 1990, Exil-Studien, 1993—, Christa Wolf: The Author's Dimension, 1993, 2d edit., 1995, Themes and Structures, 1997, Uwe Johnson: Speculations about Jakob and Other Writings, 2000, Early 20th Century German Fiction, 2003, Anna Seghers, Die Entscheidung, 2003; co-editor: Studies in GDR Culture and Society, 1981—90, Schreiben im Exil, 1985, The New Sufferings of Young Werther and Other Stories from the GDR, 1997, Rot=Braun? Brecht Dialog, 2000, Nationalsozialismus und Stalinismus bei Brecht und Zeitgenossen, 2000, Jeans, Rock und Vietnam. Americanische Kultur in der DDR, 2002; co-prodr.: (TV documentaries) Im Visier des FBI, 1995, Das FBI und Marlene Dietrich, 2000, Das FBI und Brechts Telephon, 2002, Exilanten und das OSS, 2002, Thomas Mann und der CIA, 2002. Grantee, Humboldt Found., 1988, 1994, 1998—99, 2002—03, Guggenheim Found., 1989, Feuchtwanger Meml. Libr., 1998, German Acad. Exch. Svcs., 1993, 1997, NEH, 1974, 1984, 1997, Am. Coun. Learned Socs., 1976, 1977, 1984, Am. Philos. Soc., 1979, 1981, 1992, Weichmann Stiftung, 1998. Mem.: German PEN, German Assn. for Am. Studies, German Studies Assn., Internat. Anna Seghers Soc., Soc. Exile Studies. Office: Ohio State U Dept Germanic Lang/Lit 314 Dieter Cunz Hall Columbus OH 43210-1229 Office Phone: 614-247-6068.

STEPHAN, EGON, SR., cinematographer, film equipment company executive; b. Leipzig, Germany, Nov. 25, 1933; came to U.S., 1952; 1 child, Egon Jr. Engr. Reeves Sound, Inc., N.Y.C., 1952-55, Camera Equipment Co., N.Y.C., 1955-57; instr. U.S. Army Signal Corps., 1957-59; camera rental mgr. F&B Ceco, Miami, Fla., 1959-66; freelance cinematographer, 1966—; owner, pres. Cine Video Tech., Inc., Miami, 1968—. Recipient Cine Golden Eagle award Coun. on Internat. Nontheatrical Events, 1973, Gold Camera award U.S. Indsl. Film Festival, 1974, Emmy award Nat. Acad. TV Arts and Scis., 1981, Fisher Meml. award South Fla. Film and Tape Prodrs. Assn., 1981. Mem. Soc. Motion Picture and TV Engrs., Fla. Motion Picture and TV Assn. (chmn. 1978), Internat. Assn. Theatrical Stage Employees. Office: Cine Video Tech Inc 7330 NE 4th Ct Miami FL 33138-5005 E-mail: cinecamera@earthlink.net.

STEPHAN, JOHN, finance educator; m. Anne Schmutz, Dec. 16, 1978. PhD, Columbia U., N.Y.C. Asst. prof. Fla. Atlantic U., Ft. Lauderdale, 2003—. Recipient Roethlisberger Meml. Award, Jour. of Mgmt. Edn., 2003. Mem.: Acad. of Mgmt. Achievements include research in Published several scholarly articles in journals such as. Avocations: jazz, theater. Office: Florida Atlantic University Askew Twr 111 E Las Olas Blvd Fort Lauderdale FL 33065

STEPHAN, JOHN JASON, historian, educator; b. Chgo., Mar. 8, 1941; s. John Walter and Ruth (Walgreen) S.; m. Barbara Ann Brooks, June 22, 1963. BA, Harvard U., 1963, MA, 1964; PhD, U. London, 1969. Rsch. assoc. Social Sci. Ctr., Waseda U., Tokyo, 1969-70; mem. faculty U. Hawaii, Honolulu, 1970—, prof. history, 1977-2001, emeritus prof. history, 2001—, chmn. East Asian studies program, 1973-74, dir. program on Soviet Union in Pacific-Asia region, 1986-88. Rsch. prof. Japan Found.; fellow U. Hokkaido, 1976-77; vis. prof. Inst. of Far East, Moscow, 1982, Inst. Econ. Rsch., Khabarovsk, USSR, 1982-83, Stanford U., 1986, Kennan Inst. for Advanced Studies, 1987; adj. rsch. assoc. East-West Ctr., 1988-92; Sanwa disting. lectr. Tufts U. Fletcher Sch. Law and Diplomacy, 1989. Author: Sakhalin: A History, 1971, The Kuril Islands: Russo-Japanese Frontier in the Pacific, 1974, The Russian Fascists, 1978, Hawaii Under the Rising Sun, 1984, Soviet-American Horizons on the Pacific, 1986, The Russian Far East, 1994. Sr. assoc. mem. St. Antony's Coll., Oxford (Eng.) U., 1977; Bd. dirs. Library Internat. Relations, Chgo., 1976-87; Hawaii rep. U.S.-Japan Friendship Commn., 1980-83. Recipient Kenneth W. Baldridge prize Hawaii chpt. Phi Alpha Theta, 1996; Fulbright fellow, 1967-68; Asia Found. grantee, 1974. Mem. AAUP, Am. Hist. Assn., Am. Assn. Advancement Slavic Studies, Assn. Asian Studies, Authors Guild, Internat. House of Japan, Can. Hist. Assn. Home: 4334 Round Top Dr Honolulu HI 96822-5021 Office: U Hawaii Dept History 2530 Dole St Honolulu HI 96822-2303 Office Phone: 808-956-6762. Business E-Mail: stephan@hawaii.edu.

STEPHAN, KENNETH C. judge; b. Omaha, Oct. 8, 1946; m. Sharon Ross, Apr. 19, 1969; children: Alissa Potocnik, Karen Borchert, Charles. BA, U. Nebr., 1968, JD with high distinction, 1972. Bar: Nebr. Former pvt. practice atty., 1973-97; judge Nebr. Supreme Ct., Lincoln, 1997—. With U.S. Army, 1969—71. Mem.: Am Col Trial Lawyers (jud fellow), Lincoln Bar Asn (former trustee), Nebr State Bar Asn (former chmn young lawyers sect, former mem house delegs). Office: Nebr Supreme Ct State Capitol Bldg Rm 2211 PO Box 98910 Lincoln NE 68509-8910 Office Phone: 402-471-3737. E-mail: kstephan@nsc.state.ne.us.

STEPHAN, PAULA ELIZABETH, economics educator, university official; b. Menomonie, Wis., Mar. 31, 1945; d. A. Stephen and Margaret (Shaffer) S.; m. William D. Amis, July 27, 1974; 1 child, David. BA, Grinnell Coll., 1967; MA, U. Mich., 1970, PhD, 1971. Asst. prof. econs. Ga. State U., Atlanta, 1971-76, assoc. prof. econs., 1976-81, prof. econs., 1981—, assoc. dean Andrew Young Sch., 1996—2001. Vis. scholar Sci. Ctr., Berlin, 1992, 93, 94; mem. com. on equal opportunities in Sci. NSF, 1999-2002; mem. adv. bd. SBE, 2001—; mem. various coms. NRC. Author: Striking the Mother Lode in Science, 1992; contbr. over 40 articles to profl. jours. Mem. bd. dirs. Paideia Sch. Endowment, Atlanta, 1983—, chair, 1991-98. Grantee, Alfred P. Sloan Found., 1993—95, 1999, 2002, Andrew Mellon Found., 1995, 2000, NSF, 1983—85, 1990—91, 2000—02, 2002—04. Avocations: reading, travel. Home: 2101 Black Fox Dr NE Atlanta GA 30345-4124 Office: Ga State Univ Andrew Young Sch 33 Gilmer St SE Atlanta GA 30303-3083 E-mail: pstephan@gsu.edu.

STEPHANI, NANCY JEAN, social worker, journalist; b. Garden City, Mich., Feb. 19, 1955; d. Ernest Helmut Schulz and Margaret Mary Fowler Thompson; m. Edward Jeffrey Stephani, Aug. 29, 1975; children: Edward J., Margaret J., James E. AA, Northwood Inst., Midland, Mich., 1975; student in theology, Boston Coll., 1991; BS summa cum laude, Lourdes Coll., Sylvania, Ohio, 1992; MSW, Ohio State U., 1995. Lic. ind. social worker; cert. cognitive behavioral therapist, master addictions counselor. Profl. facilitator Parents United, Findlay, Ohio, 1989-94; contbg. writer Cath. Chronicle, Toledo, 1988-93; mem. ministry formation faculty Cath. Diocese of Toledo, 1992-96; crisis intervention specialist John C. Hutson Ctr., 1994-98; contbg. writer Sunset Gazette, Findlay, Ohio, 1996-98; mgr. Century Health Svcs., Findlay, Ohio, 1998, dir. emergency mental health svcs., 1998—, co-chair strategic planning action team, 1999-00; prof., field coord. MSW program Ohio State U., Lima, 2000—. Social work clinician Family Svc. Hancock County, coord. clin. svcs. Family Svc., 1997—98, Blanchard Valley Home Health Social Svc.; trustee, bd. dirs. Hope House for Homeless, Findlay, 1990—99, v.p., 1996—97, pres., 1997—99, mem. Hancock County Cluster on Elderly; v.p., pres. parish coun. St. Michael Parish, Findlay, 1985—89, adult edn. coord., 1986—93, mem. strategic plan core com., 1989—91; program planning com. Family Life Conf., Cath. Diocese, 1994—95, mem. accreditation com. ministry formation dept.; profl. facilitator Hope Plus Program through Hancock County Common Pleas Ct., 1996—; coord. critical incident stress mgmt. team Hancock County, 1997—; profl. facilitator Hancock County Survivors of Suicide group, 1997—2000; coord. Hancock County Survivors of Suicide Group, 1997—; field instr. dept. social work U. Findlay, Ohio, 1996—, mem. social work adv. coun., 1998—; adj. faculty U. Findley, Ohio; field instr. Capital U., Bowling Green State U., Heidelberg U., 1997—98; mem. adj. faculty Owens Tech. Coll., Findlay; trustee City Mission, 2000—04; co-program coord., field edn. coord. MSW program Ohio State U., Lima, 2001—; adj. faculty U. of Findlay, 2003—. Founder Food Coop., MPBA, Findlay, 1981; founding mem. Chopin Hall, Findlay, 1983; mem. Hancock County AIDS Task Force, 1994-98; strategic planning com. mem., co-chair goal setting com. Findlay Pub. Schs., 1994, steering com., Call to Action Northwest Ohio, 1997—; trustee City Mission, 1999—. Nat. Inst. Food Svcs. grantee, 1974; Diocese of Toledo grantee, 1991; Ohio State U. Coll. Social Work grantee, 1994. Mem. NOW, NASW (ethics com. Ohio 1997—, v.p. bd. trustees 2000-02, nat. com. on nominations and leadership 2001—, region VII rep. nat. leadership identification com. 2001-04, treas.-elect 2003—, program planning com., Social Worker of Yr. Region 1, 2000), AAUW (legis. chair Findlay chpt.), Internat. Critical Incident Stress Found., Am. Assn. on Child Abuse, Transpsychol. Assn., Friends of Creation Spirituality, Cognitive/Behavioral Profl. Soc., Call to Action, Pax Christi, Women in Ch. Leadership. Avocations: jogging, hiking, cooking, travel. Home: 2615 Goldenrod Ln Findlay OH 45840-1025 Office Phone: 419-422-3711. E-mail: NancyStephani@hotmail.com.

STEPHANOPOULOS, GEORGE ROBERT, political reporter; b. Fall River, Mass., Feb. 10, 1961; s. Robert and Nikki C. Stephanopoulos; m. Alexandra Wentworth, Nov. 20, 2001; 1 child, Elliott Anastasia. AB in Polit. Sci. summa cum laude, Columbia U., 1982; M Theology, Oxford U., 1986. Adminstrv. asst. rep. Edward Feighan, Washington; dep. comm. dir. Dukakis Bentsen campaign, 1988; exec. floor mgr. to House Majority leader Gephardt, Washington; dir. comm. Clinton/Gore campaign, Little Rock, The White House, Washington, 1997—, sr. advisor to the Pres. of U.S., 1993-96; vis. prof. polit. sci. Columbia U., N.Y.C., 1997; contbr., correspondent ABC News, 1997—; anchor This Week, 2002—. Author: All Too Human, 1999; contbr. to Newsweek Mag., 1997—. Recipient medal of Excellence Columbia U., 1993; Rhodes scholar Oxford U. Mem. Phi Beta Kappa. Democrat. Greek Orthodox. Address: 47 W 66th St Fl 6 New York NY 10023-6201

STEPHEN, JOHN ERLE, lawyer, consultant; b. Eagle Lake, Tex., Sept. 24, 1918; s. John Earnest and Vida Thrall (Klein) S.; m. Gloria Yzaguirre, May 16, 1942; children: Vida Leslie Stephen Renzi, John Lauro Kurt. LLB, JD, U. Tex., 1941; postdoctoral, Northwestern U., 1942, U.S. Naval Acad. Postgrad. Sch., Annapolis, 1944; cert. in internat. law, U.S. Naval War Coll., Newport, R.I., 1945; cert. in advanced internat. law, U.S. Naval War Coll., 1967. Bar: Tex. 1946, U.S. Ct. Appeals (D.C. cir.) 1949, U.S. Tax Ct. 1953, U.S. Supreme Ct. 1955, U.S. Dist. Ct. D.C. 1956, U.S. Ct. Appeals (2nd cir.) 1959, U.S. Ct. Appeals (7th cir.) 1964, U.S. Dist. Ct. (so. dist.) N.Y. 1964, U.S. Dist. Ct. (so. dist.) Fla. 1969, D.C. 1972, U.S. Dist. Ct. (no. dist.) Ill. 1974, U.S. Dist. Ct. (we. dist.) Wash. 1975, Mich. 1981, U.S. Dist. Ct. (we. dist.) Mich. 1981, U.S. Dist. Ct. (so. dist.) Tex. 1981. News editor Tex. Broadcasting Sys., 1937; grad. asst./instr. radio-TV broadcasting U. Tex., 1938—41; dir. news & spl. events Capital Boradcasting Co. Sta. KTBC, Austin, Tex., 1941; gen. mgr., corp. counsel Sta. KOPY, Houston, 1946; gen. atty., exec. asst. to pres. Tex. Star Broadcasting Co. and affiliated cos., Houston, 1947-50; ptnr. Hofheinz & Stephen, Houston, 1950—56; sr. v.p., gen. counsel TV Broadcasting Co., Tex. Radio Corp., Gulf Coast Network, Houston, 1953—56; spl. counsel, exec. asst. Mayor, City of Houston, 1953-57; spl. counsel Houston C. of C., 1953—57; sr. v.p., gen. counsel Air Transp. Assn. Am., Washington, 1958-70; v.p., gen. counsel Amway Corp. and affiliated cos., Ada, Mich., 1971-82; counsellor, cons. Austin, Tex., 1983—. Chief protocol City of Houston, 1953-56; advisor Consulates Gen. of Mex., San Antonio, Houston, New Orleans, Washington, 1956-66; cons. Internat. Air Transport Assn., Montreal and London, 1957-69, chair, counsel aviatin indistries joint com. nevigable airspace worldwide, 1958-69; legal advisor Interagy. Group on Internat. Aviation, Washington, 1958-69; mem. exec. com. global airlines supersonic/high-capacity jets insurer Soc. Préparatoire pour Air Transport Ins., S.A., Zurich, 1967-70; atty. Gen. Creighton W. Abrams Jr., Comdr. U.S. Mil. Assistance Command, Vietnam, Saigon/Washington, 1970-71; mem. editl. adv. bd. Jour. of Air Law and Commerce, 1966-72; vis. lectr. Harvard Bus. Sch., Pacific Agribus. Conf., The Southwestern Legal Found., Inter-Am. Law Conf., Inst. Aerospace Law; apptd. by Pres. of U.S. legal advisor, del. U.S. Diplomatic Dels. to Internat. Treaty Confs., Paris, London, Rome, Tokyo, Madrid, Bermuda, Guadalajara, Dakar, 1958-69, Internat. Air-Rte. Dels. to U.K., France, Spain, Portugal, Belgium, The Netherlands, Japan, Rep. of Korea, Mex., Australia, Argentina, Soviet Union, and Brazil, 1958-69; legal advisor, del. U.S. dels. to UN Specialized Orgns., Montreal, Geneva, 1964-71; U.S. rep. Internat. Conf. on Aircraft Disturbance and Sonic Boom, London, 1966; hon. faculty mem., vis. lectr. sch. of law, sch. of bus., U. Miami, 1968—; accredited corr. UN, Rep. and Dem. Nat. Convs.; exec. officer USNR Pub. Affairs Co. 8-7, 1950-57. Author, editor, media prodr. Chief comm. and transp. group Harris County/Houston CD, 1952-56; chmn. legal com. Nat. Aircraft Noise Abatement Coun., Washington; mem. adv. bd. Mus. Fine Arts Houston, 1953-57; bd. dirs. Contemporary Arts Assn. and Mus., Houston, 1952-57; mem. exec. com. Tex. Transp. Inst., 1964-72; apptd. conferee Global Strategy Conf., U.S. Naval War Coll., 1958. Comdr. USNR, 1941-46, PTO and S.E. Asia; mem. staff Supreme Allied Comdr. Atlantic, NATO. Recipient Jesse L. Lasky award RKO Pictures-CBS, Hollywood, Calif., 1939, H.J. Lutcher Stark prize U. Tex., 1939, 40, Walter Mack award PepsiCo, U. Tex., 1941, Best U.S. Pub. Svc. Broadcasts award CCNY, 1946, First-FM (West) award Frequency Modulation Assn., Houston, 1947, Tex. State Network award mobile coverage Nat. Presdl. Convs., Phila., 1948, Chgo., 1952, Trusonic Wireless Microphone award Acad. Motion Picture Arts & Scis., Beverly Hills, 1951, Frank White award, Mutual Broadcasting Sys., N.Y., 1953, H.M.S. SHEFFIELD citation Brit. Royal Navy U.S. Cruise, 1954, C.R. Smith Aviation Devel. award Am. Airlines, N.Y., 1955, Universal Internat./Interstate Theaters world premiere ceremonial award, Houston, 1955, KLM Royal Dutch Airlines Super Constellation Transatlantic award, Washington, 1956, Capt. Eddie Rickenbacker Air Transport Advancement award Eastern Air Lines, N.Y., 1956, Padre Alvarez award Boys Town Chorale Internat. Tour, Canavati Industries, Monterrey, 1957, Allied Rod & Gun Club Triple Crown trophy, Gander, Nfld., 1958, Iron

Duke award No. Va. Lit. Soc., Arlington, 1962, Pres.'s Outstanding commendation internat. law U.S. Naval War Coll., Newport, 1967, IBM Corp. Exec. Computer Concepts prize, San Jose, Calif., 1976, M.Y. ENTERPRISE Cruise award Peter Island, Brit. V.I., 1978, Glacier Bay Cruise award M.V. MALIBU, Sitka, Alaska, 1980. Mem. ABA (chmn., coun. sect. pub. utility, comms. and transp. law, standing com. on aero. law, chmn. sect. adminstrv. law aviation com.), The Am. Law Inst. (advisor Restatement (2d) of Torts), World Peace Through Law Ctr. Geneva (chmn. internat. aviation law com., advisor world air piracy and hijacking treaty), The Fed. Bar Assn. (D.C. chpt., exec. com. transp. coun., comm. coun.), The D.C. Bar, State Bar Tex. (50 Yr. Meritorious Practice award 1996), State Bar Mich., Fed. Comm. Bar Assn. (frequency modulation broadcasting com., tall-TV towers com.), Assn. ICC Practitioners, Am. Judicature Soc., Washington Fgn. Law Soc. (vis. lectr. 1967-68), USS ST. PAUL Assn. (life, CA-73) Assn., Japanese Air Law Soc. (hon.), Venezuelan Air and Space Law Soc. (hon.), SOVEDAE (hon.), USS PRESIDENT ADAMS Assn. (hon.), Naval Submarine League, Naval War Coll. Found., Internat. Club (Washington), Houston Polo Club, Lake Shore Club (Chgo.), Nat. Aviation Club (Washington), Saddle and Cycle Club (Chgo.), Breakfast Club (Houston), Execs. Club (Houston), Order Ky. Cols., Tex. Navy Adm., Flying Col., Phi Eta Sigma, Delta Sigma Rho (pres. Tex. chpt. 1940). Home: 6904 Ligustrum Cv Austin TX 78750-8352

STEPHEN, MICHAEL, psychologist; BA in Psychology, U. Okla., 1973; MS, Okla. State U., 1977, PhD in Counseling Psychology, 1986. Lic. psychologist, Okla. Pvt. practice specializing in comm., relationships, children, Oklahoma City, 1991—. Mem. univ. faculty; active staff Mercy Hosp.; spkr. in field. Author: Cherry Lane: The Power of Abuse; Sex, Love, and God; and Healing, a woman's story; The Mental States Examination for Beginning and Advanced Professionals, Hypoglycemia: A Disease of the Mind, Biochemical/Systemic Treatment to Mental Health. Vol. child abuse prevention and related polit. issues. Mem. APA, Christian Athletes Assn., Okla. Thoroughbred Assn. Okla. Psychol. Assn., Christian Assn. Psychol. Studies, numerous civic and arts orgns. Avocations: athletics, race horse training, ranching, film and acting.

STEPHENS, B. CONSUELA, minister, consultant; b. Bklyn., May 12, 1947; d. Bernadine Whitley and Montiphus DeReyes (Mortimer King). PhD in Religion, Clayton Theological Inst., 1983. Pastor Chenaniah Missionary Ch., Hollis, NY, 1986—. Cons. Chenaniah Missionary Ch., Hollis, United States, 1986—. Author: (book) Behold, I Shew You A Mystery, 1998. Dir. CASE Group, Inc., 2003—. Avocation: gardening. Home: 18625 Henderson Ave Hollis NY 11423-3132 Office: Chenaniah Missionary Ch 18625 Henderson Ave Hollis NY Office Phone: 212-412-7097. Business E-Mail: Consuela.Stephens@cwt.com. E-mail: earthling512@msn.com.

STEPHENS, BART NELSON, former foreign service officer; b. Norfolk, Va., May 29, 1922; s. Bart Dannelly and Lura Lee (Cannon) S.; m. Barrett Krausz, Jan. 7, 1950; children: Tracey Rainier, Schuyler Barrett, Holly Cannon, Sinah Kendall Lee. AB, Duke, 1943; grad., USNR Midshipman Sch., Notre Dame, 1944; A.M., Harvard, 1947; lang. tng., Fgn. Service Inst., 1962, 66, 76. Divisional asst. Greece-Turkey-Iran sect., pub. affairs overseas program staff Dept. State, 1948-49; asst. pub. affairs officer Thessaloniki, Greece, 1950; asst. info. officer Athens, 1950-51; pub. affairs officer Patras, Greece, 1951-54 and, Thessaloniki, 1954; dir. Amerika Haus, Nuernberg, Germany, 1955-59; mem. cultural council City of Nuernberg, 1958-59; mgmt. analyst USIA, Washington, 1959-61; cultural attache Am. Embassy, Warsaw, Poland, 1963-65; dir. Am. Cultural Center, Saigon, Vietnam, 1967-68; 1st sec., regional projects officer Am. Embassy, Vienna, Austria, 1968-70; consul, pub. affairs officer Am. consulate gen. Stuttgart, Germany, 1970-73; area coordinator (Europe) USIA, Washington, 1973, seminar-conf. Programming officer, 1973-74; dep. dir. Office Internat. Arts Affairs, Dept. State, 1974-76; counselor cultural affairs officer Am. Embassy, Bangkok, 1977-82; counselor Sr. Fgn. Service. Contbr. articles to profl. jours. Vice chmn., bd. dirs. Thailand-U.S. Ednl. Found., 1977-82; bd. dirs. John F. Kennedy Found., Thailand, 1977-82, John E. Peurifoy Found., 1979-82, Lynchburg Symphony Orch., 1992-93; exec. sec. Eisenhower Exch. Fellowship Selection Com., Thailand, 1977-82; mem. winter forums com. Sweet Briar Coll., 1990-96. Lt. (j.g.) USNR, 1944-46, PTO. Decorated Bronze Star with combat V, Purple Heart.; recipient Meritorious Svc. award USIA, 1956, medal for civilian service in Vietnam, 1968, Civilian award U.S. European Command, 1973. Mem. Am. Fgn. Svc. Assn., Soc. Lees of Va., Siam Soc., Phi Beta Kappa, Omicron Delta Kappa, Phi Eta Sigma, Pi Kappa Phi. Home: 501 V E S Rd Apt C210 Lynchburg VA 24503 *Personal responsibility should be an essential principle for all of us, in the family, job and community. My 34 years in the U.S. Foreign Service gave me a wonderfully stimulating and rewarding career and a profound belief: the diplomatic service is America's first line of defense.*

STEPHENS, BESS, computer company executive; Grad., Tuskegee Inst. Govt. and pub. affairs mgr. Hewlett Packard Co., human resources mgr., v.p. and global dir. philanthropy and edn., 2002—. Pres., exec. dir. Hewlett Packard Co. Found. Trustee Western Govs. U., Salt Lake City, Bay Area Sch. Reform Collaborative; mem. bd. fellows Santa Clara U., 1991—. Mem.: Nat. Bd. for Profl. Tchg. Stds. (bd. mem.), Gifts in Kind Internat. (bd. dirs.). Office: Hewlett Packard Co MS 1029 3000 Hanover St Palo Alto CA 94304

STEPHENS, BILLIE LOWELL, information assurance manager; b. Eunice, N.Mex., Apr. 4, 1950; children: Michael, David. BS in Mgmt., Calif. Coast U., 1994, MBA, 1997. Microsoft cert. engr. Chief network engr. Def. Info. Security Agy., Washington, 1999—2000; instr. nat. learning ctr. IRS, Austin, Tex., 2000—01; info. assurance mgr. SAIC, Columbia, Md., 2001—. Author: Coastal Del Rey and Mesa De Lagrimas, 2001, The Dome, 2002. Bd. dirs. Writers League Tex., Austin, 2001—01. With U.S. Army, 1969—81. Mem.: Writers League of Tex. (bd. dirs., v.p. 2002—), Tex. Assn. for Hist. Preservation (pres. 2001—02). Baptist. Avocations: golf, writing, travel, history. Home: RR 4 Box 606A Lampasas TX 76550 Personal E-mail: sierrav8@hotmail.com.

STEPHENS, BOB, electronic executive; Pres., CEO Adaptec, Inc., Milpitas, Calif. Office: Adaptec Inc 691 S Milpitas Blvd Milpitas CA 95035-5484

STEPHENS, BOBBY GENE, college administrator, consultant; b. Glendale, S.C., Mar. 8, 1935; s. Dewey and Bertha Cordelia (Mott) S.; m. Sandra Elizabeth White, June 27, 1957; children: Elaine, Ward, Todd, Adam. BS, Wofford Coll., 1957; MS, Clemson U., 1961, PhD, 1964; LHD (hon.), MacMurray Coll., 1987. Textile chemist Reeves Bros., Fairforest, S.C., 1957-58; grad. asst. Clemson (S.C.) U., 1960-63; instr. chemistry Wofford Coll., Spartanburg, S.C., 1963-64, asst. prof., 1964-67, assoc. prof., 1967-72, prof., v.p. acad. affairs, 1972-80; pres. MacMurray Coll., Jacksonville, Ill., 1980-86; v.p. research and enrollment Wofford Coll., Spartanburg, S.C., 1986-91, v.p. sci. and tech., 1991—, prof. chemistry emeritus, 2000—. Project dir. Howard Hughes Med. Inst., 1992—; cons. colls. and industry Contbr. articles to sci. jours.; inventor extractions with propylene carbonate, 1975; producer: TV series The Psychology of Interpersonal Behavior, 1974. Co-chmn. Daniel Morgan Restoration Com., 1986-88; vice chmn. Spartanburg County Pollution Control Authority, 1970-74; bd. dirs. S.C. Lung Assn., Spartanburg, 1970-75, Comms. Svcs., Inc., 1977-80; sect. maj. United Way, 1975-77. 1st lt. U.S. Army, 1958-60. Recipient Jefferson award S.C. Acad. Sci., 1969; recipient 1st prize graphics div. 2d Edit. Art Contest, 1971, 2d and 3d prizes Lawson's Fork Creek Photography Contest, 1978, Alumni Disting. Svc. award Wofford Coll., 2001; USPHS grantee; NSF grantee Mem. Am. Chem. Soc., Nat. Assn. Gifted Children, Assn. Ednl. Communications and Tech., Phi Beta Kappa. Methodist. Home: 460 S Fairview Ave Spartanburg SC 29302 Office: Wofford College 429 N Church St Spartanburg SC 29303-3663 E-mail: stephensbg@wofford.edu.

STEPHENS, BRENDA WILSON, librarian; b. Durham, N.C., Oct. 22, 1952; d. Leroy Thomas and Lucy Mae (Umstead) Wilson; m. Gregory Frederick Stephens, Mar. 6, 1977; children: Seth, Sara. Student, Vincennes U., 1970-71; BA, Winston-Salem State U., 1974; MLS, N.C. Cen. U., 1981. Cert. pub. libr., N.C. From bookmobile coord. to county libr. Orange County Pub. Libr., Hillsborough, N.C., 1976-92, regional libr. dir., 1992—. Sec. United Way of Greater Orange County, 1991—93; elected mem. Orange County Sch. Bd., 1998—, chair, 2001—03, vice chair, 2003—; sec. Lipscomb Bapt. Ch., 1998—2002. With U.S. Army, 1974—76. Mem.: ALA, N.C. Pub. Libr. Dirs. Assn. (officer, pres. 2001), N.C. Libr. Assn. (chair adult sect. 1987—93, co-chair 1985—87, lit. com. 1983—85), A.L. Stanback Mid. Sch. PTO (pres. 1991—92), Kiwanis Club (pres. 1992—93). Democrat. Baptist. Avocation: quilting. Home: 5807 Craig Rd Durham NC 27712-1008 Office: Orange County Pub Libr 300 W Tryon St Hillsborough NC 27278-2438

STEPHENS, BROOKE, financial commentator, writer; BA, Fisk U.; MA, Western Mich. U.; mktg. and fin. student, Harvard Bus. Sch. Cert. fin. planner, stockbroker, registered investment adv.; cert. insurance agent. Internat. trade officer Chase Manhattan Bank; sr. investment cons. Citicorp Investment Svcs., NY; personal fin. adv.; personal fin. commentator NPR's The Tavis Smiley Show, PBS's Nightly Bus. Report, Bloomberg Morning Report. Regular guest CNBC's Power Lunch, CNNfn's It's Only Money, CNN's Your Money with Stuart Varney; former weekly personal fin. expert FX Cable's Breakfast Time; tchr. fin. seminars Am. Mgmt. Assn., Inst. Internat. Rsch., Everywoman's Money Conf., Coalition Black Investors, Coalition 100 Black Women, Nat. Alliance Black Sch. Educators, Nat. Black MBA Assn., Nat. Assn. Black Journalists. Author: Talking Dollars & Making Sense: A Wealth Building Guide for African-Americans, 1996, Men We Cherish: African-American Women Praise the Men in their Lives, 1997, Wealth Happens One Day at a Time: 365 Days to a Brighter Future, 1999; contbr. articles to profl. pubs. including Black Enterprise, Essence, Self, and MS. Mem.: NY Soc. Cert. Fin. Planners (former bd. dirs.), Girls, Inc. (mem. adv. bd., chairwoman econ. lit. com.). E-mail: stephensnn@aol.com.

STEPHENS, CARSON WADE, minister; b. San Angelo, Tex., Mar. 12, 1950; s. Allison Carson and Betty Jo Justice (Ellis) S.; m. Jeanette Martha Zett, June 19, 1971; children: Jennifer Hope, Bethany June. MusB, U. Tex., 1974; DMin, Drew U., 1991; postdoctoral, Tex. A&M U., 1996; postdoctoral fellow, U. Tex., Austin, 1996. Tchr. Manor (Tex.) Ind. Schs., 1970-73; minister Three Rivers (Tex.) Ch. of Christ, 1976-77, East Main Ch. of Christ, Holdenville, Okla., 1977-83, Sharpstown Ch. of Christ, Houston, 1983-86, Clear Lake Ch. of Christ, Houston, 1986-99; pres. Austin (Tex.) Grad. Sch. Theology, 2001—03; dir. devel. Lifeline Chaplaincy, Houston, 2003—. Guest lectr. Fred-Hardeman U., Henderson, Tenn., 1992, Pepperdine U., 1996; dir. devel. Lifeline Chaplaincy Tex. Med. Ctr., Houston, Tex., 1999-2000. Author: Evangelization, 1991, In the Beginning, Vol. 1, 1992, Vol. 2, 1993. Mem. Mayor's Com. for Drug Prevention, Houston, Pasadena Mcpl. Band, Pasadena Mcpl. Orch.; past pres. Summer Repertoire Theatre. Mem. Rotary (youth chair Space Ctr. chpt. 1988-89, bd. dirs. 1990, Presdl. award 1989, 90, chmn. drug awareness program, 1989, 992-93, 93-94, Paul Harris fellow 1993). Avocations: music composition and performance, drama, writing, reading. Home: 112 Mountain Laurel Way Bastrop TX 78602-7468 Office: Lifeline Chaplaincy 1415 Southmore Blvd Houston TX 77004

STEPHENS, D. RICHARD, manufacturing executive; married; 2 children. BS in chem. engring., U. Akron, 1972; MBA, Bowling Green U., 1990; grad. advanced mgmt. program, Harvard Bus. Sch., 1997. Pres. Cooper Tire & Rubber Co., Findlay, Ohio, 2001—, truck devel. chemist, 1978—79, compound devel. mgr., 1979—85, product devel. mgr., 1985—90, dir. tech., 1990—94, v.p. tech., 1994—2000, v.p. tech. and comm. tire oper., 2000; pres. Cooper Tire & Rubber Co., Internat. Tire Dvsn., 2000—01. Mem. bd. trustees U. Findlay, 2000—; mem. Findlay-Hancock County C. of C., 1992; mem. bd. trustees Vennard Coll. Fin. Com., 1994—96. Office: Cooper Tire Rubber Co 701 Lima Ave Findlay OH 45840

STEPHENS, DEBORAH LYNN, health company executive; b. Newton, Iowa, May 30, 1952; d. Clarence Harry and Nancy Elizabeth (Gass) Wright; m. David K. Brender, Dec. 18, 1971 (div.); m. Michael E. Stephens, May 21, 1988 (div.). BS, U. Iowa, 1974; postgrad., U. Wis., Milw., 1978-80, U. Calif., Berkeley, 1987. Asst. to dean of fin. U. Iowa Coll. Medicine, Iowa City, 1975-77; contract audit acct. Miller Brewing Co., Milw., 1977-79; asst. contr. Unicare Health Facilities, Milw., 1979-81; v.p. fin. Sacred Heart Rehab. Hosp., Milw., 1981-84; COO, exec. v.p. Sacred Heart Rehab. Hosp., Med. Rehab. Inst., Milw., 1984-88; CEO, prin. founding mem., chmn. bd. Behavioral Health Sys., Birmingham, Ala., 1989—, also bd. dirs. Cons. on rehab., fin., multi-corp. planning and zero-base budgeting 1988; founding mem. Am. Rehab. Network, Inc., Washington, 1986-87; mem. oral exam. bd. City of Milw., 1984-86, Jefferson County, Ala., 1995; mem. prospective payment adv. com. HHS, Washington, 1986; nat. presenter on zero-base budgeting, corp. reorgns., managed care, and planning. Contbr. articles to profl. jours. Mem. healthcare cost containment com. Bus. Coun. Ala., Rotary Club of Birmingham. Named one of Top 5 Thriving Bus. Women in Birmingham, Bus. to Bus., 1995, one of Top 78 nat. Entrepreneurs, Entrepreneur mag., 1996; featured in Healthwatch, Open Minds, Entrepreneur mag., Birmingham Post Herald, Birmingham News. Mem. Hosp. Fin. Mgmt. Assn. (governing bd. 1981-88), Nat. Forensic League (life), Nat. Assn. Accts., Nat. Assn. Rehab. Facilities (prospective payment adv. bd. 1986-88, com. on med. oriented facilities 1983-88), Ga. Managed Care Assn. (bd. dirs. 1995), Birmingham C. of C. (Small Bus. Person of Yr. award 1995), Venture Club, Kappa Kappa Gamma. Avocations: dance, skiing, jogging, travel, reading. Office: Behavioral Health Systems 2 Metroplex Dr Ste 500 Birmingham AL 35209-6812 Office Phone: 205-879-1150. E-mail: deborahlstephens@aol.com., dstephens@bhs-inc.com.

STEPHENS, DONALD L., JR., lawyer; b. New Orleans, Sept. 30, 1949; s. Donald L. and Charline Stephens; m. Barbara A. Beran, Aug. 5, 1978. BS, Calif. State U., Fullerton, 1976; JD, Northwest Sch. Law, Lewis and Clark Coll., 1990. Bar: Oreg. 1990, US Patent and Trademark Office 1989. With U. Wis. McArdle Lab. for Cancer Rsch., 1976—80; project engr. Crystal Specialties, Inc., Portland, Oreg., 1981—82; tech. affairs mgr. Pirdy, Inc., 1987; engr. CD Med., Inc., 1982—88; tech. cons. Klarquist Sparkman LLP, 1988—89, patent agent, 1989—90, assoc. attorney, 1990—95, partner, 1995—. Contbr. articles prof. jours. Recipient Eagle Scout, Boy Scouts of Am., 1964, Nat. Rsch. Svc. award, NIH, 1976—78; Grad. fellowship finalist, NSF, 1976. Mem.: Am. Optical Soc., Soc. Photo-Optical Instrumentation Engrs., NY Acad. of Scis. Avocations: history, architecture, art, music. Office: Klarquist Sparkman LLP 121 SW Salmon St Ste 1600 Portland OR 97204 Office Phone: 503-226-7391. E-mail: donald.stephens@klarquist.com.

STEPHENS, DONALD R(ICHARDS), investor; b. San Francisco, June 28, 1938; s. Donald Lewis and Anona Marie (O'Leary) S.; m. Christina Brinkman, Sept. 11, 1971 (div. 1996); m. Patricia Hamilton, Oct. 21, 2000; children: Lane B., Justin H., Nicholas W., Adam H. BS, U. So. Calif., 1961; JD, Hastings Coll., 1969. Pres. Campodonico & Stephens, San Francisco, 1963-65; pres., owner Union Investment Co., San Francisco, 1966-69; assoc. Law Offices of Louis O. Kelso, 1969-72; pres. D.R. Stephens & Co., San Francisco, 1972—. Chmn., CEO Bank of San Francisco Co., 1978-91, also bd. dirs.; chmn. N.Am. Trust REIT, also bd. dirs.; bd. dirs. Charles Schwab Family of Funds Inc. Bd. dirs. Bay Area Coun.; trustee St. Francis Meml. Hosp., San Francisco, 1976-82; mem. policy adv. bd. U. Calif., 1985—. Mem. Urban Land Inst., World Bus. Coun., Bohemian Club, Mayacana Golf Club, Reserve Palm Desert, Napa Valley Reserve. Republican. Presbyterian. Avocations: tennis, golf, bridge. E-mail: drs1220@aol.com.

STEPHENS, EDWARD CARL, communications educator, writer; b. L.A., July 27, 1924; s. Carl Edward and Helen Mildred (Kerner) S.; children: Edward, Sarah, Matthew. AB, Occidental Coll., 1947; MS, Northwestern U., 1955. Advt. exec. Dancer-Fitzgerald-Sample Inc., N.Y.C., 1955-64; prof. Medill Sch. Journalism, Northwestern U., Evanston, Ill., 1964-76; prof., chmn. dept. advt. S.I. Newhouse Sch. Pub. Communications, Syracuse U., N.Y., 1976-80, dean, 1980-89; prof. comms. S.I. Newhouse Sch. Pub. Comms. Syracuse U., 1990-92, prof. emeritus, 1992—. Cons. Foote, Cone & Belding Communications Author: (novels) A Twist of Lemon, 1958, One More Summer, 1960, Blow Negative!, 1962, Roman Joy, 1965, A Turn in the Dark Wood, 1968, The Submariner, 1974, (nonfiction) Submarines, 1960. Mem. George Polk Awards Com. With USN, 1943-46, 1950-53. Capt. USNR (ret.). Decorated Purple Heart Mem. Am. Acad. Advt. (pres. 1976-77), Assn. Edn. Journalism and Mass Communication, The Army and Navy Club, Authors League, Century Club of Syracuse, Alpha Tau Omega. Episcopalian. Personal E-mail: stephens@dreamscape.com.

STEPHENS, ELISA, college president; Pres. Acad. of Art Coll., San Francisco, 1992—. Office: 79 New Montgomery St 6th Fl San Francisco CA 94105-3410

STEPHENS, ELTON BRYSON, bank executive, service and manufacturing company executive; b. Clio, Ala., Aug. 4, 1911; s. James Nelson and Clara (Stuckey) S.; m. Alys Varian Robinson, Nov. 28, 1935; children: James Thomas, Jane Stephens Comer, Elton Bryson Jr., Dell Stephens Brooke. BA, Birmingham-So. Coll., 1932, LLD (hon.), 1977; LL.B., U. Ala., 1936, LHD (hon.), 1990; grad., Advanced Mgmt. Program, Harvard U., 1960; LHD (hon.), Faulkner U., 1992. Bar: Ala. 1936. Regional dir. Keystone Readers Service, Birmingham, 1937-43; partner, then founder and pres. Mil. Service Co., Inc. (predecessor of EBSCO Industries, Inc.), Birmingham, 1943-58; founder EBSCO Industries, Inc., and affiliates, 1958, since pres., chmn. bd.; now chmn. bd. EBSCO Industries, Inc. and affiliates, Birmingham. Bd. dirs. R.A. Brown Ins. Agy. Ltd., 1966—; chmn. EBSCO Investment Svc., Inc., 1959—, Canebsco Subscription Svc., Toronto, Ont., Can., 1972—; founder, chmn. Ala. Bancorp divsn. Highland Bank; founder EBSCO Savs. and Profit Sharing Trust, Ala. Bancorp Savs. and Profit Sharing Trust. Mem. fin. and investment com., past chmn. bd. trustees, chmn. exec. com. Birmingham-So. Coll.; trustee So. Research Inst.; former pres., chmn. bd. trustee Birmingham Met. YMCA; mem. bd., chmn. econ. pension com. Tenn.-Tombigbee Waterway Authority; founder % Clubs of Ala., founder United Art Fund/Met. Arts Council; vice chmn., bd. dirs., hon. chmn.; vice chmn. Am. Coun. Arts, 1990-95; fundraiser Rebirth Symphony, Birmingham. Elton B. Stephens Expressway named in his honor, 1970, Elton B. Stephens Library, Clio, 1979. Mem. Birmingham C. of C. (bd. dirs.), The Club, Birmingham Press Club, Summit Club, Mountain Brook Country Club (Ala.), Rotary (pres. Homewood, Ala. 1979-80, Paul Harris fellow), Ala. Symphonic Assn. (chmn., CEI, prin. fund raiser), Ala. Acad. Honor, Alpha Tau Omega (past chmn. nat. found.), Omicron Delta Kappa, Phi Alpha Delta. Methodist. *Invest/reinvest earnings to create employment/profits for growth/expansion. Support worthwhile projects including but not limited to: education, health, religion, needy, cultural, arts, boys/girls clubs, law enforcement, conservation, nature, water resources. Share profits and protect the welfare and health of your employees with a major catastrophic medical program. These philosophies built a company I started in 1943 with capital of $5,000 and sales under $1,000,000 with under 20 employees to annual sales of over $860,000,000 and 3400 employees with adequate capital from earnings and borrowing to continue growth. EBSCO operates world wide.*

STEPHENS, GARY RALPH, American literature and journalism educator; b. Wichita, Kans., Mar. 4, 1943; s. Hubert Hal and Iris Lenore (Edgar) S.; m. Swati Niru Desai, May 13, 1978; children: Anaar, Joshua. AB, Wichita State U., 1965; MA, Brandeis U., 1969, PhD, 1972. Asst. prof. English, Queens Coll., CUNY, Flushing, 1971-75, N.Y. Inst. Tech., Old Westbury, 1976-81, assoc. prof., 1982-88, chmn. dept., 1979—93; prof. NY Inst. Tech., Old Westbury, 1989—, chmn. dept. NYC, 1999—2003; assoc. in journalism Grad. Sch. Journalism, Columbia U., N.Y.C., 1986-97. Cons. in field. Contbr. articles to profl. publs. J.W. Fulbright fellow India, 1993; fellow Woodrow Wilson Found., 1965, Rockefeller Found., 1966, NEH, 1981. Office: NY Inst Tech 1855 Broadway New York NY 10023-7692

STEPHENS, GEORGE EDWARD, JR., lawyer; b. Lawrence, Kans., Mar. 26, 1936; s. George Edward and Mary Helen (Houghton) Stephens; m. Gretel Geiser, Dec. 31, 1965; children: Thaddeus Geiser, Edward Houghton, Mary Schoentgen. Student, U. Colo., Boulder, 1954-57, U. Colo., Denver, 1957-59; LLB, Stanford U., 1962. Bar: Calif. 1963, U.S. Dist. Ct. (cen. dist.) Calif. 1963, U.S. Ct. Appeals (9th cir.) 1971. Law clk. to judge U.S. Dist. Ct., L.A., 1962-64; assoc. ptnr. Pollock & Palmer, L.A., 1964-69; ptnr. Gates, Morris, Merrill & Stephens, L.A., 1969-72, Paul, Hastings, Janofsky & Walker LLP, L.A., 1972—. Mem. Coordinating Coun. on Lawyer Competence, Conf. Chief Justices, 1983-86; chmn. probate sect. L.A. County Bar Assn., 1979-80. Nat. chmn. Stanford (Calif.) U. Law Fund Quad Program, 1980-87; mem. bd. visitors Stanford Law Sch., 1982-85; founder mus. Contemporary Art, L.A., 1982; bd. dirs. Pacific Oaks Coll., 1990-94. Recipient Stanford Assocs. award, 1982. Fellow: Fellows of Contemporary Art (bd. dirs. 1991—92), Internat. Acad. Probate and Trust Law, Am. Coll. Trust and Estates Counsel, Am. Bar Found.; mem.: Stanford Law Soc. (pres. 1972—73, chmn. 1998—99), ABA (chmn. standing com. specialization 1979—82, standing com. lawyer referral svcs. 1969—76, consortium delivery legal svcs. and the pub. 1979—82), The Athenaeum, Valley Hunt (Pasadena, Calif.), Annandale Golf (Pasadena, Calif.), Chancery (L.A.). Episcopalian. Office: Paul Hastings Janofsky & Walker LLP 515 S Flower St 25th Fl Los Angeles CA 90071-2300

STEPHENS, JACK EDWARD, civil engineer, consultant; b. Eaton, Ohio, Aug. 17, 1923; s. Harry M. and Mary Elizabeth (Galloway) S.; m. Virginia May Ives, June 19, 1948; children: Jay Edward, Jerry Edward, Jill Louise, Jana Lynn. BS in Engring., U. Conn., 1947; MS in Engring., Purdue U., 1955, PhD, 1959. Registered profl. engr., Conn. Jr. hwy. engr. Conn. Dept. Hwys., New Haven, 1949-50; instr. U. Conn., Storrs, 1947-48, asst. prof., then assoc. prof. civil engring., 1950-62, prof. civil engring., 1962-88, head civil engring. dept., 1965-72, prof. emeritus, 1989—, dir. Conn. Advanced Pavement Lab., 1995—2004; sr. rsch. advisor Conn. Advanced Pavement Lab., 2004—. Soils cons. A.J. Macchi Engrs., Hartford, Conn., 1958-65; pavement cons. Conn. Dept. Hwys., Hartford, 1962-63, Consumers Union Auto Test Facility, Colchester, Conn., 1991—; prin. Jack E. Stephens Soil and Materials Test Lab., Storrs, 1958—. Contbr. jour. articles to Procs. Assn. Asphalt Paving Tech., Transp. Rsch. Bd., others. Cpl. U.S. Army, 1943-46, ETO. Fellow Automobile Safety Found., Washington, 1958-59; recipient citation for tchg. excellence Western Electric Fund, Washington, 1974. Mem. ASCE (life, B. Wright award Conn. sect. 1989), NSPE, AAUP, Assn. Asphalt Paving Tech. (life), Conn. Acad. Sci. and Engring. (chmn. transp. com. 1984-94), Conn. Soc. Profl. Engrs., Am. Rd. and Transp. Builders Assn., Transp. Rsch. Bd., Am. Assn. Engring. Edn., Am. Soc. for Photogrammetry and Remote Sensing, Sigma Xi. Office: U Conn Transp Inst Box U-202 Storrs Mansfield CT 06269-5202 E-mail: jack.stephens@uconn.edu.

STEPHENS, JAMES T. publishing executive; b. 1939; married. BA in Bus. Adminstrn., Yale U., 1961; MBA, Harvard U., 1964. With Ebsco Industries Inc., Birmingham, Ala., 1961—, asst. v.p., 1966-67, v.p., 1967-70, exec. v.p., 1970—71, now pres., also bd. dirs., 1971—. Office: EBSCO Industries Inc 5724 Highway 280 E Birmingham AL 35242-6818 also: PO Box 1943 Birmingham AL 35201-1943

STEPHENS, JAY B. lawyer, manufacturing executive; b. Akron, Iowa, Nov. 5, 1946; s. Lyle R. and Marie (Borchers) S. BA magna cum laude, Harvard U., 1968, JD cum laude, 1973. Bar: D.C. 1973, U.S. Supreme Ct., 1979. Assoc. Wilmer, Cutler & Pickering, Washington, 1973-74; asst. spl. prosecutor Watergate Spl. Prosecution Force, Washington, 1974-75; assoc. gen. counsel Overseas Pvt. Investment Corp., Washington, 1976-77; asst. U.S. atty. Dept. Justice, Washington, 1977-81, spl. counsel to asst. atty. gen., 1981-83, dep. assoc. atty. gen., 1983-85, assoc. dep. atty. gen., 1985-86; dep. counsel to Pres. Reagan, 1986-88; U.S. atty. for D.C. Office U.S. Atty., 1988-93; ptnr. Pillsbury Madison & Sutro, Washington, 1993-97; v.p. and dep. gen. counsel Honeywell, Morristown, NJ, 1997—2001; assoc. atty. gen. U.S. Dept. Justice, Washington, 2001—02; sr. v.p., gen. counsel Raytheon Co., Lexington, Mass., 2002—. Dir. Nat. Legal Ctr. for Non Pub. Interest, New Eng. Legal Found. Contbr. articles to profl. publs. Knox fellow Oxford, Eng., 1968-69. Mem. D.C. Bar Assn., Asst. U.S. Atty. Assn., Nat. Assn. Former U.S. Attys., Federalist Soc., Supreme Ct. Hist. Soc., Phi Beta Kappa. Republican. Presbyterian. Office: Raytheon Co 870 Winter St Waltham MA 02451 Office Phone: 781-522-5096. Office Fax: 781-522-6471.

STEPHENS, JAY MARTIN, business owner; b. Indpls., May 10, 1942; s. Walter Eugene and Mary Ann (Murray) S.; m. Rosalind Cabuco Espedido, Febr. 16, 1995; children: James, Jon, Christopher. BS, Ind. U., Bloomington, 1981. Major Ind. State Police, Indpls., 1966-86; cons. Govt. U.S. Virgin Islands, 1987-94; bus. owner Stephens Enterprises, Bloomington, 1995—. Com. chair Navy League of the U.S., St. Thomas, 1989—; mem. bd. dirs. United Svc. Orgn., St. Thomas, 1989-90, Rotary Club II, 1988-94, United Way, 1988-94. Mem. Indpls. Athletic Club, Fraternal Order Police, Ancient Order Hibernians, Knights of Columbus, Navy League of the U.S., Ind. U. Alumni Assn. Avocations: fishing, sailing, travelling/. Office: PO Box 5111 Bloomington IN 47407-5111

STEPHENS, JERRY WAYNE, librarian, library director; b. Birmingham, Ala., Sept. 10, 1949; s. William Larkin and Odell (Kerr) S.; m. Lisa Brown, June 2, 1972; children— Jeramy Wayne, Elizabeth Ashley, John Larkin BS in Acctg., U. Ala.-Birmingham, 1974, MBA, 1976; M.L.S., U. Ala., 1977, PhD in Adminstrn. Higher Edn., 1982. Svc. mgr. Hammond Organ Studios, Birmingham, 1973-74; acct. Mervyn Sterne Libr., U. Ala., Birmingham, 1974-75, asst. to dir., 1975-76, asst. dir., 1976 85, libr., dir., 1985—, interim fiscal officer Univ. Coll. U. Ala., Birmingham, 1982, interim asst. v.p. for acad. affairs, 1989-91. Vice chmn. Network Acad. Librs., 1985-86, 95-96, chmn., 1986-88, 96, 2000-01; cons. Birmingham Pub. Libr., 1977—; cons. Southeastern Libr. Assn., Atlanta, 1979-80; bd. dirs. Southeastern Libr. Network, treas., 1992-93, chmn., 1993-94; mem. user's coun. Online Computer Libr. Ctr., 1997—, pres.-elect, 2000-01, pres., 2001-2002, bd. trustees, 2002—. Contbr. articles to profl. publs. Sponsored exec. United Way, Birmingham, 1978, sr. exec., 1982; foster parent Dept. Pensions and Securities, Birmingham, 1982-83, elder Homewood Cumberland Presbyn. Ch., Birmingham, 1982-84, 88-90. With USN, 1972-73 Named one of Outstanding Young Men Am., U.S. Jaycees, 1978, 79 Mem. ALA, SE Libr. Assn., Ala. Libr. Assn. (treas. 1977-78), Am Mgmt. Assn. Avocations: camping; softball. Home: 2621 Kemp Ct Birmingham AL 35226-1982 Office: U Ala-Birmingham Mervyn H Sterne Libr University Sta Birmingham AL 35294-0001 Office Phone: 205-934-6360. E-mail: jerry@beowulf.mhsl.uab.edu., jerryw@uab.edu.

STEPHENS, JOSEPH, psychiatrist, researcher; b. Frederick, Md., Apr. 9, 1927; s. Joseph Snyder and Mazie Naomi Stephens. BA, John Hopkins U., 1948, MD, 1952, MusM, 1959. Assoc. prof. psychiatry John Hopkins U., 1967. Contbr. articles to profl. jours. Lt. USNR, 1954—56. Recipient Honorary Denison Strong Fellow, 1952. Fellow: Am. Psychiat. Assn. (life); mem.: Parlovian Soc., Am. Psychopathology Assn. Avocation: music. Home: 1616 Bolton St Baltimore MD 21217

STEPHENS, KITTY FRANCES, academic administrator; b. Thomasville, N.C. d. Willie Edward and Dorothy Lee Harper; children: Rodney, Jamel. BS, Livingstone Coll., 1970; MPA, U. Balt., 1981. Unit adminstr. Hosp. U. Md., Balt., 1971-79, asst. to dir. ops. Hosp., 1979-82, bus. mgr. Sch. Medicine, 1991-93; asst. to chief solid waste Howard County Govt., Ellicott City, Md., 1984-90; customer svc. rep. Am. W. Airlines, Balt., 1990-93; budget analyst MD. State Dept. Human Resources, Balt., 1993-95; adminstrv. officer Md. Income Maintenance Adminstrn., Balt., 1995; ops. mgr. Cmty. Inst. Behavioral Svcs., Balt., 1995-96; office asst. N.C. A&T State U., Greensboro, 1997; grants and contracts mgr. Bennett Coll., Greensboro, 1997-99; asst. v.p. devel. Johnson C. Smith U., Charlotte, N.C., 1999—. Kresge fellow Kresge Found. and So. Edn. Found., 2000. Mem. Coun. Advancement and Support Edn., Nat. Assn. Title III Adminstrs., Nat. Sponsored Programs Adminstrs. Alliance, Delta Sigma Theta. Democrat. Methodist. Avocations: travel, reading. Office: Johnson C Smith U 100 Beatties Ford Rd Charlotte NC 28216-5398 Fax: 704-378-3521. E-mail: kstephens@jcsu.edu.

STEPHENS, LARRY DEAN, engineer, consultant; b. Sterling, Colo., Sept. 1, 1937; s. John Robert and Shirley Berniece (Rudel) S.; m. Carol Ann Wertz, Sept. 1, 1957 (div. May 1975); children: Deborah Lynn, Janell Diane, Dana Larry, Hilary Elizabeth Melton; m. Neslihan Ozlen, Aug. 18, 2000. BS in Engring., Colo. State U., 1960; MBA, U. Colo., 1967. Registered profl. engr., Colo. Engr. Bur. Reclamation, Denver, 1960-90, cons., 1991—. Exec. v.p. U.S. Com. on Irrigation and Drainage, Denver, 1971—; exec. dir. U.S. Soc. on Dams, Denver, 1986—. V.p. Internat. Commn. on Irrigation and Drainage, 1989-92. With USNG, 1961-62. Mem. Am. Soc. Agrl. Engrs., Assn. State Dam Safety Ofcls., Colorado River Water Users Assn., Coun. on Engring. and Sci. Soc. Execs., Univ. Club Denver. Republican. Methodist. Home: 1625 Larimer St Apt 1505 Denver CO 80202-1532 Office: USCID 1616 17th St Ste 483 Denver CO 80202-1277 E-mail: stephens@uscid.org.

STEPHENS, LAURENCE DAVID, JR., linguist, investor, oil industry executive; b. Dallas, July 26, 1947; s. Laurence D. Sr. and Amy Belle (Schickram) S.; m. Susan Leigh Foutz, Apr. 16, 1988; 1 child, Laurence David III. MA, Stanford U., 1972, PhD, 1976. Cert. minerals mgr. Nat. Assn. Royalty Owners, 2003. Vis. fellow Yale U., New Haven, summer 1979; rsch. fellow U. S.C., Columbia, 1980; asst. prof. U. N.C., Chapel Hill, 1982-88, assoc. prof., 1989—; pres. Colgate Mgmt. Co., Inc., Dallas, 1997—; gen. ptnr. Moorman, Schickram & Stephens, Ltd., Dallas, 1997—; mgr. Stephens Resources, LLC, 2004—; v.p., mgr. 4025 Colgate LLC, 2004—, 3712 Wentwood, LLC, 2004—. Mgr. Stephens Resources LLC; mgr. to v.p. Colgate LLC. Co-author: Two Studies in Latin Phonology, 1977, Language and Metre, 1984, The Prosody of Greek Speech, 1994, Discontinuous Syntax, 1999: editor ann. vol. L'Année Philologique, 1987-92; contbr. numerous articles to profl. jours. Mem. Univ. Pk. Cmty. League, Park Cities Hist. Soc., Nat. Trust for Hist. Preservation, Washington, 1989—, The Dallas Symphony Assn. Ann. Fund, Metro. Opera Guild, N.Y.C., 1992—, Wythe County VA Hist. Soc., 1998—. Grantee L'Année Philologique, NEH, 1987-89, 89-91, 91-93. Mem. Am. Philol. Assn., Greek and Latin Linguistic Assn. (chmn. 1987-92), N.Y. Acad. Scis., Indogermanische Gesellschaft, Internat. Soc. Bibliographic Classique, Arabian Horse Assn., Sigma Xi. Achievements include discovery of language universal regularities concerning labiovelar phonemes, and rules of palatalization, the law of catathesis in Greek (pitch lowering), and grammatical, semantic, pragmatic (information structure) regularities of discontinuous constituency and nonconfigurational syntactic structures in Greek; co-developer of Justeson-Stephens probability distribution for cognates between unrelated languages, Justeson-Stephens probability distribution of the numbers of vowels, consonants, and total phonological inventory size in the languages of the world; research on the law of the quantitative form of diachronic polysemy growth, semantic universals of aspect and modality, universals of writing systems and their evolution. Office: Univ NC Chapel Hill Dept Classics Cb 3145 212 Murphey Hl Chapel Hill NC 27599-0001 Address: Moorman Schickram & Stephens Ltd 3319 Greenbrier Dr Dallas TX 75225 Home: PO Box 538 3286 Austinville Rd Max Meadows VA 24360-0538 Office Phone: 276-228-1276. Personal E-mail: lsteph8694@aol.com.

STEPHENS, MARTIN R. state official; b. Ogden, Utah, Mar. 26, 1954; m. Carole Stephens. BSin Bus. Adminstrn., Webder State U. Mayor Farr West City, Utah, 1986-88; mem. hos. reps. State of Utah, 1988—. house speaker, 1999—. Coun. mem. Farr West City, 1984-85, vice chair Weber Area Coun. of Govts., 1986-87, chair, 1988, elected Utah rep. White House Conf. Small Bus., Washington, 1986, majority leader, 1993-94, chair legis. mgmt. com., judiciary standing com., govt. ops. standing com., retirement com., exec. appropriations com. (chair 1993-94), commerce and revenue appropriations com., 1999—. Recipient Roy B. Gibson Freedom of Information award Soc. Profl. Journalists, 1991. Office: Utah Legis 318 State Capitol Salt Lake City UT 84114 also: 3159 N Higley Rd Farr West UT 84404-9380

STEPHENS, MICHAEL DEAN, hospital administrator; b. Salt Lake City, May 1, 1942; married. B, Columbia U., 1966, MHA, 1970. Adminstrv. resident Mt. Sinai Med. Ctr., N.Y.C., 1969-70; asst. adminstr. Greenville (S.C.) Gen. Hosp., 1970-71, assoc. adminstr., 1971-72, adminstr., 1972-75; pres., ceo. Hoag Meml. Hosp.-Presbyn., Newport Beach, Calif., 1975—. Trustee Am. Hosp. Assn. Mem. Am. Coll. Healthcare Execs. Home: 900 Alder Pl Newport Beach CA 92660-4121 Office: Hoag Meml Hosp Presbyn 1 Hoag Blvd PO Box 6100 Newport Beach CA 92658-6100

STEPHENS, MICHAEL THORYNE, librarian; b. Cedartown, Ga., June 14, 1955; s. Thomas Herschel and Bertie (Moncrief) S.; m. Cindy Yvonne Coley July 1, 1977 (div. Apr. 1986); children: Jada, Joey. AA, Floyd Coll., 1993; BA, Jacksonville State U., 1996. Mgr. Rite Aid Corp., Rome, Ga., 1993—94, Revco Drug Co., Rome, 1996; libr., reference serials specialist Rome-Floyd County Libr., Rome, 1999—. Mem. Ga. Libr. Assn., Pi Sigma Alpha, Omicron Delta Kappa. Democrat. Baptist. Avocations: fishing, hiking, climbing, darts. Home: 233 Houseal St Cedartown GA 30125-2831 Office: Sara Hightower Regional Library 205 Riverside Pky Rome GA 30161 Fax: 706-236-4605. E-mail: stephen_m76@hotmail.com.

STEPHENS, NORVAL BLAIR, JR., marketing consultant; b. Chgo., Nov. 20, 1928; s. Norval Blair and Ethel Margaret (Lewis) S.; m. Diane Forst, Sept. 29, 1951; children: Jill E., John G., Sandra J. (dec.), Katherine B., James N. BA, DePauw U., 1951; MBA, U. Chgo., 1959. Asst. to v.p. ops. Walgreen Drug Co., Chgo., 1953-56; with Needham, Harper Worldwide (formerly Needham, Harper & Steers), Chgo., 1956-86, v.p., 1964-70, sr. v.p., 1970-72, exec. v.p. internat., 1972-74, exec. v.p., mng. dir., 1974-75; exec. v.p. Chgo. office Needham, Harper & Steers, 1975-82, exec. v.p. internat., 1982-86; also dir.; pres. Deltacom, N.Y.C., 1971-76; pres. Norval Stephens Co., 1987—90; exec. dir. Internat. Comms. Agy. Network, 1988-98. Recipient Rector award DePauw U., 1976, Old Gold Goblet award for outstanding svc. DePauw U., 1994, Outstanding Greek Vol. award N.Am. Interfraternity Conf., 2001, Carol Bese award Barrington Area C. of C., 2004; named Young Man of Yr., Arlington Heights Jaycees, 1964, Barrington Area Citizen of Yr., 1999; named to Sr. Hall of Fame, Barrington, Ill., 2002. Mem. DePauw Alumni Assn. (pres. 1977-79), Phi Beta Kappa, Delta Tau Delta (bd. dirs. edn. found. 1987—, vice chmn. 1994-95, chmn. 1995—, 2d v.p. Arch chpt. 1988-90, 1st v.p. 1990-92, pres. 1992-94). Republican. Methodist. Home: 107 Fox Hunt Trail Barrington IL 60010-3418 Personal E-mail: norval@norvalstephens.com. *I view my life not as a passage but a daily renewing challenge: to be better; to be a better father, husband, brother, son; to return each day an honest day's work; to bear witness to my beliefs and my faith; to serve my fellowman. I seek a whole life and a life of rewarding parts, each a lesson and an experience.*

STEPHENS, OTIS HAMMOND, JR., political science and law educator; b. East Point, Ga., Sept. 20, 1936; s. Otis Hammond and Mary Margaret (Fisher) S.; m. Linda Duren, June 18, 1960 (dec. July 1988); children: Ann S. Henderson, Carol S. Frazier; m. Mary Torpey Ballard, Oct. 21, 1989. AB cum laude, U. Ga., 1957, MA, 1958; PhD, Johns Hopkins U., 1963; JD with high honors, U. Tenn., 1983, Bar: Tenn. 1984. Grad. rsch. asst. U. Ga., 1957-58; jr. instr. Johns Hopkins U., 1959-61; asst. prof. to prof. Ga. So. Coll., 1962-67; assoc. prof. U. Tenn., Knoxville, 1967-71, prof., 1971—, Lindsay young prof., 1981-82, alumni disting. svc. prof. polit. sci., 1983—, acting head dept., 1986-88; Russell Sage Found. resident in law and social sci. Harvard Law Sch., 1975-76; assoc. dean Coll. of Arts and Scis. Univ. Tenn., 1996—2000; resident scholar of Constitutional Law Coll. Law, Univ. Tenn., 2000—. Lectr. U.S. Govt. Mgmt. Devel. Ctr., 1972-96; panel mem., chmn. various assns. Author: The Supreme Court and Confessions of Guilt, 1973; co-author: (with Gregory J. Rathjen) The Supreme Court and the Allocation of Constitutional Power, 1980; (with John M. Scheb, II) American Constitutional Law: Essays and Cases, 1988, American Constitutional Law, 1993, 3d edit., 2003; contbr. articles to profl. jours., chpts. to books. Pres. Nat. Accreditation Coun. for Agys. Serving the Blind and Visually Handicapped, 1979-83; pres. Am. Coun. of Blind, 1987-89; trustee Am. Found. for Blind, 1987-99, exec. com., 1992-99; mem. Gov.'s Adv.Com. on Fair Employment Opportunity, State of Tenn., 1987-95. Ford Found. pub. affairs grantee, 1961, faculty rsch. grantee summers 1968, 69, 70, 74, 91, Coll. of Law, 2003, 04; recipient Migel medal Am. Found. Blind, 2001; grad. fellow Am. Found. Blind, 1962, Johns Hopkins U., 1958-62; liberal arts fellow law and polit. sci. Harvard Law Sch., 1975-76; recipient Acad. Achievement award Recording for the Blind, Inc., 1962, Alumni Assn. Outstanding Teaching award U. Tenn., 1977, 84, L.R. Hesler award, 1998-99, Macebearer, 2001-02. Mem. AAUP (pres. U. Tenn. chpt. 1985-86), ABA, Am. Polit. Sci. Assn. (exec. coun. pub. law sect. 1990-92), Tenn. Polit. Sci. Assn. (pres. 1991-92), So. Polit. Sci. Assn., Tenn. Bar Assn., Knoxville Bar Assn., Phi Beta Kappa (pres. Epsilon of Tenn. chpt. 1981-82), Golden Key, Order of Coif, Omicron Delta Kappa, Phi Kappa Phi, Pi Sigma Alpha. Home: 1141 Southgate Rd Knoxville TN 37919-7647 Office: U Tenn Coll of Law Ste 377 1505 W Cumberland Ave Knoxville TN 37996

STEPHENS, PAUL ALFRED, dentist; b. Muskogee, Okla., Feb. 28, 1921; s. Lonny and Maudie Janie (Wynn) S.; m. Lola Helena Byrd, May 7, 1950; children: Marsha Stephens Wilson, Paul Alfred Jr., Derek M. BS cum laude, Howard U., 1942, DDS, 1945. Instr. dentistry Howard U., Washington, 1945-46; gen practice dentistry Gary, Ind., 1947—; chmn. bd. Assocs. Med. Ctr., Inc., Gary. Sec. Gary Ind. Sch. Bldg. Corp., 1967-85; pres. Bd. Health, 1973-81; Ind. State Bd. Dental Examiners, 1975-83. Mem. adv. bd. Ind. U.-Purdue U. Calumet Campus, 1973; bd. dirs. Urban League Northwest Ind.; pres. Gary Ednl. Devel. Found., 1990—. With AUS, 1942-44. Fellow Internat. Coll. Dentists, Acad. Dentistry Internat., Acad. Gen. Dentistry (pres. chpt. 1973, nat. chmn. dental care com. 1977, Midwestern v.p., nat. bd. dirs. 1984-89, v.p. 1990-91, pres. 1992-93), Am. Coll. Dentists; mem. ADA, Nat. Dental Assn., N.W. Ind. Dental Assn. (bd. dirs., pres. 1976-77, Disting. Svc. award 1993), Am. Soc. Anesthesia in Dentistry, Am. Acad. Radiology, Gary C. of C., Alpha Phi Alpha (pres. Gary Ednl. Found. 1988, pres. Gary Ednl. Devel. Found. 1990—), Acad. Gen. Dentistry (pres. 1992-93). Baptist. Home: 1901 Taft St Gary IN 46404-2759 Office: 2200 Grant St Gary IN 46404-3439

STEPHENS, RALPH RENNE, massage therapy educator; b. Vinton, Iowa, Apr. 19, 1948; s. E.O. and Carrie D. S.; m. Sara Ann Beckley. BS in Indsl. Edn., Iowa State U., 1971; Natural Therapeutics Splst., N Mex. Sch. Natural Therapeutics, 1986. Lic. massage therapist Iowa, N.Mex., massage therapy instr. N.Mex., cert. therapeutic massage and bodywork Nat. Cert. Bd. Therapeutic Massage and Bodywork, St. John method neuromuscular therapy. Pvt. practice Helping Hands Body Therapy Ctr., Iowa City, 1986-92; staff instr. Carlson Coll. Massage Therapy, Cedar Rapids, Iowa, 1987-92; instr. St. John Neuromuscular Therapy Seminars, 1991-99; pvt. practice Ralph Stephens Seminars, Cedar Rapids, 1992—; mem. tchg. staff Himalayan Inst. Yoga Sci. and Philosophy of U.S.A., Honesdale, Pa., 2001—. Dir. sports massage Iowa City Annual Hospice Road Race Com., 1986-88; cons., sys. engr., equipment supplier to workshop and seminar presenters Helping Hands Audio/Video, 1989-94; chairperson Iowa Bd. Examiners Massage Therapy, Des Moines, 1995-2000; sec. Iowa Bd. Examiners Massage Therapy, Des Moines, 1992-95; presenter in field. Author: Massage Therapy Principles and Practice, 1999, 2d edit., 2003; contbr. articles to profl. jours.; prodr. videos Seated Therapeutic Massage, Vol. 1, Back and Neck, 1995, Vol. 2, Shoulder, 1996, Vol. 3, Forearm, Wrist and Hand, 1996, Feel Great Hands on Health Series (4 tapes) Feel Great Every Day, Posture Yourself and Move Right, Massage Made Easy, Stretching that Works, 1998, Event Sports Massage, 1998, Side-Lying Therapeutic Massage, 1999, Therapeutic Sports Massage for the Lower Extremity, 1999, Anatomy of the Lower Extremity, 1999, Medical Massage for the Cervical Region, 2001, Medical Massage for the Lumbar Region, 2002, Golf-Flexology, 2003; monthly editl. columnist Massage Today, 2000—, quar. columnist Up Close and Personal Newsletter, 2002-. Trustee Am. Massage Therapy Assn. Found., 1990-93, 95-96; chairperson Walford (Iowa) Disaster Preparedness Com., 1999. Mem. Am. Massage Therapy Assn. (cert. sports massage therapist, registered massage therapist cert., organizer, chair Iowa sports massage team 1986-88, 1st v.p., convention coord. Iowa chpt. 1988-89, edn. chair Iowa chpt. 1988-89, pres. Iowa chpt. 1989, ctrl. dist. rep. nat. bd. dirs. 1990-93, media spokesperson nat. media rels. team 1991-96, nat. nominating com. 1994, mem.-at-large nat. bd. dirs. 1995-96, nat. nominating commn. 1998-99, Disting. Nat. Officer award 1993, 96, Meritorious award Iowa chpt. 1997, Nat. Meritorious award 1997), Himalayan Inst. Yoga Sci. and Philosophy, tchg. staff, 2000. Republican. Avocations: golf, yoga, meditation. Home: PO Box 8267 Cedar Rapids IA 52408-8267 Office: Ralph Stephens Seminars LLC PO Box 8267 Cedar Rapids IA 52408-8267 Office Phone: 319-350-1590. Business E-Mail: ralph@ralphstephens.com.

STEPHENS, RICHARD H. retired prosecutor; Adj. prof. SMU Sch. of Law & Cox Sch. of Bus.; asst. dist. atty. under Henry Wade; military judge US Navy; private practice Dallas; US Atty., 1993, Northern Dist., Tex. Office: US Attorney 1100 Commerce St 3rd Fl Dallas TX 75242-1699

STEPHENS, ROBERT DAVID, environmental engineering executive; b. La Follette, Tenn., Nov. 8, 1949; s. Robert Oscar and Billie Jean (Maples) S.; m. Donna Jean Reece, July 11, 1970 (div. Apr. 1984). BA in Biology, Berea (Ky.) Coll., 1971; postgrad., U. Cin., 1973-74. Cert. environ. assessor Fla., environ. trainer, registered environ. property assessor, environ. mgr. Environ. specialist Ky. Dept. Health, Ludlow, 1971-74; project mgr. Pedco Environ. Specialists, Cin., 1974-77; environ. control mgr. Mobil Chem. Corp., Richmond, Va., 1978-84; v.p. Environ. Analysis Corp., Richmond, 1984-85; mgr. Environ. Rsch. and Tech. Group GSX Corp., Greensboro, N.C., 1985-86; mgr. regulatory affairs and cmty. rels. Internat. Tech. Corp., Knoxville, Tenn., 1986-88, mgr. environ. studies Tampa, Fla., 1988-90; gen. mgr. First Environment, Inc., Tampa, 1990-91; co-owner Bruder Stephens, Inc., Tampa, 1991—. Faculty Fla. C. of C. Environ. Seminars, 1988—; adj. faculty U. Fla. Treeo Ctr., adj. faculty U. South Fla. Coll. Pub. Health; expert witness in environ. mgmt., sampling and analysis, environ. risk mgmt., indoor air quality, mold & mildew. Contbr. articles to profl. jours. Co-founder Berea Community Theater, 1970; bd. dirs. So. Waste Info. Exch., Inc.; mem. adv. bd. Ctr. for Environ./Occup. Risk Analysis and Mtmg., U. South Fla. Coll. Pub. Health. Mem. Fla. Bar Assn. (assoc., environ and land use sect.), Fla. Environ. Assessors Assn. (pres. 1996-97, bd. dirs. 1993—), Internat. Soc. Tech. & Environ. Profls. (exec. dir.), Water Polution Control Fedn., Va. Orchid Soc. (pres. 1980-85, del. World Orchid Congress, Miami 1984), Ridge Orchid Soc., Tampa Club (bd. dirs. 1999-2002), Outback Bowl (bd. dirs. 2001—). Republican. Avocations: orchid horticulture, guitar. Home: PO Box 145 Mango FL 33550-0145 Office: 14409 N Nebraska Ave Ste A Tampa FL 33613-2226 E-mail: robert@bruderstephens.com.

STEPHENS, ROBERT ERNEST, retired educator; b. Whitley City, Ky., Feb. 9, 1921; s. Arthur and Jewell Reed Stephens; m. Helen Carmack (div. 1972); children: Monty N'Neal, Randy Craig, Robert James; m. Beatrice Lawson, Nov. 8, 1973; 1 child, Robert Ernest Jr. BA, U. Louisville, 1972, MEd, 1974; LLB, Blackstone Sch. Law, 1959. Cert. secondary sch. supr., Ky. Commd. USMC, 1941, advanced through grades to 1st lt.; accountable officer Marine Corp Air Sta., Cherry Point, N.C., 1952; navy supply officer Marine Aircraft Group, Po Hang Dong, Korea, 1953-56; helicopter liaison officer Aviation Supply Office, Phila., 1960-62; ret., 1962; supply chief 47th Rifle Co. Marine Corps Tng. Ctr., Louisville, 1970-72; fin. officer McCreary County Schs., Whitley City, 1972, prin., 1975-79; math. and sci. tchr. Valley High Sch., Louisville, 1973-75; indsl. engr., pers. officer Devoe & Reynolds Co. Chmn. provisioning Sikorsky Helicopters, Bridgeport, Conn., 1961. Author: Historical and Cemetery Inventories, 1996-98 (Genealogy Soc. award 1997), (play) Princess Cornblossom Maiden of the River, 1998, (history) A Lost Heritage for a Changing People, 1999. Sec. Big South Fork Devel., Ky. and Tenn., 1976; chmn., sec., treas. McCreary County Sportsman Club, Whitley City, 1978; chmn. McCreary County Farm Bur., Whitley City, 1980s; mem. Com. to Prepare Ky. Health Plan, Frankfort, 1982, chmn. bd. suprs. McCreary County Soil Conservation Dist., Whitley City, 1983-95; chmn. Rural Abandoned Mine Reclamation Com., Ky., 1994-97; candidate for county judge McCreary County Rep. Primary. Recipient Cert. of Appreciation, East Ky. Health Sys. Agy., Inc., 1982, Outstanding Svc. award McCreary Farm Bur., 1984, Disting. Svc. award McCreary County Conservation Dist., 1994. Mem. VFW, Ky. Ret. Tchrs. Assn., Ky. Farm Bur., Orie S. Ware Lodge (sec. 1990-94). Republican. Baptist. Avocations: hiking, gardening, farming, reading, photography. Home: 1200 Lick Creek Rd Whitley City KY 42653-4109

STEPHENS, SHAND SCOTT, lawyer; b. Pasadena, Calif., Mar. 25, 1949; s. Elmer Shand and Gladys Joy (Baker) S.; m. Marcia Pizzo, July 25, 1982 (div. Dec. 1985); m. Kieran Candy, Feb. 6, 1999; children: Sofia, Shannon, Shand BA, Yale U., 1971; JD, U. Calif., San Francisco, 1975. Bar: Calif. 1975, U.S. Dist. Ct. (no., so., ea. and cen. dists.) Calif. 1975, U.S. Ct. Appeals (9th cir.) 1975. Assoc. Bronson, Bronson & McKinnon, San Francisco, 1978-82, ptnr., 1982—93; nat. litigation counsel Aon Corp., 1993—2004; ptnr. Piper Rudnick LLP, 2004—. Gen. counsel San Francisco State U. Found., 1987-93; gen. counsel Westamerica Bank, San Rafael, Calif., 1987-93, Valley Bank, 1993—; bd. dirs. Russian Art Found., Kydsncars Recipient Calie Lawyer of the Year, 1998. Mem. ABA, Calif. Bar Assn., Order of Coif. Avocations: american civil war history and archaeology, skiing, tennis. Office: Piper Rudnick LLP 333 Market St 32nd Fl San Francisco CA 94105-2150 E-mail: shand.stephens@piperrudnick.com.

STEPHENS, SHIRLEY LYNNE, writer, editor; b. Glendale, Ariz., Mar. 11, 1934; d. Burrell G. and Kathryn Sullivan Anderson; m. William H. Stephens; children: Laura, Paula Baker, Greg, Carol. BA, Grand Canyon U., Phoenix, AZ, 1958; MDiv, So. Bapt. Theol. Sem., Ft. Worth, TX, 1967. Contract writer, editor Lifeway Christian Resources, Nashville, 1968—94; writer self-employed, Nashville, 1968—2002; v.p. Authors Book Nook, Brentwood. Co-author Under the SS Shadow, 1976; author: A New Testament View of Women, 1980, Breaking Crime's Vicious Cycle, 1993, From the Cell to the Cross, 1999, (book) My Daughter Susan Smith, 2000, Great Truths from Jesus' Conversations With Women, 2003. Avocations: sports, movies, esl teaching. Office: Authors Book Nook PO Box 513 Brentwood TN 37024-0513 E-mail: w-s.stephens@earthlink.net.

STEPHENS, SIDNEY DEE, human resources specialist, retired chemical manufacturing company executive; b. St. Joseph, Mo., Apr. 26, 1945; s. Lindsay Caldwell and Edith May (Thompson) S.; m. Ellen Marie Boeh, June 15, 1968 (div. 1973); m. Elizabeth Ann Harris, Sept. 22, 1973; 1 child, Laura Nicole. BS, Mo. Western State U., 1971; MA, U. Houston, 1980; advanced cert. employment law, Inst. Applied Mgmt. and Law, 1998. Cert. Stephen Covey programs facilitator, 1997. Assoc. urban planner Met. Planning Commn., St. Joseph, 1967-71; prodn. acctg. assoc. Quaker Oats Co., St. Joseph, 1971-72, office mgr., pers. rep. Rosemont, Ill., 1972-73, employee and cmty. rels. mgr. New Brunswick, N.J., 1973-75, Pasadena, Tex., 1975-80; mgmt. cons., Houston, 1981—; regional mgr. human resources Syngenta Crop Protection Inc., 2001—, ret., 2004—; pvt. advisor human resources/adminstrn. Ross Estates Investments, Ltd., Houston, 2004—. Contbr. articles to profl. jours. With USNR, 1963-65. Mem. ASTD, Nat. Soc. for Human Resources Mgmt., Houston Human Resources Mgmt. Assn. (cmty. and govtl. affairs com. 1984-85, 85-86). Republican. Methodist. Home and Office: 16446 Longvale Dr Houston TX 77059-5420 Office Phone: 281-488-2379. Fax: 281-488-8912. E-mail: elsid45@aol.com.

STEPHENS, STEVE ARNOLD, real estate broker; b. Irby, Cheshire, Eng., May 25, 1945; came to U.S., 1983; s. Harold Dennis George and Hilda Leonora (Howell) S.; m. Lynn Williams, Apr. 14, 1983. Student, Manchester U., Eng., 1967-69. Lic. pvt. detective, Ill.; cert. comml. investment. From cadet to detective Cheshire (Eng.) Police, 1961-69; acting detective sgt. Merseyside (Eng.) Police, 1969-75; acting sgt. Hampshire (Eng.) Police, 1975-77; retail store owner Horsham, West Sussex, Eng., 1977-79; pvt. detective Carratu Internat., London, 1979-83, D.A.C. Stephens, Aurora, Ill., 1983-86; broker Coldwell Banker Comml.-Primus Realty, Oswego, Ill., 1986-98; broker, owner Stephens Comml. Real Estate, Aurora, Ill., 1998—. Bd. dirs. Aurora Crimestoppers, pres., 1995-96. Recipient Rep. Legion of Merit award, Rep. Order of Merit award. Mem. Nat. Assn. Realtors (CCIM), CCIM Inst. (cert., bd. dirs. Ill. CCIM chpt. 1992-97, sec.-treas. 1994, v.p. 1995, pres. 1996, v.p. region 7 1999-2001, nat. bd. dirs. 1999—), No. Ill. Comml. Assn. Realtors (dir. 1995-97), Soc. Indsl. and Office Realtors, Internat. Assn. Chiefs Police, Ill. Assn. Realtors, Greater Aurora C. of C., Aurora Country Club. Avocations: travel, literature, golf. Home: 7 Saddlewood Ct Aurora IL 60506-9175 Office: 518 N Lake St Aurora IL 60506-3135 Office Phone: 630-906-9900. E-mail: sstephens@ccim.net. *Work hard. Tell the truth and shame the Devil!.*

STEPHENS, THOMAS G. automotive executive; BS in Mech. Engring., U. Mich., 1971. With General Motors, Mich., 1969—; experimental engr., staff project engr. GM Cadillac Motor Car Div., Detroit, 1971—80, supr. product

engring., 1980—82, staff engr. emission, transmissions, 1982—85; sr. staff engr. transmission, powertrain controls GM Buick-Oldsmobile-Cadillac Powertrain Div., 1985—88; plant mgr. GM Buick-Oldsmobile-Cadillac Powertrain Livonia Engine Plant, 1988—90; dir. engring GM Engine Div., 1990—91; dir. engine engring. GM Powertrain, 1991—93, engring ops gen. mgr. Pontiac, 1993—94; v.p. GM Corp., Detroit, 1994; v.p., group dir. engring. ops. GM Truck Group., 1996—2000; v.p. vehicle integration GM Corp., 2001; group. v.p. GM Powertrain, 2001—. Mem.: U. Mich. Nat. Adv. Coun., Detroit Sci. Ctr. (bd. trustees). Office: GM Corp 300 Renaissance Ctr PO Box 300 Detroit MI 48265-3000

STEPHENS, THOMAS M(ARON), education educator; b. Youngstown, Ohio, June 15, 1931; s. Thomas and Mary (Hanna) S.; m. Evelyn Kleshock, July 1, 1955. BS, Youngstown Coll., 1955; MEd, Kent State U., 1957; EdD, U. Pitts., 1966. Lic. psychologist, Ohio. Tchr. Warren (Ohio) public schs., 1955-57, Niles (Ohio) public schs., 1957-58; psychologist Montgomery County, Ohio, 1958-60; dir. gifted edn. Ohio Dept. Edn., Columbus, 1960-66; assoc. prof. edn. U. Pitts., 1966-70; prof. edn. Ohio State U., 1970—, chmn. dept. exceptional children ., 1972-82, chmn. dept. human services edn., 1982-87, assoc. dean Coll. Edn., 1987-92, prof., 1987-92, prof. emeritus, 1992—; clin. prof. edn. U. Dayton, Ohio, 1993—; exec. dir. Sch. Study Coun. Ohio, Columbus, 1993—. Mem. Higher Edn. Consortium for Spl. Edn., chmn., 1976-77; pub., pres. Cedars Press, Inc. Author: Directive Teaching of Children with Learning and Behavioral Handicaps, 2d edit, 1976, Implementing Behavioral Approaches in Elementary and Secondary Schools, 1975, Teaching Skills to Children with Learning and Behavioral Disorders, 1977, Teaching Children Basic Skills: A Curriculum Handbook, 1978, 2d edit., 1983, Social Skills In The Classroom, 1978, 2d edit., 1991, Teaching Mainstreamed Students, 1982, 2d edit., 1988, Social Behavior Assessment Scale, 1991; dir.: Jour. Sch. Psychology, 1965-75, 80—; exec. editor: The Directive Tchr.; assoc. editor: Spl. Edn. and Tchr. Edn., Techniques, Behavioral Disorders, Spl. Edn. and Remedial Edn.; contbr. articles to profl. jours. Named to Ohio State U. Coll. of Edn. Hall of Fame, 1999; U.S. Office of Edn. fellow, 1964-65. Mem. APA, NASP (charter), State Dirs. for Gifted (pres. 1962-63), Coun. for Exceptional Children (gov., Tchr. Educator of Yr. tchr. edn. divsn. 1985), Coun. Children with Behavioral Disorders (pres. 1972-73). Home: 551 E Cooke Rd Columbus OH 43214-2813 Office: Sch Study Coun of Ohio 4807 Evanswood Dr # 300 Columbus OH 43229-6294

STEPHENS, WILLIAM THEODORE, lawyer, business executive; b. Balt., Mar. 31, 1922; s. William A. and Mildred (Griffin) S.; m. Arlene Alice Lesti, June 2, 1958; children: William Theodore Jr., Renée Adena. Grad., Balt. City Coll., 1941; student, U. Md., 1946-47; AB, JD, George Washington U., 1950, postgrad., 1951. Bar: D.C. 1951, Md. 1950, Va. 1959. Assoc. J.L. Green, Washington, 1950-51; with J.M. Cooper, Washington, 1952-54; sr. ptnr. Stephens Law Firm, Washington, 1955—. Gen. counsel Exotech, Inc., Gaithersburg, Md.; prin. owner BARBCO, Inc., Va., Fairfax Raquet Club; gen. counsel various nat. corps. and assns. Author: Rental Contracts - Contracts for the Rental of Personal Property, 2000. 1st lt. AUS, 1941-45. Mem. ABA, D.C. Bar Assn. (sect. taxation 1959—, sect. corps, banking and bus. law 1960—), Bar Assn. D.C. (sec. taxation 1959-68), XVI Corps Assn. (pres. 1967), Commonwealth Club, Univ. Club, Capitol Hill Club, Army-Navy Country Club, Regency Sport and Health Club, Jockey Club, LaCosta Country Club, Racquet Club Internat., Kappa Alpha (preceptor, ct. of honor, James Ward Wood Province 1988-91), Delta Theta Phi. also: 881 Ocean Dr Key Biscayne FL 33149-2609 Home: PO Box 1169 Rancho Santa Fe CA 92067-1169 E-mail: billstephens@cox.net.

STEPHENSON, ALAN CLEMENTS, lawyer; b. Wilmington, NC, Nov. 7, 1944; s. Abram Clements and Ruth (Smith) S.; children: Edward Taylor, Anne Baldwin. AB in Hist., U. N.C., 1967; JD, U. Va., 1970. Bar: NY 1971. Assoc. Cravath, Swaine & Moore, N.Y.C., 1970-78, ptnr., 1978-88; mng. dir. Wasserstein, Perella and Co. Inc., N.Y.C., 1988-92; ptnr. Cravath, Swaine & Moore, N.Y.C., 1992—. Mem. external adv. bd. undergrad. honors program U. N.C., 1998—. Trustee Cold Spring Harbor Lab., 2003-. Morehead scholar, John M. Morehead Found., 1963. Mem. NY State Bar Assn., Assn. of Bar of City of NY, Brook Club, Links Club, Tuxedo Club, Union Club, Meadow Brook Club, Farmington Country Club, Phi Beta Kappa. Home: 116 Central Park S Apt 15N New York NY 10019 Office: Cravath Swaine & Moore 825 8th Ave 47th Fl New York NY 10019-7475

STEPHENSON, ARTHUR EMMET, JR., corporate and investment company executive; b. Bastrop, La., Aug. 29, 1945; s. Arthur Emmet (dec.) and Edith Louise Stephenson; m. Toni Lyn Edwards, June 17, 1967; 1 child, Tessa. BS in Fin. magna cum laude, La. State U., 1967; MBA (Ralph Thomas Sayles fellow), Harvard U., 1969. Chartered fin. analyst. Adminstrv. aide to U.S. Sen. Russell Long of La., Washington, 1966; security analyst Fidelity Funds, Boston, 1968; chmn. bd., pres. Stephenson & Co., Denver, Stephenson Mcht. Banking Inc., Circle Corp.; sr. ptnr. Stephenson Ventures, Stephenson Properties; founder, chmn. Gen. Comm., Inc., Denver; founder, chmn. bd. dirs. StarTek, Inc. Bd. dirs. Danaher Corp.; co-founder Pub. Network, Inc.; founder Charter Bank and Trust, chmn., 1980-91; mem. adv. bd. First Berkshire Fund, 1984-2002, Capital Resources Ptnrs., L.P., 1987-2004; former pub. Law Enforcement Product News, Colo. Book, Pub. Safety Product News, 1990-98, Colo. Book, Denver mag., Denver Bus. mag. Past mem. assocs. coun. Templeton Coll. at Oxford U., Eng.; past nat. trustee Nat. Symphony Orch. at John F. Kennedy Ctr. for Performing Arts, 1995-98; past mem. nat. steering com. Norman Rockwell Mus., Stockbridge, Mass.; past mem. Colo. small bus. coun.; del. White House Conf., 1980. Recipient Hall of Fame award Inc. mag., 1994, Albert Einstein Tech. medal, 1999; named to Hall of Distinction, La. State U. Coll. Bus. Adminstrn., 1998. Mem. Harvard U. Bus. Sch. Assn. (internat. pres. 1987-88), Chief Execs. Orgn., World Pres.'s Orgn., Colo. Investment Advisors Assn. (treas., bd. dirs. 1975-76), Denver Soc. Security Analysts (bd. dirs. 1975-77), Colo. Press Assn., Colo. Harvard Bus. Sch. Club (pres. 1980-81, chmn. 1981-82), Thunderbird Country Club (Rancho Mirage, Calif.), Annabel's (London), Jonathan Club (L.A.), Pinnacle Club, Harvard Bus. Sch. Clubs (Colo. and So. Calif.), Omicron Delta Kappa, Phi Kappa Phi, Beta Gamma Sigma, Kappa Sigma, Delta Sigma Pi. Office: 100 Garfield St Denver CO 80206-5597

STEPHENSON, ARTHUR G. aerospace engineer; m. Loa J. Stehenson; 2 children. BS in Elec. Engring., U. Redlands, Calif., 1964; postgrad., UCLA, 1988. Design engr. TRW, Redondo Beach, Calif., 1964-72, mgr. telecomm. dept., 1972-79, mgr. advanced systems, 1979-80, mgr. solar array programs, 1980-82, mgr. space sta. mission and user requirements analysis study, 1982-83, mgr. orbital maneuvering vehicle project, 1983-84, mgr. orbital maneuvering vehicle Phase B study program, 1984-85, mgr. orbital vehicle sys. engring. and integration, 1985-88, mgr. orbital maneuvering vehicle advanced systems, 1988-90, dir. space transp. and servicing advanced programs, 1990-92; v.p., gen. mgr. Oceaneering Space Systems, Houston, 1992-97, pres., 1997-98; dir NASA Marshall Space Flight Ctr., Huntsville, Ala., 1998—. Chmn. Bay Area United Way Campaign, 1997. Mem AIAA (mem. space systems, space ops., space automation and robotics), Nat. Contract Mgmt. Assn., Nat. Space Soc. Achievements include management of space craft subsystems, spacecraft and entire launch vehicles. Office: Marshall Space Flight Ctr Mail Code C0-70 Huntsville AL 35812

STEPHENSON, DONALD GRIER, JR., political science professor; b. DeKalb County, Ga., Jan. 12, 1942; s. Donald Grier and Katherine Mason (Williams) Stephenson; m. Ellen Claire Walker, Aug. 15, 1967; children: Todd Grier, Claire Walker. AB, Davidson Coll., N.C., 1964; MA, Princeton U., 1966, PhD, 1967. Research assoc. Nat. War Coll., Washington, 1968-70; from asst. prof. to assoc. prof. govt. Franklin and Marshall Coll., Lancaster, Pa., 1970—81, prof., 1981—, Charles A. Dana prof., 1989—, dept. chair, 1976—79, 1999—2002. Mem. adv. coun. to dean of the chapel Princeton U., 1974—85; Commonwealth lectr. Pa. Humanities Coun., Phila., 1987—88, Phila., 1990, Phila., 1992—95, Phila., 1998—99. Co-author: American Constitutional Development, 1977, American Government, 1992, 2d edit., 1994, American Constitutional Law, 2002; author: The Supreme Court and the American Republic, 1981, An Essential Safeguard, 1991, Campaigns and the Court, 1999, The Waite Court, 2003; contbr. articles to profl. jours. Judge Pa. Constl. competition Dickinson Coll., 1988—94; elder, mem. session 1st Presbyn. Ch., Lancaster, 1973—76, 1996—99. Capt. U.S. Army, 1968—70. Woodrow Wilson fellow, 1964—65, 1966—67, NEH grantee, 1972, 1985—89. Mem.: Supreme Ct. Hist. Soc. (Editl. award 1990, 2002), Pa. Polit. Sci. Assn. (mem. editl. bd. Polity 1972—78), Am. Polit. Sci. Assn. (mem. Corwin award com. 1978, mem. nominating com. Law and Cts. sect. 1995). Home: 62 Oak Ln Lancaster PA 17603-4762 Office: Franklin and Marshall Coll PO Box 3003 Lancaster PA 17604-3003 Office Phone: 717-291-3961. E-mail: grier.stephenson@fandm.edu.

STEPHENSON, DOROTHY GRIFFITH See GRIFFITH, DOTTY

STEPHENSON, FRANK ALEX, engineer, consultant; b. Helena, Mont., May 4, 1940; s. Alex Banning and Phyllis Jean (Smith) S.; m. Lorann Marcella Berg, July 9, 1962 (div. Aug. 1970); children: Patty Jo, Scott Alex, Ashley L.; m. Brenda Mae Vitales, June 21, 1986; 1 child, Jennifer Jean. BS in Civil Constrn. Engring., Mont. State U., 1967; MS in Sanitary Engring., Delft U., 1973; PhD in Environ. Engring., Exeter U., 1975. Registered profl. engr., Ariz., Mont., S.D., Colo., N.Mex., Wyo., Kans. Constrn. engr. Al Johnson Co., Mpls., 1967-70; sr. engr. Stearns Roger Inc., Denver, 1975-79; ptnr. Thomas Group Inc., San Jose, Calif., 1979-85; sr. engr. CH2M Hill Inc., San Jose, Calif., 1985-87; dir. engring. western divsn. Dames & Moore, Phoenix, 1987-93; dir. techs. Terranext, Phoenix, 1993-97; sys. engr. Sumitomo-Sitix, Phoenix, 1997-98; v.p. Hyperion Internat., Tempe, Ariz., 1998—2000; parts mgr. Hunter Contracting, Gilbert, Ariz., 2000—. Recipient Ernest Cook Rsch. fellowship Royal Acad. Sci., London, 1973. Mem. AIChE, Hazardous Waste Soc., diplomate Am. Coll. Forensic Engrs. Presbyterian. Achievements include development of technology for on-line total organic carbon analysis using ultraviolet light and resistivity changes; design and installation of first reverse osmosis unit used in a nuclear (electric power) reactor. Home: 1702 E Aurelius Ave Phoenix AZ 85020-5508 Office: Hunter Contracting 701 N Cooper Rd Gilbert AZ 85299-0900 Office Phone: 480-892-0521.

STEPHENSON, HERMAN HOWARD, retired banker; b. Wichita, Kans., July 15, 1929; s. Herman Horace and Edith May (Wayland) S.; m. Virginia Anne Ross, Dec. 24, 1950; children: Ross Wayland, Neal Bevan, Jann Edith. BA, U. Mich., 1950; JD with distinction, U. Mo., Kansas City, 1958, LLD (hon.), 1993. Bar: Kans. 1958. With City Nat. Bank, Kansas City, Mo., 1952-54, City Bond & Mortgage Co., Kansas City, 1954-59, Bank of Hawaii, Honolulu, 1959-94, CEO, 1989-94, ret. chmn., 1994—. Bd. dirs. Friends of Cancer Rsch. Ctr. Hawaii. Bd. dirs. Maunalani Found.; With U.S. Army, 1950-52. Mem.: Pacific Forum/CSIS (bd. govs.), Navy League U.S., Waialae Country Club, Oahu Country Club, Eagle Bend Country Club, Rotary, Pi Eta Sigma, Kappa Sigma.

STEPHENSON, IRENE HAMLEN, biorhythm analyst, consultant, editor, educator; b. Chgo., Oct. 7, 1923; d. Charles Martin and Carolyn Hilda (Hilgers) Hamlin; m. Edgar B. Stephenson, Sr., Aug. 16, 1941 (div. 1946); 1 child, Edgar B. Author biorhythm compatibilities column Nat. Singles Register, Norwalk, Calif., 1979-81; instr. biorhythm Learning Tree Open U., Canoga Park, Calif., 1982-83, instr. biorhythm personality analysis, 1980—, instr. biorhythm compatibility, 1982—; owner, pres. matchmaking svc. Pen Pals Using Biorhythm, Chatsworth, Calif., 1979—. Editor newsletter The Truth, 1979-85, Mini Examiner, Chatsworth, 1985—; rschr. biorhythm personality and compatibility, 1974—, biorhythm columnist Psyhic Astrology Horoscope, 1989-94, True Astrology Forecast, 1989-94, Psychic Astrology Predictions, 1990-94, Con Artist Types, 1995, Pedophile (child molester) Types, 1995-2000, Personality Types, 1996, Trouble-Addict (Suicide) Types, 1997, Domineering/Nag Types, 1998, Con Artists, Sweetheart Swindlers, Super Con Artist Types, 1998, Bully types, 2000, Deadly Compatibility Combination, 2000, Fatal Attraction Types, 2000, Sadism, Sadistic, Sadistic Predators, 2000, Salesperson, Practical Joker Types, 2000, Doormat Types, 2000, Famous/Queen Bee/Rescuer Types, 2000, Prostitution, 2000. Author: Learn Biorhythm Personality Analysis, 1980, Do-It-Yourself Biorhythm Compatibilities, 1982; contbr. numerous articles to mags. Office: PO Box 3893 Chatsworth CA 91313-3893

STEPHENSON, LARRY KIRK, stategic planner, geography educator; b. Seattle, Sept. 22, 1944; s. Norman Eugene and Virginia Dare (Frost) S.; m. Margery Alsever, Aug. 15, 1992; children: Matthew Alan, Leah Anela. BS, Ariz. State U., 1966, MA, 1971; PhD, U. Cin., 1973. Manpower rsch. analyst Employment Security Commn. of Ariz., 1969-70; asst. prof. geography U. Hawaii, Hilo, 1973-76, assoc. prof., 1976-78, chmn. dept. geography, 1975-77; planner Ariz. Dept. Health Svcs., Phoenix, 1978-84; strategic planner City of Glendale, Ariz., 1984-92; pub. health analyst Gila River Indian Comty., Ariz., 1992-98, econ. devel. planner, 1998—. Vis. lectr. dept. geography Ariz. State U., 1978, adj. assoc. prof., 1979—; vis. assoc. prof. dept. geography, area devel. and urban planning U. Ariz., 1978; mem. faculty U. Phoenix, 1979—; adj. prof. Golden Gate U., 1981—; ptnr. Urban Rsch. Assocs., Phoenix, 1981—; adj. prof. Coll. St. Francis, 1982—; mem. faculty Troy State U., 1990—. Author: Statistics for Health Managers, 1981; co-author: Student Study Guide and Instructor's Manual to accompany Geography: A Modern Synthesis, 4 edits., 1975-83; editor: Kohala keia: Collected Expressions of a Community, 1977; contbr. articles to profl. jours., chpts. to textbooks. Mem. Hawaii Island Health Planning Coun., 1974-78, Glendale Comty. Colls. Pres.'s Coun., 1986-92. With U.S. Army, 1966-68. NDEA fellow 1971-72. Mem. Am. Inst. Cert. Planners, Am Planning Assn., Assn. Am. Geographers, Ariz. Planning Assn. (pres. 1987—), S.W. Profl. Geog. Assn., Lambda Alpha. Unitarian Universalist. Home: HC 4 Box 28K Payson AZ 85541 Office: PO Box 97 Sacaton AZ 85247-0097 Personal E-mail: Lstephe739@aol.com.

STEPHENSON, MASON WILLIAMS, lawyer; b. Atlanta, May 29, 1946; s. Donald Grier and Katherine Mason (Williams) S.; m. Linda Frances Partee, June 13, 1970; children: Andrew Mason, Walter Martin. AB cum laude, Davidson Coll., 1968; JD, U. Chgo., 1971. Bar: Ga. 1971, U.S. Dist. Ct. (no. dist.) Ga. 1985. Assoc. Alston, Miller & Gaines, Atlanta, 1971-76, ptnr., 1976-77, Trotter, Bondurant, Griffin, Miller & Hishon, Atlanta, 1977-82, Bondurant, Miller, Hishon & Stephenson, Atlanta, 1982-85, King & Spalding, LLP, Atlanta, 1985—, mng. ptnr. Atlanta office, 2001—. Mem. fin. com. Atlanta Olympic Organizing Com., 1988-90. Mem. ABA (sect. bus. law, real property, probate and trust sect.), Am. Coll. Real Estate Lawyers, State Bar Ga. (exec. com., real property law sect. 1989-97, chair intangible rec. tax com. 1994-97), Atlanta Bar Assn. (chair real estate sect. 1981-82), Causeway Club, Capital City Club, Phi Beta Kappa, Phi Delta Phi. Avocations: boating, skiing, jogging. Office: King & Spalding LLP 191 Peachtree St NE Ste 4900 Atlanta GA 30303-1740

STEPHENSON, PATRICIA ANN, public health researcher, educator; b. Washington, July 21, 1954; arrived in Sweden, 1990; d. Stanley Edwin and Mary Virginia (Brenneman) S.; m. Marsden Grigg Wagner, Dec. 14, 1990. BS, Calif. State U., Hayward, 1979; ScD, Johns Hopkins U., 1986. RN. Asst. prof. Sch. Pub. Health U. Wash., Seattle, 1986-90, adj. asst. prof. Sch. Nursing, 1987-90; sr. rschr. Ctr. for Pub. Health Rsch., Karlstad, Sweden, 1990-94; cons. health policy analyst, ops. rschr. Copenhagen, 1990-97; sr. advisor health and research USAID, Washington, 1998—. Vis. assoc. prof. Sch. Pub. Health U. Mich., Ann Arbor, 1995-96; cons. WHO, 1989, UNICEF, 1990—, World Bank, 1995-96. Mng. editor, co-founder European Jour. Pub. Health, 1991-94; author, editor: Tough Choices - InVitro Fertilization and the New Reproductive Technologies, 1993; contbr. articles to profl. publs. Women's health policy fellow John D. and Catherine T. MacArthur Found., 1995; recipient Commendation for work in fertility U.K. Parliament/House of Commons, 1989. Mem. APHA, Global Health Council, Delta Omega. Avocations: equestrian sports, dressage, show jumping, ballet, opera. Home: 123 Sherman Ave Takoma Park MD 20912 E-mail: pstephenson@usaid.gov.

STEPHENSON, RANDALL, communications executive; Sr. v.p., fin. SBC Comm., Inc., San Antonio, 1982—2001, exec. v.p., CFO, 2001—. Chmn. Cingular Wireless L.L.C., 2003—. Office: SBC Comm Inc 175 E Houston San Antonio TX 78205-2233

STEPHENSON, RICHARD ISMERT, lawyer; b. Augusta, Kans., Oct. 13, 1937; s. Paul Noble and Dorothy May (Ismert) S.; m. Mary Lynn Bryden, July 2, 1967 (div. 1973); 1 child, Richard William; m. Linda Cox, Apr. 5, 1976. BA, U. Kans., 1958; JD, U. Mich., 1965. Bar: Kans. 1965, U.S. Dist. Ct. Kans. 1965, U.S. Ct. Appeals (10th cir.) 1965. Assoc. Fleeson, Gooing, Coulson & Kitch, Wichita, Kans., 1965-72, ptnr., 1973-95; gen. counsel RAGE Inc. and Affiliated Cos., Wichita, 1995—. Lt. (j.g.) USNR, 1959-62. Recipient Hilden Gibson award U. Kans., 1958. Mem. ABA (forum on franchising), Def. Rsch. Inst., Internat. Assn. Def. Counsel, Kans. Bar Assn., Wichita Bar Assn., Wichita Country Club, Pi Sigma Alpha, Beta Theta Pi. Avocations: golf, fishing. Home: 9203 Killarney Wichita KS 67206-4027 Office: RAGE Inc 1313 N Webb Rd Ste 200 Wichita KS 67206-4077 Office Phone: 316-634-1888.

STEPHENSON, ROSCOE BOLAR, JR., state supreme court justice; b. Covington, Va., Feb. 22, 1922; AB, Washington and Lee U., 1943, JD, 1947, LL.D. (hon.), 1983. Bar: Va. 1947. Ptnr. Stephenson & Stephenson, Covington, 1947-52; commonwealth's atty. Alleghany County, Va., 1952-64; ptnr. Stephenson, Kostel, Watson, Carson and Snyder, Covington, 1964-73; judge 25th Jud. Cir. Ct. Commonwealth Va., Covington, 1973-81; justice Va. Supreme Ct., Richmond, 1981-97, sr. justice, 1997—. Recipient Covington Citizen of Yr. award, 1973, Outstanding Alumni award Covington H.S., 1973, Disting. Alumnus award Washington and Lee U., 1997. Fellow Am. Coll. Trial Lawyers; mem. Va. State Bar (council 1969-73), Va. Bar Assn., Va. Trial Lawyers Assn., Order of Coif, Omicron Delta Kappa. Home: North Ridge Hot Springs VA 24445 Office: Va Supreme Ct 214 W Main St PO Box 198 Covington VA 24426-0198 also: Va Supreme Court Supreme Court Bldg 100 N 9th St Richmond VA 23219-2335

STEPHENSON, SAMUEL EDWARD, JR., retired physician; b. Bristol, Tenn., May 16, 1926; s. Samuel Edward and Hazel Beatrice (Walters) S.; m. Janet Sue Spotts, May 16, 1970; children: Samuel Edward III, William Douglas, Dorothea Louise, Judith Maria. BS, U. S.C., 1946; MD, Vanderbilt U., 1950. Intern Butterworth Hosp., Grand Rapids, Mich., 1950-51; instr. to asso. prof. surgery Vanderbilt U., 1955-67; prof. surgery U. Fla., 1967-95, emeritus prof. clin. surgery, 1995—. Chmn. dept. surgery Univ. Hosp., Jacksonville, 1967-78 Asst. editor So. Med. Jour., 1968-88; contbr. articles to profl. jours. Co-chmn. Fla. Burn and Trauma Registry, 1974-77. Served with USNR, 1944-45. Fellow ACS; mem. So. Surg. Assn., Masons. Home: 10553 Scott Mill Rd Jacksonville FL 32257-6227

STEPHENSON, SHERRY MADELINE, trade economist; d. Joe Harrell and Bettie Beasley Stephenson; children: Matthew Hector Travis, Corinne Louis Madeline. MA, NYU, 1974; PhD, Grad. Inst. Internat. Studies, Geneva, 1987. Trade specialist UNCTAD, Geneva, 1978—80; trade specialist Gen. Agreement Tariffs and Trade GATT, Geneva, 1980—82; prin. adminstr. Trade Directorate OECD, Paris, 1983—91; advisor Ministry of Trade, Jakarta, Indonesia, 1992—95; prin. trade specialist Trade Unit OAS, Washington, 1995—2000, dep. dir. for trade, 2000—. Cons. Pacific Econ. Cooperation Coun., Singapore, 1993—2000, Asian Devel. Bank, Manila, 1993—96, World Bank, Washington, 1995—97, USAID, 1997—2000. Editor: (academic books) Services Trade in the Western Hemisphere, 2000, Services Trade Liberalization and Facilitation, 2002. Mem.: European Inst., Internat. Trade and Fin. Assn., Pacific Econ. Cooperation Coun., Inter-American Dialogue, Cosmos Club. Office: Orgn Am States 1889 F St NW Washington DC 20006 Office Phone: 202-458-3342. E-mail: sstephenson@oas.org.

STEPHENSON, TONI EDWARDS, publishing executive, investment management executive, communications executive; b. Bastrop, La., July 23, 1945; d. Sidney Crawford and Grace Erleene Little; m. Arthur Emmet Stephenson Jr., June 17, 1967; 1 child, Tessa Lyn. Grad. owner/pres. mgmt. program, Harvard Bus. Sch. Pres., dir. Gen. Comm., Inc., Denver; sr. v.p., founder Stephenson & Co., Denver, 1971—; gen. ptnr. Viking Fund; ptnr. Stephenson Properties, Stephenson Ventures, Stephenson Mgmt. Co. Past. pres. Children's Hosp. Assn. Vols.; past troop leader Girl Scouts Am.; v.p. Anchor Ctr. for Blind Children; past dir. The Children's Hosp., St. Joseph's Hosp., Cherry Creek H.S. Parent Tchr. Conf. Orgn. Mem. Harvard Bus. Sch. Club Colo., DAR, Delta Gamma, Jonathan Club, Annabel's (London), Thunderbird Country Club, Pinnacle Club.

STEPHENSON, VIVIAN M. former retail executive; B Math., NYU; MBA, U. Havana. Mgmt. positions Rand Info. Sys., Occidental Petroleum Corp., Assoc. Credit Burs. Svcs., Inc.; dir. info. sys. devel. Mervyn's, 1989-90, v.p. MIS, 1990-94, sr. v.p., 1994-95; sr. v.p., chief info. officer Dayton Hudson Corp., Mpls., 1995-2000; exec. v.p., chief info. officer Target Corp., Mpls., —2000; ret., 2000. Bd. dirs. MobiNetrix Sys. Inc.; mem. info. sys. customer adv. coun. IBM; mem. Tandem Americas Customer Coun. Chair bd. dirs. San Francisco AIDS Found.; mem. Nat. Retail Fedn. Info. Sys. Bd. Mem. Calif. C. of C. Office: Target Corp 1000 Nicollet Mall Minneapolis MN 55403-2467

STEPNER, DONALD LEON, lawyer; b. Boston, Apr. 23, 1939; s. Neil and Sadie (Adelman) S.; m. Beth Klass, Aug. 14, 1965 (div. Dec. 1985); children: David, Jeff. AA, Wentworth Inst., Boston, 1958; BA, Ky. Wesleyan U., 1963; JD, U. Ky., 1966. Bar: Ky. 1966, U.S. Dist. Ct. Ky. 1966, U.S. Ct. Appeals (6th cir.) 1966, U.S. Supreme Ct. 1971. Assoc. Charles Adams, Covington, Ky., 1966-69; ptnr. Adams, Stepner, Woltermann & Dusing, Covington, 1969—. Pres. Ky. State Ethics Com. Bd. dirs. Boys Club. Recipient Human Rels. award NCCJ, 1986. Fellow Am. Coll. Trial Lawyers; mem. ABA, Ky. Bar Assn. (pres. 1999-2000), No. Ky. Bar Assn. (judiciary com., ethics and unauthorized procedure com.), Ky. Def. Rsch. Inst., Kenton County Bar Assn. (pres. 1973-74, Merit award 1973, Gavel award 1973), U.S. Soccer Fedn. (cert. referee, pres. 1980-85), Ky. High Sch. Referees Assn., No. Ky. Soccer Assn. (ofcl. pres. 1980—). Avocations: golf, jogging, biking. Office: Adams Stepner Woltermann & Dusing PO Box 12861 Covington KY 41012-0861

STEPONAITIS, VINCAS PETRAS, archaeologist, anthropologist, educator; b. Boston, Aug. 10, 1953; s. Vincas and Elena (Povydis) S.; m. Laurie Cameron, Dec. 31, 1976; children: Elena Anne, Lillian Kazimiera. AB in Anthropology magna cum laude, Harvard U., 1974; MA in Anthropology, U. Mich., 1975, PhD in Anthropology, 1980. From lectr. to assoc. prof. dept. anthropology SUNY, Binghamton, 1979-87; assoc. prof. U. N.C., Chapel Hill, 1988-94, prof., 1995—, dir. Rsch. Labs. Archaeology, 1988—. Guest worker Nat. Bur. Standards, 1979; adj. lectr. dept. anthropology SUNY, Binghamton, 1979; lectr. and presenter in field. Author: Ceramics, Chronology, and Community Patterns, An Archaeological Study at Moundville, 1983, Archaeology of the Moundville Chiefdom, 1998, (CD-Rom) Excavating Occaneechi Town, 1998; editor Southeastern Archaeology, 1984-87; regional editor Investigations in Am. Archaeology, 1987-91; mem. editl. bd. Prehistory Press, 1990-97, Southern Cultures, 1992—, Am. Archaeology, 1996-2000; contbr. articles to profl. jours. Smithsonian Instn. fellow, 1978-79; grantee NSF, 1978-80, 83, 89-92, 94, 2000, Wenner-Gren Found., 1981, 86-88, Nat. Geographic Soc., 1987-88, Z. Smith Reynolds Found., 1992-94. Fellow Am. Anthrop. Assn.; mem. Soc. Am. Archaeology (Presdl. Recognition award 1993-94, exec. com. 1983-84, treas. 1992-94, pres. 1997-99), Archaeological Conservancy (bd. dirs. 2000—, chmn. 2003—), Ctr. for Maya Rsch. (bd. dirs. 2002-), Southeastern Archaeol. Conf. (editor 1984-87, pres. 1990-92), N.C. Archaeol. Soc. (exec. sec. 1988-91, sec. 1991-96), N.C. Archaeol. Coun. (exec. com. 1988-92), Archaeol. Soc. S.C., Ala. Archaeol. Soc., Miss. Archaeol. Soc., La. Archaeol. Soc., Tenn. Anthrop. Assn. Office: U NC Rsch Labs Archaeology Alumni Bldg Cb 3120 Chapel Hill NC 27599-3120

STEPP, CATHY, state senator; b. Aug. 17, 1963; married. Supr., New Home Consultants First Stepp Builders, Inc., Racine, Wis.; state sen. Wis. State Senate, Madison, 2002—. 3-time judge Met. Milw. Area Parade of Homes; chair Parade of Homes, 1998—99; apptd. dept. natural resources bd. former Gov. Tommy Thompson, 2000—; bd. dirs. Girl Scouts of Racine County. Mem.: Wis. Builders Assn. (bd. dirs. 1996—), Racine-Kenosha Builders Assn. (pres. 1998—99, past sec.), Nat. Assn. Home Builders (bd. dirs. 1999—). Office: State Capitol Rm 7 S PO Box 7882 Madison WI 53u70-7882

STEPP, JAMES MICHAEL, business executive; b. Huntington, W.Va., Apr. 26, 1944; s. James Dial and Helen (Shelton) S.; m. Lillian Arlene Radeker, Jan. 3, 1970; children: James Michael, Scott Adams, John Radeker. BS, U.S. Mil. Acad., 1966; MBA, Stanford U., 1972. Commd. lt. C.E. U.S. Army, 1966, advanced through grades to capt., 1968, served in Vietnam, resigned, 1970; asst. v.p. Bank of Am., San Francisco, 1972-75, v.p. N.Y.C., 1975-81; v.p., treas. Fotomat Corp., Wilton, Conn., 1981-83, Emhart Corp., Hartford, Conn., 1983-89; pres. Am. Corp. Fin. Group Inc., West Hartford, 1989-92; exec. v.p., CFO Purolator Products Co., Tulsa, Okla., 1992—, bd. dirs. Adv. dir. Conn. Nat. Bank, 1986-92. Bd. dirs. Jr. Achievement, North Cen. Conn., 1986-92. Decorated Silver Star, Bronze Star, Purple Heart, Army Commendation medal, Air medal. Mem. Fin. Execs. Inst., Stanford Bus. Sch. Alumni Assn., West Point Soc. of N.Y. Republican. Episcopalian. Avocations: tennis, fishing, jogging, golf. Home: 1900 E Valley Rd Bloomfield Hills MI 48304-2155*

STEPP, LAURA SESSIONS, journalist; b. Ft. Smith, Ark., July 27, 1951; d. Robert Paul Sessions and M. Rae Barnes; m. Carl Sessions Stepp; children: Ashli, Amber, Jeffrey. BA, Earlham Coll., 1973; MA, Columnia U., 1974. Reporter Palm Beach Times, West Palm Beach, Fla., 1974; MA Columbia U., Phila., 1975; projects editor The Charlotte (N.C.) Observer, 1979-81, asst. editorial page editor, 1981-82; Md. editor The Washington Post, 1982-86, religion editor, 1987-92, writer Style sect., 1992—. Bd. advisors U. Md. Casey Journalism Ctr. Children and Families, College Park. Recipient Nat. Reporting award Religion Writers Am., Feature Writing award AAUW, 1994. Mem. Investigative Reporters and Editors (bd. dirs. 1986-90). Office: Washington Post Co 1150 15th St NW Washington DC 20071-0002

STEPP, WAYLON GENE, management consultant, retired municipal official; b. Springdale, Ark., Feb. 27, 1968; s. Bill Wayne and Leona Ruth Stepp; m. Shawn R. Buckner, Dec. 28, 1966; children: Destiny Victoria, Brittany Elizabeth, William Jared. AA in Criminal Justice, Summit U., Baton Rouge, La.; BS in Criminal Justice Mgmt., La Salle U., Mandeville, La.; MS in Criminal Justice Mgmt., La Salle U., Mandeville; PhD in Pub. Adminstrn., Pacific Western U., L.A. Police officer to detective, pr dir. Springdale Police Dept., Springdale, Ark., 1988—94; chief of police West Helena Police Dept., West Helena, 1994—96; city mgr. City of Lowell, Lowell, 1996—97; spl. asst. to supt. Agra Pub. Sch. Dist., Agra, Okla., 1999—2001; pres. and lead cons. Dr. Trigger Enterprises, Inc., Cedar Rapids, Iowa, 1997—. Chmn. Ark. Police and Fire Retirement Sys., Little Rock, 1990—94; exec. bd./vice pres. Ark. Mcpl. Police Assn., Heber Springs, 1990—96; exec. bd. Nat. Fire and Police Pension Fund Assn., Boca Raton, Fla., 1992—94; regional v.p. Ark. Chiefs of Police Assn., Little Rock, 1994—96. Contbr. articles to profl. jour. Co-founder N.W. Ark. chpt. Nat. Family Partnership. Recipient Cert. of Appreciation, Nat. Crime Prevention Coun., U.S. Dept. of Justice, 1992. Democrat. Home: 2805 Newcastle Rd Marion IA 52303 Office: Dr Trigger Enterprises inc PO Box 10163 Cedar Rapids IA 52410-0163 Office Phone: 319-730-1215. Office Fax: 319-398-3684. E-mail: drtrigger@prodigy.net.

STEPPE, STEPHEN, management consultant; Sr. v.p. RREEF Mgmt. Co., San Francisco, mng. prin. Office: RREEF Mgmt Co 26th Fl 101 California St San Francisco CA 94111*

STEPS, BARBARA JILL, lawyer; b. Springfield, Mo., June 19, 1945; d. Louis Edward and Margaret Pearl (Stiver) Bredeman; m. Robert William Steps, Dec. 21, 1968; children: Rebecca Harper, Aaron Andrew, Jessica Anne. BA in Psychology, St. Louis U., 1966; JD, U. Mo., 1969; MBA, U. Conn., 1983. Atty. Ralston Purina Co., St. Louis, 1969; law clerk U.S. Dist. Ct., St. Louis, 1969-72; assoc. Stone, Keck & Staser, Evansville, Ind., 1973-75, Cline & Callahan, Indpls., 1975-77, Law Office, Herbert V. Camp, Ridgefield, Conn., 1978-81; from comml. counsel to corp. counsel, sec. Framatome Connectors USA, Inc. (now FCI USA, Inc.), Fairfield, Conn., 1981-93; v.p., counsel, sec. FCI USA, Inc. (formerly Framatome Connectors USA, Inc.), Etters, Pa., 1993—2002, sr. v.p. adminstrn., counsel, sec., 2002—. Mem.: ABA, Am. Corp. Counsel Assn. Home: 23 Emlyn Ln Mechanicsburg PA 17055-8017 Office: FCI USA Inc 825 Old Trail Rd Etters PA 17319-9392

STEPTOE, MARY LOU, lawyer; b. Washington, July 15, 1949; d. Philip Pendleton and Irene (Hellen) S.; m. Peter E. Carson, Sept. 1986; children: Elizabeth Maud, Julia Grace. BA, Occidental Coll., 1971; JD, U. Va., 1974. Bar: Va., 1974, Supreme Ct., 1987, D.C. 1996. Staff atty., Bur. of Competition FTC, Washington, 1974-79, atty. advisor to commr., 1979-86, exec. asst. to chmn., 1988-89, assoc. dir., Bur. of Competition, 1989-90, dep. dir., 1990-92, acting dir., 1992-95, dep. dir., 1995-96; ptnr. Skadden Arps Slate Meagher & Flom LLP, Washington.

STEPTOE, SONJA, journalist; b. Lutcher, La., June 16, 1960; d. Eldridge Willie and Rosa Jane Steptoe. BA in econs., B in journalism, U. Mo., 1982; JD, Duke U. Law Sch., 1985. Staff reporter Wall St. Jour., NYC, 1985—90; sr. editor Sports Illustrated, NYC, 1990—2001, People Mag., NYC, 2001—02; nat. corr, CNN Sports, NYC, 1999—2001; corr. HBO Sports, 1995—2001; sr. corr. Time Mag., Los Angeles, 2002—. Editl. adv. bd. U. Mo. Alumni Mag., Columbia, Mo., 1991—96; alumni bd. Duke U. Law Sch., Durham, NC, 1996—98; mem. U. Mo. Strategic Develop. Bd., 1988—. Co-author: (book) Guide to Women's Golf, 1993, A Kind of Grace" The Autobiography of the World's Greatest Female Athlete, 1997. Bd. mem. Alvin Ailey Dance Sch., NYC, 2001—02, Assoc. Black Charities, NYC, 1989—97. Recipient Emmy award, Nat. Assn. TV Arts and Sci., 1998, Nat. Headliner award, Press Club of Atlantic City, 1999, Disting. Alumni award, U. Mo., Duke Law Sch. Young Alumni award, 1994, 2000. Mem.: ABA, Nat. Assn. Black Journalists, World Affairs Coun. Office: Time Inc Mag 11766 Wilshire Blvd Los Angeles CA 90025

STERBENZ, JAMES PHILIP GUENTHER, computer network scientist; s. Bertram L. Jr. and Lois Sterbenz; m. Kristine L.G. Sterbenz; 1 child, Katarina. BSEE, BSCS, ABEcon, Wash. U., 1981, MS, 1986, DSc, 1991. Adv. engr., scientist IBM Rsch., Milford, Conn., Hawthorne, N.Y.; prin. MTS GTE Labs., Waltham, Mass.; sr. network scientist BBN Technologies, Cambridge, Mass., mgr. mobile wireless and active networking. Chair steering com. Protocols for High-Speed Networks, 2000—; chair Internat. Working Conf. on Active Networks, 2002. Author: High Speed Networking, 2001; editor Protocols for High Speed Networks, 1999-2001, Active Networks, 2002; mem. editl. bd. IEEE Network, Computer Networks, 1999—, Jour. Comm. and Networks, 2000—. Mem.: IEEE (sr.; chmn. ComSoc TCGN 1994—99, steering com. 1999—), Protocols for High-Speed Networks (keynote address 1994, program chair 1999, steering com. chair 2000—), Internat. Fedn. Info. Processing Soc., Interplanetary Chpt. Internet Soc., Assn. Computing Machinery (vice chair SIGCOMM 99 conf.). Avocation: railway signaling. Home: PO Box 187 Hopkinton MA 01748-0187 Office: BBN Technologies 10 Moulton St Cambridge MA 02138-1191 E-mail: jpgs@acm.org.

STERKINA, SOFIYA, writer; b. Neshin, Ukraine, Aug. 5, 1962; arrived in U.S., 1998; d. Aaron Sterkin and Zinaida Gornaya. RN, Med. Coll., Ukraine, 1985. Nurse Kiev Railroad Hosp., 1985—89, Kiev Hosp., 1989—91, Kiev Med. U., 1991—93, Irpen Mil. Hosp., 1993—97; nurse asst. trng., 1998—99; author, 2001—. Author: (children's books) With the Secret for All World, Dragonfly, Baby, Magicians, Circus, Tobik Bobik and Me, The Little Brothers, Unusual Adventure of the Small Duck, On the Children's Ground, (book) Inspiration, (book of poems) Holidays of Jewish Nation, short stories. Served Irpen Mil. Hosp., 1993—97, Ukraine. Jewess. Avocations: reading, swimming, badminton. Home: 491 31st Ave Apt #518 San Francisco CA 94121

STERLING, ARTHUR JAMES, legal assistant; b. Pineville, La., July 27, 1944; s. Leon Henry and Dorothy Mae Sterling; children: Hope, Monique, Heather. Student, U. Southern Calif., 1988-89. With U.S. Naval Weapons Sta., Seal Beach, Calif., 1979-83, Norwalk Superior Ct., 1991; law clk.; guidance counselor, 2000—02. Dave Holt Meml scholar, K.T. Skula meml. scholar, Johnson Controls, Inc. Fund scholar, Amy Welch Meml. scholar. Mem. Soc. for Advancement of Mgmt., Phi Beta Lambda. Democrat. Avocations: computers, cooking, reading. Home: 4216 Carlin Ave #C Lynwood CA 90262-5208

STERLING, CHARLOTTE B. hotel executive; b. San Francisco, June 2, 1946; d. Robert and Lee Butler; m. James Campbell Sharf; children: Elizabeth, Stephanie. AA, BA, Stephens Coll., Columbia, Mo.; MA in Journalism, U. Mo. Journalist Bolivar (Mo.) Herald Free Press, 1967-73, v.p. mktg. svcs. Hill & Knowlton, Washington, 1973-83; v.p. pub. affairs Fannie Mae, Washington, 1984-96; exec. v.p. comms. Marriott Internat., Washington, 1996—. Bd. dirs. Fed. City Coun., Washington, 1998—, Studio Theatre, Washington, 1995. Mem. Press Club (bd. dirs. Washington chpt. 1985), Econs. Club (bd. dirs. Washington chpt. 1998—). Avocation: painting. Office: Marriott Internat Marriott Dr Washington DC 20058-0001

STERLING, CHRISTOPHER H. telecommunications educator; b. Washington, D.C., 1943; m. Ellen Sterling; children: Jennifer, Robin. BS in Polit. Sci., U. Wis., 1965, MS in Comm., 1967, PhD in Comm., 1969. Asst. prof. speech U. Utah, Salt Lake City, 1969—70; prof. comms. Temple U., Phila., 1970—80; spl. asst. FCC, Washington, 1980—82; dir. Ctr. for Telecomms. Studies, 1982—84; prof. dept. comm. and theater, 1984—89; dir. grad. telecomm. program, 1984—94; acting chmn. dept. comm., 1989—91; assoc. dean for grad. affairs Columbian Sch. Arts and Scis., 1994—2001; dir. grad. telecomm. program, prof. Sch. Media and Pub. Affairs George Washington U., 1982—94, 2001—03. Cons., lectr., presenter in field. Author: Electronic Media: A Guide to Trends In Broadcasting and Newer Technologies 1920-1983, 1984; co-author: Who Owns the Media? Concentration of Ownership in the Mass Communications Industry, 1978, Who Owns the Media? Concentration of Ownership in the Mass Communications Industry, 2d edit., 1982, History of Telecommunication Technology: An Annotated Bibliography, 2000, Stay Tuned: A Concise History of American Broadcasting, 2002; editor: International Telecommunications and Information Policy, 1984, (CD-ROM) Focal Guide to Electronic MEdia, 1998, Encyclopedia of Radio, 3 vols., 2004; co-editor: Mass News: Practices, Controversies, Alternatives, 1973, Decision to Divest: Major Documents in U.S. V. AT&T, 4 vols., 1986—88, Broadcasting in America: A Survey of Electronic Media, Telecommunications Research Resources: An Annoteted Guide, 1995, Mass Communication Research Resources: A Annotated Guide, 1998; contbr. articles, monographs, revs., chpts., report to profl. publs.; mem. editl. bd. (jour.) Comm. Law and Policy; mem. editl. bd.: jour. Jour. Broadcasting and Electronic Media, Jour. Media Econs., Journalism and Mass Comms. Avocations: history of passenger ocean liners, history of medieval castles and fortifications, works by and about Winston Churchill, second-hand bookshops. Office: George Washington U MPA Bldg 407 Ste 400 805 21st St NW Washington DC 20052

STERLING, DONALD T. professional basketball team executive; b. Chgo. m. Shelly Stein; 3 children. Lawyer L.A. (formerly San Diego) Clippers, Nat. Basketball Assn., owner, 1981—, also chmn. bd. Office: c/o Los Angeles Clippers 1111 S Figueroa st ste 1100 Los Angeles CA 90015

STERLING, ERIC EDWARD, lawyer, legal policy advocate; b. N.Y.C., Oct. 25, 1949; s. Bowen and Helen (Champnella) S.; m. June S. Beittel, Oct. 1996; 1 child, Maya Rebecca. BA, Haverford Coll., 1973; JD, Villanova (Pa.) U., 1976. Bar: Pa. 1976, U.S. Supreme Ct. 1980. Asst. pub. defender Del. County, Media, Pa., 1976-79; asst. counsel sub. on criminal justice U.S. Ho. Reps., Washington, 1979-81, counsel subcom. on crime, 1981-89; pres. The Criminal Justice Policy Found., Washington, 1989—. Cons. Dem., Rep. and Libertarian Party orgns. and candidates, 1982—; cons. The Brookings Instn., 1990, Office of Pers. Mgmt., 1990, GAO, 1992, Nat. News Media, 1989—; lectr. Am. U. Sch. Pub. Affairs, Washington, 1984-86, U. Colo. Conf. on World Affairs, 1990-99, others. Founder, dir. Nat. Drug Strategy Network, 1989-2000; mem. D.C. Mayor's Adv. Com. on Drug Abuse, 1990, Baltimore Mayor's Task force on Drug Policy, 1993; mem. steering com. D.C. Safe Streets Project, 1990-91; bd. dirs. Families Against Mandatory Minimums Found., 1991—, Forfeiture Endangers Am. Rights, 1993-95, William Penn House, 1992-98, Marijuana Policy Project, 1995—, Vol. Com. of Lawyers, 1995—. Recipient Cert. of Appreciation, U.S. Bur. Alcohol, Tobacco and Firearms, 1982, U.S. Postal Inspection Svc., 1988, Justice Gerald LeDain award for achievement in law Drug Policy Found., 1999. Mem. ABA (individual rights and responsibility sect.). Mem. Soc. Of Friends. Avocations: swimming, bicycling, hiking. Office: The Criminal Justice Policy Found 8730 Georgia Ave Ste 400 Silver Spring MD 20910-3649 E-mail: esterling@cjpf.org.

STERLING, JOHN, consulting firm executive; 2 children. Grad., Jackson State U. Founder, pres., CEO Synchronous Solutions, Inc., Chgo., 1998—. Active Boy Scouts Am., The Woodlawn Orgn., Chgo. Pub. Schs., Urban League Boys and Girls Club. Office: Synchronous Solutions INc Ste 2150 200 W Madison St Chicago IL 60606*

STERLING, KEIR BROOKS, historian, educator; b. N.Y.C., Jan. 30, 1934; s. Henry Somers and Louise Noel (de Wetter) S.; m. Anne Cox Diller, Apr. 3, 1961; children: Duncan Diller, Warner Strong, Theodore Craig. BS, Columbia U., 1961, MA, 1963, profl. diploma, 1965, PhD, 1973. Asst. to dean Sch. Gen. Studies Columbia U., N.Y.C., 1959-65; rsch. grantee Eng., 1965-66; instr. history Pace U., N.Y.C. and Pleasantville, N.Y., 1966-71, from asst. prof. to assoc. prof., 1971-77, adj. prof., 1977-83; ordnance br. historian U.S. Army Ordnance Ctr. and Sch., Aberdeen Proving Ground, Md., 1983-94, Ft. Lee, Va., 1994-98; historian U.S. Army Combined Arms Support Command, Ft. Lee, 1998—. Lectr. gen. counseling Bklyn. Coll., CUNY, 1967-68; asst. acad. dean, adj. asst. prof. history, coord. Am. studies program, dir. summer session Marymount Coll., Tarrytown, N.Y., 1968-71; asst. dean Rockland C.C., SUNY, Suffern, 1971-73; vis. prof. Mercy Coll., Westchester C.C., King's Coll., Nyack Coll., U. Wis., 1971, 75, 78-80, 83, Harford (Md.) C.C., 1987-94; adj. instr. Army Logistics Mgmt. Coll., Ft. Lee, 1995—; co-project dir. Am. Ornithologists Union Centennial Hist., Project, 1976-89; cons. Arno Press, Inc., 1973-78, Coun. State Colls. of N.J., 1984-85, NSF, 1983—, Am. Trust for Brit. Libr., 1986-89; active Columbia U. Seminar on History and Philosophy of Sci., 1976-83; archivist, historian mem. steering com. sect. mammalogy Internat. Union Biol. Scis., 1985—; judge Ann. Nat. History Day Competition U. Md., 1993-; grant reviewer Teaching Am. History Program U.S. Dept. Edn., 2003-. Author: Last of the Naturalists: The Career of C. Hart Merriam, 1974, 77; editor: Notes on the Animals of North America (B.S. Barton), 1974; assoc. editor: Am. Nat. Biog., 1989-98; editor, contbr.: Natural Sciences in America, 1974, 68 vols., 1974, Biologists and Their World, 1978, 77 vols.; gen. editor, contbr.: The International History of Mammalogy, 1987—; sr. editor, contbr. (with R. Harmond, G. Cevasco, and L. Hammond) Biographical Dictionary of American and Canadian Naturalists and Environmentalists, 1997; contbg. author: Ground Warfare: An International Encyclopedia, 2002, Dictionary of Am. History, 3d edit., 2003, Encyclopedia of World Environmental History, 2003; editor, contbr. to numerous works in history, Am. natural scis., and Am. mil. history. With U.S. Army, 1954—56. Grantee Theodore Roosevelt Meml. Fund, Am. Mus. Natural History, 1967, Nat. Geog. Soc., 1977, NSF/Am. Soc. Mammalogists, 1978, NSF, 1981-82, IREX, 1982; recipient Editor's Quill Award, Internat. Assn. of Torch Clubs, 2003. Mem.: History of Sci. Soc., Orgn. Am. Historians, Am. Hist. Assn., Assn. Bibliography of History (mem. coun. 1994—), Am. Soc. Environ. History (sec., mem. governing bd., editor newsletter), Am. Ornithologists Union (co-chmn. centennial hist. com., mem. archives com., grantee 1976, 1977), Am. Soc. Mammalogists (mem. archives com., mem. 75th ann. com.), Phi Delta Kappa, Sigma Tau Delta, Phi Alpha Theta. Democrat. Episcopalian. Home: 7104 Wheeler Rd Richmond VA 23229-6939 Office: 3901 A Ave Ste 100 Fort Lee VA 23801-1807 E-mail: kbs1934@cs.com., sterlink@lee.army.mil.

STERLING, RAYMOND LESLIE, civil engineering educator, researcher, consultant; b. London, Apr. 19, 1949; came to U.S., 1966; s. Richard Howard and Joan Valeria (Skinner) S.; m. Linda Lee Lundquist, Aug. 8, 1970 (div. Sept. 1982); children: Paul, Juliet, Erika; m. Janet Marie Kjera, Aug. 20, 1983; 1 child, Zoey. B in Civil and Structural Engring. with 1st class honors, U. Sheffield, Eng., 1970; MS in Geol. Engring., U. Minn., 1975, PhDCE, 1977. Registered civil engr., Minn.; chartered structural engr., Eng. Engr. trainee Met. Water Bd., London, 1968; civil engr. Egil Wefald and Assocs., Cons. Engrs., Mpls., 1969-71; structural engr. Husband and Co., Cons. Engrs., Eng., 1971-73; rsch. asst. U. Minn., Mpls., 1973-77, dir. Underground Space Ctr., 1977-95, asst. prof. dept. civil and mineral engring., 1977-83, assoc. prof., 1983-95; project. coord., structural engr. Setter, Leach and Lindstrom, Inc., Mpls., 1976-77; prin. cons. Itasca Cons. Group, Inc., Mpls., 1981-94; prof. civil engring. La. Tech. U., Ruston, 1995—, dir. Trenchless Tech. Ctr., 1995—. Vice-chmn. U.S. Nat. com. on tunneling tech. NRC, NAS, 1990-91, chmn 1992-94, com. on infrastructure, 1991-93, bd. infrastructure and the constructed environment, 1994-96; acting co-dir. Minn. Cold Climate Bldg. Rsch. Ctr. U. Minn., 1987-89, co-dir. Bldg. Energy Rsch. Ctr., 1986, speaker's bur., other u. coms.; energy adv. com. Legis. Com. on Minn. Resources, 1989-95; com. on moisture control in bldgs. U.S. Bldg. Thermal Envelope Coordinating Coun., 1985-86; program planning com. on bldg. founds. U.S. Dept. Energy, 1985-95; adv. bd. for energy efficient residence demonstration project Nat. Assn. Home Builders, 1980; mem. Gov's. Exxon Oil Overcharge Adv. Task Force, 1986, Mpls. Energy Future Com., 1980-81, Scientist's Inst. for Pub. Info., N.Y.; cons. U.S. Army Corps. Engrs., UN, N.Y., Opus Corp., Mpls., Dames & Moore Internat., London, City of Mpls., Larson Engring., White Bear, Minn., Pilsbury Co., Mpls., Colgate Divsn. Sch., Rochester, N.Y., others; adv. prof. Chongqing Jianzhu U., Sichuan, People's Republic China, 1985—; vis. rschr. Nat. Inst. Pollution and Resources MITI, Japan, 1991; vis. prof. U. Mo., Rolla, 1979; Shimizu prof. civil and mineral engring., U. Minn., 1988-95; adv. prof. Tongji U., Shanghai, 1996—; mem. eminent speaker program Instn. Engrs., Australia, 1993; hon. prof. Changsha Rwy. U., China, 1998—, Xian U. Arch. and Tech., China, 1999; lectr., presenter in field. Author: Earth Sheltered Housing Design: Guidelines, Examples and References, 1978, transl. into Chinese, French, Spanish and Russian, 2d. edit., 1985, (with others) Earth Sheltered Community Design: The Design of Energy-Efficient Residential Communities, 1980 (award for Best Book in Architecture and Urban Planning Profl. and Scholarly div. Assn. Am. Pubs. 1981), transl. into Spanish, 1981, Underground Building Design, 1983, translated into Japanese and Russian, others, Building Foundation Handbook, 1988, Underground Space Design, 1993, others; editor: (with others) Key Questions in Rock Mechanics: Proc. 29th U.S. Symposium on Rock Mechanics, 1988; contbr. articles to profl. jours. including Jour. Agrl. Engring., Internat. Jour. Rock Mechanics and Mining Scis., Exptl. Mechanics, many others. Named Most Valuable Profl., Gulf Coast Trenchless Assn., 1999; recipient Young Engr. of Yr. award, Minn. Fedn. Engring. Soc., 1982, Applied Rsch. award in rock mechanics, NRC, 1993, elected fgn. mem., Acad. Engring. of Russian Fedn., 1993, Person of Yr. award, Trenchless Tech. mag., 2001; grantee Shimizu Constrn. Co., 1987—93, Nat. Assn. Homebuilders, 1989, U.S. Dept. Energy, 1989—90, NSF, 1991, Minn. Dept. Transp., 1991, ASHRAE, 1991—92, many others. Fellow: ASCE (bd. dirs. 1985—92, pres. Minn. sect. 1990—91, Young Civil Engr. of Yr. award 1982, Stephen D. Bechtel Pipeline Engring. award 2003), Royal Soc. Arts, Mfrs. & Commerce, Inst. Structural Engrs., Instn. Civil Engrs.; mem.: NSPE, Internat. Soc. Trenchless Tech. (vice chmn. 1999—2002, chmn. 2002—), N. Am. Soc. Trenchless Tech. (bd. dirs. 1996—, treas. 1997, internat. rep. 1998—, vice chmn. 1999, chmn. 2000), Internat. Tunneling Assn. (coordinating editor jour. 1986—95, co-sr. editor 1996—, animateur working group on direct/indirect advantages of underground structures 1997—2000), Am. Underground Constrn. Assn. (Award of Distinction 2000). Achievements include research in underground construction, underground space utilization, trenchless technology, rock mechanics, and energy use in buildings. Office: Trenchless Technology Ctr Louisiana Tech U PO Box 10348 Ruston LA 71272-0046

STERLING, RICHARD LEROY, English and foreign language educator; b. Atlantic City, Feb. 18, 1941; s. Richard Leroy and Anne (Bass) S. BA, Am. U., 1968; MA, Cath. U., 1971; PhD, Howard U., 1990. Head Start tchr. DC Pub. Schs., summer 1968, tchr. French and English, adult and continuing edn., 1969-71, 76-83; instr. French Howard U., Washington, 1973-76, grad. tchg. asst., 1983-85, instr., lectr. in French, 1985-89; tchr. English Cmty.-Based Orgns., DC Pub. Schs., 1989-91; asst. prof. French and English Bowie (Md.) State U., 1991-97, assoc. prof. French, 1997—. Tchr. summer enrichment program for gifted children Sch. Edn., Howard U., summers 1985, 86; tchr. ESL, DC Pub. Schs., summer, 1989, 94; asst. coord. Humanities Immersion Program, Project Access for H.S. Students, Bowie State U., summer 1997-98; vice-chmn. World Centennial Conf.; French, Am. and Planetary Dimensions of Saint-John Perse, U. DC, 1987; mem. adv. coun. Northeast Conf. Tchg. Fgn. Langs; NAACP-ACT-SO competition humanities judge 1997-2000; adj. assoc. prof. English, Southeastern U., Washington, summer 1998—; judge DC Pub. Schs. World Langs. Festival, 2001; presenter, book reviewer in field. Author: The Prose Works of Saint-John Perse: Towards an Understanding of His Poetry, 1994; contbg. editor MaComere Rev., 2003—; contbr. articles to profl. jours. Active Assn. Democratique des Francais a L.Etranger, 1988—, Senegal friendship com. Office Cmty. and Ethnic Affairs, Prince George's County Govt., Md., 1993-94, Inst. for Haitian Cultural and Sci. Affairs, 1992-94, local arrangements com. Conf. Coll. Composition and Communication, Washington, 1995, Friends of the Corcoran, 1999; membership com. and outreach com. St. John's Ch., Washington, 1993, ch. growth com., 1995. With U.S. Army, 1964-66. Mem. MLA, Coll. Lang. Assn., Mid. Atlantic Writers Assn. (chmn. essay contest com. 1995-2000, bd. dirs. 2000—), Samuel Beckett Soc., Societe des Professeurs Francais et Francophones d'Amerique, Zora Neale Hurston Soc., Am. Assn. Tchrs. French (sec.-treas. Washington chpt. 1986-90), Nat. Cathedral Assn., Md. Fgn. Lang. Assn. (bd. dirs. 1997-2001, 2003—), Coun. Internat. d'Etudes Francophones, Friends DC Superior Ct. (bd. dirs. 1996—), Univ. Club (Washington), Pi Delta Phi, Sigma Tau Delta. Democrat. Episcopalian. Avocations: classical music, history, travel. Office: Bowie State U Dept English & Modern Langs Bowie MD 20715 E-mail: rsterling@bowiestate.edu.

STERLING, ROBERT LEE, JR., investment company executive; b. Cleve., June 12, 1933; s. Robert Lee and Kathryn (Durell) S.; children from previous marriage: Robert Livingston, William Lee, Cameron Platt; m. Joyce Lanier Milner, June 4, 1994. Student, U. Edinburgh, Scotland, 1955; BA, Brown U., 1956; MBA, Columbia U., 1962. Corp. rsch. analyst Morgan Guaranty Trust, N.Y.C., 1962-63; asst. comptr. Western Hemisphere CPC Internat., N.Y.C., 1963—76; v.p. White, Weld & Co., Inc., N.Y.C., 1976—78, Merrill Lynch Asset Mgmt., 1978-80, Wood, Struthers & Winthrop Mgmt. Corp., N.Y.C., 1980-83; sr. v.p. Shearson Lehman Bros. Asset Mgmt., 1983-88; v.p., sr. portfolio mgr. Chase Manhattan Bank, 1988-93; exec. v.p., sr. portfolio mgr. Melhado, Flynn & Assocs., Inc., N.Y.C., 1993—; mng. ptnr. Winthrop Asset Mgmt., 1995—. Mem. adv. bd. Mus. Modern Art, Oxford U., Eng.; trustee Soc. of the Four Arts, Palm Beach, Norton Mus. of Art, Palm Beach, Preservation Soc., Palm Beach, Game Coservancy, U.S. Mem. New Eng. Soc. (past pres., J.P. Morgan medal), St. Nicholas Soc., Pilgrims, N.Y. State Soc. of Cin. (past pres.), Univ. Club (N.Y.C.), Everglades Club (Palm Beach, Fla.), Bath and Tennis Club (Palm Beach, Fla.), Anabell's (London), Alpha Delta Phi, Alpha Kappa Psi. Home: 200 Regent Park Palm Beach FL 33480 Office: Melhado Flynn & Assocs Inc 530 5th Ave New York NY 10036-5101 Office Phone: 212-764-3648.

STERLING, STEVE, professional athletics coach; m. Francesca Sterling; 2 children. Degree, Boston (Mass.) U. Head coach hockey team Babson Coll., Mass., 1978—83, 1985—93, athletic dir., 1986—97; head coach Providence Coll., 1983—85; scout N.Y. Islanders, 1997—98, head coach, 2003—; asst. coach Lowell Lock Monsters, 1998—2000; head coach Bridgeport Sound Tigers, 2001—03. Mailing: 1535 Old Country Rd Plainview NY 11803*

STERLING, WARREN MARTIN, engineering director; b. Chgo., Jan. 4, 1947; s. Harold D. and Ruth Sterling; m. Barbara A. Marbell, Aug. 21, 1977; 1 child, Reuben. BSEE, U. Ill., 1968; MSEE, Carnegie-Mellon U., 1970, PhD, 1974. Sys. engr. Westinghouse, Pitts., 1968-74; sr. mem. rsch. staff Xerox Parc, El Segundo, Calif., 1974-82; dir. engring. Teradata, El Segundo, 1982-92, AT&T, El Segundo, 1992-97, Teradata, a divsn. of NCR, El Segundo, 1997—. Instr. UCLA, 1975-82; mem. engring. adv. bd. Calif. State U., Long Beach, 1990—; mem. sci. adv. bd. U. So. Calif., L.A., 1996—; bd. chmn. NIST-sponsored Nat. Med. Knowledge Bank Project, 1996-2000, European Union-sponsored Artiste Project, 2000-02. Contbr. papers to profl. jours. Mem. IEEE, Tau Beta Pi. Achievements include 4 patents in field; leader design and implementation of world's first massively parallel computer for business applications (DBC/1012). Office: Teradata a Divsn of NCR 100 N Sepulveda Blvd El Segundo CA 90245-4359

STERLING, WILLIAM CARLISLE, physician assistant; b. Toledo, Ohio, Oct. 18, 1942; s. Robert Kelso and Maryellen Ruth S.; m. Christina A. Clark, June 1, 1995; children: Sean Carlisle, Lyle Brent, Nelson Anthony. Student, U. Toledo, 1960-61, 65-69. Physician asst. Grand Rapids (Ohio) Med. Clinic, 1969-76, GM, Toledo, Ohio, 1983-93, Brownville (Tex.) Cmty. Health, 1993-98, Excalibur Health Assocs., Brownsville, 1998—. Med. dir. Brownsville Cmty. Health, 1995-97; founder, dir. Emergency Squad Unit, Inc., Grand Rapids, 1973-83. With USN, 1961-65. Decorated Commendation medal. Mem. Am. Acad. Physicians Assts., Am. Assn. Physician Assts. Occupational Medicine (v.p.), Ohio Assn. Physician Assts., Tex. Assn. Physician Assts. Home: 805 Rose Ct Pemberville OH 43450-9437

STERMER, DUGALD ROBERT, designer, illustrator, writer, consultant; b. Los Angeles, Dec. 17, 1936; s. Robert Newton and Mary (Blue) S.; children: Dugald, Megan, Chris, Colin, Crystal. BA, UCLA, 1960. Art dir., v.p. Ramparts mag., 1965-70; freelance designer, illustrator, writer, cons. San Francisco, 1970—; founder Pub. Interest Communications, San Francisco, 1974; chmn. illustration dept. Calif. Coll. Arts and Crafts, 1994—, disting. prof., 1994—. Bd. dirs. Am. Inst. Graphic Arts, Illustration Partnership Am.; mem. San Francisco Art Commn., 1997—. Cons. editor: Communication Arts mag., 1974-90; designer: Oceans mag., 1976-82; editor: The Environment, 1972, Vanishing Creatures, 1980; author: The Art of Revolution, 1970, Vanishing Creatures, 1980, Vanishing Flora, 1994, Birds and Bees, 1994; designer 1984 Olympic medals; illustration exhbn. Calif. Acad. Scis., 1986; one-man show Jernigan Wicker Gallery, San Francisco, 1996. Mem. Grand Jury City and County San Francisco, 1989; bd. dirs. Delancey St. Found., 1990—. Recipient various medals, awards for design and illustration nat. and internat. competitions. Office: 600 The Embarcadero # 204 San Francisco CA 94107-2121 Office Phone: 415-777-0110. Business E-Mail: ds@dugaldstermer.com.

STERN, ANDREW L. labor union administrator; St. social svc. worker, mem. Local 668 Svc. Employees Internat. Union, 1973—80, mem. internat. exec. bd., 1980—, org. field svc. programs, 1984—96, internat. pres., 1996—. Bd. dirs. AFL-CIO Housing and Bldg. Investment Trust, Medicare Rights Ctr., Aspen Inst. Mem.: Am. Hosp.Assn. (commn. on workforce for hosps. and health systems.), Nat. Acad. Social Ins. Office: Svc Employees Internat Union 1313 L St NW Washington DC 20005-4101*

STERN, ANDREW MILTON, public relations executive; b. Cleve., Mar. 22, 1949; s. Sidney Harrison Stern, Jr. and Sue (Friedlander) Miller; m. Sabina R. Bobzin, Feb. 28, 1971; children: David Patrick, Eric Thomas. BA, U. Del., 1970. Press sec. to mayor City of Wilmington, Del., 1970-73; dir. pub. affairs Wilmington Med. Ctr., 1973-75; staff asst. to pres. The White House, Washington, 1975-77; dir. pub. relations and advt. Wylain, Inc., Dallas, 1977-80; sr. v.p. Assocs. Corp. N.Am., Dallas, 1980-82; chmn., chief exec. officer Sunwest Communications, Inc., Dallas, 1982—. Founder, dir. Dallas Nat. Bank. Chmn. Med. City Dallas Hosp., Dallas County Hist. Found. Mem. Pub. Rels. Soc. Am., North Dallas C. of C. (past chmn.). Clubs: Salesmanship, Prestonwood, Park City, Press (Dallas). Republican. Jewish. Home: 5916 Club Oaks Dr Dallas TX 75248-1124 Office: Sunwest Communications Inc 5420 Lyndon B Johnson Pwy 1475 Dallas TX 75240-6265

STERN, ARLENE HELEN, human resources specialist; b. Bklyn., Nov. 7, 1950; d. Irving and Shirley Judith (Koretz) Stern. BS in Labor Rels., U. Bridgeport, 1971; postgrad., Pace U., 1972—75. From Pers. asst. to dir. human resource planning Pathmark, Woodbridge, NJ, 1971—77, dir. pers. and labor rels. Phila., 1977—81; v.p. human resources Howland-Steinbach-Hochschild's, White Plains, NY, 1981—85; sr. v.p. human resources and distbn. P.A. Bergner & Co., Milw., 1985—89, exec. v.p. human resources and distbn., 1989—. Mem. Frederick Atkins Pers. Adv. Bd., NYC, 1981—86, chmn., 1984. Women's divsn. Wis. State of Israel Bonds, 1988, Milw. Jewish Fedn., 1987—, Milw. Jewish Coun., 1987—; bd. dirs. Clavis Theatre, 1986—. Mem.: ASTD, Am. Soc. Pers. Adminstrs. Home: 628 West Rd New Canaan CT 06840-2513 Office: Gantos Inc Soundview Plz 1266 E Main St 5th Fl Stamford CT 06902

STERN, ARTHUR PAUL, electronics company executive; b. Budapest, Hungary, July 20, 1925; arrived in U.S., 1951; s. Leon and Bertha (Frankfurter) Stern; m. Edith M. Samuel; children: Daniel, Claude, Jacqueline. Diploma in Elec. Engring., Swiss Fed. Inst. Tech., Zurich, 1948; MSEE, Syracuse U., 1955. Mgr. electronic devices and applications lab. GE, Syracuse, N.Y., 1957-61; dir. engring. Martin Marietta Corp., Balt., 1961-64; dir. ops. Bunker Ramo Corp., Canoga Park, Calif., 1964-66; v.p., gen. mgr. advanced products divsn. Magnavox, Torrance, Calif., 1966-79; pres. Magnavox Advanced Products and Systems Co., Torrance, 1980-90; vice chmn., dir. Magnavox Electronics Systems Co., Ft. Wayne, Ind., 1987—90; pres. Ea. Beverly Hills Corp., 1991—. Pres. Calif.-Israel C. of C., 1994—98, chmn. bd. dirs., 1998—2000; mem. governing coun. Am.-Jewish Congress, 1997—98; bd. dirs. Jewish Coun. Pub. Affairs, 1996—2002; v.p. Progressive Jewish Alliance, 1999—; non-resident staff mem. MIT, 1956—59; instr. GE Bus. Mgmt., 1955—57. Co-author: (book) Transistor Circuit Engineering, 1957, Handbook of Automation, Computation and Control, 1961; contbr. articles to profl. jours. Mem. adv. bd. dept. elec. engring. U. Calif., Santa Barbara, 1980—92; mem. Sch. Engring. Adv. and Devel. Coun. Calif. State U., Long Beach, 1985—90; chmn. bd. dirs. Calif. Humanitarian Found. for Holocaust Survivors, 2000—; regional co-chmn., bd. dirs. Ams. for Peace Now, 2002—; bd. dirs. So. Calif. Ams. for Dem. Action, 2000—04; chmn. engring. divsn. United Jewish Appeal, Syracuse, 1955—57; bd. dirs. Bur. Jewish Edn., L.A., 1995—, chmn. investment com., 2000—; vice-chmn. Jewish Cmty. Rels. Com. of Jewish Fedn. of L.A., 1998—2003; bd. dirs. Jewish Fedn. Greater L.A., 2003—. Recipient Justice-Tzedek award, Labor Zionist Alliance, 2001. Fellow: IEEE (pres. 1975, bd. dirs., officer 1970—77, guest editor spl. issue IEEE Trans. on Circuit Theory 1956, invited guest editor spl. issue Procs. IEEE on Integrated Electronics 1964, Centennial medal 1984, Millennium medal 2000, Haraden Pratt award 2001), AAAS; mem.: Eta Kappa Nu Assn. (eminent mem.). Achievements include patents in field.

STERN, BRIAN E. consumer products company executive; b. London, Nov. 8, 1947; B in History, U. East Anglia, Norwich, Eng., 1969; MBA, Harvard U., 1973. Corp. v.p. Xerox Corp., Stamford, Conn., 1993—95, sr. v.p., 1995—, pres. supplies bus. group, 2001—. Office: Xerox Corp 800 Long Ridge Rd Stamford CT 06904

STERN, BRUCE H. lawyer; b. Washington, Apr. 13, 1956; s. Harvey L. and Carol (Bash) S.; m. Linda Korsen, May 23, 1981. BA cum laude, Duke U., 1977; JD cum laude, Rutgers U., Camden, N.J., 1981. Bar: N.J. 1981, Pa. 1982, U.S. Dist. Ct. N.J. 1981, U.S. Ct. Appeals (3rd cir.) 1982, U.S. Dist. Ct. (ea. and so. dists.) N.Y. 1983. Assoc., Trenton, N.J., 1982-85, 1985-88, Stark & Stark, Lawrenceville, N.J., 1988-89, ptnr., 1989—. Mem. Supreme Ct. Com. on Spl. Civil Practice, 1987-90, Supreme Ct. Com. Model Jury Charge Civil, 1990-94. Mem. editorial bd. N.J. Lawyer, 1989-91, Neurolaw Letter Trial Lawyer; assoc. editor: Nat. Trial Lawyer; state editor N.J. Trial Lawyer; contbr. articles to legal jours. Mem. Mercer County Bar Assn. (pres. 1997-98, trustee 1988-94) Trial Lawyers of N.J., N.J. State Bar Assn. (exec. bd. civil trial sect.), Assn. Trial Lawyers Am. (exec. bd. traumatic brain injury litigation group), Assn. Trial Lawyers N.J. (bd. govs., treas. 1997-98, 2d v.p. 1999—, 1st v.p. 2000-01, pres. elect 2001-02, pres. 2002-03), Internat. Brain Injury Assn. (treas. 2001—), Brain Injury Assn. N.J. (trustee), Brain Injury Assn. North Am. Brain Injury Soc. (treas. 2003—). Office: Stark & Stark PC 992 Lenox Dr CN 5315 Princeton NJ 08543-5315 Office Phone: 609-896-9060. E-mail: bstern@stark-stark.com.

STERN, CARL LEONARD, former news correspondent, federal official; b. N.Y.C., Aug. 7, 1937; s. Hugo and Frances (Taft) S.; m. Joy Elizabeth Nathan, Nov. 27, 1960; children: Lawrence, Theodore. AB, Columbia U., 1958, MS, 1959; JD, Cleve. State U., 1966, JD (hon.), 1975, New Eng. Coll. Law, 1977. Bar: Ohio 1966, D.C. 1968, U.S. Supreme Ct. 1969. Law corr. NBC News, Washington, 1967-93; dir. Office of Pub. Affairs U.S. Dept. Justice, Washington, 1993-96; Shapiro Prof. of Media and Pub. Affairs George Washington U., 1996—. Lectr. Nat. Jud. Coll.; adj. prof. George Washington U., Stanford U. Editorial bd.: The Dist. Lawyer. Mem. Dept. Transp. Task Force on Assistance to Families in Aviation Disasters, 1997; mem. nat. adv. coun. Cleveland-Marshall Law Sch. Recipient Peabody award, 1974, Emmy award, 1974, Gavel award, 1969, 74, Headliner Club award, 1991, Edmond J. Randloph award U.S. Dept. Justice. Mem. ABA (vice chmn. criminal justice sect. com. on criminal justice and the media, gov., forum com. on communications law, working group intelligence requirements and criminal code reform, mem. standing com. on strategic comms.), AFTRA (nat. exec. bd. 1984-86, first v.p. Washington, Balt. chpt. 1985-87). Home: 2956 Davenport St NW Washington DC 20008 Office: George Washington U #400 805 21st St NW Washington DC 20052 Office Phone: 202-994-1464. Personal E-mail: sterncarl@aol.com. Business E-Mail: cstern@gwu.edu.

STERN, CARL WILLIAM, JR., management consultant; b. San Francisco, Mar. 31, 1946; s. Carl William and Marjorie Aline (Gunst) S.; m. Karen Jaffe, Sept. 7, 1966 (div. Mar. 1972); 1 child, David; m. Holly Drick Hayes, Mar. 21, 1985; children: Kenneth, Matthew. BA, Harvard U., 1968; MBA, Stanford U., 1974. Cons. Boston Cons. Group, Inc., Menlo Park, Calif., 1974-77, mgr., 1977-78, London, 1978-80, v.p. Chgo., 1980-87, sr. v.p., 1987-97, pres., CEO, 1998—2003, co-chmn. bd., 2004—. Lt. USNR, 1968-71. Office: Boston Consulting Group Inc 200 S Wacker Dr Ste 2700 Chicago IL 60606-5846

STERN, CLAUDIO DANIEL, medical educator, embryological researcher; b. Montevideo, Uruguay, Feb. 9, 1954; came to U.S., 1994; s. Erico and Trude Stern. BSc with honors, U. Sussex, 1975, DPhil, 1978; MA, U. Oxford, 1985, DSc, 1994. Asst. prof. anatomy dept. Cambridge (England) U., 1984-85; assoc. prof. dept. human anatomy U. Oxford (England), 1985-93; prof., chmn. dept. genetics and devel. Coll. Physicians and Surgeons Columbia U., N.Y.C., 1994—. Contbr. articles to profl. jours.; mng. editor Mechanisms of Devel.; mem. editorial adv. bd. Devel.; mem. editorial bd. Internat. Jour. Devel. Biology, Cell. Rsch. fellow U. Coll. London, 1978-84, fellow Christ Ch. Coll., 1985-93. Office: Columbia U Dept Genetics & Devel 701 W 168th St Dept & New York NY 10032-2704

STERN, DANIEL, author, executive, educator; b. N.Y.C., Jan. 18, 1928; s. Morris and Dora (Hochman) S.; m. Gloria Shapiro, Nov. 9, 1963; 1 son, Eric Branfman. Sr. v.p., mng. dir., mem. bd. mgmt. McCann-Erickson Advt., Inc., N.Y.C., 1964-69; v.p. advt. and publicity worldwide, also dir. Warner Bros., 1969-72; v.p., dir. mktg. Longchamps, Inc., N.Y.C., 1972-73; v.p., creative dir. Lubar-Southard, Inc., N.Y.C., 1973; fellow Ctr. for Humanities, Wesleyan U., 1969, vis. prof. letters and English, 1976-79; v.p. promotion East Coast CBS Entertainment, N.Y.C., 1979-86; pres. entertainment divsn. McCaffrey & McCall, Advt., N.Y.C., 1986; prof. English and creative writing U. Houston, 1992—, Cullen disting. prof. English, 1993—. Dir. Humanities, 92nd St. YMHA, 1988. Author: Girl with Glass Heart, 1953, The Guests of Fame, 1955, Miss America, 1959, Who Shall Live, Who Shall Die, 1963 (Internat. Remembrance award for fiction Bergen Belsen Assn. 1973), After the War, 1967, The Suicide Academy, 1968, The Rose Rabbi, 1971, Final Cut, 1975, An Urban Affair, 1980, Twice Told Tales, 1989 (Richard and Hinda Rosenthal Fiction award AAAL 1990), Twice Upon a Time, 1992, One Day's Perfect Weather, 1999, In the Country of the Young, 2001, A Little Street Music: Novella and Stories, 2004. With U.S. Army, 1946-47. Recipient Brazos prize for best short story Tex. Inst. Letters, 1996, Fiction prize Tex. Rev. Press, 2003. Mem. PEN, Nat. Book Critics Circle, Author's League.

STERN, DAVID JOEL, National Basketball Association Commissioner; b. N.Y.C., Sept. 22, 1942; s. William and Anna (Bronstein) Stern; m. Dianne Bock, Nov. 27, 1963; children: Andrew, Eric. BA, Rutgers U., 1963; LLB, Columbia U., 1966. Bar: N.Y. 1963. Assoc. Proskauer Rose Goetz & Mendelsohn, N.Y.C., 1966—74, ptnr., 1974—78; gen. counsel Nat. Basketball Assn., N.Y.C., 1978—80, exec. v.p. bus. and legal affairs, 1980—84, commr., 1984—. Mem. Martin Luther King Jr. Fed. Holiday Commn., 1988—; White House Conf. for a Drug-Free Am., 1988; bd. dirs. NAACP, 1990—93; trustee Beth Israel Med. Ctr., 1985—, Rutgers U. Found., 1987—, Columbia U., 1992—. Mem.: ABA, Assn. Bar City N.Y. (chmn. com. on entertainment and sports 1983—86), N.Y. State Bar Assn. Office: NBA Olympic Tower 645 5th Ave Fl 10 New York NY 10022-5986

STERN, DAVID MARK, dean, educator; s. Robert and Florence Stern; m. Kathleen Shirley Stern; children: Eric David, Alan Robert. BS, Yale U., 1973; MD, Harvard U., 1978. Mem. faculty Coll. Physicians and Surgeons, Columbia U., NYC, 1983—2002, named Gerald & Janet Carrus Prof. of Surg. Sci., 1998, dir. Ctr. Vascular and Lung Pathobiology, dir. Juvenile Diabetes Rsch. Ctr.; dean sch. medicine, sr. v.p. clin. activities Med. Coll. Ga., Augusta, 2002—. Mem.: Am. Assn. Physicians, Am. Soc. Clin. Investigation. Office: 1120 15th St Augusta GA 30912 Business E-Mail: dstern@mail.mcg.edu.

STERN, DONALD KENNETH, lawyer; BA, Hobart Coll., 1966; JD, Georgetown U., 1969; LLM, U. Pa., 1973. Intern Dist. Atty.'s Office, Mineola, N.Y., 1967, Citizen's Adv. Ctr., Washington, 1968; staff atty. Defender Assn. Phila., Cmty. Legal Svcs., Phila., 1969-71; adj. prof. law, supervising atty. Boston Coll. Law Sch., Boston Coll. Legal Assistance Bur., 1971-73, asst. prof. law, dir. clin. programs, supervising atty., 1973-75; asst. atty. gen., dir. atty. gen. clin. program, Mass. Atty. Gen.'s Office, Boston Coll. Law Sch., 1975-77, asst. prof. law, dir. atty. gen. clin. program, spl. asst. atty. gen., 1977-78, asst. atty. gen., dir. atty. gen. clin. program, 1978-79; chief govt. bur. Mass. Atty. Gen.'s Office, 1979-82; assoc. Hale and Dorr, Boston, 1982-85, jr. ptnr., 1985-87, sr. ptnr., 1987, 91-93, of counsel, 1990-91; chief legal counsel to Gov. Mass., 1987-90; U.S. atty. Dist. Mass., 1993—2001; ptnr. Bingham McCutchen, LLP, 2001—; lectr. Harvard Law Sch., 2002—. Office: Bingham McCutchen LLP 150 Federal St Boston MA 02210-1726 Office Phone: 617-951-8250. E-mail: donald.stern@bingham.com.

STERN, EDITH LOIS, counselor, hypno-therapist; b. Paterson, N.J., Apr. 20, 1928; d. Meyer Zenack and Helen Rebecca (Jarvis) Zenack-Kollin; m. Eugene Stern, June 23, 1949 (div. Dec. 1978); children: Michael, Jonathan, Andrew. BA in Edn., Bklyn. Coll., 1949; MS in Counseling, C.W. Post U., 1971. Cert. counselor, N.Y. Tchr. Pub. Sch. 70, Bklyn., 1949-53; counselor Jericho (N.Y.) H.S., 1972, Farmingdale (N.Y.) H.S., 1973, 75, Uniondale (N.Y.) H.S., 1974; dir. New Directions, Massapequa, N.Y., 1971-91. Mem. adv. bd. Mid-Queens Cmty. Coun., Jamaica, N.Y., 1957-64, Peacesmith's, Inc., Massapequa, 1972-75, Nassau Women's Polit. Caucus, Mineola, 1973-80; dir. Kaplan Meml. Libr., Mineola, N.Y., 1968-80; counselor Nassau County CETA, Hempstead, N.Y., 1977-81; tax agt. N.Y. State Dept. Taxation, Hempstead, 1982-92. Editor (editl.) Temple Judea Newsletter, 1967. Pres. PTA Pub. Sch. 165, Flushing, N.Y., 1962-64; committeewoman Nassau County Dem., Massapequa, 1965-85; campaign mgr. Krupsak for Lt. Gov., Nassau County, 1974. Mem. NOW, Am. Pers. and Guidance Assn., Am. Assn. Ret. Persons, N.Y. State Ret. Pub. Employees Assn., Hawaiian Gardens Women's Club (v.p. 1995-97, pres. 1997-99), Ilana Hadassah (corr. sec. 1995-97, pres. 1997—). Jewish. Avocations: reading, attending the theatre, writing. Home: Apt D210 5041 W Oakland Park Blvd Fort Lauderdale FL 33313-1517

STERN, EDWARD ABRAHAM, physics educator; b. Detroit, Sept. 19, 1930; s. Jacob Munich and Rose (Kravitz) S.; m. Sylvia Rita Sidell, Oct. 30, 1955; children: Hilary, Shari, Miri. BS, Calif. Tech., 1951, PhD, 1955. Post-doctoral fellow Calif. Tech., Pasadena, 1955-57; asst. prof. U. Md., College Park, 1957-61, assoc. prof., 1961-64, prof., 1964-65, U. Wash., Seattle, 1965—2000, emeritus, 2000—. Contbr. over 200 articles to profl. jours.; editor; three books. Recipient B. Warren award Am. Crystallography Assn., 1979, Outstanding Achievement award Internat. XAFS Soc., 2000; named Guggenheim fellow, Cambridge, Eng., 1963-64, NSF Sr. Post-doctoral fellow, Haifa, Israel, 1970-71, Fulbright fellow, Jerusalem, Israel, 1985-86. Fellow AAAS, Am. Physical Soc. Achievements include patent for x-ray focusing device; development of x-ray absorption fine structure technique; research on surface plasmons, nonlinear reflection from surfaces, electronic properties of alloys, structural phase transition. Office: U Wash Dept Physics PO Box 351560 Seattle WA 98195-1560 E-mail: stern@phys.washington.edu.

STERN, ELIZABETH ESPIN, lawyer; b. Prince Georges County, Md., June 21, 1961; d. Cesar A. and M. Cecilia (Salvador) E.; m. Michael L. Stern, May 16, 1992; 1 child, Alexander. BA magna cum laude, U. Va., 1983, JD, 1986. Bar: Va. 1986, U.S. Dist. Ct. (ea. dist.) Va., D.C. 1988. Ptnr. comml. immigration Shaw, Pittman, Potts & Trowbridge, Washington, 1986—. Past chair young lawyers sect. Vol. Bar Assn. D.C. Recipient Martin Preis award Vol. Bar Assn. D.C., 1992; named one of top 75 lawyers in Washington, Washingtonian Mag. Mem. NAFE, Am. Immigration Lawyers Assn., Va. Bar Assn., D.C. Bar Assn. (internat. sec. 1986—, del. to ABA, chair young lawyers sect. 1992-93, Young Lawyer of Yr. 1994), Immigration Tech. Assn. Am. Republican. Avocation: journalism. Home: 8529 Century Oak Ct Fairfax Station VA 22039-3343 Office: Shaw Pittman Potts & Trowbridge 2300 N St NW Fl 5 Washington DC 20037-1172

STERN, EMANUEL, real estate developer; s. Leonard N. and Judith Stern. Grad., Tufts U.; M in Pub. Affairs, Columbia U. Joined The Hartz Group, Inc., N.Y.C., 1991—, pres., COO Hartz Mountain Industries, 1997—. Trustee N.Y. Hist. Soc., N.Y.C., Citizens Budget Commn. N.Y.C.; mem. exec. bd. Urban Justice Ctr. Office: Hartz Mountain Industries Inc PO Box 1515 400 Plaza Dr Secaucus NJ 07096 also: The Hartz Group 667 Madison Ave New York NY 10021*

STERN, FRITZ RICHARD, historian, educator; b. Breslau, Germany, Feb. 2, 1926; came to U.S., 1938, naturalized, 1947; s. Rudolf A. and Catherine (Brieger) S.; m. Margaret J. Bassett, Oct. 11, 1947 (div. 1992); children: Frederick P., Katherine Stern Brennan; m. Elisabeth Niebuhr Sifton, Jan. 1, 1996. BA, Columbia U., 1946, MA, 1948, PhD, 1953; DLitt (hon.), Oxford U., 1985; LLD (hon.), New Sch. for Social Rsch., 1997, Columbia U., 1998; LLD (hon.), U. Wroclaw, 2002. Lectr., instr. Columbia U., 1946-51, faculty, 1953—, prof. history, 1963—, Seth Low prof. history, 1967-92, univ. prof., 1992-96, provost, 1980-83; acting asst. prof. Cornell U., 1951-53; univ. prof. emeritus Columbia U., 1997—; tchr. Free U. Berlin, 1954, Yale U., 1963; permanent vis. prof. U. Konstanz, West Germany, 1966—; sr. adviser U.S. Embassy, Bonn, 1993-94. Élie Halévy prof. U. Paris, spring 1979; Phi Beta Kappa vis. scholar, 1979-80; Tanner lectr. Yale, 1993. Author: The Politics of Cultural Despair, 1961, The Failure of Illiberalism-Essays in the Political Culture of Modern Germany, 1972, rev. edit., 1992, Gold and Iron: Bismarck, Bleichroeder and the Bldg. of the German Empire, 1977 (recipient Lionel Trilling award Columbia U.), Dreams and Delusions: The Drama of German History, 1987, rev. edit. 1999, Einstein's German World, 1999; editor: The Varieties of History, 1956, 71, (with L. Krieger) The Responsibility of Power, 1967; mem. editorial bd. Foreign Affairs, 1978-92; contbr. articles to profl. jours.; reviewer Fgn. Affairs, 1963-95. Trustee German Marshall Fund, 1981-99, Aspen Inst. of Berlin, 1983—; senator Deutsche Nationalstiftung, 1994—; mem. Trilateral Commn., 1983-90. Decorated Officer's Cross Order of Merit Fed. Republic of Germany; fellow Center Advanced Behavioral Scis., 1957-58; fellow Social Sci. Research Council, 1960-61; fellow Am. Council Learned Socs., 1966-67; fellow Netherlands Inst. Advanced Study, 1972-73; mem. Nuffield Coll., Oxford, 1966-67, Inst. Advanced Study Princeton, 1969-70; Guggenheim fellow, 1969-70; Ford Found. grantee, 1976-77; vis. scholar Russell Sage Found., 1989, spring 1993; recipient Leopold-Lucas-prize Evang. Faculty U. Tübingen, 1984, Peace prize German Book Trade Frankfurt Book Fair, 1999, Bruno Snell medal U. Hamburg, 2002. Mem. Am. Hist. Assn., AAAS, Am. Philos. Soc., Coun. Fgn. Rels., Deutsche Akademie für Sprache und Dichtung (corr.), Berlin Brandenburgische Akademie der Wissenschaften (corr.), Orden Pour le Mérite, Germany, Phi Beta Kappa (senator-at-large 1973-78). Clubs: Century (N.Y.C.). Home: 15 Claremont Ave New York NY 10027-6802 E-mail: fs20@columbia.edu.

STERN, GAIL FRIEDA, historical association director; b. Atlantic City, May 18, 1950; d. Herbert and Faith (Beldegreen) Stern; m. Irwin Allen Popowsky (div.); m. Shawn Paul Aubitz (div.); 1 child, Jonathan. Student, Brown U., 1972; postgrad., U. Pa., 1973. Asst. in decorative arts Phila. Mus. Art, 1972-75; asst. curator Wheaton Mus. Glass, Millville, N.J., 1973-74; assoc. dir. Pa. Humanities Coun., Phila., 1976-79; mus. curator The Balch Inst. for Ethnic Studies, Phila., 1979-83, mus. dir., 1984-93; dir. Hist. Soc. Princeton, N.J., 1993—. Chair Pa. Task Force on Folk Arts and Culture, 1981-82; vice chmn. crafts panel Pa. Coun. on the Arts, Harrisburg, 1988-89; chair cultural conservation com., Pa. Heritage Affairs Commn., Harrisburg, 1990-92; participant Internat. Partnership in Mus., Singapore, 1991. Recipient pub. programming award, NJ Coun. Humanities, 1996, award for outstanding contbns. to NJ history, NJ Hist. Commn., 1999. Mem. Mus. Coun. Phila. (v.p. 1982-83), Am. Assn. Mus./Internat. Coun. Mus. (bd. dirs. 1991-97), N.J. Mus. Assn. (bd. dirs., sec. 1993-98, John Cotton Dana award 2000), Am. Assn. for State and Local History Awards (N.J. chair 1994-95, 2002-03), Mid-Atlantic Assn. Mus. (bd. dirs. 1997-98). Home: 41 Lafayette Street Hopewell NJ 08525 Office: Hist Soc Princeton 158 Nassau St Princeton NJ 08542-7006 Office Phone: 609-921-6748. E-mail: gailfstern@aol.com.

STERN, GEOFFREY, lawyer, disciplinary counsel; b. Columbus, Ohio, Nov. 29, 1942; s. Leonard J. and Anastasia (Percin) S.; m. Barbara Shnider; children: Emily Staheli, Elizabeth Leskowyak; stepchildren: Courtney, Jennifer, Brian Feuer. Student, Williams Coll., 1960-63; BA cum laude, Ohio State U., 1965, JD summa cum laude, 1968. Bar: Ohio 1968. Assoc. Alexander, Ebinger, Holschuh & Fisher, Columbus, Ohio, 1968-72; ptnr. Folkerth, Calhoun, Webster & O'Brien, Columbus, Ohio, 1972-80, Arter & Hadden, Columbus, Ohio, 1980-93; disciplinary counsel Supreme Ct. of Ohio, 1993-97; counsel Kegler, Brown, Hill & Ritter, Columbus, 1997-2000, dir., 2000—. Nat. coordinating counsel for asbestos litigation Combustion Engring. Inc. and Basic, Inc., 1985-93; lectr. on legal ethics and profl. responsibility; mem. Spl. Commn. to Review Ohio Ethics Rules, 1995-98, Spl. Commn. on Legal Edn., 1995-98; mem. symposium on ethics and Chinese legal sys., Shanghai, 1998; keynote spkr. Faith and Law Symposium, 1999; spl. investigator Bd. Commrs. Character and Fitness Ohio Supreme Ct., 1998. Sr. editor Ohio State Law Jour., 1967-68. Pres. Bexley (Ohio) City Coun., 1977-80, mem., 1973-80, mem. Bexley Civil Svc. Commn., 1983-85; v.p., trustee Creative Living, Columbus, 1981-89, Ohio Citizens Com. for Arts, Columbus, 1982-88; mem. Nat. Def. Com. on Asbestos in Bldgs. Litigation, 1986-92; pub. mem. Ohio Optical Dispensers Bd., Columbus, 1978-82. Recipient Am. Jurisprudence Evidence award Ohio State U. Coll. Law, 1967. Fellow Am. Bar Found., Columbus Bar Found., Ohio State Bar Found.; mem. Ohio State Bar Assn. (com. on legal ethics and profl. conduct, sec. 1981-90, vice chmn. 1990-92, chmn. 1992-93), Columbus Bar Assn. (profl. ethics com. 1975-86, 90-93, Liberty Bell award for Cmty. and Profl. Svc. 1998), Order of Coif, Phi Beta Kappa, Pi Sigma Alpha. Home: 278 Crossing Crk N Columbus OH 43230-6108 Office: Kegler Brown Hill & Ritter 65 E State St Ste 1800 Columbus OH 43215-4213 Office Phone: 614-462-5400. Business E-Mail: gstern@keglerbrown.com.

STERN, GERALD MANN, lawyer; b. Chgo., Apr. 5, 1937; s. Lloyd and Fannye (Wener) S.; m. Linda Stone, Dec. 20, 1969; children: Eric, Jesse, Maia. BS in Econs., U. Pa., 1958; LL.B. cum laude, Harvard, 1961. Bar: D.C. 1961, Calif. 1991, U.S. Supreme Ct. 1971. Trial atty. civil rights div. U.S. Dept. Justice, 1961-64; assoc. firm Arnold & Porter, Washington, 1964-68, ptnr., 1969-76; founding ptnr. Rogovin, Stern & Huge, Washington, 1976-81; exec. v.p., sr. gen. counsel Occidental Petroleum Corp., Washington, 1981—92; spl. counsel fin. instn. fraud and health care fraud U.S. Dept. Justice, Washington, 1993-95; ind. legal cons. pvt. practice, Washington, 1995—; cons. Antitrust divsn. U.S. Dept. Justice, 1998—2001. Bd. dirs. Oceania Cruises, Inc. Author: The Buffalo Creek Disaster, 1976; co-author: Southern Justice, 1965, Outside the Law, 1997. Trustee Facing History and Ourselves, 1996—. Mem. ABA. Home and Office: 3322 Newark St NW Washington DC 20008-3330 Fax: 202-364-2595. Office Phone: 202-253-2257., 202-362-2078. E-mail: GMS37@aol.com.

STERN, GRACE MARY, former state legislator; b. Holyoke, Mass., July 10, 1925; d. Frank McLellan and Marguerite M. (Nason) Dain; m. Charles H. Suber, June 21, 1947 (div. 1959); children: Ann, Peter, Thomas, John; m. Herbert L. Stern, May 13, 1962; stepchildren: Gwen, Herbert III, Robert. Student, Wellesley Coll., 1942-45; LLD (hon.), Shimer Coll., 1984. Asst. supr. Deerfield Twp., Lake County, Ill., 1967-70; county clk. Lake County, Ill.,

1970-82; mem. Ill. Ho. of Reps., Springfield, 1984-92, Ill. State Senate, 1993-95. Author: With a Stern Eye, 1967, Still Stern, 1969. Candidate lt. gov. State of Ill., 1982. Democrat. Presbyterian. Home: 140 S Dearborn St Ste 1400 Chicago IL 60603-5208

STERN, GUY, German language and literature educator, writer; b. Hildesheim, Germany, Jan. 14, 1922; came to U.S., 1937, naturalized, 1943; s. Julius and Hedwig (Silberberg) S.; m. Judith Owens, June 16, 1979; 1 child, Mark. BA in Romance Langs., Hofstra Coll., 1948; MA in Germanic Langs. with honors, Columbia U., 1950, PhD with honors, 1953; Dr. (hon.), Hofstra U., 1998. Grad. asst., then instr. Columbia U., 1948-55; asst. prof., then assoc. prof. Denison U., Granville, Ohio, 1955-63; prof. German, dept. head U. Cin., 1964-73, dean univ., 1973-76; prof., chmn. Germanic and Slavic dept. U. Md., College Park, 1976-78; v.p., provost Wayne State U., Detroit, 1978-80, disting. prof. German, 1980—. Guest prof. Goethe Inst., Freiburg U., summers 1963-66, 84, Frankfurt U., 1993, Leipzig U., 1997, Potsdam U., 1998, Munich U., 1999; adv. editor langs. and linguistics Dover Publs. Co-author: Brieflich Erzaehlt, 1956, Listen and Learn German, 1957, Say It in German, 1958, Uebung macht den Meister, 1959, An Invitation to German Poetry, 1960, Hints on Speaking German, 1961, Quick Change Pattern Drills, vol. I, 1962, vol. II, 1963, Hoer zu und Rat mit, 1964; author: Efraim Frisch: Zum Verstaendnis des Geistigen, 1964, War, Weimar and Literature, 1971, Alfred Neumann (anthology with biography), 1979, Literatur im Exil, 1989, Nazi Book Burning and the American Response, 1989,; Literarische Kultur im Exil (essay collection), 1997, Fielding, Wieland, Goettle and the Rise of the Novel, 2003; editor: Konstellationen: Die besten Erzaehlungen des Neuen Merkur, 1964; co-editor: Nelly Sachs Ausgewaehlte Gedichte, 1968; assoc. editor: Lessing Yearbook, 1970-72, edit. bd. 1972—; sr. editor, 1979-81; co-editor (Jurt Weill) Aufdem Wegzum Weg der Verheissung; contbr. articles on 18th and 20th century German lit. to profl. jours., also chpts. to books; mem. edit. bd. CG, 1976. Bd. dirs. Kurt Weill Found., sec., 1990—; bd. dirs. Leo Baeck Inst., 1967—, mem. exec. bd., 1978—; bd. dirs., chair acad. adv. com. Holocaust Meml. Mus. Greater Detroit; co-founder, pres. Lessing Soc., 1975-77; bd. dirs. Detroit Am. Jewish Com., 1988—; mem. pub. bd. Aufbau, 1997—. With AUS, 1942-45. Decorated Bronze Star; Fulbright Rsch. grantee U. Munich, 1961-63; recipient Order of Merit 1st Class, 1968, Friendship award, 1983, Germany, 1987, Grand Order of Merit, Festschrift in Honor of Guy Stern; Exile and Enlightment, 1987, Goethe medal, 1989, Presdl. award for Excellence in Tchg., 1992, Disting. Alumni award Hofstra U., 1993, Disting. Grad. Faculty award Wayne State U., 1998. Mem. Am. Assn. Tchrs. German (pres. 1970-72, Disting. Germanist of Yr. 1985, hon. mem. 1989), AAUP, Internat. PEN Club, MLA, South Atlantic MLA, Soc. for Exile Studies (v.p. 1981—). Home: 6197 Forest Grv West Bloomfield MI 48322-1375 E-mail: ad5422@wayne.edu.

STERN, HERBERT JAY, lawyer; b. N.Y.C., Nov. 8, 1936; s. Samuel and Sophie (Berkowitz) S.; children: Jason Andrew and Jordan Ezekiel (twins), Samuel Abraham, Sarah Kathrine. BA, Hobart Coll., 1958; JD (Ford Found. scholar), U. Chgo., 1961; LL.D. (hon.), Seton Hall Law Sch., 1973, Hobart Coll., 1974; L.H.D. (hon.), Newark State Coll., 1973; D.C.L. (hon.), Bloomfield Coll., 1973; Litt.D. (hon.), Montclair State Coll., 1973. Bar: N.Y. 1961, N.J. 1971. Asst. dist. atty., New York County, 1962-65; trial atty. organized crime and racketeering sect. Dept. of Justice, 1965-69; chief asst. U.S. atty. Dist. of N.J., Newark, 1969-70, U.S. atty., 1971-74, U.S. dist judge, 1974-87; ptnr. Stern & Kilcullen, Roseland, NJ, 1990—. Adv. com. U. Chgo. Law Sch. Author: Judgment in Berlin, 1984 (Valley Forge award Freedoms Found. 1984, Torch of Learning award Am. Friends of Hebrew U. 1987), Trying Cases to Win, Vol. I, 1991, Vol. II, 1992, Vol. III, 1993, Vol. IV, 1995; co-author: Trying Cases to Win, Anatomy of A Trial, 1999, Trying Cases to Win: Evidence Weapons for Winning, Vol. I, 2000, Vol. II, 2003; subject of book Tiger in the Court, 1973. Trustee Hobart and William Smith Colls. Named One of America's 10 Outstanding Young Men U.S. Jr. C. of C., 1971; Swartzer scholar U. Chgo. Law Sch., 1985; recipient Dean's Club award U. Akron Sch. Law, 1986, medal of excellence Hobart Coll., 1990, Citizen's award N.J. Acad. Medicine, 1997. Fellow ABA, Am. Law Inst. (Clarence Darrow award), Internat. Platform Assn.; mem. ABA, N.J. Bar Assn., Fed. Bar Assn. (past pres. Newark chpt., recipient William J. Brennan, Jr. award 1987), Essex County Bar Assn., Am. Judicature Soc., Phi Alpha Delta. Achievements include being subject of book Tiger in the Court, 1973. Office: 75 Livingston Ave Roseland NJ 07068-3701 E-mail: dpenna@sgklaw.com.

STERN, HOWARD ALLAN, radio personality, television show host; b. Jackson Heights, N.Y., Jan. 12, 1954; s. Ben and Rae S.; m. Alison Berns, 1978 (div. 2001); children: Emily, Debra, Ashley Jade. BA in Comm., Boston U., 1976. Disc jockey Sta. WRNW, Briarcliff Manor, N.Y., 1976-78, Sta. WCCC, Hartford, Conn., 1978-79, Sta. WWWW, Detroit, 1979-80, Sta. WWDC, Washington, 1980-82, Sta. WNBC, N.Y.C., 1982-85, Sta. WXRK, N.Y.C., 1985—, numerous other markets, 1986—. Author: Private Parts, 1993, Miss America, 1995; TV shows include The Howard Stern Show (WOR-TV), 1990-92, The Howard Stern Interview (E!), 1992-93, The Howard Stern Show (E!), 1994—; actor (films) Private Parts, 1997; writer, exec. prodr., voice Doomsday, 2000; writer, exec. prodr. (TV series) Son of the Beach, 2000-02; recordings include 50 Ways To Rank Your Mother, 1982, Crucified by the FCC, 1991; pay-per-view spls./videos include: Howard Stern's Neglige and Underpants Party, U.S. Open Sores, Butt Bongo Fiesta, The Miss Howard Stern New Year's Eve Pageant. Libertarian candidate for gov. State of N.Y., 1994. Rest Stop on I-295 in N.J. named in his honor, 1995. Address: The Howard Stern Show WXRK-FM/Infinity Broadcasting 401 W 57th St New York NY 10019-1701 also: care Don Buchwald & Associates 10 E 44th St New York NY 10017-3601

STERN, JAMES ANDREW, investment banker; b. N.Y.C., Oct. 1, 1950; s. Arthur and Lenore (Oppenheimer) S.; m. Jane Yusem, April 13, 1975; children: Peter, David. BS, Tufts U., 1972; MBA, Harvard U., 1974. Assoc. Lehman Bros. Inc., N.Y.C., 1974-79, v.p., 1979-82, mng. dir., 1982-94; chmn. The Cypress Group, N.Y.C., 1994—. Dir. Lear Corp., Southfield, Mich., Amtrol, Inc., West Warwick, R.I., Wesco Inc. Trustee Tufts U., Medford, Mass., 1982-, chmn. bd. trustees 2003-, Jewish Mus., N.Y.C.; bd. dirs. Cystic Fibrosis Found. Mem. Quaker Ridge Golf Club, Beach Point Club. Clubs: Quaker Ridge Golf (Scarsdale, N.Y.), Beach Point (Mamaroneck, N.Y.). Avocations: golf, reading. Office: The Cypress Group Inc 65 E 55th St New York NY 10022-3219 Business E-Mail: jstern@cypressgp.com.

STERN, JOAN NAOMI, lawyer; b. Phila., Mar. 7, 1944; d. Clarence J. and Diana D. (Goldberg) S. BA, U. Pa., 1965; JD, Temple U., 1977. Bar: Pa. 1977. Assoc. Blank, Rome LLP, Phila., 1977—83, ptnr., 1983—, co-chair pub. fin. group, 1983-92, chair pub. fin. group, 1993, chair pub. fin. dept., 1994—. Cons. counsel Phila. Charter Commn., 1993-94. Contbr. articles to profl. jours. Mem. Sch. Dist. Task Force on Regulatory Reform, Phila., 1987, Tax Policy and Budget Com., Phila., 1989, Phila. Mayor's Fiscal Adv. Com., 1990; chair Sch. Dist. of Phila. Task Force on Alternate Financing Strategies, 1995; bd. mgrs. Moore Coll. Art and Design, Phila., 1993—, vice chair bd. trustees, bd. mgrs., 1995—; bd. dirs. Police Athletic League, Phila., 1994—, Jewish Fedn. of Greater Phila., 2000—, Am. Jewish Congress, 1995—, Urban Tree Connection, 2000—, Mother Bethel Found., 2002—; bd. trustees The Franklin Inst., 2004—. Fellow Am. Bar Found. (life); mem. ABA, Nat. Assn. Bond Lawyers, Phila. Bar Assn., Phila. Bar Assn. (chmn. mcpl. govt. com. 1983-97), Pa. Assn. Bond Lawyers. Office: Blank Rome LLP One Logan Square Philadelphia PA 19103-6998 Office Phone: 215-569-5526. E-mail: stern@blankrome.com.

STERN, JOSEPH SMITH, JR., former footwear manufacturing company executive; b. Cin., Mar. 31, 1918; s. Joseph S. and Miriam (Haas) S.; m. Mary Stern, June 14, 1942; children: Peter Joseph, William Frederick, Peggy Ann Graeter. AB, Harvard U., 1940, MBA, 1943; HHD (hon.), Xavier U., 1988; DSc(hon.), U. Cin., 1989. With R. H. Macy & Co., N.Y.C., 1940-41; with U.S. Shoe Corp., Cin., 1941-68, v.p., 1951-65, pres., 1965-66, chmn. bd., chief exec. officer, 1966, chmn. exec. com., 1966-68, dir., 1956-70. Prof. bus. policy emeritus U. Cin. Pres. bd. trustees Cin. and Hamilton County Pub. Libr.; chmn. Cin. Bicentennial Com., Greater Cin. Tall Stacks Commn.; trustee Cin. Music Hall Assn., Cin. Hist. Soc., Children's Hosp. Med. Center, Cin. Symphony Orch., Cin County Day Sch., 1956-72, Family Svc., Cin., 1964-82; trustee, pres. Cin. Mus. Festival Assn.; pres. bd. trustees Children's Convalescent Hosp., Cin., 1972-75; bd. overseers vis. com. univ. libr. Harvard U. Served to lt. USNR, 1943-46. Recipient Disting. Community Svc. award NCCJ, 1986, Great Living Cincinnatian award Cin. C. of C., 1989, Disting Svc. award U. Cin. Coll. Bus., 1992. Mem. Am. Footwear Industries Assn. (life; dir.) Jewish (past pres. temple). Clubs: Literary (Cin.), Harvard (Cin.) (pres. 1965), Queen City (Cin.), Queen City Optimists, Harvard (N.Y.C.). Home: 3 Grandin Pl Cincinnati OH 45208-3402

STERN, JUDITH SCHNEIDER, nutritionist, researcher, educator; b. Bklyn. d. Sidney and Lillian (Rosen) Schneider; m. Richard C. Stern; 1 child, Daniel Arthur. BS, Cornell U., 1964; MS, Harvard U. Sch. Pub. Health, 1966, ScD, 1970. Rsch. asst., dept. food sci. and nutrition MIT, Cambridge, 1964-65; rsch. assoc. dept. human behavior and metabolism The Rockefeller U., NYC, 1969-72, asst. prof. dept. human behavior and metabolism, 1972-74; contbg. editor Vogue Mag., Conde Nast Publs., NYC, 1974; asst. prof. nutrition U. Calif., Davis, 1975-77, assoc. prof. dept. nutrition, 1977-82, dir. food intake lab. group, 1980—2001, prof. dept. nutrition, 1982—, prof. divsn. endocrinology, clin. nutrition and vascular biology, 1988—, disting. prof. 2003 . Mem. edit. bd. Internat. Jour. Obesity, 1976-85, Appetite, 1990, Obesity Rsch., 1993—, Nutrition Today, 1999—. Bd. sci. advisors Am. Coun. Sci. and Health, 1980—; mem. U.S. Dept. Agr. Dietary Guidelines Adv. Com., 1983—85; mem. obesity task force NIDDK, 1996—2002, AAAS; mem. expert com. U.S. Pharmacopeia Bioavailability and Nutrient Absorption, 2000—; mem. adv. bd. USDA Nat. Agrl. Rsch. Ext., Edn. and Econs., 2000—03. Recipient Sec.'s Honor award USDA, 2004; NIH tng. grantee, 1979—. Fellow Am. Heart Assn.; mem. Am. Soc. Clin. Nutrition (pres. 1995-96), Am. Dietetic Assn., Am. Diabetic Assn., Am. Obesity Assn. (v.p. 1995-), N.Am. Assn. for Study of Obesity (pres. 1992-93), Inst. Medicine of NAS, Inst. Food Technologists, Am. Soc. Nutrition Sci. (chair pub. info. com. 1992-94), Sigma Xi, Delta Omega. Office: U Calif Dept Nutrition 1 Shields Ave Davis CA 95616-5271 Office Phone: 530-752-6575. Personal E-mail: sternhome@aol.com. Business E-Mail: jsstern@ucdavis.edu.

STERN, LEO G. lawyer; b. Mpls., Apr. 10, 1945; s. Philip J. and June I. (Monasch) S.; m. Christine E. Lamb, June 29, 1968; children: Alison M., Zachary A. BA, U. Calif., Davis, 1967; JD cum laude, U. Minn., 1970. Bar: Minn. 1970, U.S. Dist. Ct. Minn. 1971, Calif. 1971, U.S. Ct. Appeals (6th, 7th and 8th cirs.) 1985, U.S. Supreme Ct. 1993, Wis. 1999; cert. mediator and arbitrator, Minn. Ptnr. Cox, King & Stern, Mpls., 1970-77, Wright, West & Diessner, Mpls., 1977-84, Fredrikson & Byron, P.A., Mpls., 1984—. Mem. Minn. Bar Assn. (governing coun. environ. and natural resources law sect. 1989-95, governing coun. litigation sect. 1995-99), Am. Arbitration Assn. (arbitrator, mediator). Avocations: sailing, jogging. Home: 206 Central Ave S Wayzata MN 55391-1818 Office: Fredrikson & Byron PA 4000 Pillsbury Ctr 200 S 6th St Minneapolis MN 55402 Office Phone: 612-492-7061. Business E-Mail: lstern@fredlaw.com.

STERN, LEONARD BERNARD, television and motion picture production company executive; b. N.Y.C., Dec. 23, 1923; s. Max and Esther (Marton) S.; m. Gloria Jane Stroock, Aug. 12, 1956; children: Michael Stroock, Kate Jennifer. Student, NYU, 1944. Dir. TV, L.A., 1946-53; writer, dir., producer Jackie Gleason Show/Honeymooners, Sergeant Bilko, Steve Allen Show N.Y.C., 1953-60; founder Price-Stern-Sloan, L.A., 1959-64, v.p., 1964-69, dir., 1969-80; pres. Heyday Prodns., L.A., 1962-69, 75-97; v.p. Talent Assocs./Norton Simon, L.A. and N.Y.C., 1965-75; pres. Tallfellow Prodns., L.A., 1997—. Author: (with Roger Price) Mad Libs, 1958, What Not to Name the Baby, 1960, Dear Attila the Hun, 1985; (with Roger Price and Larry Sloan) The Baby Boomer Book of Names, 1985, (with Diane L. Robison) A Martian Wouldn't Say That, 1994; writer, dir.: (motion pictures) Just You and Me, Kid, 1979, Target, 1985, Missing Pieces, 1990; creator, writer, dir. 21 TV series, including Get Smart, McMillan and Wife and He and She, 1953-89; media editor Dialogue newsletter. Mem. adv. coun. Sch. of Arts, NYU; bd. dirs. Nat. Coun. for Families and TV, Inst. for Mental Health Initiatives. Recipient Peabody award U. Ga., Writers Guild award 1956, 66, Nat. Assn. TV Arts and Scis. award 1956, 66-67, Emmy award 1956, 1966. Mem. Writers Guild Am., Dirs. Guild Am., Caucus for Producers, Writers and Dirs. (co-chmn., Mem. of Yr award 1987, Disting. Svc. award 1987), Producers Guild Am. (pres.), Bd. Motion Picure and TV Fund Found. Office: Tallfellow Prodns 1180 S Beverly Dr Ste 320 Los Angeles CA 90035-1154

STERN, LEONARD NORMAN, real estate developer, former pet supply manufacturing company executive; b. N.Y.C., Mar. 28, 1938; s. Max and Hilda (Lowenthal) Stern; m. Judith Stern (div.); children: Emanuel Theodore, Edward Julius, Andrea Caroline; m. Allison Maher, 1987. BS cum laude, NYU, 1956, MBA, 1957; DHL (hon.), Yeshiva U., 1985; LLD (hon.), Fairleigh Dickinson, 1995. Formerly pres., dir., now chmn., CEO Hartz Group, Inc., 1959—, sold pet div., 1999; chmn., CEO Hartz Mountain Industries Inc., 1966—; founder Stern Pub., 1986—99; owner 667 Madison Ave., NYC, Tribeca Grand Hotel, NYC, SoHo Grand Hotel, NYC, Harmon Cove, Secaucus, NJ, Lincoln Harbor, Weehawken, NJ, Colgate Ctr., Jersey City, Journal Square, Jersey City. Mem. adv. bd. Chem. Bank, N.Y.C., 1970-; active real estate constrn., devel. Bd. dirs. Manhattan Day Sch., Jewish Ctr., N.Y.C.; founder Albert Einstein Coll. Medicine, 1958; mem. N.Y.C. Holocaust Meml. Commn.; founder Homes for the Homeless, 1986-; trustee NYU, 1976-1996, former chmn. fin. com. Named Graduate and Undergraduate Schs. of Bus. The Leonard N. Stern Sch. Bus., NYU, 1984; recipient Albert Gallatin medal. Office: Hartz Group 667 Madison Ave 26th Floor New York NY 10021*

STERN, LOUIS WILLIAM, marketing educator, consultant; b. Boston, Sept. 19, 1935; s. Berthold Summerfield Stern and Gladys (Koch) Cohen (deceased); m. Rhona L. Grant; children: Beth Ida, Deborah Lynn. AB, Harvard U., 1957; MBA in Mktg, U. Pa., 1959; PhD in Mktg, Northwestern U., 1962. Mem. staff bus. research and consumer mktg. sects. Arthur D. Little, Inc., Cambridge, Mass., 1961-63; from asst. prof. bus. orgn. to prof. Ohio State U., Columbus, Ohio, 1963—70, prof. mktg., 1970—73; from prof. mktg. to A. Montgomery Ward prof. mktg. Northwestern U., 1973—83, John D. Gray disting. prof. mktg., 1983—2001, John D. Gray disting. prof. emeritus mktg., 2001—; on leave as exec. dir. Mktg. Sci. Inst., Cambridge, Mass., 1983-85; Thomas Henry Carroll Ford Found. vis. prof. Harvard U. Grad. Sch. Bus. Adminstrn., 1984-85; Dorinda and Mark Winkelman Disting. Scholar sr. fellow, co-dir. Jay H. Baker Retailing Initiative, The Wharton Sch., U. Pa., 2004—. Mem. staff Nat. Commn. on Food Mktg., Washington, 1965-66; vis. assoc. prof. bus. adminstrn. U. Calif., Berkeley, 1969-70; guest lectr. York U., U. Minn., U. Ky., UCLA, Ohio State U., U. N.C., Duke U., U. Wis., U. Pitts., U. Chgo., MIT, U. Mich., U. Pa., Cornell U., U. Mo., Norwegian Sch. Econs. and Bus. Adminstrn.; faculty assoc. Hernstein Inst., Vienna, Austria, 1976-77, Mgmt. Centre Europe, 1988-96; faculty assoc. Gemini Cons. Inc., Montvale, N.J., 1977-96, mem. midwest adv. bd., 1989-94; Xerox rsch. prof. Northwestern U., 1981-82; cons. to FTC, 1973, 80; vis. scholar U. Calif., Berkeley, 1997-2001; mem. faculty adv. bd. CSC Index, 1997-98; co-dir. Jay H. Baker Retailing Initiative Wharton Sch., U. Pa., 2004. Author: Distribution Channels: Behavioral Dimensions, 1969, (with Frederick D. Sturdivant and others) Managerial Analysis in Marketing, 1970, Perspectives in Marketing Management, 1971, (with John R. Grabner, Jr.) Competition in the Marketplace, 1970, (with Anne T. Coughlan, Erin Anderson and Adel I. El-Ansary) Marketing Channels, 6th edit., 2001, (with Thomas L. Eovaldi) Legal Aspects of Marketing Strategy: Antitrust and Consumer Protection Issues, 1984; (with Adel I. El-Ansary and James R. Brown) Management in Marketing Channels, 1989; mem. editl. bd. Jour. Mktg. Rsch., 1976-82, Jour. Mktg., 1979-83, Mktg. Letters, 1988-94; contbr. articles on mktg. to profl. jours. Mem. exec. com. Northwest Area Coun. on Human Rels., Columbus, 1971—72. Rsch. grantee Ohio State U., 1964-73, Mktg. Sci. Inst., 1976-77, 88-90, 92-94; recipient Harold H. Maynard award best article Jour. Mktg., 1980, Kellogg's Spl. Lifetime Achievement Award for Tchg. Excellence, 1999; named Mktg. Educator of Yr. Sales and Mktg. Execs. Internat., 1989, also Chgo. chpt. 1990, Outstanding Profl. of Yr. award, 1992, and named One of Top 6 Profs. in Kellogg Sch., Northwestern U., Grad. Mgmt. Assocs., 1984-94, (named 6 times Outstanding Prof. Exec. Masters Program), One of Top 12 Tchrs. in U.S., U.S. Bus. Schs., Bus. Week; named Dorinda and Mark Winkelman Disting. scholar, Sr. fellow Wharton Sch., U. Pa., 2004. Mem. AAUP, Am. Mktg. Assn. (mem. program com. educators conf. 1971, chmn. com. 1978, Paul D. Converse award 1986, Richard D. Irwin Disting. Mktg. Educator of Yr. 1994), Hellenic Inst. Mktg. (hon.), Beta Gamma Sigma. Home: 522 Church St Apt 2D Evanston IL 60201-4575 Office: Northwestern U Kellogg Sch Mgmt Dept Mktg Evanston IL 60208-2001 Office Phone: 847-491-2718. E-mail: lwstern@kellogg.northwestern.edu.

STERN, MADELEINE BETTINA, rare books dealer, author; b. N.Y.C., July 1, 1912; d. Moses Roland and Lillie (Mack) S. BA, Barnard Coll., 1932; MA, Columbia U., 1934. Tchr. English N.Y.C. High Schs., 1934-43; ptnr. Leona Rostenberg Rare Books, N.Y.C., 1945—, Leona Rostenberg and Madeleine B. Stern Rare Books, N.Y.C., 1980—. Lectr. history of book, feminism, pub. history, lt. Author: We Are Taken, 1935, The Life of Margaret Fuller, 1942, Louisa May Alcott, 1950, new edit., 1996, Purple Passage: The Life of Mrs. Frank Leslie, 1953, Imprints on History: Book Publishers and American Frontiers, 1956, We the Women: Career Firsts of Nineteenth Century America, 1962, new edit., 1994, So Much in a Lifetime: The Story of Dr. Isabel Barrows, 1965, Queen of Publishers' Row: Mrs. Frank Leslie, 1966, The Pantarch: A Biography of Stephen Pearl Andrews, 1968, Heads and Headlines: The Phrenological Fowlers, 1971, Books and Book People in 19th-Century America, 1978, Antiquarian Bookselling in the United States: A History from the Origins to the 1940s, 1985, Nicholas Gouin Dufief of Philadelphia Franco-American Bookseller, 1776-1834, 1988, The Life of Margaret Fuller: A Revised Second Edition, 1991, Louisa May Alcott: From Blood & Thunder to Hearth & Home, 1998; (with Leona Rostenberg) Old and Rare: Forty Years in the Book Business, 1974, rev. edit. 1988, Between Boards: New Thoughts on Old Books, 1978, Bookman's Quintet: Five Catalogues about Books, 1980, Quest Book-Guest Book: A Biblio-Folly, 1993, Connections: Our Selves-Our Books, 1994, Old Books in the Old World: Reminiscences of Book Buying Abroad, 1996, Old Books, Rare Friends: Two Literary Sleuths and Their Shared Passion, 1997, New Worlds in Old Books, 1999, Books Have Their Fates, 2001, Bookends: Two Women, One Enduring Friendship, 2001, From Revolution to Revolution: Perspectives on Publishing and Bookselling, 2002; editor: Women on the Move, 4 vols., 1972, Victoria Woodhull Reader, 1974, Louisa's Wonder Book-An Unknown Alcott Juvenile, 1975, Behind a Mask. The Unknown Thrillers of Louisa May Alcott, 1975, new edit., 1995, Plots and Counterplots: More Unknown Thrillers of Louisa May Alcott, 1976, Publishers for Mass Entertainment in 19th-Century America, 1980, A Phrenological Dictionary of 19th-Century Americans, 1982, Critical Essays on Louisa May Alcott, 1984, A Modern Mephistopheles and Taming a Tartar by Louisa May Alcott, 1987, Louisa May Alcott Unmasked: Collected Thrillers, 1995, Modern Magic by Louisa May Alcott, 1995, The Feminist Alcott: Stories of a Woman's Power, 1996, Louisa May Alcott: Signature of Reform, 2002; co-editor: Selected Letters of Louisa May Alcott, 1987, A Double Life: Newly Discovered Thrillers of Louisa May Alcott, 1988, The Journals of Louisa May Alcott, 1989, Louisa May Alcott: Selected Fiction, 1990, (co-editor) Freaks of Genius: Unknown Thrillers of Louisa May Alcott, 1991, From Jo March's Attic: Stories of Intrigue and Suspense, 1993 (Victorian Soc. award), The Lost Stories of Louisa May Alcott, 1995. Guggenheim fellow, 1943-45; recipient Medalie award Barnard Coll., 1982, Victorian Soc. award, Disting. Alumna award Barnard Coll., 1997. Mem. Antiquarian Booksellers Assn. Am. (gov. 1966-68, 78-80), Internat. League Antiquarian Booksellers, MLA, Am. Printing History Assn. (co-recipient award 1983), Authors League, Manuscript Soc. (former trustee), Phi Beta Kappa. Jewish. Home: 40 E 88th St New York NY 10128-1176

STERN, MARGARET BASSETT, retired special education educator, author; b. Bklyn., June 6, 1920; d. Preston Rogers and Jeanne (Mordorf) Bassett; m. Fritz R. Stern Oct. 11, 1947 (div. Dec. 1992); children: Frederick Preston, Katherine Stern Brennan. BA, Wellesley Coll., 1942; MEd, Bank Street Coll. Edn., N.Y.C., 1943, MEd, 1974. Propr. Castle Sch., N.Y.C., 1944-51; dir. Mothers' Coop. Nursery Sch., Ithaca, N.Y., 1952-54; tchr. sci. and math. The Brearley Sch., N.Y.C, 1956-57. Cons., lectr. Head Start, Tuskegee, Ala., 1964; cons. in math. The Gateway Sch., N.Y.C., 1967-90; spl. lectr. Columbia U. Tchrs. Coll., N.Y.C., 1990-94; condr. workshops in Eng., 1960-88. Author: (with Catherine Stern and Toni Gould) Structural Reading Program, Workbooks and Teachers Guides A through E, 1963, 3d edit., 1978, Structural Arithmetic Workbooks and Teachers Guides Grades 1-3, 1965, 2d edit., 1966, (with Stern) Children Discover Arithmetic, 1971, (with Gould) Spotlight on Phonics, Four Workbooks and Teachers Guides, 1980, Sound/Symbol Activities and Decoding Activities, 1980, 2d edit., 1994; Experimenting with Numbers, 1988, Structural Arithmetic, 1-3, 1992. Recipient award, Orton Dyslexia Soc. N.Y., 1989, Bank St. Coll. Edn., 1998. Mem.: Nat. Coun. Tchrs. Math., Internat. Dyslexia Assn. Home: 3204 River Crescent Dr Annapolis MD 21401 E-mail: structuralarith@aol.com.

STERN, MARILYN, photographer, writer, picture editor; b. Detroit, Nov. 8, 1953; d. Julian and Phyllis Stern. BA, Brown U., 1976. Photographer's asst., N.Y.C., 1976-82; freelance photographer, 1976—; freelance writer, 1985—; picture editor Across the Board mag., N.Y.C., 1990-96; faculty Internat. Ctr. of Photography, 2001, NYU, 2004. Photographer, organizer: (book) Masked Culture: The Greenwich Village Halloween Parade, 1994; author, photographer: Kval! Die Walfänger der Lofoten, 1990; solo exhbns. Profil Gallery, Bratislava, 2001, Scandinavia House, N.Y.C., 2003; several group exhbns., 1976--; represented in permanent collection Detroit Inst. Arts, also numerous pvt. collections. Travel Study grantee Royal Norwegian Consulate to Norway in the U.S., 1987, Am.-Scandinavian Found., 1986.

STERN, MICHAEL DAVID, dentist; b. Cleve., Feb. 26, 1946; s. Milton B. and Harriette (Hoffman) S.; m. Ellen Weiner, June 9, 1968; children: Gregory, Stephanie, Jeffrey. BS, Ohio State U., 1968, DDS, 1972; cert., L.I. U., N.Y.C., 1981. Cert. pain mgmt., Am. Acad. Pain Mgmt., instruction in temporomandibular joint disfunction syndrome, L.I. U. Staff dentist Office of Drs. Rhodes and Rinaldi, Cleve., 1972-73; assoc. dentist Office of William Rothkopf, DDS, Cleve., 1973-75; practice dentistry specializing in temporomandibular joint disorders Wickliffe, Ohio, 1975-93, Willoughby Hills, Ohio, 1993—; resident in cranio facial pain Coll. Dentistry U. Fla., Gainsville, 1989. Media spokesperson Morning Exch. WEWS-TV, Cleve., 1981—85, WJW-TV, Cleve., 1996—; cons. Richmond Hts. (Ohio) Hosp., 1983; adj. grad. lectr. Cleve. State U., 1983—84; preceptorship lectr. Case Western Res. U., Cleve., 1986—95; mem. staff Pain Ctr. South Pointe Hosp., Cleve. Clinic Health Sys., Cleve., 1991—; TMJD and facial pain cons. Sound Health Alternatives, Inc., Bio-Acoustics, Athens, Ohio, 1996—99; chair bd. trustees North Coast Spring Dental Meeting, 2001—. Fellow Am. Endodontic Soc., Acad. Gen. Dentistry, Internat. Coll. Craniomandibular Orthopedics; mem. ADA, Ohio Dental Assn. (state del. 2000), N.E. Ohio Dental Soc. (pub. rels. chmn. 1979-83, sec. 1996-98, v.p. 1999, pres. 2000), Am. Acad. Craniofacial Pain, Acad. Laser Dentistry. Avocations: bicycling, automobiles, music, gardening. Office: 34950 Chardon Rd Ste 209 Willoughby OH 44094-9162 Office Phone: 440-975-8444. E-mail: dentist@nodrillingfillings.com.

STERN, MICHAEL LAWRENCE, psychologist; b. N.Y.C., July 3, 1948; s. Abraham Isaac and Etta (Silverberg) S.; m. Karen Beth Rivard, July 26, 1981; children: Joshua Ethan, Rachel Lynn. BA, Calif. State U., Long Beach, 1970; PhD, U. Wash., 1977. Diplomate Am. Bd. Med. Psychotherapists; cert. employee assistance profl., sex therapist. Intern St. Elizabeth's Hosp. NIMH, Washington, 1973-74; instr. dept. psychology U. Wash., Seattle, 1975-77; rsch. assoc. dept. psychiatry U. Tenn. Med. Sch., Memphis, 1977-78; clin. dir. drug abuse program Fed. Correction Inst., Danbury, Conn., 1978-85, chief psychologist, 1985-86; dir. outpatient recovery ctr. Briarcliff Manor, N.Y., 1986-88; pvt. practice clin. psychology, 1981-86; cons. Addiction Recovery Corp, Westchester, 1987-88; adj. faculty Fairfield U., 1981-86; dir. OMNI Health Assn. U. Tenn. postdoctoral fellow, 1977-78. Mem. Am. Psychol. Assn. (cert. addictions), Assn. Advancement Behavior Therapy, Am. Assn. Sex Educators, Counselor, and Therapists, Conn. Psychol. Assn. Family Firm Inst. Cons. editor TSA News, 1977-78. Home: Saw Mill Ridge Rd Newtown CT 06470 Office: Green Knoll Profl Ctr 60 Old New Milford Rd Brookfield CT 06804-2430

STERN, MITCHELL, broadcast executive; B, U. Pa., 1976; MBA, U. Chgo., 1978. With CBS TV Stas. Divsn., 1978—86, dir. planning and adminstrn. WCBS-TV, dir. planning and adminstrn. WBBM-TV Chgo., fin. analyst corp. office; v.p., CFO Fox TV Stas., L.A., 1986—90, v.p., sta. mgr. KTTV-Fox 11, 1990—92, sr. v.p., 1990—92, exec. v.p., COO, 1992—93, pres., COO, 1993—98, chmn., CEO, 1998—, Twentieth TV, L.A., 1998—. Office: Fox TV Stas Inc 205 E 67th St New York NY 10021

STERN, MORT(IMER) P(HILLIP), journalism and communications educator, academic administrator, consultant; b. New Haven, Feb. 20, 1926; s. Bernard and Louise Eleanor (Spiro) S.; m. Patricia Ruth Freeman, Jan. 10, 1946; children: Susan C., Margaret L. AB, U. Ark., 1947; MS, Columbia U., 1949; postgrad., Harvard U., 1954—55; PhD, U. Denver, 1969. Reporter S.W.-Am., Ft. Smith, Ark., 1946-47; night bur. mgr. UPI, Little Rock, 1947-48; reporter, polit. writer, state editor Ark. Gazette, Little Rock, 1949-51; reporter, rewrite man Denver Post, 1951-53, night city editor, 1953-54, asst. editor Rocky Mountain Empire sect., 1955-56, mng. editor, 1956-58, assoc. editor, 1958, editl. page editor, 1958-65, asst. to pub., 1965-70, editl. page editor, 1971-73; dean Sch. Pub. Communication U. Ala., 1973-74; dean Sch. Journalism U. Colo., Boulder, 1974-77; lectr. journalism U. Denver, 1953-54, adj. prof., 1970, exec. dir. pub. affairs, 1977-78, exec. asst. to chancellor, 1978-84; prof., chmn. dept. journalism and mass communication U. No. Colo., Greeley, 1985-90; pres. P. Paty & Co., Georgetown, Colo., 1989—. Atwood prof. journalism U. Alaska, Anchorage, 1981-82. With USAAF, 1944-45. Mem. Georgetown Bd. of Selectmen, 1997-99; mem. Georgetown Bd. Adjustment, 2001-. Nieman fellow Harvard U., 1954-55; named Disting. Alumnus dept. journalism U. Ark., 1999; inducted to Fulbright Coll. Alumni Acad. U. Ark., 1999. Mem.: Georgetown Libr. Assn. (v.p. 1999, pres. 2001—04, bd. dirs.), Phi Beta Kappa, Sigma Delta Chi, Omicron Delta Kappa. Baptist. Home: PO Box 549 Georgetown CO 80444-0549

STERN, MYLES STEVEN, information technology educator, consultant; b. Detroit, Mich., May 12, 1945; s. Adeline Edyce and Albert Alfred Stern; m. Laura Ann Waisbren, Aug. 24, 1951; children: Karen, Jonathan; 1 child, Rebecca Klausner. PhD, Mich. State U., East Lansing, Mich., 1968—74; MBA, The U. of Mich., Ann Arbor, Mich., 1966—68, A.B., 1963—66. Assoc. prof. Wayne State U., Detroit, 1978—, asst. prof., 1971—78. Pres. MIS Resources, Inc., Southfield, Mich., 1985—. Author: (article) Relating Benefits from Using IS to Orgnl. Characteristics: Comparing Results from Two Countries, Computer-Based Document Mgmt. Systems, How to Select Application Software, A Data Base Primer for Accountants, Comparison of Methods of Predicting Burn Mortality, Data for Comparative Study from a Burns Ctr., Methods of Burn Treatment: Comparison by Probit Analysis. Recipient Cert. of Disting. Performance, Inst. of Cert. Mgmt. Accountants, 1972. Mem.: Assn. for Info. Systems. Jewish. Office: Wayne State Univ 100 Rands House Detroit MI 48202 E-mail: m.stern@wayne.edu.

STERN, PAULA, international trade advisor; b. Chgo., Mar. 31, 1945; d. Lloyd and Fan (Wener) Stern; m. Paul A. London; children: Gabriel Stern London, Genevieve Stern London. BA, Goucher Coll., 1967; MA in Middle Eastern Studies, Harvard U., 1969; MA in Internat. Affairs, MA in Law and Diplomacy, Fletcher Sch. of Law and Diplomacy, 1970, PhD, 1976; D Comml. Sci. (hon.), Babson Coll., 1985; LLD (hon.), Goucher Coll., 1985. Legis. asst., sr. legis. asst. to U.S. Sen. Gaylord Nelson U.S. Senate, Washington, 1972—74, 1976; guest scholar Brookings Inst., Washington, 1975-76; policy analyst Pres. Carter-V.P. Mondale Transition Team, Washington, 1977-78; fellow Council on Fgn. Relations, Washington, 1977-78; commr. U.S. Internat. Trade Commn., Washington, 1978-87, chairwomen, 1984-86; sr. assoc. Carnegie Endowment for Internat. Peace, Washington, 1986-88. Chmn. internat. bus. and econs. Hamline U., 1994—2000; chairwomen Stern Group, Inc., 1988—; bd. dirs. Avaya, Inc., Avon Products, Inc., Hasbro, Inc.; mem., sr. advisor U.S. trade policy coun. Competition Policy Inst., 1991—93; sr. fellow Progressive Policy Inst., 1994—95; pub. vice chairwoman Atlantic Coun. U.S.; trustee Com. Econ. Devel.; mem. Inter-Am. Dialogue, Coun. Fgn. Rels.; past co-chair Internat. Competition Adv. Com.; past chmn. antitrust div. U.S. Dept. Justice; past chmn. Import-Export Bank; past mem. U.S. Pres. Adv. Com. on Trade Policy and Negotiation; bd. dirs. Carnegie Coun. Ethics and Internat. Affairs., Inter-Am. Found., 1980—81. Author: Water's Edge--Domestic Politics and the Making of American Foreign Policy, 1979; contbg. author newspapers; contbr. articles to profl. jours. Recipient Journalism award, Alicia Patterson Fund, 1971, Joseph Papp Award for Racial Harmony, Found. Ethnic Understanding, 2004. Democrat. Jewish. Avocations: sculpting, tennis, dance. Office: 3314 Ross Pl NW Washington DC 20008-3332 Office Phone: 202-966-7894. Business E-Mail: pstern@sterngroup.biz.

STERN, PETER R. lawyer; b. East Orange, N.J., Nov. 2, 1947; s. Ralph and Jacqueline Rene (Piot) S. BA, Columbia U., 1969, JD, 1972. Bar: N.Y. 1973, U.S. Dist. Ct. (so. and ea. dists.) 1973, U.S. Ct. Appeals (2d cir.) 1975, U.S. Ct. Appeals (3d cir.) 1995, U.S. Ct. Appeals (D.C. cir.) 2001, U.S. Supreme Ct. 1979. Law clk. to judge U.S. Dist. Ct., N.Y.C., 1972-74; assoc. Winthrop, Stimson, Putnam & Roberts, N.Y.C., 1974-80; founding ptnr. Berger, Steingut, Weiner, Fox & Stern, N.Y.C., 1980-85; ptnr. Berger & Steingut, N.Y.C., 1986-90, Berger Steingut Tarnoff & Stern, N.Y.C., 1990-93, Berger, Steingut & Stern, N.Y.C., 1993-94, Berger, Stern & Webb, LLP, N.Y.C., 1994—2004; counsel McLaughlin & Stern, 2004—. Bd. dirs. Kitchen Ctr., N.Y.C., 1978-90; bd. advisors Franklin Furnace, 1984-97; law adv. coun. Internat. Found. for Art Rsch., 1988—. Bd. dirs. Vol. Lawyers for Arts, 1995—, chmn. 1999—. Mem. ABA, N.Y.C. Bar Assn., Fed. Bar Coun., N.Y. State Bar. Office: 260 Madison Ave New York NY 10016 E-mail: pstern@mclaughlinstern.com.

STERN, PHYLLIS NOERAGER, nursing educator; b. San Mateo, Calif., Sept. 2, 1925; d. Philip Julius and Grace Ann (Zoellen) Noerager; m. David Arthur Hungerford, May 20, 1949 (div. Sept. 1956); 1 child, Paula Ann; m. Milton Stern, July 5, 1960 (dec. Jan. 2001). AA, Coll. San Mateo, 1968; BS magna cum laude, San Francisco State U., 1970; MS, U. Calif., San Francisco, 1971, D of Nursing Sci., 1976; LLD (hon.), Dalhousie U., Can., 2003. Asst. prof. Calif. State U., Hayward, 1971-76, U. Calif., San Francisco, 1976-80; prof. Northwestern State U. La., Shreveport, 1980-82; prof., dir. Dalhousie U., Halifax, N.S., Can., 1983-87, prof., 1987-91; prof., dept. chair Ind. U., Indpls., 1991-96, prof., 1996—. Editor, author: Women Health and Culture, 1986; editor: Childbirth and Childcare, 1988, Lesbian Health Care, 1991; editor-in-chief: Health Care for Women Internat., 1983-2001; co-editor: (with R.S. Schrecber) Grounded Theory for Nurses (Am. Jour. Nursng Book of Yr. award 2001), 2001. Health educator Battered Women's Shelter, Indpls., Salvation Army, Indpls., 1994-96. Named Disting. Alumna U. Calif., San Francisco, 1995; rsch. grantee Ind. U., 1995; Glenn W. Irwin Jr. Rsch. scholar, 1999; recipient Lifetime Achievement award for contbns. to women's health internationally Internat. Soc. Qualitative Rschrs. Fellow Am. Acad. Nursing (mem. expert panel 1989-96), Am. Acad. Practice Coun. (Disting. Practitioner 1992), Coun. Gen. Internat. on Women's Health Issues (co-founder 1984, coun. gen. emeritus 2002—), Sigma Theta Tau. Avocations: film, reading, walking, mentoring. Office: Ind U 1111 Middle Dr Indianapolis IN 46202-5243 Office Phone: 317-274-0032. Personal E-mail: pnstern@comcast.ne. Business E-Mail: pstern@iupui.edu.

STERN, RICHARD DAVID, investment company executive; b. New Rochelle, N.Y., Nov. 5, 1936; s. Leo and Grace Marjorie (Phillips) S.; m. Phyllis Marlene Edelstein, Nov. 20, 1966; children: Marjorie Anne, Andrew Howard. AB, Princeton U., 1958; MBA, Harvard U., 1962. CFA. 1st v.p. Newburger, Loeb & Co., N.Y.C., 1962-74, also bd. dirs., 1969-74; sr. investment officer Ctrl. Trust Co., Cin., 1974-76, owner bus. valuation cons. co., 1976-78; v.p. Gt. Western Bank & Trust Co. (now Wells Fargo Bank), Phoenix, 1978-84; pres. Stern, Ludke & Co. (now Stellar Capital Mgmt. LLC.), Phoenix, 1984—, mng. mem., 2000—. Co-author: Air Cushion Vehicles, 1962. Trustee endowment trust Phoenix Chamber Music Soc., 1982-91; v.p., 1986-90, bd. dirs., 1982-91, 93-94; pres. Cen. Ariz. chpt. Arthritis Found., 1982-84, chmn. planned giving com., 1986-91, mem. nat. planned giving com., 1987-89; chmn. endowments and trusts com. Temple Beth Israel, Phoenix, 1980-83; dir., investment com. Endowment Found., Temple Solel, Paradise Valley, 1990-92; pres. Am. Jewish Com., Phoenix, 1983-84, bd. dirs., 1980-84, adv. bd., 1985—; bd. dirs. Asian Arts Coun., Phoenix Art Mus., 1987-93, v.p., 1989-90, pres., 1990-92; trustee Ariz. Theatre Co., 1990-97, mem. regional nominating com., 1995-97, chmn., 1995-96, asst. treas., 1996-97; panelist Phoenix Office of Arts and Culture, 2002. Mem. Assn. for Investment Mgmt. and Rsch., Phoenix Soc. Fin. Analysts (chmn. profl. conduct com. 1980-83, membership com. 1990-91, bd. dirs.), Anti-Defamation League (dir. Ctrl. Ariz. chpt. 1986—, exec. bd. 1989—, chair nominating com. 1990-94, 2001—, chair bd. devel. 1993-94, treas. 1994—, assoc. nat. commr. 1998—), Princeton Alumni Assn. No. Ariz. (alumni schs. com. 1992—), Univ. Club Phoenix (bd. dirs. 1990-92, fin. com. 1990-91), Harvard Bus. Sch. Club Ariz. (bd. dirs. 1991—, pres. 1993-95, treas. 1995—). Republican. Home: 7547 N Lakeside Ln Paradise Valley AZ 85253-2857 Office: 2200 E Camelback Rd Ste 130 Phoenix AZ 85016-3455 E-mail: rstern@stellarmgt.com.

STERN, RICHARD GUSTAVE, writer; b. N.Y.C., Feb. 25, 1928; s. Henry George and Marion (Veit) S.; m. Gay Clark, Mar. 14, 1950 (div. Feb. 1972); children: Christopher Holmes, Kate Macomber, Andrew Henry, Nicholas Clark; m. Alane Rollings, Aug. 9, 1985. BA, U. N.C., 1947; MA, Harvard U., 1950; PhD, State U. Iowa, 1954. Mem. faculty U. Chgo., 1955—, prof. English, 1965—, Helen Regenstein prof. English, 1990—2002, prof. emeritus, 2002. Author: Golk, 1960, Europe and Up and Down with Baggish and Schreiber, 1961, In Any Case, 1962, Teeth, Dying and Other Matters, 1964, Stitch, 1965, 1968: A Short Novel, An Urban Idyll, Five Stories and Two Trade Notes, 1970, The Books in Fred Hampton's Apartment, 1973, Other Men's Daughters, 1973, Natural Shocks, 1978, Packages, 1980, The Invention of the Real, 1982, A Father's Words, 1986, The Position of the Body, 1986, Noble Rot: Stories, 1949-88, 1989 (book of yr. award Chgo. Sun-Times 1990), Shares and Other Fictions, 1992, One Person and Another, 1993, A Sistermony, 1995 (Heartland award, nonfiction book of year), Pacific Tremors, 2001, What Is What Was, 2002, Collected Stories, 2004; editor: Honey and Wax, 1966. Recipient Longwood Found. award, 1960, Friends of Lit. award, 1963, fiction award Nat. Inst. Arts and Letters, 1968; Nat. Coun. Arts and Humanities fellow, 1967-68, Carl Sandburg award for fiction, 1979, Arts Coun. awards, 1979, 81, Am. Acad. and Inst. of Arts and Letters medal of Merit for Novel, 1985; Rockefeller fellow, 1965, Guggenheim fellow, 1973-74. Fellow Ctr. Advanced Studies in the Behavioral Scis.; mem. Am. Acad. Arts and Scis. Office: U Chgo Dept English Chicago IL 60637 E-mail: rstern@uchicago.edu.

STERN, RICHARD HENRY, advertising executive; b. N.Y., Sept. 9, 1936; s. Henry Leo and Harriet Caroline (Koll) S.; m. Alicia Bishko, May 7, 1960; children: Jeffrey, Steffan, Elizabeth. BS, Fordham U., 1958. Mgr. advt. devel. Consol. Edison Co., N.Y., 1959-66; account exec. Reach McClinton & Co., N.Y., 1966-73; account supr. Bozell & Jacobs, Inc., N.Y., 1973-78, group v.p. Union, N.J., 1980-84; account supr. Marsteller, Inc., N.Y., 1978-80; advt. sales promotion mgr. Automatic Switch Co., N.J., 1985-99; ret., 1999; owner Dee Ess Comm., Towaco, N.J., 1984-87. Mem. adv. bd. Nat. Mfg. Week. Dep. mayor Montville Twp., 1988-89, mayor, 1990, councilman, 1976-87; mem. Montville Twp. Planning Bd., 1981-90; mem. Montville Twp. Zoning Bd., 2001—; pres. bd. trustees Montville Twp. Pub. Libr.; legis. Aide, N.J. State Assembly, 1996-99, N.J. State Senate, 1973-77. Republican. Roman Catholic. Avocations: decoy carving, woodworking, gardening, travel. Home: 5 Tumbling Brook Dr Towaco NJ 07082-1021: 254 Pompano Dr Loveladies NJ 08008 E-mail: rdeeess@aol.com.

STERN, ROBERT, psychiatrist; b. Aug. 12, 1928; BS, Swiss Fed. Inst. Tech., Zurich, 1951; MS, Yale U., 1953, PhD, 1956; MD, Case Western Res. U., 1966. Diplomate Am. Bd. Psychiatry and Neurology; lic. physician, Conn. Asst. prof. chemistry Wesleyan U., Middletown, Conn., 1957—58, Conn. Coll., New London, 1959-60; supr. bio-organic chem. rsch. Arthur D. Little, Inc., Cambridge, Mass., 1960-62; vis. fellow medicine Mass. Gen. Hosp., 1964; rsch. assoc. biol. chemistry Harvard Med. sch., Boston, 1964, tchg. fellow psychiatry, 1967-68; intern medicine King County Hosp./U. Wash., Seattle, 1966-67; resident in psychiatry McLean Hosp., Belmont, Mass., 1967-68; jr./sr. asst. resident internal medicine Yale-New Haven Hosp., 1968-70, clin. fellow medicine, 1970-71; postdoctoral fellow psychiatry Yale U. Sch. Medicine, 1971-73, asst. clin. prof. psychiatry, 1974-86, assoc. clin. prof. psychiatry, 1986—; pvt. practice New Haven, 1973—. Cons. Child Guidance clinic of Southeastern Conn., New London, 1973-82; cons. CHAMPUS peer reviewer Qualidigm, Inc., Middletown, 1994—; lectr. in field. Contbr. articles to profl. jours. Fellow Am. Psychiat. Assn. (Disting. life fellow); mem. New Haven Individual Practice Assn. (co-chmn. psychiatry panel 1985-98, quality assurance com. 1989-98, bd. dirs. 1986-89), Conn. Psychiatry Soc. (councilor-at-large 2001—, councilor 2000-2001, pres. New Haven/Middlesex chpt. 1999-2000, treas. 1996-99). Conn. State Med. Soc., New Haven County Med. Assn., New Haven pvt. practice com. 1995—. Office: 340 Whitney Ave New Haven CT 06511-2317

STERN, ROBERT ARTHUR MORTON, architect, educator, writer; b. N.Y.C., May 23, 1939; s. Sidney S. and Sonya (Cohen) S.; m. Lynn G. Solinger, May 22, 1966 (div. 1977); 1 child, Nicholas S.G. BA, Columbia U., 1960; MArch, Yale U., 1965. Registered architect, Calif., Colo., Conn., Fla., Hawaii, Ill., Ind., Maine, Mass., Mich., N.H., N.J., Ohio, S.C., Tex., N.Y., D.C., Ga. Program dir. Archtl. League N.Y., 1965-66; designer Office Richard Meier, Architect, N.Y.C., 1966; cons. Small Parks Program, Dept. Parks, N.Y.C., 1966-70; urban designer, asst. to asst. adminstr. housing and devel. adminstrn. N.Y.C., 1967-70; ptnr. Robert A.M. Stern & John S. Hagmann, Architects, N.Y.C., 1969-77; prin. Robert A.M. Stern, Architects, 1977-89, sr. ptnr., 1989—. Bd. dirs. Walt Disney Co.; cons. Eye on New York TV documentary, CBS-TV, 1966-67; mem. architecture com. Whitney Mus. Am. Art, 1970-76, adv. commn., archtl. sect. Venice Biennale, 1980; lectr. architecture Columbia U., 1970-72, asst. prof. 1973-77, assoc. prof., 1977-82, prof. 1982—; vis. fellow Inst. for Architecture and Urban Studies, 1974-76, trustee, 1983-85; dir. Temple Hoyne Buell Ctr. for Study Am. Architecture, 1984-88, dir. Hist. Preservation Program, 1991-98; vis. lectr. Yale U., 1972, 73; vis. critic R.I. Sch. Design, 1976, U. Pa., 1977, N.C. State U., Raleigh, 1978; William Henry Bishop vis. prof. architecture Yale U., fall 1978; editorial cons. Archtl. History Found., 1979-83; dean Yale Sch. Arch., 1998—, J.M. Hoppin prof. arch., 2000—. Author: New Directions in American Architecture, 1969, rev. edit., 1977, George Howe: Toward a Modern American Architecture, 1975, (with Deborah Nevins) The Architect's Eye, 1979, (with John M. Massengale) The Anglo-American Suburb, 1981, (with Thomas Catalano) Raymond Hood, 1982, East Hamptons Heritage, 1982, (with John M. Massengale and Gregory Gilmartin) New York 1900, 1983, Pride of Place, 1986, (with Gregory Gilmartin and Thomas Mellins) New York 1930, 1987, (with Raymond Gastil) Modern Classicism, 1988, The House That Bob Built, 1991, The American Houses of Robert A.M. Stern, 1991, (with Thomas Mellins and David Fishman) New York 1960, 1995, (with Thomas Mellins and David Fishman) New York 1880, 1999. Mem. N.Y.C. Mayor's Task Force on Urban Design, 1966-67, architects selection com. N.Y. Conv. Ctr., 1979; trustee Am. Fedn. Arts, 1967-79, Inst. for Architecture and Urban Studies, 1983-85; v.p. Cunningham Dance Found., 1969-73; bd. dirs. Preservation League N.Y., 1984—, Historic Landmarks Preservation Ctr., 1995—; trustee Nat. Bldg. Mus., 1999—, Trust for Historic Preservation, 2000—. Recipient numerous awards for archtl. works including Nat. Hon. awards of AIA, 1980, 85, 90, John Jay award Columbia Coll., 1991. Fellow AIA (bd. dirs. N.Y. chpt. 1976-78, Disting. archtl. award N.Y. chpt. 1982, 84, 85, 87, medal of honor 1984), Soc. Archtl. Historians (bd. dirs. 1975-78), Archtl. League N.Y. (pres. 1973-77, exec. com. 1977—), N.Y. State Assn. Architects (excellence in design cert. 1985), Am. Architecture Found. (bd. regents 1989-91), Skidmore, Owings and Merrill Found. (bd. dirs. 1984-90), Chgo. Inst. for Architecture and Urbanism (bd. dirs. 1990-93), Century Assn., Coffee House Club. Office: 460 W 34th St Fl 18 New York NY 10001-2320

STERN, ROBERT C. pediatrician, medical educator; b. NYC, Dec. 13, 1938; s. Samuel and Lily S. BA, Drew U., 1959; MD, Albert Einstein Coll. Medicine, 1963. Diplomate Nat. Bd. Med. Examiners, Am. Bd. Pediat., Am. Bd. Pediatric Pulmonology. Intern pediat. U. Hosps. Cleve., Babies and Childrens Hosp. Divsn., 1963-64, jr. asst. resident pediat., 1964-65; sr. asst. resident pediat. Bronx Mcpl. Hosp. Ctr., N.Y.C., 1965-66; fellow cystic fibrosis/pediat. pulmonary diseases Case Western Res. U. Sch. Medicine, Cleve., 1968-70; sr. instr. pediat. Case Western Res. U., Cleve., 1970-71, asst. prof., 1971-77, assoc. prof., 1977-83, prof., 1983—. Cons. Cystic Fibrosis Founds. various countries, 1990—, various pharm. and med. tech. cos., 1990—. Author: Treatment of Hospitalized Cystic Fibrosis Patients, 1998, Treatment of Cystic Fibrosis, 2000; contbr. numerous chpts. to Nelson's Textbook of Pediatrics, 1979—, also over 100 articles to med. jours. Pres., CEO, Children's Lung Found., Cleve., 1983—. Capt. USAF, 1966-68. Recipient David Stuckert award Cystic Fibrosis Rsch. Inst., San Francisco, 1997. Mem. Am. Thoracic Soc., Soc. Pediat. Rsch. Achievements include introduction of heparin lock for intermittent administration of intravenous drugs; research in cystic fibrosis. Home: 2300 Overlook Rd Apt 406 Cleveland Heights OH 44106-2391 Office: Univ Hosp Cleve 11100 Euclid Ave Cleveland OH 44106-1736 Office Phone: 216-844-3267. E-mail: rcs1@prodigy.net.

STERN, ROBERT D. publishing executive; b. N.Y.C., Sept. 30, 1929; s. Morris and Jean (Gordon) S.; m. Natalie Greenberg, Sept. 5, 1952 (div. 1978); children: Mitchell, Bradley; m. Roslyne Paige, June 5, 1978. BA, Syracuse U., 1950; JD, NYU, 1953, LLM, 1958. Bar: N.Y. 1955, U.S. Dist. Ct. (D.C. cir.) 1953, U.S. Supreme Ct. 1967. Ptnr. Fink, Weinberger, Levin & Gottschalk, N.Y.C., 1957-59, 1957—72; chmn. Rudor Consol. Industries, 1972—99, Dance Mag., Inc., 1985—2001, AGC/Sedgwick Inc., Princeton, NJ, 1990—2001. Bd. dirs. Ctr. for Graphic Comms. Mgmt. and Tech., NYU, N.Y.C., 1979—; chmn. bd. dirs. AGC Sedgwick, Princeton, N.J., Rudor Consol. Ind. Inc.; pub. Stern's Performing Arts Directory, 1989-98. Bd. dirs. YMCA, N.Y.C., 1987-90 Mem. ABA, N.Y. State Bar Assn., Sheldrake Yacht Club (Mamaroneck, N.Y.), Birchwood Country Club (Westport, Conn.). Avocations: tennis, skiing, sailing. Home: 2 Imperial Lndg Westport CT 06880-4934

STERN, ROBERT MORRIS, gastrointestinal psychophysiology researcher, psychology educator; b. N.Y.C., June 18, 1937; s. Irving Dan and Nellie (Wachstetter) S.; m. Wilma Olch, June 19, 1960; children: Jessica Leigh, Alison Rachel. AB, Franklin and Marshall Coll., 1958; MS, Tufts U., 1960; PhD, Ind. U., 1963. Research assoc. dept. psychology Ind. U., 1963-65; asst. prof. psychology Pa. State U., 1965-68, assoc. prof., 1968-73, prof., 1973—, disting. prof., 1992—, head dept., 1978-87. Author (with W.J. Ray): Biofeedback, 1977; author: (with W.J. Ray and C.M. Davis) Psychophysiological Recording, 1980; author: (with K.L. Koch) Electrogastrography, 1985; author: (with W.J. Ray and K.S. Quigley) Psychophysiological Recording, 2nd edit., 2001; author: (with K.L. Koch) Handbook of Electrogastrography, 2004; contbr. articles. Recipient Nat. Media award Am. Psychol. Found., 1978 Mem. Am. Psychol. Soc., Aerospace Med. Assn., Soc. Psychophysiol. Rsch., Am. Gastroent. Assn., Internat. EGG Soc., Functional Brain-Gut Rsch. Assn., Internat. Brain-Gut Soc. Home: 1360 Greenwood Cir State College PA 16803-3232 Office: Pa State U 512 Moore Bldg University Park PA 16802-3105 Office Phone: 814-865-1712. Business E-Mail: RS3@psu.edu.

STERN, ROSLYNE PAIGE, magazine publisher; b. Chgo., May 26, 1926; d. Benjamin Gross and Clara (Sniderman) Roer; m. William E. Weber, May 3, 1944 (div. Mar. 1956); m. Richard S. Paige, June 28, 1958 (div. Apr. 1978); children: Sandra Weber Porr, Barbara Paige Kaplan, Elizabeth Paige (dec.); m. Robert D. Stern, June 5, 1978. Cert., U. Chgo., 1945. Profl. model, singer, 1947-53; account exec. Interstate United, Chgo., 1955-58; sales mgr. Getting To Know You Internat., Great Neck, N.Y., 1963-71, exec. v.p., 1971-78; pub. After Dark Mag., N.Y.C., 1978-82; assoc. pub. Dance Mag., N.Y.C., 1978-85, pres., pub., 1985—2001, pres. emeritus, 2001—. Bd. dirs. Rudor Consol. Industries, Inc., N.Y.C., AGC/Sedgwick, Inc., Princeton, N.J. Founding pres. Dance Mag. Found., N.Y.C., 1984-86 chmn. Dance Mag. awards, 1986-; life mem. nat. women's com. Brandeis U., Waltham, Mass., 1958—; bd. dirs. Westport Arts Ctr.; The Internation Com. for Dance Libr. of Israel. Recipient Disting. Svc. award Dance Notation Bur., 1996, Am. Coll. Dance Festival award, 1998, Pres.'s award Dance Masters of Am., Inc., 1998, Documents of Dance award Dance Library of Israel, 1999. Mem. Pub. Relations Soc. Am., LWV, Am. Theatre Wing, Nat. Arts Club. Democrat. Jewish. Avocations: dance, theater, opera, visual arts, travel. Home: 2 Imperial Lndg Westport CT 06880-4934 Office: 60 W 66th St Ste 26A New York NY 10023

STERN, SAMUEL ALAN, lawyer; b. Phila., Jan. 21, 1929; AB, U. Pa., 1949; LLB, Harvard U., 1952. Bar: Mass. 1952, D.C. 1958. Ptnr. Wilmer, Cutler & Pickering, Washington, 1962-88, Dickstein, Shapiro & Morin, Washington, 1988-92; pvt. practice law and bus. Washington and St. Petersburg, Russia, 1992-94; counsel Rogers & Wells, Washington, N.Y.C., 1994-97; pvt. practice law and bus. Washington, 1997-98; gen. counsel Global Energy Investors, Inc., Washington, 1997-2000; ptnr. Hills & Stern LLP, Washington, 1999—; pres. Hills Enterprises, 1999—; counselor Hills & Co., 1999—. Vis. prof. law Harvard Law Sch., Cambridge, Mass., 1976; dir. Internat. Law Inst. Georgetown U., 1971—, adj. prof. law, 1979—92; asst. counsel Warren Commn., 1964; cons. UN, 1984—96; bd. dirs. Hills Enterprises, Ltd., Warp Broadband Corp., Verihealth, Macrobuild.com, Lexsite.com, India, Pan-Asia Media, VeriPay, Marshall & Swifty Boeckh, Target World Ltd., Commonwealth Shore Power, Beijing Security Alarm & Monitoring Co., Marshall & Swift/Boeckh, LLC; lectr. profl. confs. on project fin., privatization, cross-border investment and dispute resolution. Contbr. articles to legal jours. Mem. ABA, Am. Law Inst., Internat. Bar Assn., D.C. Bar Assn. Home: 210 Lee Ct Alexandria VA 22314 Office: 901 15th St NW Washington DC 20005 Office Phone: 202-822-1638. E-mail: sastern@hillsandstern.com.

STERN, SANDOR, film writer, director; b. Timmins, Ont., Can., July 13, 1936; s. Stephen Mendel and Ann (Gurevitch) S.; m. Marlene Greenstein, May 19, 1957 (div. 1976); children: Shawn, Mark, Adam, Jamie; m. Kandy Lea Cave, Jan. 26, 1980; children: Lauren, Seth. BA, U. Toronto, 1957, MD, 1961. Intern New Mount Sinai Hosp., Toronto, 1961-62; physician Toronto, Can., 1962-68; writer L.A., 1968—; dir., 1974—. Writer (films) The Amityville Horror, 1978, Fastbreak, 1979 (NAACP Image award); writer, dir. (film) Pin, 1988, (TV films) Web of Deceit, 1990, Deception: A Mother's Secret, 1991, Dangerous Pursuit, 1989, John and Yoko, 1985, Muggable Mary: Street Cop, 1981, (TV miniseries) Woman on the Run: The Lawrencia Bembeneck Story, 1992-93; dir. (TV films) Glitz, 1988, Passions, 1984, Heart of a Child, 1993, The Stranger Beside Me, 1995, Gridlock, 1995, Badge of Betrayal, 1996, In My Sister's Shadow, 1997; co-writer, dir. (TV films) Jericho Fever, 1992, Duplicates, 1992, A Child's Cry for Help, 1994, (episodes for TV shows) Touched by an Angel, 1997, 98, 99, Promised Land, 1997, 98, 99, Early Edition, 2000, Leap Years, 2001. Mem. Writers Guild Am., Dirs. Guild Am., Producers Guild Am. Office: Jamson Prodns Inc 9472 Rembert Ln Beverly Hills CA 90210-1720 E-mail: sandorstern@sbcglobal.net.

STERN, STANLEY, psychiatrist; b. N.Y.C., Apr. 5, 1933; s. Frank and Gussie S.; children: Marcus F., David S. BA cum laude, N.Y. U., 1953; MD, SUNY, 1957. Intern Ohio State U. Hosp., Columbus, 1957-58; resident in psychiatry Inst. Living, Hartford, Conn., 1958-60, Austen Riggs Ctr., Stockbridge, Mass., 1960-61; psychoanalytic tng. We. New Eng. Inst. for Psychoanalysis, New Haven, Conn., 1965-73; asst. clin. prof. psychiatry Yale U., New Haven, Conn., 1975-81; assoc. clin. prof. psychiatry U. Calif., San Diego, 1982-84; pvt. practice New Haven, 1965-82, La Jolla, Calif., 1982-84, Phoenix, 1984—. Mem. faculty San Diego Psychoanalytic Inst., 1980-84; pres. Ariz. Psychoanalytic Study Group, Phoenix, 1986-88, Phoenix Psychoanalytic Study Group, 1986-88; tng. and supervising analyst So. Calif. Psychoanalytic Inst., 1989; chmn. edn. com. Ariz. Pyschoanalytic New Tng. Facility, 1990-91; lectr., presenter, participant seminars and confs. in field. Contbr. article to profl. jours. Trustee, Gesell Inst., New Haven, 1986-88, Ctr. for the Exceptional Patient, New Haven; bd. dirs. ACLU. Capt. USAF, 1961-63. Mem. Am. Coll. Psychoanalysts, Am. Psychoanalytic Assn. (cert.), Am. Psychiat. Assn., Am. Acad. Psychoanalysts, Irene Josselyn Group Advancement of Psychoanalysis, So. Calif. Psychoanalytic Inst. and Soc. (faculty), San Diego Psychoanalytic Inst., Council for the Advancement of Psychoanalysis (treas. 1972-73, pres.-elect 1973-74, pres. 1974-75, councillor 1975-80), Phi Beta Kappa, Beta Lambda Sigma, Psi Chi. Home and Office: 3104 E Camelback Rd # 601 Phoenix AZ 85016 Address: 4438 E Arlington Rd Phoenix AZ 85018-1262 Office Phone: 602-840-5614. *Personal philosophy: "Be a little kinder to each other" Aldous Huxley.*

STERN, STEPHEN JEFFREY, lawyer; b. L.A., Dec. 31, 1940; s. M.E. and Jane (VanDement) S.; m. Betsy Stern, June 16, 1962 (div. 1974); children: Christopher, Jeffrey; m. Sheila Duckworth, Apr. 23, 1976. BS in Econs., U. Calif., 1962; JD, U. San Francisco, 1965. Bar: Calif., N.Y. Ptnr. O'Melveny & Myers, L.A., 1973—. Lectr., chmn. N.Y. Law Jour., Calif. League of Cities, Mcpl. Fin. Officers Assn. Mem. ABA, Calif. State Bar Assn., N.Y. State Bar Assn., Nat. Assn. Bond Lawyers, Bel Air Bay Club. Office: O'Melveny & Myers 3 Finsbury Sq London EC2A 1LA England Office Phone: 011 44 20 7256 8451.

STERN, STEVEN ALAN, sports development owner; b. Chgo., Dec. 5, 1943; s. Sidney J. and Leona (Bernstein) S.; m. Helena Kerner, July 12, 1975; children: Jeremy, Jessica. BA, Brandeis U., 1965; postgrad., Columbia U., 1965-66. CPCU, Ill. Trust officer First Nat. Bank Chgo., 1966-69; ptnr. Equicon, Inc., Chgo., 1970-74; coord. Singer for Mayor, Chgo., 1974-75; mgr. underwriting policy CNA Ins., Chgo., 1976-79; project dir. Gov.'s Blue Ribbon Panel, Denver, 1979-81; dir. capital budget State of Colo., Denver, 1981-82; exec. dir. Ctr. Bus. and Econ. Forecasting U. Denver, 1982—85; v.p. pub. fin. Kirchner Moore Divsn. George K. Baum & Co., Denver, 1986—93; sr. v.p. pub. fin. Donaldson, Lufkin & Jenrette Securities Co., 1993—95, William R. Hough & Co., 1995—99; mng. dir. Scheer Game Sports Devel., 1999—, CEO, 2002—; mng. dir. Coll. Town, LLC, 2003—. Sr. fin. cons. Greenville (S.C.) Auditorium Dist., 1994-98, City of Greenville, 2004, U. Akron, 2003—, Stamfair Sports, 1996-99, City of Manchester, N.H., 1997-2001, City of Jacksonville, Fla., 2001-04, Morris Comm. Inc., 2001-04, St. Louis U., 2003, Harbor Devel. Co., 1999-2000, Met. Denver Major League Baseball Stadium Dist., 1989-92, Augusta Entertainment LLC, 2004—, adv. task force to capital devel. com. Colo. Gen. Assembly, 1985-87, chmn. adv. task force subcom. on privatization, 1986-87; adv. coun. Colo. Advanced Tech. Inst., 1986-90; guest lectr., 1982, 93; adv. task forces on capital budgeting, transp. Denver C. of C., 1980-91; co-chmn. Bond Buyer Ann. Stadium and Arena Fin. Conf., 1998; prin., program mgr. arena and ballpark projects City of Jacksonville, Fla., 2001-04; spkr. in field. Author: Colorado Capital Investment Budget, 1982, (with others) Colorado: Investing in the Future, 1981; editor: Techniques of Economic Research, 1981. Spkr. Adopt-A-Sch., Denver Pub. Schs., 1983, 86, Brandeis U. Alumni Admissions Coun., 1990-93, numerous other orgns.; participant Leadership Denver, 1983-84; sec.-treas. Colo. Student Obligation Bond Authority, 1984-86, also bd. dirs.; bd. dirs. Circus Arts Found., 1985-86; chmn. devel. com. Stanley Brit. Primary Sch., Denver, 1984; mem. Denver Baseball Commm., 1987-89; bd. dirs., chmn. corp. gifts Epilepsy Found., Chgo., 1977-79. Mem. Brandeis U. Alumni Assn. Jewish. Office: 2215 S 3d St Ste 203 Jacksonville FL 32250-6827 Business E-Mail: sstern@scheergame.com.

STERN, T. NOEL, political scientist, educator; b. Pitts., July 7, 1913; s. Leon Thomas (LeFevre) and Elizabeth Gertrude (Limburg) S.; m. Katherine Frances Kirk, Dec. 28, 1940; children: S. Yolanda, Roland Craig, Ellen Cornog, Joan Thrush. *T. Noel Stern's family has long American roots, with a unique, challenging and complex history. His ancestors arrived between 1656 and 1876. Three grandparents were Protestant, one Catholic. Some forbears were Quaker. His parents were born illegitimately and lived for part of their early years with Jewish foster families. Both parents took assumed identities, frequently modified. Stern writes on those changes in family identity in his autobiography, Secret Family. The end result, for Stern, has been a liberal and universalist Quaker outlook, which he shares with his wife and children.* BA with honors, Swarthmore Coll., 1934; postgrad., U. Lyons, France, 1934-35; MA in Polit. Sci. U. Pa., 1940, PhD in Polit. Sci. 1942. Tchr. Lycée des Garçons, Roanne, France, 1934-35; prof., acting chmn. dept. govt. Boston U., 1945-53; Fulbright prof. U. Rennes, U. Strasbourg, 1952; dir. Fondation des Etats-Unis, U. Paris, France, 1953-56; acting chief UN Pub. Adminstrn. Mission to Ethiopia, 1956-57; dir. research and stats. Pa. Dept. Revenue, 1957-60; pres. West Chester State Coll., Pa., 1960-61; research prof. govt. African Studies program Boston U., 1962-63; also chief pub. adminstrn. team Boston U./US Aid, Guinea, West Africa; prof., founding chmn. dept. polit. sci. U. Mass., Dartmouth, 1964-69, prof., 1969-85, prof. emeritus, 1985—, also past chmn. acad. coun. Frequent guest on radio, Boston, 1948-53, New Bedford, Fall River and Providence, 1964-2000. *T. Noel Stern's professional life in the United States, France and Africa has been marked by his universalist Quakerism. In his teaching he has unabashedly expressed his social idealism and his admiration for figures such as Socrates, William Penn, John Dewey-to the delight of many students. He has written on figures such as Albert Camus, William Penn and Plato for professional publications and Quaker journals. In retirement, Stern has written on his life story, local government reform, casino gambling, pacifism, the United States Constitution, and impeachment.* Author: Community Forests in Pennsylvania for U.S. Allegheny Forest Experiment Station, 1941, Secret Family, 1988, Your Guide to Dartmouth Town Government, 1991; past mem. editl. bd. Internat. Rev. History and Polit. Sci., Revue de la Cité, Paris; contbr. to Boston U. Law Rev., Sch. and Society, New Republic, Progressive mag., Christian Sci. Monitor, Friends Jour., Quaker Life, Quaker History, Boston Globe, Providence Jour.-Bull, New Bedford Standard-Times, U. Pa. Gazette, Pitts. Post-Gazette, Indiana (Pa.) Gazette, Johnstown (Pa.) Tribune-Dem., others; collective writings deposited in Archives of Friends Hist. Libr., Swarthmore Coll. and Libr. U. Mass., Dartmouth; frequent contbr. to internet discussion groups Quaker-Spectrum and Quaker-List. Past mem. permanent bd. New Eng. Yearly Mtg. of Friends; past mem. exec. com. Friends Gen. Conf., Phila.; past mem. adminstrv. bd. William Penn House, Washington; past clk. North Dartmouth Friends Mtg., past presiding clk. Sandwich Quar. Mtg. of Friends; trustee, chmn. Dartmouth Town Librs., 1992-98; bd. dirs. Cmty. Ctr. for Non-Violence, New Bedford, Mass., 1994-98; mem. governing com. New England Friends Home, Hingham, Mass., 1996-98. Mem. AAUP (past pres. U. Mass.-Dartmouth chpt.), Am. Polit. Sci. Assn., LWV (acting pres. New Bedford-Fall River area 1990-91). Home: The Village House 1155 Indian Springs Rd Indiana PA 15701

STERN, WALTER EUGENE, neurosurgeon, educator; b. Portland, Oreg., Jan. 1, 1920; s. Walter Eugene and Ida May (McCoy) S.; m. Elizabeth Naffziger, May 24, 1946; children: Geoffrey Alexander, Howard Christian, Eugenia Louise, Walter Eugene III. AB cum laude, U. Calif., MD, 1943. Diplomate Am. Bd. Neurol. Surgery (vice chmn. 1975-80). Surg. intern, asst. resident surgery and neurol. surgery U. Calif. Hosp., 1943-46, asst. resident neurol. surgery and neuropathology, 1948; clin. clk. Nat. Hosp. Paralyzed and Epileptic, London, 1948-49; Nat. Rsch. fellow med. sci. Johns Hopkins, Balt., 1949-50; asst. resident, resident U. Calif. Svc., 1951; clin. instr. U. Calif., 1951; asst. prof. neurosurgery UCLA, 1952-56, assoc. prof., 1956-59, prof., 1959—87, prof. emeritus, 1987—, chief divsn. neurosurgery, 1952-85, chmn. dept. surgery, 1981-87; NIH spl. fellow univ. lab. physiology Oxford (Eng.) U., 1961-62. Cons. neurosurgery Wadsworth VA Hosp. Former mem., chmn. editl. bd. Jour. Neurosurgery; contbr. articles to sci. jours., chpts. to books. Lt. to capt. M.C. AUS, 1946-48. Fellow ACS (sec.); mem. AMA, Am. Surg. Assn., Pacific Coast Surg. Assn., L.A. Surg. Soc. (pres. 1978), Am. Assn. Neurol. Surgeons (pres. 1979-80, Cushing medalist, 1992), James IV Assn. Surgeons, Western Neurosurg. Soc. (past pres.), Soc. Neurol. Surgeons (past pres., Disting. Svc. award 1999), Neurosurg. Soc. Am., Am. Neurol. Assn., Soc. Univ. Surgeons, Soc. Brit. Neurol. Surgeons (hon.), Calif. Assn. Neurol. Surgery (Disting. Svc. award 2004), Phi Beta Kappa, Sigma Xi, Alpha Omega Alpha. Republican. Episcopalian. Home: 435 Georgina Ave Santa Monica CA 90402-1909

STERN, WALTER PHILLIPS, investment executive; b. N.Y.C., Sept. 26, 1928; s. Leo and Marjorie (Phillips) S.; m. Elizabeth May, Feb. 12, 1958; children: Sarah May, William May, David May. AB, Williams Coll., 1950; MBA, Harvard U., 1952. With Lazard Freres & Co., N.Y.C., 1953-54; assoc. Burnham & Co., Inc. (predecessor firm to Drexel Burnham Lambert Group, Inc.), N.Y.C., 1954-60, ptnr., 1960-71, sr. exec. v.p., 1972-73; vice-chmn., mng. dir. Ea. ops. Capital Rsch. Co., 1973-95; chmn. bd. New Perspective Fund, Inc., 1973—2003, vice chmn., 2003—; chmn. Capital Internat. Inc., 1973—2002, vice chmn., 2002—. Chmn. Europacific Growth Fund, Inc., 1984—99; chmn. bd. dirs. Emerging Markets Growth Fund Capital Group Internat., Inc., chmn., 1984—2002; mem. Mcpl. Securities Rulemaking Bd., 1984—87; trustee Fin. Analysts Rsch. Found., 1975—2003; chmn. bd. trustees Hudson Inst.; instr. investment mgmt. and fin. NYU, 1956—62; mem. adv. bd. South African Growth Fund, 1996—2002, CyberCity Capital LLC, 1999—2002. Contbr. articles to profl. jours. Dir. Jewish Cmty. Rels. Coun. N.Y.; mem. Coun. Fgn. Rels.; chmn. fin. adv. com. Haddassah; trustee Am. Jewish Com., Tel Aviv U., Jaffee Inst. Strategic Studies, Tel Aviv; mem. publ. com. Commentary, 1995—; editl. adv. bd., Moment, 1998—; dir. Am.-Israel Friendship League, 1996—; gov. Anti-Defamation League; bd. dirs. Am. Friends of Tel Aviv U.; v.p., mem. exec. com. Washington Inst. Near East Policy; chmn. steering com. Freedom Trade with Israel; adv. bd. Am. Committees on Fgn. Rels., 1998—; bd. visitors Monterrey Inst., 2001—; trustee The Jewish Pol. Ctr. Mem. N.Y. Soc. Security Analysts (bd. dirs.), Fin. Analysts Fedn. (pres. 1971-72, bd. dirs.), Inst. Chartered Fin. Analysts (pres. 1976-77, bd. dirs.), Assn. Investment and Mgmt. Rsch. (bd. dirs., exec. com. 1990-92), Harvard Club, Econ. Club, Sunningdale Country Club, Calif. Club, Phi Beta Kappa. Jewish. Home: 450 Fort Hill Rd Scarsdale NY 10583-2413 Office: Capital Group Inc 630 5th Ave New York NY 10111-0100 also: Capital Group Inc 333 S Hope St Los Angeles CA 90071-1406 E-mail: wps@capgroup.com.

STERN, WALTER WOLF, III, lawyer; b. Cin., Mar. 25, 1946; s. Walter W. Jr. and Harriet Louise Stern; m. Judith M. Looker, Jan. 4, 1974; 1 child, Rachael Louise. BA, Carthage Coll., 1969; JD, Marquette U., 1974. Bar: Wis. 1974, U.S. Dist. Ct. (ea. and we. dists.) Wis. 1974, U.S. Ct. Appeals (7th cir.) 1981, U.S. Supreme Ct. 1983. Pvt. practice, Kenosha, Wis., 1974-82, 85-91; sr. ptnr. Joling Rizzo Willems Stern & Burroughs, Kenosha, 1982-85; pvt. practice Union Grove, Wis., 1991—. Lectr. criminal law Carthage Coll., Kenosha, Wis., 1976—. Educator, Domestic Violence Project, Kenosha, 1983-94; hearing examiner Gen. Relief, Kenosha, 1990-95. Fellow Am. Acad. Forensic Scis. Avocations: fishing, hunting, jogging, reading, creative writing. Office: Atty at Law PO Box 64 Union Grove WI 53182-0064

STERNBACH, NANCY SAPORTA, language educator, researcher; b. NYC, Apr. 5, 1949; d. Sheldon and Claire Saporta Sternbach; children: Rafael, Tobias. BA, U. Wis. Madison, 1971; MA, Middlebury Coll., Madrid, Spain, 1973; PhD, U. Ariz., Tucson, 1984. Asst. prof. Hamilton Coll., Clinton, NY, 1984—85; prof. Smith Coll., Northampton, Mass., 1985—. Co-author: (books) Stages of Life, 2001; co-editor: Puro Teatro, 1999, Breaking Boundaries, 1989. Mem.: Modern Lang. Assn. (del. 1995—96).

STERNBERG, ESTHER MAY, neuroendocrinologist, immunologist, rheumatologist; b. Montreal, May 9, 1951; came to U.S., 1980, naturalized, 1991; d. Joseph and Ghitta (Wexler) Sternberg; 1 child, Penny Rebecca Herscovitch. BSc with great distinction, McGill U., 1972, MD, 1974. Diplomate Nat. Bd. Med. Examiners; lic. physician, Can., Mo. Intern Royal Victoria Hosp./McGill U., Montreal, 1974-75, resident II in medicine, 1977-78, clin. fellow rheumatology, 1978-79, clin. and rsch. fellow rheumatology, 1979-80; gen. practice medicine Mount Royal, Que., 1975-77; rsch. assoc. divsn. allergy/clin. immunology Washington U., St. Louis, 1981-83, rsch. assoc. Howard Hughes Med. Inst., 1983-84, assoc. Howard Hughes Med. Inst., 1984-86, instr. divs. rheumatology, 1984-86; attending physician Barnes Hosp., St. Louis, 1981-86; tenured sr. scientist NIMH/NIH, Bethesda, 1991—, med. officer, chief unit on neuroendocrine immunology, 1991-95, assoc. br. chief clin. neuroendocrinology br., 1994-2000, med. officer, chief sect. neuroendocrine immunology, 1995—, dir. integrative neural-immune program, 1999—. Vis. scientist Nat. Inst. Arthritis Musculoskeletal and Skin Disease, NIH and head Inter-Inst. Unit on Neuroendocrine Immunology and Behavior, NIMH and Nat. Inst. Arthritis, Musculoskeletal and Skin Diseases, Bethesda, 1989-90; rsch. full prof. Am. U., Washington, 1995—; temporary advisor WHO, 1991; ad hoc mem. NIH/NIMH/Libr. Congress Human Genome Project liaison com., 1990-91; invited expert CDC, Atlanta, 1989-93; spl. cons. Inst. Health (Hygienic) Scis., Min. of Health, Japan, 1992-94; med. adv. bd. Scleroderma Fedn., 1993-95; cons. John D. and Catherine T. MacArthur Found. Network on Mind-Body Interactions, 1994—; participant WHO/Pan Am. Health Orgn. Collaborating Ctr. for Health of the Elderly Work Group meeting, 1995; mem. com. on military nutrition rsch. Inst. of Medicine of NAS, 1998—; advisor Nat. Libr. of Medicine Planning Com., Breath of Life: An Exhbn. on Asthma, 1997-98, NIMH/NIH Ctr. for Sci. Rev., 1998; reviewer FDA's Office of Women's Health, 1998; co-dir. Exhibition on Emotions and Disease Nat. Libr. Medicine, 1996-97, others; dir. NIMH Program on Integrative Neural-Immune, 1999—; co-chair/chair/organizer numerous confs. Author: The Balance Within. The Science Connecting Health and Emotions; editl. bd. Brain, Behavior and Immunity, Jour. Neuroimmunology, Neuroimmunomodulation, Molecular Psychiatry, Immunologic Rsch.; invited guest series editor Jour. Clin. Investigation, 1997; reviewer Jour. Clin. Investigation, New Eng. Jour. Medicine, Jour. Immunology, Endocrinology, Jour. Clin. Endocrinology and Metabolism, Arthritis and Rheumatism, Am. Jour. Physiology, Jour. Neuroimmunology, Brain, Behavior and Immunity; editor: Stress: Mechanisms and Clinical Implications, 1995, Neuroimmune Interactions: Molecular, Integrative Systems and Clinical Implications, 1998; assoc. editor Brain, Behavior and Immunity, Neuroimmunomodulation; contbr. chpts. to books and articles to profl. jours.; patentee in field. Recipient Arthritis Found. Met. Washington William R. Felts award for excellence in rheumatology rsch. pubs., 1991, FDA's Commr.'s Spl. Citation, 1991, USPHS Superior Svc. award, 1994; McGill U. scholar, 1967-68, 68-71; Am. Acad. Allergy/Schering Travel grantee, 1982, United Scleroderma Found. grantee, 1985-86, 86-87, Scleroderma Found. Greater Washington, 1987, 88; NIH New Investigator awardee, 1985-88, others. Fellow Am. Coll. Rheumatology; mem. AAAS, Soc. Neurosci., Am. Soc. Clin. Investigation, Am. Assn. Immunologists, N.Y. Acad. Scis., Can. Med. Assn., Internat. Soc. Neuroimmunology (mem. internat. adv. com. 1995), PsychoNeuroImmunology Rsch. Soc. (councillor 1997—), Soc. for Neuroimmunomodulation (sec. 1997-99, pres. 1999—). Office: NIMH/NIH Bldg 10 10 Center Dr MSC-1284 Bethesda MD 20892-1284 Fax: 301-496-6095. E-mail: ems@codon.nih.gov.

STERNBERG, JEFFREY, research manager; PhD, U. Ill., 1987. Chemistry rsch. mgr. E.I. DuPont de Nemours, Newark, Del., 1998—. Achievements include invention of of several crop protection chemicals and chemical synthesis processes.

STERNBERG, ROBERT JEFFREY, psychology educator, researcher; b. Newark, Dec. 8, 1949; s. Joseph Sternberg and Lillian Myriam (Politzer) Weingast; m. Elena Grigorenko, 2003; children from previous marriage: Seth, Sara. BA summa cum laude, Yale U., 1972; PhD in Psychology, Stanford U., 1975; D honoris causa, Complutense U., Madrid, 1994, U. Cyprus, 2000, U. Paris, 2000, U. Leuven, Belgium, 2001, Constantine the Philosopher U., Nitra, Slovakia, 2004. Mem. faculty dept. psychology Yale U., New Haven, 1975—, asst. prof., 1975—80, assoc. prof., 1980—83, prof. psychology, 1983-86, dir. grad. studies, 1983—88, IBM prof. psychology and edn., 1986—, acting chmn. dept. psychology, 1992, dir. Yale Ctr. Psychology of Abilities, Competencies and Expertise, 2000—. Editor-in-chief Ency. of Human Intelligence, Psychol. Bull., 1991-96, Contemporary Psychology, 1999-2004; cons. editor Learning and Individual Differences, 1992—, Intelligence, 1977—, Devel. Rev., 1987-91, Jour. Personality and Social Psychology, 1989-91, Psychol. Rev., 1989-91; author: Intelligence, Information Processing and Analogical Reasoning, 1977, Beyond IQ, 1985, The Triarchic Mind, 1988, Metaphors of Mind, 1990, In Search of the Human Mind, 1995, 98, (with T. Lubart) Defying the Crowd, 1995, Successful Intelligence, 1997, Pathways to Psychology, 1997, Thinking Styles, 1997, Intelligence, Heredity and Environment, 1997, Love is a Story, 1998, Cupid's Arrow, 1998, Handbook of Intelligence, 2000, Wisdom, Intelligence, and Creativity Synthesized, 2003. Recipient award for Excellence Mensa Edn. and Rsch. Found., 1989, Disting. Lifetime Contbn. to Psychology Conn. Psychology Assn., 1999, Disting. Scientist and Scholar award Positive Psychology Network, 2002, Anton Jurovsky award, Slovak Psychol. Soc., 2004; Guggenheim Found. fellow, 1985-86. Fellow AAAS, APA (bd. dirs. 2002-04, pres. 2003, past pres. divsns. 1, 10, 15, 24, bd. trustees ins. trust 2004, McCandless Young Scientist award divsn. devel. psychology 1982, Disting. Sci. award for early career contbn. 1981, pres. 2003, Farnsworth award, Arthur W. Staats award, E.L. Thorndike award 2003), Am. Acad. Arts and Scis., Am. Psychol. Soc., Soc. Exptl. Psychologists; mem. Am. Ednl. Rsch. Assn. (Rsch. Rev. award 1986, Outstanding Book award 1987, Sylvia Scribner award 1996, James McKeen Cattell award 1999), Soc. Multivariate Exptl. Psychology (Cattell award 1982), Nat. Assn. Gifted Children (Disting. Scholar award 1985), Phi Beta Kappa, Kappa Delta Pi (Laureate chpt. 2003). Achievements include theory of successful intelligence; balance theory of wisdom. Avocations: physical fitness, travel, reading, cello. Home: 105 Spruce Bank Rd Hamden CT 06518-2233 Office: Yale Univ PACE Ctr PO Box 208358 New Haven CT 06520 Office Phone: 203-432-4633. Business E-Mail: robert.sternberg@yale.edu.

STERNBERG, SEYMOUR, insurance company executive; b. Bklyn., June 24, 1943; s. Max and Mollie Sternberg; m. Roslyn Jacobowitz, June 14, 1965 (div.); children: Jodi, Donna; m. Laurette Zolty, Sept. 14, 1980; 1 child, Matthew. BSEE, CCNY, 1965; MSEE in Computer Sci., Northeastern U., 1968. Mgr. Raytheon Co., Bedford, Mass., 1965-73; mgr. Data Architects, Waltham, Mass., 1973-75; dir. info. svcs. Mass. Mut. Life Ins. Co., Springfield, 1975-76, 2d v.p., 1976-77, v.p. info. svcs., 1977-81, sr. v.p. group life and health divsn., 1981-84, exec. v.p. group life and health divsn., 1984-87, sr. exec. v.p., 1987-88; sr. v.p. group ops. N.Y. Life Ins. Co., 1989, exec. v.p., 1991, vice chmn., pres., COO, 1995-97, chmn., pres., CEO, 1997—2002, chmn., CEO, 2002—. Bd. govs. United Way Tri-State; bd. trustees Hackley School, Tarrytown, NY, Big Bros./ Big Sisters of NYC, Northeastern U., Boston, 2004—; bd. dirs. Express Scripts Inc. Mem.: CUNY Bus. Leadership Coun., NYC Partnership and C. of C. (bd. mem.), BRT, ACLI (bd. dir.). Avocations: stamp collecting; tennis. Office: NY Life Ins Co 51 Madison Ave Rm 1304 New York NY 10010

STERNBERGER, LUDWIG AMADEUS, neurologist, educator; b. Munich, May 26, 1921; s. Hugo and Emy (Wolinger) S.; m. Nancy Jeanne Hoy, Dec. 13, 1961. BA, Am. U. Beirut, 1941, MD, 1945. Fellow Sloan Kettering Meml. Cancer Ctr., N.Y.C., 1948-50; sr. med. biochemist N.Y. State Dept. Health, Albany, 1950-54; asst. prof. medicine Northwestern U., Chgo., 1954-55; chief basic scis. div. Med. Research Labs., Edgewood Arsenal, Md., 1957-78; prof. brain research U. Rochester Med. Ctr. (N.Y.), 1978-86; prof. neurology, pathology and anatomy U. Md., Balt., 1986-92; sci. co-dir., treas. Sternberger Monoclonals, Inc., Balt., 1992—. Author: Immunocytochemistry, 1974, 3d edit, 1986; mem. editoral bd. Cell and Tissue Research, Histochemistry, Jour. Histochemistry and Cytochemistry, Jour. Neurosci. Methods, Jour. Neuroimmunology, Histochem. Jour., Electron Microscopy in Biology. Served to maj. M.C., U.S. Army, 1955-57. Recipient Paul A. Siple prize, 1972; recipient Humboldt prize for sr. U.S. scientists, 1980, Classic Author citation Inst. Sci. Info., 1983; Senator Jacob K. Javits neurosci. investigator award, 1984; 25th most frequently cited author in sci. lit. of 1984; author of one of 17 Newcomer Superstar papers among 100 most cited of all time. Mem. Histochem. Soc. (pres. 1977-78), Am. Soc. Neurochemistry (program com. 1983-84), Am. Assn. Immunologists, Endocrine Soc., Am. Acad. Allergy, Am. Assn. Neuropathologists Lutheran. Home: 10 Burwood Ct Lutherville Timonium MD 21093-3502

STERNE, JOSEPH ROBERT LIVINGSTON, newspaper editor, educator; b. Phila., Apr. 25, 1928; s. Robert Livingston and Edith Eisner (Heymann) S.; m. Barbara Adele Greene, Feb. 10, 1951; children: Robert Greene, Paul Livingston, Edward Joseph, Adam Heymann, Lee Winslow Greene. BA cum laude, Lehigh U., 1948; MS, Columbia U., 1950. Reporter Salt Lake Telegram, Salt Lake City, 1948-49, Wall Street Jour., N.Y.C., 1950-51, Dallas Morning News, 1951-53; reporter Balt. Sun, 1953-72, editorial page editor, 1972-97; sr. fellow Inst. for Policy Studies Johns Hopkins U., 1997—. Mem. Am. Soc. Newpaper Editors, Hamilton St. Club, Phi Beta Kappa. Home: PO Box 599 Sparks MD 21152-0599 Office: Johns Hopkins U Inst Policy Studies 3400 N Charles St Baltimore MD 21218-2680 E-mail: sterne@jhunix.hcf.jhu.edu.

STERNER, FRANK MAURICE, industrial executive; b. Lafayette, Ind., Nov. 26, 1935; s. Raymond E. and Maudelene M. (Scipio) S.; m. Elsa Y. Rasmusson, June 29, 1958; children: Mark, Lisa. BS, Purdue U., 1958, MS, 1959, PhD, 1962. Sr. staff specialist Gen. Motors Inst., Flint, Mich., 1962-63; dir. personnel and orgnl. research Delco Electronics, Milw., 1963-66, dir. personnel devel. and research, 1966-68; partner Nourse & Sterner, Inc., Milw., 1968-69; pres., 1969-73; assoc. dean, prof. Krannert Grad. Sch. of Mgmt., Purdue U., West Lafayette, Ind., 1973-79; v.p. strategic mgmt. Johnson Controls, Inc., Milw., 1979-89; pres., chief exec. officer E.R. Wagner Mfg. Co., 1989—; pres., owner Ridgeway Devel. Inc., Milw., 1993—. Bd. dirs. Wausau Homes, Inc., E.R. Wagner Mfg. Co., Ridgeway Devel. Inc., Fullerton Cos., Inc., Greenheck Fan Corp. Mem. rsch .com. Am. Lung Assn., Wis.; bd. dirs. Children's Hosp. of Wis. Found. Home: 1440 E Standish Pl Milwaukee WI 53217-1958 Office: ER Wagner Mfg Co 4611 N 32nd St Milwaukee WI 53209-6000 Office Phone: 414-449-8204. E-mail: frank.sterner@erwagner.com.

STERNER, MICHAEL EDMUND, international affairs consultant; b. N.Y.C., Dec. 26, 1928; s. Harold Walther and Leonie (Knoedler) S.; m. Courtenay Read, Mar. 30, 1957; children: Lucian, Marcellin. AB, Harvard Coll., 1951. Govt. rels. rep. Arabian-Am. Oil Co., Dhahran, Saudi Arabia, 1951-54; joined Fgn. Svc., 1956; vice consul Aden, 1957-58; polit. officer Cairo, 1960-64; desk officer Near Eastern Affairs Dept. State, 1964-70, dir. Egyptian affairs, 1970-74; amb. to United Arab Emirates Abu Dhabi, 1974-76; dep. asst. sec. state for Near East and South Asian affairs, 1977-81; mng. dir. The IRC Group, Inc., 1982—. Mem. bd. govs. Mid. East Inst. With AUS, 1954-56. Mem. Coun. Fgn. Rels. Home: 2712 36th St NW Washington DC 20007-1421 Office Phone: 202-337-4369. E-mail: sternerm@starpower.net.

STERNFELD, MARC HOWARD, finance educator; b. N.Y.C., July 12, 1947; s. Joseph and Jeane (Richstein) S.; m. Arleen Estelle Weinreb, Aug. 25, 1968; children: Joshua, Jonathan. BA, Queens Coll., 1968; MS, NYU, 1970; MBA, Columbia U., 1971; student, Jewish Theol. Sem., 2001—. Spacecraft programmer Grumman Aero., 1968-70; fin. analyst CBS, N.Y.C., 1971-72; rsch. asst. Nat. Bur Econ. Rsch., 1970-71; sr. analyst N.Y.C. Police Dept., 1972-75; ptnr. Arthur Andersen & Co., N.Y.C., 1975-88; prin. Morgan Stanley, N.Y.C., 1987-94; mng. dir. Salomon Bros., N.Y.C., 1994-96; pres. Trans-Form L.L.C., N.Y.C., 1995—2001; mng. dir. Deutsche Bank Global Ops. and Tech., 1996—2001; CEO Settlement.com, 2000—01. Asst. prof. Columbia U. Internat. bd. dirs., exec. com. United Synagogue Conservative Judaism; past pres. Marlboro Jewish Ctr.; v.p. World Counsel of Synagogues; dean's coun. Tisch Sch. Arts; bd. dirs. Hillel. Mem. Jazz Vt. Avocation: piano. Home: 13 Evan Dr Morganville NJ 07751-1062

STERNHAGEN, FRANCES, actress; b. Washington, DC, Jan. 13, 1930; Student, Vassar Coll., Perry-Mansfield Sch. Theatre; studied with Sanford Meisner, NY. Tchr. Milton Acad., Cath. U. Ams., Mass.; actress Arena Stage, Washington, DC, 1953-54. Debut Thieves Carnival, NY, 1955; plays include The Carefree Tree, The Admirable Bashville (Clarence Derwent award, Obie award), Ulysses in Night Town, Red Eye of Love, Misalliance, The Return of Herbert Bracewell, Laughing Stock, The Displaced Person, The Pinter Plays (Obie award); Broadway shows include The Skin of Our Teeth, Viva Madison Avenue, Great Day in the Morning, The Right Honorable Gentleman, The Cocktail Party, Cock-a-Doodle Dandy, Playboy of the Western World, The Sign in Sidney Brustein's Window, The Good Doctor (Tony award 1973), Equus (Drama Desk award), Angel, On Golden Pond (Drama League award), The Father, Grownups, Summer, You Can't Take It With You, Home Front, Driving Miss Daisy, Remembrance, A Perfect Ganesh, The Heiress (Tony award 1995), Long Day's Journey into Night, 1998, The Exact Center of the Universe, 1999, Morning's at Seven, 2003; actress (films) Up The Down Staircase, 1967, Starting Over, 1979, Outland, 1981, Independence Day, 1983, Romantic Comedy, 1983, Bright Lights, Big City, 1988, See You in the Morning, 1989, Communion, 1989, Misery, 1990, Doc Hollywood, 1991, Raising Cain, 1992, Curtain Call, Land Fall, 1997, The Rising Place, 1998; (TV series) Love of Life, The Doctors, Secret Storm, Cheers, Golden Years, Under One Roof, The Road Home, E.R., Sex and the City; (TV movies) Who Will Save Our Children?, 1978, Prototype, 1982, Resting Place, 1986, Follow Your Heart, 1990, She Woke Up, 1992, Labor of Love: The Arlette Schweitzer Story, 1993, Reunion, 1994, Tales from the Crypt, Outer Limits, Law and Order, 1990, 96, The Con, 1997, To Live Again, 1997, New York: A Documentary Film, 1999, The Laramie Project, 2001.*

STERN-LAROSA, CARYL M. advocate, educational association administrator; BA in Studio Art, SUNY, Oneonta; MD in Student Personnel Adminstrn., We. Ill. U.; postgrad., Loyola U. Dean students Polytecn. U.; former sr. mgmt. World of Difference Inst., 1991, former dir. spl. tng. program, dir. edn. divsn. Anti-Defamation League. Nat. chairperson Nat. Assn. Campus Activites; former chairperson Boroughof Bklyn. Unity Task Force. Co-author: Future Perfect: A Model for Professional Development. Recipient Founder's award, Nat. Assn. Campus Activities, 1992, Borough of Bklyn. Unity award, Borough of Queen's Citation for Contbn. to Racial and Religious Harmony, Oneonta Alumni Recognition award, SUNY, Alumni Achievement award, We. Ill. U., Senn award for profl. excellence. Office: Anti-Defamation League 823 United Nations Plz New York NY 10017

STERNLICHT, BARRY STUART, hotel executive; b. 1960; married; 3 children. BA magna cum laude, Brown U., 1982; MBA with distinction, Harvard U., 1986. Chmn., CEO Starwood Hotels and Resorts Trust, Phoenix; pres., CEO Starwood Capital Group, LLC, Phoenix, 1991—. Trustee Equity Residential Trust; bd. dirs. Starwood Fin. Trust, U.S. Franchise Systems and Comm.; mem. Urban Land Inst., Nat. Multi-Family Housing Coun, Young Presidents Org., World Travel & Tourism Council, Council for the U.S. and Italy. Bd. dirs. Com. to Encourage Corp. Philanthropy, Bus. Com. for the Arts, Inc., Channel 13/WNET, Nat. Leadership Advocacy Program for Juvenile Diabetes Rsch. Found. Internat., Kids in Crisis, Fairfield County Jr. Achievement, Ctr. for Christian-Jewish Understanding; bd. govs. NAREIT. Named Man of the Year, Juvenile Diabetes Rsch. Found. Internat.; recipient Preston Robert Tisch Disting. Industry Leadership award, NYU Sch. Hospitality, Tourism & Travel Admin. Office: Starwood Hotels and Resorts Worldwide 1111 Westchester Ave White Plains NY 10604-3520*

STERNLICHT, BENO, research and development company executive; b. Nowy Sacz, Poland; arrived in U.S., 1949, naturalized, 1950; s. Hugo Charles and Helena (Anisfield) Sternlicht; m. Lisa Spilberg; children: Mark David, Eric Alan, Joshua Hugh, Aaron Jonathan. BSEE, Union Coll., Schenectady, N.Y., 1950; MS, Columbia U., 1951, PhD, 1954, DSc (hon.), 1970. Staff engr. thermal power sys., gen. engring. lab. GE, 1951-54, specialist applied mechanics, 1954-58, cons. engr., 1958-61; co-founder, 1961; since chmn. bd., tech. dir. Mech. Tech., Inc., Latham, NY; pres. Benjosh Mgmt. Corp., NY, 1983, Ameast, N.Y.C., 1981—, Arben Internat. LLC, N.Y.C., 1994—. Dir. Small Diesels Ltd., India, New Ea. India Ltd., Plub Power LLC; pres. Vols. Internat. Tech. Assistance, 1965—71, chmn. bd. dirs., 1971—73; chmn. con. energy tech. and space propulsion NASA, 1969—72, mem. rsch. adv. coun., 1970—72; mem. Nat. Energy Task Force, 1981; pres. Comfortex Corp., 1995—; cons. to PRC, Israel. Advisor to Pres. Carter, to Pres. Reagan, Pres. Bush. Fellow: ASME (Machine Design award 1966); mem.: AIAA, Am. Soc. Lubrication Engrs., Nat. Acad. Engring., Navy League, Sigma Xi, Tau Beta Pi. Achievements include patents in field. Address: 123 Partridge Run Schenectady NY 12309-1321 E-mail: LISBEN26@aol.com.

STERNLICHT, SANFORD, English and theater arts educator, writer; b. N.Y.C., Sept. 20, 1931; s. Irving Stanley and Sylvia (Hilsenroth) S.; m. Dorothy Hilkert, June 4, 1956 (dec. 1977); children: David, Daniel. BS, SUNY, Oswego, 1953; MA, Colgate U., 1955; PhD, Syracuse U., 1962. Instr. SUNY, Oswego, 1959-60, asst. prof., 1960-62, prof. and dir. grad. studies in English, 1962-72, chmn. dept. theater, 1972-84; adj. prof. English Syracuse (N.Y.) U., 1981—. Leverhulme vis. prof. English, U. York, Eng., 1965-66; Fulbright sr. specialist, vis. prof. English, U. Pecs, Hungary, 2004. Author: Gull's Way, 1961, The Blue Star Commodore, 1961, Love in Pompeii, 1967, John Webster's Imagery and the Webster Canon, 1972, John Masefield, 1977, McKinley's Bulldog, 1977 (Mil. Book Club award, Saturday Evening Post Book Club award), C.S. Forester, 1981, Padraic Colum, 1985; (with E.M. Jameson) The Black Devil of the Bayous, 1971; (with E.M. Jameson) U.S.F. Constellation: Yankee Racehorse, 1981, John Galsworthy, 1986, R.F. Delderfield, 1988, Stevie Smith, 1990, Stephen Spender, 1992, Siegfried Sassoon, 1993, All Things Herriot: James Herriot and His Peaceable Kingdom, 1995, Jean Rhys, 1997, A Reader's Guide to Modern Irish Drama, 1998, C.S. Forester and the Hornblower Saga, 1999, Chaim Potok: A Critical Companion, 2000, A Reader's Guide to Modern American Drama, 2002, A Student Companion to Elie Wiesel, 2003; editor: The Selected Short Stories of Padraic Colum, 1985, The Selected Plays of Padraic Colum, 1986, The Selected Poems of Padraic Colum, 1988, In Search of Stevie Smith, 1991, New Plays from the Abbey Theatre, 1993-1995, 96, 96-98, 99, 99-2001, 2003. Lt. (j.g.) USN, 1955-59, comdr. USNR, ret. Recipient New Poets award Writer mag., 1960, Chancellor's award SUNY, 1974; fellow Poetry Soc. Am., 1964; rsch. grantee SUNY, 1963-70; named Tchr. of Yr. Syracuse U., 1986. Mem. MLA, PEN, Shakespeare Assn. Am., Am. Conf. Irish Studies. Democrat. Jewish. Home: 128 Dorset Rd Syracuse NY 13210-3048 Office: Syracuse U Dept English Syracuse NY 13244-0001 Office Phone: 315-443-9480. Business E-Mail: svsternl@syr.edu.

STERNMAN, JOEL W. lawyer; b. N.Y.C., Oct. 20, 1943; s. Abraham and Sarah (Simon) S.; children: Mark S., Cheryl A.; m. Barbara E. Shiers, March 31, 1985; children: Matthew S., Julia S. AB, Dartmouth Coll., 1965; LLB, Yale U., 1968. Bar: N.Y. 1970, U.S. Dist. Ct. (so. and ea. dists.) N.Y. 1971, U.S. Ct. Appeals (2d cir.) 1972, U.S. Supreme Ct. 1984, U.S. Ct. Appeals (6th cir.) 1985, U.S. Ct. Appeals (9th cir.) 1994, U.S. Tax Ct. 1996, U.S. Dist. Ct. (ea. dist.) Mich. 1997. Law clk. to judge U.S. Dist. Ct., New Haven, 1968-69; assoc. Rosenman Colin Freund Lewis & Cohen, N.Y.C., 1969-77; ptnr. Rosenman & Colin LLP, N.Y.C., 1977—2002, Katten Muchin Zavis Rosenman, 2002—. Editor Yale Law Jour., New Haven, 1966-68. Mem. Phi Beta Kappa. Office: Katten Muchin Zavis Rosenman 575 Madison Ave New York NY 10022-2585 Office Phone: 212-940-7060. Business E-Mail: j.sternman@kmzr.com.

STERNS, HARVEY LEONARD, psychologist, gerontologist; b. Waterville, Maine; s. Frederick James and Sarah (Hoos) S.; m. Ronni Susan Small, Nov. 14, 1964; children: Anthony Alexander, Randy Rose, George Herbert. Bachelor, Bard Coll., 1965; Master, SUNY, Buffalo, 1968; PhD, W.Va. U., 1971. Lic. psychologist. Prof. psychology U. Akron, Ohio, 1971—, dir. Inst. Life-Span Devel. and Gerontology, 1975—; rsch. prof. gerontology Northeastern Ohio Univs. Coll. Medicine, Rootstown, 1978—. Prin. Creative Action Inc., Akron, 1988—. Editor: Gerontology in Higher Education: Perspectives and Issues, 1978, Gerontology in Higher Education: Building Institutional and Community Strength, 1979; contbr. chpts. to books and articles to profl. jours. Bd. trustees Ohio Presbyn. Retirement Communities, Columbus, 1989-2000, Sumner Home, Akron; pres. Jewish Family Svcs., Akron, 1991-93, Mature Svcs., Inc., Akron, 1998—; chair City of Akron Sr. Citizens Adv. Commn., Akron, 1995-2003. Recipient award Andrus Found., 1976, 77, 78, award Dept. HEW, 1977-79, award Nat. Inst. Disability and Rehab. Rsch., 1992-2003, award Ohio Dept. Aging, 1993. Fellow APA (charter; mem.-at-large 1983-87, editor Adult Devel. and Aging News 1997-2002, pres. 2002—), Assn. Gerontology in Higher Edn. (pres. 1983-84, Clark Tibbitts award 1994), Gerontol. Soc. Am. (mem.-at-large Behavioral and Social Sci. 1988-90), Ohio Acad. Sci. (v.p. psychology sect. 1973-74), Sigma Phi Omega (life, nat. pres. 1985-86). Democrat. Jewish. Avocations: sailing, old house restoration, old car restoration. Home: 680 N Portage Path Akron OH 44303 Office: Univ Akron Inst Li-Span Dev&Geron Arts & Scis Bldg Ste 340 Akron OH 44325-4307 Home Fax: 330-867-6899; Office Fax: 330-972-5174. E-mail: hsterns@uakron.edu.

STERNS, JOEL HENRY, lawyer; b. N.Y.C., Apr. 13, 1934; s. Barney and Yvetta S.; m. Joanne Glickman, Nov. 19, 1961; children: Racel, Leslie, David. BS in Journalism, 1956; MPA, Princeton U., 1958; JD, NYU, 1967. Bar: N.J., D.C. Exec. asst. to commr., acting commr. N.J. Dept. Conservation and Econ. Devel., 1958-61; exec. asst. to adminstr. Bur. Security and Consular Affairs, U.S. Dept. State, 1961-62; regional programs coord. Alliance for Progress, 1962-64; exec. asst. to pres. Export-Import Bank U.S., 1964; dep. commr. N.J. Dept. Cmty. Affairs, 1967-68; counsel to gov. N.J., 1968-70; pres. firm Sterns, Herbert & Weinroth (P.A.), Trenton, N.J., 1970-88; mem. exec. com., compensation com. and mktg. com. Sterns, Herbert & Weinroth (merged with Hannoch-Weisman 1988), Roseland, N.J., 1988-91; pres. Hannoch-Weisman, Roseland, 1991-93, Sterns & Weinroth, Trenton, 1994—. Mem. lawyers adv. com. U.S. Dist. Ct. N.J., 1995—. Mem. ABA, Am. Law Inst., Am. Judicature Soc., N.J. Bar Assn. (trustee), Mercer County Bar Assn., Assn. Princeton U. Grad. Alumni (trustee 1975-77), NYU Alumni Assn. N.J. (Disting. Alumni award 1987). Home: 28 Heritage Hills Dr Washington Crossing PA 18977 Office: Sterns & Weinroth PO Box 1298 50 W State St Ste 1400 Trenton NJ 08607 Office Phone: 609-392-2100. E-mail: jsterns@sternslaw.com.

STERNSTEIN, ALLAN J. lawyer; b. Chgo., June 7, 1948; s. Milton and Celia (Kaganove) Sternstein; m. Miriam A. Dolgin, July 12, 1970 (div. July 1981); children: Jeffery A., Amy R.; m. Beverly A. Cook, Feb. 8, 1986 (div. 2004); 1 child, Julia S. B.S., U. Ill., 1970; M.S., U. Mich., 1972; J.D., Loyola U., Chgo., 1977. Bar: Ill. 1977, U.S. Dist. Ct. (no. dist.) Ill. 1977, U.S. Dist. Ct. (no. dist.) Ohio 1977, U.S. Dist. Ct. (ea. dist) Mich. 1986, U.S. Dist. Ct. (we. dist.) Mich. 1990, U.S. Ct. Customs and Patent Appeals 1978, U.S. Ct. Appeals (7th cir.) 1979, U.S. Ct. Appeals (Fed. cir.) 1982, U.S. Dist. Ct. (ea. dist.) Wis. 2003, U.S. Ct. Appeals (5th cir.) 2003. Patent agt. Sunbeam Corp., Oak Brook, Ill., 1972—76; ptnr. Neuman, Williams, Anderson & Olson, Chgo., 1976—84; divsn. patent counsel Abbott Labs., North Chgo., Ill., 1984—87; ptnr. Brinks Hofer Gilson & Lione, Chgo., 1987—, mng. ptnr., 1996—99. Adj. prof. law U. Ill., 1992—; lectr. Oxford (Eng.) U., 2003. Co-author: Designing an Effective Intellectual Property Compliance Program; contbr. articles to profl. jours. Legal advisor Legal Aid Soc., Chgo., 1974—76, Pub. Defender's Office, Chgo., 1974. Mem.: ABA, Licensing Execs. Soc., Am. Intellectual Property Law Assn., Patent Law Assn. Chgo. (com. chmn. 1982), Chgo. Bar Assn., Phi Eta Sigma, Sigma Gamma Tau, Sigma Tau, Tau Beta Pi. Jewish. Office: Brinks Hofer Gilson & Lione Ste 3600 455 N Cityfront Plaza Dr Chicago IL 60611-5599 Office Phone: 312-321-4228.

STERRETT, JAMES KELLEY, II, lawyer; b. St. Louis, Nov. 26, 1946; s. James Kelley and Anastasia Mary (Holzer) S.; 1 child, Brittany. AB, San Diego State U., 1968; JD, U. Calif., Berkeley, 1971; LLM, U. Pa., 1973. Bar: Calif. 1972, U.S. Dist. Ct. (so. dist.) Calif. 1972. From assoc. to ptnr. Gray, Cary, Ames & Frye, San Diego, 1972-83; ptnr. Lillick, McHose & Charles, San Diego, 1983-90, Pillsbury, Madison & Sutro, San Diego, 1991-96, Dostart Clapp Sterrett & Coveney, LLP, 1996-99; sole practice, 1999—. Contbr. articles to profl. jours. Bd. dirs. Holiday Bowl, San Diego, 1980—, Mus. Photog. Arts, San Diego, 1985-88, San Diego Internat. Sports Coun., 1980—, pres., 1990, chmn., 1992. Capt. USAFR, 1972. Fellow U. Pa. Ctr. Study Fin. Instns., 1971-72. Mem. ABA, Calif. Bar Assn., San Diego County Bar Assn. Clubs: Fairbanks Ranch Country (Rancho Santa Fe) (bd. dirs. 1985-87). Republican. Episcopalian. Avocations: golf, college football, hiking. Office: Ste 291 3525 Del Mar Heights Rd San Diego CA 92130

STERRETT, SAMUEL BLACK, lawyer, former judge; b. Washington, Dec. 17, 1922; s. Henry Hatch Dent and Helen (Black) S.; m. Jeane McBride, Aug. 27, 1949; children: Samuel Black, Robin Dent, Douglas McBride. Student, St. Albans Sch., 1933-41; grad., U.S. Mcht. Marine Acad., 1945; BA, Amherst Coll., 1947; LLB, U. Va., 1950; LLM in Taxation, NYU, 1959. Bar: D.C. 1951, Va. 1950. Atty. Alvord & Alvord, Washington, 1950-56; trial atty. Office Regional Counsel, Internal Revenue Service, N.Y.C., 1956-60; ptnr. Sullivan, Shea & Kenney, Washington, 1960-68; municipal cons. to office vice pres. U.S., 1965-68; judge U.S. Tax Ct., 1968-88, chief judge, 1985-88; ptnr. Myerson, Kuhn & Sterrett, Washington, 1988-89; of counsel Vinson & Elkins, Washington, 1990—2002; pvt. practice Law Offices of Samuel B. Sterrett, Washington, 2002—. Bd. mgrs. Chevy Chase Village, 1970-74, chmn., 1972-74; 1st v.p. bd. trustees, mem. exec. com. Washington Hosp. Center, 1969-79, chmn. bd. trustees, 1979-84, mem. bd. trustees, 1999—; chmn. bd. trustees Washington Healthcare Corp., 1982-87; chmn. bd. trustees Medlantic Healthcare Group, 1987-89; mem. audit com. Medstar Health, 1990—; mem. Washington Cathedral, 1973-81, 99—, mem. fin. com., 1998—, chmn., 1999—; mem. governing bd. St. Albans Sch., 1977-81; trustee Louise Home, 1979-89. Served with AUS, 1943; Served with U.S. Mcht. Marine, 1943-46. Fellow Am. Bar Found. (life); mem. ABA, D.C. Bar Assn., Am. Coll. Tax Counsel, Soc. of the Cincinnati, Coun. for Future, Am. Inns. of Ct., Chevy Chase Club (bd. govs. 1979-84, pres. 1984), Met. Club, Lawyers Club, Alibi Club, Alfalfa Club, Ch. of N.Y. Club, Beta Theta Pi. Episcopalian. Office: Law Offices of Samuel B Sterrett Ste 600 1455 Pennsylvania Ave NW Fl 7 Washington DC 20004-1013 Office Phone: 202-639-6665. Business E-Mail: ssterrettalv@law.com.

STERRETT, STEVEN E. real estate company officer; From various positions to exec. v.p., CFO Simon Property Group, Inc., Indpls., 1989—2001, exec. v.p., 2001—, CFO, 2001—. Office: Simon Property Group Inc National City Ctr 115 W Washington St Indianapolis IN 46204*

STERTZ, STEPHEN ALLEN, historian, educator; b. N.Y.C., Aug. 2, 1944; s. Philip Bernard and Anne (Herman) S. BS, Columbia U., 1968; PhD, U. Mich., 1974. Rschr. Bronx (N.Y.) County Hist. Soc., 1978-82, 83—. Adj. asst. prof. history Rutgers U., Newark, 1980—82, 1986, Dowling Coll., Oakdale, NY, 1991—, Beverly Coll., Bronx, 1996—; vis. asst. prof. classics U. Ill., Urbana, 1982—83; adj. lectr. classics and history St. Peter's Coll., Jersey City, 2000—, Fordham U., N.Y.C., 2000, Montclair State Coll., Upper Montclair, NJ, 2002—. Author: Jonathan Swift's Gulliver's Travels, 1996; editor: Concordantia in Orationem Quae Aristidis Fertur Eis Basilea, 1996; contbr articles to profl. jours. Candidate N.Y. State Legislature, 1970. Travel to Collections grantee NEH, Washington, 1984; rsch. grantee Wilbur Found., Mecosta, Mich., 1992, Soc. Farsaratul, L.I. City, N.Y., 1992, Richter Found., N.Y.C., 1996. Mem. Am. Hist. Assn., Am. Philol. Assn., Archaeol. Instn. Am. (nat. coun. 1977-78). Avocations: reading, book collecting. Office: Montclair State Univ Dept Classics and Gen Humanities Montclair NJ 07043 E-mail: sstertz@pipemail.mercy.com.

STERZER, FRED, research physicist; b. Vienna, Nov. 18, 1929; came to U.S., 1947, naturalized, 1952; s. Karl and Rosa (Trumer) S.; m. Betty Distel, Sept. 5, 1964 (dec.). BS in Physics, CCNY, 1951; MS in Physics, NYU, 1952, PhD in Physics, 1955. With RCA, 1954-87, RCA Labs., David Sarnoff Research Center, Princeton, N.J., 1956-87, dir. microwave tech. center, 1972-87; dir. microwave research lab. David Sarnoff Research Ctr., 1987-88; pres. MMTC, Inc., Princeton, 1988—. Herbert J. Kayser research prof., City Coll., CUNY, 1986-87. Contbr. numerous articles to profl. publs. Fellow IEEE; mem. Am. Phys. Soc., Nat. Acad. Engring., Sigma Xi, Phi Beta Kappa. Achievements include condr. research on optical components, microwave solid-state devices and circuits, med. microwave tech. Home: 4432 Province Line Rd Princeton NJ 08540-4368 Office: MMTC Inc 12 Roszel Rd Princeton NJ 08540-6234 E-mail: sterzer@mmtc.com.

STETLER, DAVID J. lawyer; b. Washington, Sept. 6, 1949; s. C. Joseph and Norine (Delaney) S.; m. Mary Ann Ferguson, Aug. 14, 1971; children: Brian, Christopher, Jennifer. BA, Villanova U., 1971, JD, 1974. Bar: U.S. Supreme Ct. 1978, Ill. 1988, U.S. Ct. Appeals (7th cir.) 1988, U.S. Ct. Appeals (3d cir.) 1992, U.S. Dist. Ct. (ctrl. dist.) 1994, U.S. Ct. Appeals (8th cir.) 1994. Atty. IRS, Washington, 1974-79; spl. atty. tax divsn. Dept. Justice, Washington, 1975-79; asst. atty. U.S. Atty.'s Office, Chgo., 1979-88, dep. chief spl. prosecutions div., 1985-86, chief criminal receiving and appellate divsns., 1986-88; ptnr. McDermott, Will & Emery, Chgo., 1988-98; prin. Stetler & Duffy, Ltd., Chgo., 1998—. Lectr. Atty. Gen. Trial Advocacy Inst., Washington, 1977—. Fellow Internat. Soc. Barristers, Am. Coll. Trial Lawyers; mem. ABA (chmn. midwest subcom. White Collar Crime com. 1991-93), Wong Sun Soc. San Francisco. Office: 140 S Dearborn St Chicago IL 60603-5202 Office Phone: 312-338-0200. E-mail: dstetler@stetlerandduffy.com.

STETLER, RUSSELL DEARNLEY, JR., private investigator; b. Phila., Jan. 15, 1945; s. Russell Dearnley and Martha Eleanor (Schultz) S. BA with honors in Philosophy, Haverford (Pa.) Coll., 1966; postgrad., New Sch. Social Research, 1966-67. Research asst. to Bertrand Russell, 1967; lectr. Hendon Coll., London, 1968-69; pres. Archetype, Inc., Berkeley, Calif., 1971-78; pub. Westworks, Berkeley, 1977-80; pvt. investigator, 1980-90; chief investigator Calif. Appellate Project, 1990-95; dir. of investigation and mitigation N.Y. State Capital Defender Office, N.Y.C., 1995—. Cons., dir. Ramparts Press, Palo Alto, 1971-80; editorial cons. Internews, Berkeley, 1973-78; faculty Caribbean Sch., Ponce, P.R., 1978-80 Author: The Battle of Bogside, 1970; co-editor: The Assassinations: Dallas and Beyond, 1976. Research grantee Atlantic Peace Found., 1969-70 Mem. Calif. Assn. Lic. Investigators, Nat. Assn. Legal Investigators, Calif. Soccer Referees Assn.-North (treas. Marin County chpt. 1982-90), Amigos de las Americas (pres. Marin chpt. 1985-88). Clubs: Mill Valley Soccer (dir. 1981), Albany-Berkeley Soccer (pres. 1977-78). Office: Capital Defender Office 217 Broadway Fl 9 New York NY 10007-2909 E-mail: rstetler@nycdo.org.

STETLER-STEVENSON, WILLIAM GEORGE, pathologist; b. Trenton, N.J., Nov. 27, 1953; BS in Biochemistry cum laude, Albright Coll., 1975; PhD in Biochemistry & Molecular Biology, Northwestern U., 1983, MD, 1984. Diplomate Am. Bd. Pathology. Mem. house staff anatomic pathology McGaw Med. Ctr., 1984-87; sr. staff fellow NIH, 1987-91, med. officer, rschr., 1991—, chief extracellular matrix pathology sect., 1993—. Editl. bd. Diagnostic Molecular Pathology, Am. Jour. Pathology, Invasion & Metastasis; contbr. articles to profl. jours. Kemper Found. Med. scholar, 1978-79. Mem. Am. Soc. Biochemistry and Molecular Biology, Am. Chem. Soc., Am. Soc. Investigative Pathology (Warner-Lambert/Parke-Davis award 1996). Office: Nat Cancer Inst Lab Pathology Extracellular Matrix Pathology Sect Bldg 10 Rm 2A33 10 Ctr Dr Bethesda MD 20892

STETSON, EUGENE WILLIAM, III, film producer; b. Norwalk, Conn., Mar. 31, 1951; s. Eugene William Jr. and Grace Stuart (Richardson) S.; m. Jane White Watson, June 14, 1993. AB, Harvard U., 1982, postgrad. in Sch. Arts and Scis., 1986. Assoc. exec. dir. Conn. River Watershed Coun., Easthampton, Mass., 1978-81; v.p. Fairhill Oil & Gas Corp. (Fairhill Oil Ltd.-Can.), N.Y.C., Calgary, Alta., Can., 1981-84, pres., 1984-92; film and TV writer and producer, 1991—. Bd. dirs. Piedmont Fin. Co., Greensboro, N.C., 1978-80, Chisolm Mgmt. Corp., N.Y.C., 1983—; supr. Ottauquechee Conservation Dist., Woodstock, Vt., 1978-82; pres. Boatwright Found., N.Y.C., 1981—; exec. com. Westminster Sch., Simsbury, Conn., 1984-86; gov. Smith Richardson Found., N.Y., 1984—; trustee Proctor Acad., Andover, N.H., 1985—; co-founder River Watch Network, Montpelier, Vt., 1987—; pres. bd. dirs. Vt. Film Commn., 1996—. Mem. Vt. Gov.'s Coun. of Environ. Advisors, 1992—, Vt. Gov.'s Coun. on Bus. and the Environment, 1994—; pres. Vt. Film Commn., 1996—. Mem. Harvard-Radcliffe Club Vt. (v.p. 1994—), Harvard Club N.Y.C., Hasty Pudding Club. Home: 139 Elm St Norwich VT 05055-9445

STETSON, JOHN BATTERSON, IV, construction executive; b. Phila., Dec. 21, 1936; s. John Batterson Stetson III and Winifred (Walton) Todd; m. Solveig Weiland, Nov. 23, 1963; children: John Batterson V, Eric Weiland, Scott Walton. BA, Yale U., 1959, MArch, 1966; postgrad., U. Pa., 1969-73. Registered architect, Pa., Mass., Fla. Staff architect Bower & Fradley, Architects, Phila., 1966-68, Young & Exley, Architects, Phila., 1968-69; project architect Day & Zimmerman Assocs., Phila., 1969-71, mgr. tech. staff, 1974-76; project mgr. Schnadelbach & Braun, Phila., 1971-74; project exec. Bldg. Scis., Inc., Balt., Kinshasa, Zaire, 1976-77; project mgr. Bldg. Scis., Inc., Balt., 1977-78; sr. cons., v.p., pres. MDC Sys. unit Day and Zimmermann, Inc., Phila., 1978-95, v.p. transp. svcs. unit, 1996-99; cons., Construction Project, 1999. Active Haverford (Pa.) Civic Assn., 1981-84. Comdr. USNR, 1959-81. Mem. Constrn. Mgmt. Assn. Am. (bd. dirs. 1986—), Am. Arbitration Assn., Constrn. Specifications Inst., Haverford Sch. Alumni Assn. Clubs: Merion Cricket (Haverford). Republican. Avocations: music, sailing. Home: 7 Druid Ln Malvern PA 19355-2825

STETSON, PETER BRAILEY, astronomer; b. Middleboro, Mass., Aug. 30, 1952; s. George Robert and Estelle Marie (Ives) Stetson; m. Frances Eileen Bogucki, Aug. 5, 1979; children: Whitney Ann, Brailey Marie, Garrett Wilson, Leete Anthony. BA, MA, Wesleyan U., 1974; MS, Yale U., 1975, PhD, 1979. Postdoctoral astronomy dept. Yale U., New Haven, 1979-80; Carnegie fellow Mt. Wilson and Las Campanas Obs., Pasadena, Calif., 1980-83; rsch. assoc. Dominion Astrophys. Obs., Victoria, Canada, 1983-84, asst. rsch. officer, 1984-86, assoc. rsch. officer, 1986-89, sr. rsch. officer, 1989—2002, prin. rsch. officer, 2003—; adj. prof. U. Victoria, 1988—. Contbr. articles to Astrophys. Jour., Jour. of Royal Astron. Soc. Can., Ann. Revs. of Astronomy and Astrophysics, Astron. Jour., Nature, Publ. Astron. Soc. Pacific. Recipient R.M. Petrie prize lectr. Can. Astron. Soc., 1991, Gold medal Sci. Coun. B.C., 1994, Maria and Eric Muhlmann award Astron. Soc. Pacific, 2000. Office: Dominion Astrophys Obs 5071 W Saanich Rd Victoria BC Canada V9E 2E7 E-mail: peter.stetson@nrc.gc.ca.

STETSON, ROBERT FRANCIS, retired metallurgist; b. N.Y.C., Oct. 20, 1928; s. Ralph Jerome and Margaret Mary Stetson; m. Rita Marie Jubach, Dec. 30, 1950 (dec. May 31, 1994); 1 child, Barbara A.; m. Mary Jane McKinney, June 10, 1999. CE in Metallurgy, Pa. State U., 1955. ICET A NSPE. Lab. technologist & inspection Babcock & Wilcox Co., Beaver Falls, Pa., 1949—58; tech. specialist materials sci. Gen. Atomics, San Diego, 1958—86, cons., 1986—98; ret., 1998; cons. NASA Marshall Space Flight Ctr., 2002—03. With AC U.S. Army, 1945—47, ETO. Recipient Nat. Engring. Assocs. Achievement award, Am. Soc. Metals, 1979, James F. Lincoln Arc Welding Found. award, 1979. Fellow: Am. Soc. Metals Internat. (exec. bd. San Diego chpt. 1964—96, chmn. San Diego chpt. 1972—73). Achievements include patents for plasma orifice tip. Avocation: genealogy. Home: 6317 North Bond Fresno CA 93710

STETTLER, STEPHEN F. performing company executive; b. Phila., May 1, 1952; s. Wallace Frederick and Catherine Sue (Brill) S. AB summa cum laude, Kenyon Coll., 1974; MFA in Directing, Cath. U. Am., 1982; MLitt in Theatre, Lincoln Coll., Oxford, Eng., 1983. Dir. dramatics Westminster Sch., Simsbury, Conn., 1975-80; acting coach Hartke Conservatory Cath. U., Washington, 1982; chair drama dept. St. Albans and Nat. Cathedral Schs., Washington, 1980-84; dir., instr. acting Nat. Theatre Inst. O'Neill Theater Ctr., Waterford, Conn., 1984-93; artistic dir. TNT/New Theatre Bklyn., 1985-90; producing dir. Weston (Vt.) Playhouse, 1988—. Lit. asst. Arena Stage Co., Washington, 1983-84; site evaluator theatres Nat. Endowment for Arts, Washington, 1990—; panelist Vt. Coun. Arts, Montpelier, NEA, Washington, D.C.; mem. capital grants com. N.Y.C. Dept. Cultural Affairs; guest instr. directing Teatret Vart, Norway. Dir.: Who's Afraid of Virginia Woolf?, Dancing at Lughnasa, Animal Fair, Rough Crossing, Nora, Donkeys' Years, Floyd Collins (Moss Hart award for best prodn. in New Eng.), Sweeney Todd, Six Degrees of Separation, A Midsummer Night's Dream (Best Play award Folger Shakespeare Libr. competition). Mem. Phi Beta Kappa. Office: Weston Playhouse 703 Main St Weston VT 05161 E-mail: sstettler@westonplayhouse.org.

STETTNER, EDWARD A. political science educator; b. N.Y.C., Feb. 18, 1940; s. Frederick Albert and Celia Carolyn S.; m. Laura Gagliardi, July 17, 1966; children: Victoria, Jeffrey, Thomas. BA, Brown U., 1962; MA, Princeton U., 1964, PhD, 1968. Lectr. polit. sci. Rutgers U., New Brunswick, N.J., 1965-66; instr. polit. sci. Wellesley (Mass.) Coll., 1966—68, asst. prof. polit. sci., 1968—74, assoc. prof., 1974—80, prof. polit. sci., 1980-95, Ralph Emerson and Alice Freeman Palmer prof. polit. sci., 1995—, assoc. dean of the coll., 1977-86, dean of the faculty, 1986—88. Author: Shaping Modern Liberalism: Herbert Croly and Progressive Thought, 1993; editor: Perspectives on Europe, 1970. Trustee Mount Ida Coll., Newton, Mass., 2000—. Mem. AAUP (mem. nat. coun. 1970-73, pres. Mass. State Conf. 1975-77), Am. Polit. Sci. Assn., New Eng. Polit. Sci. Assn., Phi Beta Kappa. Democrat. Episcopalian. Home: 67 Carriage Hill Cir Southborough MA 01772 Office: Wellesley College 106 Central St Wellesley MA 02481 Office Phone: 781-283-2198. E-mail: estettner@wellesley.edu.

STETTNER, JERALD W. retail drugs stores executive; b. Miami, Fla., Mar. 31, 1952; s. Richard A. and LeJean D. (Haberman) S.; m. Linda G. Day, Dec. 22, 1978; children: Kelly R., Jarrod M., Zachary A. BS in Behavioral Mgmt., Ga. Inst. Tech., 1974. Various mgmt. positions Eckerd Drug Co., Clearwater, Fla., 1974-87; regional v.p. Eckerd Corp., Clearwater, Fla., 1987-98, sr. v.p., 1998—. Mem. Ga. Tech. Alumni Assn., Phi Delta Theta. Avocations: tennis, golf, skiing. Office Phone: 727-395-7115. Personal E-mail: JWStettner@aol.com.

STEUBEN, NORTON LESLIE, lawyer, educator; b. Milw., Feb. 14, 1936; s. Benjamin and Ria (Beerman) S.; m. Judith Ann Dickens, June 21, 1958; children: Sara Ann, Marc Nelson. AB, U. Mich., 1958, JD with distinction, 1961. Bar: N.Y. 1962, Colo. 1975. Assoc., then ptnr. Hodgson, Russ, Andrews, Woods & Goodyear, Buffalo, 1961-68; mem. faculty U. Colo. Law Sch., Boulder, 1968—2002, prof. law, 1974—2002, Nicholas Rosenbaum prof., 1997—2002, Nicholas Rosenbaum prof. emeritus, 2002—; of counsel Ireland, Stapleton, Pryor & Pascoe, Denver, 1980-97, 1999—. Lectr. Law Sch., SUNY, Buffalo, 1961-68; officer Buffalo-Niagara Indsl. Devel. Corp., 1963-68, Buffalo Opportunities Devel. Corp., 1966-68; vis prof. law U. Puget Sound. Sch. Law, 1992-93; resident tax policy advisor to the govt. of Ukraine, Treas. Dept., 1997-99. Author: Cases and Materials on Real Estate Planning, 1974, 3d edit., 1989; co-author: Problems in the Fundamentals of Federal Income Taxation, 1985, 3d edit. 1994, Problems in the Federal Income Taxation of Business Enterprises, 1985, 3d edit., 1996; co-editor: Bittker, Fundamentals of Federal Income Taxation, 1983; editor Jour. Affordable Housing & Cmty. Devel. Law, 1994-97; contbr. articles to profl. jours. Mem. Boulder Human Rights Commn., 1969-72, chmn., 1972-74; mem. Boulder Landlord-Tenant Com., 1973-74; trustee Boulder Open Space Bd., 1976-81, vice chmn., 1978-79, chmn., 1979-81; trustee Congregation Har Ha Shem, Boulder, 1978-79, v.p., 1979-81, pres., 1982-84; mem. Boulder Housing Authority, 1982-89, vice chmn., 1984-85, chmn., 1985-88; mem. legal and advocacy com. Am. Tinnitus Assn., 2002—. Recipient S.I. Goldberg award Alpha Epsilon Pi, 1957, Disting. Svc. to Community award Buffalo Area C. of C., 1966, John W. Reed award U. Colo. Law Sch., 1970; Teaching Recognition award U. Colo.-Boulder, 1972, Teaching Excellence award, 1982; Commendation for Exceptional Assistance to Govt. of Ukraine, 1999; Presdl. Teaching scholar, U. Colo., 1989, Fulbright Scholar, 2003-04. Mem. ABA, N.Y. State Bar Assn., Colo. Bar Assn., Boulder County Bar Assn., Am. Law Inst., AAUP, Scribes (officer, editor Scrivener 1975-76, dir. 1979-82), Barristers Soc., Order of Coif, Tau Epsilon Rho. Democrat. Home: 845 8th St Boulder CO 80302-7408 Office: U Colo 418 Fleming Law Bldg Boulder CO 80309-0001 Office Phone: 303-492-7963.

STEUER, GARY PAUL, art association administrator; b. Newport, R.I., Nov. 28, 1955; s. Irwin And Wilma S.; m. Renee Perez, Dec. 30, 1983; children: Rachel, Emma. BA, NYU, 1977, M in Arts Adminstrn., 1981. Aide Congressman Ted Weiss, N.Y.C., 1976-79; dir. programs Alliance Resident Theatres, N.Y.C., 1981-84; mng. dir. Vineyard Theatre, N.Y.C., 1984-88; mgr. Capital Funding Initiative N.Y. State Coun. on Arts, N.Y.C., 1988-91; exec. dir. Nat. Actors Theater, N.Y.C., 1991-92; pres., CEO Arts & Bus. Coun., Inc., N.Y.C., 1993—. Bd. dirs. Early Stages, Inc., N.Y.C., Alliance for Nonprofit Mgmt., Washington; mem. steering com. N.Y.C. Arts Coalition, Arts Action for NY State, 1999—. Contbr. articles to profl. jours.; spkr. in field. Office: Arts & Bus Coun Inc Ste 319 520 Eighth Ave New York NY 10018 E-mail: gsteuer@artsandbusiness.org.

STEUER, RICHARD MARC, lawyer; b. Bklyn., June 19, 1948; s. Harold and Gertrude (Vengar) S.; m. Audrey P. Forchheimer, Sept. 9, 1973; children: Hilary, Jeremy. BA, Hofstra U., 1970; JD, Columbia U., 1973. Bar: N.Y. 1974, U.S. Dist. Ct. (ea. and so. dists.) N.Y. 1974, U.S. Ct. Appeals (2d cir.) 1974, U.S. Supreme Ct. 1979, U.S. Dist. Ct. (no. dist.) N.Y. 1984, U.S. Dist. Ct. (we. dist.) N.Y. 1997, U.S. Ct. Appeals (3d cir.) 1987, U.S. Ct. Appeals (5th cir.) 1995. Ptnr. Kaye Scholer LLP, N.Y.C., 1973—2002, chair antitrust practice group, 1996—2002; ptnr. Mayer, Brown, Rowe and Maw LLP, N.Y.C., 2002—. Adj. assoc. prof. law NYU, 1985; adj. prof. law St. John's U., 2003; lectr. in field; neutral evaluator U.S. Dist. Ct. Ea. Dist. N.Y, 1994-96. Author: A Guide to Marketing Law: Law and Business Inc., 1986; contbr. articles to profl. jours. Fellow: Am. Bar Found. (others); mem.: ABA (lectr. 1969, 1978, chmn. monograph com. refusals to deal and exclusive distributorships 1983, editl. bd. antitrust devel. vol. 1984—86, lectr. 1985, vice-chmn. program com. 1988—91, lectr. 1989, chmn. spring meeting program com. 1991—92, Sherman Act sect. 1 com. 1991—93, coun. sect. antitrust law 1993—96, chmn. publs. com. 1996—98, lectr. 1997, 1998, editl. chmn. Antitrust mag. 1998—2001, lectr. 1999, 2000, coun. sect. antitrust law 2001—, lectr. 2002, 2003), Assn. Bar City N.Y. (chmn. antitrust and trade regulation 1995—98, antitrust and trade regulation, internat. trade, lectures and CLE coms). Office: Mayer Brown Rowe and Maw LLP 1675 Broadway New York NY 10019-5820 E-mail: rsteuer@mayerbrownrowe.com.

STEVANOVIC, MILAN V. surgeon; Resident, sports medicine U. Belgrade, resident, orthopedic surgery, resident, orthopedic surgery I; resident, hand surgery U. So. Calif. Med. Ctr.; resident, hand and microvascular surgery Duke U. Med. Ctr.; surgeon, dept. orthopedics Children's Hosp., L.A. Office: 1510 San Pablo St #322 Los Angeles CA 90033*

STEVENS, ALICE MARIE, educational consultant; b. Colorado Springs, Colo., Jan. 18, 1954; d. Charles C. and Gladys Marie (Craft) S. BS, S.W. Bapt. U., 1976; MEd, U. Mo., 1983; PhD, Purdue U., 2001. Cert. tchr. reading, learning disabilities, Mo. Sci. tchr. Lincoln County R-IV Schs., Winfield, Mo., 1976-78; sci. instr. Ricks Inst., Monrovia, Liberia, West Africa, 1978-79; learning specialist Total Learning Clinic, Columbia, Mo., 1982-89; homebound instr. Rusk Rehab. Ctr., Columbia, Mo., 1988-91; instr. Columbia Coll., Columbia, Mo., 1989, 91; learning disabilities specialist Columbia (Mo.) Pub. Schs., 1989-91; tchr., rsch. asst. Purdue U., West Lafayette, Ind., 1991-98; ednl. cons. West Lafayette, Ind., 1991-97; asst. dir. Cerebral Palsy Assn. Greater Lafayette, 1993-94; instr. Frostburg (Md.) State U., 1998-2000; dir. prevention programs Brain Injury Assn., Alexandria, Va., 2000—. Asst. dir. Cerebral Palsy Assn. Greater Lafayette, 1993-94. Mem. ASCD, AAE, Nat. Sci. Tchrs. Assn. (conf. presenter 1993), Coun. for Exceptional Children (conf. presenter), Soc. for Prevention Rsch., Kappa Delta Pi, Phi Delta Kappa. Office: Brain Injury Assn 105 N Alfred Alexandria VA 22314 Home: 1200 First St Apt 1520 Alexandria VA 22314-1688 E-mail: amstevens@biausa.org.

STEVENS, ART, public relations executive; b. N.Y.C., July 17, 1935; m. Eva Sandberg, Mar. 19, 1972. BA, CCNY, 1957. Pub. relations dir. Prentice Hall, Inc., Englewood Cliffs, N.J.; account exec. William L. Safire Public Relations Inc., N.Y.C., 1966-69, v.p., 1967-68, pres., 1968-69, Lobsenz-Stevens Inc., N.Y.C., 1970—99; instr. Fairleigh Dickinson U.; chmn. & CEO Publicis Dialog, N.Y.C., 1999—2002; cons., 2003—; mng. ptnr. Stevens Gould Ptnrs., LLC, 2003—. Weekly humor commentator WINK-TV, Ft. Myers, Fla. Author: The Persuasion Explosion, 1985, Sanibel Shell Shocked, 1992; weekly columnist Sanibel-Captiva (Fla.) Islander; contbr. articles to profl. jours. Bd. dirs. United Way of Putnam County, N.Y.; trustee Gotthelf Lupus Rsch. Inst. Inducted City Coll. N.Y. Comms. Alumni Hall Fame, 2001. Mem.: Public Relations Soc. Am. (nat. bd., pub. rels. com., chair-elect tri-state dist., exec. com., chmn. eligibility com., counselors acad. sect., sec. 2003), Publicity Club N.Y. (Disting. Svc. award 1969), Gipsy Trail (pres., chmn. Carmel, N.Y.). Home: 201 E 21st St New York NY 10010-6401 E-mail: artstevens@att.net. *Life is not an accident. The events in one's life are not accidents either. When I look back at what I have done and the lives that have been interwined with mine, it's as though it's all been scripted by a higher power.*

STEVENS, BERTON LOUIS, JR., data processing manager; b. Chgo., Apr. 4, 1951; s. Berton Louis Sr. and Mary Cover (Kochavaris) S.; m. Janet Alene Madenberg, May 20, 1990. Student, Ill. Inst. Tech., Chgo., 1969-73. Systems and applications programmer Judge & Dolph, Ltd., Elk Grove Village, Ill., 1978-91, mgr. data processing, 1991-99; bus. sys. coord. Meml. Med. Ctr., Inc., 2000-2001, lead sys. analyst, 2001—02; svc. ctr. mgr. Siemens Health Sys., 2002—. Instr. Adler Planetarium and Astron. Mus., Chgo., 1980-86; dir. Desert Moon Observatory #448. Editor and author newsletter Bert's Bull., 1987-90; editor newsletter No. Lights, 1990-98. Recipient Regional award North Ctrl. Region Astron. League, 1989. Mem. Nat. Assn. Sys. Programmers, Internat. Occulation Timing Assn. (sec. 1975-78), Chgo. Computer Soc., Chgo. Astron. Soc. (pres. 1977, 80, 84), Racine Astron. Soc. (pres. 1979), Astron. League (exec. sec. 1993-95, webmaster 1995-02), Desert Moon Observatory (dir.), Astron. Soc. Las Cruces (pres, 2001). Personal E-mail: bstevens@zianet.com. Business E-Mail: Berton.Stevens@siemens.com.

STEVENS, CLARK VALENTINE, lawyer; b. Detroit, Nov. 28, 1933; s. Valentine W. and Florence Mary (Potrykus) S.; m. Kathleen Rose Tobosky, Sept. 1, 1956; children: Mark, Glenn. B.S. in Acctg., U. Detroit, 1958; J.D., Wayne State U., 1967. C.P.A., Mich.; bar: Mich. 1967. Auditor, City of Detroit, 1958-60, IRS, 1960-65; tax mgr. Ernst & Ernst, 1965-69; mem. firm Regan & Stevens, 1969—; sec., dir. Mich. Rivet Corp., Warren, 1974—; bd. dirs. Tuff Machine Co., Warren, Mich. Mem. Mich. Bar Assn., Mich. Assn. C.P.A.s. Republican. Roman Catholic. Club: Grosse Pointe Yacht. Office: CV Stevens Prof Corp 23409 Jefferson Ave Ste 104 Saint Clair Shores MI 48080-3449

STEVENS, CONNIE, actress, singer; b. Bklyn., Aug. 8, 1938; d. Peter and Eleanore (McGinley) Ingolia; m. Maurice Elias; m. Edwin Jack Fisher (div.); children: Joely, Tricia Leigh. Pres. Forever Spring Cosmetics; founder Windfeather Foundation. Show bus. debut as vocalist with, The Three Debs, Hollywood, at age 16; appeared in: Finians Rainbow for Hollywood Repertory Co.; numerous motion pictures, including Way, Way Out, Scorchy, Eighteen and Animals, Young and Dangerous, Drag Strip Riot, Rock-a-bye Baby, Parish, Susan Slade, Palm Springs Weekend, The Grissom Gang, Never Too Late, Grease II, 1983, Back to the Beach, 1987, Bring Me the Head of Dobie Gillis, 1988, Love Is All There Is, 1996; starred in TV series Wendy and Me and TV series Hawaiian Eye, 1959-62, Head Over Heals, 1997, Titus, 2000-02, TV films for ABC-TV Movie-of-the-Week; Call Her Mom, 1972, Playmates, Mister Jericho, Cole Porter in Paris, The Sex Symbol, 1974, Starting From Scratch, 1988, James Dean: Live Fast, Die Young, 1997; guest star on TV with, Bob Hope, Red Skelton, Englebert Humperdinck, Tom Jones, Perry Como and Laugh-In; TV appearance comedy spl. Harry's Battles; headliner at Flamingo Hotel, Las Vegas, also, Hilton Internat., Sands Hotel, Desert Inn, Aladdin, MGM, Sahara, 1969-76; stage appearances include The Wizard of Oz at Carousel Theatre in So. Calif., Any Wednesday at Melodyland, Anaheim, Calif.; made Broadway debut in Star Spangled Girl, 1967; accompanied Bob Hope around world on his Christmas tour, 1969, Persian Gulf Christmas tour, 1987; dir., prodr., writer, editor, cinematographer: A Healing, 1997 (Santa Clarita Internat. Film Festival Award, 1998); created line of cosmetics called Forever Spring and opened the Garden Sanctuary day spa in Los Angeles Bd. dirs. Ctr. for Plastic and Reconstructive Surgery, South Vietnam. Recipient Lady of Humanities Award, Shriners Hospital, 1991, Humanitarian of the Year, Sons of Italy, 2001, Distinguished Civilian Service Medal, 2002.

STEVENS, CURTIS, consumer products company executive; BA in Econs., MBA, U. Calif., LA, Calif. Sr. fin. exec. Planar Sys., Inc., 1984—97; v.p., treas. CFO La.-Pacific Corp., Portland, Oreg., 1997—2002, exec. v.p. adminstrn., 2002—, CFO, 2002—. Office: Louisiana Pacific Corp 805 SW Broadway Ste 1200 Portland OR 97205-3303*

STEVENS, DAVID ALEC, medical educator; b. N.Y.C., June 3, 1940; m. Julie Anne Teece, Aug. 15, 1964; children: Joseph John, Emily Beth Stevens Marsh. BA, Cornell U., 1960; MD, U. Rochester, 1965. Diplomate Nat. Bd. Med. Examiners, Am. Bd. Internal Medicine; med. lic. Wis., Calif. Intern, asst. resident dept. medicine U. Wis. Hosps., Madison, 1965 67; rsch. assoc. Nat. Cancer Inst., Bethesda, Md., 1967-69; resident dept. medicine UCLA Med Ctr., 1969-70; fellow divsn. infectious diseases, dept. medicine Stanford (Calif.) U., 1970-72, asst. prof. divsn. infectious diseases dept. medicine, 1972-78; chief divsn. infectious diseases Santa Clara County-Valley Med. Ctr., San Jose, Calif., 1972—, assoc. chief dept. medicine, 1972—, epidemiologist, 1972—; assoc. prof. divsn. infectious diseases, dept. medicine Stanford U., 1978-85, assoc. prof. divsn. geographic medicine, dept. medicine, 1984-85, prof., 1985—. Co-dir. microbiology lab. Santa Clara Valley Med. Ctr., 1972—; prin. investigator Infectious Diseases Rsch. Lab., Calif. Inst. Med. Rsch., San Jose, 1973—, bd. regents, 1978-90, 92—, sec.-treas., 1979-81, sci. dir. coun., 1986-88, pres., 1992—; mycology ref. lab. Pub. Health Lab. Svcs. Dept. Microbiology, U. London, 1979; dir. clin. labs. Calif. Inst. Med. Rsch., 1980—; co-dir. AIDS program Santa Clara Valley Med. Ctr., 1986-88, assoc. dir., 1988-98; lectr. fourth ann. O.J. Farness lecture, U. Ariz., Tucson, 1999. Author: (with others) Coccidioidomycosis, 1980; Contbr. articles to profl. jours; patentee in field. With USPHS, 1967-69. Rhoda Benham Medal, Med. Mycology Soc. Ams., 1999; Ian Murray Meml. lectr. British Soc. Mycopathology, Canterbury, Eng., 1985. Fellow ACP, Am. Soc. Microbiology (chair mycology 1992-93), Infectious Diseases Soc. Am., Am. Acad. Microbiology; mem. AMA, AAUP, AAAS, Am. Fedn. Clin. Rsch., Am. Soc. Clin. Investigation, Fedn. Am. Scientists, Med. Mycology Soc. Ams., Calif. Med. Assn., Western Assn. Physicians, Calif. Collaborative Treatment Group, Santa Clara County Med. Soc., Internat. Soc. Human and Animal Mycology (clin. mycology com. 1985-91). Avocations: jazz, running, stamps. Home: 19070 Portos Dr Saratoga CA 95070-5169 Office: Santa Clara Valley Med Ctr 751 S Bascom Ave San Jose CA 95128-2699

STEVENS, DAVID BOYETTE, law educator; b. Augusta, Ga., Jan. 31, 1923; s. Henry Boyette and Floreid Elizabeth (Miller) S.; m. Willa King Horner, July 18, 1942; children: David Boyette, Caroline Elizabeth, Paul King. BS in Bus., U. N.C., 1949, JD, 1951; LLM, Duke U., 1956. Bar: N.C. 1951, U.S. Ct. Mil. Appeals 1965, U.S. Supreme Ct. 1967. Commd. 2d lt. U.S. Army Air Force, 1944; advanced through grades to col. USAF, 1968; asst. prof. internat. law U.S. Air Force Acad., Colorado Springs, Colo., 1959-63; judge adv., acting dir. U.S. Air Force Judiciary, Washington, 1963-70; ret., 1970; asst. prof. bus. East Carolina U., Greenville, N.C., 1970-74, prof., 1984—, dir. EEO Office, 1974-81, univ. atty., 1970—. Divsn. chmn. United Fund Svc., East Carolina U., 1972; mem. Greenville Bd. Adjustments, 1983—. Recipient Meritorious Achievement award USAF, 1970, Outstanding Svc. award East Carolina U. Law Soc., 1978. Mem. Fed. Bar Assn., N.C. Bar Assn., Pitt County Bar Assn., Nat. Assn. Coll. and Univ. Attys., Kiwanis (pres. Greenville 1976-77, lt. gov. 1979-80, Disting. Lit. Gov. ward 1981), Delta Theta Phi. Democrat. Baptist. Home: 304 Francis Asbury Ln Greenville NC 27858

STEVENS, DENNIS MAX, audit director; b. Jersey City, Sept. 3, 1944; m. Susan Gail Brown, Mar. 15, 1969; children: Julie Ayn, Daniel Ross. BBA, Rutgers U., 1966; MA in Acctg., U. Mo., 1968. CPA, Mo. Staff Peat, Marwick, Mitchell and Co., St. Louis, 1968-80, ptnr., 1980-84; sr. v.p. and internal auditor Southwestern States Bankcard Assn., Dallas, 1985-86, sr. v.p. and chief fin. officer, 1986-89; corp. planner NCH Corp., Irving, Tex., 1989-95, dir. corp. audit, 1995—2002; auditor Alamo Group, Seguin, Tex., 2002—. Contr. articles to profl. jours. 1st lt. U.S. Army, 1969-70. Mem. AICPA (mem. electronic data processing auditing stds. com. 1979-84), Inst. Internal Auditors, Beta Gamma Sigma, Beta Alpha Psi. Home: 23711 Legend Gln San Antonio TX 78258-4316 E-mail: den.stevens@attglobal.net.

STEVENS, DIANA LYNN, elementary school educator; b. Waterloo, Iowa, Dec. 12, 1950; d. Marcus Henry and Clarissa Ann (Funk) Carr; m. Paul John Stevens; 1 child, Drew Spencer. BS, Mid Am. Nazarene Coll., 1973; M in Liberal Arts, Baker U., 1989. Elem. tchr. Olathe (Kans.) Sch. Dist. #233, 1975—. Artwork appeared in traveling exhibit ARC/Nat. Art Edn. Assn., 1968, Delta Kappa Gamma Bull., 2001. Pres. Artists' League, Olathe, 1990—. Olathe Sch. Dist. Action grantee, 1996-97. Mem. NEA, Kans. Edn. Assn., Olathe Edn. Assn. (social com.), Nat. Art Edn. Assn., Delta Kappa Gamma (profl. affairs com. mem.), Coll. Ch. of the Nazarene. Avocations: portrait art, reading biographies, power walking, exhibiting artwork. Home: 217 S Montclaire Dr Olathe KS 66061-3828

STEVENS, DONALD KING, retired aeronautical engineer, consultant; b. Danville, Ill., Oct. 27, 1920; s. Douglas Franklin and Ida Harriet (King) S.; m. Adele Carman de Werff, July 11, 1942; children: Charles August, Anne Louise, Alice Jeanne Stevens Kay. BS with high honors in Ceramic Engring., U. Ill., 1942; MS in Aeros. and Guided Missiles, U. So. Calif., 1949; grad., U.S. Army Command and Staff Coll., 1957, U.S. Army War Coll., 1962. Staff mem. Ill. State Geol. Survey, 1938—40; commd. 2d lt. U.S. Army, 1942, advanced through grades to col., 1963, air def. officer in Eng., North Africa, Italy, 1942—44, regimental staff officer 473d Inf. Rgt., 1944—45; ceramic engr. Harbison-Walker Refractories Co., Pitts., 1945—46; with Ft. Bliss Arty. Sch. U.S. Army, Tex., 1949—52, supr. unit tng. and Nike missile firings, 1953—56; mem. weapons sys. evaluation group Office Sec. Def., Washington, 1957—61; chief Plans Br, J2 UN Command/US Forces U.S. Army, Korea, 1962—63; comdr. Niagara-Buffalo Def. 31st Arty. Brigade, Lockport, NY, 1963—65; dir. USA ballistics Missile def. studies Sec. Def., Washington, 1965—66; chief Air Def. and Nuc. War Plans divsn. ODCSOPS, Washington, 1965—67; chief strategic forces divsn. Office Dep. Chief of Staff Mil. Ops. U.S. Army, Washington, 1967—69, chief spl. weapons plans, J5, U.S. European Command, 1969-72, ret., 1972. Guest lectr. U.S. Mil. Acad., 1958-59; cons. U.S. Army Concepts Analysis Agy., Bethesda, Md., 1973-95; cons. on strategy Lulejian & Assocs., Inc., 1974-75; cons. nuc. policy and plans to Office Asst. Sec. of Def., 1975-80, 84-93; cons. Sci. Applications, Inc., 1976-78. Contbr. articles to profl. jours. Asst. camp dir. Piankeshaw Area coun. Boy Scouts Am., 1937; mem. chancel choir, elder First Christian Ch., Falls Church, Va., 1957-61, 65-69, 72-2002; elder, trustee Presbyn. Ch., Niagara Falls, N.Y., 1963-65. Decorated D.S.M., Legion of Merit, Bronze Star. Mem. Am. Ceramic Soc., Assn. U.S. Army, U. Ill. Alumni Assn., U. So. Calif. Alumni Assn., Rotary, Keramos, Niagara Falls Country Club, Ill. Club (Washington), Terrapin Club, Sigma Xi, Sigma Tau, Tau Beta Pi, Phi Kappa Phi, Alpha Phi Omega. Achievements include pioneer in tactics and deployment plans for Army surface-to-air missiles. Address: 5916 5th St N Arlington VA 22203-1010 Personal E-mail: dkstevens@starpower.net.

STEVENS, ELISABETH GOSS (MRS. ROBERT SCHLEUSSNER JR.), writer, journalist, graphic artist; b. Rome, N.Y., Aug. 11, 1929; d. George May and Elisabeth (Stryker) Stevens; m. Robert Schleussner, Jr., Mar. 12, 1966 (dec. 1977); 1 child, Laura Stevens BA, Wellesley Coll., 1951; MA with high honors, Columbia U., 1956. Editl. assoc. Art News Mag., 1964-65; art critic and reporter Washington Post, Washington, 1965-66; freelance art critic and reporter Balt., 1966—; contbg. art critic Wall Street Jour., N.Y.C., 1969-72; art critic Trenton (NJ) Times, 1974-77; art and architecture critic The Balt. Sun, 1978-86; critic-at-large Madyradio.com, 2004—. Author: Elisabeth Stevens' Guide to Baltimore's Inner Harbor, 1981, Fire and Water: Six Short Stories, 1982, Children of Dust: Portraits and Preludes, 1985, Horse and Cart: Stories from the Country, 1990, The Night Lover: Art & Poetry, 1995, In Foreign Parts, 1997, Household Words, 1999, 2000, Eranos, 2000, Cherry Pie & Other Stories, 2001; one-woman shows include Coll. Notre Dame of Md., 1997, Galerie Francoise, Lutherville, Md., 2000, exhibited in group shows at The Corcoran Gallery of Art, Washington, Towson State U., Balt., Atelier A/E, N.Y.C., Stephen Gang Gallery, Govt. Ho., Annapolis, U. Minn., Morris, Cooperstown (N.Y.) Art Assn., Armory Art Ctr., West Palm Beach, Fla., Venice (Fla.) Art Ctr., Ft. Meyers (Fla.) Alliance for the Art, Katharine Butler Gallery, Sarasota, Fla., 2004; contbr. articles, poetry and short stories to jours., nat. newspapers and popular mags. Recipient A.D. Emmart award for journalism, 1980, Critical Writing citation Balt.-Washington Newspaper Guild, 1980, fiction awards Md. Poetry Rev., 1992, 93, 94, 2d prize Lite Circle, 1994, 1st prize in fiction Lite Circle, 1995, 96, Balt. Writers Alliance Play Writing Contest award, 1994; art critics' fellow NEA, 1973-74, fellow MacDowell Colony, 1981, Va. Ctr. for Creative Arts, 1982-85, 88-90, 92, 93, 95, 97, 2000, Ragdale Found., 1984, 89, Yaddo, 1991, Villa Montalvo, 1995; Work in-Progress grantee for poetry Md. Art Coun., 1986, Creative Devel. grantee for short fiction collection Balt. Mayor's Com. on Art and Culture, 1986. Mem. Coll. Art Assn., Authors Guild, Fla. Printmakers Assn., Poetry Soc. Am., Am. Soc. Graphic Artists, Nat. Book Critics Circle, Women Contemporary Artists Sarasota. Home: Bards Castle 5353 Creekside Trail Sarasota FL 34243

STEVENS, ELLIOTT WALKER, JR., allergist, cardiologist, pulmonologist; b. Wilmington, N.C., Sept. 11, 1940; s. E. Walker Sr. and Margaret Ardelle (Hester) S.; m. Blanche Bonner, July 10, 1965; children: Elliott W. III, Margaret Baker. AB in French, U. N.C., 1962, MD, 1966. Diplomate Am. Bd. Internal Medicine, Am. Bd. Allergy and Immunology, Am. Bd. Pulmonery Diseases. Intern U. N.C. Hosp., Chapel Hill, N.C., 1966-67; resident Duke U., Durham, N.C., 1969-70, fellow Allergy and pulmonary diseases, 1970-72; allergist and pulmonologist Greensboro Chest Disease and Allergy Associates, Greensboro, N.C., 1972—. Capt. USAF, 1967-69. Fellow Am. Coll. Allergy and Immunology, Am. Coll. Chest Physicians. Republican. Episcopalian. Avocations: skiing, sailing. Home: 4 Round Hill Ct Greensboro NC 27408-3709 Office: Greensboro Chest Diseases and Allergy Assocs and Allergy Assocs 1018 N Elm St Greensboro NC 27401-1488 E-mail: wstev7970@aol.com.

STEVENS, GARY, retired jockey; Jockey, 1991. Named winner, Breeder's Cup Turf Race, 1990, Breeder's Cup Juvenile, 1993, Breeder's Cup Distaff, 1994. Achievements include Top money winner, 1991. Office: Jockey's Guild Inc PO Box 150 Monrovia CA 91017-0150

STEVENS, GARY LEE, state senator; b. McMinnville, Oreg., Aug. 21, 1941; m. Rita Stevens; children: Anna, Matthew, Natalie. BA, Linfield Coll., 1963; MFA, U. Oreg., 1965, PhD, 1984. Dir. Kodiak Oral History Project; gen. mgr. No. Processors Inc., 1970—75; mayor Kodiak, Kodiak Island Borough; mem. Alaska Ho. of Reps., 2000—02, Alaska Senate, 2003—04. Prof. U. Alaska, Kodiak, Alaska, 1975—2000. Pres. Kodiak Sch. Bd.; presiding officer Borough Assembly; bd. dirs. Alaska Humanities Forum, Alaska Mcpl. League, Alaska Conf. Mayors. 1st lt. U.S. Army, 1966—69. Decorated Army Commendation medal, Nat. Def. medal. Mem.: Nat. Assn. Counties (edn. steering com.), Alaska Hist. Soc. (pres.), Rotary (gov.). Republican. Office: Rm 417 State Capitol Juneau AK 99801-1182 E-mail: senator_gary_stevens@legis.state.ak.us.

STEVENS, GEORGE ALEXANDER, real estate broker; b. Loma, Mont., Nov. 10, 1923; s. Otto Oliver and Josephine (Dale) S.; m. Martha Evie Fultz, Sept. 16, 1944 (div. 1978); children: Gary, Kathleen, Arlene, Tina; m. Arleen Dorothea Largent, Nov. 14, 1978. A in Bus Admisntrn., SUNY, 1992. Prin. George Stevens Farm, Loma, Mont., 1946-93, George Stevens, Real Estate Broker, Loma, Mont., 1957-93; pres. George A. Stevens Corp., Loma, 1976-93, Gold and Silver Realty, Inc., Great Falls, Mont., 1993—, Cowboys n Plowboys, Inc., Great Falls, 2000—. Trustee Sch. Dist. # 32, Loma, 1947-50; election judge Precinct # 7, Loma, 1953-88. With USN, 1944-46, PTO. Mem.: VFW (life), Eagles Lodge (life), Elks (life), Am. Legion (life). Democrat. Lutheran. Home: 810 8th Ave N Great Falls MT 59401-1036

STEVENS, GEORGE RICHARD, business consultant, public policy commentator; b. Chgo., Sept. 6, 1932; s. George and Irene (Kaczmarek) S.; m. Jeanne E. Sowden, Aug. 2, 1957; children: Stacey, Samantha, Pamela. BS with honors, Northwestern U., 1954. CPA, Ill. With Arthur Andersen & Co., 1954-78, mng. ptnr. Brussels, 1957—71, ptnr. Chgo., 1971-78; pres. Daubert Industries, Oak Brook, Ill., 1978-80, G.R. Stevens Group, 1981—; founder, pres. Stevens Ctr. for Pub. Policy Studies, 1981—. Commr. Ill. Ednl. Facilities Authority, 1989-04. Commr. Ill. State Scholarship Commn., 1981-87; vice chmn. Ill. Ind. Higher Edn. Loan Authority, 1982-88. Home and Office: 22615 N Las Lomas Ln Sun City West AZ 85375-2022

STEVENS, GLADSTONE TAYLOR, JR., industrial engineer; b. Brockton, Mass., Dec. 16, 1930; s. Gladstone Taylor and Blanche Ruth S.; m. Jane A. Crouch, July 20, 1953; children— Robert, Bartlett. BSM.E., U. Okla., 1956; MSM.E., Case Inst. Tech., 1962; PhD in Indsl. Engring, Okla. State U., 1966. Registered profl. engr., Tex., Okla. Project engr. E.I. duPont, Orange, Tex., 1956-59; research engr. Thompson-Ramo-Wooldridge, Cleve., 1960-62; asst. prof. mech. and indsl. engring. Lamar U., Beaumont, Tex., 1962-64; asst. prof. to assoc. prof. indsl. engring. Okla. State U., Stillwater, 1966-75; prof., chmn. dept. indsl. engring. U. Tex., Arlington, 1975-98. Author: (with J.E. Shamblin) Operations Research: A Fundamental Approach, 1974, Economic and Financial Analysis of Capital Investments, 1993; Engineering Economy, 1983. Served with AUS, 1948-52. Recipient E.L. Grant award, 1974, AMOCO Teaching award, 1979, Wellington award, 1992. Fellow Am. Inst. Indsl. Engrs.; mem. Sigma Xi, Alpha Pi Mu (nat. pres.), Tau Beta Pi, Sigma Tau, Omicron Delta Kappa. Home: 2501 Spanish Trl Apt 212 Arlington TX 76016-1410 Office: U Tex Indsl Engring Arlington TX 76019-0001 Office Phone: 817-272-3092.

STEVENS, HELEN JEAN, music educator; b. Nevada, Iowa, July 11, 1934; d. Paul Ellison and Helen Margaret (Ives) Stevens. MusB, U. So. Calif., 1956. Cert. secondary music tchr. Calif. Tchr. San Francisco Sch. Dist., 1956-58; prin. oboist Marin Symphony Orch., San Rafael, Calif., 1956-94, Santa Rosa (Calif.) Symphony, 1956-86; tchr. Santa Venetia Mid. Sch., San Rafael, 1958-83; asst. prof. music Sonoma State Coll., Rohnert Park, Calif., 1963-76; tchr. Davidson Mid. Sch., San Rafael, 1984-89; pvt. tchr. oboe. Oboist Eveings on the Roof Series, L.A., 1953—56, Debut TV Show, L.A., 1954—56, Carmel (Calif.) Bach Festival, 1954—82; prin. oboist Light Opera Curren Theatre, San Francisco, 1966—67, Marin Opera Co., San Rafael, 1980—84. Leader Sonoma County 4-H Guide Dog Project Guide Dogs for Blind, Inc., 1974—87; organist, choir dir. Korean Meth. Ch., L.A., 1953—56, United Meth. Ch., St. James, Mo., 2002—. Named Outstanding Tchr., Marin Edn. Found., 1986; recipient Svc. award, PTA, 1974, Golden Bell award, Marin County Office Edn., 1984, Continuing Svc. award, Calif. Congress Parents, Tchrs. and Students, Inc., 1989. Mem.: German Shepherd Dog Club Am. Avocations: computers, animals. Home: 14713 State Rt BB Saint James MO 65559 E-mail: stevfam@fidnet.com.

STEVENS, HERBERT FRANCIS, lawyer, law educator; b. Phila., Nov. 19, 1948; s. Herbert F. and Lois Marie (Kenna) S.; m. Jane Pickard, 1994; children: Sarah, Ben. SB, MIT, 1970; JD, Catholic U. Am., 1974; ML in Tax, Georgetown U, 1983. Bar: D.C., 1975; U.S. Supreme Ct., 1980. Law clk Md. Ct. of Spl. Appeals, 1974-75; with Morgan, Lewis & Bockius, Washington, 1975-78, Lane & Edson, P.C., Washington, 1979-89, Kelley Drye & Warren, Washington, 1989-93, Nixon Peabody LLP, Washington, 1993—; adj. prof. Georgetown U. Law Ctr., 1983-98. Spkr. in field. Editor: Real Estate Aspects of the 1984 Tax Law, 1984; author: Real Estate Taxation: A Practitioner's Guide, 1986, Developer's Guide to Low Income Housing Tax Credit, 4th edit., 2000. Bd. dirs. Ctr. for Mental Health, Inc., 1987—, exec. com.; bd. dirs. Nat. Fund for U.S. Botanic Garden, 1992—, exec. com. Mem. ABA, D.C. Bar Assn. Democrat. Presbyterian. Home: 8301 Hackamore Dr Potomac MD 20854-3877 Office: Nixon Peabody LLP 401 9th St NW Washington DC 20004-2128 Office Phone: 202-585-8811. E-mail: hstevens@nixonpeabody.com.

STEVENS, JAMES HERVEY, JR., retired financial advisor; b. Balt., June 22, 1944; s. James H. and Hilda (Pearce) S.; m. Patricia Carol Donohue, Aug. 27, 1967 (div. Mar. 1983); children: James III, Carol; m. Lisa Gay Landrum, Apr. 29, 1984. BA, Duke U., 1966; MS in Fin. Scis., Am. Coll., Bryn Mawr, Pa., 1981. CLU; ChFC; CFP; registered health underwriter. Supr. New Eng. Life, Overland Park, Kans., 1969-75, agt., 1969—; v.p., treas. Creative Planning, Inc., Overland Park, 1980-95; pres. Hokanson, Lehman & Stevens, Inc., Overland Park, 1982-95; founder, chmn. Wings Over Mid-Am., Inc., 1995-97, chmn. emeritus, 1997—; chmn. Air Care Alliance, 1997—; chmn. emeritus Wings Over Mid-Am., Inc., 1997—; founder, chmn. Angel Flight Ctrl., Inc., Kansas City, Mo. Contbg. editor monthly tax topics Kansas City Bus. Jour.; contbg. editor Pvt. Pilot Mag.; contbr. articles to profl. jours. Bd. dirs. Mo. divsn. Am. Cancer Soc., Kans. and Mo., 1982-84, Ctrl. United Meth. Ch., Kansas City, Mo., 1990-92, North Cross United Meth., 1991—; bd. dirs. Apple Valley Homes Assn., Overland Park, 1990—, pres. 1992; co-founder Kansas City Friends of Gilda's. Recipient Outstanding Young Man award, 1977; named one of Top 200 Fin. Advisors, Money Mag., 1987, Boss of Yr., Kansas City LICOMA, 1983. Mem. Kansas City Life Underwriters (pres. 1980-82, Herbert A. Hedges award 1987), Kansas City CLU & ChFC Soc. (pres. 1981-83), Mo. Life Underwriters (pres. 1984-86), Am. Soc. CLU & ChFC (vice chmn., bd. dirs.). Republican. Avocations: model railroading, collecting post-war "lionel", airline transport pilot, instrument flight instr. Home: 5200 W 98th Ter Shawnee Mission KS 66207-3221 Office: Angel Fly Ctrl Inc 10 Richards Rd Kansas City MO 64113 E-mail: wuffer2@cs.com.

STEVENS, JANE, advertising executive; Exec. v.p., exec. media dir. Bernstein-Rein Advertising Inc, Kansas City, Mo., 1990—. Office: Bernstein-Rein Advertising Inc 4600 Madison Ave Ste 1500 Kansas City MO 64112-3016

STEVENS, JEROME HEBERT, entrepreneur; b. Paris, Apr. 24, 1959; came to U.S., 1991; s. Francois Hébert-Stevens and Claude Arthaud; m. Valerie Travert, Dec. 28, 1996; children: Arthur, Leopold, Aurelieu. MD, U. Paris VII, 1987; diploma in health economics, U. Paris V, 1989; MBA, U. Pa., 1994. Attending physician Hosp. de Paris, 1987-90; med. dir. Lyonnaise Santé, Paris, 1989-92; cons. CSC Healthcare, N.Y.C., 1994-99; founder Direct Medica, Paris, 2000—. Co-author: Reengineering the Operating Room, 1996; participant med. TV series Entretiens de Bichat, 1990. Bd. dirs. GERO 92 Geriat. Assn., Paris, 1989-92. With French Army, 1985-86. Mem. Am. Coll. Physician Execs. Avocations: sailing, golf, modern art. Home: 666 5th Ave No 239 New York NY 10103-0001 E-mail: jstevens@directmedica.com.

STEVENS, JILL WINIFRED, project expediter; d. William Horace Routledge and Winifred Mabel (Richards) S. Governess pvt. home, Hillsboro, Calif., 1965; adminstrv. asst. Cambridge U., England, 1966—78; expediter, buyer, technician Bechtel Petroleum Inc., San Francisco, 1979—83, control sys. technologist Houston, 1983—84; technologist, sub-group lead Bechtel Power, Limerick Nuclear Generating Sta., Sanatoga, Pa., 1988—96; material planner/elec. and control sys. Union Carbide/Bechtel Corp., Houston; control sys. expediter multi-project acquisition group Bechtel Corp., Houston, 1997—99; project expediter Bechtel Nat., Inc., Houston, 1999-2000; field project expeditor mustard gas destruction project Aberdeen Proving Ground, Md., 2000—04; buyer/expediter Pueblo Chemical Depot, Colo., 2004—. Recipient awards in English lang. and English lit. with honors, Royal Soc. Arts and Scis., City of London Day Coll. Mem. Instrument Soc. Am., Soc. Women Engrs. (assoc.). Home: 1823 Mohawk Rd Pueblo CO 81001 Office: Pueblo Chemical Agent Destruction Pilot Plant Project Pueblo Chemical Depot PSB 45825 Hwy 96 E Pueblo CO 81006 Office Phone: 719-549-4931. E-mail: jwsteven@bechtel.com., Jill4465@webtv.net.

STEVENS, JOANN A. textile, political leader, author, minister; b. Snow Hill, N.C., May 15, 1957; d. Moses Lee and Annie Iola Artis; m. Willard Ray Stevens, Apr. 3, 1993; children: Thyais Artis, Jorel, Shakira. Student, Wayne C.C., Goldsboro, N.C., 1983; student in criminal justice, Lenoir C.C., Kinston, N.C., 1984. Ordained elder Bapt. Ch., 1983; cert. substance abuse counselor N.C., 1986, Min. Inst. Shaw Divinity Sch., 1987, protective intervention Caswell Ctr., Dept. Human Resource, 1988, Safety E.I. Dupont, 1989. Founder, owner JoAnn's Christian Supply, Bibile and Bookstore, Snow Hill, NC, 1989—93; incorporator Spectrum for Living, Snow Hill, NC, 1990—93; founder, counselor Spectrum's Substance Abuse, N/A, A/A Group, Snow Hill, NC, 1991—94. Founder Rosenwald Ctr. Cultural Enrichment, 2001—; co-founder Power of Prayer Bible Inst. and Sem., 2002—. Author: The Holy Spirit, Is He a Stranger in Your House?, 1997 (1999), Could it Be I'm Chosen? (Fear, Peer Pressure, Rejection), 1999; host (TV Show) Appearances on various morning TV shows., 2002—03; singer: You Can Love Again, 1985; author: Fear, Peer Pressure Rejection- Could it be I'm Chosen. Policy coun. chair person Greene Lamp Headstart Inc., Kinston, NC; v.p. Greene County Interfaith Vols., Snow Hill, NC, 1999—2001; press sec. Com. To Elect Don Davis for Mayor, Snow Hill, NC, 2002; sec. Snow Hill Dem. Party, Snow Hill, NC; asst. regional chmn. Dem. Get Out to Vote Campaign, 2002; coord. ticket sales Mal Williams Gospel World Tour, Germany, 1996; bd. dirs. Legal Aide, NC, 2002—. Recipient Cert. of Achievement, Goshen Rubber Co., 1984, Cert. of Award, Snow Hill Primary Sch., 1985, Cert. of Appreciation, State of NC, Dept. of Correction & Human Resources, 1985 -1986, Award of Merit, East Carolina U. Sch. of Medicine / Project Concern Internat., 1988 - 1990, Cert. of Recognition, Self Image Bldg. Program, 1989, Letter of Appreciation, First Lady Hillary Rodham Clinton, 1998, Letter of Recognition, N.C. Gen. Assembly - Marian McLawhorn 9th Dist., 1999 -2001, Friends of Project Head Start award, 1999, cert. of Excellence, N.C. Hist. Preservation Office, 2003. Mem.: N.C. Ctr. for Non Profit Gifts In Kind Internat., Nat. Trust. for Hist. Preservation, Greene County Arts & Hist. Soc. (bd. dirs. 2001—03, neighborhood affairs com., vice chmn. hist. commn. 2002—03). Achievements include initiated process of Nat. Register Nomination for Snow Hill Colored, Greene Co. Sch. Avocations: travel, reading, counseling, research, history. Home: PO Box 343 Snow Hill NC 28580 Office Phone: 252-560-6221. Personal E-mail: Outreachjs@aol.com. E-mail: sajoann@earthlink.net.

STEVENS, JOHN PAUL, judge; b. Chgo., Apr. 20, 1920; s. Ernest James and Elizabeth (Street) Stevens; m. Elizabeth Jane Sheeren, June 7, 1942; children: John Joseph, Kathryn Stevens Jedlicka, Elizabeth Jane Stevens Sesemann, Susan Roberta Stevens Mullen; m. Maryan Mulholland, Dec. 1979. AB, U. Chgo., 1941; JD magna cum laude, Northwestern U., 1947. Bar: Ill. 1949. Practiced in, Chgo.; law clk. to Hon. Wiley Rutledge U.S. Supreme Ct., 1947—48; assoc. Poppenhusen, Johnston, Thompson & Raymond, 1949—52; assoc. counsel sub-com. on study monopoly power, com. on judiciary U.S. Ho. of Reps., 1951; ptnr. Rothschild, Stevens, Barry & Myers, 1952—70; judge U.S. Cir. Ct., 1970—75; assoc. justice U.S. Supreme Ct., 1975—. Lectr. anti-trust law Northwestern U. Sch. Law, 1952—54, U. Chgo. Law Sch., 1955—58; mem. Atty. Gen.'s Nat. Com. to Study Anti-Trust Laws, 1953—55. With USNR, 1942—45. Decorated Bronze Star. Mem.: Am. Law Inst., Fed. Bar Assn., Ill. Bar Assn., Am. Bar Assn., Chgo. Bar Assn. (2d v.p. 1970), Order of Coif, Phi Delta Phi, Psi Upsilon, Phi Beta Kappa. Office: US Supreme Ct Supreme Court Bldg 1 First St NE Washington DC 20543

STEVENS, JOSEPH CHARLES, psychology educator; b. Grand Rapids, Mich., Feb. 28, 1929; s. Joseph, Jr. and Anne Katheryn Stevens. AB, Calvin Coll., Grand Rapids, 1950; MA, Mich. State U., 1953; PhD, Harvard U., 1957. Instr., asst. prof. psychology Harvard U., 1957-66; fellow emeritus John B. Pierce Found. Lab., sr. rsch. scientist Yale U., 1966—. Cons. in field. Author: Laboratory Experiments in Psychology, 1965; co-editor: Sensation and Measurement, 1974; mem. editl. bds. profl. jours.; contbr. numerous articles to profl. jours. Grantee NSF; Grantee NIH, Air Force Office Sci. Rsch. Fellow AAAS, Am. Psychol. Soc., NY Acad. Scis.; mem. Acoustical Soc. Am., Optical Soc. Am., Soc. Neuroscience, Ea. Psychol. Assn., Gerontol. Soc. Am. Office: 290 Congress Ave New Haven CT 06519-1403 Business E-Mail: jstevens@jbpierce.org.

STEVENS, JOYCE ANN, author, publisher, writer, speaker; d. Peter Joseph and Vera Ester Stevens. Degree in Bus. Adminstrn., Springfield Tech. C.C., 1978. Cert. nurse asst., Mass., Conn., Med. coding and billing specialist. Propr., sales and mktg. for Divine Power Pub., Springfield, 2000—. Author: FROM THE HEART, Conversations, Visions and Answers from God's Angels and Saints, 2000, revised edit., 2003. Mem.: Am. Health Info. Mgmt. Assn. Office: Divine Power Pub 126 Columbia St Chicopee MA 01020 Business E-Mail: joyceannstevens@aol.com.

STEVENS, JOYCE WEST, social worker, educator, researcher; b. Clayton, Mo., Mar. 15, 1936; d. John Lawrence and Gertrude M. West; children: Janet, Melinda Stevens-Ademuyiwa. BS, Loyola U., Chgo., 1960, MSW, 1964, PhD, 1993. LCSW, Acad. Cert. Social Workers. Social worker, counselor Cook County Dept. Pub. Aid, Chgo., 1960—66; project dir. YMCA Met. Chgo., 1969—71; social work counselor, cons. Lake Bluff Chgo. Homes for Children, 1972—73; counselor, psychotherapist U. Ill., Chgo., 1973—74; faculty advisor Chgo. State U., 1974—75; program coord., counselor Michael Reese Hosp. and Med. Ctr., Chgo., 1974—91; field work instr. U. Chgo. Social Svc. Adminstrn., 1979—82; clin. field work instr. DePaul U., Chgo., 1990—91; instr. Loyola U. Chgo., 1990—92; asst. prof. Boston U. Sch. Social Work, 1993—2001, assoc. prof., 2001—; pvt. clin. practice Boston, 1993—. Mem. ETA Creative Arts Found. Aux., 1976—92, Chgo. Urban League Women's Bd., 1977—94; clin. cons. St. Philip Neri Parish, Chgo., 1989—91; adj. prof. Smith Coll. Sch. Social Work, Northampton, Mass., 1991—92; mem. Beethoven Project adv. bd. Ctr. for Successful Child Devel., 1991—94; trustee Family Svc. Greater Boston, 2000—02; rsch. cons. Mass. Dept. Social Svcs. Teen Living Program Network Evaluation Study, Boston; mem. instnl. rev. bd. Family Svc. Grater Boston and Latino Health Inst. Author: Smart and Sassy: The Strengths of Inner City Black Girls, 2002 (2002 Black Adminstrs. Child Welfare Scholars award, 1997); editor, book rev. editor: Child and Adolescent Social Work Jour., 1993, 2002, editor, consulting editor: Social Work Jour., 1999, 2002, Families in Society, 1998, 2002; contbr. chapters to books, articles to profl. jours. Minority Fellow grant, Nat. Inst. Drug Abuse, 1999—, African Am. Women's Study grant, 1999—2002. Avocation: book collecting. Office: Boston Univ Sch Social Work 264 Bay State Rd Boston MA 02215

STEVENS, KENNETH ALLEN, retired defense department worker; b. Exeter, N.H., June 21, 1933; s. Albert Howard and Helen Susan (Sewall) S. BA, U. N.H., 1961. With Dept. Def., 1961-88. Bd. dirs. Columbia (Md.) Dem. Club, 1988-90; mem. Howard County (Md.) Dem. Ctrl. Com., 1990-94; vol. Office Human Rights, Howard County, 1989-2001; mem. Howard County Charter Rev. Commn., 2003-. Staff sgt. USAF, 1953-57. Mem. ACLU (coord. Howard County chpt. 1988-98). Democrat. Avocations: computer games, crossword puzzles.

STEVENS, KENNETH NOBLE, electrical engineer, educator; b. Toronto, Ont., Can., Mar. 23, 1924; arrived in U.S., 1948, naturalized, 1962; s. Cyril George and Catherine (Noble) Stevens; m. Phyllis Fletcher, Jan. 19, 1957 (div. 1979); children: Rebecca, Andrea, Michael Hugh, John Noble; m. Sharon Manuel, Jan. 14, 1994; 1 child, Kendra Wenyu Manuel. BASc., U. Toronto, 1945, MASc., 1948; Sc.D., MIT, 1952. Instr. U. Toronto, 1946—48; faculty MIT, Cambridge, 1948—, prof. elec. engring., 1963—, Clarence J. LeBel prof., 1977—. Vis. fellow Royal INst. Tech., Stockholm, 1962—63; cons. to industry, 1952—; vis. prof. phonetics U. Coll., London, 1969—70; mem. Nat. Adv. Coun. on Neurol. and Communicative Disorders and Stroke, NIH, 1982—86. Author (with A.G. Bose): Introductory Network Theory; author: Acoustic Phonetics, 1998; contbr. articles to profl. jours. Trustee Buckingham Browne and Nichols Sch., 1974—80. Recipient Quintana award, Voice Found., 1992, medal, European Speech Comm. Assn., 1995, Nat. Medal of Sci., 1999; fellow, Guggenheim, 1962. Fellow: IEEE, Am. Acad. Arts and Scis., Acoustical Soc. Am. (exec. com. 1963—66, v.p. 1971—72, pres.-elect 1975—76, pres. 1976—77, Gold medal 1995); mem.: NAE, NAS. Home: 7 Larchwood Ln Natick MA 01760 Office: MIT 77 Massachusetts Ave Cambridge MA 02139-4307

STEVENS, KENNETH T. personal care industry executive; b. 1952; At, U. Redlands; MBA, U. So. Calif. Former ptnr. McKinsey & Co.; former sr. v.p. and treas. Pepsico; exec. v.p. mktg. Taco Bell divsn. of Pepsico, 1993—94, pres. and COO, 1994—97; chmn. and CEO Bank One Retail Group, 1997—2000; pres. and COO inChord Comm., 2000—01; exec. v.p. and COO Bath & Body Works divsn. of Ltd. Brands, Inc., 2002, pres., 2003—. Bd. mem. Spartan Stores, 2002—. Mailing: Bath & Body Works Seven Ltd Pkwy Reynoldsburg OH 43068

STEVENS, LAUREN ROGERS, writer, environmentalist; b. Phila., May 3, 1938; s. Lewis Miller and Elizabeth (Morgan) Stevens; m. Beverly Decker, June 20, 1964 (div. Dec. 1987); children: Rebecca Fasciano, Jeffrey L., Jennifer B.; m. Peggy Brooks, June 26, 2004. BA, Princeton U., 1960; MA, U. Iowa, 1962. Tchr. English lang. & environ. studies Williams Coll., Williamstown, Mass., 1963-81, dean of freshmen, 1970-81; founder, pub., editor Advocate Newsweekly, Williamstown, Mass., 1981-83. Writer, freelance, Williamstown, 1983—. Author: The Double Axe, 1961, Skiing: Downhill and Cross Country, 1991; co-author (with Deborah Burns): Most Excellent Majesty, 1988; co-author: (with Richard W. Babcock) Old Barns in the New World: Reconstructing History, 1996; author: The Berkshire Book, 2003; columnist: Berkshire Eagle; author: Hikes and Walks in the Berkshire Hills, 2004; contbr. articles to mags. and newspapers. Founder Hoosic River Watershed Assn., Williamstown, 1986, co-pres., 1994—96, exec. dir., 1997—2002; leader Mahican-Mohawk Trail, N.Y., Vt., Mass., 1992—; co-founder Greylock A Better Chance, Williamstown, 1968; deacon First Congl. Ch., Williamstown, 1985—, moderator, 2000—03. Mem.: The Trustees of Reservations, Phi Beta Kappa. Democrat. Avocations: hiking, canoeing, cross country skiing. Home: 235 Lesure Rd Stamford VT 05352

STEVENS, LEONARD BERRY, educational consultant; b. Fall River, Mass., Sept. 19, 1938; s. Henry Bennett and Manetta (Berry) S.; m. Elizabeth Holihen, Aug. 17, 1963; children: Lisa M., Christopher M., Andrew B., Rosa B. A. BS, Boston U., 1960; EdD, U. Mass., 1978. Cert. supt., Mass. Edn. writer Providence Jour.-Bull., 1963—67; sr. editor Cowles Comm., Inc., N.Y.C., 1967—68; exec. editor Change in Higher Edn. Mag., N.Y.C., 1968—70; spl. asst. to Chancellor N.Y.C. Bd. Edn., 1970—73; rsch. asst. U. Mass., Amherst, 1973—76; dir. Greater Cleve. Project, 1976—78; dir. Office Sch. Monitoring and Cmty. Rels. U.S. Dist. Ct. (no. dist.) Ohio, Cleve., 1978—88; dir. Compact for Ednl. Opportunity, Milw., 1988—90; race-related sch. planning cons. Sarasota, Fla., 1990—. Cons. as racial/cultural diversity and sch. desegregation planning expert and analyst to state edn. depts., pub. sch. dists., parties in litigation; expert witness in over 25 sch. desegregation cases; lectr. in field at univs. and seminars. Co-author: Make Your Schools Work, 1975; contbr. articles to profl. jours. and mass media publs. Trustee Inst. Child Advocacy, Cleve.; bd. dirs. Com. on Cath. Cmty. Action, Cleve., 1981-88. Lt. (j.g.) USN, 1960-63. Office: PO Box 2479 Sarasota FL 34230 Office Phone: 941-355-5258.

STEVENS, LEOTA MAE, retired elementary education educator; b. Waverly, Kans., Mar. 27, 1921; d. Clinton Ralph and Velma Mae (Kukuk) Chapman; m. James Oliver Stevens, Nov. 7, 1944 (dec.); children: James Harold, Mary Ann Hooker Tibbits. BA, McPherson Coll., 1954; MS, Emporia U., 1964, postgrad., 1969-77, Wichita U., 1977. Educator Pleasant Mound Sch., Waverly, 1940-41; prin. educator Halls Summit Sch., Waverly, 1941-42; educator Waverly Grade Sch., 1942-43, Ellinwood (Kans.) Jr. H.S., 1943-45, Hutchinson (Kans.) Grade Sch., 1945-48, Lincoln Sch., Darlow, Kans., 1948-49; educator prin. Mitchell-Yaggy Consol. Sch., Hutchinson, 1949-57; educator elem. Hutchinson Sch. Dist. 308, 1957-85, ret., 1985. V.p. Reno County Tchrs. Assn. Hutchinson, 1956-57, pres. Assn. Childhood Edn. Internat., 1978-79. Author of numerous poems; compiler The Alexander-Kukuk Descendants: 1754 to 1998. Mem. Worker ARC Blood Mobile, 1986—2000, Hutchinson Cmty. Concerts, 1970—; historian Women's Civic Ctr., 1988—92, art com. chmn, 1992—96; den mother Cub Scouts, 1963—66; leader Girl Scouts Ellinwood, 1944—45; bell ringer ARC Blood Mobile, 1986—2000; ch. sch. tchr. Trinity United Meth. Ch., 1959—71, attendance chair, 1994. Mem. AAUW (news reporter 1984-87, legis. chmn. program com. 1991-94, 2d v.p., 1994-95), Ret. Nation State and Local Edn. Assn., Reno County Tchrs. Assn. (v.p. 1956-57), Assn. Childhood Edn. Internat. (pres. 1978-79), Reno County Extension Homemaker Coun. (rep. 1987—), Rainbow Extension Club (pres. 1986-92), Hutchinson Area Ret. Tchrs. Assn. (historian 1996-99), Am. Legion Aux., Friends of Preservation, Delta Kappa Gamma (sec., v.p. 1972-80, grant chmn. 1980-88, publicity com. 1990-93, legis. chmn. 1994-2000). Republican. Avocations: art, music, travel, gardening, camping, genealogy. Home: 426 S Tulip St Mcpherson KS 67460-4935

STEVENS, LINDA DOREEN, intensive care nurse; b. Reedley, Calif., May 9, 1964; d. Frank Henry and Ruth Ann (Unruh) R.; m. Patrick B. Stevens, July 15, 1995. BSN, Calif. State U., Fresno, 1987. RN, Calif.; cert. pediatric advanced life support instr. Neurology nurse Fresno Community Hosp.; orthopedics nurse Sierra Community Hosp., Fresno; surg. clin. nurse USAF, Mather AFB, Calif.; nurse neonatal ICU Keesler Med. Ctr., Keesler AFB, Miss., Valley Children's Hosp., Fresno; nurse neonatal spel. care unit Kaiser Hosp., Fresno, 1996—. Capt. USAF, 1992.

STEVENS, MARILYN RUTH, editor; b. Wooster, Ohio, May 30, 1943; d. Glenn Willard and Gretchen Elizabeth (Ihrig) Amstutz; m. Bryan J. Stevens, Oct. 11, 1969; children: Jennifer Marie, Gretchen Anna. BA, Coll. Wooster, 1965; MAT, Harvard U., 1966; JD, Suffolk U., 1975. Bar: Mass. 1975. Tchr. Lexington (Mass.) Pub. Schs., 1966-69; with Houghton Mifflin Co., Boston, 1969—, editl. dir. sch. depts., 1978-81, editl. dir. math. scies. sch. divsn., 1981-84, mng. editor sch. pub., 1984—. Mem.: Cosmopolitan Neighborhood Assn. Office: Houghton Mifflin 222 Berkeley St Fl 7 Boston MA 02116-3764

STEVENS, MARK, banker; b. Chgo., May 24, 1947; s. Joseph K. and Phoebe (Copeland) S.; m. Joyce Sue Skinner, Aug. 22, 1970; children: Mark Benjamin, Katherine Joyce. BA, W.Va. U., 1969, JD, 1972. V.p. Continental Ill. Nat. Bank & Trust Co., Chgo., 1972-79, No. Trust Co., Chgo., 1979-81; pres., CEO, No. Trust Bank Fla., Sarasota, 1981-87, chmn., pres., CEO, 1987-96; exec. v.p. No. Trust Co. & No. Trust Corp., 1996-98, pres. personal fin. svcs., 1998—. Pres. No. Trust Fla. Corp., Miami, 1987-96, chmn., 1996—. Trustee Ctr. Fine Arts, 1988-94, 1988-94, Miami Children's Hosp. Found., 1993-96, South Fla. Performing Arts Ctr. Found., 1993—, U. Miami, 1994, Beacon Coun., 1990—; mem. U. Miami Citizens Bd., 1988-89, Young Pres.'s Orgn., 1988—; bd. dirs. Miami Coalition and Task Force, 1988—, New World Symphony, 1991—; charter mem. Coun. of 100 Fla. Internat. Univ. Found., 1990—; hon. bd. dirs. Audubon House; mem. Orange Bowl Com., 1994. Mem. Young Pres. Orgn., Riviera Country Club, Miami Club. Office: The No Trust Co 50 S Lasalle St Chicago IL 60603-1006

STEVENS, MARK, publishing executive; m. Trish Stevens; children: Kyle, Kevin. BS in Commerce, U. Toronto, 1981. With Spicer MacGillivray, 1981—85; mgr. fin. reporting Nabisco Brands Ltd., 1985—88; from asst. controller to pub., CEO Toronto (Can.) Sun, 1988—2000, pub., CEO, 2000—01; v.p., CFO Houston (Tex.) Post, 1991—95; v.p. corp. comms. Sun Media, 1999—2000; group pub. Rogers Pub., Toronto, 2001—04; pub. Press-Telegram, Long Beach, Calif., 2004—. Office: Press Telegram 6th and Pine Ave Long Beach CA 90802*

STEVENS, MARTIN BRIAN, publisher; b. N.Y.C., Dec. 29, 1957; s. David Robert and Shirley Stevens. Grad. high sch. Advt. artist Unitron Pubs., N.Y.C., 1977, Westchester Publs., Elmsford, N.Y., 1978; pub. Retailers Forum, Centerport, N.Y., 1981—, Swap Meet mag., Centerport, 1990—; founder, CEO, Forum Pub. Co., Centerport, 1981—. Pub. 8 bus. directories, rep. 6 bus. book pubs.; founder Rodeo Dr. Limousine Svc., 1990-93, Mercedes-Benz Limousine Svc., 1990-93. Named Top Mail Order Dealer, Nat. Mail Dealers Counsel, 1978. Mem. Mail Order Bus. Bd. (pres. 1978-80), Better Bus. Bur., Nat. Assn. Self-Employed, Nat. Assn. Desktop Pub., L.I. Assn., Can. Direct Mail Assn. Avocations: weight training, reading. Office: Forum Pub Co 383 E Main St Centerport NY 11721-1538

STEVENS, MARY ANN, state legislator; b. West, Miss. m. A.J. Stevesn, III; 1 child, Elizabeth Ann. Grad., West H.S. Mem. Miss. Ho. of Reps., 1981—, chmn. ins. com., mem. appropriations com., jud. com., juvenile justice com.; former banker; landowner; project dir. West Primary Health Care Clinic. Former mayor, former alderman Town of West. Mem. West Garden Club (past pres.), Miss. Women's Club. Democrat. Methodist. Office: Miss State Senate State Capitol PO Box 1018 Jackson MS 39215-1018

STEVENS, MAY, artist; b. Boston, June 9, 1924; d. Ralph Stanley and Alice Margaret (Dick) S.; m. Rudolf Baranik, June 5, 1948; 1 child, Steven. BFA, Mass. Coll. Art, 1946; postgrad., Academie Julian, Paris, 1948-49, Art Students League, 1948. Mem. faculty Sch. Visual Arts, N.Y.C., 1964-96, Skowhegan Sch. Painting and Sculpture, 1992, Vt. Studio Ctr., 1997, Santa Fe Art Inst., 2000, 2003. Lectr. Royal Coll. Art, London, 1981, U. Wis.-Racine, 1973, Coll. Art Assn., Washington, 1975; sole juror Am. Drawing Biennial, Coll. William and Mary, Williamsburg, Va., 2000; lectr. Coll. Santa Fe, 1998, Santa Fe Art Inst., 2003. One-woman shows: Terry Dintenfass Gallery, N.Y.C., 1971, Cornell U., 1973, Douglass Coll., Rutgers U., 1974, Lerner-Heller Gallery, N.Y.C., 1975, 76, 78, 81, Clark U., 1982, Boston U. Art Gallery, 1984, Frederick S. Wight Gallery, UCLA, 1985, U. Md., College Park, 1985, Real Art Ways, Hartford, Conn., 1988, New Mus. Contemporary Art, 1988, Orchard Gallery, Derry, No. Ireland, 1988, Kenyon Coll., Gambier, Ohio, 1988, Greenville County (S.C.) Art Mus., 1991, Herter Gallery, U. Mass., Amherst, 1991, U. Colo., Boulder, 1993, U. N.Mex., Albuquerque, 1996, Mary Ryan Gallery, N.Y.C., 1996, 97, 99, 2001, 03, Mus. Fine Arts, Boston, 1999, Lew Allen Contemporary, Santa Fe, 1998; exhibited in numerous group shows including most recently: Santa Fe Art Inst., 2002, Mus. Fine Art, Sante Fe, 2002, Guild Hall, East Hampton, N.Y., 2002, Hobart & William Smith Colls., 2002, We. Wash. U. Bellingham, 2002, UBS Paine Webber Art Gallery,

N.Y.C., 2002, Deutsche Bank, N.Y.C., 2002, Bass Mus. Art, Miami Beach, Fla., 2002, Bklyn. Mus., 2003, Nat. Mus. Women in the Arts, Washington, 2003, Danese Gallery, N.Y.C., 2003, Tamarind Inst., Albuquerque, N.Mex., 2004, Harwood Mus., Taos, N.Mex., 2004, Ctr. Contemporary Arts Warehouse, Santa Fe, N.Mex., 2004, Nat. Acad. Design, N.Y.C., 2004; represented in permanent collections: Met. Mus. Art, N.Y.C., Mus. Modern Art, N.Y.C., Moca, L.A., San Francisco Mus. Art, New Mus. Contemporary Art, Whitney Mus., Bklyn. Mus., Herbert F. Johnson Mus., Cornell U., Mus. Fine Arts Boston, De Cordova Mus., Lincoln, Mass., Harwood Mus., Taos, N.Mex., Joslyn Art Mus., Omaha; contbr. articles to various mags. Recipient Childe Hassam Purchase awards Nat. Inst. Arts and Letters, 1968, 69, 75, N.Y. State Coun. on Arts award, 1974, Disting. Alumna award Mass. Coll. Art, 1997, Disting. Artist award Coll. Art Assn., 2001, Edsin Palmer Meml. prize NAD, 2004; Andy Warhol Found. grantee for project space Headlands Ctr. for Arts, Sausalito, Calif., 2001; MacDowell Colony fellow, 1971, 72, 74, 75, 81, 82, 84, Bunting Inst. fellow Radcliffe Coll., 1988-89; Line Assn. grantee for artists books, 1978; grantee NEA, 1983, Guggenheim, 1986; honoree Women's Caucus for Art, 1990. Mem. NAT, Coll. Art Assn.

STEVENS, PAUL, newspaper editor; Bur. chief AP, Kansas City, Mo., 1980—. Office: 215 W Pershing Rd Kansas City MO 64108-4317

STEVENS, PAUL G., JR., brokerage house executive; b. 1944; With Saul Lerner Co., N.Y.C., 1968-71, Lombard Street Inc., N.Y.C., 1971-72, Ragner Option Corp., N.Y.C., 1975-89, Am. Stock Exch., N.Y.C., 1989—, pres., COO, treas.; pres. Options Clearing Corp., Chgo., 1989—. Office: Options Clearing Corp 440 S La Salle St Ste 2400 Chicago IL 60605-1028

STEVENS, PAUL IRVING, manufacturing executive; b. Lawrence, Kans., Mar. 22, 1915; s. Ira F. and Ida M. S.; m. Artie Faye Womack, Nov. 10, 1935; children: Richard Irving, Constance Irene. Student bus. adminstrn., Pasadena (Calif.) Coll., 1933-35. Indsl. engr. Consol. Aircraft Co., San Diego, 1940-49; founder, prin. stockholder, pres. United Machine Co., Ft. Worth, 1950-61; exec. v.p. Clary Corp., San Gabriel, Calif., 1962-65; pres., owner Stevens Corp., Ft. Worth, 1965-69; pres., chief exec. officer Waltham Industries, N.Y.C., 1969-71, Stevens Industries, La Jolla, Calif., 1972—, Campbell Industries, San Diego., 1976-79; chmn., pres. Stevens Air Systems, El Cajon, Calif., 1974-81; pres. Womack Motors, Inc., El Centro, Calif., 1982-90. Chmn. bd. dirs., CEO Stevens Graphics Corp., Ft. Worth, 1986-95; bd. dirs. Rancho Santa Fe Nat. Bank, Calif., 1982-85, chmn. 1985-95; chmn., CEO Stevens Internat., Inc., 1995—; bd. dirs. Rancho Santa Fe. Mem. Nat. Mgmt. Assn. (exec. com.), Presidents Assn., Civic Round Table, La Jolla Country Club, Colonial Country Club, Canyon Country Club, University Club, Ft. Worth Club, Shady Oaks Country Club. Republican. Methodist. Home: 2585 Calle Del Oro La Jolla CA 92037-2005 Office: PO Box 950 La Jolla CA 92038-0950

STEVENS, PAUL SCHOTT, lawyer; b. New Orleans, Nov. 19, 1952; s. Miles Gordon and Rosemary Louise (Schott) S.; m. Joyce Lynn Pilz, Aug. 18, 1979; Paul Schott Jr., Alexander Holmes, Andrew Colby, Carl Bernard. BA magna cum laude, Yale U., 1974; JD, U. Va., 1978. Bar: D.C. 1979, U.S. Dist. Ct. D.C. 1979, U.S. Ct. Appeals (D.C. cir.) 1979, U.S. Ct. Appeals (fed. cir.) 1983, U.S. Supreme Ct. 1982. Assoc., prin. Dickstein, Shapiro & Morin, Washington, 1978-85, ptnr., 1989-93; dep. dir., gen. counsel Pres.'s Blue Ribbon Commn. on Def. Mgmt., Washington, 1985-86; legal adviser NSC, Washington, 1987, exec. sec., 1987-89; spl. asst. to Pres. for nat. security affairs The White House, Washington, 1987-89; exec. asst. to Sec. of Defense, Washington, 1989; sr. v.p., gen. counsel Investment Co. Inst., Washington, 1993-97; sr. v.p., gen. counsel Mut. Funds and Internat. Enterprise, Charles Schwab & Co., Inc., San Francisco, 1997-99; ptnr. Dechert LLP, Washington, 1999—2004; pres. Investment Co. Inst., 2004—. Bd. dirs. ICI Mutual Ins. Co.; lectr. law Washington Coll. Law, Am. U., Washington, 1980-83; trustee M.G. Stevens Corp., New Orleans, 1978—; quality of markets com. NASDAQ Stock Market, Inc., 1997, investment cos. com. NASD Regulation, Inc., 1999; adv. bd. Ctr. Banking & Fin. Law, Boston U., 1996—. Author: U.S. Armed Forces and Homeland Defense: The Legal Framework, 2001. Chmn. bd. dirs. Student Conservation Assn., Charlestown, N.H., 1986-87, bd. dirs., 1985-91, 94-96, sec., gen. counsel, 1991-93. Recipient medal for disting. pub. svc. Dept. Def., 1989; Bates fellow Yale U., 1973, Scholar of House, 1973-74; Rotary Internat. Found. grad. fellow, 1978, U.S.-Japan Leadership fellow Japan Soc., 1989-90, assoc. fellow Saybrook Coll., Yale U., 1993—. Mem.: ABA (chmn. standing com. law and nat. security 1995—98), Coun. Fgn. Rels., Federalist Soc. (vice chmn. internat. and nat. security law practice group), Internat. Bar Assn., DC Bar Assn., Soc. of Sons of the Am. Revolution, Soc. of Mayflower Descendants, Soc. War 1812, Jamestowne Soc., Cosmos Club, Elizabethan Club, Yale Club, Met. Club. Republican. Roman Catholic. Office: Dechert 1775 Eye St NW Washington DC 20006-2402 Office Phone: 202-326-5800. E-mail: paul.stevens@dechert.com., paul.stevens@ici.org.

STEVENS, RHEA CHRISTINA, lawyer; b. Chgo., Dec. 25, 1964; d. Samuel Nowell and Rhea Mae (Lipham) S.; m. Peter Linzer, June 20, 1992; 1 child, Grayson Nowell. BS in Psychology, U. Houston, 1989; MEd, Cambridge Coll., 1987; JD, U. Houston, 1992. Bar: Tex. 1992. Instr., client liaison Hippocrates Health Inst., Boston, 1985-86; reorganization cons. Psychotechnics, Inc., Cary, Glenview, Ill., 1987-88; pvt. practice law Houston, 1992—. Founder, owner Aristic Enterprises I and II, 1995, breeder Great Danes, Anatolian Shepherds, Papillons and Dobermans for svc. orgns. and show-August Kennels, 1988—; canine behaviorist; founder DemiSance Ctr., 1999. Rep. mid-Am. chpt. ARC to Nat. Conv., 1980; bd. dirs., treas. Clark Rd. Found., Houston, 1990-92, Houston ACLU, 1990-92; counsellor Boston Area Rape Crisis Ctr., 1986-87. Recipient cert. commendation ARC, 1979-80. Mem. State Bar Tex. (disability issues com. 1996—, Pro Bono Coll. 1995—). Avocations: training and exhibiting dogs, locksmithing, computer consulting. Office: 6655 Arabia Ln Ste 100 Sealy TX 77474

STEVENS, RICHARD GORDON, political scientist, educator; b. Chgo., Dec. 29, 1925; s. Philip Jacob and Almyra (DeVillery) Solomon; m. Norma Jean Duncan, Oct. 14, 1949; children: Dennis Gordon, Laura Louise, Patricia Jean. AM in Polit. Sci., U. Chgo., 1956, PhD in Polit. Sci., 1963. Asst. prof. Coll. William and Mary, Williamsburg, Va., 1959-62; tutor honors divsn. U. Santa Clara, Calif., 1963-66; asst. prof. U. Wash., Seattle, 1966-69; assoc. prof. U. Waterloo, Ont., Can., 1969-73; prof., chmn. Rockford (Ill.) Coll., 1973-75; prof. Georgetown U., Washington, 1981-85; prof., assoc. dean Def. Intelligence Coll., Washington, 1984-92; prof. Nat. Def. U., Washington, 1992-94; lectr. Inst. World Politics, Washington, 1994-2000; adj. prof. Am. U., Washington, 1994—. Cons. Pub. Adminstrn. Svc., McLean, Va., 1975—, Office Sec. Def., Washington, 1977; Fulbright prof. law U. Hong Kong, 1986-87. Author: The American Constitution and Its Provenance, 1997, Frankfurter and Due Process, 1987, Sober as a Judge, 1999; co-author: American Political Thought, 1973, 83; contbr. articles to profl. jours. Comdr. USNR, 1943—85. Carnegie fellow in law and govt. Harvard Law Sch., Cambridge, Mass., 1962-63; Salvatori fellow Free Congress Found., Washington, 1994-95. Mem. Am. Polit. Sci. Assn., Nat. Assn. Scholars, Naval Res. Assn., Assn. Former Crewmembers USS Intrepid, Harvard Law Sch. Assn., Mil. Officer's Assn. of Am. Home: 8350 Greensboro Dr # 307 Mc Lean VA 22102 E-mail: stevensrg@aol.com.

STEVENS, RICHARD YATES, state senator; b. Raleigh, N.C., Dec. 12, 1948; s. Floyd L. and Luna (Yates) Stevens; m. Jere Ann Gilmore, Sept. 13, 1980; children: Charles Andrew, Katherine Elizabeth. BA in Polit. Sci., U. N.C., 1970, JD, 1974, MPA, 1978. Bar: N.C. 1974. Asst. dean men U. N.C., Chapel Hill, 1970-71, asst. residence dir., 1971-75, asst. Office Student Affairs, 1973-75; pvt. practice Chapel Hill, 1974-76; adminstrv. asst. City of Durham, NC, 1975-76, budget officer, 1976-78, dir. adminstrn., 1978-79, dir. fin. and program devel., 1979-80; asst. county mgr. Wake County, NC, 1980-84, county mgr., 1984-2000; mem. N.C. State Senate, 2003—. Coord. N.C. State Govt. intern program, Inst. Govt., 1971; adj. prof. polit. sci. N.C. State U., 1980, 92, 94; sr. budget advisor N.C. Gov.'s Transition Team, 2000—01. Bd. visitors U. N.C., Chapel Hill, 1991—95, trustee, 1995—2003, chmn., 1997—99; chmn. bd. dirs. U. N.C. Endowment Fund, 1997—99; chmn. U. N.C. Found., 1997—99. Mem.: ASPA (Nat. Pub. Svc. award 2000), N.C. Mus. Natural Scis. Soc. (bd. dirs. 1987—88, treas. 1988—89, pres.-elect 1989—90, pres. 1990—91), N.C. City-County Mgmt. Assn. (bd. dirs. 1991—92, 2d v.p. 1997—98, 1st v.p. 1999—99, pres. 1999—2000), N.C. Bar, Nat. Assn. County Adminstrs. (bd. dirs. 1989—92), Internat. City-County Mgmt. Assn. (life), Yates Mill Assn. (bd. dirs.), Cary Acad. (bd. dirs.), U. N.C. Gen. Alumni Assn. (dir. 1978—80, 1983—88, treas. 1988—98, chmn.-elect 1999—2000, chmn. 2000—01, Disting. Svc. medal 1994), U. N.C. Pub. Adminstrn. Alumni Assn. (pres. 1977—79, dir. 1982—84, Disting. Pub. Svc. award 1998), Carolina Club (vice chmn. 1993—94, chmn. 1994—98, 2002—). Home: 132 Lochwood Dr W Cary NC 27511-8301 Office: NC Gen Assembly Rm 515 Legislative Office Bldg Raleigh NC 27601-2808 Office Phone: 919-733-5653.

STEVENS, RISË, performing arts company administrator; b. N.Y.C. m. Walter Surovy; 1 child, Nicolas. Student, Juilliard Sch.; Hon. Degree Smith Coll., Coll. of Senecas, Russell Sage Coll., Rider Coll., U. Pa., Baylor U., Rice U., Mercy Coll., Mannes Coll Music, Hobart Coll., Cleve. Inst. Music, Va. Commonwealth U. Co-gen. mgr. Met. Opera Nat. Co., N.Y.C., 1980-88; pres. The Mannes Coll. Music, N.Y.C., 1975-78; mng. dir. Met. Opera Bd. Performer Prague Opera, Vienna State Opera, Royal Opera, NY Met. Opera, 1938 61; starred in films, concerts, TV, and radio. Mem. Nat. Endowment for Arts (co-chair music panel 1981-83), N.Y. State Coun. on Arts (chmn. music panel), Met. Opera Guild (bd. dirs.), Wagnerian Soc. Buenos Aires, Sigma Alpha Iota. Office: Met Opera Assn Lincoln Ctr New York NY 10023

STEVENS, ROBERT BOCKING, lawyer, educator; b. U.K., June 8, 1933; naturalized, 1971; s. John Skevington and Enid Dorothy (Bocking) S.; m. Katherine Booth, Dec. 23, 1985; 1 child, Robin; children by previous marriage: Carey, Richard. BA, Oxford U., 1955, BCL, 1956, MA, 1959, DCL, 1984; LLM, Yale U., 1958; LLD (hon.), N.Y. Law Sch., 1984, Villanova U., 1985, U. Pa., 1987; D.Litt. (hon.), Haverford Coll., 1991. Bencher, Gray's Inn, 1999. Barrister-at-law, London, 1956; tutor in law Keble Coll. Oxford U., 1958-59; asst. prof. law Yale U., 1959-61, assoc. prof., 1961-65, prof., 1965-76; provost, prof. law and history Tulane U., 1976-78; pres. Haverford Coll., 1978-87; chancellor, prof. history U. Calif., Santa Cruz, 1987-91; counsel Covington and Burling, Washington and London, 1991—; master Pembroke Coll., Oxford, 1993-2001; mem. Essex Court Chambers, 1966—; sr. rsch. fellow Univ. Coll., London, 2001—. Vis. prof. U. Tex., 1961, U. East Africa, 1962, London Sch. Econs., 1963, Stanford U., 1966, Brookings Instn., 1967-68, U. Coll. London, 1991-94, U. Hong Kong, 1998, Yale U., 1999, George Washington U., 2003; cons. UN, HEW, U.S. Dept. State; hon. fellow, Keble Coll., Oxford U., 1985, Pembroke Coll., 2001. Author: The Restrictive Practices Court, 1965, Lawyers and the Courts, 1967, In Search of Justice, 1968, Income Security, 1970, Welfare Medicine in America, 1974, Law and Politics, 1978, The Law School, 1983, The Independence of the Judiciary, 1993, The English Judges, 2002, From University to Uni, 2004. Chair Marshall Memorial Commn., 1994—2001; mem. Nat. Humanities Coun., 1982—86. Fellow Russell Sage Found., 1967—68, NEH, 1973—74; grantee, Rockefeller Found., 1962—64, Ford Found., 1962—64, 1973—74, NEH, 1973—74, Nuffield Found., 1975. Home: Mill Bank Northleach GL54 3HJ England Office: Covington and Burling 265 Strand London WC2R 1BH England Office Phone: 011-44-20-7067-2213. Personal E-mail: rstevens@cov.com.

STEVENS, ROBERT DAVID, librarian, educator; b. Nashua, NH, Aug. 11, 1921; s. David Philip and Ruth (Ackley) S.; m. Helen Medora Conrad, Jan. 16, 1943; children: Ruth Wilson Robertson, Hope Conrad. AB magna cum laude, Syracuse U., 1942; BS in L.S. with honors, Columbia, 1947; MA, Am. U., 1955, PhD, 1965. Employed Libr. Congress, Washington, 1947-64, coord. pub. law, 480 programs, 1962-64; dir. Libr. East West Ctr., Honolulu, 1964-65; dean Grad. Sch. Library Studies U. Hawaii, 1966-75; chief cataloging div. Copyright Office, 1975-80, coordinator copyright collections, 1980; lectr. grad. Sch. Libr. Studies, U. Hawaii, 1981-91; chief exec. officer Molesworth Inst. West, Inc., 1984-91, chmn., 1991-96. Fulbright lectr. U. Indonesia, 1971; US del. Intergovtl. Conf. Planning Nat. Libraries Infrastructures, 1974 Author: Role of the Library of Congress in International Exchange of Government Publications, 1955, Toshokan Kyoryoku, 1970, Documents of International Organizations, 1974, Japanese and US Research Libraries at the Turning Point, 1977, Short History of the School of Library and Information Studies, 1991; contbr. articles to profl. publs. Served to lt. USNR, 1943-46. Mem. Hawaii Library Assn. (pres. 1966-67), ALA (mem. council 1967-70, mem. US, Japan adv. com. 1972-79, chmn. 1974-76, Rlms policy and rsch. com. 1977-81), Assocs. U. Hawaii Library (vice chmn. 1981-84), Japan Library Assn., Hui Dui, Phi Beta Kappa, Pi Sigma Alpha. Clubs: 15 (Honolulu). Home: 3-3400 Kuhio Hwy Apt C208 Lihue HI 96766-1084

STEVENS, ROBERT EDWARD, engineering company executive; b. Kansas City, Mo., Oct. 30, 1957; s. Kenneth E. and Nina (France) S. BS in Chem. Engring., U. Mo.-Rolla, 1980, MS in Engring. Mgmt., 1985. Process design engr. The Pritchard Corp., Kansas City, Mo., 1981-83; process engr. Procter & Gamble, Cape Girardeau, Mo., 1986-87, tech. mgr., 1987-90; from project engring. mgr. to site mgr. Bechtel, 1990—99, engring. mgr. Mex., 1999-2000, project mgr., 2000-01, resident engring. mgr. Egypt, 2001, sys. engring. mgr. Hanford, 2002—. Contbr. to Properties of Gases and Liquids, 1987. Chmn. bd. dirs. Wesley Found., St. Louis, 1993-98; corp. devel. coun. U. Mo., Rolla, 1995-2003, chair benchmarking com., 1996-2000, chair distance learning com., 2001-03, mem. chem. engring. indsl. adv. bd. Acad. Chem. Engrs., 2002—. Recipient Stan Adams Reliability award P & G Paper Div., 1990, Pres.'s award for team excellence Shell Oil Co., 1994; Nat. Merit scholar, 1976. Mem. AIChE, Nat. Fire Protection Assn., Project Mgmt. Inst., Am. Soc. Engring. Mgmt., George C. Marshall Inst., Chem. Heritage Found./Robert Boyle Soc., U. Mo. Rolla-Wesley Found. Alumni Assn. (pres. 1988-97, Outstanding Contbr. 1983, 88), Order of the Golden Shillelagh, Alpha Chi Sigma (expansion com. 2002—, ednl. found. bd. dirs., Cert. Appreciation 1991), Tau Beta Pi. Methodist. Home and Office: 11220 W Florissant # 369 Florissant MO 63033-6741

STEVENS, ROBERT EDWIN, bank executive, former insurance company executive; b. Hartford, Feb. 12, 1927; s. Horace and Anna E. (Lauritzen) S.; m. Betty L. Hippler, June 30, 1951; children— Paul, Lynn, Peter. BA, Wesleyan U., 1949. Various positions bond and common stock divs. Conn. Mut. Life Ins. Co., Hartford, 1951-71, v.p., treas., 1972-74, sr. v.p., 1974-76, exec. v.p., 1976-89; pres. Conn. Mut. Investment Accounts, Inc., 1980-89; chmn. bd. dirs. Liberty Bank, Middletown, Conn., 1989-95. Bd. dirs. Freedom Fin. Svcs. Bd. dirs. Hartford Hosp.; trustee emeritus Jacob L. and Lewis Fox Scholarship Found.; trustee emeritus Wesleyan U.; corporator Middlesex Hosp.; mem. investment com. Hartford Found. Pub. Giving. With USNR, World War II. Mem. Hartford Soc. Fin. Analysts (past pres.). Home: 46 Keighley Pond Rd PO Box 361 Cobalt CT 06414-0361

STEVENS, ROBERT J. aerospace transportation executive; b. McKeesport, Pa. BS summa cum laude, Slippery Rock U., 1976; grad., Dept. Def. Sys. Mgmt. Coll.; M in Engring. and Mgmt., Polytechnic U. N.Y.; M in Bus., Columbia U. With Fairchild Republic Co.; gen. mgr. to v.p., CFO Loral Sys. Manufacturing Co. (acquired by Lockheed Martin), 1987—93; exec. v.p., sr. v.p., CFO, air traffic mgmt. Lockheed Martin, 1993—96; pres., air traffic mgmt. Lookheed Martin, 1996—98; pres., COO energy and environ. bus Lockheed Martin, 1998—99, v.p. strategic devel., 1998—99, exec. v.p., CFO, 1999—2001, pres., COO, 2000—04, pres., CEO, 2004—, also chmn. bd. dirs., 2004—. Commr. Commn. Future of US Aerospace Industry, 2001—02; chmn., bd. dirs. Sandia Corp.; presiding dir., bd. dirs. Monsanto Co., 2002—; assoc. fellow Am. Inst. Aeronautics and Astronautics; mem., internat. adv. bd British-American Business Coun. Served USMC. Recipient Disting. Alumni award, 2003, Exec. Yr., Nat. Mgmt. Assn., 2004; fellow Fairchild Fellowship. Fellow: Am. Astronautical Soc.; mem.: Aerospace Industries Assn. (mem. exec. com.).*

STEVENS, ROBERT JAY, magazine editor; b. Detroit, July 25, 1945; s. Jay Benjamin and Louise Ann (Beyreuther) S.; m. Dahlia Jean Conger, Aug. 15, 1970; children— Sandra Lee, Julie Ann. Student, Huron (S.D.) Coll., 1963-66, Wayne State U., 1968-71. Sr. staff writer Automotive News, Detroit, 1968-71; editor Excavating Contractor mag., Cummins Pub. Co., Oak Park, Mich., 1971-78, Chevrolet's Pro Jour., Sandy Corp., Southfield, Mich., 1978—79, Cars and Parts mag., Cars and Parts Corvette mag. Amos Press, Sidney, Ohio, 1979—; truck editor Automotive Design & Devel. mag., 1971-78. Lectr., speaker in field. Author articles, poems. Served with AUS, 1966-68, Vietnam. Decorated Air medal, Bronze star, Commendation medal; recipient Alphomega Publs. award, 1965—, Robert F. Boger Meml. award for outstanding constrn. journalism, 1975, U.L.C.C. nat. editl. award, Am. Pub. Works Assn., 1978, Moto award for outstanding automotive journalism, Internat. Automotive Media Conf., 1997, 1998, 1999, 2000, 2001, Internat. Automotive Media Conf., 2002, Best of Divsn. award, Internat. Automotive Media Conf., 2001, Folio mag. Editl. Excellence award, 2001. Mem. Detroit Auto Writers (past dir.), Internat. Motor Press Assn., Antique Automobile Club Am. Republican. Presbyterian. Home: 653 Ridgeway Dr Sidney OH 45365-3432 Office: PO Box 482 911 Vandemark Rd Sidney OH 45365 E-mail: bstevens@carsandparts.com.

STEVENS, ROGER TEMPLETON, writer; b. Syracuse, N.Y., Jan. 11, 1927; s. Raymond Alfred and Mabel Eunice Stevens; m. Mildred Lorraine Hasbrouck, June 12, 1948 (dec. Aug. 1978); children: Margaret Ann, David Keith; m. Barbara Ann Wilkinson, July 14, 1979. AB in English, Union Coll., Schenectady, N.Y., 1949; MA in Math., Boston U., 1959; MS in Systems Engring., Va. Inst. Tech., 1975; PhD in Elec. Engring., Calif. We. U., 1978. Tech. writer Raytheon Mfg. Co., Waltham, Mass., 1950—51; engr. Lab. for Electronics, Boston, 1951—55; sr. engr. Spencer Kennedy Labs., Boston, 1955—56, Avco Mfg. Co., Boston, 1956—57, Electronics Systems, Inc., Boston, 1957—60; supr., video and display Sanders Assocs., Nashua, NH, 1960—65, mem. tech. staff The Mitre Corp., Bedford, Mass., 1965—67; sr. rsch. engr. The Dikewood Corp., Albuquerque, 1967—70; mem. tech. staff The Mitre Corp., Bedford, Mass., 1970—74; sr. rsch. engr. The Dikewood Corp., 1974—81; sect. head EG & G Inc., Albuquerque, 1981—83; mem. tech. staff The Mitre Corp., Bedford, Mass., 1983—92. Author: Operational Test and Evaluation, 1979, Graphics Programming in C, 1988, Fractal Programming with C, 1989, Fractal Programming with Turbo Pascal, 1990, Advanced Fractal Programming in C, 1990, Fractal Programming and Ray Tracing with C++, 1991; author: (with Christopher Watkins) Advanced Graphics Programming in C and C++, 1991, Advanced Graphics Programming with Turbo Pascal, 1991; author: The C Graphics Handbook, 1992, Learning C with Fractals, 1993, Quick Reference Guide to Computer Graphics Terms, 1993, Object Oriented Graphics Programming in C++, 1994, Using PCX Graphics Files, 1995, Understanding Self-Similar Fractals, 1995, The C++ Graphics Handbook, 1996, Graphics Programming with Java, 1997, Computer Graphics Dictionary, 2002. With USN, 1945—46, Pacific. Mem.: AF and AM, Shriners. Avocations: computers, photography. Home: 17 Castle Rock Rd Rio Rancho NM 87124

STEVENS, ROSEMARY A. medicine and public health historian, artist; b. Bourne, Eng. came to U.S., 1961, naturalized, 1968; d. William Edward and Mary Agnes (Tricks) Wallace; m. Robert B. Stevens, Jan. 28, 1961 (div. 1983); children: Carey, Richard; m. Jack D. Barchas, Aug. 9, 1994 BA, Oxford (Eng.) U., 1957; Diploma in Social Adminstrn., Manchester (Eng.) U., 1959; MPH, Yale U., 1963, PhD, 1968; LHD (hon.), Hahnemann U., 1988; DSc (hon.), Northeastern Ohio U. Coll. Medicine, 1995. Various hosp. adminstrv. positions, Eng., 1959-61; rsch. assoc. Med. Sch. Yale U., 1962-68, asst. prof. Med. Sch., 1968-71, assoc. prof. Med. Sch., 1971-74, prof. pub. health Med. Sch., 1974-76; master Jonathan Edwards Coll., 1974-75; prof. dept. health systems mgmt. and polit. sci. Tulane U., New Orleans, 1976-78, chmn. dept. health systems mgmt., 1977-78; prof. history and sociology of sci. U. Pa., Phila., 1979—2002, chmn. dept., 1980-83, 86-91, UPS Found. prof., 1990-91, dean Sch. Arts and Scis., Thomas S. Gates prof., 1991-96, Stanley I. Sheerr prof., 1997—2001, prof. emeritus, 2002—. Prof. emeritus U. Pa., Phila., 2002-; vis. lectr. Johns Hopkins U., 1967-68; guest scholar Brookings Instn., Washington, 1967-68; acad. visitor London Sch. Econs., 1962-64, 1973-74. Author: Medical Practice in Modern England: The Impact of Specialization and State Medicine, 1966, new edit., 2003, American Medicine and the Public Interest, 1971, rev. edit., 1998, In Sickness and in Wealth: American Hospitals in the Twentieth Century, 1989, rev. edit., 1999, (with others) Foreign Trained Physicians and American Medicine, 1972, Welfare Medicine in America, 1974, new edit., 2003, Alien-Doctors: Foreign Medical Graduates in American Hospitals, 1978. Bd. dirs. Milbank Meml. Fund. Rockefeller Humanities fellow, 1982-83, Guggenheim fellow, 1984-85; Bellagio Study and Conf. scholar, 1984; recipient Frohlich medal Royal Soc. Medicine, London, 1986, Baxter Found. prize distinction in health svcs. rsch., 1990, James A. Hamilton Book award Am. Coll. Healthcare Execs. best book, 1990, Welch medal distinction in history of medicine Am. Assn. History Medicine, 1990, Arthur Viseltear award history pub. health Am. Pub. Health Assn., 1990, Nicholas E. Davies award Piedmont Hosp., Atlanta, 1997, Investigator award in health policy rsch. Robert Wood Johnson Found., 1998-2003, Carlson award for extraordinary contbns. to history of medicine Cornell U., Weill Med. Coll., 2000., Lifetime Achievement award Am. Assn. History Medicine, 2002. Fellow Am. Acad. Arts and Scis.; mem. AAAS (chmn. sect. history and philosophy of sci., 2002-03), Inst. Medicine of Nat. Acad. Sci., Am. Sociol. Assn., Am. Assn. for History of Medicine, Coll. Physicians of Phila.Am. Bd. Med. Specialties (pub. mem., exec. com.), Cosmopolitan Club. Home: 1900 Rittenhouse Sq # 18 A Philadelphia PA 19103-5767 Office: U Pa 303 Logan Hall 249 South 36th St Philadelphia PA 19104-6304 Office Phone: 215-898-7601. Business E-Mail: rstevens@sas.upenn.edu.

STEVENS, ROY W. sales and marketing executive; b. Ottumwa, Iowa, Oct. 28, 1924; s. Manley O. and Ruth (Worrell) S.; m. Donna R. Borman, June 7, 1952 (dec. Jan. 1973); children: Katharine Anne Stevens Dillon, Thomas W., John M.; m. Beth A. Murphy, Apr. 20, 1974; children: Carrie Theresa, Elizabeth Mary. BSC., U. Iowa, 1948. With Coca-Cola Co., 1948-54, Gen. Foods Corp., 1954-67; exec. v.p. Riviana Foods, Houston, 1967-73; v.p. mktg. Hiram Walker Inc., Detroit, 1973-75, pres., 1975-80, Maidstone Wine & Spirits Inc., L.A., 1980-91, Kahlua Group (Allied Domecq), 1987-91; exec. v.p. The Century Coun., Los Angeles, 1991-98. Bd. dirs., past chmn. Detroit Met. YMCA; bd. dirs. L.A. Met. YMCA. Lt. (j.g.) USN, 1943-46. Mem. Sigma Alpha Epsilon, Jonathan Club, Annandale Golf Club (Pasadena, Calif.). Episcopalian. Home: 1444 S Marengo Ave Pasadena CA 91106-4228

STEVENS, ROY W. microbiologist, researcher; BS, State Univ. of N.Y., Albany, 1956, MS, 1958; PhD, Albany Med. Coll., 1965. Diplomate Am. Bd. Med. Microbiology. Rsch. scientist Wadsworth Ctr., N.Y. State Dept. Health, Albany, 1967—70, assoc. rsch. scientist, 1970—73, prin. rsch. scientist, 1973—79, dir. lab. diagnostic immunology, 1979—85, dir. retrovirology and immunology lab., 1985—91; adj. prof. microbiology and immunology Albany Med. Coll., 1982—92; assoc. prof. sch. pub. health State Univ. N.Y., Albany, 1988—98; pres. Bio-med. Resource Group, Albany, 1991—. Trustee Bender Sci., Albany, 1986-98; chair Bender Sci. Ltd. Cmty. Found., Albany, 2002—; chair Univ. Libr. Devel. Com. State Univ. of N.Y., Albany, 2003. Fellow Am. Acad. Microbiology, emeritus 2002, Assn. Med. Lab. Immunologists (pres. 1989), Am. Soc. Microbiology (chmn. clin. and diagnostic immunology divsn. 1997-98). Home: 507 Acre Dr Schenectady NY 12303-5226 Office: Bio-med Resource Group PO Box 12393 Albany NY 12212-2393

STEVENS, SCOTT, professional hockey player; b. Kitchener, Ont., Canada, Apr. 1, 1964; Player Washington Capitals, 1982—90, St. Louis Blues, 1990—91; capt. NJ Devils, 1991—. Played in NHL All-Star Game, 1985, 89, 91-94, 96; mem. Stanley Cup Championship Team, 1995, 2000, 2003; named to NHL All-Rookie Team, 1982-83, Sporting News All-Star Second Team, 1987-88, NHL All-Star First Team, 1987-88, 93-94, 2004, NHL All-Star Second Team, 1991-92, Sporting News All-Star First Team, 1993-94. Office: c/o NJ Devils Continental Airlines Arena PO Box 504 East Rutherford NJ 07073-0504

STEVENS, SHANE, novelist; s. John and Caroline (Royale) S. MA, Columbia U. Mem. numerous writers confs. including Bread Loaf, Santa Barbara Writers Conf. Author: Go Down Dead, Way Uptown in Another World, Dead City, Rat Pack, By Reason of Insanity, The Anvil Chorus; (as

J.W. Rider) Jersey Tomatoes (Best Novel award), Hot Tickets; contbr. articles to pubs. including N.Y. Times, Life, Washington Post; screenwriter: By Reason of Insanity, The Me Nobody Knows. Mem. Authors Guild, Writers Guild Am.

STEVENS, SHEILA MAUREEN, retired teachers union administrator; b. Glendale, Calif., Nov. 1, 1942; d. Richard Chase and Sheila Mary (Beatty) Flynn; m. Jan Whitney Stevens, Sept. 12, 1964; children: Ian Whitney, Bevin Michelle. AA in Liberal Arts, Monterey Peninsula Coll., Calif., 1963; BA in Anthropology, Calif. State U., Long Beach, 1969; postgrad. studies in Edn., U. Guam, 1976-77. Tchr. U.S. Trust Territory of the Pacific, Koror, Palau Island, 1968-72, Kolonia, Ponape Island, 1972-76, Dept. Edn., Agana, Guam, 1976-79; newspaper editor Pacific Daily News (Gannett), Agana, 1979-83; comm. dir. Guam Fedn. of Tchrs., Agana, 1983-84, exec. dir., 1984-85, Alaska Fedn. Tchrs., Anchorage, 1985-87; labor rels. specialist N.Y. State United Tchrs., Watertown, 1987-93, regional staff dir. Potsdam, 1993—2003; ret., 2003. Mem. Gov.'s Blue Ribbon Panel on Edn., Agana, Guam, 1983-85; leadership devel. coord. Am. Fedn. Tchrs., Washington, 1983—; trainer positive negotiations program Situation Mgmt. Sys., Hanover, Mass., 1988—. Author, editor: Pacific Daily News, 1981-83 (Guam Press Club awards 1981, 82, 83); contbr. articles to mags. and jours. Mem. task force on labor policy, com. on self determination, Govt. of Guam, Agana, 1984-85, Adult Basic Edn. Planning Com., 1985; mem. labor studies adv. bd., Anchorage, Alaska, 1989, regional compact coalition N.Y. State Edn. Dept., Albany, 1994; del. NY State Labor Religion Coalition. Named Friend of Edn., Carthage (N.Y.) Tchrs. Assn., 1990. Mem. NOW, ACLU, ASCD, AAUW, Am. Fedn. Tchrs. Comm. Assn. (Best Editorial award 1984), Indsl. Rels. Rsch. Assn. Democrat. Methodist. Avocations: travel, reading, free-lance writing, cross country skiing. Personal E-mail: seawings49@hotmail.com.

STEVENS, STANLEY DAVID, historian, researcher, retired librarian, archivist; b. San Francisco, Nov. 10, 1933; s. David Franklin and Ellen Myrtle (Wixson) S.; m. Carli Ann Lewis, Sept. 3, 1960; adopted children: Alexander Lewis, Nikolas Harriman, Brooke Cayton Stevens. BA, San Jose (Calif.) State U., 1959. Conf. officer polit. and security com. 14th Gen. Assembly, UN, NYC, 1959; map libr. U. Calif., Santa Cruz, 1965-93, ret., 1993, coord. Hihn-Younger Archive, Univ. Libr., 1994—. Mem. Cartographic Users Adv. Coun., 1976-86, chmn., 1982-86; presenter in field; adj. prof. libr. sci. San Jose State U., 1989, 91. Author: Index to Guinn's Biographical Record of Santa Cruz, San Benito, Monterey and San Luis Obispo Counties, Catalog of aerial photos by Fairchild Aerial Surveys, Inc. now in the collections of the Dept. Geography, UCLA, 1982, Correspondence of Charles B. Younger Sr. and Charles B. Younger Jr., Santa Cruz, California Attorneys and Counsellors at Law, vols. 1-13, 1996—, indexed edit. Santa Cruz County, Calif., 1997; editor, Santa Cruz County History Jour., 1994-96, 98; also 10 others related to Hihn-Younger Archive; prodn. editor: Index to Boulder Creek Mountain Echo, 1896-1916, 1999; contbr. over 100 articles to profl. jours. Mem. adv. com. archaeol. program Cabrillo Coll., Aptos, Calif., 1985—; bd. dirs. Santa Cruz County Hist. Soc., 1985-94, chmn. publs. com., 1985-96, mem. programs adv. coun., 1994-95; mem. Santa Cruz Orgn. for Progress and Euthenics, 1987—; bd. dirs. Friends of U. Calif.-Santa Cruz Libr., 1994-97; founding mem. Rschr. Anonymous, Santa Cruz, 1993—; mem. U. Calif.-Santa Cruz Emeriti Group, sec.-treas. 1996—; mem. collections adv. com. Santa Cruz City Mus. Natural History, 1995—. With U.S. Army, 1954-56. Recipient honors award geography and map divsn. for outstanding achievement in map librarianship Spl. Librs. Assn., 1981, cert. of commendation Santa Cruz Hist. Soc., 1986, appreciation cert. for svcs. Assn. Info. and Image Mgmt., 1989, Proclamation of Honor, Santa Cruz County Bd. Suprs., 1998, Historian of Yr. award History Forum of Santa Cruz Mus. of Art and History, 2001; grantee Librs. Assn. U. Calif., 1981-82, rsch. grantee Office of Pres., U. Calif., 1985-86. Mem. ALA (publs. com. Map and Geography Round Table 1985-86, editl. bd. Meridian 1989-2000, honors award Map and Geography Round Table 1992), ACLU (chmn. bd. dirs. Santa Cruz County chpt. 1962-68, bd. dirs. No. Calif. br. 1973-76), Western Assn. Map Librs. (hon. life, founding pres. 1967-68, treas. 1968-89, editor Info. Bull. 1969-84, Exec. Com. award 1984, Stanley D. Stevens Hon. Map presented at 30th anniversary meeting 1997), Calif. Hist. Soc., Calif. Map Soc., Pájaro Valley Hist. Assn., Santa Cruz County Geneal. Soc., Capitola Hist. Soc., El Paso de Robles Hist. Soc. (life). Democrat. Avocations: researching local history, listening to jazz and classical music. Home: 231 13th Ave Santa Cruz CA 95062-4831 Office: U Calif Dean E McHenry Libr Santa Cruz CA 95064 E-mail: sstevens@library.ucsc.edu.

STEVENS, TERRY L. realty company executive; b. Johnstown, Pa., June 20, 1948; s. Owen G. and Marian A. S.; m. Dianna J., Aug. 22, 1970; children: Rebecca, Amy. BS, Juniata Coll., 1970; MBA, U. Pa., 1971. CPA. Ptnr. Price Waterhouse, Balt., 1983-90; audit & fin. dir. Allied-Signal, Inc., Morristown, N.J., 1990-94; chief acctg. officer, then CFO Crown Am. Realty Trust, Johnstown, 1994—. Fin. and audit com. Conemaugh Health Sys., Johnstown, 1996—. V.p. Johnstown Symphony Orch., 2000—; bd. dirs. Penns Wood Coun. BSA, Johnstown, 1998—. Office: Crown Am Realty Trust Pasquerilla Plz Johnstown PA 15901 E-mail: TStevens@crownamerican.com.*

STEVENS, THEODORE FULTON, senator; b. Indpls., Nov. 18, 1923; s. George A. and Gertrude (Chancellor) S.; m. Ann Mary Cherrington, Mar. 29, 1952 (dec. 1978); children— Susan B., Elizabeth H., Walter C., Theodore Fulton, Ben A.; m. Catherine Chandler, 1980; 1 dau.; Lily Irene. BA, U. Calif. at Los Angeles, 1947; LL.B., Harvard U., 1950. Bar: Calif., Alaska, D.C., U.S. Supreme Ct. bars. Pvt. practice, Washington, 1950-52, Fairbanks, Alaska, 1953; U.S. atty. Dist. Alaska, 1953-56; legis. counsel, asst. to sec., solicitor Dept. Interior, 1956-60; pvt. practice law Anchorage, 1961-68; mem. Alaska Ho. of Reps., 1965-68, majority leader, speaker pro tem, 1967-68; U.S. senator for Alaska, 1968—; asst. Rep. leader U.S. Senate, 1977-85; chair Senate Appropriations com., 1997—2001, 2003—; pres. pro tempore U.S. Senate, 2003—. Chmn. appropriations com. US Senate, 1997—2001, 2003—. Served as 1st lt. USAAF, World War II. Mem. ABA, Alaska Bar Assn., Calif. Bar Assn., D.C. Bar Assn., Am. Legion, VFW. Lodges: Rotary, Pioneers of Alaska, Igloo #4. Republican. Home: PO Box 100879 Anchorage AK 99510-0879 Office: US Senate 522 Hart Senate Bldg Washington DC 20510-0001

STEVENS, VAL, state legislator; m. Keith Stevens; 2 children. Mem. Wash. Senate, Dist. 39, Olympia, 1996—; mem. senate agr. and rural econ. devel. com. Wash. Legislature, Olympia, Wash. state chair Am. Legis. Exch. Coun., mem. agr. and rural econ. devel. com., mem. human svcs. and corrections com., mem. natural resources, parks and recreation com., mem. child abuse investigation work group, mem. joint selection com. on DNA, mem. family policy coun., mem. civil justice task force subcom. on Y2K, mem. Gov.'s coun. on substance abuse. Mem. Northshore Christian Ch.; bd. dirs. 1991 Concerned Women for Am.; past mem. Gov.'s Task Force for Natural Death Act; charter mem. Better Govt. Bur.; mem. ad hoc bd. dirs. Naval Aux. Air Sta. Mus. Recipient 100 Percent Voting Record award Wash. State Farm Bur., gold medal Ind. Bus. Assn., Sentinel award Wash. State Law Enforcement Assn., 1996, Outstanding Support Voc. Tech. Edn. award WAVA, 1996, Cornerstone award Assn. Wash. Bus., Outstanding Support award Wash. Retail Assn., 1996, Guardian of Small Bus. award Nat. Fedn. Ind. Bus., Pub. Safety award Snohomish County Law Enforcement, 1993. Mem. Christian Armed Svcs. Assn. Republican. Office: 105 Irving Newhouse Ofc Olympia WA 98504-0001

STEVENS, WARREN, actor; b. Clark's Summit, Pa., Nov. 2, 1919; s. Albert Clifford and Helen Dodd (Blakeslee) S.; m. Barbara Helen Fletcher, Sept. 9, 1969; children— Adam Fletcher, Matthew Dodd; 1 son by previous marriage, Laurence Blakeslee. Student, U.S. Naval Acad., 1939-40. Appeared on: New York stage in Gallileo, 1947, Sundown Beach, 1948, Smile of the World, 1949, Detective Story, 1949; appeared in numerous motion pictures, since 1950, including, Barefoot Contessa, Forbidden Planet; appeared on: numerous television shows, including Richard Boone Rep. With USN, 1937-40; with USAAF, 1942-46. Mem. Actors Studio.

STEVENS, WENDELL CLAIRE, retired anesthesiology educator; b. Mason City, Iowa, June 28, 1931; s. Lloyd Leroy and Amy Luella (Hodson) S.; m. Lola C. Claycomb, July 27, 1958; children: Amy P., Eric C., Mitchell L. AA, Mason City Jr. Coll., 1951; MD, U. Iowa, 1956. Diplomate Am. Bd. Anesthesiology. Intern City Hosp., Cleve., 1956-57; resident in gen. surgery U. Iowa Hosp., Iowa City, 1957-58, 60-61, resident in anesthesia, 1961-63; assoc. in anesthesia U. Iowa Coll. Medicine, Iowa City, 1963, asst. prof. anesthesia dept., 1963-67; asst. prof. U. Calif. Sch. Medicine, San Francisco, 1967-72, assoc. prof., 1972-77, prof., 1977; prof., chmn. anesthesia dept. U. Iowa Coll. Medicine, Iowa City, 1978-82, Oreg. Health Scis. U., Portland, 1982-92, prof., 1992-96, prof. emeritus, 1996—. Contbr. papers and book chpts. to profl. publs. Lt. USNR, 1958-60. Recipient anesthesiology rsch. grant U. Calif., San Francisco NIH, 1969-78. Mem. Oreg. Soc. Anesthesiologists, Am. Soc. Anesthesiologists, Oreg. Med. Assn., AMA, Christian Med. Soc. Republican. Baptist. Avocation: church related activities. Office: Oreg Health Scis Ctr Dept Anesthesiology 3181 SW Sam Jackson Park Rd Portland OR 97201-3011

STEVENS, WILBUR HUNT, accountant; b. Spencer, Ind., June 20, 1918; s. John Vosburgh and Isabelle Jane (Strawser) S.; m. Maxine Dodge Stevens, Sept. 28, 1941; children: Linda Maxine Piffero, Deborah Anne Augello. BS, MBA, U. Calif., Berkeley, 1949. CPA, Calif.; cert. fraud examiner, fin. svcs. auditor; diplomate Am. Bd. Forensic Acctg. Staff acct. McLaren, Goode, West & Co., San Francisco, 1949-52; mng. ptnr. Wilbur H. Stevens & Co., Salinas, Calif., 1952-70; regional ptnr. Fox & Co., CPAs, Salinas, 1970-73, nat. dir. banking practice Denver, 1973-80; pres., chmn. Wilbur H. Stevens, CPA, PC, Salinas, 1980-94; chmn. Stevens, Sloan & Shah, CPAs, 1994—. Adj. prof. acctg. U. Denver, 1975-78; faculty mem. Assemblies for Bank Dirs., So. Meth. U., Dallas, 1976-81, Nat. Banking Sch., U. Va., Charlottesville, 1979-87; chmn., dir. Valley Nat. Bank, 1963-71, Pacific Ag Credit, Inc., 1997—; dir. World Travel, Inc.; v.p., dir. Dirs. Coun. Ind. Banks, Global Uplift, Inc. Editor Issues in CPA Practice, 1975; contbr. articles to profl. jours. Capt. AUS, 1942-53. Decorated Bronze Star; Frank G. Drum fellow U. Calif., Berkeley, 1949. Mem. AICPA (v.p. 1971), Am. Acctg. Assn., Am. Assembly Collegiate Schs. Bus. (accreditation coun. 1975-78, 81-84), Nat. Assn. State Bds. Accountancy (pres. 1976-77, strategic initiatives com. 1997-99), Inst. Internal Auditors (fin. svcs. group), Am. Acad. Cert. Consultants and Experts, Calif. Soc. CPAs (pres. 1968-69, Disting. Svc. award 1988), Acctg. Rsch. Assn. (pres. 1973-75), Acad. Acctg. Historians, Assn. Cert. Fraud Examiners, Am. Coll. Forensic Examiners, Ctrl. Calif. Past Masters Assn. (pres. 1998), Burma Star Assn., CBI Vets. Assn., 14 AF Assn., Hump Pilots Assn., Salinas C. of C. (pres. 1960), Commonwealth Club Calif., Masons (master 1992, 97, Hiram award 1998, grand lodge com. taxation), Knight Templar (comdr. 2000), Royal Arch (high priest 1998, grand chpt. inspector 1999-2000), Cryptic Masons (illus. master 2000), Knight Masons Am., Royal Order Scotland, 32 degree Scottish Rite, Nat. Sojourners (pres. Monterey Bay chpt. 1996), Heroes of '76 (comdr. John C. Fremont chpt. 1996-97), Fed. for Collingwood Libr. and Mus., Red Cross of Constantine, Salinas High Twelve Club (pres. 1995), Philalethes Soc., QCCC, London, Rotary (dist. gov. 1983, chmn. internat. fellowship accounts 1994-96, Paul Harris fellow 1973), Phi Beta Kappa, Beta Gamma Sigma (v.p. 1949), Beta Alpha Psi. Republican. Methodist. Home: 38 Santa Ana Dr Salinas CA 93901-4136 Office: 975 W Alisal St Ste D Salinas CA 93901-1148

STEVENS, WILLIAM C., JR., pharmaceutical executive; b. Portsmouth, Va., June 30, 1967; s. William C. and Shelby B. Stevens; m. Bess M. Stevens. PhD, U. Va., 1996. Postdoctoral trainee Mpls. Med. Rsch. Found., 1997-99; sr. scientist ArQule-Pfizer, Medford, Mass., 1999—2002, X-ceptor Therapeutics, Inc., San Diego, 2002—. Mem. Am. Chem. Soc. Avocation: surfing. Office: X-ceptor Ste 200 4757 Nexus Ctr Dr San Diego CA 92121 Fax: 617-551-3431. E-mail: combinatorial@telocity.com.

STEVENS, WILLIAM DOLLARD, consulting mechanical engineer; b. Bayonne, N.J., Aug. 4, 1918; s. William B. and Beatrice (Dollard) S.; m. Mary E. King, Oct. 12, 1940; children: Sandra A. (Mrs. Jeffrey N. Melin), Barbara E. (Mrs. Dennis Gallagher), William K. BSME, Rensselaer Poly. Inst., 1940; postgrad., Case Inst. Tech., 1958; DSc (hon.), N.J. Inst. Tech., 1986. Various engring. and mgmt. positions Babcock & Wilcox Co., N.Y.C., 1940-62; v.p. equipment div. Foster Wheeler Corp., Livingston, N.J., 1962-73, sr. v.p., 1972-74, exec. v.p., 1974-78, chmn. bd., 1978-81, dir., 1974-86, dir. emeritus, 1986-90; bd. of dir. Am. Soc. for Macro Engring., 1992—2001. Instr. Pratt Inst., 1946-47; bd. overseers N.J. Inst. Tech., 1978-94. Contbr. articles to profl. jours.; patentee in field Chmn. fund drive ARC, Hackensack, N.J., 1956; planning commr., Hackensack, 1955-58; trustee Bergen County Mental Health Consultation Ctr., 1955-58; bd. dirs. Metals Properties Coun.; mem. coun. Rensselaer Polytech. Inst., 1983—. Lt. USNR, 1943-45. Fellow ASME; mem. Nat. Acad. Engring., Sigma Xi, Tau Beta Pi, Phi Kappa Tau, Pi Tau Sigma. Methodist. Home and Office: 4 Stonybrook Dr North Caldwell NJ 07006-4025 E-mail: wmdstevens@aol.com.

STEVENSON, A. BROCKIE, retired artist; b. Montgomery County, Pa., Sept. 24, 1919; s. Alfred Brockie and Caroline Lansdale (Sill) Stevenson; m. Jane Merriman Mackenzie, Dec. 23, 1978. Student, Pa. Acad. Fine Arts, 1940-41, 46-50, Barnes Found., 1946-48, Skowhegan Sch., Maine, 1950. Instr. Sch. Fine Arts, Washington U., St. Louis, 1960-62; head dept. painting and drawing Corcoran Sch. Art, 1965-81, from assoc. prof. to prof. design, painting, drawing & watercolor, 1965-98; ret., 1998. One-man shows include War Paintings, London and Salisbury, Eng., 1944, Instituto Cultural Peruano-Norteamericano, Lima, Peru, 1953, Art Ctr., Miraflores, Peru, 1958, 1960, Assn. Cultural Peruano-Britanica, Lima, 1959, Mickelson Gallery, Washington, 1970, Pyramid Galleries Ltd., 1973, No. Va. C.C., 1974, Fendrick Gallery, Washington, 1978, 1984, 1988, exhibited in group shows at Nat. Gallery Art, London, 1944, Pa. Acad. Fine Arts, Phila., 1948—51, Sociedad Bellas Artes del Peru, Lima, 1953—56, SUNY, Potsdam and Albany, 1971, Columbia (S.C.) Mus. Art, 1971, EXPO '74, Spokane, Wash., 1974, Corcoran Gallery, Washington, 1980, retrospective, Villanova (Pa.) U., 2002, Strathmore Hall Arts Ctr., Bethesda, Md., 2004, Represented in permanent collections Corcoaran Gallery Art, Washington, Dept. Def., Nat. Mus. Am. Art, Phillips Collection, Fed. Res. Bank, Richmond, Va., Woodward Found., Washington, Ogunquit (Maine) Mus. Art, Brown U. Libr. Milit. Coll., Providence, one-man shows include Villanova U., 2002. With U.S. Army, 1941—45, ETO. Home: 6106 Yale Ave Glen Echo MD 20812-1122

STEVENSON, ADLAI EWING, III, lawyer, former senator; b. Chgo., Oct. 10, 1930; s. Adlai Ewing and Ellen (Borden) S.; m. Nancy L. Anderson, June 25, 1955; children: Adlai Ewing IV, Lucy W., Katherine R., Warwick L. Grad., Milton Acad., 1948; AB, Harvard U., 1952, LL.B., 1957. Bar: Ill. 1957, D.C. 1977. Law clk. Ill. Supreme Ct., 1957-58; assoc. Mayer, Brown & Platt, Chgo., 1958-66, ptnr., 1966-67, 81-83, of counsel, 1983-91; treas. State of Ill., 1967-70; U.S. senator from Ill., 1970-81; chmn. SC&M Internat. Ltd., Chgo., 1991-95, pres., 1995-98, chmn. of bd., 1998—. Mem. Ill. Ho. of Reps., 1965-67; Dem. candidate for gov. of Ill., 1982, 86. Capt. USMCR, 1952-54. Office: 2117 N Fremont St Chicago IL 60614 Office Phone: 773-281-3578.

STEVENSON, ALEXANDRA, professional tennis player; b. San Diego, Calif., Dec. 15, 1980; d. Samantha. Student, U. Colo. Mem. U.S. Fed Cup Team, 2003. Winner ITF/Midland, Mich., 1998, 13 of 15 grass court matches, 1999; semifinalist Wimbledon, 1999, U.S. Open, 1999; mem. U.S. Pan Am Games Team, 1999; jr. competition winner U.S. Open Jr., 1997, USTA Nat. Girls' 18s, 1997; jr. competition singles finalist USTA Nat. Girls' 18 Clay Courts, 1996; named Roles Rookie of the Yr., Tennis Mag., 1999. Avocations: singing, ballet, swimming, dance. Office: WTA 1266 E Main St Ste 4 Stamford CT 06902-3546

STEVENSON, AMANDA (SANDY STEVENS), librettist, composer, document examiner; b. Bklyn., Oct. 24, 1943; d. Haakon and Grace Svendsen. Grad., Bay Ridge H.S., Bklyn., 1961. Cert. Nat. Bur. Document Examiners. Composer, librettist, Nellie Bly, Victorine, (screenplay) The Last Assignment Mem. Actors Equity Assn., GMI, Songwriters Guild. Democrat. Unitarian Universalist. Avocations: chess, art history, pen pals. Home and Office: 3543 84th St Apt 327 Jackson Heights NY 11372

STEVENSON, BEN, artistic director; b. Portsmouth, Eng., Apr. 4, 1936; came to U.S., 1968; s. Benjamin John and Florence May (Gundry) S.; m. Joan Toastivine, Jan. 6, 1968. Grad., Arts Ednl. Sch., London, 1955. Dir. Houston Ballet Acad. Mem. dance panel Tex. Commn. Arts, 1977; guest tchr. Am. Ballet Theatre, Joffrey Ballet, Royal Ballet, London, Beijing Dance Acad. Dancer Theatre Arts Ballet, London, 1952-54, Sadler's Wells Theatre Ballet, 1955-56, Royal Ballet, 1956-60, London Festival Ballet, 1960-62; appearances in Wedding in Paris, 1954-55, Music Man, London, 1962-63, Half a Sixpence, also, Boys in Syracuse, London, 1964; prin. dancer, ballet master, London Festival Ballet, 1964-68; artistic dir. Harkness Ballet Youth Dancers, 1968-71, Chgo. Ballet, 1974-75, Houston Ballet, 1976-2003, artistic dir. emeritus, 2003—; co-dir. Nat. Ballet, Washington, 1971-74; prin. ballets choreographed include Three Faces of Eve, 1965, Cast Out, 1966, Sleeping Beauty (full length), 1967, 71, 76, 78, Fervor, 1968, Three Preludes, 1968, Forbidden, 1969, Cinderella (full length), 1969, 71, 73, 74, 76, Bartok Concerto, 1970, Nutcracker (full length), 1972, 76, Symphonetta, 1972, Courant, 1973, Swan Lake (full length), 1977, L, 1978, Britten Pas de Deux, 1979, Four Last Songs, 1979, Space City, 1980, Peer Gynt (full length), 1981, Zheng Ban Qiao, 1982, The Prince of Pagodas, 1986 Recipient 1st prize London Choreographic competitions, 1965, 66, 67, 1st prize modern ballet choreography Internat. Ballet Competition, Varna, Bulgaria, 1972, Gold medal for choreography Internat. Ballet Competition, 1982, Dance mag. award, 2000; named Order of Brit. Empire, 1999. Asso. mem. Royal Acad. Dancing (Adeline Genee Gold medal 1955) Office: Tex Ballet Theatre 6845 Green Oaks Rd Fort Worth TX 76116

STEVENSON, BRUCE WARREN, food products executive, researcher; b. San Bernadino, Calif., Apr. 28, 1954; s. Leslie D. and Cathern N. Stevenson; m. Ronda M. Grounds, Aug. 23, 1980. BBA in Fin. & Mgmt., Mesa State Coll., Grand Junction, Colo., 1988. Intelligence analyst U.S. Govt., Seattle, 1973—83, large contract negotiator, 1989—91; pres. Seattle Coffee Co., Inc., Little Rock, 1995—2003. Bd. dirs. Seattle Coffee Co., Inc., Little Rock, 1995—2003. Author: (book series) The Dawn of Man: Revelations From God, 1999—2003. Mem.: Christian Writers Guild. Avocations: hiking, travel, writing. Home: 1517 N 25th St Colorado Springs CO 80904

STEVENSON, BRYAN ALLEN, lawyer; b. Milton, Del., Nov. 14, 1959; s. Howard Carlton and Alice Gertrude (Golden) S. BA, Eastern Coll., St. Davids, Pa., 1981; MPP, Kennedy Sch. Govt., Cambridge, Mass., 1985; JD, Harvard U., 1985. Bar: Ga. 1985, Ala. 1987. Staff atty. So. Prisoners Def. Com., Atlanta, 1985-89; exec. dir. Ala. Capital Representation Resource Ctr., Montgomery, 1989-95; dir. Equal Justice Initiative of Ala., Montgomery, 1995—. Vis. prof. law NYU Sch. Law, 1997, U. Mich. Law Sch., 1995. Contbr. articles to publs. Recipient MacArthur Found. award, Thurgood Marshall medal of justice, Nat. Human Rights award Reebol Human Rights Found., 1989, ACLU Medal of Liberty, 1991, ABA Wisdom Award for Pub. Svc., 1991; Harvard Law Sch. Pub. Interest fellow, 1985. Avocations: music, piano and keyboards. Office: Equal LJustice Initiative of Alabama 122 Commerce St Montgomery AL 36104-2538

STEVENSON, DENISE L. business executive, banking consultant, realtor; b. Washington, Sept. 18, 1946; d. Pierre and Alice (Mardrus) D'Auga; m. Walter Henry Stevenson, Oct. 17, 1970 (div. 1990). AA, Montgomery Coll., 1967; BA in Econs./Bus. Mgmt., N.C. State U., 1983; cert. legal asst., Meredith Coll., 1989; cert. in Mgmt., Fin. Women Internat., 1990. Lic. ins. agt.; ABR Nat. Assn. of Realtors, GRI, SRES, e-PRO. Savs. counselor Perpetual Bldg. Assn. (now Crestar Bank), Washington, 1968—70; regional asst. v.p. 1st Fed. Savs. (now Centura Bank, Rocky Mount), NC, 1971—83; pres., owner Diversified Learning Svcs., Raleigh, 1983—; pres., treas. Daily Life Svcs., Inc., 1994—99; realtor Prudential Carolinas Realty, 2002—. Instr. Inst. Fin. Edn., Raleigh, 1983—89, Am. Inst. Banking, 1986. Mem. Am. Bus. Women's Assn. (Woman of Yr. 1982), Fin. Women Internat. (cert. leader 1987, Mem. of Yr. award 1992, N.C. Woman of Yr. 1992), Laurel Hills Women's Club (pres. 1974-75, Raleigh), Omicron Delta Epsilon. Avocation: fishing. Office: Diversified Learning Svcs PO Box 33231 Raleigh NC 27636-3231 E-mail: divlrnserv@aol.com.

STEVENSON, EDWARD WARD, retired physician, surgeon, otolaryngologist; b. Chester, S.C., Jan. 9, 1926; s. Thomas M. and Annie Lou (Ward) S.; m. Dorothy Giles, Sept. 2, 1947; children: Sally Anne Stevenson Yeilding, Laura Stevenson Healy, Nancy Stevenson Schonbeger (dec.), Molly Stevenson Walker. B in Medicine, Duke U., 1945; MD, U. Md., Balt., 1949. Intern Bapt. Meml. Hosp., Memphis, 1949-50; resident Med. Coll. Va. Hosp., Richmond, 1953-55; fellow Ochsner Found. Hosp., New Orleans, 1955-56; staff otolaryngologist Ochsner Clinic, 1956-57; pvt. practice Birmingham, 1957-60, 65-94, 1965—94; instr., clin. asst. prof. surgery U. Ala., 1957-94; pvt. practice Decatur, 1960-65; ret., 1994. Faculty Tulane U. Sch. Medicine, 1956-57; staff Bapt. Med. Ctr.-Montclair, Birmingham. Contbr. articles to profl. jours. Bd. dirs. So. Mus. Flight, Birmingham, 1989—, Ala. Aviation Hall of Fame, chmn. pres, 2003, bd. dirs., 2003—; pres. Birmingham Aero Club, 1996. Lt. M.C. USNR, 1949—53. Mem. AMA, ACS, Am. Laryngol., Rhinol. and Otol. Soc. (sec.- treas. so. sect. 1990-93, v.p. so. sect. 1993-94), Am. Soc. Head and Neck Surgery, Am. Acad. Otolaryn., Jefferson County Med. Soc., Ala. Otolaryn. Soc. (founder, pres. 1971), Med. Assn. State Ala., Morgan County Med. Soc. (pres. 1964-65), Tri-State Otolaryn. Assembly (co-founder), Birmngham Otolaryn. Soc. (pres. 1984), Birmingham Downtown Rotary Club. Methodist. Avocations: aerobatic flying, world travel. Home: 4249 Antietam Dr Birmingham AL 35213-3221 E-mail: edstevenson@bellsouth.net.

STEVENSON, FRANCES KELLOGG, museum program director; b. Boston; d. Charles Summers and Alice deGueldry (Stevens) S.; m. James Richard Wein, 1971 (div. 1989). BA, Wells Coll., Aurora, N.Y., 1967; MA, Oxford U., 1972; MBA, U. Pa., 1992. Publs. officer Nat. Portrait Gallery Smithsonian Instn., Washington, 1974—2001, strategic planning officer, 2001—. Mem. St. John's Episcopal Ch., Lafayette Sq. James E. Webb fellow Smithsonian Instn., 1988-89. Mem. Sulgrave Club. Home: 2724 Ordway St NW Apt 4 Washington DC 20008-5047 Office: Smithsonian Instn Nat Portrait Gallery PO Box 37012 Victor Bldg MRC 973 Washington DC 20013-7012

STEVENSON, GARTH, social sciences educator; b. Montreal, Que., Can., Apr. 7, 1943; s. Andrew Archibald Stevenson and Ruth Graham (Scott) Swinton; m. Carol Barbara Krell, Aug. 10, 1968 (div. 1983); children: Colin, Fiona, Moira; m. Yvonne Brown, Aug. 5, 1983; 1 child, Jacqueline. BA, McGill U., Montreal, 1963, MA, 1965; PhD, Princeton U., 1971. Asst. prof. Carleton U., Ottawa, 1968—76, assoc. prof., 1976—78, U. Alberta, Edmonton, Canada, 1978—82, prof., 1982—87, Brock U., St. Catharines, Canada, 1987—, chmn. dept. polit. sci., 2003—. Vis. prof. Duke U., Durham, NC, 1992—93. Author: The Politics of Canada's Airlines, 1987, Ex Uno Plures, 1993, Community Besieged, 1999. Candidate in Canadian Gen. Election New Democratic Party, Edmonton North, 1984. Mem.: Internat. Polit. Sci. Assn., Midwest Polit. Sci. Assn., Canadian Polit. Sci. Assn. (bd. dirs. 1998—2000), Am. Polit. Sci. Assn. Anglican Ch. Of Canada. Home: 35 October Dr Saint Catharines ON Canada Office: Brock U 500 Glenridge Ave Saint Catharines ON Canada L2S 3A1 Address: Brock U Polit Sci Dept PO Box 1600 Lewiston NY 14092-5000 Business E-Mail: stevensn@spartan.ac.brocku.ca.

STEVENSON, HAROLD WILLIAM, psychology educator; b. Dines, Wyo., Nov. 19, 1924; s. Merlin R. and Mildred M. (Stodick) S.; m. Nancy Guy, Aug. 23, 1950; children: Peggy, Janet, Andrew, Patricia. BA, U. Colo., 1947; MA, Stanford U., 1948, PhD, 1951; DS (hon.), U. Minn., 1996. Asst. prof. psychology Pomona Coll., 1950-53; asst. to asso. prof. psychology U. Tex., Austin, 1953-59; prof. child devel. and psychology, dir. Inst. Child Devel., U. Minn., Mpls., 1959-71; prof. psychology, fellow Center for Human Growth and Devel., U. Mich., Ann Arbor, 1971—; dir. program in child devel. and social policy U. Mich., 1978-93. Adj. prof. Tohoku Fukushi Coll., Japan, 1989—, Peking U., 1990—, Inst. Psychology Chinese Acad. Scis.; mem. tng. com. Nat. Inst. Child Health and Human Devel., 1964-67; mem. personality and cognition study sect. NIMH, 1975-79; chmn. adv. com. on child devel. Nat. Acad. Scis.-NRC, 1971-73; exec. com. div. behavioral scis. NRC, 1969-72; mem. del. early childhood People's Republic of China, 1973, mem. del. psychologists, 1980; mem. vis. com. Grad. Sch. Edn., Harvard U.,

1979-86; fellow Center Advanced Studies in Behavioral Scis., 1967-68, 82-83, 89-90. Recipient J.M. Cattell Fellow award in applied psychology Am. Psychol. Soc., 1994, William James Fellow award, 1995, Quest award Am. Fedn. Tchrs., 1995. Fellow Am. Acad. Arts and Scis., Nat. Acad. Edn.; mem. APA (pres. divsn. devel. psychology 1964-65, G. Stanley Hall award 1988, Bronfenbrenner award 1997, Dist. Sci. award Applications of Psychology 1997), Soc. Rsch. Child Devel. (mem. governing coun. 1961-67, pres. 1969-71, chmn. long-range planning com. 1971-74, mem. social policy com. 1977-85, mem. internat. affairs com. 1991-94, Disting. Rsch. award 1993), Internat. Soc. Study Behavioral Devel. (mem. exec. com. 1972-77, pres. 1987-91), Phi Beta Kappa, Sigma Xi. Home: 4001 Glacier Hills Dr # 322 Ann Arbor MI 48105-2847 E-mail: hstevens@umich.edu.

STEVENSON, HOWARD HIGGINBOTHAM, business educator; b. Salt Lake City, June 27, 1941; s. Ralph Shields and Dorothy Dee (Higginbotham) S.; m. Fredericka O'Connell; children: William, Charles, Andrew. BS, Stanford U., 1963; MBA, Harvard U., 1965, DBA, 1969. From asst. prof. to prof. Harvard U., Cambridge, Mass., 1968—82, prof., 1982—, sr. assoc. dean for fin. adminstrn., 1991-94, sr. assoc. dean external rels., 2000—04, faculty chair, sr. assoc. provost resources and planning, 2004. Owner, pres., mgr. Program in Exec. Edn., 1998—2000; chmn. publs. rev. bd. Harvard Bus. Sch. Press, 1999—2000; faculty chmn. Latin. Am. Adv. Bd., 1999—2001; v.p. Simmons Assocs., Boston, 1970—72; v.p. fin. adminstrn. Preco Corp., West Springfield, Mass., 1978—81; bd. dirs. Landmark Comms., Norfolk, Va., Camp Dresser and McKee Inc., Cambridge, The Baupost Group, Inc., Boston, Commonwealth Capital Ptnrs., Boston. Co-author: Policy Formation and Administration, 1984, New Business Ventures and the Entrepreneur, 1985, 89, 94, 5th edit., 1999, Entrepreneurial Ventures, 1992, 2d edit., 1999, Do Lunch or Be Lunch: The Power of Predictability in Creating Your Future, 1997, (with David Amis) Winning Angels: The Seven Fundamentals of Early Stage Investing, 2001, (with David Amis) Winning Angels: Mentors in a Network of Success, 2003, (with Laura Nash) Just Enough: Tools for Creating Success in Your Work and Life, 2004. Trustee Rural Land Found., Lincoln, Mass., 1973-78, Boston Ballet, Suffield Land Conservancy, Conn., 1978-82; dir. Sudbury Valley Trustees, 1991—, pres. bd. trustees, 96-2000; trustee Nat. Pub. Radio Found., 1998-2003, Mass. Chpt. Nature Conservancy; bd. dirs. Nat. Pub. Radio, 2004. IBM Nat. Merit scholar, 1959; Ford Found. fellow, 1965. Mem. Fin. Execs. Inst., Acad. Mgmt., Harvard Club (N.Y.C.). Office: Harvard Bus Sch Rock Ctr 314 Boston MA 02163

STEVENSON, IAN, psychiatrist, educator; b. Montreal, Que., Can., Oct. 31, 1918; s. John Alexander and Ruth Cecilia (Preston); m. Octavia Reynolds, Sept. 13, 1947 (dec. Nov. 1983); m. 2d, Margaret H. Pertzoff, Nov. 29, 1985. Student, U. St. Andrews, Scotland; BS, McGill U., 1942, MD, CM, 1943. Cert. Am. Bd. Psychiatry, 1952. Asst. prof. psychiatry La. State U., New Orleans, 1949-52, assoc. prof. psychiatry, 1953-57; prof. psychiatry, chmn. U. Va. Sch. Medicine, Charlottesville, 1957-67, Carlson prof. psychiatry, head divsn. of personality studies, 1967—2002, rsch. prof. psychiatry, 2001—; assoc. mem. Darwin Coll., U. Cambridge, 1981-96. Author: The Diagnostic Interview, 1960, Twenty Cases Suggestive of Reincarnation, 1966, Reincarnation and Biology, 1997, 10 other books; contbr. 250 articles to profl. jours. Fellow: Am. Psychiat. Assn. (life disting. fellow); mem.: Soc. for Sci. Exploration (founding com.), Am. Soc. for Psychical Rsch., Soc. for Psychical Rsch. London (coun. and pres. 1988—89), Oxford and Cambridge Club, Colonnade Club. Office: U of Va Health Sys PO Box 800152 Charlottesville VA 22908-0152 Business E-Mail: ips6r@virginia.edu.

STEVENSON, JAMES D(ONALD), JR., psychologist, counselor; b. Ft. Wayne, Ind., July 6, 1943; s. James Donald Sr. and Charlotte Eileen (Starnes) S.; m. Sharon Sue Kearns, Nov. 26, 1965 (div. 1978); 1 child, E. Willow; m. Diane Kulesza, Apr. 13, 1980 (div. 1987); 1 child, James Wesley; m. Christine Berthold, Aug. 8, 1992. BA, Whittier (Calif.) Coll., 1965; MA, Calif. State U., Northridge, 1974; PhD, Calif. Coast U., 1986. Lic. counselor, Calif. Auditor State Compensation Ins. Fund, Arcadia, Calif., 1965-66, supervising auditor, 1969-74; dir. social svcs. Buena Vista Acad., Ventura, Calif., 1974-76, benefits counselor, 1976-77; counselor Calif. Dept. of Rehab., Thousand Oaks, 1977-82, vocat. psychologist Mt. Diablo, 1982—2003. Prin. James Stevenson Pub., 1994—, Career Interest Testing Svc., Ventura and Contra Costa Counties, 1980-83; instr. Ventura Coll., 1975; cons. Ctr. for Career Evaluation, Oakland, Calif., 1986-87, St. Vincent DePaul Soc., Pittsburg, Calif., 1986-97, Allied Fellowship Svcs., Oakland, 1990. Contbr. articles to profl. jours. Bd. dirs. Solano County (Calif.) Hist. Records Commn., pres., 1997-99, v.p., 1999-2001, pres., 2001-03. With U.S. Army, 1965-67, ETO. Mem. AACD, Nat. Rehab. Assn. (exec. bd. San Francisco chpt. 1986-93, pres. San Francisco East Bay divsn. 1991-92), Ventura County Mental Health Assn. (bd. dirs. 1978-81), Los Padres Rehab. Assn. (pres. Ventura chpt. 1978-79), Sons Am. Revolution, Napa County Hist. Soc., Solano County Geneal. Soc. Avocations: genealogy, hiking. Office: James Stevenson Publ 1500 Oliver Rd Ste K-109 Fairfield CA 94533-

STEVENSON, JAMES LARAWAY, communications engineer, consultant; b. Detroit, Oct. 25, 1938; s. Joseph Morley and Kittie Harriet (Laraway) S.; m. Jeanie Lorraine Minkstein, Aug. 7, 1965; children: Amy Jean, Brian Morley. AAS, U.S. Armed Forces Inst., 1958; BSEE, MIT, 1960, MSEE, 1962, PhD in Electronics and Computer Engring., 1994. Cert. master radio and telecommunications engr. Nat. Assn. Radio and Telecomm. Engrs., Inc.; 1st class cert. of competency Associated Pub. Safety Comm. Officers, Inc. With USN Mercury Space Project, 1957-63, Office of Naval Rsch., 1962—63; engr. Sta. WBCM-FM, Bay City, Mich., 1964-65; chief engr. Sta. WCRM, Clare, Mich., 1965-66, Sta. WSMA, Marine City, Mich., 1966; engr. Sta. WWJ-AM-FM-TV, Detroit, 1966-79; owner, mgr. Twin Oaks Comms. Engring. (name now Twin Oaks Comms. Engring. P.C.), North Branch, Mich., 1972—. Charter pilot, flight & ground instr. G. B. DuPont Co., Almont Marlette Aviation Inc., 1977-82; cons. electronics engr. various cos., 1968—; expert legal witness, 1968—; mem. corp. edn. dean's adv. coun. Colls. Bus. Adminstr., Sci., Engring. & Tech., Saginaw Valley State U., 1997—; mem. curriculum adv. com. ITT Tech. Inst., Canton, Mich., 2002—. Mem. editl. advisory panel: eWeek Mag., 2004; contbr. articles to profl. jours. Sr. divsn. judge Detroit Met. Sci. and Engring. Fair, 1975—, Mich. State Sci. & Engring. Fair, 2000—; spl. awards judge Intel Internat. Sci. & Engring. Fair, Detroit, 2000; search & rescue pilot, mission comdr., capt. Mich. wing CAP, 1961-81; cubmaster Pack 457 Boy Scouts Am., North Branch, 1983-85; mem. adv. bd. jacknabbit.com., Issaquah, Wash., 1999-2001; hon. state chmn. bus. adv. coun. Rep. Congl. Com., 2002—; mem. Tri-County Econs. club Saginaw Valley State U., 2002—. Recipient appreciation award CAP, 1980, North Branch Area Schs., 1985, Century award Boy Scouts Am., 1984, Intl. Scientist of the Year award, IBC, Cambridge, 2002. Mem. AIAA, IEEE (sr., chmn. N.E. Mich. sect. 1987-88, 95—, bd. dirs. 1984—), NSPE, Am. Soc. for Engring. Edn. (profl. mem.), Nat. Assn. Radio Telecomm. Engrs. (sr.), Am. Inst. Physics (assoc.), Mich. Soc. Profl. Engrs. (flint chpt.), Saginaw Valley Engring. Coun. (chmn. 1990-91, 2000-01, sec.-treas. 1992-95, Outstanding Leadership award 1991, 2001), Engring. Soc. Detroit (profl.), Profl. Activities Coun. Engrs. (chmn. U.S. activities bd. 1985—), Nat. Pilots Assn. (sr. pilot citation, safe pilot award 1978), Aircraft Owners and Pilots Assn., North Branch C. of C. (charter), Tri-County Econs. Club, Am. Legion, Lions (pres. North Br. club 1990-91), Radio Club Am. Avocations: computers, amateur radio, flying. Office: Twin Oaks Comms Engring PC 2465 Johnson Mill Rd PO Box 340 North Branch MI 48461-0340 Office Phone: 810-688-2633. Personal E-mail: stepthe8@aol.com.

STEVENSON, JAMES RICHARD, radiologist, lawyer; b. Ft. Dodge, Iowa, May 30, 1937; s. Lester Lawrence and Esther Irene (Johnson) S.; m. Sara Jean Hayman, Sept. 4, 1958; children: Bradford Allen, Tiffany Ann, Jill Renee, Trevor Ashley. BS, U. N.Mex., 1959, JD, 1987; MD, U. Colo., 1963. Diplomate Am. Bd. Radiology, Am. Bd. Nuc. Medicine, Am. Bd. Legal Medicine, 1989; Bar: N.Mex. 1987, U.S. Dist. Ct. N.Mex. 1988. Intern U.S. Gen. Hosp., Tripler, Honolulu, 1963-64, resident radiology Brook, San Antonio, 1964-67; radiologist, ptnr. Van Atta Labs., Albuquerque, 1970-88, Radiology Assocs. of Albuquerque, 1988—, pres., 1994-96. Radiologist, ptnr. Civerolo, Hansen & Wolf, Albuquerque, 1988-89; adj. asst. prof. radiology U. N.Mex., 1970-71; pres. med. staff AT & SF Meml. Hosp., 1979-80, chief of staff, 1980-81, trustee, 1981-83. Author: District Attorney manual, 1987. Participant breast screening Am. Cancer Soc., Albuquerque, 1987-88; dir. profl. divsn. United Way, Albuquerque, 1975. Maj. U.S. Army, 1963-70, Vietnam; col. M.C. USAR, 1988—. Decorated Bronze Star; Allergy fellow, 1960; Med.-Legal Tort scholar, 1987. Fellow Am. Coll. Radiology (councilor 1980-86, mem. med. legal com. 1990-96), Am. Coll. Legal Medicine, Am. Coll. Nuc. Medicine, Am. Coll. Nuc. Physicians, Radiology Assn. Albuquerque; mem. AMA (Physicians' Recognition award 1969—), Am. Soc. Law & Medicine, Am. Arbitration Assn., Albuquerque Bar Assn., Soc. Nuc. Medicine (v.p. Rocky Mountain chpt. 1975-76), Am. Inst. Ultrasound in Medicine, N.Am. Radiol. Soc. (chmn. med. legal com. 1992-95), N.Mex. Radiol. Soc. (pres. 1978-79), N.Mex. Med. Soc. (chmn. grievance com.), Albuquerque-Bernalillo County Med. Soc. (scholar 1959), Nat. Assn. Health Lawyers, ABA (antitrust sect. 1986—), N.Mex. State Bar, Albuquerque Bar Assn., Sigma Chi, Albuquerque Country Club, Elks, Masons, Shriners. Republican. Methodist. Home: 3333 Santa Clara Ave SE Albuquerque NM 87106-1530 Office: Med Arts Imaging Ctr A6 Med Arts Sq 801 Encino Pl NE Albuquerque NM 87102-2612

STEVENSON, JO ANN C. federal bankruptcy judge; b. 1942; AB, Rutgers U., 1965; JD cum laude, Detroit Coll. Law, 1979. Bar: Mich. 1979. Law clk. to Vincent J. Brennan, Mich. Ct. Appeals, Detroit, 1979; law clk. to Cornelia G. Kenendy, U.S. Ct. Appeals for 6th Cir., Detroit, 1980; assoc. Hertzberg, Jacob & Weingarten, P.C., Detroit, 1980-87; judge U.S. Bankruptcy Ct., Grand Rapids, Mich., 1987—. Office: US Bankruptcy Ct PO Box 3310 Grand Rapids MI 49501-3310

STEVENSON, JOHN W. lawyer; b. June 19, 1947; BA, Centre Coll. Ky.; JD, U. Ky. Bar: Ky. 1947. Atty. Connor, Neal, Stevenson & Mitchell, LLP, Owensboro, Ky. Mem.: Ky. Bar Assn. (pres.-elect). Office: Connor Neal Stevenson and Mitchell Corp Ctr Bldg D Ste 102 401 Frederica St Owensboro KY 42301

STEVENSON, JOSIAH, IV, management consultant; b. Jamaica, N.Y., Oct. 4, 1935; s. Josiah and Ruth Lillian (Leech) S.; m. Jane Margaret Kupfer, Sept. 1, 1957; children: Josiah V., Todd Sander. AB, Dartmouth Coll., 1957; MBA, Amos Tuck Sch. Bus., 1958. Instr. U. Md.-Far East, 1959-61; account supr. Benton & Bowles, Inc., N.Y.C., 1961-66; group product mgr., gen. mgr. Japan Chesebrough-Pond's Inc., Greenwich, Conn., 1967-77; dir. devel. Dartmouth Coll., 1977-84, Boston Symphony Orch., 1984-95; v.p. Curtis Inst. Music, Phila., 1995—2003; mng. ptnr. Dover Stevenson & Assocs., 1987—. With USAF, 1958-61. Mem. U.S. C. of C., Assn. Fund Raising Profls. (Mass. chpt. bd. dirs., v.p. 1993-95, Greater Phila. chpt. bd. dirs., v.p. fin. 1996-2003), Dartmouth Club, Tokyo Lawn Tennis Club, Yale-Dartmouth Club (N.Y.C.), Badminton and Tennis Club (Boston). Independent. Presbyterian. Home: 23 Spring Pond Rd PO Box 1810 Norwich VT 05055-1810 E-mail: jstevenson@valley.net.

STEVENSON, JUDY G. instrument manufacturing executive, Bookkeeper Magnetrol, Naperville, Ill., 1964-65, accounting supr./mgr., 1965-76, treas./admin. v.p., 1967-75, pres., 1975-78, owner, 1978—. Bd. trustees N. Ctrl. Coll.; established Harold E. Meiley, Judy G. Stevenson, African Scholarship Funds; supports Naperville Heritage Soc., Edward Hosp., the Riverwalk, Millennium Carillon Found., Good Samaritan Hosp., DuPage Intergenerational Village. Recipient YWCA Businesswoman Yr. DuPage Co., 1985, YWCA Outstanding Woman Leader DuPage Co., 1997, Top 500 Woman-Owned Businesses, Working Woman Mag., 1998. Mem. Chief Exec. Officers Club, Nat. Assn. Women Bus. Owners, Nat. Assn. Female Execs., Eastern Star. Avocations: gardening, gourmet cooking, music, ballet, horses. Office: Magnetrol Internat 5300 Belmont Rd Downers Grove IL 60515-4499

STEVENSON, KAREN, lawyer; b. Bay Shore, N.Y., Oct. 02; BA summa cum laude, UCLA, 1971; JD, U. Calif., 1970. Bar: Calif. 1980, U.S. Dist. Ct. (no. dist.) Calif. Law clk. Judge William W. Schwarzer U.S. Dist. Ct. (no. dist.) Calif., 1980-81; v.p., assoc. gen. counsel Transam. Corp., 1987-88, v.p. law, sec., 1989-90; v.p., gen. counsel Knight-Ridder, Inc., San Jose, Calif. Mem. jury instrns. com. U.S. Ct. Appeals (9th cir.), 1983-84. Assoc. editor Calif. Law Rev., 1978-79, articles editor, 1979-80. Regents fellow, 1978-79. Mem. State Bar Calif. (mem. corps. com. 1991-94, legis. liaison 1991-92, vice-chair 1992-93, chair 1993-94), Phi Beta Kappa, Pi Gamma Mu. Office: 50 W San Fernando St Ste 1500 San Jose CA 95113-2434

STEVENSON, KATHERINE HOLLER, federal agency administrator; b. Jan. 20, 1948; d. Jacob W. and Sheila Holler; m. Donald Stevenson, aug. 14, 1982; 2 children. BA, Skidmore Coll., 1969; MA, U. Del., 1971. Researcher Nat. portrait Gallery, Smithsonian Inst., Washington, 1971; with Nat. Park Svc., Washington, 1972-80, Denver, 1980-87, Phila., 1987-95, assoc. dir. Washington, 1995—. Co-author: Houses by Mail, 1983. Recipient Meritorious Svc. award Dept. Interior, 1994. Office: Nat Park Svc Cultural Resource 1849 C St NW Washington DC 20240-0001 E-mail: Kate_Stevenson@nps.gov.

STEVENSON, KENNETH LEE, chemist, educator; b. Ft. Wayne, Ind., Aug. 1, 1939; s. Willard Henry and Luella Marie (Meyer) S.; m. Virginia Grace Lowe, Dec. 26, 1959 (dec. Mar. 1991); children: Melinda Anne, Jill Marie; m. Carmen Ramona Kmety, May 9, 1992; 1 child, Sarah Ann. BS, Purdue U., 1961, MS, 1965; PhD, U. Mich., 1968. Tchr. Ladoga High Sch., Ind., 1961-63; tchr. Central High Sch., Pontiac, Mich., 1963-65; prof. chemistry Ind.-Purdue U., Ft. Wayne, 1968—, chmn. dept. chemistry, 1979—86, 1987—2003, acting dean Sch. Sci. and Humanities, 1986-87. Sabbatical visitor Solar Energy Research Inst., Golden, Colo., 1980; vis. faculty N.Mex. State U., Las Cruces, 1975-76 Author: Charge Transfer Photochemistry of Coordination Compounds, 1993, also numerous rsch. papers. Mem. Am. Chem. Soc. (chmn. Northeastern Ind. sect. 1978-79, Chemist of Yr. 1979, 93), Inter-Am. Photochem. Soc., Phi Kappa Phi, Sigma Xi. Office: Ind U-Purdue U Dept Chemistry Fort Wayne IN 46805 E-mail: stevenso@ipfw.edu.

STEVENSON, LAURA CAROLINE, writer, educator; b. Ann Arbor, Mich., Sept. 8, 1946; d. Charles Leslie and Louise Ellen (Destler) S.; m. Michael William O'Connell, Sept. 27, 1969 (div. July 1981); children: Katharine O'Connell, Margaret O'Connell; m. Franklin D. Reeve, Dec. 22, 1997. AB with highest honors, U. Mich., 1968; MPhil, Yale U., 1971, PhD, 1974. Lectr. history U. Calif., Santa Barbara, 1970-71; prof. humanities Bradford Coll., Haverhill, Mass., 1980-83, Marlboro (Vt.) Coll., 1986—. Author: Praise and Paradox, 1984, 2d edit., 2002, Happily After All, 1990, The Island and the Ring, 1991, All the King's Horses, 2001, A Castle in the Window, 2003. Recipient Grant-in-Aid, Am. Coun. Learned Socs., 1975; Andrew W. Mellon Faculty fellow Harvard U., 1982-83, Rsch. fellow NEH, 1996-97. Mem.: AAUW, Windham County Farm Bur., Vt. Natural Resources Coun., Authors Guild, Royal Oak Found., Beatrix Potter Soc., Assn. Late-Deafened Adults, Phi Beta Kappa. Soc. Of Friends. Avocations: gardening, farming. Home: PO Box 14 Wilmington VT 05363-0014 Office: Marlboro Coll Dept Humanities Marlboro VT 05344 Office Phone: 802-257-4333. Business E-Mail: lsteve@marlboro.edu.

STEVENSON, LAWRENCE N. retail executive; CEO Chapters and Chapters Online Inc.; pres., CEO Pathfinder Capital Inc.; CEO Pep Boys, Phila. Bd. dir. CAE, Inc., SNC-Lavalin Group Inc., Sobeys Inc., chmn. compensation com. Office: The Pep Boys 3111 W Allegheny Ave Philadelphia PA 19132*

STEVENSON, NANCY NELSON, museum executive; b. Annapolis, Md., Oct. 23, 1950; d. Perry Waldemar and Grace Anne Nelson; m. Roger Stevenson Jr., Nov. 18, 1972; children: Jennifer Loren, Matthew Austin. BA, Sarah Lawrence Coll., 1972. Tchr. Montgomery County (Md.) Pub. Schs., 1972—76; bd. dirs. Jr. League of Washington, 1988—89, 1990—92; trustee Nat. Mus. Women in the Arts, Washington, 1996—, sec. bd. of trustees, 1997—98, treas. bd. of trustees, 1998—2002, v.p. bd. trustees, 2002—04, pres. bd. trustees, 2004—. Co-author French immersion curriculum, 1974. Pres. Country Pl. Citizens Assn., Potomac, Md., 1983-84. Office: Nat Mus Women in the Arts 1250 New York Ave NW Washington DC 20005-3970

STEVENSON, PAUL MICHAEL, physics professor, researcher; b. Denham, Eng., Oct. 10, 1954; came to U.S., 1983; s. Jeremy and Jean Helen (Jennings) S. BA, Cambridge (Eng.) U., 1976; PhD, Imperial Coll., London, 1979. Rsch. assoc. U. Wis., Madison, 1979-81, 1983-84; fellow European Orgn. for Nuclear Rsch., Geneva, 1981-83; sr. rsch. assoc. Rice U., Houston, 1984-86, asst. prof. physics, 1986-89, assoc. prof., 1989-93; prof. physics, 1993—. Contbr. articles to profl. jours. Avocation: music. E-mail: stevenson@physics.rice.edu.

STEVENSON, ROBERT BRUCE, lawyer; b. Detroit, Jan. 28, 1951; s. Allan M. and Rose A. (Ferriole) S.; m. Sharon A. Buslepp, Mar. 19, 1982; children: Ruth, Kate. BA with highest honors, Mich State U., 1973; JD, U. Mich., 1976. Bar: Mich. 1976. Assoc. Hill, Lewis, Adams, Goodrich & Taft, Detroit, 1976-82, ptnr., 1982-86; assoc. Rose, Schmidt, Chapman, Duff & Hasley, Ann Arbor, Mich., 1986-87; ptnr. Stevenson Keppelman Assocs., Ann Arbor, 1987—. Author: Incorporating the Small Business - A Systems Approach, 1983. Fellow: Am. Coll. of Employee Benefits Counsel (charter); mem.: State Bar Mich. (chmn. employment benefits com., tax sect. 1987—89). Avocations: skiing, coaching lacrosse. Office: 444 S Main St Ann Arbor MI 48104-2304 Office Phone: 734-747-7050.

STEVENSON, ROBERT EDWIN, microbiologist, consultant; b. Columbus, Ohio, Dec. 2, 1926; s. Arthur Edwin and Mary Lucille (Beman) S. BS, Ohio State U., 1947, MS, 1950, PhD, 1954. Cert. Am. Bd. Microbiology. Virologist USPHS, Cin., 1954-58; head cell culture sect., Tissue Bank U.S. Naval Med. Sch., Bethesda, Md., 1958-60; head cell culture and tissue material sect. Nat. Cancer Inst., Bethesda, 1960-63, chief viral carcinogenesis br., 1963-67; mgr. biolog. scis., corp. devel. dept. Union Carbide Corp., Tarrytown, N.Y., 1967-72; v.p., gen. mgr., Frederick (Md.) div. Litton Bionetics, 1972-80; dir. Am. Type Culture Collection, Rockville, Md., 1980-93; dir. emeritus, 1993. Dir. Large Scale Biology, Inc., Rockville, 1984-90; cons. Am. Assn. Tissue Banks, 1999—; chmn. biotech. adv. com. Dept. Commerce, Washington, 1985-93. With USN, 1944-45. Recipient Hyatt award, AATB, 2004. Fellow Inst. for Soc., Ethics & Life Scis.; mem. Tissue Culture Assn. (pres. 1988-90), World Fedn. Culture Collections, U.S. Fedn. Culture Collections (pres. 1988-90), Am. Soc. Micrbiology, Cosmos Club (Washington). Episcopalian. Avocations: painting, cross country skiing. Home: 27 Evart's Ln Madison CT 06437 Office Phone: 703-827-9582.

STEVENSON, ROBERT MURRELL, music educator; b. Melrose, N.Mex., July 3, 1916; s. Robert Emory and Ada (Ross) S. AB, U. Tex., El Paso, 1936; grad., Juilliard Grad. Sch. Music, 1938; MusM, Yale, 1939; PhD, U. Rochester, 1942; STB cum laude, Harvard U., 1943; BLitt, Oxford (Eng.) U.; Th.M., Princeton Theol. Sem.; DMus honoris causa, Cath. U. Am., 1991; LHD honoris causa, Ill. Wesleyan U., 1992; LittD honoris causa, Universidade Nova de Lisboa, 1993. Instr. music U. Tex., 1941-43, 46; faculty Westminster Choir Coll., Princeton, NJ, 1946-49; faculty rsch. lectr. UCLA, 1981, mem. faculty to prof. music, 1949—. Vis. asst. prof. Columbia, 1955-56; vis. prof. Ind. U., Bloomington, 1959-60, U. Chile, 1965-66, Northwestern U., Chgo., 1976, U. Granada, 1992; adj. prof. Cath. U. Am., 1991—; cons. UNESCO, 1977; Louis Charles Elson lectr. Libr. of Congress, Washington, 1969; inaugural prf. musicology Nat. U. Mex., 1996; spkr. Dumbarton Oaks Pre-Columbian Music Workshop, 1998, Internat. Colonial Music Congress, Lima, Peru, 2000; lectr. Tureck Bach Rsch. Found., Oxford U., 2000; hon. prof. Conservatorio Nacional, Peru, 2000; hon. lectr Royal Conservatory, Madrid, 2004; keynote spkr. Morales Colloquium, Oxford U., 2004. Author: Music in Mexico, 1952, Patterns of Protestant Church Music, 1953, La musica en la catedral de Sevilla, 1954, 85, Music Before the Classic Era, 1955, Shakespeare's Religious Frontier, 1958, The Music of Peru, 1959, Juan Bermudo, 1960, Spanish Music in the Age of Columbus, 1960, Spanish Cathedral Music in the Golden Age, 1961, La musica colonial en Colombia, 1964, Protestant Church Music in America, 1966, Music in Aztec and Inca Territory, 1968, Renaissance and Baroque Musical Sources in the Americas, 1970, Music in El Paso, 1970, Philosophies of American Music History, 1970, Written Sources for Indian Music Until 1882, 1972, Christmas Music From Baroque Mexico, 1974, Foundations of New World Opera, 1973, Seventeenth Century Villancicos, 1974, Latin American Colonial Music Anthology, 1975, Vilancicos Portugueses, 1976, Josquin in the Music of Spain and Portugal, 1977, American Musical Scholarship, Parker to Thayer, 1978, Liszt at Madrid and Lisbon, 1980, Wagner's Latin American Outreach, 1983, Spanish Musical Impact Beyond the Pyrenees, 1250-1500, 1985, La Música en las catedrales españolas del Siglo de Oro, 1993; contbg. editor: Handbook Latin Am. Studies, 1976—; editor Inter-Am. Music Rev., 1978—; contbr. to New Grove Dictionary of Music and Musicians, 17 other internat. encys. Served to capt. U.S. Army, 1943-46, 49. Decorated Army Commendation ribbon; fellow Ford Found., 1953-54, Gulbenkian Found., 1966, 81, Guggenheim Found., 1962, NEH, 1974, Comité Conjunto Hispano-Norteamericano (Madrid), 1989; recipient Fulbright rsch. awards, 1958-59, 64, 70-71, 88-89, Carnegie Found. tchg. award, 1955-56, Gabriela Mistral award OAS, 1985, Heitor Villa Lobos Jury award OAS, 1988, OAS medal, 1986, Cert. Merit Mexican Consulate San Bernardino, Calif., 1987, Silver medal Spanish Ministry Culture, 1989, Gold medal Real Conservatorio Superior, 1994, 97, 1st Lifetime Achievement award Sonneck Soc., 1999. Mem. Am. Musicol. Soc. (hon. life, Pacific SW chpt.), Real Academia de Bellas Artes, Hispanic Soc. Am., Am. Liszt Soc. (cons. editor), Heterofonia (cons. editor), Brazilian Musicol. Soc. (hon.), Portuguese Musicol. Soc. (hon.), Argentinian Musicol. Soc. (hon.), Venezuelan Musicol. Soc. (hon.), Am. Musicol. Soc. (hon.), Orden Andrés Bello, Primera Clase, Venezuela, 1992. Avocation: playing piano. Office: UCLA Dept Music 405 Hilgard Ave Los Angeles CA 90095-9000

STEVENSON, THOMAS HERBERT, management consultant, writer, executive coach; b. Covington, Ohio, Oct. 16, 1951; s. Robert Louis and Dolly Eileen (Minnich) S.; m. Jackie Lowe, June 1, 1997. BA in Econs./Comm., Wright State U., 1977; MA in Psychology, Cleve. State U., 2001. Cert. regulatory compliance mgr. Am. Bankers Assn., 1990, Gestalt Practitioner Gestalt Inst., Cleve., 1999, Diversity Profl. NTL, 2001. Teaching asst., rsch. asst. Wright State U., Dayton, Ohio, 1975-77; teaching asst. Bowling Green (Ohio) State U., 1978; loan officer Western Ohio Nat. Bank & Trust Co., 1979-80, asst. v.p. adminstrs., 1981-82, v.p. mgmt. svcs. div., 1983-85; bank mgmt. cons. Young & Assocs., Inc., Kent, Ohio, 1985-86, exec. v.p., 1987-2000; mem. faculty Gestalt Inst. Cleve., 2001—, Cleve. State U., 2002—; pres., CEO, Cleve. Cons. Group, Inc., 2002—. Legis. impact analyst Community Bankers Ohio, 1985-94, Community Bankers Ga., 1988-94; mem. exec. com. Owl Electronic Banking Network 1981-85; mem. faculty Gestalt Inst. Cleve., 2001—. Author: Compliance for Community Banks, 1987, Compliance Deskbook, 1988, Internal Audit for Community Banks, 1989, Truth in Lending for the Community Bank, 1989, Bank Protection for the Community Bank, 1989, Community Reinvestment Act for the Community Bank, 1989, Executive Management Guide to an Effective Board of Directors, 1990, The Board of Directors, 1990, The Home Mortgage Disclosure Guide, 1990, A Guide to Flood Insurance, 1990, Insider Lending, 1990, A Guide to the Equal Credit Opportunity Act, 1990, Investment Management, 1990, Contingency Planning, 1990, Insider Conduct, 1990, Currency Transaction Reporting Deskbook, 1990, Property Appraisal Deskbook, 1991, Bank Protection Deskbook, 1991, Regulatory Management Deskbook, 1991, Record Retention Deskbook, 1991, Environmental Deskbook for Financial Institutions, 1992, Deposit Compliance Deskbook, 1992, Fair Housing Deskbook, 1992, Insider Lending Deskbook, 1992, CRA Deskbook, 1992, Investment Mgmt. Deskbook, 1992, Internal Audit Deskbook, 1993; contbr. articles to profl. jours. Mem. adv. bd. Upper Valley Joint Vocat. Sch. for Fin. Instns., 1981-85, Am. Indian Edn. Ctr., Cleve. Cpl. USMC, 1972-73. Recipient George Washington medal of Honor Freedom's Found., 1974. Mem. Nat. Mus. Am. Indian (charter), Am. Inst. Banking (adv. bd. 1982-85), Native Am. Heritage Assn., Inst. Noetic Scis., Eagles Club, Gestalt Inst. Cleve. Republican. Mem. Ch. of Brethren. Home and Office: 3750 Chagrin River Rd Chagrin Falls OH 44022-1130 E-mail: herb@clevelandconsultinggroup.com.

STEVENSON, THOMAS RAY, plastic surgeon; b. Kansas City, Mo., Jan. 22, 1946; s. John Adolph and Helen Ray (Clarke) S.; m. Judith Ann Hunter, Aug. 17, 1968; children: Anne Hunter, Andrew Thomas. BA, U. Kans., 1968, MD. Diplomate Am. Bd. Plastic and Reconstructive Surgery, Am. Bd. Surgery.

Resident in gen. surgery U. Va., Charlottesville, 1972-78; resident in plastic surgery Emory U., Atlanta, 1980-82; asst. prof. surgery U. Mich., 1982-88, assoc. prof. surgery, 1988-89. Chief plastic surgery Ann Arbor VA Hosp., 1982—, U. Calif., Davis, 1989—. Served to maj. USAR, 1978-80. Fellow ACS; mem. Am. Soc. Plastic and Reconstructive Surgery. Office: UC Davis Divsn Plastic Surg 2221 Stockton Blvd 2d Fl Sacramento CA 95817-2214

STEVENSON, WILLIAM ALEXANDER, retired justice of Supreme Court of Canada; b. Edmonton, Alta., Can., May 7, 1934; s. Alexander Lindsay and Eileen Harriet (Burns) S.; m. Patricia Ann Stevenson; children: Catherine, Kevin, Vivian, James. BA, U. Alta., Edmonton, 1956, LLB, 1957; LLD (hon.), U. Alta., 1992. Called to Alta. bar, 1958. Ptnr. Hurlburt Reynolds Stevenson & Agrios, Edmonton, 1957-68; prof. U. Alta., 1968-70; ptnr. Reynolds Stevenson & Agrios, Edmonton, 1970-75; judge Dist. Ct. Alta., Edmonton, 1975-79; justice Ct. of Queens Bench Alta., Edmonton, 1979-80, Ct. of Appeal Alta., Edmonton, 1980-90, Supreme Ct. Can., Ottawa, Ont., 1990-92. Officer Order of Can., 1997. Co-author: Civil Procedure Guide, 1995. Mem. Can. Bar Assn., Can. Inst. for Adminstrn. Justice (pres. 1983-85, hon. dir.), Nat. Jud. Inst. (hon. dir.). Home: 7 Laurier Pl Edmonton AB Canada T5R 5P4

STEVENSON, WILLIAM EDWARD, chemical engineer; b. Farmington, Mo., Apr. 21, 1938; s. Herbert Coleman and Mary Jeannetta (Harrington) S.; m. Ramona Ann Shrum, Aug. 29, 1959; children: Marjorie Ellene, Gretchen Faithe. BS in ChemE, Washington U., St. Louis, 1971. Lab tchnician Internat. Oil Burner, St. Louis, 1959-61; maintenance supt. Lever Brothers Co., St. Louis, 1961-74; mgr. hose dept. Haywood Co., Brownsville, Tenn., 1974-95, safety mgr., 1995—. Pres. Haywood County Band Boosters, 1981-83, Haywood County Edn. Task Force, 1985-86; chmn. Haywood County Indsl. Com., 1989-91, mem., 1994—; chmn. Haywood County Job Svc. Employers Com., 1991—, Haywood County Ptnrs. in Edn. Com., 1987-94, Haywood County Rep. Com., 1995—; pres. bd. elders Luth. Ch., 1987-90; chmn. bd. edn. Concordia Luth. Ch. and Sch., 1990-93; v.p. Haywood County Arts Coun., 1994, 95, pres., 1995-96; mem. distbn. com. United Way, 1996-97; bd. dirs. Jackson Tenn. Symphony, 1999. Mem. ASSE, Haywood County C. of C., Brownsville Rotary (pres. elect 1996, pres. 1998). Avocations: fishing, golf, gardening. Home: 127 Hillcrest St Brownsville TN 38012-2702 Office: Haywood Co 751 Dupree Rd Brownsville TN 38012-6255

STEVENTON, ROBERT WESLEY, marketing executive; b. Allentown, Pa., Nov. 2, 1948; s. Robert Wesley and Catherine May (Feineur) S; m. Deborah Damon Barrett, Aug. 29, 1977; children: Calvin Nathaniel, Alexander MacAuley. BA, Pa. State U., 1970; MA, U. Minn., 1975; Cert. Resident, Cambridge U., Eng., 1992. Mktg. specialist U.S. Bur. of Census, Washington, 1975-77; mktg. mgr. Am. Chem. Soc., Washington, 1978-83; account exec. Kreitlow & Assocs., Silver Spring, Md., 1983-84; sr. account exec. Mktg. Gen., Inc., Washington, 1984-85, v.p. Alexandria, Va., 1985-89, sr. v.p., 1989-94; pres. AB&C Mktg., McLean, Va., 1994-2000; mng. ptnr. iMark Comms. Ltd., Fairfax, Va., 2000—. Dir. Intelmark Corp., 1995—, Immedia Corp., 1999—, InfoQuest Comms. Corp., 1999—, InfoQuest Comm. Corp., 2000—; advisor Euro Broadcasting Corp., 1996-99; lectr. Direct Mktg. Assn., Washington, 1988-92, Coun. Engring. and Sci. Soc. Execs., N.Y.C., 1988-98; gen. chmn. Direct Mktg. Days Conv. Com., Washington, 1988. Mem. com. econ. devel. bur. Greater Washington Bd. Trade, 1989-92, bus. mktg. com., 1993-96; mem. Greater Washington Initiative, 1999—; vol. Christ House, Alexandria, Va., 1987—. With U.S. Army, 1970-73. Recipient Capital award Nat. Leadership Coun., 1992. Mem. Am. Soc. Assn. Execs. (membership com. 1989—), Am.-European Cmty. Assn., Brit. Am. Bus. Assn., Direct Mktg. Assn. Washington (bd. dirs. 1983-85), Soc. for Assn. Mktg. Internat. (pres. 1991-94), Assn. Svcs. Group (chmn. bd. 1996-2000), Order St. Etheldreda (officer 1993), Manorial Soc. Gt. Britain (life), Army and Navy Club Washington, Salisbury Club (U.K.), Kappa Tau Alpha. Republican. Episcopalian. Avocations: downhill skiing, bicycling, golf. Office: iMark Comm Ltd Ste 380 13135 Lee-Jackson Hwy Fairfax VA 22033-1907 Home: 103 Wolfe St Alexandria VA 22314-3831

STEVER, DONALD WINFRED, lawyer; b. Altoona, Pa., Jan. 25, 1944; s. Donald Winfred and June Lily (Bargfrede) S.; m. Betsy Jean Seaman, May 28, 1968 (div. Oct. 1975); 1 child, Heather Elene; m. Margo Leaman Taft, July 30, 1976; children: David Whittaker, James Taft. BA, Lehigh U., 1965; JD, U. Pa., 1968. Bar: Conn. 1968, N.H. 1969, D.C. 1983, N.Y. 1983, U.S. Dist. Ct. N.H. 1969, U.S. Dist. Ct. Conn. 1986, U.S. Dist. Ct. (so. dist.) N.Y. 1985, U.S. Dist. Ct. (no. and we. dists.) N.Y. 1990, U.S. Ct. Appeals (1st cir.) 1974, U.S. Ct. Appeals (10th cir.) 1980, U.S. Ct. Appeals (5th, 11th and Fed. cirs.) 1982, U.S. Ct. Appeals (2d cir.) 1990, U.S. Supreme Ct. 1972. Atty. Aetna Life & Casualty co., Hartford, Conn., 1968-69, Office of N.H. Atty. Gen., Concord, 1969-72, asst. atty. gen., chief environ. protection, 1972-77; atty. pollution control sect. U.S. Dept. Justice, Washington, 1978-79, chief pollution control sect., 1979-80, chief environ. def. sect., 1980-82; prof. Pace U. Sch. Law, White Plains, N.Y., 1982-87, adj. prof. environ. law, 1987-92; ptnr. Sidley and Austin, N.Y.C., 1987-93, Dewey Ballantine, N.Y.C., 1993—2004, Kirkpatrick and Lockhart LLP, 2004—. Bd. dirs. Environ. Law Inst., Washington, chmn., 1996-97, 99-2003; bd. dirs. Hudson Valley Writers Ctr. Inc., Sleepy Hollow, N.Y., Friends of Rockefeller State Park Preserve, Inc. Author: Seabrook and The Nuclear Regulatory Commission, 1980; Law of Chemical Reation and Hazardous Waste, 1986; editor: Environmental Law & Practice, 1992; co-editor Environmental Law & Practice, 1992. Bd. dirs. Biddeford Pool (Maine) Improvement Assn., 1989-93; mem. conservation adv. com. Village of North Tarrytown, N.Y., 1989-93; trustee Village of Sleepy Hollow, 1998—. Mem. Biddeford Pool Yacht Club (treas. 1989-92, sec. 1992-2000, rear commodore 2000-02, vice commodore 2002—), Sleepy Hollow Country Club, Abenakee Club, Mill Reef Club. Avocations: golf, tennis, sailboat racing, early music. Home: 157 Millard Ave Sleepy Hollow NY 10591-1412 Office: Kirkaptrick & Lockhart LLP 599 Lexington Ave New York NY 10022-6030

STEVER, EDWARD W. writer, English language educator; b. Amityville, NY, Feb. 17, 1955; s. Edward Francis and Therese Stever; m. Linda Stever; children: Sandra, Caitlyn, Kimberly. A in Liberal Studies, Suffolk Coll., Selden, NY, 1984—89; BA in English, Empire State Coll., Saratoga Springs, 1991—94; MA in Liberal Studies, Empire State Coll., Saratoga Springs, NY, 1995—99. Author: (plays) The Third Pulpit, Shakespeare, Time Warps and Black Holes (First Pl., Oxford Ten-Minute Play Competition, 2000), (poetry) Propulsion, Transparency; dir.: (plays) Private Lives, As Bees in Honey Drown, A Prelude to a Kiss, The Beauty Queen of Leenane, The Third Pulpit, Clare Rose Playhouse; actor: Private Lives; (films) Duncan's Blues. Mem.: Theatre Comm. Group. Home: 41 Park Dr Rocky Point NY 11778-8858 Personal E-mail: edliam@verizon.net. E-mail: edward.stever@usps.gov.

STEVER, HORTON GUYFORD, aerospace scientist and engineer, educator, consultant; b. Corning, N.Y., Oct. 24, 1916; s. Ralph Raymond and Alma (Matt) Stever; m. Louise Risley Floyd, June 29, 1946; children: Horton Guyford, Sarah, Margarette, Roy. AB, Colgate U., 1938, ScD (hon.), 1958; PhD, Calif. Inst. Tech., 1941; LLD, U. Pitts., 1966, Lehigh U., 1967, Allegheny Coll., 1968, Ill. Inst. Tech., 1975; DSc, Northwestern U., 1966, Waynesburg Coll., 1967, U. Mo., 1975, Clark U., 1976, Bates Coll., 1977; DH, Seton Hill Coll., 1968; D.Engring., Washington and Jefferson Coll., 1969, Widener Coll., Poly. Inst. N.Y., 1972, Villanova U., 1973, U. Notre Dame, 1974; DPS, George Washington U., 1981. Staff radiation lab. MIT, Cambridge, Mass., 1941—42, asst. prof., 1946—51, assoc. prof. aero. engring., 1951—56, prof. aero. and astro., 1956—65, head depts. mech. engring., naval architecture, marine engring., 1961—65, assoc. dean engring., 1956—59, exec. officer guided missiles program, 1946—48; chief scientist USAF, 1955—56; pres. Carnegie-Mellon U., Pitts., 1965—72; dir. NSF, Washington, 1972—76; sci. adviser, chmn. Fed. Council Sci. and Tech., 1973—76; dir. Office Sci. and Tech. Policy, sci. and tech. adviser to Pres., 1976—77, sci. cons., corp. trustee, 1977—. Secretariat guided missiles com. Joint Chiefs of Staff, 1945; sci. liaison officer London Mission, OSRD, 1942—45; guided missiles tech. evaluation group Rsch. and Devel. Bd., 1946—48; sci. adv. bd. to chief of staff USAF, 1947—69, chmn., 1962—69; steering com. tech. adv panel on aeros. Dept. Def., 1956—62; chmn. spl. com. space tech. NASA, chmn. rsch. adv. com. missile and spacecraft aerodynamics, 1959—65; mem. Nat. Sci. Bd., 1970—72, ex-officio, chmn. exec. com., 1972—75; mem. Def. Sci. Bd., 1962—68; adv. panel U.S. Ho. Reps. Com. Sci. and Astronautics, 1959—72; mem. Pres.'s Commn. on Patent System, 1965—67; chmn. U.S.-USSR Joint Commn. Sci. and Tech. Cooperation, 1973—77, Fed. Council Arts and Humanities, 1972—76; Pres. com. Nat. Sci. medal, 1973—77. Author: Flight, 1965, In War and Peace: My Life in Sci and Tech, 2002; contbr. articles to profl. jours. Past trustee Colgate U., Shady Side Acad., Sarah Mellon Scaife Found., Buckingham Sch; trustee Univ. Rsch Assn., 1977—, pres., 1982—85; trustee Woods Hole Oceanographic Inst., 1980—, Sci. Svc., 1982—, Univ. Corp. for Atmospheric Rsch., 1980—83; bd. dirs. Saudi Arabia Nat. Ctr. for Sci. and Tech., 1978—81; bd. govs. U.S. Israel Binat. Sci. Found., 1972—76, chmn., 1972—73; mem. Carnegie Commn. on Sci., Tech. and Govt., 1988—93. Recipient Pres.'s Cert. of Merit, 1948, Exceptional Civilian Svc. award, USAF, 1956, Scott Gold medal, Am. Ordinance Assn., 1960, Disting. Pub. Svc. medal, award, Dept. Def., 1969, NASA, 1988, Nat. Medal of Sci., 1991. Fellow: AAAS, AIAA (hon.; pres. 1960—62), Am. Phys. Soc., Royal Soc. Arts, Am. Philos. Soc., Am. Acad. Arts and Scis., Royal Aero. Soc.; mem.: NAE (chmn. aero. and space engring. bd. 1967—69, fgn. sec. 1984—88), NAS (chmn. assembly engring. 1979—83, chmn. policy divsn. 1995—97), Royal Acad. of Engring. of Great Britain (fgn. mem.), Acad. Engring. of Japan (fgn. mem.), Bohemian, Cosmos Club, Phi Beta Kappa, Tau Beta Pi, Sigma Gamma Tau, Sigma Xi. Episcopalian. Office Phone: 301-216-5689.

STEVES, GALE C. marketing professional, writer, editor-in-chief, publishing executive; b. Mineola, N.Y., Dec. 20, 1942; d. William Harry and Ruth (May) S.; m. David B. Stocker, Mar. 31, 1972 (div. Apr. 1978); m. Philip L. Perrone, Aug. 14, 1983. BS, Cornell U., 1964; MA, NYU, 1966. Editorial asst. Ladies Home Jour., N.Y.C., 1966-69; seafood consumer specialist U.S. Dept. Commerce, N.Y.C., 1969-73; editor food Homelife mag., N.Y.C., 1973-74; editor food and equipment Co-Ed mag., N.Y.C., 1974-76, Am. Home mag., N.Y.C., 1976-78; editor kitchen design and equipment Woman's Day mag., N.Y.C., 1979-83; editor-in-chief Woman's Day Spls., N.Y.C., 1983-91; v.p., editor-in-chief Home Mag. Group, N.Y.C., 1991—2001; pres. Open House Prodns., N.Y.C., 2001—03; v.p., editl. dir., pub. AMI Mini Mags. Group, N.Y.C., 2003—. Bd. dirs. Les Dames d'Escoffier, N.Y.C., Coun. Sr. Ctrs. and Svcs. of N.Y.C., 1982-98, The Catskill Ctr. for Cons. and Econ. Devel.; mem. editl. bd. Sr. Summary, N.Y.C., 1982-88; co-chmn. Alder Lake Restoration Soc. Author: Game Cookery, 1974, The International Cook, 1980, Creative Microwave Cooking, 1981, (with Lee M. Elman) Country Weekend Cooking, Home Magazine's Best Little Houses, 1998. Chmn. alumni adv. bd. Coll. Human Ecology, Cornell U., 1993-97, mem. univ. coun., 1996-2000, mem. Pres.'s Coun. for Cornell Women, 1992-2001; mem. adv. bd. Cornell Plantations. Mem. Internat. Furnishings and Design Assn., Am. Soc. Mag. Editors, Garden Writers Assn. Am., Acad. of Women Achievers at YWCA of N.Y.C. Address: 185 West End Ave Ste 26C New York NY 10023-5551

STEWARD, ALETA JOANNA, fine artist, digital artist; b. Bethpage, N.Y., Dec. 18, 1957; d. John L. and Loretta Rossi; m. Steve M. Steward, June 10, 1978; children: Luke, Bill, Nathan. Student, Art Students League, 1977. Artist, Alturas, Calif., 1979-87, Cape Cod, Mass., 1987—; owner Deco Graphics. One woman show including Trees Place, Orleans, Mass., 1995—, Cape Cod Mus. of Natural History, 1988, 90; exhibited in group exhibitions Schaff Gallery, Cin., 1996, Gallery 503, Klamath Falls, Oreg., 1986-87, Marine Arts Gallery, Salem, Mass., 1996-97. Recipient multiple nat., regional and local art awards, 1985—. Mem. Nat. Assn. Photoshop Profls. Republican. Avocations: astronomy, photography, interior design, digital imaging. Home: 57 Colonial Way Harwich MA 02645-1456 E-mail: decographics@earthlink.net.

STEWARD, ALFRED, education educator, researcher; b. Greensburg, La., Feb. 10, 1918; s. Ebbie and Ada Thomas Stewart; m. Iona Jones Stewart, Aug. 23, 1943; children: Rosalyn, Myralyn, E. Alfred, Danita. BS, SU, 1949; MS, La. State U., 1956, PhD, 1969. Tchr. agrl. Ascension Parish Sch., Donaldsville, La., 1949—65; supr. dir. of programs La. State Edn. Agy., Baton Rouge, 1966—72; tchr./rsch. Alcorn State U., Lorman, Miss., 1972—83. Dir. disadvantage programs La. State Edn. Agy., Baton Rouge, 1968—72, dir. vocat. ednl. professions develop., 1969—72. Mem. Baker Improvement Org., Baker, La., 1978—2003. Cpl. U.S. Army, 1941—45, So. Pacific. Democrat. United Meth. Avocations: organ, reading, writing, bible study, computers. Home: 4206 Daveco St Baker LA 70714

STEWARD, DAVID L. technology company executive; b. Clinton, Mo. m. Thelma Steward; children: David, Kimberly. BS, Ctrl. Mo. State U., 1973. Various sales and mktg. positions Wagner Elec., Mo. Pacific Railroad, Fed. Express; founder, chmn. World Wide Tech., Maryland Heights, Mo., 1990—. Named 14th Best Am. Entrepreneur, Success Mag., 1998, Minority Small Bus. Person of Yr., Small Bus. Adminstrn., 1997—98, #1 African-Am.-Owned Bus. in US, Black Enterprise Mag., 2000; named to Small Bus. Adminstrn. Hall of Fame, 2001. Office: World Wide Tech Inc 127 Weldon Pkwy Maryland Heights MO 63043-3108

STEWARD, JAMES BRIAN, lawyer, pharmacist; b. Cleve., Mar. 25, 1946; s. Louis Fred and Helen Elaine Steward; m. Betty Kay Krans, Dec. 14, 1968; children: Christina Lynn, Brian Michael. BS in Pharmacy, Ferris State Coll., 1969; JD, U. Mich., 1973. Bar: Mich. 1973, U.S. Dist. Ct. (we. dist.) Mich. 1979, U.S. Ct. Appeals (6th cir.) 1980, U.S. Supreme Ct. 1986, cert.: elder law atty., Nat. Elder Law Found. Pharmacist Revco Pharmacies, Grand Rapids, Mich., 1969-70, Coll. Pharmacy, Ypsilanti, Mich., 1970-73; assoc. Bridges & Collins, Negaunee, Mich., 1973-80; ptnr. Steward, Peterson, Sheridan & Nancarrow, Ishpeming, Mich., 1980-94, Steward & Sheridan, Ishpeming, 1995—. Mem., chmn. Negaunee Commn. on Aging, 1974-86; mem., chmn., sec. Marquette County Commn. on Aging, 1976-82; trustee, v.p., pres. Negaunee Bd. Edn., 1984-88, 91-95; mem., chmn., adv. bd. trustee Greater Ishpeming Area Cmty. Fund, 1995—; mem. combined ad hoc com. Marquette County Commn. on Aging, 1996; bd. mem. Noquemanon Trails Network, 2000—; mem. econ. restructuring com. Ishpering Main St. program, 2004. Mem.: Am. Soc. for Pharmacy Law, Marquette County Bar Assn. (sec.-treas., v.p., pres.), Mich. Bar Assn. (chmn. awards com. 1996—2004), Nat. Acad. Elder Law Attys., Wawonowin Country Club, Greater Ishpeming Cross County Ski Club, Superiorland Cross Country Ski Club, Rho Chi, Phi Delta Chi. Avocations: cross country ski racing, downhill and water skiing, running, mountain bike racing, classic cars. Office: 205 S Main St Ishpeming MI 49849-2018

STEWARD, JERRY WAYNE, air transportation executive, consultant; b. Tulia, Tex., Mar. 22, 1945; s. Joe M. and Mary Evelyn (Boggs) S.; m. Peggy L. Thomas, Nov. 18, 1978; children: Eric, Chalynda, Julie. AMT, Spartan Aeronautics, Tulsa, 1965. Designated Airworthiness Rep., U.S. FAA. Dir. quality control Braniff, Dallas, Orlando, Tex., Fla., 1966-90; dir. tech. svcs. Polaris Aircraft Leasing, San Francisco, 1990-94; cons. Roanoke, Tex., 1994—. With U.S. Army, 1966-69. Avocations: hunting, fishing, travel. Home and Office: 1820 Summer Ln Roanoke TX 76262-4921 E-mail: planerep@aol.com.

STEWARD, MARSH, JR., obstetrician, gynecologist; b. Plano, Ill. s. Charles Marsh and Louise (Warnock) S.; m. Huguette Gabriell Dulondel, Nov. 14, 1964 (div. Jan. 1991); children: Lewis Olivier, John Jacques. BS, Northwestern U., 1945, MD, 1948; JD, Western State U., 1987. Diplomate Am. Bd. Ob-Gyn. Intern Cook County Hosp., Chgo., 1948-49, resident, 1953-55; mem. staff St. Jude Hosp., Fullerton, Calif., Placentia (Calif.)-Linda Hosp.; pvt. practice Fullerton. Clin. prof. ob-gyn. U. Calif.-Irvine. Fellow Am. Coll. Legal Medicine, ACOG, Calif. Assn. Ob-Gyn. (pres. 1980); mem. AMA, Calif. Med. Assn., Orange County Ob-Gyn. Soc. (pres. 1967). Office: PO Box 5977 Fullerton CA 92838-0977 E-mail: msmdjd@aol.com.

STEWARD, OSWALD, neuroscience educator, researcher; b. Sept. 12, 1948; m. Kathy L. Pyle; children: Jessica, Oswald IV. BA in Psychology magna cum laude, U. Colo., 1970; PhD in Psychobiology, U. Calif., Irvine, 1974. Asst. prof. neurosurgery and physiology U. Va. Sch. Medicine, Charlottesville, 1974-79, assoc. prof., 1979-84, prof., 1984-86, acting chmn. neurosci. dept., 1986-88, chmn., 1998-99; dir. Reeve Irvine Rsch. Ctr. U. Calif., Irvine, Calif., 1999—. Assoc. editor Journal of Comparative Neurology. Author: Principles of Cellular, Molecular, and Developmental Neuroscience, 1989, Functional Neuroscience, 2000; contbr. over 200 articles and revs. to profl. publs. Predoctoral fellow NIMH, Bethesda, Md., 1971-74; rsch. career devel. grantee NIH, 1978-83, Jacob Javitts neurosci. grantee NIH, 1987-94, Disting. Investigator award, Nat. Alliance for Rsch. on Schizophrenia & Depression. Mem. Soc. Neurosci. (chmn. chpts. com. 1985-87), Am. Assn. Anatomists, Am. Soc. Cell Biology, Cajal Club. Office: Reeve-Irvine Rsch Ctr 1105 Gillespie Neurosci Rsch Facility Irvine CA 92697-4292 E-mail: osteward@uci.edu.

STEWARD, SHERRY ANN, information technology executive, educator; b. Ft. Campbell, Ky., Aug. 22, 1959; d. Vincent John Nappa and Mary Emma Woodward; m. J.R. Hooper, June 1977 (div. Oct. 1982); children: Amanda Renee Hooper, James Robert Hooper; m. W.H. Steward, Dec. 4, 1992. BA in English, Rollins Coll., 1996; MA in English and Tech. Writing, U. of Ctrl. Fla., 1999; MS in Info. Tech., Barry U., 2001; PhD in Texts and Tech., U. of Ctrl. Fla., 2004—. Sr. logistics specialist Harris Corp., Palm Bay, Fla., 1981—89; sr. documentation specialist Ea. Test Range, Malabar, Fla., 1989—93; sr. tech. writer DME Corp, Orlando, Fla., 1993—96; program mgr. Dimensions Internat., Inc., Orlando, 1996—. Technologist Dimensions Internat., 1996—. Contbr. articles to profl. jours. Mem.: IEEE (adcom 2000—03, 2004—), Armed Forces Comm. Electronics Assn. (v.p. publicity 2002—03), Nat. Def. Indsl. Assn., Soc. for Tech. Comm. Democrat. Roman Catholic. Office: Dimensions International Inc 3452 Lake Lynda Dr Ste 345 Orlando FL 32817 Personal E-mail: sasteward@earthlink.net. Business E-Mail: ssteward@dimen-intl.com.

STEWARD, WELDON CECIL, architecture educator, architect, consultant; b. Pampa, Tex., Apr. 7, 1934; s. Weldon C. and Lois (Maness) S.; m. Mary Jane Nedbalek, June 9, 1956; children: Karen A., W. Craig. Cert. in architecture and planning, Ecole des Beaux Arts, Fontainebleu, France, 1956; B.Arch., Tex. A&M U, 1957; MS in Architecture, Columbia U., 1961; LHD (hon.), Drury Coll., 1991. Registered architect, Tex., Nebr. Designer Perkins & Will, Architects, White Plains, N.Y., 1961-62; asst. prof. architecture Tex. A&M U., College Station, 1962-67, assoc. chmn. Sch. Architecture, 1966-69, assoc. dean, prof. Coll. Environ. Design, 1969-73; dean, prof. Coll. Architecture U. Nebr., Lincoln, 1973-2000, emeritus dean, prof. arch. and planning, 2000—; founding pres. Joslyn Castle Inst. Sustainable Cmtys., Omaha, 1996—; W. Cecil Steward dist. chair sustainable arch. U. Nebr., Lincoln, 2000—02; founding dir. Nebr. Ctr. for Sustainable Constrn., 2003; editor-in-chief Greensource Report, Atlanta, 2002—04. Adj. prof. Sch. Arch. U. Hawaii, 1999—; ednl. cons. People's Republic of China, 1979--; project dir. Imo State U. Planning, Nigeria, 1981-88; vis. prof. Tong ji U., Shanghai; 1984; hon. prof. N.W. Inst. Architects Engrs., Xian, 1989; specialist Design USA, USSR, 1990; co-chmn. nat. coordination com. AIA Nat. Coun. Archtl. Registration Bd. Intership, Washington, 1980-81; bd. visitors Drury Coll., 1980-97, Coll. Arch. U. Miami, Fla., 1993-96, Judson Coll., 1998-2000; mem. nat. design rev. bd. GSA, Washington, 1994—; mem. founding bd. dirs. East/West Pacific Arch., U. Hawaii, 1995—; vice chmn. Design Futures Coun., Reston, Va., 1995—; sr. fellow Design Futures Coun., 1999. Designer, Quinnipiac Elem. Sch., New Haven, Conn., 1961 (Am Assn. Sch. Adminstrs. Exhibit 1969), J.J. Buser Residence, Bryan, Tex., 1969, Steward Urban Residence, Lincoln, Nebr., 1994. Mem. Lincoln Architects, Engrs. Selection Bd., 1979-88; mem. Nat. Com. for U.S.-China Rels., N.Y.C., 1981—, Nebr. Capitol Environ. Commn., 1989-97; bd. dirs. Downtown Lincoln Assn., 1996—, KZUM Pub. Radio, 1997-2001; mem. Lincoln/Lancaster County Planning Commn., 1996-2004, chmn., 2003-04; co-chmn. steering com. City of Lincoln Downtown Master Plan, 2004—; bd. dirs. Lincoln Children's Mus., 1996-2001; profl. adviser nat. design competition Wick Alumni Ctr., Lincoln, 1981; steering com. Internat. Coun. Tall Bldgs., 1992-96. Recipient T.R. Russel award for Newsletters, 2003; named Disting. Alumnus, Tex. A&M U., 1998; Grad. fellow Columbia U., 1960. Mem. AIA (pres. Brazos chpt. 1969, chmn. profl. devel. com. 1979, bd. dirs. 1979-90, dir. Cen. States 1987-90, nat. pres. 1991-92, Coll. of Fellows 1983, Tri-Nat. com. 1991-02, Nebr. Gold medal 1997, nat. AIA/ACSA Topaz award for excellence in architecture 1999); mem. Am. Planning Assn. (chair Dubai Internat. award for sustaining cmty. 2000), Nebr. Soc. Architects (bd. dirs. 1977-2000), Archtl. Found. Nebr. (bd. dirs. 1981-94, treas. 1981-94), Assn. Collegiate Schs. Architecture (bd. dirs. 1975-79), Nat. Archtl. Accrediting Bd. (bd. dirs. 1986-89, pres. 1988-89), Kazakhstan Union Architecture, Assn. Siamese Architects, Royal Inst. Canadian Architects, Fedn. Mexican Architects, Japan Inst. Architects (hon.), Tau Sigma Delta (medal 1999), Phi Kappa Phi, Phi Beta Delta. Home: 125 N 11th St Lincoln NE 68508-3605 Office: U Nebr Coll Architecture Lincoln NE 68588 Office Phone: 402-472-0087. E-mail: csteward1@unl.edu.

STEWART, ALEC THOMPSON, physicist, educator; b. Windthorst, Sask., Can., June 18, 1925; s. Arthur and Nelly Blye (Thompson) S.; m. Alta Aileen Kennedy, Aug. 4, 1960; children: A. James Kennedy, Hugh D., Duncan R. BSc, Dalhousie U., Halifax, N.S., Can., 1946, MSc, 1949; PhD, Cambridge U., Eng., 1952; LLD, Dalhousie U., Halifax, N.S., Can., 1986. Research officer Atomic Energy Can., Chalk River, Ont., Can., 1952-57; assoc. prof. Dalhousie U., Halifax, 1957-60; assoc. prof. to prof. U. N.C., Chapel Hill, 1960-68; head physics Queen's U., Kingston, Ont., 1968-74, prof. physics, 1968-90, prof. physics emeritus, 1990—. Vis. prof. various univs., Can., Europe, Japan, China, Hong Kong. Author 2 books; contbr. over 100 articles to profl. jours. Decorated officer Order of Can.; recipient CAP medal for achievement in physics, 1992, Canada 125 medal, 1992, Queen Elizabeth II Golden Jubilee medal 2002. Fellow Am. Phys. Soc., Royal Soc. Can. (pres. Acad. Sci. 1984-87), Japan Soc. for Promotion Sci.; mem. Can. Assn. Physicists (pres., other offices 1970-74). Achievements include research in solid state physics, behavior of phonons, electrons, positrons and postronium in crystals and liquids, public service: nuclear reactor safety, possible hazards of power frequency electric and magnetic fields, emergency measures following a nuclear accident, state of nuclear technology in Canada. Office: Queens U Dept Physics Kingston ON Canada K7L 3N6

STEWART, ALEX, finance educator; b. Montreal, Can., June 24, 1950; m. Marjory S. Watt, Jan. 6, 1959; children: Benjamin A., Ian A., M. Arden. MA, MBA, PhD, York U., Toronto, 1984. Assoc. prof. Tex. Tech U., Lubbock, Tex., 1990—2000; chmn. Entrepreneurship Dept. Marquette U., Milw., 2000—. Co-convener Orgn. Sci. Winter Conf., 2004—. Author: Team Entrepreneurship, The Ethnographer's Method. Office: Marquette University David Straz Hall Milwaukee WI 53201-1881 Business E-Mail: alex.stewart@marquette.edu.

STEWART, ALEXANDER CONSTANTINE, medical technologist; b. N.Y.C., Nov. 3, 1957; s. Dudley Constantine and Lillian Eunice (Mills) S.; m. Shirlene Denise Keys, June 22, 1985; children: Shechianh Faith, Akilah Danielle, Omari Joseph Constantine. Student, Herbert H. Lehman Coll., 1975-77; BS in Med. Tech., U. Kans., 1979; BTh, Northgate Bible Coll., 1989; ThM, Parkersburg Bible Coll., 2002. Cert. med. technologist Am. Soc. Clin. Pathologists. Chemistry technologist White Plains (N.Y.) Med. Ctr., 1979-89, Mt. Vernon (N.Y.) Hosp., 1987-89; chemistry supr. St. Agnes Hosp., White Plains, 1989-92, Westchester Sq. Med. Ctr., Bronx, N.Y., 1992-93; med. technologist Richland Meml. Hosp., Columbia, S.C., 1993—. Instr. W. L. Bonner Bible Coll., 1995-97. Co-author: (with Sherry Sherrod DuPree) The Silent Spokesman, 1994, (with Shirlene Stewart) Write the Vision, 1996. Asst. historian Ch. of Our Lord Jesus Christ, 1989—; deacon Refuge Temple, Ch. of Our Lord Jesus Christ, 1993—, chmn. bd. trustees, 1993—; bd. dirs. New and Living Way Ministries, 1999-2000. Mem. Soc. Pentecostal Studies (editl. com. 1992-99), Pentecostal Hist. Soc., African Am. Genealogical Soc., S.C. African Am. Hist. e Geneal. Soc. (sec. 1999-2001). Democrat. Pentecostal. Avocation: research and storage of african american pentecostal materials. Home: 801 Riverwalk Way Irmo SC 29063-9375 also: Refuge Temple 4450 Argent Ct Columbia SC 29203-5901 also: 4159 Grace Ave Bronx NY 10466-2015 E-mail: stewart_alexande@hotmail.com.

STEWART, ALLAN FORBES, lawyer; b. Kansas City, Kans., Nov. 14, 1947; s. Ernest William and Elizabeth Jeannette (Forbes) S. BA, U. Mo., St. Louis, 1969; JD, St. Louis U., 1972. Bar: Mo. 1972, Ill. 1979, Md. 1986, U.S.

Dist. Ct. (we. dist.) Mo. 1973, U.S. Dist. Ct. (ea. dist.) Mo. 1978, U.S. Dist. Ct. (so. dist.) Ill. 1978, U.S. Ct. Appeals (8th cir.) 1975, U.S. Supreme Ct. 1976. Staff atty. Legal Aid Soc., Clayton, Mo., 1972-76; ptnr. Braun, Newman, Stewart, Clayton, Mo., 1976-81, Braun & Stewart, Clayton, Mo., 1981-82; pres. Braun, Stewart & Anderson, Inc, and predecessor firms, Clayton, Mo., 1982-97; ptnr. Beach, Burcke, Helfers, Mittleman & Stewart, St. Louis, 1997-99; prin. Beach, Stewart, Heggie, Mittleman LLC, St. Louis, 1999—. Contbr. chpts. to books. With Army N.G., 1970-76. Fellow am. Acad. Matrimonial Lawyers, Am. Acad. Adoption Attys.; mem. Mo. Bar Assn. (chmn. juvenile sect. 1982—, Pres. award 1983), St. Louis County Bar Assn. (chmn. family law sect. 1979-81). Home: 1077 Jackson Ave Saint Louis MO 63130-2226 Office: 222 S Central Ave Ste 900 Saint Louis MO 63105-3575 Office Phone: 314-863-8484. E-mail: VADM22825@aol.com.

STEWART, ARDEN RUTH, automotive aftermarket manufacturing executive; b. Wheeling, W.Va., Sept. 29, 1930; d. Oliver Shaw and Helen (Neitzel) Stewart; children: Mark, Todd. BA, Baldwin Wallace Coll., 1952. Trainee GM, Cleve., 1952-57; tchr. Elyria (Ohio) City Bd. Edn., 1967-85; pres., CEO AAR, Inc., Cleve., 1984—, also chmn. bd. dirs. Pres. Elyria Schs. PTA, 1967; treas. Homeowners Assn., North Ridgeville, Ohio, 1988-89; mem. adv. com. bus. and tech. Cuyahoga C.C. Recipient Weatherhead 100 award Case Western Res. U., 1990, 91, 92, 93, 94, 95. Republican. Episcopalian. Avocations: music, scuba diving, dance. Home: 32889 Brownstone Ln PO Box 39359 North Ridgeville OH 44039-0359 Office: AAR Inc 34999 Mills Rd North Ridgeville OH 44039-1366 Personal E-mail: arden9201@aol.com.

STEWART, ARLENE JEAN GOLDEN, designer, stylist; b. Chgo., Nov. 26, 1943; d. Alexander Emerald and Nettie (Rosen) Golden; m. Randall Edward Stewart, Nov. 6, 1970, 1 child, Alexis Anne. BFA, Sch. of Art Inst. Chgo., 1966, postgrad., Ox Bow Summer Sch. Painting, Saugatuck, Mich., 1966. Designer, stylist Formica Corp., Cin., 1966-68; with Armstrong World Industries, Inc., Lancaster, Pa., 1968-96, interior furnishings analyst, 1974-76, internat. staff project stylist, 1976-78, sr. stylist Corlon flooring, 1979-80, sr. exptl. project stylist, 1980-89, sr. project stylist residential DIY flooring floor divsn., 1989-96, master stylist DIY residential tile, 1992-96; creative dir. Stewart Graphics, Lancaster, Pa., 1996—. Mem. Exhibitions include Art Inst. Chgo., 1966, Ox-Bow Gallery, Saugatuck, Mich., 1966. Home and Office: 114 E Vine St Lancaster PA 17602-3550 Personal E-mail: stewartgraphics@redrose.net.

STEWART, ARTHUR IRVING, III, (ART STEWART), management consultant; b. Plainfield, N.J., Aug. 1, 1958; s. Arthur Irving Jr. and Audree Claire (Rollerson) S. BS in Mass Communication, Emerson Coll., 1982; profl. devel. cert. sr. exec leadership, Georgetown U., 2004. Intern Sta. KYW Newsradio/TV, Phila., 1977; news anchorman, reporter Sta. WLBR-WUFM-FM, Lebanon, Pa., 1984; ops. mgr. Sta. WMSP-FM, Harrisburg, Pa., 1984-86; sr. account exec. mktg. and sales promotion Sta. WFCC-FM, Chatham, Mass., 1987-88; account mgr. Vizwiz Film-Video, Inc., Brookline, Mass., 1989-90; pub. rels. account exec. The Interface Group, Needham, Mass., 1991-92; sr. account exec. pub. rels. Mullen Advt., 1992-93; pres., sr. counsel Stewart Strategies Group, LLC, Wayne, Pa., 1993—. Dir. mktg. and pub. rels. Cape and Islands Chamber Music Festival, Cape Cod, Mass., 1988; asst. organist The United Parish, Brookline, 1982-84. Producer (radio concert broadcasts) Harrisburg Symphony Orch., 1984-86, documentary on U.S. debut tour of Westminster Cathedral Choir of London, 1985, investigative report on acid rain, 1985 (Excellence in Broadcasting award), documentary on Nat. Cathedral Washington, 1986 (Excellence in Broadcasting award). Editor OUTREACH newsletter Trinity Ch., Boston, 1990-94; staff media rels. 72d genl. conv. Episcopal Ch. U.S.A., 1997. Recipient Excellence in Broadcasting award Pa. Assn. Broadcasters. Mem. Pub. Rels. Soc. Am., Greater Wash. Bd. Trade, Leadership, Inc., Phila., Assn. Corp. Growth, Pub. Affairs League, Am. Guild Organists, Edn. Com., Pub. Relations Com., Anti Defamation League. Episcopalian. Avocations: running, bicycling, travel, the arts, politics. E-mail: results@stewartgrp.com.

STEWART, BARBARA DEAN, writer, musician, educational consultant; b. Rochester, NY, Sept. 17, 1941; d. George Adgate and Louise (Griswold) Dean; children: Allison, Whitney. AB, Cornell U., 1962; MS, Simmons Coll., 1964; diploma with honors in flute, Eastman Sch. Music., 1958; MFA in Playwriting, Columbia U., 1993; postgrad. minority exec. program, Dartmouth Coll., 2000—01. Asst. law libr. Cornell U., Ithaca, N.Y., 1963-64; writer, performer Kazoophony, N.Y., 1972-90; pub. rels. dir. Margaret Woodbury Strong Mus., 1978; pres. Stewart Assocs. Ednl. Sys. Group, Rochester, 1979-85; pres., CEO SWI, Fairport, N.Y., 1985—. Flutist La Jolla Civic Orch., 1966-68; exec. assoc. Tony Randall's Nat. Actors Theatre, N.Y.C., 1991, co. dramaturg, asst. to artistic dir., 1992-93; faculty U. Phoenix, 2000—. Author: How To Kazoo, 2003, Squash Raquets: Pro and Khan, From Camera to Finished Print, Ghost Tales and Trails of the Erie Canal, Sydney the Sea Squid; (plays) Sound Barriers, Platypus Rex, (musical) The Magic Fruit. Founding chmn. jr. devel. U.S. Squash Racquets Assn.; pres. bd. dirs. Rochester Chamber Orch.; bd. dirs. Rochester chpt. English Spkg. Union, 1982-85; pole vault coach Pittsford (N.Y.) H.S., 1999, Robert Wesleyan Coll., 1999; pres. Share Arts Found., 1989—; non-govtl. orgn. del. UN Human Rights Subcom., Geneva, 1998; mem. president's coun. on athletics Cornell U. Fellow Yale Sch. Drama, 1989-90; Recipient 68 nat. championships and 2 world championships in 20 different masters track and field events, holder 14 Am. and 6 world records, 5 MAC achievement awards Met. Athletics Congress, N.Y.C., 1986, 88, 90; 1st ofcl. world, U.S., Can. women's pole champion masters; Soviet women's pole vault record, 1990; named to Cornell U. Athletic Hall of Fame, Greater Rochester track Club Hall of Fame. Mem.: ASCAP, Nat. Tng. Sys. Assn., Nat. Def. Indsl. Assn., Nat. Classification Mgmt. Soc., Dramatist Guild, Am. Fedn. Musicians, N.Y. State Track Ofcls. Assn., U.S.A. Track and Field Ofcls., Ibsen Soc., Players Club (N.Y.C.), Yale Club N.Y.C. Office: 11 W Church St Ste 101 Fairport NY 14450-2111

STEWART, BOBBY GENE, laboratory director; b. Jesse, W.Va., Apr. 18, 1940; s. Leonard Mart and Zeta Marie Stewart; m. Linda May Smith, Mar. 17, 1961; children: Barbara Lynn, Ramona Jean Stewart Pinkerman. Cert. in med. tech., Army Med. Svc. Sch., 1960; cert. blood banking specialist, 10th Med. Rsch. Lab., Landstuhl, Germany, 1961. Lic. nursing home adminstr. Mo., cert. clin. lab. scientist, bioanalytical lab. mgr. Med. and x-ray technologist Oceana (W.Va.) Med. Ctr., 1962-68; clin. mgr., med. technologist Sigourney (Iowa) Med. Clinic, 1968-69; staff med. and x-ray technologist Van Buren County Hosp., Keosauqua, Iowa, 1969; dir. lab. and x-ray svcs. Scotland County Hosp., Memphis, Mo., 1969-71; dir. lab. svcs. Keller Meml. Hosp., Fayette, Mo., 1971-95, Regional Med. Assocs., Fayette, 1995-97; med. technologist Boyce and Bynum Pathology Labs., 1998-99, Mo. Cancer Assocs., Columbia, 1999—. Mem. city coun. City of Fayette, 1977—85, mayor pro-tem, 1980—85, chmn. parks and recreation com., 1977—80, chmn. elec. dist. com., 1981—85. With U.S. Army, 1959—62. Mem.: Mo. State Soc. of AMT (v.p. 1973—74, pres. 1975—76, legis. chmn. 1975—90, v.p. 1989—90, Med. Technologist of Yr. 1977, Pres.'s award 2001), Am. Med. Technologists (dist. councillor 1977—81, 1988—93, nat. bd. dirs. 1993—2002, nat. treas. 1994—96, nat. v.p. 1996—97, nat. pres. 1997—99, 2001—02, nat. sch. liaison 2002—, Disting. Achievement award 1976, Exceptional Merit award 1981, Nat. Silver Svc. award 1997, Nat. Pillar award 1998, Nat. Order Golden Microscope award 2000, Technologist of Yr. 2002). Avocations: tennis, golf, swimming. Office: Mo Cancer Assocs Keene St Columbia MO 65201 Home: 91-1012 Wahipana St Kapolei HI 96707-2922 E-mail: bgslms@verizon.net.

STEWART, BURTON GLOYDEN, JR., retired banker; b. Clayton, N.C., Mar. 14, 1933; s. Burton Gloyden and Evelyn I. (Stallings) S.; m. Patricia Taylor, June 16, 1956; children: Burton Gloyden III, H. Taylor. AB, Duke U., 1955; grad., Sch. Banking of the south, 1970; exec. program, U. N.C., 1975. With Allstate Ins. Co., 1957-66, regional sales mgr., 1964-66; with Branch Banking and Trust Co., Wilson, N.C., 1966-98, sr. v.p., mgr. corp. planning and mktg. divsn., 1972-81, dir. investor rels., 1981-98, ret., 1998. Dir. Branch Corp., 1974-82; dir. N.C. Payments System, 1980-89, v.p., 1983-86, chmn. bd. 1986-89; bd. dirs., chmn. Electronic Fin. Svcs., Inc., 1988-90. Bd. dirs., treas. Wilson Arts Coun., 1969-71; bd. dirs. Wilson Heart Assn., 1968, Wilson United Way, 1974-80, 86-89, campaign chmn., 1977, pres., 1979, chmn. strategic planning com., 1986-90; mem. N.C. Gov.'s Efficiency Study Commn., 1985, N.C. Goals and Policy Bd., 1985-93; local com. Cypress Glen Retirement Cmty., 1991—, chmn., 1999-2001; fin. com., trustee United Meth. Ret. Homes, Inc., 1999—, chmn., 2002—, trustee UMRH Found., 1999—, chmn., 2002—. Lt. USNR, 1955-57. Mem. Bank Investor Rels. Assn. (bd. dirs. 1984-98, v.p. 1984-87), Wilson Country Club, Dunes Club. Methodist. Address: 1107 Salem St NW Wilson NC 27893-2139

STEWART, CARL E. federal judge; b. Shreveport, LA, 1950; BA magna cum laude, Dillard U., 1971; JD, Loyola U., New Orleans, 1974. Atty. Piper & Brown, Shreveport, La., 1977—78; staff atty. La. Atty. Gen. Office, Shreveport, 1978—79; asst. U.S. atty. Office U.S. Atty. (we. dist.) La., Shreveport, 1979—83; prin. Stewart & Dixon, Shreveport, 1983—85; spl. asst. dist. atty., asst. prosecutor City of Shreveport, 1983—85; judge La. Dist. Ct., 1985—91, La. Ct. Appeals (2d cir.), 1991—94, U.S. Ct. Appeals (5th cir.), 1994—. Adj. instr. dept. mgmt. and mktg. La. State U., Shreveport, 1982—85. Mem. chancellor's adv. bd. La. State U., Shreveport, 1983—89, chmn., 1988—89; mem. black achievers program steering com. YMCA, 1990. Capt. JAGC other, 1974—77, Ft. Sam Houston, Tex. Mem.: La. State Bar Assn. (bench/bar liaison com.), La. Conf. Ct. Appeal Judges, Black Lawyers Assn. Shreveport-Bossier, Am. Inns of Ct. (Harry Booth/Henry Politz chpt. Shreveport), Nat. Bar Assn., Omega Psi Rhi (Rho Omega chpt.). Office: US Ct Appeals 5th Cir 300 Fannin St Ste 2299 Shreveport LA 71101-3124

STEWART, CARLETON M. bank executive, director; b. Chgo., 1921; s. Carleton Merrill and Margaret (Lyon) S.; m. Alicia Dewar (dec.); 3 children; m. Kathryn White. Student, Stanford U., 1939-42; grad. in indsl. adminstrn., Harvard U., 1943, MBA, 1947. With Citibank, 1947-76, v.p., 1960-67, sr. v.p. in charge of Asia Pacific area, 1967-69, sr. v.p. in charge of South Asia, Middle East and Africa, 1969-73, sr. officer London, 1973-76; dir. Grindlay's Bank Ltd., London, Banque Internat. pour L'Afrique Occidentale, Paris, 1973-76; chmn. bd., chief exec. officer Am. Security Corp. and Am. Security Bank, Washington, 1976-80; chmn. bd. Internat. Bank Miami, 1983-85; dir. Travelers Asset Mgmt. Internat. Corp., N.Y.C., 1985-87. Mayor Longboat Key, Fla., 1987-88, town commr., 1984-90, ethics com., 1990-99, chmn. 1992-94; mem. Planning Commn., Sarasota County, Fla., 1990-92. Capt. AUS, 1943-46.

STEWART, CHARLES LESLIE, lawyer; b. Fayetteville, Ark., Aug. 12, 1919; s. Charles Leslie and Ruth (Ward) S.; m. Edalee Esther Gastrock, Aug. 30, 1941; children: William Paul, Thomas Alan, Katherine Jean, Robert Edward. AB, U. Ill., 1940; MA, La. State U., 1941; student, George Washington U. Law Sch., 1944-45; JD, U. Chgo., 1947. Bar: Ill. 1948, U.S. Supreme Ct. 1954. Economist, Dept. Agr., 1941-42; adminstrv. asst. OPA, 1942-43, Bd. Econ. Warfare, 1943; exec. dir. Chgo. div. ACLU, 1946-47; practiced law Chgo., 1948-91, Glencoe, Ill., 1991-98; assoc. Mayer, Brown, Rowe & Maw, Chgo., 1947-55, ptnr., 1956-67, 70-71, resident ptnr. charge European office, Paris, 1967-70; v.p., gen. counsel Hart Schaffner & Marx, Chgo., 1971-73, v.p., sec., gen. counsel, 1974-83, Hartmarx Corp., Chgo., 1983-84, v.p., sec., sr. counsel, 1984, of counsel legal dept., 1985-89; arbitrator Mandatory Arbitration Program Cir. Ct. Cook County, Ill., 1990—. Mem. Am. Law Inst., 1983-90. Mem. Glencoe (Ill.) Bd. Edn., 1965-66; mem. planning com. Corp. Counsel Inst., Northwestern U. Sch. Law and Ill. Inst. Continuing Legal Edn., 1978-84, vice-chmn., 1983, chmn., 1984; mem. Glencoe Union Ch. Served with OSS, AUS, 1943-45. Mem. ABA, Ill. State Bar Assn., Chgo. Bar Assn. (com. devel. of law 1977-91, vice chmn. 1984-85, chmn. 1985-86, corp. law com. 1981-91, corp. law depts. com. 1981-83, sr. lawyers com. 1987-92), Am. Soc. Corp. Secs. (adv. com. Chgo. regional group 1978-83, vice chmn. 1979-80, chmn. 1980-81, nat. dir. 1981-84, exec. com. 1983-84, corp. practices com. 1982-87, assoc. mem. 1986-91), Skokie Country Club, Rotary, Delta Phi. Avocations: genealogy, history, bridge. Home: 2525 Mayapple Ct Northbrook IL 60062-6531

STEWART, CHARLES TODD, JR., retired economist; b. NYC, May 13, 1922; s. Charles Todd and Leonor Pereira (de Magalhaes) S.; m. Nancy Thayer, Jan. 24, 1953; children: Eileen, David, Jocelyn. BA, George Washington U., 1946, MA, 1948, PhD, 1954. Asst. prof. econs. Utah State U., Logan, 1947-49; rsch. assoc. George Washington U., 1951—52, prof. econs., 1963—92, prof. emeritus, 1992—; sr. rsch. analyst Georgetown U. Grad. Sch., 1953—58; rsch. economist, dir. econ. rsch. U.S. C. of C., 1958—63. Cons. Interam. Devel. Bank, Washington, 1978-79, NSF, Washington, 1970-71, 73-78, OAS, Washington, 1968-69, U.S.-P.R. Commn. on Status, San Juan, 1965-67, Litton Industries, 1965, Atlantic Rsch. Corp., 1967, NASA, 1969-70, Econ. Devel. Adminstrn., 1968-72, Nat. Bur. Stds., 1975-76. Author: Low Wage Worker in an Affluent, 1974, Air Pollution, Human Health, 1979, Technology Transfer and Human Factors, 1987 (Ohira award 1987), Healthy, Wealthy, or Wise, 1995, Inequality and Equity, 1998, Around the World in Eighty Years, 2000; co-author: Employment Effects of Minimum Wages, 1969, From Basic Economics to Supply-Side, 1983; contbr. articles to profl. jours. With inf. U.S. Army, 1942-45. Mem. AAAS, Am. Econ. Assn. Avocations: painting, poetry.

STEWART, CHRISTINE SUSAN, Canadian government official; b. Jan. 3, 1941; d. Morris Alexander Leishman and Laura Anne Doherty; m. David Ian Stewart, Aug. 24, 1963; children: Douglas Alexander, John David, Catherine Anne. Ed., Neuchatel Jr. Coll., Switzerland, U. Toronto, Ont., Can. Nurse; mem. Ho. of Commons, 1988—, mem. standing com. for external affairs and internat. trade, assoc. critic for human rights; official opposition critic Can. Internat. Devel. Agy.; sec. state L.Am. and Africa Cabinet of Prime Min. Jean Chrétien, Ottawa, 1993-97, min. environ., 1997—. Founding exec. dir. Horizons of Friendship. Liberal. Roman Catholic. Office: House of Commons Confederation Bldg Rm 232 Ottawa ON Canada K1A 0A6

STEWART, C(ORNELIUS) VAN LEUVEN, lawyer; b. Balt., Sept. 22, 1936; s. Charles Morton and Lillie Emerson (Van Leuven) S.; m. Clare Wright Horsley, June 18, 1960; children: Clare Winston, Lillie Elliotte, Jenett Ten Eyck (dec.). BA, Yale U., 1958; LLB, U. Va., 1961. Bar: Md. 1962, D.C. Bar 1982. Assoc. in law U. Calif. Law Sch., Berkeley, 1961-62; assoc. Venable, Baetjer & Howard, Balt., 1962-69, ptnr., 1970-91, Stewart, Plant & Blumenthal, LLC, Balt., 1991—. Bd. dirs., past pres. Irvine Natural Sci. Ctr.; past bd. overseers Balt. Sch. for the Arts; past bd. dirs. Pks. and People Found., Balt. Symphony Orch. Assn., Internat. Visitors Coun. of Balt., Roland Park Country Sch., Magic Me; past pres. Md. Ballet Co., Met. Balt. Mental Health Assn. Mem. ABA, State Bar Assn., Balt. City Bar Assn., D.C. Bar Assn., Am. Coll. Trust and Estate Counsel (Md. chpt., past state chair), Internat. Acad. of Estate and Trust Law, Balt. Estate Planning Coun. (pres. 1987). Republican. Episcopalian. Office: 7 Saint Paul St Ste 910 Baltimore MD 21202-1672 E-mail: cvstewart@spblaw.com.

STEWART, DAVID MARSHALL, librarian; b. Nashville, Aug. 1, 1916; s. David and Mary (Marshall) Stewart; m. Gladys Carroll, June 9, 1947; 1 child, James Marshall. BA, Bethel Coll., 1938; BSLS, George Peabody Coll., 1939. Circulation asst. Vanderbilt U. Library, 1938-39; county librarian Ark. Library Commn., 1939-40; Tenn. supr. WPA library service projects, 1940-42; librarian Memphis State U., 1942-46; spl. asst. to chief card div. Library of Congress, Washington, 1947; librarian CIA, Washington, 1948-60; chief librarian Nashville Pub. Library, 1960-85; Instr. Peabody Library Sch., 1966-80. Bd. dirs. Coun. Cmty. Agys., Nashville, Friends Chamber Music, Nashville, Traverlers Aid, Nashville; v.p. Friends Mid.-E. Tenn. Arthritis Found. Served to lt. comdr. USNR, 1942—46. Mem.: ALA, Pub. Libr. Assn. Am. (chmn. stds. com. 1964—65, pres. 1966—67), Southeastern Libr. Assn., Tenn. Libr. Assn. (chmn. legis. com. 1961—65, v.p. 1965, pros. 1966, Honor award 1983), Alumni Assn. Bethel Coll. (dir., Disting. Alumni award 1992), Coffe House Club (Nashville), Kiwanis. Democrat. Mem. Ch. Of Christ. Home: 6342 Torrington Rd Nashville TN 37205-3157

STEWART, DAVID PENTLAND, lawyer, educator; b. Milw., Dec. 24, 1943; s. James Pentland and Frederica (Stockwell) S.; children from previous marriage: Jason, Jonathan; m. Jennifer Kilmer, June 21, 1986; children: Daniel, Mary Elizabeth. AB, Princeton U., 1966; JD, MA, Yale U., 1971; LLM, N.Y.U., 1975. Bar: N.Y. 1972, U.S. Dist. Ct. (ea. and so. dists.) N.Y. 1973, U.S. Ct. Appeals (2d cir.) 1973, D.C. 1976. Assoc. Donovan, Leisure, Newton & Irvine, N.Y.C., 1971-76; atty. adviser, office of legal adviser U.S. Dept. State, Washington, 1976-82, asst. legal adviser, 1982—. Adj. prof. law Georgetown U., Washington, 1984—, Am. U., Washington, 1985-86, Johns Hopkins U. Sch. Advanced Internat. Studies, 2000—; vis. lectr. Sch. Law U. Va., 1993-96, Nat. Law Ctr., George Washington U., 1993—. Contbr. articles to profl. jours. Served to maj. USAR, 1970-87. Mem. ABA, Fed. Bar Assn., Am. Soc. Internat. Law., Internat. Law Assn. (adv. coun. procedural aspects internat. law inst.). Office: US Dept State Office Legal Adviser Washington DC 20520-6310 E-mail: stewartdp@state.gov.

STEWART, DAVID WAYNE, marketing educator, psychologist, consultant; b. Baton Rouge, Oct. 23, 1951; s. Wesley A. Stewart, Jr. and Edith L. (Richhart) Moore; m. Lenora Francois, June 6, 1975; children: Sarah Elizabeth, Rachel Dawn. BA, N.E. La. U., 1972; MA, Baylor U., 1973, PhD, 1974. Rsch. psychologist HHS, La., 1974-76; rsch. mgr. Needham, Harper & Steers Advt., Chgo., 1976-78; assoc. prof. Jacksonville (Ala.) State U., 1978-80, Vanderbilt U., Nashville, 1980-86, sr. assoc. dean, 1984-86; prof. U. So. Calif., L.A., 1986-90, Ernest W. Hahn prof. mktg., 1990-91, Robert Brooker rsch. prof. mktg., 1991—, chmn. dept. mktg., 1995-99, dep. dean faculty, 1999-2001, dep. dean, 2001—04. Mgmt. cons., 1978—. Author, co-author: Secondary Research: Sources and Methods, Effective Television Advertising: A Study of 1000 Commericals, Consumer Behavior and the Practice of Marketing, Focus Group: Theory and Practice, Attention, Attitude, and Affect in Repsonse to Advertising, Nonverbal Communication and Advertising; editor: Jour. of Mktg., 1999-2002; contbr. articles to profl. jours.; editor: Jour. of Mktg., 1999-2002; mem. edtl. bd. Jour. Mktg. Rsch., Jour. Consumer Mktg., Jour. Pub. Policy & Mktg., Jour. Mktg., Jour. Advt., Jour. Promotion Mgmt., Current Issues and Rsch. in Advt., Jour. Internat. Consumer Mktg., Jour. Managerial Issues, Jour. Promotion Mgmt.; past pres. policy bd. Jour. Consumer Rsch., Acad. Mgmt. Fellow APA (coun. rep.), Am. Psychol. Soc. (charter); mem. Soc. for Consumer Psychology (past pres.), Inst. Mgmt. Scis., Decision Sci. Inst., Am. Mktg. Assn. (pres. acad. coun. 1997-98, v.p. fin. 1998-99), Assn. for Consumer Rsch., Am. Statis. Assn. (chair sect. on stats. in mktg. 1997), Acad. of Mgmt., Acad. Mktg. Sci. (bd. govs. 2004—). Republican. Baptist. Office: U So Calif Marshal Sch Bus Office Dep Dean HOH 802C Los Angeles CA 90089-1428 Office Phone: 213-740-5037. Business E-mail: david.stewart@marshall.usc.edu.

STEWART, DAVID WITHERINGTON, aerospace engineer; b. Marion, Ind., Feb. 9, 1939; s. Edgar Allen Jr. and Faye Maxine (Cummings); m. Ruth Ada Valk, Aug. 26, 1961, (div.); m. Annette Louise Witherington, Dec. 17, 1962 (dec. Aug. 1999); children: Edna (dec.), Geoffrey. BS in Physics, U. Fla., Gainesville, 1959. Sr. engr. Atlas Gen. Dynamics/Convair, Cape Canaveral, Fla., 1959-63; lead engr. Gemini-Titan Martin Canaveral, Cape Canaveral, 1963-66; lead engr. Sprint Martin-Orlando, Orlando, Fla., 1966-67; lead engr. Apollo Rockwell Internat., Kennedy Space Center, Fla., 1967-74, lead engr. avionics, 1975-78, prime system integ. engr. shuttle, 1978-79, supr. orbiter software, 1979-81, project mgr. software, 1982-84, project mgr. design, 1984-85, project mgr. adv. programs, 1985-89, mgr. adv. program, 1989-91, project mgr. adv. program and bus. devel., 1991-92, program devel. mgr. Fla. ops. space sys. divsn., 1992-96; pres. L&D Consulting, Titusville, Fla., 1996—. Pres. Rockwell Fla. Chpt. NMA, 1985-87. Author: Edie and the Gobie, 1966. Pres. North Brevard Environ. Action Com., Titusville, 1970-73; chmn. Marine Resources Coun. East Fla., 1996-97, 2000—; pres.-elect Space Coast Devel. Commn., 1995-96; sec. Space Coast Grant Profls. Network, 1997-99; pres. Brevard Adult Literacy Vols., Inc., 2000—. Mem. Inst. Cert. Prof. Mgrs. (cert. mgr.), Am. Cons. League (accredited profl. cons.). Republican. Unitarian Universalist. Home: PO Box 5869 Titusville FL 32783-5869 Office: Bus Devel Cons 609 Garden St Titusville FL 32796 Fax: 321-264-1885. E-mail: bizplnz@aol.com.

STEWART, DEBORAH CLAIRE, dean; b. Freeport, Ill., Sept. 14, 1951; Student, Monterey Peninsula Coll., 1969-71; BS in Zoology, U. Calif., Davis, 1973; MD, U. Calif., San Francisco, 1977. Diplomate Am. Bd. Peds. Intern Children's Hosp. L.A., 1977-78, resident in peds., 1978-79, fellow in adolescent medicine, 1979-81, attending physician emergency med. svcs., 1980-81; med. dir. comprehensive adolescent program dept. ob-gyn. Charles R. Drew Postgrad. Med. Sch., L.A., 1981-83; asst. prof. dept. ob-gyn. UCLA/Charles R. Drew Postgrad. Med. Sch., 1982-83; mem. ped. staff Children's Hosp. of Orange County, Orange, Calif., 1983-86, U. Calif. Irvine Med. Ctr., Orange, 1983-99; assoc. prof. ob-gyn., assoc. prof. medicine U. Calif., Irvine, 1983-99, dir. child sexual abuse program, 1983-99, assoc. prof. clin. peds., chief divsn. gen. peds., dir. adol, 1988-95, assoc. dean for med. student and resident affairs, 1992-99; med. dir. child protection ctr. Meml. Miller Children's Hosp., Long Beach, Calif., 1995-99; assoc. dean med. edn. program U. Calif.-San Francisco, Fresno, 1999—. Project dir. South Ctrl. L.A. Sexual Trauma Program, 1983; med. cons. L.A. Commn. on Assaults Against Women, 1982-84, Calif. Children's Svcs., 1980-85, Sexual Assault Protocol Office of Criminal Justice Planning, 1984-86, Sexual Assault Protocol L.A. County, 1984-86; med. dir. Child Abuse Svcs. Team County of Orange, 1987—; physician mem. Calif. State Atty. Gen.'s Investigative Pilot Projects Rsch. and Evaluation Adv. Panel; cons. County of Orange Coroner's Office, 1994-99. Contbr. articles to profl. jours.; presenter in field; reviewer: Ped. and Adolescent Gyn., 1988—, Jour. Adolescent Health Care, 1986—, Peds., 1988—, Am. Jour. Obs. and Gyn., 1991— Mem. med. adv. bd. Planned Parenthood, 1983-94. Fellow Am. Acad. Pediatrics (pres. Dist. IX Chpt. 4, 1995-97, sec. chpt. IV, chair chpt. IV com. on child abuse 1983—); mem. N.Am. Soc. Pediatric And Adolescent Gynecology (co-chair collaborative rsch. com. 1988—), Orange County Ped. Assn. Office: U Calif San Francisco-Fresno Med Edn Program 2615 E Clinton Ave Fresno CA 93703-2223 E-mail: deborah.stewart@ucsfresno.edu.

STEWART, DEBRA WEHRLE, academic administrator; b. Petersburg, Va., May 22, 1943; BA in Philosophy and Polit. Sci., Marquette U., 1965; MA in Govt., U. Md., 1967; PhD in Polit. Sci., U. N.C., 1975. Instr. polit. sci. European divsn. U. Md., Nuremberg, Germany, 1967-69; instr. polit. sci. and pub. adminstrn. N.C. State U., Raleigh, 1974-75, asst. prof., 1975-78, assoc. prof., 1979-83, prof., 1984—, acting dir. MPA program, 1978, assoc. dean Grad. Sch., 1983-86, interim vice provost and dean Grad. Sch., 1986-88, dean Grad. Sch., 1988-2000, vice provost, 1995-98, vice chancellor, dean Grad. Sch., 1998-2000; pres. Coun. Grad. Schs., Washington, 2000—. Interim chancellor U. N.C., Greensboro, 1994; mem. com. on assessment of rsch. doctorate NRC, 1992-95; mem. Grad. Record Exam. Bd., 1992-96, chmn.-elect, 1994-95, chmn., 1995-96; bd. dirs. Coun. Grad. Schs., 1990—, chmn.-elect, 1992-93, chmn., 1993-94; mem. Test English as Fgn. Lang. Bd., 1992-95; councilor Oak Ridge Assoc. Univs., 1988-92, bd. dirs., 1993—, chair-elect 1997—; bd. dirs. Nat. Phys. Scis. Consortium, 1998—; mem. exec. com. Coun. So. Grad. Schs., 1989-91; trustee Triangle U. Ctr. for Advanced Studies, 1989—; mem. Commn. on Peer Rev. and Accreditation, Nat. Assn. of Schs. of Pub. Affairs and Adminstrn., 1997-99. Author: The Women's Movement in Community Politics: The Role of Local Commissions on the Status of Women, 1980, (with G. David Garson) Organizational Behavior and Public Management, 1983, 3d edit. (with Vasu and Garson), 1998; editor: Women in Local Politics, 1980; mem. editl. bd. Rev. Pub. Pres. Adminstrn., 1981-89, Annals Pub. Adminstrn., 1982-84, Women and Politics, 1980-88, Politics and Policy, 1983-86; contbr. articles to profl. jours., chpts. to books. Recipient edn. award YWCA Acad. Women, 1988 Mem. Nat. Assn. State Univs. and Land-Grant Colls. (bd. dirs. 1992-94, exec. com. coun. on rsch. policy and grad. edn. 1989-92, chmn. 1990-91), Am. Soc. for Pub. Adminstrn. (com. on status of women in pub. adminstrn. 1976-78, com. on profl. stds. and ethics 1980-89, chmn. com. on whistle blowing and dissent channels of profl. stds. and ethics com. 1985-86, Burchfield award 1976), So. Polit. Sci. Assn. (nominating com. 1978, coord. pub. adminstrn. sect. 1979), Women's Forum N.C., Phi Kappa Phi, Pi Sigma Alpha, Pi Alpha Alpha. Office: Coun Grad Schs Grad Sch 1 Dupont Cir NW Ste 430 Washington DC 20036-1136

STEWART, DONALD GEORGE, musician, composer, music industry executive; b. Sterling, Ill., Jan. 8, 1935; s. Donald Balmer and Elinore Maud (Denison) S.; m. Susan Ann Trainer, June 13, 1963 (div. 1979); 1 child, Elizabeth Ann. MusB, Ind. U., 1960; postgrad., Manhattan Sch., 1960-62;

student, Sch. of Jazz, 1958-60; studied with Roy Harris, Bernhard Heiden, Gunther Schuller. 2d clarinetist Birmingham (Ala.) Symphony, 1954-56, Fla. Symphony, Orlando, 1963; musician with numerous jazz groups including Ornette Coleman, David Baker, Sammy Davis, 1957-65; woodwind player Orch. USA, N.Y.C., 1963-65; libr. Harkness Ballet, N.Y.C., 1967-72; founder, clarinetist Boehm Quintette, N.Y.C., 1968-88; music asst. N.Y. State Coun. on the Arts, N.Y.C., 1972-75; freelance copyist N.Y.C., 1958-88; founder, pres. Trillenium Music Co., 1986—, clarinetist, saxophonist, 1958—; pres. Opera North, Norwich, Vt., 1987-89. Founder, treas. Chamber Music Am., N.Y.C., 1977-81; panelist Vt. Coun. on the Arts, 1976-78. Composer Piccolo Concerto, 1973, August Lions for Youth Orch., 1978, Song of Arion, 1985 (2d prize Am. Harp Soc.), First Blue Symphony, 1988, Book of Sliding Things, 1989, Green Mountain Christmas Card (opera), 1995, Never Seek to Tell Thy Love (voice and ensemble), 1998, Duo for Violin and Cello, 1999, Flute Quartet, 2003; others; transcriber wind chamber music; composer, arranger for G. Schirmer, Boosey and Hawkes, Carl Fischer, Trillenium Music Co.; recs. for Columbia, Orion, New World, Margun and Marlboro, 1964—; participant Marlboro Festival, Vt., 1966-68, Berkshire Festival, Mass., summer 1965, 68. Vt. Coun. on the Arts fellow, 1985, Nat. Endowment for Arts grant, 1978—. Mem. ASCAP, Am. Fedn. Musicians, Am. Soc. Music Copyists (bd. dirs. 1970-87, treas. 1984-87), Am. Music Ctr., Music Pub.'s Assn. Democrat. Congregationalist. Office: Trillenium Music PO Box 88 Tunbridge VT 05077-0088

STEWART, DONALD W. lawyer; Ptnr. Stewart, Falkenberry & Whatley, Birmingham, Ala. Office: 2100 16th Ave S Ste 305 Birmingham AL 35205-5021

STEWART, DORIS MAE, biology professor; b. Sandsprings, Mont., Dec. 12, 1927; d. Virgil E. and Violet M. (Weaver) S.; m. Felix Loren Powell, Oct. 8, 1956; children: Leslie, Loren. BS, Coll. Puget Sound, 1948, MS, 1949; PhD, U. Wash., 1953. Instr. U. Mont., Missoula, 1954-56, asst. prof., 1956-57, U. Puget Sound, Tacoma, 1957-58; head sci. dept. Am. Kiz Lisesi, Istanbul, Turkey, 1958-62; rsch. asst. prof. U. Wash., Seattle, 1963-67, rsch. assoc. prof., 1967-68; assoc. prof. Cen. Mich. U., Mt. Pleasant, 1970-72, U. Balt., 1973-81, prof., 1981-95, prof. emeritus, 1995—. Contbr. numerous articles to profl. jours. Mem. Am. Physiol. Soc., Sigma Xi. Home: 1103 Frederick Rd Baltimore MD 21228-5032

STEWART, DOROTHY K. librarian; b. Bristol, Conn., Sept. 28, 1928; d. Robert and Anna Esther (Schwitz) Konopask; m. David Benjamin Stewart, Sept. 27, 1952 (div. Nov. 1979); children: Douglas Neil, Diane Alison. BA in Romance Langs. and Lit. cum laude, Boston U., 1950; MSLS, Cath. U. Am., 1959. Children's libr. Brookline (Mass.) Pub. Libr., 1953-55, Takoma Park (Md.) Libr., 1955-57; reference libr. U.S. Geol. Survey, 1961; libr. Washington Internat. Sch., 1979-80, Office Sea Grant NOAA, Rockville, Md., 1980-82; info. specialist Life Ring, Inc., Silver Spring, Md., 1983-84; pub. svc. libr. Urban Inst., Washington, 1984-85; user svcs. coord. ERIC Clearinghouse on Tchg. and Tchr. Edn., Washington, 1985-97; ret., 1997. Active, past pres. PTA, Rockville, Md., 1973-78; chmn., mem. com. Potomac (Md.) Libr. Adv. Com., 1975-85. Mem. Capital PC User Group, French lang. clubs, Phi Beta Kappa, Beta Phi Mu. Democrat. Avocations: travel, hiking, birding, microcomputers. Personal E-mail: dkstewart1@netzero.net.

STEWART, DOROTHY MARY HANTON, literature and writing educator; b. Santa Monica, Calif., Nov. 13, 1922; d. Thomas Rhea Hanton and Dora Catherine Prior; m. Arvel Stewart, Aug. 15, 1942; children: Sheila, Paul, David, Kathleen. BA, U. No. Colo., 1963, MA, 1965; postgrad., Cambridge U. Tchr. Ault Grade Sch., Colo., 1943—45, Windsor HS, Colo., 1963—65, Highland HS, Ault, 1965—67; prof. Aims C.C., Greeley, Colo., 1967—94, prof. emeritus, 1995—. Bd. dirs. Aims Found., Greeley, 1994—. Mem. Human Rels. Commn., Greeley, 1986—93. Mem.: NEA, Colo. Edn. Assn., Nat. Genealogy Soc., Pi Lambda Theta. Democrat. Roman Catholic. Avocations: genealogy, reading, Irish history, travel.

STEWART, E(DWARD) NICHOLSON, investment management executive; b. Bronxville, N.Y., Sept. 28, 1940; s. Edward Nicholson and Helen (Davis) S.; m. Mary Patricia Hunter, Aug. 8, 1964; children: Pamela S. Burke, Wendy S. Leary. Student, Hamilton Coll., 1959-62; BA, New Sch. Social Rsch., 1965. Dir. membership Investment Co. Inst., N.Y.C., 1968; v.p. Lord, Abbett & Co., N.Y.C., 1969-74; pres. Trevor Stewart Burton & Jacobsen Inc., N.Y.C., 1974-95, CEO, 1990—, chmn., 1995—. Pres., bd. dirs. Robert Hampton Tapp Found., 1993—. Co-founder, editor Hackley Rev., 1963-68. Trustee Hackley Sch., 1971-87, treas., 1972-87, v.p. 1980-87; pres. Hackley Alumni Assn., Inc., 1967-69. Mem. USN League (Marine Corps com. N.Y. 1986—), Naval War Coll. Found. (life), Marine Corps Univ. Found. (assoc.), U.S. Naval Inst., Nat. Def. Indsl. Assn. (life), Union League Club (bd. govs. 1985-87, 95-97, vice-chmn. 1987, pres. 1989-90), Pendennis Club (Louisville), Sleepy Hollow Country Club (bd. govs. 1993-96, sec. 1995, 2001-2003, asst. sec. 2000, v.p. 2003—), Econ. Club N.Y., The 200 Club (bd. dirs.), Delta Kappa Epsilon. Republican. Office: 90 Park Ave New York NY 10016-1301

STEWART, FRANK MAURICE, JR., federal agency administrator; b. Okalona, Miss., Apr. 1, 1939; s. Frank Maurice Stewart and Henryne Annette (Walker) Goode; m. Regina Diane Mosley, Dec. 26, 1964; children: Lisa Ann, Dana Joy. BA, Wesleyan U., 1961, MA in Teaching, diploma further study, Wesleyan U., 1963; postgrad., Am. U., 1982-84. Dir. urban edn. corps N.J. State Dept. Edn., Trenton, 1969-70; dir. urban teaching intern program Sch. Edn. Rutgers U., New Brunswick, N.J., 1970-71; staff asst. White House Conf. on Aging, Washington, 1971-73; chief program devel. U.S. Office of Equal Edn. Opportunity, Washington, 1973-74; chief policy analysis U.S. Adminstrn. on Aging, Washington, 1974-75; asst. exec. sec. U.S. HEW, Washington, 1975-77; dir. govt. programs U.S. Dept. Energy, Washington, 1977-80, dir. instnl. conservation programs, 1980-84, dir. state and local assistance programs, 1984-90, dep. asst. sec. for tech. and fin. assistance, 1990-93; acting asst. sec. for energy efficiency and renewable energy, 1993-94; mgr. Golden (Colo.) Field Office, U.S. Dept. Energy, 1994—. Bd. dirs. Renewable Energy for African Devel., 1992-94; mem. U.S. Presdl. Del. on Sustainable Energy Devel. to South Africa, 1995, U.S. Del. to African-African-Am. Summit, Dakar, Senegal, 1995; bd. advisors Internat. Sustainable Tech. Bus. Ctr. Bd. dirs. Urban League of Met. Denver. Recipient Svc. Recognition award Assn. Phys. Plant Adminstrs., Washington, 1982, Svc. Appreciation award Nat. Assn. State Energy Officials, Washington, 1987, Midwest Rsch. Inst., 1996; named Energy Exec. of Yr. Assn. Energy Engrs., Atlanta, 1988. Mem. Sr. Execs. Assn., Nat. Assn. of Black Environmentalists (bd. dirs.), Am. Assn. of Blacks in Energy (bd. dirs. Denver chpt.), Denver Fed. Exec. Bd. Episcopalian. Home: 202 S Madison St Denver CO 80209-3010 Office: US Dept Energy Field Office 1617 Cole Blvd Golden CO 80401-3305 E-mail: frank_stewart@nrel.gov.

STEWART, GEORGIANA LICCIONE, writer; b. Mount Vernon, N.Y., May 18, 1943; d. Arthur Alfred and Grace Marie (Zuzzolo) Liccione; m. William Lawrence Stewart, July 18, 1975. BA, Columbia U., 1971; MA, Columbia Tchr.'s Coll., N.Y.C., 1973; MAT, Manhattanville Coll., 1973. Author, cons. Kimbo Ednl., Long Branch, N.J., 1970—; spl. edn. tchr. Bronxville (N.Y.) H.S., 1989—. Cons. NAEYC, SACUS, 1975-89, Pres.'s Coun. on Physical Fitness, 1979-81. Author: (69 children's musical activity records and books including) Adaptive Motor Learning, 1982, Bean Bag Activities, 1983, Preschool Aerobic Fun, 1989, Children of the World, 1991, ulticultural Rhythm Stick Fun, 1992, Toddlerific, 1993, World of Parachute Play, 1997, Children's Folk Dances, 1998, Moving with Mozart, 1999 (Early Childhood Dir.'s Choice award NAEYC), Nursery Rhyme Time, 2000, Cool Aerobics for Kids, 2001, Musical Scarves, 2002, Circle Time, 2004. Recipient Student Advocacy Overcoming the Odds award, 1997. Mem. AAHPERD, Nat. Assn. for Edn. of Young Children, So. Assn. for Children Under Six, Faculty Dance Educators Am., Assn. for Retarded Citizens, Columbia Club, Women's Nat. Rep. Club. Avocations: Heatsong music and art therapy program, organizing local benefit programs. Home: 81 Pondfield Rd # 328 Bronxville NY 10708-3818 Office: Kimbo Ednl PO Box 477 Long Branch NJ 07740-0477

STEWART, GORDON CURRAN, association executive; b. Chgo., July 22, 1939; s. Henry Stewart and Evangeline (Williams) Bolton; m. Elizabeth Knorr, June 19, 1965 (div. 1968); m. Zanne Early, Dec. 20, 1995; 1 child, Katarina Guadalupe Hadley. BA, Oberlin Coll., 1960; MA, U. Chgo., 1962; student, U. Vienna, Austria, 1963; MFA, Yale U., 1967. Instr. Amherst (Mass.) Coll., 1967-68; dir. Bus. Comm. for Arts, N.Y.C., 1969-71; exec. asst. Mayor of N.Y.C., 1971-73; dir., writer N.Y.C., L.A., U.K., 1973-78; dep. chief speechwriter President of U.S., Washington, 1978-81; instr. Bus. and Govt. Acad. forums, U.S. and fgn. countries, 1981-82; v.p. AMSE, N.Y.C., 1982-89; exec. v.p. Ins. Info. Inst., N.Y.C., 1989-91, pres., 1991—. Cons. Am. Bus. Conf., Washington, 1982-89, Internat. Commn. for Ctrl. Am., Washington, 1986-88, Coun. on Competitiveness, Washington, 1987-88, Def. Sci. Bd., Washington, 1988-89. Writer films: The Store, 1978, Joey, 1978, Gallery, 1978; dir. (play) The Elephant Man (1st U.S. prodn.), 1977, Jesse, 1975, Cowboy Mouth, 1976, Sleep, 1977, (films) The Blazers, 1975; condr. Beggar's Opera, 1969, West Side Story, 1970. Dir. N.Y. Urban Coalition, N.Y.C., 1984-88; dir. policy Samuels for Gov., N.Y., 1974; speechwriter numerous dem. campaigns, 1974-81; mem. fin. coun. Dem. Nat. Com., 1984-88; mem. adv. coun. Dem. Leadership Coun., 1984-90. Woodrow Wilson fellow Woodrow Wilson Found., 1961. Mem. Writers Guild Am. (west), Judson Welliver Soc. of Chief Presdl. Speechwriters (sec.-treas.), Coun. Fgn. Rels., Century Assn., Phi Beta Kappa, Yale Club. Avocations: politics, music.

STEWART, GORDON MEAD, architect; b. Leonardtown, Md., May 18, 1959; s. William Nelson and Eileen Marie (Mead) S.; m. Jacqueline Joelle Le Moigne, Apr. 5, 1986; children: Gavin, Lauriane. BArch, BA in Urban Studies, U. Md., 1982. Registered architect, Md. Architect-intern sys. mgr. Wat & Assocs., Arlington, Va., 1981-84; architect prodn. mgr. RTKL, Balt., 1984-92; architect sys. mgr. MK Ferguson, Columbia, Md., 1992-93, CRSS Architects, Washington, 1993-94; architect project mgr., mem. tech. bd. HOK Inc., Washington, 1994-96, Jacob-Sverdrup/CRSS, Arlington, 1996—. Pres. bd. dirs. Bowie (Md.) Regional Arts Vision Assn., 1995—. Designer child care ctr. IRS, Martinsburg, W.Va., 1996; author (bus. plan) Vision 2000, 1997. Recipient 1st pl. residential design competition So. Homes Showcase, Balt., 1992, Olympic Design Competition award Bentley/Microstation, Atlanta, 1995; named Bowie Outstanding Citizen, 2000. Mem.: Washington Area Microstation Cmty., Mid-Atlantic Region Intergraph LUG (sec., treas. 1983—95), AIA. Avocations: soccer, windsurfing, reading, photography. Home: 2830 Belair Dr Bowie MD 20715-2154 Office: Sverdrup-CRSS Jacobs Engring 1100 N Glebe Rd #500 Arlington VA 22201

STEWART, GREGORY WALLACE, physician; b. Balt., July 8, 1961; s. Don Milton and Martha (Davis) S.; divorced; 1 child, Lauren Elizabeth; m. Bonnie Marie Johnson, June 8, 1991; children: Tess Marie, Shaid Michael. BS in Biology, Chemistry and Para-Med. Sports Therapy, Houston Baptist U., 1982; MD, U. Tex. Med. Br. Sch. of Medicine, 1986. Diplomate Am. Bd. Phys. Medicine and Rehab. Resident in phys. medicine and rehab. La. State U./Charity Hosp. in New Orleans, 1986-90; instr. and asst. residency Sect. Phys. Medicine and Rehab. La. State U. Sch. Medicine in New Orleans, 1990-92; clin. asst. prof. Dept. Orthop. Tulane U. Sch. Medicine, 1990-95; asst. prof. and residency program dir. Sect. of Phys. Medicine La. State U. Sch. Medicine in New Orleans, 1992-95; assoc. prof. orthopedics Tulane U. Sch. Medicine, 1995—, chief divsn. phys. medicine and rehab., 1995—, med. dir. Tulane Ctrs. for Phys. Medicine and Rehab., 1996—, co-dir. Tulane Inst. Sports Medicine, 1995—. Team physician New Orleans Night Arena Football Team, 1991-92, Tulane U., 1990—, Hahnville H.S., 1987—; physician Ballet Hysell, New Orleans; coord. sports medicine St. Charles and Plaquemines Parish Sch. Dists.; assoc. coord. sports medicine St. Bernard and Orleans Parish Sch. Dists.; mem. adv. coun. La. Sports Medicine and Safety; mem. U.S. Olympic Track and Field Trials Sports Medicine Staff, 1992; mem. sports medicine organizing com. NCAA Track and Field Championships, 1993. Contbr. numerous articles to med. jours. Mem., chmn. task force on disabling violence La. Adv. Coun. on Disability Prevention, 1990-93, mem. com. on prevention of secondary disabilties; med. cons. Weiss Rehab. Ctr.; chmn. divsn. of rehab. svcs. head injury tech. assistance com. State of La.; mem. adv. com. for phys. therapy asst. program Delgado C.C.; reviewer Medicine and Sci. in Sports and Exercise Jour. of Orthopaedic and Sports Phys. Therapy; abstract reviewer Nat. Head Injury Found.; grant reviewer Nat. Inst. Disability Rsch. and Rehab., prin. investigator, 1997-2001. Recipient Study of Personal Care Attendants for Indigent Quadriplegics grant Am. Assn. of Spinal Cord Injury Psychologists and Social Workers, 1991-93, Rehab. Long Term Tng. -Rehab. Medicine grant Rehab. Svcs. Adminstrn., 1993-95, La. Disability Prevention Program grant Sports Injury Surveillance in La., 1993-94. Fellow Am. Coll. Sports Medicine; mem. AMA, Am. Acad. Phys. Medicine and Rehab., Am. Congress Rehab. Medicine, Nat. Athletic Trainers Assn., S.E. Athletic Trainers Assn., La. State Med. Soc., La. Athletic Trainers Assn., Orleans Parish Med. Soc., La. Sports Medicine Soc. (edn. chmn. 1994-2002). Avocations: gardening, genealogy. Home: 4905 Clearlake Dr Metairie LA 70006-1112 Office: Dept Orthopaedics SL32 1430 Tulane Ave New Orleans LA 70112-2699 E-mail: gstewart@tulane.edu.

STEWART, HAROLD BROWN, biochemist; b. Chatham, Ont., Can., Mar. 9, 1921; s. John Craig and Margaret Gertrude (Brown) S.; m. Audrey Pauline Blake, Oct. 14, 1950; 1 dau., Ann Margaret. MD, U. Toronto, 1944, PhD, 1950, Cambridge (Eng.) U., 1955. Prof. biochemistry U. Western Ont., London, 1956—; chmn. dept. biochemistry U. Western Ont., 1964-72, dean grad. studies, 1972-86, prof. emeritus, 1986—. Med. Research Council Can. vis. scientist dept. biochemistry U. Cambridge, Eng., 1971-72 Contbr. articles in biochemistry to sci. jours. Served with Royal Canadian Navy, 1945-46. Mem. Canadian, U.K. biochem. socs., Canadian Physiol. Soc., Am. Soc. Biochemistry and Molecular Biology, Coll. Physicians and Surgeons of Ont. Home: 118 Baseline Rd E London ON Canada N6C 2N8

STEWART, HAROLD SANFORD, real estate investment and supply executive; b. Cookeville, Tenn., Nov. 22, 1949; s. Willie Sanford and Margaret Eula (Wassom) S.; m. Diana Gail Law, May 3, 1968; children: Rhonda Gail, Scott Harold. Diploma, Nashville Vocat.-Tech. Sch., 1969. Cert. ACCA-EPIC instr., Air Conditioning Contractors of Am. Sales and part mgr. Scotsman Supply Co., Nashville, 1967-73; salesman Brock-McVey Supply Co., Bowling Green, Ky., 1973-76; pres., gen. mgr. Eds Supply Co., Bowling Green, 1976-79, Nelsco Supply Co., Bowling Green, 1979-80; pres. Air Supply Co., Inc., Bowling Green, 1980-88; sales mgr. One Stop Supply, Inc., Bowling Green, 1988-89; pres. Bilt-Rite Constrn., Inc., Bowling Green, 1989-92; sec., treas. K&H Enterprises, Inc., Bowling Green, 1989-93; pres., gen. mgr. H.S. Properties, Bowling Green, Ky., 1989—; pres., gen. mgr., stockholder Stewart Supply, Inc., Bowling Green, 1993—. Chmn. Ky. State Vocat. HVAC Craft Com., Frankfort, 1987, Bowling Green Vocat. HVAC Craft Com., 1980-88, 1993-; nat. adv. coun. Thermaflex Mfg. Co., Kansas City, Mo., 1986-87. City clk. and trustee City of Plum Springs, Ky., 1975-79; treas. Bowling Green Civitan Club, 1973-78; trustee Jackson Grove Bapt. Ch., Bowling Green, 1975-86. Named Civitan of Yr., Bowling Green Club, 1973-75, Col., Hon. Order of Ky. Cols. Mem. Masons, Optimist. Avocations: reading, computers, tennis, jogging, dance. Office: 300 W 6th St Bowling Green KY 42101-1878 Home: 536 Detour Rd Bowling Green KY 42101 Office Phone: 270-843-4545. Business E-Mail: hstewartbg@insightbb.com.

STEWART, JACK, artist, educator, writer; b. Atlanta, Jan. 27, 1926; s. Jack Thomas and Lilly Ruth (Hemperley) S.; m. Margot S. Stewart (div.); 1 child, Brandon Burns; m. Regina Serniak, Dec. 10, 1976. BFA, Yale U., 1951; MA, NYU, 1975, PhD, 1989. Mem. faculty Columbia U. Grad. Sch. Art, N.Y.C., 1966—76; chmn. dept. art Cooper Union Sch. Art, N.Y.C., 1971—74; v.p., provost R.I. Sch. Design, Providence, 1976—77. Academician Nat. Acad., 1995. Exhibited at George Binet Gallery, N.Y.C., 1950, Pa. Acad. Phila., 1953, Grippi and Waddell Gallery, N.Y.C., 1963-64, Collegeo Raffaello, Urbino, Italy, 1973, La Scuola di Teodora, Venice, Italy, 1976, Sheldon Swope Gallery, Terre Haute, Ind., 1978, Broome St. Gallery, N.Y.C., 1990, 92, 96, 2001, Nat. Acad. Mus., 1995-2003, Galeria Tonalli, Mexico City, 1997, Anita Shapolski Gallery, 1997, Silvermine Galleries, Conn., 1998, others; works include mosaic murals at Versaile Hotel, Miami Beach, Fla., mosaics on Grace Line's SS Santa Paula, 1957, Facade of Aruba (Netherlands Antilles) Carib Hotel, 1958, mosaic murals in Pub. Sch. 28, N.Y.C., 1958, stained glass Robin Internat. Cinarama, 1962, Cluett Shirt Group, Atlanta, 1990; editor: Modern Mosaic Techniques, 1967; author articles in encys. and mags; inventor laminated stained glass. Sgt. inf. U.S. Army, 1944—46, ETO. Mem.: Fine Arts Fedn. N.Y. (v.p. 2002, pres. 2003), Nat. Soc. Mural Painters (pres. 1996—2000), N.Y. Artists Equity Assn. (pres. 1987—89). Baptist. Home: Stewart Studio 31 E 7th St New York NY 10003-8001

STEWART, JACK M. management consulting firm executive; b. Oneida, N.Y., Feb. 20, 1926; s. E. Jerome and Frieda Freeman (Holz) S.; m. Tudy Newman Stewart, June 26, 1955; children: Eileen Jan Guttman, Leslie Ann, Ralph Edward. BME, Syracuse U., 1946, MSIE, 1950. cert. mgmt. cons., cert. profl. material handling, cert. profl. material mgmt.; registered profl. engr. Rsch. engr. Martin-Marietta Co. (name now Lockheed-Martin), Balt., 1946-47; chief/indsl. engr. Syracuse (N.Y.) Ornamental Co., Inc., 1947-49; instr. Syracuse U., N.Y., 1949-50; asst. mgr. mfr. engring. General Electric Co., Syracuse & Auburn, N.Y., 1950-53; v.p. Wheeler Associates, Inc., Cleve., 1953-57; pres. Research for Industry, Inc., Cleve., 1960-88, Indsl. Technol. Assocs., Inc., Cleve., 1957--. Panel of Arbitrators Am. Arbitration Assoc., N.Y.C., 1986-2001. Contbr. numerous articles to profl. jours. Precinct Committeeman and mem. cen. com. Republican Party, Pepper Pike, Ohio, 1970-; pres. Pepper Pike Civic League, 1990-92. Mem. Internat. Material Mgmt. Soc., Am. Foundrymen's Soc., Am. Defense Preparedness Assoc., Solon (Ohio) C. of C., Chagrin Valley Shrine Club, Al Koran Temple, Interstate Scottish Rite 32 Club of Cleve. (pres. 1975-76), Ancient Accepted Scottish Rite, Forest City Lodge (Free & Accepted Masons), Am. Soc. Mech. Engrs., Inst. Packaging Profl., Inst. Mgmt. Cons. (pres.-N.E. Ohio, 1988-91), Coll. of Firm Prins., Syracuse U. Alumni Assn. (chmn. rep. program N.E. Ohio, Nat. v.p. 1964, Alumnus of Yr., 1973, Outstanding Alumni Rep. 1991). Republican. Avocations: organization work, gardening, biking, golf. Office: Indsl Tech Assocs 28326 Belcourt Rd Cleveland OH 44124-5622 E-mail: tns.jms@juno.com., ita12@juno.com.

STEWART, JAMES BREWER, historian, writer, college administrator; b. Cleve., Aug. 8, 1940; s. Richard Henry and Marion Elizabeth (Brewer) S.; m. Dorothy Ann Carlson; children: Rebecca Ann, Jennifer Lynn. BA, Dartmouth Coll., 1962; PhD, Case Western Res. U., 1968. Asst. prof. history Carroll Coll., Waukesha, Wis., 1968-69, Macalester Coll., St. Paul, 1969-79, James Wallace prof. history, 1979—, provost, 1986-89. Cons. Am. Coun. of Learned Socs., N.Y.C., 1988-92. Author: Joshua R. Giddings & the Tactics of Radical Politics, 1970, Holy Warriors: Abolitionists & Slavery, 1976, rev. editon 1997, Liberty's Hero: Wendell Phillips, 1986 (Best Biography award, Soc. Midland Authors 1986), William Lloyd Garrison and the Challenge of Emmancipation, 1992, To Heal the Scourge of Prejudice: The Life and Writings of Hosea Easton, 1999, Race and the Construction of the Republican State, 2000. Rsch. fellow NEH, 1973, Am. Coun. Learned Socs., 1984. Mem. Am. Hist. Assn., Orgn. Am. Historians (nom. com. 1988-92), Soc. Historians of the Early Republic (exec. com. 1987-94, editl. bd. 1999—, pres.-elect 2003—), Phi Beta Kappa. Avocations: camping, gardening, furniture restoration. Home: 1924 Princeton Ave Saint Paul MN 55105-1523 Office: Macalester Coll Dept Of History Saint Paul MN 55105 E-mail: stewart@macalester.edu.

STEWART, JAMES GATHINGS, insurance company executive; b. Fort Wayne, Ind., Oct. 5, 1942; s. Gathings and Mary (Sieber) S.; children: John, David, Mitchell, Rebecca. BA, DePauw U., 1964; MAS., U. Mich., 1965. Various fin. positions Conn. Gen. Life Ins. Co., Hartford, Conn., 1966-77, v.p., 1977-82; exec. v.p., CFO CIGNA Corp., Phila., 1983—. Fellow Soc. Actuaries; mem. Am. Acad. Actuaries Republican. Office: Cigna Corp 1 Liberty Pl PO Box 7716 1650 Market St Philadelphia PA 19192

STEWART, JAMES IAN, agricultural water scientist, cropping system developer, consultant; b. San Diego, Jan. 9, 1928; s. Castle Elmore and Myrtle Catherine (Hasty) S.; m. Robbie Nell Oliver, Mar. 23, 1975; children: Virginia Lane Stewart Carton, Ian Castle Stewart, Kevin Scott Overby. BSc, U. Calif., Berkeley, 1950; PhD, U. Calif., Davis, 1972. Farm advisor Agrl. Extension Svc., U. Calif., Stockton and Merced, 1950-61; extension expert Irrigation, FAO UN, Nicosia, Cyprus, 1962-66; assoc. rsch. water scientist U. Calif., Davis, 1966-77; supervisory soil scientist USDA/Office for Internat. Cooperation and Devel., Nairobi, Kenya, 1977-83; team leader, agrometeorologist USAID/Kenya Mission, 1977-83; founder, pres. Found. for World Hunger Alleviation Through Response Farming (WHARF), Davis, 1984—. Cons. sustainable agrl. devel. and resource mgmt. for ecol. balance AID, USDA, World Bank, FAO/UNDP, 37 countries of Ams., Europe, Asia, Africa, Australia, 1965—; sci. convocations, 17 internat. countries, 1969—. Author: Response Farming in Rainfed Agriculture, 1988; creator (computer programs) Wharf, Wharfdat, 1993; contbr. numerous articles to profl. jours. Mem. Internat. Soil Sci. Soc., World Assn. Soil and Water Conservation, Internat. Com. for Irrigation and Drainage (life, U.S. com.), Indian Soc. Dryland Agr. (life), Sigma Xi, Phi Delta Theta. Achievements include research in crop water requirements; soil water extraction capabilities of crops; impacts of water deficits in different growth periods; relations between crop yeild and water evapotranspired; development of FAO world standard linear and weighted growth stage models for estimating crop yields from actual evapotranspiration; four-growth-period linear model est. crop water requirements; response farming methodology for design of dryland cropping systems based on historical rels. between season rainfall onset dates and subsequent season rainfall behavior; seasonal flexibility in dryland cropping sys. mgmt. based on realtime rainfall season date of onset defined to meet crop establishment requirements. Home: 640 Portsmouth Ave Davis CA 95616-2738 Office: World Hunger Allev Through Response Farming PO Box 1158 Davis CA 95617-1158 Office Phone: 530-753-1422. Personal E-mail: wharf@cal.net. Business E-Mail: ian@responsefarming.org.

STEWART, JAMES MALCOM, lawyer; b. Aberdeen, Wash., May 8, 1915; s. Malcolm M. and Ethel Lucille (Hinman) S.; m. Dorothy Vera Gilardi, Sept. 16, 1945; children: Barbara Jane, Robert Bruce, William James. BA, U. Wash., 1939, JD, 1941. Bar: Wash., 1941, U.S. Dist. Ct. (we. dist.) Wash., 1998, U.S. Supreme Ct., 1948. Dep. prosecuting atty. Grays Harbor County, Wash., 1945-48; pvt. practice Montesano, Wash., 1952-99. Author: 90 Day Naval Wonder, 2002. Pres., dir. Gray Harbor Coll. Found., Aberdeen, 1955-95; bd. dirs. St. Joseph Hosp., Aberdeen, 1972-87; organizer Gray Harbor Cmty. Found., Aberdeen, 1993. Lt. USNR, 1942-45, PTO, admirality officer, 1945-46, lt. comdr., 1950-52, Korea, ret. Decorated 16 Battle Stars, 2 Silver Stars, Gold Star. Mem. Am. Judicature Soc., Wash. State Bar Assn. (hon.; 50 Yr. award 1991), Gray Harbor Bar Assn. (pres. 1953), Aberdeen Pioneers Assn. (pres., dir. 1948-98), Lions (Melvin Jones award 1997), Elks, Sigma Nu, Phi Delta Phi. Republican. Episcopalian. Avocations: tree farming, hiking, horseback riding, tennis. Home: 711 3rd St N # D Montesano WA 98563-1625

STEWART, JAMES MICHAEL, engineer; b. Woodbury, NJ, Feb. 5, 1958; s. Frankin Andrew and Dorothy Mae Stewart; children: Kathleen Elizabeth, Matthew Baraw. AAS, U. Alaska, 1990; BA, Colo. State U., 1993, MSc, 1994; M of pub. health, U. No. Colo., 1999. Corp. indsl. engr. Con Agra Red Meat Co., Greeley, Colo., 1994—95; facility safety mgr. Manfort Inc., Greeley, 1995—97; complex sfety mgr. Longmart Food, 1992—98; corp. ergonomist US West, Denver, 1998—2000; dir. R&D, sr. ergonomist ESP/Office Safe, 2000—. Cw2 U.S. Army, 1987—94. Cath. Home: 2218 Arikaree Ct Loveland CO 80538

STEWART, JAMES MONTGOMERY, retired bank executive; b. Detroit, May 31, 1939; s. Albert Edwin and Dagny Winter (Jensen) S.; m. Kathleen Williams, Sept. 27, 1940; children— Laura, Wendy, Kathleen BBA, U. Mich., 1962, MBA, 1963. Asst. sec. Irving Trust Co., N.Y.C., 1966-68, asst. v.p., 1968-70, v.p., 1970-81, sr. v.p., 1981-86; regional gen. mgr. Copenhagen Handelsbank, 1986-90; gen. mgr. Danske Bank, N.Y.C., 1990—2001, sr. advisor, 2002—04, ret., 2004. Trustee, treas. Am. Scandinavian Found. Mem. Anglers, Links Club, Country Club New Canaan. Republican. Avocations: fishing, golf, jazz. Home: 130 Ramhorne Rd New Canaan CT 06840-3007

STEWART, JANE, psychology educator; b. Ottawa, Ont., Can., Apr. 19, 1934; d. Daniel Wallace and Jessie Stewart; m. Dalbir Bindra, Aug. 5, 1959 (dec. 1981). BA with honours, Queen's U., Kingston, Ont., 1956; PhD, U. London, 1959; DSc (hon.), Queen's U., 1992. Sr. rsch. biologist Averst Labs., Montreal, Que., 1959-63; part-time instr. psychology Sir George, Montreal, 1962-63; assoc. prof. psychology Williams U., Montreal, 1963-69; prof., chmn. psychology SGW Univ. (now Concordia U.), Montreal, 1969-75; prof. psychology Concordia U., Montreal, 1975—. Dir. Ctr. for Studies in Behavioral Neurobiology, Concordia U., Montreal, 1990-97. Fellow: APA, AAAS, Can. Psychol. Assn., Royal Soc. Can.; mem.: NY Acad. Sci., Soc. for Neurosci. Office: Concordia Univ 7141 Sherbrooke St W Montreal QC Canada H4B 1R6

STEWART, JANE, former Canadian government minister; b. Brantford, Ont., Can., Apr. 25, 1955; d. Robert Nixon; 2 sons. BS with honors, Trent U., 1978. Chair Nat. Liberal Caucus, 1994-96; Human Resources profl., to 1994; min. nat. revenue Govt. of Can., 1996-97, min. Indian Affairs and No. Devel., 1997-99, min. Human Resources devel., 1999—2003. Chair Econ. Union, 2002—. Liberal Party Can. Office: 1 Market St N3T6C8 Brantford ON Canada E-mail: stewaj@parl.gc.ca.

STEWART, JANICE MAE, federal judge; b. Medford, Oreg., Feb. 13, 1951; d. Glenn Logan and Eathel Mae (Jones) S.; m. F. Gordon Allen III, Aug. 10, 1975; children: Benjamin Stewart, Rebecca Mae. AB in Econs., Stanford U., 1972; JD, U. Chgo., 1975. Bar: Ill. 1976, Oreg. 1977, U.S. Dist. Ct. Oreg. 1977, U.S. Ct. Appeals (9th cir.) 1978. Assoc. Winston & Strawn, Chgo., 1975-76, McEwen, Gisvold, Rankin & Stewart, Portland, Oreg., 1976-81, ptnr., 1981-93; U.S. Magistrate Judge Portland, 1993—. Mem. Multonomah County Profl. Responsbility Com., Portland, 1979-82, Oreg. Profl. Responsibility Bd., 1982-85, Oreg. State Bar Practice and Procedure Com., 1985-88, Profl. Liability Fund Def. Panel, Portland, 1985-93, Multnomah County Jud. Selection Com., 1985-88, Oreg. State Bar Professionalism Com., 1989-91, Oreg. State Bar Fed. Practice and Procedure Com., 1996-99, 2004-, Coun. Ct. Procedures, 1991-93, lawyer rep. 9th Cir. Jud. Conf., 1990-93, Multnomah County Professionalism Com., 1997-2000. Mem. ABA, Am. Arbitration Assn. (arbitrator 1990-93), Oreg. Bar Assn., Multnomah County Bar Assn. (dir. 1990-93), Phi Beta Kappa. Democrat. Office: 1027 US Courthouse 1000 SW 3rd Ave Portland OR 97204-2930 Office Phone: 503-326-8260.

STEWART, JEFFREY VINCENT, III, information technology educator; b. Asmara, Ethiopia, Apr. 27, 1970; s. Jeffrey Vincent Jr. and Sandra Wilkie Stewart; m. Laura Ann Leslie, Mar. 9, 1996. BS, Western Carolina U., 1992; MA, U. Ala., 1994, PhD, 2001. Cert. athletic trainer. Athletic trainer Atlanta Braves, 1995; head athletic trainer Mercer U., Macon, Ga., 1995—99; asst. prof. info. tech. Macon State Coll., 2001—, interim chair divsn. info. tech., 2003—. Mem. exec. com. SIG-ITE, 2002—. Bd. dirs. Am. Cancer Soc., Macon, 2002—04. Named Outstanding Young Man of Am., 1998. Mem.: Nat. Athletic Trainers Assn. (com. 1998—, Multimedia Software award 2000), Assn. Computing Machinery (exec. com. 2001—), Kappa Delta Epsilon. Office: Macon State Coll 100 College Station Dr Macon GA 31206 E-mail: jstewart@mail.maconstate.edu.

STEWART, JOAN HINDE, academic administrator; b. N.Y.C., Aug. 11, 1944; d. Wade and Dorothy (Ronning) H.; m. Philip Robert Stewart, Jan. 31, 1970; children: Anna Faye, Justin. Student, Université Laval Summer Sch, Quebec, 1963, Middlebury Coll. Summer Sch., 1964-65; BA summa cum laude, St. Joseph's Coll., 1965; student, Salzburg Summer Sch., Austria, 1966; MPhil, Yale U., 1969, PhD, 1970. Tchg. assoc. French Yale U., New Haven, 1967—69, acting instr. French, 1969—70; instr. French Wellseley (Mass.) Coll., 1970—71, asst. prof. French, 1971—72, N.C. State U., Raleigh, 1973—77, assoc. prof. French, 1977—81, prof. French, 1981—99, asst. head dept. fgn. langs. and lits., 1978—82, asst. dean rsch. and grad. programs, 1983—85, acting head dept. fgn. langs. and lits., 1984—85, head dept. fgn. langs. and lit., 1985—97; prof., dean liberal arts U. S.C., 1999—2003; pres., prof. French Hamilton Coll., Clinton, NY, 2003—. Author: The Novels of Mme Riccoboni, 1976, Colette, 1983, 1996, Gynographs: French Novels by Women of the Late Eighteenth Century, 1993; editor: Mme Riccoboni's Lettres de Mistriss Fanni Butlerd, 1979; co-editor: Isabelle de Charrière's Lettres de Mistriss Henley, 1993, Marie Riccoboni's Histoire d'Ernestine, 1998. Chmn. N.C. Humanities Coun., 1988-89. Fellow Camargo Found., Cassis, France, 1979, Nat. Humanities Ctr., 1982-83, (sr.) ctr. for humanities Wesleyan U., 1990; NEH summer seminar fellowship, Princeton U., 1980; NEH fellowship Coll. Tchrs. and Ind. Scholars, 1990-91, 1994-95; fellow Ctr. d'Etude du XVIII Siecle, U. Paul Valery, Montpellier, France, 1995, Liguria Study Ctr. for the Arts and Scis., Bogliasco, Italy, 1997, Beinecke Rare Book and Manuscript Libr., Yale U., 1997; stipend younger humanists NEH, 1973; travel grantee ACLS, 1983; travel to collections grantee NEH, 1984; vis. scholar European Humanities Rsch. Ctr., Oxford U., 1995. Mem. AAUP, MLA, Am. Assn. Tchrs. French.

STEWART, JOANNE, retired director; b. Vancouver, Wash., Mar. 10, 1944; d. Edward Charles and Claudine Marie Spencer; m. William Lemley Stewart, Sept. 2, 1966 (dec. June 1983); children: Amy Diane Stemple, Nicholas William. BS, Wash. State U., 1966, MA, 1973. Cert. tchr., Mont., Idaho, Wash., Calif. Tchr. foods Seaside High Sch., Monterey, Calif., 1966-67; tchr. home econs. Marysville (Wash.) High Sch., 1967-68, Palouse (Wash.) High Sch., 1968-73, Ennis (Mont.) High Sch., 1973-76, Genesee (Idaho) High Sch., 1976-77; instr. young family Missoula (Mont.) County High Sch., 1983-84; tchr. home econs. Woodman Sch., Lolo, Mont., 1985-86; travel cons. Travel Masters, Missoula, 1984-87; ticketing mgr. Blue Caboose Travel, Missoula, 1987-91; tchr. family and consumer scis. Victor (Mont.) High Sch., 1991-2001; dir. Victor 21st Century Learning Ctr., 2001—04, After Sch. Learning Ctr. Project dir. sch.-to-work implementation Victor Sch. Reaching Out for Positive Ednl. Success (ROPES), 1996—2002, project dir. Op. Green Thumb, gender equity Carl Perkins grant, 1997—98. Co-pres. Lolo PTO, 1980-81; v.p. Lolo Community Ctr., 1981; sec. Lolo Mosquito Control Bd., 1988—; mem. telecommunications com. Conrad Burns & Gov. Racicot; sec. state supt. edn. task force on vocat. edn., 1995-96; coord. Health Rocks!, Nat. 4-H Program, 2000-01. Marysville Edn. Assn. scholar, 1962, Future Homemakers Am. scholar, 1962. Mem. AAUW (sec. 1986, program chmn. 1987), Forestry Triangle (pres. 1981, editor cookbook 1982), Washington State Future Homemakers Am. (hon. mem.), Am. Family and Consumer Scis. Assn., Mont. Family and Consumer Scis. Assn. (bylaws chair 1994, pres. elect 1995-96, pres. 1996-97, Profl. of Yr. 1997), Mont. Vocat. Tchrs. Assn. (returning Rookie of Yr. 1992, Am. Federated Tchrs., Mont. Vocat. Family and Consumer Scis. Tchrs. (v.p. 1993-94, pres. 1994-95, Tchr. of Yr. 1998). Republican. Methodist. Avocations: homemaking, swimming. Home: 1200 Lakeside Dr Lolo MT 59847-9705

STEWART, JOHN EDWARD, psychologist, researcher; AB, U. NC, 1966; PhD, U. Ga., 1973. Sr. rsch. psychologist Army Rsch. Inst., Fort Rucker, Ala., 1989—; asst. prof. Mercyhurst Coll., Erie, Pa., 1973—79; rsch. psychologist Army Rsch. Inst., Alexandria, Va., 1985—89, Air Force Rsch. Lab., Mesa, Ariz., 1984—85; rsch. analyst State of Ariz., Phoenix, 1980—84. Ari liaison officer Asst. Sec. Army (L&T), Arlington, Va., 2002—03; adj. faculty Troy State U., Dothan, Ala., 1990—98. Contbr. articles to prof. jours. Recipient R & D Achievement award, U.S. Army, 2002. Mem.: S.E. Psychological Assn., Am. Psychological Soc., Human Factors and Ergonomics Soc. Office: Army Rsch Inst Building 5100 Fort Rucker AL 36362-5354

STEWART, JOHN HARGER, music educator; b. Cleve., Mar. 31, 1940; s. Cecil Tooker and Marian (Harger) S.; m. Julia Wallace, Aug. 14, 1977; children: Barbara, Cecily Bronwen. BA, Yale U., 1962; MA, Brown U., 1972; cert., New Eng. Conservatory, 1965. With various operas including Santa Fe Opera, N.Y.C. Opera, Met. Opera, U.S. and Europe, 1965—; lectr. Mt. Holyoke Coll., South Hadley, Mass., 1988-90; dir. vocal activities Washington U., St. Louis, 1990—, dir. Friends of Music. Office: Dept Music Washington U Campus Box 1032 One Brookings Dr Saint Louis MO 63130-4899 Office Phone: 314-935-5597. E-mail: jstewart@wustl.edu.

STEWART, JOHN LINCOLN, university administrator; b. Alton, Ill., Jan. 24, 1917; s. Frederick William and Hilda (Denovan) S.; m. Joan Elsdon Guthridge, Sept. 23 1939 (div. 1964); children: Leslie Cythera Stewart Chalmers, Ann Guthridge Stewart Nutt; m. Ruth Peabody Quinn, July 11, 1964; stepchildren: Geoffrey Cornelius Quinn, Andrew Dean Quinn. AB, Denison U., 1938, ArtsD (hon.), 1964; MA, Ohio State U., 1939, PhD, 1947. From tchg. asst. to instr. Ohio Sate U., Columbus, 1939-47; instr. UCLA, 1947-49; from asst. prof. to prof. English Dartmouth Coll., Hanover, N.H., 1949-64; prof. Lit. U. Calif., San Diego, 1964-87, provost John Muir Coll., 1965-87. Author: Exposition for Science and Technical Students, 1950, The Essay, 1952, John Crowe Ransom, 1962, The Burden of Time, 1965; (with others) Horizons Circled, 1974, Ernst Krenek, 1990; contbr. articles to profl. jours. Assoc. dir. Hopkins Ctr. for Arts, 1961-64; dir. Mandeville Ctr. for Arts, 1974-76; mem. Dartmouth Community Symphony Orch., 1949-58; trustee Kinhaven Music Sch., 1960-64, Fla. West Coast Symphony, 1958, Oakland Cmty. Orch., 1997-2002; bd. dirs. Theater and Arts Found. San Diego County, 1970; pres. La Jolla (Calif.) Friends Sch. Music, 1971-73, Friends of Music, U. Calif., San Diego. Served with Aus, 1942-45. Howard Found. fellow, 1953-54, Dartmouth Coll. fellow, 1962-63. Democrat. Avocation: performer with music ensembles. Home: 2361 E 29th St Oakland CA 94606-3511

STEWART, JOHN MILLER, behavioral scientist, psychobiologist, educator; b. Bradford, Pa., Sept. 27, 1938; s. James A. and Virginia G. (Essington) S.; m. Sharon Stewart, Sept. 7, 1963; 1 child, David Dylan. Student, U. Birmingham, Eng., 1969; PhD in Psychobiology, Bowling Green State U., 1971. NIMH postdoctoral fellow Jackson Lab., Bar Harbor, Maine, 1971-75; staff fellow NIMH, Bethesda, Md., 1975-77; clin. asst. prof. U. Md., Balt., 1978-79; co-founder, chief rsch. and evaluation Regional Inst. for Children, Rockville, Md., 1980-88; clin. assoc. prof. Georgetown U., Washington, 1983-92; assoc. faculty Johns Hopkins U., Balt., 1986-92; prof., chair dept. psychology Northland Coll., Ashland, Wis., 1992—, dir. Wolf Rsch. Team, 1992—. Mem. Bd. Sci. Integrity, State of Md., Balt., 1990-92, mem. Instnl. Rev. Bd., 1986-92; mem. Wolf Monitoring Team, State of Wis., Madison, 1992-2002. Contbr. chpts. to books, numerous articles to sci. jours. Pres. bd. dirs. Frederick County Librs., Frederick, Md., 1982-88, New Horizons North, Ashland, 1993-98, Chequameque Humane Assn., Ashland, 2001—; trustee Washburn (Wis.) Edn. Found., 1998—; scoutmaster Boy Scouts Am. Fellow NCI, NSF, NICHD, NATO, 1963-71; grantee W.T. Grant Found., NIMH, NICHD, NATO, 1968-80. Fellow Internat. Soc. for Rsch. on Aggression (charter); mem. APA, Animal Behavior Soc. Achievements include being recognized expert in the development of social behavior in domestic dogs and wolves in the wild. Home: 810 Washington Ave Washburn WI 54891-9488 Office Phone: 715-682-1284. E-mail: jstewart@ncis.net., jstewart@northland.edu.

STEWART, JOHN MURRAY, retired bank executive; b. Summit, N.J., Apr. 2, 1943; s. Robert John Stewart and Mary Catherine Yoder; m. Sandra Meyers Frazier, 1966 (div. 1997); children: Jennifer Bricar Crone, Catherine Dorothy Lochead; m. Rebecca Marie Mellen, July 10, 1998. BA, U. Va., 1965; MBA, NYU, 1983. Trust officer, v.p. Bankers Trust Co., N.Y.C., 1965-82, Morgan Guaranty Trust Co., N.Y.C., 1982-83; mgr., pres., dir. Morgan Trust Co. Fla., Palm Beach, 1983-89; pres., dir. Bankers Trust Co. Fla., 1989-93; founder, pres. pvt. capital group SunTrust Bank, Orlando, Fla., 1993-96; pres., dir. Harris Trust/Bank of Montreal, West Palm Beach, 1996—2001, Fla. Trust Co., Ft. Lauderdale, Fla., 2002—03. Campaign chmn. Palm Beach Cmty. Chest, 1985, 1986; mem. exec. com. Palm Beach County Local Initiatives Support Corp.; vestryman Bethesda By the Sea Ch., Palm Beach, 1986—89, 1992—94, treas., 1986—87, Cathedral Ch. of St. Luke, Orlando, 1996; bd. dirs. Orlando Opera Co., 1994—96, Palm Beach Opera Co., 1996—2001. Mem. Fla. Bankers Assn. (chmn. trust bus. devel. com. 1989, planning commn., chmn. trust legis. com. 1990), N.Y. State Bankers Assn. (mem. trust bus. devel. com. 1978-82), N.Y. Yacht Club (N.Y.C.), St. Petersburg Yacht Club, Monmouth Boat Club (Red Bank, N.J.), SAR (pres. Palm Beach chpt. 1997, 98). Home: 621 Riviera Isle Dr Fort Lauderdale FL 33301 E-mail: uva1965@msn.com.

STEWART, JOHN TODD, economist, consultant; AB, Stanford U., 1961; MA, Tufts U., 1962, MALD, 1970. With Am. Fgn. Svc., 1962-98; U.S. amb. to Republic of Moldova, 1995-98; dep. head U.S. diplomatic missions to Can., Costa Rica and Jamaica; dir. office maritime and land transport Dept. of State, Washington; dir. GATT affairs Pres.'s Spl. Rep. for Trade Negotiations; dep. dir. Inst. Internat. Econs., Washington, 1998—2002; diplomat-in-residence Am. U., 2003—04. Vis. fellow Inst. Internat. Econs., 2002—. Home and Office: po bOX 3200 Sun Valley ID 83353 E-mail: stewartconsult@aol.com.

STEWART, JOHN WRAY BLACK, college dean; b. Coleraine, Northern Ireland, Jan. 16, 1936; s. John Wray and Margaret Reid (Black) S.; m. Felicity Ann Patricia Poole, Aug. 7, 1965; children: J.W. Matthew, Hannah Louise. BSc with honors, Queen's U., Belfast, Northern Ireland, 1958, BSA with honors, 1959, PhD, 1963, DSc, 1988. Registered profl. agrologist. Sci. officer chem. rsch. divsn. Ministry of Agr., Belfast, 1959-64; asst. prof. soil sci. dept. U. Sask., Saskatoon, Canada, 1966-71, assoc. prof., 1971-76, prof., 1976-81, dir. Sask. Inst. Pedology, 1981-89, dean Coll. Agr., 1989-99, prof. emeritus, 1999—, dean emeritus, 1999—, interim dir. Inter-Am. Inst. for Global Change Rsch., 2002. Tech. expert, cons. FAO/IAEA, U.N.D.P., Vienna, 1971, Vienna, 1974—75; mem. program com. Can. Global Change, 1985—98; sec.-gen. Sci. Com. on Problems of Environ., Paris, 1988—92, pres., 1992—95, editor-in-chief, 1999—; cons. UNESCO, Paris, 1990; trustee Internat. Inst. Tropical Agr., Nigeria, 1991—97; chair sci. adv. com. Inter-Am. Inst. for Global Change Rsch., 1994—2001. Contbr. articles to profl. publs., chapters to books. Fellow Can. Soc. Soil Sci., Berlin Inst. Advanced Study, Am. Soc. Agronomy, Soil Sci. Soc. Am., Agrl. Inst. Can.; mem. Brit. Soc. Soil Sci., Internat. Soc. Soil Sci. Avocations: golf, tennis. E-mail: Jwbstew@island.net.

STEWART, JON (JONATHAN STEWART LEIBOWITZ), comedian, actor; b. N.Y.C., Nov. 28, 1962; m. Tracy McShane, 2000. BS in Psychology, Coll. William and Mary, 1984. Actor: (TV films) Since You've Been Gone, 1998; (films) Mixed Nuts, 1994, Wishful Thinking, 1997, Half Baked, 1998, The Faculty, 1998, Playing by Heart, 1998, Big Daddy, 1999, The Office Party, 2000, Jay and Silent Bob Strike Back, 2001, Death to Smoochy, 2002; host: (TV series) Short Attention Span Theater, 1989; You Wrote It, You Watch It, 1992; The Daily Show, 1999—; (TV Special) The Daily Show with Jon Stewart: Indecision 2000, 2000 (Emmy award, 2001); exec. prodr., writer: (TV series) The Daily Show, 1996—; writer, host The Jon Stewart Show, 1993; writer (TV series) The Sweet Life, 1989. Office: Lee Stollman/James Dixon William Morris Agency One William Morris Place Beverly Hills CA 90212*

STEWART, JONATHAN TAYLOR, psychiatrist, educator; b. Bethpage, N.Y., Mar. 15, 1956; s. Allen Theodore and Vivian (Dreiblatt) S.; m. Linda Sue Irvin, Oct. 27, 1984; children: Jacob Zachary, Aaron Joshua. BA with honors, Rollins Coll., 1976; MD, U. South Fla., 1979. Diplomate Am. Bd. Psychiatry and Neurology, Geriatric Psychiatry, Nat. Bd. Med. Examiners. Resident in psychiatry U. Fla. Coll. Medicine, Gainesville, 1979-83, assoc. prof. psychiatry, 1983-94; asst. chief psychiatry VA Med. Ctr., Gainesville, 1987-94; prof. psychiatry U So. Fla. Coll. Medicine, 1994—; chief geropsychiatry sect. Bay Pines (Fla.) VA Med. Ctr., 1994—. Contbr. articles to profl. jours., 1985—. Mem. Head Injury Adv. Coun. State of Fla., 1985-90. Fellow: Am. Geriatrics Soc., Am. Psychiat. Assn. (disting. fellow); mem.: Fla. Geriatrics Soc., Fla. Psychiat. Soc. Jewish. Avocations: cooking, cycling, skin diving, traveling. flying. Office: VA Med Ctr Psychiatry Service 116A Bay Pines FL 33744

STEWART, JOSEPH TURNER, JR., retired pharmaceutical company executive; b. N.Y.C., Apr. 30, 1929; s. Joseph Turner and Edna (Pride) S.; m. Carol Graham, Aug. 7, 1954; children: Lisa D., Alison D. BS with honors, U.S. Mcht. Marine Acad., 1951; MBA, Harvard U., 1954. Systems analyst Warner Lambert Co., Morris Plains, N.J., 1954-56, budget dir. internat., 1956-60, asst. div. controller consumer products group, 1960-62, div. controller group, 1962-66; dir. adminstrn. and fin. Proprietary Drug div. Warner Lamber Co., 1966; dir. Lactona Products div. Warner Lamber Co., 1967; controller Beech-Nut subs. Squibb Corp., N.Y.C., 1968, v.p. fin., 1968-71, v.p. planning, corp. staff parent corp., 1971-79, v.p. fin. and planning parent co., 1979-82, sr. v.p. corporate affairs parent co., 1982-89; also bd. dirs.; cons. Johnson & Johnson, 1990-98. Bd. dirs. Gen. Am. Investment Corp. 1987-. Trustee Tax Found., 1985-89; commr. N.J. State Commn. on Income and Expenditures, 1985-88; mem. adv. com. Grad. Sch. Indsl. Adminstrn., Carnegie Mellon U., 1986-91; trustee New Sch. for Social Rsch., 1990-98, U. Medicine and Dentistry of N.J. Found., 1989—; bd. dirs. Liposome Co., 1995-2000; vis. coun. Marine Biol. Lab., 1995—; bd. advisors U.S. Mcht. Marine Acad., 2002—. John Hay Whitney Opportunity fellow, 1952-54. Mem.: Harvard (N.Y.C.). E-mail: kingpin497@aol.com.

STEWART, KENT KALLAM, analytical biochemistry educator; b. Omaha, Sept. 5, 1934; s. George Franklin and Grace S.; m. Margaret Reiber, June 10, 1956; children: Elizabeth, Cynthia, Richard, Robert. Student, U. Chgo., 1951-53; AB, U. Calif., Berkeley, 1956; PhD, Fla. State U., 1965. Guest investigator Rockefeller U., N.Y.C., 1965-67, research assoc., 1967-68, asst. prof., 1968-69; research chemist U.S. Dept. Agr., Beltsville, Md., 1970-75, lab. chief Nutrient Composition Lab., 1975-82; prof., head dept. food sci. and tech. Va. Poly. Inst. and State U., Blacksburg, 1982-85, prof. biochemistry, anaerobic microbiology, food sci./tech., 1985—96, prof. emeritus of biochemistry; adj. prof. dept. chemistry and biochemistry U. Tex., Austin, 1996—. Editor Jour. Food Composition and Analysis, 1987-97, also 3 books; contbr. articles to profl. jours., co-author book; patentee in field. Capt. USMCR, 1956-59. Fellow Inst. Food Technologist, AAAS; mem. Am. Chem. Soc. Home: 3900 Glengarry Dr Austin TX 78731-3812 Office: Dept Chemistry and Biochemistry Mail Code A5300 1 University Sta U Tex Austin TX 78712 E-mail: kkstewart@mail.utexas.edu.

STEWART, KIRK T. public relations executive; b. 1951; BA in polit. sci., U. So. Calif., 1973; MA in pub. rels./journalism, 1976. Account exec. Burson-Marsteller, 1976—79; pub. affairs dir. Info. Svcs. Dir. TRW, 1979—81; group supr. Manning Selvage & Lee, 1981—82, v.p., 1982—83, exec. v.p., 1983—84; exec. v.p., mng. dir. Manning Selvage & Lee/L.A., Calif., 1984—89; pres. Manning, Selvage & Lee Inc., N.Y.C., 1989—91, pres., CEO, 1992; chmn., CEO Manning, Selvage & Lee, Inc., N.Y.C., 1993—97; v.p. corp. comms. Nike Inc., Beaverton, Oreg., 1997—. Office: Nike Inc 1 Bowerman Dr Beaverton OR 97005-6453

STEWART, KORDELL, professional football player; b. New Orleans, La., Oct. 16, 1972; Student, U. Colo. Quarterback Pitts. Steelers, 1995—2003, Chgo. Bears, 2003—04. Achievements include playing in Super Bowl XXX, 1995; AFC championship game, 1995, 97.

STEWART, LUCILLE MARIE, retired special education educator; b. Pitts., Feb. 24; d. William H. and Edna (Hoffman) S. BEd, Duquesne U.; MEd, U. Pitts.; postgrad., Columbia U., U. Calif., Calif. State U. Cert. elem. and secondary tchr., spl. edn. tchr., supr., adminstr. Tchr., group leader mentally retarded Ednl. Alliance, N.Y.C., 1950—53; tchr. Lincoln (Ill.) State Sch., 1953; tchr., program leader, sec. Edn. Alliance, N.Y.C., 1954 58; tchr. mentally retarded Ramapo Ctrl. Sch. Dist., Spring Valley, N.Y., 1958-60, tchr. seriously emotionally disturbed, 1960-64, supr. presch. program for educationally disadvantaged, 1965-67; program dir. Pomona (N.Y.) Camp for Retarded, summers 1960-63; tchr. mentally retarded Stockton Sch., San Diego, 1964-65; tchr. mentally retarded sch. Cathedral City Sch., 1967-78; program specialist spl. edn. Palm Springs (Calif.) Unified Sch. Dist., 1978-95; prin. elem. summer schs. Palm Springs (Calif.) Unified Sch. Dist., 1971-72; tchr. elem. mentally retarded sch. Palm Springs (Calif.) Unified; prin.-tchr. Summer Extended Sch. for Spl. Students, summer 1979-99. Exec. com. U. Calif. Extension, area adv. com.; spl. edn. surrogate parent Palm Springs Unified Sch. Dist. Mem. NEA, AAUW, ASCD, Calif. Adminstrs. Spl. Edn. (desert cmty. mental health childrens com.), Coun. Exceptional Children (adminstrn. divsn., early childhood-learning handicap divsns.), Am. Assn. Childhood Edn., Autism Soc., Coachella Valley, Learning Disabilities Assn., Creative Desert, Desert Theater League, Alpha Kappa Alpha, Phi Delta Kappa, Delta Kappa Gamma.

STEWART, MAC A. educator; b. Forsyth, Ga., July 7, 1942; s. Alonzo and Zillia (Watson) S.; m. Tena Clemons, June 4, 1967; children: Bruce Kifle, Justin Che. BA, Morehouse Coll., 1963; MA, Atlanta U., 1965; PhD, Ohio State U., 1973. Lic. psychologist, Ohio. Tchr., counselor Jasper County Tng. Sch., Monticello, Ga., 1963—64; tchr. Crispus Attucks High Sch., Indpls., 1965-66; dir. student fin. aid Morehouse Coll., Atlanta, 1966-70, dir. upward bound, 1967-70; dir. residence hall Ohio State U., Columbus, 1970-71, grad. adminstrv. assoc. student fin. aid, 1971-73, asst. dean Univ. Coll., 1973-75, assoc. dean Univ. Coll., 1975-90, assoc. prof., 1991-98, assoc. provost for undergrad. studies, 1998—, dean Univ. Coll., 1998-2001, vice provost Minority Affairs, 2001—. Contbr. articles to profl. jours.; mem. editl. bd. The Negro Ednl. Rev., 1983—, editor-in-chief, 1999—. Bd. trustees The Columbus Acad., Gahanna, Ohio, 1990-96, Buckeye Boys Ranch, Grove City, Ohio, 1978-84, Mt. Carmel Coll. Nursing, 1998—, Internat. Found. Edn. & Self-Help, 1998—; adv. coun. Internat. Found. Edn. and Self-Help, Phoenix, 1992—, bd. dirs., 1998—; bd. dirs. Urban Edn., Rsch. and Human Devel. Inst., Columbus, 1977-80. Mem. ASCD, Ohio Acad. Sci., Nat. Assn. Equal Opportunity in Health Edn., United Negro Coll. Fund, Phi Kappa Phi, Phi Beta Sigma, Sigma Pi Phi. Avocations: reading, collecting insulators, travel, jogging, weightlifting. Home: 930 Notchbrook Dr Delaware OH 43015-8996 Office: Ohio State U Bricker Columbus OH 43201-1806

STEWART, MARGARET MCBRIDE, biology professor, researcher; b. Guilford County, N.C., Feb. 6, 1927; d. David Henry and Mary Ellen (Morrow) S.; m. Paul C. Lemon, June 1962 (div. 1968); m. George Edward Martin, Dec. 19, 1969. AB, U. N.C.-Greensboro, 1948; MA, U. N.C.-Chapel Hill, 1951; PhD, Cornell U., 1956; DSc (hon.), U. P.R., Mayaquez, 1996. Instr. biology Greensboro Evening Coll. U. N.C., Greensboro, 1950-51; instr. biology Catawba Coll., Salisbury, N.C., 1951-53; extension botanist Cornell U., Ithaca, N.Y., 1954-56; asst. prof. biology SUNY, Albany, 1956-59, assoc. prof., 1959-65, prof. vertebrate biology, 1965-97, disting. tchg. prof., 1977—, disting. tchg. prof. emerita, 1997; dir. Program in Biodiversity Conservation and Policy, 1997-2000. Faculty rsch. participant Oak Ridge Assoc. Univs., 1983. Author: (with A.H. Benton) Keys to the Vertebrates of the Northeastern States, 1964, Amphibians of Malawi, 1967; contbr. numerous articles and revs. to profl. jours. Bd. dirs. E.N. Huyck Nature Preserve, Rensselaerville, N.Y., 1976-86; bd. dirs. Ea. N.Y. chpt. Nature Conservancy, 1983-88, 90-96, 97-2004, N.Y. State chpt., 1987-90; mem. Albany Pine Bush Commn., 1993-1004. Recipient Citizen Laureate award SUNY Found., 1987, Oak Leaf award Nature Conservancy, 1997; Am. Philos. Soc. rsch. grantee, 1975, 81, NSF grantee, 1978-80, Oak Ridge Assocs. Univs. grantee, 1983-97. Fellow Herpetologists League (bd. dirs. 1978-80); mem. Soc. for Study of Amphibians and Reptiles (pres. 1979), Am. Soc. Ichthyologists and Herpetologists (bd. govs. 1975-80, 87-90, 96—, herpetology editor 1983-85, pres. 1996, historian 1999—), Ecol. Soc. Am., Assn. for Tropical Biologists, Soc. Study of Evolution, III World Congress of Herpetology (mem. exec. com. 1995-01), Sigma Xi, Sigma Delta Epsilon, Phi Kappa Phi. Democrat. Presbyterian. Avocations: photography, gardening, reading, travel. Office: SUNY Dept Biol Scis 1400 Washington Ave Albany NY 12222-1000

STEWART, MARK THOMAS, gas industry executive; b. Butler, Pa., June 9, 1948; s. Paul William and Donna Ruth (Wonderly) Stewart; m. Judith Lynne Christie, Aug. 12, 2967; children: Andrew Paul, Elizabeth Christie. BA, Indiana U. Pa., 1969; MAT, Duquesne U., 1972; cert. in orthodox theology, St. Stephen Coll., 1996. Cert. tchr. Pa., master balloon artist Nat. Assn. Balloon Artists. Tchr. Butler (Pa.) Cath. Sch., 1970-74; acct. George F. Pott, CPA, Gibsonia, Pa., 1974-76; field rep. Republican State Com., Harrisburg, Pa., 1976; exec. dir. Harmony (Pa.) Mus., 1977-78; foreman Pullman Std. Co., Butler, 1978-82; mgr. P. W. Stewart Welding Supply, West Sunbury, Pa., 1982-84; balloon design cons., dir. Stewart & Stewart, Inc., West Sunbury, 1984—, v.p., 1984-87, pres., 1987—. Originator balloon art techniques. Bd. dirs. Montieau Sch. Dist., West Sudbury, 1982—85; mem. campaign staff, writer, rschr. Rep. campaigns Bulter and Allegheny Counties, Pa., 1974—87. Recipient 3d pl. award internat. design competition, Nat. Assn. Balloon

Artists, 1989. Mem.: NRA (life), Nat. Propane Gas Assn., Nat. Fedn. Ind. Bus., Masons. Mem. Orthodox Ch. Avocations: reading, writing, hunting. Home: 1675 Oneida Valley Rd Chicora PA 16025-4123 Office: PO Box 248 West Sunbury PA 16061-0248

STEWART, MARSHA BEACH, performing arts educator; b. Memphis, Jan. 17, 1952; d. Bruce Charles and Marjorie Hudson (Campbell) Stewart; 1 child, Myra Grace. BBA in Internat. Bus., U. Tex., 1982; MFA in Arts Adminstrn./Dance Mgmt., Yale U., 1985; MS in Ednl. Adminstrn., CUNY, 2004. Mng. dir. Yale Cabaret, New Haven, 1984-85; agt. Columbia Artists Mgmt., Inc., NYC, 1985-90; v.p., dir. sales SATRA Arts Internat. (formerly Classical Artists), NYC, 1990-92; pres. Beach Internat. Enterprises, Inc., NYC, 1993—95; tchr. NYC Dept. Edn., 1999—, Fulbright Meml. Fund, 2003—. Dancer with Louisville Ballet (formerly Civic Ballet), 1967-70, Actor's Theatre of Louisville, 1972, Arena Stage, Washington, 1972, Disney on Parade, NBC, S.Am., Europe, Africa, 1974, 75, 76, Geneva Ballet Co., 1975, 76; dance chairwoman cultural entertainment com. U. Tex., Austin, 1981-82. NEA fellow, 1983, assoc., 1984. Mem. Yale U. Alumni Assn., Kentuckians of NYC, Scottish Heritage Soc., NY Caledonian Club. Avocations: travel, languages.

STEWART, MARVIN LEWIS, human resources professional; b. Fairmont, W.Va., June 30, 1953; s. Charles T. and Edna W. (Jones) S.; m. Phyllis A. Mitchell, July 7, 1973; children: Autumn Nicole, Kristen Leighann, Danielle Denise, Matthew Lewis. BS in Bus. Adminstrn., Fairmont State U., 1976; MS in Econs., W.Va. U., 1984. Preload supr. United Parcel Svc., western Pa., 1974-76, pers. supr., 1976-82, packaging ctr. mgr., 1982-85, employment mgr., 1985-86, spl. assignment, 1987, employment mgr., 1989, human resources div. mgr. Air Dist., Pa., 1989—. Loaned exec. United Way, Phila., 1989, dist. coord., 1990; chmn. activity bd. dirs. Marion Parks and Recreation, Fairmont, 1983-84; mem. Leadership Marion, Fairmont, 1984-85. Baptist. Avocations: tennis, golf, singing (gospel choir), travel. Office: United Parcel Svc 1 Hog Island Rd Philadelphia PA 19153-3996 Home: 730 Shagbark Dr West Chester PA 19382-1506

STEWART, MELINDA JANE, judge; b. Merced, Calif., Apr. 10, 1949; d. Donald Joel and Betty Yvonne S.; m. Bruce G. Wilbur, Aug. 1998; children from previous marriage: Alexa Marie, Julienne Rose, Robert Patrick; stepchildren: Michelle, Keith, Kelly, Kevin. BA, Stanford U., 1972; JD, Golden Gate Law Sch., 1975. Bar: Calif. 1975, U.S. Dist. Ct. (no. dist.) Calif. 1975. Dep. dist. atty. Santa Clara County Dist. Atty., San Jose, Calif., 1976—80; atty. Miller & Hinkle Law Offices, San Jose, 1980; pvt. practice Tondreau & Goodman, San Jose, 1980—83; referee Santa Clara County Superior Ct., San Jose, 1983—89, judge, 1989—2000; judge on assignment Superior Ct., 2001—. Faculty Calif. Ctr. for Jud. Edn. and Rsch., 1983—. Bd. dirs. Eastfield Ming Quong Childrens Ctr., 1993-98, pro bono project of Santa Clara County, 1992-95, YWCA Kids Connection, 1993-95, Hillbrook Sch., 1993-98; adv. bd. Santa Lucia Preserve, 2001—. Named Calif. State Bar Assn. Family Law Judge of Yr., 1995; recipient Henry B. Collada Meml. award, 1995. Mem. Calif. Judges Assn., Assn. Family and Conciliation Cts. (Calif. chpt. bd. dirs.). Avocations: tennis, cross country skiing, golf. Office: Superior Ct Santa Clara County 191 N 1st St San Jose CA 95113-1001

STEWART, MICHAEL B. lawyer, mechanical and aerospace engineer; b. Royal Oak, Mich., Nov. 5, 1963; s. Colin M. and Jacqueline P. Stewart; m. Katherine Hewitt, May 1987; children: Elizabeth and Caitlin. BSME, BA in English, U. Mich, 1987, MS in Aerospace Engring., 1988, JD, 1991. Assoc. Dykema Gossett PLLC, Bloomfield Hills, Mich., 1991-96; mnging. ptnr. Rader, Fishman & Grauer PLLC, Bloomfield Hills, 1996—. Contbr. articles to profl. jours. Named 40 Under 40 Honoree Crain's Detroit Bus., 1998. Mem. ABA, Intellectual Property Law Assn., Mich. Patent Law Assn., Mich. Bar Assn., Oakland County Bar Assn. (chmn. continuing legal edn. subcom. for IP com. 1998), Optimists (bd. dirs. 1993-97), Delta Theta Phi (dean., bd. govs., Detroit alumni senate). Avocations: bicycling, woodworking. Office: Rader Fishman & Grauer PLLC 39533 Woodward Ave Ste 140 Bloomfield Hills MI 48304-5098 E-mail: mbs@raderfishman.com.

STEWART, MICHAEL GLENN, otolaryngologist, educator; b. Bowling Green, Ky., Sept. 17, 1962; s. Michael Joseph and Barbara (Weisser) S. B in Engring. summa cum laude, Vanderbilt U., 1984; MD, Johns Hopkins U., 1988; MPH, U. Tex., 1996; Gen. Surgery, Baylor Coll. Medicine, 1990, Otolaryngology, 1994. Diplomate Am. Bd. Otolaryngology. Asst. prof. Baylor Coll. Medicine, Houston, 1994-99, assoc. prof., 1999—, dir. residency edn. dept. otolaryngology, 1996—, asst. dean clin. affairs, 1998-2000, gen. dir. affil. med. svc., 1999—, assoc. dean clin. affairs, 2000—. Chief otolaryngology Ben Taub Gen. Hosp., 1994—; chmn. med. bd. Harris County Hosp. Dist., Houston, 1999-2000. Editor Rev. Head and Neck, 1994—; reviewer Archive Otolaryngology-Head and Neck, 1997—, Jour. Trauma, 1998—, Otolaryngology-Head and Neck Surgery, 1998—, Cancer, 2001—; assoc. editor Am. Jour. Rhinology, 2003—. Recipient Outstanding Clin. Rsch. award Kelsey-Seybold Found., 1992, 93. Fellow: ACS, Am. Rhinologic Soc., Am. Laryngol., Rhinol. and Otol. Soc., Am. Triological Soc., Am. Acad. Otolaryngology Head and Neck Surgery (chmn. outcomes rsch. subcom., Disting. Svc. award). Office: Baylor Coll Medicine Dept Otolaryngology 1 Baylor Plz # Na102 Houston TX 77030-3411

STEWART, MICHAEL MCFADDEN, professional speaker; b. Eupora, Miss., Aug. 24, 1938; s. Judge Ernest and Billie Rivers (McFadden) S.; m. Barbara Ann Dickerson, June 2, 1962; children: Michael Jr., Mark Robert (dec. Dec. 1997). BS, La. State U., 1961. Cert. speaking profl. Nat. Spkrs. Assn., 1996. Cons. E.K. Williams & Co., Birmingham, Ala., 1964-66, br. mgr., 1966-68, Miami, Fla., 1968-69, Marcoin, Inc., Balt., 1969-73, dist. mgr. Falls Church, Va., 1973-74; v.p. Marcoin Western Ops., Inc., Houston, 1974-77; dir., v.p. Marcoin, Inc., Atlanta, 1977-85; ptnr. Cherokee/G & S Assocs., Atlanta, 1985-88; pres. Stewart & Stewart, Inc., Dunwoody, Ga., 1988—. The Sales Power Resource Group, Inc., Atlanta, 1991-95. Cons., speaker AMA, N.Y.C., 1989—, Duffy-Vinet Inst., Langhorne, Pa., 1987-92, The Sullivan Group, Guilford, Conn., 1990-92; guest speaker SBA, Bell South Success Symposium Series, 1990-91. Author: How to Get Started with a Small Business Computer, 1984, Quality Customer Service, 1990, Using Your Financial Statements to Boost Your Bottom Line Profits, 1990, Computerizing Your Business, 1991, The Magic of Customer Service, 1991, Bring Home the Bacon, 1992, Customer Service Excellence: How to Implement a Corporate-wide Program, 1992, Strategic Relationship Selling, 1992, Transition into Sales Management, 1992, Sales Managememt Call Reluctance Workshop, 1992, Negotiating with Style, 1992, Meeting Today's Competitive Challenges, 1992, Creative Management in Tough Economic Times, 1993, Relationship Empowered Technical Selling, 1993, Consultative Relationship Selling, 1993, Customer-Centered Sales Management Leadership, 1993, Customer Centered Selling, 1993, Being Different in a Niche Market, 1993, Moving, Shaking and Prospecting, 1993, 50/250 The Smart Way, 1993, Customer-Centered Relationship Selling, 1994, Working Sucessfully with Others, 1994, Fundamentals of Quality Customer Service, 1994, Sales Are The Life-Blood Service is the Heart Beat, 1994, Customer-Centered Value Selling, 1994, Customer-Centered Sales Management, 1994, Make the Number by Selling Value, 1995, Hiring Smart, 1995, Customer-Centered Sales Management, 1995, Live the Spirit, 1996, Sell Value, Not Price, 1996; contbg. author: Chicken Soup for the Soul at Work, 1996, Relationship Centered Value Selling, 1997, Professional Sales Skills, 1997, Sales Negotiation for Higher Profits, 1998; contbg. author: Reach for the Stars, 1998, Close More Sales!, 1999, Close More Sales With Premise, 2000, Developing A Productive Sales Orientation, 2000, Motivational Sales Management, 2000, Basic Sales Training Boot Camp, 2001, DNA of Sales Success: Hiring and Motivating Blue-Chip Sales Persons, 2002, Leading Explosive Growth-Encouraging Passionate Sales Performance, 2002, others; co-author: Embracing Change-Understanding and Managing Transitions in Life and Work, 2002; contbr. articles to profl. jours. Fin. officer Atlanta Colts Youth Assn., 1979; vol. speaker Am. Cancer Soc., 1994—. Capt. U.S. Army, 1961-64. Recipient Silver award Carlson Learning Co., Mpls., 1990, numerous other awards. Mem. Ga. Speakers Assn. (past pres., past dir., Mem. of Yr. 1996), Nat. Spkrs. Assn. (cert. speaking profl.), Dunwoody Country Club, Dunwoody Gridiron Club (pres. 1981), Lambda Chi Alpha. Episcopalian. Avocation: golf. Home: 490 Tavern Cir Atlanta GA 30350-4455 Business E-Mail: mike@mikestewartseminars.com.

STEWART, MILTON ROY, lawyer; b. Clovis, N.Mex., Dec. 16, 1945; s. Virgil Maurice and E. Marie (Collins) S. BA, Ind. U., 1968, JD summa cum laude, 1971. Bar: Oreg. 1971, U.S. Ct. Appeals (9th cir.) 1971, U.S. Dist. Ct. (no. dist.) Oreg. 1971. Assoc. Davies, Biggs et al, Portland, Oreg., 1971-75; v.p., gen. counsel U.S. Datacorp, Portland, 1975-77; pvt. practice Portland, 1977-86; bus. devel. ptnr. Davis, Wright, Tremaine, Portland, 1987—. Bd. dir. Lex Mundi assn. internat. law firms. Past chmn., mem emeritus Oreg. chpt. Nat. Multisclerosis Soc., 1994—; bd. dirs. Nat. Multiple Sclerosis Soc.; emeritus bd. visitors Ind. U. Law Sch.; active Bd. Ind. U. Found. Capt. U.S. Army, 1968-78. State Farm Found. fellow, 1970, John H. Edwards fellow Ind. U. Found., 1971. Mem. Oreg. State Bar Assn., Wash. State Bar Assn., Multnomah Athletic Club, Astoria Golf and Country Club. Office: Davis Wright Tremaine 1300 SW 5th Ave Ste 2200 Portland OR 97201-5667 Business E-Mail: miltstewart@dwt.com.

STEWART, MIMI (MIRIAM) (KAY) (MIMI STEWART), state legislator, educator; b. Sarasota, Fla., Jan. 27, 1947; d. Wilbur H. Stewart and Alice Miriam Beck; children: Boris Nathan Margolin, Hannah Beck Margolin. BA cum laude, Boston U., 1971; MS, Wheelock Coll., 1977. Spl. educator, 1977—2004; mem. N.Mex. Ho. of Reps., Albuquerque, 1994—. Democrat. Address: 313 Moon St NE Albuquerque NM 87123-1151

STEWART, MURRAY BAKER, retired lawyer; b. Muskogee, Okla., May 16, 1931; s. Francis and Fannie Penelope (Murray) S.; m. Roseanna Furgason; children: Melinda, Jeffrey, Cheryl. BA, U. Okla., 1953, JD, 1955; postgrad., Georgetown U., 1958-59. Bar: Okla. 1955; CLU, ChFC. Judge adv. U.S. Army, 1955-59; ptnr. Stewart & Stewart, Tulsa and Muskogee, Okla., 1955, 62-72; asst. v.p. First Nat. Bank and Trust Co. of Tulsa, 1959-62, 77-78; mem. Hutchins, Stewart, Stewart & Elmore, Tulsa, 1972-77; atty. cons. advanced underwriting Metlife Ins. Co., N.Y.C., 1978-94; assoc. Metlife Securities, Inc., SEC Registered Investment Advisors, 1984-94; of counsel Brumley & Bishop, Tulsa, 1997-99; ret., 1999. Cons., lectr. in field. Contbr. articles to profl. and hist. jours.; prodr. texts and videos on history, investment and bus. Fellow Life Mgmt. Inst.; mem. Okla. Bar Assn., Okla. Indian Bar Assn., Sons Confederate Vets. (judge advocate Army of Trans-Mississippi 1998-2000, Kans. divsn. 2002—), Civil War Roundtable Tulsa. Office: PO Box 1000 Broken Arrow OK 74013-1000

STEWART, NANCY SUE SPURLOCK, education educator; b. Phoenix, Dec. 31, 1933; d. Ernest Neal and Ethel Ora (Boothe) Spurlock; m. Biven Stewart, Dec. 31, 1953 (div. 1962); 1 child, Sally K. BA in Edn., Ariz. State U., 1961, MA in Edn., 1968, Reading Specialist Cert., 1970. Cert. tchr. 1-12, Ariz. Elem. tchr., reading specialist Chandler (Ariz.) Pub. Schs. Dist. 80, 1961-92; instr. Greater Phoenix Area Writing Project Ariz. State U. and Chandler Unified Sch. Dist. 80, 1983—. Mem. AAUW, NEA, Chandler Edn. Assn., Ariz. Edn. Assn., Delta Kappa Gamma Soc. Internat., Kappa Delta. Mem. Ch. of Christ. Avocations: crafts, reading. Home: 4308 E Ahwatukee Dr Phoenix AZ 85044-2702

STEWART, PAMELA L. lawyer; b. Bogalusa, La., Mar. 13, 1953; d. James Adrian and Patricia Lynn (Wood) Lloyd; m. Steven Bernard Stewart, Aug. 31, 1974 (div. July 1980); 1 child, Christopher. BA, U. New Orleans, 1986; JD, U. Houston, 1990. Intern La. Supreme Ct., New Orleans, 1984, Councilman Bryan Wagner, New Orleans, 1984-85; legal asst. Clann, Bell & Murphy, Houston, 1988-89, Tejas Gas Corp., Houston, 1989-90; atty. Law Offices of Pamela L. Stewart, Houston, 1991—. Bd. dirs. Alliance for Good Govt., New Orleans, 1983-84, Attention Deficit Hyperactivity Disorder Assn. Tex., 1989-90; vol. Houston Vol. Lawyers Program, Houston, 1992—; mem. Planned Giving Coun.; bd. dirs. West Lane Place Civic Assn., sec., 2001-2003, v.p., 2003—; mem. com. Lawyers Against Waste, Habitat for Humanity; apptd. Harris County Appraisal Rev. Bd. Innsbruck scholar, U. New Orleans, 1985. Fellow Inst. Politics; mem. ABA, Tax Freedom Inst., Nat. Assn. Consumer Bankruptcy Attys., Nat. Assn. Elder Law Attys., Am. Networking Trust Planning Attys., Houston Bar Assn., Nat. Assn. of Chpt. 13 Trustees (assoc.), Katy Bar Assn. (3d v.p. 1997-98), Houston Assn. Debtors Attys. (pres. 1996-98), Upper Kirby Dist. Optimist Club (v.p. 2000-01, pres. 2001-02), Planned Giving Coun., Feng Shui Guild, Feng Shui Basics (pres.), Nat. Assn. Consumer Advs. Methodist. Avocations: music, cooking, swimming, politics. Home: 24503 Alexander Crossing Ln Katy TX 77494 Office: 4265 San Felipe St Ste 1100 Houston TX 77027-2998 E-mail: plsatty@swbell.net.

STEWART, PATRICIA CANUP, vocal music and performing arts educator; b. Salisbury, N.C., July 15, 1944; d. Robert Lamont and Hazel Loretta (Heggie) Canup; (div.); children: Jeffrey Scott, J. Levi. BA, Greensboro (N.C.) Coll., 1966; cert. in teaching, U. N.C., 1969; MA, Appalachian State U., 1974; Cert. of Advanced Study, U. N.C., Greensboro, 1992; PhD, Am. State U., 1998. Buyer, mgr. music dept. Andrews Music Co., Charlotte, N.C., 1966-68; prof. Caldwell Community Coll., Lenoir, N.C., 1972-74; chmn. music dept. Charlotte Cath. High Sch., 1975-80, Catawba Sch., Rock Hill, S.C., 1983-86; dir. choral music Iredell/Statesville (N.C.) Schs., 1985-93, 98—, Balt. County Schs., Timonium, Md., 1993—98; choral and drama dir. Mooresville (NC) City Schs., 2000—. Choral dir. chs., 1964-88. Mem. ASCD, Am. Choral Dirs. Assn., Music Educators Nat. Conf., N.C. Music Educators, Pi Kappa Lambda. Home: 305 Windsor Dr Salisbury NC 28144-7725 Office: 659 E Center Ave Mooresville NC 28115

STEWART, PATRICIA CARRY, foundation administrator; b. Bklyn., May 19, 1928; d. William J. and Eleanor (Murphy) Carry; m. Charles Thorp Stewart, May 30, 1976. Student, U. Paris, 1948—49; BA, Cornell U., 1950. Fgn. corr. Irving Trust Co., N.Y.C., 1950-51; with Janeway Rsch. Co., N.Y.C., 1951-60, sec., treas., 1955-60; with Buckner & Co. and successor firms, N.Y.C., 1961-73, ptnr., 1962-70, v.p., treas., 1970-71, pres., treas., 1971-73, Knight, Carry, Bliss & Co., Inc., N.Y.C., 1971-73, G. Tsai & Co., Inc., 1973; v.p. Edna McConnell Clark Found. Inc., 1974-92. Dir. Cmty. Found. Palm Beach and Martin Counties, 1993-2001, chair, 1998, 2000; allied mem. N.Y. Stock Exch., 1962-73; past mem. nominating com. Am. Stock Exch., N.Y. Stock Exch., N.Y.C. Fin. Svcs. Corp.; dir. emeritus, past chmn. Investor Responsibility Rsch. Ctr. Trustee emerita, vice chair Cornell U., mem. bd. life overseers Cornell Med. Coll.; mem. vis. com. Grad. Sch Bus., Harvard U., 1974-80; bd. dirs. NOW Legal Def. and Edn. Fund, 1984-92, Women in Founds./Corp. Philanthropy, 1980-86; v.p. fin. com. Women's Forum, 1982-90; vice chmn. CUNY, 1976-80; bd. dirs. United Way of Tri-State, 1977-81, Inst. for Edn. and Rsch. on Women and Work; voting mem. Blue Cross and Blue Shield Greater N.Y., 1975-82; trustee N.Y. State 4-H Found., 1970-76, Intenrt. Inst. Rural Reconstrn., 1974-79; mem. N.Y.C. panel White House Fellows, 1976-78; mem. bus. adv. coun. The Hosp. Chaplaincy. Recipient Elizabeth Cutter Morrow award YWCA, 1977, Catalyst award Women Dirs. in Corps., 1978, Trustee medal CUNY, 1983, Acomplishment award Wings Club N.Y. 1984, Women's Funding Coalition Innovators for Women$hare award, 1986, Banking Industry Achievement award Nat. Assn. Bank Women, 1987, Cert. Disting. Accomplishments Barnard Coll., 1989; named to YWCA Acad. Women Achievers. Mem. Fin. Women's Assn. N.Y., Country Club of Fla. (bd. dirs.), Univ. Club (N.Y.C), Gullane Golf Club (Scotland), North Berwick Golf Club (Scotland), Dunbar Golf Club (Scotland), St. Andrews Club (Delray Beach, Fla.), Phi Beta Phi. Home and Office: 2613 N Ocean Blvd Delray Beach FL 33483-7367 also: Halfland Barns North Berwick EH395PW Scotland E-mail: stewartpc@aol.com.

STEWART, PATRICIA RHODES, former clinical psychologist, researcher; b. Vallejo, Calif., Feb. 11, 1910; d. Butler Young Rhodes and Sarah Virginia (Ryan) Rhodes; m. John Kenneth Stewart (div.); children: John K., Nancy Rush. AB summa cum laude, Stanford U., 1930; MA, San Jose State U., 1959; PhD, U. London, 1963. Tchg. asst. San Jose State U., 1959-60; staff psychologist Napa State Hosp., 1964-77; pvt. practice in psychotherapy Berkeley, Calif., 1978-94; pvt. rsch. in adolescent deviance, 1979-85. Staff psychologist Westwood Mental Health Facility, Fremont, Calif., 1985-88. Author: Children in Distress: American and English Perspectives, 1976. Chair criminal justice com. No. Calif. region Am. Friends Svc. com., San Francisco, 1977-80, chair exec. com. 1970-74, 80-83, bd. dirs., 1980-83; bd. dirs. Friends Com. on Legis., Sacramento, 1985-88, No. Calif. Ecumenical Coun., Oakland, Calif., 1989-95. Mem. APA, AAAS, Phi Beta Kappa. Mem. Soc. Of Friends. Home: 1225 Monterey Ave Berkeley CA 94707-2718

STEWART, PATRICK, actor; b. Mirfield, Eng., July 13, 1940; s. Alfred and Gladys (Barraclough) S.; m. Sheila Falconer, 1966, div., 1990; 2 children; m. Wendy Neuss, 2000, div., 2003. Trained, Bristol Old Vic Theatre Sch. Performed in (theatre) Treasure Island (U.K., debut), 1959, (U.S.) A Midsummer Night's Dream (Broadway debut), 1970, A Christmas Carol, 1991, 92, 94; (TV series) Star Trek: The Next Generation, 1987-94, (mini series) I, Claudius, 1977, Tinker, Sailor, Soldier, Spy, 1979, Smiley's People, 1982, Playing Shakespeare, 1983, When the Lion Roars, 1992, (TV movies) The Gathering Storm, 1974, Anthony and Cleopatra, 1974 (Olivier award best supporting actor), The Madness, 1976, Hamlet, Prince of Denmark, 1980, Little Lord Fauntleroy, 1980, John Paul II, 1984, The Devil's Disciple, 1987, Death Train, 1993, In Search of Dr. Seuss, 1994, (also co-prodr.) The Canterville Ghost, 1996, Moby Dick, 1997, Safe House, 1998, (voice) Animal Farm, 1999, (also exec. prodr.) A Christmas Carol, 1999, (also exec. prodr.) King of Texas, 2002, The Lion in Winter, 2003; (TV series) Fall of Eagles, 1974, North and South, 1975, Maybury, 1981, 500 Nations, 1995; host on Saturday Night Live, 1994; actor (films) Hennessy, 1975, Hedda, 1975, Excalibur, 1981, The Plague Dogs (voice) 1982, Dune, 1984, Uindii, 1984, Lifeforce, 1985, Code Name: Emerald, 1985, Wild Geese II, 1985, The Doctor and the Devils, 1985, Lady Jane, 1986, L.A. Story, 1991, Robin Hood: Men in Tights, 1993, Gunmen, 1994, Star Trek: Generations, 1994, The Pagemaster, 1994 (voice), Jeffrey, 1995, Let It Me Be (aka Love Dance), 1995, Star Trek: First Contact, 1996, Conspiracy Theory, 1997, Safe House, 1997, Dad Savage, 1997, Master Minds, 1997, (voice) Prince of Egypt, 1998, X-Men, 2000, (voice) Jimmy Neutron: Boy Genius, 2001, Star Trek: Nemesis, 2002, X-Men 2, 2003; assoc. prodr. Star Trek IX: Insurrection, 1998; assoc. artist with Royal Shakespeare Co., 1967—; recording: Prokofiev: Peter and the Wolf (Grammy award best spoken word album for children 1996). Office: Flying Freehold Productions 2219 Wilshire Blvd Ste 600 Santa Monica CA 90401 also: William Morris Agy 151 El Camino Dr Beverly Hills CA 90212*

STEWART, PETER BEAUFORT, retired beverage company executive; b. Montreal, Que., Can., Aug. 23, 1923; s. Harold Beaufort and Mary W. (Martin) S.; m. Yolande Winifred Powell, June 1955; children— Thomas B., Angus B. B.Comm., McGill U.; MBA, Harvard U. With Bldg. Products Ltd., Toronto, Ont., Can., 1947-62; dir., v.p. mktg. Molson Breweries Ltd., Montreal, 1962-66; pres. Molson Western Breweries Ltd., Calgary, Alta., Can., 1966-70; exec. v.p., pres. Molson Breweries Ltd., Montreal, 1970-75; exec. v.p. The Molson Cos. Ltd., Toronto, 1975-88.

STEWART, PETER J. general surgery, trauma and critical care physician; b. Oxford, Eng., May 1, 1957; came to U.S., 1959; m. Huyen V. Cao; children: Daniel, Mai, Ian. BS, SUNY, Brockport, 1979; MD, U. Wis., 1983. Diplomate Am. Bd. Surgery. Intern in surgery St. Luke's-Roosevelt Hosp., N.Y.C., 1983-84, resident in surgery, 1984-88; trauma fellow U. Md. R. Adams Cowley Shock Trauma Ctr., 1988—89; attending surgeon SUNY Health Scis. Ctr., Bklyn., 1989-90; attending surgeon-trauma Kings County Hosp., Bklyn., 1989-90; dir. trauma svc. St. Luke's Roosevelt Hosp., N.Y.C., 1990-93; dir. trauma svc., dir. surg. critical care St. Joseph's Hosp. and Med. Ctr., Paterson, N.J., 1993—. Chair trauma com. St. Joseph's Hosp., 1993—, chair trauma quality assurance com., 1993—, chair critical care com., 1997—. Recipient award Eastman Kodak, Rochester, N.Y., 1978. Fellow ACS; mem. AMA, Am. Trauma Soc., Soc. Critical Care Medicine, Sigma Xi. Democrat. Roman Catholic. Office: St Joseph's Hosp and Med Ctr 703 Main St Paterson NJ 07503-2621

STEWART, PRISCILLA ANN MABIE, art historian, educator; b. Iowa City, Sept. 21, 1926; d. Edward Charles and Grace Frances (Chase) Mabie; m. Thomas Wilson Stewart, Aug. 28, 1949 (dec. Mar. 1996). BA, U. Iowa, 1948; MA, U. South Fla., 1971; EdS, Fla. Atlantic U., 1983. Coord. elem. art Manatee County, Fla., 1953-59; prof. art history, intercultural humanities and photography Manatee C.C., Bradenton, Fla., 1959—. Organizer, dir. Pelican Perch Wild Bird Hosp., Bradenton, 1953-85; participant Women's Archives U. Iowa Librs. Apptd. charter mem. of adv. bd. to dean of Liberal Arts, U. Iowa, 1999. Mem. AAUP, Pres.'s Club U. Iowa, Fla. Assn. C.Cs., Sarasota-Manatee Phi Beta Kappa Assn. (pres. 1984-86), Phi Beta Kappa, Alpha Xi Delta, Phi Kappa Phi. Episcopalian. Home: 2705 Riverview Blvd Bradenton FL 34205-4335 Office: Manatee Community Coll Dept Art and Humanities 5840 26th St W Bradenton FL 34207-3522 E-mail: stewarp@aol.com., stewarp@mccfl.edu.

STEWART, RICHARD A. former mayor; m. Susan B. Stewart. Postgrad, Air War Coll.; BA, Calif. State U., 1965; MA, No. Mich. U., 1972; JD, Calif. So. Law Sch., 1982. Mayor City of Moreno Valley, Calif., 1996—2000; ptnr. Gellar Stewart and Foley, Riverside, Calif., 1995—; mem. Moreno Valley City Coun., 1990—. Active Res. Deputy Riverside County Sheriff's Dept., 1992—. Office: Law Offices of Gellar Stewart and Foley 6301 Day St Ste 106 Riverside CA 92507: 3430 Bundy Ave Ste 107 March Air Force Base CA 92518 E-mail: richards@moval.org.

STEWART, RICHARD ALFRED, business executive; b. Hartford, Conn., Nov. 2, 1945; s. Charles Alfred and Theresa (Procopio) S. BS, Valley Coll., 1967. Account exec. Bank Printing Inc., Los Angeles, 1967-70; pres. Carpet Closet Inc., Los Angeles, 1970-73; western sales mgr. Josten's, Los Angeles, 1973-84; pres. Western Internat. Premiums, Los Angeles, 1984-87; dir. corp. sales Tiffany and Co., Beverly Hills, Calif., 1987-90, dir. major program sales, 1990-92, dir. regional sales N.Y.C., 1992-93, dir. major programs, 1992-93; v.p. sales mktg. and recognition divsn. Jostens, Memphis, 1993—; prin. The Stewart Group Sales & Mktg. Cons., 1994—. V.p. sales & mktg. Am. Gem Corp.; recognition cons. L.A. Olympic Com., 1983-84. Contbr. articles to profl. mags.; developer medals for 1984 summer Olympics. Chmn. bd. dirs. Athletes and Entertainers for Kids. Avocations: tennis, basketball, photography.

STEWART, RICHARD BURLESON, law educator; b. Cleve., Feb. 12, 1940; s. Richard Siegfreid and Ruth Dysert (Staten) Stewart; m. Alice Peck Fales, May 13, 1967 (div. June 1992); children: William, Paul, Elizabeth; m. Jane Laura Bloom, Sept. 20, 1992; children: Emily, Ian. AB, Yale U., 1961; MA (Rhodes scholar), Oxford (Eng.) U., 1963; LLB, Harvard U., 1966; D (hon.), Erasmus U., Rotterdam, 1993. Bar: DC 1968, U.S. Supreme Ct. 1971. Law clk. to Hon. Potter Stewart U.S. Supreme Ct., 1966-67; assoc. Covington & Burling, Washington, 1967-71; asst. prof. law Harvard U., 1971-75, prof., 1975-82, Byrne prof. adminstrv. law, 1982-89, assoc. dean, 1984-86; asst. atty. gen. environment and natural resources div. Dept. Justice, Washington, 1989-91; prof. law NYU Law Sch., N.Y.C., 1992-94, Emily Kempin prof. law, 1994—2002, John Edward Sexton prof. law, 2002—, univ. prof., 2002—; of counsel Sidley & Austin, 1992—. Spl. counsel U.S. Senate Watergate Com., 1974; vis. prof. U. Calif., Berkeley Law Sch., 1979—80, U. Chgo. Law Sch., 1986—87, Georgetown U., 1991—92, Europen U. Inst., 1995; dir. Ctr. Environ. and Land Use Law, Health Effects Inst.; mem. adv. bd. Environ. Def. Author: (book) The Reformation of American Administrative Law (in Chinese), 2002; author: (with P. Menell) Environmental Law and Policy, 1994; author: (with S. Breyer, C. Sunstein and M. Spitzer) Administrative Law and Regulation, 1979, Administrative Law and Regulation, 5th edit., 2002; author: (with E. Rehbinder) Integration Through Law: Environmental Protection Policy, 1985, Integration Through Law: Environmental Protection Policy, paper edit., 1987; author: (with R. Revesz) Markets v. Environment?, 1995; author: (with R. Revesz and P. Sands) Environment, the Economy, and Sustainable Development, 2001; author: (with J. Wiener) Reconstructing Climate Policy, 2003; editor (with R. Revesz): (book) Analyzing Superfund: Economics, Science, and Law, 1995. Fellow: Am. Acad. Arts and Scis.; mem.: ABA, Am. Law Inst. Office: NYU Law Sch 40 Washington Sq S New York NY 10012-1099 Office Phone: 212-998-6170. E-mail: stewartr@juris.law.nyu.edu.

STEWART, RICHARD DONALD, internist, educator, writer; b. Lakeland, Fla., Dec. 26, 1926; s. LeRoy Hepburn and Zoa Irene (Hachet) S.; m. Mary Leeuw, June 14, 1952; children: R. Scot, Gregory D., Mary E. AB, U. Mich., 1951, MD, 1955, MPH, 1962; MA, U. Wis. Milw., 1979; PhD in English, U. Wis., Milw., 1997. Diplomate Am. Bd. Internal Medicine, Am. Bd. Med. Toxicology, Acad. Toxicol. Scis. Intern Saginaw (Mich.) Gen. Hosp., 1955-56; resident in internal medicine U. Mich. Med. Ctr., Ann Arbor, 1959-62; dir. med. rsch. sect. Dow Chem. Co., Midland, Mich., 1962-66; staff physician Midland Hosp., 1962-66; assoc. prof. preventive medicine Med. Coll. Wis., Milw., 1966-68, prof., chmn. dept. environ. medicine, 1969-78, adj. prof. dept. pharmacology and toxicology, 1978—. Cons. Children's Hosp. Wis., 1989-93, Internal Medicine St. Mary's Hosp., Racine, Wis., 1983-93; prof., dir. med. toxicology fellowship Dept. Emergency Medicine Milw. Regional Med. Ctr., 1989-91; sr. attending staff, 1967-90; staff Internal Medicine St. Luke's Hosp., Racine, 1983-93; med. dir. Poison Control Ctr. Southeastern Wis., 1989-93; corp. med. advisor S.C. Johnson & Son, Inc., Racine, 1971-78, corp. med. dir., 1978-89. Mem. adv. med. staff Milw. Fire Dept., 1975—. Cadet USAF, 1945-46. Fellow ACP, Am. Coll. Occuptl. Medicine, Am. Acad. Clin. Toxicology, Acad. Toxicological Scis.; mem. AMA, Soc. Toxicology, Wis. State Med. Soc., Racine Acad. Medicine, Rotary Internat., Phi Theta Kappa, Phi Kappa Phi, Sigma Tau Delta. Achievements include invention of medical devices including the hollow fiber artificial kidney and capillary artificial lung; being leader of team that performed first human dialyses with the Hollow Fiber Artificial Kidney, beginning Aug.4, 1967. This artificial kidney is universally used for long-term dialysis. Avocations: history of medicine, wilderness hiking, literature, creative writing. Home and Office: 5337 Wind Point Rd Racine WI 53402-2322 Office Phone: 262-639-6483.

STEWART, RICHARD EDWIN, insurance consulting company executive; b. Washington, Nov. 4, 1933; s. Irvin and Florence Elsie (Dezendorf) S.; m. Barbara Lewis Dickson, Oct. 29, 1993. BA, W.Va. U., 1955; BA (Rhodes scholar), Oxford (Eng.) U., 1957, MA, 1961; JD, Harvard, 1959. Bar: N.Y. 1960. Assoc. Royall, Koegel & Rogers, N.Y.C., 1960-63; asst. counsel to Gov. of N.Y., 1963-64, 1st asst. counsel, 1965-66; supr. ins. N.Y. State Ins. Dept., 1967-70; sr. v.p., gen. counsel First Nat. City Bank, N.Y.C., 1971-72; sr. v.p., dir. Chubb & Son Inc., N.Y.C., 1973-81; sr. v.p. Chubb Corp., N.Y.C., 1973-81, CFO, 1974-81; gov. N.Y. Ins. Exch., N.Y.C., 1979-81; chmn. Stewart Econs., Inc., N.Y.C., 1981-90, Chapel Hill, NC, 1990—. Mem. adv. com. HUD, 1968-72; mem. Adminstrv. Conf. U.S., 1970-74; bd. dirs. Am. Arbitration Assn., 1970-80; mem. UN panel experts on Transnational Bank failure, 1991. Co-author: Automobile Insurance...For Whose Benefit?, 1970, Watergate: Implications for Responsible Government, 1974, Medical Malpractice, 1977, Managing Insurer Insolvency, 1988, Insurance Insolvency Quarantees, 1990, A Brief History of Underwriting Cycles, 1991, Niche Insurance Companies, 1997, Information Technology and Insurance Agent Licensing, 1998, The Loss of the Certainty Effect, 2002, Managing Insurer Insolvency, 2003; author: Reason and Regulation, 1972, Insurance and Insurance Regulation, 1980. Trustee Coll. Ins., N.Y., 1970-78, Am. Coll. Life Underwriters, 1990-93; mem. Mayor's Com. on Taxi Regulation, 1979-82, ABA Com. to Improve Liability Ins. System, 1989; mem. panel experts on transnat. bank failure UN, 1991; mem. spl. panel U.S. Senate Com. on Presdl. Campaign Practice, 1974. Served with AUS, 1959. Mem. Nat. Acad. Pub. Adminstrn., Nat. Acad. Social Ins., Cosmos Club of Washington, Century Club of N.Y.C., Phi Beta Kappa Assn. Home and Office: 7600 Talbryn Way Chapel Hill NC 27516-7862

STEWART, RICHARD WILLIAMS, lawyer; b. Harrisburg, Pa., Aug. 21, 1948; s. Alexander H. and M. Winifred (Williams) S.; m. Mary A. Simmonds, June 7, 1975; 1 child, Anne W. AB cum laude, Franklin and Marshall Coll., 1970; JD, Duke U., 1973. Bar: Pa. 1973, U.S. Dist. Ct. (mid. dist.) Pa. 1975, U.S. Tax Ct. 1984. Assoc. Stone & Sajer, New Cumberland, Pa., 1973-77; ptnr. Stone, Sajer & Stewart, New Cumberland, 1977-87, Johnson, Duffie, Stewart & Weidner, Lemoyne, Pa., 1987—. V.p. Secured Land Transfers, Inc., Camp Hill, Pa., 1985-2000, pres., 2000—; solicitor West Shore Sch. Dist., Lemoyne, Pa., 1977-93, No. York County Sch. Dist., Dillsburg, Pa., 1984—, Camp Hill Sch. Dist., 1986—, Fairview Twp., 1987-98; v.p. Cedar Cliff Abstract Agy., 1980-87. Chmn. Cumberland County Rep. Com., 1981-84; mem. Rep. State Com. Pa., 1990—. Mem. ABA, Pa. Bar Assn., Cumberland County Bar Assn., Supreme Ct. of Pa. (disciplinary bd. 1998—, vice chmn. 2003, chmn. 2004), Ctrl. Pa. Estate Planning Coun. (bd. dirs. 1983-85), Pa. Sch. Solicitors Assn. (pres. 1995), Rotary (bd. dirs. West Shore). Presbyterian. Home: 1811 Warren St New Cumberland PA 17070-1148 Office: 301 Market St Lemoyne PA 17043-1628

STEWART, RITA JOAN, academic administrator; b. Muncie, Ind., June 6, 1945; d. John Marion and Crystalee Masterson; children: Jon Lewis, Robert Forrest. BS, Ball State U., 1967, MA, 1974. Tchr. Blue River H.S., Mt. Summit, Ind., 1968-69, Sunnyside Elem. Sch., New Castle, Ind., 1967-68; copywriter, announcer Sta. WTIM, Taylorville, Ill., 1974-75; dir. Kitselman Conf. Ctr. Ball State U., Muncie, Ind., 1978-2000, dir. conf. and spl. events, 2000—. Contbr. articles to profl. jours. Precinct committeewoman Henry County Dem. Party, New Castle, Ind., 1969-70; precinct chmn. March of Dimes, New Castle, Ind., 1974-75; chmn. edn. com. West Viwe Sch. Coun., Muncie, 1987-88; sec., bd. dirs. PAL Club, Muncie, 1988-93; pres., bd. dirs. Altrusa Club Found., Muncie, 1997-98, v.p., 2001-01, pres., 2002. Mem.: AAUW (v.p. 1984—85), Ind. Conf. Dirs. Assn., Assn. Collegiate Conf. and Event Dirs. Internat. (dir. region 8 1999—2000, internat. bd. dirs., Mentor Yr. award 2004), Altrusa Club of Muncie (pres. 2002—03), Kappa Delta Pi (Disting. Svc. award 1995). Methodist. Office: Ball State U Confs and Spl Events Muncie IN 47306 Home: # 1-203 4501 N Wheeling Ave Muncie IN 47304-1277 Office Phone: 765-285-1396. Office Fax: 765-285-5457. Business E-Mail: conferences@bsu.edu.

STEWART, ROBERT FORREST, JR., lawyer; b. Niagara Falls, N.Y., Oct. 25, 1943; s. Robert Forrest and Margaret Joanne (Mahoney) Stewart; m. Tara Campbell Mescal, Aug. 27, 1966; children: Jane Margaret, Laura Campbell, Rebecca Forrest. BS, Coll. Holy Cross, Worcester, Mass., 1965; JD, Georgetown U., 1968; LLM in Labor, Temple U., 1978. Bar: DC 1968, Del. 1969, Pa. 1976. Law clk. to presiding judge U.S. Dist. Ct. Del., Wilmington, 1968-69; judge adv. USAF, 1969-72; assoc. Morris, Nichols, Arsht & Tunnell, Wilmington, 1972-76, Obermayer, Rebmann, Maxwell & Hippel, Phila., 1976-80, ptnr., 1981-85, Duane, Morris & Heckscher, Phila., Wilmington, 1985-92, Dilworth Paxson LLP, Phila., Wilmington, 1992—. Pub. mem. Coun. Engring. and Sci. Splty. Bd., 1991—. Author: (book) At-Will Termination in Pennsylvania, 1983, Emerging Employee Rights, 1984, At-Will Termination in New Jersey, 1985, Legal Issues of Managing Difficult Employees in Delaware, 1988, Personnel and Employment Law in Pennsylvania/New Jersey/Delaware, 1990, Sexual Harassment, 1993, Employer's Guide to Delaware and Federal Employee Relations Laws and Regulations, 1998. Mem. N.E. regional coun. United Way, 1993—97; bd. dirs., 1st vice chair Assoc. United Ways, 1996—97; chmn. Common Cause Del., 1974—75, 1979—80, 1997—; bd. dirs., vice chmn. United Way, Del., 1994—97; bd. dirs. Del. Citizens Opposed to Death Penalty, 1993—, Bayard Ho., 1993—98, Cath. Schs. Diocese of Wilmington, 1998—2001, 18th St. Devel. Corp., 2002—; mem. exec. com. Del. Employer Coun., 1998—; mem. adv. bd. Seton Villa, Siena Hall and Children's Home, 1992—; pres. adv. bd. Cath. Charities, Diocese of Wilmington, 1976—90. Named Vol. of the Yr., United Way Del., 1984; recipient Fellowship award, 1993. Mem.: ACLU (bd. dirs. Del. chpt. 1972—76, 1992—95), ABA, Del. Contractors Assn., Assoc. Builders & Contractors (co-chmn. govt. rels. legal rights com. Del. chpt. 1999), Phila. Bar Assn., Pa. Bar Assn., Del. State Bar Assn., Del. C. of C. (labor advisor 1980—, chmn. com. employee rels. 1987—), Port of Wilmington Maritime Soc. (bd. dirs., pres. 1999—), Holy Cross Varsity Club (bd. dirs. 1981—), Du Pont Country Club. Democrat. Roman Catholic. Office: Dilworth Paxson LLP 3200 Mellon Bank Ctr 1735 Market St Philadelphia PA 19103-7501 also: Ste 500 First Federal Plaza Wilmington DE 19801 E-mail: rstewart@dilworthlaw.com.

STEWART, ROBERT GORDON, former museum curator; b. Balt., Mar. 5, 1931; s. Kenneth Elsworth and Ruth (Chambers) S. Student, Gilman Sch., 1946-49; B.F.A., U. Pa., 1954. Architect Ind. Nat. Hist. Park, Phila., 1954, Nat. Park Service, Phila., 1956-57; architect, curator Jefferson Barracks Hist. Park, St. Louis, 1958-61; dir. properties Nat. Trust for Historic Preservation, Washington, 1961-64; sr. curator Nat. Portrait Gallery, Smithsonian Instn., Washington, 1964-94, sr. curator emeritus, 1994—. Cons. Loyalist Homestead, St. John's, N.B., Can., 1960; vis. lectr. George Washington U., 1967-70 *John Stewart was granted land in Maryland January 8, 1668, was a captain in Maryland militia 1678. His three times great grandson, John Trevillian Stewart, signed the oath of allegiance to the state of Maryland February 16, 1778. His son Levin Stewart was appointed lieutenant, 48 Maryland regimen June 21, 1813. Levin Stewart manumitted all 22 of his slaves July 28, 1817 in Maryland. Robert Gordon Stewart is his great grandson.* Author: Nucleus for a National Collection, 1965, Recent Acquisitions, 1966, A Nineteenth-Century Gallery of Distinguished Americans, 1969, Henry Benbridge (1743-1812): American Portrait Painter, 1971, Robert Edge Pine, A British Artist in America 1784-1788, 1979. Dir. Landmarks of St. Louis, 1959-61; adjudicator Jamaican Nat. Art Competition, 1971; cons. The Papers of George Washington, 1990-98; bd. dirs. Washington Studio Sch., 1997-99. Served with U.S. Army, 1954-56. Mem. Md., Dorchester County, Lewes hist. socs., Walpole Soc., Assn. of Historians of Am. Art, Zeta Psi. Episcopalian.

STEWART, ROBERT LEE, retired career officer, astronaut; b. Washington, Aug. 13, 1942; s. Lee Olin and Mildred Kathleen (Wann) S.; m. Mary Jane Murphy; children: Ragon Annette, Jennifer Lee. BS in Math., U. So. Miss., 1964; MS in Aerospace Engring., U. Tex., 1972; grad., U.S. Army Air Def. Sch., 1964, grad. advanced course, guided missile systems officers course, 1970. Commd. 2d lt. U.S. Army, 1964, advanced through grades to brig. gen., 1986, fire team leader armed helicopter platoon 101st Aviation Bn., instr. pilot Primary Helicopter Sch., 1967 69, bn. ops. officer, bn. exec. officer 309th Aviation Bn., 1972-73, exptl. test pilot Aviation Engring. Flight Activity Edwards AFB, Calif., 1974-78; astronaut candidate NASA, 1978, mission specialist Space Shuttle Mission 41-B, 1984; mission specialist STS-51J, 1985; dep. comdr. U.S. Army Strategic Def. Command, Huntsville, Ala., 1987-89; dir. of plans U.S. Space Command, 1989-92. Decorated D.S.M., (2) Legion of Merit, (4) DFC, (2) Purple Hearts, Bronze star, Def. Superior Svc. medal, others; recipient NASA Space Flight medal, 1984, 85, Fineburg Meml. award Am. Helicopter Soc., 1984, Herman Oberth award AIAA, 1990; named Army Aviator of Yr., 1984. Mem. Soc. Exptl. Test Pilots, Assn. U.S. Army, Army Aviation Assn. Am., Assn. Space Explorers. Avocations: photography, woodworking, skiing. Home and Office: 815 Sun Valley Dr Woodland Park CO 80863-7729

STEWART, RODERICK DAVID, singer; b. North London, Eng., Jan. 10, 1945; m. Alana Collins, Apr. 6, 1979 (div. 1984); children: Alana, Sean; child with Kelly Emberg: Ruby Rachel; m. Rachel Hunter, Dec. 15, 1990, child, Renée. Singer with Jeff Beck Group, 1968-69, Faces, 1969-75; albums include (with Jeff Beck Group) Truth, 1968, Beck-Ola, 1969; (with Faces) The First Step, 1970, Long Player, 1971, A Nod Is As Good as a Wink...To a Blind Horse, 1971, Ooh La La, 1973, Coast to Coast/Overture & Beginners, 1973, Snakes and Ladders/The Best of Faces, 1976; (solo) An Old Raincoat Won't Ever Let You Down, 1969, Gasoline Alley, 1970, Every Picture Tells a Story, 1971, Never a Dull Moment, 1972, Sing it Again Rod, 1973, Smiler, 1974, Atlantic Crossing, 1975, The Best of Rod Stewart, 1976, The Best of Rod Stewart Vol. II, 1976, A Night on the Town, 1976, Foot Loose & Fancy Free, 1976, Blondes Have More Fun, 1978, Greatest Hits Vol. I, 1979, Tonight I'm Yours, 1981, Absolutely Live, 1981, Camouflage, 1984, (with Jeff Beck) Get Workin', 1985, Out of Order, 1988, Storyteller: The Complete Anthology 1964-1990, 1990, Downtown Train, 1990, Vagabond Heart, 1991, You Wear It Well, 1992, The Mercury Anthology, 1992, Once In A Blue Moon Vintage, 1993, Ridin High, The Rod Stewart Album, Unplugged...And Seated, 1993 (Grammy nomination, Best Pop Male Vocal for "Have I Told You Lately"), Spanner in the Works, 1995, Handbags and Gladrags, 1996, When We Were the New Boys, 1998; films include Rod Stewart - The Best of Rod Stewart, Rod Stewart and The Faces - The Final Concert, 1974, Rod Stewart and Faces, 1975, Rod Stewart Live at Los Angeles Forum, 1980, Rod Stewart-Tonight He's Yours, short and long versions, 1981, The Rod Stewart Concert Video, 1984, Rod Stewart -Storyteller 1984-91, 1991, Rod Stewart - Vagabond Heart Named Rock Star of Year Rolling Stone mag., 1971; recipient British Rock and Pop Lifetime Achievement award, 1992; inducted into the Rock & Roll Hall of Fame, 1994. Office: Warner Bros Records 3300 Warner Blvd Burbank CA 91505-4694

STEWART, ROY J. communications executive; BA, U. Va., 1960; JD, Cornell U., 1963. Chief mass media FCC, Washington, 1989—. Office: FCC 455 12th St SW Rm 2C337 Washington DC 20554-0001

STEWART, SANDRA KAY, music educator; b. New Albany, Ind., Dec. 24, 1947; d. Dale F. and June V. (Martin) Byrne; m. William Lee Stewart, June 25, 1971. B Music Edn., Ind. U., 1969; MusM, Norfolk State U., 1992; D Mus. Arts, U. S.C., 1995. Cert. vocal music tchr., N.Y., Mo.; nat. cert., state cert. piano tchr. Vocal music tchr., choral dir. Ritenour Sch. Dist., St. Louis, 1969-75, Sch. Dist. # 54, Chgo., 1975-76, Waverly (N.Y.) Jr./Sr. H.S., 1977-78, Clarence (N.Y.) H.S., 1978-82; piano instr., show choir dir. Inst. Fine Arts, Reading, Pa., 1982-85; piano accompanist Berks Grand Opera Co., Reading, Pa., 1982-85, Va. Opera Co., Norfolk, 1986, U. S.C., Columbia, 1992-95, Jacksonville Masterworks Sr. Chorale, 1996-99, Bolles Sr. H.S., 1996-98, Pinewood Presbyn. Ch., 1996-98; piano and music theory instr. Acad. of Music, Virginia Beach, Va., 1986-91, 2002—03; piano instr., choral dir., vocal jazz dir., accompanist Jacksonville (Fla.) U., 1995—2000; chair vocal music dept. Douglas Anderson Sch. of Arts, 1998—2000; prof. music U. North Fla., Jacksonville, 2000—. Editor: Florida Music Teacher, 1999-2000; contbr. articles to profl. publs. Mem. Virginia Beach Pops Orch., 1989-91. Recipient Fla. First Lady's Art Scholar award, 2000. Mem. AAUW (numerous offices 1975—), Am. Choral Dirs. Assn., Coll. Music Soc., Nat. Piano Found., Music Educators Nat. Conf., Nat. Guild Piano Tchrs., Music Tchrs. Nat. Assn., Delius Assn. Fla. (bd. dirs. 1997-99), Phi Kappa Lambda, Mu Phi Epsilon, Delta Kappa Gamma Soc. Internat., TRI-M Music Honor Soc. Home: 4782 Harpers Ferry Ln Jacksonville FL 32257-4544

STEWART, SARAH, elementary school educator; BS in Edn., Ohio State U., 1963; MS, U. N.C., 1978. Reading recovery/reading resource tchr. McDougle Elem. Sch., Chapel Hill, NC, 1998—. Recipient N.C. Gov.'s Long Leaf Pine award, 1992. Mem.: Am. Fedn. Tchrs. in N.C. (past pres.), Nat. Bd. for Profl. Tchg. Stds. (bd. mem.). Office: Chapel Hill-Carrboro City Schs-McDougle 900 Old Fayetteville Rd Chapel Hill NC 27516

STEWART, SHIRLEY ANNE, educational administrator; b. Bridgeville, Del., June 8, 1957; d. James Elliott and Pearline (Jacobs) Stewart. BS in Spl. Edn., U. Del., 1979, MEd in Curriculum and Instrn., 2001; MEd in Spl. Edn., Temple U., 1981. Cert. tchr., Del. Spl. edn. tchr. Caesar Rodney Sch. Dist., Camden, Del., 1979, Indian River Sch. Dist., Frankford, Del., 1980—; tchr. Frankford Elem. Sch., 1980-91, Sussex Ctrl. Mid. Sch., Millsboro, Del., 1991-94; asst. prin. Woodbridge Elem. Sch., Greenwood, Del., 1994-96, Pleasantville Elem. Sch., New Castle, Del., 1996-98, McCullough Elem. Sch., New Castle, 1998—2001; prin. Martin L. King Jr. Elem. Sch., Wilmington, Del., 2001—03; asst. prin. George Read Mid. Sch., Newcastle, Del., 2003—. Mem. Gov.'s Adv. Coun. for Exceptional Citizens, Dover, Del., 1986-91; mem. Coun. Exceptional Children, Dover, 1986—; mem. Statewide Multicultural Com., 1989-90; instr. Del. Tchr. Ctr., 1990; mem. mid. sch. adv. coun. State Del., 1990-91, adv. coun. on multicultural edn., 1991-92, Mid. Sch. Reading Com., 1992, Indian River Sch. Dist. Recruitment/Critical Shortage Com., 1992, instructional materials rev. com. 1993—; pres. Garden Cmty., Inc., 1999—. Mem. black recruitment com. U. Del., 1987; mem. Minority Action Com., Dover, 1985-87, chmn. Martin L. King Jr. Writing Contest, 1987-88, mem. exec. bd., 1988-89, chmn. black history com., 1986-87, sec. local minority action com., 1985-88; mem. attendance com. Indian River Sch. Dist., 1987-88, recruitment & retention com., 1992, mid. sch. reading com., 1992, mem. materials rev. com., 1993—; chmn. Del. State Edn. Minority Action Com., 1989-90; mem. strategic planning com. Del. State Edn. Assn., 1989-90, issues for the 90's com., 1991; active Dept. Pub. Instrn. Multicultural Inst. Tng., 1989; mem. middle sch. com. State of Del., 1991; mem. Statewide Multicultural Adv. Com., 1991—; vol. Saturday Sch. Com., 1992-93; mem. New Directions Com., 1992-93, Del. Prin.'s Leadership Acad., 1995-96; mem. tech. task force Colonial Sch. Dist., 1998-99; pres. Garden Cmty. Inc., 1999-2000. Recipient Instrnl. Profl. Devel. award Minority Action Com., 1987, Del. Tchr. Ctr. Svc. award, 1989, Instrnl. Profl. Devel. award Del. State Edn. Assn., 1990, Outstanding Black Woman award Nat. Polit. Congress of Black Women, Inc., 1997, 21st Century award for Positive Sch. Leadership, 2003. Mem. NEA, NAACP, ASCD, Nat. Elem. Sch. Prins. Assn., Del. Assn. Sch. Adminstrs., Del. Elem. Sch. Prins. Assn., Del. State Edn. Assn. (chairperson minority action com. 1988-91, Instrnl. Profl. Devel. award 1991, Human and Civil Rights award 1992), Indian River Edn. Assn. (treas. 1989-91, chairperson minority action com. 1990-93), Adults and Children with Learning Disabilities. Democrat. Pentacostal/Apostolic. Avocations: reading, poetry. Home: 224 Becks Woods Dr Bear DE 19701-3831 E-mail: sstew63598@aol.com.

STEWART, SUE S. lawyer; b. Oct. 9, 1942; d. Fraizer McVale and Carolyn Eliabeth (Hunt) S.; m. Arthur L. Stern, III, July 31, 1965 (div.); m. children: Anne, Mark Alan; m. John A. Ciampa, Sept. 1, 1985 (div.); m. Stephen L. Raymond (dec.). BA, Wellesley Coll., 1964; postgrad., Harvard U. Law Sch., 1964-65; JD, Georgetown U., 1967. Bar: N.Y. 1968. Clk. to judges Juvenile Ct., Washington, 1967-68; mem. Nixon, Hargrave, Devans & Doyle (now Nixon Peabody LLP), Rochester, N.Y., 1968-74, ptnr., 1975—2001, mng. ptnr., 1998—2001, ret., 2001; v.p., gen. counsel U. Rochester, 2003—. Lectr. in field; trustee Found. of Monroe County (N.Y.) Bar, 1976-78; v.p. & Gen. Counsel Univ. Rochester, NY, 2003-. Author: Charitable Giving and Solicitation. Sec., dir. United Cmty. Chest of Greater Rochester, 1973-87, 1992-; trustee, sec. Internat. Mus. Photography at George Eastman House, Rochester, 1974-97, 2000-03, Genesee Country Mus., Mumford, N.Y., 1976-2002; bd. dirs. Ctr. for Govtl. Rsch., 1990-97; trustee, chmn. United Neighborhood Ctr. of Greater Rochester Found., 1991-2003; trustee, chmn. exec. com. Nat. Ctr. Edn. and Economy, 1997-; dir. Canandaigua (N.H.) Nat. Bank, 2000-. Mem. ABA (chmn. task force on charitable giving, exempt orgns. com. tax sect. 1981-2003), N.Y. State Bar (exec. com. tax sect. 1974-76, chmn. com. exempt orgns. 1975-76), Monroe County Bar Assn. (trustee 1974-75), BNA Portfolio, Pvt. Found. Distbns. (Athena award 2000, de Tocqueville award 2003). Office: Office of Counsel 266 Wallis Hall PO Box 270040 Rochester NY 14627-0040

STEWART, SUSAN, writer; b. 1952; BA, Dickinson Coll., 1973; MA, Johns Hopkins U., 1975; PhD, U. Pa., 1978. Asst. prof. dept. English Temple U., Phila., 1978—81, assoc. prof., 1981—85, prof., 1986—87; Regan prof. English U. Pa., Phila., 1997—. Vis. scholar Getty Ctr. for the History of Art and the Humanities, Santa Monica, Calif., 1995. Author: Nonsense: Aspects of Intertextuality in Folklore and Literature, 1979, On Longing: Narratives of the Miniature, the Gigantic, the Souvenir, the Collection, 1984, Crimes of Writing: Problems in the Containment of Representation, 1991, poetry. Recipient Individual Writer's award, Lila Wallace-Reader's Digest Found., 1996; fellow, Nat. Endowment for the Arts, 1982, 1990, Pa. Coun. on the Arts, 1984, 1988, John Simon Guggenheim Meml. Found., 1987; MacArthur fellow, 1997. Office: Univ Pa Dept English 119 Bennett Hall 3340 Walnut St Philadelphia PA 19104-6273*

STEWART, THOMAS CLIFFORD, trading and investment company executive; b. Portland, Oreg., Oct. 25, 1950; s. Jack Fry Stewart and Naomi June Gedney Cuyler; m. Susan Elizabeth Sample; children: Andrew, Tommy, MacKenzie, Cortny. Student, U. Gothenburg, Sweden, 1971; BS, U. Oreg., 1974; MBA, UCLA, 1982. Exec. dir. Morgan Stanley & Co., N.Y.C., 1982-90; pres. Cort MacKenzie & Co., Portland, 1990-2000; dir. Acrymed, Lake Oswego, Oreg., 1995-96, Morley Fin. Svcs., Lake Oswego, Oreg., 1995-97. Dir. NCAA Leadership Adv. Bd., 2003—. Contbr. articles to profl. jours. Trustee U. Oreg. Found., 1994-2004; dir. Oreg. Air and Space Mus., 2001-2004; chmn. U. Oreg. Pres.'s Assn., 1997-99; exec. com., Lundquist Coll. of Bus., Univ. Oregon, 1998-2001, 2003-04, bd. advisors Coll. Bus., U. Oreg., 1990—, Athletic Dept., Bd. Advisors, Univ. Oregon, 1998—; Oreg. State Commn. on Higher Bus. Edn., 1992-94; mem. leadership coun. U. Oreg., 1995-99; bd. dirs. Lake Oswego Sch. Found., 1996-2000; treas. adv. cabinet State of Oreg., 1993-94; adv. bd. Sec. of Navy Nat. Naval Res. Policy Bd., Washington, 1987-89; mem. edn. specification com. Eugene 4J, Oreg., 2001-2004. Comdr. USN, 1974-80, USNR, 1980-91. Decorated Air medal, Navy Commendation for Valor; Baker scholar, 1981. Mem. Naval Res. Assn. (Jr. Officer of Yr. 1988), U.S. Navy League, ROA, Am. Legion, VFW, Beta Gamma Sigma, Beta Alpha Psi, Alpha Mu Alpha, Skull & Dagger.

STEWART, THOMAS J. wholesale distribution executive; b. Mar. 28, 1945; CEO Svcs. Group Am., 1985—. Office: Svcs Group of Am 4025 Delridge Way SW Ste 500 Seattle WA 98106-1271

STEWART, THOMAS JAMES, JR., baritone; b. San Saba, Tex., Aug. 29, 1928; s. Thomas James and Gladys Naomi (Reavis) S.; m. Evelyn Lear, Jan. 8, 1955; children: Jan Lear, Bonni Lear. Mus.B., Baylor U., 1953; postgrad., Juilliard Sch. Music, 1953-54, Berlin Hochschule for Music, 1957-58. Appeared with, Met. Opera, Chgo. Opera, San Francisco Opera, Bayreuth Festival, Salzburg Festival, Vienna State Opera, Royal Opera Covent Garden, Grand Opera Paris, Deutsche Oper Berlin, La Scala, Milan, Budapest Opera, Prague Opera, 1960—, also major orchs., throughout the world. Mem. hon. coun. IVS S'hertogenbosch, The Netherlands, 1996; artistic advisor Vocal Arts Soc., Washington, 1995; mem. hon. adv. bd. George London Found. for Singers, N.Y.C., 1994. Served with USAF, 1945-49. Recipient Kammersaenger of Berlin, 1964; Richard Wagner medal, 1965; San Francisco Opera medal, 1985, Am. Artist citation N.Y. Singing Tchrs. Assn., 1995; Fulbright grantee, 1957-58.

STEWART, TONY, professional race car driver; b. Rushville, Ind., May 20, 1971; Recipient Hoosier Auto Racing Fans 1st-Yr. Driver award, 1989, USAC Sprint Rookie of Yr. award, 1991, Indpls. Speedrome midget series Rookie of Yr. award, 1991. Achievements include Internat. Kartin Found. Grand nat. champion, 1983; World Karting Assn. nat. champion, 1987; 1st USAC victory, Indpls., 1991; 1st USAC nat. midget victory, Hut Hundred, Terre Haute, Ind., 1993; finished 5th in points, finished 2d Copper World Classic, Phoenix; NASCAR Busch Series Grand Nat. divsn. debut, 1999; winner Pennzoil 400, 1999; Checker Auto Parts/Dura-Lube 500, 1999; Exide NASCAR 4000, 1999. Office: c/o Joe Gibbs Racing 13415 Reese Blvd W Huntersville NC 28078-7933

STEWART, VERLINDSEY LAQUETTA, accounting educator; b. Birmingham, Ala., Dec. 27, 1965; d. Nathan Jr. and Shirley Ruth Brown; m. Kelvin Lorenzo Stewart I, June 22, 1991 (div. Feb. 1999); 1 child, Kelvin Lorenzo II. BS in Acctg., Ala. A&M U., 1988, MS in Bus. Edn., 1995, AA Cert. in Bus. Edn., 1997; EdD in higher edn. leadership, Nova Southeastern Univ., 2004. Cert. tchr. bus. grades 7-12, Ala. Jr. acct. Childress Acctg., Huntsville, Ala., 1990-93; acctg. clk. Appeal Beauty Salon, Huntsville, 1988-94; receptionist Coop. Ext., Normal, Ala., 1992-94; grad. asst. Ala. A&M U., Normal, 1995; student tchr. J.O. Johnson H.S., Huntsville, Ala., 1995; acctg. instr. J.F. Drake State Tech., Huntsville, 1996—. Cons. Jr. Achievement, Huntsville, 1995—96. Post-reviewer: (book) College Accounting 9th, 1999 (Honorarium 1999). Vol. Habitat for Humanity, Huntsville, 1995-97; vol. asst. leader Girl Scouts North Ala., Huntsville, 1995-96. Recipient Adminstrv. Acad. award Rust Coll., 1999, Emerging Leaders Sch. award Ala. Edn. Assn., 1994, Ala. Master Tchr. Seminar, 2001. Mem. Nat. Bus. Edn., Ea. Star Mitzpah Ctr., Phi Beta Lambda (adviser 1998—), Delta Sigma Theta. Democrat. Baptist. Avocations: aerobics, weights, reading, listening to jazz music. Office: JF Drake State Tech Coll 3421 Meridian St N Huntsville AL 35811-1544 Personal E-mail: vbdst28@aol.com.

STEWART, WARREN EARL, chemical engineer, educator; b. Whitewater, Wis., July 3, 1924; s. Earl Austin and Avis (Walker) S.; m. Jean Durham Potter, May 24, 1947; children— Marilyn, David, Douglas, Carol, Margaret, Mary Jean. BS in Chem. Engring. U. Wis., 1945, MS in Chem. Engring, 1947; Sc.D. in Chem. Engring, Mass. Inst. Tech., 1951. Project chem. engr. Sinclair Research Labs., Harvey, Ill., 1950-56, cons., 1956-83; from asst. prof. to prof. chem. engring. dept. U. Wis., Madison, 1956—96, chmn. dept., 1973-78, McFarland-Bascom prof., 1983-96, prof. emeritus, 1997—; pres. Stewart &

Assoc. Engring. Software, Inc., 1998—. Cons. Engelhard Industries, Inc., Newark, 1956-58; instr. spl. courses transport phenomena Chemstrand Corp., Pensacola, Fla., 1962, Nat. U. La Plata, Argentina, 1962, Esso Rsch. & Engring. Co., 1963, 66, Phillips Petroleum Co., 1963, Am. Inst. Chem. Engrs., 1965, 68-69, Inst. Tec. Celaya (Mex.), 1983, U. Autonoma de Mex., 1985; Reilly lectr. Notre Dame U., 1993. Author: (with R.B. Bird and E.N. Lightfoot) Transport Phenomena, 1960, 2d edit., 2002, Special Topics in Transport Phenomena, 1965, (with R.B. Bird, E.N. Lightfoot and T.W. Chapman) Lectures in Transport Phenomena, 1969; editl. adv. Latin Am. Applied Rsch., Computers and Chem. Engring., 1977—. Recipient Benjamin Smith Reynolds teaching award, 1981, Byron Bird rsch. award, 1991. Fellow Am. Inst. Chem. Engrs. (Computing in Chem. Engring. award 1985); mem. NAE, Am. Chem. Soc. (Murphree award 1989), Am. Soc. for Engring. Edn., (Chem. Engring. Lectureship award 1983), Wis. Acad. Scis., Arts and Letters, Phi Beta Kappa, Sigma Xi, Alpha Chi Sigma (Rsch. award 1981), Phi Eta Sigma, Tau Beta Pi, Phi Lambda Upsilon, Phi Kappa Phi. Conglist. (deacon, moderator). Home: 734 Huron Hill Madison WI 53711-2955 Business E-Mail: stewart@wisc.engr.edu.

STEWART, WILLIAM A. medical educator, neurosurgeon; b. Liberty Center, Ohio, Apr. 6, 1933; s. Cyrus Byron Stewart, Ardis Marjory Hicks; m. Nancy Newell Travis, June 18, 1960; children: Katherine, Elizabeth, Janet, Sarah, Heather, Alexandra. AB, Miami U., Oxford, Ohio, 1954; MD, Ohio State U., 1958. Diplomate Am. Bd. Neurosurgery. Resident in gen. surgery/neurosurgery SUNY-Upstate Med. Univ., Syracuse, 1958—65; prof. clin. neurosurgery SUNY-Upstate Med. Ctr. Inst. Med. Humanities; team dir. Project Hope, Ile Ife, Nigeria, 1974—75. Bd. Prof. Med. Conduct N.Y. State Dept. Health, 1977—98, chmn., NY, 1989—91, adminstrn. rev. bd., 1992—98. Lt. comdr. M.C. USNR, 1955—72, with M.C. USN, 1965—67, Vietnam. Fellow: FACS; mem.: AMA, Congress of Neurologic Surgeons, Am. Assn. Neurologic Surgeons, Coalition for Physician Enhancement. Presbyterian. Avocations: gardening, coin collecting/numismatics. Home: 7595 Hunt Ln Fayetteville NY 13066

STEWART, WILLIAM THOMAS, communications educator; b. Bryan, Tex., Sept. 29, 1934; s. Simeon Brooks and Bess Maude (McGee) S.; m. Roswitha Form Stewart, June 19, 1959; children: Terri M., Erin K. BA in History, U. Tex., Austin, 1957; MA in Speech and Drama, Calif. State U., Sacramento, 1969. Cert. tchr., Calif. Mgmt. trainee S.W. Bell Tel. Co., Houston, 1960—61; tchr. San Juan Unified Sch. Dist., Carmichael, Calif., 1962—99; instr. We. Career Coll., Sacramento, 1999—; student tchr. supr. Nat. U., Sacramento, 2000—, Chapman U., 2001—. Author: International Film Necrology, 1981, Ronald Reagan: A Bibliography, 1988; contbr. plays and poetry to profl. jours. With U.S. Army, 1957-63. Mem. NEA. Mem. Ch. Christ. Avocations: play directing and writing, reading, extra work in films. Home: 7101 Falcon Rd Fair Oaks CA 95628 E-mail: bvstew@pacbell.net.

STEYER, THOMAS FAHR, investment company executive; Grad., Yale U.; MBA, Stanford U., 1983. Mng. dir. Hellman & Friedman LLC, 1986—; sr. mng. mem. Farallon Capital Mgmt. LLC, 1986—; assoc. risk arbitrage dept. Goldman, Sachs & Co.; with mergers and acquisitions dept. Morgan Stanley & Co. Bd. dirs CapitalSource, Chevy Chase, Md. Office: Hellman & Friedman LLC One Maritime Plz 12th Fl San Francisco CA 94111*

STIASSNY, MELANIE L.J. curator; BSc in Zoology with honors, U. London, 1976, PhD in Zoology, 1980. Fellow Rijksuniversiteit and Rijksmuseum, Leiden, Netherlands, 1980—83; asst. prof. dept organismic and evolutionary biology Harvard U., 1983—87; asst. curator dept. herpetology and ichthyology Am. Mus. Natural History, N.Y.C., 1987—92, assoc. curator dept. herpetology and ichthyology, 1992—97, Herbert R. and evelyn Axelrod rsch. curator, curator-in-charge dept. ichthyology, 1997—. Adj. prof. CUNY, 1992—, Ctr. for Environ. Rsch. and Conservation, NY, 1999—; sci. adv. World Wildlife Fund for Nature, Conservation Internat., World Resources Inst., Internat. Found. for Sci. Contbr. articles to profl. jours. Grantee, NSF, 1993—2001, Nat. Geog. Soc., 1997—98, Am. Mus. Natural History, 1997—99. Office: Am Mus Natural History Dept Ichthyology Central Park West at 79th St New York NY 10024

STIBBE, AUSTIN JULE, accountant; b. St. Paul, Mar. 29, 1930; s. Austin Julius and Agnes Dorothea (Delaney) S.; m. Mary Elizabeth King, May 29, 1952; children: Anne Marie, Craig Jule, David King, Karen Lee. BSB in Acctg., U. Minn., 1952. CPA, Minn., Wis. Tax acct. Ernst & Ernst, Mpls., 1955-60; corp. tax mgr. EcoLab, Inc., St. Paul, 1960-65; audit mgr. Coopers & Lybrand, Mpls., 1965-74; v.p. Wilkerson, Guthmann & Johnson, Ltd., St. Paul, 1974-93, of counsel, 1993—. Exec. officer Twin Cities Squadron, U.S. Naval Sea Cadet Corps, Mpls., 1974-80; bd. dirs., treas., mem. Twin Cities coun. Navy League, 1970—, pres., 1979-81, treas., 1975-79, 81-91; mem. adv. coun. to dept. acctg. U. Minn., Mpls., 1983-86; bd. dirs., chmn. audit com. St. Paul Area Coun. Chs., 1985-87; mem. adv. bd. Headwaters Soc., 1987-88; mem. fin. reporting com. United Way St. Paul Area, 1981-93, mem. audit com., 1991-93; dist. commr. staff Indianhead coun. Boy Scouts Am., 1962-65. Lt. USN, 1952-55. Mem. Minn. Soc. CPAs (life), U.S. Naval Inst. (life), Belle Taine Lake Assn. (dir. 1995-2001, treas. 1996-2001), Hubbard County COLA Print Com., 1995-98, Friends of Heritage, 1996—, Hubbard County Works of Improvement (steering com. 2001), VFW (life), Am. Legion. Presbyterian. Avocations: music, boating, history. Home: PO Box 41 Nevis MN 56467-0041

STIBER, JULIE ANNE, social worker; b. Binghamton, N.Y., May 1, 1962; d. Max Linwood and Ruth Mary S. BA, Albertus Magnus, New Haven, Conn., 1984; MSW, So. Conn. State U., New Haven, Conn., 1991. LCSW Conn., 1993, DCSW Conn., 1996. Asst. dir. Coord. Coun. Children in Crisis, New Haven, 1996—99; clin. coord. social work Priority Care, New Haven, Bridgeport and Norwalk, Conn., 1999—2000; dir. social work svcs. New Eng. Home Care, Conn., 2000—; clin. cons. Dept. Children & Families, State of Conn. Mem.: Nat. Assn. Social Workers (children's com. 2001—, diplomate in clin. social work 1996). Democrat. Episcopalian. Avocations: running, painting, drawing, jewelry, cooking. Office: State of Conn Dept Children & Families 1 Long Wharf New Haven CT 06511

STICE, DWAYNE LEE, broadcasting company executive; b. Paducah, Ky., Aug. 10, 1956; s. Freeman D. and Dorris Olive (Lee) S. AA, Paducah Community Coll., 1976; BS, Murray State U., 1977; MS, Southern Ill. U., 1983. Lic. funeral dir., Ky. Dir. Johnson-Lambert Funeral Home, Calvert City, Ky., 1974-81; gen. mgr. Paducah Area Transit System, 1980-92; pres. Sta. WCCK-FM, Stice Comm., Inc., Calvert City, 1990—2001; human resources, programming WPSD-TV, Paducah, Ky., 2001—. Adj. bus. instr. Paducah Community Coll., 1979—, Lindsey Wilson Coll., Columbia, Ky., 1991; adj. reporter CBS Radio Network, 1997-2000. Contbr. articles to profl. jours. Bd. dirs. Calvert Area Mentoring Program; mem. Calvert Area Devel. Assn.; transp. com. Purchase Area Devel. Dist. Outstanding grantee Ky. Transp. Cabinet, 1985, 86. Mem. Ky. Pub. Transit Assn. (pres. 1988-91), Ky. Broadcasters Assn. (bd. dirs. 1997-2000), Marshall C. of C. (bd. dirs., vice chmn. govt. affairs 1998), Paducah C.C. Alumni Assn. (pres. 1983), Hon. Order Ky. Cols., Travelers Protective Assn. (pres. Paducah chpt. 1989-90), Lions, Masons (master Calvert City 1984), Shriners, Order Ea. Star, Phi Kappa Phi, Phi Theta Kappa. Methodist. Avocations: organist, travel, baseball, antique clocks, automobiles. Home: 647 S Main St Calvert City KY 42029-8385 Office: WPSD-TV 100 TV Ln Paducah KY 42003

STICH, JUNE JEACOMA, psychotherapist; b. Mineola, N.Y., June 27, 1939; d. John Daniel and Mercedes (Serrano) Jeacoma; m. William Thomas Lloyd, Sept. 16, 1961 (div. 1967); m. Edward Stich, July 6, 1974 (div. 1999); 1 child, Edward John. AA, Nassau C.C., 1967; BS, Empire State Coll., 1981; MSW, Adelphi U., 1990; postgrad., Hunter Coll., 1986-87. Cert. social worker. Welfare examiner I Dept. Social Svcs., Mineola, N.Y., 1971-74; pres., founder Happy Marriage League, Long Beach, N.Y., 1974-81; asst. coord. St. Mary Roman Cath. Ch., Long Beach, N.Y., 1980-82; social worker, case mgr. Cath. Charities, Lynbrook, N.Y., 1985-87; social worker, counselor Peninsula Counseling Ctr., Woodmere, N.Y., 1988-89, Jewish Assn. of Svcs. to Aged, Long Beach, 1989-90; social worker, psychotherapist Winter Park (Fla.) Home Health Care, 1991-92, Margaret Tietz Nursing Home, Jamaica, NY, 1992—94, Fla. Hosp. Ctr. Psychiatry, Orlando, 1995—96, Shands Homecare, Orlando, Fla., 1997—99, pvt. practice, Winter Park, Fla., 1998—2000, Mayfair Care Ctr., Hempstead, NY, 2001—, pvt. practice, Rockville Center, NY, 2001—, N.Y.C., 2002—. Held several bereavement groups & stress mngmt. groups, NY, 1999—. Narrator, writer audio tape: Think Thin, 1985. Coord. retreats L.I. Charismatic Renewal, 1985, 86. Recipient Silberman award Scholarship Com. of Hunter Coll., 1986; recipient 4 vol. svc. awards VA, 1988-89. Mem. Am. Assn. for Counseling and Devel., Nat. Assn. Social Workers, N.Am. Assn. of Christians in Social Wk. Roman Catholic. Avocations: painting, dance, walking, gardening. Home: 111 West 71st St Apt 2B New York NY 10023

STICH, STEPHEN PETER, philosophy educator; b. N.Y.C., May 9, 1943; s. Samuel Joseph and Sylvia Lucille (Siegel) S.; m. Judith Ann Gagnon, Dec. 20, 1971; children: Jonathan Andrew, Rebecca Elizabeth. BA summa cum laude with distinction, U. Pa., 1964; PhD, Princeton U., 1968. Teaching asst. Princton U., 1965; asst. prof. U. Mich., 1968-73, assoc. prof., 1973-78, dir. grad. studies in philosophy, 1973-74, assoc. chmn. dept. philosophy, 1975-76; assoc. prof. U. Md., 1978-81, prof., 1981-86, dir. grad. studies in philosophy, 1982-83; prof. U. Calif., San Diego, 1986-89, dir. cognitive sci. program, 1988-89; prof. philosophy and cognitive sci. Rutgers U., New Brunswick, 1989—, acting chair dept. philosophy, 1992-93, dir. rsch. group on evolution and higher cognition, 1997—, bd. govs. prof., 1998—. Prof. Linguistic inst., Linguistic Soc. Am., summer 1982; dir. Summer Seminar for Coll. Tchrs. NEH, 1983, 89; vis. sr. lectr. U. Sydney, 1984-85; vis. fellow Australian Nat. U., 1992; Jemison prof. humanities U. Ala., Birmingham, 1993; adj. prof. CUNY Grad. Ctr., 1994-97; Erskine fellow Canterbury U., Christchurch, New Zealand, 1996; cons. Pres. Commn. for Nat. Priorities in the Eighties, Pres. Commn. on Ethics in Medicine and Biomed. and Behavioral Rsch.; mem. selection com. Mellon Fellowships in the Humanities, 1983-84; mem. Fulbright Selection Com., 1981-83, chair, 1983; vis. fellow Australian Nat. U., Rsch. Sch. Social Scis., 1992. Author: From Folk Psychology to Cognitive Science, 1983, The Fragmentation of Reason, 1990, Deconstructing the Mind, 1996, Mindreading, 2003; editor: Innate Ideas, 1975; (with others) The Recombinant DNA Debate, 1979, Philosophy and Connectionist Theory, 1991, Mental Representation, 1994; editor Evolution and Cognition Series; mem. editl. bd. Linguistics and Philosophy, 1984—, Mind and Language, 1985—, Cognitive Sci., 1990—, Minds and Machines, 1991—, Pragmatics and Cognition, 1991—, Philosophical Studies, 1992—, Philosophy of Sci., 1992—, Cognition, 1993—, Neural Network Modeling and Connectionism; mem. editl. adv. bd. Studies in Cognitive Sys.; contbr. articles to profl. jours., chpts. to books. Woodrow Wilson Nat. Fellowship Found. fellow, 1964-65, Woodrow Wilson dissertation fellow, 1967, Danforth grad. fellow, 1964-67, H.H. Ford fellow Princeton U., 1967, Coun. Philos. Studies Summer Inst. fellow, 1971, Am. Coun. Learned Socs. fellow, 1978-79, Rutgers U. competitive fellow, sch. liberal arts fellow U. Otago, Dunedin, New Zealand, 2001; recipient fellowships NEH, 1974, 83-84, 96, Ctr. for Advanced Study in Behavioral Scis., Stanford, Calif., 1983; Fulbright sr. rsch. scholar, Bristol (U.K.) U., 1978-79; grantee U.S.-Israel Ednl. Found., 1979, NRC and U.S. Nat. Com. for Internat. Union of History and Philosophy of Sci., Hannover, West Germany, 1979, NSF, 1981-82. Mem. Am. Philos. Assn., Soc. for Philosophy and Psychology (pres. 1982-83, exec. com. 1980-82, 83-84, chair program com. 1979-80), Philosophy of Sci. Assn., Brit. Soc. for Philosophy of Sci., Fulbright Alumni Assn. Office: Rutgers U Philosophy Dept Davison Hall Douglass Campus New Brunswick NJ 08901-2882 E-mail: stich@ruccs.rutgers.edu.

STICHNOTH, JOHN A. corporate lawyer; V.p. gen. counsel Union Carbide Corp., Danbury, Conn. Office: Old Ridgebury Rd Danbury CT 06817-0001

STICHT, J. PAUL, retired food products and tobacco company executive; b. Clairton, Pa, 1917; BA, Grove City Coll., 1939; postgrad., U. Pitts. With US Steel Corp., 1939-44; pers. dir. Trans World Airlines, 1944-48; v.p. Campbell Soup Co., 1947-57, pres. internat., 1957-60; from exec. v.p. to pres. Federated Dept. Stores, Inc., 1960-72; chmn. exec. com., COO R.J. Reynolds Industries, Inc., Winston-Salem, NC, 1972-73, pres., CEO, 1978-79, chmn. bd., 1979-85; chmn. RJR Nabisco, Inc., Winston-Salem, 1987-89, acting chmn., CEO, 1989; pres. Castle Springs, LLC, Winston-Salem, 1992—2002, chmn., 2002—03. Mem. Bd. Trustees Grove City Coll., former chmn; mem. bd. visitors Wake Forest U. Med. Sch., former chmn. bd. visitors; mem. bd. visitors Fuqua Sch. Bus. Duke U. Office: 119 Brookstown Ave Winston Salem NC 27101-5245

STICK, MICHAEL ALAN, lawyer; b. Elizabeth City, N.C., June 2, 1954; s. David and Phyllis (Stapells) S.; m. Debra Joan Braselton, May 22, 1993. BA, Davidson Coll., 1976; JD, U. N.C., 1981. Bar: Ill. 1981, U.S. Dist. Ct. (no. dist.) Ill. 1982, U.S. Ct. Appeals (7th cir.) 1983, U.S. Ct. Appeals (8th cir.) 1986. Assoc. Jenner & Block, Chgo., 1981-84, Butler, Rubin, Newcomer, Saltarelli & Boyd, Chgo., 1984-87; ptnr. Butler, Rubin, Saltarelli & Boyd, Chgo., 1988—. Co-author: Environmental Law Handbook, 1988, Environmental Law in Illinois, 1993; mem. staff U. N.C. Law Rev., 1979-80. Chmn. spl. gifts divsn. United Way Crusade of Mercy, Chgo., 1993-94. Me. ABA, Chgo. Bar Assn. Democrat. Methodist. Avocations: travel, skiing, art. Home: 616 E Hickory St Hinsdale IL 60521-2413 Office: Butler Rubin Saltarelli & Boyd Three First Nat Pla # 1800 Chicago IL 60602

STICK, THOMAS HOWARD FITCHETT, corporate architect, construction litigation consultant; b. Balt., Feb. 28, 1938; s. Gordon M. F. and Anne Howard (Fitchett) S.; m. Rosalie Wade Reynolds, 1959 (div. 1982); children: H. Edward M., Alexander W., David F.; m. Joyce Yeargin Carr, 1982 (div. 1989); m. Alyce C. Cushing, 1989. BA in Psychology, Yale U., 1960; postgrad., Md. Inst., 1962, U. Pa. Grad. Sch. Arch., 1964. Registered arch., Pa., Md., Del., N.J., Va., Maine, N.Y., D.C., Mass., N.H., N.C., Vt., Tenn., Okla., Colo., Ind., Ga., Ill., Mich., Ky., Kans., Ohio, Peoples Republic of China; cert. recommendation Nat. Coun. Archtl. Registration Bds. Arch. Vincent G. Kling & Ptnrs., Phila., 1964-74, B.J. Hoffman & Assocs., Berwyn, Pa., 1974; ptnr. Grim & Stick, Ardmore, Pa., 1975-77; prin. Stick Assocs., Gladwyne, Pa., 1977-80; corp. arch. Gino's Inc., King of Prussia, Pa., 1980-81; mgr. constrn. adminstrn. Ballinger Co., Phila., 1981-83; sr. constrn. claims cons. MDC Sys. Corp., Phila., 1984-85; chief arch. Day & Zimmermann Inc., Phila., 1985—, discipline mgr., 1987—, corp. arch., 1995—; dir. Day & Zimmermann Internat. Corp., Phila., 2000—. V.p. F-S Found., 1986, also bd. dirs. One-man show in photography Ea. Camera Gallery, 1972. Named Arch. of Best Food Plant of Yr., Food Engring. Mag., 1992. Mem. AIA, Pa. Soc. Archs., Bldg. Ofcls. and Code Adminstrs. Internat., Internat. Conf. Bldg. Ofcls., So. Bldg. Code Congress Internat., Constrn. Specifications Inst., Nat. Fire Protection Assn., Soc. War of 1812 (sec. 1977-82), Soc. of Cincinnati, Soc. Colonial Wars, SR, Descs. of Lords of the Md. Manors, Mil. Order of Loyal Legion of U.S., Huguenot Soc., Am. Clan Gregor Soc., St. Andrew's Soc. of Balt., St. George's Soc. of Balt., Merion Cricket Club (Haverford, Pa.), Yale Club, Sovereign Mil. of Temple of Jerusalem (comdr.), Sovereign Order of St. John of Jerusalem (Knight of Justice), Knights Malta, Zeta Psi. Home: 1501 Monticello Dr Gladwyne PA 19035-1206 Office: Day & Zimmermann Internat 240 Continental Dr Newark DE 19713-4328

STICKEL, FREDERICK A. publishing executive; b. Weehawken, N.J., Nov. 18, 1921; s. Fred and Eva (Madigan) S.; m. Margaret A. Dunne, Dec. 4, 1943; children— Fred A., Patrick F., Daisy E., Geoffrey M., James E., Bridget A. Student, Georgetown U., 1939-42; BS, St. Peter's Coll., 1943. Advt. salesperson Jersey Observer daily, Hoboken, N.J., 1945-51; retail advt. salesperson Jersey Jour., Jersey City, 1951-55, advt. dir., 1955-66, publisher, 1966-67; gen. mgr. Oregonian Pub. Co., Portland, Oreg., 1967-72, pres., 1972-86, publisher, 1975—. Bd. regents U. Portland; adv. bd. Portland State U., St. Vincent's Hosp.; bd. dirs. Portland Rose Festival Assn., United Way Oreg.; chmn. Portland Citizens Crime Commn. Capt. USMC, 1942-45. Mem. Assn. for Portland Progress (dir.), Portland C. of C. (dir.), Oreg. Newspaper Pubs. Assn. (past pres.), Pacific N.W. Newspaper Assn. (past pres.), Newspaper Assn. Am., University Club, Multnomah Athletic Waverley Country Club, Arlington Club, Rotary. Office: Oregonian Pub Co 1320 SW Broadway Portland OR 97201-3499

STICKEL, PATRICK FRANCIS, publishing executive, newspaper; b. Hoboken, N.J., Apr. 17, 1950; s. Fred A. and Margaret (Dunne) Stickel; m. Debra Isaak, May 10, 1986. Degree in bus. mgmt., U. Portland, 1975. With advt. dept. Jersey Jour., Jersey City, 1966—67; with Oregonian Pub. Co., Portland, 1967—68, 1970—75, pressman, with retail advt. dept., 1975—77, with retail & circulation depts., 1980—86, adminstrv. asst., 1987—89, gen. mgr., 1990—94, pres., 1994—; project mgr. Times Picayune, New Orleans, 1986—87. Mem. exec. com. Oreg. Forum, Portland. 1st lt. USMC, 1977—80. Mem.: Pacific N.W. Newspapers Assn. (bd. dirs.), Multnomah Athletic Club, Univ. Club, Waverley Country Club. Avocation: golf. Office: The Oregonian 1320 SW Broadway Portland OR 97201-3499

STICKLE, DAVID WALTER, microbiologist; b. Boston, Apr. 18, 1933; s. Harold Edwards and Lucille Margaret (Magee) S.; m. Mary Elizabeth DeLong, July 29, 1972. BS in Chemistry, Biology, Tufts U., 1955; MS in Pharmacy and Health, Northeastern U., Boston, 1968; MPH, U. N.C., 1969, DrPH, 1971. Bacteriologist Mass. Dept. Pub. Health, Boston, 1959-63, supr. immunology unit, 1963-68; UNC/CDC lab. dir.'s program Ctrs. for Disease Control, Atlanta, 1968-71; chief, clin. lab. improvement program Divsn. Med. Labs./Minn. Dept. Health, Mpls., 1971-82, acting dir., 1977-78, asst. dir., 1978-88. Ex-officio mem. Minn. Soc. Clin. Pathologists Exec. Com., Mpls., 1977-78; mem. Proficiency Testing Com., Minn. Acad. Family Physicians, Mpls., 1977-83; adj. asst. prof. U. Minn., Mpls., 1977-88; assoc. prof. emeritus, U. Minn., 1988—. Editor: Med. Lab. Forum periodical, 1973-88. Proctor Nat. Registry of Microbiology, Mpls. Examinations for Minn., 1987-92; instr. Edina Community Edn. Programs, Minn., 1992. With U.S. Army, 1955-57. Lab. tng. grantee Ctr. for Disease Control, HEW, Atlanta, 1977-78, 1978-80, 1979-81. Mem. Am. Soc. Microbiology, Phi Sigma, Sigma Xi. Achievements include serologic tests for systemic candidiasis which were in use for many years by the Ctrs. for Disease Control, U.S. Dept. of Health and Human Svcs.

STICKLER, DANIEL LEE, health care management consultant; b. Fairmont, W.Va., Jan. 4, 1938; s. Elmer Daniel and Ruby Lee (Ball) S.; m. Donna Lou Johnson, Apr. 16, 1960; children— Dwight Lorne, Dwayne Lee, Douglas Lynn BS in Civil Engring., W.Va. U., 1960; M.P.H. in Health Adminstrn., U. Pitts., 1970. Registered profl. engr., Tex. Asst. dir. Presbyn.-Univ. Hosp., Pitts., 1970-71, assoc. dir., 1971-72, adminstr., chief operating officer, 1972-76, exec. dir., chief exec. officer, 1976-83, pres., chief exec. officer, 1983-86; pres., CEO, The Cedars Med. Ctr., Miami, Fla., 1986-91; pres. DLS Assocs., Inc., Miami, 1991-95; sr. v.p. The Hunter Group, 1996—. Adj. assoc. prof. Grad. Sch. Pub. Health, U. Pitts., 1976-86. Fellow Am. Coll. Hosp. Adminstrn.; mem. Palmaire Country Club. Methodist. Avocations: golf, gardening. Home and Office: 5803 Fairwoods Cir Sarasota FL 34243-3821 E-mail: dstickle@tampabay.rr.com.

STICKLER, GUNNAR BRYNOLF, pediatrician; b. Petershirchen, Germany, June 13, 1925; came to U.S., 1951, naturalized, 1958; s. Fritz and Astrid (Wennerberg) S.; m. Duci M. Kronenbitter, Aug. 30, 1956; children: Katarina Anna, George David. MD, U. Munich, Germany, 1949; PhD, U. Minn., Mpls., 1957. Diplomate Am. Bd. Pediatrics, ofcl. examiner and mem., 1965-95. Resident in clin. pathology Krankenhaus III Orden, Munich, 1950; resident in pathology U. Munich, 1950-51; intern Mountainside Hosp., Montclair, N.J., 1951-52; fellow in pediatrics Mayo Grad. Sch., Rochester, Minn., 1953-56; sr. cancer research scientist Roswell Park Meml. Inst., Buffalo, 1956-57; asst. to staff Mayo Clinic, Rochester, 1957-58, cons. in pediatrics, 1959-89, head sect. pediatrics, 1969-74; prof. pediatrics, chmn. dept. pediatrics Mayo Clinic and Mayo Med. Sch., 1974-80. Mem. test com. III Nat. Bd. Med. Examiners, 1973-75; vis. prof. at various univs and instns., including U. Dusseldorf (Germany) and U. Munich, 1971, Pahlavi U., Iran, 1975, Olga Hosp., Stuttgart, Germany, 1978, Martin Luther King Hosp., Los Angeles, 1979, U. Man., 1981; mem. emeritus staff Mayo Clinic, 1989. Mem. editl. bd. Clin. Pediatrics, 1968-76, 79-97, European Jour. Pediatrics, 1976-84, Pediatrics, 1983-89; contbr. more than 290 articles to med. publs. Active parent support groups in field of cyclic vomiting syndrome; life pres. Stickler Syndrome support group, 1997—. Recipient Humanitarian award Chgo. region chpt. Nat. Found. Ileitis and Colitis, 1978, award for excellence of subject matter and presentation So. Minn. Med. Assn., 1978 Mem. Am. Acad. Pediatrics (Disting. Svc. award Minn. chpt. 1999), Soc. Pediatric Rsch., Am. Pediatric Soc., Nat. Coun. Reliable Health Info., Midwest Soc. Pediatric Rsch. (coun. 1967-69, pres. 1970-71, Founders award 1996), N.W. Pediatric Soc. (pres. 1973-74) Achievements include description of hereditary progressive arthropthalmopathy in 1965, now called Stickler syndrome; and the treatment otitis media, hypophosphatemic rickets, renal disease; research in areas of parents' fears and the need of routine physical examinations in adolescents, and the excesses of "alternative medicine.". Office: Mayo Clinic Emeritus Ctr Rochester MN 55905

STICKLES, BONNIE JEAN, retired nurse; b. Waukesha, Wis., Nov. 24, 1944; d. Donald William and Betty Jane S. BSN, U. Wis., 1967; MSN in Midwifery, Columbia U., 1974. Mem. nursing staff Grace Hosp., Detroit, 1970-73; mem. faculty and staff U. Minn. Sch. Nursing and Nurse-Midwifery Svc., Mpls., 1974-76; chief nurse-midwife, clin. instr. St. Paul-Ramsey Med. Ctr., 1976-84; midwifery supr. IHS/PHS Chinle Hosp., 1984-85; program mgr. maternal health sect. N.Mex. Dept. Health and Environ., 1985-90, Lovelance Med. Ctr., 1990-91, St. Vincent's Hosp., 1991-94, NMC Dialysis Divsn., 1994-95; blackjack dealer, 1995-97; nurse CMS Penitentiary, N.Mex., 1997—2002; ret. Author articles in field; patentee tchg. model. Mem. FDA Anesthetics, Life Support Adv. com.; adv. bd. Childbirth Edn. Assn., 1980-85. Served with USNR, 1965-70. Mem. Am. Coll. Nurse-Midwives (chmn. profl. affairs com. 1975-80), Nurses Assn. Am. Coll. Obstetricians and Gynecologists (charter), Aircraft Owners and Pilot Assn., Gt. Plains Perinatal Orgn., Alpha Tau Delta.

STICKNEY, JESSICA, former state legislator; b. Duluth, Minn., May 16, 1929; d. Ralph Emerson and Claudia Alice (Cox) Page; m. Edwin Levi Stickney, June 17, 1951; children: Claudia, Laura, Jeffrey. BA, Macalester Coll., St. Paul, Minn., 1951; PhD (hon), Rocky Mtn. Coll., Billings, Mont., 1986. Rep. State of Mont., 1989-92. Mem. Gov.'s Commn. on Post-Sec. Edn., Mont., 1973-75. Mem. Sch. Bd. Trustees, Miles City, Mont., 1968-74; mem., chmn. zoning bd., Miles City, 1975-89; mem. Govt. Study Commn., Miles City, 1974-76, United Ch. Christ Bd. Homeland Ministries, 1975-81; chmn., conf. moderator United Ch. Christ Bd. Mont.-Northern Wyo. Conf., 1980-82; chmn. Town Meeting on the Arts, Mont., 1980; mem., chmn. Miles Community Coll. Bd., 1975-89, chmn. 1978-80. Mem. Mont. Arts Coun. (chmn. 1982-85), Western States Arts Found. (vice chmn. 1984), Nat. Assembly State Arts Agys. (bd. dirs. 1982-88), AAUW (pres. 1964-66). Democrat. Avocations: writing, sewing, painting, reading.

STICKNEY, JOHN MOORE, lawyer; b. Cleve., Apr. 8, 1926; s. Isaac Moore and Alicia Margaret (Burns) S.; m. Elfriede von Rebenstock, Oct. 4, 1958; children: Michaela B., Alicia J., Thomas M. AB, Western Res. U., 1948, LLB, 1951. Bar: Ohio 1952. Sole practice, Cleve., 1952-79; ptnr. Burgess, Steck, Andrews & Stickney, Cleve., 1979-88; of counsel Weston, Hurd, Fallon, Paisley & Howley, Cleve., 1988-90, sole practice, 1990—; pres. Scranton-Averell, Inc., Cleve., 1979—. Trustee Cleve. Music Sch. Settlement, 1967—, Salzedo Sch. Harp, Cleve., 1962—, Bishop Brown Fund, Cleve., 1981—, Flats Oxbow Assn., Lake Erie Sci. & Nature Ctr., 1996—, also pres., 1970-72; co-trustee Margaret & Edwin Griffiths Trusts, Cleve., 1968—. Served with USNR, 1945-46. Mem. ABA, Ohio State Bar Assn., Cleve. Bar Assn., Hermit Club (Cleve.), Rowfant Club (Cleve.). Republican. Episcopalian.

STICKNEY, NANCY CARVER, state legislator; b. Bethel, Maine, July 20, 1936; d. Irving L. and Ruth W. (Homsted) Carver; m. Wallace E. Stickney, 1957; children: Peter, Christopher J., Daniel C., Adam K. BS, U. N.H., 1960. Mem. NH Ho. of Reps. (dist. 26), Concord, Maine, 1997—2000. Methodist. Home: PO Box 177 North Salem NH 03073-0177 Office: NH State Legis State House Concord NH 03301

STICKNEY, ROBERT ROY, fisheries educator; b. Minneapolis, July 2, 1941; s. Roy E. and Helen Doris (Nelson) S.; m. LuVerne C. (Whiteley), Dec. 29, 1961; children: Robert Roy, Marolan Margaret. BS, U. Nebr., 1967; MA, U. Mo., 1968; PhD, Fla. State U., 1971. cert. fisheries scientist. Rsch. assoc. Skidaway Inst. Oceanography, Savannah, Ga., 1971—73, asst. prof., 1973—75, Tex. A and M U., Coll. Sta., 1975—78, assoc. prof., 1978—83, prof., 1983—84; prof. zoology, dir. Fisheries Rsch. Lab., So. Ill. U., Carbondale, 1984—85; dir. Sch. of Fisheries U. Wash., Seattle, 1985—91, prof., 1985—86; dir. Sea Grant Coll. program Tex. A&M U., Coll. Sta., 1996—. Chmn. S-168 com. So. Regional Coop. Rsch. Project, 1981-84. Author: Principles of Warm Water Aqua-culture, 1979, Estuarine Ecology of the Southeastern U.S. and Gulf of Mex., 1984; editor: Culture of Non Salmonid Freshwater Fishes, 1986, 1992, Flagship: A History of Fisheries at the U. of Washington, 1989; co-editor: Fisheries: Harvesting Life from Water, 1989, Culture of Salmonid Fishes, 1992, Fisheries: Harvesting Life from Water, 1995, Principles of Aqua Culture, 1994, Fish Culture in the United States: A Hist. Survey, 1996, Responsible Marine Aqua-culture, 2002; editor: revs. in Fisheries Sci., Ency. of Aqua-culture, World Aqua-culture mag.; contbr. articles to profl. jour. Served in USAF, 1959-63. Mem.: Sea Grant Assn. (pres. 2004—). Personal E-mail: rrstickney@aol.com. E-mail: stickney@tamu.edu.

STIDHAM, LUCAS WESLEY, music educator; b. Lakeside, Ariz., Jan. 27, 1979; s. Nancy Ellen and Clayton Randall Stidham. BA in Music, No. Ariz. U., 2001. Cert. secondary edn. tchr. Ariz., 2004. Dir. of bands Blue Ridge Sch. Dist., Lakeside, Ariz., 2001—. Bassoonist Silver Creek Regional Symphony Orch., Snowflake, Ariz., 1993—; regional gov.-elect Ariz. Music Educator's Assn., N.E. Region, Ariz., 2003—. Adjudicator, in visual and general effect cations Winterguard Ariz., 2004; senator Sch. of Performing Arts, Associated Students of No. Ariz. U., Flagstaff, 2000—01; v.p. Silver Creek Regional Symphony Orch., Snowflake, Ariz., 2003—04. Recipient Regional Honor Orch. Clinician award, Ariz. Music Educator's Assn., 2004. Mem.: NEA (local chpt. treas. 2002—04), Blue Ridge Edn. Assn. (treas. 2002—04), Music Educator's Nat. Conf., Golden Key Honor Soc., Kappa Kappa Psi (pres. 1999—2001). Republican. Pentacostal. Achievements include design of Outstanding Visual Performance Award for Marching Band Drill Design Arizona Band and Orchestra Director's Association State Marching Band Festival 2001. Avocations: music, private lessons, travel, movies, video games. Home: PO Box 927 Lakeside AZ 85929 Office: Blue Ridge Sch Dist 1200 W White Mountain Blvd Lakeside AZ 85929 Personal E-mail: lstidham@kkpsi.org. Business E-Mail: lstidham@brusd.k12.az.us.

STIDHAM, SHALER, JR., operations research educator; b. Washington, Dec. 4, 1941; s. Shaler and Gladys (Ruddick) S.; m. Carolyn Jean Noble, Apr. 6, 1968; children: Christiane Wilson, Dana Claire, Ann-Elise. BA, Harvard U., 1963; MS, Case Inst. Tech., 1964; PhD, Stanford U., 1968. Asst. prof. dept. ops. rsch. Cornell U., Ithaca, N.Y., 1968-75; assoc. prof., prof. dept. indsl. engring. N.C. State U., Raleigh, 1975-86; prof. dept. ops. rsch. U. N.C., Chapel Hill, 1986—2002, chmn. dept. ops. rsch., 1990-95. Lectr. Aarhus (Denmark) U., 1971-72; guest prof. Tech. U., Denmark, Lyngby, 1976-77; vis. fellow Statis. Lab., Cambridge (Eng.) U., 1982-83; cons. Bell Telephone Labs., 1981; vis. scholar Stanford (Calif.) U., 1975, 79, Australian Nat. U., 2001; invited prof. Inst. Nat. Rsch. Informatique et en Automatique, Sophia Antipolis, France, 1991-92; keynote spkr. to profl. confs., The Netherlands, Germany, Poland, France and Japan, 1977—. Co-author (with M. El-Taha): Sample-Path Analysis of Queueing Systems, 1999 (Best Publ. award Applied Probability Soc. 1999). Bd. dirs. Friends of Coll., Raleigh, 1979—82, chmn. program com., 1981—82; bd. dirs. N.C. Symphony Found., Raleigh, 1990—, pres., 2003—; bd. dirs. N.C. Mus. of Art Found., Raleigh, 1996—; mem. faculty coun. U. N.C., Chapel Hill, 1995—98; bd. deacons Pullen Meml. Ch., 1995—98. Overseas fellow Churchill Coll., Cambridge, 1982—. Mem. Inst. for Ops. Rsch and Mgmt. Scis. (chmn. applied probability tech. sect. 1990-91, program co-chmn. internat. meeting Osaka, Japan 1989), Sigma Xi (Young Scientist Rsch. award 1978). Home: 10428 Whitestone Rd Raleigh NC 27615-1236 Office: U NC Dept Ops Rsch Cb 3180 Smith Bldg Chapel Hill NC 27599-0001

STIEBER, TAMAR, journalist; b. Bklyn., Sept. 15, 1955; d. Alfred and Florence (Spector) Stieber. Student, Rockland C.C., 1972—75, West London (Eng.) Coll., 1973—74; BA in Film cum laude, U. Calif., Berkeley, 1985, postgrad. in comparative lit., 1985—86; grad. Police Res. Acad. cum laude, Napa Valley Coll., 1988. Office mgr., confidential sec. AP, San Francisco, 1981—83; stringer Daily Californian, Berkeley, Calif., 1983—84; film rsch. tchg. asst. U. Calif., Berkeley, 1984—86; libr. and rsch. asst. Pacific Film Archive, Berkeley, 1984—86; intern San Francisco Examiner, 1984; reporter Sonoma (Calif.) Index-Tribune, 1987—88, Vallejo (Calif.) Times-Herald, 1988—89, Albuquerque Jour., 1989—94, freelancer, 1994—. Recipient Pulitzer Prize for specialized reporting, 1990, 1st pl. pub. svc. divsn., N.Mex. Press Assn., 1990, Pub. Svc. award, Albuquerque Press Club, 1990, 1st pl. newswriting, N.Mex. Press Assn., 1991, Hon. Mention, AP Mng. Editors, 1994. Mem.: AAUW, Phi Beta Kappa. Home: PO Box 9835 Santa Fe NM 87504-9835

STIEF, LOUIS JOHN, chemist; b. Pottsville, Pa., July 26, 1933; s. Louis Norman and Dorothy Elizabeth (Bassler) S.; m. Kathleen J. Talbot, Nov. 30, 1963 (div. 1980); children— Andrew, Lorraine. BA, La Salle Coll., 1955; PhD, Catholic U. Am., 1960. Nat. Acad. Scis.-NRC postdoctoral rsch. assoc. Nat. Bur. Standards, Washington, 1960-61; NATO postdoctoral fellow, ind. researcher chemistry dept. Sheffield (Eng.) U., 1961-63; sr. scientist, sr. chemist Melpar, Inc., Falls Church, Va., 1963-68; NAS-NRC sr. postdoctoral rsch. assoc. NASA/Goddard Space Flight Ctr., Greenbelt, Md., 1968-69, astrophysicist, 1969-76, head br. astrochemistry, 1976-90, sr. scientist, 1990—2004, emeritus scientist, 2004—. Adj. prof. chemistry Cath. U. Am. Research: numerous publs., especially in Jour. Chem. Physics and Jour. Phys. Chemistry. Recipient Alumni Achievement award Cath. U. Am., 1985; NASA fellow Queen Mary Coll., U. London, 1981-82 Fellow: Washington Acad. Sci.; mem.: Am. Astron. Soc. (divsn. planetary sci.), Am. Geophys. Union, Royal Soc. Chemistry, Am.Chem. Soc. (Hillebrand prize Chem. Soc. Washington 2002), Sigma Xi.

STIEFEL, ETHAN, dancer; b. Tyrone, Pa. s. Alan and Mima Stiefel. Studied with Mikhail Baryshnikov, Sch. Classical Ballet, 1987; student, Fordham U., 1995—. From mem. to prin. dancer N.Y. City Ballet, 1989-95, prin. dancer, 1995-96, Am. Ballet Theatre, N.Y.C., 1997—; artistic dir. Stiefel and Stars, 2002—. With Zurich Ballet, 1992-93; guest artist N.Y.C. Ballet, 1998-99, Atlanta Ballet, 1999, Royal Ballet, 1999—. Dancer prin. roles include Le Corsaire, Romeo & Juliet, Giselle, Les Patineurs, Onegin, Swan Lake, Theme and Variations, Raymonda, Don Quixote, A Midsummer Night's Dream, La Bayadere, The Dream, The Four Temperaments, Apollo, Stars and Stripes, Harlequinade, Tarantella, Tchaikovsky Pas de Deux, Chaconne, Prodigal Son, La Fille Mal Gardee, The Nutcracker, Robbins' ballets Dances at a Gathering, West Side Story Suite, The Goldberg Variations, The Cage, Quiet City, Martins' ballets Fearful Symmetries, Ash, Tchaikovsky Pas de Quatre, The Sleeping Beauty, others; appeared in PBS TV prodn. Le Corsaire, 1999, Born to be Wild, 2002, The Dream, 2004; artistic dir. Steifel & Stars, 2001—, artistic dir Performance Project, 2004; guest artist Teatro Colon, 1999, Hamburg Ballet, 2000, Kirov Ballet, 2001, 04, Verona, Italy, 2003, Washington Opera, 2003, Budapest Opera, 2003, others; starring role: (film) Center Stage, 2000. Recipient Silver medal Prix de Lausanne, 1989, Statue award Princess Grace Found., 1999; emerging dance artist grantee Princess Grace Found. U.S.A., 1991-92 Office: care Peter S Diggins Assoc 133 W 71st St Ste 8-B New York NY 10023 Personal E-mail: festspiel@aol.com.

STIEFEL, LINDA SHIELDS, lawyer; b. Syracuse, N.Y., Nov. 14, 1948; d. Harold F. and Ellen (Brown) Shields; m. John L. Stiefel, Sept. 20, 1969; 1 child, John L. BS, Tusculum Coll., 1988; JD, Akron Sch. Law, 1991. Bar: Ohio 1992, D.C. 1993, N.Y. 1998, U.S. Dist. Ct. (no. dist.) Ohio 1993, U.S. Supreme Ct. 1997. Judicial law clk. Stark County Common Pleas, Canton, Ohio, 1991-94; pvt. practice Louisville, Ohio, 1992-97, Cape Vincent, N.Y., 1998—. Trustee, mem. exec. com. Am. Handweaving Mus., 1997-2001. Mem. ABA, NOW, N.Y. State Bar Assn., Jefferson County Bar Assn. Methodist.

STIEGEL, MICHAEL A. lawyer; b. Greenfield, Mass., Sept. 15, 1946; s. Sid James and Ida Eleanor (Solomon) S.; m. Marsha Palmer, Sept. 10, 1983. BA, U. Ariz., 1968; JD cum laude, Loyola U., Chgo., 1971. Bar: Ill. 1971, U.S. Dist. Ct. Ill. 1971, U.S. Ct. Appeals (7th cir.) 1971, U.S. Ct. Appeals (6th cir.) 1975, U.S. Supreme Ct. 1975, Wis. 1985, Fla. 1987. Law clk. to fed. judge William Lynch U.S. Dist. Ct. Ill., Chgo., 1971—72; mng. ptnr. Arnstein & Lehr, Chgo., 1985-98; ptnr. Michael Best and Friedrich, 1998—. Adj. prof. law Northwestern U.; faculty Nat. Inst. Trial Advocacy, La. State U. Trial Advocacy Program, 1995; co-chmn. litigation group Michael Best and Friedrich, 1998-2003, mem. mgmt. com., 2003—. Contbr. articles to profl. jours. Mem. fin. com. Lynn Martin for Senate, Ill., 1989-90. Mem. ABA (sects. on litigation, bus. law, and labor and employment law, vice chmn. trial evidence com. litigation sect. 1990-91, co-chmn. trial evidence com. 1991-95, lawyers conf. standards for admissibility of technologically sophisticated evidence com., co-chair nat. CLE programs 1995-97, coun. 1997-2000, mem. exec. com. 2000—, budget officer 2000-02, revenue officer, 2002—, litigation sect. advisor, uniform laws commn., drafting com. on Model Punitive Damages Act), Ill. Bar Assn., Fla. Bar Assn., Wis. Bar Assn., Chgo. Bar Assn. (chair large firm com.), 410 Club, Econ. Club. Avocations: sports, reading, horse racing syndications. Office: Michael Best & Friedrich 401 N Michigan Ave Ste 1900 Chicago IL 60601-1635 E-mail: mastiegel@mbf-law.com.

STIEHL, RUTH RASCO, nursing educator; b. Miami, Fla., Oct. 31, 1939; d. Russell Austin and Beatrice (Tanner) Rasco; m. Paul A. Stiehl, June 5, 1959; children: Mark Russell, Kristin Stiehl Murray, Eric Paul. BS, U. Miami, 1961; MA, U. South Fla., 1972, PhD, 1977; MN, U. Fla., 1989. RN, Fla. Staff nurse ob/gyn Bapt. Hosp., Miami, 1961-62; staff nurse pediatrics Broward Gen. Hosp., Ft. Lauderdale, Fla., 1963-65; staff nurse dialysis Tampa (Fla.) Gen. Hosp., 1967-70; faculty Coll. Nursing, U. South Fla., Tampa, 1973-76; nursing edn. dir. Fla. Bd. Nursing, Jacksonville, 1977-82; dir. Sch. Nursing, Jacksonville (Fla.) U., 1982—; exec. dir. Florida Board of Nursing, Jacksonville, 1997—. Mem. examination com. Nat. Coun. State Bds. of Nursing, Chgo., 1978-82. Bd. dirs. Cypress Village Retirement Community, Jacksonville, 1990—, Mayor's Commn. on Status of Women, Jacksonville, 1985-92, Gateway Coun. Girl Scouts U.S.A., 1989—, S.E. Heart Assn., Jacksonville, 1986-88, N.E. Fla. Easter Seals, Jacksonville, 1982-86; mem. task force Women and AIDS, Jacksonville, 1991—; treas. Fla. Commn. on Future of Nursing, 1987-91. Mem. ANA, Fla. Nurses Assn., Nat. League for Nursing, Sigma Theta Tau. Avocations: reading, jogging, cross-stitch, singing. Office: Jacksonville Univ 2800 University Blvd N Jacksonville FL 32211-3394 Address: Florida Bd of Nursing 4080 Woodcock Dr Ste 202 Jacksonville FL 32207-2723

STIEHL, WILLIAM D. federal judge; b. 1925; m. Celeste M. Sullivan; children: William D., Susan M. Student, U. N.C., 1943-45; LLB, St. Louis U., 1949. Pvt. practice, 1952-78; ptnrs. Stiehl & Hess, 1978-81; ptnr. Stiehl & Stiehl, 1982-86; judge, former chief judge U.S. Dist. Court, (so. dist.) Ill., East Saint Louis, 1986—96, sr. judge, 1996—. Spl. asst. atty. gen. State of Ill., 1970-73. Mem. bd. Belleville Twp. High Sch. and Jr. Coll., 1949-50, 54-56, pres., 1956-57, Clair County, Ill., county civil atty., 1956-60. Mem. Ill. State Bar Assn., St. Clair County Bar Assn. Office: US Dist Ct 750 Missouri Ave East Saint Louis IL 62201-2954

STIEHM, E. RICHARD, pediatrician, educator; b. Milw., Jan. 22, 1933; s. Reuben Harold and Marie Dueno S.; m. Judith Hicks, July 12, 1958; children: Jamie Elizabeth, Carrie Eleanor, Meredith Ellen. BS, U. Wis., 1954, MD, 1957. Diplomate Am. Bd. Pediat., Am. Bd. Allergy and Clin. Immunology (bd. dirs. 1977-83), Am. Bd. Diagnostic Lab. Immunology. Intern Phila. Gen. Hosp., 1957-58; fellow in physiol. chemistry U. Wis., 1959-61, asst. prof. pediat., 1968-69, assoc. prof., 1969-72; med. officer USNR, Johnsville, Pa., 1961-63; resident in pediat. Babies Hosp., NYC, 1963-65; rsch. fellow in pediat. immunology U. Calif., San Francisco, 1965-68; assoc. prof. UCLA, 1972-78, prof., 1978-87, chief divsn. immunology, allergy and rheumatology, 1972—2003, assoc. dir. Ctr. for Interdisciplinary Rsch. in Immunologic Diseases, 1981-82, co-dir. Cystic Fibrosis Ctr., 1988—95, vice chair acad. affairs dept. pediat., 1989—99; vis. scientist metabolism br. Nat. Cancer Inst., Bethesda, Md., 1982-88. Vis. prof. Yale U., Mayo Clinic, U. Cin., Great Ormond St. Hosp., U.K., U. Wis.; bd. sci. dirs. Immune Deficiency Found., 1981—, Eczema Found., 1988—, Pediat. AIDS Found., 1989-99; task force on pediatric allergy NIH, 1977; mem. gen. clin. rsch. ctr. study sect. NIH, 1978-82, 84-88; adv. com. Hartford Fellowship, 1984-88; co-dir. LA Pediatric AIDS Consortium, 1988—. Editor: Immunologic Disorders in Infants and Children, 1972, 80, 89, 96; Am. editor: Pediatric Rsch., 1984-89; assoc. editor: Pediat. Update, 1978-85; mem. editl. bd. Pediat., 1972-78, Pediat. in Rev., 1978-81, Jour. Allergy and Clin. Immunology, 1976-80, Jour. Clin. Immunology, 1985-89, Jour. Asthma Pediatric Allergy and Immunology, 1987-91, Am. Jour. Diseases of Children, 1987-97, Contemporary Pediat., 1991-96, Am. Jour. Clin. Nutrition, 1992-97; contbr. articles to profl. jours. Commr. HHS Commn. on Childhood Vaccines, 1988-90; mem. clin. rsch. adv. com. Nat. Found. March of Dimes, 1992-97, 2004—. Recipient Career Devel. award Nat. Inst. Allergy and Infectious Diseases, 1967-69, E. Mead Johnson award for Pediat. Rsch., 1974, Alumni Citation award U. Wis. Med. Sch., 1988, Lifetime Achievement award Immune Deficiency Found., 1995, Med. Sci. award UCLA Med. Alumni, 1999, Disting. Alumni award Babies and Children's Hosp. Alumni Assn., N.Y., 1999; Markle scholar, 1967-72. Fellow AAAS; mem. Am. Assn. Immunologists, Western Soc. Pediat. Rsch. (coun. 1977-80, pres. 1983, Ross Rsch. award 1971), Soc. Pediat. Rsch., Am. Pediat. Soc., Am. Acad. Allergy, Asthma and Clin. Immunology, Am. Acad. Pediat. (infectious diseases com. 1971-77), Am. Soc. Clin. Investigation, Clin. Immunology Soc., Phi Beta Kappa, Alpha Omega Alpha. Office: UCLA Dept Peds Divsn Immunology 10833 Le Conte Ave Los Angeles CA 90095-3075 Business E-Mail: estiehm@mednet.ucla.edu.

STIEHM, JUDITH HICKS, university official, political science educator; b. Madison, Wis., Oct. 9, 1935; d. Stratton Elson and Eleanor Spencer (Kilbourn) Hicks; m. E. Richard Stiehm, July 12, 1958; children: Jamie Elizabeth, Carrie Eleanor, Meredith Ellen. Student, Oberlin Coll., 1953; BA in E. Asian Studies, U. Wis., 1957; MA in Am. History, Temple U., 1961; PhD in Polit. Theory, Columbia U., 1969. Dir. resident hons. program U. So. Calif., Los Angeles, 1970-73, asst. prof., 1970-74, assoc. prof., 1974-83, dir. program for study of women and men in soc., 1975-81, prof. polit. sci., 1983, vice provost, 1984-87; provost Fla. Internat. U., Miami, 1987-91, prof. polit. sci., 1987—. Vis. prof. U. Wis., 1994, U.S. Army Peacekeeping Inst., U.S. Army War Coll., 1995-96, U.S. Army Strategic Studies Inst., U.S. Army War Coll., 1996, U. So. Calif., 2002-; lectr. U. Wis., Madison, 1966-69, UCLA, 1969-70; vis. lectr. San Francisco State U., 1965-66; affiliate NAS Project, 1981-82; cons. UN Div. for the Advancement of Women, Calif. Elected Women, Dept. HEW, AAUW, LWV L.A., UN Lessons Learned Unit, Dept. Peacekeeping Ops. Author: Nonviolent Power: Active and Passive Resistance in America, 1972, Bring Me Men and Women..., 1981, Arms and the Enlisted Woman, 1989, The U.S. Army War College: Military Education in a Democracy, 2002; editor: The Frontiers of Knowledge, 1976, Women and Men's Wars, 1983, Women's Views of the Political World of Men, 1984, It's Our Military, Too!, 1996, The U.S. Army War College: Military Education in a Democracy, 2002; mem. editorial bd. Western Polit. Quar., 1972-75, Signs, 1981-84, Women and Politics, 1986-88, 2000-. Mem. Calif. Postsecondary Edn. Commn., 1978, Calif. Adv. Coun. on Vocat. Edn., 1978-82, Def. Adv. Com. on Women in Svcs., 1979-82; bd. dirs. So. Calif. and Miami chpts. ACLU. Named Woman of Yr., Santa Monica YWCA, 1981; recipient Outstanding Civilian Svc. medal U.S. Army, 1996. Mem. Am. Polit. Sci. Assn. (exec. coun. 1989, sec. 2000), Western Polit. Sci. Assn. (pres. 1986), Women's Caucus Polit. Sci. (pres. 1996-97), Nat. Council for Research on Women (exec. council 1982), Council on Fgn. Relations, Phi Beta Kappa, Phi Kappa Phi (Victoria Schuck Book award 1990). Avocations: tennis, skiing, stained glass. Home: 434 24th St Santa Monica CA 90402-3102 Office: Fla Internat U Dept Polit Sci Tamiami Trl Miami FL 33199-0001 E-mail: stiehmj@fiu.edu.

STIENSTRA, STEPHANI ANN, editor, writer; b. Baytown, Tex., Aug. 6, 1955; d. Herbert Howard and Janice Faye (Stowe) Cruickshank; m. George Keyston III, Oct. 8, 1983 (div. Mar. 1997); children: Jeremy George, Kristopher Samuel; m. Thomas Frank Stienstra, Dec. 4, 1998. AA with honors, Merced (Calif.) Coll., 1975; BA in Journalism with distinction, San Jose State U., 1976. Reporter Fresno (Calif.) Bee, 1974-75; reporter, photographer Merced (Calif.) Sun Star, 1974-77; pub. info. officer Fresno City Coll., 1977—80; dir. comms. Aerojet Tactical Sys. Co., Sacramento, 1980—83; co-owner, v.p. Keyco Landscape Contractor Inc., Loomis, Calif., 1984—96; co-owner Stienstra Outdoor Books, Inc., 2003—. Co-author (with Tom Stienstra): (book) Northern California Cabins and Cottages, 2002 (Hon. Mention Book award Outdoor Writers Assn. Calif., 2002), Washington Camping, 2002. Co-coord. Aeroject United Way Campaign, 1981; Aeroject Tactical Sys. Co. coord. West Coast Nat. Derby Rallies, 1981-83; co-founder, pres. Calif. Lion Awareness. Mem. Internat. Assn. Bus. Communicators (dir. Sacramento chpt. 1983), Citrus Heights C. of C. (v.p. 1983). Office: PO Box 151 Mount Shasta CA 96067-0151 E-mail: stienstra@jps.net.

STIER, EDWIN H. lawyer; b. Newark, Nov. 2, 1939; BA, Rutgers U, 1961, LLB, 1964. Bar: NJ 1965. Asst. atty. US Supreme Ct., 1979; asst. US atty. Fed. Ct., Newark, 1965—69; chief criminal div. US Atty. Office, Newark, 1967—69; asst. atty. gen., dir. criminal justice State of NJ, Trenton, NJ, 1969—82; ptnr. Kirsten, Friedman & Cherin, Newark, 1982—. Author: (book) White Collar Crime, 1981. Office: Trucking Employees 707 Summit Ave Union City NJ 07087-3463

STIER, MARY P. publishing executive; b. Memphis, Tennessee, Nov. 9, 1956; m. Jeff Stier; 2 children. Grad. in comm., broadcasting, U. Iowa. With Gannett Co., 1982—; retail advt. mgr. Iowa City Press-Citizen, 1982—84, advt. dir., 1984—87, pres., pub., 1987—91; v.p. Ctrl. Region Newspaper Divsn., 1990—93; pres., pub. Rockford (Ill.) Register Star, 1991—2000; pres. Midwest Newspaper Group, 1993—2000; pres., pub. The Des Moines Register, 2000—; sr. group pres. Midwest Newspaper Group, 2000—. Bd. trustees Drake U. Mem.: The Greater Des Moines Partnership, Am. Press Inst., Iowa Newspaper Assn., Newspaper Assn. Am., Phi Beta Kappa. Office: Des Moines Register PO Box 957 Des Moines IA 50304-0957*

STIER, ROGER EDWIN, chemist, researcher; b. Hackensack, N.J., Dec. 23, 1946; s. Edwin Richard and Irmtraut Margaret Stier; m. Nancy Louise Stier, Oct. 5, 1969; children: David Roger, Brian Roger, Kathlean Ann. BS magna cum laude, Fairleigh Dickinson U., 1968; PhD in Chemistry, Stafford U, 2003. Technician Burroughs Wellcome Co., Tuckahoe, N.Y., 1968-70; analytical chemist Schering, Union, N.J., 1970-73; rsch. assoc. Beecham Products Rsch., Parsippany, N.J., 1973-97; sr. chemist Noville, South Hackensack, N.J., 1997—, tech. dir., 2003—. Cons. Proctor & Gamble, Cin., 1999—, Smith Klein Beecham, Parsippany, 1997—, Diamond Products, Tampa, Fla., 1997—. Author and inventor in field. Asst. scout master Boy Scouts Am., Eagle Scout, 1961, Clifton, N.J., 1957-64; minister New Apostolic Ch., Clifton, 1967—. Named Outstanding Citizen, B'nai B'rith, 1968. Mem. AAAS, Am. Chem. Soc., Soc. Cosmetic Chemists, Internat. Assn. Dental Rsch., Am. Assn. Pharmaceutical Scientists, Sigma Xi, Phi Zeta Kappa, Phi Omega Epsilon. Republican. Avocations: playing and teaching organ, reading, writing poems. Home: 265 Washington Ave Clifton NJ 07011 Office: Noville 3 Empire Blvd South Hackensack NJ 07606 Business E-Mail: rstier@noville.com.

STIER, WILLIAM FREDERICK, JR., academic administrator, educator; b. Feb. 22, 1943; m. Veronica Ann Martin, 1965; children: Mark, Missy, Michael, Patrick, Willy III. BA, St. Ambrose Coll., 1965; MA, Temple U., 1966; EdD, U. S.D., 1972; postdoct., Marquette U., 1976-77, U. Wis., summer 1977. Grad. asst. Coll. Edn. Temple U., Phila., 1965-66; various faculty positions dept. health, phys. edn., recreation, 1968-74; pres., CEO Fla. Breeders, Inc., Largo and St. Petersburg, 1974-76; treas. Charolais of Fla., Inc., St. Petersburg and Ft. Myers, 1975-76; adminstrv. campus Cardinal Stritch Coll., Milw., 1976-80; chmn. dept. profl. health and phys. edn., athletic dir. Ohio No. U., Ada, 1980-83; chmn., prof. phys. edn. and sports dept. SUNY, Brockport, 1983-86, dir. intercollegiate athletics, 1983-90, grad. coord. sport mgmt., 1990—, pres. faculty senate, 1992-93, grad. coord., 1994—, Disting. Svc. prof. Pres., CEO Ednl. and Sport Mgmt. cons., N.Y. and Ohio, 1980—; chmn. bd. dirs. Kreative Kids Learning Ctrs., Inc., 1978—; bd. dirs. Cretive Children Child Care Ctrs.; cons. MacMillan Pub. Co., Inc., 1981-83, Sport Fedn., Hong Kong, Singapore and Malaysia, 1987, 88, Nat. Coll. Sport Coaches, Mexico City, 1990; speaker numerous confs. and convs. Author of 17 books and contbr. to several compendiums in field; contbr. more than 274 articles to profl. jours.; mem. editl. bd. and reviewer profl. jours.; editor The Phys. Educator, 1998—, Internat. Jour. Sport Mgmt., 1999—. Active ARC, 1975-90, Boy Scouts Am., 1955-59; mem. greater Milw. REgional day Care adv. Com., 1979-81; adv. bd. Nat. Ctr. Exploration Human Petential, Del Mar, Calif., 1981-84; nat. basketball coach, St. Kitts-Nevis, 1984; cons. on basketball, Mex., 1982, 90. Brockport scholar, 1984-86, 92, 93, 94, 98, 99. Mem. AAHPERD (reviewer jour. 1984—), N.Y. Assn. Health, Phys. Edn., Recreation and Dance (higher edn. sect. 1983—, pres. 1985-86, 87-88), Nat. Assn. sport and Phys. Edn., Nat. Assn. Girls and Women's Sports, Nat. Assn. Phys. Edn. in Higher Edn., Nat. Assn. Phys. Edn. in Higher Edn., Nat. Assn. Athletic Mktg. and Devel. Dirs., Nat. Assn. Collegiate Dirs. Athletics, Internat. Soc. Comparative Phys. Edn. and Sports, N.Am. Sport Mgmt., Eta Sigma Gama, Phi Epsilon Kappa, Phi Kappa Phi, Phi Epsilon Omega. Office: SUNY-Brockport Dept Phys Edn and Sport Brockport NY 14420 E-mail: bstier@brockport.edu.

STIERLE, LINDA J. military officer; BSN magna cum laude, Incarnate Word Coll., 1978; grad., Air Command and Staff Coll., 1980; MSN with honors, U. Calif., San Francisco, 1983; grad., Air War Coll., 1986; grad. Interagy. Inst. Healthcare Execs., George Washington U., 1993; grad. CAPSTONE, Nat. Def. U., 1996. Commd. 2d. lt. USAF, 1970, advanced through grades to brigadier gen., 1995; staff nurse med. unit Wiesbaden (West Germany) USAF Med. Ctr., 1974-76, asst. charge nurse surg. unit, 1976; charge nurse female med. unit David Grant USAF Med. Ctr., Travis AFB, Calif., 1978-81, edn. coord. dept. nursing, 1981; divsn. chief, sr. mgmt. cons. mgmt. strategies/edn. dir. Leadership and Mgmt. Devel. Ctr., Maxwell AFB, Ala., 1984-86; asst. chmn. dept. nursing David Grant USAF Med. Ctr., Travis AFB, 1986-88; chief nurse 48th Tactical Fighter Wing Hosp., RAF, Lakenheath, England, 1988-90; dep. chief divsn. nursing Wilford Hall USAF Med. Ctr., Lackland AFB, Tex., 1991-93; command nurse Office of Command Surgeon Air Mobility Command, Scott AFB, Ill., 1993-95; dir. nursing svds. Office of Air Force Surgeon Gen., Bolling AFB, DC, 1995, dir. Med. Readiness Doctrine and Planning and Nursing Svcs., 1995—99; CEO ANA, Washington, 2000—. Decorated Legion of Merit with oak leaf cluster, Meritorious Svc. medal with 3 oak leaf clusters, D.S.M. USAF. Mem. Am. Soc. Assn. Execs., Soc. Air Force Nurses, Am. Orgn. of Nurse Execs., Md. Nurses Assn., Sigma Theta Tau. Office: ANA Ste 100W 600 Maryn Ave SW Washington DC 20024 Business E-Mail: lstierle@ana.org.

STIERS, DAVID OGDEN, actor, conductor; b. Peoria, Ill., Oct. 31, 1942; s. Kenneth Truman and Margaret Elizabeth (Ogden) S. Diploma drama div., Juilliard Sch., 1973. Actor, Actors Workshop, 1962, Calif. Shakespeare Festival, 1963-68, mem., The Committee, 1968-70, San Francisco (revue)/Broadway season City Center Acting Co., N.Y.C., 1974; Broadway appearances include Ulysses in Nighttown, 1974, The Magic Show, 1974-75; other stage appearances include King Lear, 1981; regular on TV series MASH 1977-83; other TV appearances include Mary Tyler Moore Show, Rhoda, Two Guys, a Girl, and a Pizza Place, Murder, She Wrote, The Dead Zone, Lilo & Stitch: The Series (voice); TV film appearances include Charlie's Angels, 1976, A Circle of Children, 1977, A Love Affair: The Eleanor and Lou Gehrig Story, 1978, Sergeant Matlovich Vs. the US Air Force, 1978, Breaking Up Is Hard To Do, 1979, Damien: The Leper Priest, 1980, The Day the Bubble Burst, 1982, Anatomy of an Illness, 1984, The First Olympics-Athens 1896, 1984, The Bad Seed, 1985, North and South, 1985, North and South Book II, 1986, Mrs. Delafield Wants to Marry, 1986, Perry Mason: Case of the Notorious Nun, 1986, Perry Mason: Case of the Shooting Star, 1986, The Kissing Place, 1990; film appearances include: Drive, He Said, 1972, Oh God!, 1977, The Cheap Detective, 1978, Magic, 1978, The Man With One Red Shoe, 1985, Creator, 1985, Better Off Dead, 1985, The Accidental Tourist, 1988, Another Woman, 1988, Doc Hollywood, 1991, Beauty and the Beast (voice), 1991, Iron Will, 1994, The Toolshed, 1994, Bad Company, 1995, Pocahontas (voice), 1995, Steal Big, Steal Little, 1995, Mighty Aphradite, 1995, Everyone Says I Love You, 1996, The Hunchback of Notre Dame

(voice), 1996, Meet Wally Sparks, 1997, Jungle 2 Jungle, 1997, Beauty and the Beast: The Enchanted Christmas (voice), 1997, Justice League of America, 1997, Belle's Magical World (voice), 1997, Reagan, 1998, Krippendorf's Tribe, 1998, Pocahontas: Journey to a New World (voice), 1998, MacArthur, 1999, Love & Money, 1999, The Stand-In, 1999, Tomcats, 2001, Atlantis: The Lost Empire (voice), 2001, The Majestic, 2001, The Assistant, 2001, Lilo & Stitch (voice), 2002; artistic assoc. The Acting Co., N.Y.C.; prin. guest condr. Yaquina Orch., 1989; now resident condr. Yaquina Chamber Orch.; guest condr. 70 orchs. including San Diego Symphony, Dallas Symphony Orch., Utah Symphony Orch., Chgo. Symphony Orch., Va. Symphony Orch., N.C. Symphony Philharm., Ft. Wayne Philharm., Calif. Symphony Orch., also orchs. in Honolulu, Portland, Maine, Grand Rapids, Mich., Peoria, Ill. Mem. NARAS, Conductors Guild, Am. Symphony Orch. League, Internat. Horn Soc., Magic Castle, Players Club. Office: Susan Smith and Assocs 121 N San Vicente Blvd Beverly Hills CA 90211-2303*

STIFEL, FREDERICK BENTON, minister, biochemist, nutritionist; b. St. Louis, Jan. 30, 1940; s. Carl Gottfried and Alma J. (Clark) Stifel; m. Gail Joane Stewart, Aug. 10, 1963; children: Tim, Faith, Seth, Elizabeth. BS, Iowa State U., 1962, PhD, 1967; MDiv., Melodyland Sch. Theol., Anaheim, Calif., 1979. Ordained to ministry Evang. Presbyn. Ch., 1981. Lab. supr., research chemist U.S. Army Med. Research and Nutrition Lab., Denver, 1968-74, Letterman Army Inst. Research, San Francisco, 1974-76; intern pastor Melodyland Christian Ctr., Anaheim, 1979-80; assoc. pastor Faith Presbyn. Ch., Aurora, Colo., 1980—, moderator bd. deacons, 1997—; pastor Outreach and Missions, 1999—. Chmn. care candidates com. Presbytery of West, Denver, 1985—88, Denver, 1991—94, Denver, 2003—; v.p. Love Inc. Metro Denver, 1987—90; regional coord. Nat. Assn. Single Adult Leaders, 1987—90, coord. Denver area, 1990—95; mem. Denver Seminary Commn., 1995—, mem. world outreach com., 1998—99; regional coord. Colo. Pregnancy Ctrs., Inc., 1992—94, Rocky Mountain Prayer Network, 1994—96, Christian Family Svcs., 1990—; bd. dirs. St. James Bible Coll., faculty, Ukraine; bd. dirs. Profl. Publs.; faculty Life of Jesus Bible Coll., Yellow Water, Ukraine; bd. dirs. Internat. Project Adv. Bd. Contbr. articles to profl. jours. Young Life leader Hinkley HS, Aurora, 1968—74; vice chmn. Young Life com. Marin County, Calif., 1974—76; mem. parent adv. coun. IMPACT drug intervention team Rangeview HS, Aurora, 1985—89, mem. accountability com., 1989—96; mem. Friends of Arts, 1992—96; del. Iowa and Colo. State Rep. Conv., Denver, 1984, Colorado Springs, 2002. Capt. Med. Svc. Corps U.S. Army, 1967—70. Recipient Sci. Achievement award, U.S. Army Sci. Conf., 1968, 1970, Parents of the yr. award, Rangeview HS, 1992—93; Ralston Purina Rsch. fellow, 1962—63, Borden Agrl. scholar, 1962. Mem.: Am. Sci. Affiliation, Am. Soc. Clin. Nutrition, Am. Soc. Nutritional Scis., Evang. Theol. Soc., Sigma Xi, Kappa Sigma, Gamma Sigma Delta, Alpha Zeta, Phi Kappa Phi, Phi Eta Sigma. Avocations: reading, hiking, swimming, poetry, gardening. Home: 3492 S Blackhawk Way Aurora CO 80014-3909 Office: Faith Presbyn Ch 11373 E Alameda Ave Aurora CO 80012-1023 Office Phone: 303-364-7271.

STIFF, PATRICK JOSEPH, internist, hematologist, oncologist, educator; b. Toledo, Nov. 27, 1950; BS, U. Toledo, 1972; MD, Loyola U., 1975. Intern Cleve. Clinic, 1975-76, resident in medicine, 1976-78; fellow in hematology and oncology Meml. Sloan-Kettering Med. Ctr., N.Y.C., 1978-81; asst. prof. medicine Sch. Medicine So. Ill. U., 1981-86; asst. prof. medicine Loyola U. Med. Ctr., Maywood, Ill., 1986-92; assoc. prof. medicine Loyola U. Med. Ctr.-Stritch Sch. Medicine, Maywood, Ill., 1992-96; prof. medicine and pathology Loyola U. Med. Ctr., Maywood, Ill., 1996—, dir. Cardinal Bernardin Cancer Ctr., 2003—, dir. divsn. hematology and oncology, 2003—. Chair transplant subcom. Ill. State Med. Adv. Com., 1999—. Mem. Internat. Soc. Exptl. Hematology, Internat. Soc. Hematotherapy and Graft Engrs., S.W. Oncology Group, Am. Soc. Clin. Oncology, Am. Soc. Hematology. Office: Loyola Univ Med Ctr 2160 S 1st Ave Maywood IL 60153-3304 Office Phone: 708-327-3148. Business E-Mail: pstiff@lumc.edu.

STIFF, ROBERT MARTIN, newspaper editor; b. Detroit, Aug. 25, 1931; s. Martin L. and Gladys (Mathews) S.; m. Cindy Rose, Aug. 30, 1980; children: David Alan, Amy Anne, Kirsten Marie. BA in Radio and Journalism, Ohio State U., 1953. Reporter, bur. chief, city editor Painesville (Ohio) Telegraph, 1953-61; deskman, asst. city editor, sports editor, city editor, day editor, state editor, asst. mng. editor St. Petersburg (Fla.) Times, 1961-67; editor St. Petersburg Evening Ind., 1967-84; dir. St. Petersburg Times Pub. Co., 1969-84; exec. editor, v.p. Tallahassee Democrat, 1985-91; pres. Bob Stiff & Assocs., Tallahassee, 1991-95; exec. editor JMT Assocs., 1991—92, 1994—95; mng. editor About Fla., 1991-94; editor Lexington (N.C.) Dispatch, 1995—. Mem. Pulitzer Prize Jury, 1982-83; dir. devel. and pub. rels. Fla. Taxwatch Inc., 1992-94; bd. dirs. N.C. AP News Coun., 1995-2001, v.p., 1997-99, pres., 1999-2000; pres. Empty Stocking Fund, 1995—. Bd. dirs. Cancer Svcs. Davidson County, 1996-2004, N.C. First Amendment Coalition, 2004-, U. N.C., Chapel Hill, Sch. Journalism Found., 2004-; pres. Capital Press Assn., 1998-2001, N.C. Daily Newspaper Assn., 1995-, v.p., 1998-99, pres., 1999-2000. Mem. AP Assn. Fla. (pres. 1970-71), Am. Soc. Newspaper Editors (dir. 1981-87), Am. Soc. Newspaper Editors Found. (bd. dirs., treas. 1986-90), Fla. Soc. Newspaper Editors (pres. 1975-76, dir. 1971-84, 90-93), Fla. Bar Found. (bd. dirs. 1990-92), AP Mng. Editors Assn., Sigma Delta Chi (pres. West Coast chpt. 1970-71, N.C. Press Assn. (bd. dirs. 1999-2000, 02--), Nat. Coun. Editl. Writers, Lexington Kiwanis (bd. dirs. 1996-2000, 2003—). Office Phone: 336-249-3981. Business E-Mail: bob.stiff@the-dispatch.com.

STIFFLER, JACK JUSTIN, electrical engineer; b. Mitchellville, Iowa, May 22, 1934; s. John Justin and Helen Irene (Roorda) S.; m. Ardis Ann Ackerman, Aug. 21, 1955; 1 child, Julia Alise; m. Sally Voris Burns, Apr. 20, 1989. AB magna cum laude in Physics, Harvard U., 1956; MS in E.E, Calif. Inst. Tech., 1957, PhD, 1962; postgrad., U. Paris, 1957-58. Engr. Hughes Aircraft Corp., Culver City, Calif., 1956-57; mem. tech. staff Jet Propulsion Lab., Pasadena, Calif., 1959-67; cons. scientist Raytheon Corp., Sudbury, Mass., 1967-81; co-founder, exec. v.p. Sequoia Systems, Inc., Marlborough, Mass., 1981—97; cons., 1997—. Lectr. Calif. Inst. Tech., U. So. Calif., UCLA, Northeastern U. Author: Theory of Synchronous Communications, 1971; contbr. chpts. to books, articles to profl. jours. Fellow: IEEE; mem.: Sigma Xi, Phi Beta Kappa. Personal E-mail: stiffler@capecod.net.

STIFLER, VENETIA CHAKOS, dancer, educator, choreographer; b. Chgo., Feb. 27, 1950; d. Theodore and Ruth (Pastirsky) Chakos; m. John G. Stifler, Jan. 28, 1972 (dec. 1977); m. Michael Hugos, 1994. BA, U. Ill., Chgo., 1983; MFA equivalency, Union Inst., Cin., 1987, PhD, 1992. Tchr. workshops Urban Gateways, Chgo., 1977; tchr. Chgo. Dance Ctr., Chgo., 1971-78, Smith Coll., Northampton, Mass., 1975, Wilson Coll., Chambersburg, Pa., 1984; guest tchr., artistic dir. composition/improvisation U. Wis., Madison, 1980-81, 85, 87; tchr. modern, jazz and ballet Venetia Stifler & Concert Dance, Inc., Chgo., 1978—; tchr. choreography workshop Bell Elem. Sch., Chgo., 1987; tchr./artist in residence Mundelein Coll., Chgo., 1982-90; asst. prof., chair dance program Northeastern Ill. U., Chgo., 1987—; tchr. modern technique So. Ill. U., Carbondale, 1975. Lectr. Mundelein Coll., Chgo., 1983, 84, 85, 86, Mayor's Office of Spl. Events, Chgo., 1980program dir. and choreogrpaher spl. programs Chgo. Symphony Orch., 1985, 87; pres. bd. dirs. Chgo. Dance Arts Coalition, 1983-85; adv. dance panel Ill. Arts Coun., 1983-85, Chgo. Office of Fine Arts, 1983-86; guest speaker Chgo. Office of Fine Arts, 1987; choreographer Sears Fashion Files, BoMay Prodns., 1983, 84, 86; prodn. asst. Audio Visual Prodns., 1970-71; artistic dir. Ruth Page Dance Series, 1992—; centennial dir. Ruth Page Found. Centennial, 1999; exec. dir. Ruth Page Found., 2001. Choreographer Between Us, 1991, Magic Spaces, 1985, 86, Fugues, 1981, 82, Corporate Cases, 1988, Private places, 1987, Bell School Scrimmage, 1987, Blessings, 1986, Don't Dance with Your Back to the Moon, 1986, Imagery & Concept in the Dances of Venetia Stifler, 1985, Rhymes, 1984, Arriving at Onion, 1984, Pulse, 1983, Haiku, 1982, Mundelein Madness, 1981, Solo Crane, 1981, Tales of a Winter's Night, 1980, Jackson Park-Howard, 1979, La Gaite Parisienne (opera), 1976, Chicago Sketches, 1995, Veils, 1996, Over Weight Over Wrought Over You, 1997, Three German Songs, 1999, Shenandoah. Recipient Ruth Page award; named for Outstanding Artistic Achievement, Chgo. Dance Coalition, 1985. Avocations: voice, film, art. Office: Northeastern Ill U 5500 N Saint Louis Ave Chicago IL 60625-4679 E-mail: venetia@ruth.

STIGALL, PHYLLIS GRAHAM, retired librarian; b. Ft. Wayne, Ind., Oct. 3, 1917; d. Edwin James and Mary Josephine (Palmer) Graham; m. Richard Patten Pooley, Apr. 4, 1943 (dec. Dec. 1950); 1 child, Samuel Graham Pooley; m. William Jasper Stigall Jr., Aug. 11, 1956 (dec. Sept. 2001). AA, Stephens Coll., 1937; AB, Northwestern U., 1939; MALS, U. Mich., 1952. Asst. counselor Stephens Coll., Columbia, Mo., 1939-42; asst. to dir. USO-YWCA Clubs, various locations, 1942-46; co-dir. U. Mich. Cmty. Ctr., Ann Arbor and Willow Run, 1946-47; libr., dean, instr. Lincoln (Ill.) Coll., 1952-66; mgr. publs. and librs. IBM Rsch. Ctr., Yorktown Heights, N.Y., 1966-88; ret. Author: Notes on 46 Women Writers, 1991, Journeys of the Brave, 1992, Ireland: Reader's Guide. Women, 1995; co-editor: I Couldn't be Better, 2002. Mem. AAUW, LWV (chpt. bd. dirs., pres. 1947-66). Democrat. Episcopalian. Avocations: photography, research, biography, history, genealogy. Home: PO Box 211 Scarborough NY 10510

STIGLER, STEPHEN MACK, statistician, educator; b. Mpls., MInn., Aug. 10, 1941; s. George Joseph and Margaret (Mack) S.; m. Virginia Lee, June 27,1964; children: Andrew, Geoffrey, Margaret, Elizabeth. BA, Carleton Coll., 1963; PhD, U. Calif., Berkeley, 1967. Asst. prof. U. Wis., Madison, 1967-71, assoc. prof., 1971-75, prof., 1975-79, U. Chgo., Ill., 1979—; chmn. dept., 1986-92; Ernest DeWitt Burton Disting. Svc. prof. U. Chgo., Ill., 1992—. Trustee Ctr. for Advanced Study in the Behavioral Scis., Stanford, Calif., 1986-92, 93-99, 2000—, chmn., 1995-99, 2002--. Author: The History of Statistics, 1986, Statistics on the Table, 1999; contbr. articles to jours. in field. Guggenheim Found. fellow, 1976-77; Ctr. for Advanced Study in Behavioral Scis. fellow, 1978-79. Fellow: AAAS, Royal Statis. Soc. (Fisher lectr. 1986), Am. Statis. Assn. (editor Jour. 1979—82), Inst. Math. Stats. (Neyman lectr. 1988, pres. 1993—94), Am. Acad. Arts and Scis. (mem. coun. 1995—99); mem.: Brit. Soc. for History Sci., History of Sci. Soc., Bernoulli Soc., Statis. Soc. Can., Internat. Statis. Inst. (mem. coun. 1999—2001, pres. 2003—), Quadrangle Club, Phi Beta Kappa, Sigma Xi. Office: U Chgo Dept Statistics 5734 S University Ave Chicago IL 60637-1514

STIGLITZ, JOSEPH EUGENE, economist, educator; b. Gary, Ind., Feb. 9, 1943; s. Nathaniel David and Charlotte (Fishman) Stiglitz; children: Siobhan, Michael, Edward, Julia. BA, Amherst Coll., Mass, 1964; DHL, Amherst Coll., 1974; PhD in Econs., MIT, 1966; MA (hon.), Yale U., 1970; D in Econs. (hon.), U. Leuven, 1994. Asst. prof. econs. MIT, 1966—67; asst. prof. Cowles Found., Yale U., New Haven, 1967—68, assoc. prof., 1968—70, prof. econs., 1970—74; vis. fellow St. Catherine's Coll., Oxford, England, 1973—74; Joan Kenney professorship Stanford U., 1974—76, prof. of economics and senior fellow, Hoover Inst., 1988—2001; Oskar Morgenstern dist. fellow Inst. Advanced Studies Math., Princeton, NJ, 1978—79; Drummond prof. polit. economy Oxford U., England, 1976—79; prof. econs. Princeton U., 1979—88; sr. v.p., chief economist World Bank, Washington, 1995—2000; sr. fellow Brookings Inst., Washington, 2000; Stern visiting prof. Columbia U., 2000; prof. of economics and finance Columbia U. Grad. Sch. of Bus., Dept. of Econ. and Sch. of Internat. and Public Affairs, 2001—; prof. of exec. MBA programs Columbia U. Tapp rsch. fellow Gonville and Caius Coll., Cambridge, England, 1966—70; vis. prof. dept. econs. U. Canterbury, Christchurch, New Zealand, 1967; sr. rsch. fellow social sci. divsn. Inst. for Devel. Studies U. Coll. Nairobi, 1969—71; mem. Pres.'s Coun. Econ. Advisers, 1993—95, chmn. coun. econ. advisers, 1995—97, sr. v.p. devel. econs. and chief econs., exec. dir.; cons. World Bank, State of Alaska, Seneca Indian Nation, Bell Comm. Rsch. Editor: Jour. Econ. Perspectives, 1986—93; Am. editor: Rev. of Econ. Studies, 1968—76, assoc. editor: Am. Econ. Rev., 1968—76, Energy Econs., Managerial and Decision Econs., mem. editl. bd.: World Bank Econ. Rev.; author: Whither Socialism?, 1996, Frontiers of Development Economics: The Future in Perspective, 2000, New Ideas About Old Age Security: Toward Sustainable Pension Systems in the 21st Century, 2001; author: (with C.E. Walsh) Principles of Macroeconomics, 2002, Economics, 2002; author: (with R. K. Sah) Peasants Versus City-Dwellers: Taxation and the Burden of Economic Development, 2002; author: Globalization and Its Discontents, 2002, The Rebel Within: Joseph Stiglitz and the World Bank, 2002; author: (with B. Greenwald) Towards a New Paradigm in Monetary Economics, 2003; author: The Roaring Nineties, 2003. Recipient John Bates Clark award, Am. Econ. Assn., 1979, Internat. prize, Accademia Lincei, 1988, Union des Assurances de Paris prize, 1989, The Nobel Prize in Economic Sciences, 2001, Rechtenwald Prize, Germany, 1998; fellow, Guggenheim, 1969—70; scholar guest, The Brookings Inst., Washington. Fellow: Inst. for Policy Rsch. (sr. 1991—93), Brit. Acad. (corr.); mem.: NAS (fellow, 1988), Econometric Soc., Am. Acad. Arts and Scis.(fellow, 1983), Am. Econ. Assn. (exec. com. 1982—84, v.p. 1985). Office: Columbia U Uris Hall Rm 814 Broadway and 116th St New York NY 10027 E-mail: jes322@columbia.edu.

STIGWOOD, ROBERT COLIN, theater, movie, television and record producer; b. Adelaide, Australia, Apr. 16, 1934; came to Eng., 1956; s. Gordon and Gwendolyn (Burrows) S. Student, Sacred Heart Coll., Adelaide. Worked as copywriter for advt. agy., Adelaide; held series of jobs, including mgr. provincial theater and halfway house for delinquents in Cambridge; opened talent agy. London, 1962; liquidated firm, 1965; became bus. mgr. for group Graham Bond Orgn.; became co-mng. dir. NEMS Enterprises, 1967; prin. Robert Stigwood Orgn., 1967; formed RSO Records, 1973; dir. Polygram, 1976; co-founder (with Rupert Murdoch) R&R Films, 1979. Founder Music for UNICEF. 1st ind. record producer in Eng. with release of single Johnny Remember Me; producer: films, including Jesus Christ Superstar, 1973, Bugsy Malone, Tommy, 1975, Survive, 1976, Saturday Night Fever, 1977, Grease I, 1978, Grease II, 1982, Moment By Moment, 1978, Sergeant Pepper's Lonely Hearts Club Band, The Fan, 1981, Times Square, 1980, Gallipoli, 1980, Staying Alive, 1983, Evita, 1996; stage musicals in Eng. and U.S., including, Hair, Oh! Calcutta, The Dirtiest Show in Town, Sweeney Todd, Pippin, Jesus Christ Superstar, Evita, Grease, Saturday Night Fever; TV producer in Eng. and U.S.; prodns. include The Entertainer (dramatic spl.); All in the Family (series), The Prime of Miss Jean Brodie (dramatic series). Bd. dirs. Police Athletic League, N.Y.C.; patron Australian Nat. Art Gallery. Recipient Tony award for best musical (Evita); named Internat. Producer of Yr. ABC Interstate Theatres, Inc., 1976, Knight of St. John of Jerusalem, Malta, 1985. Mem. Royal Bermuda Yacht Club. Clubs: Royal Bermuda Yacht. Avocations: yachting, tennis. Home: Barton Manor East Cowes Isle of Wight England

STILES, GARY LESTER, cardiologist, molecular pharmacologist, educator; b. N.Y.C., May 22, 1949; s. Robert L. and Vivian M. (Cano) S.; m. Alexis H. Stiles; children: Heather B., Wendy A. BS in Chemistry, St. Lawrence U., 1971; MD, Vanderbilt U., 1975. Diplomate Am. Bd. Internal Medicine, sub.-bd. Cardiovascular Medicine. Resident in internal medicine Vanderbilt U., Nashville, 1975-78; from fellow in cardiology to prof. Duke U., Durham, NC, 1978—90, prof. medicine, 1990—; CMO, v.p. Duke Health Sys., 1999—2004; exec. v.p. Wyeth Pharms., Collegeville, Pa., 2004—, chief med. officer, 2004—. Mem. sci. adv. coun. Alta. Heritage Found., Edmonton, Can., 1990—; mem. pharmacology study sect. NIH, Bethesda, Md., 1988-91. Mem. editl. bd. Jour. Biol. Chemistry, 1990-95, Molecular Pharmacology, 1991-99. Recipient Katz prize Am. Heart Assn., 1983, award Am. Fedn. Clin. Rsch., 1989; grantee Am. Heart Assn., 1987-90. Fellow Am. Coll. Cardiology (award 1993); mem. Internat. Churchill Soc., Assn. Am. Physicians, Am. Soc. Clin. Investigation. Republican. Achievements include patent in field. Office: D6106 Wyeth Pharms 500 Arcola Rd Collegeville PA 19426 Office Phone: 484-865-8700. Business E-Mail: stilesg@wyeth.com.

STILES, JULIA, actress; b. N.Y.C., Mar. 28, 1981; Student, Columbia U., 2000—. Actor: (TV films) Before Women Had Wings, 1997, The '60s, 1999; (films) I Love You, I Love You Not, 1996, The Devil's Own, 1997, Wicked, 1998, Wide Awake, 1998, 10 Things I Hate About You, 1999, Down to You, 2000, Hamlet, 2000, State and Main, 2000, Save the Last Dance, 2001, The Business of Strangers, 2001, O, 2001, The Bourne Identity, 2002, A Guy Thing, 2003, Carolina, 2003, Mona Lisa Smile, 2003, The Prince & Me, 2004, The Bourne Supremacy, 2004; TV guest appearances include Ghostwriter, 1992, Promised Land, 1996, Chicago Hope, 1994. Voted one of, People Mag.'s 50 Most Beautiful People, 2001. Office: Clare Ryu c/o United Talent Agy 9560 Wilshire Blvd Beverly Hills CA 90212

STILES, MARY ANN, lawyer, author, lobbyist; b. Tampa, Fla., Nov. 16, 1944; d. Ralph A. and Bonnie (Smith) S.; m. Barry Smith. AA, Hills Community Coll., 1973; BS, Fla. State U., 1975; JD, Antioch Sch. Law, 1978. Bar: Fla. 1978. Legis. analyst Fla. Ho. of Reps., Tallahassee, 1973-74, 74-75; intern U.S. Senate, Washington, 1977; v.p., gen. counsel Associated Industries Fla., Tallahassee, 1978-81, gen. counsel, 1981-84, spl. counsel, 1986-97; assoc. Deschler, Reed & Crichfield, Boca Raton, Fla., 1980-81; founding ptnr. Stiles, Taylor, & Grace, P.A., Boca Raton, Tampa, Orlando, Jacksonville, Talahassee, and Miami, Fla., 1982—, shareholder, dir. Tampa; gen. counsel Associated Industries Ins. Co., Inc., 1996—, Associated Industries Fla., Inc., 1997—, Associated Industries Ins. Svcs., Inc., 1997—. Shareholder, dir. Six Stars Devel. Co. of Fla., Inc. Platnum Bank; dr. Eclipse, Inc.; owner, pres. Styles by Stiles; shareholder, pres. 42nd St., The Bistro; mem. Workers' Compensation Task Force, 2000-01. Author: Workers' Compensation Law Handbook, 1980-94 edit. Bd. dirs., sec. Hillsborough C.C. Found., Tampa, 1985-87, 94-96; bd. dirs. Hillsborough Area Regional Transit Authority, Tampa, 1986-89, Boys and Girls Club of Tampa, 1986—, The Spring, 1992-93, What's My Chance, 1992-94; mem. Gov.'s Oversite Bd. on Workers' Compensation, 1989-90, Workers' Compensation Rules Com., Fla. Bar, 1990-95, 2000—, Workers' Compensation Exec. Counsel Fla. Bar, 1990-95, Jud. Nominating Commn. for Workers' Compensation Cts., 1990-93, trustee Hillsborough Cmty. Coll., 1994-99, vice-chair, 1995-96, chair, 1996-97; bd. dirs. Seminole Boosters, Inc., Fla. State U., 1996—. Mem. ABA, Fla. Bar Assn., Hillsborough County Bar Assn., Hillsborough Assn. Women Lawyers, Fla. Assn. Women Lawyers, Fla. Women's Alliance, Hillsborough County Seminole Boosters (past pres.), Tiger Bay Club (Tampa, past. pres., sec.). Republican. Baptist. Avocations: boating, reading. Office: 315 S Plant Ave Tampa FL 33606-2325 also: 317 N Calhoun St Tallahassee FL 32301-7605 also: PO Box 310397 Miami FL 33231-0397 Address: PO Box 294349 Boca Raton FL 33429 also: PO Box 48190 Jacksonville FL 32247

STILES, RYAN, actor; b. Seattle, Apr. 22, 1959; s. Sonny and Irene Stiles; m. Pat McDonald, 1989; children: Mackenzie, Sam. Actor (films) Rainbow War, 1985, Hot Shots!, 1991, Hot Shots! Part Deux, 1993, Courting Courtney, 1997, (tv series) Whose Line Is It Anyway, 1998— (Emmy award nominee 2002), The Drew Carey Show, 1995—; prodr.: Whose Line Is It Anyway?, 1998; tv guest appearances include: The Magic Hour, 1998, The Hitchhiker, 1983, Mad TV, 1995, The Beachcombers, 1971, Parker Lewis Can't Lose, 1990, The John Larroquette Show, 1993, Mad About You, 1992, Weird Science, 1994, Murphy Brown, 1988, Dharma & Greg, 1997, Rendez-View, 2001, The Sweet Spot, 2002. Office: ABC Inc care Drew Carey Show 500 S Buena Vista St Burbank CA 91521-4551

STILES, THOMAS BEVERIDGE, II, retired investment banking executive; b. Easton, Pa., Oct. 4, 1940; s. Ezra Martin and Vivien (de Fay) S.; m. Elaine Ann Patyk, July 2, 1966 (div. Oct. 1980); children— Thomas Beveridge III, Jonathan Ezra; m. Barbara Toll Alexander, Mar. 7, 1981. BA, Yale U., 1963; MBA, Harvard U., 1968. V.p. Laird, Inc., N.Y.C., 1968-73; sr. v.p., dir. Smith Barney Harris Upham and Co., Inc., N.Y.C., 1973-82; exec. v.p., dir. E.F. Hutton & Co. Inc., N.Y.C., 1982-87; chmn., CEO Shearson Lehman Advisors Asset Mgmt. Co., N.Y.C., 1988-90, 99—, Bernstein Macaulay, N.Y.C., 1988-90; CEO, chmn. Greenwich Street Advisors, N.Y.C., 1990-97; mng. dir. Smith, Barney, Inc., N.Y.C., 1993-99, retired, 1999—. Bd. dirs., pres. Cedar Lawn Cemetery, Paterson, N.J., 1973—. Bd. dirs., v.p., mem. collections com., devel. com., fin. com., pers. com. Laguna Art Mus., Laguna Beach, Calif.; bd. dirs. Sanford C. BErnstein Fund, 2003—. 1st lt. M.I., U.S. Army, 1963-66. Fellow Fin. Analysts Fedn.; mem. N.Y. Soc. Security Analysts, Spring Lake Bath and Tennis Club (N.J.), El Niguel Country Club (Calif.). Republican. Presbyterian. Avocations: political science, tennis, swimming. E-mail: tom.stiles@cox.net.

STILES, VIRGINIA FORD, data processing executive, poet; b. Memphis, June 3, 1961; d. Margaret Berry and John Edward Ford, Mattie Virginia Martin; m. Allen Wesley Stiles, Aug. 9, 2003; children: Lakeisha Lashun Williams, Teresita Louise Cornelius. Lic. Tax Preparer, H&R Block Tax Sch., 1992. Data entry clk. H&R Block, LA, 1992—93; ms mgmt. specialist USN, Norfolk, Va., 1996. Tax examiner IRS, Memphis, 1987—88. Singer (author): (anthology) Memphis Miracle (Editor's Choice award, 2000); author: I Think (Best Poet, 2002). Recipient Veterans Integrity, Patrotism Recognition, Am. Legions, 2000, Pub. greeting cards, anthology, and CD, Internat. Libr. of Poetry, 2001. Mem.: Phi Theta Kappi Honor Soc. (hon.). Personal E-mail: virginiallen@aol.com.

STILL, CHARLES HENRY, SR., lawyer; b. Lubbock, Tex., Sept. 22, 1942; s. Charles Alphonso and Henri Sue S.; m. Frances Eugenia Odell, Apr. 29, 1967; children: Charles Henry Jr., Kathryn Elizabeth. BBA in Acctg., Tex. Tech. U., 1965; JD with honors, U. Tex., 1968. Bar: Tex. 1968. Assoc. Fulbright & Jaworski, Houston, 1968-75, ptnr., 1975—, head corp. dept., 1984-99, mem. exec. com., 1992-99. Speaker numerous confs. and meetings; bd. dirs. Oyo Geospace Corp., TrueTime Inc. Comment editor Tex. Law Rev., 1967-68. Bd. dirs. Alley Theatre, Houston, 1980-81, St. Luke's Episcopal Hosp., Houston, 1991—, Free Enterprise Inst., Houston, 1993—, Catalyst Found., Houston, 1992--; mem. vestry Christ Ch. Cathedral, Houston, 1981-84, sr. warden, 1983, chancellor, 1986-2002. Fellow Am. Bar Found., Tex. Bar Found., Houston Bar Found.; mem. ABA (bus. law sect. 1968—, corp. laws com. 1983-89, fed. regulation of securities com. 1976—, com. on legal opinions 1989—, adminstrv. law sect. 1981—, law firms com. 1990—, chmn. 1998-2000, ethics 2000 task force 1999-2002, multiple disciplinary practice task force 1998—, profl. conduct com. 2002--), Am. Law Inst., State Bar Tex. (chmn. bus. law sect. 1984-85, mem. coun. 1982-86, chmn. securities law com. 1981-83, com. on corp. laws 1985—), Forest Club, Petroleum Club, Order of Coif, Phi Delta Phi, Phi Kappa Phi, Gamma Phi Beta, Beta Alpha Psi, Phi Delta Theta, Phi Eta Sigma. Avocations: hunting, reading, photography. Home: 3734 Locke Ln Houston TX 77027-4006 Office: Fulbright & Jaworski 1301 Mckinney St Ste 5100 Houston TX 77010-3095

STILL, CHARLES NEAL, neurologist, consultant; b. Richmond, Va., Apr. 15, 1929; s. Charles Wright and Ruth (Kemp) S.; m. Dorothy Lee Varn, Dec. 27, 1958; children: Charles Herbert, Carl Nelson, Sara Alice. BS in Chemistry, Clemson U., 1949; MS in Biochemistry, Purdue U., 1951; MD, Med. U. S.C., 1959. Diplomate Am. Bd. Psychiatry and Neurology. Instr. chemistry Clemson (S.C.) U., 1951-52; rotating intern U. Chgo. Clinics, 1959-60; neurology fellow Sch. Medicine Johns Hopkins U., Balt., 1960-63; resident in neurology Johns Hopkins-Balt. City Hosp., 1960-63; NIH rsch. fellow Harvard U.-McLean Hosp., Belmont, Mass., 1963-65; chief neurology svcs. William S. Hall. Psychiat. Inst., Columbia, S.C., 1965-81, assoc. dir. gen. psychiatry and neurology, 1989-92; dir. C. M. Tucker Human Resources Ctr., Columbia, 1981-88; clin. prof. neuropsychiatry USC Sch. Medicine, Columbia, S.C., 1981-88, prof. neuropsychiatry, 1989—. Instr. chemistry U.S. Mil. Acad., West Point, N.Y., 1953-55; assoc. clin. prof. neurology Med. U. S.C., Charleston, 1973-92; assoc. prof. neuropsychiatry U. S.C. Sch. Medicine, Columbia, 1976-78, prof. neuropsychiatry, 1978-81. Author: (with others) Handbook of Clinical Neurology, 1976, Neurologic Clinics, 1984, Movement Disorders, 1986; editor The Recorder Columbia Med. Soc., 1991-2003, editor emeritus, 2003—; mem. editl. bd. Jour. S.C. Med. Assn., 1980—, Jour. Applied Gerontology, 1983-88; contbr. articles to profl. jours. Chmn. grants rev. bd. S.C. Dept. Mental Health, Columbia, 1973-78; mem. exec. bd. Alzheimer's Assn. Columbia, 1985-93, pres. Mid-State chpt. Alzheimer's Assn., 1991-92; med. dir. Alzheimer's Disease Registry, Columbia, 1989-92, Alzheimer's Daycare Ctr., Columbia, 1989-92; mem. Gov.'s Adv. Coun. to Alzheimer's Disease and Related Disorders Resource Coordination Ctr., 1995-99. 1st lt. U.S. Army, 1952-55. Fellow: Am. Geriatrics Soc., Am. Acad. Neurology, Gerontol. Soc. Am., Am. Inst. Chemists (life); mem.: AMA (life), Am. Chem. Soc. Baptist. Avocations: writing, photography. Home: 2 Culpepper Cir Columbia SC 29209-2234 Office: WJB Dorn VA Med Ctr Psychiatry Svc Columbia SC 29209-1639 Personal E-mail: cndstill@aol.com.

STILL, DAVID BARNES, banker, lawyer; b. Abington, Pa., June 2, 1949; s. Harold Ferguson and Virginia (Barnes) S.; m. Sheridan Shepherd, Nov. 1, 1984; 1 child, Meredith Susan Lynn; children by previous marriage: David Jr., Mark L. BA, St. Lawrence U., Canton, N.Y., 1971; MBA, U. Pa., 1972; JD, Temple U., 1987. Bar: Pa. 1989. V.p. Shawmut Nat. Bank, Boston, 1972-78; sr. v.p. Phila. Nat. Bank, 1978-84, CoreStates Fin. Corp., Phila., 1984—. Vice chmn., trustee Curtis Inst. Music, Phila., 1982—; trustee Mary Louis Curtis Bok Found., Phila., 1984—. Mem. Robert Morris Assocs., Pine Valley (N.J.) Golf Club, Merion Golf Club. Republican. Episcopalian. Office: CoreStates Fin Corp Broad & Chestnut Sts Philadelphia PA 19101

STILL, JOHN C., III, insurance agent, state legislator; b. Dover, Del., Oct. 27, 1952; s. John Clifton Jr. and Kathleen (Nichols) S.; m. Kathleen Heron, Mar. 6, 1982. AA, Wesley Coll., Dover, 1972; BS in Edn., U. Del., 1974. CLU, registered health underwriter, chartered fin. cons. Math. & sci. tchr. Newark (Del.) Sch., 1974-77; ins. agt. Dover, 1976—; mem. Dist. 17 Del. Senate, Dover, 1988—. Recipient Pub. Svc. award March of Dimes, 1982, 83. Mem. Nat. Assn. Life Underwriters, Nat. Assn. Health Underwriters, Cen. Del. C. of C., Rotary. Republican. Methodist. Avocations: skiing, walking, travel. Office: Still Ins Agy PO Box 1401 Dover DE 19903-1401 also: Still Ins Agy 872 Walker Rd Ste C Dover DE 19904-2700

STILLER, BEN, actor, director; b. NYC, Nov. 30, 1965; s. Jerry Stiller and Anne Meara. m. Christine Taylor, 2000, 1 child. Student, UCLA. Actor: (Broadway plays) The House of Blue Leaves, 1985; (films) Hot Pursuit, 1987, Empire of the Sun, 1987, Fresh Horses, 1988, Next of Kin, 1988, That's Adequate, 1989, Elvis Stories, 1989, Stella, 1990, Highway to Hell, 1992, Reality Bites, 1994, Heavyweights, 1995, Happy Gilmore, 1996, Flirting With Disaster, 1996, Zero Effect, 1998, There's Something About Mary, 1998, Your Friends and Neighbors, 1998, Permanent Midnight, 1998, Nobody Knows Anything, 1998, The Suburbans, 1999, McClintock's Peach, 1999, Black and White, 1999, Mystery Men, 1999, The Independent, 2000, Keeping the Faith, 2000, Meet the Parents, 2000, The Royal Tannenbaums, 2001, Orange County, 2002, Duplex, 2003, Nobody Knows Anything, 2003, Along Came Polly, 2004, Starsky & Hutch, 2004, Envy, 2004; actor, dir. (films) Reality Bites, 1994, The Cable Guy, 1996, Zoolander, 2001; actor, prodr. (films) Dodgeball: A True Underdog Story, 2004; actor (TV series) Kate McShane, 1975, Kate & Allie, 1986, Miami Vice, 1987, The Ben Stiller Show (also writer, dir.)(Emmy award for writing), 1992-93, Frasier, 1993, Duckman, 1995, Friends, 1997, Saturday Night Live, 1998, 2000, Freaks and Geeks, 2000, The Simpsons (voice only), 2002, Undeclared, 2002, The King of Queens, 2002, Curb Your Enthusiasm, 2004.*

STILLER, JENNIFER ANNE, lawyer; b. Washington, May 4, 1948; d. Ralph Sophian and Joy (Dancis) S. AB in Econs. and History, U. Mich., 1970; JD, NYU, 1973. Bar: Pa. 1973, U.S. Dist. Ct. (mid. dist.) Pa. 1977, U.S. Supreme Ct. 1978, Ill. 1979, U.S. Dist. Ct. (no. dist.) Ill. 1979, U.S. Dist. Ct. (ea. dist.) Pa. 1983, U.S. Ct. Appeals (3rd cir.) 1983, U.S. Ct. Appeals (D.C. cir.), 1996. Dep. atty. gen. Pa. Dept. Justice, Harrisburg, 1973-75, Pa. Dept. Health, Harrisburg, 1975-78; sr. staff atty. Am. Hosp. Assn., Chgo., 1978-80, mgr., dept. fed. law, 1980-81; gen. counsel Ill. Health Fin. Authority, 1981-82; sr. assoc. Berriman & Schwartz, King of Prussia, Pa., 1983-85, Wolf, Block, Schorr & Solis-Cohen, Phila., 1985-88, Montgomery, McCracken, Walker & Rhoads, LLP, Phila., 1988-90; ptnr. Montgomery, McCracken, Walker & Rhoads, Phila., 1990-2000, chair health law group, 1991-2000; sr. counsel Tenet Healthcare Corp., Phila., 2000-2001; pvt. practice Haverford, Pa., 2001—. Contbr. health law articles to profl. jours. Mem. ABA (gov. com. Health Law Forum 1994-95), Am. Health Lawyers Assn. (bd. dirs. 1997-2003, exec. com. 2002-03), Pa. Soc. Healthcare Attys. (pres. 1995). Avocations: gardening, bicycling, hiking, music. Office: Law Office Jennifer A Stiller 625 Haydock Ln Haverford PA 19041-1207 Office Phone: 610-642-3366. E-mail: stiller@healthregs.com.

STILLER, JERRY, actor; b. N.Y.C., June 8, 1927; s. William and Bella S.; m. Anne Meara, Sept. 14, 1953; children: Amy, Benjamin. BS in Speech and Drama, Syracuse U., 1950. Actor with nat. co. of Peter Pan, 1951, also at Henry St. Playhouse, 1941, Cherry Lane Theatre, N.Y.C., 1947, Billy Barnes Showboat, Chgo., 1950, Erie (Pa.) Playhouse, 1951, 52, Memphis Arena Theatre, 1952, Phoenix Theatre, 1954, 55, 56, Shakespeare Festival Theatre, Stratford, Conn., 1955, Compass Players, 1959, mem. Shakespeare Co. in Central Park, N.Y.C., 1957, 71, Two Gentlemen, 1971, Much Ado, 1988; Broadway appearances include The Golden Apple, 1954, The Ritz, 1975, Unexpected Guests, 1977, Hurlyburly, 1985, Three Men on a Horse, 1993, What's Wrong With This Picture?, 1994, The Three Sisters, 1997; film appearances include The Taking of Pelham 1-2-3, 1974, Airport '75, 1975, The Ritz, 1976, Those Lips, Those Eyes, 1979, Nadine, 1986, That's Adequate, 1986, Hairspray, 1986, Shoeshine (Acad. award nomination, short subject 1989), A Pair of Jokers, 1990, The Pickle, 1992, Stag, 1996, Camp Stories, 1996, The Deli, 1997, Die Story Von Monty Spinnerratz, 1997, The Fish in the Bathtub, 1998, The Independent, 2001, On the Line, 2001, Serving Sara, 2002, Zoolander, 2003; Off-Broadway appearances include Boubouroche, 1971, Passione, 1980, Prairie du Chien, 1985, After-Play, 1995-96; mem. comedy team, Anne Meara, 1961—, Ed Sullivan Show 36 appearances; night club appearances include Compass Players, St. Louis, 1957, Happy Medium, Chgo., 1960, also Village Gate, Village Vanguard, Blue Angel, Bon Soir and, Phase Two, N.Y.C., Mr. Kelly's, Chgo., Hungry I, San Francisco, The Establishment, London, The Sands, Flamingo, Las Vegas, Harrah's, Reno and Lake Tahoe, Trump Plaza, QE II; co-star: daily TV series Take Five with Stiller and Meara, 1977-78; actor TV series Joe and Sons, 1975, Tattinger's, 1987, The Detective, The Sunset Gang, PBS, 1991, Seize the Day, 1990, The Hollow Boy, American Playhouse, 1991, Seinfeld, 1993-98, Subway Stories, Tales From the Underground, 1997, King of Queens, 1998—; commercials: Blue Nun, United Van Lines, Amalgamated Bank, Vermeer Liquor, Nike, AT&T, Glad Bags, Total Cereal; AOL, Video (co-host with Anne Meara): So You Want to be an Actor?; animation: Teachers Pet "Pretty Boy", 2000-02, Lion King III, 2003, Lion King 1Y2, 2004; author: (book) Married to Laughter (Grammy nomination for audio), 2000. Recipient Disting. Alumnus award Syracuse U., 1973, Voice of Imagery award, 1975, Arents Pioneer Medal, 1979, 1st Biffy award Balt. Internat. Film Festival, Entertainment Father of Yr. award, 1977, Syracuse Walk of Stars, 1994, Syracuse U. award for Achievement in the Arts, Am. Comedy award for role in Seinfeld, 1998, Fourth Ann. Alan King award in Jewish humor (with Anne Meara), Am. Comedy award Seinfeld, 1998, Productive Aging award Jewish Coun. Aging, 2004; nominated Emmy award for role in Seinfeld, 1997, Ellis Island Medal of Honor, 2000.

STILLER, SHALE DAVID, lawyer, educator; b. Rochester, N.Y., Feb. 23, 1935; s. Maurice Aaron and Dorothy (Salitan) S.; m. Ellen M. Heller; children: Lewis B., Michael J., Kenneth R.; stepchildren: William Heller, Lawrence Heller. BA, Hamilton Coll., 1954; LLB, Yale U., 1957; MLA, Johns Hopkins U., 1977. Bar: Md. 1957. Ptnr. Piper & Marbury, Balt., 1992—. Lectr. U. Md. Law Sch., 1963—. Contbr. articles to profl. jours. Trustee Johns Hopkins U., Assn. Jewish Charities, Peabody Inst., Weinberg Found.; trustee, vice chmn. Johns Hopkins Sch. Medicine; mem. adv. bd. Tax Mgmt., 1972-93; chmn. Jud. Nominating Commn., Balt., 1979-83; officer, bd. dirs. Park Sch., 1973-79, pres., 1982-86; pres. Jewish Family Agy., 1972-74. Mem. ABA, Am. Law Inst., Am. Coll. Tax Counsel, Am. Coll. Trust and Estate Counsel, Order of Coif, 14 W. Hamilton St. Club (Balt.). Democrat. Jewish. Home: 807 St Georges Rd Baltimore MD 21210-1408 Office: Piper Marbury Rudnick & Wolfe 6225 Smith Ave Baltimore MD 21209-3600

STILLINGER, FRANK HENRY, chemist, educator; b. Boston, Aug. 15, 1934; s. Frank Henry and Gertrude (Metcalf) S.; m. Dorothea Anne Keller, Aug. 18, 1956; children: Constance Anne, Andrew Metcalf. BS, U. Rochester, 1955; PhD, Yale U., 1958. NSF postdoctoral fellow Yale U., 1958-59; with Bell Telephone Labs., Murray Hill, N.J., 1959-2001, head chem. physics dept., 1976-79; disting. mem. tech. staff Bell Labs., 1982-2001. Mem. evaluation panel Nat. Bur. Stds., 1975-78; mem. adv. com. for chemistry NSF, 1980-83, mem. adv. com. for advanced sci. computing, 1984-86, mem. adv. com. material and phys. sci. directorate, 1992-94; disting. lectr. chemistry U. Md., 1981; Karcher lectr. U. Okla., 1984; Trumbull lectr. Yale U., 1984; Washburn Meml. lectr. U. Nebr., 1986; Gucker lectr. Ind. U., 1987; W.A. Noyes lectr. U. Tex., 1988; Regents lectr. UCLA, 1990; Meek indsl. lectr. Ohio State U., 1990; McElvane lectr. U. Wis., 1992; Gomberg lectr. U. Mich., 1992; vis. faculty mem. Princeton U., 1996—. Assoc. editor Jour. Stat. Physics, Jour. Chem. Physics, Phys. Rev., Jour. Mathematical Physics, Procs. Nat. Acad. Scis.; contbr. articles to profl. jours. Recipient Elliott Cresson medal Franklin Inst., 1978, Hildebrand award Am. Chem. Soc., 1986, Peter J. Debye award Am. Chem. Soc., 1992, Onsager medal Norwegian U. Sci. and Tech., 2002; Welch Found. fellow, 1974. Fellow AAAS, Am. Phys. Soc. (Langmuir award 1989); mem. Nat. Acad. Scis. Home: 216 Noe Ave Chatham NJ 07928-1548 Office: Princeton U Chemistry Dept Princeton NJ 08544 E-mail: fhs@princeton.edu.

STILLINGS, DENNIS OTTO, research association administrator, consultant; b. Valley City, N.D., Oct. 30, 1942; s. Harlow Cecil and Ruth Alice (Wolff) S. BA, U. Minn., 1965. Tchr. Henry (S.D.) Pub. Schs., 1965-66, Darby (Mont.) Pub. Schs., 1966-68; tech. rsch. libr., then mgr. hist. dept. Medtronic, Inc., Mpls., 1968-79; instr. humanities U. Minn., Mpls., 1970-72; founding dir., then curator Bakken Libr., Mpls., 1976-80; ind. antiquarian hist. cons. Mpls., 1979-81; sole proprietor Archaeus Project, Kamuela, Hawaii, 1981—; exec. dir. Five Mountain Med. Cmty., 1996-97, also bd. dirs., 1996—. Cons. Ctr. for Sci. Anomalies Rsch., Ann Arbor, Mich., 1993—; bd. nutrition Kahala Ctr., 2001—; bd. dirs. Dan Carlson Enterprises, Mpls. Columnist Med. Progress Through Technology, 1974-76; columnist Med. Instrumentation, 1973-76, guest editor, 1975; editor: Cyberphysiology: The Science of Self-Regulation, 1988, Cyberbiological Studies of the Imaginal Component in the UFO Contact Experience, 1989, The Theology of Electricity: On the Encounter and Explanation of Theology and Science in the 17th and 18th Centuries, 1990, Project 2010: On the Current Crisis in Health and Its Implications of the Hospital for the Future, 1992; founding editor: (jours.) Artifex, 1981-93, Archaeus, 1982-84, Healing Island. Fellow Am. Inst. Stress; mem. Assn. Sci. Study Anomalous Phenomena, Bioelectromagnetics Soc., Soc. Sci. Exploration. Avocations: jungian psychology, golf, fishing, travel. E-mail: dstillings@archaeusproject.com.

STILLINGS, IRENE ELLA GRACE CORDINER, ret.foundation executive; b. Boston, Aug. 17, 1918; d. Matthew Wilson and Susan F. (Mason) Cordiner; m. Gordon A. Stillings, May 13, 1945; children: David Gordon, Susan Irene. Student, Radcliffe Coll., 1936-39; diploma, Burdett Coll., 1941. Sec., bookkeeper Boston Refrigerator Co., 1941-42; sec., tchr. Burdett Coll., 1942-44; sec., bookkeeper Gertrude Rittenburg, Boston, 1944-46. Town chmn. Heart Fund, Woodland, Maine, 1953-61; Brownie leader Girl Scouts U.S., 1954-58; pres. Woodland Woman's Club 1961-63; sec. PTA, 1961-62; chmn. Baileyville Superintending Sch. Com., 1962-64; chmn. women's activities Nat. Found., East Washington County, 1959-61; pres. Hosp. Aid, 1961-63; chmn. Newcomers Coll. group YWCA, 1965-66, chmn. theatre group, 1968-70, pres. Suburbanites, 1970-71; Stamford (Conn.) chmn. Expt. in Internat. Living, 1965-68; bd. dirs. YWCA of Stamford, 1969-78, chmn. antique show, 1960-77, chmn. devotion, 1970-92, ann. Antique Show benefit, 1970-77; pres. New Suburbanites, Stamford, 1994-95, ret. 1996. Mem. Mass. Hort. Soc., St. Luke's Guild (treas. 1954-63), Radcliffe Club, Stamford Woman's Club (treas. 1975-79, program com., co-chmn. Am. home dept. 1974, 75, pres. 1981-83, bd. dirs. 1981—, 2d v.p. fin. 1979-81, 83-85, 87-89, chmn. bldg. investment 1979-81, parliamentarian 1990—, pres., newcomers/suburbanites, 1994-95), Theta Alpha Chi. Episcopalian. Home: 277 W Hill Rd Stamford CT 06902-1708

STILLMAN, ALFRED WILLIAM, JR., electrical engineer; b. Biloxi, Miss., Sept. 11, 1942; s. Alfred William and Marie Ann (Hengen) S.; children: Shannon Lynn, Laura Marie. AA, Am. River Coll., 1966; BSEE, BS in Applied Math., Calif. Poly. State U., 1970, MS in Applied Math., 1973; ME in Indsl. Engring., Tex. A&M U., 1976; postgrad. studies in Elec. Engring., N.J. Inst. Tech., 1977; PhD in Mgmt., Calif. Coast U., 1984. Cert. profl. logistician, instr. Calif. C.Cs. Engring. intern U.S. Army Material Command, Texarkana, Tex., 1973-75, electronic sys. staff maintenance engr. Fort Monmouth, N.J., 1975-77; mgr. mil. tactical data sys. integrated logistics support Office of Project Mgr. ARTADS, Fort Monmouth, 1977-78; tactical ADP ILS mgr., ILS dir. CORADOM, Fort Monmouth, 1978-79; engring. mgr. regional dist. office Office of Project Mgr. Firefinder Hughes Aircraft Co., Fullerton, Calif., 1979-80; prof. sys. acquisition mgmt. Dept. Def. Sys. Mgmt. Coll., Ft. Belvoir, Va., 1980-82; integrated logistics support engring. specialist advanced sys. divsn. Northrop Corp., Poco Rivera, Calif., 1982-83; program mgmt. rep. space sys. group Rockwell Internat., Downey, Calif., 1983-84; product assurance project engr. Space Sta. Sys. divsn. Rockwell Internat., Downey, 1984-85, mgr. product support, 1985-86; sr. mgr. ILS Amex Sys., Inc., Compton, Calif., 1986-88; dir. ILS NavCom Def. Electronics, Inc., Huntington Beach, Calif., 1988-91. Pres. AWS Assocs. Calif., Inc., El Monte, 1983—; corp. v.p., divsn. pres. HOPE Assocs., Inc., Huntington Beach, 1983—. With USAF, 1962-66. Mem. IEEE, Am. Mgmt. Assn., Am. Inst. Indsl. Engrs. (sr.), Soc. Logistics Engrs. (sr.), Am. Def. Preparedness Assn., Am. Security Coun., Acacia, Tau Beta Pi. Presbyterian. Home: 12020 226th St Unit B Hawaiian Gardens CA 90716-1379 Office: 7071 Warner Ave Ste F202 Huntington Beach CA 92647-5495 E-mail: aes@genesis1st.com., bill@stillman.cc.

STILLMAN, ANDREA L. state legislator; b. N.Y.C. BA, Calif. State U., Northridge. Mem. Conn. Ho. of Reps., Hartford, 1993—. Rep. town meeting, 1980-83; mem. Bd. Fin., 1984-92; bd. dirs. Conn. Resource Recovery Authority, 1988-92, Conn. Low Level Radioactive Waste Adv. Coun., 1992; mem. Waterford Dem. Town Com., Waterford Hist. Soc., Citizen's Task Force on Substance Abuse, 1996. Mem. AAUW, LWV, Nat. Women's Political Caucus, Nat. Assn. Women, Lions Club. Democrat. Jewish. Address: 5 Coolidge Ct Waterford CT 06385-3309 Office: Conn Ho of Reps State Capitol Hartford CT 06106

STILLMAN, JEANNE BETSOCK, public health administrator, consultant; b. Bethlehem, Pa., Dec. 15, 1942; d. Paul Thomas and Juliana Habera Betsock; m. David George Stillman, 1965; children: J. Alexander, Gregory D., Juliana E. C. BA, Am. U., 1964; MSPH, U. N.C., 1971; postgrad., Columbia U. Sch. Pub. Health, 1979-81. Assoc. dir. Quaker Svc./AFSC, Lome, Togo, 1969-70; from instr. to lectr. health adminstrn. Sch. Pub. Health U. N.C., Chapel Hill, 1971-74, rsch. assoc. Population Ctr., 1971-74; staff assoc., Tunisia project mgr. The Population Coun., N.Y.C., 1982-83; dir. N.Y. office Inst. for Devel. Tng., N.Y.C., 1989-93; Nigeria project mgr. The Africa-Am. Inst., N.Y.C., 1993-96; prin. Strategies for Devel., Inc., Hastings-on-Hudson, N.Y., 1998—. Dep. dir. devel. The Children's Village, Dobbs Ferry, 2002; mem. adv. com. UN Population Fund, N.Y.C., 1998; cons. in field. Assoc. editor, contbr. International Encyclopedia of Population, 2 vols., 1982; editor: (tng. manuals) Training Course in Women's Health, 2nd edit., 11 vols., 1993; editor, writer: UNHCR Manual for Health Services in Afghan Refugee Camps, 1985; project dir.: (video) Population and People of Faith, 1991 (N.Y. Internat. Film Festival Bronze medal 1992). Ch. coord. Habitat for Humanity, Hastings-on-Hudson, 1997—2000; vol. Internat. Microcredit Summit Meeting of Couns., N.Y.C., 1998; bd. sec. Greater Westchester Youth Orch. Assn., Valhalla, N.Y., 1997-99; parent fund vol. Phillips Exeter Acad., 1998-; mem. Ch. Vestry, 2001—; vol. Bus. Coun. of Westchester, 2002—; vol. emergency preparedness ARC, 2002—. Mem. APHA, Assn. Devel. Officers (bd. dirs. 2003—), UN Assn. USA (Westchester chpt., bd. dirs. 2002—), Am. Freedom Assn. (hon. bd. dirs. 2003-). Democrat. Episcopalian. Avocations: reading, theater, music. Office: Strategies for Development Inc 166 Edgars Ln Hastings On Hudson NY 10706-1108 Office Fax: 914-478-7859. Business E-Mail: jbs@stratdev.com.

STILLMAN, MARGARET D. library director; m. Peter R. Stillman; children: Lindsay H. and Walker H. Forehand. BA in Edn., U. Richmond, 1973; MA in Edn., Va. Commonwealth U., 1974; MLS, U. Md., 1977. Mem. staff to dir. Chesapeake (Va.) Pub. Libr. Sys., 1975-85, dir., 1985—. Chmn. State Adult Literacy Initiative, 1989-95; mem. Govs. Rural Econ. Devel. Task Force, 1990-92, U. Va. Continuing Edn. Ctr. Council, 1990-94; bd. dirs. United Way Hampton Rds., 1995—, Vol. Hampton Rds., 1996-98, Va. Stage Co., 1979-85 (v.p. 1981-82), Colonial Girl Scouts, 1993-95, Cultural Alliance, 1985-91, Tidewater Red Cross, 1980-83. Recipient Outstanding Young Career Woman of Va. award, 1978, Outstanding Profl. Woman, 1993. Mem. Pub. Libr. Assn. (bd. dirs. 1997-98, chmn. leadership dev. com. 1997), Libr. Va. Found. (bd. dirs. 1996—), WHRO Found. (bd. dirs. 1997—). Office: Chesapeake Public Library 298 Cedar Rd Chesapeake VA 23322-5598 Home: 3924 Oak Dr E Chesapeake VA 23321-5905

STILLMAN, MARTIN J. physical science research administrator, bioinorganic chemist; b. London, June 4, 1947; Can. citizen; BSc, U. East Anglia, 1969, MSc, 1970, PhD in Chemistry, 1973. Fellow in chemistry U. Alta., Edmonton, Can., 1973-75; from asst. prof. to assoc. prof. U. Western Ont., London, Can., 1975-86, prof. chemistry, 1986—, dir. Ctr. Chemistry and Physics, 1994—. Mem. Can. Inst. Chemistry, Am. Chem. Soc. Office: Univ Western ON Ctr Chem Phys P&A Bldg Rm 102 London ON Canada N6A 3K7 E-mail: stillman@uwo.ca.

STILLMAN, NINA GIDDEN, lawyer; b. NYC, Apr. 3, 1948; d. Melvin and Joyce Audrey (Gidden) S. AB with distinction, Smith Coll., 1970; JD cum laude, Northwestern U., 1973. Bar: Ill. 1973, U.S. Dist. Ct. (no. dist.) Ill. 1973, U.S. Dist. Ct. (ea. dist.) Wis. 1979, U.S. Dist. Ct. (no. dist. trial bar) Ill. 1983, U.S. Ct. Appeals (7th cir.) 1974, U.S. Supreme Ct. 1981, U.S. Dist. Ct. (ctrl. dist.) Ill. 1994, U.S. Dist. Ct. (ea. dist.) Tex., 1996, U.S. Dist. Ct. (Colo.), 1999, U.S. Dist. Ct. (ND) 2002. Assoc. Vedder, Price, Kaufman & Kammholz, Chgo., 1973-79, ptnr., 1980—2004, Morgan, Lewis and Bockius, LLP, Chgo., 2004—. Adv. bd. occupational health and safety tng. program U. Mich., Ann Arbor, 1980-83; adj. faculty Inst. Human Resources and Indsl. Rels., Loyola U., Chgo., 1983-86, bd. advisors, 1986—. Author: (with others) Women, Work, and Health: Challenge to Corporate Policy, 1979, Occupational Health Law: A Guide for Industry, 1981, Employment Discrimination, 1981, Personnel Management: Labor Relations, 1981, Occupational Safety and Health Law, 1988; contbg. author: Occupational Medicine: State of the Art Reviews, 1996; contbr. articles to profl. jours. Legal advisor, v.p. Planned Parenthood Assn. Chgo., 1979—81; sec. jr. governing bd. Chgo. Symphony Orch., 1983; trustee Merit Sch. Music, 2000—, vice chmn. bd. trustees, 2001—. Recipient Svc. award Northwestern U., 1994. Mem.: ABA (occupl. safety and health law com. 1978—), Human Resources Mgmt. Assn. Chgo. (bd. dirs. 1986—88, officer), Am. Inns of Ct. (v.p. Wigmore chpt. 1988—89), Chgo. Bar Assn. (chmn. labor and employment law com. 1986—87), Northwestern U. Sch. Law Alumni Assn. (pres. 1991—92), Univ. Club Chgo. (bd. dirs. 1988—2001, sec. 1999—2000, v.p. 2000—01), The Chgo. Com., Econ. Club Chgo., Lawyers Club, Smith Coll. Club Chgo. (pres. 1972). Avocations: travel, reading, the arts, collecting art. Office: Morgan Lewis and Bockius LLP 77 W Wacker Dr Ste 600 Chicago IL 60601 Business E-Mail: nstillman@morganlewis.com.

STILLMAN, RICHARD JOSEPH, retired army officer, consultant, publisher, writer; b. Lansing, Mich, Feb. 20, 1917; m. Darlene Slater, Nov. 15, 1941 (dec. Oct. 1992); children: Richard, Thomas, Ellen. BS, U. So. Calif., 1938; postgrad., Harvard U., 1938-39; MS, Syracuse U., 1950, PhD, 1955; postgrad., Command and Gen. Staff Sch., 1943, Army War Coll., 1959-60, NATO Def. Coll., 1960-61. Commd. 2d lt. US Army, 1938, advanced through grades to col., 1955, ret., 1965; faculty mem. NATO Def. Coll., 1961-63; dir. Ctr. for Econ. Opportunity. and Mgmt. Devel., Ohio U., Athens, 1965-67; prof. bus. adminstrn. Ohio U., 1965-67; prof. mgmt. U. New Orleans, 1967-82; pres. R.J. Stillman Co., New Orleans, 1982—. Author: (novels) US Infantry: Queen of Battle, 1965, Do It Yourself Contracting to Build Your Own Home, 1974, Your Personal Financial Planner, 1981, Small Business Management, 1981, Dow Jones Indus. Average: History and Role in an Investment Strategy, 1986; co-author (with J. Page): How to Use Your Personal Computer to Manage Your Personal Finances, 1987; author: Guide to Personal fin., 5th edit., 1988, Gen. Patton's Timeless Leadership Principles, 1997—98, (video), 1999; co-author (with M.F. Riggs): Gen. Patton's Best Friend: The Story of G.S. Patton, Jr. and His Beloved Dog, Willie, 2001; contbr. articles, Gen. Patton's Secret Missions, Intriguing Experiences of Old Blood and Guts, 2004. Mem. Mayor's Mill Adv. Com., New Orleans; apptd. spl. advisor on mil. affairs New Orleans region C. of C., 2001. Decorated Legion of Merit, Bronze star, Luxembourg Order of the Crown, Cross of Merit La. N.G., 2001; named to Hon. Order Ky. Cols.; Maxwell scholar, 1949-50; recipient Paratrooper Badge, Plaque Nat. D-Day Mus., State Scouters award Boy Scouts Am., 1955, Stillman prize and professorship named in his honor U. New Orleans, 6 Gold and a Silver medal Louisiana State Sr. Olympics, 2002, Outstanding Tchr. award U. New Orleans, 2000, Gen. Patton award Gen. Patton Meml. Mus., 2001, honoree 60th Anniversary La. Maneuvers, 2001; jogging track named in his honor U. New Orleans, 2002. Mem. Army Navy C.C., Plimsoll Club of World Trade Ctr. Avocations: swimming, jogging, public speaking.

STILLMAN, ROBERT DONALD, government official; b. Chgo., Sept. 27, 1929; s. Arthur Joseph and Grace Ellen (McLean) S.; m. Joan Ellen Caspersen, 1963 (dec. May 1993); children: Nancy, Barbara, John. BE in Chem. Engring., Yale U., 1950; MBA, Harvard U., 1952. With orgn. planning dept. FMC Corp., San Jose, Calif., 1954-57; assoc. Payson & Trask, N.Y.C., 1957-62, gen. ptnr., 1962-72; exec. v.p., treas., dir. AEA Investors Inc., N.Y.C., 1972-92; assoc. adminstr. for investment U.S. SBA, Washington, 1994-95; v.p. investment funds Overseas Pvt. Investment Corp., Washington, 1995—. Lt. USAF, 1952-54. Mem. Univ. Club (Washington and N.Y.C.), Yale Club (N.Y.C.), Tau Beta Pi, Sigma Xi, Alpha Chi Sigma. Office: Overseas Pvt Investment Corp 1100 New York Ave NW Washington DC 20527-0001

STILLS, STEPHEN, musician, vocalist, composer; b. Dallas, Jan. 3, 1945; Vocalist, guitarist Buffalo Springfield band, 1966-68, Crosby, Stills & Nash, 1968-69, 77, 82, Crosby, Stills, Nash, & Young, 1969-71, solo career, 1971—. Albums include Stephen Stills, 1970, Stephen Stills II, 1971, Stephen Stills, 1975, Illegal Stills, 1976, Thoroughfare Gap, 1978, Right by You, 1984, (with Buffalo Springfield) Buffalo Springfield, 1967, (with Buffalo Springfield) Buffalo Springfield Again, 1967, Last Time Around, 1969, (with Crosby, Stills, Nash, & Young) Deja Vu, 1970, Four Way Street, 1972, (with Crosby, Stills, Nash, Young) So Far, 1974, American Dream, 1989, (with Crosby, Stills, Nash) Crosby, stills and Nash, 1969, Crosby, Stills and Nash, 1977, Daylight Again, Live It Up, Replay (best of), After The Storm, 1994, (with Manassas) Manassasm 1972, Down The Roadm 1973; singles include (solo) Love the One You're With, 1971, Super Session, (with Buffalo Springfield) For What It's Worth, 1967, (with Crosby, Stills, Nash, & Young) Woodstock, Ohio, Teach Your Children, 1970, Stills Alone, 1991. Inducted into Rock and Roll Hall of Fame, 1997. Office: Vision Records 13385 W Dixie Hwy North Miami FL 33161-4134

STILLWAGON, GARY BOULDIN, radiation oncologist; b. Memphis, Dec. 30, 1951; s. Jack Wright and Ida Jean (Bouldin) S.; m. Leta Fern Miller, Jan. 20, 1979. BS in Physics, Ga. Inst. Tech., 1974, MS in Nuclear Engring., 1975, PhD, 1978; MD, U. Tenn., 1983. Diplomate Nat. Bd. Med. Examiners, Am. Bd. Radiology in Radiation Oncology; cert. FLEX, 1983. Med. physicist Meth. Hosp., Memphis, 1974; rsch. asst. Ga. Inst. Tech., Atlanta, 1975-78; radiation safety officer, physicist VA Med. Ctr., Memphis, 1978-80, cons. radiation safety, 1980-83; fellow in radiation oncology Johns Hopkins U. and Hosp., Balt., 1983-87; asst. prof. oncology and radiology Johns Hopkins U. Sch. Medicine, Balt., 1987—. Vis. rschr. radiobiology lab. U. Utah, 1978; com. mem., site visitor, radiation therapy oncology group, coop. group Nat. Cancer Inst., 1989—; cons. in field. Contbr. articles to profl. jours. Active Boy Scouts Am., Bapt. Ch. Sunday Sch. Dept. of Energy fellow, 1976-78, Clin. fellow Am. Cancer Soc., 1986-87. Fellow Am. Coll. Radiology; mem. AAAS, AMA, Health Physics Soc., Am. Assn. Physicists in Medicine, Am. Nuclear Soc., Am. Soc. Therapeutic Radiology and Oncology, Am. Soc. Clin. Oncology, Sigma Xi. Republican. Home: 655 River Chase Rdg NW Atlanta GA 30328-3568 Office: 1000 Johnson Ferry Rd Atlanta GA 30342

STILSON, WALTER LESLIE, radiologist, educator; b. Sioux Falls, S.D., Dec. 13, 1908; s. George Warren and Elizabeth Margaret (Zager) S.; m. Grace Beall Bramble, Aug. 15, 1933 (dec. June 1984); children: Carolyn G. Palmieri, Walter E., Judith A. Stirling; m. Lula Ann Birchell, June 30, 1985. BA, Columbia Union Coll., 1929; MD, Loma Linda U., 1934. Diplomate Am. Bd. Radiology, Nat. Bd. Med. Examiners. Intern White Meml. Hosp., Los Angeles, 1933-34; resident radiology Los Angeles County Gen. Hosp., 1934-36; instr.

radiology Loma Linda (Calif.) U. Sch. Medicine, 1935-41, asst. prof., 1941-49, exec. sec. radiology, 1945-50, assoc. prof., 1949-55, head dept. radiology, 1950-55, prof. radiology, 1955-83, chmn. dept. radiology, 1955-69, emeritus prof., 1983—. Chief radiology service White Meml. Hosp., Los Angeles, 1941-65, Loma Linda U. Med. Ctr., 1966-69; chmn. dept. radiologic tech. Sch. Allied Health Professions, 1966-75, med. dir. dept. radiologic tech., 1975-83. Contbr. articles to health jours. Fellow Am. Coll. Radiology; mem. AAAS, Los Angeles Radiol. Soc. (sec. 1960-61, treas. 1961-62, pres. 1963-64), Radiol. Soc. N.Am., Am. Roentgen Ray Soc., N.Y. Acad. Sci., Inland Radiol. Soc. (pres. 1971), Alpha Omega Alpha. Republican. Adventist. Avocations: photography, classical music, travel. Home: 25045 Crestview Dr Loma Linda CA 92354-3414 Office: Loma Linda Radiol Med Group 11234 Anderson St Loma Linda CA 92354-2804

STILWELL, WILLIAM EARLE, III, psychology educator, retired military officer; b. Cin., Ohio, July 28, 1936; s. William Earle Jr. and Frances (Hunt) S.; m. Doris Ann Nowak; children: Jane Belen Stilwell Angel, William Earle IV. AB, Dartmouth Coll., 1958; MS, San Jose State U., 1966; PhD, Stanford U., 1969. Lic. counseling psychologist, Ky.; cert. profl. qualification in psychology Assn. State of Provincial Psychology Bds. Rsch. assoc. Am. Inst. Rsch., Palo Alto, Calif., 1967-69; prof. psychology U. Ky., Lexington, 1969—. V.p. Ednl. Skills Devel., Lexington, 1969-85. Author: Psychology for Teachers and Students, 1981; mem. editl. bd. Counsel Edn. and Supervision, 1980-87; contbr. numerous (25) articles to profl. jour., chpts. to books. Assigned to patron nine, USNR, 1960-63, active res. in Alameda, Calif., Washington area, 1965-83, exec. officer, 1979-82. Recipient Natl. Def. and Armed Forces Res. with cluster, Tchr. Who Make a Difference Awd., UK Coll. of Edn., 1998, 2002, Svc. award, Coun. Univ. Depts. Clin. Psychology, 1998, Study Web Academic Excellence Awd., 1999, 2000, Web Homework Spot award, 2000. Mem. APA (life), Coun. Counseling Psychology Tng. Programs (Svc. award 2001), Am. Ednl. Rsch. Assn. (v.p. 1980-82), Ky. Psychol. Assn., Ky. Sch. Counseling Assn. (v.p. 1979-80, 81-82), Ohio Soc. of the Colonial Wars, Hon. Order Ky. Cols., Res. Officers Assn. US (life), Stanford Alumni Assn. (life). Avocations: hypertext mark up language, fishing in ontario. Home: 1919 Williamsburg Rd Lexington KY 40504-3013 Office Phone: 859-257-3395. E-mail: westil3@uky.edu.

STIMAC, JOHN ANTHONY, small business owner, poet, cartoonist, inventor; b. Kansas City, Kans., Nov. 12, 1946; s. Max George and Lola Mae Stimac; m. Sherry Lynn Stimac, Apr. 30, 1965; children: Mary Ann, John Anthony, Christopher John. Union painter Local 43, Leavenworth, Kans., 1973—79; owner Heritage Painting Co., Kansas City, Kans., 1979—85, J-Duncan's Painting Co., Kingsville, Mo., 1985—2001, John Stimac Painting Co., Kingsville, 2001—. Cartoons, Highlights for Children, 1983; author: poetry. With U.S. Army, 1963—65. Recipient Editors Choice awards, Internat. Libr. of Poetry, 2001—02. Mem.: Soc. of Poets (Merit award). Achievements include invention of inventive systems minor images. Avocations: guitar, instrumental music. Home and Office: 13 NW 1621 Rd Kingsville MO 64061 Office Phone: 816-682-6757.

STIMMEL, BARRY, cardiologist, internist, educator, university dean; b. Bklyn., Oct. 8, 1939; s. Abraham and Mabel (Bovit) S.; m. Barbara Barovick, June 6, 1970; children: Alexander, Matthew. BS, Bklyn. Coll., 1960; MD, SUNY, Bklyn., 1964. Diplomate: Nat. Bd. Med. Examiners, Am. Bd. Internal Medicine. Resident Mt. Sinai Hosp., N.Y.C., 1964-65, 67-69; asst. dean admissions and student affairs Mt. Sinai Sch. Medicine, CUNY, 1970-71, assoc. dean, 1971-81, asst. prof. medicine, 1972-75, assoc. prof., 1975-83, prof. medicine and med. edn., 1984—, assoc. dean acad. affairs, 1975-81, assoc. attending physician, 1975-83, acting chmn. dept. med. edn., 1979-94, dean admissions, acad. affairs and student affairs, 1981-94, dean grad. med. edn., 1994—, attending physician, 1984—, Katherine and Clifford Goldsmith prof. medicine (cardiology), 1998—. Mem. com. planning, priorities and evaluation N.Y. Met. Regional Med. Program, 1971-73; adv. com. Nat. Ctr. Urban Problems CUNY, 1970-71; adv. com. methadone maintenance Office of Drug Abuse Svcs. State N.Y., 1976-79; sci. adv. bd. Nat. Coun. Drug Abuse, 1978-84, N.Y. State Bd. Profl. Med. Conduct, 1983-97; bd. dirs. Am. Soc. Addiction Medicine, N.Y. State Coun. on Grad. Med. Edn., Greater N.Y. Hosp. Assn. Task Force on Health Manpower. Author: Heroin Dependency: Medical Social and Economic Aspects, 1975, Cardiovascular Effects Mood Altering Drugs, 1979, Pain, Analgesia, Addiction, 1984, Ambulatory Care, 1983, The Facts about Drug Use, 1993, Drugs Abuse and Social Policy in America: The War That Must Be Won, 1996, Pain and Its Relief Without Addiction, 1997, Alcoholism, Drug Addiction and the Road to Recovery: Life on the Edge, 2002; editor Advances in Alcohol and Substance Abuse, 1980-91, Jour. Addictive Diseases, 1991—; assoc. editor Am. Jour. Drug and Alcohol Abuse, 1979-85; contbr. chpts. to books, articles to profl. jours. Served with M.C. USNR, 1965—67. Mem. AAUP, Am. Assn. Physicians Assts. (adv. bd. 1972-73), Am. Assn. Higher Edn., Soc. Study of Addiction to Alcohol and Other Drugs, Assn. Med. Edn. and Rsch. Substance Abuse, Inst. Study of Drug Addiction, Am., N.Y. heart assns., Am., N.Y. State socs. internal medicine, Soc. Internal Medicine County of N.Y. (dir.), Am. Coll. Cardiology, Greater N.Y. Coalition on Drug Abuse, NYS Coun. on Grad. Medical Edn., N.Y. Acad. Medicine, Nat. Coun. Alcoholism, Rsch. Soc. on Alcoholism, Am. Ednl. Research Assn., Am. Fedn. Clin. Rsch., Am. Soc. Addiction Medicine. Office: Mt Sinai Sch Med 5 E 98th St Fl 3 New York NY 10029-6501 Office Phone: 212-241-6694. E-mail: barry.stimmel@mssm.edu.

STIMPERT, MICHAEL ALAN, agricultural products company executive; b. Madisonville, La., Aug. 21, 1944; s. Warren Eugene and Louisa (Beale) S.; m. Kim Kathleen Agee, Apr. 17, 1970 (div. 1985); 1 child, Kelly Kathleen; m. Helen Marie Evans, June 27, 1987; children: Katherine Helen, Michael Adam. Student, Washburn U., 1962-64, U. Copenhagen, 1964; BA, Western Res. U., 1967; MBA, Harvard U., 1974. Asst. to group v.p. Gold Kist Inc., Atlanta, 1974, mgr. internat. div., 1975-80, dir. spl. markets and staff services, 1980-81, group v.p., 1982-86; v.p. ops. and govt. affairs Golden Peanut Co., Atlanta, 1986-89, exec. v.p., 1989-95; sr. v.p. Gold Kist Inc., Atlanta, 1996—. Chmn. bd. dirs. Sunpower, Inc., Athens, Ohio, G.C. Properties, Atlanta, Luker Engring. Inc., Augusta, Ga., GKX Inc., Agana, Guam, Fundatropicos, Turrialba, Costa Rica; immediate past chmn. Global Health Action, Atlanta; chmn. Agra Trade Financing, Inc., Atlanta. Mem. adv. bd. dirs. Internat. Svc. Assn. for Health Devel. Edn. Project, 1982-91; bd. dirs. Global Health Action. Lt. (j.g.) USN, 1967-72, Vietnam. Mem. Assn. for Corp. Growth, Japan-Am. Soc. Ga., Harvard Bus. Sch. Club Atlanta, Cherokee Town and Country Club. Democrat. Roman Catholic. Office: Gold Kist Inc 244 Perimeter Center Pkwy NE Atlanta GA 30346-2397

STIMPSON, CATHARINE ROSALIND, English language educator, writer; b. Bellingham, Wash., June 4, 1936; d. Edward Keown and Catharine (Watts) Stimpson. AB, Bryn Mawr Coll., 1958; BA, MA, Cambridge U., Eng., 1960; PhD, Columbia U., 1967. Mem. faculty Barnard Coll., N.Y.C., 1963—80; prof. English, dean of grad. sch., vice provost grad. edn. Rutgers U., New Brunswick, NJ, 1980—92, univ. prof., 1991—; chmn. bd. scholars Ms. Mag., N.Y.C., 1981—92; dir. fellows program MacArthur Found., 1994—97; univ. prof., dean Grad. Sch. Arts and Sci. NYU, N.Y.C., 1998—. Author: Class Notes, 1979, Where the Meanings Are, 1988; editor: Signs: Jour. Women in Culture and Soc., 1974—81, Women in Culture and Society book series, 1981; contbr. Change Mag., 1992—93. Chmn. N.Y. Coun. Humanites, 1984—87, Nat. Coun. Rsch. on Women, 1984—89; trustee Bates Coll., 1990—; pres. Assn. Grad. Schs., 2000—01; bd. dir. Stephens Coll., Columbia, Mo., 1982—85, Legal Def. and Edn. Fund, 1991—96. Fellow, Woodrow Wilson Found., 1958, Fulbright fellow, 1958—60, Nat. Humanities Inst., 1975—76, Rockefeller Humanities fellow, 1983—84. Mem.: PBS (bd. dirs. 1994—2000), NOW, AAUP, PEN, MLA (exec. coun., chmn. acad. freedom com., 1st v.p., pres. 1990). Democrat. Home: 29 Washington Sq W Apt 15C New York NY 10011-9199 Office: NYU 6 Washington Sq N New York NY 10003-6668 Office Phone: 212-998-8040. Business E-Mail: catharine.stimpson@nyu.edu.

STIMPSON, PATRICIA, software company executive; BA in Math. and Physics cum laude, Wheaton Coll.; MA in Math., U. Mich.; grad. exec. edn. program, Babson Coll. Various mgmt., cons. and engring. positions Camex, Inc., Data Resources, Inc., Nixdorf Computer, Wang Labs, Inc.; sr. devel. positions, dir. Lotus Devel. Corp., until 1995; v.p. R & D, Silknet Software, Inc., Manchester, N.H., 1995—. Office: Silknet Software Inc Gateway Bldg 50 Phillippe Cote St Ste 301 Manchester NH 03101-1186 Fax: 603-625-0428.

STINCHCOMB, ALBERT MONROE, producer, designer/realtor; b. Battle Creek, Mich., Apr. 6, 1944; s. Loid Monroe and Barbara Hough (Parks) S. Student, U. Mich., CUNY. Chmn. Stinchcomb and Monroe, Inc., N.Y.C., N.J., 1979—, Majestic Entertainment, Ltd., Jersey City, 1984—; pres. 275 Corp., Jersey City, N.J., 1983-95, Majestic Devel. Corp., Jersey City, 1989-95; exec. v.p. The Gyncyn Corp., 1994—, CJS Mgmt., 1996—. Owner Majestic Theatre, 1980-95. Appeared in numerous prodns. including Life With Father, 1954, Wizard of Oz, 1955, She Stoops to Conquer, 1985; produced numerous prodns. including Macbeth, 1986, Royal Shakespear Co., 1987, The Golden Handshake, 1987, Why Father Won't Come Home, 1987, Scarpa the Magician, Liberty, The Ballet, 1988, The Adams Letters, 1988. Pres. Liberty Ctr. for Performing Arts, Jersey City, 1984-94; bd. dirs. Fraunces Tavern Mus., 1977-94, Acad. of Art, 1987—, Ednl. Art Team, 1988-95; active Preservation N.J. Mem. Nat. Film Inst., Am. Soc. Interior Designers, Sons of Revolution, Soc. Colonial Wars, Saint Nicholas Soc., N.J. Assn. Realtors (Burgdorff Realtors Million Dollar Club). Home: Grove Cottage PO Box 487 Jersey City NJ 07303 E-mail: amsa@dellnet.com.

STINCHCOMBE, MAXWELL B. economist, educator; BA, U. Calif., Berkeley, 1978, MA, 1984, PhD, 1986. Asst. prof. dept. econs. U. Calif., San Diego, 1986—92, assoc. prof. dept. econs., 1992—93, U. Tex., Austin, 1994—98, prof. dept. econs., 1998—. Mem. editl. bd.: Jour. Math. Econs., 1995—97, referee: Econometrica, Jour. Econ. Theory; referee: Games and Econ. Behavior; referee: Jour. Nonlinear Sci., others. Named McCarty Centennial prof. Achievements include research in game theory; econometrics; examination of different senses in which stochastic processes that satisfy central limit theorems are dense in the set of all stochastic processes; investigation of statistical problem of sequentially monitoring data for changes in the dynamics. Office: U Tex-Austin Dept Econs BRB 2 118 Austin TX 78712-1173

STINCHFIELD, JOHN EDWARD, lawyer; b. Alameda, Calif., July 31, 1947; s. John Eastwood and Pauline Finch (Acker) S.; m. Niall O'Melia, May 15, 1976; children: John Ryan, Noel O'Neil. BA, Wesleyan U., Middletown, Conn., 1969; JD, U. Calif., 1973. Bar: Calif. 1974, D.C. 1980. Atty. advisor Divsn. Corp. Fin. U.S. SEC, 1974-76, Divsn. Investment Mgmt. SEC, 1976-77; atty., advisor Bur. of Competition U.S. FTC, 1977-79; corp. counsel, sec. The Donohoe Cos., Inc., Washington, 1979—, also bd. dirs. Mem. ABA, D.C. Bar Assn., State Bar Calif., Columbia Country Club (Chevy Chase, Md.), Tenley Sport and Health Club. E-mail: johns@donohoe.com.

STINE, EARLE JOHN, JR., radiologist; b. Feb. 21, 1932; s. Earle John and Ione Genevieve (Best) Stine; m. Bernita Evelyn Emerson, Aug. 27, 1954; children: Renee Evelyn, Mark Earle, John Emerson. AB, Albion Coll., 1954; MD, Wayne State U., 1958. Diplomate Am. Bd. Radiology, Am. Bd. Nuc. Radiology. Intern Bon Secours Hosp., Grosse Pointe, Mich., 1958-59, gen. surgery resident, 1959-61; pvt. practice Pigeon, Mich., 1961-62, Marcus, Iowa, 1962-65, Ida Grove, Iowa, 1965-75; resident radiology U. Iowa, Iowa City, 1975-78; staff radiologist St. Joseph Med. Ctr., Ponca City, Okla., 1978-80; med. dir. radiology Jackson County Meml. Hosp., Altus, Okla., 1980-95; med. missions Karaganda, Kazakhstan, 1995-98; locum tenens radiology, 1998—. Mem.: AMA. Republican. Methodist. Avocations: loom-weaving, painting. Office: Diagnostic Imaging Cons 1203 Canterbury Blvd PO Box 679 Altus OK 73522-0679 Office Phone: 580-482-6570. Business E-Mail: earle@stinesystems.com.

STINE, GORDAN BERNARD, dentist, educator; b. Charleston, SC, Feb. 10, 1924; s. Abe Jack and Helen (Pinosky) S.; m. Barbara Berlinsky, Jan. 20, 1951; children: Steven Mark, Robert Jay. BS in Chemistry, Coll. of Charleston, 1944; DDS, Emory U., 1950; DHL (hon.), Coll. of Charleston, 1999. Lic. dentist, Ga., S.C. Pvt. practice gen. dentistry, Charleston, 1953-87; spl. asst. to pres. Med. U. S.C., Charleston, 1983-97, clin. assoc. prof. cmty. dentistry, 1983-97, dir. Dental Continuing Edn., 1984-97, dental cons., 1997—, bd. visitors, 1982, 83, chmn., 1982, chmn. Cultural Projects Coun., 1984-97, mem. continuing edn. adv. com., 1986-89; dental coord. Area Health Edn. Ctrs., 1987-97. Dental cons., 1997—. Trustee Coll. Charleston, 1988—, vice-chmn., 1992-98, emeritus trustee, 1999—; instr. Trident Tech. Coll., 1981; trustee State Coll., 1987-88; dental adv. com. Divsn. Dental Health SC State Bd. Health, 1967-68; regional adv. group S.C. Regional Med. Program, 1974-75; chmn. S.C. Dental Polit. Action Com., 1973-74, 76-84, bd. dirs., 1973-85, chmn., 1973-83; bd. dirs. Coastal Carolina Fair Assn., 1957-61, 63-65, pres., 1965-66; bd. dirs. Charleston Symphony Assn., 1963-68, pres., 1965, pres.'s coun., 1983-84; bd. dirs. Charleston Civic Ballet, 1968, S.C. Art Alliance, 1973-74, Charleston Concert Assn., 1967-73, Charleston R.R. Hist. Soc., 1967-68; bd. dirs. Coastal Carolina coun. Boy Scouts Am., 1972, 74-75, 82-84, v.p. for So. Regional Coun. Exec. Com. Programs, 1985-86, pres., 1990-91, adv. com., 1972, 74-75, 82-85, chmn. Kiawah Dist., 1982, Gordan B. Stine Health Ctr., 1995, Boys Coun., 2001-2003; chmn. Coll. Prep. Sch., 1963-67, vice chmn., 1964-66, regional bd., 1992—; mem. Task Force for Martin Luther King Jr. Legal Holiday, YMCA of Greater Charleston, 1974-75; founder Charleston Mini Parks, 1969, bd. dirs., 1969-71, chmn., 1969, 71; bd. dirs. Charleston Pride, 1986-2003, chmn., 1973-75, 83-85; chmn. dental divsn. Trident United Way, 1962, 69, bd. dirs., 1970-76, 78—, cmty. welfare planning coun., 1967-68, chmn. pub. svc. sect., 1993, pres., 1982, chmn. fund drive, 1977, exec. com., 1977-79, 81-84; chmn. fundraising dental divsn. Cancer Soc., 1956, 61, 66, 70-71; chmn. Charleston County Dems., 1968-72; Charleston County councilman, 1975-84, chmn., 1979-80; alderman Ward 13 City of Charleston, 1971-75; active pub. svc. coms. including S.C. Assembly on Growth, 1981, Trident Devel. Coun., 1972; legis. com. S.C. Assn. Counties, 1979, 81-82, Charleston Waterfront Park Adv. Com., 1982-83, Charleston Neighborhood Housing Svcs. Bd., 1984; state senatorial candidate, 1975; vice chmn. Berkeley-Charleston-Dorchester Coun. of Govts., 1983—, sec., 1985-90, chmn., 1991-95, chmn. exec. bd. dirs., 1995—, mem. & chmn. various coms.; exec. com. Charleston Mus., 1980, bd. dirs., 1977-78, steering com., 1978-80; chmn. Charleston Bicentennial Com., 1972-75; bd. dirs. Carolina Art Assn., 1978; fund drive chmn. Roper Hosp., 1973; bd. dirs. Coastal Fed. Credit Union, 1979-80, pres., 1979; exec. com. Greater Charleston Safety Coun., 1976-85, v.p., 1986-88, pres., 1989; bd. dirs. Trident Area Found., 1977-80, adv. bd., 1981-82, life mem. bd. dirs., 1995; steering com. Charleston campaign United Negro Coll. Fund, 1972-73; bd. dirs. Robert Shaw Boys Ctr., 1975-77, Mil. Svcs. Ctr., 1979-82, Trident 100, 1980-81; chmn. State Health Fair Adv. Bd. for Nat. Health Screening Coun., 1984-85; pres. adv. coun. Winthrop Coll., 1984-85; extension adv. bd. Clemson U., 1985-86, chmn., 1987-89, statewide cmty. devel. adv. com., 1985; bd. mem. Hebrew Benevolent Soc., 1968—, pres., 1970, 71; mem. Hebrew Orphan Soc., 1972—, v.p., 1988-89, pres., 1990-92; trustee Congregation Beth Elohim, 1959-64, pres., 1967-68, Brotherhood pres., 1960, chmn. 250th ann. yr. 2001; pres. Jewish Welfare Bd., 1970-71, com. mem. With USMC, 1942, with USN, 1945-46, 51-53, res., 1953-72, res. ret., 1971-84. Named Coll. of Charleston Alumnus of Yr., 1966, Cmty. Leader Am., 1968-71; recipient Hettie Rickett Cmty. Devel. award, 1979, award adv. dental bd. Carolina Continental Ins. Co., 1983-84, Gov.'s Order of Palmetto award, 1985, 94, 96, Joseph P. Riley Leadership award, 2002. Fellow ACD, Royal Soc. Health; mem. ADA, APHA, Coastal Dist. Dental Soc. (pres. 1954), Charleston Dental Soc. (pres. 1957-58, Dentist of Yr. 1992), S.C. Acad. General Dentistry (Dentist of Yr. 1998, newsletter editor 1995—), Nat. Assn. Regional Couns. (bd. dirs. 1991-95), Israel Dental Assn., Hebrew Orphan Soc. (pres. 1991, 92, 93), Pierre Fauchard Acad. (state chmn. 1991, 93, State Dentist of Yr. 1994, trustee S.E. region U.S. 1997—), S.C. Dental Assn. (pres. 1974-75, edn. com. 1985-90, Cmty. Svc. award 1995), S.C. Downtown Devel. Assn. (bd. dirs. 1983—, pres. 1992-93), Charleston Trident C. of C. (pres. 1972, bd. dirs. 1968-74, 80), S.C. Assn. Regional Couns. (pres. 1986-87), Exch. Club Charleston (pres. 1962), S.C. State Exch. Club (bd. dirs. 1965-68), Alpha Omega (pres. 1949-50, Disting. Svc. award 1976-77, pres. Southeastern group 1960-78, charter mem., emeritus mem. 1993), Tau Epsilon Phi (chpt. pres. 1943). Avocations: gardening, community service. Home: 27 Wraggborough Ln Charleston SC 29403-6362 Office: 171 Ashley Ave Charleston SC 29425-0001

STINE, KATIE KRATZ, state legislator; b. Dec. 6, 1956; BS, U. Cin.; JD, No. Ky. U. Atty.; mem. Ky. Ho. of Reps., Frankfort, 1995-98, Ky. Senate, Frankfort, 1999—, mem. econ. devel. & tourism, health & welfare, judiciary com. Active Jr. League Cin., Episcopal Ch. Women, No. Ky. Right to Life, Johnson Elem. Sch. PTA; former vice chair Ft. Thomas Bd. Adjustments. Mem. DAR, Ky. Bar Assn., Ft. Thomas Garden Club. Republican. Office: Ky Senate 24th Dist 702 Capitol Ave Rm 225 Frankfort KY 40601-3448 Home: 15 Cliffview Ave Fort Thomas KY 41075-1102

STINE, RICK D. editor; Mng. editor Dow Jones News Svc., Jersey City, 1999—. Office: Dow Jones News Svc Harborside Fin Ctr 800 Plaza Two Jersey City NJ 07311-1199

STINE, ROBERT HOWARD, retired pediatrician, allergist; b. Nov. 1, 1929; s. Harry Raymond and Mabel Eva (Newhard) S.; m. Lois Elaine Kihlgren, Oct. 22, 1960; children: Robert E., Karen E., Jonathan N. BS in Biology, Moravian Coll., 1952. Diplomate Am. Bd. Pediatrics, Am. Subbd. Pediatric Allergy, Cojoint Bd. Allergy and Immunology. Intern St. Luke's Hosp., Bethlehem, Pa., 1960-61, resident in surgery, 1961-62; physician Jefferson Med. Coll., Phila., 1956-60; resident in pediatrics U. N.Y., Syracuse, 1962-64; resident in allergy Robert A. Cooke Inst. Allergy Roosevelt Hosp., N.Y.C., 1964-65; clin. instr. pediatrics U. Ill., Chgo., 1965-71; mem. courtesy staff Proctor Community Hosp., Peoria, Ill., 1966-77, mem. active staff, 1977—, chmn. dept. medicine, 1988—89; pres. elect. med. staff, 1990-91; pres. med. staff, 1991-92; mem. teaching staff St. Francis Hosp., Peoria, 1969—2002; clin. instr. pediatrics Rush-Presbyn. St. Luke's Hosp., Chgo., 1971—2002; ret. Vol. Heartland Cmty. Health Clinic, Peoria, Ill., 2002—. Lt. (j.g.) USN, 1953—56. Fellow Am. Acad. Pediatrics, Am. Acad. Allergy Asthma and Immunology, Am. Coll. Allergy and Asthma, Am. Assn. Cert. Allergists; mem. Ill. Soc. Allergy and Clin. Immunology, Peoria Med. Soc. (pres.-elect 1993, pres. 1994), Christian Med. and Dental Soc. Home: 105 Hollands Grove Ln Washington IL 61571-9623

STINE, R(OBERT) L(AWRENCE), children's book author; b. Columbus, Ohio, Oct. 8, 1943; s. Lewis and Anne (Feinstein) S.; m. Jane Waldhorn, June 22, 1969. BA, Ohio State U., 1965. Assoc. editor Jr. Scholastic, N.Y.C., 1969-71; editor Search, N.Y.C., 1972-75, Barnas, N.Y.C., 1972-83, Maniac, N.Y.C., 1984-85. Author: The Time Raider, 1982, The Golden Sword of Dragonwalk, 1983, Horrors of the Haunted Musuem, 1984, Instant Millionaire, 1984, Through the Forest of Twisted Dreams, 1984, Indiana Jones and the Curse of Horror Island, 1984, Indiana Jones and the Giants of the Silver Tower, 1984, Indiana Jones and the Cult of the Mummy's Crypt, 1985, The Badlands of Hark, 1985, The Invaders of Hark, 1985, Demons of the Deep, 1985, Challenge of the Wolf Knight, 1985, Conquest of the Time Master, 1985, Cavern of the Phantoms, 1986, Operation: Deadly Decoy, 1986, Mystery of the Imposter, 1986, Blind Date, 1986, Twisted, 1986, The Baby-Sitter, 1989, Phone Calls, 1990, Curtains, 1991, Broken Date, 1991, Baby-Sitter II, 1991, Beach House, 1992, Dead Girlfriend, 1993, Halloween Night, 1993, Hitchhiker, 1993, Be Careful What You Wish For, 1993, Baby-Sitter III, 1993, Call Waiting, 1994, The Beast, 1994; (series) Fear Street, Fear Street Super Chiller, Fear Street Saga, Fear Street Cheerleaders, Ninety-Nine Fear Street: The House of Evil, Thrillers, Space Cadets, Goose Bumps; (as Jovial Bob Stine) The Absurdly Silly Encyclopaedia and Flyswatter, 1978, How to Be Funny: An Extremely Silly Guidebook, 1978, The Complete Book of Nerds, 1979, The Dynamite Do-It-Yourself Pen Pal Kit, 1980, Dynamite's Funny Book of the Sad Facts of Life, 1980, Going out! Going Steady! Going Bananas!, 1980, The Pigs' Book of World Records, 1980, The Sick of Being Sick Book, 1980, Bananas Look at TV, 1981, The Beast Handbook, 1981, The Cool Kids' Guide to Summer Camp, 1981, Ghastly Gnomes, 1981, Don't Stand in the Soup, 1982, Bored with Being Bored!: How to Beat the Boredom Blahs, 1982, Blips! The First Book of Video Game Funnies, 1983, Everything You Need to Survive: Brothers and Sisters, 1983, Everything You Need to Survive: First Dates, 1983, Everything You Need to Survive: Homework, 1983, Everything You Need to Survive: Money Problems, 1983, Jovial Bob's Computer Joke Book, 1985, Miami Mice, 1986, One Hundred and One Silly Monster Jokes, 1986, The Doggons Dog Joke Book, 1986; (as Eric Affabee) G.I. Joe and the Everglades Swamp Terror, 1986, Attack of the King, 1986; (as Zachary Blue) The Petrova Twist, 1987, The Jet Fighter Trap, 1987.

STINEHART, ROGER RAY, lawyer; b. Toledo, Jan. 27, 1945; s. Forrest William and Nettie May (Twyman) S.; m. Martha Jean Goodnight, Sept. 19, 1970; children: Amanda Jean, Brian Scott. BS, Bowling Green (Ohio) State U., 1968; JD, Ohio State U., 1972. Bar: Ohio 1972. Fin. analyst Gen. Electric, Detroit, 1968-69; assoc. Gingher & Christensen, Columbus, Ohio, 1972-76, ptnr., 1976-80; sr. v.p., gen. counsel, sec. G.D. Ritzy's, Inc., Columbus, 1983-85; ptnr. Jones, Day, Reavis & Pogue, Columbus, 1980-83, 85—. Adj. prof. law Capital U., Columbus, 1976-79; mem. adv. com. Ohio securities divsn. Dept. Commerce, Columbus, 1979—; fellow Columbus Bar Found., 1992—; adv. bd. The Entrepreneurship Inst., 1992-95. Contbr. Ohio State U. Coll. Law Jour., 1970-72. Gen. counsel, trustee Internat. Assn. Rsch. on Leukemia and Related Diseases, 1975—; v.p., trustee Hospice of Columbus, 1978-80; trustee Cen. Ohio chpt. Leukemia Soc. of Am., Columbus, 1983-93, v.p., 1985-87; trustee Ohio Cancer Rsch. Assocs., Columbus, 1983—, v.p., 1990—. With USMCR, 1963-68. Mem. ABA (bus. law com., franchise law com.), Ohio State Bar Assn. (corp. law com., franchise law com.), Columbus Bar Assn. (securities law com., chmn. 1981-83, bus. law com., franchise law com.), Rotary Club (Columbus), Sigma Tau Delta, Beta Gamma Sigma. Home: 2155 Waltham Rd Columbus OH 43221-4149 Office: Jones Day Reavis & Pogue 1900 Huntington Ctr Columbus OH 43215-6103

STINES, BETTY IRENE, artist; b. Stinesville, Ind., May 3, 1918; d. Claude Everett Parham and Helen Bryan Acuff Parham; m. Willard Russell Elliott, Oct. 11, 1936 (dec. Aug. 1969); children: Jerry Lee Elliott, Gillespie-Kathy Lyn Elliott Holtsclaw, Willard Keith Elliott; m. Edmond Glen Stines, Feb. 19, 1972. Grad. high sch., Bloomington, Ind. Organizer, mem. Hoosier Hills Art Guild, Bloomington, Ind., 1963—80; organizer Hoosier Hills Art Guild Ann. Student Art Exhibit, 1963—73; floral designer Unique Florist Shoppe, Ellettsville, Ind., 1963—69. Oil and water color paintings, 1950—2001, exhibited in group shows at Ind. U., Manchester Coll., Swope Art Gallery, Terre Haute, Ind., Hoosier Hills Art Gallery, Bloomington, Ind., Owen County Art Gallery, Spencer, Ind., Represented in permanent collections, exhibited in group shows at Ind. State House Art Salon. Chmn., co-chair art exhibits Monroe County Festival, Ellettsville, Ind., 1950—60; Sunday sch. tchr. Gave Chalk Talks Bapt. Ch., 1950; leader Brownie Scouts, 1943—47. Recipient numerous First, Best in Show and Champion Exhibitor awards. Mem.: Ind. Women in Arts, Nat. Mus. Women in Arts. Baptist. Avocations: genealogy, antiques. Home: 7935 W Ratliff Rd Bloomington IN 47404-9685

STINES, FRED, JR., publisher; b. Newton, Iowa, Mar. 16, 1925; s. Fred and Nella (Haun) S.; m. Dorothy G. McClanahan, Sept. 5, 1953 (dec.); children: Steven, Scott, Ann; m. Mary K. Devin, Sept. 12, 1989. B.C.S., U. Iowa, 1949. With Meredith Corp., Des Moines, 1949-90, sales promotion and mdse. mgr., 1955-63, advt. dir., 1963-66, pub., 1966-73, pub. dir. mag. div., 1973-76, v.p., gen. mgr. books and newspapers, 1976-83, sr. v.p., 1983-87, pres. book pub., 1986-90, corp. v.p. spl. projects, 1988-90; pres., prin. Concepts in Mktg., 1990—. Cert. instr. Dale Carnegie courses, 1958-63. Bd. dirs. Des Moines Ballet Assn., North Am. Outdoor Group, Mpls., 1992-95; bd. dirs., v.p. Jr. Achievement of Ctrl. Iowa. Served with AUS, 1946-49. Named Farm Marketing Man of Year, 1972 Mem. Future Farmers Am. Found. (nat. chmn. 1971), Rotary Internat., Des Moines Golf and Country Club, Phi Gamma Delta (sect. chief 1983, nat. bd. dirs. 1985-89), Alpha Kappa Psi, Alpha Delta Sigma. Clubs: Des Moines Golf and Country (dir., pres. 1981, pres. Ednl. Found.). Home and Office: 8401 E Del Camino Dr Scottsdale AZ 85258-2438

STING, (GORDON MATTHEW SUMNER), musician, songwriter, actor; b. Newcastle Upon Tyne, Eng., Oct. 2, 1951; s. Ernest Matthew and Audrey (Cowell) Sumner; m. Frances Eleanor Tomelty, May 1, 1976 (div. Mar. 1984); children: Joseph, Fuschia Katherine; m. Trudie Styler, Aug. 22, 1992, children: Brigette, Michael, Jake, Eliot, Paulina, Giacomo Luke. Grad., Warwick U., Coventry, Eng.; hon. doctorate, Northumbria U., 1992; hon. degree, Berklee Coll. Music, Boston, 1994. Schoolmaster, Newcastle Upon Tyne, Eng., 1975-77; songwriter, singer, bass player with rock group The Police, 1977-86; mng. dir. Kaliedescope Cameras, London, from 1982; singer, songwriter, 1986—. Albums (with The Police) Outlandos D'Amour, 1978, Reggatta De Blanc, 1979, Zenyatta Mondatta, 1980, Ghost in the Machine, 1981, Synchronicity, 1983, singles Every Breath You Take, 1986; appearance: (Broadway plays) Three Penny Opera, 1989; solo (albums) The Dream of the Blue Turtles, 1985, Bring On The Night, 1986, Nothing Like the Sun, 1987, The Soul Cages, 1991, Ten Summoner's Tales, 1993 (Grammy award, Best Long Form Music Video, 1994), Demolition Man, soundtrack, 1993, Brand New Day, 1999, Sacred Love, 2003 (Grammy award, Best Pop Collaboration With Vocals for song "Whenever I Say Your Name" with Mary J. Blige, 2003), appeared (films) Quadrophenia, 1979, The Secret Policeman's Other Ball, 1981, Brimstone and Treacle, 1982, Dune, The Bride, Plenty, 1985, Julia and Julia, 1987, Stormy Monday, 1988, Resident Alien, 1990, The Grotesque, 1995, Lock, Stock and Two Smoking Barrels, 1998, voice artist (TV series) Captain Planet and the Planeteers, 1990—92, rec. soundtracks (films) Brimstone and Treacle, Party, Party, The Secret Policeman's Other Ball, 1982, The Emperor's New Groove, 2000. Recipient 15 Grammy awards with The Police and as solo artist, 13 BMI awards, 4 Brit awards, Downbeat mag. Readers' Poll Pop/Rock Musician of Yr. award, 1989, Downbeat mag. Readers' Poll Pop/Rock group award, 1989, Internat. Rock award for Video Legend, 1991, Star on the Hollywood Walk of Fame, 2000, Golden Globe award Kate and Leopold, 2001. Mem.: Rainforest Found. (co-founder), Amnesty Internat., Performing Rights Soc. also: Firstars 3520 Hayden Ave Culver City CA 90232-2413 also: A & M Records Inc 70 Universal City Plz Universal City CA 91608-1011 Office: KSM 826 Broadway Fl 4 New York NY 10003-4826

STINGER, FANCHON, newscaster; d. Edward and Zelma Stinger; m. Tony Camilleri. BA in English and Comm., U. Mich., 1993. Reporter WJBK-TV, Detroit, 1997—, editor and co-anchor 5:30pm news, 2000—. Recipient 5 Emmy awards, NATAS, 1998—, Best Reporter award, AP-Mich., 2000, Insp. Gen.'s Integrity award, U.S. Dept. HHS, 2002. Office: WJBK-TV Fox 2 PO Box 2000 Southfield MI 48037-2000

STINGLEY, KRISTI JO, writer; b. Ogallala, Nebr., Apr. 12, 1960; d. Carlin R. and Ruth E. (Rohlfing) Frerichs; m. Todd G. Stingley, June 9, 1985 (div. June 1996). BS in Engring., N.Mex. Inst. Mining & Tech., 1982; JD, Southwestern U., 1998. Bar: Calif. Spl. projects engr. Arco Oil and Gas Co., Denver, 1982—86; sr. engr. Arco Internat. Co., L.A., 1986—91, 1986—91, 1986—91; assessment mgr. Arco Environ., L.A., 1991—93; mgr. environ. & regulatory affairs Arco Pipeline Co., Long Beach, 1993—95; mgr. contracting & purchasing Arco Marine, Inc., 1995—97; mgr. OSP Arco Products Co., L.A., 1997—2000; atty. pvt. practice, Ft. Collins, Colo., 2001—03. Author: Chaos Rules? Finding Meaning in Chaos, 2004. Mem.: ABA, Soc. Petroleum Engrs. Republican. Lutheran. Avocations: reading, hiking, cards, backgammon. E-mail: kjstingley@aol.com.

STINI, WILLIAM ARTHUR, anthropologist, educator; b. Oshkosh, Wis., Oct. 9, 1930; s. Louis Alois and Clara (Larsen) S.; m. Mary Ruth Kalous, Feb. 11, 1950; children: Patricia Laraine, Paulette Ann, Suzanne Kay. BBA, U. Wis., 1960, MS, 1967, PhD, 1969. Planner cost acct. Kimberly-Clark Corp., Niagara Falls, NY, 1960-62; from asst. prof. to assoc. prof. Cornell U., Ithaca, NY, 1968-73; assoc. prof. U. Kans., Lawrence, 1973-76; prof. anthropology U. Ariz., Tucson, 1976—, prof. family and cmty. medicine, 1978—; panelist anthropology program NSF, 1976-78; cons. NIH, 1974—. Mem. Ariz. Cancer Ctr., 1995—; adj. prof. Nutritional Scis., 1997—; head dept. anthropology U. Ariz., 1980-89, prof. pub. health, 1998—; panelist NRC/NSF Grad. Fellowship Program, 1991-95. Author: Ecology and Human Adaptation, 1975, Nature, Culture and Human History - A Biocultural Introduction to Anthropology (with Davydd J. Greenwood), 1977, Physiological and Morphological Adaptation and Evolution, 1979 (with Frank E. Poirier and Kathy B. Wreden) In Search of Ourselves: An Introduction to Physical Anthropology, 1990, 5th edit., 1994; field editor phys. anthropology The Am. Anthropologist, 1980-83; editor-in-chief Am. Jour. Phys. Anthropology, 1983-89; assoc. editor Nutrition and Cancer, 1981-95; cons. editor Collegium Antropologicum, 1985—. Mem. Gov.'s Adv. Coun. on Aging, State of Ariz., 1980-83. Nat. Inst. Dental Rsch. tng. grantee, 1964-68; Clark Found. grantee Cornell U., 1973; Nat. Dairy Coun. grantee, 1985-88; Wenner-Gren Found. grantee, 1991—; fellow Linacre Coll., Oxford, 1985; vis. fellow U. London, 1991. Fellow AAAS (steering group sect. H 1987-91), Am. Anthrop. Assn., N.Y. Acad. Scis.; mem. Am. Assn. Phys. Anthropologists (exec. com. 1978-81, pres. 1989-91), Human Biology Assn. (exec. com. 1978-81), Soc. for Study Social Biology, Am. Soc. Nutritional Scis., Am. Soc. on Aging, Sigma Xi. Home: 6240 N Camino Miraval Tucson AZ 85718-3025 Office: U Ariz Dept Anthropology Tucson AZ 85721-0001 Office Phone: 520-621-8206. Business E-Mail: stini@u.arizona.edu.

STINN, BRADLEY J. jewelry retailer; CEO Friedman's Inc., 1992-97, pres., CEO, 1999—; CEO Crescent Jewelers, Inc., 1999. Chmn. exec. com. Friedman's Inc. Office: Friedman's Inc 4 W State St Savannah GA 31401-3696

STINNETT, TERRANCE LLOYD, lawyer; b. Oakland, Calif., July 22, 1940; s. Lloyd Monroe and Gertrude (Hyman) S. BS, Stanford U., 1962; JD magna cum laude, U. Santa Clara, 1969. Bar: Calif. 1970, U.S. Dist. Ct. (no. dist.) Calif. 1970, U.S. Dist. Ct. (ea. ctrl. and so. dists) Calif. 1975, U.S. Ct. Appeals (9th cir.) 1970, U.S. Supreme Ct. 1975. Law clk. to judge Calif. Ct. Appeals, San Francisco, 1969-70; assoc. Hyman, Rhodes & Aylward, Fremont, Calif., 1970-71, Glicksberg, Kushner & Goldberg, San Francisco, 1972-77; mem. Goldberg, Stinnett Meyers & Davis, San Francisco, 1977—. Bd. dirs. Fremont Bancorp, Fremont Bank, vice-chmn. bd., 1998-2000. Mem. ABA, Bar Assn. San Francisco (chmn. bench bar liaison com. for U.S. Bankruptcy Ct., No. Dist. of Calif. 1997). Republican. Roman Catholic. Home: 131 Alamo Hills Ct Alamo CA 94507-2243 Office: Goldberg Stinnett Meyers & Davis 44 Montgomery St Ste 2900 San Francisco CA 94104-4803 Office Phone: 415-362-5045. E-mail: tstinnett@gsmdlaw.com.

STINSMUEHLEN-AMEND, SUSAN, artist; b. Balt., Nov. 5, 1948; d. William I. and Geraldine S. (Dodds) Hamilton; m. Richard E. Amend, Nov. 27, 1987; children: Jason Stinsmuehlen, Wyatt Amend. Student, Hood Coll., U. Tex. Designer, owner Renaissance Glass Co., Austin, 1973-87; artist dba. Impresa, Inc., L.A. and Ojai, Calif., 1987—. Mem. Art in Pub. Places Panel, Austin, 1986-87; cons. Nat. Endowment for the Arts, Washington, 1986, 87, Cmty. Redevel. Agy., L.A., 1990-92; artist trustee Am. Craft Coun., 1988-92; lectr., lead artist Hollywood Blvd. Streetscape Team, Hollywood, Calif., 1991-94; mem. Arts Commn., Ojai, Calif., 2000—; mem. Hollywood Art and Design Adv. Panel, 1994-2003; educator in field. One-woman shows include Mattingly Baker Gallery, Dallas, 1984, Kurland Summers Gallery, L.A., 1985, 88, 90, 92, Traver Sutton Gallery, Seattle, 1986, Habatat Galleries, Detroit, 1991, The Nest Gallery, Ojai, Calif., 1997, The Glass Gallery, Bethesda, Md., 2000, Carnegie Mus. Art, Oxnard, Calif., 2004; exhibited in group shows at Whatcom Mus., Bellingham, Wash., 1992-94, Finegood Art Gallery, West Hills, Calif., 1993-94, Miller Gallery, N.Y.C., 1994, The Wignall Mus., Chaffey Coll., Rancho Cucamonga, Calif., 1995, Traver Gallery, Seattle, 1995, Smithsonian Inst. Travelling Exhbn., 1999, Muckenthaler Cultural Arts Ctr., Calif., 1999, Loveland (Colo.) Mus. Gallery, 1998, 99, Fresno Art Mus., 1998, SOFA Chgo., 1998, Santa Cruz Mus. Art and History, 1999, Smithsonian Inst., 1998-2000, L.A. County Mus. Art, 1999, Orange County Mus. Art, 1999, L.A. Mcpl. Art Gallery, 2003, Reynolds Gallery, Richmond, Va., 2003, others; represented in permanent collection Am. Airlines, Dallas, Renwick Gallery Nat. Mus. Art, Washington, The Jewish Mus., N.Y.C., The Corning (N.Y.) Mus. Glass, Detroit Inst. Arts, Leigh Yawkey Woodson Mus., Wausau, Wis., Oakland (Calif.) Mus., Wagga Wagga City Art Gallery, NSW, Australia, Nishida Mus., Toyoma, Japan, Pilchuck Glass Ctr., Stanwood, Wash., Am. Craft Mus., N.Y.C., L.A. (Calif.) County Mus. Art, Radisson Hotel, Austin, AT&T, Dallas, AT&T, N.Y.C., Marshall Fields Corp. Collection, Chgo., City of L.A., Mus. Am. Art/Smithsonian Instn., Carnegie Art Mus., others plus numerous pvt. collections. Nat. Endowment for the Arts grantee, Washington, 1982, 88; Hauberg fellow Pilchuck Glass Sch., 2001. Mem. Glass Art Soc. (hon. life; bd. dirs. 1982-86, pres. 1984-86), Mus. Contemporary Art (L.A.), L.A. County Mus. Avocations: gardening, swimming, walking, hiking, golf. E-mail: impresa@pobox.com.

STINSON, ANDREA MARIA, professional basketball player; b. Mooresville, N.C., Nov. 25, 1967; BA, N.C. State U., 1991. Guard Charlotte Sting, 1997—. Named Kodak All-Am., 1990, 1991, MVP, ACC Tournament, ACC Player of Yr., 1991, lead scorer, Charlotte Sting, 1997—2001; named to All-ACC Tournament Team, Italian League All-Star Team, Ea. Conf. All-Star Team, 2001; recipient Gold medal, 1992 Jones Cup Team, Bronze medal, 1991 Pan Am. Team playing overseas for Thiene in Italy, 1996—97. Office: Charlotte Sting 100 Hive Dr Charlotte NC 28208-7707*

STINSON, DEANE BRIAN, financial executive, consultant; b. Ottawa, Ont., Can., Nov. 12, 1930; s. Earl Minto and Clara Edna (Acres) S.; m. Patricia Ann Paynter, Aug. 25, 1956; children: Steven Wayne, Brian Richard, Andrew Alan. Chartered acct. With Arthur A. Crawley & Co., Ottawa, 1949-58; staff chartered acct. KMPG, Sault Ste. Marie, Ont., 1958-59, audit ptnr., 1960-79, mng. ptnr., 1980-86, sr. exec. ptnr., 1986-88; mem. Ont. Regional Mgmt. Coun.; ptnr. in charge Grant Thornton, Sault Ste. Marie, 1988-93. Pres., CEO Tille Investments Ltd., Tolstar Mgmt. Inc., 985875 Ont. Ltd., dir. No. Breweries Ltd.; Viscount Energy Corp., CGAN. Fellow Inst. Chartered Accts. Ont.; mem. Can. Inst. Chartered Accts. (pres. chpt. 1965), Rotary (pres. 1978). Conservative. Anglican. Home: 15 Atlas Ave Sault Sainte Marie ON Canada P6A 4Z2 also: 34 White Lane Rd Jones Landing ON Canada

STINSON, KENNETH E. construction and mining company executive; b. Chgo, May 24, 1946; BS in Civil Engring., U. Notre Dame; MS in Civil Engring., Stanford U. Pres. Kiewit Constrn. Group Inc., Omaha, 1992-93, chair., pres, 1993-96; chmn., CEO Peter Kiewit Sons' Inc., Omaha, 1996—. Bd. dir. ConAgra Foods, Inc., Omaha, 1996—, Valmont Industries, Inc., Omaha, 1996—. Recipient Outstanding Projects and Leaders awards, ASCE, 2003. Office: Peter Kiewit Sons Inc 1000 Kiewit Plaza Omaha NE 68131 Office Phone: 402-342-2052. Office Fax: 402-271-2939.*

STINSON, MARION DENNIS, lawyer, land use planner, judge; b. Alton, Ill., Aug. 19, 1953; s. George Washington and Clara Alevia (Keene) S.; m. Shirley Joan Cartwright, Feb. 13, 1971; children: Casey René (dec.), Marion David. AA magna cum laude, Rogers State Coll., Claremore, Okla., 1992; BA summa cum laude, Northeastern State U., Tahlequah, Okla., 1997; JD, Oklahoma City U., 2002. Leadman Stresscon Inc., Tulsa, 1971-74; crane operator Gardner-Denver, Pryor, Okla., 1974-79; laborer Lone Star Industries, Pryor, 1979-88; owner, mgr. sml. bus. Pryor, 1988-90; concrete finisher Unifed Bridge Constrn., Joplin, Mo., 1990-91; sec. Grand Gateway Econ. Devel. Assn., Vinita, Okla., 1991-93; coord. cmty. devel. Grand Gateway Econd. Devel. Assn., Vinita, Okla., 1993-94, dir. cmty. devel., 1994-95, dir. cmty./econ. devel. Big Cabin, Okla., 1995—, dep. exec. dir., 1999—2003. Bd. trustees Town of Salina, 1990-91; com. chmn. MESTA, Pryor, 1995-98; citizen's adv. com. chmn. Mayes County Commrs., Pryor, 1997-98; mem. oversight com. Multiple Local Govts., Delaware/Adair County, Okla., 1995-99; mem. Salina (Okla.) Bd. Edn., 1995-98, v.p., 1996-97, pres., 1997-98; precinct chmn. Dem. Party, Salina, 1996; chmn. bd. N.E. Okla. Little League, Salina, 1994-96; bd. dirs. Pryor Sr. Citizens, Inc., 1996, Cmty. Devel. Soc., 1995—; com. mem. Okla. Dept. Commerce, 1994-96, bd. govs., O.D. Mayor Found. Recipient Acad. Achievement award Northeastern State U., 1997, scholarship Okla. Scholar Leadership Enchancement Program, 1996, Cert. of Achievement, Okla. Mcpl. League, 1995, 96, 97, 98. Mem. Okla. Floodplain Mgmt. Assn. (cert. floodplain mgr., sec. com. 1996-98), Am. Planners Assn., Salina Area C. of C. (bd. dirs. 1996), Phi Theta Kappa, Alpha Chi. Democrat. Baptist. Avocations: boating, golf, movies, family time. Office: Stinson Law Firm PO Box 922 Pryor OK 74362 E-mail: stinsonlawfirm@sbcglobal.net.

STINSON, MARY FLORENCE, retired nursing educator; b. Wheeling, W.Va., Feb. 11, 1931; d. Rolland Francis and Mary Angela (Voellinger) Kellogg; m. Charles Walter Stinson, Feb. 12, 1955; children: Kenneth Charles, Karen Marie Wiberg, Kathryn Anne Kartye. BSN, Coll. Mt. St. Joseph, 1953, postgrad., 1983; MEd, Xavier U., Cin., 1967; postgrad., U. Cin., 1981. Staff nurse contagious disease ward Cin. Gen. Hosp., 1953-54, asst. head nurse med. and polio wards, 1955, acting head nurse, clin. instr., 1955-56; instr. St. Francis Hosp. Sch. Practical Nursing, Cin., 1956-57, Good Samaritan Hosp. Sch. Nursing, Cin., 1957—66; instr. refresher courses for nurses Cin. Bd. Edn. and Ohio State Nurses Assn. Dist. 8, 1967-70; coord. sch. health office Coll. Mt. St. Joseph, Ohio, 1969-72, instr. dept. nursing, 1974-79, asst. prof., 1979-89; RN assessor Passport program Coun. on Aging Southwestern Ohio, 1989-90, quality assurance coord. Passport program, 1990-93; quality assurance supr. Passport and Elderly Svcs. Program, 1993-94; quality assurance mgr. Coun. Aging Southwestern Ohio, 1995-2000; ret., 2000. Staff nurse St. Francis/St. George Hosp., Cin., 1988-89. Charter mem. Adoptive Parents Assn. St. Joseph Infant and Maternity Home; women's com. for performing arts series Coll. Mt. St. Joseph; chmn. by-law com. Coll. Mt. St. Joseph Nursing Honor Soc., 1996—98; active St. Antoninus Rosary Altar and Sch. Soc., St. Antoninus Athletic Club, com. chmn., 1969—70; bd. dirs. Coll. Mt. St. Joseph Alumni Assn., 1982—84, sec., 1968—69, v.p., 1969—70, pres., 1970—71, chmn. revision of constn., 1976—77; homecoming chmn. Coll. Mt. St. Joseph, 1970, co-chmn., 1977, co-chair com. to celebrate 75 years of nursing edn., 2001—02; mem. com. to plan 50th ann. of graduation Coll. Mt. St. Joseph Alumni Assn. Democrat. Roman Catholic. Mem. River Squares Club (v.p. 1967), Sigma Theta Tau (charter Omicron Omicron chpt. 1998—). Home: 5549 Cleander Dr Cincinnati OH 45238-4266 Personal E-mail: fiostinson@fuse.net.

STINSON, MELANIE A, freelance/self-employed writer; d. Robert Edwin and Nilda Judith Stinson. BA, Bowling Green State U., Ohio, 1971—78. Lic. massage therapist NY State Licensing Bd., 1993, Reiki 1 Reiki Master Dina Kushnir, NY, 1992, Reiki 1 & 2 Reiki Master Laura Galliger, Ohio, 2002, Reiki Master Reiki Master Steve Murray, Calif., 2003. Dir. NYC Ballet Guild, 1986—87, assoc. dir., 1982—86; freelance writer/ editor/ assoc ed NYC Ballet, 1987—96; adminstrv. assoc. Assn. for the Help of Retarded Children, 1996—99; freelance writer Bowling Green State U. - various magazines. Writing/drawing/nature/relaxation workshops Worlds of Wonder, Bowling Green; adv. bd. mem. Big Bros. Big Sisters of NW Ohio, 1999—2002. Author: (middle grade novel) Nattie in Search of Adventure (Mary Ann Pfenninger Award, 2003); actor(extra): (Columbia Pictures film) Center Stage; author: (magazine fiction) Highlights for Children, Sharanda's Voice (Hon. Mention, Writers Digest Writing Competition, 2001); adaptor (musical) Alley; contbr. independent feature film; author: (dance screenplay) Encore (Top 10% of Nicholl Screenwriting Fellowships, 2003). Mentor, relaxation tchr. - at risk youth WIA, 2003—03. Mem.: SCBWI. Avocations: pottery, design.

STINSON, NANCY, military officer; b. Royal Oak, Mich., Dec. 1, 1957; d. Paul J. Petrits and Shirley J. Burke; m. Thomas J. Stinson, Feb. 10, 1990; 1 child, Katherine Anne. B in Radio/TV Journalism, U. Ariz., 1983; M in Def. Mgmt., Amu U., 1996. Commd. 2d lt. USAF, 1988, advanced through grades to lt. col., 1998. Keader San Antonio Girl Scouts Am., 2000—03. Mem.: Nat. Def. Industry Assn., Logistics Officers Assn. Democrat. Roman Catholic. Home: 3202 Sable Creek San Antonio TX 78259 Office: HQ ATEC 11GMT 555 E St East Randolph A F B TX 78150

STINSON, RICHARD FLOYD, retired horticulturist, educator; b. Cleve., Feb. 4, 1921; s. Floyd Earl and Helen M. (Schiemann) S.; m. Lois D. Stinson; children: Leigh, Laurie, Glenn, Paul, Cathy. BS, Ohio State U., 1943, MS, 1947, PhD, 1952. Instr. floriculture SUNY, Alfred, 1947-48; asst. prof. floriculture U. Conn., Storrs, 1948-55; asst. prof. horticulture Mich. State U., East Lansing, 1955-59, assoc. prof. horticulture, 1959-67; assoc. prof. agrl. edn. and horticulture Pa. State U., University Park, 1967-73, prof., 1973-89, sr. faculty mem., 1979-89, prof. emeritus, 1990—. Cons. in field. Contbr. articles to profl. jours. Lt. (j.g.) USNR, 1943-46. Mem. N.Am. Assn. Colls. and Tchrs. Agr. (E.B. Knight Jour. award 1992), Sigma Xi, Alpha Tau Alpha, Gamma Sigma Delta, Phi Delta Kappa. Office: Pa State U 323 Agrl Adminstrn Bldg University Park PA 16802-2601 E-mail: rfs5@psu.edu.

STIPE, EDWIN, III, mechanical contracting company executive; b. Easton, Pa., Aug. 22, 1931; s. Edwin and Rose Mildred (Blackburn) S.; m. Jean Elizabeth Boyer, Aug. 14, 1954; children: Daniel McMichael, Kelly Jean. AAS, SUNY, Binghamton, 1958. Chief engr. Joseph E. Biro & Assocs., Easton, 1958-61; with ITT Nesbitt, 1961-72, br. mgr., 1965-67, Boston, 1967-70, N.Y.C., 1970-72; v.p. Byko-Stipe Assocs., Morristown, N.J., 1972-77; pres. Edwin Stipe, Inc., Easton, 1973—, Thermogetics, Inc., Morristown, 1977-80. Bd. dirs. Easton Heights Cemetery, 1986—, Valley Health Employee Health Network, Valley Health Svcs. Served with USN, 1951-55. Mem. ASHRAE, Assn. Energy Engrs., Two Rivers Area C. of C. (chmn. small bus. coun. 1989-91, chmn. 1991-93), Pomfret Club, Harker's Hollow Golf Club, Kiwanis. Lutheran. Office: 999 Conroy Pl Easton PA 18040-6646 Home: 33 Pinewild Dr Pinehurst NC 28374-9735

STIPE, MICHAEL, musician; b. Decatur, Ga., Jan. 4, 1960; Student, U. Ga. Singer R.E.M., 1980—; owner C-OO. Albums (with R.E.M.) Chronic Town, 1982, Murmur, 1983 (Gold record, Rolling Stone Critics Poll Best Album of Yr., 1983), Reckoning, 1984 (Gold record, 1984), Fables of the Revolution, 1985 (Gold record, 1985), Life's Rich Pageant, 1986 (Gold record, 1986), Dead Letter Office, 1987 (Gold record, 1987), Document, 1987 (Platinum record, 1987), Eponymous, 1988 (Platinum record, 1988), Green, 1989 (Platinum record, 1989), Out of Time, 1991 (Platinum record, 1991, 7 Grammy nominations, 1992, Best Pop Vocals Grammy award for group, 1992), Automatic for the People, 1992 (Platinum record, 1992, 4 Grammy nominations, 1992), Monster, 1994, Songs That Are Live (4 song CD), 1995, New Adventures in Hi-Fi, 1996, Up, 1998, Reveal, 2001, In Time: The Best of R.E.M., 2003, guest artist for following groups 10,000 Maniacs, 1987, Indigo Girls, 1989, soundtrack Man on the Moon, 1999. Named Rolling Stone Critics Poll Best New Group, 1983, Rolling Stone Group Artist of Yr., 1992, Rolling Stone Male Vocalist of Yr., 1992; recipient MTV Video Music Video of Yr. award, 1992, MTV Best Direction, Best Editing, Best Cinematography, and Breakthrough Video awards for "Everybody Hurts", 1994. Address: REM PO Box 8032 Athens GA 30603-8032

STIPE, ROBERT EDWIN, design educator; b. Easton, Pa., July 18, 1928; s. J. Norwood and Ethel M. Stipe; m. Josephine Davis Weedon, 1952; children: Daniel W. Stipe, Frederick Norwood Stipe. AB in Econ., Duke U., 1950, LLB, 1953; MRP, U. N.C., 1959. Urban planning cons. City and Town Planning Assocs., Chapel Hill, N.C., 1956-57; asst. dir., prof. pub. law and govt. U. N.C. Inst. Govt., Chapel Hill, N.C., 1957-74; sr. Fulbright rsch. fellow London U., 1968-69; dir. Divsn. Archives and History N.C. Dept. Cultural Resources, Raleigh, N.C., 1974-75; vis. prof. U. N.C., Chapel Hill, 1975-77; prof. design N.C. State U., Raleigh, 1976-89, emeritus prof. design, part time prof. design, 1989—2000. Lectr. Inst. Advanced Studies, Bratislava, Slovak Republic, 1992-96; bd. trustees U.S. com. Internat. Coun. on Monuments and Sites, Preservation Action, Nat. Coun. on Preservation Edn., Hist. Preservation Fund N.C., Alliance for Preservation Hist. Landscapes, Old Salem Inc., Stagville Ctr. for Preservation Tech.; emeritus trustee Nat. Trust for Hist. Preservation; mem. bd. adv. Nat. Alliance Preservation Commn. Author, editor more than 100 articles and publs. in fields of historic preservation, landscape conservation, design, urban planning and planning law. Mem. Chapel Hill Design Review Bd.; trustee Chapel Hill Preservation Soc.; founder, trustee Chapel Hill HIstorical Soc. Fellow U.S. Com. Internat. Coun. on Monuments and Sites, 1986; recipient Disting. Svc. award Ruth Coltrane Cannon award, N.C. Soc. for Preservation of Antiquities, 1973, Sec. of Interior's Disting. Conservation Svc. award, 1978, Spl. award outstanding contbns. to landscape architecture Am. Soc. Landscape Archiects, N.C. chpt., 1985, Louise DuPont Crowninshield award for Superlative Lifetime Achievement in Historic Preservation, Nat. Trust for Historic Preservation, 1988, Dist. Svc. and Profl. Leadership award Nat. Coun. for Preservation Edn., 1989, Charles S. Murphy award, Duke U. Law Sch. Alumni Assn., 2003. Mem. Cosmos Club (Washington), Sigma Pi Kappa (First Disting. mem. 1994), Sigma Lambda Alpha (disting. mem. 1996), Phi Delta Phi. Home: 100 Pine Ln Chapel Hill NC 27514-4331

STIPEK, DEBORAH, education educator, dean; BS in Psychology, U. Wash., 1972; PhD in Devel. Psychology, Yale U., 1977. Prof. Grad. Sch. Edn. UCLA, 1977—2000; co-dir. NIMH Tng. Program in Applied Human Devel.; dir. Corinne Seeds U. Elme. Sch., Urban Edn. Studies Ctr.; I. James Quillen dean, prof. edn. Stanford (Calif.) U., 2001—. Mem. bd. on children, youth and families NRC; dir. MacArthur Found. Network on Tchg. and Learning. Author: Motivation to Learn: From Theory to Practice, 2002; author: (with A. Bohart) Constructive and Destructive Behavior: Implications for Family, School, and Society, 2001; author: (with K. Seal) Motivated Minds: Raising Children to Love Learning, 2001. Congl. Sci. fellow, Soc. for Rsch. in Child Devel., Office Senator Bill Bradley, 1983—84. Office: Stanford Univ Sch Edn 485 Lasuen Mall Stanford CA 94305-3096

STIREWALT, JOHN NEWMAN, coal company executive; b. Springfield, Ill., July 14, 1931; s. Newman Claude and Genevieve (Henton) S.; m. Joan Marie McCarthy, Dec. 26, 1957; children: Genevieve, Janice, James, Christopher. AB, U. Miami, 1953; grad. execs. program, Carnegie Mellun U., 1978. Salesman Kaiser Aluminum, Indpls., 1957-63; dist. sales mgr. Consol. Coal, Detroit, 1963-67, Cleve., 1967-73, gen. sales mgr. Detroit, 1973-76, asst. v.p., 1976-79; v.p. mktg. Youghiogheny and Ohio Coal Co., St. Clairsville, 1979-81; v.p. mktg. Crown Coal and Coke Co. Pitts., 1981-85, Arch Mineral, 1985-90; sr. v.p. Crown Coal & Coke Co., 1990—. Exec. reservist U.S. Dept. Interior emergency solid fuels adminstrn., 1971, U.S. Energy Dept., 1991-97. Chmn. coun. Cub Scouts, Highland, Mich., 1976; mem. Mich. Energy Task Force, 1966; pres. bd. trustees Wheeling Country Day Sch., 1980-84; trustee Wheeling Symphony; bd. dirs. Teen Challenge for New Life Inc. Served with U.S. Army, 1954-56. Mem.: Vinyard Christian Fellowship, Symposiarchs, Wheeling Country Club, Sigma Chi. Home: 130 Spring Hill Ln Wheeling WV 26003-7746 Office: Crown Coal and Coke Co Pittsburgh PA 15220 Office Phone: 412-920-1908.

STIRITZ, WILLIAM P. food company executive; b. Jasper, Ark., July 1, 1934; s. Paul and Dorothy (Bradley) Stiritz; m. Susan Ekberg, Dec. 4, 1972; children: Bradley, Charlotte, Rebecca, Nicholas. BS, Northwestern U., 1959; MA, St. Louis U., 1968. Mem. mktg. mgmt. staff Pillsbury Co., Mpls., 1959—62; staff Gardner Advt. Co., St. Louis, 1963; with Ralston Purina Co., St. Louis, 1963—97, pres., CEO, chmn., 1981—97; chmn., CEO Agribrands Internat., St. Louis, 1997—. Bd. dirs. Am. Freightways, Angelica Corp., Ball Corp., Boatmen's Bancshares, Inc., Gen. Am. Life Ins. Co., May Dept. Stores, S.C. Johnson & Son, Reins. Group Am., Vail Resorts; bd. dirs., chmn. Ralston Purina, Ralcorp.; chmn. Westgate Equity Group, LLC. Served USN, 1954—57.

STIRLING, ALEXANDRA LUCERO, science administrator, writer; b. New York, NY, Aug. 31, 1969; d. Hector and Martha Lucero; m. James Stirling, June 28, 1997. B in pharmacy, St John's U., 1992; PharmD, Mass. Coll. of Pharmacy, 1996. Asst. clin. prof. St John's U., 1997—2001; sci. dir. Cerebrio, NYC, 2001—. Office: Corlett Accel Healthcare Group 30 Irving Pl 11th Floor New York NY 10003 E-mail: alexandra_stirling@accelhealth.com.

STIRLING, D. LESLIE, corporate financial executive; b. Lake Forest, Ill., July 26, 1976; d. James Paulman and Ellen Adair Stirling. BA, Princeton Univ., Princeton, N.J., 1998; MBA, Kellogg Sch. of Mgmt., Chgo., Ill., 2004. Sale rep. Kraft Foods. Inc., Boston, 1998—99, customer category mgr. I, 1999—2000, customer category mgr. II, 2000—01, customer category mgr. III, 2001—03, retail sales mgr., 2003—. Team leader Kraft Region Roundtable, Addsion, Ill., 2003. Young alumni chair Princeton Club of Chgo., Ill.,

2001—; vol. Jr. achievement, Addison, Ill., 2000—; mem. of aux. bd. Shedd Aquarium. Mem.: Young Exec. Club. Avocations: running, writing, hiking, reading, volunteering. Home: 441 W Barry Ave # 528 Chicago IL 60657

STIRLING, ELLEN ADAIR, retail executive; b. Chgo., June 21, 1949; d. Volney W. and Ellen Adair (Orr) Foster; m. James P. Stirling, June 6, 1970; children: Elizabeth Ginevra, Diana Leslie, Alexandra Curtiss. Student, U. Chgo., 1970-71; BA, Wheaton Coll., Norton, Mass., 1971; postgrad., U. London, 1974. Pres., CEO, The Lake Forest Shop, 1986—. Bd. dirs. Lake Forest Bank and Trust. Founder, v.p. aux. bd. Art Inst. Chgo., 1972-91; dir. Friends of Ryerson Woods, 1992—; mem. women's bd. Lyric Opera, Chgo., 1992—, Lake Forest Coll., 1989—; mem. adv. bd. Hope C. McCormick Costume Ctr., Chgo. Hist. Soc.; trustee Nat. Louis U., 1999—. Mem. Onwentsia Club, Racquet Club, Chgo. Club. Office: The Lake Forest Shop 165 E Market Sq Lake Forest IL 60045

STIRLING, JAMES PAULMAN, investment banker; b. Chgo., Mar. 30, 1941; s. Louis James and Beverly L. (Paulman) S.; m. Ellen Adair Foster, June 6, 1970; children— Elizabeth Ginevra, Diana Leslie, Alexandra Curtiss. AB, Princeton U., 1963; MBA, Stanford U., 1965. Chartered fin. analyst. Vice pres. corp. fin. Kidder, Peabody & Co. (now UBS), N.Y.C. and Chgo., 1965-71, 84-86, sr. v.p. corp. fin., 1987—; asst. to sec. U.S. Dept. Commerce, Washington, 1976-77. Chmn. bd. Northwestern Meml. Mgmt. Corp., Chgo., 1989—; trustee Northwestern Meml. Hosp., Chgo., 1985—. Pres. jr. bd. Chgo. Symphony, 1968—70; mem. exec. coun. Chgo. Metropolis 2020; trustee Chgo. Symphony, 1970—75, Tchrs. Acad. for Math. Sci., 1991—95. Mem. Investment Analysts Soc. (dir.), Bond Club of Chgo., Nat. Econ. Hon. Soc. Clubs: Chicago, Racquet (Chgo.); Onwentsia (Lake Forest, Ill.). Office: UBS Tower One N Wacker Dr Ste 2500 Chicago IL 60606-4302 Business E-Mail: James.Stirling@ubs.com.

STIRRAT, WILLIAM ALBERT, electronics engineer; b. Syracuse, Nov. 5, 1919; s. Robert William and Doris (White) S.; m. Bernice Amelia Wilson, July 13, 1958; children: Valerie Lynne, Dorothy Grace, William Ellsworth. Student, Yaddo's Triuna Arts of the Theatre Sch., 1936, Saratoga Eastman Sch Bus., 1936-37; BS in Physics, Rensselaer Poly. Inst., 1942, postgrad. in aerodynamics, 1949-50; postgrad. in electronics, Rutgers U., 1951-58; postgrad., Fairleigh Dickinson U., 1971. Elecs. engr. GE, Schenectady, N.Y., 1941-44; instr. physics Clarkson Coll. Tech., 1947-49; electronic engr. rsch. and devel. U.S. Army, Fort Monmouth, N.J., 1950-87; prin. engr. Eagle Tech. Logicon, Inc., Northrop Grumman Corp., Eatontown, N.J., 1987-92; prin. Stirrat Arts & Scis., Freehold, NJ, from 1992. Author: (with Alex North) Unchained Melody, 1936 (Top song of Yr. 1955, ASCAP Song of Yr. 1990, a Top Song of the Century, Acad. award nomination 1955, Top ASCAP love song of the 50s decade, Gareth Gates debut single (named U.K. Record of the Year, 2002 by popular vote), Why 3? (Annual Sys. Analysis award US Army, 1985); assoc. editor IEEE Transactions on Electromagnetic Compatability, 1970-76; contbr. articles to profl. jours.; patentee in field. Chmn. pub. rels. Battleground dist. Monmouth coun. Boy Scouts Am., 1970-77; mem. Rep. Congl. Leadership Coun., 1989-91; mem. Rep. Campaign Coun., 1992-93, Rep. Nat. Com., 1992-99. Mem. SAR, IEEE (editor N.J. Coast sect. Scanner 1974-75), Internat. Songwriters Assn., Palgrave Soc., Am. Soc. of Composers, Authors and Publishers. Achievements include origination at Schenectady New York of "rock" in 1941; brought emanation security to a White House television communication system in 1961; circumvented a standard violation of mathematical discipline and originated in 1964 the binomial pulse as a powerful breakthrough in bandwidth reduction, correction in 1971 to texts on electromagnetic field theory, control of interference in design of SYNCOM 1 ground stations, deception control in Tactical Fire Control System. Died July 2, 2004.

STIRRUP, JOHN T. metal products executive; Pres., COO Bway Corp., Atlanta, pres. Brockway std. divsn., 1998—. Office: 8607 Roberts Dr Ste 250 Atlanta GA 30350-2230

STITES, SUSAN KAY, writer, human resources consultant; b. Colorado Springs, Colo., Sept. 20, 1952; d. William Wallace and Betty Jane (Kosley) Stites; m. Gerald Frederick Simon, Aug. 14, 1988. BA, Wichita State U., 1974; MA, Northwestern U., 1979. Benefits authorizer Social Security Adminstrn., Chgo., 1974-77; trainer Chgo. Urban Skills Inst., 1977-79; human resources mgr. Montgomery Ward, Chgo., 1979-83; mgr. tng. Lands' End, Dodgeville, Wis., 1983-87; dir. human resources Ctrl. Life Assurance, Madison, Wis., 1988-90; owner Mgmt. Allegories, Madison, 1987—. Author: Delegating for Results, 1992, Business Communications, 1992, Managing with a Quality Focus, 1994, Training and Orientation for the Small Business, 1994, Powerful Performance Management, 1994, Safety Management Techniques, 1995, Teaching First Aid and CPR, 1995, Alive at 25, 1995, Strategic Thinking and Planning, 1995, Teaching Alice at 25, 1996, Fundamentals of Industrial Hygiene, 1996, Recruiting, Developing and Retaining Volunteers, 1996, Creating a Credit Union University: An Administrator's Guide, 1997, 2d edit., 2001, Creating a Corporate University, 1997, Strategic Thinking for the Automotive Industry, 1997, Managing Sales and Service, 1997, Sales and Service Management in Credit Unions, 1997, Provide Training Without Straining Your Budget, 1997, Car America Sales Training manual, 1998, Introduction to Community Organizing, 1998, Car America Leader's Guide, 1998, Effective Loan Interviewing, 1999, Driven to Extremes, 2000, Safety Inspections, 2001, Job Safety Analysis, 2001, Incident Investigations, 2001, Ergonomics for the Small Business, 2003, Creating a Safety Culture; Strategies for Small Business, 2004, The Nine Elements of Safety Managment System, 2004; editor: Backstay, 1999-2001. Vol. tutor Japanese students in English, Evanston, Ill., 1977-80; reader to the blind Chgo. Coun. for the Blind, 1974-76. Named Outstanding Woman of Yr. Wichita State U., 1974. Mem. ASTD (chpt. pres. 1988, v.p. membership 1986, region V awards chair 1992), Soc. Applied Learning Tech., Madison Area Quality Improvement Network, Assn. for Quality and Participation, Rotary (vol. fundraiser), Mendota Yacht Club (treas. 1990-94). Avocations: sailing, boardsailing, gardening, cooking, travel. Office: Mgmt Allegories 3788 Highridge Rd Madison WI 53718-6206

STITH, KENNETH, federal agency administrator; Dir. Office Fin. Mgmt. NIH, Bethesda, Md., 2000—. Office: Nat Inst Health 31 Center Dr Rm B1C-23 Bethesda MD 20892-2054

STITH, LAURA DENVIR, state supreme court justice; b. St. Louis, Oct. 30, 1953; BA magna cum laude, Tufts U., 1975; JD magna cum laude, Georgetown U., 1978. Law clk. to Hon. Robert E. Seiler, Mo. Supreme Ct., 1978—79; assoc. Shook, Hardy & Bacon, Kansas City, Mo., 1979—84, ptnr., 1984—94; judge. Mo. Ct. Appeals (we. dist.), 1994—2001; judge Supreme Ct. Mo., 2001—. Office: Supreme Ct Mo PO Box 150 Jefferson City MO 65102

STITH, MARY BETH (RAE), marketing professional for graphic design; b. St. Louis, Jan. 19, 1945; d. William King and Ella Roe Barnett; 1 child, Elliot King. BA in Am. Studies, Grinnell Coll., 1966. Dir. spl. events March of Dimes, Chgo., 1982-86; dir. mktg. Gerhardt & Clemons, Chgo., 1986-95, v.p., 1995—. Home: 2650 W Belden Ave Chicago IL 60647-3039 E-mail: rae@gerhardtclemons.com.

STITLEY, JAMES WALTER, JR., food manufacturing executive; b. York, Pa., May 23, 1944; s. James Walter and Geraldine Salome (Horn) S.; m. Tresa Rose Adkins, 1996. BS in Chemistry, Millersville U., 1970. Med. technician York Hosp., 1962-66; rsch. biochemist Carter-Wallace, Inc., Cranbury, N.J., 1970-75; mgr. Ward Labs. divsn. Ward Foods, East Orange, N.J., 1975-77; mgr. tech. svcs. Pepperidge Farms, Inc., Norwalk, Conn., 1977-86; dir. tech. devel. Am. Inst. Baking, Manhattan, Kans., 1986-88; dir. baking and cereal sci. rsch. and biscuit product devel. internat. Campbell Soup Co., Camden, N.J., 1988-90; nat. dir. rsch. and tech. Domino's Pizza, Inc., 1990-91, divsn. v.p. consumer and product rsch., 1992—; pres., CEO TechnoVation Network, Inc., 1992—; dir. new product innovation Weider Nutrition Internat., Salt Lake City, 1999—. Cons. biochemistry and toxicology. Contbr. articles to profl. jours.; patentee in field. Asst. scoutmaster Boy Scouts Am. Mem. AAAS, Am. Chem. Soc., Am. Mgmt. Assn., Am. Assn. Cereal Chemists, Am. Inst. Baking (ednl. adv. com. 1978—), Instrument Soc. Am. (assoc. dir.-food industry liaison), Am. Astron. Rsch. Group, York Astron. Soc. (v.p. 1960). Home: 9295 S Vista West Dr West Jordan UT 84088-8842 Office: Weider Nutrition Internat 2002 S 5070 W Salt Lake City UT 84104 E-mail: sitf2000@yahoo.com.

STITT, DOROTHY JEWETT, journalist; b. Houston, Sept. 4, 1914; d. Harry Berkey and Gladys (Norfleet) Jewett; m. James Wilson Stitt, Feb. 14, 1939; children: James Harry (dec. 1999), Thomas Paul. AB, Rice U., 1937; MS, Columbia U., 1938. Reporter Houston Post, 1936-38, asst. city editor, 1938; editor of publs. Jewett Family of Am., 1971-94, editor emeritus, 1994—. Spl. asst. to pub. Jewett Genealogy Vols. III and IV, 1995-97; Jewett family Dir.-for-Life, 1995—; gen. chair Jewett Family Reunion, 1996; exec. com. Jewett 2000 Millennium Reunion. Author, editor: The 100th Anniversary Yearbook and History of the George Taylor Chapter, DAR, 1895-1995, 1994, Easton Red Cross Fiftieth Anniversary Booklet and History—Fifty Years of Service, 1967. Adv. bd. Easton Salvation Army, pub. chmn., 1956—, chmn. bd. dirs., 1964, bd. treas., 1981; bd. dirs., pub. chmn. Easton chpt. ARC, 1952-67, vol. Lehigh Valley chpt., 1995-96, 98; founding chmn., pres. Easton JC Wives, 1950-53; mem. fin. com. Little Stone House Mus. Assn., 1974-76, 80, organizing bd. dirs. sec. and pub. chmn., 1974-91; bd. dirs. Easton United Comty. Chest/United Way, 1957-60, publicity chmn. for 1st campaign, 1960; active Easton Civil Def. Comms., 1956-60; charter mem. bd. Montgomery County Pa. Girl Scouts USA, 1946-48, publicity chmn., initiator and editor county newsletter; den mother cub scouts Easton Boy Scouts Am., 1948-55; capt. renovation campaign area YWCA, 1956; mem. March Sch., Easton PTA, 1948-57, sec., 1952-54, v.p., 1954-56, bylaws chmn., 1953, Easton H.S., 1954-61, membership chmn., 1955-57, 59-60; bd. dirs. Easton Young Woman's Christian Assn., 1965-68, publicity chmn. Y-Teen com., 1953-68; sponsoring dir. Easton area H.S. Students weekly TV 30-minute news program, 1955-56; class agent 60th reunion Pulitzer Grad. Sch. Journalism Class of 1938 Columbia U., 1998. Recipient plaques Salvation Army, 1982, 91, Jewett Family of Am., 1993, cited for Outstanding Svcs., Easton chpt. ARC, 1967, cert. for Outstanding Svc. and Support, 1997, citation Hist. and Geneal. Soc. Northampton County for outstanding svc. in restoration and pub. of Little Stone House Mus., 1993, citation United Way of Easton, 1960, Molly Pitcher gold medal of appreciation SAR, 1980. Mem. AAUW (treas. Easton br. 1950-52, newsletter initiator and editor 1951-60, rep. of br. to UN N.Y.C. conf. 1961-68, internat. rels. chair 1960-68; Pa. achievement award 2000), UDC (Jefferson Davis chpt./Houston), DAR (George Taylor chpt. regent 1974-80, 89-95, vice regent 1980-83, historian 1971-74, 95—, pub. chair 1969—, Pa. state chair vol. svcs. 1995-98, DAR chmn. Kressler Meml. Garden, Easton, 1999—), DAR, PEO (chpt. AF Houston), Easton Tavern House Soc., World Affairs Coun. Phila., Woman's Club of Easton (pres. 1961-64, bd. dirs. 1957—, pub. chair 1952-68, 70-82, 92-96, parliamentarian 1984-92, 2000—, spl. fin. chair 1969-78, legis. chair 1982-84, internat. affairs chair 1996-2000, history update chair 1997—, Outstanding Woman of Yr. 1992, Gold Medal of Honor 1992), Pa. Northeastern Dist. Regents Club (pres. 1980-83, treas. 1997—), Northampton Country Club (Niners' Golf chair 1957-91), Women's Golf Assn. (constn. and bylaws chair, publicity chmn. 1957-92, parliamentarian 1960-92), Libr. of Congress Assn. (founding nat. mem., charter assoc.). Republican. Episcopalian. Avocations: antiques, historical research, golf, swimming, grandmothering. Home: 110 Upper Shawnee Ave Easton PA 18042-1356

STITT, FRANK, food service executive; Chef Highlands Bar & Grill, Ala., 1982—. Named Best Chef: Southeast, Am. Express, 2001—01. Office: Highlands Bar & Grill 2011 11th Ave Birmingham AL 35201

STIVENDER, DONALD LEWIS, mechanical engineering consultant; b. Chgo., May 8, 1932; s. Paul Macon and Grace (Larsen) S.; m. Margaret Ann Lourim, Apr. 14, 1956; children— Anne, Robert, Carole. BS in Engring, U.S. Coast Guard Acad., 1954; MS, U. Mich., 1959. Registered profl. engr., Mich. R & D engr. Rsch. Labs., GM Corp., Warren, Mich., 1959-92, sr. rsch. engr., 1968-92; owner, consulting engr. Stivender Engring. Assos., 1980—. Cons. engine, thermodynamics, emissions and systems engring. disciplines. Contbr. articles tech. jours. on diesel, gas turbine and spark ignition engine combustion, emission, constrn. and electronic control aspects. Engring. officer USCG, 1950-58. Fellow Soc. Automotive Engrs. (Arch T. Colwell award 1968, 69, 79, governing bd. 1971-73); mem. NAS (naval studies bd. 1990-92), ASME, NRC, Combustion Inst., Sigma Xi. Achievements include inventions of internal combustion engines and electronic control systems. Home: 1730 Hamilton Dr Bloomfield Hills MI 48302-0221 Office Phone: 248-334-7622. E-mail: stive@umich.edu.

STIVER, JAMES FREDERICK, pharmacist, health physicist, administrator, scientist; b. Elkhart, Ind., Jan. 27, 1943; s. Melvin Hugh and Pauline Anna (Schrock) S.; m. Joan Louise Trindle, Aug. 14, 1965; children: Gregory James, Richard Frederick, Kristin Louise, Elizabeth Ann. BS in Pharmacy and Pharm. Scis., Purdue U., 1966, MS, 1968, PhD, 1970. Lic. pharmacist, Ind., N.D. Asst. prof. N.D. State U., Fargo, 1969—73, radiol. safety officer, 1969—76, assoc. prof., 1973—76; radiation safety officer KMS Fusion Inc., Ann Arbor, Mich., 1976—80; mgr., pharmacist Kroger Sav-On Pharmacy Co., Elkhart, Ind., 1980—81; pharmacist Elkhart Gen. Hosp., 1981; environ. regulatory affairs adminstr. Upjohn Co., Kalamazoo, 1981—88, patent liaison scientist, 1988—92, sr. patent liaison scientist, 1992—94; pharmacist, asst. mgr. Judd Drugs, Elkhart, 1994—95; pharmacist Meijer Pharmacy, Goshen, Ind., 1995—99; pharmacist, asst. mgr. Wal-Mart Pharmacy, Elkhart, 1999—2000, mgr., 2000, K-Mart Pharmacy, Elkhart, 2000—02, Plymouth, Ind., 2002—. Cons., lectr. Contbr. articles, abstracts to publs. Named to Hon. Order Ky. Cols. Fellow Am. Inst. Chemists; mem. AAAS, Am. Pharm. Assn., Am. Chem. Soc., Health Physics Soc., Internat. Radiation Protection Assn., Am. Biol. Safety Assn., Ind. Pharmacists Assn., N.D. Pharm. Assn., Order Ky. Cols., Kappa Psi, Rho Chi, Phi Lambda Upsilon, Sigma Xi. Home: 505 Skyview Dr Middlebury IN 46540-9427 Office: KMart Plymouth IN 46563

STOB, MARTIN, physiology educator; b. Chgo., Feb. 20, 1926; s. Cornelius and Theodora (Sluis) S. BS, Purdue U., 1949, MS, 1951, PhD, 1953. Mem. faculty Purdue U., Lafayette, Ind., 1953—, assoc. prof. animal scis., 1958-63, prof., 1963-92; ret., 1992—. Contbr. articles to profl. jours. Patentee prodn. of fermentation estrogen Served with USN, 1944-46; ETO, PTO Name Best Tchr. Sch. Agr., 1970, Best Counselor Sch. Agr., 1977, Best Counselor Purdue U., 1977 Fellow AAAS; mem. Am. Inst. Biol. Scis., Am. Soc. Animal Sci., Soc. Study of Reprodn., Soc. Study of Fertility Episcopalian. Home: 6218 W Rd 75 N West Lafayette IN 47906

STOBAUGH, ROBERT BLAIR, business educator, business executive; b. McGehee, Ark., Oct. 15, 1927; s. Robert B. and Helen (Parris) S.; m. Beverly Ann Parker, Oct. 18, 1947 (dec. 1990); children: Blair, Susan, William (dec.), Clay; m. June Gray Milton, Dec. 7, 1991. BS in Chem. Engring., La. State U., 1947; DBA, Harvard Bus. Sch., 1968. Refinery engr. Exxon Corp., Baton Rouge and Venezuela, 1947-52; engring. mgr. Caltex Oil Co., N.Y., Bahrain, London, 1952-59; mgr. econ. evaluation Monsanto Co., Houston, 1959-65; lectr. Harvard Bus. Sch., Boston, 1967-70, assoc. prof., 1970-71, prof., 1972-83, Charles E. Wilson prof., 1984-96, Charles E. Wilson prof. emeritus, 1996—, chmn. doctoral programs, 1984-89, dir. energy project, 1972-83, chmn. tech. and ops. mgmt. area, 1981-83. Bd. dirs. 11 cos. Co-author: Money in the Multinational Enterprise, 1973, Energy Future (best-seller list N.Y. Times and Time mag.), 1979, How To Build an Effective Small-Company Board, 1996; author: Nine Investments Abroad and Their Impact at Home, 1976, Innovation and Competition, 1988; co-editor: Technology Crossing Borders, 1984; contbr. articles on corp. governance to profl. publs. Mem. bd. advisors Instituto de Estudios Superiores de la Empresa, Barcelona, Spain, 1973-80; co-chmn. The Dumbarton Oaks Symposium on Energy Efficiency, Washington, 1979; bd. dirs. Alliance to Save Energy, Washington, 1979-94; expert testimony Congress; advisor to cabinet-level depts. of White House and UN; trustee French Libr. and Cultural Ctr., Boston, 1995—. Named to Hall of Distinction, La. State U., 1987. Fellow Acad. Internat. Bus. (pres. 1979-80), Coun. on Fgn. Rels., Am. Econ. Assn., Nat. Assn. Corp. Dirs. (bd. dirs. 1996—, Blue Ribbon commn. on dir. professionalism 1996, chair compensation 1995, co-chmn. role of bd. in corp. strategy 2000, vice chmn. risk oversight 2002, vice chmn. exec. compensation 2003), Belmont Hill Club (Mass.), Harvard Club (N.Y.), Forest Club (Houston). Episcopalian. Office: Harvard Bus Sch Soldiers Field Rd Boston MA 02163-1317 E-mail: rstobaugh@hbs.edu.

STOBBE, MICHAEL, reporter; b. Lexington, Ky., May 10, 1966; s. Edward Michael and Patricia Ann (Quealy) Stobbe. BS in Polit. Sci., BA in Journalism, Northwestern U., MA in Journalism, 1988; MA in Pub. Health, U. Mich., 1994. Reporter The Sun Herald, Biloxi, 1988-89; health and environment writer The Flint (Mich.) Journal, 1989-94; health and human svcs. writer The Fla. Times-Union, Jacksonville; healthcare and medicine reporter The Tampa Tribune, Fla.; healthcare writer The Charlotte Observer, NC. Case We. Res. U. fellow, Cleve., 1995; recipient award Mich. Emergency Mgrs. Assn., 1990, Internat. Assn. Firefighters award, 1990; hon. mention, best news story Miss. Press Assn., 1989. Mem.: Assn. of Health Care Journalists (bd. dirs. 2001—, chair membership com.). Office: The Charlotte Observer 600 S Tryon St Charlotte NC 28202

STOBERSKI, MICHAEL EDWARD, lawyer; b. Troy, N.Y., Oct. 18, 1966; s. John S. and Winifred A. S.; m. Holly S. Sedarat, Oct. 21, 1994. BA, U. San Diego, 1988, JD, 1991. Bar: Calif. 1991, Nev. 1992, U.S. Dist. Ct. (so. dist.) Calif. 1991, Nev. 1992, U.S. Ct. Appeals (9th cir.) 1992. Shareholder Rawlings, Olson, Cannon, Gormley & Desruisseaux, Las Vegas, Nev., 1991—. Counsel Clark County Pro Bono Project, Las Vegas, 1992-96, named Rookie of Yr. 1992-93. Mem. ABA, Def. Rsch. Inst., Clark County Bar Assn. Avocations: golf, skiing, scuba diving. Office: Rawlings Olson Cannon Et Al 9950 W Cheyenne Ave Las Vegas NV 89129

STOBO, JOHN DAVID, dean, educator, physician; b. Somerville, Mass., Sept. 1, 1941; BA, Dartmouth Coll., 1963; MD, SUNY, Buffalo, 1968. Intern Osler Med. Services, Johns Hopkins, Balt., 1968-69, asst. med. resident, 1969-70, chief med. resident, 1972-73; research assoc. NIH, Bethesda, 1970-72; asst. prof. Mayo Clinic and Research Found., Rochester, Minn., 1973-76; assoc. prof. Moffitt Hosp., San Francisco, 1976-82, prof., head section rheumatology, clin. immunology, 1982-85; William Osler prof. medicine, chmn. dept. medicine John Hopkins Hosp. and Univ., Balt., 1985-94, vice dean clin. sci., assoc. v.p. medicine, 1994—97; v.p. Johns Hopkins Health System, Balt., 1994—97; chmn., CEO Johns Hopkins Healthcare LLC, Balt.; pres. U. Tex. Med. Br., Galveston, 1997—. Mem. transp. and immunobiology adv. com. NIAID, 1976—81; vice chmn. rsch. com. Arthritis Found., 1982—84, chmn. rsch. com., 1984—86, sr. investigator, 1974—77; mem. bd. sci. counselors Nat. Cancer Inst., 1982—; mem. sci. adv. bd. exec. com. Lupus Rsch. Inst.; mem. rsch. adv. bd. DuPont Co., 1987—94. Mem. editl. bd.: Jour. Immunology, 1981—86, Jour. Lab. and Clin. Investigation, 1977—82, Arthritis and Rheumatism, 1980—85, Jour. Reticuloendothelial Soc., 1982—84, Jour. Clin. Investigation, 1981—86, Jour. Clin. Immunology, 1982—87, Jour. Molecular and Cellular Immunology, 1984—86, Rheumatology Internat., 1984—86, Jour. Immunology, 1875—1987; contbr. numerous articles to profl. jours. Recipient Merck award, 1967, Maimonides Med. Soc. award, 1968. Fellow: ACP, Am. Clin. and Climatol. Assn.; mem.: AAAS, Assn. Profs. Medicine (sec.-treas. 1991—92, pres. 1994—95), Am. Soc. Clin. Investigation, Am. Fedn. Clin. Rsch., Assn. Am. Physicians, Am. Assn. Immunologists, Am. Rheumatism Assn. (sec., treas., 1st v.p. 1985—89), Am. Coll. Rheumatology (pres. 1989—90), Inst. Medicine, Md. Soc. Internal Medicine, Interurban Clin. Club, Balt. City Med. Soc., Alpha Omega Alpha. Office: U Texas Med Br Pres Office 301 University Blvd Galveston TX 77555-5302

STOCK, ANN, federal official; m. Stuart C. Stock; 1 child. Grad., Purdue U. Dep. press sec. to V.p. Walter F. Mondale, 1980, 84; regional dir. pub. rels. Bloomingdales Dept. Stores, 1982-88, dir. br. stores, 1988-92, v.p. pub. rels., 1988-93; dep. asst. to Pres. and Social Sec. The White House, Washington, 1993-97; v.p. institutional affairs The Kennedy Ctr., Washington, 1997—. Asst. sec. Kennedy Ctr. Bd. Trustees; bd. dirs. Young Concert Artists, Cultural Alliance Greater Washington, United Artists. Mem. Capital Children's Mus. (co-founder), The Women's Forum, N.Y. Fashion Group (former program chmn.), Washington Woman Roundtable (founder), "Race for the Cure" (co-founder). Office: Institutional Affairs The Kennedy Ctr Washington DC 20566-0001

STOCK, DAVID EARL, mechanical engineering educator; b. Balt., Feb. 2, 1939; s. Walter E. and Minnie H. (Bauer) S.; m. Mary R. Wilford, Aug. 4, 1962; children: Joseph W., Katherine W. BS, Penn State U., 1961; MS, U. Conn., 1965; PhD, Oreg. State U., 1972. Test engr. Pratt & Whitney Aircraft, East Hartford, Conn., 1961-65; vol. Peace Corps, Ghana, 1965-68; prof. Wash. State U., Pullman, 1972—, chair faculty senate, 1997-98. Contbr. articles to profl. jours. Fellow ASME (chair multiphase flow com. 1988-90, Freeman scholar 1994, chair exec. com. fluid engring. divsn., 2000-01). Office: Wash State U Sch Mech Materials Engr PO Box 642920 Pullman WA 99164-2920 Office Phone: 509-335-3223. E-mail: stock@wsu.edu.

STOCK, MARGARET DEBORAH, lawyer; b. Boston, 1961; m. Neil Thomas O'Donnell, June 6, 1992. BA, Harvard-Radcliffe U., 1985; JD, Harvard U., 1992, MPA, 2001. Bar: Alaska 1993, U.S. Dist. Ct. Alaska 1993, U.S. Ct. Appeals (9th cir.) 1996. Assoc. Atkinson Conway & Gagnon, Anchorage, 1992-98; pvt. practice, Stock & Moeller, LLC, Anchorage, 1998—; asst. prof. Dept. Law U.S. Mil. Acad., West Point, NY. Editor-in-chief Harvard Jour. Law and Pub. Policy, 1991-92. Col. Y, 1982. Mem. ABA, Alaska Bar Assn. (chair immigration law sect. 1995-96), Anchorage Bar Assn. (pres. young lawyers sect. 1995-96), Am. Immigration Lawyers Assn., Federalist Soc. Office: Dept Law US Military Acad West Point NY 10996 Office Phone: 845-938-5818. E-mail: margaret.stock@us.army.mil.

STOCK, PEGGY A(NN), college president, educator; b. Jan. 30, 1936; married; 5 children. BS in Psychology, St. Lawrence U., 1957; MA in Counseling, U. Ky., 1963, EdD, 1970. Lic. psychologist, Ohio. Instr., rsch. asst. dept. psychology and spl. edn. U. Ky., Lexington, 1958-59, 63-67, staff psychologist Med. Ctr., 1964-66; dir. edn. United Cerebral Palsy of the Bluegrass, Lexington, 1962-64; exec. dir. Community Council for Physically Handicapped and Mentally Retarded, Lexington, 1964-66; dir. clin. program No. Ky. Regional Cmty. Mental Health Ctr., Covington, 1969-71; pres. Midwest Inst. Tng. and Edn., Cin., 1971-75; assoc. prof., counseling psychologist Mont. State U., Bozeman, 1975-79, asst. dean Office of Student Affairs and Service, 1977-79; spl. asst. to pres. U. Hartford, Conn., 1979-80, assoc. prof. Coll. Edn., 1980-85, v.p. adminstrn., 1981-86; prof., pres. Colby-Sawyer Coll., New London, N.H., 1986-95; pres. Westminster Coll., Salt Lake City, 1995—. Mem. wild horse and burro adv. bd. Bur. Land Mgmt./Dept. Interior, 1997—2000; bd. dirs. BMW Bank of N.Am., Pacificorp, Fed. Res. Bank, Salt Lake City; trustee St. Mark's Hosp., 2000—. Contbr. chpts. to books, articles to profl. jours. Mem. adv. com. Rowland Hall-St. Mark's Sch., 1999—; chair Utah selection com. Rhodes Scholarships, 1995—; mem. program com. Coun. Ind. Coll., 1996—2000; bd. dirs. Utah Partnership for Edn. and Econ. Devel., 1996—; hon. bd. dirs. Big Bros./Big Sisters, 1999—. Recipient Disting. Alumna award, St. Lawrence U., 1989, Athena Pathfinder award, 2001; fellow, U. Ky., 1966—68, Am. Coun. Edn., 1979—80, United Jewish Com., 1981; grantee, George I. Alden Trust, Helene Fuld Health Trust, Surdna, Cogswell, U.S. Dept. Edn., numerous others. Mem. Am. Coun. on Edn., Am. Assn. for Higher Edn., Advancement Women in Higher Edn., Nat. Assn. Ind. Colls. and Univs. (bd. dirs. 1998—), Am. Assn. Pres.'s Ind. Colls. and Univs. (bd. dirs. 1996—), Salt Lake Area C. of C. (bd. govs. 1996-99), Utah Info. Techs. Assn. (trustee 1998-99). Avocations: breeding arabian horses, reading, fishing. Office: Westminster Coll 1840 S 1300 E Salt Lake City UT 84105-3617

STOCK, STEPHEN MICHAEL, broadcast journalist; b. Colorado Springs, May 16, 1961; s. Ray Kesecker and Juanita Madeline (Keller) Stock; m. Lynn Victoria Peithman, July 20, 1985; 1 child, Michael Stephen Ray. BA, U.N.C., 1983. From engring. tech. to gen. assignment reporter WDBJ-TV, Roanoke, Va., 1983-86; from investigative reporter to weekend anchor, producer WECT-TV, Wilmington, N.C., 1986-87; bur. chief Anderson, S.C. WYFF-TV, Greenville, S.C., 1987-91; investigative reporter-bur. chief Ocala, Fla. WESH-TV, Orlando, 1991—; standby SE corr. NBC NewsChannel, 1995—. Guest

lecr. Marion County Sheriff's Office, Ocala, 1993—98, U. Fla. Press Club, Gainesville, 1993; participant Media Studies Initial Advanced Power Reporting Seminar The Poynter Inst., 1998, participant Getting Wired Seminar, 2001. Adv. bd. mem. Jack Eckerd Youth Camp E-Kel-Etu, Silver Springs, Fla., 1996—; founder Ocala/Marion County Town Mtg. on Violence, 1996; adv. bd. mem Fla. Environthon, Ocala/Silver Springs, 1993; v.p., bd. dirs. Ocala Habitat for Humanity, 1996—99; elder First Presbyn. Ch., Ocala, 1996—99. Named TV Journalist of Yr., RTNDA of Carolinas, 1989; recipient TV Agrl. News Coverage award, S.C. Agr. Co., 1989, Fla. Media award, Fla. Emergency Mgmt. Assn., 1997, 5 Emmy awards, 2003, Alfred I. DuPont Columbia U. Silver Baton, 2004, George Foster Peabody award, 2004, award, Signa Delta Chi, 2003, 1st Pl. Individual Achievement award, Associated Press, 2004; Ethics fellow, Poynter Inst. Media Studies, 2004. Mem.: Ctrl. Fla. Press Club (Best Gen. News 1994, Merit Recognition for Spot News 1995, Best Spot News award 1996, Merit Gen. News award 1996, Best Investigative Report award 1996), Investigative Reporters and Editors Assn., Soc. Profl. Journalists (Finalist Non-deadline News 1999, 1st pl. TV Investigations Market 1-100 Green Eyeshade award 2000, Fla. Sunshine State award for best investigative reporting 2000, Sunshine State award finalist 2001, RTNDA Communicator award of distinction). Avocation: Avocations: wine collecting, photography, sports, gardening, carpentry. Office: WESH-TV Bur Chief 7 E Silver Springs Blvd Ocala FL 34470-6634 Office Phone: 352-622-2222. E-mail: sstock@hearst.com.

STOCK, STUART CHASE, lawyer; b. St. Louis, July 19, 1946; s. Sheldon Harry and Muriel Cecile (Lovejoy) S.; m. Judith Ann Stewart, July 18, 1970; 1 child, Frederick Chase. BS with highest distinction, Purdue U., 1968; JD magna cum laude, Harvard U., 1971. Bar: Mo. 1971, Ind. 1973, D.C. 1974. Law clk. to Chief Judge Henry J. Friendly U.S. Ct. Appeals 2d cir., New York, 1971-72, law clk. to Justice Thurgood Marshall U.S. Supreme Ct., Washington, 1972-73; assoc. Covington & Burling, Washington, 1974-78, ptnr., 1978—. Lectr. law U. Va., Charlottesville, 1987-90. Mem. Am. Law Inst. Office: Covington & Burling PO Box 7566 1201 Pennsylvania Ave NW Washington DC 20044

STOCKAR, HELENA MARIE MAGDALENA, artist; b. Bratislava, Czechoslovakia, Mar. 22, 1933; came to the U.S., 1968; d. Arnost J. and Helen R. (Strakova) Kubasek; m. Ivo J. Stockar, Oct. 31, 1959; children: David, Laura Bates. Diploma, Graficka Skola, Prague, 1952, Music Conservatory, 1954. Piano tchr. Music Sch., Prague, 1954-68; company pianist State Ballet/Breacrest Sch., R.I., 1968-74; piano tchr. Music Tchr. Assn., R.I., 1968-86. One-woman shows include Warwick (R.I.) Mus., 1986, Brown U., Providence, 1987, Westerly (R.I.) Art Gallery, 1987, Westerly Art Gallery/Morin-Miller, 1988, 1989, Galerie Horizon, Paris, 1989, Barnes & Noble, Warwick, 1999, 2000, Bohemian Gallery, N.Y.C., 1999, Hoxie Gallery, Westerly, 2000, Happy White Gallery, Barrington, R.I., 2000, C.C. R.I., Lincoln, 2000, Pittenweem Art Festival, Scotland, 2001, Pawtucket Congl. Ch., 2002, Bell St. Chapel, Providence, 2002, Courthouse Ctr. Arts, West Kingston, R.I., 2003, two-person shows at: R.I. State Com. Nat. Mus. Women in the Arts, Triboro Studio, R.I., 1995, Bush Gallery, Bryce Studio, Providence, 1995, Monserat Gallery, Soho, 2002, Courthouse Ctr. for the Arts, West Kingston, R.I., 2002, De Blois Gallery, Newport, 2002, Stonington Vineyards Gallery, Conn., 2002, Teichman Gallery, Cape Cod, Mass., 2003, Gallery Z, Providence, 2003, exhibited in group shows at World Congress Czechoslovak Soc. Art and Sci., Washington, 1988, Prague, 1992, Morin-Miller Internat., N.Y.C., 1989, Ariel Gallery, Soho, N.Y.C., 1989, Art Expo N.Y.C., 1989, New Eng. Internat. Art Expo, 1993, R.I. State Com. Nat. Mus. Women Arts, 1995, Providence Art Club, 1996—97, Sarah Doyle Galery, Brown U., Providence, 1997, Visions, Newport, 2001, 2002, Gallery Z, Providence, 2003, 2004, Krause Gallery, 2003, Breslin Fine Arts, Inc., Warwick, RI, 2003, exhibited in group shows, Warwick Mus., 2003, Represented in permanent collections; featured on TV shows. Participant Art in Public Places: Convention Ctr., Providence, 1994. Recipient Second prize Nat. Competition of Children's Book Illustration, Prague, 1965; named finalist Internat. Art Competition, L.A., 1984. Mem.: Czechoslovak Soc. Art and Sci. Avocations: travel, gardening.

STOCKARD, JAMES ALFRED, lawyer; b. Lake Dallas, Tex., Aug. 4, 1935; s. Clifford Raymond and Thelma Gladys (Gotcher) S.; m. Mary Sue Hogan, Aug. 17, 1956; children— Bruce Anthony, James Alfred, Paul Andrew. BA with honors, N. Tex. State U., Denton, 1956; LLB magna cum laude, So. Methodist U., 1959. Bar: Tex. 1959. Pvt. practice, Dallas, 1959-62; with Employers Casualty Co., Dallas, 1962-65; v.p. Southland Life Ins. Co., Dallas, 1965-77, sr. v.p., gen. counsel, dir., 1977-87; exec. v.p., gen. counsel, sec. Southland Fin. Corp., Dallas, 1978-87; dir. Tex. Life, Accident, Health and Hosp. Svc. Ins. Guaranty Assn., 1978-84, chmn. bd., 1980-84; ptnr. Butler & Binion, Dallas, 1987-2000; pvt. practice Dallas, 2000—; gen. counsel Employers Gen. Ins. Group, Inc., 1994—. Bd. dirs. Ins. Systems Am., Atlanta; pres., bd. dirs. Dallas County Mcpl. Utility Dist. 1, Irving, Tex.; gen. counsel, bd. dirs. Lone Star Life Ins. Co., 1988-99. Contbr. legal jours. Mem. exec. com., precinct chmn. Dallas County Dem. Com., 1971. Mem. Am., Tex., Dallas Bar Assn., Assn. Life Ins. Counsel. Methodist. Home: 3607 Asbury St Dallas TX 75205-1848 Office: 7501 Inwood Rd Dallas TX 75209-4019 E-mail: jastockard@sbcglobal.net.

STOCKARD, SUSAN See CHANNING, STOCKARD

STOCKBAUER, ROGER LEWIS, physicist, researcher; b. Victoria, Tex., Feb. 3, 1944; s. Fred Ferdinand and Elizabeth (Nitschman) S.; m. Catherine Pauline Jones, June 10, 1972; children: Robbin Renee, Kathryn Elizabeth, Marc Daniel. BA, Rice U., 1966; MS, U. Chgo., 1968, PhD, 1973. Rsch. assoc. U. Chgo., 1972-73; rsch. physicist Nat. Inst. Standards and Tech., Gaithersburg, Md., 1973-89; prof. physics La. State U., Baton Rouge, 1989—. Editor: High Tc Superconducting Thin Films, 1990; contbr. articles to profl. jours. Recipient Silver medal US Dept. Commerce, 1983; NRC fellow, 1973-75. Fellow Am. Phys. Soc., Am. Vacuum Soc.; mem. AAAS, AAUP, Materials Rsch. Soc., Sigma Xi. Office: La State U Dept Physics 215 Nicholson Hl Baton Rouge LA 70803-4001 Office Phone: 225-578-1263. Business E-Mail: stockbauer@lsu.edu.

STOCKBURGER, JEAN DAWSON, lawyer; b. Scottsboro, Ala., Feb. 4, 1936; d. Joseph Mathis Scott and Mary Frances (Alley) Dawson; m. John Calvin Stockburger, Mar. 23, 1963; children: John Scott, Mary Staci, Christopher Sean. Student, Gulf Park Coll., 1954-55; BA, Auburn U., 1958; M in Social Work, Tulane U., 1962; JD, U. Ark., Little Rock, 1979. Bar: Ark. 1979, U.S. Dist. Ct. (ea. dist.) Ark. 1980. Assoc. Mitchell, Williams, Selig, Gates & Woodyard and predecessor, Little Rock, 1979-85, ptnr., 1985-94, of counsel, 1994—. Bd. dirs., sec. Cen. Ark. Estate Coun., Little Rock, 1984-85, 2d v.p., 1985-86, pres. 1987-88. Assoc. editor U. Ark. Law Rev., 1978-79. Bd. dirs. Little Rock Cmty. Mental Health Ctr., 1994—, v.p., 1996—99, pres., 1999—2001; bd. dirs. Sr. Citizens Activities Today, Little Rock, 1983—88, treas., 1986—88; bd. dirs. Vol. Orgn. for Ctrl. Ark. Legal Svcs., 1986—91, sec., 1987—88, chmn., 1989—91, H.I.R.E. Inc., 1994—2001. Mem. ABA, Ark. Bar Assn. (chmn. probate and trust law sect. 1986-88), Pulaski County Bar Assn. (bd. dirs. 1994-97), Ark. Bar Found., Am. Coll. Trust and Estate Counsel. Democrat. Methodist. Office: Mitchell Williams Selig Gates & Woodyard 425 W Capitol Ave Ste 1800 Little Rock AR 72201-3525

STOCKDALE, JAMES BOND, writer, research scholar, retired naval officer; b. Abingdon, Ill., Dec. 23, 1923; s. Vernon Beard and Mabel Edith (Bond) S.; m. Sybil Elizabeth Bailey, June 28, 1947; children: James Bond, Sidney Bailey, Stanford Baker, Taylor Burr. BS, U.S. Naval Acad., 1946; MA, Stanford U., 1962; LLD (hon.), Brown U., 1979; LHD (hon.), U. R.I., 1980; 9 other hon. degrees. Commd. ensign USN, 1946, advanced through grades to vice admiral, served as naval aviator, test pilot sch. instr., squadron comdr. of supersonic fighters, air wing comdr.; prisoner of war (sr. naval service POW) North Vietnam, 1965-73; pres. Naval War Coll., Newport, R.I., 1976-79; retired USN, 1979; pres. The Citadel, Charleston, S.C., 1979-80; sr. research fellow The Hoover Instn., Stanford U., 1981-96, emeritus, 1996; independent candidate V.P. U.S. running mate of Ross Perot, 1992. Author: A Vietnam Experience, 1985 (Freedoms Found. at Valley Forge hon. prize 1985), (with Sybil Stockdale) In Love and War, 1984, Thoughts of a Philosophical Fighter Pilot, 1995 (Freedoms Found. Valley Forge George Washington honor medal). Mem. acad. adv. bd. U.S. Naval Acad., Annapolis, 1981-94. Decorated D.F.C. (2), D.S.M. (3), Silver Star (4), Medal of Honor; inducted Carrier Aviation Hall of Fame, 1993; enshrined U.S. Naval Aviation Hall of Honor, 1996. Fellow Soc. Exptl. Test Pilots (hon.); mem. Lincoln Acad. Ill. (laureate), Congl. Medal of Honor Soc., Soc. of Cincinnati, SAR, Bohemian Club (San Francisco). Episcopalian. Home: 547 A Ave Coronado CA 92118-1917

STOCKDALE, RUSSELL, information technology executive; BSc, Stanford U.; MBA, U. Pa. Mgr. Anderson Con.; from mgr. end-user mktg. to corp. v.p. Microsoft, Redmond, Wash., 1991, corp. v.p. knowledge worker solutions group. Office: One Microsoft Way Redmond WA 98052-6399

STOCKDALE, SALLY BOYD, artist, real estate agent; b. Coral Gables, Fla., Apr. 20, 1941; d. Grant Stockdale and Alice Boyd (Magruder) Proudfoot; m. David Michael deWilde, Dec. 21, 1968 (div. 1978); children: Holland Stockdale, Christian duCroix; m. Mariano Eduardo Munoz-Lopez, Mar. 26, 1981. AA, Bennett Coll., Millbrook, N.Y., 1961; postgrad., Trinity Coll., Dublin, Ireland, 1962; B.F.A., Am. U., 1979; postgrad., Corcoran Sch. Art, Washington, 1980-93; grad., Realtor Inst., 1994. Lic. realtor, Washington, Md., Va. Realtor Pardoe Real Estate ERA, Washington, 1987—. One-woman shows include: Tahiti Gallery, Marbella, Spain, 1978, Dumbarton Series, Washington, 1982; commd. murals include Children's Hosp., Washington; represented Folger Library, Washington; portraits state and fed. legislators, others; illustrator Holiday Mag., 1963-68, Spanish Jour., 1979, The Dreadful Day, 1981, Patrick, 16 Centuries, 1983. Mem. Nat. Trust for Historic Preservation. Work featured in Washington Evening Star, Washington Post, New York Times; recipient Top Prodr. award Washington Assn. Realtors, 1987-99. Mem. Nat. Mus. Women in Arts, Capital Spkrs., Club Nautico de Altea. Home: 4719 Chesapeake St NW Washington DC 20016-4465

STOCKER, ARTHUR FREDERICK, classics educator; b. Bethlehem, Pa., Jan. 24, 1914; s. Harry Emilius and Alice (Stratton) S.; m. Marian West, July 16, 1968. AB summa cum laude, Williams Coll., 1934; A.M., Harvard U., 1935, PhD, 1939. Instr. Greek Bates Coll., 1941-42; asst. prof. classics U. Va., 1946-52, assoc. prof., 1952-60, prof., 1960-84, prof. emeritus, 1984—, chmn. dept., 1955-63, 68-78, assoc. dean Grad. Sch. Arts and Scis., 1962-66; vis. asst. prof. classics U. Chgo., summer 1951. Editor: (with others) Servianorum in Vergilii Carmina Commentariorum Editio Harvardiana, Vol. II, 1946, Vol. III, 1965; assoc. editor: Classical Outlook. Served with USAAF, 1942-46; col. (ret.). Sheldon traveling fellow from Harvard, 1940-41 Mem. Va. Classical Assn. (pres. 1949-52), Mid. West and South Classical Assn. (pres. So. sect. 1960-62, pres. 1970-71), Nat. Huguenot Soc. (pres. gen. 1989-91), Am. Philol. Assn., Mediaeval Acad. Am., Poetry Soc. Va. (pres. 1966-69), Soc. Colonial Wars in the State of Va., Sons of the Revolution, S.A.R. (chpt. pres. 1972, 91), Huguenot Soc. Va. (pres. 1981-83), Raven Soc. (Raven award 1977), Phi Beta Kappa, Omicron Delta Kappa. Republican. Presbyterian (elder). Clubs: Masons, Red-Land (Charlottesville, Va.), Colonnade (Charlottesville, Va.), Farmington Country (Charlottesville, Va.), Commonwealth (Richmond, Va.), Williams (N.Y.C.), Army and Navy (Washington). Home: 250 Pantops Mountain Rd Charlottesville VA 22911-8694

STOCKER, GREGG, quality assurance professional, writer; BA, Mich. State U., 1981; MBA, U. Houston, 1990. Cert. purchasing mgr. Inst. for Supply Mgmt., 1985, quality mgr. Am. Soc. for Quality, 1995. Prodn. planning mgr. Ruska Instrument Corp., Houston, 1981—92; quality dir. 3P-USA, Houston, 1992—97, Anderson Greenwood Crosby, Stafford, Tex., 1997—2000; global quality dir. Daniel Industries, Inc., Houston, 2001—03, ICO Polymers, Inc., Houston, 2003—. Cons., Richmond, Tex., 2000. Author: (book) The Six Warning Signs of Organizational Decline; contbr. articles to profl. jours. Vol. Citizens for Animal Protection, Houston, 2000. Recipient Shelter Vol. of Yr. award, Citizens for Animal Protection, 2001. Mem.: Am. Soc. for Quality.

STOCKER, JOYCE ARLENE, retired secondary school educator; b. West Wyoming, Pa., May 13, 1931; d. Donald Arthur and Elizabeth Mae (Gardner) Saunders; m. Robert Earl Stocker, Nov. 26, 1953; children: Desiree Lee Stocker Stackhouse, Rebecca Lois Stocker Genelow, Joyce Elizabeth Stocker Scrobola. Grad. cum laude, Coll. Misericordia, Dallas, 1953; Master's equivalency diploma, Pa. Dept. Edn., 1991. Cert. tchr., Pa. Tchr. music and lang. arts West Pittston (Pa.) Sch. Dist., 1953-60; tchr. music and choral Wyoming Area Sch. Dist., Exeter, Pa., 1970-78, tchr. English composition, 1978-93, chmn. lang. arts dept., 1982-90, dir. nat. history day activities, 1982-93. State cons. Nat. History Day, 1996—. Organist, choir dir. United Meth. Ch., Wyo., 1958—; dir. W. Wyo. Centennial Choir, 1998; mem. adminstrv. bd. West Wyo., 2000—; mem. worship com. United Meth. Ch. and Interch. Coun., Wyo. and West Wyo. Recipient DAR Tchr. of Yr. award, 1992-93, Wilkes U., 1990; named Outstanding Educator, Times Leader, 1993; honoree Wyo. United Meth. Ch. Choir, 1999. Mem. NEA, Pa. Edn. Assn., Wyo. Edn. Assn., N.E. Pa. Writing Coun., Nat. Coun. Tchrs. English, Women Educators Internat., Orgn. Am. History, Pa. Music Educators Assn., Music Educators Nat. Coun., Nat. Coun. Social Studies, Pa. Assn. Sch. Retirees (Vol. of Yr. 1998), Pa. Sch. Employees Retirement Sys. (social svcs. com.), Pa. Retired Pub. Sch. Employees Assn. (Luzerne-Wyoming counties chpt.), Pa. Coun. Social Studies, Delta Kappa Gamma (recording sec. 1991—, accompanist Pa. state chorus, 1999—, 2000—), Phi Mu Gamma. Methodist. Avocations: reading, writing, sewing, hunting, fishing. Office: Wyoming Area Sch Dist 20 Memorial St Exeter PA 18643-2659

STOCKER, MICHAEL AUBREY, health insurance company executive; b. Mpls., 1942; Degree, U. Notre Dame; MD, Med. Coll. Wis., 1968; MPH, U. Mich., 1987. Intern Milw. County Gen. Hosp.; resident Mayo Clinic, U. Calif., San Joaquin Gen. Hosp.; assoc. chmn. dept. family practice Cook County Hosp., Chgo., 1975—80; med. dir. ANCHOR Rush Presbyn. St. Luke's Med Ctr., Chgo., 1980—85; exec. v.p., gen. mgr. N.Y. area market US Healthcare, 1985—92; pres. CIGNA Health Plans, 1993—94; pres., CEO Empire Blue Cross and Blue Shield (subs. WellChoice Inc.), NYC, 1994—; CEO WellChoice Inc., NYC, 2002—, pres., 2003—. Bd. dirs. Nat. Quality Forum, Am. Assn. Health Plans, Coun. Affordable Quality Healthcare, Sec.'s Coun. for Pub. Health Preparedness, HHS, 2002—. Bd. dirs. Arthur Ashe Inst. Served U.S. Army. Mailing: WellChoice 11 W 42nd St New York NY 10036*

STOCKGLAUSNER, WILLIAM GEORGE, accountant; b. St. Louis, Dec. 25, 1950; s. William George and Mary Virginia (Lopez) S.; m. Vickie Kay Mackler, Nov. 17, 1973 (div. Dec. 1999); children: Tyson Marshall, Jacob Cameron. BS summa cum laude, Columbia (Mo.) Coll., 1985. CPA, Mo. Staff acct. Wright-Price Inc., Jefferson City, Mo., 1974-77, Williams-Keepers CPAs, Columbia, 1977-81, supr. acctg. svc., 1981-85, auditor, 1985-86; acct. Don Landers & Co. CPAs, Columbia, 1986-89, ptnr., 1990-99; founder, pres. William. G. Stockglausner CPA, PC, Columbia, 1999—; ptnr. Ashland Manor Properties, 2001—. Coach Daniel Boone Little League, Columbia, 1986-90, 94-99, Diamond Coun., 1994-99, Columbia Soccer Club, 1988-90, 94-2000, divsn. coord., 1991-92; campaign vol. United Way, 1991-94, 97-98; fin. adv. com. City of Columbia, 1996—. Mem. AICPA, Mo. Soc. CPAs (tech. standards rev. com. 1989-90), Lions (sec. Columbia club 1983-85, bd. dirs. 1986-88). Republican. Roman Catholic. Avocations: fishing, photography, running, music/guitar, mem. Low-Water Crossing bluegrass band. Office: 601 W Nifong Blvd Ste 1E Columbia MO 65203-6804 E-mail: wstock139@att.net.

STOCKING, GEORGE WARD, JR., anthropology educator; b. Berlin, Dec. 8, 1928; came to U.S., 1929; s. George Ward and Dorothé Amelia (Reichhard) S.; m. Wilhelmina Davis, Aug. 19, 1949 (div. 1965); children: Susan Hallowell, Rebecca, Rachel Louise, Melissa, Thomas Shepard; m. Carol Ann Bowman, Sept. 29, 1968. BA, Harvard U., 1949; PhD, U. Pa., 1960. From instr. to assoc. prof. history U. Calif., Berkeley, 1960-68; assoc. prof. anthropology and history U. Chgo., 1968-74, prof. anthropology, 1974—2000, Stein-Freiler Disting. Svc. prof., 1990—, prof. emeritus, 2000—, dir. Fishbein Ctr. for History Sci. and Medicine, 1981-92. Vis. prof. U. Minn., Mpls., 1974, Harvard U., Cambridge, Mass., 1977, Stanford U., Palo Alto, Calif., 1983, U. Ill., Urbana, 1999. Author: Race, Culture and Evolution, 1968, Victorian Anthropology, 1987, The Ethnographer's Magic, 1992, After Tylor, 1995, Delimiting Anthropology, 2001; author, editor: The Shaping of American Anthropology, 1974; editor History of Anthropology, 1983-97. Active labor union and radical polit. activity, 1949-56. Fellow Ctr. for Advanced Study in Behavioral Scis., 1976-77, John Simon Guggenheim Meml. Found., 1984-85, Inst. for Advanced Study, 1992-93; Getty Ctr. for History of Art and Humanities scholar, 1988-89, Dibner Inst., MIT, 1998. Fellow Am. Anthropol. Assn. (Franz Boas award 1998), Am. Acad. Arts and Scis.; mem. Royal Anthropol. Inst. (Huxley medal 1993), History Sci. Soc. Avocation: needlepoint. Office: Univ Chicago Dept Anthropology 1126 E 59th St Chicago IL 60637-1580 E-mail: g-stocking@uchicago.edu.

STOCKING, VALERIE, playwright; b. Waterbury, Conn., Aug. 18, 1954; d. Anson Gilbert and Harriett Margaret (Keller) Stocking. BA in Speech and Drama, Cath. U., Washington, 1974; MA in Cinema Studies, NYU, 1991. Rsch. analyst Corinthian Broadcasting, NYC, 1977—80, SRI, NYC, 1980—83; freelance photographer NYC, 1983—86; recruitment mgr., copywriter TempsAmerica, NYC, 1986—89; office mgr. Richard Rice Arch., NYC, 1989—92; editor audio books Sunset Prodn., Santa Fe, 1992—99; pvt. practice Santa Fe, 1999—. Performer: (readings) Santa Fe Playhouse, 1998, Santa Fe HS, 2000, Los Alamos (N.Mex.) Little Theatre, 2001, Gargoyle Theatre, 2001—03, Lake County Rep Theatre, 2002, Last Frontier Theatre Conf., 2003; author: The End, 2003. Daye & Drake scholar, Miami-Dade Jr. Coll., 1970. Mem.: Internat. Ctr. for Women Playwrights, Dramatists Guild. Avocations: films, reading, crossword puzzles, chess. Home: 2963 Plaza Blanca Santa Fe NM 87507

STOCKMAN, DAVID ALAN, investment banker; b. Ft Hood, Tex, Nov. 10, 1946; s. Allen and Carol (Bartz) S. BA in Am. History cum laude, Mich. State U., East Lansing, 1968; postgrad., Harvard U. Div. Sch., 1968—70. Spl. asst. to Congressman John Anderson, 1970-72; exec. dir. Rep. Conf., Ho. of Reps., 1972-75; mem. 95th Congress from 4th Dist. Mich., Interstate and Fgn. Commerce Com., Adminstrn. Com.; chmn. Rep. Econ. Policy Task Force, 1977-81; dir. Office of Mgmt. and Budget, Washington, 1981-85; mng. dir. Salomon Bros., NYC, 1985-88; sr. mng. dir. The Blackstone Group, NYC, 1988-99; founder Heartland Indsl. Ptnrs., 1999—; CEO Collins & Aikman, 2003—. Mem. Nat. Commn. on Air Quality, 1978. Author: The Triumph of Politics: Why the Reagan Revolution Failed, 1986. Fellow, Inst. Politics, 1974. Mem. Coun. on Fgn. Rels. Office: Heartland Indsl Ptnrs 55 Railroad Ave Greenwich CT 06830 Office Phone: 203-861-2622. Business E-Mail: david.stockman@heartlandpartners.com.

STOCKMAN, JAMES ANTHONY, III, pediatrician; b. Phila., 1943; MD, Jefferson Med. Coll., 1969. Diplomate Am. Bd. Pediat. Intern Childrens Hosp. Pa., 1969—70, resident in pediat., 1970—72; fellow in pediatric hematology/oncology SUNY, Syracuse, 1972—74; now clin. prof. Duke U.; also with U. N.C., Chapel Hill; pres. Am. Bd. Pediat., Chapel Hill. Office: Office of the Pres Am Bd Pediatrics 111 Silver Cedar Ct Chapel Hill NC 27514-1512

STOCKMAYER, WALTER H(UGO), chemistry professor; b. Rutherford, N.J., Apr. 7, 1914; s. Hugo Paul and Dagmar (Bostroem) Stockmayer; m. Sylvia Kleist Bergen, Aug. 12, 1938 (dec. Oct. 2002); children: Ralph, Hugh. SB, MIT, 1935, PhD, 1940; BSc (Rhodes scholar), Oxford U., 1937; DSc (hon.), U. Louis-Pasteur, Strasbourg, France, 1972; LHD (hon.), Dartmouth Coll., 1983; DSc (hon.), U. Mass., 1996. Instr. MIT, 1939—41, asst. prof., 1943—46, assoc. prof., 1946—52, prof., 1952—61; Albert W. Smith prof. chemistry Dartmouth Coll., 1961—79, prof. emeritus, 1979—; instr. Columbia U., 1941—43. Cons. E.I. duPont de Nemours & Co., Inc., 1945—98; vis. com. Nat. Bur. Stds., 1979—84. Author (with others): Polymer Phase Diagrams, 2001; contbr. articles on phys. and macromolecular chemistry to sci. jours. Recipient Nat. medal of Sci., 1987, MCA Coll. Chemistry Tchr. award, 1960, Hermann Staudinger prize, Soc. German Chemists, 2000; fellow Guggenheim, 1954—55, hon. fellow Jesus Coll., Oxford (Eng.) U., 1976, Alexander von Humboldt, 1978—79. Fellow: Am. Phys. Soc . (Polymer Physics prize 1975), Am. Acad. Arts and Scis.; mem.: NAS, Soc. Plastics Engrs. (Internat. award 1991), Soc. Polymer Sci. Japan (hon.), Am. Chem. Soc. (assoc. editor Macromolecules 1968—74, 1976—94, chmn. polymer chem. divsn. 1968, Polymer Chemistry award 1965, Peter Debye award 1974, T.W. Richards medal 1988, polymer divsn. award 1988, Oesper award 1992), Appalachian Mountain Club, Sigma Xi (William Procter prize 1993). Office: Dartmouth Coll Chemistry Dept Dept Chemistry Hanover NH 03755 E-mail: walter.stockmayer@dartmouth.edu.

STOCKMEYER, NORMAN OTTO, law educator, consultant; b. Detroit, May 24, 1938; s. Norman O. and Lillian R. (Hitchman) S.; m. Marcia E. Rudman, Oct. 1, 1966; children: Claire, Kathleen, Mary Frances. AB, Oberlin Coll., 1960; JD, U. Mich., 1963. Bar: Mich. 1963, U.S. Ct. Appeals (6th cir.) 1964, U.S. Supreme Ct. 1974. Legis. grad. fellow Mich. State U., 1963; legal counsel Senate Judiciary Com., Mich. Legislature, 1964; law clk. Mich. Ct. Appeals, 1965, commr., 1966-68, rsch. dir., 1969-76; assoc. prof. law Thomas M. Cooley Law Sch., 1977-78, prof., 1978—. Vis. prof. Mercer U. Sch. Law, 1986, Calif. Western Sch. Law, 1993; lectr. Mich. Judicial Inst., 1995. Editor Mich. Law of Damages, 1989; contbr. numerous articles to state and nat. legal jours. Named one of 88 Greats, Lansing State Jour., 1988. Fellow Am. Bar Found. (life); mem. ABA (chmn. Mich. membership 1972-73, ho. of dels. 1988-92, editl. bd. Compleat Lawyer 1990-99), Nat. Conf. Bar Founds. (trustee 1985-90, sec. 1988-89), Mich. State Bar Found. (pres. 1982-85, trustee 1971-92), State Bar Mich. (chmn. Young Lawyers sect. 1971-72, rep. assembly 1972 79, bd. commrs. 1985-93), Ingham County Bar Assn. (bd. dirs. 1981-85), Mich. Assn. Professions (bd. dirs. 1981-84, Profl. of Yr. 1988), Thomas M. Cooley Legal Authors Soc. (pres. 1982-83), Scribes (bd. dirs. 1994—, pres.-elect, 2003-), Delta Theta Phi (dean Christiancy Senate 1962, Outstanding Prof. 1984). Address: PO Box 13038 Lansing MI 48901-3038 Office Phone: 517-371-5140. E-mail: stockmen@cooley.edu.

STOCKTON, ANDERSON BERRIAN, electronics company executive, consultant, genealogist; b. Lithonia, Ga., Oct. 7, 1943; s. Berrian Henry and Mary Grace (Warbington) S.; m. Linda Arlene Milligan, June 9, 1963; 1 child, Christopher Lee. Cert. in cryptographic engrng., USAF Acad., Wichita Falls, Tex., 1963. Supr. Western Union Telegraph Co., East Point, Ga., 1965-67; mgr. RCA Corp., Cherry Hill, N.J., 1967-72; v.p. Universal Tech., Inc., Verona, N.J., 1972-76; v.p. engring. Siemens Ag., Anaheim, Calif., 1976-84, Concorde, El Toro, Calif., 1984-85, Data Card Troy, Inc., Santa Ana, Calif., 1985-86; dir. laser engring. div. ITT, San Jose, Calif., 1986-87; v.p. S.T.A.R. Ricoh Corp., San Jose, 1988-93; v.p. mktg. QMS, Inc., Mobile, Ala., 1993-94; mng. gen. dir. IDT, Inc., Santa Clara, Calif., 1994-98; gen. mgr. HDTV engring. Philips Semicondrs., Sunnyvale, Calif., 1998-99; COO. Mediagate Inc., Orlando, Fla., 1999—. Cons. Hutchinson (Minn.) Tech. Corp., 1984-87, Xerox, 1993, Hewlett Packard, 1993, NEC, 1997-98. Author: Polled Network Communications, 1976, A Quest for the Past, 1991; patentee in field. With USAF, 1961-65. Mem. IEEE, Am. Electronics Assn. Avocations: classic car collecting, genealogical and historical research, sword, coin and stamp collecting. Home: PO Box 1380 Flagler Beach FL 32136-1380 Office: Mediagate Inc Ste 300 PO Box 1380 Flagler Beach FL 32136-1380 E-mail: absto@vfemail.net.

STOCKTON, JOHN HOUSTON, retired professional basketball player; b. Spokane, Wash., Mar. 26, 1962; m. Nada Stepovich, Aug. 16, 1986; 1 child, John Houston. Grad., Gonzaga U., 1984. With Utah Jazz, Salt Lake City, 1984—2003. Mem. U.S. Olympic Basketball Team, 1992. Named All-Star Co-Most Valuable Player, NBA, 1993; named to All-Star team, 1989—94, All-NBA 1st team, 1994. Achievements include being NBA Assists leader, 1987-92; sharing single-game playoff record for most assists, 24, 1988; leading NBA in most assists per game, 1988-93; leading NBA with highest steals per game avg., 1989, 92; being NBA Steals leader, 1989, 92; being holder of NBA single season rec. most assists, 1991.

STOCKTON, KEVIN W. insurance and investment professional; b. Ariz., Oct. 1, 1967; m. Suzanne M. (Tadra), June 13, 1992; children: Reilly G., Paige R. BS magna cum laude, U. Colo., 1992. CLU; ChFC; CFP; registered health underwriter. Sales rep. Merck Human Hlth. Div., Warren, Mich., 1992-94; agent, registered rep. Northwestern Mutual Life/Baird Sec., Troy, Mich., 1994, Denver, 1995-98; dir. mktg. The Madison Group, Inc., Denver, 1998—. Fin. vice chmn., Boy Scouts of Am., Troy, Mich., 1992-94, U.S. Trnsplt. Games Steering Comm., Natl. Kidney Found., Ann Arbor, Mich, 1992-94, fin. comm., Denver, 1995, Distinguished Citizen Dinner Steering Comm., Boy Scouts of Am., Boulder, Colo., 1995-97, pres., chmn. bd. Gatsbys Cigar Merchants, Inc., Denver, 1996-97. Contrib. articles to profl. magazines, 1995. Cadet, Army, West Point, N.Y., 1985-87. Mem. Am. Soc. CLU's and ChFC, Internat. Assn. Fin. Planners, Nat. Assn. Life Underwriters, Inst. Cert. Fin. Planners, Million Dollar Round Table, Beta Gamma Sigma (life). Avocations: travel, exercise, family, music, reading. Office: The Madison Group Inc 4582 S Ulster St Ste 1300 Denver CO 80237-2639

STOCKTON, RALPH MADISON, JR., lawyer; b. Winston-Salem, N.C., June 22, 1927; s. Ralph Madison and Margaret (Thompson) S.; m. Frances Bowles, July 15, 1950 (dec. Apr. 27, 1994); children: Mary Ellen Sartin, Ralph Madison III, David Anderson, James Alexander; m. Margaret Norfleet, Mar. 3, 1995. BS, U. N.C., 1948, LL.B. cum laude, 1950; LL.D. (hon.), Winston-Salem U., 1983. Bar: N.C. 1950. Assoc. firm Dwight, Royal, Harris Koeger & Caskey, Washington, 1950-51; with Petree Stockton, Winston-Salem, Charlotte, N.C. and Raleigh, N.C., 1951—, ptnr., 1956—, chmn. exec. com., 1980—. Permanent mem. jud. conf. U.S. Ct. Appeals (4th cir.), 1958—. Trustee Winston-Salem State U., 1958-84, vice chmn., 1973-84; trustee Forsyth County Legal Aid Soc., 1966-70, pres., 1969; trustee Meth. Children's Home, 1966-84, chmn. exec. com., 1969-75, pres. bd. trustees, 1975-84; bd. mgrs. Meth. Home, Charlotte, N.C., 1967-70; bd. dirs. Winston-Salem Found., 1979-86, chmn. bd., 1985-86; mem. Leadership Winston-Salem, 1984-85, alumni council, 1987-88; co-chmn. N.C. Legis. Com. on Evidence and Comparative Negligence, 1980-82; mem. Gov.'s Jud. Nominating Com., 1982-85; chmn. adminstrv. bd. local United Meth. Ch., 1984-86. Mem. ABA (Ho. of Dels. 1986-91, standing com. fed. judiciary 1989-92), N.C. Bar Assn. (bd. govs. 1957-60, chmn. comml. banking and bus. law com. 1958-60, chmn. appellate rules study com. 1973-75, pres. 1976-77, named to Hall of Fame 1993), Forsyth County Bar Assn. (pres. 1965-66), Am. Coll. Trial Lawyers (state chmn. 1984-86), regent 1987-91), Nat. Conf. Bar Presidents, Fellows of Am. Bar Found., Supreme Ct. Hist. Soc. (state chmn. 1989-91, cir. rep. nat. membership 1991-93), Law Alumni Assn. U. N.C. (pres. 1964, dir. gen. 1970-73, Disting. Alumni award 1994), Order of Coif, Phi Delta Phi. Lodges: Rotary (pres. Winston-Salem 1965-66). Democrat. Methodist. Office: Kilpatrick Stockton LLP 1001 W Fourth St Winston Salem NC 27101

STOCKWELL, ROBERT PAUL, linguist, educator; b. Oklahoma City, June 12, 1925; s. Benjamin P. and Anna (Cunningham) S.; m. Lucy Louisa Floyd, Aug. 29, 1946; 1 child, Paul Witten. BA, U. Va., 1946, MA, 1949, PhD, 1952. Instr. English, Oklahoma City U., 1946-48; mem. linguistics staff Sch. Langs., Fgn. Service Inst., State Dept., 1952-56; mem. faculty UCLA, 1956-94, prof. English, 1962-66, prof. linguistics, 1966—94, chmn. dept., 1966-73, 80-84, prof. emeritus, 1994—. Mem. com. lang. programs Am. Coun. Learned Socs., 1965-69 Author: (with J.D. Bowen) Patterns of Spanish Pronunciation, 1960, Sounds of English and Spanish, 1965, (with J. D. Bowen, J.W. Martin) The Grammatical Structures of English and Spanish, 1965, The Major Syntactic Structures of English, 1973, (with P.M. Schachter, B.H. Partee) Foundations of Syntactic Theory, 1977, Workbook in Syntactic Theory and Analysis, 1977, (with Donka Minkova) English Words: History and Structure, 2001; also numerous articles.; editor: (with R.S.K. Macaulay) Linguistic Change and Generative Theory, 1972, (with Donka Minkova) Studies in the History of the English Language: A Millennial Perspective, 2003; assoc. editor: Lang., 1973-79, Festschrift: Rhetorica, Phonologica, Syntactica: A Festchrift for Robert P. Stockwell, 1989. Served with USNR, 1943-45. Am. Coun. Learned Socs. fellow, 1963-64. Mem. Linguistic Soc. Am. (exec. com. 1965-68), Philol. Assn. Great Britain. Home: 4000 Hayvenhurst Ave Encino CA 91436-3850 Office: UCLA Linguistics Dept Los Angeles CA 90025 E-mail: stockwel@ucla.edu.

STOCKWELL, WILLIAM F. fundraiser, management consultant; b. Belmont, Mass., Oct. 1, 1948; s. Fred F. and Marjorie (Werner) Stockwell; m. Sara Gray Stockwell, June 16, 1973; children: Quentin F., Carl W. BA, Rutgers U., 1971; MEd, Boston U., 1975. Dir. devel. Eaglebrook Sch., Deerfield, Mass., 1980-83, Hyde Sch., Bath, Maine, 1983-84, Western Regional Coun. on Alcoholism, Lewiston, Maine, 1992-94; dealer Target/1 Fundraiser, Auburn, Maine, 1985-95, Campagne Assn., Manchester, N.H., 1999—; cons. William F. Stockwell Fundraising and Nonprofit Mgmt. Cons., Waterford, Maine, 1984—. Dir. numerous workshops, presentations, retreats and studies including Arthur Griffin Ctr. for Photographic Art, Winchester, Mass., 1997, Shaw House, Bangor, Maine, 1998, Bear Mountain Learning Cmty., South Waterford, Maine, 1998, Cary Med. Ctr., Caribou, Maine, 1998, Deertrees Found., Ltd., Harrison, Maine, 1998, Calais Regional Hosp., 1998, Bridgton (Maine) Pub. Libr., 1998, Watershead Ctr. for Ceramic Arts, Nobleboro, Maine, 1999, Lincoln Home, Newcastle, Maine, 1999, Carriage and Driving Ctr., Skyline Farm, North Yarmouth, Maine, 1999, USM-Sr. Coll., Portland, Maine, 1999, Maine Bar Found., Augusta, 2000, Hyde Sch., Bath, Me., 2001, Eagle Hill Sch., Hardwick, 2001, among others. Trustee Western Maine Health, Norway, Maine, 1990—; dir., pres. Oxford Hills Assn. Devel. Corp., Norway, 1985-94; corporator Norway Savs. Bank, 1986—, Maine HEalth, 1999—; mem. annual fund steering com., parent vol. Eagle Hill Sch., 1999—. Mem. Maine Hosp. Assn. (healthcare governance coun. 1991—), Kiwanis (dir. Norway-Paris chpt. 1986-88). Republican. Avocations: semi-precious gems, gardening. Home: PO Box 84 264 Passaconaway Rd Waterford ME 04088-0084 Office: PO Box 84 Waterford ME 04088 E-mail: fndrsr@megalink.net.

STODDARD, ALEXANDRA, designer, writer, lecturer; b. Weston, Mass., Nov. 8, 1941; d. Robert Powell and Barbara Rutledge (Green) Johns; m. Brandon Stoddard (div.); children: Alexandra Brandon, Brooke Goodwin; m. Peter Megargee Brown, May 18, 1974. Diploma in design, N.Y. Sch. Interior Design, 1961. Designer McMillen, Inc., N.Y.C., 1963-77; pres., CEO Alexandra Stoddard Inc., N.Y.C., 1977—. Founder, pres. Design & Art Soc., Ltd., N.Y., 1987—. Author: Style for Living: How to Make Where You Live You, A Child's Place: How to Create a Living Environment for Your Child From Birth through Adolescence, Reflections on Beauty: Lectures and Notes on Interior Design, The Postcard as Art: Bring the Museum Home (Cert. of Merit award 1986), Living a Beautiful Life: 500 Ways to Add Elegance, Order, Beauty and Joy To Every Day of Your Life, Alexandra Stoddard's Living Beautifully Together, Alexandra Stoddard's Book of Color, Gift of a Letter, Daring to be Yourself, Creating a Beautiful Home, Grace Notes, Making Choices, Alexandra Stoddard's Tea Celebrations, The Art of the Possible, Mothers: A Celebration, Gracious Living in a New World, The Decoration of Houses, Open Your Eyes - 1000 Simple Ways to Bring Beauty into Your Home and Life Each Day, Feeling at Home - Defining Who You are and How You Want to Live, Choosing Happiness: Keys to a Joyful Life, Things I Want My Daughters to Know - A Small Book About the Big Issues in Life; contbg. editor Country Antiques and Collectibles, Decorating with Americana; back page columnist Design Times - The Art of Interiors; columnist McCall's mag.; contbr. articles to profl mags. and jours. Founding mem., chmn. spiritual direction com. Ch. of Heavenly Rest, 1975-77; former mem. bd. regents Cathedral St. John the Divine; dame Am. Soc. of Order of St. John Hosp. of Jerusalem. Recipient Burlington prize, 1975, award for design Greenwich Arts Coun., 1985, Interior Design award Brandeis U., 1986, cert. of spl. merit Graphic Art Inst., Designer of Yr. award Kips Bay Boys and Girls Club, 1997, Disting. Womans' award Northwood U., 1999, Lit. Lion, 100th Anniversary prize 2000 Stonington (Conn.) Libr. Mem. English Speaking Union, Decorators Club, Coral Beach and Tennis Club (Paget, Bermuda), New Eng. Soc. Republican. Episcopalian. Home: 1125 Park Ave New York NY 10128-1243 Office: John Rathbone House 87 Water St Stonington CT 06378-1432 also: 1125 Park Ave Ste 6A New York NY 10128-1243 Office Phone: 212-289-5509.

STODDARD, ALLAN LEE, writer, musician; b. Perry, Okla., Sept. 1, 1944; s. Leland Luellan and Lena Ethel Stoddard; m. Katherin Ann Gilpen, Apr. 28, 1974; m. Diana Elizabeth Doyle, Apr. 21, 1973 (div. Sept. 1973). Musician The Intruders, Okla., 1959—67; band leader The Shirelles, 1967—71; prin., owner Cherokee Heart Pub. Co., Shawnee, Okla., 1967—. Musician The Drifters, 1966—67, The Olympics, 1966—67; band leader Mickey Hargitay, 1966—67, Wolfman Jack, 1966—67; prodr. for Mel Fender and Ashley Fender. Author: Oklahoma Trade Tokens & Baggage Checks, 2003, Oklahoma Territory and Indian Territory Collectibles, 2003; music video writer: Hit and Run Lover, 1990. Vol. Okla. Cystic Fibrosis Found., 2003; musician benefit fundraiser REST Homeless Shelter, Okla. City, 2000; bd. dirs. Washington Irving Mus., Stillwater, Okla., 2000—03. With Nat. Guard, 1961—67. Mem.: We. Heritage Assn. Republican. Baptist. Avocations: metal detecting, treasure hunting, writing songs. Home: 1615 East Main Shawnee OK 74801 Office Phone: 405-878-0355.

STODDARD, ANNE MAHER, biostatistician, researcher, educator; b. Rochester, NY, Mar. 26, 1946; d. Robert Williamson and Mary Jane Gunter Maher; children: Joshua Forrest, Nathan Edward. AB, Hollins Coll., Roanoke, VA, 1964—68; MS, Harvard Sch. of Pub. Health, Boston, MA, 1971—73, ScD, 1973—78. Instr. in pub. health U. Mass., Amherst, 1977—78, asst. prof. pub. health, 1978—89, assoc. prof. pub. health, 1989—2003, assoc. prof. emerita, 2003—; sr. rsch. scientist New England Rsch. Inst., Watertown, Mass., 2003; dir. Ctr. for Statis. Analysis and Rsch., 2004—. Dir. UMASS/ Baystate Ctr. for Rsch. and Edn. in Women's Health, Amherst, Mass., 1997—2003; adj. lectr. Harvard Sch. of Pub. Health, Boston, 1997—; vis. scientist Dana Farber Cancer Inst., Boston, 2001—02. Fulbright Sr. Specialists grantee, 2004. Office: NERI 9 Galen St Watertown MA 02472 E-mail: astoddard@neri.org.

STODDARD, GEORGE EARL, investment company financial executive; b. Perry, Oreg., Jan. 7, 1917; s. G. Earl and Elthira (Thomas) S.; m. Elma Skelton, Feb. 4, 1942; children— Evan, Jean, Robert, Patricia. AB, Brigham Young U., 1937; MBA, Harvard U., 1939; LL.B., Fordham U., 1954. Investment analyst Central Hanover Bank & Trust Co., N.Y.C., 1939-42; v.p. investment ops. Equitable Life Assurance Soc. U.S., N.Y.C., 1945-79; chmn. fin. com. W. P. Carey & Co., N.Y.C., 1979—, also dir. Bd. dirs. United Fund of Bronxville-Eastchester, N.Y., 1960-61; pres. Home Sch. Assn., Eastchester, 1962. Served to lt. USNR, 1942-45. Mem.: Univ. Club (N.Y.C.), Harvard Bus. Sch. Club (N.Y.C.). Home: 11 Cedar Pl Eastchester NY 10709-5703 Office: 50 Rockefeller Plz New York NY 10020-1605

STODDARD, M. ANITA, psychiatric nurse; b. Spartanburg, S.C., July 7, 1946; d. David Dupree and Maudie (Johnson) S. BSN, U. S.C., 1968; MSN, U. N.C., 1972. RN, S.C.; cert. clin. specialist in adult psychiatric and mental health nursing, lic. marriage and family therapist, S.C. Staff nurse in psychiatry S.C. Bapt. Hosp., Columbia, 1968; staff nurse Columbia Area Mental Health Ctr., 1968-70; dir. nursing Spartanburg Area Mental Health Ctr., 1972-87, asst. dir., 1987-2000, part-time spl. svcs. coord., 2001—. Mem. summer faculty U. S.C. Sch. Nursing, Columbia, 1971-72; adj. faculty Mary Black Sch. Nursing, U. S.C., Spartanburg, 1980-93; adv. bd. women's program Spartanburg Tech. Coll., 1987-2000; presenter at profl. meetings. Mem. Spartanburg Symphony/Festival Chorus, 1972—, Spartanburg County Emergency Preparedness, 1988-99. Mem. ANA (local bd. dirs. 1987-92, pres. 1974-76, Excellence in Practice award 1990), Am. Assn. Marriage and Family Therapy, Sigma Theta Tau. Methodist. Avocations: music, needlecrafts, day trips, walking, reading.

STODDARD, PATRICK CLARE, retired military systems consultant, computer engineer; b. June 13, 1941; s. Frank Eudaly and Mary Clarann (Burns) Stoddard; m. Anneliese Barg, Sept. 18, 1963; children: Patrick Frank, Conni Maryann. Student, Cleve. Inst. Electronics, 1967—68, U. Md., 1961—63. Enlisted USAF, 1959, radar technician, 1959—67, resigned, 1967; asst. engr. Univac divsn. Sperry Rand, Minn., 1967—68, field engr., 1968; sys. engr. Hydrospace Challenger Rsch., Inc., Md., 1968—73; sr. engr. Control Data Corp., Arlington, Va., 1973—74, prin. engr. computer scis., 1974—78, mil. sys. cons., 1978—; ret., 2002. Contbr. numerous studies in support of mil. sys. devel. Recipient Bill Norris Shark Club award, Control Data Corp., 1978. Roman Catholic. Achievements include patents for electronic oil slick control. Home: 55 Mohegan Rd Groton CT 06340-5537 Office Phone: 860-445-4902. Personal E-mail: thames1@mindspring.com.

STODDARD, PETER HAWKINS, education educator, consultant; b. Biloxi, Miss., June 10, 1949; s. Richard Williams Stoddard and Winifred Gertrude Hawkins; 1 child, Matthew Richard. BA, Hiram Coll., 1967—71; MSW, San Francisco State U., 1979—81; PhD, Case Western Res. U., 1981—83. Reporter Charlotte Observer, NC, 1971—73; transp. mgr. Jesica/Gunne Sax, Ltd., San Francisco, 1973—74; news editor Alameda Times Star, Calif., 1975—77; social worker San Francisco Welfare Dept., 1977—79; aid to the mayor City of San Francisco, 1979—81; prof. of social work Moorhead State U., Moorhead, Minn., 1983—84, U. of Tenn. Grad. Social Work Sch., Knoxville, 1984—88, Austin Peay State U., Clarksville, Tenn., 1988—. Dir. Ctr. for Social Rsch./ Coun. of Cmty. Services, Nashville, 1986—89; founder and exec. dir. Montgomery County Coun. of Cmty. Services, Clarksville, 1993—94; founder and dir. APSU Cmty. Outreach Partnership Ctr., Clarksville, 1992—96, Vol. Ctr. of Clarksville, Tenn., 1995—96; co-founder Family Guidance Ctr., Clarksville. Author: (book) An Atlas of Montgomery County, Tennessee; contbr. articles to profl. jours. Bd. mem. Nat. Assn. of Planning Councils, Dallas; governor's task force on social svc. block grants State of Tenn., 1996—97; task force mem. Governor's Task Force on Manpower Needs in Mental Health, Nashville, 1987—89, SF Mayor's Task Force on Housing Needs, San Francisco, 1980—81; sec. and bd. mem. Red River Improvement Corp., Clarksville, Tenn.; pres. Cmty. Services Orgn., Clarksville, Tenn., 1993—96, AAUP Austin Peay State U. Chpt., Clarksville, Tenn., 2000—03. Fellow NIMH fellowship, NIMH, 1981—82; grantee Austin Peay State U. Tower grant, Austin Peay State U., 1989. Mem.: Austin Peay State U. Faculty Senate (senator 1998—2002), Coun. on Social Work Edn. Accreditation Com. (licentiate; u. accreditation team insp. 1998—2003), AAUP (life; chpt. pres. 2000—03). Democrat-Npl. Unitarian Universalist. Office: Austin Peay State Univversity College St Clarksville TN 37040 Personal E-mail: stoddardp@apsu.edu.

STODDARD, PHILIP HENDRICK, foreign affairs analyst, consultant, writer; b. Iowa City, Apr. 30, 1929; s. George Dinsmore and Margaret (Trautwein) S.; m. Carol Cannon, Jan. 19, 1952 (div. 1959); children: Michele, Christopher, Eric; m. Doris Joyce Mills, Dec. 26, 1960; children: Leah, Evan. BA, U. Ill., 1950; MA, Princeton U., 1955, PhD, 1963. Asst. prof. SUNY New Paltz, 1958-60; analyst, 1963-80; with U.S. Dept. State, Washington, dep. asst. sec., 1980-83; exec. dir. Middle East Inst., Washington, 1983-87; cons. Nat. Intelligence Coun., Washington, 1988-90, dir., analytic group, 1990-94; ret., 1994; mem., dir. Ctrl. Intelligence's Sr. Rev. Panel, 1996-97. Author: Teskilat-i Mahsusa, 1993; editor: Change and the Muslim World, 1981; editor, co-translator: The Turkish Battle at Khaybar, 1997 (in English and Turkish); contbr. articles to profl. jours. State Dept. fellow Coun. Fgn. Rels., 1979-80. Sgt. USMC, 1951-53. Named Disting. Fed. Exec., U.S. Govt.; recipient Nat. Intelligence Disting. Svc. medal. Mem. Middle East Inst., Middle East Studies Assn., Turkish Studies Assn., Am. Fgn. Svc. Assn., Phi Beta Kappa, Sigma Chi. Home: 6000 Springfield Dr Bethesda MD 20816-1232 E-mail: phstoddard@aol.com.

STODDARD, ROBERT H. geography educator; b. Auburn, Nebr., Aug. 29, 1928; s. Hugh P. and Nainie L. (Robertson) S.; m. Sally E. Salisbury, Dec. 10, 1955; children: Martha, Andrew R., Hugh A. BA, Nebr. Wesleyan, Lincoln, 1950; MA, U. Nebr., 1960; PhD, U. Iowa, 1966. Instr. Nebr. Wesleyan, 1961-63, asst. prof., 1963-67, U. Nebr., Lincoln, 1967-71, assoc. prof., 1971-81, prof., 1981—2001. Vis. prof. Tribhuvan U., Kathmandu, Nepal, 1975-76, U. Colombo, Sri Lanka, 1986; inst. instr. Okla. State U., Stillwater, 1966; TV instr. Nebr. Ednl. TV Higher Edn., Lincoln, 1969; instr. Career Opportunity Program, Lincoln, 1973; dir. Geog. Edn. of Nebr., Lincoln, 1989-95. Author: Field Techniques, 1982; contbg. author: Human Geography, 2d edit., 1989; editor: Sacred Places, 1997. Mem. subcom. Lincoln-Lancaster Planning Com., 1974-78. Mem. Assn. Am. Geographers, Nat. Coun. for Geog. Edn. (Disting. Tchg. Achievement award 1992). Democrat. Unitarian Universalist. Office: U Nebr Geog Program Lincoln NE 68588-0368

STODDARD, ROGER ELIOT, librarian; b. Boston, Dec. 2, 1935; s. Merton Edgar and Helen (Bonney) S.; m. Helen Louise Heckel, May 24, 1958; children— Alison Louise, Christopher Paine AB, Brown U., 1957. Asst. curator Harris Coll. Am. Poetry and Plays, Brown U., Providence, R.I., 1961-63, curator, 1963-65; asst. to librarian Harvard U. Houghton Library, Cambridge, Mass., 1958-61, asst. librarian, 1965-69, assoc. librarian, 1969-85; sr. curator, 1995—; curator rare books Harvard Coll. Library, Cambridge, Mass., 1985—; lectr. English Harvard U., Cambridge, Mass., 1984-86, sr. lectr., 1986—. Faculty mem. Columbia U. Rare Book Sch., N.Y.C., 1984-85; sec. Friends of Harvard Coll. Libr., Cambridge, Mass., 1983-98. Author: Catalogue of Books & Pamphlets Unrecorded in Wegelin's Early American Poetry, 1969, The Houghton Library 1942-82, 1982, Poet & Printer in Colonial & Federal America, 1983, The Parkman Dexter Howe Library, part 1: Early New England Books, 1983, Marks in Books, Illustrated and Explained, 1985 (N.E. Book Show award, 1986, Am. Libr. Assn. award, 1987), Put a Resolute Hart to a Steep Hill: William Gowans Antiquary and Bookseller, 1990; editor: A Glance at Private Libraries, 1991, Edmond Jabès in Bibliography, 1998, 2001, John Laurent, Maine Painter: An Annotated Register of Paintings, Prints and Drawings, 2000, Julian Offray de La Mettrie, 1709-1751: A Bibliographical Inventory, 2001, A Library-Keeper's Business: Essays, 2002; contbr. articles to profl. jours. Mem. Records and Archives Com., Concord, Mass., 1985-87; bd. dirs. Louisa May Alcott Meml. Assn., Concord, 1983— Huntington Library fellow, San Marino, Calif., 1978; W. F. Milton fellow Harvard U. Med. Sch., Boston, 1978-80; D.W. Bryant fellow Harvard U., 1992. Mem. Bibliog. Soc. Am. (coun. mem. 1982-88, Bibliography of Am. Lit. supervisory com. chmn. 1982-91, pres. 1996-2000), Am. Antiquarian Soc. (coun. mem. 1989-93), Assn. Internat. de Bibliophilie, Book Club Calif., Colonial Soc. Mass. (corr. sec. 1993-97), The Johnsonians, Bibliog. Soc. London (hon. sec. for Am. 1992—), Bibliog. Soc. Va., Grolier Club (N.Y.C.), Harvard Club (N.Y.C.), Odd Vols. Boston Club (exec. com. 1985-87), Soc. of Printers Boston. Home: 9 Birchwood Ln Lincoln MA 01773-4907 Office: Harvard Univ Houghton Library Harvard Yard Cambridge MA 02138-6502

STODDARD, SANDOL, freelance/self-employed writer; b. Birmingham, Ala., Dec. 16, 1927; d. Carlos French and Caroline (Harris) S.; m. Felix M. Warburg (div. 1966); children: Anthony, Peter, Gerald, Jason; m. Peter R. Goethals, May 1, 1984. BA magna cum laude, Bryn Mawr Coll., 1959. Author 26 books including: Growing Time, 1971, The Doubleday Children's Bible, 1983 (Lewis citation 1983), The Hospice Movement: Updated and Expanded Edition, 1992, Prayers, Praises and Thanksgivings, 1992. Bd. dirs., co-founder Hospice of Kona, Kailua-Kona, Hawaii, 1985; co-founder Kona Theol. Inst., 1990; bd. dirs. Choice in Dying, N.Y.C. Recipient Humanitarian Svc. award Forbes Health System, 1979, Notable Book award Am. Libr. Assn., 1964. Mem. AAUW, Nat. Writer's Guild, Cosmpolitan Club. Democrat. Episcopalian. Home and Office: 78-6646 Mamalahoa Hwy Holualoa HI 96725-9734

STODDARD, STEPHEN DAVIDSON, ceramic engineer, former state senator; b. Everett, Wash., Feb. 8, 1925; s. Albert and Mary Louise (Billings) S.; m. Joann Elizabeth Burt, June 18, 1949 (dec. Oct. 1993); children: Dorcas Ann, Stephanie Kay; m. Barbara L. Seitz, Feb. 18, 1995. Student, Tacoma Coll., 1944, Conn. Coll., 1946; BS, U. Ill., 1950. Asst. prodn. supr., asst. ceramic engr. Coors Porcelain Co., Golden, Colo., 1950-52; ceramics-powder metallurgy sect. leader Los Alamos (N.Mex.) Sci. Lab., U. Calif., 1952-82; pres., treas. Materials Tech. Assocs., Inc., 1978-94; cons. Ceramic Age Mag., 1958-60; Cons. Nuclear Applications for Ceramic Materials, 1958-60; Jury commr. Los Alamos County, 1969; justice of peace, 1956-62; mem. Los Alamos Sch. Adv. Council, 1966; mcpl. judge, 1976-77; chmn. Los Alamos Ordinance Rev. Com., 1958; Mem. Republican County and State Central Com., 1955—; county commr. Los Alamos, N.Mex., 1966-68; mem. Los Alamos County Planning Commn., 1962-63, N.Mex. Senate, 1980-92. Bd. dirs. Los Alamos Econ. Devel. Corp., U. N.Mex. Los Alamos Found. Patentee in field. Vestryman Episcop. Ch., 1999—2002; bd. dirs. Sangre de Cristo coun. Girl Scouts U.S.A., 1965—71; N.Mex. chpt. Nature Conservancy, 1988—97, v.p., 1993—94, disting. trustee, 2001; bd. dirs. Southwestern Assn. on Indian Affairs, Inc., 1987—91, chmn., 2000—02; chmn. bd. dirs. Los Alamos Vis. Nurses, 1995—2004; chmn. Gov.'s Commn. in Nat. and Cmty. Svc., 2001, Los Alamos County 50th Anniversary Com., 1998—99; trustee, vice chmn. Valles Caldera Nat. Preserve, 2000—02; chmn. Los Alamos Vis. Nurses, 2000—; mem. Los Alamos Edn. Group, 1995—. With AUS, 1943—46. Decorated Bronze Star, Purple Heart, Combat Infantry Badge; recipient disting. alumni award U. Ill. Coll. Engring., 1986, Leopold Conservation award N.Mex. Nature Conservancy, 1988, Cmty. Svc. award. Fellow Am. Inst. Chemists, Am. Ceramic Soc. (treas. 1972-74, pres. 1976-77, disting. life 1984); mem. Nat. Inst. Ceramic Engrs. (PACE award 1965, Greaves Walker award 1984), Am. Soc. Metals, N.Mex. Soc. Profl. Engrs. (Ingeniero Veterano de Neuvo Mejico award 1992), Los Alamos C. of C. (citizen of yr. award 1992), Living Treasure of Los Alamos, Masons, Shriners (pres. 1994-95), Elks (dist. dep. grand exalted ruler 1968-69), Los Alamos Golf Assn. (dir. 1964-66), Am. Legion (nat. legis. coun. 1992-94), Kiwanis (pres. 1964, lt. gov. 1968-69), Sigma Xi, Alpha Tau Omega. Episcopalian. Home: 4557 Trinity Dr Los Alamos NM 87544-1862 E-mail: sbstoddard@msn.com.

STOEBNER, JOHN MARTIN, physician; b. Burlington, Tex., 1933; s. Alfred Walter Richard and Mary Evaleen (Martin) S.; m. Julia Bryan Fisher, Aug. 7, 1971; children: J. Eric, Richard, William Scott, Julia M., Kristin. BS, Loyola U., New Orleans, 1956; MD, U. Tex. Med. Br., Galveston, 1959. Intern Fitzsimons Gen. Hosp., Denver, 1959-60; resident Walter Reed Gen. Hosp., Washington, 1965-68; prof. Tex. A&M Coll. Medicine. Vice-chmn. radiology Scott & White Clin., Temple, Tex., 1986-92, chmn. 1992-96. Comdr. 94th Gen. Hosp. USAR, Dallas, 1972-82. Mem. Am. Coll. Radiology, Texas Radiol. Soc. Office: Scott & White Clin Radiology Temple TX 76508-0001

STOEBUCK, WILLIAM BREES, law educator; b. Wichita, Mar. 18, 1929; s. William Douglas and Donice Beth (Brees) S.; m. Mary Virginia Fields, Dec. 24, 1951; children: Elizabeth, Catherine, Caroline. BA, Wichita State U., 1951; MA, Ind. U., 1953; JD, U. Wash., 1959; SJD, Harvard U., 1973. Bar: Wash. 1959, U.S. Supreme Ct. 1967. Pvt. practice, Seattle, 1959—64; asst. prof. law U. Denver, 1964—67; assoc. prof. U. Wash., Seattle, 1967—70, prof., 1970—95, Judson Falknor prof., 1995—99, prof. emeritus, 1999—; of counsel Karr, Tuttle, Campbell, Seattle, 1988—. Author: Washington Real Estate: Property Law, 1995, 2d edit., 2004, Washington Real Estate: Transactions, 1995, 2d edit., 2004, Basic Property Law, 1989, Law of Property, 1984, 3d edit., 2000, Nontrespassory Takings, 1977, Contemporary Property, 1996, 2d edit., 2002; contbr. articles to profl. jours. Bd. dirs. Cascade Symphony Orch., 1978-83, Forest Park Libr., 1975-80. 1st lt. USAF, 1951-56. Mem. Am. Coll. Real Estate Lawyers, Am. Coll. Mortgage Attys., Wash. State Bar Assn., Assn. Am. Law Schs., Order of Coif, Seattle Yacht Club. Home: 3515 NE 158th Pl Lk Forest Park WA 98155-6649 Office: Sch Law Univ Washington William H Gates Hall Seattle WA 98195-3020 Office Phone: 206-543-4917.

STOECKER, DAVID THOMAS, banker; b. St. Louis, June 8, 1939; s. John Garth and Marie (Zahler) S.; m. Ann E. Conrad, Aug. 18, 1962; children— Lisa Ann, Susan Jane. BS, Ind. U., 1963. Sr. v.p. comml. loans Mercantile Trust Co. N.Am., St. Louis, 1965-80; pres. Gravois-Merc. Bank, St. Louis, 1980-87; pres., chief exec. officer Bank of South County, St. Louis, 1987-95; chmn. bd., CEO Ctrl. West End Bank, St. Louis, 1996—. Served to 1st lt. AUS, 1963-65. Mem. Robert Morris Assos. (pres. St. Louis 1980), Sunset Country Club. Methodist. Office: 415 Debaliviere Saint Louis MO 63112

STOELTING, CURTIS W. consumer products company executive; BS in Acctg., U. Ill. From v.p. fin. and ops. to CEO RC2 Corp., Bolingbrook, Ill., 1996—2003, CEO, 2003—, bd. dir. Office: RC2 Corp 800 Veterans Pkwy Bolingbrook IL 60440*

STOERMER, EUGENE FILMORE, biologist, educator; b. Webb, Iowa, Mar. 7, 1934; s. Edward Filmore and Agnes Elizabeth (Ekstrand) S.; m. Barbara Purves Ryder, Aug. 13, 1960; children: Eric Filmore, Karla Jean, Peter Emil. BS, Iowa State U., 1959, PhD, 1963. Assoc. rsch. scientist, rsch. scientist U. Mich., Ann Arbor, 1965-79, assoc. prof., 1979-85, prof., 1985—. Editl. advisor Jour. Paleolimnology. Contbr. over 225 articles to profl. jours. Fellow Acad. Natural Scis., Phila., 1980; recipient Darbaker prize, Bot. Soc. Am., 1993. Mem. Phycological Soc. Am. (pres. 1988-89), Internat. Assn. for Diatom Rsch. (pres. 1992-94). Home: 4392 Dexter Ave Ann Arbor MI 48103-1636 Office: U Mich Sch Nat Resources Ann Arbor MI 48109 E-mail: stoermer@umich.edu.

STOESEN, ALEXANDER RUDOLPH, retired history educator; b. Austin, Texas, Apr. 9, 1932; s. Andrew Robert William and Laura Tomine (Thompson) S.; m. Carol Annette Cronk, Aug. 22, 1959 (dec. Feb. 1999); children: Robert Andrew, William Darden, Carolyn Anne. BA, The Citadel, 1954; MA, U. Rochester, 1958; PhD, U. N.C., 1965. Tchr. Washington Sq. Reading Ctr., NYC, 1958-59; asst. prof. history Newberry Coll., SC, 1964-66; from asst. to prof. history Guilford Coll., Greensboro, NC, 1966-99, chmn. dept. history, 1972-77, 82-84, 90-91; Lilly fellow Duke U., Durham, NC, 1976-77 Mem., past chair NC Hwy. Hist. Market Adv. Commn., Raleigh, 1986-91, 94-98, 2001—; v.p. So. Assn. Pre-Law Advisers, 1989-91, pres., 1991-93; mem. Pre-Law Advisers Nat. Coun., 1991-93, cons., 1993—. Author: Guilford College: On the Strength of 150 Years, 1987, Guilford County Since 1890, Part II of History of Guilford County, 1981, Guilford County: A Brief History, 1993; author: (with others) The North Carolina Experience, 1984, Encyclopedia of Southern History, 1979; contbr. articles to profl. jours. and reviews to newspapers. Mem. Greensboro Sit-Ins Twentieth Anniversary Com., 1979-80, 13th Anniversary Com., 1989-90, 40th Ann. Com., 1999-2000; chmn. bd. trustees Unitarian Ch. of Greensboro, 1979-81; trustee Greensboro Hist. Mus., 1997-99; vol. Habitat for Humanity, various countries, 2001—; vol. Quaker workteam in Ramallah, Palestine, 1999, 2001. 1st lt. U.S. Army, 1955-57, capt. USAR, 1969. 1st lt. USAR, 1955—57, capt. USAR, 1969. Recipient Congl. Leadership award Thomas Jefferson dist. Unitarian-Universalist Assn., Excellence in Tchg. Award, Guilford Coll., 1995, Appreciation award Guilford County Bd. of Pub. Health, 2000, Christopher Crittenden award State NC, 1990, 2000; grantee NEH, 1975, 82. Mem. Am. Hist. Assn., Hist. Soc. NC (coun. 1988-90, sec. 1990-96, v.p. 1997-98, pres. 1998-99, Hugh T. Lefler undergrad. history award com. 1983, chmn. 1984), N.C. Lit. and Hist. Assn. (Mayflower Cup book prize com. 1987, 91), So. Hist. Assn., Orgn. Am. Historians (chmn. membership com., 1991-96), Assn. of Citadel Men (life). Democrat. Avocations: bicycling, bicentennial memorabilia collector, gardening, bird watching, whitewater rafting. Personal E-mail: astoesen@aol.com.

STOESSINGER, JOHN GEORGE, political science educator; b. Vienna, Oct. 14, 1927; came to U.S., 1947; s. Oscar and Irene Stoessinger; m. Carolyn Stoessinger, 1966 (div. 1985); children: Richard Victor, Anna. BA, Grinnell Coll., 1950, LLB (hon.), 1970; MA, Harvard U., 1952, PhD, 1954; LLB (hon.), Am. Coll. in Switzerland, Leysin, 1981. Prof. polit. scis. CUNY, N.Y.C., 1957-83; dir. polit. affairs divsn. UN, N.Y.C., 1967-74; disting. prof. internat. affairs Trinity U., San Antonio, 1983-2000; disting. prof. global diplomacy U. San Diego, 2000—. Teaching fellow Harvard U., Cambridge, Mass., 1952-54; asst. prof. polit. sci. Wellesley (Mass.) Coll., 1954-56; vis. prof. internat. affairs Columbia U., N.Y.C., 1963-67, Princeton (N.J.) U., 1978. Author: The Might of Nations, 1962, 10th edit., 2000 (Bancroft prize 1963), Nations at Dawn, 1979, 6th edit., 1996, Henry Kissinger, 1979, Why Nations Go To War, 1983, 9th edit., 2004. Active UNA-USA, NY, 1960—. Mem. Coun. on Fgn. Rels. (book rev. editor Fgn. Affairs 1968-78). Jewish. Avocation: classical music. Home: 418 Neptune Ave Encinitas CA 92024 Office: U San Diego 5998 Alcala Park San Diego CA 92110 Office Phone: 760-632-8682. E-mail: jgs@johngstoessinger.com.

STOFER, BOYD B. real estate company executive; b. Cleve. With Gerald D. Hines Interests, Houston, 1975—78; joined United Properties, Mpls., 1978, dir. real-estate devel. activities, exec. v.p., pres., COO United Properties' subsidiaries, 1990—95; pres., CEO United Properties - ONCOR Internat., 1995—. Bd. mem. AmberJack, Northland/Marquette Capital Group, Inc., St. Paul Capital City Partnership, Ctr. for Urban Land Econs. Rsch., U. Wis. Bd. dirs. Boys & Girls Clubs of the Twin Cities. Mem.: Urban Land Inst., Nat. Assn. Indsl. and Office Properties (bd. dirs., past pres. Minn. chpt., Pres. award of excellence 1999). Office: United Properties-ONCOR Internat 3500 W 80th St #200 Minneapolis MN 55431*

STOFF, JEFFREY S. physician, educator; b. Oct. 20, 1942; BS, Hobart Coll., Geneva, N.Y., 1964; MD, SUNY, Buffalo, 1968. Dir. renal medicine U. Mass. Meml., Worcester, 1983—, dir. transplantation medicine, 1983—; prof. medicine/physiology U. Mass. Med. Sch., Worcester, 1983—; assoc. prof. Harvard Med. Sch., Boston, 1982-83; asst. physician Beth Israel Hosp., Boston, 1974—. Editor: Jour. Intensive Care Medicine; editl. bd. Transplant Jour.; contbr. articles in profl. jours. Bd. trustees New England Organ Bank, 1996-98, councilor United Network Organ Sharing, Richmond, Va., 1998-2002. Office: Medicine Dept/Renal Medicine U Mass Meml 55 Lake Ave N Worcester MA 01655-0317 Office Phone: 508-856-3156. Business E-Mail: stoffj@ummhc.org.

STOFFERSON, TERRY LEE, financial officer; b. Omaha, Apr. 22, 1957; s. Dale Leslie and Alma Rose (Flores) S. BSBA, U. Nebr., Omaha, 1980; MBA, DBA, Calif. Coast U., Santa Ana, 1998. Auditor Alexander Grant & Co., CPA's, Omaha, 1979-81; budget mgr. Archbishop Bergan Mercy Hosp., Omaha, 1981-86; controller Lafayette (La.) Gen. Med. Ctr., 1986-87; chief fin. officer Opelousas (La.) Gen. Hosp., 1987-89; assoc. adminstr. fin. County of Fresno Valley (Calif.) Med. Ctr., 1989-94; v.p. fin. Trinity Med. Ctr., Minot, N.D., 1994-96; exec. v.p. St. Catherine Hosp., Garden City, Kans., 1996-2001; sr. v.p. Provena St. Joseph Hosp., Elgin, Ill., 2001—02; v.p. adminstrn. La Rabida Children's Hosp., Chgo., 2003—. Cons. in field. Mem. Healthcare Fin. Mgrs. Assn. (advanced), Nat. Assn. Accts. (contr.'s coun. 1988, 89), Am. Hosp. Assn., Am. Coll. Healthcare Execs Lodges: Optimist (pres. 1988). Republican. Presbyterian. Avocations: fishing, electronics, photography. E-mail: drterrbear@aol.com.

STOFFLE, CARLA JOY, university library dean; b. Pueblo, Colo., June 19, 1943; d. Samuel Bernard and Virginia Irene (Berry) Hayden; m. Richard William Stoffle, June 12, 1964; children: Brent William, Kami Ann. AA, So. Colo. State Coll., Pueblo, 1963; BA, U. Colo., 1965; MLS, U. Ky., 1969; postgrad., U. Wis., 1980. Head govt. publ. dept. John G. Crabbe Library, Eastern Ky. U., Richmond, 1969-72; from head pub. svcs. to asst. chancellor edn. svcs. U. Wis. Parkside Libr., Kenosha, 1972—85; dep. dir. U. Mich. Libr., Ann Arbor, 1986—91; prof. libr. sci. U. Ariz., Tucson, 1991—, dean librs. and ctr. for creative photography, 1991—, acting dir. Sch. Info. Resources and Libr. Sci., 1999—2001. Adv. bd. Bowker Librs., NY, 1985—90; bd. dirs. Trejo Foster Found., 2000—; state adv. com. Ariz. State Dept. of Libr. Archives and Pub. Records, 2000—; adv. com. U. Mich. Sch. Libr. Sci., 1986—92, OCLC Rsch. Librs., 1995—2000. Co-author: Administration of Government Documents Collection, 1974, Materials and Method for History Research, 1979, Materials and Methods for Political Science Research, 1979; mem. editl. bd. The Collection Bldg., 1978—95, The Bottom Line, 1989—95, Internet and Higher Edn., 1998—99, The Univ. Ariz. Press, 1992—. Vol. Peace Corps, Barbados, West Indies, 1965—67. Named Outstanding Alumnus, Coll. Libr. and Info. Sci., U. Ky., 1989; recipient Miriam Dudley Bibliographic Instruction Libr. of Yr. award, 1991, Academic Libr. of Yr., 1992, Pres.'s award, Ariz. Ednl. Media Assn., 1993, YWCA Tucson Outstanding Women of 1992: A Women on the Move award, 1992, Ariz. Libr. of Yr. award, 2000. Mem.: ALA (councilor 1983—93, exec. bd. dirs. 1985—93, treas. 1988—93, endowment trustee 1988—93, endowment campaign com. 1989—93, pres. adv. com. 1993—96, legis. com. 1994—96, nominations com. 1997, Lippincott award com. 1997, spectrum scholarship com. 1998—2002, endowment trustee 2001—, chair com. accreditation 2002—03, libr. and outreach svcs. adv. com. 1997-99, chair 1997-98, Elizabeth Futas Catalyst Change award 2002, Equality award 2003, Loleta Fyan award Jury 2003—04), Ctr. Rsch. Librs. (budget and fin. com. 1994—2001, exec. com., bd. dirs. 1998—, treas. 1999—2000, vice chair, bd. dirs. 2001—03, chair, bd. dirs. 2003), Ariz. State Libr. Assn., Assn. Coll. Rsch. Librs. (bd. dirs. 1978—84, mem. exec. com. 1981—84, pres. 1982—83, Planning Com. 1993—95, chair nat. conf. planning com. 1995—97, Excellence Acad. Librs. award 2001), Assn. Rsch. Librs. (chair com. stats. and measurement 1994—2003, bd. dirs. 1997—2001, mem. steering com. Scholarly Pub. and Acad. Resource Coalition 1998—2001, mem. govt. documents digitization project work group 2004—, info. policies com. 2004—). Office: U Arizona Main Libr 1510 E University Blvd Tucson AZ 85721-0055

STOFFLET, MARY KIRK, museum curator, writer; b. Long Branch, N.J., Dec. 23, 1942; d. Norman Kirk and Virginia (Birdsall) S. BA in Art History, Skidmore Coll., 1964; MA in Art History, NYU, 1969. Coord. intern program Fine Arts Museums of San Francisco, 1977-80; asst. curator San Francisco Internat. Airport, 1982-85; edn. curator San Diego Mus. Art, 1985-88, modern art curator, 1988-97, asst. dir. edn. and publs. San Francisco Airport Mus., 1998—. Editor newsletter Western Assn. Art Museums, Oakland, Calif., 1974-77; contbg. editor Artweek, Oakland, 1974-81, Images & Issues, L.A., 1980-85; author, coordinating editor (exhbn. catalog) California Cityscapes, 1991; essayist, coordinating editor (exhbn. catalog) Latin American Drawings Today, 1991; author (exhbn. catalogs) Dr. Seuss From Then to Now, 1987, Deborah Butterfield, 1996; editor (book) Correspondence Art, 1984. Rockefeller/NEA fellow in mus. edn., 1975-76; recipient Critic's Grant, NEA, 1981. Mem. MLA, Internat. Assn. Art Critics, Am. Assn. Museums, Coll. Art Assn., ArtTable. Avocation: writing mystery novels. Office: San Francisco Airport Mus 1766 El Camino Real Burlingame CA 94010-3206

STOHL, ESTHER A. senior citizen advocate; b. Olympia, Wash., Apr. 13, 1919; d. James Vernon and Anna Marie (Rixe) Snodgrass; m. Edwin F. Crowell, Sept. 4, 1938 (div. Apr. 1958); children: John Steven Crowell, Charles Edwin Crowell; m. Donald L. Stohl, Oct. 16, 1960 (dec. 1983). Grad. high sch., Olympia. Asst. to sales mgr. Ga.-Pacific Plywood, Olympia, 1937-41, 46-54; adminstrv. asst. Wash. Fedn. State Employees, Olympia, 1954-79; senate healthcare com. aide Wash. State Legislature, Olympia, 1980; office mgr. Sr. Citizens Lobby, Olympia, 1980-83, 84-89; office asst. Wash. State Ret. Tchrs. Assn., Olympia, 1989-95. Pres. Srs. Educating Srs., Olympia, 1984-96; chmn. Area Agy. on Aging Adv. Coun., 1991-92. Author, editor Srs. Educating Srs. jour., 1984-96. Consumer advocate Wash. State Long Term Care Commn., Olympia, 1989-90. Mem. AFSCME (life), Wash. Fedn. State Employees (life), Am. Assn. Ret. Persons (lobbyist 1988-94), Sr. Citizens Lobby Wash., Ret. Pub. Employees Wash. Democrat. Lutheran. Avocations: reading, cooking, gardening, visiting in nursing homes. Home: 1347 Pear St NE Olympia WA 98506-3945

STOHLER, CHRISTIAN S. dental educator, dean; DMD, U. Bern, Switzerland, 1972, DrMedDent, 1975. Cert. in oral surgery U. Bern, 1976, in prosthodontics U. Bern, 1979. Vis. asst. prof. U. Mich., 1979—81; assoc. prof. prosthodontics U. Bern, 1981—83; vis. assoc. prof. U. Mich. Sch. Dentistry, 1983—84, assoc. prof., 1984—90, prof., 1990—95; rsch. scientist Ctr. for Human Growth and Devel., U. Mich., 1991—98; dir. rsch. U. Mich. Sch. Dentistry, 1994—97; chair dept. biologic and material sci. U. Mich., 1995—2003, William R. Mann prof., 1997—2002, Robert and Natalie Roberts prof., 2002—03; dean Balt. Coll. Dental Surgery, U. Md., 2003—. Mem. bd. scientific counselors Nat. Inst. Dental and Craniofacial Rsch., 2000—. Assoc. editor: Journal of Orofacial Pain. Office: U Maryland Baltimore Coll Dental Surgery 666 W Baltimore St Baltimore MD 21201

STOHR, DONALD J. federal judge; b. Sedalia, Mo., Mar. 9, 1934; s. Julius Leo and Margaret Elizabeth (McGaw) Stohr; m. Mary Ann Kuhlman, July 31, 1957; 5 children. BS, St. Louis U., 1956, JD, 1958. Bar: Mo. 1958, U.S. Dist. Ct. (ea. dist.) Mo. 1958, U.S. Ct. Appeals (8th cir.) 1966, U.S. Supreme Ct. 1969. Assoc. Hocker Goodwin & MacGreevy, St. Louis, 1958-63, 66-69; asst. counselor St. Louis County, 1963-65, counselor, 1965-66; U.S. atty. Ea. Dist. Mo., St. Louis, 1973-76; ptnr. Thompson & Mitchell, St. Louis, 1969-73, 76-92; judge U.S. Dist. Ct. (ea. dist.) Mo., St. Louis, 1992—. Mem. ABA, Mo. Bar Assn., Am. Judicature Soc., St. Louis Met. Bar Assn. Office: 111 S 10th St Rm 16 182 Saint Louis MO 63102

STOIA, VIOREL G. life underwriter; b. Aberdeen, S.D., Feb. 13, 1924; s. John and Seana (Biliboca) S.; m. Donna Marie Maurseth Stoia, Sept. 10, 1949; children: Marsha Jo, Nancy Kay, Gregory Allen, Thomas John, James Vincent. BBA, U. Minn., 1949; D in Pub. Svc. (hon.), No. State U., 2002. CLU, ChFC, Am. Coll. Sr. agt. Northwestern Mut. Life, Milw. Co-founder, chmn. bd. Student Loan Fin. Corp., 1978—2003; co-founder, mng. ptnr. Tel Serv, 1983—97; co-founder Northwest Regional Health and Fitness Ctr., 1999—. Co-founder, pres. Northeastern Mental Health Ctr., 1957-59, North Plains Hospice, 1980-84; sec. Edn. Asst. Corp., 1978-97; bd. dirs. S.D. Crippled Children's Hosp., Avera Health Sys., 1996-2003; trustee Aberdeen YMCA, 1969-73, St. Luke's Hosp., 1969-96; co-founder, trustee Northern State U. Found., 1972-99; co-founder Great Plains Edn. Found., 1999—, Aberdeen Downtown Assn., 1999, Blackstone Devel. Corp., 2000. USN, C.P.O., 1942-46. Named Outstanding Civic Leader of Am., 1967; recipient, Jefferson award Nat. Inst. of Pub. Svc., Sioux Falls, 1980, George award Aberdeen C. of C., Aberdeen, 1979, 94, Gov.'s award for Excellence in Econ. Devel., 2000, Disting. Trustee award S.D. Assn. Healthcare Orgns., 2002. Mem. Aberdeen Devel. Corp. (pres. 1972-87), Aberdeen Jr. C. of C. (pres. 1956), S.D. Soc. CLU's (co-founder, pres. 1958-59), Nat. Assn. Life Underwriters, Aberdeen Dist. Life Underwriters (pres. 1953-54), S.D. Assn. Life Underwriters (pres. 1959-60), Million Dollar Round Table (life), Moccasin Creek Country Club (v.p. 1969-75). Republican. Roman Catholic. Avocations: jogging, hunting, reading. Home: 1022 N Main St Aberdeen SD 57401-2426 Office: Stoia Kusler & Assoc PO Box 98 304 1/2 S Main St Aberdeen SD 57401-4146 E-mail: stoia@nvc.net.

STOIBER, CARLTON RAY, nuclear law consultant, retired federal official; b. Vallejo, Calif., July 5, 1942; s. Raymond F. and Grace (Fairhurst) S.; m. Susanne Alexander, Sept. 10, 1966. BA summa cum laude, U. Colo., 1964, LLB, 1969; diploma cum laude, Hague Acad. Internat. Law, 1975. Bar: Colo.1969, D.C.1970, U.S. Supreme Ct. 1973. Atty. U.S. Dept. Justice, Washington, 1969-71, dir. Office of Indian Rights, 1972-74; asst. gen. counsel U.S. NRC, Washington, 1975-80, U.S. Arms Control and Disarmament Agy., Washington, 1980-81; dir. Office Nuclear Export Control U.S. Dept. State, Washington, 1981-85, dir. Office Nuclear Non-Proliferation Policy, 1988-91, dir. Office Nuclear Tech. and Safeguards, 1991-93; counselor U.S. Mission to UN Agys., Vienna, Austria, 1985-88; dir. Internat. Programs Internat. Programs USNRC, 1993-99; cons. Sci. Applications Internat. Corp., 1999—. Rhodes scholar, 1964, Norlin award for disting. achievement U. Colo., 1994. Mem. Reform Club, Am. Soc. Internat. Law, Phi Beta Kappa. Avocations: cartooning and caricaturing, mountain climbing, birding.

STOIBER, SUSANNE A. health science organization administrator; BA, MPA, U. Colo.; MS, London Sch. Econs. Principal analyst for health care fin. programs Congressional Budget Office; adminstr. of clinical research Nat. Inst. of Health; dir. divsn. soc. and econ. studies NRC US Dept. HHS, 1990-94, various sr. positions, 1994—98; exec. officer Inst. Medicine, 1998—. Contbr. articles to profl. jours. Recipient NIH Directors Award, 1985, Presidential Rank Award for lifetime achievement in Senior Exec. Service. Office: Inst Medicine 500 5th St NW Washington DC 20418-0007 Fax: 908-771-8618.*

STOICHEFF, BORIS PETER, physicist, researcher; b. Bitol, Macedonia, June 1, 1924; s. Peter and Vasilka (Tonna) S.; m. Lillian Joan Ambridge, May 15, 1954; 1 child, Richard Peter. BSc, U. Toronto, 1947, MA, 1948, PhD, 1950, DSc (hon.), 1994, U. Skopje, Macedonia, 1981, York U., 1982, U. Windsor, 1989. McKee-Gilchrist postdoctoral fellow U. Toronto, Canada, 1950-51; postdoctoral fellow NRC Can., Canada, 1951-53, sr. rsch. officer, 1954-64; vis. scientist MIT, 1963-64; prof. physics U. Toronto, Canada, 1964-89, univ prof., 1977-89, univ. prof. emeritus, 1989—, chmn. engring. sci., 1972-77, H.L. Welsh lectr., 1984; sr. fellow Massey Coll., 1979—; exec. dir. Laser and Lightwave Rsch. Ctr., Canada, 1988-91. Mem. NRC Can., 1977-83; govt. appointee to coun. Assn. Profl. Engr. Ont., 1985-91; vis. sci. Stanford U., 1978; Walter E. Kaskan lectr. SUNY, Binghamton, 1980; Elizabeth Laird Meml. lectr. U. Western Ont., 1985; UK/Can. Rutherford lectr., 1989; v.p. Internat. Union Pure and Applied Physics, 1994-96. Author: Gerhard Herzberg: An Illustrious Life in Science, 2002; contbr. articles to profl. jours. Decorated officer Order of Can., 1982; I.W. Killam scholar, 1977-79; Geoffrey Frew fellow Australian Acad. Sci., 1980. Fellow Royal Soc. Can. (co-fgn. sec. 1995-2000, Henry Marshall Tory medal 1989), Royal Soc. London, Am. Phys. Soc., Optical Soc. Am. (pres. 1976, William F. Meggers award 1981, Frederic Ives medal 1983, Disting. Svc. award 2002), Indian Acad. Sci. (hon.), Macedonian Acad. Sci. and Arts (hon.), Am. Acad. Arts and Sci. (fgn. hon.); mem. Can. Assn. Physicists (pres. 1984, Gold medal 1974). Achievements include develop. of techniques for high resolution Raman spectroscopy of gases and determination of geometrical structures many molecules; use of lasers in spectroscopic investigations including Brillouin and Raman scattering and two photon absorption; observation of stimulated Raman absorption and stimulated Brillouin scattering resulting in generation of intense hypersonic waves in solids; use of Brillouin spectra to measure elastic constants of rare gas crystals; generation of tunable coherent VUV radiation for use in atomic and molecular spectroscopy. Home: 66 Collier St Apt 6B Toronto ON Canada M4W 1L9 Office: U Toronto Dept Physics Toronto ON Canada M5S 1A7 Office Phone: 416-978-2948.

STOKAN, LANA J. LADD, state legislator; b. El Dorado, Ark., Sept. 5, 1958; children: Garrett, Adair. BA, MA in Secondary Edn. and History, So. Ill. U. Rep. dist. 76 State of Mo. Office: 625 Wilshire Dr Florissant MO 63033-3824 also: State Capital Rm 305A Jefferson City MO 65101

STOKELY, JOHN E. food distribution executive; Cfo Richfood Holdings, Inc., Richmond, Va., 1990-93, v.p. fin., adminstrn., 1993-95, pres., 1995—, CEO, 1997-1999, chmn., 2000, also bd. dirs. Dir. Performance Food Group Co. Office: Richfood Holdings Inc 4860 Cox Rd Ste 300 Glen Allen VA 23060-9250 also: 8258 Richfood Rd Mechanicsville VA 23116-2008

STOKES, ARCH, lawyer, writer; b. Atlanta, Sept. 2, 1946; s. Mack B. and Rose Stokes; m. Maggie Mead; children: Jennifer Jean, Austin Christopher, Susannah Rose, Travis, Emmarose. BA, Emory U., 1967, JD, 1970. Bar: Ga. 1970, U.S. Dist. Ct. (no. dist.) Ga. 1970, U.S. Ct. Appeals (5th cir.) Ga. 1970, U.S. Ct. Mil. Appeals 1971, U.S. Ct. Appeals (9th cir.) Ga. 1980, (2d cir.) Ga. 1990, U.S. Supreme Ct. 1981, U.S. Dist. Ct. (no. dist.) Calif. 1981, U.S. Ct. Appeals (11th cir.) Calif. 1982, U.S. Ct. Appeals (7th cir.) Calif. 1986, U.S. Ct. Appeals (1st cir.) Calif. 1992, U.S. Ct. Appeals (8th cir.) Calif. 1991, U.S. Dist. Ct. (no. dist.) N.Y. 1991, U.S. Dist. Ct. (ea. dist.) Mich. 1986. Ptnr. Stokes Lazarus & Carmichael, Atlanta, 1972-92, Stokes & Murphy, Atlanta, 1992—, San Diego, Pitts., 1992—, Las Vegas, Ithaca, NY, 2001—. Author: The Wage & Hour Handbook, 1978, rev. edit., 2000, The Equal Employment Opportunity Handbook, 1979, The Collective Bargaining Handbook, 1981. Founding mem. adv. bd. William F. Harrah Hotel Coll., U. Nev., Las Vegas, also vis. spkr.; vis. spkr. Cornell U., Johnson and Wales U., U. Houston, Ga. State U. Recipient Hal Holbrook award Internat. Platform Assn., 1990. Mem. ABA, ATLA, Union Internat. des Avocats, Internat. Soc. Hospitality Cons., Confrérie de la Chaîne des Rotisseurs, Am. Hotel and Lodging. Office: Stokes & Murphy PC 3593 Hemphill St College Park GA 30337-0468 E-mail: astokes@stokesmurphy.com.

STOKES, B. R. retired transportation consultant; b. Anadarko, Okla., Feb. 20, 1924; s. Robert Allan and Ethel Nan (James) S.; m. Joan Pringle, Oct. 22, 1950; children: Timothy, Leigh, Lindsey, Celia. Student, U. Okla., 1941-44; BA, U. Calif., Berkeley, 1947. Reporter, writer Oakland (Calif.) Tribune, 1946-58; dir. info. San Francisco Bay Area Rapid Transit Dist., 1958-61, asst. gen. mgr., 1961-63, gen. mgr., 1963-74; exec. v.p. Am. Public Transit Assn., Washington, 1974-80; sr. v.p. internat. ATE Mgmt. and Service Co., Inc., 1980-95. Dir. gen. Saudi Arabian Public Transport Co., 1980-81 Served with USNR, 1942-46. Recipient Salzberg medal Syracuse U., 1975; inductee Am. Pub. Transit Assn. Transit Hall of Fame, 1996; Reid Found. fellow, 1954. Office: 1911 Fort Myer Dr Arlington VA 22209-1603

STOKES, CHARLES EUGENE, JR., wool merchant, textile executive; b. Temple, Tex., Oct. 11, 1926; s. Charles Eugene and Esther Annette (Lawlis) Stokes. BBA, U. Tex., 1948; MA, U. Tex., El Paso, 1968; PhD, Tulane U., 1974. Apprentice, then asst. wool buyer Conant & Co., Inc., Boston, 1946-48; wool buyer and dir. Stokes & Co., Ltd., Puno, Peru, 1949-55; pres., treas. Stokes Bros., Inc., New Braunfels, Tex., 1955-59; mng. ptnr. Stokes Bros. & Co., Peru, Uruguay and San Antonio, 1959-94; owner Merino Ranch, Ft. McKavett, Tex., 1994—, Stokes Bros. & Co., Ft. McKavett, Tex., 1994—; pres., treas. Stokeswool LLC, Ft. McKavett. Wool mktg. and processing advisor Ministry Agr., La Paz, Bolivia, 1961—63. Author: (book) The Amazon Bubble: World Rubber Monopoly, 2000. Recipient Fulbright fellowship, Tulane U., Bolivia and Brazil, 1970—71. Mem.: Sons Rep. of Tex. (life), Phi Alpha Theta. Republican. Episcopalian. Avocations: sheep and cattle ranching, Latin American history. Home: Merino Ranch PO Box 7 Fort Mc Kavett TX 76841-0007 Office: Stokeswool LLC 7029 FM 864 at FM 1674 Fort Mc Kavett TX 76841

STOKES, CONNIE, state legislator; m. James Stokes; children: Bernard, Jason, Marcus. AA, Art Inst. Atlanta; BBA, Ga. State U. Owner, pres. First Choice Travel Agy.; co-owner Remax Pacesetters Real Estate; mem. Ga. Senate, Atlanta; vice chmn. consumer affairs com.; mem. banking and fin. instn., health and human svcs. coms.; also ins. and labor, judiciary, appropriations coms.; mem. state commn. on family violence. Mem. bd. dirs. Regional Leadership Found.; mem. women's coun. NAREB; active St. Phillip's AME Ch., DeKalb. Recipient Hall of Fame award for Cmty. Svc. Mem. Coalition 100 Black Women, Women's Polit. Caucus, Nat. Polit. Congress Black Women (devel. coord.), Leadership DeKalb, Leadership Atlanta. Democrat. Office: Rm 319 Legis Office Bldg Atlanta GA 30334 also: PO Box 360350 Decatur GA 30036-0350

STOKES, HENRY ARTHUR, journalist; b. Jacksonville, Fla., Dec. 9, 1944; s. Henry Jasper and Waneta Marian (Lord) S.; m. Carolyn Elizabeth Morley, Aug. 6, 1966; children: Elizabeth, Virginia, Katherine. AA, St. Johns River Jr. Coll., Palatka, Fla., 1966; BS in Journalism with high honors, U. Fla., 1969. Reporter Daytona Beach (Fla.) News-Jour., 1966, Palatka (Fla.) Daily News, 1966-69, Fla. Times-Union, Jacksonville, 1969-71, night city editor, 1972; various editing positions Detroit News, 1972-88; asst. mng. editor Comml. Appeal, Memphis, 1988-92, mng. editor, 1992—2002, dir. adminstrn. and planning, 2003—. Mem. Memphis Literacy Coun., 1989-97, chmn., 1993, 94; bd. dirs. Friends Memphis/Shelby Co. Libr., 1991-2003, Found. for the Libr., 2003—; mem. pres. adv. coun. LeMoyne-Owen Coll., 1992-2000; bd. dirs. Memphis Downtown YMCA, 2001—. Recipient Emig award Coll. Journalism U. Fla., 1970. Mem. Soc. Profl. Journalists, Tenn. Press Assn. (bd. dirs. 2003-04, v.p. 2004—), The Egyptians, Rotary (bd. dirs. Memphis chpt. 2002-04). Episcopalian. Avocations: ornithology, fly fishing. Office: Comml Appeal 495 Union Ave Memphis TN 38103-3221 Office Phone: 901-529-2301. Business E-Mail: stokes@commercialappeal.com.

STOKES, JAMES PORTER, II, music educator; b. Spartanburg, S.C., Dec. 10, 1951; s. James Porter and Marjorie (Ussery) Stokes; m. Barbara Hill, Oct. 11, 1975; children: James Porter Stokes III, Joshua Preston. BA in Music Edn., U. S.C., 1975, MusM, 1977; D of Musical Arts, U. Cin., 1993. Instr. choral Lakeview Mid. Sch., Greenville, SC, 1978—80, J.L. Mann H.S., Greenville, 1980—81; faculty Music North Greenville Coll., Tigerville, SC, 1980—85, Erskine Coll, Due West, SC, 1988—98, Presbyn. Coll., Clinton, SC, 1998—. Chancel choir dir. 1st Presbyn. Ch., Greenwood, SC, 2003—. Artistic dir. Augusta Choral Soc., 1999—. Mem.: S.C. Music Educators Assn., Music Educators Nat. Conf., Nat. Assn. Schs. Music, Nat. Assn. Tchrs. Singing, Am. Choral Dirs. Assn. (S.C. pres. 1993—95), Presbyn. Assn. Musicians. Home: 105 York St Clinton SC 29325 Office: Presbyterian Coll 503 S Broad St Clinton SC 29325 Office Phone: 864-833-8468.

STOKES, JAMES SEWELL, lawyer; b. Englewood, N.J., Jan. 24, 1944; s. James Sewell III and Doris Mackey (Smith) S.; m. Esther Moger, Aug. 19, 1967; children: Jessica Neale, Elizabeth Sewell BA, Davidson (N.C.) Coll.,

1966; LLB, Yale U., 1969. Bar: Ga. 1969. Asst. to gen. counsel Office Gen. Counsel of the Army, Washington, 1969-72; assoc. Alston, Miller & Gaines, Atlanta, 1972-77; ptnr. Alston & Bird (previously Alston, Miller & Gaines), Atlanta, 1977—, chmn. environ. group, 1987—96, chmn. bus. devel. com., 1983-85, 93-94, 96—; mem. ptnr.'s com. Alston & Bird, Atlanta, 1995-98; chmn., 1998. Speaker on environ. matters to various seminars and meetings; mem. Gov.'s Environ. Adv. Coun., 1991—, chmn., 1997-99; chmn. Gov.'s Conf. on Pollution Prevention and the Environment, 1997. Contbr. articles to profl. jours. Mem. Metro Atlanta Chamber Clean Water Initiative, 2000, chair Metro Atlanta Chamber Water Com., 2002; mem. Trust for Public Land Ga. Bd., 1986-91; co-chmn. Spotlight on Ga. Artists V, 1986; mem. City of Atlanta Zoning Rev. Bd., 1978-85, chmn., 1984-85; bd. dirs. Brookwood Hills Civic Assn., 1975-77, pres., 1977; bd. dirs. Nexus Contemporary Arts Ctr., Atlanta, 1987-92, vice chmn. capital campaign, 1989, chmn. nominating com., 1988, chmn. fundraising com., 1987-88; bd. dirs. Butler St. YMCA N.W. br., 1973-75, Dynamo Swim Club, 1988-91, Arts Festival Atlanta, 1994-98; trustee Inst. Continuing Legal Edn., Athens, 1980-81, Trinity Sch., Atlanta, 1988, 97—, Charles Loridans Found., 1994—; mem. session Trinity Presbyn. Ch., 1986-89, 97—, clk. of session, 1988-89, chmn. cmty. concerns com., 1987-88, chmn. pers. com., 1989-90, 99—, chmn. assoc. pastor search com., 1991-92; bd. dirs. The Hambidge Ctr., 2000—; bd. dirs. Park Pride, 1992; bd. dirs. Ga. C. of C., 1998—, chmn. environ. com., 1987-92, environ. legal counsel, 1981-87; mem. spl. program Leadership Atlanta, 1979-80, Leadership Ga., 1985; mem. Ga. bd. advisors Trust for Pub. Land, 1986-91. Capt. U.S. Army, 1969-72. Decorated D.S.M.; recipient Spl. award Atlanta chpt. AIA, 1988, Mayor Andrew Young, 1985. Mem. ABA (natural resources sect.), State Bar Ga. (chmn. environ. law sect. 1979-82), Atlanta Bar Assn., City of Atlanta Hist. Preservation (policy steeering com. 1989), Ga. C. of C. (bd. dirs. 1998—), Atlanta C. of C. (water resources task force 1982-87, solid waste task force 1989, air quality task force 1993-97, environ. affairs com. 1998—), Ga. Indsl. Developers Assn. (hazardous waste com. 1983-84), Phi Beta Kappa, Omicron Delta Kappa. Avocations: swimming, bird watching, community activities. Home: 129 Palisades Rd NE Atlanta GA 30309-1532 Office: Alston & Bird One Atlantic Ctr 1201 W Peachtree St LLP Atlanta GA 30309-3424

STOKES, JEANETT BARRETT, editor; Mng. editor Gannett News Svc., Arlington, Va., 2000—. Office: USA Today 7950 Jones Branch Dr Mc Lean VA 22108-0001

STOKES, JEFFERY DAVID, Spanish language educator; b. Ogden, Utah, July 25, 1947; s. Arch Junior Stokes and Dauna Gayle Stokes Seager; m. Jill L. Parker Nagy, May 12, 1998; children: Aaron David, Jana Coates, Kimberly Kay Nagy, Emily Lewis, Julianne Baker. BA, Weber State Coll., Ogden, Utah, 1975; MA, U. of Utah, 1977; PhD, Ind. U., 1981. Asst. prof. of Spanish Millikin U., Decatur, Ill., 1980—85; prof. of Spanish Weber State U., Ogden, Utah, 1985—. Founder, pres., exec. bd. mem. Golden Spike Empire Lang. Alliance, Ogden, Utah, 1987—2001; oral proficiency interviewer Am. Coun. on the Tchg. of Fgn. Langs., Yonkers, NY, 1986—92, Utah State Office of Edn., Salt Lake City, 1989—2003. Contbr. articles to profl. jours. Sgt. U.S. Army, 1971—74. Mem.: Utah Fgn. Lang. Assn (pres.-elect 2003—04, pres. 2004—), Am. Assn. of Tchrs. of Spanish and Portuguese, Am. Coun. on the Tchg. of Fgn. Langs. Avocations: camping, hiking, music. Home: 1386 E 5875 St Ogden UT 84405 Office: Weber State Universtiy 1403 University Cir Ogden UT 84408-1403 Personal E-mail: jstokes1@weber.edu. E-mail: jstokes1@weber.edu.

STOKES, JIM D. psychotherapist; b. Koseiuske, Miss., Sept. 7, 1941; s. Louis Franklin and Gurtha Bell Stokes; children: Diana, Jim Jr. BME, Delta State U., 1967, MEd, 1970; EdD, East Tex. State U., 1973. Instr. psychology, rsch. asst. Delta State U., Cleveland, Miss., 1965—68; instr. psychology East Tex. State U., Commerce, 1970—73; dir. psychol. testing Sulphur Springs Pub. Schs., 1972—; asst. prof. psychology Sam Houston State U., 1970—73; pvt. practice Arlington, Tex., 1977—80; asst. dir. psychol. svcs. and hostage negotiations Houston Police Dept., 1982—90; asst. prof. Houston C.C., 1984—88; pvt. practice Houston, 1998—2003; dir. psychol. svcs. Airline House, Houston, 1998—2003, Turning Point Ctr., Houston, 2003—. Band dir. Lexington Public Schs., Miss., 1961—63, Phila. Public Schs., 1963—64, Newton Public Schs., 1964—65; choir dir. Yale St. Bapt. Ch., Cleveland, Miss., 1965—68, Elkins Lake Bapt. Ch., 1973—76; adv. hostage negotiation Houston Police Dept., 1983—90; bd. mem. Airline House, 2000—03. Author: Survival Guide to Step-Parenting, 1993. Mem.: Tex. Personnel and Guidance (TPGA). Republican. Baptist. Avocations: golf, racquetball, power walking. Office: The Turning Point Ctr 1701 Jacquelyn Dr Houston TX 77055

STOKES, JOHN LEMACKS, II, clergyman, retired university official; b. Songdo, Korea, Aug. 23, 1908; s. Marion Boyd and Florence Pauline (Davis) S.; m. Alda Grey Beaman, June 20, 1933; children: John Lemacks III, Mary Anne (foster dau.). AB, Asbury Coll., 1930; postgrad., Asbury Theol. Sem., 1930-31; M.Div., Duke U., 1932; PhD, Yale U., 1936; LL.D., Pfeiffer Coll., 1975. Ordained to ministry Meth. Ch., 1931. Pastor Meth. chs., Randleman, Franklin and Elkin, N.C., 1936-45, Rock Hill, St. John's, S.C., 1945-50; sec. religion higher edn., div. ednl. instns. Bd. Edn. Meth. Ch., Nashville, 1950-53, del. jurisdictional conf., 1952, 60, 68; pres. Pfeiffer Coll., Misenheimer, N.C., 1953-68; exec. sec. Quadrennial Emphasis, United Meth. Ch., 1968-69; asso. dir. N.C. Bd. Higher Edn., Raleigh, 1969-71, acting dir., 1972; asso. v.p. U. N.C., Chapel Hill, 1972-75, spl. asst. in acad. affairs, 1976-93. Dir. numerous out-of-state programs in health professions, 1972-94; mem. Govs. Commn. Citizens for Better Schs. N.C., 1956-60, N.C. Com. on Nursing and Patient Care, 1956-64, N.C. Higher Edn. Facilities Edn., 1964-68, N.C. Com. on Drug Abuse, 1970-76, N.C. Com. on Aero. Edn., 1971-86; chmn. N.C. adv. com. Farmers Home Adminstrn., 1967-69, Marine Sci. Coun., 1969-72; dir. N.C. Inst. Undergrad. Curricular Reform, 1972-78; coordinator Fort Bragg-Pope Grad. Program, 1973-77; adv. com. Nat. Four-year Servicemens Opportunity Coll., 1973-78. Author: Recollections of a Nonagenarian, 2003; contbr. articles to profl. jours. Bd. dirs. ARC, 1940-48, YMCA, 1946-50; vice chmn. Western N.C. Conf. Bd. Missions, 1960-64; trustee Asbury Coll., 1945-51. Recipient Outstanding Svc. award N.C. Optometric Assn., 1988, Merit award So. Coun. Optometrists, 1990. Mem. Aircraft Owners and Pilots Assn., U.S. Lawn Tennis Assn., Am. Assn. Higher Edn., So. Srs. Golf Assn., NEA, Nat. Christian Edn. Assn., So. Philos. Soc., Woman's Soc. Christian Svc., Echo Farms Country Club, Masons, Shriners, Rotary, Civitan, Lions. Address: 2298 S 41st St Unit 309 Wilmington NC 28403-5407

STOKES, KIMBERLY ANN, counselor; b. Wilkes-Barre, Pa., Sept. 17, 1972; d. Leonard Robert and Nancy Joan Tuzinski; m. Richard Douglas Stokes, Oct. 12, 1996. BA, Kings Coll., 1994; MS in Cmty. Counseling, U. Scranton, 2000. Nat. cert. counselor. Psychologist Allied Svcs. John Heinz Inst. Rehab. Medicine, Wilkes-Barre, 1999—. Mem.: ACA, Pa. Counseling Assn. Home: 276 Jackson Rd Shavertown PA 18708 Office: Allied Svcs John Heinz Inst Rehab Medicine 150 Mundy St Wilkes Barre PA 18702

STOKES, LORI, newscaster; Attended, Ohio State U.; grad., Howard U. Weekend anchor, med. reporter CBS affiliate WCIA-TV, Champaign-Urbana, Ill.; weekend anchor CBS affiliate WBTC, Charlotte, NC, 1988—90; reporter Fox station WBFF, Balt., 1991—92; anchor evening news for 6pm and 11pm broadcasts WJLA-TV, Wash., DC, 1992—96. Achievements include credited with breaking the Gianni Versace's murder story. Office: 7 Lincoln Sq New York NY 10023

STOKES, LOUIS, lawyer, former congressman; b. Cleveland, Ohio, Feb. 23, 1925; s. Charles and Louise (Stone) S.; m. Jeanette Francis, Aug. 21, 1960; children: Shelley, Louis C., Angela, Lorene. Student, Case Western Res. U., 1946-48; JD, Cleve. Marshall Law Sch., 1953; 26 hon. doctorate degrees, 1953-2001. Bar: Ohio 1953. Mem. 91st-105th Congresses from 11th (formerly 21st) Ohio dist., Washington, 1969-99; sr. counsel Squire, Sanders and Dempsey, Washington, 1999—. Former chmn. appropriations subcom. on Vets. Affairs, HUD & Ind. Agys.; sr. vis. scholar Mandel Sch. Applied Social Scis. Case Western Res. U., 1999—. Served with AUS, 1943-46. Decorated Congl. DSM; recipient numerous awards for civic activities including Disting. Svc. award Cleve. br. NAACP; Certificate of Appreciation U.S. Commn. on Civil Rights. Mem. ABA, ACLU, Cuyahoga County Bar Assn., Cleve. Bar Assn., Urban League, Am. Legion, Masons, Kappa Alpha Psi. Democrat. Office: Squire Sanders & Dempsey 1201 Pennsylvania Ave Washington DC 20044-0407 Office Phone: 202-626-6697. Business E-Mail: lstokes@ssd.com.

STOKES, MACK BOYD (MARION BOYD STOKES), bishop; b. Wonsan, Korea, Dec. 21, 1911; arrived in U.S., 1959; s. Marion Boyd and Florence Pauline (Davis) Stokes; m. Ada Rose Yow, June 19, 1942; children: Marion Boyd III, Arch Yow, Elsie Pauline. Student, Seoul Fgn. High Sch., Korea; AB, Asbury Coll., 1932; BD, Duke, 1935; postgrad., Boston U. Sch. Theol., 1935-37, Harvard, 1936-37; PhD, Boston U., 1940; LLD, Lambuth U., Jackson, Tenn., 1963; DD, Millsaps Coll., 1974. Resident fellow systematic theology Boston U., 1936-38, Bowne fellow in philosophy, 1938-39; ordained to ministry Meth. Ch., deacon, 1938, elder, 1940; vis. prof. philosophy and religion Ill. Wesleyan U., 1940-41; prof. Christian doctrine Candler Sch. Theology, Emory U., 1941-56, asso. dean, Parker prof. systematic theology, 1956-72, chmn. exec. com. div. of religion of grad. sch., 1956-72; acting dean Candler Sch. Theology, Emory U. (Candler Sch.), 1968-69; bishop-in-residence Peachtree Rd. United Meth. Ch. Atlanta, 1988—. Faculty mem. Inst. Theol. Studies Oxford U., 1958; del. Meth. Ecumenical Conf., 1947, 52, 61, 71, Holston, Gen. confs., S.E. Jurisdictional Conf., 1956, 60, 64, 68, 72; chmn. com. ministry Gen. Conf. Meth. Ch., 1960; nat. com. Nature Unity We Seek, 1956—; mem. gen. com. ecumenical affairs theol. study com. United Meth. Ch., 1968—72, com. on Cath.-Meth. rels., 1969—, bishop, 1972—. Author: (book) Major Methodist Beliefs, 1956, Major Methodist Beliefs, rev. 15th edit., 1990, The Evangelism of Jesus, 1960, The Epic of Revelation, 1961, Our Methodist Heritage, 1963, Crencas Fundamentals Dos Methodistas, 1964, Study Guide on the Teachings of Jesus, 1970, The Bible and Modern Doubt, 1970, Major United Methodist Beliefs, 1971, Major United Methodist Beliefs, Korean transl., 1977, Major United Methodist Beliefs, rev. with added study guide, 1998, The Holy Spirit and Christian Experience, 1975, The Holy Spirit and Christian Experience, Korean transl., 1985, Twelve Dialogues on John's Gospel, 1975, Jesus, The Master-Evangel, 1978, Can God See the Inside of an Apple?, 1979, Questions Asked by United Methodists, Philippine transl., 1980, The Bible in the Wesleyan Heritage, 1981, Respuestas A Preguntas Que Hacen Los Metodistas Unidos, 1983, The Holy Spirit in the Wesleyan Heritage, 1985, The Holy Spirit in the Wesleyan Heritage, Spanish transl., 1992, The Holy Spirit in the Wesleyan Heritage, Korean transl., 1992, Scriptural Holiness of the United Methodist Christian, 1988, Talking with God: A Guide of Prayer, 1989, Theology for Preaching, 1994, Questions and Answers about Life and Faith, 2000. Trustee Emory U., Millsaps Coll., Rust Coll., Wood Jr. Coll. Methodist. Home: PO Box 497 Waynesville NC 28786 *Faith in God and basic trust in people. Knowing the direction in which to go, and moving with divine assistance toward it with persistence, resourcefulness, imagination and patience.*

STOKES, PATRICK T. brewery company executive; b. Washington, 1942; married. BS, Boston Coll., 1964; MBA, Columbia U., 1966. Fin. analyst Shell Oil Co., 1966-67; v.p. materials acquisitions Anheuser-Busch Cos. Inc., St. Louis, 1979-81, v.p., group exec., 1981—; pres. Anheuser-Busch Inc., St. Louis, 1990—; COO Campbell Taggart Inc. (subs. Anheuser-Busch Cos. Inc.), Dallas, 1986-90, CEO, 1990—; pres. Anheuser-Busch Inc.; chmn. Anheuser-Busch Internat.; CEO, sr. exec. v.p. Anheuser-Busch Cos. Inc., 2000—02, pres., 2002—. Served to 1st lt. U.S. Army, 1967-69. Office: Anheuser-Bush Co Inc 1 Busch Place Saint Louis MO 63118-1852*

STOKES, PAUL MASON, lawyer; b. Miami Beach, Fla., July 16, 1946; s. Walter Johnson and Juanita (Hemperley) S.; m. Carol Crocker, Sept. 12, 1970; children: Macon Lanford, Walter Ashley, Mary Juanita. BA, Duke U., 1968; JD, U. Chgo., 1971. Bar: Fla. 1971. Law clerk to hon. Milton Pollack U.S. Dist. Ct. (so. dist.) N.Y., N.Y.C., 1971-72; assoc. Smathers and Thompson, Miami, Fla., 1972-77, ptnr., 1977-88, Kelley Drye & Warren L.L.P., Miami, 1988-99, Stokes McMillan & Maracini P.A., Miami, 1999—. Adj. prof. law U. Miami, Coral Gables, Fla., 1987-94; pub. defender City of Miami Springs, Fla., 1974, City of Hialeah, Fla., 1974-75. Mem. Code Enforcement Bd. Miami Springs, 1990-92; regent Trinity Internat. U., Deerfield, Ill., 1989-98; mem. Permanent Jud. Commn., Presbytery of Tropical Fla., 1997-2000; bd. dirs. Greater Miami Youth for Christ, 2000—. Fellow Am. Coll. Trust and Estate Coun.; mem. Dade County Bar Assn. (probate and guardianship ct. com. 1988—, bd. dirs. 1989-92, 94-2000, 2004—), Fla. Bar (cert. wills, trusts and estates), Phi Beta Kappa, Order of Coif. Democrat. Presbyterian. Office: Stokes McMillan & Marcini PA One SE 3d Ave Ste 1750 Miami FL 33131 Office Phone: 305-379-4008. E-mail: pstokes@smpalaw.com.

STOKES, ROBERT JAMES, retired materials scientist; b. Devizes, Wiltshire, Eng., Oct. 15, 1928; arrived in U.S., 1955; s. Ernest and Marie A.J. Stokes; m. Audrey Lovell Rogers, July 14, 1955; children: Neil, Sandra. BSc with honors, U. Bristol, Eng., 1952; PhD, U. Birmingham, Eng., 1955. Rsch. scientist, asst. prof. Univ. Calif., Berkeley, 1955—57; rsch. scientist Honeywell, Inc., Mpls., 1957—64, tech. mgr., 1965—82; sec. head NSF, Washington, 1982—84; staff scientist Honeywell, Inc., Mpls., 1986; vis. prof. U. Minn., Mpls., 1987—99; hon. prof. Warwick U., Coventry, England, 1988—98; vis. prof. N.C. State U., Raleigh, 1988—90; ret. Mem. adv. bd. Nat. Bur. Standards, Gaithersburg, Md., 1965—70; rsch. advisor U.S. Army Rsch. Office, Durham, NC, 1970—80; Ford Disting. vis. prof. Carnegie Mellon U., 1964—65; G.T. Piercy disting. vis. prof. U. Minn., 1987. Author: Fundamental of Interfacial Engineering, 1998; co-author: Ceramics Processing Engineering; editor: Jour. Am. Ceramic Soc., 1966—70; contbr. more than 60 articlees to profl. jours. Pres. Condominium Assn., Minnetonka, 1988—98. Mem.: Am. Ceramic Soc. (Sosman lectr. 1976). Avocations: travel, photography, golf, campanology. Home: 3000 St Albans Mill Rd #315 Minnetonka MN 55305

STOKES, SUSAN, political science educator; MA in Anthropology, Stanford U., 1985, MA in Polit. Sci., 1986, PhD, 1988. Assoc. prof. polit. sci. U. Chgo. Contbr. articles to profl. jours.; author: Social Movements and the State in Peru, 1995, Neoliberalism by Surprise in Latin America; editor: Political Support for Market Reforms in New Democracies, 2001; co-editor: Democracy, Accountability, and Representation. Recipient Guggenheim fellowship, 2003. Office: U Chgo Dept Polit Sci Pick Hall 414 5828 S University Ave Barkhamsted CT 06063

STOKKE, DIANE REES, lawyer; b. Kansas City, Mo., Jan. 29, 1951; d. William James and Marybeth (Smith) Rees; m. Larry Ernst Stokke, June 9, 1973; children: Michelle, Megan, Carly. AB magna cum laude, Gonzaga U., 1972; JD with high honors, U. Wash., 1976. Bar: Wash. 1976, U.S. Dist. Ct. (ea. dist.) Wash. 1976, U.S. Dist. Ct. (we. dist.) Wash. 1976, U.S. Ct. Appeals (9th cir.) 1980. Assoc. Preston, Thorgrimson, Ellis & Holman, Seattle, 1976-83; ptnr. Preston, Gates & Ellis LLP, Seattle, 1983—. Atty. Seattle Ctr. Found., 1977-83. Trustee Seattle Infant Devel. Ctr., 1984-86, Fremont Pub. Assn., 1994-2001, 03—. Gonzaga U. scholar, 1968. Mem. ABA, Wash. State Bar Assn. (spl. dist. counsel 1985-88), Seattle-King County Bar Assn., Wash. Women Lawyers, Order of Coif, Wash. Women Real Estate Lawyers, Am. Coll. of Mortgage Attys., Comml. Real Estate Women. Roman Catholic. Office: Preston Gates & Ellis LLP 925 Fourth Ave Ste 2900 Seattle WA 98104-1158 Office Phone: 206-623-7580. E-mail: dianes@prestongates.com.

STOKLOSA, GREGORY A. paper company executive; BS, U. Mich.; MA in Mgmt., Northwestern U. Various fin. positions Kraft Gen. Foods, Inc.; from asst. treas. global corp. fin. to exec. v.p., CFO RR Donnelley & Sons, Chgo., 1993—2000, exec. v.p., 2000—, CFO, 2000—. Office: RR Donnelley & Sons 77 West Wacker Drive Chicago IL 60601-1696

STOKOE, KENNETH H., II, civil engineer, educator; BSCE, U. Mich., 1966, MSCE, 1967, PhD, 1972. Jennie C. and Milton T. Graves chain in engring. U. Tex., Austin. Mem. NAE. Office: U Tex ECJ 9 227 Dept Civil Engring Austin TX 78712

STOKSTAD, MARILYN JANE, art history educator, curator; b. Lansing, Mich., Feb. 16, 1929; d. Olaf Lawrence and Edythe Marian (Gardiner) S. BA, Carleton Coll., 1950; MA, Mich. State U., 1953; PhD, U. Mich., 1957; postgrad., U. Oslo, 1951-52; LHD (hon.), Carleton Coll., 1997. Instr. U. Mich., Ann Arbor, 1956-58; mem. faculty U. Kans., Lawrence, 1958—, assoc. prof., 1961-66, prof., 1966-80, Univ. Disting. prof. art history, 1980-94, Judith Harris Murphy disting. prof. art, 1994—, dir. mus. art, 1961-67, research assoc., summers 1965-66, 67, 71, 72; assoc. dean Coll. Liberal Arts and Scis., U. Kans., 1972-76; research curator Nelson-Atkins Mus. Art, Kansas City, Mo., 1969-80, consultative curator medieval art, 1980—. Bd. dirs. Internat. Ctr. Medieval Art, 1972-75, 81-84, 88-96, v.p., 1990-93, pres., 1993-96, sr. advisor, 1996-97; cons., evaluator North Ctrl. Assn. Colls. and Univs., 1972—, commr.-at-large, 1984-89. Author: Santiago de Compostela, 1978, The Scottish World, 1981, Medieval Art, 1986, Art History, 1995, rev. edit., 1999, Art: A Brief History, 2000. Recipient Disting. Service award Alumni Assn. Carleton Coll., 1983, Kans. Gov.'s Arts award, 1997; Fulbright fellow, 1951-52; NEH grantee, 1967-68 Fellow AAUW; mem. AAUP (nat. coun. 1972-75), Archeol. Inst. Am. (pres. Kans. chpt. 1960-61), Midwest Coll. Art Conf. (pres. 1964-65), Coll. Art Assn. (bd. dirs. 1970-80, pres. 1978-80), Soc. Archtl. Historians (chpt. bd. dirs. 1971-73). E-mail: stokstad@ku.edu.

STOLARIK, M. MARK, history professor; b. St. Martin, Slovak Republic, Apr. 22, 1943; s. Imrich and Margita (Vavro) S.; m. Anne Helene Ivanco, June 15, 1968; children: Roman Andrej, Matthew Mark. BA, U. Ottawa, 1965, MA, 1967; PhD, U. Minn., 1974. Ast. prof. history Cleve. State U., 1972-76; hist. rschr. Nat. Mus. of Man, Ottawa, Ont., Can., 1977-78; pres. Balch Inst. for Ethnic Studies, Phila., 1979-91; prof. history, chair dept. Slovak history and culture U. Ottawa, 1992—. Cons. Harvard Ency. Ethnic Groups, Cambridge, Mass., 1976-80; advisor State Hist. Records Bd., Harrisburg, Pa., 1982-91; cons. Ency. Canada's Peoples, 1991—99. Author: film documentary Vianoce-Slovak Christmas, 1978 (2d prize 1979), Slovaks in Bethlehem, Pa., 1985, The Slovak Experience, 1870-1918, 1989. Mem. Pa. adv. com. to U.S. Commn. on Civil Rights, 1985-91. Lehigh U. fellow, 1976. Mem. 1st Cath. Slovak Union, Nat. Slovak Soc., Can. Slovak League (pres. 1994-99). Roman Catholic. Office Phone: 613-562-5800 ext 1286. Business E-Mail: stolarik@uottawa.ca.

STOLBA, K. MARIE, music educator; d. John Nickalos and Elsie Helena Marie Stolba. BA magna cum laude, Monmouth Coll., 1944, DHL (hon.), 1990; MA, U. No. Colo., 1952; PhD, U. Iowa, 1965. Cert. tchr. Iowa. H.S. tchr. Sperry (Iowa) Consol. Schs., 1946—48; H.S. and music tchr. West Burlington (Iowa) Pub. Schs., 1948—64; asst. prof. music Kellogg C.C., Battle Creek, Mich., 1965—67, Ft. Hays (Kans.) State Coll., 1967—71; music tchr. Grace Coll. and Word, Inc., Winona Lake, Ind., 1972—73; full prof. Ind.-Purdue U., Ft. Wayne, 1973—89; vis. prof. Colo. Christian U., Lakewood, 1990—. Permissions/royalties Rodeheaver Co./Word Music, Inc., Winona Lake, Ind., 1972—78; music dir. North Highlands Presbyn. Ch., Ft. Wayne, 1989—96, Grace Presbyn. Ch., Ft. Wayne, 1996—2004; lectr. in field. Author: A History of the Violin Etude, 1967, 1978, Bruni: Caprices & Airs Varies and Cinquante Etudes, 1982, Facsimile of Manscript of J.S. Bach's Sonaten und Partiten fur Violine Allein, 1982, Development of Western Music: History, 1990, 1994, 1998, Development of Western Music: An Anthology, 1990, 1994, 1998, Sigma Alpha Iota (Centenial History), 2003; contbr. articles to profl. jours. Mem.: PEO (pres.), Bach Collegium-Ft. Wayne (bd. dirs., pres. 2002—), Sigma Alpha Iota, Pi Kappa Lambda. Presbyterian. Avocation: violin. Home: 5621 Joyce Ave RR12 Fort Wayne IN 46818 Office Phone: 260-489-9726.

STOLFI, THOMAS EDWARD, advertising executive; b. Bethpage, N.Y., July 30, 1963; s. John Michael and Catherine Rita (Reitano) S.; m. Jacqueline Laguardia, June 27, 1987; children: Jessica Marie, Thomas Patrick. BS summa cum laude, St. John's U. Assoc. media planning, acct. mgr. SFM Media Corp., N.Y.C., 1986, media planner, acct. mgr., 1987-88, sr. media planner, acct. mgr., 1988-90, acct. planning dir., rsch. dir., 1990-93, v.p., acct. planning dir., dir. planning rsch., 1993-98, sr. v.p., planning dir., dir. planning rsch., 1998—. Recipient Silver Effie for Advt. Effectiveness, Am. Mktg. Assn. Republican. Roman Catholic. Home: 267 Harbor Ln Massapequa Park NY 11762-4012 Office: SFM Media LLC Ste 2001 1180 Avenue Of The Americas Fl 10 New York NY 10036-8405

STOLINA, MARINA, immunologist, research scientist; b. Kiev, Ukraine, Feb. 28, 1960; d. Galina Stolina and Roman Stolin; m. Sergey Prikhodko, Aug. 14, 1985. PhD in Biol. Sciences, Inst. of Molecular Biology and Genetics, Kiev, Ukraine, 1989—94. Rsch. fellow Inst. of Molecular biology and Genetics, Kiev, Ukraine, 1989—95; vis. scientist Univ. So. Calif., Norris cancer Ctr., L.A., Calif., 1995—96; post-doctoral fellow UCLA Med. Sch., L.A., Calif., 1996—2000; rsch. scientist Amgen, Inc, Thousand Oaks, Calif., 2000—. Author: (rsch.) The effects of chronic low-doze irradiation on reproductive functions of lab. mice from Chernobyl exptl. population (Internat. Sci. Found. individual sci. grant award, 1993); contbr. rsch. (Young Investigator's Award, 88th Ann. Meeting of Am. Assn. for Cancer Rsch., 1997), (Am. Lung Assn. Nat. rsch. grant-award, 1998); author: (rsch.) Specific inhibition of cyclooxygenase 2 restores antitumor immunity by altering the balance of IL-10 and IL-12 synthesis (Am. Lung Assn. Nat. Career Rsch. grant-award, 1999). Recipient grant for young scientists award, NAS of Ukraine, 1994—95; fellow tng. grant, NIH, 1996—97; grantee Nat. rsch. grant-award, Am. Lung Assn., 1998—2000, 1998 Tobacco Related Disease Rsch. Program individual rsch. grant-award, 1998—2000. Mem.: N.Y. Acad. Sci., Am. Assn. for Cancer Rsch., Am. Assn. of Immunologists. Achievements include invention of NNT-1 Stimulates Osteoblast Activity Incuding IL-6 Production and Bone Formation. Office: Amgen Inc One Amgen Ctr Dr Thousand Oaks CA 91320

STOLL, HOWARD LESTER, JR., dermatologist; b. Buffalo, June 13, 1928; s. Howard L. and Margaret (Kahler) S.; m. Jacklyn Fay Straight, June, 1948; children— Shelley, Margaret, Amy, Howard III AB, Harvard U., 1948; MD, U. Pa., 1952. Diplomate Am. Bd. Dermatology. Intern E.J. Meyer Hosp., Buffalo, 1952, resident in dermatology, 1953-55; sr. cancer research surgeon Roswell Park Meml. Inst., Buffalo, 1958-59, assoc. cancer research dermatologist, 1959-67, chief, sect. dermatology, 1984-92; mem. courtesy staff Mercy Hosp., Buffalo, 1958-70; asst. in dermatology E.J. Meyer Meml. Hosp., Buffalo, 1962-72. Clin. assoc. prof. dermatology Sch. Medicine, SUNY-Buffalo, 1976-91, clin. prof., 1991—. Served to capt. U.S. Army, 1955-57 Mem. Am. Acad. Dermatology, Soc. Investigative Dermatology, Buffalo-Rochester Dermatologic Soc. Office: Roswell Park Meml Inst Elm & Carlto Sts 666 Elm St Buffalo NY 14263-0002

STOLL, NEAL RICHARD, lawyer; b. Phila., Nov. 7, 1948; s. Mervin Stoll and Goldie Louise (Serody) Stoll Wilf; m. Linda G. Seligman, May 25, 1972; children: Meredith Anne, Alexis Blythe. BA in History with distinction, Pa. State U., 1970; JD, Fordham U., 1973. Bar: N.Y. 1974, U.S. Dist. Ct. (ea. dist.) N.Y. 1974, U.S. Ct. Appeals (2d cir.) 1974, U.S. Ct. Appeals (11th cir.) 1982, U.S. Dist. Ct. (ea. dist.) Mich. 1983, U.S. Dist. Ct. (so. dist.) N.Y. 1974, U.S. Supreme Ct. 1986. Assoc. Skadden, Arps, Slate, Meagher & Flom, LLP, N.Y.C., 1973-81, mem., 1981—. Lectr. Practicing Law-Inst., N.Y.C. Author: (with others) Aquisitions Under the Hart Scott Rodino Antitrust Improvements Act, 1980; contbr. articles to profl. pubs. Mem. Assn. Bar City of N.Y. (mem. trade regulation com. 1983-85), ABA, N.Y. State Bar Assn. Democrat. Office: Skadden Arps Slate Four Times Sq New York NY 10036-6522 E-mail: nstoll@skadden.com.

STOLL, RICHARD G(ILES), lawyer; b. Phila., Oct. 2, 1946; s. Richard Giles and Mary Margaret (Zeigler) S.; m. Susan Jane Nicewonger, June 15, 1968; children: Richard Giles III, Christian Hayes. BA magna cum laude, Westminster Coll., 1968; JD, Georgetown U., 1971. Bar: D.C. 1971, U.S. Dist. Ct. D.C. 1971, U.S. Ct. Appeals D.C. 1971, U.S. Ct. Appeals (4th cir.) 1977. Assoc. Arent, Fox, Kintner, Plotkin & Kahn, Washington, 1971-73; atty. Office of Gen. Counsel EPA, Washington, 1973-77, asst. gen. counsel, 1977-81; dep. gen. counsel Chem. Mfrs. Assn., Washington, 1981-84; ptnr. Freedman, Levy, Kroll & Simonds, Washington, 1984-2001, Foley & Lardner, Washington, 2001—. Instr. environ. law and policy U. Va., Charlottesville, 1981-90. Co-author: Handbook on Environmental Law, 1987, 88, 89, 91, Practical Guide to Environment Law, 1987; contbr. articles to profl. jours.; moderator, panelist legal ednl. TV broadcasts and tapes ABA and Am. Law Inst. Elder Georgetown Presbyn. Ch.; bd. dirs. Georgetown Ministry Ctr., 2004—. Capt., USAR, 1968-76. Recipient Alumni Achievement award Westminster Coll.,

1998. Mem. ABA (sect. environment, energy and resources, chmn. water quality com. 1980-82, hazardous waste com. 1983-85, coun. mem. 1985-88, sect. chmn. 1990-91, sect. adminstrv. law co-chmn. rulemaking com. 2004—, chair sponsorship com. 2004—), Washington Golf and Country Club, Cosmos Club. Avocations: piano, golf, music composition. Office: Foley & Lardner 3000 K St NW Washington DC 20007 Office Phone: 202-295-4021. E-mail: rstoll@foley.com.

STOLL, WILHELM, mathematics professor; b. Freiburg, Germany, Dec. 22, 1923; arrived in U.S., 1960; s. Heinrich and Doris (Eberle) S.; m. Marilyn Jane Kremser, June 11, 1955; children: Robert, Dieter, Elisabeth, Rebecca. PhD in Math, U. Tübingen, Fed. Republic Germany, 1953, habilitation, 1954. Asst. U. Tübingen, 1953-59, dozent, 1954-60, ausserplanmássiger prof., 1960; vis. lectr. U. Pa., 1954-55; temp. mem. Inst. Advanced Study, Princeton, 1957-59; prof. math. U. Notre Dame, 1960-88, Vincent J. Duncan and Annamarie Micus Duncan prof. math., 1988-94, prof. emeritus, 1994—, chmn. dept., 1966-68, co-dir. Ctr. for Applied Math., 1992. Vis. prof. Stanford U., 1968-69, Tulane U., 1973, U. Sci. and Tech., Hefei, Anhui, People's Republic of China, summer, 1986; adviser Clark Sch., South Bend, Ind., 1963-68; Japan Soc. Promotion Sci. fellow, vis. prof. Kyoto U., summer 1983. Publs. in field. Fellow: AAAS. Achievements include research complex analysis several variables. Home: 54763 Merrifield Dr Mishawaka IN 46545-1519 Office: U Notre Dame Dept Math Notre Dame IN 46556

STOLL, WILLIAM HERMANN, real estate company executive; b. Aug. 7, 1944; s. Gottfried Alois and Mary Elizabeth (Lochrie) Stoll; m. Elizabeth Anne Stoll, Aug. 5, 1967. BBA, U. Ark., Fayetteville, 1966; MA (grad. fellow), U. Tex., Austin, 1970. Budget examiner Tex. Gov.'s Office, 1967—71; fin. grants adminstr. City Mgrs. Office, Austin, Tex., 1971—73; dir. program devel. Tex. Dept. Cmty. Affairs, Tex., 1973—78; gen. mgr. AIS Data Sys., Inc., Austin, 1978—81; pres. Submariner, Inc., Austin, 1981—86; sales mgr. Better Homes & Gardens, Austin, 1986—97; sales counselor Standard Pacific Homes, Austin, 1997—. Chmn. Southwest Nat. Bank, Austin, 1980—82, also bd. dirs.; chmn. Austin Bd. Realtors, Austin, 1987. Author (digest): Texas Water Plan, 1967. Chmn. North Austin Mental Health/Mental Retardation Com., 1975—76; rep. Goals for Austin Tomorrow, 1974—75; chmn. Allandale Neighborhood Assn., 1975—76; mem. LBJ Librarry Found.; mem. selection com. Austin Most Worthy Citizen award, 1993—94; mem. pledge com. Muscular Dystrophy Ann. Campaign, Williamson County, 1999—2001; mem. fin. com. KLRO-TV PBS sta., 1994—95; presiding judge Travis County Election Commn., Austin, 1976—79; fin. chmn. Travis County Dem. Party, 1977—78; vice chmn. Austin Planning and Zoning Commn., 1976—80. Mem.: Austin Soc. Pub. Adminstrn., Austin C. of C., Exch. Park Toastmasters, U. Tex.-Austin Ex-students' Assn., Men's Polit Club Austin (co-founder), Young Men's Bus. Club, Kiwanis, Sigma Phi Epsilon (advisory dir. alumni assn. 1984—88). Home: 8704 Azalea Trl Austin TX 78759-7503

STOLLAR, BERNARD DAVID, biochemist, educator; b. Saskatoon, Sask., Can., Aug. 11, 1936; came to U.S., 1960; s. Percy and Rose (Direnfeld) S.; m. Carol A. Singer, Oct. 7, 1956; children: Lawrence, Michael, Suzanne. BA, U. Sask., Saskatoon, 1958, MD, 1959. Intern U. Sask. Hosp., 1959-60; postdoctoral fellow Brandeis U., Waltham, Mass., 1960-62; asst. prof. dept. pharmacology Tufts U. Schs. Medicine and Dental Medicine, Boston, 1964-67, asst. prof. dept. biochemistry, 1967-68, assoc. prof. biochemistry/pharmacology, 1968-74, prof., 1974—, acting chmn. dept. biochemistry and pharmacology, 1984-86, chmn. dept. biochemistry, 1986-2001; dean ad interim Sackler Sch. Grad. Biomed Sci., Tufts U., 2002—04. Vis. prof. internat. course in immunology and immunochemistry Mexico City, 1971; sr. fellow Weizmann Inst. Sci., Rehovot, Israel, 1971-72; vis. prof. chemistry Wellesley (Mass.) Coll., 1976, U. Tromsö, Norway, 1981; Dozor vis. prof. Ben-Gurion U. Sch. Medicine, Beer Sheva, Israel, 1986; cons. USAF Office Sci. Rsch., 1966-69, Seragen, Inc., 1983-88, Cetus, 1982-85, Gene-Trak, 1986-89, Alkermes, Inc., 1989-94, Catalytic Antibodies, Inc., 1993-98; 3d ann. alumni lectr. U. Sask. Coll. Medicine, 1989; mem. allergy/transplantation rsch. com. NIH/NIAID, 1990-94; mem. sci. vis. com. Okla. Med. Rsch. Found., 1996-98; mem. panel Israel Cancer Rsch. Found., 1996-2000. Contbr. over 200 articles to profl. jours., chpts. to books; exec. editl. bd. Analytical Biochemistry, 1988—; editl. bd. Jour. Immunology, 1981-85, Molecular Immunology, 1980-95, Arthritis and Rheumatism, 1986-89, Jour. Immunological Methods, 1988—. Mem. adult edn. com. Temple Reyim, Newton, Mass., v.p., 2001—. Capt. USAF, 1962-64. Recipient (with Carol Stollar) 2d Century award Jewish Theol. Sem. and Temple Reyim, 1997; rsch. grantee NSF, NIH, 1964—; sr. fellow Weizmann Inst. Sci., 1971-72. Mem. AAAS, Am. Assn. Immunologists, Am. Soc. Biochemistry and Molecular Biology, Am. Coll. Rheumatology, Clin. Immunology Soc., N.Y. Acad. Sci. Office: Tufts Univ Sch Medicine Dept Biochemistry 136 Harrison Ave Boston MA 02111-1800 Office Phone: 617-636-2948. Business E-Mail: david.stollar@tufts.edu.

STOLLER, CLAUDE, architect; b. N.Y.C., Dec. 2, 1921; s. Max and Esther (Zisblatt) S.; m. Anna Maria Oldenburg, June 5, 1946 (div. Oct. 1972); children: Jacob, Dorothea, Elizabeth; m. Rosemary Raymond Lax, Sept. 22, 1978. Student, Black Mountain Coll., N.C., 1942; M.Arch., Harvard U., 1949. Architect Architects Collaborative, Cambridge, Mass., after 1949, Shepley, Bulfinch, Richardson & Abbot, Boston, 1951; co-founder, partner firm Marquis & Stoller, San Francisco, 1956; pvt. practice architecture N.Y.C. and San Francisco, 1974-78; founder, partner Stoller/Partners, Berkeley, Calif., 1978, Stoller, Knoerr Archs., 1988-95. Mem. faculty Washington U., St. Louis, 1955-56, U. Calif., Berkeley, 1957-91, prof. arch., 1968-92, acting chmn. dept., 1965-66, chair grad. studies, 1984-91; mem. Berkeley Campus Design Rev. Bd., 1985-91, chmn., 1992-93; commr. Calif. Bd. Archtl. Examiners, 1980-90, mem. exam. com., 1985-88; mem. diocesan commn. arch. Episcopal Diocese Calif., 1961-98; vis. arch. Nat. Design Inst., Ahmedabad, India, 1963; planning commr. City of Mill Valley, 1961-66, Marin County Planning Commn., 1966-67; mem. pub. adv. panel archtl. svcs. GSA, 1969-71; citizens urban design adv. com. City of Oakland, Calif., 1968; vis. com. nat. archtl. accrediting bd. U. Minn. and U. Wis., Milw., 1971; coun. Harvard Grad. Sch. Design Assn., 1976 77; mem. design rev. com. The Sea Ranch, Calif., 1990-2002. Prin. works include St. Francis Sq. Coop. Apts., San Francisco, 1961, Pub. Housing for Elderly, San Francisco, 1974, Learning Resources Bldg, U. Calif., Santa Barbara, 1975, Menorah Park Housing for Elderly, San Francisco, 1979, San Jose State U. Student Housing Project, 1984, Delta Airlines Terminal, San Francisco Internat. Airport, 1988. Served with AUS, 1943-46. Recipient numerous awards including AIA Honor awards, 1963, 64, AIA Bay Region Honor award, 1974, Concrete Reinforced Steel Inst. award, 1976, AIA award, 1976, CADA Site I Solar Housing award Sacramento, Calif., 1980, State of Calif. Affordable Housing award, 1981, PG&E Suntherm award, 1981, San Francisco Housing Authority award, 1983, Orchid award City of Oakland, 1989, Citation for achievement and svc. U. Calif., Berkeley, 1991, Design award Berkeley Design Advocates. Fellow AIA. Home: 2816 Derby St Berkeley CA 94705-1325 Office: Claude Stoller FAIA Arch 1818 Harmon St Berkeley CA 94703-2472 E-mail: stoller@uclink.berkeley.edu.

STOLLER, JOHN R. lawyer; b. N.Y.C., Oct. 16, 1948; BA, Valparaiso U., 1970, JD, 1973. Bar: Minn. 1973, Colo. 1978, Mich. 1993. Editor-in-chief Calparaiso U. Law Rev., 1972—73; law clk. to Justice Walter F. Rogscheske Minn., 1973—74; assoc. HArstad & Rainbow, 1974—78; spl. asst. atty. gen. Minn. Dept. Transp., 1974—78; atty. The Mountain States Telephone and Telegraph Co., 1978—83; v.p., gen. counsel, sec. Beta West Properties, Inc., 1984—90; gen. counsel, sec. Pulte Homes, Inc., Bloomfield Hills, Mich., 1990—, sr. v.p., 1999—. Mem.: ABA, Am. Soc. Corp. Secs., Am. Corp. Counsel Assn., State Bar Mich., Denver Bar Assn., Colo. Bar Assn., Minn. Bar Assn. Office: Pulte Homes Inc 100 Bloomfield Hills Pky Ste 300 Bloomfield Hills MI 48304

STOLLER, ROSE, think-tank executive; With N.D. Dept. Human Svcs.; exec. dir. Mental Health Assn., ND, The Consensus Coun., Bismarck, ND, 2002—. Chairperson Bismarck Human Rels. Com.; vol. Mo. Slope United Way; grad. leadership program Bismarck C. of C. Recipient Mental Health Svcs. award, N.D. Psychiat. Soc., Welcome Back award, Eli Lilly Co. Office: The Consensus Coun Inc Ste 7 1003 E Interstate Ave Bismarck ND 58503-0500*

STOLLERMAN, GENE HOWARD, physician, educator; b. N.Y.C., Dec. 6, 1920; s. Maurice William and Sarah Dorothy (Mezz) S.; m. Corynne Miller, Jan. 21, 1945 (dec. Mar. 1997); children: Lee Denise Stollerman Meyburg, Anne Barbara Stollerman DiZio, John Eliot; m. Vita Mark, Nov. 9, 1997. AB summa cum laude, Dartmouth Coll., 1941; MD, Columbia U., 1944. Diplomate Am. Bd. Internal Medicine. Clin. tng. Mt. Sinai Hosp., N.Y.C, 1944-46, chief med. resident, 1948; Dazian research fellow microbiology NYU Med. Sch., 1949-50, mem. dept. medicine, 1951-55; med. dir. Irvington House for Cardiac Children, 1951-55; prin. investigator Sackett Found. Research in Rheumatic Diseases, 1955-64; asst. prof. medicine Northwestern U., 1955-57, assoc. prof., 1957-61, prof. medicine, 1961-65; prof., chmn. dept. medicine U. Tenn., 1965-81, Goodman prof., 1977-81; physician-in-chief City of Memphis Hosps., 1965-81; prof. medicine Boston U. Sch. Medicine, 1981-95, prof. pub. health, 1991-95, prof. medicine and pub. health emeritus, 1996—. Chief sect. gen. internal medicine Univ. Hosp., Boston U. Med. Ctr., 1983-86; Disting. physician VA Med. Ctr., Bedford, Mass., 1986-89; assoc. chief of staff Geriatrics and Extended Care, 1989-92; clin. dir. Bedford div. Geriatric Rsch., Ednl. and Clin. Ctr., 1989-92; dir. VA Health Svcs. Rsch. Field, 1990-93; chmn. research career program com. NIAMD-NIH, 1967-70, mem. commn. streptococcal and staphylococcal diseases U.S. Armed Forces Epidemiol. Bd., 1956-74; adv. bd. immunization practices Center for Disease Control, 1968-71; expert adv. panel cardiovascular disease WHO, 1966—; mem. Am. Bd. Internal Medicine, 1967-73, chmn. cert. exam. com., 1969-73, mem. exec. com., 1971-73; chmn. Panel on Bacterial Vaccines, FDA, 1973-80; mem. nat. adv. council Nat. Inst. Allergy and Infectious Diseases, NIH, 1978-82; mem. Dept. Health & Human Services nat. vaccine adv. com. Editor-in-chief Advances in Internal Medicine, 1968-93, Jour. Am. Geriatric Soc., 1984-88; co-editor Hosp. Practice, 1990 , editor, 1998—; contbr. chpts. to Braunwald's Textbook of Cardiology, Harrison's Textbook of Medicine, Cecil & Loeb Textbook of Medicine, others; contbr. articles to profl. jours. Served as capt. M.C., AUS, 1946-48. Recipient Bicentennial award in internal medicine Columbia U., 1967, Disting. Alumnus award Mt. Sinai Hosp., 1989, Thewlis award Am. Geriatric Soc., 1990, Mentor award Infectious Disease Soc. Am., 2004. Master ACP (bd. regents 1978, v.p. 1984, Bruce medal for preventive medicine 1985), Am. Coll. Rheumatology; mem. Am. Heart Assn. (mem. exec. com., pres. coun. on rheumatic fever and congenital disease 1965-67), Am. Fedn. Clin. Rsch., Am. Rheumatism Assn., Am. Soc. Clin. Investigation, Cen. Soc. Clin. Rsch. (v.p. 1973-74, pres. 1974-75), Assn. Profs. Medicine (pres. 1975-76), Am. Assn. Immunologists, Assn. Am. Physicians, Infectious Disease Soc. Am. (coun. 1968-70), Phi Beta Kappa, Alpha Omega Alpha. E-mail: gstollerman@valley.net.

STOLLERY, ROBERT, construction company executive; b. Edmonton, Alta., Can., May 1, 1924; s. Willie Charles and Kate (Catlin) S.; m. Shirley Jean Hopper, June 11, 1947; children: Carol, Janet, Douglas. BSc in Engring., U. Alta., 1949, LLD (hon.), 1985, Concordia U., Montreal, Que., 1986, St. Stevens Coll., 1999. Field engr. Poole Constrn. Ltd., Edmonton, 1949-54, project mgr., 1954-64, v.p., 1964-69, pres., 1969-81; chmn. bd. PCL Constrn. Group Inc., Edmonton, 1979-93; chmn. PCL Constrn. HOldings, Edmonton, 1993—. Bd. dirs. Melcor Devels. Ltd., Edmonton, Alta. Chmn. Edmonton Community Found. Decorated Order of Can.; recipient Exec. of Yr. award Inst. Cert. Mgmt. Cons. of Alta., 1988, Can. Businessman of Yr. award U. Alta., 1993, Golden Jubilee medal 2002. Fellow Can. Acad. Engring.; mem. Assn. Profl. Engrs. (Frank Spragins Meml. award 1981), Engring. Inst. Can. (Julian C. Smith medal 1990), Conf. Bd. Can. (vice chmn. 1980-82), Constrn. Assn. Edmonton (pres. 1972, Claude Alston Meml. award), Can. Constrn. Assn. (v.p. 1970, Can. Businessman of the Yr. award 1993). Conservative. Mem. United Ch. of Canada. Club: Mayfair Golf and Country (Edmonton). Office: PCL Constrn Group Inc 5410 99 St Edmonton AB Canada T6E 3P4

STOLLEY, ALEXANDER, advertising executive; b. Coethen Anhalt, Germany, May 12, 1922; came to U.S., 1923, naturalized, 1929; s. Mihail and Tatiana (Rainich) Stolarevsky; m. Patricia Martin, June 26, 1944 (dec. Aug. 1970); children: Christopher, Peter, Laura Stolley Smith, Annabel Stolley Hetzer, Megan Stolley Berry; m. Bette Scott Vogt, June 15, 1973. ME, U. Cin., 1948. With Cin. Milacron, Inc., 1941-50, dir. employee relations, 1948-50; with Northlich, Stolley, Inc., Cin., 1950-89, exec. v.p., 1959-67, pres., 1967-84; chmn. Northlich, Stolley, LaWarre, Inc. (formerly Northlich, Stolley, Inc.), Cin., 1984-89. Mem. exec. com. Cincinnatus Assn., 1968-73, sec., 1970-71, v.p., 1971-72, pres., 1972-73; mem. Cin. Council on World Affairs, 1969—; chmn. Contemporary Arts Center, Cin., 1966-67; mem. exec. com. Cin. Conv. and Visitors Bur., 1975, chmn. long range planning com., 1983; trustee Cin. Symphony Orch., 1969-75. Served to 1st lt. AUS, 1943-46. Mem. Bus., Profl. Advt. Assn., Greater Cin. C. of C. (exec. com. 1982-83) Clubs: Cin. Country, Literary, Gasparilla Beach, Lemon Bay Golf, Boca Bay Pass. Home: 135 Garfield Pl Apt 514 Cincinnati OH 45202-5737 also: PO Box 1339 Boca Grande FL 33921-1339

STOLLEY, PAUL DAVID, medical educator, researcher; b. Pawling, NY, June 17, 1937; s. Herman and Rosalie (Chertock) Stolley; m. Jo Ann Goldenberg, June 13, 1959; children: Jonathan, Dorie, Anna. BA, Lafayette Coll., 1957; MD, Cornell U., 1962; MPH, Johns Hopkins U., 1968; MA (hon.), U. Pa., 1976. Diplomate Am. Coll. Preventive Medicine, Am. Coll. Epidemiology. Intern U. Wis. Med. Ctr., 1962—63, resident in medicine, 1963—64; med. officer USPHS, Washington, 1964—67; asst. prof. Johns Hopkins Sch. Pub. Health, Balt., 1968—71, assoc. prof., 1971—76; Herbert C. Rorer prof. medicine U. Pa. Sch. Medicine, Phila., 1976—91; prof. dept. epidemiology U. Md. Sch. Medicine, Balt., 1991—2002; staff epidemiologist Public Citizen Health Rsch. Group, 2002—04. Co-author: Foundations of Epidemiology, 3d edit., 1995, Epidemiology: Investigating Disease, 1995 (Am. Med. Writers Assn. award, 1996); contbg. author: Case-Control Studies, 1982, mem. editl. bd.: New Eng. Jour. Medicine, 1989—93, Millbank Quar., Health and Soc., 1986—, assoc. editor: Clin. Pharmacology and Therapeutics, 1987—93; contbr. articles to med. jours. Charter mem. Physicians for Social Responsibility, 1961—. Lt. comdr. USPHS, 1964—67. Fellow: ACP; mem.: Johns Hopkins Soc. Scholars, Internat. Epidemiol. Assn. (treas. 1982—84), Am. Epidemiol. Soc. (pres. 1994—), Soc. Epidemiol. Rsch. (pres. 1982—84), Inst. Medicine of NAS, Am. Coll. Epidemiology (pres. 1987—89). Home: 6424 Brass Knob Columbia MD 21044-4019 Office Phone: 410-706-3610. Personal E-mail: pstolley@aol.com.

STOLLEY, RICHARD BROCKWAY, journalist; b. Peoria, Ill., Oct. 3, 1928; s. George Brockway and Stella (Sherman) S.; m. Anne Elizabeth Shawber, Oct. 2, 1954 (div. 1981); children: Lisa Anne, Susan Hope, Melinda Ruth, Martha Brockway; m. Lïse Jane Hilboldt, 1997. BS in Journalism, Northwestern U., 1952, MS, 1953; LLD, Villa Maria Coll., 1976. Sports editor Pekin (Ill.) Daily Times, 1944-46; reporter Chgo. Sun-Times, 1953; mem. staff weekly Life mag., 1953-73, bur. chief, 1961-64, Washington, 1964-68, sr. editor, 1968-70, asst. mng. editor, 1971-73; mng. editor monthly Life mag., N.Y.C., 1982-86; founding mng. editor People mag., N.Y.C., 1974-82, Picture Week mag., N.Y.C., 1985-86; dir. spl. projects Time Inc., N.Y.C., 1987-89; editl. dir. Time Inc. Time Warner Inc., N.Y.C., 1989-93, sr. editl. adviser, 1993—. Author: Sinatra: An Intimate Portrait of a Very Good Year, 2002; introd. to Leigh A. Wiener, Marilyn: A Hollywood Farewell: The Death and Funeral of Marilyn Monroe, 1990; editor People Celebrates People: The Best of 20 Unforgettable Years, 1994, rev. edit., 1996, Life: Our Century in Pictures, 1999, Life: Century of Change, America in Pictures, 1900-2000, 2000, LIFE: World War 2, 2001; exec. prodr. (TV show) Extra, 1995-96; editl. cons. Our American Century series Time-Life Books, 1998-99. Chmn. Twins Found., Providence; bd. govs. Nat. Parkinson Found., Miami, Fla.; trustee N.Y.C. Citizens Crime Commn. With USN, 1946-48. Recipient Alumni merit award Northwestern U., 1977, Alumni medal Northwestern U., 1994, Henry Johnson Fisher award for lifetime achievement in mag. pub., 1997, Mag. Profl. of Yr. award Assn. for Edn. in Journalism and Mass Comm., 2002; inducted into Am. Soc. Magazine Editors' Hall of Fame, 1996, Hall of Achievement Medill Sch. Journalism Northwestern U., 1997. Mem. Am. Soc. Mag. Editors (pres. 1982-84), Nat. Press Club (pres. 2004—), Overseas Press Club, Century Assn., Kappa Tau Alpha, Sigma Delta Chi.

STOLLMAN, ISRAEL, city planner; b. N.Y.C., Mar. 15, 1923; s. Philip and Yetta (Strelchik) S.; m. Mary Florence Callahan, Dec. 27, 1953; children—Susan Elisabeth, Katharine Rachel, Sarah Ellen. BS in Social Sci, CCNY, 1947; M. City Planning, MIT, 1948. Planner Cleve. Planning Commn., 1948-51; planning dir. Youngstown, Ohio, 1951-57; prof., chmn. div. city and regional planning Ohio State U., 1957-68; exec. dir. Am. Soc. Planning Ofcls., 1968-78, Am. Planning Assn., Washington, 1978-93, cons., 1994—. Lectr. Western Res. U., 1949-51, U. Chgo., 1968-69, U. Va., 1994—2002; pres. Assn. Collegiate Sch. Planning, 1966-67; chmn. Charles E. Merriam Center Pub. Adminstrn., 1977-93. Trustee Alfred Bettman Found.; bd. govs. Met. Housing and Planning Council Chgo., v.p., 1969-79. Served with USAAF, 1943-45. Fellow Am. Inst. Cert. Planners (exec. dir. emeritus), Internat. Fedn. Housing and Planning (bur. mem. 1988-98), Soc. for Am. City and Regional Planning History (trustee 1996—2001), Lambda Alpha. Avocation: stereoscopy. Home and Office: 1708 Swann St NW Washington DC 20009-5535

STOLOV, WALTER CHARLES, medicine physicist, physiatrist, educator; b. N.Y.C., Jan. 6, 1928; s. Arthur and Rose F. (Gordon) S.; m. Anita Carvel Noodelman, Aug. 9, 1953; children: Nancy, Amy, Lynne. BS in Physics, CCNY, 1948; MA in Physics, U. Minn., 1951, MD, 1956. Diplomate Am. Bd. Phys. Med. and Rehab., Am. Bd. Electrodiagnostic Medicine. Physicist U.S. Naval Gun Factory, Nat. Bur. Stds., Washington, 1948-49; teaching and rsch. asst. U. Minn., Mpls., 1950-54; from instr. to assoc. prof. U. Wash., Seattle, 1960-70, prof., 1970-99, prof. emeritus, 1999—, also chmn., 1987-99, prof. emeritus, 1999—. Editl. bd. Archives Phys. Medicine and Rehab., 1967-78, Muscle and Nerve, 1983-89, 92-95; cons. Social Security Adminstrn., Seattle, 1975—; sec. Am. Bd. Electrodiagnostic Medicine, 1995—. Co-editor: Handbook of Severe Disability, 1981; contbr. articles to profl. jours. Surgeon USPHS, 1956-57. Recipient Townsend Harris medal CCNY, 1990. Fellow: AAAS, Am. Heart Assn.; mem.: Am. Spinal Cord Injry Assn., Am. Assn. Electrodiagnostic Medicine (pres. 1987—88, Lifetime Achievement award 2001), Assn. Acad. Physiatrists, Am. Congress Rehab. Medicine (Essay award 1959), Am. Acad. Phys. Medicine and Rehab. (Disting. Clinician award 1987). Avocations: dance, singing. Office: U Wash Box 356490 1959 NE Pacific St Seattle WA 98195-0001 Office Phone: 206-543-7065.

STOLPER, EDWARD MANIN, secondary school educator; b. Boston, Dec. 16, 1952; s. Saul James and Frances A. (Liberman) S.; m. Lauren Beth Adoff, June 3, 1973; children: Jennifer Ann, Daniel Aaron. AB, Harvard U., 1974, PhD, 1979; MPhil, U. Edinburgh, Scotland, 1976. Asst. prof. geology Calif. Inst. Tech., Pasadena, 1979-82, assoc. prof. geology, 1982-83, prof. geology, 1983-90, William E. Leonhard prof. geology, 1990—, chmn. divsn. geol. and planetary sci., 1994—2004, acting provost, 2004—. Marshall scholar Marshall Aid Commemoration Commn., 1974-76; recipient Newcomb Cleve. prize AAAS, 1984, F.W. Clarke medal Geochem. Soc., 1985, Arthur Holmes medal European Union Geosci., 1997; Geochemistry fellow Geochem. Soc. and The European Assn. for Geochemistry, 1997. Fellow Meteoritical Soc. (Nininger Meteorite award 1976), Am. Geophys. Union (James B. Macelwane award 1986), Mineral Soc. Am., Am. Acad. Arts and Scis.; mem. NAS, Geol. Soc. Am. (Arthur L. Day medal 2004), Sigma Xi. Office: Calif Inst Tech Div Geol Planetary Sci Pasadena CA 91125-0001

STOLPER, PINCHAS ARYEH, religious organization executive, rabbi; b. Bklyn., Oct. 22, 1931; s. David Bernard and Nettie (Rosch) S.; m. Elaine Liebman, Nov. 22, 1955; children: Akiva Psachia, Michal Hadassah Cohen, Malka Tova Kaweblum. BA, Bklyn. Coll., 1952; MA, New Sch. for Social Rsch., 1971. Rabbinical ordination Chaim Berlin-Gur Aryeh Rabbinical Acad., 1956; dir. L.I. Zionist Youth Commn., 1956-57; dir. public relations, adminstrv. dean, adviser to English-speaking students Ponevez Yeshiva, Bnai Brak, Israel, 1957-59; also prin.; instr. English and Talmud Naehalim Bnai Akiva H.S., 1959-77; nat. dir. youth div. Union Orthodox Jewish Congregations Am., Nat. Conf. Synagogue Youth, N.Y.C., 1959-76, founder NCSY, Torah Fund, Ben Zakai Honor Soc., 1959-76; editor Jewish Youth Monthly, 1967—; exec. v.p. Union Orthodox Jewish Congregations Am., 1976-94, sr. exec., 1994—. Adj. prof. Jewish studies Touro Coll., N.Y., 1975—; mem. publs., Israel, campus commns., staff mem. responsible for edn., Talmud Torah, day sch. commns. Union Orthodox Jewish Congregations Am., 1965—; del. White House Conf. on Children and Youth, 1961; cons. N. Am. Jewish Youth Conf., 1967— Author: Tested Teen Age Activities, 1961, rev. edit., 1964, Day of Delight, 1961, Tefilah, Text and Source Book, 1963, Revelation What Happened on Sinai, 1966, Prayer, The Proven Path, 1967, The Road to Responsible Jewish Adulthood, 1967, Jewish Alternatives in Love, Dating and Marriage, 1985, The Sacred Trust, Love, Dating and Marriage, The Jewish View, 1996, Beyond Belief, Revelation for the Modern Jew, 1996, Living Beyond Time: The Mystery and Meaning of the Jewish Festivals, 2003, Purim in A New Light: Mystery, Grandeur and Depth, 2003; contbr. numerous articles, plays, and revs. to Jewish publs.; columnist The Jewish Press, 1994. Nat. dir. Nat. Conf. Synagogue Youth, 1995-98; bd. dirs. Chaim Berlin Torah Schs.-Mesivta Rabbi Chaim Berlin-Rabbinical Acad., 1965—. Recipient Alumi Amudim award Mesivta Rabbi Chaim Berlin-Gur Aryeh Inst., 1967, award Assn. Orthodox Jewish Tchrs., 1975, citation Rabbinical Coun. Am., 1984, Jabotinsky medal, 1990, Alumnus of Yr. award Flatbush Yeshiva, 1989, Joseph K. Miller Achdut Yisrael award Shaalvim Yeshiva, 1993. Mem. Rabbinical Coun. Am. Jewish. Home: 603 Twin Oaks Dr Lakewood NJ 08701-7147 Office: Union Orthodox Jewish Cong of Am 11 Broadway New York NY 10004-1303 E-mail: PinchasStolper@aol.com.

STOLPIN, WILLIAM ROGER, artist, printmaker, retired engineer; b. Flint, Mich., June 25, 1942; s. William and Dorothy Florence (Mitchell) S.; m. Kathleen Diane Poyner, Aug. 14, 1970; children: Krishna Ann, James Mitchell. B of Mech. Engring., Kettering U., Flint, 1965; AA, Charles Stewart Mott C.C., Flint, 1978; postgrad., Ea. Mich. U., 1992. Jr. reliability engr. GM Corp., Flint, 1968-76, sr. reliability engr., 1976-80, quality control supr., 1980 83, product assurance mgr., 1983-89, asst. staff engr. Warren, Mich., 1990-93; printmaker, print pub. Flint, 1969-80; printmaker, print pub., co-founder DAS Print Co., Holly, Mich., 1980—. Resident artist Robert T. Longway Planetarium, Flint, 1975— Printmaker: (lithograph) ...And the Santa Maria, 1969 (Smithsonian permanent collection 1973), (serigraph) One Giant Leap For Mankind, 1970 (Smithsonian permanent collection 1973), numerous pub. serigraphs, lithographs, intaglio prints and woodcuts, 1969—. Grant reviewer Greater Flint Arts Coun., 1989-90, 2000-02, v.p., 1973-74, programming and planning, 1988, mktg. and pub. rels., 1999—, bd. dirs., 1999—; pres. Buckham Fine Arts Project, Flint, 1993-94, bd. dirs., 1993-2000; bd. dirs. Whaley Hist. House, Flint, 1997-2000; adv. com. U. Mich. Flint Art Gallery, 1997-2000, Shiawassee Arts Coun., 1999-2000, Alma Coll., 1999-2001; accessions and collections com. Flint Inst. Arts, 2000—; grant reviewer Oakland County Office Arts, Culture and Film, 2002—. Recipient 1st in Graphics award Internat. Platform Assn., 1969, Koegler Meml. award Left Bank Gallery, 1991, 1st in Overall Attitude, Mich. Renaissance Festival, 1998, 99, 1st prize all media award Left Bank Gallery, 1998, purchase prize Saginaw Art Mus., 1994, 98, hon. mention Ann Arbor Art Ctr., 2003, 04, 1st prize Flint (Mich.) Art Fair, 2004; Fed. Design and Art in Transp. grantee, 2002. Mem. AAAS, AIAA, Internat. Assn. for Astron. Arts, Am. Soc. for Quality, Nat. Stereoscopic Assn., Soc. Automotive Engrs., Soc. Am. Graphic Artists, Flint Artist's Market, Left Bank Gallery, Detroit Artist's Market, Assn. Sci. Fiction and Fantasy Artists, Mich. Assn. Printmakers, Am. Print Alliance, Mid Am. Print Coun., Internat. Ctr. for the Print, Wood Engravers Network, Mich. Guild Artists and Artisans, Renaissance Artisans Guild. Avocations: directing community theater, participant in michigan renaissance festival, stereoscopic imaging. Studio: DAS Print Co 12201 Gage Rd Holly MI 48442-8339

STOLTE, LARRY GENE, marketing executive, former computer and publishing company executive; b. Cedar Rapids, Iowa, Sept. 17, 1945; s. Ed August and Emma Wilhelmina (Tank) S.; m. Rebecca Jane Tappmeyer, June, 1970; children: Scott Edward, Ryan Gene. BBA with highest distinction, U. Iowa, 1971; MBA, Trinity U., 2000. CPA Ill., Mo., Minn., Mich., Wis., personal fin. specialist, Ill., Mo., Minn., Mich., Wis., cert. mgmt. acct., Inst. Mgmt. Accts., profl. cons. to mgmt., Nat. Bur. Profl. Mgmt. Cons., mktg. exec., Sales and Mktg. Execs. Internat., mgmt. cons., Inst. Cert. Mgmt. Cons. Tax and auditing acct. McGladrey Pullen & Co., Cedar Rapids, 1971—73; v.p., gen. mgr. TLS Co. (subs. CCH Computax Inc.), Cedar Rapids, 1973—92;

re-engrng. cons. CCH, Inc., Riverwoods, Ill., 1992—94; nat. dir. mktg. McGladrey & Pullen, Cedar Rapids, 1994—97; sr. v.p., mng. dir. Web Site Dynamics & Stolte Enterprises, Cedar Rapids, 1997—2000; ptnr. NY Life Ins. Co. & NY Life Securities, Inc., Cedar Rapids, 2001—03; personal fin. advisor Lincoln Savs. Bank, 2003—04. Sgt. USMC, 1964-67. Mem. AICPA, Nat. Assn. Computerized Tax Processors (pres.), Am. Mgmt. Assn., Am. Mktg. Assn., Inst. Mgmt. Accts. (cert.), Nat. Bur. Profl. Mgmt. Cons. (cert.), Sales and Mktg. Execs. Internat. (cert. mktg. exec., cert. sales exec.), Inst. Cert. Mgmt. Cons. (cert.). Methodist. Address: 3000-A Towne House Dr NE PO Box 0489 Cedar Rapids IA 52406-0489 Office Phone: 319-378-4697. E-mail: larrystolte@hotmail.com.

STOLTMAN, CLAUDIA JILL, performing arts educator; d. Alan and Henrietta (Siegel) Stoltman; m. Brian Leahy Doyle, Aug. 8, 1998. BA, Brown U., Providence, 1980; MA, Columbia U., NYC, 1991. Program coord., prof. Marymount Coll., Tarrytown, NY, 1995—97; program chair, dance educator Convent Sacred Heart, Greenwich, Conn., 1997—2001; dance educator The Ballet Class, Rye, NY, 2002—, Conservatory of Dance, Wilton, Conn., 2003—. Adv. bd. Croton Coun. Arts, Croton, NY, 1985—87; pres., founder, artistic dir. Hudson Valley Ctr. Dance., Inc., Hastings On Hudson, NY, 2001—. Performer: Jacob's Pillows 65th Anniversary Season, 1997, Lincoln Ctr., 1999, Portland Ballet, 2002. Alumnae rep., area interviewer Brown Alumni Schs. Com., Providence, 2002—. Imagination Celebration dance grant, Westchester Arts Coun., 1989, 1993.

STOLTZFUS, VICTOR EZRA, retired university president; b. Martinsburg, Pa., Mar. 24, 1934; s. Ira Mark and Elsie Rebecca (Shenk) S.; m. Marie Histand Althouse, June 19, 1955; children: Kristina, Rebecca, Malinda. BA in Social Sci., Goshen Coll., 1956; BD, Goshen Bibl. Sem., 1959; MA in Sociology, Kent State U., 1964; PhD in Sociology, Pa. State U., 1970. Pastor North Lima (Ohio) Mennonite Ch., 1959-66; instr. Youngstown (Ohio) U., 1964-66, Pa. State U., University Park, 1966-70; prof. Eastern Ill. U., Charleston, 1970-81; dean Goshen (Ind.) Coll., 1981-84, pres., 1984-96. Contbr. articles to profl. jours. Mem.: Rotary. Avocation: raquetball. Home: 607 College Ave Goshen IN 46526-4911

STOLTZMAN, RICHARD LESLIE, clarinetist; b. Omaha, July 12, 1942; s. Leslie Harvey and Dorothy Marilyn (Spohn) S.; m. Lucy Jean Chapman, June 6, 1976; children: Peter John, Margaret Anne. MusB summa cum laude, Ohio State U., 1964; MusM magna cum laude, Yale U., 1967; postgrad., Columbia U. Tchrs. Coll., 1967-70. Mem. faculty Calif. Inst. Arts, 1970-75, New Eng. Conservatory, 1996. Western regional dir. Young Audiences, Inc., 1972-74, mem. nat. bd. Appeared in concerts throughout U.S., Europe, Japan, Hong Kong, Australia, 1976—; rec. artist, 1974—; debut LaScala, Milan, 1981, Carnegie Hall, N.Y.C., 1982; appeared in world premiere of Einar Englund concerto Helsinki Festival, 1991, Toru Takemitsu concerto (Fantasma/Cantos) Wales BBC, 1991, U.S. premiere of Lukas Foss concerto L.A. Philharm. Orch., 1991, Copland concert, 1993 (Emmy award for best performing arts video 1993), world premiere of Leonard Bernstein sonata for clarinet and orch. Pacific Music Festival, Sapporo, Japan, 1994, world premiere of Steven Hartke concerto PBS, Tenn., 2001, world premiere of Thomas McKinley concerto 9 Shades of Lament, Boston Civic Orch., 2001, of Einohuhani Rautavaara Concerto, Nat. Symphony, Carnegie Hall, 2002. Recipient Horatio Parker award Yale U., 1966, Avery Fisher prize, 1977, Martha Baird Rockefeller award, 1973, Grammy award, 1983, 95, Avery Fisher artist award, 1986, Disting. Alumnus award Ohio State U., 1990. Home: 6 Lincolnshire Way Winchester MA 01890-3048 Office: 201 W 54th St Apt 4C New York NY 10019-5521 *Be mindful of the breath. It gives life to the sound which sends music to the soul.*

STOLWIJK, JAN ADRIANUS JOZEF, physiologist, biophysicist; b. Amsterdam, Netherlands, Sept. 29, 1927; came to U.S., 1955, naturalized, 1962. s. Leonard and Cornelia Agnes (Van Der Bijl) S.; m. Deborah Rose, 1990. BS, Wageningen U., Netherlands, 1948, MS, 1951, PhD, 1955. Biophysicist John B. Pierce Found., New Haven, 1957-61; assoc. fellow John B. Pierce Found. Lab., 1961-64, fellow, 1964, assoc. dir., 1974-89; instr. dept. physiology Yale U. Sch. Medicine, New Haven, 1962-63, asst. prof., 1964-68, asst. prof. epidemiology, 1968-69, assoc. prof., 1969-75, prof., 1975-99, dir. grad. studies, dept. epidemiology and pub. health, 1992-99, chmn. dept. epidemiology and pub. health, 1982-89; rsch. fellow Harvard U., 1955-56. Cons. divsn. disease prevention Conn. Health Dept., 1977-99; cons. vehicle inspection program Dept. Motor Vehicles, 1979-83; mem. sci. adv. bd. EPA, 1985-93; mem. tech. adv. bd. Dept. Commerce, 1972-77. Mem. Am. Physiol. Soc., Biophys. Soc., Aerospace Med. Soc., Am. Pub. Health Assn., AAAS, Internat. Biometeorol. Soc., Soc. Occupl. and Environ. Health, Am. Conf. Govt. Indsl. Hygienists, ASHRAE, Conn. Acad. Sci. and Engring., Cosmos Club. Home: 4414 Harbour Town Dr Beltsville MD 20705-1081 E-mail: stolwijk@prodigy.net.

STOLZ, ALAN JAY, youth camp executive; b. NYC, May 7, 1931; s. Irving H. and Pearl (Maltz) S.; m. Sandra Stolz (div.); m. Gail C. Stolz; children: Maryann Stolz Levanti, Gary M. AB, Wabash Coll., 1953; LHD (hon.), London Inst., 1973. Cert. lifetime camp dir. Colo. Outdoor Inst., state instr. emergency med. svc. Pres. Camp Cody, Inc., Freedom, NH; ptnr., prin. 72d St Assocs. Real Estate Corp., NYC. Cons., profl. witness U.S. Senate and Ho. Reps., White House, Washington; cons. youth camp health various govtl. agys., Washington; guest spkr. Am. Free Enterprise program, Moscow and St. Petersburg, Russia, 1993; spkr. Internat. Youth Conf., Toronto, Ont., Can., 1994, Orlando, 1995, Washington, 2002; pres. Alanor, Inc., Fla., 1994—; apptd. consumer affairs specialist NH Atty. Gen. Office, Dept. of Justice, Fraud and Anti-Trust Bur. Author: National Camp Directors Guide, 1990; contbr. articles to profl. jours. Founding mem. USAF Mus. in Britain; primary instr. EMS, Westport, Conn., v.p., 1996—, bd. dirs.; vol. staff lectr. Maritime Aquarium, Norwalk, Conn., 2000—; instr. trainer ARC, 1999, Conn. and NH; advisor explorer adv. coun. Boy Scouts Am.; justice of peace State of NH, quorum mem.; bd. govs. Judaica Mus., Riverdale, NY, 1994—; vol. dist. coord. NH marine patrol Aux. State Dept. Safety, 1991—; mem. Am. Friends Brit. Mus., 1998—. Sgt. U.S. Army, 1955-57. Recipient honor award Emergency Med. Svcs., 1989, 97, 99, Environ. Youth Honors award White House-EPA, 1994, Citation for 55 yrs. svc. to Boy Scouts Am., Conn. State Legislature, 1994, Gov.'s Exec. Coun., NH, 1995, Cold War Recognition cert. U.S. Dept. Def., 1999, numerous awards Boy Scouts Am., honored for safety patrol svc., 1996, White House Med. Corps Secret Svc. citation for svcs. on presdl. visit, 1999, Congressional Record Congratulations citation for a quarter century EMS vol. leadership, 1999, Congratulations citation from Conn. Gov., State Legislature and Town Mayor, 1999, ARC Unsung Heroes award, 2000, 2003, EMS Vol. of Yr. award, 2000; named Conn. Vol. of Yr., Carosel Mag., 1990, Conn. Man of Yr., Spotlight Mag., 1991, Disting. Svc. award EMS, Conn. State, 2001, 1st Pl. Nat. Gold award, EMS Vols., 2001, Nat. Disting. Svc. Lifetime Achievemnt award Assn. Ind. Camps Divsn., Colo. Internat. Camping Conf., 2003. Mem. Am. Camp Assn. (life, nat. legis. chmn. 1970-86, nat. bd. dirs. 1972-84, nat. v.p. 1984-86), NH Camp Dirs. Assn. (pres. 1974-76, state sec./hon. bd. mem. 1976—, Nat. Lifetime Disting. Svc. award 2003), Am. Legion, Kiwanis. Republican. Jewish. Avocations: archeology, photography, aviation, history, medical research. Office: 5 Lockwood Cir Westport CT 06880-1640 Home: 46 Gailan Rd Freedom NH 03836

STOLZBERG, MARK ELLIOTT, psychologist; b. NYC, Apr. 30, 1944; s. Seymour and Ruth (Petesky) S.; m. Marilyn Goldberg, Mar. 18, 1972; children: Susan Beth, David Jonathan, Daniel Jason. BA, Hofstra U., 1966, PhD, 1986; MA in Exptl. Psychology, C.W. Post Coll., 1970; postgrad. in clin. psychology, SUNY, Albany, 1973. Intern in clin. psychology Maimonides Hosp., Bklyn., 1972-73; pres. Stolzberg Rsch., LLC, Stony Brook, NY, 1976—. Adj. lectr. Bklyn. Coll., 1973; faculty Coll. Optometry, SUNY, 1985-86; cons. clin. psychologist to numerous nursing homes, 1994—. Contbr. articles to profl. jours. Co-pres. North Shore SEPTA, 1999-2001. Grad. fellow C.W. Post Coll., 1968-70, SUNY, Albany, 1970-72, N.Y. State War Svc. scholar; recipient Disting. Achievement award for Rsch., N.Y. State Optometric Assn., 1983. Mem. Ind. Practitioners of Geropsychology (founder, past pres.), N.Y. State Psychol. Assn. (pres. divsn. on aging 2004), Aircraft Owners and Pilots Assn., Nat. Aeronautics Assn. Achievements include setting a transcontinental speed record for piston-engine aircraft in the U.S. Home and Office: 3 Seabrook Ct Stony Brook NY 11790-3305 Personal E-mail: mstolzbe@optonline.net.

STOLZENBERG, ROSS MARK, sociology educator; b. N.Y.C., Dec. 19, 1946; s. Seymour and Edith Richman Stolzenberg; m. Linda Joan Waite; children: Shana Anat, Nava Rachel. AB, Columbia U., 1968; MA, U. Mich., 1971, PhD, 1973. Asst. prof. sociology Harvard U., Cambridge, Mass., 1972-73; asst. prof. social rels. Johns Hopkins U., Balt., 1973-76, asst. prof. population dynamics, 1975-76; asst. prof., then assoc. prof. sociology U. Ill., Urbana, 1976-81, assoc. prof. program in applied stats., 1980-81; social scientist Rand Corp., Santa Monica, Calif., 1980-83; v.p. rsch. and test devel. Grad. Mgmt. Admission Coun., Santa Monica and L.A., 1983-91; prof. sociology U. Chgo., 1991—. Spl. agt., cons. U.S. Bur. Census, Washington, 1975-77, mem. adv. com. of profl. orgns., 1995-2001; cons. Rand Corp., 1983-2000; mem. editl. bd. sociol. Methodology, 1998-2001, Sociol. Methods and Rsch., 1974-80, 98—, Am. Jour. Sociology, 1990—, Social Forces, 1995-98, Rsch. on Social Stratification and Mobility, 1999-04; dep. editor Am. Sociol. Rev., 1977-79; mem. bd. cons. editors Am. Jour. Sociology, 1977-79; assoc. editor Social Sci. Rsch., 1974—. Contbr. articles to profl. jours.; author monographs in field. Trustee Sonia Shankman Orthogenic Sch., Chgo., 1997—, Hyde Park Sch. for Learning Disabled Children, Chgo., 1999—. Recipient citation for valor ARC, 1966, Rsch. Scientist Career Devel. award, NIMH, 1979; rsch. grantee U.S. Dept. Labor, 1971, NSF, 1978. Mem. Sociol. Rsch. Assn., Am. Sociol. Assn., Population Assn. Am. Democrat. Jewish. Home: 899 Kimball Rd Highland Park IL 60035 Office: U Chgo Dept Sociology 1123 E 57th St Chicago IL 60637 Business E-Mail: r-stolzenberg@uchicago.edu.

STOLZER, LEO WILLIAM, bank executive; b. Kansas City, Mo., Oct. 14, 1934; s. Leo Joseph and Lennie Lucille (Hopp) S.; m. Eleanor Katherine Griffith, Aug. 17, 1957; children: Joan Ellen Stolzer Bolen, Mary Kevin Stolzer Giller. BS in Acctg., Kans. State U., 1957. Teller Union Nat. Bank & Trust Co., Manhattan, Kans., 1960-62, asst. cashier, 1962-63, asst. v.p., 1963-64, v.p., 1964-69, exec. v.p., 1969-72, pres., 1972-80, chmn., CEO, 1980-95; chmn., 1995—. Bd. dirs. Commerce Bankshares Inc., Commerce Bank-Manhattan; chmn., CEO Griffith Lumber Co., Cmty. Bancorporation of N.Mex., Inc. Trustee, past treas., past vice-chair Kans. State U. Found.; trustee Midwest Rsch. Inst.; chmn. Riley County Savs. Bond. Capt. USAF, 1957-60. Recipient Disting. Service award Manhattan Jr. C. of C., 1968, Kans. State U. Advancement award. Fellow Coll. Bus. Adminstrn. Alumni; mem. Am. Bankers Assn. (past treas., past exec. com., past bd. dirs.), Assn. U.S. Army (bd. dirs. Ft. Riley Ctl. Kans. chpt., past chair), Kans. U. Alumni Assn. (devel. com.), Newcomen Soc. in N.Am. (past Kans. chmn.), KC, Beta Theta Pi. Avocation: skiing. Office: Commerce Bank 727 Poyntz Ave Manhattan KS 66502-0118

STOMBERG, ERIC W, musician; b. Vero Beach, Fla., Dec. 13, 1971; Mus D, Cin. College-Conservatory of Music, 1994—2003. Bassoonist Ky. Symphony Orch., 1996—2000, Cin. Chamber Orch., 1997—2002; instr. of bassoon Interlochen Arts Acad., Interlochen, Mich., 2001—, Interlochen Arts Camp, Interlochen, Mich., 2001—; bassoonist ProMusica Chamber Orch. of Columbus, Columbus, Ohio, 2002—; asst. prof. of bassoon Ohio U., Ohio, 2000—. Office: Ohio University School of Music 440 Athens OH 45701 E-mail: stomberg@ohio.edu.

STOMFAY-STITZ, ALINE MARIA, education educator; b. Newark, N.J. d. Adolph and Irene (Badowska) Wegrocki; m. Emery Stomfay-Stitz (dec.); children: Peter, John, Robert. BA, Barnard Coll.; MA, Case Western Reserve U.; EdD, No. Ill. U., 1984. Asst. prof. Coll. St Scholastica, Duluth, Minn., 1984-85, St. Leo (Fla.) Coll., 1985-87, Nicholls State U., Thibodaux, La., 1989-91; assoc. prof. edn. Christopher Newport U., Newport News, Va., 1991-96. Vis. prof., assoc. prof. edn. U. No. Fla., Jacksonville, 1996-2003; assoc. editor Joun. Early Childhood Tchr. Edn. Author: Peace Education in America 1828-1990, 1993; author (book chpt.): Toward Education That is Multicultural, 1992, Multicultural Education for the 21st Century, 1993; contbr. articles to profl. jours. Mem.: Internat. Peace Rsch. Assn., Nat. Assn. for Early Childhood Tchrs. Educators, Am. Ednl. Rsch. Assn. (SIG exec. com.).

STONE, ALAN, container company executive; b. Chgo., Feb. 5, 1928; s. Norman H. and Ida (Finkelstein) S.; m. Joanie B. Stone; children: Christie-Ann Stone Weiss, Joshua. BSE., U. Pa., 1951. Trainee, salesman Stone Container Corp., Chgo., 1951-53, dir. mktg. service, 1954-64, gen. mgr., regional mgr., 1964-72, sr. v.p. adminstrn., gen. mgr. energy div., 1972—, also dir., sr. v.p. purchasing and transp.; pres. North La. and Gulf R.R./Ctrl. La. and Gulf R.R., 1985-92, Atlanta St. Andrews and Bay Line R.R., 1992-94, Abbeville-Grimes R.R., 1992-94, Apache R.R., 1992-94. Bd. dirs., exec. com. Stone Container Corp., 1960—; cons. Chgo. Mfg.; pres. No. La. Gulf Railroad, 1985, Ctrl. La. Gulf Railroad, 1985. Pres. Jewish Vocat. Svc., Chgo., 1975-77; v.p. Sinai Temple, Chgo., 1977-84; bd. dirs. Jewish Fedn. Chgo.; vice chmn. Roycemore Sch., Evanston, Ill., 1982-87; pres. Emergency Fund for Needy People, 1993-2003, chmn., 2003—; trustee Brewster Acad., Wolfeboro, N.H.; vol. exec. for overseas needs Citizen's Democracy Corps; vol. cons. for non-profit agys., schs. and librs. Exec. Svc. Corps., 1992—, project mgr., 1997, bd. dirs., 2002—; bd. dirs. Gastrointestinal Rsch. Found., Intermodal Transp. Inst., U. Denver, 1997—; mem. cancer adv. bd. Northwestern U. Mem. Standard Club, Tavern Club, Bryn Mawr Country Club, Tamarisk Country Club, Long Boat Key Club, Beta Alpha Psi, Phi Eta Sigma, Zeta Beta Tau. Avocations: golf, sports, reading, travel, cultural activities. Office: Stone Container Corp 645 N Michigan Ave Ste 800 Chicago IL 60611-3775 Office Phone: 312-981-5016. Personal E-mail: alanstone3@aol.com.

STONE, ALAN ABRAHAM, law and psychiatry educator, psychiatrist; b. 1929; AB, Harvard U., 1950; MD, Yale U., 1955. Lectr. Harvard U., 1966-72, asst. prof. psychiatry, 1966-69, assoc. prof., 1969-72, prof. law, psychiatry, 1972—, Touroff-Glueck prof. law, psychiatry, 1982—. Adv. com. project mentally Ill Am. Bar Found., 1967-71; com. revision criminal code Mass. Gov., 1968-72; com. mentally disabled ABA, 1973-77; chmn. Mass. Com. Psychosurgery, 1974-75; Tanner lectr. Stanford U., 1982; mem. Justice Panel on Waco, 1993. Author: (with Onque) Longitudinal Studies of Child Behavior, 1961, Mental Health and Law: A System in Transition, 1975, Law, Psychiatry and Morality: Essays and Analysis, 1984; editor: (with Sue Stone) Abnormal Personality Through Literature, 1966. Capt. M.C., U.S. Army, 1959-61. Recipient Manfred S. Guttmacher award, Isaac Ray award, 1982; Ctr. Advanced Study Behavioral Sci. fellow Stanford U., 1980-81. Mem. Am. Psychiat. Assn. (trustee, v.p., pres., chmn. com. jud. action 1974-79), Group Advancement Psychiatry. Office: Harvard U Law Sch 1575 Massachusetts Ave Cambridge MA 02138-2801

STONE, ALAN JAY, retired academic administrator; b. Ft. Dodge, Iowa, Oct. 15, 1942; s. Hubert H. and Bernice A. (Tilton) S.; m. Jonieta J. Smith; 1 child, Kirsten K. Stone Morlock. BA, Morningside Coll., 1964; MA, U. Iowa, 1966; MTh, U. Chgo., 1968, DMin, 1970; PhD (hon.), Kyonggi U., Korea, 1985; LLD, Stillman Coll., 1991, Sogong U., Korea, 1992, Alma Coll., 2001; HD, Morningside Coll., 2001. Admissions counselor Morningside Coll., Sioux City, Iowa, 1964-66; dir. admissions, asso. prof. history George Williams Coll., Downers Grove, Ill., 1969-73; v.p. coll. relations Hood Coll., Frederick, Md., 1973-75; v.p. devel. and fin. affairs W.Va. Wesleyan Coll., Buckhannon, 1975-77; dir. devel. U. Maine, 1977-78; pres. Aurora (Ill.) U., 1978-88, Alma (Mich.) Coll., 1988-2000; pres., CEO Alzheimer's Assn., Chgo., 2001—02; ret., 2002. Home: 28897 N 94th Pl Scottsdale AZ 85262 E-mail: stone5613@earthlink.net.

STONE, ALAN JOHN, manufacturing company executive, real estate executive; b. Dansville, N.Y., Sept. 9, 1940; s. Guthrie Boyd and Doris Irene (Wolfanger) S.; m. Sandra Barber, Aug. 22, 1964; children: Teri, Timothy, Michael. BSME, Rochester Inst. Tech., 1963; MBA, U. Pitts., 1964. Engring. aide Xerox Corp., Webster, N.Y., 1960-63; gen. mgr. mech. component divsn. Stone Conveyor Co., Inc., Honeoye, N.Y., 1964-67, v.p. sales, 1968; co-founder, CEO Stone Constrn. Equipment Inc., Honeoye, 1969-86, also cons., bd. dirs., 1969—; founder, pres. Canandaigua Apts. Inc., N.Y., 1968-83; pres. Wildtrak, Inc., 1983—; founder, gen. ptnr. Stone Properties, 1986—2002; mng. mem. Stone Family Properties, LLC, 2002—. Dir., co-founder Baker Rental Svc., Inc., 1973-75; met. adv. bd. Chase Lincoln Bank, 1981-84; co-founder, dir. Royal Lines Ltd., 1989-91; v.p. Naples Biol. Rsch. Sta. Inc., 1996-98; bd. dirs. Canandaigua Nat. Bank & Trust Co., chmn. 1994-2004; mng. mem., City Mini Storage, LLC, 2001-. Patentee in field. Mem. Town of Richmond (N.Y.) Planning Bd., 1970-75, chmn., 1970-71; mem. Honeoye Ctrl. Sch. Bd. Edn., 1971-76, pres., 1974-75; com. chmn. pack 10 Boy Scouts Am., 1975-78; mem. Ontario County Overall Econ. Devel. Com., 1976-81; bd. dirs. F.F. Thompson Hosp., 1987-91; chmn. fin. com. United Meth. Ch., Allens Hill, 1995—2001; trustee Honeoye Pub. Libr., 1998-2002. Mem. Honeoye C. of C., Constrn. Industry Mfrs. Assn. (exec. mem. new bus. challenges coun. 1980-83), Honeoye Valley Assn. (dir. 1991-95, treas. 1993-95), Griswold and Cast Iron Collectors Assn. (treas. 1994-96, chmn. fin. com. 1996-2002), Honeoye Area Hist. Soc. (bicentennial com. 1989), Grand Slam Club, Safari Internat., Found. N.Am. Wild Sheep. Methodist. Home and Office: Box 500 4638 County Rd 33 Honeoye NY 14471-0500

STONE, ALLAN DAVID, economics professor; b. Joliet, Ill., Jan. 9, 1937; s. William E. and Leona V. (Frieh) S.; m. Peggy J. Carter, Jan. 11, 1958; children: David, Richard. BA, Beloit Coll., 1961; MA, U. Okla., 1964, PhD, 1973. Asst. prof. econs. U. Tex., El Paso, 1963-65; instr. econs. Wartburg Coll., Waverly, Iowa, 1965-66; asst. prof. econs. Oklahoma City U., 1966-72; prof. econs. S.W. Mo. State U., Springfield, 1972—2001, dept. head, 1985-87, emeritus prof., 2001—. Served with U.S. Army, 1956-58. NSF grantee. Mem. Am. Econ. Assn., Mo. Coun. Econ. Edn. (bd. dirs. 1977-80), Phi Beta Kappa, Phi Kappa Phi. Home: 820 E Cherokee St Springfield MO 65807-2708

STONE, AMY, reporter; b. Brunswick, Maine; m. Paul Stone. B in Comm. and Film, U. Mich., 1989. Prodr. Sta. WDIV-TV, Detroit; reporter New Eng. Sports Network, Boston, 1991—94; anchor SportsChannel, 1994—97; reporter Sta. WMAQ-TV, Chgo., 1997—2000, Sta. WCBS-TV, N.Y.C., 2000—. Recipient Emmy, 1999, 2000. Office: CBS 524 W 57th St New York NY 10019

STONE, ANDREW GROVER, lawyer; b. L.A., Oct. 2, 1942; s. Frank B. and Meryl (Pickering) S.; 1 child, John Blair; m. Susan Anselmo, Feb. 14, 2003. BA, Yale U., 1965; JD, U. Mich., 1969. Bar: D.C. 1970, U.S. Dist. Ct. D.C. 1970, U.S. Ct. Appeals (D.C. cir.) 1972, Mass. 1981. Assoc. Rogers & Wells, Washington, 1969-71; atty. Bur. Competition, FTC, Washington, 1971-80; antitrust counsel Digital Equipment Corp., Maynard, Mass., 1980-83, mgr. N.E. law group, 1983-86, mgr. headquarters sales law group, 1986-88; asst. general counsel U.S. (acting), 1987, 88; corp counsel, 1988-90; corp. counsel, pub. sect. mktg. Thinking Machines Corp., Cambridge, Mass., 1990-91, corp. counsel, 1992-95; pvt. practice on-site legal svcs. Marblehead, Mass., 1995—. Corp. mem. Tenacre Country Day Sch., Wellesley, Mass., 1981-88. Mem. ABA (bus. law sect.), Mass. Bar Assn. (internat. law steering com. 1993-94), Boston Bar Assn. (membership com. 1998-2000, chair corp. counsel com. 1995-98, chair gen. counsel forum 1995—), Am. Arbitration Assn. (comml. arbitrator), New Eng. Corp. Counsel Assn., Assn. Ind. Gen. Counsel.

STONE, ANN ELIZABETH, marketing agency executive, consultant; b. Bridgeport, Conn., Aug. 9, 1952; d. Jack Reginald and Edith Pauline (Christiansen) Wesche; m. Roger J. Stone, June 15, 1974 (div. Dec. 1990). BA, George Washington U., 1974; postgrad., Wharton Sch. Bus., Washington, 1975-76. Mktg. mgr. Human Events, Washington, 1974-76; v.p. polit. div. The Viguerie Co., Falls Church, Va., 1976-82; chmn. Capstone Lists, Alexandria, Va., 1983—, Unique Graphics, Alexandria, 1985—; vice chmn. George Washington Nat. Bank, Alexandria, 1988—; ptnr. Weintraub-Stone Direct, Inc., Woodland Hills, Calif., 1991—; pres. Ann E.W. Stone & Assocs., Alexandria, 1982—. Contbr. articles to profl. jours. Chmn. D.C. Young Reps., Washington, 1975-77; fin. dir. Alexandria Rep. Party, 1989-92; Republican candidate for mayor, Alexandria, 1991; chmn. Reps. for Choice, Alexandria, 1989—; bd. dirs. Campaigns and Elections Mag., Washington, 1987—, Am. Heart Assn., 1990—, chmn., 1993-94. Mem. Direct Mktg. Assn. Washington (bd. dirs. 1974—), Renaissance Women (bd. dirs. 1985—), Alexandria C. of C. (bd. dirs. 1982), Lions Club, Alexandria Seaport Fedn. Lutheran. Avocations: reading, travel, historical renovation, rock collecting, music. Office: Ann EW Stone & Assocs 2900 Eisenhower Ave # 200 Alexandria VA 22314-5223 Home: Ste 250 2760 Eisenhower Ave Alexandria VA 22314-4569

STONE, CAROLINE FLEMING, artist; b. N.Y.C., Mar. 26, 1936; d. Ralph Emerson and Elizabeth (Fleming) Stone; m. Oakleigh B. Thorne, June 1956 (div. 1969); children: Oakleigh, Henry; m. John Roderick Keating, July 2002. Student, Art Students' League, 1954-57, 71-72, Pratt Graphics, 1973-74. One-woman shows include Washington Art Assn., Conn., Ella Sharp Mus., Mich., 1980, San Diego Pub. Library, 1981, Trustman Gallery Simmons Coll., Boston, 1985, Mary Ryan Gallery, N.Y.C., 1989, Boston Pub. Libr., 1994, Messiah Coll., 1995; two-person shows include Mary Ryan Gallery, 1985, Katonah Gallery, N.Y., 1986, Davidson Gallery, Seattle, 1990, The Millbrook (N.Y.) Gallery, 1993; juried shows include Silvermine Nat. Printmaking, Conn., 1978, Print Club, Phila., 1981, Trenton State (Nat. Print Exhibn. Purchase award), 1982, Minot State Coll., N.D., 1985, Boston Printmakers (Jurors Commendation), 1986; group shows include Mus. N.Mex., 1984, De Cordova and Dana Mus., Nat. Acad. Art, N.Y.C., Boston Pub. Libr., Mus. Contemporary Hispanic Art, N.Y.C., 1987, World Print Exhbn., San Francisco, Smith Coll. Gallery, Northampton, Mass., Mary Ryan Gallery, 1988, Virginia Lynch Gallery, R.I., 1989, 91, Accent on Paper, Lintas, N.Y., 1991, Women Printmaker's Nat. Touring Show, Boston Pub. Libr. 1991, The Tenth Anniversary Show Virginia Lynch Gallery, 1993; represented in permanent collections Art Inst. Chgo., Mid-West Mus. Am. Art, Ind., Mus. N.Mex., Nat. Mus. Am. Art, Boston Pub. Library, U. Chgo., U. Mich., The Portland Art Mus. Mem.: The Kitchen (bd. dirs.). Home and Office: C Stone Press 80 Wooster St New York NY 10012-4347

STONE, DAVID M. federal agency administrator, retired career military officer; m. Cynthia Faith Voth, 1977. Diploma, U.S. Naval Acad., 1974; MS in Nat. Security Affairs, U.S. Naval Postgrad. Sch., 1977; MA in Nat. Security/Strategic Studies, U.S. Naval War Coll., 1986; MS in Mgmt., Salve Regina Coll. Commd. ensign USN, 1974, advanced through ranks to rear adm., ret., 2002, various assignments to comdr. Middle East Force and Destroyer Squadron 50, 1994-96; chief of staff U.S. Sixth Fleet, 1996-98; comdr. NATO's Standing Naval Force Mediterranean, 1998-99; deputy director surface warfare USN, 99-00, Nimitz battlegroup comm., 2000-01; dir., environ. protection, safety & occupational health Office of the Chief of Naval Ops., Washington, 2001—02; fed. security dir. LA Internat. Airport, 2002—03; dep. chief of staff Transp. Security Adminstrn., US Dept. Homeland Security, 2003—04, acting administr., 2004; asst. sec. for transp. security US Dept. Homeland Security, 2004—. Decorated Legion of Merit (3 times), Def. Meritorious Svc. medal (2 times), Meritorious Svc. medal (3 times), Navy Commendation medal (3 times), Navy Achievement medal, others. Office: US Dept Homeland Security 601 S 12th St Rm 1203N E Bldg Washington DC 22202-4220*

STONE, DAVID MARK, plastic surgeon; b. Chgo., Jan. 11, 1956; MD, U. Ill., 1981. Diplomate Am. Bd. Otolaryngology, Am. Bd. Facial Plastic & Reconstructive Surgery. Intern U. Ill./Metro Group Hosps., Chgo., 1981-82, resident in gen. surgery, 1982-83; resident in otolaryngology, head and neck surgery Northwestern U., Chgo., 1983-86; fellow in facial plastic surgery Am. Acad. Facial Plastic and Reconstructive Surgery, Birmingham, 1986-87; head, neck and facial plastic surgeon Van Buren, Ark.; asst. clin. prof. dept. otolaryngology/head and neck surgery U. Calif., Irvine. Fellow ACS; mem. AAOHNS, AMA, Am. Acad. Facial Plastic and Reconstructive Surgery. Office: 2010 Chestnut Ste D Van Buren AR 72956

STONE, DAVID PHILIP, lawyer; b. N.Y.C., Sept. 11, 1944; s. Robert and Laura Stone; m. Arlene R. Stone, June 11, 1966; children: Aaron J., Rachel E. AB, Columbia U., 1967; JD, Harvard U., 1970. Bar: N.Y. 1971. Assoc. Cahill, Gordon & Reindel, N.Y.C., 1970-74, Baer & McGoldrick, N.Y.C., 1974-76, Weil, Gotshal & Manges, L.L.P., N.Y.C., 1976-79, ptnr., 1979—. Office: Weil Gotshal & Manges LLP 767 5th Ave New York NY 10153-0119 Business E-Mail: david.stone@weil.com.

STONE, DEE WALLACE, actress; b. Kansas City, Mo., Dec. 14, 1948; d. Robert Stanley and Maxine (Nichols) Bowers; m. Christopher Stone, June 28, 1980 (dec.); m. Skip Belyea. BA, U. Kans., 1971. Actress feature films The Christmas Visitor, Secret Admirer, Cujo, E.T., Jimmy the Kid, The Howling, 10; actress ABC movies of the week Eminent Domain, Hostage Flight, A Whale for a Killing; actress CBS movies of the week An Enemy Among Us, Sin of Innocence, The Sky is No Limit, Happy, Surprise, Surprise, The Five of Me, Young Love, First Love; actress NBC movies of the week Wait Til Your Mother Gets Home, Child Bride of Short Creek, Skeezer; actress CBS After School Special Dad's Out of a Job; actress ABC After School Special Run Don't Walk; actress CBS series Police Story, Together We Stand/Nothing is Easy, Lou Grant; actress stage prodns. including Annie Get Your Gun, Oklahoma, My Fair Lady, Applause, Butterflies are Free, Middle of the Night. Spkr. in field; mgr. DWS Acting Studio, Burbank, Calif. Appeared in films including Nevada, 1997, Mutual Needs, 1997, Black Circle Boys, 1997, Bad As I Wanna Be: The Dennis Rodman Story, 1998, Flamingo Dreams, 1998, To Love, Honor and Betray, 1999, Invisible Mom II, 1999, Pirates of the Plain, 1999, Out of the Black, A Month of Sundays, Dead Canaries, others. Fundraiser Actors and Others for Animals, L.A., 1980—, Amanda Found., L.A., 1986, 87; co-host, fundraiser Children's Hospital Telethon, Sta. KCET, L.A., 1985—; spokesperson Nat. Assn. of Children of Alcoholics, 1987—. Mem. Screen Actors Guild, Actors Equity, AFTRA. Methodist. Avocations: dance, singing.

STONE, DONALD DIAMOND, investment and sales executive; b. Chgo., June 25, 1924; s. Frank J. and Mary N. (Miller) Diamondstone; m. Catherine Mauro, Dec. 20, 1970; 1 child, Jeffrey. Student, U. Ill., 1942-43; BS, DePaul U., 1949. Pres. Poster Bros., Inc., Chgo., 1950-71, Revere Leather Goods, Inc., Chgo., 1953-71; owner Don Stone Enterprises, Chgo., 1954—; v.p. Horton & Hubbard Mfg. Co. Inc. div. Brown Group, Nashua, N.H., 1969-71, Neevel Mfg. Co., Kansas City, Mo., 1969-71. Mem. adv. bd. San Diego Opera; founder Don Diego Meml. Scholarship Fund; mem. bd. overseers U. Calif., San Diego, chancellor's assoc.; mem. exec. bd. Chgo. Area council Boy Scouts of Am. Served with U.S. Army, 1943-46. Clubs: Bryn Mawr Country (Lincolnwood, Ill.) (dir.), Carlton, La Jolla Beach and Tennis, La Jolla Country, Del Mar Thoroughbred. Home: 8240 Caminito Maritimo La Jolla CA 92037-2204

STONE, DONALD JAMES, retired retail executive; b. Cleve., Mar. 5, 1929; s. Sidney S. and Beatrice (Edelman) S.; m. Norma Fay Karchmer, Oct. 26, 1952; children— Michael, Lisa, Angela. BBA, U. Tex., Austin, 1949. With Foley's, Houston, 1949-75, v.p., gen. mdse. mgr., 1960-75; chmn., chief exec. officer Sanger-Harris, Dallas, 1975-80; vice chmn. Federated Dept. Stores, Inc., Cin., 1980-88. Bd. dirs. M Corp., Fossil, Inc., Bloom Agy., Dallas, XTEC Corp., Cin. Pres. Dallas Symphony Soc., 1980-82, 88—, chmn. Found. bd., 1989—; chmn. exec. com. Dallas Ballet, 1979; bd. dirs. Dallas Mus. Fine Art, 1979-81; mem. adv. coun. Coll. Bus. Adminstrn. U. Tex., 1981—, chmn., 1990-92; bd. dirs. Cin. Ballet, 1982-87, Cin. Symphony, 1983-88, pres., 1987; bd. Cin. overseers, chmn., 1988-92; bd. govs. Hebrew Union Coll., 1988—; bd. dirs. Aspen Inst. Humanistic Studies, 1988-94. Mem. Dallas C. of C. (chmn. cultural com. 1979-81), Assoc. Mdse. Corp. (bd. dirs., exec. com.). Democrat. Jewish. Home: 3601 Turtle Creek Blvd Dallas TX 75219-5522

STONE, DONALD RAYMOND, lawyer; b. Madison, Wis., Mar. 6, 1938; s. Donald Meredith and June Dorothy (Graffenberger) S.; m. Dorothy Tetzlaff, June 23, 1962; children: Randall, Brian. BS in Physics, U. Wis., 1960, JD, 1963. Bar: Minn. 1963, D.C. 1987, U.S. Supreme Ct. 1987. Patent atty. Honeywell, Inc., Mpls., 1963-66; patent atty. firm Burd, MacEachron, Braddock, Bartz & Schwartz, Mpls., 1966-68; with Medtronic, Inc., Mpls., 1968-87, v.p., then sr. v.p. product assurance and regulation, 1973-77, sr. v.p., sec., gen. counsel, 1977-80, sr. v.p., 1980-85, v.p., 1985-87; ptnr., mem. Burditt, Bowles & Radzius, Chartered, Washington, 1987-90; ptnr. McKenna & Cuneo, L.L.P., Washington, 1990-2001, Kirkpatrick & Lockhart LLP, Washington, 2001—03, of counsel, 2003; ret., 2003. Condr. seminars, 1974—. Contbr. articles to profl. jours. Bd. dirs., 1st v.p. East Side Neighborhood Services, Inc., Mpls., 1976-80; bd. dirs. Guthrie Theater Found., 1979-85; mem. allocations com. United Way Mpls., 1979-86, chmn. allocations com., 1985, bd. dirs. 1985-86; mem. Citizens League of Twin Cities, 1965-86. Mem. ABA, D.C. Bar Assn., Fed. Bar Assn., Hennepin County Bar Assn., Am. Soc. Quality, Am. Intellectual Property Law Assn., Advanced Med. Tech. Assn. (past chmn. legal and regulatory sect., std. sect., 1975-87), Nat. Elec. Mfrs. Assn. (past chmn. med. electronics sect., 1970-76), Minn. State Bar Assn., Minn. Intellectual Property Law Assn. (past sec.), Minn. Corp. Counsel Assn., Order of Coif, Phi Delta Phi, Kappa Sigma. Episcopalian.

STONE, DUANE SNYDER, school psychologist, clergyman; b. Turon, Kans., Nov. 10, 1935; s. Herman and Neva F. (Snyder) S.; m. Nancy R. Castillo, July 12, 1958; children: Patricia L. Stone Davis, Christopher D. AA, Graceland Coll., 1953; BA, San Jose State U., 1959, MA, 1961; EdS, Wichita State U., 1985. Ordained to ministry Reorganized LDS Ch., 1951. Tchr., adminstr., supt. Santa Clara County Schs., San Jose, Calif., 1959-63; commd. 2d lt. USAF, 1963, advanced through grades to maj., 1974, security police officer, 1963-66, instr. Officer Tng. Sch. Lackland AFB, Tex., 1966-69, base def. officer 35 TRW Phan Rang Air Base, Vietnam, 1969-70; asst. prof. aerospace sci. Memphis State U. AFROTC, 1970-73; comdr. security police squadron USAF, Minot AFB, N.D., 1973-76; clin. psychologist 91st Regional Hosp. USAF, Minot AFB, 1976-83; ret., 1983; sch. psychologist Wichita (Kans.) Pub. Schs., 1985-86, Butler County Sch. Bd., El Dorado, Kans., 1986—. Pres. Reality Theapy Assocs., Wichita, 1983—. Author: The Ministry of Health and Healing, 1986, Ministry to Persons with Debilitating Lifestyles, 1988. Treas. Springhaven, Andover, Kans., 1955—. Recipient award Reorganized LDS Ch., 1995. Mem. NASP (cert.), DAV, NRA, Ret. Officers Assn. Avocations: flying, photography. Home: 1112 S Kansas St Wichita KS 67211-2724 Office: Butler County Sch Bd 1518 W 6th Ave El Dorado KS 67042-1425

STONE, EDWARD C. physicist, researcher; b. Knoxville, Iowa, Jan. 23, 1936; s. Edward Carroll and Ferne Elizabeth (Baber) Stone; m. Alice Trabue Wickliffe, Aug. 4, 1962; children: Susan, Janet. AA, Burlington Jr. Coll., 1956; MS, U. Chgo., 1959, PhD, 1964, DSc (hon.), 1992, Washington U., St. Louis, 1992, Harvard U., 1992; BA (hon.), U. So. Calif., 1998. From rsch. fellow in physics to prof. Calif. Inst. Tech., Pasadena, Calif., 1964—94, David Morrisroe prof. physics, 1994—, v.p., 1964—91, Voyager project scientist, 1972—, chmn. divsn. physics, math. and astron., 1983—88, dir. jet propulsion lab., 1991—2001, mem. Draper Lab., 2001, vice provost for spl. projects, 2004—. Cons. Office of Space Sci., NASA, 1969—85, adv. com. outer planets, 1972—73; high energy astrophysics mgmt. oper. working group NASA, 1976—84, cosmic ray program working group, 1980—82, outer plantets working group, 1981—82, solar sys. exploration com., 1981—82, U. rels. study group, 1983; exec. com. Com. on Space Rsch. Interdisciplinary Sci. Commn., 1982—86; com. on space astronomy and astrophysics Space Sci. Bd., 1979—82, steering group study on maj. directions for space sci., 1984—85; mem. Space Sci. Bd., NRC, 1982—85; commn. on phys. sci., math. and resources NRC, 1986—89; adv. com. vis. sr. scientist program NASA/Jet Propulsion Labs., 1986—90; com. on space policy NAS/NAE, 1988—89; chmn., chief sci. advisor The Astronomers, KCET, 1989—91; chmn. adv. panel NAS/WQED TV program "Sail on, Voyager!", 1989—90; v.p. COSPAR Bur., 2001—. Mem. editl. bd. Space Sci. Instrumentation, 1975—81, Space Sci. Rev., 1982—85, Astrophysics and Space Sci., 1982—, Sci. mag. Bd. dir. W.M. Keck Found., 1994—. Named an asteroid Edward C. Stone in his honor, 1996; named to Hall of Fame, Aviation Week and Space Tech., 1997, Hall of Honor, Burlington Comm., 1999; recipient medal for exceptional sci. achievement, NASA, 1980, Am. Edn. award, 1981, Disting. Svc. medal, 1981, 1998, 2001, Dryden award, 1983, Disting. Pub. Svc. medal, 1985, Outstanding Leadership medal, 1986, 1995, Achievement award, Soc. for Tech. Comm., 1984, Space Achievement award, AIAA, 1986, Oppenheimer Mem. Lecture Aviation Week and Space Tech. Aerospace Laureate, 1989, Sci. Man of Yr. award, ARCS Found., 1991, Nat. Medal of Sci., 1991, Golden Plate award, Am. Acad. Achievement, 1992, COSPAR award, 1992, LeRoy Randle Grumman medal, 1992, Disting. Pub. Svc. award, Aviation/Space Writers Assn., 1993, Internat. von Karman Wings award, 1996, Space Flight Award, Am. Astron. Soc., 1997, Alumni award, S.E. C.C., Burlington, Iowa, 1997, CEO of Yr. award, ARC, 1998, Allan D. Emil Meml. award, Internat. Astronautical Fedn., 1999, Carl Sagan award, Am. Astronautical Soc. and Planetary Soc., 1999, Prof. Achievement award, Alumni, U. Chgo., 2002, Nat. Award for Op., Assn. for Unmanned Sys., Nat. Medal of Sci., Pres. Bush; fellow Sloan Found., 1971—73. Fellow: AAAS (award 1993), AIAA (assoc.; Calif. coun. sci. and tech. 1996—2001, Space Sci. award 1984, von Karman lectureship in astronautics 1999), Internat. Astron. Union, Am. Geophys. Union, Am. Phys. Soc. (exec. com. 1974—76, chmn. cosmic physics divsn. 1979—80); mem.: NAS, Sci. Edit. Bd., Comm. of Phys. Sci., Math., and Applications, NRC, Am. Philos. Soc., Calif. Assn. Rsch. in Astronomy (bd. dirs., vice-chmn. 1986—88, vice-chmn. 1986—2003, bd. dirs., vice-chmn. 1991—94, chmn. bd. dirs. 1994—97, bd. dirs., vice-chmn. 1997—2000, chmn. bd. dirs. 2000—03), Astron. Soc. Pacific (hon.), Royal Aero. Soc., Nat. Space Club (bd. govs., Sci. award 1990), Am. Philos. Soc. (Magellanic award 1992), Am. Astron. Soc. (divsn. planetary sci. com. 1981—84, Space Flight award 1997), Internat. Acad. Astronautics (trustee 1989—2001, v.p. 2001—). Office: Calif Inst Tech Space Radiation Lab M/C 220-47 Pasadena CA 91125

STONE, EDWARD HARRIS, II, landscape architect; b. Lanesboro, Pa., Aug. 28, 1933; s. Frank Addison and Beth Lee (Brennan) S.; m. Diane Gertrude Berg, June 11, 1955; children: Randel Harris, Deborah Dee. BS, SUNY, 1955. Landscape architect Harmon, O'Donnell & Henninger, Denver, 1955-56, U.S. Forest Service, Colo., 1958-61; regional landscape architect Alaska, 1961-64; regional landscape architect, Colo., 1964—65; chief landscape architect U.S. Forest Service, U.S. Dept. Agr., Washington, 1966-79, asst. dir. for recreation, 1979-85; ret., 1985; with C-3 Co., Bowie, Md., 1986—. Served with AUS, 1956-57. Recipient Arthur S. Flemming award for outstanding fed. govt. service U.S. Jr. C. of C., 1969 Fellow Am. Soc. Landscape Architects (pres. 1975-76); mem. Sigma Lambda Alpha (hon.) Home and Office: 13200 Forest Dr Bowie MD 20715-4390

STONE, EDWARD HERMAN, lawyer; b. July 20, 1939; s. Sidney and Ruth Stone; m. Penni G. Gray (dec. 1990); children: Andrew, Matthew; m. Elaine Ornitz, Dec. 22, 1995. BS in Acctg., U. Ill., 1961; JD, John Marshall Law Sch., 1967. Bar: Ill. 1967, Calif. 1970, cert.: Calif. (specialist probate, estate planning, and trust law). With IRS, 1963-71; assoc. Eilers, Baranger, Myers & Smith, 1971-72; pvt. practice Newport Beach, Calif., 1972—88, Santa Ana, Calif., 1988-89; mem. Davis, Samuelson, Goldberg & Blakely (formerly Cohen, Stokke & Davis), Santa Ana, 1984-88; ptnr. Edward H. Stone A Law Corp., Irvine, Calif., 1990—. Instr. income and estate taxes Western States U. Sch. Law, 1971—72; mem. joint adv. com. CEB, Calif.; judge pro tem, jud. arbitrator Orange County Superior Ct.; moderator, spkr. Calif. Trust and Probate Litig. CEB, 1999; mediator IRS ADR tax cases in appeals, 2000—; moderator, spkr. postmortem trust adminstrn. CEB, Calif., 2002, Calif., 04; moderator, spkr. Calif. Trust and Probate Litig. CEB, 2001, 04. Contbr. articles to profl. jours. Pres. Jewish Family Svcs. Orange County, 1975; v.p., bd. dirs. Jewish Fedn. Orange County, 1985—88; bd. dirs. Heritage Points Orange County, 1992—95, Eastbluff Homeowners Cmty. Assn., Newport Beach, 1980—82, pres., 1981—82. Mem.: Orange County Bar Assn. (vice-chmn. estate planning probate and trust law sect. 1976—77, chmn. sect. 1977—78, instr. Probate Clinic 1980, chairperson ADR com. 1996, spkr. in substantive law, dir. 1977—82, past chmn. profl. edn. coun., chmn.del. real property and probate sect, chmn. del. real property and probate sect. state bar conv. 1992—), Phi Alpha Delta (pres. alumni chpt. 1975—76).

STONE, EDWARD LUKE, private equity investor, realtor; b. Englewood, N.J., Jan. 18, 1937; s. James and Anna (Druskin) S.; m. Cassandra Reeve, Mar. 15, 1969. BA, Yale U., 1958; postgrad., Cambridge U., Eng., 1959; MBA, Harvard U., 1966. Dir. fin. planning Yale U., New Haven, 1966-69; pres. HDC, Inc., Boston, 1969-77; ptnr. Dane, Falb, Stone, Boston, 1977-81; exec. dir. White House Preservation Fund, Washington, 1981-90; trustee Newport Art Mus., 1991-94; chmn. Stone and Cranwell, Newport, R.I., 1995-99; pres. Hogan and Stone, Newport, 1996-99; broker Benchmark Assocs., Middletown, RI, 1999—2001; chmn. Edward L. Stone Realty llc, Newport, 2002—. Cons. Booz Allen Hamilton, Bethesda, Md., 1987-88. Trustee Nat. Mus. of Women in the Arts, Washington, 1988-90, Tudor Pl. Found., Washington, 1988-95, The Washington Home, 1988-95, Touro Synagogue Friends, 1996—; gov. Newport Health Care Corp., 1997—; co-chmn. The Isaac Bell House, 1995—. Mem. Newport Reading Rm., Spouting Rock Beach Assn., Somerset Club, Elizabethan Club, Phi Beta Kappa. Avocation: early 19th century american decorative arts. Home: The Poplars 12 Leroy Ave Newport RI 02840-4106 Office Phone: 401-849-9262. E-mail: estone3137@aol.com.

STONE, ELAINE MURRAY, author, composer, television producer; b. NYC, Jan. 22, 1922; d. H. and Catherine Fairbanks Murray-Jacoby; m. F. Courtney Stone, May 30, 1944; children: Catherine Gustavson, Pamela Webb, Victoria Mattson. Student, Juilliard Sch., 1939-41; BA, N.Y. Coll. Music, 1943; licentiate in organ, Trinity Coll. Music, London, 1947; student, U. Miami, 1952, Fla. Inst. Tech., 1963; PhD (hon.), World U., 1985, Oxford (Eng.) U., 1998. Organist, choir dir. St. Ignatius Episc. Ch., 1940-44; accompanist Strawbridge Ballet on Tour, N.Y.C., 1944; organist All Saints Episc. Ch., Ft. Lauderdale, 1951-54, St. John's Episc. Ch., Melbourne, Fla., 1956-59, First Christian Ch., Melbourne, 1962-63, United Ch. Christ, Melbourne, 1963-65, piano studio, Melbourne, 1955-70; editor-in-chief Cass Inc., 1970-71; dir. continuity radio Sta. WTAI, AM-FM, Melbourne, 1971-74; mem. sales staff Engle Realty Inc., Indialantic, Fla., 1975-78; v.p. pub. relations Consol. Cybertronics Inc., Cocoa Beach, Fla., 1969-70; writer, producer Countdown News, Sta. KXTX-TV, Dallas, 1978-80; assoc. producer Focus News, Dallas, 1980. Host producer TV show, Focus on History, 1982-94, Episc. Digest, 1984-90; judge Writer's Contest sponsored Brevard Cmty. Coll., 1987; v.p. Judges Fla. Space Coast Writer's Conf., 1985—, chmn., 1987. Author: The Taming of the Tongue, 1954, Love One Another, 1957, Menéndez de Avilés, 1968, Bedtime Bible Stories, Travel Fun, Sleepytime Tales, Improve Your Spelling for Better Grades, Improve Your Business Spelling, Tranquility Tapes, 1970, The Melbourne Bi-Centennial Book, 1976, Uganda: Fire and Blood, 1977, Tekla and the Lion, 1981 (1st pl. Nat. League Am. Pen Women), Brevard County: From Cape of the Canes to Space Coast, 1988, Kizito, Boy Saint of Uganda, 1989 (2d pl. Nat. League Am. Pen Women 1990), Christopher Columbus: His World, His Faith., His Adventures, 1991 (1st pl. Nat. League Am. Pen Women 1992), Elizabeth Bayley Seton: An American Saint, 1993 (3d pl. Nat. League Am. Pen Women 1994), Dimples The Dolphin, 1994 (1st pl. Fla. Space Coast Writer's Guild, 1994), Brevard at The Edge of Sea and Space, 1995, The Widow's Might, 1996 (1st pl. Space Coast Writer's Contest), Carter G. Woodson Father of Black History, 1997 (1st pl. Am. Heritage Contest Nat. Soc. Daus. of Am. Revolution 1997), Maximilian Kolbe: Saint of Auschwitz, 1997 (Cath. Bestseller list 1997), Albert's Jungle Piano, 1997 (1st pl. Nat. League Am. Pen Women 1997, 2d pl., Nat. League of Am. Pen Women, 1999), Mother Teresa: A Life of Love, 1999, The Taming of the Tongue, 1999, C.S. Lewis: Creator of Narnia, 2001 (3d place Nat. League Am. Pen Women 2001), Mary and the Apparitions of Guadalupe, Lourdes and Fatima, 2003, A Saint and His Lion The Story of Tekla of Ethiopia, 2003, A New Life (1st place Fla. Assn. Univ. Women 2003), Saints of the Americas, 2004, Dorothy Day: Champion of the Poor, 2004; composer: Christopher Columbus Suite, 1992 (1st pl. Pen Women Music Awards 1992, 2d pl. 1993), Florida Suite for cello and piano, 1993, Two Crowns of St. Maximilian, 1998 (1st pl. in music Nat. League Am. Pen Women 1997), Pastorale, 2000 (1st pl. Nat. League Am. Pen Women, Washington, 2000), Anima Christi, 2000 (hon. mention Nat. League Am. Pen Women, Washington, 2000); contbr. articles to mags., newspapers including N.Y. Herald Tribune, Living Church, Christian Life, Episcopal Life; space corr. Religious News Service, Kennedy Space Ctr., 1962-78. Exec. bd. Women's Assn., Brevard Symphony, 1967—; heritage com. Melbourne Bicentennial Commn.; mem. Evangelism Commn. Episc. Diocese Cen. Fla., 1985-94; v.p. churchwomen group Holy Trinity Episcopal Ch., Melbourne, 1988-89, Stephen minister, 1988 , pres. churchwomen group, 1989—; bd. dirs. Fla. Space Coast Council Internat. Visitors, Fla. Space Coast Philharm., 1989—, Aid for the Arts, 1994; appointee Hist. Preservation Com., Melbourne, Fla., 2003. Recipient 1st place for piano Ashley Hall, 1935-39, S.C. State Music Contest, 1939, 1st place for piano composition Colonial Suite, Constitution Hall, Washington 1987, 88, 89, 3d place for vocal composition, 1989, honorable mention for article, 1989, 2nd place for piano composition, 1989, award lit. contest Fla. AAUW, 1989, 1st place award Fla. State PEN Women, 1990, 1st Place award Nat. Black History Essay Contest, 1990, 2d place Nat. League Am. Pen Women, 1999, 2d place for music composition, 1999, named Woman of Achievement, 1999, Disting. Author of Yr. plaque Fla. Space Coast Writers Guild, 1992, 96, Woman of Achievement plaque AAUW, 1997, Martha Ingram award Excellence in Arts, Ashley Hall, Charleston, 2004; honoree Nat. Polish Alliance, 3d place award for essay "Remembering C.S. Lewis" Mount Dora Festival of Music and Literature, 2001. Mem. ASCAP, Nat. League Am. PEN Women (1st place awards Tex. 1979, 1st place award for duet, Washington, 2000, pres. Dallas br. 1978-80, organizing pres. Cape Canaveral br. 1969, pres. 1988-90, 96—), Women in Comms., DAR (Fla. state chmn. music 1962-63), Colonial Dames Am. (organizing pres. Melbourne chpt. 1994), Nat. Soc. DAR (organizing regent Rufus Fairbanks chpt. 1981-85, vice regent 1987—, historian 1989—, Fla. state chmn. Am. Heritage), Children Am. Revolution (past N.Y. state chaplain), Am. Guild Organists (organizing warden Ft. Lauderdale), Space Pioneers, Fla. Press, Aid for the Arts, Space Coast Writers Guild (past v.p.). Home: 1945 Pineapple Ave Melbourne FL 32935-7656 E-mail: stonebooks@mailstation.com.

STONE, ELIZABETH CECILIA, anthropology educator; b. Oxford, Eng., Feb. 4, 1949; d. Lawrence and Jeanne Cecilia (Fawtier) S.; m. Paul Edmund Zimansky, Nov. 5, 1976. BA, U. Pa., 1971; MA, Harvard U., 1973; PhD, U. Chgo., 1979. Lectr. anthropology SUNY, Stony Brook, 1977-78, asst. prof., 1978-85, assoc. prof., 1985-95, prof., 1995—2002. Participated archaeol. in Eng., Iran, Iraq, Afghanistan; dir. archaeol. projects Ain Dara, Syria, Tell Abu Duwari, Iraq, Ayanis Survey, Turkey. Author: Nippur Neighborhoods, 1987; co-author: (monograph) Old Babylonian Contracts from Nippur 1, 1976, Adoption in Old Babylonian Nippur and the Archive of Mannum-meshulissur, 1991, The Iron Age Settlement at Ain Dara, Syria, 1999, The Anatomy of a Masopotamian City: Survey and Soundings of Mashkan-Shapin, 2004; co-editor: The Cradle of Civilization Recent Archaeology in Iraq-Biblical Archaeologist, 1992, Velles Paraules: Ancient Near Eastern Studies in Honor of Miguel Civil on the Occasion of His 65th Birthday, 1991; mem. editl. bd. Bull. Am. Schs. Oriental Rsch., 1993-95, 99—; contbr. articles to profl. jours. Assoc. trustee Am. Schs. of Oriental Rsch., 1983-90. Recipient P.E. MacAllister Field Archaeology award Am. Sch. Oriental Rsch., 2002; named Woman of the Yr. in Sci., Three Village Cmty., 2004; Fulbright fellow, 1986-87; rsch. grantee Ford Found., 1974, Nat. Geog. Soc., 1983, 84, 88, 90, 97-99, 2002, 03, Am. Schs. of Oriental Rsch., 1987, 88, NSF, 1989-95, 2000—, NEH, 1989-93, Andrew Mellon Found., 2003, USAID, 2003-4. Office: SUNY Dept Anthropology Stony Brook NY 11794-0001 Office Phone: 631-632-7627. Business E-Mail: estone@notes.cc.sunysb.edu.

STONE, F. L. PETER, lawyer; b. Wilmington, Del., Feb. 24, 1935; s. Linton and Lorinda (Hamlin) S.; m. Therese Louise Hannon, Apr. 7, 1969; 1 child, Lisa Judith. AB, Dartmouth Coll, 1957; LLB, Harvard U., 1960. Bar: Del. Supreme Ct. 1960, U.S. Ct. Appeals (3d cir.) 1964, U.S. Supreme Ct. 1965, U.S. Ct. Appeals (fed. cir.) 1983. Assoc. Connolly, Bove & Lodge, Wilmington, 1960-64; dep. atty. gen. State of Del., Wilmington, 1965-66; atty. Del. Gen. Assembly, Dover, 1967-68; counsel Gov. Del., Dover, 1969; U.S. atty. Dist. of Del., Wilmington, 1969-72; ptnr. Connolly, Bove, Lodge, & Hutz, Wilmington, 1972-97; counsel Trzuskowski, Kipp, Kelleher & Pearce, Wilmington, 1997—98, 2001—02; dep. atty. gen., counsel to ins. dept. State of Del., 1998-2001; dep. commr. Del. Ins. Dept., 2002—. Mem. Del. Agy. to Reduce Crime, 1969-72, Del. Organized Crime Commn., 1970-72, State Drug Abuse Coun., 1990-93, State Judicial Nominating Commn., 1991-93, State Coun. Corrections, 1992-99; co-founder, adj. prof. criminal justice progra, West Chester (Pa.) U., 1975-79; chmn. Gov.'s Harness Racing Investigation Com., 1977, Del. Jai Alai Commn., 1977-78, Del. Govs. Corrections Task Force, 1986-88. Contbr. articles to profl. jours. Chmn. UN Day, Del., 1989; mem. Del. Gov.'s Task Force on Prison Security, 1994—95; trustee Leukemia Soc. Am., N.Y.C., 1972—74, Marywood Coll., Scranton, Pa., 1974—79, Ursuline Acad., Wilmington, 1974—80; bd. dirs. Boys and Girls Club Del., 1997—, Seamen's Ctr., Port of Wilmington, 2001—; Rep. candidate for atty. gen. Del., 1990; mem. Rep. exec. com. Wilmington region, 1991—2000; chmn. reelection campaign Del. Ins. Commr., 1996. Mem. Port of Wilmington Maritime Soc. (bd. dirs., chair 1998-2000), Wilmington Country Club, Rehoboth Beach Country Club, Lincoln Club Del. (pres. 1994), Wilmington Rotary (bd. dirs. 1995-97), Nat. Assn. Former U.S. Attys. (bd. dirs. 1995-98). Roman Catholic. Avocations: hiking/mountaineering, tennis, golf, music. Office: Del Ins Dept 841 Silver Lake Blvd Dover DE 19904 E-mail: peter.stone@deins.state.de.us. *My major accomplishment has been establishing and maintaining a close relationship with my family, first and foremost, regardless of what activities and accomplishments were pursued in my professional, political and community life.*

STONE, FLORENCE SMITH, film festival executive, consultant; b. Balt., June 15, 1938; d. Howard Chandler and Mary (Burnam) Smith; m. Roger David Stone; 1 child, Leslie Burnam. BA, Vassar Coll., 1960; cert. Inst. Arts Adminstrn., Harvard U., 1978. Asst. to v.p. for pub. rels. Transam. Corp., San Francisco, 1962-64; newsletter editor U.S. Embassy, Rio de Janeiro, 1964-66; coord. cmty. rels. Am. Mus. Natural History, N.Y.C., 1970-79, coord. spl. progrm, 1977-84; dir. Washington Office Earthwatch, Washington, 1985-90; ind. cons. to mus. and ednl. orgns. Washington, 1990—; coord., founder Environ. Film Festival, Washington, 1993—. Co-chmn. Margaret Mead Film Festival, 1977-84. Trustee The Textile Mus., Washington, 1994—, Laura Boulton Found., N.Y.C., 1980-99, Mus. of the Hudson Highlands, Cornwall-on-Hudson, N.Y., 1974-96; mem. adv. com. Margaret Mead Film Festival, N.Y.C., 1992—; chmn. Trees for Georgetown Com., Washington, 1996-2004. Mem.: Textile Soc., Women in Film and Video, Ind. Film and Video Assn., Internat. Documentary Assn., Am. Assn. Mus., Cosmos Club, Cosmopolitan Club, Georgetown Garden Club. Democrat. Avocations: textiles, film, trees, performing arts, outdoor activities. Office: Environ Film Festival 1228 1/2 31st St NW Washington DC 20007-3402 Office Phone: 202-342-2564. Business E-Mail: flostone@igc.org.

STONE, FRANK BRUCE, contractor; s. Ronald Eugene and Gisela Maria Stone; m. Melody Sue Crawford, Sept. 8, 1973; children: Jennifer Lynn Evans, Nichole Katherine. Lic. gen. contractor Ala. Owner Melody Homes, Huntsville, Ala., 1996—. Bd. dirs. Builders Assn., Huntsville, 1987—88. Served with U.S. Army, 1970—73. Home and Office: Melody Homes 111 Pine Valley Cir Madison AL 35758 E-mail: mel2510@knology.net.

STONE, FRANK BUSH, lawyer; b. Houghton, Mich., Dec. 18, 1913; s. John Grover and Helen Grace (Ball) S.; m. Meryl A. Pickering, Aug. 26, 1939 (dec. 1991); children: Andrew G., William D.; m. Patricia A. Fath, Jan. 25, 1993. (dec. 2002). AB, Yale U., 1935; JD, U. Mich., 1938. Bar: Mich. 1939, N.Y. 1941, D.C. 1942, Calif. 1943. Assoc. Chadbourne, Wallace, Parke & Whiteside, Washington, L.A., N.Y.C., 1938-43; resident counsel N.Am. Aviation, L.A., 1943-45; assoc. Chadbourne, Parke, Whiteside, Wolff & Brophy, N.Y.C., 1945-55, ptnr., 1955-83; of counsel Chadbourne & Parke, LLP, N.Y.C., 1983—. Vestryman, sr. warden St. Andrew's Episcopal Ch., Murray Hill, N.J., 1976-79. Mem. Old Guard of Summit (dir. 1991). Avocation: genealogy. Home: 24 Ramsey Dr Summit NJ 07901-3015

STONE, FRED LYNDON, retired human resources administrator; b. High Point, N.C., Mar. 30, 1941; s. Charlie Edward and Minnie (Killingsworth) S. AB, High Point U., 1963. Field epidemiologist USPHS, Raleigh, N.C., 1963-66; supr. tng. Manhattan Shirt Co., Lexington, N.C., 1966-68; mgr. tng. Manhattan Industries, Salisbury, Md., 1968-72; mgr. pers. Silver Springs Sportswear, Ocala, Fla., 1972-74; v.p. human resources Citrus Meml. Hosp., Inverness, Fla., 1974—2001; ret., 2001. Coord. nursing scholarships Ctrl. Fla.

C.C., Ocala, 1974-96, Marion County Sch. Radiol. Tech., Ocala, 1985-99. Author: Heritage of Healing, 1995. Mem. Am. Soc. Healthcare Human Resources, Fla. Soc. Healthcare Human Resources, ACLU, Fla. Trust Hist. Preservation, Fla. Hist. Soc. Episcopalian. Home: 11471 W Dixie Shores Dr Crystal River FL 34429-5283

STONE, FRED MICHAEL, lawyer; b. Bklyn., Jan. 20, 1943; s. Nathan and Rose (Silverman) Stone; m. Bonnie B. Dobkin, Aug. 14, 1965; children: Jonathan, Jennifer. AB cum laude, Bklyn. Coll., 1964; JD, Harvard U., 1967; LLM, NYU, 1971. Bar: N.Y. 1968. Assoc. Cadwalader, Wickersham & Taft, N.Y.C., 1967-69; asst. gen. counsel Standard & Poor's/Intercapital, Inc., N.Y.C., 1969-71; v.p., gen. counsel Neuwirth Funds, 1971-73, Mocatta Metals Corp., N.Y.C., 1973-76; sr. v.p., gen. counsel Am. Stock Exch., Inc., N.Y.C., 1976-86, artbitrator, 1986—; exec. v.p., gen. counsel Jamie Securities Co., Caronan Ptnrs., N.Y.C., 1986-88; sr. v.p., gen. counsel, sec. M.D. Sass Assocs., Inc., N.Y.C., 1989-2000; chmn. exec. com. Amex Commodities Exch., 1980-81; dir. Am. Gold Coin Exch., Inc., 1981-85; exec. v.p., dir. Revere Copper and Brass, Inc., 1986-88; dir. Ea. Electric Motor Co., Inc., 1987-88; mng. dir. Chase & M.D. Sass Ptnrs., 1998-2000; mng. dir., gen. counsel Millennium Ptnrs., L.P., N.Y.C., 2000—. Ofcl. advisor drafting com. to Revise Uniform Securities Act Nat. Conf. Uniform State Law Commrs., 1981—85; sec. rules com. Investment Co. Inst., 1989—92; sec., treas. steering com. Taxaple Mcpl. Bondholders Protective Com., 1990—95; mem. task force pvt. investment entities, 1994—; lectr. various legal seminaries. Mem. Manalapan (N.J.) Twp. Zoning Bd. Adjustment, 1975—86, 2000—03, chmn., 2001—02; mem. N.J. regional exec. com. Anti-Defamation League of B'nai B'rith, 1991—; vice chmn. Manalapan Dem. Com., 1988—96; Dem. candidate Manalapan Twp. Com., 1989, 1993. Mem.: ABA, Nat. Futures Assn. (mem. nominating com. 1986—88), Nat. Assn. Securities Dealers (arbitrator 1986—), Assn. Bar City of N.Y. (mem. chorus), Harvard U. Law Sch. Assn. Democrat. Jewish. Home: 15 Kingsley Dr Manalapan NJ 07726-3134 Office Phone: 212-841-4124. E-mail: fstone@mlp.com.

STONE, GEOFFREY RICHARD, law educator, lawyer; b. Nov. 20, 1946; s. Robert R. and Shirley (Weliky) S.; m. Nancy Spector, Oct. 8, 1977; children: Julie, Mollie. BS, U. Pa., 1968; JD, U. Chgo., 1971. Bar: N.Y. 1972. Law clk. to Hon. J.S. Kelly Wright U.S. Ct. Appeals (D.C. cir.), 1971-72; law clk. to Hon. William J. Brennan, Jr. U.S. Supreme Ct., 1972-73; asst. prof. U. Chgo., 1973-77, assoc. prof., 1977-79, prof., 1979-84, Harry Kalven Jr. disting. svc. prof., 1984—, dean Law Sch., 1987-93, provost, 1994—2002. Author: Constitutional Law, 1986, 4th edit., 2001, The Bill of Rights in the Modern State, 1992, The First Amendment, 1999, Eternally Vigilant: Free Speech in the Modern Era, 2001; editor The Supreme Ct. Rev., 1991—; contbr. articles to profl. jours. Bd. dirs. Ill. divsn. ACLU, 1978-84; bd. advisors Pub. Svc. Challenge, 1989; bd. govs. Argonne Nat. Lab., 1994—. Fellow AAAS; mem. Chgo. Coun. Lawyers (bd. govs. 1976-77), Am. Law Inst. Assn. Am. Law Schs. (exec. com. 1990-93), Legal Aid Soc. (bd. dirs. 1988), Order of Coif. Office: U Chgo 1111 E 60th St Chicago IL 60637-5418

STONE, GEORGE, artist, art educator; BA, Calif. State U., Long Beach, 1972; MFA, R.I. Sch. Design, 1974. Instr. R.I. Sch. Design, Providence, 1972-74; instr. sculpture Portsmouth (R.I.) Abbey Sch., 1973-74, Wayne State U., Detroit, 1974-75; vis. lectr., sculpture dept. Ohio U., Athens, 1976-77; instr., found. dept. Otis/Parsons Sch. Design, L.A., 1982-83; vis. lectr., sculpture dept. UCLA, 1986; assoc. prof. fine arts Art Inst. So. Calif., Laguna Beach, 1989-93; assoc. prof. visual art U. La Verne, Calif., 1994-2000. Vis. artist Calif. State U. Long Beach, 1986, Crossroads H.S. for Arts and Sci., Santa Monica, 1987, Claremont (Calif.) Grad. Sch., 1987, 88, U. Calif. Santa Barbara, 1989, Art Ctr. Coll. Design, Pasadena, Calif., 1991, Yale U., New Haven, 1992, Chatham Coll., Pitts., 1992, Calif. State U. San Francisco, 1993; commd. artist City of West Hollywood, 1986, City of L.A. Cmty. Redevel. Agy., 1987, Metro Art L.A. County Met. Transp. Auth., 1990-97, City of L.A. Cultural Affairs Dept., 1995-97. Solo exhbns. include Forsythe Bldg., Detroit, 1975, Cline Bldg., Athens, Ohio, 1976, Lake Hope, Athens, 1977, Otis/Parsons Gallery, 1981, East Gallery Claremont Grad. Sch., 1985, Calif. State U. Long Beach Art Mus., 1986, Meyers/Bloom Gallery, Santa Monica, Calif., 1988, 91, Laguna Art Mus., Costa Mesa, Calif., 1990, Capp St. Project, 1991, New Langton Arts, San Francisco, 1991, Ruth Bloom Gallery, Santa Monica, 1993, Pitts. Ctr. Arts, 1994; 2-person exhbns. L.A. Contemporary Exhbns., 1985, Claremont Grad. Sch. Gallery, 1988; group exhbns. include Lehigh U. Art Gallery, Bethlemen, Pa., 1975, Wayne State U., 1975, U. Calif. Santa Cruz, 1978, Vanguard Gallery, L.A., 1979, L.A. Inst. Contemporary Art, 1979, NYU Art Gallery, N.Y.C., 1980, Charles Kobler and Assoc. Architects, L.A., 1983, Design Ctr. L.A., 1984, Univ. Art Mus. Calif. State U. Long Beach, 1985, IDM Corp. and Pub. Corp. Arts, Long Beach, 1985, CRA, L.A., 1987, Newport Harbor Art Mus., Newport Beach, Calif., 1988, Meyers/Bloom Gallery, 1989, Galerie Antoine Candeau, Paris, 1990, Sezon Mus. Art, Tokyo and Osaka, Japan, 1991, Muckenthaler Cultural Ctr., Fullerton, Calif., 1991, Contemporary Arts Ctr., New Orleans, 1993, Next Thread Waxing Space, N.Y.C., 1993, Contemporary Arts Forum, Santa Barbara, 1996, Armand Hammer Mus. Art and Cultural Ctr., UCLA, 1997, others; subject numerous catalogs, publs., and revs., 1984—. Home: 1815 Laurel Canyon Blvd Los Angeles CA 90046-2028 Fax: 323-654-3012.

STONE, GLENDA LEE, librarian, genealogist; b. Cleburne, Tex., July 27, 1948; d. Herbert Roy Johnson and Ida Corene Roe; m. Ray Stone, Oct. 28, 1977; children: Jason Alan Smith, Dennis Ray, Julia Lee. BS, Tarleton State U., 1969; MLS, Tex. Woman's U., 1986. Clk. typist Dick Smith Libr. Tarleton State U., Stephenville, Tex., 1970—72, libr. asst., 1972—88, libr., 1988—91, libr. III, 1991—2002, libr. IV, head cataloging dept., 1991—. Presenter on local history, genealogy, Stephenville area. Co-author: Thomas Getzendanner of Maryland and South Carolina. Developer Cross Timbers Hist. Images Project. Recipient Cert. for support of today's youth, Stephenville H.S. History Honor Soc., 1999; grantee Cross Timbers Hist. Images digitization project, Tex. Coun. for the Humanities, 2002—03, Ralph and Dossie Rogers Collection digitization project, Tex. State Libr. Tex Treasures, 2002—03. Mem.: Tex. Libr. Assn., ALA, Erath County Geneal. Soc. (exec. officer, ex-officio advisor 2003—04). Methodist. Avocations: local history, genealogy, arts and crafts, travel.

STONE, HARRY H. retail executive; b. Cleve., May 21, 1917; s. Jacob and Jennie (Kantor) Sapirstein; m. Lucile Tabak, Aug. 10, 1960; children: Phillip, Allan, Laurie (Mrs. Parker), James Rose, Douglas Rose. Student, Cleve. Coll., 1935-36. With Am. Greetings Corp., Cleve., 1936-44, v.p., 1944-58, exec. v.p., 1958-69, vice chmn. bd., chmn. finance com., chmn audit com., 1969-78, dir., 1944—2003, dir. emeritus, 2004—. Mem. Ofcl. U.S. Mission to India and Nepal, 1965; cons. U.S. Dept. Commerce, U.S. Dept. State; adviser U.S. del. 24th session UN Econ. Commn. for Asia and Far East, Canberra, Australia, 1968; cons. Nat. Endowment for Arts, Nat. Council on Arts. Treas. Criminal Justice Co-ordinating Council., 1968-82; trustee emeritus Brandeis U., also univ. fellow. Mem. Rotary (hon. pres.). Office: The Courtland Group Inc 1621 Euclid Ave Ste 1600 Cleveland OH 44115-2195

STONE, HAZEL ANNE DECKER, artist; b. Salt Lake City, Oct. 30, 1934; d. Carl Marcellus and Hazel Sheets (Van Cott) Decker; m. William Samuel Stone, July 20, 1956; children: Cynthia Anne Stone Barkanic, Lisa Marie. BS, RN, U. Utah, 1956; postgrad. in arts and humanities, Ariz. State U., 1979-81; studied with various artists, Ariz., N.Mex., 1985—. Nurse out-patient dept. Salt Lake County Hosp., 1956-57; instr. med.-surg. nursing U. Utah Coll. Nursing, 1957-59; watercolor fine artist. One-woman show Sun Cities Mus. of Art, Sun City, Ariz., 1997; exhibited in group shows at Depot Rd. Aberdare, Wales, 2004, Springfield (Mo.) Art Mus., 2004, Plains Art Mus., Fargo, ND, 2004, AIS, Seattle, 2004, Beverly Arts Ctr., Chgo., 2003 (Merit award), Art Ctr., Grand Junction, Colo., 2003, Cynon Valley Mus., Aberdare, Wales, 2003, Pitts. Watercolor Soc. Aqueous Open, 2003, John Stobart's Three Rivers Gallery, Pitts., 2003, Beverly Arts Ctr., Chgo., 2003, Albuquerque Art Mus., 2002, Pikes Peak Watercolor Soc., 2001, 03, Tubac, Ariz., Ctr. Arts, 2003, Ariz. Watercolor Assn., 2000, Pa. Watercolor Soc., 2000, Woodmere Art Gallery, 2000, Chandler Ctr. Arts, 1999, Watercolors Gallery, Pitts., 2000, Farmington (N.Mex.) Mus., 1999, Wenatchee (Wash.) Valley Coll., 1997, 99-2000, Tubac (Ariz.) Ctr. for Arts, 1999, Sangre de Cristo Arts Ctr., Pueblo, Colo., 1999, Watercolors Gallery, Pitts., 1999, Gallery '76, Wenatchee, 1999-2000, West Valley Art Mus., Surprise, Ariz., 1999, Van Vechten-Lineberry Taos (N.Mex.) Art Mus., 1997, Chandler (Ariz.) Ctr. for the Arts, 1997, Stables Gallery, Taos, 1996, Walton Arts Ctr., Fayetteville, Ark., 1995, Bareiss Gallery, Taos, 1995, Foothills Art Ctr., 1994, Sun Cities (Ariz.) Art Mus., 1994, Golden, Colo., Vistas, 1989, 91, 93, Tucson Mus. Art, 1988, Vision Gallery (2d pl. award Chandler Ostrich Festival Fine Arts Print Contest 1998), others; two person shows include Gallery Nineteen, Phoenix, 1996, Ch. of the Beatitudes, Phoenix, 1995; commd. Chandler Ctr. Arts, 1999; TV interview includes Open My Album: A Collection of Watercolor Paintings and Stories Connecting Generations Channel 20 Ednl. TV Chandler Unified Sch. Dist., Ariz., 1997. Docent Phoenix Art Mus., 1979-80, master docent, 1989-96; mem. Ariz. Women's Caucus Art, 1988-91. Mem. Am. Watercolor Soc. (assoc.), Calif. Watercolor Assn., Internat. Soc. Exptl. Artists, Nat. Coll. Soc.Ariz. Artists Guild, Ariz. Watercolor Assn. (Coatimundi Honor Soc., Royal Scorpion, Award of Merit, 97 Merchant award 1994, 2003, bd. dirs. 1994-2001, co-chair nat. watercolor exhbn. 1999, chair nat. watercolor exhbn. 2002, gen. chair, 2002-03), Contemporary Watercolorists Ariz. (signature, chair spl. exhbns. 1998, chair, exhbn. chair 2002-04, Merit award 1998, Award of Excellence 1997, 2000), Q Artists (chair exhbns. 1995-99), Waterworks Artists, Internat. Soc. Exptl. Artists, Nat. Watercolor Soc. (assoc.), Pa. Watercolor Soc., Phila. Watercolor Soc. (signature), La. Watercolor Soc. (assoc.), N.W. Watercolor Soc. (assoc.), San Diego Watercolor Soc. (assoc.), Taos Soc. Watercolorists (signature), Watercolor Art Soc. Houston, Watercolor West, Mo. Watercolor Soc., Internat. Soc. Exptl. Artists (Merit award), others. Home: 3621 E Pasadena Ave Phoenix AZ 85018-1511

STONE, HERBERT MARSHALL, architect; b. N.Y.C., July 12, 1936; s. Irving and Rose (Gelb) S.; m. Linda Ann Baskind, May 30, 1960; children: Ian Howard, Matthew Lloyd. BArch, Pratt Inst., N.Y.C., 1958, postgrad., 1958-59. Registered architect, N.Y., Iowa, Kans., Ill., Wis., Minn. Designer Henry Dreyfuss Indsl. Design, N.Y.C., 1960-63; architect Max O. Urbahn Architect, N.Y.C., 1963-66; project architect Brown Healey Bock, P.C., Cedar Rapids, Iowa, 1966-73; ptnr. Brown Healey Stone & Sauer, Cedar Rapids, Iowa, 1973—, pres., 1994—. Guest lectr. U.S. Inst. Theatre Tech., Seattle, 1978; speaker on design of pub. librs. ALA Nat. Conv., Miami, Fla., 1994. Prin. works include Strayer-Wood Theatre, 1978, KUNI radio sta. U. No. Iowa, 1978, Cedar Rapids Pub. Libr., 1984, Greenwood Terr. Sr. Citizen Housing, 1986, Iowa State Hist. Mus., 1988, Nat. Hot Air Balloon Mus., 1988 (Spectrum Ceramic Tile Grand award 1989), Student Ctr. Grinnell Coll., 1992, Hall of Pride, Iowa H.S. Athletic Assn., 1995. Pres. Cedar Rapids Trust for Hist. Preservation, 1981—; bd. dirs. Art in Pub. Places Com., Cedar Rapids, 1988, Cedar Rapids/Marion Arts Coun., 1988, Jane Boyd Community House, Cedar Rapids, 1988; mem. Cedar Rapids Hist. Commn. Mem. AIA, Am. Mus. Assn. Avocations: bicycling, skiing, reading, ceramics. Home: 3411 Riverside Dr NE Cedar Rapids IA 52411-7405 Office: Brown Healey Stone & Sauer PC 800 1st Ave NE Cedar Rapids IA 52402-5002

STONE, HERMAN HULL, internist; b. Noble, Ill., Dec. 12, 1915; s. Roy Edson and Carrie (Michels) S.; m. Marie Carlson Christensen; children, Patricia Marie Soln, Richard Allen. BS, U. Ill., 1937, MD, 1941. Resident in internal medicine U.S. VA Hosp., Hines, Ill., 1946-49; chief of medicine VA Hosp., Oklahoma City, 1949-50; with Riverside (Calif.) Med. Clinic, 1950-91; dir. Med. Libr., 1991—; clin. prof. medicine Loma Linda (Calif.) U., 1963—. Founder, dir. Patients' Info. Libr., Riverside, 1991—; pres. citizens univ. com. U. Calif. Riverside, 1979-81; trustee Calif. Blue Shield, 1960-66. Served to maj. M.C., AUS, 1942-46. Recipient Laureate ACP Ca. Region II, 2003, Outstanding award Nat. Soc. Fund Raising Execs., 1996. Fellow ACP (life), Paul Harris Fellow; mem. AMA (Calif. del. 1971-78),L.A. Acad. Medicine (trustee), Rotary Club, Omega Beta Pi, Phi Rho Sigma. Avocations: golf, books, travel. Office: Patients Info Libr 3660 Arlington Ave Riverside CA 92506-3912 Mailing: Roverside Med Found PO Box 2605 Riverside CA 92516 E-mail: rmfpil@aol.com.

STONE, JAMES HOWARD, management consultant; b. Chgo., Mar. 4, 1939; s. Jerome H. and Evelyn Gertrude (Teitelbaum) S.; m. Carole Marlen David, Apr. 21, 1972; children: Margaret Elisa, Emily Anne, Phoebe Jane. AB cum laude, Harvard U., 1960, MBA, 1962. Cert. mgmt. cons., CMC, 1977. From staff analyst to exec. com. Stone Container Corp., Chgo., 1962—83, exec. com., 1983—96; founder, owner, CEO, pres. Stone Mgmt. Corp., Chgo., 1969—2002; pres. Jemp, Inc., Chgo., 2002—. Mem. strategic alliance Boston Cons. Group, 1990—; trustee, sec., exec. com. Roosevelt U., Chgo., 1983—, exec. com. edn. alliance, 1994—; co-chmn. commn. fgn. and domestic affairs Northwestern U., Evanston, Ill., 1981-85, bus. plan judge Kellogg Grad. Sch. Mgmt., 1994—; mem. vis. com. libr., lectr. U. Chgo., 1980—, The Chgo. Com., 1986—, Mid-Am. Com., Chgo., 1993-98; bd. overseers, lectr. IIT Stuart Sch. Bus., 1993—; bd. dirs. Cinema Chgo., Pilgrim Chamber Players. Mem. Chgo. Coun. Fgn. Rels., 1967, bd. dirs., 1974-78; bd. dirs., mem. exec. com. NCCJ, Chgo., 1985, presiding co-chmn., 1990-97; trustee Hadley Sch. Blind, Winnetka, Ill., 1985-96, chmn. planning com., 1989-96, Hadley life trustee, 1996—; vice chmn. fin. com. North Shore Congregation Israel, 1995-98; bd. dirs. Suzuki-Orff Sch., 1997—; pres. Pilgrim Chamber Players, 2002—. Mem. Coun. Logistics Mgmt. (dir. Roundtable-Chgo. 1990-94), The Exec. Club Chgo., Econs. Club, Harvard Club Chgo. (dir. 1995—), Harvard Bus. Sch. Club Chgo. (dir. 1992—, pres. 1997-99), Traffic Club Chgo., Standard Club, Northmoor Country Club, Mid-Day Club, The Casino, Arts Club, Menttium 100, Juvenile Protective Assn. (trustee 1999—), The East Bank Club, Internat. Longevity Ctr. Avocations: family-centered activities, reading, golf, travel.

STONE, JAMES ROBERT, surgeon; b. Greeley, Colo., Jan. 8, 1948; s. Anthony Joseph and Dolores Concetta (Pietrafeso) S.; m. Kaye Janet Friedman, May 16, 1970; children: Jeffrey, Marisa. BA, U. Colo., 1970; MD, U. Guadalajara, Mex., 1976; MBA, Madison U., 2002. Diplomate Am. Bd. Surgery, Am. Bd. Surg. Critical Care, Am. Bd. Forensic Medicine. Intern Md. Gen. Hosp., Balt., 1978-79; resident in surgery St. Joseph Hosp., Denver, 1979-83; pvt. practice Grand Junction, Colo., 1983-87; staff surgeon, dir. critical care Va. Med. Ctr., Grand Junction, 1987-88; dir. trauma surgery and critical care, chief surgery St. Francis Hosp., Colorado Springs, Colo., 1988-91; pvt. practice Kodiak, Alaska, 1991-92; with Summit Surg. Assocs., 1992-96; asst. dir. trauma Tristate Trauma System, Erie, Pa., 1996-99; med. dir. LifeStar Aeromed, Erie, Pa., 1997-99; dir. trauma, sr. assoc. physician, med. dir. emergency svcs. ISJ Mayo Health, 1999—2001; clin. prof. surgery U. Minn. Med. Sch., Mpls., 1999—2001, dir. trauma/EMS med. dir., sr. assoc.; gen., thoracic and vascular surgery Caylor-Nickel Clinic, Bluffton, Ind., 2001—02, Emergency Medicine of Ind., Bluffton, Ind., 2002—. Asst. clin. prof. surgery U. Colo. Health Sci. Ctr., Denver, 1984-96; pres. Stone Aire Cons., Grand Junction, 1988—; owner, operator Jjnka Ranch, Flourissant, Colo.; spl. advisor CAP, wing med. officer, 1992-96; advisor med. com. unit, 1990-92; advisor Colo. Ground Team Search and Rescue, 1994-96; cons. Am. Med. Forensic Specialists, Berkeley, Ca., 2002-. Contbr. articles to profl. jours.; inventor in field. Bd. dirs. Mesa County Cancer Soc., 1988-89, Colo. Trauma Inst., 1988-91. Colo. Speaks out on Health grantee, 1988; recipient Bronze medal of Valor Civil Air Patrol. Fellow Denver Acad. Surgery, Southwestern Surg. Congress, Am. Coll. Chest Physicians, Am. Coll. Surgeons (trauma com. Colo. chpt.), Am. Coll. Critical Care; mem. Am. Coll. Physician Execs., Soc. Critical Care (task force 1988—), Assn. Air Med. Physicians. Roman Catholic. Avocations: horse breeding, hunting, fishing. Office Phone: 260-413-6465. E-mail: jr.stone@att.net.

STONE, JEREMY JUDAH, public interest activist; b. N.Y.C., Nov. 23, 1935; s. I.F. and Esther (Roisman) S.; m. Betty Jane Yannet, June 16, 1957. BS magna cum laude, Swarthmore Coll., 1957, LL.D. (hon.), 1985; PhD, Stanford U., 1960. Research mathematician Stanford Research Inst., 1960-62; mem. profl. staff Hudson Inst., Croton-on-Hudson, 1962-64; research asso., arms control and disarmament Harvard Ctr. Internat. Affairs, 1964-66; asst. prof. math., lectr. polit. sci. Pomona Coll., Claremont, Calif., 1966-68; pres. Fedn. Am. Scientists, Washington, 1970-2000, Catalytic Diplomacy, 1999—. Author: Containing the Arms Race; Some Concrete Proposals, 1966, Strategic Persuasion, 1967, "Every Man Should Try." Adventures of a Public Interest Activist, 1999. Recipient award for pub. svc. Forum on Physics and Soc., Am. Phys. Soc., 1979, Fedn. of Am. Scientists Pub. Svc. award, 1994; Social Sci. Rsch. Coun. fellow in econs. Stanford U., 1968-69, Coun. Fgn. Rels. internat. affairs fellow, 1969-70. Mem. Coun. Fgn. Rels., Internat. Inst. Strategic Studies, Phi Beta Kappa. Home and Office: 5615 Warwick Pl Bethesda MD 20815-5503 E-mail: Jstone@catalyticdiplomacy.org.

STONE, JOHN MCWILLIAMS, JR., electronics executive; b. Chgo., Nov. 4, 1927; s. J. McWilliams and Marion (Jones) S.; m. Cheryl Johansen Cullison, Dec. 18, 1976; children: Jean Stone, Lee Stone Nelson, John III (dec.), Michael (dec.), Shannon Bergman, Tamra Downing. BA, Princeton U., 1950. Salesman A.B. Dick Co., Milw., 1950-51; prodn. supr. Dukane Corp., St. Charles, Ill., 1951-56, exec. v.p., 1956-62, pres., 1962-70, pres., chmn. bd., 1970—, chmn. bd., pres., CEO, 1991-97. Trustee The Elgin (Ill.) Acad. (recipient Elgin medal 1984, emeritus 1985—), Phillips Exeter (N.H.) Coun., 1985—. Three Rivers Coun. Boy Scouts Am., St. Charles; mem. Delnor Cmty. Hosp. Men's Found., St. Charles. Named Exec. of Yr. Valley chpt. Profl. Secs. Internat., Aurora, 1981. Mem. Commonwealth Club of Chgo., Econ. Club of Chgo., Princeton Club of Chgo., Execs. Club of Chgo., Dunham Woods Riding Club (pres. 1967-68, 78-79, 89-90). Republican. Episcopalian. Avocation: tennis. Home: PO Box 755 Wayne IL 60184-0755 Office: Dukane Corp 2900 Dukane Dr Saint Charles IL 60174-3395

STONE, JOHN TIMOTHY, JR., writer; b. Denver, July 13, 1933; s. John Timothy and Marie Elizabeth (Briggs) S.; m. Judith Bosworth Stone, June 22, 1955; children: John Timothy III, George Williams. Student, Amherst Coll., 1951-52, U. Mex., 1952; BA, postgrad., U. Miami, 1955, U. Colo., 1959-60. Sales mgr. Atlas Tag, Chgo., 1955-57; br. mgr. Household Fin. Corp., Chgo., 1958-62; pres. Janeff Credit Corp., Madison, Wis., 1962-72, Recreation Internat., Mpls., 1972-74, Continental Royal Svcs., N.Y.C., 1973-74; dir. devel. The Heartlands Group/Tryon Mint, Toronto, Ont., Can., 1987-89; spl. cons. Creative Resources Internat., Madison, 1988-90, Pubs. Adv. Group, 1990—; spl. cons. art and antiques Treasure Hunt Assocs., 1994—. Bd. dirs. Madison Credit Bur., Wis. Lenders' Exch. Author: Mark, 1973, Going for Broke, 1976, The Minnesota Connection, 1978, Debby Boone So Far, 1980, (with John Dallas McPherson) He Calls Himself "An Ordinary Man", 1981, Satiacum, The Chief Who's Winning Back the West, 1981, Runaways, 1983, (with Robert E. Gard) Where the Green Bird Flies, 1984, The Insiders Guide to Buying Art, 1993, Anyone's Treasure Hunt, 1995; syndicated columnist The Great American Treasure Hunt, 1983-87. Served with CIC, U.S. Army, 1957-59. Mem. Minarani Club, African First Shotters Club, Sigma Alpha Epsilon. Presbyterian. Office Phone: 608-271-9211.

STONE, KAREN, theater director; b. Horsforth, Yorkshire, England, 1952; Degree, Royal Academy of Music, 1970—73, Conservatorio di Musica "Santa Celilia", 1973—76. Asst. dir. Freiburg Opera, 1982—85; dir. English Nat. Opera, 1985—86; prod. and dir. various organizations including Maggio Musicale Fiorentino (Italy), Brighton Festival (Eng.), Royal Opera House (Covent Garden), Teatro Lirico di Parma (Italy), Glyndebourne Festival Opera (Eng.), et al, 1986—94; dep. dir. Cologne Opera, Germany, 1995; gen. mgr. Theaters of Graz, Austria, 2000—03; gen. dir. Dallas Opera, 2003—. Office: Dallas Opera 909 1st Ave Dallas TX 75210

STONE, LARRY DEAN, management executive; b. North Wilkesboro, N.C., July 18, 1951; s. Clyde D. and Irene (Mamess) S.; m. Diane Adams, Aug. 23, 1969; children: Larry Jr., Chris. Student in bus., Wilkes Community Coll., Wilkesboro, N.C., 1971. With mailroom and printshop Lowe's Cos., Inc., North Wilkesboro, 1969-70, area gen. mgr., 1986-89; office trainee Lowe's of Hickory, N.C., 1970-71; office and credit mgr. Lowe's of Raleigh, N.C., 1971-75, sales mgr., 1975-78; store mgr. Lowe's of Cary, N.C., 1978-83, Lowe's of North Wilkesboro, 1983-86; v.p. store merchandising Lowe's Cos., North Wilkesboro, 1989-92; v.p. merchandising, 1992-95; sr. v.p. sales opers., 1995-96; exec. v.p. store opers., 1996—. Bd. dirs. North Wilkesboro Mchts. Assn., 1985, North Wilkesboro Homebuilders Assn., 1985. Served with Army N.G., 1970-76. Mem.: Rotary (treas. North Wilkesboro chpt. 1982-84), Elks. Republican. Baptist. Avocations: golf, swimming. Home: 825 Elledge Mill Rd North Wilkesboro NC 28659-9237

STONE, LAWRENCE D. software company executive; BS in Math., Antioch Coll., 1964; MS in Math., Purdue U., 1966, PhD in Math., 1967. With Daniel H. Wagner Assocs., 1967—85; v.p. Metron, Inc., Reston, Va., 1986—89, sr. v.p., COO, 1990—2003, CEO, 2004—. Author: Theory of Optimal Search (Ops. Rsch. Soc. Lanchester prize), 1975, Bayesian Multiple Target Tracking, 1999. Mem. NAE. Office: Metron Inc 11911 Freedom Dr Ste 800 Reston VA 20190-5602 Fax: 703-787-3518. Office Phone: 703-787-8700. E-mail: stone@metsci.com.

STONE, LAWRENCE MAURICE, lawyer, educator; b. Malden, Mass., Mar. 25, 1931; s. Abraham Jacob and Pauline (Bernstein) S.; m. Anna Jane Clark, June 15, 1963; children: Abraham Dean, Ethan Goldthwaite, Katharine Elisheva. AB magna cum laude, Harvard U., 1953, JD magna cum laude, 1956. Bar: Mass. 1956, Calif. 1958. Rsch. asst. Am. Law Inst., Cambridge, Mass., 1956-57; assoc. Irell and Manella, L.A., 1957-61, ptnr., 1963, 79-96, of counsel, 1997—; internat. tax coordinator U.S. Treasury Dept., Washington, 1961-62, tax. legis. counsel, 1964-66; prof. law U. Calif., Berkeley, 1966-78. Vis. prof. law Yale U., New Haven, 1969, Hebrew U. Jerusalem, 1973-74, U. So. Calif., L.A., 1984; mem. adv. group to commr. IRS, Washington, 1973-74; mem. President's Adv. Commn. on Tax Ct. Appointments, Washington, 1976-80; tax advisory bd. Little Brown Co., 1994-96. Author: (with Doernberg) Federal Income Taxation of Corporations and Partnerships, (with Klein, Bankman and Bittker) Federal Income Taxation; bd. editors Harvard Law Rev., 1955-56. Fellow Am. Coll. Tax Counsel; mem. ABA, Am. Law Inst., Internat. Fiscal Inst., Am. Arbitration Assn., L.A. County Bar Assn. (recipient Dana Latham award 1995), Phi Beta Kappa. Office: Irell & Manella 1800 Avenue Of The Stars Los Angeles CA 90067-4276 Office Phone: 310-203-7525.

STONE, LAWRENCE MYNATT, publishing executive; b. Balt., June 24, 1945; s. David G. and Clara Ruth (Coxey) S.; m. Lois V. Smith, June 10, 1967; children: Bradley Michael, Geoffrey David. BA, U. Iowa, 1968. Prof. Northeastern Bible Coll., Essex Fells, N.J., 1968-69; missionary Africa Evangelical Fellowship, Ndola, Zambia, 1969-71; asst. to production mgr. Am. Bible Soc., N.Y.C., 1971-72; book club mgr. Iversen-Norman Assocs., N.Y.C., 1972-75; editl. v.p. Thomas Nelson Pubs., Nashville, 1976-85; pres. Rutledge Hill Press, Nashville, 1985-99, pub., 1999—. Book and libr. adv. com. U.S. Info. Agency, Washington, 1984-88; editor in field; ghost writer. Office: Rutledge Hill Press PO Box 141000 Nashville TN 37214-1000 Personal E-mail: larryrhp@aol.com. Business E-Mail: lstone@rutledgehillpress.com.

STONE, LEON, banker; b. Rockdale, Tex., Feb. 27, 1914; s. Harley J. and Ella (Strelsky) S.; m. Bess Northington, Aug. 19, 1939; children— Pebble Stone Moss, Cherry J. Stone McKinnon. Student, Blinn Coll., Brenham, Tex., 1932, Sul Ross Coll., Alpine, Tex., 1934, U. Tex., 1935, Rutgers U., 1954. With Brown & Root, Houston, 1936-37; Guggenheim-Goldsmith, Austin, Tex., 1937-38; with Austin Nat. Bank, 1938—, pres., 1963-84; also dir. Bd. dirs. First State Bank, Burnet, Tex.; chmn. Southwestern Grad. Sch. Banking, So. Meth. U. Dallas Vice chmn. Tchr. Retirement System Tex., 1956-77; Bd. dirs. Presbyn. Theol. Sem., 1958—, Seton Hosp., 1966—, Mental Health and Mental Retardation Assn., 1965—. Served to lt. col. U.S. Army, ETO. Named Boss of Year, Credit Women of Austin, 1966 Mem. Am. Bankers Assn. (regional v.p. 1965—, exec. com. 1966—), Tex. Bankers Assn. (pres. 1973), Am. Inst. Banking (past pres.), Austin C. of C. (pres. 1968), Tex. Taxpayers Assn. (pres.) Clubs: Rotarian, Mason, Shriner (Jester). Office: Bank of Am PO Box 908 Austin TX 78781-0001

STONE, MARC J. lawyer; b. N.Y.C., Dec. 21, 1960; m. Amy Siobayne Wheeler Solt, Mar. 23, 2002; children: Alexandra Paige, Justin Alexander, Dylan Mackenzie. AB, Brown U., 1982; JD, U. Calif., Berkeley, 1985. Bar: N.Y., Fla. Assoc., corp. dept. Rubin Baum Levin Constant & Friedman, N.Y.C., 1985-87, Rubin Baum Levin Constant Friedman & Bilzin, Miami, Fla., 1987-92, ptnr., 1993-97; v.p., gen. counsel, sec. TradeStation Group, Inc.,

Plantation, Fla., 1997—. Mem.: ABA, Fla. Bar Assn., NY State Bar Assn. Avocations: theater, film, reading, team sports, tennis. Office: TradeStation Group Inc 8050 SW 10th St Plantation FL 33324 E-mail: mstone@tradestation.com.

STONE, MARVIN JULES, physician, educator; b. Columbus, Ohio, Aug. 3, 1937; s. Roy J. and Lillian (Bedwinek) S.; m. Jill Feinstein, June 29, 1958; children: Nancy Lillian, Robert Howard. Student, Ohio State U., 1955-58; SM in Pathology, U. Chgo., 1962, MD with honors, 1963. Diplomate Am. Bd. Internal Medicine, (Hematology, Med. Oncology). Intern ward med. svc. Barnes Hosp., St. Louis, 1963-64, asst. resident, 1964-65; clin. assoc. arthritis and rheumatism br. Nat. Inst. Arthritis and Metabolic Diseases, NIH, Bethesda, Md., 1965-68; resident in medicine, ACP scholar Parkland Meml. Hosp., Dallas, 1968-69; fellow in hematology-oncology, dept. internal medicine U. Tex. Southwestern Med. Sch., Dallas, 1969-70, instr. dept. internal medicine, 1970-71, asst. prof., 1971-73, assoc. prof., 1974-76, clin. prof., 1976—, chmn. bioethics com., 1979-81; mem. faculty and steering com. immunology grad. program, Grad. Sch. Biomed. Scis., U. Tex. Health Sci. Ctr., Dallas, 1975, adj. mem., 1976—. Dir. Charles A. Sammons Cancer Ctr., chief oncology, dir. immunology, co-dir. divsn. hematology-oncology, attending physician Baylor U. Med. Ctr., Dallas, 1976—; v.p. med. staff Parkland Meml. Hosp., Dallas, 1982. Contbr. chpts. to books, articles to profl. jours. Chmn. com. patient-aid Greater Dallas/Ft. Worth chpt. Leukemia Soc. Am., 1971-76, chmn. med. adv. com., 1978-80, bd. dirs., 1971-80; mem. v.p. Dallas unit Am. Cancer Soc., 1977-78, pres., 1978—; mem. adv. bd. Baylor U. Med. Ctr. Found. With USPHS, 1965-68. Recipient Wings of Eagles award, Baylor Health Care Sys., 2001, Disting. Svc. award, U. Chgo., 2002. Master ACP (gov. No. Tex. 1993-97, laureate Tex. chpt. 2000); fellow Royal Soc. Medicine (London); mem. AMA, Am. Assn. Immunologists, Am. Soc. Hematology, Internat. Soc. Hematology, Coun. Thrombosis, Am. Heart Assn. (established investigator 1970-75), Am. Soc. Clin. Oncology (edn. com. 2002—, career devel. com. 2002—), Am. Osler Soc. (bd. govs. 1997-2000, v.p. 2001-03, pres. 2003-04), Am. Assn. for Cancer Rsch., So. Soc. Clin. Investigation, Tex. Med. Assn., Dallas County Med. Soc., Clin. Immunology Soc., Phi Beta Kappa, Sigma Xi, Alpha Omega Alpha. Office: Baylor U Med Ctr Charles A Sammons Cancer Ctr 3500 Gaston Ave Dallas TX 75246-2096 E-mail: marvins@baylorhealth.edu.

STONE, MATT, animator; b. Houston, May 26, 1971; Student, U. Colo. Actor: (films) Orgazmo, 1997, BASEketball, 1998, South Park: Bigger, Longer, and Uncut, 1999 (MTV Movie award Best Musical Performance, 1999), Bowling for Columbine, 2002; writer, prodr.: That's My Bush, 2001; creator, writer, dir., prodr., actor (TV series) Spirit of Christmas (now South Park), 1992, South Park, 1997—, also voices of characters Kyle Broslofski, Kenny McCormick, Terrance Henry Stoot, Pip Pirrup, Leopold "Butters" Stotch, Saddam Hussein, Stuart McCormick, Jesus Christ, others, —. Nominee Emmy Awards for Best Animated Program (South Park), 1998, 2000, 2002. Achievements include appearances include The Tonight Show with Jay Leno, MTV Movie Awards, The Emmy Awards. Office: c/o Comedy Central 10th Fl 1175 Broadway New York NY 10019*

STONE, MERRILL BRENT, lawyer; b. Jersey City, N.J., Aug. 16, 1951; s. Leonard and Claire (Orlean) S.; m. Geri Ellen Satkin, Nov. 24, 1976; children: Jacqueline Blair, Erica Lauren. AB summa cum laude, Rutgers U., 1973; JD, Columbia U., 1976. Bar: N.J. 1976, N.Y. 1977, Fla. 1981, U.S. Dist. Ct. N.J. 1976, U.S. Dist. Ct. (so. dist.) N.Y. 1977, U.S. Dist. Ct. (so. dist.) Fla. 1983. Assoc. Kelley Drye & Warren, N.Y.C., 1976-84, resident Miami, 1983-85, ptnr. N.Y.C., 1985—, mng. ptnr., 1992—2003. Editor: (comments section) Columbia Human Rights Law Rev., N.Y.C., 1975-76. Trustee Greater Miami C. of C., 1984-85. Named Harlan Fiske Stone Scholar, Columbia Law Sch., N.Y.C., 1975-76. Mem. ABA (bus. bankruptcy com. sect. on bus. law, banking law com.), Am. Soc. Corp. Secs., Fla. Bar Assn., Club 101, Phi Beta Kappa, Pi Sigma Alpha. Office: Kelley Drye & Warren LLP 101 Park Ave New York NY 10178-0002 Office Phone: 212-808-7543. E-mail: mstone@kelleydrye.com.

STONE, MICHAEL JOHN, music educator, conductor; b. Jacksonville, NC, Dec. 11, 1953; s. Burton and Ruth Stone; m. Sugako Yoshimura, Oct. 20, 1990; children: Miku Yoshimura, Mei Yoshimura, Reina Yoshimura. MusB in Theory/Composition, U. of Iowa, 1975, MA, 1977; DMA in Orchestral Conducting, Ctrl. Pacific U., Honolulu, 2002. Asst. dir. of bands U. of Wis., Milw., 1978—79; dir. adirondack philharm. orch. Adirondack C.C., Glens Falls, NY, 1979—85, chair dept. of music, 1979—85; conducting faculty Hartt Sch. of Music, U. of Hartford, Conn., 1985—87; dir. symphony orch. Manatee C.C., Bradenton, Fla., 1989—99, chair dept. of music, 1989—99; dir. symphonic band McAllen Town Band Assn., Tex., 1999—; chair dept. of music South Tex. C.C., McAllen, 1999—2003; dir. orchestral activities U. of Tex., Brownsville, 2001—; asst. prof., dir. of bands Tex. A&M Internat. U., Laredo, 2003—. Musician: Hilversum (2d Pl. at SW Mo. State U. Jazz Competition, 1977). Mem.: Coll. Music Soc., Tex. Music Educators Assn. Conservative. Avocations: swimming, bicycling, camping, running, basketball. Home: 716 Bluebird McAllen TX 78504-2772 Office: Tex A&M Internat Univ Fine and Performing Arts Ctr Rm 233B 5201 University Blvd Laredo TX 78041-1900 Personal E-mail: maestros@peoplepc.com. Business E-Mail: mjstone@utb.edu. E-mail: mstone@tamiu.edu.

STONE, NIKKI, motivational speaker, retired Olympic athlete; b. Princeton, N.J., Feb. 4, 1971; BS in Psychology magna cum laude, Union Coll., 1997. Motivational spkr. Podium Enterprises. Freestyle aerial skier. Winner Olympic Gold Medal in aerials, Nagano, 1998, World Championship Gold Medal, 1995, World Cup title, 1995, 1 World Cup events. Address: PO Box 680332 Park City UT 84068-0332 E-mail: nikkistone@compuserve.com.

STONE, OLIVER, screenwriter, director; b. N.Y.C., Sept. 15, 1946; s. Louis and Jacqueline (Goddet) S. Student, Yale U., 1965; BFA, NYU Film Sch., 1971. Tchr., Cholon, Vietnam, 1965-66; wiper U.S. Mcht. Marine, 1966; taxi driver N.Y.C., 1971. Screenwriter Midnight Express, 1978 (Acad. award for screenplay, Writers Guild Am. for screenplay); screenwriter, dir.: The Hand, 1981, (with John Milius) Conan, the Barbarian, 1982 (writer), Scarface, 1983, (writer with Michael Cimino) Year of the Dragon, 1985, (writer with David Lee Henry) 8 Million Ways to Die, 1986; dir., writer (with Richard Boyle) Salvador, 1986, Platoon, 1986 (Acad. award, Dirs. Guild award, British Acad. award); co-writer, dir.: Wall Street, 1987, Talk Radio, 1988, The Doors, 1991, Any Given Sunday, 1999; screenwriter, prodr., dir.: Born on the Fourth of July, 1989 (Acad. award 1990), Heaven & Earth, 1993, Comandante, 2003; co-writer, prodr., dir.: JFK, 1991, Natural Born Killers, 1994, Nixon, 1995 (Acad. award nominee for best screenplay with Stephen J. Rivele and Christopher Wilkinson 1996); co-prodr. Reversal of Fortune, 1990; prodr.: South Central, 1992, Zebrahead, 1992, The Joy Luck Club, 1993, The New Age, 1994, The Corruptor, 1999, (TV mini-series) Wild Palms, 1993; exec. prodr. Killer: A Journal of Murder, 1996, (HBO) Indictment: The McMartin Trial, 1995 (Emmy award), Freeway, 1996, The People vs. Larry Flynt, 1996, Evita, 1996, (writer), U-Turn, 1997; dir. Persona Non Grata, 2003 Served with inf. U.S. Army, 1967-68, Vietnam. Decorated Purple Heart with oak leaf cluster, Bronze Star. Mem. Writers Guild Am., Dirs. Guild Am., Acad. Motion Picture Arts and Scis. Office: 1207 4th St PH 1 Santa Monica CA 90401-1340

STONE, PAMELA ANN, accountant; b. Flint, Mich., Jan. 10, 1954; d. Leslie Elwood and Aloha Augusta (Wegener) S. AS in Acctg., Baker Bus. U., 1980; BS in Acctg., Detroit Coll. Bus., 1981; AS in Computer Programming, Baker Jr. Coll., 1983; MS in Profl. Accountancy, Walsh Coll., 1986; MS in Info. Sys. Mgmt., Ferris State U., 1996; PhD in Counseling, Universal Life Ch., 2003. Acct., bus. mgr. Drury Bros. Inc., Durand, Mich., 1982-85; instr. Pontiac (Mich.) Bus. Inst., 1985-86; software tng. mgr. Gateway, 1999—2001; founder, pres. Bright Futures Bus. Sch., Flint, 2001—. Pvt. practice, Flint, 1985—; instr. Baker Coll., Flint, 1986-99, Detroit Coll. Bus., Flint; vocat. edn. tchr. Shiawassee Intermediate Sch. Dist. Avocations: piano, organ, tennis, bowling, needlepoint. Office: Bright Futures Bus Sch PO BOx 7906 G3490 Miller Rd Ste 12 Flint MI 48507 Office Phone: 810-732-5420. Business E-Mail: brightfutures@aol.com.

STONE, R. DARY, real estate company executive; JD, Baylor U. Campaign mgr. Re-election of Gov. Clements; dir. Tex. Office State-Fed. Rels. in Washington, D.C.; counsel former Tex. Gov. Bill Clements; joined Cousins, 1999, pres. Tex. ops., head properties svcs.; pres., CEO Cousins Properties Inc., 2001—03; vice chmn. Cousins Properties, Dallas, 2003—. Former chmn. Tex. Fin. Commn.; former regional bd. mem. Resolution Trust Corp.; bd. dirs. Lone Star Bank, Tolleson Pvt. Bank, Real Estate Round Table; former dir. Baylor Med. Ctr. Found., Tex. Econ. Devel. Found., Cistercian Prep. Sch., Real Estate Coun., Dallas; former mem. Govs. Strategic Planning Com., Tex. Commn. on Jud. Efficiency, North Tex. Regional Transp. Task Force. Mem.: Urban Land Inst., State Bar Tex., Young Pres. Orgn., Dallas Assembly. Office: Cousins Properties Ste 1100 5215 N OConnor Blvd Irving TX 75039*

STONE, RALPH KENNY, lawyer; b. Bainbridge, Ga., Aug. 7, 1952; s. Ralph Patrick and Joyce (Mitchell) S.; m. Julie Ann Waldren, Aug. 24, 1974; children: Laura Lee, Rebecca, Michael. BBA magna cum laude, U. Ga., 1974, JD cum laude, 1977. Bar: Ga. 1977, U.S. Dist. Ct. (so. dist.) Ga. 1977, U.S. Supreme Ct. 1980, U.S. Ct. Appeals (11th cir.) 1981. Staff acct. Price Waterhouse & Co., Columbia, S.C., 1974; assoc. Calhoun & Donaldson, Savannah, Ga., 1977; ptnr. Franklin & Stone, Statesboro, Ga., 1977-88, Edenfield, Stone & Cox, Statesboro, Ga., 1988-94; pres. R. Kenny Stone, P.C., 1994—. Instr. taxation Ga. So. Coll., Stateboro, 1979-80. Sect. chmn. United Way S.E. Ga., campaign chmn., 1989, pres. 1991; charter pres. Leadership Bulloch, Inc., 1984; chmn. Bulloch County Dem. Com., 1984-90, Bulloch 2000 Com., 1986-88; alt. del. Dem. Nat. Conv., 1988; sec. Ga. Assn. Dem. County Chairs, 1985-89, pres. 1989-91; dist. chmn. Boy Scouts Am., 1985; pres. Forward Bulloch Inc., 1986; participant Leadership Ga., 1986; mem. Ga. Bd. Industry Trade & Tourism, 1991-96. Mem. ABA, State Bar Ga., Bulloch County Bar Assn. (pres. 1982-83), Statesboro-Bulloch C. of C. (pres. 1986, chmn. bd. dirs. 1987, chmn. devel. authority Bulloch County 1991-2001), Rotary (Statesboro; pres., 2004-2005), Optimist Club (pres. 1980-81, dist. lt. gov. 1981-82), East Ga. Regional Med. Ctr. (bd. dirs., 2000-), Business Adv. Coun. Coll. of Business Adminstrn. (Ga. So. Univ.), Phi Kappa Phi, Beta Alpha Psi. Baptist. Home: 319 Dogwood Trl Statesboro GA 30461-4253 Office: R Kenny Stone PC PO Box 681 Statesboro GA 30459-0681

STONE, RICHARD JAMES, lawyer; b. Apr. 30, 1945; s. Milton M. and Ruth Jean (Manaster) S.; m. Lee Lawrence, Sept. 1, 1979; children: Robert Allyn, Katherine Jenney, Grant Lawrence. BA in Econs., U. Chgo., 1967; JD, UCLA, 1970. Bar: Calif. 1971, Oreg. 1994, D.C., 2000. Assoc. O'Melveny & Myers, L.A., 1971-77; dep. asst. gen. counsel U.S. Dept. Def., Washington, 1978-79; asst. to sec. U.S. Dept. Energy, Washington, 1979-80; counsel Sidley & Austin, L.A., 1981, ptnr., 1982-88; ptnr., head litig. dept. Milbank, Tweed, Hadley & McCloy, L.A., 1988-94; mng. ptnr. Zelle & Larson, LLP, L.A., 1994-97; counsel Ball Janik LLP, Portland, Oreg., 1998—. Gen. counsel and staff dir. Study of L.A. Civil Disturbance for Bd. Police Commrs., 1992; adj. prof. law Lewis and Clark Northwestern Sch. Law, 1998-99; lawyer rep. 9th Cir. Jud. Conf., 1998-99; mem. legal ethics com. Oreg. State Bar, 2002-03, com. on spl. rules, 2002-03. Editor-in-chief: UCLA Law Rev., 1970. Mem. Pub. Sector Task Force, Calif., State Senate Select Com. on Long Range Policy Planning, 1985-86, U.S. del. Micronesian Polit. Status Negotiations, 1978-79; mem. U.S. Mil. Acad. at West Point, Oreg. Field Force, 2003—; mem. adv. panel Coun. Energy Resource Tribes, 1981-85; mem. vestry St. Aidan's Episcopal Ch., 1990-93, 97-98, sr. warden, 1998; dir. Legal Aid Found. L.A., 1991-99, officer, 1994-98, pres., 1997-98; dir. Portland City United Soccer Club, 1999-2000; classic coach, 2002-. Recipient Amos Alonzo Stagg medal and Howell Murray Alumni medal U. Chgo., 1967; honoree Nat. Conf. Black Mayors, 1980; recipient spl. citation for outstanding performance Sec. Dept. Energy, 1981. Fellow Am. Bar Found.; mem. ABA, Fed. Bar Assn., Calif. Bar Assn., Oreg. Bar Assn., L.A. County Bar Assn. (trustee 1986-88), Assn. Bus. Trial Lawyers, Multnomah County Bar Assn., Phi Gamma Delta. Home: 3675 NW Gordon St Portland OR 97210-1285 Office: Ball Janik LLP 101 SW Main St Portland OR 97204-3228 Office Phone: 503-228-2525. Business E-Mail: rstone@bjllp.com.

STONE, ROBERT ANTHONY, author; b. N.Y.C., Aug. 21, 1937; s. C. Homer and Gladys Catherine (Grant) S.; m. Janice G. Burr, Dec. 11, 1959; children: Deidre M., Ian A. Student, N.Y. U., 1958-59; Stegner fellow, Stanford, 1962. Editorial asst. N.Y. Daily News, N.Y.C., 1958-60; former actor New Orleans; former advt. copywriter N.Y.C.; writer Nat. Mirror, N.Y.C., 1965-67; novelist, 1960—. Mem. faculty Johns Hopkins U., Balt., 1993-94, Yale U., 1994—; free-lance writer London, Hollywood, Calif., South Vietnam, 1967-71; writer-in-residence Princeton U., 1971-72; faculty Amherst Coll., 1972-75, 77-78, Stanford U., 1979, U. Hawaii-Manoa, 1979-80, Harvard U., 1981, U. Calif.-Irvine, 1982, NYU, 1983, U. Calif.-San Diego, 1985, Princeton U., 1985. Author: (novels) A Hall of Mirrors, 1967, Dog Soldiers, 1974 (Nat. Book award 1975), A Flag for Sunrise, 1981, Images of War, 1986, Children of Light, 1986, Outerbridge Reach, 1992, Bear and His Daughter, 1997, Damascus Gate, 1998, (screenplays) WUSA, 1970, (with Judith Rascoe) Who'll Stop the Rain, 1978; contbg. author: Best American Short-stories, 1970, 88. Served with USN, 1955-58. Recipient William Faulkner prize, 1967, John Dos Passos prize for lit., 1982; award in lit. Am. Acad. and Inst. Arts and Letters, 1982, grantee, 1988-92; Guggenheim fellow, 1971, NEH fellow, 1983. Mem. PEN (exec. bd.) also: care Donadio & Ashworth 121 W 27th St Ste 704 New York NY 10001-6207

STONE, ROBERT ELDRED, small business owner, museum director; b. Chester, N.H., July 26, 1929; s. Harold I. and Anna L. (Ahlberg) S.; m. Dorothy Harriette Fullonton, Feb. 3, 1951 (div. 1977); children: Dennis Wayne, Kathy Ann. Electronic Technician, USCG Tng. Ctr., Groton, Conn., 1952; A. in Electronic Engring., Merrimac Coll., Andover, Mass., 1957. Crew chief N.H. Permastone Corp., Londonderry, 1948, 49; quality assurance technician Western Elec. Corp. (AT&T), Lawrence, Mass., 1953-57, assoc. engr., 1957-83; owner, pres. America's Stonehenge, North Salem, N.H., 1957—. Coach, Little League Basketball, Derry, N.H.; chmn. Cub Scouts, Derry; past mem. vestry Episc. Ch. of Transfiguration, Derry, past chmn. fin. com. With USCG, 1949-52. Mem. N.H. Archaeol. Soc., New England Antiquities Rsch. Assn. (founder, pres. 1964-76, rsch. dir. 1976-78), The Gungywamp Soc. Avocations: archaeology, history, acrylic painting, reading, tv documentaries. Office: Am's Stonehenge PO Box 84 North Salem NH 03073-0084

STONE, ROGER DAVID, environmentalist; b. N.Y.C., Aug. 4, 1934; s. Patrick William and Kathleen Mary Stone; married; 1 child. BA in English, Yale U., 1955. Asst. to pub. Time Mag., 1959-61, corr., news bur. chief, 1961-68; asst. to pres. Time Inc., N.Y.C., 1968-70; v.p. internat. dept. Chase Manhattan Bank, N.Y.C., 1970-74; pres. Ctr. for Inter-Am. Rels., N.Y.C., 1975-82; v.p. World Wildlife Fund, 1982-86, sr. fellow, 1986-90; vis. fellow, cons. on environ. issues Coun. on Fgn. Rels., 1990-92; vice chmn. ECO Inc., Washington, 1992-96; pres. Sustainable Devel. Inst., Washington, 1993—. Vis. lectr. Yale Ctr. for Internat. and Area Studies, 1994-95. Author: Dreams of Amazonia, 1985, The Voyage of the Sanderling, 1990, Wildlands and Human Needs, 1991, The Nature of Development: Reports from the Rural Tropics on the Quest for Sustainable Economic Growth, 1992, Fair Tide: Sailing Toward Long Island's Future, 1996, Tropical Forests and the Human Spirit = Journeys to the Brink of Hope, 2001; contbr. chpts. to books; contbr. articles to Time, Life, Life en Espanol, Fgn. Affairs, N.Y. Times, Internat. Herald Tribune, Christian Sci. Monitor, Harvard Bus. Rev., USA Today Mag., Cruising World, Conservation Found. Letter, numerous others. Bd. dirs. Astrolabe, Inc., Cintas Found.; v.p. Armand G. Erpf Fund, Sotterley Found.; former bd. dirs. U. Andes Found.; former bd. dirs. and exec. com. World Wildlife Fund-U.S., Ctr. for Inter-Am. Rels., Ams. Found., Accion Internat., Arts Internat., others. Lt. (j.g.) USN, 1956-59. Mem.: Century Assn. Democrat. Episcopalian. Avocation: sailing. Home: 1527 30th St Nw # B-32 Washington DC 20007 Fax: 202-337-9639. E-mail: susdev@igc.org.

STONE, ROSS GLUCK, orthopedic surgeon; b. Pottsville, Pa., May 14, 1951; s. Jerome M. and Alma (Gluck) S.; m. Wendy E. Reiner, March 21, 1987; children: Melissa, Logan. BA in Philosophy, Yale U., 1973; MD, Columbia U., 1977. Diplomate Am. Bd. Orthopaedic Surgery. Intern, resident Harvard U., 1977-79; resident, vis. clin. fellow Columbia U., 1979-83; pvt. practice Atlantis, Fla., 1983—. Clin. fellow in surgery Harvard Med. Sch., 1978-79; expert med. advisor Fla. Dept. Labor & Employment, 1995-97, 97—; editl. adv. bd. Am. Jour. Pain Mgmt., 1992—; chmn. surg. rev. com. Palm Beach Regional Hosp., 1995, chmn. instnl. rev. com. John F. Kennedy Med. Ctr., 1995-02; chmn. divsn. ortho. surgery Columbia Hosp., 1994—; chmn. dept. surgery Palms West Hosp., 1998—. Contbr. chpt. to book and articles to profl. jours.; invented tension headache reliever device. Trustee Palms West Hosp., Loxahatchee, Fla., 1985-88. Recipient Physician's Choice award So. Med. Assn. 88th Assembly, 1994, Scientific Poster recognition So. Med. Assn. 88th Assembly, 1994, 89th Assembly, 1995, Sr. Resident award Eastern Ortho. Assn. 14th ann. meeting, 1983, Rsch. Manuscript award Assn. for the Advancement of Med. Instrumentation, 1996. Mem.: Ea. Orthop. Assn. (Fla. state rep. 2001—), Palm Beach County (Fla.) Med. Soc. (emergency med. svc. and disaster relief plan coms. 1994—95, health and human svcs. com. 1994—95, pub. rels. com. 1995—98, legis. com. 1995—99, del. Fla. Med. Assn. 1995—2002, bd. dirs. 1995—, chmn. pub. rels. com. 1996—98, sec. 1998, 2d v.p. 1999, chmn. bd. censors and mediation 1999, sec. MEDPAC bd. dirs 1999 , 1st v.p. 2000, treas. MEDPAC bd. dirs. 2000, chmn. membership 2000, pres.-elect 2001, pres. 2002, editor Jour. 2003, sec.-treas. 2003, bd. dirs. FLAMPAC Fla. med. polit. action com. 2003, bd. trustees 2003, chmn. other coms.). Republican. Jewish. Avocations: weightlifting, aerobic conditioning, reading, tennis, golf. Office: 120 John F Kennedy Dr Ste 124 Lake Worth FL 33462-6623

STONE, RUSSELL A. sociology educator; b. Medicine Hat, Alta., Can., Feb. 8, 1944; came to U.S., 1966; s. Ben and Clara G. (Gibbs) S.; m. S. Rala Stollar, Aug. 18, 1965; children: Peter H., Mira Beth. BA, McGill U., Montreal, Que., Can., 1965; PhD, Princeton U., 1971. Asst. to assoc prof. sociology SUNY, Buffalo, 1970-84, prof., 1984-91, chmn. dept. sociology, 1985-88; prof. sociology Am. U., Washington, 1991—, assoc. dean for grad. affairs, 1991—96, chmn. dept. sociology, 2002—. Vis. rsch. assoc. Israel Inst. Applied Social Rsch., Jerusalem, 1977-78; vis. assoc. prof. Ben Gurion U. of the Negev, Beersheba, Israel, 1978; vis. prof. Hebrew U., Jerusalem, 1977-78. Author: Social Change in Israel: Attitudes and Events, 1982; co-author: Political Elites on Arab North Africa, 1982; editor: OPEC and the Middle East, 1977; co-editor: Change in Tunisia, 1976, Critical Essays on Israeli Social Issues and Scholarship, 1994, chmn. editorial bd. SUNY Press, 1987-90, series editor; contbr. articles to profl. jours. Mem. Am. Sociol. Assn., Middle East Studies Assn., Assn. for Israel Studies (sec., treas. 1989-93, adminstrv. officer 1998—). Office: Am U Dept Sociology 4400 Massachusetts Ave NW Washington DC 20016-8003 E-mail: rstone@american.edu.

STONE, SHARON, actress; b. Meadville, Pa., Mar. 10, 1958; d. Joe and Dorothy S; m. Michael Greenburg, 1984 (div. 1987); m. Phil Bronstein, 1998; 1 son. Student, Edinboro U. Model Eileen Ford Modeling Agy. Appeared in films Stardust Memories, 1980, Deadly Blessing, 1981, Irreconcilable Differences, 1984, King Solomon's Mines, 1985, Allan Quatermain and the Lost City of Gold, 1986, Cold Steel, 1987, Police Academy 4, 1987, Action Jackson, 1988, Above the Law, 1988, Beyond the Stars, 1989 (Personal Choice award), Total Recall, 1990, Year of the Gun, 1991, Diary of a Hitman, 1991, He Said/She Said, 1991, Scissors, 1991, Basic Instinct, 1991, Where Sleeping Dogs Lie, 1992, Last Action Hero, 1993, Sliver, 1993, Intersection, 1994, The Specialist, 1994, (also co-prodr.) The Quick and the Dead, 1995 (also co-prodr.), Casino, 1995 (Golden Globe award for best actress in film 1996, Acad. award nominee for best actress 1996), Diabolique, 1996, Last Dance, 1996, Sphere, 1998, The Mighty, 1998 (Golden Global nominee), Antz, 1998 (voice), Gloria, 1999, The Muse, 1999, Simpatico, 1999, Beautiful Joe, 2000, Picking Up the Pieces, 2000, Cold Creek Manor, 2003; TV appearances include Not Just Another Affair, 1982, Bay City Blues, 1983, Calendar Girl Murders, 1984, The Vegas Strip Wars, 1984, War and Remembrance, 1988, Tears in the Rain, 1988, (guest) The Larry Sanders Show, 1994, Big Guns Talk: The Story of the Western (tv spl.), 1997; narrator: Harlow: The Blond Bombshell, 1993, If These Walls Could Talk 2, 2000, Harold and the Purple Crayon, 2001, Cold Creek Manor, 2003, A Different Loyalty, 2004, Catwoman, 2005. Office: Care Guy McElwaine PO Box 7304 North Hollywood CA 91603-7304

STONE, STEVEN M. consumer products company executive; BBA, Appalachian State U. Sr. mgr. info. tech. consulting Ernst & Young; v.p. info. resources Lowe's Cos., Inc., 1997—99, v.p. MIS ops., 1999—2002, v.p. info. tech. strategy, 2002—03, sr. v.p., chief info. officer, 2003—. Office: 1605 Curtis Bridge Rd Wilkesboro NC 28697

STONE, STUART LEE MORRISON, librarian, language educator; b. St. Louis, June 4, 1949; s. Norwood Lee Stone and Antoinette Aubouchon Engle. BS in Edn., The U. Mo., 1971; M of Libr. and Info. Sci., The Cath. U. Am., 1979, postgrad., 1980—82. Cert. secondary edn. U. Mo., 1971, English as a fgn. lang. tchr. The Cambridge Sch., Ltd., London, 1982. Quadri-lingual rsch. asst. The Inter-Am. Def. Coll. / OAS, Washington, 1972—75; tchr. French, Spanish, & history The Wash. Ethical Soc. H.S., 1975—77; sr. staff asst. The U.S. Ho. Subcom. Postal Pers. and Modernization, 1980—82; tchr. English and Am. history The Am. Lang. Inst., Lisbon, Portugal, 1982—86; asst. libr. IMF, Washington, 1986—87; sr. cataloger, Portuguese-French-Spanish-Gaelic Libr. Congress, 1987—2002, recommending officer Scots-Gaelic, 1997—, sr. acquisitions specialist Europe and L.Am., 2000—. Instr. beginning Scots-Gaelic The Am. Gaelic Soc. (ACGA), Alexandria, Va., 1999—. Translator (seminar instr. / U. Sao Paulo): (international library online networking) Training Manual / MARC Name Authorities; author: (ednl. discussion kit) Inauguration: An American Beginning (Presdl. Inaugural Com. award, 1981). Ward rep. bldgs. and grounds com. Fairlington Villages, Arlington, Va., 2003—. With U.S. Army, 1972—75. Decorated Joint Svc. Commendation medal Sec. Def. Pentagon. Fellow: Soc. Antiquaries Scotland; mem.: Libr. Congress Pa., The Am. Gaelic Soc. Am. (Gaelic instr. & newsletter editor asst. 1997—), Am. Legion. Home: 3079 S Buchanan St C-2 Arlington VA 22206

STONE, SUSAN A. lawyer; BA summa cum laude, Yale U., 1983; JD cum laude, Harvard U., 1987. Bar: Calif. 1987, U.S. Dist. Ct. (no. dist.) Calif. 1987, U.S. Ct. Appeals (9th cir.) 1987, U.S. Dist. Ct. (ctrl. dist.) Calif. 1988, Ill. 1990, U.S. Dist. Ct. (no. dist.) Ill. 1990, U.S. Ct. Appeals (7th cir.) 1990. Asst. U.S. atty. U.S. Dept. Justice, L.A.; law clk. to Judge William J. Orrick, U.S. Dist. Ct. for No. Dist. Calif.; ptnr. Sidley & Austin, Chgo. Former adj. prof. trial practice DePaul U. Coll. Law, Chgo. Named one of Top Young Litigators Under 40, Ill. Legal Times. Mem. Ill. Bar Assn., Calif. State Bar, Phi Beta Kappa. Office: Sidley & Austin 1 S First National Plz Chicago IL 60603-2000 Fax: 312-853-7036. E-mail: sstone@sidley.com.

STONE, SUSAN RIDGAWAY, marketing educator; b. Coronado, Calif., Oct. 30, 1950; d. Lester Jay and Marguerite Ridgaway (King) Stone; m. Martin Zachary Sipkoff, Oct. 27, 1984; 1 child, Benjamin. AB, Wilson Coll., 1977; MBA, Shippensburg U., 1980; DBA, George Washington U., 1992. Assoc. prof. mgmt. and mktg. Shippensburg (Pa.) U., 1983—; dir. mktg. VSP Wastewater Tech., Gettysburg, Pa., 1982; pres. Ridgaway Rose Internat., Inc., 1999—. Mktg. cons. Svcs. Unltd., Gettysburg, 1975—; lectr. in field. Author: (with Stephen J. Holoviak) Managing Human Productivity: People are Your Best Investment, 1987, 2nd printing 1991; contbr. articles to profl. jours. Recipient Excellence in Tchg. award, Corning Found., 1993, Outstanding Svc. award, 1994, 2002, Sprint Tchg. Excellence award, 1998, Orrston Bank Tchg. Excellence award, 2001, Panhellenic Coun. Tchg. award, 1999, Martin Babinee Outstanding Adv. award, 2003; fellow John L. Grove Rsch. fellow, 2002. Mem.: DAR, NOW, Southwest Acad. of Mgmt., S.E. Acad. Mgmt., Am. Mktg. Assn., Acad. Mktg. Sci., Survivors, Inc. (chmn. bd., personnel), Mensa, Adams County Literacy Coun., Nat. Hist. Trust, Kappa Kappa Gamma, Beta Gamma Sigma. Democrat. Episcopalian. Avocations: gardening, writing, sailing. Office: Shippensburg Univ 1871 Old Main Dr Shippensburg PA 17257-2299 E-mail: srston@ship.edu.

STONE, THERESA M. communications executive; b. Boston, 1944; Grad., Wellesley Coll.; grad. studies Cornell U.; MS, Sloan Sch. Mgmt., Mass. Inst. Tech., 1976. With Chubb Corp., 1990—97; pres., CEO Chubb Life Ins. Co. Am., 1994—97; with Morgan Stanley & Co., 1976—90; pres. Jefferson Pilot Comm., Greensboro, NC, 1997, exec. v.p., CFO, 1997—. Mem.: Burlington

Industries Bd., Fed. Res. Bd., Richmond Br., MIT Corp., Greensboro United Way 1999 Campaign (pacesetters chair), Greensboro C. of C. Office: Jefferson Pilot Corp PO Box 21008 Greensboro NC 27420

STONE, THOMAS D. music educator, composer; b. Oshkosh, Wis., Oct. 3, 1957; s. Leslie H. and Marian E. (Wearing) Stone; m. Jennifer M. Dowd, Oct. 4, 2003. MusB, Lawrence U., 1979; MusM, DePaul U., Chgo., 1983; MusD, U. Cin., 1996. Cert. tchr. wis. Dir. bands Cambria (Wis.)-Friesland Schs., 1979—81, Lincoln Sch., Chgo., 1981—83, Latin Sch. Chgo., 1983—89, Bolles Sch., Jacksonville, Fla., 1989—92; dir. inst. music Centenary Coll., Shreveport, La., 1995—. Pres. First Coast Wind Ensemble, Jacksonville, 1990—92; conductor Prevailing Winds, Shreveport, La., 1995—2002. Composer: Shadows of Eternity, 1990; composer: (for brass) Centennial Fanfare, 1988; editor (folk songs): Gilmore, 2002. Summer Band grant, Cmty. Found., 2000, Shreveport Arts Coun., 2000. Mem.: Broadcast Music, Inc., Coll. Band Dirs. Nat. Assn., Tex. Music Educators. Avocation: chess. Office: Centenary Coll 2911 Centenary Blvd Shreveport LA 71134-1188

STONE, THOMAS RICHARDSON, management consultant; b. Milw., Feb. 1, 1939; s. Thomas S. and Ann Louise (Taplin) S.; m. Cynthia White Hutchinson, July 20 1963; children: Sarah, Thomas. BS, U.S. Mil. Acad., 1961; MA, Rice U., 1971, PhD, 1974. Commd. 2d lt. field artillery U.S. Army, 1961, advanced through grades to col., 1988; v.p. medicare support svcs. Pa. Blue Shield, Camp Hill, 1988-90; dir. devel. and fin. Metro Arts of the Capital Region, Harrisburg, Pa., 1990-93; founding pres., CEO Whitaker Ctr. for Sci. & the Arts, 1993—2002; prin. The Franklin Cons. Group, 2002—. Author: The Second World War: Europe and the Mediterranean, Vol. II, 1980; contbr. articles to profl. publs. Mem. Pa. Heritage Soc., Cumberland-Perry Assn. for Retarded Citizens, 1980—, bd. dirs., 1980—82, 1986—97, 2002—, pres., 1984—86; mem. preservation com. Pa. Monuments at Gettysburg Battlefield, 1999—2000; bd. dirs. Capital Area Sch. for the Arts, 2000—; founding dir. Modern Transit Partnership, 2000—; bd. dirs. Cmty. Action Commn., 2002—, Susquehanna Art Mus., 2002—; deacon St. Paul's United Ch. Christ, Mechanicsburg, Pa., 1987—90, pres. of consistory, 1989—92, elder, 1990—92. Decorated Bronze Star, Legion of Merit; grantee Rice U., 1971-72; recipient Cmty. Svc. award, Am. Legion, Carlisle, Pa., 1987. Mem.: Nat. Soc. Fund Raising Execs. (bd. dirs. ctrl. Pa. chpt. 1994—2000, 2002—, cert., Outstanding Fund Raising Exec. Ctrl. Pa. chpt. award 1997), Cosmopolitan Diabetes Found. (dir. 1988—91, 1997—2003, chmn. 1999—2002), Assn. U.S. Army, Capital Fedn. Cosmopolitan Internat. Club (pres. 1980—82, lt. gov. 1983—86, gov.-elect 1986—87, gov. 1987—88, internat. 2d v.p. 1991—92, internat. 1st v.p. 1992—93, internat. pres.-elect 1993—94, internat. pres. 1994—95, Cosmo of Yr. award 1981—82, Patrick J. Hodgins award 1999). Home: 6319 Stephens Xing Mechanicsburg PA 17050-2347 Office: The Franklin Cons Grp PO Box 414 Mechanicsburg PA 17055-0414 E-mail: tom.stone@ix.netcom.com.

STONE, VAN COURTRIGHT, not-for-profit developer; b. Deland, Fla., June 22, 1946; s. Wilfred Arthur and Catherine Louise Stone; m. Nancy M. Stone, July 19, 1969 (div. 1989); 1 child, Edana A. Stone Neundorf; m. Lisa L. Stone, Dec. 22, 1990; children: Melisa A., Wesley Alan. BA, Wichita State U., 1968; JD, Washburn U., 1974. Exec. v.p., officer S.W. State Bank, Topeka, Kans., 1974-81; pres. Nat. Bank of Andover, Kans., 1985-87; corp. atty. various corps., 1987-91; COO Gerber Bus. Devel. Corp., Petaluma, Calif., 1991-94; exec. dir. Lions of Ill. Found., Sycamore, 1995—. Bd. dirs. Ill. Sch. for the Visually Impaired, Jacksonville, Ill. Eye Fund, Chgo., mng. dir. Lions of Ill. Endowment Fund, 1995—; pres., N.Am. Conf. of Lions Founds., 2000-2004. Author: (newsletter) Lions Share, 1995—; contbr. articles to profl. jours. Capt. U.S. Army, 1968-71. Decorated 3 Bronze Stars; recipient Presl. medal of honor Ill. Coll. of Optimetry, 1999, Meritorious Svc. award Deicke Ctr., 1999; Lions of Ill. Found. fellow laureate, 2002. Mem. VFW, No. Aurora Lions Club, Andover C. of C. (pres. 1986), Phi Sigma Rho, Tau Kappa Alpha, Phi Alpha Delta. Republican. Methodist. Avocations: golf, running, bridge, writing, bowling. Office: Lions Ill Found 2814 Dekalb Ave Sycamore IL 60178-3117 Office Phone: 815-756-5633 227.

STONE, WILLIAM CHARLES, software executive, consultant; b. Evansville, Ind., Apr. 9, 1955; s. Norbert Joseph and Patricia Mary (Browning) S.; m. Mary Ruth O'Daniel, Nov. 17, 1979; children: Robert Samuel, Justine Rosalie. Student, U. Hawaii, 1974-75; BS, Marquette U., 1977. CPA. Acct. KPMG Peet Merwick, St. Louis, 1977-79, Hartford, Conn., 1979-80; v.p. Advest, Inc., Hartford, 1980-85; cons. KPMG Peet Merwick, Hartford, 1985-86; chief exec., founder, pres. Securities Software & Cons., Inc., Bloomfield, Conn., 1986—. Office: SS & C 80 Lamberton Rd Windsor CT 06095-2150*

STONE, WILLIAM EDWARD, academic administrator, consultant; b. Peoria, Ill., Aug. 13, 1945; s. Dean Proctor and Katherine (Jamison) S.; m. Deborah Ann Duncan; children: Jennifer, Allison, Molly. AB, Stanford U., 1967, MBA, 1969. Asst. dean Stanford U., 1969-71, asst. to pres., 1971-77; exec. dir. Stanford Alumni Assn., 1977-90, pres., CEO, 1990-98; pres., dir. Stanford Alumni Assn. divsn. Stanford U., 1998-2001, Stanford Sierra Programs LLC, South Lake Tahoe, Calif., 1998-2001, Alpine Chalet, Inc., Alpine Meadows, Calif., 1987-2001; pres.-emeritus Stanford Alumni Assn. Stanford U., 2001—, cons. in ednl. advancement, 2001—; prin. eAdvancement Consortium, 2001—. Dir. Coun. Alumni Assn. Execs., 1989-93, v.p., 1990-91, pres., 1991-92; trustee Coun. for Advancement and Support of Edn., 1988-91; bd. dirs. Univ. ProNet, Inc., chmn., 1990-92, sec. 1996-2000. Bd. dirs. North County YMCA, 1975-76; bd. dirs., chmn. nominating com. faculty club Stanford U., 1979-81; trustee Watkins Discretionary Fund, 1979-82; mem. cmty. adv. bd. Resource Ctr. for Women; dir. Stanford Hist. Soc., 2002—, v.p., 2003—. Recipient K.M. Cuthbertson award Stanford U., 1987, Tribute award Coun. for Advancement and Support of Edn., 1991, Steuben Apple award, 2002. Mem.: Stanford Assocs., Stanford Faculty Club. Home: 1061 Cathcart Way Stanford CA 94305-1048 E-mail: westone@stanford.edu.

STONE, WILLIAM ROSS, research and development company executive, physicist; b. Aug. 26, 1947; s. William Jack and Winifred S.; m. Susan Letitia Lane, Aug. 8, 1970; 1 child, Ann Michele. AB in Earth Sci., U. Calif., San Diego, 1967, MS in Applied Physics, 1973, PhD in Applied Physics, 1978. Rsch. asst. U. Calif., San Diego, 1967-69; sr. physicist Gen. Atomic, La Jolla, Calif., 1969-72; sr. engr. engring. divsn. Gulf Gen. Atomic, La Jolla, 1972-73; sr. scientist Megatek Corp., San Diego, 1973-80; pres. stoneware, Ltd., La Jolla, 1976—; prin. physicist, inverse scattering group leader IRT Corp., San Diego, 1980-86, rsch. advisor, 1986-87; chief scientist McDonnell Douglas Tech., 1989—90, Expersoft Corp., 1990-91; exec. dir. Fund for Internat. Sci. Interchange, 1992-98. Dir., chmn. Samaritan Inst., San Diego, 1984-89. Editor: Vol. New Methods for Optical, Quasioptical, Acoustic and Electromagnetic Synthesis, 1981; contbr. articles to profl. jours. Recipient medal San Diego Soc. Tech. Writers and Pubs., 1962. Fellow: IEEE (3d Millennium medal), Chinese Inst. Electronics; mem.: Soc. Photooptical Instrumentation Engrs., Soc. Indsl. and Applied Math., Assn. Computing Machinery, Soc. Exploration Geophysics, Acoustical Soc. Am., Optical Soc. Am., Internat. Radio Soc. Union (asst. sec. gen., publs. 2001—, editor Radio Sci. Bull. 2001—), IEEE Antennas and Propagation Soc. (coord. profl. activities 1980—83, editor-in-chief Antenna Propagation Mag. 1984—, Outstanding Svc. award 2003), Phi Eta Sigma. Home: 1446 Vista Claridad La Jolla CA 92037-7839 Office Phone: 858-459-8305.

STONECIPHER, CHARLES H. information technology executive; BSME, MSME, Stanford U.; MBA, Harvard U. Former engr. Boeing Co.; former mgr. Bain & Co.; v.p. fin. and adminstrn., CFO Interpoint, 1994—95; COO Advanced Digital Info. Corp. (ADIC), Redmond, Wash., 1995—, pres., 1997—. Mem.: Phi Beta Kappa. Office: ADIC PO Box 97057 Redmond WA 98073-9757 also: ADIC Corp Hdqs 11431 Willows Rd NE Redmond WA 98052

STONECIPHER, DAVID A. insurance company executive; b. 1941; m. Nancy Berend; 4 children. Degree, Vanderbilt U., 1962; M Agrl. Sci., Ga. State U., 1967. With Life Ins. Co. Ga., Altanta, 1967-92, sr. v.p., actuary Atlanta, 1978—84, exec. v.p., 1984—89, pres., COO, 1989—91, CEO, 1991—92, Southland Life Ins. Co, Altanta, 1991—92; CEO elect Jefferson-Pilot Corp., Greensboro, NC, 1992; pres., CEO Jefferson Pilot Corp., Greensboro, NC, 1993—2004, Jefferson-Pilot Life Ins. Co., 1993—2004; chmn. Jefferson-Pilot Corp., Greensboro, NC, 1998—. Bd. dirs. Jefferson-Pilot Corp., Bassett Furniture Industries, Inc., McKenney's Corp., Internat. Home Furnishings Ctr., Inc., Fin. Services Roundtable. Bd. dirs. McCallie Sch. Served U.S. Army, 1962—64. Fellow, Soc. of Actuaries, 1970. Mem.: Am. Acad. Actuaries, Soc. Actuaries, Am. Coun. Life Insureres (past chmn.). Office: Jefferson-Pilot Corp PO Box 21008 100 N Greene St Greensboro NC 27420*

STONECIPHER, HARRY CURTIS, aerospace transportation executive; b. Robbins, Tenn., May 16, 1936; s. Harry Sheldon and Jennie Mae Stonecipher; m. Joan Stonecipher; 2 children. BS, Tenn. Poly. Inst., 1960; DSc (hon.), Washington U., 2002. With GE, 1960—61, 1962—79, Martin Aircraft Co., 1961-62; v.p., gen. mgr., comml. & mil. transp. ops. GE, 1979—84, v.p., gen. mgr., aircraft engine ops., 1984—87; exec. v.p. Sundstrand Corp., 1987, pres., COO, 1987-88, pres., CEO, 1988-94, chmn., 1991-94, also past bd. dirs.; pres., CEO McDonnell-Douglas Corp., St. Louis, 1994-97; pres., COO The Boeing Co., 1997—2001, vice chmn., 2001—02, pres., CEO, 2003—. Bd. dirs. PACCAR, Inc., The Boeing Co., 1997-. Recipient John R. Allison award, 1996, Rear Adm. John J. Bergen Leadership medal Navy League, 1996, Wings Club Disting. Achievement award, 2001, John W. Dixon award, U.S. Army Assn., 2002 . Follow Royal Aero. Soc., 1998. Office: The Boeing Co 100 N Riverside Plz Chicago IL 60606-2609*

STONEHILL, ERIC, lawyer; b. Rochester, N.Y., Feb. 27, 1950; BA with distinction, Northwestern U., 1970; JD, Cornell U., 1973, MBA, cert. hosp. and health svc. adminstrn., Cornell U., 1981. Bar: N.Y. 1974, D.C. 1981, U.S. Dist. Ct. (we. dist.) N.Y. 1974, U.S. Dist. Ct. (no. dist.) N.Y. 1976. Assoc. Harris Beach LLP, Rochester, 1973—81, ptnr., 1982—. Adj. instr. Rochester Inst. Tech., 1990-92. Contbr. articles to profl. jours. Bd. dirs. Rochester Eye and Human Parts Bank, 1983-91, 92-2001, pres., 1987-90. Mem. Am. Health Lawyers Assn., N.Y. State Bar Assn. (mem. health law sect.), D.C. Bar Assn., Monroe County Bar Assn., Sloan Alumni Assn., Phi Beta Kappa. Office: Harris Beach LLP 99 Garnsey Rd Pittsford NY 14534 Office Phone: 585-419-8641.

STONEHILL, LLOYD HERSCHEL, gas industry executive, mechanical engineer; b. South Bend, Ind., May 20, 1927; s. Charles Myers and Louise Mary (Reed) S.; m. Jean Carole Herzer, Dec. 30, 1961; children: Mark, Bill, John, Rob. BSME, Purdue U., 1949. Registered profl. engr., La. Chief engr. Rothschild Boiler & Tank Works, Shreveport, La., 1949-54; chmn. bd. dirs. Frankfort (Ind.) Bottle Gas, Inc., 1956—. Patentee in field. Founding prs. Clinton County Hosp. Authority, Frankfort, 1974; membership chmn. Clinton County Hosp. Found., Frankfort, 1982-83, 89. With U.S. Army, 1954-56. Recipient Heroism award Elks Lodge, Frankfort, 1959. Mem. Nat. Propane Gas Assn. (mktg. awards 1986, 87), Am. Legion, Purdue Alumni Assn. (Clinton County Chpt. mem. pres.' coun.), Hudson Inst., Rotary (sec. 1963-65, Paul Harris fellow), Lambda Chi Alpha (sec. 1946-47). Republican. Mem. Christian Ch. Avocations: collecting old violins, sailing, reading. Home: 1258 Forest Dr Frankfort IN 46041-3230 Office: Frankfort Bottle Gas Inc 1555 McKinley Ave Frankfort IN 46041-1805

STONEHOUSE, JAMES ADAM, lawyer; b. Alameda, Calif., Nov. 10, 1937; s. Maurice Adam and Edna Sigrid (Thuesen) S.; m. Marilyn Jean Kotkas, Aug. 6, 1966; children: Julie Aileen, Stephen Adam. AB, U. Calif., Berkeley, 1961; JD, U. Calif., San Francisco, 1965. Bar: Calif. 1966; cert. specialist probate, estate planning and trust law. Assoc. Hall, Henry, Oliver & McReavy, San Francisco, 1966-71; ptnr. Whitney Hanson & Stonehouse, Alameda, 1971-77; pvt. practice Alameda, 1977-79; ptnr. Stonehouse & Silva, Alameda, 1979—. Judge adv. Alameda coun. Navy League, 1978-98. Founding dir. Alameda Clara Barton Found., 1977-80; mem. Oakland (Calif.) Marathon-Exec. Com., 1979; mem. exec. bd. Alameda coun. Boy Scouts Am., 1979—, pres., 1986-88, endowment chair area III, 1996—; trustee Golden Gate Scouting, 1986-95, treas., 1989-91, v.p., 1991-92, pres., 1993-95, v.p. area III western region, 1990-95, bd. dirs. western region, 1991—. Alemeda (Calif.) Boy Scouts Found., 2003—; bd. dirs. Lincoln Child Ctr. Found., 1981-87, 94-98, pres., 1983-85; pres. Robert L. Lippert Found., 1990—; mem. sch. bd. St. Joseph Notre Dame, 1994-2000, pres., 1997-2000. Recipient Lord Baden-Powell Merit award Boy Scouts Am., 1988, Silver Beaver award, 1991, Silver Antelope award, 1999, Citizen of Yr. award City of Alameda, 1999; named Boss of Yr., Alameda Jaycees, 1977; Coro Found. fellow, 1961-62. Mem. ABA, Alameda County Bar Assn. (vice chmn. com. office econs. 1977-78), Commonwealth Club, Rotary (dir. 1976-78, trustee Alameda Rotary Found. 1991—, treas. 1994-98, pres. 1998-2000), Elks (past exalted ruler, all state officer 1975-76, all dist. officer 1975-77, 78-79). Republican. Roman Catholic. Home: 2990 Northwood Dr Alameda CA 94501-1606 Office: Stonehouse & Silva 512 Westline Dr Ste 300 Alameda CA 94501-5870

STONEMAN, WILLIAM, III, physician, educator; b. Kansas City, Mo., Sept. 8, 1927; s. William and Helen Louise (Bloom) S.; m. Elizabeth Johanna Wilson, May 19, 1951; children: William Laurence, Sidney Camdon (dec.), Cecily Anne Erker, Elizabeth Wilson, John Spalding. Student, Rockhurst Coll., 1944-46; BS, St. Louis U., 1948, MD, 1952. Diplomate: Am. Bd. Surgery, Am. Bd. Plastic Surgery. Intern Kansas City Gen. Hosp., 1952-53; resident in surgery St. Louis U., 1953-57, resident in plastic surgery, 1957-59, mem. faculty, 1959—, assoc. prof. surgery, assoc. prof. community medicine, 1975-84, prof. surgery, community medicine, 1984-94, prof. surgery, community medicine emeritus, 1994, assoc. dean Sch. Medicine, 1973-76; exec. assoc. dean St. Louis U. (Sch. Medicine), 1976-82, dean, 1982-95, dean emeritus, 1995—, assoc. v.p. med. ctr., 1983-95. Mem. adj. faculty Washington U. Sch. Medicine, St. Louis, 1968-74; chief exec. officer Bi-State Regional Med. Program, 1968-74; bd. dirs. St. Louis Office Mental Retardation/Developmentally Disabled Resources, 1980-82, Combined Health Appeal of Mo., 1990-94. Editor: Parameters, 1976-94; contbr. articles on plastic surgery, health care delivery planning to profl. jours. Served with AUS, 1946-47. Fellow ACS; mem. AMA (chmn. sect. on med. schs. 1987-88, sect. alt. del. 1989-91, del. 1992-94), Mo. Med. Assn., Mem. St. Louis Met. Med. Soc., St. Louis Surg. Soc., Am. Soc. Plastic and Reconstructive Surgeons, Midwestern Assn. Plastic Surgeons. Roman Catholic. Clubs: University. Office: St Louis U Sch Medicine 1316 Carr Lane Ave Saint Louis MO 63104-1011 E-mail: stoneman@slu.edu.

STONER, JAMES LLOYD, retired foundation executive, clergyman; b. Point Marion, Pa., Apr. 23, 1920; s. Martin Clark and Bess (Hare) S.; m. Janice Faller Evans, Aug. 28, 1943; children: Thomas Clark, James Douglas and Geoffrey Lloyd (twins). BS, Bethany Coll., 1941, DD (hon.), 1958; BD, MA, Yale U., 1944. Ordained to ministry Christian Ch., 1943; minister in Hamden, Conn., 1942-44; assoc. exec. sec. U. Tex., YMCA, 1944-45; dir. Student Christian Fellowship, Bowling Green State U., 1945-47, Univ. Christian Mission, Fed. Council Ch. and Nat. Council Chs., 1947-56; minister North Christian Ch., Columbus, Ind., 1956-66; asst. gen. sec. for exec. operations Nat. Council Chs., 1966-72; sr. minister Central Christian Ch., Austin, Tex., 1972-80; dep. exec. dir. Found. for Christian Living, Pawling, N.Y., 1980-83, exec. dir., 1983-87. Chmn. com. recommendations Internat. Conv. Christian Chs., 1962-65; bd. mgrs. United Christian Missionary Soc., 1956-63; mem. adv. bd. Am. Bible Soc., 1966-72; life mem. coun. Christian Unity, Christian Ch.; a founder, 1st pres. LINK Award, Ridgewood, N.J., 1966-72; mem. Austin Conf. Chs., pres., 1973-75; rep. Tex. Conf. Chs., 1976-80; mem. goals com. Austin Tomorrow; mem. adv. bd. 1st Comml. Bank of Lakeway, Austin, Tex., 1990-95. Author: Down-to-Earth Meditations That Give You a Lift, 2000; contbr. articles to profl. publs. A founder, bd. dirs. Fellowship Christian Athletes, Kansas City, Mo., 1956-68; trustee Tougaloo (Miss.) Coll., 1968-74; trustee emeritus Lakeway Ch.; v.p., mem. exec. com. Ecumenical Ctr. Continuing Edn., Yale, 1966-72; mem. exec. com. Boy Scouts Am., Austin, 1980, Dutchess County council, 1981-82; bd. mgrs. New Milford Hosp., 1983-88; bd. dirs. Holiday Hills YMCA, 1983-87; com. mem. Town of Pawling 200th Anniversary, 1985-88, Lakeway Ecumenical Ch.; co-founder Holy Week Palm Observance, Lakeway,Tex. Mem. Pawling C. of C. (exec. com. 1984-87), Fellowship of Christian Athletes (nat. adv. bd. 1994—), Masons (32 degree), Pawling Rotary Club (pres. 1983-84, dist. gov.-elect 1991-92, dist. gov. 1992-93, Paul Harris fellow), Shriners, Austin Rotary Club (spl. lifetime mem.), Lake Travis/Lakeway Rotary Club (hon.), Alpha Psi Omega, Beta Theta Pi. Home: 1134 Challenger Austin TX 78734-3802 *Fill every day with rainbow colors, and punctuate life with a positive outlook... Even the Cross of Christ is a positive sign.*

STONER, JOHN RICHARD, federal government executive; b. Ypsilanti, Mich., May 11, 1958; s. Richard P. and Marjorie G. Stoner; m. Diane Leslie Snow. BA in Govt., B in Music Edn., Lawrence U., 1981; MS in Mgmt., U. Md., 2004. Staff asst. Senator Robert Kasten Jr., Washington, 1981-82; staff assoc. Wis. Office Fed.-State Rels., Washington, 1982-83; intergovtl. rels. officer U.S. Dept. Transp., Washington, 1983-86, congl. rels. officer, 1989-91; dir. Office of Program and Policy Support, Rsch. and Spl. Programs Adminstrn., Dept. Transp., Washington, 1991-93; exec. dir. Republican Nat. Lawyers Assn., 1993-97; rep. Primerica Fin. Svcs., 1993-97, mortgage banker, 1998—; state govt. rels. mgr. Am. Trucking Assn., Inc., Alexandria, Va., 1986-88; researcher George Bush for Pres. Com., 1988; staff asst. Office of Pres.-Elect, Washington, 1988-89; state dir. The Century Coun., Washington, 2000—03. Admissions contact Washington area Lawrence U., 1986-87; softball team mgr. Montgomery County Recreation League. Recipient Eagle Scout award Boy Scouts Am., 1972; Mortar Bd. scholar, 1980; Senate Rep. Policy Com. Legis. fellow, 1993-96. Republican. Mem. Ch. of Christ, Scientist. Avocations: water-skiing, organ. Home: 10409 Brunswick Ave Silver Spring MD 20902-4845 Office: The Century Coun 1310 G St NW Washington DC 20005-3000

STONER, LEONARD D. automotive parts company executive; b. Galion, Ohio, Feb. 19, 1950; s. Kenneth M. and Delores I. (Fix) S.; m. Katharine I. Wiese, Feb. 14, 1980; children: Elisha, Cameron, Aaron. AS in Electronics Engring. Tech., Bell Howell U., 1974-76; student, U. Nebr., 1976-80; BS of Bus. Adminstrn. in Tech. Svcs., Bellevue U., 1995. Maintenance stores Keeper Control Data Corp., Omaha, 1978-85; prodn. control mgr. Douglas and Lamason, Richmond, Mich., 1986-87; ops. mgr. Johnson Controls, Lapeer, Mich., 1987-89; project mgr. Dohrman Machine Prodn. Inc., Omaha, 1990-92; mgr. prodn. and inventory control Stuart Entertainment, Inc., Council Bluffs, Iowa, 1995-96; materials control mgr. Sears Mfg., Davenport, Iowa, 1996-98; prodn. control mgr. Nishikawa Standard Co., Topeka, 1998-2000; materials mgr. RoMech, Red Oak, Iowa, 2000—. Assoc. cons. Internat. Purchasing Svc., Dearborn. With USAF, 1970-77. Mem. Am. Prodn. & Inventory Control Soc., Am. Radio Relay League. Avocations: amateur radio, camping, boating, woodworking, car repair. Office: RoMech 2700 N Broadway Red Oak IA 51566 Home: 14884 320th St Council Bluffs IA 51503-3948 E-mail: LeonardStoner@msn.com.

STONESIFER, PATRICIA Q. foundation administrator; b. Indpls., 1956; m. Michael Kinsley. BA, Ind. U., 1982. Editor-in-chief Que Corp., Indpls.; sr. mgr. Microsoft Press, 1988-89; gen. mgr. Microsoft Can., 1989-90; gen. mgr., then v.p. product support svcs. consumer divsn. Microsoft Corp., Redmond, Wash., 1990-93, sr. v.p. consumer divsn., 1993—96; chairwoman, pres. Gates Learning Found., 1997—99; co-chair, pres. Bill & Melinda Gates Found., Seattle, 2000—. Mem. US delegation to UN Gen. Assembly Spl. Session on AIDS; mem., bd. dirs. Viacom Inc., 2000—, The Seattle Found., Amazon.com. Office: Bill & Melinda Gates Found PO Box 23350 Seattle WA 98102

STONEY, GEORGE CASHEL, film educator; b. Winston-Salem, N.C., July 1, 1916; s. George Henry Cashel Stoney and Kate Crenshaw; m. Mary Forthrop Bruce, July 14, 1945 (div. 1961); children: Kate Cashel(dec.), Mary Louise, James Bruce. AB in English, U. N.C., 1937. Feature writer Raleigh (N.C.) News and Observer, 1937, Survey Graphic Mag., N.Y.C., 1938—39; assoc. info. officer Farm Security Adminstrn., Montgomery, Ala., 1940—41; filmmaker So. Edn. Film Prodn. Svc., Athens, Ga., 1946—50; chair Film Inst. CCNY, N.Y.C., 1946—47; filmmaker Assn. Am. Med. Coll., Washington, 1950—56; dir., prodr. Stoney Assocs., N.Y.C., 1946—90; prof. film/TV Tish Sch. Arts, NYU, N.Y.C., 1970—. Adj. faculty film Columbia U., N.Y.C., 1948—53; filmmaker in residence Stanford U., Palo Alto, Calif., 1965—67; guest exec. prodr. Can. Nat. Film Bd., Montreal, Que., Canada, 1968—70; co-founder Alt. Media Ctr., NYU, 1972—76; Fulbright prof. film Cath. U., Rio de Janeiro, 1989. Bd. dirs. Manhattan Neighborhood Network, N.Y.C., 1992—. Capt. USAF, 1942—46, ETO. Named Paulette Goddard Prof. Cinema, N.Y.C., 1994—, Disting. Alumnus, U. N.C., Chapel Hill, 1997. Mem.: Alliance Cmty. Media (founder). Democrat. Episcopalian. Home: 240 Waverly Pl #45 New York NY 10014 Office: NYU Tisch Sch Arts 721 Broadway New York NY Office Phone: 212-998-1718.

STONG, JOHN ELLIOTT, retail electronics company executive; b. Elkater, Iowa, Sept. 20, 1921; s. Elliott Sheldon and Nora Elizabeth (Daly) S.; m. Olive Miriam Foley, Dec. 11, 1943; children: Mary Myers, Jon, Miriam Koza. Student U. Colo., 1939-43. Salesman, Purucker Music, Medford, Oreg., 1946-48, dept. mgr., 1949-56, store mgr., 1957, partner, 1958-61, owner, 1962-64; pres. Purucker Music Houses, Medford, 1965-67, Music West, Inc., Eugene, Oreg., 1968-70, Magnavox Centers, Medford, 1971-99, exec. asst., Consultants Internat., 1972—. Served with USAF, 1943-45. Decorated Air medal. Mem. Nat. Assn. Music Mchts. (dir. 1969-72), Scull Mchts. Rsch. Group (dir., chmn.). Republican. Roman Catholic. Home: PO Box 129 Junction City OR 97448-0129

ST-ONGE, DENIS ALDERIC, geologist, research scientist; b. Ste-Agathe, Man., Can., May 11, 1929; s. Adolphe and Jeanne M (Ritchot) St-Onge; m. Jeanne Marie Behaegel, Jan. 7, 1955; children: Marc R, Nicole J M. BA, Coll. St-Boniface, 1951; Lic. Sci., U. Louvain, Belgium, 1957, DSc, 1962, U. Man., 1990. Research scientist Geol. Survey, Ottawa, Ont., Can., 1958-68, sect. head, 1982-85; chief sub. div. Quaternary Geology, 1985-87, dir. terrain scis. div., 1987-91, sci. advisor Polar Continental Shelf Project, 1991-97; prof. geography U. Ottawa, 1968-82, chmn. geography, 1974-77, vice dean grad. studies, 1977-80, prof. emeritus, 1998—, bd. govs., 2000—; scientist emeritus Geol. Survey Can., 1997—. Chmn. bd. dirs. Fluxnet Can., 2002—, Arctic Net, 2003—04. Author: (book) Geomorphologie Ellef-Ringes Island, 1965, Quaternary Geology, Inman River Region, N.W.T. Canada, 1995; contbr. articles to profl jours. Pres Ont Francophone PTA, 1967—69. Decorated Officer Order of Can; recipient medal, Queen Elizabeth II, 1979, Commemorative medal, Govt. of Can., 1992, Medal of Honor, Univ Liege, Belgium, 1980, medal, A Cailleux, 1991, Can 125, 1992, Royal Scottish Geog. Soc, 1994, Golden Jubilee medal, Queen Elizabeth II, 2002. Fellow: Arctic Inst. N.Am., Royal Can. Geog. Soc. (bd dirs 1980—2001, pres 1992—98, chmn Partnership Group Sci Eng 1999—2001), Geol. Assn. Can. (pres 1984—85, J W Ambrose Medal 2001); mem.: Can. Geosci. Coun. (pres 1996—97), Assn. Quebecoise pour l'etude du Quaternaire (hon.), Internat. Union Quaternary Rsch. (hon.), Can. Quaternary Assn., Can. Assn. Geographers (pres 1979—80, Award for Serv to the Profession 2000). Avocations: swimming, skiing, photography. Home: 1115 Sherman Dr Ottawa ON Canada K2C 2M3 Office: Geolog Survey of Canada 601 Booth St Ottawa ON Canada K1A OE8 Office Phone: 613-947-1652. Business E-Mail: dstonge@nrcan.gc.ca.

STONINGTON, EMILY S. state legislator; b. Oak Park, Ill., Jan. 12, 1947; m. Tim Swanson; 2 children. BA, Bennington Coll.; MA, U. Calif., Berkeley. Mem. Mont. Ho. of Reps., Mont. Senate, Dist. 15, Helena, 1996—. Home: 15042 Kelly Canyon Rd Bozeman MT 59715-9625 Office: Mont Ho of Reps State Capitol Helena MT 59620

STONNER, DAVID MOORE, foundation administrator; b. Boonville, Mo., Jan. 11, 1948; s. Hadley Pershing and Mary Magdeline Stonner; m. Anne Laura Schwartz, Apr. 20, 1991; children: Julia Elizabeth, Hope Alina. BA, U. Mo.; MA, U. Mo.; PhD, U. Mo., 1970. Asst. prof. Oakland U., Rochester, Mich., 1974—78; program officer Office of Naval Rsch., Arlington, Va., 1979—82; legislative dir. Rep. Claudine Schneider, Washington, 1982—90; sect. head congl. affairs NSF, Arlington, 1991—. Contbr. articles to profl. jours., chapters to books. Charter bd. dirs. NSF Child Devel. Ctr., Arlington, 1995—99. Mem.: AAAS (Swiss fellow 2000). Office: NSF 4201 Wilson Blvd Arlington VA 22230

STONNINGTON, HENRY HERBERT, physician, medical executive, educator; b. Vienna, Feb. 12, 1927; arrived in U.S., 1969; m. Constance Mary Leigh Hamersley, Sept. 19, 1953. MB, BS, Melbourne U., Victoria, Australia, 1950; MS, U. Minn., 1972. Diplomate Am. Bd. Phys. Medicine and Rehab., 1973. Pvt. practice, Sydney, N.S.W., Australia, 1955-65; clin. tchr. U. N.S.W., Sydney, 1965-69; resident in Phys. Medicine and Rehab. Mayo Clinic, Rochester, Minn., 1969-72, mem. staff, 1972-83; assoc. prof. Mayo Med. Sch., Rochester, 1975-83; chmn. dept rehab. medicine Med. Coll. Va., Va. Commonwealth U., Richmond, 1983-88, prof. rehab. medicine, 1983-89, dir. rsch. tng. ctr., 1988-89; v.p. med. svcs. Sheltering Arms Hosp., Richmond, 1985-92; prof. and chmn. dept. phys. medicine and rehab. U. Mo., Columbia, 1992-94; med. dir. Meml. Rehab. Ctr., Savannah, Ga., 1994-97; clin. prof. rehab. medicine Emory U., Atlanta, 1997—2000; clin. prof. medicine sect. phys. medicine and rehab. La. State U., 2001—. Med. dir. rehab. svcs. Meml. Hosp., Gulfport, Miss., 1998—; clin. prof. phys. med. and rehab. La. State U. Med. Sch., 2001—. Editor: Brain Injury, 1987—2001, Pediatric Rehabilitation, 1997—2000; contbr. articles to profl. jours. Recipient award Rsch. Tng. Ctr. Model Sys., Nat. Inst. Disability and Rehab. Rsch., Washington, 1987, 88, Disting. Clinician award Am. Acad. Phys. Medicine and Rehab., 2002. Fellow Australian Coll. Rehab. Medicine, Australasian Faculty Rehab. Medicine, Royal Coll. Physicians Edinburgh (Scotland), Am. Acad. Phys. Medicine and Rehab. (named Disting. Physician 2002), Am. Coun. Rehab. Medicine, Am. Assn. Acad. Physiatrists; mem. Internat. Brain Injury Assn. (v.p. for sci. affairs 1998—, bd. govs., Founder's award 2004). Office Phone: 228-865-3423. Personal E-mail: hencon2731@aol.com.

STOOKEY, NOEL PAUL, folksinger, composer; b. Balt., Dec. 30, 1937; s. George William and Dorothea (St. Aubrey) S.; m. Mary Elizabeth Bannard, Sept. 4, 1963; children: Elizabeth Drake, Katherine Darby, Anna St. Aubrey. Student, Mich. State U., 1955-58; HHD (hon.), Husson Coll., 1978. Prodn. mgr. Cormac Chem. Corp., N.Y.C., 1959-60; artist in residence Northfield Mount Hermon Sch., 1999. Released album of songs Birds of Paradise, 1954; sang professionally, master ceremonies events, Mich. State U., 1955-58; profl. singer, Greenwich Village, N.Y.C., 1960-61; mem. folksinging group, Peter, Paul and Mary, 1961—; solo rec. artist for Warner Bros., 1971-74; producer folk albums for Scepter Records, Verve/Folkway Records; founder, Neworld Media, rec. studio Neworld Records, 1977-81; rec. artist: Paul And, 1971, One Night Stand, 1972, Real to Reel, 1976, Something New and Fresh, 1978, Band and Bodyworks, 1979, Wait'll You Hear This, 1982, There is Love, 1985, State of the Heart, 1985, In Love Beyond Our Lives, 1990; host Maine Pub. TV broadcasting series "E-Maine", 1997. Mem. AFTRA, Screen Actors Guild, ASCAP, Delta Upsilon. Clubs: St. Botolph's (Boston). Personal E-mail: stook@celestat.com. Business E-Mail: neworld@celestat.com.

STOOKEY, STANLEY DONALD, chemist; b. Hay Springs, Nebr., May 23, 1915; s. Stanley Clarke and Hermie Lucille (Knapp) Stookey; m. Ruth Margaret Watterson, Dec. 26, 1940; children: Robert Alan, Margaret Ann, Donald Bruce. BA, Coe Coll., 1936, LLD, 1959, DSc (hon.), 1963; MSc, Lafayette Coll., 1937; PhD in Phys. Chemistry, MIT, 1940; DSc (hon.), Alfred U., 1984. With Corning Glass Works Rsch., NY, 1940—79, dir. fundamental chem. rsch., 1970—79, ret., 1987. Contbr. articles to profl. jours.; patentee field of photosensitive glasses, glass ceramics, photochromatic and polychromatic glasses; published: Journey to the Center of the Crystal Ball, 1985. Named Inventor of Yr., George Wash. U., 1970; recipient John Price Wetherill award, Franklin Inst., 1953, 1962, Toledo Glass and Ceramic award, 1964, Beverly Myers Achievement award, Ednl. Found. in Opthalmic Optics, 1973, Phoenix award of the Glass Industry, 1975, Achievement award, Indsl. Rsch. Inst., 1979, Disting. Inventor award, Central NY Patent Law Assn., 1984, World Materials Congress award, 1988, Nat. medal of Tech., 1986, 1994, Wilelm Eitel medallion for Excellence in Silicate Sci., 1993. Fellow: Am . Inst. Chemists, Am. Ceramic Soc. (Ross Coffin Purdy award 1960, E.C. Sullivan award, Corning Sect. 1971, Samuel Giejsbeek award, Pacific Coast Sect. 1982, named disting. life mem. 1989); mem.: NAE, Am. Chem. Soc. (Award for Creative Invention 1971), Sigma Xi. Republican. Methodist. Achievements include invention of Corning Ware cookware, the company's first consumer product; other inventions include glass that darkens and fades in response to light (for Photogray eyeglasses) and glass that can be etched with light; discovery of how to control crystal formation in glass by melting and forming glass products, then use heat to regulate crystal growth and transform the products into fine-grained ceramics; this concept has been used to make missile nose cones, cooking surfaces, hot plates, capacitors, insulators, and floor tile. Office: Corning Corp c/o Paul Rogoski One River Front Plaza Corning NY 14831*

STOOLMAN, HERBERT LEONARD, public relations executive; b. Newark, Apr. 6, 1917; s. Abe C. and Ida H. (Sinar) S.; AB, Catawba Coll., 1937; BS, Temple U., 1939; postgrad. Harvard U., 1938; m. Sarah Janice Cutler, Apr. 6, 1944; children: Cathy Lynn (Mrs. Richard Schwartz), Robert Henry. Pub., East Camden Newspapers, 1941-57; pres. Stoolman Assos., Camden, N.J., 1946—; dir. public relations Camden County, N.J., 1953-86. Mem. Camden County Econ. Devel. Commn., 1963—, Camden County Cultural and Heritage Commn., 1973—. With USAF, 1942-46. Recipient Nat. award Nat. Assn. Counties, 1969, 72, 78, 79; Nat. award Am. Indsl. Devel. Council, 1963. Mem. Am., N.J. hosps. public relations assns., S. Jersey, Phila. public relations assns., Am. Assn. County Public Relations Officers, N.J. Press Assn., Phila. Press Assn. Lodge: Lions (dir. pub. relations). Home and Office: 6 S Mansfield Ave Margate City NJ 08402-2514

STOOPES, GARY ROBERT, technical consultant, geoscientist; b. Eugene, Ore., Aug. 28, 1953; s. William Gerald and Jacqueline Stoopes. BSc, U. Ore., 1985; MSc, Ariz. State U., 1991. Geologist U.S. Geol. Survey, Vancouver/Wash., 1985—87; geoscientist Roy. F. Weston, Inc., Albuquerque, 1991—2001, Aurora Tech. Svcs. Inc., Los Alamos, N.Mex., 2001—03; tech. cons. Self-Employed, Los Alamos, 2003—. Republican. Avocations: skiing, fly fishing, hiking, reading. Home and Office: 505 Oppenheimer Dr #311 Los Alamos NM 87544 Business E-Mail: garys@cnsp.com.

STOOPLER, MARK BENJAMIN, physician; b. N.Y.C., Sept. 29, 1950; s. Alex and Blanche Sylvia (Kappel) S.; m. Lynn Sara Fruchter, Jan. 10, 1982; children: David Andrew, Emily Rachel, Jesse Bryan. BS, Tulane U., 1971; MD, Cornell U., 1975. Diplomate Am. Bd. Internal Medicine, Am. Bd. Oncology. Intern and resident in internal medicine North Shore U. Hosp., Manhasset, N.Y., 1975-78, Meml. Sloan-Kettering Cancer Ctr., N.Y.C., 1975-78, asst. chief resident in medicine, 1978, fellow in med. oncology, 1978-80; asst. attending physician Presbyn. Hosp., N.Y.C., 1980-93, assoc. attending physician, 1993—; asst. clin. prof. medicine Columbia U. Coll. of Physicians and Surgeons, N.Y.C., 1980-93; assoc. clin. prof. medicine, 1993—. Contbr. articles to profl. jours. Recipient U. scholar Tulane U., 1970-71; named one of America's Top Doctors, A Castle Connolly Guide, 2003, 2004. Fellow ACP; mem. Am. Soc. of Clin. Oncology, Am. Fedn. for Clin. Research, Internat. Assn. for the Study of Lung Cancer, Phi Beta Kappa. Office: Columbia-Presbyn Med Ctr 161 Fort Washington Ave New York NY 10032-3713

STOPFORD, MICHAEL JOHN, university administrator; b. June 22, 1953; MA in English Lang. and Lit., Oxford (Eng.) U., 1975. With U.K. Diplomatic Svc., London, N.Y.C. and Vienna, 1975-79; sec. UN, N.Y.C. and Geneva, 1980-95, dir. Info. Ctr. Washington, 1992-95; chief media and pub. rels. Internat. Fin. Corp., Washington, 1996-97; sr. asst. to pres. Am. U., Washington, 1997—. Office: Am U 4400 Massachusetts Ave NW Washington DC 20016 E-mail: mjs@american.edu.

STOPP, DONALD L. retired educator, retired business owner; b. Allentown, Pa., Mar. 15, 1928; s. Marcus Martin and Dorothy May; m. Jacklin Talmage Stopp, Dec. 22, 1967. AB, Duke U., 1954; postgrad. in MBA program, U. Buffalo, 1973—74. Social Studies cert., East Stroudsburg Univ., East Stroudsburg, PA, 1957, Buffalo Univ., Buffalo, NY, 1972. Tchr. Kennett Square High School, KennettSquare, PA, 1957-58; social studies tchr. The Gow School, South Wales, NY, 1958-60; sales position Marquis Who's Who, Chicago, IL, 1960-61; caseworker Erie County Dept. Social Svcs., Buffalo, 1961-63; driving instr. Three Buffalo Schs., Buffalo, 1964-66; rememdial math tchr. Buffalo Public Schs., Buffalo, 1966-70; owner, distr. Thesaurus Wholesale Maps, Lockport, NY, 1975-91. Dept. head, Montgomery Ward, Springfield, IL, 1955-56, econs. instr., Leelanau Schs., Leelanau, Mich., 1965, sales, pub. rels., Goodwill Industries, Buffalo, NY, 1972-73, owner, founder, Pac-N-Ship, Buffalo, NY, 1980-84, Erie Canal TV series: Vision Construction, Effects, 2002; spkr. and lectr. in field. Bd. dirs. Niagara Coutny Hist. Soc., 1997—2001. Mem. Kiwanis Club of Lockport, Niagara County Hist. Soc.(bd dirs. 1997-2001), Canal Task Force C. of C. Avocations: history, past, present, future applications, the cold war past and residual effects.

STOPPARD, TOM (TOMAS STRAUSSLER), playwright; b. Zlin, Czechoslovakia, July 3, 1937; s. Eugene and Martha (Stoppard) Straussler; m. Jose Ingle, 1965 (div.); m. Miriam Moore-Robinson, 1972 (div.); 4 children. MLitt (hon.), U. Bristol, Eng., 1979, Brunel U., 1979, U. Sussex, 1980. Journalist Western Daily Press, Bristol, Eng., 1954-58, Evening World, Bristol, 1958-60; free-lance reporter, 1960-63. Bd. dirs. Royal Nat. Theatre, London, 1989—. Author: (plays) The Gamblers, 1965, Rosencrantz and Guildenstern Are Dead, 1966 (Plays and Players Best Play award 1967, Best Play Tony award 1968), Enter a Free Man, 1968, The Real Inspector Hound, 1968, Albert's Bridge, 1969 (Prix Italia 1968), If You're Glad I'll Be Frank, 1969, After Magritte, 1970, Dogg's Our Pet, 1971, Jumpers, 1972 (Evening Standard Best Play award 1972, Plays and Players Best Play award 1972), Travesties, 1974 (Evening Standard Best Play award 1974, Best Play Tony award 1976), Dirty Linen and New-Found-Land, 1976, Every Good Boy Deserves Favor, 1974, Night and Day, 1978 (Evening Standard Best Play award 1978), Dogg's Hamlet, Cahoot's Macbeth, 1979, The Real Thing, 1982 (Evening Standard Best Play award 1982, Best Play Tony award 1984, Best Fgn. Play Tony award 1984), Hapgood, 1988, Artist Descending a Staircase, 1988, Arcadia, 1993 (Evening Standard Best Play award 1993, Oliver award 1994), Indian Ink, 1995, Invention of Love, 1997 (Evening Standard Best Play award 1997); (play adaptations) Tango by Slawomir Mrozek, 1966, The House of Bernarda Alba by Federico Garcia Lorca, 1973, Undiscovered Country (based on Das Weite Land by Arthur Schnitzler), 1979, On the Razzle (based on Einen Jux will er sich machen by Johann Nestroy), 1981, Rough Crossing (based on The Play's the Thing by Ferenc Molnar), 1984, Dalliance (based on Liebelei by Arthur Schnitzler), 1986; (radio plays) The Dissolution of Dominic Boot, 1964, M is for Moon Among Other Things, 1964, If You're Glad I'll Be Frank, 1966, Albert's Bridge, 1967, Where Are They Now?, 1970, Artist Descending A Staircase, 1972, The Dog It Was That Died, 1982, In the Native State, 1991, also episodes of radio serials The Dales, 1964, A Student's Diary, 1965; (screenplays) The Romantic Englishwoman, 1975, Despair, 1978, The Human Factor, 1980, (with Terry Gilliam and Charles McKeown) Brazil, 1985 (Best Screenplay Acad. award nominee 1985, Best Screenplay L.A. Critics Circle award 1985), Empire of the Sun, 1987, The Russia House, 1990; (author, dir.) Rosencrantz and Guildenstern Are Dead, 1990 (Grand prize Venice Film Festival 1990), Billy Bathgate, 1991, (with Marc Norman) Shakespeare in Love, 1998 (Golden Globe award and Oscar for best screenplay); (teleplays) A Walk on the Water, 1963, A Separate Peace, 1966, Teeth, 1967, Another Moon Called Earth, 1967, Neutral Ground, 1968, The Engagement (based on his radio play The Dissolution of Dominic Boot), 1970, One Pair of Eyes, 1972, (with Clive Exton) Boundaries, 1975, Three Men in a Boat, 1975, Professional Foul, 1977, Squaring the Circle: Poland 1980-81, 1985; (translator) Largo Desolato by Vaclav Havel, 1987; (novel) Lord Malquist and Mr. Moon, 1966; contbr. short stories to Introduction 2, 1964. Decorated knight comdr. Order Brit. Empire; Ford Found. grantee, 1964; recipient John Whiting award Arts Coun. Great Britain, 1967, Evening Standard Most Promising Playwright Drama award, 1972, Shakespeare prize Hamburg, Germany, 1979. Fellow Royal Soc. Literature. Office: Peters Fraser Dunlop Drury Ho 34-43 Russell St London WC2B 5HA England

STORANDT, MARTHA, psychologist; b. Little Rock, June 2, 1938; d. Farris and Floy (Montgomery) Mobbs; m. Duane Storandt, Dec. 15, 1962; 1 child, Eric AB, Washington U., St. Louis, 1960, PhD, 1966. Lic. psychologist, Mo. Staff psychologist VA, Jefferson Barracks, Mo., 1967-68; asst. prof. to prof. Washington U., St. Louis, 1968—. Mem. nat. adv. council on aging Nat. Inst. on Aging, 1984-87; editor-in-chief Jour. Gerontology, 1981-86 Author: Counseling and Therapy with Older Adults, 1983; co-author: Memory, Related Functions and Age, 1974; co-editor: The Clinical Psychology of Aging, 1978, The Adult Years: Continuity and Change, 1989, Neuropsychological Assessment of Dementia and Depression in Older Adults: A Clinician's Guide, 1994. Recipient Disting. Service award Mo. Assn. Homes for the Aging, 1984. Fellow APA (pres. divsn. 20 1979-80, council rep. 1983-84, 86-88, Disting. Sci. Contbn. award divsn. adult devel. and aging 1988, Master Mentor award divsn. adult devel. and aging 2000, Disting. Contbns. to Clin. Geropsychology divsn. clin. psychology 2002), Gerontol. Soc. Am. Office: Washington U Dept Psychology Saint Louis MO 63130

STORB, URSULA BEATE, molecular genetics and cell biology educator; b. Stuttgart, Germany; came to U.S., 1966; d. Walter M. Stemmer and Marianne M. (Kämmerer) Nowara. MD, U. Freiburg, Germany, 1960. Asst. prof. dept. microbiology U. Wash., Seattle, 1971-75, assoc. prof., 1975-81, prof., 1981-86, head. div. immunology, 1980-86; prof. dept. molecular genetics and cell biology U. Chgo., 1986—. Mem. editl. bd. Immunity, Current Opinion in Immunology, Internat. Immunology, Immunol. Revs.; contbr. articles to sci. jours. Grantee NIH, NSF, Am. Cancer Soc., 1973—. Fellow Am. Acad. Arts and Scis.; mem. AAAS, Assn. Women in Sci., Am. Assn. Immunologists. Office: U Chgo 920 E 58th St Chicago IL 60637-5415 E-mail: stor@midway.uchicago.edu.

STORCH, ARTHUR, theater director; b. Bklyn., June 29, 1925; s. Sam and Bessie (Goldner) S.; children: Max Darrow, Alexander English, Bess Martin. BA, New Sch. Social Research, 1949. Actor in Broadway prodns. End as a Man, 1953, Time Limit, 1955, Girls of Summer, 1956, Look Homeward, Angel, 1957, Night Circus, 1958, The Long Dream, 1960, The Best Man, 1961; motion pictures The Strange One, 1956, Girls of the Night, 1959, The Exorcist, 1974; dir. off-Broadway Two by Saroyan, 1961, Three by Three, 1962, Talking to You (London debut), 1962, The Typists and the Tiger, 1963, The Owl and the Pussycat, 1964, The Impossible Years, 1965, The Local Stigmatic, 1970, Under the Weather, 1965, Golden Rainbow, 1967, The Chinese and Dr. Fish, 1969, Promenade All, 1970, 42 Seconds from Broadway, 1973, Tribute, 1978, Twice Around the Park, 1982, Clarence, 1986; Of Mice and Men, 1988; dir. nat. tour The King and I, 1989; dir. Syracuse Stage Waiting for Lefty, Noon, Of Mice and Men, 1974, 75, La Ronde, The Butterfingers Angel. Mornings at Seven, Dynamo, 1975-76, A Quality of Mercy, The Seagull, 1976-77, 1976-77, Love Letters on Blue Paper, End of the Beginning, 1977-78, Loved, 1978, Naked, 1979, The Comedy of Errors, 1980, The Impromptu of Outremont, 1982, The Double Bass, 1984, Arms and the Man, Handy Dandy, Cyrano de Bergerac, Romeo and Juliet, 1986, Of Mice and Men, N.Y.C., 1987, Fugue, 1988, Seven By Beckett, 1988, Look Homeward Angel, Wait Unitl Dark, Dangerous Corner, 1990, A Walk in the Woods, 1989, Finding Donis Ann, 1990, Androcles and the Lion, 1991; Lend Me a Tenor, 1992; Awake and Sing, 1993; dir., actor Love Letters, 1992. Founder, producing artistic dir. Syracuse Stage; chmn. drama dept. Syracuse U., 1974-92, Arthur Storch Theatre, 1992. Home: 400 W 43d St Apt 21H New York NY 10036

STORCH, DAVID, manufacturing executive; Degree, Ithaca (N.Y.) Coll., 1975. Pres. AAR Aircraft Turbine Ctr.; pres., COO AAR Corp., Wood Dale, Ill., 1989—, CEO, 1996—. Bd. dirs. AAR Corp., Whittman-Hart Inc., Prentice Women's Hosp. Bd. trustees Ithaca (N.Y.) Coll., 2000—. Mem.: Young Pres. Org. Internat., Econ. Club Chgo. Office: AAR Corp 1100 North Wood Dale Rd Wood Dale IL 60191*

STORCH, GERALD L. retail executive; BA cum laude, JD magna cum laude, MBA with hons., Harvard U. With McKinsey & Co., Boston, 1982—93; sr. v.p. strategic planning Dayton Hudson Corp., Mpls., 1993—98; pres. fin. svcs. and new bus. Target Corp., Mpls., 1999—2001, vice chmn., 2001—. Office: Target Corp 1000 Nicollet Mall Minneapolis MN 55403

STORCH, SUSAN BOROWSKI, lawyer; b. Jersey City, June 23, 1961; d. Raymond Edward and Clara Mary (Stryzek) Borowski; m. Michael John Storch, Feb. 9, 1985; children: Samantha Clare, Michael John Jr. BA, Rutgers U., 1983; JD, Seton Hall U., 1990. Bar: N.J. 1991. Corp. trust adminstr. Mfrs. Hanover Trust Co., N.Y.C., 1983-86; law clk. Congressman Dean Gallo, Washington, 1988, N.J. Supreme Ct. Com. on Complementary Dispute Resolution, Trenton, N.J., 1988; law clk. to asst. atty. gen. legis. affairs U.S. Dept. Justice, Washington, 1989; assoc. Rodino & Rodino, East Hanover, NJ, 1991—92; sr. assoc. Fragomen, Del Rey & Bernsen, Iselin, NJ, 1992—98, ptnr., 1998—2000; ptnr., chair corp. immigration practice group Sills Cummis Radin Tischman Epstein & Gross, Newark, 2000—. Lectr. in field. Bd. dirs. Players Forum, N.Y.C., 1993-94; coord. Corp. Giving Coun., N.J. Women's Polit. Caucus, 1995; active various polit. fundraising campaigns. Recipient Commendation award Essex County Bd. Chosen Freeholders, N.J., 1990; Lyndon B. Johnson Congl. scholar, 1988. Mem.: ABA (labor and employment law sect. 1994—95), Exec. Women N.J. (nominations com.), Ctr. Study of Presidency, Psychology Assn. Am., Inst. Cont. Legal Edn. and Info. (N.J.), Coun. Internat. Personnel, Am. Immigration Lawyer Assn. (former press sec., former sec.), N.J. Bar Assn. (exec. bd. programs ctr. 1994—95). Democrat. Avocations: writing, sailing, golf. Office: Stills Cummis Radin Tischman Epstein & Gross PA One Riverfront Plaza Newark NJ 07102-5400

STORER, MARYRUTH, law librarian; b. Portland, Oreg., 1953; d. Joseph William and Carol Virginia Storer; m. David Bruce Bailey, 1981; children: Sarah, Allison. BA in History, Portland State U., 1974; JD, U. Oreg., 1977; M in Law Librarianship, U. Wash., 1978. Bar: Oreg. 1978. Assoc. law libr. U. Tenn., Knoxville, 1978-79; law libr. O'Melveny & Myers, L.A., 1979-88; dir. Orange County Pub. Law Libr., Santa Ana, Calif., 1988—. Mem. Am. Assn. Law Librs. (exec. bd. 1999-2002), So. Calif. Assn. Law Librs. (pres. 1986-87), Coun. Calif. County Law Librs. (sec./treas. 1990-94, pres. 1994-96), Arroyo Sero Libr. Network (chair 2000-03). Democrat. Episcopalian. Office: Orange County Public Law Library 515 N Flower St Santa Ana CA 92703-2304

STORER, NORMAN WILLIAM, sociologist, educator; b. Middletown, Conn., May 8, 1930; s. Norman Wyman and Mary Emily (House) Storer; m. Ada Joan Van Valkenburg, Aug. 19, 1951 (div. Feb. 1975); children: Martin Wilson, Thomas Wyman; m. Mary Ashton Pott Hiatt, Mar. 7, 1975. AB, U. Kans., 1952, MA, 1956; PhD, Cornell U., 1961. Lectr., asst. prof. Harvard U., Cambridge, Mass., 1960-66; staff assoc. Social Sci. Rsch. Coun., N.Y.C., 1966-70; prof. sociology CUNY-Baruch Coll., N.Y.C., 1970-88, prof. emeritus, 1989—, dept. chmn., 1970-85, chmn. faculty senate, 1981-84. Author: (book) The Social System of Science, 1966, Focus on Society, 1973, Focus on Society, 2d edit., 1980, A Leer of Limericks, 1990; author: (with William Flores) Domestic Violence in Suburban San Diego, 1994; editor: The Sociology of Science, 1973; column editor: San Diego Writers' Monthly, 1992—94. Vol. San Diego Sheriff's Dept., 1992—2002; mem. San Diego Hate Crimes Registry Mgmt. Team, 1993—2003. Sgt. U.S. Army, 1953—55. Mem.: Sigma Xi (newsletter editor 2000—03, sec. chpt. 2001—02), Phi Beta Kappa. Democrat. Home: 1417 Van Buren Ave San Diego CA 92103-2339 E-mail: normwstorer@earthlink.net.

STOREY, BRIT ALLAN, historian; b. Boulder, Colo., Dec. 10, 1941; s. Harold Albert and Gladys Roberta (Althouse) S.; m. Carol DeArman, Dec. 19, 1970; 1 child, Christine Roberta. AB, Adams State Coll., Alamosa, Colo., 1963; MA, U. Ky., 1965, PhD, 1968. Instr. history Auburn (Ala.) U., 1967-68, asst. prof., 1968-70; dep. state historian State Hist. Soc. Colo., Denver, 1970-71, acting state historian, 1971-72, rsch. historian, 1972-74; hist. preservation specialist Adv. Coun. on Hist. Preservation, Lakewood, Colo., 1974-88; sr. historian Bur. Reclamation, Lakewood, 1988—. Contbr. articles to profl. publs. Mem. Fed. Preservation Forum (pres. 1990-91), Nat. Coun. Pub. History (sec. 1987, pres.-elect 1990-91, pres. 1991-92), Orgn. Am. Historians (com. 1983-86, chmn. 1985-86), Victorian Soc. Am. (bd. dirs. 1977-79), Western History Assn. (chmn. com. 1982-86), Colo.-Wyo. Assn. Mus. (sec. 1974-76, pres. 1976-77), Cosmos Club (Washington). Avocation: birding. Home: 7264 W Otero Ave Littleton CO 80128-5639 Office: Bur Reclamation Denver Fed Ctr D 5300 Bldg 67 Denver CO 80225-0007

STOREY, CHARLES PORTER, lawyer; b. Austin, Tex., Dec. 4, 1922; s. Robert Gerald and Frances Hazel (Porter) S.; m. Helen Hanks Stephens, Oct. 14, 1950; children: Charles Porter, Harry Stephens, Frederick Schatz. BA, U. Tex., 1947, LLB, 1948; LLM, So. Methodist U., 1952. Bar: Tex. 1948. Pvt. practice law, Dallas, 1948—; sr. counsel Carrington Coleman Sloman & Blumenthal, LLP. Pres. Dallas Day Nursery Assn., 1958, Greater Dallas Coun. Chs., 1970-71; chmn. Internat. Com. YMCA, 1969-71; nat. bd. dirs. U.S. YMCA, 1964-75; pres. Children's Devel. Ctr., Dallas, 1959; trustee Baylor Coll. Dentistry, 1981-90, Hillcrest Found., 1994—; trustee emeritus Southwestern Legal Found., chmn. 1980-90; dir. Zale Lipshy U. Med. Ctr., 1999—. 1st lt., pilot USAAF, 1943-45, ETO. Decorated Air medal. Master emeritus Dallas Inn of Ct. (pres. 1991-93); fellow Am. Coll. Trial Lawyers, Am. Bar Found., Tex. Bar Found.; mem. ABA, Tex. Bar Assn. (bd. dirs. 1976-79), Dallas Bar Assn. (pres. 1975), Philos. Soc. Tex., Dallas Country Club, Crescent Club, Idlewild Club, Phi Delta Phi, Phi Delta Theta. Mem. Christian Ch. (Disciples Of Christ). Home: 5855 Farquhar Ln Dallas TX 75209 Office: 200 Crescent Ct Ste 1500 Dallas TX 75201-7839 Fax: 214-855-1333. E-mail: cstorey@ccsb.com.

STOREY, FRANCIS HAROLD, business consultant, retired bank executive; b. Calgary, Alberta, Can., June 20, 1933; s. Bertwyn Morrell and Hilda Josephine (Masters) S.; m. Willomae Saiter, Apr. 25, 1954; children: Daryl, Elizabeth, Brian, Shelley. Student, Gonzaga U., 1953, Pacific Coast Bankers Sch., 1974-76. Designated Certified Profl. Cons. Bank trainee Wash. Trust Bank, Spokane, 1950-56; owner Storey & Storey, Spokane, 1956-64; agt. Bankers Life Nebr., Spokane, 1964-67; sr. v.p. Old Nat. Bank, Spokane, 1967-87, U.S. Bank of Wash., Spokane, 1987-90; pvt. practice cons. Spokane, 1990—. Bd. dirs. Output Tech. Corp. Bd. dirs. Spokane Bus. Incubator, 1985-96, United Way of Spokane, 1987-95; bd. dirs., treas., fin. chair, gen. conv. dep. Episc. Diocese Spokane Dep., 1969-2001; trustee Spokane Symphony Soc., 1986-93, Spokane Area Econ. Devel. Coun., 1982-89; mem. adv. bd. Intercollegiate Ctr. Nursing Edn., 1990-96, chair, 1996; bd. dirs. Coalition for Women on Streets, treas., fin. chmn., 1999-2001. Mem.: Inland N.W. Soc. Consulting Profls., Acad. Profl. Consultants and Advisors, Spokane Club, Spokane Rotary (bd. dirs. Spkane Rotary Club 21 2003—, trustee Spokane Rotary Found. 2004—). Episcopalian. Avocations: golf, reading, travel. Home: 214 E 13th Ave Spokane WA 99202-1115 E-mail: fhstorey@comcast.net.

STOREY, GREGORY DEAN, publisher, editor; b. Denver, Sept. 16, 1950; s. Harold Robert and Grace Alberta (Wright) S.; m. Charlene Komar, May 28, 1983. Student, U.S. Mcht. Marine Acad., 1968-70; BA with honors, U. Conn., 1973; MS in Journalism, So. Ill. U., 1984. Reporter, editor Norwich (Conn.) Bull., 1973-76; press dir. Vt. Pres. Ford Com., Burlington, 1976; reporter Naples (Fla.) Star, 1977; freelance writer, copy editor Ill., 1978-79; maritime reporter Jour. Commerce, N.Y.C., 1980-82, editl. writer, 1982-84, editor west coast San Francisco, 1984-86; dir. pub. rels., corp. sec. N.Y. Shipping Assn., N.Y.C., 1986-95, v.p. corp. rels., 1995—; ed. dir. Jour. of Commerce, N.Y.C.; columns editor Daily Deal, 2000—. Contbr. articles to profl. jours. Mem. Soc. of the Silurians, Phi Kappa Phi, Kappa Tau Alpha. Avocations: maritime history, N.Y.C. history, Irish interests.

STOREY, J. BENTON, horticulturist, educator; BS in Horticulture, Tex. A&M U., 1949, MS, 1952; PhD in Botanical Sci. and Plant Physiology, U. Calif., LA, Calif., 1957. Prof. Tex. A & M Univ., College Station, 1950—. Editor: The Pecan Quar., 1967—81. Recipient Outstanding Grad. Educator award, 1992. Office: Texas A&M University Dept Horticultural Scis College Station TX 77843-0001

STOREY, JAMES MOORFIELD, lawyer; b. Boston, Apr. 12, 1931; s. Charles Moorfield and Susan Jameson (Sweetser) S.; m. Adair Miller, Aug. 28, 1954 (div. 1973); children: Barbara Sessums Storey McGrath, Mary Sweetser Storey Meley, Susan Adair Storey Frank, Eliza Allison Tebo Storey Anderson,

Alice Leovy Storey Wille; m. Isabelle Helene Boeschenstein, May 17, 1973. AB, Harvard U., 1953, LL.B., 1956. Bar: Mass. 1956. Atty. SEC, Washington, 1956-57, legal asst. to chmn., 1957-59; assoc. Gaston, Snow, Motley & Holt, Boston, 1959-62; ptnr. Gaston, Snow, Motley & Holt (name changed to Gaston Snow & Ely Bartlett), Boston, 1962-87, Dechert Price & Rhoads, Boston, 1987-94, ret., 1994, profl. trustee, corp. dir., 1994—. Trustee Mt. Auburn Cemetery, Cambridge, Mass., 1980-. Co-author: Mutual Fund Law Handbook, 1998, The Uneasy Chaperone, 2000. Mem. ABA, Boston Bar Assn., Tavern Club Boston (pres. 1985-87), Century Assn. of N.Y. Unitarian Universalist. Home: 89A Mt Vernon St Boston MA 02108-1330 Office: 5 Boylston Pl Boston MA 02116 Office Phone: 617-728-0429.

STOREY, KENNETH BRUCE, biology professor; b. Taber, Alta., Can., Oct. 23, 1949; s. Arthur George and Madeleine Una (Mawhinney) S.; m. Janet Margaret Collicutt, June 6, 1975; children: Jennifer, Kathryn. BSc with honors, U. Calgary, Alta., 1971; PhD, U. B.C., Vancouver, Can., 1974. Asst. prof. Duke U., Durham, N.C., 1975-79; assoc. prof. Carleton U., Ottawa, Ont., Can., 1979-85, prof., 1985—, Can. Rsch. chair, 2001—. Invited lectr. numerous confs., univs.; chmn. rsch. molecular physiology, Canada. Editor Cell and Molecular Responses to Stress; mem. editl. bd. Jour. Comparative Physiology, 1995—; contbr. over 400 articles to profl. jours. Recipient E.W.R. Steacie award Nat. Sci. and Engring. Rsch. Coun. Can., 1984-86, Killam Sr. Rsch. fellow, 1993-95. Fellow AAAS, Royal Soc. Can.; mem. Can. Biochem. Soc. (Ayerst award 1989), Can. Soc. Zoology, Soc. Cryobiology, Nat. Sci. and Engring. Rsch. Coun. Avocations: movies, music, renaissance art. Office: Carleton U Dept Biology 1125 Colonel By Drive Ottawa ON Canada K1S 5B6 E-mail: kenneth_storey@carleton.ca.

STOREY, NORMAN C. lawyer; b. Miami, Fla., Oct. 11, 1943; BA cum laude, Loyola-Marymount U., L.A., 1965; JD, U. Ariz., 1968. Bar: Ariz. 1968. Law clk. to Hon. James A. Walsh U.S. Dist. Ct. Ariz.; ptnr. Squire, Sanders & Dempsey, L.L.P., Phoenix. Mem.: Am. Arbitration Assn. (comml. dispute panelist), State Bar Ariz. Office: 40 N Central Ave Ste 2700 Phoenix AZ 85004-4498

STOREY, SUSAN, investment banker; b. Dublin; 1 child. Student, U. Coll. Dublin, York U., Toronto, Can. Fgn. exch. trader CIBC Wood Gundy, 1982—87, v.p., 1987—88, with bank derivatives group, 1988—90, derivatives mgr. Toronto, 1990—96, head global derivatives trading, 1996—, mng. dir., head global trading DCM. Former chair Can. Com. for Professionalism; past pres. Forex Can.; voting mem. Fed. Res. Bank, N.Y. Fgn. Exch. Com.; ex-officio mem. Can. Fgn. Exch. Com. Bank Can. Chair CIBC Wood Gundy Children's Miracle Found.; vice chair Children's Aid Found.; bd. mem. Ireland Fund. Named one of 25 Most Powerful Women in Banking, U.S. Banker, 2003. Office: 161 Bay St BCE Pl PO Box 500 Toronto ON Canada M5J 2S8*

STORHOFF, DIANA CARMACK, research scientist; b. Anderson, Ind., Sept. 10, 1946; d. William Paul and Elsie Bernice (Wilson) Carmack; m. Bruce Norman Storhoff, July 25, 1970 (div. Mar. 1990); children: Damon Anthony, James Justin. BS, Ball State U., 1969, MS in Chemistry, 1973; MS, U. Fla., 1996; PhD, Northwestern U., 1999. Sec. Carmack's Inc., 1962; tchg. asst. Ball State U., Muncie, Ind., 1971-73, chemistry prof., 1981-82, 83-87; chemistry tchr. Delta H.S., Muncie, 1982-83; rsch. scientist Boehringer Mannheim Corp., Indpls., 1987-98, Roche Diagnostics, 1999. Author: (poetry) Live Again, 1995, A Rose Upon The Mist, 1997, Where Eagles Dare Not Soar, 1998. Natural resources chair LWV, Muncie, 1981-97; chmn. conservation Audubon Soc., Muncie; bd. dirs. Mayors Task Force, Muncie. Named Internat. Poet of Merit. Mem. Am. Chem. Soc. Office: Roche Diagnostics 9115 Hague Rd Indianapolis IN 46256-1045 Home: 1728 Billings St Sarasota FL 34231-8817 E-mail: donyasol@aol.com.

STORHOFF, JAMES JUSTIN, scientist; b. Muncie, Ind., July 13, 1973; s. Bruce Norman and Diana Faye Storhoff. PhD, Northwestern U., 1995—2000. Scientist Nanosphere, Northbrook, Ill., 2000—. Author: (sci. pub.) Nature (BFGoodrich Collegiate Inventors Award, 1997). Grantee Rapid Assay for the I1307K Mutation of the APC Gene, NIH, 2000 - 2003, Staphylococcus Speciation and Methicillin Resistance Assay, 2001-2002, Nanoparticle Probe Assay for Biol. Threat Agents, 2002-2003. Mem.: Am. Chem. Soc. Achievements include invention of nanoparticles having oligonucleotides attached thereto and uses therefore. Office: Nanosphere 4100 Commercial Ave Northbrook IL 60062 Personal E-mail: jstorhoff@attbi.com.

STORIN, MATTHEW VICTOR, academic administrator, educator, retired editor; b. Springfield, Mass., Dec. 24, 1942; s. Harry Francis and Blanche Marie S.; m. Keiko Takita, Aug. 1, 1975; 1 child, Kenyatta; children by previous marriage: Karen, Aimee, Sean. BA, U. Notre Dame, 1964. Reporter Springfield Daily News, 1964-65, Griffin-Larrabee News Bur., Washington, 1965-69; Washington corr., city editor, Asian corr., nat. editor, asst. mng. editor, dep. mng. editor, mng. editor Boston Globe, 1969-85; dep. mng. editor U.S. News & World Report, Washington, 1985-86; editor, sr. v.p. Chgo. Sun-Times, 1986-87; editor The Maine Times, Topsham, 1988-89; mng. editor N.Y. Daily News, 1989-91, exec. editor, 1991-92, Boston Globe, 1992-93, editor, 1993—2001; assoc. v.p., prof. Am. studies U. Notre Dame, 2002—. Recipient Disting. Polit. Reporting award Am. Assn. Polit. Sci., 1969, Yankee Quill award New Eng. Chpt. Sigma Delta Chi, 1997. Home: 1333 Oliver Cir South Bend IN 46614-7218 Office Phone: 574-631-8696. E-mail: mstorin@nd.edu.

STORING, PAUL EDWARD, retired foreign service officer; b. Ames, Iowa, Oct. 24, 1929; s. James Alvin and Edith Nora (Ryg) S.; children: Mimi Storing Harlan, Felice Storing Kite. Student, U Oslo, Norway, 1950-51; BA, Allegheny Coll., 1952; MA with honors, Colgate U., 1956; postgrad., U. Wis., Madison, 1955-59. Fgn. service officer Dept. State, Washington, Mex. and Scandinavia, 1960-80; spl. asst. U.S. Sect. Internat. Boundary and Water Commn. U.S. And Mex., Washington, 1980-99; ret. Contbr. articles to profl. jours. Served to cpl. U.S. Army, 1953-55 Fellow U. Wis., 1957-58; Fulbright fellow U. Oslo, 1959-60 Mem. Am. Fgn. Svc. Assn., Fulbright Assn., Phi Beta Kappa, Delta Tau Delta (pres. Alpha chpt. 1949-50). Baptist. Avocations: music, photography, travel. Home: 9006 Opera Alley Manassas VA 20110 Office Phone: 703-530-6197. E-mail: storingpe@netscape.net.

STORK, DONALD ARTHUR, advertising executive; b. Walsh, Ill., June 17, 1939; s. Arthur William and Katherine Frances (Young) S.; m. Joanna Gentry, June 9, 1962; 1 child, Brian Wesley. BS, So. Ill. U., 1961; postgrad., St. Louis U., 1968-69. With Naegele Outdoor Advtsg., Mpls. and St. Louis, 1961-63; acct. exec. Richard C. Lynch Advtsg., 1963-64; media exec. Gardner Advtsg. co., 1964-69; v.p. mktg. Advanswers Media/Programming, 1975-79; pres. Advanswers divsn. Wells/BDDP, N.Y.C., 1979-98; pres. Advanswers unit Omnicom, St. Louis, 1998—2002, pres. PHD unit, 2002—, chmn., 2004. Bd. dirs. Trailblazers, Inc.; corp. devel. St. Louis Art Mus., 1999. Pres. Signal Hill Sch. Assn. Parents Tchrs. Capt. Mo. Air N.G., 1961-67. Recipient Journalism Alumnus of Yr. award So. Ill. U., Alumni Achievement award. Mem. St. Louis Advtsg. Club, Mensa, Mo. Athletic Club, St. Clair Country Club (bd. dirs. 2001), Alpha Delta Sigma (Aid to Advtg. Edn. award). Home: 27 Symonds Dr Belleville IL 62223-1905 Office: PHD 10 S Broadway Saint Louis MO 63102-1712 Office Phone: 314-444-2036. Business E-Mail: don.stork@phdus.com.

STORK, GILBERT, chemistry educator, investigator; b. Brussels, Dec. 31, 1921; s. Jacques and Simone (Weil) Stork; m. Winifred Stewart, June 9, 1944 (dec. May 1992); children: Diana, Linda, Janet, Philip. BS, U. Fla., 1942; PhD, U. Wis., 1945; DSc (hon.), Lawrence Coll., 1961, U. Paris, 1979, U. Rochester, 1982, Emory U., 1988, Columbia U., 1993, U. Wis., 1997. Sr. rsch. chemist Lakeside Labs., 1945—46; instr. chemistry Harvard U., 1946—48, asst. prof., 1948—53; assoc. prof. Columbia U., N.Y.C., 1953—55, prof., 1955—67, Eugene Higgins prof., 1967—92, prof. emeritus, 1992—, chmn. dept., 1973—76. Lectr. and cons. in field; chmn. Gordon Steroid Conf., 1958—59. Recipient Baekeland medal, 1961, Harrison Howe award, 1962, Edward Curtis Franklin Meml. award, Stanford, 1966, Gold medal, Synthetic Chems. Mfrs. Assn., 1971, Nebr. award, 1973, Roussel prize in steroid chemistry, 1978, Edgar Fahs Smith award, 1982, Nat. Medal of Sci., 1982, Linus Pauling award, 1983, Tetrahedron prize, 1985, Remsen award, 1986, Cliff S. Hamilton award, 1986, Mony Ferst award, Sigma Xi, 1987, George Kenner award, 1992, Robert Robinson award, 1992, Chem. Pioneer award, Am. Inst. Chemists, 1992, Welch Found. award in chemistry, 1993, Allan R. Day award, 1994, Wolf prize, 1996, Phila. Chemists Club award, 1998, Barton Gold medal, U.K., 2002, Ryoji Noyori award, Soc. Synthetic Organic Chemistry Japan, 2003; fellow, Guggenheim, 1959. Fellow: NAS (award in chem. sci. 1982), Am. Philos. Soc., Am. Acad. Arts and Scis., Royal Soc., French Acad. Scis., Royal Soc. Chemistry (Barton Gold medal 2002); mem.: Am. Chem. Soc. (chmn. organic chemistry divsn. 1967, award in pure chemistry 1957, award for creative work in synthetic organic chemistry 1967, Nichols medal 1980, Arthur C. Cope award 1980, Willard Gibbs medal 1982, Roger Adams award in organic chemistry 1991), Chem. Soc. Japan (hon.), Pharm. Soc. Japan (hon.), Chemists Club (hon.). Home: 188 Chestnut St Englewood Cliffs NJ 07632-1908 Office: Columbia U Dept Chemistry Chandler Hall New York NY 10027 E-mail: gjs8@columbia.edu.

STORM, HANNAH, newscaster; b. Oak Pk., Ill., June 13, 1962; B in Polit. Sci. and Comm., U. of Notre Dame, 1983. Sports anchor, reporter KTXH-TV, Houston; Home Sports Entertainment; KNCN-FM Radio, Corpus Christi, Tex., WNDU-TV, South Bend, Ind., 1982—88; sports reporter, anchor WPQC-TV, Charlotte, NC, 1988—89; anchor CNN Sports Tonight, 1989—92; anchor, reporter NBC Sports, 1993—2002; anchor The Early Show, 2002—. Host NBC coverage of the NBA, 1997—2002, NBC coverage of Major League Baseball, 1995—2002, NBC coverage of Major League Baseball World Series, 1995, 97, 99. Author: (sports guide for parents) Go Girl!, 2002. Recipient Gracie Allen award, Am. Women in Radio and TV. Office: CBS News 524 W 57th St New York NY 10019

STORM, JACKIE, nutritionist, health education specialist; b. Halifax, N.S., Can., Sept. 20, 1943; d. Jack Charles Stone and Kathleen (Clow) Devisser. BA, NYU, 1979, MA, 1982, PhD, 1995. Cert. nutrition specialist. Nutrition educator N.Y. Health and Racquet Club, N.Y.C., 1973—; tchr. New Sch. Social Rsch., N.Y.C., 1980-87. Adj. prof. Kingsborough C.C., Bklyn., 1987-2001, St. Francis Coll., Bklyn., 1987; tchr. Acad. Med. Sys., 2001-. Author: There's No Such Thing As A Fattening Food!, 1983. Mem. Am. Coll. Nutrition, Am. Nutraceutical Assn., Soc. nutrition Edn. Avocations: gardening, weightlifting. Office: 115 E 57th St New York NY 10022-2049 Office Phone: 212-220-0773. E-mail: jackiestorm@jackiestorm.com.

STORM, JANET S. psychiatric social worker; b. Indpls. d. Charles R. and Evelyn M. (Seitz) Howard; children: Beth A., Mary J. BSW with high distinction, Ind. U., 1982, MSW, 1984. Cert. ACSW; lic. clin. social worker; lic. marriage and family therapist; cert. diplomate in psychotherapy. Pvt. indsl. social work therapist Supportive Systems Inc., Indpls.; med. social worker Wishard Meml. Hosp., Indpls.; social work cons. State of Ind., Indpls.; psychiat. sr. mental health clinician Community Hosp., Indpls.; pscyhiat. social worker Adult and Child Mental Health Ctr., Indpls.; psychiat. social worker St. Francis Counseing Ctr.; pvt. practice Indpls. Mem. NASW, Sigma Pi Alpha. Home: PO Box 47461 Indianapolis IN 46247-0461 E-mail: sto340@aol.com.

STORM, SUZANNE, state representative; b. Spokane, Wash., July 17, 1941; 1 child, Carmen. BA, William Jewell Coll., 1963; MS, U. Kans., 1984. Tchr. pub. schs., 1964—78; tchr., 1978—92; mem. Kans. Ho. of Reps., 1996—. Mem.: Shawnee Mission Edn. Found., Mainstream Coalition (bd. dirs. 1990—), Kans. Nat. Edn. Assn. (bd. dirs. 1990—96), NEA (pres. 1992—96). Democrat. Baptist. Office: 272-W State Capitol 300 SW 10th Ave Topeka KS 66612 Address: 8145 Mackey Overland Park KS 66204-3121

STORMER, CINDY HODGE, lawyer, educator; b. Ponca City, Okla, May 22, 1956; d. Lloyd John and Clara Louise (Reisch) Hodge; m. Kenneth John Stormer; 1 child, Julia Lauren Stormer. AA, Tarrant County Jr. Coll., Hurst, Tex., 1981; BA, U. Tex., 1983; JD, So. Tex. Coll. Law, 1986. Bar: U.S. Dist. Ct. (no. dist.) Tex. 1991, U.S. Dist. Ct. (ea. dist.) Tex. 1992, U.S. Supreme Ct. Peace officer City of Dallas, 1978-79, Tarrant County Jr. Coll., Hurst, 1979-86; asst. dist. atty. Tarrant County Dist. Atty.'s Office, Ft. Worth, 1986-89; chief atty., asst. city atty. Dallas Police Dept., 1989-90; sole practice Gainesville, Tex., 1990—; prof. North Ctrl. Tex. Coll., Gainesville, 1991—, mem. legal curriculum adv. bd., 1994-96. Mem. pro bono com. West Tex. Legal Svc., Gainesville. Contbr. articles to profl. jour. Pres. Cooke County Child Welfare Bd., Gainesville, 1993-96. Mem. LWV, Tex. Trial Lawyers Assn.; pres. Cooke County Bar. Office: 102 Elm Gainesville TX 76240

STÖRMER, HORST LUDWIG, physicist; b. Frankfurt-Main, Fed. Republic Germany, Apr. 6, 1949; arrived in U.S., 1977; s. Karl-Ludwig and Marie (Ihrig) S.; m. Dominique A. Parchet, 1982. PhD, U. Stuttgart, 1977. From tech. staff to dir. phys. rsch. lab. AT&T Bell Labs., Murray Hill, NJ, 1977—97; prof. physics and applied physics Columbia U., N.Y.C., 1998—. Adj. physics dir. Lucent Tech., 1997—. Decorated Officier de la Legion d'Honneur France, Grosses Verdienstkreuz Mit Stern Germany; recipient Otto Klung prize, 1985, Benjamin Franklin medal in physics, 1998, Nobel prize in Physics, 1998, N.Y.C. Mayor's award for excellence in sci. and tech., 2000; fellow Bell Labs., 1983. Fellow: NAS, Am. Acad. Arts and Scis., Am. Phys. Soc. (Buckley prize 1984). Office: Columbia U Dept Physics 538 W 120th St New York NY 10027-6601 also: Lucent Technologies 700 Mountain Ave New Providence NJ 07974-1208

STORMER, JOHN ANTHONY, minister emeritus, author, publisher; b. Altoona, Pa., Feb. 9, 1928; s. Regis Walter and Mary Ann (Forr) S.; m. Elizabeth Ruth Lewis, July 2, 1951; 1 child, Holly. BS in Journalism, San Jose (Calif.) State U., 1954; DLitt (hon.), Manahath Sch. Theology, Hollidaysburg, Pa., 1965; LittD (hon.), Shelton Coll., 1976. Ordained to ministry Bapt. Ch., 1968. Pastor Heritage Bapt. Ch., Florissant, Mo., 1968-86; supt. Faith Christian Acad., Florissant, 1968—99; owner Liberty Bell Press, Florissant, 1963—. Bd. dirs. Internat. Coun. Christian Chs., 1965-87; dir. I Chronicles 12:32 Ministry, Florissant, 1985-2003; leader bible studies for legislators, Jefferson City, Mo., 1977—. Author: None Dare Call It Treason, 1964, The Death of a Nation, 1968, Growing of God's Way, 1984, NDCIT—25 Years Later, 1990, None Dare Call It Education, 1999. Mem. rep. state com., state chmn. Mo. Young Reps., 1962-64, state del. Rep. Nat. Conv., San Francisco, 1964; tchr. legis. bible studies Mo. State Capital, Jefferson City, Mo., 1977-2003. With USAF, 1950-53. Mem. Coun. for Nat. Policy. Office: PO Box 32 Florissant MO 63033 *Through the resurrected life of the Lord Jesus Christ, individuals who have received Him have everything they need to be and do all that God the Father calls them to.*

STORMES, JOHN MAX, instructional systems developer; b. Manila, Oct. 7, 1927; s. Max Clifford and Janet (Heldring) S.; m. Takako Sanae, July 29, 1955; children: Janet Kazuko Stormes-Pepper, Alan Osamu. BS, San Diego State U., 1950; BA, U. So. Calif., 1957, MA, 1967. Cert. secondary and community coll. tchr., sr. profl. human resources. Editing supr. Lockheed Propulsion Co., Redlands, Calif., 1957-61; proposals supr. Rockwell Internat., Downey, Calif., 1961-62; publs. dir. Arthur D. Little, Inc., Santa Monica, Calif., 1962-63; publs. coord. Rockwell Internat., Downey, 1963-68; project dir. Gen. Behavioral Systems, Inc., Torrance, Calif., 1969-73; tng. and comm. cons. Media Rsch. Assocs., Santa Cruz, Calif., 1973—; instrl. design supr. So. Calif. Gas Co., L.A., 1985-2001; adj. assoc. prof. Alliant U., Alhambra, Calif., 2001—02. Lectr. Calif. State U., Northridge, 1991-2003; tng. cons. Nat. Ednl. Media, Chatsworth, Calif., 1966-81, comm. cons. Opinion Rsch. Calif., Long Beach, 1974-. Co-author: TV Communications Systems For Business and Industry, 1970; contbg. author: ASTD's In Action series of casebooks, 1996-99. Curriculum adv. bd. communications dept. Calif. State U., Fullerton, 1964-78. Sgt. U.S. Army, 1953-55, Japan. Mem. Soc. Tech. Communication (sr. mem., 2nd v.p. Orange County chpt. 1962-63), Internat. Soc. Performance and Instruction (v.p. L.A. chpt. 1989, pres. 1990). Democrat. Episcopal. Avocations: photography, sailing. Home and Office: 136 Alamo Ave Santa Cruz CA 95060 E-mail: jmstormes@comcast.net.

STORMONT, RICHARD MANSFIELD, hotel executive; b. Chgo., Apr. 4, 1936; s. Daniel Lytle and E. Mildred (Milligan) S.; m. Virginia Louellen Walters, Nov. 21, 1959; children: Stacy Lee Freeman, Richard Mansfield, John Frederick. BS, Cornell U., 1958. Cert. hosp. adminstrn.; cert. hosps. industry profl. Food cost analyst, sales rep. Edgewater Beach Hotel, Chgo., 1957-58; asst. sales mgr. Marriott Hotels, Inc., Washington, 1962-64, dir. sales Atlanta, 1964-68, resident mgr., 1969-71; gen. mgr. Marriott Hotel, Dallas, 1971-73, Phila., 1973-74, Atlanta, 1974-79; pres. Hardin Mgmt. Co., 1979-80; v.p. Marriott Franchise div. Marriott Corp., Washington, 1980-83, v.p. ops. Courtyard by Marriott, 1981-83; pres. The Stormont Cos. Inc., Atlanta, 1984-92; chmn. bd. dirs. Stormont Trice Corp., Atlanta, 1993-2000; chmn. Stormont Noble Devel. LLC (formerly Stormont Hospitality Group LLC), Atlanta, 2001—. Bd. dirs. Lenbrook Square Found., Inc. Pres. Atlanta Conv. and Visitors Burs., 1975-76, chmn. bd., 1976-77, vice chmn., 1996-97, chmn. bd. exec. com., 1998-2000; trustee Young Harris Coll.; bd. dirs. Better Bus. Bur.; exec. com. Ctrl. Atlanta Progress, 1979-80; exec. coun. Boy Scouts Am.; bd. dirs., chmn. tourism divsn. Ga. Dept. Industry, Trade and Tourism, 1999-2001. Recipient Disting. Salesman of Yr. award Marriott, 1967, Obi T. Brewer award for Decade of Outstanding Svc., 1979. Mem. Sales and Mktg. Execs. (exec. v.p. 1969-70, pres. Atlanta 1970-71), Am. Hotel-Motel Assn. (exec. com., bd. dirs. 1993-95, Most Valuable Vol. Ga. 1999), Ga. Hospitality and Travel Assn. (founder 1975, bd. dir., pres. 1989-90, chmn. bd. 1991-92, Hotelier of Yr. award 1977, Hall of Fame 2001), Ga. Bus. and Industry Assn. (bd. dirs.), Atlanta Hotel Assn. (pres. 1976), So. Innkeepers Assn., Atlanta C. of C. (v.p. 1978-79), Gwinnett C. of C. (bd. dirs.), Cornell Soc. Hotelmen (pres. Ga. chpt. 1976, regional v.p. 1989-91), Rotary Club of Atlanta (chmn. program com. 1998, bd. dirs. 1999-2002, chmn. membership com., 2003, Paul Harris fellow Rotary Internat., 2003). Home and Office: 2980 Nancy Creek Rd NW Atlanta GA 30327-2000 Business E-Mail: rstormont@stormont.noble.com.

STORMS, CLIFFORD BEEKMAN, lawyer; b. Mount Vernon, N.Y., July 18, 1932; s. Harold Beekman and Gene (Pertak) S.; m. Barbara H. Grave, 1955 (div. 1975); m. Valeria N. Parker, July 12, 1975; children: Catherine Storms Fischer, Clifford Beekman. BA magna cum laude, Amherst Coll., 1954; LLB, Yale U., 1957. Bar: N.Y. 1957. Assoc. Breed, Abbott & Morgan, N.Y.C., 1957-64; with CPC Internat., Inc., Englewood Cliffs, N.J., 1964-97, v.p. legal affairs, 1973-75, v.p., gen. counsel, 1975-88, sr. v.p., gen. counsel, 1988-97, atty. alternate dispute resolution, corp. dir., 1997—; pvt. practice Greenwich, Conn., 1997—. Bd. dirs. Corn Products Internat., Inc., Atlantic Legal Found.; mem. Conn. Alternate Dispute Resolution panel Ctr. for Pub. Resources. Trustee emeritus Food and Drug Law Inst. Mem. ABA (com. of corp. gen. counsel), Am. Arbitration Assn. (panel arbitrators large complex case program), Assn. Gen. Counsel (pres. 1992-94), Assn. Bar City N.Y. (sec., com. on corp. law depts. 1979-81), Indian Harbor Yacht Club, Phi Beta Kappa. Home: 19 Burying Hill Rd Greenwich CT 06831-2604 Office: Ste 100 Two Sound View Dr Greenwich CT 06830 E-mail: cbstorms@aol.com.

STORMS, LESTER C. retired veterinarian; b. Camas, Wash., Oct. 13, 1920; s. Roy Lester and Helen Violet (Belshe) S.; m. Marjorie Louise Hudson, Apr. 10, 1943 (div.); children: Marjorie Maureen, Terry Jo, Sandra Diane. BS in Animal Husbandry, Wash. State U., 1951, DVM, 1952. Intern, Portland, 1952; gen. practice vet. medicine Camas, 1952-54; dr.'s asst. pvt. practice vet. office, Hollywood, Calif., 1954, L.A., 1954, Whittier, Calif., 1954, vet. in charge Artesia, Calif., 1955-56; owner, pvt. practice vet. medicine Buena Park, Calif., 1956-86; ret., 1986. Mem. adv. bd. Guide Dogs for Blind, San Rafael, Calif., 1957-58; mem. steering com. Children's Hosp., Fullerton, Calif., 1960-61. With USN, 1940-51, PTO. Decorated Air medal with 3 gold stars, DFC.; recipient Pappy Pedigoe Meml. Trophy Calif. Sports Car Racing Assn., 1965. Mem. NRA, So. Calif. Vet. Medicine Assn. (life), Am. Vet. Medicine Assn., Orange County Vet. Medicine Assn. (pres. 1958), Olde '78 Fraser's Highlanders (chief-of-staff), Explorer's Club, Adventurer's Club L.A. (sec. 1984, bd. dirs., 1980-82, 95-97), Long Beach Yacht Club, Rotary (Paul Harris fellow, pres. Buena Park chpt. 1963), Masons, Shriners (capt., pres. 1999—, Legion of Honor, capt. Legion of Honor Shrine). Avocations: race car driving, sailing, fishing, shooting. Home: 78th Frasers Highlanders 4316 Latona Ave Los Angeles CA 90031-1426

STORMS, WILLIAM WALLACE, physician; b. Racine, Wis., May 18, 1942; m. Bette Bear, Aug. 14, 1965; children: Cathy, Trisha, Jenny. BA, Northwestern U., 1964; MD, U. Wis., 1968. Diplomate Am. Bd. Internal Medicine, Am. Bd. Allergy and Immunology. Intern San Francicso Gen. Hosp., 1968-69; resident in internal med. U. Wis. Hosps., Madison, 1969-70, 73-73, fellow in allergy/immunology, 1973-75; prof. medicine Health Scis. Ctr. U. Colo., Denver, 1981—; practice medicine specializing in immunology Allergy Assocs., Colorado Springs, Colo., 1975—. Mem. bd. regents Am. Coll. Allergy and Immunology, 1990-93. Contbr. articles to profl. jours. Vestryman Chapel Our Saviour Episcopal Ch., Colorado Springs, 1978-81. Served with U.S. Army, 1970-72. Fellow ACP, Am. Acad. Allergy, Am. Coll. Allergists, Coll. Chest Physicians; mem. Am. Thoracic Soc., Western Soc. Allergy and Immunology (exec. coun. 1983-88, pres. 1987-88), Colo. Allergy Soc. (pres. 1988-90). Republican. Avocations: skiing, tennis, golf, fly fishing. Office: Allergy Assocs 2709 N Tejon St Colorado Springs CO 80907-6291 Office Phone: 719-473-0872. Business E-Mail: sneezedoc@aacos.com.

STORPER, DAVID H. bank executive; b. N.Y.C., Aug. 27, 1965; s. Stanley Arnold and Vivian Cecile (Schwartz) S. BS in Applied Math., Columbia U., 1987, MBA in Acctg./Fin., 1989. Corp. banking officer Wells Fargo Bank, N.Y.C., L.A.; rsch. analyst Libra Investments, Credit Suisse First Boston Corp.; mng. dir. WL Ross LLC, N.Y.C., sr. mng. dir., 2000—. Mem. Tau Beta Pi. Office: WL Ross & Co LLC Manhattan Tower 101 E 52nd St New York NY 10022*

STORR, ROBERT, curator, art educator; b. Portland, Maine, Dec. 28, 1949; s. Richard J. and Virginia V. Storr; m. Rosamund Helen Morley, Sept. 1, 1979; children: Katharine, Susannah. BA, Swarthmore Coll., 1972; postgrad., Sch. Art Inst. of Chgo., 1975-78; MFA, Skowhegan (Maine) Sch. Painting and Sculpture, 1978. Assoc. dean N.Y. Studio Sch., NYC, 1987-88; asst. prof. Tyler Sch. Art, Phila., 1989; Avery prof. Bard Coll., Annandale On Hudson, NY, 1990-91; sr. curator painting and sculpture Mus. Modern Art, NYC, 1991—2002; Rosalie Solow prof. of modern art NYU Inst. of Fine Arts, NYC, 2002—. Vis. artist Cooper Union, N.Y.C., 1988-89; vis. artist, critic R.I. Sch. Design, Providence, 1988; lectr. art mus., univs. and art schs. in U.S. and abroad; coordinating curator at Moma, 1995. Author: Philip Guston, 1986; co-author: Chuck Close, 1987, (with Lars Hitue) Susan Rothenberg 15 Years a Survey, 1990, (with Kirk Varnedoe) From Bauhaus to Pop: Masterworks Given By Phillip Johnson, 1996; also exhbn. catalogues; contbg. editor Art in Am.; mem. editorial bd. Art Jour.; contbr. articles to profl. jours.; exhibitions include Inst. Contemporary Art Phila., 1991, Moma, 1991, 93, 94, 95, 96. Penny McCall Found. grantee, 1988, Peter Norton Family Found. grantee, 1990. Mem. Internat. Assn. Art Critics. Office: NYU Inst Fine Arts James B Duke House 1 E 78th St New York NY 10021

STORRER, WILLIAM ALLIN, consultant; b. Highland Park, Mich., Mar. 22, 1936; s. Fredrick Ray and Margaret Ann (Pitts) S.; m. Carol A. Tuthill, Nov. 6, 1964 (div. June 1969); 1 child, Kirsten; m. Patricia Alice Whalley, Dec. 30, 1976. Student, Albion Coll., 1954-56; AB in Engring. Scis., Harvard U., 1959; MFA in Theatre Arts, Boston U., 1962; PhD in Comparative Arts, Ohio U., 1968. Electronics engr. Raytheon Co., Wayland, Mass., 1958-60; tech. dir. small stage Boston Arts Festival, 1961, 62; dir. dramatics Melrose (Mass.) H.S., 1962-63; dir. playhouse and repertory theatre, instr. drama-speech Hofstra U., 1963-66, instr. opera, 1965; asst. prof. theatre, dir. univ. theatre, U. Toledo, 1968-69; assoc. prof. theatre and film, dir. Southampton Coll., L.I. U., 1969-73; asst. prof. cinema studies and still photography Ithaca (N.Y.) Coll., 1973-76; assoc. prof. media arts U. S.C., Columbia, 1976-82; pres. MINDaLIVE Creative Mind Enhancement, Newark, 1980—. Assoc. prof. theater and speech World Campus Afloat, Chapman Coll., 1972; edn. media specialist Newark Bd. Edn., 1990-94, Linden Bd. Edn., 1994-95, Harrison Bd. Edn., 1995-96, Rosa Parks Fine and Performing Arts H.S., Paterson, N.J., 1996-2004, dir. Storrer/Storre/Storer Family Inst., adj. prof. U. Tex., 2004-. Author: The Architecture of Frank Lloyd Wright, 1974, 3d edit.

2002, The Frank Lloyd Wright Companion, 1993; contbr. articles to popular mags. and profl. jours. Grantee Graham Found. for Advanced Studies in Fine Arts, 1987, 94. Home: Frankfort MI 49635-9309 Office: 424 Corning Ave Frankfort MI 49635 E-mail: MINDaLIVE@aol.com.

STORRS, ALEXANDER DAVID, astronomer; b. Idaho Falls, Idaho, May 30, 1960; s. Charles Lysander and Betty Lou (Wood) S.; m. Jean Elizabeth Seitzer, Nov. 4, 1989; 1 child, Matthew. BS, MIT, 1982; MS, U. Hawaii, 1985, PhD, 1987. Postdoctoral fellow NASA/Goddard Space Flight Ctr., Greenbelt, Md., 1987-89, U. Tex., Austin, 1989-91; assoc. scientist Space Telescope Sci. Inst., Balt., 1991—. Mem. AAAS, Am. Astron. Soc. (divsn. planetary scis.), Smithsonian Air and Space Mus. Office: Space Telescope Sci Inst 3700 San Martin Dr Baltimore MD 21218-2464

STORRS, ELEANOR EMERETT, research institute consultant; b. Cheshire, Conn., May 3, 1926; d. Benjamin Porter and Alta Hyde (Moss) S.; m. Harry Phineas Burchfield, Jr., Nov. 29, 1963; children: Sarah Storrs, Benjamin Hyde. BS with distinction in Botany, U. Conn., 1948; MS in Biology, NYU, 1958; PhD in Chemistry, U. Tex., 1967. Asst. biochemist Boyce Thompson Inst. for Plant Rsch., Yonkers, N.Y., 1948-62; rsch. scientist Clayton Found. Biochem. Inst., U. Tex., Austin, 1962-65; biochemist Pesticides Rsch. Lab., USPHS, Perrine, Fla., 1965-67; dir. dept. biochemistry Gulf South Rsch. Inst., New Iberia, La., 1967-77; adj. prof. chemistry U. Southwestern La., Lafayette, 1974-77; rsch. prof. biology Fla. Inst. Tech., Melbourne, 1977-94, cons. on leprosy-armadillo programs, 1975-94, mem. Faculty Senate, 1979-84, prof. emeritus, 1994—. Cons. in rehab. and prevention deformities leprosy Pan Am. Health Orgn., WHO, Venezuela, Argentina, Brazil, Mex., 1972-90; dep. v.p. Coll. Hansenology in Endemic Countries, 1980-85. Author: (with H.P. Burchfield) Biochemical Applications of Gas Chromatography, 1962, (with Burchfield, D.E. Johnson) Guide to the Analysis of Pesticide Residues, 2 vols, 1965; also articles, book chpts. Grantee NIH, 1968-88, CDC, 1969-73, WHO, 1973-93, Leprosy Program, 1978-93, German Leprosy Relief Assn., 1973-78, Nat. Coun. Episc. Ch., 1975-77, Brit. Leprosy Relief Assn., 1981-88; recipient plaque La. Health Dept., 1972, Disting. Alumni award U. Conn., 1975, Gold award Am. Coll. Pathologists and Am. Soc. Clin. Pathologists, 1974, Gerard B. Lambert award for spl. recognition, 1975. Fellow AAAS; mem. AAUW, Internat. Leprosy Assn., Am. Recorder Soc., Early Music Assn., Sigma Xi. Episcopalian (vestryman). Clubs: Appalachian (Boston); Green Mountain (Bear Mountain, N.Y.). Achievements include pioneering devel. leprosy in exptl. animal (armadillo) reproduction. Home: 72 Riverview Ter Melbourne FL 32903-4640 *Children display interests early in their lives, and in my life, this early interest - in animals, and the beauty of nature - is one which I have never lost, but one which seems to become more important now with the passing of years. Parents can help mold a child, but should mold the child in the child's interests as my parents did, not in a mold designed by them.*

STORRS, IMMI CASAGRANDE, sculptor; b. Aug. 2, 1945; d. Leo and Carla Maria Annie (Busch) Casagrande; m. Thomas Austin Storrs, Dec. 19, 1971 (div. 1983); 1 child, A. Maya. BA, U. Denver, 1968. Nessa Cohen grantee, 1981, 82, E.D. Found. grantee, 1989, 96; recipient Purchase award, Art Students League N.Y., Chaim Gross Found. award, 1989, Nat. Acad. Mus. Speyer prize, 1992. One-woman shows include Gallery 2, Woodstock, Vt., 1973, Fairwinds Gallery, Ferrisburg, Vt., 1974, Congress Hall, Timmendorferstrand, Germany, 1976, Amerika Haus, Hamburg, Germany, 1976, Cambridge Art Assn., Mass., 1978, Goethe Inst., Boston, 1980, 83, Sutton Gallery, N.Y.C., 1981, 82, 83, 86, Madison Gallery, 1987, Bologna-Landi Gallery, Easthampton, N.Y., 1987, 93, Vorpal Gallery, N.Y.C., 1989, 91, 92, La Posada, Santa Fe, 1989, Ruth Volid Gallery, Chgo., 1990, Bachelier-Cardonsky Gallery, Kent, Conn, 1996, Hurlbutt Gallery, Greenwich, Conn., 1997, Dillon Gallery, N.Y.C., 1997, 00; group shows include Fleming Mus., Burlington, Vt., 1973, ARtist Choice Mus., N.Y.C., 1983, Nat. Acad. Mus., N.Y.C., 1988, 92, 94, 95, 97, 99, 2001, 2003, Provincetown Art Assn. & Mus., Mass., 1988, Nat. Scultpure Soc., N.Y.C., 1989, 91, Elaine Benson Gallery, bridgehampton, N.Y., 1993, Sculptors Guild, Kyoto, Japan & Washington, 1993, N.Y.C., 1994, Cline Fine Art Gallery, Sante Fe, 1994, 95, Stamford Mus., Conn., 1996, Bachelier-Cardonsky Gallery, 1996, The White House, Washington, 1996, 97; represented in permanent collections at The Nat. Mus. Women in Arts, Washington, The Snite Mus., Nat. Acad. Mus., The Herbert Johnson Mus. at Cornell, numerous pvt. collections. Mem. Nat. Acad. Mus., Century Assn., Sculptors Guild. Avocations: skiing, tennis. Home: 169 E 78th St New York NY 10021-0485

STORTZ, THOMAS C. lawyer, communications executive; b. 1951; BBA, U. Iowa; JD, Creighton U. Bar: Nebr. 1976. Atty. Peter Kiewit Sons', Inc., 1981—91, v.p., gen. counsel, 1991—98, Kiewit Constrn. Group, Inc., 1991—98; group v.p. Level 3 Comms., Inc., Broomfield, Colo., 1998—, gen. counsel, 1998—, sr. v.p., 1998—. Bd. dir. RCN Corp., C-TEC Corp., Kiewit Diversified Group, Inc., CCL Industries, Inc. Bd. dir. Nebr. Meth. Hosp. Found. Office: Level 3 Communications Inc 1025 Eldorado Blvd Broomfield CO 80021

STORY, ELLEN, state legislator; m. Ronald Story; 2 children. BA, U. Tex.; postgrad., U. Wis., SUNY, Stony Brook; MA, Cambridge Coll. County coord. Family Planning Coun. Western Mass., 1973, asst. exec. dir., 1981, assoc. exec. dir., 1984-92; mem. Mass. Ho. of Reps., Boston, 1992—. Founding mem. Hampshire County Human Svcs., Mass., 1974, past mem. prof. adv. com.; organizer Western Mass. Dems. and Independents for Frank Hatch for Gov., 1978; chmn. Barbara Griffith for Amherst Selectbd., 1982; coord. Evelyn Murphy for Lt. Gov., 1982; mem. Amherst Town Meeting, Mass.; pres., bd. dirs. Hampshire County Coun. Social Agencies, Mass.; bd. dirs. Hampshire Youth 2000 Coalition; charter mem. Friends of Amherst Recreation; co-founder, dir. Concerned Citizens for Quality Edn. Recipient Spl. Recognition award Hampshire County Coun. Social Agencies, 1991. Mem. Amherst Club, Rotary. Democrat. Office: Mass Ho of Reps State House Rm 167 Boston MA 02133

STORY, JULIE ANN, English educator; b. Muncy, Pa., Aug. 6, 1959; d. Phillip Mason Story and Mary Lee Peters. BA in English, Lock Haven U., 1982; MA in English, Ind. U. Pa., 1984. Assoc. dir. undergrad. writing ctr., lectr. English Pa. State U., Univ. Pk., 1987—2003; English instr. Juniata Coll., Huntingdon, Pa., 1987—89; dir. writing ctr., writing specialist Lock Haven U., Pa., 1998, 2003—. Internship coord. writing ctr. Pa. State U., University Park; cons. in field; faculty advisor Dangling Modifier. Mem. Pa. State Commn. for Women, University Park. Grantee, Ctr. Excellence Learning and Tchg., 2001. Mem.: NOW, Nat. Coun. Tchrs. English, Conf. Coll. Composition Comm., Ctrl. Pa. Writing Ctrs. Assn. (bd. dirs.), Nat. Conf. Peer Tutoring in Writing (adv. bd.), Mid-Atlantic Writing Ctrs. Assn. (v.p. 2003—), Internat. Writing Ctrs. Assn., Sigma Tau Delta, Phi Kappa Phi (life). Democrat. Avocations: gardening, walking, photography, reading, movies. Home: 33 Julia Dr Lock Haven PA 17745 Office: Lock Haven Univ Pa 411 Raub Hall Lock Haven PA 17745 Personal E-mail: jstory@csrlink.net. Business E-Mail: jstory@crslink.net.

STORY, KENDRA, wholesale distribution executive; CFO Am. Bldrs. & Contrs. Supply Co., Inc., Beloit, Wis. Office: Am Bldrs & Contrs Supply One ABC Pkwy Beloit WI 53511 Office Fax: (608) 362-6215.

STOSS, FREDERICK WARREN, librarian, educator; b. Gloversville, NY, Aug. 12, 1950; s. Dayton Robert and Katherine Gretchen (Ruzicka) Stoss; m. Dorothy Katherine Holderle, Aug. 24, 1974; 1 child, Kaeti Elizabeth. BA in Biology, Hartwick Coll., 1972; MS in Zoology, SUNY, Brockport, 1974; MLS, Syracuse U., 1982. Tech. rsch. assoc. U. Rochester Med. Ctr., NY, 1974—78; rsch. assoc. Syracuse Rsch. Corp., 1978—82; libr. dir. Ctr. for Environ. Info., Rochester, 1982—90; rsch. assoc. U. Tenn., Knoxville, 1990—96; scis. libr. U. Buffalo, 1996—. Lab. instr. U. Rochester, 1975—78; adj. lectr. Syracuse U., 1983—85; vis. lectr. U. Buffalo, 1997—; mem. editl. adv. bd. Environment Abstracts, 1988—, Electronic Green Jour., 1990—, Counterpoise, 1999—. Assoc. editor: Information Resources in Toxicology, 2001. Pres. Seth Green chpt. Trout Unlimited, Rochester, 1989—90. Mem.: ALA (chair task force on the environment 1995—99, coord. social responsibilities round table 1999—2002, team trainer Librs. Build Sustainable Cmtys. Team), Spl. Librs. Assn. (pres. So. Appalachian chpt. 1994—95, chair environ. info. divsn. 1988, Outstanding Divsn. Mem. award, Environ. Resource Mgmt. divsn., Environment and Resource Mgmt. Divsn. 1994), Nat. Sci. Tchrs. Assn., NY Libr. Assn., SUNY Libr. Assn., Sierra Club (chair environ. edn. com. 2001—), Sigma Xi (Outstanding Grad. Rsch. award 1974). Democrat. Luth. Avocations: fly fishing, nature photography. Office: Univ Buffalo Sci Eng Libr 228-B Capen Hall Buffalo NY 14260 Office Phone: 716-645-2947 224.

STOSSEL, THOMAS PETER, medical educator, medical researcher, director; b. Chgo., Sept. 10, 1941; m. Kerry Maguire, 1997. AB, Princeton U., 1963; MD, Harvard U., 1967, U. Linkoping, Sweden, 1989, U. Geneva, 2004. Diplomate Am. Bd. Internal Medicine. Ho. staff medicine Mass. Gen. Hosp., Boston, 1967-69, chief hematology-oncology, 1976-90; staff assoc. NIH, Bethesda, Md., 1967-71; fellow to sr. assoc. Med. Ctr. Children's Hosp., Boston, 1971-76; prof. medicine Harvard Med. Sch., Boston, 1982—; chief divsn. exptl. medicine Brigham Women's Hosp., Boston, 1991—, co-dir hematology divsn., 1998. Sci. bd. Biogen Corp., 1987—2002, Dyax Corp., 1996—2002; clin. rsch. prof. Am. Cancer Soc., 1987—; bd. dirs. Zymequest, Inc. Author (with B. Babior): (book) 2d edit., 1984, Hematology, A Pathophysiological Approach, 1994; editor (with R. Handin and S. Lux): Blood, Principles & Practice of Hematology, 1995, 2d edit., 2003; contbr. articles to profl. jours. Lt. comdr. USPHS, 1969—71. Mem.: NAS, Am. Acad. Arts and Scis., Assn. Am. Physicians, Am. Soc. Cell Biology, Am. Soc. Hematology (pres. 1997, Damashek prize 1983, Thomas prize 1993), Am. Soc. Clin. Investigation (pres. 1987), Am. Fedn. Clin. Rsch., Inst. Medicine. Achievements include patents in field. Office: Brigham & Womens Hosp 75 Francis St BCCH6 Boston MA 02115 Office Phone: 617-355-9001. Business E-Mail: tstossel@rics.bwh.harvard.edu.

STOTLER, ALICEMARIE HUBER, federal judge; b. Alhambra, Calif., May 29, 1942; d. James R. and Loretta M. Huber; m. James Allen Stotler, Sept. 11, 1971. BA, U. So. Calif., 1964, JD, 1967. Bar: Calif. 1967, U.S. Dist. Ct. (no. dist.) Calif. 1967, U.S. Dist. Ct. (ctrl. dist.) Calif. 1973, U.S. Supreme Ct. 1976; cert. criminal law specialist. Dep. Orange County Dist. Attys. Office, 1967-73; mem. Stotler & Stotler, Santa Ana, Calif., 1973-76, 83-84; judge Orange County Mcpl. Ct., 1976-78, Orange County Superior Ct., 1978-83, U.S. Dist. Ct. (ctrl. dist.) Calif., L.A., 1984—. Assoc. dean Calif. Trial Judges Coll., 1982; lectr., panelist, numerous orgns.; standing com. on rules of practice and procedure U.S. Jud. Conf., 1991-98, chair, 1993-98; chair 9th cir. Pub. Info. and Cmty. Outreach, 2000-; mem. exec. com. 9th Cir. Jud. Conf., 1989-93, Fed. State Jud. Coun., 1989-98, jury com., 1990-92, planning com. for Nat. Conf. on Fed.-State Jud. Relationships, Orlando, 1991-92, planning com. for We. Regional Conf. on State-Fed. Jud. Relationships, Stevens, Wash., 1992-93; chair dist. ct. symposium and jury utilization Ctrl. Dist. Calif., 1985, chair atty. liaison, 1989-90, chair U.S. Constn. Bicentennial com., 1986-91, chair magistrate judge com., 1992-93; mem. State Adv. Group on Juvenile Justice and Delinquency Prevention, 1983-84, Bd. Legal Specializations Criminal Law Adv. Commn., 1983-84, victim/witness adv. com. Office Criminal Justice Planning, 1980-83, U. So. Calif. Bd. Councilors, 1993-2001; active team in tng. Leukemia Soc. Am., 1993, 95, 97, 2000; legion lex bd. dirs. U. So. Calif. Sch. Law Support Group, 1981-83. Winner Hale Moot Ct. Competition, State of Calif., 1967; named Judge of Yr., Orange County Trial Lawyers Assn., 1978, Most Outstanding Judge Orange County Bus. Litig. Sect., 1990. Mem. ABA (jud. adminstrn. divsn. and litig. sect. 1984—, nat. conf. fed. trial judges com. on legis. affairs 1990-91), Am. Law Inst., Am. Judicature Soc., Fed. Judges Assn. (bd. dirs. 1989-92), Nat. Assn. Women Judges, U.S. Supreme Ct. Hist. Soc., Ninth Cir. Dist. Judges Assn., Calif. Supreme Ct. Hist. Soc., Orange County Bar Assn. (mem. numerous coms., Franklin G. West award 1984), Calif. Judges Assn. (mem. com. on jud. coll. 1978-80, com. on civil law and procedure 1980-82, Dean's coll. curriculum commn. 1981), Calif. Judges Found. Office: Ronald Reagan Fed Bldg & Courthouse 411 W 4th St Santa Ana CA 92701-4500

STOTLER, EDITH ANN, retired grain company executive, financial planner; b. Champaign, Ill., Oct. 11, 1946; d. Kenneth Wagner and Mary (Odebrecht) S. Student, Mary Baldwin Coll., 1964-66; BA, U. Ill., 1968. Asst. v.p. Harris Trust and Savs. Bank, Chgo., 1969-83; mgr. Can. Imperial Bank of Commerce, Chgo., 1983, sr. mgr., 1983-85, asst. gen. mgr. group head, 1985-88, v.p., dir. utilities, 1988-90; ptnr. Stotler Grain Co., Champaign, Ill., 1990—2002; pres. Homer Grain Co., Champaign, 1990-2000; pres., bd. dirs. S&I Grain Co., 1990-2000, SEMCO Energy Inc., 1987—2004. Bd. dirs., audit com., fin. com. SEMCO Energy Inc.; compensation com. Strategic Capital Bancorp, Inc., 2002—03. Past pres. liberal arts and scis. constituent bd., mem. pres.'s coun. U. Ill.; trustee, mem. fin. com. Countryside Sch., 1997—2000; dean's bus. coun. and exec. com. U. Ill. Bus. Coll., 1998—; bd. dirs. Champaign County YMCA, 2000—03; bd. dirs., treas. bd., chair investment and fin. coms. Champaign Pub. Libr. Found.; past mem. investment com., bd. trustees 4th Presbyn. Ch. Mem.: U. Ill. Found., Art Club (past pres., v.p.), Krannert Art Mus. Coun., Champaign Country Club (chair house com.), U. Ill. Found., Book Club. Avocations: needlepoint, reading, tennis, golf, cooking. Home: 900 N Lake Shore Dr Apt 2106 Chicago IL 60611-1522

STOTT, BRIAN, software company executive, consultant; b. Eccles, Eng., Aug. 5, 1941; came to U.S., 1983; s. Harold and Mary (Stephens) S.; m. Patricia Ann Farrar, Dec. 3, 1983. BSc, Manchester U., 1962, MSc, 1963, PhD, 1971. Asst. prof. Middle East Tech. U., Ankara, Turkey, 1965-68; lectr. Inst. Sci. and Tech., U. Manchester (Eng.), 1968-74; assoc. prof. U. Waterloo (Ont., Can.), 1974-76; cons. Electric Energy Rsch. Ctr. Brazil, Rio de Janeiro, 1976-83; prof. Ariz. State U., Tempe, 1983-84; chmn. Power Computer Applications Corp., Mesa, Ariz., 1984-2000. Cons. in field. Contbr. numerous articles to rsch. publs. Fellow IEEE (Millennium medal). Home and Office: 10222E Southwind Lane #1004 Scottsdale AZ 85262 E-mail: brianstott@ieee.org.

STOTT, DON S. precious metals products executive; b. Washington, Feb. 17, 1934; s. Marion McClelland Stott and Mabelle Louise (Maidem) Vanice; m. Dorothy Greene, June 21, 1962 (div.); children: David Michael, Melissa Ann; m. Bonnie Jean Peltomen, Dec. 4, 2002. Owner DS Theatres, DC and Phila., 1956—67, Bijou Iced Creme Parlours, Phila., 1967—71; hotel owner Wyman, Alma House and Grand Imperial Hotels, Silverton, Colo., 1971—94; pres. Colo. Gold, Montrose, 1977—. Author: Where the Mountains Meet the Sky, Three Feet to Silverton, Trails Among the Columbines, Consequences, numerous newspaper columns. Past pres. Montrose Hist. Soc., Valley Symphony, Kiwanis Club, Early Words Toastmasters, Am. Theatre Organ Soc., Silverton C. of C.; bd. dirs. Ariz. Opera. Republican. Avocations: trains, antiques, architecture. E-mail: gold@gwe.net.

STOTT, GRADY BERNELL, lawyer; b. Bailey, N.C., Sept. 19, 1921; s. William Willard and Zettie Harriett (Bissette) S.; m. Mays Beal, May 9, 1952; children: Sue J., Caroline Beal. AB, Duke U., 1947, JD, 1952. Bar: N.C. 1952. Dist. atty. 27th Jud. Dist., Gastonia, N.C., 1957-62; partner firm Stott, Hollowell, Palmer & Windham, Gastonia, 1960—. Served with USMC, 1943-48. Fellow Am. Bar Found., Am. Coll. Trial Lawyers; mem. N.C. State Bar (pres. 1978-79), Am. Bar Assn. (del. 1980), N.C. Bar Assn., Assn. Ins. Attys. Clubs: Masons. Democrat. Methodist. Office: 401 E Franklin Blvd Gastonia NC 28054-7152 Office Phone: 704-846-3425. Personal E-mail: gbs@shpw.com.

STOTT, PETER WALTER, forest products company executive; b. Spokane, Wash., May 26, 1944; s. Walter Joseph and Rellalee (Gray) S.; m. Julie L. Neupert, Oct. 12, 1996; 1 child, Preston. Student, Portland State U., 1962-63, 65-68, U. Americas, Mexico City, 1964-65. Founder, chmn. bd. dirs. Market Transport Ltd., Portland, Oreg., 1969—. Bd. dirs., pres., CEO, prin. Crown Pacific; bd. dirs. Liberty Northwest, CNF Inc. Mem. pres.'s adv. bd. for athletics Portland State U.; trustee Lewis & Clark Coll.; mem. adv. bd. Cascade Pacific coun. Boy Scouts Am. With USAR, 1966-72. Mem. Nat. Football Found. and Hall of Fame, Oreg. Sports Hall of Fame (lifetime), Stop Oreg. Litter and Vandalism (founders' circle), Arlington Club, Mazamas Club, Multnomah Athletic Club, Portland Golf Club, The Racquet Club, Univ. Club, Waverly Country Club, Valley Club. Republican. Roman Catholic. Office: Crown Pacific 805 SW Broadway Ste 1500 Portland OR 97205

STOTTER, HARRY SHELTON, banker, lawyer, savings and loan association executive; b. N.Y.C., Aug. 28, 1928; s. Jack and Adele (Sgel) S.; m. Marilyn H. Knight, Nov. 7, 1954; children: Jeffrey Craig, Cheryl dee. Student, L.I. U., 1948-49; JD, St. John's U., 1952; postgrad., NYU Law Sch., 1956-57. Bar: N.Y. 1952, N.J. 1974, U.S. Supreme Ct. 1983. Pvt. practice in, N.Y.C., 1952-53, 54-56; atty. U.S. Dept. Def., 1953; with trust div. Bank of N.Y., 1956-63; exec. v.p., sr. mgmt. com. Summit Bank (now Fleet Boston Bank), NJ, 1963-84; exec. v.p. Chase Manhattan Bank, N.Y.C., 1984-94; dir., vice chmn. Chase Manhattan Trust Co. Fla., Palm Beach, Fla., 1984-87; pvt. trust and estates law practice N.J., 1974-2000; former mem. probate com. N.J. Supreme Ct. Jud. Conf. Mem. N.Y.C. and Bergen County estate planning couns.; former pres. Bergen County coun. Girl Scouts Am.; bd. dirs., pres., chief exec. officer Bergen County United Way; treas. 2d Century Fund, Hackensack Hosp.; bd. dirs. Holy Name Hosp., Teaneck, N.J. With USN, World War II; brig. gen. Army N.G. Mem. ABA (co-chmn. nat. conf. lawyers and corp. trustees 1991-93), Am. Bankers Assn. (chmn. trust counsel com. 1991-93), N.Y. Bar Assn., N.J. Bar Assn., N.Y. County Lawyers Assn., Bergen County Bar Assn. (former trustee, former chmn. probate and estate planning com.), Fed. Bar Assn., N.Y. Militia Assn.

STOTTER, LAWRENCE HENRY, lawyer; b. Cleve., Sept. 24, 1929; s. Oscar and Bertha (Lieb) S.; m. Ruth Rapoport, June 30, 1957; children: Daniel, Jennifer, Steven. BBA, Ohio State U., 1956, LLB, 1958, JD, 1967. Bar: Calif. 1960, U.S. Supreme Ct. 1973, U.S. Tax Ct. 1976. Pvt. practice, San Francisco, 1963—; ptnr. Stotter and Coats, San Francisco, 1981-97; sole practitioner, 1997—; mem. faculty Nat. Judicial Coll.; mem. Calif. Family Law Adv. Commn., 1979-80. Editor in chief: Am. Bar Family Advocate mag, 1977-82; TV appearances on Phil Donahue Show, Good Morning America. Pres. Tamalpais Conservation Club, Marin County, Calif.; U.S. State Dept. del. Hague Conf. Pvt. Internat. Law, 1979-80; legal adv. White House Conf. on Families, 1980— . Served with AUS, 1950-53. Mem. ABA (past chmn. family law sect.), Am. Acad. Matrimonial Lawyers (past nat. v.p.), Calif. State Bar (past chmn. family law sect.), San Francisco Bar Assn. (past chmn. family law sect.), Calif. Trial Lawyers Assn. (past chmn. family law sect.) Home: 2244 Vistazo St E Belvedere Tiburon CA 94920-1970 Office: 1255 Columbus Ave # 200 San Francisco CA 94133-1326 Office Phone: 415-928-5050. Personal E-mail: lhstotter@aol.com.

STOTTLEMYER, DAVID LEE, government official; b. Waynesboro, Pa., June 1, 1935; s. Omar Samuel and Miriam (Noll) S.; m. Jane Ann Hembree, Aug. 26, 1961; children: Todd Andrew, Kristen Elizabeth, Kathryn Ann. AB, Miami U., Oxford, Ohio, 1959; M. Pub. and Internat. Affairs (NDEA fellow), U. Pitts., 1964, also postgrad. Program and budget analyst Exec. Office of Pres., Office of Mgmt. and Budget, Washington, 1964-69; sr. mgmt. officer UN, N.Y.C., 1969-70; adviser internat. orgn. affairs U.S. Mission to UN, N.Y.C., 1971-72, counsellor internat. orgn. affairs, 1973-75, counsellor UN resources mgmt., 1976-77; also mem. U.S. del. 26th-31st gen. assemblies, mem. UN Com. on Contbns., 1971; mem. UN Adv. Com. on Adminstrv. and Budgetary Questions, 1973-77; dir. policy mgmt. staff Bur. Internat. Orgn. Affairs, U.S. Dept. State, Washington, 1977-80, exec. asst. to asst. sec. of state for internat. orgn. affairs, 1980; mem. staff Office of Vice-Pres., Washington, 1981-83; dir. adminstrv. mgmt. service UN, N.Y.C., 1984-85; exec. asst., dir. Office of Under-Sec.-Gen. for Adminstrn. and Mgmt., UN, N.Y.C., 1986-87; pvt. practice as cons., 1987-90; dir. industry rels. NASA, Washington, 1990-91, dir. office nat. svc., 1992-93; retired, 1993; cons. pvt. practice, 1993—. Served with AUS, 1953-56. Recipient Superior Honor award State Dept., 1975 Mem. Am. Fgn. Svc. Assn. Home and Office: 5920 Sherborn Ln Springfield VA 22152-1035 Office Phone: 703-644-7348. Personal E-mail: dave.stot@verizon.net.

STOTZKY, GUENTHER, microbiologist, educator; b. Leipzig, Germany, May 24, 1931; came to U.S., 1939; s. Moritz Stotzky and Erna (Angres) Kester; m. Kayla Baker, Mar. 17, 1958; children: Jay, Martha, Deborah. BS, Calif. Poly. State U., 1952; MS, Ohio State U., 1954, PhD, 1956. Spl. sci. employee Argonne Nat. Lab. USAEC, Lemont, Ill., 1955; rsch. assoc. dept. botany U. Mich., Ann Arbor, 1956-58; head soil microbiology Ctrl. Rsch. Labs. United Fruit Co., Norwood, Mass., 1958-63; chmn., microbiologist Kitchawan Rsch. Labs. Bklyn. Botanic Garden, Ossining, NY, 1963-68; assoc. prof. dept. biology NYU, 1967-70, prof. dept. biology, 1970—, chmn. dept. biology, 1970-77. Editor: Soil Biochemistry, 1990-2000; series editor Marcel Dekker, Inc., 1986-92; contbr. over 280 articles to profl. jours., chpts. to books. With USCG, 1957. Recipient Selman A. Waksman Hon. Lecture award Theobald Smith Soc., 1989, Honored Alumnus of Yr. award Calif. Poly. State U., 1992, fellowship Japanese Soc. for Promotion of Sci., 1996; named Disting. Vis. Scientist, U.S. EPA, 1986-89. Fellow AAAS, Am. Soc. Agronomy, Soil Sci. Soc. Am.; mem. Am. Acad. Microbiology, Am. Soc. Microbiology (Fisher Co. award for applied and environ. microbiology 1990, Excellence in Tchg. award N.Y.C. br. 1994). Jewish. Avocations: gardening, reading, music. Office: NYU Dept Biology 1009 Silver Ctr New York NY 10003 Office Phone: 212-998-8268. E-mail: gs5@nyu.edu.

STOUCK, JERRY, lawyer; b. Washington, Mar. 24, 1955; s. Alex and Eileen Marion (Tepper) S.; m. Mindy A. Buren, Feb. 18, 1984; children: Danielle, David, Rachel. BA magna cum laude, Wesleyan U., 1977; JD, NYU, 1980. Bar: U.S. Dist. Ct. D.C. 1981, U.S. Ct. Fed. Claims 1981, D.C. Ct. Appeals, 1981, Md. Ct. Appeals 1983, U.S. Ct. Appeals (4th cir.) 1983, U.S. Dist. Ct. Md. 1985, U.S. Ct. Appeals (fed. cir.) 1992, U.S. Supreme Ct. 1993, U.S. Ct. Appeals (D.C. cir.) 1997. Law clk. to Hon. Pettine U.S. Dist. Ct. R.I., 1980-81; assoc. McKenna, Conner & Cuneo, Washington, 1981-83, Spriggs & Hollingsworth, Washington, 1983-84, 87-89, ptnr., 1989—; assoc. Shulman, Rogers, Gandel, Rockville, Md., 1984-87. Mem. Phi Beta Kappa. Office: Spriggs & Hollingsworth 1350 I St NW Ste 900 Washington DC 20005-3399 E-mail: jrstouck@spriggs.com.

STOUDEMIRE, AMARE CARSARES, professional basketball player; b. Lake Wales, Fl, Nov. 16, 1982; Player Phoenix Suns, 2002—. Mem. US Olympic Basketball Team, Athens, Greece, 2004. Named NBA Rookie of the Year, 2003, MVP, Rookie Challenge, 2004; named to NBA All-Rookie Team, 2003. Achievements include The only high school student slected in the 2002 NBA Draft. Office: c/o Phoenix Suns 201 E Jefferson St Phoenix AZ 85004

STOUDT, HOWARD WEBSTER, biological anthropologist, human factors specialist, consultant; b. Pitts., May 13, 1925; s. Howard Webster and Harriet Catharine (Powers) S.; m. Jean Gorey Henderson, Feb. 14, 1953; children: Katharine Webster, Roberta Henderson. AB, Harvard Coll., 1949; MA, U. Pa., 1953, PhD, 1959; SM in Hygiene, Harvard U., 1963. Rsch. asst. Harvard Sch. Pub. Health, Boston, 1952-55; rsch. specialist Air U., U.S. Air Force, Montgomery, Ala., 1955-57; rsch. assoc. Harvard Sch. Pub. Health, Boston, 1957-66, asst. prof., 1966-73; prof. community medicine Mich. State U., East Lansing, 1973-88, chmn. dept., 1973-78, prof. emeritus, 1988—; cons. Stoudt Assocs., Bath, Maine, 1988—. Cons. U.S. Army, USAF, NASA, USPHS, VA, NRC, NAS, pvt. industry, 1952—. Author: Physical Anthropology of Ceylon, 1961; co-author: Human Body in Equipment Design, 1971; contbr. over 40 articles to profl. jours. Sgt. U.S. Army, 1943-46, Europe. Harrison fellow U. Pa., Phila., 1951-52, USPHS fellow, Boston, 1961-62. Fellow Human Biology Coun.; mem. AAAS, Am. Assn. Phys. Anthropologists, Human Factors and Ergonomics Soc. Democrat. Home and Office: 4 Schooner Ridge Rd Ste 4 Bath ME 04530-1662

STOUGHTON, W. VICKERY, healthcare executive; b. Peoria, Ill., Mar. 1, 1946; s. Warner Vickery and Mary Olive (McNamara) S.; m. Anne Stoughton; children: Zachary Benjamin, Samantha. BS, St. Louis U., 1968; MBA, U. Chgo., 1973. Asst. dir. Boston Hosp. for Women, 1973-74, Peter Bent Brigham Hosp., Boston, 1975-77, dir., 1978-80; pres. The Toronto Hosp., Ont., Can.; asst. prof. U. Toronto, 1982-90, assoc. prof., 1991; vice chancellor health affairs, chief exec. officer Duke U. Hosp., Durham, N.C., 1991-92; pres.

Smithkline Beecham Clin. Labs., Collegeville, Pa., 1992-95, Smithkline Beecham Diagnostic Systems, King of Prussia, Pa., 1996; chmn., CEO Careside, Culver City, Calif., 1996—; dir. Biomira, 1988—. Bd. dirs. Sun Life Assurance Co. Bd. dirs. Toronto Symphony, 1983-86, Toronto United Way, 1988-91. Served to capt. AUS, 1969-72. Fellow Am. Coll. Hosp. Adminstrs. Home: 8820 Lookout Mountain Ave Los Angeles CA 90046-1820 Office: Box 366 11288 Ventura Blvd Studio City CA 91604-3149

STOUP, ARTHUR HARRY, lawyer; b. Kansas City, Mo., Aug. 30, 1925; s. Isadore and Dorothy (Rankle) S.; m. Kathryn Jolliff, July 30, 1948; children: David C., Daniel P., Rebecca Ann, Deborah E. Student, Kansas City Jr. Coll., Mo. 1942-43; BA, U. Kansas City, 1950; JD, U. Mo., Kansas City, 1950. Bar: Mo. 1950, D.C. 1979, U.S. Dist. Ct. (we. dist.) Mo., U.S. Dist. Ct. Kans., U.S. Dist. Ct. Ariz. Pvt. practice law, Kansas City, 1950—. Chmn. U.S. Jud. Merit Selection Com. for Western Dist. Mo., 1981. Chmn. com. to rev. continuing edn. U. Mo., 1978—79; mem. dean search com. U. Mo. Law Sch., Kansas City, Mo., 1979, 1994—95; trustee U. Mo.-Kansas City Law Found., 1972—, pres., 1979—82; trustee U. Mo., Kansas City, 1979—2001, hon. trustee, 2001—. With USNR, 1942—45. Recipient Alumni Achievement award, U. Mo., Kansas City, 1975, Law Found. Svc. award, U. Mo.-Kansas City Law Found., 1987, Lifetime Achievement award, 2002. Fellow Internat. Soc. Barristers (state mem. chmn.), Am. Bar Found. (life mem.); mem. ABA (ho. dels. 1976-80), Kansas City Met. Bar Assn. (pres. 1966-67, Dean of Trial Bar award 1991, mem. exec. com. 2003-), Mo. Bar (bd. govs. 1967-76, v.p. 1972-73, pres. elect 1973-74, pres. 1974-75), Lawyers Assn. Kansas City Mo., Mo. Assn. Trial Attys. (sustaining), Assn. Trial Lawyers Am. (sustaining), So. Conf. Bar Pres.'s (life), Mobar Research Inc. (pres. 1978-86), Phi Alpha Delta Alumni (justice Kansas City area alumni 1955-56). Lodges: Optimists (pres. Ward Pkwy. 1961-62, lt. gov. Mo. dist. internat. 1963-64), Sertoma, B'nai B'rith. Home: 9002 Western Hills Dr Kansas City MO 64114-3566 Office: Palace Bldg Ste 230 1150 Grand Blvd Kansas City MO 64106-2317 Fax: 816-474-0714.

STOUT, DONALD EVERETT, real estate developer, environmental preservationist; b. Dayton, Ohio; s. Thorne Franklin and Lovella Marie (Sweeney) S.; m. Gloria B. McCormick; children: Holly Sue, Scott Kenneth. BS, Miami U.; postgrad., Appraisal Inst. Lic. real estate broker, Ohio, U.S. V.I.; cert. gen. appraiser, Ohio. Pres. various real estate groups. Developer 1st transp. ctr. for trucking Ohio; pres. Falls Estates, Wright Gate Tech. Ctr., Edglo Land Recycle, Donald E. Stout, Inc.; developer, instr. real estate courses. Contbr. articles to profl. jours. With U.S. Army and USN. Named Outstanding Real Estate Salesmen State, Ohio Bd. Realtors. Mem. Nat. Assn. Real Estate Bds., Appraisal Inst. (sr. real estate analyst, sr. residential appraiser), Soc. Indsl. Office Realtors, Dayton Area Bd. Realtors (co-founder, 1st pres. salesman divsn.), U.S. Naval Res. Officers Assn., Raymond M. Hughes Soc., Exhausted Roosters, Masons (32d degree), Shriner, Phi Delta Theta. Office: 1344 Woodman Dr Dayton OH 45432-3442 E-mail: stoutde@sbcglobal.net.

STOUT, MARY WEBB, education program specialist; b. Richmond, Va., Dec. 24, 1947; d. Frank Edmond Webb and Edith Diuguid (Harris) Webb Steger; m. Teddy Alvin Stout, July 8, 1972. BA, Mary Washington Coll., 1970; MEd, U. Va., Charlottesville, 1972; Edn. Specialist, Coll. William and Mary, 1991, EdD, 1995; cert. in Multimedia Devel., George Mason U., 2003. Tchr. Harrisonburg City Sch., Va., 1970-71, Buckingham County Sch., Va., 1972-73; guidance counselor So. European Task Force US Army, Vicenza, Italy, 1973-78, edn. specialist Quartermaster Sch. Ft. Lee, Va., 1978-80, edn. specialist Tng. Support Ctr. Ft. Eustis, Va., 1980-82; edn. specialist Hdqs. Tng., Doctrine Command, Ft. Monroe, Va., 1982-83; edn. svc. specialist Combined Arms Ctr., Ft. Leavenworth, Kans., 1983-88; instrnl. systems specialist Hdqs. TRADOC, Ft. Monroe, 1988-98; supervisory edn. svc. specialist Hdqs. US Army Pers. Command, Alexandria, Va., 1998-2000; edn. program specialist OSD Office of Chancellor Edn. and Profl. Devel., Arlington, Va., 2000—03; online faculty U. Phoenix, 2002—; edn. program specialist OSD Civilian Pers. Mgmt. Services, Arlington, 2003—. Mem. devel. bd. Sch. Edn. Coll. William and Mary, 2002—. Legis. affairs rep. Running Man Homeowners Assn., Yorktown, Va., 1996—98; treas. Massanetta Springs Alumni Assn., Harrisonburg, Va., 1988—2002, membership chmn., 1998—2002, pres., 2002—. Recipient Alumni award Massanetta Springs Alumni Assn., 1996. Mem.: Am. Soc. for Tng. and Devel., Assn. for Instnl. Rsch., Am. Assn. for Adult and Continuing Edn., Mary Washington Coll. Alumni Assn., U. Va. Alumni Assn., Coll. William and Mary Alumni Assn., Assn. Advancement of Computing in Edn., Assn. Ednl. Comm. and Tech., Am. Assn. Higher Edn., Assn. Study Higher Edn., Kappa Delta Pi. Presbyterian. Avocations: running, red cross water safety instructor. Home: 6006 River Dr Mason Neck VA 22079-4127 Office: Dept Def Civilian Pers Mgmt Svcs 1400 Key Blvd Ste B-200 Arlington VA 22209 Personal E-mail: MSTOUT8895@aol.com.

STOUT, MICHAEL W. communications executive; BSBA, U. Colo. Various mgmt. pos. United Airlines, Covia Partnership, and Galileo Internat.; v.p., chief tech. and info. officer GE Capital, 1995—2003; exec. v.p., chief info. officer Sprint Corp., Overland Park, Kans., 2003—. Office: Sprint Corp 6200 Sprint Pkwy Overland Park KS 66251

STOUT, NEIL RALPH, retired history educator; b. Marietta, Ohio, Aug. 12, 1932; s. Ralph Plumly and Carrie Baker Stout; m. Marilynn Blumenstiel, Sept. 8, 1956; children: Hilary Ann, Peter Neil. BA, Harvard U., 1954; MS, U. Wis., 1958, PhD, 1961. Asst. prof. Tex. A&M U., Hist. Dept., College Station, 1961—64; prof. U. Vt., Hist. Dept., Burlington, Vt., 1964—2000, prof. emeritus, 2000—. Editor Vt. Hist. Soc., Montpelier, 1993—94; pres. New Eng. Hist. Assn., Worcester, Mass., 1979—80. Author: Royal Navy in America, 1760-1775, 1973, The Perfect Crisis, 1976, The History Student's Vade Mecum (4 editions). Historian Vt. State Hist. Preservation Adv. Coun., Montpelier, 1990—94. With U.S. Army, 1954—56, France. Home: 129 Robinson Pkwy Burlington VT 05401 Personal E-mail: vze34ppp@verizon.net.

STOUT, PATRICIA A. communications educator; BA in Anthropology, U. Ariz., 1979; postgrad., U. Minn., 1979-81; PhD in Comm., U. Ill., 1985. Advt. mgr. alumni publ. U. Mont., Missoula, 1978-79; acct. mgmt. Judge Advt., Pub. Rels., Helena, Mont., 1979; tchg. asst., Sch. Journalism & Mass Comm. U. Minn., Mpls., 1979-80; project asst. Minn. Cmty. Prevention Program, 1980-81; vis. lectr. dept. advt. U. Ill., Urbana, 1981-84; asst. prof. dept. advt. U. Tex., Austin, 1984-90, assoc. prof. dept. advt., 1990—, assoc. dean acad. affairs Coll. Comm., 1996—. Vis. rsch. prof. Ctrs. for Disease Control and Prevention, Atlanta, 1993-94; vis. assoc. prof. dept. mktg. and internat. bus. U. Auckland, New Zealand, 1994; chmn. 5 doctoral coms., numerous masters theses, profl. reports U. Tex., Austin, mem., reader numerous others; dir. grad. studies dept. advt. U. Tex., Austin, Fall 1990, Summer 1993; ad hoc reviewer Jour. Advt., Jour. Consumer Rsch., Jour. Pub. Policy & Mktg., Journalism Quar., Critical Studies in Mass Comm., Jour. Bus. Rsch. Author: (with John D. Leckenby and Nugent Wedding) Advertising Management, (with Michael Solomon and Kim Rotzoll) The Advertising Around Us: A Consumer Perspective on Marketing Communications; editor procs. of 1990 Am. Acad. of Advt. Conf.; contbr. tech. papers, procs., articles to profl. jours.; presenter in field. Recipient cartoon caption contest first place award Olympia Beer Distbrs., Missoula, Mont., 1978-79, Jour. Advt. best article award Am. Acad. Advt., 1993, vis. rsch. prof. intergovernmental pers. act award Nat. AIDS Edn. and Info. Program, Ctrs. for Disease Control and Prevention, Atlanta, 1993-94; Pub. Health Svc. Tng. fellow Lab. Physiological Hygiene, U. Minn., 1980-81, Houston Harte Centennial Comm. fellow U. Tex., Austin, 1987-88, Am. Acad. Advt. Industry fellow Advt. Rsch. Found, N.Y., 1993-94; dissertation rsch. grantee U. Ill., 1984-85, summer rsch. grantee U. Tex., Austin, 1984-85, direct support grantee U. Tex., 1985-86, 86-87, rsch. grantee Am. Acad. Advt., 1985-86, rsch. grantee Teh Ogilvy Ctr. Rsch. and Devel., San Francisco, 1985-86, U. Rsch. Inst. spl. rsch. grantee U. Tex., 1988-89, 95-96, Columbia U. Tech. Studies Seminar grantee Freedom Forum Media Studies Ctr., 1992-93, immunization of Tex. children co-investigator grantee Tex. Dept. Health, 1995-96, an exploratory study on appropriate internet content and use standards for children co-investigator grantee Hogg Found. for Mental Health, 1996-97. Mem. Internat. Comm. Assn. (ad hoc reviewer), Am. Acad. Advt. (treas. 1989, v.p. 1990, pres. elect 1991, pres. 1992, past pres. 1993, publs. com. 1997—, ad hoc reviewer), Assn. Consumer Rsch. (ad hoc reviewer), Assn. Edn. in Journalism and Mass Comm., Soc. Consumer Psychology, Phi Kappa Phi, Kappa Tau Alpha, Alpha Delta Sigma. Home: 5508 Great Divide Dr Austin TX 78738-6123 Office: Univ Tex Dept Advt CMA 7142 Austin TX 78712

STOUT, RANDALL, architect; BArch (with hons.), U. Tenn., 1981; MArch, Rice U., 1989. Registered Calif., Tex., Tenn. With Frank O. Gehry & Assocs., sr. assoc., then lead; with Skidmore Owings & Merrill, Houston; intern FKP, Inc., Houston; with solar design group TVA; pres. Randall Stout Archs., LA, 1993—. Adj. prof., lectr. U. Tex., Austin, 2001; adj. prof. UCLA, 2001, recruitment com., 02, admissions rev. com., 02. Recipient Design award, TAAST, 1981, Cmty. Svc. award, Houston Proud, 1985, Graphic Design award, Tex. Soc. Arch., 1988, Progressive Arch. award, 1993, Innovation in Tech. award, SOLTEC Germany, 1998; fellow Pittman fellow, Rice U., 1988; scholar Gen. Shale scholar, 1980. Fellow: AIA (environment com. 1997—, Henry Adams medal 1981, Honor award 1992, 1995, 1998, 2000, Merit award 1998, Design citation 2000). Office: 12964 Washington Blvd Los Angeles CA 90066

STOUTENBOROUGH, J. TODD, architect; BA in Arch., Calif. State Polytechnic U. Lic. D.C. Sr. prin. LPA, Inc., Irvine, Calif.; prin. Stoutenborough, Inc., 1992—2002, Perkowitz & Ruth, Newport Beach, Calif., 2002—. Mem. Internat. Coun. Shopping Ctrs. Mem.: AIA. Office: Perkowitz & Ruth 15 Corporate Plaza Ste 200 Newport Beach CA 92660*

STOUTENBURG, JANE SUE WILLIAMSON, nurse practitioner, fund raiser, actress; b. Davenport, Iowa, Mar. 10, 1949; d. George Baker and Hazel Elaine (Kline) W.; m. Noel Wayne Stoutenburg, Aug. 25, 1979 (div. July 1996); 1 child, Karen Elaine. AS with honors, Black Hawk Jr. Coll., East Moline, Ill., 1970; BA, BS, Augustana Coll., 1973, 75; Cert. in Fire Sci. with honors, Harper Coll., Palatine, Ill., 1982; AS in Nursing with high honors, Elgin Community Coll., 1987. EMT; cert. paramedic; cert. tchr. Rsch. technologist Rush-Presbyn. St. Luke's Med. Ctr., Chgo., 1974-75; acct. supr., pvt. investigator Per Mar Security Inc., Davenport, Iowa, 1975-77; pre-trial release investigator 7th Jud. Ct. Dist., Davenport, Iowa, 1976-77; pharm. rep. Bristol Labs., Syracuse, N.Y., 1977-80; dir. safety tng. Zee Med., Irvine, Calif., 1981-83; tng. specialist ARC, Chgo., 1983-86, Lake County Fire Rescue, Barrington, Ill., 1981—; nurse practitioner Boy Scouts of Am., St. Charles, Ill., 1990—; nurse trainer Buehler YMCA, Palatine, Ill., 1990-94. Emergency med. svc. coord. Robbins (Ill.) Fire Dept., 1985—; bd. dirs. Barrington Area Devel. Coun., 1981-90; EMS coord. Lake Counte Fire Rescue, 1980—, owner, Snail's Pace Gifts, Barrington, IL, 1997—, pres. Karyn Etcetera Inc., 1997—. Author: Academy of Science, 1967, (poetry), 1970, actress: ER, 1997—, First Edition, 1998—, Backdraft, A Normal Life, Relic, My Best Friends Wedding. Troop leader Girl Scouts, Barrington, 1990-95; book fair chmn. Lines Sch. PTO, Barrington, 1991-94; camp nurse Boy Scouts Am., Camp Big Timber, Ill., YMCA Camp Duncan, Fox Lake, Ill.; pageant judge Miss Am. System, 1995—.bd. dirs. Elgin C.C., 1998—, NW Suburb Chgo. Vol. Bur., 1998—. Recipient Ill. EMT of the Yr. award, 1989-90, Disting. Svc. award ARC, 1989, Disting. Svc. key Alpha Phi Omega, 1989, Key, Phi Theta Kappa, 1989, Vol. of the Yr. award Chgo. Vol. Bur., 1993, J.C. Penney Golden Flame award, 1993. Mem. Am. Soc. Safety Engrs., Am. Trauma Soc., Am. Acad. Sci., Internat. Soc. Fire Sci. Instrs., Prehosp. Care Providers of Ill., Alpha Phi Omega (mem. bd. dirs. 1995—, publicity com.), P.E.O. Sisterhood. Episcopalian. Avocations: poetry, camping, firefighting, girl scouts, dixieland jazz. Office: Lake County Fire Rescue 618 W Northwest Hwy Ste 213 Barrington IL 60010-2730

STOVAL, LINDA, political party official; b. Wyo. m. Tony Stoval. Ran 2 campaigns former Dem. Gov. Mike Sullivan; owner Solutions, Wyo.; chairperson Wyo. Dem. Party, 2001—. Office: 737 Kirk Ave Casper WY 82601-3324 Business E-Mail: stoval@trib.com.

STOVALL, APRIL LEANNE, music educator; b. Aurora, Ill., Apr. 19, 1968; d. Vernon Albert and Bobette Lee Shoger; m. James Brian Stovall, Nov. 24, 1990. MusM Edn., Bob Jones U., S.C., 1990. Cert. Svc. Playing Am. Guild of Organists, 1999. Pvt. piano tchr., bus. owner Artistry by Apr. Studios, North Aurora, Ill., 1990—; accompanist St. Charles Singers, Ill., 1999—2002; assoc. organist Baker Meml. United Meth. Ch., St. Charles, Ill., 1999—; music faculty Waubonsee C.C., Sugar Grove, Ill., 1999—; dir. music, choirmaster, organist St. Charles Episcopal Ch., Ill., 2002—. Local bd. mem., fox valley chpt. Am. Guild of Organists, Batavia, Ill., 2001—; nat. steering com. mem. Chgo. AGO Nat. Conv., 2001—; accompanist Elgin Choral Union, Ill., 2003—. Musician: (musical recording) Live at Cambridge U., Eng. Tour, 2000, Lenten Artists Series, Baker United Meth. Ch. Accompanist, world tours St. Charles Singers, Ill., 2000; dir., children's chorus St. Charles Episcopal Ch., Ill., 2002. Recipient Superior Rating, Nat. Piano Guild, 1990. Mem.: Ill. State Music Tchrs. Assn. (life; music educator 1990), DAR. Conservative. Avocations: travel, art, reading, skiing, mountain biking. Home: 209 April Ln North Aurora IL 60542-1205 Office: St Charles Episcopal Ch 994 N Fifth Ave Saint Charles IL 60174 Personal E-mail: jimapril1124@earthlink.net. E-mail: stcharles@anet.com.

STOVALL, CARLA JO, former state attorney general; b. Hardner, Kans., Mar. 18, 1957; d. Carl E. and Juanita Joe (Ford) Stovall. BA, Pittsburg (Kans.) State U., 1979; JD, U. Kans., 1982, MPA, 1993. Bar: Kans. 1982, U.S. Dist. Ct. Kans. 1982. Pvt. practice, Pitts., 1982—85; atty. Crawford County, Pitts., 1984—88; gov. Kans. Parole Bd., Topeka, 1988—94; atty. gen. State of Kans., Topeka, 1995—2002. Lectr. law Pittsburg State U., 1982—84. Mem. bd. govs. U. Kans. Sch. Law; Nat. Ctr. Missing and Exploited Children; Am. Legacy Found.; Nat. Crime Prevention Coun.; Coun. State Govts.; mem. bd. govs. Kans. Children's Cabinet; pres. NAAG, 2001—02, chmn. exec. com. midwest region, sexually violent predator com., 1995—96; Bd. dirs., sec. Pittsburg Family YMCA, 1983—88. Named Outstanding Atty. Gen., Nat. Assn. Attys. Gen., 2001, Topeka Fraternal Order of Police's Amb. to Law Enforcement; recipient Champion award, Campaign Tobacco Free Kids, 2002, Adam Walsh Children's Fund Rainbow award, Nat. Ctr. Missing and Exploited Children, 2001, Kelley-Wyman award, Nat. Assn. Attys. Gen., 2001, Person of the Yr., Kans. Peace Officer Assn.'s Law Enforcement, Morton Baud Allied Profl. award, Nat. Orgn. Victim Assistance, Father Ken Czillinger award, Nat. Parents Murdered Children, Disting. Svc. to Kans. Children award, Kans. Children's Svc. League, Woman of Achievement award, Miss Kans. Pageant. Mem.: NAAG (pres. 2001—02), AAUW (bd. dirs. 1983—87), ABA, Bus. and Profl. Women Assn. (Young Careerist award 1984), Nat. Coll. Dist. Attys., Kans. County and Dist. Attys. Assn., Crawford County Bar Assn. (sec. 1984—85, v.p. 1985—86, pres. 1986—87), Kans. Bar Assn., Kans. Assn. Commerce and Industry (Leadership Kans. award 1983), Pittsburg Area C. of C. (bd. dirs. 1983—85, Leadership Pitts. award 1984), Pittsburg State U. Alumni Assn. (bd. dirs. 1983—88). Republican. Methodist. Avocations: travel, photography, tennis. Home: 138 S Blue Bells Ct Garden Plain KS 67050-9225

STOVALL, JULIA CONNOR, industrial engineer; d. John Joseph and Anne Kestler Connor; m. Thomas Bruce Stovall, Jr., Dec. 28, 1973; 1 child, Elizabeth Martha. BS, Ohio U., 1981. Indsl. and sys. engr. NCR, Cambridge, Ohio, 1979—84, Exide Electronics, Raleigh, NC, 1984—85; sr. engr. Northrop Grumman, Raleigh, NC, 1998—. Spkr. in field. Contbr. articles to profl. jours. Mem.: Human Factors and Ergonomics Soc. Personal E-mail: julia-stovall@nc.rr.com.

STOVALL, RICHARD L. retired academic administrator; b. Springfield, Mo., Mar. 28, 1944; s. Wilbern Lee and Ernestine Patricia (Putman) S.; m. Susannah K. Young; children: Richard Christopher, Stacy Suzanne. BA, SW Mo. State U., 1966; MA, C.W. Post Coll. L.I. U., 1969; PhD, Ohio State U., 1975. Instr. SW Mo. State U., Springfield, 1969-72; asst. prof. U. S.C., Columbia, S.C., 1975-77; prof., asst. dept. head SW Mo. State U., Springfield, 1977—2003, ret., 2003. Cons. Cedar Hills High Sch., Dallas, 1986, Andrews Ins. Agy., 1984, Mo. Cosmetology Assn., 1983-84, Springfield Pers. Assn., 1982, Syntex Corp. 1981-82; pub. rels. Halcyon of Dallas, 1988-96, Hawthorne Group of Washington, 1995-96, The Harrell Group, Dallas, 1999. Contbr. articles to profl. jours. Tabulation room coord. for MSHSAA Dist. Speech Festival; lectr. Springfield Pub. Schs., City Utilities Citizens Adv. Bd.; pres. Boy Scouts Am. With ES USNR-TAR, 1962-69. Mem. Pub. Rels. Soc. Am., Am. Forensics Assn., Speech Communication Assn. Am., So. Speech Communication Assn., Pub. Rels. of the Ozarks, Pub. Rels. Soc. Mid-Mo., Cen. States Speech Assn., Speech and Theatre Assn. Mo., Cherokee Homeowners Assn. (past pres.). Episcopal. Home and Office: 3 Whiterock Ln Kimberling City MO 65686 E-mail: richardstovall@msn.com.

STOVALL-BROOKS, PATRICIA, elementary school educator, writer; b. Gillett, Ark., Mar. 8, 1951; d. Ambrose Poke and Addie Britton Stovall; 1 child, Sheldon Leon Brooks. BS in Edn. cum laude, Ark. Bapt. Coll., 1972; MS, Nat. Louis U., 1982. Cert. tchr. Ill., 1981. Tchr. Chgo. Pub. Schs., 1973—. Cons. U.S. Dept. Edn., Washington, 2002. Author: Except The Lord Builds The House/Relationships. Rec. sec. Women Empowered For Change, Chgo., 1999—2003; choir mem. mass choir and gospel choir Chancel Choir/Du Page A.M.E.Ch., Lisle, Ill.; active mem. Women's Missionary Soc., Lisle, 2002—03. Recipient Disting. Svc. award, Greater Instnl. A.M.E. Ch., 1999, Dedicated Svc. award, Greater Instl. Guild, 2002. Avocations: singing, cooking, writing. Home: 433 Marshall Ave Bellwood IL 60104 Office: Chicago Public Schs 125 S Clark St Chicago IL 60605 Office Phone: 630-886-8711. Personal E-mail: pbstovall@aol.com.

STOVEKEN, JAMES E., JR., paper packaging and chemical company executive; CFO, sr. v.p. Westvaco Corp., N.Y.C.; sr. v.p., controller, 2001—. Office: Westvaco Corp 1 High Ridge Pk Stamford CT 06905

STOVER, CARL FREDERICK, foundation executive; b. Pasadena, Calif., Sept. 29, 1930; s. Carl Joseph and Margarete (Müller) S.; m. Catherine Swanson, Sept. 3, 1954; children: Matthew Joseph, Mary Margaret Stover Marker, Claire Ellen Stover Herrell; m. Jacqueline Kast, Sept. 7, 1973. BA magna cum laude, Stanford U., 1951, MA, 1954. Instr. polit. sci. Stanford U., 1953-55; fiscal mgmt. officer Office Sec. Dept. Agr., 1955-57; assoc. dir. conf. program pub. affairs Brookings Instn., 1957-59, sr. staff govtl. studies, 1960; fellow Center Study Democratic Instns., Santa Barbara, Calif., 1960-62; asst. to chmn. bd. editors Ency. Brit., 1960-62; sr. polit. scientist Stanford Research Inst., 1962-64; dir. pub. affairs fellowship program Stanford U., 1962-64; pres. Nat. Inst. Pub. Affairs, Washington, 1964-70, Nat. Com. U.S.-China Relations, 1971-72; pres., dir. Federalism Seventy-Six, Washington, 1972-74; dir. cultural resources devel. Nat. Endowment Arts, 1974-78; pres., dir. Cultural Resources, Inc., Washington, 1978-85; bd. dirs. H.E.A.R. Found., 1976-86, treas., 1976-80, pres., 1980-86. Bd. dirs. Ctr. for World Lit., pres., 1987-90, chmn., 1990-92; pvt. profl. cons., 1970—; scholar-in-residence Nat. Acad. Pub. Adminstrn., 1980-82; cons. in field. Author: The Government of Science, 1962, The Technological Order, 1963; Founding editor: Jour. Law and Edn., 1971-73; pub. Delos mag., 1987-92. Treas. Nat. Com. U.S.-China Rels., 1966-71, 82-87, 89-94, bd. dirs., 1966-74, 79-98, dir. emeritus, 1998—; bd. dirs. Coord. Coun. Lit. Mags., 1966-68, H.E.A.R. Found., 1976-86, treas., 1976-80; trustee Inst. of Nations, 1972-76, Nat. Inst. Pub. Affairs, 1967-71, Kinesis Ltd., 1972-78; vol. Nat. Exec. Svc. Corps, 1984-89. Fellow AAAS, Phi Beta Kappa (hon. lectr. 1972-87); mem. Am. Soc. Pub. Adminstrn., Fedn. Am. Scientists, Soc. Internat. Devel., Jordan Soc. (dir. 1982-84), Nat. Acad. Pub. Adminstrn. (hon.), Md. U. Club, Internat. Soc. Panetics (pres. 1991-95, chmn. 1995-98, chmn. emeritus 1999—, bd. govs. 1991—, founding mem. 1991—). Democrat. Presbyterian. Home and Office: 4109 Metzerott Rd College Park MD 20740-2082 Office Phone: 301-935-5263. E-mail: carlfstover@aol.com.

STOVER, ELLEN L. health scientist, psychologist; b. Bklyn., Nov. 21, 1950; d. Ralph and Charlotte (Tulchin) Simon; m. Alan B. Stover, June 3, 1973; children: Elena Randall Simon, Randall Alan Simon, Samantha Anne Simon. BA with honors, U. Wis., 1972; PhD, Catholic U., 1978. Cons. NIMH, Rockville, Md., 1972-74, exec. sec. drug abuse rsch. review com., 1974-76, spl. asst. to assoc. dir. extramural programs, 1976-77, chief, small grants program, 1977-79, asst., acting & chief rsch. resources br., 1980-85, dep. dir., div. basic scis., 1985-88, dir. office AIDS, 1988-97, dir. divsn. mental disorders, behavioral rsch. and AIDS, 1997—; dir. Ctr. Mental Health Rsch. on AIDS. Co-chmn. AIDS rsch. behavioral coordinating com. NIH, 1993—. Recipient Superior Svc. award USPHS, 1987, 92, 93, Dir.'s award NIH, 1996, Presdl. Rank award, 2001. Mem. APA, Am. Psychol. Soc. Avocations: gardening, dance. Office: NIMH 6001 Executive Blvd Rm 6217 Bethesda MD 20892-0001

STOVER, JAMES HOWARD, retired real estate executive; b. Forest Hill, W.Va., Oct. 20, 1911; s. Charles William and Zora (Goode) S.; m. May Simmons, Oct. 21, 1939 (dec.); children: Ann, Robert Bruce; m. Elizabeth J. Cobb, Dec. 27, 1977 (dec.). Student, Benjamin Franklin U., 1936-38; grad., Advanced Mgmt. Program, Harvard U., 1959, Exec. Devel. Program Ind. U., 1960, Inst. Mgmt. Northwestern U., 1960. Asst. purchasing agt. Woodward & Lothrop, Washington, 1932-35; asst. chief field supervision div., central accounts office Bur. Accounts Treasury Dept., 1935-41, asst. chief Treasury Budget sect., 1941-42, fiscal acct. Office Commr. Pub. Debt, 1946-51, chief treasury mgmt. analysis staff, 1951-63, dir. Office Mgmt. and Orgn., 1963-66, regional commr. customs Miami Region IV, 1966-72; real estate sales assoc., mgmt. cons., 1972-75; pres. Bay Realty of Fla., Inc., 1975-99; ret., 1999. Chmn. Inter-agy. Mgmt. Analysis Conf., 1958-59; mem. orgn. and mgmt. adv. com. Dept. Agr. Grad. Sch., 1956-63. Chmn. adv. coms. orgn. and procedure and legislative program Arlington (Va.) County Bd., 1958-63; pres. Tuckahoe Recreation Club, 1957; chmn. Greater Miami Fed. Exec. Coun., 1968-69; mem. exec. adv. coun. Coll. Bus. and Pub. Adminstrn., Fla. Atlantic U., 1969-80. 2d lt. to maj. AUS, 1942-46. Recipient Rockefeller Pub. Svc. award, 1959, Spl. Svc. award Treasury Dept., 1963, Exceptional Svc. award, 1965, other treasury awards, 1969, 70, 71, 72. Home: 2335 Biscayne Blvd Miami FL 33137-4513

STOVER, JOHN FORD, railroad historian, educator; b. Manhattan, Kans., May 16, 1912; s. John William and Maud (Ford) S.; m. Marjorie Ellen Filley, Aug. 21, 1937; children: John Clyde, Robert Vernon (dec.), Charry Ellen Stover. AB, U. Nebr., 1934, MA, 1937; PhD, U. Wis., 1951. Instr. social studies Arcadia (Nebr.) H.S., 1936-37; instr. history and govt. Bergen (N.J.) Jr. Coll., 1937-41; grad. asst. history U. Wis., 1941-42, 46-47, Univ. fellow, 1946; from instr. to assoc. prof. Purdue U., Lafayette, Ind., 1947-59, prof. history, 1959-78, prof. emeritus, 1978—, Purdue Rsch. Found. XL grantee, summer 1957, 59, fellow in Coll.-Bus. Exch. Program, I.C. R.R., summer 1962. Chmn. Pres.'s adv. coun. on retirement Purdue U., 1980-81. Author: The Railroads of the South, 1865-1900, 1955, American Railroads, 1961, rev. edit., 1997, A History of American Railroads, 1967, Turnpikes, Canals and Steamboats, 1969, The Life and Decline of the American Railroad, 1970, Transportation in American History, 1970, History of Illinois Central Railroad, 1975, Iron Road To The West, 1978, Sixty-Five Years of Kiwanis in Indiana, 1981, History of the Baltimore & Ohio Railroad, 1987, Seventy-Five Years of Kiwanis and Indiana, 1990, The Routledge Historical Atlas of the American Railroads, 1999; contbr. to hist. jours., books, numerous encys., including Americana and Academic Americana, and biog. works. Chmn. edn. com., mem. exec. com. Ind. Sesquicentennial Commn., 1962-67; hon. mem. Indiana Am. Revolution Bicentennial commn., 1972-82; mem. adv. council Centennial History of Ind. Gen. Assembly, 1979-83; pres. Lafayette Kiwanis Found., 1977-78. Served to capt. USAAF, 1942-46; Res., 1946-53, ret., 1953. George F. Hixson fellow, 1996; named Sagamore of the Wabash Gov. Ind., 1978; recipient Alumni Achievement award U. Nebr., 1985. Fellow Soc. Am. Historians; mem. Ind. Acad. Social Scis., Western History Assn., Bus. History Conf. (trustee 1973-76), Am. Hist. Assn., So. Ind. Hist. Assn. (com. on libr. 1975-91), Nebr. Hist. Assn., Tippecanoe County Hist. Assn. (pres. 1972-74), Lexington Group (R.R. historians), AAUP, Ind. History Tchrs. Assn. (pres. 1958-59), Orgn. Am. Historians, Newcomen Soc. N.Am., Rlwy. and Locomotive Hist. Soc. (editl. adv. bd. for R.R. History jour., 1970-94, Sr. Achievement R.R. History award 1983), Soc. Ind. Pioneers, Civil War Round Table of Nebr., Nat. Ry. Hist. Soc., Phi Beta Kappa (hon.), Phi Alpha Theta, Delta Sigma Rho. Clubs: Fortnightly, Lincoln Open Forum. Lodges: Kiwanis (local pres. 1973-74, disting. lt. gov.

1978-79, historian Ind. dist. 1980-81, 83-90. 91-92). Republican. Congregationalist. Avocations: golf, model railroading, stamps. Home: Apt 318 Grand Lodge 4400 S 80th St Lincoln NE 68516

STOVER, KENNETH ALAN, sales executive; b. Lynn, Mass., Aug. 27, 1952; s. Homer Nelson and Elizabeth Ann (Dryer) Stover. BA, Boston U., Mass., 1978. Chemist Stohler Isotope Chemicals, Waltham, Mass., 1979—85, Strem Chemicals Inc., Newburyport, Mass., 1985—96; cons. sales assoc. Sears, Roebuck & Co., Peabody, Mass., 1998—2004. Mem.: North Shore Computer Soc.

STOVER, LEON (EUGENE STOVER), anthropology educator, writer, critic; b. Lewistown, Pa., Apr. 9, 1929; s. George Franklin and Helen Elizabeth (Haines) S.; m. Takeko Kawai, Oct. 12, 1956. BA, Western Md. Coll., 1950, LittD (hon.), 1980; MA, Columbia U., 1952, PhD, 1962. Instr. Am. Museum Natural History, N.Y.C., 1955-57; asst. prof. Hobart and William Smith Colls., Geneva, N.Y., 1957-63; vis. asst. prof. Tokyo U., 1963-65; assoc. prof. Ill. Inst. Tech., Chgo., 1966-74, prof. anthropology, 1974-94, prof. emeritus, 1995—. Founder, 1st chmn. John W. Campbell Meml. Award, 1972; guest lectr. Brit. Film Inst., 1986; humanities cons. Champaign (Ill.) Pub. Library H.G. Wells Traveling Exhbn., 1986. Author: La Science Fiction Americaine, 1972, The Cultural Ecology of Chinese Civilization, 1974, China: An Anthropological Perspective, 1976, The Shaving of Karl Marx, 1982, The Prophetic Soul: A Reading of H.G. Wells's "Things to Come", 1987, Robert A. Heinlein for Twayne's United State Authors Series, 1987, Harry Harrison for Twayne's United States Authors Series, 1990, The Annotated H.G. Wells: The Time Machine, 1996, The Annotated H.G. Wells: The Island of Docotor Moreau, 1996, The Annotated H.G. Wells: The Invisible Man, 1998, The Annotated H.G. Wells: The First Men in the Moon, 1998, The Annotated H.G. Wells: When the Sleeper Wakes, 2000, The Annotated H.G. Wells: The War of the Worlds, 2001, The Annotated H.G. Wells: The Sea Lady, 2001, Science Fiction from Wells to Heinlein, 2002, The Annotated H.G. Wells: Man Who Could Work Miracles, 2002, Stonehenge City: A Reconstruction, 2003, Imperial China and the State Cult of Confucius, 2004; sr. author: Stonehenge: The Indo-European Heritage, 1979; co-author: Stonehenge: Where Atlantis Died, 1983; sr. editor: Apeman, Spaceman, 1968; co-editor: Above the Human Landscape, 1972; sci. editor: Amazing, Stories, 1967-69; cons. editor: Contemporary Authors, 1987. Recipient Chris award for best ednl. film, 1974; recipient Cine award Internat. Council Non-Theatrical Events, 1973; named Disting Faculty Lectr. Sigma Xi, 1978; honored with Stover Day Western Md. Coll., 1981 Mem. H.G. Wells Soc., Sci. Fiction Writers Am. Home: 3100 S Michigan Ave Apt 602 Chicago IL 60616-3825

STOVER, WILBUR G., JR., manufacturing executive; BSBA, Wash. State U., 1975. Audit mgr. Cooper & Lybrand; with Micron, 1989, dir. subs. sales; v.p. fin., CFO, Micron Semiconductor, 1992; v.p. fin., CFO Micron Tech., Inc., Boise, Idaho, 1994—. Office: Micron Tech Inc PO Box 6 8000 S Federal Way Boise ID 83707-0006

STOWE, CHARLES ROBINSON BEECHER, management consultant, educator, lawyer; b. Seattle, July 18, 1949; s. David and Edith Beecher (Andrade) Stowe; m. Laura Everett, Mar. 9, 1985. BA, Vanderbilt U., 1971; MBA, U. Tex., Dallas, 1975; JD, U. Houston, 1982; PhD, U. Warsaw, Poland, 1998. Bar: Tex. 1982, US Dist. Ct. (so. dist.), Tex. 1984, US Tax Ct. 1984. Acct. exec. Engleman Co., Dallas, 1974-75; dir. Productive Capital Assoc., 1975-81; instr. Richland Coll., Dallas, 1976; acct. Arthur Andersen and Co., 1976-78; pres. Stowe and Co., 1978—; asst. prof. dept. gen. bus., fin. Coll. Bus. Adminstrn., Sam Houston State U., 1982—, dir. office internat. programs, 1997-2001; part-time pub. rels. cons. Bd. dir., office internat. programs Sam Houston State U., Tex.; adminstrv. intern asst. to pres., 1985. Editor: (book) Houston Journal International Law, 1981—82, ACET Journal of Computor Education and Research, 2002—; co-editor: Knowledge Cafe for Intellect Product and Intellectual Entrepreneurship, 2001, Knowledge Cafe for Intellectual Entrepreneurship, Intellectual Product, Intellectual Capital, 2001; author: (book) Bankruptcy I Micro-Mash Inc., 1989, 1995, The Implications of Foreign Financial Institutions on Poland's Emerging Entrepreneurial Economy, 1999; co-author: CPA; contbr. articles to profl. jour. Team chief, US Mil. liaison, Rep., 1994; founder Young Am.'s Found., 1969—; mem. Trustee Stowe-Day Found., 1979—80; vol., faculty State Bar Tex., Profl. Devel. Program, 1988—; vol., mediator Dispute Resolution Ctr., Montgomery County; mediator so. dist. US Dist. Ct., Tex., 1993; pub. affairs officer George C. Marshall European Ctr. Security Studies, 1997. Capt. Res. USNR, 1971—74. Decorated Navy Achievement medal, Gold Star Navy, US, Def. Meritorious Svc. medal (oak leaf cluster), Navy Meritorious Svc. award; recipient Legion of Merit, Freedoms Found. award; fellow Summer Fellow Tex. Coordinating Bd., 1988, Prince-Babson Fellow Entrepreneurship Symposium, 1991. Mem.: Res. Officers Assn., Naval Res. Assn., Tex. Assn. Realtors, Pub. Rels. Soc. Am., Assn. Computer Educators Tex. (bd. dirs. 2000—03), Tex. State Bar Coll. (bd. dirs. 2001—), Walker County Bar Assn. (pres. 1987—88), State Bar Tex. (vol. faculty profl. devel. program 1988—90, vice chmn. profl. efficiency and econ. rsch. com. 1993, chmn. law office mgmt. com. 1993—94, bd. dirs. 2002—), Am. Arbitration Assn., ABA, US Navy League, Dallas Vanderbilt Club (pres. 1977—78). Office: PO Box 2144 Huntsville TX 77341-2144

STOWE, MADELEINE, actress; b. L.A., Aug. 18, 1958; m. Brian Benben, 1982; 2 children. Films: Stakeout, 1987, Worth Winning, 1989, Tropical Snow, 1989, Revenge, 1990, The Two Jakes, 1990, Closetland, 1991, Unlawful Entry, 1992, The Last of the Mohicans, 1992, Another Stakeout, 1993, Short Cuts, 1993 (Best Supporting Actress award Nat. Soc. Film Critics), China Moon, 1993, Blink, 1994, Bad Girls, 1994, Twelve Monkeys, 1995, The Proposition, 1998, Playing By Heart, 1998, Dancing About Architecture, 1999, Impostor, 1999, The General's Daughter, 1999, We Were Soldiers, 2002, Avenging Angelo, 2002; TV movies: The Nativity, 1978, Beulah Land, 1980, The Gangster Chronicles: An American Story, 1981, Blood and Orchids, 1986, Magnificent Ambersons, 2002, Black Orchid (miniseries). Office: UTA care David Schiff 9560 Wilshire Blvd Ste 500 Beverly Hills CA 90212-2427

STOWE, ROBERT LEE, III, textile company executive; b. Charlotte, N.C., July 3, 1954; s. Robert Lee Jr. and Ruth Link (Harding) S.; m. Christine Ruth Edwards, Jan. 15, 1983; children: Christine Ruth, Lillian Rhyne. BA, Davidson (N.C.) Coll., 1976. Dir., mgmt. trainee R.L. Stowe Mills, Inc., Belmont, N.C., 1976-77, v.p., 1977-79, exec. v.p., 1979-84, chmn. bd., 1984—. Sec., treas. Lakeview Farms, Inc.; pres. Robrt Lee Stowe Jr. Found., Belmont, 1978—; bd. mgrs. Wachovia Bank of N.C., Gaston County; mem.-mgr. McAdams & Stowe, LLC. Trustee Belmont Abbey Coll., 1987-90, Mint Mus. Art, Charlotte, 1989-92, Crossnore (N.C.) Sch., 1987-98, Sci. Museums, Charlotte, 1989-91, Gaston Day Sch., 1994-97, Gaston County C. of C., 1992-95, Mis. of New South; trustee Daniel Jonathan Stowe Conservancy, 1990, pres., 1996-2000, vice-chmn., 2000; deacon, elder local Presbyn. Ch.; bd. dirs. Downtown Belmont, Inc., Gaston County Edn. Found., Gaston County YMCA; bd. trustees Presbyn. Hosp. Found., Charlotte, N.C. Named one of Outstanding Young Men Am., 1979. Mem. Am. Textile Mfrs. Inst. (bd. dirs. 1989-92), Newcomen Soc. U.S., N.C. Textile Found. (bd. dirs. 1986—), Met. Club N.Y., Charlotte Country Club, Gaston Country Club. Republican. Avocations: golf, boating, church activities. Home: 135 N Main St PO Box 232 Belmont NC 28012-0232 Office: RL Stowe Mills Inc 100 N Main St Belmont NC 28012-3104 Office Phone: 704-825-5314. Business E-Mail: rlstowe@rlstowe.com.

STOWELL, CHRISTOPHER R. artistic director, choreographer, retired dancer; b. N.Y.C., June 8, 1966; s. Kent and Francia (Russell) S. Student, Pacific N.W. Ballet Sch., 1979-84, Sch. Am. Ballet, 1984-85. Entered corps de ballet San Francisco Ballet, 1986, promoted to soloist, 1987, prin., 1990—2001; freelance choreographer for ballet and opera cos., 2001—; ballet master Balanchine Trust, 2001—. Guest artist Ballet Met, Ohio, Pacific N.W. Ballet, Seattle, and with Jean Charles Gil, Marseilles, France, Asami Maki Ballet, Tokyo. Created leading roles in Handel-A Celebration, Con Brio, The Sleeping Beauty, New Sleep, Connotations, Pulcinella, Meistens Mozart; other roles include Calcium Light Night, Rubies, The Sons of Horus, The Four Temperaments, Hearts, Tarantella, Flower Festival, La Fille Mal Garde, Haffner Symphony, Forgotten Land, The End, Agon, In the Middle Somewhat Elevated, Le Quattro Stagioni, Swan Lake, Job, Company B, Tchaikousky Pas de Deux, Maelstrom, Mercutio in Romeo and Juliet, The Dance House, Stars and Stripes, Ballo Della Regina, Drink to me Only With Thine Eyes, Pacific; performed in Reykjavik Arts Festival, Iceland, 1990, San Francisco Ballet at the Paris Opera Garnier, 1994, Bolshoi Theatre, Moscow, 1998; artistic dir. Oreg. Ballet Theatre, Portland, 2003—. Avocations: cooking, reading, camping. Office: 818 SE 6th Ave Portland OR 97214

STOWELL, JOSEPH, III, academic administrator; Pres. Moody Bible Inst., Chgo., 1987—. Office: Moody Bible Inst 820 N La Salle Dr Chicago IL 60610-3263 also: Sta WKES-FM PO Box 8888 Saint Petersburg FL 33738-8888

STOWELL, KENT, ballet director; b. Rexburg, Idaho, Aug. 8, 1939; s. Harold Bowman and Maxine (Hudson) S.; m. Francia Marie Russell, Nov. 19, 1965; children: Christopher, Darren, Ethan. Student, San Francisco Ballet Sch., Sch. Am. Ballet; Lead dancer San Francisco Ballet, 1957-62, N.Y.C. Ballet, 1962-68; ballet dir., ballet master Frankfurt (Fed. Republic Germany) Opera Ballet, 1973-77; artistic dir. Pacific N.W. Ballet, Seattle, 1977—; prof. dance Ind. U., Bloomington, 1969-70; bd. dirs. Sch. of Am. Ballet, Dance/USA, Washington, 1986—. Choreographer: Silver Lining, Cinderella, Carmina Burana, Coppelia, Time & Ebb, Faure Requiem, Hail to the Conquering Hero, Firebird, Over the Waves, Nutcracker, The Tragedy of Romeo and Juliet, Delicate Balance, Swan Lake, Time and Ebb, Through Interior Worlds, Quaternary, Orpheus. Bd. dirs. Sch. of Am. Ballet, N.Y.C., 1981—; mem. Goodwill Games Arts Com., Seattle, 1987—; chmn. dance panel NEA, 1981-85. Grantee NEA, 1980, 85; fellow NEA, 1979. Recipient Arts Service award King County Arts Commn., 1985, Outstanding Contbn. to Pacific N.W. Ballet State of Was., 1987, Best Dance Co. award The Weekly Newspaper, Seattle, 1987, Gov. Arts award, 1988, Dance Mag. award, 1996. Office: Pacific NW Ballet 301 Mercer St Seattle WA 98109-4600*

STOWELL, LINDA, communications executive; Bur. chief Phila. AP, 1996. Office: Ste 250 One Franklin Plz Philadelphia PA 19102

STOWELL, ROBERT EUGENE, pathologist, retired educator; b. Cashmere, Wash., Dec. 25, 1914; s. Eugene Francis and Mary (Wilson) S.; m. Eva Mae (Chambers), Dec. 1, 1945; children: Susan Jane, Robert Eugene Jr. Attended, Whitman Coll., 1932-33; BA, Stanford Univ., 1936, MD, 1941; PhD, Washington Univ., 1944. Fellow in cytology Wash. U. Sch. Medicine, St. Louis, 1940-42; rsch. fellow Barnard Free Skin and Cancer Hosp., St. Louis, 1940-42, rsch. assoc., 1942-48; asst. resident in pathology Barnes, McMillan, St. Louis Children's Hosps., St. Louis, 1942-43, resident in pathology, 1943-44, asst. pathologist, 1944-48; instr. in pathology Washington U. Sch. Medicine, St. Louis, 1943-45, asst. prof., assoc. prof., 1948; advanced med. fellow Inst. for Cell Rsch., Stockholm, 1946-47; chmn. dept. oncology U. Kans. Med. Ctr., Kans. City, Kans., 1948-51, prof. pathology and oncology, dir. cancer rsch., 1948-59, chmn., 1951-59; sci. dir. Armed Forces Inst. Pathology, Washington, 1959-67; chmn. dept. pathology Sch. of Medicine U. Calif., Davis, 1967-69, asst. dean Sch. Medicine, 1967-72, prof. pathology Sch. Medicine, 1967-82, prof. emeritus, 1982—; dir. div. pathology Sacramento Med. Ctr., 1967-69. Vis. prof. U. Md. Sch. Medicine, Balt., 1960-67; acting dir. Nat. Ctr. for Primate Biology, U. Calif., Davis, 1968-69, dir., 1969-71; cons. U.S. Atomic Energy comm., Los Alamos, N.Mex., 1949-54; NIH, 1949-74; Cancer Control Div. USPHS, 1949-59, others; mem. adv. med. bd. Leonard Wood Meml. found., Washington, 1965-67, numerous univs.; prin. investigator, chmn. Expert Panel on Authentication Review of Selected Materials Submitted to the FDA Relative to Application of Searle Lab. to Market Aspartame, 1977-78; Assessment of the Practical Risk to Human Health from Nitrilotriacetic Acid in Household Laundry Products, 1984-85. Contbr. 121 articles, 34 abstracts to jour. in field; editor 35 biomed. books, monographs and conf. reports, 1941-88; mem. editorial bd. Cancer Rsch., 1949-59, Lab. Investigation, 1952-71, editor, 1967-71. Recipient Meritorious Svc. Award, Dept. Army, 1963; Exceptional Civilian Svc. Award, Dept. Army, 1965; Disting. Svc. Award U. Calif., 1988, Robert E. Stowell ann. Med. Student Award Outstanding Excellence in Pathology, 1981—; Robert E. Stowell ann. lectureship established U. Calif. Sch. Medicine, 1991 and Am. Registry of Pathology, Washington, 1991; endowed Robert E. Stowell professorship, 2002-. Mem. AMA; Am. Registry of Pathology (bd. dir. 1976-83, exec. com. 1976-82, v.p. 1976-78, pres. 1978-79, Disting. Svc. Award 1995), Am. Assn. Cancer Rsch., Am. Assn. Pathologists (Gold-headed Cane Award 1990), Am. Assn. Pathologists and Bacteriologists (councilor 1965-72, v.p. 1969-70, pres. 1970-71); Am. Soc. Clin. Pathologists; Am. Soc. Exptl. Pathology (councilor 1962-66, v.p. 1963-64, pres. 1964-65); Calif. Med. Soc.; Calif. Soc. Pathologists; Binford-Dammin Soc. Infectious Disease Pathologists; Coll. Am. Pathologists; Histochem. Soc.; Internat. Acad. Pathology (councilor 1954-61, pres.-elect 1958-59, pres. 1995-60); Disting. Svc. Award 1970; Diamond Jubilee Award 1981; Stowell-Orbison Award established 1982—); Soc. Cryobiology (bd. gov. 1968-71); Soc. Exptl. Biology and Medicine; U.S. and Can. Acad. Patholog;, Yolo County Med. Soc.; Assn. Mil. Surgeons U.S. (sustaining membership award 1965), Univ. Associated for Rsch. and Edn. in Path. (bd. dir. 1975-90, sec.-treas. 1978-82, hon. dir. 1990-2002); Sigma Xi; Alpha Omega Alpha. Home: 44752 N El Macero Dr El Macero CA 95618-1090

STOWERS, CARLTON EUGENE, writer; b. Brownwood, Tex., Apr. 14, 1942; s. Ira Milton and Fay Eloise (Stephenson) S.; m. Patricia Ann Folks, Mar. 2, 1981; children: Anson, Ashley. Student, U. Tex., Austin, 1961-63. Sportswriter Abilene (Tex.) Reporter News, 1963-64; sports editor Roswell (N.Mex.) Daily Record, 1964-65; sportswriter Lubbock (Tex.) Avalanche Jour., 1965-67; sports editor Amarillo (Tex.) Globe News, 1967-72; reporter, columnist Dallas Morning News, 1972-81; freelance writer Cedar Hill, Tex., 1981—. Editor Dallas Cowboys Weekly, 1985-89. Author: The Randy Matson Story, 1971, Spirit, 1973, (with E.B. Hughes) Doc, 1976, (with Trent Jones) Where the Rainbows Wait, 1978, pub. softcover as Terlingua Teacher, 1982, (with Wilbur Evans) Champions, 1978, The Overcomers, 1978, (with Roy Rogers and Dale Evans) Happy Trails, 1979 (book clubs awards, Christian Herald Family Bookshelf main selection, selected for talking book program Nat. Library Svc. for Blind and Handicapped), The Unsinkable Titanic Thompson, 1982, softcover, 1988, Journey to Triumph, 1988, (with Steve Perkins and Greg Aiello) Dallas Cowboys Bluebook III, 1982 (Spanish lang. edit. 1982), Partners in Blue: The 100-Year History of the Dallas Police Department, 1983, Friday Night Heroes, 1983, Just One Kiss Baby, 1983, (with Greg Aiello) Dallas Cowboys Bluebook IV, 1983 (Spanish lang. edit. 1983), (with Billy Olson) Reaching Higher, 1984, The Dallas Cowboys: The First 25 Years, 1984, The Cowboy Chronicles, 1984, (ghosted for Pam Lontos) Don't Tell Me It's Impossible Until I've Already Done It, 1988, Careless Whispers, 1986 (Edgar Allen Poe award Mystery Writers Am., Oppie award S.W. Booksellers Assn.), The Cotton Bowl: The First 50 Years, 1986, (with Jarret Bell) Dallas Cowboys Bluebook IX, 1988, (with William C. Dear) Please...Don't Kill Me: The True Story of the Milo Murder, 1989 (Literary Guild selection), (with Larry Wansley) The FBI Undercover: The True Story of Special Agent 'Mandrake', 1989, Innocence Lost, 1990, A Hero Named George, 1991, Hard Lessons, 1994, Open Secrets, 1994, Sins of the Son, 1995, Marcus (with Marcus Allen), 1997, To the Last Breath, 1998 (Edgar Allen Poe award Mystery Writers Am. 1999), (with Rev. Carroll Pickett) Within These Walls, 2002, Scream at the Sky, 2003, Death in a Texas Desert, 2003. Recipient Katie awards Dallas Press Club, 1985-92, Stephen Philben awards Dallas Bar Assn., 1987-92, other journalism awards. Home: 1015 Randy Rd Cedar Hill TX 75104-3035 Office Phone: 972-291-4831. E-mail: cstowers1@comcast.net.

STOWERS, JAMES EVANS, JR., investment company executive; b. Kansas City, Mo., Jan. 10, 1924; s. James Evans Sr. and Laura (Smith) S.; m. Virginia Ann Glasscock, Feb. 4, 1954; children: Pamela, Kathleen, James Evans III, Linda. AB, U. Mo., 1946, BS in Medicine, 1947. Chmn. bd. Am. Century Investment Mgmt. Inc., Am. Century Cos., Inc.; Am. Century Group of Mutual Funds, Kansas City, 1958—. Author: Why Waste Your Money on Life Insurance, 1967, Principles of Financial Consulting, 1971, Yes, You Can...achieve financial independence, 1992. Co-founder, chmn. Stowers Inst. for Med. Rsch., Kansas City, 1995—. Capt. USAAF, 1943-45; with USAFR, 1945-57. Mem. Kansas City C. of C., Sigma Chi Republican. Office: Am Century Svcs 4500 Main St Kansas City MO 64111-1816

STOWERS, JAMES W., III, data processing executive; b. 1958; With Twentieth Century Svcs., Kansas City, Mo., 1979—, pres.; CEO Am. Century Cos., Kansas City, Mo. Office: Am Century Investments 4500 Main St Kansas City MO 64111-1816

STOWERS, MARK DAVID, chemicals executive; b. Houston, Tex., Feb. 9, 1957; s. Charles Henry Stowers, Jr. and Eleanor Ann (Schutz) Fowler; m. Sarah Kent Upham, Sept. 2, 1984; children: Rosemary Diane, Samuel Huntington, Elizabeth Ann. BS in Biology, Appalachian State U., Boone, N.C., 1977; MS in Microbiology, N.C. State U., 1980, PhD in Microbiology, 1982. Postdoctoral assoc. Cornell U., Ithaca, N.Y., 1982-83; sr. project leader NPI, Inc., Salt Lake City, 1983-86; head, biol. scis. rsch. Eastman Kodak Co., Rochester, N.Y., 1986-89; bus. dir. Monsanto Co., St. Louis, 1989-95, v.p. ops. Naples, Fla., 1995—96; v.p. mktg. Seminic Inc., Oxnard, Calif., 1996—98, v.p. bus. devel., 1998—2000; pres., CEO, MBI Internat., Lansing, Mich., 2000—. Bd. dirs. BioPlastics Inc., Natura, Inc., MBI Internat. Bd. dirs. Pierce Coll. Found., 2000—01. Rsch. grantee NSF, 1984, AID, 1985, Dept. Energy, 2001—, EPA, 2001-03, USDA, 2002—. Mem. AAAS, Am. Soc. for Microbiology, Soc. for Indsl. Microbiology, Assn. Univ. Tech. Mgrs., Coun. of Logistic Mgmt., Am. Mgmt. Assn., Inst. Food Technologists, Comml. Devel. Assn., Produce Mktg. Assn., United Fresh Fruit and Vegetable Assn. (sci. and tech. com.), Fla. Fruit and Vegetable Assn. (bd. dirs.). Conservative. Methodist. Achievements include patents for use of a protease in the extraction of Chlamydial, Gonococcal and Herpes Antigens. Avocations: golf, cross country skiing, basketball, fly fishing. Home: 480 Juneberry Ln Okemos MI 48864-4126 Office: MBI Internat 3900 Collins Rd Lansing MI 48910 Office Phone: 517-336-4612. Personal E-mail: mdstowers@yahoo.com.

STOWERS, RUSSELL BRENT, physical therapy educator; b. Amarillo, Tex., July 23, 1969; s. Larry Travis Stowers and Jan Boothe Beck. AAS, Amarillo Coll., 1988—90; BS, Abilene Christian U., 1992—94; MS, Tex. A&M U., 1994. Bd. dirs. Tex. Phys. Therapy Assn., Austin, Nat. Assembly APTA, Wash. D.C. Sr. leadership adv. City of Corpus Christi, Tex. E-S USN, 1987—94. Mem.: Am. Physical Therapy Assn., Am. Legion. Home: 1046 Burkshire Corpus Christi TX 78412 Office: Del Mar Coll 101 Baldwin Corpus Christi TX 78404 Office Phone: 361-698-1847. Business E-Mail: rstowers@delmar.edu.

STOYTCHEVA, LILIA STEFANOVA, concert pianist, educator; b. Sofia, Bulgaria, July 13, 1962; arrived in US, 1995; d. Stefan Sotirov Stoytchev and Liliana Georgieva Sarafova. M in Piano summa cum laude, Bulgarian State Conservatory, 1987; M of Music summa cum laude, Winthrop U., 1997; doctorate in piano-performance, U. Iowa, 1997—. Instr. piano Bulgarian State Conservatory, Sofia, 1988—92; asst. prof. piano Sofia's U. Kliment Ohridski, 1988—90; prof. piano State Conservatory, Czech Republic, 1992—95; asst. prof. Ctrl. State U., Wilberforce, Ohio, 2003—. Composer: 1300 Anniversary Bulgaria, 1981; musician (solo pianist): Symphony Orch. of the Bulgarian State Conservatory, 1987; musician: (orchestral pianist) Symphony Orchestra of Biel/Bienne, 1992, The Jihoceske Chamber Orchestra of South Bohemia, 1992, Hancher Auditorium, 2002; musician: (pianist) Harper Hall, 2001, Clapp Hall, 2001—02, Rudolf Steiner House and St. Cyprianus Ch. Eng., 2001, Concert Hall at the Conservatory of Stravanger, 2002, Salle Munch at Ecole Normal de Musique, 2002, others. Recipient award, Nat. Composition Competition, Bulgaria, 1981, Internat. Piano Competition, Italy, 1988, Maia Quartet Competition, 2001, John Simms award, 1998—99, 2001; fellow Internat. Master Classes with Norma Fisher, London, UK, 2001, Internat. Master Classes with Nelson Delle-Vigne, John Perry, Phillippe Entremont and Einar Nokleberg, Paris, 2002; grantee, George Soros Found. Open Soc., Sofia, 1992; scholar, Internat. Piano Workshop, 2002, Walter Hautzig Piano Master Classes, 1995—96, Piano Master Classes with Rudolf Buchbinder and Victor Merzhanov, 1992—93; Grad. Coll. scholar, U. Iowa, 2001. Mem.: Studio of the Young Musician, Coll. Music Soc., Phi Kappa Phi. Avocations: travel, movies, painting, sculpting, languages. Personal E-mail: lstoytch@hotmail.com.

STRAATSMA, BRADLEY RALPH, ophthalmologist, educator; b. Grand Rapids, Mich., Dec. 29, 1927; s. Clarence Ralph and Lucretia Marie (Nicholson) S.; m. Ruth Campbell, June 16, 1951; children: Cary Ewing, Derek, Greer. Student, U. Mich., 1947; MD cum laude, Yale U., 1951; DSc (hon.), Columbia U., 1984; JD cum laude, U. West LA, 2002. Diplomate Am. Bd. Ophthalmology (vice chmn. 1979, chmn. 1980). Intern New Haven Hosp., Yale U., 1951-52; resident in ophthalmology Columbia U., N.Y.C., 1955-58; spl. clin. trainee Nat. Inst. Neurol. Diseases and Blindness, Bethesda, Md., 1958-59; assoc. prof. surgery/ophthalmology UCLA Sch. Medicine, 1959-63, chief div. ophthalmology, dept. surgery, 1959-68, prof. surgery/ophthalmology, 1963-68, prof. ophthalmology, 1968—2001, dir. Jules Stein Eye Inst., 1964-94, chmn. dept. ophthalmology, 1968-94, prof. emeritus, 2001—; ophthalmologist-in-chief UCLA Med. Ctr., 1968-94. Lectr. numerous univs. and profl. socs. 1971—; cons. to surgeon gen. USPHS, mem. Vision Research Tng. Com., Nat. Inst. Neurol. Diseases and Blindness, NIH, 1959-63, mem. neurol. and sensory disease program project com., 1964-68; chmn. Vision Research Program Planning Com., Nat. Adv. Eye Council, Nat. Eye Inst., NIH, 1973-75, 75-77, 85-89; mem. med. adv. bd. Internat. Eye Found., 1970-79; mem. adv. com. on basic clin. research Nat. Soc. to Prevent Blindness, 1971-87; mem. med. adv. com. Fight for Sight, 1960-83; bd. dirs. So. Calif. Soc. to Prevent Blindness, 1967-77, Ophthalmic Pub. Co., 1975-93, v.p. 1990-93, Pan-Am. Ophthalmol. Found., 1985-95; chmn. sci. adv. bd. Ctr. for Partially Sighted, 1984-87; mem. nat. adv. panel Found. for Eye Research, Inc., 1984-94; mem. cons. com. Palestra Oftalmologica Panamericana, 1976-81; coord. com. Nat. Eye Health Edn. Program, 1989; mem. sci. adv. bd. Rsch. to Prevent Blindness, Inc., 1993—2003. Editor-in-chief Am. Jour. Ophthalmology, 1993-2002; mem. editorial bd. UCLA Forum in Med. Scis., 1974-82, Am. Jour. Ophthalmology, 1974-91, Am. Intra-Ocular Implant Soc. Jour., 1978-79, EYE-SAT Satellite-Relayed Profl. Edn. in Ophthalmology, 1982-86; mng. editor von Graefe's Archive for Clin. and Exptl. Ophthalmology, 1976-88; contbr. over 500 articles to med. jours. Trustee John Thomas Dye Sch., Los Angeles, 1967-72. Lt. USNR, 1952-54. Recipient William Warren Hoppin award N.Y. Acad. Medicine, 1956, Univ. Service award UCLA Alumni Assn., 1982, Miguel Aleman Found. medal, 1992, Benjamin Boyd Humanitarian award Pan Am. Assn. Ophthalmology, 1991, Lucian Howe medal, Am. Ophthalmological Soc., 1992, Internat. Gold Medal award 3rd Singapore Nat. Eye Ctr. Internat. Meeting and 11th Internat. Meeting on Cataract, Implant, Microsurgery and Refractive Keratoplasty, 1998, award of merit in retinal rsch. Retina Rsch. Found., 2002, Jose Rizal gold medal Asia-Pacific Acad. Ophthalmology, 2003. Fellow Royal Australian Coll. Ophthalmologists (hon.); mem. Academia Ophthalmologica Internationales (pres. 1998-2002), Am. Acad. Ophthalmology (bd. councillors 1981, Life Achievement award 1999), Found. of Am. Acad. Ophthalmology (trustee 1989, chmn. bd. trustees 1989-92), Am. Acad. Ophthalmology and Otolaryngology (pres. 1977), Am. Soc. Cataract and Refractive Surgery, AMA (asst. sec. ophthalmology sect. 1962-63, sec. 1963-66, chmn. 1966-67, coun. 1970-74), Am. Ophthalmol. Soc. (coun. 1985-90, v.p. 1992, pres. 1993), Assn. Rsch. in Vision and Ophthalmology (Mildred Weisenfeld award 1991), Assn. U. Profs. of Ophthalmology (trustee 1969-75, pres.-elect 1973-74, pres. 1974-75), Assn. VA Ophthalmologists, Calif. Med. Assn. (mem. ophthalmology adv. panel 1972-94, chmn. 1974-79, sci. bd. 1973-79, ho. of dels. 1974, 77, 79), Chilean Soc. Ophthalmology (hon.), Columbian Soc. Ophthalmology (hon.), Glaucoma Soc. Internat. Congress of Ophthalmology (hon.), Heed Ophthalmic Found. (chmn., bd. dirs. 1990-98), Hellenic Ophthalmol. Soc. (hon.), Internat. Coun. Ophthalmology (bd. dirs. 1993—), Internat. Coun. Ophthalmology Found. (pres. 2002—), LA County Med. Assn., LA Soc. Ophthalmology, Pan-Am. Assn. Ophthalmology (coun. 1972—, pres. elect 1985-87, pres. 1987-89), Peruvian Soc. Ophthalmology (hon.), Retina Soc., Barraquer Inst. Ophthalmology (pres. 1996—), Academia Ophthalmol. Internat. (pres. 1998-2002), Internat. Coun. Ophthalmology (pres. Found. 2002—,

Jules Francois medal 2002), The Jules Gonin Club. Republican. Presbyterian. Avocations: music, scuba diving. Home: 3031 Elvido Dr Los Angeles CA 90049-1107 Office: UCLA 100 Stein Plz Los Angeles CA 90095-7065

STRACHER, DOROTHY ALTMAN, education educator, consultant; b. N.Y.C., May 11, 1934; d. Joseph and Gussie (Newman) Altman; m. Alfred Stracher, July 4, 1954; children: Cameron Altman, Adam Reed, Erica Terri. BA, Bklyn. Coll., 1955; MA, Columbia U., 1957; postgrad., U. Copenhagen, 1958-59; acad. vis., Oxford (Eng.) U., 1973-74; PhD, Hofstra U., 1979. Cert. English and social sci. tchr., N.Y. Coordinator secondary reading Cen. Moriches (N.Y.) Sch. Dist., 1974-78; coordinator reading Ea. Williston (N.Y.) Sch. Dist., 1978-79; specialist reading and writing SUNY, Old Westbury, 1979-81; adj. prof. dept. reading Hofstra U., Hempstead, N.Y., 1979-82; asst. prof. edn. L.I. U., Bklyn., 1982-83, Coll. New Rochelle, N.Y., 1983-85; sr. learning diagnostic specialist child devel. div. L.I. Jewish Hosp., Bklyn., 1985-86; prof. Dowling Coll., Oakdale, N.Y., 1986—, acad. chair Sch. Edn., 1991-93, coord. elem. edn. dept., 2000-01, acad. chair Sch. Edn., 2001—; vis. prof. U. East London, London, 1994. Cons. Johnson & Johnson, Inc., Princeton, N.J., 1982—, Sanford (Fla.) Sch. Dist., 1983, Lawrence (N.Y.) Sch. Dist., 1984, Sch. Dist. 7, N.Y.C., 1984—. Author: (with others) First the Fundamentals, 1980, What Do You Call a Well-Behaved Martian?, A Manual For Thinkers' Parents, 1981, Integrating Assessment, 1982; editor: Differentiated Curricula, 1986, A Literature Based Integrated Curriculum: Grades Pre-K-, 1989, Successful Strategies for Learning Disabled College Students: Reading, Writing and Reasoning, 1991, Cognitive Development Through Literacy for Inner City Students: A Curriculum Staff Development Project in the South Bronx in Commitment to Excellence, 2002; contbg. author: Immortal Longings, 2003; contbr. articles to profl. jours. Bd. dirs. Roslyn (N.Y.) Sch. Dist., 1975-84, v.p., 1980-82, pres., 1982-84; mem. adv. bd. Children's Sch. Sci., Woods Hole, Mass., 1976-82. Mem. Coun. for Exceptional Children, Orton Soc., Internat. Reading Assn., Nat. Assn. for Gifted Edn., LWV (bd. dirs. 1961-70), NOW, Kappa Delta Pi. Avocations: reading, writing, traveling. Home: 47 The Oaks Roslyn NY 11576-1704 Office Phone: 631-244-3306. E-mail: strached@dowling.edu., dastracher@cs.com.

STRACK, HAROLD ARTHUR, retired electronics company executive, retired air force officer, planner, analyst, author, musician; b. San Francisco, Calif., Mar. 29, 1923; s. Harold Arthur and Catheryn Jenny (Johnsen) S.; m. Margaret Madeline Decker, July 31, 1945; children: Carolyn, Curtis, Tamara. Student, San Francisco Coll., 1941, Sacramento Coll., 1947, Sacramento State Coll., 1948, U. Md., 1962, Indsl. Coll. Armed Forces, 1963. Commd. 2d lt. USAAF, 1943; advanced through grades to brig. gen. USAF, 1970; comdr. 1st Radar Bomb Scoring Group Carswell AFB, Ft. Worth, 1956-59; vice comdr. 90th Strategic Missile Wing SAC Warren AFB, Cheyenne, Wyo., 1964; chief, strategic nuclear br., spl. studies group Joint Chiefs of Staff, 1965-67, dep. asst. to chmn. JCS for strategic arms negotiations, 1968; comdr. 90th Strategic Missile Wing SAC Warren AFB, Cheyenne, 1969-71; chief Studies, Analysis and Gaming Agy. Joint Chiefs Staff, Washington, 1972-74, ret., 1974; v.p., mgr. MX Peacekeeper Program v.p. strategic planning Northrop Electronics Divsn., Hawthorne, Calif., 1974-88; ret., 1988. 1st clarinetist, Cheyenne Symphony Orch., 1969-71. Mem. Cheyenne Frontier Days Com., 1970-71. Decorated D.S.M., Legion of Merit, D.F.C., Air medal, Purple Heart, Presdl. citation, Army, Air Force and Joint Svc. Commendation medals. Mem. Inst. Nav., Am. Def. Preparedness Assn., Air Force Assn., Aerospace Edn. Found., Am. Fedn. Musicians, Orde Pour le Merite, Cheyenne Frontier Days "Heels". Home: 707 James Ln Incline Village NV 89451-9612 *The precepts which have guided me recognize the dignity of the individual and human rights. I believe that living by the Golden Rule contributes to the quality of life by making us better and more useful citizens while favorably influencing others. Integrity, ideals, and high standards reinforce one's own character. While taking pride in accomplishment, show gratitude for opportunity and humility for success. Lead by example and always do your best. Service to humanity and country is the highest calling, and the satisfaction of a job well done, approbation, respect and true friendship are one's greatest rewards.*

STRACK, STEPHEN NAYLOR, psychologist; b. Rome, NY, Nov. 13, 1955; s. Ralph and Grace (Naylor) S.; m. Leni Ferrero. BA, U. Calif., Berkeley, 1978; PhD, U. Miami, Fla., 1983. Psychologist L.A. County Dept. Mental Health, 1984-85; staff psychologist VA Outpatient Clinic, L.A., 1985—, dir. tng., 1992-97. Clin. assoc. U. So. Calif., L.A., 1986-95; adj. prof. Calif. Sch. Profl. Psychology, L.A., 1989—; clin. prof. Fuller Grad. Sch. Psychology, Pasadena, Calif., 1986—. Author (test): Personality Adjective Check List, 1987; co-author (book): Differentiating Normal and Abnormal Personality, 1994, Death and the Quest for Meaning, 1997, Essentials of Million Inventories Assessment, 1999, 2d edit., 2002; cons. editor Jour. Personality Disorders, N.Y.C., 1992—, Omega, 1997—; Jour. Personality Assessment, 1999—. U.S. Dept. VA grantee, 1986-93, 96-2000. Fellow APA, Soc. for Personality Assessment; mem. Internat. Soc. for the Study of Personality Disorders, Calif. Psychol. Assn., Soc. for Interpersonal Theory and Rsch., Soc. for Rsch. in Psychopathology, Western Psychol. Assn., Sigma Xi. Office: VA Outpatient Clinic 351 E Temple St Los Angeles CA 90012-3328 E-mail: snstrack@aol.com.

STRADER, JAMES DAVID, lawyer; b. Pitts., June 30, 1940; s. James Lowell and Tyra Fredrika (Bjorn) S.; m. Ann Wallace, Feb. 8, 1964; children: James Jacob, Robert Benjamin. BA, Mich. State U., 1962; JD, U. Pitts., 1965. Bar: Pa. 1966, US Dist. Ct. (we. dist.) Pa. 1966, US Dist. Ct. (ea. dist.) Pa. 1973, US Dist. Ct. (mid. dist.) Pa. 1985, US Ct. Appeals (4th and 5th cirs.) 1977, US Ct. Appeals (3d and 11th cirs.) 1981, US Supreme Ct. 1982, W.Va. 1996. Assoc. Peacock, Keller & Yohe, Washington, 1967-68; atty. US Steel Corp., Pitts., 1968-77, gen. atty. worker's compensation, 1977-84; assoc. Caroselli, Spagnolli & Beachler, Pitts., 1984-87; ptnr. Dickie, McCamey & Chilcote, Pitts., 1987—. Pres. bd. trustees Mt. Lebanon Pub. Libr., 2002—; del. Dem. Mid-Yr. Conv., 1974; mem. Dem. Nat. Platform Com., 1976; commr. Mt. Lebanon, Pa., 1974—78. Capt. U.S. Army, 1965—67. Mem. ABA (sr. vice-chmn. worker's compensation com. 1978-94), Pa. Bar Assn. (chmn. worker's compensation law sect. 1994-95), Pa. Bar Inst. (bd. dirs. 2001-),State Bar W.Va., Allegheny County Bar Assn., Valley Brook Country Club. Democrat. Presbyterian. Office: Dickie McCamey & Chilcote 2 PPG Pl Ste 400 Pittsburgh PA 15222-5491 Office Phone: 412-392-5419. E-mail: stradej@dmclaw.com.

STRADLEY, WILLIAM JACKSON, lawyer; b. Houston, Oct. 27, 1939; s. Samuel and Mary Stradley; m. Emmalee H. Stradley, Apr. 16, 1960; children: Lisa D., William M. BS, U. Houston, 1964, JD, 1967. Bar: Tex. 1967, U.S. Dist. Ct. (so. dist.) Tex. 1967, U.S. Ct. Appeals (5th cir.) 1967, U.S. Supreme Ct. 1970, cert.: (civil trial law), Tex. Bd. Legal Specialization (personal injury trial law). Of counsel Mithoff & Jacks, L.L.P.; mem. faculty trial advocacy course Law Sch. U. Houston, 1982. Pres. Police Adv. Com., 1981—84, sec., 1980—81; bd. dirs. Houston Coun. Human Rels., 1982—84; mem. adminstrv. bd. St. Luke's United Meth. Ch.; co-chair fed. judiciary appts. com. State Bar Tex., 1991, mem. cont. legal edn. com., 1991, adminstrn. justice com., spl. com. professionalism. Recipient Pub. Svc. award, Houston Police Dept., 1984. Mem.: Assn. Trial Lawyers Am., Tex. Trial Lawyers Assn. (dir. emeritus, chmn. ethics com., by-laws com.), Houston Bar Assn. (chmn. tort and compensation sect. 1980—81, chmn. cont. legal edn. com., com. on professionalism), Houston Trial Lawyers Assn. (bd. dirs. 1980—82, v.p. 1983—84, pres. 1985—86), Am. Bd. Trial Advocates (pres., treas. 1980—82, v.p. Houston 1983—84), Houston Bar Found. (charter), The Houstonians Club, Houston Club. Home: 64 E Broad Oaks Dr Houston TX 77056-1226 Office: 3450 One Allen Ctr Houston TX 77002

STRAFACI, SAMUEL ANTHONY, academic administrator, consultant; b. N.Y.C., July 6, 1952; s. Sam Strafaci and Mildred Ciulla; m. Susan K. Parker, Sept. 28, 1985. BA in English, Calif. State U., Long Beach, 1975, MPA, 1979. With McDonnell Douglas Corp., Long Beach, Huntington Beach, Calif., 1979—85; lectr. Calif. State U., Dominguez Hill, 1984, dir. employee rels. Office Chancellor Long Beach, 1990—93, sr. dir. labor rels., 1993—2001, interim vice chancellor human resources divsn., 1996—99, asst. vice chancellor human rels., 2000—. Mem. bd. advisors Calif. Pub. Employee Rels. Reporter; contbr. articles to profl. jours. Mem.: Indsl. Rels. Rsch. Assn., Coll. and Univ. Pers. Adminstrs., Nat. Acad. Academic Pers. Adminstrs. (sec.-treas. 1998—99, v.p. 1999—2000, pres. 2000—01), Nat. Ctr. Study Collective Bargaining Higher Edn. and Professions (mem. nat. adv. com.). Avocations: golf, skiing, reading, travel, cooking. Home: 235 Pomona Ave Long Beach CA 90803 Office: Calif State U 401 Golden Shore 4th Fl Long Beach CA 90802-4210 Office Phone: 562-951-4400. Office Fax: 562-951-4890. Business E-Mail: sstrafaci@calstate.edu.

STRAHAN, MICHAEL, professional football player; b. Houston, Nov. 21, 1971; m. Jean Strahan. Student, Tex. State U. Defensive end N.Y. Giants, 1993—. Co-chair Meet the Giants Fundraisers. Named First Team All-American, 1992, NFL Defensive Player of the Yr., 2001; named to NFL Pro-Bowl, 1997—99, 2001—03. Achievements include set NFL single season sack record (22.5), 2001. Office: Giants Stadium East Rutherford NJ 07073

STRAHILEVITZ, MEIR, inventor, researcher, psychiatry educator; b. Beirut, July 13, 1935; s. Jacob and Chana Strahilevitz; m. Aharona Nattiv, 1958; children: Michal, Lior. MD, Hadassah Hebrew U. Med. Sch., 1963. Diplomate Am. Bd. Psychiatry and Neurology, Royal Coll. Physicians and Surgeons Can. Asst. prof. Washington U. Med. Sch., St. Louis, 1971-74; assoc. prof. So. Ill. U., Springfield, 1974-77, U. Chgo., 1977, U. Tex. Med. Br., Galveston, 1978-81; chmn. dept. psychiatry Kaplan Hosp., Rehovot, Israel, 1987-88; clin. assoc. prof. U. Wash., Seattle, 1981-88; prof. U. Tex. Med. Sch., Houston, 1988-92. Contbr. articles to profl. jours. Fellow Am. Psychiat. Assn., Royal Coll. Physicians and Surgeons Can. Achievements include patents for immunological and affinity adsorption methods and devices for removing species from the blood circulatory system; specific adsorption devices with automatic regeneration of adsorbent utilized in automated fluid purification and analytical and preparatory applications; for treatment methods for psychoactive drug dependence; for immunological methods for treating psychoactive drug intoxication; methods of improved targeting of drugs and visualization ligands, particularly in the treatment and diagnosis of cancer; invention of use of antibodies to receptors and their fragments as drugs, of immunoadsorption treatment of hyperlipidemia, cancer, autoimmune disease, atherosclerosis and coronary artery disease; immunoassay methods for psychoactive drugs; discovery of the protective effects of Nitric Oxide (NO) on psychiatric patients. Office: PO Box 25008 Seattle WA 98165-1908

STRAHM, SAMUEL EDWARD, veterinarian; b. Fairview, Kans., Feb. 9, 1936; s. Silas Tobias and Martha Mary (Beyer) S.; m. Barbara Jean Wenger, June 1, 1958; children: Gregory Lee, Bryan Scott, Andrea Marie Enloe. BS, DVM, Kansas State U., 1959. Owner Osage Animal Clinic Inc., Pawhuska, Okla., 1959—, pres., 1985—. Bd. dirs. 1st Nat. Bank, Pawhuska, Okla.; bd. cons. Profl. Exam Svc., 1990-2000; adv. bd. USDA Users, 1991-95; adv. com. Pew Nat. Health Profession Vet. Medicine, 1991; state adv. coun. Okla. Coop. Extension Svcs., 2000—, chmn.-elect, 2000-01, chmn., 2001-04. Bd. dirs. Okla. Sch. Bd. Assn., 1977-98, 2d v.p., 1993, 1st v.p., 1994, pres., 1996; active Okla. All-State Sch. Bd., 1993, Pawhuska Sch. Bd., 1974-98, 2001—, pres., 1991-98, 2003—; active Pawhuska Planning Commn., 1965-70, Okla. State U. Centennial Commn., Stillwater, 1986-91; bd. dirs. Nat. Sch. Bd. Assn., 1996-98, exec. com., 1997-99, western reg. chmn., 1996. Recipient Disting. Alumni award Coll. Vet. Medicine Kans. State U., 1994, Fairview HS, 2004, Outstanding Svc. award Nat. Sch. Bds. Assn., 1997, Disting. Svc. award Nat. Bd. Exam. Com., 2000, Friend of Yr. award Okla. Coop. Extension, 2002. Mem. AVMA (pres. 1989-90, coun. on govt. affair 1992-98, coun. on edn. 2002—, AVMA award 1986), Am. Vet. Med. Found. (chmn. 1995-98, vice chair 2003—), Am. Assn. Theriogenealogy, Am. Assn. Bovine Practitioners (Practioner of Yr. award 2002), Am. Assn. Vet. State Bds., Am. Assn. Food Hygiene Vets. (bd. dirs. 2000—), Nat. Bd. Vet. Med. Examiners (Disting. Svc. award 2000), Okla. Vet. Med. Assn. (all offices from 1959, Veterinarian of Yr. 1990, Disting. Svc. award 1998), Kans. Vet. Med. Assn., Okla. Bd. Vet. Med. Examiners (pres.), Pawhuska C. of C. (pres. 1968), Pawhuska Jaycees (all offices 1959-69), Toastmasters Club. Republican. Baptist. Avocations: gardening, fishing, flying. Home: PO Box 1256 Pawhuska OK 74056-1256 Office: Osage Animal Clinic Inc PO Box 1209 Pawhuska OK 74056-1209

STRAIGHT, CATHY, editor; Dep. mng. editor Nashville Tennessean; with editor-development program Pioneer Press divsn. Knight Ridder; mng. editor features and sports St. Paul Pioneer Press, 2002—. Recipient Newsroom Supr. Recognition award, Gannett, 1999. Office: St Paul Pioneer Press 345 Cedar St Saint Paul MN 55101*

STRAIGHT, ELSIE HOSKING, retired art librarian, sculptor; b. Moresby, Cumberland, Eng., 1914; arrived in U.S., 1923, naturalized, 1926; d. Thomas E. and Anne (Molyneaux) Hosking; 1 child, Elaine W. Sanders. AA, Art Inst. Pitts., 1940, NY Sch. Applied Design, 1941; BA, Roger Williams Coll., 1969; MLS, U. RI, 1974. Libr. St. Raphael Acad., Pawtucket, RI, 1960—68, Elmhurst Acad., Portsmouth, RI, 1968—74; libr. dir. Ringling Sch. Art and Design, Sarasota, Fla., 1974—81; ret.; cons. U. South Fla., Sarasota, 1981—. Manatee Art League, Bradenton, Fla., 1980—82, 1983, 1984, Plaza Art Show, Sarasota, 1983, Longboat Key Art Ctr., 1984; author: (novels) Between the Dark and the Daylight, 2001, Land of the Dead, 2002. Mem.: Manatee Writers Guild, Fla. West Coast Writers, Ringling Sch. Art Libr. Assn., Longboat Key Art Ctr., Art League Manatee County, Art Librarian's Soc. (dir. 1980). Avocation: writing. Home: 435 Edwards Dr Sarasota FL 34243-2038

STRAIGHT, RICHARD COLEMAN, photobiologist, natural philosopher; b. Rivesville, W.Va., Sept. 8, 1937; BA, U. Utah, 1961, PhD in Molecular Biology, 1967. Asst. dir. radiation biology summer inst. U. Utah, 1961-63; supervisory chemist med. svc. VA Hosp., 1965—; dir. VA Venom Rsch. Lab., 1975—; adminstrv. officer rsch. svc. VA Ctr., 1980—; dir. Dixon laser inst. U. Utah, Salt Lake City, 1985-90; pres. Western Inst. for Biomed. Rsch., Salt Lake City, 1990—2003. Dir. Utah Ctr. for Photo Medicine, Salt Lake City, 1993-; assoc. chief of staff for rsch. VA Salt Lake City Health Care Sys., 1997-2003; chmn. bd. dirs. VAMCU FEd. Credit Union, 1980-; cons. to NIH, NSF, Dept. Def., 1985-. Assoc. editor Lasers in Surgery and Medicine, 1990-95, Jour. Biomed. Optics, 1998—. Mem. AAAS, Am. Chem. Soc., Am. Soc. Photobiology, Biophysics Soc., Am. Soc. for Laser Medicine and Surgery, Utah Life Sci. Industries Assn. (charter). Achievements include research in photodynamic action on biomonomers and biopolymers, tumor immunology, effect of antigens on mammary adenocarcinoma of C3H mice, biochemical changes in aging, venom toxicology, mechanism of action of photoactive drugs, optical imaging and spectroscopy. Office: Prothérics-Utah Univ Utah PO Box 58663 Salt Lake City UT 84158 Office Phone: 801-913-4799. E-mail: rcsrcsrcs3@aol.com.

STRAIN, JAMES ARTHUR, lawyer; b. Alexandria, La., Oct. 11, 1944; s. William Joseph and Louise (Moore) S.; m. Cheryl Sue Williamson, Aug. 19, 1967; children: William Joseph, Gordon Richard, Elizabeth Parks. BS in Econs., Ind. U., 1966, JD, 1969. Bar: Ind. 1969, U.S. Dist. Ct. (so. dist.) Ind. 1969, U.S. Ct. Appeals (7th cir.) 1972, U.S. Supreme Ct. 1975, U.S. Ct. Appeals (5th cir.) 1978. Instr. Law Sch. Ind. U., Indpls., 1969-70; law clk. to Hon. John S. Hastings 7th Cir. Ct. Appeals, Chgo., 1970-71; assoc. Cahill, Gordon & Reindel, N.Y.C., 1971-72; law clk. to Hon. William H. Rehnquist U.S. Supreme Ct., Washington, 1972-73; assoc. Barnes, Hickam, Pantzer & Boyd, Indpls., 1973-75; ptnr. Barnes, Hickam, Pantzer & Boyd (name changed to Barnes & Thornburg), 1976-96, Sommer & Barnard, PC, Indpls., 1996—. Adj. asst. prof. law Ind. U. Sch. Law, 1986-92. Mem., bd. dirs. The Penrod Soc., Indpls., 1976—, Indpls. Symphonic Choir, 1988-91, Festival Music Soc., Indpls., 1990-96. Mem. 7th Cir. Bar Assn. (meetings chmn. Ind. chpt. 1979-88, portraits 1988-89, bd. govs. 1989—, 1st v.p. 1995, pres. 1996). Avocations: photography, music. Office: Sommer Barnard Ackerson PC Ste 3500 One Indiana Sq Indianapolis IN 46204 Office Phone: 317-713-3460. Business E-Mail: strain@sbalawyers.com.

STRAIN, JAMES ELLSWORTH, pediatrician, retired association administrator; b. Lincoln, Nebr., Apr. 23, 1923; s. Elmer Ellsworth and Tessa Elizabeth (Stevens) Strain; m. Ruby Lee Shepard; children: James A., John D., Janet M. Strain McKinney, Jeffrey Lee Phillips-Strain. AB, Phillips U., Enid, Okla., 1945; MD, U. Colo., Denver, 1947. Diplomate Am. Bd. Pediat. (examiner 1984-89, mem. 1989-93, emeritus mem. 1993—). Intern Mpls. Gen. Hosp., 1947—48; resident in pediat. Denver Children's Hosp., 1948—50, pres. med. staff, 1964, dir. genetic unit, 1982—86; pvt. practice specializing in pediat. Denver, 1950—86; exec. dir. Am. Acad. Pediat., Elk Grove Village, Ill., 1986—93, ret., 1993. Pres. med. bd. Colo. Gen. Hosp., 1969—70; clin. prof. pediat. U. Colo. Med. Ctr., 1969—86, 1993—, U. Chgo., 1987—93; mem. Colo. Med. Adv. Coun. for Title 19, 1968—75, chmn., 1968—71; mem. Task Force on Iowa Health Care Stds. Project, 1984—85; presenter numerous profl. confs. Editl. bd. Pediat. in Rev., reviewer Jour. Pediat.; contbr. articles to profl. publs. Mem. Colo. Commn. on Children and Youth, 1971—75; trustee Phillips U., 1974—. Capt. U.S. Army, 1953—55. Recipient Disting. Alumnus award, Phillips U., 1974, Florence Sabin award, U. Colo., 1984, Excellence in Pub. Svc. award, U.S. Surgeon Gen., 1988, Abraham Jacobi award, AMA and Am. Acad. Pediat., 1994, James E. Strain Child Advocacy award established in his name, Denver Children's Hosp., 1983. Fellow: Am. Acad. Pediat. (Clifford Grulee award 1985); mem.: AMA, APHA, Inst. Medicine NAS, Ambulatory Pediatric Assn., Can. Pediatric Soc., Denver Med. Soc., Colo. Med. Soc., Alpha Omega Alpha. Republican. Mem. Christian Ch. (Disciples Of Christ). Avocations: fishing, sports, reading.

STRAIN, LUCILLE BREWTON, education educator, researcher; b. Florence, S.C. d. William O. and Jurheutha (Gibbs) Brewton; m. Winston M. Strain (dec. 1984); 1 child, Rada Ruth Higgins. BA, Benedict Coll., 1943; MEd, Ohio State U., 1954, PhD, 1965. Cert. elem., secondary teaching, adminstrn., supervision. Tchr. Columbus (Ohio) Pub. Schs., 1950-62; prof. various U., 1965-79; policy analyst Nat. Ctr. Edn. Stats., Washington, 1979-83; from coord. to prof. and chmn. dept. edn. Bowie (Md.) State U., 1983-89, prof. edn., coord. grad. reading edn., 1989—. Nat. policy fellow Inst. Edn. Leadership, Washington, 1979-80; mem. adv. coun. edn. stats. Nat. Ctr. Edn. Stats., Washington, 1982-85. Author: Accountability in Reading Instruction, 1976; contbr. articles to profl. jours. Recipient grant, U.S. Dept. Edn., Washington, 1989, Bowie State U., 1989, President's Tchg. award, 2003. Mem.: Am. Assn. Colleges for Fla. Edn. (AACTE), Am. Edn. Rsch. Assn. (AERA), Nat. Coun. Tchr. of English (membership com. 1999—), Nat. Assn. Multicultural Edn., Assn. Tchr. Educators (corp. by-laws com. 1990—93, meetings com. 1998—2002, planning com. 2003—), Internat. Reading Assn. (tchrs. rsch. com. 1991—93, chmn. internat. projects and activities com. State of Md. chpt.), Phi Delta Kappa, Pi Lambda Theta. Home: 5508 Vantage Point Rd Columbia MD 21044-2632 Business E-Mail: lstrain@bowiestate.edu.

STRAIR, ROGER K. oncologist; MD, Albert Einstein Coll. Med., 1981. Diplomate Am. Bd. Internal Medicine. Intern Brigham & Womens Hosp., Boston, 1981—82, resident in internal medicine, 1982—84; fellow in hematology/oncology Harvard Med. Sch., Boston, 1985—88; physician Cancer Inst. N.J., New Brunswick. Office: Cancer Inst NJ 195 Little Albany St New Brunswick NJ 08903

STRAIT, NICK EDWARD, elementary school educator; b. Huntington, Ind., Aug. 21, 1967; s. Dane and Patricia Sue (Gensic) Strait; m. Beth Armstrong; 1 child, Jacob Luke. BS in Edn., Purdue U., 1989. Tech. tchr. Montpelier Mid. Sch., 1990—97, Blackford H.S., 1997—98, Huntington North H.S., 1998—99; archaeologist Ind. State U. Field Lab., 1999—2000; archaeologist, field supr. Cojeen Archaeol. Svcs., 2000—01; tchr. Carroll H.S., Ft. Wayne, Ind., 2001—03, Alexandria (Ind.) Mid. Sch., 2003—. Cert. hunting guide, Wyo. Achievements include supervised largest seismic archaeological survey in Oklahoma (Eufala Lake). Avocations: fishing, archaeology. Home: 922 N County Line Rd Markle IN 46770

STRAIT, VIOLA EDWINA WASHINGTON, librarian; b. El Paso, Tex., Aug. 29, 1925; d. Leroy Wentworth and Viola Edwina (Wright) Washington; m. Freeman Adams, Mar. 6, 1943; 1 child, Norma Jean (Mrs. Louis Lee James); m. Clifford Moody, Jan. 8, 1950; 1 child, Viola Edwina III (Mrs. Paul M. Cunningham); m. Amos O. Strait, Dec. 9, 1972. Bus. cert., Tillotson Coll., 1946, BA, 1948; MS in Libr. Sci., U. So. Calif., 1954. Substitute tchr. El Paso Pub. Schs., 1948; sec., bookkeeper U.S.O.-YWCA, El Paso, 1948-50; libr. asst. Spl. Svcs. Libr., Ft. Bliss, Tex., 1950-53, libr., 1954-71; equal employment opportunity officer Ft. Bliss, 1971-72; dep. equal employment opportunity officer Long Beach (Calif.) Naval Shipyard, 1972-85; with Temp. Job Mart, Torrance, Calif., 1986-87; substitute tchr. Ysleta Ind. Sch. Dist., 1988-89; profl. libr. Eastwood Hts. Elem. Sch., 1989-90; sec. Shiloh Bapt. Ch., El Paso, 1991-92; br. mgr. El Paso Pub. Libr., 1992-96, retired, 1996. Host, prodr. (gospel music video with Viola Washington Strait), Time Warner TV, Cable Channel 15, 2003—04. Sec. Sunday sch. Bapt. Ch., 1956-66, 92-96, min. music, 1958-72, supr. young adult choir, 1966-72, pres. sr. choir, 1969-71; disc jockey Sta. KELP, El Paso, 1970-72; host radio show Sta. KTEP, U. Tex., El Paso, 1994-2004; hon. chmn. for ann. observance of Nat. Libr. Week, City of El Paso, 1970. Mem. ALA, Border Region Libr. Assn. (chmn. scholarship com. 1970), NAACP (sec. 1996), Alpha Kappa Alpha. Democrat. Baptist. Avocations: playing the piano and organ, public speaking, reading, ocean view dining. Home: 210 E Ocean Blvd Unit 1209 Long Beach CA 90802-4861

STRAJA, SORIN RADU, chemical engineer, mathematician, computer programmer; b. Bucharest, Romania; s. Radu and Sonica Straja; m. Mihaela Cirstea, Mar. 26, 1982. MS, Poly. Inst., Bucharest, 1979, PhD, 1987. Chem. engr. Plastics Processing, Bucharest, 1979-81; rsch. and devel. cons. Chem. and Biochem. Energetics Inst., Bucharest, 1982-89; cons., vol. USDA, Washington, 1991-92; chemist U. Md., Balt., 1992-93; dir. occupl. health and safety dept. Temple U., Phila., 1993—95, asst. prof. stats., 1994—2001; v.p. Inst. Regulatory Sci., Columbia, Md., 1996—. Cons. Montgomery Investment Tech., Radnor, 1995—. *Over twenty years experience working with the industry, academia, and government agencies in the United States and Europe. Proven expertise in mathematical modeling and software development applied in chemical and biochemical engineering, risk analysis, financial engineering, environmental and health sciences. Author of two books and over fifty scientific papers published in internationally recognized and refereed journals. Editor of Environment International and contributing editor of Technology (formerly Jour. of the Franklin Institute). Received the "Nicolae Teclu" prize of the Romanian Academy of Sciences, a certificate of appreciation for teaching from Temple University and a certificate of appreciation from the United States Department of Agriculture for significant volunteer contributions.* Editor: Environmental International, 1993-99; contbg. editor: Technology, 1996—; contbr. numerous articles to profl. jours. Recipient Nicolae Teclu award Romanian Acad. Scis., 1983. Mem. AIChE, ACS, N.Y. Acad. Sci., Soc. Risk Analysis. Avocations: history, geography. Office: Inst Regulatory Sci Ste 200 5457 Twin Knolls Rd Columbia MD 21045-3297 Office Phone: 301-596-8263. Business E-Mail: straja@nars.org.

STRAKA, LASZLO RICHARD, publishing consultant; b. Budapest, Hungary, June 22, 1934; came to U.S., 1950, naturalized, 1956; s. Richard J. and Elisabeth (Roeck) S.; m. Eva K. von Viczian, Jan. 20, 1962 (div. May 1981); children: Eva M., Monika E., Viktoria K. BA cum laude, NYU, 1959. Acct. Greatrex Ltd., N.Y.C., 1952-53; pres. Maxwell Macmillan Internat. Pub. Group, N.Y.C., 1991-92; with Pergamon Press, Inc., Elmsford, N.Y., 1954-90, v.p., 1964-68, exec. v.p., treas., 1968-74, pres., 1974-75, 80-88, chmn. bd., 1975-77, 88-90, vice chmn. bd., 1977-80, 88-89, also dir.; vice chmn. bd. Pergamon Books Ltd., Oxford, Eng., 1986-88; group v.p. Macmillan Inc., N.Y.C., 1989-91; pub. cons., 1992—. Treas. Brit. Book Centre, Inc., N.Y.C., 1956-67; pres. Pergamon Holding Corp., 1981-86; chmn. bd. Microforms Internat., Inc., 1971-87. D. dirs., sec. Szechenyi Istvan Soc., N.Y.C., 1967-80, 89-93. Mem. Phi Beta Kappa. Home and Office: 80 Radnor Ave Croton On Hudson NY 10520-2610 Office Phone: 914-271-8180. E-mail: laszlo.straka@verizon.net.

STRAKA, MARTIN, professional hockey player; b. Pizen, Czech Republic, Sept. 3, 1972; Center Pitts. Penguins, 1992—95, 1997—, Ottawa Hockey Team, 1994—96, N.Y. Islanders, 1995—96, Fla. Panthers, 1995—97. Mem. Czech Republic Olympic Hockey Team, Nagano, Japan, 1998. Office: Pittsburgh Penguins Mellon Arena 66 Mario Lemieux Place Pittsburgh PA 15219

STRAKA, THOMAS JAMES, forester, educator; b. Chippewa Falls, Wis., Dec. 17, 1949; s. James Otto and Elieen Helen S.; m. Patricia Casciere, Feb. 14, 1976. BS, U. Wis., 1972, MS, 1973; MBA, U. S.C., 1978; PhD, Va. Tech. U., 1981. Registered forester, S.C., Miss. Porject forester Internat. Paper Co., Georgetown, S.C., 1974-78; grad. rsch. asst. Va. Tech. U., Blacksburg, 1978-81; assoc. prof. Miss. State U., Mississippi State, 1982-89; prof. Clemson U., S.C., 1989—. Mem. Appalachian Soc. Am. Foresters (chair 2000), Miss. Soc. Am. Foresters (chair 1987), Miss. Forestry Assn. (bd. dirs. 1984-89), Forest Products Soc., Lions, Kiwanis, Xi Sigma Pi, Sigma Xi. Republican. Episcopalian. Home: 130 Timber Trl Westminster SC 29693-5366 Office: Clemson U Dept Forestry & Natural Resources PO Box 340317 Clemson SC 29634-0317

STRALEY, JOSEPH WARD, retired molecular spectrascopist, retired science educator; b. Paulding, Ohio, Oct. 6, 1914; s. Ozro Elbert and Stella Marie Straley; m. Lucy Gertrude Whittlesey, Jan. 28, 1914; children: Joseph Paul, David Lee, Lesley Mae. BSc in Edn., Bowling Green (Ohio) State U., 1936; MSc, Ohio State U., 1937, PhD, 1941. Instr. physics Heidelberg Coll., Tiffin, Ohio, 1938—39; asst. prof. U. Toledo, 1941—44; prof. physics U. N.C., Chapel Hill, 1944—80, ret., 1980. Dir. Piedmont Crescent Energy Project, Chapel Hill, 1976—80. Contbr. articles to profl. jours. Mem. town coun. Town of Chapel Hill, 1980—84. Recipient Guggenheim award, 1953. Mem.: Am. Phys. Soc. Democrat. Unitarian Universalist. Achievements include research in structure of methanes. Avocations: reading, writing. Home and Office: 53 Davie Circle Chapel Hill NC 27514 Home Fax: 919-942-1694. Personal E-mail: jstraley@email.unc.edu. E-mail: jwstraley@earthlink.net.

STRALING, PHILLIP FRANCIS, bishop; b. San Bernardino, Calif., Apr. 25, 1933; s. Sylvester J. and Florence E. (Robinson) S. BA, U. San Diego, 1963; MS in Child and Family Counseling, San Diego State U., 1971. Ordained priest Roman Catholic Ch., 1959, consecrated bishop Roman Catholic Ch., 1978. Mem. faculty St. John Acad., El Cajon, Calif., 1959—60, St. Therese Acad., San Diego, 1960—63; chaplain Newman Club, San Diego State U., 1960—72; mem. faculty St. Francis Sem., San Diego, 1972—76; pastor Holy Rosary Parish, San Bernardino, 1976—78; bishop Diocese of San Bernardino, 1978—95; pub. Inland Cath. newspaper, 1979—95; chmn. com. on lay ministry U.S. Cath. Conf./Nat. Cath. Conf. Bishops, 1993—; bishop of Reno, Nev., 1995—. Bd. dirs. Calif. Assn. Cath. Campus Mins., 1960; exec. sec. Diocesan Synod II, 1972—76; Episcopal vicar San Bernardino Deanery, 1976—78. Mem.: Nat. Cath. Campus Ministries Assn. (bishop rep. 1992—98). Office: Ste 200 290 S Arlington Reno NV 89501

STRAMPEL, WILLIAM DERKEY, dean, medical educator; b. Saugatuck, Mich., Feb. 8, 1948; married; 3 children. BA, Hope Coll., 1970; DO, Chgo. Coll. Osteopathic Medicine, 1976. Intern Madigan Army Med. Ctr., Fort Lewis, Wash., 1976—77, resident in medicine, 1977—79; fellow in pulmonary disease Fitzsimons Army Med. Ctr., Aurora, 1980—82; staff internal medicine svc. and dir. intensive care 121 Evacuation Hosp., Seoul; pulmonary staff and dir. intensive care Fitzsimons Army Med. Ctr., Aurora, Colo.; divsn. surgeon First Infantry Divsn. Irwin Army Cmty. Hosp., Fort Riley, Kans., dep. comdr., dir. med. edn., Evans Army Cmty. Hosp., Fort Carson, Colo.; chief Quality Assurance Divsn., Dept. of Army, Office Surgeon Gen., 1991—94; dir. med. edn. Brooke Army Med. Ctr., 1994—96; comdr. Brooke Army Med. Ctr. and Great Plains Med. Command, 1996—97; dir. quality mgmt. Office Sec. Def.; chief med. officer Tricare Mgmt. Activity; spl. asst. for ops. and readiness to U.S. surgeon gen.; leader Mich. State U. Health Team; sr. assoc. dean Mich. State U., Coll. Osteo. Medicine, 1999—2002, prof. internal medicine, 2001—, acting dean, 2001—02, dean, 2002—. Served to col. U.S. Army. Office: A314 E Free Hall East Lansing MI 48824-1316*

STRANAHAN, PATRICIA, dean; d. John Quay and Carol Scott Stranahan; m. Edward J.M. Rhoads, June 10, 1994. BA, Westminster Coll., 1971; MA, U. Pa, 1974, PhD, 1979; MBA, U. Pitts., 1992. Asst. prof. history Tex. A&M U., College Station, 1980—86, assoc. prof. history, 1986—97; prof. history U. Pitts., 1997—2001, dir. Asian studies program, 1997—2001; provost, dean faculty Hobart and William Smith Coll., Geneva, NY, 2001—; interim v.p. acad. affairs Chatham Coll., Pitts., 2000. Exec. dir. Com. Scholarly Comm. with China, Washington, 1995—96. Author: Molding the Medium: the Chinese Communist Party and the Liberation Daily, 1990, Yan'an Women and the Communist Party, 1983, Underground: the Shanghai Communist Party and the Politics of Survival, 1927-1937, 1998; editl. bd.: CCP Rsch. Newsletter, 1997—2000. Bd. dirs. Global Rsch. Consortia, 1997—99. Recipient Sr. Rsch. fellow, Am. Coun. of Learned Societies, 1996; fellow Naomi Lewis fellow, Tex. A&M U., 1986—88. Mem.: LWV (bd. dirs. 2002—), Assn. of Am. Colleges and Universities (assoc.), Assn. of Asian Studies (assoc.), Penn Club (assoc.). Office: Hobart and William Smith Colleges Office of the Provost Geneva NY 14456

STRAND, CURT ROBERT, hotel executive; b. Vienna, Nov. 13, 1920; naturalized Am. citizen, 1943; m. Fleur Lillian Emanuel, June 14, 1946; 1 child, Karen. BS, Cornell U., 1943. Supt. service Plaza, N.Y.C., 1947-49; asst. to v.p. Hilton Hotels Corp., 1949-53; v.p. Hilton Internat. Co., N.Y.C., 1953-64, exec. v.p., 1964-67, pres., chief exec. officer, 1967-86, chmn., 1986-87. Sr. v.p., dir. Trans World Air Lines, Inc.; lectr. Cornell U. Sch. Hotel Adminstrn., Ecole Superieure de Scis. Econs., Paris, NYU, Houston U.; sr. cons. Am. Express; mem. adv. panel com. Am. Hotel and Motel Assn.; dir. Sherry Netherland Corp.; mem. exec. com. Bd. Exec. Svc. Corps, Aspen. Mem. coun. Cornell U.; adv. bd. Aspen Found.; bd. govs. Snowmass Resort Assn., also pres.; fellow Aspen Inst. Mem. Cornell Soc. Hotelmen (Hotelier of Yr. 1986), Nat. Arts Club. Home: PO Box 6359 Snowmass Village CO 81615

STRAND, JOAN H. law educator; b. 1950; BA, George Washington U., JD, 1975. Bar: D.C. 1976. Prof. law Nat. Law Ctr. George Washington U., Washington. Mem. ABA, D.C. Bar Assn. (pres.-elect, sec. 1993-94, bd. govs., family law sect., pub. svc. activities com.), D.C. Bar Found. (Jerrold Scoutt prize 1997). Office: George Washington U Nat Law Ctr Washington DC 20052-0001

STRAND, MARK, poet; b. Summerside, P.E.I., Can., Apr. 11, 1934; came to U.S., 1938. s. Robert Joseph and Sonia (Apter) S.; m. Antonia Ratensky, Sept. 14, 1961 (div. June 1973); 1 dau., Jessica; m. Julia Rumsey Garretson, Mar. 15, 1976; 1 son, Thomas Summerfield. BA, Antioch Coll., 1957; BFA, Yale, 1959; MA, U. Iowa, 1962. Instr. English U. Iowa, 1962-65; asst. prof. Mt. Holyoke Coll., 1967; assoc. prof. Bklyn. Coll., 1971-72; Bain-Swiggett lectr. Princeton, 1973; Hurst prof. poetry Brandeis U., 1974-75; prof. U. Utah, 1981-93; U.S. poet laureate Library of Congress, Washington, 1990-91; prof. Johns Hopkins U., 1994—97; Andrew MacLeish disting. svc. prof. U. Chgo., 1997—. Fulbright lectr. U. Brazil, Rio de Janeiro, 1965-66; adj. assoc. prof. Columbia U., 1969-72; vis. prof. U. Wash., 1968, 70, U. Va., 1977, Wesleyan U., 1979, Harvard U., 1980; vis. lectr. Yale, 1969-70, U. Va., 1976, Calif. State U., Fresno, 1977, U. Calif., Irvine, 1979. Author: Sleeping with One Eye Open, 1964, Reasons for Moving, 1968, Darker, 1970, The Story of Our Lives, 1973 (Edgar Allan Poe award Acad. Am. Poets 1974), The Sargeantville Notebook, 1974, The Monument, 1978, Elegy for My Father, 1978, The Late Hour, 1978, Selected Poems, 1980, The Planet of Lost Things, 1982, The Night Book, 1983, Mr. and Mrs. Baby and Other Stories, 1985, Rembrandt Takes a Walk, 1986, William Bailey, 1987, The Continuous Life, 1990, Dark Harbor, 1993, Hopper, 1994, Blizzard of One (Pulitzer Prize); Editor: The Contemporary American Poets, 1968, New Poetry of Mexico, 1970, 18 Poems from Quechua, 1971, The Owl's Insomnia, 1973, The Best American Poetry 1991, The Golden Ecco Anthology, 1994; co-author: 89 Clouds, 1999; co-editor: Another Republic: Seventeen European and South American Writers, 1976, The Art of the Real, 1983, Traveling in the Family, 1987; translator: Souvenir of the Ancient World, 1976. Recipient award Am. Acad. and Inst. Arts and Letters, 1975, Utah Gov.'s award in arts, 1992, Bobbitt Nat. prize for poetry, 1992, Bollingen prize for poetry Yale Univ. Libr., 1993; Fulbright scholar in Italy, 1960-61; Ingram Merrill Found. grantee, 1966; Nat. Endowment for Arts grantee, 1967-68, 78-79, 86-87; Rockefeller Found. grantee, 1968-69; Guggenheim fellow, 1975-76; Acad. Am. Poets fellow, 1979; MacArthur Found. fellow, 1987; Pulitzer Prize in Poetry, Blizzard of One, 1999. Fellow Acad. Am. Poets; mem. Am. Acad. and Inst. Arts and Letters.

STRAND, MELFORD LIEN, anesthesiologist; b. La Crosse, Wis., Aug. 15, 1940; BS in Pharm., U. Wis., 1963; MD, U. Iowa, 1967. Diplomate Am. Bd. Anesthesiology. Intern Sacramento County Hosp., 1967—68; resident U. Colo. Med. Ctr., Denver, 1970—72; asst. clin. prof. of Anesthesia U. Colo., 1972—76; pvt. practice, 1976—. With U.S. Army, 1968—70. Mem.: Colo. Soc. Anesthesiologists, Colo. Med. Soc., Denver Med. Soc., Am. Soc. Anesthesiologists. Office: Met Denver Anesthesiology PO Box 481710 Denver CO 80248-1710

STRAND, ROGER GORDON, federal judge; b. Peekskill, N.Y., Apr. 28, 1934; s. Ernest Gordon Strand and Lisabeth Laurine (Phin) Steinmetz; m. Joan Williams, Nov. 25, 1961. AB, Hamilton Coll., 1955; LLB, Cornell U., 1961; grad., Nat. Coll. State Trial Judges, 1968. Bar: Ariz. 1961, U.S. Dist. Ct. Ariz. 1961, U.S. Supreme Ct. 1980. Assoc. Fennemore, Craig, Allen & McClennen, Phoenix, 1961-67; judge Ariz. Superior Ct., Phoenix, 1967-85, U.S. Dist. Ct. Ariz., Phoenix, 1985—. Assoc. presiding judge Ariz. Superior Ct., 1971-85; lectr. Nat. Jud. Coll., Reno, 1978-87; mem. jud. conf. U.S. com. on info. tech., 1996-2002. Past pres. cen. Ariz. chpt. Arthritis Found. Lt. USN, 1955-61. Mem. ABA, Ariz. Bar Assn., Maricopa County Bar Assn., Nat. Conf. Fed. Trial Judges, Phi Delta Phi, Aircraft Owners and Pilots Assn. Lodges: Rotary. Avocations: computer applications, golf, fishing. Home: 5825 N 3rd Ave Phoenix AZ 85013-1537 Office: Sandra Day O'Connor US Courthouse SPC 57 401 W Washington Phoenix AZ 85003-2156

STRANDBERG, JOHN DAVID, comparative pathologist; b. Alexandria, Minn., Aug. 28, 1939; s. Winfred Carl and Evelyn Joyce (Studlien) S. AB, Johns Hopkins U., 1960; DVM, Cornell U., 1964, PhD, 1968. Diplomate Am. Coll. Vet. Pathologists. USPHS NIH postdoctoral fellow Cornell U., Ithaca, N.Y., 1964-67; fellow, resident in pathology Sch. Medicine, Johns Hopkins U., Balt., 1966-67; instr. dept. pathology/divsn. animal medicine Sch. Medicine Johns Hopkins U., Balt., 1967-68, asst. prof. pathology/divsn. lab. animal medicine, 1968-75, dir. comparative pathology tng. program Sch. Medicine, 1973—, asst. prof. pathobiology Sch. Hygiene and Pub. Health, 1974-77, acting dir. divsn. lab. animal medicine Sch. Medicine, 1974-76, assoc. prof. pathology and comparative medicine, 1975—, joint appointment pathobiology Sch. Hygiene and Pub. Health, 1977-99, dir. divsn. comparative medicine sch. medicine, 1983-99. Vis. scientist Marine Biol. Lab., Woods Hole, Mass., 1993; cons., panelist, presenter in field; mem. peer rev. group Nat. Zool. Park, 1987, 88, 90; chmn. Md. Coun. on Sci. Use of Animals, 1989-93; mem. adv. con. Nat. Ctr. for Rsch. Resources NIH, 1991-96; mem. adv. bd. Nat. Aquarium in Balt., 1986—, Ctr. for Alternatives to Animal Testing, Balt., 1985-90; dir. comparative medicine Nat. Ctr. Rsch. Resources NIH, 1999—. Mem. editorial rev. bd. The Biomedical Investigator's Handbook, 1987; contbr. articles to profl. publs. V.p. Balt. Zool. Soc., 1978-82, chmn. med. com., 1973-86. Mem. AAAS, AMVA, Am. Coll. Vet. Pathologists (com. on tng. programs 1976-82), U.S. and Can. Acad. Pathology, Am. Assn. Pathologists, Md. State Vet. Med. Assn. (com. on liaison to humane orgns. 1986-88, com. on registration of vet. technicians 1977), Med. Zool. Soc., Wildlife Disease Assn., Am. Soc. Lab. Animal Practitioners, Phi Beta Kappa, Phi Kappa Phi, Phi Zeta.

STRANDBERG, MALCOM WOODROW PERSHING, physicist; b. Box Elder, Mont., Mar. 9, 1919, s. Malcom and Ingeborg (Riestad) S.; m. Harriet Elisabeth Bennett, Aug. 2, 1947 (dec.); children— Josiah R.W., Susan Abby, Elisabeth G., Malcom B. S.B., Harvard Coll., 1941; PhD, M.I.T., 1948. Research asso. M.I.T., Cambridge, 1941-48, asst. prof. physics, 1948-53, asso. prof., 1953-60, prof., 1960-88, prof. emeritus, 1988—. Author: Microwave Spectroscopy, 1954; patentee in field. Fellow Am. Phys. Soc., Am. Acad. Arts and Scis., IEEE, AAAS; mem. Am. Assn. Physics Tchrs. Episcopalian. Home: 82 Larchwood Dr Cambridge MA 02138-4639 Office: Mass Inst Tech 26-351 Cambridge MA 02139 Office Phone: 617-253-2563. Business E-Mail: mwpstr@mit.edu.

STRANDJORD, M. JEANNINE, telecommunications industry executive; B in Acctg. and Bus. Adminstrn., U. Kans. CPA. V.p. fin. Macy's Midwest; with Kans. city Power & Light Co., Ernst and Whinney; v.p. fin. and distrbn. AmeriSource, Inc. (subs. Sprint), 1985—90, controller, 1986—90, sr. v.p., treas., 1990—98, sr. v.p. fin. global markets group, 1998—2003; sr. v.p. fin. svcs. Sprint Corp., 2003, sr. v.p., chief integration officer, 2003—. Bd. dirs. Am. Century Mutual Funds, DST Sys., Inc., Euronet Worldwide. Trustee Rockhurst U. Office: 6200 Spring Pkwy Overland Park KS 66251

STRANG, JAMES DENNIS, editor; b. Ashtabula, Ohio, June 23, 1945; s. Delbert Devoe and Mildred Edith (Green) S.; m. Margaret Florence Littell, Aug. 25, 1974; children: Megan Lisbeth, Amy Colleen, Benjamin Jefferson. BS in Journalism, Kent State U., 1969. Cert. firearms instr. Reporter The Star-Beacon, Ashtabula, Ohio, 1966, The Record-Courier, Kent, Ohio, 1966-69, The Cleve. Press, 1969-71; cons. Tom Rall & Assocs., Washington, 1971-72; reporter, editor The Plain Dealer, Cleve., 1973-75, assoc. editor, 1975—. Instr. journalism Lorain County C.C., Elyria, Ohio, 1973-74. Recipient Nat. Comdrs. award DAV, 1980, Best Editorial award AP Soc. Ohio, 1988. Mem. Nat. Conf. Editorial Writers, Soc. Profl. Journalists, Nat. Rifle Assn. (life). Unitarian-Universalist. Avocation: shooting sports. Office: The Plain Dealer 1801 Superior Ave E Cleveland OH 44114-2198

STRANG, RUTH HANCOCK, pediatric educator, pediatric cardiologist, priest; b. Bridgeport, Conn., Mar. 11, 1923; d. Robert Hallock Wright and Ruth (Hancock) S. BA, Wellesley Coll., 1944, postgrad., 1944-45; MD, N.Y. Med. Coll., 1949; MDiv, Seabury Western Theol. Sem., 1993. Diplomate Am. Bd. Pediat.; ordained deacon Episc. Ch., 1993, priest, 1994. Intern Flower and Fifth Ave. Hosp., N.Y.C., 1949-50, resident in pediat., 1950-52; mem. faculty N.Y. Med. Coll., N.Y.C., 1952-57; fellow cardiology Babies Hosp., N.Y.C., 1956-57, Harriet Lane Cardiac Clinic, Johns Hopkins Hosp., Balt., 1957-59, Children's Hosp., Boston, 1959-62; mem. faculty U. Mich., Univ. Hosp., Ann Arbor, 1962-89, prof. pediatrics, 1970-89, prof. emeritus, 1989—; priest-in-charge St. Johns Episcopal Ch., Howell, Mich., 1994—. Dir. pediat. Wayne County Gen. Hosp., Westland, Mich, 1965-85; mem. staff U. Mich. Hosps., 1962-89; mem. med. adv. com. Wayne County chpt. Nat. Cystic Fibrosis Rsch. Found., 1966-80, chmn. med. adv. com. nat. found., Detroit, 1971-78; cons. cardiology Plymouth (Mich.) State Home and Tng. Sch., 1970-81; diocesan coun. Diocese Mich., 2003-, mem. com. on noms. and elections Diocesan Conv., 2003, chmn. conf. com., 2004. Author: Clinical Aspects of Operable Heart Disease, 1968; contbr. numerous articles to profl. jours. Mem. citizen's adv. coun. Juvenile Ct., Ann Arbor, 1968—76; mem. med. adv. bd. Ann Arbor Continuing Edn. Dept., 1968—77; v.p. Am. Heart Assn. Mich., 1989, pres., 1991; bd. dirs. Livingston Cmty. Hospice, 1995—99, Emrich Episcopal Conf. Ctr., 1998—; mem. Diocesan Com. for World Relief, Detroit, 1970—72; trustee Episcopal Med. Chaplaincy, Ann Arbor, 1971—96; mem. bishop's com. St. Aidan's Episc. Ch., 1966—69, sec., 1966—68, vestry, 1973—76, 1978—80, 1984—86, 1990—91, sr. warden, 1975—76, 1978, 1986, 1990; del. Episc. Diocesan Conv., 1980, 1991; mem. Congl. Life Circle Episcopal Diocese Mich., 1995—2001, mem. loans and grants com., 1995—99, mem. com. on reference ann. diocesan conv., 1995-98, chmn., 1996; mem. Diocese Mich. Clergy Family Project, 1996—98; co-dean Huron Valley area coun. Diocese Mich., 1998—2000; bd. trustees Ecumenical Theol. Sem., 1996—, chair acad. affairs com., 2000—; mem. Congl. Devel. Commn., 2001—03. Mem. AMA, Am. Acad. Pediat., Am. Coll. Cardiology, Mich. Med. Soc., Washtenaw County Med. Soc., N.Y. Acad. Medicine, Am. Heart Assn., Women's Rsch. Club (membership sec. 1966-67), Ambulatory Pediat. Assn., Am. Assn. Child Care in Hosps., Am. Assn. Med. Colls., Assn. Faculties of Pediat. Nurse Assn./Practitioners Programs (pres. 1978-81, exec. com. 1981-84), Episc. Clergy Assn. Mich., Northside Assn. Ministries (pres. 1975, 76, 79-80). Home: 4500 E Huron River Dr Ann Arbor MI 48105-9335 Personal E-mail: sjec@cac.net.

STRANG, SANDRA LEE, airline official; b. Greensboro, N.C., Apr. 22, 1936; d. Charles Edward and Lobelia Mae (Squires) S. BA in English, U. N.C., 1960; MBA, U. Dallas, 1970. With Am. Airlines, Inc., 1960—, mgr. career devel. for women, 1972-73, dir. selection and tng., 1974-75, sr. dir. selection, tng. and affirmative action, 1975-79, sr. dir. compensation and benefits Dallas/Ft. Worth, 1979-84, dir. passenger sales tng. and devel., 1984—, regional sales mgr. Rocky Mt. region Denver, 1985—. Pres. The SLS Group, Inc., (DBAs) Sales Leadership Seminars, Inc., Sr. Leadership Svcs., Inc., Svc. Leadership Seminars, Inc., Speakers, Lectrs., and Seminars, Inc. 1988—. Mem. Am. Mgmt. Assn., Assn. Advancement of Women into Mgmt., Am. Soc. Tng. and Devel., Am. Compensation Assn., Internat. Platform Assn., AARP. Office: PO Box 7609 Horseshoe Bay TX 78657-7609 E-mail: slstrang@compaq.net.

STRANGE, CURTIS NORTHROP, professional golfer; b. Norfolk, Va., Jan. 30, 1955; s. Thomas Wright Strange Jr. and Nancy (Ball) Neal; m. Sarah Jones; children: Thomas Wright III, David Clark. Student, Wake Forest U., 1974-76. Winner of Southeastern Amateur, 1973, NCAA, 1974, Western Amateur, 1974, Eastern Amateur, 1975, 76, North and South Amateur, 1975, 76, Va. State Amateur, 1976, World Amateur Cup, 1975, Walker Cup, 1974, Pensacola Open, 1979, Michelob-Houston Open, Mfrs. Hanover Westchester Classic, 1980, Panama Open, 1980, Sammy Davis Jr.-Greater Hartford Open, 1983, LaJet Classic, 1984, Honda Classic, Panasonic-Las Vegas Invitational, Canadian Open, 1985, Houston Open, 1986, Canadian Open, Fed. Express St. Jude Classic, NEC World Series of Golf, 1987, Ind. Ins. Agent Open, Meml. Tournament, U.S. Open, 1988, 89, Nabisco Championships, 1988. Named to Collegiate Golf Hall of Fame, 1987, Wake Forest Hall of Fame, 1988, PGA Player-of-the-Yr., 1988; recipient Golf Writers Player-of-the-Yr. award, 1985, 87, 88, ABC Cup Japan, 1986, PGA Leading Money Winner 1985, 87-88. Avocations: hunting, fishing. Office: PGA America PO Box 109601 100 Ave of The Champions Palm Beach Gardens FL 33410

STRANGE, DONALD ERNEST, health care company executive; b. Ann Arbor, Mich., Aug. 13, 1944; s. Carl Britton and Donna Ernestine (Tenney) Strange; m. Lyn Marie Purdy, Aug. 3, 1968 (div. Mar. 2001); children: Laurel Lyn, Chadwick Donald. BA, Mich. State U., 1966, MBA, 1968. Asst. dir. Holland (Mich.) City Hosp., 1968-72, assoc. dir., 1972-74; exec. dir. Bascom Palmer Eye Inst./Anne Bates Leach Eye Hosp., U. Miami, Fla., 1974-77; v.p. strategic planning and rsch. Hosp. Corp. Am., Nashville, 1977-80, group v.p. Boston, 1980-82, regional v.p., 1982-87; chmn., chief exec. officer HCA Healthcare Can., Toronto, 1985-87; exec. v.p. Avon Products, Inc., N.Y., 1987-89; chmn. Sigecom, Ltd., Greenwich, Conn., 1989-94, U.S. HomeCare Corp., 1990-91; exec. v.p., COO, dir. EPIC Healthcare Group, Dallas, 1991-93; chmn, CEO TransCare Corp., Dallas, 1993-95; chmn., CEO First New Eng. Dental Ctrs., Inc., Boston, 1996-98; pres., CEO Behavorial Healthcare Ptnrs., Inc., Quincy, Mass., 2000; sr. v.p. Bon Secours Health Sys. Inc., Mariottsville, Md., 2001—. Mem. Harvard Club (Boston), Nat. Arts Club (N.Y.). Episcopalian. Office: Bon Secours Health Sys Inc 1505 Marriottsville Rd Marriottsville MD 21104-1399

STRANGE, HENRY HAZEN, judge; b. Oleary, P.E.I., Can., July 26, 1939; s. Henry Hazen and Marion Yvonne (Copp) S.; m. Heather Susan Carson, July 30, 1966; children: Elizabeth Marion, Jennifer Jody. BBA, U. N.B., Fredericton, 1961, BA, 1963, B in Civil Laws, 1964. Pvt. practice barrister, solicitor, N.B., 1964-66; spl. asst. to dir. of pub. rels. Centennial Commn., Ottawa, Ont., Can., 1966-67; crown prosecutor Dept. Justice, Fredericton, N.B., 1967-71, dir. pub. prosecutions, 1971-81; judge Provincial Ct., N.B., 1981—, chief judge, 1987-97. Chmn. Can. Coun. Chief Judges, 1995. Apptd. as Queen's Counsel, N.B., 1977. Avocations: salmon fishing, sports. Home: 664 Woodstock Rd Fredericton NB Canada E3B 5N7 Office: Provincial Ct PO Box 6000 Fredericton NB Canada E3B 5H1 Office Phone: 506-453-2120. E-mail: hazen.strange@gnb.ca.

STRANGE, J. LELAND, computer company executive; b. Dallas, May 15, 1941; s. James Alton and Ola (Johnson) S.; m. Jane Hendrix Strange, Aug. 28, 1965; children— Mark, Cary, Ryan. BS Indsl. Mgmt., Ga. Tech. U., 1965, MBA, Ga. State U., 1968. Gen. mgr. Colonial Film & Equipment Co., Atlanta, 1967-69; pres. Cheese Villa Stores, Inc., 1969-74, Quadram Corp., 1981-83, Intelligent Systems Corp., 1983— (all Atlanta); prof. mktg. Mercer U., 1976-83; bd. dirs. Healthdyne Corp., Atlanta, Intelligent Systems Corp., Wave Air Corp, IQ Software Corp. Republican. Baptist. Office: Intelligent Systems Corp 4355 Shackleford Rd Norcross GA 30093-2948

STRANGFELD, JOHN R., JR., diversified financial services company executive; Various mgmt. pos. Prudential Fin., 1977—89, chmn., PRICOA Capital Group Europe, 1989—95, sr. mng. dir., Pvt. Asset Mgmt. Group, 1995—96, exec. in charge of Global Asset Mgmt. Group, 1996—2000, chmn., CEO Prudential Securities, 2000—01, CEO, Prudential Investment Mgmt. of Prudential Ins., 2001—02, exec. v.p., 2001—02, vice chmn., 2002—. Office: Prudential Financial Inc 751 Broad St Newark NJ 07102-3777

STRANGHOENER, LARRY W. manufacturing executive; BS, St. Olaf Coll., Northfield, Minn.; MBA, Northwestern U. CFA. Investment analyst Dain Bosworth, Mpls.; with Honeywell, Inc., 1983—99; dir. investor rels., dir. mktg./internat. sales Honeywell Centra, Germany, dir. corp. fin. planning/bus. analysis, asst. treas., 1992—93; v.p. fin. Honeywell Indsl. Automation and Control, Phoenix, 1993—96; v.p. bus. devel. Honeywell, Inc., Mpls., 1996—97, v.p., CFO, 1997-99; exec. v.p., CFO Techies.com, Edina, Minn., 2000—01; CFO Lutheran Brotherhood, 2001—02, Thrivent Financial for Lutherans (formerly Lutheran Brotherhood). Mpls., 2002—. Office: 325 Fourth Ave S Minneapolis MN 55415-1624*

STRAS, PENNY LYNN, director; b. Fergus Falls, Minn., Sept. 13, 1951; d. Orville James and Mildred Georgia Stras; m. Wade Elson Olson, Dec. 19, 1974 (div. Sept. 1977); 1 child, J. D. Olson. AA, Yankton Coll., 1981, BA, 1982, U. Mont., 1991, MPA, 1993. From adminstrv. asst. to case mgr. Vietnam Vets. Childrens Asst. Program, Missoula, Mont., 1989—92; advocacy specialist Mont. Advocacy Program, Helena, 1992—93; child devel. specialist Comprehensive Devel. Ctr., Missoula, 1993—95; pvt. practice acct. Libby, Mont., 1995—99; asst. dir. Missoula Head Start, 1999—2000; bus. office coord. Ashby (Minn.) Care Ctr., 2001; dir. Grand Portage (Minn.) Head Start, Grand Portage, 2001—03, SEMCAC Head Start, Rushford, Minn., 2003—. Grant writer Dept. HHS, 1989—93. Vol. Spl. Olympics, Yankton, SD, 1981—82, Missoula, Mont., 1991—93. Grantee Fed. grant, Dept. Health & Human Svcs., 2001. Avocations: refinishing furniture, latch hook rugs. Home: 301 River St Rushford MN 55971 Office: SEMCAC Head Start 204 S Elm Rushford MN 55971 E-mail: nvrtool8@yahoo.com.

STRASBAUGH, WAYNE RALPH, lawyer; b. Lancaster, Pa., July 20, 1948; s. Wayne Veily and Jane Irene (Marzolf) S.; m. Carol Lynne Taylor, June 8, 1974; children: Susan, Wayne T., Elizabeth. AB, Bowdoin Coll., 1970; AM, Harvard U., 1971, PhD, 1976, JD, 1979. Bar: Ohio 1979, Pa. 1983, U.S. Tax Ct. 1980, U.S. Ct. Fed. Claims 1980, U.S. Ct. Appeals (fed. cir.) 1982, U.S. Dist. Ct. (no. dist.) Ohio 1979, U.S. Dist. Ct. (ea. dist.) Pa. 1983. Assoc. Jones Day Reavis & Pogue, Cleve., 1979-82, Morgan Lewis & Bockius, Phila., 1982-84, Ballard Spahr Andrews & Ingersoll, LLP, Phila., 1984-88, ptnr., 1988—, chmn. tax group, 2001—. Mem. ABA (tax sect., chmn. com. 1992-94), Am. Coll. Tax Counsel (regent 2003—)., Phila. Bar Assn. (tax sect., chmn. fed. tax com. 1992, coun. mem. 1995, sec.-treas. 1996, vice-chmn. 1997-98, chmn. 1999-2000). Episcopalian. Office: Ballard Spahr Andrews & Ingersoll LLP 1735 Market St Ste 5100 Philadelphia PA 19103-7599 Personal E-mail: strasbaugh@ballardspahr.com.

STRASBURG, WILLIAM EDWARD, retired newspaper publisher; b. Lima, Ohio, June 8, 1927; s. Dewey Edward and Helen Mae Strasburg; m. Sylvia Schultz Schweiker, July 14, 1951; children: Bruce Edward, Scott Alan, Mark Douglas, Barbara Lee. BA, Ohio Wesleyan U., 1950; MA, Am. U., 1952; LittD (hon.), Lycoming Coll., 1970; LLD (hon.), Beaver Coll., 1979. Corr., Washington and Africa, 1950-52; pres., pub. Montgomery Pub. Co., Ft. Washington, Pa., 1952-90; v.p. Ind. Publs., Bryn Mawr, Pa., 1976-93; chmn. Meadowood Corp., Worcester, Pa., 1982-95; ret. dir. exec. com., chmn. compensation com. Harleysville (Pa.) Ins. Cos., 1970-2000, ret.; assoc. dir. U.S. Info. Agy., Washington, 1969-70. Pres. Ambler Pub. Libr., 1960-62, Rotary Club, Ambler, Pa., 1960-61, YMCA, Phila., 1976-77, Pa. Newspaper Assn., Harrisburg, 1968-69; chmn. Found. Montgomery County C.C., Blue Bell, Pa., 1994-96. Recipient Amos award Nat. Newspaper Assn., 1970, Alumni award Ohio Wesleyan U., 1974, Dean Lesher award Suburban

Newspapers Am., 1990, Leadership award Pa. News Assn., 1999. Mem. Soc. Profl. Journalists (chpt. pres. 1968), King of Prussia C. of C. (pres. 1978), Omicron Delta Kappa, Delta Sigma Rho, Phi Delta Epsilon, Phi Gamma Delta, Bonita Bay Club. Home: PO Box 419 Gwynedd Valley PA 19437-0419

STRASBURGER, VICTOR C. pediatrician; b. Balt., Oct. 7, 1949; s. Arthur Charles and Marjorie (Cohen) S.; m. Alison Reeve, Aug. 18, 1984; children: Max, Katya. BA summa cum laude, Yale U., 1971; MD, Harvard U., 1975. Intern Children's Hosp.- U. Wash., Seattle, 1975-76, residency, 1976-77, Boston Children's Hosp., 1977-78; dir. adolescent medicine Bridgeport (Conn.) Hosp., 1979-86; vis. lectr. St. Mary's Hosp. Med. Sch., London, 1986-87; chief div. adolescent medicine sch. medicine U. N.Mex., Albuquerque, 1987—, prof. pediats., 1997—. Cons. Nat. PTA, Washington and Chgo., 1978-86. Author: Rounding Third and Heading Home, 1974, Adolescent Medicine: A Practical Guide, 1991, 2d edit., 1998, Getting Your Kids to Say No in the '90's When You Said Yes in the '60's, 1993, (with B. Wilson) Children, Adolescents, and the Media, 2002; editor: Basic Adolescent Gynecology, 1990; editor-in-chief Adolescent Medicine: State of the Art Revs., 1989—. Recipient Adele Hofmann award, 2000. Fellow Am. Acad. Pediatrics (Holyroyd-Sherry award 2000), Soc. for Adolescent Medicine; mem. Phi Beta Kappa. Office: U NM Sch Medicine Dept Pediatrics MSC10 5590 1 Univ New Mexico Albuquerque NM 87131-0001 Office Phone: 505-272-0338. Business E-Mail: vstrasburger@salud.unm.edu.

STRASFOGEL, IAN, stage director, playwright; b. N.Y.C., Apr. 5, 1940; s. Ignace and Alma (Lubin) S.; m. Judith Hirsch Norell, Feb. 15, 1973; children: Daniella Elizabeth, Gabrielle Sandra. BA, Harvard U., 1961. Adminstrv. asst. N.Y.C. Opera Co., 1962-64, stage dir., 1964—; tchr. music Julliard Sch. Music, N.Y.C., 1965-66, Augusta (Ga.) Coll., 1967-68; founder, previous artistic dir. Augusta Opera Co., from 1967; chmn. dept. opera New Eng. Conservatory, Boston, 1968-72; prof. opera U. Mich., Ann Arbor, 1980; freelance opera dir., playwright Rosenstone & Wander Agency, N.Y.C., 1982—. Stage dir. Balt. Civic Opera, Kansas City Lyric Theatre, Netherlands Opera Co., 1973—, N.Y.C. Opera, San Francisco Opera, Stuttgart Opera, Alte Oper Frankfurt, Edinburgh Festival, Aix-en-Provence Festival, Aspen Music Festival; dir. music theatre project Tanglewood Festival, Lenox, Mass., 1971-73; gen. dir. Opera Soc. Washington, 1972-75; artistic cons. Phila. Lyric Opera, 1973; dir. New Opera Theatre, Bklyn. Acad. Music, 1976-79. Author: Il Musico (music by Larry Grossman), 1990-91 The Caregiver (play), 1999, Jewish Ensemble Theatre, Detroit; editor: Ba-Ta-Clan, 1970. Served with AUS, 1966-68. Henry Russell Shaw travelling fellow, 1961-62; Ford Found. internship in performing arts, 1962-64; grantee: Internat. Inst. Edn., 1965, Berrillon Kerr Found., 1997 (for The Caregiver). Mem. Phi Beta Kappa. Home: 915 W End Ave New York NY 10025-3535

STRASSBURGER, JOHN ROBERT, academic administrator; b. Sheboygan, Wis., Apr. 6, 1942; s. J. Robert and Elizabeth (Mathewson) S.; m. Gertrude Hunter Mackie, Aug. 24, 1968; children: Sarah Electa, Gertrude Hunter. BA, Bates, 1964; Honours degree, Cambridge (Eng.) U., 1966; PhD, Princeton U., 1976. Faculty Hiram (Ohio) Coll., 1970-82; program officer NEH, Washington, 1982-84; prof. history, exec. v.p., dean Coll., Knox Coll., Galesburg, Ill., 1984-94; pres. Ursinus Coll., Collegeville, Pa., 1995—; CEO Philip & Muriel Berman Mus. Art at Ursinus Coll., Collegeville, Pa. Mem. commn. govt. rels. Am. Coun. Edn., 1997—. Contbr. articles to profl. jours. Bd. trustees Perkiomen Sch., 1997—. Mem. Am. Conf. Acad. Deans (chair 1990-91), Sunday Breakfast Club (Phila.). Office: Ursinus Coll Office of Pres PO Box 1000 Collegeville PA 19426-1000

STRASSER, GABOR, management consultant; b. Budapest, Hungary, May 22, 1929; s. Rezso and Theresa (Seiler) S.; m. Linda Casselman Pemble, Aug. 16, 1958 (div. 1976); children: Claire Margaret, Andrew John; m. Joka Verhoeff, Feb. 2, 1978; children: Steven Verhoeff, Tessa Christina. BCE, City Coll. N.Y., 1954; MS, U. Buffalo, 1959; PMD, Harvard, 1968; MDiv, Va. Theol. Sem., 1992. Research engr. Bell Aircraft Co., Buffalo, 1956-61; project leader Boeing Airplane Co., Seattle, 1961-62; dept. head Mitre Corp., Bedford, Mass., Washington, 1962-68; v.p. Urban Inst., Washington, 1968-69; tech. asst. to pres.'s sci. adviser White House, 1969-71, exec. sec. pres.'s sci. and tech. policy panel, 1970-71; dir. planning Battelle Meml. Inst., Columbus, Ohio, 1971-73; pres. Strasser Assocs., Inc., Washington, 1973-92. Author, editor: Science and Technology Policies-Yesterday, Today, Tomorrow, 1973; Contbr. articles to profl. jours. and theol. lit. Served to 1st lt., C.E. USAR. Recipient 1st nat. award Gravity Research Found., 1952 Mem. AIAA, AAAS (chmn. indsl. sci. sect. 1974), Cosmos Club (Washington), Harvard Club (Washington), Sigma Xi.

STRASSER, JOEL A. public relations executive, engineer, executive producer; b. N.Y.C., Aug. 8, 1938; s. Albert Gerson and Nellie (Singer) S.; children: Alison Debra, Andria Jocelyn, Jon Fredric. BS, CCNY, 1961. News editor Electronic Design mag., N.Y.C., 1962; space electronics editor Electronics mag. McGraw-Hill, N.Y.C., 1963-65; account exec. Lescarboura Advt., Inc., Briarcliff Manor, N.Y., 1965-67; bur. chief Aerospace Tech. mag., N.Y.C., 1967-68; syndicated sci. columnist N.Am. Newspaper Alliance, N.Y.C., 1974-80; sr. v.p., founding dir. indsl. and sci. communications svcs. Hill & Knowlton, Inc., N.Y.C., 1968-83; exec. v.p. Thomas L. Richmond, Inc., N.Y.C., 1983-85; sr. v.p., mng. dir. Dorf & Stanton Tech. Communications, N.Y.C., 1985-91; pres. Joel A. Strasser & Assocs., 1991—; dir. corp. comms. People's Choice TV Corp., 1993-96; v.p. mktg. and corp. comms. Digital Broadcast Corp., 1996—; exec. prodr. WCN Radio, Worldwide Corp. Network, Inc., 1998-2000. Adj. asst. prof. NYU, 1988—; adj. instr. Marymount Coll., Tarrytown, N.Y., 1981—; course leader, guest lectr. Am. Mgmt. Assn., 1976—, Am. Med. Writers Assn., 1983—, Ecole Francais des Affaires Publique, 1988-90; speaker and program coord. in field. Transmitted 1st color photograph by communications satellite, 1963; conducted 1st press interview by communications satellite, 1963; regular columnist High-Tech Mktg., Atlantic Tech., O'Dwyer's PR Svcs. Report, The Counselor; contbr. numerous articles to profl. jours. V.p., Citizens of Ramapo, 1969-70, Jewish Temple, 1980-83. Fellow AIAA (assoc.), Pub. Rels. Soc. Am. (accredited, N.Y. chpt. pres., founding nat. chmn. tech. sect. 1985—, Silver Anvil award 1980, John W. Hill award 1989, Presdl. citations 1986, 87); mem. IEEE (sr.), Am. Astron. Soc., Nat. Assn. Sci. Writers, Internat. Solar Energy Soc., Internat. Assn. Bus. Communicators, Am. Med. Writers Assn. (guest lectr. 1983—). Office: PO Box 203 Tallman NY 10982-0203 Office Phone: 845-357-5946. E-mail: jjas888@aol.com.

STRASSER, ROBERT, architectural firm executive; Grad., City U. Joined Swanke, Hayden, Connell Archs., N.Y.C., 1989, prin., CFO, 1993—, ptnr., 1998—. Mem.: AIA (CFO large firm roundtable), Fin. Execs. Internat. (pres. N.Y. chpt.). Office: SHCA 295 Lafayette St New York NY 10012*

STRASSLER, MARC A. corporate lawyer; Gen. counsel Supermarkets Gen. Corp., Woodbridge, N.J., sr. v.p., gen. counsel. Office: Pathmark Stores Inc PO Box 5301 200 Milik St Carteret NJ 07008-1102

STRASSMANN, W. PAUL, economics professor; b. Berlin, July 26, 1926; s. Erwin Otto and Ilse (Wens) S.; m. Elizabeth Marsh Fanck, June 27, 1952; children— Joan, Diana, Beverly BA magna cum laude, U. Tex., Austin, 1949; MA, Columbia U., 1950; PhD, U. Md., 1956. Econ. analyst Dept. Commerce, 1950-52; instr. U. Md., 1955; mem. faculty Mich. State U., East Lansing, 1956—, assoc. prof. econs., 1959-63, prof., 1963—. Sr. research dir. ILO, Geneva, 1969-70, 73-74; cons. World Bank, AID Author: Risk and Technological Innovation, 1959, Technological Change and Economic Development, 1968, The Transformation of Housing, 1982, (with Jill Wells) The Global Construction Industry, 1988. Served with USN, 1944-46 Mem. Am. Econ. Assn., Latin Am. Studies Assn., Am. Real Estate and Urban Econs. Assn., Assn. Evolutionary Econs., European Housing Rsch. Network, Phi Beta Kappa. Office: Mich State Univ Dept Econs East Lansing MI 48824 E-mail: strassma@msu.edu.

STRASSNER, HOWARD TAFT, JR., obstetrician, educator; b. Tulsa, Okla., Dec. 2, 1948; Undergrad. degree, U. Chgo., MD, 1974. Diplomate Am. Bd. Ob-gyn. Intern Columbia Presbyn. Med. Ctr., N.Y.C., 1974, resident ob-gyn., 1974—78; fellow maternal fetal medicine L.A. County-U. So. Calif. Med. Ctr., 1978—80; physician, dir. sect. maternal fetal medicine Rush-Presbyn.-St. Luke's Med. Ctr., Chgo., 1980—, co-dir. Rush Perinatal Ctr. John M. Simpson prof. dept. ob-gyn. Rush Med. Coll., Chgo., chmn. dept. ob-gyn. Office: Rush Med Ctr 1653 W Congress Pkwy Chicago IL 60612 Office Phone: 312-997-2229.

STRATAKIS, CHRIST, lawyer; b. Chios, Greece, June 6, 1928; s. John and Sophie S.; m. Mary C. Skinitis, Oct. 25, 1959; children: Sophia, John, Irene. BS in Econs., Drexel U., 1951; JD, NYU, 1955. Bar: N.Y. 1956, U.S. Dist. Ct. (so. and ea. dists.) 1957, U.S. Ct. Appeals (2d cir.) 1958, U.S. Ct. Customs 1965, U.S. Supreme Ct. 1970. Gen. counsel Nat. Shipping & Trading Corp., N.Y.C., 1955-59; with Poles, Tublin, Patestides & Stratakis (now Poles, Tublin, Stratakis, Gonzalez & Weickert), N.Y.C., 1960—61, ptnr., 1961—62, sr. ptnr., 1962—. Chmn. adv. coun. Ctr. Byzantine and Modern Greek Studies/Queens Coll., Flushing, N.Y., 1990—; treas., sec., vice-chmn., bd. dirs. Drexel U., 1990-96, 98—; cons., lectr. in field. Contbr. articles to profl. jours. Chmn. sch. bd. Sch. of the Transfiguration, Corona, N.Y., 1967-78; adv. coun. N.Y. dist. SBA, 1971-73; archon nat. coun. legal counsellor Order of St. Andrew the Apostle; chmn., legal com. Archdiocesan Coun. Greek Orthodox Archdiocese Am., 1998-2000. Decorated knight Holy Sepulchre of Jerusalem; recipient St. Pauls award Greek Orthodox Archdiocese N.Am. and S.Am., 1976, Laymans award, 1991, Medal of Merit award Govt. of Greece, 1974, Medal of Honor Ellis Island Found., 2001; inducted to Drexel 100, 2003. Mem. ABA, Maritime Law Assn. U.S., United Chios Socs. Am. (supreme legal advisor 1960-82), Greek-Am. Dem. of Queens Club (chmn. law com. 1960-74), Sigma Rho, Phi Alpha Delta. Greek Orthodox. Office: 5th Floor 46 Trinity Pl Fl 5 New York NY 10006-2207

STRATAS, TERESA (ANASTASIA STRATAKI), opera singer, soprano; b. Toronto, Ont., Can., May 26, 1938; Student, of Irene Jessner, 1956-59; grad., Faculty Music, U. Toronto, 1959; LLD (hon.), McMaster U., 1986, U. Toronto, 1994; hon. degree, Juilliard Sch. Music, 1995, Eastman Sch. Music, 1998, U. Rochester, 1998. Winner Met. Opera auditions, 1959; major roles in opera houses throughout world include: Mimi in La Bohème; Tatiana in Eugene Onegin; Susanna in The Marriage of Figaro; Nedda in Pagliacci; Marenka in The Bartered Bride; Three Heroines in Il Trittico; Violetta in La Traviata; title role in Rusalka; Jennie in Mahagonny; created title role in completed version of Lulu (Alban Berg), Paris Grand Opera, 1979; film appearances Kaiser von Atlantis, Seven Deadly Sins; Zefirelli's La Traviata, Salome, Lulu, Paganini, Zarewitsch, Eugene Oregin; Broadway debut in Rags, 1986; creator the role of Marie Antoinette Ghosts of Versailles world premiere Met. Opera, 1992; sang both female leading roles Il Tabarro, Pagliacci double bill opening Met. Opera, 1994, numerous recs. including Richard Strauss' Salomé, Songs of Kurt Weill. Decorated Order of Can.; recipient 3 Grammy awards, Emmy award, Drama Desk award, 1986, 3 Grammy nominations, Tony nomination, 1986, Tiffany award, 1994, Highest Paedeia award, 1996, Gemini award, 1997; named Performer of Yr., Can. Music Council, 1979. Address: The Ansonia 2109 Broadway New York NY 10023-2106

STRATE, LANCE ADAM, communications educator; b. N.Y.C., Sept. 17, 1957; s. Benjamin and Betty (Bogomolny) S.; m. Barbara Deborah Gold, Dec. 29, 1991; children: Benjamin Lewis, Sarah Gabrielle. BS, Cornell U., 1978; MA, CUNY, Flushing, 1981; PhD, NYU, 1991. Adj. lectr. CUNY, Flushing, 1979—80, Adelphi U., Garden City, 1984—87, U. Conn., Stamford, 1985—88; instr. William Patterson U., Wayne, NJ, 1988—89; adj. prof. NYU, N.Y.C., 1988—94; from instr. to assoc. prof. Fordham U., Bronx, 1989—96, assoc. prof., 1996—, assoc. chair, 1996—98, chair dept. comm. media studies, 1998—2001. Bd. dirs. Donald McGannon Ctr. Comm. Rsch. Author (chpt.): Inter/Media, Interpersonal Communication a a Media World, 1982, 1986, This Thing of Ours, 2003; author: Men, Masculinity, and the Media, 1992, A Rhetorical Analysis of Popular American Film, 1993, American Heroes in a Media Age, 1994, The Emerging Cyberculture, 2000, Academic American Ency., 1990, 2001, Grolier Multimedia Ency., 2000; co-editor: Communication and Cyberspace: Social Interaction in an Electronic Environment, 1996, 2003, Critical Studies in Media Commercialism, 2000, Explorations in Media Ecology, 2002; editor: Speech Comm. Annual, 2000, 2001; mem. editl. bd. N.J. Jour. Comm., 1995—2003, Media Ecology, 1996—, Interpersonal Computing Tech., 1996—, Qualitative Rsch. Reports, 1999—, Jour. Comm. Culture, 2001—; mem. editl. bd.: Etc., 2003—, supervisory editor: Hampton Press, 1994—; reviewer Acad. Am. Ency., 1989, New Dimension Comm., 1992, Comm. Rsch., 1995, scriptwriter Area Arts, 1982; scriptwriter Adventures of Galaxy Rangers, 1985—86; contbr. articles; dir., actor: Area Arts, 1982. Advisor Mothers Onward Search for Autism Intervention and Cure, 1999—; bd. dirs. Temple Beth Elohim, Hasbrouck Heights, N.J., 1994-96, co-chair publ. com., co-editor newsletter. John F. Wilson fellow N.Y. State Comm. Assn., 1998; grantee Am. Automobile Assn. Found. Traffic Safety Rsch., 1987, Fordham U., 1996, 97, Can. Consulate, 1998-2002. Mem. Internat. Comm. Assn., Internat. Soc. Gen. Semantics, Nat. Comm. Assn. (nominating com., comm. comm. in future 1997-98, local arrangements com., chair conv. registration com. 1998), Am. Comm. Assn., Autism Soc. Am., Ctr. Outreach Svcs. Autistic Cmty., Ea. Comm. Assn. (assoc. program contbr. 1999-2000), N.J. Comm. Assn. (bd. dirs. 1997-99), Media Ecology Assn. (founding pres. 1998—), N.Y. State Speech Comm. Assn. (v.p. 1997-98, pres. 1998-99), Kappa Delta Pi. Democrat. Jewish. Home: 519 Fourth St Palisades Park NJ 07650 Office: Dept Comm Media Studies Fordham U Bronx NY 10458 E-mail: strate@fordham.edu.

STRATIGOS, WILLIAM NARGE, computer company executive; b. Huntington, N.Y., Mar. 14, 1946; s. Narge G. and Portia R. (Kleros) Stratigos; m. Deborah Feller, Jan. 4, 1981; children: Stephanie, Elena. BA in Biology cum laude, NYU, 1972, DDS, 1977. Lic. dentist N.Y. Mgr. div. Med. Ctr. NYU, N.Y.C., 1966-74; mng. ptnr., dentist Stratigos et al, N.Y.C., 1978-88; pres. Sigma Imaging Sys. Inc., N.Y.C., 1988-95; also bd. dirs. Sigma Imaging Sys., Inc., N.Y.C., NY; v.p. Wang Software, N.Y., Inc., N.Y.C., 1995-97, Eastman Software, Inc., N.Y.C., 1997; v.p., bd. dirs. R2K, Inc., N.Y.C., 1997—; pres. Comfidex Corp., N.Y.C., 1998—. Bd. dirs. Animal Med. Ctr. Author: (book) Hot Spot, 1993. Fellow: NYU Acad. Oral Rehab.; mem.: First Dist. Dental Soc., Dental Soc. State of N.Y., Assn. Image & Info. Mgmt. Internat. (bd. dirs., treas. exec. com., chmn. accreditation com.), Omicron Kappa Upsilon. Greek Orthodox. Achievements include patents in field. Avocations: writing, chess, bowling. Office: R2K Inc 83 Maiden Ln New York NY 10038 E-mail: wstratigos@aol.com.

STRATING, SHARON L. elementary school educator, professional staff developer, educational consultant; b. Jamestown, ND, Jan. 20, 1949; d. Walter and Evelyn Darlene (Lang) Remmick; m. Rick Donald Strating, Dec. 24, 1978 (presently divorced); children: Heather Dawn, Amber Nicole, Ashley Renee. BS in Secondary Edn., S.W. Mo. State U., 1971; MEd in Sci. Edn., N.W. Mo. State U., 1992. Cert. elem. tchr., Mo. Tchr. Cassville R-III Sch., 1971-76, Savannah R-III Sch. Sys., Mo., 1976-91; instr. 4th grade Horace Mann Lab. Sch., Maryville, Mo., 1991—2003; profl. staff developer Regional Profl. Devel. Ctr., N.W. Mo. State U., Maryville, 2003—. Facilitator for Environ. Edn. Pilot Project Kans. U., Lawrence; co-chair EPA Pollution Prevention Adv. Task Force; mem. biol. sci. curriculum study Elem. Tchr. Module Project, 1993; instr. for coll. practicum students; Map 2000 Sr. Leader for performance-based assessment sys., Mo., 1994—. Author: Living the Constitution Through the Eyes of the Newspaper, 1987, Tabloid Teaching Tool, 6 edits., 1986-91; tchr. guides in lit. revised editions for Sadako and the Thousand Paper Cranes, The Kid in the Red Jacket, Missing Gator of Gumbo Limbo, Owls in the Family, Where the Waves Break: Life at the Edge of the Sea, 2000-2001; author: Open the Eyes of Children to the World of Literacy Through Comprehensive Literacy, Prof. Develop. Program, 2002. Chairperson March of Dimes, 1972-76, Cystic Fibrosis, 1972-78; scout leader Brownies, 1976-77; exec. bd. dirs. PTA, 1976-82, fund raising chairperson, 1976-83; program chairperson presch. PTA, 1976-80;chairperson community environ. activities, 1976—, Adopt a Hwy. Program, 1976-91; mem. Mo. Stream Team Effort, 1976—. Recipient Nat. Pres. Environ. Youth award, 1988, 89, Presdl. award State of Mo., 1992, 93, Nat. Presdl. award, 1992-93; named Mo. State Tchr. of Yr., 1990-91, Disney Salutes the Am. Tchr. award, 1995. Mem. Nat. Hist. Soc., Internat. Reading Assn., Nat. Bd. for Profl. Tching. Standards and Mid.-Age Child in Sci., Nat. Sci. Tchrs. Assn., Nat. Assn. Lab. Schs. (sec. 1994-95), Sci. Tchrs. Mo. Lutheran. Avocations: travel, ecology, creative writing, motivational speaking, arts and crafts. Office: Northwest Mo State U McKemy Ctr for Lifelong Learning Maryville MO 64468 Home: 3A Faustiana Pl Maryville MO 64468 Office Phone: 660-562-1515.

STRATMAN, DEBORAH, filmmaker, film and video educator; BFA, Sch. of the Art Inst. of Chgo., 1990; MFA, Calif. Inst. of the Arts, 1995. Adj. asst. prof. Film, Video and New Media, 1998; filmmaker and adj. asst., prof. film and video Sch. of Art Inst. of Chgo., 1998—. John Simon Guggenheim Meml. Found., 2003. Office: 37 South Wabash Chicago IL 60603-3103

STRATMAN, JOSEPH LEE, retired petroleum refining company executive, consultant, chemical engineer; b. Louisville, Oct. 15, 1924; s. Dominic Herman and Mary Ann (Wolf) S.; m. Elizabeth Jewell Doyle, July 1, 1950; children: Joseph Lee, Mary Elizabeth, Sharon Ann, Judith Ann. BChemE, U. Louisville, 1947. Registered profl. engr., Tex. Chem. engr. Pan Am. Refining Corp., Texas City, Tex., 1947-55, operating supr., 1955-61; mgr. Texas City Refining, Inc., Texas City, Tex., 1961-69, v.p., 1969-80, sr. v.p., 1980-88; pvt. practice, 1988-2001. Bd. dirs., exec. com., treas., chmn. Galveston County ARC, 1966-73; bd. dirs., exec. com., chmn. Texas City Jr. Achievement, 1966-73; treas. Texas City Refining Good Govt. Fund., 1983-88. With USNR, 1945-46. Mem. AIChE. Roman Catholic.

STRATMANN, HENRY GEORGE, cardiologist; b. Dec. 1, 1953; s. Henry George Sr. and Helen Catherine (Schrader) S.; m. Maryellen Amato, May 12, 1984; children: Henry, Joseph. BA in Chemistry, St. Louis U., 1974; MD, So. Ill. U., 1977. Diplomate Am. Bd. Internal Medicine and Cardiology. Intern St. Louis U. Group Hosps., 1977-78, resident in internal medicine, 1978-80; fellow in cardiology, 1980-82; mem. staff John Cochran VA Hosp., St. Louis, 1982—, St. John's Regional Health Ctr., 2002—; prof. medicine St. Louis U. Sch. Medicine, 1997—. Contbr. articles to profl. jours. Cardiology fellowship St. Louis U. Group Hosps., 1980-82. Fellow Am. Coll. Physicians, Am. Coll. Angiology, Am. Coll. Cardiology, Am. Coll. Chest Physicians. Office: 1900 S National Ste 3600 Springfield MO 65804 E-mail: hstratmann@aol.com.

STRATON, JOHN CHARLES, JR., investment banker; b. Warwick, N.Y., Apr. 18, 1932; s. John Charles and Helen (Sanford) S.; m. Sally M. Strawhand (div. Mar. 1970); children: John Charles III, Sara; m. Marion S. Holder, Feb. 18, 1974 (div. Mar. 1997); 1 child, Ashley Holder Straton; m. Donna S. DeCoursey, June 24, 1998. BA, U. Va., 1954. With Jas. H. Oliphant and Co., N.Y.C., 1956—, gen. ptnr., 1962—, 1st v.p., 1972-75; v.p. Spencer Trask & Co., Inc., N.Y.C., 1975-77, Hornblower, Weeks, Noyes & Trask, N.Y.C., 1977-78, Loeb Rhoades, Hornblower & Co., 1978-79, Shearson Loeb Rhoades, 1979-81; v.p., fin. cons. Shearson Lehman Bros., N.Y.C., 1981-93; sr. v.p. Smith Barney, N.Y.C., 1993—, Saloman Smith Barney, N.Y.C., 1997—, Smith Barney, N.Y.C., 2004—. Assessor Village of Tuxedo Park, N.Y., 1963-70. Vestryman St. Mary's, Tuxedo, N.Y. Served to maj. AUS, 1954-56; ret. Mem. U. Va. Alumni Assn. N.Y. (pres., treas. 1973-90), Mil. Order Fgn. Wars (comdr. 1981-86, treas. 1986—), Pilgrims of U.S., Tuxedo Park Club, Sigma Phi Epsilon. Home: 2 Ledge Rd Tuxedo Park NY 10987 Office: 250 Park Ave New York NY 10177-0001

STRATT, RICHARD MARK, chemistry researcher, educator; b. Phila., Feb. 21, 1954; s. Stanford Lloyd and Florence Clair (Sussman) S. SB in Chemistry, MIT, 1975; PhD, U. Calif., Berkeley, 1979. Postdoctoral rsch. assoc. U. Ill., Champaign, 1979-80; NSF postdoctoral rsch. assoc., 1980; asst. prof. chemistry Brown U., Providence, 1981-85, assoc. prof., 1986-88, prof., 1988—, dept. chair, 1996—99, Harrison S. Kravis prof., 1999—2000. Mem. editl. bd. Jour. Chem. Physics, 2002—, Molecular Physics, 2003—; mem. adv. bd. Jour. Phys. Chemistry, 1999—; contbr. articles to profl. jours. Alfred P. Sloan fellow, 1985-89; Fulbright scholar Oxford U., 1991-92. Fellow Am. Phys. Soc.; mem. Am. Chem. Soc. (chmn.-elect theoretical chem. subdivsn. 1997-98, chair 1998-99, program chair phys. chem. divsn. 2000-01, chair 2001-02), Sigma Xi, Phi Lambda Upsilon. Office: Brown U Dept Chemistry Providence RI 02912-0001 Office Phone: 401-863-3418. Business E-Mail: Richard_Stratt@brown.edu.

STRATTON, EVELYN LUNDBERG, judge; b. Bangkok, Feb. 25, 1953; came to U.S., 1971 (parents Am. citizens); d. Elmer John and Corrine Sylvia (Henricksen) Sahlberg; children: Luke Andrew, Tyler John; m. Jack A. Lundberg. Student, LeTourneau Coll., Longview, Tex., 1971-74; AA, U. Fla., 1973; BA, U. Akron, 1976; JD, Ohio State U., 1978. Bar: Ohio 1979, U.S. Dist. Ct. (so. dist.) Ohio 1979, U.S. Ct. Appeals (6th cir.) 1983. Assoc. Hamilton, Kramer, Myers & Cheek, Columbus, 1979-85; ptnr. Wesp, Osterkamp & Stratton, 1985-88; judge Franklin County Ct. Common Pleas, 1989-96; justice Ohio State Supreme Ct., 1996—. Vis. prof. Nat. Jud. Coll., 1997—; spkr. legal seminars. Contbr. articles to profl. jours. Trustee Ohio affiliate Nat. Soc. to Prevent Blindness, 1989—, bd. dirs., trustee Columbus Coun. World Affairs, 1990-99, chmn. bd. dirs., 1999—; bd. dirs., trustee Dave Thomas Adoption Found., 1996—, ArChSafe Found., 1997—; mem. women's bd. Zephyrus League Cen. Ohio Lung Assn., 1989—; mem. Alliance Women Cmty. Corrections, 1993—. Recipient Gold Key award LeTourneau Coll., Gainesville, Fla., 1974, Svc. commendation Ohio Ho. of Reps., 1984, Scholar of Life award St. Joseph's Orphanage, 1998. Mem. ABA, ATLA, Columbus Bar Assn. (bd. govs. 1984-88, 90—, lectr.), Ohio Bar Assn. (jud. adminstrv. and legal reform com., coun. dels. 1992-96, Ohio Cmty. Corrections Orgn. (trustee 1995—), Columbus Bar Found. (trustee 1986-91, officer, sec. 1986-87, v.p. 1987-88), Am. Inns of Ct., Women Lawyers Franklin County, Phi Alpha Delta (pres. 1982-83). Office: Supreme Ct Ohio 30 E Broad St Fl 3 Columbus OH 43215

STRATTON, GREGORY ALEXANDER, computer specialist, administrator, mayor; b. Glendale, Calif., July 31, 1946; s. William Jaspar and Rita Phyllis (Smith) S.; m. Yolanda Margot Soler, 1967 (div. 1974); 1 child, Tiffany Schwarzer; m. Edith Carter, Sept. 27, 1975; stepchildren: Paul Henkell, D'Lorah Henkell Wismar. Student, Harvey Mudd Coll., 1964-65; BS in Physics, UCLA, 1968; MBA, Calif. Luth. U., 1977. Elec. engr. Naval Ship Weapon System Engring. Sta., Port Hueneme, Calif., 1968-73; sr. staff mem. Univac, Valencia, Calif., 1973-74; v.p. Digital Applications, Camarillo, Calif., 1974-75; cons. Grumman Aerospace, Point Mugu, Calif., 1975-76; F-14 software mgr. Pacific Missle Test Ctr., Pt. Mugu, 1976-84; software mgr. Teledyne Systems, Northridge, Calif., 1984-92, dir. engring. software dept., 1992-93; dep. dir. software engring. Teledyne Electronic Systems, Northridge, Calif., 1993-94; software mgr. Litton Guidance and Controls, Woodland Hills, Calif., 1995-2001, Northrop/Grumman Nav. Sys., Woodland Hills, Calif., 2001—. Mem. strategic planning Simi Valley Hosp. Mem. City Coun., City of Simi Valley, Calif., 1979-86, mayor, 1986-98; mem. Rep. County Cen. Com., Ventura County, 2000—; mem. Rep. State Cen. Com., Calif., 1990—; bd. dirs. Simi Valley Hosp., 1987-2001; pres. Simi Valley Cultural Arts Found., 1999—; trustee Simi Valley Unified Sch. Dist, 2002—. Mem. Rotary (Paul Harris award Simi Sunrise chpt. 1989), Jaycees (pres. Simi Valley chpt. 1974-75, nat. bd. dirs. 1975-76, v.p. Calif. state 1976-77). Republican. Lutheran. Home: 2003 Tulip Ave Simi Valley CA 93063 Office: Northrop Grumman Navigation Sys 5500 Canoga Ave Woodland Hills CA 91367-6698 E-mail: gastratton@sbcglobal.net., greg.stratton@ngc.com.

STRATTON, JESSIE GRAY, state legislator; b. Swarthmore, Pa., Feb. 18, 1947; d. Caleb Allen and Jeannette (Poole) S.; m. Richard Arthur Stratton, 1970; children: Christopher Caleb, Susan Elise, David Pickett. BA, Earlham Coll., 1969. Tchr. social studies Olney Friends Sch., Barnesville, Ohio, 1970-76; mem. Canton Dem. Town Com., 1982—, vice chmn., 1987—; mem. Conn. Ho. of Reps., Hartford, 1989—. Del. Dem. Nat. Conv., 1984, 88. Del. Dem. Nat. Conv., 1984, 88; bd. dirs.,mem. exec. com. Sane/Freeze Campaign for Global Security, 1985-89. Home: 33 Bahre Corner Rd Canton CT 06019-2230 Office: Conn Ho of Reps State Capitol Hartford CT 06106

STRATTON, JOHN ALFRED, electrical engineer, educator; b. Rochester, N.Y., Sept. 12, 1941; s. Burton Elbridge and Alice Adele (Howie) Stratton; m. Lois Averett; children: Thomas C., Linda S. Palmer, Ann-Marie Giannosa. AAS, Rochester Inst. Technology, 1962, BS, 1964; MSEE, Rensselaer Poly. Inst., Troy, N.Y., 1966. Profl. engr. Sys. planning engr. N.Y. State Elec. & Gas, Binghamton, 1966—69; asst. prof. Alfred State Coll., NY, 1969—71; from prof. elec. engring. tech. to chair dept., assoc. dean Rochester Inst. Tech., 1971—99, chair mfg. & mech. engring. technology, pckg. sci., 1999—2003, prof. elec./mech. engring., 2003—. Cons. in field. Mem. IEEE, Inst. Power Engring. Soc., Am. Soc. Engring. Edn. Avocation: riding trains. Home: 43 Queensway Rd Rochester NY 14623-4627 Office: Rochester Inst Technology 78 Lomb Memorial Dr Rochester NY 14623-5604 Office Phone: 716-475-2017. E-mail: jasite@rit.edu.

STRATTON, KATHLEEN R. medical association administrator; PhD. Dir. divsn. health promotion and disease prevention Inst. Medicine NAS, sr. program officer, 1999—2002; study dir. Immunization Safety Rev. Comm., Inst. of Medicine, 2002—. Office: Inst Medicine Foundry Bldg 1055 Thomas Jefferson St NW Washington DC 20007-5259 also: 2101 Constitution Ave NW Washington DC 20418-0007

STRATTON, MARIANN, retired naval nursing administrator; b. Houston, Apr. 6, 1945; d. Max Millard and Beatrice Agnes (Roemer) S.; m. Lawrence Mallory Stickney, nov. 15, 1977 (dec.). BSN, BA in English, Sacred Heart Dominican Coll., 1966; MA in Mgmt., Webster Coll., 1977; MSN, U. Va., 1981. Cert. adult nurse practitioner. Ensign USN, 1966, advanced through grades to rear adm., 1991; patient care coord. Naval Regional Med. Ctr., Charleston, S.C., 1981-83; nurse corps plans officer Naval Med. Command, Washington, 1983-86; dir. nursing svcs. U.S. Naval Hosp., Naples, Italy, 1986-89, Naval Hosp., San Diego, 1989-91; chief pers. mgmt. Bur. Medicine & Surgery, Washington, 1991-94; dir. USN Nurse Corps, Washington, 1991-94; ret. Oct. 1, 1994 USN, 1994. Decorated Disting. Svc. medal, Meritorious Svc. medal with two stars, Naval Achievement medal. Mem. Interagy. Inst. of Fed. Health Care Execs., Am. Volksporting Assn., Tex. Wanders, D'Vine Women, Garden Vols. of South Tex.

STRATTON, ROBERT, retired electronics executive; b. Vienna, Aug. 14, 1928; came to U.S., 1959, naturalized, 1966; s. Kenneth Kurt and Eugenie (Schwatzer) S.; m. Elfriede Karlberger, Jan. 11, 1980; children: David Alexander, Valerie Pam. B.Sc. in Physics, Manchester U., 1949, PhD in Theoretical Physics, 1952. Rsch. physicist Met. Vickers Elec. Co., Manchester, Eng., 1952-59; with Tex. Instruments, Inc., Dallas, 1959-94, dir. physics rsch. lab., 1963-71, assoc. dir. cen. rsch. labs., 1971-72, dir. semiconductor R & D, 1972-75, dir. cen. rsch. labs., 1975-77, asst. v.p., dir. cen. rsch. labs., 1977-82, v.p. corp. staff, dir. cen. rsch. labs., 1982-94; dir. Indsl. Outreach Elec. Materials Sci. Tech. Ctr., dir. Engring. and Tech. Inst., U. Tex., Austin, 1994-96. Contbr. articles to profl. jours. Bd. dirs. Indsl. Rsch. Inst., 1985-88, Coun. on Superconductivity for Am. Competitiveness, 1987-90; adv. bd. dirs. Tex. Ctr. for Superconductivity, 1989-2000. Fellow IEEE, Inst. Physics (U.K.), Am. Phys. Soc.; mem. NAE. Personal E-mail: rstratton@comcast.net.

STRATTON, WALTER LOVE, lawyer; b. Greenwich, Conn., Sept. 21, 1926; s. John McKee and June (Love) S.; children: John, Michael, Peter (dec.), Lucinda; m. DeAnna Weinheimer, Oct. 1, 1994. Student, Williams Coll., 1943; AB, Yale U., 1948; LL.B., Harvard U., 1951. Bar: N.Y. 1952. Assoc. Casey, Lane & Mittendorf, N.Y.C., 1951-53; assoc. Donovan, Leisure, Newton & Irvine, N.Y.C., 1956-63, ptnr., 1963-84, Gibson, Dunn & Crutcher, 1984-93, Andrews & Kurth, N.Y.C., 1993-95, of counsel, 1996—. Asst. U.S. atty. So. Dist. N.Y., N.Y.C., 1953-56; lectr. Practising Law Inst. Served with USNR, 1945-46. Fellow: Am. Coll. Trial Lawyers; mem.: ABA, N.Y. State Bar Assn., Fed. Bar Coun., Greenwich Riding and Trails Assn. (chmn.), Colo. Arlberg Club, Indian Harbor Yacht Club. Home: 434 Round Hill Rd Greenwich CT 06831-2639 also: Andrews & Kurth 450 Lexington Ave 15th Fl New York NY 10017-3911 Office Phone: 212-850-2821. Business E-Mail: walterstratton@akllp.com.

STRATTON-CROOKE, THOMAS EDWARD, financial consultant; b. NYC, June 28, 1933; s. Harold and Jeanne (Stifft); children: Karen, John Ryland; m. Suzanne Williams, Oct. 21, 1989. Student, Hunter Coll., 1951-52; BS in Marine Engring. and Transp., U.S. Maritime Acad., 1952-56; student, Washington U., St. Louis, 1961; MBA in Internat. Mktg., Banking and Fin., NYU, 1967. Commd. ensign USN, 1956, advanced through grades to lt., 1957; with Goodyear Internat. Corp., Akron, Ohio, 1960-63, Esso Internat., N.Y.C., 1958-60; dir. market info. and devel. Hotel Corp. Am., Boston, 1964-68; with Continental Grain Co., N.Y.C., 1968-72; dir. charter contracts Conoco, Stamford, Conn., 1973-75; cons. A. T. Kearney, Cleve., 1976-81; investment banker E. F. Hutton, Cleve., 1981-83, AG Edwards and Sons, Inc., Cleve., 1983-89; sr. fin. advisor, registered investment advisor, asst. v.p., sr. fin. cons. Merrill Lynch, Cleve., 1989—. Chmn. Indsl. Devel. Resch. Coun., Atlanta, 1970, Indsl. Devel. Resch. Coun., Snow Mass, Colo., 1971; lectr. bus. U. R.I., Kingston, 1968-70, tchr. Bus. Coll. Internat., 1986-89. Contbr. articles to profl. jours. Mem. Findley Lake (N.Y.) Hist. Soc.; mem. Nat. Task Force Reps. for Pres. Reagan, Cleve., 1982—. Officer (ret.) USN. Mem. Naval Res. Officers Assn., Naval Res. Assn., Great Lakes Hist. Soc., Soc. Naval Architects/Engrs., Navy League, Civil War Roundtable, NYU Alumni Assn., U.S. Coast Guard Club (Cleve.), Univ. Club, Circumnavigators Club (life), Internat. Shipmasters Assn., Propeller Club, Army Club, Navy Club, French Creek Hist. Soc., Town Club (Jamestown, N.Y.), Masons, Shriners, Cleve. City Club, Kings Point Alumni Assn., Civil War Round Table, U.S. Mcht. Marine Acad., English Speaking Union (chpt. bd. dirs.). Avocations: sailing, skiing, bird watching, gardening, sports car enthusiast. Office: Merrill Lynch One Cleveland Ctr 1375 E 9th St Cleveland OH 44114-1798 Office Phone: 216-363-6717. E-mail: tommyesc@aol.com.

STRAUB, CHESTER JOHN, judge; b. Bklyn., May 12, 1937; s. Chester and Ann (Majewski) Straub; m. Patricia Morrissey; children: Chester, Michael, Christopher, Robert. AB, St. Peter's Coll., 1958; JD, U. Va., 1961. Bar: N.Y. 1962, U.S. Dist. Ct. (so. and ea. dists.) N.Y. 1963, U.S. Ct. Appeals (2d cir.) 1967, U.S. Supreme Ct. 1978. Assoc. Willkie Farr & Gallagher, N.Y.C., 1963—71, ptnr., 1971—98; mem. N.Y. State Assembly, 1967—72, N.Y. State Senate, 1973—75, Dem. Nat. Com., 1976—80; judge U.S. Ct. Appeals (2d cir.), 1998—. Past mediator U.S. Dist. Ct. (so. dist.) N.Y.; neutral evaluator U.S. Dist. Ct. (ea. dist.) N.Y.; chmn. jud. screening com. State of N.Y., 1988—94, first dept. jud. screening com., 1983—94, Senator Moynihan's jud. selection com., 1976—98. Trustee Lenox Hill Hosp.; Cardinal's com. laity Cath. Charities, NY. With U.S. Army, 1961—63. Mem.: ABA, Assn. of Bar of City of N.Y.C., N.Y. State Bar Assn., Kosciuszko Found. Office: US Ct Appeals Second Circuit 500 Pearl St New York NY 10007-1316

STRAUB, LINDA CATHERINE, poet; b. Tampa, Fla., Sept. 12, 1948; d. Martin James and Alvena Mae (Carwile) Estep; m. Robert E. Straub, May 23, 1970 (div. Mar. 1991); children: Robert Jeffrey, Amy Catherine, Kyle Martin. Cert. exec. sec., Lansdale (Pa.) Sch. Bus., 1968. Mgr. adminstrv. br. Navy Resale and Support Svcs., Mechanicsburg, Pa., 1987-90; exec. sec. A.Z. Ritzman Assocs., Harrisburg, Pa., 1990-95; adminstrv. asst. HealthAm. of Pa., Harrisburg, 1996—. Contbr. poetry and short stories to lit. jours. and comml. mags. Mem. Acad. Am. Poets, IWWG, Pennwriters. Avocations: guitar, reading, photography.

STRAUB, PETER FRANCIS, novelist; b. Milw., Mar. 2, 1943; s. Gordon Anthony and Elvena (Nilsestuen) S.; m. Susan Bitker, Aug. 27, 1966; children: Benjamin Bitker, Emma Sydney Valli. BA, U. Wis., 1965; MA, Columbia U., 1966. English tchr. Univ. Sch., Milw., 1966-68. Author: Marriages, 1973, Julia, 1975, If You Could See Me Now, 1977, Ghost Story, 1979, Shadowland, 1980, Floating Dragon, 1983, Leeson Park and Belsize Square, 1984, Wild Animals, 1984, Blue Rose, 1985, Koko, 1988, Mystery, 1989, Houses Without Doors, 1990, Mrs. God, 1991, The Throat, 1993, The Hellfire Club, 1996, Mr. X, 1999, Pork Pie Hat, 1999, Magic Terror, 2000, Lost Boy Lost Girl, 2003, In the Night Room, 2004; (with Stephen King) The Talisman, 1984, Black House, 2001; editor: Peter Straub's Ghosts, 1995, Conjunctions #39, 2002. Recipient Brit. Fantasy award, August Derleth award, 1983, World Fantasy awards World Fantasy Conv., 1989, 93, World Horror Assn. awards, 1993, 98, 99, 2000, 03, Grand Master award, World Horror Conv., 1997, award Internat. Horror Guild, 1999, 2003. Mem. PEN, Horror Writers Assn. Avocations: jazz, opera, classical music. E-mail: pstraub@nyc.rr.com.

STRAUB, PETER THORNTON, lawyer; b. St. Louis, Mar. 27, 1939; s. Ralph H. and Mary Louise (Thornton) S.; m. Wendy B. Cubbage, Dec. 29, 1964; children: Karl Thornton, Philip Hamilton, Ellen Elizabeth. AB, Washington and Lee U., 1961, LLB, 1964. Bar: Mo. 1964, Va. 1964, U.S. Dist. Ct. (ea. dist.) Mo. 1967, U.S. Circuit Ct. Appeals (8th cir.) 1969, U.S. Supreme Ct. 1970. U.S. Circuit Ct. Appeals (D.C. cir.) 1971, Ct. Mil. Appeals 1970, U.S. Tax Ct. 1971, U.S. Bankruptcy Ct. 1991. Assoc. Evans & Dixon, St. Louis, 1966-68; asst. pub. defender St. Louis County, St. Louis, 1968-69; asst. U.S. Atty. St. Louis, 1969-71; trial atty. internal security div. Dept. Justice, Washington, 1971-72, atty.-adviser office of dep. atty. gen., 1972-73, dir. office criminal justice, spl. asst. to atty. gen., 1974; minority counsel com. on judiciary U.S. Ho. of Reps., Washington, 1973-74; gen. counsel SSS, Washington, 1974-76; pvt. practice Law Offices of Peter T. Straub, Alexandria, Va., 1976—. Pres., gov. bd. Alexandria Cmty. Mental Health Ctr., 1982—95; mem. No. Va. Estate Planning Coun., 1981—; mem. pres.'s coun. Trinity Coll., Washington, 1980—87; mem. adv. bd. Am. Heart Assn., Alexandria, 1991—92, Salvation Army, Alexandria, 1991—, v.p., 1994—96, chmn., 1997—99, Alexandria Cmty. Shelter Adv. Bd., 1995—97; Va. escheat atty. City of Alexandria, 1994—2002; dist. chmn. Boy Scouts Am., 1998—2001; mem. adv. bd. Hospice No. Va., 2000—; bd. dirs. Friends of the Washington and Old Dominion Trail, 2002—, Parc East Condominium, 1990—, sec., 1992—; bd. dirs. Sigma Nu Ednl. Found., Inc., 2000—; charter mem. bd. dirs. Alexandria Country Day Sch., 1983—90. Recipient certificate of award Dept. Justice, 1970, certificate of appreciation Law Enforcement Assistance Adminstrn. Dept. Justice, 1974, Silver Beaver award Boy Scouts Am., Washington, 1987, Collins award Alexandria Coun. Persons with Disabilities, 1993, Cmty. Svc. award Am. Indian Alliance, 1995. Mem.: FBA, ABA, Va. Trial Lawyers Assn., Alexandria Bar Assn., Mo. Bar Assn., Bar Assn. Met. St. Louis, Va. State Bar Assn., Optimists (bd. dirs., pres. Alexandria chpt. 1984, lt. gov. Nat. Capitol Va. Dist. 1987—89, treas. 1999—2001), Nat. Eagle Scout Assn., Nat. Lawyers Club, Sigma Nu. Republican. Congregationalist. Avocations: scouting, reading, bicycling. Office: 1225 Martha Custis Dr # 103 Alexandria VA 22302-2040 Fax: 703-820-8602. Office Phone: 703-820-3600. E-mail: straublaw@erols.com.

STRAUB, SUSAN MONICA, special education educator; b. Tampa, Fla., Jan. 31, 1954; d. Paul Ferdinand and Betty Hew (Wellacott) S. AA, Hillsborough Community Coll., 1975; BA, U. S. Fla., 1978. Lifeguard, swimming instr. Tampa Recreation Dept., 1970-74 summers, pool mgr., 1975-76 summers, office asst. sec., 1977-78 summers; tchr. Hillsborough Assn. Retarded Citizens, Tampa, 1978-79, Hillsborough County Sch. Bd., Tampa, 1979—, Sch. of Hope, 1979-81, Mango Elem. Sch., 1981-85, Lopez Elem Sch., Seffner, Fla., 1985-93, Wilson Elem. Sch., Plant City, Fla., 1993-98, Mann Mid. Sch., Brandon, Fla., 1998-2000, Armwood H.S., Seffner, Fla., 2000—. Coach Spl. Olympics, Tampa, 1980, 2000—, games ofcl., 1982, steering com., Hillsborough County, 1984-92. Sec., treas. Superstar Bowling League for Handicapped, Tampa, 1988-89, 1st v.p., 1989-91. Recipient Spl. Olympics award Hillsborough County, State of Fla., 1980; named Vol. of Yr. Mass. Mutual, 1982, Coach of Yr. Hillsborough County Spl. Olympics, 1982, Tchr. of Yr. U. So. Fla. Alumni Assn., 1990. Mem. Coun. Exceptional Children (hospitality chair, Dept. Exceptional Student Edn. Person of Yr. 1987-88, Chpt. Tchr. of Yr. 1990), Soroptimist Internat. (1st v.p., 2d v.p. 1990-91, Team Leader 1985-91, 92-93). Democrat. Roman Catholic. Avocations: soccer, swimming. Home: 517 Somerstone Dr Valrico FL 33594 Office: Lithia Springs Elem Lynx Paw Tr Valrico FL 33594 E-mail: straubsl@gte.net.

STRAUCH, BERISH, plastic surgeon, hand and cosmetic surgeon; b. New York City, Sept. 19, 1933; m. Rena (Feuerstein), June 12, 1955; children: Robert, Laurie. BS, Columbia U., 1955, MD, 1959. Diplomate Am. Bd. Surgery, Am. Bd. Plastic Surgery, qualification in hand surgery. Intern Bellevue Hosp., N.Y.C., 1959—60; resident gen. surgery Montefiore Med. Ctr., Bronx, NY, 1960—63; hand surgery fellow Roosvelt Hosp., N.Y.C., 1961; resident plastic surgery Stanford U., Palo Alto, Calif., 1966—67, chief resident, 1967—68; asst. prof. plastic surgery Albert Einstein Coll. Medicine, Bronx, NY, 1970—76, assoc. prof., 1976—81; chief plastic surgery svc. Montefiore Med. Ctr. and Albert Einstein Coll. Medicine, Bronx, NY, 1978—87; prof. plastic surgery Albert Einstein Coll. Medicine and Montefiore Med. Ctr., Bronx, NY, 1981—; acting chmn. dept. Montefiore Med. Ctr. and Albert Einstein Coll. Medicine, Bronx, NY, 1987—89, chmn., 1989—. Instr. Stanford U., 1967-68; vis. plastic surgeon Sing Sing Prison, N.Y., 1968-75. Co-author: (with others) Atlas of Microvascular Surgery: Anatomy and Operative Approaches, 1993 (Best Healt Sci. Book, Doody's Rating Svc. 1993); co-editor: Textbook on Microsurgery, 1976, (with others) Grabb's Encyclopedia of Flaps, 3 vols., 1990, (Outstanding Publ. in Clin. Medicine, Assn. Am. Pub. 1990), 2d edit. 1997; contbr. articles to profl. journals. and 20 chpts. to sci. books; assoc. editor Plastic and Reconstructive Surgery, 1982-88; founder, editor-in-chief Jour. Reconstructive Microsurgery, 1984—. Capt. Med. Corp. U.S. Army, 1964-66, Mem. AAAS, ACS, Am. Soc. for Reconstructive Microsurgery (founder, past sec., treas., pres., chmn. Founder's Lectr. 1988), Am. Assn. Plastic Surgeons, Internat. Soc. Reconstructive Microsurgery (chmn. founding coun. 1983-84, pres. 1984-85). Med. Soc. State of N.Y., Am. Trauma Soc. (founding mem.), N.Y. Acad. Sci., Am. Soc. for Peripheral Nerve Surgery (pres. 1993-94), and others. Office: Montefiore Med Pk 1625 Poplar St Ste 200 Bronx NY 10461-2653 Office Phone: 718-405-8444. Business E-Mail: bstrauch@montefiore.org.

STRAUCH, JOHN L. lawyer; b. Pitts., Apr. 16, 1939; s. Paul L. and Delilah M. (Madison) S.; m. Gail Lorraine Kohn, Dec. 5, 1991; children: Paul L., John M., Lisa E. BA summa cum laude, U. Pitts., 1960; JD magna cum laude, NYU Sch. Law, 1963. Law clk. to Judge Sterry Waterman U.S. Ct. Appeals (2d cir.), St. Johnsbury, Vt., 1963-64; assoc. Jones, Day, Reavis & Pogue, Cleve., 1964-70, ptnr., 1970—, mem. adv. com., partnership com., chmn. litigation group. Mem. Statutory Com. on Selecting Bankruptcy Judges, Cleve., 1985-88; mem. lawyers com. Nat. Ctr. for State Cts. Editor-in-chief: NYU Law Rev., 1962-63; contbr. chpt. to book. Pres., trustee Cleve. Task Force on Violent Crimes, 1985-88; trustee Legal Aid Soc., Cleve., 1978, Cleve. Greater Growth Assn., 1985-86, Citizens Mental Health Assembly, 1989-90, lawyers com. Nat. Ctr. for State Cts., 1989—. Fellow Am. Coll. Trial Lawyers (life); mem. ABA, Ohio Bar Assn., Cleve. Bar Assn. (trustee 1980-83, pres. 1985-86), Fed. Bar Assn. (trustee Cleve. chpt. 1978-79, v.p. Cleve. chpt. 1979-80), Sixth Fed. Jud. Conf. (life), Ohio Eighth Jud. Conf. (life), Order of Coif, Inns of Ct., Oakmont Country Club, The Country Club, Kiawah Island Club, Phi Beta Kappa. Home: 28149 N Woodland Rd Cleveland OH 44124-4522 Office: Jones Day Reavis & Pogue N Point 901 Lakeside Ave E Cleveland OH 44114-1190

STRAUGHAN, WILLIAM THOMAS, engineering educator; b. Shreveport, La., Aug. 2, 1936; s. William Eugene and Sara Chloetilde (Harrell) S.; m. Rubie Ann Barnes, Aug. 20, 1957; children: Donna Ann, Sara Arlene, Eugene Thomas. BS, MIT, 1959; MS, U. Tex., 1986; PhD, Tex. Tech. U., 1990. Registered profl. engr., Fla., Ill., Iowa., La., Tex., Wash. Project engr. Gen. Dynamics Corp., Chgo., 1959—60; chief project, design engr. Gen. Foods Corp., Kankakee, Ill., 1960—64; mgr. plant engring. Std. Brands Inc., Clinton, Iowa, 1964—66; regional mgr. Air Products & Chems., Inc., Creighton, Pa., 1966—68; gen. mgr. Skyline Corp., Harrisburg, NC, 1968—70; cons. Charlotte, NC, 1970—72; dir. engring. and Fla. ops. Zimmer Homes Corp., Pompano Beach, 1972—73; v.p. engring. and mfg. Nobility Homes, Inc., Ocala, Fla., 1973—78, Moduline Internat., Inc., Lacey, Wash., 1978—85; rsch. engr. U. Tex., Austin, 1985—86; lectr., rschr. Tex. Tech. U., Lubbock, 1987—90; assoc. prof. U. New Orleans, 1990—92; asst. prof. dept. civil engring. La. Tech. U., Ruston, 1992—98. Tchr. 26 different courses, 1987—; adj. prof. Coll. Engring., La. Tech. U., 2001-; cons. in field, Dubach, La., 1992—; condr. workshops in field; apptd. spokesman Mfrd. Housing Industry before U.S. Congress. Contbr. articles to profl. jours. Vol. engring. svcs. Lubbock Fire Safety House, 1990; judge sci. fair Ben Franklin H.S., New Orleans, 1990. Recipient T.L. James Svc. award La. Tech. U., 1994; grantee Urban Waste Mgmt. and Rsch. Ctr., New Orleans, 1991, Shell Devel. Co., 1993, La. Edn. Quality Support Fund, Insituform Techs., Inc., Trenchless Tech. Ctr., PABCO, Inc., InLiner USA, Inc., 1995, others; numerous grants in field. Mem. ASME (life), ASCE (Student chpt. Tchr. of Yr. award 1995, 98), Phi Kappa Phi, Sigma Xi, Chi Epsilon. Achievements include design, construction and management of first plant for the production of intermediate moisture pet food (Gainesburgers) in the world; organization and direction of all activities to allow Clinton, Iowa plant with a 1 mile shoreline to continue operations during the greatest flood of the upper Mississippi River in 1965. Avocations: flying, skiing, backpacking, golf, photography. Home: 199 Sellers Rd Dubach LA 71235-3218 Personal E-mail: drtomstraughan@msn.com.

STRAUGHN, JOANNA MARZIA, poet; b. Abilene, Tex., Jan. 9, 1969; d. Harold Kent and Carole Frances (Stone) Straughn; m. Victor Hugo Gener, Aug. 14, 1999; 1 child, Sophia Isabella Gener. MFA, U. Utah, 2002. Presenter in field. Author poetry. Recipient Ellipsis prize, Ellipsis Mag., 2003. Mem.: Acad. Am. Poets. Democrat. Unitarian Universalist. Home: Apt 3 652 E 700 S Salt Lake City UT 84102

STRAULMAN, ANN THERESE, retired English language educator; b. Kansas City, Mo., Apr. 26, 1933; d. Francis Wilson and Theresa Irene (Greene) S. AB, Wellesley Coll., 1955; MA in English, U. Mo., Kansas City, 1962; PhD in English, U. Wis., 1968. Life cert. English tchr., Mo. Tchr. English Sunset Hill Sch., Kansas City, 1960-62; from asst. to assoc. prof. English U. Western Ont., London, Can., 1966-93, prof. emeritus, 1993—. Adv. editor restoration and 18th Century theatre rsch. Loyola U. Chgo., 1990-2000. Trustee, mem. mus. com. Liberty Meml., Kansas City, 1993—, treas. 1998—; bd. dirs., docent Union Cemetery Hist. Soc., Kansas City, 1996—. Seven Coll. Conf. nat. scholar Wellesley Coll., 1951-55. Mem. MLA (life, mem. del. assembly 1975-77), Am. Soc. for 18th Century Studies (life), Samuel Johnson Soc. Ctrl. Region (v.p. 1976-77, pres. 1977-78), Jackson County Hist. Soc., Kemper Mus. Contemporary Art and Design,Friends of Art, Nelson-Atkins Mus. Art, Art. Inst. Chgo., Archaeol. Inst. Am., Kansas City Wellesley Club. Avocations: local history, archaeology, world travel.

STRAUMANIS, JOAN, academic administrator; b. N.Y.C., Feb. 10, 1937; d. Herbert S. and Mollie (Brandt) Cole; m. Irwin H. Pomerantz, June 25, 1956 (div. 1969); children: Rebecca, Joel; m. Eric R. Straumanis, June 7, 1969 (dec. 1996); 1 child, Andrei. BA Polit. Sci., Math., Antioch Coll., 1957; MS math., U. Colo.; PhD Philosophy, U. Md., 1974. Prof. Denison U., Granville, Ohio, 1971-82; acad. dean, prof. Kenyon Coll., Gambier, Ohio, 1982-86; dean faculty, prof. Rollins Coll., Winter Park, Fla., 1986-92; program officer Fund for Improvement of Postsecondary Edn. U.S. Dept. Edn., Washington, 1992—95; dean arts and scis. Lehigh U., Bethlehem, Pa., 1995—98; program officer Fund for Improvement of Postsecondary Edn. U.S. Dept. Edn., Washington, 1998—2002; pres. Antioch Coll., Yellow Springs, Ohio, 2002—. Office: Antioch Coll Pres Office 795 Livermore St Yellow Springs OH 45387 Office Phone: 202-777-1937.

STRAUS, DAVID A. architectural firm executive; b. Medford, Oreg., 1943; m. Sherry Straus; 2 children. BArch, U. Oreg., 1967. Registered architect, Oreg. Founding ptnr. Skelton, Straus & Seibert, Medford, 1989—. Mem Oreg Transp Comn, Rogue Valley Area Comn Transp. Past pres Medford Arts Comn, Arts Coun Southern Oreg; coach Rogue Valley Soccer Asn; leader Boy Scouts Am; bd dirs, past pres Schneider Mus Art SOSC; bd dirs Medford YMCA, Rogue Valley Art Asn. Lt USNR, Vietnam. Mem.: AIA (pres. so. Oreg. chpt.), Archit Found Oreg (past bd. dirs.), Medford/Jackson County CofC (past bd. dirs., Mem of the Yr 2000), Univ Oreg Alumni Asn, Oreg Club Southern Oreg (past pres.), Univ Club Medford (past pres.), Rotary. Office: Skelton Straus & Seibert Arch 26 Hawthorne St Medford OR 97504-7114 Office Phone: 541-779-4363. E-mail: dstraus@sssarchitects.com.

STRAUS, FRANCIS HOWE, pathologist, educator; b. Chgo., Mar. 16, 1932; s. Francis Howe and Elizabeth (Kales) S.; m. Helen Lorna Puttkammer, June 11, 1955; children: Francis H., Helen E., Christopher M., Michael W. AB, Harvard Coll., 1953; MD, U. Chgo., 1957, MS, 1964. Intern U. Chgo. Hosp., 1957-58; resident dept. pathology U. Chgo., 1958-60, resident, 1960-62, USPH fellow, 1958-60, chief resident, 1962-63, instr. dept. pathology, 1962-65, asst. prof., 1965-71, assoc. prof., 1971-78, prof., 1978—2003, prof. emeritus, 2003—. Author: Hyperparathyrodism, 1973, Essentials of Surgical Pathology, 1974. Chmn. profl. edn. com. Ill. divsn. Am. Cancer Soc., 1980-88, v.p., 1984-88, pres., 1988-90, nat. del., bd. dirs., 1988-92; mem. Inst. of Medicine of Chgo., 1969—, Ill. Coun. on Continuing Med. Edn., 1984-86; bd. dirs. S.E. Chgo. Commn., Chgo., 1970—; pres. Beaumont Emergency Operating Rm. Bd., Mackinac Island, Mich., 1985-2002. Fellow Am. Cancer Soc., 1962-63, clin. fellow, 1965-68. Mem. Chgo. Pathology Soc., Am. Soc. for Investigative Pathology, Internat. Acad. Pathology, Am. Soc. Exptl. Pathologists, Chgo. Lit. Club, Cliffdwellers Club, Sigma Xi, Alpha Omega Alpha (hon.). Avocations: gardening, travel, boating, music appreciation, art appreciation. Office: U Chgo Dept Pathology 5841 S Maryland Ave Chicago IL 60637-1463

STRAUS, JOZEF, manufacturing executive; b. 1946; Various rsch. and mgmt. positions in fiber optic tech. Bell-No. Rsch. Ltd. and No. Telecom Ltd.; bd. dirs. JDS FITEL, 1981, v.p. sales and mktg., 1990-93, CEO, pres., 1993-99; co-chmn., CEO JDS Uniphase Corp. (merged with JDS FITEL), San Jose, Calif., 2000—. Office: 163 Baypointe Pkwy San Jose CA 95134 Fax: 408-954-0760.

STRAUS, KATHLEEN NAGLER, education administrator, consultant; b. N.Y.C., Dec. 3, 1923; d. Maurice and Mildred (Kohn) Nagler; m. Everet M. Straus, May 29, 1948 (dec. Nov. 1967); children: Peter R., Barbara L. BA in Econs., Hunter Coll., 1944; postgrad., Columbia U., 1944-45, Am. U., 1946-47, Wayne State U., 1976-78. Various positions, 1944-50, 66; dep. dir. Model Neighborhood Agy., City of Detroit, 1968-70; dir. social svcs. Southeastern Mich. Coun. Govts., Detroit, 1970-74; staff coord. Edn. Task Force, Detroit, 1974-75; exec. dir. People and Responsible Orgns. for Detroit, 1975-76; staff dir. edn. com. Mich. Senate, Lansing, 1976-79; assoc. exec. dir. Mich. Assn. Sch. Bds., Lansing, 1979-86; dir. community rels. and devel. Ctr. for Creative Studies, Detroit, 1986-87, pres., 1987-91; mem. Mich. Bd. Edn., 1992—, pres., 2003. Mem. Mich. Bd. for Pub. Jr. and C.C.s, Lansing, 1980-92, v.p., 1989, pres., 1991; cons. Met. Columbus (Ohio) Schs. Com., 1975-76; mem. steering com. Mich. Edn. Seminars, 1979-86; mem. Adv. Com. on Higher Edn. Needs in S.W. Mich., 1971-72, Ad Hoc Com. on Equal Access to Higher Edn., 1970-71, Citizens Action Com. on Sch. Fin. Contbr. articles to profl. jours. Active numerous civic orgns.; vice chmn. downtown br. Met. Detroit YWCA, 1970-74; bd. dirs. Citizens for Better Care, Inc., 1973-78; mem. edn. com. New Detroit, Inc., 1972—; trustee Detroit Sci. Ctr., Inc., 1975—; founder, pres. Mich. Tax Info. Coun., 1982—; v.p. bd. dirs. Univ. Cultural Ctr. Assn., 1986-91; trustee Comprehensive Health Planning Coun. Southeastern Mich., 1977-78; mem. Wayne County Art and History Commn., 1988; co-chmn. Nat. Arts Program, 1987-88. Recipient Amity citation Congress, Detroit, 1966, Disting. Community Svc. award Am. Jewish Com., 1988, Disting. Community Svc. award Common Coun., Detroit, 1976, resolution Mich. Ho. of Reps., 1986, Mich. Senate, 1988, Educator of Yr. Wayne State U., 1999, Disting. Warrior award Detroit Urban League, 2000; named to Mich. Edn. Hall of Fame, 1997; inducted into Mich. Women's Hall of Fame, 2000, Lifetime Achiev. award Anti Defamation League, 2004, Multi Cultural Edn. award Nat. Conf. Community and Justice, 2004. Mem. LWV (pres. Detroit 1961-63), Alpha Chi Alpha. Democrat. Avocations: travel, theater, concerts. Home: 8801 Kingswood St Detroit MI 48221-1569 Office: State Bd Edn PO Box 30008 Lansing MI 48909-7508

STRAUS, LAURA, photographer, art association administrator; b. N.Y.C., Nov. 25, 1966; d. Roger William and Nina Pelikan Straus. Bachelors, Wesleyan U., Conn., 1988. Photo editor Magnum Photos, N.Y.C., 1989—93; photography dir. Abbeville Press, N.Y.C., 1994—98; stills photographer New Line TV, N.Y.C., 2000—01; artist in residence, tchr. N.Y. Found. for the Arts, N.Y.C., 2002. Rights adminstr. Artists Rights Soc., N.Y.C., 1998—. Author:

(photography book/monograph) A Child's World; photography book, What Fathers Are, What Love Is, What Mothers Are, What Girlfriends Do, The Bride's Book of Weddings, Girls Girls Girls, Fathers and Daughters, For Dad with Love. Recipient Photo 2000 Black and White Photography, Brush Art Gallery, 2000; Photography Fellow, N.Y. Found. for the Arts, 2001—02. Mem.: Am. Soc. Picture Profls.

STRAUS, LEON STEPHAN, physicist; b. Takoma Park, Md., May 29, 1943; s. Sidney and Ruth Straus; m. Cheryl Sarran Straus, Apr. 4, 1970; children: Jonathan, Jennifer. BS in Physics, Antioch Coll., Yellow Springs, Ohio, 1965; M Physics, Georgetown U., 1970, PhD in Physics, 1971. Mem. rsch. staff Ctr. Naval Analyses, Alexandria, Va., 1973-75, field rep. CTF 69 Naples, Italy, 1975-77, project mgr. Alexandria, 1977-79, field rep. CTF 69 and CTF 66/67 Naples, Italy, 1979-82, assoc. dep. dir. Alexandria, 1982-85, field rep. CTF 72 Kamiseya, Japan, 1985-87, program mgr. Alexandria, 1987-90, field rep. COMSIXTHFLT Gaeta, Italy, 1990-92, project mgr. Alexandria, 1992-95, tech. dir. spl. projects, 1995-97, dep. dir. info. ops. warfare team, 1997-2000; pvt. contractor, 2001—. Asst. AEC, Germantown, Md., 1968-71. Contbr. articles to profl. jours. Vol. Jewish lay leader USN, Naples, 1975-77, 79-82. Recipient Fellowship Georgetown U., Washington, 1965-68. Mem. Acoustical Soc. Am., Navy Submarine League. Jewish. Achievements include planning, evaluating and documenting tests/exercises and conducting studies associated with U.S. Navy and joint strategy, tactics, communication and technology. Office Phone: 954-298-2513. Personal E-mail: strausconsult@aol.com.

STRAUS, LORNA PUTTKAMMER, biology professor; b. Chgo., Feb. 15, 1933; d. Ernst Wilfred and Helen Louise (Monroe) Puttkammer; m. Francis Howe Straus II, June 11, 1955; children: Francis, Helen, Christopher, Michael. BA magna cum laude, Radcliffe Coll., 1955; MS, U. Chgo., 1960, PhD, 1962. Rsch. assoc. dept. anatomy U. Chgo., 1962-64, instr., 1964-67, asst. prof., 1967-73, assoc. prof., 1973-87, prof., 1987—, asst. dean, then dean students Coll., 1967-82, dean admissions Coll., 1975-80, univ. marshal, 1999—. Trustee Radcliffe Coll., Cambridge, Mass., 1973-83; chmn. Cmty. Found., Mackinac Island, Mich., 1994—. Recipient silver medal Coun. for Advancement and Support Edn., 1987. Mem.: North Ctrl. Assn. (commr. 1998—, pres.-elect 2001—02, pres. 2002—04), Harvard U. Alumni Assn. (bd. dirs. 1980—83), Phi Beta Kappa. Avocations: travel, gardening. Home: 5642 S Kimbark Ave Chicago IL 60637-1606 Office: U Chgo 5845 S Ellis Ave Chicago IL 60637-1476 E-mail: l-straus@uchicago.edu.

STRAUS, OSCAR S., II, foundation executive; b. N.Y.C., Nov. 6, 1914; s. Roger Williams and Gladys (Guggenheim) S.; m. Marion Miller Straus, 1941 (div. 1982); 1 child, Oscar S. III.; m. Joan Sutton, 1982. AB, Princeton U., 1936; postgrad., U. Dijon, summer 1936, Sch. Bus. Adminstrn. Harvard U., 1938. Pvt. sec. Internat. Labor Office, Geneva, 1937-38; U.S. fgn. svc. officer, 1940-42; divisional asst. Dept. State, 1942-43, 44-45; treas., dir., v.p., chmn. fin. com. Am. Smelting & Refining Co., 1945-59; ptnr. Guggenheim Bros., 1959-83; pres., dir. Guggenheim Exploration Co., Inc., 1963-73; gen. ptnr. Straus Minerals, 1973-88; chmn., bd. dirs. Daniel and Florence Guggenheim Found., N.Y.C. Chmn., bd. dirs. Fred L. Lavanburg Found.; chmn., bd. dirs. Mut. of Omaha, Companion Life Ins. Co., United of Omaha. Trustee emeritus Am. Mus. Natural History, Mystic Seaport, Conn.; hon. chmn. Rensselaerville (N.Y.) Inst.; trustee Congregation Emanu-El. Mem.: Coun. Fgn. Rels., River Club of N.Y., L.I. Wyandanch Club Inc., Knickerbocker Club, Doubles Club, Megantic Fish and Game Club, Cruising Club Am. Jewish. Home: 40 S Howells Point Rd Bellport NY 11713 Office: 950 3rd Ave New York NY 10022 Office Phone: 212-755-4431.

STRAUS, ROBERT, behavioral sciences educator; b. New Haven, Jan. 9, 1923; s. Samuel Hirsh and Alma (Fleischner) Straus; m. Ruth Elisabeth Dawson, Sept. 8, 1945; children: Robert James, Carol Martin, Margaret Dawson, John William. BA, Yale U., 1943, MA, 1945, PhD, 1947. Asst. prof. Yale U., 1948—51, rsch. assoc. applied physiology, 1951—53; acting dir. Conn. Child Study and Treatment Home, New Haven, 1952—53; assoc. prof. preventive medicine SUNY Upstate Med. Ctr., 1953—56; prof. med. sociology U. Ky., Lexington, 1956—59, prof. dept. behavioral sci. Coll. Medicine, also chmn. dept., 1959—87; dir. for sci. devel. Med. Rsch. Inst. San Francisco, 1991—93. Vis. fellow Yale U., 1968—69; vis. prof. U. Calif., Berkeley, 1978, 86; sec. Com. Med. Sociology, 1955—57; chmn. Coop. Com. Study Alcoholism, 1961—63, Nat. Adv. Com. on Alcoholism, 1966—69; mem. Nat. Adv. Coun. on Alcohol Abuse and Alcoholism, 1984—87; trustee Med. Rsch. Inst. San Francisco, 1988—93; mem. Calif. Pacific Med. Ctr. Rsch. Coun., 1993. Author: Medical Care for Seamen, 1950; author: (with S.D. Bacon) Drinking in College, 1953; author: Alcohol and Society, 1973, Escape From Custody, 1974, A Medical School is Born, 1996; co-editor: Medicine and Society, 1963; mem. editl. bd.: Jour. Studies on Alcohol, 1950—2000. Pres. Bluegrass R.R. Mus., 1980. Mem.: Inst. Medicine NAS, Acad. Behavioral Medicine Rsch., Am. Pub. Health Assn. (lifetime achievement award sect. on alcohol, tobacco and other drugs 1993), Assn. Behavioral Scis. and Med. Edn. (pres. 1974), Am. Sociol. Assn. (chmn. med. sociology sect. 1967—68, Leo G. Reeder award Disting. Contbn. to Med. Sociology 1998), Sigma Xi, Phi Beta Kappa. Home: 656 Raintree Rd Lexington KY 40502-2874

STRAUS, STEPHEN EZRA, biomedical researcher; b. N.Y.C., Nov. 23, 1946; s. Samuel Lieb and Dora Beatrice (Drattel) S.; m. Barbara Ellen Portnoy, June 24, 1973; children: Kate, Julie, Benjamin. BS, MIT, 1968; MD, Columbia U., 1972. Diplomate Am. Bd. Internal Medicine with subspecialty Bds. in Infectious Diseases. Intern and resident in internal medicine Washington U., St. Louis, 1972-73, 75-76; sr. investigator Nat. Inst. Allergy and Infectious Diseases, Bethesda, Md., 1979—, chief Lab. Clin. Investigation, 1991—2003; dir. Nat. Ctr. Complementary and Alternative Medicine, NIH, Bethesda, Md., 1999—. Contbr. over 375 articles to profl. jours. Med. dir. USPHS, 1973-75, 79-2000. Recipient 5 medals USPHS, 1983, 87, 90, 98, 2000. Mem. Assn. Am. Physicians, Am. Soc. for Clin. Investigation, Infectious Diseases Soc. Am. Achievements include research and fundamental discovery on treatment and pathogenesis of human viral infections and immunological disorders. Office: Dept Health & Human Svcs/Nat Ctr Complementary and Alternative Medicine 31 Center Drive Bethesda MD 20892-0001

STRAUSBERG, ROBERT L. federal agency administrator; Head, sequencing tech. br. Nat. Ctr. for Human Genome Rsch., NIH, 1994—96; dir., office of cancer genomics Nat. Cancer Inst., NIH, 1999—; v.p., rsch. The Inst. for Genomic Rsch., 2003—. Office: Office of Cancer Genomics Nat Cancer Inst 31 Center Dr Bethesda MD 20892-2586*

STRAUSE, RANDALL SCOTT, judge; b. Louisville, June 13, 1963; s. James L. and Charlotte Ray (Motherhead) S.; m. Rene Marie Ricci, Aug. 7, 1987; children: Randall Scott Jr., James Austin. BA, Ind. U., 1985; JD, U. Louisville, 1988. Bar: Ky. 1989, U.S. Dist. Ct. (ea. and we. dists.) Ky. 1992, U.S. Ct. Appeals (6th cir.) 1992. Atty. pvt. practice, Louisville, 1989-90; law clk. to Hon. Joseph M. Hood U.S. Dist. Ct. (ea. dist.) Ky., Pikeville, 1990-92; atty. Alagia, Day, Trautwein & Smith, Louisville, 1992-94; prin. asst. to commr. dept. medicaid svcs. Commonwealth of Ky., Frankfort, 1994-95, chief adminstrv. law judge cabinet health svcs., 1995-99. Dir. Strategic Mktg., Inc., Louisville, 1995-96. Bd. dirs. Louisville Tennis Assn., 1996-99, Kentuckiana Children's Ctr., 1998—. Rsch. grantee Tort & Litigation, 1987. Mem. ABA, Am. Health Lawyers Assn., Assn. Trial Lawyers Am., Nat. Assn. Adminstrv. Law Judges, Nat. Assn. Hearing Ofcls. (bd. dirs.), Ky. Bar Assn., S.C. Bar Assn., Nat. Assn. Securities Dealers (arbitrator 1998—), Ky. Real Estate Commn., Louisville Bar Assn., Kappa Sigma, Delta Theta Phi, Omicron Delta Kappa, Order of Ky. Cols. Republican. Episcopalian. Avocation: tennis. Home: 10107 Falling Tree Way Louisville KY 40223-3736 Office: One Riverfront Plz Ste 1400 Louisville KY 40202

STRAUSER, ROBERT WAYNE, lawyer; b. Little Rock, Aug. 28, 1943; s. Christopher Columbus and Opal (Orr) S.; m. Atha Maxine Tubbs, June 26, 1971 (div. 1991); children: Robert Benjamin, Ann Kathleen; m. Terri D. Seales, Oct. 17, 1998. BA, Davidson (N.C.) Coll., 1965; postgrad., Vanderbilt U., Nashville, 1965-66; LLB, U. Tex., 1968. Bar: Tex. 1968, U.S. Ct. Mil. Appeals 1971. Staff atty. Tex. Legis. Coun., Austin, 1969-71; counsel Jud. Com., Tex. Ho. of Reps., Austin, 1971-73; chief counsel Jud. Com., Tex. Constl. Conv., Austin, 1974; exec. v.p. and legis. counsel Tex. Assn. Taxpayers, Austin, 1974-85; assoc. Baker & Botts, Austin, 1985-87, ptnr., 1988—. Assoc. editor Tex. Internat. Law Jour., 1968. Mem. Tex. Ho. Speakers Econ. Devel. Com., Austin, 1986-87; assoc. dir. McDonald Obs. Bd. Visitors, 1988—; bd. dirs. Tex. Assn. Bus. and C. of C., 2000-2002; mem. Dean's Roundtable, U. Tex. Law Sch.; bd. dirs. Austin Symphony Orch. Soc., 1985—, v.p., 1993-94, nominating com., 1998-2002, mem. exec. com., 2003—. Capt. USNR, ret. Named Rising Star of Tex., Tex. Bus. Mag., 1983. Fellow Tex. Bar Found.; mem. State Bar of Tex. (tax sect.), Travis County Bar Assn., Travis County Bar Found., Headliners Club (Austin). Home: 3312 Gilbert St Austin TX 78703-2102 Office: Baker & Botts 1600 San Jacinto Blvd Austin TX 78701

STRAUSER, SUSAN PARKYN, performing arts educator, singer; d. Harold Mann and Helen Ruth (Knapp) Parkyn; m. George John Strauser; 1 child, Andrew. BS in Music Edn., West Chester U., Pa., 1964; MEd in Music, West Chester U., 1967; postgrad., Ind. U., 1976—80. Profl. singer, 1959—; prof. voice William Paterson U., Wayne, NJ, 1974—75; artistic dir. Vocal Arts Studio, Wallkill, NY, 1985—; voice seminar dir. Delaware Valley Opera, Narrowsburg, NY, 1985—86; prof. voice SUNY, Orange/Middletown, 1990—2004, voice program dir. Ulster/Stone Ridge, 2000—. Seminar presenter in field; artistic dir. Empire Artists of N.Y., Wallkill, 1992—; appeared with N.J. Symphony Orch., Hudson Valley Philharmonic Orch., West Chester Symphony, Ind. U. Philharm. and Opera Theatre; guest artist West Islip Symphony Orch. of L.I.; performances with opera and musical theatre cos. as well as in concert, oratorio and recital presentations include numerous leading roles; numerous appearances for cable TV Lunch N Listen series, Heroines-Women of the Musical Stage. Contbr. articles to profl. jours. Bd. dirs. Delaware Valley Opera, 1986. Recipient U.S. Congl. Citation in the Benjamin Gilman Congress, 1995, Theodore Presser Found. award, Westchester U., 1962, N.J. Opera Festival winner, Nat. Arion award. Avocation: genealogy. Home and Office: PO Box 412 37 DuBois St Wallkill NY 12589

STRAUSFELD, NICHOLAS JAMES, neurobiology and evolutionary biology researcher, educator; b. Claygate, England, Oct. 22, 1942; BSc in Zoology, Univ. Coll. London, 1965, PhD in Neurophysiology, 1968; Habilitation, U. Frankfurt, Germany, 1985. Prof. neurobiology, ecology, evolutionary biology, entomology, anatomy U. Ariz., Tucson, also adj. prof. art. Author: Atlas of an Insect Brain, 1976, Neuroanatomical Techniques, Insect Nervous System, 1980, Functional Neuroanatomy, 1983. Fellow, John Simon Guggenheim Found., 1994, MacArthur Found., 1995. Office: U Arizona PO Box 210077 Tucson AZ 85721-0077 also: Gould Simpson Bldg Rm 415 Tucson AZ 85721-0001

STRAUSS, ALBERT JOHN, JR., pediatrician; b. Jersey City, July 16, 1938; s. Albert John and Marjorie Elizabeth (Boyd) S.; m. Mary Maddry, Oct. 12, 1963 (div. Jan. 1997); children: Alexandra, Stephanie, Albert III; m. Kelli Alisa Strauss, Jan. 31, 1997; 1 child, John Tyler. BA, U. Va., 1960, MD, 1964. Intern Duke, Durham, NC, 1964-65; resident U. Va., Charlottesville, 1965-67; ptnr., owner The Children's Doctor, Hagerstown, Md., 1969—. Past vice chief of staff Washington County Hosp., Hagerstown. Bd. dir. Dream Come True, Hagerstown, 1998—; co-founder Partners for Acad. and Creative Excellence, Hagerstown, 1985. Capt. USAF, 1967—69. Decorated Air Force Commendation medal. Fellow Am. Acad. of Pediatrics; mem. AMA, Washington County Med. Soc. (pres. 1979), Med. and Chirigical Soc. of Md. (del., councillor 1975-85), Southern Med. Assn. Republican. Avocations: gardening, hunting, fishing, birding. Home: 18916 Geeting Rd Keedysville MD 21756-1476 Office: The Childrens Doctors 319 E Antietam St Hagerstown MD 21740-5701 Office Phone: 301-790-3620. E-mail: kidoc67@yahoo.com.

STRAUSS, DAVID J. lawyer; b. Chgo., Jan. 26, 1943; BBA, U. Iowa, 1964, JD, 1967. Bar: Iowa 1967, Ohio 1967. Ptnr. Baker & Hostetler, Cleve. Mem. Phi Delta Phi, Order of Coif. Office: Baker & Hostetler 3200 Nat City Ctr 1900 E 9th St Ste 3200 Cleveland OH 44114-3475

STRAUSS, DOROTHY BRANDFON, marriage and family therapist; b. Bklyn. BA, Bklyn. Coll., 1932; MA, NYU, 1937, PhD, 1963. Diplomate Am. Bd. Sexology, Am. Psychotherapy Assn. Instr. Hunter Coll./CUNY, 1960-63; prof. Kean U., 1963-77; pvt. practice Bklyn. and, N.J., 1970—. Clin. prof. psychiatry Downstate Med. Ctr., SUNY, Bklyn., 1974-88; assoc. dir. Ctr. for Human Sexuality, 1974-82; mem. NIMH rsch. team U. Pa., 1973-82; guest lectr. Menninger Clinic, 1990. Contbr. chpts. to Understanding Human Behavior in Health and Illness; contbr. articles to profl. jours. and self help and psychol. web mags. Fellow Am. Assn. Clin. Sexologists (founding); mem. APA, Am. Assn. for Marital and Family Therapy (clin. mem. 1971—, supr. 1981—, presenter nat. confs., accreditation site vis.), Am. Assn. Sex Therapists, Counselors and Educators (chair task force on supervision 1984-86, chair supr. cert. com. 1986-93, chair cert. steering com. 1992-98, Disting. Svc. award 1998), Soc. for Clin. and Exptl. Hypnosis, Internat. Soc. Poets (Disting. Mem.), Kappa Delta Pi.

STRAUSS, ERIC JAMES, urban planning educator, lawyer, consultant; b. Chgo., Apr. 14, 1947; s. Harold Richard and Irene (Jacobson) S.; m. Emily Jane Fisher, July 3, 1971; children: Rebecca, Janet, Karen. BA, U. Wis., 1968, PhD, 1981; JD, Northwestern U., Chgo., 1971. Bar: Tex. 1971, Wis. 1972, Kans. 1987. Specialist U. Wis. Extension, Madison, 1971-78; prof. urban planning U. Kans., Lawrence, 1978—2001; prof. urban and regional planning Mich. State U., East Lansing, 2001—. Vis. lectr. Queen's U., Belfast, No. Ireland, 1983, U. Wis.-Madison, 1993—, Ind. U., Bloomington, 1995; cons. City of Eudora, Kans., 1988—, City of Hillsboro, Kans., 1992—; site vis. Planning Accrediation Bd., 1986—. Contbr. articles to profl. jours. Recipient Energy Ordinance award City of Lawrence, 1981, Govtl. Tng. award State of Kans., 1984, Profiles of Innovations award Am. Pub. Power Assn., 1986, Pub. Svc. award City Attys. Assn. of Kans., 1992. Mem. Am. Inst. Cert. Planners, Am. Planning Assn. (v.p. Kans. chpt. 1983-85). Democrat. Jewish. Avocations: arts and crafts fairs, gardening. Office: 101 UPLA Bldg East Lansing MI 48824 E-mail: strausse@msu.edu.

STRAUSS, GARY JOSEPH, lawyer; b. N.Y.C., July 6, 1953; s. Stanley Vinson and Frieda (Fischoff) S. BA magna cum laude, City Coll. of N.Y., 1974; JD, NYU, 1977. Bar: NY 1978, Fla. 1980. Assoc. Finley, Kumble, Wagner, Heine & Underberg, N.Y.C., 1977—79; ptnr. Phillips, Nizer, Benjamin, Krim & Ballon, N.Y.C., 1979—87, Gaston & Snow, N.Y.C., 1987—88; pvt. practice N.Y.C., 1988—2002; ptnr. Gerstein Strauss & Rinaldi LLP, N.Y.C., 2002—. Mem. ABA (chmn. N.Y. com. current literature and real property law 1977), Fla. Bar Assn., N.Y. State Bar Assn. Home: 57 W 38th St Fl 9 New York NY 10018-5500 Office Phone: 212-398-7900.

STRAUSS, HARLEE SUE, environmental consultant; b. New Brunswick, N.J., June 19, 1950; d. Robert Lemuel and Helene (Marcus) S. BA, Smith Coll., 1972; PhD, U. Wis., 1979. Postdoctoral fellow dept. biology MIT, Cambridge, 1979-81; congrl. sci. fellow U.S. House of Reps., Washington, 1981-83; spl. asst. Am. Chem. Soc., Washington, 1983-84; spl. cons. Environ. Corp., Washington, 1984-85; rsch. assoc. Ctr. for Tech., Policy and Indsl. Devel. MIT, Cambridge, 1985-86, rsch. affiliate, 1986-92; sr. assoc. Gradient Corp., Cambridge, 1986-88; pres. H. Strauss Assocs., Inc., Natick, Mass., 1988—. Exec. dir. Silent Spring Inst., Inc., 1994-95; adj. assoc. prof. Sch. Pub. Health, Boston U., 1990-94; lectr. Sch. Medicine, Tufts U., Boston, 1988-95; mem. steering com. Boston Risk Assessment Group, 1986-95. Co-editor, author: Risk Assessment in Genetic Engineering, 1991; author: Biotechnology Regulations, 1986; author book chpts. in field. Active Instl. Biosafety Com., Army Rsch. Lab., Natick, 1989—94, Army Sci. Bd., 1994—2001. Mem. AAAS, Am. Chem. Soc., Am. Soc. Microbiology, Assn. for Women in Sci. (chmn. com. New England chpt. 1986-88, co-chmn. legis. com. 1985-93), Biophys. Soc. (chmn. com. 1983-84, Congl. Sci. fellow 1981-83), Soc. for Risk Analysis (pres. New England chpt. 1991-92, pres.-elect 1995-2000). Jewish. Avocations: travel, hiking. Office: H Strauss Assocs Inc 21 Bay State Rd Natick MA 01760-2942 Business E-Mail: h.strauss@rcn.com. E-mail: hstrauss@aol.com.

STRAUSS, HERBERT LEOPOLD, chemistry professor; b. Aachen, Germany, Mar. 26, 1936; came to U.S., 1940, naturalized, 1946; s. Charles and Joan (Goldschmidt) S.; m. Carolyn North Cooper, Apr. 24, 1960; children: Michael Abram, Rebecca Anne, Ethan Edward. AB, Columbia U., 1957, MA, 1958, PhD, 1960; postgrad, Oxford U., 1960-61. Mem. faculty U. Calif., Berkeley, 1961—, prof. chemistry, 1973—2003, prof. grad. divsn., 2003—, vice chmn. dept. chemistry, 1975-81, 92-95, asst. dean. Coll. Chemistry, 1986-92, assoc. dean, 1995—. Vis. prof. Indian Inst. Tech., Kanpur, 1968-69, Fudan U., Shanghai, 1982, U. Tokyo, 1982, U. Paris du Nord, 1987; mem. IUPAC Commn. I.1, 1994—. Author: Quantum Mechanics, 1968; assoc. editor Ann. Rev. Phys. Chemistry, 1976-85, editor, 1985-2000. Recipient Bomen-Michaelson award Coblentz Soc., 1994, Ellis Lippincott award Optical Soc. Am., 1994, The Berkeley citation, 2003; Alfred P. Sloan fellow, 1966-70. Fellow Am. Phys. Soc., AAAS; mem. Am. Chem. Soc., Sigma Xi, Phi Beta Kappa, Phi Lambda Upsilon. Achievements include research in elucidation of vibrational spectra associated with large amplitude molecular motion in gases, liquids and solids. Home: 2447 Prince St Berkeley CA 94705-2021 Office: U Calif Dept Chemistry Berkeley CA 94720-1420 Office Phone: 510-642-7114. Business E-Mail: hls@cchem.berkeley.edu.

STRAUSS, JEROME FRANK, III, reproductive endocrinologist, educator; b. Chgo., May 2, 1947; s. Jerome Frank (Jr.) and Josephine (Newberger) Strauss; m. Catherine Blumlein, June 20, 1970; children: Jordan L., Elizabeth J. BA, Brown U., 1969; MD, U. Pa., 1974, PhD, 1975. Asst. prof. Sch. of Medicine U. Pa., Phila., 1976—83, assoc. prof. Sch. of Medicine, 1983—85, prof. Sch. of Medicine, 1985—, assoc. chair Sch. of Medicine, 1987—, assoc. dean Sch. of Medicine, 1990—98; Luigi Mastroianni jr. prof. and founding dir. Ctr. Rsch. on Women's Health and Reproduction, Phila., 1990—94; prof. Inst. of Medicine NAS, 1994—. Biochem. endocrinology study sect. NIH, 1983—87, Nat. Adv. Child Health and Human Devel. Coun., 2002—; chmn. population rsch. com. Nat. Inst. Child Health and Human Devel., 1989—92; chair Reproductive Scientist of the Ams. Network, 1995—; dir. Ctr. Excellence in Women's Health, 1996—2002; co-chair Indo-U.S. Joint Working Group on Reproductive Sci. and Contraceptive Tech., 1999—; bd. dirs. Burroughs Wellcome Fund, 2003—. Editor: Lipoprotein and Cholesterol Metabolism in Sterodogenic Tissues, 1985, Current Topics in Membrane Research, 1987, Uterine and Embryonic Factors in Early Pregnancy, 1991, New Achievements in Research of Ovarian Function, 1995, Cell Death in Reproductive Physiology, 1997, Molecular Biology in Reproductive Medicine, 1999, Ovarian Function Research: Present and Future, 1999, Reproductive Medicine Molecular, Cellular and Genetic Fundamentals, 2002, New Frontiers in Contraceptive Research, 2004, Yen and Jaffe's Reproductive Endocrinology, 2004, Steroids jour., 1993—; assoc. editor Ency. of Reproduction, 1998—, assoc. editor, mem. editl. bd. Jour. Lipid Rsch., 1982—90, corr. editor Jour. Steroid Biochem. and Molecular Biology, 1990—99, mem. editl. bd. Endocrinology, 1986—90, 1997—2000, Biology of Reprodn., 1986—90, 1999—2003, Jour. of Women's Health, 1991—, Jour. Soc. Gynecologic Investigation, 1993—, Placenta, 1995—98, Trends in Endocrinology and Metabolism, 1999—, Reference en Gynecologie Obstetrique, 1999—, Seminars in Reproductive Endocrinology, 2000—, Jour. Endocrinology, 2000—, Human Reproduction Update, 2001—; editor: Yen and Jatte's Reproductive Endocrinology, 2004. Recipient Transatlantic medal, Brit. Endocrine Soc., 1998. Fellow: Internat. Acad. Human Reproduction; mem.: Perinatal Rsch. Soc., Am. Soc. for Reproductive Medicine, Soc. for Study of Reproduction (bd. dirs. 1989—91, Rsch. award 1992), Endocrine Soc., Soc. Gynecologic Investigation (pres. 2003, Pres.'s Achievement award 1990), Am. Physiol. Soc., Am. Assn. Pathologists. Office: U Pa Dept Ob/Gyn 421 Curie Blvd Philadelphia PA 19104-4218 Office Phone: 215-898-0147. Business E-Mail: jfs3@mail.med.upenn.edu.

STRAUSS, JEROME MANFRED, lawyer, banker; b. Milw., Nov. 7, 1934; s. Emanuel and Loraine (Goetz) S.; m. Susan Jean Kauffman, Dec. 30, 1967; children: Martha Lynn, Jared Lee, David Aaron. BA with honors, Ind. U., 1956; JD, NYU, 1959. Bar: Ind. 1959, Fla. 1996, U.S. Dist. Ct. (so. dist.) Ind. 1959, U.S. Tax Ct. 1965, U.S. Ct. Appeals (7th cir.) 1969. Lawyer Ice Miller Donadio & Ryan, Indpls., 1959—93, ptnr., 1969-93; sr. v.p. and regional trust mgr. Merrill Lynch Trust Co., 1993-95; with Mershon, Sawyer, Johnston, Dunwody & Cole, Miami, Palm Beach, Naples, 1995-96; established Wollman, Strauss & Assocs., P.A., 1997—2002; with Galbraith Assoc., P.A., Naples, Fla., 2003—; founder Midwest Tax and Estate Planning Inst., Indpls., 2003—. Co-author: Marital Deduction Trusts, 1963, Real Estate in an Estate, 1963, Durable Powers of Attorney, 1993; contbr. articles to profl. jours. Bd. dirs. Orton Soc., Indpls., 1970-72, Indpls., 1970-72, Indpls. Hebrew Congregation, 1979-85, Planned Giving Group of Ind., Indpls., 1988-95, Ind. Continuing Legal Edn. Forum, 1989-94; devel. com. Collier County, Fla. Cmty. Found., 1995-2002; mem. Planned Giving Com. of Lee County, Fla., 1995-2002, Fla. Planned Giving Coun., 1995—; planning coun. Naples, Fla. Estate, 1996—. Fellow Am. Coll Trust and Estate Counsel (charitable com., estate and gift tax com. 1996-2001), Am. Coll. Tax Counsel; mem. ABA (vice-chmn. marital deduction com. real estate property, probate and trust sect. 1988-90), Internat. Acad. Estate and Trust Law (academician 1987—), Ind. State Bar Assn. (sec. 1979-80, chmn. probate, trust and real property sect. 1970-71), Ind. Estate Planning Coun. (pres. 1970-71), Fla. State Bar Assn., Internat. Assn. of Fin. Planners of S.W. Fla., Collier County Bar Assn. Home: 1056 Diamond Lake Cir Naples FL 34114-9211 Office: 9115 Galleria Ct Ste 2 Naples FL 34109 E-mail: rv-atty@lawyer4u.com.

STRAUSS, JOHN STEINERT, dermatologist, educator; b. New Haven, July 15, 1926; s. Maurice Jacob and Carolyn Mina (Ullman) Strauss; m. Susan Thalheimer, Aug. 19, 1950; children: Joan Sue, Mary Lynn. BS, Yale U., 1946, MD, 1950. Intern U. Chgo., 1950-51; resident dermatology U. Pa., Phila., 1951-52, 54-55, fellow dermatology, 1955-57, instr., 1956-57; mem. faculty Boston U. Med. Sch., 1958-78, prof., 1966-78; head dept. dermatology U. Iowa, Iowa City, 1978-98, prof. dermatology, 1978-00, prof. emeritus, 2000—. Mem. editl. bd.: Archives of Dermatology, 1970—79, Jour. Am. Acad. Dermatology, 1979—89, Jour. Investigative Dermatology, 1977—82; contbr. articles to profl. jours. With USNR, 1952—54. Fellow James H. Brown Jr., 1947—48, USPHS, 1955—57; grantee. Fellow: Am. Acad. Dermatology (pres.); mem.: Internat. Com. Dermatology (pres. 1992—97), Internat. League Dermatol. Socs. (pres. 1992—97), 18th World Congress Dermatology (pres.), Am. Bd. Med. Spltys. (exec. com. 2001—04), Coun. Med. Splty. Socs. (pres.), Am. Fedn. Clin. Rsch., Ctrl. Soc. Clin. Rsch., Assn. Am. Physicians, Am. Dermatol. Assn. (sec., pres.), Am. Bd. Dermatology (bd. dirs., pres., assoc. exec. dir., exec. cons.), Dermatology Found. (pres.), Soc. Investigative Dermatology (sec.-treas., pres.). Achievements include research in sebaceous glands and pathogenesis of acne. Office: U Iowa Hosp & Clinics Dept Dermatology 200 Hawkins Dr # BT2045-1 Iowa City IA 52242-1009

STRAUSS, JON CALVERT, academic administrator; b. Chgo., Jan. 17, 1940; s. Charles E. and Alice C. (Woods) S.; m. Joan Helen Bailey, Sept. 19, 1959 (div. 1985); children: Susan, Stephanie; m. Jean Anne Sacconaghi, June 14, 1985; children: Kristoffer, Jonathon. BSEE, U. Wis., 1959; MS in Physics, U. Pitts., 1962; PhD in E.E., Carnegie Inst. Tech., 1965; LLD (hon.), U. Mass., 1996. Assoc. prof. computer sci., elec. engring. Carnegie Mellon U., Pitts., 1966-70; dir. computer ctr., prof. computer sci. Tech. U. Norway, Trondheim, Norway, 1970; vis. assoc. prof. elec. engring. U. Mich., Ann Arbor, 1971; assoc. prof. computer sci. Washington U., St. Louis, Mo., 1971-74, dir. computing facilities, 1971-73; dir. computing activities U. Pa., Phila., 1974-76, faculty master Stouffer Coll. House, 1978-80, prof. computer, info. scis., prof. decision sci. Wharton Sch., 1974-81, exec. dir. Univ. Budget, 1975-78, v.p. for budget, fin., 1978-81; prof. elec. engring. U. So. Calif., Los Angeles, 1981-85, sr. v.p. adminstrn., 1981-85; pres. Worcester Poly. Inst., Mass., 1985-94; v.p., chief fin. officer Howard Hughes Med. Inst., Chevy Chase, Md., 1994-97; pres. Harvey Mudd Coll., Claremont, Calif., 1997—. Cons. Electronics Assocs., Inc., 1965, IBM Corp., 1960-64, Westinghouse Elec. Corp., 1959-60; bd. dirs. Transamerica Income Fund, Variable Ins. Fund, United Educators Ins. Contbr. articles on computer systems and university mgmt. to profl. jours.; co-holder patent. Bd. dirs. Presbyn.-U. Pa. Med. Ctr., Phila., 1980-81, U. So. Calif. Kenneth Norris Jr. Cancer Hosp., L.A., 1981-85, Med. Ctr. of Ctrl. Mass., 1986-94, Worcester Acad., 1986-91, Mass. Biotech. Rsch. Inst., 1985-94. Mem. New. Eng. Assn. Schs. and Colls., Inc., Commn. on

Instns. of Higher Edn., Nat. Collegiate Athletic Assn. (pres.'s commn. 1990-94). Avocations: rowing, running, sailing, swimming. Office: Harvey Mudd Coll 301 E 12th St Claremont CA 91711-5901

STRAUSS, PETER L(ESTER), law educator; b. N.Y.C., Feb. 26, 1940; s. Simon D. and Elaine Ruth (Mandle) S.; m. Joanna Burnstine, Oct. 1, 1964; children: Benjamin, Bethany. AB magna cum laude, Harvard U., 1961; LLB magna cum laude, Yale U., 1964. Bar: D.C. 1965, U.S. Supreme Ct. 1968. Law clk. U.S. Ct. Appeals D.C. Cir., 1964-65, U.S. Supreme Ct., 1965-66; lectr. Halle Selassie U. Sch. Law, Addis Ababa, Ethiopia, 1966-68; asst. to solicitor gen. Dept. Justice, Washington, 1968-71; assoc. prof. law Columbia U., 1971-74, prof., 1974—, Betts prof., 1985—, vice-dean, 1996, 2001—02. Gen. counsel NRC, 1975-77, Adminstrv. Conf. U.S., 1984-95; Byrne vis. prof. Sch. Law Harvard U., Cambridge, Mass., 1994; bd. dirs. Ctr. for Computer Assisted Legal Instrn., 2002—. Mem. adv. bd. Lexis Electronic Author's Press, 1995-99; editor: SSRN Administrative Law Abstracts, 1997—; author: (with Abba Paulos translator) Fetha Negast: The Law of the Kings, 1968; (with others) Administrative Law Cases and Comments, 2003, Administrative Justice in the United States, 2002; contbr. articles to profl. jours. Recipient John Marshall prize Dept. Justice, 1970, Disting. Svc. award NRC, 1977 Mem. ABA (chair sect. administrv. law and regulatory practice 1992-93, Disting. Scholarship award 1988), Am. Law Inst. Office: Columbia U Law Sch 435 W 116th St New York NY 10027-7201 Office Phone: 212-854-2370. Business E-Mail: strauss@law.columbia.edu.

STRAUSS, ROBERT PHILIP, economics professor; b. Cleve., May 11, 1944; s. Harry and Carrie S.; m. Celeste G. Meade, Jan. 11, 1980; children: Sarah Elizabeth, David Anthony, Elena Nicole. AB in Econs., U. Mich., 1966; MA, U. Wis., 1968, PhD in Econs., 1970. Fellow Inst. Research on Poverty, 1968-69; asst. prof. econs. U. N.C., Chapel Hill, 1969-73, assoc. prof., 1973-79; econ. policy fellow Brookings Instn., Washington, 1971-72; economist U.S. Congress Joint Com. Taxation, 1975-78; prof. econs. and pub. policy Carnegie-Mellon U., Pitts., 1979—, assoc. dean Sch. Urban and Pub. Affairs, 1981-83, dir. Ctr. for Pub. Fin. Mgmt., 1984-91; dir. research Pa. Tax Commn., 1979-81. Vis. prof. econs. and pub. policy U. Rochester, 1992-94. Mem. Pa. Local Tax Reform Commn., 1987; sec. faculty Carnegie-Mellon U., 1991-92. Recipient Exceptional Service award U.S. Treasury, 1972, Disting. Service award Pitts. Tax Execs. Inst., 1987, Georgescu Roegen award, 1998; named to Alumni Hall of Fame, Cleveland Heights H.S., 2004; grantee NSF, U.S. Dept. Labor, U.S. Treasury, HUD, Social Security Adminstrn. Mem. Am. Econ. Assn., Econometric Soc., Nat. Tax Assn., Pub. Choice Soc., Assn. for Pub. Policy and Mgmt., Am. Soc. for Pub. Adminstrn., Nat. Tax Assn. (bd. dirs. 1995-98). Clubs: Cosmos. Home: 2307 Country Pl Export PA 15632-9059 Office: 5000 Forbes Ave Pittsburgh PA 15213-3890 Office Phone: 412-268-4798. E-mail: rpstrauss@att.net.

STRAUSS, ROBERT SCHWARZ, lawyer, former ambassador; b. Lockhart, Tex., Oct. 19, 1918; s. Charles H. and Edith V. (Schwarz) S.; m. Helen Jacobs, 1941; children: Robert A., Richard C., Susan. LL.B., U. Tex., 1941. Bar: Tex. 1941, D.C. 1971. Spl. agt. FBI, 1941-45; ptnr. Akin, Gump, Strauss, Hauer & Feld, Dallas, 1945-77, 81—; Dem. nat. committeeman from Tex., 1968-72; mem. exec. com. Dem. Nat. Com., 1969-77, treas., 1970-72, chmn., 1972-77; spl. rep. for trade negotiations with rank of ambassador Office of Pres., 1977-79; chmn. Pres. Carter's reelection campaign, 1979-81; Pres.'s personal rep. for Mid. East negotiations, 1979-81; U.S. amb. to Russia, 1991-93. Bd. dirs. Archer-Daniels-Midland Co., Decatur, Ill., Gulf Stream Corp., Savannah, Ga., Gen. Instruments, N.Y.C. Co-chmn. Nat. Econ. Commn., 1988—. Recipient Presdl. medal of freedom, 1980 Mem. ABA, Dallas Bar Assn., D.C. Bar Assn. Jewish. Office: care Akin Gump Strauss Hauer & Feld 4100 First City Ctr Dallas TX 75201 also: Ste 400 1333 New Hampshire Ave NW Washington DC 20036-1532

STRAUSS, SIMON WOLF, chemist, materials scientist; b. Bedzin, Keltz, Poland, Apr. 15, 1920; arrived in U.S., 1929; s. Israel Calvin and Anna (Hops) S.; m. Mary Jo Boehm, Dec. 27, 1957; children: Jack Calvin, Ruth Ann. BS in Chemistry, Poly. Inst. Bklyn., 1944, MS in Chemistry, 1947, PhD in Chemistry, 1950. Rsch. chemist Nat. Bur. Stds., Washington, 1951-55; from phys. chemist to head chem. metallurgy sect. Naval Rsch. Lab., Washington, 1955-63; sr. staff scientist Air Force Systems Command, Washington, 1963-80; ind. tech. cons. Washington, 1980—. Mem. bd. civil svc. examiners for sci. and tech. pers. U.S. Naval Dist. of Washington, 1959-63; mem. air force panel expert tech. reviewers patents for secrecy considerations Office Air Force Judge Adv. Gen., Washington, 1965-80; co-chair com. on career planning and appraisal of sci. and engrs. Air Force Sys. Command, Washington, 1966-67; air force mem. in-house com. mgmt. rev. tech. info. program, Dept. Def., 1967; chair rsch. steering com. Air Force Dir. of Sci. Tech., Washington, 1976-80; mem., chair editl. adv. com. Washington Acad. Jour., 1983-87, chair com. on scholarly activities, 1984-88. Author: Advanced Composites: An Historical Perspective, Retiring Presidential Lecture, 1987; prin. compiler 75 Years of Scientific Thought, 1987; mem. bd. reviewers Jour. Chem. Engring. Data, 1965-66; contbr. articles to profl. jours. Judge Internat. Sci. Engring. Fair, 1970, 72, 73; nat. evaluator space shuttle student involvement program NSTA, NASA, Washington, 1984, 85. With U.S. Army, 1944-45. Recipient Air Force Exceptional Civilian Svc. medal, 1980, first Disting. Career in Sci. award Wash. Acad. Scis., 1988, Disting. Svc. award, 1990. Fellow AAAS, Wash. Acad. Scis. (first Disting. Scholar-in-Residence 1984-89, pres.-elect 1985-86, pres. 1986-87, life mem. fund trustee 1988—), Am. Inst. Chemists; mem. Math. Assn. Am., Air Force Assn., Cosmos Club, Air Force Materials Lab. (hon. life), Sigma Pi Sigma, Phi Lambda Upsilon, Sigma Xi. Achievements include 3 patents for electrodeposition of Cadmium on high strength steel; research and development of advanced composites technology; the development of equations for the estimation of surface tensions, viscosities and densities of liquid metals as a function of temperature. Home: 4506 Cedell Pl Temple Hills MD 20748-3805 *Living a life not just for oneself contributes not only to the elevation of humankind, but also to the ennoblement and enrichment of one's own life.*

STRAUSS, STANLEY ROBERT, lawyer; b. N.Y.C., June 3, 1915; s. Maurice M. and Blanche Anna (Danciger) S.; m. Margaret Inglis Forbes, Mar. 13, 1944 (div. 1950); m. Helen Anne Cummings, Dec. 31, 1975 (dec. 1980). BA cum laude, Williams Coll., 1936; LLB, Columbia U., 1940. Bar: N.Y. 1941, D.C. 1964, U.S. Ct. Appeals (1st cir.) 1977, U.S. Ct. Appeals (3d cir.) 1986, U.S. Ct. Appeals (4th cir.) 1974, U.S. Ct. Appeals (5th cir.) 1970, U.S. Ct. Appeals (6th cir.) 1977, U.S. Ct. Appeals (8th cirs.) 1975, U.S. Supreme Ct. 1965. Assoc. Howard Henig, N.Y.C., 1940-41; atty. NLRB, Washington, 1946-52, supervising atty., 1953-59, chief counsel, 1959-63; assoc. Vedder, Price, Kaufman & Kammholz, Washington, 1963-65, ptnr., 1965-90; of counsel Ogletree, Deakins, Nash, Smoak & Stewart, Washington, 1990—. Co-author: Practice and Procedure Before the National Labor Relations Board, 3d edit., 1980, 4th edit., 1987, 5th edit., 1996. Officer U.S. Army, 1941-45, PTO. Decorated Bronze Star; Horn scholar Columbia U. Law Sch., 1937-40. Mem. ABA, Fed. Bar Assn., D.C. Bar Assn., Kenwood Country Club. Avocations: golf, tennis. Home: 4956 Sentinel Dr Bethesda MD 20816-3594 Office: Ogletree Deakins Nash 2400 N St NW Fl 5 Washington DC 20037-1154 E-mail: stanleystrauss@odense.com.

STRAUSS, SUSAN GAYLE, linguistics educator; d. David and Beatrice E. Strauss. PhD, UCLA, 1998. Asst. prof. Pa. State U., State College, Pa., 1998—. Author: Japanese/Kiren Linguistics, 1996, vol. 7, 1998; editor: Japanese/Korean Linguistics, vols. 5, 7, 10; author: vol. 10, 2002; contbr. articles to profl. jours. Fellow, Japan Found., 1994—95; grantee, Sociol. Initiatives, 2001. Mem.: Linguistics Soc. Am. Achievements include research in cross-linguistic research on Japanese, Korean, Spanish, and French; cognitive linguistics; cross-cultural studies on school bullying (Japan, Korea, United States). Office: Pa State U University Park Campus State College PA 16802 Personal E-mail: sgs9@psu.edu.

STRAUSS, ULRICH PAUL, chemist, educator; b. Frankfurt, Germany, Jan. 10, 1920; s. Richard and Marianne (Seligmann) S.; m. Esther Lipetz, June 20, 1943 (dec. Sept. 1949); children— Dorothy, David; m. Elaine Greenbaum, Nov. 23, 1950; children— Elizabeth, Evelyn. AB, Columbia U., 1941; PhD, Cornell U., 1944. Sterling fellow Yale U., 1946-48; faculty Rutgers U., New Brunswick, N.J., 1948—, prof. phys. chemistry, 1960-90, prof. emeritus, 1990—; also dir. Sch. Chemistry, 1965-71, chmn. dept. chemistry, 1974-80. Prof. emeritus Rutgers U., 1990—. Mem. editorial bd. Macromolecules, 1990-93; contbr. articles to profl. jours. Recipient Sci. achievement award Johnson Wax Co., 1986; NSF sr. fellow Nat. Center Sci. Research, Strasbourg, France, 1961-62; Guggenheim fellow U. Oxford, Eng., 1971-72 Fellow N.Y. Acad. Scis.; mem. Am. Chem. Soc. (chmn. phys. chemistry group N.J. sect. 1956, councillor 1961-72, honored by 1-day symposium at nat. meeting N.Y.C. 1986, Excellence in Edn. award N.J. sect. 1994). Home: 227 Lawrence Ave Highland Park NJ 08904-1837 Office: Rutgers U Dept Chemistry New Brunswick NJ 08903 E-mail: strauss@rci.rutgers.edu.

STRAUSS, WILLIAM VICTOR, lawyer; b. Cin., July 5, 1942; s. William Victor and Elsa (Lovitt) S.; m. Linda Leopold, Nov. 9, 1969; children: Nancy T., Katherine S. AB cum laude, Harvard U., 1964; JD, U. Pa., 1967. Bar: Ohio 1967. Pres. Security Title and Guaranty Agy., Inc., Cin., 1982—, Strauss & Troy, Cin., 1995—. Trustee Cin. Psychoanalytic Inst., 1990—, Cin. Contemporary Arts Ctr., 1997-2004. Mem. ADA, Nat. Assn. Office and Indsl. Parks, Ohio State Bar Assn., Cin. Bar Assn., Ohio Land Title Assn., Cincinnatus Assn. Home: 40 Walnut Ave Wyoming OH 45215-4350 Office: Strauss & Troy Fed Res Bldg 150 E 4th St Fl 4 Cincinnati OH 45202-4018 Office Phone: 513-629-9416.

STRAUSSLER, TOMAS See STOPPARD, TOM

STRAUTINS, VILNIS, flute educator, past symphony orchestra executive; b. Lubana, Madona, Latvia, Dec. 28, 1939; s. Fricis Strautins and Emma (Bundzis) Strautina; m. Dzidra Markevica, Dec. 31, 1964; children: Ineta, Peteris. MA, Latvian Music, Riga, 1965. Prin. flutist Latvian Nat. Symphony Orch., Riga, 1961-89, mng. dir., 1989-97; prof. flute Latvian Music Acad., Riga, 1971—. Mem.: Latvian Correspondence Chess Fedn. (pres. 2001—). Lutheran. Avocation: correspondence chess. Office: Latvian Music Acad Kr Barona 1 LV-1050 Riga Latvia E-mail: vstrautins@apollo.lv.

STRAVALLE-SCHMIDT, ANN ROBERTA, lawyer; b. NYC, Jan. 2, 1957; Grad. cum laude, Phillips Exeter Acad., 1975; student, Occidental Coll., 1975-78, Oxford Coll., Eng., 1976-77; BS cum laude, Boston Coll., 1980; JD, Boston U., 1987; MBA, Rensselaer Poly. Inst., 2002. Bar: Conn. 1987, U.S. Dist. Ct. Conn. 1988, U.S. Supreme Ct. 1993. Consulting staff Arthur Andersen, Boston, 1980-82; supr. CID ops. Aetna Life & Casualty, Hartford, Conn., 1982-84; summer intern US Atty.'s Office, Boston, 1985; jud. clk. Hon. Judge Thayer III NH Supreme Ct., 1987-88; trial lawyer Day, Berry & Howard, Hartford, Conn., 1988-91; sr. lawyer comml. litig. and appellate practice Berman & Sable, Hartford, Conn., 1991-96; dir. maj. case unit Travelers Property and Casualty Corp., Hartford, Conn., 1996-98; sr. atty. Robinson & Cole, Hartford, Conn., 1998-2000; dir. legal svcs., gen. counsel Conn. Resources Recovery Authority, Hartford, Conn., 2000—. Brief judge Nat. Appellate Advocacy Competition, 1996; online faculty U. Phoenix, 2002—, moot court judge, U. Conn., 1992, 2004. Mem. editl. bd. Conn. Bar Jour., 1990-99, contbr. articles to profl. jours. Mem. Hebron Dem. Town Com., Hebron Bd. Fin., 1995-99, Hebron Sch. Bldg. Com., 1997-99; justice of peace, 1997-99; apptd. mem. Hebron Bldg. Com., 1997-99; bd. dirs. Lawyers Without Borders, 2004; mem. adv. bd. Discovery Ctr., 2004—; mgr. Lawyers at Risk and Neutral Obseavea Program. Hennessey scholar Boston U. Sch. Law, 1987. Mem. ABA, Conn. Bar Assn. (founder, chair appellate practice com. litigation sect. 1994-96, mem. exec. com. litigation sect., pro bono exec. com, 2004, chair pro bono initiative, corp. counsel sect. 2004). Home: 7 Don St Plainville CT 06062-1111 Office: Conn Resources Recovery Authority 100 Constitution Plz Ste 1700 Hartford CT 06103-1719 Office Phone: 860-757-7788. Personal E-mail: astravalle@comcast.net.

STRAWDERMAN, WILLIAM E. statistics educator; b. Westerly, R.I., Apr. 25, 1941; s. Robert Lee and Alida Browning (Dow) S.; m. Susan Linda Grube; July 20, 1985; children: Robert Lee, William Edward, Heather Lynne. BS, U. R.I., 1963; MS, Cornell U., 1965, Rutgers U., 1967, PhD, 1969. Mem. tech. staff Bell Tel. Labs., Holmdel, NJ, 1965-67; vis. asst. prof. Stanford (Calif.) U., 1969-70; instr. Rutgers U., New Brunswick, NJ, 1967-69, prof. stats., 1970—. Contbr. more than 140 articles to profl. jours. Fellow Inst. Math. Stats., Am. Statis. Assn. Office: Rutgers U Statistics Dept Hill Ctr-Busch Campus New Brunswick NJ 08903 Office Phone: 732-445-2697. E-mail: straw@stat.rutgers.edu.

STRAWHECKER, PAUL JOSEPH, fundraising consultant; b. Oct. 31, 1947; s. John Leslie and Leone Francis (Kalamaja) S.; m. Margaret Ellen Baumann, Aug. 31, 1974; children: Risa Nicole, Ryan John. Student, St. Joseph's Sem., 1963-67, Blessed John Neumann Coll., 1968-68; BA, Creighton U., 1970, postgrad. Law Sch., 1971-73; MPA, U. Nebr., 1980. Advanced cert. fundraising exec. Assn. Fundraising Profls. Rsch. specialist mayor's office City of Omaha, 1970, spl. asst. to mayor, 1971, mgr. spl. programs, 1972-73; dir. spl. resources Father Flanagan's Boys Home, Boys Town, Nebr., 1974-81; v.p. for devel. Luth. Hosps. and Homes Soc. Am., Fargo, N.D., 1982-86; asst. adminstr. Sacred Heart Gen. Hosp., Eugene, Oreg., 1986-87; v.p. Northwood U., Midland, Mich., 1987-94; pres. Paul J. Strawhecker, Inc., Omaha, 1995—. Adj. prof. U. Nebr., Omaha, 1995—; treas. Credit Union, 1975; clk., treas., liaison officer Village of Boys Town, 1974-81; writer Am. Soc. Planning Ofcls.; past owner The Wooden Spoon Ltd., Omaha.; exec. com. Assn. Philanthropic Counsel. Author: Fund Raising, 1997, Capital Campaigns, 1998, Resource Development, 1999. Chmn. Met. Area Planning Agy. Coun. Ofcls. Goals Com. for Human Svcs., 1976; mem. Omaha/Douglas County Criminal Justice Commn., 1977-80; mem. adv. com. Douglas County Office ChildrenYouth, Midland County Cmty. Corrections, 1991-92; bd. dirs. "Say Yes" to Youth, 1990-92; chmn. urban affairs com. Met. Area Planning Agy. Mem. Assn. Fundraising Profls. (cert., pres. N.D. area chpt., bd. dirs. 1994-95, pres. Mich. chpt. bd. dirs. 1987-90, pres. Nebr. chpt. bd. dirs. 1997-99, vice chair nat. bd. 1991, nat. found. bd. 2000—, bd. mem. Internat. Found.), Nat. Assn. Hosp. Devel. (spkr. 1983), Internat. City Mgmt. Assn. (spkr. 1971), Multi Hosp. Devel. Assn. (pres. 1986), Leadership Midland (alumni and steering com. 1990-92), Phi Kappa Psi. Roman Catholic. Home: 3424 N 129th Cir Omaha NE 68164-4240 Office: Paul J Strawhecker Inc 4913 Dodge St Omaha NE 68132-2917 E-mail: paul@pjstraw.com.

STRAWN, FRANCES FREELAND, real estate executive; b. Waynesville, N.C., Nov. 18, 1946; d. Thomas M. and Jimmie (Smith) Freeland; m. David Updegraff Strawn, Aug. 30, 1974; children: Trisha, Kirk, Laurel. Cert. real estate broker, cert. residential specialist; grad. Realtor Inst.; LTG. Realtor, broker, pres. Advance Am., Inc., Orlando, Fla., 1982-89; assoc. Ann Cross, Inc., Winter Park, Fla., 1988-99, Coldwell Banker, Winter Park, 1999—2002, Fannie Hillman & Assocs., Inc., 2002—. Contbr. articles to Fla. Realtor, Communique. Co-chmn. fundraiser Black Tie Walk on the Wild Side, 1992; co-ticket chmn. Art and Arch. Orlando Regional Hosp.; mem. steering com. Fla. Heritage Homecoming, Orlando, 1987; chmn. Horizon Exec. Bd., 1989; rec. sec. Women's Bus. Edn. Coun., 1988, mem. adv. bd., 1987, bd. dirs., 1988—90; lectr. Jr. Achievement, 1988—93; mem. steering com. scholarship dinner Crummer Bus. Coll., Rollins Coll., 1992; mem. adv. bd. Ronald McDonald House, 2001—; program chmn. Young Rep. Women, Orlando, 1983; bd. dirs. Vol. Ctr. Ctrl. Fla., rec. sec., 1989; bd. dirs. Ctrl. Fla. Zoo, 1989—92, Women's Resource Ctr., 1989—90. Mem. Creative Bus. Ownership for Women (adv. bd. 1986-88, vice chair grievence com. 1989), Nat. Assn. Realtors. Orlando Bd. Realtors (lectr. Sucess Series), Women's Coun. Realtors (bd. dirs., program co-chair 1998), Women's Exec. Coun., Citrus Club (Orlando) (bd. dirs. 1990-95). Episcopalian. Avocations: travel, skiing, reading. Home: 735 Yale Rd Deland FL 32724 Office: Fannie Hillman & Assocs Inc 205 W Fairbanks Ave Winter Park FL 32789 Office Phone: 800-283-6235.

STRAWSER, JERRY, dean; BBA in accounting, Tex. A&M U., 1983, MS in accounting, 1984, PhD in accounting, 1985. CPA Tex., 1985. Asst. prof. La. State U., 1985—90, Arthur Andersen & Co. rsch. fellow, 1989—90; assoc. prof. Conn. Bauer Coll. Bus., U. Houston, 1990—97, assoc. dean acad. and rsch. programs, 1997—2001, prof. and Arthur Anderson & Co. alumni prof. acctg. and taxation, 1997—2001, interim dean, 1999—2001; dean, devel. coun. chair bus., prof. acctg., Leland/Weinke chair accounting Mays Bus. Sch., Tex. A&M U., 2001—. Bd. govs. Houston Chpt. Inst. Internal Auditors, 1993—95; bd. dirs. Better Bus. Bureau, 1999—2001. Co-author: (books) Auditing Theory and Practice, 1985—2001, Managerial Accounting, 1990—2000, Auditing & Assurance Services, 2004; mem. editl. bd.: Advances in Acctg., 1991—2000, The Internal Auditor, 1993—, Jour. Bus. Rsch., 1994—95, Advances in Acctg. Behavioral Rsch., 1997—99, Issues in Acctg. Edn., 1998—. Mem. bd. advisors Chin. U. Hong Kong, 1995—2001. Recipient Outstanding Tchg. award, Alpha Kappa Psi, 1985, George W. Fair award for tchg. excellence, 1986, Melcher award for rsch. excellence, 1992, 1995, Master Tchg. award, NationsBank, 1994, Disting. Faculty award, Exec. MBA Alumni Assn., 2000; Arthur Andersen rsch. fellowship, 1989, Melcher tchg. fellow, 1991, Melcher svc. fellow, 1993. Office: Mays Bus Sch Tex A&M Univ 4113 TAMU College Station TX 77843-4113 Office Phone: 979-845-4712. Business E-Mail: jstrawser@tamu.edu.

STRAX, THOMAS E. physiatrist; b. N.Y.C., N.Y., Mar. 5, 1942; MD, NYU Sch. Medicine, 1967. Diplomate Am. Bd. Phys. Medicine and Rehab. Intern Jewish Hosp.-Med. Ctr., Bklyn, 1967—68; resident phys. medicine and rehab. NYU, 1968—71; med. dir. Moss Rehab. Hsop., Phila., NJ, 1974—85, JFK Johnson Rehab Inst., Edison, NJ, 1985—. Attending physician Salr Hosp./Clinic. Mem.: AACerPal, ACRM, AAP, Am. Acad. Phys. Medicine and Rehab. (pres. 2002—). Office: JFK Johnson Rehab Inst Edison NJ 08818

STRAYER, BARRY LEE, federal judge; b. Moose Jaw, Sask., Can., Aug. 13, 1932; s. Carl John and Nina Naomi Strayer; m. Eleanor Lorraine Staton, July 2, 1955; children: Alison Lee, Jonathan Mark, Colin James. BA, U. Sask., Can., 1953, LLB, 1955; BCL, Oxford U., Eng., 1957; SJD, Harvard U., 1966. Bar: Sask., 1959. Crown solicitor Gov. Sask., Regina, 1959-62; prof. law U. Sask., 1962-68; dir. constitutional rev. Gov. Can., Ottawa, 1968-72, dir. constitutional law, 1972-74, asst. dep. minister justice, 1974-83; judge trial divsn. Fed. Ct. Can., Ottawa, 1983-94; jud. mem. Competition Tribunal Can., Ottawa, 1986-93; judge Fed. Ct. Appeal of Can., 1994—2004; chief justice Ct. Martial Appeal Ct. of Can., 1994—2004. Sessional lectr. U. Ottawa, 1973-78; constitutional advisor Rep. Seychelles, 1979; adviser Hongkong Govt. Bill of Rights, 1989. Author: Judicial Review of Legislation, 1968, Canadian Constitution and the Courts, 1983, 3d edit., 1988; contbr. articles to profl. jours. Mem.: Commonwealth Lawyers Assn., Larrimac Golf Club, Rideau Club. Office: Fed Ct Kent & Wellington Sts Ottawa ON Canada K1A 0H9

STRAYHORN, CAROLE KEETON, comptroller; b. Sept. 13, 1939; d. Page Keeton; m. Barr McClellan (div. 1977); m. Hill Rylander (div. 1995); m. Ed Strayhorn, 2003; children from previous marriage: Mark, Scott, Brad, Dudley 1 stepchild. Govt. hons. grad., U. Tex., Austin. Pub. sch. tchr.; sch. bd. mem., pres., 1972—77; mayor, 1977—83; mem. Tex. R.R. Commn., 1994—98; state comptr. of rep. accounts Tex., 1998—. Recipient Friends of Tex. Taxpayers award, Citizens for a Sound Economy, 1999, Friend of Edn. award, Tex. Classroom Tchrs. Assn. Office: Tex Comptroller Capitol Station PO Box 13528 Austin TX 78711-3528

STREAM, ARNOLD CRAGER, lawyer, writer; b. N.Y.C. s. Mervyn and Sophia (Hyams) S.; m. Barbara Bloom, Oct. 1, 1967; children by previous marriages: Jane, Abigail. BA, CCNY, 1936; LLD, St. Lawrence U., 1940. Bar: N.Y. 1940, D.C. 1942. Asst. U.S. Atty. N.Y.Dist., 1940-43; ptnr. Amen, Weisman & Butler, N.Y.C., 1948-55; exec. v.p., gen. counsel C & C TV Corp., 1955-60, Hazel Bishop, Inc., 1955-60; trial lawyer, 1960-91; sr. ptnr. Monasch, Chazen & Stream, N.Y.C., 1973-82, Blum, Gersen & Stream, N.Y.C., 1982-93; ret., 1993. Former trial counsel Gulfstream Aerospace Corp., Twentieth Century-Fox Film Corp., French Embassy, N.Y.C.; spl. counsel to TV industry; vis. lectr. Tauro Coll. Law; spkr. on lit. topics for Gt. Neck Libr.; archivist Palace of the Govs. and Mus. Fine Arts, Sante Fe; tutor lit. and bus. law Santa Fe C.C. Author: (novels) The Third Bullet, Until Proven Guilty, Nemo; (short story) Sudi, others; contbr. book revs., tax series, series on constl. law, articles to profl. jours. Served with JAGD, AUS, 1943-46. Mem. Bar of Assn. of City of N.Y. *A lawyer standing in the courtroom provides the ultimate buffer against importunate government.*

STREAN, BERNARD M. retired naval officer; b. Big Cabin, Okla., Dec. 16, 1910; s. Ralph Lester and Maude (Hopkins) S.; m. Janet Lockey, June 12, 1935 (dec. 1978); children: Bernard M., Richard Lockey, Judy (Mrs. William S. Graves); m. Susan Noble Webb, 1978. BS, U.S. Naval Acad., 1933; grad., Armed Forces Staff Coll., 1949, Nat. War Coll., 1958. Commd. ensign USN, 1933, advanced through grades to vice adm., 1965; designated naval aviator, 1935, assigned USS Pennsylvania, 1933-35, assigned Naval Air Sta., 1935-36, assigned USS Saratoga, 1936-38, assigned San Diego Naval Air Sta., 1938-39, assigned Pearl Harbor Naval Air Sta., 1939-40, assigned Naval Air Sta., 1940-42, comdr. Fighter Squadron 1, USS Yorktown, 1943-44, comdr. Air Group 98, 1944-45, comdr. Air Group 75, 1945-46, head tech. tng. program sect. Office Chief Naval Ops., 1950-51, comdg. officer Air Transp. Squadron 8, 1951-54, comdg. officer Pre-Flight Sch., 1954-56, comdg. officer USS Kenneth Whiting, 1956-57, comdg. officer USS Randolph, 1958-59, chief staff, aide to comdr. Naval Air Force, U.S. Atlantic Fleet, 1959-60, comdr. Fleet Air Whidbey, 1960-61, comdr. Patrol Force 7th Fleet, also U.S. Taiwan Patrol Force, 1961-62, asst. chief naval ops. for fleet ops. Operation Navy, High Command of Navy, Comdr. Naval ops., 1962-64, comdr. Carrier Div. 2, Atlantic Fleet, 1964-65, comdr. World's 1st All-Nuclear Naval Task Force, 1964, comdr. round the world cruise; dep. asst. chief for pers., Bur. Naval Pers. Dept. Navy, Washington, 1965-68, chief naval air tng. Naval Air Sta. Pensacola, Fla., 1968-71; ret., 1971; v.p. O.S.C. Franchise Devel. Corp., 1971-75; chmn. bd. Solaray Corp., 1975-80; v.p. Huet-Browning Corp., Washington. Bd. dirs. U.S. Olympic Com., 1965-68; trustee No. Va. Community Colls., 1978-82. Decorated Navy Cross, (2) D.F.C. with 2 gold stars, Air medal with 7 gold stars, Legion of Merit, D.S.M., numerous area and campaign ribbons; Disting. Svc. medal (Greece); medal of Pao-Ting (Republic of China). Mem. Mil. Order World Wars, Loyal Order Carabao, Early and Pioneer Naval Aviators Assn. (pres. 1977-79), Arlington County Tax Assn. (vice chmn. 1978-80), Md. Aviation Hist. Soc. (founder, bd. dirs. 1978-82), U.S. Naval Acad. Alumni Assn. (pres. Class 1933, 1973-88), Army Navy Club (Washington), N.Y. Yacht Club, Washington Golf and Country Club (Arlington), L.A. Country Club. Home: 10858 Meadow Pond Ln Oakton VA 22124-1446

STREAR, JOSEPH D. public relations executive; b. N.Y.C., Nov. 5, 1933; s. Morris and Betty (Birenbaum) S. BA, CCNY, 1955. Pres. AC&R Pub. Relations, Inc., N.Y.C., 1972-82; mng. ptnr. Kanan, Corbin, Schupak & Aronow, Inc., N.Y.C., 1982-84; pres. Strear, David & Mitchell, Inc., N.Y.C., 1984-91; prin. Joseph Strear Pub. Rels., N.Y.C., 1992—. 1st lt. U.S. Army, 1955-57. Mem. Pub. Relations Soc. Am. Avocation: sports. Office: 408 W 57th St New York NY 10019-3053

STREATOR, EDWARD, retired diplomat, management consultant; b. N.Y.C., Dec. 12, 1930; s. Edward James and Ella (Stout) S.; m. Priscilla Craig Kenney, Feb. 16, 1957; children: Edward James, III, Elinor Craig Garcia-Garcia, Abigail Merrill Squance. AB, Princeton U., 1952. Commd. fgn. service officer Dept. State, 1956; assigned ICA, 1956-58; 3d sec. embassy Addis Ababa, Ethiopia, 1958-60; 2d sec. embassy, 1960-62; intelligence research specialist Office Research and Analysis for Africe, Dept. State, Washington, 1962-63, staff asst. to sec. state, 1964-66, chief polit.-mil. affairs unit, 1966-67; dep. dir. polit.-mil. affairs, 1967-68; dep. dir. polit. affairs U.S. Mission to NATO, 1968-69; dep. dir. Office NATO and Atlantic Polit.-Mil. Affairs, Dept. State, 1969-73; dir. office, 1973-75; dep. U.S. permanent rep. to NATO, dep. chief U.S. Mission to NATO, 1975-77; minister, dep. chief of mission Am. embassy, London, 1975-84; ambassador, U.S. rep. OECD Paris, 1984-87. Bd. dirs. South Bank, 1991-99; chmn. New Atlantic Initiative, 1996—. U.S. dels. NATO and OECD Ministerial Meetings, 1964, 66, 69-75, 85-87; mem. 10th SEATO Coun. Min. Meeting, 1965; 2d spl. Inter-Am. Conf., 1965, Conf. Security and Coop., Europe, 1973; mem. Coun., Royal United Svcs. Inst., 1987-92, vice patron, 1991—; exec. com. The Pilgrims, U.K., 1988—, Internat. Inst. Strategic Studies, 1988-99; coun. mem. Royal United

Svcs. Inst. Def. Studies, 1988-1992; gov. Ditchley Found., 1988—, English Speaking Union, 1988-94; pres. Am. C. of C., U.K., 1988-94; chmn. European Coun. Am. C. of C., 1992-94; bd. dirs. Brit-Am. Arts Assn., 1987-99; dir. Brit. Mus. Natural History Internat. Found.; devel. com. Nat. Gallery, U.K., 1991-95; adv. bd. Inst. U.S. Studies-U. London, 1993-99; mem. coun. Oxford Inst. Am. Studies, 1989-2001; adv. com. Fulbright Commn., 1995-2001; trustee Northcote Parkinson Fund, 2004—. Recipient Presdl. Meritorious Svc. award, 1986, Wilbur Carr award Dept. of State, 1987, Benjamin Franklin medal Royal Soc. Arts, 1992. Mem. Knickerbocker Club (N.Y.), Pilgrims (N.Y.), Met. Club (Washington), Beefsteak Club, Garrick Club, White's Club (London), Mill Reef Club (Antigua). Episcopalian. Address: Chateau de St Aignan 32480 La Romieu France Mailing: 535 Park Ave New York NY 10021 Office Phone: 212-486-6688.

STREB, PAUL GERARD, arbitrator; b. Balt., Dec. 8, 1945; s. Edwin and Marie (W.) S.; m. Mary Ament, Nov. 16, 1973. AB in Philosophy, Mount St. Mary's Coll., 1967; JD, U. Balt., 1973. Bar: Md. 1973, U.S. Ct. Appeals (Fed. cir.) 1986. Adminstrv. judge U.S. Civil Svc. Commn. and U.S. Merit Systems Protection Bd., Washington, 1973-83; atty. U.S. Merit Systems Protection Bd., Washington, 1983-90, dep. dir. regional ops., 1990-91; adminstrv. law judge U.S. Dept. HUD, Washington, 1991-94; chief adminstrv. law judge U.S. Merit Systems Protection Bd., Washington, 1994-2001; bd. dirs. fgn. svc. grievance bd. U.S. Dept. State, Washington, 2001—03. Sec. Fed. Administrative Law Judges Conf., 1993-94; arbitrator Fed. Mediation and Conciliation Svc, 2002-. Vol. atty. for Homeless Persons Representation Project, Balt., 1990-91. Lt. U.S. Army, 1967-70, Vietnam. Decorated Purple Heart, U.S. Army; recipient Chmn.'s Legal Excellence award Merit Systems Protection Bd., 1987. Avocations: running, swimming, biking, travel, the arts.

STRECKER, AL, energy executive; With OGE Energy Corp., Oklahoma City, 1971—, sr. v.p. fin. and adminstrn., 1994—98, exec. v.p., COO, 1998—. Bd. govs. Okla. State U. Found., 1996—. Mem.: Rotary (pres. Edmond, Okla. chpt. 2003—). Office: OGE Energy Corp PO Box 321 321 N Harvey Oklahoma City OK 73101

STRECKER, DAVID EUGENE, lawyer; b. Carthage, Mo., Nov. 29, 1950; s. Eugene Albert and Erma Freida (Wood) S.; m. Katherine Ann Pugh; children: Charles David, Carrie Christina. BA, Westminster Coll., 1972; JD, Cornell U., 1975, M in Indsl. Labor Rels., 1976. Bar: N.Y. 1976, Okla. 1981, U.S. Dist. Ct. (no. dist.) N.Y. 1976, U.S. Dist. Ct. (ea. dist.) Okla. 1984, U.S. Dist. Ct. (we. dist.) Okla. 2000, U.S. Dist. Ct. (we. and ea. dists.) Ark. 2000, U.S. Ct. Appeals (no. dist.) Okla. 1981, U.S. Ct. Appeals (10th cir.) 1982, U.S. Ct. Appeals (6th cir.) 1990, U.S. Supreme Ct. 1991. Assoc. Conner & Winters, Tulsa, 1980-85, ptnr., 1985-91, Shipley, Inhofe & Strecker, Tulsa, 1991-95, Strecker & Assocs. P.C., Tulsa, 1995—. Instr. paralegal program Tulsa Jr. Coll., 1985—, mem. adv. com., 1986-91; mem. Cornell Secondary Schs. Com., Tulsa, 1985—; adj. instr. labor rels. Okla. State U., 1995—; master Am. Inns of Ct. Bd. dirs., v.p. Tulsa Sr. Svcs., 1988-91; mem. pers. com. Philbrook Art Mus. Capt. JAGC, U.S. Army, 1976-80. Mem. ABA, Okla. Bar Assn. (chmn. labor sect. 1990-91), Tulsa County Bar Assn. (continuing legal edn. com. 1981—), Soc. for Human Resource Mgmt., Tulsa Area Human Resources Assn. (gen. counsel 1989-2000, v.p. 1994-98, bd. dirs. family and children's svcs. 2000—04), Kappa Alpha. Democrat. Episcopalian. Avocations: jogging, golf. Home: 5112 E 107th St Tulsa OK 74137-7238 Office: Midcontinent Tower 401 S Boston Ste 2150 Tulsa OK 74103-4009 E-mail: destreck@juno.com.

STRECKER, JUDY ELLEN, music educator; d. Robert Joseph and Tressie Eulala Gibson; m. Jerome John Strecker, Dec. 28, 1990. MusB, Incarnate Word U., 1965; MA, Eastman Sch. Music, 1971; D of Musical Arts, U. Colo., 1979. Chair music dept. Incarnate Word Coll., San Antonio, 1971—76; dir. music St. Alphonsus Ch., Greenwell Springs, La., 1985—87; chair music dept. St. Mary of Plains Coll., Dodge City, Kans., 1987—90, Frank Phillips Coll., Borger, Tex., 1992—. V.p. faculty assoc. Frank Phillips Coll., 1996—98; adjudicator Nat. Guild Piano Tchrs., 1990—; organist 1st Meth. Ch., Pampa, 1992—94. Musician: (albums) Afternoon of Jazz, 1998, Recorder Music. Regional dir. Tex. Jr. Colls. Choral Festival, San Antonio, 1997—98; organist various chs., Borger, 1992—. Recipient NISOD Excellence award, U. Tex., Austin, 1998; fellow, Eastman Sch. Music, Rochester, N.Y., 1976—79. Mem.: Am. Coll. Musicians (piano judge 1990—), Tex. Assn. Music Schs., Tex. Music Educators Assn. Home: Box 835 Fritch TX 79036 Office: Frank Phillips Coll 1301 W Roosevelt Borger TX 79008

STREEB, GORDON LEE, diplomat, economist; b. Windsor, Colo., Dec. 24, 1935; s. Gerhard O. and Amelia (Martin) S.; m. Alice Junette Thomas, Aug. 11, 1962; children: Kurt, Kent, Kerry-Lynn. BSBA, BSChemE, U. Colo., 1959; PhD in Econs., U. Minn., 1978. Fgn. service officer U.S. Dept. State, Berlin, 1963-65; vice consul Am. Consulate, Guadalajara, Mex., 1965-67; instr. econs. U. Minn., 1968; examiner Bd. Examiners, 1972-73; internat. economist for trade policy Bur. Econ. and Bus. Affairs, Washington, 1973-77; econ. counselor U.S. mission European Office of the UN and other internat. orgns., Geneva, 1977-80; exec. asst. to undersec. of state on econ. affairs Washington, 1980-81; dep. asst. sec. state for econ. and social affairs Bur. Internat. Orgn. Affairs, Washington, 1981-84; dep. chief mission Am. Embassy, New Delhi, India, 1984-88; sr. inspector Dept. State, Washington, 1988-90; amb. to Zambia Am. Embassy, Lusaka, 1990-93; diplomat-in-residence The Carter Ctr., Atlanta, 1994-95, assoc. exec. dir. peace program, 1995—. Mem. Coun. on Fgn. Rels. Bd., Friendship Force Internat. Bd. Friendship Force Internat. Home: 2680 Churchwell Ln Tucker GA 30084-2402 Office: The Carter Ctr One Copenhill Atlanta GA 30307 E-mail: gstreeb@emory.edu.

STREEK, DAN, corporate financial executive; BBA, U. Nev., Las Vegas; MBA, Rockhurst Coll. CPA. With mgmt. Arthur Andersen LLP; v.p., asst. controller Aquila, CFO, treas., 2001—. Mem.: Fin. Execs. Inst. Office: Aquila 20 W Ninth St Kansas City MO 64105

STREEM, JAMES KENNETH, musician, educator; b. Cleve., Jan. 15, 1934; s. Irving Earl and Geraldine W. Streem; m. Prudence Vitale, July 4, 1968 (dec. June 29, 2000). BS, Juilliard, 1956, MS, 1959. Mem. piano faculty Cleve. Music Sch. Settlement, 1960—68; prof. piano Fla. State U., Tallahassee, 1968—; concert debut Carnegie Hall, N.Y.C., NY, 1966. Lectr. in field. Composer: (film score) Double Stop, 1967; author: 125 Pianists on the Legend of Vladimir Horowitz, 1996; performer: Steinway concert series, Kosciusko Found., Alice Tully Hall, numerous recitals throughout U.S.; soloist: with symphony orch. Trustee Temple Israel, Tallahassee, 1975—82, 1987—93. With U.S. Army, 1958—63. Home: 2604 Stonegate Dr Tallahassee FL 32308 E-mail: jks1115@aol.com.

STREEP, MERYL (MARY LOUISE STREEP), actress; b. Summit, N.J., June 22, 1949; d. Harry, Jr. and Mary W. Streep; m. Donald J. Grummer, 1978. BA, Vassar Coll., 1971; MFA, Yale U., 1975, DFA (hon.), 1983, Dartmouth Coll., 1981. Co-founder Mothers & Others for a Livable Planet. Appeared with: Green Mountain Guild; actress: (Broadway plays) Trelawny of the Wells, 1975; (plays) 27 Wagons Full of Cotton (Theatre World award); A Memory of Two Mondays; Henry V; Secret Service; The Taming of the Shrew; Measure for Measure; The Cherry Orchard; Happy End; Wonderland; Taken in Marriage; Alice in Concert (Obie award, 1981); (films) Julia, 1977; The Deer Hunter, 1978 (Best Supporting Actress award nat. Soc. film Critics, Acad. award nomination, 1978); Manhattan, 1979; The Seduction of Joe Tynan, 1979; Kramer vs. Kramer, 1979 (N.Y. Film Critics' award, Los Angeles Film Critics' award, both for best actress, Golden Globe award, Acad. award for best supporting actress); The French Lieutenant's Woman, 1981 (Los Angeles Film Critics award for best actress, Brit. Acad. award, Golden Globe award, Acad. award nomination, 1981); Sophie's Choice, 1982 (Acad. award for best actress, Los Angeles Film Critics award for best actress, Golden Globe award, 1982); Still of the Night, 1982; Silkwood, 1983 (Acad. award nomination); Falling in Love, 1984; Plenty, 1985; Out of Africa, 1985 (Los Angeles Film Critics award for best actress, Golden Globe award, 1985); Heartburn, 1986; Ironweed, 1987 (Acad. award nomination); A Cry in the Dark, 1988 (named Best Actress N.Y. Film Critics' Circle, 1988, Best Actress Cannes Film Festival, 1989, Acad. award nomination); She-Devil, 1989; Postcards From the Edge, 1990; Defending Your Life, 1991; Death Becomes Her, 1992; The House of Spirits, 1993; The River Wild, 1994; The Bridges of Madison County, 1995 (Acad. award nominee for best actress, 1996); Before and After, 1996; Marvin's Room, 1996; Dancing at Lugnasa, 1998; One True Thing, 1998; Music of the Heart, 1999 (Acad. award nominee for best actress); The Hours, 2002; Adaptation, 2002 (Southeastern Film Critics Assn. award for best supporting actress, 2002, Chgo. Film Critics Assn. award for best supporting actress, 2003, Golden Globe for best supporting actress, 2003); The Manchurian Candidate, 2004; (TV films) The Deadliest Season, 1977; Alice at the Palace, 1982; (TV miniseries) Holocaust, 1978; Angels in America, 2003 (Golden Globe for best actress, 2004, Screen Actors Guild Award for best actress, 2004); (TV dramatic spls.) Uncommon Women and Others, 1979; First Do No Harm, 1997; Secret Service, 1977; voice: (films) Artificial Intelligence, 2001; narrator: (TV films) A Vanishing Wilderness, 1990; The Velveteen Rabbit, 1984 (Emmy award Best Children's Rec.). Recipient Mademoiselle award, 1976, Woman of Yr. award, B'nai Brith, 1979, Hasty Pudding Soc., Harvard U., 1980, Best Supporting Actress award, Nat. Bd. of Rev., 1979, Best Actress award, 1982, Star of Yr. award, Nat. Assn. Theater Owners, 1983, People's Choice award, 1983, 85, 86, 87, 1990, Women in Film Crystal award, 1998, Gotham award for Lifetime Achievement, 1999, Bette Davis Lifetime Achievement award, 1999. Office: Creative Artists Agy 9830 Wilshire Blvd Beverly Hills CA 90212-1825*

STREET, DAVID HARGETT, investment company executive; b. Oklahoma City, Dec. 4, 1943; s. Bob Allen and Elizabeth Anne (Hargett) S.; m. Betty Ann Nichols, Oct. 1, 1966; children: Elizabeth Ann, Randall Hargett, Jeffrey David. BA in English, U. Okla., 1965; MBA in Fin., U. Pa., 1970. Vice pres. SEI Corp., 1970; v.p., prin. Street & Street, Inc., N.Y.C., 1970-74; v.p., mgr. San Francisco regional office First Nat. Bank Chicago, 1974-78; sr. v.p., CFO, treas. Bangor Punta Corp., Greenwich, Conn., 1978-84; v.p., treas. Penn Cen. Corp., Greenwich, 1984-86, v.p. fin., 1986-87, sr. v.p. fin. Cin., 1987-92; exec. v.p. Gen. Cable Corp., Highland Heights, Ky., 1992-94, also bd. dirs.; pres., CEO Street Capital Group, Duluth, Ga., 1994—. Mem. adv. bd. Mfrs. Hanover Trust Co., 1982-88. 1st lt. M.I. U.S. Army, 1966—67. Mem. St. Ives Country Club. Republican. Presbyterian. Home and Office: 103 Villamoura Way Duluth GA 30097-2068

STREET, DEBORRA LYNN, director of fine arts; b. Ft. Payne, Ala., Feb. 25, 1953; d. John M. and Mary (Adams) Long. B in Music Edn., Troy State U., 1976, MEd, 1982, EdS, 1994; student, Birmingham U. Sch. Law. Tchr. music S. Hall Jr. High Sch., Oakwood, Ga., 1976-77, Slocomb (Ala.), 1977-79, U.S. Collegiate Wind Bands European (summer) Tours, 1978-88, Judson Coll., Marion, Ala., 1980—, Marion Mil. Inst., 1980—, Marion Acad., 1987-88. Band camp instr. 22 U.S. Univs., 1968—; band judge U.S. music festivals, 1977—; asst. conductor U.S. Collegiate Wind Bands European Tours, 1979; sponsor Drama Soc., Marion, 1985—. Prodr.(over 30 musicals and plays):. Sunday sch. tchr. United Meth. Ch., Marion, 1987-88; chmn. Marion Mil. Inst. Fine Arts Coun., 1989-90; mem. steering com. Citizens for a Better Community, Marion, 1990-91; conductor Community Instrumental Ensemble, Marion, 1990—. Mem. Nat. Band Assn., Music Educators Nat. Conf., Women Band Dirs. Nat. Assn. (Indsl. chmn. 1988), DAR, Perry County Hist. Soc., Am. Legion Aux. (Americanism award 1971), Delta Kappa Gamma, Perry County Arts and Humanities Council, AAUW, Tau Beta Sigma, Kappa Kappa Psi, Delta Gamma. Avocations: music, drama, swimming. Home: 803 Washington St Marion AL 36756-3027 Office: Marion Mil Inst Washington St Marion AL 36756-1822

STREET, JOHN CHARLES, linguistics educator; b. Chgo., Apr. 3, 1930; s. Charles Larrabee and Mary Louise (Rouse) S.; m. Eve Elizabeth Baker, June 4, 1975. BA, Yale, 1951, MA, 1952, PhD, 1955. Asst. prof. English Mich. State U., 1957-59; asst. prof. linguistics and Mongolian langs. Columbia, 1959-62; vis. asst. prof. linguistics U. Wash., 1962-63; assoc. prof. linguistics U. Wis., Madison, 1963-65, prof. linguistics, 1965-92, prof. emeritus, 1992—. Author: The Language of the Secret History of the Mongols, 1957, Khalkha Structure, 1963, The Journal of Oliver Rouse, 1983, An Ellis Family of Devon and Newfoundland, 1994, A Genealogy of the Rouses of Devon, 2002. Research asso. Am. Council Learned Socs., 1959-62. Served with AUS, 1955-57.

STREET, JOHN F. mayor; b. Norristown, Pa., 1943; m. Naomi Street; children: Sharif, Rasida, Lateef, Akeem. BA, Oakwood Coll., 1966; JD, Temple U., 1975. City councilman City of Phila., 1979-98, coun. pres., 1992-98, past chmn. licenses and inspections, appropriations coms., chmn. Whole, Rules & Fiscal Stability, Intergovt. coop. com., 1992—; mem. Phila. Gas Commn., 1984-89, chmn., 1992—; mayor City of Phila., 2000—. Of counsel Ross & Goldstein.

STREET, PICABO, Olympic athlete; b. Triumph, Idaho, Apr. 3, 1971; Downhill skier U.S. Ski Team, 1994—. Biography Picabo: Nothing to Hide. Named World Cup Downhill Women's Champion, 1995, 1996; recipient Silver medal Women's Downhill Alpine Skiing, Plympic Games, Lillehammer, 1994, Bronze and Gold medals, World Championships, 1996, Gold medals (3) Woman's Super Giant Slalom Alpine Skiing, Nagano, Japan, 1998, Gold medal Super 6 Slalom, Winter Olympics, Nagano, Japan, 1998.

STREET, ROBERT LYNNWOOD, civil, mechanical and environmental engineer; b. Honolulu, Dec. 18, 1934; s. Evelyn Mansel and Dorothy Heather (Brook) S.; m. Norma Jeanette Ensminger, Feb. 6, 1959; children: Brian Clarke (dec.), Deborah Lynne, Kimberley Anne. Student, USN ROTC Program, 1952-57; MS, Stanford U., 1957, PhD (NSF grad. fellow 1960-62), 1963. Mem. faculty Sch. Engring. Stanford U., 1962—, prof. civil engring., assoc. chmn. dept. Sch. Engring., 1970-72, chmn. dept. Sch. Engring., 1972-80, 94-95, prof. fluid mechanics and applied math. Sch. Engring., 1972—, founding dir. environ. fluid mechanics lab. Sch. Engring., 1985-91, assoc. dean rsch. Sch. Engring., 1971-83, vice provost acad. computing and info. sys., 1983-85, vice provost, dean rsch. and acad. info. sys., 1985-87, v.p. for info. resources, 1987-90, acting provost, 1987, v.p. librs. and info. resources, 1990-92, vice provost, dean of librs. and info. resources, 1992-94, William Alden and Martha Campbell prof. Sch. Engring., 1997—. Vis. prof. U. Liverpool, Eng., 1970-71, Ctr. for Water Rsch., U. Western Australia, 1985; vis. prof. mech. engring. James Cook U., Australia, 1995; trustee Univ. Corp. Atmospheric Rsch., 1983-94, chmn. sci. programs evaluation com., 1981, treas. corp., 1985, vice chmn. bd., 1986, chmn. bd., 1987-91; bd. dirs., sec.-treas. UCAR Found., 1987-91; bd. govs. Rsch. Libr. Group, 1990-91; chmn. Com. Preservation Rsch. Libr. Materials, Assn. Rsch. Librs., 1993; mem. higher edn. adv. bds. computer corps., 1983-94; mem. basic energy sci. adv. com. U.S. Dept. Energy, 1993-96; bd. dirs. Stanford U. Bookstore, Inc., 1993-98. With C.E.C., USN, 1957-60. Sr. postdoctoral fellow Nat. Center Atmospheric Research, 1978-79; sr. Queen's fellow in marine sci., Australia, 1985; fellow N.E. Asia-U.S. Forum on Internat. Policy at Stanford U., 1985-89. Fellow: AAAS; mem.: ASME (R.T. Knapp award 1986), ASCE (chmn. publs. com. hydraulics divsn. 1978—80, Walter Huber prize 1972, Hilgard Hydraulic Engring. prize 2002), Nat. Acad. Engring., Am. Meteorol. Soc., Oceanographic Soc., Am. Geophys. Union, Phi Beta Kappa, Tau Beta Pi. Office: Stanford U Environ Fluid Mechs Lab Dept Civil/Environ Engring Stanford CA 94305-4020 Office Phone: 650-723-4969. Business E-Mail: street@stanford.edu.

STREET, SUSAN LEE, elementary school educator; b. Kansas City, Kans., Aug. 4, 1955; d. Charley E. Taylor and Betty Lee Milum; m. Thomas D. Street, Dec. 20, 1980; children: Amanda Lee, Jordan Thomas. BS in Elem. Edn., Ark. Tech. U., 1977. Tchr. kindergarten Jasper (Ark.) Elem.; tchr. elem. Woodland Heights Sch., Harrison, Ark. Tchr. Bible Sch. Home: RR 6 Box 60K Harrison AR 72601-8808

STREET, WALTER SCOTT, III, lawyer; b. Richmond, Va., May 20, 1944; s. Walter Scott Jr. and Margaret (Hoyt) S.; m. Virginia Mapes, Aug. 23, 1967; children: Walter Scott IV, Christopher F., Elizabeth M. BA, Hampden-Sydney Coll., 1965; LLB, U. Va., 1968. Bar: Va. 1968, U.S. Ct. Appeals (4th cir.) 1968, U.S. Dist Ct. (ea. dist.) Va. 1968, U.S. Supreme Ct. 1974. Assoc. atty. Bremner, Byrne & Baber, Richmond, Va., 1968-70; house coun. Blue Cross Va., Richmond, 1970-71; ptnr. Wood & Street, Richmond, 1971-80, Williams, Mullen, Clark & Dobbins, Richmond, 1980—. Sec.-treas. Va. Bd. Bar Examiners, Richmond, 1972—; commr. in chancery Chesterfield Cir. Ct., Va., 1970—. Trustee Hargrave Mil. Acad., Chatham, Va., 1988-92. Fellow Am. Bar Found., Va. Law Found.; mem. ABA (mem. ho. of dels. 2002—), Nat. Conf. Bar Examiners (chmn. adminstrs. com. 1980-81), Richmond Bar Assn., Va. State Bar (bar coun. 1991-2001, chmn. com. on legal edn. and admission to the bar 1991-93, exec. com. 1994-2001, pres.-elect 1998-99, pres. 1999-2000), Country Club Va. Office: Williams Mullen Christian & Dobbins 2 James Center 1021 E Cary St Richmond VA 23219-4000

STREET, WILLIAM MAY, beverage company executive; b. Louisville, 1938; Grad., Princeton U., 1960; MBA, Harvard U., 1963. V.p. Brown-Forman Corp., Louisville, 1969, dir., mem. exec. com., 1971, sr. v.p., 1977, vice chmn., 1983, pres., 2000; pres., COO Brown-Forman Beverage Co. Divsn., Louisville, 1986-94; pres., CEO Brown-Forman Beverages Worldwide Divsn., 1994—; pres. Brown-Forman Corp., 2001—. Office: Brown-Forman Beverages Worldwide 850 Dixie Hwy Louisville KY 40210-1038

STREETEN, BARBARA WIARD, ophthalmologist, medical educator; b. Candia, N.H., Mar. 3, 1925; d. Robert Campbell Wiard and Gertrude Sarah Matheson; m. David Henry Palmer Streeten, Aug. 2, 1952; children: Robert Duncan, Elizabeth Anne, John Palmer. AB magna cum laude, Tufts U., 1945, MD cum laude, 1950. Diplomate Am. Bd. Ophthalmology. Jr. resident in gen. pathology Mallory Inst., Boston City Hosp., 1951-52; fellow in ophthalmic pathology Mass. Eye and Ear Infirmary, Boston, 1952-53; resident in ophthalmology Wayne County Gen. Hosp., Eloise, Mich., 1953-56; from jr. to sr. clin. instr. ophthalmology U. Mich. Med. Sch., Ann Arbor, 1956-60; from asst. prof. to prof. ophthalmology SUNY Health Sci. Ctr. (now called SUNY Upstate Med. U.), Syracuse, 1964—, dir. eye pathology lab., 1966—; from asst. prof. to prof. pathology SUNY Health Sci. Ctr., Syracuse, 1968—. Contbr. more than 114 articles to profl. jours., chpts. to textbooks. Mem. vision study sect. Nat. Eye Inst., NIH, Bethesda, Md., 1977-80, mem. bd. sci. counselors, 1982-86; mem. editl. bd., mem. editl. adv. com. Ophthalmology jour., 1982-94; gen. editor Investigative Ophthalmology and Visual Sci., 1979-82, mem. editl. bd., 1987-92. Grantee Nat. Eye Inst., NIH, 1975—2002. Mem. Am. Assn. Ophthalmic Pathologists (charter, past pres., bd. dirs., Zimmerman medal 1997), Am. Acad. Ophthalmology (honor award 1990), Verhoeff Ophthalmic Pathology Soc. (past pres.), Assn. for Rsch. in Vision and Ophthalmology (past sect. chmn.), Internat. Soc. Ophthalmic Pathology (co-v.p. N.Am. 1990-92), Phi Beta Kappa, Alpha Omega Alpha. Episcopalian. Achievements include establishment of elastic system nature of the suspensory ligament of the ocular lens; ultrastructural and immunopathologic contributions to diseases of the ocular connective tissue matrix, particularly those related to cataract and glaucoma. Home: 334 Berkeley Dr Syracuse NY 13210-3000 Office: SUNY Upstate Med Univ WH Rm 2107 766 Irving Ave Syracuse NY 13210-1602 Office Phone: 315-464-7156.

STREETER, JOHN WILLIS, information systems manager; b. Topeka, Sept. 3, 1947; s. Jack and Edith Bernice (Vowels) S.; m. Nancy Ann Buck, June 15, 1968 (div. 1985); children: Sarah Beth, Timothy Paine; m. Linda Lea Wenrich Weisbender, Sept. 13, 1986; stepchildren: Michael Leon Weisbender II, Debra Ann Weisbender Johnson, Dawn Marie Weisbender. BS in Computer Sci., Kans. State U., 1973, MBA in Mgmt., 1974; postgrad., Harvard U., 1992. Computer programmer U.S.M.C., 1965-70, Kans. State U., Manhattan, 1970-74; cons., mgr., prin. Am. Mgmt. Systems, Inc., Arlington, Va., 1974-83; systems planning analyst Fed. Nat. Mortgage Assn., Washington, 1983-85; assoc. dir. computing and telecomm. Kans. State U., Manhattan, 1985-91, dir. info. systems, 1991—. Mem. State of Kans. Info. Tech. Adv. Bd., 1997-98. Author: Streeter Genealogy, 1985. Staff sgt. USMC, 1965-70. Recipient Navy Achievement medal in data processing Sec. Navy, 1971. Mem. SR, KC, Am. Inst. Cert. Computer Profls., Educause, Inc. (Kans. State U. voting mem. rep. 1987—), Streeter Family Assn. (bd. dirs. 1988—, v.p. 1990-95), Am. Legion. Republican. Roman Catholic. Avocations: genealogy, history, book collecting. Home: 6765 Salzer Rd Wamego KS 66547-9636 Office: Kans State U Info Sys 2323 Anderson Ave Ste 215 Manhattan KS 66502-2912

STREETER, KEVIN D. management consultant; b. Birmingham, Jan. 26, 1956; s. Martin Freeman and Mamie Ruth (Cross) Streeter. AA, Ga. Mil. Coll., 1976; BA, Houston Bapt. U., 2000—. Cons. Pneuma Consulting, Houston, 2001—. Author: (poetry) Made In His Loveness (Poet of Yr., 2002). Scholar Full Scholarship, Ga. Mil. Coll., 1974—76, RSMIS Scholarship, Tex. Ind. Coll. Fund, 2002—. Avocations: cooking, archery, exercise. Home: PO Box 2001 Bellaire TX 77402 Personal E-mail: kdstreet@swbell.net.

STREETER, LINCOLN HOWARD, retired sales executive; b. Northampton, Mass., May 31, 1939; s. Lincoln Lucius and Clara Cecilia Streeter; m. Janet Helena Forfa, Jan. 28, 1942; children: Carolyn Thersa Mirek, Michael Lincoln, Jennifer Elise, Julie Marie Mosley, Matthew Scott, Jefferson Edward. BA, St. Michael's Coll., Colchester, Vt., 1957—61. Account exec. Estabrook & Co., Inc., Boston, 1966—67; accounts mgr. GE Lighting, West Haven, Conn., 1975—82, nat. accounts mgr. Cleveland, 1982—85, regional accounts Meriden, Conn., 1985—95, Milford, Conn., 1995—2001. Town treas. Town of South Windsor, Conn., 1993—95; chmn. Rep. Town Com., South Windsor, 2001—04; pres. & bd. mem. Rotary Club, South Windsor, 1978; genealogy assn. Streeter Family Assn., Northampton, Mass., 1984—2004; mayor Town of South Windsor, Conn., 1989—93; pres. Nat. Alumni Assn., Colcester, Vt., 1980—81; mem. Direct Descendants of Mayflower, Plymouth, Mass., 2001. Capt. USAF, 1961—66, Dover, DE; Vietnam. Recipient Alumnus of the Yr., St. Michael's Coll., 1981. Mem.: Rotary Club (pres. & bd. mem. 1990—2004, Paul Harris Fellowship Award 1985). R-Consevative. Catholic. Avocations: genealogy studies, travel, golf, politics, social planner. Home: 56 Bramblebrae South Windsor CT 06074

STREETER, OSCAR EDWARD, JR., radiation oncologist; b. Roanoke, Va., May 20, 1955; s. Oscar Edward Sr. and Betty (Richardson) S.; m. Paulette Y. Saddler; 1 child, Rebecca. BS in Biology, USC; MD, Howard U., 1982. Diplomate Am. Bd. Med. Examiners. Intern U. Calif., Irvine, 1983-85; resident Howard U. Med. Ctr., Washington, 1986-89; resident tng. program dir. dept. radiation oncology U. So. Calif. Sch. Medicine, L.A., 1990-94, asst. prof. radiation oncology, 1990-95, asst. prof. clin. radiation oncology, 1995-97, assoc. prof. clin. radiation oncology, 1997—; dept. radiation oncology chief physician LAC, U. So. Calif. Med. Ctr., 1992-94, U. So. Calif. Norris Cancer Ctr., 1994—. Chair cancer com. U. So. Calif. Sch. Medicine, L.A., 1997, med. exec., 1995—, acad. tech. adv. com., 1997; mem. leadership coun. U. So. Calif. Cancer Ctr., 1995—. Contbr. articles to profl. jours. Chmn. NBLIC/Western Region, L.A., 1995—; adv. bd. Wellness Com. Foothills, Pasadena, Calif., 1995—; bd. dirs. Real Men Cook Found., L.A., 1993—, Women of Color Breast Cancer Survivors Project, L.A., 1995—; mem. Real Men Cook Found., 1994; mem. Maxine Waters-35th Dist. Com. Svc., Mem. of Congress; mem. health svcs. Office of Willie Brown Jr. Spkr. of Assembly 13 Dist. Grantee U. So. Calif., 1993, 93-96, U. Calif., 1993-95, Biotech. Comms., L.A., 1995; named one of Top 100 Black Physicians in Am., Black Enterprise Mag., 2001. Office: 1441 Eastlake Ave Los Angeles CA 90089-0112

STREETER, ROBERT DAVENPORT, electrical engineer, consultant; b. Springfield, Mass., Sept. 17, 1941; s. William Allen Streeter and Muriel Ethel Davenport; m. Carole Janet Riley; children: John Riley, Susan Streeter Billian. B in Elec. Engring., Ohio State U., 1964; MSEE, Purdue U., 1968. Registered profl. engr., Ind. Engr. WBNS Radio-TV, Columbus, Ohio, 1961—64, Ohio State U. Rsch. Found., Columbus, 1962—64, The Magnavox Co., Fort Wayne, Ind., 1965—82; pres. A M Stereo, Inc., Fort Wayne, 1982—; engring. fellow Raytheon, Fort Wayne, 1985—. Contbr. articles to profl. jours. Mem.: IEEE, Armed Forces Comm. and Electronics Assn., Eta Kappa Nu (life). Achievements include invention of AM stereo, microelectromechanical systems. Avocations: private pilot, amateur radio, bicycling. Home: 6111 Eagle Creek Dr Fort Wayne IN 46814-3213 Office: Raytheon 1010 Production Rd Fort Wayne IN 46808 Personal E-mail: r.streeter@ieee.org.

STREETER, STEPHANIE ANNE, printing company executive; b. Boston, Sept. 19, 1957; d. Andrew Geoffrey Galef and Suzanne Jane (Cohen) Sidy; m. Edward Stanley Streeter, Feb. 22, 1980. BA in Polit. Sci., Stanford U., 1979. Mgr. market analysis Xerox Small Bus. System, Sunnyvale, Calif., 1980-81; regional sales mgr. Xerox Office Products Divsn., Sunnyvale, Calif., 1981-83; product mgr. Decision Data Computer Corp., Horsham, Pa., 1983-85; sr. product mgr. Avery Dennison Corp., Covina, Calif., 1985-88, bus. mgr. indexes, 1988-89, bus. mgr. computer supplies, 1989-90, dir. mktg., computer products, 1990-91, v.p. gen. mgr. label divsn. Diamond Bar, Calif., 1991-93, v.p., gen. mgr., Avery Dennison Brands, 1993—96, worldwide group v.p., 1996—2000; COO idealab!, Pasadena, Calif., 2000; pres., COO Banta Corp., Menasha, Wis., 2001—02, dir., 2001—, pres., CEO, 2002—04, chmn., pres., CEO, 2004—. Bd. dirs. Wis. Mfrs. and Commerce. Fellow Internat. Women's Forum. Democrat. Avocations: bicycling, skiing. Office: Banta Corp 225 Main St Menasha WI 54952*

STREETER, THOMAS WAYNE, music educator; b. Kokomo, Ind., Apr. 26, 1943; s. Claude Clive Streeter and Zoe Alberta Blossey; m. Christine Elizabeth Pfeiffer, July 13, 1968; children: Carrie Elizabeth, Bradley Thomas, Geoffrey Scott, Troy David, Tiffany Leigh, Cynthia Dawn. B in Music Edn., Ind. U., 1965, M in Music Edn., 1967; D of Musical Arts, Cath. U. of Am., 1971. Bass trombonist Airmen of Note USAF, Washington, 1967—71; prof. music Ill. Wesleyan U., Bloomington, 1971—. Adj. prof. trombone Bradley U., Peoria, Ill., 1972—73, Ill. State U., Normal, 1980—81; chmn. instrumental dept. Ill. Wesleyan U., 1981—; program dir. Birch Creek Music Ctr., Door County, Wis., 1981—2000; dir. Ill. Wesleyan U. Jazz Festival, Bloomington, 1975—, Ill. Wesleyan U. Summer Music Camps, Bloomington, 1982—85; adminstr. Nat. Stage Band Camps, Bloomington, 1978—81. Bass trombonist Andy Williams tours, tours with Henry Mancini, orch. performances with maj. artists, recitalist premier of Trilogy for Bass Trombone and Band, by Tom Dossett, premier of works by Abram Plum, premier of bass trombone pieces by Robert Bankert, premier of bass trombone pieces by Chris Dedrick, premier of bass trombone work by Bedford Watkins. Bishop LDS Ch., Normal, 1991—97, br. pres., 2000—04. Tech. sgt. USAF, 1967—71. Mem.: Music Educators Nat. Conf. (assoc.), Internat. Trombone Assn. (assoc.; treas. 1973—78), Internat. Assn. Jazz Educators (assoc.; Ctrl. Divsn. coord. 1986—2000), Phi Mu Alpha (assoc.). Mem. Lds Ch. Avocations: gardening, bicycling. Office: Sch Music Ill Wesleyan U Box 2900 Bloomington IL 61702-2900

STREETMAN, BEN GARLAND, electrical engineering educator; b. Cooper, Tex., June 24, 1939; s. Richard E. and Bennie (Morrow) S.; m. Lenora Ann Music, Sept. 9, 1961; children: Paul, Scott. BS, U. Tex., 1961, MS, 1963, PhD, 1966. Fellow Oak Ridge Nat. Lab., 1964-66; asst. prof. elec. engring. U. Ill., 1966-70, assoc. prof., 1970-74, prof., 1974-82; rsch. prof. Coordinated Sci. Lab., 1970-82; prof. elec. engring. U. Tex., Austin, 1982—, dir. Microelectronics Rsch. Ctr., 1984—, Dula D. Cockrell Centennial chair engring., 1989-96, dean Coll. Engring., 1997—. Bd. dirs. Nat. Instruments, Zix Corp. Author: Solid State Electronic Devices, 5th edit., 2000. Recipient Frederick Emmons Terman award Am. Soc. Engring. Edn., 1981, AT&T Found. award, 1987; named Disting. Alumnus, U. Tex. at Austin, 1998. Fellow IEEE (Edn. medal 1989), Electrochem. Soc.; mem. NAE, Am. Acad. Arts and Scis., Tau Beta Pi, Eta Kappa Nu, Sigma Xi. Office: U Tex at Austin Dean of Engring 1 University Sta C2100 Austin TX 78712-0284 Office Phone: 512-471-1166.

STREETMAN, JOHN WILLIAM, III, museum official; b. Marion, N.C., Jan. 19, 1941; s. John William, Jr. and Emily Elaine (Carver) S.; children: Katherine Drake, Leah Farrior, Burgin Eaves. BA in English and Theatre History, Western Carolina U., 1963; cert. in Shakespeare studies, Lincoln Coll., Oxford (Eng.) U., 1963. Founding dir. Jewett Creative Arts Ctr., Berwick Acad., South Berwick, Maine, 1964-70; exec. dir. Polk Mus. Art, Lakeland, Fla., 1970-75; dir. Mus. Arts and Sci., Evansville, Ind., 1975—; chmn. mus. adv. panel Ind. Arts Commn., 1977-78. Mem. Am. Assn. Museums, Assn. Ind. Museums (bd. dirs.) Episcopalian. Office: Evansville Mus Arts History and Sci 411 SE Riverside Dr Evansville IN 47713-1037

STREETT, WILLIAM BERNARD, retired university dean, engineering educator; b. Lake Village, Ark., Jan. 27, 1932; s. William Bernard and Marie Louise (Pfeffer) S.; m. Jackie Lou Heard, June 8, 1955 (dec. Jan. 14, 1999); children— Robert Stuart, David Alexander, Kathleen Ann, Michael Richard; m. Mary J. Sansalone, Oct. 23, 1999. BS, U.S. Mil. Acad., 1955; MS, U. Mich., 1961, PhD, 1963. Commd. 2d lt. U.S. Army, 1955; founder, first dir. Sci. Rsch. Lab., U.S. Mil. Acad., West Point, N.Y., 1968-78, asst. dean, 1968-78, ret. col., 1978; sr. rsch. assoc. Cornell U., Ithaca, N.Y., 1978-81, prof. chem. engring., 1981-95, dean engring., 1984-93; v.p. Impact-Echo Cons., Ithaca, 1995; founder, pres. Impact-Echo Instruments, LLC, 1997—. Contbr. articles to profl. jours. Postdoctoral fellow NATO, 1966, Guggenheim fellow Oxford U., 1974 Mem. Am. Concrete Inst., Tau Beta Pi, Sigma Xi. Home: 105 Oak Hill Pl Ithaca NY 14850-2323 Office: Cornell U Coll Engring Hollister Hall Ithaca NY 14850 E-mail: wbs3@cornell.edu.

STREFF, WILLIAM ALBERT, JR., lawyer; b. Chgo., Aug. 12, 1949; s. William Albert Streff Sr. and Margaret (McKeough) Streff Fisher; m. Kathleen Myslinski, Sept. 29, 1984; children: Amanda, William III, Kimberly. BSME, Northwestern U., 1971, JD cum laude, 1974. Bar: Ill. 1974, U.S. Dist. Ct. (no. dist.) Ill. 1974, U.S. Dist. Ct. (no. dist.) N.Y. 1987, U.S. Dist. Ct. (no. dist.) Calif. 1988, U.S. Ct. Appeals (7th cir.) 1980, U.S. Ct. Appeals (9th cir.) 1988, U.S. Ct. Appeals (fed. cir.) 1982, U.S. Ct. Customs and Patent Appeals, 1978, U.S. Ct. Appeals (3rd cir.), 1992, U.S. Ct. Internat. Trade, 1996, U.S. Dist. Ct. (ea. dist.) Mich., 1999. Legal writing instr. Law Sch. Northwestern U., Chgo., 1973-74; assoc. Kirkland & Ellis, Chgo., 1974-80, ptnr., 1980—. Lectr. Ill. Inst. Continuing Legal Edn., 1984; adj. prof. Northwestern U. Law Sch., 1992-94, 97-99, Chgo. Kent-IIT Law Sch., 1998, John Marshall Law Sch., 2000-03. Contbr. articles to profl. jours. Mem. adv. bd. Ill. Inst. Tech./Chgo.-Kent, 1983-86; trustee Northwestern U., Evanston, 1984-86, mem. vis. com. Law Sch., Chgo., 1988-94. Mem. ABA. Office: Kirkland & Ellis 200 E Randolph Dr Chicago IL 60601-6636

STREGE, KAREN, library director; State libr. Mont. State Libr., Helena, 1996—. Office: Mont State Library 1515 E 6th Ave PO Box 201800 Helena MT 59620

STREICHER, JAMES FRANKLIN, lawyer; b. Ashtabula, Ohio, Dec. 6, 1940; s. Carl Jacob and Helen Marie (Dugan) S.; m. Sandra JoAnn Jennings, May 22, 1940; children: Cheryl Ann, Gregory Scott, Kerry Marie. BA, Ohio State U., 1962; JD, Case Western Res. U., 1966. Bar: Ohio 1966, U.S. Dist. Ct. (no. dist.) Ohio 1966. Assoc. Calfee, Halter & Griswold, Cleve., 1966-71, ptnr., 1972—. Bd. dirs. Provider Gateway, Inc., Sensir Technologies, Stamford, Conn., Mid Am. Consulting; mem. Divsn. Securities Adv. Bd., State of Ohio; lectr. Case Western Res. U., Cleve. State U.; mem. pvt. sector com. John Carroll U. Former trustee Achievement Ctr. for Children, Western Res. Hist. Soc., Make-A-Wish Found. Endowment. Mem. ABA, Fed. Bar Assn., Ohio State Bar Assn., Assn. for Corp. Growth, Ohio Venture Assn., No. Ohio Venture Assn. (trustee), Greater Cleve. Bar Assn. (founding chmn. corp., banking, bus. law sect.), Ohio State U. Alumni Assn., Case Western Res. U. Alumni Assn., Newcomen Soc., Bluecoats Club (Cleve.), Mayfield Country (bd. dirs. 1985-89), Union Club, The Pepper Pike Club, The Tavern Club, Beta Theta Pi, Phi Delta Phi. Roman Catholic. Republican. Fax: 216-241-0816. Office Phone: 216-622-8234. E-mail: jstreicher@calfee.com.

STREICKER, JOHN H. real estate company executive; Pres. Sentinel Real Estate Corp., N.Y.C., 1989—. Office: Sentinel Real Estate Corp Rm 3403 1251 Avenue Of The Americas Fl 35 New York NY 10020-1104*

STREIFF, ARLYNE BASTUNAS, business owner, educator; b. Sacramento, Calif., Nov. 04; d. Peter James and Isabel (Gemnas) Bastunas; children: Peter Joshua, Joshua Gus. BS, U. Nev., 1965; postgrad., U. Calif., Davis, 1965-68, Calif. State U., Chico, 1968, 71. Cert. elem. tchr., Calif., Nev., cert. in English-specially designed lang. acad. instrn. devel. in English. Tchr. reading, lang. and kindergarten Enterprise Elem. Sch. Dist., Redding, Calif., 1965-98, tchr. kindergarten, 1988-98; owner, pres. Arlyne's Svcs., Redding, Calif., 1990—. Author: Niko and His Friends, 1989, Niko The Black Rottweiler, 1995, Color-Talk-Spell. Mem. Rep. Women, Five County Labor Coun., Redding, 1976 93, Calif. Labor Fedn., 1974-97, AFL-CIO, 1974-97. Named Tchr. of Yr., Enterprise Sch. Dist., 1969. Mem. AAUW, Am. Fedn. Tchrs., Calif. Tchrs. Assn. (bargaining spokesperson 1968-72, exec. bd. dirs.), United Tchrs. Enterprise (pres. 1979-80, chmn. lang. com.), Calif. Reading Assn., Enterprise Fedn. Tchrs. (pres. 1974, pres.-elect 1995-97), Calif. State Fedn. Tchrs. (v.p. 1974-75, exec. bd. 1995-97), Redding C. of C., Women of Moose, Elks. Avocations: home interior design, real estate, construction, creative writing, educational advancement. Office: Arlynes Svcs 1468 Benton Dr Redding CA 96003-3116

STREIFFER, JENNY, former soccer player; b. Metairie, La., May 25, 1978; Student, U. Notre Dame. Alt. U.S. Women's Olympic Soccer Team, 1996; mem. U-20 Nat. Team Nordic Cup championship, Denmark, 1997. Named Big East Rookie of Yr. and NSCAA 3d Team All-Am., freshman yr., U. Notre Dame. Achievements include scoring winning goal U-20 Nat. Team Nordic Cup championship, Denmark; midfield Notre Dame, NCAA championship freshman yr., undefeated regular season sophomore year. Office: US Soccer Fedn 1801-1811 S Prairie Ave Chicago IL 60616

STREIKER, SUSAN L. law librarian; b. Phila., Dec. 11, 1959; d. Lowell Dean and Lois Suzanne Streiker. BA, Brigham Young U., 1981, MLS, 1983. Reference and media asst. Law Sch. Libr. Brigham Young U., Provo, Utah, 1981—83; instr. in legal rsch., reference and media libr. Sch. of Law Southwestern U., L.A., 1984—89; reference libr. Paul, Hastings, Janofsky & Walker, LLP, 1989 91, head law libr., 1991—. Fellow ABA; mem. Am. Assn. Law Librs., Southern Calif. Assn. Law Librs., Phi Alpha Theta. Avocations: music, travel, painting, gardening, ballooning. Office: Paul Hastings Janofsky & Walker LLP 515 S Flower St Fl 25 Los Angeles CA 90071-2300

STREISAND, BARBRA JOAN, singer, actress, director; b. Bklyn., Apr. 24, 1942; d. Emanuel and Diana (Rosen) S.; m. Elliott Gould, Mar. 1963 (div.); 1 son, Jason Emanuel; m. James Brolin, July 1, 1998. Grad. high sch., Bklyn.; student, Yeshiva of Bklyn. N.Y. theatre debut Another Evening with Harry Stoones, 1961; appeared in Broadway musicals I Can Get It for You Wholesale, 1962, Funny Girl, 1964-65; motion pictures include Funny Girl, 1968, Hello Dolly, 1969, On a Clear Day You Can See Forever, 1970, The Owl and the Pussy Cat, 1970, What's Up Doc?, 1972, Up the Sandbox, 1972, The Way We Were, 1973, For Pete's Sake, 1974, Funny Lady, 1975, The Main Event, 1979, All Night Long, 1981, Nuts, 1987; star, prodr. film A Star is Born, 1976; prodr., dir., star Yentl, 1983, The Prince of Tides, 1991, The Mirror Has Two Faces, 1996 (ASCAP Award for score, 1996); exec. prodr.: (TV movie) Serving in Silence: The Margarethe Cammermeyer Story, 1995; TV spls. include My Name is Barbra, 1965 (5 Emmy awards), Color Me Barbra, 1966; actress, prodr., dir. The Mirror Has Two Faces, 1996; rec. artist on Columbia Records; Gold record albums include People, 1965, My Name is Barbra, 1965, Color Me Barbra, 1966, Barbra Streisand: A Happening in Central Park, 1968, Barbra Streisand: One Voice, Stoney End, 1971, Barbra Joan Streisand, 1972, The Way We Were, 1974, A Star is Born, 1976, Superman, 1977, The Stars Salute Israel at 30, 1978, Wet, 1979, (with Barry Gibb) Guilty, 1980, Emotion, 1984, The Broadway Album, 1986, Til I Loved You, 1989; other albums include: A Collection: Greatest Hits, 1989, Just for the Record, 1991, Back to Broadway, 1993, Concert at the Forum, 1993, The Concert Recorded Live at Madison Square Garden, 1994, The Concert Highlights, 1995, Higher Ground, 1997, A Love Like Ours, 1999, Christmas Memories, 2001, The Essential Barbara Streisand, 2002. Recipient Emmy award, CBS-TV spl. (My Name Is Barbra), 1964, Acad. award as best actress (Funny Girl), 1968, Golden Globe award (Funny Girl), 1969, co-recipient Acad. award for best song (Evergreen), 1976, Georgie award AGVA 1977, Grammy awards for best female pop vocalist, 1963, 64, 65, 77, 86, for best song writer (with Paul Williams), 1977, 2 Grammy nominations for Back to Broadway, 1994; Nat. Acad. of Recording Arts & Sciences Lifetime Achievement Award, 1994, Cecil B. Demille Lifetime Achievement Award, 2000, Liberty & Justice Award, Rainbow/PUSH Coalition, 2001. Office: Barbra Streisand c/o Martin Erlichman Assoc Inc 5670 Wilshire Blvd Ste 2400 Los Angeles CA 90036 also: Nigro Karlin Segal 10100 Santa Monica Blvd Ste 1300 Los Angeles CA 90067

STREIT, MICHAEL J. state supreme court justice; b. Sheldon, Iowa; married; 1 child. BA, U. Iowa, 1972; grad., U. San Diego Sch. Law, 1975. Cert.: (U.S. Ct. Appeals) 1996. Asst. atty. Lucas County, atty.; dist. ct. judge, 1983; Supreme Ct. justice Iowa State Supreme Ct., 2001—. Mem.: Blackstone Inn of Ct., Supreme Ct. Jud. Tech. Com., Iowa Jud. Inst., Judges Assn. Edn. Com., Supreme Ct. Edn. Adv. Com. Office: State House Des Moines IA 50319

STREITWIESER, ANDREW, JR., chemistry professor; b. Buffalo, June 23, 1927; s. Andrew and Sophie Streitwieser; m. Mary Ann Good, Aug. 19, 1950 (dec. May 1965); children: David Roy, Susan Ann; m. Suzanne Cope Beier, July 29, 1967. AB, Columbia U., 1949, MA, 1950, PhD, 1952; postgrad. (AEC fellow), MIT, 1951-52. Faculty U. Calif., Berkeley, 1952-92, prof. chemistry, 1963-92, prof. emeritus, 1993—. Researcher on organic reaction mechanisms, application molecular orbital theory to organic chemistry, effect chem. structure on carbon acidities; cons. to industry, 1957— Author: Molecular Orbital Theory for Organic Chemists, 1961, Solvolytic Displacement Reactions, 1962, (with J.I. Brauman) Supplemental Tables of Molecular Orbital Calculations, 1965, (with C.A. Coulson) Dictionary of Pi Electron Calculations, 1965, (with P.H. Owens) Orbital and Electron Density Diagrams, 1973, (with C.H. Heathcock and E.M. Kosower) Introduction to Organic Chemistry, 4th edit., 1992, A Lifetime of Synergy with Theory and Experiment, 1996; also numerous articles; co-editor: Progress in Physical Organic Chemistry, 11 vols., 1963-74. Recipient Humboldt Found. Sr. Scientist award, 1976, Humboldt medal, 1979, Berkeley citation, 1993. Fellow AAAS; mem. NAS, Am. Chem. Soc. (Calif. sect. award 1964, award in Petroleum Chemistry 1967, Norris award in phys. organic chemistry 1982, Cope scholar award 1989), Am. Acad. Arts and Scis., Bavarian Acad. Scis. (corr.), Phi Beta Kappa, Sigma Xi. Office: U Calif Dept Chemistry Berkeley CA 94720-1460 Office Phone: 510-642-2204. Business E-Mail: astreit@socrates.berkeley.edu.

STREKOWSKI, LUCJAN, chemistry professor; b. Grabowo, Poland, June 21, 1945; came to U.S., 1981; s. Antoni and Janina (Chrapowicz) S.; m. Alewtina Smirnova, Oct. 14, 1967; children: Rafal, Anna. BS in Polymer Chemistry with distinction, Mendeleev Inst. Chemistry, Moscow, 1967; PhD in Organic Chemistry, Polish Acad. Scis., 1972; DSc in Chemistry, Adam Mickiewicz U., Poznan, Poland, 1976. Instr. organic chemistry Adam Mickiewicz U., Poznan, 1971-72, asst. prof. dept. chemistry, 1972-78, assoc. prof. dept. chemistry, 1978-81; rsch. assoc. dept. chemistry U. Fla., Gainesville, 1981-84; asst. prof. dept. chemistry Ga. State U., Atlanta, 1984-89, assoc. prof. dept. chemistry, 1989-96, prof. dept. chem., 1996—. Vis. prof. U. Fla., Gainesville, 1979-80, 81, Australian Nat. U., 1980, U. Kans., Lawrence, 1972-73. Editor: Pyridine-Metal Complexes, Vol. 14, Part 6, 1985; N.Am. editor Heterocyclic Comms.; mem. editl. bd. Arkivoc; contbr. more than 220 articles to profl. jours.; patentee in field. Recipient award, Polish Ministry Sci., 1997, Polish Chem. Soc., 1973, Polish Acad. Scis., 1972, Ga. State U., 1993; grantee Am. Chem. Soc.-Petroleum Rsch. Fund, 1985—, Solvay Pharms., 1992—93, Nat. Diagnostics, 1991—93, NIAID/NIMH, 1988—89, Rohm and Hass Co., 1988, Am. Cancer Soc., 1987—89, Rsch. Corp., 1985—94, Milheim Found. Cancer Rsch., 1985—86, DuPont Co., 1996—2000, Small Bus. Innovation Rsch. Program, 2000—02, Coley Pharms., 2003—, FBI, 2002—. Mem. Am. Chem. Soc., Internat. Soc. Heterocyclic Chemistry, Internat. Acad. Scis. of Nature and Soc. (mem. presidium). Avocation: classical music. Office: Ga State Univ Dept Chemistry Atlanta GA 30303 Personal E-mail: lucjan@gsu.edu.

STRELAU, RENATE, historical researcher, artist; b. Berlin, Feb. 1, 1951; came to U.S., 1960; d. Werner Ernst and Gerda Gertrud (Bargel) S. BA, U. Calif., Berkeley, 1974; cert. Arabic lang. proficiency, Johns Hopkins U., 1976; MA, Am. U., 1985, MFA, 1991. Rsch. asst. Iranian Embassy, Washington, 1976-80. One-woman shows include Cafe Espresso, Berkeley, 1973, Riggs Bank, Arlington, Va., 1994-95; exhibited in group shows at Watkins Gallery, Washington, 1999, Khoja Gallery, Arlington, 2002; represented in permanent collections C. Law Watkins Meml. Collection, Am. U. Mem. Am. Hist. Assn., Orgn. Am. Historians, Soc. for Historians Am. Fgn. Rels. (life). Office: PO Box 12655 Arlington VA 22219-2655 Office Phone: 703-862-9000. Business E-Mail: strelau@renatestrelau.com.

STRELLA, EVE G. industrial engineer, consultant; d. Robert Marshall and Evelyn (Ashenfelter) Johnston; m. David Strella (dec.). BS in Indsl. Engring., Rochester Inst. Tech., 1986. Cert. expanded duties dental asst. Dental asst. Dr. Rappaport, Balt., 1976—78, Dr. Sherman, Balt., 1978—79, Dr. Henry Rohner, Rochester, NY, 1979—81; mgmt. engr. Park Ridge Health Sys., Rochester, 1983—98; v.p. indsl. engring. XLR8 Team, Rochester, 1998—2001; CEO Illuminate of Rochester, Inc., Pittsford, NY, 2001—03, Strella and Assoc., Pittsford, 2003—. Cons., presenter, spkr. in field. Author: Quality Care, 1997. Named Adult Amateur, Am. Horse Show Assn., 1990; recipient Horse of the Yr. award, 1990, Champion in the Zone award, US Dressage Fedn., 1990. Mem.: Inst. Indsl. Engrs., Rochester Acad. Sci., Pittsford Art Group. Avocations: astronomy, horseback riding, art, photography, cooking. Home and Office: Strella and Assoc 15 Stuyvesant Rd Ste 100 Pittsford NY 14534 Fax: 585-385-9699. E-mail: estrella@rochester.rr.com.

STRENA, ROBERT VICTOR, university research laboratory manager; b. Seattle, June 28, 1929; s. Robert Lafayette Peel and Mary Oliva (Holmes) S.; m. Rita Mae Brodovsky, Aug. 1957; children: Robert Victor, Adrienne Amelia. AB, Stanford U., 1952. Survey mathematician Hazen Engring., San Jose, Calif., 1952-53; field engr. Menlo Sanitary Dist., Menlo Park, Calif., 1954-55; ind. fin. reporter Los Altos, Calif., 1953-59; asst. dir. Hansen Labs. Stanford U., 1959-93, asst. dir. emeritus Ginzton Lab., 1993—. Ind. fin. cons., Los Altos, 1965—; mem. restoration adv. bd., Moffett Fed. Airfield, 1994—. Active Edn. System Politics, Los Altos, 1965-80, local Boy Scouts Am., 1968-80, Maj. USAR, 1948-70. Mem. AAAS, Mus. Soc., Big X (Los Altos), Cherry Chase Golf Club. Republican. Avocations: golf, sailing. Home: 735 Raymundo Ave Los Altos CA 94024-3139 Office: Stanford U Ginzton Lab Stanford CA 94305 Office Phone: 650-923-0200.

STRENG, WILLIAM PAUL, lawyer, educator; b. Sterling, Ill., Oct. 17, 1937; s. William D. and Helen Marie (Conklen) S.; children: Sarah, John. BA, Wartburg Coll., 1959; JD, Northwestern U., 1962. Bar: Iowa 1962, Ill. 1962, Ohio 1964, Tex. 1975. Law clk. to U.S. circuit judge Lester L. Cecil, Cin., 1963-64; asso. firm Taft, Stettinius & Hollister, Cin., 1964-70; atty.-advisor Office Sec. Tax Policy, Office Tax Legis. Counsel, Dept. Treasury, Washington, 1970-71; dep. gen. counsel Export-Import Bank U.S., Washington, 1971-73; prof. law Sch. Law, So. Methodist U., Dallas, 1973-80; vis. prof. Coll. Law Ohio State U., Columbus, 1977; partner firm Bracewell & Patterson, Houston, 1980-85; Vinson & Elkins prof. of law U. Houston Law Ctr, 1985—. Vis. prof. Rice U., NYU Law Sch., 1990, U. Tex. Sch. Law, 2002; disting. vis. prof. U. Hong Kong Law Faculty, 1992; Fulbright prof. U. Stockholm Law Faculty, 1993; vis. fellow law faculty Victoria U., Wellington, New Zealand, 1996; vis. law lectr. U. Leiden, The Netherlands, 1997, The Netherlands, 98, The Netherlands, 2000; cons. Bracewell & Patterson, 1985—; lectr. various confs. Am. Law Inst., World Trade Inst., Practicing Law Inst., Internat. Fiscal Assn., ABA, Tex. State Bar. Author: International Business Transactions-Tax and Legal Handbook, 1978, Estate Planning, 1991, 1997, International Business Planning: Law and Taxation, 6 vols., 1982, 2004, Tax Planning for Retirement, 2001, revised edit., 2004, Doing Business in China, 1990, 1996, Federal Income Taxation of Corporations and Shareholders--Forms, 1995, 2004, Choice of Entity, 1994, 1999, U.S. International Estate Planning, 1996, revised, 2004. Served with USMC, 1962. Lutheran. Home: 1903 Dunstan Rd Houston TX 77005-1619 Office Phone: U Houston Law Ctr Houston TX 77204-6060 Office Phone: 713-743-2148. E-mail: wstreng@uh.edu.

STRENGTH, JANIS GRACE, management executive, educator; b. Ozark, Ala., Jan. 31, 1934; d. James Marion and Mary Belle (Riley) Grace; m. Robert Samuel Strength, Sept. 12, 1954; children: Stewart A., James Houston (dec.), Robert David (dec.), James Steven (dec.) BS in Home Econs. and Edn., Auburn U., 1956; MA in Edn., Washington U., St. Louis, 1978, MA in Adminstrn., 1980. Home economist Gulf Power Co., Pensacola, Fla., 1956-59; tchr. sci. Northside Jr. High Sch., Greenwood, S.C., 1961-68; tchrs. home econs. Greenwood High Sch., 1968-70; chairperson dept. sci. Parkway West Jr. High Sch., Chesterfield, Mo., 1975-82; tchr. sci. Parkway West High Sch., Chesterfield, 1982-88; v.p.-sec. Product Safety Mgmt. Inc., Gulf Breeze, Fla., 1989—2001; ret., 2001. Chairperson dist. Phys. Scis. Curriculum Com., 1978-85, Sci. Fair Placement Com., 1978-82, Gifted Edn., 1983-84; leader Phys. Sci. Summer Workshops, Safety Sci. Lab. Workshop; sponsor Nat. Jr. Honor Soc., Parkway West Jr. Class. Supt. youth dept. Sunday sch. Greentrails Meth. Ch., sponsor summer camp; vol. fundraiser March of Dimes, Cerebral Palsy, Multiple Schlorosis, Cancer funds; judge Parkway/Monsanto/St. Louis Post Dispatch Sci. Fairs, 1978—; mem. citizens action com. Parkway Sch. Bd., 1980-84; v.p. United Meth. Women, 2000, pres. 2004. Mem. NEA, Nat. Sci. Tchrs. Assn., Ladies Golf Assn. (sec. 1998-99, 2003—), Santa Rosa Women's Club (pres. 1998-2000), Tiger Point Country Club (Gulf Breeze), Raintree Country Club (Hillsboro, Mo.). Republican. Methodist.

STRENSKI, JAMES B. retired communications executive; b. Jan. 2, 1930; m. Jane E.; 5 children. Grad., Marquette U. Pub. info. officer USN, NATO; with Pub. Communications Inc., Chgo.; chmn., chief exec. officer Pub. Communications Inc, Tampa, Fla. Cons. to nonprofit, health care and social agys., pub. and pvt. corps., fin. and acad. instns.; lectr. to industry groups, trade assns., bus. orgns. Contbr. more than 70 articles on pub. rels. to jours. in field. Mem. Tampa Jesuit High Sch. Found., Tampa Downtown Partnership Bd., Hillsborough County Affordable Housing Com., Bus. Adv. Coun., Coll. of Journalism of Marquette U.; bd. dirs. Chgo. Leadership Coun. for Met. Open Communities, Tampa Goodwill Industries-Suncoast; program chmn. Tampa Pkwy. Assn.; pub. rels. chmn. Paint Your Heart Out, Tampa, U. Tampa Bd. Fellows. Mem. Worldcom Group, Inc. (founder, exec. com.). Home: 1200 Gulf Blvd Apt 1205 Clearwater Beach FL 33767-3700

STRENSKI, ROBERT FRANCIS, lawyer; b. Chgo., Oct. 10, 1947; s. Bernard F. and Harriet L. (Prokopiak) S. BS, U. Ill., 1969; JD, Washington U., St. Louis, 1973; postgrad., U. Colo., 1975. Bar: Mo. 1973, Colo. 1974. Acct. Motorola, Inc., Chgo., 1970, City and County of Denver, 1973-74, asst. city atty., 1974—. Precinct committeeman Denver Dem. Com., 1976-78, dist. fin. chmn., 1977-78; arbitrator Better Bus. Bur., Denver, 1977—; mediator Ctr. for Dispute Resolution, Denver, 1980 Mem. Colo. Bar Assn., Denver Bar Assn., Nat. Inst. Mcpl. Law Officers (ethics com. 1985-88), Am. Arbitration Assn. (arbitrator). Democrat. Roman Catholic. Home: 410 Pearl St Denver CO 80203-3808 Office: Law Dept City & County Denver 201 W Colfax Ave Dept 1207 Denver CO 80202 Office Phone: 720-913-3281. Business E-Mail: robert.strenski@ci.denver.co.us.

STRETCH, JOHN JOSEPH, social work educator, management and evaluation consultant; b. St. Louis, Feb. 24, 1935; s. John Joseph and Theresa Carmelita (Fleming) S.; children: Paul, Leonmarie, Sylvan, Adrienne, Sharonalice; m. Barbara Ann Stewart, Mar. 16, 1985; children: Margaret, Thomas. AB, Maryknoll Coll., Glen Ellyn, Ill., 1957; MSW, Washington U., St. Louis, 1961; PhD, Tulane U., 1967; MBA, St. Louis U., 1980. LCSW 1990. Instr. Tulane U., 1962—68, asst. prof., 1968; assoc. prof. social work St. Louis U., 1968—71, prof., 1972—; asst. dean Sch. Social Service, 1976-87, dir. doctoral studies, 1976-94, dir. MSW. program, 1985-86, bd. dirs., mem. exec. com. Ctr. for Social Justice, 1987—, mem. instnl. rev. bd. Sch. Social Svc., 1987—92; dir. rsch. Social Welfare Planning Coun. Met. New Orleans, 1962—68. Cons. to United Way Met. St. Louis, Cath. Charities of Archdiocese of St. Louis, Cath. Svcs. for Children and Youth, Full Achievement, Mo. Province of S.J., Cath. Commn. on Housing, Cath. Family Svcs., Youth Emergency Svcs., Mo. State Dept. Social Svcs., U. Mo. Extension Svc., St. Joseph's Home for Boys, Marian Hall Ctr. for Adolescent Girls, Boys Town-Girls Town of Mo., A World of Difference, Anti Defamation League of B'nai Brith, Prog. Youth Ctr., Foster Care Coalition of Greater St. Louis, Rankin-Jordan Children's Rehab. Hosp., 1999-2000, Ill. St. Claire County Sch. Sys.'s Old Man River Project, 2002—; expert witness on homeless U.S. House Select Com. on Families, Children and Youth, 1987; mem. resource spl.

task force on homeless Office of Sec. U.S. Dept. HUD, 1989; survey design cons. U.S. Office of The Insp. Gen., 1990; methodology expert on homelessness U.S. Census Bur., 1989; expert homeless policy GAO hearings, 1992; chair Mo. Assn. for Social Welfare Low Income Housing, 1982—; mem., chmn. St. Louis Low Income Housing Preservation Com., 1985; mem. Comprehensive Housing Affordabiltiy Strategies (CHAS) Mo. Statewide Planning Group, Mo. Housing Devel. CHAS citizen's com., State of Mo. Affordable House Task Force, Mo. Housing Devel. Corp., 1998-2002, Mo. Inst. Psychiatry, 1995, University City Sch. Dist., 1990; mgmt. cons. People's Issues Task Force Agrl. div. Monsanto Chem. Inc., 1992, regional office NCCJ, 1990-92; vis. prof. Nat. Cath. U. Am. Sch. Social Svcs., 1991, 92, U. Bristol, Eng., 1992, U. Calif. Sch. Pub. Health, Berkeley, 1990; cons. Mo. Speaker of the Ho. statewide legis. task force, 1990-92, Russian Am. Summer U., 2000; statewide grant project reviewer emergency shelter grant program Mo. Dept. Social Svcs., 1989—, chair, 2000—; homeless svcs. grant reviewer City of St. Louis, 1996-97. Mem editl. bd. Social Work, 1968-74, Health Progress, 1988—01, Social Work Administration, 2003—; manuscript referee Jour. Social Svc. Rsch., 1977-99; mgmt. and evaluation content referee Wadsworth Press, Human Svcs. Press, Allyn and Bacon Press; editor, contbr. books and profl. jours. and books. Bd. dirs. Beyond Housing, Inc. 1985—, pres., 1993-95, St. Louis U. Ctr. for Social Justice, 1990—, Housing Comes First, 1995-99, Adequate Housing for Missorians, 2002—, Neighborhood Housing Svc., 2004—, Nat. Coalition for Homeless, 2004—; mem. Mo. Assn. Social Welfare, 1980—, DuBourg Soc. of St. Louis U., 1989; mem. Salvation Army Family Haven, 1987, 2000—, mem. adv. bd., 1988-92; bd. dirs., exec. com. Cmty. Asset Mgmt. Co.; chmn. United Way of Greater St. Louis venture grant com., 1988-91, vice chmn. day care allocation com., 1985-95, mem. process and rev. com., 1991-93, inter-orgnl. priorities com., 1991-93; mem. leadership coun. Success By Six, 1990—; organizer Mo. State Nat. Coalition for the Homeless, 1989; appointee instl. representation nat. Jesuits social concern group St. Louis U., 1993—; mem. exec. and support tng. group, St. Louis U., 1987-92; mem. instnl. rev. bd., 1979-99. NIMH Career Leadership Devel. fellow, 1965-67, Fed. Ednl. grantee Ill. Sch. Sys., 2002; recipient Scholar of Yr. award Sch. Social Svc., St. Louis U., 1987; named Vol. of Yr. Ecumenical Housing Prodn. Corp., 1990; Presdl. scholar Sch. Social Svc., 1992. Mem. AAUP (St. Louis U. chpt. exec. com. 1990—, pres. 1994—), ACLU, Acad. Cert. Social Workers (charter mem.), Nat. Assn. Social Workers, Mo. Assn. for Social Welfare (bd. dirs., Outstanding State-Wide Mem. of Yr. 1987), Coun. on Social Work Edn., Common Cause, Amnesty Internat., Nat. Consumer's Union (com. on vital and health stats.), U.S. Census Bur. (subcom. on health stats. for minorities and other spl. populations of U.S. 1988—). Democrat. Roman Catholic. Home: 9100 Litzsinger Rd Saint Louis MO 63144-2214 Office: 3550 Lindell Blvd Saint Louis MO 63103-1021 Office Phone: 314-977-2715. *My entire professional life has been in the field of social work. My personal and professional values are derived from a dual commitment to empower the uniqueness of individuals and to enhance the development of caring communities. These goals have organized and directed my professional practice, teaching and writing. I believe that the profession of social work has a unique and singular mission in society. That mission is to advocate for and consciously bring about the social development of all people.*

STREVEY, TRACY ELMER, JR., army officer, surgeon, physician executive; b. Shorewood, Wis., Apr. 24, 1933; s. Tracy Elmer and Margaret (Rees) S.; m. Victoria Crowley (div.); children: Virginia Ann, Tracy Elmer III, Andrew Victor; m. Elizabeth Sommers; children: Stephanie Jean, James Sommers. Student, Pomona Coll., 1951-54; MD, U. So. Calif., 1958; student, Armed Forces Staff Coll., 1970-71, U.S. Army War Coll., 1977-78. Diplomate Am. Bd. Surgery, Am. Bd. Thoracic Surgery. Intern Los Angeles County Gen. Hosp., 1958-59; commd. officer U.S. Army, 1959, advanced through grades to maj. gen., 1983; resident in gen. surgery Letterman Gen. Hosp., San Francisco, 1962-66; resident in thoracic and cardiovascular surgery Walter Reed Gen. Hosp., Washington, 1968-70; comdg. officer 757 Med. Detachment OA, Ludwigsburg, Germany, 1959-61; ward officer orthopaedic svc. 75th Sta. Hosp., Stuttgart, Fed. Republic Germany, 1961-62; chief profl. svc., chief surgery 85th Evacuation Hosp., Qui Nhon, Vietnam, 1967; comdg. officer 3d Surg. Hosp., Dong Tam, Vietnam, 1967-68; asst. chief thoracic and cardiovascular surgery service Fitzsimons Army Med Ctr., Denver, 1971-73, chief thoracic and cardiovascular surgery service, 1973-75; asst. dir. med. activities and dir. Profl. Edn. Gorgas Hosp., Panama Canal Zone, 1975-77; chief dept. surgery Walter Reed Army Med. Ctr., Washington, 1978-81; comdr. Brooke Army Med. Ctr., Ft. Sam Houston, Tex., 1981-83, Tripler Army Med. Ctr., Hawaii, 1983-86, U.S. Army Health Svcs. Command, San Antonio, 1986-88; ret. U.S. Army, 1988; CEO Nassau County Med. Ctr., 1988-93; pres., CEO N.Y. Hosp Med. Ctr. Queens, N.Y.C., 1993-94; v.p. N.Y. Hosp. Care Network, N.Y.C., 1994-95; v.p. for med. affairs Sisters of Mercy Health Sys., St. Louis, 1995-99; prin. Strevey Cons. Assocs., LLC, 1999—2003. Asst. clin. prof. surgery U. Colo. Med. Ctr., Denver, 1973-75; prof. surgery Uniformed Services U. Health Scis., Bethesda, 1978-2003, vice chmn. dept. surgery, 1978-81 Contbr. articles to profl. jours. Mem. reg. bd. Am. Heart Assn. Decorated D.S.M., Legion of Merit with 2 oak leaf clusters, Meritorious Service medal with 2 oak leaf clusters, Purple Heart, Army Commendation Medal for Valor, Vietnam Cross of Gallantry with Palm; recipient Outstanding Service award U. So. Calif. Med. Alumni Assn., 1983 Fellow ACS, Am. Coll. Chest Physicians, Am. Coll. Cardiology, Am. Coll. Physician Execs. (disting.); mem. Assn. Mil. Surgeons U.S., Soc. Thoracic Surgeons, Western Thoracic Surg. Assn., Am. Assn. Thoracic Surgery, Masons. Avocations: ham radio; scuba diving; golf; computer science. Home and Office: 1509 Woodgate Dr Saint Louis MO 63131-4724

STRICK, JEREMY, curator; BA in History of Art with highest honors, U. Calif., Santa Cruz, 1977; postgrad., Harvard U. Asst. curator 20th Century art Nat. Gallery Art, Washington, 1986-89, assoc. curator 20th Century art, 1989-93, acting dept. dept 20th Century art, 1992-93, curator Nat. Sculpture Garden project, 1989-93; curator modern art St. Louis Art Mus., 1993-96; Frances and Thomas Dittmer curator 20th Century painting and sculpture Art Inst. Chgo., 1996-99; dir. Mus. Contemporary Art, L.A., 1999—. Curator N.Y. Interpreted: Joseph Stella and Alfred Stieglitz, Nat. Gallery Art, 1987, Milton Avery, 1990, Mark Rothko: The Spirit Myth, 1990-95, asst. curator A Century of Modern Sculpture: The Patsy and Raymond Nasher Collection, 1987, co-curator Twentieth-Century Art: Selections for the Tenth Anniversary of the East Building, 1987; curator Brice Marden: A Painting, Drawings, Prints, St. Louis Art Mus., 1993, Currents 58: Susan Crile—The Fires of War, 1994, Louise Bourgeois: The Personages 1946-1954, 1995, Currents 60: Jerald Ieans, 1994, Masterworks from Stuttgar: The Romantic Age in German Art, 1995, Currents 66: Michael Byron, 1996, Currents 67: Leonardo Drew, 1996; curator The Sublime Is Now: The Early Work of Barnett Newman, Walker Art Ctr., Mpls., Pace Gallery, N.Y.C., 1994; curator In the Light of Italy: Corot and Early Open-Air Painting, Nat. Gallery Art, Bklyn. Mus., St. Louis Art Mus., 1996; lectr., symposia participant and organizer, 1980—; juror Showhegan awards, 1995. Contbg. author: Works by Antoine-Louis Barye in the Collection of the Fogg Art Museum, Vol. IV, 1982; contbr. articles to exhbn. catalogs, newspapers, mags., ency. Instnl. fellow Samuel H. Kress Found., Paris, 1983-85, fellow Mrs. Giles Whiting Found., 1985-86. Office: Mus Contemporary Art Dept 20th Century Painting 250 S Grand Ave Los Angeles CA 90012-3021 Home: 261 N Bundy Dr Los Angeles CA 90049-2825

STRICKER, STEVE, professional golfer; b. Edgerton, Wis., Feb. 23, 1967; m. Nicki Stricker; 1 child, Bobbi Maria. Student, U. Ill. Named winner, Kemper Open, 1996, Motorola Western Open, 1996, Victoria Open, Can., 1990, Can. PGA, 1993, WGC-Accenture Math Play Championship, 2001. Office: c/o PGA Tour 112 PGA Tour Blvd Ponte Vedra Beach FL 32082

STRICKLAND, ANTHONY, state representative; b. Fort Ord, Calif., Feb. 17, 1970; m. Audra Strickland. Student, Cochise C.C., Ariz.; BA in Polit. Sci., Whittier Coll. Calif. Mem. Calif. Assembly, 1998—. Mem. adv. bd. Food Share; founding pres. So. Calif. Taxpayers' Alliance; hon. bd. dirs. Doris Tate Crime Victims' Bur.; bd. dirs.Go N Strong Basketball Camp; hon. bd. dirs. Moorpark Boys & Girls Club; bd. dirs. Ventura County United Way. Republican. Office: PO Box 942849 Rm 4098 Sacramento CA 94249 Address: 2659 Townsgate Rd Westlake Village CA 91361

STRICKLAND, ARVARH EUNICE, history professor; b. Hattiesburg, Miss., July 6, 1930; s. Eunice and Clotiel (Marshall) S.; m. Willie Pearl Elmore, June 17, 1951; children: Duane Arvarh, Bruce Elmore. BA, Tougaloo Coll., 1951; MA, U. Ill., 1953, PhD, 1962. Tchr. Hattiesburg Schs., 1951-52; instr. Tuskegee Inst., 1955-56; prin. supr. Madison County Schs., Canton, Miss., 1956-59; asst. prof. history Chgo. State U., 1962-65, assoc. prof. history, 1965-68, prof., 1968-69, U. Mo., Columbia, 1969-96, prof. emeritus, 1996—, chmn. dept. history, 1980-83, interim dir. black studies program, 1994-96, sr. faculty assoc., Office of V.P. acad. affairs, 1987-88, assoc. v.p. acad. affairs, 1989-91. Author: History of the Chicago Urban League, 1966, reprint, 2001, (with Reich and Biller) Building the United States, 1971, (with Reich) The Black American Experience to 1877, 1974, The Black American Experience since 1877, 1974; editor: Working with Carter G. Woodson, (with Lorenzo J. Greene) The Father of Black History: A Diary, 1928-1930, 1989, Selling Black History for Carter G. Woodson: A Diary, 1930-33, 1996, (with Robert E. Weems) The African American Experience: A Historiographical and Bibliographical Guide, 2000. Commr. Planning and Zoning, Columbia, Mo., 1977-80, Boone County Home Rule Charter, 1982, Mo. Peace Officers Standards and Tng. Commn., 1988-89; co-chmn. Mayors Com. to Commemorate Contbns. of Black Columbians, Columbia, 1981; mem. exec. subcom. Mayor's Ad Hoc Election '82 Com., 1982; bd. dirs. Harry S. Truman Library Inst., 1987-96, U. of Mo.-Columbia Health Sys., 2003—. Recipient Disting. Svc. award Ill. Hist. Soc., 1957, Byler Disting. Prof. award U. Mo., 1994, St. Louis Am.'s Educator of Yr. award, 1994, Disting. Faculty award U. Mo.-Columbia Alumni Assn., 1995, Tougaloo Coll. Alumni Hall of Fame, 1995, Alumni Achievement U. Ill. Coll. Liberal Arts and Scis., 1997, Disting. Svc. award State Hist. Soc. Mo., 1997. Mem. Orgn. Am. Historians, Am. Hist. Assn., Assn. Study Afro-Am. Life and History (Carter Godwin Woodson Scholars medallion 1999), So. Hist. Assn., State Hist. Soc. Mo. (Disting. Svc. award 1997), Boone County Hist. Soc. (bd. dirs. 1998-2002, 2d v.p. 1999, 1st v.p. 2000-02), Kiwanis, Alpha Phi Alpha, Phi Alpha Theta (internat. v.p. 1991-93, pres. 1994-95, chair adv. bd. 1996-97, Disting. Svc. award 1997). Democrat. Methodist. Home: 4100 Defoe Dr Columbia MO 65203-0252 Office: U Mo Dept History 101 Read Hall Columbia MO 65211-7500

STRICKLAND, BONNIE RUTH, psychologist, educator; b. Louisville, Nov. 24, 1936; d. Roy E. and Billie P. (Whitfield) S. BS, Ala. Coll., 1958; MS, Ohio State U., 1960, PhD (USPHS fellow), 1962. Diplomate: clin. psychology Am. Bd. Examiners in Profl. Psychology. From asst. to asso. prof. psychology Emory U., Atlanta, 1962-73, dean of women, 1964-67; prof. emeritus psychology U. Mass., Amherst, 1973—, chmn. dept. psychology, 1976-77, 78-82, assoc. to chancellor, 1983-84. Mem. adv. coun. NIMH, 1984-87; Sigma Xi nat. lectr., 1991-93. Adv. editor numerous psychology jours., acad. pub. houses; contbg. author texts personality theory.; contbr. of numerous articles on social personality and clin. psychology to profl. jours.; contbg. author of two citation classics. Recipient Outstanding Faculty award Emory U., 1968-69; Chancellor's medal disting. service U. Mass., 1983. Fellow APA (pres. divsn. clin. psychology 1983, pres. divsn. gen. psychology 2005, chmn. bd. profl. affairs 1980-83, chmn. policy and planning bd. 1983-85, pres. 1987, bd. dirs. 1986-87, Outstanding Leadership award 1992, Disting. Contbns. and Psychology in the Pub. Interest award 1999, Presdl. Citation 2001), Am. Psychol. Soc. (founder 1988, bd. dirs. 1989-93), New Eng. Psychol. Assn. (Disting. Contbns. award 2002), Am. Assn. Applied and Preventive Psychology (founder 1990, bd. dirs. 1990-94, pres. 1992-94), Acad. Clin. Psychology (chmn. 1982-83). Home: 558 Federal St Belchertown MA 01007-9754 Office: U Mass Dept Psychology Amherst MA 01003-7710

STRICKLAND, DOROTHY, education educator; BS, Newark State Coll.; MA, PhD, NYU. Elem. sch. tchr. N.J. pub. sch. sys., reading cons., learning disabilities specialist; prof. edn. Rutgers U., New Brunswick, NJ, 1985—, Samuel DeWitt Proctor Prof. Edn., 2002—. Active in numerous state and nat. adv. bds. Author: Language Literacy and the Child, Process Reading and Writing: A Literature Based Approach, The Administration and Supervision of Reading Programs, Educating Black Children: America's Challenge, Family Storybook Reading, Listen Children: An Anthology of Black Literature, Families: An Anthology of Poetry for Young Children, Teaching Phonics Today, 1998, Beginning Reading and Writing, 2000, Supporting Struggling Readers and Writers, 2002, Preparing Our Teachers, 2002, (Language Arts) Preparing Our Tchr., 2003, Learning & Tchg., 2004. Inducted into the Reading Hall of Fame, pres., 1997-98. Mem. Nat. Coun. Tchrs. English (Rewey Belle Inglis award for Outstanding Woman in English Education Annual Conv., rsch. award, Outstanding Educator in Lang. Arts award 1998), Internat. Reading Assn. (past pres., Outstanding Tchr. Educator of reading award). Home: 131 Coccio Dr West Orange NJ 07052-4121 Office: Rutgers U Dept Edn Grad Sch Edn New Brunswick NJ 08903

STRICKLAND, HUGH ALFRED, lawyer; b. Rockford, Ill., May 3, 1931; s. Hugh and Marie (Elmer) S.; m. Donna E. McDonald, Aug. 11, 1956; children: Amy Alice, Karen Ann. AB, Knox Coll., 1953; JD, Chgo. Kent Coll. Law, 1959. Bar: Ill. 1960. Partner firm McDonald, Strickland & Clough, Carrollton, Ill., 1961—; asst. atty. gen. Ill., 1960-67; spl. asst. gen., 1967-69; pres. McDonald Title Co. Mem. Greene County Welfare Svcs. Com., 1963—, Ill. Heart Assn., 1961-65; trustee Thomas H. Boyd Meml. Hosp., 1972-95; pres. Long Lake Assn. Vilas County, Inc., 2002—. With AUS, 1953-55. Recipient award for meritorious service Am. Heart Assn., 1964 Fellow Ill. Bar Found. (charter); mem. ABA, Ill. Bar Assn., Greene County Bar Assn. (past pres.), Southwestern Bar Assn. (past pres.), Ill. Def. Counsel, Am. Judicature Soc., Def. Rsch. Inst., Elks Club, Westlake Country Club (v.p. 1968-70, dir.), Big Sand Lake Country Club, Phi Delta Theta, Phi Delta Phi. Methodist. Home: 827 7th St Carrollton IL 62016-1421 Office: 524 N Main St PO Box 71 Carrollton IL 62016-1027 Office Phone: 217-942-3115. E-mail: has3@irtc.net., lawyers@irtc.net.

STRICKLAND, JEFFERY, medical products executive; b. Russellville, Ala., Dec. 13, 1958; s. Orvil and Earlene (Clevland) S.; m. Norma Kay Fennel, June 9, 1979; children: Jeffery Andrew, April Kay. BS, U. North Ala., 1981. CPA, Ala. Staff acct. Smither Talley Mauldin CPA, Decatur, Ala., 1981-83, Atrion Corp., Allen, Tex., 1983-87; asst. contr. Ala.-Tenn. Natural Gas, Florence, Ala., 1987-89, dir. planning, 1989-90, asst. sec.-treas., 1990-92, v.p., 1992-97, CFO, 1997—; CFO, v.p., treas. & sec. Atrion Corp., Allen, Tex. Home: 3102 Saint Germain Dr Mc Kinney TX 75070-4726

STRICKLAND, JENNIFER LAURA, engineer; d. Lee Arthur and Julieta Strickland. AA, N.Mex State U., Alamagordo, 1997; BA in Psychology, N.Mex State U., Las Cruces, 1999, MA in Exptl. Psychology, 2003. Usability cons. psychology dept. N.Mex. State U., Las Cruces, 2000—01, rsch. asst. psychology dept., 2001—; usability engr. intern Microsoft, Mountain View, Calif., 2001. Author: (poster) The Object Superiority Effect: Is the Effect Limited to Object-Like Contexts? (1st Pl. Grad. Rsch. and Arts Symposium, 2003), An Examination of Information Portrayal in Static and Dynamic Visual Weather Displays (1st Pl. Grad. Rsch. and Arts Symposium, 2002), The Object Superiority Effect Within and Between Geons (2nd Pl., 2001). Mem.: Human Factors and Ergonomics Soc. (assoc.), Golden Key Nat. Honor Soc. (life), Alpha Chi (life). Democrat. Roman Catholic. Avocations: Latin dancing, rock hounding, coin collecting/numismatics, drawing, piano. Office: NMex State U PO Box 30001 Las Cruces NM 88003 Personal E-mail: jestrick@nmsu.edu.

STRICKLAND, JOHN ARTHUR VAN, minister; b. Detroit, Sept. 25, 1952; s. Maurice Alexander and Irma (Surovy) S.; m. Constance Fillmore, Dec. 24, 1976 (div. Aug. 1984); m. Brenda Cecile Bunch, Nov. 23, 1985. BA cum laude, Ga. State U., 1974; ministry program, Unity Ministerial Sch., 1974-76. Ordained to Assn. Unity Chs., 1976. Minister Unity Ch. Christianity, Santa Rosa, Calif., 1976-77, min. Jacksonville, Fla., 1978-79; dir. prayer ministry Unity Sch. Christianity, Unity Village, Mo., 1979-90, mem. task force, 1984-87, mem. adv. council, 1987—; min. Unity Ctr., N.Y.C., 1990-91, Unity Ch., Hawaii, 1991—. Trustee Assn. Unity Chs., 1994—, mem. exec. com., 1995—, chmn. bd., 1998—; coord. Internat. Youth of Unity, Unity Village, 1975-76; vol. chaplain Jackson County Jail, Kansas City, 1974-75. Contbr. articles to profl. jours. Trustee, Kans. Children's Mus.; vol. Unity Help Line, Unity Village, 1975-76. Named one of Outstanding Young Men Am., 1982. Mem. Rotary (youth svcs. com., chmn. invocation com. 1988-89, Paul Harris fellow). Avocations: running, physical fitness, hiking, music. Home: 1517 Makiki St Apt 1407 Honolulu HI 96822-4526 Office: Unity Ch Hawaii 3608 Diamond Head Cir Honolulu HI 96815-4430

STRICKLAND, MARSHALL HAYWARD, bishop; b. Rome, Ga., Oct. 8, 1933; s. Albert A. Strickland and Elzie Greer Strickland Morton; 1 child, Marshall H. II. BA, Livingstone Coll., 1951; PhD, St. Mary's Theol. Sem., Balt.; MDiv, Hood Theol. Sem., 1955, DD (hon.), Allen U. Pastor Patten Meml. AME Zion Ch., Chattanooga, David Stan AME Zion Ch., Lancaster, SC, Hood Meml. AME Zion Ch., Bristol, Tenn., Big Zion AME Ch., Mobile, Ala., Pa. Ave. AME Zion Ch., Balt.; bishop Mid Atlantic I dist. AMEZ Ch., Balt., sec.; Bishop AMEZ, Balt., 1992—. Bd. bishops AME Zion Ch., chmn. commn. judiciary, chmn. Am. Bible Soc., 1st vice chair brotherhood pension svc., 1st vice chair Christian edn., 2d vice chair bicentennial commn., trustee Livingstone Coll.; past mem. Ala. Consultation Ch. Union; guest pastor Gen. Conf. AME Ch., St. Paul Cathedral, others; spkr. in field; guest on various radio and TV stas. Author: William E. Fine: Kennedy-The Dreamer, Church and State: Not Separate, Our Heritage is Our Religion, The Black Church: Black America's Salvation, The Black Church: Solving Black America's Crisis, Health Care: Preaching Prevention from the Pulpit, Rebuilding Our Cities in Partnership with the Black Church: A Master Plan; contbr. articles to profl. jours. Former chmn. bd. dirs. Mobile Community Action Authority; past mem. Commn. Organic Union; founder Zion Outreach Ctr., Balt. Recipient Humanitarian award, Zion Outreach Svcs. Associated Black Charities, Econ. Devel. award, HUB, Flood Relief Support award, Jamaican Assn. Md. Mem.: NAACP (past pres. Bristol chpt., Recognition awards Bristol and Balt. chpts.). Office: 2000 Cedar Circle Dr Baltimore MD 21228-3743

STRICKLAND, ROBERT LOUIS, former retail company executive; b. Florence, S.C., Mar. 3, 1931; s. Franz M. and Hazel (Eaddy) S.; m. Elizabeth Ann Miller, Feb. 2, 1952; children: Cynthia Anne, Robert Edson. AB, U. N.C., 1952; MBA with distinction, Harvard U., 1957. Bd. dirs. Lowe's Cos., Inc., North Wilkesboro, N.C., 1961-2000, sr. v.p., 1970-76, exec. v.p., 1976-78, chmn. bd., 1978-98, chmn. exec. com., 1988-98, mem. office of pres., 1970-78, chmn. emeritus, 1999; founder Sterling Advt., Ltd., 1966. V.p., mem. adminstrv. com. Lowe's Profit-Sharing Trust, 1961-87, chmn. ops. com., 1972-78; mgmt. com. Lowe's ESOP Plan, 1978-97; bd. dirs. Lowe's Cos., Wilkesboro, NC, T.Rowe Price Assocs., Balt., 1991-2001, Hannaford Bros. Co., Portland, Maine, Krispy Kreme Corp., Winston-Salem, NC, Revelstoke Co., Calgary, Can., Wholesale Club, Indpls., Summit Comms., Atlanta; panelist investor rels. field, 1972-99; spkr., panelist employee stock ownership, 1978-2000; spkr. on investor rels., London, Edinburgh, Glasgow, Paris, Zurich, Frankfurt, Milan, Vienna, Singapore, Tokyo. Author: Lowe's Cybernetwork, 1969, Lowe's Living Legend, 1970, Ten Years of Growth, 1971, The Growth Continues, 1972, 73, 74, Lowe's Scoreboard, 1978; contbr. articles to profl. jours. Mem. N.C. Ho. of Reps., 1962-64, Rep. Senatorial Inner Circle, 1980-95; exec. com. N.C. Rep. Com., 1963-73; trustee U. N.C., Chapel Hill, 1987-95, chmn. bd., 1991-93; dir., dep. chmn. Fed. Res. Bank of Richmond, 1996-98; com. on bus. laws and the economy N.C., 1994-97; dir. U.S. Coun. Better Bus. Burs., 1981-85; bd. dirs., v.p. Nat. Home Improvement Coun., 1972-76; bd. dirs. N.C. Sch. Arts Found., 1975-79, N.C. Bd. Natural and Econ. Resources, 1975-76; bd. dirs., govt. affairs com. Home Ctr. Inst.; trustee, sec. bd. Wilkes C.C., 1964-73; chmn., pres. bd. dirs. Do-It-Yourself Rsch. Inst., 1981-89; pres. Hardware Home Improvement Coun. City of Hope Nat. Med. Ctr., L.A., 1987-89. With USN, 1952-55, lt. Res. 1955-62. Named Wilkes County N.C. Young Man of Yr., Wilkes Jr. C. of C., 1962; recipient Bronze Oscar of Industry award Fin. World, 1969-74, 76-79, Silver Oscar of Industry award, 1970, 72-74, 76-79, Gold Oscar of Industry award as best of all industry, 1972, 87, Excellence award in corp. reporting Fin. Analysts Fedn., 1970, 72, 74, 81-82, cert. of Distinction Brand Names Found., 1970, Retailer of Yr. award, 1971, 73, Disting. Mcht. award, 1972, Spirit of Life award City of Hope, 1983, Free Enterprise Legend award Students Free Enterprise, 1994; named to Home Ctr. Hall of Fame, 1985. Mem. Nat. Assn. Over-Counter Cos. (bd. advisers 1973-77), Newcomen Soc., Employee Stock Ownership Assn. (pres. 1983-85, chmn. 1985-87), James Madison Club, Federalist Soc., Forsyth Country Club, Piedmont City Club, Roaring Gap Club (N.C.), Ponte Vedra Inn and Club (Fla.), Scabbard and Blade, Phi Beta Kappa, Pi Kappa Alpha. Home: 226 N Stratford Rd Winston Salem NC 27104-3132 also: apt GH 721 5th Ave New York NY 10022 Office: 2000 W 1st St Winston Salem NC 27104-4225 E-mail: lowchair@aol.com.

STRICKLAND, RODNEY, professional basketball player; b. Bronx, N.Y., July 11, 1966; Grad., DePaul U., 1988. Basketball player N.Y. Knicks, 1988—90, San Antonio Spurs, 1990—92, Portland (Oreg.) Trailblazers, 1992—96, Washington Wizards, 1996—. Named to NBA All-Rookie Second Team, 1988—89. Avocations: bowling, basketball. Office: Miami Heat Suntrust Internat Ctr One SE 3rd Ave Ste 3200 Miami FL 33131

STRICKLAND, TED, congressman, clergyman, psychology educator, psychologist; b. Lucasville, Ohio, Aug. 4, 1941; m. Frances Smith. BA in History, Asbury Coll., 1963; MDiv, Asbury Seminary, 1967; PhD in Psychology, U. Ky., 1980. Clergyman; dir. social svcs. Ky. Meth. Home; consulting psychologist Southern Ohio Correctional Facility, 1985-92, 94-96; prof. psychology Shawnee State U., 1988-92, 94-96; mem. U.S. Congress from 6th Ohio dist., Washington, 1993-94, 97—; mem. energy and commerce com.; mem. Vet. Affairs Com. Mem. numerous coms. in fields of: edn. and labor, postsecondary edn. and tng., labor standards, occupational health and safety, small bus., rural enterprise, exports and environ. Democrat. Office: US Ho of Reps 336 Cannon House Office Bldg Washington DC 20515-3506

STRICKLAND, WILLIAM JESSE, lawyer; b. Newport News, Va., Mar. 21, 1942; BSBA, U. Richmond, 1964, JD, 1970. Bar: Va. 1969, U.S. Dist. Ct. (ea. and we. dists.) Va., U.S. Ct. Claims, U.S. Tax Ct., U.S. Ct. Appeals (4th cir.). Exec. com. coord. dept., mng. ptnr. McGuire Woods LLP, Richmond, Va., 1969—. Bd. dirs. Cableform Inc., Zion Crossroads, Va., Eimeldingen Corp., Indpls. Bd. dirs. Va. Found. Rsch. and Econ. Edn., Inc.; mem. coun. Va. Inst. Marine Scis.; founder Marine Corps Heritage Found. Capt. USMC 1964-67, Vietnam. Mem. ABA, Va. Bar Assn., Richmond Bar Assn., Nat. Assn. Bond Lawyers, Va. Govt. Fin. Officers Assn., Local Govt. Attys. Assn., Va. Bond Club. Office: McGuire Woods LLP 901 E Cary St Richmond VA 23219-4057

STRICKLAND, WILTON L. lawyer; b. Ft. Myers, July 1, 1942; s. Lorenzo Strickland and Mary Voncille Singletary; m. Barbara Hathaway Lahna (div. July 1984); children: Amy Beth Strickland-Quattlebaum, Wilton Hathaway Strickland. BA, U. Fla., 1964; JD, Stetson U., 1969. Bar: Fla. 1969, U.S. Dist. Ct. (so. dist.) Fla. 1969, Trial Bar (so. dist.) Fla. 1983, U.S. Dist. Ct. (mid. dist.) Fla. 1988, U.S. Ct. Appeals (5th cir.) 1978, U.S. Ct. Appeals (11th cir.) 1981, U.S. Supreme Ct. 1977. Ptnr. Howell, Kirby, Montgomery et al, Ft. Lauderdale, Fla., 1969-73, Ferrero, Middlebrooks & Houston, Ft. Lauderdale, 1974-77, Ferrero, Middlebrooks & Strickland, Ft. Lauderdale, 1977-91, Strickland & Seidule, Ft. Lauderdale, 1991-98; pvt. practice Wilton L. Strickland, P.A., Ft. Lauderdale, 1998—. Chmn. bd. Hospice Care Broward County, Inc.; bd. dirs. Salvation Army Broward County; mem. Helping Abandoned and Dependent Youth. Mem. ABA, ATLA, Fla. Bar (mem. ethics com.), Acad. Fla. Trial Lawyers (dir. 1980-84), Broward County Trial Lawyers Assn. (past pres. 1981), Broward County Bar Assn., Am. Bd. Trial Advs. (founder Broward County chpt.), Million Dollar Advocates Forum, The Bar Register of Preeminent Lawyers, Phi Alpha Delta (former pres. Brewer chpt.). Democrat. Presbyterian. Avocations: winter skiing, reading, hiking, boating, white water rafting. Home: 2897 NE 25th St Fort Lauderdale FL 33305-1722 Office: # 303 1401 E Broward Blvd Ste 303 Fort Lauderdale FL 33301-2100

STRICKLER, IVAN K. dairy farmer; b. Carlyle, Kans., Oct. 23, 1921; s. Elmer E. and Edna Louise (James) S.; m. Madge Lee Marshall, Aug. 7, 1949; children— Steven Mark, Thomas Scott, Douglas Lee. BS, Kans. State U., 1947. Owner, mgr. dairy farm, Iola, Kans., 1947—; tchr. farm tng. to vets. World War II, 1947-54; judge 1st and 2d Nat. Holstein Show, Brazil, 1969-70, Internat. Holstein Show, Buenos Aires, 1972, Nat. Holstein Show, Ecuador, 1978, 10th Nat. Holstein Show, Brazil, 1980, Holstein Show, Australia, Mex. and Argentina, 1981, 1984, Adelaide (Australia) Royal Show, 1987; pres Mid-America Dairymen, Inc., Springfield, MO, 1981—. Appointed chmn.

Nat. Dairy Bd., 1985-90; dairy leader 4-H Club, 1962-75; dir. Iola State Bank; rep. U.S. Internat. Dairy Symposium, 1994, Belo Horinzote, Brazil. Author: Wholly Cow We Did It, 1996 (Centennia Honor roll 1997). Trustee Allen County Community Jr. Coll.; mem. agr. edn. and rsch. com. Kans. State U (recipient Medallion-highest honor, 2000), U.S. Agrl. Trade and Devel. Mission, Algeria and Tunisia, 1989. With USN, 1942-46, PTO. Recipient Silver award Holstein Friesian Assn. Brazil, 1969, Top Dairy Farm Efficiency award Ford Found., 1971, Master Farmer award Kans. State U. and Kans. Assn. Commerce and Industry, 1972, Gold award Holstein Friesian Assn. Argentina, 1972, Richard Lynng award Nat. Dairy Bd., 1990, award of merit Gamma Sigma Delta, 1987, Alumni medallion Kans. State U., 1999; named Man of Yr. World Dairy Exposition, 1978; portrait in Dairy Hall of Fame Kans. State U., 1974; Guest of Hon. Nat. Dairy Shrine, 1985; selected First Dairy Leader of Yr., 1996; inductee Kans. Co-op Hall of Fame, 1999. Mem. Mid Am. Dairymen (sec. corporate bd. 1971-81, pres. 1981-95), Holstein Friesian Assn. Am. (nat. dir. 1964-72), Dairy Shrine (nat. dir. 1971-81), United Dairy Industry Assn. (dir. 1971-79), Nat. Holstein Assn. Am. (pres. 1979-80), Alpha Gamma Rho (highest honor 1989, Hall of Fame 1998). Mem. Christian Ch. (elder, bd. dirs.). Club: Nat. Dairy Shrine (pres. 1978). Home: PO Box 365 Iola KS 66749-0365 Office: Mid America Dairymen Inc 1641 N Dakota Rd Iola KS 66749

STRICKLER, JEFFREY HAROLD, pediatrician; b. Mpls., Oct. 14, 1943; s. Jacob Harold and Helen Cecelia (Mitchell) S.; m. Karen Anne Stewart, June 18, 1966; children: Hans Stewart, Liesl Ann. BA, Carleton Coll., 1965; MD, U. Minn., 1969. Diplomate Am. Bd. Pediatrics. Resident in pediatrics Stanford (Calif.) U., 1969-73; pvt. practice Helena, Mont., 1975—; chief staff Shodair Children's Hosp., Helena, 1984-86. Dir. maternal-child health Lewis and Clark County, Helena, 1978-88; chief of staff St. Peters Hosp., Helena, 1994-96; bd.chmn. Helena Health Alliance, 1996-99. Mem. Mont. Gov.'s Task Force on Child Abuse, 1978-79; mem. steering com. Region VIII Child Abuse Prevention, Denver, 1979-82; bd. dirs. Helena Dist. 1 Sch. Bd., 1982-88, vice chmn., 1985-87. Maj. M.C., USAF, 1973-75. Fellow: Am. Acad. Pediatrics (vice chmn. Mont. chpt. 1981—84, chmn. 1984—87, mem. nat. nominating com. 1987—90, chmn. 1989—90, coun. on govt. affairs 1990—96, future of pediatric edn. II 1996—2000, Wyeth award 1987); mem.: Am. Bd. Pediatrics (PMCP-G practice performance com. 2001—), Rotary (youth exch. chmn. dist. 539 1984—88, pres. Helena 1988—89, polio plus chair dist. 5390 1996—, asst. gov. dist. 5390 2002—, dist. gov. nom.). Avocations: skiing, hiking. Office: Helena Pediatric Clinic 1122 N Montana Ave Helena MT 59601-3513 Home: 41A Stony Brook Dr Clancy MT 59634 Office Phone: 406-449-5563. E-mail: j.strickler@bresnan.net.

STRICKLER, MATTHEW M. lawyer; b. Bryn Mawr, Pa., June 27, 1940; s. Charles S and Mary Webster (Cornman) S.; m. Margaret Renshaw, Sept. 3, 1966; children: Matthew David, Andrew Kellogg, Timothy Webster, Edward Charles. AB, Haverford Coll., 1962; JD, Harvard U., 1965. Bar: Pa. 1965, U.S. Supreme Ct. 1975. Assoc. Ballard, Spahr, Andrews & Ingersoll, Phila., 1965-74, ptnr., 1974—2002, sr. counsel, 2003—; dir. legal affairs Sch. Medicine Temple U., Phila., 2003—. Adj. prof. Temple U. Sch. Law, Phila., 1993—. Editor: Representing Health Care Facilities, 1981. Bd. dirs. Phila. chpt. Girl Scouts Am., 1978-96, v.p., 1984-90, 94-96; bd. dirs. Kardon Inst. Arts, 2000—, treas., 2003—. Mem. Union League Phila., Pocono Lake Preserve. Office: Temple Univ School Medicine 3420 N Broad St Rm 107 Philadelphia PA 19140 Business E-Mail: mstrick@temple.edu.

STRICKLER, STEVE P, theater educator; m. Laci D Osmus, Oct. 16, 1999; 1 child, Hannah Grace. BA in speech theatre Edn., Southwestern Okla. State U., 1988; MA in theater, Okla. State U., 1990. Instr. of communication arts, theatre Southwestern Okla. State U., Weatherford, 1992—. Dir.: (theatre production) Blood Knot (Directors' Choice award, 2003), Fuddy Meers (Directors' Choice award, 2002), Medea: A Noh Cycle Based On The Greek Myth (Directors' Choice, Respondent's Choice, Excellence in Directing, advancement to Reginal theatre festival award, 2001), A Question Of Mercy (Respondent's Choice award, 2001), The Cover Of Life (Directors' Choice, Respondents' Choice, Excellence in Directing, Advancement to Regional theatre festival with KCACTF award, 1999), Kindertransport (Respondent's Choice Award, Excellence in Directing, 1996). Mem. Weatherford Arts Coun., Okla., First United Meth. Ch., Weatherford. Mem.: Kennedy Ctr. Am. Coll. Theatre Festival (state chair 1998—2003), Okla. Speech Theatre Assn. Achievements include Kennedy Center American College Theatre Festival Bronze Medallion for Service. Office: Southwestern Okla State U 100 Campus Dr Weatherford OK 73096

STRICKLIN, HUT, race car driver; b. June 24, 1961; m. Pam Stricklin; children: Taylor, Tabitha. Racecar driver NASCAR, 1982—84, Bobby Allison, 1990—95, Stavola Bros. Racing, 1996—98; crew chief Triad Motorsports team, 1998—99; racecar driver SBII Motorsports, 1999, Junie Donlavey Racing, 2000—01, Bill Davis Racing, 2002—. Named champion, Ala. Ltd. Sportsman, 1978—79, Winston Cup Racing Series, 1982, 1984, Dash Series, 1986, Most Popular Driver, All Am. Challenge Series, 1984, Bud Pole winner, 1995, BGN Bud Pole winner, 1999—2000; recipient 2d pl., Southern 500, 1991, 1996, Rockingham, 1995, 14th pl., Brickyard 400, 2000, 11th pl., NAPA 500, 2001, 6th pl., Kmart 400, 2001. Office: c/o Bill Davis Racing 300 Old Thomasville Rd High Point NC 27620-8190

STRICKON, HARVEY ALAN, lawyer; b. Bklyn., Nov. 9, 1947; s. Milton and Norma (Goodhartz) S.; m. Linda Carol Meltzer, July 2, 1972; children: Joshua Andrew, Meredith Cindy, Erica Stacey. BBA, CCNY, 1968; JD, NYU, 1971. Bar: N.Y. 1972, U.S. Dist. Ct. (so. and ea. dists.) N.Y. 1973, U.S. Ct. Appeals (2d cir.) 1973, U.S. Supreme Ct. 1975, U.S. Dist. Ct. (no. dist.) N.Y. 1980, U.S. Dist. Ct. (we. dist.) N.Y. 1981, U.S. Dist. Ct. Ariz. 1991, U.S. Dist. Ct. Conn., 1996. Law clk. U.S. Dist. Ct. (ea. dist.) N.Y., Bklyn., 1971-73; assoc. Moses & Singer, N.Y.C., 1973-80; from assoc. to ptnr. Kaye, Scholer, Fierman, Hays & Handler, N.Y.C., 1980-91; from ptnr. to counsel Paul, Hastings, Janofsky & Walker LLP, N.Y.C., 1991—. Mem. complaint mediation panel, departmental disciplinary com. appellate div., 1st dept. Supreme Ct. State N.Y.; mem. mediation panel U.S. Dist. Ct. (ea. dist.) N.Y.; mem. mediation register U.S. Bankruptcy Ct. (so. and ea. dists.) N.Y. Co-author: Enforcing Judgments and Collecting Debts in New York, 1996. Mem. Nassau County Rep. Com., Great Neck, N.Y., 1982—; chmn. bd. dirs. Flushing Community Vol. Ambulance Corps. Inc., N.Y., 1981-86, vice chmn., 1987-92. Mem. ABA, N.Y. State Bar Assn., Assn. Bar City N.Y. (chmn. complaint mediation panel com. on profl. discipline), Am. Judicature Soc., Assn. Comml. Fin. Attys., N.Y. Law Inst., Bankruptcy Lawyers Bar Assn., (bd. govs. 1987-89, corr. sec. 1989—), Am. Bankruptcy Inst. Republican. Jewish. Home: 11 West Brook Rd Great Neck NY 11024-1219 Office: Paul Hastings Janofsky & Walker LLP 75 E 55th St New York NY 10022-3205 Office Phone: 212-318-6380. E-mail: harveystrickon@paulhastings.com., hastrick@optonline.net.

STRIDER, MARJORIE VIRGINIA, artist, educator; b. Guthrie, Okla. d. Clifford R. and Marjorie E. (Schley) S. BFA, Kansas City Art Inst., 1962. Faculty Sch. Visual Arts, N.Y.C., 1970-2001; artist-in-residence City U. Grad. Ctr. Mall, N.Y.C., 1976, Fabric Workshop, Phila., 1978, Grassi Palace, Venice, Italy, 1978. One-woman shows of sculpture, drawings and/or prints include Pace Gallery, N.Y.C., 1963-64, Nancy Hoffman Gallery, N.Y.C., 1973-74, Weather Spoon Mus., U.N.C., Chapel Hill, 1974, City U. Grad. Center Mall, 1976, Clocktower, N.Y.C., 1976, Sculpture Center, N.Y.C., 1983, Steinbaum Gallery, N.Y.C., 1983, 84, Andre Zarre Gallery, 1993, 95, Outdoor Installation, N.Y.C., 1997, Selby Gallery, Ringling Sch. of Art, Sarasota, Fla., 1998, Neuherzer Mus., Purchase, N.Y., 1999; exhibited in group shows at The Sculpture Center, N.Y.C., 1981, Drawing Biennale, Lisbon, Portugal, 1981, Newark Mus., 1984, William Rockhill Nelson Mus., Kansas City, 1985, Danforth Mus., Framingham, Mass., 1987, Delahoyd Gallery, N.Y.C., 1992; represented in permanent collections Guggenheim Mus., N.Y.C., U. Colo., Boulder, Albright-Knox Mus., Buffalo, Des Moines Art Center, Storm King (N.Y.) Art Center, Larry Aldrich Mus., Ridgefield, Conn., City U. Grad. Center, N.Y.C., Hirschhorn Mus. and Sculpture Garden, Washington, Santa Fe (N. Mex.) Mus. of Art, also pvt. collections. Nat. Endowment for Arts grantee, 1973, 80, Longview Found. grantee, 1974, Pollock-Krasner Found. grantee, 1990, Florsheim Art Fund grantee, 1998, 2000; Va. Ctr. for Creative Arts fellow, 1974, 92, Millay Colony for Arts fellow, 1992, Yaddo Colony, 1996, 97.

STRIDIRON, IVER ALLISON, attorney general; m. Priscilla Blyden; 4 children. BA Lincoln U., 1969; JD, Howard U. Sch. of Law, 1974. Atty. U.S. Nuclear Regulatory Commn., U.S. Commn. on Civil Rights, Washington, 1974—77; pvt. practice St. Thomas, 1977—99; mem. V.I. Legis., 1981—83, 1985—89; atty. gen. V.I., 1999—. Democrat. Office: Dept Justice 48B-50C Kronprindsens Gade GERS Bldg 2nd fl Charlotte Amalie VI 00802

STRIEFSKY, LINDA A(NN), lawyer; b. Carbondale, Pa., Apr. 27, 1952; d. Leo James and Antoinette Marie (Carachilo) S.; m. James Richard Carlson, Nov. 3, 1984; children: David Carlson, Paul Carlson, Daniel Carlson. BA summa cum laude, Marywood Coll., 1974; JD, Georgetown U., 1977. Bar: Ohio 1977. Assoc. Thompson Hine LLP (formerly Thompson, Hine & Flory), Cleve., 1977-85, ptnr., 1985—. Loaned exec. United Way N.E. Ohio, Cleve., 1978; trustee ideastream, Mus. Theater Edn. Programming. Mem. ABA (real estate fin. com. 1980-87, vice chmn. leader liability com. 1993-97, mem. non-traditional real estate fin. com. 1987—), Am. Bar Found., Am. Coll. Real Estate Lawyers (bd. govs. 1994-98, treas. 1999), Internat. Coun. Shopping Ctrs., Nat. Assn. Office and Indsl. Parks, Urban Land Inst. (chmn. Cleve. dist. coun. 1996-2000), Cleve. Real Estate Women, Ohio Bar Assn. (bd. govs. real property sect. 1985-97), Greater Cleve. Bar Assn. (chmn. bar applicants com. 1983-84, exec. coun. young lawyers sect. 1982-85, chmn. 1984-85, mem. exec. coun. real property sect. 1980-84, Merit Svc. award 1983, 85), Pi Gamma Mu. Democrat. Roman Catholic. Home: 2222 Delamere Dr Cleveland OH 44106-3204 Office: Thompson Hine LLP 3900 Key Ctr 127 Public Square Cleveland OH 44114-1216 E-mail: linda.striefsky@thompsonhine.com.

STRIER, KAREN BARBARA, anthropologist, educator; b. Summit, N.J., May 22, 1959; d. Murray Paul and Arlene Strier. BA, Swarthmore Coll., 1980; MA, Harvard U., 1981, PhD, 1986. Lectr. anthropology Harvard U., Cambridge, Mass., 1986-87; asst. prof. Beloit (Wis.) Coll., 1987-89, U. Wis., Madison, 1989-92, assoc. prof., 1992-95, prof., 1995—, dept. chair, 1994-96. Panel mem. U.S. Dept. Edn., Washington, 1989—92. Author: (book) Faces in the Forest, 1999, Primate Behavioral Ecology, 2d edit., 2003; co-author: Planning, Purposing, and Presenting Science Effectively; mem. editl. bd.: Internat. Jour. Primatology, 1990—, Primates, 1991—, Yearbook of Phys. Anthropology. Recipient Presdl. Young Investigator award, NSF, 1989—94. Fellow: AAAS (coun. del. anthropology sect. 1998—2000), Am. Anthropol. Assn.; mem.: Animal Behavior Soc., Internat. Primatological Soc., Am. Assn. Phys. Anthropologists. Office: U Wis Dept Anthropology 5403 Social Sci Bldg 1180 Observatory Dr Madison WI 53706-1320 E-mail: kbstrier@facstaff.wisc.edu.

STRIFLER, STANLEY, former business solutions executive; Grad., So. Meth. U. Sys. engr. IBM; founder Strifler Group, 1984; group v.p. tech. Technology Solutions Co.; CEO ePartners, 1998—. E-mail: sstrifler@epartnersolutions.com.

STRIGL, DENNIS F. telecommunications industry executive; BBA, Canisius Coll.; MBA, Dickinson U. With N.Y. Telephone Co., 1968, AT&T; v.p. product mgmt. network svcs. Bell Atlantic, 1989—91; pres., CEO Bell Atlantic Mobile and Bell Atlantic Global Wireless, 1991—97, Bell Atlantic Global Wireless, 1997—2000, Verizon Wireless Joint Venture, 2000—; exec. v.p. Verizon Comm., Inc., Bedminster, NJ, 2000—. Office: Verizon Wireless 180 Washington Valley Rd Bedminster NJ 07921

STRIKER, CECIL LEOPOLD, archaeologist, educator; b. Cin., July 15, 1932; s. Cecil and Delia (Workum) S.; m. Ute Stephan, Apr. 27, 1968. BA, Oberlin Coll., 1956; MA, NYU, 1960, PhD, 1968; MA (hon.), U. Pa., 1972. From instr. to asst. prof. Vassar Coll., 1962-68; assoc. prof. U. Pa., Phila., 1968-78, prof. history of art, 1978—, chmn. dept. history of art, 1980-87; field archaeologist Dumbarton Oaks Center for Byzantine Studies, 1966-80, fellow, 1972-73. Adj. prof. Sabanci U., 1999—; dir. survey and excavation, Myrelaion, Istanbul, 1965-66; co-dir. Kalenderhane Archaeol. Project, Istanbul, 1966-78, Aegean Dendrochronology Project, 1977-88; gen. archaeol. cons. Istanbul Metro and Bosphorus Tunnel Project, 1985-87; dir. Archtl. Dendrochronology Project, 1988—; cons. Integrated Study of Hagia Sophia Structure, 1991-95. Mem. editorial bd. Architectura: Zeitschrift für Geschichte der Architektur, 1986—. Adv. bd. Ctr. for Advanced Study in the Visual Arts, 1986-88, Samuel H. Kress Found. Art History Fellowship Program, 1986-87. With U.S. Army, 1954-57. Fulbright grant in Germany, 1960-62, NEH grant, 1985-86; art historian in residence Am. Acad. in Rome, 1973. Mem. Archaeol. Inst. Am., Coll. Art Assn., Am. Rsch. Inst. in Turkey (fellow 1965-66, pres. 1978-84, hon. dir. 2002), Coun. Am. Overseas Rsch. Ctr. (chmn. 1980-84), Soc. Archtl. Historians, Turkish Studies Assn., U.S. Nat. Com. for Byzantine Studies, Koldewey Gesellschaft, German Archaeol. Inst. (corr.). Office Phone: 215-898-3249. E-mail: cstriker@sas.upenn.edu.

STRIMBAN, ROBERT, graphic designer; b. N.Y.C., Aug. 18, 1923; s. Max and Yetta (Spencer) S.; m. Irma Ferguson, Aug. 1, 1959. Diploma, Pratt Inst., 1942. Ptnr., designer Strimban Design, N.Y.C., 1946-59, designer, self-employed, 1959-90; sculptor N.Y.C. and Cutchogue, N.Y., 1959—. Designer: (book jacket) The Sea Around Us, 1970s (Art Dir.'s Club award 1970s), The Golden Bough, 1970s (Aiga award 1970s); designer/illustrator: (mag. covers) Forbes, 1980s (Art Dir.'s Club award 1980s), N.Y. Times, 1970s-80s; group exhbns. include Springs Invitational Show, Elaine Benson Gallery, Bridgehampton, 1995-96, Jimmy Ernst Springs Invitational, 1995, 97, 98, Greenport Internat. Outdoor Sculpture Exhibit, 1997, Artist's Woods, Amagansett, L.I., 2001; commd. sculptures Greenway Plaza Indsl. Park, Farmingdale, 1999. With USAF, 1942-45, China, Burma, India. Home: 1925 Eugenesro Cutchogue NY 11935

STRIMBU, VICTOR, JR., lawyer; b. New Philadelphia, Ohio, Nov. 25, 1932; s. Victor and Veda (Stancu) S.; m. Kathryn May Schrote, Apr. 9, 1955 (dec. 1995); children: Victor Paul, Michael, Julie, Sue; m. Marjorie Bichsel, Oct. 23, 1999. BA, Heidelberg Coll., 1954; postgrad., Western Res. U., 1956-57; JD, COlumbia U., 1960. Bar: Ohio 1960, U.S. Supreme Ct. 1972. With Baker & Hostetler LLP, Cleve., 1960—, ptnr., 1970—. Bd. dirs. North Coast Health Ministry; mem. Bay Village (Ohio) Bd. Edn., 1976-84, pres., 1978-82; mem. Bay Village Planning Commn., 1967-69; life mem. Ohio PTA; mem. Greater Cleve. Growth Assn.; trustee New Cleve. Campaign, 1987-94—, North Coast Health Ministry, 1989-2001, Heidelberg Coll., 1996—; mem. indsl. rels. adv. com. Cleve. State U., 1979—, chmn., 1982,1999, vice chmn., 1998. With AUS, 1955-56. Mem. ABA, Ohio Bar Assn., Greater Cleve. Bar Assn., Ohio Newspaper Assn. (minority affairs com. 1987-90), Ct. of Nisi Prius Club. Republican. Presbyterian. Office: Baker & Hostetler LLP 3200 National City Ctr 1900 E 9th St Ste 3200 Cleveland OH 44114-3485

STRINER, HERBERT EDWARD, economics educator; b. Jersey City, Aug. 16, 1922; s. Harry and Pearl (Strynar) S.; m. Erma Steinert, Dec. 9, 1943 (div. 1970); children: Richard Alan, Deborah Jane; m. Iona V. Meredith. AB, Rutgers U., 1947, MA, 1948; PhD (Maxwell fellow 1949-50), Syracuse U., 1951. Asst. prof. Syracuse U., 1951; economist Interior Dept., 1951-54; program dir. NSF, 1954-55, Nat. Planning Assn., 1955-57; sr. analyst Operations Research Office, Johns Hopkins, 1957-59; program dir. Brookings Inst., 1959-61, Stanford Research Inst., 1961-62; program devel. dir. Upjohn Inst., Washington, 1962-69; dean Coll. Continuing Edn. Am. U., Washington, 1969-72, dean Coll. Bus., 1974-81, prof. econs. and mgmt., 1981-89; cons. Los Alamos Nat. Lab., 1990-91; chief planning and policy NIH, 1972-73; pres. U. Research Corp., 1973-74; assoc. faculty mem. Johns Hopkins U., 1997. Chmn. bd. dirs. NetTalon Corp. Inc., 2002—. Author: Toward a Fundamental Program for the Training, Employment and Economic Equality of the American Indian, 1968, Continuing Education as a National Capital Investment, 1972, Regaining The Lead: Policies for Economic Growth, 1984; co-author: Local Impact of Foreign Trade, 1960, Civil Rights, Employment and the Social Status of American Negros, 1966; Contbr. profl. jours. Mem. rev. panel Pres.'s Cabinet Com. Juv. Delinquency, 1961-63, D.C. Youth Employment Com., 1963, Pres.'s Task Force Am. Indians, 1967, White House Conf. Aging, 1971, bd. dirs. Opportunities Industrialization Ctr., NAACP, Washington. Officer inf. U.S. Army, 1943-46. Decorated Breast Order of Yun Hui with Ribbon, World War II Govt. China. Home: 4979 Battery Ln Bethesda MD 20814-4986

STRINGEL, GUSTAVO, pediatric surgeon; b. Mier, Mex., Sept. 29, 1945; s. Gustavo Sr. and Magdalena (Toledo) S.; m. Lina Guertin, Dec. 29, 1978; children: Gustavo, Mariana, Virginia, Patricia, Alexander. MD, U. Mex., 1969. Intern Hispana Benevolent Soc., Mexico City, 1969; rotating intern Hosp. Espanol de Mex., Mexico City, 1971; resident in pediatrics Hosp. Infantil de Mex., Mexico City, 1971-72; rotating intern St. Michael's Hosp., Toronto, 1972-73; resident in gen. surgery Gallie Course, U. Toronto, 1973-77; resident in pediatric surgery Hosp. for Sick Children, 1977-79; asst. prof. surgery U. Ottawa, Can., 1979-85; assoc. prof. surgery U. Tex., Dallas, 1985-92, SUNY, Stony Brook, 1992-94; prof. surgery N.Y. Med. Coll., Valhalla, 1994—. Fellow ACS, Am. Acad. Pediatrics, Royal Coll. Physicians and Surgeons of Can., Am. Coll. of Physician Executives; mem. AMA, Am. Pediatric Surg. Assn., Can. Assn. Pediatric Surgeons, Larchmont Yacht Club. Roman Catholic. Home: 21 Addison St Larchmont NY 10538-2744 Office: Westchester Co Med Ctr Valhalla NY 10595

STRINGER, C. VIVIAN, college basketball coach; b. Edenborn, Pa. m. William D. Stringer (dec.); children: David, Janine, Justin. Grad., Slippery Rock State Coll. Head coach Cheyney State Coll., 1971—83, U. Iowa, 1983—95, Rutgers U., 1995—. Head coach US Select Team tour China, 1980, World U. Games, Kobe, Japan, 1985, World Championship Zone Qualification Tournament, San Paulo, Brazil, 1989, US Pan-American Games, Havana, Cuba, 1991. Finalist Naismith Nat. Coach of Year award, 2000, 2001, 2003; named to Women's Basketball Hall of Fame, 2001; recipient Phila. Sportswriters' Coach of Year, 1980, Phila. Sportswriters' Coach of Year, 1981, NCAA, Wade Trophy Women's Nat. Coach of Year, 1982, Converse Women's Nat. Coach of Year, 1988, Naismith award, Converse, Sports Illustrated, USA Today, Los Angeles Times and Black Coaches Assn. Women's Coach of the Year, 1993. Mem. Amateur Basketball Assn. U.S. (bd. dirs.). Achievements include 1st person (male or female) to lead 3 different schools to the NCAA final four.*

STRINGER, CHARLES COLUMBUS, JR., minister, protective services official, writer; b. Clarksdale, Miss., Oct. 21, 1944; s. Charles Columbus, Sr. and Vivian Nelson Stringer; m. Helen Jean Perkins, Dec. 17, 1964; children: Charles Columbus III, Natalie Nicole. BA, Calif. State U., Seaside, 2002. Funeral dir. Stringer Funeral Home, Clarksdale, Miss., 1964—75; pvt. investigator N. Delta Security, Clarkesdale, Miss., 1965—75; law enforcement officer Clarksdale Police Dept., Miss., 1969—75; pvt. investigator Stringer & Assocs., Seaside, Calif., 1975—2003; min. various Baptist chs., Seaside, Calif., 1977—2003; investigator Pebble Beach Co., Calif., 1984—94; patrolman Federal Police Dept., Calif., 1985—. Adv. bd. mem. City of Seaside, Calif., 1980—; chmn., redress com. NAACP, Clarksdale, Miss., 1994—96; writer, asst. editor Seaside Post News Sentinel, Calif., 2002—. Author: Diary of a Dixie Cop, 1986. Candiddate for sheriff Coahoma County, Miss., 1975; candidate for mayor City of Clarksdale, Miss., 1996. SP/4 U.S. Army, 1961—64, Ft. Hood, Tex. Mem.: Am. Legion, VFW. Democrat. Baptist. Avocations: hiking, weightlifting, training dogs, reading. Home: PO Box 1398 Marina CA 93933 Office: Seaside Post News Sentinel 1201 Echo Ave Seaside CA 93955 E-mail: jwlcharles@wmconnect.com., dltphnsl@aol.com.

STRINGER, EDWARD CHARLES, judge, lawyer; b. St. Paul, Feb. 13, 1935; s. Philip and Anne (Driscoll) S.; m. Mary Lucille Lange, June 19, 1957 (div. Mar. 1991); children: Philip, Lucille, Charles, Carolyn; m. Virginia L. Ward, Sept. 10, 1993. BA, Amherst Coll., 1957; LLD, U. Minn., 1960. Bar: Minn. Ptnr. Stringer, Donnelly & Sharood, St. Paul, 1960-69, Briggs & Morgan, St. Paul, 1969-79; sr. v.p., gen. counsel Pillsbury Co., Mpls., 1980-82, exec. v.p., gen. counsel, 1982-83, exec. v.p., gen. counsel, chief adminstrv. officer, 1983-89; gen. counsel U.S. Dept. Edn., Washington, 1989-91; chief of staff Minn. Gov. Arne H. Carlson, 1992-94; assoc. justice Minn. Supreme Ct., St. Paul, 1994—2002. Mem. ABA, Minn. State Bar Assn., Ramsey County Bar Assn. (sec. 1977-80), Order of Coif, Mpls. Club. Congregationalist. Home: 712 Linwood Ave Saint Paul MN 55105-3513 Office: W-2200 First Nat Bank Bldg Saint Paul MN 55101-

STRINGER, HOWARD, media executive; b. Cardiff, Wales, Feb. 19, 1942; arrived in U.S., 1965, naturalized, 1985; s. Harry and Marjorie Mary (Pook) Stringer; m. Jennifer Kinmond Patterson, July 29, 1978; children: David, Ridley, Harriet, Kinmond. BA, MA, Oxford (Eng.) U., 1964; PhD (hon.), London Inst., 2003. Prodr., dir. CBS News, N.Y.C., 1973—76; exec. prodr. CBS Reports, 1976—81, Evening News, 1981—84; exec. v.p., 1984—86; pres. CBS News, 1986—88, CBS Broadcast Group, 1988—95; chmn., CEO Tele-TV, 1995—97, Sony Canada, 1997—; chmn. Sony Electronics, 1998—; chmn., CEO Sony Am., 1998—; dir. Sony Corp., 1999—; pres. Sony Broadband Entertainment, 2000—; vice chmn. Sony Corp., 2003—. Bd. dirs. Sony Corp., Intercontinental Hotel Group. Chmn. Am. Film Inst.; bd. dirs. Am. Theatre Wing; trustee NY Presbyn. Hosp., Mus. Radio and TV, Teach for Am. Sgt. U.S. Army, 1965—67, Vietnam. Decorated knight bachelor Eng.; named hon. fellow Merton Coll., Oxford, 2000, hon. fellow Welsh Coll. Music and Drama, 2001; named to Broadcasting and Cable Hall of Fame, 1996, Royal TV Soc., Wales, 1999; recipient Emmy award, NATAS, 1973, 2 Emmy awards, 1979, 1981, 4 Emmy awards, 1983, Columbia Dupont award, Columbia Journalism Sch., 1979, 1981, Overseas Press Club awards, 1974, 1979, 1982, IRTS Found. award, 1994, First Amendment Leadership award, Radio and TV News Dirs. Found., 1996, Britannia award for contbns. to worldwide entertainment, BAFTA, 2003, Gold medal, St. George Soc., 2004. Mem.: Coun. on Fgn. Rels. Presbyterian. Office: Sony Corp of Am 550 Madison Ave New York NY 10022-3211 E-mail: howard_stringer@sonyusa.com.

STRINGER, L. E. (DEAN STRINGER), retired lawyer; b. Sayre, Okla., June 22, 1936; s. Rex Herman and Bessie (Morris) S.; m. Carol Ann Woodson, Aug. 31, 1963; children: Craig Woodson, Laura DeAnn. BA, Okla. State U., 1958; LLB, Harvard U., 1961. Bar: Okla. 1961, U.S. Ct. Appeals (10th cir.) 1962, U.S. Dist. Ct. (we. dist.) 1963, U.S. Supreme Ct. 1972. Assoc. Crowe, Boxley, et al (now Crowe & Dunlevy), Oklahoma City, 1961-68, mem., dir., 1968-2000, chmn. bd., 1999-2000; ret., 2000. Pres. Crowe & Dunlevy, P.C., 1979-81, chmn. litigation dept., 1987-2000; bd. dirs. Okla. Inst. for Child Advocacy, 2003-, v.p., 2004-. Pres. Okla. State U. Alumni Assn., 1972-73; bd. regents Okla. State U. and A&M Colls., Stillwater, 1986-94, vice-chmn., 1989-90, chmn., 1990-91; chmn. Okla. State U. Found., Stillwater, 1982-85; pres. Friends of the Libr., Okla. State U., 2000—; bd. dirs. Okla. Heritage Assn., 1995-2000; pres. adv. com. Okla. State U./OKC, 1998—, chmn., 2000—; mem. regents edn. adv. com. Okla. State Regents for Higher Edn., 1995-2001; trustee Youth Svcs. Oklahoma County, Inc., 2001—, vice chmn. 2002-04, chmn. 2004—. Maj. Okla. N.G., 1961-71. Recipient Disting. Alumnus award Okla. State U., 1979; inducted Hall of Fame Okla. State U. Alumni Assn, 1998. Fellow Am. Bar Found. (adv. rsch. com. 1996-2000); mem. Okla. Bar Assn. Democrat. Methodist. Home: 325 NW 17th St Oklahoma City OK 73103-3424

STRINGER, MARY EVELYN, art historian, educator; b. Huntsville, Mo., July 31, 1921; d. William Madison and Charity (Rogers) S. AB, U. Mo., 1942; AM, U. N.C., Chapel Hill, 1955; PhD (Danforth scholar), Harvard U., 1973. From asst. prof. art to prof. Miss. State Coll. for Women (now Miss. U. for Women), Columbus, 1947-91, prof. emeritus, 1991—. Regional dir. for Miss., Census of Stained Glass Windows in Am., 1840-1940. Bd. dirs. Mississippians for Edn. Broadcasting; mem. Miss. com. Save Outdoor Sculpture, 1992-93. Recipient Medal of Excellence award Miss. U. Women, 2003; named Honored Artist Miss. Chpt. Nat. Mus. Women in Arts, 2003; scholar Fulbright Found., 1955-56; grantee Harvard U., 1966-67, NEH, 1980. Mem. AAUW (Medal of Excellence award Miss. chpt., 2003), Coll. Art Assn., Southeastern Coll. Art

Conf. (dir. 1975-80, 83-89, Disting. Svc. award 1992, Miss. Hist. Soc. (Merit award 1995), Internat. Ctr. Medieval Art, Am. Birding Assn., Audubon Soc., The Nature Conservancy, Sierra Club, Phi Beta Kappa, Phi Kappa Phi. Democrat. Episcopalian.

STRINGER, WILLIAM JEREMY, university official; b. Oakland, Calif., Nov. 8, 1944; s. William Duane and Mildred May (Andrus) S.; m. Susan Lee Hildebrand; children: Shannon Lee, Kelly Erin, Courtney Elizabeth. BA in English, So. Meth. U., 1966; MA in English, U. Wis., 1968, PhD in Ednl. Adminstrn., 1973. Dir. men's housing Southwestern U., Georgetown, Tex., 1968-69; asst. dir. housing U. Wis., Madison, 1969-73; dir. residential life, assoc. dean student life, adj. prof. Pacific Luth., Tacoma, 1973-78; dir. residential life U. So. Calif., 1978-79, asst. v.p., 1979-84, asst. prof. higher and post-secondary edn., 1980-84; v.p. student life Seattle U., 1984-89, v.p. student devel., 1989-92, assoc. provost, 1989-95, assoc. prof. edn., 1990—, chair ednl. leadership, 1994—97, chair strategic planning, 1997—2000, chair profl. studies, 2001—. Author: How to Survive as a Single Student, 1972, The Role of the Assistant in Higher Education, 1973. Bd. dirs. N.W. Area Luth. Social Svcs. of Wash. and Idaho, pres.-elect, 1989, pres., 1990-91; bd. dirs. Seattle Coalition Ednl. Equity. Recipient John Hubbard Leadership award, 1984; Danforth Found. grantee, 1976-77. Mem. AAUP, Am. Assn. Higher Edn., Nat. Assn. Student Pers. Adminstrs. (bd. dirs. region V 1985-97, mem. editl. bd. Jour. 1995-2001, Disting. Svc. to Profession award 2000, faculty fellow 2002-), Am. Coll. Pers. Assn., Phi Eta Sigma, Sigma Tau Delta, Phi Alpha Theta, Lambda Chi Alpha. Lutheran. Home: 4553 169th Ave SE Bellevue WA 98006-6505 Office: Seattle U Dept Edn Seattle WA 98122 E-mail: stringer@seattleu.edu.

STRINGER, WILLIAM WARNER, physician; BA, U. Calif., La Jolla, San Diego, 1979; MD, U. Calif., San Diego, 1984. Chair, dept. of medicine Harbor-UCLA Med. Ctr., Torrance, Calif., 2000—. Office: Harbor-UCLA Med Ctr 1000 W Carson St Bin 400 Torrance CA 90509 E-mail: stringer@ucla.edu.

STRINGFELLOW, CHARLES, automotive executive; CFO Brown Automotive Group Ltd. (formerly Mid-Atlantic Cars), Fairfax, Va. Office: Brown Automotive Group Ltd 10287 Lee Hwy Fairfax VA 22030-2202

STRINGFELLOW, GERALD B. engineering educator; b. Salt Lake City, Apr. 26, 1942; s. Paul Bennion and Jean (Barton) S.; m. Barbara Farr, June 9, 1962; children: Anne, Heather, Michael. BS, U. Utah, 1964; PhD, Stanford U., 1968. Staff scientist Hewlett Packard Labs., Palo Alto, Calif., 1967-70, group mgr., 1970-80; disting. prof. elec. engring., materials sci. U. Utah, Salt Lake City, 1980—, chmn., 1994-98, adj. prof. physics, 1988—, dean Coll. Engring., 1998—2003. Cons. Tex. Instruments, Dallas, 1995-97, AT&T-Bell Labs., Holmdel, N.J., 1986-90, Brit. Telecom., London, 1989-92; editor-in-chief Phase Diagrams for Ceramics, Vol. IX. Author: Organometallic Vapor Phase Epitaxy, 1989, 2d edit., 1999; editor: Metal Organic Vapor Phase Epitaxy, 1986, 2004, American Crystal Growth, 1987, Alloy Semiconductor Physics and Electronics, 1989, Phase Equilibria Diagrams-Semiconductors and Chalcogenides, 1991, High Brightness LEDs, 1997; prin. editor Jour. Crystal Growth, 1998-2003; letters editor Jour. Electronic Materials, 1992-99; contbr. over 360 articles to profl. jours. Recipient U.S. Sr. Scientist award Alexander von Humboldt Soc., Bonn, Germany, 1979, Gov.'s Sci. Tech. medal State of Utah, 1997, John Bardeen award TMS, 2003; guest fellow Royal Soc., London, 1990. Fellow IEEE, Japan Soc. Promotion of Sci.; mem. Am. Phys. Soc., Electronic Materials Com. (pres. 1985-87), Nat. Acad. Engring. Achievements include pioneering development of organometallic vapor phase epitaxy, development of theories of thermodynamic properties of alloy semiconductors; discovery of phenomenon of compositional latching in alloy semiconductor layers grown by epitaxial techniques. Office: U Utah Dept ECE 3280 MEB Salt Lake City UT 84112-1109 E-mail: stringfellow@coe.utah.edu.

STRINGFIELD, CHARLES DAVID, hospital administrator; b. Nashville, May 11, 1939; s. Ernest Jake Stringfield and Lucille (Lovelace) Birthright; m. Ruth Dvorak, Aug. 25, 1962; children— David Fisher, John Lovelace BA, Vanderbilt U., 1961; cert. tchr., George Peabody Coll., 1962, MA in Sch. Adminstrn., 1964; MA in Hosp. Adminstrn., Washington U., St. Louis, 1966. Tchr. Sch. Dist. No. 11, Colorado Springs, Colo., 1962-64; adminstrv. asst., adminstrv. resident Milwaukee County Instns., Milw., 1965-66; exec. dir. Tenn. Nursing Home Assn., Nashville, 1966-67; asst. dir. Tenn. Hosp. Assn., Nashville, 1966-68; adminstrv. dir. Bapt. Hosp., Inc., Nashville, 1968-70, exec. v.p., 1970-82, exec. v.p., chief exec. officer, 1981-82, pres., chief exec. officer, 1982—. Pres. dedication of C. David Springfield Bldg. to Bapt. Hosp.; mem. governing bd. Mid.-Tenn. Eye Bank Found.; bd. dirs. NationaBank/Ctrl. South, Nashville Health Care Mgmt. Found./Comprehensive Care Ctr., 1993. Author: Hospital Administrator - Physician Relationships. Recipient 1st Ann. Arthritis Found. Tribute, 1989, C. David Stringfield Dedicatory plaque Bapt. Women's Pavillion East at Mid. Tenn. Med. Ctr., Disting. Svc. award Tenn. Secondary Sch. Athletic Assn., 1993; named one of Nashville's 100 Most Influential Leaders, SOURCEBOOK, 1991, 92, one of Nashville's 100 Most Powerful People, Bus. Nashville, 1994, 95, 96, 97. Fellow Am. Coll. Hosp. Adminstrs.; mem. Am. Hosp. Assn., Vol. Hosps. of Am. (bd. dirs.). Lodges: Kiwanis. Office: Bapt Hosp 2000 Church St Nashville TN 37236-0002

STRINGFIELD, HEZZ, JR., contractor, financial consultant; b. Heiskell, Tenn., Oct. 4, 1921; s. Hezz and Cecil Willie (Williams) S.; m. Helen Louise Hinton, Mar. 20, 1939; children— Carolyn Mae Joyce (Mrs. James M. Corum), Don Wayne, Gail Louise (Mrs. John D. Gamble), Debra June (Mrs. Patrick T. Cassidy). Grad. bus. adminstr., Draughon Coll., 1939; student finance and bus., U. Tenn. Fin. and bus. adminstrn. exec. Clinton Engr. Works, E.I. duPont de Nemours & Co., 1943-44; Manhattan Dist. metall. project U. Chgo., 1944-45, Monsanto Chem. Co., 1945-48; nuclear div. Union Carbide Corp., 1948-77; ind. bldg. contractor, real estate developer, 1946—; cons. gen. bus., real estate financing, 1946—; pres. FBF, Inc., 1977—2002; with U.S. AID Mission to Middle East. Cons. with industry, govt. and edn. in developing nations, 1965; bd. dirs. Found. Mgmt. Edn., Advanced Mgmt. Council, Council for Internat. Progress in Mgmt., Inc., Found. for Internat. Progress in Mgmt.; mem. Adv. Council Univs. and Colls. Fellow Soc. Advancement Mgmt. (Profl. Mgr. citation 1963, v.p. 1958-62, exec. v.p. 1962-63, pres. 1963-64, chmn. bd. 1964-65); mem. Am. Mgmt. Assn., Am. Inst. Accountants Baptist. Home: 5314 Ball Rd Knoxville TN 37931-3501

STRINGFIELD, SHERRY, actress; b. Colorado Springs, Colo., June 24, 1967; m. Larry Joseph, 1998; 1 child. BFA, SUNY, Purchase, 1989. Theater appearances include Goose and Tom Tom, Hurly Burly, Devil's Disciple, A Dream Play, Hotel Baltimore, The Kitchen, Tom Jones; appeared in (TV series) Guiding Light, 1989-92, NYPD Blue, 1993, ER, 1994-96, 2001- (Emmy nominee Outstanding Lead Actress in a Drama Series, 1995), Going Home, 2000; (films) Burnzy's Last Call, 1995, 54, 1998, Borderline, 1998, Autumn in New York, 2000, Viva Las Nowhere, 2001; (TV movies) Border Line, 1999, Going Home, 2000; (TV appearances) Touched by an Angel, 1999, Third Watch, 2002.

STRINGHAM, LUTHER WINTERS, economist, administrator; b. Colorado Springs, Colo., Dec. 14, 1915; s. Luther Wilson and Fern (Van Duyn) S.; m. Margret Ann Pringle, Dec. 1, 1942 (dec. May 1998); 1 child, Susan Jean; m. Kathryn Cochran Baehr, June 19, 1999. BA summa cum laude, U. Colo., 1938, MA in Econs, 1939; Rockefeller fellow pub. adminstrn., U. Minn., 1939-40, Nat. Inst. Pub. Affairs, 1940-41. Economist Dept. Commerce, also OPA, 1941-43; intelligence officer Def. Dept., 1946-55; program analysis officer Office of the Sec. HEW, 1956-63, chmn. sec.'s com. mental retardation, 1961-63; exec. dir. Nat. Assn. for Retarded Children, 1963-68; intergovtl. relations officer HEW, 1968-77; planning dir. Central Va. Health Systems Agy., 1977-83. Dir. TV series Healthy Virginians, 1981-83. Mem. Pres.'s Com. Employment Handicapped, 1963-68; pres. Music for People, Inc., 1971-74; lectr. CUNY, 1971-76; mem. nat. coun. Boy Scouts Am., 1963-83; co-founder Older Virginians for Action, 1983-84; bd. dirs. Capital Area Agy. Aging, 1984-87; Midlothian Dist. rep. Keep Chesterfield Clean Corp. Capt. AUS, 1943-46; lt. col. USAFR, 1946-56. Mem. Am. Econ. Assn., Greater Richmond C. of C. (mem. quality coun. 1993-94), Phi Beta Kappa, Pi Gamma Mu, Delta Sigma Rho, Va. Hist. Soc., 2001—. Home: 2500 Durhamshire Pl Cheltenham Midlothian VA 23113

STRINGILE, MARIE ELIZABETH, educational administrator; b. Bayonne, N.J., May 13, 1954; d. Orlando Salvatore and Amelia Mary (Prisco) S. BA in edn., Jersey State Coll., 1976; MA in adminstrn., St. Peter's Coll., 1988; PhD in Edn. Adminstrn., 1976. Cert. elem. tchr., prin./supr., sch. adminstr., N.J. Tchr. St. James Sch., Newark, N.J., 1976-79; remedial math tchr. Ind. Child Study Teams, Jersey City, N.J., 1979-88, assoc. dir., 1988-90, adminstr., 1990—97, dir. ednl. programs, rsch. and evaluation mgr., 1997—2000; edn. program devel. specialist N.J. Dept. Edn., 2000—. Data documentation monitor Ind. Child Study Teams, Jersey City, 1990—, testing and curriculum specialist, 1990—, staff inservices, 1990—, data collection on all eligible remedial students, 1990—; cons. Devel. Remedial Math. Curriculum, 1993, resource room, 1985-88. Bd. dirs. O.L. Assumption Sch. Bd., 1991-93. Mem. ASCD, Sisters of St. Joseph of Peace (assoc.), Nat. Coun. Tchrs. Math., Internat. Reading Assn., Disabled Vets. Am., Medic Alert Found., Handyman Club Am., Black Seal Boiler Operator, Phi Delta Kappa. Avocations: carpentry, gardening, reading, mechanics, educational research. Home: 133 W 25th St Bayonne NJ 07002-1715 Office: NJ State Dept Edn Program Improvement 240 S Harrison St South Orange NJ

STRINKO, THOMAS EDWARD, medical services administrator; b. Middletown, Ohio, June 20, 1943; s. Thomas John and Mary Earlene (Taylor) S.; m. Vanna Om Strinko, Dec. 23, 1978; 1 child, Sontha Sue. Student, U. So. Calif., 1961-63; BS in Edn., Bowling Green State U., 1965; MA, Antioch U., 1968. Vol. Peace Corps, Nepal, 1965-67; fgn. svc. officer U.S. Dept. State, Vietnam, Peru and Washington, 1969-74; dir. Peace Corps, Micronesia, 1976-79; state dir. Action, Columbus, Ohio, 1979-87; child care coord. U.S. Army, European Divsn., Germany, 1987-94; program adminstr. Children's Med. Svcs., Miami, 1994—. Prodr. (record) The Bloody Boys at Phnom Penh, 1974. Founder Cambodian Mut. Assistance Assn., Columbus, Ohio, 1980; bd. dirs. Patches, Miami, Me Boun Found., Palm Beach, Fla., Wings of Valor, Miami, Vietnam Vets. Am., Dayton, 1974-75; cand. for U.S. Congress, 8th dist. Ohio, 1974, cand. for Miami-Dade County Commr., 1998. Mem. Longan and Lychee Growers of Miami-Dade, Human Svc. Coalition of Miami-Dade, State of Fla. Health Adminstrs., Early Intervention Coalition, Phi Alpha Theta, Phi Kappa Pi. Democrat. Avocations: stamp collecting/philately, cambodian stamp collecting, gardening, sports, travel, languages. Home: 8120 SW 178th St Miami FL 33157 Office: Childrens Med Svcs 1500 NW 12th Ave Miami FL 33136 E-mail: tesvos@aol.com.

STRIPLING, KAYE, school system administrator; BS in Health and Phys. Edn., Tex. Woman's U., 1962; EdM in Spl. Edn., U. Houston, 1967, ED in Curriculum and Instrn., 1985. Tchr. spl. edn. Houston Ind. Sch. Dist., 1964—75, prin. elem. and mid. schs., 1975—87, supt. Adminstrv. Dist. XIV, 1987—90, asst. supt. staff devel., 1990—94, supt. S.W. Adminstrv. Dist., 1995—2001, acting supt. schs., 2001, supt. schs., 2001—. Named Disting. Alumna, Tex. Woman's U., 2002. Office: Houston Ind Sch Dist 3830 Richmond Ave Houston TX 77027

STRIPLING BYER, KATHRYN, poet; Grad., Wesleyan Coll., Macon, Ga.; MFA, U. N.C., Greensboro. Poet-in-residence Western Carolina U., Cullowhee, NC. Author: The Girl in the Midst of the Harvest, 1986, Wildwood Flower, 1992 (Lamont Poetry Selection, 1992), Black Shawl, 1998; contbr. poems to jours., reviews and anthologies. Recipient Writing fellowship, Nat. Endowment for Arts, N.C. Arts Coun. Office: Western Carolina Univ Dept English Coulter Bldg Cullowhee NC 28723

STRIPPOLI, WILLIAM PETER, academic administrator; b. Camden, N.J., June 15, 1952; s. Frank and Rose Mildred (DiCarmine) S. BS, Rutgers U., 1975; MBA, Drexel U., 1977; MS, U. Pa., 1990. CPA, N.J. Sr. loan clk. Heritage Bank N.A., Camden, 1972-75; sr. acct. Moss Rehab. Hosp., Phila., 1975-76; instr. acctg. Rider U., Lawenceville, N.J., 1976-79; instr. of acctg. Ocean County Coll., Toms River, N.J., 1979-81; mgr. of budgeting and fin. analysis Thomas Jefferson U., Phila., 1981-86, dir. of budgeting and fin. analysis, 1986-87, exec. assoc., 1988-90; sr. adminstrv. officer U. So. Calif., L.A., 1990—. Project adminstr.: The NAMES Project AIDS Meml. Quilt, displayed at U. So. Calif., 1992 (Display Excellence award 1993). Democrat. Avocations: writing, bicycling, travel, performing comedy. Home: 2031 W Pacific Ave Burbank CA 91506-1036 Office: U So Calif Bovard Adminstrn Bldg Los Angeles CA 90089-0001 E-mail: strippol@usc.edu.

STRITTERMATTER, WARREN J. science educator, health science association administrator; MD, Duke U., 1973. Intern Emory-Grady Hosp.; neurology resident Duke U.; rsch. assoc. pharmacology-toxicology program NIH, 1977—79; asst. prof. depts. neurology and biochemistry Baylor Coll. Medicine, 1979—91, prof., co-dir. Alzheimer's Disease Rsch. Ctr.; with divsn. neurology Duke U., 1991—95; dir. Deane Lab., 1995; prof., chief divsn. neurobiology Duke Clin. Rsch. Inst., Durham, NC, 1998—. Achievements include research in Alzheimer's disease; CAG-triplet repeat diseases. Office: Duke Clin Rsch Inst Dept Neurobiology 227H Bryan Rsch Bldg Box 2900 Durham NC 27710

STRITTMATTER, PETER ALBERT, astronomer, educator; b. London, Eng., Sept. 12, 1939; came to U.S., 1970. s. Albert and Rosa S.; m. Janet Hubbard Parkhurst, Mar. 18, 1967; children— Catherine D., Robert P. BA, Cambridge U., Eng., 1961, MA, 1963, PhD, 1967. Staff scientist Inst. for Astronomy, Cambridge, Eng., 1967-70; staff scientist dept. physics U. Calif.-San Diego, La Jolla, 1970-71; assoc. prof. dept. astronomy U. Ariz., Tucson, 1971-74, prof. dept. astronomy, 1974—, Regent's prof., 1994—. Dir. Steward Observatory, Tucson, 1975—; mem. staff Max Planck Inst. Radioastronomy, Bonn, W. Germany, 1981— Contbr. articles to profl. jours. Recipient Sr. award Humboldt Found., 1979-80, Karl Schwarzschild medal, 1998. Fellow Royal Astron. Soc.; mem. Am. Astron. Soc., Astronomische Gesellschaft. Office: U Ariz Steward Obs Tucson AZ 85721-0001

STRIZ, ALFRED GERHARD, aerospace engineer, educator; b. Rosenheim, Bavaria, Germany, July 25, 1952; arrived in U.S., 1975; s. Alfons Johann and Gertraud Maria Striz; m. Elise Ann Carpenter, Jan. 4, 1983; children: Leonhard Christopher, Anneliese Christina, Andrea Verena. Vordiplom in mech. engring., Technische U., Munich, 1974; BS in Aeronautics and Astronautics, MS in Aeronautics and Astronautics, Purdue U., 1976, PhD in Aeronautics and Astronautics, 1981. Summer faculty rsch. fellow Eglin AFB, Ft. Walton Beach, Fla., 1982; summer sr. project engr. GM, Warren, Mich., 1985, 1986; summer rsch. and engring. scholar Air Force Inst. Tech., Dayton, Ohio, 1988; summer vis. scientist Wright-Patterson AFB, Dayton, Ohio, 1989, 1990, summer faculty rsch. fellow, 1996; summer faculty fellow NASA Langley Rsch. Ctr., Hampton, Va., 1994, 1995, 2004; prof. U. Okla., Norman, 1981—, L.A. Comp Chair in Mech. and Aerospace Engring., 2002—. Cons. in field, Norman; bd. dirs. Casmeo, Oklahoma City; panel and com. mem. NRC NASA Rev. Program, Washington, 2003. Contbr. articles to profl. jours. Pres. Flaming Oaks Home Owners Assn., Norman, 1995, 2002; karate instr. USA Stars, Moore, Okla., 1996—; mate Sea Scout Ship 5790, Norman, 1998—. With German Air Force, 1971—72. Recipient Ralph R. Teetor award, Soc. Automotive Engrs., 1984; grantee in field. Fellow: AIAA (assoc.; vice chair tech. com.); mem.: Internat. Soc. Structural and Multidisciplinary Optimization, Thunderbird Sailing Club. Democrat. Roman Catholic. Achievements include first computational flutter analysis in transonic flow; development of differential quadrature method for structures; displacement based multilevel structural optimization. Avocations: sailing, martial arts, singing, hiking, remote control airplanes. Home: 6415 Oak Grove Dr Norman OK 73026-0875 Office: Univ Okla FH 206 865 Asp Ave Norman OK 73019-1052 Office Phone: 405-625-1730. E-mail: striz@ou.edu.

STROBEL, PAMELA B. energy executive; b. Chgo., Sept. 9, 1952; BS highest honors, U. Ill., 1974, JD cum laude, 1977. Bar: Ill. 1977, U.S. Dist. (ctrl. and no. dists.) Ill. 1977, U.S. Ct. Appeals (7th cir.) 1981, U.S. Claims Ct. 1983, U.S. Ct. Appeals (fed. cir.) 1985. Ptnr. Sidley & Austin, Chgo., 1988-93; exec. v.p., gen. counsel Commonwealth Edison Co., Chgo., 1993—2000; exec. v.p. Exelon Corp., Chgo., 2000—, exec. v.p., chief adminstrv. officer, 2003—; pres. Exelon Energy Delivery Co., Chgo., 2000—, vice-chair, 2000—01, CEO, vice-chair, 2001—02, chmn., CEO, 2002—03. Mem. Kappa Tau Alpha (staff 1975-77). Office: Exelon Corp PO Box 805398 Chicago IL 60680-5398

STROBEL, RUSS M. lawyer; b. N.Y.C., May 2, 1952; BA, Northwestern U., 1974; JD magna cum laude, U. Ill., 1977. Bar: Ill. 1977. Ptnr. Jenner & Block, Chgo., Friedman & Koven; sr. v.p., gen. counsel, & sec. Nicor Inc., Naperville, Ill., 2000—02, exec. v.p., 2002—03; pres. Nicor Gas, Naperville, Ill., 2002—, CEO, 2003—. Mem. ABA, Ill. State Bar Assn., Chgo. Bar Assn. Office: Nicor Inc 1844 Ferry Rd Naperville IL 60563-9600*

STROBELL, DAN F. bank executive, writer; b. Whittier, Calif., Dec. 16, 1951; s. Joseph B. Strobel and Maxine G. Tuttle; m. Cindy L. Boggs, May 5, 1998; m. Michele C. Cooper, Feb. 21, 1975 (dec. Feb. 3, 1992); children: Amanda C. Bird, Tim J., Scott F., Ken D., Kevin C. BA, Brigham Young U., Provo, Utah, 1975. V.p. US Bank, St. George, Utah, 1992—2000; chief adminstr. officer SunFirst Bank, St. George, Utah, 2000—. Author: (religious) Justice & Mercy. Pres. La Casita Found., St. George, Utah, 1998—2004. Mem.: Rotary (pres. 1990—91, Rotarian of the Yr. 1984, 2000). Lds. Avocations: travel, international service projects. Office: SunFirst Bank 146 E St George Blvd Saint George UT 84770

STROBER, MYRA HOFFENBERG, education educator, consultant; b. N.Y.C., Mar. 28, 1941; d. Julius William Hoffenberg and Regina Scharer; m. Samuel Strober, June 23, 1963 (div. Dec. 1983); children: Jason M., Elizabeth A.; m. Jay M. Jackman, Oct. 21, 1990. BS in Indsl. Rels., Cornell U., 1962; MA in Econs., Tufts U., 1965; PhD in Econs., MIT, 1969. Lectr., asst. prof. dept. econs. U. Md., College Park, 1967-70; lectr. U. Calif., Berkeley, 1970-72; asst. prof. grad. sch. bus. Stanford (Calif.) U., 1972-86, assoc. prof. sch. edn., 1979-90, prof. edn., 1990—, assoc. dean acad. affairs, 1993-95, interim dean, 1994; program officer in higher edn. Atlantic Philanthropic Svcs., Ithaca, N.Y., 1998-2000. Organizer Stanford Bus. Conf. Women Mgmt., 1974; founding dir. ctr. rsch. women Stanford U., 1974-76, 79-84, dir. edn. policy inst., 1984-86, dean alumni coll., 1992, mem. policy and planning bd., 1992-93, chair program edn. adminstrn. and policy analysis, 1991-93, chair provost's com. recruitment and retention women faculty, 1992-93, chair faculty senate com. on coms., 1992-93; mem. adv. bd. State of Calif. Office Econ. Policy Planning and Rsch., 1978-80; mem. Coll. Bd. Com. Develop Advanced Placement Exam. Econs., 1987-88; faculty advisor Rutgers Women's Leadership Program, 1991-93. Author: (with others) Industrial Relations, 1972, 1990, Sex, Discrimination and the Division of Labor, 1975, Changing Roles of Men and Women, 1976, Women in the Labor Market, 1979, Educational Policy and Management: Sex Differentials, 1981, Women in the Workplace, 1982, Sex Segregation in the Workplace: Trends, Explanations, Remedies, 1984, The New Palgrave: A Dictionary of Economic Theory and Doctrine, 1987, Computer Chips and Paper Clips: Technology and Women's Employment, Vol. II, 1987, Gender in the Workplace, 1987, Challenge to Human Capital Theory: Implications for the HR Manager, American Economic Review, 1995, Rethinking Economics Through a Feminist Lens, Feminist Economics, 1995, Making and Correcting Errors in Economic Analyses: An Examination of Videotapes, (with Agnes M.K. Chan) The Road Winds Uphill All the Way: Gender, Work, and Family in the U.S. and Japan, 1999, (with Jay M. Jackman) Fear of Feedback, 2003; editor (with Francine E. Gordon) Bringing Women Into Management, 1975, (with others) Women and Poverty, 1986, Industrial Relations, 1990, Challenges to Human Capitol Theory: Implications for HR Managers, 1995, (with Sanford M. Dornbusch) Feminism, Children and the New Families, 1988, Rethinking Economics Through a Feminist Lens, 1995, (with Agnes M.K. Chan) The Road Winds Uphill All The Way: Gender Work and Family in the U.S. and Japan, 1999, (with Jay M. Jackman) Fear of Feedback, 2003, Application of Mainstream Economics Constructs to Education: A Feminist Analysis, 2003; mem. bd. editors Signs: Jour. Women Culture and Soc., 1975-89, assoc. editor, 1980-85; mem. bd. editors Sage Ann. Rev. Women and Work, 1984—; mem. editorial adv. bd. U.S.-Japan Women's Jour., 1991—; assoc. editor Jour. Econ. Edn., 1991—; contbr. chpt. to book, articles to profl. jours. Mem. rsch. adv. task force YWCA, 1989—; chair exec. bd. Stanford Hillel, 1990-92; bd. dirs. Resource Ctr. Women, Palo Alto, Calif., 1983-84; pres. bd. dirs. Kaider Found.; Mountain View, Calif., 1990-96; bd. trustees Mills Coll. Fellow Stanford U., 1975-77, Schiff House Resident fellow, 85-87. Mem.: NOW (bd. dirs. legal def. and edn. fund 1993—98), Ctr. Gender Equality (bd. dirs. 2000—), Internat. Assn. Feminist Econs. (assoc. editor Feminist Econs. 1994—, pres. 1997), Indsl. Rels. Rsch. Assn., Am. Ednl. Rsch. Assn., Am. Econ. Assn. (mem. com. status of women in profession 1972—75). Office: Stanford U School Edn Stanford CA 94305 E-mail: myra.strober@stanford.edu.

STROBER, SAMUEL, immunologist, educator; b. N.Y.C., May 8, 1940; s. Julius and Lee (Lander) S.; m. Linda Carol Higgins, July 6, 1991; children: William, Jesse; children from a previous marriage: Jason, Elizabeth. AB in Liberal Arts, Columbia U., 1961; MD magna cum laude, Harvard U., 1966. Intern Mass. Gen. Hosp., Boston, 1966-67; resident in internal medicine Stanford U. Hosp., Calif., 1970-71; rsch. fellow Peter Bent Brigham Hosp., Boston, 1962-63, 65-66, Oxford U., Eng., 1963-64; rsch. assoc. Lab. Cell Biology Nat. Cancer Inst. NIH, Bethesda, Md., 1967-70; instr. medicine Stanford U., 1971-72, asst. prof., 1972-78, assoc. prof. medicine, 1978-82, prof. medicine, 1982—, Diane Goldstone Meml. lectr., 1978-97, John Putnam Merrill Meml. lectr., chief div. immunology & rheumatology, 1978-97. Investigator Howard Hughes Med. Inst., Miami, Fla., 1976-81; bd. dirs. La Jolla Inst. for Allergy and Immunology; founder Dendreon, Inc. Assoc. editor: Jour. Immunology, 1981-84, Transplantation, 1981-85, 99—, Internat. Jour. Immunotherapy, 1985—, Transplant Immunology, 1992—, Biol. Bone Marrow Transplantation, 1999—; contbr. articles to profl. jours. Served with USPHS, 1967-70. Recipient Leon Reznick Meml. Rsch. prize Harvard U., 1966. Mem. Am. Assn. Immunology, Am. Soc. Clin. Investigation, Am. Coll. Rheumatology, Transplantation Soc. (councilor 1986-89), Am. Soc. Tranplantation Physicians, Western Soc. Medicine, Am. Assn. Physicians, Clin. Immunology Soc. (pres. 1996), Alpha Omega. Home: 405 Minoca Rd Portola Valley CA 94028-7740 Office: Stanford U Sch Medicine 300 Pasteur Dr Palo Alto CA 94304-2203

STROBLE-THOMPSON, COLETTE MARY HOULE, plastering and stucco company executive; b. Manchester, N.H., Aug. 10, 1947; d. George Albert and Mary Agnes (Sala) Houle; children: B.J., Danielle, Alden; m. Dennis W. Thompson. Student, CAP Regional Staff Coll. Tex., 1985, 86. Lic. real estate agt., stucco/plasterer. Switchboard operator Leavitt's Dept. Store, Manchester, N.H., 1965-66, with credit office, 1966-67, merchandizer, advertiser, 1966-69; advt. marketer Ariz. wide K-Mart, Mesa; owner, mgr. Colette's Boutique, Mesa, 1980-82; co-founder, CEO, pres. Stroble Plastering, Gilbert, Ariz., 1977—. Cons. area wide constrn. firms, Phoenix, 1979—; contractor plastering and stucco, Phoenix, 1987-90; realtor personal real estate property, Phoenix, 1988-90. Author, editor Wing Tips, 1985-86; co-inventor, electronic locator transmitter. Maj., squadron leader, fin. officer, personnel officer CAP, Mesa, 1990; active Dept. Disabled/Disadvantaged, Phoenix, 2000. Recipient Humanitarian award Dept. Econ. Security, Mesa, 1989, Letters of Appreciation, Leper Colony, Mexico, 1989. Mem. Nat. Assn. Search and Rescue (life), World Wing Kung Fu Assn., Rosicrucian Order Amorc (dep. master, master). Avocations: collector of masks & fetishes of all cultures, fishing, travel, real estate, boating. Office: Stroble Plastering & Stucco 721 N Monterey St Ste 103 Gilbert AZ 85233-3835

STROCK, CARL A. career military officer; b. GA; BCE, Va. Military Inst.; MCE, Miss. State U. Registered profl. engr., Mo. Commd. 2d. lt. U.S. Army, 1972, advanced through grades to lt. gen., 2004; various assignments Columbus AFB, 1980—83; with 307 Engr. Battalion, 82nd Airborne, Ft. Bragg, NC, 1983—86; sr. tactics instr. British Royal Sch. Military Engring.; cols. assignment officer, personnel staff officer Office of Dep. Chief Staff for Personnel Hdqs. Dept. Army, 1991—94; comdr. engr. brigade 24th Infantry

Divsn., Ft. Stewart, Ga., 1994—96; chief of staff US Army Engr. Training Ctr., Ft. Leonard Wood, Mo., 1996—97; comdr., divsn. engr. Pacific Ocean Divsn. U.S. Army Corps Engrs., Ft. Shafter, Hawaii, 1997—99; comdr., Northwestern Divsn. US Army Corps of Engineers, Portland, Oreg., 1999—2001, dir. military programs Washington, 2001—03, dir. civil works, 2003—04, chief of engineers/commdg. gen., 2004—; dep. dir. ops. Coalition Provisional Authority, Iraq, 2003. Decorated Legion of Merit with one oak leaf cluster, Bronze Star with one oak leaf cluster, Meritorious Svc. medal with two oak leaf clusters, Southwest Asia Svc. medal with three battle stars. Office: US Army Corps of Engineers 441 G St NW Washington DC 20314*

STROCK, HERBERT LEONARD, motion picture producer, director, editor, writer; b. Boston, Jan. 13, 1918; s. Maurice and Charlotte Ruth (Nesselroth) S.; m. Geraldine Polinger, Dec. 25, 1941; children: Leslie Carol, Genoa Ellen, Candice Dell. BA, U. So. Calif., 1941, MA, 1942. Asst. editor Metro-Goldwyn-Mayer, Culver City, Calif., 1941-42; prodr., dir. IMPPRO, Culver City, 1946-51; dir., film editor Hal Roach Studios, Culver City, 1951-53, Ivan Tors Prodns., Culver City, 1931-58; prodr., dir. ZIV Prodns., Hollywood, Calif., 1956-61; dir. Warner Bros., Burbank, Calif., 1958-63; ind. dir., pres. Herbert L. Strock Prodns., Hollywood, Calif., 1963—. Pres., chmn. bd. Hollywood World Films Inc., lectr. U. So. Calif. Producer, dir.: I Led Three Lives, Mr. District Attorney, Favorite Story, Corliss Archer, Science Fiction Theater, Highway Patrol, Dr. Christian, Man Called X, Harbor Command, 1954; dir. Battle Taxi; assoc. producer, dir.: Tom Swift series,(TV shows) Mann of Action, Red Light and Siren Sky King; Maverick, Alaskans, Colt 45, Bronco, Cheyenne, 77 Sunset Strip, Bonanza, Hans Brinker Spl., Decisions-Decisions, (feature pictures) Perfect World of Rodney Brewster, I Was a Teenage Frankenstein, Blood of Dracula, How to Make a Monster, Rider on a Dead Horse, Strike Me Deadly, Search the Wild Wind, Magnetic Monster, Riders to the Stars, Gog - Storm Over Tibet; editor, dir.: The Crawling Hand, One Hour of Hell; editorial supr. Shark; writer, dir. Brother on the Run; editor: So Evil My Sister, Chamber-Mades; co-producer Small Miracle; editor, dir. (documentary) They Search for Survival; supervising film editor Hunger Telethon; editor (spl.) The Making of America, co-writer, film editor Hurray for Betty Boop; dir., chief prodn. coordinator for Miss World, 1976; editor (documentary) UFO Journals, UFO Syndrome, Legends, all 1979, Neighbor hood Watch; co-dir., film editor Witches Brew, 1979; writer, film editor (TV series) Flipper, 1981. Editor post prodn. services: China--Mao to Now, Eucatastrophe, Tibet, El Papa, Night Screams, King Kung Fu; dir., editor Deadly Presence; producer, writer, dir. (med. documentary) A New Lease on Life; editor Snooze You Lose, Olympic Legacy, Water You Can Trust, Distance, Fish Outta Water; dir., editor Gramma's Gold; co-editor Infinity, Peaceful Sabbath; producer, writer, dir. (fund raising documentary) Combined Federal Campaign; co-dir., editor Detour; editor (experimental film) This Old Man..., Sidewalk Motel; author: Picture Perfect, 2000. Served with U.S. Army, 1940-41. Mem. Acad. Motion Picture Arts and Scis., Dirs. Guild Am., Am. Cinema Editors (dir., bd. mem. 1984-85), Motion Picture Editors Guild, Delta Kappa Alpha (pres. 1941-65), Editors Guild. Democrat. Avocation: photography. E-mail: herbstrock@earthlink.net.

STROCK, JAMES MARTIN, communications executive, writer, mediator; b. Austin, Tex., Aug. 19, 1956; s. James Martin Strock Sr. and Augusta (Tenney) Mullins. AB, Harvard U., 1977, JD, 1981; postgrad, New Coll. Oxford U., 1981-82. Bar: Colo. 1983. Tchg. asst. Harvard U., 1980-81; spl. cons. to majority leader U.S. Senate, Washington, 1982-83; spl. asst. to adminstr. EPA, Washington, 1983-85, asst. adminstr. for enforcement, 1989-91; spl. counsel U.S. Senate Com. on Environment and Pub. Works, Washington, 1985-86; atty. Davis, Graham & Stubbs, Denver, 1986-88; acting dir., gen. counsel U.S. Office Pers. Mgmt., Washington, 1988-89; sec. for environ. protection State of Calif., Sacramento, 1991-97; prin. James Strock & Co., San Francisco, 1997—; sr. fellow, exec. edn. R.H. Smith Sch. bus. U. Md., 2003—. Adj. prof. U. So. Calif., 1996-97, mem. adv. bd. Global Nature Fund 1998—; Ctr. for the Study of The Presidency, 2002-03; mem. Intergovtl. Policy Adv. Com., rep. U.S. Trade, 1991-97; mem. Calif. State Pers. Bd., 1998; guest prof. U. Konstanz, 1998; bd. dir. Raoul Wallenberg com. of the U.S.; mem. Calif. State Personnel Bd., 1997-99. Author: Reagan on Leadership, 1998, Theodore Roosevelt on Leadership, 2001; contbr. articles to profl. jours. Capt. JAGC USAR, 1987—96. Recipient Ross Essay award ABA, 1985, Environ. Leadership award Calif. Environ. Bus. Coun., 1994, Fed. Republic Germany Friendship award, 1996; Environ. Soc. India fellow, 1997, commendation Calif. Dist. Attys. Assn., 1997; Rotary Internat. scholar, 1981-82. Mem. Coun. Fgn. Rels., Pacific Coun. on Internat. Policy, Nat. Spkrs. Assn., Am. Arbitration Assn., Authors' Guild, Phi Beta Kappa. Republican. Office: 400 Spear St Ste 107 San Francisco CA 94105-1691 E-mail: jms@jamesstrock.com.

STROCK, ROBERT S. retired education educator; b. Sewickley, Pa., Oct. 19, 1921; s. Paul Blazier and Jessie Serene Strock. BS, Geneva Coll., 1947; EdM, Shippensburg U., 1964; postgrad., Colo. State U., 1965, U. Tenn., 1966, U. Miami, 1968, Ind. U., 1969. Cert. tchr. Dept. Pub. Instrn., Pa., Nat. Coun. Bus. Schs. Acctg. tchr. Duffs Iron City Coll., Pitts., 1947—50; stock control clk. H.H. Robertson Co., Inc., Ambridge, Pa., 1950—57; tchr. Baden (Pa.)-Economy Sch. Dist., 1957—67; asst. prof. Slippery Rock (Pa.) U., 1967—72; assoc. prof. Indiana U. Pa., 1972—99; ret. Mem. bd. elections Beaver (Pa.) County Election Bur., 1982—84; councilman Ind. Boro Coun., 1991—94. Staff sgt. USAF, 1943—45. Recipient Outstanding Prof. award, Student Pa. State Edn. Assn., 1992, Patriotic Achievement award, Mil. Order of the World Wars Chpt. 200, 1993. Mem.: Beaver Heritage Soc. (bd. trustees), Beaver County Geneal. Soc., Am. Legion, Alpha Phi Omega, Delta Pi Epsilon (treas. Beta Alpha chpt. 1973—76), Theta Xi (past advisor Beta Lambda chpt. 1972—75). Republican. Methodist. Avocations: genealogy, travel, collecting miniature bottles, collecting postcards, parade consultant. Home: 222 Fourth St Beaver PA 15009

STRODE, GEORGE K. sports editor; b. Amesville, Ohio, Nov. 10, 1935; s. Mac and Edith M. (Murphey) S.; m. Jennifer Lanning (div. 1973); m. Ruth E. Wingett, July 15, 1973. BJ, Ohio U., 1958. Sports editor Zanesville (Ohio) Times Reporter, 1958, Athens (Ohio) Messenger, 1958-62; sports reporter Dayton (Ohio) Daily News, 1962-63, Columbus (Ohio) Citizen Jour., 1963-69; Ohio sports editor AP, Columbus, 1969-85; sports editor Columbus Dispatch, 1985—, exec. sports editor, 1999—. Mem. Ohio AP Sports Writers Assn. (v.p. 1984—), U.S. Golf Writers Assn., U.S. Harness Writers Assn. (pres. Ohio chpt. 1968-69). Republican. Methodist. Avocations: golf, horse racing. Office: Columbus Dispatch 34 S 3rd St Columbus OH 43215-4241

STRODE, JOSEPH ARLIN, lawyer; b. DeWitt, Ark., Mar. 5, 1946; s. Thomas Joseph and Nora (Richardson) S.; m. Carolyn Taylor, Feb. 9, 1969; children: Tanya Briana, William Joseph. BSEE with honors, U. Ark., 1969; JD, So. Meth. U., 1972. Bar: Ark. 1972. Design engr. Tex. Instruments Inc., Dallas, 1969-70; patent agent Tex. Instruments, Dallas, 1970—72; assoc. Bridges, Young, Matthews, Drake, Pine Bluff, Ark., 1972-74, ptnr., 1975—. Chmn. Pine Bluff Airport Commn., 1993; bd. dirs. United Way Jefferson County, Pine Bluff, 1975-77, campaign chmn., 1983, pres., 1986, exec. com., 1983-87; bd. dirs. Leadership Pine Bluff, 1983-85. Mem. Ark. Bar Assn., Jefferson County Bar Assn. (pres. 1995), Pine Bluff C. of C. (dir. 1981, 84, 94, 97), Ark. Wildlife Fed. (dir. 1979-81), Jefferson County Wildlife Assn. (dir. 1973-80, pres. 1974-76), Kiwanis (lt. gov. Mo.-Ark. divsn. 1983-84, chmn. lt. govs. 1983-84), Order of Coif, Tau Beta Pi, Eta Kappa Nu. Home: 7600 Jay Lynn Ln Pine Bluff AR 71603-9387 Office: 315 E 8th Ave Pine Bluff AR 71601-5005 E-mail: joestrode@bridgesplc.com.

STRODE, SCOTT K. communications educator; b. Avon, Ill., Nov. 3, 1936; s. Everette L. and Susanna K. Strode; m. Joanna Melyn Ward, May 5, 1963; children: Kyle, Susanna, Paul. BA, U. Puget Sound, Tacoma, Wash., 1959; MA, U. Wash., Seattle, 1966; PhD, Ind. U., Bloomington, 1974. Asst. prof. Creighton U., Omaha, 1963—67, Rutgers U., Newark, 1971—74; prof. Manchester Coll., Ind., 1974—. Actor; creative dir. Recipient, Lilly Endowment, 2003, 2004; grantee, 2001. Mem.: Assn. Asian Performance, Am. Theatre in Higher Edn. Democrat. Avocations: music, theater. Office: Manchester Coll 604 E Coll Ave North Manchester IN 46962

STRODE, WILLIAM HALL, III, photojournalist, publisher; b. Louisville, Aug. 6, 1937; s. William Hall and Margaret (Diehl) S.; m. Elizabeth Ann Wheeler, Nov. 26, 1960 (div. 1973); children: Alissa Michelle, Erin Hall; m. Hope Powel Alexander, Nov. 12, 1977 (div. 1997); children: Hope Ives, Charlotte Alexander. BS, Western Ky. U., 1959. News photographer Courier Jour. and Louisville Times, 1960-64, asst. dir. photography, 1968-75; photographer Courier Jour. mag., 1964-77; formed William Strode Assocs., photog. and pub. co., Louisville, 1978—, Harmony House pubs., 1984—. Author 23 books; exhbns. include Fine Arts III, 1961, Profile in Poverty, Smithsonian Instn., 1966, Documerica, in Corcoran Gallery, Washington, 1972, 73, Picture of the Year Travelling Exhibits; one man show includes Speed Mus. Active local Boy Scouts Am.; founder Nat. Press Photographers Found., 1975. Served with AUS, 1959. Recipient Headliners best photojournalism award, 1965; award for excellence for best mag. photog. reporting Overseas Press Club, 1967; co-recipient Pulitzer Prize for pub. service Courier Jour., 1967, for feature photography, 1976; Art Dirs. Gold medal, 1980, World Press Photog. Arts and Scis. award, 1985 Mem. Nat. Press Photographers Assn. (nat. ednl. chmn. 1966-68, v.p. 1973, pres. 1974, Photographer of Yr. 1966, Newspaper Mag. Picture Editor of Yr. 1968), Am. Soc. Mag. Photographers, Soc. Profl. Journalists, Masons (32 deg.), Scottish Rite, Knights Templar, Soc. Colonial Wars, Sigma Chi, Kappa Alpha Mu. Methodist. Home and Office: 1008 Kent Rd Goshen KY 40026-9768 Office Phone: 502-228-4446.

STROH, GUY WESTON, philosophy educator; b. Elizabeth, N.J., Mar. 28, 1931; s. Galusha Amos and Hanna Isabel Stroh; m. Marion Lorraine Kopec, Aug. 13, 1966. AB, Princeton U., 1953, AM, 1955, PhD, 1957. Asst. prof. philosophy Rider U., Lawrenceville, N.J., 1956-63, assoc. prof. philosophy, 1963-66, prof. philosophy, 1966—. Author: Plato and Aristotle, 1964, American Philosophy Edwards to Dewey, 1968, American Ethical Thought, 1979, American Ethics: A Source Book, 2000. Recipient Disting. Tchg. award Lindback Found., 1966. Mem. AAUP (pres. N.J. state conf. 1969-71). Avocation: tennis. Home: 501 Parkway Ave Trenton NJ 08618-2542 Office: Rider U 2083 Lawrenceville Rd Lawrenceville NJ 08648-3099

STROH, RAYMOND EUGENE, retired personnel executive; b. Bloomington, Ill., Aug. 13, 1942; s. Harry William and Felcie Cleo (Weaver) S.; m. Peggy Jane Whitacre, June 12, 1966 (dec. Jan. 2002); children: Rebecca Jane, David Ray. BA, So. Ill. U., 1966, U. Ill., 1977. Pers. technician Ill. Dept. Mental Health, Springfield, Ill., 1966-67; pers. officer Andrew McFarland Mental Health Ctr., Springfield, 1967-68, Manteno (Ill.) State Hosp., 1968-69; chief pers. officer Ill. Dept. Law Enforcement, Springfield, 1969-75, Ill. Dept. Revenue, Springfield, 1975-81, Ill. Dept. Mental Health, Springfield, 1981-82; pers. exec. Ill. Dept. Cen. Mgmt. Svcs., Springfield, 1982-2001; ret. State govt. chmn. U.S. Savs. Bond Campaign, Springfield, 1978-82. Bd. dirs. Consumer Credit Counseling Svc., Springfield, 1988-94, sec., 1994; coun. exec. bd. Boy Scouts Am., Springfield, 1987—, v.p., 1987-99, dist. commr., 1979-86, unit commr., 1970-79; bd. dirs. Ill. State Employees Credit Union, 1984-85. Recipient Patriotic Svc. awards U.S. Treasury Dept., 1979-82, Silver Beaver award Boy Scouts Am., 1987, Dist. award of merit, 1981, Area Pres. awards, 1985, 86, Scouters Key award, 1976, Order of the Arrow Vigil Honor, 1998, James E. West Fellowship award, 1998. Mem. NRA, U. Ill. Alumni Assn., So. Ill. U. Alumni Assn., Exptl. Aircraft Assn., Aircraft Owners and Pilots Assn., Cessna Owner Orgn., Ponce De Leon Inlet Lighthouse Assn., Nat. Geog. Soc., Cornell U. Lab. of Ornithology, Abraham Lincoln Gun Club, Appalachian Trail Conf., Union County (Tenn.) Hist. Soc., Wabash R.R. Hist. Soc., Am. Rose Soc., Theta Delta Chi. Republican. Lutheran. Avocations: aviation, hunting, fishing, bird watching, model railroading. Home: 2111 Warwick Dr Springfield IL 62704-4147

STROHECKER, LEON HARRY, JR., orthodontist; b. Schuylkill Haven, Pa., Aug. 14, 1932; s. Leon Harry and Anna (Fabian) S.; m. Juanita Mary Puyoou, Apr. 13, 1957; children: Sandra Lee Strohecker Beckett, Leon Harry III. Student, U. Pa., 1950-53, DDS, 1957, orthodontic cert., 1960. Bd. cert. Am. Bd. Orthodontics. Pres., pvt. practice, Lansdale, Pa., 1961—; dir. Face Head & Neck Pain and Trauma Ctr., Lansdale, 1987-99. Bd. dirs. Artman Home Retirement Ctr., Ambler; treas., bd. dirs. Valley Ctr. Mental Health Clinic, Lansdale, 1984—2002; guest lectr. in field. Pres. Lansdale Rotary Club, 1967-68; coun. mem. Trinity Luth. Ch., Lansdale, 1977-85, chmn. fin. com., 1980-85. Lt. (j.g.) USN, 1957-59. Named Internat. Health Profl. of Yr., Internat. Biographical Ctr., 2003; recipient Spoke award, Jr. C. of C., 1963, Spark Plug award, 1963, Widsom award of Honor, Best Orthodontist vote, 2 Lansdale area newspapers, One Thousand Great Ams. award, Internat. Biographical Ctr., 2001, 2002. Mem. ADA, Internat. Acad. Head, Neck and Facial Pain, Internat. Coll. Cranio-Mandibular Orthopedics, Am. Acad. Pain Mgmt. (diplomate), Am. Assn. for Functional Orthodontics, Am. Profl. Practice Assn., Am. Soc. Dentistry for Children, Am. Acad. Oral Medicine, Am. Assn. Orthodontists, Am. Assn. Stomatologists, Am. Acad. Oral Medicine, Middle Atlantic Orthodontic Soc., Pa. Orthod ontic Soc., Phila. Orthodontic Soc., Pa. Dental Assn., Second Dist. Dental Assn., Montgomery-Bucks Dental Soc., Alpha Omega, Omicron Kappa Epsilon. Avocations: tennis, travel, bridge, water sports. Home: 1512 Cedar Hill Rd Ambler PA 19002-1406 Office: 456 E Hancock St Lansdale PA 19446-3803 Office Phone: 215-855-7717. Personal E-mail: lstrohecker@hotmail.com.

STROHM, BRUCE C. real estate company executive; b. 1955; BS, U. Ill.; JD, Northwestern U. Ptnr. Rosenberg & Liebentritt, PC, Chgo.; exec. v.p., gen. counsel, sec. Equity Residential, Chgo., 1995—. Office: Equity Residential 2 N Riverside Plaza Chicago IL 60606*

STROHM, DAVID, venture capitalist; BA, Dartmouth Coll.; MBA, Harvard Bus. Sch. Gen. ptnr. Greylock Partners, Waltham, Mass., 1980—83, gen. ptnr., opened Palo Alto office, 1983—. Bd. dirs. Legato Systems, Inc., 1988—2003, AccelClip, AtHoc, Successfactors, CoWare, Decru, DoubleClick, EMC Corp., Internet Security Systems, Mobile Automation, Wily Technol. Office: Greylock Ptnrs 2929 Campus Dr Ste 400 San Mateo CA 94403 Office Phone: 650-493-5525. Office Fax: 650-493-5575. Business E-Mail: dstrohm@greylock.com.*

STROHMAIER, THOMAS EDWARD, designer, educator, photographer; b. Cin., Aug. 26, 1943; s. Charles Edward and Margaret Mary (Meyers) S.; m. Margaret Ann Haglage, June 7, 1980; children: Paige Maura, Edward Michael, Phoebe Greer, Michael Thomas. BFA, U. Cin., 1969, MFA, 1973. Asst. prof. design U. Cin., 1973—; City Outreach Program, 1975-76; instr. in design U. Dayton, Ohio, 1976-80, asst. prof. design, 1980-83; pres. Strohmaier Design Group, Cin., 1983—. Cons. City Arts Corp., Cin., 1977-78, City Beautiful Program, Dayton, 1982; adj. prof. design U. Cin., 1983—, mem. lecture outreach program, 1995, developed digital design program in photography, 1999-2000. Designer urban wall projects Ohio Arts Council, Columbus, 1974, Corbet award, Cin., 1977; patentee in field. U. Dayton grantee, 1980. Mem. Contemporary Arts Ctr., Design, Architecture, Art and Planning Alumni Com., Internat. Freelance Photographers Orgn., Associated Photographers Internat., U. Cin. Decade Club. Clubs: Decade. Democrat. Roman Catholic. Avocations: running, bicycling. Home: 7311 Redondo Ct Cincinnati OH 45243-1247 Office: Strohmaier Design Group 5274 Ridge Ave Cincinnati OH 45213-2542 E-mail: ts@sdg.com.

STROHMENGER, THOMAS C, lawyer; BA, Fordham U.; JD, St. John's U. Sch. of Law; M, NYU. Bar: Conn., Fla., NY. Counsel Am. Ins. Assn.; with Aetna, 1978—; v.p. and chief compliance officer Aetna Inc., 2001—. Office: Aetna Inc 151 Farmington Ave Hartford CT 06156

STROHMEYER, JOHN, writer, former editor; b. Cascade, Wis., June 26, 1924; s. Louis A. and Anna Rose (Saladunas) S.; m. Nancy Jordan, Aug. 20, 1949 (dec. 2000); children: Mark, John, Sarah; m. Sylvia Ciernick Broady, Oct. 25, 2003. Student, Moravian Coll., 1941—43; AB, Muhlenberg Coll., 1947; MA in Journalism, Columbia U., 1948; LHD (hon.), Lehigh U., 1983. With Nazareth (Pa.) Item, 1940-41; night reporter Bethlehem (Pa.) Globe-Times, 1941-43, 45-47; investigative reporter Providence Jour.-Bull., 1949-56; editor Bethlehem Globe-Times, 1956-84, v.p., 1961-84, dir., 1963-84. African-Am. journalism tchr. in Nairobi, Freetown, 1964; Atwood prof. journalism U. Alaska, Anchorage, 1987-88, writer-in-residence, 1989—; Clendinen Prof., U. S. Fla., 2001. Author: Crisis in Bethlehem: Big Steel's Struggle to Survive, 1986, Extreme Conditions: Big Oil and The Transformation of Alaska, 1993, Historic Anchorage, 2001. Lt. (j.g.) USNR, 1943-45. Pulitzer Traveling fellow, 1948; Nieman fellow, 1952-53; recipient Comenius award Moravian Coll., 1971; Pulitzer prize for editl. writing, 1972; Alicia Patterson Found. fellow, 1984, 85. Mem. Am. Soc. Newspaper Editors, Pa. Soc. Newspaper Editors (pres. 1964-66), Anchorage Racquet Club. Home: 6633 Lunar Dr Anchorage AK 99504-4550 E-mail: jstroh@gci.net.

STROJNIK, TADEJ, neurosurgeon, researcher; b. Ljubljana, Slovenia, July 11, 1963; s. Franc and Marija (Petrič) S.; m. Irena Šurca, June 6, 1987; children: Tom, Maša. MD, U. Ljubljana, 1989, MSc, 1994, PhD, 1998. Physician Health Ctr., Ptuj, Slovenia, 1989-90; resident in neurosurgery Univ. Clinic Neurosurgery, Ljubljana, 1995—96, Tchg. Hosp., Maribor, Slovenia, 1990-95, neurosurgeon, 1996—; asst. prof. U. Ljubljana, 2002—. Aitken Clin. Rsch. fellow, 1998-99. Mem. Med. Chamber Slovenia, Slovene Med. Soc., Slovenian Neurosurg. Soc. (sec. 1997-2001), European Assn. Neurosurgeons, Ctrl. European Neurosurg. Soc. (bd. dirs.). Roman Catholic. Avocations: photography, fishing, reading. Office: Tchg Hosp Dept Neurosurgery Ljubljanska 5 2000 Maribor Slovenia E-mail: t.strojnik@siol.net.

STROJNY, JOAN ELIZABETH, writer; b. Chgo., Jan. 2, 1941; d. Julius Steven and Florence Rose Strojny; children: Gerald Thomas, Pamela Ferraro, Jill Miller. BS, U. Md., 1973. Reporter McGraw-Hill Info. Svcs., San Francisco, 1980—82; mng. editor Battle Mountain (Nev.) Bugle, 1982—83; reporter, featured writer Porterville (Calif.) Recorder, 1983—84; polit. action adminstr., editor, writer, 1985—88. Bd. dirs. Bexar County Rep. Women, Cibolo, 2004—. Author: The Mapmaker. Mem.: McNey Mus. Arts, Assn. Am. Poets. Home: 141 Westerly Pl Cibolo TX 78108 E-mail: stropro@satx.rr.com.

STROKE, HINKO HENRY, physicist, researcher; b. Zagreb, Croatia, June 16, 1927; came to U.S., 1943, naturalized, 1949; s. Elias and Edith (Mechner) S.; m. Norma Bilchick, Jan. 14, 1956; children: Ilana Lucy, Marija Tamar. BEE, N.J. Inst. Tech., 1949; MS, MIT, 1952, PhD, 1955. From rsch. asst. to rsch. assoc. Princeton (N.J.) U., 1954-57; rsch. staff lab. electronics, lectr. dept. physics MIT, 1957-63; assoc. prof. physics NYU, N.Y.C., 1963-68, prof., 1968—. Dept. chmn. NYU, 1988-91; prof. associé. U. Paris, 1969-70, Ecole Normale Supérieure, 1976; vis. scientist Max Planck Inst. für Quantenoptik, Garching, U. Munich, 1977-78, 81-82, 93; cons. Atomic Instrument Co., MIT Sci. Translation Svc., Tech. Rsch. Group, Cambridge Air Force Rsch. Ctr., Am. Optical Corp., ITT Fed. Labs., NASA, others; mem. com. on line spectra of elements NAS-NRC, 1976-82; sci. assoc. CERN, Geneva, 1983—. Contbg. author: Nuclear Physics, 1963, Atomic Physics, 1969, Hyperfine Interactions in Excited Nuclei, 1971, Francis Bitter: Selected Papers, 1969, Atomic Physics 3, 1973, Nuclear Moments and Nuclear Structure, 1973, A Perspective of Physics, Vol. 1, 1977, Atomic Physics 8, 1983, Lasers in Atomic, Molecular, and Nuclear Physics, 1989—, Symposium on Probing Luminous and Dark Matter, 2000; editor: Comments on Atomic, Molecular and Optical Physics, The Physical Review-The First Hundred Years. Mem. Chorus Pro Musica, 1951—54, 1957—63, Münchener Bach-Chor, Munich, 1977—82, 1992; Choeur pro Arte Lausanne, 1983—; mem. Collegiate Chorale, NY, 1964—94, Dessoff Choirs, 1994—, Westchester Oratorio Soc., 2001—. Recipient Sr. U.S. Scientist award Alexander von Humboldt Found., 1977; NATO sr. fellow in sci., 1975 Fellow Am. Phys. Soc. (publs. oversight com. 1991-93), Optical Soc. Am., AAAS; mem. IEEE, European Phys. Soc., Soc. Française de Physique, Sigma Xi, Tau Beta Pi, Omicron Delta Kappa. Office: NYU Dept Physics 4 Washington Pl New York NY 10003-6621 E-mail: henry.stroke@nyu.edu.

STROM, BRIAN LESLIE, internist, educator; b. N.Y.C., N.Y., Dec. 8, 1949; s. Martin and Edith (Singer) S.; m. Elaine Marilyn Moskowitz, June 4, 1978; children: Shayna Lee, Jordan Blair. BS, Yale U., 1971; MD, Johns Hopkins U., 1975; MPH, U. Calif., Berkeley, 1980. Diplomate Am. Bd. Internal Medicine, Am. Bd. Epidemiology. Intern in medicine U. Calif., San Francisco, 1975-76, resident in medicine, 1976-78, research fellow in clinical pharmacology, 1978-80; from asst. prof. to assoc. prof. medicine and pharmacology U. Pa., Phila., 1980-93, prof. medicine, 1993—, prof. biostatistics & epidemiology, 1995—. Adj. asst. prof. clin. pharmacy Phila. Coll. of Pharmacy and Sci., 1981-90, adj. assoc. prof., 1990-93, adj. prof., 1993—; mem. U. Pa. Cancer Ctr., 1981—; attending staff Hosp. U. Pa., 1980—, co-dir Clin. Epidemiology Unit, 1980-91, dir., 1991-2001; dir. Clin. Pharmacology Cons. Svc., 1981-82; dir. Ctr. for Clin. Epidemiology and Biostats., 1993—, chair dept. biostats. and epidemiology, 1995—; lectr. in field; George S. prod. pub. health and preventive medicine, 2002—; cons. CDC, 1981, Coun. for Internat. Orgn. of Med. Scis., Geneva, Switzerland, 1981-83, Office of Tech. Assessment, Congress of U.S., 1980-81, Aging Rev. Com., Nat. Inst. Aging, 1982, Ministry of Pub. Health, State of Kuwait, 1982, Royal Tropical Inst., Amsterdam, 1983, others. Editl. cons. Johns Hopkins U. Press, J.B. Lippincott; referee Annals of Internal Medicine, Archives of Internal Medicine, Clin. Pharmacology and Therapeutics, Digestive Diseases and Sci., Internat. Jour. Cardiology, Internat. Jour. Epidemiology, Jour. AMA, Jour. Gen. Internal Medicine, Med. Care, Primary Care Tech., Sci.; editor Pharmaepidemiology and Drug Safety; mem. editl. bd. 7 jours.; contbr. numerous articles to profl. jours. Nat. Acad. Scis. grantee, Rockefeller Found. grantee, NIH grantee, many others. Fellow ACP, Am. Coll. Epidemiology, Am. Epidemiology Soc.; mem. Am. Fedn. Med. Rsch., Am. Pub. Health Assn., Am. Soc. Clin. Pharmacology and Therapeutics, Am. Soc. Clin. Investigation, Am. Assn. Physicians, Internat. Soc. Pharmacoepidemiology, Internat. Epideliol. Assn., Soc. for Epidemiologic Rsch., Soc. Gen. Internal Medicine, Inst. Medicine, Inst. Medicine. Democrat. Jewish. Avocations: hiking, biking, camping, skiing. Home: 332 Hidden River Rd Narberth PA 19072-1111 Office Phone: 215-898-2368. Business E-Mail: bstrom@cceb.med.upenn.edu.

STROM, DAVID J. lawyer, labor union administrator; Assoc. atty. Highsaw, Mahoney & Clarke, Washington; gen. counsel Am. Fedn. Tchrs., Washington, 1993—. Office: Am Fedn Tchrs 555 New Jersey Ave NW Washington DC 20001

STROM, J. PRESTON, JR., lawyer; b. May 21, 1959; s. Grace and J.P. Sr. S.; m. Donna Savoca, Oct. 5, 1985; children: Margaret, Caroline. BA, U. S.C., 1981, JD, 1984. Bar: S.C. 1984, U.S. Dist. Ct. S.C., 1984, U.S. Ct. Appeals (4th cir.) 1984. Asst. solicitor 5th Jud. Cir., S.C., 1985-86; ptnr. Leventis, Strom & Wicker, 1986-88, Strom Law Firm, 1988-90, Bolt, Popowski, McCulloch & Strom, 1990-93; acting U.S. atty. Office U.S. Atty., S.C., 1993, U.S. atty., 1993-96; atty. Strom Law Firm, LLC, Columbia, S.C., 1996—. Chmn. Law Enforcement Coord. Com.; chmn. juvenile justice and child support enforcement subcom. U.S. Dept. Justice; active Atty. Gen. Adv. Com. Mem. S.C. Bar, S.C. Trial Lawyers Assn., Richland County Bar Assn. (chmn. criminal law sect.). Office: Strom Law Firm LLC 1501 Main St Ste 700 Columbia SC 29201

STROM, KRISTINA CHASE, writer, consultant; b. Schenectady, Ny, Dec. 28, 1948; d. Raymond Olaf and Lois Moulton Strom; children: Kia Strom Kuresman, Kamala Strom Kuresman, Kimberly Strom Kuresman, Kara Strom Kuresman. PhD, Universal Life Sem. Lic. Insurance OH; Ordained Clergy OH. Asst. buyer, buyer Hess's Dept. Store, Allentown, Pa., 1968—69; educator Xavier U., New Orleans, 1970; columnist Denver Free Press, 1972; co-founder, owner New World Ctr. Bookshop and Foodshop, 1973—74; tchr. Beth Adam Religious Sch., Cin., 1981—88, art dir., 1987—89, prin., 1988—89; editor Beth Adam Newsletter, Cin., 1982—86; designer Del Favero Enterprises, Cin., 1984—90; store mgr. B. Dalton Books, Cin., 1990—91; systems operator TriStateOnline Greater Cin. Consortium Colls. and Univs., 1999, adminstr., 1999; pvt. practice Glendale, Ohio, 1968—; freelance artist, 1970—; designer and bus. cons., 1985—. Columnist, staff writer Silent Messages, Cin., 1996—99; moderator Wells List, 1995—; owner, mgr. CelestialPerspectives.com, Cin., 1999—. Great Lakes Great Quilts travelling exhibit, Mich. State U., 2003—04; designer and co-creator fiber art, four innovative torah covers, artist (fiber wall hanging) Millennium Challenge; author: Denim and Lace, An historical mystery of first love, timeless love; co-editor, contbr. From Eulogy to Joy, A Heartfelt Anthology, Feathered Star:

Monkey Wrench New Quilts from an Old Favorite; contbr. articles to profl. jours., poems to jours. Pres. Kindervelt #17 Cin. Children's Hosp. Aux., 1983—85. Mem.: Smithsonian Nat. Mus. Am. Indian, Nat. Ctr. for Preservation of Medicinal Herbs, The Nature Conservancy, Nat. Audubon Soc., Am. Quilter's Soc., Sierra Club, Twilight Club Ctr. Evolutionary Ethics. Avocations: gardening, genealogy, book collecting, anthropology, archaeology. Home: 171 West Sharon Road Glendale OH 45246-4334 Personal E-mail: kristinastrom@celestialperspectives.com.

STROM, LYLE ELMER, judge; b. Omaha, Nebr., Jan. 6, 1925; s. Elmer T. and Eda (Hanisch) Strom; m. Regina Ann Kelly, July 31, 1950 (dec.); children: Mary Bess, Susan Frances(dec.), Amy Claire, Cassie A., David Kelly, Margaret Mary, Bryan Thomas. Student, U. Nebr., 1946-47; AB, Creighton U., 1950, JD cum laude, 1953. Bar: Nebr. 1953. Assoc. Fitzgerald, Brown, Leahy, Strom, Schorr & Barmettler and predecessor firm, Omaha, 1953-60, ptnr., 1960-63, gen. trial ptnr., 1963-85; judge U.S. Dist. Ct. Nebr., Omaha, 1985-87, chief judge, 1987-94, sr. judge, 1995—. Adj. prof. law Creighton U., 1959-95, clinical prof., 1996—; mem. com. pattern jury instrns. and practice and proc. Nebr. Supreme Ct., 1965-91; spl. legal counsel Omaha Charter Rev. Commn., 1973; chair gender fairness task force U.S. Ct. Appeals (8th cir.), 1993-97. Exec. com. Covered Wagon Coun. Boy Scouts Am., 1953—57, bd. trustees, exec. com. Mid-Am. Coun., 1988—; chmn. bd. trustees Marian H.S., 1969—71; mem. pres. coun. Creighton U., 1990—. With U.S. Maritime Svc., 1943—46. Fellow Am. Coll. Trial Lawyers, Internat. Acad. Trial Lawyers; mem. Nebr. Bar Assn. (ho. of dels. 1978-81, exec. coun. 1981-87, pres. 1989-90), Nebr. Bar Found. (bd. trustees 1998—), Omaha Bar Assn. (pres. 1980-81), Am. Judicature Soc., Midwestern Assn. Amateur Athletic Union (pres. 1976-78), Rotary (pres. 1993-94), Alpha Sigma Nu (pres. alumni chpt. 1970-71). Republican. Roman Catholic. Office: US Dist Ct Roman Hruska Courthouse 111 S 18th Plz Ste 3190 Omaha NE 68102

STROM, MILTON GARY, lawyer; b. Rochester, N.Y., Dec. 5, 1942; s. Harold and Dolly (Isaacson) S.; m. Barbara A. Simon, Jan. 18, 1975; children: Carolyn, Michael, Jonathan. BS in Econ., U. Pa., 1964; JD, Cornell U., 1967. Bar: N.Y. 1968, U.S. Dist. Ct. (W. dist.) N.Y. 1968, U.S. Ct. Claims 1969, U.S. Ct. Mil. Appeals 1969, U.S. Ct. Appeals (D.C. cir.) 1970, U.S. Supreme Ct. 1972, U.S. Dist. Ct. (so. dist.) N.Y. 1975. Atty. SEC, Washington, 1968-71; assoc. Skadden, Arps, Slate, Meagher & Flom, N.Y.C., 1971-76, ptnr., 1977—. Served with USCGR, 1967-73. Mem. ABA, N.Y. State Bar Assn. (corp. law sect.), Assn. of Bar of City of N.Y., Internat. Bar Assn., Beach Point Club. Republican. Jewish. Avocations: tennis, skiing, golf. Office: Skadden Arps Slate Meagher & Flom 4 Times Sq Fl 42 New York NY 10036-6522 E-mail: mstrom@skadden.com.

STROM, ROBERT DUANE, psychologist, educator; 2 children. BS, Macalester Coll., 1958; MA, U. Minn., 1959; PhD, U. Mich., 1962. Prof. U. Conn., Storrs, 1962—64, Ohio State U., Columbus, 1964—69, Ariz. State U., Tempe, 1969—. Author: (book) Teaching In The Slum School, 1965, Mental Health And Achievement, 1965, The Inner-City Classroom, 1966, Psychology For The Classroom, 1969, Experiences In Educational Psychology, 1970, Values And Human Development, 1972, Education For Affective Achievement, 1973, Parent And Child In Fiction, 1977, Parent And Child Development, 1978, Growing Through Play, 1981, Edcutional Psychology, 1982, Human Development And Learning, 1989, Grandparent Education, 1991, Becoming A Better Grandparent, 1991, Achieving Grandparent Potential, 1992, (measurement instruments) Grandparent Strengths and Needs Inventory, 1993, Parent As a Teacher Inventory, 1995, Parent Success Indicator, 1998, (book) Teaching Adolescents and Learning From Them, 2005, (measurement instruments) Interpersonal Intelligence Inventory, 2002. Scholar, Fulbright Found., 1975, 1976, 1985. Office: Coll Education Arizona State Univ Tempe AZ 85287-0611 E-mail: bob.strom@asu.edu.

STROMAN, SUSAN, choreographer, theater director; b. Wilmington, Del., Oct. 17, 1954; d. Charles and Frances Stroman; m. Mike Ockrent, 1996 (dec. Dec. 2, 1999); stepchildren: Ben, Natasha. Grad., U. Del. Choreographer Flora Roberts Inc. Dancer Chgo., 1977—78, Whoopee!, 1979, Richard III, 1980, Peter Pan, 1983, choreographer (off-Broadway) Broadway Babylon, 1984, Sayonara, 1987, Flora, the Red Menace, 1987, Shenandoah, 1988, Slasher, 1988, Rhythm Ranch, 1989, The Roar of the Greaspaint-The Smell of the Crowd, 1990, Gypsy, 1991, And the World Goes 'Round, 1991 (Outer Critics' Cir. award for choreography, 1991), A Christmas Carol, 1994, (Broadway plays) Crazy for You, 1992 (Tony award for best choreography, 1992, Drama Desk award for choreography, 1992, Outer Critics' Cir. award, 1992, Laurence Olivier award for choreography, 1993), Picnic, 1994, Show Boat, 1994 (Tony award for best choreography, 1995, Astaire award Theatre Devel. Fund, 1995), Big, 1996 (Tony nomination for best choreography, 1996), Oklahoma, 2002 (Laurence Olivier Award for choreography, 2002, Tony nomination for best choreography, 2002), (Operas) Don Giovanni, 1989, A Little Night Music, 1990, 100 in the Shade, 1992, (spl.) Liza Minnelli: Stepping Out at Radio City Music Hall, 1991 (Emmy nomination for choreography, 1993); choreographer, conceiver (Broadway plays) Steel Pier, 1997 (Tony nomination for best choreography, 1997), dir., choreographer The Music Man, 2000 (Tony nomination for best choreography, 2000, Tony nomination for best dir., 2000), The Producers, 2001 (Tony award for best choreography, 2001, Tony award for best dir., 2001, Drama Desk Award for best dir. musical, 2001), The Frogs, 2004, dir., choreographer, conceiver Contact, 2000 (Tony award for best choreography, 2000, Lucille Lortel Award for outstanding direction, 2000, Tony nomination for best dir., 2000), Thou Shalt Not, 2001; dir.: (Broadway plays) The Frogs, 2004; co-conceiver Trading Places, Equity Libr. Theatre Informals, 1983, dir., co-conceiver (off-Broadway) Living Color, 1986, co-conceiver, choreographer (TV spl.) Sondheim-A Celebration at Carnegie Hall, 1992, asst. dir., asst. choreographer (Broadway plays) Musical Chairs, 1980; dir.(TV spl.): An Evening With the Boston Pops-A Tribute to Leonard Bernstein, 1989. Recipient Disting. Achievement in Musical Theatre award, Drama League, 2001. Address: Flora Roberts Agy Penhouse A 157 W 57th St New York NY 10019-2210*

STROMBERG, CLIFFORD DOUGLAS, lawyer; b. NYC, June 1, 1949; s. George M. and Greta (Netzow) S.; m. Ava S. Feiner, June 25, 1972; children: Kimberly, Eric. BA summa cum laude, Yale U., 1971; JD, Harvard U., 1974. Bar: N.Y. 1975, D.C. 1975, U.S. Dist. Ct. (so. and ea. dists.) N.Y. 1975, U.S. Ct. Appeals (D.C. cir.) 1975, U.S. Ct. Appeals (2nd cir.) 1975, U.S. Supreme Ct. 1980. Law clk. to judge U.S. Dist. Ct. (ea. dist.) N.Y., 1974-75; assoc. Arnold & Porter, Washington, 1975-78, 80-83; dep. exec. sec. HHS, Washington, 1978-80; cons. FTC, Washington, 1980; ptnr. Dorsey & Whitney, Washington, 1983-84, Hogan & Hartson, Washington, 1984—. Adj. asst. prof. emergency medicine George Washington U. Sch. Medicine, 1991-97. Co-author: Mental Health and Law: A System in Transition, 1975, Alternatives to the Hospital: Ambulatory Surgery Centers and Emergicenters, 1984, Entrepreneurial Health Care: How to Structure Successful New Ventures, 1985, The Psychologist's Legal Handbook, 1988, Access to Hospital Information: Problems and Strategies: 4 Frontiers of Health Services Management 3-33, 1987, Healthcare Provider Networks: Antitrust Issues and Practical Considerations in Devels. in Antitrust Law, 1990, Healthcare Credentialing: Implications for Academic Medical Centers, 1991; mem. editl. bd. Harvard Law Rev., 1972-73; editor in chief Healthspan: The Report of Health Business and Law, 1984-87; cons. editor: Managed Care Law Strategist, 1999-2002; contbr. articles to profl. jours. Bd. dirs. Nat. Children's Eye Care Found., Washington, 1985-87. Teaching fellow in govt. Harvard U., 1973-74. Fellow Am. Bar Found.; mem. ABA (chair working group health care reform 1993-96, state membership chmn. 1984, bd. dirs. forum com. health law 1987-90, adv. com. govt. affirs 1993-98, governing bd., individual rights and responsibilities sect., exec. coun., 1980-90, sec. 1984-87, chair-elect 1987-88, chair 1988-89, legal aid and indigent defendants com. 1982-87), Am. Health Lawyers Assn., Nat. Assn. Coll. and Univ. Attys., Phi Beta Kappa. Office: Hogan & Hartson 555 13th St NW Washington DC 20004-1161 Office Phone: 202-637-5699. E-mail: cdstromberg@hhlaw.com.

STROMBERG, GREGORY, printing ink company executive; b. Milw., Feb. 10, 1948; s. Clifford Norman and Margaret Betty (Hoover) S.; m. Gail Elizabeth Steinbach, Aug. 22, 1970; children: Christopher, Brian, Ellen. BS, Marquette U., Milw., 1970. Office contact salesman Continental Can Co., Milw., 1970-78; sales rep. Sun Chem. Co., Milw., 1978-82; v.p., gen. mgr. Acme Printing Ink Co., Milw., 1982—; exec. v.p. Can. ops. Acme Printing Ink Can. Ltd., 1985—, pres., 1990—, v.p. sales/mktg. metal divsn., 2000—. Bd. dirs. Can. Ops. Acme Inks of Can.; pres. Toobee Internat., Inc., Milw., 1981—; v.p., dir. mktg. and internat. sales INX Internat. Ink Co., 1991—. Author: Toobee Air Force Flight Training Manual, 1983. Advisor Milw. Jr. Achievement, 1974; sponsor Muscular Dystrophy, 1983; asst. mem. com. toys for Tots, Children's Hosp., Milw., 1983; active United Meth. Men. Mem. Am. Mktg. Assn., Sales and Mktg. Execs. of Milw., Am. Mgmt. Assn., Am. Soc. Quality Control, Nat. Metal Decorators Assn., Nat. Assn. Printers and Lithographers, Nat. Assn. Printing Equipment and Suppliers. Home: N69w23448 Donna Dr Sussex WI 53089-3245 E-mail: mitze@execpc.com.

STROMBERG, JEAN WILBUR GLEASON, lawyer; b. St. Louis, Oct. 31, 1943; d. Ray Lyman and Martha (Bugbee) W.; m. Gerald Kermit Gleason, Aug. 28, 1966 (div. 1987); children: C. Blake, Peter Wilbur; m. Kurt Stromberg, Jan. 3, 1993; 1 child, Kristoffer Stromberg. BA, Wellesley Coll., 1965; LLB cum laude, Harvard U., 1968. Bar: Calif. 1969, D.C. 1978. Assoc. Brobeck, Phleger & Harrison, San Francisco, 1969-72; spl. counsel to dir. div. corp. fin. SEC, Washington, 1972-76, assoc. dir. div. investment mgmt., 1976-78; of counsel Fulbright & Jaworski, Washington, 1978-80, ptnr., 1980-96; dir. fin. instns. and market issues GAO, Washington, 1996-97; cons. Washington, 1997—. Mem. adv. panel on legal issues GAO, 1992—96; mem. NASD select com. on NASDAQ, 1994—96; trustee AARP Intestment Program and AARP Scudder Mut. Funds, 1997—2000; bd. dirs. Scudder Mut. Funds., Svc. Source, Inc., Mut. Fund Dirs. Forum. Dir. William and Flora Hewlett Found., 2000—; overseer Wellesley Ctrs. Women, 2003-. Mem. ABA (chmn. subcom. on securities and banks, corp. laws com., bus. sect. 1982-93), D.C. Bar Assn. (chmn. steering com. bus. sect. 1982-84), FBA (chair exec. coun., securities com. 1993-95), Am. Bar Retirement Assn. (bd. dirs. 1986-90, 94-96), Phi Beta Kappa. Home and Office: 3816 Military Rd NW Washington DC 20015-2704

STROMBERG, ROSS ERNEST, lawyer; b. Arcata, Calif., May 5, 1940; s. Noah Anders and Anne Laura (Noyes) S.; m. Toni Nicholas, Dec. 16, 1961; m. Margaret Telonicher, Oct. 3, 1965; children: Kristin, Matthew, Gretchen, Erik. BS, Humboldt State U., 1962; JD, U. Calif., Berkeley, 1965. Bar: Calif. 1966, U.S. Dist. Ct. (no. dist.) Calif. 1966, U.S. Ct. Appeals (9th cir.) 1966. Assoc. Hanson Bridgett, San Francisco, 1965-70, ptnr., 1970-85, Epstein Becker Stromberg & Green, San Francisco, 1985-90, Jones Day, San Francisco, 1990—. Chmn. Jones Day's Healthcare Specialized Industry Practice; pres. Shyster Creek Vineyards, Healdsburg, Calif., 2002—. Author: Economic Joint Venturing, 1985, Acquisition and Enhancement of Physician Practices, 1988. Bd. dirs. Sutter Med. Ctr., Santa Rosa, 2001—; pres. Am. Acad. Hosp. Attys. of Am. Host. Assn., Chgo., 1978; chair Sutter Med. Ctr., Santa Rosa, 2003—, Pediat. Dental Initiative of the North Coast, Healdsburg, Calif., 2004; pres. East Bay AHEC, Oakland, Calif., 1984—87; bd. dirs. Am. Cancer Soc., Oakland, 1984—95, Wildflowers Inst., San Francisco, 1984—. Mem. Am. Health Lawyers Assn. Democrat. Office: Jones Day 555 Calif St 26th Fl San Francisco CA 94104 Office Phone: 415-875-5724.

STROMBOM, DAVID GLEN, designer; b. Pullman, Wash., Apr. 18, 1951; s. Donald A. and Dona S. (Bell) S.; m. Cathy J. (Powers), June 17, 1972; 1 child, Paul Davis. Student, Whitman Coll., 1968—70; BS in Architecture, Wash. State U., 1973; MArch, Harvard U., 1977. Registered arch., Wash. Vol. U.S. Peace Corps, Marrakech, Morocco, 1973-75; designer Seattle, 1978-82; prin. The Strombom Architects, Seattle, 1982-91; dir. David Roberts Bowman, Ltd., 1991—; assoc. Internat. Devel. Bus. Cons., Washington, 1996—, Islamabad, Pakistan, 1996, Port au Prince, Haiti, 1997-99, Bali, Indonesia, 1999, Chiang Mai, Thailand, 1999, Venice, Italy, 2002. Fulbright scholar Ahmedabad, India, 1977-78; vis. prof. Ahmedabad Sch. Architecture; designer Ctr. Devel. Studies and Activities, Pune, India. Office Phone: 206-283-1023.

STROME, MARSHALL, otolaryngologist, educator; b. Lynn, Mass., Apr. 27, 1940; s. David and Rose (Cantor) S.; m. Deena Lazarov, Sept. 23, 1962; children: Scott Eric, Randall Alan. Degree, U. Mich., 1960, MD, 1964, MS, 1970. Resident in otolaryngology U. Mich., Ann Arbor, 1966-70; asst. prof. U. Conn., Hartford, 1971, Beth Israel-Harvard, Boston, 1972-77, chief otolaryngology, 1977-93; prof., chmn. otolaryngology Cleve. Clinic Found., 1993—. Sr. surgeon Brigham & Women's Hosp., Boston, 1982-93; assoc. prof. harvard Med. Sch., Boston, 1989-93, Longwood ORL coord., 1982-90; mem. cons. bd. Xomed Treace Corp., Jacksonville, Fla., 1987-90; advisor SLT Laser Corp., Oaks, Pa., 1994—; dir. Great Comebacks, Gresham, Oreg.; prof. otolaryngology Cleve. Clinic Found. Health Scis. Ctr. Ohio State U., 1994; hon. guest, prin. spkr. Turkish Otolaryngol. Soc., 1997; Qgura lectr., 2000; mem. sci. adv. bd. Somnus Corp.; pres. Soc. Univ. Otolaryngologists, 2002—. Mem. editl. bd. Harvard Health News Letter, 1976-85; author: Differential Diagnoses in Pediatric ORL, 1975; editor: Manual of Otolaryngology, 1985, Complications of Laser Surgery of the Head and Neck, 1986; transplanted 1st total human larynx, 1998. Mem. fund raising com. Belmont Hill (Mass.) Sch., 1984. Capt. U.S. Army, 1965-71. Recipient Medal City of Paris, 1987, Sword of Saudi Arabia, 1991, Cert. of Appreciation, Ministry of Health-Singapore, 1995, Presdl. citation Coll. Physicians and Surgeons of Pakistan, Classic Telly award, 1999; named One of Best Doctors in Cleve., Cleve. Mag., 1995—, One of Best Drs. in Am., 1996—, Outstanding People of 20th Century, 1999, Medical Hero Guiness Book of World Records, 2000. Mem.: Triological Soc. (v.p. 1990—91), Cartesian Soc. (pres. 1999), Soc. Univ. Otolaryngologists (pres. 2003), Am. Soc. Head and Neck Surgery, Am. Acad. Otolaryngology (Honor award 1987, one of nine recognized for conbtn. to medicine in last 250 years 1999, Internat. Scientist of Yr. 2002), Am. Acad. Facial Plastic Reconstructive Surgery (Medallion of Honor 1989), U. Mich. Med. Ctr. Alumni Soc. (coord. New Eng. Fund. Raising 1992, chair bd. govs. 1992—93, Cleve. Clinic tchr. of yr. 2002). Avocations: bicycling, skiing, sculling, sea kyacking, tennis. Office: Cleve Clinic Found 9500 Euclid Ave Cleveland OH 44195-0001

STROME, STEPHEN, distribution company executive; b. Lynn, Mass., June 20, 1945; s. David and Rose (Cantor) S.; m. Phyllis Ruth Fields, Jan. 14, 1967; children: Michael, Rochelle. BA, Hillsdale (Mich.) Coll., 1967; MBA, Wayne State U., 1968. Trainee KMart Corp., Detroit, 1968-69, mgr. work measurement Troy, Mich., 1970-73; mgr. tng., edn. Fruehauf Corp., Detroit, 1974-76, regional mgr. labor relations, 1976-78; dir. ops. Handleman Co., Clawson, Mich., 1978-80, account exec., 1980-82, v.p. computer software div. Troy, 1983-85, pres. computer software/video div., 1986-87, exec. v.p., 1987-89, exec. v.p., chief oper. officer, 1990, pres., CEO, 1991-2001, chmn., CEO, 2001—. Home: 4597 Kiftsgate Bnd Bloomfield Hills MI 48302-2331 Office: Handleman Co 500 Kirts Blvd Troy MI 48084-4142

STROMINGER, JACK LEONARD, biochemist; b. N.Y.C., Aug. 7, 1925; AB, Harvard U., 1944; MD, Yale U., 1948; DSc (hon.), Trinity Coll., Dublin, 1975, Washington U., 1988. From asst. prof. to prof. pharmacology sch. med. Washington U., St. Louis, 1955-61, prof. pharmacology and microbiology, 1961-64; prof. pharmacology and chem. microbiology med. sch. U. Wis., Madison, 1964-68; prof. biochemistry Harvard U., 1968-83, chmn. dept. biochemistry and molecular biology, 1970-73, Higgins prof. biochemistry, 1983—; head tumor virol. divsn. Dana-Farber Cancer Inst., Boston, 1977—. Recipient John J. Abel award, 1960, Paul-Lewis Lab award, 1962, Rose Payne award Am. Soc. Histocompat. & Immunogen., 1986, Hoechst-Roussel award, 1990, Pasteur medal, 1990, Albert Lasker Award for Basic Med. Rsch., 1995; named Passano Found. laureate, 1993. Mem. NAS (mem. inst. medicine, Microbiology award 1968, Selman Waxman award 1968), AAAS, Am. Soc. Biol. Chemists, Am. Soc. Pharmacology & Exptl. Therapeutics, Am. Assn. Immunologists, Am. Soc. Microbiologists, Am. Chem. Soc., Am. Acad. Arts & Sci., European Molecular Biol. Orgn., Sigma Xi. Address: Harvard U Dept Molecular & Cell Bio 7 Divinity Ave Cambridge MA 02138-2019 Office: Dana Farber Cancer Inst Dept Biochem 44 Binney St Boston MA 02115-6084

STROMME, GARY L. law librarian; b. Willmar, Minn., July 8, 1939; s. William A. and Edla A. Stromme; m. Suzanne Readman, July 21, 1990. BA, Pacific Luth. U., 1965; BLS, U. B.C., Vancouver, Can., 1967; JD, U. Calif., San Francisco, 1973. Bar: Calif. 1973, U.S. Supreme Ct. 1977. Serials libr. U. Minn. St. Paul. Campus Libr., 1967-69; asst. libr. McCutchen, Doyle, Brown and Enerson, San Francisco, 1970-71, Graham & James, San Francisco, 1971-73, ind. contracting atty., 1973-74; law libr. Pacific Gas and Electric Co., San Francisco, 1974-95; cons., 1995—. Lectr. in field. Author: An Introduction to the use of the Law Library, 1974, 76, Basic Legal Research Techniques, 1979. With USAF, 1959-63. Mem. ABA (chmn. libr. com. of sect. econs. of law practice 1978-82), Am. Assn. Law Librs. (chmn. com. on indexing of legal periodicals 1986-88), Western Pacific Assn. Law Librs., No. Calif. Assn. Law Librs., Pvt. Law Librs., Corp. Law Librs. Home: 6106 Ocean View Dr Oakland CA 94618-1841 E-mail: stromme1@earthlink.net.

STROMMEN, MERTON PETER, research psychologist, clergyman; b. Calumet, Mich., Mar. 31, 1919; s. Peter Andrew and Nellie (Framstad) S.; m. Irene Anna Huglen, June 23, 1944; children: Peter, Timothy, James, John, David. BA, Augsburg Coll., Mpls., 1942; BTh, Augsburg Theol. Sem., Mpls., 1944; MA, U. Minn., 1956, PhD, 1960. Ordained to ministry Luth. Ch., 1944; cert. cons. psychologist, Minn. Nat. youth dir. Luth. Free Ch., Mpls., 1944-58; parish pastor Calvary Luth. Ch., Mora, Minn., 1943-47; campus pastor Augsburg Coll., 1947-58; exec. dir. Search Inst., Mpls., 1958-85, Augsburg Inst., Mpls., 1986-90; rsch. psychologist Mpls., 1990—. Author: Profiles of Church Youth, 1963, Bridging the Gap, 1973, Five Cries of Youth, 1988, The Innovative Church, 1997; co-author: A Study of Generations, 1972, Ministry in America, 1980, How Church Related Are Church-Related Colleges?, 1980, Five Shaping Forces, 1982, Ten Faces of Ministry, 1979, Five Cries of Parents, 1985, Five Cries of Grief, 1990; editor: Research on Religious Development: A Comprehensive Handbook, 1971, Passing on the Faith, 2000, Transformational Youth Ministry, 2000, The Church and Homosexuality: Searching for Middle Ground, 2001, Augsburg Gospel Quartets: A Mission-Driven Story, 2004. Mem. bd. regents Augsburg Coll., 1980-88; mem. Richfield (Minn.) Sch. Bd., 1970-80. Recipient Preus award Luth. Brotherhood, Mpls., 1956; named Disting. Alumnus, Augsburg Coll., 1970. Fellow APA (William James award 1983). Democrat. Avocations: piano, choral directing, reading, hiking, sports. Home: 7005 Garfield Ave Minneapolis MN 55423-3057

STROMQUIST, KENNETH JAMES, JR., pilot, retired military officer; m. Edna Dyrud; children: Virginia, Paul. BBA, U. Minn., 1968; grad., USMC Weapons, Tactics Instrn., 1969, Air Command Staff Coll., 1979, Air War Coll., 1993. Commd. 2d lt. USAF, 1968, forward air controller, 1969-70; pilot instr. T-41, T-33 USAF Acad. Aerospace Defense Command, Peterson AFB, Colo., 1970-73; pilot, flight comdr., unit plans officer, officer in charge of alert forces Duluth (Minn.) Air Nat. Guard, 1973-90; comdr. detachment 1, 148 Fighter Wing USAF, Tyndall AFB, Fla., 1990-93; advisor Air Nat. Guard NORAD/USSPACECOM, Peterson AFN, Colo.; air comdr. 148 fighter wing Duluth Air Nat. Guard Base, 1995-98, wing comdr. 148 fighter wing, 1997-98; vice comdr. First Air Force USAF, Tyndall AFB, Fla., 1998-99, ret.; pilot Frontier Airlines, Denver. Past Minn. State pres. Nat. Guard Assn. U.S. Decorated Legion of Merit, Disting. Flying Cross, Purple Heart, Air medal, Meritorious Svc. medal.

STRONACH, BELINDA, former retail executive; b. Newmarket, Ont., Can., May 2, 1966; d. Frank Stronach; m. Donald Walker, 1990 (div. 1995); children: Nikki 2 children; m. Johann Olov Koss, 2000 (div. 2003). Student, York U., Toronto; JD (hon.), McMaster U. With Magna Internat. Inc., Aurora, Canada, 1985—2004, CEO, 2001—04, pres., 2002—04. Mem., bd. dirs. Magna Internat. Inc., 1988—2004, U.S. Chamber of Commerce; mem., Dean's Coun. J.F.K. Sch. Govt., Harvard U.; mem., Dean's Advisory Coun. Joseph L. Rotman Sch. Mgmt., U. Toronto; ran for leadership of Can. Conservative Party, 2004. Named Most Powerful Businesswoman in Can., Nat. Post, 2001.

STRONACH, CAREY ELLIOTT, physicist, researcher; b. Boston, Aug. 8, 1940; s. Ralph Howard and Frances Burns (Maynard) S.; m. Joan Alice Louise Venner, Aug. 20, 1966; children: John Maynard, Howard Stanley. BS, U. Richmond, Va., 1961; MS, U. Va., 1963; PhD, Coll. William and Mary, 1976. Instr. physics Va. State U., Petersburg, 1965-66, asst. prof., 1966—76, assoc. prof., 1976—80, prof., 1980—. Dir. Muon Spin Rotation Rsch. Program, 1977—, Superconducting Materials Rsch. Program, 1988-97, Nanostructured Materials Rsch. Program, 1997-2001, Galactic Cosmic Radiation Rsch. Program, 1993-97, U.S.-France Joint Muon Spin Rotation Rsch. Program, 1985-91, Magnetic Materials Lab. Devel. Program, 1999-2001; radiation safety officer; mem. Solid State Physics Rsch. Inst., 1983-87; founding dir. Ctr. Interactive Micromagnetics, 2001—; vis. assoc. prof. U. Alta, 1978-79; guest scientist Brookhaven Nat. Lab.; organizing com. Internat. Symposium on the Electronic Structure and Properties of Hydrogen in Metals, 1982, Internat. Symposium on the Physics and Chemistry of Small Clusters, 1986, From Clusters to Crystals, 1991, Sci. and Tech. Atomically Engineered Materials, 1995, Internat. Symposium on Cluster and Nanostructure Interfaces, 1999, Internat. Symposium Clusters and Nano-Assemblies: From Physical to Life Sciences, 2003; adv. com. Internat. Conf. on Muon Spin Rotation, 1996-99; sci. adv. com. European Workshop on the Spectroscopy of Subatomic Species in Non-Metallic Solids, 1985, govs. com. on Superconducting Supercollider, 1987; TV physics lectr., 1991-94; chair adv. com. Internat. Conf. on Muon Spin Rotation, 1999-2002. Contbr. numerous articles to publs. in field; playwright. Pres. Petersburg area chpt. Va. Coun. Human Rels., 1965—67; active Petersburg Commn. Cmty. Rels. Affairs, 1974—77; long-range transp. adv. com. City of Petersburg, 1994—98; steering com. Gilmore for Gov., 1997; active Dramatists Guild; sec. adv. coun. bds. and commns. Commonwealth Coun., 1998—2002; active Richmond Playwrights Forum, 1999—, Virginians for Warner, 2001; corr. sec. Petersburg Dem. Com., 1974—77, active, 1972—85, vice chmn., 1981—85. Fellow duPont Corp., 1961-63, NSF, 1971-72, NASA, 1976; recipient Patrick Henry award Va. Gov. James C. Gilmore III, 2001. Mem.: AAUP (chpt. pres. 1968—70), AAAS, Air Force Assn., Internat. Soc. on Muon Spectroscopy (founding mem.), WWII Meml. Soc. (charter), Sci. Netlinks Adv. Bd., N.Y. Acad. Scis., Planetary Soc., High Speed Rail/Maglev Assn. (govt. rels. com. 1992—97, Maglev task force 1994—97), Va. Assn. Scholars (bd. govs. 1999—, pres. 2004—), Southeastern Univs. Rsch. Assn. (site sel. com. 1980—81, materials sci. com. 1983—86, trustee 1983—98, sci. and tech. com. 1986—88, rules com. 1988—92, edn. com. 1992—94, new projects com. 1994—95, Jefferson Lab. com. 1995—98), Va. Acad. Sci. (sec. astronomy, math. and physics sect 1983—84, chmn. 1984—85, pres. 2004—), Nat. Assn. Scholars, Am. Assn. Physics Tchrs., Am. Phys. Soc., Va. Inst. Public Policy (assoc.), Tri-univ. Meson Facility Users Group, Richmond Area Free Thinkers, Coun. Secular Humanism (assoc.), Pi Mu Epsilon, Sigma Pi Sigma, Sigma Xi (chpt. sec. 1977—78, chpt. pres. 1980—84, 1987—88), Phi Beta Kappa. Achievements include co-devel. of low-energy muon beam line at the AGS of Brookhaven Nat. Lab.; rsch. in pion-nucleus interactions, heavy-ion reactions, muon spin rotation studies of high-temperature superconductors and related materials, fullerenes, heavy-fermion materials, ferromagnetic metals, metal hydrides, fatigue in metals and other materials; participation in the establishment of the Southeastern Universities Research Association and the Thomas Jefferson Nat. Accelerator Facility; discovery of formation of muonium and muonated radicals in Buckminsterfullerene; discovery of simultaneous high-temp. superconductivity and magnetic ordering in strontium yttrium ruthenate. Home: 2241 Buckner St Petersburg VA 23805-2207 Office: Va State U PO Box 9325 Petersburg VA 23806-0001 Office Phone: 804-524-5915. Business E-Mail: cstronac@vsu.edu.

STRONE, MICHAEL JONATHAN, lawyer; b. N.Y.C., Feb. 26, 1953; s. Bernard William and Judith Semel (Sogg) S.; m. Andrea Nan Acker, Jan. 27, 1979; children: Noah Gregory, Joshua Samuel. BA cum laude, Colby Coll., 1974; JD, Fordham Law Sch., 1978. Bar: N.J. 1978, N.Y. 1979, Conn. 1988, U.S. Ct. Appeals (2d and 3d cirs.) 1979, U.S. Dist. Ct. (so. and ea. dists.) N.Y. 1979, U.S. Dist. Ct. N.J. 1979. Assoc. Ratheim Hoffman et al, N.Y.C., 1978-80, Botein Hays et al, N.Y.C., 1980-84; v.p., assoc. gen. counsel, asst. sec. GE Investment Corp., Stamford, Conn., 1984-2000; v.p., gen. counsel real estate GE Asset Mgmt. Inc., 2000—02, sr. cons., 2002—; pres., CEO Oracle Investment Advisors, LLC, 2002—; CEO Oracle Fin., LLC, 2004—. Cons. First Am. Title Ins. Co., 2002—. Bd. dirs. N.Y. chpt. Juvenile Diabetes Found., N.Y.C., 1981-89, vice chmn., 1981-88; mem. fin. com. Juvenile Diabetes

Found. Internat., 1981-86; asst. prin. bassist Westchester Symphony Orch., Scarsdale, N.Y., 1982-2000, pres., 1982-87, chmn. bd., 1982-90, exec. mng. dir., 1990-93; vice chmn. ann. dinner NCCJ, 1987; bd. dirs. Parkinson's Disease Found., 1989-96, chmn. merger com., 1991-96; bd. dirs. Parkinson's Action Network, 1994-98, trustee Jewish Cmty. Ctr. of Harrison, 1996—2003, mem. ritual com., 1996—, chmn., 2000-03, chmn. alt. svcs. com., lay cantor, 1997—; chmn. county United Way Campaign, 1999, bd. dirs., gen. coun. Harrison Little League, 2001—; bd. dirs., v.p., gen. counsel Mariners Hockey, Inc., 2003—, v.p. adminstrn., 2004—; mem. zoning bd. appeals, Village of Harrison, 2003—. Recipient Gerald I. Phillippe award for dist. cmty. svc., Juvenile Diabetes Found., 1994, Lifetime Achievement award, 2003. Mem. ABA (chmn. pension plan investments 1989-91, chmn. asset mgmt. 1992-94, 95-97, significant legis. coms. 1985-92, chmn. subcom. on joint ventures 1988-90), Am. Coll. Real Estate Lawyers (com. professionalism 1994—, vice chmn. 1999-2000), Am. Polit. Items Collectors, The Corp. Bar Assn., Nat. Assn. Real Estate Investment Mgrs. (sr. legal officers adv. com. 1993-2003, ann. forum chair 1997), Colby Coll. Alumni Coun. (nominating com. 1994-97), Fordham Law Alumni Assn., The Internat. Netsuke Soc., Jewish Geneal. Soc. Republican. Home: 10 Genesee Trail Harrison NY 10528-1802 Office: PO Box 6 Harrison NY 10528-0006 Office Phone: 914-899-9000. Personal E-mail: mstrone@oracleinvest.com. Business E-Mail: michael@strone.org.

STRONG, DOROTHY SWEARENGEN, school system administrator; b. Feb. 3, 1934; d. John Harrison and Willie Beatrice (Hawkins) Swearengen; m. Joseph Nathaniel Strong, Mar. 19, 1953; 1 child, Joronda Ramette Crawford. BS in Edn., Chgo. State U., 1958, MA in Math. Edn., 1964; EdD, Nova U., 1985. Elem. and secondary tchr. Chgo. Pub. Schs., 1958-65, dir. math., 1976-94; co-prin. investigator Access 2000, 1991-93, dir. NSF Urban Systemic Initiative, 1993-94, regional coord., 1994-96; dir. Bimathematics Project, 1996—2001; pres. Edn. Support Group, Chgo., 2001—. Dir. Pre-Algebra Devel. Ctrs., 1967—84; instr. Chgo. State U., 1969—71; mem. Commn. Tchr. Edn., Task Force Math. Urban Ctrs., Ill. Basic Skills Adv. Coun., Nat. Inst. Edn. Conf. Basic Skills; mem. coun. acad. affairs Coll. Bd., v.p., 1983—86; mem. in-svc. handbook com. Allendale Sch. Boys, 1972, bd. dirs., 1974—, mem. com. educating tchrs. math., 1974—77, mem. ann. regional meeting, 1977—84. Author: (book) Modern Mathematics Structure and Use-Spirit Masters, 1977, Pre-Algebra Unit Packs: Ratios and Proportions, Fractions, Decimals, Percent, Measurements; co-author: Bible Mathematics Book I, 1995, Algebra for Everyone; contbr. articles to profl. jours. Co-leader People-to-People South African Amb. team, 2000; pres. United Pentecostal coun. Assemblies of God, 1995—2002, v.p., midwest dir., dir. Christian edn. Home: 2820 Paris Rd Olympia Fields IL 60461-1826 Personal E-mail: dorothyss@aol.com.

STRONG, GARY EUGENE, librarian; b. Moscow, Idaho, June 26, 1944; s. Authur Dwight and Cleora Anna (Nirk) S.; m. Carolyn Jean Roetker, Mar. 14, 1970; children: Christopher Eric, Jennifer Rebecca. BS in Edn., U. Idaho, 1966; AMLS, U. Mich., 1967. Adminstrv. and reference asst. U. Idaho, 1963-66; extension librarian Latah County Free Library, Moscow, 1966; head librarian Markeley Residence Library, U. Mich., 1966-67; library dir. Lake Oswego (Oreg.) Public Library, 1967-73, Everett (Wash.) Public Library, 1973-76; asso. dir. services Wash. State Library, Olympia, 1976-79, dep. state librarian, 1979-80; state librarian Calif. State Library, Sacramento, 1980-94; dir. Queens Borough Pub. Libr., Jamaica, 1994—2003; dir. emeritus Calif. State Library Found., 1994—; Univ. libr. UCLA, 2003—. Adj. prof. Queens Coll. Grad. Sch. of Libr. and Info. Scis., 2000-03; chief exec. Calif. Libr. Svcs. Bd., 1980-94; founder, bd. dirs. Calif. State Libr. Found., 1982-94, Calif. Literary Campaign, 1984-94, Calif. Rsch. Bur., 1992; bd. dirs. No. Regional Libr. Bd., 1983-94, Queens Libr. Found., 1994-2003; mem. adv. bd. Ctr. for Book in Libr. of Congress, 1983-86; mem. nat. adv. com. Libr. of Congress, 1987-89; chmn. adv. bd. Calif. Libr. Constrn. and Renovation Bond Act Bd., 1989-94; vis. lectr. Marylhurst Coll., Oreg., 1968, Oreg. Divsn. Continuing Edn., 1972, San Jose State U. Sch. Libr. Svc., 1990; mem. N.Y. State Adv. Coun. Librs., 1996-97; mem. chancellor's task froce ednl. tech. and librs. CUNY, 1996-97; convenor Archons of the Colophan, 1997-98; regents adv. coun. librs. N.Y. State, 1999-2003; lectr. and cons. in field. Host, producer: cable TV Signatures Program, 1974-76, nationwide videoconfs. on illiteracy, censorship, 1985; author: On Reading-in the Year of the Reader, 1987, U.S. Patriot's Act: Protecting Patron's Rights, 2002; editor Calif. State Library Found. Bull., 1982-94 (H.W. Wilson Periodical award 1988), Western Americana in the Calif. State Library, 1986, On Reading-In the Year of the Reader, 1987, Chinatown Photographer: Louis J. Stellman, 1989, Local History Genealogical Resources, 1990, Literate America Emerging, 1991; curator Queens Libr. Gallery, 1998; contbr. articles to profl. jours.; editor, designer and pub. of various books. Bd. dirs., v.p. Pacific N.W. Bibliog. Ctr., 1977-80; bd. dirs. Thurston Mason County Mental Health Ctr., 1977-80, pres., 1979-80; bd. dirs. Coop. Library Agy. for Sys. and Svcs., 1980-94, vice chmn., 1981-84; bd. dirs. Sr. Svcs. Snohomish County, 1973-76, HISPANEX (Calif. Spanish lang. database), 1983-86; bd. govs. Snohomish County Hist. Assn., 1974-76; mem. psychiat. task force St. Peters Hosp., Olympia, 1979-80; co-founder Calif. Ctr. for the Book, bd. dirs., 1987-94; mem. adv. bd. Calif. State PTA, 1981-86, Gov.'s Tech. Conf., 1993-94; mem. adv. com. Sch. Libr. Sci., UCLA, 1991-94, Sch. Libr. and Info. Studies, U. Calif., Berkeley, 1991-94, Libr. Sch. Queens Coll., 1996-2003, libr. sch. St. John's U., 1996-98; mem. Oreg. Coun. Pub. Broadcasting, 1969-73, Calif. Adult Edn. Steering Com., 1988-94, N.Y. State Adv. Coun. on Librs., 1996-97; chmn. collaborative coun. Calif. State Literacy Resource Ctr., 1993-94; bd. dirs. Queens coun. Boy Scouts Am., 1994-2003; v.p. 100 Yr. Assn. N.Y., 1996-2003; mem. Chancellor's Task Force on Ednl. Tech. and Librs., CUNY, 1996-97; participant N.Y. Pub. Libr. Conf. of World Libr. Leaders, 1996; trustee Flushing Cemetery Assn., 1998-2003; mem. com. on intellectual property rights and the engring. info. infrastructure Nat. Rsch. Coun., 1998-2000; chair organizing com. China-U.S. Libr. Conf., 2001. Oreg. Libr. scholar, 1966; recipient Disting. Alumnus award U. Mich., 1984, Disting. Svc. award Calif. Literacy Inc., 1985, Spl. Achievement award Literacy Action, 1988, Assn. Specialized and Coop. Libr. Agys. Exceptional Achievement award 1992, Gov.'s award of Achievement Govt. Tech. Conf., 1994, Advancement of Literacy award Pub. Libr. Assn., 1994, John Cotton Dana award Libr. Adminstrn. and Mgmt. Assn., 1994, Chartie Robinson award PLA, 2002; named Libr. of Yr. Calif. Assn. Libr. Trustees and Commrs., 1994, Disting. Svc. award Chinese Am. Libr. Assn., 1996, 21st Century Libr. award Syracuse U., 2002, Bus. Person of Yr., Queens C. of C., 2002. Mem.: Assn. Specialized and Coop. Libr. Agys., Western Coun. State Librs. (pres. 1989—91), Chief Officers of State Libr. Agys. (pres. 1984—86), Calif. Libr. Assn. (govt. rels.com. 1980—94), Pacific N.W. Libr. Assn. (hon. life mem., pres. 1978—79), Oreg. Libr. Assn. (hon. life mem., pres. 1970—71), N.Y. Libr. Assn., Libr. Adminstrn. and Mgmt. Assn. (bd. dis. 1980—88, pres. 1984—85), Am. Printing History Assn., ALA (legis. com. 1980—82, Commn. on Freedom and Equality of Access to Info. 1983—86, legis. com. 1995—97, chair intellectual property subcom. 1995—98, chmn. conf. librs. Beijing 1996, rep. Internat. Fedn. of Libr. Assn. nat. organizing com. 1996—2001, intellectual property com. 1998—2001, Fedn. of Libr. Assn. UN rep. 2001—03, Humphrey award for Internat. Librarianship 2003), METRO (bd. dirs. 1994—2003, treas. 1996—99, 1st v.p. 1999—2001), Queens County C. of C. (bd. dirs. 1996—2003, named Bus. Person of Yr. 2002), Jamaica Devel. Corp., Everett Area C. of C. (bd. dirs. 1974—76), The Typophiles, Guild of Book Workers, Grolier Club, The Book Collectors Club of L.A., Roxburghe Club, Sacramento Book Collectors Club, Book Club of Calif. Office: UCLA Lirb Box 951575 Los Angeles CA 90095-1575 E-mail: gstrong@library.ucla.edu.

STRONG, GEORGE GORDON, JR., litigation and management consultant; b. Toledo, Apr. 19, 1947; s. George Gordon and Jean Boyd (McDougall) S.; m. Annsley Palmer Chapman, Nov. 30, 1974; children: George III, Courtney, Meredith, Alexis. BA, Yale U., 1969; MBA, Harvard U., 1971; JD, U. San Diego, 1974. Bar: Calif. 1974, U.S. Dist. Ct. (cen. dist.) Calif. 1974; CPA, Calif., Hawaii, cert. mgmt. cons. Contr. Vitredent Corp., Beverly Hills, Calif., 1974-76; sr. mgr. Price Waterhouse, L.A., 1976-82, ptnr., 1987—2001, mng. ptnr. west region dispute analysis and corp. recovery, 1993—99, mem. policy bd., bd. dirs., 1995-98, combination bd., 1997-98; bd. ptnrs., prin Pricewaterhouse Coopers LLP, L.A., 1998-2001, global oversight bd., 1998—2001; exec. v.p., COO Internat. Customs Service, Long Beach, Calif., 1982-84; CFO Uniform Software Systems, Santa Monica, Calif., 1984-85; exec. v.p., COO Cipherlink Corp., 1986; pres. Woodleigh Lane, Inc., Flintridge, Calif., 1985-87; mng. dir., gen. counsel Cornerstone Rsch., 2002—. Chmn. bd. dirs. L.A. SPCA; bd. dirs. Pasadena Pops Orch. Mem. ABA, AICPA, Calif. State Bar, Calif. Soc. CPAs, Andover Abbott Alumni So. Calif. (bd. dirs., treas.), Inst. Mgmt. Cons., Harvard Bus. Sch. Alumni Assn. (bd. dirs. 1996-99), Harvard Bus. Sch. Assn. So. Calif. (chmn. bd. trustees scholarship fund 1992—, pres. 1988-89, dir. 1996-99, 2001-03), Harvard Club N.Y., Harvard Club Boston, Yale Club N.Y., Lincoln Club, Calif. Club, Jonathan Club, Annandale Golf Club, Coral Beach and Tennis Club, Mid Ocean Golf Club, Royal Bermuda Yacht Club, Valley Hunt Club, Tuckers Point Golf Club (Bermuda). Republican. Presbyterian. Avocations: golf, tennis, bridge. Home: 5455 Castle Knoll Rd La Canada Flintridge CA 91011-1319 Office: 555 S Flower St #2750 Los Angeles CA 90071-2300 Office Phone: 213-553-2500. Personal E-mail: gstrong@cornerstone.com.

STRONG, GEORGE HOTHAM, private investor, consultant; b. Johnstown, Pa., July 15, 1926; s. George Hite and Mary Elizabeth (Hotham) S.; m. Mary Louise Lyon, Sept. 19, 1953; children: Cynthia Strong Hibbard, Dexter, Sarah Strong Bornstein. AB magna cum laude, Allegheny Coll, 1949; MBA, Harvard U., 1951. V.p. Smith Barney & Co., NYC & Boston, 1951-67, Norlin Corp., NYC, 1967-73, Am. Medicorp, Bala-Cynwyd, Pa., 1974-78; cons. A.D. Little, Cambridge, Mass., 1973-74; sr. v.p., dir. Universal Health Svcs., King of Prussia, Pa., 1978-84; pvt. practice investor NYC, 1985—. Served on 16 pub. and pvt. corp. bds. Served to sgt. U.S. Army, 1944—46, Italy. Mem. Harvard Club (NYC), Union League Club (Phila.), Seabright (NJ) Lawn Tennis Club, Seabright Beach Club, Rumson (NJ) Country Club, Phi Beta Kappa. Republican. Episcopalian. Home: 946 Navesink River Rd Rumson NJ 07760-2330

STRONG, HENRY, foundation executive; b. Rochester, NY, Oct. 6, 1923; s. L. Corrin and Alice (Trowbridge) S.; m. Malan Swing, June 30, 1951; children: Sigrid Anne, Barbara Kirk, Dana Elizabeth, Henry Lockwood. AB, Williams Coll., 1949; LHD, Mt. Vernon Coll., 1999. Joined Fgn. Service, 1950; with State Dept., 1950-51; vice consul The Hague, 1951-54, Washington, 1954-55; 2d sec. US Embassy, Copenhagen, 1955-58, State Dept., 1958-62, Djakarta, Indonesia, 1962-64; resigned, 1968; chmn. bd., pres. Hattie M. Strong Found., 1968—. Mem. D.C. Commn. Arts, 1968-75; mem. DC Bd. Higher Edn., 1973-76; vice chmn. bd. trustees J.F. Kennedy Ctr. for Performing Arts, 1975-90, hon. trustee, 1991—; bd. dir. Nat. Symphony Orch., Pomfret Sch., 1967-1990, M.M. Post Found. DC, Community Found. of Greater Washington, 1974-91, Mt. Vernon Coll., 1969-88, 91-98, Nat. Capital chpt. ARC, 1994—. Lt. (j.g.) USNR, 1943-46. Mem.: Chevy Chase; Metropolitan (Washington); Gibson Island (Md.). Republican. Episcopalian. Home: 5039 Overlook Rd NW Washington DC 20016-1911 Office: Hattie M Strong Found 1620 I St NW Ste 700 Washington DC 20006-4005

STRONG, JACK PERRY, pathologist, educator; b. Birmingham, Ala., Apr. 27, 1928; m. Mihoko Strong; 4 daus. BS, U. Ala., 1948; MD, La. State U., 1951. Diplomate Am. Bd. Pathology (trustee 1980-92, sec. 1985-87, v.p. 1988-89, pres. 1990-92, rep. residency rev. com. pathology 1980-84). Rotating intern Jefferson Hillman Hosp., Birmingham, 1951-52; practice medicine, specializing in pathology New Orleans, 1952—. Cons. pathology S.W. Found. for Research and Edn., 1954-55; assigned to Prof. J.N. Morris social medicine research unit Med. Research Council, London, Eng., 1962-63; asst. vis. pathologist Med. Ctr. La. at New Orleans-Charity Hosp., 1952-53, 55-58, vis. pathologist, 1958-66; sr. vis. pathologist, pathologist-in-chief La. State U. divsn., 1966—; asst. dept. pathology La. State U. Sch. Medicine, 1952-53, instr. pathology, 1955-57, asst. prof., 1957-60, asso. prof., 1960-64, prof., 1964—, head dept. pathology, 1966—, Boyd prof., 1980, med. dir. Med. Tech. Program, 1993—; chmn. med. ctr. planning and devel. com. La. State U. Sch. Medicine, 1969—; mem. Pathology A study sect. USPHS, 1965-67, chmn., 1967-69; cons. VA Hosp., New Orleans, 1967—; mem. epidemiology and biometry adv. com. NIH, 1971-78; mem. sci. adv. bd. cons. Armed Forces Inst. Pathology, 1971-79, chmn., 1977-78; mem. panel on geochemistry of water in relation to cardiovascular disease U.S. Nat. Com. for Geochemistry, Nat. Acad. Scis., 1976-79 Mem. editorial bd. Exptl. and Molecular Pathology, 1977—, Atherosclerosis, 1978—; contbr. articles on atherosclerosis, coronary heart disease to med. jours.; editor, co-editor, author chpts. in books on atherosclerosis; contbr. chpts. on pathology to med. rev. books. Pres. Bissonet Elem. PTA, 1961; v.p. Jefferson Com. for Better Schs., 1964. Served to capt., M.C. USAF, 1953-55. Recipient Research Career Devel. award USPHS, 1962-64; USPHS sr. research fellow, 1957-62 Fellow Am. Soc. for Study Arteriosclerosis, Am. Heart Assn. (council on epidemiology, chmn. com. on myocardial and coronary artery lesions Council on Arteriosclerosis 1970, exec. com. 1979—); mem. Internat. Acad. Pathology (council 1976-78, pres. 1988—), Internat. Soc. Cardiology, Internat. Acad. Pathology (coun. 1968-70, v.p. 1976-77, pres. 1978 U.S.-Can. divsn., pres.-elect 1986), AMA (alt. del. 1978-79, del. 1980—, rep. residency rev. com. pathology 1977-79, coun. on sci. affairs 1985-94), Am. Assn. Pathologists and Bacteriologists (asst. sec. 1959-62), Am. Soc. Exptl. Pathology, Am. Soc. Clin. Pathologists (councilor for La. 1966-68), Coll. Am. Pathologists, Assn. of Pathology Chairmen, Inc. (v.p. 1969, pres. 1970), La. Heart Assn. (vice chmn. research com. 1964-71), Phi Beta Kappa, Alpha Omega Alpha, Phi Kappa Phi, Sigma Chi (Significant Sig award 1983). Office: La State U Health Scis Ctr 1901 Perdido St New Orleans LA 70112-1328

STRONG, JOHN DAVID, insurance company executive; b. Cortland, N.Y., Apr. 12, 1936; s. Harold A. and Helen H. Strong; m. Carolyn Dimmick, Oct. 26, 1957; children: John David, Suzanne. BS, Syracuse U., 1957; postgrad., Columbia U., 1980. With Kemper Group, 1957-90, Kemper Corp., 1990-96, Empire sales divsn. mgr., 1972-74, CEO, 1988-93, chmn. bd., 1989-93; vice chmn. Millikin Assocs., 1993-96, chmn., 1996; exec. v.p., dir. Facilitators, Inc., 1995-98. Mem. adv. coun. Sch. Bus., Millikin U., 1975-79, 84—; bd. dirs. United Way of Decatur and Macon County, Ill., 1976-83, campaign chmn., 1978-79, pres. bd. dirs., 1979-81; pres. United Way of Ill., 1981-83; bd. dirs. DMH Commn. Svcs. Corp., 1985-97, chmn., 1988-90; bd. dirs. Decatur-Macon County Econ. Devel. Found., 1983-88, DMH Health Systems, 1987-94, Richland C.C. Found., 1987-90, Symphony Orch. Guild of Decatur, 1992-96, DMH Found., 1988-97; bd. dirs. Ill. Ednl. Devel. Found., 1983-90, pres., 1986-87; bd. dirs. Decatur Meml. Hosp., 1985-94, vice chmn., 1988, chmn., 1990-92; bd. dirs. Ctrl. Ill. Health Assocs., Inc., 1994, vice chmn., 1994-96; mem. steering com. Decatur Advantage, 1981-93, pres., 1988-93. Capt. USAR, 1958-69. Mem. Metro Decatur C. of C. (bd. dirs. 1977-80, chmn. 1983-84), Decatur Club (bd. dirs. 19080-83, pres. 1983), Country Club of Decatur (bd. dirs. 1993-99, pres. bd. 1995-97), Alpha Kappa Psi. E-mail: jack@strongs.net.

STRONG, JOHN OLIVER, plastic surgeon, educator; b. Montclair, N.J., Feb. 1, 1930; s. George Joseph and Olivia (LeBrun) S.; m. Helen Louise Vrooman, July 19, 1958 (dec. Mar. 1973); m. Deborah Sperberg, May 20, 1978; children: John Jr., Jean LeB., Andrew D. BS, Yale U., 1952; MD, U. Pa., 1957. Cert. vol. paleontologist Calif. Practice medicine specializing in plastic and reconstructive surgery, Santa Ana, Calif., 1964-97; asst. clin. prof. plastic and reconstructive surgery U. Calif., Irvine, 1970—. Chief of staff Western Med. Ctr., Santa Ana, 1996-97, interim chmn. bd., 1996-97, bd. dirs.; bd. dirs. United Western Med. Ctrs., Healthcare Found. Orange County, CFO; vol. Anya-Bottego Desert State Pk., steering com., 1998-2003. Vol. Anza -Borrego Desert State Pk. Fellow ACS; mem. Calif. Med. Assn. (chmn. sci. adv. panel 1983-89), Calif. Soc. Plastic Surgeons (pres. 1991-92). Republican. Office: PO Box 94 Borrego Springs CA 92004-0094

STRONG, JOHN WILLIAM, lawyer, educator; b. Iowa City, Aug. 18, 1935; s. Frank Ransom and Gertrude Elizabeth (Way) S.; m. Margaret Waite Cleary, June 16, 1962; children— Frank Ransom, Benjamin Waite. BA, Yale U., 1957; JD, U. Ill., 1962; postgrad, U. N.C., 1966-67. Bar: Ill. 1963, Oreg. 1976. Assoc. firm LeForgee, Samuels, Miller, Schroeder & Jackson, Decatur, Ill., 1963-64; asst. prof. law U. Kans., 1964-66; assoc. prof. Duke U., 1966-69; prof. U. Oreg., 1969-75; legal counsel Oreg. Task Force on Med. Malpractice, 1976; prof. U. Nebr., 1977-84, dean, 1977-82, vice chancellor for acad. affairs, 1981-84; Rosenstiel Disting. prof. law U. Ariz., 1984-98, prof. emeritus, 1998—. Nat. sec.-treas. Order of the Coif, 1992-98; cons. Nat. Judicial Coll. Author: (with others) Handbook on Evidence, 5th edit., 1999. Served with U.S. Army, 1957-59. Mem. Ill. Bar Assn., Oreg. Bar Assn., ABA, Am. Law Inst., Phi Delta Phi. Independent. Congregationalist. Home: 3220 E 3rd St Tucson AZ 85716-4233 Office: U Ariz Coll Law Tucson AZ 85721-0001 E-mail: strong@law.arizona.edu.

STRONG, JUDITH ANN, chemist, educator; b. June 19, 1941; d. Philip Furnald and Hilda Bernice (Hulbert) S. BS cum laude, SUNY, Albany, 1963; MA, Brandeis U., 1966, PhD, 1970. Asst. prof. chemistry Moorhead State U., Minn., 1969—73, assoc. prof., 1973—81, prof., 1981—, chmn. chemistry dept., 1984—86, dean social and natural scis., 1986—97, assoc. v.p. acad. affairs, 1997—. Recipient Gov.'s Acts of Kindness Vol. award, 1997; fellow, NSF, 1965—67. Mem.: Minn. Acad. Sci., Assn. Women in Sci., Am. Chem. Soc., Soroptimist Internat. (gov. North Ctrl. region 2002—), Sigma Xi. Home: 1209 12th St S Moorhead MN 56560-3707 Office: Minn State U Moorhead Academic Affairs Moorhead MN 56563-0001

STRONG, LOUISE CONNALLY, geneticist; b. San Antonio, Apr. 23, 1944; d. Ben Clarkson and Sarah Nell (Allen) Connally; m. Beeman Ewell Strong III, Jan. 10, 1970; children: Beeman Connally, Larkin Louise. BA, U. Tex., 1966; MD, U. Tex. Med. Br., Galveston, 1970. Diplomate Tex. State Bd. Med. Examiners. Faculty Grad. Sch. Biomed. Scis. U. Tex. Health Sci. Ctr., Houston, 1972—, rsch. assoc. Med. Genetics Ctr., 1972-73; asst. prof. pediatrics and biology, asst. geneticist U. Tex. M.D. Anderson Cancer Ctr., 1976-79, assoc. prof. exptl. pediatrics, assoc. geneticist, 1979—, Sue and Radcliffe Killam prof., 1981—. Part-time asst. prof. U. Tex. Health Sci. Ctr., 1973-78; vis. prof. pediatrics, U. Tex. Med. Sch., U. Tex. Health Sci. Ctr., 1988-95; nat. adv. bd. Dept. Health and Human Svcs., Nat. Cancer Inst., NIH, Bethesda, Md., 1984—, bd. scientific counselors Div. Cancer Etiology, Nat. Cancer Inst., 1981-84, mem. search com. for dep. dir. Div. Extramural Activities, Nat. Cancer Inst., speaker in field, others. Contbr. articles to profl. jours., books and abstracts. Named Warren E. Wheeler Vis. Prof., Children's Hosp., Columbus, Ohio, 1989; recipient Marjorie W. Margolin Award for Outstanding Achievement in Retina Rsch., Retina Rsch. Found., Houston, 1987, Outstanding Achievement in Field of Oncology, State Pres.'s BPW award Tex. Fedn. Bus. and Profl. Women's Clubs, 1984, several scholarships; grantee NIH, 1984-92, John S. Dunn Rsch. Found., 1989-91, Retina Rsch. Found., 1982-90, Joe and Jessie Crump Fund Med. Rsch., 1982-83, Kelsey-Leary Found., others. Mem. AAAS, Am. Assn. Cancer Rsch. AMA, Am. Med. Women's Assn., Am. Men and Women in Sci., Am. Soc. Human Genetics, Am. Soc. Preventive Oncology, Environ. Health Inst., Tex. Genetics Soc., Phil. Soc. Tex.; GM Adv. Council, Cancer Rsch. Found. Avocation: tennis. Office: 1515 Holcombe Blvd HMB Box #209 Houston TX 77030

STRONG, MAURICE FREDERICK, hydro-electric power company executive, former United Nations official; b. Oak Lake, Man., Can., Apr. 29, 1929; s. Frederick Milton and Mary (Fyfe) S.; m. Hanne Marstrand, 1981; children by previous marriage— Frederick Maurice, Maureen Louise, Mary Anne, Kenneth Martin. 35 hon. degrees. Fin. analyst James Richardson & Sons, Winnipeg, Man., and Calgary, 1948-51, asst. to pres., 1951-52; mktg. asst. Caltex (Africa) Ltd., Nairobi, Kenya, 1953-54; v.p., treas. Dome Petroleum Ltd., Calgary, 1955-59; pres. Canadian Indsl. Gas Ltd., Calgary, 1959-64, Power Corp. Can., Montreal, 1962-66, Canadian Internat. Devel. Agy. Ottawa, 1966-70; exec. dir. environment program UN, also sec.-gen. UN Conf. Human Environment, N.Y.C., 1971-75; chmn. bd. Petro-Can., 1975-78; chmn. Internat. Devel. Research Centre, 1977-78, Procor, Inc., AZL Resources, Inc., Phoenix, 1978-83, Internat. Energy Devel. Corp., 1980-83; dir., vice chmn. Can. Devel. Corp., 1981-84, chmn., 1982-84; dir. Massey Ferguson, 1984; exec. coord. UN Office for Emergency Ops. in Africa, 1985-86; pres. World Fedn. UN Assocs., 1987-91; sec.-gen. UN Conf. on Environ. and Devel. (Earth Summit), 1990-92; chmn., CEO Ontario Hydro, 1992-95; spl. advisor UN devel. programme, 1992—. Former chmn. Internat. Union for Conservation of Nature and Natural Resources; chmn. Coun. World Econ. Forum, Baca Resources Ltd., Am. Water Devel. Inc., North-South Roundtable, SID, Strovest Holdings; dir. World Soc., First Color. Corp., Baca Corp., Consolidated Press Holdings; chmn. exec. com. Société Générale pour l'Energie et les Ressources; mem. adv. bd. York U., Toronto, 1969-70, vis. prof. govt. adminstrn., 1969; alt. gov. Internat. Bank for Reconstrn. and Devel., Asian Devel. Bank, 1968-70, Caribbean Devel. Bank, 1970; gov. Internat. Devel. Research Centre, 1970-71, 77-78; bd. dirs. Centre D'Etudes Industrielles, Geneva, Switzerland, Aspen Inst. Humanistic Studies; mem. World Com. Environ. and Devel., 1983-87; co-chmn. InterAction Policy Bd. Trustee Rockefeller Found., Fitzer Found.; Pres. Nat. Council YMCA's Can., 1967-68; chmn. com. extension and inter-movement aid World Alliance YMCA's, 1963-65; mem. joint com. soc. justice peace World Council Chs., Vatican, 1969-71; Montague Burton prof. Internat. Relations U. Edinburgh, 1973. Decorated officer Order of Can., 1976; recipient Blue Planet Prize, Asahi Glass Foundation, 1995, Pub. Welfare medal NAS, 2003. Fellow Royal Soc. (U.K.), Royal Soc. Can.; mem. Century Assn., Queen's Privy Coun. Can., Yale Club, Univ. Club, Vancouver Club. Office: Ontario Hydro 700 University Ave Ste 19 A27 Toronto ON Canada M5G 1X6*

STRONG, MICHAEL CORRIN, publishing executive, writer; b. Washington, Dec. 16, 1950; s. Trowbridge and Alice Wadsworth Strong; children: Mary Alice, Cecelia Anna, Corinna Alana, Edward Trowbridge. BA, SUNY Geneseo, 1975—77; JD, Albany Law Sch., 1977—80. Member of Bar (retired): NYS Appelate Div. 4th Dept. 1981. Pub. Clarion Publications, Geneseo, NY, 1990—. Author: (collection of weekly columns) Writing for Myself (and ticking everybody else off!). Dir. Geneseo Found., Geneseo, NY, 1999—2003; state committeeman NYS Rep. Party, Geneseo, NY, 1994—2000; dir. Genesee Valley Conservancy, Geneseo, NY, 1994—2003. Mem.: NY Press Assn. Home: 17 Avon Road Geneseo NY 14454 Office: Clarion Publications Inc 38 Main Street PO Box 9 Geneseo NY 14454

STRONG, ROBERT THOMAS, former mayor, middle school educator; b. N.Y.C., June 16, 1936; s. Joseph A. and Pauline R. (Manger) S.; m. Evelyn Ann Repasky, Aug. 23, 1958; children: Robyn, Robert Jr. BS, SUNY, Oswego, 1958; MLS, SUNY, Stony Brook, 1976. Social studies tchr. South Country Sch. Dist., Bellport, N.Y., 1958-66, asst. prin. middle sch., 1966-72, tchr., chmn. social studies dept., 1972-91. Student coun. adviser Bellport Middle Sch., 1968-91; prin. Infant Jesus Religious Sch., Port Jefferson, 1966-68. Trustee Village of Port Jefferson, 1991-95, code commr., 1991-99, dep. mayor, 1993-95, mayor, 1995-99; mem., chmn. Zoning Bd. Appeals, Port Jefferson, 1978-91; liaison to pub. safety adv. bd. Village of Port Jefferson, 1991-95; charter mem. Friends of St. Charles Hospice; grad. Suffolk County Citizens Police Acad.; 2d v.p. Suffolk County Village Ofcls., 1998-99; mem. Port Jefferson Harbor Complex Harbor Mgmt. Group; founder, pres. Suffolk County Citizens Police Alumni Assn.; chmn. Village of Port Jefferson Harbor Front Com.; bd. dirs. Port Jefferson Civic Assn. Mem. N.Y. State Tchrs. Assn., Bellport Tchrs. Assn. (treas. 1974-76, bldg. rep. 1989-91), L.I. Coun. for Social Studies, South Country Ret. Educators Assn. (founder, v.p. 1996—), Moose, Kiwanis, S.C.C. Pa. Alumni Assn. (pres.). Roman Catholic. Avocations: skiing, travel, ice skating. Home: 8 Shady Tree Ln Port Jefferson NY 11777

STRONG, STEPHEN ANDREW, lawyer; b. Longview, Tex., June 13, 1960; s. Jack B. and Rose N. (Otts) S.; m. LeAnn Troop, Aug. 6, 1983; children: Mark Andrew, Lindsey Michelle. BBA, Baylor U., 1983, JD, 1984. Bar: Tex. 1984. Assoc. Boyd, Veigel & Hance, Dallas, 1984-87, Liddell, Sapp, Zivley, Hill & LaBoon, Dallas, 1987-90; v.p., sr. counsel AmWest Savs. Assn., Dallas, 1990-94; sr. v.p., sr. counsel 1st Am. Bank Tex., SSB, Bryan, 1994—. Adv. dir. Briarcrest Ins. Agy., Inc., Bryan, Tex., 1991-97, SALSCO, Inc., Bryan, 1990-97; adv. Rutherford Inst., Dallas, 1991—. Co-author: Southern Methodist U.—Mortgages in Depth, 1991. Adv. dir. Internat. Crusades Found., Inc., Dallas, 1988—; chmn. policy com. Brazos Christian Sch., 1997-98; chmn. Carrollton (Tex.)/Farmers Br. Christian Network, 1990-94; bd. dirs., fin. chmn. Concerned Parents Tex., Inc., Dallas, 1991—; deacon, dir. Sunday schs., Ctrl. Baptist Bryan; chmn. Pub. Sch. Awareness com. Citizens for Excellence in Edn., 1992—. Mem. Tex. Bar Assn., Baylor Bear Found., Tex. Eagle Forum. Avocations: family, church, golf, tennis. Office: 1st Am Bank Tex SSB 2800 S Texas Ave Bryan TX 77802-5343

STRONG, SUSAN CLANCEY, writer, communication consultant, editor; b. Cin., Nov. 10, 1939; d. William Power and Elizabeth (Browne) Clancey; m. Oliver Swigert, 1957 (div. 1972); children: Silvia, David Mack; m. Richard Devon Strong, 1977. BA, Northwestern U., 1965; MA, U. Calif., Berkeley, 1972, PhD, 1979. Tchr. Helen Bush Parkside Sch., Seattle, 1965-66, Taipei (Taiwan) Lang. Inst., 1967-68; acting instr. U. Calif., Berkeley, 1972-78, teaching fellow, 1979, lectr., 1979-84, St. Mary's Coll., Moraga, Calif., 1982-85; pvt. practice Orinda, Calif., 1985-90, 97—; sr. rsch. assoc. Ctr. for Econ. Conversion, 1990-96. Mem. Contra Costa County Conflict Resolution Panels, Calif., 1987-90; affiliate Support Ctr./CTD, San Francisco, 1987-90; del. UN Conf. on Econ. Conversion, Moscow, 1990; co-founder "The Who's Counting?" Project, 1996; founder The Metaphor Project, 1997. Author: The GDP Myth: How It Harms Our Quality of Life, and What Communities are Doing About It, 1995; editor Deficit Delirium, 1993, Shaping A New Conversion Agenda, 1995; author poetry; columnist, book reviewer, film reviewer. Mem. Bay Area Global Tomorrow Com., 1986; co-founder Peace Economy Working Group, 1988; co-founder Peace Economy Campaign, 1988; mem. Peace Action Nat. Strategy Com., 1989-95, co-chair strategy com., 1992-93; conf. co-chmn. Nat. Sane/Freeze Congress, 1989-90, rep. nat. bd. advisors Nat. Peace Action, Washington, 1989-95; mem. bd. advisors Peace and Environ. Project, San Francisco, 1986-88; chmn. No. Calif. Sane Freeze, San Francisco, 1985-89; co-convenor The Natural Step Open Space Com. Conf., San Francisco, 1997. Mem. Phi Beta Kappa. Democrat. Episcopalian. Avocations: music, gardening. Mailing: PO Box 892 Orinda CA 94563-2124 Fax: 925-254-3304. E-mail: sstrong@metaphorproject.org.

STRONG, VIRGINIA WILKERSON, freelance writer, former educator; b. Vernal, Utah, Mar. 19, 1935; d. Arbun C. and Mildred (Wyman) Wilkerson; m. David Smith, Oct. 6, 1950 (div. Jan. 1960); children: Anna Smith Blyton, Dorothy Smith Wolf, Wendell Lee Smith, Ava Smith Eatman, Karen Smith Ritter; m. Lawrence D. Strong, June 1961 (div. May 1973); children: Lawrence D. Jr., Jeffrey A. BA, U. Miss., 1970, MEd, 1972; PhD, Ohio U., 1985. Cert. elem. edn. tchr., spl. edn. K-12 tchr., ednl. adminstrn. Rsch. asst. U. Miss., University, 1968-70, Utah State U., Logan, 1974-78; tchr. spl. edn. various schs., nr. Oxford, Miss., 1969-74; instr. spl. edn., project coord., rsch. asst. Ohio U., Athens, 1978-82; supr. spl. edn. Meigs County Bd. Edn., Pomeroy, Ohio, 1982-84; tchr. spl. edn., dept. chmn. L.A. Unified Sch. Dist., 1986-93, co-faciliator alcohol drug abuse, 1990-93; freelance writer, owner, mgr. Fenix Devel., Long Beach, Calif., 1990—. Early childhood adv. Utah Bd. Edn., Salt Lake City, 1976, evaluator edn. programs, Salt Lake City and Logan, 1976-77; acting dir. edn., cons. North Miss. Retardation Ctr., Oxford, 1993-94; curriclum developer Meigs County, 1982-84; dir. gifted edn. workshop Ohio U., 1980. Author: The Role of the Special Education Supervisor, 1985, (screenplays) To See the Elephant, Dark Encounters; contbr. articles to newspapers. Elector Dem. Party, Logan, 1976; religious instr. LDS Ch., various locations, 1953-97; docent Thoroughbred Hall of Fame, 2003—. U.S. Dept. Edn. grantee Utah State U., 1976. Mem. ASCD, Kappa Delta Pi, Phi Delta Kappa. Avocations: genealogy, gemology, photography, history buff, travel.

STRONGIN, BONNIE LYNN, English language educator; b. Chgo., Sept. 27, 1943; d. Arthur Caroll and Jennie Grace (Coffler) Bondy; m. Barry Michael Woldman, Jan. 27, 1965 (div. Aug. 1979); children: Scott, Erika, Jonathan; m. Stuart Jeffrey Strongin, Jan. 26, 1992. BA, Roosevelt U., 1964; MA, Concordia U., 1990. Cert. sec. English tchr., Ill. Core tchr. Dist. 15, Rolling Meadows, Ill., 1964—65, 1979—2004; English tchr., chair freshman level Leyden Twp. H.S., Franklin Park, Ill., 1965-69. Ednl. cons. French Internat. Sch. of Chgo., 1995; spkr. in field. Contbg. editor Collage Mag., 1980-82; contbr. articles to Collage Mag., Chgo. Tribune; guest Phil Donahue Show, 1984. Recipient Golden Apple State finalist award Golden Apple Found., Chgo., 1993, Excellence in English award English Speaking Union, Chgo., 1994, Tchrs. Who Care Enough to Challenge Award Ill. Math. and Sci. Acad., 2002. Fellow: Internat. Biographical Assn.; mem.: Ill. Assn. Tchrs. English, Ill. Edn. Assn., ASCD, NOW, NEA. Avocations: theater, opera, travel, film, art. Office: Plum Grove Jr HS 2600 Plum Grove Rd Rolling Meadows IL 60008-2042

STRONGIN, JONATHAN DAVID, physician; b. Kingston, N.Y., June 19, 1951; s. Jack and Thelma (Kaufman) S.; m. Ellen Wells Seely, June 11, 1983; children: Jessica, Matthew. BA, Columbia Coll., 1973; PhD, MD, Columbia U., 1982. Diplomate Am. Bd. Internal Medicine, Am. Bd. Pulmonary Disease, Am. Bd. Critical Care Medicine. Intern, resident Cambridge (Mass.) Hosp., 1982-84; med. resident Beth Israel Hosp., Boston, 1984-85; pulmonary fellow Mass. Gen. Hosp., Boston, 1985-97; physician Pulmonary Assocs. of Greater Boston, 1994—96. Pres. med. staff Whidden Meml. Hosp., Everett, Mass., 1995-97; trustee Melrose Wakefield Health Care Corp., 1996-98; med. dir. respiratory care Cambridge Health Alliance. Fulbright scholar, 1976-77. Fellow Am. Coll. Physicians, Am. Coll. Chest Physicians. Avocation: running.

STRONG-TIDMAN, VIRGINIA ADELE, marketing professional; b. July 26, 1947; d. Alan Ballentine and Virginia Leona (Harris) Strong; m. John Fletcher Tidman, Sept. 23, 1978. BS, Albright Coll., Reading, Pa., 1969; postgrad., U. Pitts., 1970-73, U. Louisville, 1975-76. Exec. trainee Pomeroy's divsn. Allied Stores, Reading, 1969-70; mktg. rsch. analyst Heinz U.S.A., Pitts., 1970-74; new products mktg. mgr. Ky. Fried Chicken, Louisville, 1974-76; dir. Pitts. office M/A/R/C, 1976-79; assoc. rsch. dir. Henderson Advt., Inc., Greenville, S.C., 1979-81; sr. v.p., dir. rsch. Bozell, Jacobs, Kenyon & Eckhardt, Inc., Dallas, 1981-86, 1981-86, sr. v.p., dir. rsch. and strategic planning Atlanta, 1986-88; sr. v.p., dir. mktg. svcs. Bozell, Inc., Atlanta, 1988-91; sr. v.p., mng. ptnr. Henderson Adv., Inc., 1991-95; prin. Ender-Ptnr., Inc., 1995-96; v.p. mktg. Booth Rsch. Svcs., Inc., 1996-98; COO Moore & Symons, Inc., 1998—. Cons. mktg. rsch. Greenville Zool. Soc., 1981; adj. prof. So. Meth. U., 1984-85. Mem. Am. Mktg. Assn. (Effie award N.Y. chpt. 1982). Republican. Episcopalian. Home: 146 Northshores Dr Seneca SC 29672

STROOBANDT, DIRK RUDY, research scientist, educator; b. Oost-Vlaanderen, Belgium, Jan. 21, 1972; s. Roger F. and Brigitta (DeClercq) S.; m. Mieke Marleen Roelens, May 12, 1995. Electrotech. Engr., U. Ghent, 1994, PhD in Applied Scis., 1998. Rsch. asst. Fund Scientific Rsch.-Flanders/U. Ghent, 1994-98, postdoct. fellow, 1998—2002; prof. Ghent U., 2002—. Contbr. article to profl. jour. Office: Sint-Pietersnieuwstraat 41 Gent Oost-Vlaanderen B-9000 Belgium Fax: 32 9 264.35.94. E-mail: dstr@elis.ugent.be.

STROOCK, MARK EDWIN, II, public relations company executive; b. N.Y.C., Nov. 6, 1922; s. Irving Sylvan and Blanche (Loeb) S.; m. Hanna Marks Eiseman, June 24, 1945 (dec. May 2003); children— Mark E., Carolyn E. BA, Bard Coll., 1947. Reporter The New York Journal of Commerce, 1947-50; writer Barrons, N.Y.C., 1950-51; mng. editor Fairchild Publ., N.Y.C., 1952-53; bus. editor World Mag., N.Y.C., 1953-54; contbg. editor Time Mag., N.Y.C., 1954-56; with Young & Rubicam Inc., N.Y.C., 1956-87, sr. v.p., dir. corp. rels., cons., 1987—. Bd. trustee N.Y. Urban League, 1971-78, Alvin Ailey Dance Theatre, N.Y.C., 1977-84, Friends of the Theatre Mus. City N.Y., 1977-85, Arts Horizons, N.Y.C., 1998—; vice-chmn. Covenant House, N.Y.C., 1978-90; exec. com., mktg. and communications com., assoc. nat. commr. Anti-Defamation League, 1992—. With U.S. Army, 1943-46. Democrat. Jewish. Home: 50 Park Ave Apt 11B New York NY 10016-3075 Office: Young & Rubicam Inc 285 Madison Ave New York NY 10017-6486

STROOCK, THOMAS FRANK, oil and gas company executive; b. N.Y.C., Oct. 10, 1925; s. Samuel and Dorothy (Frank) S.; m. Marta Freyre de Andrade, June 19, 1949; children: Margaret, Sandra, Elizabeth, Anne. BA in Econs., Yale U., 1948; LLB (hon.), U. Wyo., 1995; PhD (hon.), Universidad del Valle, Guatemala, 2001. Landman Stanolind Oil & Gas Co., Tulsa, 1948-52; pres. Stroock Leasing Corp., Casper, Wyo., 1952-89, Alpha Exploration, Inc., 1980-89; ptnr. Stroock, Rogers & Dymond, Casper, 1960-82; dir. First Wyo. Bank, Casper, 1967-89; mem. Wyo. Senate, 1969-89, chmn. appropriations com., 1983-89, co-chmn. joint appropriations com., 1983-89, mem. mgmt. and audit com., pres., 1988-89; mem. steering com. Edn. Commn. of States; amb. to Guatemala Govt. of U.S., 1989-93; pres. Alpha Devel. Corp., 1992—; prof. pub. diplomacy U. Wyo., Laramie, 1993—2002, chmn. internat. adv. bd., 2001—. Dir. Wyo. Med. Ctr., 1996—. Rep. precinct committeeman, 1960-68; pres. Natrona County Sch. Bd., 1966, 69; pres. Wyo. State Sch. Bds. Assn., 1965-66; chmn. Casper Cmty. Recreation, 1955-60; chmn. Natrona County United Fund, 1963-64; chmn. Wyo. State Rep. Com., 1975-78, exec. com. 1954-60; del. Rep. Nat. Conv., 1956-76, 92; regional coord. campaign George Bush for pres., 1979-80, 87-88; chmn. Western States Rep. Chmn. Assn., 1977-78; chmn. Wyo. Higher Edn. Commn., 1969-71; mem. Nat. Petroleum Coun., 1972-77; chmn. trustees Sierra Madre Found. for Geol. Rsch., New Haven; chmn. Wyo. Nat. Gas Pipline Authority, 1987-88; bd. dirs. Ucross Found., Denver; mem. Nat. Pub. Lands Adv. Coun., 1981-85; chmn. Wyo. Health Reform Commn., 1993-95; trustee Nature Conservancy, 1993—; chmn. Universidad del Valle Found., Guatemala City, 1995-2000, trustee, 2000—; chmn. Wyo. Health Access Task Force, 2003—. Sgt. USMC, 1943-46. Mem. Rocky Mountain Oil and Gas Assn., Petroleum Assn. Wyo., Kiwanis, Casper Country Club, Casper Petroleum Club, Yale Club N.Y. Republican. Unitarian Universalist. Home and Office: PO Box 2875 Casper WY 82602-2875

STROSCIO, MICHAEL ANTHONY, physicist, researcher; b. Winston-Salem, NC, June 1, 1949; s. Anthony and Norma Lee (Sidbury) S.; children: Elizabeth de Clare, Charles Marshall Sidbury, Gautam Dutta. BS, U. N.C., 1970; MPhil in Physics, Yale U., 1972, PhD in Physics, 1974. Physicist Los Alamos Sci. Lab., N.Mex., 1975-78; sr. staff mem. Johns Hopkins U. Applied Physics Lab., Laurel, Md., 1978-80; prof. mgr. for electromagnetic research Air Force Office of Sci. Research, Washington, 1980-83; spl. asst. to research dir. Office of Under Sec. Def., Washington, 1982-83; policy analyst White House Office of Sci. and Tech. Policy, Washington, 1983-85; prof. dir. for microelectrons, prin. scientist U.S. Army Research Office, Research Triangle Park, NC, 1985—2001; adj. prof. depts. physics and elec. and computer engrng. N.C. State U., Raleigh, 1985—; prof. depts. bioengrng. and elec. computer engrng., univ. scholar, dir. grad. studies in bioengrng. U. Ill., Chgo., 2001—, dir. grad. studies, 2002—. Adj. prof. depts. elec. engrng. and physics Duke U., Durham, 1986—, dept. physics U. Ill., Chgo., Ill., 2002—; vis. prof. dept. of elec. engring. U. Va., Charlottesville, 1990-95, U. Md., College Park, 1996-97; mem. congrl. coun. Duke U. Chapel, 1989-91; lectr. UCLA, 1987, U. Mich., 1988; cons. U.S. Dept. Energy, Washington, 1985-90; vice-chmn. White House Panel on Sci. Communication, Washington, 1983-84; chmn. Dept. Def. Rsch. Instrumentation Com., Washington, 1982; assoc. mem. Adv. Group on Electron Devices, 1985-91, liaison Nat. Laser Users Facility, Rochester, N.Y., 1984; liaison Panel on Sci. Comm. and Nat. Security, NAS, 1982, Panel on Materials for High-Density Electron Packaging, 1987-90; U.S. Army liaison to JASON, 1991—; mem. U.S. Govt. coord. com. on Semiconductor Rsch. Corp., 1992—; reviewer Irish Sci. Found. Author: Positronium: A Review of the Theory, 1975, Onslow Families, 1977, Quantum Heterostructures: Microelectronics and Optoelectronics, 1999, Phonons in Nanostructures, 2001, Biological Nanostructures and Applications of Nanostructures in Biology, 2004; editor: Quantum-Based Electronic Devices and Systems, 1998, Advanced Semiconductor Lasers and Applications to Optoelectronics, 2000, Advanced Semiconductor Heterostructures, 2003; reviewer: Army Rsch. Office, NSF, Office of Naval Rsch., Dept. Commerce and the Natural Scis., Engring. Rsch. Coun. Can., 1981—, Irish Sci. Found., 2003, referee jours.; contbr. articles to profl. jours. Capt. USAF, 1974-75. Grantee Los Alamos Sci. Lab., 1977, Air Force Office Sci. Rsch., 2002—, Army Rsch. Office, 2003—, Def. Advanced Rsch. Projects Agy., 2002—, NSF, 2004—. Fellow AAAS, IEEE (exec. com. for plasma sci. 1983—, Harry Diamond Meml. award 1998), Yale Sci. and Engring. Assn. (exec. bd. dirs. 1983—), Army Rsch. Lab.; mem. Am. Phys. Soc., Phi Beta Kappa, Nat. Geneal. Soc. Achievements include patents in field. Home: 2045 Central Ave Wilmette IL 60091-2383 Office: U Ill Dept Elec and Computer Engring MC154 851 S Morgan St Chicago IL 60607 Office Phone: 312-413-5968. E-mail: stroscio@uic.edu., m.stroscio@gte.net.

STROSNIDER, JOHN, dean; b. Owosso, Mich., Oct. 29, 1947; m. Jo Ann Strosnider; children: John Adam, Alisha, Paul. BS Gen. Sci., Northeast Mo. State U., 1971; DO, Kans. City Coll., 1975; rotating intern, Lakeside Osteo. Hosp., 1976; student, Continuing Med. Edn., 1976—. V.p., ptnr. Family Care, Inc., Kansas City, Mo., 1976—91; dir. med. edn., med. dir. Lakeside Osteo. Hosp., Kansas City, Mo., 1978—90; v.p., med. dir. Med. Rev. Cons., Inc., Independence, Mo., 1985—92; assoc. dean acad. affairs/clin. scis. U. Health Scis. Coll. Osteo. Medicine, Kansas City, Mo., 1991—95; dean Pikesville Coll. Sch. Osteo. Medicine, 1992—. Mem. bd. trustees Lakeside Hosp., Inc., 1987—93; mem. bd. dirs. Med. Rev. Cons., 1985—92, v.p., 1985—92; mem. Ctr. Dist. #58 Bd. Edn., 1992—95. Recipient MAOPS Medallion award, outstanding achievement in osteo. med. edn., 1993, Mo. Ho. Reps. Resolution 304, promotion osteo. medicine Mo., 1991, Mo. Senate Resolution 220, leadership in osteo. med. edn. Mo., 1991, MAOPS Ho. Dels. REsolution, outstanding leadership osteo. medicine, 1992. Mem.: Ky. Osteo. Med. Assn. (ad hoc bd. trustees 1996—), Soc. Tchrs. Family Medicine, Nat. Sch. Bds. Assn., Assn. Osteo. Med. Dirs. and Educators, Am. Coll. Osteo. Family Physicians, Jackson County Osteo. Assn. (pres. 1981—82, bd. trustees 1978—84), Mo. Assn. Osteopathy Physicians and Surgeons (pres. 1919—92, bd. trustees 1988—94, chmn. mem. com. 1992—96), Am. Osteo. Assn. (bd. trustees 1992—, chmn. dept. bus. affairs 1994—96, chmn. bur. student affairs 1994—96, exec. com. bd. 1994—97, chmn. dept. ednl. affairs 1996—97, bur. ins. 1997—, vice chair bur. small states' concerns 1997—, vice chair com. on memberships 1997—, com. strat. planning 1997—, task force healthcare facilities accreditation 1997—, adv. task force osteo. medicine accreditation). Avocations: reading, fishing, travel, political debate, golf. Office: 214 Sycamore St Pikeville KY 41501

STROSS, JEOFFREY KNIGHT, internist, educator; b. Detroit, May 2, 1941; s. Julius Knight and Molly Ellen (Fishman) S.; m. Ellen Nora Schwartz, May 22, 1965; children: Wendy, Jonathan. BS in Pharmacy, U. Mich., 1962, MD, 1967. Diplomate Am. Bd. Internal Medicine. Intern Univ. Mich. Hosp., Ann Arbor, 1967-68, resident in internal medicine, 1971-73; instr. internal medicine U. Mich., Ann Arbor, 1973-74, asst. prof., 1974-79, assoc. prof., 1979-87, prof., 1987—. Contbr. numerous articles to med. jours. Served to maj. USAF, 1969-71. Nat. Heart, Lung and Blood Inst. grantee, 1975—. Fellow ACP; mem. Soc. for Gen. Internal Medicine (regional chmn. 1984-86). Jewish. Home: 824 Asa Gray Dr Ann Arbor MI 48105-2853 Office: U Mich Med Sch 3119 Taubman Ann Arbor MI 48109-0376 E-mail: jstross@umich.edu.

STROSSEN, NADINE, legal association administrator, law educator; b. Jersey City, Aug. 18, 1950; d. Woodrow John and Sylvia (Simicich) S.; m. Eli Michael Noam, Apr. 25, 1980. AB, Harvard U., 1972, JD magna cum laude, 1975; LHD (hon.), U. Vt., 1992, U. R.I., 1992; JD (hon.), San Joaquin Coll. Law, 1996; LHD (hon.), Rpcky Mountain Coll., 1996, Mass. Sch. Law, 2000. Jud. clk. Minn. Supreme Ct., St. Paul, 1975-76; assoc. Lindquist & Vennum, Mpls., 1976-78, Sullivan & Cromwell, N.Y.C., 1978-83; prof. clin. law, supervising atty. Civil Rights Clinic, Sch. Law, NYU, 1984-88; prof. law N.Y. Law Sch., N.Y.C., 1988—; adj. prof. Columbia U., 1990—; pres. ACLU, N.Y.C., 1991—. Editor Harvard Law Rev., 1975; contbr. book chpts., articles to profl. jours.; author: In Defense of Pornography: Free Speech and the Fight for Women's Rights, 1995. Mem. Coun. Fgn. Rels., 1994—. Recipient Outstanding Young Person award Jaycees Internat., 1986; named one of Ten Outstanding Young Ams., U.S. Jaycees, 1986; adj. fellow Yale U. Calhoun Coll., 1997-. Mem. ACLU, Nat. Coalition Against Censorship (bd. dirs. 1988—), Human Rights Watch (exec. com. 1989-91), Harvard Club (N.Y.C.). Avocations: travel, skiing, singing. Office: NY Law Sch 57 Worth St New York NY 10013-2960 also: ACLU 125 Broad St 18th Fl New York NY 10004 E-mail: nstrossen@aclu.org.*

STROTHER, ALLEN, biochemical pharmacologist, researcher; b. Nolan County, Tex., Feb. 20, 1928; s. Henry Allen and Minnie Etta (Taylor) S.; m. Julia Ann Gutch, Feb. 7, 1957; children: Wesley Allen, Lori Ann. BS, Tex. Tech U., 1955; MS, U. Calif., 1957; PhD, Tex. A&M U., 1963. Rsch. asst. Tex. A&M, Coll. Sta., 1959-63; rsch. biochemist FDA, Washington, 1963-65; asst. prof. pharmacology Loma Linda (Calif.) U., 1965-70, assoc. prof., 1970-75, prof., 1975-95, retired, vol. faculty, 1995—, prof. emeritus Physiology and Pharmacology, 1997—. Cons. WHO, Geneva, 1982-86. Contbr. numerous articles to profl. jours.; chpt. to WHO Bull. Pilot CAP/USAF Search and Rescue San Bernardino, Calif., 1967-95; pilot examiner CAP Air Force Aux., Norton AFB, 1970-86. Named Investigator of Yr. Walter E. McPherson Soc., Loma Linda U., 1984, Basic Sci. Fellow of Yr., 1986, Outstanding Faculty Rschr. of Yr. award, 1997. Mem. Am. Soc. Pharmacology and Exptl. Therapeutics, Am. Chem. Soc., Xzenobiotic Soc. Avocations: flying, golf. Home: 74448 Nevada Cir E Palm Desert CA 92260-2269 Office: Loma Linda U Sch Medicine Dept Physiology and Pharmacology Loma Linda CA 92354

STROTHMAN, JAMES EDWARD, editor; b. Pitts., Mar. 27, 1939; s. Edward Charles and Harriet Hope (Jones) S.; m. Eleanor Shawfield Jacobs, Sept. 9, 1961; children— Joseph, Jill, Stuart. BA in Journalism, Pa. State U., 1961. Asst. city editor, city hall reporter Williamsport Grit, Pa., 1961-64; with Miami Herald, Fla., 1964-67; aerospace writer AP, Cape Kennedy, Fla., 1967-69; reporter Los Angeles bur. Electronic News, 1969-71, sr. editor computer news sect., 1971-73, mng. editor, 1973; sr. info. rep. corp. hdqrs., then program adminstr. data processing divsn. hdqrs. IBM Corp., 1973-77, mgr. ea. area comm. data processing divsn., 1977-79, field comm. mgr. data processing divsn., 1979-81, mgr. comm. rsch. divsn., 1981; free-lance writer and cons. Strothman Assocs., 1981-82; editor-in-chief MIS Week, N.Y.C., 1982-88; free-lance writer, cons., 1988-89; editor-in-chief Computer Pictures, Chappaqua, NY, 1989-94; news editor ISA On Line Instrument Soc. Am. (ISA), Research Triangle Park, NC, 1994-2000. Online editor, eCommerce Bus. Mag., 2000-01; assoc. editor InTech Mag., 2001-02; freelance writer, mktg. comm. cons., 2003—. Episcopalian.

STROTHMAN, WENDY JO, book publisher; b. Pitts., July 29, 1950; d. Walter Richard and Mary Ann (Hodtum) S.; m. Mark Kavanaugh Metzger, Nov. 25, 1978; children: Andrew Richard, Margaret Ann. Student, U. Chgo., 1979-80; AB, Brown U., 1972. Copywriter, mktg. U. Chgo. Press, 1973-76, editor, 1977-80, gen. editor, 1980-83, asst. dir., 1983; dir. Beacon Press, Boston, 1983-95; v.p., pub. adult, trade and reference Houghton-Mifflin, Boston, 1995-96, exec. v.p. trade and reference divsn., 1996—2002, lit. agent, 2003—. Trustee Brown U., 1990-96, Deerfield Acad., 2003-; fellow Brown U., 1999-. Edtl. adv. bd. Scholarly Pub., 1993-94; bd. editors Brown Alumni Monthly, 1983-89; chmn., 1986-89. Bd. dirs. Editorial Project for Edn., trustee, 1987-91, treas., 1988-90. Fellow Brown U., 1997—. Mem. Renaissance Soc. (bd. dirs. 1980-83), Assn. Am. Pubs. (Freedom to Read com.), Pubs. Lunch Club (N.Y.C.), PEN New Eng. (adv. bd.), Examiner Club, NacRe Reins. Corp. (bd. dirs.). Office: The Strothman Agy LLC One Faneuil Hall Marketplace Third Fl Boston MA 02109

STROUCKEN, ALBERT P.L. chemical company executive; Exec. v.p. industrial chemicals divsn. Bayer Corp.; gen. mgr. inorganic chemicals divsn. Bayer AG; chmn., pres./CEO H.B. Fuller Co., St. Paul, Minn., 1998—. Office: HB Fuller Co 1200 Willow Lake Blvd Saint Paul MN 55110

STROUD, BETSY DILLARD, artist; b. Roanoke, Va., Aug. 12, 1940; d. Peter Hairston Dillard and Alice Elizabeth (Fitch) Madden; m. Ethan Beden Stroud, Dec. 29, 1979 (div. Mar. 1986); 1 child, John Hatcher Ferguson, III. BA, Radford Coll., 1968; MA, U. Va., 1970. Assoc. editor Internat. Artist mag., Scottsdale, Ariz., 1998-2001; prof. artist. Tchr. workshops throughout U.S.; judge art shows including those in Farmington, N.Mex., 1999, The Adirondacks Nat. Watermedia Exhbn., Old Forge, N.Y., 1996, Contemporary Watercolorists of Ariz., 1998, others. Contbr. articles to Am. Artist mag., 1987— and other profl. jours. Mem. S.W. Watercolor Soc. (pres. 1988-89, Edgar A. Whitney award 1989), Am. Watercolor Soc. (High Winds medal 1992, Artist Mag. award 1995), Nat. Watercolor Soc., Rocky Mountain Nat. Honor Soc. (Brass Cheque award 1992), Knickerbocker Artists, Ariz. Watercolor Soc. Avocations: piano, bridge, Scrabble, movies. E-mail: betsydillart@uswest.net.

STROUD, HERSCHEL LEON, retired dentist; b. Peabody, Kans., Sept. 21, 1930; Student, U. Kans., 1948-50; BS, U. Mo., Kansas City, 1952; OD cum laude, Ill. Inst. Tech., 1954; DDS magna cum laude, U. Mo., Kansas City, 1961. Diplomate Nat. Dental Bd. Officer, founder Topeka Dental Lab., Inc., 1971; ptnr. Gage Ctr. Dental Group, P.A., Topeka, 1979-98. Pres., bd. dirs. Delta Dental Ins. of Kans. Corp., 1974-92; mem. dental staff St. Francis Hosp. and Med. Ctr., Topeka, 1963—, C.F. Menninger Meml. Hosp., Topeka, 1964—; cons., lectr. civil war medicine. Contbr. articles to profl. publs.; co-partner Kings of Swing Big Band. Vesteryman St. David's Episcopal Ch., 1966-68, composer/dir. Jubilee Mass, dir. Rejoice folk mass, 1967-74, mem. choir; dir. music for blessing of animals Friends of Topeka Zoo, 1983—; mem. U. Kans. Alumni Marching Band; founder/dir. Kans. U. Pep Band, Topeka Club; re-enactor surgeon Maj. Frontier Brigade, 1st Fed. Divsn., Union Army, Civil War, officer Kans. City Civil War Round Table. With USNR, 1950-54; capt. USAF, 1954-57, USAR, 1957-70. Fellow Am. Coll. Dentists, Internat. Coll. Dentists; mem. Soc. Preservation Oral Health (bd. dirs. 1965, exec. sec.-treas. 1966-70), Kans. State Dental Assn. (chmn. coun. on dental care plans 1972-76, state peer rev. com. 1974-76), Am. Dental Assn., Chgo. Dental Soc., Midwest Soc. Peridontology, Am. Prosthodontic Soc., Am. Equilibration Soc., Acad. Gen. Dentistry, Am. Pain Soc., Soc. for Preservation Barbershop Quartet Singing Am. (chorus dir.), Rip Chords babershop quartet, Shawnee Yacht Club, Masons, Shriner, Associated Club Spkrs of Am., Knife and Fork Club Inc., Tau Kappa Epsilon, Tau Kappa Nu, Xi Psi Phi. Avocations: scuba diving, skiing, sailboat racing, marching band. Home: 3640 SW Drury Ln Topeka KS 66604-2550

STROUD, JACQUELINE LUCILLE, medical supply company executive; b. Carthage, Mo., Jan. 5, 1932; m. Herschel L. Stroud; children: Susan K. Stroud Milash, John L. Student, U. Mo., Kansas City, 1949-50, Sarachon Hooley Sec. Sch., 1950-51; BA in Spanish magna cum laude, Washburn U., Topeka, 1980. Pvt. sec. Recordak Corp., Chgo., 1951-54, Vance AFB, Okla., 1954-57, Hallmark Cards, Kansas City, Mo., 1957-61; adminstrv. asst., translator, export mgr. Munns Med. Supply (now MedVentures Internat. Inc.), Topeka, 1980—. Hist. lectr. Mid-19th Century Women, Civil War Medicine, U.S. San. Commn., recreation of Civil War era personages, 1995—; lectr. Associated Club Spkrs. Am., Knife and Fork Club, Inc. Officer, bd. mem. Internat. Ctr. Topeka, 1980's; bd. dirs. Girls' Club Topeka, 1980's; panelist Panel of Am. Women, 1967-75; Spanish translator Topeka Police Dept., 1981—; choir mem. St. David's Episcopal Ch., 1961—; participant, co-organizer Rejoice, Jubilee and Godspell folk masses, Blessing of the Animals at Topeka Zoo, 1968-96; columnist Westboro Neighborhood newsletter, 1975-98; mem. St. Francis Hosp. Aux. Recipient Outstanding Vol. award Jr. League Topeka, 1973, 1st pl. Mother-Dau. Nat. Equitable Ski Challenge, Keystone, Colo., 1972-73 Mem. ADA, Nat. Mus. Civil War Medicine, Am. Soc. Civil War Surgeons, Frontier Brigade of the 1st Western Divsn., Kans. Dental Auxs., Topeka Knife and Fork Club (pres. 1989-90), Minerva Lit. and Music Club (treas. 1999-2000), Kans. State Hist. Soc., Topeka Hist. Soc., Shawnee County Hist. Soc., N.E. Kans. Civil War Round Table, Kansas City Round Table (officer), Victorian Carthage. Avocations: hostess for kings of swing big band, skiing, spanish conversation classes, scuba diving, photography, civil war reenacments, church choir. Address: 3640 SW Drury Ln Topeka KS 66604-2550

STROUD, JAMES STANLEY, retired lawyer; b. Wimbledon, N.D., Jan. 26, 1915; s. Herbert Montgomery and Amanda Getchell (Longfellow) S.; m. Marjorie Marsh Hovey, Sept. 11, 1940; children: Jay Stanley, Steven Hovey. AB, Jamestown Coll., 1936; JD, U. Chgo., 1939. Bar: Ill. 1939, U.S. Supreme Ct. 1945, D.C. 1972. Counsel Ill. Mcpl. Code Commn., Chgo., 1939-40; bill drafter Ill. Legis. Ref. Bur., Springfield, 1941; from assoc. to ptnr. Mayer, Brown & Platt, Chgo., 1941-71, ptnr.-in-charge Washington, 1972-80, ret., 1982. Bd. dirs. Chgo. Community Renewal Found., 1962-70; mem. adminstrv. bd. Nat. United Meth. Ch., Washington, 1982-84; coord. Extended Family Program, 1981-82. Capt. AUS, 1943-46. Home: Cottage 304 3300 Darby Rd Haverford PA 19041-1063

STROUD, JOHN FRED, JR., judge; b. Hope, Ark., Oct. 3, 1931; s. John Fred and Clarine (Steel) S.; m. Marietta Kimball, June 1, 1958; children: John Fred III, Ann Kimball, Tracy Steel. Student, Hendrix Coll., 1949-51; BA, U.

Ark., 1959, LLB, 1960. Bar: Ark. 1959, Tex. 1988, U.S. Supreme Ct. 1963. Ptnr. Stroud & McClerkin, 1959-62; city atty. City of Texarkana (Ark.), 1961; legis. asst. to U.S. Senator John L. McClellan, 1962-63; ptnr. Smith, Stroud, McClerkin, Dunn & Nutter, 1963-79, 81 95; assoc. justice Ark. Supreme Ct., Little Rock, 1980; judge Ark. Ct. Appeals, Little Rock, 1996—2001, chief judge, 2001—04. Chmn. Texarkana Airport Authority, 1966-67, Texarkana United Way Campaign, 1988; pres. Caddo area coun. Boy Scouts Am., 1971-73; former trustee Ark. Nature Conservancy; former bd. dirs. Ark. Cmty. Found.; former pres. Red River Valley Assn.; former commr. Red River Compact Commn.; past vice chmn. Ark. Water Code Study Commn.; chmn. bd., chmn. coun. ministries Meth. Ch. Lt. col. USAF, 1951-56, Res. ret. Recipient award of exceptional accomplishment Ark. State C. of C., 1972, 86, Silver Beaver and Disting. Eagle awards Boy Scouts Am.; named Outstanding Young Man of Texarkana, 1966, One of Five Outstanding Young Men of Ark., 1967, Outstanding Alumnus of U. Ark. Law Sch., 1980. Fellow Am. Bar Foune.; mem. ABA, Ark. Bar Assn. (chmn. exec. coun. 1979-80, pres. 1987-88, Presdl. award of excellence and Charles L. Carpenter Meml. award 1997-98), Four States Area Estate Planning Coun. (past chmn.), State Bar Tex., Miller County Bar Assn. (past pres.), Texarkana Bar Assn. (pres. 1982-83), Ark. Bar Found. (chmn. 1974-75, chmn. trust com. 2003—), Am. Coll. Trust and Estate Counsel (chmn. Ark. chpt. 1986-91), S.W. Ark. Bar Assn., Texarkana C. of C. (pres. 1969, C.E. Palmer award 1979), U. Ark. Law Alumni Soc. (bd. dirs.), Texarkana Country Club (pres. 1990-92), Rotary (pres. Texarkana 1965-66). Avocations: tennis, golf, hunting, fishing. Office: Ark Ct Appeals 625 Marshall St Little Rock AR 72201-1075 Office Phone: 501-682-7977.

STROUD, PATRICIA TYSON, writer; b. Phila., Dec. 22, 1932; d. George Peterson and Jane (Chapman) Huber; m. Noel J. Tyson, Sept. 8, 1956 (dec. July 1982); children: John Tyson II, Peter H. Tyson, Lisa Tyson Ennis; m. Morris Wistar Stroud III, Mar. 11, 1989 (dec. Apr. 1990); m. Alexander McCurdy III, Nov. 16, 1991. AB, Smith Coll., Northampton, Mass., 1955. Writer, pub. rels. releases First Pa. Bank, Phila., 1968-69; editor, Frontiers Acad. Natural Scis., Phila., 1979-82; writer pvt. practice, Phila., 1982—. Author: Thomas Say: New World Naturalist, 1992, The Emperor of Nature: Charles Lucien Bonaparte and His World, 2000; contbr. articles to profl. jours. Pres. bd. dirs. Ga. Farm Found., 1990—; bd. dirs. Hist. Bartram's Garden, 1992—98, U. Pa. Press, 1999—2003. Avocations: reading, gardening, piano. Home: PO Box 15 East Blue Hill ME 04629-0015 E-mail: fdaza@earthlink.net.

STROUD, RHODA M. elementary school educator; Tchr. Webster Magnet Elem. Sch., St. Paul. Apptd. mem. Minn. Bd. Edn. for State of Minn. Recipient State Tchr. of Yr. Elem. award Minn., 1992. Office: Webster Magnet Elem Sch 707 Holly Ave Saint Paul MN 55104-7126

STROUD, ROBERT ARLEN, medical equipment company executive; b. Lake Charles, Ill., Nov. 26, 1937; s. Grover Cleveland Stroud and Dolly Lucille (Mericle) S.; m. Mary Erin Coge, Oct. 1, 1965; children: Shannon Dene Stroud Dowden, Robert Arlen II. BS, La. State U., 1962. Sales rep. Chemetron Corp. Nat. Cylinder Gas, Inc., New Orleans, 1962-64; SE regional mgr. Orthopedic Equipment Corp., New Orleans, 1964; dist. mgr. Ohio Med. Products, Inc. Airco, New Orleans, 1964-75; v.p. sales and mktg. Med. Equipment Co. Inc., New Orleans, 1975-76, pres., CEO, 1976—. Pres., CEO Clin. Svcs. Inc., New Orleans, 1983-99. Contbr. papers to profl. jours. Chmn. bd. dirs. New Eng. Presch. Acad., Windsor Locks, Conn., 1992-99; chmn. bd. civil svc. bd. City of Slidell, La., 1977-97; state bd. adv. coun. La. Dept. Edn., Baton Rouge, 1977-82; adv. bd., small bus. coun. La. Assn. Bus. and Industry, Baton Rouge, 1985-96. Mem. Internat. Camellia Soc. (bd. dirs. 2000—), Am. Camellia Soc. (bd. dirs. 1989-99, dir.-at-large 1991-96, v.p. 1997-99, endowment bd. 1993-99, pres. 2002—), Gulf Coast Camellia Soc. (pres., v.p., treas. 1985-99, Dedication award 1996), Camellia Club (pres., v.p. 1992-99, Dedication award 1996). Republican. Avocation: camellia hobbyist. Home: 2 Oak Grove Way Slidell LA 70458-5328 E-mail: bobcamelia@aol.com.

STROUP, ELIZABETH FAYE, librarian; b. Tulsa, Mar. 25, 1939; d. Milton Earl and Lois (Buhl) S. BA in Philosophy, U. Wash., 1962, MLS, 1964. Intern Libr. of Congress, Washington, 1964-65; asst. dir. North Cen. Regional Libr., Wenatchee, Wash., 1966-69; reference specialist Congl. Reference div. Libr. of Congress, Washington, 1970-71, head nat. collections Div. for the Blind and Physically Handicapped, 1971-73, chief Congl. Reference div., 1973-78, dir. gen. reference, 1978-88; city libr., chief exec. officer Seattle Pub. Libr., 1988-96; exec. dir. Wash. Literacy, Seattle, 1996-99; reference coord. Timberland Regional Libr., Olympia, Wash., 1999—. Cons. U.S. Info. Svc., Indonesia, Feb. 1987. Mem. adv. bd. KCTS 9 Pub. TV, Seattle, 1988—; bd. visitors Sch. Librarianship, U. Wash., 1988—; bd. dirs. Wash. Literacy, 1988—. Mem. ALA (pres. reference and adult svcs. div. 1986-87, div. bd. 1985-88), Wash. Libr. Assn., D.C. Libr. Assn. (bd. dirs. 1975-76), City Club, Ranier Club. Avocations: gardening, mountain climbing, reading. Office: Wash Literacy 220 Nickerson St Seattle WA 98109-1622

STROUP, KALA MAYS, educational alliance administrator, former state higher education commissioner; BA in Speech and Drama, U. Kans., 1959, MS in Psychology, 1964, PhD in Speech Comm. and Human Rels., 1974; EdD (hon.), Mo. Western State Coll., 1996; LHD (hon.), Harris-Stowe State Coll., 2000. V.p. acad. affairs Emporia (Kans.) State U., 1978-83; pres. Murray State U., Ky., 1983-90, S.E. Mo. State U., Cape Girardeau, 1990-95, Am. Humanics, Kansas City, Mo., 2002—; commr. higher edn., mem. gov.'s cabinet State of Mo., Jefferson City, 1995—2002. Pres. Mo. Coun. on Pub. Higher Edn.; mem. pres.'s commn. NCAA; cons. Edn. Commn. of States Task Force on State Policy and Ind. Higher Edn.; adv. bd. NSF Directorate for Sci. Edn. Evaluation; adv. com. Dept. Health, Edn. and Welfare, chair edn. com.; citizen's adv. coun. on state of Women U. S. Dept. Labor, 1974-76. Mem. nat. exec. bd. Boy Scouts Am., nat. exploring com., former chair profl. devel. com., mem. profl. devel. com., exploring com., Young Am. awards com., 1986-87, north ctrl. region strategic planning com., bd. trustees, nat. mus. chair; mem. Gov.'s Coun. on Workforce Quality, State of Mo.; bd. dirs. Midwestern Higher Edn. Commn.; chair ACE Leadership Commn.; mem. bd. visitors Air U.; v.p. Missourians for Higher Edn.; bd. dirs. St. Francis Med. Ctr. Found., 1990-95, Cape Girardeau C. of C., 1990-95, U. Kans. Alumni Assn.; pres. Forum on Excellence, Carnegie Found.; adv. bd. World Trade Ctr., St. Louis, Svc. Mems. Opty. Colls., 1997—; mem. Mo. Higher Edn. Loan Authority, 1995—, depts. econ. devel. & agrl. Mo. Global Partnership, 1995—, Mo. Tng. & Employment Coun., 1995-2002, Concordia U. Sys. Advancement Cabinet, State Higher Edn. Exec. Officers, 1995—, mem. com. workforce edn. and tng., 1996; bd. govs. Heartland's Alliance Minority Participation, 1995-2002; chair, mem. workforce devel. com. NPEC coun. U.S. Office of Edn., 1997—; bd. dirs. Midwestern Higher Edn. Commn. Distributed Learning Workshop, 1998-2002, Dept. Natural Resources Minority Scholarship Adv. Bd.; chair Show Me Results sub-cabinet Educated Missourians; mem. Pub. Policy Initiative Stakeholder Com., 1999—; mem. Coun. Higher Edn. transfer and pub. interest com.; mem. access/diversity com. State Higher Edn. Exec. Officers; trustee, mem. adv. coun. Assn. Governing Bds. of Univs. and Colls. Ctr. for Pub. Edn., 2000—. ACE fellow; recipient Alumni Honor Citation award U. Kans., Award Distinction Profl. Black Men's Club, S.E. Mo., 1990, Dist. Svc. to Edn. award Harris-Stowe State Coll., 1996; named to U. Kans. Womans Hall of Fame, Ohio Valley Conf. Hall of Fame, 1997. Mem. Am. Assn. State Colls. and Univs. (past bd. dirs., mem. Pres.'s Commn. on Tchr. Edn., Task Force on Labor Force Issues and Implications for the Curriculum), Mortar Board, Phi Beta Kappa, Omicron Delta Kappa, Phi Kappa Phi, Rotary (found. Ednl. awards com.). Office: Am Humanics 4601 Madison Ave Kansas City MO 64112

STROUP, SALLY, federal agency administrator; b. Harrisburg, Pa. Grad., Ind. U. Pa., Loyola U. From staff atty. to sr. v.p. legal svcs. and chief counsel Pa. Higher Edn. Agy.; mem. profl. staff com. on edn. and the workforce U.S. Ho. of Reps., 1993—2001; dir. industry and govt. affairs Apollo Group Inc./U. Phoenix; asst. sec. postsecondary edn. Dept. Edn., Washington, 2001—. Office: Dept Edn Office Postsecondary Edn 1990 K St NW Washington DC 20006

STROUP, STANLEY STEPHENSON, lawyer, educator; b. LA, Mar. 7, 1944; s. Francis Edwin and Marjory (Weimer) S.; m. Sylvia Douglass, June 15, 1968; children: Stacie, Stephen, Sarah. AB, U. Ill., 1966; JD, U. Mich., 1969. Bar: Ill. 1969, Calif. 1981, Minn. 1984. Atty. First Nat. Bank Chgo., 1969-78, asst. gen. counsel, 1978-80, v.p., 1980; sr. v.p., chief legal officer Bank of Calif., San Francisco, 1980-84; sr. v.p., gen. counsel Norwest Corp., Mpls., 1984-93, exec. v.p., gen. counsel, 1993-98, Wells Fargo & Co., San Francisco, 1998—2003. Adj. faculty Coll. Law, William Mitchell Coll., St. Paul, 1985-98; mem. Regulatory Affairs Coun., Bank Adminstrn. Inst., 1996—2003. Bd. dirs. San Francisco Zool. Soc., 2000—, Legal Aid Soc. San Francisco, 1999—2003. Mem. ABA, Ill. Bar Assn., State Bar Calif., Minn. Bar Assn., Bar Assn. San Francisco (bd. dirs. 2000-02). E-mail: stan_stroup@yahoo.com.

STROUSE, JEAN, writer; b. L.A., Sept. 10, 1945; d. Carl David and Louise (Friedberg) S. BA, Radcliffe Coll., 1967. Editl. asst. N.Y. Rev. of Books, 1967-69; freelance writer N.Y.C., 1969-72; editor Pantheon Books, N.Y.C., 1972-75; freelance writer N.Y.C., 1975-79, 1983—2003; book critic Newsweek Mag., N.Y.C., 1979-83; dir. Cullman Ctr. for Scholars and Writers N.Y. Pub. Libr., N.Y.C., 2003—. Selection com. J.S. Guggenheim Found., N.Y.C., 1995-97, trustee, 1987-94, 2001—04, fellow, 1977, 86; exec. coun. Authors Guild; Ferris prof. journalism Princeton U., 1998; John J. Rhodes chair in Am. instns. and pub. policy Barrett Honors Coll., Ariz. State U., 2003. Author: Alice James, A Biography, 1980, Morgan American Financier, 1999; editor: Women & Analysis: Dialogues on Psychoanalytic Views of Femininity, 1974. Fellow NEH, 1976, 92, John D. and Catherine T. MacArthur Found., 2002—; recipient Bancroft prize Columbia U., 1981. Mem. Soc. Am. Historians (pres. 2001-02), Am. Acad. Arts and Scis., Am Philos Soc, The Century Assn., Phi Beta Kappa (vis. scholar 1996-97).

STROUSE, WAYNE STEVEN, physician; b. Phila., Nov. 11, 1954; s. Albert and Selma (Friedman) s.; m. Janet Lisa Lewis, June 1, 1986; 1 child, Kelsey Lynn. BA cum laude, U. PA., 1976; MD, Med. Coll. Va., 1986. Diplomate Am. Bd. Family Practice. Intern Charleston (S.C.) Naval Hosp., 1986-87; resident Kingsport (Tenn.) Family Practice, Holston Valley Hosp., Kingsport, Tenn., 1992-94, attending physician, 1994-95, Soldiers and Sailors Meml. Hosp., Penn Yan, NY, 1995—; asst. prof. East Tenn. State U., Johnson City, 1994-95, U. Rochester, 1995-96, asst. clin. prof., 1997—. Recipient Mead-Johnson award. Fellow: Am. Bd. Family Practice; mem.: AMA, Am. Acad. Family Physicians. Democrat. Jewish. Office: Main St Family Health 108 Kimball Ave Penn Yan NY 14527 Office Phone: 315-536-2273. Business E-Mail: pennyandoc@medscape.com.

STROUTH, BARON HOWARD STEVEN, geologist, mining engineer; b. Frankfurt, Germany, Sept. 28, 1919; arrived in U.S., 1941; s. Baron Karl Siegfried and Ida (Morck) von Strauss; m. Penelope Ann Creamer-Osteen, Nov. 3, 1951. BSc, U. Sorbonne, 1939; PhD in Engring., Bretton Woods U., 1965; PhD in Engring. (hon.), Rochedale U., Can., 1970. Asst. mgr. Drexel Bros. Ltd., N.Y.C., 1941—43; pres. Std. Mining, N.Y.C., 1951-58, Stanleigh Uranium Mine, Toronto, Can., 1954-61; mng. dir. Norsul Oil and Mining Quito, Ecuador, 1961-71; dir., officer Mining and Oil Cos., various locations; founder, operator Stanleigh Uranium and Norsul Oil. Sr. trustee Weingueter Baron K. S. von Strauss, Erben Trust, Vaduz, 1954—. Translator: The Cornet (Rilke), 1950; author: A Window to the Morrow, 1963, A Sonata for Frankfurt, 1987, Cities of the Break of Dawn, 1988, Beauty is Forever, 1996; patentee in mining and oil porcesses. Maj. USAR, 1943-69, ret. Recipient Conspicuous Svc. Cross, Gov. Dewey, 1947, French, Czech, Cambodian decorations. Fellow Explorers Club; mem. Can. Inst. Mining Engrs. (life), Am. Inst. Mining Engrs. (sr.), St. James Club (London), Ontario Club Toronto. Avocations: collector, antique books, pre-colombian art, antique maps.

STROYD, ARTHUR HEISTER, lawyer; b. Pitts., Sept. 5, 1945; 1 child, Elizabeth. AB, Kenyon Coll., 1967; JD, U. Pitts., 1972. Bar: Pa. 1972, U.S. Dist. Ct. (we. dist.) Pa. 1972, U.S. Ct. Appeals (3d cir.) 1972. Law clk. to judge U.S. Ct. Appeals (3d cir.), Phila., 1972—75; with Reed, Smith, LLP, Pitts., 1975—, mng. ptnr., Allegheny Region, 1997—2001. Mem. Nat. Adv. Coun. on Child Nutrition, U.S. Dept. Agriculture, 1984-85. Mem. Mt. Lebanon Zoning Hearing Bd., 1978-81; pres. bd. dirs. Mt. Lebanon Sch. dist., 1981-87; solicitor Allegheny County Rep. Com., 1988-95; pres. bd. dirs. Ctr. for Theatre Arts, Pitts., 1984-93; grad. Leadership Pitts., 1991-92; chair bd. dirs. Mt. Lebanon Hosp. Authority, 1993-2001; bd. dirs. U. Pitts. Cancer Inst., 1993—; mem. alumni coun. Kenyon Coll., 1996-2000; bd. trustees Historical Soc. of Western Pa., 1999—; bd. dirs. Edn. Policy and Issues Ctr., 2000-03. Lt. USNR, 1969-71. Fellow Am. Coll. Trial Lawyers; mem. ABA, Pa. Bar Assn., Allegheny County Bar Assn. (pres., bd. govs., past chair civil litig. sect., past chmn. judiciary com.), Acad. Trial Lawyers (v.p., bd. govs.), mem. Pa. Supreme Ct. Civil Procedural Rules Com., Duquesne Club, Pitts. Golf Club, Western Pa. Hist. Soc. (bd. dirs. 1999—). Episcopalian. Avocations: skiing, motorcycling, golf. Office: Reed Smith LLP 435 6th Ave Pittsburgh PA 15219-1886 Office Phone: 412-288-3110. Business E-Mail: astroyd@reedsmith.com.

STRUBBE, THOMAS R. insurance industry executive; b. Ft. Wayne, Ind., Mar. 30, 1940; s. Rudolph C. and Maverne E. (Wagoner) S.; children: Tracy Lynn, Patrick Thomas, Christina Lee. BS, Ind. U., 1962; JD, Tulane U., 1965. Bar: Ind. 1965, Ill. 1969. Atty. Lincoln Nat. Life Ins. Co., Ft. Wayne, Ind., 1965-66, asst. counsel, 1967-68; with Washington Nat. Corp., Evanston, Ill., 1968-90, counsel, 1968-73, gen. counsel, 1973-79, corp. sec., 1970-84, v.p., 1975-79, sr. v.p., 1979-83, exec. v.p., 1983-84, pres., 1984-90, also bd. dirs., mem. exec. com.; pres., CEO Osborn Labs. Inc., Olathe, Kans., 1990-98, Guarantee Res. Life Ins. Co., Chgo., 1998-99, also bd. dirs., ret., 2000. V.p., bd. dirs., exec. com. Chgo. chpt. Epilepsy Found. Am., 1975—79; trustee Glencoe (Ill.) Union Ch., 1984—87; Stephen min. Trinity Luth. Ch., 2003—; bd. dirs. Assn. Retarded Citizens Ill., 1985—89, Northlight Theater, 1984—89. Lt. USNR, 1965—71. Lincoln Found. grantee, 1964. Mem. ABA, Assn. Life Ins. Counsel, Nat. Investor Rels. Inst., Am. Soc. Corp. Secs., Home Office Life Underwriters Assn., Ind. Bar Assn., Ill. Bar Assn., Skokie Country Club (Ill.), Shadow Glen Golf Club (Kans.), Hallbrook Country Club (Kans.), Hideaway Beach Club (Fla.). Home (Summer): 9210 Oak Valley Dr De Soto KS 66018-7994 E-mail: thomstrubbe@aol.com.

STRUBEL, DEBORAH WEAVER, think-tank associate; b. Ephrata, Pa., May 29, 1957; d. Arthur Martin and Ruth F. (Bollinger) Weaver; m. Kenneth Eugene Strubel, Nov. 10, 1979; children: Benjamin J., Elizabeth A. BA in English, Nyack Coll., 1979. Freelance editor and writer, Lancaster, Pa., 1994—99; editor Starburst Pub., Lancaster, 1999—2001, sr. editor, 2001—02; assoc. agent Big Score Prodns. Literary Agy., Lancaster, 2002—03; dir. found. rels. Inst. Am. Values, N.Y., 2003—. Co-author: Single, Whole and Holy, 1996, Beautiful Places, Spiritual Spaces: The Art of Stress-free Interior Design, 2004; editor: Bible Seeds, 2001. Judge Writers Digest Self-Published Book Awards, 2003—; dir. Smoketown (Pa.) Elem. Reading Incentive Program, 1991—92. Mem.: Lancaster (Pa.) Literary Guild, Advanced Writers and Speakers Assn. Republican. Presbyn. Avocations: reading, gardening, quilting. Home: 2467 Creek View Dr Lancaster PA 17602 Office: Inst American Values 1841 Broadway Ste 211 New York NY 10023 Office Phone: 212-246-3942. Business E-Mail: deb@americanvalues.org.

STRUBEL, ELLA DOYLE, advertising executive, public relations executive; b. Chgo., Mar. 14, 1940; d. George Floyd and Myrtle (McKnight) D.; m. Richard Craig G'sell, Apr. 26, 1969 (div. 1973); m. Richard Perry Strubel, Oct. 23, 1976; stepchildren: Douglas Arthur, Craig Tollerton. BA magna cum laude, U. Memphis, 1962; MA, U. Ill., 1963. Staff asst. Corinthian Broadcasting Co., N.Y.C., 1963-65; dir. advt. and pub. rels. WANE-TV, Ft. Wayne, Ind., 1965-66; asst. dir. advt. WBBM-TV, Chgo., 1966-67, mgr. sales promotion, 1967-69, dir. advt. sales promotion and info. svcs., 1969-70; dir. pub. rels. Waltham Watch Co., Chgo., 1973-74; mgr. advt. promotion and pub. rels. WMAQ-TV, Chgo., 1974-76; v.p. corp. rels. Kraft, Inc., Glenview, Ill., 1985-87; sr. v.p. corp. affairs Leo Burnett Co., Inc., Chgo., 1987-92, exec. v.p., 1992-98; mng. dir. EllaQuent Designs, 2002—. Mem. vis. com. U. Chgo. Harris Sch. Pub. Policy; pres. women's bd. Rehab. Inst. Chgo., 1982—84; chair Chgo. Network, 1994—95; trustee 4th Presbyn. Ch.; chair Rehab. Inst. Chgo., 1998—2001; vice chair Chgo. Pub. Libr. Found.; bd. dirs. Rehab. Inst. Chgo. Named Outstanding Woman in Comms. in Chgo., YWCA, 1995, one of 100 Most Influential Women in Chgo., Crain's Chgo. Bus., 1996, Who's Who in Chgo. Bus., 2002. Mem. Casino Club, Econ. Club. Democrat. Presbyterian. Home: 55 W Goethe St Chicago IL 60610-7406 Office: 737 N Michigan Ave Ste 1405 Chicago IL 60611-6654 Office Phone: 312-255-0235. E-mail: estrubel@aol.com.

STRUBEL, RICHARD PERRY, Internet company executive; b. Evanston, Ill., Aug. 10, 1939; s. Arthur Raymond and Martha (Smith) S.; m. Linda Jane Freeman, Aug. 25, 1961 (div. 1974); children: Douglas Arthur, Craig Tollerton; m. Ella Doyle G'sell, Oct. 23, 1976. BA, Williams Coll., 1962; MBA, Harvard U., 1964. Assoc. Fry Cons., Chgo., 1964-66, mng. prin., 1966-68; with N.W. Industries, Inc., Chgo., 1968-83, v.p. corp. devel., 1969-73, group v.p., 1973-79, exec. v.p., 1979-83, pres., 1983; chmn. bd., pres. Buckingham Corp., N.Y.C., 1972-73; pres., chief exec. officer Microdot Inc., Chgo., 1983-94; mng. dir. Tandem Ptnrs. Inc., Chgo., 1990-99; with UNext Inc., Deerfield, Ill., 1999, pres., COO, 1999—2004, vice chmn., dir., 2004—. Trustee Mut. Funds of The No. Trust Co., Chgo., and various mutual funds of Goldman Sachs Asset Mgmt., N.Y.C.; bd. dirs. Gildan Activewear, Inc., Montreal, Que., Can. Trustee U. Chgo.; mem. visiting com. Divinity Sch., U. Chgo.; mem. adv. bd. Martin Marty Ctr. Mem. Casino Club, Chicago Club, Comml. Club, Racquet Club of Chicago, Commonwealth Club, Econ. Club. Presbyterian. Office: UNext Inc Ste 150 500 Lake Cook Rd Deerfield IL 60015

STRUBLE, DAN, academic administrator; m. Karen Brown Struble; children: Amanda, Benjamin. BS with merit, U.S. Naval Acad., 1983; MA in Comparative Politics, U. So. Calif., 1989, PhD in Am. Politics, 1993. Asst. prof. pub. adminstrn. Navy ROTC Dept. U. So. Calif., 1987—93; from asst. to assoc. to acting dir. Major and Planned Giving Office Occidental Coll., L.A., 1993—95; v.p. prin. gifts U.S. Naval Acad., 1995—2004; pre. Montreat (N.C.) Coll. Active Christ Our Anchor Presbyn. Ch. Commdr. USNR. Office: Montreat Coll PO Box 1267 Montreat NC 28757*

STRUBLE, JAMES CURTIS, ambassador; b. Visalia, Calif., Oct. 29, 1953; s. Arthur James and Ezella Ruby (Meek) S.; m. Susan Mary Briggs, Dec. 9, 1976; children: Peter James, Dale. BA in Slavic Lang. & Lit., BA in History, U. Calif., Berkeley, 1975. Vice consul Am. Consulate Gen., Monterrey, Mex., 1977-79; consul Am. Embassy USSR, Moscow, 1981-83; first sec. Am. Embassy Spain, Madrid, 1983-86; consul gen. Am. Embassy Honduras, Tegucigalpa, 1986-88; program assoc. Hoover Institution, Stanford, Calif., 1988—89; gen. consul Am. Embassy Thailand, Bangkok, 1994—96; dep. chief of mission Am. Embassy Ecuador, Quito, 1996—99; dir., office of Brazilian and So. cone affairs U.S. Dept. State, Washington, 1999—2001, dep. asst. sec., bureau of western hemisphere affairs, 2001—02, prin. dep. asst. sec., 2002, acting asst. sec., 2002—03, U.S. amb. to Peru Lima, 2003—. Mem. Am. Fgn. Svc. Assn. Avocations: coin collecting/numismatics, history. Office: Am Embassy APO Lima AA 34031-5000 Peru

STRUBLE, SUSAN C. artist, volunteer art therapist; b. N.Y.C., Jan. 4, 1939; d. Calvert Horton and Catherine (Snell) Crary; m. Robert Musser Struble, Mar. 30, 1985. BA, Carleton Coll., 1960. Art therapist Skills Inc., State College, Pa., 1995—, Adult Day Activities Ctr., State College, 1995—, adv. com., 2001—. Vol. art therapist Centre County Youth Ctr., Pa., 1990-93, Laurelton State Sch. and Hosp., 1973-74. Artist: works include Reclining Figure (1st prize Art Alliance Ctrl. Pa.), 1999. Asst. English tchr. Internat. Hospitality Coun., State Coll., 1995—; bd. dirs. friends Palmer Mus. of Art, Pa. State U., 1999—, sec., 2000—. Named Vol. of Yr. Ctrl. Counties Youth Ctr., 1993, Internat. Hospitality Coun., 1999, Adult Day Activities Ctr., 1999. Mem.: State Coll. Woman's Club (sec. art dept. 1998—99), Pa. Watercolor Soc. (sig. mem.), Am. Art Therapy Assn., Antique Automobile Club Am. Republican. Presbyterian. Avocations: art, music. E-mail: rmstruble@webtv.net.

STRUCK, NORMA JOHANSEN, artist; b. West Englewood, N.J., Feb. 17, 1929; d. Hans Christian and Amanda (Solberg) Johansen; m. H. Walter Struck, Aug. 21, 1955; children: Steven, Laurie. Student, N.Y. Phoenix Sch. Design, 1946-50, Art Students' League, N.Y.C., 1976-77. Staff artist Norcross, Inc., N.Y.C., 1950-60, free-lance artist, 1967-75; artist portraits, prints Scafa-Tornabene, Nyack, N.Y., 1976—; artist portraits, paintings U.S.N., U.S. Coast Guard, Washington, 1976—. Com. bd. mem. Navy Art Coop. Liaison, N.Y.C., 1976-80, Coast Guard Art Program, N.Y.C., 1980—, Navy Hist. Mus., Washington. One-woman shows include Valley Cottage Gallery, N.Y., Bergen Co. Playhouse, Oradell, N.J., N.Y. Yacht Club, 2003, Nabisco Co., Fairlawn, N.J., 1987; exhibited in group shows Navy Hist. Mus., Washington, 1976, Navy Combat Art Gallery, Washington, World Trade Ctr., 1979, USCG, New Eng. Air Mus., Windsor Locks, Conn., 1984, Fed. Hall, N.Y.C., 1986, 93, 94, 95, 96, 97, Salmagundi Club, N.Y.C., Officers Club, Governor's Island, Hudson Valley Show, White Plains, N.Y., Intrepid Mus., N.Y.C., Alexander Hamilton U.S. Custom House, Newington-Cropsey Mus., N.Y., Bergen County Mus. Art & Sci., N.J.; represented in permanent collections U.S. Pentagon, Washington, Henie-Onstad Mus., Oslo, World Figure Skating Hall of Fame and Mus., Colorado Springs, Alexander Hamilton custom House, N.Y.C. Recipient Louis E. Seley award, Navy Art Program, 1979; Grumbacher award, Catherine Lorillard Wolfe, Nat. Arts Club, N.Y.C., 1978; George Gray award Coast Guard Art Program, Governors Island, N.Y., 1983, 89. Fellow Am. Artists Profl. League (pres.'s award 1979); mem. Portrait Soc. Am., Art Students League (life), Hudson Valley Assn. (bd. dirs. 1985-88, M. Dole award 1980), Soc. Illustrators, Salmagundi Club, Portrait Soc. Am., Inc. Avocations: antique collecting, gourmet cooking. Home: 910 Midland Rd Oradell NJ 07649-1904 E-mail: njstruck99@cs.com.

STRUDLER, ROBERT JACOB, real estate development executive; b. N.Y.C., Sept. 22, 1942; m. Ruth Honigman, Aug. 29, 1965; children: Seth, Keith, Craig. BS in Indsl. and Labor Relations, Cornell U., 1964; LLB, Columbia U., 1967. Bar: N.Y. 1967, Fla. 1973. Assoc. firms in, N.Y.C., 1967-71; v.p., chmn. operating com. U.S. Home Corp., Clearwater, Fla., 1972-76, v.p. legal affairs, 1976-77, v.p. ops., 1977-79, sr. v.p. ops. Houston, 1979-81, sr. v.p. acquisitions, 1981-84, pres., chief operating officer, 1984-86, CEO, 1986-2000; vice-chmn. & COO Lennar Corp., Miami, 2000—. Pres., trustee Sch. for Young Children; mem. pres.' adv. coun. U. St. Thomas. Co-recipient Builder of Yr. award Profl. Builder Mag., 1994, Bronze award Wall Street, 1995, Hearthstone Builder Lifetime Pub. Svc. award, 2003, Legend of Residential Mktg. award Nat. Sales and Mktg. Coun., 2004; elected to Nat. Housing Hall of Fame, 2000. Mem. ABA, N.Y. State Bar Assn., Fla. Bar Assn., Cornell Real Estate Coun., Nat. Assn. Homebuilders (chmn. high prodn. coun. 1991-93). Office: Lennar Corp 10707 Clay Rd Houston TX 77044

STRUELENS, MICHEL MAURICE JOSEPH GEORGES, political science educator, foreign affairs consultant; b. Brussels, Mar. 10, 1928; m. Godelieve De Wilde, Aug. 2, 1949; children: Alain, Patricia, Brigitte, Bernard, Jean Paul (dec.). BA, Coll. St. Pierre, Brussels, 1944; MA, Antwerp U., Belgium, 1949; PhD, Am. U., Washington, 1968. Insp. econ. affairs Congo Govt., Leopoldville, 1950-54, chief insp. econ. affairs, 1954-55, dep. commr. transp., 1955-57; dir. Info. and Public Relations Office for Congo, Brussels, 1957-58, Congo Tourism Pavillion, Internat. World's Fair, Brussels, 1958-59; dir. gen. Belgian Congo and Ruanda Urundi Tourist Office, Congo, 1959; chmn. African Commn. Internat. Union Ofcl. Travel Orgns., Geneva, 1959-60; ofcl. Katanga rep. in U.S., N.Y.C., 1960-63; dir. gen. Internat. Inst. for African Affairs in Can., 1963-64; spl. asst. to prime minister Democratic Republic Congo, fgn. affairs minister, adviser to Congo UN del., adviser Congo embassy, 1964-66; dir. Eurafrica, Consultants on Fgn. Affairs, Washington, 1966—; prof. polit. sci., French, internat. bus. Am. U., 1968-93; prof. emeritus, 1993; dir. Ctr. Rsch and Documentation on European Community Am. U., 1971—, chmn. faculty rels. com., 1986-87, chmn. grad. studies com., SIS, 1989-90; dir. E.C. Inst. in Europe, 1978-93, U. Antwerp Exchange Program, 1979-83. Dir. EPSCI/ESSEC (France) Exchange Program, 1980-84, chmn. internat. bus. dept., 1980-84; dir. exchange program Bus. Sch. of Poly., U. Madrid, 1981-84; investment adviser, 1977—; adminstr. French Parish, 1974-75, Ctr. Studies on Internat. Relations, 1987-96, Econs. and Bus., La Rochelle, France, 1987-96; exec. v.p. Eglise St. Louis Corp., French-Speaking

Union, Washington, 1974-75; mgr. by agreement with European Communities, European Documentation Ctr. (CERDEC), accessing by satellite EC Data Banks, 1985— and providing through WCL Libr. of Am. U., On Line Pub. Access Cataloging, 1991—. Author: (with Inforcongo) Congo Belge et Ruanda-Urundi, 1958; monograph Le Canada à l'Heure de l'Afrique, 1964; The United Nations in the Congo - or ONUC and International Politics, 1976. Recipient Internat. Union Ofcl. Travel Orgns. Poster award Brussels, 1958, Etoile de Service en Argent King of Belgium, 1956; chevalier de l'Ordre Royal du Lion, 1957; Faculty award for outstanding contbn. to acad. program devel. Coll. Bus. Adminstrn., Am. U., 1979; Faculty award for outstanding teaching, 1980, 82, 84; Faculty award for outstanding service to Am. U., 1981 Mem. Golden Key, Phi Sigma Alpha. Clubs: Cosmos (Washington); Bukavu Royal Sports (founder 1950, pres. 1951-54, hon. pres. 1957) (Congo). Lodges: Rotary. Home: 1374 Woodside Dr Mc Lean VA 22102-1536 Office: Am U 4400 Mass Ave NW Washington DC 20016-8071 *"Ad Augusta per Angusta". Using Latin, French writer Victor Hugo said it all! Nothing comes easy and "success," a very personal perception indeed, requires a great deal of luck, perseverance and hard work. True success, though, is directly related to the pursuit of happiness, which in turn is a state of mind. If and when I reach eternity, I'll then be able to tell how successful I was during my passage on earth.*

STRUGGLES, JOHN EDWARD, management consultant; b. Wilmette, Ill., Nov. 29, 1913; s. William George and Sarah Adell (Chambers) S.; m. Dorothy Eloise Goetz, Oct. 23, 1937; 1 child, John Kirk. Student, Miami U., Oxford, Ohio, 1932-34. Supt. Consol. Biscuit Co., Chgo., 1934-37; sales rep. Pillsbury Mills, Chgo., 1937-41; various personnel and operating positions Montgomery Ward & Co., Chgo., Kansas City, Denver, 1941-50, v.p. personnel, 1950-53; co-founder, co-chmn. Heidrick & Struggles, Inc., Chgo., 1953—. With USNR, World War II. Republican. Home: 505 Sheridan Rd Winnetka IL 60093-2639 Office: Heidrick Struggles Inc 233 S Wacker Dr Chicago IL 60606-6306

STRUHL, STANLEY FREDERICK, real estate developer; b. Bklyn., Oct. 10, 1939; s. Isidore and Yvette (Miller) Struhl; m. Patricia Joyce Wald, Feb. 26, 1966; children: Marc Howard, Lisa Lynn. BS in Engring. with honors, UCLA, 1961, MBA in Data Processing, 1963. Tech. staff Hughes Aircraft Co., Fullerton, Calif., 1963—65; sr. assoc. Planning Rsch. Corp., LA, 1965—70; mgr. corp. info. sys. Logicon, Inc., Torrance, Calif., 1970—73; mgr. ops. analysis Sys. Devel. Corp., Santa Monica, Calif., 1973—77; gen. ptnr. TST Developers, Canyon Country, Calif., 1977—81; pres. Struhl Enterprises, Inc., Northridge, Calif., 1977—85; owner Struhl Properties, West Hills, 1977—2003. Planning sub. com. 12th Coun. Dist., LA, 1986—98; Lic. real estate broker, Calif. Mem.: Trail Dusters, Tau Beta Pi, Beta Gamma Sigma, Alpha Phi Omega. *Personal philosophy: Word(s) to live by; "Think"!.*

STRUHL, THEODORE ROOSEVELT, surgeon; b. N.Y.C., Jan. 5, 1917; s. Samuel and Florence (Kossoy) S.; m. Ruth Brand, Oct. 19, 1941; children: Karsten, Wendy. BA, NYU, 1936; MS, 1938; MD, NY Med. Coll., 1942; MS in Surg., 1947; grad., Juliard Conservatory of Music, 1933. Dipl. Am. Bd. Abdominal Surg., Am. Bd. Surg.; spl. expert Agy. Health Care Adminstrn., Bd. Medicine, Fla. Int. Queens Gen. Hosp., Jamaica, NY, 1942-43; res. VA Hosp., Newington, CT, 1947-48, Cumberland Med. Ctr., Brooklyn, NY, 1948-51; prac. med. specializing in surg. Miami, FL, 1951—; staff mem. Mt. Sinai Med. Ctr., Miami Beach, FL, Jackson Meml. Hosp., Cedars of Lebanon Health Care Ctr., Variety Chldrns. Hosp., South Shore Hosp., Miami Beach, FL, Victoria Hosp.; former instr. in anatomy L.I. Coll. Med., NY; instr. in surg., instr. in anatomy and surg. anatomy U. Miami; instr. in surg. anatomy and surg. Mt. Sinai Med. Ctr. Mem. adv. ARC of Dade County, Fla.; chief med. examiner Miami Beach Boxing Commn.; med. adv. World Martial Arts, Judo and Karate; mem. Am. Bd. Quality Assurance and Utilization Rev. Physicians; formerly instr. in diving med. Underwater Demolition Team Sch., U.S. Navy, Key West, Fla.; spl. expert Bd. of Medicine of the State of Fla.; lectr., instr. in scuba diving, diving med.; lectr. med. and surg., cancer, artificial respiration, anatomy, hypnosis, boxing, weight lifting, judo, skin and scuba diving, swimming, water skiing; spl. expert AHCA Bd. Medicine, State of Fla., Agy. for Health Care Adminstrn. Contbr. articles to profl. jours. Active ARC, 1936—, now bd. dirs., chmn. safety svcs. ARC of Dade County, bd. trustees; instr./trainer in CPR, instr. in advanced cardiac life support Am. Heart Assn.; former mem. N.Y. div. Olympic Wrestling Com. Served to maj. M.C., U.S. Army, World War II; ETO. Fellow ACS, Internat. Coll. of Surgeons (vice-regent Fla.), Am. Coll. Angiology, Internat. Acad. Proctology; mem. AMA, So. Med. Assn., Fla. Med. Assn., Dade County Med. Assn., Israeli Med. Assn., Fla. Assn. Gen. Surgeons (charter), Med. Hypnosis Assn. Dade County Med. Assn., Israeli Med. Assn., Fla. Assn. Gen. Surgeons (charter), Med. Hypnosis Assn. Dade County (past pres.), Am. Coll. Angiology, Pan Am. Med. Assn., Am. Soc. Abdominal Surgeons, Am. Soc. Contemporary Med. and Surg., Med. Aspects of Atomic Explosion, Assn. Mil. Surgeons U.S., Am. Coll. Sports Med., Fla. Bar Ass. (appointed bd. govs. 1990-94, mem. unlicensed practice of law 1997—, mem. pub. info. com. 1997—, grievance com.), Dade County Bar Assn. (mem. grievance com. 1987-90, 94-97), Commodore Longfellow Soc., Miami Beach Power Squadron (charter), Am. Canoe Assn., Am. White Water Assn., Underwater Med. Soc., Photog. Soc. Am., Contin. Hon. Soc. of N.Y. Med. Coll., Phi Delta Epsilon (past pres. chpt.). Democrat. Jewish. Avocations: judo (3rd degree black belt), karate (black belt, 4th degree). Home: 44 Star Island Dr Miami FL 33139-5146 Office: 1444 Biscayne Blvd Ste 304 Miami FL 33132-1423 Office Phone: 305-379-8601.

STRUHS, DAVID B. state agency administrator; BA in Journalism and Polit. Sci., Ind. U., 1982; MA in Pub. Adminstrn., Harvard U. Exec. asst. to region 1 adminstr. Michael Deland EPA, 1986—89, chief of staff coun. on environ. quality, 1989—95; commr. Mass. Dept. Environ. Protection, 1995—99; sec. Fla. Dept. Environ. Protection, 1999—. Office: Fla Dept Environ Protection 3900 Commonwealth Blvd Tallahassee FL 32399

STRUIF, L. JAMES, lawyer; b. Alton, Ill., Sept. 18, 1931; s. Leo John and Clara Lillie (Bauer) S.; m. Shirley Ann Spatz, Mar. 24, 1965; children: Scott B., Jamie Lynn Pehowski, Susan Marie Bazzell, Jeffrey James. BS, Northwestern U., 1953; JD, U. Ill., Champaign, 1960. Bar: Ill. 1960, U.S. Dist. Ct. (so. dist.) Ill. 1960. Gen. counsel So. Ill. U., 1960-64; pvt. practice Struif Law Offices, Alton, Ill., 1964—. Lectr. So. Ill. U., Edwardsville, 1960-65. Author: Guide to Law for Laymen, Field Guide to 150 Prairie Plants of S.W. Ill. Scoutmaster Boy Scouts Am., Alton, 1966-69; active civil rights worker, Miss., 1964; trustee The James and Aune Nelson Found. With USN, submarines 1953-57, Pacific. Recipient Chmns. award Madison County Urban League, Blazing Star award The Nature Inst. Democrat. Mem. United Ch. of Christ. Avocations: nature, gardening, science, piano, mathematics. Office: The Struif Law Offices 2900 Adams Pkwy Alton IL 62002-4857 Office Phone: 618-463-0700.

STRUKOFF, RUDOLF STEPHEN, retired music educator; b. Rostov, Don, Russia, July 18, 1935; came to U.S., 1951; s. Stephen and Olga (Flemming) S.; m. Donna Lee Hill, May 31, 1959; children: Rudolf Stephen, Jr., Robbin Stanley, Regan Stuart. B Music Edn., Andrews U., 1960; MusM, Mich. State U., 1964, PhD in Music, 1970. Instr. music Mich. State U., East Lansing, 1963-65; asst. prof. Ind. State U., Terre Haute, 1966-69; assoc. prof. Andrews U., Berrien Springs, Mich., 1969-76; prof. music Gov's. State U., Univ. Park, Ill., 1977-97. Chorus master Ill. Philharm. Chorus, Park Forest, Ill., 1982-84; music dir. Univ. Cmty. Chorale, Univ. Park, Ill., 1978-96, Chamber Orch., Univ. Park, 1978-96. Composer: The Greatest of These, 1970, Childhood Sketches, 1973; singer (opera) Attila by Verdi, 1979; condr. Christmas Oratorio by Saint-Saens, 1986, Stabat Mater by Rossini, 1988, German Requiem by Brahms, 1989, Requiem by Mozart, 1990, Mass in C by Beethoven, 1991, Mass in E Flat by Schubert, 1992, Requiem in C Minor by Cherubini, 1993, Cathedral Series, Joliet, Ill., Mass in B Flat by Haydn, St. Liborius, Steger, Ill., 1994, Symphony #2 (Hymn of Praise), Temple Anshe Sholom, 1994, Olympia Fields, Ill., Requiem by Mozart, St. Liborius, Steger, Ill., 1995, Messiah by Handel, Ctr. for Performing Arts, University Park, Ill., 1995, Concert Overture and Requiem by Cherubini, 1996; rec. artist (CD) How Great Thou Art, 2003, My Native Land, 2003. Lectr. Lyric Opera, Chgo., 1979-89, Libr. Lectr. Series, Park Forest, 1982, Career Days, Chgo., 1982-97, Symposium on Soviet Russia, Univ. Park, 1985, Ill. Philharmonic Workshop Series, 1991-96. Mem. ASCAP, Chgo. Singing Tchrs. Guild (pres. 1984-86, 91-93, bd. dirs. 1986-96), Am. Choral Dirs. Assn., Nat. Assn. Tchrs. Singing, Nat. Assn. Schs. Music, Pi Kappa Lambda. Avocations: antiques, golf, reading.

STRUL, GENE M. communications executive, former television news director; b. Bklyn., Mar. 25, 1927; s. Joseph and Sally (Chartoff) S.; m. Shirley Dolly Silber, Aug. 7, 1949 (dec.); children: Ricky, Gary, Eileen. Student journalism, U. Miami, 1945-47. News dir. Sta. WIOD AM-FM, Miami, 1947-56; assignment editor, prodr. Sta. WCKT-TV, Miami, 1956-57; news dir., 1957-79; dir. broadcast news Miami News, 1957; v.p. Hernstadt Broadcasting Corp., 1980-81; dir. corp. comm. Burnup & Sims, 1981-90; dir. comm. Printing Industry South Fla., 1990-92, Printing Assn. Fla., 1992—. Free-lance writer newspapers and mags.; cons. dept. comm. U. Miami, 1979, dir. public relations, 1979-80. Comm. dir. United Way Dade County, 1981. Served with AUS, 1945. Recipient Peabody award, 1975, Preceptor award Broadcast Industry conf., San Francisco State U., Abe Lincoln awards (2) So. Bap. Radio-TV Conf., Nat. Headliners awards (5); led Sta. WSVN (formerly WCKT) to more than 200 awards for news, including 3 Peabody awards, Emmy award. Mem. Nat. Acad. TV Arts and Scis. (past gov. Miami chpt.), Radio-TV News Dirs. Assn., Fla. AP Broadcasters (past pres.), Greater Miami C. of C., Nat. Broadcast Editl. Assn., Sigma Delta Chi (2 nat. awards). Home: 145 SW 49th Ave Miami FL 33134-1228

STRULL, GENE, technology consultant, retired electrical manufacturing company executive; b. Chgo., May 15, 1929; s. Albert and Helen (Wolf) S.; m. Joyce Landsbaum, July 6, 1952; children— David Jay, Brian Lee. BSEE, Purdue U., 1951; MS, Northwestern U., 1952, PhD in Elec. Engring, 1954. With Westinghouse Electric Corp., Pitts., later Balt., 1954-93, supervisory engr., adv. engr., mgr. solid state tech.-aerospace, 1958-68, mgr. sci. and tech. systems devel. div., mgr. advanced tech. labs., 1968-78, dep. gen. mgr. systems devel. div., 1979-81, gen. mgr. advanced tech. div., 1981-93, exec. dir. tech., 1987-93. Cons. Army Sci. Bd., 1979-83, NRC-NAS, 1980-82, Def. Sci. Bd., 1981-83, NSF, 1992—; cons. NASA, 1967-87, com. chmn., 1976-78; adv. com. panel USNR, 1989. Contbg. author: Integrated Electronic Systems, 1970, Integrated Circuit Technology, 1967; contbr. articles to profl. jours.; patentee in field. Gene Strull Tech. Ctr. at Westinghouse Electric Corp. Advanced Tech. Labs. named in his honor, Balt., 1993; named Outstanding Elec. Engr. award Purdue U., 1994. Fellow IEEE (life, Govt. Industry Svc. award 1987, Frederik Philips award 1991); mem. Md. Acad. Scis. (chmn. 1978-80). Home: One Gristmill Ct # 606 Baltimore MD 21208

STRULL, JAMES RICHARD, lawyer; b. NYC, Oct. 31, 1946; s. Abraham Arthur and Beverly Ann (Lamot) Strull; m. Catherine Koziel, Sept. 25, 1983. BBA, St. Johns U., N.Y.C., 1971; JD, N.Y. Law Sch., 1974. Bar: N.J. 1974, U.S. Dist. Ct. N.J. 1974, N.Y. 1980, U.S. Dist. Ct. (southeastern dist.) N.Y. 1980, U.S. Supreme Ct. 1983, U.S. Tax Ct. 1986. Ins. broker Strull Garber Corp., N.Y.C., 1967—74; assoc. Ludmer & Slaff, Wood-Ridge, NJ, 1974; ptnr. Ludmer & Strull, Wood-Ridge, 1975—81, LaFianza & Strull, Wood-Ridge, Hackensack, NJ, 1981—90, Uscher Quiat Uscher & Strull, Hackensack, 1990—95, Rubenstein, Rudolph, Meyerson, Blake & Strull, Oakland, NJ, 1995—99, Kudman Trachten LLP, Hackensack, 1999—2004, N.Y.C., 1999—2000; pvt. practice Hackensack, 2004—. Bd. dirs. Bergen County (N.J.) Cath. Youth Orgn., 1984—90. Mem.: Lions (pres. 1979). Office: Continental Plaza III 2nd Fl 433 Hackensack Ave Hackensack NJ 07601 Office Phone: 201-968-1700. Business E-Mail: james@strull.com.

STRUM, BRIAN J. real estate executive; b. Bklyn., Nov. 27, 1939; s. Max J. and Beatrix (Galitzky) S.; m. Mickey Weiss, Nov. 19, 1966; children: Ira, Howard, Beth. BA, Bklyn. Coll., 1960; LLB, NYU, 1963. Bar: N.Y. 1964, N.J. 1969; CLU; counselor of real estate. Atty. Gilbert, Segall and Young, N.Y.C., 1963-65; assoc. res. atty. Prudential Ins. Co. Am., N.Y.C., 1965-67, various positions, law dept., 1967-75, v.p. real estate investments, 1975-86; chmn. Prudential Property Co., Newark, 1986—94; CEO Prudential Realty Group, Newark, 1992-94; Silverstein chair of real estate devel. NYU, 1995-98. Pres., trustee Prudential Realty Trust, 1985-94; mem. adv. bd. Chgo. Title & Trust Co., N.Y.C., 1982-96. Editor: Financing Real Estate in the Inflationary Eighties, 1981; contbr. articles to profl. jours. With USAR, 1963-69. Recipient Disting. Cmty. Svc. award Brandeis U., 1983, Urban Leadership award NYU, 1990, Good Scout award N.Y.C. coun. Boy Scouts Am., 1991, Nat. Achievement awrd D.A.R.E. Am., 1993. Fellow Anglo Am. Real Property Inst. (charter); mem. ABA (chmn. real property, probate and trust law sects. 1984-85), N.Y. State Bar Assn. (chmn. real property sect. 1975-76), Urban Land Inst. (coun. mem.), Am. Coll. Real Estate Lawyers (charter), Am. Soc. Real Estate Counselors. Home: 435 Pine Ln Haworth NJ 07641-1308 Office Phone: 201-384-1400. E-mail: mstrum77@aol.com.

STRUM, JAY GERSON, lawyer; b. N.Y.C., July 6, 1938; s. John and Dorothy (Chaikind) S.; m. Patricia Ann Burtis, Jan. 25, 1969; children: Daniel, Jennifer. BA in polit. sci. magna cum laude, CCNY, 1959; LLB, Harvard U., 1962. Bar: N.Y. 1963, U.S. Dist. Ct. (so. and ea. dists.) N.Y. 1963, U.S. Ct. Appeals (2d cir.) 1965, U.S. Supreme Ct. 1979. Trial atty. SEC, N.Y.C., 1963-65; ptnr. Coon, Dubow, Kleinberg & Strum, N.Y.C., 1965-67; assoc. Kaye, Scholer, Fierman, Hays & Handler, N.Y.C., 1967-70, ptnr., 1971—. Mem. ABA, Assn. of Bar of City of N.Y., Harvard Club (N.Y.C.), Phi Beta Kappa. Clubs: Harvard (N.Y.C.). Office: Kaye Scholer Fierman Hays & Handler LLP 425 Park Ave New York NY 10022-3506

STRUNA, NANCY L. social historian and American studies educator; b. Painesville, Ohio, May 24, 1950; d. Edward A. and Betty J. (Hoffacker) S. BS, U. Wis., 1972; PhD, U. Md., 1979. Social studies tchr. The Andrews Sch., Willoughby, Ohio, 1972-74; grad. asst. U. Md., College Park, 1974-76; tchr. 1-8 grades St. Mark's Elem., Adelphi, Md., 1976-78; instr. U. Md., College Park, 1978-80; asst. prof. U. Minn., Mpls., 1980-82; prof. dept. Am. Studies U. Md., College Park, 1982—, acting chair, 2001, exec. dir. univ. gen. edn., 2002—03. Spl. asst. to pres. women's issues, 1998-2000, fellow Acad. Affairs, 1998-99, campus legis. liaison, 1999. Author: People of Prowess, Sport, Leisure and Labor in Early America, 1996; contbr. articles to profl. jours., chpts. to books. Chair Pres. Commn. on Women's Issues U. Md., 1996—98; mem. Omohundro Inst. for Early Am. History, Culture and Soc. Named Disting. scholar Nat. Assn. Phys. Edn. in Higher Edn., 1993. Fellow Am. Acad. Kinesiology, N.Am. Soc. Sport History (pres. 1995-97), Orgn. Am. Historians, Am. Hist. Assn., Am. Studies Assn., U.S. Capitol Hist. Assn. Office: U Md 1102 Holzapfel Hall Coll College Park MD 20742-5620 Business E-Mail: nlstruna@umd.edu.

STRUPP, HANS HERMANN, psychologist, educator; b. Frankfurt am Main, Germany, Aug. 25, 1921; came to U.S., 1939, naturalized, 1945; s. Josef and Anna (Metzger) S.; m. Lottie Metzger, Aug. 19, 1951; children: Karen, Barbara, John. AB with distinction, George Washington U., 1945, AM, 1947, PhD, 1954; MD (hon.), U. Ulm, Fed. Republic of Germany, 1986. Diplomate in clin. psychology Am. Bd. Profl. Psychology; lic. clin. psychologist, Tenn. Research psychologist Human Factors Ops. Research Labs., Dept. Air Force, Washington, 1949-54; supervisory research psychologist, personnel research br. Adj. Gen.'s Office, Dept. of Army, Washington, 1954-55; dir. psychotherapy research project Sch. Medicine, George Washington U., Washington, 1955-57; dir. psychol. services, dept. psychiatry U. N.C. Sch. Medicine, Chapel Hill, 1957-64, asso. prof. psychology, 1957-62, prof., 1962-66; prof. dept. psychology Vanderbilt U., Nashville, 1966-76, dir. clin. tng., dept. psychology, 1967-76, disting. prof., 1976-94, Harvie Branscomb disting. prof., 1985-86; disting. prof. emeritus, 1994—. Mem. editorial adv. bd. Psychotherapy: Theory, Research and Practice, 1963-97, Jour. Cons. and Clin. Psychology, 1964—, Jour. Nervous and Mental Disease, 1965—, Jour. Am. Acad. Psychoanalysis, 1972—, Jour. Contemporary Psychotherapy, 1972-86, Psychiatry Research, 1979-86, Jour. Profl. Psychology, 1976-89; founding editor Psychotherapy Rsch., 1990-95; others; contbr. chpts. to books, articles and revs. to profl. jours. Recipient Helen Sargent meml. prize Menninger Found., 1963; Alumni Achievement award George Washington U., 1972; Disting. Profl. Achievement award Am. Bd. Profl. Psychology, 1976, Disting. Profl. Contbns. to Knowledge award Am. Psychol. Assn., 1987; others Fellow Am. Psychol. Assn. (mem. exec. council 1964, exec. bd. 1969-72, council of reps. 1970-73, chmn. com. on fellows div. psychotherapy 1970-74, pres. div. clin. psychology 1974-75, recipient Disting. Profl. Psychologist award 1973, Disting. Scientist award 1979), Tenn. Psychol. Assn., AAAS; mem. Eastern Psychol. Assn., Southeastern Psychol. Assn., Am. Psychopathol. Assn., Am. Psychoanalytic Assn. (hon.), Soc. for Psychotherapy Research (pres. 1972-73, Career Contbr. award 1986), Psychologists Interested in Advancement of Psychoanalysis, Phi Beta Kappa, Sigma Xi. Home: 4117 Dorman Dr Nashville TN 37215-2404 *As a refugee from Nazi Germany, I remain deeply grateful for the opportunities my adopted country has provided me.*

STRUPP, JOHN ALLEN, oncologist; b. Chapel Hill, N.C., Dec. 13, 1958; s. Hans Hermann and Lottie (Metzger) S.; m. Dana Morris, Oct. 20, 1984; children: Emily, Joshua, Suzanne. BA, U. N.C., 1980; MD, U. Tenn., 1985. Diplomate Nat. Bd. Med. Examiners. Intern, resident in internal medicine U. Pitts. Hosp., 1985-88; fellow in med. oncology Vanderbilt U., Nashville, 1988-90; med. oncologist St. Thomas Med. Group, Nashville, 1990—. Chief divsn. hematology/oncology St. Thomas Hosp., Nashville, 1994—; med. dir. Response Oncology, Inc., 1991—; asst. clin. prof. dept. medicine Vanderbilt U. Sch. Medicine, 1993—; bd. dirs. Alive Hospice, Inc., chmn. quality improvement com., 1997; med. adv. bd. Coram Healthcare, Inc., 1994—. Campaign chmn. physician's divsn. Nashville Jewish Fedn., 1994-95, 95-96; bd. dirs. Nashville chpt. Am. Jewish Com., 1994-96; parents com. Univ. Sch. Nashville Capital Campaign, 1996. Mem. Am. Coll. Physicians, Am. Soc. Clin. Oncology, Tenn. Med. Assn. (alt. del.), Nashville Oncology Soc., Nashville Acad. Medicine, Phi Beta Kappa. Office: St Thomas Med Group 4230 Harding Rd Ste 400 Nashville TN 37205-4900 Home: 57 Whitworth Blvd Nashville TN 37205-5019

STRUTHERS, MARGO S. lawyer; BA, Carleton Coll., 1972; JD cum laude, U. Minn., 1976. Atty., shareholder Moss & Barnett, P.A. and predecessor firms, Mpls., 1976-93; ptnr. Oppenheimer Wolff & Donnelly, LLP, Mpls., 1993—. Mem. Am. Health Lawyers Assn., Minn. State Bar Assn (bus. law sect., former chair nonprofit com., former chair and former mem. governing coun. health law sect.). Office: Oppenheimer Wolff & Donnelly LLP Plaza VII 45 S 7th St Ste 3300 Minneapolis MN 55402-1614 E-mail: mstruthers@oppenheimer.com.

STRUTTON, LARRY D. former newspaper executive; b. Colorado Springs, Colo., Sept. 12, 1940; s. Merril and Gladys (Sheldon) Strutton; m. Carolyn Ann Croak, Dec. 3, 1960; children: Gregory L., Kristen. AA in Electronics Engring., Emily Griffith Electronics Sch., 1968; BS in Bus. Mgmt. and Systems Mgmt., Met. State Coll., 1971; diploma in Advanced Mgmt. Program, Harvard U., 1988. Printer Gazette Telegraph, Colorado Springs, 1961—64; prodn. dir. Rocky Mountain News, Denver, 1964—80, pres., 1990, pres., CEO, 1991—2001, former pub.; exec. v.p. ops. and advt. Detroit Free Press, 1981—83; v.p. ops. Los Angeles Times, 1983—85, exec. v.p. ops., 1986—90. Mem. adv. com. Rochester Inst. Tech., 1984—. Mem.: Am. Newspaper Pubs. Assn. (chmn. 1987, chmn. TEC com. 1985—86), R&E Coun. (rsch. and engring. coun. Graphic Arts Industry Inc.), Lakeside Golf Club (L.A.).

STRUTZ, WILLIAM A. lawyer; b. Bismarck, N.D., May 13, 1934; s. Alvin C. and Ina Vee (Minor) S.; m. Marilyn Seagly, Aug. 31, 1957; children: Heidi Jane Mitchell, Colin Christopher, Nathaniel Paul. Student, Drake U., 1952-53; BA, North Ctrl. Coll., 1956; postgrad., Washington and Lee U., 1956-57; JD, U. N.D., 1959. Bar: N.D. 1959, U.S. Dist. Ct. N.D. 1959, U.S. Ct. Appeals (8th cir.) 1961. Atty., pres. Fleck, Mather & Strutz, Ltd., Bismarck, N.D., 1959—. Mem. grievance com. N.D. Supreme Ct., Bismarck, 1974-77, chmn. supreme ct. svcs. com., 1979—. Bd. dirs. Vets. Meml. Pub. Libr., Bismarck, Shiloh Christian Sch., Bismarck, 1978—; pres. student body North Ctrl. Coll., 1956. Recipient Herbert Harley award Am. Judicature Soc., 1991. Mem. ABA, Am. Bd. Trial Advs. (adv.), Lions Club. Methodist. Avocations: reading, rare book collecting, music, sports. Home: 1238 W Highland Acres Rd Bismarck ND 58501-1259 Office: Fleck Mather Strutz Ltd 400 E Broadway Ave Bismarck ND 58501-4038

STRUVE, GUY MILLER, lawyer; b. Wilmington, Del., Jan. 5, 1943; s. William Scott and Elizabeth Bliss (Miller) S.; m. Marcia Mayo Hill, Sept. 20, 1986; children: Andrew Hardenbrook, Catherine Tolstoy, Frank Leroy Hill, Guy Miller, Beverly Marcia Wise Hill (dec.), Elena Wise Struve-Hill. AB summa cum laude, Yale U., 1963; LLB magna cum laude, Harvard U., 1966. Bar: N.Y. 1967, D.C. 1986, U.S. Dist. Ct. (so. dist.) N.Y. 1970, U.S. Dist. Ct. (ea. dist.) N.Y. 1973, U.S. Dist. Ct. (no. dist.) Calif. 1979, U.S. Dist. Ct. D.C. 1987, U.S. Dist. Ct. (no. dist.) N.Y. 2000, U.S. Ct. Appeals (2d cir.) 1969, U.S. Ct. Appeals (D.C. cir.) 1973, U.S. Ct. Appeals (8th cir.) 1976, U.S. Ct. Appeals (9th cir.) 1979, U.S. Supreme Ct. 1971, U.S. Dist. Ct. (we. dist.) N.Y. 1991. Law clk. Hon. J. Edward Lumbard, Chief Judge United States Ct. Appeals for 2d Circuit, 1966-67; assoc. Davis Polk & Wardwell, N.Y.C., 1967-72, ptnr., 1973—. Ind. Counsel's Office, 1987-94. Mem. ABA, N.Y. State Bar Assn., Assn. of Bar of City of N.Y. (chmn. com. antitrust and trade regulation, 1983-86, chmn. com. fed. cts. 1998-2001), Am. Law Inst. Home: 116 E 63rd St New York NY 10021-7325 Office: Davis Polk & Wardwell 450 Lexington Ave Fl 31 New York NY 10017-3982

STRUYK, PIETER M. music educator; b. Arlington, Va., June 9, 1970; s. Raymond Jay Struyk; m. Ali Kathleen Prime, July 29, 2000. Bachelor of Music Performance, U. Mich., 1992; studied with, Michael Udow, Salvatore Rabbio, Albert Merz, Gerald Cleaver. Percussion instr. and clinician Performing Arts Sch. Worcester, Mass., 2000—; percussion specialist Northborough Pub. Schs., Mass., 2001—. Artist endorser Sabian Cymbals, 1997—; percussion cons. Coll. Holy Cross, Worcester, 2001—; adj. prof. percussion Worcester Polytechnic Inst., 2001—, Anna Maria Coll., Paxton, Mass., 2001—. Contbr. articles to mags.; musician: (recs. with Big Dave and the Ultrasonics) Love and Money, 1993, No Sweat Live!, 1996, Big Dave and the Ultrasonics, 1999; percussionist Algonquin H.S. Wind Ensemble, Northboro, Mass., 2002, Ann Arbor Symphony Orch., 1992—98, Adrian Symphony Orch., Mich., 1996—99, Greg Piccolo and Heavy Juice, Bradford, R.I., 1999—, Coll. Holy Cross, Worcester, 2000—, Worcester Chorus Orch., 2001—, New Bedford Symphony Orch., Mass., 2001—, Jim Dower Trio, Boston, 2001—, Chorus N. Shore, Danvers, Mass., 2002—, appearances include (TV series) Much Music Lunch TV, 1995, (radio) House of Blues Radio Show, L.A., 1999. Mem.: Boston Musicians Assn., Am. Fedn. Musicians, Percussive Arts Soc. Democrat. Avocations: martial arts, ballroom dancing. Home: 19 Brookfield Cir Framingham MA 01701-4036

STRUYK, ROBERT JOHN, lawyer; b. Sanborn, Iowa, May 17, 1932; s. Arie Peter and Adriana (VerHoef) S.; m. Barbara Damon, Sept. 7, 1963; children: Arie Franklin, Damon Nicholas, Elizabeth Snow. BA, Hope Coll., 1954; MA, Columbia U., 1957; LLB, U. Minn., 1961. Bar: Minn., U.S. Dist. Ct. Minn. Secondary tchr. Indianola (Iowa) Pub. Schs., 1957-58; assoc., then ptnr. Dorsey & Whitney, Mpls., 1961—. Mem.: Mpls., Minikahda. Episcopalian. Office: Dorsey & Whitney 50 S 6th St Ste 2200 Minneapolis MN 55402-1498

STRYER, LUBERT, biochemist, educator; b. Tientsin, China, Mar. 2, 1938; BS with honors, U. Chgo., 1957; MD magna cum laude, Harvard U., 1961; DS (hon.), U. Chgo., 1992. Helen Hay Whitney fellow Harvard U., also Med. Research Council Lab., 1961-63; from asst. prof. to assoc. prof. biochemistry Stanford U., 1963-69; prof. molecular biophysics and biochemistry Yale U., 1969-76; Winzer prof. neurobiology Stanford U. Sch. Medicine, 1976—2004, chmn. dept. structural biology, 1976-79, prof. emeritus, 2004—; chmn. sci. adv. bd. Affymetrix, Inc., 1993—; chmn., chief sci. officer Senomyx, Inc., La Jolla, Calif., 1999-2001, chmn. sci. adv. bd., 2001—. Cons. NIH, NRC; pres., sci. dir. Affymax Rsch. Inst., Palo Alto, Calif., 1989-90; mem. sci. adv. bd. Jane Coffin Childs Fund, 1982-90, Rsch. to Prevent Blindness, 1984-93, Pew Scholars Profs. in Biomed. Scis.; chmn. sci. adv. bd. Affymetrix, Inc., 1993—. Mem. editorial bd.: Jour. Molecular Biology, 1968-72, Jour. Cell Biology, 1981-84; assoc. editor: Annual Revs. Biophysics and Bioengineering, 1970-76. Trustee Helen Hay Whitney Found., 1997—2001, McKnight Endowment for the Neuroscis., 1999—. Recipient Am. Chem. Soc. award in biol. chemistry Eli Lilly & Co., 1970, Alcon award in vision Alcon Rsch. Inst.,

1992, Molecular Bioanalytics award German Soc. Biochemistry and Molecular Biology, 2002. Fellow AAAS (Newcomb Cleveland prize 1992), Am. Acad. Arts and Scis.; mem. NAS, Am. Chem. Soc., Am. Soc. Biol. Chemists, Biophys. Soc., Phi Beta Kappa. Office: Stanford Sch Medicine Fairchild Ctr D221 Stanford CA 94305-5125

STRYKER, JAMES WILLIAM, retired automotive executive, former military officer; b. Grand Rapids, Mich., Apr. 20, 1940; s. John Alvin and Marian (Anderson) S.; m. Eleanor Marie Finger, Sept. 26, 1964; children: James William II, Marian Marie Jenkins, Kathryn Alison Greenbauer. BS, U.S. Mil. Acad., 1963; student, Def. Lang. Inst., 1968—69; MA, U. Mich., 1972; postgrad., U.S. Army Command and Gen. Staff Coll., 1978. Commd. 2d lt. U.S. Army, 1963, battery exec. officer 6th/20th field arty., 1964-65, advisor JUSMAG, 1965—66, battery comdr. 4th/3d field arty., 1967-68, advisor TMAG, 1969—70; S-3 ops. officer 1st/7th F.A., Ft. Riley, Kans., 1972-73; assoc. prof. history U.S. Mil. Acad., West Point, N.Y., 1973-77; chief nuc. ops. Ctrl. Army Group NATO, Heidelberg, Germany, 1978-81; dir., project mgr. tank-automotive command U.S. Army, Warren, Mich., 1981-86, ret., 1986; program mgr. military vehicles operation GMC Truck, Pontiac, Mich., 1987-95; cross brand portfolio mgr. Pontiac GMC Divsn. GM Corp., Detroit, 1996-98, asst. brand mgr. product full size and mid size vans, 1999-2001, asst. brand mgr. product alternative fuels and mobility, 2001—02, product mgr. alternative fuels and mobility, 2002—04; ret., 2004. Author: (with others) Encyclopedia of Southern History, 1977; co-author: Early American Wars, 1978. Torch bearer Olympic Winter Games, Salt Lake City, 2002. Decorated Legion of Merit, Bronze Star medal, Def. Meritorious Svc. medal, Meritorious Svc. medal with oakleaf cluster, Army Commendation medal with oakleaf cluster, U.S. Army/Vietnamese Cross of Gallantry with palm and gold star; Olympic torchbearer Winter Olympics, 2002. Mem.: NRA (endowment), Nat. Def. Indsl. Assn. (dir. Detroit chpt. 1991—97, 2d v.p. 1995, 1st v.p. 1995—96, pres. 1996—97, adv. 1997—2000), Trout Unltd., Ruffed Grouse Soc. (banquet com. Detroit 1998—2003), Assn. U.S. Army (dir. Detroit chpt. 1990—95), Ducks Unltd., Pheasants Forever, Nodrog Setter Club Mich., Gordon Setter Club Am. Avocations: hunting, skeet shooting, trout fishing, field training english and gordon setters. Home: 168 First St Romeo MI 48065-5000 E-mail: bbillstryker@aol.com.

STRYKER, STEVEN CHARLES, lawyer; b. Omaha, Nebr., Oct. 26, 1944; s. James M. and Jean G. (Grannis) S.; m. Bryna Dee Litwin, Oct. 20, 1972; children: Ryan, Kevin, Gerrit, Courtney. BS, U. Iowa, 1967, JD with distinction, 1969; postgrad. studies, Northwestern U. Grad. Sch. Bus, 1969-70, DePaul U., 1971. Bar: Iowa 1969, Tex. 1986; CPA Ill., Iowa. Sr. tax acct. Arthur Young & Co., Chgo., 1969-72; fed. tax mgr. Massey Ferguson, Des Moines, 1972-74; fed., state tax mgr. FMC Corp., Chgo., 1974-78; gen. tax atty. Shell Oil Co., Houston, 1978-81, asst. gen. tax counsel, 1981-83, gen. mgr., 1983-86, v.p., gen. tax counsel, 1986—. Mem. ABA, AICPA, Tex. Bar Assn., Iowa Bar Assn., Ill. Soc. CPAs, Iowa Soc. CPAs, Tax Execs. Inst., Am. Petroleum Inst. Home: 2121 Kirby Dr Unit 124 Houston TX 77019-6068 Office: Shell Oil Co 1 Shell Plz Ste 4570 Houston TX 77001

STRYKER, TERENCE WAYNE, secondary school educator; b. Daytona Beach, Fla., Nov. 21, 1956; s. Judson Phillip and Irene Lillian Stryker; m. Lynn Lyda. B in Music Edn., Fla. State U., 1980; M in M in Music Edn., PhD in Music Edn., Trinity Coll., 2001. Cert. network engr.; music tchr. grades K-12 Fla. Choral dir. Port St. Joe (Fla.) H.S., Port St. Joe, 1985—89; band dir. Wewahitchka (Fla.) H.S., 1989—. Named All USA Tchr. Team, USA Today, 1999, Tchr. of Yr., Gulf County Schs., 2000. Mem.: Fla. League Arts Tchrs., Fla. League Tchrs., Music Educator's Nat. Conf., Fla. Music Educator's Assn., Fla. Bandmaster's Assn. Baptist. Avocations: coin collecting/numismatics, auto restoration, woodworking, technology. Home: 4801 Sunset Dr Panama City FL 32404 Office: Wewahitchka HS One Gator Circle Wewahitchka FL 32465 Personal E-mail: stryker_t@firn.edu. Business E-Mail: tstryker@wewahigh.com.

STRYSICK, MICHAEL OTTO, terrestrial ecologist, physicist, microbiologist; b. Sheboygan, Wis., Jan. 13, 1931; s. Michael Sr. and Agnes (Czaja) S.; m. Carol Ann Greiner, June 25, 1955 (dec. July 1992); children: Peter Michael, Mary Susan. Terrestrial ecologist, rschr., Sheboygan, Wis., 1954—. Cons. Master Gardner program U. Wis. Ext. Svcs., Sheboygan Falls, Wis., 1988—; rschr. Neem Oil Margosan-O, 1992. Cubmaster to commr. Boy Scouts Am.; treas. Cath. Com. Scouting, Sheboygan, 1970-97. With U.S. Army, 1952-54, Korea. Recipient St. George medal Boy Scouts Am., 1984. Mem. AAAS, Korean War Vets. Assn., VFW, Am. Legion. Achievements include Neem Oil development in the 1980s and field studies; Hanta Virus verification in Ams. as med. problem, 1990—; researcher in Myology 2000, a post-genome 30 protein complex of the nucleus of human cells; cell protein atom chemistry in female cumulus cell; Krebs/Calvincycle phenomena citric TNF alpha beta gamma omega role of un P un Ca polarity to transfat and uric acid lactic acidosis in human diabetes; symbiotic GUT thermobacteria excess citric acid as source of H3 and of NH3 and to NO and excess uric acid and E. coli or salmonella muntation, or UVB radiation induced cancers; including all life forms cycle of reproduction avoidance of overpopulation and evolutionary adaptation; and use of woodchip mulch, adverse effects in anerobic conditions in 1970-80. Home and Office: 1002 N 16th St Sheboygan WI 53081-3825 E-mail: gardnersenvy@bytehead.com.

STUARD, SUSAN MOSHER, education educator; b. Rochester, N.Y., Apr. 15, 1935; d. Charles Hull and Doris Sherman Mosher; m. Ian Donald Stuard, June 10, 1957; children: Ian, Charles, Susan. BA, Smith Coll., Northampton, Mass., 1957; MA, U. Rochester, 1961; MS, SUNY, 1961; PhD, Yale U., 1971. Instr. Washington U., St. Louis, 1966—68; part time instr. U. Rochester, 1968—69; asst. prof. history SUNY, 1970—77, assoc. prof. history, 1975—85; vis. assoc. prof. history Haverford Coll., Pa., 1983—84, 1986—88, prof. history, 1988—2000, prof. history emeritus, 2001—. Coun. mem. Medieval Acad. Am., Boston, 1995—98; del. to Am. Coun. of Learned Socs., New York, 2002—; elected mem., prof. div. Am. Hist. Assn., Washington, 2001—. Author: (book) State Deference, 1992; author: (editor) Becoming Visible, 2nd edit., 1997, 3d edit., 1998. Grantee Newly Co-ed Institutions, Ford Found., 1987—88, Mellon Found., 2004—; Grant for Rsch. in Venice, Delmas Found., 1999—2000. Mem.: Am. Hist. Assn. (program com. 1996—), Am. Acad. of Rome (selection com. 1996—97), Medieval Acad. of Am. (coun. 1995—98). Democrat. Achievements include Helped pioneer history of medieval women with Women in Medieval Soc., 1976. Home: 1507 Greenhill Rd West Chester PA 19380 Office: Haverford Coll 370 Lancaster Ave Haverford PA 19041 Office Phone: 610-896-2904. Business E-Mail: sstuard@haverford.edu.

STUART, ALICE MELISSA, lawyer; b. NYC, Apr. 7, 1957; d. John Marberger and Marjorie Louise (Browne) S. BA, Ohio State U., 1977; JD, U. Chgo., 1980; LLM, NYU, 1982. Bar: NY 1981, Ohio 1982, Fla. 1994, U.S. Dist. Ct. (so. dist.) Ohio, 1983, U.S. Dist. Ct. (so. and ea. dists.) NY 1985. Assoc. Schwartz, Shapiro, Kelm & Warren, Columbus, Ohio, 1982-84, Paul, Weiss, Rifkind, Wharton & Garrison, NYC, 1984-85, Kassel, Neuwirth & Geiger, NYC, 1985-86, Phillips, Nizer, Benjamin, Krim & Ballon, NYC, 1987—92; pvt. practice NYC, 1992—98; atty. LeBoeuf, Lamb, Greene & MacRae, NYC, 1998—. Adj. prof. So. Coll., Orlando, Fla., 1997-98. Surrogate Speakers' Bur. Reagan-Bush Campaign, NYC, 1984; mem. Lawyers for Bush-Quayle Campaign, NYC, 1988; bd. dirs. Mayflower Soc. in State of NY, 1998-, counsellor, 2002-. Mem. ABA, NY State Bar Assn., Winston Churchill Meml. Libr. Soc., Jr. League, Soc. Mayflower Descs. in State of NY (bd. dirs. 1999-, counselor 2002-), Phi Beta Kappa, Phi Kappa Phi, Alpha Lambda Delta. Republican. Office: LeBoeuf Lamb Greene & MacRae 125 W 55th St New York NY 10019-5369 Office Phone: 212-424-8000. E-mail: astuart@llgm.com.

STUART, ANN, academic administrator, writer, educator; b. Madisonville, Ky., Dec. 22, 1935; d. Peter Frank and Laura (Hatchett) S.; m. Raymond R. Poliakoff, Aug. 22, 1980. BA in Edn., U. Fla., 1958; MA in English, U. Ky., 1962; PhD in English, So. Ill. U., 1976. Tchr. Maderia Beach Jr. High Sch., St. Petersburg, Fla., 1958-59, Bourbon County High Sch., Paris, Ky., 1959-60, Henry Clay High Sch., Lexington, Ky., 1960-62; prof. of English and tech. writing U. Evansville, Ind., 1962-89, asst. dean Coll. Arts and Scis., 1979-81, 86-87, adminstrv. coordinator writing programs, 1984-86; dean Sch. Arts and Scis. East Stroudsburg (Pa.) U., 1989-90; provost, v.p. acad. affairs Alma (Mich.) Coll., 1990-93; pres. Hartford (Conn.) Grad. Ctr., 1994—. Lectr. various regional and nat. profl. orgns.; dir. computer edn. Vanderburgh Sch. Corp., U. Evansville, Ball Communications, Inc., Evansville, 1985—; adminstrv. coordinator writing programs U. Evansville, 1985—; cons. various local, nat. bus., 1982—; vis. prof. computer tech. Purdue U., West Lafayette, Ind., 1987-88. Author: Writing and Analyzing Effective Computer System Documentation, 1984, Corresponding with Customers, 1985, The Technical Writer, 1987, Communication Guide For Corresponding with Students, Parents, Alumni and Donors, 1988. Bd. dirs. Evansville Arts and Edn. Council, 1972-75, Harlaxton Soc., Evansville, 1981-85. Mem. MLA, Ind. Corp. Sci. and Industry, Nat. Council Tchrs. English, Assn. Tchrs. Tech. Writing, Am. Coun. Edn., Am. Assn. Higher Edn., Am. Assn. Univ. Adminstrs., Rotary, Phi Kappa Phi, Delta Kappa Gamma. Clubs: Musicians of Evansville (pres. 1972-78). Avocations: art museums, performing arts, architecture. Office: Hartford Grad Ctr 275 Windsor St Hartford CT 06120-2910

STUART, CAROLE, publishing executive; b. N.Y.C., Feb. 22, 1941; d. Frank and Sally (Stern) Rose; m. Lyle Stuart, Feb. 4, 1982; 1 child, Jennifer Susan Livingston. Student, Bklyn. Coll. Pub. Lyle Stuart, Inc., Secaucus, N.J.; assoc. pub. Carol Pub. Group, N.Y.C.; pub. Barricade Books, Inc., N.Y.C. Author: Why Was I Adopted?, To Turn You On, 39 Sex Fantasies for Women, (with Claire Ciliotta), Why Am I Going to the Hospital?, I'll Never Be Fat Again, How To Lose 5 Pounds Fast, The Thank You Book. Mem. Authors Guild, Women's Media Group, Wine and Food Soc. N.Y.. Home: 1530 Palisade Ave Apt 6L Fort Lee NJ 07024-5402 Office: Barricade Books Ste 308A 185 Bridge Plz N Fort Lee NJ 02024

STUART, CHARLES EDWARD, electrical engineer, oceanographer; b. Durham, N.C., Feb. 9, 1942; s. Charles Edward and Wilma Kelly Stuart; m. Margaret Ann Robinson, Jan. 9, 1982; children: Marjorie Kelly, Heather Alison. BSEE, Duke U., 1963. Engr. Westinghouse Electric Corp., Balt., 1963-65; sr. engr. Booz Allen Hamilton, Chevy Chase, Md., 1966-68; rsch. dir. B-K Dynamics Inc., Huntsville, Ala., 1969-78; oceanographer Office of Naval Rsch., Arlington, Va., 1979-84; dir. Maritime System Office Advanced Rsch. Projects Agy., Arlington, 1985-98; with def. programs U.S. Dept. Energy, Washington, 1998-99; pres. Competitive Enterprise Solutions, LLC, Arlington, 2000—. Contbr. 12 papers on ocean acoustics, unmanned systems and maritime tech. to profl. jours. Recipient Am. Def. Preparedness Assn. award, Bushnell award for career contbns. to undersea warfare, 1996. Mem. IEEE (sr., ad. com. 1991-93), Assn. Unmanned Vehicle Systems (trustee 1989-93). Methodist. Achievements include leading work in antisubmarine warfare, cybersecurity and unmanned undersea vehicle technology. Office: Competitive Enterprise Solutions LLC 901 N Nelson St # 809 Arlington VA 22203

STUART, CYNTHIA MORGAN, university administrator; b. Harrisburg, Pa, June 29, 1949; d. Paul William and Bernice Leona (Boyer) M.; m. David Edward Stuart, June 14, 1971. Student, Elizabethtown (Pa.) Coll., 1967-69; BA, U. N.Mex., 1971, MPA, 1982, ABD in Ednl. Leadership, 2003. Admissions counselor U. N.Mex., Albuquerque, 1974-77, asst. dir. admissions, 1977-80, assoc. dir. admissions, 1980-83, dir. admissions, 1983—, Univ. articulation officer, 1989—, dir. student outreach svc. (secondary appointment), 1991-95, enrollment mgmt. team mem., 1998—. Mem. N.Mex. Coordinating Coun. Secondary Sch. and Coll., 1983-92; chair Coun. for Common Concerns, Albuquerque, 1987-95; mem. N.Mex. Articulation Com., Santa Fe, 1983-95; mem. adv. bd. Albuquerque Tech. Vocat. Inst., 1991—. Compiler, editor Statewide Statistical Profile Report, N.Mex. HS, 1983-90; cover photographer Prehistoric New Mexico, 2d edit., 1994, Glimpses of the Ancient Southwest, 1995. Coord. United Way, Albuquerque, 1980-81; elected del. N.Mex. Dem. Conv., 1982; mem. issues and advocacy com. Albuquerque Bus. Edn. Compact, 1991-93; mem. Am. Indian Edn. Initiative, Albuquerque, 1992—; Coll. Bd. del., 1991—. Recipient sys. devel. grant Commn. on Higher Edn., Santa Fe, 1995. Mem. Am. Assn. Collegiate Registrars and Admissions Officers (reporting officer of transfer credit N.Mex. 1979—), Rocky Mountain Assn. Collegiate Registrars and Admissions Officers (v.p. 1979-81, pres. 1983-84), N.Mex. Assn. Collegiate Registrars and Admissions Officers (sec.-treas. 1978-82, pres. 1991-92, Outstanding Svc. award 1990), N.Mex. Am. Coll. Testing Coun. (chair 1996-97, state rep. 1997—, trustee Am. Coll. Testing 1999-2002, del. to Coll. Bd. 1991—). Democrat. Avocations: photography, travel, drawing, music. Home: 423 Tulane Dr SE Albuquerque NM 87106-1417 Office: Univ New Mex Office of Admissions Student Svc Ctr Albuquerque NM 87131-0001 E-mail: cstuart@unm.edu.

STUART, DABNEY, poet, author, English language educator; b. Richmond, Va., Nov. 4, 1937; s. Walker Dabney Jr. and Martha (vonSchilling) S.; m. Sandra Westcott, Jan. 20, 1983; children: Martha, Nathan vonSchilling, Darren Wynne AB, Davidson Coll., 1960; AM, Harvard U., 1962. Instr. Coll. William and Mary, Williamsburg, Va., 1961-65; prof. English Washington and Lee U., Lexington, Va., 1965—2002, S. Blount Mason Jr. prof. English, 1991—2002. Vis. prof. Middlebury (Vt.) Coll., 1968-69, Ohio U., Athens, 1975, U. Va., Charlottesville, 1981-83. Author: The Diving Bell, 1966, A Particular Place, 1969, The Other Hand, 1974, Friends of Yours, Friends of Mine, 1974, Round and Round, 1976, Nabokov: The Dimensions of Parody, 1978, Rockbridge Poems, 1981, Common Ground, 1982, Don't Look Back, 1987, Narcissus Dreaming, 1990, Sweet Lucy Wine, 1992, Light Years: New and Selected Poems, 1994, Second Sight: Poems for Paintings by Carroll Cloar, 1996, Long Gone, 1996, The Way to Cobbs Creek, 1997, Settlers, 1999, Strains of the Old Man, 1999, No Visible Means of Support, 2001, The Man Who Loves Cezanne, 2003, Family Preserve, 2004. Recipient Dylan Thomas prize Poetry Soc. Am., 1965, Gov.'s award State of Va., 1979; NEA lit. fellow, 1975, 82, Guggenheim fellow, 1987-88, Individual Artist fellow Va. Commn. for Arts, 1995, resident fellow Rockefeller Study and Conf. Ctr., Bellagio, Italy, 2000. Avocations: food, travel, painting. Home: 30 Edmondson Ave Lexington VA 24450-1904

STUART, DAVID EDWARD, anthropologist, writer, educator; b. Calhoun County, Ala., Jan. 9, 1945; s. Edward George and Avis Elsie (Densmore) S.; m. Cynthia K. Morgan, June 14, 1971. BA, W.Va. Wesleyan Coll., 1967; MA in Anthropology, U. N.Mex., 1970, PhD, 1972, postdoctoral student, 1975-76; LHD, W.Va. Wesleyan Coll., 2001. Rsch. assoc. Andean Center, Quito, Ecuador, 1970; continuing edn. instr. anthropology U. N.Mex., 1971-72; asst. prof. Eckerd Coll., St. Petersburg, Fla., 1972-74; rsch. archeologist Office Contract Archeology U. N.Mex., 1974, rsch. coord., 1974-77, asst. prof. anthropology, 1975-77, assoc. prof. anthropology, 1984-99, prof. anthropology, 1999—, asst. v.p. acad. affairs, 1987-95, assoc. v.p. acad. affairs, 1995-99, assoc. provost, 1999—, prof. architecture and planning, 2001—. Cons. archeologist right-of-way divsn. Pub. Svc. Co. N.Mex., Albuquerque, 1977-78; cons. anthropologist Bur. Indian Affairs, Albuquerque, 1978, Historic Preservation Bur. N.Mex., Santa Fe, 1978-81, Nat. Park Svcs., 1980, Albuquerque Mus., 1981; sr. rsch. assoc. Human Sys. rsch., Inc., 1981-83, Quivira Rsch. Ctr., Albuquerque, 1984-86; bd. dirs. Table Ind. Scholar, 1979-83, pres., bd. dirs. Rio Grande Heritage Found., Albuquerque and Las Cruces, 1985-87; advisor Human Sys. Rsch., Ind., Tularosa, N.Mex., 1978-80, Albuquerque Commn. on Hist. Preservation, 1984-86. Co-author: Archeological Survey: 4 Corners to Ambrosia, N.Mex., 1976, A Proposed Project Design for the timber Management Archeological Surveys, 1978, Ethnoarcheological Investigations of Shepherding in the Pueblo of Laguna, 1983; author: Prehistoric New Mexico, 1981, 2d edit., 1984, 3rd edit., 1989, Glimpses of the Ancient Southwest, 1985, The Magic of Bandelier National Monument, 1989, Power and Efficiency in Eastern Anasazi Architecture, 1994, Anasazi America, 2000, The Guaymas Chronicles, 2003, others; columnist New Mexico's Heritage, 1983-87, others; editor: Archeological Reports, No. 1, 1975, No. 2, 1982. Grantee Eckerd Coll., 1973, Historic Preservation Bur., 1978-80; recipient Essayist award N.Mex. Humanities Coun., 1986. Mem. Am. Anthrop. Assn., N.Mex. Archeol. Coun., Albuquerque Archeol. Soc. (pres. 1986-88), Descs. Signers Declaration Independence, Sigma Xi, Phi Kappa Phi. Office: U NMex Dane Smith Hall Rm 220 Albuquerque NM 87131-0001 Office Phone: 505-277-0896. Business E-Mail: dstuart@unm.edu. *Personal philosophy: In academics, as in life, reliabilty, integrity, and compassion are far more precious than mere intellectual brilliance.*

STUART, FRANK ADELL, county official; b. Tahoka, Tex., Dec. 18, 1928; s. John Franklin and Mary Elizabeth (Reed) S.; m. Mary Louise Wheat Crelia, Feb. 2, 1962; children: Rita, Donna, Franklin, Burce, Susan, Mary, Chris. BBA, Tex. Tech U., 1979. Asst. cashier Am. State Bank, Lubbock, Tex., 1949-52, Citizen Nat. Bank, Lubbock, 1953-59; acct. in pvt. practice Lubbock, 1960-63; asst. mgr. Gibson Discount Ctr., Lubbock, 1964-77; tax. assessor and collector Lubbock County, Lubbock, 1979-94, ret., 1994. Served to col. Tex. State Guard, 1988-98. Mem. Tax Assessor-Collectors Assn. Tex., Lubbock C. of C., Masons, YorkRite, Scottish Rite, Shriners, Yellow House Lodge, Daylight Lodge. Baptist. Home: 2704 57th St Lubbock TX 79413-5605 E-mail: stuart2704@aol.com.

STUART, GERARD WILLIAM, JR., investment company executive, city official; b. Yuba City, Calif., July 28, 1939; s. Gerard William and Geneva Bernice (Stuke) S.; m. Lenore Frances Lorona, 1981. Student, Yuba Jr. Coll., 1957-59, Chico State Coll., 1959-60; AB, U. Calif., Davis, 1962; MLS, U. Calif., Berkeley, 1963. Rare book libr. Cornell U., 1964-68; bibliographer scholarly collections Huntington Libr., San Marino, Calif., 1968-73, head acquisitions libr., 1973-75; sec.-treas., dir. Ravenstree Corp., 1969-80, pres, chmn. bd., 1980—, William Penn Ltd., 1981—. Councilman City of Yuma, 1992-96, deputy mayor, 1995; bd. dirs Ariz. Humanities Coun., 1993-99, Yuma Libr. Found., 1997, chmn., 1997-98, 99-2001. Lilly fellow Ind. U., 1964-63. Mem. Bibliog. Soc. Am., Rolls-Royce Owners Club, Grolier Club (N.Y.C.), Zamorano Club (L.A.), Phi Beta Kappa, Alpha Gamma Sigma, Phi Kappa Phi.

STUART, GLORIA, actress; b. Santa Monica, Calif., July 14, 1910; m. Arthur Shekman, July 29, 1934 (dec. 1978); children: Blair Gordon Newell, Cylvia. Student, U. Calif., Berkeley. Film appearances include The Old Dark House, The Invisible Man, The Kiss Before the Mirror, My Favorite Year, 1982, Mass Appeal, 1984, Wildcats, 1986, Titanic, 1997 (Acad. award nomination for best supporting actress, Saturn award for best supporting actress, Golden Globe award for best performance by an actress in a supporting role, SAG award for outstanding performance by a female actor in a supporting role); appeared in numerous stage prodns.; one women shows (painting) in N.Y., Austria, Italy. Hollywood Walk of Fame-2000. Office: SAG 5757 Wilshire Blvd Los Angeles CA 90036-3635

STUART, HAROLD CUTLIFF, lawyer, business executive; b. Oklahoma City, July 4, 1912; s. Royal Cutliff and Alice (Bramlitt) S.; m. Joan Skelly, June 6, 1938 (dec. 1994); children: Randi Stuart Wightman, Jon Rolf; m. Frances Langford, Nov. 18, 1994. JD, U. Va., 1936. Bar: Okla. 1936, DC 1952. Ptnr. Stuart, Biolchini, Turner & Givray, Tulsa; judge Common Pleas Ct., 1941-42; asst. sec. USAF, 1949-51; chmn. bd. 1st Stuart Corp., radio, oil, real estate and investments, Tulsa; dir. Lowrance Electronics, Inc., Tulsa. Spl. cons. to sec. Air Force, 1961-63; mem. Okla. Hwy. Commn., 1959-63; bd. dirs. Great Empire Broadcasting Inc., Wichita, Kans. Trustee emeritus Lovelace Found., Albuquerque; trustee N.Am. Wildlife Fedn; mem. Nat. Eagle Scout Coun. Boy Scouts Am., Disting. Eagle Scout; past pres. Air Force Acad. Found., chmn. bd. Served from 1st lt. to col. USAAF, 1942-46, ETO. Decorated Bronze Star and 6 battle stars; comdr. Order of St. Olav; King Haakon 7th Victory medal; medal of Liberation (Norway); Croix de Guerre (Luxembourg); named to Okla. Aviation and Space Hall of Fame, Okla. Hall of Fame. Mem. ABA, Okla. Bar Assn., DC Bar Assn., Air Force Assn. (dir., nat. pres., chmn. bd. 1951-52), Tulsa C. of C., Tulsa Headliner, Falcon Found. (vice chmn.), Ducks Unltd. (trustee), Southern Hills Country Club, The Boston Club (Tulsa), Burning Tree Club (Washington), Willoughby Golf Club, The Amb. Club (Stuart, Fla.), Delta Kappa Epsilon. Democrat. Home: PO Box 96 2460 Palmer St Jensen Beach FL 34958-0096 also: Ste 600 2431 E 61st St Tulsa OK 74136-1235 E-mail: stuar28@adelphia.net.

STUART, JAY WILLIAM, retired engineer; b. L.A., Aug. 26, 1924; s. Jay William and Mamie Marie (Pollock) S.; m. Nancy Giovinazzo, July 28, 1951; children: Tani Lynn Stuart Robertson, Joel Vanni Stuart. BSME, Caltech, 1946, MS in Aero. Engring., 1948, profl. degree in Aero. Engring., 1951. Registered profl. engr., Calif. Various engring. and sci. positions, Calif., 1943—; aerospace engr. Jet Propulsion Lab., Pasadena, Calif., 1963-71; contract engr. fluid mech. GE Atomic Energy, San Jose, Calif., 1972; engring. specialist, hydro/aero. Aerojet Gen., Surface Effect Ship, Tacoma, 1973; engring. specialist Lockheed Missile Space/Surface Effect Ship, Sunnyvale, Calif., 1973-74; contract engr., prin. aero. Rohr Marine, Surface Effect Ship, San Diego, 1974-76; engring. specialist, heat exch. Aerojet Mfg. Co. AMCO, Fullerton, Calif., 1976-77; contract engr., aero. Hughes Missiles, AMRAM, Canoga Park, Calif., 1977-78; mem. tech. staff Jet Propulsion Lab., Pasadena, 1978-80; sr. spacecraft specialist TDRSS ABACUS Programming Corp./TRW, Redondo Beach, Calif., 1980-82; prin engr. Spacecom Contel divsn. TDRSS/TRW, Redondo Beach, Calif., 1982-86; contract engr., aero. sci. Rockwell Internat., Shuttle, Downey, Calif., 1986-88, contract engr., systems safety, 1989-90. Contbr. articles to profl. jours. Leader YMCA, Gardena, 1965-72. Scholarship Douglas Aircraft, 1947, 49. Mem. AIAA (mem. subcom. on ednl. tech. L.A. sect. 1969-71), NSPE (mem. skill conversion team dept. labor 1971-72, del. to Ministry of Machine Bldg., China 1986), Am. Def. Preparedness Assn., Heat Transfer and Fluid Mechanics Inst., Caltech Alumni Assn., U.S. Badminton Assn., Sigma Xi, Lambda Delta Lambda. Achievements include research in improved solution of the Falkner and Skan boundary-layer equation, low-drag specification of surface irregularities, complete spectra of the velocity fluctuations in the wake of a stalled aircraft; derivation of geophysical-Coriolis form of the Orr-Sommerfeld stability equation. Home: 17502 Vlaymeer Ave Gardena CA 90248-3356

STUART, JOAN MARTHA, fund raising executive; b. June 2, 1945; d. Ervin Wencil and Flora Janet (Applebaum) S. Student, Boston U., 1963-67. Cert. fund raising exec. Prodn. asst. Random House, N.Y.C., 1968-69; book designer Simon & Schuster, N.Y.C., 1969-71; feature writer Palm Beach (Fla.) Post, 1971-72; co-founder, comm. dir. Stuart, Gleimer & Assocs., West Palm Beach, 1973-84, pres., 1982—. Fin. devel. dir. YWCA Greater Atlanta, 1984-86, Ctr. for the Visually Impaired, Atlanta, 1986-90; ea. divsn. dir. City of Hope, 1990-94; devel. dir. Jewish Family Svcs., Atlanta, 1994-99, Ctr. for Visually Impaired, 1999-2002; dir. advancement The Epstein Sch., 2002—. Contbr. articles to profl. jours. Mem. crusade com. Am. Cancer Soc. Bd., 1981—; bd. dirs. Theatre Arts Co., 1980-81; cmty. svcs. chmn., bd. dirs. B'nai B'rith Women, 1980-82; chmn. publicity Leukemia Soc. Atlanta Polo Benefit, 1983; com. chmn. Atlanta Zool. Beastly Feast Benefit, 1984; mem. Atlanta Symphony Assocs.; chmn. Salute to Women of Achievement, 1987-90; founder, advisor Lauren's Run, 1992—; grad. Leadership Midtown, 2001. Recipient Nat. award B'nai B'rith Women, 1978, Regional award, 1979, Cert. of Merit, Big Bros./Big Sisters, 1976. Mem. Nat. Soc. Fund Raising Execs. (cert.), Diabetes Assn. (bd. dirs. 1990—), Jerusalem House (bd. dirs. 1991-94), Parent to Parent (bd. dirs. 1993-95). Democrat. Jewish. Office: 335 Colewood Way NW Atlanta GA 30328 Office Phone: 404-250-5636. E-mail: jstuart@epsteinatlanta.org.

STUART, JOHN E. Internet company executive; BBS, MBA, Pace U. CEO Alco Standard; chmn., CEO Ikon Office Solutions, 98; founder, CEO Tesla Group, West Chester, Pa., 1999—; chmn. Logic Stream, Inc., Exton, Pa., 2000—. Bd. dirs. Foster-Wheeler Corp. Bd. dirs. Coaches vs. Cancer, Police Athletic League West Chester. Office: Logic Stream Inc 412 Creamery Way Exton PA 19341-2500

STUART, JOSEPH MARTIN, art museum administrator; b. Seminole, Okla., Nov. 9, 1932; s. Arch William and Lillian (Lindsey) S.; BFA in Art, U. N.Mex., 1959, MA in Art, 1962; m. Signe Margaret Nelson, June 18, 1960; 1 dau., Lise Nelson Stuart. Dir., Roswell (N.Mex.) Museum and Art Center, 1960-62; curator U. Oreg. Mus. Art, 1962-63; dir. Boise (Idaho) Gallery Art, 1964-68, Salt Lake (City) Art Ctr., 1968-71, S.D. Art Mus., Brookings, 1971-93; prof. art S.D. State U., 1971-93; represented in permanent collec-

tions: Civic Fine Arts Ctr., Sioux Falls, S.D., Coll. Idaho, Eureka Coll., Salt Lake Art Ctr., Sioux City (Iowa) Art Ctr., U. N.Mex. Art Mus., West Tex. State U. With USN, 1951-55. Mem. Phi Kappa Phi. Unitarian. Author: Index of South Dakota Artists, 1974; Art of South Dakota, 1974, Harvey Dunn: Son of the Middle border, 1984, Art for a New Century, 1989; The Legacy of South Dakota Art, 1990; author numerous exhbn. catalogs.

STUART, LORI AMES, public relations executive; b. Hempstead, N.Y., Oct. 23, 1957; d. Henry Aschner and Janet (Hackel) Goldman; m. John Robert Ames, Jan. 30, 1982 (div. July 1990); 1 child, Robert Walter Ames; m. Robert John Stuart, July 27, 1991. BA, Hofstra U., 1979. Publicist Jane Wesman Pub. Rels., N.Y.C., 1980-84, v.p., 1991—; publicist, publicity mgr. William Morrow & Co., N.Y.C., 1984-89, publicity dir., 1989-90. Lectr., mentor NYU, 1994—. Jewish. Avocations: fishing, travel, reading, writing. Office: Jane Wesman Public Rels 322 8th Ave Ste 1702 New York NY 10001-6766

STUART, LYLE, publishing company executive; b. N.Y.C., Aug. 11, 1922; s. Alfred and Theresa (Cohen) Stuart; m. Mary Louise Strawn, Sept. 26, 1946; children: Sandra Lee Strawn, Rory John Strawn; m. Carole Livingston, Feb. 4, 1982; 1 child, Jennifer Susan. Student pub. schs., N.Y.C.; PhD (hon.), State of Calif. Reporter Internat. News Service, 1945, Variety, 1945-46; script writer Dept. State, Voice of Am., 1946; editor Music Bus. mag., 1946-48; founder Expose, 1951; pub. The Independent, 1951-75; bus. mgr. MAD mag., 1952-54; pres. Citadel Press, 1970-89; founder Lyle Stuart, Inc., 1956; pres. University Books, Inc., 1983—, Hot News, 1983, Barricade Books, 1990—. Founder North Bergen (N.J.) Pub. Library. Prodr. Chinese Festival of Music, 1952-62; author: God Wears A Bowtie, 1949, The Secret Life of Walter Winchell, 1953, Mary Louise, 1970, Casino Gambling for the Winner, 1978, Lyle Stuart on Baccarat, 1983, 2d edit., 1997, Winning at Casino Gambling, 1995. Served with AUS, 1942-44. Mem.: Silurians, Nat. Acad. TV Arts and Scis., Soc. Ky. Cols., NY Zool. Soc. Home: 1530 Palisade Ave Apt 6L Fort Lee NJ 07024-5402 Office: Barricade Books Inc 185 Bridge Plaza N Fort Lee NJ 07024 Office Phone: 201-944-7600. Business E-Mail: lyle@barricadebooks.com.

STUART, LYN (JACQUELYN L. STUART), judge; b. Sept. 23, 1955; m. George Stuart; children: Tucker, Shepard, Kelly. BA in Sociology and Edn., Auburn U., 1977; JD, U. Ala., 1980. Asst. atty. gen. State of Ala.; exec. asst. to commr. and spl. asst. atty. gen. Ala. Dept. Corrections; asst. dist. atty. Baldwin County; dist. judge, 1988—97; judge Ala. Cir. Ct., 1997—2001; justice Ala. Supreme Ct., 2001—. Republican. Office: 300 Dexter Ave Rm 3-215 Montgomery AL 36104-3741

STUART, MARIE JEAN, physician, hematologist, researcher; b. Bangalore, India, Sept. 11, 1943; came to U.S., 1967; d. Norman and Dorothy (Dias) S. BS, MB, Madras (India) U. Asst. prof. pediatrics SUNY Health Sci. Ctr., Syracuse, 1972-76, assoc. prof., 1976-81, prof. pediatrics, 1981-87; prof. chief hematology and oncology div. St. Christophers Hosp. for Children and Temple U., Phila., 1987-97; prof. thrombosis rsch. Temple U., 1987-97; dir. NIH Comprehensive Sickle Cell Ctr. Thomas Jefferson U., Phila., 1998—. Mem. nat. child health com. Nat. Inst. Child Health and Human Devel., Bethesda, Md., 1982-86; mem. nat. heart, lung and blood rsch. tng. com., NIH, Bethesda, 1993-2000; mem. NIH Sickle Cell Disease Adv. Coun., 2000—; mem. NIH Erythrocyte and Leucocyte Biology Study Sect., 2003—. Mem. editl. bd. Biology of the Neonate, 2000—; contbr. chpts. to books, articles to profl. jours. Docent in tng. Phila. Mus. Art. Recipient Rsch. award Temple U., 1997. Mem. Am. Fedn. Clin. Research. Am. Pediatric Soc., Soc. for Pediatric Research. Avocations: music, art. Home: 10B W Society Hill Towers Philadelphia PA 19106

STUART, NANCY GIOVINAZZO, secondary school educator; b. L.A., Aug. 8, 1931; d. Joseph and Carmelita Mary (Frontino) Giovinazzo; m. Jay William Stuart, Jr., July 28, 1951; children: Tani Lynn Stuart Robertson, Joel Vanni; 1 foster child, Hilary Davis. AA, UCLA, 1952, BS, 1954, MS, 1967. Tchr. Washington High Sch., L.A. Unified Sch. Dist., 1954-60, tchr. Gardena High Sch., 1960-63, tchr. Carson High Sch., 1963-91, chair dept. health, master tchr., 1970—91, retired, 1991, preferred substitute tchr., 1992—; mentor Calif. Acad. Math. and Sci. at Calif. State U., Dominguez Hills, 1993—2000. Drill team-pep units sponsor, 1968-81. Author teaching guides on dance, CPR, adapted phys. edn., family life edn. Tchr. rep. L.A. Unified Sch. Dist. on City of L.A. Drug Commn., 1968-69. Grantee State of Calif., 1985. Mem. Calif. Assn. for Health, Phys. Edn., Recreation and Dance (Health Edn. Tchr. of Yr. 1988), AAUW, Delta Kappa Gamma, Alpha Delta Kappa. Home: 17502 Valmeyer Ave Gardena CA 90248-3356 Office: Carson High Sch 22328 Main St Carson CA 90745-4599 Office Phone: 310-835-0181. E-mail: ngs54@earthlink.net.

STUART, NANCY RUBIN (NANCY ZIMMAN STETSON), journalist, author, writer, producer; b. Boston, Nov. 25, 1944; d. Stuart Wendell and Ethel (Rabinovitz) Zimman; m. William W. Stetson, Apr. 28, 2001; children: Elisabeth, Jessica. BA, Tufts U., 1966; MA in Teaching, Brown U., 1967; PhD (hon.), Mt. Vernon Coll., 1995. Playwright, dir. Equity Library Theatre, Roundabout, Joseph Jefferson and St. Clement's theaters, N.Y.C., 1971-74; freelance reporter Westchester-Gannett newspapers and mags., 1975-77, N.Y. Times, N.Y.C., 1977—. Faculty affiliate Bush Ctr. in Child Devel., Yale U., New Haven, 1981-86; mem. Westchester County Women's Adv. Bd., chair, 1988; bd. dirs. Women Writing Women's Lives Seminar; mem. faculty SUNY, Purchase, 1994-95, Fordham U., N.Y.C., 1996-99. Author: The New Suburban Women, Beyond Myth and Motherhood, 1982, The Mother Mirror: How a Generation of Women is Changing Motherhood in America, 1984, Isabella of Castile: The First Renaissance Queen, 1991, American Empress: The Life and Times of Marjorie Merriweather Post, 1995, Club Dance: The Show, The Steps, The Spirit of Country, 1998; writer, assoc. prodr: TV series America's Castles for A&E Network, 1996—99 (Telly award, 1999, Telly award (3), 2001, Writing Communicator award, 1999), The Gold Coast for The Grand Tour A & E TV, 1997, writer prodr., prodr.: TV series Restore America, 1999; writer prodr., prodr. (TV series) Restore America, 2001 (3 Telly awards); writer/assoc. prodr.: TV series Eccentrics, 1999 (Crystal award, Telly award), The N.Y. Times, 1977—2001, contbg. editor: Parents mag., 1987—91,: McCalls, Savvy, Travel & Leisure, Ladies Home Jour., 1980—92; theater critic: Stamford Advocate, 1994—96. Recipient Washington Irving award Westchester Libr. Assn., 1993, Telly award finalist, 2001; Time, Inc.-Bread Loaf Writers' Colony scholar, 1979. Fellow MacDowell Colony; mem. Author's Guild, Am. Soc. Journalists and Authors (Author of Yr. award 1992), PEN, Nat. Arts Club. Avocations: skiing, sailing, ballet and jazz dancing, classical music.

STUART, NED, film producer; b. Milan, June 13, 1945; s. Edward Stuart and Elizabeth McClery-Hollis; children: Alexandra, Catherine, Charles. MS in Chemistry, Acad. Sci., Rome; MusB, Trinity Coll., Cambridge, Eng. Prodr., exec. prodr. Lang Syne Films, Inc., N.Y.C., Prodrs. Group, N.Y.C. Office: 1501 Broadway New York NY 10036 Office Phone: 212-944-9090.

STUART, PAMELA BRUCE, lawyer; b. N.Y.C., Feb. 13, 1949; d. J. Raymond and Marion Grace (Cotins) S. AB with distinction, Mt. Holyoke Coll., 1970; JD cum laude, U. Mich., 1973. Bar: N.Y. 1974, D.C. 1975, U.S. Dist. Ct. D.C. 1979, U.S. Ct. Appeals (D.C. cir.) 1980, U.S. Supreme Ct. 1980, U.S. Dist. Ct. Md. 1989, Md. 1992, Va. 1993, U.S. Ct. Appeals (4th cir.) 1993, Fla. 1994, U.S. Dist. Ct. (ea. dist.) Va. 1994, U.S. Dist. Ct. (no. dist.) N.Y. 1996, U.S. Dist. Ct. (so. dist.) Fla. 1998, U.S. Dist. Ct. (so. dist.) N.Y. 1999, U.S. Dist. Ct. (ea. dist.) N.Y. 1999, U.S. Dist. Ct. (mid. dist.) Fla. 2001. Trial atty., deputy asst. dir. Bur. of Consumer Protection, FTC, Washington, 1973-79; asst. U.S. atty. U.S. Atty's Office, Washington, 1979-85; sr. trial atty. Office of Internat. Affairs, U.S. Dept. Justice, Washington, 1985-87; atty. Ross, Dixon & Masback, Washington, 1987-89; mem. Lobel, Novins, Lamont & Flug, Washington, 1989-92; pvt. practice, Washington, 1992—. Instr. Nat. Inst. for Trial Advocacy, Atty. Gen.'s Advocacy Inst., Legal Edn. Inst., Fed. Practice Inst.; mem. Jud. Conf. D.C., 1985-88, 1991-2004; mem. Jud. Conf., D.C. Cir., 1996, 98, 2000; assoc. mem. Consular Corps Washington; legal analyst CNN, MSNBC, Fox News, other TV networks. Author: The Federal Trade Commission, 1991; contbr. articles to profl. jours. Bd. dirs. Anacostia Econ. Devel. Corp., 1993—, Anacostia Holding Co., Inc., Anacostia Mgmt. Co., Inc., 1997—. Mem. ABA (internat. criminal law com., chmn., 1993-96, chmn. fed. crime rules subcom. white collar crime com. sect. criminal justice 1997-99), Bar Assn. D.C. (bd. dirs. 1995-2001, 03-04), Asst. U.S. Attys. Assn. D.C. (exec. coun. 1993-99, pres. 1998-99), Assn. Trial Lawyers Am., Women's Bar Assn. D.C., Fla. Bar (exec. coun. real property probate and trust law sect. 1999—), Alumnae Assn. Mt. Holyoke Coll. (bd. dirs. 1986-89, 92-95, Alumnae medal of honor 1990), Edward Bennett Williams Inn of Ct. (master of bench), Fed. City Club (bd. govs. 1992—), Cosmos Club. Avocations: writing, interior design, investments, piano, art. Home: 5115 Yuma St NW Washington DC 20016-4336 Office: The J Raymond Stuart Bldg 1750 N Street NW Washington DC 20036 also: 111 Johns Island Dr Apt 7 Vero Beach FL 32963-3274 Office Phone: 202-835-2200. Personal E-mail: pamstuart@aol.com.

STUART, ROBERT, container manufacturing executive; b. Oak Park, Ill., Aug. 3, 1921; s. Robert S. and Marie (Vavra) Solinsky; m. Lillian C. Kondelik, Dec. 5, 1962 (dec. May 1978); m. Lila Winterhoff Peters, May 21, 1982. BS, U. Ill., 1943; LLD, U. Ill., Chgo., 1982. Sec.-treas., gen. mgr. Warren Metal Decorating Co., 1947-49; asst. to gen. mgr. Cans, Inc., 1950-52; asst. to v.p., then v.p. Nat. Can Corp., Chgo., 1953-59, exec. v.p., 1959-63, pres., 1963-69, chief exec., 1966-69, chmn. bd., chief exec. officer, 1969-73, chmn. bd., 1973-83, chmn. fin. com., 1983, mem. corp. devel. com., until 1986, chmn. emeritus, 1986—. Past pres., bd. dirs. Corp. Responsibility Group of Greater Chgo. Past pres., bd. dirs. Chgo. Crime Commn.; past dir. Nat. Crime Prevention Coun.; founding chmn. Nat. Minority Supplier Devel. Coun., 1972-73, Lloyd Morey Scholarship Fund: Freedoms Found. at Valley Forge, past trustee; past mem. adv. bd. Salvation Army, Broader Urban Involvement and Leadership Devel.; chmn. emeritus World Federalist Assn.; past bd. dirs., past moderator Millard Congl. Ch.; trustee, past pres. Ctrl. Ch. Chgo. Congregationalist; chmn. emeritus Assn. to Unite the Democracies; numerous other civic activities. Capt. AUS, 1943-46. Mem. Chgo. Club, Comml. Club, Yacht Club, Little Ship Club (London), Mason (32 degree, Red Cross of Constantine), Rotary (past pres. Chgo. club, past dist. gov.), Alpha Kappa Lambda (past nat. pres.). Home and Office: 233 SW 43d Ter Cape Coral FL 33914 Office Phone: 239-540-3657.

STUART, ROBERT KENNETH, internist, oncologist, hematologist, educator; b. Baton Rouge, July 6, 1948; s. Walter Bynum and Rita Bess (Kleinpeter) S.; m. Gail Elaine Wiscarz, June 12, 1971 (div. Dec. 1988); children: R. Morgan, Elaine C.; m. F. Charlene Gates, Nov. 2, 1991. BS, Georgetown U., 1970; MD, Johns Hopkins U., Balt., 1974. Diplomate Am. Bd. Internal Medicine. Resident in medicine Johns Hopkins Hosp., Balt., 1974-76, oncology fellow Oncology Ctr., 1976-78; rsch. fellow Sloan-Kettering Inst., N.Y.C., 1978-79; asst. prof. Johns Hopkins U., Balt., 1979-84, assoc. prof., 1984-85; prof. medicine Med. U. S.C., Charleston, 1985—; assoc. dir. Hollings Cancer Ctr., Charleston, 1993-97; chmn. dept. oncology King Faisal Specialist Hosp and Rsch. Ctr., Riyadh, Saudi Arabia, 1997-2001; prof. medicine Med.U. S.C., Charleston, 2001—. Bd. dirs. Aplastic Anemia Found., Balt., 1982-93, med. adv. bd., 1993—. Democrat. Roman Catholic. Office: Medical Univ of South Carolina 171 Ashley Ave Charleston SC 29425-0100 E-mail: stuartrk@musc.edu.

STUART, SPENCER RAYMOND, management consultant; b. Balt., Sept. 25, 1922; s. William Moore Stuart and Helen Lenore Raymond; m. Eugenia Presler Birdsall, Sept. 24, 1949; children: Spencer Raymond Stuart Jr., Cooper B., Eugenia Anne. BS, Haverford Coll., 1947. Mgr. mktg. and advt. Martin Senour Paint Co., Chgo., 1947—52; cons. Booz Allen and Hamilton, Chgo., 1952—55; prin. Heidrick and Struggles, Chgo., 1955; founder, CEO Spencer Stuart, Exec. Search Consultants, Chgo., 1956—74, founder, chmn. N.Y.C., 1974—, Dean Witter Coun. of Mgmt. Advisors, N.Y.C., 1990—92; mgmt. cons., corp. dir. Palm City, Fla., 1974—2001. Dir., chmn. compensation and mgmt. succession com., chmn. corp. governance com. Enhance Fin. Svcs. Group, N.Y.C., 1986—2001; dir., chmn. audit com., mem. compensation stock option and mgmt. succession com. UST, Inc., Greenwich, Conn., 1977—97; dir., mem. audit and compensation com. U.S. Timberlands Co., L.P., N.Y.C., 1997; dir., mem. exec. com., chmn. compensation and mgmt. succession com. Western Airlines, L.A., 1984—87; dir., chmn. compensation and corp. strategy coms. Allegheny Internat., Pitts., 1984—89; panelist Am. Mgmt. Assn., Presidents Assn., N.Y.C., 1960—72; exec. compensation Blue Ribbon com. Nat. Assn. Corp. Dirs., Washington, 1974—97; past dir. Assn. Exec. Recruiting Consultants, N.Y.C.; dir. Mass. Co./Keystone Custodian Funds, Boston, 1982—97. Contbr. articles to newspapers and profl. jours. Reception com. Econ. Club. Chgo., 1956—65; chmn. exploring divsn. Boy Scouts Am., Stamford, Conn., 1974—86, founder, chmn. corp. adv. bd. Fairfield County, Conn., 1975—86; trustee, pres. Silvermine Guild of Artists, New Canaan, Conn., 1972—79; trustee Green Mountain Coll., Poultney, Vt., 1980—84; chmn. fundraising dinner com., athlete of decade program Am. Cancer Soc., N.Y.C., 1977—82; panelist Aspen (Colo.) Inst. Humanistic Studies, 1948—58; mem. Conf. Christians and Jews, Conn., 1960—68. 1st lt. AUS, 1943—46, ETO. Decorated Bronze Star, Purple Heart; recipient Wm. H. Splurgen III award for disting. svc., Nat. Exploring Coun., Boy Scouts Am., 1978, Profl. Leadership award, Newcomen Soc. Am., 1981, Heidrick award, Assn. Exec. Search Consultants, 1995. Mem.: Hassayampa Golf Club, The Sky Club, Eldorado Country Club, Univ. Club N.Y.C. Avocations: golf, exercise, writing, computers, art. Home: 948 Winding Spruce Way Prescott AZ 86303-6912

STUART, TARA, international business intelligence advisor; b. Passaic, N.J., Aug. 2, 1966; d. Stanton and Carol Stuart. BA in Polit. Sci., Kean U., 1988; M Internat. Rels. and Diplomacy, Schiller Internat. U., Paris, 1989; M Econs. and Social Studies, Inst. Etudes Econ. et Sociales, Paris, 1995; PhD in Bus. Adminstrn., Harrington U., London, 1999. Sr. cons. internat. bus. devel. Palco Group Ltd., London, 1989-98; exec. mgr. western Europe UPI, Paris, 1994-97; mgr. profiling desk, office of chmn. Deloitte & Touche LLP, N.Y.C., 1999—. Country chmn. France, Republicans Abroad Internat., Washington, 1997-2000. Mem.: NAFE, UN Assn. U.S.A., Fgn. Policy Assn., Acad. Polit. Sci., Soc. Competitive Intelligence Profls. Office: Deloitte & Touche LLP 2 World Financial Ctr New York NY 10281 Home: 4302 Martinique Cir Apt L2 Coconut Creek FL 33066-1422

STUART, WALTER BYNUM, III, banker; b. Baton Rouge, Oct. 5, 1922; s. Walter Bynum and Rosa (Gauthreaux) S.; m. Rita Kleinpeter, May 20, 1944; children— Walter Bynum IV, Robert, Douglas, Ronald, Scott. BS, La. State U., 1943. Adminstrv. mgr. Kaiser Aluminum & Chem. Corp., 1946-63; v.p. First Nat. Bank Commerce, New Orleans, 1963-65, sr. v.p., 1965, exec. v.p., 1965-73; vice chmn. bd., dir. 1st Nat. Bank Commerce, New Orleans, 1973-78; exec. v.p. 1st Commerce Corp., New Orleans, 1972-73, pres., 1973-75, vice-chmn. bd., 1975-78, dir., 1973-78; pres. Am. Bank & Trust Co., Lafayette, La., 1978-86, cons. Assoc. dir., mem. faculty Sch. Banking La. State U., 1973-75, dir., 1975-78; mem. Faculty Assemblies for Bank Dirs. Campaign group chmn. industry com., mem. United Fund for Greater New Orleans Area, 1974; mem. research com. Pub. Affairs Research Council La., 1973-76, v.p., trustee, 1973-76; bd. dirs. Bur. Govtl. Research, 1973-77, Council Better La., 1975—; pres. New Orleans Indsl. Devel. Bd., 1973-75. Served to lt. (j.g.) USNR, 1943-46. Mem. C. of C. of Greater New Orleans Area (v.p. 1973-75, bd. dirs.), Am. Bankers Assn., La. Bankers Assn. (pres. 1977), Am. Mgmt. Assn., Kappa Alpha, Delta Sigma Pi, Beta Gamma Sigma. Democrat. Roman Catholic. Office: Jefferson at Lee Lafayette LA 70501 Home: 10100 Hillview Dr Apt 2109 Pensacola FL 32514-5481 *Recognizing that life is the experiencing of reality, and that reality is simply a continuing series of problems, I long ago decided that I would treat a problem as an opportunity. Every incident of difficulty has always invited my intense interest as a challenge, and my thoughts have been immediately marshalled for positive effort. My life has been most rewarding because I believe that "a problem is an opportunity!".*

STUART, WILLIAM CORWIN, judge; b. Knoxville, Iowa, Apr. 28, 1920; s. George Corwin and Edith (Abram) S.; m. Mary Elgin Cleaver, Oct. 20, 1946; children: William Corwin II, Robert Cullen, Melanie Rae, Valerie Jo. BA, State U. Iowa, 1941, JD, 1942. Bar: Iowa 1942. Pvt. practice, Chariton, 1946-62; city atty., 1947-49; mem. Iowa Senate from, Lucas-Wayne Counties, 1951-61; justice Supreme Ct. Iowa, 1962-71; judge U.S. Dist. Ct., So. Dist. of Iowa, Des Moines, 1971-86, sr. judge, 1986—. With USNR, 1943-45. Recipient Outstanding Svc. award Iowa Acad. Trial lawyer, 1987, Iowa Trial Lawyers Assn., 1988, Spl. award Iowa State Bar Assn., 1987, Disting. Alumni, U. Iowa Coll. Law, 1987. Mem. ABA, Iowa Bar Assn., Am. Legion, All For Iowa, Order of Coif, Omicron Delta Kappa, Phi Kappa Psi, Phi Delta Phi. Clubs: Mason (Shriner). Presbyterian. Home: 216 S Grand St Chariton IA 50049-2139

STUBBE, JOANNE, chemistry professor; Novartis prof. chemistry and biology MIT, Cambridge. Arthur C. Cope scholar award Am. Chemistry Soc., 1993. Mem. NAS. Office: MIT Dept Chemistry 77 Massachusetts Ave Dept Cambridge MA 02139-4307

STUBBE, RAY WILLIAM, minister, writer; b. Milw., Aug. 15, 1938; s. Clarence Arnold and Ruby Otillie (Mueller) Stubbe. *Grandfather, Julius F. Mueller, emigrated in 1889 from Germany at age 4. Although schooled only through 8th grade and losing both his parents, his subsequent employment in a cast iron foundry saw him eventually rise to become superintendent of that foundry. In later years, his innovative techniques drew inquires from numerous foreign foundry men and, upon retirement, he traveled to Sao Paulo, Brazil where he successfully modernized a foundry. His boundless energy and value on education saw him flying bi-planes in the 1920's, building a reflecting telescope in the 1930's, singing in a civic male chorus, and visiting by car every state as well as Canada and Mexico on vacations.* BA, St. Olaf Coll., 1962; MDiv, Northwestern Luth. Theol. Sem., 1965; postgrad., U. Chgo., 1967. Ordained to ministry Evang. Luth. Ch. Am., 1965. Mission devel. bd. Am. missions Luth Ch. in Am., Oak Creek, Wis., 1965-66; organizer, pastor All Saints Luth Ch., Oak Creek, 1966-67; enlisted USN, 1955; commd. ensign USNR, 1963, advanced through grades to lt., comdr. chaplain corps, 1971; augmented to USN, 1971; chaplain, 1967-85; ret. USN, 1985. Interviews on national televised programs. *Subject of numerous nationally televised programs, including: "Vietnam: A Soldier's Story" aired on The Learning Channel, Sep 6, 1998, " War Stories with Oliver North: Khe Sanh," Aired on Fox News, Oct 28, 2001, "Atmospheres: War and Weather," aired on The Weather Channel, Mar 3, 2002.* Author: Inside Force Recon, 1989, Khe Sanh Chaplain, 1970, Paddles, Parachutes, Patrols, 1979, Aarugha, 1989, Valley of Decision, 1991, The Final Formation, 1995, Khe Sanh and the Mongol Prince, 2002, numerous poems; editor: Khe Sanh Veteran/Red Clay, 1996—98; contbr. articles to profl. jours. Founder, pres. emeritus Khe Sanh Vets., Inc., 1988—; spkr. numerous vet. assemblies; chaplain Wis. Vietnam Vets., Milw., 1984—, 3d Marine Divsn. Assn., 1988. Decorated Bronze Star with combat V; recipient Legion of Honor award, Chapel Four Chaplains. Mem.: DAV (life), VFW (life), Wis. Acad. Scis., Arts and Letters (life), Spl. Ops. Assn. (life), 3d Marine Divsn. Assn. (life), Spl. Forces Assn. (life), Force Reconnaissance Assn. (life), Soc. Bibl. Lit., Vietnam Vets. Am. (life), Wis. Vietnam Vets. (life), Mil. Officers Assn. Am. (life), Marine Corps Hist. Found. (life), Pi Kappa Delta. Lutheran. Avocation: boxing. Home: 8766 Parkview Ct Wauwatosa WI 53226-2729 Office: Redeemer Luth Church 631 N 19th St Milwaukee WI 53233-2152 Office Phone: 414-771-9987. *The most powerful Words of God have always been communicated to me by the occasional people encountered in life's pathways. These are the quiet ones whose very being reflect possibilities of being the image of God we all are; living Words of God who make us know we are free, forgiven, loved, blessed with value and future; heroes, who at great risk and pain to themselves, transform negatives into positives; great, good people who empty themselves into servants and incarnate love into all human conditions. When the vision they offer becomes life's task of who to become, all of life becomes a gift of everdeepening wells which nourish everything living with the deep underground stream, which is God.*

STUBBEN, DOLUS JANE (D. J. STUBBEN), advertising executive; b. Clovis, N.Mex., Sept. 12, 1951; d. Joseph P. Harmon and Maurine Yvonne (Simmons) McDonald; m. Ronald Patrick Day, Apr. 11, 1970 (div.); m. John David Stubben, Sept. 23, 1979 (div.); 1 child, Patricia Joan. Student, West Tex. State U., 1969-70. Instr. Amarillo (Tex.) Coll., 1971-73; advt. cons. Amarillo, 1976-78; advt. mgr. Montgomery Ward, Amarillo, 1978-80; musician Furr's Cafeteria, Amarillo, 1978-80; piano bar musician, comedienne Quigley's Restaurant, Eugene, Oreg., 1980-81, Jolly's Comedy Club, Amarillo, 1986-88, Sheraton Towers Amarillo, 1988-89. Owner, mgr. Welcome Pardner!, Amarillo, 1981—; arbitrator Better Bus. Bur., Amarillo, 1978-79 Author: #555 Death Row, 1981 (Nat. Press Women 2nd place award 1982), Dog Pause..., 1981 (Nat. Press Women 2nd place award 1982, Hon. Mention award 1987), It's a Secret, I Can't Tell You, 1984, poems; songwriter. Media chmn. Am. Cancer Soc., Amarillo, 1978-79; media dir. Bralley's 45h of July Picnic, Amarillo, 1977-78; media rels. com. St. Jude's Hosp. Tex. Com., Amarillo, 1983; publicity chmn. Miss Amarillo Area, 1993—; nominating com. Tex. plains Girl Scouts U.S.A., 1999; bd. dirs. Panhandle Ind. Living Ctr., 1999—, High Plains Food Bank, 2001; active Panhandle Film Commn., 1999—. Top 10 Winner Am. Mktg. Awards, 1996; recipient Rookie award 1989, Entrepreneur award Center City BPW, 1999, BPW Achievement of the Decade award, 1999, Hall of Fame award Tex. Panhandle Broadcasters, 2003. Mem.: Tex. Panhandle Broadcasters Assn. (treas. 1998—99), Tex. Press Women (v.p. 1982, state treas. 1986, membership chmn. 1986, First Pl. (2) awards 1988), Lions Club (chmn. pub. rels. com. 1990—, Rookie of Yr. Downtown 1989—90, Lions Fellow award 1999). Office: Welcome Pardner PO Box 30926 Amarillo TX 79120-0926 E-mail: stubben@amaonline.com.

STUBBERUD, ALLEN ROGER, electrical engineering educator; b. Glendive, Mont., Aug. 14, 1934; s. Oscar Adolph and Alice Marie (LeBlanc) S.; m. May B. Tragus, Nov. 19, 1961; children: Peter A., Stephen C. BS in Elec. Engring, U. Idaho, 1956; MS in Engring, UCLA, 1958, PhD, 1962. From asst. prof. to assoc. prof. engring. UCLA, 1962-69; prof. elec. engring. U. Calif., Irvine, 1969—, assoc. dean engring., 1972-78, dean engring., 1978-83, chair elec. and computer engring., 1993-98, interim dean engring., 1994-96; chief scientist U.S. Air Force, 1983-85. Dir. Elec. Communications and Systems Engring. divsn. NSF, 1987-88. Author: Analysis and Synthesis of Linear Time Variable Systems, 1964, (with others) Feedback and Control Systems, 2d edit., 1990, (with others) Digital Control System Design, 2d edit., 1994; contbr. articles to profl. jours. Recipient Exceptional Civilian Svc. medal USAF, 1985, 90, Meritorious Civilian Svc. medal, 1996. Fellow IEEE (Centennial medal 1984, Millennium medal 2000), AIAA, AAAS, NYAS; mem. INFORMS, Sigma Xi, Sigma Tau, Tau Beta Pi, Eta Kappa Nu. Office: U Calif Dept Ece Irvine CA 92697-0001 E-mail: arstubbe@uci.edu.

STUBBINS, HUGH A(SHER), JR., architect; b. Birmingham, Ala., Jan. 11, 1912; s. Hugh Asher and Lucile (Matthews) S.; m. Diana Hamilton Moore, Mar. 3, 1938 (div. 1960); children: Patricia, Peter, Hugh Asher III, Michael; m. Colette Fadeuilhe, Sept. 1960 (dec. 1992); m. June M. Kootz, 1994 (dec. July, 2001). BS in Architecture, Ga. Inst. Tech., 1933; MArch, Harvard U., 1935. Pvt. practice, Boston, 1935-38, 41—; formed partnership, 1938-40; pvt. practice, 1940; assoc. prof. Grad. Sch. Design Harvard U., 1946-52, chmn. dept. architecture, 1953, mem. vis. com. Grad. Sch. Design, 1958-72; pres. Hugh Stubbins & Assocs., Inc., 1957-83, also chmn. bd. dirs., 1983-92. Vis. critic-in-residence, Yale U., 1948-49, U. Oreg., 1950; sec. Rotch travelling Scholarship, 1971-80; Thomas Jefferson prof. architecture U. Va., 1979; mem. adv. coun. Sch. Architecture, Princeton U., 1962-65; mem. Harleston Parker Medal Com., 1973. Designer Berlin Congress Hall, 1957, Countway Libr. Medicine, Harvard U., Fed. Res. Bank, Boston, U. Va. Law Sch., Citicorp Ctr., N.Y.C., St. Peter's Ch., N.Y.C., Fifth Ave. Pl., Pitts., 1988, Bank One, Indpls., 1989, Landmark Tower, Minoto-Mirai 21, Yokohama, Japan, 1989, Ronald Reagan Presdl. Libr., 1990, numerous other bldgs.; exec. architect Phila. Stadium; one-man show Norton Sculpture Gallery, West Palm Beach, 1997-98. Hon. mem. Boston Archtl. Ctr.; chmn. design adv. com. Boston Redevel. Authority, 1964-76; mem. design rev. panel Worcester Redevel. Authority, 1966-70; mem. adv. com. Office Fgn. Bldgs. Ops., U.S. Dept. State, 1979-82; bd. dirs. Benjamin Franklin Found.; mem. arts and archtl. com. Kennedy Meml. Libr.; mem. Fgn. Bus. Coun., Commonwealth of Mass., 1978-79; mem. nat. adv. bd. Ga. Inst. Tech., 1978-81; trustee Tabor Acad., 1974-78; mem. adv.

bd. Whitney Libr. Design, 1976-78. Recipient Alpha Rho Chi medal, 1933, 3d prize at competition Nat. Smithsonian Gallery of Art, 1939, Progressive Architecture 1st Design award, 1954, Arcadia Achievement award, 1957, Rodgers and Hammerstein award, 1961, award Am. Inst. Steel Constrn., 1970, award Archtl. Record, 1971, award Prestressed Concrete Inst., 1971, award of merit Inst. So. Affairs and So. Acad. Letters, Am. Acad. Arts and Scis., 1973, citation Am. Assn. Sch. Adminstrs., 1974, award for environ. design, 1975, award of merit Libr. Bldgs. award for Nathan Marsh Pusey Libr., Harvard U./AIA/ALA, 1976, Spl. Energy award for Shiraz Tech. Inst., Am. Assn. Sch. Adminstrs./AIA, N.E. Regional Coun. award Fed. Res. Bank, 1979, Thomas Jefferson Meml. medal U. Va., 1979, R.S. Reynolds Meml. award Citicorp, 1981, numerous other awards. Fellow AIA (v.p. 1964-65, jury fellows 1974-75, chmn. Nat. Honor award com. 1966, 79-80, Merit award 1970, Honor award 1979, Firm award 1967), Mexican Soc. Archs. (hon.), AAAS; mem. NAD (academician), Mass. Assn. Archs., Boston Soc. Archs. (pres. 1969-70, Honor award 1988), Archl. League NY (Silver medal 1958), Harvard Club, Laurel Brook Club, Malapan Yacht Club, The Little Club (Gulf Stream, Fla.), Century Club (NYC), Delray Beach Yacht Club, Beta Theta Pi, Omicron Delta Kappa. Home: 6110 N Ocean Blvd Boynton Beach FL 33435-5248 also: 199 Brattle St Cambridge MA 02138-3345

STUBBLEFIELD, JOHN K., JR., food products company executive; m. Sharon Stubblefield; 2 children. BBA in Acctg., U. Houston, 1970. V.p. adminstrn. Langazorta Internat., 1976-84; controller Sysco Corp., Houston, 1984-86, v.p. fin. Denver, 1986-92, v.p., controller, sr. v.p. Houston, 1993—99, CFO, 1994—, sr. v.p. fin. & admin., 1999—2003, exec. v.p. fin. and adminstrn., 2003—, also bd. dirs., 2003. Office: Sysco Corp 1390 Enclave Pkwy Houston TX 77077-2099

STUBBLEFIELD, J(OSEPH) STEPHEN, lawyer; b. Jackson, Miss., Mar. 28, 1947; s. Joseph Murat and Mary Alice (Ragland) S.; m. Mary Margaret McRae, Mar. 7, 1970; children: Mary Lindsay, David Stephen. BS, Miss. State U., 1969; JD, U. Miss., 1974. Bar: Miss. 1974. Estate tax atty. IRS, Jackson, 1974-78; assoc. Peterson, Harper & Bellan, Jackson, 1978-82; ptnr. Wells, Moore, Simmons, Stubblefield & Neeld, Jackson, 1982-91, Stubblefield & Assocs., Jackson, 1991-97, Stubblefield & Yelverton, PLLC, Jackson, 1997—. Mgr. Fiduciary Mgmt. Co., LLC, Jackson, 1995—. Mem. Belhaven Estate Planning Council, 2000—, Miss. State U. Planned Gifts Council, 1999—. 1st lt. U.S. Army, 1970-72. Mem. Fin. Planning Assn. (sec., treas. 1992-94), Nat. Lawyers Assn., Miss. Coll. Estate Planning Coun. (exec. bd.), Miss. Estate Planning Counsel, Miss. State Bar Assn., Phi Delta Phi. Republican. Baptist. Avocations: fishing, hiking, boating. Home: 340 Sherborne Pl Jackson MS 39232 Office: 3900 Lakeland Dr Ste 401 PO Box 320399 Jackson MS 39232 Office Phone: 601-936-4910. E-mail: srj0201@aol.com.

STUBBLEFIELD, ROBERT F. travel agency executive; married Judy Stubblefield; children: Matt, Rob, Kaarin, Erik. BSBA, U. Nebr. Enlisted U.S. Army, served to inf. capt., ret.; former asst. gen. merchandise mgr. Brandeis & Co.; pres. AAA, Omaha, 1976—. Active Nebr. Spl. Olympics; mem. North Hill Hunt Club, bd. dirs. numerous civic bds.; active Mid-Am. Coun. Boy Scouts. Office: AAA 10703 J St Omaha NE 68127-1023

STUBBLEFIELD, THOMAS MASON, agricultural economist, educator; b. Taxhoma, Okla., Apr. 16, 1922; s. Temple Roscoe and Martha Lacy (Acree) Stubblefield; m. Martha Lee Miller, Mar. 7, 1943; children: Ellen Damron, Paula Culbertson, Thommye Zingsheim. BS, N.Mex. State Coll., 1948; MS, A. and M. Coll. Tex., 1951; PhD, A. and M. Coll. Tex., 1956; postgrad., U. Ariz., 1954. Specialist cotton mktg. N.Mex. State Coll., 1948; extension economist then asst. agrl. economist U. Ariz., Tucson, 1951—58, from assoc. prof. to prof., 1958—64, prof. and agrl. economist, 1964—83, emeritus prof., 1983—, acting asst. dir. agrl. expt. sta., 1966—68, asst. to dir. sta., 1973—74, chief party Brazil contract, 1968—70. Author bulls. in field. Mem. Pima Coun. Aging, 1974—77, 1980—90, Ret. Sr. Vol. Program, Pima County, 1974—2004, chmn. adv. com., 1974—77, 1980—90; chmn. bd. Saguaro Home Found., 1980—85; mem. adv. bd. Unified Cmty., 1994—2004. With U.S. Army, 1942—45. Home: 810 W Calle Milu Tucson AZ 85706-3925

STUBBS, DONALD CLARK, retired secondary school educator; b. Providence, Mar. 6, 1935; s. Edward J. and Margaret Eleanor (Clark) S.; m. Lorraine Alice Thivierge, Apr. 3, 1969 (dec. Jan. 1986); 1 child, Derek C.; m. Sarah E. Andrews, Apr. 23, 1999. AB, Cath. U. Am., Washington, 1959, MS, 1966; postgrad., St. John's U., N.Y.C., 1960. Tchr. Bishop Loughlin Meml. High Sch., Bklyn., 1959-61, Bishop Bradley High Sch., Manchester, N.H., 1961-66; tchr., sci. dept. chair LaSalle Mil. Acad., Oakdale, N.Y., 1966-69, Ponaganset Regional High Sch., Glocester, R.I., 1969-2000; ret., 2000. Home: 35 Shove St Woonsocket RI 02895-5741 E-mail: naddad@aol.com.

STUBBS, GERALD, biochemist, educator; b. Hobart, Australia, May 9, 1947; came to the US, 1976; m. Rebecca Lynn Harris; children: Andrew, Tamsin, Anneliese, Rachel. BSc, Australian Nat. U., 1968; DPhil, Oxford U., 1972. Sci. asst. Max Planck Inst., Heidelberg, Germany, 1973-76; rsch. assoc. Brandeis U., Waltham, Mass., 1976-83; asst. prof. Vanderbilt U., Nashville, 1983-87, assoc. prof., 1987-90, prof., 1990—. Contbr. articles to profl. jour. Achievements include determination of molecular structure of tobacco mosaic virus. Office Phone: 615-322-2018. E-mail: gerald.stubbs@vanderbilt.edu.

STUBBS, JEFFREY MATTHEW, research scientist; b. Nashua, NH, Oct. 14, 1974; s. Lawrence Walter and Theresa Marie Stubbs; m. Amanda Caitlin Weld, July 14, 2001; children: Dakota, Julia. BS in chem. engring., U. N.H., 1996, MS in chem. engring., 2000. Rsch. scientist U. of N.H., 2001—. Contbr. articles. Recipient A. L. Hendry award, Fedn. of Socs. for Coatings Tech. Avocations: soccer, snowboarding. Office: U NH G106 Parsons Hall Durham NH 03824 Office Fax: 603-862-3617.

STUBBS, JOHN HOWELL, architectural educator, preservationist; b. Monroe, La., Apr. 26, 1950; s. William King and Sue (Graves) S.; m. Jane Kelley, Dec. 30, 1983 (div. Aug. 1998); m. Linda Karsteter, Apr. 9, 1999. BS in Archtl. Tech., La. State U., 1972; MS in Arch., Preservation and Planning, Columbia U., 1974; cert., Internat. Ctr. Conservation of Cultural Property, Rome, 1977. Asst. prof. La. State U. Sch. Architecture, 1974-77; hist. arch. Tech. Preservation Svcs. U.S. Nat. Park Svc., Washington, 1977-78; pres. Stubbs Books and Prints Inc., N.Y.C., 1978-98; assoc. Beyer Blinder Belle Archs., N.Y.C., 1979-89; assoc. prof. Columbia U., N.Y.C., 1989—; v.p. programs World Monuments Fund, N.Y.C., 1989—. Advisor Abagail Adams Smith House, N.Y.C., 1983-95; advisor gallery coun. N.Y. Sch. Interior Design, 1988-91; mem. adv. coun. U. Fla. Sch. Landscape Architecture, 1997-98. Contbg. author: Conservation on Archaeological Sites, 1984, 93, Five Centuries of Great Architectural Books, 1997; editor: Architecture of W.K. Stubbs, 1994; also articles. Trustee Met. Hist. Structures Assn., 1990-94, James Marston Fitch Charitable Trust, 1992, Archaeol. Inst. Am., Boston, 1999—. UNESCO fellow, Rome, 1977, fellow Salzburg (Austria) Seminar, 1990, travel fellow S.H. Kress Found., Sri Lanka, 1993. Mem. Internat. Coun. on Monuments and Sites, Coll. Art Assn., Soc. Archtl. Historians, Columbia U. Preservation Alumni Assn. (pres. 1981-82), Century Club, Nat. Trust Hist. Pres. Forum. Avocations: books, rare books, antiques, travel. Office: World Monuments Fund 95 Madison Ave New York NY 10016-7801

STUBBS, KENDON LEE, retired librarian; b. Washington, Apr. 6, 1938; s. Donald Harrison and Rosalee Adelia (Brown) S.; m. Patricia Townsend, June 3, 1961; children: Christopher, Peter, Timothy. BA, St. John's Coll., Annapolis, Md., 1960; MA, U. Va., 1964; MS, Columbia U., 1965. Sr. asst. in manuscripts U. Va. Libr., Charlottesville, 1965, reference libr., 1966-76, acting acquisitions libr., 1967-68, assoc. univ. libr., 1976-87, assoc. univ. libr. for pub. svcs., 1987-92, acting univ. libr., 1993, assoc. univ. libr., 1994-98, dep. univ. libr., 1998—2003, ret., 2003. Cons. US Dept. Edn., Washington, 1982—84. Author: Quantitative Criteria for Academic Research Libraries, 1984; editor: Cumulated Assn. Research Libraries Statistics, 1981, Rsch. Libr. Statistics, 1990, ARL Statistics, 1992-95, Japanese Text Initiative on World Wide Web, 1995—; contbr. articles on library stats., rsch. to profl. publs., Internet. Mem. Assn. of Rsch. Librs. (mem. stats. com., vis. program officer 1995-97), Bibliog. Soc. U. Va. (pres. 1975-78, v.p. 1978-99).

STUBBS, SUSAN CONKLIN, retired statistician; b. Washington, July 26, 1935; d. Maxwell Robertson and Marcia (Nye) Conklin; m. LeRoy Carter Hostetter, May 20, 1975 (div. 1988); m. Joel Richard Stubbs, Sept. 20, 1992. BA, Pa. State U., 1957. Economist Bur. of Census, Suitland, Md., 1973-74, Bur. of Labor Statistics, Washington, 1974-78, supervisory economist, 1978-84; statistician IRS, Washington, 1984-95, chief rschr. stats. of income divsn., 1989-92, coord. for indsl. classification, 1994-95; ret., 1995. Cons. joint com. on taxation U.S. Congress, 1992-94; OPM legis. fellow, 1988. Contbr. articles to profl. jours.; editor govtl. statis. publs. Leader, del., bd. dirs., v.p., chmn. nominating com. Nation's Capital coun. Girl Scouts U.S., 1968—; sec.-treas. Middlesex Beach Assn., Bethany, Del., 1991—94; jobs. editor Caucus for Women in Stats., Washington, 1992—95; mentor Mentors Inc., Washington, 1992—94; treas. Smith Point Sea Rescue, 1997—2003; docent Reedville Fisherman's Mus., 1997—, treas., 2003, chmn. fin., 2003; active Boy Scouts Am. Campaign for Family Values; tutor and mentor People Helping People; fin. chmn., Christmas on Cockrell's Creek Reedville Fisherman's Mus., 2002; mem. Tax Economist Forum, 1990—97; treas. Rappahannock C.C. Found., 2003—; mentor Northumberland Middle Sch. in Tobacco grant program; treas. Region II, Episc. Diocese of Va., 1999—; bd. dirs. Rice's Hotel/Hughlett's Tavern Found., 1998—2000. Mem.: Northumberland Assn. for Progressive Stewardship (mem. edn. com. 1997—), Am. Statis. Assn., St. Stephen's Episcopal Ch. ECW (vice pres. 2002, treas. 2003—04), Bus. and Profl. Women Essex County and No. Neck (sec. 1999—2001), Va. Federated Women's Clubs (pres. Northumberland County chpt. 1996—98, pres Ea. area Lee dist. 1998—2000), Rivers Bend Assn. (v.p., bd. dirs. 1996—98, chair bylaws com., chair long range planning com., chair fin. com. 1998—2001, v.p., bd. dirs., bd. mem. 2001—). Avocations: sailing, swimming, gardening, reading. Home: 776 Riverview Ln Heathsville VA 22473-4011

STUBBS, WILL, JR., pharmaceutical company manager; b. Birmingham, Ala., Feb. 26, 1955; s. Will, Sr. and Elizabeth S.; 1 child, Will III. BS in Mgmt. and Econs. cum laude, Fisk U., 1977. Sys. engr. Procter & Gamble, Jackson, Tenn., 1977-78, prodn. team mgr., 1978-80; large parenterals labeling/packaging supr. Abbott Labs., Rocky Mount, N.C., 1980-81, large parenterals terminal sterile filling supr., 1981-85, aseptic sterilization supr., 1985-88, small parenterals terminal sterile fill supr., 1988-90, aseptic filling supr., 1990-93, sr. prodn. supr., 1993-95, pharm. prodn. mgr., 1995-2001, terminal sterile filling prodn. mgr., 2001—02, small volume parenterals labeling/packaging prodn. mgr., 2002—. Contbr. poetry to Fisk Herald. Mem. econ. growth task force Rocky Mount City Coun., 1992-94; bd. dirs. Nash Edgecombe Econ. Devel. Inc., Rocky Mount, 1994-99, vice chmn. bd. dirs., 1998, chmn., 1999; mem. Adult Basic Edn. Bd., 1980-84; pres. Rocky Mount Pan Hellenic Coun., 1991-93. Named to Outstanding Young Men of Am., Jaycees, 1983, 5th Dist. Scholar of the Yr., Omega Psi Phi, 1977; recipient internship Mobil Oil Corp. Mem. Omega Psi Phi (Vice-Basileus grad. chap. 1989-91). Democrat. Baptist. Avocations: community service, travel, music, swimming, jogging. Home: 1028 Niblick Dr Rocky Mount NC 27804-9655 Office: 4285 N Wesleyan Blvd Rocky Mount NC 27804-8612 Office Phone: 252-977-5961.

STUBER, CHARLES WILLIAM, genetics educator, researcher; b. St. Michael, Nebr, Sept. 19, 1931; s. Harvey John and Minnie Augusta (Wilks) S.; m. Marilyn Martha Cook, May 28, 1953; 1 child, Charles William Jr. BS, U. Nebr., 1952, MS, 1961; PhD, N.C. State U., 1965. Vet., agrl. instr. Broken Bow HS, 1956-59; rsch. asst. U. Nebr., Lincoln, 1959-61; rsch. geneticist Agrl. Rsch. Svc., USDA, Raleigh, NC, 1962-75, supervisory rsrch. geneticist, rsch. leader, 1975-98, collaborator, 1998—; prof. genetics & crop sci. NC State U., Raleigh, 1975-98, prof. emeritus, 1998—. Assoc. editor Crop Sci. Jour., 1979-82, tech. editor, 1984-86, editor, 1987-89; contbr. over 200 articles to profl. jour., chpt. to books. Chmn. coun. on ministries and numerous offices Highland United Meth Ch., Raleigh. Lt. USN, 1952-56. Named Outstanding Sci. of Yr., USDA-ARS, 1989; recipient Genetics and Plant Breeding award Nat. Coun. Comml. Plant Breeders, 1995, Award of Merit, U. Nebr. Alumni Assn., 1997; inductee USDA-Agrl. Rsch. Svc. Sci. Hall of Fame, 1999; Vol. 45 of MAYDICA dedicated to Charles W. Stuber, 2000. Fellow: Crop Sci. Soc. Am. (editor-in-chief 1987—91, pres. 1992—93, Crop Sci. Rsch. award 1995, DeKalb Genetics Crop Sci. Disting. Career award 1999), Fellow Am. Soc. Agronomy (pres. 2002); mem.: Am. Genetic Assn. (sec. 1984—86), Genetics Soc. Am., Phi Kappa Phi, Sigma Xi. Avocations: windsurfing, water-skiing, sailing. Home: 1800 Manuel St Raleigh NC 27612-5510 Office: USDA-ARS NC State U Dept Genetics PO Box 7614 Raleigh NC 27695-0001 Personal E-mail: cstuber2@aol.com. Business E-Mail: cstuber@ncsu.edu.

STUBER, SCOTT, film company executive; Past mktg. dept. Universal Pictures; exec. Donner/Schuler-Donner Prodns.; v.p. prodn. Universal Pictures, Universal City, Calif., 1997—2000, exec. v.p. prodn., 2000—01, co-pres. prodn., 2001—03, vice chmn., worldwide prodn., 2003—. Office: Universal Pictures 100 Universal City Plaza Universal City CA 91608

STÜBGEN, JOERG-PATRICK, neurologist; b. Tripoli, Libya, Sept. 07; s. Fritz Hans Georg and Marie-Louise Hildegard Stübgen. MD, U. Pretoria, South Africa, 1983. Diplomate Am. Bd. Psychiatry and Neurology. Intern Grey's Hosp., Pietermaritzburg, South Africa; neurology resident U. Pretoria, South Africa, 1984—89, neuromuscular fellow, asst. prof. dept. neurology, 1990—91, assoc. prof., 1991—92; asst. prof. Cornell U., N.Y.C., 1995—99, assoc. prof. dept. neurology, 2000—. Contbr. over 30 articles to profl. jours., 6 chpts. to books. Named one of Best Doctors in Am., 2003—04. Fellow: Royal Coll. Physicians and Surgeons of Can., Coll. Physicians of South Africa; mem.: AMA, Am. Acad. Neurology. Lutheran. Avocations: road running, travel. Office: Cornell Univ Med College 525 E 68th St New York NY 10021

STUCK, ROGER DEAN, electrical engineering educator; b. Ventura, Calif., Nov. 6, 1924; s. William Henry and Marian Grace (Ready) S.; m. Opal Christine Phillips, July 25, 1948; children: Dean, Phyllis, Sandra. BSEE, Calif. Inst. Tech., 1947; MSEE, N.C. State U., 1957. Elec. engr. Warren Wilson Coll., Swannanoa, N.C., 1947—, instr. elec. engring. physics, 1948-69, dean students, 1969-72, instr. physics, elec. engr., 1972-86. Author: (charts) The Periodic Table of Physical Concepts, 1977, The Periodic Table of Physical Concepts with Economic Concepts, 1980; (book) The Periodic Table of Physical Concepts Book of Definitions, 1980. Lt. (j.g.) USNR, 1942-46. Mem. Sigma Xi. Republican. Presbyterian. Achievements include an elliptical response for the creative theory and the identification of gravitational inductance, capacitance and splendor (MVVV) and energy-spread (hc) as a fundamental initial concept of physical creation relating mass and charge which is fundamental to any Grand Unification Theory; the statement of a quantized conservation law for energy-spread to establish an internal and external structure for neutrons, protons, electrons and neutrinos. Home: 65 Green Forest Rd Swannanoa NC 28778-2246

STUCKEY, JAMES P. real estate company executive; b. Bklyn., Feb. 15, 1954; s. John McRae and Ethel Lilian Stuckey; m. Deborah Marie Stuckey, Apr. 6, 1974; children: Nicole Marie, James P. Jr., Danielle Antionette. BS, St. John's U., 1975, MA, 1977, St. Joseph Seminary and Coll., 2002. Various Office Econ. Devel., 1977-80, N.Y.C. Pub. Devel. Corp., 1980-86, pres., CEO, 1986-89, also bd. dirs.; mng. dir. Gronich & Co., Inc., 1990-93; exec. v.p., dir. comml. and residential devel. Forest City Ratner Cos., S.I., 1994—. Lectr. Columbia U., Yale U., St. John's U., NYU, John Jay Coll., Pratt Inst. Mem. Westside Task Force, N.Y.C. Mcpl. Water Fin. Authority, Ctr. Family Life, Nat. Trust Historic Preservation, Art Commn. N.Y.C.; vice chmn. Cmty. Bd. 2, S.I.; chmn. Ctr. Against Domestic Violence Mem. Nat. Assn. Corp. Real Estate Execs., Urban Land Inst., Coun. Urban Econ. Devel., Inst. Urban Design (mem. regional adv. coun.), Am. Assn. Individual Investors. Avocations: music, bicycling, racquetball, golf. Office: Forest City Ratner Corp 1 Metrotech Center Brooklyn NY 11201-3831 E-mail: jstuckey@fcrs.com.

STUCKY, GALEN D. chemist, biochemist, educator; PhD in Phys. Chemistry, Iowa State U., 1962. Postdoctoral assoc. Dept. Physics MIT, Mass., 1962—63; from asst. prof. in inorganic chemistry to prof. U. Ill., Urbana-Champaign, 1964—72, prof., 1972—80; rschr. Sandia Nat. Lab. DuPont Ctrl. R&D, 1980—85; prof. Dept. Chemistry and Biochemistry U. Calif., Santa Barbara, 1985—. Mem. Interdepartmental Program in Biochemistry and Molecular Biology U. Calif.; spkr. in field. Contbr. over 470 articles to profl. jours. Recipient Humboldt Rsch. prize, 2000; fellow, NSF, 1963. Fellow: AAAS; mem.: Internat. Soc. Optical Engrs., Materials Rsch. Soc. (mem. numerous editl. bds.), Am. Chemical Soc. (chmn. solid state divsn. 1999—, assoc. editor Jour. of Inorganic Chemistry). Office: USCB Dept Chyem and Bio Chemistry 3623D Physical Scis North Santa Barbara CA 93106

STUCKY, JEAN SEIBERT, lawyer; b. Berkeley, Calif., Feb. 9, 1951; d. Edward Raymond and Frances Selma (Berg) S.; m. Scott Wallace Stucky, Aug. 18, 1973; children: Mary-Clare, Joseph. BA in Econs., Wellesley (Mass.) Coll., 1973; JD, Cornell U., 1978; MA in Econs., Trinity U., San Antonio, 1980; postgrad., George Washington U., 1991—95. Bar: DC 1978. Atty.-advisor Adminstrv. Conf. US, Washington, 1978-79, Divsn. Advice, NLRB, Washington, 1979-94; contractor labor counsel US Dept. Energy, Office Gen. Counsel, Washington, 1994—. Mem. Washington Cathedral Altar Guild, 1988—. Mem. DC Bar, Dames of Loyal Legion of US, Washington Wellesley Club (pres. 1992-94), Wellesley Coll. Alumnae Assn. (regional chmn. 1995-97). Republican. Episcopalian. Avocations: gardening, flower arranging. Home: 11004 Homeplace Ln Potomac MD 20854-1406 Office: US Dept Energy Office Gen Counsel 1000 Independence Ave SW Washington DC 20585-0001

STUCKY, NANCY L. special education educator; Tchr. spl. edn. Sandstone Elem., Billings, Mont. Recipient State Tchr. of Yr. Spl. Edn. award Mont., 1992.

STUCKY, SCOTT WALLACE, lawyer; b. Hutchinson, Kans., Jan. 11, 1948; s. Joe Edward and Emma Clara (Graber) S.; m. Jean Elsie Seibert, Aug. 18, 1973; children: Mary-Clare, Joseph. BA summa cum laude, Wichita State U., 1970, JD, Harvard U., 1973; MA, Trinity U., 1980; LLM with high honors, George Washington U., 1983; postgrad., Nat. War Coll., 1993. Bar: Kans. 1973, U.S. Dist. Ct. Kans. 1973, U.S. Ct. Appeals (10th cir.) 1973, U.S. Ct. Mil. Appeals 1974, U.S. Supreme Ct. 1976, D.C. 1979, U.S. Ct. Appeals (D.C. cir.) 1979. Assoc. Ginsburg, Feldman & Bress, Washington, 1978-82; chief docketing and svc. br. Nuclear Regulatory Commn., Washington, 1982-83; legis. counsel U.S. Air Force USAF, Washington, 1983-96, gen. counsel sen. com. on armed svcs., 1996—2001, 2003—, prin. minority counsel, 2001—03. Lectr. bus. law Maria Regina Coll., Syracuse, N.Y., 1977; congrl. fellow Office Senator John Warner, 1986; res. judge adv. USAF Res., Washington, 1982-2003; col. Appellate Mil. Judge, USAF Ct. Criminal Appeals, 1991-95, 97-98, 2001-03; sr. reservist USAF Judiciary, 1995-97, Air Res. Pers. Ctr., 1998-99, Air Force Legal Svcs. Agy., 1999-2001. Contbr. articles to profl. jours. Capt. USAF, 1973-78. Decorated Legion of Merit, Air Force Meritorious Svc. medal with two oak leaf cluster. Mem. Fed. Bar Assn., Judge Advs. Assn. (bd. dirs. 1984-88), Res. Officers Assn., Wichita State U. Alumni Assn. (pres. chpt. 1981-86, nat. bd. dirs. 1986-92), Adoption Svc. Info. Agy. (bd. dirs. 1998-2002, 2004—), Army and Navy Club (Washington), Mil. Order of Loyal Legion U.S. (state comdr. and recorder 1984-92, nat. treas. 1987-89, nat. vice comdr. 1989-93, nat. comdr.-in-chief 1993-95), Sons of Union Vets Civil War (chpt. vice-comdr 1986-88), Phi Delta Phi, Phi Alpha Theta, Phi Kappa Phi, Omicron Delta Kappa, Sigma Phi Epsilon. Republican. Episcopalian. Home: 11004 Homeplace Ln Potomac MD 20854-1406 Office: Sen Armed Svcs Com 228 Senate Office Bldg Washington DC 20510-0001

STUCKY, STEVEN (EDWARD), composer, conductor; b. Hutchinson, Kans., Nov. 7, 1949; s. Victor Eugene and Louise Doris (Trautwein) S.; m. Melissa Jane Whitehead, Aug. 22, 1970; children: Maura Catharine, Matthew Steven. MusB, Baylor U., 1971; MFA, Cornell U., 1973, DMA, 1978. Vis. asst. prof. Lawrence U., Appleton, Wis., 1978-80; prof. Cornell U., Ithaca, N.Y., 1980—, chmn. dept. music, 1992-97; vis. prof. Eastman Sch. of Music, 2001—02; Ernest Bloch vis. prof. U. Calif., Berkeley, 2003. Composer-in-residence L.A. Philharm. Orch., 1988— Author: Lutoslawski and His Music, 1981 (Deems Taylor award ASCAP 1982); composer: Sappho Fragments, 1982, Voyages, 1984, Boston Fancies, 1985, Dreamwaltzes, 1986, Concerto for orch., 1987, Son et Lumière, 1988, Angelus, 1990, Impromptus, 1991, Four Poems of A.R. Ammons, 1992, Ancora, 1994, Double Flute Cto., 1994, Fanfares and Arias, 1994, Pinturas de Tamayo, 1995, Music for Saxophones and Strings, 1996, Cradle Songs, 1997, Concerto Mediterraneo, 1998, Ad Parnassum, 1998, American Muse, 1999, Nell'ombra, nella luce, 1999, Etudes, 2000, Pastorale-Partita, after J.S.B., 2000, Concerto for Percussion and Wind Orchestra, 2001, Skylarks, 2001, Colburn Variations, 2002, Whispers, 2002, Album Leaves, 2002, Spirit Voices, 2003, Jeu de timbres, 2003, Second Concerto for Orchestra, 2003, Sonate en forme des preludes, 2004; received commn. from Nat. Endowment for Arts, 1982, Koussevitzky Found., 1991, Meet the Composer, 1995. Bd. advisors Barlow Endowment, 1993-97; bd. dirs. MacDowell Colony, 1993-95. Fellow Guggenheim Found., Nat. Endowment for the Arts, Bogliasco Found., Goddard Lieberson fellow Am. Acad. Arts and Letters. Office: Theodore Presser Co care One Presser Pl Bryn Mawr PA 19010 Office Phone: 607-277-8938. E-mail: stevenstudky@mac.com.

STUDDARD, RUBEN (CHRISTOPHER RUBEN STUDDARD), singer; b. Birmingham, Ala., July 14, 1978; s. Kevin Studdard Sr. and Emily Studdard. Graduated, Ala. A&M U., 2000. Singer, jazz and soul band Just a Few Cats; singer, gospel group God's Gift. Backup singer: American Idol: The Search for a Superstar, 2002; singer, 2003 (named American Idol, 2003), (single) Flying Without Wings, 2003, (albums) Soulful, 2003; singer: (with various artists) American Idol Season 2: All Time, 2003; cameo Scooby Doo 2: Monsters Unleashed, 2004; nominee commentator: I Wanna Thank My Mama: The BET Awards 2004 Nomination Special; performer: American Idol Tour, 9th Annual Walk of Fame Honoring Aretha Franklin, 2003, Fromage, 2003, American Idol Christmas, 2003, 3rd Annual BET Awards, 2003, Good Morning America, 2004; guest appearances Oprah Winfrey Show, 2003, 2004, Making the Video, Ruben Studdard: Flying Without Wings, 2003, American Juniors, 2003, Sharon Osbourne Show, 2003, Late Show with David Letterman, 2004, Ellen: The Ellen DeGeneres Show, 2004, Mad TV, 2004, One on One, 2004, Jimmy Kimmel Live, 2004. Nominee Grammy award for best male vocal R&B performance. He was nicknamed the 'Velvet Teddy Bear' by the legendary soulful diva Gladys Knight. During the competition he acknowledged his home state of Birmingham, Alabama by wearing a t-shirt adorned with the state's area code "205." The state declared March 11 'Ruben Studdard Day'. Office: J Records 745 5th Ave New York NY 10151 Office Phone: 646-840-5600.*

STUDDERT, ANDREW PAUL, air transportation executive; married; 3 children. BS, San Francisco State U., 1979. Various exec. positions First Interstate Bancorp, L.A., exec. v.p.; sr. v.p. info. svcs. divsn., chief info. officer United Airlines, Chgo., sr. v.p. fleet ops., 1997—99, COO, 1999—. Office: UAL Corp and United Airlines World Hqrs PO Box 66100 Chicago IL 60666-0100

STUDDS, SUSAN MARTIN, education educator; b. Cincinatti, Ohio, Jan. 30, 1954; d. David Morgan and Junne Erickson Martin; m. Jeffrey Lynn Studdes, May 31, 1980. BA, Hanover Coll., 1976; MS, Miami U., 1978; PhD, U. Md., 1990. Dir. of student life Wash. Ctr. Internships, Wash., DC, 1983—84; resident dir. U. Md., 1984—85, rsch. asst., 1986—89; special asst. to provost Geo Mason U., Fairfax, Va., 1989—91; dir. ctr. for equal opportunity Am. Assn. State Coll. and Univ., Wash., DC, 1991—92; prof. edn. Nat. Def. U., 1993—95, asst. vp. acad. affairs, 1995—. Trustee Moravian Coll., Bethlehem, Pa., 2000—; adj. prof. of human behavior Indsl. Coll. Armed Forces, Wash., DC, 1996—2003. Actor: Side Door Coffee House, 2000—. Treas. Univ. Hills Civic Assn., 1991—93. Democrat. Presbyn. Avocations: theater, choir. Home: 7203 Wells Pkwy Hyattsville MD 20782 Office: Nat Def U 71 Lesley McNair Washington DC 20319

STUDEBAKER, IRVING GLEN, mining engineering consultant; b. Ellensburg, Wash., July 22, 1931; s. Clement Glen and Ruth (Krause) S.; (widowed); children: Ruth, Betty, Raymond, Karl, Donna. BS in Geol. Engring., U. Ariz., 1957, MS in Geology, 1959, PhD in Geol. Engring., 1977. Registered profl. engr., Wash., Nev., Ariz., Colo., Mont. Geophys. engr. Mobil, 1959-61; civil engr. City of Yakima, Wash., 1964-66; instr. Yakima Valley Coll., 1962-67; sr. rsch. geologist Roan Selection Trust, Kalulushi, Zambia, 1967-72; sr. mining engr. Occidental Oil Shale, Grand Junction, Colo., 1974-81; prof. Mont. Coll. Mining Sch., Butte, 1982-96; prof. emeritus, 1996—. Cons. in field. Sgt. U.S. Army, 1951-54, Korea. Mem. N.W. Mining Assn., Geol. Soc. Am., Soc. for Mining and Metall. Engring., Soc. Econ. Geologists, Sigma Xi (pres. Mont. tech. chpt. 1990-91). Avocations: golf, travel. Home and Office: 34222 1st Pl S Apt C Federal Way WA 98003-6537

STUDEBAKER, JOHN MILTON, utilities engineer, consultant, educator; b. Springfield, Ohio, Mar. 31, 1935; s. Frank Milton and Monaruth (Beatty) S.; m. Virginia Ann Van Pelt, Mar. 12, 1960; 1 child, Jacqueline Ann Allcorn. BS in Law, LaSalle U., Chgo., 1969; MS and PhD in Indsl. Engring., Columbia Pacific U., San Rafael, Calif., 1984. Cert. plant engr. Am. Inst. Plant Engrs., profl. cons. Acad. Profl. Cons. & Advisors. Indsl engr. Internat. Harvest Co., 1957-60, supr. indsl. engring., 1960-66, gen. supr. body assembly, 1967-68, mgr. indsl. engring., 1968-70; mgr. manufacturing engring. Lamb Electric Co., 1970—76, Cascade Corp., 1976—88; engring. mgr. Bundy Tubing Corp., Winchester and Cynthia, Ky., 1988—98; chmn. The Studebaker Group, Inc., Alexandria, Va., 1998—; pres. Studebaker Energy Cons., LLC, 1998—. Instr. numerous univs. including Boston U., Clemson U., Cornell U., Harvard U., Duquesne U., U. Ala., U. Ill., U. Wis., Ga. State U., James Madison U., Tex. Tech. U., U. Calif., Calif. State U., Columbia U., Fairleigh Dickinson U., San Francisco State U.; instr. Am. Mgmt. Assn., Rochester Inst. Tech., Ctr. for Profl. Advancement. Author: Slashing Utility Costs Handbook, Natural Gas Purchasing Handbook, Electricity Retail Wheeling Handbook, Electricity Purchasing Handbook, Utility Negotiation Handbook, ESCO Handbook. Mem. NSPE, Am. Inst. Facility Engrs. (cert.), Assn. Energy Engrs. (instr.). Republican. Home and Office: PO Box 708 Winchester KY 40392-0708 Office Phone: 859-744-1018. Business E-Mail: jstudebaker@studebakerenergy.net.

STUDER, CAROL A. creative director, graphic designer, photographer, consultant; b. Joliet, Ill. BA in Design with honors and distinction, U. Ill., Chgo., 1975. Photographer Motorola Inc., Schaumburg, Ill., 1977-78; photographer, designer Revell/MONOGRAM, Morton Grove, Ill., 1978-80; sr. graphic designer Bank of Am., Chgo., 1980-88; graphic design mgr. Strombecker Corp./TOOTSIETOY, Chgo., 1988-98. Pvt. practice design cons. Carol Studer Design/Photographer, Oak Park, Ill., 1987—. Inventor (children's toy) Mr. Bubbles, Finger Wands, 1991. Democrat. Avocations: downhill skiing, gardening, international child welfare issues, the arts.

STUDER, JAMES EDWARD, geological engineer; b. Aurora, Colo., Sept. 1, 1961; s. Fredrick Ernest and Patricia Dora (McWilliams) S.; m. Anita Louise Palmer, Apr. 19, 1986; 1 child, Matthew Bernard. BS in Geol. Engring., U. Mo., Rolla, 1984, MS in Geol. Engring., 1985. Registered profl. engr., Kans., Fla., Tex., N.Mex., Okla., Ariz.; registered geologist, Ky. (inactive). Engring. aide engring. divsn. pub. works City of Kansas City, Mo., 1981-83; civil engr. tech. U.S. Army Corps Engrs., Kansas City, 1984; staff engr. Woodward-Clyde Cons., St. Louis, 1985, staff to asst. project engr. Overland Park, Kans., 1986-89, project engr., 1989-90; grad. teaching asst. U. Mo., Rolla, 1985; sr. project engr. Coastal Remediation Co., Norman, Okla., 1990-92; program dir. Hall Southwest Corp., Austin, Tex., 1992-93; S.W. region program mgr. Envirogen, Inc., Austin, 1993-94; sr. engr. Duke Engrg. and Svcs., Albuquerque, 1995-98, sect. mgr., 1998-2000; founder, prin. Cons. and Funding Resources LLC, 1997—. Lectr. grad. sch. seminars, 1987-96, Nat. Seminar on RCRA Corrective Action, 1990, Internat. Symposium on Bioremediation, 1995, 97, 99, Superfund Conf., 1996, U.S. EPA Tech. Transfer Conf., 1996, 98, Internat. Symposium on Chlorinated and Recalcitrant Compounds, 1998, 2000; adv. bd. Albuquerque Tech.-Vocational Inst., 1995-99; youth soccer coach, 1997-2001. Contbr. articles on environ. sci. and engring. to profl. jours. and books. Environ. adv. bd. City of Round Rock, Tex., 1993. Eagle Scout Boy Scouts Am. Mem. ASCE, Waste Edn. and Rsch. Consortium, Am. Cash Flow Assn., Assn. Ground Water Scientists and Engrs., N.Mex. Optics Industry Assn., Coronado Venture Forum, N.Mex. Entrepreneurs Assn., N.Mex. Biotech. and Biomed. Assn., Sigma Gamma Epsilon (W.A. Tarr award 1984). Roman Catholic. Achievements include leading first full-scale vadose zone partitioning interwell tracer test for in-situ quantification of dense non-aqueous phase liquid (DNAPL); leading design of first US EPA-permitted arid-land final cap for hazardous waste landfill; on team that discovered and mapped previously unrecorded cave in Missouri; devel. of innovative technologies for characterization and restoration of hazardous waste sites and water resources. Office: Cons and Funding Resources LLC 9900 Lorelei Ln NE Albuquerque NM 87111-1246 E-mail: funding_resource@msn.com.

STUDER, JEANNETTE R. dean; m. Mike Studer. MS, U. of Wyo., 1972. Assoc. dean of instrn. Pima C.C., Tucson, 1997—99, instrnl. divsn. dean, 1999—. Judge U.S. Synchronized Swimming Assn., Tucson. Recipient Next Steps, Nat. Inst. for Leadership Devel., 2002.

STUDER, LOUIS, priest, religious organization administrator; b. Algona, Iowa, Oct. 24, 1949; s. Paul Otto and Marcella Bertha (West) Studer. BA in Sociology, Lewis U., 1971; MDiv in Theology, Weston Coll. Sch. Theology, 1975; MS in Edn. Adminstrn. and Supervision, So. Ill. U., 1979; PhD in Philosophy of Edn., St. Louis U., 1984. Assoc. pastor St. Patrick's Parish, McCook, Nebr., 1976—77; prin. St. Henry's Seminary, Belleville, Ill., 1977—84; dir. campus ministry U. Minn., Duluth, Minn., 1984—86; dir. Pre-Novitiate Program, Omaha, 1986—89, St. Louis, 1989—91; vocation dir. Oblate House Theology, Chgo., 1991—96; sabbatical program Jerusalem, Israel, Cambridge, Mass., 1996—97; dir. Shrine of Our Lady of the Snows & Missionary Assn. of Mary Immaculate, Belleville, 1997—. Provincial coun. mem. Oblates of Mary Immaculate, St. Paul, 1990—99. Author: (book) The High School Seminary in U.S. Today, 1984. Bd. dirs. Bethany Place, Belleville, 1998—. Home: 442 S De Mazenod Dr Belleville IL 62223 Office: Nat Shrine of Our Lady of the Snows 442 S DeMazenod Dr Belleville IL 62223

STUDER, PATRICIA S. psychologist; b. Ft. Scott, Kans., Sept. 3, 1942; d. Herb E. Studer and Mary Edith (McElroy) Cook; children: Mary Paige, Catherine Ann. BS, Cen. Mo. State U., Warrensburg, 1964; MS, Pittsburg (Kans.) State U., 1975; PsyD, U. Minn., 1999. Lic. psychologist, N.Y.; cert. elem. tchr., Mo. Supervisory tchr. Cen. Mo. State U., 1966; tchr. Consolidated Sch. Dist. 1, Hickman Mills, Mo., 1964-68; clin. psychologist Nevada (Mo.) State Hosp., 1977-80, chief unit psychologist, 1980-83; dir. psychology dept., staff psychologist Raphael Ctr. Hosp., Nevada, 1982-83; exec. dir., psychologist Nevada Counseling Ctr., 1983-91; adj. med. staff Nevada Regional Med. Ctr., 1983-99; exec. dir. Ctr. for Human Devel., Nevada, Mo., 1992-95. Practicum supr. Pittsburg State U., 1980-95; clin. supr. Cmty. Counseling Cons., Clinton, Mo., 1987-88; cons. psychologist Barton County Meml. Hosp., 1993-95, Heartland Hosp., Nevada, 1995, South Oaks Hosp., L.I., 1999-2000, Clin. PsychAssocs., N.Y.C., 2000—; mem. Com. for Drug Free Schs., Nevada, 1988-95, cons. psychologist, 1988-90; cons. psychotherapist Nevada Child Abuse Coun., 1981-82; pvt. practice, Long Island, N.Y., 2001. Mem. The Nelson-Adkins Mus. Art; mem. Mo. Regional Adv. Coun. on Alcohol and Drug Abuse, 1985-94, v.p., 1988, 92; bd. dirs. Mental Health Adv. Bd., 1993-95, Sch. Health Adv. Com., 1994-95. Mem. APA (assoc.)., Mo. Psychol. Assn., Soroptimist Internat. of Nevada (pres. 1992-93), Rotary Internat., Nevada Vernon County C. of C. Avocations: gardening, interior decorating, environmental issues. Home: 1424 W Altheimer Dr Fayetteville AR 72704-6897

STUDER, WILLIAM ALLEN, county official; b. Chgo., July 27, 1939; s. William Gotlieb and Annette Elizabeth (Bruzek) S.; m. Donna Barnes Bray, Dec. 26, 1961; children: Scott, Shannon. BS in Indsl. Mgmt., Ga. Inst. Tech., 1961; MS in Guidance and Counseling, Troy State U., 1975, MS in Mgmt., 1978; student, Air War Coll., Maxwell AFB, Ala., 1980-81. Commd. 2d lt. USAF, 1961, advanced through grades to maj. gen., 1989; legis. liaison U.S. Senate, Washington, 1981-83; dir. fighter ops./tng. USAF Hdqrs. Europe, Ramstein AB, Fed. Republic Germany, 1983-84; vice comdr. 10th Tactical Reconnaissance Wing RAF USAF, Alconbury, Eng., 1984-85, comdr. 10th Tactical Reconnaissance Wing RAF, 1985-86, comdr. 81st Tactical Fighter Wing RAF Bentwaters, Eng., 1986-87, comdr. 316th Air Div/Kaiserslautern Ramstein AB, Fed. Republic Germany, 1987-88, vice comdr. 12th Air Force/U.S. So. Command Bergstrom AFB, Tex., 1988-90, comdr. 13th Air Force Clark AFB, The Philippines, 1990-91; dir. ops. CENTCOM/J-3, MacDill AFB, Fla., 1992-94; ret. USAF, 1994; dir. pub. safety dept. Hillsborough County, Tampa, Fla., 1994—. Decorated D.S.M., Legion of Merit with oak leaf cluster, DFC with three oak leaf clusters, Bronze Star, Air medal with 35 oak leaf clusters; Legion of Honor, Bronze Cross medal (The Philippines). Mem. Daedalians, Quiet Birdmen, Rotary. Avocations: golf, reading. Home: 5309 Bayshore Blvd Tampa FL 33611 Office: Hillsborough County Pub Safety Dept Tampa FL 33610 Office Phone: 813-272-6408. Personal E-mail: studerdm@aol.com. Business E-Mail: studerw@hillsboroughcounty.org.

STUDER, WILLIAM JOSEPH, library educator; b. Whiting, Ind., Oct. 1, 1936; s. Victor E. and Sarah G. (Hammersley) S.; m. Rosemary Lippie, Aug. 31, 1957; children: Joshua E., Rachel Marie. BA, Ind. U., 1958, MA, 1960, PhD (Univ. fellow), 1968. Grad. asst. divsn. libr. sci. Ind. U., 1959-60, reference asst., 1960-61; spl. intern Libr. of Congress, 1961-62, reference libr., sr. bibliographer, 1962-65; dir. regional campus librs. Ind. U., Bloomington, 1968-73, assoc. dean univ. librs., 1973-77; dir. librs. Ohio State U., Columbus, 1977-2000, prof. emeritus libr. sci., 2000—, coord. univ. oral history program, 2001—. Mem. Libr. Svcs. and Constrn. Act Adv. Com. of Ind., 1971-76; mem. Adv. Coun. on Fed. Libr. Programs in Ohio, 1977-85, chmn., 1980-81; adv. coun. Libr. Svcs. and Tech. Act, 1997-99; mem. ARL Office Mgmt. Studies Adv. Com., 1977-81, ARL Task Force on Nat. Libr. Network Devel., 1978-83, bd. dirs., 1981-84, chmn., 1981-83, com. on preservation, 1985-88, vice-chmn., 1989-90, chmn., 1991-92, task force on scholarly comm., 1983-87, com. stats. and measurement, 1993-99, chmn., 1997-98; network adv. com. Libr. Congress, 1981-88; libr. study com. Ohio Bd. Regents, 1986-87; mem. steering com. Ohio Libr. and Info. Network (OhioLINK), 1987-90; vice-chmn. Ctr. Rsch. Librs., 1993-94, chmn., 1994-95, sec., chmn. membership com., 1990-93; adv. coun. OhioLink Libr., 1992-2000, chmn., 1991-92, policy adv. coun., governing bd., 1991-92. Contbr. articles to profl. jours. Trustee Online Computer Libr. Ctr. Inc., 1977-78; del. Online Computer Libr. Ctr. Users Coun., 1983-91; rsch. librs. adv. com. Online Computer Libr. Ctr., 1989-95, vice-chmn., chmn.-elect, 1993-94, chmn., 1994-95; bd. dirs. Ohio Network of Librs. Ohionet, 1977-87, chmn., 1980-82, 86-87, treas., 1983-86; mem. Columbia U. Sch. Libr. Svc. Conservation Programs, vis. com., 1987-90; nat. adv. coun. to commn. on preservation and access, 1989-92; treas. Monroe County (Ind.) Mental Health Assn., 1966-76; budget rev. com. United Way, 1975-77; bd. dirs. Mental Health Assn. Recipient citation for participation MARC Insts., 1968-69, Disting. Alumni award Ind. U., 1978, OhioLINK Founders award, 2002. Mem. ALA, Ohio Libr. Assn. (bd. dirs. 1980-83), Assn. Coll. and Rsch. Librs. (bd. dirs. 1977-81, com. on activities model for 1990, 1981-82, chmn. libr. sch. curriculum task force 1988-89), Ohio State U. Retirees Assn. (pres.-elect 2004—), Acad. Libr. Assn. Ohio, Torch Club (pres. 1993-94), Phi Kappa Phi (pub. rels. officer 1982-83, sec. 1983-85), Phi Eta Sigma, Alpha Epsilon Delta, Beta Phi Mu. Home: 724 Olde Settler Pl Columbus OH 43214-2924 Office: Ohio State U William Oxley Thompson Meml Libr 1858 Neil Ave Columbus OH 43210-1286 Office Phone: 614-688-0204. Business E-Mail: studer.2@osu.edu.

STUDEVANT, LAURA, medical association administrator; Pres. Nat. Environ. Health Assn., Denver; regional health mgr. Amtrak, Chgo. Address: Regional Pub Health Mgr Amtrak 210 S Canal Chicago IL 60606 Office: National Environ Health Assn 720 S Colorado Blvd Ste 970S Denver CO 80246-1925

STUDIN, JAN, publishing executive; From acct. mgr. to v.p. Woman's Day, 1982—95, v.p., advt. dir., 1995—96; v.p., pub. Woman's Day Hachette Filipacchi Mags., Inc., N.Y.C., 1996—2002; v.p., pub. G+J USA's Parents Group, 2002—. Office: G+J USA Publishing 375 Lexington AVe New York NY 10017-5514

STUDLEY, JAMIENNE SHAYNE, lawyer, educator; b. N.Y.C., Apr. 30, 1951; d. Jack Hill and Joy (Cosor) Studley; m. Gary J. Smith, July 14, 1984. BA magna cum laude, Barnard Coll., 1972; JD, Harvard U., 1975. Bar: DC 1975, U.S. Dist. Ct. DC 1978. Assoc. Bergson, Borkland, Margolis & Adler, Washington, 1976—80; spl. asst., sec. U.S. HHS, 1980—81; assoc. Weil, Gotshal & Manges, Washington, 1981—83; assoc. dean law sch. Yale U., New Haven, 1983—87, lectr. law, 1984—87; syndicated columnist Am. Lawyer Media, 1990—91; exec. dir. Nat. Assn. for Law Placement, Washington, 1987—90, Calif. Abortion Rights Action League, 1992—93; dep. gen. counsel U.S. Dept. Edn., 1993—99, acting gen. counsel, 1997—99; pres. Skidmore Coll., Saratoga Springs, NY, 1999—2003; scholar-in-residence Carnegie Found. for the Advancement of Tchg., Palo Alto, Calif., 2003—04; pres. Pub. Advocates, Inc., 2004—. Vis. scholar adj. faculty U. Calif., Berkeley Law Sch., 1992; vis. com. Harvard Law Sch.; bd. dirs. Assn. Am. Colls., Urban Sch., Adirondack Trust Co., 1999—2003; vice chair for program The Annapolis Group, 2001—03; chair legis. com. Commn. on Ind. Colls. and Univs. N.Y. State, 2002—03. Pres. Conn. Women's Ednl. and Legal Fund, Hartford, 1986—87; co-founder Washington Area Women's Found., 1997; founding bd. dirs. Wood Art Collectors; mem. Jacob Javits fellowship bd. U.S. Dept. Edn., 2000—03; mem. policy com. Campus Compact, 2002—; bd. dirs. The Urban Sch., San Francisco, 2004—, San Francisco Mus. Crafts and Design, 2004—. Mem.: ABA (commn. on women in the profession 1991—94, chair editl. bd. Perspectives 1991—99, chair coord. coun. legal edn. 1996—97, com. on loan repayment and forgiveness 2001—03), Nat. Adv. Coun., First Book, Nat. Assn. for Ind. Colls. and Univs. (accountability com. 1999—2002), DC Bar Assn., Adv. Com. Ann.Giving, Assn. Alumnae Barnard Coll. (bd. dirs. 1978—81), Barnard in Washington (pres. 1977—78), Mus. Craft and Design, Urban Sch. Bd., Phi Beta Kappa. Office: 131 Steuart St # 300 San Francisco CA 94105-1241 Office Phone: 415-431-7430.

STUDNESS, CHARLES MICHAEL, economist; b. Mpls., Nov. 2, 1935; s. Leo C. and Alma (Mehus) S.; m. Harriet Leah Katz, Oct. 27, 1968; children: Erica, Lisa, Roy. BA, U. Minn., 1957, MA, 1958; PhD in Econs., Columbia U., 1963. Lectr. CCNY, 1961-64, U. Minn., Mpls., 1964-65; economist Fed. Res. Bank N.Y., N.Y.C., 1965-67, N.Y. Stock Exchange, N.Y.C., 1967-68, Eastern Airlines, N.Y.C., 1968-70, Baker Weeks, N.Y.C., 1970-76, E.F. Hutton, N.Y.C., 1976-79; pres. Studness Rsch., Manhasset, N.Y., 1979—; lectr. Baruch Coll., N.Y.C., 1968-74. Contbg. editor Public Utilities Fortnightly, 1990—. Columnist, Pub. Utilities Fortnightly, 1979—. Personal E-mail: studness@optonline.net.

STUDWELL, WILLIAM EMMETT, librarian, writer; b. Stamford, Conn., Mar. 18, 1936; s. Alfred Theodore and Mary Alice (Baker) S.; m. Ann Marie Stroia, Aug. 28, 1965 (dec. 2003); 1 child, Laura Ann. BA, U. Conn., 1958, MA, 1959; MLS, Cath. U. Am., 1967. Tech. abstracter Libr. Congress, Washington, 1963-66, asst. editor decimal classification office, 1966-68; head libr. Kirtland C.C., Roscommon, Mich., 1968-70; head/prin. cataloger No. Ill. U., DeKalb, 1970-2000; freelance writer, editor, 2001—. Mem. U.S. Adv. Com. to Chemistry Sects., Universal Decimal Classification, 1968-72; chmn. adv. group Libr. Rsch. Ctr., Urbana, Ill., 1982-84. Author: Chaikovskii, Delibes, Stravinskii, 1977, Christmas Carols, 1985, Adolphe Adam and Leo Delibes, 1987, Ballet Plot Index, 1987 (named One of Outstanding Acad. Books by Choice Mag. 1988-89), Cataloging Books, 1989, Library of Congress Subject Headings, 1990, Opera Plot Index, 1990, Christmas Card Songbook, 1991, Subject Access to Films and Videos, 1992, Popular Song Reader, 1994, Christmas Carol Reader, 1995, National and Religious Song Reader, 1996, Americana Song Reader, 1997, Minor Ballet Composers, 1997, State Songs of the United States, 1997, Publishing Glad Tidings, 1998, College Fight Songs, 1998, Barbershops, Bullets, and Ballads, 1999, Circus Songs, 1999, The End of the Year, 1999, The Classic Rock and Roll Reader, 1999, They Also Wrote, 2000, The Big Band Reader, 2000, The Clandestine Classical Music Reader, 2000, Forward! Forward! Is the Word, 2000, College Fight Songs II, 2001, Lest We Forget, 2001, A Fable, A Fantasy, and a Farewell, 2002, The French Violin School, 2002, Suzannah's Redemption, or The Devil Gets His Due, 2003, The Man Who Invented God and Other Fantastic Tales, 2004; asst. editor Western Assn. of Map Librs. Info. Bull., 1989-94; editor Music Reference Svcs. Quarterly, 1991-99, Resources in Music History Book Series, 1999—; text editor (Christmas music) The Millennia Collection, 2000—; contbg. editor Technicalities, 1996—; contbr. nearly 390 articles to profl. jours.; over 610 radio, TV and print media appearances. U.S. expert on Christmas Carols; internat. recognized expert on Am. Coll. fight songs; internat. leader to devel. standardization code for libr. congress subject headings; leading internat. proponent multinat., multicultural and multilingual subject access sys. Named most productive author among librs. in U.S., Coll. and Rsch. Librs. Mag., 1983-87, 93-97, Outstanding Alumnus, Sch. Libr. and Info. Sci., Cath. U. Am., 2002. Mem. Ill. Assn. Coll. and Rsch. Librs. (exec. bd. 1980-85, newsletter editor 1980-85, lifetime achievement award 1992), Ill. Libr. Assn., Librs. for Social Responsibility (editor newsletter 1986-87, bd. dirs. 1986-94). Home: 3332 S Forrester St Bloomington IN 47401-7115

STUDZINSKI, JOHN JOSEPH PAUL, investment banking executive; b. Mass., Mar. 19, 1956; arrived in Eng., 1984; s. Alfred and Jennie S. AB, Bowdoin Coll., 1978; MBA, U. Chgo., 1980. Investment banker Morgan Stanley & Co. Ltd., N.Y.C., 1980; head, corp. fin. Morgan Stanley Internat. Inc., London, 1989—92, head, mergers & acquisitions European bus., 1992—97, head, investment banking Europe, 1997—2001, dep. chmn, 2001—03; co-chief exec., corp. investment banking, and markets (CIBM) HSBC Holdings, 2003—. Chmn. Bus. Action on Homelessness, London, 1999—; founder Passage Day Centre, London, 2000—; trustee Tate Gallery, 1998—; life trustee Sir John Soane Mus., 1999—; trustee Human Rights Watch, N.Y.C., 1999—, Bowdoin Coll. Named to Knight of the Order of St. Gregory, Pope John Paul II, 2001; recipient Prince of Wales Ambassador's award, 2000, dist. alumnus, U. Chgo., 2002. Avocations: performing arts, hiking, outdoor survival. Office: HSBC Holdings 8 Canada Sq London E14 5HQ England*

STUEBING, EDWARD WILLIS, research scientist; b. Cin., Sept. 9, 1942; s. Edward Norman and Ruth Marcella (Glass) S.; m. Mary Ann Brown (div. 1980); children: Barbara Jean, Jennifer Jane. BS with high honors, U. Cin., 1965; PhD, Johns Hopkins U., Balt., 1970. Rsch. scientist U.S. Army Frankford Arsenal, Phila., 1971—77, U.S. Army, Edgewood R&D Ctr., Aberdeen Proving Ground, Md., 1977—; joint svcs. bus. area mgr. CB Def. Supporting Sci. and Tech., 1994—2003, chief scientist for physical scis., 1999—2001, team leader aerosol sci., 1992—. Adj. prof. Drexel U., Phila., 1973-1976. Contbr. articles to profl. jours. Dir. Civic Assn., Kingsville, Md., 1989-92; pres. Gunpowder Valley Conservancy, Md., 1990-94, treas., 1995—; elder Presbyn. Ch., Franklinville, Md., 1993—. Capt. U.S. Army, 1970-71. Recipient Army R&D Achievement award, 1974, 85, medal for Meritorious Civilian Svc., 1984, The Outstanding Fed. Profl. of 1984 award Fed. Exec. Bd., 1984, William H. Walker award, 1989. Mem. Am. Assn. for Aerosol Rsch. (chmn. nat. meeting 1983, dir. 1998—2001), Am. Chem. Soc., Am. Phys. Soc., Phi Beta Kappa, Sigma Xi. Avocations: trombone, sailing. Home: PO Box 233 Gunpowder MD 21010-0233 Office: Attn AMSRD ECB RT TA Bldg E5951 5183 Blackhawk Rd Aberdeen Proving Ground MD 21010-5424 Office Phone: 410-436-3089.

STUEBNER, ERWIN AUGUST, JR., internist; b. Phila., Oct. 9, 1944; s. Erwin August and Frances Badge (Quinn) S.; m. Jane Sigrid Christensen, Sept. 21, 1968; children: Eric Jay, Andrew Todd, Scott August. AB, Dartmouth Coll., 1966; MD, Northwestern U., Chgo., 1970. Diplomate Am. Bd. Internal Medicine. Intern, resident U. Mich., Ann Arbor, 1970-74; physician Williamstown (Mass.) Med. Assocs., 1976—; chmn. dept. medicine North Adams (Mass.) Regional Hosp., 1991—2003. Corporator North Adams Regional Hosp., 1992-; bd. dirs. Med. Profl. Mut. Ins. Co., Boston, 1995-. Fundraising chmn. Campaign for New Athletic Field, Williamstown, Mass., 1995-96. Maj. U.S. Army, 1974-76; trustee No. Berkshire Health Sys., 2002—. Mem. ACP, Am. Heart Assn. (exec. com. 1978-94), Mass. Med. Soc. (trustee 1988-94, 2000—, alt. trustee 1994-2000), Berkshire Dist. Med. Soc. (pres. 1984-86, exec. com. 1982-). Avocations: classical music, hiking, tennis, adventure vacation. Office: Williamstown Med Assn 197 Adams Rd Williamstown MA 01267-2930

STUEBNER, JAMES CLOYD, real estate developer, contractor; b. Phila., Dec. 15, 1931; s. Erwin A. and Frances (Quinn) Stuebner; children: Kathleen, Stephen, James, Susan, Elizabeth. BA, Dartmouth Coll., 1953. Sales engr. Rohm & Haas Co., Phila., 1956-69; pres. Structural Plastics Corp., Mpls., 1961-69; pres., gen. ptnr. Stuebner Properties, Mpls., 1969—; pres. Northland Inn and Exec. Conf. Ctr., 1988—; CEO Five Star Realty and Devel. Co., Mpls., 1992—, Boone 94 Properties (Sleep Inn Hotel), 1998. Mem. Minn. Conv. Ctr. Commn., St. Paul, 1988; commr. Minn. Econ. Devel. Commn., St. Paul, 1985; bd. dirs. Bach Soc. of Minn., Mpls., 1986—, Minn. Orchestral Assn., Mpls., 1988-91. Sgt. U.S. Army, 1953-55. Mem. Nat. Assn. Office and Indsl. Parks (bd. dirs. Minn. chpt. 1976-85, 81-90, pres. 1978-80, 92-93, nat. pres. 1983-84, v.p. 1981-81, Developer of Yr. award 1987, Minn. Bus. Person of Yr. award 1990, vice chmn. indsl. devel. forum 1996, chmn. 1997). Avocations: sailing, running, singing. Office: Stuebner Properties 7000 Northland Dr N Minneapolis MN 55428-1502 Office Phone: 763-535-5093. Business E-Mail: jstuebner@quest.net.

STUECK, WILLIAM NOBLE, small business owner; b. Elmhurst, Ill., May 20, 1939; s. Otto Theodore and Anna Elizabeth (Noble) S.; m. Martha Lee Hemphill Stueck, June 2, 1963; children: Matthew Noble, Erika Lee. BS, U. Kans., 1963. Owner, pres. Suburban Lawn & Garden, Inc., Overland Park, Kans., 1953—. Chmn. bd. Mark Twain Bank South, Kansas City., Mo., 1984—. Bd. dirs. Ronald McDonald House, Kansas City; ambassador Am. Royal, Kansas City, 1983. Mem. Am. Assn. Nurserymen, Mission Valley Hunt Club (master 1986—), Leavenworth Hunt Club, Saddle & Sirloin Club. Office: PO Box 480200 Kansas City MO 64148-0200 also: Suburban Lawn & Garden Inc 13635 Wyandotte St Kansas City MO 64145-1516

STUEHRENBERG, PAUL FREDERICK, librarian; b. Breckenridge, Minn., Mar. 14, 1947; s. Henry Ernest Frederick and Marian Violet (Sandberg) S.; m. Suzanne Elaine Draper, June 14, 1969 (div. Apr. 1982); m. Carole Lee DeVore, Aug. 1, 1983. BA, Concordia Sr. Coll., 1968; MDiv, Concordia Sem., 1972; STM, Christ Sem., 1974; MA, U. Minn., 1978, PhD, 1988. Asst. libr. U. Minn., Mpls., 1974-82; monographs libr. Yale Divinity Libr., New Haven, 1982-91, div. libr., 1991—; adj. assoc. prof. in theol. lit. Yale Divinity Sch., New Haven, 1993—. Asst. pastor Christ Meml. Luth. Ch., Plymouth, Minn., 1974-82; adj. pastor Bethesda Luth. Ch., New Haven, 1984—; sec. Luth. Student Found., Mpls., 1978-81. Contbr. articles to profl. jours. Sec. North Haven (Conn.) Libr. Bd., 1989-2003. Mem. Am. Theol. Libr. Assn., Soc. Bibl. Lit., Am. Acad. Religion, North Haven Meml. Libr. Assn. Home: 280 Bayard Ave North Haven CT 06473-4307 Office: Yale U Div Sch Libr 409 Prospect St New Haven CT 06511-2167 E-mail: paul.stuehrenberg@yale.edu.

STUEWE, ISABEL, elementary school educator; BS in English, Concordia U. 5th grade tchr. St. John's Luth. Sch., Orange, Calif. Mem.: Luth. Edn. Assn. (past pres. Luth. elem. tchrs. dept.), Western Assn. Schs. and Colls. (commr.), Nat. Bd. for Profl. Tchg. Stds. (bd. mem. 1992—). Avocations: fishing, camping, reading. Office: St Johns Luth Sch 154 S Shaffer St Orange CA 92866

STUFANO, THOMAS JOSEPH, criminologist, author, inventor; b. Newport, R.I., July 23, 1955; s. Thomas and Zoe (Halsey) S.; 1 child, Christine Anne; m. Rene Ellen Goldfarb, Nov. 10, 1994. BSc in Criminal Justice, Pacific Western U., 1988; PhD in Criminal Justice, Clayton U., 1992; disting. grad., U.S. Air U., 2000; postgrad., Eurotech. Rsch. U., 1997; MBA in Mil. Scis., Touro U., 2001. Legis. rschr. R.I. Ho. of Reps., Providence, R.I., 1978-79; sub com. investigator U.S. Ho. of Reps., Washington, 1979-81; law enforcement staff rschr. State of Fla., 1981-88; intelligence officer, cons. U.S. Govt., Washington, 1988-96; exec. dir. Diversified Technologies and System Inc., 1989—; CEO U.S. Dept. Homeland Security, 2002—. Cons. crime

commn. State of Fla., 1986-87, U.S. Govt., Washington, 1990-92, State of R.I., 1979-80; mem. Pres.' Commn. on Aviation Security and Terrorism. Author: Human Element in Business, 1992, Combating Terrorism, 1994, Investigators Pretext Investigation Manual, 1998, BEA Training Manual, 1998; Applied Impact Theory patentee, 1999; contbr. articles to profl. jours. Mem. Rep. Senatorial Inner Circle, Washington, 1992—; instr. ARC, Fla., 1994—; mem. adv. bd. Nat. Civil Def., Washington, 1988—; mem. Presdl. Round Table. Recipient Presdl. Commendation Pres. of U.S., 1988, 91, 94, Commendation U.S. Ho. of Reps. and Senate, 1982, 91, 94, commendation Prime Minister Lady Margaret Thatcher, 1991, Citation R.I. Ho. of Reps., 1980, Gov. of Mass., 1980, Tenn., Fla., Ky., 1990, Commendation U.S. Dept. of State, 1992, Min. Intelligence Security, Eng., 1996, Meritorious Achievement award for global antiterrorism, 1997, 20th Century Achievement award ABI, 1998, Millennium Hall of Fame award, 1998, 500 Leaders of Influence award IBI, 1998. Mem. Air Force Assn., Internat. Narcotic Enforcement Officers Assn., Res. Officers Assn., World Assn. of Investigators, Internat. Assn. Counter Terrorism and Security Profls., USAF/SARCAP (instr. search/rescue command pilot), Aircraft Owners and Pilots Assn., Profl. Assn. of Diving Instrs. (instr., Platnuim Diving award 1989), Am. Shorin Kempo Karate Assn. (5th degree blackbelt), Order of Ky. Cols. Roman Catholic. Avocations: scuba diving, airplane pilot, parachuting, bicycling, Karate. E-mail: Intel6Dig@aol.com.

STUFFLEBEAM, DANIEL LEROY, education educator; b. Waverly, Iowa, Sept. 19, 1936; s. LeRoy and Melva Stufflebeam; m. Carolyn T. Joseph; children: Kevin D., Tracy Smith, Joseph. BA, State U. Iowa, 1958; MS, Purdue U., 1962, PhD, 1964; postgrad., U. Wis., 1965. Prof., dir. Ohio State U. Evaluation Ctr., Columbus, 1963-73; prof. edn. Western Mich. U. Evaluation Ctr., Kalamazoo, 1973—, dir., 1973—2002, Beula McKee prof. edn. Western Mich. U., 1997—, disting. univ. prof., 2002—. Author monographs and 15 books; contbr. chpts. to books, articles to profl. jours. Served with U.S. Army, 1960. Recipient Paul Lazersfeld award Evaluation Rsch. Soc., 1985, Jason Millman award Consortium for Rsch. on Ednl. Accountability and Tchr. Evaluation, 1999. Mem.: Am. Evaluation Assn. Baptist. Office: Western Michigan Univ The Evaluation Ctr Kalamazoo MI 49008-5237 Fax: 269-387-5923. Personal E-mail: dlstfbm@aol.com.

STUHAN, RICHARD GEORGE, lawyer; b. Braddock, Pa., July 1, 1951; s. George and Pauline Madeline (Pavlocik) S.; m. Mary Ann Cipriano, Aug. 23, 1975; children: Brendan George, Sara Katherine, Brian Christopher, Caitlin Emily. BA summa cum laude, Duquesne U., 1973; JD, U. Va., 1976. Bar: Va. 1976, D.C. 1977, U.S. Ct. Appeals (D.C. cir.) 1977, U.S. Ct. Appeals (4th cir.) 1977, U.S. Claims Ct. 1979, U.S. Supreme Ct. 1980, U.S. Ct. Appeals (3d cir.) 1981, U.S. Ct. Appeals (11th cir.) 1982, U.S. Dist. Ct. (no. dist.) Ohio 1985, Ohio 1986. Assoc. Arnold & Porter, Washington, 1976-84; of counsel Jones Day, Cleve., 1984-86, ptnr., 1987—. Pres. Womankind Maternal and Prenatal Care. Mem. Va. Law Review, 1974-76. Recipient Gold Medal for Gen. Excellence, Duquesne U., 1973; named Ohio Super Lawyer, Law and Politics Media, Inc. Mem. Cleve. Bar Assn., Internat. Assn. Def. Counsel, Order of Coif. Democrat. Roman Catholic. Avocations: tennis, swimming, basketball, home repair. Home: 2865 Falmouth Rd Shaker Heights OH 44122-2838 Office: Jones Day 901 Lakeside Ave Cleveland OH 44114-1190 Office Phone: 216-586-7148. Business E-Mail: rgstuhan@jonesday.com.

STUHL, OSKAR PAUL, scientific and regulatory consultant; b. Dec. 23, 1949; s. Johannes Alexander and Johanna Wilhelmine (Hoelling) S. S. Dipl. Chem., U. Duesseldorf, 1976, Dr.rer.nat., 1978. Tutor Inst. Organische Chemie U. Duesseldorf, 1975-76, sci. assoc., 1976-79; mgr. product devel. Drugofa GmbH, Cologne, Fed. Republic of Germany, 1980; mgr. sci. rels. RJRN, Cologne, 1981-88, mgr. sci. svcs., 1989-94; co-founder, co-owner WRKM Internat., 1996—. Cons. in field, 1995—. Mem. editl. bd. Beitraege zur Tabakforschung Internat., 1986-96; contbr. articles to profl. jours.; patentee in field. Mem. Duesseldorf Mus. Verein, Verein der Freunde des Hetjens-Museums, Verein der Freunde des Stadtmuseums Duesseldorf, Met. Mus. Art, N.Y.C., Friends Royal Acad. Arts, London, Friends of Tate Gallery, London, Art Soc. of Rheinlande and Westfalen, Gesellschaft der Freunde der Kunstammlung NRW, Gesellschaft der Freunde und Foerderer der Univ. Duesseldorf, Zuercher Kunstgesellschaft, Freundeskreis Theatermuseum, Duesseldorf, Foerderverein NRW-Stiftung, Forum fuer Film, Duesseldorf, Freunde und Foerder der Akademie fuer Kommunikations Design, Duesseldorf, Deutsch-Japanische-Gesellschaft. Mem. AAAS, Gesellschaft Deutscher Chemiker, Gesellschaft Deutscher Naturforscher und Aerzte, Max-Planck-Gesellschaft, Deutsche Gesellschaft fuer Arbeits hygiene, Am. Chem. Soc. (including various divsns.), Chem. Soc. Japan, N.Y. Acad. Scis., Royal Soc. Chemistry, Am. Pharm. Assn., Acad. Pharm. Rsch. and Sci., Internat. Union Pure and Applied Chemistry, Am. Soc. Pharmacognosy, Fedn. Internat. Pharmaceutic, Christlich Demokratische Union, Vereinigung AC Club Duesseldorf, PCL Club (London), KDStV Burgundia-Leipzig Club, Golf Club Velbert. CDU-Mittelstands und Wirtschaftsvereinigung. Roman Catholic. Office: PO Box 140544 D-40075 Düsseldorf Germany

STUHLDREHER, GEORGE WILLIAM, lawyer; b. Mansfield, Ohio, Nov. 20, 1923; s. George Henry and Clara Sophia (Gabel) S.; m. Fay McClurg, Jan. 7, 1956 (div.); children: Karen Louise, Diane Marie; m. Norah Constance Burran, July 1, 1978. Student, Kans. State Coll., 1943-44, U. Detroit, 1946-47; BA, Ohio State U., 1948, JD summa cum laude, 1951. Bar: Ohio 1951, U.S. Dist. Ct. (no. dist.) Ohio 1953, U.S. Ct. Appeals (6th cir.) 1955, U.S. Supreme Ct. 1979; diplomate Am. Bd. Profl. Liability Attys. Atty., ptnr. Gallagher, Sharp, Fulton & Norman and predecessor firms, Cleve., 1951—. Dir. Bulkley Bldg. Co., Cleve.; bd. govs. Am. Bd. Profl. Liability Attys., 1991—97. Editor-in-chief Ohio State Law Jour., 1951. Mem. Citizens League Cleve. Served to cpl. U.S. Army, 1943-46. Mem. ABA, Am. Judicature Soc., Internat. Assn. Def. Counsel, Def. Rsch. Inst., Ohio Bar Assn., Ohio Assn. Civil Trial Attys., Cleve. Bar Assn., Cleve. Assn. Civil Trial Attys. (pres. 1973), Phi Sigma Kappa, Phi Delta Phi, Order of Coif. Home: 6 Edgewater Sq Cleveland OH 44107-1808 Office: Gallagher Sharp Fulton & Norman 630 Bulkley Bldg Cleveland OH 44115

STUHLINGER, ERNST, physicist; b. Niederrimbach, Germany, Dec. 19, 1913; came to U.S., 1946, naturalized, 1955. s. Ernst and Pauline (Werner) S.; m. Irmgard Lotze, Aug. 1, 1950; children: Susanne, Tilman, Hans Christoph. PhD, U. Tuebingen, Germany, 1936. Asst. prof. Technische Hochschule, Berlin, Germany, 1936-41; guidance and control equipment rocket Devel. Center, Peenemuende, Germany, 1943-45; with Guided Missile Devel. Office, Ft. Bliss, Tex., 1946-50; physicist Ordnance Missile Labs., Huntsville, Ala., 1950-56, Army Ballistic Missile Agy., 1956-60; dir. Space Scis. Lab., George C. Marshall Space Flight Center, NASA, Huntsville, Ala., 1960-68; assoc. dir. for sci. George C. Marshall Space Flight Center, NASA, 1968-76; sr. research scientist, adj. prof. U. Ala. at Huntsville, 1976-84; sr. research assoc. Teledyne Brown Engring. Corp., Huntsville, 1984-88; cons. aerospace cos. Vis. scientist Tech. U. Munich, W. Germany, 1978, Max Planck Inst. Nuclear Physics, Heidelberg, 1983-85; cons. Teledyne-Brown Engring., 1984-90. Author: Ion Propulsion for Space Flight, 1964; co-author: Skylab, A Guidebook, 1973, Project Viking, 1976, Aufbruch in Den Weltraum, 1992, Wernher von Braun, Crusader for Space, 1994. Served with German Army, 1941-43, Russian Campaign. Recipient Humboldt prize Tech. U. Munich, 1978, Rainer Bauer award Ala.-Germany Partnership, 2002; induction Ala. Aviation Hall of Fame, 2001. Fellow Am. Astronautical Soc., Am. Rocket Soc. (dir.), AIAA (tech. dir.); mem. Internat. Acad. Astronautics, Von Braun Astron. Soc. (dir.), Austrian Astron. Soc. (hon.), Deutsche Roentgengesellschaft (hon.), Deutsche Physikalische Gesellschaft, Deutsche Gesellschaft Fuer Luft und Raumfahrt (hon.), Hermann Oberth Gesellschaft (hon.), Internat. Foerderkreis fuer Raumfahrt (hon. pres.). Rsch. cosmic rays, nuclear physics, 1934-41, electric space propulsion, 1947—, studies on manned missions to Mars, 1954—. Home: 3106 Rowe Dr SE Huntsville AL 35801-6151

STUHR, DAVID PAUL, business educator, consultant; b. Ridgewood, N.J., Oct. 10, 1938; s. Edward Philip and Theresa Alma (Cherny) S. B Engring., Yale U., 1960; MS, Rensselaer Poly. Inst., 1962; PhD, NYU, 1972. Research fellow Fed. Res. Bank of N.Y., N.Y.C., 1968-69, cons. economist, 1969-92; assoc. in bus. Columbia U. Grad. Sch. Bus. Adminstrn., N.Y.C., 1969-72, asst. prof. fin., 1972-73; assoc. prof. fin. Rutgers U. Grad. Sch. Bus. Adminstrn., Newark, N.J., 1973-77, Fordham U., Faculty of Bus., N.Y.C., 1977—, acting dean faculty, 1984-85; assoc. dean Fordham U. Coll. Bus. Adminstrn., Bronx, N.Y., 1980-83, dean, 1983-87; pres. faculty senate Fordham U., Bronx, N.Y., 1994-95, assoc. v.p. for acad. affairs, 1995—. Mem. bus. faculty com. Regents Coll., Albany, 1987-97. Contbr. articles to profl. jours. Mem. Exec. bd. Bergen coun. Boy Scouts Am., 1979-95, No. N.J. coun., 2003—; mcpl. chmn. Ho-Ho-Kus (N.J.) Rep. Com., 1968-2002; chair fin. com. St. Gabriel the Archangel Ch., Saddle River, N.J., 1986-, trustee Notre Dame School, N.Y.C., 1998-. Mem. Am. Econ. Assn. (life), Am. Fin. Assn. (life), Fin. Mgmt. Assn., Phila. Soc. (founding mem., trustee 1977-80, treas. 1979—). Republican. Roman Catholic. Avocations: backpacking, camping, skiing. Office: Fordham Univ Office of Academic Affairs Bronx NY 10458

STUHR, ELAINE RUTH, state legislator; b. Polk County, Nebr., June 19, 1936; m. Boyd E. Stuhr, 1956; children: Cynthia (Stuhr) Zluticky, Teresa (Stuhr) Robbins, Boyd E., Jr. BS, U. Nebr. Tchr. jr. and sr. vocat. h.s. Nebr. schs.; senator Nebr. Unicameral, Lincoln, 1994—; chmn. Nebr. retirement sys. com.; vice chair natural resources com., commr. edn. com. of states; farmer. Former asst. instr. U. Nebr., Lincoln; participant farmer to farmer assignment to Russia with Winrock, Internat., 1993, to Lithuania with Vol. Overseas Coop. Assistance, 1993; former pres. Agrl. Womens Leadership Network; former mem. bd. dirs. Feed Grains Coun., Nebr. Corn Bd.; agrl. adv. com. for Congressman Doug Bereuter. Past pres., bd. dirs. Found. for Agrl. Edn. and Devel.; former mem. exec. com. and bd. dirs. Agrl. Coun. Am.; nat. pres. Women Involved in Farm Econs., state pres.; mem. adv. com. Nebr. Extension Sv.; bd. dirs. Heartland Ctr. for Leadership Devel.; past chmn. Nebr. Agrl. Leadership Coun. Republican. Office: Nebr State Capitol Dist # 24 Lincoln NE 68509 E-mail: estuhr@unicam.state.ne.us.

STUKEL, JAMES JOSEPH, academic administrator, mechanical engineer, educator; b. Joliet, Ill., Mar. 30, 1937; s. Philip and Julia (Mattivi) S.; m. Mary Joan Helpling, Nov. 27, 1958; children: Catherine, James, David, Paul. BS in Mech. Engring, Purdue U., 1959; MS, U. Ill., Urbana-Champaign, 1963, PhD, 1968. Research engr. W.Va. Pulp and Paper Co., Covington, Va., 1959-61; mem. faculty U. Ill., Urbana-Champaign, 1968—, prof. mech. engring., 1975—, dir. Office Coal Research and Utilization, 1974-76, dir. Office Energy Research, 1976-81, dir. pub. policy program Coll. Engring., 1981-84, assoc. dean Coll. Engring. and dir. Expt. Sta., 1984-85; dean Grad. Coll., vice chancellor for research U. Ill. at Chgo., 1985-86, exec. vice chancellor, vice chancellor academic affairs, 1986-91, interim chancellor, 1990-91, chancellor, 1991-95, pres., 1995—. V.p. Chgo. Tech. Park Corp., 1985-88. pres., 1990-91; exec. sec. midwest Consortium Air Pollution, 1972-73, chmn. bd. dirs., 1973-75; mem. adv. bd. regional studies program Argonne (Ill.) Nat. Lab., 1975-76; adv. com. Energy Resources Commn., 1976; chmn. panel on dispersed electric generating techs. Office Tech. Assessment, U.S. Congress, 1980-81; chmn. rev. adv. bd. tech. rev. dist. heating and combined heat and power systems Internat. Energy Agy, OECD, Paris, 1982-83; cons. in field. Contbr. articles to profl. jours. Pres. parish council Holy Cross Roman Cath. Ch., Urbana, 1967-68. Mem. ASCE (State-of-the-Art of Civil Engring. award 1975), ASME, AAAS, Sigma Xi, Phi Kappa Phi, Pi Tau Sigma. Home: 2650 N Lakeview Ave Apt 1610 Chicago IL 60614-1819 Office: 364 Henry Adm Bldg M/C 346 Urbana IL 61801

STUKENBERG, MICHAEL WESLEY, lawyer; b. Freeport, Ill., Feb. 22, 1951; s. Wesley W. and Nancy Jack (Baker) S.; m. Amanda Reed Eggert, July 21, 1973; children: Sarah Reed, William Robinson. BA, Princeton U., 1973; JD, Vanderbilt U., 1976. Bar: Tex. 1977, U.S. Tax Ct. 1977, U.S. Dist. Ct. (so. dist.) Tex. 1982. Assoc. firm Matthews & Branscomb, Corpus Christi, Tex., 1976-81, shareholder, 1981—. Gov. Art Mus. South Tex., Corpus Christi, 1990-96; dir., pres. Corpus Christi Estate Planning Coun., 1989-98; trustee, chair bd. trustees YMCA Corpus Christi, 1997-. Fellow Am. Coll. Trust and Estate Counsel; mem. ABA, Tex. Bar Assn. (tax sect.), Tex. Acad. of Probate and Trust Lawyers, Coll. of State Bar of Tex. Clubs: Corpus Christi Yacht, Causeway (Southwest Harbor, Maine). Episcopalian. Home: 3502 Aransas St Corpus Christi TX 78411-1302 E-mail: mstukenberg@mattbran.com.

STUKENHOLTZ, LARRY LEE, music educator; b. Broken Bow, Nebr., Apr. 5, 1957; s. Rollan Wirth and Mary Elaine Stukenholtz; m. Lien Phoung Nguyen, June 10, 2000; 1 child, Amy Lien. MusB, Wichita State U., 1981; MusM, U. Mich., 1982, Mus D, 1987. Chair music dept. St. Louis C.C., Kirkwood, 2001—. Mem.: Music Educators Nat. Conf., Am. Choral Dir. Assn. E-mail: lstukenholtz@stlcc.edu.

STULL, GARY EVAN, secondary school educator, writer; b. Waynesboro, Pa., Aug. 4, 1947; s. Mark McKean and Evelyn Rebecca Stull; m. April Lee Walker, Mar. 21, 1970; 1 child, Andrew Evan. BS, Ohio State U., 1969, MA, 1984, postgrad., 1986. Tchr. Mohawk Jr.-Sr. H.S. Columbus City Schs., Columbus, Ohio, 1970—71, tchr. Ridgeview Jr. H.S., 1971—79, tchr. Ridgeview Mid. Sch., 1980—. Named Educator of Yr., PTA, 1985, 1995. Mem.: NEA, Ohio Edn. Assn., Columbus Edn. Assn. Presbyterian. Avocations: writing, travel, photography, carpentry, reading. Office: Ridgeview Mid Sch 4241 Rudy Rd Columbus OH 43214 E-mail: gstull@columbus.rr.com.

STULL, MIKE, personal care industry executive; CFO Optiva Corp., Bellevue, Wash. Office: Optiva Corp PO Box 5000 Snoqualmie WA 98065-5000

STULL, ROBERT L. trucking executive; BA in Polit. Sci., Miami U. Former dispatcher, terminal manager Roadway Express, Inc., former dist. mgr., Portland, Oreg., v.p. Western divsn., 1994—99, v.p. new venture commerce, 1999—2003, pres., CEO, 2003—. Office: Roadway Express Inc 1077 Gorge Blvd Akron OH 44309*

STULTS, WALTER BLACK, management consultant, former trade organization executive; b. Hightstown, N.J., Oct. 25, 1921; s. C. Stanley and Nettie M. (Black) S.; m. Ann D. Haynes, June 28, 1947 (dec. 2002); children: Andrew Haynes, Thomas Stanley; m. Jean Morris Curtin, 2003. BA, Williams Coll., 1943; MA (Woodrow Wilson fellow), Princeton U., 1949. Teaching asst. Princeton (N.J.) U., 1946-49; legis. asst. to U.S. Senator Robert Hendrickson, Washington, 1949-50; staff dir. U.S. Senate Small Bus. Com., Washington, 1950-61; pres. Nat. Assn. Small Bus. Investment Cos., Washington, 1961-86; prin. W.B. Stults, Cons., Chapel Hill, N.C., 1979-99. Dir. Pardee & Curtin Lumber Co., Pardee Resources Co., Phila.; chmn. Coun. Small and Ind. Bus. Assns., 1976-81. Pres. Carol Woods Residents Assn.; dir. Carol Woods Retirement Comty., 1995-97, 2001—. With USAAF, 1943-46. Mem. Am. Soc. Assn. Execs., The Exchequer Club, Masons. Congregationalist.

STULTZ, NEWELL MAYNARD, retired political science educator; b. Boston, June 13, 1933; s. Irving Washburn and Marjorie May (MacEachern) S.; m. Elizabeth Petronella Olckers, Apr. 6, 1958; children: Elliot Andries, Amy Elizabeth. AB, Dartmouth Coll., 1955; MA, Boston U., 1960, PhD, 1965; MA hon., Brown U., 1968. Fulbright exchange scholar U. Pretoria, South Africa, 1955-56; asst. prof. polit. sci. Northwestern U., Evanston, Ill., 1964-65; asst. prof. to prof. polit. sci. Brown U., Providence, 1965—2003, assoc. grad. dean, 1970-74, assoc. dean of faculty, 1993-98, assoc. provost, 1998-2000; ret., 2003. Vis. fellow Yale U.-South African Research Program, 1977; vis. prof. U. South Africa, Pretoria, 1980; James Gathings lectr. Bucknell U., Lewisburg, Pa., 1980 Author: Afrikaner Politics in South Africa, 1974, Who Goes to Parliament?, 1975, Transkei's Half Loaf, 1979, (bibliography) South Africa, 1989, 2d edit., 1993; co-author: South Africa's Transkei, 1967; co-editor: Governing in Black Africa, 1970, 2d edit., 1986 V.p. World Affairs Council R.I., 1983. Served as lt. (j.g.) USN, 1956-59. Fulbright fellow, 1955-56; NDEA grantee, 1959-62; Ford Found. fellow, 1962-64; Rockefeller Found. fellow, 1976-77 Unitarian Universalist. Home: 371 New Meadow Rd Barrington RI 02806-3729 Office: Brown U Dept Polit Sci PO Box 1844 Providence RI 02912-1844 Office Phone: 401-863-1567. E-mail: newell_stultz@brown.edu.

STULZ, KARIN M. educator; d. Kyle R. and Joan M Ericson; m. Warren Kevin Stulz, Feb. 24, 1965; children: Emily C., Connor W. MAE, No. Mich. U., 1990, MOS Word Core Microsoft, 2001, MOS Access Core Microsoft, 2001, MOS PowerPoint Microsoft, 2001, MOS Excel Core Microsoft, 2002, MOS Word Expert Microsoft, 2002. Instr. No. Mich. U., Marquette, 1992—2003, asst. prof., 2003—. Author: (textbook) Procedures & Theory for Administrative Professionals, (online training module) Online Training for the Office Professional; contbr. textbook. Recipient Post-Secondary Tchr. of the Yr. award, Mich. Bus. Edn. Assn., 2001, Outstanding Tchg. award, Walker L. Cisler Coll. of Bus., 2001. Mem.: Mich. Bus. Edn. Assn., Nat. Bus. Edn. Assn. Home: Office: No Mich Univ Coll of Bus Marquette MI 49855

STUMBLES, JAMES RUBIDGE WASHINGTON, security firm executive; b. Harare, Zimbabwe, Aug. 13, 1939; arrived in U.S., 1980; s. Albert R.W. and Mary Dallas (Atherstone) S.; m. Vyvienne Clare Shaw, Dec. 19, 1964; children: Christopher, Timothy, Jonathan. BA, U. Cape Town, South Africa, 1960, LLB, 1962. Adv. Supreme Ct. of S. Africa. Mng. dir. Rennies Confirming & Fin. Proprietary Ltd., Johannesburg, 1971-72; group mng. dir., chmn. subsidiaries Pritchard Svcs. Group South Africa, Proprietary Ltd., 1972-80; dir. security, pres. subs. Pritchard Svcs. Group Am., Columbus, Ohio, 1980-83; exec. v.p., pres. subs. Mayne Nickless/ Loomis Corp., Seattle, 1984-87; v.p. N.W. Protective Svc. Inc., 1987-91, pres. and CEO, 1991—, N.W. Protective Svc.-Imprimis, Inc., Spokane, 1991—, Northwest Protective Svc. Inc.-Oreg., Portland, 1992—. Chmn. Clarington Inc., 1996—, Washington Law Enforcement Exec. Forum, 1999-2001. Sec. Boy Scouts, Johannesburg, 1978-80. Mem. Rand Club, Rainier Club, Rotary, Kiwanis, Round Table (officer 1969-80). Avocations: tennis, boating, fishing. Office: NW Protective Svc Inc 2700 Elliott Ave Seattle WA 98121-1189 Business E-Mail: jim.stumbles@nwprotective.com. *Personal philosophy: Love thy God, love thy neighbor, and be true unto thyself.*

STUMBO, GREGORY D. state attorney general; b. Huntington, W.Va., Aug. 14, 1951; s. Harold James and Pluma Jean (Martin) S.; m. Mary Henderson, Aug. 18, 1973; children: Brooks, Elizabeth Morgan. B Gen.Sci., U. Ky., Lexington, 1973; JD, U. Louisville, 1975. Asst. county atty. Floyd County, Prestonsburg, Ky., 1976-78; trial commr. to dist. ct. Adminstrv. Office of Cts., State Ky., Prestonsburg, 1978-79; mem. Ky. Ho. of Reps., Frankfort, 1980—2003, majority fl. leader, 1985—2003; attn. gen. state of Ky., 2003—. Bd. dirs. First Guaranty Nat. Bank, Martin, Ky. Mem. Gov.'s Task Force on Coal Transp., Frankfort, 1983, Ky. Lottery Commn., Frankfort, 1988, Ky. Task Force on Edn. Reform, 1989—. Recipient Disting. Svc. award Ky. Cir. Judges Assn., 1980, Cert. of Appreciation, Western Ky. U., Bowling Green, 1982, Disting. Aumni award, U. Louisville, 1985. Mem. ABA, Ky. Bar Assn. Democrat. Baptist. Avocations: hunting, fishing, golf. Address: Fred's Fork Prestonsburg KY 41653 Office: Office of the Attorney General State Capitol Suite 118 Frankfort KY 40601

STUMBO, JANET LYNN, state supreme court justice; b. Prestonsburg, Ky. d. Charles and Doris Stanley Stumbo; m. Ned Pillersdorf, children: Sarah, Nancee, Samantha. BA, Morehead State U., 1976; JD, U. Ky., 1980. Bar: Ky. 1980, W.Va. 1982. Staff atty. to Judge Harris S. Howard Ky. Ct. Appeals, 1980—82; asst. county atty. Floyd County, 1982—85; ptnr. Turner, Hall & Stumbo, P.S.C., 1982—88; prosecutor Floyd Dist. Ct. and Juvenile Ct.; ptnr. Stumbo, DeRossett & Pillersdorf, 1989; judge Ct. Appeals, Ky., 1989—93, Supreme Ct. of Ky., 1993—. Named to Morehead State U. Alumni Assn. Hall of Fame, 1990, U. Ky. Coll. Law Alumni Hall of Fame, 1999; recipient Justice award, Ky. Women Advocates, 1991, Outstanding Just award, 1995, Bull's Eye award, Women in State Govt. Network, 1995. also: 311 N Arnold Ave Ste 502 Prestonsburg KY 41653-1279

STUMER, MARK BRADLEY, lawyer, business consultant, restaurateur; b. NYC, May 31, 1969; s. Nathan and Roberta Adele (Klau) S. LLB, SUNY, Albany, 1991; JD, N.Y. Law Sch., 1995. Bar: N.Y. 1995, U.S. Dist. Ct. (ea. and so. dists.) N.Y., 1995. Pres. Marker Entertainment, Inc., 1992—95, Mark B. Stumer & Assoc., P.C., N.Y.C., 1995—; owner Tja! Restaurant, N.Y.C., 1999—; pres. Soho Consulting Group, N.Y.C., 1996—. Gen. counsel Tribeca Ventures, Inc., Abaya, Inc., Lima's Taste, Inc., KC Enterprises, Inc., Bella Inca, Bubbys, Inc., Pinch, Inc., Sage, Inc., others; lectr. in field. Contbr. articles to profl. jours. including Nat. Restaurant Assn., Restaurant Law, The Legal Monitor, and The Restaurateur; pub. Restaurant Law newsletter, Restaurant and Bar Law newsletter, Entertainment Law & Fin., Bus. Lawyer, Civil Rights Jour. Mem. ABA, N.Y. State Bar Assn. (former chmn. copyright sect. student divsn. 1993-94, Civil Rights com.), Nat. Assn. Trial Lawyers, Nat. Employment Lawyers Assn. (N.Y. chpt.), Young Entreprenuers Orgn., Nat. Restaurant Assn., N.Y. State Restaurant Assn., N.Y. County Lawyers Assn. Office: Mark B Stumer & Assocs PC 200 Park Ave S New York NY 10003-1008 Office Phone: 212-633-2225. E-mail: mstumer@newyorklawfirm.org.

STUMP, E. GORDON, association administrator; m. Marie Stump; children: Scott, Traci Wills. B of Mech. Engring., U. Akron. V.p. automotive engring. Michelin Tire Corp., ret.; commd. 2d lt. USAF, 1965, advanced through grades to, 1969; with Ohio Air N.G., 1970—73, Wolverine State's N.G., Mich., 1973—91, adj. gen., 1991—; v.p. air N.G. Assn. U.S., 1996—98, pres., 1998—. Office: NG Assn of US 1 Massachusetts Ave NW Washington DC 20001

STUMP, EARL SPENCER, psychologist; b. Parkersburg, W.Va., Dec. 12, 1943; s. Amos Earl Stump and Harriet Gertrude (White) Stiff; m. Ann Chadwick, Sept. 30, 1967 (div. 1985); 1 child, Andrea Renee; m. Joan Irene Croft, Sept. 28, 1985. BA, Ohio State U., 1966; MS in Corrections, Xavier U., 1971; PhD, Ohio U., 2000. Lic. psychologist, Ohio, profl. clin. counselor; cert. rehab. counselor. Psychiat. aide Harding Hosp., Worthington, Ohio, 1965-67; psychology trainee Athens (Ohio) State Hosp., 1966-67; psychologist Ohio Dept. Rehab. and Correction, Columbus, 1967-97; supr. psychology and clin. dir. Chillicothe (Ohio) Correctional Inst., 1977-97. Pvt. practice psychology Columbus Mental Health Clinic, Columbus, 1976-77; instr. psychology Hocking Tech. Coll., Chillicothe, 1973-78; asst. prof. Ohio U., Athens, 2002; psychologist Scioto Point Valley Mental Health Ctr., Chillicothe. Mem.: ACA, APA, Nat. Rehab. Assn. Home: 15 N May Ave Athens OH 45701-1817 E-mail: estump@eurekanet.com.

STUMP, JOHN SUTTON, retired lawyer; b. Clarksburg, W.Va., Aug. 7, 1929; s. John Sutton and Helen (Mannix) S.; m. Elaine Claire Scammahorn, Sept. 14, 1968; children— John Sutton IV, James Felix. Student, Washington and Lee U., 1946-47, LL.B., 1957; BS in Commerce, U. N.C., 1951. Bar: W.Va. 1957, Va. 1957, D.C. 1983. Assoc. Jackson, Kelly, Holt & O'Farrell, Charleston, W.Va., 1957-58, Boothe, Dudley, Koontz & Boothe, Alexandria, Va., 1958-61, Boothe, Dudley, Koontz & Blankingship, Fairfax and Alexandria, Va., 1962-63; ptnr. Boothe, Dudley, Koontz, Blankingship & Stump, Fairfax and Alexandria, 1963-71, Boothe, Prichard & Dudley, 1971-87, McGuire, Woods, Battle & Boothe LLP, 1987-99. Served to lt. comdr. USNR, 1951-54, 61-62. Fellow Am. Coll. Trial Lawyers; mem. Am. Law Inst. Home: 8329 Weller Ave Mc Lean VA 22102-1717 Office: 1750 Tysons Blvd Mc Lean VA 22102-4208

STUMP, M. PAMELA, sculptor; b. Detroit, July 8, 1928; d. Clarence Homer S. and Gladys Greening Bogue; m. David Everet Walsh, Aug. 1950 (div. 1975); children: Kimberly Klaerr, Sara Greening Walsh Munro, John Klaerr II; m. Richard Taylor White, March, 1989. B of Design, U. Mich., 1950, M of Design, 1951. Educator Ann Arbor (Mich.) Adult Edn., 1950-51, Saginaw (Mich.) Mus. Sch., 1963-68, Birmingham (Mich.) Bloomfield Art Assn., 1969, Washtenaw C.C., Ypsilanti, Mich., 1968-69, Cranbrook Ednl. Cmty., Bloomfield Hills, Mich., 1969-90. One-woman shows include Cranbrook Kingswood, Bloomfield Hills, 1969-90, Mich. Women's Hist. Ctr. & Hall of Fame, Lansing, 1994, Swann Gallery, Detroit, 1997; exhibited in group shows at Cranbrook Kingswood, 1950, 70, 87, City Art Mus., St. Louis, 1951, Terry Art Inst., Miami, Fla., 1951, Temple Israel, Detroit, 1951, 58, Ceceile Gallery, N.Y.C. (3rd prize), 1956, Pa. Acad. Fine Arts, Phila., 1958, Horace H. Rackham Sch. Grad. Studies, Detroit, 1960, Detroit Artists Market, 1961, R

and R Robinson Gallery, Naples, Fla., 1962, Rubiner Gallery, West Bloomfield, Mich., 1963, Mich. Fine Arts Competition (Juror's award), 1983, 87, Slusser Gallery, U. Mich., 1989, Outdoor Sculpture II, III, Southfield, Mich., 1990, 91, N.Y. Acad. Scis., N.Y.C., 1991, Oakland U., 1991-92, Urban Park, Detroit, 1991, 92, Arc Gallery, Chgo., 1992, 1 Heritage Place, Southgate, Mich., 1993, Art Ctr., Sarasota, Fla.; prin. works include courtyard sculpture Kingswood Sch., steel sculpture Sister City, Tokushima, Japan, 10 bronze sculptures for Cranbrook Schs., Bloomfield Hills, Civic Ctr., Saginaw, bronze fountain at Presbyn. Ch., Grosse Ile, Mich, bronze sculpture of history of U. of Mich. Women, Ann Arbor, Mich. Bell Telephone Co., Saginaw, bronze sculpture at Providence Hosp., Southfield, meml. for poet T. Roethke Saginaw Valley State U., bronze sculpture at First Presbyn. Ch., Pompano Beach, Fla., Rochester Hills Libr., Saginaw Mus., Western Mich. U., Kalamazoo, numerous others. Mem. Emily's List, Planned Parenthood. Mem. ACLU, NOW, LWV, Nat. Assn. Women Artists, Nat. Mus. Women in Arts (charter), Detroit Artist Market, Detroit Inst. Arts Founders Soc., Internat. Sculptors. Avocations: reading, writing. Home: 19629 Parke Ln Grosse Ile MI 48138-1024 E-mail: mpamelastump@gatecom.com.

STUMPE, WARREN ROBERT, county official, retired scientific, engineering and technical services company executive; b. Bronx, N.Y., July 15, 1925; s. William A. and Emma J. (Mann) S.; children: Jeffrey, Kathy, William. BS, U.S. Mil. Acad., 1945; MS, Cornell U., 1949; MS in Indsl. Engring, N.Y. U., 1965; grad., Command and Gen. Staff Coll., 1972, Army War Coll., 1976; PhD (hon.), Milw. Sch. Engring., 1982. Registered profl. engr., N.Y., Fla., Wis. Commd. 2d lt., C.E. U.S. Army, 1945, advanced through grades to capt., 1954; with (65th Engr. Bn.), 1945-48; asst. prof. mechanics U.S. Mil. Acad., 1951-54; resigned, 1954; from capt. to col. Res., 1958-79; dep. gen. mgr., gen. engring. div. AMF, Stamford, Conn., 1954-63; exec. v.p. Dortech, Inc., Stamford, 1963-69; dir. systems mgmt. group Mathews Conveyor div. REX, Darien, Conn., 1969-71; dir. research and devel. Rexnord, Inc., Milw., 1971-73, v.p. corp. research and tech., from 1973, v.p. bus. devel. sector, 1981-83, v.p., chief tech. officer, 1983-86; pres. Rexnord Techs., Milw., 1986-87; v.p. Radian Corp., Milw., 1987—90; civilian aide to sec. army for State of Wis., 1981-85; alderman City of Mequon, 1994—97, pres. coun., 1996—97, county supr., 1998—. Mem. adv. bd. technology transfer program U. Wis.-Whitewater. Contbr. articles to profl. jours. Founder, pres. No. Little League, Stamford, 1965-69; pres. Turn of River Jr. High Sh. PTA, 1967-68; vice chmn. for Wis. Dept. Def., Nat. Com. Employer Support Guard and Res.; bd. regents Milw. Sch. Engring.; mem. liaison coun. Coll. Engring., U. Wis., also mem. indsl. adv. coun.; mem. adv. coun. Marquette U.; mem. Wis. Gov.'s Task Force on Energy, Coun. Great Lakes Govs.' Regional Econ. Devel. Commn., 1987-88; bd. dirs. MRA-Inst. Mgmt., Inc. Mem. Am. Water Pollution Control Fedn., Indsl. Rsch. Inst. (pres., dir.), Wis. Assn. Rsch. Mgrs. (founder), West Point Soc. Wis., Tau Beta Pi, Phi Kappa Phi. Clubs: Wis., Ozaukee Country. Office Phone: 262-241-9560.

STUMPF, DAVID ALLEN, pediatric neurologist; b. L.A., May 8, 1945; s. Herman A. and Dorothy F. (Davis) S.; children: Jennifer F., Kaitrin E.; m. Elizabeth Dusenbery, Feb. 2, 1989; children: Todd Coleman, Shilo Walker. BA, Lewis and Clark Coll., 1966; MD cum laude, PhD, U. Colo., 1972. Pediatric intern Strong Meml. Hosp., Rochester, N.Y., 1972-73, resident, 1973-74; resident in neurology Harvard Med. Sch., Boston, 1974-77; dir. pediatric neurology U. Colo. Health Sci. Ctr., Denver, 1977-85; chief neurology Children's Meml. Hosp., Chgo., 1985-89; chmn. neurology, Benjamin and Virginia T. Boshes prof. Northwestern U., 1989-98, prof. neurology and pediatrics, 1999—; pres. and CEO Oyxis, LLC, 1999—. Mem. sci. adv. com. Muscular Dystrophy Assn., 1981-87; bd. dirs. North-Western Meml. Corp., Chgo. Mem. editl. bd. Neurology, 1982-87; contbr. articles to sci. jours. Recipient Lewis and Clark Coll. Disting. Alumni award, 1991; NIH grantee, 1979-84; Muscular Dystrophy Assn. grantee, 1977-89; March of Dimes grantee, 1983-85. Fellow Am. Acad. Neurology; mem. Child Neurology Soc. (counsellor 1982-84, pres. 1985-87), Am. Neurol. Assn., Am. Pediatric Soc., Soc. Pediatric Rsch., Internat. Child Neurology Assn. (v.p. 1998—). Presbyterian. Office: 540 Judson Ave Evanston IL 60202-3084 Mailing: Northwestern U Dept Neurology Abbott Hall 710 N Lakeshore Dr Chicago IL 60611-3006 E-mail: david@stumpf.org.

STUMPF, FELIX FRANKLIN, law educator; b. Boston, Feb. 10, 1918; s. Karl Heinrich and Annette (Schreyer) S.; m. Martha Wickland, May 29, 1948; m. Betty-Jo Volberg, Aug. 5, 1959; children: Eric, Kenneth, Kirk, Mark, Paul. AB magna cum laude, Harvard U., 1938, LLB, 1941. Bar: Mass. 1941, Calif. 1946, Nev. 1975, U.S. Dist. Ct. (no. dist.) Calif. 1946, U.S. Dist. Ct. Nev. 1981, U.S. Ct. Appeals (9th cir.) 1948, U.S. Supreme Ct. 1967. Assoc. Hale & Dorr, Boston, 1941-42, McCutchen, Thomas, Matthews, Griffiths & Greene, San Francisco, 1946-50, Livingston, Leeker & Feldman, San Francisco, 1950-53; adminstr. Calif. Continuing Edn. Bar/U. Calif. Extension, Berkeley, 1953-70; staff atty. U.S. Dist. Ct. No. Dist. Calif., San Francisco, 1971-73; acad. dir. Nat. Jud. Coll. U. Nev., Reno, 1973-84, jud. rsch. cons., 1988—; prof. Old Coll. Nev. Sch. Law, Reno, 1984-85, dean, 1985—88. Of counsel White Law, chartered, Reno, 1988—. Contbr. articles to profl. jours. Past trustee Washoe Legal Svcs. 1st lt. U.S. Army, 1942—46. Recipient First Harrison Tweed award Assn. Continuing Legal Edn. Adminstrs., 1969, Francis Rawle award, 2000, Lifetime Achievement award State Bar Nev., 2001. Mem. ABA, Nev. Bar Assn., Washoe County Bar Assn., Nev. Bar Found.(past trustee). Democrat. Home: 4205 Slide Mountain Dr Reno NV 89511-6529 Office: U Nev Nat Judicial Coll Reno NV 89503 also: White Law Chartered Reno NV 89503 Office Phone: 775-327-8214. Business E-Mail: stumpf@judges.org.

STUMPF, HEINRICH J. psychometrician, research consultant; b. Cologne, Germany, Dec. 10, 1951; came to U.S., 1991; s. Friedrich Hubert and Johanna Luise (Bauer) Stumpf; m. Doris Elisabeth Hoffmann, May 10, 1990. Diploma in Psychology, U. Bonn, Germany, 1975, PhD, 1978. Sci. employee German Nat. Scholarship Found., Bonn, Germany, 1978-91; sr. rsch. assoc. Ctr. for Talented Youth, Johns Hopkins U., Balt., 1991-95; rsch. cons. Ctr. for Talented Youth Johns Hopkins U., Balt., 1996—. Contbr. to German Encyclopedia of Psychology. Mem. German Psychol. Assn., Am. Psychol. Soc., N.Y. Acad. Scis. Achievements include: sr. author of the Cube Perspective Test of Spatial Ability, 1983, the German Personality Research Form, 1985 and the Spatial Test Battery of the Ctr. for Talented Youth; contbr. to German Ency. Psychology; contbr. about 50 scientific publications. E-mail: stumpfhj@aol.com.

STUMPF, JOHN G. bank executive; b. Minn. B of Acctg., St. Cloud U.; M in Fin., U. Minn. Sr. v.p., chief credit officer Norwest Bank, Minn., 1982—89; exec. v.p. Southwestern Banking, 1988; regional pres. Norwest Bank, Colo., 1990—94, head, 1994—2000; exec. v.p. Western Banking, 2000—02; group exec. v.p. cmty. banking Wells Fargo & Co., 2002—. Bd. dirs. VISA U.S.A., San Francisco Zool. Soc.; Bay Area chpt. Jr. Achievement; treas. Office: Wells Fargo & Co 420 Montgomery St San Francisco CA 94163

STUMPF, PAUL KARL, biochemistry educator emeritus; b. N.Y.C., Feb. 23, 1919; s. Karl and Annette (Schreyer) S.; m. Ruth Rodenbeck, June 1947; children: Ann Carol, Kathryn Lee, Margaret Ruth, David Karl, Richard Frederic. AB, Harvard Coll., 1941; PhD, Columbia U., 1945. Instr. pub. health U. Mich., Ann Arbor, 1946-48; faculty U. Calif., Berkeley, 1948-58, prof., 1956-58, Davis, 1958-84, prof. emeritus, 1984—. Chief scientist Competitive Rsch. Grants Office USDA, Washington, 1988-91; cons. Palm Oil Rsch. Inst., Kuala Lumpur, Malaysia, 1982-92; mem. sci. adv. bd. Calgene, Inc., Davis, 1990-93; mem. sci. adv. panel Md. Biotech. Inst., 1990-92; Inaugural lectr. Tan Sri Dato'Seri B. Bek-Nielsen Found., Kuala Lumpur, 1996. Co-author: Outlines of Enzyme Chemistry, 1955, Outlines of Biochemistry, 5th edit., 1987; co-editor-in-chief Biochemistry of Plants, 1980; exec. editor Archives of Biochemistry/Biophysics, 1965-88; contbr. over 250 articles to profl. jours. Planning commn. City of Davis, 1966-68; bd. dirs. Internat. House, Davis, 2002—. Guggenheim fellow, 1962, 69; recipient Lipid Chemistry award Am. Oil Chemists Soc., 1974, Sr. Scientist award Alexander von Humboldt Found., 1976, Superior Svc. Group award USDA, 1992, Award of Excellence, Calif. Aggie Alumni Found., 1996. Fellow AAAS; mem. NAS, Royal Danish Acad. Scis., Am. Soc. Plant Physiologists (pres. 1979-80, chmn. bd. trustees 1986-90, Stephen Hales award 1974, Charles Reid Barnes Life Membership award 1992), Internat. Ho. (mem. bd. dirs. 2002-). Avocation: golf. Home: 764 Elmwood Dr Davis CA 95616-3517 Office: U Calif Molecular & Cellular Biology Davis CA 95616 Business E-Mail: pkstumpf@ucdavis.edu.

STUMPF, WALTER ERICH, cell biology educator, researcher; b. Oelsnitz, Sachsen, Germany, Jan. 10, 1927; arrived in U.S., 1963; m. Ursula Emily Schwinge, May 20, 1961; children: Andrea, Martin, Carolin, Silva. MD summa cum laude, Humboldt U., Berlin, 1952; PhD in Pharmacology, U. Chgo., 1967; D of Human Biology (hon.), U. Ulm, Germany, 1987. Resident in neurology and psychiatry Humboldt U., Berlin, 1954-57, U. Marburg, Germany, 1957-61, resident in radiobiology, 1961-62; rsch. assoc. U. Chgo., 1963-67, asst. prof., 1967-70; assoc. prof. U. N.C., Chapel Hill, 1970-73, prof., 1973-95, mem. labs. for reproductive biology and neurobiology program, mem. Cancer Rsch. Ctr., Carolina Population Ctr., mem. curriculum in toxicology. Vis. psychiatrist Maudsley Hosp., London, 1959; vis. prof. Max-Planck Inst. for Cell Biology, Wilhelmshaven, Germany, 1975, U. Ulm, 1981, U. Sao Paulo, Brazil, 2000-02; rsch. advisor Chugai Pharm. Co., Ltd., Tokyo, 1992-95; lectr. U. São Paulo, 1997, 2000, Ain Shams U., Cairo, 1998; cons. Harris Mfg. Co., North Billerica, Mass., Rsch. Triangle Inst., Chemistry and Life Scis. Divsn., Rsch. Triangle Park, N.C., Merck Sharp and Dome, Westpoint, Pa., Glaxo Wellcome, Rsch. Triangle Park; exec. com. NRC, Inst. of Lab. Animal Resources, NAS, 1979-81, coun. Inst. of Lab. Animal Res., 1978-81, com. Soc. for Exptl. Biology and Medicine, 1987-92, founder Internat. Inst. Drug Distbn. Cytopharmacology and Cytoxicology, Chapel Hill, 1995—. Editor: Autoradiography of Diffusible Substances, 1969, Anatomical Neuroendocrinology, 1975, Autoradiography and Correlative Imaging, 1995; author: Drug Localization in Tissues and Cells, 2003; mem. editl. bd. Neuroendocrinology Letters, 1979-87, Exptl. Aging Rsch., 1975-85, Jour. Histochemistry and Cytochemistry, 1982-90, Cell and Tissue Rsch., 1982-88, Molecular and Cellular Neurosci., 1989-94, Biomed. Rsch., 1991-94, Histochemistry, 1992-96; contbr. articles to profl. jours. Recipient Humboldt Found. award, 1989. Mem. AAAS, Am. Assn. Anatomists, N.Y. Acad. Scis., Soc. for Exptl. Biology and Medicine, Soc. for Neurosci., Endocrine Soc., Internat. Brain Rsch. Orgn., Am. Soc. Zoologists, Histochem. Soc. (coun. 1977-81), Histochem. Gesellschaft (Feulgen lectureship 1982), Internat. Soc. Study Xenobiotics (charter), Internat. Inst. Drug Distbn. Cytopharmacology and Cytotoxicology (founder). Home: U NC Sch Medicine 2612 Damascus Church Rd Chapel Hill NC 27516-8043 Office: Internat Inst Drug Distribution Cytopharmacology & Cytotoxicology Chapel Hill NC 27516

STUMPFF, ROBERT THOMAS, academic administrator; b. Lewistown, Pa., June 25, 1945; s. Harry Clarence and Marjorie Louise (Bossinger) Stumpff; m. Sylvia Simmons, Apr. 22, 1972; children: Robert Dale, Cherie Lynn Stumpff Zimmer. BS, U. Md., 1968; cert., U. Ky., 1978. Asst. dir. athletics U. Md., College Park, 1968-69, asst. dir. Md. student union, 1969-72, assoc. dir. Md. student union, 1973-80, acting dir. Md. student union, 1974-75, bus. mgr. athletics, 1980-81, asst. athletic dir., 1982-88, asst. dir. gen. svcs., facilities mgmt., 1988—. Cons. U.S. Naval Acad. Athletic Assn., Annapolis, Md., 1984. Author, editor: Maryland Wrestling, 1964—65, 1968—69, asst. editor: Maryland Basketball, 1964—65, 1968—69, Maryland Football Guide, 1965—69. Asst. min. St. Paul's Luth. Ch., Fulton, Md., 1996—; mem. ch. coun. Abiding Savior Luth. Ch., Columbia, Md., 1986—87; mem. Luth. campus ministry bd. U. Md., 1995—. Mem.: Assn. Phys. Plant Adminstrs., Coll. and Univ. Recycling Coun., Nat. Recycling Coalition, Md. Recylcers Coalition (bd. dirs. 1997—), Md.-Del. Solid Waste Assn., Nat. Solid Wastes Mgmt. Assn., Solid Waste Assn. N.Am. (bd. dirs. Mid-Atlantic chpt. 1992—94, cert. mcpl. solid waste mgr.), Am. Pub. Works Assn., U. Md. M Club Found. (life; bd. dirs. 1970—, past pres.), U. Md. Alumni Assn. (life), U. Md. Terrapin Club, Omicron Delta Kappa (Sigma chpt. faculty sec.-treas. 1972—76, faculty adviser 1976—91, faculty coord. 1991—). Avocations: reading, sightseeing. Home: 8206 Bubbling Spring Laurel MD 20723-1079 Office: Univ Md Facilities Mgmt Dept Bldg & Landscape Svcs 1300 Service Building College Park MD 20742-6055 Office Phone: 301-405-7085. Business E-Mail: rs76@umail.umd.edu.

STUNKARD, ALBERT JAMES, psychiatrist, educator; b. N.Y.C., Feb. 7, 1922; s. Horace Wesley and Frances (Klank) Stunkard. BS, Yale U., 1943; MD, Columbia U., 1945, U. Edinburgh, 1992. Intern in medicine Mass. Gen. Hosp., Boston, 1945—46; resident physician psychiatry Johns Hopkins Hosp., 1948—51, rsch. fellow psychiatry, 1951—52; 1rsch. fellow medicine Columbia U. Svc., Goldwater Meml. Hosp., N.Y.C., 1952—53; Commonwealth rsch. fellow, then asst. prof. medicine Cornell U. Med. Coll., 1953—57; mem. faculty U. Pa., 1957—73, 1976—, prof. psychiatry, 1962—73, 1976—, Kenneth Appel prof. psychiatry, 1968—73, chmn. dept., 1962—73; prof. psychiatry Med. Sch., Stanford U., 1973—76. Contbr. more than 400 articles on psychol., physiol., sociol., therapeutic and genetic aspects of obesity to profl. jours. Capt. M.C. AUS, 1946—48. Recipient Disting. Svc. award, Am. Psychiat. Assn., 1994, Goldberger award, AMA, 1990, Willendorf award for clin. rsch., Internat. Assn. for Study of Obesity, 1998; fellow, Ctr. for Advanced Study in Behavioral Scis., 1971—72. Mem.: Soc. Behavioral Medicine (past pres.), Assn. Rsch. in Nervous and Mental Diseases (past pres.), Am. Psychosomatic Soc. (past pres.), Acad. Behavioral Medicine Rsch. (past pres.), Am. Assn. of Chmn. of Depts. of Psychiatry (past pres.), Inst. of Medicine of NAS. Achievements include contributions to the behavioral and pharmacological treatment of obesity and to understanding of sociological, physiological, psychological and genetic aspects of the disorder; contributions also to nosology and treatment of the eating disorders. Office: U Pa Sch Medicine Dept Psychiatry 3535 Market St 3rd Flr Philadelphia PA 19104-2641 E-mail: stunkard@mail.med.upenn.edu.

STUNTEBECK, CLINTON A. lawyer; b. Hibbing, Minn., May 25, 1938; s. Robert F. and S. Mary Stuntebeck; m. Mary Joan Carmody; children: Robin, M. Alison, Susan, John, William. BA in Psychology, U. Minn., 1960; LLB, U. Maine, 1968. Bar: Pa. 1969, U.S. Dist. Ct. (ea. dist.) Pa. 1969. Ptnr. emeritus, chmn. corp. fin. and securities, mem. exec. com. Schnader, Harrison, Segal & Lewis, Phila. Bd. dirs. Markel Corp., Greater Phila. First Partnership for Econ. Devel.; lectr. corp. and securities law. Contbr. articles to profl. jours. Pres. Radnor (Pa.) Twp. Bd. Commn., 1981—83, 1992—2001; founder, bd. dirs. Radnor Enhancement Cmty. Trust; bd. visitors U. Maine Sch. Law; trustee Cabrini Coll.; bd. dirs. Am. Heart Assn., Ctr. for Responsible Leadership and Governance, Villanova U. Capt. USAF, 1960—68. Mem. ABA, Am. Law Inst., Pa. Bar Assn., Phila. Bar Assn., Securities Industry Assn. (law and compliance com.), Nat. Assn. Corp. Dirs., U. Maine Law Alumni Assn. (pres. 1974-76), Federalist Soc., Union League Phila., Phila. Country Club, Sunday Breakfast Club, Corinthian Yacht Club. Avocations: sailing, skiing, golf. Office: Schnader Harrison Segal 1600 Market St Ste 3600 Philadelphia PA 19103-7287 Office Phone: 215-751-2034. E-mail: cstuntebeck@schnader.com.

STUNZ, JOHN HENRY, JR., retired physician; b. Freeland, Pa., May 20, 1921; s. John Henry and Anna Amelia (Gross) S.; m. Geraldine Kutz, July 2, 1944; children: Beverly A. Stunz Boyd, Geri Stunz Konstantin. BA, U. Pa., 1943, MD, 1946. Diplomate Am. Bd. Occupational Medicine. Intern U.S. Naval Hosp., Saint Albans, N.Y., 1946-47; pvt. practice Freeland, 1949-50; plant physician Harrison Radiator div. Gen. Motors Corp., Lockport, N.Y., 1950-52, med. dir., 1952-78, Cadillac Motor Car div. Gen. Motors Corp., Detroit, 1978-86; occupational medicine cons. Preferred Med. Assocs., Southfield, Mich., 1987-98, ret., 1998. Pres. Niagara County (N.Y.) Bd. Health, 1966; acting commr. health Niagara County, 1972-73. Lt. (j.g.) M.C., USNR, 1946-49. Fellow Am. Coll. Occupl. and Environ. Medicine; mem. Mich. State Med. Soc., Oakland County Med. Soc. (environ. health com. 1988), Mich. Occupl. and Environ. Med. Assn. (bd. dirs. 1985-88), Detroit Occupl. Physicians Assn. Republican. Presbyterian. Avocations: stamp collecting/philately, boating, golf. Home: 735 Ardmoor Dr Bloomfield Hills MI 48301-2417

STUPAK, BART T. congressman, lawyer; b. Feb. 29, 1952; m. Laurie Ann Olsen; children: Ken, Bart Jr. (dec.). AA in Criminal Justice, Northwestern Mich. C.C., Traverse City, 1972; BS in Criminal Justice, Saginaw Valley State Coll., 1977; JD, Thomas M. Cooley Law Sch., 1981. Patrolman Escanaba City Police Dept., 1972-73; state trooper Mich. Dept. State Police, 1973-84; instr. State Police Tng. Acad., 1980-82; atty., 1981-84, Hansley, Neiman, Peterson, Beauchamp, Stupak, Bergman P.C., 1984-85; ptnr. Stupak, Bergman, Stupak P.C., 1985-88; mem. Mich. Ho. of Reps., 1989-90; prin. Bart T. Stupak P.C., 1991—; mem. 103rd-108th Congresses from 1st Mich. dist., 1993—. Mem. commerce subcom. on health & environment. Nat. committeeman Boy Scouts Am., coach Menominee Youth Baseball Assn., Little League; active Wildlife Unltd., Menominee Woods and Streams Assn., Menominee County Hist. Soc.; adv. com. Bay Pines Juv. Detection Ctr. Mem. Nat. Rifle Assn., Sons of the Am. Legion, Knights of Columbus, Elks Club, State Employees Retirees Assn., fin. com. Holy Spirit Catholic Ch. Democrat. Office: US Ho of Reps 2352 Rayburn Ho Office Bldg Washington DC 20515-2201 E-mail: stupak@mail.house.gov.

STURCKOW, FREDERICK W. (RICK), astronaut; b. La Mesa, Calif., Aug. 11, 1961; s. Karl H. and Janette R. Sturckow; m. Michele A. Street. BS in Mech. Engring., Calif. Poly. State U., 1984. Commd. 2d lt. USMC, 1984, advanced through grades to lt. col.; with MCAS, Beaufort, SC, Sheik Isa Air Base, Bahrain; mission comdr. Operation Desert Storm; with Naval Air Warfare Ctr.-Aircraft Divsn., Patuxent River, Md.; astronaut NASA, Houston, 1994—, with Vehicle Systems and Ops. Br. Decorated Single Mission Air medal with combat "V", 4 Strike/Flight Air medals. Mem.: Marine Corps Assn. Achievements include logged 4,000 flight hours in over 50 different aircraft; logged 568 hours in space; pilot STS-88 Endeavour (1998) and STS-105 Discovery (2001). Avocations: flying, physical training. Office: Astronaut Office/CB NASA Johnson Space Ctr Houston TX 77058

STURDEVANT, WAYNE ALAN, education and providertechnical services; b. Portland, Oreg., Apr. 3, 1946; s. Hervey Sturdevant and Georgia Bright; m. Helen F. Radbury, Sept. 24, 1976; children: Wayne Jr., Stephen, John, Brian, Daniel. BS in Edn., So. Ill. U., 1980. With USAF, 1964—85, chief on-job-tng. ops., 1982-85; lead engr. McDonnell Douglas Corp., 1985-88; br. mgr. Southeastern Computer Cons., Inc., 1988-2000; pres., COO Apollo Software/eSaba Systems, 2000-01; CEO Sturdevant Assocs., Austin, 2001—. Dir. tech. svcs. PRO Fin. Group, Austin, 2003—. Contbr. articles to profl. jours. Bishop LDS Ch., 1983-84, 98-2002, stake presidency, 1990-96; exec. bd. Boy Scouts Am., 1986-2003. Recognized for leadership in multi-nat. programs; recipient Citation of Honor Air Force Assn., 1980, Silver Beaver award Boy Scouts Am., 1998; named Internat. Man of Yr., Internat. Biog. Ctr., 1992. Republican. Achievements include development of advanced concepts in tech. mgmt; program and media design; formal quality sys. Avocations: genealogy, lighthouses. Home: 9214 Independence Loop Austin TX 78748-6312

STURGELL, ROBERT A. government agency administrator; b. 1959; m. Lynn Sturgell; 1 child. BS, US Naval Acad.; JD, Univ. of Va., Va. Bar: 1994. Chmn. primary advisor and coord. Nat. Trans. Safety Bd.; flight op. super. and line pilot flying the B-757 and B-767 United Airlines; atty. for aviation law Shaw Pittman, Wash., DC; naval aviator instr. on F-14, F-18, F-16 and A-4 aircraft Navy Fighter Weapons Sch. (Topgun); Ret. Comdr. US Naval Reserves. Achievements include The Senate has confirmed Robert A. Sturgell as Deputy Administrator of the Fed. Aviation Admin. Office: Federal Aviation Admin Dept of Transportation 800 Independence Ave SW Rm 1010 Washington DC 20591

STURGEON, JOHN ASHLEY, insurance company executive; b. Alliance, Nebr. B degree, Midland Luth. Coll., 1962. Ptnr. Arthur Andersen & Co., 1962—82; exec. v.p., gen. comptroller The Mutual of Omaha Ins. Cos., Omaha, 1982—97, pres., 1997—98, pres., COO, 1998—; pres. United World Life Ins. Co., 1997—. Bd. dirs. Kirkpatrick, Pettis, Smith, Polian Inc., Companion Life Ins. Co., United World Life Ins. Co., The Omaha Indemnity Co., Mut. of Omaha Structured Settlement Co., KFS Corp., Mut. of Omaha Holdings, Inc., Mut. of Omaha Ins. Co., Health Ins. Assn. Am., Creighton U., Mut. of Omaha Investor Svcs., Inc.; chmn. Omaha Property and Casualty Ins. Co., 1996—, Innowave Inc., 1998—. Consultation com. U.S. Strategic Command; bd. trustees Mid-Am. Coun. Boy Scouts Am. Office: The Mutual of Omaha Ins Co Mutual of Omaha Plz Omaha NE 68175

STURGES, JOHN SIEBRAND, management consultant; b. Greenwich, Conn., Feb. 12, 1939; s. Harry Wilton and Elizabeth Helen Sturges; m. Anastasia Daphne Sturges, May 6, 1967; children: Christina Aurora, Elizabeth Athena. AB, Harvard U., 1960; MBA, U. So. Calif., 1965; postgrad., NYU, 1972, U. Mich., 1982; PhD, Columbia U., 1997; ThD, Am. Coll., 1997, PhD, 2000. Cert. profl. mgmt. cons., sr. profl. in human resources; cert. mgmt. cons. With Equitable Life Assurance Soc. U.S., N.Y.C., 1965-79, mgr. sys. devel., 1965-70, dir. compensation and benefits, 1971-75, v.p. pers. and adminstrv. svcs., 1975-79; sr. v.p. pers. Nat. Westminster Bank U.S.A., N.Y.C., 1979-82; corp. sr. v.p. adminstrn. and human resources Willis-Corroon Corp., N.Y.C., 1982-84; mng. dir. human resources Marine Midland Bank, N.Y.C., 1984-87; mng. dir. Siebrand-Wilton Assocs., N.Y.C., 1986-87, pres., 1987—. Lay reader, Stephen minister St. Peters Episcopal Ch., Freehold, N.J., 1972—. Lt. USNR, 1960-65. Fellow Am. Coll.; mem. Internat. Found. Employee Benefit Plans, Strategic Leadership Forum, Commerce Assocs., Soc. for Human Resource Mgmt. (dir. 1979—), Am. Compensation Assn., Human Resource Planning Soc., Inst. Mgmt. Cons. (bd. dirs. 1992-2001), Cons. Bur., Harvard Club (N.Y.C., Boston, Princeton; dir. 1991-97), Nassau Club, Monmouth Boat Club, Beta Gamma Sigma (dir. N.Y. 1978—), Phi Kappa Phi. Republican.

STURGES, LYNN H. lawyer, sociologist; b. New York, NY, July 2, 1966; d. Albert and Constance E. Rosenthal; m. Peter B. Sturges, May 20, 1989; children: Jessica, Rachel. BA Magna Cum Laude, Boston U., Mass., 1988; JD, Case Western Rosene, Cleve., 1992. Bar: (Ohio), (Ga.) 2003. Assoc. counsel Akan Aluminum Corp., Mowfield Heights, Ohio, 1992—97; atty. self employed, Cleve., 1997—98, Buckley, King & Bluso, Cleve., 1998—2000, Holden & Assoc., Tucker, Ga., 2000—. Guardian ad litem Bar Assn., SC, 1994, Cuyahoga County, Ohio, 1997—98; pro bono atty. Legal Aid, Ga., 1993. Vol. Safe Place, Buford, Ga., 2003—04. Mem.: Ga. Bar Assn., Am. Bar Assn. Avocations: writing, exercise, musical theater. Office: Holden & Associates 2100 East Exchange Place Tucker GA 30084 Office Phone: 770-270-6983. Office Fax: 770-270-6986.

STURGES, SHERRY LYNN, recording industry executive; b. Long Beach, Calif., Dec. 11, 1946; d. Howard George and Alice Myrtle Fairbairn; m. Jeffery Alan Sturges, Dec. 30, 1969; children: Allisun Malinda, Jay. Grad. high sch., Las Vegas, Nev. V.p. Soultime, Inc., Las Vegas, 1968-69, Universe, Inc., Las Vegas, 1971-76; co-developer, owner Fun Trax Music Video and Audio Recording Studios, Westwood, Calif., 1986—. Creative cons. John Debella Show, 1990, M.T.V., L.A., 1990, KCET-TV, L.A., 1990,KTLA-TV, L.A., 1991. Co-writer song The Sharing of Love for TV series Murder, She Wrote, 1996, feature film The Ride, 1997; song writer (film) The Ride, 1997. Officer PTA, Woodland Hills, Calif., 1977-86, pres., 1984-86; vol. Connie Stevens Charity Orgn., Beverly Hills, Calif., 1980-84; vol. Crossroads Sch. for Arts and Sci., Westwood Meth. presch., West L.A. Bapt. Sch., Northridge United Meth. Ch., St. Vincent's Parents Coun., St. Joseph the Worker Sch., Chatsworth H.S., Sepulveda Nursery Sch., Nat. Neurofibromatosis Found., Life Steps Found., Westwood Village Assn., San Joaquin Valley Actors Repertory Co., 1997—. Recipient Outstanding Contribution award L.A. Unified Sch. Dist., Oxnard Unified Sch. Dist., 1998, 99. Mem. Am. Soc. Composers, Authors and Pubs. Republican. Avocations: collecting dolls, plates and figurines. Home: 29468 Sequoia Rd Santa Clarita CA 91387-6246

STURGES, SIDNEY JAMES, pharmacist, educator, investment and development company executive; b. Kansas City, Mo., Sept. 29, 1936; s. Sidney Alexander and Lenore Caroline (Lemley) S.; m. Martha Grace Leonard, Nov. 29, 1957 (div. 1979); 1 child, Grace Caroline; m. Gloria June Kitch, Sept. 17, 1983. BS in Pharmacy, U. Mo., 1957, post grad.; MBA in Pharmacy Adminstrn., U. Kans., 1980; PhD in Bus. Adminstrn., Pacific Western U., 1980; cert. in Gerentology, Avila Coll., 1986. Registered pharmacist, Mo., Kans.; registered nursing home adminstr., Mo.; cert. vocat. tchr., Mo. Pharmacist, mgr. Crown Drugs, Kansas City, Mo., 1957-60; pharmacist,

owner Sav-On-Drugs and Pharmacy, Kansas City, 1960-62; ptnr. Sam's Bargain Town Drugs, Raytown, Mo., 1961-62; pharmacist, owner Sturges Drugs DBA Barnard Pharmacy, Independence, Mo., 1962—; pres., owner Sturges Med. Corp., Independence, Mo., 1967-1977, Sturges Investment Corp., Independence, 1967-1978, Sturwood Investment Corp., Independence, 1968—, Sturges Agri-Bus. Co., Independence, 1977—, Sturges Devel. Co., 1984—; bd. dirs. Comprehensive Mental Health Corp., Truman Med. Ctr., 1992; instr. pharmacology Penn Valley C.C., 1976-92; instr., lectr. various clubs and groups. Contbr. articles to profl. jours. Bd. dirs. Independence House, 1981-83; mem. Criminal Justice Adv. Commn., Independence, 1982—. Recipient Outstanding award Kans. City Alcohol and Drug Abuse Council, 1982. Mem. Mo. Sheriffs Assn., Mo. Pharm. Assn. (pharmacy dr. 1981, Pharmacists Against Drug Abuse award 1989), Mo. Found. Pharm. Care, U. Mo. Alumni Assn. Home and Office: Sturges Co 16805 E Cogan Rd Ste B Independence MO 64055-2815 Office Phone: 816-478-0764.

STURGILL, JUDITH LYNN, education educator, lawyer; b. Akron, Ohio, May 14, 1947; d. John Wayne and Betty Jo (Timmons) Harr; m. Jerry L Sturgill, Mar. 20, 1989 AA, Polk Cmty. Coll., 1978; BS in edn., Kent State U., 1969; JD, U. Akron, 1985. Bar: Ohio 1985. Asst. prosecutor Richland County, Mansfield, Ohio, 1989—98; magistrate Richland County of Common Pleas, Mansfield, 1992—98; assoc. prof./program dir. North Ctrl. State Coll., Mansfield, 1998—. Dem. precinct chairperson Richland County. Office: North Central State Coll Mansfield OH 44901 Office Phone: 419-755-4778. Office Fax: 419-755-4750. Business E-Mail: jsturgil@ncstatecollege.edu.

STURGULEWSKI, ARLISS, state legislator, director; b. Blaine, Wash., Sept. 27, 1927; BA, U. Wash.; LLD (hon.), U. Alaska, Anchorage, 1993. Mem. Assembly Municipality of Anchorage; interim exec. dir. Alaska Sci. and Tech. Found., 1995. Vice chmn. New Capital Site Planning Commn., mem. Capital Site Selection Com.; chmn. Greater Anchorage Area Planning and Zoning Commn.; mem. Alaska State Senate, 1978-93; Rep. nominee Office Gov. Alaska, 1986, 90. Home: 2957 Sheldon Jackson St Anchorage AK 99508-4469 Office: 3201 C St Ste 405 Anchorage AK 99503-3967 Business E-Mail: a.sturgulewski@swallingcpas.com.

STURKEN, CRAIG, retail executive; Sr. v.p. Big Star Food Stores, 1989—90; chmn. Can. ops. Spartan Stores Inc., 1990—93, group v.p. Mich. ops., then pres. A&P Mich., 1993—97, chmn., CEO midwest region, 1997—2000, pres., CEO atlantic region, 2000—. Office: PO Box 8700 850 76th St SW Grand Rapids MI 49518-8700*

STURM, CHRISTOPHER DOUGLAS, neurosurgeon; b. San Diego, June 20; s. Douglas and Marianna (Barr) Sturm; m. Janet Lee Griffin, Aug. 20, 1997; children: Kaci, Faith. BA in Biology, Washington U., 1987; MD summa cum laude, St. Louis U., 1992. Lic. physician Ill., Wis. Intern St. Louis U. Hosp., 1992—93, resident neurol. surgery, 1993—98; neurosurgeon, med. dir. Mercy Regional Neurosurgery Ctr., Janesville, Wis., 2002—. Cons. in field. Contbr. articles to profl. jours. Maj. U.S. Army, 1998—2002. Mem.: Wis. Med. Assn., Congress Neurol. Surgeons, Am. Assn. Neurol. Surgeons, St. Louis Sch. Medicine Med. Alumni Assn., Alpha Omega Alpha, Alpha Sigma Nu. Avocation: golf. Office: Mercy Health Sys 1000 Mineral Point Ave Janesville WI 53548 Business E-Mail: csturm@mhsjvl.org.

STURM, JOHN F. trade association administrator; Grad., U. Notre Dame; grad. in Law, Ind. U. Bar: U.S. Supreme Ct. From asst. to chmn. FCC, Washington; atty. NBC, Washington; v.p. govt. affairs CBS, Washington; sr. v.p. pub. policy, gen. counsel Newspaper Assn. Am., Vienna, Va., 1991—95, pres., CEO, 1995—. Office: Newspaper Assn Am 1921 Gallows Rd Ste 600 Vienna VA 22182-3900

STURM, WILLIAM CHARLES, lawyer; b. Milw., Aug. 4, 1941; s. Charles William and Helen Ann (Niesen) S.; m. Kay F. Sturm, June 10, 1967; children: Patricia, Elizabeth, Katherine, William, Susan. BS in Bus. Adminstrn., Marquette U., 1963; JD, 1966. Bar: Wis. 1966, U.S. Dist. Ct. (ea. dist.) Wis. 1966, U.S. Supreme Ct. 1980. Sole practice, Milw., 1966—77; ptnr. Rausch, Hamell, Ehrle & Sturm, S.C., Milw., 1977—81, Rausch, Hamell, Ehrle, Sturm & Blom, Milw., 1981-83, Rausch, Hamell, Ehrle & Sturm, 1983-95, Rausch, Hamell, Sturm & Israel S.C., 1995-98, Rausch, Sturm, Israel & Hornik, S.C., 1999—, Asst. prof. Marquette U., 1982-91; lectr. U. Wis., Milw., 1991-97, sr. lectr. 1997-2002. Contbr. articles to profl. jours. Mem. adv. bd. Pallotine Order, 1985—; bd. dirs. Pius XI H.S., 2002-2004. Recipient Editors award Wis. Med. Credit Assn., 1980, Recipient Outstanding Alumni Pius XI H.S., 2002. Mem. ABA, Wis. Bar Assn., Comml. Law League Am. (exec. council midwestern dist. 1981-83, 86-88, chmn. state membership com. 1981-88, nat. nominating council 1984-86, 1988-89, sec., 2d v.p. midwestern dist. 1989-90, 1st v.p. midwestern dist. 1990-91, chmn. 1991-92, nat. bd. govs. 1997-2000, pres. elect, 2000-01, pres. 2001-02, past pres. 2002-), Acad. Legal Studies in Bus., Midwest Bus. Law Assn. (sec. 1988-89, v.p. 1989-90, pres. 1990-91), Healthcare Fin. Mgmt. Assn., Beta Alpha Psi (faculty v.p. Psi chpt. 1985-88, Eta Theta chpt. 1992-99), Midwest Bus. And Health Assn. (v.p. procs. 1987-88, v.p. program 1988-89, pres. 1989-90). Clubs: Westmoor Country (Milw.); Kiwanis (pres. 1979, lt. gov. div. 5, 1980) (Wauwatosa, Wis.). Office: 2448 South 102nd St Milwaukee WI 53227 Office Phone: 414-328-1400. E-mail: wsturm@wiscollect.com.

STURMAN, DEBORAH MUSCHA, lawyer, columnist; d. Herman Getzie and Gladys Freiman Sturman; 1 child, Rachel Zipporah. Prix D'Excellence, Royal Brussels Conservatory of Music, Belgium, 1992; JD, UCLA, 1995. Bar: Calif. 1995, D.C. 1999, NY 2000. Of counsel Milberg Weiss Bershad Hynes & Lerach LLP, N.Y.C., 1995—2001, Milberg, Weiss, Bershad, & Schulman, 2001—. Legal columnist Mgr. Magazin, Hamburg, Germany, 2003—. French horn soloist, Telemann Konzerte; Mozart Chamber Music; etc.; dir.(prodr.): (radio and television broadcasts) Lieder und Schwenke aus der Kloster Schenke, Aus dem Leben eines Taugenichts. Mem. Calif. Holocaust Era Ins. Oversight Com., Sacramento, 2000—. Democrat. Jewish. Avocations: music, writing. Office: Milberg Weiss Bershad & Schulman One Pennsylvania Plaza New York NY 10119-0165 Office Phone: 212-594-5300. E-mail: deborah.sturman@blbglaw.com., dsturman@milbergweiss.com.

STURMAN, GEORGE, poet; b. N.Y., Oct. 19, 1914; s. Benny and Anna Sturman; m. Mary Kruse, Oct. 18, 1953 (dec. June 27, 1993). Student, C.C. N.Y. Adminstr. officer U.S. Gen. Svc. Adminstrn., Washington, 1935—78. Editl. adv. Truth Seeker; pub. rels. Rancho Bernardo Sun, Poway, Calif. Author: (poetry) A Sonnet to Pavarotti; contbr. articles to profl. jour.; prof. listener (Royal Caribbean cruise line). Vol. Marriott's Remington Ret. Facility, San Diego, 1998—. Recipient Vol. of the Yr., Marriotts Remington Ret. facility., 2002. Home: 11098 Picaza Pl San Diego CA 92127

STURMAN, GLORIDA J. lawyer; b. Cortez, Colo., June 26, 1957; BS cum laude, Ariz. State U., 1979, JD, 1982. Bar: Ariz. 1982, Nev. 1983. Atty. Edwards, Hale, Sturman, Atkin & Cushing, Ltd., Las Vegas. Mem.: ABA, So. Nev. Assn. Women Attys. (pres. 1988—89), Clark County Bar Assn. (pres. 1994), State Bar Nev. (pres. 2002—03, bd. govs.), State Bar Ariz. Office: Edwards Hale Sturman et al 415 S Sixth St Ste 300 Las Vegas NV 89101-6937

STURROCK, PETER ANDREW, space science and astrophysics educator; b. South Stifford, Essex, England, Mar. 20, 1924; came to U.S., 1955; s. Albert Edward and Mabel Minnie (Payne) S.; m. Marilyn Fern Stenson, June 29, 1963; children: Deirdre, Colin; 1 child from previous marriage, Myra. BA, Cambridge (Eng.) U., 1945, MA, 1948, PhD, 1951. Scientist Telecommunications Rsch. Establishment, Malvern, Eng., 1943-46, Nat. Bur. Standards, Washington, 1949-50, Ecole Normale Superieure, Paris, 1950-51, Atomic Energy Rsch. Establishment, Harwell, 1951-53; fellow St. John's Coll., Cambridge U., 1952-55; rsch. assoc. Stanford (Calif.) U., 1955-61, prof. dept. applied physics, dept. physics, 1961-98, dir. Inst. for Plasma Rsch., 1964—74, 1980—83; dep. dir. Ctr. for Space Sci. and Astrophysics, 1983-92, dir., 1992-98. Author: Static and Dynamic Electron Optics, 1955, Plasma Physics, 1993, The UFO Enigma, 1999; editor: Plasma Astrophysics, 1967, Solar Flares, 1980, Physics of the Sun, vols. I, II, III, 1986. Recipient Gravity prize Gravity Found., 1967, Hale prize Am. Astron. Soc., 1986, Henryk Arctowski medal NAS, 1990, Space Sci. award AIAA, 1992; European Ctr. for Nuclear Rsch. fellow, 1957-58. Fellow AAAS, Royal Astron. Soc., Am. Phys. Soc.; mem. Internat. Astron. Union, Internat. Acad. Astronautics, Soc. for Sci. Exploration (pres. 1982-2001). Office: Stanford U Dept Physics Varian Bldg Rm 302G Stanford CA 94305 Home: 1850 Sand Hill Rd Apt 29 Palo Alto CA 94304-2147 E-mail: sturrock@stanford.edu.

STURTEVANT, BRERETON, retired lawyer, former government official; b. Washington, Nov. 24, 1921; d. Charles Lyon and Grace (Brereton) S. BA, Wellesley Coll., 1942; JD, Temple U., 1949; postgrad., U. Del., 1969-71. Bar: D.C. 1949, Del. 1950. Research chemist E.I. duPont DeNemours & Co., 1942-50; law clk. Del. Supreme Ct., 1950; gen. practice law Wilmington, Del., 1950-57; partner Connolly, Bove & Lodge, Wilmington, 1957-71; examiner-in-chief U.S. Patent and Trademark Office Bd. Appeals, Washington, 1971-88. Adj. prof. law Georgetown U., 1974-79 Trustee Holton-Arms Sch., Bethesda, Md., 1977-96, chmn. or mem. all coms., trustee emerita, 1997—. Mem. ABA, Exec. Women in Govt. (charter mem., chmn. 1978-79) Clubs: Wellesley College, Washington-Wellesley (pres. 1982-84). Episcopalian. Achievements include first woman law clerk, Delaware Supreme Court; first woman patent examiner-in-chief. Home: 1227 Morningside Ln Alexandria VA 22308-1042

STURTEVANT, PETER MANN, JR., television news executive; b. Northampton, Mass., Feb. 27, 1943; s. Peter Mann and Katharine Bryan (Hobson) S.; m. Anne Elizabeth Fitzpatrick, July 12, 1969 (div. Dec. 1984); 1 child, Amanda Hadden; m. Toni F. Siegel, Apr. 14, 1985; 1 child, Gillian Lee. BA, Wilmington Coll., 1965, MA, U. Iowa, 1967. Assoc. prodr. CBS News, Washington, 1967-71, bur. chief Viet Nam Saigon, 1971-73, nat. news editor N.Y.C., 1974-80, asst. v.p. spl. events, 1981-83, producer 60 Minutes, 1984-85; exec. bus. news editor CNN, N.Y.C., 1985-86; prodr. Today's Bus. Buena Vista TV, N.Y.C., 1987; dir. news coverage CNBC, Fort Lee, N.J., 1988-90, v.p., mng. editor Ft. Lee, N.J., 1991-94; sr. v.p. Internat. Bus. News NBC, 1994-98; disaster relief, instr. Am. Red Cross, 1999—. Tutor, mentor Children's Aid Soc., 2001—; trustee Wilmington Coll., 2000—. Named Disting. Alumnus, Wilmington Coll., 1975, 97; named to Journalism Hall of Fame, U. Iowa Grad. Sch. Journalism, 1988; named to Wilmington Coll. Sports Hall of Fame, 1997. Mem. Nat. Acad. Cable Programming (nominated ACE award 1992, 93, 94), Soc. Profl. Journalists, Deadline Club N.Y., The Asia Soc., Overseas Press Club (bd. dirs.). Episcopalian. Avocations: racquet sports, landscaping, travel, stamp collecting/philately, parenting. Home: 90 Riverside Dr New York NY 10024-5306

STURTEVANT, RUTHANN PATTERSON, anatomy educator; b. Rockford, Ill., Feb. 7, 1927; d. Joseph Hyelmun and Virginia (Wharton) P.; m. Frank Milton Sturtevant Jr., Mar. 18, 1950; children: Barbara (dec.), Jill Sturtevant Rovani, Jan Sturtevant Cassidy. BS, Northwestern U., 1949, MS, 1950; PhD, U. Ark., 1972. Instr. life scis. Ind. State U., Evansville, Ind., 1965—72, asst. prof., 1972—74; asst. prof. anatomy Ind. U. Sch. Medicine, Evansville, 1972—74, U. Evansville, 1972—74; lectr. anatomy Northwestern U., Chgo., 1974—75; asst. prof. anatomy and surgery Loyola U., Maywood, 1975—81; assoc. prof. Loyola U. Sch. Medicine, Maywood, 1981—88, prof., 1988—90, prof. emerita, 1990—. Contbr. articles to profl. jours.; editorial bd. Chronobiology Internat., 1988-90; reviewer numerous profl. jours. Mem. Mayor's Task Force on High Tech. Devel., Chgo., 1983-85; exec. bd. Anatomical Gifts Assn. Ill., Chgo., 1978-89. Grantee Pott's Found., NIH, others, 1978—88. Mem. Am. Assn. Anatomists, So. Soc. Anatomists (councillor 1978-80), Internat. Soc. Chronobiologists, Am. Soc. Pharmacology and Exptl. Therapeutics, Soc. for Exptl. Biology and Medicine, Am. Assn. Clin. Anatomists, League of Underwater Photographers, Sarasota Scuba Club, Sigma Xi. Avocations: underwater photography, scuba diving, flying, digital imaging. Address: 5760 Midnight Pass Rd Unit 610-D Sarasota FL 34242 E-mail: patty5760@comcast.net.

STURTS, DONNA JEAN, music educator; b. Shelby, Ohio, Feb. 11, 1940; d. Charles Gilbert Burky and Martha Mabel Schwert; m. Delmar Dean Sturts, Apr. 8, 1961; children: Erica Lynn, Erin Elizabeth, Blair Alan. Cert. music tchr. Am. Coll. Musicians, 2002. Bank teller Citizens Bank, Shelby, Ohio, 1958—64; choir dir. Ctrl. Meth. Ch., Mansfield, Ohio, 1982—2000; piano tchr. Sturts Studio of Music, Mansfield, 1974—; vocal soloist various area churches, Mansfield, 1962—. Gold cup chmn. Fedn. of Music Clubs, Dist. IV, Ohio, 1999—. Recipient Service award, Centra United Meth. Ch., 1986, 1996. Mem.: Am. Coll. Musicians, Ohio Music Teachers Assn. (25 Yr. award 2002), North Ctrl. Dist., Ohio Music Teachers Assn., Music Teachers Nat. Assn. (ribbon festival chmn., Richland County 1997—), Nat. Fedn. Music Clubs, Mansfield Music Study Club. Avocations: painting, woodworking, needlecrafts, travel. Home: 92 Stewart Ave Mansfield OH 44906

STURTZ, DONALD LEE, physician, educator, naval officer; b. Coshocton, Ohio, Apr. 18, 1933; s. Walter Raymond and Helene Josephine (Kubic) S.; m. Alice Marie McGuire, June 11, 1955; children: Jimalee, Janel. BS, U.S. Naval Acad., Annapolis, Md., 1955; MD, U. Pa., 1965; diploma med. care catastrophe, Soc. Apothecaries London, 1996. Diplomate Am. Bd. Surgery. Surg. resident USN, Phila., 1965-70, ship's surgeon, 1970-71; staff surgeon Bethesda Naval Hosp., USN, 1971-80; chief of surgery San Diego Naval Hosp., USN, 1980-84; exec. officer Oakland (Calif.) Naval Hosp., USN, 1984-85; prof. clin. surgery USN, Bethesda, Md., 1985-87, commd. Naval Med. Command, 1987-88, Atlantic fleet surgeon, Supreme Allied Command surgeon, 1989-91; prof. surgery USUHS, Bethesda, Md., 1991—. Contbr. articles to profl. jours. Recipient B.D. Larrey award for Surgical Execellence, Surgical Dept. USUHS, Bethesda, 1988, Exceptional Svc. medal Uniformed Svcs. U., 1998. Fellow ACS (gov. 1985-88); mem. Am. Assn. for Surgery of Trauma, Assn. Mil. Surgeons, USN Inst. Republican. Presbyterian. Avocations: travel, gardening, antiquing, music, reading. Office: USUHS Dept Surgery 4301 Jones Bridge Rd Bethesda MD 20814-4799

STURZL, ALICE A. school library administrator; b. Marshfield, Wis., May 22, 1949; d. Aloysius F. and Lorraine R. (Wolk) Beyerl; m. Bruce R. Sturzl, Sr., June 9, 1973; stepchildren: Bruce R., Scott, Daniel, Ann, Todd, Timothy. BA, U. Wis., Oshkosh, 1971. Cert. tchr., Wis. Elem. libr. Sts. Peter and Paul Parish, Oshkosh, 1970-71; libr. Sch. Dist. of Laona, Wis., 1971-73; tchr. math. Our Lady of Perpetual Help, Glendale, Ariz., 1974-75, Most Holy Trinity Parish, Sunnyslope, Ariz., 1975-76; substitute tchr. Sch. Dists. of Laona and Wabeno, Wis., 1976-77; K-12 instructional media specialist Sch. Dist. of Laona, 1977—. Mem. Northeastern Wis. In-Sch. Telecomms. Adv. Bd., Green Bay, 1987-97, pres. 1989-97; trustee, v.p., pres. Wisconsin Valley Libr. Svc. Bd., Wausau, 1984-89, 2000—. Mem. Econ. Devel. Com., Town of Laona, 1987—; mem. parish coun. St. Leonard's Cath. Ch., Laona, intermittently 1983—; active Cmty. Soup and Homecoming/Laona Lions Club, 1983—. Mem. ALA, NEA, Wis. Libr. Assn. (sec. 1993-94, v.p. 1996, pres. 1997, past pres. 1998), Laona Edn. Assn. (sec.-treas.), Wis. Edn. Assn. (No. Tier UniServ), Wis. Ednl. Media Assn., Wis. Libr. Assn. Found. (v.p., sec.). Roman Catholic. Avocations: bowling, reading, travel, helping others, working with numbers. Home: 5170 E Silver Lake Rd Laona WI 54541-9255 Office: Sch Dist of Laona PO Box 100 5216 Forest Ave Laona WI 54541

STUTMAN, LEONARD JAY, research scientist, cardiologist; b. Boston, Apr. 8, 1928; s. Herbert Hyman and Nellie (Wiener) S.; BS, MIT, 1948; MA, Boston U., 1949; MD, U. Rochester, 1953; m. Jeanne Ann Soblen, Dec. 23, 1951; children: Peter, David, Marc, Robin. Intern, resident medicine Bellevue Hosp., 1953-57; chief, med. services br. WPAFB, Dayton, Ohio, 1957-59; spl. advanced research fellow NIH, Nat. Heart Inst. 1959-61; instr. in clin. medicine N.Y. U. Coll. Medicine, 1956-61, asst. prof. pathology, 1961-65; assoc. prof. clin. medicine N.Y. Med. Coll., 1980—; head coagulation research lab. St. Vincent's Hosp. and Med. Center, N.Y., 1965—; attending physician St. Vincent's Hosp.; sr. attending physician medicine, sr. cardiologist Nyack (N.Y.) Hosp.; med. dir. Presdl. Life Ins. Co., Nyack; bd. dirs. Metriplex, Inc. Cambridge, Mass., 1992—. Contbr. articles to profl. jours. Dir. cardiac epidemiology study Ford Found. Vera Inst.; mem. Internat. Com. on Thrombosis and Hemostasis. Capt. USAF, 1957-59. Fellow Am. Coll. Cardiology, ACP, N.Y. Acad. Medicine; mem. Am. Soc. Hematology, N.Y. Med. Soc., Sigma Xi. Home: 250 Townline Rd West Nyack NY 10994-2824 Office: 153 W 11th St New York NY 10011-8305

STUTTS, WILLIAM FLOYD, JR., lawyer, educator; b. El Dorado, Ark., Nov. 8, 1952; s. William Floyd and Marilyn Martin Stutts; m. Susan P. Campbell, May 16, 1992. BA, U. Tex., 1973; JD, U. Va., 1976. Bar: Tex. 1976, U.S. Dist. Ct. (we. dist.) Tex. 1992. Law clk. U.S. Ct. Appeals (5th cir.), Austin, 1976-77; assoc. Baker & Botts, Houston, 1978-85; ptnr. Baker Botts, Austin, 1987—, Clark, Thomas, Winters, Austin, 1985-87. Adj. prof. U. Tex. Law Sch., Austin, 1997—; instr., cons. Internat. Law Inst., Washington, 1998, 2001. Bd. dirs. Ballet Austin, 1988-96, Austin Oita Sister City Com., 1990—, Travis County Bar Assn., 1995-96, Capital Area Coun. Boy Scouts Am., Austin, 1996—. Fellow Am. Coll. Investment Counsel, Tex. Bar Found. (life); mem. ABA, Am. Bankruptcy Inst., Comml. Law League of Am. Lutheran. Home: 1405 Hardouin Ave Austin TX 78703 Office: Baker Botts 98 San Jacinto Blvd # 1300 Austin TX 78701

STUTZ, PEARL HEWLETT, retired photojournalist; b. Rochester, N.Y., Apr. 28, 1927; d. Herbert Henry Hewlett and Carolyn Amanda Brockmann; m. Peter Swan Stutz, May 23, 1953 (dec. July 1988); children: Eric Edward, Carolyn Edith Stutz Kourofsky. BA in Journalism, Ohio State U., 1949; MLS, SUNY, Geneseo, 1971. Cert. profl. libr. and media specialist, N.Y. Reporter Pampa (Tex.) Daily News, 1949, Great Falls (Mont.) Tribune, 1950; staff photographer Democrat and Chronicle, Rochester, 1950-56; libr. dir. Irondequoit Pub. Libr., Rochester, 1976-91; ret., 1991. Libr. cons. Cancer Action, Inc., Rochester, 1992-01. Named Disting. Communicator, Women in Comms., 1996. Achievements include first woman press photographer for large-city newspaper.

STUTZMAN, L. LEE, pastor; b. Clinton, Okla., June 13, 1953; s. Clamens L. Stutzman and Viola Darlene (Waters) Bonn; m. Connie R. Stutzman, June 3, 1972; children: Elizabeth, Jonathan, Rebecca. BA in Theology, MS in Theol. Studies, D in Ministry, Vision Christian U. With traveling ministry, 1972-78; founder Liberty Temple, Lima, Ohio, 1978-88, Christ Cathedral, 1988—; with nat. traveling ministry; apostle Liberty Network of Chs., Dayton, Ohio, 1986—. Author: From the Ground Up, 1987; producer (TV show) Foundation for Faith, 1985—; motivational spkr., Sci. of Empowered Living Forum. Author: From the Ground Up, 1987, Order Out of Chaos, 1995, Spiritual Gifts, 1992; prodr. (TV show) Life Without Limit, 1985—. Republican. Office: Christ Cathedral 295 E Salem St Clayton OH 45315-9719 *The greatest key to Godly success: you've got to start where you're at to get where you're going.*

STUTZMAN, SANDRA LOUISE, advanced nurse practitioner; b. Ashland, Pa., Nov. 10, 1953; d. Mary (Tersavige) S. Diploma, Sacred Heart Hosp. Sch., Norristown, Pa., 1979; LPN, Pottstown Meml. Med. Ctr.; diploma, St. Joseph Sch. Nursing, Reading, Pa., 1983; BS, Pa. State U., Reading, 1991; MS, U. South Fla., 1994. Advanced RN practitioner. Staff nurse Pottstown Meml. Med. Ctr., 1983—91; advanced RN practitioner Infectious Disease Ctr., Tampa (Fla.) Gen. Hosp., 1995—98; advanced RN practitioner EverCare, Tampa, Fla., 1998-99, Sergio H. Vallejo, M.D., Lakeland, Fla., 1999—2002, Advent Christian Village, Dowling Park, Fla., 2002—. Mem. Am. Acad. Nurse Practitioners, Fla. Nurses Assn., Sigma Theta Tau.

STUTZMAN, THOMAS CHASE, SR., lawyer; b. Portland, Oreg., Aug. 1, 1950; s. Leon H. and Mary L. (Chase) S.; m. Wendy Jeanne Craig, June 5, 1976; children: Sarah Anne, Thomas Chase Jr. BA with high honors, U. Calif., Santa Barbara, 1972; JD cum laude, Santa Clara U., 1975. Bar: Calif. 1976; cert. family law specialist. Pvt. practice, San Jose, Calif., 1976-79; pres., sec., CFO Thomas Chase Stutzman, PC, San Jose, 1979—. Instr. San Jose State U., 1977—78. Bd. dirs. Santa Cruz Campfire, 1978-80, Happy Hollow Park, 1978-80, 83-86, Pacific Neighbors, pres., 1991-92. Mem. Calif. Bar Assn., Santa Clara County Bar Assn. (chmn. environ. law com. 1976-78, exec. com. family law), Assn. Cert. Law Specialists, San Jose Jaycees (Dir. of Yr. 1976-77), Rotary, Lions (dir. 1979-81, 2d v.p. 1982-83, 1st v.p. 1983-84, pres. 1984-85), Scottish Rite, Masons, Phi Beta Kappa, Alameda Valley Rotary Club. Congregationalist. Office: 1625 The Alameda Ste 626 San Jose CA 95126-2207 Office Phone: 408-294-4600. E-mail: stutzman@tomstutzman.com.

STUVER, FRANCIS EDWARD, former railway car company executive; b. Greenville, Pa., Aug. 22, 1912; s. Willard Seeley and Anna Katherine (Henry) S.; m. Jessie Lucile Bright, Jan. 26, 1938; children: Robert Edward, Nancy (Mrs. Randolph Patrick Mutdosch). Grad. high sch. With Greenville Steel Car Co. (subsidiary Pitts. Forgings Co.), 1937—, chief accountant, 1944-46, asst. treas., 1946-54, asst. sec., 1948-56, treas., 1956-61, v.p., 1956-61, exec. v.p., 1961-75, ret., 1975; pres. Greenville Savs. & Loan Assn., 1977-83, dir., 1949-83, Greenville Steel Car Co., 1961-74, Pitts. Forgings Co., 1975-80. Bd. dirs. Municipal Authority Borough Greenville, 1946-74, treas., 1946-73; bd. dirs., mem. exec. com. Mercer County br. Pa. Economy League, 1949-64; bd. dirs., treas., chmn. finance com. Greenville Hosp., 1953-59. Mem. Am. Ry. Car Inst. (dir. 1964-75) Clubs: Masons, Elks, Moose, KP, Greenville Country. Home: 46 Chambers Ave Greenville PA 16125-1856

STUZIN, JAMES M. plastic surgeon; b. Miami, Fla., June 1, 1952; BA, U. Fla., Gainesville, 1974, MD, 1978. Cert. in gen. surgery 1985, in plastic surgery 1989. Intern, gen. surgery U. Wash. Hosps., Seattle, 1978—79, resident, gen. surgery, 1979—83; fellow, plastic surgery NYU Hosps., N.Y.C., 1984—86; craniofacial fellow U. Miami Hosps., Fla., 1986, UCLA Sch. Medicine, 1987, asst. clin. prof., plastic surgery, 1987; clin. instr., dept. plastic surgery U. Miami Sch. Medicine, Fla., 1989—95, clin. asst. prof., plastic surgery, 1995—. Mem. editl. bd. Annals of Plastic Surgery, 1993—. Mem.: Am. Soc. for Aesthetic Plastic Surgery (treas.), Alpha Omega Alpha, Phi Beta Kappa. Office: 1501 S Miami Ave Miami FL 33129-1102*

STWALLEY, BRIAN DAVID, pharmacist; b. Greencastle, Ind., Aug. 1, 1972; s. David Earl and Norma Jean Stwalley; m. Diane Marie Stwalley, Oct. 21, 1995; children: Andrew, Lauren. BS in Pharmacy, PharmD, Phila. Coll. Pharmacy Sci., 1996. Cert. geriatric pharmacist. Pharmacy mgr. Managed Care Rx, Lemoyne, Pa., 1996-98; v.p. clin. svcs. Continuing Care Rx, Camp Hill, Pa., 1998—. Fellow: Am. Soc. Cons. Pharmacists (pres. Pa. chpt. 2002); mem.: Am. Med. Dirs. Assn. Avocations: musician, reading, golf. Home: 6 N Alydar Blvd Dillsburg PA 17019 Office: Continuing Care Rx 5775 Allentown Blvd Ste 202 Harrisburg PA 17112 E-mail: bdsrph@adelphia.net.

STYCOS, JOSEPH MAYONE, retired demographer, educator; b. Saugerties, N.Y., Mar. 27, 1927; s. Stravos and Clotilda (Mayone) S.; m. Maria Nowakowska, Nov. 25, 1964; children: Steven Andrew, Christina Mayone (by previous marriage), Marek. AB, Princeton U., 1947; PhD, Columbia U., 1954. WithBur. Applied Social Rsch. Columbia U., 1948-50, lectr. sociology, 1951-52; project co-dir. U. P.R., 1952-53; postgrad. PC fellow U. N.C., 1954-55; assoc. prof. sociology St. Lawrence U., 1955-57; faculty Cornell U., Ithaca, N.Y., 1957-2000, prof. emertius, 2000, prof. sociology, 1963—, chmn. dept., 1966-70, dir. Latin Am. program, 1962-66, dir. internat. population program, 1962-88, prof. rural sociology, 1987-2001, dir. population and devel. program, 1988-92. Fulbright-Hayes Disting. prof. U. Warsaw, Poland, 1979; external examiner U. Ife, Nigeria, 1973; Cons. AID, 1962-64; sr. cons. Population Council, 1963-74, 77-79; cons. Airlie Found., 1972-73, Inst. for Research in Social Behavior, 1974, Clapp & Mayne, Inc., 1974, Ford-Rockefeller Population Program, 1977, Nat. U. Costa Rica, 1979, U. P.R., 1979; trustee Population Reference Bur., 1964-68, cons., 1968-74; mem. exec. com. Internat. Planned Parenthood Fedn., West Hemmis, 1965-71, cons., 1971-77; adv. com. population and devel. OAS, 1968-70; mem. bd. Population Assn. Am., 1968-71, editorial cons. demography, 1965-69; adv. panel population Nat. Inst. Child Health and Human Devel., Dept. Health, Edn. and Welfare, 1969; co-chmn. population task force U.S. Nat. Commn. for UNESCO, 1972-73; adv. council, interdisciplinary communications program Smithsonian Instn., 1974-76; cons. Pan Am. Health Orgn., WHO, 1975; cons.

steering com., acceptability task force WHO, 1978-85; cons. UNESCO, 1978-79, UN Fund for Population Activities, 1979-82, WHO, 1987-90; co-dir. Spanish family life project U. Complutense de Madrid, 1978-80; internat. adv. coun. Internat. Ctr. Photography, 1979-95; Fulbright-Hays prof. Nat. U. Costa Rica, spring 1986; chmn. U.S. Census Adv. Com. on Population Stats., 1983-84; mem. Fulbright-Hays program Nat. Screening Com. Cen. Am., 1989-92; population rsch. team Environ. & Natural Resources Policy & Tng. Project, 1992-96; planning com. Global Omnibus Environ. Survey (GOES) Human Dimensions of Global Environ. Change Program, 1993—, chair, 1996-97. Author: (with Hussein Abdel Aziz Sayed, Roger Avery and Samuel Firdman) Community Development and Family Planning: An Egyptian Experiment, 1988; mem. editl. bd. Human Orgn., 1962-64; editor: Demography as an Interdiscipline, 1989. Mem. council Cornell U., 1969-70. Mem. Rural Sociological Soc., Population Assn. of Am., Internat. Union for the Scientific Study of Population. Home: 28 Twin Glens Rd Ithaca NY 14850-1041 Office: Cornell U Population & Devel Program Warren Hall Ithaca NY 14853-7801

STYER, JANE M. computer consultant; b. Bethlehem, Pa., Apr. 14, 1957; d. LeRoy V. and Pauline M. (Diehl) S. Assoc in Gen. Edn., NCACC, 1977, Assoc in Applied Sci., 1979; BS in Computer Sci., St. Francis de Sales Coll., 1985, cert. profl. legal sec., 1986. PC technician A+ cert. 1997. Legal sec., asst. Lower Saucon Police Dept.; asst. to treas., bookkeeper Lehigh Valley Motor Club, Allentown, Pa.; title ins. agt., real estate and probate paralegal, office mgr. various attys., Lehigh & Delaware Valleys, Pa., 1976—92; owner, mgr. Abstractors' Svcs., Bingen, Pa., 1982—; quality control theory checker, tax preparer H & R Block, 1992—2002. Mem. exec. com., comptr. Northampton County Drop In Ctr., 2003—. Mem. NAFE, Nat. Assn. Legal Secs. (Continuing Legal Edn. Recognition award 1988), Lehigh-Northampton Counties (chmn. continuing legal edn. com. 1984-88, seminar chmn. 1985-88), Pa. Assn. Notaries, Single Sq. Dancers U.S.A. (nat. sec. 1986-87), Bachelors and Bachelorettes, Internat. (sec. Mid-Atlantic region 1980-84). Avocations: camping, square and round dancing, horseback riding. Home and Office: Abstractors' Svcs 3228 Bingen Rd Bethlehem PA 18015-5707

STYLER, ANDA JASAMINE, artist, educator; b. Norfolk, Va., Sept. 25, 1952; d. Franklin Merritt Brown and Edith Kathrine Knox; m. Richard James Barbera, Aug. 13, 1978 (div. Dec. 18, 1992); children: Melonie Ann Carroll. Student, Western State U., 1979-80; BFA, Parsons Sch. Design, 1983. Asst. art dir. Altamount Advtg., N.Y.C., 1983-84, Bell Yellow Pages, Elmsford, N.Y., 1984-86; art dir. Dellwood Pub., N.Y.C., 1986-93; freelance artist Wire Focus, Danbuy, Conn., 1994-98; tchr. various workshops, 1992—. Judge art work, show Watertown Art League, Conn., 1999, Soc. Creative Artists, Newtown, Conn., 2000, Memphis Art League, Tenn., 2000; tchr. The Art Ctr., Danbury, Conn. 1990; selected artist Gibson Card Co., 1994, 97; designer artwork Accent on Home, 1994; cover designer Women's Forum Mag. Using Quilts, 1993. One woman show at Bay State Med. Ctr., Springfield, Mass., 1995; exhibited in group shows at Nat. Congress Art Show, 1988, Art Horizons Show, 1989 (cert. excellence), Houstatonic Art League Show, 1989 (1st pl. award), Bethel Art League Show, 1989, 90, 91 (1st pl. award 1989, 91, 2d pl. award 1990), Richter Assn. Arts Show, 1989, 90, Housatonic Art League Summer Show, 1989, The Gallery Card, Kent, Conn., 1989, Ariel Gallery, N.Y.C., 1989, Soc. Creative Artisits Newton, 1990 (2d pl. award), Kent Gallery, Paris, N.Y., 1990, Hartford Architecture Conservancy, 1991, Conn. Capital Bldg., 1991, Aetna Gallery, Hartford, Conn., 1991, Gallery 7, Danbury, 1991 (featured painting), Christi Gallery, Washington, 1992, The Artist Son Gallery, Boston, 1993, The Madison Ave. Art Gallery, Memphis, 1995, Beaux Art Gallery, Southbury, Conn., 1996, The Birchstone Gallery, Egg Harbor, Wis., 1996, Springfield Mus. Fine Art, 1997, Birchstone Gallery & Studio, Egg Harbor, 1997, 98, 2000, Beaux Arts, Woodbury, 1998, 99, Food for Thought Gallery, New Milford, 2000; represented in permanent collections Morales Art Gallery, Nags Head, N.C., Beaus Art Gallery, Woodbury, Conn., Peel Gallery, Danby, Vt., Fleck Worner Fine Art, West Palm Beach, Fla., Barn Gallery, New Fairfield, Conn., Bay State Hosp., Springfield, Mass., St. Frances Hosp., Hartford, Conn., St. Vincents Hosp., Bridgeport, Conn., GTE Corp., Stamford, Conn., Bank Boston, Dean Witter, West Palm Beach. Recipient Honor award The Artist Mag., 1995. Mem. Husdon Valley Art Assn. (hon. mention award 1989), Richter Assn. Arts (bd. dirs. 1989, 91, two 2d pl. award 1989, 1st pl. acrylics award 1990, judge 1990, 91, 1st pl. award 1992), Avocations: quilting, gardening, collecting salt glaze pottery, cooking.

STYLES, ANGELA B. federal agency administrator; BA with distinction, U. Va.; JD with honors, U. Tex. Legis. aide Congressman Joe Barton, Washington; counsel Miller & Chevalier, Washington; wigh gen. svcs. adminstrn. Office Govt.-Wide Policy and Pub. Bldgs. Svcs., 2001; counselor to the dir. Office Mgmt. and Budget; adminstr. for fed. procurement policy Exec. Office of the Pres., Washington, 2001—. Articles editor: Am. Jour. Criminal Law. Mem.: ABA (chair legis. coordinating com. sect. pub. contract law, vice chair acctg., cost and pricing com.), Order of the Coif. Republican. Office: Exec Office of the Pres Fed Procurement Policy EEOB 17th & Pennsylvania Ave NW Washington DC 20503

STYLES, BEVERLY (JUANITA ROBINS CARPENTER), entertainer, composer, musician; b. Richmond, Va., June 6, 1923; d. John Harry Kenealy and Juanita Russell (Robins) Carpenter; m. Wilbur Cox, Mar. 14, 1942 (div.); m. Robert Marascia, Oct. 5, 1951 (div. Apr. 1964). Studies with Ike Carpenter, Hollywood, Calif., 1965—98; student, Am. Nat. Theatre Acad., 1968—69; studies with Paula Raymond, Hollywood, 1969—70; diploma, Masterplan Inst., Anaheim, Calif., 1970. Freelance performer, musician, 1947-81; owner Beverly Styles Music, Yucca Valley, Calif., 1971—. V.p. spl. programs Lawrence Program of Calif., Yucca Valley, Calif.; talent coord., co-founder Quiet Place Studio, Yucca Valley, 1994; mem. exec. bd., awards dir. Am. chpt. Diogenes Process Group, 1996—. Composer, lyricist: (songs) Joshua Tree, 1975, Wow, Wow, Wow, 1986, World of Dreams, 1996, Thank You God, 1996, (music for songs) I'm Thankful, 1978, The Whispering, 1994; piano arrangements include Colour Chords and Moods, 1995, Desert Nocturne, 1996; records include The Perpetual Styles of Beverly, 1978; albums include The Primitive Styles of Beverly, 1977; tape cassettes include Gospel Diamonds, 1996; author: A Special Plan to Think Upon, The Truth as Seen by a Composer, 1978, A Special Prayer to Think Upon, 1983. Mem. ASCAP (Gold Pin award), Profl. Musicians Local 47 (life), Internat. Platform Assn. Republican. Avocation: creating abstract art. Home and Office: 7839 Aster Ave Yucca Valley CA 92284-4130

STYLES, MARGRETTA MADDEN, nursing educator; b. Mount Union, Pa., Mar. 19, 1930; d. Russell B. and Agnes (Wilson) Madden; m. Douglas F. Styles, Sept. 4, 1954; children: Patrick, Michael, Megan. BS, Juniata Coll., 1950; M. in Nursing, Yale U., 1954; Ed.D., U. Fla., 1968; hon. doctorate, Valparaiso U., 1986, U. Athens, Greece, 1991. Staff nurse VA Hosp., West Haven, Conn., 1954-55; instr. Bklyn. Hosp. Sch. Nursing, 1955-58; supr. North Dist. Hosp., Pompano Beach, Fla., 1961-63; dir. nursing edn. Broward Community Coll., Ft. Lauderdale, Fla., 1963-67; assoc. prof. Sch. Nursing Duke U., Durham, N.C., 1967-69, dir. undergrad. studies, 1967-69; prof., dean Sch. Nursing U. Tex., San Antonio, 1969-73; dean, prof. Coll. Nursing Wayne State U., Detroit; prof. nursing U. Calif., San Francisco, 1977—, dean Sch. Nursing, 1977-87; chairperson Com. for Study of Credentializing in Nursing, 1976-79; mem. adv. group div. nursing HEW, 1977. Asst. dir. nursing svcs. U. Calif. Hosps. and Clinics, 1978-87; mem. Nat. Commn. Nursing, 1980—; mem. Calif. Bd. Registered Nursing, 1985—; mem. Sec.'s Commn. on Nursing HHS, 1988—. Author: On Nursing: Toward a New Endowment (Am. Jour. Nursing Book of Yr. award 1982); co-author (with A. Affara) From Principle to Power: A Guidebook to Regulation in Nursing, 1992. Recipient Disting. Alumna award Yale U. Sch. Nursing, 1979; Am. Nurses' Found. 1st disting. scholar, 1983 Fellow Am. Acad. Nursing; mem. Nat. Acad. Scis., Am. Nurses Assn. (pres. 1986-88), Internat. Coun. Nurses (bd. dirs. 1989—), Sigma Theta Tau. Office: U Calif Sch Nursing PO Box N531C San Francisco CA 94143-0001

STYMIEST, BARBARA, stock exchange executive; MBA, Richard Ivey Sch. Bus. Audit ptnr., Fin. Svcs. Group Ernst & Young, 1978—87; exec. v.p., CFO Nesbitt Burns Corp., Ltd., Canada, 1992—99; chair, bd. govs. Toronto Stock Exch. (now TSX Group Inc.), 1997—99, CEO, 1999—, also. bd. dirs. Mem. ICAO Task Force, 1996; gov. Can. Investor Protection Fund, 1996; chair Joint Industry Coord. Com., 1995—97; alt. gov. Can. Securities Inst., 1995, gov., 1997—; mem. task force on std. setting CICA, 1996—98. Mem. ofcl. Bd. Forest Hills United Ch., 1984; bd. mem. Rehab. Inst. Toronto, 1996, Hincks Dellcrest Children's Ctr., 1990—97, chair, bd. dirs., 1993—96. Fellow: Inst. Chartered Accts. Ont. Office: TSX Group Exch Tower 130 King St W Toronto ON Canada M5X 1J2*

STYNE, DENNIS MICHAEL, physician, educator; b. Chgo., July 31, 1947; s. Irving and Bernice S.; m. Donna Petre, Sept. 5, 1971; children: Rachel, Jonathan, Juliana, Aaron. BS, Northwestern U., 1969, MD, 1971. Diplomate Am. Bd. Pediat. Intern in pediatrics U. Calif., San Diego, 1971-72, resident in pediatrics, 1972-73, Yale U., New Haven, 1973-74; fellow in pediatric endocrinology U. Calif., San Francisco, 1974-77, asst. prof. pediatrics, 1977-83, assoc. prof. Davis, 1983-90, prof., 1990—, chair pediatrics, 1989-97; now prof., sect. chief pediatric endocrinology U. Calif. Davis Med. Ctr., Sacramento. Author numerous book chpts., contbr. articles to profl. jours. Mem. Endocrine Soc., Soc. Pediat. Rsch., Am. Pediat. Soc., Am. Acad. Pediat., Lawson Wilkins Soc. for Pediat. Endocrinology, Western Assn. of Physicians. Avocations: sailing, music. Office: UC Davis Med Ctr Dept Pediat 2516 Stockton Blvd Fl 3 Sacramento CA 95817-2208

STYNE, MARLYS MARSHALL, retired English educator; b. Whitewater, Wis., Oct. 12, 1932; d. Clifford William and Violet Marie (Uhl) Marshall; m. Robert Carter Clark, Feb. 14, 1959 (div. Sept. 1964); m. Julian Harold Styne, June 27, 1970 (dec. Mar. 2000). BA, Luther Coll., 1954; MA, U. Minn., 1957; postgrad., U. Wis., 1958-59. Instr. English W.Va. U., Morgantown, 1956-58; tchg. asst. U. Wis., Madison, 1958-59; instr. English Wilbur Wright Coll., Chgo., 1959-65, asst. prof., 1965-76, assoc. prof., 1976-87, prof. English, 1987-99, chair. dept. English, 1993-99; ret., 1999. Adj. faculty dept. English, Wilbur Wright Coll., Chgo., 2000-03. Contbr. articles to profl. jours. Recipient Outstanding C.C. Faculty award Ill. C.C. Trustees Assn., 1996, Excellence award Nat. Inst. Staff and Orgnl. Devel., Austin, Tex., 1996. Avocations: travel, opera, classical music, writing. E-mail: mstyne@aol.com.

STYNES, STANLEY KENNETH, retired chemical engineer, educator; b. Detroit, Jan. 18, 1932; s. Stanley Kenneth and Bessie Myrtle (Casey) S.; m. Marcia Ann Meyers, Aug. 27, 1955; children: Peter Casey, Pamela Kay, Suzanne Elizabeth. BS, Wayne State U., 1955, MS, 1958; PhD, Purdue U., 1963. Lab. asst. U. Chgo., 1951; instr. Purdue U., 1960-63; asst. prof. chem. engring. Wayne State U., Detroit, 1963-64, assoc. prof., 1964-71, prof., 1971-92, dean engring., 1972-85, prof. emeritus, 1992—. Dir. Energy Conversion Devices, Inc., Troy, Mich., MacMedia, Holland, Mich.; cons. Schwayder Chem. Metallurgy Co., 1965, chemistry dept. Wayne State U., 1965—66, Claude B. Schneible Co., Holly, Mich., 1968. Contbr. engring. articles to profl. jours. Mem. coun. on environ. strategy S.E. Mich. Coun. Govts., 1976—81; sec.-treas. Mich. Ednl. Rsch. Info. Triad; trustee Sci. Ctr. Met. Detroit, 1980—92; mem. ops. com. MACTV, 2000; sec. Friends of Herrick Dist. Libr., 2003; bd. dirs. Program for Minorities in S.E. Mich., Sci. and Engring. Fair of Met. Detroit, pres., 1983; bd. dirs. Midwest Program for Minorities in Engring., Friends of Herrick Dist. Libr.; treas. bd. dirs. Mac Media, 2002—; bd. dirs. Hope Acad. Sr. Profls., 2004. Ford Found. fellow, 1959-63; DuPont fellow, 1962-63; Wayne State U. faculty research fellow, 1964-65 Fellow: AIChE (past chmn. Detroit sect.), Mich. Soc. Profl. Engrs. (pres. 1987—88), Engring. Soc. Detroit (past bd. dirs.); mem.: Adult Learning Inst. (bd. dirs. 1994—99), Engring. Sci. Devel. Found. (pres. 1992—94), Am. Chem. Soc., Hope Acad. Sr. Profls. (bd. dirs. 2004—), Phi Lambda Upsilon, Omicron Delta Kappa, Tau Beta Pi, Sigma Xi. Presbyterian. Home: 145 Columbia #609 Holland MI 49423-2980 Personal E-mail: stynes@macatawa.org.

STYRON, ROSE, human rights activist, poet, journalist; b. Balt., Apr. 4, 1928; d. Benjamin Bernei and Selma (Kann) Burgunder; m. William Styron, May 4, 1953; children: Susanna, Polly, Thomas, Alexandra. BA, Wellesley Coll., 1950; MA, Johns Hopkins U., 1952; LHD (hon.), Briarcliff Coll., 1976, SUNY, Purchase, 1991, Trinity Coll., 2000. Bd. dirs. Amnesty Internat., USA, N.Y.C., 1973-83, chair nat. adv. coun., 1984-94. Author: (poems) From Summer to Summer, 1965, Thieves' Afternoon, 1973, By Vineyard Light, 1995; co-author, translator: Modern Russian Poetry, 1972; contbr. editorials, profiles, articles, book revs. and poetry to maj. newspapers and mags. Chair, judge Robert F. Kennedy Meml. Human Rights Award, 1983—; mem. adv. bd. Reebok Found. for Human Rights, 1987—; mem. exec. bd. Human Rights Watch, N.Y.C., 1975-94; bd. dirs. Acad. of Am. Poets, 1995—, Equality Now, 1993—; chmn. adv. coun. Roxbury (Conn.) Libr., 1990-92; bd. dirs. N.Y. Found. for Arts, N.Y.C., 1986-94, Lawyers Com. for Human Rights, N.Y.C., 1981—, Rainforest Found., 1989-95, Assn. to Benefit Children, 1993—, Folger Shakespeare Libr., 1994-00; bd. overseers NYU Faculty of Arts and Scis., 1994—. Mem. P.E.N. (chair freedom-to-write com. 1983-89, bd. dirs. 1983-93), Coun. Fgn. Rels., Vineyard Haven Yacht Club. Democrat. Home: 12 Rucum Rd Roxbury CT 06783-1906

STYRON, WILLIAM, writer; b. Newport News, Va., June 11, 1925; s. William Clark and Pauline Margaret (Abraham) S.; m. Rose Burgunder, May 4, 1953; children: Susanna Margaret, Paola Clark, Thomas, Claire Alexandra. Student, Christchurch Sch., Davidson Coll.; Litt.D., Davidson Coll., 1986; AB, Duke U., 1947, Litt.D., 1968. Fellow Am. Acad. Arts and Letters at Am. Acad. in Rome, 1953; fellow Silliman Coll., Yale, 1964-99. Jury pres. Cannes Film Festival, 1983. Author: novels Lie Down in Darkness, 1951, The Long March, 1953, Set This House on Fire, 1960, The Confessions of Nat Turner, 1967 (Pulitzer prize 1968, Howells medal Am. Acad. Arts and Letters 1970), Sophie's Choice, 1979 (Am. Book award 1980), In the Clap Shack (play), 1972, This Quiet Dust, 1982, Darkness Visible, 1990, A Tidewater Morning, 1993; also articles, essays, revs.; editor: Best Stories from the Paris Rev., 1959; adv. editor: Paris Rev., 1953—; mem. editorial bd. The Am. Scholar, 1970-76. Decorated Commandeur de l'Ordre des Arts et des Lettres, Commandeur Legion d'Honneur (France); recipient Duke U. Disting. Alumni award, 1984, Conn. Arts award, 1984, Prix Mondial del Duca, 1985, Elmer Holmes Bobst award for fiction, 1989, Edward MacDowell medal for excellence in the arts, 1988, Nat. Mag. award, 1990, Nat. medal of Arts, 1993, Medal of Honor, Nat. Arts Club, 1995, Common Wealth award, 1995, F. Scott Fitzgerald award, 1996. Mem. Am. Acad. Arts and Scis., Am. Acad. Arts and Letters, Soc. Am. Historians, Signet Soc., Harvard, Académie Goncourt, Phi Beta Kappa. Democrat.

STYSLINGER, LEE JOSEPH, JR., manufacturing executive; b. Birmingham, Ala., June 28, 1933; s. Lee Joseph and Margaret Mary (McFarl) S.; m. Catherine Patricia Smith, Apr. 30, 1960; children: Lee Joseph III, Jon Cecil, Mark Joseph. Student, U. Ala., 1952. Pres., chief exec. officer Altec, Inc. and predecessors, truck equipment mfrs., Birmingham, 1956-89, chief exec. officer, chmn. bd., 1989-92, chmn., 1992—. Bd. dirs. Jemison Investment Co., Birmingham, Ala., Electronic Healthcare Systems. Mem. Country Club Birmingham, Mountain Brook Club, Shoal Creek Club, Willow Point Golf and Country Club, Jupiter Island Club (Hobe Sound, Fla.), Seminole Golf Club (Juno Beach, Fla.), Rotary. Roman Catholic. Home: 3260 E Briarcliff Rd Birmingham AL 35223-1305 Office: 210 Inverness Center Dr Birmingham AL 35242-4834 Office Phone: 205-991-7733.

SU, DONGWEI, economist, educator; b. Xiamen, Fujian, People's Republic China, Dec. 12, 1970; s. Jinyu Su and Yuande Lin; m. Nan Chi. BA, Xiamen U., 1992; MA, Ohio State U., 1993, PhD, 1997. Asst. prof. U. Akron, 1997—. Expert Inst. of Fin. Rsch. and Edn., McGill U., Montreal, Can., 1997—. Contbr. articles to profl. jours. Dir. Chinese Fin. Assn. in Am., Columbia U., 1996. Rsch. fellow Sandra-Ann Morsillis Pacific-Basin Capital Markets Rsch. Ctr., 1997—. Avocations: biking, cooking, reading, movies, classical music. Office: Univ of Akron Dept Econs Akron OH 44325-0001 Home: 330 Union Pl Akron OH 44304-1315 E-mail: su@uakron.edu.

SU, GEORGE SHENGHUI (SHENG-HUI SU), chemist, medical researcher, educator; b. Shanghai, Mar. 9, 1941; came to U.S., 1992; s. Cheng-Ye and Zao-Fu (Hwang) S.; m. Qi Qi Zhang, Mar. 8, 1967; 1 child, Junjie. BS in Pharmacy, Shanghai Med. U., 1962, PhD in Med. Chemistry, 1966. Vis. rsch. fellow Inst. Microbial Chemistry, Tokyo, 1981-83; v.p., R & D dir. Shanghai Inst. Pharm. Industry, 1983-89, rsch. prof., 1989-92; rsch. scientist BioGenex Labs., San Ramon, Calif., 1992-95, sr. rsch. scientist, mgr. R & D, 1995-99, dir. R & D, 2000—. Guest prof. Shanghai Inst. Pharm. Industry, 1993—. Contbr. articles to profl. jours. Mem. AAAS, Am. Chem. Soc., Chinese Am. Chem. Soc., Sino-Am. Pharm. Assn. Achievements include patents in field; development of novel synthetic process for antibiotics Amikacin, Tobramycin, cephalosporins and penicillins; invention and development of novel technology for DNA synthesis applied in oligonucleotide labeling and signal amplification. Home: 2 Craydon Ct San Ramon CA 94583-3906 Office: BioGenex Labs 4600 Norris Canyon Rd San Ramon CA 94583-1320 E-mail: geoshsu@hotmail.com., g.su@biogenex.com.

SU, HUI FANG HUANG, mathematician, educator; b. Taichung, Taiwan, Sept. 7, 1955; came to U.S., 1966; d. Bau-Duan and Chia Mei Huang; m. Tsung-Chow Joe Su, Dec. 26, 1976; children: Julius Tsu-Li, Jonathan Tsu-Wei, Tsu-Te Judith, Jessica Tsu-Yun. BA, CUNY, 1977; MEd, Tex. A&M U., 1978, MS, 1979; EdD, Nova U., 1991. Tchr. Pine Grove Elem., Delray Beach, Fla., 1985-98; instrnl. specialist Sch. Dist. Palm Beach County, West Palm Beach, Fla., 1998-99, math. specialist, 1999—2001; program prof. Nova Southeastern U., 2001. Adj. prof. Nova Southeastern U., Ft. Lauderdale, Fla., 1996-2001; presenter in field. Author: Some Ways To...in Mathematics, 1996, Strategies? Tricks? See..., 1997. Bd. dirs. Somerset Neighborhood Charter Sch., 1998—. Recipient NSF Presdl. award, 1998, William T. Dwyer award, Econ. Coun. PBC, 1996, Gov's Points of Light award, 2004; Annenberg Challenge grantee, Fla., 1998—; named one of 50 Most Successful Bus. Women in S. Fla., Fast Track Mag., 2001; named Women of Distinction, Broward County March of Dimes, 2003 Mem. ASCD, Nat. Coun. Suprs. Math., Nat. Coun. Tchrs. Math., Presdl. Awardees Assn., Soroptimist Internat. (Women of Distinction award 1999, Broward County Women of Distinction award 2003). Achievements include development of Math Is Not Difficult. Avocations: piano, hiking, teaching, reading, dining. Home: 2150 Areca Palm Rd Boca Raton FL 33432-7994 Office: 1750 NE 167th St North Miami Beach FL 33162 Office Phone: 561-866-7430. Personal E-mail: huifangt@aol.com. Business E-Mail: shuifang@nsu.nova.edu.

SU, HUNG-JUE, mechanical engineer, educator; b. TsinChu, Taiwan; PhD, U. Mich., 1988. Prof. Tex. A&M U., College Station, 2002—03; dir. Polymer Tech. Ctr., 2003—. Dir. Scratch Behavior Polymers Consortium, College Station, 2001—. Contbr. articles to profl. jours. Fellow, Tex. Engring. Exptl. Sta., 2000—02, 2002—03, Tex. A&M U., 2002—. Mem.: Materials Rsch. Soc., Am. Chem. Soc., Sigma Xi, Alpha Sigma Mu. Achievements include patents for Method for Improving the Impact Resistance and Scratch Resistance of Polymetric Systems.

SU, JUDY YA HWA LIN, pharmacologist; b. Hsinchu, Taiwan, Nov. 20, 1938; came to U.S., 1962; d. Ferng Nian and Chiu-Chin (Cheng) Lin; m. Michael W. Su; 1 child, Marvin. BS, Nat. Taiwan U., 1961; MS, U. Kans., 1964; PhD, U. Wash., 1968. Asst. prof. dept. biology U. Ala., Huntsville, 1972-73; rsch. assoc. dept. anesthesiology U. Wash., Seattle, 1976-77, acting asst. prof. dept. anesthesia, 1977-78, rsch. asst. prof., 1978-81, rsch. assoc. prof., 1981-89, rsch. prof., 1989—. Mem. surg. anesthesiology & trauma study sect. NIH, 1987-91; vis. scientist Max-Planck Inst. Med. Rsch., Heidelberg, West Germany, 1982-83; vis. prof. dept. anesthesiology Mayo Clinic, Rochester, Minn., Med. Coll. Wis., 1988; editorial bd. cons. Jour. Molecular & Cellular Cardiology, London, 1987—, European Jour. Physiology, Berlin, Germany, Muscle & Nerve, Kyoto, Japan, 1989—, Anesthesiology, Phila., 1987—, Molecular Pharmacology, 1988—, Jour. Biol. Chemistry, 1989—, Am. Jour. Physiology, 1990—; mem. rsch. study com. Am. Heart Assn., 1992-95. Contbr. articles to profl. jours. Grantee Wash. Heart Assn., 1976-77, 1985-87, Pharm. Mfrs. Assn. Found., Inc., 1977, Lilly Rsch. Labs, 1986-88, Anaquest, 1987—, NIH, 1978—; recipient Rsch. Career Devel. award NIH, 1982-87; rsch. fellowship San Diego Heart Assn., 1970-72, Max-Planck Inst., 1982-83. Mem. AAAS, Biophys. Soc., Am. Soc. for Pharmacology and Exptl. Therapeutics, Am. Physiol. Soc., Am. Soc. Anesthesiologists. Home: 13110 NE 33rd St Bellevue WA 98005-1318 Office: U Wash Dept Anesthesiology PO Box 356540 Seattle WA 98195-6540

SU, JULIE, legal association administrator; BA, Stanford U., 1991; JD, Harvard U., 1994. With Asian Am. Legal Ctr., L.A., 1994—, dir. litig. Recipient Reebok Internat. Human Rights award, 1996, Individual Award of Achievement, State Bar Calif., 1996, Am. Spirit award, Changing Images in Am., 1997, Adv. award, Nat. Asian Women's Health Orgn., 1998, Achievement award for pub. svc., YWCA, 1998; fellow Skadden fellow, 1994—96. Office: Asian Pacific Am Legal Ctr 1145 Wilshire Blvd Fl 2 Los Angeles CA 90017

SU, KENDALL LING-CHIAO, engineering educator; b. Fujian, China, July 10, 1926; came to U.S., 1948; s. Ru-chen and Sui-hsiong (Wang) S.; m. Jennifer Gee-tsone Chang, Sept. 10, 1960; children: Adrienne, Jonathan. BEE, Xiamen U., Peoples Republic China, 1947; MEE, Ga. Inst. Tech, 1949; PhD, Ga. Inst. Tech., 1954. Jr. engr. Taiwan Power Co., Taipei, Republic China, 1947-48; asst. prof. Ga. Inst. Tech., Atlanta, 1954-59, assoc. prof., 1959-65, prof., 1965-70, Regents prof., 1970-94, Regents' prof. emeritus, 1994—. Mem. tech. staff Bell Labs., Murray Hill, N.J., 1957. Author: Active Network Synthesis, 1965, Time-Domain Synthesis of Linear Networks, 1969, Fundamentals of Circuits, Electronics, and Signal Analysis, 1978, Handbook of Tables for Elliptic-Function Filters, 1990, Fundamentals of Circuit Analysis, 1993, Analog Filters, 1996. Fellow IEEE (life); mem. Sigma Xi (pres. Ga. Inst. Tech. chpt. 1968-69, 72-73, Faculty Rsch. award 1957), Phi Kappa Phi, Eta Kappa Nu. Methodist. Office: Ga Inst Tech Sch Elec & Comp Engring Atlanta GA 30332-0250 E-mail: ksu@ece.gatech.edu.

SU, SUNYU, MRI scientist; b. Jinjiang, Fujian, China, Apr. 8, 1955; s. Guangjun Su and Linfeng Wang; m. Rong Luo, Dec. 29, 1986; children: Charles, Robin. MSc, U. of NB, 1986; PhD, U. of Toronto, 1991. Postdoctal fellow U. of Toronto, 1991—93; rsch. assoc. NRC Can., Winnipeg, 1993—96; MRI scientist Toshiba Am. MRI, Inc., South San Francisco, 1996—2000; mgr., open MRI coils GE Med. Systems, USA Instruments, Inc., Aurora, Ohio, 2000—03; open segment program mgr. GE Med. Sys.-USA Instruments, Inc., Aurora, 2003—. Cons. Toshiba Am. MRI, Inc., South San Francisco, 2000—02. Contbr. 32 articles to profl. jours. Mem.: Internat. Soc. of Magnetic Resonance in Medicine. Achievements include development of solenoidal array concept for vertical field magnetic resonance imaging; patents for sandwiched solenoidal array coil; flexible, region-selectable inherently decoupled sandwiched solenoidal array coil; uneven counter-rotational coil; double counter-rotational coil; quadreture detection coil for interventional MRI; open structure breast coil and support arrangement for interventional MRI; patents pending in field. Office: GE Med Systems - USA Instruments Inc 1515 Danner Dr Aurora OH 44202 Office Phone: 330-995-8586. Personal E-mail: sunyusu@hotmail.com.

SU, WEI, electrical engineer; s. Shao-Zhong Su and Ling Zhang; m. Elaine Y. Yu, Feb. 11, 1988; 1 child, Robin. BS, Shanghai U. of Sci. and Tech., China, 1983; MS, Shanghai Jaio Tong U., China, 1987; ME, CUNY, 1991, PhD, 1992. Sr. engr. GEO Ctrs., Inc, Eatontown, 1991—94; electronics engr., project leader U.S. Army RDECOM, Fort Monmouth, NJ, 1994. Contbr. articles to profl. jours. Recipient Nat. Significant R & D Contbn. award, The Nat. Bur. Edn. China, 1988, Cert. of Appreciation, Office of the Sec. of Def. of U.S., 1994, Cert. of Recognition for supporting worldwide sci. and tech. activities, U.S. Army Material Command, 2000, Thomas Alva Edison Patent award, R&D Coun. N.J., 2002, R&D award, Assn. Electronic Warfare and Info. Operation, 2004, Assn. Old Crows, 2004. Achievements include patents for Recursive Frequency Aging Estimation and Prediction Devices, Methods and Computer Programs for Crystal Oscillators; Phase Magnitude Compensated Tuning for Suppression of Vibration Induced Phase Noise of Crystal Oscillator with Varying Vibration Frequencies; Method and Apparatus to Process Drawing Images; Methods and Computer Programs for Minimizing Logic Circuit Design Using Identity Cells; Built-in Self Testing for the Identification of Faulty Integrated Circuit Chips in A Multichip Module;

Method for Generating Computer Aided Design Programming Circuit Designs from Scanned Images of The Design; Method for Generating Test Files from Scanned Test Vector Pattern Drawings; Method and Apparatus For Rapid And Precision Detection of Omnidirectional Postnet Barcode Location. Home: 40 Marc Dr Englishtown NJ 07726 Office: US Army RDECOM CERDEC AMSRD-CER-IW-II Bldg 600 Fort Monmouth NJ 07703 Office Phone: 732-427-6332. E-mail: wei.su@us.army.mil.

SUAREZ, BENJAMIN, consumer products company executive; Pres., CEO Suarez Corp. Office: Suarez Corp 7800 Whipple Ave NW Canton OH 44767-0002

SUAREZ, GEORGE MICHAEL, urologist; b. Havana, Cuba, Apr. 21, 1955; came to U.S., 1955; s. Miguel Angel and Elena (Sanchez) S. BA, Heideberg U., 1976; MD, U. Dominica, Portsmouth, 1980, Rutgers U., 1980. Diplomate Am. Bd. Urology; lic. physician, Ind., Fla., La. Intern straight gen. surgery Columbus-Cuneo-Cabrini Med. Ctr., Northwestern U. Med. Sch., Chgo., 1980-81, resident gen. surgery, 1981-82; urology rsch. fellow Tulane U. Sch. Medicine and Delta Regional Primate Ctr., New Orleans, 1982-83; resident, chief resident urology Tulane U. Sch. Medicine, New Orleans, 1983-87; attending urologist, dir. urodynamics lab. spinal cord unit VA Med. Ctr., Miami, Fla., 1987-90; attending urologist U. Miami Hosp. and Clinics, 1987-90, dir. Urodynamics Lab., Jackson Meml. Med. Ctr., 1987-90, dir. urology rehab. rsch. program Bantle Rehab. Rsch. Ctr., 1987—; attending urologist Jackson Meml. Hosp., Miami, 1987—; asst. prof. dept. urology U. Miami Sch. Medicine, 1987-90. Cons. Sylvester Comprehensive Cancer Ctr., Miami, 1987—, Childrens Med. Svcs., Miami, 1987—, Avalon Technologies, Indpls., Mentor Corp., Santa Barbara, Calif., Cook Urol., Spence, Ind., Teknar Ultrasound, Inc., Santa Barbara, Schering Labs. N.J., Rorer Pharms., Ft. Washington, Pa.; attending urologist Doctors Hosp., Bat. Hosp., Childrens Hosp., South Miami Hosp., Larkin Hosp., Mercy Hosp., Victoria Hosp., West Gables Hosp., Cedars Med. Ctr., Kidney Stone Ctr. Contbr. articles to profl. jours. Founder, pres. For the Love of Life Found. Recipient Urology Rsch. award Touro Infirmary Hosp., New Orleans, 1983-84, award of excellence Video Urology, 1989. Mem. ACS, AMA, Am. Acad. Pediatrics, Am. Fertility Soc., Am. Med. Polit. Action Com., Am. Soc. Andrology,. Am. Urol. Assn., Colegio Interam. de Medicos y Cirujanos, Am. Confederation Urology, Cuban Am. Urol. Soc., Dade County Med. Assn., European Urologic Soc., Fla. Med. Assn., Fla. Urol. Soc., Internat. Continence Soc., Greater Miami Urol. Soc., N.Y. Acad. Scis., So. Med. Assn., World Med. Assn., Urodynamics Soc., Surg. Aid to Children of the World, Internat. Soc. Urology. Office: Miami Urologic Inst PO Box 143167 Coral Gables FL 33114-3167

SUAREZ, MICHAEL ANTHONY, civil engineer, consultant; b. Havana, Cuba, Dec. 14, 1948; came to U.S., 1961, naturalized, 1973; s. Miguel Angel and Elena Felicia (Sanchez) Suarez. BS in Civil Engring., U. Miami, 1973, postgrad., 1974. Registered profl. engr., Fla.; lic. gen. contractor, Fla. Civil engr. Bert Saul Cons. Engr., Miami, 1969-72, De-Zarraga & Donnell Cons. Engrs., Coral Gables, Fla., 1972-76; spl. cons. Cadillac Fairview-Southeastern Fla. Properties, Miami, 1976 80; pres., dir. Michael A. Suarez & Assocs., Inc. Cons. Engrs., Miami, 1980—. Pres. Summa Devel. Corp., Real Devel. Corp., United Capital Group, Inc.; spl. cons. to chmn. of the bd. Ashland Oil Co.; pres. Gulfstream Petroleum Co., Brit. Oil Refining Co., Ltd. Mem. nat. adv. bd. Am. Security Coun.; chmn.'s adviser U.S. Congl. Adv. Bd.; mem. Rep. Presdl. Task Force, Rep. Nat. Com., Fgn. Affairs Coun. Recipient Presdl. Achievement award. Mem. Nat. Engring. and Physics Honor Socs. Republican. Roman Catholic.

SUAREZ-MURIAS, MARGUERITE C. retired language educator, retired literature educator; b. Havana, Cuba, Mar. 23, 1921; arrived in U.S., 1935, naturalized, 1959; d. Eduardo R. and Marguerite (Vendel) Suarez-Murias. AB, Bryn Mawr Coll., 1942; MA, Columbia U., 1953, PhD, 1957. Lectr. in Spanish Columbia U., 1954-56; pub. rels. officer med. divsn. Johns Hopkins U., 1957-58; asst. prof. Spanish and French Sweet Briar Coll., 1958-59; asst. prof. Hood Coll., 1960-61; lectr. Cath. U., 1960-63, asst. prof., summers 1960-62, assoc. prof., summers 1964-66; asst. prof. dept. langs. and linguistics Am. U., 1961-63, assoc. prof., 1963-66; prof. dept. classical and modern langs. Marquette U., Milw., 1966-68; prof. Spanish and Portuguese U. Wis., Milw., 1968—83, chmn., 1972-75; ret., 1983. Guest Milw. prof. U. South Africa, Pretoria, 1980. Author: (book) La Novela Romántica en Hispanoamérica, 1963, Antología Estilística de la Prosa Moderna Española, 1968, Essays on Hispanic Literature/Ensayos de Literatura Hispana, 1982; editor: Gironella's Los Cipreses Creen en Dios, 1969; contbr. articles to profl. jours.;. Mem.: Nat. Trust Historic Preservation. Roman Catholic. Achievements include designing, building and landscaping two homes. Home: 1315 Cold Bottom Rd Sparks MD 21152-9518

SUAREZ RIVERA, ADOLFO ANTONIO CARDINAL, retired archbishop; b. San Cristobal de las Casas, Mexico, Jan. 9, 1927; Ordained priest Roman Cath. Ch., 1952. Bishop of, Tepic, 1971—80, Tlalnepantla, 1980—83; archbishop of Monterrey, Mexico, 1984—2003; elevated to cardinal Coll. of Cardinals, Monterrey, Mexico, 1994—. Office: Porfirio Barba Jacob No 906 Col Anahuac CP 66450 San Nicolas de Graza Nuevo Leon Mexico also: Apt Postal 7 Loma Larga 2429 con Sierra Madre 6400 Monterrey Nuero Leon Mexico

SUBA, STEVEN ANTONIO, obstetrician, gynecologist; b. Columbia, Mo., July 4, 1957; s. Antonio Ronquillo and Sylvia Marie (Karl) S.; m. Brenda Charlene Crosby, Aug. 9, 1986; children: Bethany Caroline, Sarah Marie. BA in Biology, St. Mary's U., San Antonio, 1979; MD, Tex. Tech U., 1984. Diplomate Am. Bd. Ob.-Gyn. Resident ob-gyn. Tex. Tech. U., Lubbock, Tex., 1984-87; chief resident ob-gyn. John Peter Smith Hosp., Ft. Worth, 1987-88; pvt. practice ob-gyn. Ft. Worth, 1988—. Fellow Am. Coll. Ob.-Gyn., mem. AMA, Tex. Med. Assn. Office: 6100 Harris Pky Ste 245 Fort Worth TX 76132-4107

SUBAK, JOHN THOMAS, lawyer; b. Trebic, Czechoslovakia, Apr. 19, 1929; came to U.S., 1941, naturalized, 1946; s. William John and Gerda Maria (Subakova) S.; m. Mary Corcoran, June 4, 1955; children: Jane Kennedy, Kate, Thomas, Michael. BA summa cum laude, Yale U., 1950, LLB, 1956. Bar: Pa. 1956. From assoc. to ptnr. Déchert, Price & Rhoads, Phila., 1956-76, v.p., gen. counsel, dir., 1976-77; group v.p., gen. counsel, dir. Rohm and Haas Co., Phila., 1977-93; counsel Dechert Price & Rhoads, Phila., 1994—2001. Editor: The Bus. Lawyer, 1982-83. Bd. dirs. Am. Cancer Soc., 1982-95; trustee Smith Coll., 1991-2001; pres. Gasparilla Island Conservation and Improvement Assn., 2001-03. Lt. (j.g.) USN, 1950-53. Mem. ABA (chmn. corp. and bus. law sect. 1984-85), Am. Law Inst. (coun. mem.), Defender Assn. of Phila. (v.p., bd. dirs. 1982-95), Merion Cricket Club, Lemon Bay Club. Democrat. Roman Catholic. Office: Dechert Price & Rhoads 4000 Bell Atlantic Tower Philadelphia PA 19102-2793 E-mail: johnsubak@aol.com.

SUBAK-SHARPE, GERALD EMIL, electrical engineer, educator; b. Vienna, June 15, 1925; came to U.S., 1959, naturalized, 1967; s. Robert and Nelly (Brull) S.; m. Genell Jackson, Nov. 23, 1963; children: David, Sarah and Hope (twins). BS with 1st class honors, Univ. Coll., London, 1951; PhD, U. London, 1965; ScD, Columbia U., 1969. Rsch. engr. Brit. Telecommunications Rsch., Taplow, Eng., 1951-58; mem. tech. staff Bell Labs., Murray Hill, N.J., 1959-64, cons., 1977-78; assoc. prof. elec. engring. Manhattan Coll., Bronx, N.Y., 1966-68; prof. elec. engring. CCNY, N.Y.C., 1968—; v.p. G.S. Sharpe Communications Inc., 1981—. Author: (with A.B. Glaser) Integrated Circuit Engineering, 1978; contbr. articles on network structure and semicondr. theory to profl. jours. Served as lt. Royal Warwickshire Regt., 1944-47. Recipient Prof. of Yr. award Eta Kappa Nu/CCNY, 1985-86. Fellow Instn. Elec. Engrs. (London); mem. IEEE (sr.), N.Y. Acad. Scis., Nat. Trust for Historic Preservation. Home: 606 W 116th St Apt 71 New York NY 10027-7024 Office: CCNY Dept Elec Engring Convent Ave New York NY 10027 also: Knollcroft East Chatham NY 12060

SUBER, DIANNE BOARDLEY, educational administrator; b. Tallahassee, May 22, 1949; d. John Wilkerson and Barbara Ann (Baker) Boardley; BS with honors, Hampton Inst., 1971; ME., U. Ill., 1973; postgrad. Hampton U.; MEd, Old Dominion U., doctoral studies Va. Poly. Insst. and State U.; children: Nichole Reshan, Raegan Latrese; m. Robert B. Suber. Elem. tchr. Greensboro (N.C.) Public Schs., 1971-72; tchr. Newport News (Va.) Public Schs., 1973-77, asst. prin., 1977-79, 80-82, acting prin., 1979-80; elem. prin. Williamsburg, Va., 1982-85; prin. Newport (Va.) News, 1986-89, 91—, program devel. specialist, 1989-91; owner/prin. DBS and Assocs.; adj. instr. Hampton U. grad. sch. edn., 1986—; owner Child Care Resources Inc.; guest lectr. Coll. William and Mary, Williamsburg; owner human resources devel. cons. DBS & Assoc. Mem. Coalition for Good Govt. Mem. Nat. Assn. Elem. Sch. Prins., Nat. Assn. Edn. Young Children, Assn. Supervision and Curriculum Devel., Nat. Alliance Black Sch. Educators, Hampton Crusade for Votes League, Black Child Inst.; presenter nat. conf. Am. Assn. Sch. Adminstrs. State Dept. Edn., Va. and N.C. Mem. Am. Assn. Sch. Adminstrs. Democrat. Roman Catholic. Home: 12208 Penrose Trl Raleigh NC 27614-6804

SUBER, ROBIN HALL, former medical and surgical nurse; b. Bethlehem, Pa., Mar. 14, 1952; d. Arthur Albert and Sarah Virginia (Smith) Hall; m. David A. Suber, July 28, 1979; 1 child, Benjamin A. BSN, Ohio State U., 1974. RN, Ariz., Ohio. Formerly staff nurse Desert Samaritan Hosp., Mesa, Ariz. Lt. USN, 1974-80. Mem. ANA, Sigma Theta Tau.

SUBIN, ELI HAROLD, lawyer; b. Phila., June 25, 1935; s. Benjamin and Freda (Kalen) S.; m. Suzon Bette Rosenbluth, Oct. 21, 1962; children: Andrea Beth Craig, Ben William. BA, U Pa., 1957; LLB, U. Miami, Coral Gables, Fla., 1961. Bar: Fla., 1961, U.S. Dist. Ct. (mid. dist.) Fla., 1961, U.S. Supreme Ct., 1964, U.S. Ct. Appeals (5th, 11th cirs.), 1966. Trial atty. antitrust divsn. U.S. Dept. Justice, Phila., 1962-63; rsch. aide Dist. Ct. Appeal (1st dist.) Fla., Tallahassee, 1963-64; atty. Roth Segal & Levine, Orlando, Fla., 1964-72, Subin Shams, et. al. P.A., Orlando, 1972-96; city atty. City of Orlando, 1980-82; atty. Maguire, Voorhis & Wells, P.A., Orlando, 1997-98, Holland & Knight LLP, Orlando, 1998—. Referee Supreme Ct. Fla., Tallahassee, 1975; mem. Fla. Bd. Bar Examiners, 1982-87, chmn., 1986-87. Mem. exec. com. Seminole County Dems., Sanford, Fla., 1970-74; mem. jud. nominating com. 9th cir. Fla., 1976-79; dir. Fla. Bar Found., Orlando, 1992-00. 1st lt. USAR, 1957-64. Mem. Am. Law Inst., Am. Bd. Trial Advs. (assoc.), Orange County Bar Assn. (dir. 1968-71). Jewish. Office: Holland & Knight LLP PO Box 1526 Orlando FL 32802-1526 E-mail: esubin@hklaw.com.

SUBIRATS, EDUARDO, language educator; b. Barcelona, Feb. 24, 1947; arrived in US, 1993; s. Pedro Subirats and Loly Ruggeberg. PhD, U. Barcelona, Spain, 1980. Prof. dept. Spanish and Portuguese NYU, NYC; prof. Princeton U., São Paulo, Mexico, Madrid. Author: Da vanguarda ao pós-moderno, 1989, Culturas virtuales, 2001, A flor e ó cristal, 1988, El continente vacío, 1995, Linterna Mágica, 1997, One Last Vision of Paradise, 2001; contbr. articles various profl. jours. Office: NY U 19 U Pl New York NY 10003

SUBLER, EDWARD PIERRE, advertising executive; b. Shelby, Ohio, Mar. 24, 1927; s. Leo John and Dorotha (Armstrong) S.; m. Alice Ellen Carpenter, Sept. 8, 1956; children: Leo, Scott, Dorotha. BA, Denison U., 1950; grad. advanced mgmt. course, Emory U. Mgr. product advt. Westinghouse Electric Co., Mansfield, Ohio, 1950-65; mgr. advt. and sales promotion Bell & Howell Co., Chgo., 1965-69; v.p. mdsg. Westinghouse Consumer Products Co., 1969-76; sr. v.p. Ketchum Advt., Pitts., 1976-92, ret., 1992; v.p. Pacific Garden Co., Millheim, Pa., 1998—, sec., bd. dir. Trustee BCB Anglers, Baie Jeanne Assn., Tanglewood Assn. Served with USN, 1945-46. Mem. Am. Mktg. Assn., Am. Assn. Advt. Agencies (regional chmn.), Catawba Island Club, Bus./Profl. Adv. Assn. (Pitts. Advt. Exec. of Yr. 1988), U.S. Power Squadron, Baie Jeanne Assn. (bd. dirs.). Home: 2465 Circleville Rd Unit 122 State College PA 16803-3390 E-mail: esubler@yahoo.com.

SUBLETT, CARL CECIL, artist, educator; b. Johnson County, Ky., Feb. 4, 1919; s. T.T. and Beulah F. S.; m. Helen C. Davis, Aug. 20, 1942; children: Carol, Eric. Student, Western Ky. U., 1938-40, Univ. Center, Florence, Italy, 1945, U. Tenn., 1955-56. Indsl. engr., draftsman Enterprise Wheel & Car Corp., Bristol, Va., 1946-49; staff artist Bristol, Va.-Tennesean & Herald Courier, 1950-52; artist, asst. mgr. Bristol Art Engravers, 1952-54; art dir. Charles S. Kane Co., Knoxville, Tenn., 1954-65; prof. art U. Tenn., Knoxville, 1966-82; juror Watercolor Soc. Ala., Birmingham, 1979, Jacksonville U. Ann., 1980. Juror Bristol Art Guild 8th ann. juried exhbn., 1993. Artist prize-winning watercolors, 1964, Drawing Soc. Nat. Exhbn., 1965, Artists U.S.A., 1971-72, 73-74, 74-75; one-man shows in oil and watercolors, 1995—; numerous exhbns. art in embassies program, 1964—; solo exhibition Greenville Mus. Art, Greenville, SC, 2002-03; featured in publs. Taipei Fine Arts Inst. including Allied Publs. Inc.; numerous exhbns. in catalogs Tenn. State Mus., Nashville, Artist U.S.A., others; retrospective exhbn. Knoxville Mus. Art, 1991, Ewing Gallery, U. Tenn., 2000; invitational show Hampton III Gallery, Ltd., Taylors, S.C., 1992, Union U., Jackson, Tenn., 1991, Collector's Gallery, Nashville, 1960, 93, 96, 2000, Bennett Galleries, Knoxville, 1992-93, 95; featured in Watercolor Impressions, 1999. Hon. mem. Oak Ridge Tenn.Community Art Ctr. Served with U.S. Army, 1943-45. Recipient Purchase Mead Corp. Painting of Yr., Atlanta, 1963, Grumbacher Washington Watercolor Club, 1964, Rudolph Leach Am. Watercolor Soc., N.Y.C., 1972, Purchase Watercolor U.S.A., Springfield, Mo., 1975, Lifetime Achievement award Knoxville Arts Coun. and Knoxville Mus. of Art, 1994, Disting. Alumni award U. Tenn. and Cmty. Adv. Bd., 2000. Mem. NAD (Alfred Easton poor prize 1995), Bristol Art Guild (treas. 1951-54), Tenn. Watercolor Soc. (gold medal 1973, award of merit 1974, 75, 77, 78, 81, 84, 85), Knoxville Watercolor Soc., Port Clyde (Maine) Arts and Crafts Soc., Watercolor USA Soc., Knoxville Mus. Art, Oak Ridge Cmty. Art Ctr. (hon.). Methodist. Home: 2104 Lake Ave Knoxville TN 37916-2802 *We are creatures of history; credit your helpers, share your successes, and the future will reward your time.*

SUBPRASOM, KITTI, civil engineer; b. Phetchabun, Thailand, Feb. 8, 1974; s. Chuan and Vanich Subprasom. B in civil engring., King Mongkut's U. of Tech. Thonburi, 1993—97; MS in civil and environ. engring., Utah State U., 1998—2000. Civil engr. Dept. of Hwy., Thailand, 1997—98; spl. lectr. King Mongkut's U. of Tech. Thonburi, Thailand, 1997—98; rsch. assoc. Utah State U., Dept. of Civil and Environ. Engring., 1999—2000, PhD candidate, 2000—. Contbr. articles to profl. jours. Royal Thai Govt. scholarship, Royal Thai Govt., 1998, 2000. Master: Thai Student Assn.; mem.: Inst. for Ops. Rsch. and Mgmt. Sci. (corr.), Inst. of Transp. Engineers Student Chapters (assoc.). Office: Utah State U Dept Civil and Environ Engring Logan UT 84322-4110 E-mail: sls9r@cc.usu.edu.

SUBRA, WILMA ALPHA, chemist, environmentalist; b. Morgan, La., Aug. 14, 1943; BS, U. Southwestern La., 1965, MS, 1966. Microbiologist, biostatistician Gulf South Rsch. Inst., 1967-74, chemist, 1972-81; founder Subra Co., Inc., 1981. Lectr. Harvard U.; mem. common sense initiative petroleum refinery subcom. and com. on toxic data reporting, EPA. Office: Subra Co PO Box 9813 New Iberia LA 70562-8813

SUBRAMANIAM, SHIVAN SIVASWAMY, insurance company executive; b. Madras, India, Feb. 15, 1949; came to U.S., 1970; s. Kodaganullor Sivaswamy and Seethalakshmi S. B.E. in Mech. Engring. with honors, Birla Inst. Tech., Pilani. India, 1970; MS in Ops. Research, Poly. Inst. Bklyn., 1972; S.M. in Mgmt., MIT, 1978. Indsl. engr. Midland Container Corp., Ridgewood, N.J., 1971-74; mgmt. sci. analyst Allendale Ins. Co., Johnston, R.I., 1974-76, sr. mgmt. sci. analyst, 1976-77, sr. fin. staff officer, 1978-80, v.p., treas., 1980-83, sr. v.p. fin., chief fin. officer, 1983-91, exec. v.p., 1991-92, pres., 1992-93, pres., CEO, 1993-95, chmn., pres., CEO, 1995—. Mem. Fin. Execs. Inst. (membership chmn. 1982-84, Providence chpt. pres. 1985-86), Nat. Assn. Corp. Treas. Office: Allendale Ins Co PO Box 7500 Johnston RI 02919-0750

SUBRAMANIAN, VALAVANUR A. surgeon, director, thoracic surgeon; b. Cuddalore, India, Oct. 4, 1939; MD, Madras Med. Coll., India, 1962. Cert. Surgery, 1972, Thoracic Surgery, 1974. Intern U. Minn. Hosp., 1963—64, resident, 1964—68, NY Hosp., 1968—72; prior appt. NY Hosp. Cornell Med. Ctr., NY; fellow St. Luke's Hosp., Wis.; chief, cardiothoracic surgery Lenox Hill Hosp., 1987—96, dir., chmn., sr. cardiac surgeon, dept. of cardiovascular and thoracic surgery, divsn. of gen. surgery, 1995—; clin. prof. surgery SUNY, Health Sci. Ctr., Brooklyn, NY, 1999—. Mem.: Soc. Thoracic Surgeons (coun. on edu. and mem. services-new tech. assessment), Am. Assn. for Thoracic Surgery (com. on New Tech. Assessment), Internat. Soc. for Minimally Invasive Cardiothoracic Surgery (bd. dirs., devel., officer), European Assn. for Cardio-Thoracic Surgery, Cardiothoracic Surgery Network. Achievements include pioneer of noninvasive surgeries including beating heart (off-pump bypass surgery), coronary artery bypass, mitral valve repair, robotic (Da Vinci Sugical Sys.) and left ventricular aneursym repair; first physician in the country to conduct a procedure known as "midcab", mininmally invasive direct coronary-artery bypass). Avocation: financial investing. Office: Lenox Hill Hosp Dept Cardiovascular and Thoracic Surgery 130 E 77th St 4th Fl New York NY 10021 Office Phone: 212-434-3000. Office Fax: 212-434-4559. Business E-Mail: vsubramanian@lenoxhill.net.

SUCHENEK, MAREK ANDRZEJ, computer science educator; b. Warsaw, May 2, 1949; arrived in US, 1986, naturalized, 1999; s. Tadeusz Aleksander and Barbara Krystyna (Zych) Suchenek; m. Ewa Aleksandra Czerny, July 30, 1974 (div. 1991); m. Cynthia M. Vincent, July 6, 2001. MSc in Math. Engring., Warsaw Tech. U., 1973, PhD in Tech. Scis. with distinction, 1979. Instr. Warsaw Tech. U., 1973-79, asst. prof., 1979-88; assoc. Nat. Inst. for Aviation Rsch., Wichita, 1987-90; vis. asst. prof. Wichita (Kans.) State U., 1986-88, assoc. prof., 1988-89, assoc. prof., chair, 1989-90; prof. Calif. State U.-Dominguez Hills, Carson, 1990—, co chair, 1996—97, chair, 1997-98, 2001—02. Adj. prof. Pepperdine U., Malibu, Calif., 1999; mem. organizing com. Internat. Symposium on Methodologies for Intelligent Sys., 1989-90; program com. Ann. Ulam Math. Conf., 1990-91, Internat. Conf. on Computing and Info., 1992-94; referee NSF, 1990-92, Annals of Math. and Artificial Intelligence, 1992-93, Jour. Logic Programming, 1992-94; presenter in field. Author: (with Jan Bielecki) ANS FORTRAN, 1980, (with Jan Bielecki) FORTRAN for Advanced Programmers, 1981, 2nd edit., 1983, 3rd edit., 1988 (Minister of Sci. Higher Edn. and Techs. prize 1982); reviewer Zentralblatt fur Mathematik, 1980-89, Math. Revs., 1989-91, Jour. Symbolic Logic, 1998-2000; mem. editl. bd. Ulam Quar., 1990—; contbr. articles to profl. jours. Rsch. grantee Polish Govt., 1974-76, 85-86, FAA, 1988-90, NASA, 1997. Avocations: cats, collectibles, swimming, target shooting. Office: Calif State U Dominguez Hills 1000 E Victoria St Carson CA 90747-0001 Home: 5605 Van Gogh Way Yorba Linda CA 92887-5604 E-mail: suchenek@csudh.edu.

SUCHER, CHERYL PEARL, writer; b. Bklyn., July 23, 1957; d. Philip and Fay Sucher; m. William John Macready. BA, Wesleyan U., 1978; MFA, U. Iowa, 1982. Mgr. Muswell Hill Bookshop, London, 1983—85, Endicott Booksellers, N.Y.C., 1985—87; rschr. Pacific St. Design and Prodn. Group, N.Y.C., 1985—89; asst. to entertainment atty./prodr. David Singer, N.Y.C., 1987—90; ind. writer/prodr., 1990—94; editl. asst. Paris Rev., N.Y.C., 1987—91; assoc. publicist Lee Gross Assocs., N.Y.C., 1994—99; feature writer, book reviewer various newspapers, New Zealand, 2001—02. Contbr. fiction and poetry to lit. jours. and mags. (Emily Dickinson Poetry prize finalist, 1997, McGinnis award, 1992, Kenyon Rev. Emerging Writer award, 1990, Lawrence Found. prize, 1984); author: The Rescue of Memory, 1997; contbr. to lit. anthologies. NEA Creative Fellow in Fiction, 1995. Mem.: Author's Guild, Nat. Writer's Union, N.Y. Choral Soc.

SUCHOFF, BENJAMIN, music educator; b. N.Y.C., Jan. 19, 1918; s. Aaron and Sadie (Leishin) S.; m. Eleanor Rosen, Nov. 16, 1949; children: Michael Alan, Susan Carol, Deborah Ann. BS, Cornell U., 1940; postgrad., Juilliard Sch. Music, 1940-41, 46-47; MA, N.Y. U., 1949, Ed.D., 1956. Dir. music Hewlett-Woodmere Union Free Sch. Dist., Hewlett, N.Y., 1950-78; dir. spl. collections and computer program Center for Contemporary Arts and Letters, SUNY, Stony Brook, 1973-84, prof. arts and letters. Lectr. Columbia Tchrs. Coll., 1973; cons. computer applications for music research. Author: Guide to the Mikrokosmos of Bela Bartok, 1970, Curriculum Guide to Electronic Music, 1973, Electronic Music Techniques, 1975, Béla Bartók: A Celebration, 1981; editor: Rumanian Folk Music (Bartok), vols. 1-3, 1967, vols. 4, 5, 1976, Turkish Folk Music from Asia Minor (Bartok), 1975, Bela Bartok Essays, 1976, Yugoslav Folk Music (Bartok), vols. 1-4, 1978, The Hungarian Folk Song, 1981, The Bartók Archive Edition, 1981; Composer, arranger works for choruses, symphonic band, orch., instrumental ensemble. Bd. dirs. N.Y. Bartok Archive, Cedarhurst, N.Y., 1953—; trustee Estate of Bela Bartok, Cedarhurst. Served to capt. AUS, 1941-45. Recipient Founders Day award N.Y. U., 1954; Am. Council Learned Socs. grantee in aid computerized music research, 1966 Mem. ASCAP, Am. Musicol. Soc., Soc. for Ethnomusicology, Music Educators Nat. Conf., Coll. Music Soc., Assn. for Computing Machinery, Internat. Folk Music Council, Music Library Assn., N.Y. State Sch. Music Assn., Soc. Am. Archivists. Office: Center for Contemporary Arts and Letters Suny Stony Brook NY 11794-0001

SUCKIEL, ELLEN KAPPY, philosophy educator; b. June 15, 1943; d. Jack and Lilyan Kappy; m. Joseph Suckiel, June 22, 1973 AB, Douglass Coll., 1965; MA in Philosophy, U. Wis., 1969, PhD in Philosophy, 1972. Lectr. philosophy U. Wis., Madison, 1969-71; asst. prof. philosophy Fla. State U., Tallahassee, 1972-73, U. Calif., Santa Cruz, 1973-80, assoc. prof., 1980-95, prof., 1995—, provost Kresge Coll., 1983-89, provost Stevenson Coll., 2004—. Author: The Pragmatic Philosophy of William James, 1982, Heaven's Champion: William James's Philosophy of Religion, 1996, also articles, book introductions and chpts. Mem. Am. Philos. Assn., Soc. for Advancement Am. Philosophy Office: U Calif Provost's Office Stevenson Coll Santa Cruz CA 95064 Office Phone: 831-459-2328. Business E-Mail: suckiel@ucsc.edu.

SUDAK, HOWARD STANLEY, physician, psychiatry educator; b. Cleve., Nov. 13, 1932; s. Sol and Leona (Simms) S.; m. Diane M. Ressler, Dec. 25, 1955 (dec.); children: Ellen, Nancy, Janet, David; m. Donna M. Miller, Mar. 25, 1995. AB in Chemistry magna cum laude, Case Western Res. U., 1954, MD, 1958. Diplomate Am. Bd. Psychiatry and Neurology (sr. examiner 1991—). Intern in medicine Univ. Hosps. Cleve., 1958-59, resident in psychiatry, 1959-62; clin. assoc. NIMH, Bethesda, Md., 1962-64; chief psychiatry Cleve. VA Med. Ctr., 1964-84; asst. prof. psychiatry Case Western Res. U., Cleve., 1964-74, assoc. prof., 1974-82, prof., 1982—, vice dean Med. Sch., 1985-92; chmn. dept. psychiatry The Pa. Hosp., Phila., 1992-2001; psychiatrist-in-chief Inst. of Pa. Hosp., Phila., 1992-96; clin. prof. psychiatry U. Pa. Sch. Medicine, 1993-94, 97—; prof. psychiatry, vice chmn. psychiatry/human behavior Thomas Jefferson U., Phila., 1994-96; project supr. AFSF Evidence-Based Suicide Prevention Programs, 2003—. Mem. profl. adv. coun. Youth Suicide Nat. Ctr., Washington, 1986—; com. mem. Ctrs. for Disease Control, Atlanta, 1990-91. Editor: Suicide in the Young, 1984, Clinical Psychiatry, 1985; cons. editor Suicide and Life Threatening Behavior, 1988—; contbr. numerous articles to profl. jours., chpt. to books. Dir. Inst. for Urban Health, Cleve., 1990-92. Grantee NIMH, 1972-73, 83-86. Fellow Am. Psychiat. Assn., Am. Coll. Psychiatrists, Am. Coll. Psychoanalysts; mem. Am. Assn. Suicidology (trustee 1988-90), Am. Suicide Found. (trustee 1987—, pres. 1989-91), Phi Beta Kappa, Alpha Omega Alpha. Avocations: biking, sailing, reading, skiing, jazz and classical music. Home: 321 S Lawrence Ct Philadelphia PA 19106-4220 Office: Mezzanine Fl 210 W Washington Sq Philadelphia PA 19106-3514 Office Phone: 215-238-0409. Business E-Mail: hsudak@afsp.org.

SUDANOWICZ, ELAINE MARIE, government executive; d. John Anthony and Helen Mary Sudanowicz. Student, Fontbonne Acad., Milton, Mass., 1974; BA, Boston State Coll., 1978; MPA, Suffolk U., Boston, 1986; grad. Exec. Leadership Devel. Program, Dept. of Def., 1993. Cert. level 2 contractor, level 3 in program mgmt., Mass. Pub. rels. office mgr. MacDonald & Evans Inc. Litho., Dorchester, 1974-78; rsch. asst. Nat. Commn. Neighborhoods, Washington, 1978; polit. cons. various nat., state and local polit. campaigns, 1974-86; telephonist supr., cons. ARC, Boston, 1980-81; adminstrv. asst. Suffolk County Courthouse Commn., Boston, 1981-82; exec. asst. sheriff Suffolk County Sheriff's Office, 1982-86; presdl. mgmt. intern ESD/PK Air Force Systems Command, Hanscom AFB, Mass., 1986-89, advanced copper CAP Andrews AFB, Md., 1989-90; contract negotiatior Hdqrs., Electronic Systems divsn. Joint STARS Program, Hanscom AFB, Mass., 1990-92;

program mgr. Hdqrs., Electronic Sys. Ctr., EN-1, Hanscom AFB, 1992-95; asst. program dir. bus. acquisition re-engring. Elec. Sys. Ctr., Hanscom AFB, 1994-95; dep. commr. for transp. City of Boston, 1995—. Mayor's interagency liaison Boston Emergency Mgmt. Agy., 1995—; guest spkr. Armed Forces Comm. and Elecs. Assn., 2000-; guest lectr. Suffolk U., Sawyer Sch. Mgmt., 2001-; panelist Neighborhood Issues Forum, 2002. Author: Constitutional Vignette, Separation of Powers and Contracting in the Bureaucrat, 1987; contbr. PMInformer, 1989—; also articles; agt., cons Theatre Arts-Play 1988—. Vol., cons. City & State Pub. Agys.-Pub. Sector, Boston; literacy vol., 1988-89; task force Transp. Rsch. Bd. on Critical Transp. Infrastructure Security, 1999—. Recipient Spl. Achievement award U.S. Dept. Transp., 1989, Outstanding Alumnus award Suffolk U., 1990 Mem. Am. Soc. Pub. Adminstrn. (coun. mem. 1996—, mem. exec. bd. emergency and crisis mgmt. sect. 1999—), Nat. Contract Mgmt. Assn. (bd. dirs. 1996—, photographer No. Va. chpt. 1989-90, cert. profl. contracts mgr., nat. chair program mgmt. spl. topics com.), Presdl. Mgmt. Alumni Group (nat. bd. dirs. 1989-90, N.E. field bd. dirs. 1990—, Outstanding Alumnus award 1990), Trustees of Reservations Mass., Dept. Def. Sr. Profl. Women's Assn., Boston Network for Women in Govt. and Politics, Pi Alpha Alpha (pres. Suffolk U. chpt.). Democrat. Roman Catholic. Avocations: art, cross country and downhill skiing, hiking, outdoors, gardening.

SUDARSKY, JERRY M. industrialist; b. Russia, June 12, 1918; s. Selig and Sara (Ars) S.; m. Mildred Axelrod, Aug. 31, 1947; children: Deborah, Donna (dec.). Student, U. Iowa, 1936-39; BS in Chem. Engrging., Poly. U. Bklyn., 1942; DSc (hon.), Poly. U. N.Y., 1976; PhD Hebrew U. Jerusalem (hon.), 2002. Founder, CEO Bioferm Corp., Wasco, Calif., 1946-66; cons. to Govt. of Israel, 1966-67; founder, chmn. Israel Chems., Ltd., Tel Aviv, 1967-72; chmn. I.C. Internat. Cons., Tel Aviv, 1971-73; vice chmn., bd. dirs. Daylin, Inc., L.A., 1972-76; pres., chmn. J.M.S. Assocs., L.A., 1976—; vice chmn. bd. dirs. Jacobs Engring. Group Inc., Pasadena, Calif., 1982-94; chmn., CEO Health Sci. Prop. Holding Corp., 1994-97; chmn. Alexandria Real Estate Equities Inc., Pasadena, 1997—. Mem. sci. adv. bd. Calif. Tech. Ventures, Pasadena, 2000—. Patentee in field of indsl. microbiology. Bd. govs. Hebrew U., Jerusalem; trustee Polytechnic U. N.Y., 1976—; bd. dirs. Mgmt. Edn. Assn., UCLA, 1990-99. Served with USNR, 1943-46. Mem. AAAS, Am. Chem. Soc., Brentwood Country Club, Sigma Xi.

SUDBRINK, JANE MARIE, sales and marketing executive; b. Sandusky, Ohio, Jan. 14, 1942; niece of Arthur and Lydia Sudbrink. BS, Bowling Green State U., 1964; postgrad., Kinderspital-Zurich, Switzerland, 1965. Field rep. Random House and Alfred A. Knopf Inc., Mpls., 1969-72, Ann Arbor, Mich., 1973, regional mgr. Midwest and Can., 1974-79, Can. rep., mgr., 1980-81; psychology and ednl. psychology adminstrv. editor Charles E. Merrill Pub. Co. div. Bell & Howell Corp., Columbus, Ohio, 1982-84; sales and mktg. mgr. trade products Wilson Learning Corp., Eden Prairie, Minn., 1984-85; fin. cons. Merrill Lynch Pierce Fenner & Smith, Edina, Minn., 1986-88; sr. editor Gorsuch Scarisbrick Pubs., Scottsdale, Ariz., 1988-89; regional mgr. Worth Publs., Inc. - von Holtzbrinck Pub. Grp., N.Y.C., 1988-97; mktg. assoc. Harcourt Brace Coll. Pubs., Northbrook, Ill., 1997-98, cons. midatlantic region, 1998—; mktg. assoc. W.W. Norton & Co., Ill., Ind., Ohio, 1998—. Lutheran. Home and Office: 3801 Mission Hills Rd Northbrook IL 60062-5729 E-mail: jsudbrink@wwnorton.com.

SUDBURY, JOHN DEAN, religious foundation executive, petroleum chemist; b. Natchitoches, La., July 29, 1925; s. Herbert J. and Mary Flora S.; m. Jean Elizabeth Jung, July 18, 1947; children: John Byron, James Vernon (dec.), Linda Gail. BS, U. Tex., Austin, 1943, MA, 1947, PhD, 1949; DHL (hon.), Okla. Christian U., 2003. Registered profl. engr., Okla. With Conoco Inc., various locations, 1949-83, asst. to v.p. tech. N.Y.C., 1970-72, v.p. coal research Conoco Coal Devel. Co. subs. Pitts., 1972-83; pres. Ea. European Mission and Bible Found., Houston, 1983-98, pres. emeritus, 1999—. Author: Oil Well Corrosion, 1956; contbr. articles to profl. jours.; patentee in energy field. Mem. Ponca City (Okla.) Sch. Bd., 1965-67; trustee Okla. Christian U., 1968—; bd. dirs. Am. Christmas Village, 2003—. Served with USN, 1943-45. Recipient Frank Newman Speller award Nat. Assn. Corrosion Engrs., 1967 Mem. Am. Chem. Soc., N.Y. Acad. Scis., AAAS, Sigma Xi. Republican. Mem. Ch. of Christ. Home and Office: 3 Devon Mill Pl The Woodlands TX 77382-5304 Home Fax: 281-440-1955. Personal E-mail: jejs@evi.net.

SUDDABY, GLENN T. lawyer; b. 1956; Grad., SUNY, Syracuse U. Asst. dist. atty. Onondaga County Dist. Atty.'s Office, 1986—89; assoc. Menter, Rudin & Trivelpiece, Syracuse, NY, 1989—92; chief asst. dist. atty. Onondaga County Dist. Atty.'s Office, 1992, 1st chief asst. dist. atty.; U.S. atty. No. Dist. N.Y., 2002—. Office: PO Box 7198 100 S Clinton St Syracuse NY 13261

SUDDOCK, FRANCES SUTER THORSON, grief educator, writer; b. Estelline, S.D., Oct. 23, 1914; d. William Henry and Anna Mary (Oakland) Suter; m. Carl Edwin Thorson, July 6, 1941 (dec. Apr. 1976); children: Sarah Thorson Little, Mary Frances Thorson; m. Edwin Matthew Suddock, Aug. 7, 1982 (dec. Sept. 1986). BA, Iowa State Tchrs. Coll., 1936; postgrad., Syracuse U., 1940-41, U. Iowa, 1946; MA, Antioch U., San Francisco, 1981. Cert. tchr. Tchr. various high schs., Correctionville and Eagle Grove, Iowa, 1936-38, 38-40, 41-43, 45-47; chief clk. War Price and Rationing Bd., Eagle Grove, 1943-45; instr. (part time) Eagle Grove Jr. Coll., 1953-61; adminstr. Eagle Grove Pub. Libr., 1961-77; facilitator Will Schutz Assocs., Muir Beach, Calif., 1987-88. Author: Whither the Widow, 1981. Vol. Nat. Trainer Widowed Persons Svc. Am. Assn. Retired Persons, 1989-2002, ret. sr. vol. program, Anchorage, 1988—; pres., bd. dirs. Anchorage Widowed Persons Svc., 1992-94; bd. dirs. North Iowa Mental Health Ctr., Mason City, Iowa, 1959-76, Eagle Grove Cmty. Chest, 1960, Help Line, Inc., Ft. Dodge, Iowa, 1976-77; chmn. Cmty. Mental Health Fund, Eagle Grove, 1966-73; charter pres. Eagle Grove Concerned, Inc., 1973-77; active various civic orgns. Mem. AAUW (charter pres. Eagle Grove br. 1973-75), Alaska Assn. Gerontology (treas. 1992-94), Anchorage Woman's Club, P.E.O., Kappa Delta Pi. Home: 333 M St Apt 404 Anchorage AK 99501-1902

SUDHIVORASETH, NIPHON, pediatrician, allergist, immunologist; b. Bangkok, 1940; MD, Chulalongkorn Hosp. U., Bangkok, 1966. Diplomate Am. Bd. Pediatrics, Am. Bd. Allergy and Immunology. Intern Ch. Home Hosp., Balt., 1967-68; resident in pediatrics St. Lukes Hosp., N.Y.C., 1968-69, Beth Israel Hosp., N.Y.C., 1969-70; fellow in allergy Metro Hosp., N.Y. Med. Coll., N.Y.C., 1970-72; staff Marshall Meml. Hosp., Tex., 1978—; pvt. practice. Mem. AMA, Am. Acad. Allergy, Asthma, and Immunology, Am. Acad. Pediats., Am. Coll. Allergy and Immunology. Office: PO Box 2087 705 S Grove St Marshall TX 75670-5220

SUDHOF, THOMAS CHRISTIAN, molecular genetics educator, neuroscientist; b. Göttingen, Germany, Dec. 22, 1955; Degree in medicine, RWTH, Aachen, Germany, 1977; MD, Georgia Augusta U., Göttingen, Germany, 1982. Postdoctoral fellow Max-Planck-Inst. Biophysikallsche Chemie, Göttingen, 1982-83; postdoctoral fellow dept. molecular genetics U. Tex. Southwestern Med. Ctr., Dallas, 1983-85, asst. prof. dept. molecular genetics, 1987-89; asst. investigator U. Tex. Southwestern Med. Ctr., Howard Hughes Med. Inst., Dallas, 1986-89, assoc. prof. dept. molecular genetics, 1989-91, prof. dept. molecular genetics, 1991—, Gill disting. chair neurosci. rsch., 1995—, dir. center for neurosci., 1998—. Loyd B. Sands disting. chair in neurosci.; mem. molecular, cellular and devel. neurobiology rev. com. NIMH, 1995—. Mem. editl. bd. Jour. Biol. Chemistry and of Neuron; contbr. numerous articles to profl. publs. Recipient W. Alden Spencer award Columbia U., 1993, Wilhelm Feldberg award, 1994, Molecular Biology award NAS, 1997. Office: Howard Hughes Med Inst 5323 Harry Hines Blvd Dallas TX 75390-7208

SUDKAMP, THOMAS, science educator; b. Elkhorn, Wis., Sept. 8, 1953; s. Donald J. and Mary Sudkamp; m. Janice Edwards Sudkamp, Jan. 8, 1993; 1 child, Elizabeth Regina. BS, U. Wis., 1974; MS, U. Notre Dame, 1978, Wright State U., 1981; PhD, U. Notre Dame, 1978. Prof. Wright State U., Dayton, 1982—. Assoc. editor IEEE Trans. on Fuzzy Systems, IEEE Trans. on Systems, Man, and Cybernetics. Author: Languages and Machines: An Introduction to the Theory of Computer Science; co-author: (monograph) Similarity and Compatibility in Fuzzy Set Theory. Mem.: Internat. Fuzzy Systems Assn. (v.p. 2003—), North Am. Fuzzy Info. Processing Soc. (pres. 2000—02). Office: Wright State U 3640 Colonel Glenn Hwy Dayton OH 45435 Office Phone: 937-775-5118. E-mail: tsudkamp@cs.wright.edu.

SUDWEEKS, JAY DEAN, lawyer; b. Ft. Peck, Mont., June 10, 1940; s. Harold D. and Rachel N. Sudweeks; m. Isabell Murray, Feb. 25, 1966. AA, Ricks Coll., 1960; BS, Brigham Young U., 1966; JD, U. Utah, 1969. Bar: Idaho 1969, U.S. Supreme Ct. 1973. Ptnr. May, Sudweeks & Browning, Twin Falls, Idaho, 1969—. Bd. dirs. United Way, Twin Falls. Mem.: Idaho Trial Lawyers Assn. (pres. 5th jud. dist. 1975—76), Idaho Bar Assn. (bd. dirs. bankruptcy sect. 1984—90). Office: 516 2d St E PO Box 1846 Twin Falls ID 83303-1846

SUE, ALAN KWAI KEONG, dentist; b. Honolulu, Apr. 26, 1946; s. Henry Tin Yee and Chiyoko (Ohata) S.; m. Ginger Kazue Fukushima, Mar. 19, 1972; 1 child, Dawn Marie. BS in Chemistry with honors, U. Hawaii, 1968; BS, DDS, U. Calif., San Francisco, 1972. Film editor, photographer Sta. KHVH-TV ABC, Honolulu, 1964-71; staff dentist Strong-Carter Dental Clinic, Honolulu, 1972-73; dentist Waianae Dental Clinic, Honolulu, 1972-73; pvt. practice Pearl City, Hawaii, 1973—; chief exec. officer Dental Image Specialists, Pearl City, 1975—; dental dir. Hawaii Dental Health Plan, Honolulu, 1987—; dental cons. Calif. Dental Health Plan, Tustin, 1987—, Pacific Group Med. Assn., The Queen's Health Care Plan, Honolulu, 1993—. Dental cons. Pacific Group Med. Assn., 1994—; cons. Hawaii Mgmt. Alliance Assn., 1996—; bd. dirs. Kula Bay Tropical Clothing Co., Hawaiian Ind. Dental Alliance; mem. exec. bd. St. Francis Hosp., Honolulu, 1976-78, chief dept. dentistry, 1976-78; mem. expert med. panel Am. Internat. Claim Svc., 1995—. Mem. adv. bd. Health Svcs. for Sr. Citizens, 1976—; mem. West Honolulu Sub-Area Health Planning Coun., 1981-84; mem. dental task force Hawaii Statewide Health Coordinating Coun., 1980, mem. plan devel. com., 1981-84; vol. oral cancer screening program Am. Cancer Soc.; v.p. Pearl City Shopping Ctr. Merchants Assn., 1975-84, 92-93, pres., 1994—. Regents' scholar U. Calif., San Francisco, 1968-72. Fellow Pierre Fauchard Acad., Acad. Gen. Dentistry; mem. ADA, Acad. Implants and Transplants, Am. Acad. Implant Dentistry, Hawaii Dental Assn. (trustee 1978-80), Honolulu County Dental Soc. (pres. 1982), Am. Acad. and Bd. Head, Facial, Neck Pain and TMJ Orthopedics, Intertel, Internat. Platform Assn., Mensa, Porsche Club, Pantera Owners Club, Mercedes Benz Club. Democrat. Avocations: cars, tennis, photography, gardening. Office: Dental Image Specialists 850 Kam Hwy Ste 116 Pearl City HI 96782-2691 Office Phone: 808-455-4191.

SUE, HUNG-JUE, engineer, educator; b. Tsin Chu, Taiwan;, US, 1983; BE, Chung Yuan Christian U., 1981; MSE, U. Mich., 1987, PhD, 1988. Rsch. staff Dow Chemical USA, Freeport, Tex., 1988—95; vis. assoc. prof. Hong Kong UST and INSA, France, 1997, 1999; vis. prof. City U. of Hong Kong, 2001; dir. Polyole Films Consortium, Coll. Sta., Tex., 1998—2001; assoc. prof. Dept. Mech. Engring., Coll. Sta., 1995—2002; vis. prin. fellow Inst. of Materials Rsch. and Engring., Singapore, 2001—02; co-dir. Polymer Tech. Ctr., Coll. Sta., Tex., 2000—03; dir. Scratch Behavior in Polymers Consortium, Coll. Sta., 2001—; prof. Dept. Mech. Engring., Coll. Sta., 2002—; dir. Polymer Tech. Ctr., 2003—. Fellow Tex. A&M U., 2002—; sr. fellow Tex. Engring. Exptl. Sta., 2002—03, fellow, 2000—02. Co-author: (book) Thermal Degradation of Polyamide and Clay Narocomposites, 2003, Mogohology and Compression After Impact Strength Relationship in Interleaud, 2003, Transport Behavior of PMMA/Expanded Graphite Nanocomposites, 2002. Mem.: Materials Rsch. Soc., Am. Chem. Soc., Sigma Xi Soc., Alpha Sigma Mu. Achievements include patents for. Home: 4605 Valleybrook College Station TX 77843

SUE, MICHAEL ALVIN, allergist; b. L.A., Apr. 15, 1956; MD, U. Chgo., 1980. Diplomate Am. Bd. Internal Medicine, Am. Bd. Allergy and Immunology. Intern, resident and fellow West Los Angeles VA Med. Ctr., L.A., 1980-86; allergist Kaiser Permanente, Panorama City, Calif., 1986—. Fellow Am. Coll. Allergy, Asthma, and Immunology; mem. Am. Acad. Allergy, Asthma, and Immunology. Office: Kaiser Permanente 13652 Cantara St Panorama City CA 91402-5497

SUEDFELD, PETER, psychologist, educator; b. Budapest, Hungary, Aug. 30, 1935; emigrated to US, 1948, naturalized, 1952; s. Leslie John and Jolan (Eichenbaum) Field; m. Gabrielle Debra Guterman, June 11, 1961 (div. 1980); children: Michael Thomas, Joanne Ruth, David Lee; m. Phyllis Jean Johnson, Oct. 19, 1991. Student, U. Philippines, 1956-57; BA, Queens Coll., 1960; MA, Princeton U., 1962, PhD, 1963. Rsch. assoc. Princeton U.; lectr. Trenton State Coll., 1963-64; vis. asst. prof. psychology U. Ill., 1964-65; asst. prof. psychology Univ. Coll. Rutgers U., 1965-67, assoc. prof., 1967-71, prof., 1971-72, chmn. dept., 1967-72; prof. psychology U. B.C., Vancouver, 1972-2001, head dept., 1972-84, dean faculty grad. studies, 1984-90, disting. scholar-in-residence, P. Wall Inst. Adv. Studies, 2000, dean and prof. emeritus, 2001—. Disting. vis. scholar Ohio State U., 2000—03; cons. in field; chmn. Can. Antarctic Rsch. Program, 1994—98; lectr. in field. Author: Restricted Environmental Stimulation: Research and Clinical Applications, 1980; editor: Attitude Change: The Competing Views, 1971, Personality Theory and Information Processing, 1971, The Behavioral Basis of Design, 1976, Psychology and Torture, 1990, Restricted Environmental Stimulation: Theoretical and Empirical Developments in Flotation REST, 1990, Psychology and Social Policy, 1991, Light from the Ashes, 2001; editor Jour. Applied Social Psychology, 1975-82;assoc. editor Environment and Behavior, 1992—; contbr. articles to profl. jour. Served with US Army, 1955-58. Recipient Antarctica svc. medal, 1994, Zachor award, 2000, Donald O. Hebb award, 2001, Harold D. Lasswell award, 2001; grantee, NIMH, 1970—72, Can. Coun., 1973—, Nat. Rsch. Coun. Can., 1973—90, NIH, 1980—84, Can. Space Agy., 2003—. Fellow Royal Soc. Can., Can. Psychol. Assn. (pres. 1998-99), APA, Am. Psychol. Soc., Acad. Behavioral Medicine Resch., Soc. Behavioral Medicine, NY Acad. Sci.; mem. Internat. Soc. Polit. Psychol. (v.p. 1999-2001), Soc. Exptl. Social Psychology, Phi Beta Kappa, Sigma Xi. Office: U BC Dept Psychology Vancouver BC Canada V6T 1Z4 Office Phone: 604-822-5713.

SUELTO, CONSUELO QUILAO, retired nursing educator; b. The Philippines, June 27, 1924; d. Catalina Pamplona; m. Anacleto T. Suelto, Apr. 28, 1952; children: Ramona, Anacleto Q. Jr. Diploma, U. Philippines Sch. Nursing, Manila, 1949; BS in Nursing Edn., Philippine Women's U., Manila, 1955, EdD, 1983; MA in Nursing, U. Philippines, Quezon City, 1960; EdD, P.W. U., 1983. Staff nurse U. Philippines-Philippine Gen. Hosp., 1949-50, instr. Sch. Nursing, 1950-61; adminstrv. officer, asst. dean Philippine Women's U., 1961-68; prin. St. Jude Sch. Nursing, Manila, 1968-73, Lipa City (The Philippines Sch. Nursing, 1976-80; dean Lipa City Coll. Nursing, 1980-84, Golden Gate Coll. Coll. Nursing, Batangas City, The Philippines, 1980-84; coord., instr. St. James Mercy Hosp. Sch. Nursing, Hornell, N.Y., 1973-75, 84-94. Mem. adv. bd. PNA of Fla., 1995. Mem. Philippines Nurses Assn. (life, bd. dirs.), Nurses Assn. of the Am. Assn. of Ob-Gyn.

SUELTZ, PATRICIA C. computer company executive; BA in Polit. Sci., Occidental Coll. With Installation and Repair Divsn. Pacific Telephone and Telegraph Co.; from various tech. positions to gen. mgr. Java Software IBM Corp., 1979—98, gen. mgr. Java Software, 1998—99; exec. v.p., gen. mgr. Software Sys. Group Sun Microsystems Inc., 1999—2002, exec. v.p. Enterprise Svcs. Group, 2002—04; pres. mktg., tech. and sys. Salesforce.com Inc., San Francisco, 2004—, exec. v.p., 2004—. Bd. dir. Delphi Automotive Sys., Amgen Inc. Named one of 50 Most Powerful Women in Bus., Fortune Mag., 2000; fellow, Rockefeller Found.*

SUEN, CHING YEE, computer scientist and educator, researcher; b. Chung Shan, Kwang Tung, China, Oct. 14, 1942; s. Stephen and Sin (Kan) S; m. Sheung Ling Chan, May 12, 1970; children: Karwa, Karnon. BSc in Engring., U. Hong Kong, 1966, MSc in Engring., 1968; MASc., U. B.C., 1970, PhD, 1972. Asst. prof. computer sci. Concordia U., Montreal, Can., 1972-76, assoc. prof., 1976-79, prof., 1979—, chmn., 1980-84, dir. Centre for Pattern Recognition and Machine Intelligence, 1988—, assoc. dean faculty engring. and computer sci., 1993-97, disting. chair artificial intelligence and pattern recognition, 2001—. Vis. scientist Rsch. Lab. of Electronics, MIT, Cambridge, 1975, 76, 78-79; invited prof. Ecole Polytechnique Fédérale de Lausanne, Switzerland, 1979, Institut de Recherche d'Informatique et d'Automatique, Rocquencourt, France, 1976, 78, 79, founder, Vision Interface, 1986; founder, co-chmn. Internat. Conf. on Document Analysis and Recognition, St.-Malo, France, 1991, Tsukuba Sci. City, Japan, 1993, chmn., Montreal, Can., 1995; founder, chmn. Internat. Workshop on Frontiers in Handwriting Recognition (hon. chair, 2002), gen. chair Internat. Conf. on Pattern Recognition, Quebec City, Canada, 2002; organizer numerous confs. Author: Computational Analysis of Mandarin, 1979, Computational Studies of the Most Frequent Chinese Words and Sounds, 1986, (with Z.C. Li, T.D. Bui, Y.Y. Tang) Computer Transformation of Digital Images and Patterns, 1989; editor: (with R. De Mori) Computer Analysis and Perception Vol. 1, Visual Signals, 1982, Computer Analysis and Perception Vol. 2, Auditory Signals, 1982, (with R. De Mori) New Systems and Architectures for Automatic Speech Recognition and Synthesis, 1985, (with R. Plamondon and M.L. Simner) Computer Recognition and Human Production of Handwriting, 1989, Frontiers in Handwriting Recognition, 1990, Operating Expert System Applications in Canada, 1992, (with P.S.P. Wang) Thinning Methodologies for Pattern Recognition, 1994; assoc. editor Signal Processing, 1979—, Pattern Recognition Letters, 1982—, Pattern Recognition, 1983—, IEEE Transactions on Pattern Analysis and Machine Intelligence, 1986-89, Internat. Jour. Pattern Recognition and Artificial Intelligence, 1986—, Pattern Analysis and Applications, 1998—, Internat. Jour. on Document Analysis and Applications, 1998—; founder, editor-in-chief Computer Processing of Chinese and Oriental Langs., 1982-93; adviser IEEE Transactions on Pattern Analysis and Machine Intelligence, 1989-92; author more than 300 publs.; patentee in field. Recipient award Fedn. Chinese Can. Profls., 1988; rsch. fellow Concordia U., 1998; Swire scholar U. Hong Kong, 1967, ITAC/NSERC award Info. Tech. Assn. Can. and Natural Scis. and Engring. Rsch. Coun. Can., 1992. Fellow IEEE (advisor Computer Soc.), Royal Soc. Can., Internat. Assn. for Pattern Recognition; mem. (life) Chinese Lang. Computer Soc. (v.p. 1987-90, pres. 1990-93, award 1988), Can. Image Processing and Pattern Recognition Soc. (pres. 1984-90, award 1997). Office: Concordia U Dept Computer Sci 1455 Maisonneuve W Ste GM-606 Montreal QC Canada H3G 1M8 Office Phone: 514-848-2424 x3006.

SUENRAM, ANDY, lawyer; b. Lakeport, Calif., May 24, 1961; BA in Econs., U. Calif., Santa Cruz, 1985; JD, U. Mont., 1988. Bar: Mont. 1988, U.S. Dist. Ct. Mont. 1988. Atty. Erb & Suenram, Dillon. Mem.: ABA (econs. of law practice, natural resources law sects.), State Bar Mont. (exec. com. 1997—, pres.-elect 2001—02), Beaverhead County C. of C. (dir. 1990—91). Office: Erb and Suenram PO Box 1366 134 E Reeder St Dillon MT 59725-1366

SUER, MARVIN DAVID, architectural consultant; b. Phila., Apr. 4, 1923; m. Gertrude Litvin, 1947; children: Marsha Suer Clark, Sharon, Deborah Suer Berman. BArch, U. Pa., 1950. Registered architect, Pa. Ptnr. Suer & Livingston, 1961-62, Suer, Livingston & Demas, 1962-69; dir. tech. prodn. Eshbach, Pullinger, Stevens & Bruder, Phila., 1969-74; assoc. Ballinger, Phila., 1974-79, Bartley Long Mirenda, Phila., 1979-85, S.T. Hudson Internat., Phila., 1986-95; archtl. cons., 1996—. Archtl. works include State Hosp. for Crippled Children addition, 1964, Huey Elem. Sch., Phila., 1964, Dist. No. 4 Health Ctr., Phila., 1967, Stephen Smith Towers, 1969, Foxchase Br. Libr., 1969. Chmn. bd. trustees Phila. Found. for Architecture, 1980-81. With C.E., AUS, 1943-46. Fellow AIA (pres. Phila. chpt. 1968, 125th Yr. citation 1982); mem. Tau Sigma Delta. Home: 305 Overlook Ave Willow Grove PA 19090-2806

SUERO, JOSÉ AGUSTIN, company executive; b. Santo Domingo, Dominican Republic, May 3, 1947; s. Justiniano Vasquez and Amelia Suero; m. Josefina Cuello, Mar. 19, 1972; children: Juan Carlos, Arlene Suero Cuello. Student, Mahatmagandy, Santo Domingo, 1967-68, Corp. Argentina de Production, Buenos Aires, 1970, NYU, 1983, 84, Ctrl. Ednl. Caribe, N.Y.C., 1987. Mgr. prodn. Super Maquet Domincano, Santo Domingo, 1966-71; pres. adminstrn. Products Gaucho, Santo Domingo, 1971-76; mgr. meat Fedco Foods, Bronx, N.Y., 1976-82, Pioneer Super Marquet, 1982-84, Associated Super Marquet, 1984-87, Read Apple Super Marquet, N.Y.C., 1987—. Bd. mem. Esperanza Ctr., 1974-94, Dominican Parade, 1981-84, La Gran Parade of Bronx, 1990; v.p. Ceduca Centro Ednl. Caribe, 1976-90, 34 Police Precinct coun., 1989-92; active Presdl. Commn. Am. Agenda. Mem. U.S. Families of Am., Lions Club. Republican. Roman Catholic. Office: High Power Coalition 580 W 161st St Apt 26 New York NY 10032-6210

SUESS, JAMES FRANCIS, retired psychiatry educator; b. Rock Island, Ill., Nov. 27, 1919; s. Joseph John and Elizabeth Ida (Dalton) S.; m. Rae Love Miller, Mar. 24, 1946; children: Rae Anne, James Francis, John Randall. B Med. Sci., Northwestern U., 1950, MD, 1952; postgrad., Coll. Physicians and Surgeons, Columbia U. and N.Y. Psychiat. Inst., 1958. Diplomate Am. Bd. Psychiatry and Neurology (examiner various times). Intern USPHS Hosp., New Orleans, 1952-53; resident in psychiatry Warren (Pa.) State Hosp., 1953-56, clin. dir., 1956-62; asst. prof. psychiatry U. Miss. Med. Sch., Jackson, 1962-65, assoc. prof., 1965-69, prof., 1969-82; prof. emeritus, 1982—; chmn. dept., 1967-69, 73-75; asst. dean, 1978-82. Assoc. chief staff for edn. VA Med. Ctr., Jackson, 1978-82; vis. prof. Inst. Psychiatry, London, 1977, 83; referee editl. bd. Am. Jour. Psychiatry, Washington. Contbr. articles to med. jours., including Am. Jour. Psychiatry, Jour. Med. Edn., chpts. to books. Capt. U.S. Army, 1941-45. Fellow Am. Psychiat. Assn., So. Psychiat. Assn. (edn. com. 1973-77), Miss. Psychiat. Assn. (pres. 1968-69); mem. Am. Assn. Dirs. Psychiat. Tng. (a founder, exec. bd. 1969-71). Avocations: piano, organ, golf, duplicate bridge. Home: 1415 Radcliffe St Jackson MS 39211-4824 E-mail: jamespsychman@cs.com.

SUFALKO, DYNAH NAOMI JULIETTE, marketing professional; b. Harrogate, York, England, July 18, 1964; arrived in U.S.A., 1967; d. Robert Duncan White and Lesley Marigold Elizabeth Nordyke; m. Arnold Felix Sufalko, Aug. 11, 1990 (div. Oct. 1998). Basic vocat. specialist in mgmt. mktg., AS, Elgin C.C., Ill., 1993; BS in Bus. Adminstrn., Roosevelt U., Chgo., 1999, MS in Integrated Mktg. and Comm., 2002. Cert. trade show marketer, San Francisco State U.; cert. mgr. of exhibits Trade Show Exhibitors Assn. Office mgr. Ko-Pack Corp. of Am., Bensenville, Ill., 1982—86; midwest rep. LDC Am. divsn. Pioneer Electronics, Rosemont, Ill., 1986—87; sales rep. Contamination Control and Devices, Dundee, Ill., 1987—94; project mgr. Star Displays, Elgin, 1994—95; exhibit mgr. Richardson Electronics, LaFox, Ill., 1995—97; account mgr. exhibit group, Giltspur, Roselle, Ill., 1997—99; sr. corp. account exec. Contempo Design, Libertyville, Ill., 1999; mktg. comm. mgr. Gen. Exhibit and Display, Chgo., 2000, Gen. Exhibits and Design, Inc., Chgo., 2000; promotions dir. Gen. Motors R*Works, Detroit, 2003. Records coord., fin. officer Windy City chpt. Operating Coun. Tradeshow Exhibitors Assn., Chgo.; advisor, rev. com. mem. Cert. Trade Show Marketers Program, Boulder, Colo. Scholastic scholar Roosevelt U., Chgo., 1993-99. Mem. Phi Theta Kappa, Mu Alpha Theta. Republican. Methodist. Avocations: dance, theater, golf, pets. Home: 29149 Minton St Livonia MI 48150-3121 Office: Gen Motors R*Works 535 Griswold Ste 500 Detroit MI 48226 Office Phone: 313-596-9155.

SUFLAS, STEVEN WILLIAM, lawyer; b. Camden, NJ, Oct. 7, 1951; s. William V. and Dorothy (Stafre) S.; m. Rochelle B. Volin, Apr. 15, 1978; children: Allison, Rebecca, Whitney. BA, Davidson Coll., 1973; JD with honors, U. N.C., 1976. Bar: N.J. 1976, Pa. 1978, U.S. Dist. Ct. N.J., U.S. Ct. Appeals (3d cir.). Field atty. NLRB, Phila., 1976-80; assoc. Archer & Greiner P.C., Haddonfield, NJ, 1980-86, ptnr., 1986—2002, Ballard, Spahr, Andrews & Ingersoll LLP, Voorhees, NJ, 2002—. Fellow Coll. of Labor and Employment Lawyers; mem. ABA, Pa. Bar Assn., Phila. Bar Assn., NJ Bar Assn. (exec. com. labor and employment law sect. 1985—, chmn. 1999-2001), Order of Coif, Omicron Delta Kappa. Office: Ballard Spahr Andrews & Ingersoll Plaza 1000 Ste 500 Main St Voorhees NJ 08043-4636 Office Phone: 856-761-3466.

SUGAHARA, BYRON MASAHIKO, transportation company executive; b. Jan. 22, 1940; s. Kay and Yone (Kuwahara) S.; m. Nancy Shaw Hall, June 5, 1977; children: Christopher, Abigail, Alexandra. BA, Harvard Coll., 1962. From v.p. to pres. Gt. Am. Lines, Roseland, N.J., 1985—. Mem. Am. Bur. of Shipping. Bd. dirs. The Peck Sch., Morristown, N.J., 1993-95. 1st Lt. U.S. Army, 1963-65, Korea. Mem. Henryville Conservation Club. Tokyo Club. Avocations: fly fishing, golf. Home: Blue Mill Rd Morristown NJ 07960 Office: Great American Lines 5 Becker Farm Rd Ste 4 Roseland NJ 07068-1779

SUGAR, RONALD D. aerospace executive; BSEE summa cum laude, UCLA, 1968, MS, 1969, PhD, 1971. Dir. advanced R & D programs TRW Inc., Cleve., 1981-83, chief engr., dep. program mgr. Milstar Satellite payload program, 1983-87, v.p., gen. mgr. space comms. divsn., 1987-92, v.p. strategic bus. devel. space and def. sector, 1992-94, exec. v.p., CFO, 1994-96, exec. v.p., gen. mgr. automotive electronics group, 1996-98, exec. v.p. spl. projects, 1998-99, pres., COO space and info. sys. sector, 1999-2000; pres., COO Litton Industries, Inc., Woodland Hills, Calif., 2000—01, Northrop Grumman Corp., L.A., 2001—03, pres., CEO, 2003—, chmn., 2003—. Office: Northrop Grumman Corp 1840 Century Park E Los Angeles CA 90067-2199

SUGARBAKER, STEPHEN PHILIP, surgeon, educator; b. Jefferson City, Mo., Mar. 13, 1956; s. Everett Dornbush and Geneva Irene (Van Dyke) S.; m. Clera Jane Perdue, June 24, 1995; 1 child, Stephen James. BS in Biology cum laude, Wheaton Coll., 1978; MD, Cornell U., 1982. Cert. in surgery, specialty in surg. critical care. Intern Vanderbilt U. Med. Ctr., Nashville, 1982-83, resident in gen. surgery, 1983-84, 86-87, Kaiser Found. Hosp., San Francisco, 1988-91; fellow Brigham and Women's Hosp., Boston, 1984-86; clin. fellow in nutrition Dana Farber Cancer Ctr., Boston, 1985-86. Asst. prof. surgery U. Mo.-Columbia Sch. Medicine, 1991-94, clin. asst. prof. surgery, 1994-97; mem. tumor bd., cancer com., critical care com. Capitol Region Med. Ctr., Jefferson City, 1994-98. Fellow: ACS; mem.: Southwestern Surg. Congress, Soc. Critical Care Medicine. Southern Baptist. Office: 603 Ne Brookwood Ct Apt D Blue Springs MO 64014-2918

SUGARMAN, ALAN WILLIAM, educational consultant, national speaker; b. Boston, Sept. 26, 1924; s. Henry and Dorothy (Adams) S.; m. Alice Mulhall, 1974; children: Michael, Susan, Ellen, William, Jane, James. *Son Michael serves as a drug counselor; daughter Susan is a nurse; son William is a vocational school principal; daughter Ellie is a kindergarten teacher; daughter Jane is a social worker; son James is a bookstore manager.* BS, Boston U., 1948; MA, Columbia U., 1949, EdD, 1967; postgrad., SUNY, Albany, 1954-56. Entrance examiner Boston U., 1947-48; tchr. Public Schs. Hudson, N.Y., 1950-54, prin. jr. high sch., 1954-56, prin. sr. high sch., 1956-61; prin. Spring Valley (N.Y.) Sr. High Sch., 1961-67; dir. secondary edn. Ramapo Central Sch. Dist. No. 2, Spring Valley, 1967-69, asst. supt. instrn., 1969-73; prin. Ramapo Sr. High Sch., Spring Valley, 1969; supt. schs. Connetquot Central Sch. Dist. Islip, Bohemia, N.Y., 1973-80, Ft. Lee (N.J.) Sch. Dist., 1980—2000; nat. spkr., cons., 2000—. Adj. prof. N.Y. U., N.Y.C., U. P.R., Rio Piedras, Hofstra U., 1967—; prof. Fordham U., N.Y.C., 1969 *Since public school superintendency retirement, serving as a national speaker and consultant on school violence prevention and especially bullying presentation made throughout the country to audiences involving education and police personnel.* Athletic dir. East River Day Camp, N.Y.C., summer 1949; group worker St. John's Guild, summer 1950; asst. dir. Tenn. Work Camp, Unitarian Service Com., summer 1951; dir. spl. activities Hudson Youth Bur., Hudson, N.Y., summer 1952; exec. dir. Jewish Community Center, Hudson, 1953-56; chmn. vis. coms. Middle States Commn. Colls. and Secondary Schs., 1958-76; chmn. county leadership tng. com., mem. Rockland County exec. council Boy Scouts Am., 1956; bd. dirs. Bergen County Red Cross; corr. sec. Rockland County Negro Scholarship Fund, Inc.; pres. Spring Valley Youth Activities Com., 1956-58; bd. dirs., past campaign co-chmn. Greater Hudson Community Chest; bd. dirs., 2d v.p. Hudson Youth Recreation Center, 1958-61; bd. dirs. Rockland County br. Am. Cancer Soc., 1958-61, Columbia Meml. Hosp., 1959-61; chmn. Town of Islip Health Usage Com., 1973; bd. dirs. Am. Heart Assn. N.J. affiliate, 1993—. Served with AUS, 1944-46, ETO. Recipient Disting. Svc. award Hudson Jr. C. of C., 1960, Ft. Lee Citizen of Yr. award VFW, Bergen County Citizen of Yr. award VFW, 1989, N.J. State Elks Alcohol and Drug Prevention award, 1989, St. Michael's award, 1992, PBA Silver Life Card award, 1993, EIA award Greek Orthodox Archdiocese, 1993; named Adminstr. of Yr., Fordham U., 1990, B'nai Brith Man of Yr., 1995. Mem. Nat. Honor Soc. Secondary Schs. (hon.), Nat. PTA (hon. life), Am. Assn. Sch. Adminstrs., Assn. Supervision and Curriculum Devel., Nat. Sch. Public Relations Assn., Assn. Sch. Bus. Ofcls., Nat. Soc. Study Edn., DAV, VFW, Jewish War Vets., Rotary (bd. dirs.), Phi Delta Kappa (Adminstr. of Yr. award 1990), Kappa Delta Pi, Pi Gamma Mu. Home: 2 Jenny Lyn Dr Northfield NJ 08225 Office: 400 Fairview Ave Fort Lee NJ 07024 Office Phone: 609-646-0702. E-mail: amwsintac@msn.com.

SUGARMAN, IRWIN J. lawyer; b. Dayton, Ohio, June 17, 1943; s. Nathan and Esther (Goldstein) S.; 1 child, Alexander David Sugarman. BA, Rutgers U., New Brunswick, N.J., 1965; JD, Rutgers U., Newark, 1968. Bar: N.Y. 1968. Law clk. to Judge Edmund Palmieri U.S. Dist. Ct. for So. Dist. N.Y., N.Y.C., 1968-69; assoc. Debevoise Plimpton Lyons & Gates, N.Y.C., 1969-79; ptnr. Schulte Roth & Zabel, N.Y.C., 1979—. Bd. dirs. Santa Fe Opera, 1989-94. Office: Schulte Roth & Zabel 919 3rd Ave Fl 23 New York NY 10022-4774 E-mail: irwin.sugarman@srz.com.

SUGARMAN, JULE MEYER, children's services consultant, former public administrator; b. Cin., Sept. 23, 1927; s. Melville Harty and Rachel Wolf (Meyer) S.; m. Sheila Mary Shanley, May 20, 1956 (dec.); children: Christopher (dec.), Maryanne, Jason, James; m. Candace Sullivan, Apr. 2, 1989. Student, Western Res. U., 1945-46; AB with highest distinction, Am. U., 1951. Dir. Head Start, 1965-69; adminstr. Human Resources Adminstrn., N.Y.C., 1970-73; chief adminstrv. officer City of Atlanta, 1974-76; vice chmn. CSC, Washington, 1977-78; dep. dir. Office Personnel Mgmt., 1979-81; mng. dir. Human Service Info. Ctr., 1981-83; v.p. Hahnemann U., 1983-86; sec. Wash. State Dept. Social and Health Services, 1986-89; exec. dir. Spl. Olympics Internat., Washington, 1989-91; chmn. Ctr. on Effective Svcs. for Children, Washington, 1991—. Cons. Delotte & Touch, 1997-98. Program dir. AmeriCorps, Calven County, 2000; vice chmn. Boys and Girls Clubs So. Md., 2000-. Served with U.S. Army, 1946-48. Recipient Meritorious Service award Dept. State, 1963, Alumni Service award Am. U., 1977, Disting. Pub. Svc. award Nat. Acad. Pub. Adminstrn., 1988, Gov.'s Volunteer of Yr. award, 2001. Home and Office: 4023 Evergreen Rd Street Republic MD 20676 E-mail: jule@comcast.net.

SUGARMAN, MICHAEL, physician, rheumatologist; b. Galveston, Tex., May 26, 1945; s. Harold and Amelia Sugarman; m. Hilda Roberta Krug, Aug. 26, 1967; children: Jason, Steven. BS, U. Calif., Berkeley, 1966; MD, U. Calif., San Francisco, 1970. Diplomate Am. Coll. Physicians, Am. Coll. Rheumatology. Rheumatologist Fullerton (Calif.) Internal Medicine Ctr., Fullerton, Calif., 1976-94. Pres. St. Jude Heritage Med. Group, 1996—. Bd. trustees St. Jude Hosp. Fellow Am. Coll. Rheumatology, Orange County Rheumatism Soc.; mem. AMA, Orange County Med. Assn. Office: St Jude Heritage Med Group 433 W Bastanchury Rd Fullerton CA 92835-3404 Office Phone: 714-446-7819.

SUGARMAN, MYRON GEORGE, lawyer; b. San Francisco, Nov. 7, 1942; s. Irving Carden and Jane Hortense (Weingarten) S.; m. Cheryl Ann Struble, June 8, 1968 (div. 1993); children: Andrew, Amy, Adam; m. Cynthia Wilson Woods, Apr. 16, 1994. BS, U. Calif., Berkeley, 1964, JD, 1967. Assoc. Cooley Godward LLP, San Francisco, 1972-77, ptnr., 1977—. Served to capt. U.S. Army, 1968-71. Fellow Am. Coll. Trust and Estate Counsel, Am. Coll. Tax Counsel, Am. Bar Found.; mem. U. Calif. Alumni Assn. (bd. dirs. 1985-88), San Francisco Tax Club (pres. 1990), San Francisco Grid Club, Order of Coif, Phi Beta Kappa, Beta Gamma Sigma. Avocations: skiing, tennis. Office: Cooley Godward LLP 1 Maritime Plz San Francisco CA 94111-3404

SUGARMAN, PAUL RONALD, lawyer, educator, academic administrator; b. Boston, Dec. 14, 1931; m. Susan J. Sugarman; children: Amy J., Ellen L. AA, Boston U., 1951, JD cum laude (Law Week award 1954, asso. editor law rev. 1952-54), 1954; LLD (hon.), Suffolk U., 1989. Bar: Mass. 1954, U.S. Supreme Ct. 1965. Ptnr. Sugarman & Sugarman, Boston, 1967-90, 94—; prof. law, dean Suffolk U. Law Sch., Boston, 1990-94. Mem. Atty. Gen. Mass. Hwy. Law Study Commn., 1965, Mass. Gov.'s Select Com. on Jud. Needs, 1976; bd. bar overseers Supreme Jud. Ct., 1984-88, chmn., 1985-88; advocate Am. Bd. Trial Advocates; spl. master, commr. Boston Mcpl. Ct. Report Supreme Jud. Ct. of Mass., 1990. Trustee Mass. Bar Found., 1980-81. Served as officer AUS, 1955-58. Recipient Courageous Adv. award, Mass. Acad. Trial Attys., 1984, William O. Douglas First Amendment Freedom award, Anti-Defamation League, 1986, Silver Shingle award for svc. to legal profession Boston U. Sch. Law, 1989, Jurisprudence award Am. Orgn. for Rehab. through Tng. Fedn., 1991, Civil Justice award Am. Bd. trial Adv., 1993. Fellow: Internat. Soc. Barristers, Mass. Bar Found., Am. Coll. Trial Lawyers, Am. Bar Found.; mem.: ATLA (gov. 1966—68, pres. Mass. chpt. 1968—70), ABA, Boston U. Sch. Law Alumni Assn. (pres. 1979—80), Boston Bar Assn., Mass. Bar Assn. (pres. 1976—77, chmn. com. on recall of ret. judges 1982—86, chmn. Jud. Adminstrn. Sect. Coun., chmn. 2000—01, Task Force on Jud. Conduct Commn., Gold Medal award 1991). Office: Sugarman and Sugarman PC One Beacon St Boston MA 02108 E-mail: psugarman@sugarman.com.

SUGARMAN, ROBERT EDWARD, writer; b. Syracuse, NY, Mar. 27, 1927; s. David Bernard and Golda Sophian Sugarman; married, June 22, 1959; children: Paul, David. BA, Syracuse U., 1948; MA, Hunter Coll., NYC, 1961. Faculty Cazenovia (NY) Coll., 1963—67, Bennington (Vt.) Coll., 1969—71; asst. prof. SUNY, Albany, 1971—73; faculty So. Vt. Coll., Bennington, 1976—93; publisher Montainside Press, Shaftsbury, Vt., 2001—. Author: (book) Circus for Everyone: Circus Learning Around the World, 2001; author: (prodr.) 8 full length plays. Bd. mem. Hubbard Hall Projects, Cambridge, NY, 2003—. With USN, 1943—45. Mem.: Popular Culture Assn. (chmn. circus area 1992—). Home: PO Box 407 Shaftsbury VT 05262 E-mail: bobsugar@sover.net.

SUGARMAN, ROBERT GARY, lawyer; b. Bronx, N.Y., Sept. 3, 1939; s. Eugene Leonard and Frances (Solomon) S.; m. Brenda Harrison, Sept. 8, 1963 (div. 1984); children: Dana, Alison; m. Surie Rudoff, June 16, 1985; children: Amanda, Jason. BA, Yale U., 1960, LLB, 1963. Bar: N.Y. 1963, Fla. 1963, U.S. Supreme Ct. 1971, U.S. Dist. Ct. (so. dist.) N.Y. 1966, U.S. Dist. Ct. (ea. dist.) N.Y. 1982, U.S. Ct. Appeals (2d cir.) 1970, U.S. Ct. Appeals (10th cir.) 1971. Assoc. Sugarman, Kuttner & Fuss, N.Y.C., 1966, Sullivan & Cromwell, N.Y.C., 1966-72, Weil, Gotshal & Manges, N.Y.C., 1972-75, ptnr., 1975—. Author: (with others) Litigation Strategy and Tactics, 1979, Deposition Strategy Law and Forms, 1980, Masters of Trial Practice, 1988; contbr. articles on intellectual property law to profl. jours. Assoc. counsel N.Y. State Constl. Conv., Albany, N.Y., 1967; pres. Hillel of N.Y., 1986-88. Served to capt. U.S. Army, 1963-65. Fellow Am. Coll. Trial Lawyers; mem. Assn. of Bar of City of N.Y. (chmn. comm. and media law com. 1989-92, mem. copyright com. 1996—), B'nai Brith (internat. bd. govs. 1975-85), Anti-Defamation League (nat. commn. 1981—, vice chmn. 1997—, nat. exec. com. 1988—, vice chmn. 1990-92, chmn. intergroup rels. com. 1992-94, chmn. civil rights com. 1994-97). Democrat. Jewish. Office: Weil Gotshal & Manges 767 5th Ave Fl Concl New York NY 10153-0119

SUGARS, JANEAL M. opera singer, vocal educator; b. Wichita falls, Tex., Jan. 11, 1954; d. Thomas R. and Jane Sugars. B, U. Houston, 1977; M in music, U. Tex., Austin, 1978; profl. diploma, Juillard Sch. Music, 1982. Head voice dept. Houston Music Inst.; mem. faculty Houston Cmty. Coll. Vis. prof. Office: HMI 14511 Meml Dr Houston TX 77079

SUGAWARA, TAKU, neurosurgeon, researcher; b. Kamaishi, Japan, Oct. 12, 1963; s. Kazuro and Noriko Sugawara; m. Mikiko Ishikawa, Oct. 12, 1996. MD, Akita (Japan) U., 1989, PhD, 1995. Japanese Bd. Cert. Neurosurgeon, 1996. Neurosurgery resident Akita U., 1989-95, asst. prof. neurosurgery, 1996—. Rsch. scholar, Med. Coll. Pa., Phila., 1992-94, Stanford U., 1998—; vis. cons. neurosurgery, Kiev Neurosurg. Inst., Ukraine, 1993. Author: Maturation Phenomenon in Cerebral Ischemia, 2001; contbr. articles to profl. jours. Rsch. grantee Japanese Ministry Edn., 1996—. Mem: Soc. Neurosci., Japanese Congress Neurol. Surgeons, Japanese Neurosurg. Soc. Office: Stanford U MSLS # P 355 1201 Welch Rd Stanford CA 94305 Fax: (650) 498-4551. E-mail: taku@stanford.edu.

SUGERMAN, ABRAHAM ARTHUR, psychiatrist, educator; b. Dublin, Jan. 20, 1929; came to U.S., 1958, naturalized, 1963; s. Hyman and Anne (Goldstone) S.; m. Ruth Nerissa Alexander, June 5, 1960; children: Jeremy, Michael, Adam, Rebecca. BA, Trinity Coll., Dublin, 1950, MB, BChir, BA in Obstetrics, 1952; DSc, SUNY, Bklyn., 1962. Diplomate Am. Bd. Psychiatry and Neurology. House officer Meath Hosp., Dublin, 1952-53, St. Nicholas Hosp., London, 1953-54; sr. house physician Brook Gen. Hosp., London, 1954; registrar in psychiatry Kingsway Hosp. Derby and Kings Coll. Med. Sch., Newcastle, England, 1955-58; clin. psychiatrist Trenton (N.J.) Psychiat. Hosp., 1958-59; rsch. fellow Downstate Med. Ctr., Bklyn., 1959-61; chief investigative psychiatry sect. N.J. Bur. Rsch., Princeton, 1961-73; cons. psychiatry, 1964-80; cons. rsch., assoc. psychiatrist Carrier Clinic, Belle Mead, 1968-72, 78-90, dir. outpatient svcs., 1972-74, 77-78, med. dir., 1974-77; dir. rsch. Carrier Found., 1972-79; med. dir. addiction recovery svcs. Cmty. Mental Health Ctr., U. Medicine and Dentistry of N.J., Piscataway, 1990-93; cons. psychiatry Med. Ctr., Princeton, 1972—2001, assoc. in psychiatry, 2001—03, attending, 2003—; clin. assoc. prof. psychiatry Rutgers Med. Sch. (now Robert Wood Johnson Med. Sch.), New Brunswick, 1972-78, clin. prof., 1978—. Vis. prof. Rutgers Ctr. for Alcohol Studies, 1977-83, Hahnemann Med. Coll., Phila., 1978-93; contbg. faculty Grad. Sch. Applied and Profl. Psychology, Rutgers U., 1974-78. Editor: (with Ralph E. Tarter) Alcoholism: Interdisciplinary Approaches to an Enduring Problem, 1976, Expanding Dimensions of Consciousness, 1978; contbr. articles to profl. jours. Bd. dirs. N.J. Mental Health R & D Fund, Princeton, 1968-74; v.p. Jewish Family Svc., Trenton, 1972-78; 1st v.p. Trenton Hebrew Acad., 1972-75. Fellow AAAS, Am. Psychiat. Assn., Am. Coll. Neuropsychopharmacology, Am. Coll. Clin. Pharmacology, Am. Coll. Psychiatrists, Royal Coll. Psychiatrists; mem. AMA, Soc. Biol. Psychiatry, Assn. Rsch. Nervous and Mental Diseases. Office: 256 Bunn Dr Princeton NJ 08540-2859 Office Phone: 609-924-6711.

SUGG, DIANA K. reporter; Grad., Villanova U., 1987; M in Journalism, Ohio State U. Reporter Spartanburg (S.C.) Herald-Jour., AP, Phila.; crime reporter The Sacramento Bee, med. writer, 1993; health reporter Balt. Sun, 1995—. Tchr. Poynter Inst., Am. Press Inst., Nat. Writers' Workshops; mem. nat. adv. bd. Poynter Inst. Works featured in journalism textbooks and Harvard's Nieman Reports. Recipient Kiplinger fellowship, Ohio State U., Pulitzer prize for beat reporting, 2003, Excellence in Journalism award, Am. Psychoanalytic Assn., Robert T. Morse award, Am. Psychiatric Assn., A.D. Emmart Prize for Writing in the Humanities, ARC AL Nakkula award for Police Reporting, local, state, and nat. awards. Mem.: Phi Beta Kappa. Office: PO Box 1377 501 N Calvert St Baltimore MD 21278*

SUGG, ROBERT PERKINS, former state supreme court justice; b. Eupora, Miss., Feb. 21, 1916; s. Amos Watson and Virgie Christian (Cooper) S.; m. Elizabeth Lorraine Carroll, June 23, 1940; children: Robert Perkins, Charles William, John David. Student, Wood Jr. Coll., 1933—34, Miss. State U., 1935—37, Jackson Sch. Law, 1939—40. Bar: Miss. Practice law, 1940-51; chancery judge, 1951-71; assoc. justice Miss. Supreme Ct., 1971-83; county pros. atty. Webster County, Miss., 1949-50; spl. chancery judge Hinds, Scott and Jasper counties, Miss., 1989; sr. judge, 1990-2000. Mem. adv. coun. Nat. Ctr. for State Cts., 1973-79. Bd. govs. Miss. Jud. Coll., 1973-80; literacy missions assoc. Home Mission Bd. of So. Bapt. Conv., 1983—; tchr. internat. class First Bapt. Ch., Jackson, Miss., 1980-2004, tchr. adult Bible class, 1973-2002, mem. fin. com. 1995-98, vision com. 1996-97, legal com. 1998-2001, missions com., 1997-2001. Named Outstanding Citizen, Eupora Jr. C. of C., 1970, Alumnus of Year, Wood Jr. Coll., 1973; recipient Svc. to Humanity award Miss. Coll., 1976, Literacy Missions Svc. award Home Mission Bd. of So. Bapt. Conv., 1995. Mem. Miss. State Bar, CAP (Miss. Wing, squadron comdr. 1974-76), Am. Legion (post comdr. 1950) Democrat. Baptist (chmn. bd. deacons 1964). Home: 1067 Meadow Heights Dr Jackson MS 39206-6021

SUGGS, LEO H. transportation executive; Sr. v.p. Yellow Freight System Inc.; CEO Preston. Office: Preston Trucking Co PO Box 157 Preston MD 21655-0157

SUGGS, ROBERT CHINELLO, academic administrator, educator; b. Newport, R.I., Dec. 23, 1943; s. Lewis Clinton and Beatrice M. Suggs; m. Mary Louise Morrison, July 10, 1967; children: Lawrence Robert, Sarah Shani Dodson, Elizabeth Joy, James Lewis. BA, Gordon Coll., Wenham, Mass., 1967; MS, SUNY, Albany, 1971, EdD, 1979. Certificate in Fund Raising The Fund Raising Sch., Indpls., Ind., 2002. V.p. acad. affairs Cornerstone U., Grand Rapids, Mich., 1992—95; provost Malone Coll., Canton, Ohio, 1995—2002, Ashland U., Ohio, 2002—. Clin. asst. prof. U. of Md. Med. Sch., Balt., 1983—85; vis. prof. Daystar U., Nairobi, Kenya, 1985—86. Minister Nat. Bapt. Assn.; first v.p. Canton Urban League, Canton, Ohio, 1998—2001. Recipient Outstanding Faculty Mem., Messiah Coll., 1981; grantee Author and Adminstrator of Pew Charitable Grant, Pew Charitable Trust, 1989—94; Grad. Fellow, State U. of NY at Albany, 1971—73. Mem.: Kappa Delta Pi. Baptist. Office: Ashland Univ 401 College Ave Ashland OH 44805 E-mail: rsuggs@ashland.edu.

SUGIHARA, KENZI, publishing executive; b. Kearny, N.J., Oct. 4, 1940; s. Kyuichi and Shinobuko (Yamaguchi) S.; m. Roslyn Forbes, Dec. 1966; children: Kenichi, Takeo, Akira, Fumio; m. Nancy Elizabeth Kirsh, June 8, 1981; 1 child, Toshiro. BA, NYU, 1963. Supr. McGraw Hill, Inc., N.Y.C., 1965-67; assoc. dir. coll. product dept. Harcourt Brace Jovanovich Inc., N.Y.C., 1978-82, dir. electronic pub., 1982-83; v.p., pub. Bantam Electronic Pub. div., pub. Bantam Reference Books, Bantam Profl. Books, Bantam Doubleday Dell, N.Y.C., 1983-93; v.p., pub. Random House Reference & Electronic Pub. (Random House Inc.), N.Y.C., 1993-95; pres. Sugihara and Rose, N.Y.C., 1995—; pres., pub. ToExcel divsn. Kaleidoscope Software Corp., N.Y.C., 1998—2001; pub. Iuniverse; CEO, pres. SelectBooks, Inc., N.Y.C., 2001—. Democrat. Presbyterian. Home: 585 West End Ave Apt 15D New York NY 10024-1715 Office: SelectBooks Inc One Union Sq West Ste 909 New York NY 10003

SUGIKI, SHIGEMI, ophthalmologist, educator; b. Wailuku, Hawaii, May 12, 1936; s. Sentaro and Kameno (Matoba) S.; m. Bernice T. Murakami, Dec. 28, 1958; children: Kevin S., Boyd R. AB, Washington U., St. Louis, 1957, MD, 1961. Intern St. Luke's Hosp., St. Louis, 1961-62; resident in ophthalmology Washington U., 1962-65; chmn. dept. ophthalmology Straub Clinic, Honolulu, 1965-70, Queens Med. Ctr., Honolulu, 1970-73, 80-83, 88-90, 93-2000; clin. prof. ophthalmology Sch. Medicine U. Hawaii, 1997. Maj. M.C., AUS, 1968-70. Decorated Hawaiian N.G. Commendation medal, 1968. Fellow ACS; mem. AMA, Hawaii Med. Assn., Honolulu County Med. Soc., Am. Acad. Ophthalmology, Contact Lens Assn. Ophthalmologists, Pacific Coast Oto-Ophthal. Soc., Pan-Pacific Surg. Assn., Am. Soc. Cataract and Refractive Surgery, Am. Glaucoma Soc., Internat. Assn. Ocular Surgeons, Am. Soc. Contemporary Ophthalmology, Washington U. Eye Alumni Assn., Hawaii Ophthal. Soc., Rsch. To Prevent Blindness. Home: 2398 Aina Lani Pl Honolulu HI 96822-2024 Office: 1380 Lusitana St Ste 714 Honolulu HI 96813-2443

SUGIOKA, KENNETH, anesthesiologist, educator; b. Hollister, Calif., Apr. 19, 1920; s. Seigiro and Kameno (Takeda) S.; m. Mary Trabue Hinternhoff, June 18, 1966; children— Stephanie, Colin, Kimi (by previous marriage), Nathan, Brian. BS, U. Denver, 1945; MD, Washington U., St. Louis, 1949. Intern, resident U. Iowa, 1949-52, instr. anesthesiology, 1952; asst. prof. surgery N.C. Meml. Hosp., Chapel Hill, 1954-62, assoc. prof. surgery, 1962-64; prof. surgery, chmn. div. anesthesiology U. N.C., 1964-69, prof., chmn. dept. anesthesiology, 1969-83; prof. anesthesiology and physiology Duke U., 1985—. Vis. prof. Physiol. Inst., U. Göttingen, Fed. Republic of Germany, 1963, Kings Coll. Med. Sch., London, Max-Planck Inst. Physiology, Dortmund, Fed. Republic of Germany, 1976-77; vis. prof. Royal Coll. Surgeons, Eng., 1983-84; dir. Morgan Creek Land Co.; mem. adv. com. on anesthetic and life support drugs FDA; bd. alumni U. Denver. Author textbook of clin. anesthesiology; contbr. articles to profl. jours. Pres. Triangle Opera Theater. Served to capt., M.C. USAF, 1952-54. Recipient spl. research fellowship NIH, 1961-62 Fellow Faculty Anaesthesiologists Royal Coll. Surgeons (Eng.) (hon.); mem. Soc. Acad. Anesthesia Chairmen (past pres.) Home: 319 Bayberry Dr Chapel Hill NC 27517-9116

SUGISAKI, SHIGEMITSU, international bank official; b. 1941; married; three children. BA, U. Tokyo, 1963; M Internat. Affairs, Columbia U., 1967. Mem. Minister's Secretariate, to various banking positions Min. of Finance, Japan, 1964-76; various to dep. vice min. of finance for internat. affairs Min. of Fin., Japan, 1979-90, 90-91, dep. dir. gen. Internat. Fin. Bur., 1991-92; personal asst. to pres. Asian Devel. Bank, 1976-79; commr. Tokyo Regional Taxation Bur., 1992-93; sec. gen. Exec. Bur. Securities and Exch. Surveillance Commn., 1993-94; spl. advisor to mng. dir. IMF, Washington, 1994-97, dep. mng. dir., 1997—. Office: Internat Monetary Fund 700 19th St NW Washington DC 20431-0001

SUGIYAMA, TOKU MARY, retired school administrator; b. Sacramento, Sept. 6, 1921; d. Sakae and Kuniko (Kosaka) Koda; m. Yone J. Sugiyama, Apr. 5, 1952; m. George Y. Morishita, Mar. 23, 1942 (dec. Mar. 1949); children: Maeona, Carolyn, George. Jr. cert., U. Calif., Berkeley, 1941; BA, Towson State U., 1980, MA, 1984. Tchr. Poston Relocation Ctr., Ariz., 1941-44; purchasing agt. U.S. Dept. Def., Tokyo Ordnance Depot, 1952-56; instr. Ikebana Sogetsu Sch., Tokyo, 1956-67; exec. dir. Sogetsu USA, sch. Japanese flower arrangement, 1967-93; ret., 1993. Author: Sogetsu Ikebana Notes, 1997. Recipient Mohan Sho, Sogetsu Sch., 1960, Sofu Sho, 1967, Flower Arranger of Yr. award Nat. Coun. State Garden Clubs, 1979, 1st Sofu Teshigahara Meml. award, 1991, Japan's Ministry of Fgn. Affairs award to commemmorate 157th anniversary of U.S. and Japan's relationship, 2004. Mem. Md. Fedn. Garden Clubs, Ikebana Internat. (charter), Balt.-Kawasaki Sister City Cultural Com. Home: 959 Ellendale Dr Baltimore MD 21286-1511 E-mail: msugiy8305@aol.com.

SUGRUE, DENNIS PATRICK, clinical psychologist; b. Detroit, Oct. 28, 1949; s. Francis Michael and Diane (Reckinger) S.; m. Bernadette Tomasik, June 11, 1976; children: Dennis Patrick II, Sean Michael Francis. BA magna cum laude, Sacred Heart Sem., 1971; MA, U. Detroit, 1976; MS, Ea. Mich. U., 1976; PhD, U. Windsor, Ont., Can., 1981. Sr. staff psychologist Henry Ford Hosp., Detroit, 1979-85; clin. instr. psychiatry Med. Sch. U. Mich., 1985-92; founder, dir. Henry Ford Ctr. Human Sexuality, Farmington Hills, Mich., 1986-95; asst. clin. prof. psychiatry Med. Sch. U. Mich., Ann Arbor, 1992-93; regional clin. dir. dept. psychiatry Henry Ford Hosp., West Bloomfield, Mich., 1993-95; asoc. divsn. head outpatient psychiatry Henry Ford Health Sys., Detroit, 1995-98; pvt. practice Bloomfield Hills, Mich., 1998—. Asst. adj. prof. psychiatry Coll. Human Medicine Mich. State U., 1991; lectr. on human sexuality; cons. U. Mich. Comprehensive Gender Svcs. Program, 1994—; clin. assoc. prof. psychiatry Med. Sch. U. Mich., Ann Arbor, 1999—. Co-author: Sex Matters for Women, 2002; contbr. chpts. in books, articles to profl. jours. Den leader Farmington Hills Boy Scouts Am., 1988-91; coach South Farmington Little League Baseball, Farmington Hills, 1990-96. Mem. Harry Benjamin Internat. Gender Dysphoria Assn., Internat. Coun. Psychologists (chair counseling and psychotherapy), Internat. Soc. for Study of Women's Sexual Health, Soc. Sci. Study Sex, Am. Assn. Sex Educators, Counselors and Therapists (Mich. chair, profl. edn. chair, bd. dirs., cert. sex therapist, diplomate in sex therapy, pres.), Phi Kappa Phi. Roman Catholic. Avocations: golf, bridge, tae kwon do (1st degree black belt). Office: Affil Psychologists Mich 74 W Long Lake Ste 104 Bloomfield Hills MI 48304-2770

SUH, JINWOO, computer scientist; s. Jungwhan and Heeyul Suh; m. Chunho Suh; children: Christopher, Justin, Jessica. BS, Dongguk U., Seoul, Korea, 1988; MS, Korea Advanced Inst. Sci. and Tech., Seoul, 1990; PhD, U. So. Calif., LA, 1999. Rsch. asst. U. of So. Calif., LA, 1996—99; computer scientist U. of So. Calif. - ISI, Arlington, Va., 1999—. Scholar, DAEWOO Electronics Co., Ltd., 1994-1999. Mem.: IEEE. Achievements include research in computer architecture, algorithms, parallel processing, performance modeling and evaluations. Office: Univ of So Calif - ISI 3811 N Fairfax Dr Arlington VA 22203

SUH, JUNG SOOK KY, management consultant, educator; d. Keum Joon and Jung Ja Suh. BA, Calif. State U., Fullerton, 1996; MS in Orgnl. Psychology, Alliant Internat. U., 2001, PhD, 2003; postgrad., Oxford (Eng.) U., 2000. V.p. Packy B., Inc., Bellflower, Calif., 1995—2001; cons. Optimal Mgmt. Consulting, Long Beach, Calif., 2001—. Adj. faculty Long Beach City Coll., 2002—, Am. InterContinental U., Playa Del Rey, Calif. Mem. Peral Chorus SGI, USA, L.A., 2002—02. Mem.: ASTD (assoc.), Am. Mgmt. Assn. (assoc.), Soc. for Indsl. and Orgnl. Psychology (assoc.), Acad. Mktg. Sci. (assoc.), Acad. Mgmt. (assoc.). Office: 819 Wright Ave Apt 15 Pasadena CA 91104-4468

SUH, NAM PYO, mechanical engineering educator; b. Seoul, Apr. 22, 1936; arrived in U.S., 1954, naturalized, 1963; s. Doo Soo and Joon Joo (Lee) S.; m. Young Ja Surh; children: Mary M., Helen H., Grace J., Caroline Y. SB, MIT, 1959, SM, 1961; PhD, Carnegie-Mellon U., 1964; D of Engring. (hon.), Worcester Poly. Inst., 1986; LHD (hon.), U. Mass., Lowell, 1988; D of Tech. (hon.), Royal Inst. Tech., Sweden, 2000. Devel. engr. Guild Plastics Inc., Cambridge, Mass., 1958-60; sr. rsch. engr., project mgr. USM Corp., Beverly, Mass., 1961-65; asst. prof. U. SC, Columbia, 1965-68, assoc. prof., 1968-69; assoc. prof. mech. engring. MIT, Cambridge, 1970-75, prof., 1975—, Ralph E. and Eloise F. Cross prof., 1989—, dir. Lab. Mfg. and Productivity, 1977-84, dir. industry polymer processing program, 1973-84, dir. Mfg. Inst. (now Park Ctr. for Complex Sys.), 1989—, Cross prof., dept. head mech. engring., 1991-2001; presdl. appointee asst. dir. for engring. NSF, Washington, 1984-88. Bd. dirs. Trexell, Inc. (formerly Axiomatics Corp.), Woburn, Mass., Axiomatic Design Software, Inc., Boston, Integrated Cir. Sys., Inc., Valley Forge, Pa., Tribotek, Inc., Burlington, Mass., Parker Vision, Inc., Jacksonville, Fla., Therma Wave, Inc., Fremont, Calif.; cons. Lawrence Livermore Nat. Lab.; advisor Korea Elec. Power Rsch. Inst.; former mem. sci. and tech. rev. bd. Nat. Engring. Lab., mem. NRC rev. panel, 1986—90; mem. vis. com. (statutory) Nat. Inst. Stds. and Tech., 1990—94; mem. tech. adv. com. Alcan Aluminum Corp., 1989—90; editor advanced mfg. series Oxford U. Press; hon. prof. Univ. Hong Kong, 2003—; disting. vis. prof. Korea Advanced Inst. of Sci. and Tech., 2002—. Author (with A.P.L. Turner): Mechanical Behavior of Solids, 1975; author: The Principles of Design, 1990; author: (with others) Manufacturing Engineering, 1990; author: Axiomatic Design: Advances and Applications, 2001, Complexity: Theory and Applications, 2004; co-author: Axiomatic Design and Fabrication of Composite Structures, 2004; editor (with N. Saka): Fundamentals of Tribology, 1980; editor: (with N. Sung) Science and Technology of Polymer Procs., 1979; editor: The Delamination Theory of Wear, 1977; editor: (with B.M. Kramer) University/Industry Cooperation, 1982; former co-editor-in-chief Robotics and Computer Aided Manufacturing, contbr. over 280 articles to profl. jours. Former chmn. bd. Korean-Am. Soc. New Eng., 1979. Named Fed. Engr. of Yr., NSF/NSPE, 1987; recipient Best Paper award, Soc. Plastics Engrs., 1981, Citation Classic, Inst. for Sci. Info., 1981, F.W. Taylor Rsch. award, Soc. Mfg. Engrs., 1986, Disting. Svcs. award, NSF, 1988, Mainstream Am. award, 1991, scholarly award, Korea Broadcasting Svc., 1994, The Mensforth Internat. Gold Medal, U.K. Instn. Elec. Engrs., 2000, The Hills Millennium Internat. award, U.K. Instn. Engr. Designers, 2001; USM Corp. fellow, 1962—63. Fellow ASME (Gustus L. Larson Meml. award 1976, Blackall award 1982, W.T. Ennor Mfg. Tech. award 1993, Best Tribology Paper award 1993, Ho-Am. prize for Engring. Ho.-Am. com. 1997), Soc. Mfg. Engrs.; mem. AAAS, Am. Soc. for Engring. Edn. (Centennial medal 1993), Internat. Instn. for Prodn. Engring., Royal Swedish Acad. Engring. Sci. (fgn.), Korean Acad. Sci. and Engring., Sigma Xi, Pi Tau Sigma, Phi Kappa Phi. Achievements include holder 50 U.S. patents. Office: MIT Rm 35-237 Dept Mech Engring Cambridge MA 02139

SUHR, PAUL AUGUSTINE, lawyer; b. Sonwunri, Chonbuk, Korea, Jan. 20, 1940; arrived in US, 1966; s. Chong-ju and Oksuk (Pang) So; m. Angeline M. Kang Suhr; 1 child, Christopher. BA, Campbell Coll., Buies Creek, N.C., 1968; MA, U. N.C., Greensboro, 1970; MS, U. N.C., Chapel Hill, 1975; JD, N.C. Cen. U., 1988. Bar: N.C. 1989, U.S. Dist. Ct. (ea. and mid. dist.) N.C. 1989, U.S. Ct. Appeals D.C. 1990, U.S. Ct. Appeals (4th cir.) 1992. Bibliographer N.C. Div. of State Libr., Raleigh, 1975-78; dir. Pender County Pub. Libr., Burgaw, N.C., 1978-80; libr. Tob. Lit. Svc., N.C. State U., Raleigh, 1980-85; pvt. practice law Law Offices of Paul A. Suhr, PLLC, Raleigh and Fayetteville, N.C., 1989—. Author short stories and novelettes various lit. mags., jours. and revs. Mem. Human Resources and Human Rels. Adv. Commn., City of Raleigh, 1990-95, chmn., 1994-95. N.C. Humanities Com. grantee, 1979-80; recipient Presdl. award President of Korea, 1992. Mem. ABA, ATLA, Am. Immigration Lawyers Assn., NC Bar Assn., NC Trial Lawyers Assn., Wake County Bar Assn. (bd. dirs. 1996-97, 2003—), DC Bar Assn. Democrat. Roman Catholic. Avocations: gardening, fishing, writing. Office: 1110 Navaho Dr Ste 502 Raleigh NC 27609-7322 Office Phone: 919-876-4707. E-mail: paulsuhr@aol.com.

SUHRE, WALTER ANTHONY, JR., retired lawyer, brewery executive; b. Cin., Jan. 17, 1933; s. Walter A. and Elizabeth V. (Heimbuch) S. BS in Bus. Adminstrn., Northwestern U., 1956; LL.B. with honors, U. Cin., 1962. Bar: Ohio 1962, Mo. 1982. Assoc. Taft, Stettinius & Hollister, Cin., 1962-65; with Eagle-Picher Industries, Inc., Cin., 1965-82, v.p., gen. counsel, 1970-82; v.p., gen. counsel Anheuser-Busch Cos., Inc., St. Louis, 1982-93; ret., 1994. Served with USMC, 1956-59. Republican. Presbyterian. Home: 48 Woodcliffe Rd Saint Louis MO 63124-1336 Personal E-mail: suhre@charter.net.

SUHRHEINRICH, RICHARD FRED, federal judge; b. Lincoln City, Ind., 1936; BS, Wayne State U., 1960; JD cum laude, Detroit Coll. Law, 1963; LLM, U. Va., 1990; LLM (hon.), Detroit Coll. Law, 1992. Bar: Mich. Law clerk Stringari, Fritz & Fiott, 1963; assoc. Moll, Desenberg, Purdy, Glover & Bayer, 1963—67; asst. prosecutor Macomb County, 1967; ptnr. Rogensues, Richard & Suhrheinrich, 1967; assoc. Moll, Desenberg, Purdy, Glover & Bayer, 1967—68; ptnr. Kitch, Suhrheinrich, Saurbier & Drutchas, 1968—84; assoc. prof. of law Detroit Coll. of law, 1975—85; judge U.S. Dist. Ct. (ea. dist.) Mich., Detroit, 1984—90, U.S. Ct. Appeals (6th Cir.), Lansing, 1990—2001, sr. judge, 2001—. Law prof. Thomas M Cooley Law Sch., 2003—; mem. State of Mich. Atty. Discipline Bd., Atty. Grievance Commn. Bd. trustees Brighton Hosp. Mem.: Ingham County Bar Assn., State Bar Mich., Mich. State Univ.-Detroit (bd. trustees 1985—2003, pres. 1999—2001). Office: US Ct Appeals 6th Cir USPO & Fed Bldg 315 W Allegan St Rm 241 Lansing MI 48933-1514

SUID, LAWRENCE H. historian, writer; b. Cleve., July 13, 1938; s. Ben Suid and Regina Reiter. BA in History and English cum laude, Case Western Res. U., 1961, PhD in Am. Studies, 1980; MA in Russian History, Duke U., 1962; MFA in Theater Arts/Film, Brandeis U., 1971. Cons., presenter in field. Author: Guts & Glory: Great American War Movies, 1978, The Army's Nuclear Power Program: The Evolution of a Support Agency, 1990, A History of the Armed Forces Radio and Television Service, 1993, Sailing on the Silver Screen, 1996, Guts & Glory: The Making of the American Military Image in Film, 2002, Stars and Stripes on Screen: A Comprehensive Guide to Portrayals of the American Military in Film, 2004; contbr. articles to profl. jours., newspapers, chapters to books; editor: Air Force, 1983, Film & Propaganda in America: A Documentary History, 1991. Home: 19 C Hillside Rd Greenbelt MD 20770 Personal E-mail: lhsuid@aol.com.

SUINN, RICHARD MICHAEL, psychologist; b. Honolulu, May 8, 1933; s. Maurice and Edith (Wong) S.; m. Grace D. Toy, July 26, 1958; children: Susan, Randall, Staci, Bradley. Student, U. Hawaii, 1951-53; BA summa cum laude, Ohio State U., 1955; MA in Clin. Psychology, Stanford U., 1957, PhD in Clin. Psychology, 1959; Doctorate (hon.), Calif. Sch. Profl. Psychology, 1999. Lic. psychologist, Colo.; diplomate Am. Bd. Profl. Psychology. Counselor Stanford (Calif.) U., 1958-59, rsch. assoc. Med. Sch., 1964-66; asst. prof. psychology Whitman Coll., Walla Walla, Wash., 1959-64; assoc. prof. U. Hawaii, Honolulu, 1966-68; prof. Colo. State U., Ft. Collins, 1968-99, head dept. psychology, 1972-93, emeritus prof., 2000—. Cons. in field; psychologist U.S. Ski Teams, 1976, Olympic Games, U.S. Women's Track and Field, 1980 Olympic Games, U.S. Ski Jumping Team, 1988, U.S. Shooting Team, 1994; mem. sports psychology adv. com. U.S. Olympic Com., 1983-89; reviewer NIMH, 1977-80, 94-98. Author: The Predictive Validity of Projective Measures, 1969, Fundamentals of Behavior Pathology, 1970, The Innovative Psychological Therapies, 1975, The Innovative Medical-Psychiatric Therapies, 1976, Psychology in Sport: Methods and Applications, 1980, Fundamentals of Abnormal Psychology, 1984, 88, Seven Steps to Peak Performance, 1986, Anxiety Management Training, 1990; editorial bd.: Jour. Cons. and Clin. Psychology, 1973-86, Jour. Counseling Psychology, 1974-91, Behavior Therapy, 1977-80, Behavior Modification, 1977-78, Jour. Behavioral Medicine, 1978-83, Behavior Counseling Quar., 1979-83, Jour. Sports Psychology, 1980-91, Clin. Psychology: Science and Practice, 1994-97, Professional Psychology, 1994-97; author: tests Math. Anxiety Rating Scale, Suinn Test Anxiety Behavior Scale, Suinn-Lew Asian Self-identity Acculturation Scale. Mem. City Council, Ft. Collins, 1975-79, mayor, 1978-79; mem. Gov.'s Mental Health Adv. Council, 1983, Colo. Bd. Psychologist Examiners, 1983-86. Recipient cert. merit U.S. Ski Team, 1976, APA Career Contbn. to Edn. award, 1995; NIMH grantee, 1963-64; Office Edn. grantee, 1970-71. Fellow APA (chmn. bd. ethnic minority affairs 1982-83, chmn. edn. and tng. bd. 1986-87, policy and planning bd. 1987-89, publs. bd. 1993-97, bd. dirs. 1990-93, pres.-elect 1998, pres. 1999, vice chair membership com. 2003—, vice chmn.), Behavior Therapy and Rsch. Soc. (charter); mem. Am. Psychol. Found. (trustee 2000—), Assn. for Advancement Psychology (trustee 1983-86), Assn. for Advancement Behavior Therapy (sec.-treas. 1986-89, pres. 1992-93), Asian Am. Psychol. Assn. (bd. dirs. 1983-88), Am. Bd. Behavior Therapy (bd. dirs. 1987-2000), Phi Beta Kappa, Sigma Xi. Home: 808 Cheyenne Dr Fort Collins CO 80525-1560 Office: Colo State U Dept Psychology Fort Collins CO 80523-0001 Office Phone: 970-491-1351. Business E-Mail: suinn@lamar.colostate.edu.

SUISSA, DAVID, advertising executive; Exec. creative dir., chmn. bd. Suissa Miller Advt., L.A.

SUIT, HERMAN DAY, physician, medical educator; b. Houston, Feb. 8, 1929; BA, U. Houston, 1948; MD, Baylor U., 1952; PhD, Oxford (Eng.) U., 1956. Intern Jefferson David Hosp., Houston, 1952-53, resident in radiology, 1953-54; house surgeon registrar Churchill Hosp., Oxford, 1954, rsch. asst. radiobiol. lab., 1954-56, registrar in radiotherapy, 1956-57; sr. asst. surgeon radiation br. Nat. Cancer Inst., 1957-59; asst. radiotherapist U. Tex. M.D. Anderson Hosp. and Tumor Inst., Houston, 1959-63, assoc. radiotherapist, 1963-68, radiotherapist, 1968-71, chief sect. exptl. radiotherapy, 1962-70; prof. radiation oncology Harvard Med. Sch., 1970—; head dept. radiation oncology Mass. Gen. Hosp., Boston, 1970—2000. Mem. staff NASA Manned Spacecraft Ctr., 1969-71. Recipient Charles F. Kettering prize, GM Cancer Rsch. Found., 1997. Mem. AAAS (subcom. radiation biology), AMA, Am. Coll. Radiology, Am. Soc. Therapeutic Radiology, Am. Assn. Cancer Rsch. Office: Mass Gen Hosp Dept Radiation Therapy Boston MA 02114

SUIT, TERRIE L. state representative; b. Orleans, France, Oct. 3, 1964; m. Thomas F. Suit. Student, Southwestern C.C., Tidewater C.C. Home mortgage cons.; mem. Va. Ho. of Reps., 2000—. Mem.: Virginia Beach Farm Bur., Hampton Roads Rep. Profls. Network, Hampton Roads C. of C., Chesapeake Farm Bur., Navy League US. Republican. Presbyterian. Office: Gen Assembly Bldg PO Box 406 Richmond VA 23218

SUITER, THOMAS, advertising executive; Attended, San Diego State U., Art Ctr. Coll. Design, Pasadena, Calif. Creative dir., creative svcs. dir. Apple Computer; creative dir. Landor Assocs.; chief creative dir. CKS Partners, Cupertino, Calif.; chief creative officer US Web CKS, March First Inc., 2000—. Office: 410 Townsend St San Francisco CA 94107-1537

SUITS, BERNARD HERBERT, philosophy educator; b. Detroit, Nov. 25, 1925; s. Herbert Arthur and Helen Dorothy (Carlin) S.; m. Nancy Ruth Berr, July 3, 1952; children— Mark, Constance; m. Cheryl Ann Ballantyne, June 14, 1996. BA, U. Chgo., 1944, MA, 1950; PhD, U. Ill., 1958. Investigator venereal disease USPHS, 1950-51; personnel officer Detroit Civil Service Commn., 1952-54; instr. philosophy U. Ill., Urbana, 1958-59; asst. prof. Purdue U., 1959-66; assoc. prof. U. Waterloo, Ont., 1966-72, prof. philosophy, chmn. dept., 1971-74, assoc. dean arts for grad. affairs, 1981-84. Vis. prof. U. Lethbridge, Alta., Can., 1980, U. Bristol, Eng., 1980, disting. prof. emeritus U. Waterloo, 1995. Author: The Grasshopper: Games, Life, and Utopia, 1978, paper, 1990; contbr. to profl. jours. and books; featured guest on seven-week TV Ontario series The Academy of Moral Philosophy, 1982. Served with USNR, 1944-46. Recipient Disting. Tchg. award U. Waterloo, 1983. Mem.: Philosphic Soc. Study of Sport (pres. 1973). Office: U Waterloo Dept Philosophy Waterloo ON Canada E-mail: bernard.suits@sympatico.ca.

SUJANSKY, EVA BORSKA, pediatrician, geneticist, educator; b. Bratislava, Slovak Republic, Feb. 14, 1936; d. Stefan and Terezia (Kaiserova) Borsky; m. Eduard Sujansky, Apr. 2, 1960 (dec. Sept. 1979); children: Paul, Walter. MD, Comenius U., Bratislava, Czechoslovakia, 1959. Diplomate Am. Bd. Pediats., Am. Bd. Med. Genetics. Resident in pediats. U. Iowa, Iowa City, 1969-71; fellow in human genetics Mt. Sinai Sch. Medicine, N.Y.C., 1971-73; clin. geneticist Beth Israel Hosp., N.Y.C., 1973-74; dir. clin. genetics Sch. Medicine, U. Colo., Denver, 1974-90, assoc. prof. pediats., biochemistry, biophysics and genetics, 1981—; co-dir. divsn. genetic svcs. The Children's Hosp., U. Colo., Denver, 1990—. Contbr. articles to profl. jours. Fellow Am. Acad. Pediats., Am. Soc. Human Genetics, Am. Coll. Med. Genetics (founding fellow). Avocations: fine arts, reading, travel. Office: U Colo Med Ctr/TCH 1056 E 19th Ave Denver CO 80218-1007

SUKAPDJO, WILMA IRENE, language educator; b. Indpls., Nov. 8, 1936; d. Wilson Homer and Della Irene Warren; m. Humam Sukapdjo, Apr. 12, 1960; children: Tina, Stephen, Amye. AB, MS, Butler U. Tchr. French U. Wis., Madison, Gadjah Mada U., Jakarta, Indonesia, Plainfield High Sch., Ind., Columbus Hr. High Sch., Ben Davis High Sch., Indpls.; tchr. French, Spanish, German Iupui Continuing Edn.; tchr. French, Italian, German Wilhum Acad., Carmel; tchr. Inodnesian, Dutch, Portuguese, Japanese Oasis, Indpls. Mem. Indpls. Mus. Art, 1998—2003; vol. guide Fiteljorg Indian Mus., 1999—2000. Mem.: Tomodachi Japan-Am. Club (pres.), Phi Kappa Phi. Republican. Presbyterian. Avocation: travel. Office: Wilhum Academy of Foreign Lang 622 S Range Line Rd Ste I Carmel IN 46032-2152

SUKO, LONNY RAY, judge; b. Spokane, Wash., Oct. 12, 1943; s. Ray R. and Leila B. (Snyder) Suko; m. Marcia A. Michaelson, Aug. 26, 1967; children: Jolynn R., David M. BA, Wash. State U., 1965; JD, U. Idaho, 1968. Bar: Wash. 1968, U.S. Dist. Ct. (ea. dist.), Wash. 1969, U.S. Dist. Ct. (we. dist.), Wash. 1978, U.S. Ct. Appeals (9th cir.) 1978. Law clk. U.S. Dist. Ct. Ea. Dist., Wash., 1968—69; assoc. Lyon, Beaulaurier & Aaron, Yakima, Wash., 1969—72; ptnr. Lyon, Beaulaurier, Weigand, Suko & Gustafson, Yakima, Wash., 1972—91, Lyon, Weigand, Suko & Gustafson, Yakima, Wash., 1991—95; U.S. magistrate judge Yakima, Wash., 1971—91, 1995—2003; judge U.S. Dist. Ct., 2003—. Mem.: Phi Kappa Phi, Phi Beta Kappa. Office: PO Box 2726 Yakima WA 98907-2726

SUKONECK, IRA DAVID, lawyer; b. Newark, Jan. 20, 1947; s. Edward and Mae (Rosenkrantz) S.; m. Vicki Sherman, Oct. 29, 1972; children: Marc, Randi. BS in Pharmacy, Northeastern U., 1969; JD, Suffolk U., 1972. Bar: Mass. 1972, N.J. 1973, U.S. Dist. Ct. N.J. 1973, U.S. Supreme Ct. 1978; cert. workers compensation law atty. Assoc. ptnr. Braff, Harris & Sukoneck, Livingston, N.J., 1973—. Mem. ABA, N.J. Bar Assn., Assn. Trial Lawyers Am., Am. Inns of Ct., N.J. Workers Compensation Def. Assn. Office: Braff Harris Sukoneck 570 W Mount Pleasant Ave PO Box 657 Livingston NJ 07039-0657 E-mail: isukoneck@bhs-law.com.

SUKOPP, KARL MARTIN, sculptor, painter, graphic artist; b. Mannersdorf, Austria, Nov. 4, 1928; s. Karl and Magdalena (Rossner) S.; m. Margaretha Anna Meidl, Feb. 21, 1953; children: Krl, peter, paul, Margaretha, Barbara, Do-Hee Kim. Student graphic arts and design, Vienna, 1946-50; diploma in scultpure, Acad. Applied Arts, Vienna, 1959; MA, Acad. Applied Arts, 1984. Free-lance artist, Schwechat, Austria, 1953-74, 79—. Artistic collaborator workshops of Pub. theatre Union, Vienna, 1974-79. One man shows include Gallery ZB, Austria, 1966, Galeria Galeria de Arte, Naharro, Zaragoza, 1971, The Austria-Days, Kiev, 1974, Salzburger Kunstverein, 1980; group shows include The New Hagenbund, Warsaw, 1968, La Chaux de Fonds, 1969, House of Artists, vienna, 1973, Salzburg, 1977, Vienna, 1983, Paris, 1983, Schwechat Anniv. Exposition, 1988, Gladbeck, 1992, Schwechat Anniv. Exposition, 1998, Europe '99, Neustadt; represented in permanent collections including State Govt. Lower Austria, Fed. Ministry of Edn., Bldg. Soc. Vienna, nat. and internat. assns.; prin. works include Vietcong/resistance (Biennale Rzezby with Metalu Warzawa 1968), 1964, 3 sculptures in bronze (House of Arts prize 1973), 1969, 70, 73, dep. chmn. of the new hagenbund, Vienna, 1957, others. Recipient prize Union f Arts, 1967, Vienna Festival, 1983, Chapel of St. Laurentius' Home, 1984, 85, badge of honour in gold, 1998, ring of honor Schwechat, 1998, badge of honour in gold, 1998. Mem. House of Arts Salzburg, Union of Artists of Austria, Union of Artists. Mem. Social Dem. Party. Roman Catholic.

SUL, YI CHUL, neurologist; b. Seoul, Korea, May 5, 1947; came to U.S., 1976; s. Tae Woon Sul and Jung Sook Suh; m. Kyu Won, Nov. 21, 1976; children: Caroline, Douglas, Joseph. MD, Yonsei U., Seoul, 1972. Bd. cert. in neurology Am. Bd. Psychiatry and Neurology, subspecialty clin. neurophysiology. Clin. instr. Vanderbilt U., Nashville, 1981-82; v.p. Lakeside Neurology, PC, Grosse Pointe Woods, Mich., 1985—; asst. clin. prof. Mich. State U., Lansing, 1995—; chief neurology sect. St. John Northeast Cmty. Hosp., Detroit, 2002—03. Adj. clin. asst. prof. U. Osteo. Medicine and Health Sci., 1998-99; clin. asst. prof. Coll. Osteo. Medicine U. Health Sci., 2000-; med. mission, Thailand, 1994, China, 1997. Chairperson adminstrv. bd. Korean United Meth. Ch., Detroit, 1997-98, chairperson bd. trustees, 2001; sec. Christian Assn. for Med. Mission, Detroit, 1991-95. Capt. Korean Army, 1972-75, Korea. Grantee Muscular Dystrophy Assn., 1981-82. Fellow Am. Assn. Electrodiagnostic Medicine; mem. AMA, Am. Acad. Neurology, Am. Clin. Neurophysiology Soc., Mich. State Med. Soc., Christian Assn. for Med. Mission (pres. 1999-2001). Home: 20720 Green Ct Grosse Pointe Woods MI 48236-1459 Office: Rim and Sul MP PC 20867 Mack Ave Ste 6 Grosse Pointe Woods MI 48236-1356 Office Phone: 313-882-2922. E-mail: yisulzi@comcast.net.

SULAK, PATRICIA JANE, gynecologist, educator; b. Hillsboro, Tex., Nov. 6, 1952; m. Jeffrey Alan Waxman, Dec. 6, 1980; children: David Bartholomew Waxman, Gabriel Waxman. B in pharmacy, U. Houston, Tex., 1973—75; MD, U. Tex., San Antonio, 1976—80. Cert. MD Tex. State Bd. Medicine, 1980; Pharmacist Tex., 1975. Physician, maj. Darnall Army Cmty. Hosp., Ft. Hood, Tex., 1985—; obstetrician, gynecologist Scott and White Hosp., Temple, Tex., 1987—; prof. Tex. A&M Coll. Medicine, Temple, Tex., 1987—. Dir. Scott and White Depart of Ob/gyn, Temple, Tex., 1995—, Scott and White Sex Edn. Program, Temple, Tex., 1996—2004. Author: Worth The Wait (Hero For Children, Tex. State Bd. Edn., 1999, Am. Coll. Obstetricians and Gynecologists Dist. VII Presdl. award for Cmty. Svc., 2004). Maj. U.S. Army, 1981—87, Walter Reed Army Med. Ctr. and Darnall Army Com. Hosp. Fellow: Am. Coll. Obstetricians and Gynecologists; mem.: Am. Bd. Obstetricians and Gynecologists, Alpha Omega Alpha. Achievements include research in redesign of oral contraceptives to eliminate monthly menstruation. Office: Scott and White Hosp 2401 S 31st St Temple TX 76508 Business E-Mail: psulak@swmail.sw.org.

SULC, DWIGHT GEORGE, investment advisor; b. Oklahoma City, May 25, 1948; s. George Bennett and Hedvika (Kyzivat) S. BA, U. Tex., 1971; JD, Tuebingen U., Germany, 1979, LLD, 1983. Cert. securities and exch. commn., Paris, U.S. Investment advisor, Paris, Berlin, London, 1974-83, Oklahoma City, 1984—. Strategic planning advisor cmty. orgns., Oklahoma City, 1989. Author: A National Neighborhood Association System for America, 1991, Building A Volunteer Neighborhood Watch Patrol, A Civic Leadership Training Manual of the Council of Confederated Neighborhoods of America, 1996, Czechoslovak Society of Arts and Sciences World Congress, Brno: Strategic Management Design for the International Society of Arts Management and the Arts, 1996, Legal Commentary on Romanian Commodities Exchange Law, 1999. Chmn. strategic planning com. Federally Employed Women Assn., Tinker AFB, 1990; founder The Coun. of Confederated Neighborhoods of Am. Inc., Oklahoma City, 1991, The Internat. Soc. for the Arts Management and the Arts, Praha, Czechoslovakia/London/Oklahoma City, 1994; pres. Mil. Park chpt. Coun. Confederated Neighborhoods of Am., 1992. Rsch. grantee Fulbright, Berlin, 1980, Brusselles, 1981. Mem. Nat. Assn. Parliamentarians (pres. 1994), Okla. Assn. Parliamentarians (state sec. 1997). Presbyterian. Avocation: music. Home: 3321 N Virginia Ave Oklahoma City OK 73118-3044

SULC, JEAN LUENA (JEAN L. MESTRES), lobbyist, consultant; b. Worcester, Mass., Mar. 17, 1939; d. Emilio Beija and Julia Luena; m. Lee Gwynne Mestres, Oct. 9, 1965 (div. Dec. 1973); m. Lawrence Bradley Sulc, Nov. 4, 1983. BS in Psychology, Tufts U., 1961; M in Urban and Regional Planning, U. Colo., 1976. Lic. real estate, Va.; lic. pvt. pilot. Mem. staff U.S. fgn. svc. Dept. State, Washington, 1962-65; intern Adams County Planning Dept., Brighton, Colo., 1974-75; cons. office policy analysis City and County of Denver, 1976; program dir. Coun. Internat. Urban Liaison, Washington, 1976-79; asst., dir. internat. Cities Svc. Oil & Gas Corp., Washington, 1980-81; govt. affairs rep. Cities Svc., OXY USA Inc., Washington, 1982-89; mgr. fed. rels. OXY USA Inc., Washington, 1990-95; pres. EdgeSystem.XXI, Washington, 1996—. Chmn. govt. affairs com. L.P. Gas Clean Fuel Coalition, Irvine, Calif., 1990-92. Author, editor: (newsletter) Dayton Climate Project, 1979-80; contbr. articles to newsletters. Vol. Reagan/Bush and Bush/Quayle Presdl. Campaigns and Inaugural Coms., Washington, 1984-89; pres. Hale Found., Nathan Hale Inst., Washington, 1984-85; mem. nat. panel consumer arbitrators Better Bus. Burs., Va., 1991—. Recipient Presdl. citation Nat. Propane Gas Assn., 1992; Minority Intern grantee Denver Regional Coun. Govts., 1974-76. Mem. ASTD, ABA (assoc., arbitration sect.), Am. League Lobbyists (bd. dirs. 1994-97, 2nd v.p. 1996-97, emeritus 1999—), Assn. Image Cons. Internat. (ea. regional adv. 1998—), Greater Beaufort C. of C., Psi Chi. Episcopalian. Avocations: skiing, sports shooting.

SULENTIC, ROBERT E. real estate company executive; Various positions Trammell Crow Co., Dallas, 1984—94, pres. Trammell Crow NE, Inc., 1995—98, exec. v.p., nat. dir. devel. and investment, 1997—98, exec. v.p., CFO, 1998—2000, pres., CEO, 2000—, chmn., 2002—. Office: Trammell Crow Co Trammell Crow Ctr 2001 Ross Ave Dallas TX 75201*

SULG, MADIS, corporation executive, entrepreneur; b. Tallinn, Estonia, May 25, 1943; came to U.S., 1950; s. Hand Eduard and Erika (Turk) S.; m. Mary Diane Detellis, Dec. 30, 1967; children: Danielle Marie, Michaella Erika. SB in Engring. Mgmt., MIT, 1965, SM in Mgmt., 1967. Cons. Barss, Reitzel & Assocs., Cambridge, Mass., 1970—71; mgr. planning and research Converse Rubber Co., Wilmington, Mass., 1971—75; dir. bus. planning and devel. AMF, Inc., Stamford, Conn., 1975—79; sr. v.p. planning and devel. Bandag, Inc., Muscatine, Iowa, 1978—88; pres. Prime Investments, 1988—, Muscatine Natural Resources Corp., 1981—88; chmn., CEO Siege Auto Parts, Davenport, Iowa, 1989—93; COO Hammer's Plastic Recycling, Iowa Falls, Iowa, 1994, PURethane, Inc., West Branch, Iowa, 1994—98; COO, Bytec, Inc., Clinton Township, Mich., 1999—2001; prin. M&D Mgmt. Assocs., 1989—; mng. mem. Maddi's Gallery, LLC, 2001—. With U.S. Army, 1968-70. Presbyterian. Avocations: bridge, jogging, swimming. Home: 11238 Home Place Lane Charlotte NC 28227 Office Phone: 704-907-1289. E-mail: madissulg@aol.com.

SULICK, JOSEPH EDWARD, SR., information technology manager, retired military officer; b. Columbus, Ohio, July 31, 1945; children: Scott, Shawn, Sandra, Joseph Jr. BS in Edn., Ohio State U., 1967; grad., USAF

Squadron Officer Sch., 1971; MBA, St. Edward's U., 1973; grad., Air Command and Staff Coll., 1974, Air War Coll., 1987; MS in Nat. Resource Strategy, Nat. Def. U., 1996; grad., Info. Resources Mgmt. Coll., 2000. Comm. officer USAF, Keesler AFB, Miss., 1968, Bergstrom AFB, Tex., 1972-74, Holloman AFB, N.Mex., 1976-79; radar officer 689th Radar Squadron, Mt. Hebo, Oreg., 1968—71; spl. electronics officer USAF, Lowry AFB, Colo., 1971—72, combat ops. specialist Dover AFB, Del., 1974-76, combat sys. requirements office staff Langley AFB, Va., 1979-82; chief of frequency assignments, exec. officer USAF Frequency Mgmt. Ctr., Washington, 1982-88; ret., 1988. Mem. Frequency Assignment subcom., US Mil. Comms.-Electronics Bd. Frequency Panel, 1994—; dir. Plans and Requirements, USAF Frequency Mgmt. Agy., Alexandria, Va., 1994—, chief info. officer, 1994—. Mem.: N.Y. Acad. Scis., Air War Coll. (life), Air Force Assn. (life). Home: 2006 Peggy Stewart Way Unit 205 Annapolis MD 21401 Office: USAF Frequency Mgmt Agy 2461 Eisenhower Ave Alexandria VA 22331-1500

SULIMIRSKI, WITOLD STANISLAW, banker; b. Lwow, Poland, May 18, 1933; came to U.S., 1957; s. Tadeusz and Olga (Lepkowska) S.; m. Teresa Maria Boniecka, Dec. 28, 1957; children: Elizabeth Sulimirski Blakeslee, Adam, Edward BA with honors, Cambridge U., 1953, MA, 1957. With Irving Trust Co., N.Y.C., 1957-89, exec. v.p., 1986-89; pres. Servus Assocs., Inc., N.Y.C., 1989-95; chmn. exec. com. Intercap Investments, Inc., N.Y.C., 1989—. Chmn. Am. Bank in Poland, Warsaw, 1989-91, LBS Bank N.Y., 1990—; exec. dir. Am. Investment Initiative in Poland, Warsaw, 1992-94; bd. dirs. Octava Nat. Investmen t Fund, Warsaw, Big Bank Gdanski SA, Warsaw, Bicentennial Publs., N.Y.C. Dir. Polish Inst. Arts and Scis., Inc., N.Y.C., 1976-97; vice-chmn. Kosciuszko Found., Inc., N.Y.C., 1983-97, chmn. 1997—; chmn. Polish Assistance, Inc., N.Y.C., 1984-92; bd. dirs. Middle East Policy Coun., Washington, 1984-98, Nat. U.S.-Arab C. of C., Washington, 1987-93. Mem. Bronxville Field Club, Knights of Malta. Roman Catholic. Office: Intercap Investments Inc 29 W 57th St # 12 New York NY 10019-3406

SULKIN, HOWARD ALLEN, college president; b. Detroit, Aug. 19, 1941; s. Lewis and Vivian P. (Mandel) S.; m. Constance Annette Adler, Aug. 4, 1963; children— Seth R., Randall K. PhB, Wayne State U., 1963; MBA, U. Chgo., 1965, PhD, 1969; LHD (hon.), De Paul U., 1990. Dir. program rsch., indsl. rels. ctr. U. Chgo., 1964-72; dean Sch. for New Learning, De Paul U., Chgo., 1972-77; v.p. De Paul U., Chgo., 1977-84; pres. Spertus Inst. Jewish Studies, Chgo., 1984—. St. Paul's vis. prof. Rikkyo U., Tokyo, 1970—; cons., evaluator North Central Assn., Chgo., 1975—. Contbr. articles to profl. jours. Sec.-treas. Grant Park Cultural and Ednl. Cmty., Chgo., 1984—; bd. dirs. Chgo. Sinai Congregation, 1972—, pres., 1980-83; bd. dirs. S.E. Chgo. Commn., 1980—, United Way, 1984—, Crusade of Mercy United Way, 1990—; bd. dirs., chmn. Parliament of World's Religions, 1989—. Mem. The Standard Club, Tavern Club. Office: Spertus Inst of Jewish Studies 618 S Michigan Ave Chicago IL 60605-1901

SULLEBARGER, JOHN THOMPSON, internist, cardiologist, educator; b. Plainfield, N.J., May 2, 1957; s. Franklyn Jackson and Joanne Abbott (Aspinall) S.; m. Lorrie Jeanne Miller, June 14, 1980; children: Jeffrey Franklyn, Melissa Jeanne. Student, U. Mainz, 1977; AB, Dartmouth Coll., 1979; MD, Johns Hopkins U., 1983. Intern U. Rochester, N.Y., 1983-84, resident in medicine, 1984-86, fellow in cardiology, 1986-89, from sr. instr. to asst. prof., 1989-92; asst. prof. U. South Fla., Tampa, 1992-96, assoc. prof., 1997-99; dir. CCU Tampa Gen. Hosp., 1997—; dir. interventional cardiology Fla. Cardiovascular Inst., 1999—2004; clin. assoc. prof. U. South Fla., Tampa, 2004—. Dir. Cardiac Catheterization Lab. James Haley VA Hosp., Tampa, 1992—99; dir. interventional cardiology U. South Fla., 1994—99; attending physician Strong Meml. Hosp., Rochester, 1989—92. Author: (with others) book chapters; contrb. articles to profl. jours. Chmn. Bd. Christian Svc., 1st Bapt. Ch., Rochester, 1991-92. Fellow ACP, 1992, Am. Coll. of Cardiology, 1991, Counc. on Clin. Cardiology of Am. Heart Assn., 1991, N.Y. Cardiological Soc., 1992. Fellow ACP, Soc. Cardiac Angiography and Interventions, Am. Coll. Cardiology, N.Y. Cardiol. Soc.; mem. Am. Heart Assn. (fellow coun. on clin. cardiology), Tampa Internat. Heart Found. (founder 2004-). Avocation: music. Office: 509 S Armenia Ste 200 Tampa FL 33609 Office Phone: 813-353-1515.

SULLENBERGER, ARA BROOCKS, mathematics professor; b. Amarillo, Tex., Jan. 3, 1933; d. Carl Clarence and Ara Frances (Broocks) Cox; m. Hal Joseph Sullenberger, Nov. 2, 1952; children: Hal Joseph Jr., Ara Broocks Sullenberger Switzer. Student, Randolph-Macon Woman's Coll., 1951—52, So. Meth. U., 1952, U. Tex., Arlington, 1953, Amarillo Coll., 1953—54; BA in Math., Tex. Tech. U., 1955, MA, 1958; postgrad., Tex. Christian U., 1963—67, U. N. Tex., 1969—80, Tarrant County Coll., Fort Worth, Tex., 1972—83. Cert. tchr., Tex. Math. tchr. Tom S. Lubbock (Tex.) High Sch., 1955-56; instr. math. Tex. Tech U., Lubbock, 1956-63; teaching fellow math. Tex. Christian U., Ft. Worth, 1963-64; chmn. dept. math. Ft. Worth Country Day Sch., 1964-67; instr. math. Tarrant County Coll.-South, Ft. Worth, 1967-70, asst. prof. math., 1970-74, assoc. prof. math., 1974-95; prof. emeritus, 1995—; ret., 1995. Adj. prof. math. Tex. Christian U., 1996; cons. Project Change, Ft. Worth, 1967-68; math. scis. advisor Coll. Bd., Princeton, N.J., 1979-83; math. book reviewer for various pub. cos. including Prentice-Hall, McGraw Hill, D.C. Heath, Prindle, Weber & Schmidt, MacMillan, Harcourt, Brace Jovanovich, West, Worth, Saunders, Wadsworth. Contbr. article, book revs. to profl. publs.; author book supplement to Intermediate Algebra, 1990. Active Jr. League, Ft. Worth, 1954—73, sustaining mem., 1973—; editor newsletter Crestwood Assn., Ft. Worth, 1984, 1986, 1991, membership sec., 1985, 1990—91, 1995, 1999, pres., 1988—89, 1998—99, crime patrol capt., 1993, 2000—01, v.p., 1993, treas., 1987, 1996, 2003, sec., 1997—98, crime patrol sec., 1999, crime patrol sec.-treas., 2001—. Recipient award for excellence in teaching Gen. Dynamics, 1968. Mem. Math. Assn. Am. (life), Nat. Coun. Tchrs. Math. (life), Am. Math. Assn. Two-Yr. Colls. (life), Tex. Math. Assn. Two-Yr. Colls. (charter, v.p. 1997-99), Tex. Jr. Coll. Tchrs. Assn., Ft. Worth League Neighborhood Assn. (v.p. 1999-2000, del. 2004-05), Pi Beta Phi. Republican. Episcopalian. Avocations: grandchildren, reading, pets, walking, writing. Home: 600 Eastwood Ave Fort Worth TX 76107-1020 E-mail: halandara@aol.com.

SULLIVAN, ALFRED DEWITT, academic administrator; b. New Orleans, Feb. 2, 1942; s. Dewitt Walter and Natalie (Alford) Sullivan; m. Marilyn Janie Hewitt, Sept. 1, 1962 (div. May 1989); children: Alan, Sean; m. Dorothy Madeleine Hess, Apr. 1993. BS, La. State U., 1964, MS, 1966; PhD, U. Ga., 1969. Asst. prof. Va. Poly. Inst. and State U., Blacksburg, 1969—73; assoc. prof., then prof. Miss. State U., Starkville, 1973—88; dir. Sch. Forest Resources Pa. State U., University Park, 1988—93; dean coll. natural resources U. Minn., St. Paul, 1993—2002, vice provost Mpls., 2002—. Assoc. Danforth Found., 1981. Contbr. articles to profl. jours. Fellow, Am. Coun. Edn., 1987—88, NDEA fellow, U. Ga., 1966—69. Mem.: Soc. Am. Foresters. Office: U Minn 234 Morrill Hall 100 Church St SE Minneapolis MN 55455 E-mail: alsull@umn.edu.

SULLIVAN, AUSTIN PADRAIC, II, diversified food company executive; b. Washington, June 26, 1940; s. Austin P. and Janet Lay (Patterson) Sullivan; m. Judith Ann Raab, June 1, 1968 (dec. Oct. 1995); children: Austin P. III, Amanda, Alexander; m. Marie Elise de Golian, Aug. 1, 1997; stepchildren: Lauren Gibbons, Georgia Gibbons, Samuel Gibbons. BA cum laude(hon.), Princeton U., 1964. Spl. asst. to dep. dir. N.J. Office Econ. Opportunity, Trenton, NJ, 1956—66; prof. staff mem. Com. on Edn. and Labor, U.S. Ho. of Rep., Washington, 1967—71, legis. dir., 1971—76; dir. govt. relations Gen. Mills, Inc., Mpls., 1976—78, v.p., corp. dir. govt. rels., 1978—79, v.p. pub. affairs, 1979—93, v.p. corp. comm. and pub. affairs, 1993—94, sr. v.p. corp. rels., 1994—. Lectr. fed. labor market policies Harvard U., Mass., 1972—76, Boston U., 1972—76. Mem. Nat. Commn. on Employment and Tng., 1979—81, U.S. Sec. Agr. Adv. Com. on Agrl. Biotech., 2000—; chmn. Governor's Coun. on Employment and Tng., 1976—82; bd. dir., exec. com. Urban Coalition Mpls., 1978—80, Guthrie Theatre, Mpls., 1978—84, Minn. Citizens for the Arts, 1980—83; co chmn. Governor's Commn. on Dislocated Workers, 1988—89; chmn. Pub. Affairs Coun., 1993—94; bd. dir. Minn. C. of C., 1993—99; trustee Minn. Pub. Radio, 1999—; bd. advisors Dem. Leadership Coun., 1986—. Served in USMC, 1957—59. Recipient Eleanor Roosevelt Fellow in Interracial Rels., 1964—65. Mem.: Grocery Mfr. Assn. (govt. affairs coun. 1991—, chmn. biotech. task force 1999—), Coun. of Pub. Affairs Exec. (chmn. 1989—90), Medica (bd. dir. 2001—), Greater Mpls. C. of C. (exec. com. 1980—86, 1990—93, bd. dir.), Mpls. Club (bd. governor's 2001—). Home: 17830 County Rd 6 Minneapolis MN 55447-2905 Office: Gen Mills Inc One Gen Mills Blvd Minneapolis MN 55426

SULLIVAN, BARBARA BOYLE, management consultant; b. Scranton, Pa., Apr. 12, 1937; d. Edmund F. and Mary R. (O'Connell) Boyle; m. John L. Sullivan Jr. BS in Bus. Adminstrn., Drexel U., 1958; PhD (hon.), Newton Coll., 1975, Gwynedd Mercy Coll., 1975. With IBM, 1959-72, systems engring. mgr. Ea. and Cen. Europe, 1967-70, mgmt. devel. mgr., 1970, mgr. spl. programs, 1970-71, sales mgr., asst. br. mgr., 1971-72; pres. Boyle/Kirkman Assocs., N.Y.C., 1972-88; mng. ptnr. Innovation Assocs., Framingham, Mass., 1988-92. Bd. dirs. Ams. Fostering Latino Edn. and Culture; chair compensation com. Equitable Resources, Inc 1989-92, nominating com., 1991, mem. audit, pension trust, and compensation com.; cons. major corps. on human resoruce devl. programs, organizational change programs, changing work force; condr. exec. leadership and visionary and strategic planning awareness seminars Harvard Bus. Sch., Internat. Mgmt. Conf.; pres. Latin Am. Resource Ctr. Trustee Drexel U.; mem. Pres.'s adv. com. Gwynedd Mercy Coll., adv. com. Drexel U. Coll. Bus. Adminstrn.; vice chmn. bd. trustee Marymount Manhattan Coll., N.Y., bd. regents Mt. St. Mary's Coll., L.A., 1982-88; bd. dirs. Mary House Day Care Ctr., Glynn Hispanic Resource Ctr.; chair Tour of Homes Christ Ch. Featured in numerous mags., books, radio and TV programs, including CBS 60 Minutes; named Bus. Person of Yr. St. Johns U., 1973, One of 50 Leaders for Future, Time mag., 1979. Mem. AAUW, Women's Forum, Weston Womens' League, Rotary Womens Aux. (v.p.), Boston Club, Newcomers Club (bd. dirs.). Home: 264 Saint Andrews Saint Simons Island GA 31522-2465

SULLIVAN, BARRY, lawyer; b. Newburyport, Mass., Jan. 11, 1949; s. George Arnold and Dorothy Bennett (Furbush) S.; m. Winnifred Mary Fallers, June 14, 1975; children: George Arnold, Lloyd Ashton. AB cum laude, Middlebury Coll., 1970; JD, U. Chgo., 1974. Bar: Mass. 1975, Ill. 1975, U.S. Dist. Ct. (no. dist.) Ill. 1976, U.S. Ct. Appeals (7th cir.) 1976, U.S. Ct. Appeals (10th cir.) 1977, U.S. Supreme Ct. 1978, U.S. Ct. Appeals (11th cir.) 1986, U.S. Ct. Appeals (5th and 9th cirs.) 1987, U.S. Ct. Appeals (fed. cir.) 1993, U.S. Ct. Appeals (DC cir.) 1994, Va. 1995, U.S. Ct. Appeals (4th cir.) 1997, U.S. Ct. Appeals (2d and 3d cirs.) 2002. Law clk. to judge John Minor Wisdom U.S. Ct. Appeals (5th cir.), New Orleans, 1974-75; assoc. Jenner & Block, Chgo., 1975-80; asst. to solicitor gen. of U.S. U.S. Dept. of Justice, Washington, 1980-81; ptnr. Jenner & Block, Chgo., 1981-94, 2001—; prof. law Washington and Lee U., Lexington, Va., 1994-2001, dean, 1994-99, v.p., 1998-99; Fulbright prof. U. Warsaw, Poland, 2000—01; lectr. in law U. Chgo., 2001—02; spl. asst. state's atty. Cook County, Ill., 2002—03. Vis. fellow Queen Mary and Westfield Coll., U. London, 2001; spl. asst. atty. gen. State of Ill., 1989—90; lectr. in law Loyola U., Chgo., 1978—79; adj. prof. law Northwestern U., Chgo., 1990—92, 1993—94, vis. prof., 1992—93; vis. prof. Ctr. for Am. law studies U. Warsaw, 2002—03; Jessica Swift Meml. lectr. in constnl. law Middlebury Coll., 1991; Rufus Monroe and Sophie Payne lectr. U. Mo., Columbia, 2003. Assoc. editor U. Chgo. Law Rev., 1973-74; mem. editl. bd. Dublin U. Law Jour., 2004--; contbr. articles to profl. jours. Mem. nat. adv. bd. Ctr. for Religion, The Professions, and The Pub., U. Mo., Columbia, 2003—; trustee Cath. Theol. Union at Chgo., 1993—2003, trustee emeritus, 2003—; mem. vis. com. Irving B. Harris Grad. Sch. Public Policy Studies U., Chgo., 2001—, U. Chgo. Divinity Sch., 1987—2001; mem. adv. panel Fulbright Sr. Specialist Program, 2001—04; mem. adv. bd. Internat. Human Rights Inst. DePaul U., 2003—; trustee U. Chgo. Court Theatre, 2003—. Yeats Soc. scholar, 1968; Woodrow Wilson fellow, Woodrow Wilson Found., 1970. Mem.: ABA (chmn. coord. com. on AIDS 1988—94, standing com. on amicus curiae briefs 2004—, coun. sect. individual rights and responsibilities 1993—98, sect. legal edn. com. on law sch. adminstrn. 1994—98, chair sect. legal edn. com. on professionalism 1999—2000, co-chair sect. individual rights/responsibilities com. amicus briefs 2002—04, sect. legal edn. stds. rev. com. 2002—, co-chair sect. individual rights/responsibilities com. on bill of righ 2002—), Lawyers Club Chgo., Supreme Ct. Hist Soc. (Ill. membership chair 2002—03), Ill. State Bar Assn., Appellate Lawyers Assn., Am. Law Inst., Bar Assn. 7th Fed. Cir. (vice chmn. advminstrv. justice com. 1985—86), Va. State Bar (chair sec. on edn. of lawyers), Phi Beta Kappa (fellows). Democrat. Roman Catholic. Home: 5555 S Everett Apt A1-2 Chicago IL 60637 Office: Jenner & Block One IBM Plz Chicago IL 60611 E-mail: bsullivan@jenner.com.

SULLIVAN, BETTYE YARBOROUGH, foundation administrator; d. John Marion and Elise Barnette Yarborough; children: Elizabeth Sullivan Turello, Margaret Sullivan Harvey. BA, U. of Miss., 1960—63. Exec. dir. Wilson Rsch. Found. At Meth. Rehab. Ctr., Jackson, Miss., 1993—. Named one of Top 12 of Mississippi's Leading Bus. Women, Miss. Bus. Jour., 2001; recipient Governor's Disting. Svc. award, Gov. of Miss., 1984, Mar. of Dimes Tribute, Woman of Achievement, Mar. of Dimes, 1986, Athena award, Jackson Area Alumnae Panhellenic Assn., 1994, Salute to Vol. award, Goodwill Industries, 1987. Mem.: Miss. Arts Festival (exec. bd. of dirs. 1976—77), Miss. Symphony Orch. Bd. of Governors (exec. com. 1974—75), Miss. Rep. Women (pres. 1990—91), Rsch. Club (pres. 1991—92), Goodwill Industries of Miss. (pres. 1982—83), Goodwill Industries Internat. (pres. - volunteers 1985—87), Jackson Symphony League (pres. 1973—74), Chi Omega (Outstanding Alumna of Miss. 1986). Bapt. Avocations: reading, music, travel. Home: 1437 Sheffield Dr Jackson MS 39211 Office: Wilson Rsch Found 1350 East Woodrow Wilson Drive Jackson MS 39216

SULLIVAN, BRENDAN PAUL, state official, communications educator; b. Boston, Apr. 20, 1949; s. Francis Joseph and Margaret Rita (McDonough) S.; m. Debra Marie Fitzgerald, Feb. 11, 1988; children: Erin, Patrick. BS, Boston State Coll., 1970; MA in Comms., Fairfield U., 1976; MBA, Boston Coll., 1995. Tchr. Boston Pub. Schs., 1970-81; mgr. adminstrn. Mass. State Lottery, Braintree, 1981-91; asst. clk.-magistrate Commonwealth of Mass. Superior Ct., Brockton, 1993—. Adj. prof. Massasoit C.C., Brockton, 1996—, mem. mediation adv. bd., 1999-. Mem. Plymouth County Dem. League, Abington, Mass., 2000—. Mem.: Furnace Brook Golf Club (gov. 1976—). Democrat. Roman Catholic. Avocations: golf, fishing, coaching baseball. Home: 220 Plymouth Ave Quincy MA 02169 Office: 72 Belmont St Brockton MA 02301-5248 E-mail: brensullivan@comcast.net.

SULLIVAN, BRENDAN V., JR., lawyer; b. Providence, Mar. 11, 1942; AB, Georgetown U., 1964, JD, 1967. Bar: R.I. 1967, D.C. 1970, U.S. Dist. Ct. D.C. 1970, U.S. Ct. Appeals (D.C. cir.) 1970, U.S. Supreme Ct. 1972, U.S. Dist. Ct. Md. 1974, U.S. Ct. Appeals (4th cir.) 1981, U.S. Ct. Appeals (3d cir.) 1979, U.S. Ct. Appeals (6th cir.) 1991, U.S. Ct. Appeals (9th cir.) 1996, U.S. Ct. Fed. Claims 1998, U.S. Ct. Appeals (fed. cir.) 2003. Mem. Williams & Connolly, Washington. Lectr. Practicing Law Inst., 1981—, Md. Inst. for Continuing Profl. Edn. of Lawyers, Inc., 1979—, D.C. Criminal Practice Inst., 1975-81. Author: Grand Jury Proceedings, 1981, Techniques for Dealing with Pending Criminal Charges or Criminal Investigations, 1983, White Collar Criminal Practice Grand Jury, 1985. Fellow Am. Coll. Trial Lawyers; mem. ABA, R.I. Bar Assn., D.C. Bar. Office: Williams & Connolly 725 12th St NW Washington DC 20005-5901 Office Phone: 202-434-5800.

SULLIVAN, CHARLES, dean, educator, author; b. Boston, May 27, 1933; s. Charles Thomas and Marion Veronica (Donahue) S.; divorced; children: Charles Fulford, John Driscoll, Catherine Page; m. Shirley Ross Davis, Sept. 6, 1997. BA in English, Swarthmore Coll., 1955; MA, NYU, 1968, PhD in Social Psychology, 1973; MPA, Pa. State U., 1978. Predoctoral fellow NYU, 1964-68; postdoctoral fellow Ednl. Testing Svc., Princeton, N.J., 1973-74; asst. prof. psychology Ursinus Coll., Collegeville, Pa., 1973-78; mgmt. cons., 1978-86; adj. prof. Pa. State U., Radnor, Pa., 1978-80; prof., head dept. pub. adminstrn., dir. student svcs. Southeastern U., Washington, 1986-89; asst. dean Grad. Sch. Arts and Scis. Georgetown U., Washington, 1989-92, assoc. dean Grad. Sch. Arts and Scis., 1992-97, professorial lectr., dept. psychology, 1994-95; exec. dir. Doylestown Found., Doylestown, Pa., 1958-73; assoc. dean, prof. Coll. Profl. Studies U. San Francisco, 1997-98. Adj. prof. social and behavioral scis. U. Md., 1984-96; lectr., spkr. on lit. and art Cooper-Hewitt Mus., N.Y.C., Nat. Soc. Arts and Letters, Washington, Martin Luther King Jr. Libr., Washington, Met. Mus. Art, N.Y.C., Smithsonian Instn., Washington, Children's Book Fair, N.Y.C., Nat. Mus. Women in Arts, Lombardi Cancer Rsch. Ctr., Georgetown U., Arts Club of Washington, Phillips Collection, Corcoran Gallery of Art, U. San Francisco Multicultural Lit. Program, Nat. Mus. Am. History, New Coll. of Calif., others. Author: Alphabet Animals, 1991, The Lover in Winter, 1991, Numbers at Play, 1992, Circus, 1992, Cowboys, 1993, A Woman of A Certain Age, 1994, Out of Love, 1996, American Folk, 1998, In a Certain Place, 1999, The Lovers' Companion, 2002; editor: America in Poetry, 1988, 2d edit., 1992, 3d edit., 1996, Imaginary Gardens, 1989, Ireland in Poetry, 1990, Children of Promise, 1991, 2d edit., 2001, Loving, 1992, American Beauties, 1993, Here Is My Kingdom, 1994, Fathers and Children, 1995, Imaginary Animals, 1996, Dancing in the Wind, 2002. Trustee Folger Poetry Bd., 1988-92; Nat. Soc. Arts and Letters, 1992-94, 2002-04, Am. Acad. Liberal Edn., 1995—, San Francisco Art Inst., 2000—, Pacific Ctr. for Photog. Arts, 2003—; pres. Am. Found. Arts, 1995—; collectors com. Nat. Gallery Art, Washington, 1998—; mem. Dir.'s Cir., San Francisco Mus. Modern Art, 1998—. Recipient Best Books for Young Adults award Young Adult Libr. Svcs. Assn., 1992, 98, Best Books for Teens award N.Y. Pub. Libr., 1992, 93. Mem.: The Family Club, Cosmos Club. E-mail: artsfound@earthlink.net.

SULLIVAN, CHARLES A. food products executive; BBA, U. Toledo, 1959. With Seven-Up Co., Los Angeles, 1966-70; v.p. strategic planning Pepsi-Cola Co., Los Angeles, 1966-70; pres. Seven Up of Ind.; with Westinghouse Electric Corp., 1970-79; pres. Can. Dry of New Eng. subs. Norton Simon Co., 1979-82; sr. v.p. pres. Merita divsn. Am. Bakeries Co. subs. BCA Corp., N.Y.C., 1982-86; exec. v.p. BCA Corp., N.Y.C.; pres., exec. v.p. Merita div. Am. Bakeries Co., 1986-89; pres., CEO, Interstate Bakeries Corp., 1989-90, CEO and chmn., 1991—; pres., CEO, Interstate Brands Corp., 1989-90. Office: Interstate Brands Corp PO Box 419627 Kansas City MO 64141-6627 also: Interstate Brands Corp 12 E Armour Blvd Kansas City MO 64111-1202

SULLIVAN, COLLEEN ANNE, anesthesiologist, educator; b. Lucknow, India, Feb. 11, 1937; arrived in U.S., 1961; d. Douglas George and Nancy Irene (MacLeod) Sullivan; m. Alexander Walter Gotta, July 17, 1965; 1 child, Nancy Colleen Gotta. MB, ChB, U. St. Andrews, Scotland, 1961. Diplomate Am. Bd. Anesthesiology, Am. Coll. Anesthesiologists. Rotating intern Nassau Hosp. (now Winthrop U. Hosp.), Mineola, N.Y., 1961-62; clin. instr. Cornell U., N.Y.C., 1962-64; resident in anesthesiology N.Y. Hosp./Cornell U., 1962-64; fellow in anesthesiology Meml. Sloan-Kettering Cancer Ctr., N.Y.C., 1964-67, asst. prof. Cornell U. Med. Coll., 1978-79; assoc. dir. anesthesia St. Mary's Hosp.-Cath. Med. Ctr., Bklyn., 1968-78; clin. assoc. prof. SUNY, Bklyn., 1979-90, clin. dir. anesthesia, 1990-93, clin. prof. anesthesiology, 1990-97. Clin. dir. anesthesia Kings County Hosp., Bklyn., 1983—90, med. dir. ambulatory surg. unit, 1993—97. Contbr. chapters to books, articles to profl. jours. Mem.: N.Y. State Soc. Anesthesiologists (mem. ho. of dels. 1983—97, asst. editor Sphere 1990—95, mem. com. sci. program 1990—97), Woman's Club Great Neck (bd. dirs. 2004). Republican. Roman Catholic. Avocations: reading, cooking. Personal E-mail: colleenag@optonline.net.

SULLIVAN, CONNIE CASTLEBERRY, artist; b. Cin., Jan. 8, 1934; d. John Porter and Constance (Alf) Castleberry; m. John J. Sullivan, June 6, 1959; children: Deirdre Kelly, Margaret Graham. BA, Manhattanville Coll., 1957. Spl. lectr. Cin. Contemporary Art Ctr., 1984, Toledo Friends of Photography, 1991, U. Ky. Art Mus., 1993, Dennison U. Sch. Art, 1993, El Instituto de Estudios Norte Americanos, Barcelona, 1994, Ctr. for Photography, Bombay, India, 1997, Miami U. Art Mus., Oxford, Ohio, 1998, Alice and Harris K. Weston Gallery, Aronoff Ctr. for the Arts, Cin., 2000. One-woman shows include Contemporary Art Ctr. Cleve., 1982, Cin. Contemporary Arts Ctr., 1983, Fogg Art Mus., Cambridge, Mass., 1983, 90, Neikrug Gallery, N.Y.C., 1984, Camden Arts Ctr., London, 1987, Evanston Art Ctr., Chgo., 1987, Silver Image Gallery Ohio State U., Columbus, 1988, Jean-Pierre Lambert Galerie, Paris, 1988, 96, David Winton Bell Gallery, Brown U., Providence, 1989, Toni Burckhead Gallery, Cin., 1989, Rochester Inst. Tech., 1991, Fotomus. im Münchner Stadtmus., Munich, 1992, U. Ky. Art Mus., Lexington, 1993, Internat. Photography Hall, Kirkpatrick Mus. complex, Oklahoma City, 1993, Institut d'Estudios Fotografics de Catalunya, Barcelona, Spain, 1994, Cheekwood Art Mus., Nashville, 1994, Museo Damy di Fotografia Contemporanea, Brescia, Italy, 1995, Photography Gallery U. Notre Dame, Ind., 1995, Louisville Visual Art Assoc., Watertower, Louisville, KY, 1995, Jean-Pierre Lambert Galarie, 1996, Museo Damy, Milan, 1997, Ctr. for Photography, Bombay, India, 1997, Miami U. Art Mus., Oxford, Ohio, 1998, Aronoff Ctr. for the Arts, Cin., 2000, Vine St. Studios, Houston, 2000, Columbus Mus. Art, 2001, Visual Studies Worshop Gall. Rochester, NY, 2000, NuNatte Duo Centre Photography, OP Photo Gall., Hong Kong, 2000, FotoFest, 2000; exhibited in numerous group shows including Robert Klein Gallery, Boston, 1981, Cin. Art Mus., 1981, 84, 85, 93, Witkin Gallery, N.Y.C., 1984, Milw. Art Mus., 1986, Dayton (Ohio) Art Inst., 1987, J.B. Speed Art Mus., Louisville, 1988, Trisolini Gallery Ohio U., 1989, Ohio U., Athens, 1989, Centre Nat. Photographie, Paris, 1989, Cleve. Ctr. for Contemporary Art, 1991, Tampa Mus. Art, 1991, 93, Images Gallery, 1991, Dayton Art Inst./Mus. Contemporary Art Wright State U., Dayton, 1992, Bowling Green State U. Sch Art, 1992, Carnegie Arts Ctr., Covington, Ky., 1993, POLK Mus. Art, Lakeland, Fla., 1993, Tampa (Fla.) Mus. Art, 1993, Adams Landing Fine Art Ctr., Cin., 1995, Checkwood Mus. Art, Nashville, 1995, Photo Forum Gallery, 1995, 96, Jean-Pierre Galerie, 1996, Soros Ctr. Contemporary Art, Kiev, Ukraine, 1996, Dom Khudozhnikiv, Kharkiv, Ukraine, 1996, Wolf Photographic Galleries, Cin., 1996, Columbus Mus. Art, 1996, Mus. fine Arts, St. Petersburg, Fla., 1997, Louisville Visual Art Assn., Water Tower, 1997, Mus. Damy di Fotografia Contemporanea, Brescia, Italy, 1998, Kharkiv Mcpl. Art Gallery, Kharkiv, Ukraine, 1999, Jean-Pierre Lambert Gallery, Paris, 1999, Huntington (W.Va.) Mus. Art, 2000, Centre Socio-Cultural Galerie Pierre Tal Coat, Hunnebont, France, 2000; represented in numerous permanent collections Tampa Mus. of Art, Mûnchner Stadt Mus., Munich, Germany, Museo Damy, Brescia, Italy, Ctr. Creative Photography, Tucson, Detroit Inst. Arts, Biblioteque National, Paris, Internat. Photography Hall of Fame and Mus., Kirkpatrick Ctr. Mus. Complex, Okla. City, Nelson Gallery-Atkins Mus., Kansas City, Ctr. for Photography, Bombay, Milw. Art Mus., Mus. Photography Arts, San Diego, Musee Nat. D'Art Modern, Cin. Art Mus., High Mus., Atlanta, Mus. Fine Arts, St. Petersburg, Fla., Centre Georges Pompidou, Paris, Denver Art Mus., Boston Mus. Fine Arts, Stanford U. Mus. Art, Palo Alto, Indpls. Art Mus., New Orleans Mus. Art, Fogg Mus., Cambridge, Mass., numerous others; also pvt. collections; author: Petroglyphs of the Heart, Photographs by Connie Sullivan, 1983; work represented in numerous publs. Trustee Images Ctr. for Fine Photography, Cin., 1986-94. Named Hyde Park Living Person of Yr., 1996; recipient Juried Show, Toledo Friends Photography, 1986, Best of show, 1988, Images Gallery, 1986, Pres.'s Coun. for Arts award, Manhattanville Coll., 1991, Treasure of the Month award, Mus. Fine Arts St. Petersburg, Fla., 1995; fellow Arts Midwest fellow, NEA, 1989—90; grantee Aid to Individual Artists grantee, Summerfair, 1987, travel grantee, Ohio Arts Coun., 1995, 1997, 2000, Artist Projects, 1999. Mem. McDowell Soc. Avocations: travel, reading, gardening, music. Home: 1950 Mount Vernon Dr Fort Wright KY 41011 Fax: 513-871-6931.

SULLIVAN, D. HAROLD, retail grocery company executive; CFO DeMoulas Market Basket, Tewksbury, Mass., ret., 2001. Office: DeMoulas Market Basket 875 East St Tewksbury MA 01876-1469

SULLIVAN, DANIEL F. academic administrator, sociologist, educator; b. Jan. 19, 1944; m. Ann H. Sullivan; 3 children. BS in Math., St. Lawrence U., 1965; PhD in Sociology, Columbia U., 1971. Ctrl. office supr. N.Y. Tel. Co., Syracuse, 1966—67; rsch. assoc. Barnard Coll., 1969—73, instr. sociology, 1970—71; asst. prof. sociology, sr. rsch. assoc. Cornell U., 1974—76; asst. prof. sociology Carleton Coll., 1971—79, assoc. prof. sociology, 1979—86, dean acad. devel. and planning, 1979—81, v.p. for planning and devel., 1981—86, sec. of the coll., 1981—86; pres. Allegheny Coll., Meadville, Pa., 1986—96, prof. sociology, 1986—96; pres. St. Lawrence U., Canton, NY, 1996—, prof. sociology, 1996—. Mem. adv. com. NSF Divsn. Undergrad. Edn., 1991—; chair bd. trustees St. Lawrence Aquarium and Ecol. Ctr.,

1998—; bd. dirs. N.Y. Commn. for Ind. Colls. and Univs., mem. exec. com., 2003; trustee Commn. on Ind. Colls. and Univs., 2002—. Co-author: Research on Human Subjects: Problems and Processes of Social Control in Bio-Medical Experimentation, 1973, Applying Market Research in College Admissions, 1983, What Works: Building Natural Science Communities, 1991. Mem.: Western Pa. Hist. Soc. (trustee 1994—), Am. Assn. Colls. and Univs. (bd. dirs. 2003—). Office: St Lawrence Univ 23 Romoda Dr Canton NY 13617*

SULLIVAN, DANIEL JOSEPH, theater critic; b. Worcester, Mass., Oct. 22, 1935; s. John Daniel and Irene Ann (Flagg) S.; m. Helen Faith Scheid, 1965; children: Margaret Ann, Benjamin, Kathleen. AB, Holy Cross Coll., 1957; postgrad., U. Minn., 1957-59, U. So. Calif., 1964-65, Stanford U., 1978-79. Reporter Worcester Telegram, Mass., 1957, Red Wing Republican Eagle, Minn., 1959, St. Paul Pioneer Press, 1959-61; music and theater critic Mpls. Tribune, 1962-64; comedy writer Dudley Riggs' Brave New Workshop, 1961-64; arts reporter/theater reviewer N.Y. Times, 1965-68; theater critic L.A. Times, 1969-90. Dramaturg Eugene O'Neill Theatre Ctr., Waterford, Conn., 1972-73, 93-98; instr. O'Neill Critics Inst., Waterford, 1977-92, assoc. dir., 1993-98, dir., 1999—; adj. prof. U. Minn., Mpls., 1990—; juror theater panel Nat. Endowment for Arts, 1983; juror Pulitzer Prize for Drama, 1985, 89, 92; pres. L.A. Drama Critics Circle, 1970-71, Ctr. for Arts Criticism, St. Paul, 1992-95. Mem. Am. Theater Critics Assn. (founding). Office Phone: 612-522-9053.

SULLIVAN, DENNIS JAMES, JR., hospitality and music executive; b. Jersey City, Feb. 23, 1932; s. Dennis James and Mary Theresa (Coyle) S.; m. Constance Rosemary Shields, Jan. 31, 1953; children: Denise Sullivan Morrison, Mary Agnes Sullivan Wilderotter, Colleen Sullivan Bastkowski, Andrea Sullivan Doelling. AB, St. Peters Coll., 1953; postgrad., U. Md., 1955; MBA, U. Pa., 1973. Various line and staff positions N.J. Bell, 1955-61, N.Y. Telephone Co., 1961-64, 67-68, AT&T, N.Y.C., 1964-67, 68-76, dir. mktg., 1972-74, asst. v.p., 1974-76; v.p. mktg. Ohio Bell Telephone Co., Cleve., 1976-78; v.p. consumer info. services AT&T-Am. Bell, Parsippany, N.J., 1978-83; exec. v.p. Cin. Bell Telephone Co., 1983-84, pres., 1984-87, also bd. dirs.; exec. v.p., chief fin. officer Cin. Bell Inc., 1987-93; exec. founder Dan Pingor Pub. Rels., 1993-2000; pres., CEO Gaylord Entertainment, Nashville, Tenn., 2000—. Bd. dirs. Fifth Third Bancorp & Bank, Anthem Ins. Co., Kalthoff Internat. Author: Videotex, IEE Nat. Conf., 1981. Bd. dirs. Boy Scouts, Cin. Bd. Edn., 1993-97; gen. chmn. United Way, 1990—. Lt. (j.g.) USN, 1953-55, ret. comdr. USNR, 1976. Mem. Fin. Exec. Inst., Commonwealth Club, Cin. Country Club, Queen City Club, Legatus, Metropolitan Club. Roman Catholic. Office: Gaylord Entertainment Pinger Bldg One Gaylord Dr Nashville TN 37214 E-mail: dennissullivan@gaylordentertainment.com.

SULLIVAN, DONAL D. federal bankruptcy judge; b. 1931; Attended, Loyola U., Chgo., 1949-50, Ill. Inst. Tech., 1952-54; LLB, De Paul U., 1957. Bar: Oreg. 1957, Ill. 1958. 1st asst. U.S. atty. for Oreg., Portland, 1962-65; clk. U.S. Dist. Ct. Oreg., Portland, 1966-69, bankruptcy judge, 1969—98; ret., 1998; recalled, 1998—. Office: US Bankruptcy Ct 900 Bank of Am Plz 1001 SW 5th Ave Portland OR 97204-1147 E-mail: dds@teleport.com, 1donalsz@joimail.com.

SULLIVAN, DOROTHY RONA, state official; b. Jan. 7, 1941; d. Lewis Robert and Dorothy (Hopkins) Sullivan. BA, Boston U., 1963; MEd, State Coll. Boston, 1966; CAGS, Boston U., 1972; postgrad., Northeastern U., 1970—71, Boston Coll., 1974—78, U. Mass., 1980. Rsch. asst. Boston Lying-In Hosp., 1963—64; employment counselor Mass. Divsn. Employment Security, Boston, 1964—66, sr. employment counselor, 1966—67, prin. employment counselor, 1967—70, employment office mgr., 1970—75, supr., 1975—78, chief rsch. dept., 1978—88, dir. def. employment analysis, 1985—87; chief rsch. dept. Mass. Divsn. Employment and Tng., 1989—98, 1998—2002. Supr. cmty. counselor interns and rehab. adminstrn. interns Northeastern U. Grad. Sch. Edn., 1968—74; supr. pub. adminstrn. interns Suffolk U., 1976; supr. econ. interns Boston U., 1979, Regis Coll., 1984, U. Mass.-Boston, 1998; presenter in field. Author: Boston Employment Service Guide, 1969, Careers and Training in the Allied Health Field, 1989, Higher Skills, Higher Wages and Higher Achievement, 1997, Career Families and Career Paths, 1997, Massachusetts Cities and Towns, 1978—82, Outplacement Program, 1993, Presentation and Performance Portfolio, 1998; editor: Mass. Trends, 1978—82; mem. editl. bd. Memos to the Gov., Mgmt. Advice from the Commonwealth's Experts in Pub. Adminstrn., 2003; contbr. articles to profl. jours. Recorder Gov.'s Conf. on Rehab., 1970; mem. Gov.'s Commn. Employment of Handicapped, 1972—78, Pres.'s Com. Employment of Handicapped, 1975—78; exec. bd. Greater Boston coun. Camp Fire Girls, 1971—73; R.S.V.P. adv. bd. Boston Commn. Affairs of the Elderly, 1977—78; mem. adv. com. equal employment opportunity practices Dept. Pers. Adminstrn., 1984—85; mem. adv. group Mass. Occupl. Info. Coordinating Com., 1991—98; mem. adv. bd. Mass. Ctr. Civic Edn., 2001—; bd. dirs. Doric Dames, Mass. State Ho., 2004—. Recipient Recognition award, Nat. Occupl. Info. Coordinating Com., 1994, Exceptional Achievement award, U.S. Sec. Labor, 2003. Mem.: APGA (nat. recorder conf. 1968), ASPA, AACD, ACA (recorder), Am. Bus. Women's Assn. (del. nat. conv. 1980, 1983, pres. Boston chpt. 1982, Woman of Yr., Boston chpt. 1983), Am. Econ. Assn., Am. Acad. Polit. and Social Sci., Am. Fedn. State, County and Mcpl. Employees (exec. bd. local 164 1972—73, 1974—76), Nat. Rehab. Assn. (Mass. sec. 1971—72, exec. bd. 1972—74, v.p. 1974—75, pres. 1976—77), Nat. Career Devel. Assn., Am. Soc. Pub. Adminstrn. (life; region I-II liaison, sect. women in pub. adminstrn. 1988—90, Mass. chpt. coun., officer, treas. 1997, sec. 1998, v.p. 1998—, pres.-elect 1999, pres. 2000, nat. coun. campaign for internat. rels.), Charitable Irish Soc., Rockport Art Assn. (patron), Boston Ctr. for Internat. Visitors, Chatham Swim Club. Home: 33 Morey Rd Roslindale MA 02131-1037 also: Eldredge Sq Chatham MA 02633

SULLIVAN, E. THOMAS, law educator; b. Amboy, Ill., Dec. 4, 1948; s. Edward McDonald and Mary Lorraine (Murphy) S.; m. Susan A. Sullivan, Oct. 2, 1971. BA, Drake U., 1970; JD, Ind. U., Indpls., 1973. Bar: Ind. 1973, Fla. 1974, D.C. 1975, Mo. 1980. Law clk. to Judge Joe Eaton, U.S. Dist. Ct. for So. Dist. Fla., Miami, 1973-75; trial atty. U.S. Dept. Justice, Washington, 1975-77; sr. assoc. Donovan, Leisure, Newton & Irvine, Washington, 1977-79; prof. law U. Mo., Columbia, 1979-84; assoc. dean, prof. Washington U., St. Louis, 1984-89; dean U. Ariz. Coll. Law, Tucson, 1989-95; William S. Pattee prof. law, dean U. Minn. Law Sch., Mpls., 1995—2002, Irving Younger prof. law, 2002—. Fellow Am. Bar Found.; mem. Am. Law Inst., Am. Econ. Assn. Home: 180 Bank St SE Minneapolis MN 55414-1042 Office: U Minn Law Sch Walter F Mondale Hall Office 381 229 19th Ave S Minneapolis MN 55455

SULLIVAN, EARL LE ROY, political science educator, academic administrator; b. Anaconda, Mont., Aug. 11, 1942; s. Earl Richard Sullivan and Margaret Jones; m. Jean Ann Wendell, Aug. 10, 1963; children: Mark, Erin, Colin. BA in Polit. Sci., Seattle U., 1964; PhD in Internat. Rels., Claremont U., 1970. Asst. prof. U. Portland, Oreg., 1967-73, chair social sci., 1970-73; from asst. to full prof. Am. U., Cairo, 1973-99, chair polit. sci., 1994-97, provost, 1998—. Vis. scholar Von Grunebaum Ctr., UCLA, 1984-85, U. Utah, Salt Lake City, 1991-92. Author: Women in Egyptian Public Life, 1986, Social Background and Bureaucratic Behavior in Egypt, 1990; editor: Contemporary Study of the Arab World, 1991, Multilateral Diplomacy and the United Nations Today, 1999; chair editl. bd. Cairo Papers in Social Sci., 1982-84, 87-88. Mem. bd. trustees Cairo Am. Coll., 1974-84, chair bd. trustees, 1974-79. Mem. Am. Soc. Internat. Law, Middle East Studies Assn. Avocations: reading, hiking, camping, fishing, music. Office: Am Univ Cairo 113 Kasr el Aini Cairo Egypt E-mail: tims@aucegypt.edu.

SULLIVAN, EDMUND BERTRAM, writer; b. Salem, Mass., Jan. 28, 1928; s. Michael Lawrence and Eleanor Bertram Sullivan; m. Marie Dianne Sullivan, Aug. 28, 1954 (dec.); children: Geoffrey, David, Maura, Mark. BS in History, Mass. State Coll., 1953; MEd, Boston Coll., 1954; EdD, Boston U., 1968. Prin. New Hampton Pub. Schs., NH, 1954—56; critic tchr., instr. North Adam State Coll., North Adams, Mass., 1956—58; tchr. secondary schs. Newton, Mass., 1958—62; dean faculty Mass. State C.C., Greenfield, 1962—63; edn., grad. studies Am. Internat. Coll., Springfield, Mass., 1963—68; prof. edn. found. U. Hartford, West Hartford, Conn., 1968—85, mus. dir., cur., 1985—93, prof. emeritus, 1993—. Dir. U.S. Peace Corps, East Africa and Zaire, 1973—74; cons. NEH, Detroit, 1989; vis. lectr., scholar U. San Diego, 1996. Author: Collecting Political Americana, 1980, Hellbent for the White House, 1989, Campaigning with James M. Curley, 2000; co-author: Images of American Radicalism, 1999. Vice chmn. Conn. State Libr. Bd., Hartford, 1991—; mem. Suffield Libr. Bd., 1972—, Conn. State Mus. Adv. Bd., Hartford, 1991—; founding dir. Mus. of Am. Polit. Life, U. Hartford; tour dir. Bicentennial Tour of U.K., 1976. With USN, 1945—46, with USMC, 1950—52. Named Disting. Alumnus, Mass. State Coll., 1998; NEH grantee, 1983—85, Inst. for Mus. Svc. grantee, 1988—89. Fellow: John Dewey Soc.; mem.: Nat. Assn. Atomic Vets., New Eng. Hist. Assn., Am. Assn. Mus. Democrat. Avocations: hiking, Irish American studies. Home: 70 Valley View Dr Suffield CT 06078

SULLIVAN, EDWARD, periodical editor; b. Sharon, Pa., 1956; BA in Journalism, Johns Hopkins U., 1979. From news editor to mgr. publs. Am. Soc. Quality Control, 1979-87; acquisitions editor Panel Publishers, 1987-89; editor Trade Press Pub., Milw., 1989—. Office: Trade Press Pub Bldg Operating Mgmt Mag 2100 W Florist Ave Milwaukee WI 53209-3721

SULLIVAN, EDWARD JOSEPH, lawyer, educator; b. Bklyn., Apr. 24, 1945; s. Edward Joseph and Bridget (Duffy) S.; m. Patte Hancock, Aug. 7, 1982; children: Amy Brase, Molly Elsasser, Mary Christine. BA, St. John's U., 1966; JD, Willamette U., 1969; MA, cert. Urban Studies, Portland State U., 1973; LLM, Univ. Coll., London, 1978; diploma in law, Univ. Coll., Oxford, 1984; MA, U. Durham, 1999. Bar: Oreg. 1969, D.C. 1978, Wash. 2001, U.S. Dist. Ct. Oreg. 1970, U.S. Ct. Appeals (9th cir.) 1970, U.S. Supreme Ct. 1972. Counsel Washington County, Hillsboro, Oreg., 1969-75; legal counsel Gov. of Oreg., Salem, 1975-77; ptnr. O'Donnell, Sullivan & Ramis, Portland, Oreg., 1978-84, Sullivan, Josselson, Roberts, Johnson & Kloos, Portland, Salem and Eugene, Oreg., 1984-86, Mitchell, Lang & Smith, Portland, 1986-90, Preston Gates & Ellis, Portland, 1990—2003; owner Garvey Schubert Barer, Portland, Oreg., 2003—. Bd. dirs., pres. Oreg. Law Inst. Contbr. numerous articles to profl. jours. Chmn. Capitol Planning Commn., Salem, 1975-77, 78-81. Mem. ABA (local govt. sect., com. on planning and zoning, adminstrv. law sect.) Oreg. State Bar Assn., D.C. Bar Assn., Wash. State Bar Assn., Am. Judicature Soc., Am. Polit. Sci. Assn. Democrat. Roman Catholic. Office: Garvey Schubert Barer 121 SW Morrison Ste 1100 Portland OR 97204-3141 Office Phone: 503-228-3939. Business E-Mail: ESulliva@gsblaw.com.

SULLIVAN, ELIZABETH B. paralegal studies educator; b. Rhein Main AFB, Germany, June 19, 1955; d. Gene A. and Joyce K. Bromberg; m. Brian B. Sullivan, July 20, 1977; children: Elizabeth, Brian Jr., Charles. BA, U. of the South, 1977; JD, Tulane U., 1980. Bar: Ala. Clk. Ala. Supreme Ct., Montgomery; instr. Cumberland Sch. of Law, Birmingham, Ala.; chair paralegal studies Phillips Jr. Coll., Birmingham, dean of academics; dept. head paralegal studies Virginia Coll., Birmingham. Mem.: DAR (1st vice regent 2004—), Jr. League of Birmingham. Office: Virginia Coll 65 Bagby Dr Birmingham AL 35209

SULLIVAN, ERNEST LEE, human resources director; b. Columbus, Ohio, Dec. 17, 1952; s. Robert Lee and Emma Jane (Phillips) S. BA, Capital U., Columbus, 1980. Cert. profl. in human resources. Mgmt. trainee Bank One Corp., Columbus, 1971-73, personnel generalist, 1973-77, profl. recruiter, 1977-79, employment mgr., 1979-81, v.p. employment mgr., 1981-87; mgr. staffing, employee rels. and labor rels. Rockwell Internat., Columbus, 1988-96; v.p. of exec. selection, regional human resources dir. Banc One Corp., nat. staffing mgr., 1997—, sr. v.p. human resources. Personnel cons. Martin Luther King Ctr., Columbus, 1989—, bd. dirs.; advisor United Negro Coll. Fund, Columbus, 1983—; bus. adv. bd. Cen. State U., Wilberforce, Ohio, 1989—. Pres. bd. Jobs for Columbus Grads., 1995—, Urban Scouting Bd., 2000; pres. bd. dirs. St. Stephen's Cmty. House; bd. dirs. Ctrl. Ohio Transit Authority. Named to Hall of Fame Columbus Met. Housing, 1989-92; recipient Outstanding Bus. and Profl. award, 1993—, Pinnacle award, Eagle award, 1995, Lazarus award, 1997, Cultural Diversity Leadership award, 1998, Roosevelt Carter Cmty. Svc. award, 1999. Mem. Soc. Human Resources and Mgmt., Employment Mgrs. Assn., Personnel Soc. Columbus. Avocations: swimming, flag football, travel, japanese lang. study. Office: Bank One Corp 800 Brookedge Blvd Columbus OH 43271-0001

SULLIVAN, EUGENE JOHN JOSEPH, manufacturing executive, director; b. N.Y.C., Nov. 28, 1920; s. Cornelius and Margaret (Smith) S.; m. Gloria Roesch, Aug. 25, 1943; children: Eugene John Joseph, Edward J., Robert C., Elizabeth Ann Hansler. BS, St. John's U., 1942, D in Commerce, 1973; MBA, NYU, 1948. With chem. divsn. Borden, Inc., N.Y.C., 1946—, beginning as salesman, successively asst. sales, 1957-58, exec. v.p., 1958-64; pres. Borden Chem. Co. divsn. Borden, Inc.; v.p. Borden, Inc., 1964-67, exec. v.p., 1967-73, pres., COO, 1973-79, chmn., pres., CEO, 1979-86; prof. St. John's U., 1987—2003. Bd. dirs. W.R. Grace & Co.; chmn. bd. dirs. Hamilton Fund; trustee Atlantic Mut. Ins. Co. Trustee, vice chmn., past sec. St. John's U., chmn. bd. dirs., 1999—; trustee N.Y. Med. Coll., Cath. Health Assn., Cath. Charities U.S.A., 1999—; chmn. Commn. on Cath. Health Care. Served as lt. USNR, 1942-46; lt. Res. Mem. Coun. Fgn. Rels., Knights of Malta, Knights of Holy Sepulchre, Knights of St. Gregory, Univ. Club, Plandome Country Club.

SULLIVAN, EUGENE RAYMOND, judge; b. St. Louis, Aug. 2, 1941; s. Raymond Vincent and Rosemary (Kiely) S.; m. Lis Urup Johansen, June 18, 1966; children— Kim, Eugene II. BS, U.S. Mil. Acad., 1964; JD, Georgetown U., 1971. Bar: Mo. 1972, D.C. 1972. Law clk. to judge U.S. Ct. Appeals (8th cir.), St. Louis, 1971-72; assoc. Patton Boggs & Blow, Washington, 1972-74; asst. spl. counsel The White House, Washington, 1974; trial counsel U.S. Dept. of Justice, Washington, 1974-82; dep. gen. counsel U.S. Air Force, Washington, 1982-84, gen. counsel, 1984—86, Nat. Reconnaissance Office, 1982—86; gov. Wake Island, 1984—86; judge U.S. Ct. Appeals (Armed Forces), Washington, 1986-90, 95—, chief judge, 1990-95. Mem. Fed. Commn. To Study Honor Code at West Point, 1989-90. Trustee U.S. Mil. Acad., 1989—. With US Army, 1964-69. Decorated Bronze Star, Air medal, airborne badge, ranger badge, others. Republican. Roman Catholic. Home: 6307 Massachusetts Ave Bethesda MD 20816-1139 Office: US Ct Appeals (Armed Forces) 450 E St NW Washington DC 20442-0001 Office Phone: 202-390-5959. Business E-Mail: esullivan@gavelconsultinggroup.com.

SULLIVAN, FRANCES TAYLOR, state legislator; b. Volney, N.Y. m. Eugene Sullivan (dec.); children: Eugene III, Katharine, Margaret. BA, Keuka Coll. Assemblywoman dist. 117 N.Y. State Assembly. Sec. Rep. Conf. N.Y. State Assembly, Agriculture Com., Edn. Com., Ways and Means Com., Vet. Com. Home: 20 N 2nd St Fulton NY 13069-1248 Office: NY State Assembly State Capitol Albany NY 12248-0001 E-mail: sullivf@assembly.state.ny.us.

SULLIVAN, FRANK, JR., state supreme court justice; b. Mar. 21, 1950; s. Frank E. and Colette (Cleary) S.; m. Cheryl Gibson, June 14, 1972; children: Denis M., Douglas S., Thomas R. AB cum laude, Dartmouth Coll., 1972; JD magna cum laude, Ind. U., 1982; LLM, U. Va., 2001. Bar: Ind. 1982. Mem. staff Office of U.S. Rep. John Brademas, 1974-79, dir. staff, 1975-78; with Barnes & Thornburg, Indpls., 1982-89; budget dir. State of Ind., 1989-92; exec. asst. Office of Gov. Evan Bayh, 1993; assoc. justice Ind. Supreme Ct., 1993—. Mem. ABA, Ind. State Bar Assn., Indpls. Bar Assn. Home: 5854 Lawton Loop West Dr Indianapolis IN 46216-2009 Office: State House Rm 321 Indianapolis IN 46204-2728 Office Phone: 317-232-2548.

SULLIVAN, FRANK C. manufacturing executive; BA, U. N.C., 1983. Various comml. lending corp. fin. 1st Union Nat. Bank and Harris Bank, 1983-87; regional sales mgr. AGR Co. RPM Group, Inc., 1987-89, dir. corp. devel., 1989-91, v.p., 1991-93, CFO, 1993-98, exec. v.p., 1998-99, pres., 1999—. Morehead scholar, 1983. Office: 2628 Pearl Rd Medina OH 44256-7623

SULLIVAN, FRANK L., JR., real estate company executive; BS, Cornell U., 1969; MBA, U. Pa., 1971. Asst. v.p. real estate fin. group Provident Nat. Bank, Phila., 1971—74; v.p. real estate acquisitions Schultz Mgmt. Co., Englewood Cliffs, NJ, 1975—78; v.p. real estate investment and mgmt. dept. Citibank, N.Y.C., 1979—83; mng. dir., founding ptnr. ING Clarion Ptnrs., N.Y.C., 1984—; chmn. ING Clarion Capital. Mem. investment com. ING Clarion Ptnrs. Office: ING Clarion 12th Fl 230 Park Ave New York NY 10169*

SULLIVAN, FRANK W, judge; b. Ft. Worth, Tex., May 19, 1947; s. Frank and Marie Wooley Sullivan; m. Ann Wildemann, July 25, 2002; m. Ruth Sullivan (div. 1975); children: Lisa, Frank IV, Megan. BA, U. Tex. at Austin, 1970; JD, Tex. Tech. U., 1973. Bar: Tex. Supreme Ct. 1973. Pvt. practice, Ft. Worth, 1973—83; judge, 322d dist. ct. State of Tex., 1983—. Pres. Tex. Acad. Family Specialists, 2000; former chair Tarrant Co. Juvenile Bd., Bd. Dist. Judges. Recipient Eva Barnes award, Tarrant Co. Family Law Bar, 2000. Mem.: Tex. Acad. Family Law Specialists, Tarrant Co. Bar, State of Tex., Ridglea Country Club. Republican. Episc. Avocations: golf, scuba diving, flying. Office: 322d Dist Ct Civil Courts Bldg Fort Worth TX 76196

SULLIVAN, G. CRAIG, household products executive; b. 1940; BS, Boston Coll., 1964. With Procter & Gamble Co., 1964-69, Am. Express Co., 1969-70; regional sales mgr. Clorox Co., Oakland, Calif., 1971-76, v.p. mktg., 1976-78, mgr. food svc. sales devel., mgr. bus. devel., 1978-79, gen. mgr. food svc. products divsn., 1979-81, v.p. food svc. products divsn., 1981, v.p. household products, 1981-89, group v.p. household products, 1989-92, chmn. bd., pres., CEO, 1992-99, chmn. bd., CEO, 1999—2003; ret., 2003.*

SULLIVAN, GEORGE EDWARD, writer; b. Lowell, Mass., Aug. 11, 1927; s. Timothy Joseph and Cecilia Mary (Shea) S.; m. Muriel Agnes Moran, May 24, 1952; 1 son, Timothy. BS, Fordham U., 1952. Pub. relations mgr. Popular Library, N.Y.C., 1952-55; pub. relations dir. AMF, N.Y.C., 1955-63. Adj. prof. Fordham U. Author: The Day Man Walked on the Moon, 1989, All About Basketball, 1990, The Day They Bombed Pearl Harbor, 1991, Racing Indy Cars, 1992, Mathew Brady, His Life and Photographs, 1993, The Day Women Got the Vote, 1994, Black Artists in Photography, 1995, Alamo!, 1996, Not Guilty, 1997, Portraits of War, Civil War Photographers and Their Work, 1998, One Hundred Years in Photographs, 1999, Picturing Lincoln, 2000, The Civil War at Sea, 2001, Power Football, 2001, In Their Own Words: The Wright Brothers, 2002, Journalists at Risk, 2003, The Civil War Photographs of Mathew Brady, 2004. Served with USN, 1945-48. Mem. PEN, Authors Guild, Am. Soc. Journalists and Authors Roman Catholic. Personal E-mail: gjsbooks@aol.com.

SULLIVAN, GEORGE MURRAY, transportation consultant, former mayor; b. Portland, Oreg., Mar. 31, 1922; s. Harvey Patrick and Viola (Murray) S.; m. Margaret Eagan, Dec. 30, 1947; children: Timothy M., Harvey P. (dec. July 1996), Daniel A., Kevin Shane, Colleen Marie, George Murray, Michael J., Shannon Margaret, Casey Eagan. Student pub. schs.; D.P.A. (hon.), U. Alaska, 1981. Line driver Alaska Freight Lines, Inc., Valdez-Fairbanks, 1942-44; U.S. dep. marshal Alaska Dist., Nenana, 1946-52; mgr. Alaska Freight Lines, 1952-56; Alaska gen. mgr. Consol. Freightways Corp. of Del., Anchorage, 1956-67; mayor of Anchorage, 1967-82; exec. mgr. Alaska Bus. Council, 1968; sr. cons. to pres. Western Air Lines Inc., 1982-87; former legis. liaison for Gov. of Alaska; now cons. Past mem. Nat. Adv. Com. on Oceans and Atmosphere, Joint Fed.-State Land Use Planning Commn.; past chmn. 4-state region 10 adv. com. OEO; mem. Fairbanks City Council, 1955-59, Anchorage City Council, 1965-67, Greater Anchorage Borough Assembly, 1965-67, Alaska Ho. of Reps., 1964-65. Trustee U. Alaska Found.; chmn. Anchorage Conv. and Visitors Bur.; bd. dirs. Western council Boy Scouts Am., 1958-59. Served with U.S. Army, 1944-46. Mem. Nat. Def. Transp. Assn. (life mem., pres. 1962-63), Nat. League Cities (dir.), Pioneers of Alaska, Alaska Mcpl. League (past pres.), Anchorage C. of C. (exec. com. 1963-65, treas. 1965-66, dir.), Alaska Carriers Assn. (exec. com.), Alaska Transp. Conf. (chmn.), U.S. Conf. Mayors (exec. com.), VFW (comdr. Alaska 1952) Clubs: Elks. Home and Office: George M Sullivan Co 1345 W 12th Ave Anchorage AK 99501-4252 Office Phone: 907-272-2918. *America is truly the land of opportunity, and I feel that the success with which God has blessed my life attests to this fact. I have been blessed four times. Not only was I born in America, but I have lived my life in Alaska. My other two blessings are my wonderful and supportive wife and our eight healthy children.*

SULLIVAN, GLENN D. music educator; b. Ridgewood, NJ, Mar. 1, 1975; s. Gerald W. and Beverly Sullivan. MusB Music Mgmt., William Paterson U., 1998. Music instr. Partesi Music Svcs., Inc., South Plainfield, NJ, 1993—. Pvt. music instr. Glenn Sullivan, Wayne, NJ, 1991—. Asst. music dir. Pentecostal Lighthouse Ch., Paterson, NJ, 1990—98, Midvale Gospel Ch., Wanaque, NJ, 2000—02; asst. dir. north jersey diocesan honors band Partesi Music Svcs., Inc., South Plainfield, NJ, 1998—2003. Mem.: Music Educators Nat. Conf. Avocations: computers, music. Home: 31 Emerson Pl Wayne NJ 07470 Personal E-mail: gds3175@aol.com.

SULLIVAN, IRENE A. lawyer; b. Bklyn., 1945; AB, Mount Holyoke Coll., 1967; MA, NYU, 1970; JD cum laude, Fordham U., 1975. Bar: N.Y. 1976. Ptnr. Skadden, Arps, Slate, Meagher & Flom. Mem. Phi Beta Kappa. Office: Skadden Arps Slate Meagher & Flom 4 Times Sq Fl 24 New York NY 10036-6595

SULLIVAN, JAMES EDWARD, poet; b. Cohasset, Mass., July 11, 1928; s. James J. Jr. and E. Louise (Hyland) S.; m. Frances Elizabeth Lynch, Aug. 11, 1963 (dec. Oct. 1976); children: Julia Marietta, John Franklin Joseph. AB, Boston Coll., 1948, MA, 1950. Dir. Woods Meml. Libr., Barre, Mass., 1967-94; ptnr. Crisis and Climax, 1989—. Lectr. in history, Boston Coll., 1962-63. Author: American Town: Barre, Mass., 1774-1994, 1974, In Order of Appearance: 400 Poems, 1988; numerous poems, plays. Selectman, Town of Barre, 1986-92, bd. chmn., 1988-92. Sgt. U.S. Army, 1950-52. Mem.: Am. Legion (past comdr. Barre Post 2). Democrat. Roman Catholic. Home: PO Box 451 Barre MA 01005-0451

SULLIVAN, JAMES F. physicist, researcher; b. Cin., Mar. 7, 1943; s. James E. and Alma L. (Lienesch) S.; m. Sylvia J. Kasselmann, Aug. 16, 1969; 1 child, Robert L. BS, Xavier U., 1965, MS, 1969. Instr. physics Brebeuf Prep. Sch., Indpls., 1965-67, OMI Coll. Applied Sci., U. Cin., 1968-71, asst. prof. physics, 1971-77, assoc. prof. physics, 1977-88, prof. physics, 1988—; dept. head math., physics, computing tech. U. Cin. OMI Coll. of Applied Sci., 2002. Summer faculty researcher Solar Energy Rsch. Inst., Golden, Colo., 1980; mem. high sch. evaluation team N. Ctrl. Assn., Cin., 1983-85; vis. prof. Arcada Polytechnic Inst., Finland, (Jan-May, 2001). Author: Technical Physics, 1988; Co-author: Laboratory Manual for General Physics, 1973, 83, 90, 92, Physics for Technology Laboratory Manual, 1995, 97. Organizer of events St. Xavier H.S. Alumni, Cin., 1983—; vol. examiner Am. Radio Relay League for U.S. Fed. Comm. Commn., Newington, Conn., 1984—; judge physics category Ohio State Sci. Fair, Delaware, Ohio, 1986—; chief negotiator faculty and librs. U. Cin., 1995. Received John B. Hart award (disting. svc. to Southern Ohio sect. of Am. Assn. of Physics Tchrs.), 2001; named Faculty Mem. of Yr., Gamma Alpha chpt. Tau Alpha Phi, 1983. Fellow Ohio Acad. Sci.; mem. AAUP (v.p. U. Cin. chpt. 1994-96), Am. Assn. Physics Tchrs. (founder, past pres., assoc. sec. So. Ohio sect. 1993—, com. on instrnl. media 1994-98, chief organizer and presenter Fundamentals of Radio workshop Toronto 1985, Columbus, Ohio 1986, Bozeman, Mont. 1987, Orono, Maine 1992, Boise, Idaho 1993, South Bend, Ind. 1994, College Park, Md. 1996, Denver, 1997, com. on metric measurements, 2000-03), Ohio Valley Amateur Radio Assn. (pres. 1997—), Am. Soc. Engring. Edn. Achievements include supervising successful attempt of OMI Coll. Applied Sci. contact of shuttle Challenger during STS-51F mission, 1985. Office: Univ Cin 2220 Victory Pkwy Cincinnati OH 45206-2822

SULLIVAN, JAMES GERALD, small business owner; b. Bad Axe, Mich., Sept. 13, 1935; s. John Thomas and Frances Eugena (O'Henley) S.; m. Florence Marie Tack, Sept. 12, 1959; children: Kevin Michael, Kathleen Marie. Student, U. Detroit, 1957—58, Highland Park Coll., 1959—60. Owner

Jerry's Barber Shop, Kinde, Bad Axe, Mich., 1963-66, 79—; purchasing agt. Thumb Elec. Coop., Ubly, Mich., 1966-79, Walbro Corp., Cass City, Mich., 1979-80; sales rep. Thumb Blanket, Bad Axe, Mich., 1980-81, Sta. WLEW, Bad Axe, 1981-82; regional mgr. Pri Am. Fin. Svcs., Bad Axe, 1985—; treas. Colfax Twp., Bad Axe, 1979-90; rural letter carrier U.S. Postal Svc., Bad Axe, 1982-98, ret., 1998. Loss clk., Toplis & Harding Wagner & Gliddon, Detroit, 1959-61; inventory control clk., Carrick Products Co., Royal Oak, Mich., 1957-59. Pres. Huron County Twp. Assn., Mich., 1988—90; leader Boy Scouts Am., Bad Axe, 1975—77. With U.S. Army, 1954—56. Mem. Huron County Rural Letter Carriers Assn. (pres. 1988-2003), Armed Forces Vets. Club of the Nat. Rural Letter Carriers Assn. (Mich. divsn., state sec. 1999—), Am. Legion, 4-H Club (pres. 1948-50), Lions (pres. 1979-80), Cmty. Club (pres. 1976-77), KC (mem. coun. #1546), Ushers Club Sacred Heart Ch. Republican. Roman Catholic. Avocations: gardening, golf, swimming, snowmobiling, fishing. Home: 122 W Richardson Rd Bad Axe MI 48413-9108

SULLIVAN, JAMES KIRK, management consultant; b. Greenwood, S.C., Aug. 25, 1935; s. Daniel Jones and Addie (Brown) S.; m. Elizabeth Miller, June 18, 1960; children: Hal N., Kim J. BS in Chemistry, Clemson U., 1957, MS, 1964, PhD, 1966; postgrad. program for sr. execs., MIT, 1975; DSc (hon.), U. Idaho, 1990. Prodn. supr. FMC Corp., South Charleston, W.Va., 1957-62, tech. supt. Pocatello, Idaho, 1966-69, mktg. mgr. N.Y.C., 1969-70; v.p. govtl. and environ. affairs Boise (Idaho) Cascade Corp., 1970-98; pres., ptnr. Veritas Advisors, LLP, 1999—; exec. com., chmn. trust and investment com., dist. bd. dirs. Key Bank of Idaho, 1983—. Bd. dirs., chmn. audit com. Key Trust Co. of the West; chmn. adv. bd. U. Idaho Coll. Engring., 1966-70, 80-87, centennial campaign, 1987-89, rsch. found., 1980-82; mem. Accreditation Bd. Engring. and Tech., Inc., 1994-99; bd. dirs. Pub. Employees Retirement Sys. of Idaho, St. Al's Regional Med. Ctr., chmn. bldg. com.; chmn. Idaho State Rep. Party. Contbr. articles to profl. jours.; patentee in field. Mem. Coll. of Forest and Recreation Resources com. Clemson U., Idaho Found. for Pvt. Enterprise and Econ. Edn., Idaho Rsch. Found., Inc., Idaho Task Force on Higher Edn.; bd. dirs. Idaho Found. for Excellence in Higher Edn., Exptl. Program to Stimulate Competitive Rsch. NSF, N.W. Nazarene Coll., 1988-90, Boise Philharm., 1996-99, mem. Len B. Jordan Pub Affairs Symposium; trustee Idaho Children's Emergency Fund, 1984-90; trustee Bishop Kelly H.S., 1987-89; chmn. adv. bd. U. Idaho Coll. Engring., Am. Forest and Paper Assn., Govtl. Affairs Com., Environ. Com., Options Adv. Group, Idaho State Rep. Com.; bd. dirs. Boise Master Chorale, 1995-98; pres. Ore-Ida coun. Boy Scouts Am., St. Al's Found. 1st lt. U.S. Army, 1958-59. Recipient Presdl. Citation U. Idaho, 1990, Silver Beaver award Boy Scouts Am. Mem. AIChE, Am. Chem. Soc., Bus. Week Found. (chmn. Bus. Week 1980), Am. Forest and Paper Assn. (environ. and health coun., product and tech. com., solid waste task force), Bus. Roundtable (environ. com.), Idaho Assn. Commerce and Industry (past chmn. bd. dirs.), C. of C. of U.S. (pub. affairs com.). Republican. Home: 5206 Sorrento Cir Boise ID 83704-2347 Office: Veritas Advisors LLP 802 W Bannock St Ste 401 Boise ID 83702-5841 Office Phone: 208-385-7070. Personal E-mail: j.kirksullivan@att.net. Business E-Mail: kirk@veritasadvisor.com.

SULLIVAN, JAMES LEO, organization executive; b. Somerville, Mass., Dec. 11, 1925; s. James Christopher and Anna Agnes (Kilmartin) S.; m. Anne Dorothy Hevner, Jan. 20, 1951; children: Maura, Mark, Lianne, Christopher. BS in History and Govt. cum laude, Boston Coll., 1950, MEd in Adminstrn. and Fin., 1958; DCS (hon.), Suffolk U., 1990. Asst. town mgr., Arlington, Mass., 1957-62; town mgr. Watertown, Conn., 1962-65; chief adminstrv. officer Town of Milton, Mass., 1965-68; city mgr. Cambridge, Mass., 1968-70, 74-81, Lowell, Mass., 1970-74; sr. rsch. asst. MIT, Cambridge, 1970-71; pres. Greater Boston C. of C., 1981-91, H.M.S. Mktg., Boston, 1991—. Chmn. Mass. Gov.'s Local Govt. Adv. Com., 1978; del. to Orgn. Econ. and Coop. Devel., Paris, 1979; chmn. New Eng.-Can. Bus. Coun., 1983; pres. Careers for Later Years, 1983; bd. dirs. Input-Output Computer Svcs., Imugen Inc., Mass. Bus. Devel. Corp. Trustee Emerson Coll., 1984-88, mem. fin. and investment com., 1985-88; bd. dirs. Bunker Hill C.C. Coll. Found., 1988—; mem. Adv. Com. on Reorgn. of Mass. Ct. Sys., 1991—, chmn. budget subcom. 1991—; bd. overseers Univ. Hosp. Boston. With USN, 1943-46. Mem. Mass. League of Cities and Towns (pres. 1978), Mass. Mayors Assn., Internat. City Mgmt. Assn., Nat. League Cities, Am. C. of C. Execs. (bd. dirs. 1988—), World Trade Club (bd. govs. 1986—). Office: HMS Mktg 65 Franklin St Boston MA 02110-1303 E-mail: jls1225@aol.com.

SULLIVAN, JAMES N. retired oil industry executive; b. San Francisco, 1937; Student, U. Notre Dame, 1959. Formerly v.p. Chevron Corp., until 1988, vice chmn., dir., 1988-2000; ret., 2000. Office: Chevron Corp 575 Market St San Francisco CA 94105-2856

SULLIVAN, JAMES NELSON, physician; b. Greenville, SC, Dec. 19, 1946; s. Edgar Nelson and Henrietta Barnwell Sullivan; m. Margaret E. Sullivan, June 10, 1989; children: Frank, Lily, Emma, Julia. BA, U. of the South, 1965; MD, Vanderbilt U., 1974. Med. resident Vanderbilt Hosp., Nashville, 1974—76, 1979—81; endocrinology fellow NIH, 1976—79; instr. in medicine Vanderbilt U., Nashville, 1980-83, clin. assoc. prof. medicine, 1985—; clin. instr. Meharry Med. Coll., Nashville, 1998—, U. Tenn., Nashville, 1983—. Co-chair ethics com. Centennial Med. Ctr. 1998—. Dir. Living Will Project, Nashville, 1997-99; founder Soc. for the Preservation of the Book of Common Prayer, Nashville, 1970-74. Fellow ACP; mem. The Endocrine Soc. (comms. com. 1990-98, ethics adv. com.2003-), Nashville Acad. Medicine (bd. dirs. 1999-2002, ethics adv. com. 2003—), Tenn. Med. Assn. (bd. dirs. 2003—), Alpha Omega Alpha. Avocations: fishing, reading. Office: Nashville Med Group # 700 300 20th Ave N Ste 700 Nashville TN 37203-2117 E-mail: jsullivan@pol.net.

SULLIVAN, JAMES STEPHEN, retired bishop; b. Kalamazoo, July 23, 1929; s. Stephen James and Dorothy Marie (Bernier) S. Student, St. Joseph Sem.; BA, Sacred Heart Sem.; postgrad., St. John Provincial Sem. Ordained priest, Roman Cath. Ch., 1955, consecrated bishop, 1972. Assoc. pastor St. Luke Ch., Flint, Mich., 1955-58, St. Mary Cathedral, Lansing, Mich., 1958-60, sec. to bishop, 1960-61; assoc. pastor St. Joseph (Mich.) Ch., 1961-65, sec. to bishop, 1965-69; assoc. pastor Lansing, 1965; vice chancellor, 1969-72; aux. bishop, vicar gen. Diocese of Lansing, 1972-85, diocesan consultor, 1971-85; bishop Fargo, ND, 1985—2002; ret., 2002. Pres. World Apostolate Fatima; episc. liaison Cath. Mktg. Network; nat. episcopal liaison to the Cath. Cursillo Movement. Mem. U.S. Conf. Cath. Bishops. Roman Catholic. Office: Church of the Holy Spirit 1420 7th St N Fargo ND 58102

SULLIVAN, JANET NELSON, dermatologist, department chairman, health facility administrator; b. Salt Lake City, Feb. 3, 1950; d. Richard Knowlton Nelson, Marian Foote Nelson; m. David J. Schiller; children: Rachel Schiller, Molly Nestor; children: Naomi Schiller, Erika. BA, Antioch Coll., 1972; MD, Ohio State U., 1987. Diplomate Am. Bd. Dermatology. Resident internal medicine Mich. State U. Associated Hosp., Lansing, 1987—89; resident dermatology U. Hosp. Cleve., 1989—92; asst. clin. prof. dermatology Case Western Res. U., Coll. Medicine, Cleve., 1992—97; staff physician Ohio Permanente Med. Group, Cleve., 1992—97; asst. med. dir. Hudson Health Plan, Tarrytown, NY, 1997—98, chief med. officer, 1998—. Chair Westchester NY Diabetes Coalition, Tarrytown, NY, 2001—; chair Provider and Health Plan Coun., Nat. Quality Forum, Washington, 2003—; adv. bd. Taking On Diabetes, 2002; Ctr. for Medicaid and Medicare Svcs./AMA adv. group Electronic Performance Measurement Specifications Project, 2003. Mem. N.Y. State Dept. Health SSI Task Force, 1999—2000, Westchester County Bioterrorism Med. Adv. Com., NY, 2001; mem. validation group Pub. Health Data Standards Consortium Rev. of HL7-EHR Functional Model, 2004. Mem.: AMA, Assn. Clinicians for the Underserved, Women's Dermatology Soc., Westchester County Med. Soc., Med. Soc. State N.Y., Am. Acad. Dermatology, Alpha Omega Alpha. Office: Hudson Health Plan 303 S Broadway Ste 321 Tarrytown NY 10591-5410 Office Fax: 914-631-1615.

SULLIVAN, JERRY STEPHEN, electronics company executive; b. Havre, Mont., July 17, 1945; s. Patrick Joseph and Evangeline (O'Neil) S.; m. Sharon Lee Horton, June 17, 1967; children: Garrett, Mindy, Darren. BS, U. Colo., 1967, MS, 1969, PhD, 1970; advanced mgmt. program, Harvard U. Bus. Sch., 1986. Tech. mgr. N.V. Philips Co., Eindhoven, The Netherlands, 1971-75; group dir. N.Am. Philips Corp., Briarcliff Manor, N.Y., 1975-80; dir. Tektronix, Beaverton, Oreg., 1981-83, div. gen. mgr., 1983-85, corp. dir., 1985-88; v.p. Microelectronics & Computer Tech. Corp., Austin, Tex., 1988-92; pres., CEO, Design Techs. Inc., Austin, 1992—. Chmn. bd. MBA Techs., Inc., Phoenix; bd. dirs. Sherpa Corp., San Jose, Calif., Ontos, Inc. Boston, MBA Tech. Inc., Phoenix; mem. adv. bd. Ctr. Integrated Sys., Stanford U., Palo Alto, Calif., 1982—. Mem. adv. com. Coll. Engring., U. Tex., Austin, 1989—, bd. dirs. Edn. Found., 1990—. Mem. IEEE, Am. Phys. Soc., Assn. Computing Machinery, Am. Mgmt. Assn., Nat. Assn. Corp. Dirs. Avocations: scuba diving, golf, chess, sailing. Office: Design Techs Inc 107 Ranch Rd 620 S Austin TX 78734-3942

SULLIVAN, JERRY WARNER, educator, physician; b. Madisonville, Ky., Sept. 26, 1942; 2 children. BS, Georgetown Coll., 1964; MD, U. Louisville, 1968. Intern San Diego Naval Hosp., 1968-69; resident in surgery Med. Sch. Tulane U., New Orleans, 1971-72, resident in urology Med. Sch., 1972-76; fellow in urology Sloan Kettering Meml. Hosp., N.Y.C., 1976-77; instr. in urology Med. Sch. La. State U., New Orleans, 1977-78, asst. prof., 1978-82, assoc. prof., 1982-87, chmn. dept. urology, 1984—, prof., 1987—. Sec. La. Lithotripter, Inc., New Orleans, 1987-91; sec.-treas. med. staff Hotel Dieu Hosp., New Orleans, 1985-90, pres. med. staff, 1991-92, bd. dirs., 1990. Bd. dirs. YMCA, New Orleans, 1980—98; bd. dirs. La. State U. Clinic, 1987-95, chmn., 1990-92. Mem. AMA, ACS, Am. Urologic Assn., Soc. Surg. Oncologists, Southeastern Sect. Am. Urologic Assn., Southwest Oncology Group, Am. Soc. Clin. Oncology. Avocations: jogging, weightlifting, swimming, biking, aerobics. Office: La State U Med Sch Dept of Urology 1542 Tulane Ave New Orleans LA 70112-2825 Home: 1750 St Charles Ave # 420 New Orleans LA 70130 Office Phone: 504-568-4890. Business E-Mail: jsulli@lsuhsc.edu.

SULLIVAN, JOHN A. congressman; b. Tulsa, Okla., Jan. 1, 1965; m. Judith Marie Beck; children: Tommy, Meredith, Sydney. BBA, Northeastern Okla. State U., 1992. Real estate broker; mem. Okla. Ho. Reps., 1995—2002, U.S. Ho. Reps. from 1st Okla. Dist., 2002—. Republican. Office: 114 Cannon HOB Washington DC 20515-3601

SULLIVAN, JOHN CORNELIUS, JR., lawyer; b. Erie, Pa., Oct. 23, 1927; s. John Cornelius and Catherine J. (Carney) S.; m. Helen E. Kennedy, Feb. 3, 1951; children: John III, Timi Ann, Michael, Elizabeth. BA in Econs., Allegheny Coll., 1953; LLB, Dickinson Sch. Law, 1959. Bar: Pa. 1960, U.S. Supreme Ct. 1976. Sales rep. IBM Corp., 1953-56; mem. firm Nissley, Clecker & Fearen, Harrisburg, Pa., 1959-63; of counsel Nauman, Smith, Shissler & Hall, Harrisburg, 1964—. Asst. city solicitor City of Harrisburg, 1964-68, city solicitor, 1968-70; gen. counsel Harrisburg Redevel. Authority, 1964-68, Harrisburg Mcpl. Authority, 1964-87; solicitor Silver-Spring Twp., 1970-81; dir. accounts and fin. City of Harrisburg, 1963; mem. Pa. House of Reps., 1963-64. Assoc. editor Dickinson Law Rev., 1958-59; editor Dauphin County Reporter, 1961-63. Chmn. bd. dirs. Harrisburg Pub. Library, 1965-73; bd. dirs., sec. Harrisburg Hosp.; bd. dirs. Harrisburg Hosp. Found., 1975-89. Mem. ABA, Pa. Bar Assn., Dauphin County Bar Assn. (past. dir.), The Pa. Soc. (N.Y.C.), Phi Gamma Delta. Home: 107 Sample Bridge Rd Mechanicsburg PA 17050-1940 Office: 200 N 3rd St Fl D18 Harrisburg PA 17101-1518

SULLIVAN, JOHN DAVID, business association executive; b. Bisbee, Ariz., Jan. 13, 1948; s. Lloyd John and Marjorie Jane (Kingsbury) S.; m. Patricia Mary Mathis, 1999. BA, U. Pitts., 1969, MA, 1972, PhD, 1983. Rschr. Inst. for Econ. Rsch., L.A., 1974-75; mem. rsch. staff Pres. Ford Com., Washington, 1976; dir. bus. edn. U.S. C. of C., Washington, 1977-82; asst. dir. The Democracy Program, Washington, 1982-83; program coord. Ctr. for Internat. Pvt. Enterprise, Washington, 1984-89; dir. Washington office Internat. Ctr. for Econ. Growth, 1989-91; exec. dir. Ctr. for Internat. Pvt. Enterprise, Washington, 1991—. Trustee Internat. Devel. Conf., Washington, 1988—. Contbr. articles to jours. in field; mem. editl. bd. Econ. Reform Today, 1991—. Speechwriter, vol. Reagan-Bush campaign, Washington, 1980, 84. Mem. Internat. Studies Assn. Republican. Roman Catholic. Avocations: photography, cooking. Office: Ctr for Internat Pvt Enterprise 1615 H St NW Washington DC 20062-0001

SULLIVAN, JOHN DOMINIC, theater producer, writer; b. La Crosse, Wis., Oct. 6, 1963; s. Arthur John and Eleanor Elizabeth (Skemp) Sullivan. BFA, U. Wis., Superior, 1986. Asst. dir. Duluth Playhouse, Minn., 1985; freelance arts cons. La Crosse, Wis., 1993—; play prodr. Great River Steamboat Co., La Crosse, Wis., 1996—97; stage mgr. La Crosse Cmty. Theatre, Wis., 1997; mng. dir. Fairbanks Shakespeare Theatre, Alaska, 1997. Author: (plays) Murder on the Mississippi, 1996, The Cabaret Killer, 1997. Social concerns com. mem. St. Joseph Cathedral, La Crosse, Wis., 1995—. Democrat. Roman Catholic.

SULLIVAN, JOHN FOX, publisher; b. Phila., Oct. 19, 1943; s. Neil Joseph S. and Mary (Fox) Cullumbine; m. Beverly Knight Lilley, June 10, 1978; stepchildren: Buchanan, Brooke, Whitman, Justin Lilley. BA, Yale U., 1966; MBA, Columbia U., 1968. Staff econ. analyst U.S. Dept. Def., Washington, 1968-69; asst. to pub. Newsweek Internat., N.Y.C., 1970-73, asst. mng. dir., 1974-75; pres., pub. Nat. Jour. Group, Inc., Washington, 1975—, The Atlantic Monthly, 1999—. Mem. editl. adv. bd. Who's Who. Bd. dirs. Arena Stage. Mem.: Mag. Publs. Am. (Bd. dirs.), Yale Club (N.Y.C.). Episcopalian. Home: 22 Old Vineyard Ln Flint Hill VA 22627-1735 Office: Nat Jour Group 1501 M St NW Ste 300 Washington DC 20005-1700

SULLIVAN, JOHN LOUIS, JR., retired search company executive; b. Macon, Ga., Aug. 27, 1928; s. John Louis and Elizabeth (Macken) S.; m. Barbara Boyle, Aug. 17, 1974; children: John, Katherine, Betsy, Ted. AB in Econs., Duke U., 1950; MBA, U. Pa., 1957; postgrad. Advance Mgmt. Program, Harvard U., 1975. Br. mgr. IBM, Phila., 1962-63, mgr. edn. Endicott, N.Y., 1963-64; asst. to pres. Data Processing Div. IBM, White Plains, N.Y., 1965-67; dist. mgr. Data Processing Div. IBM, Washington, 1967-69; mgr. eastern and fed. regions Memorex Corp., 1969-71; v.p. mktg. Infonet div. Computer Sci. Corp., El Segundo, Calif., 1971-75; exec. v.p. Fin. Service Group-ADP Inc., Clifton, N.J., 1975-77; sr. v.p. Heidrick & Struggles Inc., San Francisco and Los Angeles, 1977-82, dir., 1977-82, office mgr., 1979-82; v.p., mng. dir. Korn-Ferry Internat., Los Angeles, 1982-87, v.p., mng. ptnr. Boston, 1987-94; ret., 1994. Bd. dirs., mem. exec. com. March of Dimes, Los Angeles County; bd. regents Mount St. Mary's Coll., L.A.; chmn. bd. Latin Am. Resource Ctr.; bd. dirs. Coalition St. Simons and Sea Island. Served to lt. (j.g.) USN, 1950-53. Mem. Harvard U. Bus. Sch. Alumni Assn. (dir.). Clubs: Regency (Los Angeles), Bankers (San Francisco), Atheneum (Pasadena), Mission Hills (Rancho Mirage), Calif. Yacht (Los Angeles), Harvard (Boston), Newcomers (pres.), Rotary (bd. dirs.). Democrat.

SULLIVAN, JOHN MATTHEW, mathematician, educator; b. Princeton, N.J., Feb. 25, 1963; s. Roger D. and Margaret Gummere (Peplow) S. AB summa cum laude, Harvard U., 1985; cert. of advanced studies in math., Cambridge (Eng.) U., 1986; PhD, Princeton (N.J.) U., 1990. Software cons. Marble Assocs., Waltham, Mass., 1984-91; asst. prof. math. U. Minn., Mpls., 1991-97, U. Ill., Urbana, 1977-2000, assoc. prof. math., 2000—. Contbr. articles to profl. jours. Recipient Arnold O. Beckman rsch. award, 1997-99; Henry Cambridge U. fellow, 1985-86, NSF grad. fellow, 1986-89, Alfred P. Sloan doctoral dissertation fellow, 1989-90, Geometry Computing Group postdoctoral fellow, 1990-93, Math. Scis. Rsch. Inst. postdoctoral fellow, 1993-94. Mem. Am. Math. Soc., Math. Assn. Am. Achievements include research in minimal surfaces, knot theory and computational and optimal geometry. Office: U Ill Dept Math 250 Altgeld Hall 1409 W Green St Urbana IL 61801-2943 E-mail: jms@uiuc.edu.

SULLIVAN, JOSEPH PETER, risk and insurance management consultant; b. Boston, Sept. 8, 1939; s. Joseph Francis and Mary Anna S.; m. Rachael Anne Cullen, Dec. 22, 1974; children: Philip, Sandra, Susan, Frederick. B Gen. Studies, U. Nebr., 1968; MA, U. No. Colo., 1973, Cen. Mich. U., 1976. Sr. acct. exec. Arkwright Ins., Greenwich, Conn., 1977-83; v.p. Frenkel & Co., N.Y.C., 1983-84; sr. account exec. Republic Hogg Robinson, N.Y.C., 1984-85; v.p. Alexander & Alexander, N.Y.C., 1985-92, Hugh Wood Inc., N.Y.C., 1992-93, Crawford-THG, N.Y.C., 1993-98; sr. v.p. Frontline Ins. Mgrs., Tampa, Fla., 1998—. Assoc. Miller-Heiman Internat., 1986-92; instr. Dale Carnegie and Assocs., 1980-87; ajd. prof. ins. The Coll. of Ins., N.Y.C., 1991-98. Mem. membership com. Met. Rep. Club; bd. advisors The Salvation Army. With U.S. Army, 1956—77, with ETO, Korea and Vietnam. Decorated Bronze Star. Mem. Assn. Former Intelligence Officers (life), Ret. Officers Assn. (bd. dirs. Knickerbocker chpt.), Soc. CPCU's, Am. Soc. CLU's, Nat. Assn. Health Underwriters, Profl. Liability Underwriting Soc., N.Y. Soc. Security Analysts, Soc. Competitive Intelligence Profls., Toastmasters, N.Y. Athletic Club, Rotary, Masons, Shriners. Republican. Roman Catholic. Avocations: american history, photography, collecting old photographic prints and antique photographic equipment. Home and Office: 15920 Dawson Ridge Dr Tampa FL 33647-1324 Office Phone: 873-903-8073.

SULLIVAN, KATHLEEN MARIE, former dean, law educator; b. Cornell U., 1976, Oxford (Eng.) U., 1978; JD, Harvard U., 1981. Law clk. Hon. James L. Oakes U.S. Ct. Appeals (2d cir.), 1981-82; pvt. practice, 1982-84; asst. prof. Harvard U., Cambridge, Mass., 1984-89, prof., 1989-93, Stanford (Calif.) U. Law Sch., 1993—, Richard E. Paradise fellow, 1995-96, Stanley Morrison prof., 1996—, dean, Richard E. Lang prof. law, 1999—2004. Vis. prov. U. So. Calif. Law Ctr., 1991, Stanford U., 1992; lectr., commentator on constnl. law. Co-editor: (with Gerald Gunther) Constitutional Law, 13th edit., 1997. Named one of 50 Top Women Lawyers Nat. Law Jour., 1998; recipient Albert M. Sacks-Paul A. Freund award for Teaching Excellence, Harvard, 1992, John Bingham Hurlbut award for excellence in tchg. Stanford U., 1996. Fellow Am. Acad. Arts and Scis, Am. Philosophical Soc.; bd. trustees, The Century Found. Office: Stanford U Law Sch Bldg Lawsh 559 Nathan Abbott Way Stanford CA 94305-8610 Business E-Mail: sullivan@law.stanford.edu.

SULLIVAN, KATHLEEN N. political organization administrator, lawyer; b. Manchester, N.H., June 21, 1954; Student, Georgetown U.; BA cum laude, Coll. Holy Cross, 1976; JD, Cornell U., 1981. Bar: N.H. 1981. Chair N.H. Dem. Party, Concord; with Wadleigh, Starr & Peters, Manchester, NH, 2003—. Bd. dirs. Fed. Home Loan Bank of Boston. Trustee Manchester Pub. Lib.; former mem. Mancester charter commn. N.H. Juvenile Parole Bd.; past. treas., dir. N.H. Women's Lobby; past dir. YWCA, Manchester. Mem. N.H. Bar Assn. Office: Wadleigh Starr Peters 95 Market St Manchester NH 03101 also: Democratic Party Office 2 1/2 Beacon St Concord NH 03301

SULLIVAN, KATHRYN ANN, performing arts educator; b. New Haven, Conn., May 11, 1951; d. Vincent and Helen Sullivan; m. Gregory J. Ottmar; 1 child, Chris Ottmar. Tchr. ballet NYU-Cap 21, N.Y.C., Barnard Coll., Steps on Broadway. Choreographer, co-dir. Inner Landscapes Dance Theater, N.Y.C. Performer: (ballets) Boston Ballet, Les Grands Ballet, Canadiens and Conn. Ballet. Home: 726 Washington St New York NY 10014 E-mail: kathrynsullivan100@earthlink.net.

SULLIVAN, KATHRYN D. geologist, former astronaut; b. Paterson, N.J., Oct. 3, 1951; d. Donald P. and Barbara K. Sullivan. BS in Earth Scis., U. Calif., Santa Cruz, 1973; PhD in Geology, Dalhousie U., Halifax, N.S., Can., 1978; Dr. (hon.), Halhousie, Halifax, N.S., Can., 1985, SUNY, Utica, 1990, Stevens Inst., 1992. Astronaut NASA, 1979—93, mission specialist flight STS-41G, 1984, mission specialist flight STS-31, 1990, payload comdr. flight STS-45, 1992; chief scientist NOAA, Washington, 1993—96; pres., CEO Ctr. of Science & Industry, Columbus, Ohio, 1996—. Adj. prof. Rice U., Houston, 1985-92; mem. Nat. Commn. on Space, 1985-86; mem. exec. panel Chief of Naval Ops., 1988, chair, Ohio Aerospace and Defense Adv. Coun., 2002. Comdr. USNR. Recipient Space Flight medal NASA, 1984, 90, 92, Exceptional Svc. medal, 1985, 91, Outstanding Leadership medal, 1992, Nat. Air and Space Mus. trophy Smithsonian Instn., 1985, Haley Space Flight award AIAA, 1991, AAS Prather Eva award, 1992, Flight Achievement award, 1990. Mem. AIAA, Geol. Soc. Am., Am. Geophys. Union, Soc. Women Geographers, Explorers Club. First Am. woman to walk in space. Office: COSI Columbus 333 W Broad St Columbus OH 43215

SULLIVAN, KEITH MONTGOMERY, operations research specialist; b. Stanford, Calif., Oct. 15, 1974; s. John Patrick and Jean Elizabeth Sullivan. BA in journalism, BS in math., Ind. U., 1998; MS in math., Purdue U., 2001. Rsch. asst. US Army Corps of Engineers, West Lafayette, Ind., 1998—2001; ops. rsch. analyst Naval Undersea Warfare Ctr., Newport, RI, 2001—. Recipient Spl. Act award, Naval Undersea Warfare Ctr., 2002; Jack Scott scholarship, Ind. U. Sch. of Journalism, 1996. Mem.: Mil. Ops. Rsch. Soc., Assn. for Computing Machinery, Soc. of Indsl. and Applied Math. Achievements include research in innovative ways to use queueing theory to analyze decision making. Avocations: Tae Kwon Do, photography, bicycling. Home: 3912 Penderview Dr Apt 528 Fairfax VA 22033-4719 Personal E-mail: keithsullivan31@hotmail.com.

SULLIVAN, KENNETH WAYNE, engineer; b. N.Y.C., Apr. 15, 1957; s. William A. and Helen J. Sullivan; m. Christina A. Eastwood, Sept. 10, 1983 (div. Apr. 1997); children: Daniel, Sarah. AAS, SUNY, Farmingdale, 1978, BS, 2003. Draftsman, jr. designer Cosentini Assoc., N.Y.C., NY, 1981—84; sr. designer Syska & Hennessy Engrs., N.Y.C., NY, 1984—88; project engr. Sikorski Engring. Assn., Jericho, NY, 1990—93, Lehr Assocs., N.Y.C., 1993—99, Sear Brown, Melville, NY, 1999—2003; project mgr. Estee Lauder Co., 2003—. Recipient award, Am. Sch. and Univ. Archtl. Portfolio, 1997. Mem.: ASHRAE, Nat. Trust Hist. Preservation. Roman Catholic. Avocations: reading, history, music, running. Home: 21 Ferney St Hicksville NY 11801-5147 Office: Estee Lauder Co 350 S Service Rd Melville NY 11747

SULLIVAN, KEVIN, bureau chief, reporter; m. Mary Jordan; 2 children. Grad., U. N.H., 1981; postgrad., Georgetown U., 1994—95, Stanford U., 1999—2000. Reporter Gloucester Daily Times, Mass., Providence Jour.-Bull., RI, 1986—90; reporter met. staff Washington Post, 1991—, co-bur. chief Tokyo bur., 1995—99, co-bur. chief Mexico City bur., 2000—. Co-recipient Pulitzer prize for internat. reporting, 2003; recipient John S. Knight fellowship, Stanford U., 1999—2000, award, Inter-Am. Press Assn., 1990. Office: The Washington Post 1150 15th St NW Washington DC 20071

SULLIVAN, KEVIN B. lieutenant governor, former state legislator; b. Hartford, Conn., Aug. 20, 1949; s. John (dec.) and Gwendolyn Price (Bancroft) S.; m. Carolyn Thornberry, 1985. AB, Trinity Coll., 1971; JD, U. Conn., 1982. Polit. cons. in pvt. practice, West Hartford, Conn., 1973-74; adminstrv. clk. edn. com. Conn. Ho. of Reps., Hartford, 1974-76; legis. asst. State Commr. Edn., 1976-81; atty. Byrn Slater Sandler Shulman & Rouse, Hartford, 1981—; councilman Town of West Hartford, 1981-86, mayor, 1983-85, dep. mayor, 1985-86; mem. Dist. 5 Conn. Senate, Hartford, 1986—2004, Pro Tempore, 1997—2004; lt. gov. State of Conn., 2004—. Chmn. edn. com., mem. internship and transp. coms., dep. minority leader Conn. State Senate. Mem. ABA, Hartford Bar Assn., Greater Hartford Jaycees (Man of Yr. 1983), Pi Gamma Mu. Founded State Capitol Vietnam Veterens Meml. Democrat. Office: State Capitol Rm 304 210 Capitol Ave Hartford CT 06106

SULLIVAN, KEVIN JOSEPH, mechanical engineer; b. Dover, Del., Jan. 15, 1963; s. James Joseph and Eslie La Verne Sullivan; m. Julie Erlene Adams, Sept. 15, 1985; 1 child, Nolan Joseph. BS in Mechanical Engring., U. Calif., Santa Barbara, 1985, MS in Mech. Engring., 1987. Analyst Toyon Rsch. Corp., Goleta, Calif., 1987—93, sr. analyst, 1993—2003, dir. ISR Algorithm Devel., 2000—03, v.p., 2003—. Office: Toyon Rsch Corp 75 Aero Camino Ste A Goleta CA 93117 Business E-Mail: ksullivan@toyon.com.

SULLIVAN, LARRY EDWARD, librarian; b. Chgo., June 6, 1944; s. George A. and Veronica B. (Cibulka) S.; children: Mara, Alene and Elena. BA, DePaul U., 1966; Fulbright fellow, U. Poitiers, France, 1966-67; MA, Johns Hopkins U., 1970, PhD, 1975. Asst. prof. history Western Md. Coll., Westminster, 1975-76; libr. dir. Md. State Penitentiary, Balt., 1977-78; head libr. Md. Hist. Soc., Balt., 1978-80, N.Y. Hist. Soc., N.Y.C., 1980-84; prof., chief libr.

Lehman Coll., CUNY, Bronx, NY, 1984—89; chief Rare Book and Spl. Collections div. Libr. of Congress, Washington, 1989-95, chief rare book and spl. collections divsn., 1989-95; prof., chief librarian, assoc. dean John Jay Coll. of Criminal Justice, N.Y., 1995—; prof. criminal justice Grad. Sch. and Univ. Ctr. CUNY; ind. appraiser of rare book and manuscript collections, 1995—. Mem. editl. bd. Book History, Ency. of Crime and Punishment, Crime and Justice in New York City, Handbook of Transnational Crime & Justice; editor-in-chief Ency. Law Enforcement; author/co-editor: Guide to the Research Collections of the Maryland Historical Soc., 1981, The Prison Reform Movement: Forlorn Hope, Boston, 1990, rev. edit., 2002, Library of Congress Rare Books and Special Collections: An Illustrated Guide, 1992, Pioneers, Passionate Ladies and Private Eyes: Dime Novels, Series Books and Paperbacks, 1996, Bandits and Bibles: Convict Literature in Nineteenth Century America, 2003, Encyclopedia of Law Enforcement, 3 vols., 2004; contbr. articles to profl. jours., chpts. to books in field. Fellowship NDEA, 1967-71; grantee George N. Shuster Publs., 1989. Mem. ALA, Am. Hist. Assn., Medieval Acad. Am., Am. Soc. Criminology, Am. Printing History Assn., Assn. Internat. de Bibliophilie, Grolier Club, Cosmos Club, Century Assn. Office: Sealy Libr John Jay Coll CUNY 899 10th Ave New York NY 10019-1069 E-mail: lsullivan@jjay.cuny.edu.

SULLIVAN, LAURA PATRICIA, lawyer, insurance company executive; b. Des Moines, Oct. 16, 1947; d. William and Patricia S. BA, Cornell Coll., Iowa, 1971; JD, Drake U., 1972. Bar: Iowa 1972. Various positions Ins. Dept. Iowa, Des Moines, 1972-75; various legal positions State Farm Mut. Auto Ins. Co., Bloomington, Ill., 1975-81, sec. and counsel, 1981-88, v.p., counsel and sec., 1988—; v.p., sec., dir. State Farm Cos. Found., 1985—; sec. State Farm Lloyd's, Inc., 1987—; v.p., counsel and sec. State Farm Fire and Casualty Co., 1988—, State Farm Gen. Ins. Co., 1988—, also bd. dirs.; v.p. counsel, sec., dir. State Farm Life and Accident Assurance Co.; v.p. counsel, sec. State Farm Annuity and Life Assurance Co., State Farm Life Ins. Co.; dir. State Farm Indemnity Co., Bloomington, Ill., 1995—; sec., dir. State Farm Fla. Ins. Co., 1998—. Bd. dirs. Ins. Inst. for Hwy. Safety, Nat. Conf. Ins. Guaranty Funds, chmn., 1995-97. Trustee John M. Scott Indsl. Sch. Trust, Bloomington, 1983-86, Cornell Coll., 1999—; bd. dirs. Scott Ctr., 1983-86, Bloomington-Normal Symphony, 1980-85, YWCA of McLean County, 1993-95; chmn. Ins. Inst. for Hwy. Safety, 1987-88. Mem. ABA, Iowa State Bar Assn., Am. Corp. Counsel Assn., Am. Soc. Corp. Secs. Office: State Farm Mut Automobile Ins Co 1 State Farm Plz Bloomington IL 61710-0001

SULLIVAN, LAWRENCE MATTHEW, lawyer; b. Wilmington, Del., Sept. 5, 1937; BA Philosophy, King's Coll., 1959; LLB, Cath. U. Am., 1964. Bar: US Supreme Ct./Del. 1965, US Dist. Ct./Del. 1966. Pvt. practice, 1965; asst. county atty. New Castle County, 1966—67, register of wills, 1966—70; pub. defender State of Del., 1970; instr. bus. and real estate law Wilmington Coll., 1969—78, Del Tech. and Cmty. Coll., 1978—80, Del. State Coll., 1980—82, Brandywine Coll.; vice chmn. and mem. various com., Criminal Justice Coun., Del. Co-author: (novels) Del. Fundamentals of Real Estate, 1980. Named Del. Outstanding Young Rep. of Yr., Del., 1965, Wilmington's Young Man of Yr., Wilmington Del., 1966, one of Outstanding Young Men of Am., 1968. Mem.: New Castle County Officials Assn. (pres. 1968—70), Del Trial Lawyers Assn., Del. Bar Assn., Trial Lawyers Am., Am. Arbitration Assn., ABA, Sentencing Accountability Commn., Gov. Crime Reduction Task Force, Del. Agy. to Reduce Crime, Del Supreme Ct. Commn. on Del. Ct. 2000, Del Supreme Ct. Planning and Long Range Ct. Planning Com., Phi Alpha Delta. Office: Sullivan & Bartley 1010 Concord Ave # 201 Wilmington DE 19802-3367

SULLIVAN, LOUIS WADE, former secretary health and human services, physician; b. Atlanta, Nov. 3, 1933; s. Walter Wade and Lubirda Elizabeth (Priester) S.; m. Eve Williamson, Sept. 30, 1955; children: Paul, Shanta, Halsted. BS magna cum laude, Morehouse Coll., Atlanta, 1954; MD cum laude, Boston U., 1958. Diplomate: Am. Bd. Internal Medicine. Intern N.Y. Hosp.-Cornell Med. Ctr., N.Y.C., 1958-59, resident in internal medicine, 1959-60; fellow in pathology Mass. Gen. Hosp., Boston, 1960-61; rsch. fellow Thorndike Meml. Lab. Harvard Med. Sch., Boston, 1961-63; instr. medicine Harvard Med. Sch., 1963-64; asst. prof. medicine N.J. Coll. Medicine, 1964-66; co-dir. hematology Boston U. Med. Ctr., 1966; assoc. prof. medicine Boston U., 1968—73; dir. hematology Boston City Hosp., 1973-75; also prof. medicine and physiology Boston U., 1973—75; dean Sch. Medicine, Morehouse Coll., Atlanta, 1975-89; pres. Morehouse Sch. Medicine, Morehouse Coll., Atlanta, 1981—89, 1993—2002, pres. emeritus, 2002—; sec. Dept. of Health and Human Svcs., Washington, 1989-93. Non-exec. dir. GM, 1993—; mem. sickle cell anemia adv. com. NIH, 1974-75; ad hoc panel on blood diseases Nat. Heart, Lung Blood Disease Bur., 1973, Nat. Adv. Rsch. Coun., 1977; mem. med. adv. bd. Nat. Leukemia Assn., 1968-70, chmn., 1970; researcher suppression of hematopoiesis by ethanol, pernicious anemia in childhood, folates in human nutrition. John Hay Whitney Found. Opportunity fellow, 1960-61; recipient Honor medal Am. Cancer Soc., 1991. Mem. Assn. Am. Physicians, Am. Soc. Hematology, Am. Soc. Clin. Investigation, Clin. and Climatological Soc., Inst. Medicine, Phi Beta Kappa, Alpha Omega Alpha. Episcopalian. Office: Morehouse Sch Medicine Office of the Pres Emeritus 720 Westview Dr SW Atlanta GA 30310-1458

SULLIVAN, MARCIA WAITE, lawyer; b. Chgo, Nov. 30, 1950; d. Robert Macke and Jacqueline (Northrop) S.; m. Steven Donald Jansen, Dec. 20, 1975; children: Eric Spurlock, Laura Macke, Brian Northrop. BA, DePauw U., 1972; JD, Ind. U., 1975. Assoc. Arnstein, Gluck, Weitzenfeld & Minow, Chgo., 1975-76; ptnr. Greenberger and Kaufmann, Chgo., 1976-86, Katten Muchin Zavis Rosenman, Chgo., 1986—. Adj. prof. Kent Coll. Law, Ill. Inst. Tech., Chgo., 1991—94; pres. Chgo. Real Estate Exec. Women, 2000—01. Mem. editl. adv. bd.: Real Estate Chgo., 2001—02. Mem. NNCREW Found. Grant Making Com, 2003—04. Mem. ABA, Chgo. Bar Assn. Avocations: bicycling, cross country skiing, gardening, camping. Office: Katten Muchin Zavis Rosenman 525 W Monroe St Ste 1600 Chicago IL 60661-3693 Office Phone: 312-577-8535.

SULLIVAN, MARGARET M. editor; d. John and Elaine (Saab) Sullivan; m. Charles "Bud" Anzalone; children: Alex, Grace. BA in English, Georgetown U., 1979; MS with distinction, Medill Sch. Journalism, Northwestern U., 1980. Clk. Washington bur. Gannett News Svc., 1977—80; Buffalo-area stringer N.Y. Times, 1984—89; reporter, news-feature reporter, columnist Buffalo News, 1980—87, asst. city editor, 1987—89, asst. mng. editor, 1989—98, mng. editor, 1998—99, editor, 1999—. Instr. journalism SUNY, Buffalo, 1991—93. Named One of Buffalo's Outstanding Young Bus. Leaders, Bus. 1st newspaper, 1992; named to Medill Sch. Journalism Hall of Achievement, 2003; recipient Award for Internat. Understanding, Rotary Found., 1987, Young Leadership award, YMCA, 1987. Mem.: Kappa Tau Alpha. Office: Buffalo News The News Plaza Buffalo NY 14203*

SULLIVAN, MARTIN J. insurance company executive; With fin. dept. Am. Internat. Underwriters Ltd., 1971—83, property mgr., 1983—88, London office mgr., regional mktg. mgr. for U.K. and Ireland, 1988—89, asst. mng. dir., 1989—91, CEO, 1991—93, pres., UK/Ireland div., 1993—95, pres., 1997—98; sr. v.p. Am. Internat. Group, Inc., 1995—98, exec. v.p., 1998—2002, co-COO, 2002—, vice chmn., 2002—. Office: Am Internat Group Inc 70 Pine St New York NY 10270*

SULLIVAN, MARY ANN, artist; b. Columbus, Ohio, June 17, 1952; d. Thomas Joseph and Mary Jane (neeHouck) Sullivan; 1 child, Benjamin James. BFA in illustration, Columbus Coll. of Art and Design, 1974. Designer, illustrator Gibson Greeting Cards, Cin., 1974—78; freelance comml. artist Artwear, Albuquerque, 1984—90; exhibiting fine artist Fine Arts Ctr. En Taos, Taos, N.Mex., 1984—86, Spangler Cummings Gallery, Columbus, 1984—88, El Taller Gallery, Taos, N.Mex., 1984—94, Roberta Kuhn Gallery, Columbus, 1988—92, various galleries, 1992—. Book illustrator, Songs of the Earth, 1976, exhibited in group shows at Ohio State Fair Fine Arts Exhibit, 2001, Wilmington Coll., 2001, Spangler Cummings Gallery, Ohio, Roberta Kuhn Gallery, Grand Ctrl. Galleries, N.Y.C., 1985, El Taller Gallery, N. Mex., 1988, 1990, Society of Illustrators Annual Nat. Exhibits 18, 19, 22, 27, N.Y.C., exhibited in group shows. Mem.: Ohio Art League. Avocations: books, interior decorating.

SULLIVAN, MARY ANNE, lawyer, government official; BA in Philosophy summa cum laude, Fordham U., 1973; JD, Yale U., 1976. Law clk. to Hon. Walter K. Stapleton U.S. Dist. Ct., Wilmington, Del., 1976-77; assoc. Hogan & Hartson, Washington, 1977-84, ptnr., 1985-94; dep. gen. counsel Environ. and Civilian and Def. Nuclear Programs, U.S. Dept. Energy, Washington, 1994-98; gen. counsel U.S. Dept. Energy, Washington, 1998—. Instr. Lawyers Com. for Civil Rights; spkr. in field. Contbr. articles to profl. jours. Active Dem. Party, 1982—; sr. domestic issues advisr Geraldine Ferraro in Mondale Campaign; with debate prep. team Senator Bentsen in Dukakis Campaign; counsel to Clinton Campaign and Clinton/Gore Transition Team, 1992. Office: US Dept Energy Gen Counsel Rm 6A-245 1000 Independence Ave SW Washington DC 20585-0001 Home: 2850 Allendale PL NW Washington DC 20008-1038 Fax: 202-586-1499.

SULLIVAN, MARY BROSNAHAN, advocate, social services administrator; m. John Sullivan, Apr. 21, 2001. Degree in Comm., Notre Dame U., 1983. With Universal Studios; press aide 1988 Dem. Presdl. Campaign; joined Coalition for the Homeless, N.Y.C., 1989, exec. dir., 1990—. Recipient Dr. Thomas A. Dooley award, Notre Dame U., 2002. Office: Coalition for the Homeless 129 Fulton St New York NY 10038

SULLIVAN, MARY MARGARET, state legislator; b. Marlborough, Mass., Sept. 9, 1952; d. Robert Patrick and Eileen Frances (Lawless) S.; m. Donald W. Meals; 1 child. BA in History, Trinity Coll., 1974; MS in Journalism, Boston U., 1979. Legis. asst. Office of Senator Patrick Leahy, Washington, 1975-78; reporter News Tribune, Waltham, Mass., 1979-81; reporter, editor News Limited, Sydney, Australia, 1981-82; copy editor Washington (D.C.) Post, 1982-88; legis. aide Office of Senator Doug Racine, Montpelier, Vt., 1989; writer U. Vt. Office of Pub. Rels., Burlington, 1989-91; comm. dir. Vt. Housing Fin. Agy., Burlington, 1991-92; state rep. Vt. State Legis., 1991—. Chair Chittenden County Dem. Com., 1991—; sec. Dem. State Com., Vt., 1991—; bd. dirs. Burlington (Vt.) Cmty. Land Trust, 1992—. Mem. Amnesty Internat. Home: 84 Caroline St Burlington VT 05401-4812

SULLIVAN, MARY ROSE, English language educator; b. Boston, May 13, 1931; d. John Joseph and Elinor Mary (Crotty) Sullivan BA, Emmanuel Coll., Boston, 1952; MA, Cath. U. Am., 1957; PhD, Boston U., 1964. Tchr. Woburn Pub. Schs., Mass., 1957-60; faculty Emmanuel Coll., Boston, 1960-66; prof. English U. Colo., Denver, 1966-96. Book reviewing staff San Diego Mag., 1980-90. Author: Browning's Voices in the Ring and the Book, 1969; co-editor: (3 vols.) letters of E.B. Browning to M.R. Mitford, 1836-54, 1983, Women of Letters: Selected Letters of E.B. Browning to M.R. Mitford, 1987, Crime Classics, 1990, Elizabeth Barrett Browning: Selected Poetry and Prose, 1993; editl. bd. English Lang. Notes, 1970-96. Served to capt. USNR, 1952-83. Am. Coun. Learned Socs. fellow, 1973. Mem. MLA, Boston Browning Soc., Mystery Writers of Am.

SULLIVAN, MICHAEL EVAN, investment and management company executive; b. Phila., Dec. 30, 1940; s. Albert and Ruth (Liebert) S. BS, N.Mex. State U., 1966, MA, 1967; BS, U. Tex., 1969; MBA, U. Houston, 1974; MS, U. So. Calif., 1976, MPA, 1977, PhD in Adminstrn., 1983; BS in Acctg., U. La Verne, 1981. Sr. adminstrv. and tech. analyst Houston Lighting & Power Co., 1969-74; electronics engr. U.S. Govt., Point Mugu, Calif., 1974-77; mem. tech. staff Hughes Aircraft Co., El Segundo, Calif., 1977-78; staff program adminstr. Ventura divsn. Northrop Corp., Newbury Park, Calif., 1978-79; divsn. head engring. Navastrogru, Point Mugu, 1979-82; br. head, divsn. head spl. programs head operational sys. Pacific Missile Test Ctr., Calif., 1983-90, head tech. devel. office, head capability devel., 1993-98; far west regional coord., exec. com., exec. bd. Fed. Lab. Consortium, 1998—. CNO, dir. rsch., devel. and acquisiiton The Pentagon, Washington, 1987-88, dir. rsch. devel. test and evaluation and tech., 1990-93; pres., chmn. bd. Diversified Mgmt. Sys., Inc., Camarillo, Calif., 1978—. Author: The Management of Research, Develoopment, Test and Evaluation Orgainzations; Organization Behavior Characteristics of Supervisors-Public versus Private Sectors; Self-Actualization in RDT & E Organizations: Self-Actualization in a Health Care Agency; others. V.p., bd. dirs. Ventura County Master Chorale and Opera Assn.; bd. dirs. So. Calif. Assn. of Pub. Adminstrn. (also mem. fin. com., programs com., student aid com., exec. bd., exec. com. fed. lab. consortium). Served with U.S. Army, 1958-62. Ednl. Rsch. Info. Clearing House fellow, 1965-67, Ednl. Rsch. Tng. Program fellow N.Mex. State U., 1967. Mem. IEEE, Am. Math. Soc., Math. Assn. Am., Am. Statis. Assn., IEEE Engring. Mgmt. Soc., Am. Soc. Pub. Adminstrn., So. Calif. Assn. Pub. Adminstrn. (bd. dirs., various coms.), Assn. Fedn. Tech. Transfer Execs., Fed. Mgrs. Assn., Am. Assn. Individual Investors, Mcpl. Mgmt. Assts. So. Calif., Acad. Polit. Sci., Internat. Soc. for the Sys. Scis., Assn. MBA Execs., Tech. Transfer Soc., Internat. Fedn. for Sys. Rsch., Phi Kappa Phi, Pi Gama Mu. Home: PO Box 273 Port Hueneme CA 93044-0273 Office: PO Box 447 Camarillo CA 93011-0447 Office Phone: 805-985-3792.

SULLIVAN, MICHAEL J. prosecutor; b. Oct. 3, 1954; m. Terry Sullivan, 1975; children: Joseph, Kelly, Allyson, James. Grad., Boston Coll., 1979; JD, Suffolk U., 1983. Assoc. Bolles and Pritchard, 1983—90; ptnr. McGovern and Sullivan, 1990—95; mem. Mass. Ho. Reps., 1991—95; dist. atty. Plymouth County, Mass., 1995—2001; U.S. atty. U.S. Dept. of Justice, Mass., 2001—. Rep. dist. 7 Mass. Ho. of Reps., 1990—, mem. ways and means, post audit and oversight and steering and policy coms., spl. com. on edn. reform. Office: US Attys Office US Courthouse Ste 9200 1 Courthouse Way Boston MA 02210

SULLIVAN, MICHAEL J. labor union administrator; b. Indpls., Ind., 1945; Sheet metal worker Brad Snodgrass Sheet Metal Inc., R.M. Cotton Inc., Nyland Sheet Metal Inc.; bus. rep. Sheet Metal Workers' Internat. Assn., 1973, 1976, bus. mgr. and fin. sec./treas., Local 20, 1979—94, gen. exec. coun., 1983—94, gen. sec./treas., 1994—99, pres., 1999—. Pres. Ind. Bldg. and Constrn. Trades Coun.; v.p. State AFL-CIO; mem. Ind. Workers Compensation Commn.; chmn. Labor Inst. Tng.; pres. Sheet Metal Workers' Internat. Assn.'s Mich.-Ind. Coun. Mem. Hoosier Alliance Against Drugs. Office: 1750 New York Ave NW Washington DC 20006

SULLIVAN, MICHAEL JOHN, lawyer, former ambassador; b. Omaha, Sept. 22, 1939; s. Joseph Byrne and Margaret (Hamilton) S.; m. Jane Metzler, Sept. 2, 1961; children: Michelle, Patrick, Theresa. BS in Petroleum Engring., U. Wyo., 1961, JD, 1964. Bar: Wyo. 1964, U.S. Ct. Appeals (10th cir.) 1968, U.S. Supreme Ct. 1980. Assoc. Brown, Drew, Apostolos, Barton & Massey, Casper, Wyo., 1964-67; ptnr. Brown, Drew, Apostolos, Massey & Sullivan, Casper, 1967-86, 95-98; gov. State of Wyo., Cheyenne, 1987-95; amb. to Ireland Dublin, 1998-2001; spl. counsel Rothgerber, Johnson & Lyons, LLP, Casper, Wyo., 2001—. Trustee St. Joseph's Children's Home, Torrington, Wyo., 1986-87; bd. dirs. Natrona County Meml. Hosp., Casper, 1976-86. Mem. ABA, ATLA, Wyo. Bar Assn., Wyo. Trial Lawyers Assn., Rotary (pres. Casper club). Democrat. Roman Catholic. Avocations: fly fishing, golf, tennis, jogging. Office: Casper Bus Ctr 123 W 1st St Ste 200 Casper WY 82601 Home: 1124 S Durbin St Casper WY 82601-4328 E-mail: msullivan@rothgerber.com.

SULLIVAN, MICHAEL PATRICK, food service executive; b. Dec. 5, 1934; s. Michael Francis and Susan Ellen (Doran) S.; m. Marilyn Emmer, June 27, 1964; children: Katherine, Michael, Maureen, Bridget, Daniel, Thomas. BS, Marquette U., 1956; JD, U. Minn., 1962. Bar: Minn. 1962, U.S. Dist. Ct. Minn. 1962, U.S. Supreme Ct. 1975, U.S. Ct. Appeals (8th cir.) 1978. Assoc. Gray, Plant, Mooty, Mooty & Bennett, Mpls., 1962-67, ptnr., 1968-87, mng. ptnr., 1976-87; pres., CEO Internat. Dairy Queen, Inc., Mpls., 1987-2001, chmn. bd., 2001—. Bd. dirs. The Valspar Corp., Allianz Life Ins. Co. N.Am., Opus Corp.; instr. U. Minn. Law Sch., 1962-67; lectr. continuing legal edn.; spl. counsel to atty. gen. Minn., 1971-79, 82-84; bd. dirs. Met. Mpls.YMCA, chmn. bd. dirs., 1997-99; pres. Uniform Law Commn., 1987-89. Contbr. articles to profl. jours. Bd. regents St. John's U., 2000; bd. dirs. YMCA Met. Mpls.; bd. trustees St. Paul Sem. Served with USN, 1956-59. Mem. ABA (ho. of dels., 1984-89), Minn. Bar Assn. (gov. 1974-86), Hennepin County Bar Assn. (pres. 1978-89), Am. Bar Found., Am. Law Inst., Am. Arbitration Assn. (bd. dirs.), Order of Coif. Roman Catholic. Office: Internat Dairy Queen 7505 Metro Blvd Minneapolis MN 55439-3020

SULLIVAN, MICHELLE CORNEJO, lawyer; b. St. Louis, June 29, 1958; m. Dennis Keith Sullivan, May 18, 1985. BS, U. Calif., Berkeley, 1980; JD, U. Santa Clara, 1983. Bar: Calif., 1984; U.S. Dist. Ct. (no. dist.) Calif., 1984, (so. dist.) Calif., 1985; cert. family law specialist. Legal dept. Four-Phase Computers, Cupertino, Calif., 1984; asst. dist. atty. San Benito County, Hollister, Calif., 1984-85; assoc. Walters & Ward, Rancho Bernardo, Calif., 1986-87, Law Offices of Rebecca Prater, Carlsbad, Calif., 1987-88; pvt. practice Escondido & San Diego, Calif., 1988—. Pres. Women in Networking, San Diego, 1987; western horse show judge Calif. State Horseman's Assn., 1985; adv. com. San Diego Regional Conf. on Women, trustee, 1993-95. Law Faculty scholar U. Santa Clara, 1982-83. Mem. ABA, State Bar Assn., San Diego County Bar Assn. (cert. specialist), Bar Assn. No. San Diego County (chair family law sect. 1996-98, cert. specialist), Escondido Rotary Main Club, Rancho Bernardo C. of C. (amb. 1986-87), San Diego Trial Lawyers Assn. (family law sect.), Lawyers Club (v.p. North County chpt. 1988-89). Avocations: western horseback riding, golf, sailing, scuba diving. Office: 16516 Bernardo Center Dr Ste 330 San Diego CA 92128-2518 Office Phone: 858-451-9390. E-mail: michellesullivan@sbcglobal.net.

SULLIVAN, MIKE, professional sports team executive; m. Kate Sullivan; children: Kaitlin, Kiley, Matthew. Degree, Boston (Mass.) U., 1990. Hockey player, San Diego, 1990—91, San Jose (Calif.) Sharks, 1991—94, Calgary Flames, 1994—97, Boston (Mass.) Bruins, 1997—98, Phoenix (Ariz.) Coyotes, 1998—2002; head coach Providence Bruins, 2002—03, Boston (Mass.) Bruins, 2003—. Office: 1 Fleetcenter Ste 250 Boston MA 02114*

SULLIVAN, MITZI, accountant; b. Chattanooga, Feb. 6, 1948; d. James Warren and Maysell Lucille Sullivan; m. Hassan Zayed, Sept. 27, 1975 (div. Oct. 1983); 1 child, Janine Amira Zayed. BA Liberal Arts, U. Tenn., 1971; MS Mgmt., Fla. Internat. U., 1977. French and English tchr. Hamilton County Dept. Edn., Chattanooga, 1971—75; social worker Divsn. Retardation, Miami, 1975—78; employment specialist City of Wichita, Kans., 1985—98, accountant, 1998—; owner Internat. Dairy Queen, Kingman, Kans., 1998—2000. Bd. dirs., 1st v.p. City of Wichita Deferred Compensation Bd., 1998—. Mem.: Wichita Irish Assn. (membership chmn. 1989—92), Wichita Hispanic Assn. (v.p. 1988—90). Buddhist. Avocations: writing, gardening, quilting, cooking, reading. Home: 942 S Longfellow St Wichita KS 67207-2737 Office: City Wichita Career Devel Office 444 E Wiliam Wichita KS 67202 Personal E-mail: mitzigsullivan@hotmail.com.

SULLIVAN, MORTIMER ALLEN, JR., lawyer; b. Buffalo, Sept. 19, 1930; s. Mortimer Allen Sr. and Gertrude (Hinkley) S.; m. Maryanne Calella, Nov. 20, 1965; children: Mark Allen, Michael John. BA, U. Buffalo, 1954. Bar: N.Y. 1964, U.S. Dist. Ct. (we. dist.) N.Y. 1966, U.S. Dist. Ct. (no. dist.) N.Y. 1967, U.S. Supreme Ct. 1970. Counsel liability claims Interstate Motor Freight System, Grand Rapids, Mich., 1964-82. V.p. J.P.M. Sullivan, Inc., Elmira, N.Y., 1959-67; govt. appeal agt. U.S. Selective Service System, 1967-71; dep. sci. div. Erie County (N.Y.) Sheriff's Office, 1971—, lt., 1986—. Inventor (with others) in field; creator, dir. video depiction JudiVision, 1969; composer High Flight, 1983. Chmn. com. on Constn. and Canons Episcopal Diocese of Western N.Y., 1975-96; bd. dirs. Erie County Law Enforcement Found., Inc., 1987—; bd. dirs. Orchard Park (N.Y.) Symphony Orch., 1975-97, v.p., 1977-79, 91-94. With USAF, 1954-57; spl. agt. Air Force Office of Spl. Investigations, 1972-87, col. res. ret. Decorated Legion of Merit. Mem. Erie County Bar Assn. (chmn. law and tech. com., 1970-81), Transp. Lawyers Assn., Kappa Alpha Soc. Clubs: Saturn (Buffalo); Wanakah (N.Y.) Country. Republican. Avocation: aviation. Home: 19 Knob Hill Rd Orchard Park NY 14127-3917 Office: 88 S Davis St PO Box 1003 Orchard Park NY 14127-8003 E-mail: masulaw@aol.com.

SULLIVAN, NEIL MAXWELL, oil and gas company executive; b. May 25, 1942; s. Thomas James and Jane Mason (Ginn) S.; m. Holly Abolt; children: Margaret Blair, Mason Pedrick. BS, Dickinson Coll., 1970; MS, Tulane U., 1994; postgrad., U. S.C., 1992—. Exploration geologist Bass Enterprises, Midland, Tex., 1976-77; dist. geologist ATAPCO, Midland, 1977-78; div. geologist Anadarko Prodn. Co., Midland, 1978-79, chief geologist, 1979-80, v.p. exploration, regional mgr. Houston, 1980-82; exploration ops. mgr. Valero Producing Co., San Antonio, 1982-85, v.p. exploration New Orleans, 1985-87; pres. Bluebonnet Petroleum Co., New Orleans, Eastover, S.C., 1987-97; v.p. exploration Forcenergy, Inc., Houston, 1997-98; pres. GAPCO Energy, Houston, 1998—2001; COO Tex. Keystone, Inc., Pitts., 2002—. Mem. Dept. Interior Outer Continental Shelf Com. adv. bd., 1985-87. Editor: Petroleum Exploration in Thrust Belts and Their Adjacent Forelands, 1976, Ancient Carbonate Reservoirs and Their Modern Analogs, 1977, Guadalupian Delaware Mountain Group of West Texas and Southeast New Mexico, 1979, Deep Water Sands in the Gulf Coast Region, 1988, Offshore Louisiana Geology: An Onshore Exploration Model, 1988, Risk: Evaluation and Management, 1989, Volga-Ural Basin Analysis, 1993, Northern Marginal Zone of the Pricaspian Basin, 1996. Bd. dirs. Permian Basin Grad. Ctr., Midland, 1979; com. chmn. Mus. of S.W., Midland, 1978. Served with USAF, 1964-68. Mem. Geol. Soc. Am., A. assn. Petroleum Geologists (cert. petroleum geologist), Houston Geol. Soc., New Orleans Geol. Soc. (chmn. continuing edn. com. 1987-89), South Tex. Geol. soc. (nominating com. chmn. 1985), Soc. Econ. Paleontologists and Mineralogists (pres. Permian Basin sect. 1979), Am. Inst. Profl. Geologists (cert. profl. geologist). Lodges: Elks. Home: 3894 Ash Dr Allison Park PA 15101-3103 Office Phone: 412-434-5616. Business E-Mail: nsullivan@texasKeystone.com.

SULLIVAN, NICHOLAS G. science educator, speleologist; b. Phila., Dec. 20, 1927; s. Edward James and Florence (Delaney) S. BS, Cath. U. Am., 1950; MSc, U. Pitts., 1954; PhD, U. Notre Dame, 1961. Asst. prof. U. Notre Dame (Ind.), 1961-63; asst. prof., assoc. prof., prof. La Salle Coll., Phila., 1963-78, asst. to pres., 1972-74; prof. sci. Manhattan Coll., Riverdale, N.Y., 1979—. Vis. prof. U. Alaska, Anchorage, 1961, U. NSW, Sydney, Australia, 1963; chmn. U.S. Deep Caving Team. Author: Speleology, the Study of Caves, 1962; contbr. over 200 articles on speleology to profl. jours. Trustee Gwynedd (Pa.) Mercy Coll., 1963-75, Nat. Speleological Found., Washington, 1978-84, Charles Lindbergh Found., 1989—. Fellow Nat. Speleological Soc. (hon. life, trustee 1955-79, pres. 1957-63), Royal Geog. Soc., AAAS, N.Y. Acad. Scis., Explorers Club (pres. 1989-92, trustee 1968—, Explorer's medal Phila. chpt. 1978, Sweeney medal 1979); mem. Sydney Speleological Soc. (hon. life), South African Speleological Soc. (hon. life), Rittenhouse Club, Bankstown Sports Club (Sydney).

SULLIVAN, PATRICIA A. academic administrator; b. S.I. m. Charles Sullivan. Grad., St. John's U.; MS in Biology, PhD in Biology, NYU. Tchg. fellow, NIH pre-doctoral fellow NYU; post-doctoral fellow in cell biology Upstate Med. Ctr., Syracuse, N.Y.; vis. fellow Cornell U., 1976; tchr. Wells Coll., N.Y.; dir. biology honors program Tex. Woman's U., 1979-81; dean Salem Coll., Winston-Salem, 1981-87; v.p. acad. affairs Tex. Woman's U., 1987-94, interim pres., 1993-94; chancellor U. N.C., Greensboro, 1995—. Pres. Assn. Tex. Colls. and Univs. Acad. Affairs Officers, Assn. So. Colls. for Women, N.C. Assn. Chief Acad. Officers; active numerous coms. Tex. Higher Edn. Coordinating Bd.; lectr. in field. Contbr. articles to profl. jours. Office: U NC at Greensboro Office of Chancellor PO Box 26170 Greensboro NC 27402-6170

SULLIVAN, PATRICIA W. (TERRY SULLIVAN), real estate trainer; b. Hempstead, N.Y., July 25, 1936; d. Gilbert Hudson and Vera (Morgan) Wehmann; m. Richard J. Sullivan, June 8, 1957 (div. Apr. 1982); children: Katherine, Gillian Stewart, Adam W. BS, Skidmore Coll., 1958; MS, Syracuse U., 1965. Mgr. Purtell & Wigdale, Inc., Cedarburg, Wis., Merrill Lynch Real Estate, Cedarburg; office mgr. Coldwell Banker Real Estate, Cedarburg; sales mgr. Coldwell Banker Residential Brokerage, Mequon, WI; owner, trainer, cons. Terry Sullivan Tng. and Seminars, Belgium, Wis., 1991—; sales mgr. Coldwell Banker, Mequon, Wis. Contbr. articles to profl. jours. Named Wis.

Cert. Real Estate Brokerage Mgr. of Yr., 1990. Mem. Nat. Assn. Realtors (bd. dirs. 1989-90, Omega Tau Rho award 1983, Outstanding Educator of the Year award for medium states, 1989), Nat. Women's Coun. Realtors (pres. 1990), Women's Coun. Realtors (pres. Milw. chpt. 1982, bd. dirs. 1983-90, named WCR of Yr. 1983, LTG 1985), Ozaukee Bd. Realtors (pres. 1979, bd. dirs. 1977-79, Realtor of Yr. 1979), Realtors Nat. Mktg. Inst. (dir. RS coun. 1983-86, CRS 1978, CRB 1981), Wis. Realtors Assn. (v.p. 1982-83, bd. dirs. 1983-86, Instr. of Yr. 1988, Disting. Svc. award 1992, GRI 1975), Wis. Cert. Residential Specialists (cert.; pres. 1982, Cert. Residential Specialist of Yr. 1983), Wis. Cert. Residential Brokers (cert.; pres. 1988). Address: Terry Sullivan Tng & Seminars 5342 Sandy Beach Ln Belgium WI 53004-9731

SULLIVAN, PATRICK HENRY, management consultant; b. N.Y.C., May 6, 1938; s. Patrick Henry II and Elinor Regina (Smith) S.; children: Christine E., Suzanne P., Patrick H. IV. BS in gen. engring., U.S. Navel Acad., 1960; MS in R & D mgmt., Fla. State Univ., 1969, DBA in mgmt., 1972. Rsch. engr. The Boeing Co., Cape Canaveral, Fla., 1966-69; chief fin. planning officer Fla. State Univ., Tallahassee, 1970-73; fellow, adv. to vice-chancellor Univ. Calif. Berkeley, 1973-74; asst. chancellor Univ. Calif. Santa Cruz, 1974-78; prin. cons. SRI Internat., 1973-84; v.p. MAC Group, 1984-88; pres. Sullivan & Assocs., 1998-93; chief oper. officer Law & Econs. Cons. Group, 1994; ptnr. ICM Co., 1995—2001; pres. ICM Group, Palo Alto, Calif., 2002—. Author: Value Driven Intellectual Capital, 2000; co-editor: (book) Technology Licensing, 1996; editor: (book) Profiting From Intellectual Capital, 1998. U.S. naval officer USN, 1960-66. Mem. Licensing Executives Soc. Avocations: biking, scuba, walking. Home: 250 Meadow Rd Santa Cruz CA 95060-2040 Office: ICM Group 2465 E Bayshore Rd Ste 403 Palo Alto CA 94303-3228 E-mail: psullivan@icmgroup.com.

SULLIVAN, PATRICK JAMES, lawyer; b. Orange, Calif., Sept. 17, 1943; s. Leo Charles Sullivan and Virginia (Wohosky) Souza; m. Pamela Pressler, Aug. 17, 1974; children: Shannon, Erin. BA, U. So. Calif., 1965; JD, Loyola U., Los Angeles, 1974. Bar: (Calif.) 1974, (U.S. Ct. Appeals (9th cir.)) 1978, (U.S. Supreme Ct.) 1979, U.S. Ct. Appeals (3d cir.) 1983, U.S. Tax Ct. 1986, U.S. Ct. Appeals (2d and 8th cirs.) 1989. Trial atty. U.S. Dept. Justice, Washington, 1974—75; ptnr. Sullivan, Jones & Archer, San Diego and San Francisco, 1975—83, Hewitt, Sullivan & Marshall, San Diego, 1983—87, King & Ballow, 1987—90, The Sullivan Law Firm, San Diego, 1990—. Arbitrator San Diego Superior Ct., 1979—83; lectr. U. Calif. Securities Regulations Inst., 1985; chmn. Am. Law Inst. Anti-Trust Conf., 1988, 91; mem. faculty Hastings Ctr. for Trial and Appellate Advocacy, 1989—92, Calif. Continuing Edn. of Bar, 1989—. Served to 1st lt. U.S. Army, Vietnam. Decorated Bronze Star. Fellow: Am. Bar Found. (life); mem.: ABA (litigation and anti-trust sects., ho. dels.), Am. Bd. of Trial Advocates, Nat. Inst. Trial Adv. (faculty 1986—), Am. Judiciary Soc., Am. Law Inst., Am. Inn Ct. (master 1992—2002), Rotary (Newhall, Calif.). Republican. Roman Catholic. Home: 335 Whitewood Pl Encinitas CA 92024-3137 Office: 810 Mission Ave Ste 300 Oceanside CA 92054

SULLIVAN, PAUL E. lawyer, oil industry executive; BA in acctg., U. Maine, Bangor; LLD, Boston Coll. Law Sch. Legal asst. tax dept. Exxon Corp., N.Y.C., 1969; tax counsel Esso Inter-Am., Coral Gables, Fla.; mgr. tax dept. Exxon Co. Internat., 1977; sr. tax counsel tax planning Exploration and Prodn. Divsn.Exxon Corp., N.Y.C., 1976; mgr. tax planning Exploration and Prodn. Divsn. Exxon Corp., N.Y.C., 1979; gen. tax counsel Exxon Chem. Co., Darien, Conn., 1981, Exxon Co. U.S.A., 1989—94; v.p. and gen. tax counsel Exxon Corp., 1994—. Vice chmn. tax policy com. Am. Petroleum Inst. Mem.: ABA, Tax Execs. Inst., N.Y. State Bar Assn. Mailing: ExxonMobil Corp 5959 Las Colinas Blvd Irving TX 75039-2298

SULLIVAN, PAUL WILLIAM, communications specialist; b. Brockton, Mass., Dec. 7, 1939; s. Augustus Henry and Pearl Irene (Chisholm) S.; children: Todd Andrew, Geoffrey Scott, Dustin Raymond; m. Frances Tina Brown, Jan. 23, 1989. BA cum laude, Yale U., 1961; MA, U. Fla., 1971; PhD, So. Ill. U., 1977. Gen. mgr. Chronicle Pub. Co., Stoughton, Mass., 1962-67; editor Easton Bull., N. Easton, Mass., 1963-70; pub., editor Associated Weekly Newspapers, Stoughton, 1967-70; instr. dept. mass comm. Moorhead (Minn.) State U., 1971-73; assoc. prof., chmn. dept. comm. U. Evansville, Ind., 1973-78; prof., chmn. dept. journalism Temple U., Phila., 1978-87; pvt. practice comm. cons., sales tng. cons. Indian Rocks Beach, Fla., 1986-92; pvt. practice comm. and fin. cons. Sullivan Comms., Indian Rocks Beach, 1992—; mng. gen. ptnr. Atlantis Adventure Ltd. Partnership, Largo, Fla., 1996—. Mem. rev. panel Harry S Truman Scholarship Found., 1981-86. Author: The Modern Free Press Fair Trial Precedent, 1987, monograph News Piracy, 1978; co-author, editor: The Teaching of Graphic Arts, 1977, The Art of Consulting, 1989; contbr. articles to profl. jours. Mem. Gov.'s Commn. for Pa. Lottery, 1981. Mem. Assn. for Edn. in Journalism and Mass Communications, Soc. Profl. Journalists, Pa. Soc. Newspaper Editors (bd. dirs. 1980-87), Phila. Bar Assn. (media rels. com. 1982-87), ACLU. Avocations: photographer, landscape gardening. Office: PO Box 1049 Indian Rocks Beach FL 33785-1049 *Never underestimate the power of a liberal education to keep opening doors into the future. That education coupled with what I learned from my father and keep learning from my wife has made all the difference.*

SULLIVAN, PEGGY (PEGGY ANNE SULLIVAN), librarian, consultant; b. Kansas City, Mo., Aug. 12, 1929; d. Michael C. and Ella (O'Donnell) S. AB, Clarke Coll., 1950; MS in Libr. Sci., Cath. U. Am., 1953; PhD, U. Chgo., 1972. Children's pub. libr., Mo., Md., Va., 1952-61; sch. libr. specialist Montgomery County (Md.) Pub. Schs., 1961-63; dir. Knapp Sch. Librs. Project, ALA, 1963-68, Jr. Coll. Libr. Info. Ctr., 1968-69; asst. prof. U. Pitts., 1971-73; dir. Office for Libr. Pers. Resources, ALA, Chgo., 1973-74; dean of students, assoc. prof. Grad. Libr. Sch., U. Chgo., 1974-77; asst. commr. for ext. svcs. Chgo. Pub. Libr., 1977-81; dean Coll. Profl. Studies, No. Ill. U., DeKalb, 1981-90; dir. univ. librs. No. Ill. U., 1990-92; exec. dir. ALA, 1992-94, assoc. Tuft & Assocs., 1995-98; dean Grad. Sch. Libr. and Info. Sci. Rosary Coll., 1995-97. Instr. grad. libr. edn. programs, 1958-73, UNESCO cons. on sch. librs., Australia, 1970; trustee Clarke Coll., 1969-72; sr. ptnr. Able Cons., 1987-92; cons. in field. Author: The O'Donnells, 1956, Many Names for Eileen, 1969, Problems in School Media Management, 1971, Carl H. Milam and the American Library Association, 1976, Opportunities in Library and Information Science, 1977, Realization: The Final Report of the Knapp School Libraries Project, 1968; co-author: Public Libraries: Smart Practices in Personnel, 1982. Mem.: ALA, Ill. Libr. Assn., Cath. Libr. Assn., Caxton Club, Chgo. Lit. Club. Roman Catholic. Home and Office: 2800 N Lake Shore Dr Apt 816 Chicago IL 60657-6202 E-mail: pslibcon@alumni.uchicago.edu. *Opportunities to use my abilities in a variety of public services have enriched my life, as I hope the results have enriched and empowered others.*

SULLIVAN, PHILIP G. retired obstetrician-gynecologist; b. Boston, 1932; s. Francis Albert and Catherine A. (Clark) S.; m. Valerie Lee Wood, Apr. 29, 1960; children: Deirdre, John, Maura, Kathleen. AB, Providence Coll., 1954; MD, Tufts U., 1958; MPH, Harvard U., 1971. Diplomate Am. Bd. Ob-Gyn. Intern New Eng. Ctr. Hosps., Boston, 1958-59, resident in surgery, 1959-61, resident in ob-gyn., 1961-64, med. adminstr.; clin.asst. prof. ob-gyn. Tufts U., Boston, 1972—. Fellow ACS, ACOG; mem. Mass. Med. Soc., Alpha Omega Alpha. Office: 489 Shore Rd Monument Beach MA 02553 E-mail: pgsull@aol.com.

SULLIVAN, ROBERT EDWARD, lawyer; b. San Francisco, May 18, 1936; s. Edward C. S. and Mary Jane (Sullivan); m. Maureen Lois Miles, June 14, 1958 (dec. 1972); children: Teresa Ann, Andrew Edward, Edward Braddock; m. Lynn Bryant, Aug. 28, 2002. BS, U. San Francisco, 1958; LLB, U. Calif.-Berkeley, 1961. Bar: Calif. 1962. Assoc. Pillsbury, Madison & Sutro, San Francisco, 1963-70, ptnr., 1971—2000, Pillsbury, Winthrop, LLP, 2001—. Lectr. bus. law Calif. Continuing Edn. Bar and Practicing Law Inst.; v.p., treas., dir. MPC Ins., Ltd., 1986-93. Contbr. articles to profl. jours. Bd. dirs., exec. com. mem., sec. San Francisco Opera Assn., 1993—. 1st lt. U.S. Army, 1961-63. Mem. ABA, State Bar Calif. (com. corps. 1979-82, chmn. 1981-82, mem. exec. com. bus. law sect. 1982-85, vice chmn. 1983-84, chmn. 1984-85, advisor 1985-86, mem. partnership com. 1990-92, chmn. ltd. liability co. drafting com. 1992-93), San Francisco Bar Assn., Bankers Club San Francisco (bd. dirs., sec.). Democrat. Roman Catholic. Office: Pillsbury Winthrop LLP 50 Fremont St San Francisco CA 94105-2228

SULLIVAN, ROBERT EMMET, JR., lawyer; b. Detroit, Oct. 2, 1955; s. Robert Emmett Sr. and Gloria Marie (Lamb) S. BA in Polit. Sci. and Sociology, Wayne State U., 1977; M Urban Planning, U. Mich., 1979; JD, U. Detroit, 1983; postgrad., Oxford (Eng.) U., 1981. Bar: Mich. 1984, U.S. Dist. Ct. (we. dist.) Mich. 1984, U.S. Dist. Ct. (ea. dist.) Mich. 1984, U.S. Ct. Appeals (6th cir.) 1984, U.S. Ct. Appeal (D.C. cir.) 1984, U.S. Tax Ct. 1984, D.C. 1985, U.S. Supreme Ct. 1987. Planning commr. City of Detroit, 1982-85; shareholder Sullivan, Ward, Asher & Patton, P.C., Detroit, 1984—; v.p., bd. dirs. Internat. Inst. Metro. Detroit. Contbr. articles to profl. jours. Active St. Scholastica Parish Ch., North Rosedale Park Civic Assn., Detroit Hist. Soc. Moffitt scholar, 1982, 83. Mem. AIA, Detroit Bar Assn., Am. Planning Assn., Am. Inst. Cert. Planners. Roman Catholic. Home: 7464 Wilshire West Bloomfield MI 48322-2875 Office: Sullivan Ward Asher & Patton PC 25800 Northwestern Hwy Southfield MI 48075-1000 E-mail: rsullivanjr@swappc.com.

SULLIVAN, ROBERT EMMETT, pediatric dentist, educator; b. Sioux City, Iowa, May 28, 1932; s. Joseph A. and Daisy B. (Stanieforth) S.; m. Mary Ann Haerer, Sept. 22, 1961. BA, Morningside Coll., 1954; DDS, U. Nebr., 1961, MSD, 1963. Diplomate Am. Bd. Pediat. Dentistry. Prof., chair pediat. dentistry U. Nebr. Coll. Dentistry, Lincoln, 1963—; prof. pediats. U. Nebr. Coll. Medicine, Omaha, 1969—. Contbr. articles to profl. jours. With U.S. Army. Fellow Am. Acad. Pediat. Dentistry, Am. Coll. Dentists, Internat. Coll. Dentistry; mem. ADA, VFW, Am. Soc. Dentistry for Children, N.E. Nebr. Dental Assn., Lincoln Dist. Dental Assn. Democrat. Avocation: music. Home: 2530 Ridge Rd Lincoln NE 68512-2418

SULLIVAN, ROBERT JOHN, lawyer; b. Butte, Mont., Feb. 22, 1954; s. James David and Margorie (Ostoj) S.; m. Mary R. White, Feb. 18, 1984; children: Brian Robert, Patrick Leland. BA, U. Mont., 1976, JD, 1980; attended, Nat. Inst. Trial Advocacy, 1985. Bar: Mont. 1980, U.S. Dist. Ct. Mont. 1980, U.S. Ct. Appeals (9th cir.) 1980. Dep. county atty. Missoula (Mont.) County Atty.'s Office, 1980-85, assoc. Boone Karlberg & Haddon, Missoula, 1985-87, ptnr., 1987—. Mem. ABA, Western Mont. Bar Assn. (treas. 1989, v.p. 1990, pres. 1990-91), Mont. State Bar Assn. (trustee, mem. character and fitness com., 1991-, chmn. 2001-02, pres.-elect 2002-03, pres. 2003-). Avocations: biking, skiing, outdoors. Office: Boone Karlberg & Haddon 201 W Main St Ste 300 PO Box 9199 Missoula MT 59807-9199

SULLIVAN, ROBERT S. college dean; BA in Math., Boston Coll.; MA in Prodn. Mgmt., Cornell U.; PhD in Ops. Mgmt., Pa. State U. Various U. Tex., 1976-91; dean graduate sch. Indsl. Adminstrn. Carnegie Mellon U., Pitts., 1991-95; dir. IC2 inst. U. Tex., Austin, 1995-97; dean Kenan-Flagler U. N.C., Chapel Hill, 1998—. Peace Corps. vol. Addis Ababa U., 1968-70. Office: The Kenan Flagler Business Sch Univ North Carolina PO Box 3490 Chapel Hill NC 27599-0001 E-mail: rss@unc.edu.

SULLIVAN, RUTH ANNE, librarian; b. Portland, Maine, Jan. 15, 1955; d. Lawrence P. and Mary Louise (Gilman) S.; m. Charles H. Sullivan, May 1, 1982; children: Nora J., Ian J. BA, Wheaton Coll., 1979; MLS, U. Ariz., 1980. Serials ref. Mass. Bay Community Coll., Wellesley, 1980-81; asst. dir. Bristol Community Coll., Fall River, Mass., 1981-86, chief libr., 1986—. Office: Bristol Community Coll 777 Elsbree St Fall River MA 02720-7307

SULLIVAN, SHARON LEE, mathematician, educator; m. John Patrick Sullivan, June 28, 1997; children: Jessica A., Kevin M. BS, Trinity Coll., 1994; MS, U. of Vt., 1996; PhD, U. of Ky., 2001. Grad. tchg. asst. U. of Vt., Burlington, Vt., 1994—96, U. of Ky., Lexington, Ky., 1996—2001; asst. prof. Catawba Coll., Salisbury, NC, 2001—. Course coord. Minority Coll. Awareness Program U. of Ky., 1997—2000. Recipient Phi Gamma Delta prize, Trinity Coll., 1992, 1994; fellow Tchg. fellowship, 1993. Mem.: N.C. Coun. of Tchrs. of Math., Assn. of Women in Math., Math. Assn. of Am. (fellow 2001). Office: Catawba College 2300 West Innes Street Salisbury NC 28144 E-mail: slsulliv@catawba.edu.

SULLIVAN, SHIRLEY ROSS (SHIRLEY ROSS DAVIS), art collector; b. Berkeley, Calif. d. Edwin M. Ross; m. George Freeborn (dec.); children: George, Tita, Nelly, Mary; m. Thomas Davis (dec.); m. Charles Sullivan, Sept. 6, 1997. Interior designer, Woodside, Calif., 1963-90. Tchr., lectr., Woodside, 1965-70; art collector, Woodside and San Francisco, 1968—. Trustee San Francisco Mus. Modern Art, 1986—; pres. Collectors' Art Forum, San Francisco, 1983-85; mem. collectors' com. Nat. Gallery Art, 1998—. Office: ICMS 790 Laurel St San Carlos CA 94070-3164

SULLIVAN, STUART FRANCIS, anesthesiologist, educator; b. Buffalo, July 15, 1928; s. Charles S. and Kathryn (Duggan) S.; m. Dorothy Elizabeth Faytol, Apr. 18, 1959; children: John, Irene, Paul, Kathryn. BS, Canisius Coll., 1950; MD, SUNY, Syracuse, 1955. Diplomate Am. Bd. Anesthesiology. Intern Ohio State U. Hosp., Columbus, 1955—56; resident Columbia Presbyn. Med. Ctr., 1958—60; fellow Columbia-Bellevue Hosp. Ctr., N.Y.C., 1960—61; instr. anesthesiology Columbia U. Coll. Physicians and Surgeons, N.Y.C., 1961—62, assoc., 1962—64, asst. prof., 1964—69, assoc. prof., 1969—73; prof. dept. anesthesiology UCLA, 1973—91, vice chair anesthesiology, 1974—77, exec. vice chair, 1977—90, acting chmn., 1983—84, 1987—88, 1990—91, prof. emeritus, 1991—. Capt. M.C., USAR, 1956-58. Fellow NIH, 1960-61; recipient research career devel. award NIH, 1966-69. Mem. Assn. Univ. Anesthetists, Am. Physiol. Soc., Am. Soc. Anesthesiologists. Home: 101 Foxtail Dr Santa Monica CA 90402-2047 Office: UCLA Sch Medicine Dept Anesthesiology Los Angeles CA 90095-0001

SULLIVAN, TERESA ANN, law and sociology educator, academic administrator; b. Kewanee, Ill., July 9, 1949; d. Gordon Hager and Mary Elizabeth (Finnegan) S.; m. H. Douglas Laycock, June 14, 1971; children: Joseph Peter, John Patrick. BA, Mich. State U., 1970; MA, U. Chgo., 1972, PhD, 1975. Asst. prof. sociology U. Tex., Austin, 1975-76, assoc. prof. sociology, 1981-87, dir. women's studies, 1985-87, prof. sociology, 1987—, prof. law, 1988—, assoc. dean grad. sch., 1989-90, 1992-95, chair dept. sociology, 1990-92, vice provost, 1994-95, v.p., grad. dean, 1995—2002; asst. prof. sociology U. Chgo., 1977-81; exec. vice-chancellor for acad. affairs U. Tex. System, 2002—. Pres. Southwestern Sociol. Assn., 1988-89; mem. faculty adv. bd. Hogg Found. Mental Health, 1989-92; mem. sociology panel NSF, 1983-85. Author: Marginal Workers Marginal Jobs, 1978; co-author: As We Forgive Our Debtors, 1989 (Silver Gavel 1990), Social Organization of Work, 1990, 2d edit. 1995; co-author: The Fragile Middle Class, 2000; contbr. articles and chpts. to profl. jours. Bd. dirs. Calvert Found., Chgo., 1978, CARA, Inc., Washington, 1985; mem. U.S. Census Bur. Adv. Com., 1989-95, chmn., 1991-92; mem. sociology panel NSF, 1983-85; trustee St. Michael's Acad., 1996-2001. Leadership Tex. 1994. Fellow AAAS (liaison to Population Assn. Am. 1989-91, chair sect. K 1996), Sociol. Rsch. Assn., Am. Sociol. Assn. (sec. 1995—, editor Rose Monograph Series 1988-92), Philos. Soc. Tex., Soc. Study of Social Problems (chair fin. com. 1986-87), Population Assn. Am. (bd. dirs. 1989-91, chair fin. com. 1990-91), Assn. Grad. Schs. (pres. 2001-2002). Roman Catholic. Avocations: volkssporting, sci. fiction. Office: U Tex System 601 Colorado Ste 305 Austin TX 78701 Business E-Mail: tsullivan@utsystem.edu.

SULLIVAN, TERRANCE CHARLES, lawyer; b. Neptune, N.J., Mar. 23, 1950; s. John Joseph and Marilyn Anne (DiBlasi) S.; m. Kathy Lavonne Collett, June 21, 1980; children: Jennifer Collett, Michael Charles, Cynthia Grace, Philip Gregory. BA, U. Ga., 1972; JD, U. Va., 1975. Bar: Ga. 1975. Assoc. Swift, Currie, McGhee & Hiers, Atlanta, 1975-77; assoc., ptnr. Phillips, Hart & Mozley, Atlanta, 1977-82; sr. ptnr. Hart & Sullivan, P.C., Atlanta, 1982-89, Sullivan, Hall, Booth & Smith, P.C., Atlanta, 1989-98, Butler, Wooten, Overby, Fryhofer, Daughtery and Sullivan, Atlanta, 1998—. Bd. dirs. Atlanta Coun. Younger Lawyers, 1975-77. Contbr. articles on legal edn. to profl. jours. Bd. dirs. Murphey Candler Little League, 1997—; assoc. mem. deans coun. U. Va. Law Sch., 1993—. Capt. USAF Res., 1972-80. Fellow Am. Coll. Trial Lawyers, Am. Bd. Trial Advocate's; mem. ABA, State Bar Ga., Atlanta Bar Assn., Nat. Inst. Trial Advocacy, Atlanta Inst. Trial Advocacy (co-dir. 1986-88), Atlanta Lawyers Club, Trial Lawyers Assn. Am. (conf. speaker 1988), U. Ga. Nat. Alumni Assn. (bd. dirs. 1998—), Dekalb Med. Ctr., Medallion Soc. Roman Catholic. Home: 3986 Fernway Ct NE Atlanta GA 30319-1667 Office: Butler Wooten Overby Fryhofer Daughtery and Sullivan 2719 Buford Hwy NE Atlanta GA 30324-3207 Fax: 404-321-1713.

SULLIVAN, THOMAS CHRISTOPHER, coatings company executive; b. Cleve., July 8, 1937; s. Frank Charles and Margaret Mary (Wilhelmy) S.; m. Sandra Simmons, Mar. 12, 1960; children: Frank, Sean, Tommy, Danny, Kathleen, Julie. BS, Miami U., Oxford, Ohio, 1959. Div. sales mgr. Republic Powdered Metals, Cleve., 1961-65, exec. v.p., 1965-70; chmn. bd., CEO RPM, Inc., Medina, Ohio, 1971—2002, chmn. bd., 2003—. Bd. dirs. Agil Ysys Co., Cleve., Cleve. Clinic Found., Huffy Corp., Dayton, Ohio, Kaydon Corp., Ann Arbor, Mich. Trustee emeritus Culver (Ind.) Ednl. Found.; former trustee Cleve. Tomorrow; bd. advisors Urban Cmty. Sch., Cleve., Malachi House, Cleve.; trustee City Year Cleve.; trustee Cath. Diocese of Cleve. Found. Lt. (j.g.) USNR, 1959-60. Mem.: Nat. Assn. Securities Dealers (bd. govs. 1986—88, long-range strategic planning com.), Nat. Paint and Coatings Assn. (past chmn. bd., CEO, mem. exec. com.). Roman Catholic. Office: RPM Inc 2628 Pearl Rd Medina OH 44256-7623

SULLIVAN, THOMAS JAMES, retired manufacturing company executive; b. Franklin, N.H., Mar. 26, 1923; s. James J. and Helen (Mullin) S.; m. Anne Clark, Aug. 31, 1963. AB, Holy Cross Coll., 1947; JD, Harvard U., 1949. With Gen. Dynamics Corp., 1949-61, asst. div. mgr., 1959-61; sr. assoc. Harbridge House, Cambridge, Mass., 1961-63; with Hydraulic Research & Mfg. Co., Valencia, Calif., 1963-71, v.p., 1964-68, exec. v.p., 1968-69, pres., 1969-71; v.p. Textron, Inc., Providence, 1971-73; pres. Walker/Parkersburg (W. Va.) Co., 1973-81, Sprague Meter, Bridgeport, Conn., 1981-84, Dimetrics Inc., Diamond Springs, Calif., 1984-86. Served with USAAF, 1943-46. Fellow Nat. Contract Mgmt. Assn. Home: 2186 Augusta Ct San Luis Obispo CA 93401-4500 E-mail: tsullivan0323@aol.com.

SULLIVAN, THOMAS M. federal agency administrator; BA English, Boston Coll., 1989, MA, 1993; JD, Suffolk U. Bar: U.S. Ct. Appeals (D.C. cir.), Mass. Exec. dir. Nat. Dedn. Ind. Bus. Legal Found.; chief counsel advocacy Small Bus. Adminstrn., Washington, 2002—. Office: Small Bus Adminstrn 409 3d St SW Washington DC 20416

SULLIVAN, THOMAS PATRICK, lawyer; b. Evanston, Ill., Mar. 23, 1930; s. Clarence M. and Pauline (DeHaye) Sullivan; m. Anne Landau; children from previous marriage: Margaret Mary, Timothy Joseph, Elizabeth Ann. Student, Loras Coll., Dubuque, Iowa, 1947-49; LLB cum laude, Loyola U., Chgo., 1952. Bar: Ill. 1952, Calif. 1982, N.Mex 1997. Assoc. Jenner & Block, Chgo., 1954-62, ptnr., 1963-77, 81—; U.S. atty. No. Dist. Ill., Chgo., 1977-81. Co-chair Ill. Gov.'s Commn. Capital Punishment, 2000—02. Contbr. articles to profl. jours. With U.S. Army, 1952—54. Decorated Bronze Star; named laureate, Acad. Ill. Lawyers; recipient medal of excellence, Loyola U. Law Sch., 1965, Damen award, 2004, award, Ill. Pub. Defender Assn., 1972, Justice John Paul Stevens award, 2000, Ctr. on Wrongful Convictions award, Northwestern U., 2003, Albert E. Jenner, Jr. Pro Bono award, 2003. Fellow: Am. Coll. Trial Lawyers; mem.: ABA (John Minor Wisdom Pub. Svc. and Professionalism award 2003), Chgo. Coun. Lawyers, Am. Judicature Soc., Am. Law Inst., Fed. Bar Assn., Chgo. Bar Assn., Fed. 7th Cir. Bar Assn., Ill. Bar Assn. Office: Jenner & Block 1 Ibm Plz Fl 4100 Chicago IL 60611-5697 E-mail: tsullivan@jenner.com.

SULLIVAN, THOMAS PATRICK, academic administrator; b. Detroit, July 8, 1947; s. Walter James and Helen Rose (Polosky) S.; m. Barbara Jean Fournier, Aug. 9, 1968; children: Colleen, Brendan. BA in English, U. Dayton, 1969; M. Edn. and Adminstrn., Kent State U., 1971; postgrad., U. Mich., 1988. Tchr. Resurection Elem. Sch., Dayton, Ohio, 1968-69; administr. residence hall Kent (Ohio) State U., 1969-71; program mgr. residence hall Ea. Mich. U., Ypsilanti, 1971-73, adminstrv. assoc., 1973-76, dir. housing, 1976-83; assoc. provost Wayne County Community Coll., Belleville, Mich., 1983-84, dir. budget and mgmt. devel. Detroit, 1984-85, sr. v.p. acad. affairs, acting provost, 1985-86, acting exec. dean Belleville, 1986-88, dir. budget and mgmt. devel. Detroit, 1988-89; pres. Cleary Univ., Ypsilanti, 1989—. Part-time instr. English and math. Schoolcraft Coll., Livonia, Mich., 1980-90. Home: 9835 Whisperwood Ln Brighton MI 48116-8859 Office: Cleary Univ 3601 Plymouth Rd Ann Arbor MI 48105-2659 Office Phone: 734-332-4477.

SULLIVAN, TIMOTHY, lawyer; b. Detroit, May 16, 1948; s. Paul Gilmary and Virginia (Rosier) S.; m. Marsha Rosenberg Sullivan, June 19, 1971; children: Eileen A., Hugh V. BA Journalism, U. Mich., 1970; JD, Georgetown U., 1975. Bar: Va. 1975, D.C. 1976. Contract negotiator CIA, Washington, 1973-75; assoc. Fried, Frank, Harris, Shriver & Kampelman, Washington, 1975-78; ptnr. Capell, Howard, Knabe & Cobbs P.A., Washington, 1978-83, Dykema Gossett, Washington, 1983-95, Adduci, Mastriani & Schaumberg, LLP, 1995—2001. Lectr. in field. Narrator (audio cassette) How to Negotiate Government Contracts, 1986. Citizen mem. Alexandria Commn. Persons with Disabilities, Va., 1992-99, vice-chmn. 1997-98, 98-99. Sgt. U.S. Army, 1970-73. Mem. ABA, Nat. Contract Mgmt. Assn., U. Club Washington (bd. govs. 2003-2004, sec. 2003—), Congl. Country Club (e.g. 1998-99, bd. govs. 1995-2000, pres. 1999-2000). Roman Catholic. Avocations: reading, sports. Office: Thompson Coburn LLP 1909 K St NW 6th Fl Washington DC 20006-1167

SULLIVAN, TIMOTHY JACKSON, law educator, academic administrator; b. Ravenna, Ohio, Apr. 15, 1944; s. Timotio and Margaret Elizabeth (Caris) Sullivan; m. Anne Doubet Klare, Jan. 21, 1973. AB, Coll. William and Mary, 1966; JD, Harvard U., 1969; LLD (hon.), U. Aberdeen, Scotland, 1993. Asst. prof. law Coll. William and Mary, Williamsburg, Va., 1972—75, assoc. prof., 1975—78, prof., 1978—85, Bryan prof. law, dean, 1985—92, pres., 1992—; exec. asst. for policy Office of Gov. Charles S. Robb, Richmond, Va., 1982—85; atty. Freeman, Drapers' Co., London, 1992. Vis. prof. law U. Va., Charlottesville, 1981; exec. dir. Gov.'s Commn. on Va.'s Future, Richmond, 1982—84; vice-chmn. Gov.'s Commn. on Fed. Spending, Richmond, 1986; mem. Gov.'s Fellows Selection Com., 1985—90, Gov.'s Commn. on Sexual Assault and Substance Abuse on the Coll. Campus (chmn. enforcement subcom.), 1991—92; counsel Commn. on Future of Va.'s Jud. Sys., 1987—89; mem. Livery Drapers Co., 2003. Mem. Va. State Bd. Edn., Richmond, 1987—92; chair Gov.'s Task Force on Intercollegiate Athletics, 1992—93. Decorated Bronze Star; named Outstanding Virginian, Va. 4-H Found., 1999. Fellow: Va. Bar Fedn., Am. Bar Fedn.; mem.: ABA, Va. Bar Assn., Va. State Bar, Am. Arbitration Assn. (bd. dirs. 2000—), Cosmos Club, Univ. Club (N.Y.C., Washington), Bull and Bear Club, Omicron Delta Kappa, Phi Beta Kappa. Democrat. Avocations: wine, swimming, reading, golf. Home: Pres House Williamsburg VA 23185 Office: Coll William & Mary PO Box 8795 Williamsburg VA 23187-8795

SULLIVAN, TIMOTHY PATRICK, telecommunications company executive; b. Springfield, Ill., Mar. 4, 1942; s. Jeremiah Joseph and Genevieve Anastasia (Stapleton) S.; m. Kathleen Veronica Logue, May 4, 1974; children: Timothy Patrick Jr., Michael Sean, Shannon Kathleen, Jennifer Hillary, Thomas Brendan. BSEE, U. Notre Dame, 1964; postgrad., Syracuse U., 1966-67. Tech. mgr. IBM Corp., Poughkeepsie, NY, 1964—68, Hursley, England, 1968—69, middle mgr. Poughkeepsie, San Jose, 1969—77, sr. mgr. Research Triangle Park, NC, 1977—81, corp. cons. Armonk, NY, 1981—83, product mgr. Research Triange Park, NC, 1983—85; v.p., officer No. Telecom, Richardson, Tex., 1985—92; pres., CEO Connectware, Inc., 1993—97; CEO Com World, Inc., 1997—98; pres. Optical Networking, SBU, Lucent Techs., Richardson, Tex., 1998—2000; pres. optical networking group Lucent Techs., Holmdel, NJ, 2001—03; pres., CEO Cebatech Inc., 2004—. Bd. dirs., chmn. Corp. for Open Systems, McLean, Va., 1992; bd. dirs. AXONLINK; mem. adv. bd. Monmouth U., Corrigent Sys., Reactive Nanotech., Arcana Networks, Carrius Techs.; mem. exec. adv. coun. Nat. Comms. Forum, Chgo., 1989-90;

chmn. bd. Osinet Corp., 1991. Inventor storage subsystems in field, 1969-71; author: Captain, 1974; contbr. articles to profl. jours. Adv. bd. Dallas Mus. of Art, 1988-92; mem. North Tex. Commn., Dallas, 1988-91. Republican. Roman Catholic. Avocations: creative writing, chess, golf. Home: 170 Red Hill Rd Middletown NJ 07748 Office: Cebatech Inc 87 Maple Ave Red Bank NJ 07701

SULLIVAN, WILLIAM FRANCIS, lawyer; b. San Francisco, May 6, 1952; s. Francis Michael and Jane Frances (Walsh) S.; children: Matthew, Meghan, Kathleen; m. Kait Sullivan. AB, U. Calif., Berkeley, 1974; JD, UCLA, 1977. Bar: Calif. 1977, U.S. Dist. Ct. (no. dist.) Calif. 1977, U.S. Ct. Appeals (9th cir.) 1977, U.S. Dist. Ct. (ea. dist.) Calif. 1978, U.S. Ct. Appeals (D.C. cir.) 1979, U.S. Ct. Appeals (fed. cir.) 1985, U.S. Dist. Ct. (so. dist.) Calif. 1986, U.S. Dist. Ct. (cen. dist.) Calif. 1990, U.S. Supreme Ct. 1986. Assoc. Chickering & Gregory, San Francisco and Washington, 1977-81, Brobeck, Phleger & Harrison, San Diego and San Francisco, 1981-84, ptnr., 1984—2002, mng. ptnr. San Diego, 1992-96, 2001—03, securities litigation group leader, 2002—, firmwide mng. ptnr., 1996-98; ptnr. Paul Hastings Janofsky & Walker LLP, San Diego, 2003—, co-chair nat. securities ligigation practice group, mem. litigation steering com., 2003—. Panelist Calif. Continuing Edn. Bar; instr. Fed. Practice Program, U.S. No. Dist., chair Litigation sect., 1992, U.S. Dist. Ct. (no. dist.) Calif., 1980; instr. Coll. of Advocacy, Hastings Law Sch.; adv. bd. AMICUS Info. Svcs. Mem. ABA, Assn. Bus. Trial Lawyers (bd. govs. San Diego chpt. 1993-95), Calif. Bar Assn. (litigation sect.), San Francisco Bar Assn., San Diego Bar Assn., Barristers Club San Francisco (bd. dirs. 1984-86, pres. 1985), Calif. Young Lawyers Assn. (bd. dirs. 1986-89, sec. 1987-99, 1st v.p. 1988-89). Democrat. Roman Catholic. Office: Brobeck Phleger & Harrison 1 Market St #500 San Francisco CA 94105-1521 E-mail: williamsullivan@paulhastings.com.

SULLIVAN, WILLIAM J. state supreme court justice; Student, St. Thomas Sem., 1958-59; BA in Polit. Sci., Providence Coll., 1962; B in Civil Law, Coll. William and Mary, 1965, JD, 1970. Judge Conn. Superior Ct., 1978-97, Conn. Appellate Ct., 1997-99; assoc. justice Conn. Supreme Ct., 1999-2001; chief justice, 2001—. Office: Conn Supreme Ct Supreme Ct Bldg 231 Capitol Ave Hartford CT 06106-1548

SULLIVAN, WILLIAM JOHN, osteopath; b. Pittsburg, Kans., Nov. 5, 1963; s. William Leroy and Joan Elizabeth (Prete) S.; m. Shelly Renee Lotterer, Oct. 24, 1992; 1 child, Lauren Marie. BS in Biology, Pittsburg State U., 1986; DO, U. Health Scis., Kansas City, Mo., 1990. Diplomate Nat. Bd. Osteo. Med. Examiners, Am. Bd. Internal Medicine, Am. Assn. Med. Rev. Officers. Intern Riverside Hosp., Wichita, Kans., 1990-91; resident Deaconess Hosp., St. Louis, 1991-94; pvt. practice Pittsburg Internal Medicine P.A., 1994—; active staff Mt. Carmel Med. Ctr., Pittsburg, 1994—, med. dir. occupl. health, med. dir. employee health, 1995—2002, med. dir. cardiomyopathy clinic, 1997—, chief medicine, 1998—, chief-of-staff-elect, 1999—, pres. med. staff, 2001—. Mem. adv. bd. dirs. Cmty. Nat. Bank, Pittsburg; med. staff sec. Mt. Carmel Med. Ctr., Pittsburg, 1999; clin. instr. Pittsburg State U. Sch. Nursing; participating physician Pittsburg Free Clinic; clin. adv. Pittsburg State U. Pre-Med Club; mem. health occupations adv. bd. Unified Sch. Dist. #250; physician Congl. Health Ministries. Mem. exec. bd. dirs. Pitts. Family YMCA, pres.-elect, 2003, pres., 2004—, chief internal medicine, 1995—; bd. dirs. Pitts. State U. Alumni Assn., nat. 2d v.p., 2003-04. Lt. col. Kans. Army N.G., 1988—. Fellow ACP; mem. Kans. Med. Soc., Am. Assn. Med. Rev. Officers, N.G. Assn. U.S., KC, Crawford County Med. Soc. (pres. 2000), Am. Legion, Sigma Chi (life loyal Sig program). Republican. Roman Catholic. Avocations: music, golf, stamp collecting/philately. Home: 2606 Knollview St Pittsburg KS 66762-6514 Office: Pittsburg Internal Med PA 2401 S Tucker Pittsburg KS 66762-6601 Office Phone: 620-231-8849.

SULLOWAY, FRANK JONES, social sciences educator, historian; b. Concord, N.H., Feb. 2, 1947; s. Alvah Woodbury and Alison (Green) Sulloway; 1 child, Ryan. AB summa cum laude, Harvard U., 1969, AM in History Sci., 1971, PhD in History Sci., 1978. Jr. fellow Harvard U. Soc. Fellows, 1974-77; mem. Sch. Social Sci. Inst. Advanced Study, Princeton, NJ, 1977-78; rsch. fellow Miller Inst. Basic Rsch. Sci. U. Calif., Berkeley, 1978-80, vis. Miller rsch. prof., 1999—2000, vis. prof., 2000—; rsch. fellow MIT, Cambridge, 1980-81, vis. scholar, 1989-98; postdoctoral fellow Harvard U., Cambridge, 1981-82, vis. scholar, 1984-89; rsch. fellow U. Coll., London, 1982-84; Vernon prof. biography Dartmouth Coll., Hanover, NH, 1986. Author: (book) Freud, Biologist of the Mind, 1979 (Pfizer award History Sci. Soc., 1980), Born to Rebel, 1996; contbr. articles to profl. jours. Recipient Randi award, Skeptics Soc., 1997, Golden Plate award, Am. Acad. Achievement, 1997; fellow, NEH, 1980—81, NSF, 1981—82, John Simon Guggenheim Meml. Found., 1982—83, MacArthur Found., 1984—89, Dibner Inst., MIT, 1993—94, Ctr. Advanced Study Behavioral Scis., Stanford, Calif., 1998—99. Fellow: AAAS (mem. electorate nominating com. sect. L 1988—91, 1994—97), Linnean Soc. London; mem.: History Sci. Soc. (mem. fin. com. 1987—92, mem. com. devel. 1988—92), Human Behavior and Evolution Soc., Am. Psychol. Soc. Home: 1709 Shattuck Ave Apt 205 Berkeley CA 94709-1753 Office: U Calif Dept Psychology IPSR 4125 Tolman Hall Berkeley CA 94720-1603 Office Phone: 510-642-7139. Business E-Mail: sulloway@uclink.berkeley.edu.

SULLY, IRA BENNETT, lawyer; b. Columbus, Ohio, June 3, 1947; s. Bernie and Helen Mildred (Koen) S.; m. Nancy Lee Pryor, Oct. 2, 1983. BA cum laude, Ohio State U., 1969, JD summa cum laude, 1974. Bar: Ohio 1974, U.S. Dist. Ct. (so. dist.) Ohio 1974. Assoc. Schottenstein, Garel, Swedlow & Zox, Columbus, 1974-78; atty. Borden, Inc., Columbus, 1978-80; sole practice Columbus, 1980—. Instr. Real Estate Law Columbus Tech. Inst., 1983-88; title ins. agt. Sycamore Title Agy., Columbus, 1983— . Bd. dirs. Rsch. Franklin County Celeste for Gov., Columbus, 1978; asst. treas. Pamela Conrad for City Coun., Columbus, 1979; treas. Leland for State Rep., Columbus, 1982, 84, Leland for City Atty., Columbus, 1985; active Ohio Dem. Bldg. Com., 1995-98; commentator Sta. WOSU, Columbus, 1980; trustee Ohio State U. Undergrad. Student Govt. Alumni Soc., 1997—, pres., 2000—. Mem. ABA, Ohio Bar Assn., Columbus Bar Assn., Agonis Club (Columbus). Democrat. Jewish. Avocations: running, coin collecting/numismatics. Home: 200 Reinhard Ave Columbus OH 43206-2616 Office: 844 S Front St Columbus OH 43206-2543 Office Phone: 614-443-3930.

SULPIZIO, RICHARD, communications company executive; BA in Liberal Arts, Calif. State U., L.A.; M in Systems Mgmt., U. So. Calif. Various positions including v.p. and gen. mgr. Unisys Corp.; from v.p. info. systems to sr. v.p. Qualcomm Inc., San Diego, 1991, chief operating officer, 1992-94, 95-98, pres. Omnitrac divsn., 1994-95, pres., chief operating officer, 1998—. Office: Qualcomm Inc 5775 Morehouse Dr San Diego CA 92121-1714

SULS, JERRY M. psychologist, educator; b. Washington, Jan. 9, 1947; s. Abraham Issac and Leah Suls; m. Suzzanne Bendt, Sept. 6, 1968 (div Nov. 1993); m. Rene Elizabeth Martin, May 6, 1994; 1 son, Robert. BA, Temple U., Phila., 1968, MA, 1971, PhD in Social Psychology, 1973. Asst. prof. Georgetown U., Washington, 1972—75, SUNY, Albany, 1975—78, assoc. prof., 1978—87, prof., 1987—90; prof. dept. psychology U. Iowa, Iowa City, 1990—, coord. health psychology grad. tng. area, chmn. IRB-02, 2003—. Behavioral medicine panel NIH, Bethesda, Md., 1983-86; adv. panel NSF, Washington, 1992-95. Editor: Social Comparison Processes, 1977, Social Comparison, 1991, Handbook of Social Comparison, 2000; assoc. editor Jour. Personality and Social Psychology, 1990-96; editor Personality and Social Psychology Bull., 1998-2001; contbr. articles to profl. jours., chpts. to books. Grantee NIH, 1988-94, NSF, 1996-99, Am. Heart Assn., 1996-98, NSF, 2000-04. Avocations: jazz, jazz piano. Office: U Iowa Dept Psychology E-11 SSH Iowa City IA 52242 Business E-Mail: jerry-suls@uiowa.edu.

SULTAN, CORNEL, research scientist, consultant; arrived in US, 1994; s. Ion and Sanda Sultan. MS in Aerospace Engring., Bucharest Poly. U., 1992; MS in Math., PhD in Aerospace Engring., Purdue U., 1999. Sr. rsch. engr. Tensegra Inc., Boston, 1999—2001; rsch. fellow Harvard U., Boston, 2001—03; sr. rsch. engr. Sci. Sys. Co., Inc., Woburn, Mass., 2003—. Contbr. articles to profl. jours. Recipient Spl. prize Nat. Math. Contest, Romanian Acad. Sci., 1988; fellow, NASA, 1996; Emeritus Student fellow, Ministry Edn. Romania, 1990, 1991, 1992, Puskas Meml. fellow, Purdue U., 1997, 1998. Mem.: AIAA. Achievements include research in tensegrity structures.

SULTAN, MARK R. plastic surgeon; BS, Brandeis U.; MD, Columbia U., 1982. Diplomate rgery, Am. Bd. Plastic Surgery. Resident in gen. surgery Columbia-Presbyn. Med. Ctr., N.Y.C., 1983—87, resident in plastic surgery, 1987—88, 1989—90; fellow in head and neck surgery/microvascular reconstrn. Emory U. Affiliated Hosps., Atlanta, 1988—89; chief divsn. plastic and reconstructive surgery Beth Israel Hosp.; attending physician dept. plastic surgery St. Luke's Roosevelt, N.Y. Eye and Ear Infirmary, N.Y.C., 1990—; pvt. practice plastic surgery N.Y.C. Assoc. prof. clin. surgery Columbia U. Coll. Physicians and Surgeons, N.Y.C. Mem.: Am. Soc. Reconstructive Microsurgery, Am. Soc. Plastic and Reconstructive Surgeons, Am. Soc. Aesthetic Plastic Surgery. Office: 1100 Park Ave New York NY 10128*

SULTANIK, JEFFREY TED, lawyer; b. N.Y.C., July 26, 1954; s. Solomon and Anna (Tiger) S.; m. Judith Ann Clyman, Nov. 14, 1981; children: Evan A., Sara A. BA cum laude, U. Pa., Phila., 1976; JD, Hofstra U., 1979. Bar: Pa. 1979, Fla. 1980, U.S. Dist. Ct. (ea. dist.) Pa., U.S. Ct. Appeals (3d cir.). Ptnr. Fox Rothschild, LLP, Lansdale, Pa., 1979-81; solicitor Upper Merion Sch. Dist., 1995—. Solicitor Boyertown (Pa.) Area Sch. Dist., 1981—, North Montco Vocat.-Tech. Sch., Lansdale, 1981—, Souderton (Pa.) Area Sch. Dist., 1989—, Wallingford-Swarthmore Sch. Dist., 1999—, Interboro Sch. Dist., 2002, Whitehall-Copley Sch. Dist., 2003; spl. counsel Penn Delco Sch. Dist., Aston, Pa., Kennett Consol. Sch. Dist., 1999—, Norristown Sch. Dist., 1999—, West Chester Area Sch. Dist., 2002, Hatboro-Horsham Sch. Dist., 2003; mem. pers. com., chair mktg./admissions com., trustee, bd. sec. Germantown Acad., Ft. Washington, Pa., 1991—; chair edn. law group Fox Rothschild, LLP, Lansdale, Pa.; presenter in field. Columnist Your School and the Law, 1992-2003. Mem. Nat. Sch. Bds. Assn., 2001. Mem. Nat. Assn. Sch. and Coll. Attys., Nat. Sch. Bds. Assn., Pa. Sch. Bds. Assn., Inc., Pa. Assn. Sch. Bus. Ofcls. (cert. of appreciation 1991), Pa. Bar Assn. (labor and edn. sects.), Montgomery County Bar Assn. (mcpl. law com. 1983—), Lehigh U. Law Forums, Assn. Del. Valley Ind. Schs. Republican. Jewish. Avocations: automobiles, travel. Home: 3229 Barley Ln Lansdale PA 19446-5114 Office: Fox Rothschild LLP 1250 S Broad St Lansdale PA 19446-0431 E-mail: jsultanik@foxrothschild.com.

SULTANOV, NAMIG, 2D BARONET, musician, music educator; b. Baku, Azerbaijan, May 9, 1948; arrived in USA, 2002; s. Abdulhamid Sultanov and Kubra Agalarova Sultanova; m. Sevil Agalarova Sultanova, July 10, 1970; children: Nigyar Sultanova, Narmina Sultanova. MusB piano, MusM piano, State Conservatory of Music, Moscow, Russia, 1965—70, Mus D piano, 1970—73. Faculty mem., assoc. prof. piano dept. Azerbaijan State Conservatory of Music, Baku, Azerbaijan, 1971—91, 1971—91; vis. assoc. prof. Faculty of Music and Performing Arts, Bilkent Univ., Ankara, Turkey, 1991—2002, chmn. of piano dept., 1991—2002, vice dean, 1991—2002; faculty mem., piano The Gorin Sch. of Music, Mt. View, Calif., 2002—. Named Hon. Title of State Artist, Pres. of Azerbaijan/ Baku, Azerbaijan, 1991; recipient Diploma for Student's Achievements, Third Internat. Young Pianists Compet. in Memory of v. Horowitz, 1999. Mem.: Juri mem. of Nat. and Internat. Piano Competitions., Music Tchr. Nat. Assoc. Achievements include conduct internat. master classes; Numerous students won prizes in Nat. and Internat. Piano competitions. Home: 1050 Crestview Dr Apt 216 Mountain View CA 94040-3452

SULTZBAUGH, JOHN STEPHAN, historian, educator; b. Harrisburg, Pa., July 25, 1950; s. John Leroy Sultzbaugh and Kathryn Mikailovna Sass; m. Gayle Rene Reitenbach, May 3, 1980; children: Elisabeth Yvonne, Andrew John. B.Humanities summa cum laude, Pa. State U.-Harrisburg, 1972, MA, 1975; PhD, Greenwich U., Norfolk Island, Australia, 1999. Cert. tchr. Pa. Hydrologist USGS, Harrisburg, Pa., 1973—74; hydrologic technologist Susquehana River Basin Commn., Mechanicsburg, Pa., 1974—75; history/govt. tchr. Upper Dauphin Area Sch. Dist., Lykins, Pa., 1975—. Adj. journalist and photographer Upper Dauphin Sentinal, Millersburg, Pa., 1978—88, Daily News, Lebanon, Pa., 1981—83, Sunday Pa., Lebanon, 1982, Pa. Mag., Harrisburg, 1990; mem. Nat. Jr. Honor Soc. Bd./Upper Dauphin Area Sch. Dist., 2002—; coord. student assistance program Upper Dauphin Sch. Dist., 1991—98; cons. reader Pa. History Textbook Commn., Harrisburg, 2003—. Contbr. poetry in jours. Recipient Editors award, Poetry.com, 2004. Mem.: Am. Soc. Authors, Composers and Pubs., Intersoc. Color Coun. Republican. Eastern Orthodox. Achievements include patents for variable pitch fluid impeller; research in blending colored music for instructional and theraupeutic applications; entry in Guniness Book of World Records. Avocations: aquatics, classical music, photography, philosophy. Home: 261 Romberger Ln Elizabethville PA 17023 Office: Upper Dauphin Area Sch Dist 2668 State Rt 209 Lykens PA 17048

SULTZER, BARNET MARTIN, microbiology and immunology researcher; b. Union City, N.J., Mar. 24, 1929; s. Moses Joseph and Florence Gertrude (Fischer) S.; m. Judith Ray Moreinis, Aug. 26, 1956; 1 child, Steven Bennett. BS, Rutgers U., 1950; MS, Mich. State U., 1951, PhD, 1958. Rsch. assoc. Princeton (N.J.) Labs., Inc., 1958-64; from asst. prof. to prof. microbiology SUNY, Bklyn., 1964-94, prof. emeritus, 1994—, interim chmn. dept. microbiology, 1980-82. Vis. scientist Karolinska Inst., Stockholm, 1971-72; vis. prof. Pasteur Inst., Paris, 1979-80; adj. prof. Fels Inst. of Cancer Rsch. and Molecular Biology, Temple U., Phila., 1995—; v.p. rsch. Stem Cell Therapeutics, King of Prussia, Pa., 1995-2000. Assoc. editor Jour. of Immunology, 1983-86; contbr. book chpts. and over 60 articles to profl. jours. on microbiology and immunology; mem. editl. bd. Infection and Immunity, 1980-94. Pres. Tenants Assn. Gateway Plz., Manhattan, N.Y., 1990-92; mem. Cmty. Bd. #1, Manhattan, 1989-94. 1st lt. USMC, 1952-55. Pres.'s fellow Am. Soc. Microbiology, 1957; grantee USPHS, NIH, Office of Naval Rsch., 1967-94. Mem. AAAS, Am. Soc. Microbiology, Am. Assn. Immunologists, N.Y. Acad. Sci., Harvey Soc., Internat. Endotoxin Soc., Reticuloendothelial Soc., Sigma Xi. Achievements include patent for chemical detoxification of endotoxins and discovery of the genetic basis for mammalian responses to endotoxins including immunological and pathophysiological effects; co-discoverer of a signal transduction gene controlling mammalian cellular responses to lipopolysaccharide endotoxin; developed first commercial immunological pregnancy test. Office: 375-8M South End Ave New York NY 10280 Office Phone: 212-321-2140. Personal E-mail: bsultzer@aol.com.

SULYK, STEPHEN, retired archbishop; b. Balnycia, Western Ukraine, Oct. 2, 1924; s. Michael and Mary (Denys) Sulyk. Student, Ukrainian Cath. Sem. of Holy Spirit, Fed. Republic Germany, 1945—48, St. Josaphat's Sem., 1948—52; Licentia in Sacred Theology, Cath. U. Am., 1952. Ordained priest Ukrainian Cath. Ch., 1952. Assoc. pastor, Omaha, 1952; assoc. pastor Bklyn., 1953, Minersville, Pa., 1954, Youngstown, Ohio, 1955; pastor Ch. Sts. Peter and Paul, Phoenixville, Pa., 1955, St. Michael's Ch., Frackville, Pa., 1957—61, Assumption of Blessed Virgin Mary Ch., Perth Amboy, NJ, 1962—81; sec. Archeparchy Chancery, 1956—57; adminstr. St. Nicholas, Phila., 1961; archbishop Met. of Ukraine-Rite Catholics of Archeparchy, Phila., 1981—2000; ret., 2000. Vice-chmn. Priests Senate, 1977—78, chmn.; pres. Ascension Manor, Inc.; archbishop Ukranian Rite Caths. Archeparchy Phila., Met. Ukranian-Rite Caths. U.S.A.; chmn. ad-hoc inter-rite com. Nat. Cath. Conf. Bishops/U.S. Cath. Conf., 1991. Mem.: Presidium of Synod of Ukranian Cath. Bishops (treas.), Coll. Bishops of Roman Cath. Ch., Providence Assn. Am. (Supreme Protector). Office: Archdiocese of Phila 827 N Franklin St Philadelphia PA 19123-2004

SULYOK, PAUL DAVID, music educator, composer; b. St. Johnsbury, Vt., July 14, 1958; s. Kalman Laszlo and Catherine Hagerman Sulyok. MusB in Music Edn., Westminster Choir Coll., 1981. Cert. Music Comprehensive 2100 N.J., 1981. Dir. activities Childrens' Fresh Air Home, North Wildwood, NJ, 1976—86; vocal, choral, drama tchr. East Windsor (N.J.) Schs., 1983—91, Upper Freehold Schools, Allentown, NJ, 1991—; childrens' theater dir. Green Apple Theater, Hightstown, NJ, 1993; music dir. On With The Show Bravo Cable Network, N.Y.C., 2001. Guild mem., entertainer Boheme Opera N.J., Trenton, 1993; musical dir., accompanist Off Broad St. Theater, Hopewell, 1995. Composer (and author): (musical play) Audition, 1993; composer: (author) (musical plays) Luigi's, 1995; composer: (and author) many children's musicals. Hospice vol. Hyacinth Orgn., New Brunswick, 1988—91; sch. bd. mem. Ewing Presbyn. Nursery Sch., 1998—2000; mem. choir, pianist Ewing Presbyn. Ch., 1995. Mem.: NEA, Ctrl. N.J. Orff-Schulwerk Assn., Music Educators Nat. Conf., Boheme Opera N.J. Guild (adv. bd./fundraising 1993). Democrat. Presbyterian. Avocations: piano, composing, travel, theater. Home: 27 Chippin Ct Robbinsville NJ 08691 Office: Upper Freehold Regional Schools 27 High St Allentown NJ 08501 Personal E-mail: sulyokpaul@aol.com.

SULZBACH, CHRISTI ROCOVICH, lawyer; b. L.A. BA, U. So. Calif., 1976; JD, Loyola U., 1979. Bar: Calif., 1980. Various to assoc. gen. counsel Tenet Healthcare Corp., Santa Barbara, Calif., 1983-99, exec. v.p., gen. counsel, 1999—2002, chief corp. officer, gen. counsel, 2002—. Mem. State Bar of Calif., ABA, FBA (bd. dirs. L.A. chpt.), Fedn. Am. Health Sys. (bd. dirs.), corp. adv. bd., U.S.C. Marshall Sch. Bus. Office: Tenet Healthcare Corp Corporate Office 3820 State St Santa Barbara CA 93105-3112

SULZBERGER, ARTHUR OCHS, newspaper executive; b. N.Y.C., N.Y., Feb. 5, 1926; s. Arthur Hays and Iphigene (Ochs) Sulzberger; m. Barbara Grant, July 2, 1948 (div. 1956); children: Arthur Ochs, Karen Alden; m. Carol Fox, Dec. 19, 1956 (dec. Aug. 1995); 1 adopted child, Cathy 1 child, Cynthia Fox; m. Allison Stacey Cowles, Mar. 9, 1996. BA, Columbia, 1951; LL.D., Dartmouth, 1964, Bard Coll., 1967; L.H.D., Montclair State Coll., 1972, Tufts U.; LLD (hon.), U. Scranton; L.H.D., Columbia U., 1992. With N.Y. Times, N.Y.C., 1951—, asst. treas., 1958—63, pres., 1963—79, pub., 1963—92, chmn., CEO, 1963—, chmn. emeritus, 1997—, also bd. dirs. Dir. Times Printing Co., Chattanooga. Trustee emeritus Columbia U.; trustee Met. Mus. Art, chmn. bd. trustees, 1987—. Capt. USMCR, WWII, Korea. Mem.: SAR, Met. Club (Washington), Explorers Club, Overseas Press Club. Office: NY Times Co 229 W 43rd St New York NY 10036-3959

SULZBERGER, ARTHUR OCHS, JR., newspaper publisher; b. Mt. Kisco, N.Y., Sept. 22, 1951; s. Arthur Ochs Sulzberger and Barbara Winslow Grant; m. Gail Gregg, Mar. 24, 1975; children: Arthur Gregg, Ann Alden. BA, Tufts U., 1974; grad. Prog. for Mgmt. Dev., Harvard U. Bus. Sch., 1985. Reporter The Raleigh (N.C.) Times, 1974—76; corr. AP, London, 1976—78; Washington corr. NY Times, 1978—81, city hall reporter, 1981, asst. metro editor, 1981—82, group mgr. advt. dept., 1983—84, sr. analyst corp. planning, 1985, prodn. coordinator, 1985—87, asst. pub., 1987—88, dep. pub., 1988—92, pub., 1992—; chmn. bd. dirs. NY Times Co., 1997—. Mem.: Newspaper Assn. Am. Office: The NY Times 229 W 43rd St New York NY 10036-3959

SULZER, ALEXANDER JACKSON, retired research microbiologist, educator; b. Emett, Ark., Feb. 13, 1922; s. Eugene August and Edna Jerita (Weaver) Sulzer; m. Faye Katherine Ross, Oct. 4, 1942; children: Dan L., Harry E. BA, Hardin-Simmons U., 1946—49; MS, Emory U., 1960—61, PhD, 1961—63; DHC, Univ. Peruan Cayetano Hereaia, 1977. Rsch. microbiologist Ctr. Disease Control, Atlanta, 1951—90, med. parasitologist, 1952—62, rsch. parasitologist, 1962—74; ret., 1990. Adj. prof. U. N.C., Chapel Hill, 1979—82; maleria cons. Pan Am. Health Org., 1980—90, World Health Org., 1980—90. Author: (book chpt.) Manual of Clinical Microbiology, 1995. Tech-5, medic U.S. Army, 1942—43, U.S. Recipient Sci. award, Bausch & Lomb, 1940, hon. lifetime mem., Peruvian Soc. Microbiology, 1973, Hon. Lifetime Professorship, U. Caye Heredia, Lima, Peru, 1973, 1st place, med. rsch., Inst. Hipolito Unanue, 1981; fellow rsch., Atomic Energy Commn., 1950—51, CDC-rsch., Emory U., 1959—60, Nat. Inst. Health, 1960—62. Fellow: Indian Soc. Malaria and Communicable Diseases (hon. lifetime fellow 1958—59); mem.: Nat. Registry Microbiology (life), Am. Soc. Parasitology (life), Royal Soc. Trop. Med. & Hyg. (life lifetime fellow 1957), Am. Soc. Paraistology (life), Am. Soc. Tropical Med. (life), Sigma Xi (life), Am. Acad. Microbiology (life lifetime fellow 1958). Achievements include discovery of similiar internal morphology of toxoplasma gondii and besnoitia jellisoai stained with silver protein, 1957; reproduction of toxoplasma gondii by internal budding, 1958; development of thick smear Antigen for maleria IFA tests, 1969; discovery of antigenic cross-reactions between Babesia argentina and plasmodium vivax and plasmodium falciparum, 1972; maleria and antibody patterns in primitive population in South America, 1980; indirect immunofluorescence test for human Babesia microti infections, 1986. Home: 1304 New Mexico Rd Bowden GA 30108 E-mail: asulzer@bellsouth.net.

SUMANTH, DAVID JONNAKOTY, industrial engineer, educator; b. Machilipatnam, India, Jan. 28, 1946; arrived in U.S., 1972; s. John Devraj and Nancy (David) Jonnakoty; m. Chaya J. Victor, June 26, 1974; children: John J., Paul J. BE, Osmania U., India, 1967, ME, 1969; MS in Indsl. Engring., Ill. Inst. Tech., 1974, PhD in Indsl. Engring., 1979. Tchg./rsch. asst. Ill. Inst. Tech., Chgo., 1973-78, instr., 1979; asst. prof. indsl. engring. U. Miami, Coral Gables, Fla., 1979-83, founding dir. productivity research group, 1979—, dir. grad. studies, 1980-83, assoc. prof. indsl. engring., 1983-88, Coll. Engring. coordinator MBA/MSIE, 1984-93, prof. indsl. engring., 1987—. Chmn. confs. Author: Productivity Engineering and Management, 1984, internat. student edit., 1985, Spanish edit., 1990, Indian edit., 1990, coll. custom series edit., 1994, also instrs. manual, (script) Total Productivity Management, 1985; editor: Productivity Management Frontiers-I, 1987, II, 1989, Productivity and Quality Management Frontiers III, 1991, IV, 1993, V, 1995, VI, 1997, VII, 1998, X, 2004; author: Total Productivity Management, 1998. Recipient over 65 honors, awards and recognitions including YMCA Edn. Gold medal, 1969, Freedoms Found., 1987;, Alexander Orr award of Tchg. Excellence, U. Miami, 2000; fellow U. Miami Eaton Honors Coll., 1986, fellow World Acad. Productivity Sci., 1989; gov.'s appointee as sr. judge Fla. Sterling award, 1992-93, judge, 1993-98. Mem. Am. Inst. Indsl. Engrs. (sr. mem., pres. Miami chpt. 1982-83, bd. dirs. 1983-84, nat. asst. dir. productivity mgmt. 1984—, chairperson rsch. com. 1987, Outstanding Indsl. Engr. of Yr. Miami chpt. 1983, 84); Productivity Ctr. (trustee 1985-89), Internat. Soc. for Productivity and Quality Rsch. (founder 1993, founding pres. 1993-95, chmn. 1995-97, pres. 2004—). Republican. Baptist. Avocations: reading, writing, people. Office: U Miami Productivity Rsch Group Coral Gables FL 33124 Office Phone: 305-284-2366.

SUMBERG, ALFRED DONALD, professional association executive; b. Utica, N.Y., Nov. 22, 1928; s. Samuel M. and Rachel Frances (Silverstein) S.; m. Dolly Primakow, June 26, 1955; children: Susan Diane Beldon, Laurie Darlene Sumberg. Student, Utica Coll., 1946-48, Hebrew Union Coll., 1948-50; AB, U. Cin., 1950, MA, 1951; PhD, U. Wis., 1960; LHD (hon.), U. Cin., 1994. Exec. dir., founding dir. Am. Jewish Tercentenary Com. Wis. Wis. Jewish Archives, 1954-55; instr. history U. Wis., Parkside, 1955-56; prof. history and econs. East Stroudsburg (Pa.) U., 1956-67; vis. prof. history U. Cin., Cin., 1954, 58, 67; assoc. gen. sec., dir. govt. rels. AAUP, Washington, 1967-94. Founding pres. N.E. Pa.Cmty. Fed. Credit Union, 1960-67; mem. exec. com. educator's ad hoc com. on copyright law, 1976-94, co-chair ad hoc com. for the creation of a cabinet-level dept. of edn., 1978-80, com. for edn. funding v.p.-treas., 1980-82, pres., 1982; bd. dirs. The Tuition Exch., 1988-96. Contbr. chapters to books, articles to profl. jours. Bd. dirs., chair edn. com. The Hist. Found. of Pa., 1961-67; pres. The Hist. Assn. Northeastern Pa., 1963-67, Monroe County (Pa.) Hist. Soc., 1965-67; edn. coord. Mondale-Ferraro campaign, 1984; vol. Nat. Exec. Svc. Corps, 1994-96. Mem. AAUP, Am. Hist. Assn., Nat. Trust for Hist. Preservation, U.S. Capitol Hist. Soc., Am. Econs. Assn., Nat. Economists Club, Nat. Dem. Club, U. Cin. Alumni Assn. (life, pres. Washington chpt. 1972-74), U. Wis. Alumni Assn. (life, pres. Washington chpt. 1978-80), Phi Alpha Theta, Kappa Delta Pi, Utica Coll. Alumni Assn. Democrat. Jewish. Home and Office: 1309 Fallsmead Way Rockville MD 20854-5523

SUMERS, ANNE RICKS, ophthalmologist, museum director; b. Beverly, Mass., May 8, 1957; d. David Frank and Anne Russell (Russell) Ricks; m. Elliott H. Sumers, May 31, 1983; children: Ben, Ted. BA in English Lit. with honors, U. Mich., 1979; MD, U. Cin., 1983. Diplomate Am. Bd. Ophthalmology. Intern Mt. Auburn Hosp., Cambridge, Mass., 1984; resident in ophthalmology NYU/Bellevue Hosp., 1984-87; ptnr. Ridgewood Ophthalmology, PC, NJ, 1990—; dir. NJ Childrens Mus., Paramus, NJ, 1992—; co-owner Saddle

River Market, NJ, 1995—2002. Team ophthalmologist NY Giants Football Team, 1994—, NJ Nets, 1999-2002; state coord. NJ Turn Off Your TV Week, 1994-96; Democratic candidate for US Congress (NJ-5), 2002; spkr. in field. Author: The Offical M.D. Handbook, 1983, Be A Better Mother—Today!, 1999; writer, host Channel 11/WPIX Wonder Zone, 1993; Democratic candidate for US Congress (NJ-S) 2002; interviewed on Good Morning Am., Am.'s Talking, CBS This Morning, NJN Discover NJ, Comcast Cablevision, Cablevision, Fox Channel 5 Good Day NY, 1992—, NBC Nightly News, various radio shows; contbr. articles to popular mags. Named one of 10 NJ Women of Yr., NJ Woman Mag., 1993; profiled in AMA News, Med. Econs., The NY Times, Star Ledger, Argus and other newspapers and mags. Fellow Am. Acad. Ophthalmology (media spokesperson, media info. com.); mem. AMA, Assn. Youth Museums, NJ Acad. Ophthalmology (bd. gov. 1997), Alpha Omega Alpha. Office: Ridgewood Ophthalmology PC 1200 E Ridgewood Ave Ridgewood NJ 07450-3937

SUMIDA, GERALD AQUINAS, lawyer; b. Hilo, Hawaii, June 19, 1944; s. Sadamy and Kimiyo (Miyahara) S. AB summa cum laude, Princeton U., 1966; JD, Yale U., 1969. Bar: Hawaii 1970, U.S. Dist. Ct. Hawaii 1970, U.S. Ct. Appeals (9th cir.) 1970, U.S. Supreme Ct. 1981. Rsch. assoc. Ctr. Internat. Studies, Princeton U., 1969; assoc. Carlsmith, Ball, Honolulu, 1970-76, ptnr., 1976-99; gen. counsel Asian Devel. Bank, 1999—. Mem. cameras in courtroom evaluation com. Hawaii Supreme Ct., 1984-86. Co-author: (with others) Legal, Instutional and Financial Aspects of An Inter-Island Electrical Transmission Cable, 1984, Alternative Approaches to the Legal, Instutional and Financial Aspects of Developing an Inter-Island, Electrical Transmission Cable System, 1986; editor Hawaii Bar News, 1972-73; contbr. chpts. to books. Mem. sci. and statis. com. Western Pacific Fishery Mgmt. Coun., 1979-99; mem. study group on law of armed conflict and the law of the sea Comdr. in Chief Pacific, USN, 1979-82; chmn. Pacific and Asian Affairs Coun. Hawaii, 1991, pres., 1982-91, bd. govs., 1976-96; bd. govs. ARC, 1994-2000, mem. exec. com., 1996-2000, chmn. human resources com., 1996-2000, chmn. Hawaii chpt., 1983-99, bd. dirs., 1983-99, vice chmn., 1990; chmn. Hawaii C. of C., 1997-98, bd. dirs., 1990-99; vice chmn. Honolulu Com. Fgn. Rels., 1983—; pres., dir., founding mem. Hawaii Ocean Law Assn., 1978—; mem. Hawaii Adv. Group for Law of Sea Inst., 1977-85; pres. Hawaii Inst. Continuing Legal Edn., 1979-83, dir., 1976-87; pres., founding mem. Hawaii Coun. Legal Edn. Youth, 1980-83, dir., 1983-88; chmn. Hawaii Commn. Yr. 2000, 1976-79; mem. Honolulu Cmty. Media Coun., 1976-99, exec. com., 1976-84, legal coun., 1979-83; bd. dirs. Hawaii Imin Centennial Corp., 1983-90, Hawaii Pub. Radio, 1983-88, Legal Aid Soc. Hawaii, 1984; founding gov., exec. v.p., chmn. rules and procedures Ctr. Internat. Comml. Dispute Resolution, 1987—; exec. com. Pacific Aerospace Mus., 1991—; exec. com. Pacific Islands Assn., 1988—; exec. com. Asia-Pacific Ctr. Res. Internat. Bus. Disputes, 1991-95; mem. Coun. Asia-Pacific Dispute Rsch. Ctrs., 1991-95; bd. dirs. U.S. C. of C., 1998—; mem. Pacific Basin Econ. Coun., 1993—; mem. mgmt. com. PBEC-U.S. Nat. Com., 1994-99. Recipient cert. of appreciation Gov. of Hawaii, 1979, resolutions of appreciation Hawaii Senate and Ho. of Reps., 1979; grantee Japan Found., 1979. Mem. ABA, Hawaii Bar Assn. (pres. young lawyers sect. 1974, v.p. 1984), Japan-Hawaii Lawyers Assn., Am. Soc. Internat. Law, Internat. Bar Assn., Am. Judicature Soc., Inter-Pacific Bar Assn., Internat. Law Assn., Plaza Club (Honolulu), Colonial Club (Princeton). Democrat. Office: Office Gen Coun Asian Devel Bank 6 ADB Ave 0401 Manila Mandaluyong Philippines also: Gen Coun Asian Devel Bank PO Box 789 0980 Manila Philippines E-mail: gsumida@adb.org.

SUMIDA, GREGORY ZIO, artist, photographer, musician, astronomer; b. LA; Grad., Alhambra H.S. One-man shows include Palm Springs Desert Mus., 1973, Desert S.W. Art Gallery, 1974, Pioneer Mus. and Haggin Art Gallery, 1975, Potlatch Art Gallery, 1976, Maxwell Galleries, San Francisco, 1977, Smith Gallery, N.Y.C., Troy's Gallery, Ariz., 1984, 86, 88, Zantman Galleries, Palm Desert, Calif., 1990, Legacy Gallery, 1991, 2002; group shows include Americana Gallery, Carmel, Calif., 1978, Fireside Gallery, Carmel, 1979, De Colores Gallery, Denver, 1979, Stremmel Galleries, Reno, 1980, Period Gallery West, Scottsdale, Ariz., 1981, Artist Union Gallery, 1982, 84-85, Smith Gallery, N.Y.C., 1983, Hunter Art Gallery, San Francisco, 1984, For Art Lovers Only, Denver, 1984, Classic-Am. Show, 1988-89, Legacy Gallery, Scottsdale, 1990, 2000, Zantman Galleries, Carmel, 1996, Urubamba Gallery, Paris, 1996, Artist FocusShow Legacy Gallery, Scottsdale, 2000-01, Eiteljorg Mus., 2002, Visions of the West, 2003, 2004, Legacy of the Am. West, 2003, Weatherburn Gallery, 2003, Mountain Oyster's 34th Ann. Contemporary Western Art Show, 2003—, Sylvan Gallery's Miniature Show, 2003, Trees' Place Small Works Holiday Exhbn., 2003, 2004, Big Horn Galleries, Summer Roundup, 2004, Tex. Art Gallery, Auction, 2004; represented in pub. and pvt. collections; included in publs. including S.W. Art, 1977, Contemporary We. Artists, 1982, We. Art Digest, 1986, Palm Springs Desert Life, 1987, Calif. Rev., 1989, Palm Springs Life, 1991, Am. Reference, 1991, Le Peintre Sumida, 1991, Internat. Fine Art Collector, 1992, Art West, 1999, Cowboys and Indians, 2001, Jour. Pharm. Medicine, 2001, Art Talk, 2002. Mem.: Oil Painters Am., Soc. Am. Impressionism. Office: PO Box 9210 Stockton CA 95208-1210 E-mail: ziogregory@hotmail.com.

SUMIYOSHI, TOMIKI, psychiatrist, researcher; b. Tokyo, Dec. 18, 1964; s. Hiroshi and Fusako (Naganuma) S.; m. Sawako Suemasa, Apr. 4, 1993. MB, MD, Kanazawa (Japan) U., 1989, PhD, 1993. Med. diplomate. Resident Fukui (Japan) Prefectural Psychiat. Hosp., 1990; ward adminstr., dir. neurochemistry rsch. Kanazawa (Japan) U. Hosp., 1991-93; rsch. assoc. dept. psychiatry Case Western Res. U., Cleve., 1993-95; asst. prof. dept. psychiatry, dir. psychopharmacology rsch. Saitama (Japan) Med. Sch., 1995-96; asst. prof. dept. neuropsychiatry, dir. neurochemistry rsch. Toyama (Japan) Med. and Pharmaceutical U., 1996—2000, assoc. prof. dept. neuropsychiatry, 2000—; aptd. psychiatrist Health and Welfare Ministry Japan, 1996—. Cons. Janssen, Inc., Tokyo, 1993—, Fujisawa, Inc., 1999—, Sumitomo, Inc., 2000—, Eli Lilly, Inc., 2004—; vis. prof. dept. psychiatry Vanderbilt U., Nashville, 2000—02. Author: Clinical Perspective of the New Antipsychotic Drugs, 2001, Relapse in Schizophrenia, 2002; contbr. articles to profl. jours. Rep. athlete The Nat. Athletic Meeting, Hachinohe, Japan, 1993. Recipient Psychiat Rsch. award, Saburo Matsubara Meml. Fund, Kanazawa, Japan, 1993, young investigator award, Nat. Alliance for Rsch. on Schizophrenia and Depression, Chgo., 1995, NY, 2001—03, Rsch. prize, Japanese Soc. Biol. Psychiatry, Tokyo, 1996, Meml. Travel award, Am. Coll. Neuropsychopharmacology, 2001; fellow Rsch. fellow, Min. Edn. and Sci., Japan, 2000—02; scholar, Rotary, 1994—95. Mem. Soc. Neurosci., NY Acad. Scis., World Fedn. Socs. Biol. Psychiatry, Coll. Internat. Neuropsychopharmacologicum, Japanese Soc. Psychiatry and Neurology, Japanese Soc. Biol. Psychiatry, Japanese Soc. Neuropsychopharmacology, Japanese Soc. Clin. Neuropsychopharmacology, Japanese Soc. for Brain Scis. Avocations: foreign languages, classical music, figure skating, foreign travel. Home: 144-14-B2 Nishi-araya Toyama 939-8251 Japan Office: Toyama Med & Pharm U Dept Neuropsychiatry 2630 Sugitani Toyama 930-0194 Japan E-mail: sumiyo@ms.toyama-mpu.ac.jp.

SUMMER, DONNA (LA DONNA ADRIAN GAINES), singer, songwriter, actress; b. Boston, Dec. 31, 1948; d. Andrew and Mary Gaines; m. Helmut Sommer (div.); 1 child, Mimi; m. Bruce Sudano; children: Brooklyn, Amanda. Has sold over 20 million records. Singer, 1967—; actress: (German stage prodn.) Hair, 1967-75, (Vienna Folk Opera prodns.) Porgy and Bess, (German prodns.) The Me Nobody Knows, (cable TV spl.) Donna Summer Special, 1980; recorded albums including The Wanderer, Star Collection, Love To Love You Baby, Love Trilogy, Four Seasons of Love, I Remember Yesterday, The Deep, Shut Out, Once Upon A Time, Bad Girls, On The Radio, Walk Away, She Works Hard For The Money, Cats Without Claws, All Systems Go, 1988, Another Place and Time, 1989, Mistaken Identity, 1991, Endless Summer, 1994, Christmas Spirit, 1994, I'm a Rainbow, 1996, Live & More Encore, 1999; subject My Life VH1 Concert, 1999; recorded theme song for Hunchback of Notre Dame, Disney; forerunner of disco style. Named Best Rhythm and Blues Female Vocalist, Nat. Acad. Rec. Arts and Scis., 1978, Best Female Rock Vocalist, 1979, Favorite Female Pop Vocalist, Am. Music Awards, 1979, Favorite Female Vocalist of Soul Music, 1979, Soul Artist of Yr., Rolling Stone mag., 1979; recipient Best Favorite Pop Single award, 1979, Best-selling Black Music Album for Female Artist award Nat. Assn. Record Merchandizers, 1979, Ampex Golden Reel award for album On the Radio, 1979, Best-selling Album for Female Artist, 1980, Ampex Golden Reel award for single On the Radio, 1980, Ampex Golden Reel award for album Bad Girls, Best of Las Vegas Jimmy award for best rock performance, 1980, Grammy award for best inspirational performance, 1984. Office: 2401 Main St Santa Monica CA 90405-3515

SUMMER, SHARON, marketing professional, former publisher; Nat. ad. dir. American Baby, 1989—91, pub., 1996—97; group pub. Parents Mag., Child Mag. & The Newborn Group, N.Y.C., 1997—2001; pub. Rosie Magazine, 2001, Parents Family Network, 2001—02; sr. v.p. Moda Internat. Mktg., 2003—. Office: Moda Internat Mktg 441 Lexington Ave Ste 1408 New York NY 10017*

SUMMER, THOMAS S. food products executive; BA in Econ., Harvard U., 1980; MBA, U. Chgo., 1982. CPA. Several positions, corp. fin. and internat. treasury PepsiCo, Inc., 1987—91; v.p., treas. Cardinal Health, Inc., 1991—97; sr. v.p. Constellation Brands, Inc., Fairport, NY, 1997—2000, exec. v.p., 2000—. Office: Constellation Brands Inc 300 Willowbrook Office Park Fairport NY 14450*

SUMMERALL, PAT (GEORGE ALLAN SUMMERALL), sportscaster; b. Lake City, Fla., May 10, 1931; m. Katherine Summerall; children: Susan, Jay, Kyle. Degree in Education, M. in Russain History, U. Ark. Football player Detroit Lions, 1952-53, Chgo. Cardinals, 1953-57, N.Y. Giants, 1958-61; played briefly in St. Louis Cardinals baseball orgn.; with CBS Sports, 1962-94; dir. sports Sta. WCBS Radio, N.Y.C., 1964-71, host morning program Sta. WCBS-TV, 1966-67, sportscaster early news; with CBS Radio Network; sportscaster Sports Time, Predictions, Profiles; host CBS Sports Spectacular.; lead play-by-play announcer NFL Football coverage CBS Sports, anchor golf and tennis coverage; sports commentator, football analyst Fox Network, 1994—2003. Named Sportscaster of Yr., 1977

SUMMERFIELD, JOHN ROBERT, textile curator; b. St. Paul, Feb. 21, 1917; s. Isaac and Irene (Longini) S.; m. Anne Benson, July 14, 1945. SB in Mech. Engring., MIT, 1938; MBA, U. Calif., Berkeley, 1947, PhD in Econs., 1954. Asst. prof. Sloan Sch. Mgmt., MIT, 1952-54; br. chief CIA, Washington, 1954-56; project leader The Rand Corp., Santa Monica, Calif., 1956—62; corp. economist Douglas Aircraft Co., Santa Monica, Calif., 1962—66; v.p. econ. planning Western Airlines, L.A., 1966-70; staff v.p. econ. planning Pan Am. Airways, N.Y.C., 1970-71; pres. Summerfield Assocs., Pacific Palisades, Calif., 1972-92; vis. curator Fowler Mus. Cultural History, UCLA, 1993—. Co-curator exhbns. of antique Minangkabau ceremonial textiles from West Sumatra, Textile Mus., Washington, 1990-91, Santa Barbara (Calif.) Mus. Art, 1991, Bellevue (Wash.) Art Mus., 1992, Utah Mus. Fine Art, 1992, Fowler Mus. of Cultural History, UCLA, 1999, Iris and B. Gerald Cantor Gallery, Coll. Holy Cross, 2003. Served to lt. USNR, 1942-45. E-mail: summrfld@arts.ucla.edu.

SUMMERFORD, BEN LONG, retired artist, educator; b. Montgomery, Ala., Feb. 3, 1924; s. Ben Long and Ollie Jo (Gilchrist) S.; m. Christene Morris, Jan. 30, 1951 (dec.); children: Jeffrey (dec.), Rebecca, James. Student, Birmingham-Southern Coll., 1942-43; BA, Am. U., 1948, MA, 1954; student, Ecole des Beaux Arts., Paris., 1949-50. Staff art dept. Am. U., 1950-88, chmn. dept., 1957-66, 70-86, prof., 1960-88; prof. emeritus, 1988—; artist in residence Dartmouth Coll., 1993. One-man shows include, Balt. Mus. Art, Goucher Coll., Franz Bader Gallery, Washington, Jefferson Place Gallery, Washington, Phillips Collection, Washington, Washington County Mus. Fine Arts, Hagerstown, Md.; represented in permanent collection, Watkins Gallery, Phillips Gallery Art, Corcoran Gallery Art, all Washington, numerous group shows of paintings. Served to ensign USNR, 1943-46. Fulbright fellow, France, 1949-50; J. Paul Getty scholar, Phillips Collection, 1990-91. Home: 2029 Ashley Dr Shepherdstown WV 25443 Office: Am U Dept Art Washington DC 20016

SUMMERLIN, GLENN WOOD, retired advertising executive; b. Dallas, Ga., Apr. 1, 1934; m. Anne Valley, Oct. 16, 1971; 1 child, Wade Hampton; children from previous marriage: Glenn Wood III, Edward Lee. Student, Ga. Inst. Tech., 1951-52; BBA, Ga. State U., 1956, MBA, 1967. Prodn. mgr. Fred Worrill Advt., Atlanta, 1956-65; v.p. sales Grizzard, Atlanta, 1965-74, pres., 1974-94, vice chmn., 1994-99; retired, 1999. Vice chmn. Polaris dist. Boy Scouts Am., 1967, Ga. State U. Found., 1974; chmn. distributive edn. adv. com. DeKalb Coll., 1974—76; bd. founders Geo. M. Sparks Scholarship Fund; bd. dirs. Atlanta Humane Soc., 1971—, treas., 1973, 1981—82, 1984—86, asst. treas. for capital devel., 1987—99, chmn., 2000—02, investment com., 1996—; mem. steering com. to honor Hank Aaron, 1982; lay rep. animal care com. Emory U., 1984—85; mem. adv. bd. Families in Action, 1985—86; bd. dirs. Travelers Aid Metro, Atlanta, 1989—90; mem. adv. bd. Emmaus House, 2000—03; chmn.'s coun., mem. mktg. adv. com. Crow Canyon Archaeol. Ctr., 1993—95. Recipient C.S. Bolen award Soc. Coun. Indsl. Editors, 1967; named Outstanding Young Man in DeKalb County, DeKalb Jaycees, 1967, Alumnus of Yr., Ga. State U., 1973; recipient Direct Mail Spokesman award Direct Mktg. Assn., 1973. Mem. Nat. Soc. Fund Raising Execs. (bd. dirs. Ga. chpt. 1984, cert. 1983-99), Ga. Assn. Bus. Communicators (pres. 1966-67), Ga. State Alumni Assn. (pres. 1971-72, dir. 1966-78), Sales and Mktg. Execs. Atlanta (dir. 1969-71), Ga. Bus. and Industry Assn. (bd. govs. 1975-76), Ga. Arms Collectors Assn. (dir. 1974-76, Pres.'s award 1973), Southeastern Antique Arms Collectors (charter, bd. dirs. 1978—, v.p. 1999—), Assn. Am. Sword Collectors (charter), Mid-Am. Antique Arms Soc. (charter), Mensa, Soc. Animal Welfare Adminstrs. (Disting Svc. award 2000), Travelers Aid of Atlanta (bd. dirs. 1989-90), Omicron Delta Kappa. Home: 1133 Ragley Hall Rd NE Atlanta GA 30319-2511

SUMMERLIN, WILLIAM TALLEY, allergist, immunologist, dermatologist; b. Anderson, S.C., 1938; MD, Emory U., 1964. Diplomate Am. Bd. Allergy and Immunology, Am. Bd. Dermatology, Am. Bd. Dermatopathology. Intern U. Tex. Med. Br., 1964-65; resident in dermatopathology Stanford, Palo Alto, 1967-70; resident in immunology U. Minn., Mpls., 1971-73, fellow in immunology, 1971-73; staff mem. St. Mary's Hosp., Rogers, Ark.; pvt. practice Regional Dermatology and Allergy Ctr., Rogers, Ark. Mem. AMA, Am. Acad. Dermatology, Am. Coll. Allergy and Immunology, Am. Acad. of Cosmetic Surgery, Am. Soc. for Mohs Surgery, Am. Subspecialty Bd. of Dermatopathology. Office: Regional Dermatology & Allgy PO Box 1868 Rogers AR 72757-1868

SUMMERS, ANITA ARROW, public policy and management educator; b. NYC, Sept. 9, 1925; d. Harry I. and Lillian (Greenberg) Arrow; m. Robert Summers, Mar. 29, 1953; children: Lawrence H., Richard F., John S. BA, Hunter Coll., 1945, DHL (hon.), 1995; MA, U. Chgo., 1947. Sr. econ. analyst Standard Oil Co. N.J., N.Y.C., 1947-54; asst. in econs. Yale U., New Haven, 1956-59; lectr. dept. econs. Swarthmore (Pa.) Coll., 1965-71; sr. economist Fed. Res. Bank Phila., 1971-75, research officer, 1975-79; adj. prof. pub. policy U. Pa., Phila., 1979-82, prof. pub. policy and mgmt., 1982—, dept. chair, 1983-88, univ. ombudsman, 2001—03, co-dir Wharton Urban Decentralization Project, 1987-97, dir. rsch. Wharton Real Estate Ctr., 2003—, sr. scholar Nat. Ctr. on the Edn. Quality of the Workforce, 1991—95. Expert witness schs. fin. Md., Mass., Va., 1980-85, Md., Va., 1996, Calif., 2003, bd. dirs. William Penn Found., Phila., 1993-98; chair bd. dirs. Mathematica Policy Rsch., Inc., Princeton, N.J., 1993—. Author: Economic Report on the Philadelphia Metropolitan Area, 1985, Economic Development within the Philadelphia Metropolitan Area, 1986, Local Fiscal Issues in the Philadelphia Metropolitan Area, 1987; editor: Urban Change in the United States and Western Europe, 1992, 99; contbr. articles to profl. jours. Chair econ. subcom. Pa. Three Mile Island Commn., Harrisburg, 1979; pres. Lower Merion (Pa.) LWV, 1963-65; mem. Mayor's Econ. Roundtable, Phila., 1984-88; mem. rsch. policy coun., 1992-94, Com. for Econ. Devel. Rockefeller Found. resident scholar, Bellagio, Italy, 1986. Mem. Am. Econ. Assn., Assn. for Pub. Policy and Mgmt. (policy coun. 1986), Phi Beta Kappa. Avocations: needlepoint, cooking. Home: 641 Revere Rd Merion Station PA 19066-1007 Office: U Pa Wharton Sch Dept Pub Policy and Mgmt Philadelphia PA 19104 Office Phone: 215-898-4076. Business E-Mail: summers@wharton.upenn.edu.

SUMMERS, CAROL, artist; b. Kingston, N.Y., Dec. 26, 1925; s. Ivan Franklin and Theresa (Jones) S.; m. Elaine Smithers, Oct. 2, 1954 (div. Aug. 1967); 1 son, Kyle; m. Joan Ward, May 6, 1974. BA, Bard Coll., 1951, DFA (hon.), 1974. Tchr. Hunter Coll., Sch. Visual Arts, Haystack Mountain Sch. Crafts, Bklyn. Mus. Art Sch., Pratt Graphic Art Ctr., Cheltenham Twp. Art Ctr., Valley Stream Community Art Ctr., U. Pa., Columbia Coll., U. Calif., Santa Cruz, San Francisco Art Inst., U. Utah, Logan, Art Study Abroad, Paris, Casa de Espiritus Alegres Marfil, Mex., USIS workshop tour, India, 1974, 79; folk art and textiles tour leader to Rajasthan, India, winters 1995-2004. Represented in permanent collections at, Mus. Modern Art, Bklyn. Mus., N.Y. Pub. Libr., Libr. of Congress, Nat. Gallery, Victoria and Albert Mus., London, Bibliotheque Nationale, Paris, Kunstmuseum, Basil, Lugano (Switzerland) Art Mus., Grenchen (Switzerland) Art Mus., Malmo (Sweden) Mus., Los Angeles County Mus., Phila. Mus., Balt. Mus., Seattle Mus., Boston Mus., Art Inst. Chgo., Am. embassies in Russia, Can., India, Thailand, Fed. Republic Germany and Eng.; traveling exhibit, Mus. Modern Art, 1964-66; retrospective exhbn. Brooklyn Mus., 1977, Nassau County Mus. Art, 1990, Belles Artes, San Miquel de Allende, Mex., 1992, Miami U. Art Mus., Oxford, Ohio, 1995, Egon Schiele Centrum Česky Krumlov, Czech Republic, 1997-98; 50-yr. retrospective at Mus. Art and History, Santa Cruz, 1999, Woodstock (N.Y.) Artists Assn., 1999, San Francisco Mus. Modern Art Rental Gallery, 2000. Served with USMCR, 1944-48, PTO. Named Artist of Yr., Santa Cruz County Arts Commn., 2001; Louis Comfort Tiffany Found. fellow, 1955, 60, John Simon Guggenheim Found. fellow, 1959, Fulbright fellow, Italy, 1961; Italian govt. study grantee, 1954-55, Coun. for Internat. Exch. Scholars rsch. grantee, India, 1993 94. Mem. NAD, Calif. Soc. Printmakers. Address: 2817 Smith Grade Santa Cruz CA 95060-9764 Office Phone: 831-423-0181.

SUMMERS, CATHLEEN ANN, film producer; b. Chgo. d. Paul and Elizabeth Summers; m. Patrick Crowley. BA, U. So. Calif., 1973. Film editor, comml. producer, dir.'s asst. Roman Polanski, Rome, 1972; story editor Albert S. Ruddy Prodns. Paramount Pictures, L.A., 1973-74; exec. asst. Columbia Pictures, Burbank, Calif., 1974, story editor, 1974-76; devel. exec., v.p., producer Martin Ransohoff Prodns. Columbia Pictures, 1976; sr. v.p. Tri-Star Pictures, Century City, Calif., 1984-87; motion picture producer Cathleen Summers Prodns., L.A., 1989—; ptnr. ESN, Film Prodn. Resource Co.; cons., ptnr. Estudio Network. Motion picture producer, ptnr. Summers-Kouf Prodns., Burbank, 1986-87; motion picture producer Cathleen Summers Prodns., L.A., 1987, Summers-Quaid Prodns., Century City, Culver City, Calif., 1988—. Producer: (motion picture) Stakeout, 1987, DOA, 1991, Vital Signs, 1990, Mystery Date, 1991, Dogfight, 1991, The Sandlot, 1993, Stakeout II, 1993; exec. prodr. Derivations, Who New/The Real Deal, 2003. Co-founder Diane Thomas Scholarship, UCLA, 1988—; bd. dirs. L.A. chpt. Nat. Parkinsons Found.; founding bd. dirs. U.S. Comedy Arts Festival, Aspen, Colo. Mem. Am. Film Inst. (pres. 3d Decade Coun. 1995, 96, 97).

SUMMERS, CLYDE WILSON, law educator; b. Grass Range, Mont., Nov. 21, 1918; s. Carl Douglas and Anna Lois (Yontz) S.; m. Evelyn Marie Wahlgren, Aug. 30, 1947; children: Mark, Erica, Craig, Lisa. BS, U. Ill., 1939, JD, 1942, LLD, 1998; LLM, Columbia U., 1946, JSD, 1952; LL.D., U. Leuven, Belgium, 1967, U. Stockholm, 1978, U. Ill., 1998. Bar: N.Y. 1951. Mem. law faculty U. Toledo, 1942-49, U. Buffalo, 1949-56; prof. law Yale U., New Haven, Conn., 1956-66, Garver prof. law, 1966-75; Jefferson B. Fordham prof. law U. Pa., 1975-90, prof. emeritus, 1990—. Hearing examiner Conn. Commn. on Civil Rights, 1963-71 Co-author: Labor Cases and Material, 1968, 1982, Rights of Union Members, 1979, Legal Protection for the Individual Employee, 1989, 1996, 2002; co-editor: Labor Relations and the Law, 1953, Employment Relations and the Law, 1959, Comparative Labor Law Jour., 1984—97. Chmn. Gov.'s Com. on Improper Union Mgmt. Practices N.Y. State, 1957-58; chmn. Conn. Adv. Council on Unemployment Ins. and Employment Service, 1960-72; mem. Conn. Labor Relations Bd., 1966-70, Conn. Bd. Mediation and Arbitration, 1964-72. Guggenheim fellow, 1955-56; Ford fellow, 1963-64; German-Marshall fellow, 1977-78; NEH fellow, 1977-78, Fullbright fellow, 1984-85. Mem. Nat. Acad. Arbitrators (pres. elect), Internat. Soc. Labor Law and Social Legislation. Congregationalist. Home: 753 N 26th St Philadelphia PA 19130-2429 Office: U Pa Sch Law 3400 Chestnut St Philadelphia PA 19104-6204 E-mail: csummers@law.upenn.edu.

SUMMERS, DAVID STEWART, neurologist, consultant; b. Canton, Ohio, Feb. 16, 1932; s. William Edward and Stewart (Jordan) Summers; m. Ada Ernestine Cumber, Nov. 30, 1957; children: David Stewart II, Timothy C. BS, Va. State U., 1954; MD, U. Va., 1959. Diplomate Am. Acad. Pain Mgmt. Resident in neurology SUNY, Syracuse, 1960—63; asst. prof. neurology U. Rochester, NY, 1968—72; asst. prof. U. Utah Coll. Medicine, Salt Lake City, 1972—76; staff neurologist St. Vincent Health Ctr., Erie, Pa., 1976—91, Meadville (Pa.) Med. Ctr., 1991—93; neurologist Warren (Pa.) State Hosp., 1993—2000; investor, 2000—. Cons. Reflex Sympathetic Dystrophy Assn., Erie, 1988—97; mem. adv. coun. HHS, Washington, 1974—77. Contbg. author The Black Humanist Experience, 2003; contbr. articles to profl. jours. Supporter City Mission, Erie, 1991—, Am. United Separation Ch. and State, AAAS, AAUW, Washington, 1997, NOW, ACLU, Am. Humanist Assn., People for the Am. Way, Ctr. Reproductive Law and Policy, Planned Parenthood, others; advisor to gov. Coun. Black Affairs, Salt Lake City, 1975; mem. Human Rights Campaign, Zero Population Growth. Capt. M.C. USAR, 1964—67, Landstuhl, Germany. Grantee, Nat. Med. Fellowships, 1956—59; A. A. Rockefeller scholar, Williamsburg, Va., 1951—54. Mem.: NAACP, Nat. Soc. Scabbard & Blade, NY Acad. Scis., Menninger Soc., Am. Epilepsy Soc., Nat. Med. Assn., Am. Acad. Neurology, U. Va. Alumni Assn., Am. Legion (life). Democrat. Avocations: reading, bicycling, skiing.

SUMMERS, FRANK WILLIAM, retired librarian; b. Jacksonville, Fla., Feb. 8, 1933; s. Frank Wesley and Kathleen (Gilreath) S.; 1 son, William Wesley. BA, Fla. State U., 1955; MA, Rutgers U., 1959, PhD, 1973. Libr. Jacksonville Pub. Libr., 1955, 57; sr. libr. Linden (N.J.) Pub. Libr., 1958-59; dir. Cocoa (Fla.) Pub. Libr., 1959-61; assoc. libr. Providence Pub. Libr., 1961-65; libr. Fla. State Libr., 1965-69; rsch. fellow Rutgers U., New Brunswick, N.J., 1969-70; asst. dean, prof. Coll. Librarianship, U. S.C., 1971-76, dean, 1976-85; dean Sch. Libr. and Info. Studies Fla. State U., Tallahassee, 1985-94, prof., 1994-99, dir. of librs., 2000-01. Lectr. Libr. Sch. U. R.I., 1964-95; libr. surveys in Fla., Ohio, N.Y., S.C., N.C., Ky., Tex. Contbr. profl. jours. Mem. R.I. Bd. Library Commrs., 1964-65. Served to lt. (j.g.) USNR, 1955-57. Mem. ALA (exec. bd., v.p., pres.-elect 1987-88, pres. 1988-89, Joseph W. Lippincot award 1996), R.I. Libr. Assn. (pres.), S.C. Libr. Assn. (pres.), Assn. Am. Libr. Schs. (pres.), Beta Phi Mu (exec. dir. 1996-99). Home: 505 Live Oak Plantation Rd Tallahassee FL 32312-2335 E-mail: summers.w@att.net.

SUMMERS, HARDY, state supreme court justice; b. Muskogee, Okla., July 15, 1933; m. Marilyn Summers, Mar. 16, 1963; children: Julia Summers Muchmore, Andrew Murray. BA, U. Okla., 1955, LLB, 1957. Asst. county atty. Muskogee County, 1960-62; pvt. practice law Muskogee, 1962-76; dist. judge 15th dist. Okla. Dist. Ct., 1976-85; justice Okla. Supreme Ct., Oklahoma City, 1985—, chief justice, 1999-2000. Sec. Muskogee County Election Bd., 1965-72. Capt. JAGC, USAF, 1957-62. Recipient Disting. Alumnus award, U. Okla. Coll. Law, 2000. Mem. ABA, Okla. Bar Assn., Okla. Jud. Conf. (pres. 1984). Avocations: outdoor sports, music. Office: Okla Supreme Ct Rm 202 State Capital Bldg Oklahoma City OK 73105

SUMMERS, JOSEPH FRANK, author, publisher; b. Newnan, Ga., June 26, 1914; s. John Dawson and Anne (Blalock) S.; BA in Math., U. Houston, 1942; profl. cert. meteorology, UCLA, 1943, U. Chgo., 1943; postgrad., U. P.R., 1943-44; MA in Math., U. Tex. at Austin, 1947; postgrad. Rice U., 1947-49; m. Evie Margaret Mott, July 8, 1939 (dec. May 1989); children: John Randolph, Thomas Franklin, James Mott. With Texaco Inc., Houston, 1933-42, 49-79, mgr. data processing, 1957-67, asst. gen. mgr. computer svcs. dept., 1967-79, automation cons., 1979-83; pres. Word Lab Inc., Houston, 1983—; instr. math. AAC, Ellington Field, Tex., 1941-42, U. Tex. at Austin, 1946-47. Pres. Houston Esperanto Assn., 1934-39; vol. tutor Thousand Points of Light, 1991—. Capt. AAC, 1942-46. Rice U. fellow, 1947-49. Mem. Assn. Computing Machinery (pres. 1956-58), Nat. Assn. Accts. (past bd. dir.), Am. Petroleum Inst. (mem. data processing and computing com. 1955-59), Rice U.

Hist. Soc., Rice U. Assocs., Esperanto League N.Am., Universal Esperanto Assn. Author: Mathematics for Bombadiers and Navigators, 1942, Wholly Holey Holy, An Adult American Spelling Book, 1984. Contbg. author: American Petroleum Institute Drilling and Production Practices. Home and Office: 10150 Metronome Dr Houston TX 77080-6312 E-mail: Jfranksummers@aol.com.

SUMMERS, LAWRENCE H. academic administrator, former government official; b. New Haven, Nov. 30, 1954; m. Victoria Joanne Perry, 1984; children: Pam, Ruth, Harry BS, MIT, 1975; PhD, Harvard U., 1982. Mem. faculty MIT, 1979-82; domestic policy economist Pres'. Coun. Econ. Advisors, 1982-83; v.p. devel. econs., chief economist World Bank, 1991-93; prof. econs. Harvard U., Cambridge, Mass., 1983-93, Nathaniel Ropes prof. polit. economy, 1987, pres., 2001—; under sec. for internat. affairs U.S. Dept. Treasury, Washington, 1993-95, dep. sec., 1995-99, sec., 1999-2001; Arthur Okun Disting. Fellow in Econ., Globalization, and Governance Brookings Instn., Washington, 2001. Author Understanding Unemployment, 1990; co-author Reform in Eastern Europe, 1991; editor series Tax Policy and the Economy; contbr. numerous articles to profl. jours. Recipient Alan Waterman award NSF, 1987, John Bates Clark medal, 1993, disting. achievement award Boys' & Girls' Club Greater Washington, 2000, disting. svc. award Golden Slipper Club & Charities 2000, economic patriot award Concord Coalition, 2000, Stephen P. Guggan award Inst. Internat. Edn., 2000. Fellow NAS, Econometric Soc., Am. Acad. Arts and Scis., Brookhaven Sci. Assocs. (bd. dirs.), Nat. Acad. Sci. Office: Harvard U Office of the President Massachusetts Hall Cambridge MA 02138

SUMMERS, LORRAINE DEY SCHAEFFER, retired librarian; b. Phila., Dec. 14, 1946; d. Joseph William and Hilda Lorraine (Ritchey) Dey; m. F. William Summers, Jan. 28, 1984. BA, Fla. State U., 1968, MS, 1969. Ext. dir. Santa Fe Regional Libr., Gainesville, 1969-71; pub. libr. cons. State Libr. of Fla., Tallahassee, 1971-78, asst. state libr., 1978-84; dir. adminstrv. svcs. Nat. Assn. for Campus Activities, Columbia, S.C., 1984-85; asst. state libr. State Libr. of Fla., Tallahassee, 1985—2001, ret., 2001—. Bd. dirs., sec. Southeastern Libr. Network, Inc.; cons. in field. Contbr. articles to profl. jours. Del. Pres.'s Com. on Mental Retardation Regional Forum, Atlanta, 1975; del. Fla. Gov.'s Conf. on Libr. and Info. Svcs., 1978, 90. Mem. ALA (orgn. com. 1979-83, coun. 1982-84, 93-97, resolutions com. 1983-85, mem. legislation com. 1993-95, nominating com. 1996, awards com. 1998-99, Spectrum awards jury 1999-2000), Assn. Specialized and Coop. Libr. Agys. (dir. 1976-82, chmn. planning and orgn. com. 1976-80, chmn. nominating com. 1980-81, chmn. by laws com. 1985-86, exec. bd. state libr. agy. sect. 1983-86, pres. 1987-88, chmn. stds. rev. com. 1990-92), Southeastern Libr. Assn. (exec. bd. 1976-80, v.p., pres.-elect 1994-96, pres. 1996-98, past pres. 1998-2000, nominating com. 2000-02), Fla. Libr. Assn. (sec. 1978-79, dir. 1976-80, nominating com. 1995-96), Zonta (dir. 1992-95, sec. 1999-2001). Democrat. Methodist. Personal E-mail: lorsummers@worldnet.att.net.

SUMMERS, PAUL, state attorney general; b. Somerville, Tenn., Mar. 28, 1950; BS, Miss. State U.; JD, U. Tenn. Dist. atty. gen. 25th Jud. Dist., Somerville, Tenn., 1982—90; judge Ct. of Criminal Appeals, Nashville, 1990—99; atty. gen. State of Tenn., Nashville, 1999—. Adj. prof. law U. Memphis; former adj. faculty Cumberland U.; pres. elect Tenn. Dist. Atty.'s Gen. Conf.; mem. Ct. Criminal Appeals, 1990—99; lectr. in field. Former mem. Tenn. Sentencing Commn.; col. Tenn. Army N.G. With USAF. Mem.: Tenn. Dist. Attys. Gen. Conf. (pres.), Tenn. Bar Assn. (former gov.). Democrat. Avocations: racquetball, rollerblading, Karate (black belt). Office: Office of the Attorney General 500 Charlotte Ave Nashville TN 37243-1401

SUMMERS, ROBERT, economics professor; b. Gary, Ind., June 20, 1922; s. Frank and Ella (Lipton) Samuelson; m. Anita Arrow, Mar. 29, 1953; children: Lawrence Henry, Richard Fredric, John Steven. BS, U. Chgo., 1943; PhD, Stanford, 1956; postgrad. (Social Sci. Research Council fellow), King's Coll., U. Cambridge, Eng., 1951-52. Instr. Stanford, 1949-50; mem. faculty Yale, 1952-59, asst. prof., 1956-59; staff mem. Cowles Found., 1955-59; economist RAND Corp., Santa Monica, Calif., 1959-60, cons., 1960-80. Mem. faculty U. Pa. Wharton Sch., 1959—, prof., 1967—, chmn. grad. group in econs., 1967-70, 73-76 Author: (with Lawrence R. Klein) The Wharton Index of Capacity Utilization, 1966, (with others) Strategies for Research and Development, 1967, (with others) A System of International Comparisons of Gross Product and Purchasing Power, 1975, (with others) International Comparisons of Real Product and Purchasing Power, 1978, (with others) World Product and Income, 1982; contbr. articles to profl. jours. Served with AUS, 1944-46. Ford Found. faculty rsch. fellow London Sch. Econs., 1966-67; NSF grantee 1957-59, 63-66, 80-82, 86-90, 92-94, 95-97, 97-2000, 00—03; resident scholar Rockefeller Found. Study Ctr., 1986. Fellow: AAAS, Am. Econs. Assn., Econometric Soc. Home: 641 Revere Rd Merion Station PA 19066-1007 Office: U Pa Dept Econ Philadelphia PA 19104-6297 Office Phone: 215-898-7717. Business E-Mail: rsummers@econ.upenn.edu.

SUMMERS, ROBERT SAMUEL, lawyer, author, educator; b. Halfway, Oreg., Sept. 19, 1933; s. Orson William and Estella Bell (Robertson) S.; m. Dorothy Millicent Kopp, June 14, 1955; children: Brent, William, Thomas, Elizabeth, Robert. BS in Polit. Sci., U. Oreg., 1955; postgrad. (Fulbright scholar), U. Southampton, Eng., 1955-56; LLB, Harvard U., 1959; postgrad. rsch., Oxford U., 1964-65, 74-75, 81-82, 88-89; LLD (hon.), U. Helsinki, Finland, 1990, U. Göttingen, Germany, 1994. Bar: Oreg. 1959, N.Y. 1974. Asso. King, Miller, Anderson, Nash and Yerke, Portland, Oreg., 1959-60; asst. prof. law U. Oreg., 1960-63, assoc. prof., 1964-68; vis. asso. prof. law Stanford U., 1963-64; prof. U. Oreg., 1968-69, Cornell U., 1969-76, McRoberts rsch. prof. law, 1976—. Summer vis. prof. Ind. U., 1969, U. Mich., 1974, U. Warwick, Eng., 1975, Australia Nat. U., U. Sydney, Australia, 1977; vis. Fulbright prof. U. Vienna, Austria, 1985; Goodhart vis. prof. Cambridge U., Eng., 1991-92; H. Hurst Eminent vis. scholar U. Fla., 1995; rsch. fellow Merton Coll., oxford U., 1981-82, Exeter Coll., Oxford U., 1988-89; cons. Cornell Law Project in publ. schs., N.Y., 1969-74, Law in Am. Soc. project Chgo. Bd. Edn., 1968-69; instr. Nat. Acad. Jud. Edn., 1976—; mem. faculty Salzburg Seminar in Am. Studies, 1990; ofcl. advisor Drafting commn. on New Civil Code for Russian Fedn., 1994-96. Author: Law, Its Nature, Functions and Limits, 1986; (with Hubbard and Campbell) Justice and Order Through Law, 1973; (with Bozzone and Campbell) The American Legal System, 1973; (with Speidel and White) Teaching Materials on Commercial Transactions, 1987, Collective Bargaining and Public Benefit Conferral-A Jurisprudential Critique, 1976, The Uniform Commercial Code, 1988, 4th edit., 1995; (with White) Het Pramatisch Instrumentalisme, 1981, Instrumentalism and American Legal Theory, 1982, Lon L. Fuller-Life and Work, 1984; (with Atiyah) Form and Substance in Anglo-American Law, 1987; (with Hillman) Contract and Related Obligation, 1987; (with MacCormick and others) Interpreting Statutes-A Comparative Study, 1991, Nature of Law and Legal Reasoning, 1993; contbr. book revs. and articles to profl. jours.; editor: Essays in Legal Philosophy, vol. 1, 1968, vol. 2, 1971. Social Sci. Research Council fellow, 1964-65 Mem. Am. Law Inst., Assn. Am. Law Schs. (chmn. sect. jurisprudence 1972-73), Am. Soc. Polit. and Legal Philosophy (v.p. 1976-78), Internat. Acad. Comp. Law, Internat. Assn. of Legal and Social Philosophy Am. Soc. (pres. 1989-91), Austrian Acad. of Scis., Phi Beta Kappa. Republican. Congregationalist. Office: Cornell U Sch Law Myron Taylor Hall Ithaca NY 14853

SUMMERS, RYAN CHARLES, music educator; b. Hendersonville, NC, Sept. 24, 1977; s. Kathleen Andrea and Charlie Walter Summers. B.S. in music industry studies, Appalachian State U., 1996—2001. Band dir. Lincolnton Mid. Sch., NC, 2002—. Brass instr. Carolina Crown Drum and Bugle Corps, Ft. Mill, SC, 2001—. Mem.: NC Assn. of Educators, Music Educators Nat. Conf., Phi Mu Alpha Sinfonia. Personal E-mail: summers249@yahoo.com.

SUMMERS, THOMAS CAREY, lawyer; b. Frederick, Md., Feb. 9, 1956; s. Harold Thomas and Doris Jean (Culler) S.; m. Robin Ann Stalnaker, May 12, 1990; children: Kristin, Heather, Lindsay. BA, Dickinson Coll., 1978; JD, U. Balt., 1981. Bar: Md. 1981, U.S. Dist. Ct. Md. 1981, D.C. 1986. Assoc. Ellin & Baker, Balt., 1979-89, Peter G. Angelos, Balt., Md., 1989—. Adj. prof. law U. Balt. Sch. of Law. Mem. ABA, Md. State Bar Assn., Md. Trial Lawyers Assn. Democrat. Lutheran. Avocation: golf. Office: Law Offices of P G Angelos One Charles Ctr Baltimore MD 21201

SUMMERS, VANESSA, state legislator; m. Nicholas T. Barnes. Grad., Mid-Am. Coll. Funeral Svcs. State rep., mem. aged & aging, pub. policy, ethics, vet. affairs & urban affairs coms., chmn. interstate coop. com. Ind. Ho. of Reps., Indpls., 1991—; funeral dir. Summers Funeral Chapel. Named one of Top Ladies of Distinction. Mem. Alpha Kappa Alpha, Alpha Mu Omega. Democrat. Office: 1140 Brook Ln Indianapolis IN 46202-2255

SUMMERS, WILLIAM B., JR., brokerage house executive; b. 1950; With McDonald & Co. Investments Inc., Cleve., 1971—; pres., CEO and chmn. McDonald & Co. Securities, Cleve., 1983—; chmn. McDonald Investments Inc., Cleve., 1995—; exec. v.p. KeyCorp, 1998—2000; chmn. Key Capital Partners, 1998—2000. Office: McDonald Investment Inc 800 Superior Ave E Cleveland OH 44114-2601

SUMMERS, WILLIAM COFIELD, science educator; b. Janesville, Wis., Apr. 17, 1939; s. Crosby Hungerford and Rebecca Delores (Cofield) S.; m. Wilma Jean Poos, July 24, 1965; 1 child, Emily Alexandra. BS, U. Wis., 1961, MS, 1963, PhD, MD, 1967; MA, Yale U., 1977. Post-doctoral fellow MIT, Cambridge, Mass., 1967-68; asst. prof. Yale U., New Haven, 1968-70, assoc. prof., 1970-77, prof., 1977—. Cons. NIH, Bethesda, Md., 1976—. Editor Nucleic Acids Research Jour., 1977-79, Gene jour., 1984-91; contbr. articles to profl. jours. Cons. Anna Fuller Fund, New Haven, 1973-88, Searle Scholars Program, Chgo., 1980-84; trustee Leukemia Soc. Am., N.Y.C., 1981-85, Yale-China Assn., New Haven, 1982-88, 94-98. Mem. Am. Soc. for Microbiology, History Sci. Soc., Am. Assn. History of Medicine. Office: Yale U Box 208114 New Haven CT 06520-8114 E-mail: william.summers@yale.edu.

SUMMERS, WILLIAM KOOPMANS, neuropsychiatrist, researcher; b. Jefferson City, Mo., Apr. 14, 1944; s. Joseph S. and Amy Lydia (Koopmans) S.; m. Angela Forbes McGonigle, Oct. 2, 1972 (div. Apr. 1985). Student, Westminster Coll., Fulton, Mo., 1962-64; BS, U. Mo., 1966; MD, Washington U., St. Louis, 1971. Internal medicine intern Barnes Hosp-Washington U., St. Louis, 1971—72; resident in internal medicine Jewish Hosp., St. Louis, 1972—73; resident in psychiatry Rsch. Hosp., St. Louis, 1973—76; asst. prof. U. Pitts., 1976—78, U. So. Calif., L.A., 1978—82; asst. clin. prof. rsch. UCLA, 1982—88; rschr. Arcadia, Calif., 1988—92, Albuquerque, 1992—; pres., CEO Alzheimers Corp., Albuquerque, 1999—. Mem. AMA, ACP, Am. Psychiat. Assn., Soc. Neurosci., N.Y. Acad. Scis., Am. Fedn. Clin. Rsch. Episcopalian. Achievements include holder of 8 patents in neuropharmacology and neuroceuticals. Avocation: gardening. Office: Alzheimers Corp 6000 Uptown NE Ste 308 Albuquerque NM 87110 Fax: 505-878-0211.

SUMMERS, WILLIAM LAWRENCE, lawyer; b. Ravenna, Ohio, Mar. 6, 1942; s. Samuel Long and Harriet Cordellia (Jones) S.; m. Barbara A. Herbert; children: Melinda Ann, Shannon Lea, Heather Colleen, Kelly Lynn, Michael Patrick, Kevin James. BA in Polit. Sci. and Sociology, Kent State U., 1965; postgrad., U. Miami, 1966; JD, Cleve. State U., 1969. Bar: Ohio 1969, Ky. 1988, U.S. Dist. Ct. (no. dist.) Okla. 1971, U.S. Ct. Appeals (6th cir.) 1973, U.S. Ct. Appeals (3d and 5th cirs.) 1979,, U.S. Ct. Appeals (8th and 5th cirs.) 1981, U.S. Ct. Appeals (7th cir.) 1982, U.S. Ct. Appeals (9th and 10th cirs.) 1983, U.S. Ct. Appeals (11th cir.), 1984, U.S. Supreme Ct., 1973, U.S. Tax Ct. 1973, U.S. Dist. Ct. (so. dist.) Ala. 1984, U.S. Dist. Ct. (so. dist.) Ohio 1985, U.S. Dist. Ct. (ea. and we. dists.) Ky. 1988. Ptnr. Summers & Vargas Co. LPA, Cleve. and Lexington, Ky., 1969—. Cons. on death penalty State Pub. Defender, Santa Fe, 1980-83; lectr. in field. Named one of Ten Outstanding Young Men of Cleve., Cleve. Jaycees, 1972, Five Outstanding Young Men of Ohio, Ohio Jaycees, 1972. Fellow Am. Acad. Trial Lawyers (Roscoe Pound award 1971); mem. ABA (criminal justice sect.), Ohio State Bar Assn. (ho. of dels. 1973-75, 2002-2004), Cuyahoga County Bar Assn. (trustee 1972-76, treas. 1976-79, pres. 1982-83, other coms.), Cuyahoga County Bar Assn., Cuyahoga County Criminal Ct. Bar Assn. (pres. 1977-79), Fed. Bar Assn., Portage County Bar Assn., Ohio Assn. Criminal Def. Lawyers (bd. dirs. 1988—), Ky. Assn. Criminal Def. Lawyer (bd. dirs. 1987-2000), Bar Assn. Greater Cleve., Nat. Assn. Criminal Def. Lawyers (trustee 1977-88, chmn. various coms. Pres.'s award 1981, 1986, 90, Robert C. Heeney award 1982), Am. Judicature Soc., Thoroughbred Club Am., Delta Theta Phi, Canterbury Golf Club, Elks. Roman Catholic. Avocation: thoroughbred horse breeding. Home: 17549 Merry Oaks Trl Chagrin Falls OH 44023-5643 Office: Ste 525 23240 Chagrin Blvd Cleveland OH 44122-5486 Office Phone: 216-591-0727. E-mail: wlslawyer@aol.com.

SUMMERS-POWELL, ALAN, lawyer; BA, Yale Coll., 1985; JD, U. Pa., 1988. Bar: N.Y. 1989, N.J. 1989, U.S. Dist. Ct. (fed. dist.) N.J. 1989, D.C. 1990, Fla. 1993, U.S. Dist. Ct. (mid. dist.) Fla. 1996, U.S. Ct. Appeals (11th cir.) 1996, U.S. Tax Ct. 1997, U.S. Dist. Ct. (so. dist.) Fla. 2001. Pvt. practice, Palm Harbor, Fla. Chmn. David Leasing and Devel., Inc. Office: PO Box 6043 Palm Harbor FL 34684-0643

SUMMER-STRAIT, BETH, mental health services professional; b. Kings Mountain, N.C., Apr. 21, 1963; d. Ollie Orestus and Bertha Brock Summer; m. Robert Haskell Strait, Jr., Apr. 20, 1996. BA, Lander U., Greenwood, S.C., 1981—85; MS in Edn., U. S.C., Columbia, 1998—99. Dir., prevention Union County Alcohol Drug Commn., SC; dir., mktg. & devel. Affiliated Counseling, Spartanburg, SC; opers. mgr. Upstate One Stop Career Ctr., Spartanburg, SC; exec. dir. Mental Health Assn., Spartanburg, SC. Bd. dirs., pres. Union County Habitat for Humanity, SC. Mem.: Union County Mental Health Assn. Avocations: travel, reading, photography. Home: 1234 W Springs Hwy Jonesville SC 29353 Office Phone: 864-582-3104.

SUMMERTREE, KATONAH See WINDSOR, PATRICIA

SUMMERVILLE, RICHARD M. mathematician, academic administrator; Provost Christopher Newport U. Office: Christopher Newport U Office of the Provost 1 University Pl Newport News VA 23606-2998 E-mail: rsummer@cnu.edu.

SUMMITT, PATRICIA HEAD, basketball coach; b. Henrietta, Tenn., June 14, 1952; d. Richard and Hazel Head; m. R.B. Summitt; 1 child, Ross Tyler. BS in Phys. Edn., U. Tenn., Martin, 1974; MS in Phys. Edn., U. Tenn., Knoxville, 1975. Basketball player U. Tenn., Martin, 1970—74, head women's basketball coach Knoxville, 1974—. Head coach 1st U.S. Jr. Nat. team, 1977 (2 gold medals in internat. play), U.S. Nat. team William R. Jones Cup Games, 1979, World Championships, 1979, Pan Am. Games, 1979 (2 gold medals, 1 silver medal); asst. coach U.S. Women's Olympic Basketball team, 1980-84, head coach, 1984 (gold medal); assoc. athletics dir., U. Tenn.; past v.p. USA BASKETBALL; past Olympic rep. adv. com. to USA BASKETBALL; bd. trustees Basketball Hall of Fame; bd. dirs. Women's Basketball Hall of Fame. Active Big Bros./Big Sisters; Active spokesperson United Way, Race for the Cure, Juvenile Diabetes; hon. chair Tenn. Easter Seal Soc., 1985, 87, 88, 89; Tenn. chair Am. Heart Assn., 1994. Named Naismith Coach of Yr., 1987, 1989, 1994, 1997, Naismith Coach of Century, 2000, WBCA/Converse Coach of Yr., 1983—95; named one of Women of Yr., Women in Sports and Events, 1999; named to Women's Sports Foundation Hall of Fame, 1990, Nat. Assn. for Sport and Phys. Edn., 1996, Women's Basketball Hall of Fame, 1999, Basketball Hall of Fame, 2000; recipient silver medal, Olympic Games, 1976, gold medal, Pan Am. Games, 1975, silver medal, U.S. World Univ. Games, 1973, Wooden Award, 1997, ARETE Award for Courage in Sports, 1999. Mem. Chi Omega. Achievements include coach U. Tenn. women's basketball NCAA Championship teams, 1987, 89, 91, 96, 97, 98; coach U. Tenn. women's basketball SEC Championship teams, 1980, 85, 90, 93, 94, 95, 98, 99, 2000, 01, 02, 03.*

SUMNER, DAVID GEORGE, association executive; b. Norwich, Conn., Apr. 22, 1949; s. Raymond W. and Ruth M. (Crooks) S.; m. Linda Ann Churma, June 27, 1980; 1 child, Deryn Anne. MA in Polit. Sci., Mich. State U., 1970; MBA, U. Conn., 1979. Corr. Travelers Ins. Co., Hartford, Conn., 1971-72; asst. sec. Am. Radio Relay League, Newington, Conn., 1972-76, asst. gen. mgr., 1976-82, gen. mgr., 1982-85, exec. v.p., 1985—. Bd. dirs. Windham Regional Planning Agy., Willimantic, Conn., 1991-98; mem. Coventry Dem. Town Com., 1995—; mem. spectrum planning and policy adv. com. U.S. Dept. Commerce, 1994—; sec. Internat. Amateur Radio Union, 1982-89, 99—; mem. Coventry Zoning Bd. Appeals, 1997—, chmn., 1999—. Recipient Calcutta Key, Radio Soc. Gt. Britain, 1989, Region I award Internat. Amateur Radio Union, 1989; Radio Club Am. fellow, 1991. Mem. Newington C. of C. (bd. dirs. 1988-90). Democrat. Congregationalist. Avocation: amateur radio. Office: Am Radio Relay League 225 Main St Newington CT 06111-1400

SUMNER, DAVID SPURGEON, surgery educator; b. Asheboro, N.C., Feb. 20, 1933; s. George Herbert and Velna Elizabeth (Welborn) S.; m. Martha Eileen Sypher, July 25, 1959; children: David Vance, Mary Elizabeth, John Franklin. BA, U. N.C., 1954; MD, Johns Hopkins U., 1958. Diplomate Am. Bd. Surgery; cert. spl. qualification gen. vascular surgery. Intern Johns Hopkins Hosp., Balt., 1958-59, resident in gen. surgery, 1960-61, U. Wash. Sch. Medicine, Seattle, 1961-66; clin. investigator in vascular surgery VA Hosp., Seattle, 1967, 70-73; asst. surgery U. Wash. Sch. Medicine, Seattle, 1961-66, instr. surgery, 1966-70, asst. prof. surgery, 1970-72, assoc. prof. surgery, 1972-75; prof. surgery, chief sect. peripheral vascular surgery So. Ill. U. Sch. Medicine., Springfield, 1975-84, Disting. prof. surgery, chief sect. peripheral vascular surgery, 1984-98, disting. prof. emeritus, 1998. Staff surgeon Seattle VA Hosp., 1973-75, Univ. Hosp., Seattle, 1973-75, St. John's Hosp., Springfield, 1975-98, Meml. Med. Ctr., Springfield, 1975-98; mem. VA Merit Review Bd. Surgery, 1975-78; mem. vascular surgery rsch. award com. The Liebig Found., 1990-95, chmn., 1994; bd. dirs. Am. Venous Forum Found., 1993-95; vis. prof. Cook County Hosp., Chgo., 1971, Washington U., St. Louis, 1976, U. Tex., San Antonio, 1978, Wayne State U., Detroit, 1978, U. Ind., Indpls., 1979, Ea. Va. Med. Sch., Norfolk, 1979, Case-Western Res. U., Cleve., 1980, U. Chgo., 1981, U. Manitoba, Winnipeg, Can., 1983, others; dist. lectr. Yale U., 1982; guest examiner Am. Bd. Surgery, St. Louis, 1982, assoc. examiner, 1989; lectr. in field. Author: (with D.E. Strandness Jr.) Ultrasonic Techniques in Angiology, 1975, Hemodynamics for Surgeons, 1975; (with R.B. Rutherford, V. Bernhard, F. Maddison, W.S. Moore, M.O. Perry) Vascular Surgery, 1977; (with J.B. Russell) Ultrasonic Arteriography, 1980; (with F.B. Hershey, R.W. Barnes) Noninvasive Diagnosis of Vascular Disease, 1984; (with R.B. Rutherford, G. Johnson Jr., R.F. Kempczinski, W.S. Moore, M.O. Perry, G.W. Smith) Vascular Surgery, 3d edit., 1989; (with A.N. Nicolaides) Investigation of Patients With Deep Vein Thrombosis and Chronic Venous Insufficiency, 1991; (with R.B. Rutherford, G. Johnson, K.W. Johnston, R.F. Kempczinski, W.C. Krupski, W.S. Moore, M.O. Perry, A.J. Comerota, R.H. Dean, P. Gloviczki, K.H. Johansen, T.S. Riles, L.M. Taylor Jr.) Vascular Surgery, 4th edit., 1995; (with K.A. Myers, A.N. Nicolaides Lower Limb Ischaemia, 1997; author 150 chpts. to books; mem. editl. bd. Vascular Diagnosis and Therapy, 1980-84, Appleton Davies, Inc., 1983—, Jour. Soc. of Non-Invasive Vascular Tech., 1987—, Jour. Vascular Surgery, 1987-97; series editor Introduction to Vascular Tech., 1990—; mem. exec. editl. com. Phlebology, 1987-91; mem. Internat. Editl. Adv. Bd., 1991-2000; mem. editl. com. Internat. Angiology, 1992—; contbr. over 150 articles to profl. jours. Lt. col. U.S. Army, 1967-70. Fellow in surg. rsch. Johns Hopkins U. Sch. Medicine, 1959-60, Am. Cancer Soc., Inc. fellow, 1965-66; Appleton-Century Crofts scholar, 1956, Mosby scholar, 1958. Fellow Am. Coll. Surgeons (Wash. chpt. 1971-75, Ill. chpt. counselor 1981-83), Cyprus Vascular Soc. (hon.); mem. AMA, Soc. Univ. Surgeons, Soc. Vascular Surgery (constn. and by-laws com. 1983, Wiley Fellowship com. 1990), Internat. Soc. Cardiovascular Surgery (N.Am. chpt. program com. 1985-88), Am. Surg. Assn., Am. Heart Assn. (stroke coun., cardiovascular surgery coun. 1978), Soc. Noninvasive Vascular Tech. (hon.), Vascular Surgery Biology Club, Am. Venous Forum (organizing com. 1987, founding mem. 1988, chmn. membership com. 1988-91, treas. 1992-95, pres. elect 1998, pres. 1999-2000), Cardiovascular Sys. Dynamics Soc., Internat. Soc. Surgery, Vascular Soc. So. Africa (hon.), North Pacific Surg. Assn., Ctrl. Surg. Assn., Midwestern Vascular Surg. Soc. (counselor 1977-79, pres.-elect 1980-81, pres. 1981-82), So. Assn. for Vascular Surgery, Ill. Heart Assn., Ill. Med. Soc., Ill. Surg. Soc., Chgo. Surg. Soc., Seattle Surg. Soc., Sangamon County Med. Soc., Henry N. Harkins Surg. Soc., Harbinger Soc., Phi Eta Sigma, Phi Beta Kappa, Sigma Xi, Alpha Omega Alpha. Presbyterian. Achievements include research in surgical hemodynamics and noninvasive methods for diagnosing peripheral vascular disease. Home: 2324 W Lake Shore Dr Springfield IL 62712 Office: So Ill U Sch Medicine Dept Surgery 701 N 1st St Ste D346 Springfield IL 62702 E-mail: dsumner1@aol.com.

SUMNER, GORDON, JR., retired military officer; b. Albuquerque, July 23, 1924; s. Gordon and Esstella (Berry) S.; m. Frances Fernandes, May, 1991; children: Ward T., Holly Rose. AS, N.Mex. Mil. Inst., 1943; BA, La. State U., 1955; MA, U. Md., 1963. Commd. 2d. lt. U.S. Army, 1944, advanced through grades to lt. gen., 1975, ret., 1978; founder, chmn. Cypress Internat., 1978-96; chmn. La Mancha Co., Inc., 1981-89, Sumner Assoc. Cons. U.S. Depts. State and Def; ambassador at large for Latin Am.; spl. advisor U.S. Dept. State; nat. security advisor Pres.' Bi-Partisan Commn. Cen. Am.; cons. Los Alamos Nat. Lab. Contbr. articles to profl. jours. Decorated D.S.M., Silver Star, Legion of Merit with three oak leaf clusters, Disting. Flying Cross with 13 oak leaf clusters, Bronze Star, Army Commendation medal with oak leaf cluster, Purple Heart. Mem. Phi Kappa Phi, Pi Sigma Alpha. Office: La Mancha Co 100 Cienega St Ste D Santa Fe NM 87501-2003 Office Phone: 505-984-8041.

SUMNER, GORDON MATTHEW See STING

SUMNER, MELANIE, writer, educator; b. Middletown, Ohio, Dec. 30, 1963; d. Joseph Roger and Mary Ruth (Page) S.; m. David William Marr, Mar. 31, 1996; children, Zoe Page, Sumner Rider. Student, Darlington Sch., Rome, Ga., 1982; BA, U. N.C., 1986; MA, Boston U., 1987. Instr. ESL US Peace Corps, Dakar, Senegal, West AFrica, 1988-90; instr. Cape Fear Cmty. Coll., Wilmington, N.C., 1990-93, Santa Fe Cmty. Coll., 1998-99, U. N.Mex., Taos, 1999—2001; assoc. prof. English, Shorter Coll., Rome, Ga., 2002—; writer-in-residence Berry Coll., 2003. Vis. lectr. U. N.C., Chapel Hill, 1995-96; vis. writer Berry Coll., 2003—. Author: Polite Society, 1995, The School of Beauty and Charm, 2001; contbr. articles, short stories to publs. including The New Yorker, N.Y. Times, others. Fellow Yaddo, 1992, Fine Arts Work Cetr., 1993-95; recipient Whiting award, 1996, Maria Thomas award for best Peace Corps novel, 1995. Avocations: quilting, hiking, skiing. Home: 12 Sagewood Dr Rome GA 30165

SUMNER, WILLIAM MARVIN, anthropology and archaeology educator; b. Detroit, Sept. 8, 1928; s. William Pulford Jr. and Virginia Friel (Umberger) S.; m. Frances Wilson Morton, June 21, 1952 (div. 1975): children: Jane Cassell, William Morton; m. Kathleen A. MacLean, Apr. 7, 1989. Student, Va. Mil. Inst., 1947-48; BS, U.S. Naval Acad., 1952; PhD, U. Pa., 1972. Dir. Am. Inst. Iranian Studies, Tehran, Iran, 1969-71; asst. prof. Ohio State U., Columbus, 1971-73, assoc. prof., 1974-80, prof. anthropology, 1981-89, prof. emeritus, 1989—; dir. Oriental Inst., prof. Near Eastern langs. and civilizations U. Chgo., 1989-98. Dir. excavations at Tal-e Malyan (site of Elamite Anshan) sponsored by Univ. Mus., U. Pa., 1971—; v.p. Am. Inst. Iranian Studies, 1983-86. Contbr. chpts. to books, articles and essays to profl. jours. Served to lt. comdr. USN, 1952-64. Grantee NSF, 1975, 76, 79, NEH, 1988. E-mail: sumner.1@osu.edu.

SUMNERS, LESTER FURR, lawyer; b. Blytheville, Ark., June 2, 1926; s. Chester L. and Bessie (Furr) S.; m. Mary Joyce Bonner, Feb. 12, 1956; children: Thomas Bonner, Melinda Watson, Leslie Elizabeth. BA, U. Miss., 1949, LLB, 1950. Bar: Miss. 1950. Staff atty. USDA, Washington, 1951-52; ptnr. Darden & Sumners, New Albany, Miss., 1952-76, Darden, Sumners, Carter & Trout, New Albany, 1976-83, Sumners, Carter, Trout & McMillin, New Albany, 1983-94, Sumners & Carter, P.A., New Albany, 1995—2002, Sumners, Carter & Mueller P.A., New Albany, 2002—. Assoc. editor U. Miss. Law Rev., 1950. Scoutmaster Boy Scouts Am., New Albany, 1953-75; trustee NE Miss. Jr. Coll., Booneville, 1961-66. Recipient Silver Beaver award Boy Scouts Am., 1966. Fellow Internat. Acad. Trial Lawyers, Am. Coll. Trial Lawyers; mem. Miss. Bar Assn. (commr. 1950-63, 65-67, complaint commr.

1963, 65, pres. 1971-72), Miss. Bar Found. (pres. 1979-80), U. Miss. Law Alumni Chpt. (pres. 1976-77). Office: Sumners Carter & Mueller PA PO Box 730 New Albany MS 38652-0730 Office Phone: 662-534-6326.

SUMNERS, PAMELA LAUREN, lawyer; b. Birmingham, Ala., Jan. 12, 1961; d. Walter Ishmael and Helen Kendrick Sumners. BA, Stephens Coll., 1983; MA, Syracuse U., 1984; JD, U. Va., 1991. Bar: Ala. 1993, U.S. Ct. Appeals (11th cir.) 1993, U.S. Supreme Ct. 1997. Law clk. U.S. Dist. Ct., Montgomery, Ala., 1991—92; staff atty. So. Poverty Law Ctr., Montgomery, 1992—94; pvt. practice Birmingham, Ala., 1994—2000; staff counsel, project dir. ACLU Ill., Chgo., 2000—02; dir. City at Peace, Chgo., 2002—. Pro bono counsel, legis. drafter Equality Ill., Chgo., 2001—, bd. dirs., 2002—; lectr., spkr. in field. Author: (textbook) Employment Discrimination, 2003; editor: Lexis Pennsylvania Civil Rights, 2000. Coop. atty. ACLU Ala., Birmingham, 1995—2001; Sunday sch. tchr. Pilgrim Congl. Ch., 2001—03. Recipient Board Commendation award, ACLU of Ala., 2000. Democrat. Congregationalist. Avocations: writing poetry, fiction and plays, public speaking. Office: City at Peace Chgo 5443 N Broadway Chicago IL 60640

SUMNEY, LARRY W. research company executive; Pres., CEO Semiconductor Rsch. Corp., Research Triangle Park, N.C. Address: Semiconductor Rsch Corp PO Box 12053 Research Triangle Park NC 27709-2053

SUMWALT, ROBERT LLEWELLYN, JR., retired construction company executive; b. Columbia, S.C., Dec. 29, 1927; s. Robert Llewellyn and Caroline M. (Causey) S.; m. Mary Joyce Mills, Mar. 8, 1952; children: Elizabeth Ladson, Robert Llewellyn III. BSCE, U. S.C., 1949; MSCE, MIT, 1950. Registered profl. engr., S.C. Area engr. E.I. duPont de Nemours & Co., Camden, S.C., 1950-52; constrn. engr. Columbia City Sch. Sys., 1952-58; sr. v.p., dir. McCrory-Sumwalt Constrn. Co., Inc., Columbia, 1958-77; chmn. bd., treas., dir. Sumwalt-Mashburn Engring. & Constrn. Co., Inc., Columbia, 1977-79; chmn. bd., pres., dir., CEO Sumwalt Constrn. Co., Inc., Columbia, 1979—98; ret. Bd. dirs. Columbia City Wachovia Nat. Bank. Pres. Richland County unit Am. Cancer Soc., 1956, bd. dirs. S.C. chpt., 1957; chmn. Carolina Carillon Ball, 1963; sect. chmn. United Cmty. Svcs., 1957; divsn. chmn. constrn. divsn. United Way, 1973; bd. dirs. Richland County unit ARC, 1955-56; mem. adv. bd. Salvation Army, 1982-84; mem. Bicentennial Commn. U. S.C., 1998-2001, pres. Coll. Engring. Partnership Bd., 1999—. Served to comdr. C.E.C., USNR. Named Young Man of Yr., Columbia Jr. C. of C., 1958; recipient Disting. Alumnus award Coll. Engring., 2001, Disting Alumnus award U. S.C., 2003. Mem. Carolinas Assn. Gen. Contractors Am. (chmn. bldg. divsn., dir. Carolinas br. 1977, v.p. 1986, sr. v.p. 1987, pres. Carolinas AGC 1988, nat. dir. AGC of Am. 1989, 90, pub. rels. com.), Columbia Contractors Assn. (pres. 1969), S.C. Soc. Engrs., S.C. Soc. Profl. Engrs., Assn. U.S. Army, U. S.C. Assocs. (v.p. 1997, pres. 1998), U. S.C. Alumni Assn. (circuit v.p. 1956, exec. com., 2003-), Prison Fellowship Ministries, Kiwanis (pres. 1962), Forest Lake Country Club, Tip Off Club (pres. 1981-82), Dreher H.S. Found. (pres. 1994-96), Columbia Ball Club, Centurion Club (Columbia), Litchfield Country Club (Litchfield Beach, S.C.), Springdale Hall Club (Camden), Phi Beta Kappa, Omicron Delta Kappa, Tau Beta Pi, Sigma Alpha Epsilon (chmn. S.C. Delta Housing Corp. 1999-2001). Presbyterian (chmn. bd. deacons 1968, elder, chmn. adminstrn. com. 1987, 88, adv. bd. Heathwood Hall Sch. 1995-98). Home: 445 Alexander Way Columbia SC 29206-4974 Office: PO Box 6576 Columbia SC 29260-6576

SUN, ALBERT YUNG-KWANG, biochemistry and neurochemistry educator; b. Amoy, Fukien, Peoples Republic of China, Oct. 13, 1932; came to U.S., 1959, naturalized, 1972; s. Pehcheng and SuiHo Kuo Wu; m. Grace Yen-Chi Cheung Sun, May 9, 1964; 1 child, Aggie Yee-Chun. BS in Agrl. Chemistry, Nat. Taiwan U., Taipei, 1957; PhD in Biochemistry, Oreg. State U., 1967. Postdoctoral rsch. assoc. Case-Western Res. U., Cleve., 1967-68; sr. rsch. scientist Cleve. Psychiat. Inst., 1968-74; project dir. Ohio Mental Health Rsch. Ctr., Cleve., 1972-74, rsch. prof./assoc. prof. biochemistry, 1974—91, prof. pharmacology, 1991—2003, prof. med. pharmacology, 1991—. Mem. adv. panel NSF, Washington, 1984-85. Editor: Neural Membranes, 1983, Molecular Mechanism of Alcohol, 1989. Advisor Chinese Christian Fellowship Group, Columbia, 1974—. Grantee Nat. Inst. Alcohol Abuse and Alcoholism, 1974-78, 82-98, Nat. Inst. Neurol. Communicable Disease and Stroke, 1975-79, Nat. Cancer Inst., 1979-83, EPA, 2000-2005, Nat. Inst. Aging, 2001-. Mem. Rsch. Soc. Alcoholism, Am. Soc. Neurochemistry, Am. Soc. Neurosci., Am. Soc. Biochemistry and Molecular Biology, Am. Chem. Soc. Current work: Structure-functional relationship of neural membranes using biochemical and biophysical approaches, study on the biochem.mechanism of aging and Alzheimer's Disease in the brain. Subspecialies: Biochemistry (medicine); Neurochemistry. Home: 2908 Shoreside Dr Columbia MO 65203-0941 Office Phone: 314-882-1565. Business E-Mail: suna@health.missouri.edu.

SUN, CHENGHUA, composer, music educator; b. Shao Xing, Zejiang, China, Sept. 17, 1942; arrived in U.S., 1991; s. Zhiliang Sun and Fuzhen Cai; m. Ai-Yue Ding, Jan. 17, 1968; children: Tian, Sun. Bachelors Degree in Violin Performance, Conservatory of Music, Shanghai, 1966. Group leader composition Song and Dance Theatre, Hunan, China, 1974—84; dir. song and dance group Opera & Dance Theatre, Jiangsu, China, 1986—91; founding dir. Chinese Youth Orch., Dallas, 1995—99; dir. Chinese Lucky-Star Choir, Dallas, 1995—. Advisor Little Red Flower Arts Group, Nanjing, China, 1987, Greatland Choral Soc., Dallas, 1995—2000; soloist Chinese Erhu Philharm. Symphony Orch., Irving, Tex., 1996, Voice of Change Inc., Dallas, 1998. Composer: (songs) Album of Best Songs of China Since 1949, 1980 (1st prize), violin concerto. Named Life-time Art Dir., Opera and Dance Theatre, Jiangsu, 1991; recipient Grand prize for dance music, Nat. Edn. Dept., Beijing, 1989. Mem.: Am. String Tchr.'s Assn., Chinese Muiscians Assn., Music Tchrs. Nat. Assn., Assn. Chinese Profls. (advisor 2000), Dallas Chinese Artist Assn. (dir. 1999—2003), Chinese Music Soc. Dallas (founding dir. 1994—, prodr. first Dallas Chinese Music Festival 2004). Avocations: sports, games. E-mail: sunding@juno.com.

SUN, HUN H. electrical engineering and biomedical engineering educator; b. Shanghai, Mar. 27, 1925; s. Yu F.and Tuk F. Sun; m. Nancy Liu, Jan. 30, 1951; 1 child, Elizabeth A. BSEE, Chiao-Tung U., Shanghai, 1946; MSEE, U. Wash., 1950; PhD, Cornell U., 1955. Asst. prof. elect. engring. Drexel U., Phila., 1953-56, assoc. prof., 1956-59, prof., 1959—65, dir. Biomed. Engring. and Scis. Inst., 1964-74, chmn. elec. engring. dept., 1973-78, E.O. Lange prof., 1978-95, prof. emeritus, 1995—; NIH spl. fellow MIT, Cambridge, Mass., 1963-64. Cons. Wright-Patterson AFB, Dayton, Ohio, 1963-65; mem. study com. NIH, Bethesda, Md., 1981-85; mem. adv. com. NSF, Washington, 1985-88; adj. prof. Temple U. Dept. Physiology, 1971-91. Author: Synthesis of R. C. Networks, 1967; editor in chief Annals of Biomed. Engring., 1984-94; mem. editl. bd. Automatica (London), 1974-90, Critical Rev. in Bioengring, 1978-81; cons. editor Elec. Engring. Monograph Series, 1964-67; contbr. chpts. to books, articles to profl. jours. Mem. Com. on Art and Sci. Franklin Inst., 1969-82. Recipient 1st Rsch. Achievement award Drexel U., 1973. Fellow IEEE (editor in chief Trans. Biomed. Engring. 1972-78); mem. Biomed. Engring. Soc. (founding), Sigma Xi (life). Home: 939 Hedgerow Ct Blue Bell PA 19422-2408 Office: Drexel Univ Dept Elec Engring Philadelphia PA 19104

SUN, JEFFREY C. legal educator; b. San Francisco, 1971; s. Gary and Ruth Sun. BBA, Loyola Marymount U., L.A., 1993, MBA, 1994; JD, Ohio State U., 1998; postgrad., Columbia U., 1998—. Bar: Ohio 1998. Dir. student activities Santa Monica (Calif.) Cath., 1993-95, dir. mktg. and admissions, 1993-95; assoc. Thompson, Hine & Flory, Columbus, Ohio, 1995; rsch. asst. Ohio State U., Columbus, 1997, rsch. assoc., 1998; rsch. asst. to pres. Tchrs. Coll. Columbia U., N.Y.C., 1998, instr., 1999—2004; asst. prof. U. N. Dakota, 2004—. Mem. adv. bd. St. Monica Cath., Ohio Ctr. for Law Related Edn.; adj. asst. prof. NYU, N.Y.C., 1998-2000. Mem. Ohio State Bar Assn., Coun. on Law and Higher Edn., Edn. Law Assn. Office: Tchrs Coll Columbia U 525 W 120th St Box 175 New York NY 10027 E-mail: jcs81@columbia.edu.

SUN, KAI, materials scientist, research scientist; arrived in U.S., 2000; s. Changshan Sun and Guoying Liu; m. Xiuqing Li, Jan. 20, 1995; children: Alyssa Ruoxi children: Chenxi. D of Engring., Dalian U. of Tech., Liaoning, China, 1998. Rsch. asst. Stockholm U., 1998—2000, U. Ill., Chgo., 2000—02; rsch. fellow U. Mich., Ann Arbor, 2002—03, rsch. assoc., 2003—. Contbr. articles to profl. jours. Contbr. Materials Rsch. Soc., Boston, Mass., 2000—02. Recipient Postdoctorial Rsch. fellowship, Stockholm U., 1998, postdoctoral rsch. assistantship, U. of Ill., Chgo., 2000, rsch. fellowship, U. of Mich., 2002, Outstanding Grad. fellowship, Dalian U. of Tech., 1993. Mem.: Materials Rsch. Soc. (assoc.). Achievements include research in GaMn-quasicrystals were intergreted into GaAs semiconductors; synthesis of borogermanate microporous materials were fullfilled; characterization of nuclear waste forms and nanostructured materials by analytical electron microscopy. Office: 413B Space Rsch Bldg 2455 Hayward St Ann Arbor MI 48109 Office Phone: 734-936-3353. Business E-Mail: kaisun@umich.edu.

SUN, LI, statistician; b. Changchun, Jilin, China, Aug. 5, 1957; s. Enhou Sun and Chongxin Li; m. Nancy Xiaoning Ha, Feb. 21, 1982; children: Rosy, George. BSc, U. Jilin, Changchun, Jilin, China, 1982; MSc, Acad. Sci. China, 1984; PhD, U. Toronto, 1992. Rsch. fellow U. B.C. Cancer Agy., Vancouver, 1992—2000; sr. statis. engr. Ericsson Inc, Berkeley, Calif., 2001—02; sr. statistician Edmunds.com Inc., Santa Monica, Calif., 2002—. Contbr. articles to profl. jours., chapters to books. Fellow, Natural Sci. and Engring. Rsch. Coun. Can., 1992—94; Connaught scholar, U. Toronto, 1989—92. Mem.: Am. Stats. Assn. Home: Apt 306 10615 Rose Ave Los Angeles CA 90034 Office: Edmunds.com Inc Ste 250 2401 Colorado Ave Santa Monica CA 90404 Office Phone: 310-309-4982. Personal E-mail: li_sun@comcast.net. E-mail: lsun@edmunds.com.

SUN, LIZHI, engineering educator, researcher; PhD, UCLA, 1998. Asst. prof. U. Iowa, Iowa City, 1999—. Grantee, NSF, 2000—03. Mem.: ASME, ASCE. Office: U Iowa Dept Civil and Environ Engring Iowa City IA 52242 E-mail: lizhi-sun@uiowa.edu.

SUN, NORA CHI-JUN, pathologist; b. Shanghai, June 16, 1937; came to U.S., 1966; d. K.F. and S.W. Sun; m. David T. Sung; children: Thomas C.K. Lee, Anthony D. Sung. MD, Shanghai 2d Med. Coll., 1960, MS in Pathology, U. Minn., 1973. Demonstrator U. Hong Kong, 1964-66; rsch. biologist A.H. Robins Co., Richmond, Va., 1966-67; resident Med. Coll. Va., 1967—68; clin. teaching asst. Boston U. Sch. Medicine, 1968-70; resident Mallaory Inst. Pathology, 1968—70; fellow Mayo Clinic and Grad. Sch., 1970—73; asst. prof. pathology U. So. Calif., L.A., 1973-76; staff pathologist John Wesley Hosp., L.A., 1973-76; asst. prof. UCLA Sch. Medicine, L.A., 1976-82; staff pathologist, head hematopathology Harbor-UCLA Med. Ctr., Torrance, Calif., 1976—2002; assoc. prof. UCLA Sch. Medicine, L.A., 1982-88, prof. pathology, 1988—2002, prof. emeritus, 2002—. Recipient Women Achievement award Delta Kappa Gamma, Rochester, Minn., 1972, Disting. Svc. award Am. Soc. Clin. Pathologists, 1996. Mem. Internat. Assn. Chinese Pathologists (pres.-elect 1991-93, pres. 1993-95), Harbor-UCLA Med. Ctr. Faculty Soc. (pres.-elect 1990-91, pres. 1991-92). Office: Harbor UCLA Med Ctr 1000 W Carson St Torrance CA 90502-2004 Business E-Mail: ncjsun@ucla.edu.

SUN, PETER P. neurosurgeon; b. Taipei, Taiwan, China, Oct. 6, 1965; s. Yeng C. and Yueh Y. Sun; m. Mindy Lin, Jan. 18, 1992; children: Austin, Jason. MD, Columbia U., 1991. Resident Yale U.; attending neurosurgeon Children's Hosp. of Phila., 1997-2000; dir. neurosurgery Children's Hosp. Oakland, Calif., 2000—; asst. clin. prof. U. Calif., San Francisco, 2002—. Asst. prof. U. Pa., Phila., 1997-2000. Contbr.: (books) Neurological Surgery, 1996, Principles and Practice of Pediatric Neurosurgery, 1999, Atlas of Pediatric Neurosurgery, The Unborn Patient: The Art and Science of Fetal Therapy, 2001; contbr. articles to profl. jours. NIH Rsch. Svc. awardee, 1990. Mem. Congress of Neurol. Surgeons. Office: Children's Hospital Oakland 747 52d St Oakland CA 94609 Office Fax: (510) 597-7034. E-mail: psun@mail.cho.org.

SUN, ROBERT ZU JEI, manufacturing company executive, inventor; b. Shanghai, July 5, 1948; s. David C.H. and Evelyn (Lee) S.; m. Nan Jennifer Ronis, Sept. 20, 1986; children: Matthew Nyland, Michael Elias. BS in Elec. Engring., U. Pa., 1970. Sr. project engr. Drexelbrook Engring. Co., Horsham, Pa., 1970—78; pres., chmn. bd. Suntex Internat., Inc., Easton, 1981—. Inventor 24 Math Game; Mhing Card Game; 5 patents in field. Pres. Coalition of Religious and Civic Orgns., Easton, 1979-81; mem. transition team Pa. Gov.-elect Tom Ridge, 1994; apptd. by Gov. Ridge to Pa. State Bd. Edn., 1995, Team Pa. Amb. Coun., 1999; mem. fin. comm. Moravian Acad., 2001, bd. trustees, 2004. Recipient 2 Excellence awards for Mhing pkg. Nat. Paperbox and Pkg. Assn., 1984-85. Office: 3311 Fox Hill Rd Easton PA 18045

SUN, SIAO FANG, chemistry professor; b. Shaoshing, China, Feb. 19, 1922; came to U.S., 1949; s. Yuan and Yu C. Sun; m. M. Emily Chao, June 23, 1951; children: Patricia Viane, Caroline Marie, Diana Kate. MA, U. Utah, 1950; MS, Loyola U., 1956; PhD, U. Chgo., 1958, U. Ill., 1962. Prof. math. Northland Coll., Ashland, Wis., 1960-64; asst. prof. chemistry St. John's U., Jamaica, N.Y., 1964-70, assoc. prof. chemistry, 1970-75, prof. chemistry, 1975-92, adj. prof., 1992—. Vis. scientist Nat. Ctr. Sci. Rsch., Strasbourg and Meudon-Bellevue, France, 1975-78, Carlsberg Lab., Copenhagen, 1981; staff scientist Max Planck Inst. Biophysical Chemistry, Gottingen, Germany, 1976. Author: Physical Chemistry of Macromolecules, 1994, 2d edit., 2004; contbr. articles to profl. jours. Office: St John's Univ Dept Chemistry Jamaica NY 11439-0001 E-mail: suns@stjohns.edu.

SUN, TUNG-TIEN, medical science educator; b. Chung King, Szechuan, People's Republic of China, Feb. 20, 1947; s. Chung-Yu and Wen (Lin) S.; m. Brenda Shih-Ying Bao, Aug. 14, 1971; children: I-Hsing, I-Fong. BS in Agrl. Chemistry, Nat. Taiwan U., Taipei, 1967; PhD in Biochemistry, U. Calif., Davis, 1974. Rsch. assoc. dept. biology MIT, Cambridge, 1974-78; asst. prof. depts. dermatology, cell biology and anatomy Johns Hopkins Med. Sch., Balt., 1978-81, assoc. prof. dept. cell biology and anatomy, dermatology, ophthalmology, 1981-82; assoc. prof. depts. dermatology and pharmacology NYU Med. Sch., NYC, 1982-86, prof., 1986-90, Rudolf L. Baer prof., 1990—, prof. dept. urology, 1996—, assoc. dir. Skin Disease Rsch. Ctr., 1989-93, dean's lectr., 2000. William W. Scott Meml. lectr. Johns Hopkins Med. Sch., 2001; adj. prof. Coll. Life Sci. Peking U., 1998—; hon. prof. Third Mil. Med. U., Chung King, China, 1998—; Liu lectr. Stanford Med. Sch., 1987; Swerling lectr. Harvard Med. Sch., 1991; Borden lectr. Brit. Socs. Cell Biology and Devel. Biology, 2003. Mem. editl. bd. Differentiation, 1984—, Epithelial Cell Biology, 1990-93; assoc. editor Jour. Investigative Dermatology, 1990—, Jour. Dermatol. Sci., 1992-2003; US mng. editor Molecular Biology Report, 1994-96. Recipient Career Devel. award Nat. Eye Inst., 1978-82, Monique Neill-Caulier Career Scientist award, 1984-89, Alcon award in vision rsch., 1993, Wu Jieping Urololgy Found. award Chinese Med. Assn., 1998. Fellow AAAS; mem. Academia Sinica, Am. Soc. Biol. Chemists, Am. Soc. for Cell Biology, Internat. Soc. Differentiation (bd. dir. 1985-88), Nat. Inst. Arthiritis and Musculoskeletal and Skin Diseases (bd. sci. counselors), Soc. Investigative Dermatology (Montagna lectr. 1989, bd. dir. 1993-98), Assn. Rsch. in Vision Sci. and Ophthalmology. Office: NYU Med Sch Dept Dermatology 560 1st Ave New York NY 10016-6402 E-mail: sunt01@med.nyu.edu.

SUN, WEI YUE, internist; b. Guangzhou, China, Nov. 9, 1959; came to U.S., 1990; s. Chu Yin Sun and Wei Huang; m. Xiao Jing Li, Dec. 24, 1994. MD, Sun Yat-sen U. Med. Scis., Guangzhou, 1988; MPH, U. Wis., La Crosse, 1992; M of Health Sci. Edn., U. Fla., 1995; postgrad., Columbia U., 1998—. Resident dept. medicine Sun Yat-sen U. Med. Scis. Med. Ctr., 1988-90; pub. health advisor, educator Am. Cancer Soc., La Crosse, 1990-92; rsch. and tchg. scholar dept. health sci. edn. U. Fla., Gainesville, 1995; clin./pub. health epidemiologist divsn. family health svcs. Rsch. and Devel. Unit, N.Y.C. Dept. Health, 1995-98; rsch. scholar dept. health and behavior studies Columbia U., 1998—; extendship dept. medicine Brookdale U. Hosp. and Med. Ctr., Bklyn., 1998—, resident dept. medicine, 1998—, clin. fellow in nephrology, dept. nephrology and hypertension, 2002, Nat. Kidney Found. nephrology fellow, dept. nephrology and hypertension, 2003—. Adj. asst. prof. dept. health, phys. edn. and wellness Bronx C.C. of CUNY, 1996-98; presenter in field. Author: (with W. W. Chen) Tai Chi Chuan—The Gentle Workout for Mind and Body, 1995, (with X. J. Li) Chi Kung—Increase Your Energy, Improve Your Health, 1997, New-Style Tai Chi Chuan—The Official Chinese System, 1999; contbr. articles to profl. jours. C.A. Boyd Grad. scholar U. Fla., 1994-95. Mem. AMA, APHA, Am. Sch. Health Assn., Am. Assn. Chinese Physicians. Avocations: reading, tennis, ping pong/table tennis. Home: 7 Hegeman Ave Apt 14B Brooklyn NY 11212-4744 Office: Brookdale Univ Hosp and Med Ctr 1 Brookdale Plz Brooklyn NY 11212-3139 Office Phone: 718-796-4100. E-mail: weiyuesun@yahoo.com.

SUN, ZUO, research scientist, consultant; b. Shenyang, Liaoning, China, July 3, 1970; arrived in U.S., 1996; s. Dianfu Sun and Shuxiang Liu; m. Xinxin Zhou, Jan. 7, 1975. PhD in Theoretical and Applied Mechanics, Northwestern U., 2001; MS, BS, Tsinghua U. Sr. mech. engr. Corning (N.Y.) Inc., 2001—02; rsch. scientist Va. Tech, Blacksburg, 2002—03; mech. engr. GE Global Rsch. Ctr., Schenectady, NY, 2003—. Cons. Hewlett-Packard Corp., Portland, Oreg., 2001—, State Nuc. Safety Bur. in China, Beijing, 1993—95. Contbr. articles to profl. jours. Recipient First Class award, Tsinghua U., Beijing, 1989; Grad. fellow, 1994, Grad. scholar, Northwestern U., 1997—2003. Mem.: ASME, AIAA (corr.), Sigma Xi (hon.). Achievements include development of new models to predict long term behavior and life of composite materials; design of Micro-electro-mechanical Systems; investigation of adhesion science; development of tools to characterize micro/nano scale systems. Office Phone: 518-387-5578. Personal E-mail: zuosun@yahoo.com.

SUNAGAWA, MASANORI, physiologist, researcher; b. Hirara, Okinawa, Japan, Dec. 14, 1966; s. Shotoku and Emiko Sunagawa; m. Noriko Sunagawa, Feb. 28, 1992; children: Ayano, Masataka. MD, U. Ryukyus, Nishihara, Okinawa, Japan, 1992, PhD, 1996. Tchg. asst. U. Ryukyus, Nishihara, 1994-96, asst. prof., 1996. Vis. scientist U. Cin., 1996—. Contbr. articles to profl. jours. including Jour. Vasc. Rsch., Jour. Cardiovasc. Pharmacol., Toxicon, among others. Avocations: basketball, skin diving, skating, skiing. Home: 72-3 Kakeboku Nishihara, Okinawa 903-0101 Japan Office: U Cin 231 Bethesda Ave Cincinnati OH 45267-0001

SUNAMI, JOHN SOICHI, designer; b. N.Y.C., June 10, 1949; s. Soichi and Suyeko (Matsushima) S.; m. Marialyce Norman, Apr. 21, 1973; children: Christopher Andrew-Soichi, Jennifer Kiyoko. BA, CCNY, 1969. Cert. Gemological Inst. Am. Vol. Peace Corps, Jamaica, W.I., 1969-71; jeweler N.Y.C. and Columbus, Ohio, 1971-82; dir. mktg. Knight's Inn/Cardinal Industries, Columbus, 1982; founder, exec. designer Nimbus, Columbus, 1983—. Designer/sculptor pub. artwork IntroCenter, 1990; designer logo identities for various cos.; exhibited paintings and sculpture; author poems and essays. Bd. dirs. William H. Thomas Gallery, Columbus, 1992-93; v.p., bd. dirs. South Side Settlement House, Columbus, 1982-93; mem. cultural diversity outreach com. United Way of Franklin County, 1993-01. Recipient 1st prize Macworld Gallery/Macworld Mag., 1985, Mem.: Ctrl. Ohio Machine Knitters. Avocations: music, travel. Home: 408 Fairwood Ave Columbus OH 43205-2244 Office: Nimbus 413 Fairwood Ave Columbus OH 43205-2202 Office Fax: 614-253-0453. E-mail: design@nimbus-art.com.

SUND, JEFFREY OWEN, retired publishing company executive; b. Bklyn., June 19, 1940; children: Catherine, Meredith. BA, Dartmouth Coll., 1962. Sales rep. Prentice-Hall, Englewood Cliffs, N.J., 1967-73, Houghton Mifflin, Boston, 1973-74, coll. div. editor, 1974-77, editor-in-chief, 1977-86, v.p., editorial dir., 1986-89; pres., chief exec. officer Richard D. Irwin, Burr Ridge, Ill., 1989-96; pres. McGraw-Hill Higher Edn., Burr Ridge, 1996-2000; ret. Lt. USN, 1962-66.

SUNDAR, VEERARAGHAVAN V. materials scientist; s. Manaloor Rajagopalachari and Meera Veeraraghavan; m. Claire Allison Rutiser, Dec. 3, 1999; 1 child, Ranga Nathan. B. of Tech., Indian Inst. of Tech., Madras, 1990; PhD, Pa. State U., University Park, 1996; Magistri Metaphysicae Medievalae (hon.), Miskatonic U., Arkham, Mass., 2001; MBA, Pa. State U., Malvern, 2003. Materials scientist Dentsply Ceramco, Burlington, NJ, 1998—2002; mgr., product commercialization Dentsply Prosthetics, York, Pa., 2002—. Cons. Baverstam Assocs., Wellesley Hills, Mass., 1996—98. Author: (IEEE handbook) Electrostriction; editor: (proc.) Bioceramics: Materials and Applications IV. Recipient Buonocore Silver award, Dentsply Internat.; fellow, Pa. State U. fellow, 1990—92; grantee Rsch. grantee, NSF, 1997. Mem.: Toastmasters Internat. (disting. toastmaster, Divsn. Gov. of the Yr. 1999—2000). Hindu. Avocations: reading, travel, translations. Home: 102 Cameron Rd Ste MWW Willow Grove PA 19090

SUNDARAMURTHY, CHAMUNDESWARI, finance educator, educator; d. Nagavedu and Jayalakshmi Sundaramurthy, Jayalakshmi Sundaramurthy and Sundaramurthy Nagavedu; m. Nuwan Nanayakkara, July 19, 1993; 1 child, Priyanka Nanayakkara. Law Degree, Madras U., India, 1982; Master of Bus. Adminstrv. Sci., Iowa State U., 1984; PhD, U. of Ill., 1991. Asst. prof. U. of Ky., Lexington, 1992—98; assoc. prof. U. of Cin., 1998—2003, San Diego State U., 2003—. Contbr. articles to profl. jours. Mem.: Acad. of Mgmt. (mem., rsch. com., bps divsn., aom 2002—04, Outstanding Reviewer Award, BPS Divsn., AOM 2000, 2002, 2003). E-mail: csundara@mail.sdsu.edu.

SUNDBERG, CARL-ERIK WILHELM, telecommunications executive, researcher; b. Karlskrona, Sweden, July 7, 1943; came to U.S., 1984; s. Erik Wilhelm and Martha Maria (Snaar) S. MEE, U. Lund, Sweden, 1966, PhD, 1975. Tchr., rsch. asst., lectr. U. Lund, 1966-75, rsch. prof. (docent), 1977-84; rsch. fellow European Space Agy., Nordwijk, The Netherlands, 1975-76; disting. mem. tech. staff AT&T Bell Labs., Murray Hill, N.J., 1984-96, Lucent Technologies, Bell Labs., 1997-2000; with media signal processing rsch. dept. Agere Sys., 2000—01, iBiquity Digital, Warren, NJ, 2002—03; prin., owner SundComm, Chatham, NJ, 2003—. Cons. L.M. Ericsson, Gothenburg, Sweden, 1976-77, Bell Labs., Crawford Hill, N.J., 1981-82; instr. Carl Cranz Gesellschaft, Oberpfaffenhofen, Fed. Republic Germany, 1990-93. Co-author: Digital Phase Modulation, 1986, Source-Matched Mobile Communications, 1995; contbr. articles to profl. jours.; patentee in field. Served in Swedish Navy, 1968. Fellow IEEE (Best Paper award 1986, guest editor Jour. on Selected Areas in Comm. 1988-89, 2 papers named among 50 most influential 2002), IEE Marconi Premium (Best Paper award 1989); mem. Swedish Union Radio-Scientifique Internationale. Lutheran. Avocations: travel, history, photography. Home and Office: SundComm 25 Hickory Pl Apt A11 Chatham NJ 07928-1465 Business E-Mail: cews@ieee.org.

SUNDBERG, MARSHALL DAVID, biology professor; b. Apr. 18, 1949; m. Sara Jane Brooks, Aug. 1, 1977; children: Marshall Isaac, Adam, Emma. BA in Biology, Carleton Coll., 1971; MA in Botany, U. Minn., 1973, PhD in Botany, 1978. Lab. technician Carleton Coll., Minn., 1973-74; teaching asst. U. Minn., Mpls., 1974-76, rsch. asst., 1976-77; adj. asst. prof. Biology U. Wis., Eau Claire, 1978-85, mem. faculty summer sci. inst., 1982-85; instr. La. State U., Baton Rouge, 1985-88, asst. prof. Biology, 1988-91, coord. dept. Biology, 1988-93, assoc. prof. Biology, 1991-97; prof., chair dept. biol. scis. Emporia State U., 1997—. Author: General Botany Laboratory Workbook, 5th revision, 1984, General Botany 1001 Laboratory Manual, 1986, General Botany 1002 Laboratory Manual, 1987, Biology 1002 Correspondence Study Guide, 1987, Boty 1202: General Botany Laboratory Manual, 1988, Biol 1208: Biology for Science Majors Laboratory Manual, 1988, 2d edit., 1989, Instructor's Manual for J. Mauseth, Introductory Botany, 1991; contbr. articles to profl. jours. Brand fellow U. Minn., 1976-77, Faculty Grants scholar U. Wis., 1984-85. Fellow Linnaean Soc. London; mem. NSTA, AAAS, Am. Inst. Biol. Scis. (coun. mem. at large 1992-95, edn. com. 1994-95, 98-2002), Nat. Sci. Tchrs. Assn., Assn. Biology Lab. Edn., Bot. Soc. Am. (chmn. tchg. sect. 1985-86, workshop com. tchg. sect. 1983-84, slide exch./lab. exch. tchg. sect. 1980-89, edn. com. 1991, 92, Charles H. Bessey award 1992, editor Plant Sci. Bull. 2000—), Internat. Soc. Plant Morphologists, Nat. Assn. Biology Tchrs. (Outstanding 4-Yr. Coll. Tchr. award 1997, 2003), Soc. Econ. Botany, The

Nature Conservancy, Sigma Xi (chpt. sec. 1982-84, 93-95, 2000-02, v.p. 1984-85, 96-97, pres. 1996, 99). Home: 1912 Briarcliff Ln Emporia KS 66801-5404 Office: Emporia State U Dept Biol Scis 1200 Commercial St Emporia KS 66801-5087

SUNDBORG, STEPHEN V. academic administrator; s. George and Mary Sundborg. Ordained Jesuit, 1974. Tchr. religion and Latin Gonzaga Prep. Sch., Spokane, Wash., Jesuit High, Portland, Oreg.; tchr. theology Seattle U.; rector Seattle U. Jewish Cmty., 1986-90; provincial Oreg. Province, 1990-97; pres. Seattle U., 1997—. Office: Admin Bldg 109 900 Broadway Seattle WA 98122-4340

SUNDE, DOUGLAS, plastic surgeon; b. Evanston, Ill., May 18, 1960; s. Edward Albert and Marilyn S.; m. Linda Neff, 1989; children: Samuel, Joseph. AB, Stanford U., 1982; MD, U. Calif., San Francisco, 1986. Diplomate Am. Bd. Plastic Surgery. Resident in plastic surgery Stanford (Calif.) U., 1986-92, clin. instr., 1992; fellow in aesthetic surgery Manhattan Eye Ear and Throat Hosp., N.Y.C., 1990; fellow in hand, microsurgery Davies Med. Ctr., San Francisco, 1993; pvt. practice Monterey, Calif., 1994—. Clin. asst. prof. Stanford Med. Ctr., 1998—. Contbr. articles to profl. jours. Named Nat. Merit scholar 1977. Fellow ACS; mem. Am. Bd. Plastic Surgery, Am. Soc. Plastic Reconstructive Surgery, Calif. Soc. Plastic Surgery, Alpha Omega Alpha. Office: 856 Munras Ave Monterey CA 93940-3112 Office Phone: 831-372-0200.

SUNDEEN, SANDRA JOAN, mental health nurse; b. Jamestown, N.Y., Sept. 30, 1940; d. Harold E. and Helen (Carlson) S. BS, U. Rochester, 1966; MS in Psychiat. Nursing, U. Md., 1968. Asst. prof. U. Md. Sch. Nursing; chief psychiatric nursing Md. Dept. Health and Mental Hygiene, Balt. Rsch. in field. Author several books in field. Mem. ANA, Nat. League Nursing, Md. Nurses Assn., Md. League Nursing, Sigma Theta Tau, Phi Kappa Phi. Home: 790 Dividing Rd Severna Park MD 21146-4324

SUNDEL, MARTIN, psychologist, educator, management consultant; b. Bronx, N.Y., Sept. 22, 1940; s. Louis and Pauline (Brotman) S.; m. Sandra Stone, Aug. 22, 1971; children: Adam Daniel, Jenny Rebecca, Ariel Pauline. BA cum laude, St. Mary's U., 1961; MSW., Our Lady of the Lake Univ., 1963; MA, PhD, U. Mich., 1968. Social group work supr. Valley Cities Jewish Cmty. Ctr., Van Nuys, Calif., 1963-65; asst. prof. U. Mich. Sch. Social Work, Ann Arbor, 1968-71; postdoctoral fellow Harvard U. Lab. Community Psychiatry, Boston, 1971-72; dir. rsch. and evaluation River Region Mental Health-Mental Retardation Bd., Louisville, 1972-77; adj. prof. Kent. Sch. Social Work-U Louisville, 1972-77, assoc. clin. prof. dept. psychiatry and behavioral scis., 1974-77, assoc. in psychology, 1975-77; sr. research assoc. The Urban Inst., Washington, 1977-80; pvt. practice psychology Dallas, 1980-95; Dulak Disting. prof. U. Tex., Arlington, 1980-89, prof., 1980-95, Fla. Internat. U., Miami, Fla., 1995-2000; faculty assoc. S.E. Fla. Ctr. on Aging, 1996-2000; pres. Sundel Cons. Group, 2000—. Mental health cons. UN High Commn. for Refugees in Cyprus, 1993-95; profl. adv. coun. Dallas Geriatric Rsch. Inst., 1980-89; long-range planning com. Dallas Jewish Coalition for the Homeless, 1986-95; coordinating com. Arlington Human Svcs. Project, 1981-90, Mayor's Forum on Human Svc. Needs Assessment, Ft. Worth, 1983-86; vis. prof. U. So. Calif. Sch. Social Work, spring 1985; sr. consortium rsch. fellow, Dept. Def., 1996-99. Author: (with Sandra Stone Sundel) Behavior Change in the Human Services, 1975, 5th edit., 2004; Be Assertive, 1980; co-author: Women at Midlife, 2002; co-editor: Assessing Health and Human Service Needs, 1983, Individual Change Through Small Groups, 2d edit., 1985, Midlife Myths, 1989; mem. editl. bds. and cons. to profl. jours. Fellow Prescribing Psychologists Register (diplomate), Internat. Coun. Prescribing Psychology (diplomate in psychopharmacology); mem. APA, NASW (mem. futures commn. 1979-85), Behavior Therapy and Rsch. Soc. (charter clin. fellow), Acad. Cert. Social Workers, Coun. Social Work Edn., Internat. Soc. for the Sys. Scis. Home: 3804 Barbados Ave Hollywood FL 33026-4659

SUNDEL, SANDRA STONE, social worker; b. Chgo., Oct. 8, 1948; d. Harry Bernard and Lillian (Kantor) Stone; m. Martin Sundel, Aug. 22, 1971; children: Adam Daniel, Jenny Rebecca, Ariel Pauline. BA with distinction, U. Mich., 1970; MSW, U. Louisville, 1973; PhD, U. Tex., Arlington, 1990. Lic. clin. social worker. Pvt. practice, Louisville, Ky., Bethesda, Md., 1974-80, Dallas, 1980-85; dir. Jewish Social Svc. Agy., Ft. Worth, 1982-84; exec. dir. Community Homes for Adults, Inc., Dallas, 1986-95; asst. prof. Fla. Atlantic U., 1995-97; exec. dir. Jewish Family Svc. Broward County, Plantation, Fla., 1997—. Co-author: Behavior Modification in Human Services, 1975, 2d rev. edit., 1982, 3rd rev. edit., 1993, Be Assertive, 1980, Behavior Change in the Human Services, 5th edit., 2004, Women at Midlife, 2002. Mem.: NASW, Hadassah, Nat. Coun. Jewish Women. Office: Jewish Family Svc 100 S Pine Island Rd Ste 230 Fort Lauderdale FL 33324-2664 E-mail: ssundel@aol.com.

SUNDELIUS, HAROLD W. geology educator; b. Escanaba, Mich., July 6, 1930; s. Herbert A. and Caroline (Johnson) S.; m. Charlene P. Swanson, May 21, l955; children: Karin, Kristine. AB, Augustana Coll., Rock Island, Ill., l952; MS, U. Wis., l957, PhD, l959. Geologist U.S. Geol. Survey, Washington, 1959-65; asst. prof. geology Wittenberg U., Springfield, Ohio, 1965-67, assoc. prof., 1967-74, prof., 1974-75, assoc. dean Coll., 1971-75; v.p., dean Coll., Augustana Coll., 1975-88, prof. geology, 1988-95, ret., 1995. Cons. Dow Chem. Co., Midland, Mich., l957, minerals dept. Exxon, Houston, l968-75. Contbr. articles to geol. jours., chpt. to book. Bd. dirs. Luth. Hosp., Moline, Ill., l984-89, Swenson Swedish Immigration Rsch. Ctr., Rock Island, l984—. With U.S. Army, l953-55, Korea. Fulbright fellow, Oslo, l952-53, C.K. Leith fellow, l955-57, Univ. fellow, l957-58; recipient Sweden's Order of the Polar Star, Outstanding Svc. award Augustana Alumni Assn., 1997. Fellow Soc. Econ. Geologists, Geol. Soc. Am.; mem. Nat. Assn. Geology Tchrs., Rock Island C. of C. (bd. dirs.), Augustana Hist. Soc. (bd. dirs. 1995—, pres. 1995-2000), Am.-Scandinavian Assn. (bd. dirs. 1997—), Rotary (bd. dirs. Rock Island chpt.), Phi Beta Kappa, Sigma Xi. Lutheran. Home: 2512 1st St Moline IL 61265 Office: Augustana Coll 600 38th St Rock Island IL 61201 E-mail: hwsundelius@qconline.com.

SUNDERLAND, NORMAN RAY (NORM SUNDERLAND), health physicist, nuclear engineer educator; b. Lone Wolf, Okla., Aug. 1, 1933; s. Alva Franklin and Octava Pearl (Purcell) S.; m. Marilyn Stanworth, Aug. 27, 1970; children: Melody, Larry, Derreck, Toni, James, Jo Lynn, Stacie, Thomas. BS, Okla. State U., 1960; MEd, U. Nev., Las Vegas, 1973; PhD, Columbia-Pacific U., 1985. Registered radiation protection technologist. Tchr. Ft. Morgan (Colo.) HS, 1960—61, Paxton (Nebr.) HS, 1961—66; asst. dir. environ. sci. REECO (Nev. Test Site), Mercury, Nev., 1966—77; univ. sys. radiation safety officer U. Mo., Columbia, 1977—80; prof. N.E. Mo. State, Kirksville, 1978—84; dir. environ. health, safety U. Mo., Columbia, 1980—82; nuc. power cons. AWC, Inc., Cedar Rapids, Iowa, 1982—85; asst. dir. nuc. assessment divsn. EPA, Las Vegas, 1985—91; dir. environ. health, safety Utah State U., Logan, 1991—98; dir. Envirocare of Tex., Andrews, 1998—. Chair radiation control, Utah, 1987-1992; EPA rep. to Ea. Europe (Poland, Russia), 1989-96; cons. French AEC.; lectr. Ft. Morgan (Colo.) HS, 1960-61, Paxton (Nebr.) HS, 1961-66, U. Mo., Columbia, 1977-80, 78-84, N.E. Mo. State U. and Utah State U., 1991-96. Author: Bio-Physics of Radiation, 1997; co-author: Rad Emergency Response Operations, 1968, (Jour.) Transfer of Radiocesium to Grass, 1993, Transfer of Radiocesium to Soil, 1994; patentee in field. Pres. Mo. Higher Ednl. Assoc., Columbia, 1980-81; bishop LDS Ch., Cedar Rapids, Iowa, 1982-85. With combat engring. U.S. Army, 1953-56, Alaska. Fellow Nat. Health Physics Soc. (pres. MidAm. chpt. 1981-82, Lake Mead chpt. 1988-89, Great Salt Lake chpt. 1994-95, chmn. bd., mem. membership com. 1998—), Nat. Registry Radiation Protection Technicians (sec., mem. nat. bd. 1975-98, emeritus 1992, Arthur Humm Jr. Meml. award 1998); mem. Jaycees. Republican, Democrat. Mem. LDS Ch. Achievements include TRUclean process patent which removes radioactive material from soil (now owned by Lockeed Internat.). Home: 1851 N 1600 E North Logan UT 84341-2114

SUNDERLIN, CHARLES EUGENE, consultant; b. Reliance, S.D., Sept. 28, 1911; s. Glen Eugene and Frances (Smith) S; m. Sylvia Alice Sweetman, July 8, 1936; children: Ann Elizabeth, Mary Cornelia, Katherine Patricia, William Dana. AB, U. Mont., 1933; BA, MA (Rhodes scholar), Oxford U., Eng., 1936; PhD, U. Rochester, 1939. Instr. chemistry Union Coll., 1938-41; instr., asst. prof. U.S. Naval Acad., Annapolis, Md., 1941-43, 45-46; sci. liason officer U.S. Office Naval Rsch., London, 1946-47, dep. sci. dir., 1948-49, sci. dir., 1949-51; dep. dir. NSF, Washington, 1951-57, Union Carbide European Rsch. Assocs., 1957-62; rsch. mgr. def. and space systems Union Carbide Corp., 1962-65; spl. asst. to pres. Nat. Acad. Scis., Washington, 1965-69; v.p., sec. Rockefeller U., N.Y.C., 1969-76; spl. asst. Nat. Sci. Bd., Washington, 1976-78; exec. sec., staff dir. Com. on 10th Nat. Sci. Bd. Report, Washington, 1976-78. U.S. del. 6th and 7th Gen. Assemblies Internat Coun. Sci. Unions, Amsterdam, 1952, Oslo, 1955; mem. working party on Establishment of Internat. Adv. Com. on Sci. Rsch., Paris, 1953; Meeting of Dirs. Nat. Rsch. Ctrs., Milan, 1955, Symposium on Orgn. and Adminstrn., Applied Rsch., Vienna, 1956; mem. Com. Experts on Scientists' Rights, Paris, 1953, Nat. Acad. Scis. Workshop on Indsl. Devel. Taiwan, Rep. of China, 1968; chmn. AIAA/ASME 9th Structures, Structural Dynamics and Materials Conf., 1968; treas., bd. dirs. Engrs. and Scientists Com., Inc., People to People Program. Lt. USNR, 1943-45. Fellow AAAS, Chem. Soc. (London); mem. AIAA, Am. Chem. Soc., Faraday Soc., Royal Instn. Gt. Britain, Soc. Chem. Industry, N.Y. Acad. Scis., Wadham Assn. U.S., United Oxford and Cambridge Univ. Club, Internat. Club, Sigma Alpha Epsilon. Episcopalian. Home: 3036 P St NW Washington DC 20007-3052 also: 137 E Main St Cambridge NY 12816-1208

SUNDERMAN, DUANE NEUMAN, chemist, research institute executive; b. Wadsworth, Ohio, July 14, 1928; s. Richard Benjamin and Carolyn (Neuman) S.; m. Joan Catherine Hoffman, Jan. 31, 1953; children: David, Christine, Richard. BA, U. Mich., 1949, MS, 1954, PhD in Chemistry, 1956. Researcher Battelle Meml. Inst., Columbus, Ohio, 1956-59, mgr., 1959-69, assoc. dir., 1969-79, dir. internat. programs, 1979-84; sr. v.p. Midwest Rsch. Inst., Kansas City, Mo., 1984-90, exec. v.p., 1990-94, Golden, Colo., 1990-94. Dir. Nat. Renewable Energy Lab., Golden, Colo., 1990-94, dir. emeritus, 1994—. Contbr. numerous articles to profl. jours. Bd. dirs. Mid-Ohio chpt. ARC, 1982-83, U. Kansas City, 1985-90, Mo. Corp. for Sci. and Tech., Jefferson City, 1986-90, Colo. Energy Sci. Ctr., 2000. Mem. Am. Chem. Soc. Republican. Presbyterian. Avocation: computers. E-mail: dsunderm@columbus.rr.com.

SUNDERMEYER, MICHAEL S. lawyer; b. Kansas City, Mo., Feb. 8, 1951; s. Edgar W. and Ruth (Shobe) S.; m. Susan Talarico; children: Kim Marie, Mark Shobe. BA, U. Kans., 1973; JD, U. Va., 1976. Bar: D.C., Md., Va., U.S. Dist. Ct. D.C., U.S. Dist. Ct. Md., U.S. Dist. Ct. (ea. dist.) Va., U.S. Dist. Ct. (no. dist.) Okla., U.S. Ct. Appeals (D.C. cir.), U.S. Ct. Appeals (2d, 3d, 4th, 5th, 6th, 9th and 11th cirs.). Law clk. to Hon. John Minor Wisdom U.S. Ct. Appeals (5th cir.), New Orleans, 1976-77; law clk. to Hon. Harry A. Blackmun U.S. Supreme Ct., Washington, 1977-78; assoc. Williams & Connolly, Washington, 1978-84, ptnr., 1985—. Editor-in-chief Va. Law Rev., 1975-76. Mem. ABA. Office: Williams & Connolly LLP 725 12th St NW Washington DC 20005-5901 Office Phone: 202-434-5015. E-mail: msundermeyer@wc.com.

SUNDGAARD, ARNOLD OLAF, playwright; b. St. Paul, Oct. 31, 1909; s. Olaf Johannes Sundgaard and Borghild Marie Pehrson; m. Margaret Christianson, Jan. 3, 1929 (div.); children: Joy, Jill; m. Marge Kane, Jan. 17, 1940; children: Stephen, Jeremy. Student, Yale U., 1932-35; BA, U. Wis., 1935. Resident playwright U. Tex., 1945; lectr. Columbia U., N.Y.C., 1946-49; head drama dept. Bennington (Vt.) Coll., Vt., 1949-51; staff Tanglewood, 1950. Mem. Chgo. Fed. Theatre, 1936-38, Barter Theatre, 1938, Group Theatre, 1939, Theatre Inc., 1945 (founding), Chekhov Theatre Studio, 1941, Actors Studio, 1963; playwright, lectr., assoc. prof. U. Ill., 1949; vis. lectr. in playwriting SUNY Stony Brook, 1967-68; occupied John Cranford Adams Chair in Lit., Hofstra U., 1970-71; U.S. Exchange Lectr., Trinity Coll., Dublin, 1958-59. Playwright: Spirochete, 1938, Everywhere I Roam, 1938, The First Crocus, 1941, Virginia Overture, 1946, The Great Campaign, 1947, The Kilgo Run, 1952, Forest of the Night, 1963, Of Love Remembered, 1967, (musicals) Rhapsody, 1944, Promised Valley, 1947, The Wind Blows Free, 1950, Nobody's Earnest, 1973, Winnie, 1988; librettist: (operas) Down in The Valley, 1948, Giants in the Earth, 1951, The Lowland Sea, 1952, Cumberland Fair, 1954, Gallantry, 1958, The Opening, 1970, The Truth About Windmills, Mosaic, 1988, (TV scripts) Village Incident, India, (with Leonard Bernstein) Beethoven's Fifth, Jack Be Normal, Four Flags of the Confederacy; narration, continuity (TV) Festival of Music; contbr. stories, poetry, articles to popular mags.; writer (children's books) Jethro's Difficult Dinosaur, 1977, The Lamb and the Butterfly, 1988, Jack Appleknocker, 1988, The Bear Who Loved Puccini, 1990, Ching Ching, and the Seven Golden Nightingales, 1991; (children's album with Bing Crosby) An Axe, An Apple, and A Buckskin Jacket, 1957; rec. songs include Where Do You Go, Baggage Room Blues, Douglas Mountain, Brack's Song, Sweet Lorena, Long John. Rockefeller Fellow, 1935, Dramatists Guild Fellow, 1939, Guggenheim Fellow, 1951. Mem. ASCAP, Dramatists Guild, Songwriters Guild, Authors Guild, Pen West. Clubs: Century (N.Y.). Home: 7831 Park Ln Apt 67B Dallas TX 75225-2039

SUNDHEIM, GEORGE (DUF), lawyer, political organization worker; b. Chgo., Dec. 11, 1952; m. Cheryl Sundheim; children: Jordan, Eric. BA with hons., Stanford U., 1975; JD, Northwestern U., 1980. Bar: Calif. 1981, U.S. Dist. Ct. Calif. 1981. Of counsel Doty Sundheim & Gilmore, Palo Alto, Calif.; chmn. Calif. Rep. Party, Burbank, Calif., 2003—. Guest spkr. Peninsula This Week. Fellow, State Farm. Mem.: Santa Clara Bar Assn., State Bar Calif. (trustee 1992, Wiley W. Manuel award), Palo Alto Area Bar Assn. (pres. 1992), Calif. State Bar (Pro Bono award), Bay Area Rep. Lincoln Club (pres.). Office: Doty Sundheim & Gilmore 260 Sheridan Ave Ste 200 Palo Alto CA 94306 Mailing: California Republican Party Chmn 1903 W Magnolia Blvd Burbank CA 91506*

SUNDHEIM, NANCY STRAUS, lawyer; B in History, U. Pa.; JD, Harvard U. With Arnold & Porter, Washington, Ropes & Gray, Boston, Dechert Price & Rhoads, Phila.; chief acquisitions counsel Unisys Corp., Blue Bell, Pa., 1987, dep. counsel, head corp. law group, 1990, corp. v.p., corp. sec., 1999, mem. exec. com., 1999—, sr. v., gen. counsel, 2001. Office: Unisys Corp Unisys Way Blue Bell PA 19424

SUNDICK, SHERRY SMALL, author, journalist, poet; b. Washington, July 17, 1946; d. Charles Haskell and Ruth (Behrend) Small; B.A., Am. U., 1970; m. Gary Norman Sundick, Aug. 3, 1969; children— Amy Beth, Suzanne Faye. Columnist, Today Newspapers, Rockville, Md., 1973-75; journalist The Jour. Newspapers, Chevy Chase, Md., 1975—, The Potomac Almanac, 1976-80. Recipient N.Am. Mentor Mag. Ann. Mentor Poetry award, 1973. Mem. Nat. League Am. Pen Women, Writers Center, World Poetry Soc. Jewish. Author: Celebration, 1977; (with Ruth Small) Potpourri, 1978; contbr. articles to various mags. and jours. including Md. Mag., No. Va. Mag. Design, Maine Life, Feelings, Smile, The Pen Women, Haiku Headlines, others. Address: 11809 Hunting Ridge Ct Potomac MD 20854-2152

SUNDIN, MATS JOHAN, professional hockey player; b. Sollentuna, Sweden, Feb. 13, 1971; Selected 1st round NHL entry draft Que. Nordiques, 1989; traded Toronto Maple Leafs, 1994, right wing, 1994—. Played in Europe NHL Lockout, 1994—95; mem. Swedish League All-Star Team, 1990—91, 1991—92; player NHL All-Star Game, 1996. Office: Toronto Maple Leafs Air Canada Ctr 40 Bay St Ste 300 Toronto ON Canada M5J 2X2

SUNDLOF, STEPHEN FREDERICK, veterinary administrator; DVM, PhD in Toxicology, U. Ill., 1980. Diplomate Am. Bd. Vet. Toxicology. From instr. to prof. U. Fla. Coll. Vet. Medicine, 1980-94; dir. Ctr. for Vet. Medicine, FDA, Washington, 1994—. Chmn. WHO/FAO Codex Alimentarius Com.; presenter in field. Contbr. articles to profl. jours. Recipient Presidential Rank Award, 2000. Mem. Am. Acad. Vet. Pharmacology and Therapeutics (past pres.). Office: Ctr Vet Medicine Office Dir 7500 Standish Pl Rockville MD 20855-2764 Fax: 301-827-4401.*

SUNDLUN, BRUCE, former governor; b. Providence, R.I., Jan. 19, 1920; s. Walter I. and Jan Z. (Colitz) Sundlun; m. Susan Garvin Dittelman, Jan. 1, 2000; children: Tracy, Stuart, Peter, Kara; stepchildren: Heather Conover, Max Dittelman. BA, Williams Coll., 1942; LLB, Harvard U., 1949; grad., Air Command and Staff Sch., 1948; DSBA (hon.), Bryant Coll., 1980; DBA (hon.), Roger Williams Coll., 1980; LLD (hon.), Johnson and Wales U., 1993, Williams Coll., 1993, U. R.I., 1998. Bar: R.I. and D.C. 1949. Asst. U.S. atty., Washington, 1949-51; spl. asst. to U.S. atty. gen., Washington, 1951-54; ptnr. Amram, Hahn & Sundlun, Sundlun, Tirana & Scher, Washington, 1958—76; v.p., gen. counsel, dir. Outlet Co., Providence, 1960-76, pres., CEO, 1976-84, chmn. bd., CEO, 1984-88. Pres. Exec. Jet Aviation, Inc., Columbus, Ohio, 1970—76; apptd. by Pres. Kennedy incorporator, bd. dirs. Comm. Satellite Corp., 1962—92; bd. dirs. Worthington Industries, Nat. Bank of Washington, Miriam Hosp. Mem. adv. group Nat. Aviation Goals, 1961; chmn. Inaugural Medal Com., Washington, 1961, 65; vice chmn. Inaugural Parade Com., 1961; appointed by Pres. Carter bd. visitors USAF Acad., 1978-80; mem. R.I. Capital Center Commn., 1980, R.I. Legis. Pay Commn., 1980; vice chmn. Providence Rev. Com., 1981, chmn., 1982-85; mem. Providence Sch. Bd., 1985-90; mem. Providence Housing Authority, 1987, chmn. 1987-90; elected del. Dem. Nat. Conv. 1964, 68, 80, 88, 92, R.I. Constl. Conv., 1985; Dem. candidate for gov. R.I., 1986, 88, 90, 92; gov. R.I., 1990-92, 1992-95; mem. exec. com. Dem. Gov. Assn., 1990-94; vice chmn. CONEG, 1992-94, chmn., 1994, chmn., vice chmn. Com. on Economy Nat. Gov. Assn., 1992-94, chmn. N.E. Gov. Assn., 1994; pres. Washington Internat. Horse Show, 1970-75, trustee, 1975-90; pres. Providence Performing Arts Ctr., 1978-90; bd. dirs. Friends Touro Synagogue, Newport, R.I., 1979—, Miriam Hosp., 1985-90; bd. dirs. Temple Beth El, Providence, 1979-84, v.p., 1984-88, pres., 1988-91; bd. dirs. Trinity Repertory Theater, 1980-89, chmn., 1984-89; trustee R.I. Philharm. Orch., 1981-90; trustee Providence Preservation Soc., 1981-90, v.p., 1987-90; trustee Newport Art Mus., 1985, pres., 1987-91; pres. Providence Found., 1985-86; pres. R.I. C. of C. Fedn., 1981-84, bd. dirs., 1977-81; pres. Greater Providence C. of C., 1978-81, bd. dirs. 1976-85; bd. dirs. New Eng. Coun., 1978, vice chmn., 1980-81, chmn., 1981-83; trustee Bryant Coll., 1989-98; gov.-in-residence U. R.I., 1995—; dir. Providence Facilities Mgmt. Corp., 1998—; appointed by Pres. Clinton dir. Nat. Security Edn. Bd., 2000-; dir. Sargent Rehab. Ctr., 1995—, Adams Found., 2000—. Lt. USAAF, 1941-45; col. USAFR, ret., 1980. Decorated D.F.C., Air medal with oak leaf cluster, Purple Heart; chevalier Legion d'Honneur (France); Prime Minister's medal (Israel). Mem.: Aurora Assn., Saratoga Reading Room, Spouting Rock Beach Assn., Dunes Club, Hope Club, Clambake Club, Delta Upsilon. Democrat. Home: 257 Walmsley Ln Saunderstown RI 02874-3617 Office: U RI Carlotti Bldg 1 75 Lower College Rd Kingston RI 02881

SUNDQUIST, DON, former governor, former congressman, sales corporation executive; b. Moline, Ill., Mar. 15, 1936; s. Kenneth M. and Louise (Rohren) S.; m. Martha Swanson, Oct. 3, 1959; children: Tania, Andrea, Donald Kenneth. BA, Augustana Coll., 1957. Div. mgr. Josten's, Inc., 1961-72; exec. v.p. Graphic Sales of Am., Memphis, 1972, pres., 1973-82; mem. 98th-103rd Congresses from 7th Tenn. dist., Washington, 1983-94; gov. State of Tenn., Nashville, 1995—2003. Vice chmn. bd. Bank of Germantown, Tenn. Past mem. White House Commn. Presdl. Scholars; past chmn. Jobs for High Sch. Grads. of Memphis; chmn. Congl. Steering Com. George Bush for Pres., 1988, 92; nat. campaign mgr. Howard Baker for Pres., 1979; dir. com. ops., alt. del. Republican Nat. Conv., 1980; chmn. Shelby County Rep. Party, 1975-77; alt. del. Rep. Nat. Conv., 1976; exec. com. Rep. Nat. Com., 1971-73; nat. chmn. Young Rep. Nat. Fedn., 1971-73; sec. Bedford County Election Commn., 1968-70; chmn. Tenn. Young Rep. Fedn., 1969-70; dir. Mid-South Coliseum, Am. Council Young Polit. Leaders, 1972-74, U.S. Youth Council, 1972-75; bd. govs. Charles Edison Meml. Youth Fund; nat. adv. bd. Distributive Edn. Clubs Am.; mem. U.S. del. study tour, People's Republic of China, 1978, study tour, USSR, 1975. Served with USN, 1957-59. Mem. Kiwanis. Republican. Lutheran. Mailing: PO Box 28 Townsend TN 37882

SUNDQUIST, ERIC JOHN, American studies educator; b. McPherson, Kans., Aug. 21, 1952; s. Laurence A. and Frances J. (Halene) S.; m. Tatiana Kreinine, Aug. 14, 1982; children: Alexandra, Joanna, Ariane. BA, U. Kans., 1974; MA, Johns Hopkins U., 1976, PhD, 1978. Asst. prof. English Johns Hopkins U., Balt., 1978-80, U. Calif., Berkeley, 1980-82, assoc. prof., 1982-86, prof. English, 1986-89, UCLA, 1989-97, chair dept. English, 1994-97; dean Judd A. and Marjorie Weinberg Coll. Arts and Scis. Northwestern U., Evanston, Ill., 1997—. Vis. scholar U. Kans., 1985, dir. Holmes grad. seminar, 1993; dir. NEH Summer Seminar for Coll. Tchrs., U. Calif., Berkeley, 1986, 90, UCLA, 1994; cons. Calif. Coun. for Humanities, 1986-87; prof. Bread Loaf Sch. English, Middlebury (Vt.) Coll., 1987, 89, Sante Fe, 95; mem. fellowship com. Newberry Libr., 1987, 88, 92; dir. NEH Summer Seminar for Secondary Sch. Tchrs., Berkeley, 1988; vis. prof. UCLA, 1988; Andrew Hilen vis. prof. U. Wash., 1990; Lamar Meml. lectr. in so. states Mercer U., 1991; Gertrude Conaway Vanderbilt prof. English Vanderbilt U., Nashville, 1992-93; mem. fellowship cons. Nat. Humanities Ctr., 1992, 93; acad. specialist in Am. studies Tel Aviv U., 1994; mem. adv. bd. Colloquium for the Study of Am. Culture, Claremont (Calif.) Grad. Sch. & Huntington Libr., 1994—. Author: Home as Found: Authority and Genealogy in Nineteenth-Century American Literature, 1979 (Gustave Arlt award Coun. Grad. Schs. in U.S. 1980), Faulkner: The House Divided, 1983, The Hammers of Creation: Folk Culture in Modern African-American Fiction, 1992, To Take the Nations: Race in the Making of American Literature, 1993 (Christian Gauss award Phi Beta Kappa 1993, James Russell Lowell award MLA 1993, Choice Outstanding Acad. Book 1994); co-author: Cambridge History of American Literature, Vol. II, 1995; editor: American Realism: New Essays, 1982, New Essays on Uncle Tom's Cabin, 1986, Frederick Douglass: New Literary and Historical Essays, 1990, Mark Twain: A Collection of Critical Essays, 1994, Cultural Contexts for Ralph Ellison's Invisible Man, 1995, Oxford W.E.B. DuBois Reader, 1996; mem. adv. bd. Studies in Am. Lit. and Culture, 1987-90, gen. editor, 1991-97; mem. editl. bd. Am. Lit. History, 1987—, Ariz. Quar., 1987—; assoc. editor Am. Nat. Biography, 1990—; cons. The Libr. of Am., 1992—; consulting reader African-Am. Rev., 1992—; contbr. articles to profl. jours. Am. Coun. Learned Socs. fellow, 1981, NEH fellow, 1989-90, Guggenheim fellow, 1993-94 (declined). Mem. MLA (chair adv. coun. Am. lit. sect. 1994, mem. exec. com. divsn. 19th Century Am. lit. 1994-97), Am. Studies Assn. (chair John Hope Franklin Prize com. 1993, mem. nat. coun. 1994-97, mem. fin. com. 1995-97, and other coms.), Am. Lit. Assn., Orgn. Am. Historians, So. Hist. Assn., So. Am. Studies Assn. (mem. exec. com. 1993-97), Phi Beta Kappa. Office: Northwestern U Coll Arts and Scis 1918 Sheridan Rd Evanston IL 60208-0847

SUNDQUIST, JAMES LLOYD, retired political scientist; b. West Point, Utah, Oct. 16, 1915; s. Frank Victor and Freda (Carlson) S.; m. Beth Ritchie, Dec. 25, 1937 (dec. 1982); children: Erik L., Mark L., James K.; m. Geraldine Coote, Dec. 3, 1983. Student, Weber Coll., 1932-34, HHD (hon.), 1990; student, Northwestern U., 1934-35; BS, U. Utah, 1939; MS in Pub. Adminstrn, Syracuse U., 1941; DDS (hon.), Carthage Coll., 1987. Reporter Salt Lake Tribune, 1935-39; adminstrv. analyst U.S. Bur. Budget, 1941-47, 49-51; reports and statistics officer Office Def. Moblzn., 1951-53; dir. mgmt. control European Command, U.S. Army, Berlin, 1947-49; asst. to chmn. Democratic Nat. Com., 1953-54; asst. sec. to gov. N.Y. State, 1955-56; asst. to U.S. Senator Clark, 1957-62; dep. under sec. agr., 1963-65; sr. fellow Brookings Instn., 1965-85, emeritus, 1985—, dir. govtl. studies, 1976-78; adj. prof. Smith Coll., 1975-78. Sec. platform com. Dem. Nat. Conv., 1960, 68 Author: Politics and Policy: The Eisenhower, Kennedy and Johnson Years, 1968, Making Federalism Work, 1969 (Louis Brownlow award for best pub. adminstrn. book), Dynamics of the Party System, 1973, 2d edit., 1983, Dispersing Population: What America Can Learn form Europe, 1975, The Decline and Resurgence of Congress, 1981 (Hardeman prize for best book on Congress), Constitutional Reform and Effective Government, 1986, 2d edit., 1992, Deseret Boy: Memories of a Utah Childhood, 2003; editor: Internat. Rev. Adminstrv. Scis., 1980—89, Beyond Gridlock?, 1993, Back to Gridlock?, 1995. Mem. Gov.'s Commn. on Va.'s Future, 1983-84 Recipient Exceptional Civilian Svc. award War Dept., 1945, Lifetime Achievement award Maxwell Sch. (Syracuse U.) Alumni Assn., 1994; sr. Rsch. fellow U. Glasgow, Scotland, 1972-73. Mem. Nat. Acad. Pub. Adminstrn., Am. Soc. Pub.

Adminstrn., Am. Polit. Sci. Assn. (treas. 1980, Charles E. Merriam award 1985, Eldersveld award 1994), Am. Acad. Arts and Scis. Home: 900 N Taylor St Unit 2117 Arlington VA 22203 Office Phone: 703-294-4226.

SUNDSTROM, HAROLD WALTER, public relations executive; b. Chgo., Jan. 26, 1929; s. Elmer A. and Rosalind Lillian (Busse) S.; m. Mary Olin, Oct. 1, 1955; children: Geoffrey Lee, Lori Lynn, Deborah Barron. AA, Wright Jr. Coll., 1949; BA, Mich. State U., 1952, MA, 1954. Fgn. svc. info. officer USIA, Tokyo, Jakarta, Seoul, 1955-61; sr. pub. rels. assoc. Eli Lilly and Co., Indpls., 1962-66; v.p., dir. pub. rels. Eisenhower People to People Program, Kansas City, Mo., and Copenhagen, 1966-68; govt. and pub. affairs rep. North Ctrl. States Automobile Mfrs. Assn., Kansas City, 1968-69; speechwriter, pub. rels. cons. Commdr.-in-Chief U.S. Pacific Forces, Aiea, 1969-75; pres. No. Ariz. Comm., Inc., Flagstaff, 1975-79; asst. sec., dir. pub. affairs U.S. Internat. Trade Commn., Washington, 1977-87; v.p. pub. affairs and publs. Export-Import Bank U.S., Washington, 1987-89; pres. Halamar, Inc., Manassas, Va. and Easley, S.C., 1983—, Silver Springs, Fla., 1983-98. Mem. Pres.'s Consumer Affairs Couns., 1977-89; freelance writer and poet. Author: The American West, 1956, Indonesia: Its People and Politics, 1957, Garuda, Introducing Indonesia, 1962, Faces of Asia: Korea, 1965, The Northern Arizona Scene, 1976, American Collie Champions, Vol. I, 1979, Vol. II, 1980, Vol. III, 1987, Collies - A Complete Pet Owners Manual, 1994; editor, pub. Hawaiian Dog Rev., The Alaska Cir., The Arizona Cir., Internat. Lhasa Apso Rev., Sandwich Isles Dog Gazette, 1972-76, Collie Cues, 1983-86, Travel Writer, Honolulu Sun Press, 1972-76. Active Civil War Preservation Trust, Colonial Williamsburg, Nat. Trust for Hist. Preservation, Hist. Mount Vernon, Va. With U.S. Army, 1947-48, 52-53. Recipient People to People Disting. Svc. award, 1967, George Washington Honor medal Freedom Found., 1968, Silver Beaver award Boy Scouts Am., 1975. Fellow Japan Soc. N.Y.; mem. Pub. Rels. Soc. Am. (past pres. Hawaii chpt., Silver Anvil award 1973), Dog Writers Assn. Am. (pres. 1984-92, Disting. Svc. award 1993), Dog Writers Ednl. Trust (vice chmn., chmn. 1999—), Collie Club Am. (pres. 1984-86), Collie Club Am. Found. (life, pres. 1990-92), Am. Kennel Club (del. 1986—), Pi Sigma Alpha, Phi Kappa Sigma. Republican. Avocations: pure-bred dog breeding and showing, travel, photography, conservation, preservation of historic properties. Home and Office: 11245 NW 17th Court Rd Ocala FL 34475-1339 E-mail: halamar1@aol.com.

SUNDVALL, SHEILA A. lawyer; b. Cleve., Jan. 21, 1963; BA, U. Mich., 1985, JD, 1988. Bar: Ill. 1988, U.S. Dist. Ct. (no. dist.) Ill. 1988, U.S. Ct. Appeals (7th cir.) 1989. Jud. clk. judge Richard D. Cudahy U.S. Ct. Appeals 7th Cir., Chgo., 1988-89; assoc. Sidley & Austin, Chgo., 1989-96, ptnr., 1996—. Lectr. in field. Mem. Legal Club Chgo., Phi Beta Kappa, Order of Coif. Office: Sidley & Austin 1 S First National Plz Chicago IL 60603-2000

SUNDY, GEORGE JOSEPH, JR., retired engineering executive; b. Nanticoke, Pa., Apr. 22, 1936; s. George Joseph Sr. and Stella Mary (Bodurka) S.; m. Stella Pauline Miechur, May 21, 1966; children: Sharon Ann, George Joseph III. BS, Pa. State U., 1958. Rsch. engr. Bethlehem (Pa.) Steel Corp., 1959-85; reliability engr. Flo-Con Systems, Inc. (name now Vesuvius USA), Champaign, Ill., 1985-90, reliability mgr., 1990 96, slide gate product line specialist, 1996—2001. Patentee in field. Mem. AIST, Am. Ceramics Soc., Assn. Iron and Steel Tech., Keramos, Sigma Tau. Democrat. Roman Catholic. Home: 604 E South Mahomet Rd Mahomet IL 61853-3602 Personal E-mail: gsundy@advancenet.net.

SUNIA, AITOFELE TOESE F. lieutenant governor; b. Mar. 26, 1943; JD, U. of San Francisco. Various gov. positions including asst. atty. gen., temp. dist. ct. judge Ter. of Am. Samoa, territorial treas., 1997—2003, lt. gov., 2003. Office: Office Lt Gov Terr Am Samoa Pago Pago AS 96799

SUNIA, MUAGUTUTIA FITI, American Samoa attorney general; Asst. atty. gen. Am. Samoa Govt., Pago Pago, 1997—2001, acting atty. gen., 2001—02, atty. gen., 2002—. Office: PO Box 7 Pago Pago AS 96799

SUNLEY, EMIL MCKEE, economist; b. Morgantown, W.Va., July 30, 1942; s. Emil McKee and Nelle Berniece (Traer) S.; m. Judith Evelyn Steere, Dec. 23, 1966; children: Rachel Anne, Gillian Traer, Neil Steere. BA, Amherst Coll., 1964; MA, U. Mich., 1965, PhD, 1968. Economist office tax analysis Dept. Treasury, Washington, 1968-73, assoc. dir. office tax analysis, 1973-75, dep. asst. sec. for tax policy, 1977-81; sr. fellow Brookings Instn., Washington, 1975-77; dir. tax analysis Deloitte & Touche, Washington, 1981-92; asst. dir. fiscal affairs dept. Internat. Monetary Fund, 1992—. Mem. editl. bd. Nat. Tax Jour., 1992-95. Mem. Commn. on RR Retirement Reform, 1987-90. Mem. Am. Econ. Assn., Nat. Tax Assn. (pres. 1995-96), Tax Analysts (bd. dirs. 1982-93). Episcopalian. Office: Internat Monetary Fund Fiscal Affairs Dept Washington DC 20431-0001 Business E-Mail: esunley@imf.org.

SUNSHINE, EDWARD ROBERT, theology educator; b. Tiffin, Ohio, Apr. 28, 1939; s. Thomas Newton and Kathryn Irene (Shields) S.; m. Ann Connor, May 19, 1977; 1 child, Ellen Connor. BA, Loyola U., Chgo., 1962, MA, 1965; PhD, Grad. Theol. Union, Berkeley, Calif., 1988. Tchr. secondary sch. Colegio San José, Arequipa, Peru, 1965-66, Colegio Cristo Rey, Tacna, Peru, 1966-67; lectr. Loyola U., Chgo., 1972-76; exec. dir. Food Justice Programs, Chgo., 1976-81; lectr. Santa Clara (Calif.) U., 1986-87; asst. prof. Barry U., Miami Shores, Fla., 1988-91, assoc. prof., 1991—. Cons. in field. Editor: Proc. First Global Village Conf., 1992; contbr. chpts. to books, articles to profl. jours. Mem. Am. Acad. Religion, Cath. Theol. Soc. Am., Soc. Christian Ethics, Soc. Study Christian Ethics, East-Ctrl. Am. Soc. for 18th Century Studies. Democrat. Roman Catholic. Avocation: Aikido. Office: Barry Univ Theology Dept 11300 NE 2d Ave Miami Shores FL 33161 Office Phone: 305-899-3446. Business E-Mail: esunshine@mail.barry.edu.

SUNSHINE, PHILIP, pediatrician; b. 1930; MD, U. Colo., 1955. Bd. cert. neonatal-perinatal medicine Am. Bd. Pediat. Resident Stanford Hosp. and Clinics, 1957, 1961, fellow, 1963; co-dir. MCCPOP Stanford U. Sch. Medicine, Palo Alto, Calif.; staff mem. Lucile Packard Childrens Hosp. Recipient Virgina Apgar award, Am. Acad. Pediat., 2001. Avocations: tennis, bicycling. Office: Stanford Univ Sch Medicine MC 5731 750 Welch Rd #315 Palo Alto CA 94304-1510 Office Phone: 650-723-5711. E-mail: psunshine@stanford.edu.

SUNSTEIN, CASS ROBERT, law educator; b. Salem, Mass., Sept. 21, 1954; AB, Harvard U., 1975, JD, 1978. Bar: D.C. 1980. Law clk. for Hon. Benjamin Kaplan Supreme Judicial Ct. of Mass, 1978—79; law clk. for Thurgood Marshall U.S. Supreme Ct., Washington, 1979-80; atty.-adviser, Office of Legal Counsel U.S. Dept. Justice, Washington, 1980-81; asst. prof. law U. Chgo. Sch. Law, 1981—85, prof. law, 1985—88, Karl N. Llewellyn Prof. of Jurisprudence, 1988—93, Karl N. Llewellyn Disting. Svc. Prof. of Jurisprudence, 1993—. Co-dir. Ctr. on Constitutionalism in Eastern Europe, 1992—; mem., Amer. Acad. of Arts & Sciences, 1992, Amer. Law Inst., 1990-. Author: After the Rights Revolution, 1990, The Partial Constitution, 1993, Democracy and the Problem of Free Speech, 1993 (Goldsmith Book award Harvard U.), Constitutional Law (co-author), 1995, Legal Reasoning and Political Conflict, 1996, Free Markets and Social Justice, 1997, Administrative Law and Regulatory Policy (co-author), 1998, One Case at a Time, 1999, Designing Democracy: What Constitution, 2001, Republic.com, 2001, Risk and Reason, 2002, The Cost Benefit State, 2002, Punitive Damages: How Juries Decide, 2002. Office: U Chgo Sch Law 1111 E 60th St Chicago IL 60637-2776 E-mail: csunstei@midway.uchicago.edu.

SUNTRA, CHARLES RATAPOL, surgeon, educator; b. Detroit, Dec. 4, 1968; s. Sathien and Malee Suntra. BA summa cum laude, St. Louis U., 1991, MD cum laude, 1995. Diplomate Am. Bd. Otolaryngology, bd. eligible Am. Bd. Facial Plastic and Reconstructive Surgery. Intern gen. surgery Boston U. Sch. Medicine/Boston Med. Ctr., 1995—96; resident otolaryngology-head and neck surgery Boston U. Sch. Medicine, 1996—2000; chief resident Boston Med. Ctr./Boston U., 1999—2000; fellow facial plastic and reconstructive surgery Park Ctrl. Inst./Forest Park Hosp., St. Louis, 2000—01; med. staff Forest Pk. Hosp., St. Louis, 2000—01, Sutter Gould Med. Found., Modesto, Calif., 2001—, Doctors Med. Ctr., Modesto, 2001; asst. clin. prof. Sch. Medicine U. Calif., Davis. Presenter in field. Contbr. articles to profl. jours. Fellow: ACS, Am. Bd. Otolaryngology; mem.: Thai Physicians Assn. Am., Am. Rhinologic Soc., Am. Acad. Facial Plastic and Reconstructive Surgery, Am. Acad. Otolaryngology-Head and Neck Surgery, Phi Eta Sigma, Alpha Epsilon Delta, Beta Beta Beta, Alpha Sigma Nu, Phi Beta Kappa, Alpha Omega Alpha. Office: Gould Med Group 600 Coffee Rd Modesto CA 95355 Office Phone: 209-550-4835. Business E-Mail: suntrac@sutterhealth.org.

SUNUNU, JOHN E. senator; m. Kitty Sununu; 3 children B in Mech. Engrng., M in Mech. Engrng., Mass. Inst. Tech.; MBA, Harvard Grad. Sch. Bus. Design engr. Remec, Inc., 1987-90; mgr., ops. specialist Pittiglio, Rabin, Todd & McGrath, 1990-92; chief fin. officer, dir. ops. Teletrol Sys. Inc.; cons. JHS Assocs., Ltd.; mem. U.S. Congress from 1st N.H. dist., 1997—2003; U.S. senator from N.H., 2003—. Mem. appropriations com., budget com.; previous mem. natural resources working group, house govt. reform and oversight com., house small bus. com.; vice-chmn. Nat. Econ. Growth, Natural Resources and Regulatory Affairs sub-com.; mem. Rep. Policy com. Active N.H. C. of C., N.H. Bus. and Industry Assn., N.H. High Tech Coun. Republican. Roman Catholic. Office: US Senate Russell Courtyard 4 Washington DC 20510

SUP, STUART ALLEN See ALLEN, STUART

SUPANICH, BARBARA ANN, family practice physician; b. Detroit, Sept. 24, 1952; d. Donald George and Mildred Mary (Stanovich) S. BS in Chemistry, Mercy Coll. of Detroit, 1974; MD, Mich. State U., 1980. Joined Sisters of Mercy, 1973; diplomate Am. Bd. Family Practice; lic. physician, Mich. Resident in family practice Creighton U. Affiliated Hosps., Omaha, 1980-83; family physician in pvt. practice, Eaton Rapids, Mich., 1983-86, Houghton Lake, Mich., 1986-92; fellow in clin. ethics Ctr. for Ethics, Mich. State U., East Lansing, 1992-93; asst. prof. family practice Mich. State U., East Lansing, 1993-97, assoc. chair clin. svcs., dept. family practice, 1995-99, assoc. prof., 1998, assoc. residency dir. family practice residency Munson, 1999—. Cons. Mich. Dept. Cmty. Health, Lansing, 1996-99. Contbr. chpts. to books, articles to profl. jours. Fellow Am. Acad. Family Physicians (bd. dirs., regional dir. 2000—); mem. Mich. Acad. Family Physicians, Am. Med. Women's Assn. Roman Catholic. Avocations: swimming, bicycling, mystery and science fiction novels. Home: 3525 La Casita Ave Apt 202 Traverse City MI 49684-4336 Office: Mich State U Munson Family Practice Ctr 1400 Medical Campus Dr Traverse City MI 49684-7823 E-mail: bsupanich@mhc.net., barbrsm@earthlink.net.

SUPANVANIJ, JANIKAN, finance educator; b. Bangkok, Aug. 6, 1971; arrived in U.S., 1993; d. Vitaya and Sopha Supanvanij. BBA, Thammasat U., Bangkok, 1993; MFN in Fin., St. Louis U., 1995, MBA in Fin. and Econs., 1997, postgrad., 1997—2003. Cert. tchg. skills. Internat. banking facility fgn. exch. dealer The Thai Mil. Bank, Ltd., Bangkok, 1993; instr. St. Louis U., 1997—2003; asst. prof. St. Cloud (Minn.) State U., 2003—. Contbr. articles to profl. jours. Mem.: St. Louis U. Grad. Student Assn. (webmaster 1997—2002, GSA rsch. symposium program co-chair 2001—02, pres. 2002—03), Beta Gamma Sigma, Alpha Epsilon Lambda. Office: St Cloud State U 720 4th Ave S Saint Cloud MN 56301

SUPERNEAU, DUANE WILLIAM, geneticist, physician; b. Ogden, Utah, Dec. 31, 1950; s. Richard Edwin and Mary Ellen Superneau; m. Connie A. Saltalamacchia, Apr. 21, 1978; children: Adam, Ashley, Allison. BA, Carroll Coll., 1973; MD, U. Wash., 1977. Diplomate Am. Bd. Pediat., Am. Bd. Med. Genetics. Asst. prof. dept. med. genetics U. So. Ala., Mobile, 1982-87, assoc. prof. dept. med. genetics, 1987-91; chief sect. med. genetics Ochsner Clinic, New Orleans, 1991—; clin. asst. prof. dept. biometry and genetics La. State U., New Orleans, 1992—, clin. asst. prof. dept. pediatrics, 1994—. Bd. dirs. The ARC Greater New Orleans, 1991—, pres. 1994-96; bd. dirs. ARC of La., 1994—, pres., 1999-2001; bd. dirs. Jefferson Parish Human Svcs. Authority, Jefferson Parish, La., 1992-99. Roman Catholic. Office: Ochsner Clinic Depts Pediatrics Pathology and Ob-Gyn 1514 Jefferson Hwy New Orleans LA 70121-2429 Office Phone: 504-842-3900. Business E-Mail: dsuperneau@ochsner.org.

SUPLEE, KATHERINE ANN, lawyer; b. Newark, Oct. 4, 1950; d. Frank Edward and Mary Teresa (Green) S. BA, Mt. Holyoke Coll., 1972; postgrad., Eagleton Inst. Politics, 1972-73; JD, Seton Hall U., 1977. Bar: N.J. 1978, U.S. Dist. Ct. N.J. 1978, U.S. Supreme Ct. 1983, N.Y. 1984. Assoc. Williams & Flynn, Westfield, N.J., 1978-80, Suplee, Clooney & Co., Elizabeth, NJ, 1978—2001. Atty. Union Twp. Planning Bd., Union, N.J., 1981; mem. trustee panel U.S. Trustee in Bankruptcy, Newark, 1982—; spl. counsel City of Elizabeth N.J., 1986-88; mem. adv. coun. Summit Bank, 1989-95, St. Elizabeth Hosp., 1991-2000. Fund raiser N.J. Opera Co., 1973-77, Save African Endangered Species Inc., 1980-82, Kosciusko Found.; counsel Summit chpt. Friends of Opera, 1979-84, Polish Assistance Inc., 1998-2000; bd. dirs. Westminster Ballet Co., Elizabeth, 1984-85, Union County Legal Svcs. Corp., Elizabeth, 1984-86. Mem. ABA, N.J. Bar Assn., Union County Bar Assn. (del. gen. coun. 1984, trustee 1997—), N.J. Women Lawyers (bd. dirs. 1980-87, sec. 1986-87, treas. 1988), Comml. Law League, N.J. Women in Fed. Practice (bd. dirs. 1985-98, treas. 1987-89, pres. 1995-97), Bath and Tennis Club (Spring Lake, N.J.), Spring Lake Golf Club, Suburban Golf Club (Union, N.J.), Phi Alpha Delta. Roman Catholic. Office: 1767 Morris Ave Union NJ 07083

SUPLINSKAS, RAYMOND JOSEPH, materials scientist; b. Hartford, Conn., Aug. 29, 1939; s. Paul Peter and Delina Alice (Vallieres) S.; m. Janet Hazel Mainello, Aug. 29, 1959; children: Paul, Deborah, Michael. BS, Yale U., 1961; PhD in Chemistry, Brown U., 1965. Mem. tech. staff Bell Labs., Murray Hill, N.J., 1964-65; assoc. prof. chemistry Yale U., New Haven, 1965-72; chmn. dept. chemistry Swarthmore (Pa.) Coll., 1972-77; prin. staff scientist Textron Splty. Materials, Lowell, Mass., 1977—2001; chief scientist Splty. Materials, Lowell, Mass., 2002—. Contbr. articles to Jour. Chem. Physics. Grantee NSF, 1965-72. Achievements include research in development of refractory reinforcing filaments (including SCS-6), metal matrix composites, and carbon/carbon composites; patents in field. Office: Splty Materials 1449 Middlesex St Lowell MA 01851-5199 Office Phone: 978-322-1900. E-mail: rsuplins@specmaterials.com.

SUPPA-FRIEDMAN, JANICE DESTEFANO, secondary school educator, consultant; b. Morristown, NJ, Apr. 27, 1943; d. Eugene Arthur and Isabella Vienna (Bottiglia) DeS.; m. Dennis Suppa, June 28, 1964 (div. May 1994); children: Julie Ann, Chad Dennis; m. Michael Jac Friedman, Oct. 7, 1995. BS in Edn., Bowling Green State U., 1964; MA in Edn., Va. Poly. Inst. & State U., 1977, cert. advanced grad. study, 1990. Cert. secondary tchr., Va. Tchr. English and reading Northwood (Ohio) Jr. High Sch., 1964—66; tchr. English and history Canaseraga (N.Y.) Ctrl. Schs., 1966—67; tchr. English and reading Marstellar Jr. High Sch., Manassas, Va., 1967—72; tchr. English Taylor Jr. High sch., Warrenton, Va., 1973—74; tchr. English and reading, lang. arts specialist, dept. head, lead tchr. Brentsville Dist. Mid.-Sr. High Sch., Nokesville, Va., 1975—99; reading specialist Graham Park Middle Sch., Dumfries, Va., 1999—2000; ednl. cons., 2000—; co-tchr./mentor Fredericksburg City Pub. Sch., 2004. Ednl. cons. So. Region Coll. Bd., 2001—; reader for advanced placement literature and composition exam, 1996, 1998-2003; adj. prof. Old Dominion U., 1999, No. Va. C.C., 1992-94, George Mason U., 2004. Editor newsletter Spinning Wheel, 1991-94; contbr. articles to profl. jours. Va. English Bull. Tour guide George Washington Fredericksburg Found. at Kenmore Mansion and Plantation, Ferry Farms, Va., 2001—; officer of election Stafford County, 2001—03. Grantee Va. Comm. of the Arts, 1994-95, 2000, Prince William Edn. Found., 1996, 2000, Greater Washington Reading Coun., 1999, 2000, Va. Opera Assn., 2000, So. States Southland Corp., 2000. Mem. NATE (pres. 1992-1994), Nat. Coun. Tchrs. English (coord. Va. state Achievement in Writing awards 1995-2001, Va. state liaison 2001, judge Va. state forensics finals 2000-2003, judge Va. state excellence in lit. mags. 1998-2002), Va. Assn. Tchrs. English (exec. bd. 1992—, v.p. 2001-02, pres.-elect 2002-03, pres. 2004, Svc. award 1993), Phi Delta Kappa. Avocations: reading, music, hiking, swimming, biking.

SUPPES, CHRISTINE JOHNSON, publishing executive; b. LA, Mar. 3, 1953; d. Robert and Jane Johnson; m. Patrick Suppes; children: Alexandra Christine, Michael Patrick. Copygirl/editl. asst. San Francisco Examiner, 1972—73; pres. Gravure At Home, Stanford, Calif., 1997—2001; pub., editor-in-chief www.Fashionlines.com, Stanford, Calif., 1999—; chief designer Jewels by Christine, 2002—. Advt. cons. Clarum Corp., Palo Alto, Calif., 1997—, Gravure Corp., Dallas, 1997—2000; chief designer www.jewelsbyChristine.com, Stanford, Calif., 2003—. Author: Amanda Prescott, 1984, Clinic, 1985; contbr. revs. to San Francisco Chronicle, articles to SF Moda. Organizer, Teacher's Fund Bing School, Stanford, 1995—2001; mem. Peninsula Chpt. NARAL, Palo Alto, 1997—2000; supporter ARC, Palo Alto, 2001. Recipient Angel of Fashion com. award, N.Y.C., 1999—. Mem.: Fashion Group Internat., Camera Nazionale della Moda Italiana, Federation Francaise de la Couture. Office: Fashionlines 678 Mirada Ave Stanford CA 94305

SUPPES, PATRICK, philosophy, statistics, psychology educator; b. Tulsa, Mar. 17, 1922; s. George Biddle and Ann (Costello) Suppes; m. Joan Farmer, Apr. 16, 1946 (div. 1970); children: Patricia, Deborah, John Biddle; m. Joan Sieber, Mar. 29, 1970 (div. 1973); m. Christine Johnson, May 26, 1979; children: Alexandra Christine, Michael Patrick. BS, U. Chgo., 1943; PhD (Wendell T. Bush fellow), Columbia U., 1950; LLD, U. Nijmegen, Netherlands, 1979; Dr. honoris causa (hon.), U. Rene Descartes, Paris, 1982, U. Regensburg, Germany, 1999, U. Bologna, Italy, 1999. Instr., Stanford U., 1950—52, asst. prof., 1952—55, assoc. prof., 1955—59, prof. philosophy, statistics, psychology and edn., 1959—92, prof. emeritus. Founder, CEO Computer Curriculum Corp., 1967—90. Author: Introduction to Logic, 1957, Axiomatic Set Theory, 1960, Sets and Numbers, books 1-6, 1966, Studies in the Methodology and Foundations of Science, 1969, A Probabilistic Theory of Causality, 1970, Logique du Probable, 1981, Probabilistic Metaphysics, 1984, Estudios de Filosofia y Metodologí de la Ciencia, 1988, Language for Humans and Robots, 1991, Models and Methods in the Philosophy of Science, 1993, Representation and Invariance of Scientific Structures, 2002; author: (with Davidson and Siegel) Decision Making, 1957; author: (with Richard C. Atkinson) Markov Learning Models for Multiperson Interactions, 1960; author: (with Shirley Hill) First Course in Mathematical Logic, 1964; author: (with Edward J. Crothers) Experiments on Second-Language Learning, 1967; author: (with Max Jerman and Dow Brian) Computer-assisted Instruction, 1965—66, Stanford Arithmetic Program, 1968; author: (with D. Krantz, R.D. Luce and A. Tversky) Foundations of Measurement, Vol. 1, 1971, Vol. 2, 1989, Vol. 3, 1990; author: (with M. Morningstar) Computer-Assisted Instruction at Stanford, 1966-68, 1972; author: (with B. Searle and J. Friend) The Radio Mathematics Project: Nicaragua, 1974-75, 1976; author: (with Colleen Crangle) Language and Learning for Robots, 1994; author: (with Mario Zanotti) Foundations of Probability with Applications, 1996. Served to capt. USAAF, 1942-46. Recipient Nicholas Murray Butler Silver medal, Columbia U., 1965, Disting. Sci. Contbr. award, APA, 1972, Tchrs. Coll. medal for disting. svc., 1978, Nat. medal Sci., NSF, 1990, Henry Chauncey award for disting. svc., Ednl. Testing Svc., 2003, Lakatos Book Award prize, London Sch. Econs., 2003; fellow, Ctr. for Advanced Study Behavioral Scis., 1955—56, NSF, 1957—58. Fellow: APA, AAAS, Assn. Computing Machinery, Am. Acad. Arts and Scis.; mem.: NAS, Chilean Acad. Scis., European Acad. Scis. and Arts, Norwegian Acad. Sci. and Letters (fgn.), Russian Acad. Edn. (fgn.), Am. Ednl. Rsch. Assn. (pres. 1973—74), Internat. Union History and Philosophy of Sci. (pres. divsn. logic, methodology and philosophy of sci. 1975—79), Finnish Acad. Sci. and Letters, Internat. Inst. Philosophy, Croatian Acad. Scis. (corr.), Nat. Acad. Edn. (pres. 1973—77), Acad. Internat. de Philosophie des Scis. (titular), Am. Math. Soc., Assn. Symbolic Logic, Am. Philos. Soc., Am. Philos. Assn., Math. Assn. Am., Sigma Xi. Office Phone: 650-725-6030. E-mail: psuppes@stanford.edu.

SUPRUN, HARRY ZVI, pathologist; b. San Antonio, Aug. 19, 1924; arrived in Israel, 1934; s. Joseph Jacob and Bertha Batya (Payes) S.; m. Hedva Storch-Chassidi, Mar. 26, 1950; children: Ilana Sarah, Leora Oli. BA in Medicine, Am. U. Beirut, 1948; MD, cert. med. studies, U. Lausanne, Switzerland, 1952. Rotating intern Beilinson Med. Ctr., Petah Tikvah, Israel, 1953-54; gen. practice, Affuleh, Israel, 1954-55; resident in pathology Ctrl. Emek Hosp. and Med. Ctr., Affuleh, 1955-58; resident and chief resident in anatomic pathology Tel Aviv U.-Mcpl. Tchg. Med. Ctrs., 1958-62, specialist in anatomic pathology, assoc. attending, 1961; tng. in cytopathology, rsch. fellow Sloan-Kettering Inst., N.Y.C., 1962-63; instr., asst. pathologist Ohio State U. Med. Coll., Columbus, 1963-64; instr. Tel Aviv U. Med. Sch. Tchg. Hosps., 1964-65; dir., founder dept. pathology and cytology Regional Med. Ctr. West Galilee, Nahariyya, Israel, 1965-91; lectr. gynecologic, gastrointestinal, fine needle aspiration cytology and urol. cytopathology Tel Aviv U. Postgrad. Med. Sch., 1987-92; lectr. anatomic pathology, U.S. students Tel Aviv U., 1990-92. Lectr. normal histology Technion Med. Sch., Haifa, Israel, 1977-82; mem. Internat. Bd. Cytopathology, 1986-92; head orgn. com. Israel Soc. Cytology, 1971; fellow Internat. Acad. Cytology, 1971-73. Nat. editor Acta Cytologica, 1971-93, mem. European rev. bd., 1982-93; assoc. editor The Cervix and Lower Female Genital Tract, 1987-90, mem. editl. bd., 1989-91; mem. N.Am. rev. bd. Acta Cytol, 1997--; contbr. more than 100 articles to profl. publs. Rsch. fellow Israel Cancer Rsch. Fund, 1979-82. Fellow Internat. Acad. Cytology (continuing edn. and quality assurance com. 1992—), Israel Soc. Cervical Pathology and Colposcopy (pres. 1986). Achievements include correlative study on incidence of pulmonary cancer and other lung diseases associated with squamous metaplasia of bronchial epithelium.

SUPUT, RAY RADOSLAV, librarian; b. Columbus, Ohio, May 13, 1922; s. Elias and Darinka (Balac) S.; m. Mary Grace Hansen, May 23, 1953 (dec. Nov. 1980); children: David Ray, Dorothy Mary; m. Milana Preradov, July 12, 1986. BA, Ohio State U., 1950; MSL.S., Case Western Res. U., 1951, PhD, 1972; MA, U. Chgo., 1955. Librarian Northwestern U., Evanston, Ill., 1951-52; reference and circulation librarian Law Library, U. Chgo., 1952-54, cataloger, 1954-57; asso. librarian Garrett-Evang. Theol. Sem., Evanston, 1957-58, head librarian, 1958-64; asst. dir. libraries and adj. lectr. dept. Slavic and E. European langs. Sch. Library Sci. Case Western Res. U., Cleve., 1964-67, acting dir. libraries, 1967-68; adj. instr. Case Western Res. U. (Sch. Library Sci.), 1965-69; librarian Case Western Res. U. (Freiberger Library), 1968-69; dir. univ. library, head dept. and prof. library sci. Ball State U., Muncie, Ind., 1969-78, univ. librarian, head dept. and prof. library service, 1978-81, prof. library service, also adj. prof. library sci., 1981-82, chmn. dept. library and info. sci., prof. library sci., 1982-87, prof. library sci., info. sci. emeritus, 1987—. Contbr. articles to profl. jours. Nat. Endowment for Humanities and Council on Library Resources Inc. grantee. Mem. ALA, AAUP, African Violet Soc. Am., Am. Theol. Libr. Assn., Serb Nat. Fedn., Ohio Hist. Soc. Eastern Orthodox.

SURACI, CHARLES XAVIER, JR., retired federal agency administrator, aerospace education consultant; b. Washington, Feb. 10, 1933; s. Charles Xavier and June Celcia (Hunter) Suraci; m. Florence Patricia De Mino, May 23, 1970. Cadet, Penn Mil. Coll. (now Widener U.), 1951—55; grad., Nat. Acad. Broadcasting Sch., Washington, 1959; student, Columbia Union Coll., 1962-63, 72, Catholic U., 1969; grad. extension course, CAP Staff Coll., 1974; BA, HHD (hon.), Calif. Christian Coll., 1977; grad., USAF Inspectors Gen. Sch., Eglin AFB, Fla., 1982; also grad. numerous other govt. schs. and courses. Served with USAF, 1953-57; enlisted CAP, 1957, commd. 1st lt., 1961; advanced through ranks to Col. CAP USAF Aux, 1974; co-founder Wheaton-Silver Spring Cadet Squadron; comdr. Nat. Capital Wing, 1973-76; dep. chief of staff cadet activities Middle East region, 1977-79, dir. cadet tng., 1979-82, insp. gen., 1982—. With Henry Diamond Lab. U.S. Army, Adelphi, Md., 1963—, materials publs. asst. Harry Diamond Lab., 1963—68, later asst. to motor transp. officer, now supply specialist, logistics sect.; bd. dirs. Centro Tepeyac Crisis Pregnancy Ctr., Silver Springs, Md. Mem. youth com. YMCA, Silver Spring, 1962—69, mem. bd. mgmt., 1967—; bd. dirs. Am. Youth Com.; mem. Commn. on Children and Youth Bd., Montgomery County, Md., Montgomery County Juvenile Ct. Com., 1978—86; co-chmn. Right to Life com. KC-Rosensteel Coun.; bd. dirs. Pregnancy Aid Ctr., College Park, Md.;

choir mem. Blessed Sacrament Cath. Ch., Washington. Nominee Pres.'s Vol. Action award, Pres. of U.S., 1988, 1991; named Air Man of Month, USAF, 1956, Grand Marshall Meml. Day Parade, Rockville, Md., 1971, Man of Yr. State of Md., Air Force Assn., 1993; recipient Leader and Svc. award, YMCA Silver Spring, 1968, 1969, CAP Meritorious Svc. award, Dept. Def., 1969, 1977, Cert. of Commendation, Pres. Richard Nixon, 1970, CAP Exceptional Svc. award, Congressman Lester Wolff of N.Y., 1972, award, Montgomery County C. of C., 1973, Commendation, Gov. of Tenn., 1975, Letter of Commendation, Washington Mayor Walter Washington, 1977, Outstanding Patriotic Civilian Svc. award, Dept. Def., 1977, Md. Vol. Cmty. honor award, Montgomery County, 1981, Vol. Activist award, 1984, George Washington honor medal, Valley Forge Freedom Found., 1995, Patrick Henry medal for Patriotic Achievement, Mil. Order of World Wars, 1995, Honor, Md. Ho. Dels., 1974, D.C. Govt., 1977, numerous AF and CAP ribbons and medals, Dept. of Army Spl. Act or Svc. award, Dept. of Army Superior Performance award, 1987, Cmty. Svc. award, Wheaton-Kensington News, Bethesda Chevy Chase Current, Montgomery County Press Assn., 1990, Outstanding Support Aviation Career Day Tuskegee Airmen and Commdg. Gen. of D.C., Air Nat. Guard, 1992, Spl. award for tng. over 1000 youth cadets in CAP in 31 yrs., State of Md., 1986, Plaque Name Displayed at U.S. Army-Harry Diamond Lab., Pro-Life award, KC-Rosensteel Coun., 1992, 1999—2002, Frank G. Brewer Meml. Aerospace award-CAP Mid. East Region HQ, 1984, 1991, 1992, CAP-USAF Aux. Meritorious Svc. award, Mid. East Region HQ, 1993, Cert. Appreciation Aerospace Edn. of Md., Air Force Assn., 1993—95, Exceptional Svc. award, USAF Aux., 1994—95, Sr. Officer of Yr. Mid East Region, USAF Aux.-CAP, 1998, Colonel Robinson Lifetime Leadership award, Nat. Capital Wing, 2001, Leadership award, Cen. East Region Air Force Assn., 2001, numerous others. Mem.: Md. Pvt. Industry Coun. (bd. dirs. Opportunity Skyway program), Md. Press. Assn. Montgomery County, Nat. Officers Assn., Mil. Order of World Wars (jr. vice comdr. Bethesda chpt. 1996—), Tuskegee Airmen Inc., Fed. Ret. Employees Assn., Army Aviation Assn., Navy League, Nat. Aerospace Assn., Air Force Assn. (v.p. aerospace edn. Thomas W. Anthony chpt. 1996—, pres. Thomas W. Anthony chpt. 1998—, bd. dirs., Medal of Merit 1990, Exceptional Svc. award 1991, Disting. Svc. as Inspector Gen. 1991, Exceptional Svc. award 1994, Commd. Officer of Yr. 1995, Spl. Cert. Appreciation 1996, Mem. Distinction award Thomas W. Anthony chpt. 2000—02, Cen. East Region Chpt. Pres. of Yr. for State of Md. 2002, named Outstanding Mem. 2004), Alumni Assn. Widener U., Andrews AFB Officers Club, KC (chmn. Pro-Life Father Rosensteel coun., Outstanding Leadership Pro-Life activities 1990—91, Outstanding Svc. award 1993—94, Honored Guest of Yr. 1996—97, Outstanding Cmty. award 2003, 2004), Chester Lodge. Democrat. Achievements include 2 plaques in his name displayed at Columbia Union Coll., Takoma Park, Md., Widener U. (formerly Pa. Mil. Coll.), Chester. Home: Rock Creek Hills 9817 La Duke Dr Kensington MD 20895-3156 Office: USAF Aux CAP Mid East Region Hdqrs Office of Insp Gen 9817 La Duke Dr Kensington MD 20895-3156 Office Phone: 301-585-0081.

SURACI, PATRICK JOSEPH, clinical psychologist; b. Rochester, N.Y., May 31, 1936; s. Frank and Josephine Rosalie (Marino) S. PhD in Psychology, New. Sch. for Social Rsch., N.Y.C., 1981. Cert. clin. psychologist, N.Y. Intern in clin. psychology Morrisania Neighborhood Family Care Ctr., Montefiore Hosp., N.Y.C., 1979-80; staff psychologist N.Y. Police Dept., 1981-83; pvt. practice N.Y.C., 1982—. Adj. lectr. N.Y. Inst. Tech., N.Y.C., 1975-78, John Jay Coll. Criminal Justice, CUNY, 1973-81; adj. asst. prof. dept. psychology Baruch Coll., CUNY, 1983-92; vol. Manhattan Ctr. for Living, 1994-96, Police Orgn. Providing Peer Assistance, 2001—. Author: Male Sexual Armor. Erotic Fantasies and Sexual Realities of the Cop on the Beat and the Man in the Street, 1992. Mem. The Nat. Arts Club. With U.S. Army, 1959-62. Mem. APA, N.Y. State Psychol. Assn. (task force on AIDS), Actors Equity. Office: 8 Gramercy Park S New York NY 10003-1718 Office Phone: 212-473-5966. E-mail: DrSuraci@aol.com.

SURAWICZ, BORYS, physician, educator; b. Moscow, Feb. 11, 1917; came to U.S., 1951, naturalized, 1956; s. Josef and Mathilda (Soloweczyk) S.; m. Frida G. Van Klaveren, July 19, 1946; children: Christina M., Nina M., Tanya S., Serge J. MD, Stefan Batory U., Wilno, Poland, 1939. Mem. staffs hosps., Germany, Norway, 1945-49; staff De Goesbriand Meml. Hosp., Burlington, Vt., 1951-53, Phila. Gen. Hosp., 1953-55; instr. cardiology U. Pa., Phila., 1954-55; instr. U. Vt., Burlington, 1955-57, asst. prof. clin. and exptl. medicine, 1957-62; chief div. cardiology U. Ky. Coll. Medicine, Lexington, 1962-81, asso. prof. medicine, 1962-66, prof., 1966-81; prof. medicine Ind. U. Sch. Medicine, Indpls., 1981—. Cons. VA Hosp., Indpls. Editor: (with E.D. Pellegrino) Sudden Cardiac Death, 1964, (with C. Fisch) Digitalis, 1969; (with E. Prystowsky, C.P. Reddy) Tachycardias, 1985, Electrophysiologic Basis of ECG and Cardiac Arrhythmics, 1995, Chou's Electrocardiography in Clinical Practice, 2001; mem. editl. bds. profl. jours. Mem. AMA, ACP, Am. Heart Assn., Assn. Univ. Cardiologists (pres. 1978), Am. Coll. Cardiology (master; pres. 1979), Am. Physiol. Soc., Sigma Xi. Home: 4310 E Onyx Ave Phoenix AZ 85028-4518 Office: 8333 Naab Rd Ste 400 Indianapolis IN 46260-1919 E-mail: b.surawicz@comcast.net., tscott@thecaregroup.com.

SURBAUGH, DOLORES SAYAS, accounting and professional development educator; b. Taumuning, Sept. 9, 1953; d. Feliciano Barsaga and Francisca San Nicolas Sayas. BBA Acctg./Bus. Adminstrn. magna cum laude, Chaminade U. Honolulu, 1982, MBA, 1984. CPA Tex. Tax, acct. and fin. supervisory positions Mobil Oil, Dallas, 1995-2001; nat. bank mgr. Exxon Mobil Corp., Lenexa, Kans., 1994—2002; instr. acctg. and profl. devel. Wright Bus. Sch., Overland Park, Kans., 2002—; mem. faculty U. Phoenix, 2002—. Dir. MCFC Nat. Bank, Lenexa, 1995-2001, cmty. devel., 1995-2001; dir. Mobil Oil Credit Corp., Lenexa, 1999—2002. Art instr. for physically and mentally challenged Johnson County Devel. Support, Olathe, Kans., 1999-present; vol. evening care VVUMC, 2002-2003. Recipient Cert. of Recognition, Safehome, 1999, Recognition at Fund Raiser, Met. Luth. Ministry, 2000. Mem. AICPA. Methodist. Avocations: fine art, camping, jogging. Office: Wright Bus Sch Overland Park KS E-mail: loli_surbaugh@hotmail.com.

SURBER, DAVID FRANCIS, public relations executive, consultant, television producer, journalist; b. Covington, Ky. s. Elbert and Dorothy Kathryn (Mills) Surber. BA in Physics, Thomas More Coll., 1960; LLD (hon.), London Inst. Applied Rsch., 1973. Owner P.R. Co., pub. affairs counseling, Covington, 1960—. Judge Brit. Airways Tourism Tomorrow awards, London, 2000—. Spl. corr.: Am. newspapers to Vatican II, 1965; prodr.: (TV series) Make Peace with Nature, Sta. WKRC-TV, 1973—, Strip Mining: Two Views, 1972, Energy: Where Will It Come From, How Much Will It Cost, 1975, Atomic Power for Ohio, 1976, A Conversation with the Vice President, 1976, The Bad Water, 1977, The Trans-Alaska Pipeline: A Closeup Report, 1977, Acid Rain: A World View, 1986—89, Energy Independence in the U.K., 1992, Unhappy Prospects: Acid Rain & Global Climate Change, 1995, The Kyoto Summit: Was It Global and Will It Work, 1997—98. Apptd. by Sec. of Energy to Nat. Coal Coun., 1992, 1994, 1996, 1998, 2000, 2002, 2004, chmn. comm. com., 1999—; mem. Bd. Zoning Appeals, Covington, 1964—84, chmn., 1971—84, Covington Environ. Commn., 1971—72, Commn. Strip Mining, 1967—68; pub. interest adv. com. Ohio River Valley Water Sanitation Commn., 1976—82; water quality adv. com. Ohio-Ky.-Ind. Regional Coun. Govts., 1975—82; environ. adv. coun. City of Cin., 1981—84; rehab. com. Cmty. Chest Greater Cin., 1972—78, mem. agy. admissions com., 1972—78, mem. priorities com., 1972—78; pres. bd. dirs. Cathedral Found., 1968—70; trustee Montessori Learning Ctr., 1973—75, Bklyn. Spanish Youth Choir; founding mem. Mayor's Task Force on the Environment, Cin., 1972—73; mem. Ky. Nature Preserves Commn., 1976—79; Dem. candidate for U.S. Ho. Reps., 1972. Recipient Cmty. Svc. award, Thomas More Coll., 1975. Mem.: ACLU, AFTRA, Nat. Inst. Urban Wildlife (bd. dirs. 1987—96), Tri-State Air Com. (chmn. 1973—74), Mousquetaires d'Armagnac, Izaak Walton League (pres. Ky. 1973—98, bd. dirs. Ky., nat. bd. dirs.). Office: PO Box 15555 Covington KY 41015-0555 Office Phone: 859-491-5000. Personal E-mail: surber@surber.com.

SURBER, EUGENE LYNN, architect; b. Hagerstown, Md., May 15, 1938; s. Eugene Wicker and Kathryn Gertrude (Hunt) S.; m. Margaret Ann Sparks, May 7, 1983; 1 child, James Eugene. BArch, Ga. Inst. Tech., 1964. Registered architect, Ga. Intern architect Edwards & Portman Architects, Atlanta, 1964-65, J. Robert Carlton & Assocs., Richmond, Va., 1965-66; assoc. architect Jova/Daniels/Busby Architects, Atlanta, 1966-71; prin. Surber Barber Choate & Hertlein Architects, Inc., Atlanta, 1971—. Mem. bldg com. Cath. Archdiocese Atlanta, 1990-95, chmn., 1994-95. Prin. works include N.E.-Intown YWCA (Ga. Trust award 1992), Newman Presbyn. Ch. (Ga. Trust award 1992), The Buggyworks (Fulton City Devel. award 1987), The Castle (Atlanta Urban Design award 1991), Wade Hampton Clubhouse and Cottages (So. Home awards 1990), Hillcrest Chapel (Ga. Trust award 1991), Byron Depot (Ga. Trust award 1991), Upson House (Ga. Trust award 1980), Franklin House (Ga. Trust award 1986), Acad. of Medicine (Ga. Assn. AIA award 1983, Ga. Trust award 1985). Past chmn. Ga. Nat. Register Rev. Bd., 1990; trustee Ga. Trust for Historic Preservation, 1989-95, chmn. restoration com. Lt. USN, 1961-64. Fellow AIA (sec. Atlanta chpt. 1989-90, v.p. 1990-91, Hist. Preservation award 1986, Ivan Allen Sr. award 1992, Silver medal Atlanta chpt. 1993, Bronze medal 1974), Ga. Assn. AIA (state preservation coord. 1986-98, Bronze medal 1993). Avocation: gardening. Office: Surber Barber Choate & Hertlein Archs Inc 1776 Peachtree St NW Ste 700S Atlanta GA 30309-2308

SURBER, JOE ROBERT, assistant superintendent; b. Pawhuska, Okla., Apr. 11, 1942; s. Hugh Richard and Odema (Harris) S.; m. Jo Del Novak; children: Robert Brian, Karrie Jo. BA in Edn., Northeastern State U., 1964; MS in Edn., Okla. State U., 1969, EdD, 1974. Cert. supt., sch. psychologist, sch. counselor. High sch. prin. Unity Bd. Govs., Ponca City, Okla., 1970-71; sch. psychologist Bi-State Mental Health Found., Ponca City, 1971-74; adj. prof. Okla. State U., Ponca City, 1976-84; asst. supt. Ponca City Pub. Schs., 1984—. Pub. The Blue Book of Counseling: Concrete Tools and Techniques, 1976. Past dir. ARC, Ponca City Crime Stoppers, Kay County Youth Shelter, Okla. Assn. Schs. with Impacted Svcs. Staff sgt. USAR, 1966-72. Named One of 3 Outstanding Oklahomans, 1976; recipient Disting. Svc. award, 1973, Outstanding Educator award, 1972. Pres. Okla. Dirs. Spl. Svcs. (past pres.), Okla. Sch. Psychol. Assn. (v.p.). Home: 1308 Desoto Ponca City OK 74604 Office Phone: 580-767-8000. E-mail: joejo@cableone.net.

SURDAM, ROBERT MCCLELLAN, retired banker; b. Albany, N.Y., Oct. 28, 1917; s. Burke and LeMoyne (McClellan) S.; m. Mary Caroline Buhl, July 8, 1946; children— Peter Buhl, Robert McClellan, Mary Caroline. BA cum laude, Williams Coll., 1939. With Nat. Bank Detroit, 1947-88, exec. v.p., 1964-66, pres., 1966-72, chmn. bd., 1972-82, also bd. dirs., 1966-88. Served to lt. comdr. USNR, 1941-46. Recipient, Navy and Marine Corps. medal. Mem. Detroit Club, Country Club of Detroit, Yondotega Club, Jupiter Island Club (Hobe Sound, Fla.), Jupiter Hills Club (Tequesta, Fla.), Little Traverse Yacht Club (Harbor Springs, Mich.), Rolling Rock Club (Ligonier, Pa.), Hobe Sound Yacht Club, Little Harbor Club (Harbor Springs, Mich.). Home: 396 Provencal Rd Grosse Pointe Farms MI 48236-2959

SURFACE, JAMES LOUIS, SR., trust officer, lawyer; b. Roanoke, Va., May 20, 1941; s. Thomas James and Elizabeth (Abbott) S.; m. Judith Marcia Woodford, Aug. 11, 1962; children: Susanna Elizabeth, James Louis Jr. BA cum laude, Washington & Lee U., 1963, JD cum laude, 1965. Bar: W.Va. Assoc. Spilman, Thomas, Battle & Klostermeyer, Charleston, W.Va., 1965-71; trust officer Kanawha Valley Bank, N.A., Charleston, 1971-77; v.p., trust counsel Liberty Nat. Bank & Trust Co., Louisville, 1977-84; v.p., trust officer United Va. Bank, Richmond, 1984-85; v.p., sr. trust officer First Citizens Nat. Bank, Dyersburg, Tenn., 1985-93; sr. v.p., sr. trust officer SunTrust Bank East Tenn., Johnson City, 1993—2003; retired, 2003. Mem. adminstrv. bd. First United Meth. Ch., Dyersburg, 1988-90, pres., bd. dirs. Cmty. Concert Assn., Dyersburg, 1988-93; treas., bd. dirs. Louisville-Jefferson County Youth Orch., Louisville, 1980-84; pres., bd. dirs. W.Va. Opera Theater, Inc., Charleston, 1972-77; elder First Presbyn. Ch., Johnson City, 1998-2000; bd. dirs. Tipton-Haynes Hist. Site, 2001—. Mem. ABA (chmn. subcom. on duties and responsibilities of successor trustee real property, probate and trust sect., Charleston 1974-75), W.Va. Bar Assn., Tenn. Bankers Assn. (treas. trust divsn. Nashville chpt. 1988-89, sec. 1989-90, v.p. 1990-91, pres. 1991-92), W.Va. Bankers Assn. (chmn. trust divsn. Charleston chpt. 1974-75), Rotary (bd. dirs. Dyersburg chpt. 1987-88), East Tenn. State U. Friends of Music (bd. dirs. 1994-99, 2000—). Democrat. Avocations: tennis, racquetball, photography, reading. Home: 33 Grace Meadows Ct Gray TN 37615-5214

SURFACE, STEPHEN WALTER, water treatment chemist, environmental protection specialist; b. Dayton, Ohio, Feb. 25, 1943; s. Lorin Wilfred and Virginia (Marsh) S.; m. Suzanne MacDonald, Aug. 29, 1964 (div.); 1 child, Jennifer Nalani; m. Sinfrosa Garay, Sept. 16, 1978; children: Maria Lourdes, Stephanie Alcantara. BS, Otterbein Coll., 1965; MA, U. So. Calif., 1970; postgrad., U. Hawaii, 1971. Cert. profl. chemist. Tchr. Hawaii State Dept. Edn., Honolulu, 1970-71; staff chemist Del Monte Corp., Honolulu, 1971; head chemist USNPearl Harbor, Honolulu, 1971-76; staff chemist USN Pearl Harbor, Honolulu, 1976-90; chief office installation svcs., environ. protection Def. Logistics Agy., Camp Smith, Hawaii, 1990-98, dir. adminstrv. support ctr. Pacific, 1998—. Contbr. articles to profl. jours. Recipient DuPont Teaching award, U. So. Calif., 1966. Fellow Am. Inst. Chemists; mem. Am. Chem. Soc., Am. Def. Preparedness Assn., N.Y. Acad. Scis., Nat. Def. Indsl. Assn. (life), Sigma Xeta, Phi Lambda Upsilon. Democrat. Methodist. Avocations: travel, artifact collecting, landscaping. Office: Def Logistics Agy DASC FP Camp H M Smith HI 96861-4110 Home: 17610 Deweys Run Ln Dumfries VA 22026-4546

SURI, JASJIT S. research scientist; BS in Computer Engring., Regional Engring. Coll., Bhopal, India, 1988; MS, U. Ill., Chgo., 1991; PhD in Elec. Engring., U. Wash., 1997. Lectr. dept. electronic and computer engring. Regional Engring. Coll., Bhopal, 1988-89; rsch. asst. biomed. visualization dept. U. Ill., Chgo., 1989-90; rsch. programmer image sci. group IBM Palo Alto (Calif.) Sci. Ctr., summer 1990-91; rsch. assoc. U. Wash., Seattle, 1992-97; rsch. software engr. radiation treatment planning group Siemens Med. Sys., Calif., 1991-92; rsch. scientist Gammex Inc., Middleton, Wis., 1997, Sch. Medicine, U. Wis., Madison, 1997; rsch. scientist software devel. TSI, N.Y., 1997; rsch. staff scientist image guided surgery dept. Image Processing and Computer Graphics Picker Internat., Cleve., 1999—. With Bharat Heavy Elec. Ltd., Bhopal, 1986, Larson & Tubro Ltd., Bombay, India, 1987, Nat. Info. Tech. Ltd., Bhopal, 1987; presenter in field; mem. Mayo Clinic Procs., Rochester, Minn.; rev. com. Internat. Conf. in Pattern Analysis and Applications, Plymouth, Eng., 1998. Author: (with others) Model Based Segmentation, 2d. rev. edit., 2000; mem. editl. bd. Radiology, Jour. Computer Assisted Tomography, Internat. Jour. Pattern Analysis and Applications, Internat. Conf. Pattern Analysis and Applications; contbr. over 75 articles. to profl. jours.; patentee in field. Scholar Regional Engring. Coll., 1985-88 Mem. IEEE, Assn. Computing Machinery, Artificial Intelligence, Optical Engring. Soc. Am., Engring. in Medicine and Biology Soc. (mem. editl. bd.), Am. Assn. Artificial Int., USENIX-Tcl/Tk. Office: Case Western Res U Biomed Engring Dept Cleveland OH E-mail: jsuri@adelphia.net.

SURI, JEREMI A. education educator; b. N.Y., Aug. 9, 1972; m. Alison Beth Alter, July 11, 1998. AB, Stanford U., 1994; MA, Ohio Univ., Athens, Ohio, 1996; PhD, Yale Univ., New Haven, Conn., 2001. Asst. prof. Univ. Wis., Madison, Wis., 2001—. Author: Power and Protest: Global Revolution and the Rise of Detente, 2003. Office: Dept of Hist Univ Wis 3211 Humanities Bldg Madison WI 53706 Business E-Mail: suri@wisc.edu.

SURI, ROLAND ERWIN, neuroscientist; PhD, ETH, Zurich, 1996. Rschr. Salk Inst., San Diego, 2000—02; scientist IOS, Torrance, Calif., 2002—. Rschr. USC, Los Angeles, Calif., 2001—02. Contbr. articles various profl. jours. Fellow Sci. Work, Swiss NSF, EMDO Found., ETH Zurich, 1998-2002.

SURIAN, ELVIDIO, music educator; b. Lussingrande, Istria, Italy, Jan. 10, 1940; s. Santo and Dobrilla (Ballarin) S.; m. Eugenia Venturi, Nov. 6, 1971; 1 child, Laura. BS, CUNY, 1962, MA, 1964; postgrad., NYU, 1965-70. Instr. music SUNY, Stony Brook, 1970; lectr. Lehman Coll., CUNY, N.Y.C., 1970-72; music librarian G. Rossini Music Conservatory, Pesaro, Italy, 1973-76, prof. music history, 1976—, mem. adminstrn. bd., 1986-89. Coordinator Répertoire Internat. Sources Musicales Group, Italy, 1975-83, collaboration with Répertoire Intern. de la Presse Musicale, Balt., 2002-. Author: A Checklist of Writings on 18th Century French and Italian Opera, 1970; editor: D. Cimarosa, Orazi e Curiazi, 1986, Storia della Musica in Venezia, 1987, Manuale di storia della musica, 4 vols., 1991-95, 3rd edit. 2002; contbr. articles to music jours. Mem. Internat. Musicological Soc., Am. Musicological Soc., Italian Soc. Musicology (mem. exec. council 1976-79, 82-85). Roman Catholic. Avocation: collecting stamps. Home: Via dell'iride 5 61020 Candelara (Pesaro) Italy Office: G Rossini Conservatorio Musica Piazza Olivieri 61100 Pesaro Italy E-mail: elv.surian@libero.it.

SURKIN, ELLIOT MARK, lawyer; b. Phila., Apr. 22, 1942; s. Hersh M. and Minnie (Shore) S.; m. Carol E. Foley, May 26, 1973; 1 child, Jennifer Dykema. AB, Princeton U., 1964; LLB, Harvard U., 1967. Bar: Mass. 1967. Assoc. Hill & Barlow, P.C., Boston, 1967-73, mem., 1973—2003, chmn. mgmt. com., 1988-92, chmn. real estate dept., 1996-2001; mng. ptnr. Boston Piper Rudnick LLP, 2003—. Lectr. law Harvard U., 1975-96, MIT, Ctr. for Real Estate, 1996—. Chmn. bd. Boston Ctr. Arts, 1972-81, dir., mem. exec. com., 1981-83, hon. dir., 1983—; clk., trustee, mem. exec. com. Wang Ctr. for Performing Arts, Boston, 1980—, mem. fin. com., 1995—, vice chmn. bd., 1997—; mem. New Eng. com. Legal Def. Fund NAACP, 1976-93; chmn. bd. Trustees of Reservations, 1997-2003, bd. dir., 2003—, chmn. Chappaquiddick local com. 1986-97, trustee 1985—, mem. standing com. 1994-2003, mem. exec. com. 1996-2003; dir. Sheriff's Meadow Found., 1994-97. Mem. ABA, Am. Law Inst., Am. Coll. Real Estate Lawyers, Mass. Bar Assn., Boston Bar Assn., St. Botolph Club, Harvard Club of Boston, Edgartown Yacht Club, Country Club of Brookline, Mass., Kiawah Island Club. Home: 1784 Beacon St Waban MA 02468-1434 Office: Piper Rudnick LLP One International Pl Boston MA 02110-2600 E-mail: elliot.surkin@piperrudnick.com.

SURLES, CAROL D. academic administrator; b. Pensacola, Fla., Oct. 7, 1946; d. Elza Allen and Versy Lee Smith; divorced; children: Lisa Surles, Philip Surles. BA, Fisk U., 1968; MA, Chapman Coll., 1971; PhD, U. Mich., 1978. Personnel rep. U. Mich., Ann Arbor, 1973-78, vice-chancellor-adminstrn. Flint, 1987-89; exec. asst. to pres., assoc. v.p. for human resources U. Ctrl. Fla., Orlando, 1978-87; v.p. acad. affairs Jackson State U., Miss., 1989-92; v.p. adminstrn. and bus. Calif. State U., Hayward, 1992-94; pres. Tex. Woman's U., Denton, 1994-99, Ea. Ill. U., Charleston, 1999—. Trustee Pub. Broadcasting Ch. 24, Orlando, 1985-87; bd. dirs. First State Bank, Denton, Tex., Tex.-N.Mex. Power Co., TNP-Enterprise. Recipient Outstanding Scholar's award Delta Tau Kappa, 1983. Mem. AAUW, Am. Assn. Colls. and Univs., Golden Key Honor Soc., Mortar Bd. Soc., Dallas Citizens' Coun., Dallas Women's Found., Coun. of Pres. (Austin, Tex.), Phi Kappa Phi, Alpha Kappa Alpha. Methodist. Avocation: playing piano and oboe. Office: Ea Ill U 600 Lincoln Ave Charleston IL 61920-3011

SURLES, RICHARD HURLBUT, JR., retired law librarian; b. Norfolk, Va., Mar. 28, 1943; s. Richard H. and Elda Florine (Belvin) S.; m. Judith Louise Coffin, May 29, 1964; children— Stephanie Anne, Richard H. BA, Tex. A&M U., 1963; JD, U.Houston, 1967; M.L.L., U.Wash., 1969. Bar: Colo. 1971. Asst. to law librarian U. Houston, 1966-68; asst. to law librarian King county Law Library, Seattle, 1968-69; dir. of law library, prof. law U. Denver, 1969-71, U. Tenn., Knoxville, 1971-76, U. Oreg., Eugene, 1976-81, U. Ill., Champaign, 1981—98; ret., 1998. Author: Legal Periodical Management Data, 1977 Mem. Am. Assn. Law Libraries Republican. E-mail: Beretta@KTC.com.

SURMAN, OWEN STANLEY, psychiatrist; b. Boston, Apr. 21, 1943; s. Aaron Harry and Edith Anne (Silver) S.; m. Lezlie Anne Humber, July 19, 1969 (dec. Nov. 5, 1994); children: Craig Bruce Hackett, Kathleen Bridget Lezlie; m. Amy Johnson, Oct. 1, 2000. BSc with honors, McGill U., 1964, MD, CM, 1968. Diplomate Am. Bd. Psychiatry and Neurology. Intern Balt. City Hosp., 1968-69; clin. fellow in medicine Johns Hopkins U., Balt., 1968-69; resident in psychiatry Mass. Gen. Hosp., Boston, 1969-72; clin. fellow in psychiatry Harvard Med. Sch., Boston, 1969-72; clin. asst. in psychiatry Mass. Gen. Hosp., Boston, 1975-76, asst. in psychiatry, 1977-80, asst. psychiatrist, 1980-86, assoc. psychiatrist, 1986-89, psychiatrist, 1990—; instr. psychiatry Harvard U. Med. Sch., Boston, 1975-80, asst. prof., 1980-90, assoc. prof., 1990—. Psychiat. cons. Boston Ctr. Heart Transplant, 1988-94; mem. ethics com. Mass. Ctr. Organ Transplantation, 1988—; mem. subcom. Human Studies, Mass. Gen. Hosp., 1982—, acting chmn., 1996-97, co-vice-chmn., 1999-2001, cons. transplant unit, 1975—, vice-chmn. xenotransplant adv. com., 1997-98, living related partial liver donor oversight com., 2000—; mem. Inst. for Study of Smoking Behavior and Policy, John F. Kennedy Sch. Govt., 1982-89; vis. prof. Tokyo U., 2001; mem. N.Y. State Com. on Quality Improvement in Living Liver Donation, 2002—. Contbr. articles and letters to profl. jours., chpts. to books. Bd. dirs. Unitarian-Universalist Area Ch., Sherborn, Mass., 1983-86, 93-96; advancement officer troop 1 Boy Scouts Am., Sherborn, 1983-91. Lt. comdr. M.C., USNR, 1972-75. Grantee Milton Fund, 1969-70, Upjohn Corp., 1982-84, Burroughs Wellcome Co., 1984-85, Eli Lily Corp., 1989, 90-92. Fellow Am. Psychiat. Assn. (Disting.), Am. Acad. Psychosomatic Medicine (ethics com., awards com. 1994-97); mem. AAAS, Mass. Med. Soc., N.Y. Acad. Scis., Mass. ACLU, Libr. of Boston Athenaeum, Ford Hall Forum, New Eng. Poetry Club. Avocation: creative writing. Office: Mass Gen Hosp Wang ACC 815 15 Parkman St Boston MA 02114 Office Phone: 617-724-0846. E-mail: osurman@partners.org., ossurman@partners.org.

SURMATIS, JOSEPH D. retired chemist; b. Dickson City, Pa., Mar. 22, 1913; s. George and Constance (Mickulski) Surmatis; m. Geraldine Duff, Feb. 12, 1945; 1 child, Anthony. BS, Penn. State U., 1936, MS, 1937, PhD, 1942. Instr. chemistry Penn. State U., State Coll., Pa., 1940—42; cons., rsch. G.J. Esslen, Inc., Boston, 1942—44; sr. tech. fellow Hoffman-La Roche, Nutley, NJ, 1945—78; ret., 1978. Chmn. Internat. Symposium Carotinoid Chemistry, New Mex. State U., 1969, Internat. Symposium Cartenoid Chemistry, Cluj, Romania, 1972. Contbr. scientific papers over 20; referee (Jour. of Organic Chemistry), 1978. Fellow: Am. Assn. Advancement of Sci., Am. Inst. of Chemists; mem.: NY Acad. of Sci. Achievements include patents in field of indsl. synthesis including vitamins E, A, biotin, myxin and beta-carotene (over 100). Home: 4 Sunset Rd Caldwell NJ 07006

SUROVELL, EDWARD DAVID, real estate company executive; b. Washington, Mar. 20, 1940; s. Samuel and Florence Deborah (Starfield) S.; m. Barbara Ann Bartelmes, Apr. 26, 1958 (div. Jan. 1974); children: David Alexander, Claire Katherine; m. Natalie A. Sallade, June 3, 1999. BA, Columbia U., 1962; postgrad., U. Mich., 1968-71. Lic. real estate broker, Mich. Copy editor Harcourt, Brace & World, Inc., N.Y.C., 1963-65; editor Princeton (N.J.) U. Press, 1965-67, Scott, Foresman Co., Glenview, Ill., 1967-68, U. Mich., Ann Arbor, 1968-72; real estate agt. Fletcher & Klein, Inc., Ann Arbor, 1973-75; sales mgr. Charles Reinhart Co., Ann Arbor, 1975-82; pres. Edward Surovell Realtors, Ann Arbor, 1982—. Dir. United Bank and Trust, Washtenaw, 2001—. Mem. Ann Arbor City Planning Commn., 1988-91, 95-98, Downtown Devel. Authority, Ann Arbor, 1991-95; trustee Ann Arbor Dist. Libr., 1996—, pres., 2004—; bd. dirs. Mich. Shakespeare Festival, 1999—, Jackson Symphony Orch., 2000—, Chamber Music Am., 2004—; mem. Mich. Bd. Profl. Cmty. Planners, 1988-92. Mem. Nat. Assn. Realtors, Hist. Soc. Mich. (trustee 1992—, v.p. 1996-97), Ann Arbor Area Bd. Realtors (v.p. 1984, pres. 1985, Realtor of Yr. 1990), Univ. Mus. Soc. (bd. dirs. 1992-98, trustee Mich. Ctr. for the Book 1998-2002), dir. Avocations: book collecting, arts philanthropy. Home: 1000 Forest Rd Ann Arbor MI 48105-1047 Office: Edward Surovell Realtors 1884 W Stadium Blvd Ann Arbor MI 48103-4504

SUROWIEC, ANDREW JULIUS, biophysicist, researcher; b. Lwów, Poland, Apr. 13, 1940; came to U.S., 1986; s. Jan Jakub and Maria (Knobloch) S.; m. Irene Regina Baranowski, Apr. 27, 1977; 1 child, Caroline Maria. Engr., Tech. U., Gliwice, Poland, 1962, MS, 1964; PhD, Silesian U., Katowice, Poland, 1972. Cert. elec. engring. Asst. prof. Silesien Sch. Medicine, Katowice, 1964-82; postdoctoral fellow Ctr. d'Etude L'Energie Nucleaire, Mol, Belgium, 1973-74; disting. vis. scientist U. Ottawa, Ont., Can., 1983-87; asst. prof. Bowman U. Sch. Medicine, Winston-Salem, N.C., 1987-88, U. So. Calif., L.A., 1988-93; sr. physicst Centennial Med. Ctr., Nashville, 1993—.

Peer reviewer: Cancer, Internat. Jour. Am. Cancer Soc., 1993; contbr. articles to Physics in Medicine and Biology, Bioelectromagnetics, IEEE Transactions Biomed., Internat. Jour. Hyperthermia, Biopolymers, Jour. Chem. Soc. Faraday Transactions. Grantee Nat. Sci. and Engring. Rsch. Coun., 1985. Fellow Radiation Rsch. Soc.; mem. Internat. Clin. Hyperthermia Soc., N.Y. Acad. Scis. Achievements include patent for recording system for rotating viscometer; finding of simulated materials for electromagnetic studies and cancer treatment; findings of dielectric spectroscopy of normal and cancer tissues; finding of dielectric and hydrodynamic properties of DNA. Home: 8209 Londonberry Rd Nashville TN 37221-4640 Office: Centennial Med Ctr Radiation Therapy 2300 Patterson St Nashville TN 37203-1528 Office Phone: 615-342-4850. Personal E-mail: andsur@aol.com.

SURPLUS, ROBERT WILBUR, retired music educator; b. Scranton, Pa., Sept. 1, 1923; s. Willard K. and Olive T. (Wrightson) S.; m. Jean Craig, June 25, 1976; children: Amy, Melanie. BS, Susquehanna U., 1945; MA, Columbia U., 1947, EdD, 1968. Music tchr., Mineola, N.Y., 1945-46, Butler, N.J., 1946-47; music supr. Red Lion, Pa., 1947-56; assoc. prof. Shippensburg (Pa.) State U., 1956-58; music tchr. Fox Lane Sch., Bedford, N.Y., 1958-59; instr. Columbia U., N.Y.C., 1959-61; asst. prof. U. Minn., Mpls., 1961-65; prof. music Ea. Ky. U., Richmond, 1965-94; ret., 1994. Rsch. chmn., So. Div., Music Educators Nat. Conf., 1974-80, rsch. coun. mem., 1974-80; cons. Nat. Assn. Jr. Colls., 1973-75. Author: Follow the Leader, 1962, The Alphabet of Music, 1963, The Beat of the Drum, 1963, The Story of Musical Organizations, 1963; editor: A Guidebook for State Music Education Associations, 1985, Beyond the Classroom: Informing Others, 1987; contbr. articles to profl. jours. Mem.: Ky. Alliance for Arts Edn. (pres. 1974—82, adv. bd.), Ky. Music Educators Assn. (bd. dirs., pres. 1971—73, Disting. Svc. award 1983, Citation for Svc. 2004), Music Educators Nat. Conf. (pres. so. divsn. 1982—84).

SURPRIS, JOSEPH W. research scientist; BA in biol. sciences, Hunter Coll., 1994—99. Howard Hughes student fellow Hunter Coll. Gene Ctr., NYC, 1996—2000; rsch. asst. Rockefeller U., NYC, 1998; assoc. rsch. scientist Burke Med. Rsch. Inst., Inc, White Plains, NY, 2001—. Student mentor Liberty Partnership Program, NYC, 1999; intern Cmty. Food Resource Ctr., Inc., NYC Health Rsch. Tng. Program, NYC, 1998; vol. Meml. Sloan-Kettering Cancer Ctr., NYC, 1997—98; musical dir./ch. bd. mem. Eben-Ezer French Seventh-day Adventist Ch., Bklyn, NY, 2001; vol. Project Health Care, Bellevue Hosp. Ctr., NYC, 1998—98. Howard Hughes Med. Inst. Scholar award, Howard Hughes Med. Inst., 1997—99. Mem.: NY Acad. of Sciences, AAAS, Sigma Xi, The Sci. Rsch. Soc. (assoc.), Golden Key Nat. Honor Soc. (life), Alpha Phi Omega Nat. Svc. Frat. (pub. rels. 1998—99). Seventh-Day Adventist. Achievements include research in the effects of EMF on cancer. Office: Burke Med Rsch Inst Inc 785 Mamaroneck Ave White Plains NY 10605 E-mail: jsurpris@burke.org.

SURRENCY, GARY LAWRENCE, military officer, counselor, writer; b. Blackshear, Ga., Jan. 14, 1953; s. Alfred Moses and Margaret Elizabeth Surrency; m. Millie Elizabeth Edwards-Rodriguez, June 5, 1993; children: Krystal, Brandon Witt-Surrency, Hosie Witt; m. Annette Wheeler, June 3, 1975 (div. Mar. 5, 1983); children: Gary L. Jr., James. Student, several instns., Hawaii, Fla., Alaska and Tex., 1976—94. Cert. drug and alcohol counselor, field recruiter U.S. Army, equal opportunity counselor, logistical specialist. Sgt. 1st class U.S. Army, Orlando, Fla., 1978—81, sta. comdr. Orange Pk., Fla., 1981—88, logistical support/ peace keeper Camp David accord Sinai, Israel, 1990—91. Vol. for disabled vets. rights, Jacksonville, Fla., N/A, 1994—2002. Co-author: (book) Fatal Friendship, 2002. Mentor for at risk youth, Jacksonville, 1994—2002; drug and alcohol counselor for youth, 1994—2002. Nominee Soliders Medal for act of heroism performed in 1978 at Fort Jackson, S.C., by Congresswoman Corrine Brown, 2002. Mem.: Am. Legion. Baptist. Avocations: travel, cooking. Office: 12469 Del Rio Dr Jacksonville FL 32258 Home: PO Box 217 Macclenny FL 32063-0217

SURRIDGE, STEPHEN ZEHRING, lawyer, writer; b. N.Y.C., Dec. 12, 1940; s. Robert George and Florence Elizabeth (Zehring) S.; m. Helen Frances McKenna, Mar. 15, 1969; children: Christopher S., Jonathan R., Matthew W., Martha H. BA magna cum laude, Yale U., 1962; MBA (with distinction), JD, U. Mich., 1969. Bar: Wis. 1969, Mich. 1969. Assoc. Quarles & Brady, Milw., 1969-76, ptnr., 1977-89; freelance writer, tchr., 1990—. Author: (monograph) Seven Thunders of Revelation, 1985, Revelation Revisited, 1995, Fatima's 'Third Secret' is Future Warning, 2004. 1st lt. U.S. Army, 1963-65. Mem. Phi Beta Kappa. Mem. Christian Ch. Home: 4480 N Ardmore Ave Milwaukee WI 53211-1418 E-mail: ssurridge@aya.yale.edu.

SURVILO, FRANCINE MARION, painter, sculptor; b. Toms River, NJ, Dec. 30, 1955; d. Victor and Marion Francis (Beardsley) S.; 1 child, Matthew. BFA, San Jose State U., 1998. Exhibited works at Rosicrusian Mus., San Jose, Calif., 1989, Villa Montalvo, Saratoga, Calif., 1990, Pacific Art League, Palo Alto, Calif., 1996, Coos Art Mus., Coos Bay, Oreg., 1998, Sanchez Art Ctr., Pacifica, Calif., 2003, Schoharie County Arts Coun., Cobleskill, N.Y., 2003, Sebastopol Ctr. for the Arts, 2003. Home: 957 Webster St Palo Alto CA 94301

SURWIT, RICHARD SAMUEL, psychology educator; b. Bklyn., Oct. 7, 1946; s. David and Ethel S.; m. Sandra E. Cummings, May 23, 1982; children: Daniel Alan, Sarah Jeanne. AB, Earlham Coll., 1968; PhD, McGill U., Montreal, Que., Can., 1972; postgrad., Harvard U., Boston. Postdoctoral fellow Harvard Med. Sch., 1972-74, instr., 1974-76, asst. prof., 1976-77; assoc. prof. psychiatry Duke U. Med. Ctr., Durham, NC, 1977-83, prof., 1980, 83—, vice chmn., 1993—; chief divsn. med. psychology Duke U., 1997, prof. psychology, 1991—; chmn. bd. dir. ZyCare Inc. (formerly Healthware Corp.), Chapel Hill, 1983—. Author: Fear: Learning to Cope, 1978, Behavioral Approaches to Cardiovascular Diseases, 1982, The Mind-Body Diabetes Revolution, 2004. Recipient rsch. devel. award NIMH, 1980, rsch. scientist award NIMH, 1993. Fellow APA, Soc. Behavioral Medicine (pres. 1994), Acad. Behavioral Medicine Rsch. Achievements include co-discovery in 1997, of UCP2, a novel gene related and diabetes and immunity; co-developer of the Diacare diabetes disease management system, Coag-Care anticoagulation management system. Home: 3804 Sweeten Creek Rd Chapel Hill NC 27514-9706 Office: Duke U Med Ctr PO Box 3842 Durham NC 27702-3842 E-mail: richard.surwit@duke.edu.

SURYANARAYANAN, RAJ GOPALAN, pharmacist, researcher, consultant, educator; b. Cuddalore, Tamil Nadu, India, Apr. 19, 1955; came to U.S., 1985; s. Natesan and Pushpa (Subramanian) Rajagopalan; m. Shanti Venkateswaran, Nov. 24, 1985; children: Priya Mallika Sury, Meera Sindu Sury. B in Pharmacy, Banaras Hindu U., Varanasi, India, 1976, M in Pharmacy, 1978; MS, U. BC, Vancouver, Can., 1981, PhD, 1985. Mgmt. trainee Indian Drugs and Pharms. Ltd., Rishikesh, India, 1978; supr. Roche Products, Bombay, India, 1979; tchg. asst. U. B.C., Vancouver, Can., 1979, 82-83; asst. prof. pharmaceutics U. Minn., Mpls., 1985-92, assoc. prof., 1992-99, prof., 1999—, dir. grad. studies, 1994-98. Cons. numerous pharm. cos. in U.S., 1987—. Contbr. articles to profl. jours.; patentee quantitative analysis of intact tablets. Recipient numerous grants for rsch., U.S., 1985—. Mem. Am. Assn. Pharm. Scientists, Am. Assn. Colls. Pharmacy. Hindu. Avocations: tamil literature, sports. Home: 1861 Moore St Saint Paul MN 55113-5530 Office: U Minn Coll Pharmacy 308 Harvard St SE Minneapolis MN 55455-0353 E-mail: surya001@tc.umn.edu.

SUSCHITZKY, PETER, cinematographer; Cinematographer The Skouras Agy., 1987—. Cinematographer: (films) It Happened Here, 1962, Privilege, 1967, A Midsummer Night's Dream, 1968, Charlie Bubbles, 1968, Leo the Last, 1970, Melody/Swalk, 1971, The Pied Piper, 1972, Henry VIII and His Six Wives, 1972, That'll Be the Day, 1974, All Creatures Great and Small, 1975, Lisztomania, 1975, The Rocky Horror Picture Show, 1976, Valentino, 1977, The Empire Strikes Back, 1980, Krull, 1983, Falling in Love, 1984, Dead Ringers, 1988, Where the Heart Is, 1990, Naked Lunch, 1992, The Public Eye, 1992, The Vanishing, 1993, M. Butterfly, 1993, Immortal Beloved, 1994, Crash, 1996, Mars Attacks!, 1996, eXistenZ, 1998, The Man in the Iron Mask, 1998, The Empire Strikes Back - Spl. Edition, 1999, Star Wars Trilogy-Spl. Edition, 1999, The Red Planet, 1999. Office: The Skouras Agency 1149 3rd St #3 Santa Monica CA 90403

SUSCOVICH, DAVID J. neuropsychologist, marriage and family therapist; b. Mt. Pleasant, Pa., Sept. 20, 1952; s. Joseph Anthony and Helen G. Suscovich; m. Edith P. Suscovich, May 23, 1980 (div. Sept. 15, 2001); children: Joseph Alfred, John David, Mark Andrew. BS/BA in Psychology and Sociology, U. Pitts., 1973, postgrad., 1974; MA in Marriage and Family Therapy, U. Conn., 1977; PsyD in Clin. Psychology, Antioch New Eng., 1997. Cert. marriage family therapist Conn., diplomate Am. Coll. Forensic Examiners, Nat. Bd. Addiction Examiners; cert. marriage and family therapist Am. Assn. Marriage and Family Therapists, Conn. Psychiat. clinician psychiatry dept. Waterby (Conn.) Hosp., 1974—80; pvt. practice individual and marriage and family therapy Naugatuck, Conn., 1987—. Clin. cons. Waterby Youth Svcs., Inc., 1988—, Salvation Army Youth Shelter, Waterby, 1995—, Conn. Dept. children and Famlites, 2001—03; clin. neuropsychology examiner Conn. Resource Group, LLC, Waterby, 1988—, Conn. Edn. Svcs., Middletown, 2001—; mental health cons. Danby (Conn.) Head Start, Conn., 1994—97; adj. faculty So. Conn. State U., New Haven, 1992—, Yale U., New Haven, 2002—; full adj. prof., adj. Ctrl. Conn. State U., New Britain, Conn., 1994—; presenter in field; co-facilitater G.R.A.S.P. parent advocacy and support group. Weeblos Cub Scout leader Boy Scouts Am. Pack 110, Naugatuck, 1989—98; troop com. mem. Boy Scouts Am. Troop 109, Naugatuck, 1997—. Mem.: Electroencephalography and Clin. Neurosci. Soc., Conn. Assn. Marriage and Family Therapy (chair state election com. 2002), Phi Kappa Phi. Democrat. Roman Catholic. Achievements include research in negative neurophysiological effects of stress on children and teens delaying development of executive brain functions; neurofeed back training for brain disorders. Avocations: camping, canoeing, fishing, woodworking, music. Home: 23 May St Naugatuck CT 06770 Office: 16 Orchard St Naugatuck CT 06770 Office Phone: 203-729-2565.

SUSKIN, HOWARD STEVEN, lawyer; b. Chgo., Aug. 9, 1959; BA, Northwestern U., 1980; JD, U. Mich., 1983. Bar: Ill. 1983, U.S. Dist. Ct. (no. dist.) Ill. 1983, U.S. Ct. Appeals (7th cir.) 1984, U.S. Ct. Appeals (6th cir.) 1987, U.S. Ct. Appeals (4th cir.) 1987; arbitrator Am. Arbitration Assn. Mem. staff Office Gen. Counsel, HEW, Chgo, 1978-80; mem. staff Ill. Atty. Gen. Office, Chgo, 1981; assoc. Jenner & Block, Chgo., 1983-90, ptnr., 1991—. Arbitrator Chgo Bd. Options Exch., Cir. Ct. Cook County. Editor Mich. Law Rev., 1982-83; co-author Illinois Civil Litigation Guide, 1998, 2000. Mem. ABA (arbitrator), Nat. Assn. Securities Dealers, Nat. Futures Assn., N.Y. Stock Exch., Chgo. Bar Assn. (chmn., legis. liaison mem. securities law com. 1997-98, vice chmn. class action com. 2004—), Phi Beta Kappa. Office: Jenner & Block 1 E IBM Plz Fl 4000 Chicago IL 60611-7603 Office Phone: 312-222-9350. E-mail: hsuskin@jenner.com.

SUSKIND, DENNIS A. investment banker; b. Staten Island, N.Y., Dec. 13, 1942; s. Morris and Ida (Levine) S.; m. Cynthia Ann Leverenz, Sept. 14, 1968; children— Brian, John Paul, Pamela Claire, Audrey Elizabeth. Student, Pace Coll., N.Y.C. Vice pres. J. Aron & Co., N.Y.C., 1962-81; ptnr. Goldman Sachs & Co., N.Y.C., 1981—, ltd. ptnr., 1990—. Bd. dirs. Merc. Exchange, 1972-80, Gold Inst., Washington, 1980-90; bd. dirs. Commodity Exchange, Inc., N.Y.C., 1980-87, 1st vice chmn., 1989-91; lectr. Fin. Times Conf., 1983, 84, 86-90. Bd. dirs. East End chpt. Nature Conservancy, Arthur Ashe Inst. for Urban Health, pres.; trustee Collegiate Sch., N.Y.C., Marymount Sch., N.Y.C. Mem. AIME, Silver Inst., Futures Industry Assn., Southampton Golf Club, Atlantic Golf Club (Bridgehampton, N.Y.). Home: 136 E 79th St New York NY 10021-0328 Office: Goldman Sachs & Co 85 Broad St New York NY 10004-2456

SUSKIND, RONALD STEVEN, journalist; b. Kingston, N.Y., Nov. 20, 1959; s. Walter Burton and Shirley Lila (Berman) Suskind; m. Cornelia Kennedy, May 4, 1986; children: Walter Kennedy, Harry Owen. BA in Govt. and Fgn. Affairs, U. Va., 1981; MS in Journalism, Columbia U., 1983. No. Va. field coord. Charles Robb for Gov., Alexandria, Va., 1981; campaign mgr. John Downey for U.S. Senate, New Haven, 1982; news asst., interim reporter The New York Times, 1983—85; city/state reporter The St. Petersburg (Fla.) Times, 1985—86; sr. editor Boston Bus. Mag., 1987—88, editor, 1988—90; staff reporter The Wall St. Jour., Boston, 1990—93, sr. nat. affairs writer Washington, 1993—2000, now project reporter; contr. N.Y. Times Mag., Esquire Mag. Instr. advanced journalism Harvard U., Cambridge, Mass., 1987—93; cons. Big Ideas, Inc., Boston, 1988—90; commentator Sta. WBUR, Boston, 1989—93. Author: (novels) A Hope in the Unseen, 1998, The Price of Loyalty, 2004. Recipient Pulitzer Prize for feature writing, 1995, Benjamin Fine award, Nat. Assn. Secondary Sch. Prins., 1995, Nat. Writing award, Ball State U., 1995.*

SUSKIND, SIGMUND RICHARD, microbiology educator; b. N.Y.C., June 19, 1926; s. Seymour and Nina Phillips S.; m. Ann Parker, July 1, 1951; children: Richard, Mark, Steven. AB, NYU, 1948; PhD, Yale U., 1954. Research asst. biology div. Oak Ridge Nat. Lab., 1948-50; USPHS fellow NYU Med. Sch., N.Y.C., 1954-56; mem. faculty Johns Hopkins U., Balt., 1956—, prof. biology, 1965-96, univ. prof., 1983-96, prof. emeritus, 1996—, Univ. ombudsman, 1988-91, dean grad. and undergrad. studies, 1971-78, dean Sch. Arts and Scis., 1978-83. Head molecular biology sect. NSF, 1970-71; cons. NIH, 1966-70, Coun. Grad. Schs., Mid States Assn. Colls. and Secondary Schs., 1973—, NSF, 1986; vis. scientist Weizmann Inst. of Sci., Israel, 1985; trustee Balt. Hebrew U., 1985-93; mem. adv. bd. La. Geriatric Ctr., 1990—. Author: (with P.E. Hartman) Gene Action, 1964, 69, (with P.E. Hartman and T. Wright) Principles of Genetics Laboratory Manual, 1965; editor: (with P.E. Hartman) Foundations of Modern Genetics series, 1964, 69; mem. sci. editorial bd. Johns Hopkins U. Press, 1973-76, 88-91. With USNR, 1944-46. NIH grantee, 1957-76 Fellow AAAS; mem. Am. Soc. Microbiology, Genetics Soc. Am., Am. Assn. Immunology, Am. Soc. Biol. Chemistry and Molecular Biology, Coun. Grad Schs., Assn. Grad. Schs., Northeastern Assn. Grad. Schs. (exec. com. 1975-76, pres. 1977-78). Avocation: research in microbial biochemical genetics and immunogenetics. Office: Johns Hopkins U Dept Biology and McCollum-Pratt Inst 34th and Charles Sts Baltimore MD 21218 Business E-Mail: sigr@dmv.com.

SUSLA, JEFFREY JONATHAN, English language educator; b. Bridgeport, Conn., Oct. 30, 1958; s. Nicholas Jonathan and Betty Irene (Stavnitzky) S.; m. Patricia Anne Plumb, June 25, 1995. BA in English and History, Wesleyan U., 1982, MALS, Dartmouth Coll., 1991. English tchr. U.S Peace Corps, Illassit, Kenya, 1988-89, Woodstock (Conn.) Acad., 1993—2000, Tolland H.S., 2001—. Mem. supt. search com. Town of Woodstock, 1995; co-advisor Woodstock Acad. Student Coun., 1995—2000; dir. Woodstock Acad. Theatre, 1994, 1996. Fellowship Conn. Writing Project U. Conn., 1994, Nat. Endowment for the Humanities, 1996, Fulbright Meml. Fund., Japan, 1997, Tchg. Excellence award, Kazakhstan, 1998; named Educator of Yr. 21st Century Newspaper, 1996. Avocations: reading, travel. Home: PO Box 27 140 Calkins Rd Woodstock CT 06281-0027 E-mail: jsusla@snet.net.

SUSLICK, KENNETH SANDERS, chemistry professor; b. Chgo., Sept. 16, 1952; s. Alvin and Edith Suslick. BS with honors, Calif. Inst. Tech., 1974; PhD, Stanford U., 1978. Rsch., teaching asst. Stanford (Calif.) U., 1974-78; chemist Lawrence Livermore (Calif.) Lab., 1974-75; asst. prof. U. Ill., Urbana, 1978-84, assoc. prof., 1984-88, prof. of chemistry, 1988—; prof. Beckman Inst. for Advanced Sci. and Tech., Urbana, 1989-92; prof. materials sci. and engring. U. Ill., Urbana, 1993—, William H. and Janet Lycan prof. chemistry, 1997—2004, Marvin Schmidt prof. chemistry, 2004—; founder ChemSensing, Inc., 2001—. Vis. fellow Balliol Coll., Inorganic Chemistry Lab., Oxford (Eng.) U., 1986; cons. in field. Editor: High Energy Processes in Organometallic Chemistry, 1987, Ultrasound: Its Chemical, Physical and Biological Effects, 1988, Comprehensive Supramolecular Chemistry, vol. 5, 1996; co-editor: Sonochemistry and Sonoluminescence, 1999; editl. bd. Ultrasonics, 1992-96, Ultrasonic Sonochemistry, 1996—; patentee isotope separation by photochromatography, protein microspheres, drug delivery, blood substitutes, smell-seeing, artificial olfaction; contbr. articles to profl. jours. Fellow DuPont Found., 1979-80, Sloan Found., 1985-87; A.C. Sr. Cope scholar, 2004; recipient Rsch. Career Devel. award NIH, 1985-90, NSF Spl. Creativity award 1992-94, Material Rsch. Soc. medal, 1994. Fellow AAAS, Am. Acoustical Soc. Royal Soc. Arts, Mfrs. and Commerce (Silver medal 1974); mem. Am. Chem. Soc. (chmn. sect. 1987-89, Nobel Laureate Signature award 1994, Sr. Cope Scholar award 2004). Avocations: sculpting, folk music. Office: U Ill Dept Chemistry 600 S Mathews Ave Urbana IL 61801-3602 E-mail: ksuslick@uiuc.edu.

SUSMAN, LOUIS, investment banker; b. St. Louis, Nov. 19, 1937; m. Marjorie Susman; 2 children. Grad., U. Mich., 1959, Washington U., 1962. Sr. ptnr. Thompson & Mitchell Law Firm, St. Louis; with Salomon Bros. (now Citigroup), 1989—, chmn. N.Am. customer com. Citibank's global relationship bank and Solomon Smith Barney's investment bank, 2000—; vice chmn. global corp. and investment bank Citigroup, 2000—. Mem. adv. dir. D&K Healthcare Resources, Inc., 1998—. Mem. Dem. Nat. Com., 1972—82; nat. fin. chmn. John Kerry for Pres., 2003—04; co-chmn. fin. com. Bill Bradley for Pres., 1999—2000; Mo. fin. chmn. Richard Gephardt for Pres., 1998, past dir. Cardinals Baseball. Office: Salomon Smith Barney Citigroup Inc 233 E Wacker Dr Chicago IL 60601*

SUSMAN, MILLARD, geneticist, educator; b. St. Louis, Sept. 1, 1934; s. Albert and Patsy Ruth S.; m. Barbara Beth Fretwell, Aug. 18, 1957; children: Michael K., David L. AB, Washington U., St. Louis, 1956; PhD, Calif. Inst. Tech., 1962. With microbial genetics research unit Hammersmith Hosp., London, 1961-62; asst. prof. genetics U. Wis., Madison, 1962-66, assoc. prof., 1966-72, prof., 1972—2002, prof. emeritus, 2002—, chmn. lab. genetics, 1971-75, 77-86, assoc. dean med. sch., 1986-95, acting dean Sch. Allied Health Professions, 1988-90, vice dean med. sch., 1994-95, spl. advisor to the dean med. sch., 1995; dir. Ctr. for Biology Edn., Madison, 1996—2002. Phage course instr., Cold Spring Harbor, N.Y., 1965; v.p. scis., Wis. Acad. Scis., Arts and Letters, 2000—. Co-author: Life on Earth, 2d edit., 1978, Human Chromosomes: Structure, Behavior, Effects, 3d edit., 1992; contbr. articles to sci. jours. Mem Genetics Soc. Am., AAAS, Sigma Xi, Phi Beta Kappa, Phi Eta Sigma, Omicron Delta Kapp. Home: 2707 Colgate Rd Madison WI 53705-2234 Office: 507 Genetics Blvd Madison WI 53706 Office Phone: 608-263-5075. E mail: msusman@wisc.edu.

SUSMAN, MORTON LEE, lawyer; b. Aug. 6, 1934; m. Nina Meyers, May 1, 1958; 1 child, Mark Lee. BBA, So. Meth. U., 1956, JD, 1958. Bar: Tex. 1958, U.S. Dist. Ct. (so. dist.) Tex. 1961, U.S. Ct. Appeals (5th cir.) 1961, U.S. Supreme Ct. 1961, U.S. Ct. Appeals (11th cir) 1981, D.C. 1988, U.S. Ct. Appeals (D.C. cir.) 1988, N.Y. 1990, Colo. 1996. Asst. U.S. atty., Houston, 1961-64; 1st asst. U.S. atty., 1965-66; U.S. atty., 1966-69; ptnr. Weil, Gotshal & Manges and predecessor firm Susman & Kessler, Houston, 1969-97; ret., 1998. Lt. USNR, 1958-61. Fellow Am. Coll. Trial Lawyers, Tex. Bar Found.; mem. ABA, FBA (dir., Younger Fed. Lawyer award 1968), Tex. Bar Assn. Democrat. Home: 1000 Uptown Park Blvd Ste 151 Houston TX 77056-3247

SUSMAN, SALLY, cosmetics executive; Student, London Sch. Econs.; BA, Conn. Coll. Legis. asst. U.S. Senate Com. Commerce, Sci. and Transp.; dep. asst. sec. legis. & intergovernmental affairs U.S. Dept. Commerce; pub. rels. Am. Express, 1995—97; sr. v.p. global comm. Estée Lauder Cos. Inc., N.Y.C., 2000—. Commr. N.Y.C. Commn. Women's Issues; bd. dirs. Nat. Partnership Women and Families, Parsons Sch. Design, Gina Gibney Dance; trustee Conn. Coll. Mem.: Arthur W. Page Soc. Office: Estée Lauder Co Inc 767 5th Ave New York NY 10153

SUSMAN, STEPHEN DAILY, lawyer; b. Houston, Jan. 20, 1941; m. Ellen Spencer, 1999; children: Stacy, Harry. BA magna cum laude, Yale U., 1962; LL.B. with highest honors, U. Tex., 1965. Bar: U.S. Supreme Ct. 1970, Tex. 1965, D.C. 1999, N.Y. 2000, Colo. 2002. Law clk. U.S. Ct. Appeals (5th cir.), New Orleans, 1965-66, U.S.Supreme Ct., Washington, 1966-67; ptnr. Fulbright & Jaworski, 1966-75; spl. counsel to atty. gen. Austin, Tex., 1975, Mandell & Wright, 1975-80; sr. ptnr. Susman Godfrey, Houston, 1980—. Vis. prof. law U. Tex., Austin, 1975; chmn. adv. com. on discovery Tex. Supreme Ct. Contbr. articles to profl. jours. Bd. dirs. Contemporary Arts Mus., 1988-94, 1998-2004, Yale Art Gallery, 1998—, Yale Devel. Fund, Southwest Legal Found., Inns of Ct., Houston Grand Opera, 1998—, Phoenix House, 1998-2001, Lawyers Com. for Civil Rights, 1997-, Human Rights First, 1998—, ADL, 1999-; mem. U.S. Holocaust Meml. Coun., 2000-2002 (devel. comm.), Million Dollar Advocates Forum, (life), 2000—, others. Recipient ADL Jurisprudence award, 1995; named one of Best Trial Lawyers in Am., Nat. Law Jour., 1989; named Best Litigator in World, Comml. Litigation, Go To Lawyer for Plaintiff's Comml. Litigation, Tex. Lawyer, 2002. Mem. ABA (antitrust sect., mem. coun. litigation sect., chmn. task force on fast track litigation), Houston Bar Assn., Dallas Bar Assn., D.C. Bar Assn., N.Y. Bar Assn., State Bar Tex., Am. Law Inst., Assn. Trial Lawyers Am., Am. Bar Trial Advocates, Houston Bar Assn., Southwestern Legal Found. Rsch. Fellows, Yale Club (Houston, N.Y.C.), Houston Trial Lawyers Assn. (dir.), Tex. Assn. Civil Trial and Appellate Specialists (former pres., dir.), Houston Club, Houstonian Club, Petroleum Club (Dallas), Quinnipiac Club (New Haven), Order of the Coif, Friars, Phi Delta Ph). Avocations: jogging, hiking. Office: Ste 5100 1000 Louisiana St Houston TX 77002-5096 Office Phone: 713-653-7801. Business E-Mail: ssusman@susmangodfrey.com.

SUSSBERG, MILTON JOEL, marketing professional; b. New Rochelle, N.Y., Oct. 5, 1949; s. Darwin Ralph and Carol G Sussberg; m. Linda Aland, June 27, 1971; children: Matthew H, Jordan A. BBA with distinction, U. Wis., Madison, 1971; MBA, Columbia U., 1973. Car. mktg. & sales Pearl-Wick Corp., Long Island City, N.Y., 1973-76; v.p. M. Ware Assocs., N.Y.C., 1976-79, Meteor/SKelly, Inc., Stamford, Conn., 1979-84; pres. Robot-Coupe Internat., Norwalk, Conn., 1984-86; CEO, founder Sussberg & Co., Inc., White Plains, N.Y., 1986—; owner Savannah (Ga.) Sand Gnats Baseball Club, 1991—; pres. Pearl-Wick LLC, Wallingford, Conn., 2000—. Adj. prof. mktg. Fordham U., Bronx, NY, 1996—99; mem. adv. coun. Thermoscan, San Diego, 1991—95, Sonicare, Seattle, 1996—98. Mem.: Trump Nat. Golf Club, Phi Kappa Phi. Avocations: golf, skiing. Office: Sussberg & Co Inc Ste 308W 701 Westchester Ave White Plains NY 10604

SUSSE, SANDRA SLONE, lawyer; b. Medford, Ma., June 1, 1943; d. James Robert and Georgie Coffin (Bradshaw) Slone; m. Peter Susse, May 10, 1969 (div. May 1993); 1 child, Toby. BA, U. Mass., 1981; JD, Vt. Law Sch., 1986. Bar: Mass. 1986, U.S. Dist. Ct. Mass. 1988, U.S. Ct. Appeals (1st cir.) 1995. Staff atty. Western Mass. Legal Svcs., Springfield, 1986—. Mem. ABA, Women's Bar Assn. Mass. Avocations: hiking, german literature, films, skating. Address: Western Mass Legal Serv 127 State St Fl 4 Springfield MA 01103-1905 Office Phone: 413-781-7814. E-mail: ssusse@wmls.org.

SUSSER, EZRA SAUL, psychiatry educator; b. Johannesburg, July 13, 1952; came to U.S., 1965; s. Mervyn Wilfred and Zena Athene (Stein) S.; m. Sarah Conover, July 3, 1983; children: Leah, Eli. BA in Econs., Columbia Coll., 1974; postgrad., Columbia U., 1977, MD, M.P.H. Med. Public Health, 1982, Dr.P.H. Psychiatric Epidemiology, 1992. Intern, resident in psychiatry Albert Einstein Sch. Medicine, Bronx, N.Y., 1982-87; asst. prof. dept. psychiatry Nathan Kline Inst. for Psychiat. Rsch. NYU, Orangeburg, 1987—. Presenter in field; initiator internat. study schizophrenia WHO, 1989—; cons. Policy Rsch. Assoc., 1988—, Franklin Ave. Mens' Shelter Mental Health Program, Bronx, 1985-89, other mental health programs for homeless, 1985—. Assoc. editor: Community Psychiatrist, 1987-90; contbr. numerous articles to profl. jours. Vol. social worker Native Am. Health Ctr., San Francisco, 1974, lic. vocat. nurse, 1975; health com. Coalition for Homeless, N.Y.C., 1984-88. NIMH fellow, 1984-86, Mead Johnson fellow, 1985; recipient award Nat. Alliance for Rsch. on Schizophrenia and Depression, 1987. Mem. Am. Psychiat. Assn. (com. on chronically mentally ill), Am. Assn. Community Psychiatrists (exec. bd. 1987—, assoc. editor newsletter 1987-90). Avocation: playing and coaching soccer. Address: HIV Ctr Columbia U NY State Psych Inst 722 W 168th St New York NY 10032-2603

SUSSER, MERVYN WILFRED, epidemiologist, educator; b. Johannesburg, Sept. 26, 1921; came to U.S., 1965; s. Solomon and Ida Rose (Son) S.; m. Zena Athene Stein, Mar. 28, 1949; children: Ida, Ezra, Ruth. MB, BChir, U. Witwatersrand, Union of South Africa, 1950; diploma pub. health, London Conjoint Bd., 1960; DMS (hon.), U. Witwatersrand, 1993. Med. officer, then supt. Alexandra Health Centre and Univ. Clinic, Johannesburg, 1952-55; successively lectr., sr. lectr., reader, head dept. social and preventive medicine Manchester (Eng.) U., 1957-65; also med. officer div. mental health Salford, Eng.; prof., chmn. div. epidemiology Sch. Pub. Health, Columbia U., N.Y.C., 1966-78, Gertrude H. Sergievsky prof. epidemiology, dir. Sergievsky Ctr., 1977-91; Sergievsky prof. emeritus, spl. lectr., 1992—. Hon. prof. Nat. Sch. Pub. Health, Madrid; cons. WHO, 1962, 66-72, 79, 90, NIH, NAS. Author: (with W. Watson) Sociology in Medicine, 1962, 2d edit., 1971, (with W. Watson and K. Hopper), 3d edit., 1985, Community Psychiatry: Epidemiologic and Social Themes, 1968, Causal Thinking in the Health Sciences: Concepts and Strategies of Epidemiology, 1973, (with others) Famine and Human Development: Studies of the Dutch Hungerwinter 1944-45, 1975, (with D. Rush and Z. Stein) Diet in Pregnancy: A Randomized Controlled Trial of Nutritional Supplements, 1980, Epidemiology, Health and Society: Selected Essays, 1987, (with Jennie Kline and Zena Stein) Conception to Birth: Epidemiology of Prenatal Development, 1989; editor Am. Jour. Pub. Health, 1992-98; festschrift in his honor. Pres. Com. Health in So. Africa, 1984-94. With South African Defence Force, 1940-45. Recipient Disting. Svc. award, Coll. Physicians and Surgeons, Columbia U., 1994, Jubilee medal, U. Witwatersrand, South Africa, Abraham Lilienfeld award, 1999; Belding scholar, Assn. Aid Crippled Children, 1965—66, Guggenheim fellow, 1972. Fellow: APHA (John Snow award 1994), N.Y. Acad. Medicine, Am. Epidemiol. Soc., Royal Coll. Physicians (Edinburgh), Faculty of Pub. Health Medicine of Royal Coll. Physicians U.K. (hon.), Am. Coll. Epidemiology (hon.); mem.: Physicians for Human Rights, Inst. Medicine (sr.), Soc. Pediat. Epidemiol. Rsch., Soc. Social Medicine U.K. (hon.), Soc. Epidemiol. Rsch., World Psychiat. Assn., Internat. Epidemiol. Assn. Home: 100 Pinecrest Dr Hastings On Hudson NY 10706-3702 Office: Sergievsky Ctr and Columbia U Sch Pub Health 630 W 168th St New York NY 10032-3795

SUSSKIND, EMILY H. broadcast executive; BA in Philosophy and Math., Wellesley Coll.; MBA in Fin., Wharton Sch., U. of Pa. With Salomon Brothers, Inc., 1985—96, dir.; sr. v.p., sys. devel. TELE-TV Systems, L.P., 1996—97; sr. v.p., tech. Dow Jones Markets, N.Y.C., 1997—98; sr. v.p., interactive services Sony Corp. of Am., N.Y.C., 1998—2000, pres., broadband services, 2000, exec. v.p., 2001—. Office: Sony Corp of Am 550 Madison Ave New York NY 10022

SUSSKIND, HERBERT, biomedical engineer, educator; b. Ratibor, Germany, Mar. 23, 1929; came to U.S., 1938; s. Alex and Hertha (Loewy) S.; m. E. Suzanne Lieberman, June 18, 1961; children: Helen J., Alex M., David A. BChE cum laude, CCNY, 1950; MChE, NYU, 1961. Engr., sect. supr. Brookhaven Nat. Lab., Upton, N.Y., 1950-77, biomed. engr., 1977-94, asst. to chmn. med. dept., 1989-94, rsch. collaborator, 1994—; assoc. prof. medicine SUNY, Stony Brook, 1979—. Co-inventor 3 patents in field. Co-founder, 1st pres. Huntington Twp. Jewish Forum, Huntington, N.Y., 1970-73; trustee Huntington Hebrew Congregation, 1970-78. Mem. Biomed. Engring. Soc., Soc. Nuclear Medicine, Am. Thoracic Soc., Am. Nuclear Soc. (exec. com., treas. L.I. Sect., 1978-83), Am. Inst. Chem. Engrs., CCNY Alumni Assn. (pres. 1982-84), CCNY Engring. & Architecture Alumni Assn., N.Y.C. (pres. 1963-65). Office: Brookhaven Nat Lab Box 5000 Bldg 490 Upton NY 11973-5000

SUSSKIND, LAWRENCE ELLIOTT, urban and environmental planner, educator, public dispute mediator; b. N.Y.C., Jan. 12, 1947; s. David J. and Marjorie H. (Friedman) S.; m. Miriam Mason, June 8, 1968 (div. Dec. 1982); m. Leslie Webster Tuttle, Dec. 12, 1982; children: Noah Gates, Lily Webster. AB in Sociology, Columbia U., 1968; M.C.P., MIT, 1970, PhD in Urban Planning, 1973. Asst. prof. urban and environ. planning MIT, Cambridge, 1971-74, assoc. prof., 1974-82, prof., 1982-95, Ford prof., 1995—, head dept., 1978-82, dir. MIT-Harvard Pub. Disputes Program, 1980—; exec. dir. program on negotiation Harvard Law Sch., 1984-87, visiting prof. law, 2001—. Pres. Consensus Bldg. Inst., 1993—. Author: Paternalism, Conflict and Co-Production, 1983, Proposition 1 1/2; Its Impact on Massachusetts, 1983, Resolving Environmental Regulatory Disputes, 1983, Breaking the Impasse, 1987, Environmental Diplomacy, 1994, Reinventing Congress for the 21st Century, 1995, Dealing With an Angry Public, 1996, Consensus Building Handbook, 1999, Negotiating on Behalf of Others, 1999, Negotiating Environmental Agreements, 1999, Better Environmental Policy Studies, 2001, Transboundary Environmental Negotiation, 2002; sr. editor, founder Environ. Impact Assessment Rev., 1980-96; editl. policy bd. Negotiation Jour., 1984—. Mem. Am. Inst. Cert. Planners, Assn. for Conflict Resolution. Jewish. Home: 32 Jericho Hill Rd Southborough MA 01772-1007 Office: MIT 9-330 Cambridge MA 02139 Office Phone: 617-492-1414. Business E-Mail: susskind@mit.edu.

SUSSMAN, ALEXANDER RALPH, lawyer; b. Bronx, N.Y., Sept. 24, 1946; s. Herman R. and Claire (Blumenson) S.; m. Edna Rubin, Mar. 24, 1973; children: Jason, Carl, Matthew, Eric. AB cum laude, Princeton U., 1968; JD, Yale U., 1972. Bar: N.Y. 1973, U.S. Dist. Ct. (so. and ea. dists) N.Y. 1974, U.S. Ct. Appeals (1st, 2d, 3d, 5th, 6th, 8th, 10th, and 11th cirs.) 1983, U.S. Supreme Ct. Law clk. to Hon. Constance Baker Motley U.S. Dist. Ct., N.Y.C., 1972-73; assoc. Cravath, Swaine & Moore, N.Y.C., 1974-76, Fried, Frank, Harris, Shriver & Jacobson, N.Y.C., 1977-79, ptnr., 1979—. Author: (with A. Fleischer, Jr.) Responses to Takeover Bids, 2004, Takeover Defense, 2 vols., 2004; editor Yale Law Jour., 1971-72. Bd. dirs. N.Y. Lawyers for Pub. Interest, 1983—; bd. dirs., mem. exec. com. Legal Aid Soc., 1987-93. Fulbright scholar U. Bordeaux, 1969. Mem. ABA, Am. Law Inst., N.Y. State Bar Assn., Assn. of Bar of City of N.Y. (fed. cts. com. 1984-87, jud. com. 1987-90, chmn. legal assistance com. 1988-91, Marden lectr. com. 1991-94, chmn. mergers and acquisitions com. 1995-99). Home: 20 Oak Ln Scarsdale NY 10583-1627 Office: Fried Frank Harris Shriver & Jacobson 1 New York Plz Fl 25 New York NY 10004-1980 E-mail: Alex.Sussman@ffhsj.com.

SUSSMAN, ARTHUR MELVIN, law educator, foundation administrator; b. Bklyn., Nov. 17, 1942; m. Rita Padnick; children: Eric, Johanna. BS, Cornell U., 1963; JD magna cum laude, Harvard U., 1966. Bar: N.Y. 1967, Ill. 1970. Assoc. atty. Cahill, Gordon, Reindel & Ohl, N.Y.C., 1966-67; from assoc. atty. to ptnr. Jenner & Block, Chgo., 1970-77; legal counsel So. Ill. U., Carbondale, 1977-79; gen. counsel, v.p. U. Chgo., 1979-84, gen. counsel, v.p. adminstrn., Arsonne Nat. Lab., 1984-2001, lectr. law Grad. Sch. Bus., 1986-94, bd. dirs. Lab. Schs., 1985-01; law school lecturer, 1998—; v.p. & sec. John D and Catherine T MacArthur Found., 2001—. Chmn., bd. dirs. Ency. Brit., Inc., 1995-96; presenter in field. Contr. articles to profl. jours. Mem. Ill. Sec. of State's Com. on Not-for-Profit Corp. Act, 1984-85; chair regional selection panel Harry S. Truman Scholarship Found.; bd. dirs. Chapin Hall for Children, 1996—. Capt. JAGC, U.S. Army, 1967-70. Fulbright fellow, London, 1987. Mem. Nat. Assn. Coll. and Univ. Attys., Am. Coun. Edn. Office: The MacArthur Foundation 140 S Dearborn St Chicago IL 60603 Office Phone: 312-516-1529. E-mail: asussman@macfound.org.

SUSSMAN, BARRY, author, public opinion analyst and pollster, journalist; b. N.Y.C., July 10, 1934; s. Samuel and Esther (Rosen) S.; m. Peggy Earhart, Jan. 20, 1962; children: Seena, Shari. BA, Bklyn. Coll., 1956. Reporter Herald Courier, Bristol, Va., 1960-62, mng. editor, 1962-65; editor Washington Post, 1965-69, city editor, 1970-73, spl. Watergate editor, 1972-74, pollster, pub. opinion analyst, 1975-87; co-founder, co-dir. Washington Post-ABC News poll, 1981-87; columnist Washington Post Nat. Weekly, 1983-87; mng. editor nat. affairs UPI, Washington, 1987; ind. pub. opinion analyst and pollster, 1988—. Adv. bd. Innovation news media cons. group, 1994—; editor Watchdog Project of the Nieman Found. for Journalism at Harvard U., 2003—. Author: The Great Coverup: Nixon and the Scandal of Watergate, 1974, What Americans Really Think, 1988, (with Lowell P. Weicker, Jr.) Maverick, 1995; editor: (with J.A. Giner) Innovations in Newspapers: The 1999 Global Report, 1999, The 2000 Global Report, 2000, The 2001 Global Report, 2001, 02, 03, 04. Recipient Drew Pearson award for Nat. Reporting, 1972, 1st Prize award Washington Newspaper Guild, 1973, Editor of Yr. award Washington Newspaper Guild, 1973. Mem. Am. Assn. for Pub. Opinion Rsch. (exec. coun. 1985-87). Jewish. Avocation: chess. Personal E-mail: bsussman@his.com. Business E-Mail: bsussman@niemanwatchdog.org.

SUSSMAN, DEBORAH EVELYN, designer, company executive; b. N.Y.C., May 26, 1931; d. Irving and Ruth (Golomb) S.; m. Paul Prejza, June 28, 1972. Student, Bard Coll., 1948-50, DHL (hon.), 1998; student, Inst. Design, Chgo., 1950-53, Black Mountain Coll., 1950, Hochschule für Gestaltung Ulm, Germany, 1957-58. Art dir. Office of Charles and Ray Eames, Venice, Calif., 1953-57, 61-67; graphic designer Galeries Lafayette, Paris, 1959-60; prin. Deborah Sussman and Co., Santa Monica, Calif., 1968-80; founder, pres. Sussman-Prejza and Co., Inc., Santa Monica, Calif., 1980-90, Culver City, Calif., 1990—. Spkr., lectr. UCLA Sch. Arch., Archtl. League N.Y.C., Smithsonian Inst., Stanford Conf. on Design, Am. Inst. Graphic Arts Nat. Conf. at MIT, Design Mgmt. Inst. Conf., Mass.; spl. guest Internat. Design Conf., Aspen, Colo.; Fulbright lectr., India, 1976; spkr. NEA Adv. Coun., 1985, Internat. Coun. Shopping Ctrs., 1986, USIA Design in Am. seminar, Budapest, Hungary, 1988. One-woman shows include Visual Arts Mus. Sch. Visual Arts, N.Y.C., 1995; participant exhbn., Moscow, 1989, Walker Art Ctr., Mpls., 1989; mem. editl. adv. bd. Arts and Arch. Mag., 1981-85, Calif. Mag., Arch. Calif. Fulbright grantee Hochschule für Gestaltung Ulm, 1957-58; recipient numerous awards AIA Nat. Inst. Honors, 1985, 88, Am. Inst. Graphic Arts, Calif. Coun. AIA (hon. mem., 1988), Comms. Arts Soc., L.A. County Bd. Suprs., Vesta award Women's Bldg. L.A. Fellow Soc. Environ. Graphic Design; mem. AIA (hon., Medal for XXIII Olympiad 2004), Am. Inst. Graphic Arts (bd. dirs. 1982-85, founder L.A. chpt., chmn. 1983-84, numerous awards including Legacy medal 2004), Am. Ctr. Design (hon.), L.A. Art Dirs. Club (bd. dirs., numerous awards), Alliance Graphique Internat. (elect. mem.), Archs., Designers, and Planners Social Responsibility, Calif. Women in Environ. Design (adv. d.), Trusteeship (affiliate Internat. Women's Forum, chmn.'s cir. Town Hall). Democrat. Jewish. Avocation: photography. Office: Sussman/Prejza & Co Inc 3525 Eastham Dr Culver City CA 90232 Office Phone: 310-836-3939. E-mail: dsussman@sussmanprejza.com.

SUSSMAN, GERALD, publishing company executive; b. Balt., Feb. 21, 1934; s. Hyman Jacob and Sylvia (Applebaum) S.; m. Arla Ilene Ellison, Aug. 25, 1963; children: Daniel Leonard, Andrew Louis. BA, U. Md., 1956. Co-founder, prin. Investors Service of Md., Balt., 1956-60; coll. traveller Oxford U. Press, Inc., N.Y.C., 1961-62, coll. sales mgr., 1962-69, gen. advt. mgr., 1970-73, v.p., dir. mktg., 1974-79, sr. v.p., dir. mktg., 1979-83, sr. v.p., dir. adminstrn. and planning, 1983—97; project mgr. Guide to the Sandia Mountains. Mem. Assn. Am. Pubs. (chmn. mktg. com.), Assn. Am. Univ. Presses (chmn. mktg. com. 1980-81), Pubs. Advt. Club, Phi Alpha Theta. Democrat. Jewish. Home: 10424 City Lights Dr NE Albuquerque NM 87111-7536 Office: Oxford U Press Inc 198 Madison Ave Fl 9 New York NY 10016-4341

SUSSMAN, HOWARD SIVIN, lawyer; b. NYC, Feb. 12, 1938; s. Joseph and Dora (Sivin) S. AB cum laude, Princeton U., 1958; LLB, Columbia U., 1962. Bar: N.Y. 1964, U.S. Dist. Ct. (so. and ea. dists.) N.Y. 1967, U.S. Ct. Appeals (2d cir.) 1967, U.S. Tax Ct. 1969, U.S. Dist. Ct. (no. dist.) N.Y. 1970, U.S. Supreme Ct. 1970, U.S. Ct. Appeals (5th cir.) 1982. Assoc. Chadbourne, Parke, Whiteside & Wolff, N.Y.C., 1963-71; asst. U.S. atty. So. Dist. N.Y., 1971-77; assoc. prof. law U. Houston, 1977-82; of counsel Wood, Lucksinger & Epstein, Houston, 1982-83; pvt. practice, N.Y.C., 1983-94; ptnr. Sussman Sollis Ebin Tweedy & Wood, LLP, N.Y.C., 1995—. Instr. continuing legal edn. U. Houston, Nat. Inst. for Trial Advocacy; 1985-89,Stockholm, 2003. Editor Columbia U. Law Rev., 1960-62; contbr. articles to profl. jours. Harlan Fiske Stone scholar, 1959-61, Edvard Cassels Stiftelse vis. scholar, Stockholm, 1962-63; travelling fellow Parker Sch. Fgn. and Comparative Law Columbia U., 1962-63. Mem. Assn. Bar City N.Y. (com. adminstrv. law 1974-76, profl. conf. 1979, com. fed. legis. 1984-87, com. criminal law 1987-90, com. lectr. and continuing edn. 1990-93, com. fgn. and comparative law 1993-96, arbitration com. 2002-2003), Fed. Bar Coun., Swedish Am. C. of C. (dir. N.Y. chpt. 1996—). Clubs: Princeton N.Y. Office Phone: 212-688-7373.

SUSSMAN, JEFFREY BRUCE, public relations and marketing executive; b. N.Y.C., Mar. 15, 1943; m. Suzy Hirschland-Prudden, 1964 (div. 1981); 1 child, Robert; m. Barbara Ramsay, 1984. BA in English, NYU, 1969. Pres. Suzy Prudden Studios, N.Y.C., 1975—81; v.p. Zachary and Front, N.Y.C., 1981—88; pres. Jeffrey Sussman, Inc., N.Y.C., 1988—. Instr. mktg. The New Sch. U., N.Y.C. Author: Creative Fitness for Baby and Child, 1972, Suzy Prudden's Family Fitness Book, 1975, Fit for Life, 1977, See How They Run, 1978, Suzy Prudden's Spot Reducing Program, 1979, Suzy Prudden's Pregnancy and Back-To-Shape Exercise Program, 1980, I Can Exercise Anywhere, 1981, How to Sleep Without Drugs, 1986, Power Promoting: How to Market Your Business to the Top!, 1997; book rev. editor The Manhattan Tribune, 1969-75; contbr. book revs. to N.Y. Times Book Rev., 1974; bi-monthly columnist Weight Watchers Mag., 1977-79; monthly columnist Fortune Small Business, 2000—; contbr. articles to profl. jours. including Bottom Line Bus., Independent Bus., Small Bus. Report, N.Y. Real Estate Jour., East Hampton Star, M World mag. Press sec. N.Y.C. Coun.-Henry Stern, 1981; pvt. sec. to Nobel prize winning author Isaac Bashevis Singer. Avocations: photography, writing, music, painting, drawing. Home and Office: 249 E 48th St New York NY 10017-1526 E-mail: marketingpro@aol.com.

SUSSMAN, LAUREEN GLICKLIN, junior high school educator; b. NYC, Mar. 21, 1953; d. Harry and Ruth (Goldstein) G.; m. Alan Neil Sussman, May 30, 1977; children: David Efrem, Adam Jacob, Daniel Joshua. BA, Bklyn. Coll., 1974; MS, MSc, Hofstra U., 1998. Cert. tchr. nursery-6, spl. edn. tchr. all grades. Sec. McCann-Erickson, Inc., N.Y.C., 1974-75; adminstrv. asst., tour operator EasTours divsn. Fgn. Tours, N.Y.C., 1975-78; adminstrv. asst. Alan N. Sussman, CPA, Woodmere, N.Y., 1978-96; kindergarten tchr. Hebrew Acad. Long Beach (N.Y.), 1996-97; jr. high sch. tchr. Torah Acad. Girls, Far Rockaway, NY, 1997—. Participant Instrumental Enrichment/IRI Skylight, N.Y., 1995, 98, Dynamic Assessment project Touro Coll., N.Y.C., 1996; CSE parent rep., adv. Lawrence (N.Y.) Pub. Schs., 1992-97; trainer Life Tech., Cedarhurst, N.Y., 2004. Contbr. articles to profl. jours. Mem. Spl. Edn. PTA Lawrence Schs., 1986-2003, Sisterhood Congregation Bais Tefilah, 1990-2003; mem. Sisterhood East Meadow Jewish Ctr., chairperson social action, Israel affairs, 1979-81; mem. adv. bd. Kulanu of the South Shore of Nassau County, 2000—; mem. Sisterhood Kehillah Aish Kodesh, Emunah of Am. Mem.: AMIT Women (Masada chpt.), OTSAR (founder Nassau County chpt. 1987—, nat. bd. dirs., pres. Nassau chpt. 1987—2002). Democrat. Avocations: Israeli and simcha dancing, walking, reading, needlepoint. Office: Torah Acad Girls 444 Beach 6 St Far Rockaway NY 11691 Personal E-mail: lauglick@aol.com.

SUSSMAN, LEONARD RICHARD, foundation executive; b. NYC, Nov. 26, 1920; s. Jacob and Carrie (Marks) S.; m. Frances Rukeyser, May 9, 1942 (div. 1958); m. Marianne Rita Gutmann, May 28, 1958; children: Lynne, David William, Mark Jacob. AB, NYU, 1940; MS in Journalism, Columbia U., 1941. Copy editor N.Y. Morning Telegraph, news editor radio sta. WQXR, 1941; cable editor San Juan (P.R.) World Jour., also corr. Business Week mag., 1941-42; editor fgn. broadcast intelligence svc. FCC, 1942; press sec. to Gov. of P.R., 1942-43; dir. info. in N.Y. for Govt. of P.R., 1946-49; regional dir., then nat. exec. dir. Am. Coun. Judaism, 1949-66; cons. pub. affairs cons. Nationwide Ins. Cos. (and indsl. subs.), 1955-57; mem. editorial com. Coun. Liberal Chs., 1956-59; exec. dir. Freedom House, 1967-88, 96, sr. scholar in internat. communications, 1988—; evaluator Fulbright Program Bd. Fgn. Scholarships, 1990-92; exec. dir. Willkie Meml., 1970-88. Adj. prof. journalism and mass comm. NYU, N.Y.C., 1990-99; adj. prof. Sch. for Internat. and Pub. Affairs, Columbia U., 2000-01; organizer, dir. Freedom House/Books USA, 1968-85; editor Freedom at Issue, bimonthly, 1970-81; mem. U.S. Dels. to Conf. World Communicaiton Yr./83, 1982-83; organizer acad. confs.; participant Internat. Conf. on Press Freedom, Venice, Italy, 1976, 77, Cairo, 1978, Talloires, 1981, 83, San Jose, Costa Rica, Johannesburg, and Santiago Chile, 1987, others; panel competition in space Congl. Office Tech. Assessment, 1982-83. Author: American Press-Under Siege?, 1973, Mass News Media and The Third World Challenge, 1977, Glossary for International Communications: Warning of a Bloodless Dialect, 1983, Spanish version, 1987, Power, The Press and the Technology of Freedom: The Coming of Age of ISDN, 1990, The Culture of Freedom: The Small World of Fulbright Scholars, 1992, Good News Bad News, 1994, Can A Free Press Be Responsible? To Whom?, 1995, The Press: Pressed and Oppressed, 1995, The Journalist as Pariah: Press Freedom, 1996, The Global Airscape, 1996, Democracy, Yes; Press Freedom, Maybe, 1997, Press Law Epidemic: Press Freedom, 1997, Global Warning: Press Controls Fuel the Asian Debacle, 1998, The News of the Century, 1999, Censor Dot Gov: The Internet and Press Freedom, 2000, Press Freedom in Our Genes, A Human Need, 2001, How Free? The Web and the Press, 2001, Democracy's Advocate: The Story of Freedom House, 2002, The Press at War: Marksman and Target, 2002, repub. in Freedom and Responsibility Yearbook, 2001-2002, A Global Survey of Media Independence, 2003, A Passion for Freedom: My Encounters with Extraordinary People, 2004, A Passion for Freedom: My Encounters with Extraordinary People, 2004, others; editor: Three Years at the East-West Divide, 1983, Today's American: How Free?, 1986; contbr. sects. to books, articles to profl. jours. and newspapers; project dir.: Big Story-How the American Press and Television Reported and Interpreted the Crisis of Tet-1968 in Vietnam and Washington, 1977; editor: textbook series, also quar. mag. Issues, 1953-66; mem. editl. bd. Polit. Comm. and Persuasion. Trustee Internat. Coun. on Future of Univ., 1973-84; bd. dirs. World Press Freedom Com., 1977—; chmn. Friends of Survey Mag. Charitable Trust, London, 1978-92; mem. U.S. Nat. Commn. for UNESCO, 1979-85, vice chmn., 1983-85; mem. U.S. dels. to internat. conf. on space, African Aid, UNESCO, London Info. Forum; mem. Internat. Freedom of Expression Exch., 1995-2003, mem. coun., 1997-99. 2001-2002. Decorated Legion of Merit; recipient Ann. First Amendment award N.Y. br. Soc. Profl. Journalists, 1988. Mem. Internat. Inst. Comm., Internat. Press Inst., Internat. Assn. Mass Comm. Rsch., Century Club. Home: 215 E 73d St New York NY 10021-3653 Office: 120 Wall St Fl 26 New York NY 10005-3904 E-mail: sussman@freedomhouse.org.

SUSSMAN, MARK RICHARD, lawyer; b. Bklyn., Feb. 4, 1952; s. Vincent E. and Rhoda (Urowsky) S.; m. Lisa Rosner, June 8, 1975; children: Corey, Randi, Samuel. BS in Civil Engring., Tufts U., 1974; JD, U. Pa., 1977. Bar: Pa. 1977, D.C. 1980, Conn. 1981. Trial atty. land and natural resources div. U.S. Dept. Justice, Washington, 1977-81; assoc. Murtha, Cullina, Richter & Pinney, Hartford, Conn., 1981-86, ptnr., 1987—; chmn. environ. dept. Murtha Cullina LLP, Hartford, Conn., 1990—. Gov.'s blue ribbon panel to evaluate environtl. permit programs, 1996. Chmn. conservation commn. Windsor, Conn., 1984-2000; mem. Conn. Hazardous Waste Mgmt. Service Recycling Task Force, 1986, Legis. Task Force on Environ. Permitting, 1992, Conn. State Implementation Plan Revision Adv. Com., 1984—. Mem. ABA (natural resources sect.), Conn. Bar Assn. (chmn. conservation and environ. quality sect. 1984-87, faculty continuing legal edn.), Conn. Bus. and Industry Assn. (steering com. environ. policies coun. 1990-93, 98—) Tau Beta Pi. Home: 62 Timothy Ter Windsor CT 06095-1652 Office: Murtha Cullina LLP City Pl 185 Asylum St Ste 29 Hartford CT 06103-3469 Office Phone: 203-240-6034. *Notable cases include: Mumford Cove Assn. v. Town of Groton, 786 F. 2d 530, 640 F. Supp 392, 647 F. Supp. 671, 1986, represented homeowners assn. in Clean Water Act citizens's suit to force municipality to relocate sewer discharge pipe; City of Shelton v. Commr. of Environ. Protection, 193 Conn. 506, 1984, represented the Conn. Resources Recovery Authority in obtaining and defending permits for a solid waste landfill, Conn. Coastal Fishermen's Assn. v. Remington Arms Co., Inc., 989 F 2d 1302 (2d cir. 1993), represented defendant in Clean Water Act & RCRA citizens suit which found, in part, that lead shot may be considered a hazardous waste subject to remediation under RCRA statutory definition of hazardous waste.*

SUSSMAN, MONICA HILTON, lawyer; b. N.Y.C., Apr. 2, 1952; BA cum laude, Syracuse U., 1973; JD, Hofstra U., 1977. Bar: Va. 1977, D.C. 1978. Legis. coun. N.Y. State Gov's. Office, Washington, 1977-79; spl. asst. to under sec. U.S. Dept. HUD, Washington, 1979-80, br. chief office State Agy. and Bond Fin. programs, 1980-82, office gen. counsel, 1982-83, also bd. dirs., 1988-95, v.p., 1989-93, treas. Nat. Housing Conf., 1990-93, also programs and regulations dep. gen. counsel; ptnr. McDermott, Will & Emery, Washington, Peabody & Brown, Washington, 1996-99, Nixon Peadoby LLP, Washington, 1999—. Pres. Nat. Housing Conf. Mem. D.C. Bar, Va. State Bar. Office: Nixon Peadbody LLP 401 9th St NW Ste 900 Washington DC 20004

SUSSMAN, PETER ALAN, entertainment company executive; b. Toronto, Ont., Can., July 16, 1958; came to U.S., 1992; s. Murray Sussman and Norma Weisfeld; m. Heather Ann Hartt, Sept. 30, 1993; children: Scott Oliver, Jack Elliott. BA, York U., 1979; LLB, Osgoode Hall, 1982. CEO Alliance Atlantis Entertainment Group, 1986—. Exec. prodr.: (TV miniseries) Joan of Arc, 1999 (TV Critics Best Movie or Miniseries, 13 Emmy and 4 Golden Globe nominations and 1 Emmy award), Nuremberg, 2000 (4 Emmy and Golden Globe nominations and 1 Emmy award), Life with Judy Garland: Me and My Shadows, 2001 (TV Critics Best Movie or Miniseries, 13 Emmy and 3 Golden Globe nominations, 5 Emmy awards and 1 Golden Globe award, Broadcast Film Critics Assn. award for Best Picture made for TV), more than 50 other movies and TV series. Mem., Alliance Atlantis Comms. c. (bd. dirs. 1989—). Avocations: sports, the arts. Office: Alliance Atlantis 3d Fl 808 Wilshire Blvd Fl 3D Santa Monica CA 90401-1889 E-mail: peter.sussman@allianceatlantis.com.

SUSSMAN, WENDY RODRIGUEZ, artist, educator; b. N.Y.C., June 3, 1949; BA, Empire State Coll., 1978; MFA, Bklyn. Coll., 1980. Lectr. Touro Coll., N.Y.C., 1985-86, Pratt Inst., Bklyn., 1987-89; asst. prof. U. Calif., Berkeley, 1989-96, assoc. prof., 1996—. One-woman shows include Bowery Gallery, N.Y.C., 1982, 87, John Bergruen Gallery, San Francisco, 1992, D.P. Fong Gallery, San Jose, Calif., 1994, Platt Gallery U. Judaism, L.A., 1995, Jan Baum Gallery, L.A., 1996, The Jewish Mus., San Francisco, 1996; group shows include Bowery Gallery, 1980-88, Munson-Williams-Proctor Inst. Mus. Art, 1982, Reading (Pa.) Pub. Mus. and Art Gallery, 1983, Queens Mus., N.Y.C., 1983, Colby Coll. Mus. Art, Waterville, Maine, 1983, Butler Inst. Am. Art, Youngstown, Ohio, 1983, Bklyn. Coll., 1983, Am. Acad. Inst. Arts and Letters, N.Y.C., 1984, Am. Acad. in Rome, 1987, John Berggruen Gallery, San Francisco, 1992, San Francisco Arts Commn. Gallery, 1992, 94, D.P. Fong Gallery, 1994, Boulder Mus. Art, 1995, Gallery Paule Anglin, San Francisco, 1996, 98, Jan Baum Gallery, L.A., 1996, U. Calif. San Diego Art Gallery, 1997. Rome Prize fellow in painting Am. Acad. in Rome, 1986-87, Visual Arts fellow NEA, 1989, Guggenheim fellow, 1998; Pollock-Krasner grantee Pollock-Krasner Found., 1988; recipient Max and Sophie Adler award Jewish Mus., Judah Magners Mus., 1996. Office: U Calif Berkeley Dept Art Berkeley CA 94720-0001

SUSSMANE, JEFFREY BRETT, pediatrician; BS in Chemistry, U. Miami, 1977; MD, St. Georges U., 1982; MBA, U. Miami, 2000. Pediat. residency Miami (Fla.) Children's Hosp.; pediat. critical care fellowship Children's Hosp., Pittsburgh, Pa.; pediat. pulmonary fellowship Hahnemann, Pa.; pediat. intensivist Miami (Fla.) Children's Hosp., 1988—, dir. ECLS (Extracorporel Life Support), 1988—. Mem. med. bd. Miami Childrens Hosp.; mem. Miami Childrens Hosp.-PHO. V.p. Pres. Com.; bd. dirs. Venetian Island, Miami, Deering Bay Estates, Miami. Grantee, Miami Childrens Hosp. Found., 1995, 1999, 2002. Fellow: SCCM (diplomate), ACCP (diplomate), AAP (diplomate 2000—02); mem.: Fla. Assn. Pediat. CCM (Critical Care Medicine) (pres. 1997—2002). Office: Divsn Critical Care Medicine Miami Childrens Hosp Miami FL 33155

SUSSNA, EDWARD, economist, educator; b. Phila., Nov. 26, 1926; s. Louis and Manya (Prytzycka) S.; m. Sylvia Fishman, Mar. 8, 1953; children: Audrey Francine, Ellen Sondra. BA, Bklyn. Coll., 1950; MA, U. Ill., 1952, PhD, 1954. Instr. U. Ill., 1952-54; asst. prof. Lehigh U., 1956-57; prof. bus. adminstrn. and econs. U. Pitts., 1957—; dir. ctr. for exec. edn. Grad. Sch. Bus. U. Pitts., 1983-89; dir. mgmt. program for execs. Center for Econ. Edn., Grad. Sch. Bus., acad. dir. study program in Hong Kong and Peoples Republic China, spring 1989, 95; inaugural prof. MBA program Bratislava Sch. Econs., Slovakia, 1996. Vis. Fulbright prof. U. Tehran, Iran, adviser, 1972-73; cons. Bur. of Budget, Dept. HEW, Dept. Transp., UN Indsl. Devel. Orgn., Bell

Telephone Co., Alcoa, Westinghouse Corp., NSF, Pitts. Nat. Bank, Japanese Regional Bankers Assn., others; vis. prof. UCLA, 1970, Ecole Superieure des Scis. Economiques et Commerciales, Paris, 1976-77, U. East Asia, Hong Kong and Macau, winter 1986, vis. scholar Internat. Inst. Mgmt., Berlin, spring 1982, summer sch. English tchr. grades 9-12, Butler Area Sch. Dist., 2003, Starfish Edn. Program for Students and Staff, 2003-. Contbr. articles to profl. jours. Served with U.S. Mcht. Marine, 1944-47; Served with AUS, 1954-56. Vis. prof. under Ford Found. fellowship Harvard, 1960-61; guest scholar under Ford Found. fellowship Brookings Instn., Washington, 1962-63 Mem. Am. Econ. Assn., Am. Fin. Assn., Strategic Mgmt. Inst., Beta Gamma Sigma, Omicron Delta. Home: 1538 S Negley Ave Pittsburgh PA 15217-1420 Personal E-mail: sussna@katz.pitt.edu.

SUSSO, ALHAJI PAPA, musician; b. Sotuma Sere, The Gambia, Sept. 29, 1947; came to U.S., 1985; s. Alhaji Bunka and Alhaja Mariama (Sakiliba) S.; children: Sankung, Fatoumata, Karano, Alhassan, Mariama, Binta, Muhammad, Musa, Kinda, Sarjo. BA in Bus. Adminstrn., Cuttington U., Suakoko, Liberia. Agrl. asst. Ministry of Agr., The Gambia; sr. acct. Ministry of Works, The Gambia; liaison officer Gambia Embassy, Sierra Leone, Liberia; mgr. The Bayo Co., Monrovia, Liberia; chief musician Gambia Natl. Troupe, Banjul, The Gambia; dir. Koriya Musa Ctr., Sotuma Sere, U.R.D. Address: 333 E 181st St Apt 3G Bronx NY 10457-2325

SUSTAR, T. DAVID, religious organization administrator; Pres. East Coast Bible Coll., Ch. of God, Charlotte, N.C., 1996-99; evangelism and home missions dir. Western N.C. Ch. of God, Charlotte, 1999—2002. Mem. Ch. Of God. Office: 140 Ashton Ln Anderson SC 29621 E-mail: tdsustar@aol.com.

SUSTENDAL, DIANE, media executive; Student, La. State U. With Times-Picayune, New Orleans, Fairchild Publs., N.Y.C. With N.Y. Times, N.Y.C; freelance writer, editor. Recipient award La. Press Anns., Aldo award Men's Fashion Assn. Am.

SUSTER, ZELJAN, business educator, dean; b. Split, Yugoslavia, Nov. 18, 1958; came to the U.S., 1989; s. Emil and Olga (Jelenkovic) S.; m. Sanja Grubacic, Dec. 3, 1988. BA in Econs. and Fin., U. Belgrade, Yugoslavia, 1981, MA in Econs., 1984, PhD in Econs., 1988. Rsch. assoc. Inst. Econ. Scis., Belgrade, 1983-89; assoc. prof. U. New Haven, West Haven, Conn., 1990—, chair dept. econs. and fin., 1996-97, assoc. dean Sch. Bus., 1997—. Vis. fellow Mellon Found., Yale U., 1990-91; rsch. assoc. U. Ill., Champaign-Urbana, 1995-96; sr. analyst Analytic Resources, Woodbridge, Conn., 1995—; mem. adv. bd. Charter Oak State Coll., Newington, Conn., 1996—. Author: Historical Dictionary of FR of Yugoslavia, 1999; mem. editl. bd. Serbian Studies, 1993—, Dialogue, 1998—, New Serbian Political Thought, 1998—; contbr. articles to profl. jours. Mem. N.Am. Soc. for Serbian Studies (mem. governing bd. 1993—, v.p. 1998—, pres. 1999—), Ea. Econ. Assn., Atlantic Econ. Soc., Multinational Fin. Soc., Internat. Soc. for Intercomm. of New Ideas, Am. Assn. for the Advancement of Slavic Studies, Kiwanis Internat. Avocation: chess. Office: U New Haven Sch Bus 300 Orange Ave West Haven CT 06516-1916

SUTER, ALBERT EDWARD, manufacturing executive; b. East Orange, N.J., Sept. 18, 1935; s. Joseph Vincent and Catherine (Clay) S.; m. Michaela Sams Suter, May 28, 1966; children: Christian C., Bradley J., Allison A. BME, Cornell U., 1957, MBA, 1959. Pres., chief exec. officer L.B. Knight & Assocs., Chgo., 1959-79; v.p. internat. Emerson Electric Co., St. Louis, 1979-80, pres. motor div., 1980-87, group v.p., 1981-83, exec. v.p., 1983-87, vice chmn., 1987; pres., chief operating officer, dir. Firestone Tire & Rubber Co., Akron, Ohio, 1987-88; pres., chief operating officer Whirlpool Corp., Benton Harbor, Mich., from 1988; exec. v.p. Emerson Electric Co., St. Louis, until 1990, pres., COO, 1990-92, sr. vice chmn., COO, 1992-97; CAO, 1999—2001; ret. sr. advisor, COO Emerson Electric Co., St. Louis, 2001. Bd. dirs. Furniture Brands Internat. Bd. dirs. Jr. Achievement Nat. Bd., Colorado Springs, Colo., Jr. Achievement Miss. Valley, St. Louis Sci. Ctr. Bd.; chmn. Torch div. St. Louis chpt. United Way, 1982-86. Mem. Glenview (Ill.) Country Club, St. Louis Club, Old Warson Country Club, Log Cabin Club. Republican. Episcopalian. Office: Emerson Electric Co PO Box 4100 Saint Louis MO 63136-8506

SUTER, KAREN L. former state banking department administrator; b. July 4, 1956; Grad. with honors, Rutgers U., 1978, JD, 1981. Sr. dep. atty. gen., chief sect. for dept. banking and ins. Office of Atty. Gen.; with N.J. Banking & Instns. Dept., Trenton, 1988—2000, commr., 2000—01. Office: NJ Banking & Instns Dept PO Box 325 20 W State St Trenton NJ 08625-0040

SUTERA, SALVATORE PHILIP, mechanical engineer, educator; b. Balt., Jan. 12, 1933; s. Philip and Ann (D'Amico) S.; m. Celia Ann Fielden, June 21, 1958; children: Marie-Anne, Annette Nicole, Michelle Cecile. BS in Mech. Engring, Johns Hopkins, 1954; postgrad., U. Paris, 1955-56; MS, Calif. Inst. Tech., 1955; PhD, Cal. Inst. Tech., 1960; MA (hon.), Brown U., 1965. Asst. prof. mech. engring. Brown U., Providence, 1960-65, asso. prof., 1965-68, exec. officer div. engring., 1966-68; prof. dept. mech. engring. Washington U., St. Louis, 1968-97, chmn. dept., 1968-82, 86-97, Spencer T. Olin prof. engring. and applied sci., 1997—2003, prof. biomed. engring., 1997—2003, sr. prof., 2003—. Vis. prof. U. Paris VI, 1973. Assoc. editor: Jour. Biomech. Engring., 1993-97; mem. editorial bd. Circulation Rsch., 1975-82. Pres. St. Louis-Lyon Sister Cities, Inc., 2000—. Fulbright fellow Paris, 1955; recipient Nat. Marconi Sci. award UNICO, 1999. Fellow ASME, Am. Inst. of Med and Biol. Engring. (founding); mem. Biomed. Engring. Soc. (bd. dirs. 1997-2000), Internat. Soc. Biorheology, N.Am. Soc. Biorheology (pres.-elect 1986-89, pres. 1989-90), Am. Soc. Artificial Internal Organs, Am. Soc. Engring. Edn., AAAS (Lindbergh award St. Louis sect. 1988), AIAA, European Acad. Sci., Tau Beta Pi, Pi Tau Sigma. Republican. Roman Catholic. Achievements include research in fluid mechanics, heat transfer, blood flow, rheology of suspensions. Home: 830 S Meramec Ave Saint Louis MO 63105-2539 Business E-Mail: sps@wustl.edu.

SUTHERLAND, ALAN ROY, business educator; b. N.Y.C., Jan. 15, 1944; s. Arthur Abbott and Margaret Louise (Schweitzer) S. BFA, Pratt Inst., Bklyn., 1964; MPA, NYU, 1969, PhD, 1984. Personnel dir. Manhattan Psychiat. Ctr., N.Y.C., 1966-72; dep. dir. Rockland Children's Psychiat. Ctr., Orangeburg, N.Y., 1972-74, L.I. Devel. Ctr., Melville, N.Y., 1974-78, dir., 1978-80; program dir. Vols. Am., N.Y.C., 1983-86; sr. staff officer Nat. Acad. Scis., Washington, 1986-88; dep. dir. U.S. Interagy. Coun. on Homeless, Washington, 1988-89; exec. dir. Travelers Aid Internat., Washington, 1989-91, AIDS Ctr. of Queens County, Rego Park, N.Y., 1992-96; chair dept. mgmt. studies Southeastern U., Washington, 1998-99. Prof. U. Md., College Park, 1998—. Editor: Homlessness, Health and Human Service Needs. Recipient citation N.Y.C. Coun., 1986, Stanley J. Drazak Excellence in Tchg. award U. Md., 2004. Mem. ASPA, World Futurist Soc. Lutheran. Avocation: weightlifting. Home: 1617 15th St NW Washington DC 20009-3801 Office: Univ of Maryland 3501 University Blvd E Adelphi MD 20783-7998 E-mail: arsutherland@earthlink.net.

SUTHERLAND, DONALD, actor; b. St. John, N.B., Can., July 17, 1935; m. Lois Hardwick, 1959 (div. 1966); 2d, m.Shirley Douglas, 1966. (div. 1971); children: Kiefer, Rachel; m. 3d, Francine Racette; children: Roeg, Rossif, Angus. Grad., U. Toronto, 1958. Actor: London Acad. Music and Dramatic Art, Perth Repertory Theatre, Scotland, also Nottingham, Chesterfield, Bromley, Sheffield, (plays) The Spoon River Anthology, The Male Animal, The Tempest, August for People (London debut), On a Clear Day You Can See Canterbury, The Shewing Up a Blanco Posnet, Enigma Variations, 2000, Ten Unknowns, 2001 (films) The World Ten Times Over, 1963, The Castle of the Living Dead, 1964, Dr. Terror's House of Horrors, 1965, Fanatic, 1965, The Bedford Incident, 1965, Promise Her Anything, 1966, The Dirty Dozen, 1967, Sebastian, 1968, Oedipus the King, 1968, Interlude, 1968, Joanna, 1968, The Split, 1968, Start the Revolution Without Me, 1969, The Act of the Heart, 1970, M*A*S*H, 1970, Kelly's Heroes, 1970, Little Murders, 1970, Alex in Wonderland, 1971, Klute, 1971, Johnny Got His Gun, 1971, Steelyard Blues, 1972, Lady Ice, 1972, Alien Thunder, 1973, Don't Look Now, 1973, S*P*Y*S, 1974, The Day of the Locust, 1975, End of the Game, 1976, Casanova, 1976, 1900, 1976, The Eagle Has Landed, 1977, Animal House, 1978, Invasion of the Body Snatchers, 1978, The Great Train Robbery, 1979, The Kentucky Fried Movie, 1978, Murder by Decree, 1979, Bear Island, 1979, A Man, A Woman and a Bank, 1980, Nothing Personal, 1980, Ordinary People, 1980, Eye of the Needle, 1981, Gas, 1981, The Disappearance, Blood Relative, Threshold, 1983, Max Dugan Returns, 1983, Crackers, 1984, Heaven Help Us, 1985, Revolution, 1985, The Trouble with Spies, 1987, The Wolf at the Door, 1987, Apprentice to Murder, 1988, The Rosary Murders, 1988, Lock Up, 1989, Lost Angels, 1989, A Dry White Season, 1989, Backdraft, 1991, JFK, 1991, Eminent Domain, 1991, Buffy the Vampire Slayer, 1992, Younger and Younger, 1993, Shadow of the Wolf, 1993, Six Degrees of Separation, 1993, The Puppet Masters, 1994, Quicksand, Disclosure, 1994, Outbreak, 1995, Bethune: The Making of a Hero, FTA, The Shadow Conspiracy, 1997, The Assignment, 1997, Fallen, 1997, Without Limits, 1998, Free Money, 1998, Toscano, 1999, CSS Hunley, 1999, Virus, 1999, Instinct, 1999, Panic, 2000, Space Cowboys, 2000, The Art of War, 2000, Threads of Hope(voice), 2000, Final Fantasy: The Spirit Within(voice),2001, Da wan, 2001, The Italian Job, 2003, Baltic Storm, 2003, Cold Mountain, 2003; TV shows and movies include Marching to the Sea, The Death of Bessie Smith, Hamlet at Elsinore, The Saint, The Avengers, Gideon's Way, The Champions, The Winter of Our Discontent, 1984, Ordeal By Innocence, 1985, Buster's Bedroom, Citizen X, 1995 (Emmy award), The Big Heist, 2001, Uprising, 2001, Path to War, 2002. Decorated officier dans l'Ordre des Artes et des Lettres (France); officer Order of Can. Office: c/o CAA Katherine Olin 9830 Wilshire Blvd Beverly Hills CA 90212-1804*

SUTHERLAND, DONALD GRAY, retired lawyer; b. Houston, Jan. 19, 1929; s. Robert Gray and Elizabeth (Cunningham) S.; m. Mary Reynolds Moodey, July 23, 1955; children: Stuart Gray, Elizabeth Dana. BS, Purdue U., 1954; LLB, Ind. U., Bloomington, 1954. Bar: Ind. 1954, U.S. Dist. Ct. (so. dist.) Ind. 1954, U.S. Tax Ct. 1956, U.S. Ct. Claims 1957, U.S. Ct. Appeals (7th cir.) 1981, U.S. Ct. Appeals (3d cir.) 1984, U.S. Ct. Internat. Trade 1987, U.S. Supreme Ct. 1987. Assoc. IceMiller, Indpls., 1954-64, ptnr., 1965-98, ret., 1998. Practitioner in residence Ind. U. Sch. of Law, Bloomington, 1987; trustee, pres. Pegasus Funds, Detroit, 1992-99; trustee, chmn. bd. dirs., pres. Bison Money Market Fund., Indpls., 1982-92. Contbr. articles to numerous profl. jours. Bd. dirs., v.p. Japan-Am. Soc. of Ind., Inc., Indpls., 1988-97; bd. dirs. Conner Prairie Inc., Fishers, Ind., 1988-97, v.p., 1989-90, chmn. bd., 1990-93; tennis ceremonies 10th Pan-Am. Games, Indpls., 1987; bd. dirs. The Children's Bur. Indpls., 1962-73, v.p., 1968-70, pres., 1970-72; bd. dirs. Orchard Country Day Sch., Indpls., 1970-73, Episc. Cmty. Svcs., Indpls., 1965-73, v.p., 1968, pres., 1969; trustee United Episc. Charities, Indpls., 1970-71, pres., 1971. With USMC, 1946-48. Mem.: Nat. Jr. Tennis League of Indpls. (bd. dirs. 2003—), Econ. Club (bd. dirs. Ind. chpt. 1988—94), Contemporary Club of Indpls. (pres. 2003—04), Woodstock Club. Republican. Avocations: golf, tennis, opera. Office: Ice Miller 1 American Sq Indianapolis IN 46282-0020

SUTHERLAND, DONALD WOOD, cardiologist; b. Kansas City, Mo., July 29, 1932, s. Donald Redeker and Mary Frances (Wood) S.; m. Margaret Sutherland, Sept. 11, 1954 (div. 1994); children: Kathleen Massar, Ellen Baltus, Richard, Ann, Julia McMurchie; m. Roslyn Ruggiero Elms, Mar. 31, 1995. BA, Amherst Coll., 1953; MD, Harvard U., 1957. Intern, resident Mass. Gen. Hosp., Boston, 1957-60; fellow in cardiology U. Oreg., Portland, 1961-63; pvt. practice Portland, 1963—. Assoc. clin. prof. medicine Oreg. Health Sci. U., Portland, 1967—; chief of staff St. Vincent Hosp. and Med. Ctr., Portland, 1971-72. Contbr. articles to profl. jours. Fellow Am. Heart Assn., Am. Coll. Cardiology (pres. Oreg. chpt. 1972); mem. Multnomah Athletic Club, North Pacific Soc. Internal Medicine (pres. 1985), Pacific Interurban Clin. Club (pres. 2000). Avocations: flying private planes, scuba diving. Home: 4405 SW Council Crest Dr Portland OR 97239 Office: Columbia Cardiology Assocs 9155 SW Barnes Rd Ste 233 Portland OR 97225-6629

SUTHERLAND, DOUGLASS B. former mayor, tent and awning company executive; b. Helena, Mont., May 2, 1937; s. Chris and Marie Sutherland; m. Grace Sutherland, Sept. 5, 1986; children: Karen, Scott. BA, Central Wash. U., 1959. Program specialist Boeing Co., Tacoma, Wash., 1960-71; owner, pres. Tacoma Tent & Awning, Inc., 1971-86; sec., pres., 1986-98; county exec. Pierce County, Wash. Bd. dirs. Tacoma-Pierce County Bd. Health, Tacoma-Pierce County Employment and Tng. Consortium; mayor City of Tacoma, 1982-89; pres. Puget Sound Regional Coun.; chair Urban County Caucus, Wash. Assn. of Counties. Mem. Assn. Wash. Cities, Tacoma-Pierce County C. of C. Lodges: Rotary. Republican. Avocation: sailing. Office: Pierce County Exec 930 Tacoma Ave S Rm 737 Tacoma WA 98402-2100 E-mail: dsuther@co.pierce.wa.us.

SUTHERLAND, FRANK, publishing executive, editor; b. Mt. Juliet, Tenn., May 31, 1945; s. Ernest Franklin and Fontelle (Moore) S.; m. Natilee Duning; children: Kate, Daniel. BA, Vanderbilt U., 1970. Reporter The Tennessean, Nashville, Tenn., 1963-77, zone editor, 1977-78, city editor, 1978-82, v.p. news, editor, 1989-99, sr. v.p., 1999—; editor The Shreveport (La.) Times, 1988-89; mng. editor The Hattiesburg (Miss.) Am., 1982-86; exec. editor The Jackson (Tenn.) Sun, 1986-88. Mem. Soc. Profl. Journalists (middle Tenn. chpt. pres. 1974-81, nat. bd. dirs. 1974, nat. treas. 1981, sec. 1982, pres.-elect 1983, pres. 1984-85), Am. Soc. Newspaper Editors (mem. steering com., reporters com. for freedom of press 1979-82). Office: The Tennessean 1100 Broadway Nashville TN 37203-3134

SUTHERLAND, GAIL RUSSELL, retired industrial equipment manufacturing company executive; b. Rush Lake, Wis., Dec. 20, 1923; s. Gail Marion and Edith (Grueb) S.; m. Leone Marie Witkowski, Mar. 10, 1945; children: Keith Allan, Glenn Elliott. BS in Agr., U. Wis., Madison, 1947, BSME, 1948, MS in Agrl. Engring., 1949. Div. engr. Deere & Co., Ottumwa, Iowa, 1949-63, mgr. product engring. Des Moines, 1963-77, dir. product planning Moline, Ill., 1977-80, dir. product engring. planning, 1980-83, dir. product engring., 1983-84, v.p. engring., 1984-86, v.p. engring. and tech., 1986-87. Mem. editorial adv. bd. Mfg. Engring. Mag., 1987; inventor: cotton harvester blower discharge, combine soybean header, beet harvester flail feeder, pasture renovator cutter. Bd. dirs. Bella Vista Property Owners Assn., 1992-98. Served as ensign USN, 1943-46 Mem. Nat. Acad. Engring., Am. Soc. Agrl. Engrs. (Engr. of Yr. 1980, Disting. Engr. of Yr. 1983), Soc. Automotive Engrs., Am. Nat. Standards Inst. (bd. dirs. 1984-86) Republican. Home and Office: 5109 Mueller Rd Mariposa CA 95338-9500 E-mail: gruss@sierratel.com.

SUTHERLAND, GEORGE LESLIE, retired chemical company executive; b. Dallas, Aug. 13, 1922; s. Leslie and Madge Alice (Henderson) S.; m. Mary Gail Hamilton, Sept. 9, 1961 (dec. Mar. 1984); children: Janet Leslie, Gail Irene, Elizabeth Hamilton; m. Carol Brenda Kaplan, Feb. 19, 1986. BA, U. Tex., Austin, 1943, MA, 1947, PhD, 1950. With Am. Cyanamid Co., various locations, 1951-87; asst. dir. rsch. and devel. Princeton, NJ, 1969-70; dir. rsch. and devel., agr. divsn., 1970-73; v.p. med. rsch. and devel. Pearl River, NY, 1973-86; dir. med. rsch. divsn., 1978-86; dir. chem. rsch. divsn., 1980-81; v.p. corp. rsch. tech., 1986-87. Served with USN, 1944—46. Mem. AAAS, Assn. Rsch. Dirs. (pres. 1975-76), Am. Chem. Soc. Home: 42 Sky Meadow Rd Suffern NY 10901-2519

SUTHERLAND, DAME JOAN, retired soprano; b. Sydney, Australia, Nov. 7, 1926; d. McDonald S.; m. Richard Bonynge, 1954; one son. Student, Royal Coll. Music, London, 1951. Appeared concert and oratorio performances, Australia; appeared in: opera Judith, Syndey Conservatory of Music; debut Covent Garden in Magic Flute, 1952; Italian debut in Handel's Alcina, Teatro la Fenice, Venice, 1960; Bellini's Puritani, Glyndebourne Festival, Sussex, Eng., 1960; Bellini's Beatrice di Tenda, La Scala, 1961, Rossini's Semiramide, La Scala, 1962; Meyerbeer's Les Huguenots, La Scala, 1962, N.Y. debut, Carnegie Hall, 1961; Opera debut Lucia, 1961; opened Sutherland-Williamson Opera Co. tour, Australia, 1965; appeared: Handel's Julius Caesar, Hamburg Opera, 1969; Bellini's Norma, Met. Opera, 1970; opened, Lyric Opera Chgo. with, Semiramide, 1971; San Francisco Opera with, Norma, 1972; San Francisco Opera with Trovatore, 1975; Met. Opera with I Puritani, 1976; Vancouver Opera with Le Roi de Lahore, 1977; premiered new prodn., Met. Opera in Tales of Hoffmann, 1973; first prodn. in Am. in eighty years Esclarmonde, Massenet, San Fancisco Opera, 1974; author: (with Richard Bonynge) The Joan Sutherland Album, 1986; A Prima Donna's Progress, 1997. Decorated Order of Merit, 1991; comdr. and dame comdr., Order Brit. Empire, 1979; Companion, Order Australia, 1975; recipient Grammy Award best classical vocal soloist, 1981. Fellow Royal Coll. Music. Office: Colbert Artist Mgmt 111 W 57th St New York NY 10019-2211

SUTHERLAND, JOHN BENNETT, chemical engineer; b. Burlingame, Kans., Feb. 21, 1918; s. Earl Wilbur and Edith May (Hartshorn) S.; m. Maxine Louise Turvey, Oct. 13, 1935; children: John Walter, Max Earl, Lynn Ann Sutherland Bradshaw. BS in Chem. Engring., Kans. State U., 1939, MS in Chem. Engring., 1940; PhD in Chem. Engring., U. Pitts., 1946. Rsch. engr. Texaco, Port Arthur, Tex., 1940-41; rsch. asst. Mellon Inst., Pitts., 1941-43; asst. prof. Northwestern U., Evanston, Ill., 1943-46; pres. Sutherland-Becker Lab., Burlingame, Kans., 1946-62; exec. dir. Kans State Indsl. Devel. Commn. State of Kans., Topeka, 1953-56; dir. planning and rsch. Butler Mfg. Co., Kansas City, Mo., 1956-65; dir. indsl. rsch. and ext. U. Mo. System, Columbia, 1966-80; exec. dir., v.p. Master Practitioners, Inc., Sedalia, Mo., 1983-84; prof. emeritus U. Mo., Columbia, 1980—. Cons. Kans. Indsl. Devel. Commn., 1946-53; dept. dir. econ. devel. Office Indsl. Devel. Studies Report Series, 1966; mem. Sci. Adv. Commn., Kansas City, Mo., 1962. Mem. Gov.'s Energy Adv. Com., State of Mo., 1970; treas. Pub. Sch. Dist., Burlingame, Kans., 1948. Mem. AIChE, Am. Chem. Soc., Rotary Club (pres. 1949-50). Achievements include development of new state wide technology transfer system coordinating field specialists serving manufacturers backed by a referral system, campus experts and a technical library. Home: 3021 SW Burlingame Rd Topeka KS 66611-2003

SUTHERLAND, JOHN CAMPBELL, pathologist, educator; b. Tamingfu, Hopei, People's Republic of China, Oct. 28, 1921; came to US, 1926; s. Francis Campbell and Ann Findlay (Bowman) S.; m. Eunice Lucille Kindschi, June 16, 1950; 1 child, John Mark. AB, N.W. Nazarene Coll., 1941; MD, Med. Coll. Wis., 1946. Intern Milw. Hosp., 1946-47; resident in pathology St. Francis Hosp., Wichita, Kans., 1950-52, Barnes Hosp., St. Louis, 1952-54, Stanford Med. Ctr., Calif., 1967-68; gen. practitioner Mangum Clinic, Nampa, Idaho, 1949-50; gen. med. officer Raleigh Fitkin Meml. Hosp., Manzini, Swaziland, 1955-56, Ethel Lucas Meml. Hosp., Acornhoek, South Africa, 1956-61, 62-67; acting head biology dept. N.W. Nazarene Coll., Nampa, 1961-62; head rsch. pathology dept. Balt. Cancer Rsch. Ctr., 1968-74; asst. prof. dept. pathology U. Md., Balt., 1974-76, assoc. prof., 1976-84, mem. grad. faculty, 1982-84; vis. assoc. prof. dept. surgery U. Ariz., Tucson, 1984-96; dep. med. examiner Mohave County, Ariz., 1996—2000. Co-author: Guinea Pig Doctors, 1984, Behind the Silence, 1999; contbr. articles to sci. jours. Capt. USAF, 1947-49. Mem. Alumni Assn. of N.W. Nazarene Coll. (Profl. Achievement award 1984), Toastmasters, Gideons. Republican. Mem. Wesleyan Ch. Avocations: reading, bird watching, speaking. Address: PO Box 737 Atkinson NE 68713-0737 Home: 408 W Central Atkinson NE 68713-0737 E mail: johsut@incbraska.com.

SUTHERLAND, KIEFER, actor; b. London, Eng., Dec. 21, 1966; s. Donald and Shirley Douglas S.; m. Camelia Kath, Sept. 12, 1986 (div.), m. Kelly Winn (div.); children: Sarah. Appearances include (theater) debut in Throne of Straw, 1977, (films) Max Dugan Returns, 1983, The Bay Boy, 1984 (Genie award nominee 1984), At Close Range, 1986, Crazy Moon, 1986, Stand By Me, 1986, The Lost Boys, 1987, The Killing Time, 1987, Promised Land, 1987, 1969, 1988, Bright Lights, Big City, 1988, Young Guns, 1988, Renegades, 1989, Chicago Joe and the Showgirl, 1990, Flashback, 1990, Flatliners, 1990, The Nutcracker Prince (voice), 1990, Young Guns II, 1990, Article 99, 1991, Twin Peaks: Fire Walk With Me, 1992, A Few Good Men, 1992, The Vanishing, 1993, The Three Musketeers, 1993, The Cowboy Way, 1994, Eye for an Eye, 1995, A Time to Kill, 1996, The Last Days of Frankie the Fly, 1996, Freeway, 1996, Truth or Consequences N.M, 1997, Dark City, 1997, Sweetheart of the Song Tra Bong, 1998, Ground Control, 1998, (voice) Dinosaur, 1998, The Breakup, 1998, Dark City, 1998, Woman Wanted, 1999, The Red Dove, 1999, Hearts and Bones, 1999, Beat, 2000, Picking Up the Pieces, 2000, Ring of Fire, 2000, The Royal Way, 2000, The Right Temptation, 2000, To End All Wars, 2001, Paradise Found, 2001, Desert Saints, 2002, Dead Heat, 2002, Behind the Red Door, 2002, Phone Booth, 2002, Taking Lives, 2004; (TV movies) Trapped in Silence, 1986, Brotherhood of Justice, 1986, Last Light, 1993; (TV series) 24, 2001— (Best Performance by Actor in a TV Series Drama Golden Globe award 2002, Best Performance by Actor in a Drama Series Golden Satellite award 2002, nominee Outstanding Lead Actor in Drama Series Emmy award 2002, Screen Actors Guild Award for best actor in a drama series, 2004). Office: William Morris Agency attn: Steve Dontanville 151 El Camino Dr Beverly Hills CA 90212*

SUTHERLAND, L. FREDERICK, food company executive; BS, Duke U.; MBA, U. Pitts. V.p. Chase Mahattan Bank, N.Y.C.; asst. treas. Aramark Corp., Phila., 1980-83, treas., 1983-85, v.p., treas., 1985-87, v.p. corp. fin. and devel., 1987-91, sr. v.p., 1991-93, exec. v.p. and pres. Uniform Svcs. sector, 1993-96, exec. v.p., CFO, 1997—. Office: Aramark Corp 1101 Market St Ste 45 Philadelphia PA 19107

SUTHERLAND, MALCOLM READ, JR., clergyman, educator; b. Detroit, Nov. 11, 1916; s. Malcolm Read and Edith Ione (Osborne) S.; m. Mary Anne Beaumont, Dec. 23, 1943; children: Malcolm Read III, Maryanne B. AB, Miami (Ohio) U., 1938; MS, Western Res. U., 1941; BD, Fed. Theol. Faculty U. Chgo., 1945; LLD, Emerson Coll., 1963; LHD, Meadville-Lombard Theol. Sch., 1975. Ordained to ministry Unitarian Universalist Assn., 1945. Dir. boys work Goodrich Social Settlement, Cleve., 1938-40; housing mgr. Cleve. Met. Housing Authority, 1940-41; regional housing supr. Farm Security Adminstrn., 1941-42; housing mgmt. supr. FPHA, 1942-43; pastor in Ill., Va., Mass., 1944-94; exec. v.p. Am. Unitarian Assn., 1959-61; Robert Collier prof. ch. and soc., pres., dean faculty Meadville Theol. Sch. of Lombard Coll., Chgo., 1960-75; minister Harvard (Mass.) Unitarian Ch., 1975-94, min. emeritus, 1994—; minister emeritus Thomas Jefferson Meml. Ch., Charlottesville, Va., 1985—. Adj. prof. dept. ministry Andover Newton Theol. Sch., 1992-95; exec. dir. U.S. Com. World Conf. on Religion and Peace, N.Y.C., 1980-83, internat. coun., 1984—, also v.p. U.S. exec. coun.; bd. dirs. Unitarian Universalist Svc. Com., Beacon Press; chmn. editl. adv. com. bd. Christian Register, 1955-60; field rep. Unitarian Svc. Com., Mex., 1950-51; mem. sr. secretariat World Conf. Religion and Peace, Kyoto, 1970 and del. to Louvain, 1974, Princeton, 1979, Nairobi, 1984, Melbourne, Australia, 1989, Reva del Garda, Italy, 1994, hon. pres., 1994—; cons. Niwano Peace Found., Tokyo, 1982-96; lectr., del. Japan-U.S. consultation on peace Internat. Assn. for Religious Freedom, 1970; v.p. and trustee Dana McLean Greeley Found. for Peace and Justice, 1986-94, trustee emeritus, 1994—; Thomas Minns lectr., Boston, 1955, Charlottesville, Va., 1978, Berry St., lectr., Boston, 1956; Harvard chair lectr. Warner Free Lectrs., 1985, 93; chmn. common. coun. Chgo. Cluster of Theol. Schs., inc., 1970-74; pres. Inst. on Religion in an Age of Sci., 1969, 75-77, hon. v.p., 1980—, acad. fellow, 1988—; bd. dirs., sec. Ctr. for Advanced Study Religion and Sci., Chgo., 1965—. Author: Personal Faith, 1955, Creators of the Dawn, 1979, Star Light, Star Bright, 1993; co-chmn. publs. bd. jour. religion and sci. Zygon, 1964—; also articles. Bd. govs. Harris Manchester Coll., Oxford U., 1968—, hon. fellow, 1974—. Recipient Disting. Svc. award Charlottesville (Va.) Jr. C. of C., 1949, Disting. Svc. award Internat. Assn. Religious Freedom, 1975, Disting. Svc.award Konko Kyo Chs. Am., 1975 Mem. Unitarian Universalist Ministers Assn., Phi Delta Theta, Phi Mu Alpha, Alpha Kappa Delta, Omicron Delta Kappa. Clubs: Bucks Harbor Yacht (Maine) (commodore 1979-81). Home: 14 Timothy's Ln Brooksville ME 04617

SUTHERLAND, MARIA T. marketing professional, communications executive; b. Carmel, Calif., Apr. 9, 1966; d. Frank Anthony Sutherland and Pilgrim Pauline de Hoffman; 1 child, Michael Allen Smiel-Sutherland. BA, New Sch. Social Rsch., 2000. Dir. events Silvercup Studios, L.I., 1990—92; mktg. mgr. Ian Schrager Hotels, N.Y.C., 1992—94; ptnr. Delorme Productions, 1994—98; dir. adminstrn. First Union Corp., Boston, 1998—99; mktg. cons. Carmel, Calif., 2004—, 2000—, Santa Fe, 2000—. Prodr.(writer and lyricist): (plays) Cafe Society; author (lyricist): (songs) Manhattan on the Rocks with a

Twist, Cafe Society; illustrations, Herve Pierre; contbr. articles to profl. jours. Founder Female Admirers Gay Heroic Actions, N.Y.C., 1993—94; mem. Beacon Hill Civic Assn., Boston, 1999—2000. Scholar, Harvard U., 1998—2000. Avocations: travel, culture, psychology, anthropology, art.

SUTHERLAND, MICHAEL CRUISE, librarian; b. Morgantown, W.Va., Aug. 29, 1938; s. Charles Fish and Mildred (Haymond) S. BA in English, San Fernando Valley State U., 1967, postgrad., 1968-69, UCLA, 1967, MLS, 1970. Office asst., clk. Lindsay & Hall, L.A., 1959-60; libr. asst. I, bindery clk. Biomed. Libr. UCLA, 1961-65; jr. adminstrv. asst. Dept. Pub. Works City of L.A., 1967; intermediate clk. typist San Fernando Valley State U., Northridge, Calif., 1967-69; libr. I, tchg. asst. Grad. Sch. Libr. and Info. Sci. UCLA, 1970; spl. collections libr. Occidental Coll., L.A., 1970—. Attendee numerous workshops and seminars; organizer Western Books Exhbn. at various librs. throughout the Western U.S., 1992, 96; judging organizer, 1993. Author numerous exhbn. catalog booklets; author: (with others) Encyclopedia of Library and Information Sciences, 1979, Western Books Exhibition Catalog, 1986, Striking Research Gold: Distinguished Collections in California Independent Academic Libraries, 1988; contbr. articles to profl. jours. Active Neighborhood Watch, AIDS Quilt Program. Mem. Rounce and Coffin Club (sec., treas.), Robinson Jeffers Assn., Tor House Found., Zamorano Club, Book Club Calif. Office: Occidental Coll Mary Norton Clapp Libr 1600 Campus Rd Los Angeles CA 90041-3314 Office Phone: 323-259-2852. Business E-Mail: bun@oxy.edu.

SUTHERLAND, MITCHELL ALSOBROOK, JR., mechanical engineer, consultant; b. Anderson, S.C., Oct. 18, 1960; s. Mitchell Alsobrook, Sr. Sutherland and Glendle Louise McGill; m. Jeannine Anne Jorett, Aug. 23, 1997; children: Glendle Cameron, Kyle Jameson. BSME, U. of S.C., 1985; MBA, Nova Southeastern U., Ft. Lauderdale, Fla., 2001; postgrad., Nova Southeastern U. Registered profl. engr., Calif., 1991, cert. project mgmt. specialist, Project Mgmt. Inst., 2000. Mech. engr. Asea Brown Boveri - Impell, Norcross, Ga., 1986—90; pres. Sutherland Project Controls, Inc., Chattanooga, 1990—95; project mgr. OFS-Fitel, Norcross, Ga., 1996—. Author: (publication) The German Economy in Review: Cause and Effect (Presented at the Applied Bus. Rsch. Conf., San Juan PR, 2004). Sgt. USMCR, 1979—83. Mem.: ASME, Acad. of Mgmt. Democrat. Presbyterian. Avocations: fishing, old home restoration. Home: 498 Ridgecrest Dr Norcross GA 30071

SUTHERLAND, PETER EDWARD, electrical engineer; AS in Elec. Engring. Tech., U. Maine, 1979, BSEE with honors and highest distinction, 1983; MScE, U. N.B., Fredericton, Can., 1986; PhD Electric Power Engring., Reusselaer Polytechnic Inst., 2003. Registered profl. engr., Maine, N.Y., Pa.; radiotelephone lic. FCC. Test engr. Accutest Corp., Chelmsford, Mass., 1979-80, 82, design engr., 1983-84; planning engr. Maine Pub. Svc. Co., Presque Isle, 1983; grad. tchg. and rsch. asst. U. N.B., 1984-86; power sys. engr. GE Co., Schenectady, 1987-89, 93, lead tng. specialist, 1989-92, sr. engr., 1994—2001, Super Power Inc., Schenectady, 2001—03; cons. engr. EPRI PEAC Corp., Schenectady, 2003—. Contbr. articles to profl. jours. Mem. IEEE (sr., chpt. chair Brown Book working group, chpt. co-chair Gray Book working group, power sys. protection com., London chartered engr.), IEE (London), Tau Beta Pi, Eta Kappa Nu, Phi Kappa Phi. Achievements include patents pending for; patents for power system instrumentation. Office: EPRI PEAC Corp 1462 Erie Blvd Schenectady NY 12305 E-mail: peter.sutherland@ieee.org.

SUTHERLAND, SUSAN J. lawyer; b. Canton, Ohio, 1957; BA, Denison Coll., 1979; JD, NYU, 1982. Bar: N.Y. 1983. Ptnr. Skadden, Arps, Slate, Meagher & Flom, N.Y.C. Office: Skadden Arps Slate Meagher & Flom 4 Times Sq Fl 24 New York NY 10036-6595

SUTHERLAND, WADE ALAN, music educator, director; b. Irving, Tex., Nov. 12, 1974; s. Ronald Francis and Carrilene Ann Sutherland; m. Christy Lynn Parolli, Jan. 11, 1997; children: Gabriel Wade, Olivia Joy. MusB Edn., La. State U., Baton Rouge, La, 1996, MusM, 2002. Ordained Min. King's Harvest Fellowship, State of La., 2000. Dir. bands Parkview Bapt. Sch., Baton Rouge, 1996—. Recipient Tchr. of the Yr., Parkview Bapt. Sch., 2001-2002. Mem.: La. Music Educators Assn., Nat. Band Assn., La. BandMasters Assn., Percussive Arts Soc., Music Educators Nat. Conf. Office: Parkview Bap Sch 5750 Parkview Ch Rd Baton Rouge LA 70816 Personal E-mail: wsutherland@parkviewbaptist.com.

SUTHERLAND, WILLIAM OWEN SHEPPARD, English language educator; b. Wilmington, N.C., Jan. 19, 1921; s. William Owen Sheppard and Mary Owen (Green) S.; m. Madeline Ethel Cooley, Sept. 12, 1947; children: Madeline, William, John, Thomas. AB in English with honors, U. N.C., 1942, MA, 1947, PhD, 1950. Instr. English. U. N.C., Chapel Hill, 1950-51, Northwestern U., Evanston, Ill., 1951-54; asst. prof. U. Tex., Austin, 1954-58, assoc. prof., 1958-65, prof., 1965-98, Robert A.-Thomas H. Law Centennial prof. humanities emeritus, 1998—, chmn. dept., 1983-90, faculty humanist rep. Deans of Humanities of S.W. Conf., 1980; cons. Ednl. Testing Svc. and Coll. Bd., Princeton, N.J., 1965-72, NEH, Washington, 1978—; prof. emeritus U. Tex., 1998. Author: Art of the Satirist, 1965; co-editor: The Reader, 1960, Six Contemporary Novels, 1961, An Index to 18th Century Periodicals, 1800, 1956. Served to capt. C.E. U.S. Army, 1942-45. Recipient Scarborough Excellence in Tchg. award U. Tex. Austin, 1959, Liberal Arts Pro Bene Meritis award, 1996, Pres. Assocs. Tchg. award, 1982; NEH grantee, 1978-79. Mem. MLA, South Central MLA (exec. com. 1967-69), AAUP (state v.p. 1970-71), Nat. Council Tchrs. English (dir. 1974-78) Democrat. Episcopalian. Home: 3610 Highland View Dr Austin TX 78731-4033 Office: U Tex Dept English Austin TX 78712 Business E-Mail: woss@mail.utexas.edu.

SUTHERLAND-ABEL, ANNE ELIZABETH, pediatrician; b. Milw, June 16, 1945; d. David Hollingsworth and Mildred June (Nees) Sutherland; m. Francis Lee Abel; one child, Jonathan Earl. BA, Pasadena Coll., 1967; MS, Ind. U., Indpls., 1969, MD, 1973. Diplomate Am. Bd. Pediat. Resident in pediat. Meth. Hosp., Indpls., 1973—75, Richland Meml. Hosp., Columbia, SC, 1975—76; pediatrician Moncrief Army Hosp., Ft. Jackson, SC, 1976—80; child and adolescent psychiatry fellow William S. Hall Psychiat. Inst., Columbia, SC, 1981—83, U. BC Vancouver Gen. Hosp., 1982; pvt. practice Columbia, SC, 1983—; pediatrician Children's Rehabilitative Svc., Orangeburg, SC, 1984—2000; chief med. sect. Columbia Area Mental Health Ctr., SC, 1987—92; assoc. prof. pediat., adj. assoc. prof. neuropsychiatry U. S.C., 1992—2000; mental health dir. Abuse Recovery Ctr., Columbia, SC, 1994—95; dir. Freddie Mac Child and Adolescent Protection Ctr., Children's Nat. Med. Ctr., Washington, 2001—. Cons. behavioral pediat. Epworth Children's Home, Columbia, S.C., 1983-86, 90-97; med. dir. Assessment and Resource Ctr., Columbia, 1996-2000; mem. med. adv. com., children's health rehabilitative svc. S.C. Dept. Health and Environ. Control, Columbia, 1986-92, mem. maternal and child health adv. com., 1989-91; behavioral devel. pediatrician Orangeburg Health Dept., 1994-96. Contbr. articles to profl. journals. Mem. S.C. Governor's Youth Unemployment Coun., Columbia, 1987. Recipient Alumni Award Pasadena Coll., 1977; Vol. of Yr. Award Mayor's Com. Employment Handicapped, 1988; grantee Ctr. Family Soc., U. S.C., 1993-95. Fellow Am. Acad. Pediat.; mem. AMA, Am. Profl. Soc. on Abuse of Children. Avocations: music, boating, hiking, fishing, reading. Office: U S C Dept Pediat 4 Med Pk Ste 301 Columbia SC 29203 Personal E-mail: abela616@aol.com.

SUTHERS, HANNAH LOUISE BONSEY, biologist, consultant; b. Lorain, Ohio, Oct. 4, 1931; d. William Edwin and Hannah Elisabeth Bonell B.; m. Derwent Albert Suthers, June 20, 1953 (div. Oct. 1968); children: Daniel Derwent, Hannah Marie Suthers McCabe, Edwin Bonsey. BA, Oberlin Coll., 1953, MS equivalent in biology, MA equivalent in theology, Oberlin Coll., 1998. Master permitee Bird Banding, USGS, Migratory Bird Mgmt.; cert. avian rehabilitator U.S. Dept. Interior Fish and Wildlife Svc. Sec., clk. Union Theol. Sem., NYC, 1953-54; nursery sch. tchr. Berkeley (Calif.) Unified Sch. Dist., 1954-55; sec./clk. Ch. Div. Sch. of Pacific, Berkeley, 1955; nursery sch. tchr. Edgewood People's Ch., East Lansing, Mich., 1964-65; overseas missionary Protestant Episcopal Ch., Brazil, 1965-68; lab. tech. Princeton (NJ) Labs., Inc., 1968; profl. rsch. staff Princeton U., 1968-89, profl. tech. staff, 1989-96. Reviewer Am. Jour. Botany, 1971—73, 1983, N.Am. Bird Bander, 1977—; area rep. Princeton U., 1978—80, 1982—89; coord. com. Princeton U. Women's Orgn., 1982—89; cons. Bracco Rsch. USA, Inc., Princeton, 1996—, Williams Transcontinental Gas Pipeline Corp., Lawrenceville, NJ, 1996—, FMC Corp., Princeton, 1997—2001, Allelix Neurosci., Inc., Cranbury, NJ, 1997—99, Johnson & Johnson Consumer Products, Inc., Skillman, NJ, 1998—, Purdue Pharma LP, Cranbury, 1999—, Laureate Pharma, Princeton, 2002. Contbr. articles to profl. jours. Bird bander U.S. Geol. Survey, 1953—; leader Bits and Boots 4-H Horse Club, Mercer County, NJ, 1969—75; county coach Mercer County 4-H Competitive Trail Ride and Mercer County 4-H Horse Judging Team, 1973—75; rep. Mercer County Horse Coun., 1970—75; mem. Migratory Bird Rehab. Policy and Permit Rev. Com.,, NJ, 1988—90, others; participant N.J. Audubon Breeding Bird Atlas, 1980—85, 1991—95; trainer N.Am. Banding Coun., 1998—; vol. cons. Woodrow Wilson Nat. Fellowship Found., Princeton, 1997; vol. State of N.J. Wildlife Conservation Corps, NJ, 2000—. Recipient Outstanding Layperson award Diocese of Mich. Bishop's award 1955, Frank M. Chapman Meml. award Am. Mus. Natural History, 1986, Paul A. Stewart award Wilson Ornithol. Soc., 1986, 87, Jack Gleeson Meml. Environ. award Friends Hopewell Valley Open Space, 2004; grantee Audubon/Washington Crossing Chpt., 1986-88, 94—, others. Mem. Sigma Xi. Democrat. Episcopalian. Achievements include the discovery of day-length sensitivity of Xanthium seedlings, allowing aseptic culture of sprouts for plant hormone bioassays; developed aseptic culture techniques of Xanthium hypocotyl tissue for bioassays; teammate in discovery of the chemoattractant in the cellular slime mold Polysphondylium violaceum and in the discovery of the role of ammonia in chemotaxis; discovered the transcontinental transport of cellular slime molds (Dictyostelids) by migratory songbirds.

SUTHERS, JOHN WILLIAM, prosecutor; b. Denver, Oct. 18, 1951; s. William Dupont and Marguerite A. (Ryan) S.; m. Janet Gill, May 21, 1976; children: Alison, Catherine. BA in Govt. magna cum laude, U. Notre Dame, 1974; JD, U. Colo., 1977. Bar: Colo. 1977, U.S. Dist. Ct. Colo. 1977, U.S. Ct. Appeals (10th cir.) 1979, U.S. Supreme Ct. 2003. Dep. dist. atty. 4th jud. dist. State of Colo., Colo. Springs, 1977-79, chief dep. dist. atty. 4th jud. dist., 1979-81; assoc. Sparks, Dix, Enoch, Colo. Springs, 1981-82; ptnr. Sparks, Dix, Enoch, Suthers & Winslow, Colo. Springs, 1982-89; dist. atty. 4th Jud. Dist., Colo. Springs, 1989—97; sr. counsel Sparks, Dix, 1997—99; exec. dir. Colo. Dept. Corrections, 1999—2001; US atty. US Atty.'s Office Colo. Dist., 2001—. Mem. adv. bd. Sec. of State, Denver, 1983—89; Colo. commr. Uniform State Laws, 1993—97. Author: Fraud and Deceit, 1982, How to Liquidate a Lemon, 1983. Pres., chmn. bd. dirs. Cmty. Corrections of Pikes Peak Region, Inc., 1984—87; bd. dirs. Crimestoppers, Inc., Colorado Springs, 1985—88; mem. exec. com. Colo. Dist. Atty.'s Coun., 1992—97, pres., 1994—95, treas., 1993; El Paso County Rep. Ctrl. com. Colorado Springs, 1985—2001; Colo. State Rep. Ctrl. com., 1989—2001. Zimmerman Found. scholar, 1970-74. Mem. Colo. Bar Assn. (com. chmn.), El Paso County Bar Assn. (pres. 1990-91), Notre Dame Colorado Springs (pres. 1983-84). Roman Catholic. Avocations: baseball cards, golf. Home: 573 Vista Grande Colorado Springs CO 80906 Office: US Atty 1225 17th St Ste 700 Denver CO 80202 Office Phone: 303-454-0263.

SUTIN, NORMAN, chemistry educator, scientist; b. Ceres, Republic of South Africa; came to U.S., 1956; s. Louis and Clara (Goldberg) S.; m. Bonita Sakowski, June 29, 1958; children: Lewis Anthony, Cara Ruth. B.Sc., U. Cape Town (S. Africa), 1948, M.Sc., 1950; PhD, Cambridge U. (Eng.), 1953. Research fellow Durham U. (Eng.), 1954-55; research assoc. Brookhaven Nat. Lab., Upton, N.Y., 1956-57, assoc. chemist, 1958-61, chemist, 1961-66, sr. chemist, 1966—2001, dept. chmn., 1988-95; affiliate Rockefeller U., N.Y.C., 1958-62; vis. fellow Weizmann Inst., Rehovoth, Israel, 1965; vis. prof. SUNY-Stony Brook, 1968, Columbia U., N.Y.C., 1968-69, Tel Aviv U., Israel, 1973-74, U. Calif.-Irvine, 1977, U. Tex. Austin, 1979; disting. prof. Rutgers U., 1999—2001; ret., 2001. Editor: Comments on Inorganic Chemistry Jour., 1980-87; mem. editorial bd. Jour. Am. Chem. Soc., 1985-89, Inorganic Chem., 1986-89, Jour. Phys. Chem., 1987-92; contbr. articles to profl. jours. Mem. NAS, Am. Acad. Arts and Scis., Am. Chem. Soc. (recipient award for disting. svc. in advancement of inorganic chemistry 1983). Office: Brookhaven Nat Lab Dept Chemistry Upton NY 11973 E-mail: sutin@bnl.gov.

SUTMAN, FRANCIS XAVIER, university dean; b. Newark, Dec. 20, 1927; s. Joseph L. and Ella (Joyce) S.; m. Mabel Ranagan, Apr. 1, 1956; children: Frank J., Catherine J., Elizabeth A. AB, Montclair State U., 1949, MA, 1952; EdD, Columbia U., 1956. Tchr. pub. secondary schs., N.J., 1949-55; instr. chemistry Upsala Coll., 1953-55; asst. prof. Wm. Paterson Coll., 1955-57; chmn., assoc. prof. natural scis. Inter-Am. U. P.R., 1957-58; prof. gen. edn., chmn. SUNY, Buffalo, 1958-62; prof. sci. edn., chmn. dept. secondary edn., dir. Merit Bilingual Center Temple U., Phila., 1962-82; dean Coll. Edn., Fairleigh Dickinson U., 1982-88. Tech. rsch. staff Exxon Engring. & Rsch. Lab., Linden, N.J., 1955; vis. lectr. Rutgers U.; cons. India AID Project; vis. prof., scientist Hebrew U., Israel; sr. scholar Temple U., 1988-2004, Morgan State U., 1999-2002, Richard Stockton Coll. N.J., 2004—; vis. sci. educator, program dir. edn. and human resources NSF, 1989-93; exec. dir. curriculum devel. coun., Rowan U., N.J.; sr. scholar U. Miami, 1995-2000; del. OAS Coun. Sci. Edn. and Culture, 1971; co-dir. Environ. Edn. Conf. Environ. Protection Svc., Jerusalem, 1975; cons. fed., state, local sch. dists.; dir. sci. tech. project Huazhong U., China, 1980-87; co-dir. chem. edn. conf. Tianjin Normal U., 1984. Author: Concepts in Chemistry, 1962, 2d edit., 1968, What Kind of Environment Will Our Children Have?, 1971, Chemistry in Today's Environment (U.S. and Israel), 1977, Educating Personnel for Bilingual Settings: Today and Beyond, 1979, Learning English Through Science, 1986, Improving Learning in Science and Basic Skills Among Diverse Student Populations, 1995, We need a Better Understanding of Inquiry in Instruction, Harvard Edn. Letter, 2000, Practicing Student Inquiry/Discovery in Teaching as Seen Through New Eyes: A Guidebook for Science and other Educators, 2004. Active Haddonfield (N.J.) Bd. Edn., 1976-79; v.p. alumni bd. Montclair State U., 1982-88; mem. chem. and tech. bd. Burlington County Coll., 1994—. Recipient Air Force Assn. award, 1968, N.J. Gov.'s Albert Einstein Edn. award, 1987, award Hispanic Congress of Pa., 1980, Alumni Citation Montclair State U., 1988. Fellow AAAS; mem. NSTA, Am. Chem. Soc., Am. Assn. Colls. Tchr. Edn. (chief instnl. rep. 1968-87), Nat. Assn. Rsch. Sci. Tchg. (pres.), N.J. Gov.'s Acad., Coun. Sci. Soc. Presidents, Sigma Xi, Phi Delta Kappa (pres. chpt. 2000-02). Home: 311 W Royal Ave Linwood NJ 08221-1458 Office: Richard Stockton Coll NJ PO Box 195 Pomona NJ 08240-0195 Personal E-mail: fmsutman@msn.com. *Professional success comes when one accepts the paradoxes of human activity and accepts conflict and criticism, and gives of one's self for a cause.*

SUTNICK, ALTON IVAN, dean, educator, researcher, physician; b. Trenton, N.J., July 6, 1928; s. Michael and Rose (Horwitz) S.; m. Mona Reidenberg, Aug. 17, 1958; children: Amy Sutnick Plotch, Gary Benjamin Sutnick. AB, U. Pa., 1950, MD, 1954; student in Biomed. Math., Drexel Inst. Tech., 1961—62; student in Biometrics, Temple U., 1969—70. Diplomate Am. Bd. Internal Medicine. Rotating intern Hosp. U. Pa., 1954-55, resident in anesthesiology, 1955-56, resident in medicine, 1956, USPHS postdoctoral research fellow, 1956-57; asst. instr. anesthesiology, then asst. instr. medicine U. Pa. Sch. Medicine, 1955-57; resident in medicine Wishard Meml. Hosp., Indpls., 1957-58, chief resident in medicine, 1960-61; resident instr. medicine Ind. U. Sch. Medicine, Indpls., 1957-58; USPHS postdoctoral research fellow Temple U. Hosp., 1961-63; instr., then assoc. in medicine Temple U. Sch. Medicine, 1962-65; mem. faculty U. Pa. Sch. Medicine, 1965-75, assoc. prof. medicine, 1971-75; clin. asst. physician Pa. Hosp., 1966-71; research physician, then assoc. dir. Inst. Cancer Research (now Fox Chase Cancer Ctr.), Phila., 1965-75; vis. prof. medicine Med. Coll. Pa., Phila., 1971-74; prof. medicine Drexel U. Coll. Medicine (formerly Med. Coll. Pa.), 1975—; dean Med. Coll. Pa., 1975-89, sr. v.p., 1976-89; v.p. Ednl. Commn. Fgn. Med. Grads, 1989-95; dir. internat. med. edn. Carelift Internat., 1997—. Dir. clin. devel. Am. Oncologic Hosp., Phila., 1973-75; attending physician Phila. VA Hosp., 1967-89, Allegheny U. Hosps., 1971-95; cons. in field; mem. U.S. nat. com. Internat. Union Against Cancer, 1969-72; mem. Nat. Conf. Cancer Prevention and Detection, 1973, Nat. Cancer Control Planning Conf., 1973; vice chmn. Gov. Pa. Task Force Cancer Control, 1974-76, chmn. com. cancer detection, 1974-76; mem. health rsch. adv. bd. Commonwealth of Pa., 1976-78; mem. diagnostic rsch. adv. group Nat. Cancer Inst., 1974-78; chmn. coord. com., comprehensive cancer ctr. program Fox Chase Cancer Ctr., U. Pa. Cancer Ctr., 1975; cons. WHO, Govt. of India, 1979, Govt. of Indonesia, 1980, entire S.E. Asia region, 1981, U. Zimbabwe, 1989, Minister of Health of Poland, 1992, Israel Sci. Coun., 1992, U. Autonoma de Guadalajara, Mex., 1993, Generalitat de Catalunya, Spain, 1993, Ministry of Health Russian Fedn., 1993; mem. Inst. de Pos-Graduacae Medica Carlos Chagas, 1993, Fondazione Smith Kline, Italy, 1995, Assn. Med. Schs. Europe, 1995-99, U. Jordan, 1995, U.S.-China Ednl. Inst., 1996, Georgian Postgrad. Med. Found., 1996, Instituto Universitario de Ciencias Biomedicas, Argentina, 1996, faculty of medicine, U. Saarland, Germany, 1996, Ctr. for Med. Edn., Ben Gurion U., Israel, 1996-, Hungarian Nat. Health Ins. Fund, 1996, Carelift Internat., 1997, Intercoll., Cyprus, 1997, Open Soc. Inst., 1997-99, Aieti Med. Sch., Republic of Georgia, 1997-2001, Tartu U., Estonia, 1998-99, WHO European Office, 1998, Vilnius U. and Kaunas Med. U., Lithuania, 1998-99, U. Zagreb, Croatia, 1998-99, Larnaca Hosp., Cyprus, 1998, Netherlands and Russian med. schs., Temple U., others; faculty of medicine Moldova State Med. and Pharm. U., 1997-, vis. prof., 2002, prof. assoc., 2003-; rep. for internat. med. and health scis. edn. MCP Hahnemann U. of the Health Scis., 1996-99; mem. adv. com. Open Soc. Inst. Muskie Fellowship Program, 1997, working group on implementation of presdl. policy on internat. edn., 2000, selection comm. Internat. Consortium for the Advancement of Med. Edn., 2001-. Author numerous articles in field.; Asst. editor: Annals Internal Medicine, 1972-75; editorial bd. other med. jours. Bd. dirs. Israel Cancer Rsch. Fund, 1975—95, Am. Assocs. for Democracy in Georgia, 2000—; nat. bd. dirs. Am. Assocs. Ben Gurion U., 1991—; bd. Internat. Med. Scholar Program, 1988—89, Sight Savers Internat., 1988—91; adv. commn. Internat. Participation Phila. '76, 1973—76; bd. dirs. Phila. Coun. Internat. Visitors, 1972—77; nat. bd. dirs. Phila. divsn. Am. Assocs. Ben Gurion U., 1986—, assoc. chair, 1993—95, 2000—. Capt. M.C. U.S. Army, 1958—60. Recipient Arnold and Marie Schwartz award in medicine AMA, 1976, Torch of Learning award Am. Friends of Hebrew U., 1981, medal Ben Gurion U. of Negev, Israel, 1985, medal U. Cath. de Lille, France, 1987, medal U. Belgrade, Yugoslavia, 1988, Founder's award and medal Med. Coll. Pa., 1989, St. Thomas Aquinas award Santo Tomas U. Med. Alumni Assn., The Philippines, 1989, medal Kiev Med. Inst., Ukraine, 1991, Benjamin Albagli medal Inst. de Pos-Graduacao Medica Carlos Chagas, Brazil, 1993, shield Coll. Physicians and Surgeons, Pakistan, 1993, medal Ukrainian State Med. U., 1994, medal Universidad de Cantabria, Spain, 1999, medal Hadassah-Hebrew U. Dental Sch., 1999, Negev award Am. Assocs., Ben Gurion U., 2000. Fellow ACP (internat. adv. network), Coll. Physicians Phila. (censor 1977-86, councillor 1977-86); mem. AMA, AAAS, Am. Fedn. Clin. Research (pres. Temple U. chpt. 1964-65), Am. Assn. Cancer Research, Am. Soc. Clin. Oncology, Am. Dermatoglyphics Assn., Assn. Am. Cancer Insts., Assn. Am. Med. Colls., Northeast Consortium on Med. Edn. (treas. 1983-89, chmn. 1986-87), Council of Deans of Pvt. Free-Standing Med. Schs. (co-founder, nat. chmn. 1983-85), Pa. Council Deans (chmn. 1987-89), Am. Cancer Soc. (vice chmn. service com. Phila. div. 1974-76, bd. dirs. 1974-80, chmn. awards com. 1976), Am. Lung Assn., Am. Heart Assn., NAFSA-Assn. Internat. Educators, Pan Am. Med. Assn., Phila. Coop. Cancer Assn., N.Y. Acad. Scis., Pa. Heart Assn., Heart Assn. Southeastern Pa., Pa. Med. Soc., Phila. County Med. Soc. (chmn. com. internat. med. affairs 1964-72), Pa. Lung Assn., Phila. Assn. for Clin. Trials (bd. dirs. 1980-81), Health Systems Agy. Southeastern Pa. (gov. bd., exec. com. 1983-87, sec. 1985-87), Am. Assn. Ben Gurion U. (bd. dirs. 1986—), Soc. des Medecins Militaires Français, Assn. Med. Edn. in Europe, Soc. Española de Educacion Medica, Internat. Med. Sch. Affiliates Consortium (co-founder, vice chmn. 1985-87), Phi Beta Kappa, Sigma Xi, Alpha Omega Alpha (councillor 1963-65) Achievements include discovery of association of hepatitis B surface antigen with hepatitis; performed 1st studies of pulmonary surfactant in adult human lung disease; developed cancer screening system based on risk status; pioneer in describing non-A non-B hepatitis C, pioneer in showing relationship of body iron stores to cancer susceptibility and life expectancy; organized first symposium on problems of foreign medical graduates; coined word "ergasteric" for lab.-contracted disease; responsible for advances in assessment of clinical competence. Office: Carelift Internat GSB Bldg Ste 425 One Belmont Ave Bala Cynwyd PA 19004 E-mail: alsutnick@carelift.org.

SUTOWSKI, THOR BRIAN, choreographer, educator; b. Trenton, N.J., Jan. 27, 1945; s. Walter X. and Kathryn (Tang) S.; m. Sonia Arova, Mar. 11, 1965; 1 child, Ariane. Student, San Diego Ballet, 1958-63, San Francisco Ballet, 1963-64, Nat. Ballet, 1964. Cert. solo dancer Genossenschaft Deutscher Buhnen-Angehorigen, Germany. Soloist Norwegian State Opera, Oslo, 1965-70; 1st soloist Hamburgische Staatsoper, Hamburg, Germany, 1970-71; dir. San Diego Ballet, 1971-76, Ballet Ala., Birmingham, 1978-81, State of Ala. Ballet, Birmingham, 1982-83; chmn. Ala. Sch. Fine Arts, Birmingham, 1976-96; assoc. dir. Calif. Ballet Co., San Diego, 1996-98; artistic prodr. San Diego Ballet Co., 1998-2000. Artistic advisor, choreographer Asami Maki Ballet, Toyko, 1976-79; choreographer Atlanta Ballet, 1980-87, Ballet South and State of Ala. Ballet; resident choreographer Atlanta Ballet Co., 1987-93, Calif. Ballet Co., 2001-04; dance advisor Ala. State Arts Council, Montgomery, 1977-78, Miss. Arts Council; advisor Tenn. Ballet Co.; mem. City of Atlanta Mayor's Review Fellowship panel, 1987; adj. prof. choreography U. Ala., Tuscaloosa, 1988-; prof. U. Calif., San Diego, 1998-; commd. choreograher Bavarian State Ballet-State Opera, Munich, 1994; Am. Masters choreographer Sacramento Ballet, 2001. Recipient Pub. TV Emmy award, 1976, Obelisk award for choreography, 1977, 78, 79, 80; grantee Ford Found., 1964, Nat. Endowment for Arts, 1973-74. Mem. Am. Guild. Mus. Artists. Republican. Lutheran.

SUTPHEN, HAROLD AMERMAN, JR., retired paper company executive; b. Verona, N.J., Feb. 13, 1926; s. Harold Amerman and Marion Esther (Mason) S.; m. Greta May Peterson, June 24, 1950; children— Judith Amerman, Peter Lehmann, Pamela Torrance. Grad., Phillips Exeter Acad., 1944; BS in Mech. Engring, Princeton, 1950. With Universal Oil Products Co., Chgo., 1950-51, Texaco, Inc., 1951-52; bus. research analyst Arthur D. Little, Inc., 1952-56; asst. div. mgr. adminstrn., fine papers div. W.Va. Pulp and Paper Co. (name now changed to Westvaco Corp.), 1956-60, v.p., 1967-80, sr. v.p., 1980-88, mgr. fine papers div., 1974-88, dir., 1975-88. V.p., treas. U.S. Envelope Co., Springfield, Mass., 1960-62, pres., CEO, 1962-67, chmn. bd., 1967-74; bd. dirs. Assessment Appeals, Fairfield, Conn., 1993-97, chmn., 1996-97. Served with AUS, 1944-46. Mem. Holland Soc. N.Y., Phi Beta Kappa. Clubs: Country of Fairfield (Conn.); Weston (Conn.) Gun. Home: 33 Hill Brook Ln Fairfield CT 06430-7169

SUTPHIN, JOHN E. ophthalmologist, educator; b. Atlanta, Dec. 14, 1948; s. John Everett and Elsie Eubank Sutphin; m. Emily Anne Mitchell, Aug. 29, 1970; children: Amanda, Rhett, John G. MD, Vanderbilt U., 1974. Diplomate Am. Bd. Ophthalmology. Commd. ensign USN, 1971, advanced through grades to capt., 1988; ret., 1993; intern Naval Regional Med. Ctr., San Diego, 1974-75, resident in ophthalmology, 1976-79, comprehensive ophthalmologist Orlando, Fla., 1979-82; clin. instr. Baylor Coll. Medicine, Houston, 1982-84; dir. cornea svcs. Naval Med. Ctr., San Diego, 1984-86, chmn. dept. ophthalmology, 1986-93; prof. ophthalmology U. Iowa, Iowa City, 1993—. Past advisor Surgeon Gen. of Navy, Bur. Medicine and Surgery, Washington. Fellow Am. Acad. Ophthalmology (com. chmn. 2000—, Honor award 1996). Presbyterian. Avocations: reading, hiking, biking, woodworking. Office: U Iowa Hosps and Clinics 200 Hawkins Dr Iowa City IA 52242-1091 Office Phone: 319-356-2861. Office Fax: 319-353-7996. Business E-Mail: john-sutphin@uiowa.edu.

SUTTER, DARRYL JOHN, professional hockey coach; Player Chgo. Blackhawks, 1980-86, asst. coach, 1987-88, assoc. coach, 1991-92, head coach, 1992-95, cons., 1995-97; head coach San Jose Sharks, 1997—2002, Calgary Flames, 2002—, gen. mgr., 2003—. Office: Calgary Flames P O Box 1540 Sta M T2P 3B9 Calgary AB Canada

SUTTER, ELEANOR BLY, retired diplomat; b. N.Y.C., Oct. 21, 1945; d. Samuel M. and Sylvia Gertrude Bly; children: Deborah Nelson, Willis. BA, Swarthmore Coll., 1966; MA, Am. U., 1978; diploma in strategic studies, U.S.

Army War Coll., 1997. Instr. English Thammasat U., Bangkok and Udornthani Tchr. Tng. Coll., 1967-71, Lomonosov State U., Moscow, 1973-74; rschr. Kennan Inst. for Advanced Russian Studies, 1977-79; fgn. svc. officer Office Soviet Internal Affairs Dept. of State, 1979-80, fgn. svc. officer Office of Strategic Nuc. Policy, 1986-88, fgn. svc. officer Office of Soviet Union Affairs, 1988-90, office dir., 1997-99, sr. inspector Office Inspector Gen., 1999-2001, dir. Office of Proliferation Threat Reduction, 2001—02; fgn. svc. officer U.S. Embassy, Kinshasa, 1980-82, London, 1982-85, Moscow, 1990-92, charge d'affaires ad interim Bratislava, 1993, dep. prin. officer, 1993-95, dep. chief of mission, 1995-96. Exec. dir., exec. sec., advisor U.S. Del. to Nuclear and Space Talks, Geneva, 1987-91; teaching fellow Russian lit. The Am. U., 1976-77; escort interpreter and translator Dept. of State, 1976. Co-author: Final Report of the Kennan Institute's Soviet Research Institutes Project, 1981. Founder Camp Wocsom, Moscow, 1974. Mem. Am. Fgn. Svc. Assn. Avocations: music, folk dance. Office: care of Fgn Svc Lounge Dept State Washington DC 20520

SUTTER, JANE E. editor; b. Iowa; m. Gary Brandt. B Journalism, U. Mo., 1981. Reporter, then lifestyle editor Hawk Eye, Burlington, Iowa, 1981; lifestyle writer, editor Daily Courier-News, Elgin, Ill.; features editor, then dep. city editor Bradenton (Fla.) Herald, 1987—93; assigning editor The State, Columbia, SC, 1993—95; with corp. news divsn. Knight Ridder Inc., 1995—97; mng. editor Star-Gazette, Elmira, NY, 1997—98, exec. editor, 1998—2001; mng. editor Rochester (NY) Dem. and Chronicle, 2001—. Office: Rochester Dem and Chronicle 55 Exchange Blvd Rochester NY 14614-2001 Office Phone: 585-258-2301.

SUTTER, JANE ELIZABETH, science educator, writer, lecturer, conservationist; b. St. Louis, Nov. 27, 1939; d. Richard A. and Elizabeth Henby Sutter. AB in Sociology and English, Vassar Coll., 1961; MA in Health Facilities Mgmt., Webster Coll., St. Louis, 1979. Healthcare analyst, Chgo. and St. Louis, 1966-83; asst. dir. radio, TV and motion picture dept. AMA, Chgo., 1966-67; staff coord., rsch. assoc. Chgo. water quality study and environ. health study Inst. of Medicine of Chgo., 1967-69; dir. environ. health planning Comprehensive Health Planning, Inc., Chgo., 1969-73; planning assoc., spl. asst. to med. dir. Sutter Clinic, Inc., St. Louis, 1975-84; vol. activist, educator; founder, dir. for conservation and gardening for birds Wild Birds for the 21st Century (a non-profit ednl. svc.), 1994—. Chmn. Opera Theatre of St. Louis Newsletter, Recitative, Vol. 1, No. 1, 1980, Vol. 1, No. 2, 1980; co-founder, com. mem. 1st Internat. Alewife Festival of Chgo., Chgo. Yacht Club, summer 1968; appointee Gov.'s Com. for Pure Air and Water, Chgo., 1968; spl. advocate N.Am. Migratory Birds particularly hummingbirds; mem. Ladue Chapel. Mem. Nat. Garden Clubs, Inc., Federated Garden Clubs of Mo., Inc., Clayton Garden Assn., Mo. Bot. Garden, St. Louis Artists' Guild (mem. artists' sect. 1992-95, portraitist), Inst. on Religion in an Age of Sci., Neotropical Bird Club (U.K.)., Univ. Club, Bradenton C. of C. Avocations: art, writing, gardening. Home: 7376 Pershing Blvd Saint Louis MO 63130-4206 E-mail: jesutteri@aol.com.

SUTTER, JEAN, sculptor; b. Chgo., Aug. 9, 1934; d. John H. and Lulu Kennedy Sutter; m. Paul W. Berg, Jan. 1, 1953 (dec. Mar. 1968); children: Mark, Julie, Karen;. B Visual Arts, Ga. State U., 1974, M Visual Arts, 1978. One-woman shows include: Lowe Gallery, Atlanta, 1989, U. Okla., Norman, 1984, Quinlan Art Ctr., Gainesville, Ga., 1981, Ga. State U., Atlanta, 1979, Auburn U., Ala., 1978; group shows include: Arts Connection, Atlanta, 1990, Jubilee-So. Festival of the Arts, Atlanta, 1987, Heath Gallery, Atlanta, 1985, Atlanta Arts Festival, 1980, 82, 84, Sculptural Arts Mus., 1982, Columbia Mus., S.C., 1982, Mus. of Touch, Atlanta, 1981, Am. Art Inc., Atlanta, 1981, Temple U., Phila., 1980, Cedar Crest Coll., Allentown, Pa., 1980-81, High Mus. Art, Atlanta, 1979, 78, others; collections include Ga. State U., New Life Covenant Ch., Atlanta, Macon (Ga.) State Coll., numerous pvt. parties. Home and Office: 18 Padsett Ct # 20334 Jasper GA 30143-7217

SUTTER, JOSEPH F. aeronautical engineer, consultant, retired air transportation executive; b. Seattle, Mar. 21, 1921; m. Nancy Ann French, June 14, 1943. BA, U. Wash., 1943; Doctorate, Nova Gorcia Poly. Inst., 2004. Various engring. positions Boeing Comml. Airplane Co., Seattle, 1946—65, dir. engring. for Boeing 747, 1965—71, v.p., gen. mgr. 747 div., 1971—74, v.p. program ops., 1974—76, v.p. ops. and product devel., 1976—81, exec. v.p., 1981—86, cons., 1986—87, 1987—. Chmn. aerospace safety adv. panel NASA, 1986; mem. Challenger Accident Commn., 1986. Served to lt. j.g. USN, 1943—45. Named Joseph F. Sutter professorship established in his honor, U. Wash., Boeing Co., 1992; named to, Interant. Air Cargo Assn. Hall of Fame; recipient Master Design award, Product Engring. mag., 1965, Franklin W. Kolk Air Transp. Progress award, Soc. Aero. Aerospace Coun., 1980, Elmer A. Sperry award, 1980, Nuts & Bolts award, Transport Assn., 1983, Nat. Medal Tech., U.S. Pres. Reagan, 1985, Sir Kingsford Smith award, Royal Aero. Soc. in Sydney, 1980, Wright Bros. Meml. Trophy, 1986, Alumnus Summa Laude Dignatus award, U. Wash., 2001. Fellow: AIAA (Daniel Guggenheim award 1990), Royal Aero Soc. (hon.); mem.: Internat. Fedn. Airworthiness (pres. 1989), Slovenian Acad. Engring. (hon.). Address: Boeing 7755 E Marginal Way S Seattle WA 98108-4002

SUTTER, LAURENCE BRENER, lawyer; b. N.Y.C., Feb. 5, 1944; s. Meyer and Beatrice Sutter; m. Betty A. Satterwhite, June 9, 1979. AB, Columbia Coll., 1965; JD, N.Y.U., 1976. Bar: N.Y. 1977, U.S. Dist. Ct. (so. and ea. dists.) N.Y. 1977. Assoc. Shea & Gould, N.Y.C., 1976-80, Meyer, Suozzi, English & Klein P.C., Mineola, N.Y., 1980-82; assoc. counsel publs. Gen. Media Comm., Inc., N.Y.C., 1982-96, sr. v.p., gen. counsel, sec., 1997—. With N.Y. Army N.G., 1966-72. Mem. Assn. of Bar of City of N.Y. (mem. com. on civil rights 1986-89, mem. com. on comm. and media law 1989-92, mem. com. on copyright and lit. property 1994-97), First Amendment Lawyers Assn., Nat. Arts Club, Orient (N.Y.) Yacht Club (dir. 1997-2000, sec. 2000-2001). Democrat. Jewish. Avocations: music, sailing. Office Phone: 212-702-6000.

SUTTER, LAWRENCE A. lawyer, educator; b. Barberton, Ohio, Oct. 24, 1963; BA, Glenville State Coll., 1986; JD, U. Akron, 1989. Bar: Ohio 1989, U.S. Dist. Ct. (no. dist.) Ohio 1991, U.S. Ct. Appeals (6th cir.) Tenn. 2001. Mng. ptnr. Sutter, O'Connell, Mannion & Farchione, Franklin, Tenn. Prof. U. Akron, 2001—, dir. Trial Advocacy Sch. Law. Named one of Top Ten Trial Lawyers, The Nat. Law Jour., 2002. Mem.: ABA, Ohio State Bar Assn., Cuyahoga County Bar Assn., Cleve. (Ohio) Bar Assn., Akron (Ohio) Bar Assn., Anthony D. Celebrezze Inn Ct. Office: Sutter OConnell Mannion & Farchione 217 Second Ave South Franklin TN 37064-2622*

SUTTER, MORLEY CARMAN, medical scientist; b. Redvers, Sask., Can., May 18, 1933; s. Christian Benjamin and Amelia (Duke) S.; m. Virginia Frances Mary Laidlaw, June 29, 1957; children— Gregory Robert, F. Michelle, Brent Morley. BSc, MD, U. Man., 1957, PhD, 1963. Intern Winnipeg (Man.) Gen. Hosp., Canada, 1956-57, resident, 1958-59; tchg. fellow pharmacology U. Man., 1959-63; supr. Downing Coll., Cambridge U., 1963-65; asst. prof. pharmacology U. Toronto, 1965-66, U. B.C., 1966-68, assoc. prof., 1968-71, prof., 1971-98, retired prof. emeritus, 1998—, head dept. pharmacology, 1971-87. Former mem. staff Vancouver (B.C.) Hosp. & Health Sci. Ctr., St. Paul's Hosp.; mem. Minister of Health's Adv. Com. on Drugs, Province of B.C., 1971-87. Contbr. articles to sci. jours. Recipient Gov. Gen. medal, 1950; Med. Rsch. Coun. of Can. fellow, 1959-63; Wellcome Found. Travelling fellow, 1963; Imperial Chem. Industries fellow, 1963-65; Med. Rsch. Coun. scholar, 1966-71 Mem. Brit. Pharmacol. Soc., Am. Soc. Pharmacology and Exptl. Therapeutics, Can. Pharmacol. Soc. Office: U BC Faculty Medicine Therapeutics 2176 Health Scis Mall Dept Pharmacology Vancouver BC Canada V6T 1Z3 E-mail: mcsutter@interchange.ubc.ca.

SUTTER, WILLIAM PAUL, lawyer; b. Chgo., Jan. 15, 1924; s. Harry Blair and Elsie (Paul) S.; m. Helen Yvonne Stebbins, Nov. 13, 1954; children: William Paul, Helen Blair Sutter. AB, Yale U., 1947; JD, U. Mich., 1950. Bar: Ill. 1950, Fla. 1977, U.S. Supreme Ct. 1981. Assoc. Hopkins & Sutter (and predecessors), Chgo., 1950-57, ptnr., 1957-89, of counsel, 1989—2001. Mem. Ill. Supreme Ct. Atty. Registration Commn., 1975-81 Contbr. articles on estate planning and taxation to profl. jours. Chmn. Winnetka Caucus Com., 1966-67; pres., trustee Lucille P. Markey Charitable Trust, 1983-98; precinct capt. New Trier Twp. (Ill.) Rep. party, 1960-68; asst. area chmn. New Trier Rep. Orgn., 1968-72; trustee Gads Hill Center, pres., 1962-70, chmn., 1971-80; trustee Northwestern Meml. Hosp., 1983-98, life trustee, 1998—; bd. dirs. Chgo. Hort. Soc., 1982—; mem. dean's coun. Sch. Medicine, Yale U., 1991-97; bd. visitors Waisman Ctr., U. Wis., 1996-2002; corr. sec. Yale U. Class of 1945, 1990—. Served to 1st lt. AUS, 1943-46. Fellow Am. Bar Found., Am. Coll. Trust and Estate Counsel (bd. regents 1977-83, exec. com. 1981-83); mem. ABA (ho. dels. 1972-81, chmn. com. on income estates and trusts, taxation sect. 1973-75), Ill. Bar Assn. (bd. govs. 1964-75, pres. 1973-74), Chgo. Bar Assn. (chmn. probate practice com. 1963-64), Am. Law Inst., Internat. Acad. Estate and Trust Law, Am. Judicature Soc., Ill. LAWPAC (pres. 1977-83), Order of Coif, Phi Beta Kappa, Phi Delta Phi, Chi Psi, Mid-Day Club, Indian Hill Club, Gulf Stream Golf Club, Country Club Fla., Ocean Club (Fla.) (bd. govs. 1993-99, sec. 1993-97, pres. 1997-99), Lawyers Club Chgo. Episcopalian. Home (Winter): 2 Par Club Cir Village Boynton Beach FL 33436 E-mail: wpsutter@aol.com.

SUTTERBY, LARRY QUENTIN, internist; b. North Kansas City, Mo., Sept. 11, 1950; s. John Albert and Wilma Elizabeth (Henry) Sutterby; m. Luciana Risos Magpuri, July 5, 1980; children: Leah Lourdes, Liza Bernadette. BA in Chemistry, William Jewell Coll., 1972; MD, U. Mo., Kans. City, 1976. Resident in internal medicine Mt. Sinai Hosp., Chgo., 1976-79; physician Mojave Desert Health Svc., Barstow, Calif., 1979-86; pvt. practice Barstow, 1986-2001; med. cons. State of Calif., L.A., 2001—. Med dir Mojave Valley Hospice, 1983—2001, VNA Hospice, Barstow, 1994—2001, Option-care Home Health Servs, 1995—2001. Recipient Loving Care Award, Vis Nurse Asn Inland Counties, 1988. Democrat. Roman Catholic. Avocation: astronomy. Office: 311 S Spring St Ste 900 Los Angeles CA 90013

SUTTERFIELD, JAMES RAY, lawyer; Bar: La., 1967; U.S. Dist. Ct. (ea. dist.) La., 1967; U.S. Ct. Appeals (5th cir.), 1967,; U.S. Dist. Ct. (mid. dist.) La., 1971; D.C., 1977; U.S. Supreme Ct., 1977; U.S. Dist. Ct. (we. dist.) La., 1982; U.S. Dist. Ct. (ea. dist.) Tex., 1985; Tex., 1993. Assoc. Law Offices Walter F. Marcus, New Orleans, 1967, Huddleston and Davis, New Orleans, 1968-70, ptnr., 1970-72, Sutterfield and Vickery, New Orleans, 1973-82, Carmouche, Gray, and Hoffman, New Orleans, 1982-89; sr. dir. Hoffman, Sutterfield, and Ensenat, A.P.L.C., New Orleans, 1989-97; sr. ptnr. Sutterfield and Webb, LLC, New Orleans, 1997—. Hon. consul gen. St. Vincent and The Grenadines, 1997-; faculty mem. tenth diving accident and hyperbaric oxygen treatment course Duke U.; del. Undersea and Hyperbaric Med. Soc. Nat. Oceanographic and Atmospheric Adminstrn.; speaker in field. Author: (with others) Commercial Damages, 1989; mem. editl. bd. Hull Claims Analysis; contbr. articles to profl. jour. Mem. ABA (chmn. excess surplus lines and reins. com.); La. Bar Assn., (5th Cir.) Bar Assn.; D.C. Bar Assn.; La. Assn. Def. Counsel; Internat. Assn. Def. Counsel (chmn. maritime and energy law com., class action and multiparty litigation com.); Maritime Law Assn. U.S. (chmn. marine product liability com.); Def. Rsch. Inst.; The Harmonie Group of Ind. Law Firms (pres. 1999-2001). Office: Sutterfield & Webb 650 Poydras St Fl 27 New Orleans LA 70130-6101

SUTTERLIN, JAMES SMYRL, political science educator, researcher; b. Frankfort, Ky., Mar. 15, 1922; s. Frederick J. and Agnes (Douglas) S.; m. Betty C. Berven, June 24, 1950 (dec. Jan. 1989); children: Rose E., Sabrina, Jamie Ann, James E.; m. Renate Craine, Dec. 27, 1997. BA, Haverford Coll., 1943; postgrad., Harvard U., 1949, 67; hon. degree in jurisprudence, Kyung Hee U., Seoul, Korea, 1973. Vice-consul U.S. Fgn. Svc., Berlin, 1946-48; polit. officer U.S. Mission, Berlin, 1951-54; 1st sec. U.S. Embassy, Tel Aviv, 1954-56; desk officer U.S. State Dept., Washington, 1956-60; 1st sec. U.S. Embassy, Tokyo, 1960-63, counselor Bonn, 1963-68; dir. U.S. Dept. State, Washington, 1969-72, insp.-gen., 1972-74; dir. UN, N.Y.C., 1974-87; dir. rsch. L.I. U., Bklyn., 1985-87, adj. prof., 1985—; fellow/lectr. Yale U., New Haven, 1988—. Author: Berlin—Symbol of Confrontation, 1989, UN and the Maintenance of Security, 1995, The United Nations in Iraq: Defanging the Viper, 2003. Elder Presbyn. Ch., Port Chester, N.Y., 1976-96; chmn. Samaritan House, White Plains, N.Y., 1990-95; pres. Wainwright House, Rye, 1995-96; chmn. acad. coun. on the UN Brown U., 1995-97. 1st lt. U.S. Army, 1945-46. Recipient Grosse Verdienstkreuz, Fed. Republic of Germany, 1974. Mem. UN Assn. of U.S.A., Am. Coun. on Germany, Coun. Fgn. Rels., Phi Beta Kappa. Avocation: gardening. Home: 17 N Chatsworth Ave Apt 6k-l Larchmont NY 10538-2126 Office: Yale U 34 Hillhouse Ave New Haven CT 06511-3704 E-mail: jsutter728@aol.com.

SUTTIE, JOHN WESTON, biochemist; b. La Crosse, Wis., Aug. 25, 1934; married; 2 children. BS, U. Wis., 1957, MS, 1958, PhD, 1960. Fellow biochemist Nat. Inst. Med. Rsch, England, 1960-61; asst. prof. to assoc. prof. biochemistry U. Wis., Madison, 1961-69, prof., 1969—2001, chair nutrition sci., 1988-97, Katherine Berns Van Donk Steenbock prof. nutrition, 2000, prof. emeritus, 2002—. Mem. Bd. on Agriculture & Natural Resources, 1996—2001. Assoc. editor Jour Nutrition, 1991-97; editor Jour. Nutrition, 1997—2003. Recipient Disting. Achievement in Nutrition Rsch., Bristol-Myers Squibb/Mead Johnson, 2002. Fellow Am. Heart Assn. Coun. Nutrition, Physical Activity and Metabolism, Am. Soc. for Nutrition Scis. (Osborne and Mendel award 1980, Mead Johns award 1974, Conrad Elvehjem award, 2004); mem. NAS, Am. Soc. Expl. Biology and Medicine, Am. Soc. Biochemistry and Molecular Biology, Am. Soc. Clin. Nutrition, Internat. Soc. Thrombosis and Hemostasis (Hemostasis Career award 1989). Office: U Wis Dept Biochemistry Madison WI 53706-1544 E-mail: suttie@biochem.wisc.edu.

SUTTLE, DEBORAH S. state legislator; b. Charleston, W.Va., Dec. 28, 1945; m. James H. Suttle, June 4, 1966; children: Virginia Adele, Amber Karolyn. BS, W.Va. U., 1967; postgrad., U. Nebr., Omaha, 1989-91. Former RN; mem. Nebr. Legislature from 10th dist., Lincoln, 1997—. Vol. Douglas County election commr.; mem. United Meth. Ch., Omaha, League Women Voters, 1980—, Voices for Children; former mem. Omaha 2000 Task Force, Pulling Ams. Communities Together, Omaha Pub. Sch. Supt. Adv. Com., Nebr. Partnership Com., Douglas County Corrections Adv. Com.; mem. various PTA's, Omaha, 1976-93; former pres. LWV for Greater Omaha, 1991-93, Laura Dodge Elem. Parent-Tchr. Assn., 1978-79; vol. lobbyist Omaha PTA/PTSA Coun., 1980-91, Nebr. PTA, 1986-89; v.p. Optimist Internat., 1995-96; vol. lobbyist Nebr. LWV, 1994-96; vol. lobbyist, bd. dirs. PRIDE-Omaha, 1984-96. Mem. Nebr. Nurses' Assn. Home: 6054 Country Club Oaks Pl Omaha NE 68152-2009 Office: State Capitol Dist 10 PO Box 94604 Rm 1000 Lincoln NE 68509 Fax: 402-571-6901.

SUTTLE, HELEN JAYSON, retired education educator; b. Plattsburgh, N.Y., Dec. 13, 1925; d. Harold Lincoln Jayson and Blanche Rabideau Jayson Woods; widowed, 1993; 1 child, Adolphia Helen Suttle Blanton. BA in Edn., Limestone Coll., 1961; MA in Edn., Winthrop U., 1973. Cert. tchr., S.C. Tchr. Madden Elem. Sch., Spartanburg, S.C., 1961-71, West Jr. High Sch., Gaffney, S.C., 1971-81, L.L. Vaughn Elem. Sch., Gaffney, S.C., 1981-88; substitute tchr. Gaffney Dis. 1, 1988—. Vol. SC Budget Control Bd., Upstate Carolina Med. Ctr., Meals on Wheels, Literacy Assn., local soup kitchen; chmn. Cherokee County Rep. Com.; v.p. Ch. Women's Guild, pres., 1998—; dir. religious edn. Sacred Heart Ch., 2001—; pres. Sacred Heart Sr. Citizens Club; treas. ch. com. Greenville Deanery; pres.-elect Piedmont Deanery, 2002—; Eucharistic min., lector; mem. exec. bd. SC Coun. Cath. Ch. Women, 1998—, chair family commn., 1998—; pres. Piedmont Deanery, 2002—03; trustee Limestone Coll. Named woman of Yr., S.C. Coun. Cath. Women Greenville Deanery, 1996. Fellow Internat. Biog. Assn. (life, dep. gov. Am. chpt.), Limestone Coll. Alumni Assn. (pres., chpt. pres.), Fountain Club (charter mem.), Kalosophia Honor Soc. Roman Catholic. Avocations: writing, art, gardening, crafts. Home: 201 Trenton Rd Gaffney SC 29340-3626

SUTTLE, STEPHEN HUNGATE, lawyer; b. Uvalde, Tex., Mar. 17, 1940; s. Dorwin Wallace and Ann Elizabeth Suttle; m. Rosemary Williams Davison, Aug. 3, 1963; children: Michael Barrett, David Paull, John Stewart. BA, Washington and Lee U., 1962; LLB, U. Tex., 1965. Bar: Tex. 1965, U.S. Dist. Ct. (no. and we. dists.) Tex. 1965, U.S. Ct. Appeals (5th cir.) 1967, U.S. Supreme Ct. 1970. Law clk. to Hon. Leo Brewster U.S. Dist. Ct., Ft. Worth, 1965-67; ptnr. McMahon, Surovik, Suttle, Buhrmann, Hicks, Gill & Cannon P.C., Abilene, Tex., 1970—. Pres. Abilene Boys Clubs, Inc., 1975—76; bd. dirs. Abilene Cmty. Theater, 1979—80, Abilene Fine Arts Mus., 1977—78. Fellow: State Bar Tex. (dir. 1999—2002), Tex. Bar Found., Am. Bd. Trial Advocates (pres. Tex. 2003), Am. Coll. Trial Lawyers; mem.: ABA, Tex. Bar Assn. (dir. 1999—2002), Abilene Bar Assn. (pres. 1987—88), Am. Judicature Soc. (bd. dirs. 1981—84), Tex. Young Lawyers Assn. (chmn. bd. dirs. 1976), Def. Rsch. Inst., Tex. Assn. Def. Counsel, Assn. Def. Trial Attys., Abilene Country Club. Episcopalian. Home: 1405 Woodland Trl Abilene TX 79605-4705 Office: McMahon Surovik Suttle Buhrmann Hicks Gill & Cannon PC PO Box 3679 Abilene TX 79604-3679 E-mail: ssuttle@mcmahonlawtx.com.

SUTTLES, DAVID CLYDE, educator; b. Harriman, Tenn., June 14, 1948; s. Clyde and Virginia (Stewart) S.; m. Barbara Chambers, June 3, 1968; children: Julia Kay, Robert David. BS in Bus. Adminstrn., U. Tenn., 1972, MS, 1975, MEd, 1998. Assoc. prof. Cleve. State Coll., Tenn., 1975—; news dir. WTNB-TV, 1998—99; counselor Pine Ridge Treatment Ctr., 2001—. Adj. faculty Tenn. Wesleyan Coll., 1987—; crisis intervention specialist Vol. Behavioral, 2000—01; counselor Pine Ridge Treatment Ctr., 2001. Active Cmty. Devel. Citizens Adv. Com., Cleveland, 1981; active Gov.'s Com. Employment of Handicapped, 1984; mem. Tenn. Com. on Persons with Disabilities, 1991—; lay dir. Diocese East Tenn. Episc. Cursillo Secretariat; eucharistic min. St. Luke's Episc. Ch.; bd. dirs. Friends of Libr., Cleve., 1984, Habitat for Humanity, Arthritis Found. Recipient Aciever award Gov. Tenn., 1976; cert. of appreciation Mayor of Cleveland, 1980. Mem. Coll. Media Advisors, Mensa, Phi Theta Kappa. Democrat. Office: Cleveland State Community Coll PO Box 3570 Cleveland TN 37320-3570 Personal E-mail: sudsy1948@aol.com.

SUTTON, BETTY, state legislator; married. BA, Kent State Univ., 1985; JD, Univ. Akron, 1990. Coun.-at-larte Barberton City Coun., 1990-91; v.p. Summit County Coun., 1991-92; state rep. Ohio Dist. 47, 1993—. Vice chmn. Judiciary & Criminal Justice Com., mem. Civil & Comml. Law, Ways & Means, Ins. Pub. Utilities & Elec. Twp. Com. Recipient Outstanding Performance in Const. Law Fed. Bar Assn., 1989, Am. Jurisprudence award, 1989. Mem. ABA, Akron Child Guidance Adv. Coun., Assn. Trial Lawyers Am., Ohio Acad. Trial Lawyers, Summit County Trial Lawyers, Fed. Dem. Women. Office: Ohio Ho of Reps State House Columbus OH 43215 Home: 13488 Walnut Trce Chardon OH 44024-9302

SUTTON, BETTY SHERIFF, elementary school educator; b. Orangeburg, S.C., Jan. 16, 1933; d. Luther Doyle and Mattie (White) Sheriff; m. William Bryan Nunn, June 19, 1954; 1 child, Lisbeth Sheriff Nunn (Mrs. William Reid Clark); m. James Carlton Sutton, Dec. 28, 1979 (dec., 1998). Student, Columbia Coll., 1949-52; BS, U. S.C., 1953. Tchr. grade 4 State of S.C. Pub. Sch., Blackville, 1953-54; tchr. grade 2 Dream Lake Elem. Sch., Apopka, Fla., 1954-64; tchr. spl. edn. Leon County Sch., Tallahassee, Fla., 1965-66; page mother Fla. Ho. Reps., Tallahassee, 1966-67; tchr. grade 3 Timberlane Elem. Sch./Leon County Schs., Tallahassee, 1967-71; tchr. grades 3 and 4 Golfview Elem. Sch./Brevard County Schs., Rockledge, Fla., 1972-86; tchr. grade 1 Cambridge Elem. Sch./Brevard County Schs., Cocoa, Fla., 1987-98; ret., 1998. Pres. Bits of Brevard, Inc., Rockledge. Chmn. Democrats for Conner, 1988, Keep Brevard Beautiful, 1990; active Brevard Symphony Orch. Guild, Brevard Mus. Guild, 1973—, Brevard Heritage Coun., Inc., Episcopal, St. Marks Guild. Recipient S.C. Forestry award State of S.C. Forestry Commn., 1977; ART grantee J. Paul Getty Ctr. for Edn. in the Arts, 1990. Mem. AAUW (pres. 1968-70), Apopka Woman's Club (pres. 1960-62), Apopka Garden Club, Brevard Reading Coun. (v.p. 1980-82), Am. Mothers, Inc., Columbia Coll. Column Club, Columbia Coll. Alumni Club. Ctrl. Fla., U. S.C. Alumni Club (life), Country Club of Rockledge (bd. dirs. 2002-2003, 2003-2004), Delta Kappa Gamma (pres. 1992-94). Avocations: volunteering, reading, swimming, travel, farming. Home: 2201 Royal Oaks Dr Rockledge FL 32955-5440

SUTTON, BEVERLY JEWELL, psychiatrist; b. Rockford, Mich., May 27, 1932; d. Beryl Dewey and Cora Belle (Potes) Jewell; m. Harry Eldon Sutton, July 7, 1962; children: Susan, Caroline. MD, U. Mich., 1957. Diplomate Am. Bd. Pediat., Am. Bd. Psychiatry and Neurology. Rotating intern St. Joseph Mercy Hosp., Ann Arbor, Mich., 1958; resident in child psychiatry Hawthorne Ctr., Northville, Mich., 1958-62; resident in pediat. U. Hosp./U. Mich. Med. Ctr., Ann Arbor, 1959-61; resident in psychiatry Austin (Tex.) State Hosp., 1962-64, dir. children's svc., 1964-89, dir. psychiat. residency program, 1989—, dir. tng. and rsch., 1993-98. Cons. in field. Contbr. articles to profl. jours. Active numerous civic orgns. Recipient Outstanding Achievement award, YWCA, 1989, Jackson Day award, Tex. Soc. Child and Adolescent Psychiatry, 1989, Showcase award, Tex. Dept. Mental Health/Mental Retardation, 1990. Fellow Am. Acad. Child and Adolescent Psychiatry (life), Am. Psychiat. Soc., Am. Pediatric Assn.; mem. Tex. Soc. Child and Adolescent Psychiatry (pres. 1979-80), Tex. Soc. Psychiat. Physicians (Disting. Svc. award 1990), AMA, Tex. Med. Soc., Am. Genetics Soc. Office: Seton Shoal Creek Hosp 3501 Mills Ave Austin TX 78731 Business E-Mail: bsutton@seton.org.

SUTTON, CECILIA (CECE SUTTON), bank executive; b. Charlotte, NC; B in Psychology, U. SC; MBA, Winthrop U. Branch manager First Union Corp., Raleigh and Cary, NC, consumer credit sales mgr. Charlotte, NC, 1984—86, consumer banking mgr. Greenville, SC, 1986—89, consumer bank training dir. Charlotte, NC, 1988—89, area exec. Rock Hill, SC, 1989—92, head SC Gen. Banking Group Greenville, SC, 1992—93, area exec. Rock Hill, SC, 1993—95, consumer banking exec., exec. v.p., 2001; exec. v.p., head retail Wachovia Corp. (merged with First Union Corp), Charlotte, 2001—. Office: Wachovia Corp 301 S Coll St Charlotte NC 28288-0018*

SUTTON, DOLORES, actress, writer; b. N.Y.C. BA in Philosophy, NYU. Appeared in broadway plays including Man With the Golden Arm, 1956, Career, 1958, Machinal, 1960, Rhinoceros, Liliom, She Stoops to Conquer, Hedda Gabler, Anna Karenina, Eccentricities of a Nightingale, Brecht on Brecht, Young Gifted and Black, Luv, The Friends, The Web and the Rock, The Seagull, Saturday, Sunday, Monday, The Little Foxes, What's Wrong With This Picture, The Cocktail Hour, My Fair Lady (Broadway revival), 1994, My Fair Lady (nat. tour), 1993-94; films include The Trouble With Angels, Where Angels Go, Trouble Follows, Crossing Delancey, Crimes and Misdeameanors, Tales of the Darkside; TV appearances include Studio One, Hallmark Hall of Fame Prodn. An Wilderness, Theatre Guild of the Air: Danger, Suspense, Gunsmoke, Valiant Lady, General Hospital, From These Roots, As the World Turns, Edge of Night, F. Scott Fitzgerald in Hollywood, Patty Hearst Story, All in the Family, Bob Newhart Show, All My Children, others, (TV writer) Lady Somebody, 1999, The Secret Storm, Loving; playwright: Down at the Old Bull and Bush, The Web and the Rock, Company Comin', Born Yesterday, 1995, A Perfect Ganesh, 1995, Detail of a Larger Work, 1995, The Front Page, 1996, The Exact Center of the Universe, 1997, A Drop in the Bucket, 1997, Spring Storm (newly discovered Tennessee Williams play), 1997, Signs and Wonders, 1998, It Gives Me Great Pleasure, 2001; prodns. Free Ascent, 2001, Burial Society, 2001, The Find, 2002. Mem. League of Profl. Theatre Women (bd. dirs.), Ensemble Studio Theatre (bd. dirs.).

SUTTON, ERNEST SHAW, chemical engineer; b. Burlington, N.J., May 22, 1922; s. Ernest Shaw Sr. and Elizabeth Bauer (Sholl) S.; m. Janet Gilbertson, July 1, 1950 (dec. Mar. 1974); children: Jane M., Douglas S., Andrea L.; m. Lois Williams, June 12, 1975. BSChemE, U. Pa., 1943. Analytical chemist Nat. Synthetic Rubber Corp., Louisville, 1943-44; polymer chemist Hewitt Robins, Inc., Buffalo, 1946-48, United Aircraft, Inc., Hartford, Conn., 1948-50, Thermoid Rubber Co., Trenton, N.J., 1950-53; propellant chemist Thiokol Corp., Elkton, Md., 1953-54, head R&D labs., 1954-84; head preliminary design Morton-Thiokol, Inc., Elkton, 1984-86, dir. mktg., 1986-87, v.p., gen. mgr., 1987-88; pvt. practice aerospace cons. West Grove, Pa., 1988—. Bd. dirs. Cecon, Inc., Wilmington, Del., Jenners Pond, Inc., West Grove. Author: History of Thiokol and Rockets, 1996. With U.S. Army, 1944—46. Mem. AAAS, AIAA, Am. Chem. Soc., Planetary Soc. Achievements include 8

patents in solid rocket propellants and rocket motor componants. Home: 252 Azalea Ln West Grove PA 19390-9479 Office: Cecon Inc 242 N James St Wilmington DE 19804-3168 E-mail: esutton@kennett.net.

SUTTON, FRANCIS XAVIER, social scientist, consultant; b. Oneida, Pa., July 7, 1917; s. Frank James and Rose Marie (Burns) S.; m. Ruth Jacqueline Young, Aug. 24, 1948 (dec. July 2002); children: Peter, Sean, Philip, Elizabeth. BS, Temple U., 1938; MA, Princeton U., 1940, Harvard U., 1941, PhD, 1950; DLitt (hon.), Aga Khan U., Karachi, 2023. Jr. fellow, Soc. Fellows Harvard U., Cambridge, Mass., 1946-49, asst. prof., lectr., 1949-54; program officer, overseas rep. Ford Found., N.Y.C., 1954-67, dep. v.p., acting v.p., 1968-83; cons. Ford Found. and Harvard U., 1983-85; acting pres. Social Sci. Rsch. Coun., N.Y.C., 1985-86, also bd. dirs., chmn., 1985-92; cons. Rockefeller Found, U.S. Agy. for Internat. Devel. and World Bank, N.Y.C. and Washington, 1987-92; acting dir. Rockefeller Study and Conf. Ctr., Bellagio, Italy, 1990-92; cons. Aga Khan U., 1992—. Author: The American Business Creed, 1956; editor: A World to Make/Development in Perspective, 1989; contbr. articles to profl. jours. and chpts. to books. Pres. Am. Found. for Intellectual Coop. with Europe, N.Y.C., 1987-93; mem. bd. fgn. scholarships Dept. State, Washington, 1961-63; bd. dirs. Nat. Ctr. on Adult Literacy, U. Pa., Phila., 1990-97; mem. adv. bd. Ctr. on Philanthropy, City Univ., N.Y.C., 1988—. Capt. U.S. Army Air Corps, 1941-45. Fellow AAAS; mem. Council on Fgn. Relations, Assn. for Asian Studies (Disting. Service award 1984). Clubs: Century Assn. (N.Y.C.). Democrat. Avocations: piano playing, dance, snorkeling. Home: 80 Bellair Dr Dobbs Ferry NY 10522-3504 E-mail: fxsutton@aol.com.

SUTTON, GREGORY PAUL, obstetrician, gynecologist; b. Tokyo, Dec. 12, 1948; (parents Am. citizens); s. Vernon S. And Vonna Lou (Streeter) S.; m. Judith Craigie Holt, June 26, 1977; children: Anne Craigie, James Streeter. BS in Chemistry with honors, Ind. U., 1970; MD, U. Mich., 1976. Diplomate Am. Bd. of Ob/Gyn. Prof. gynecol. oncology Ind. U. Sch. Medicine, Indpls., 1986-97; Mary Fendrich Hulman prof. Gynecologic Oncology Ind. U. Sch. Med., Indpls., 1997-2000; mem. staff St. Vincent Hosp. and Health Svcs., 2000—01. Cancer Clin. fellow Am. Cancer Soc., Phila., 1981-83; recipient Career Devel. award Am. Cancer Soc., 1986-89. Fellow: Am. Coll. Obstetrics and Gynecology (chair Ind. sect. 2000—03); mem.: ACS (com. on cancer, Ind. state liaison), Hoosier Oncology Group, Soc. of Gynecologic Oncologists, Bayard Carter Soc., Ind. State Med. Soc., Marion County Med. Soc., Gynecologic Oncology Group (cert. Spl. Competence in Gynecologic Oncology 1985). Avocations: swimming, bicycling, woodworking, sailing, crossword puzzles. Office: 8301 Harcourt Rd Ste 202 Indianapolis IN 46260-1453 E-mail: gsutton@stvincent.org.

SUTTON, HAL EVAN, professional golfer; b. Shreveport, La., Apr. 28, 1958; s. Howard Everett and Mary Alice (Rogers) S.; m. Ashley; children: Samantha, Sara, Sadie. BS in Sci., Centenary Coll. Professional golfer, 1981—. Named Player of Yr., Profl. Golf Assn., 1983; winner Disney Classic, 1982, Profl. Golf Assn. Championship, 1983, Tournament Player's Championship, 1983, 2000, Memphis Classic, 1985, Phoenix Open, 1986, Meml. Tournament, 1986, Ryder Cup Team, 1987; B.C. Open, 1995; Westin Texas Open, 1998; The Tour Championship, 1998, Bell Canadian Open, 1999, Greater Greensboro Chrysler Classic, 2000. Office: Sutton Enterprises 212 Texas St Ste 117 Shreveport LA 71101-3287 Home: 909 Trabue St Shreveport LA 71106-1114

SUTTON, HARRY ELDON, geneticist, educator; b. Cameron, Tex., Mar. 5, 1927; s. Grant Edwin and Myrtle Dovie (Fowler) S.; m. Beverly Earlene Jewell, July 7, 1962; children: Susan Elaine, Caroline Virginia. BS in Chemistry, U. Tex., Austin, 1948, MA, 1949; PhD in Biochemistry, U. Tex., 1953. Biologist U. Mich., 1952-56, instr., 1956-57, asst. prof. human genetics, 1957-60; assoc. prof. zoology U. Tex., Austin, 1960-64, prof., 1964-99, chmn. dept. zoology, 1970-73, asso. dean Grad. Sch., 1967-70, 73-75, v.p. for research, 1975-79, Ashbel Smith prof. emeritus molecular genetics and microbiology, 2000—. Mem. adv. council Nat. Inst. Environ. Health Scis., 1968-72, council sci. advs., 1972-76; mem. various coms. Nat. Acad. Scis.-NRC; cons. in field; bd. dirs. Associated Univs. for Research in Astronomy, 1975-79, Argonne Univs. Assn., 1975-79, Univ. Corp. for Atmospheric Research, 1975-79, Associated Western Univs., 1978-79 Author: Genes, Enzymes, and Inherited Disease, 1961, An Introduction to Human Genetics, 1988, Genetics: A Human Concern, 1985; editor: First Macy Conference on Genetics, 1960, Mutagenic Effects of Environmental Contaminants, 1972, Am. Jour. Human Genetics, 1964-69. Trustee S.W. Tex. Corp. Public Broadcasting, 1977-80, sec., 1979-80; bd. dirs. Ballet Austin, 1978-84, 98-2004; mem. Austin Arts Commn., 1991-95. Served with U.S. Army, 1945-46. Mem. AAAS, Am. Soc. Human Genetics (dir. 1961-69, pres. 1979), Genetics Soc. Am., Am. Soc. Biochem. and Molecular Biology, Am. Chem. Soc., Tex. Genetics Soc. (pres. 1979), Am. Genetic Assn., Headliners Club (Austin), Town and Gown Club. Achievements include research and publications in human genetics. Home: 1103 Gaston Ave Austin TX 78703-2507 Office: Univ Tex Sect Molecular Genetics & Microbiology Austin TX 78712 Business E-Mail: eldon.sutton@mail.utexas.edu.

SUTTON, HOWARD G. publishing executive; m. Kimberly G. P. Sutton; 1 child, H. J. Degree in history, Notre Dame U., 1972; MBA, Providence Coll., 1978; grad. PMD program, Harvard U., 1984. Various mgmt. positions Providence Jour. Co., 1973—, pub., pres., CEO, 1997—. V.p. devel. R.I. Philharm.; past chmn. Christmas in Apr., Providence; chmn. R.I. Acad. Decathlon, NCAA Hockey 2000; bd. dirs. Nat. Conf., Leadership R.I., Women and Infants' Hosp., Providence Coll. Pres. Coun., United Way, WaterFire Providence, First Night, The Bus. Edn. Roundtable, World Scholar Games. Mem. Greater Providence C. of C. (exec. bd.), R.I. Commodores, Hope Club, Univ. Club, R.I. Country Club, Notre Dame Club of R.I. (past pres., Man of Yr. 1993). Office: Providence Jour 75 Fountain St Providence RI 02902-0050

SUTTON, JEFFREY S. federal judge; b. Dhahran, Saudi Arabia, 1960; BA, Williams Coll., 1983; LLB, Ohio State Univ., 1990. Clk. Second Circuit Ct. for Judge Thomas Meskill, 1990—91, Supreme Ct. for Justice Scalia and ret. Justice Powell, 1991—92; assoc. Jones, Day, Reavis & Pogue, Columbus, Ohio, 1992—95; adj. law prof. Ohio State Univ., Ohio, 1994—; Solicitor Ohio State, Ohio, 1995—98; ptnr. Jones, Day, Reavis & Pogue, Columbus, Ohio, 1998—2003; judge US Ct. Appeals, (6th cir.), Cin., 2003—. Mr. Sutton's record shows him to be a leading proponent of "federalism" theories. He has written articles, given speeches and argued in several cases before the Supreme Ct. and other courts that Congress should be restricted in power to pass civil, disablility, workers' rights, and environ. laws. He also proposes that people challenging state governments to redress peoples violations of these laws should have restricted access to the courts. In other cases involving the State vs. People, Sutton argued successfully for the State supporting the federalism theory. Office: Office Clerk US Ct Appeals 6th Cir 532 Potter Stewart US Cthse 100 E 5th St Cincinnati OH 45202-3988

SUTTON, JOHN EWING, lawyer; b. San Angelo, Tex., Oct. 7, 1950; s. John F. Jr. and Nancy (Ewing) S.; 1 son, Joshua Ewing; 1 stepson, Michael Brandon Ducote. BBA, U. Tex., 1973, JD, 1976. CPA Tex.; bar: Tex. 1976, U.S. Tax Ct. 1977, U.S. Ct. Claims 1977, U.S. Ct. Appeals (5th cir.) 1978, U.S. Dist. Ct. (we. dist.) Tex. 1979, U.S. Supreme Ct. 1980. Tax specialist Peat, Marwick, Mitchell & Co., CPAs, Dallas, 1976-77; ptnr. Shannon, Porter, Johnson, Sutton and Greendyke Attys. at Law, San Angelo, 1977-87; judge 119th Dist. Ct. of Tex., 1987-99; pvt. practice Law Offices of John E. Sutton, 1999—. Treas. Good Shepherd Episcopal Ch., San Angelo, 1979-81; co-chmn. profl. divsn. United Way, San Angelo, 1980-82; trustee Angelo State U. Found., 1987-99, pres., 1988-91, 95-97, v.p., 1992-94, 98-99, sec.-treas., 1991-92. Fellow Tex. Bar Found. (life); mem. ABA, Tex. Bar Assn., Tex. Criminal Def. Lawyers Assn., Tom Green County Bar Assn. (sec.-treas. young lawyers 1977-78), AICPAs, Tex. Soc. CPAs (bd. dirs. 1980-87, pres. San Angelo chpt. 1980-81, mem. state exec. com. 1981-82, 86-87, state sec. 1986-87, chmn. profl. ethics com. 1985-86, Young CPA of Yr. 1984-85), Concho Valley Estate Planning Coun. (v.p. 1979-80, also dir.). Office: Law Office of John E Sutton 117 S Irving St San Angelo TX 76903-6419

SUTTON, JOHN F., JR., law educator, dean, lawyer; b. Alpine, Tex., Jan. 26, 1918; s. John F. and Pauline Irene (Elam) S.; m. Nancy Ewing, June 1, 1940; children: Joan Sutton Parr, John Ewing. JD, U. Tex., 1941. Bar: Tex. 1941, U.S. Dist. Ct. (we. dist.) Tex. 1947, U.S. Ct. Appeals (5th cir.) 1951, U.S. Supreme Ct. 1960. Assoc. Brooks, Napier, Brown & Matthews, San Antonio, 1941-42; spl. agt. FBI, Washington, 1942-45; assoc. Matthews, Nowlin, Macfarlane & Barrett, San Antonio, 1945-48; ptnr. Kerr, Gayer & Sutton, San Angelo, Tex., 1948-50, Sutton, Steib & Barr, San Angelo, 1951-57; prof. U. Tex.-Austin, 1957-65, William Stamps Farish prof., 1965-84, A.W. Walker centennial chair, 1984-88, emeritus, 1988—, dean Sch. Law, 1979-84. Editor: (with Wellborn) Materials on Evidence, 8th edit., 1996, (with Dzienkowski) Cases and Materials on Professional Responsibility of Lawyers, 1989, (with Schuwerk) Guideline to the Texas Disciplinary Rules of Professional Conduct, 1990, (with Dzienkowski) Cases and Materials on Professional Conduct, 2d edit., 2002; contbr. articles to profl. jours. Served to 1st lt. JAGC USAR, 1948-54. Fellow Am. Bar Found. (life), Tex. Bar Found. (life); mem. ABA (com. on ethics 1970-76), State Bar Tex. (com. on rules of profl. conduct, com. adminstrn. rules of evidence), Philos. Soc. Tex., Order of Coif, U. Tex. Club, Phi Delta Phi, San Angelo Country Club, North Austin Rotary (pres. 1969). Presbyterian. Home: 3830 Sunset Dr San Angelo TX 76904-5956 Office: U Tex Sch Law 727 E Dean Keeton St Austin TX 78705-3224

SUTTON, JOHN PAUL, lawyer; b. Youngstown, Ohio, July 24, 1934; m. Jane Williamson, Aug. 20, 1958; children: Julia, Susan, Elizabeth. BA, U. Va., 1956; JD, George Washington U., 1963. Bar: Calif. 1965. Patent examiner U.S. Patent Office, Washington, 1956, 59-62; law clk. U.S. Ct. Customs and Patent Appeals, Washington, 1962-64; assoc. Flehr, Hohbach, Test, Albritton & Herbert, San Francisco, 1964-68; ptnr. Limbach, Limbach & Sutton, San Francisco, 1969-91; spl. counsel Heller, Ehrman, White & McAuliffe, San Francisco, 1992-95; of counsel Medlin & Carroll, San Francisco, 1995, Bryan, Hinshaw & Barnet, San Francisco, 1996-99; sole practice San Francisco, 2000—. Adj. instr. Practicing Law Inst., 1968-69; continuing edn. program Calif. State Bar, 1972, 75, U. Calif. Law Sch., Berkeley, 1975, 84. Contbr. articles to legal jours. Served with USNR, 1956-59. Mem.: Am. Chem. Soc., Fedn. Internat. des Conseils en Propriete Indsl. (pres. U.S. sect. 2003—), State Bar Calif. (exec. com. patent sect. 1975—77), San Francisco Patent Law Assn. (pres. 1976), Calif. Patent Law Assn. (pres. 1975). Democrat. Episcopalian. Home and Office: 2421 Pierce St San Francisco CA 94115-1131 Office Phone: 415-929-7408.

SUTTON, JOHNNY K. lawyer; b. June 1960; B in Internat. Bus., U. Tex., 1983, JD, 1987. Criminal trial prosecutor Harris County Dist. Atty. Office; asst. dist. atty. Harris County Dist. Atty.'s Office, 1987—95; criminal justice policy dir. Gov. George W. Bush, 1995—2000; assoc. dep. atty. gen. U.S. Dept. Justice, Washington, 2001; policy coord. Bush-Cheney Transition Team, Dept. of Justice; U.S. atty. We. Dist. Tex., 2001—. Avocation: baseball (played for the Longhorns, starting lef-fielder on 1983 Nat. Championship team). Office: 601 NW Loop 410 Ste 600 San Antonio TX 78216

SUTTON, JULIA, musicologist, dance historian; b. Toronto, July 20, 1928; d. Samuel L. and Anne R. (Rubin) Sumberg. AB summa cum laude, Cornell U., 1949; MA, Colo. Coll., 1952; PhD, U. Rochester, 1962. Instr. music history New Sch. for Social Rsch., 1962-63; instr. music Queens Coll., CUNY, 1963-66; instr. music history and musicology New Eng. Conservatory Music, 1967—90, instr. and prof. musicology, 1967—90, chmn. dept. music history and musicology, 1971-90, chmn. faculty senate, 1971-73, prof. emerita, 1992. Vis. asst. prof. George Peabody Coll. for Tchrs., 1966-67; instr. NYU, summers 1963, 64; pvt. tchr. piano, 1949-65; lectr., rsch. dir. in musicology, music as related to the dance; presenter numerous workshops and summer insts. on Renaissance dance. Dance dir. N.Y. Pro Musica prodn. An Entertainment for Elizabeth, Caramoor, N.Y., Saratoga, N.Y., U. Ariz., Stanford U., UCLA, 1969, ann. nationwide tours, 1970-1973; dance dir. Descent of Rhythm and Harmony, Colorado Springs, Colo., 1970, Renaissance Revisited, Phila., 1972, An Evening of Renaissance Music and Dance, York U., Toronto, 1974; author: Jean Baptiste Besard's Novus Partus 1617, 1962; editor: Thoinot Arbeau: Orchesography 1588, 1967; translator, editor: Fabritio Caroso: Nobiltà di dame 1600, 1986, reprinted 1995; producer, co-dir. (tng. video) Il Ballarino, 1991; contbr. numerous articles to profl. jours. and Internat. Ency. of Dance, The New Grove Dictionary of Music and Musicians 1st and 2d edit., Die Musik in Geschichte und Gegenwart, 1st edit. Mem. Am. Musicological Soc., Soc. of Dance History Scholars, Phi Beta Kappa. Office Phone: 781-893-0856.

SUTTON, KAREN E. administrator; b. New Brunswick, N.J., Aug. 26, 1952; d. Alfred Michael and Carmen (Collado) Sutton; children: Sloane, Brooke, Devon, Megan, Christopher. BA, Hofstra U., 1974; postgrad., NYU, 1987—89. Asst. to dir. Mus. Am. Folk Art, N.Y.C., 1975-76, acting dir., 1976-77, bd. dirs., exec. com. officer, 1980-88, gallery dir., 1989-92, dir. ops., 1992-94, dep. dir. planning and adminstrn., 1994-95; v.p. Sotheby's, N.Y.C., 1995-96, sr. v.p. adminstrn., 1996-2001, sr. v.p. worldwide mktg., 2001—. Bd. dirs. Family Dynamics, N.Y.C., 1976-80. Mem. Cosmopolitan Club (younger members chmn.). Democrat. Episcopalian. Home: 4 Sutton Pl New York NY 10022 Office: Sotheby's 1334 York Ave New York NY 10021-4806 Office Phone: 212-606-7410. E-mail: karen.sutton@sothebys.com.

SUTTON, KEITH H. information technology executive; b. Portsmouth, Va., Aug. 28, 1961; s. Hobert Sutton and Irene Burton; m. Leslie Smith, May 5, 1984 (div. July 30, 1994); 1 child, Lauren Brooke. BSEE, Old Dominion U., Norfolk, Va., 1983; MBA, U. San Diego, 1993. Elec. design engr. Naval Electronic Systems Engring. Facility, Portsmouth, Va., 1983—84; test engr. ManTech Internat. Corp, Lexington Park, Md., 1984—87; engring. mgr. Grumman Data Sys., San Diego, 1987—96; pres. and CEO Syzygy Technologies, Inc., San Diego, 1996—. Chmn. Syzygy Technologies, Inc., San Diego. Named Best Small Company to Work for in San Diego, San Diego Bus. Jour., 2004. Mem.: IEEE (life), Armed Forces Comm. & Electronics Assn. (assoc.), Nat. Def. Indsl. Assn. (assoc.; treas. 2002—). Office: Syzygy Technologies Inc Ste 701 1450 Frazee Rd San Diego CA 92108 Office Phone: 619-297-0970 232. Home Fax: 619-297-0975; Office Fax: 619-297-0975. E-mail: ksutton@syzygy-tech.com.

SUTTON, LYNN SORENSEN, librarian; b. Detroit, July 31, 1953; d. Leonard Arthur Edward and Dorothy Ann (Steele) Sorensen. AB, U. Mich., 1975, MLS, 1976. Dir. Med. Libr. South Chgo. Cmty. Hosp., 1976-77; corp. dirs. librs. Detroit-Macomb Hosp. Corp., Detroit, 1977-86; dir. librs. Harper Hosp., Detroit, 1987-88; dir. Sci. and Engring. Libr. Wayne State U., Detroit, 1989-95, dir. undergrad. libr., 1996—2004; dir. Z. Smith Reynolds Libr. Wake Forest U., Winston-Salem, NC, 2004—. Cons. Catherine McAuley Health Sys., Ann Arbor, Mich., 1993. Contbr. articles to profl. jours. Mem. ALA, Assn. Coll. and Rsch. Librs. (budget and fin. com. 1995—), Mich. Health Scis. Librs. Assn. (pres. 1987-88), Met. Detroit Med. Libr. Group (pres. 1983-84), Phi Beta Kappa, Beta Phi Mu. Office: Z Reynolds Libr Wake Forest U Box 7777 Reynolda Station Winston Salem NC 27109

SUTTON, MARK B. diversified financial services company executive; b. Oct. 19, 1954; BSBA finance, U. Ark., 1978. With Merrill Lynch & Co., 1978—80; joined Rotan Mosely, 1980, PaineWebber Inc., 1983, office mgr., 1985—86, divsn. mgr., Rotan divsn., 1986—88; with Mitchell Hutchins Asset Mgmt., 1988—91; COO, mng. dir., investment svcs. div. Kidder, Peabody & Co., 1992—94, CEO investment svcs. divsn., CEO brokerage unit, 1994; exec. v.p. PaineWebber Inc., 1995—98, pres. pvt. client group, 1998—2000; head U.S. pvt. client group UBS Fin. Svcs., N.Y.C., 2001—02; pres., COO UBS Wealth Mgmt. USA, N.Y.C., 2002—04, CEO, 2004—. Named hon. initiate, Betta Gamma Sigma, Sam H. Walton Coll. of Bus., U. Ark., 2003. Office: UBS Fin Svcs 1285 Avenue of the Americas New York NY 10019-6028

SUTTON, PHILIP D. (PHILIP DIETRICH SUTTON), psychologist, educator; b. June 20, 1952; s. Clifton C. and Ida-Lois (Dietrich) S.; m. Kathleen E. Duffy, June 17, 1973; children: Heather, Shivonne. BA, So. Ill. U., 1974; MA, U. Chgo., 1975; PhD, U. Utah, 1979. Lic. psychologist, Colo. Psychologist VA Hosp., Salt Lake City, 1975-76; psychology intern Salt Lake Cmty. Mental Health Ctr., 1976-78; counselor, instr. Counseling Ctr. U. Utah, 1976-78; counselor, acting dir. spl. svcs. program Met. State Coll., Denver, 1978-80; staff psychologist Kaiser-Permanente Health Plan, 1980—83; pvt. practice Boulder, 1983—. Adj. prof. U. Colo., 1979-83; cons. spl. program for disacvantaged students in higher edn. HEW, 1980. Mem. APA, Biofeedback Soc., Am. Soc. Behavioral Medicine. Office: Box 1781 Nederland CO 80466 E-mail: pdsphd@aol.com.

SUTTON, ROBERT EDWARD, investment company executive; b. Burlington, Vt., July 3, 1943; s. Rollin Robert and Blanche Margaret (Deforge) S.; m. Julie Robin Levine, Feb. 1, 1975; children: Katherine Vanessa, David Robert. BA in Econs., St. Michaels Coll., 1962-66. V.p. Compretic, Inc., Beverly Hills, Calif., 1967-70; brokerage cons. Conn. Gen. Life Ins. Co., Denver, 1970-74; pres. The Core Corp., Denver, 1975-80; mng. dir. Willshire Investments & Holding Co., Denver, 1981-91; pres., chmn. Gen. Capital, Inc., Denver, 1991-93; pres, CEO WK Capital Advisors, Inc., Denver, 1994—. Dir. NAt. Assn. Indep. Contr., Denver. 1991—, Nat. Endowment Trust, Denver, 1990—, Tri Corp, Denver, 1980-89, Nat. Acceptance Corp., L.A., 1991—, Nat. Investment Holdings, L.A., 1990—; chmn. Centrix Findmiol, LLC, 1998—, EIF, Inc., 1998—. Mem. Nat. Rep. Eagles, Washington, 1986-90, Inner Circle, Washington, 1985-90, Denver Ctr. Performing Arts, 1976-86. Mem. Am. Cancer League, Glenmoor Country Club. Home: 57 Glenmoor Cir Cherry Hills Village CO 80110-7121

SUTTON, RONNIE NEAL, state legislator, lawyer; b. Pembroke, N.C., June 17, 1941; s. Willie French and Vergie Mae (Oxendine) S.; m. Genny Chavis, June 19, 1967; children: Ronette, Fonda Lynn. BA, U. West Fla., 1970; MS, Naval War Coll., 1977; MA, Ctrl. Mich. U., 1979; JD, U. N.C., 1985. Commd. ensign USN, 1958, advanced through grades to comdr., ret., 1982; atty. Sutton Law Office, Pembroke, 1985-97; rep. N.C. Ho. of Reps., Raleigh, 1993—. Bd. dirs. Lumber River Legal Svcs., Pembroke, N.C. Cancer Inst., Lumberton. Chmn. Robeson County Dem. Party, Lumberton, 1991-92. Mem. Pembroke Kiwanis Club (pres. 1991-92, Kiwanian of Yr. 1992). Democrat. Home: 2940 Philadelphus Rd Pembroke NC 28372-8308 Office: NC Ho of Reps Jones St Raleigh NC 27601 Office Phone: 910-521-4797. E-mail: rons@ncleg.net.

SUTTON, THOMAS C. insurance company executive; b. Atlanta, June 2, 1942; m. Marilyn Sutton; children: Stephen, Paul, Matthew, Meagan. BS in Math. and Physics, U. Toronto, 1965; postgrad., Harvard U., 1982. With Pacific Mut. Life Ins. Co., Newport Beach, Calif., 1963—, actuarial asst., 1966-69, successively asst. actuary, assoc. actuary, asst. v.p., 2d v.p., v.p. individual ins., 1969-80, successively v.p. individual fin., sr. v.p. corp. devel., exec. v.p. individual ins., 1980-87, pres., from 1987; now chmn. bd., CEO Pacific Life Corp., Newport Beach, Calif.; also bd. dirs. Pacific Mut. Life Ins. Co., Newport Beach, Calif. Mem. affiliates adv. bd. U. Calif. Irvine Grad. Sch. Mgmt. Trustee South Coast Repertory; bd. dirs. Ind. Colls. So. Calif. Fellow Soc. of Actuaries (mem. numerous coms.); mem. Am. Acad. Actuaries (com. on dividend prins. and practices, 1978), Pacific States Actuarial Club, L.A. Actuarial Club (sec. 1974-75, pres. 1978-79). Office: Pacific Mut Life Ins Co 700 Newport Center Dr Newport Beach CA 92660-6307

SUTTON, WILLIAM BLAYLOCK, pastor; b. Little Rock, Aug. 10, 1942; s. Richard Otto and Bettye (Blaylock) S.; m. Martha Davis, Apr. 19, 1968; children: Blake, Bryan, Stephen. BBA, Baylor U., 1964; BD, Southwestern Bapt. Theol. Sem., Ft. Worth, 1967; ThM, Internat. Theol. Sem., Orlando, Fla., 1982, DD, 1984. Ordained to ministry So. Bapt. Conv., 1965. Pastor North Hopkins Bapt. Ch., Sulphur Springs, Tex., 1965-67, 1st Bapt. Ch. Pine Hills, Orlando, 1969-77, Windsor Park Bapt. Ch., Ft. Smith, Ark., 1977-86; assoc. pastor Dauphin Way Bapt. Ch., Mobile, Ala., 1968-69; pastor 1st Bapt. Ch., McAllen, Tex., 1986—. V.p. Fla. Bapt. Pastors Conf., Orlando, 1973, So. Bapt. Conv. Tex., 2003—04; pres. Ark. Bapt. Pastors Conf., Ft. Smith, 1983; trustee fgn. mission bd. So. Bapt. Conv., Richmond, Va., 1990—. Bd. visitors Criswell Coll., Dallas, 1991. Office: 1st Bapt Ch 1200 Beech Ave Mcallen TX 78501-4687

SUTTON-STRAUS, JOAN M. journalist; b. Mimico, Ont., Can., Nov. 30, 1932; d. Frederick Edward and Anna May (Taylor) Treble; m. Walter J. Sutton, Feb. 1955 (div. 1979); children: Walter John, Deborah Anne.; m. Oscar S. Straus, Mar. 1982. Fashion editor Toronto Telegram, 1972; lifestyle editor, daily columnist Sutton's Place, Toronto Sun, 1972-79; daily commentator Sta. CFRB, Toronto, 1974-77; columnist Toronto Star, 1979; agt. gen. to U.S. Ont., 1990-91; columnist Toronto, Calgary, Edmonton and Ottawa Sun. Fin. Post, 1992-94. Author: Lovers and Others, 1974, Once More with Love, 1975, Clothing and Culture, 1975, Lovelines, 1979, All Men are not Alike, 1980, A Legacy of Caring, 1996. Former mem. adv. bd. Peggy Guggenheim Mus.; former trustee Am. Acad. Dramatic Arts; nat. gov. The Shaw Festival; trustee Am. Friends of Can., The Banff Ctr.; dir. Citizens Com. for N.Y.C. Decorated Canada medal; recipient Judy award Garment Salesmen Ont., 1964; named Can. Woman of Yr., N.Y.C., 1990; honored with Freedom of City of London.

SUTUSKY, JOHN CHARLES, higher education educator; b. Altoona, Pa., Dec. 25, 1947; s. J.C. and Mary M. (Kitko) S.; m. Kathryn Fay, Apr.5, 1975 (div.); children: Stephen C., Sarah C.; m. Rebecca Steedly, Oct. 17, 1998. BA, St. Francis Coll., 1969; MS, W.Va. U., 1972; PhD, Fla. State U., 1979. Asst. to the pres. So. W.Va. C.C., Logan, 1973-74, interim pres., 1974-75, dean learning resources, 1974-77; rsch. assoc. Fla. Dept. Edn., Tallahassee, 1977-79; coord. health affairs S.C. Commn. on Higher Edn., Columbia, 1979-82, asst. dir. health affairs, 1982-85, asst. dir. acad. affairs, 1985-88, assoc. commr., 1988-95; dir. planning Med. U. S.C., Charleston, 1995—2000, v.p. fin. and adminstrn., 2000—. Cons. in field. Recipient Kellogg fellow Fla. State U., Tallahassee, 1977. Mem. Am. Assn. for Higher Edn., Soc. for Coll. and Univ. Planning (pub. com. 1996-97, bd. dirs. 1998—). Home: 302 Ayers Cir Summerville SC 29485-3306 Office: Med U SC 141 Ashley Ave Charleston SC 29403-5808

SUVARI, MENA, actress; b. Newport, RI, Feb. 9, 1979; d. Ando and Candance Suvari; m. Robert Brinkmann, 2000. Actor: (TV films) Atomic Train, 1999; (TV series) Six Feet Under, 2004—; (films) Nowhere, 1997, Snide and Prejudice, 1997, Kiss the Girls, 1997, Slums of Beverly Hills, 1998, The Rage: Carrie 2, 1999, American Pie, 1999, American Beauty, 1999, American Virgin, 2000, Loser, 2000, Sugar & Spice, 2001, American Pie 2, 2001, The Musketeer, 2001, Sonny, 2002, Spun, 2002, Trauma, 2004. Office: c/o Gersh Agy 232 N Canon Dr Beverly Hills CA 90210

SUWYN, MARK A. building products executive; b. Denver, Aug. 8, 1942; BS in Chemistry, Hope Coll., Holland, Mich., 1964; PhD in Inorganic Chemistry, Wash. State U., 1967. From R&D to gen. mgmt. positions DuPont Co., 1967-91, sr. v.p. imaging and med. products, 1989-92; exec. v.p. Internat. Paper, Purchase, N.Y., 1992-95; CEO Louisianna Pacific Corp., Portland, 1995—. Office: Louisiana Pacific Corp 805 SW Broaday Ste 700 Portland OR 97205-3347

SUYCOTT, MARK LELAND, aerospace engineer, retired military officer; b. Riverside, Calif., Oct. 3, 1956; s. Morgan L. Suycott and Dixie L. (Drury) Bobbitt; m. Lisa Lyn Brammer, Oct. 1, 1983. BSCE, U. Mo., 1979; MS in Aero. Engring., Naval Postgrad. Sch., Monterey, Calif., 1987; test flight officer, U.S. Naval Test Pilot Sch., Patuxent River, Md., 1987; student, Def. Sys. Mgmt. Coll., Ft. Belvoir, Va., 1994. Commd. ensign USN, 1979, advanced through grades to comdr., 1995; aviation armament divsn. officer Fighter Squadron 33, Virginia Beach, Va., 1981-84; flight test project officer Pacific Missile Test Ctr., Point Mugu, Calif., 1987-89; air ops. officer Comdr. U.S. 7th Fleet, Yokosuka/Manama, Japan/Bahrain, 1989-91; ops./maintenance officer Fighter Squadron 11, San Diego, 1992-93; dep. asst. program mgr. Naval Air Sys. Command, Arlington, Va., 1994-97; prof. Def. System Mgmt. Coll., Fort Belvoir, Va., 1997-99; sr. sys. engr. SAIC Space and Def. Group, San Diego, 2000-01, prin. sys. engr. and program mgr., 2001—03, sr. project mgr., program mgr., 2004—. Asst. dist. commr. Boy Scouts Am. Decorated Def. Meritorious Svc. medal, Meritorious Svc. medal (2), Navy Commendation medal (2), Navy Achievement medal; named Outstanding Grad., U.S. Naval Test Pilot Sch.; recipient Woodbadge, Disting. Commr. and Commr.'s

Key awards, Boy Scouts Am. Mem.: VFW, AIAA (sr.), Scottish Rite, Tailhook Assn., Nat. Eagle Scout Assn. (life), Assn. Naval Aviation, Inst. Navigation, San Diego Scottish Rite, Am. Legion, Al Bahr Shrine (life), Chi Epsilon, Tau Beta Pi, Omicron Delta Kappa, Alpha Phi Omega (life). Avocations: bicycling, sailing, skiing, exercise. Address: SAIC 10260 Campus Point Dr MS c2 San Diego CA 92121-1522

SUYENAGA, ELSIE SAKAE, educator; b. Honolulu, Dec. 19; d. Shigeji Jinbo-Shimizu and Misao Jinbo; BA, Honolulu Christian Coll., 1962; AB, Pasadena Coll., 1963; postgrad. U. Hawaii, 1963-81; m. James Saburo Suyenaga; 1 son, Matthew Masao. Sec., Nuuanu Bapt. Ch., 1954-62; tchr. Ewa Beach (Hawaii) Elem. Sch., 1964-; exch. tchr. Laurel Elem. Sch., L.A. Sch. Dist., 1968-69; advisor student coun. Sec. Palisades Cmty. Assn., 1977; active polit. campaigns, 1962, 78, 80, 82, 84, 86; treas. Neighborhood Bd. Pearl City, 1982, legis. chmn. Pearl City Cmty. Assn., also treas., 1984-85; treas. local chpt. PTA. Recipient student coun. award for advisors, 1978, Dist. award PTA, 1976, cert. of merit Pearl City Cmty. Assn., 1977; Fed. grantee, 1963. Mem. Hawaii State Tchrs. Assn. (cert. of merit 1969, dir. 1981-83, sec. fin. com. 1981, vice-chmn. 1982), Leeward Tchrs. Assn. (treas., polit. action chmn. 1986—), Hawaii Edn. Assn. (bd. trustees 1986—), Am. Mus. Natural History, DAV, Alpha Delta Kappa (treas. Lambda 1980-81). Democrat. Baptist. Home: 98-099 Uao Pl Apt 1807 Aiea HI 96701-5005

SUZIEDELIS, VYTAUTAS A. engineering corporation executive; b. Kaunas, Lithuania, June 22, 1930; s. Simas and Antanina S. BS, Northeastern U., 1954; MS, N.Y. U., 1955. With Stone & Webster Engring. Corp., Boston, 1956-90, chief power engr., 1972-74, v.p., 1974-76, sr. v.p., 1976-79, exec. v.p., 1979-87, dir., 1975-87, cons., 1987-90; pres. Vasaii Corp., Brockton, Mass., 1977-91. Mem. ASME, Aircraft Owners and Pilots Assn., Pi Tau Sigma (hon.). Republican. Roman Catholic. Home: 6849 Grenadier Blvd Ph 5 Naples FL 34108-7223 E-mail: vasuziedelis@cs.com.

SUZUKI, BOB H. retired academic administrator; b. Jan. 1936; Formerly v.p. acad. affairs Calif. State Univ., Northridge; pres. Calif. State Poly. Univ., Pomona, 1991—2003; ret., 2003. Home: 3012 W Ross Ave Alhambra CA 91803

SUZUKI, HIDETARO, violinist; b. Tokyo, June 1, 1937; arrived in U.S., 1956; s. Hidezo and Humi (Sakai) S.; m. Zeyda Ruga, May 16, 1962; children: Kenneth Hideo, Nantel Hiroshi, Elina Humi. Diploma, Toho Sch. Music, Tokyo, 1956, Curtis Inst. Music, 1963. Prof. violin Conservatory Province Que., Canada, 1963-79, Laval U., Quebec, Canada, 1971-77, Butler U., Indpls., 1979—. Concertmaster Que. Symphony Orch., 1963-78, Indpls. Symphony Orch., 1978—; performed as concert violinist Can., U.S., Ea. and Western Europe, Cuba, Japan, S.E. Asia, India, USSR 1951-; guest condr. orchs. in numerous concerts, broadcasts, 1968—; mem. jury Mont. Internat. Competition, 1979, Internat. Violin Competition, 1979, Internat. Violin Competition of Indpls., 1982, 86, 90, 94; artistic dir. Suzuki and Friends chamber music series, 1980—; rec. artist (CDs, violin and piano) Dialogue, Dialogue II, Pas de deux. Office: Indpls Symphony Orch 45 Monument Cir Indianapolis IN 46204-2907 Office Phone: 317-262-1100.

SUZUKI, HOWARD KAZURO, retired anatomist, educator; b. Ketchikan, Alaska, Apr. 3, 1927; s. Goerge K. and Tsuya S.; m. Tetsuko Fujita, Sept. 12, 1952; children: Georganne, Joan, James, Stanley. BS, Marquette U., 1949, MS, 1951; PhD, Tulane U., 1955. Instr. anatomy Yale U. Sch. Medicine, 1955-58; asst. prof. anatomy U. Ark. Med. Center, Little Rock, 1958-62, asso. prof., 1962-67, prof., 1967-70; prof. anatomy, asso. dean health related professions U. Fla., Gainesville, 1970-71; prof. anatomy U. Fla. (Coll. Medicine), 1970-71; dean U. Fla. (Coll. Health Related Professions), 1971-79; prof. anatomy U. Fla. (Coll. Medicine and Health Related Professions), 1979-90, ret., 1990. Cons. NIH, VA, NASA; vis. research prof. U. Utah Sch. Medicine, 1962 Contbr. articles to profl. jours. Bd. dirs. Civitan Regional Blood Bank, 1977—; regional v.p. Fla. Retarded Citizens Assn., 1974-76; mem. Fla. Adv. Council on Vocat. Edn., 1978-86, chmn., 1981; active United Way. Fellow AAAS; mem. Soc. Exptl. Biol. Medicine, Am Assn. Anatomists, Am. Soc. Allied Health Professions, Am. Soc. Marine Artists, Sigma Xi. Episcopalian. Home: 4331 NW 20th Pl Gainesville FL 32605-3436 E-mail: hksuzuki@aol.com.

SUZUKI, ICHIRO, professional baseball player; b. Kasugai, Japan, Oct. 22, 1973; Right field Seattle Mariners, 2001—. Named Am. League Rookie of the Year, 2001, Am. League MVP, 2001; named to Am. League All-Star Team, 2001—04; recipient Am. League Gold Glove Award, 2001—03. Achievements include the second player in history to win rookie and MVP award in the same season; second in history to led in batting average and stolen bases in a season, 2001; first player in baseball history to have over 200 hits in each of his first four years. Office: Seattle Mariners PO Box 4100 Seattle WA 98104*

SUZUKI, ISAMU, microbiology educator, researcher; b. Tokyo, Aug. 4, 1930; emigrated to Can., 1962; s. Jisaku and Michie (Baba) S.; m. Yumiko Kanehira, May 16, 1962; children: Kenji, Miyo, Kohji. B.Sc.Agr., U. Tokyo, 1953; PhD, Iowa State U., 1958. NIH postdoctoral fellow Western Res. U., 1958-60; instr. Inst. Applied Microbiology, U. Toyko, 1960-62; asst. prof. mcirobiology U. Man., Winnipeg, Canada, 1964—66, assoc. prof., 1966—69, prof., 1969—99, head. dept., 1972—85, sr. scholar, 1999—2000, prof. emeritus, 2000—. Contbr. articles on sulfur-oxidizing bacteria, chemoautotrophic bacteria, mechanism of inorganic oxidation to sci. jours. NRC of Can. postdoctoral fellow, 1962-64. Mem. AAAS, Can. Soc. Microbiologists, Am. Soc. Microbiology, Can. Soc. Biochem. and Molecular Cell Biology, Sigma Xi Office: U Manitoba Dept Microbiology Winnipeg MB Canada R3T 2N2 E-mail: isuzuki@cc.umanitoba.ca.

SUZUKI, JON BYRON, medical educator, periodontist, microbiologist; b. San Antonio, July 22, 1946; s. George K. and Ruby Suzuki. BA in Biology, Ill. Wesleyan U., 1968; PhD in Microbiology magna cum laude, Ill. Inst. Tech., 1971; DDS magna cum laude, Loyola U., 1978. Med. technologist Ill. Masonic Hosp. and Med. Ctr., Chgo., 1966-67; instr. lab. in histology and parasitology Ill. Wesleyan U., Bloomington, 1967-68; med. technologist Augustana Hosp., Chgo., 1968-69; rsch. assoc., instr. microbiology Ill. Inst. Tech., Chgo., 1968-71; clin. rsch. assoc. U. Chgo. Hosps., 1970-71; clin. microbiologist St. Luke's Hosp., Columbia Coll., Physicians and Surgeons, N.Y.C., 1971-73; assoc. med. dir. Paramed Tng. and Registry, Vancouver, B.C., Can., 1973-74; dir. clin. labs. Registry of Hawaii, 1973-74; chmn. clin. labs. edn. Kapiolany Cmty. Coll., U. Hawaii, Honolulu, 1974; lectr. periodontics, oral pathology Loyola U. Med. Ctr., Maywood, Ill., 1974-90; lectr. stomatology Northwestern U. Dental Sch., Chgo., 1982-90; NIH rsch. fellow depts. pathology and periodontics Ctr. for Rsch. in Oral Biology, U. Wash., Seattle, 1978—80; prof. dept. periodontics and microbiology U. Md. Coll. Dental Surgery, Balt., 1980-90; attending faculty divsn. dentistry and oral and maxillofacial surgery Johns Hopkins Med. Inst., Balt., 1985—96; practice specializing in periodontics Balt. and Pitts.; prof., dean Sch. Dental Medicine U. Pitts., 1989—2000, prof., dir. periodontics residency program, 2002—. Cons. Dentsply Internat., York, Pa., U.S. Army, Walter Reed Med. Ctr., Washington, U.S. Army, Ft. Gordon, Ga., USN, Nat. Naval Med. Command, Bethesda, The NutraSweet Col, Chgo., FDA, Rockville, Md., 1990—, Phillips Oral Health Care, Snoqualmie, Wash.; biology/medicine study sect. NIH, Bethesda, 1985-90; nat. adv. dental rsch. coun. NIH/NIDR, Bethesda, 1994-98; vis. scientist Moscow State U., USSR, 1972, NASA, Houston, 1976-92; lectr. Internat. Congress allergology, Tokyo, 1973; lab. dir. Hawaii Dept. Health. Author: Clinical Laboratory Methods for the Medical Assistant, 1974; mem. editl. bd. Jour. Clinical Dentistry, Jour. Practical Hygiene; contbr. articles on rsch. in microbiology, immunology and dentistry to profl. jours. Instr. water safety ARC, Honolulu, 1973-90. Recipient Pres.'s medallion Loyola U., Chgo., 1977; named Alumnus of Yr., Ill. Wesleyan U., 1977, Loyola U., Chgo., 1997. Fellow Acad. Dentistry Internat., Am. Coll. Dentists, Internat. Coll. Dentists, Am. Coll. Stomatognathic Surgeons; mem. ADA (chair coun. sci. affairs 1998), AAUP, Am. Acad. Periodontology (diplomate), Am. Dental Edn. Assn., Am. Inst. Biol. Scis., Internat. Soc. Biophysics, Internat. Soc. Endocrinologists, Ill. Acad. Sci., Am. Internat. Assn. Dental Rsch. (pres. Md. chpt.), Am. Coll. Microbiology (diplomate, examiner), N.Y. Acad. Scis., Sigma Xi, Omicron Kappa Upsilon (past nat. pres., exec. sec.), Beta Beta Beta. Office: Temple Univ Dentistry Office of the Dean 3223 N Broad St Philadelphia PA 19140 Office Phone: 412-963-9000.

SUZUKI, KENJI (KEN), automotive executive; m. Yuko Suzuki; 3 children. B in Econs., U. Tokyo, 1977. Joined Toyota, 1977—, mem. overseas market rsch. and analysis dept., 1982—89; sr. exec. coord. Toyota Motor Sales, U.S.A. Inc., 1989—94; mgr. product mgmt. divsn. Toyota, 1994—97, project gen. mgr. product mgmt. divsn., 1997—2000, sr. exec. coord. rsch. and planning group, 2000; group v.p. rsch. and planning divsn. Toyota Motor N.Am., Inc., N.Y.C., NY, 2000—. Avocations: golf, basketball. Office: Toyota Motor NAm Ste 4900 Nine West 57th St New York NY 10019

SUZUKI, NOBUTAKA, chemistry professor; b. Nishio, Aichi, Japan, Nov. 8, 1942; s. Kihachiro and Masayo (Miwa) S.; m. Fumiko Sato, Mar. 21, 1971; children: Mina, Kumi. B of Chemistry, Nagoya U., Japan, 1966, D of Chemistry, 1972. Asst. prof. dept. chemistry Mie U., Tsu, Japan, 1971-88, assoc. prof., 1988; sr. rschr. Biophoton project JRDC, Sendai, Japan, 1988-90; assoc. prof. Shimonoseki (Japan) Nat. U. Fisheries, 1990-92, prof., 1993—2002, Hiroshima U., Japan, 2002—, dean dept. biol. functional chemistry, 2004—. Postdoctoral staff Johns Hopkins U., Balt., 1977-79. Author: Natural Products Chemistry, 1975, 2d rev. edit., 1983, Bioluminescence and Chemiluminescence, Current Status, 1991, Oxygen Radicals, 1992, Chemistry of Functional Dyes, Vol. 2, 1993, Bioluminescence and Chemiluminescence, Status Report, 1993, Bioluminescence and Chemiluminescence: Fundamentals and Applied Aspects, 1994, Maillard Reactions in Chemicals, Food, and Health, 1994, Food Factors: Chemistry and Cancer Prevention, 1997, Bioluminescence and Chemiluminescence, Molecular Reporting and Photons, 1997, Food Factors for Cancer Prevention, 1997, The Maillard Reaction in Foods and Medicine, 1998, Recent Research Developments in Agricultural and Biological Chemistry, Vol. 2, 1998, Advances in Shrimp Biotechnology, 1998, Dictionary of Biochemistry, 3d edit., 1998, Bioluminescence and Chemiluminescence: Perspectives for the 21st Century, 1999, Recent Development of Food Factors for the Aging Prevention, 1999, Agricultural and Biological Chemistry, Vol. 3, 1999, Future in Fisheries Science, 1999, Food Sciences, 2001, Bioluminescence and Chemiluminescence, 2000, 01, Bioluminescence and Chemiluminescence, Progress and Current Applications, 2002, Research Advances in Food Science, 2002, Trends in Comparative Biochmistry and Physiology, 2002, Near Infrared Spectroscopy, 2002; editor: The Roles of Oxygen in Chemistry and Biochemistry, 1988, (book/tape) Scientific English in Fisheries, 1992, English for Science and Technological Experiments, 1994, English for Pharmacy and Medical Science, 1995, English for International Conference, 1995, Oxidative Degradation and Antioxidative Activities of Food Constituents, 2002, Life-style Related Diseases and Food Functions, 2003, Amazing Power of Marine Foods, 2003, Biological Sciences in Foods, 2004; mem. editl. bd. ITE Letters on Batteries, New Techs. and Medicine, 2000—, award com. chmn., 2000. Recipient Rsch. award Internat. Battery Material Assn., 1997, Spl. award Internat. Tech. Exch. Soc. Internat. Battery Material Assn., 1998; grantee Naito Meml. Found., 1977, Tokai Sci. Rsch. Found., 1986, Agrl. Biol. Chemistry Japan, 1990, Kiei-Kai Sci. Rsch. Found., 1991-96, Skylark Rsch. Found., 1992, The Sci. and Tech. Agy., Japan, 1994-96, Internat. Tech. Exch. K-Found., 1996-97, Internat. Battery Material Assn., 1998—, Nakatani Electronic Measuring Tech. Assn. Japan, 1998-99, Daikin Rsch. Inst., Japan, 2002-03; grant-in-aid Sci. and Tech. Agy. of Japan, 1998—, Rsch. Devel. Corp. Japan, 1998, Small Bus. Promotion Corp., Japan, 2000, grantee Daikin Rsch. Inst., Japan, 2000—, Taki Chem. Co., 2004—. Mem. Am. Chem. Soc., Am. Soc. for Photobiology, Agrl. Biol. Soc. Japan, Chem. Soc. Japan, Japan Soc. Sci. Fisheries, Internat. Tech. Exch. Soc. (award 1995, bd. dirs. 1995—, v.p. 2000—, grantee 1998—, ITE-IBA Spl. award 1998, Kozawa award 2003). Office: Grad Sch Biosphere Sci Hiroshima Univ Higashi-Hiroshima 739-8528 Japan Office Phone: +81-82-424-7987. E-mail: suukim@hiroshimau.ac.jp.

SUZUKI, TSUNEO, molecular immunologist; b. Nagoya, Aichi, Japan, Nov. 23, 1931; s. Morichika and Toshiko (Kita) S.; widowed; children: Riichiro, Aijiro, Yozo. BS, U. Tokyo, 1953, MD, 1957; PhD, U. Hokkaido, 1967. Asst. prof. U. Kans. Med. Ctr., Kansas City, 1970-79, assoc. prof., 1979-83, prof., 1983—, interim chair, 1994-98. Mem. NIH Study Sect., Washington, 1983-87. Contbr. articles to profl. jours. Postdoctoral fellows U. Wis., 1963-66, 69-70, U. Lausanne, Switzerland, 1966-67, U Toronto, 1969; recipient Fulbright Travel award, 1962, Sr. Investigator award, U. Kans. Med. Ctr., 1990. Mem. Am. Assn. Immunologists, Am. Soc. Biological Chemists (Travel award 1988). Home: 3620 W 73rd St Prairie Village KS 66208-2903 Office: U Kans Med Ctr/Dept Microbiology Rm 3025 Wahl Hall West 3901 Rainbow Blvd Kansas City KS 66160-0001

SUZUKI, WENDY A. neural science educator; BA in Physiology and Anatomy, U. Calif., Berkeley, 1987; PhD in Neurosci., U. Calif., San Diego, 1993. Postdoctoral rschr., lab. neuropsychology Nat. Inst. Mental Health, 1993—97; assoc. prof., neural sci. NYU, N.Y.C., 1998—. Contbr. articles to profl. jours. Recipient Donald B. Lindsley prize in Behavioral Neurosci., Soc. for Neurosci., 1994, Troland Rsch. award, Nat. Acad. Scis., 2004; scholar, McKnight Found., 1998. Office: NYU Meyer 2-4 Wash Pl 1061 New York NY 10003 also: Ctr for Neural Sci NYU 4 Washington Pl Rm 809 New York NY 10003

SUZUKI, YASUHIKO, retired law educator; b. Mishima, Japan, Sept. 6, 1936; arrived in U.S., 68; s. Heijo and Hiro Suzuki; m. Kyoko Teraizumi Suzuki, May 14, 1961; children: Iori, Anri, Claude. LLB, Chuo U., Tokyo, 1960; LLM, Georgetown U., 1972. V.p. Nissan Motor Corp., Gardena, Calif., 1968—85; chmn. bd. dirs. Pacific Trade & Investment Corp., Washington, 1985—90; prof. U. Va., Charlottesville, 1991—93, Showa Joshi U., Tokyo, 1994—96, George Mason U., Fairfax, Va., 1996—2003. Vice chmn. Automobile Importers Am., Washington, 1975—85; lectr. in field. Author: Washington Lobby, 1990, The American Nation, 1999, The Constitution of the United States - The Evolving Constitution, 2000, Is the Second Amendment Anachronism? - The Right to Keep and Bear Arms, 2003. Bd. dirs. Japanese C. of C., N.Y.C., 1978—85, Washington, 1979—85. Named to Automotive Hall of Fame, 1984; recipient cert. of recognition for outstanding contbns. and efforts, Humane Soc. of Washington, DC, 1980, Youth for Understanding, 1981. Mem.: Internat. Law Inst. Japan, Acad. Polit. Sci. Home: 31242 Avenida Terramar San Juan Capistrano CA 92675

SVAHN, JOHN ALFRED, government official; b. New London, Conn., May 13, 1943; s. Albert Russell and Esther Marilu (Caffero) S.; m. Jill Weber, July 12, 1977; children: Kirsten Marie, John Alfred III. BA in Polit. Sci, U. Wash., 1966; postgrad., U. Pacific, 1970-73, Georgetown U., 1973-74. Spl. asst. to dir. Calif. Dept. Public Works, 1968-70; chief dep. dir. Calif. Dept. Social Welfare, 1971-73, dir., 1973; acting commr. Community Services Adminstrn., HEW, Washington, 1973-74; commr. Assistance Payments Adminstrn., 1973-76; dep. adminstr. Social and Rehab. Service, 1974-75; adminstr. Social and Rehab. Svcs., 1975-76; mgr. Haskins and Sells, 1976-79; pres. John A. Svahn, Inc., Annapolis, Md., 1979-81; U.S. commr. social security Balt., 1981-83; undersec. HHS, Washington, 1983-84; assst. to Pres. for policy devel. Washington, 1984-86; chmn. Maximus Inc., Washington, 1988-94; U.S. commr. Commn. for Study of Alternatives for Panama Canal, 1987-92; exec. v.p. The Wexler Group, Washington, 1995—; chmn. Captial Assocs., Inc., 1994—; bd. dirs. Logisticare, Inc., 2000—, EpicEdge, Inc., 2001—. Mem. Nat. Devel. Disability Adv. Council, 1975-76, Pres.'s Transition Team, 1980-81, Calif. Health Care Commn., 1972, pub. affairs com. United Way Am., 1987—; chmn. Govs. Commn. on Corrections Health Care, Md., 1990—; assoc. mem. Calif. Republican State Cen. Com., 1970-72; bd. dirs. Nat. Aquarium, Balt.; bd. dirs. Health Care Svcs. NAS Inst. Medicine, 1987-92; bd. dirs. Logisticare, Inc., 2001-; bd. dirs. Epic Edge, Inc., 2001-04; mem. Gov.'s Privatization Coun., 1992—. Served to lt. USAF, 1966-68. Named Outstanding Young Man in HEW, 1974; recipient Sec.'s citation, 1975, Adminstr.'s spl. citation, 1975 Mem. Phi Delta Phi, Zeta Psi. Clubs: Annapolis Yacht, Sailing of the Chesapeake. Republican. Office: 4790 Caughlin Pkwy 317 Reno NV 89509

SVAMBERA, BEATRICE ALICE, secondary school educator; b. El Paso, Tex., July 28, 1942; d. Jose Jesus Ramirez and Angelina Manilla; m. Milan Joe Svambera, Feb. 14, 1973; children: Kelli Anne, Mark Anthony. BA, U. Tex., El Paso, 1964. Speech and drama tchr. Austin H.S., El Paso, 1964—68, Jefferson H.S., El Paso, 1968—74; ESL tchr. Rusk Elem., El Paso, 1975—78, Burle Sch., 1978—79; world history tchr. Baker Jr. High, LaPorte, Tex., 1985—87; Tex. and Am. history tchr. LaPorte Jr. High, 1987—. Curator Tex. and Am. History Mus., LaPorte, 1997—; presenter in field. Sec. of edn. Tejano Preservation Assn., Houston, 1988—91. Named Am. History Tchr. of the Yr., DAR, 2002; recipient Leon Jaworsky Edn. award, State Bar Tex., 2001, Spirit of Anne Frank Educator award, Anne Frank Ctr., 2002, Robert Goldman award for Tchg. Excellence in Holocaust Edn., Jewish Found., 2002. Mem.: NEA, Tex. Coun. for the Social Studies, Tex. State Tchrs. Assn., Sons of Rep. Tex., Daus. of Rep. Tex., Tejano Preservation Assn., U. Tex. El Paso Alumni Assn., Bay Area Heritage Soc., Bay Area Vets. Assn. Home: 3207 Lazy Pine La Porte TX 77571

SVEE, GARY DUANE, newspaper editor, writer, journalist; b. Billings, Mont., Nov. 11, 1943; s. Sigvart Oluf and Beatrice Evelyn (Lund) S.; m. C. Diane Schmidt, June 26, 1966; children— Darren Kirk, Nathan Jared BA, U. Mont., 1967. Unit mgr. Midland Bank, Billings, Mont., 1967-69; reporter Billings Gazette, 1969-76, opinion editor, 1982—; pub. Bridger (Mont.) Bonanza, 1976-77; feature editor Missoulian, Missoula, Mont., 1977-81. Author: Spirit Wolf, 1987, Incident at Pishkin Creek, 1989, Sanctuary, 1990 (Best Western novel Western Writers Am. 1990), Single Tree. Vestryman St. Luke's Meml. Bd., Billings, 1989, Salvation Army, Missoula, 1980-82; vestryman Holy Spirit Parish, Missoula, 1980-82. Served to lt. USAR, 1966-72 Recipient Business Writing award U. Mo., 1974, Minority Affairs Reporting award N.W. region Sigma Delta Chi, 1980 Mem. Kiwanis (bd. dirs. Billings club 1988-89, 2d v.p. 1989, pres. 1990, 91-92), Theta Chi. Episcopalian. Avocations: fishing, golf, writing, sculpting, reading. Home: 474 Indian Trl Billings MT 59105-2706 Office: Billings Gazette PO Box 36300 Billings MT 59107-6300

SVEILICH, CAROL JOYCE, writer; d. Joseph and Blossom Sveilich; m. Don Michael Kenney, July 18, 1981. MA, Calif. State U., Carson, 2001. Comm. coord. Am. Cancer Soc., San Diego, 1981—83; acad. counselor U. of Calif., San Diego, 1983—98. Group facilitator, San Diego, 1992—98. Author: (non-fiction) JUST FINE: Unmasking Concealed Chronic Illness and Pain; photo essays, Hurry Up and Wait, photo essay, Portrait of a Portrait. Recipient Leadership award, ABC News. Democrat-Npl. Avocations: guitarist, photo essayist, photography. Personal E-mail: carol4catz@yahoo.com. E-mail: writefacefoward@yahoo.com.

SVENDSBYE, LLOYD AUGUST, college president, clergyman, educator; b. Hamlet, N.D., May 26, 1930; s. Anders A. and Gudrun J. (Birkelo) S.; m. Annelotte Frieda Erika Moertelmeyer, Dec. 20, 1958. BA, Concordia Coll., Moorhead, Minn., 1951, DD (hon.), 1983; BTh, Luther Theol.Sem., 1954; postgrad, U. Erlangen, Germany, 1954-55, Columbia U., 1959-60; ThD, Union Theol. Sem., 1966; LLD (hon.), Gettysburg Coll., 1977; LHD (hon.), Kilian C.C., 1992. Ordained to ministry, 1955; asst. pastor Our Saviours Luth. Ch., Mpls., 1955-56; adminstrv. asst. to dir. 3d Assembly Luth. World Fedn., 1956-57; asst. prof. religion Concordia Coll., 1957-59; asst. pastor Trinity Lutheran Ch., Bklyn., 1959-61; chmn. dept. religion Concordia Coll., 1962-66; editor in chief Augsburg Publ. House, Mpls., 1966-71; v.p., dean St. Olaf Coll., 1971-74; pres., prof. ch. history Luther Theol. Sem., St. Paul, 1974-82; pres. Northwestern Luth. Theol. Sem., 1976-82, Luther Northwestern Theol. Sem., 1982-87, prof. ch. history, 1982-87; pres. Augustana Coll., Sioux Falls, S.D., 1987-92. V.p. Am. Luth. Ch., 1981-87; Mem. Am. Luth. Ch.-Luth. Ch. Am. coop. com., 1974-78; Luth. World Fedn. Com. on Info. Services, 1971-76; mem. Com. on Luth. Unity, 1978-82, Commn. To Form a New Luth. Ch., 1982-86. Chmn. senate dist. 49A, Dem. Farm Labor Com., 1970-71; bd. dirs. Luth. Brotherhood, 1970-95, Luth. Gen. and Health Care Sys., Park Ridge, Ill., 1981-87; trustee Luth. Deaconess Hosp., Mpls., 1970-71, Fairview-Southdale Hosp., 1975-87, Fairview Cmty. Hosps., 1979-87. Recipient Alumni Achievement award Concordia Coll., 1974 Mem. Phi Beta Kappa. Home: 2500 Quentin Ct Minneapolis MN 55416-1900

SVENDSEN, ALF, artist, art educator; b. Bklyn., Mar. 24, 1930; s. Alf and Anna Thordina (Fjeldberg) S. BFA cum laude, Syracuse U., 1955; MFA summa cum laude, U. Notre Dame, 1965. Asst. sculptor Ivan Mestrovic, Notre Dame, Ind., 1955-56; sculptor Hall of African Man Am. Mus. Natural History, N.Y.C., 1966-68; tchr. art Mt. Anthony H.S., Bennington, Vt., 1969-71; prof. Delaware County C.C., Media, Pa., 1971-89. Exhibited work at New Sch. Social Rsch., N.Y.C., 1958, N.Y. Six Gallery, 1962, Berkshire (Mass.) Mus., 1970, Gallery 14 Sculptors, N.Y.C., 1974, Darmouth (N.H.) Coll., 1978, Deshong Mus., Chester, Pa., 1981, Art Sutton, Que., 1998, Mary Bryan Gallery, Jeffersonville, Vt., 1999. With USN, 1948-52. Home: 465 Daigle Dr Enosburg Falls VT 05450-5088

SVENDSEN, ARTHUR E. construction executive; Chair, CEO Std. Pacific Corp., Costa Mesa, Calif., 1965—. Office: 1565 W McCartha Blvd Costa Mesa CA 92626

SVENGALIS, KENDALL FRAYNE, law librarian, educator, publishing executive; b. Gary, Ind., May 16, 1947; s. Frank Anthony and Alvida Linnea (Matheus) S.; children: Hillary Linnea, Andrew Kendall; m. Ellen Christine Haffling, June 16, 2001. BA, Purdue U., 1970, MA, 1973; MLS, U. R.I., 1975. Reference librarian Roger Williams Coll., Bristol, R.I., 1975, Providence (R.I.) Coll., 1975-77; asst. law librarian R.I. State Law Library, Providence, 1976-82, state law librarian, 1982—2002. Adj. prof. libr. and info. studies U. R.I., 1987—; pres. RI Law Press, 1996— Author: The Legal Information Buyer's Guide and Reference Manual, 1996 (Best Legal Reference Book of 1996), 2004; editor: The Criv Sheet, 1988—94; contbr. articles to profl. jours. Chmn. jud. branch United Way Com. R.I., 1980; pres. Verdandi Male Chorus, 2000—. Recipient AALL Joseph L. Andrews Bibliographical awd. Mem. Am. Assn Law Librs. (state, ct. and county libr. spl. interest sect., recipient Connie E. Bolden significant publ. award 1993, 99, bd. dirs. 1986-88, 96-99), Law Librs. New Eng. (treas. 1983-85, v.p. 1985-86, pres. 1986-87), Com. on Rels. with Info. Vendors (editor 1988-94), New Eng. Law Libr. Consortium (v.p. 1990-92, pres. 1992-94), Jussi Bjorling Soc. (v.p.). Republican. Lutheran. Home: 204 Wyassup Rd North Stonington CT 06359 E-mail: ksven@comcast.net, rilawpress@comcast.net.

SVENSON, CHARLES OSCAR, investment banker; b. Worcester, Mass., June 28, 1939; s. Sven Oscar and Edahjane (Castner) S.; m. Sara Ellen Simpson, Nov. 15, 1968; children: Alicia Lindall, Tait Oscar. AB, Hamilton Coll., 1961; LL.B., Harvard U., 1964; LL.M., Bklyn. Law Sch., 1965. Bar: N.Y. 1965, U.S. Dist. Ct. (so. dist.) N.Y. 1965, U.S. Ct. Appeals (2d. cir.) 1965. Atty. Dewey, Ballantine, Bushby, Palmer & Wood, N.Y.C., 1964-68; v.p. Goldman Sachs & Co., N.Y.C., 1968-75; sr. v.p. Donaldson, Lufkin & Jenrette, N.Y.C, 1975-89, mng. dir., 1989-2000. Trustee Kirkland Coll., Clinton, N.Y., 1976-78; trustee Hamilton Coll., Clinton, 1979-83, 90—. Mem. ABA, N.Y. State Bar Assn., Assn. of Bar of City of N.Y. Clubs: Tuxedo (Tuxedo Park, N.Y.); Harvard (N.Y.C.). Home: 1185 Park Ave New York NY 10128-1308 Office: Donaldson Lufkin & Jenrette Securities Corp 277 Park Ave 16th Fl New York NY 10172-3400

SVENSSON, LARS GEORG, cardiovascular and thoracic surgeon; came to U.S., 1986; s. Karl-Georg and Marianne S.; m. Marion Frances Robinson, June 14, 1986. MB, BCh, U. Witwatersrand, Johannesburg, South Africa, 1978, MSc (Med.), 1983, PhD, 1986. Diplomate Gen., Vascular and Cardiothoracic Surgery. Resident in surgery Johannesburg Hosp., 1981-86; fellow cardiovascular surgery Cleve. Clinic Found., 1986-87, Baylor Coll. of Medicine, Houston, 1987-89, resident cardiothoracic surgery, 1989-91; attending surgeon Meth. Hosp., VA Med. Ctr., Houston, 1991-92, Lahey Clinic, Burlington, Mass., 1993—2001, dir. Aortic Surgery Ctr. and Marfan Syndrome Clinic, 1993—2001; dir. Cleve. Clinic Found., 2001—, dir. Aorta Ctr. and Marfan Syndrome Clinic, 2001—. Spkr. in field. Contbr. numerous articles to profl. jours. including Jour. Vascular Surgery, Chest, Ann. Thoracic Surgery, Jour.

Thoracic, Cardiovascular Surgery and Anesthesia.; mem. editorial bd. Annals of Thoracic Surgery, Annals of Cardiovasc. and Thoracic Surgery. Recipient Good Fellowship award Treverton Coll., 1970, Cert. of Merit South African Sugar Assn., 1972, Robert Niven award 1974-76, DeBakey Heart Fund Rsch. award 1988, 89, 90, 91, V.A. Rag Rsch. Fund award 1992; Dana Fund Rsch. fellowship, 1994, David Lurie Rsch. fellowship 1985; Davis and Geck Surg. Rsch. scholarship, 1985. Fellow Am. Coll. Surgeons, Royal Coll. Surgeons, Coll. Surgeons and Physicians of South Africa, Royal Coll. Surgeons in Can. in Vascular and Cardiothoracic Surgery, Am. Coll. Cardiology; mem. AMA, Soc. Thoracic Surgeons. Achievements include animal research to find methods of intraoperatively locating the spinal cord blood supply and methods to prevent paraplegia after aortic surgery; investigation of methods to protect the brain, spinal cord and kidneys; study of hydrogen injection to localize spinal cord supply in humans, study of intrathecal papaveine in patients undergoing aortic surgery, minimizing use of homologous blood for major aortic surgery, particularly of the ascending and aortic arch; novel operations for ascending and aortic arch surgery; first reported replacement of the entire aorta from the heart to the aortic bifurcation during a single operation; pioneered a technique for doing minimal access "keyhole" heart surgery; (with E. Stanley Crawford) wrote the first definitive textbook on the aorta entitled Cardiovascular and Vascular Disease of the Aorta; devel. an approach for minimal access to the heart for heart operations. Office Phone: 216-445-4813. Business E-Mail: svenssl@ccf.org.

SVENSSON, SVEN EILIF, civil engineer, consultant; b. Copenhagen, Dec. 15, 1945; s. Palle and Agnes Svensson; m. Dorte Merete Ahlbom, Aug. 10, 1968; children: Trine, Rikke, Jakob. MSc, Tech. U. Denmark, 1970, PhD, 1973; postgrad., Univ. Coll., London. Civil engring. Ramboel & Hannemann, Copenhagen, 1974-85, dir., 1985-90, ES Cons. Ltd., Copenhagen, 1990—. Cons. Great Belt Link Brige, Copenhagen, 1990—. Oresund Link Bridge, Copenhagen, 1993—; vis. prof. U. Coll., London, 1997—. Contbr. articles to profl. jours. Mem. ASCE, Nat. Acad. of Tech. Scis. Denmark. Avocations: music, tennis. Home: Bistrupvej 92B Birkeroed 3460 Denmark Office: ES-Consult Staktoften 20 Vedbaek DK 2950 Denmark E-mail: eilif@es-consult.dk.

SVERDLIK, SAMUEL SIMON, physiatrist, physician; b. N.Y.C., July 22, 1916; s. Simon and Fannie (Kaufman) S.; m. Norma Siegelman, June 13, 1943; children: Judy, Steven, William. BS, Alfred (N.Y.) U., 1938; MD, Hahnemann Med. Coll., Phila., 1942. Intern Jewish Hosp., Bklyn., 1942-43; residency Bellevue Hosp., N.Y.C., 1947-49; dir. rehab. medicine St. Vincent's Hosp. Med. Ctr., N.Y.C., 1949-89, emeritus dir., 1989—; clinical prof. N.Y.U. Coll. Medicine, N.Y.C., 1989—. Capt. U.S. Army, 1943-45, ETO. Decorated Bronze Star, 4 Battle Stars; Baruch fellow MIT, Cambridge, 1947. Fellow Am. Acad. Phys. Medicine and Rehab., N.Y. Acad. Medicine (chmn. sect. physical medicine rehabilitation 1965). Republican. Jewish. Office: St Vincents Hosp & Med Ctr 130 W 12th St New York NY 10011-8271 Office Phone: 239-274-7005.

SVETLIK, ROBERT WAYNE, contractor, writer; m. Antje Brinksma, Oct. 15, 1988; children: Robert Albert, Nikolas Tesla. Cert. Gen. Contr. Fla., 1986. Pres. Atlantis Rsch. Inst., Palatka, Fla., 2001—04, New Era Builders, Inc., Palatka, 2004—. Mem. code enforcement bd. City of Palatka, 2003—04. Recipient Bus. for Beauty award, City of Key West, Fla., 1989. Mem.: Northside Hist. Dist. (assoc.; vice-president 2004—04). Democrat-Npl. Achievements include patents for Automotive safety net system. Home: 511 N Third Street Palatka FL 32177 Office: New Era Builders Inc 511 N Third Street Palatka FL 32177 Personal E-mail: svetlika@bellsouth.net.

SVETLOVA, MARINA, ballerina, choreographer, educator; b. Paris, May 3, 1922; came to U.S. from Australia, 1940; d. Max and Tamara (Andreieff) Hartman. Studies with Vera Trefilova, Paris, 1930-36, studies with L. Egorova and M. Kschessinska, 1936-39; studies with A. Vilzak, N.Y.C., 1940-57; D honoris causa, Fedn. Francaise de Danse, 1988. Ballet dir. So. Vt. Art Ctr., 1959-64; dir. Svetlova Dance Ctr., Dorset, Vt., 1965-95; prof. ballet dept. Ind. U., Bloomington, 1969-92, prof. emeritus, 1992—, chmn. dept., 1969-78. Choreographer Dallas Civic Opera, 1964-67, Ft. Worth Opera, 1967-83, San Antonio Opera, 1983, Seattle Opera, Houston Opera, Kansas City Performing Arts Found. Ballerina original Ballet Russe de Monte Carlo, 1939-41; guest ballerina Ballet Theatre, 1942, London's Festival Ballet, Teatro dell Opera, Rome, Nat. Opera, Stockholm, Sweden, Suomi Opera, Helsinki, Finland, Het Nederland Ballet, Holland, Cork Irish Ballet, Paris Opera Comique, London Palladium, Teatro Colon, Buenos Aires, others; prima ballerina Met. Opera, 1943-50, N.Y.C. Opera, 1950-52; choreographer: (ballet sequences) The Fairy Queen, 1966, L'Histoire du Soldat, 1968; tours in Far East, Middle East, Europe, S.Am., U.S.; performer various classical ballets Graduation Ball; contbr. articles to Debut, Paris Opera. Mem. Am. Guild Mus. Artists (bd. dirs.), Conf. on Ballet in Higher Edn., Nat. Soc. Arts and Letters (nat. dance chmn.) Office: 2100 E Maxwell Ln Bloomington IN 47401-6119

SVEZIA, VERA TISHEFF, concert pianist; b. Alliance, Ohio; d. Thomas and Anna (Tarpov) Tisheff; m. Rudolph Svezia; children: Alexander, Alexandria. Studied with Rosina Lhevinne, Julliard Sch. Music; MusB, Mich. State U.; MusM, Eastman Sch. Music; studied with Bruce Simonds, Yale U. Creator Verex Entertainment; active as classical pianist, vocal coach, vocalist music prodr. Concert performances with leading orchs. in U.S. and Europe; solo concerts, U.S. and European cities. McDowell Music Colony scholar; recipient Martha Baird Rockefeller award Internat. Platform Assn. award, U.S. Congl. Adv. Bd. citation, various other awards. Mem. AAUW, Phi Omega Phi, Delta Omicron. Home: 130 E Hamilton Ave Englewood NJ 07631-3016

SVIGGUM, STEVEN ARTHUR, farmer, state representative; b. Minn., Sept. 15, 1951; m. Debra Beegh; children: Hans, Erik, Marit. BA in Math., St. Olaf Coll., 1973. Tchr. math., coach Belgrade (Minn.) High Sch., 1973-77, West Concord (Minn.) High Sch., 1977-78; farmer, 1973—; state rep. State of Minn., 1992—, speaker of the ho., 1999—. Bd. dirs. Riverview Manor, Inc., Wanamingo, Minn.; Rep. caucus leader Minn. Ho. of Reps., St. Paul, 1992—. Recipient Hutchinson award Am. Assn. for Mentally Retarded, 1991, Recognition of Disting. Svc. award Minn. Assn. Rehab. Facilities and Minn. Devel. Achievement Ctr. Assn., 1991, Champion of Small Bus. award Nat. Fedn. Ind. Bus. Minn., 1991; named Legislator of Yr., Assn. Retarded Citizens, 1986. Mem. Kenyon (Minn.) Lions, Kenyon Sportsmen's Club. Lutheran. Avocations: baseball, basketball, coaching. Home: 43240 90th Ave Kenyon MN 55946-3224 Office: 463 State Office Bldg Saint Paul MN 55155-0001 E-mail: rep.steve.sviggum@house.leg.state.mn.us.

SVIRSKY, MARIO ALFREDO, biomedical engineer; b. Montevideo, Uruguay, July 5, 1959; came to U.S., 1984; s. Ruben and Dora (Gilbert) S.; m. Elizabeth Fanny Sosenke, Mar. 19, 1982; children: Pablo, Daniel, Nina. B Engring., U. De La Republica, Montevideo, 1981, Engr., 1983; PhD, Tulane U., 1988. Lab. instr. U. De La Republica, Montevideo, 1981, instrumentation engr., 1983-84; asst. engr. UTE, Montevideo, 1982-83, engr., 1983-84; rsch. fellow Kresge Lab./La. State U. Med. Ctr., New Orleans, 1986-88; postdoctoral assoc. MIT, Cambridge, Mass., 1988-91, rsch. scientist, 1991-95; assoc. prof. dept. otolaryngology Ind. U. Sch. Medicine, 1995—2003, prof. dept. otolaryngology, 2003—; assoc. prof. dept. biomed. engring. Purdue U., Ind., 2000—03, prof. dept. biomed. engring., 2003—. Cons. La. State U. Med. Ctr., New Orleans, 1990-92, ATR, Japan, 1990-91, Haskins Labs., New Haven, 1990-91, Sensimetrics, Cambridge, 1991; radio commentator as Capt. Figolo Sta. WRCA 1330 AM, Cambridge, 1991-92. Reviewer Jour. Acoustical Soc. Am., 1991—, Ear and Hearing Jour., 1992—; assoc. editor for cochlear implants and aural rehab. Ear and Hearing, 1997-2001; grant reviewer Neural Protheses Program, House Ear Inst., Ohio State U.; editor in chief Ear and Hearing, 2001—. Rsch. grantee NIH, 1992-95, 99—, Deafness Rsch. Found., Motorola, Nat. Orgn. Hearing Rsch., others. Fellow: Am. Inst. for Med. and Biol. Engring., Acoustical Soc. Am.; mem.: IEEE, Collegium Oto-Rhino-Laryngologicum Amicitiae Sacrum, Am. Auditory Soc., Engring. in Medicine and Biology Soc., Am. Speech-Hearing-Lang. Assn. Achievements include development of electromagnetic midsagittal articulometer, math models of speech perception by users of cochlear implants; rsch. on the effect of cochlear implantation on speech production, speech perception by cochlear implant users, speech and language development in children with cochlear implants; establishing first cochlear implant program in Uruguay, South America. Home: 5315 E 72nd Pl Indianapolis IN 46250-2657 Office: DeVault Otologic Rsch Lab Ind Univ Rm 044 702 Barnhill Dr Indianapolis IN 46202-5128 Office Phone: 317-274-7543. Business E-Mail: msvirsky@iupui.edu.

SVOBODA, JOANNE DZITKO, artist, educator; b. Dec. 24, 1948; d. John Richard and Joanna Frances (Rygiel) Dzitko; m. Peter W. Svoboda, Sept. 3, 1972; children: Kimberly Anne, Lauren Anne. Student, Parsons Sch. Design, 1966, Kean Coll., 1970; BA, Jersey City State Coll., 1970, MA, 1975; postgrad., Tchrs. Coll., Columbia U., 1972, Chubb Inst., 1983-84. Art tchr., Jersey City, 1966-70, Henry Snyder H.S., Jersey City, 1970-80; tng. specialist Johnson & Johnson Baby Products, Skillman, N.J., 1984-89; cons., 1989—; pres. Mgmt. Strategies Internat., 1991—. Computer instr. Raritan Valley C.C., 1999—. Exhibited Courtney Gallery, Jersey City State Coll., 1970, 74, Long Valley, 1979-80; contbr. articles in fine arts to various publs. Trustee Jersey City Mus. Assn., 1973-79, chmn. fine arts dept., 1972-79; mem. curriculum revision com. Jersey City Bd. Edn., 1976; mem. Washington Twp. Shade Tree Commn., 1979-81, chmn., 1981; mem. Washington Twp. Hist. Heritage Commn., 1981-85; active encouraging establishment of hist. zone Long Valley, landmarks, Jersey City and Washington Twp. Grantee N.J. State Dept. Edn., 1973; recipient awards N.J. Fedn. Jr. Woman's Clubs: black and white photography, 1979, crafts, 1979, 1st pl. color photography, 1980, free form, 1981. Mem. Am. H.S. Assn. (asst. exec. dir. 1997-99, 2000-), Inst. Raritan Valley CC. (2000-). Office: PO Box 336 Oldwick NJ 08858-0336 Office Phone: 908-823-0909. E-mail: joan@joansvoboda.com.

SVOBODA, MARY BETH, health physicist, environmental science educator; d. Arthur Earl and Rosemary Irene S. Grad. with honors, III Corps Nuclear, Biol. and Chem. Warfare Sch., 1986; BS, U. Ariz., Tucson, AZ, 1993. Radiation safety officer Oakland U., Rochester, Mich., 1998—2001; health physicist Wayne State U., Detroit, 2001—. Adj. faculty environ. health sci. Wayne State U., Detroit, 2001—. Sgt. U.S. Army, 1984—87. Mem.: Am. Acad. of Health Physics (assoc.), Phi Theta Kappa, Golden Key. Home: PO Box 70431 Rochester Hills MI 48307 Office: Wayne State U 5425 Woodward Ave Ste 300 Detroit MI 48202 Office Phone: 313-577-0019. E-mail: aj8368@wayne.edu.

SWACKER, FRANK WARREN, lawyer; b. N.Y.C., May 18, 1922; m. Irene Maloney Michael; children: Carolyn, Frances, Michele, Ruth. BA, Union Coll., Schnectady, 1947; JD, U. Va., 1949; LLM in Internat. Law, NYU, 1961. Bar: Va. 1948, N.Y. 1950, Ohio 1962, Wis. 1969, D.C. 1977, Fla. 1991, U.S. Ct. Internat. Trade 1978, U.S. Supreme Ct. 1952. Pvt. practice, N.Y.C., 1949—54, 1964—68, Washington, 1977—84, Clearwater, Fla., 1984—89, St. Petersburg, Fla., 1994—; atty. Caltex Petroleum Corp., N.Y.C., 1955—60, Marathon Oil Co., Ohio, 1961—63; counsel Shearman & Sterling, N.Y.C., 1964—67; internat. counsel Allis-Chalmers Corp., Milw., 1968—78; sr. mem. Swacker & Assocs., P.C., Springfield, Va., 1980—84, chmn., pres. firm, sr. mem. Largo, Fla., 1989—93; vice chmn. Lasergate Sys., Inc., 1995—99. Spl. asst. dep. atty. gen. State of N.Y., 1950; govtl. adviser U.S., P.I., Algeria; lectr. Ohio No. U., 1962, N.Y. World Trade Inst., 1976; adj. prof. Stetson U. Coll. Law, St. Petersburg, Fla., 1996-2000, LLM internat. adv. coun., 1997—. Author: Business International Guide for Going Global, 1999; co-author: World Trade Without Barriers: World Trade Organization and Dispute Resolution, 1995, vol. 2, 1996; co-editor, contbr. Bus. and Legal Aspects of Latin American Trade and Investment, 1977, Reference Manual on Doing Business with Latin America, 1979; contbr. articles to legal jours. Mem. internat. bus. adv. bd. U. So. Fla., 1993-94. Lt. (j.g.) USN, 1943-46, WWII. Mem. ABA (lectr. 1978, internat. comml. arbitration com. 1991—), Nat. Law Inst., Am. Arbitration Assn. (roster of neutrals), Nat. Arbitration Forum (arbitration panel), World Intellectual Property Orgn. (arbitration panel).

SWACKHAMER, GENE L. bank executive; b. Frankfort, Ind., 1938; BS, Purdue U., 1960; MS, Cornell U., 1963; PhD, Purdue U., 1966. Pres. emeritus Farm Credit Bank Balt., Sparks, Md.; agrl. economist Kansas City Federal Reserve Bank, 1966-69; dep. gov. U.S. Govt. Farm Credit Adminstrn., 1970-76; ret. Trustee, treas. Nat. 4-H Coun., 1990-99. Lt. USN, 1962. Named Disting. Alumnus, Purdue U., 1994. Mem. World Pres. Orgn., Nat. Policy Assn., Chesapeake Pres.'s Orgn., Alpha Gamma Rho. Home: 16429 Yeoho Rd Sparks Glencoe MD 21152-9553 E-mail: ggswack@cs.com.

SWAFFORD, LESLIE EUGENE, physician assistant, consultant; b. Long Beach, Calif., Aug. 31, 1950; s. Leslie Eugene Swafford, Sr. and Kathryn Shirley (Gros) Jarvis; children: Jayson Patrick, Jonathan Allyn, Jude Christopher, Joshua Douglas; m. Cheryl Kaleen Killman, Apr. 10, 1993; 1 child, Lesli Tayte. BS in Allied Health, physician asst. degree of completion, George Washington U., 1978; postgrad. in Occupl. Medicine, U. Cin., 1994-95; M. in Physician Asst. Studies, U. Nebr., 2001. Cert. physician's asst. NCCPA, ACLS, PALS, ATLS, CDC AIDS Counselor, EBT (Alco-Sensor IV), EBT (EC/IR) QAP, TTT, lic. JBORPA. Chief EEG technologist Group Health Assn., Washington, 1974-76; physician asst. Pediat. Assocs., Frederick, Md., 1978-81, Heart Inst. for Care, Amarillo, Tex., 1981-84, Maricopa County Medicine Assocs., Avondale-Goodyear, Ariz., 1984-89; mgr. Samarital Occupl. Health Svcs. Samaritan Health System, Phoenix, 1989-98; dir. employee health/occupl. medicine, worker's comp program Maryvale Hosp. Med. Ctr., Phoenix, 1998, MRO asst., dir. adminstr. respiratory protection program, 1998-2001; Emergency Assocs. Ariz. St. Joseph's Emergency Rm. and Trauma Ctr., Phoenix, 2001—. Med. edn. and policy cons. Occupl. Health and Med. Edn. Consultants; adminstr. drug test program Samaritan Health Svcs., Phoenix, 1991—95; mem. com. Ariz. Rural Health Conf., 1992—96; adj. asst. prof. physician asst. tng. program Kirksville Coll. of Osteo. Medicine, Phoenix, 1995—; instr. Calif. Tech. Contbr. articles to profl. jours. Chmn. sex edn. com. North Ctrl. Accreditation-Aqua Fria H.S., Avondale, Ariz., 1991; physician asst. Camp Geronimo (Boy Scouts of Am.), Phoenix, 1989-94; team mem. Young People's Beginning Experience Grief Recovery Program for Children, Phoenix, 1989-93; mem. com. Ariz. Dept. Health Svcs.-Robert Wood Johnson Application, Phoenix, 1992-93. With USN, 1969-74. Recipient scholarship NIH, 1976, Squibb Pharm. Rural Physician Asst. of Yr. award honorable mention Am. Acad. Physician Assts., 1987, Dr. Paul L. Singer award for disting. cmty. svc. Samaritan Found., 1991. Fellow Ariz. State Assn. Physician Assts. (pres.-elect 1990-91, pres. 1991-92, chmn. Ariz. physician asst. tng. program task force 1990-94); mem. Am. Coll. Forensic Examiners. Republican. Roman Catholic. Avocations: fishing, hiking, softball, basketball, golf. Home: 17723 Cactus Flower Dr Goodyear AZ 85338-5232 Office: St Joseph's Hosp & Med Ctr ER 350 W Thomas Rd Phoenix AZ 85013 Office Phone: 602-406-3005.

SWAIM, C. HALL, lawyer; b. Delta, Colo., Dec. 31, 1939; s. H. Albert and Janet (Hall) S.; m. Patricia Fahey, Oct. 9, 1976; children: Caitlin Fahey, Bryan Hall. Grad. Geophys. Engr., Colo. Sch. Mines, 1961; JD, NYU, 1964. Asst. counsel Tex. Instruments Inc., Dallas, 1964-71; assoc. Hale and Dorr LLP, Boston, 1971-74, ptnr., 1974—. Served to capt. U.S. Army, 1965-67, Vietnam. Mem. ABA, Mass. Bar Assn., Boston Bar Assn., Comml. Law League Am. Office: Wilmer Cutler Pickering Hale and Dorr LLP 60 State St Boston MA 02109-1816 Office Phone: 617-526-6716. E-mail: hall.swaim@wilmerhale.com.

SWAIM, MARK WENDELL, hepatologist, molecular biologist, gastroenterologist, educator, photographer; b. Winston-Salem, N.C., Dec. 4, 1960; s. Donnie Lee and Bernice Earline (Brown) S. BA summa cum laude, U. N.C., 1983; MD, PhD with honors, Duke U., 1990. Diplomate Am. Bd. Internal Medicine, Am. Bd. Gastroenterology and Hepatology. Resident dept. medicine Duke U. Med. Ctr., Durham, NC, 1990-93, fellow gastroenterology, 1993-97, clin. med. instr., 1994-2000, fellow in advanced hepatology and endoscopy, 1997-98, attending physician, 1998-2000, Durham VA Med. Ctr., 1998-2000; asst. prof. medicine Gastrointestinal Ctr., U. Tex.-M.D. Anderson Cancer Ctr., Houston, 2000—02; dir., prin. investigator, med. dir. Regional Rsch. Inst., Jackson, Tenn., 2002—; founder Southeastern Liver Inst., Jackson, 2002—. Assoc. dept. medicine Duke U., 1998-2000; instr. clin. medicine Duke U. Sch. Medicine, 1994-2000, mem. admissions com.; asst. prof. medicine Gastrointestinal Ctr., U. Tex. M.D. Anderson Cancer Ctr., Houston; vis. med. resident Nat. Taiwan U., Taipei, 1991, 92; vis. physician Saratov (Russia) Med. U., 1995; faculty senator U. Tex. M.D. Anderson Cancer Ctr., 2000-02; book rev. panelist The Pharos of Alpha Omega Alpha; cons. physician Al-Jazeira Hosp., Abu Dhabi, United Arab Emirates. Contbr. articles to profl. jours., Ency. Brit. Great Ideas Today, 1996; photography pub. in Am. Photo. Recipient Brody award for history of medicine, 1998, Davison award for tchg. excellence, 2000; NIH Med. Sci. Tng. Program fellow, 1983-90, numerous acad. scholarships and grants. Fellow: ACP (winner assocs. competition 1994); mem.: European Assn. for Study of Liver, Houston Acad. Medicine, Tex. Med. Assn., Am. Liver Found. (bd. dirs. Tex. chpt.), Engel Soc., Am. Coll. Forensic Examiners, Reticuloendothelial Soc., Am. Assn. for Study Liver Diseases, Am. Soc. for Gastrointestinal Endoscopy, Am. Coll. Gastroenterology, Sigma Pi Sigma, Phi Lambda Upsilon, Sigma Xi, Phi Beta Kappa, Alpha Omega Alpha (pres. Duke chpt. 1989). Avocations: photography, chamber music, writing, travel. Home: 61 Valley Oak Loop Jackson TN 38305 Office: 45 Physicians Dr Jackson TN 38303 Office Phone: 731-664-2200. Personal E-mail: markswaim@msn.com.

SWAIMAN, KENNETH FRED, pediatric neurologist, educator; b. St. Paul, Nov. 19, 1931; s. Lester J. and Shirley (Ryan) S.; m. Phyllis Kammerman Sher, Oct. 1985; children: Lisa, Jerrold, Barbara, Dana. BA magna cum laude, U. Minn., 1952, BS, 1953, MD, 1955; postgrad., 1956-58. Diplomate Am. Bd. Psychiatry and Neurology, Am. Bd. Pediatrics, Am. Bd. Psychiatry and Neurology with Spl. Competence in Child Neurology. Intern Mpls. Gen. Hosp., 1955-56; resident in pediatrics, fellow in pediatrics to chief resident U. Minn. Hosp., 1956-58, spl. fellow in pediatric neurology, 1960-63, dir. pediatric neurology tng. program, 1968-94, various to interim head dept. neurology, 1994-96; chief pediatrics U.S. Army Hosp., Ft. McPherson, Ga., 1958-60; asst. prof. pediatrics, neurology U. Minn. Med. Sch., Mpls., 1963-66, prof., dir. pediatric neurology, 1969-96, mem. internship adv. coun. exec. faculty, 1966-70, interim head dept. neurology, 1994-96; postgrad. fellow pediatric neurology Nat. Inst. Neurologic Diseases and Blindness, 1960-63, assoc. prof., 1966-69. Cons. pediatric neurology Hennepin County Gen. Hosp., 1963—, Mpls., St. Paul-Ramsey Hosp., St. Paul Children's Hosp., Mpls. Children's Hosp.; vis. prof. numerous univs. including Loyola U., 1982, U. N.Mex., 1982, U. Ind. Med. Sch., 1983, U. Kyushu, Shiga, Nagoya, Tokyo, 1985, Driscoll Children's Hosp., Corpus Christi, Tex., 1986, Inst. Nacional de Pediatria, Mexico City, 1986, U. de Concepion, Chile, 1989, Beijing U. Med. Sch., 1989, Xian Med. U., China, 1989, Children's Hosp. of Mich., Detroit, 1990, Hong Kong Child Neurology Soc., 1995, Tartu, Estonia, 1997, Krem, Austria, 1997, Santiago, Chile, 1997, Kaunas, Lithuania, 1998, ICNA Ednl. Seminar, Tartu, 1998, Montevideo, Uruguay, 1999, others; lectr. in field; guest worker NIH, NICHD, Bethesda, Md., 1978-79, 79-81. Author: (with Francis S. Wright) Neuromuscular Diseases in Infancy and Childhood, 1969, Pediatric Neuromuscular Diseases, 1979, (with Stephen Ashwal) Pediatric Neurology Case Studies, 1978, 2d edit., 1984, Pediatric Neurology: Practice and Principles, 1989, 3d edit., 1999; editor: (with John A. Anderson) Phenylketonuria and Allied Metabolic Diseases, 1966, (with Francis S. Wright) Practice Pediatric Neurology, 1975, 2d edit., 1982; mem. editorial bd.: Annals of Neurology, 1977-83, Neurology Update, 1977-82, Pediatric Update, 1977-85, Brain and Devel. (Jour. Japanese Soc. Child Neurology), 1980—, Neuropediatrics (Stuttgart), 1982-92; editor-in-chief: Pediatric Neurology, 1984—; contbr. articles to sci. jours. Chmn. Minn. Gov.'s Bd. for Handicapped, Exceptional and Gifted Children, 1972-76; mem. human devel. study sect. NIH, 1976-79, guest worker, 1978-81. Served to capt. M.C. U.S. Army, 1958-60. Fellow Am. Acad. Pediatrics, Am. Acad. Neurology (rep. to nat. coun. Nat. Soc. Med. Rsch.); mem. Soc. Pediatric Rsch., Ctrl. Soc. Clin. Rsch., Ctrl. Soc. Neurol. Rsch., Internat. Soc. Neurochemistry, Am. Neurol. Assn., Minn. Neurol. Soc., AAAS, Midwest Pediatric Soc., Am. Soc. Neurochemistry, Child Neurology Soc. (1st pres. 1972-73, Hower award 1981, Founder's award 1996, chmn. internat. affairs com., 1991-96, mem. long range planning com. 1991-97, chmn. fin. com. 1995—), Internat. Assn. Child Neurologists (exec. com. 1975-79, chmn. global edn. com. 1996-99), Profs. of Child Neurology (1st pres. 1978-80, mem. nominating com. 1986-92), Japanese Child Neurology Soc. (Segawa award 1986, mem. nominating com. 1986-92, chair internat. affairs com. 1991—, mem. long range planning com. 1991-98), Soc. de Psiquiatria y Neurologia de la Infancia y Adolescencia, Internat. Child Neurology Assn. (chair internat. edn. com. 1996-99), Lithuanian Child Neurology Soc. (hon., pres. 2000—), Child Neurology Found. (pres. 2000—), Phi Beta Kappa, Sigma Xi. Office: U Minn Med Sch Dept Pediatric Neurology 1821 University Ave W Saint Paul MN 55104-2801 also: UMHC Box 486 420 Delaware St SE Minneapolis MN 55455-0374 E-mail: pncomm@uswet.net., cnfc@childneurologyfoundation.org.

SWAIN, DAVID O. manufacturing executive; b. Lizton, Ind., July 30, 1942; B of Aeronautical Engring., D, Purdue U., Rose-Hulman Inst. Tech. Engr. Gemini project McDonnell Douglas, 1954—72, engr. tactical missile programs,. tomahawk and harpoon/standoff land attack missile, 1972—87; v.p., gen. mgr. strategic bus. devel. McDonnell Douglas Astronautics Co., 1987—91; sr. v.p., c-17 program mgr. McDonnell Douglas Aerospace, 1981—94; v.p., gen. mgr. advances sys. and tech. Phantom Works McDonnell Douglas, 1994—97; v.p. engring. The Boeing Co., 1997—99; pres. Boeing Phamtom Works, 1999—2001; exec. v.p. The Boeing Co., 2002—, chief operating officer integrated defense systems, 2003—. Chmn. NASA Aerospace Tech. Adv. Com. Bd. dirs. Nat. Action Coun. Minorities in Engring., Chgo.'s Mus. Sci. and Industry. Recipient Disting. Engring. ALumnus award, Purdue U., 1993, Outstanding Aerospace Engr. award, 1999. Fellow: AIAA, Royal Aeronautical Soc.; mem.: Soc. Automotive Engrs. Office: The Boeing Co PO Box 516 Saint Louis MO 63166

SWAIN, DONALD CHRISTIE, retired university president, history educator; b. Des Moines, Oct. 14, 1931; s. G. Christie and Irene L. (Alsop) S.; m. Lavinia Kathryn Lesh, Mar. 5, 1955; children: Alan Christie, Cynthia Catherine. BA, U. Dubuque, 1953; MA in History, U. Calif., Berkeley, 1958, PhD, 1961; D (hon.), U. Louisville, 1995, Bellarmine Coll., 1995. Asst. rsch. historian U. Calif., Berkeley, 1961-63, mem. faculty Davis, 1963-81, prof. history, 1970-81, acad. asst. to chancellor, 1967-68, asst. vice chancellor acad. affairs, 1971, vice chancellor acad. affairs, 1972-75; acad. v.p. U. Calif. System, Berkeley, 1975-81; pres. U. Louisville, 1981-95, pres. emeritus, 1995—, prof. history, 1981-95; ret., 1995. Author: Federal Conservation Policy, 1921-33, 1963, Wilderness Defender: Horace M. Albright and Conservation, 1970; co-editor: The Politics of American Science 1939 to the Present, 1965. Recipient William B. Hellestine award Wis. State Hist. Soc., 1967, Disting. Tchg. award U. Calif., Davis, 1972, Wilson Wyatt award U. Louisville Alumni Assn., 1995; named Louisvillian of Yr., 1995. Democrat. Presbyterian. Office: U Louisville Alumni Ctr Louisville KY 40292-0001 E-mail: dcsandlls@aol.com.

SWAIN, JAMES BARRETT, pastor, education educator; b. Waterbury, Conn., July 29, 1932; s. Joseph Raymond and Elsie Mary (Searles) Swain; m. Doris Elizabeth Stearns, June 15, 1957; children: Suzanne Elva, Virginia Luanne, Carl Joseph. BA, Wesleyan, 1954; MA, Yale Div. Sch., 1957, U. Chgo. Div. Sch., 1968. Pastor Bethel Meth. Ch., Bridgeport, Conn., 1957—58; high sch. English tchr. Woodstock Sch., Mussoonrie, India, 1958—61; youth min. Trinity United Meth. Ch., Chgo., 1961—64; assoc. St. Johns United Meth. Ch., Chgo., 1965; pastor Englewood Meth. Ch., Chgo., 1966—70; prof. English Bariz Union Xian Coll., Batala, India, 1971—81; part time prof. English Conn. Cmty. Coll., Middletown, 1981—84; suburban and county pastorates No. Ill. Conf. United Meth. Ch., 1985—98; ret. Mem. Dem. Party of Conn., 1998, Ch. Conselling Ctr., 2000—; chmn. River Valley Services, 2002—. Democrat. United Meth. Avocations: writing, singing, painting. Home: 95 Lewis St Middletown CT 06457 Personal E-mail: dsswain1@juno.com.

SWAIN, JUDITH LEA, cardiovascular physician, educator; b. Long Beach, Calif., Sept. 24, 1948; m. Edward W. Holmes. BS in Chemistry with deptl. honors, UCLA, 1970; MD, U. Calif., San Diego, 1974. Diplomate Am. Bd. Internal Medicine, cardiovasc. disease; lic. physician Calif., Pa., N.C. Intern in medicine Duke U. Med. Ctr., 1974-75, resident in medicine, 1975-76, fellow in cardiology, 1976-80, assoc. in medicine, 1979-81, from asst. prof. medicine to assoc. prof. medicine, 1981-91, asst. prof. physiology, 1981-88, assoc. prof.

microbiology & immunology, 1988-91, Herbert C. Rorer prof. med. scis., prof. genetics, 1991-92, mem. molecular biology grad. group, 1991-92, chief cardiovasc. divsn., 1991-92; chair dept. medicine Stanford (Calif.) U., 1996—. Vis. asst. prof. dept. genetics Harvard Med. Sch., Boston, 1985-86; mem. search com. for dir. Ctr. for Aging, Duke U. Med. Ctr., 1991—, mem. exec. com. deptl. awards selection, 1992—, chmn. combined degree dir. search com., 1993, mem. clin. rsch. ctr. adv. com., 1993-94, mem. grad. student admissions com., 1993, mem. search com. for chief cardiovasc. surgery, 1992, dept. medicine intern selection com., 1992—; mem. instnl. rev. com. Pa. Muscle Inst., 1993; cardiology adv. com. Nat. Heart, Lung, & Blood Inst., 1989-93; dir. USA-Russia Cardiovasc. Rsch. Program, 1992—; mem. NIH Task Force on Heart Failure, 1992-93, dirs. standing com. on clin. rsch. NIH, 1995—; cons. Netherlands Rsch. Initiative in Molecular Cardiology, 1993; external adv. com. Ctr. for Prevention of Cardiovasc. Disease, Harvard Sch. Pub. Health, 1993—; adv. coun. NHLBI, 1995—, Friends of NHLBI com., 1996—, lectr. in field. Exec. editor: Trends in Cardiovascular Medicine, 1990-93; mem. editl. bd. Circulation Rsch., 1991—, Circulation, 1991—, Jour. Clin. Investigation, 1992—; cons. editor: Circulation, 1993—; contbr. articles to med. jours. Mem. exec. com. Coun. on Basic Sci., Am. Heart Assn., 1986-93, chmn. Katz Prize Award Com., 1989-92, rsch. rev. com., 1990-93, fellowship rsch. com., 1992—, program com., 1992—, mem. Levine Young Investigator Awards Com., Coun. on Clin. Cardiology, 1994—, mem. Basic Sci. Coun.; bd. dirs. Southeastern Pa. Heart Assn., 1992—. Recipient Bristol-Myers Squibb Cardiovasc. Achievement award, 1992, also numerous rsch. grants. Fellow Am. Coll. Cardiology (internat. edn. com. 1994—, chair cardiovasc. rsch. com. 1996—), Coll. Physicians of Phila.; mem. Assn. Univ. Cardiologists, Assn. Am. Physicians, Assn. Prof. of Cardiology, Am. Soc. Cell Biology, Am. Fedn. Clin. Rsch., Am. Soc. Clin. Investigation (pres.-elect 1994—, councilor 1991—), Internat. Soc. Heart Rsch. (councilor 1988—), Interurban Clin. Club, Clin. and Climitol. Soc., John Morgan Soc. Office: Stanford U 300 Pasteur Dr Palo Alto CA 94304-2203

SWAIN, MARY ANN PRICE, university official; b. Chardon, Ohio, Apr. 20, 1941; d. A. David and Mary A. Price; m. Donald B. Swain, June 27, 1964; children: Judy, Brenda. BA in Psychology, DePauw U., 1963; MA in Psychology, U. Mich., 1964, PhD in Psychology, 1969. Dir. Sch. Nursing Doctoral Program U. Mich., Ann Arbor, 1975—76, chmn. dept. nursing rsch., 1977—82, assoc. v.p. acad. affairs, 1983—93, interim co-dir. pers., 1986—88, interim dir. affirmative action, 1988—89, interim v.p. student svcs., 1990—92; provost and v.p. acad. affairs SUNY, Binghamton, 1993—. Evaluation site visotor U. Balt. Sch. Law, 1996—97, Tes. Wesleyan U., 1998—99, U. Va. Sch. Nursing, Charlottesville, 1994—95; chmn. coun. acad. affairs Nat. Assn. State Univs. and Land Grant Colls., 1998—99. Co-author (with H. Erickson and E. Tomlin): Modeling and Role-modeling: A Theory and Paradigm for Nursing, 1983. Chmn. campaign United Way Broome COunty, Binghamton, 1998—99; pres. bd. dirs. Vis. Nurses Assn. Huron Valley, Ann Arbor, 1989—92. Fellow Woodrow Wilson fellow, 1963. Mem.: Am. Psychol. Soc., Am. Assn. Higher Edn., Am. Soc. Quality Control, Sigma Theta Tau, Phi Beta Kappa, Golden Key Hon. Soc. Office: Couper Administration Bldg PO Box 6000 Binghamton NY 13902-6000 E-mail: mswain@binghamton.edu.

SWAIN, MARY MADGALENE, pediatrics nurse; b. Talladega, Ala., May 4, 1954; d. Quincy Jackson and Dorothy Arizona Dickerson; m. Michael Swain, May 3, 1986; children: Cassaundrian Averitte, Victor Dickerson, Tumika Shears. AAS, Gadsden State C.C., 1996; LPN, N.F. Nunnelley Tech. Coll., 1985. Lic. clin. skills observer Ala. LPN, acting unit mgr., unit coord. Northport Health Svcs., Lineville, Ala., 1987—95; case mgr. Dixie Nursing Svc., Batesville, Miss., 1995—97; DON Ball Healthcare Svc., Roanoke, Ala., 1997—2000; RN postpartum Coosa Valley Bapt. Med. ctr., Sylacauga, Ala., 2000—02; dir. parish nurse svcs. Christ Deliverance Christian Ctr., Talladega, 2001—. RN supr. Talladega Healthcare Ctr., 2002—03; staff parish nurse Sylacauga Alliance for Family Enhancement, 2002—. Author: He Has Always Been There, 2003. Avocations: writing, reading, learning. Home: 706 Glenwood Rd Talladega AL 35160

SWAIN, ROBERT, artist; b. Austin, Tex., Dec. 7, 1940; s. Robert O. and Beth (Brower) S.; m. Annette Carol Leibel, Oct. 4, 1969. BA, Am.U., 1964. Prof. fine arts Hunter Coll.; vis. artist to various schs., univs., including Bklyn. Mus. Art Sch., 1975, 77, 78; dept. architecture Harvard U. Grad. Sch. Design, 1977 One-man shows, Thenan Gallery, N.Y.C., 1965, Fischbach Gallery, N.Y.C., 1968-69, Everson Art Museum, N.Y.C., 1974, Susan Galdwell Gallery, N.Y.C., 1974, 75, 78, Tex. Gallery, Houston, 1975, Columbus (Ohio) Gallery Fine Arts, 1976, Nina Freundenhein Gallery, Buffalo, 1978, group shows include, Mus. Modern Art, N.Y.C., 1968, Grand Palais, Paris, 1968, Kunsthaus, Zurich, Switzerland, 1969, Tate Gallery, London, 1969, Corcoran Gallery Art, Washington, 1969, Whitney Mus. Am. Art, N.Y.C., 1971, Albright-Knox Gallery, Buffalo, 1971, Mus. Modern Art Internat. Circulating Exhbn.-Latin Am., 1974-75; represented in permanent collections, Corcoran Gallery Art, Walker Art Center, Mpls., Va. Mus. Fine Arts, Richmond, Everson Art Mus., Columbus Gallery Fine Arts, Detroit Inst. Art, Albright-Knox Mus., works include archtl. installations, Am. Republic Ins. Co., Des Moines, 1969, N.K. Winston Corp., N.Y.C., 1969, Schering Labs., Bloomfield, N.J., 1970, Skidmore, Owings and Merrill, N.Y.C., 1970, Kahn & Mallis Assos., N.Y.C., 1972, Harris Bank, Chgo., 1977, Powell/Kleinschmidt Chgo., 1977, Travenol Labs., Deerfield, Ill., 1977, Skidmore, Owings and Merrill, Chgo., 1977. John Simon Guggenheim Meml. Found. fellow, 1969; Nat Endowment for Arts grantee, 1976 Home and Office: 57 Leonard St Fl 4 New York NY 10013-2919

SWAIN, SUSAN MARIE, communications executive; b. Phila., Dec. 23, 1954; d. Samuel B. Swain and Marie (Baeder) Paget. BA in Comms. magna cum laude, U. Scranton, Pa., 1976, Doctorate (hon.), 2000. Reporter Sta. WDAU-TV, Scranton, 1975-76; pub. rels. staff Up With People, Inc., Tucson, 1976—78; supr. Raytheon Service Co., Cambridge, Mass., 1978-80; research assoc. Nat. Counsel Assocs., Washington, 1980-82; producer C-SPAN Cable Network, Washington, 1982-83, dir. pub. relations, 1983-87, v.p. corp. communications, mem. exec. mgmt. com., 1987-89, sr. v.p., 1989—, exec. v.p., co-chief oper. officer; also creator & host "American Writers", C-SPAN. Officer The Nat. Cable Satellite Corp.; bd. mem. C-SPAN Ednl. Found., Talbot's Inc. Moderator (TV program) C-SPAN Viewer Call-In, 1982—; editl. mgr. Booknotes, 1997, Booknotes: Life Stories, 1999, Booknotes: Stories from History, 2001. Trustee U. Scranton, 1992—2000. Recipient Alumni award U. Scranton, 1976, Disting. Achievement award, 1991. Mem. Cable Telecom. Adminstrn. and Mktg., Mus. TV and Radio, Cable TV Pub. Affairs Assn. (bd. dirs. 1986-90, sec. 1988-89), Washington Cable Club, Alpha Sigma Nu. Roman Catholic. Avocations: sailing, biking. Office: C-SPAN 400 N Capitol St NW Ste 650 Washington DC 20001-1550

SWAISGOOD, HAROLD EVERETT, biochemist, educator; b. Ashland, Ohio, Jan. 19, 1936; s. Ray Weaver and Jennie (Morr) S.; m. Janet Cromwell, Sept. 15, 1956; children: Mark Harold, Ronald Ray. BS, Ohio State U., 1958; PhD in Chemistry (NIH fellow), Mich. State U., 1963. Rsch. asst. Mich. State U., 1958-63; rsch. assoc. NIH, 1963—64; asst. prof. food sci. and biochemistry N.C. State U., 1964-67, assoc. prof., 1967-72, prof., 1972-84, William Neal Reynolds prof., 1984—2001, prof. emeritus William Neal Reynolds, 2001—, Alumni Disting. Grad. Rsch. prof., 1997. Vis. prof. U. Lund, Sweden, 1974, chmn. biotech. program, 1986-92. Editor for Ams., Comments on Agr. and Food Chemistry; assoc. editor Jour. Food Biochemistry, 1983-2000; mem. editl. bd. Jour. Dairy Sci, 1975-85, Jour. Food Sci. 1978-83; regional editor Nahrung-Food, 1995-2002; contbr. articles, chpts. to profl. publs. USPHS fellow, 1963-64; recipient Holladay medal for excellence, 1999. Fellow Am. Chem. Soc. (agriculture food chem. divsn., award advancement of application of agrl. and food chemistry sponsored by IFF 1994), Am. Dairy Sci. Assn. (pres. 1999-2000, Borden award 1987); mem. Am. Inst. Nutrition, Am. Soc. Biochemists and Molecular Biologists, AAAS, Inst. Food Technologists, Sigma Xi, Phi Kappa Phi, Gamma Sigma Delta. Democrat. Methodist. Achievements include research in protein structure, interactions, and functionality; characteristics and applications of immobilized enzymes; patents in field. Office: NC State U Dept Food Sci Raleigh NC 27695-7624 Business E-Mail: harold_swaisgood@ncsu.edu.

SWAIT, JOFFRE DAN, JR., marketing professional, educator; b. Belo Horizonte, Minas Gerais, Brazil, Jan. 17, 1954; s. Joffre Dan and Therezinha de Jesus Primo Swait; m. Carolyn B. Bernstein; children: Joffre David, Jonathan Daniel, Jennifer Denise. PhD, MIT, 1984. Prin. Advanis Inc., Gainesville, Fla., 1996—. Contbr. articles to profl. jours.; photographic exhibition. Office: Advanis Inc 12 W University Ave #205 Gainesville FL 32601 E-mail: joffre_swait@advanis.ca.

SWALLOW, FREDERICK RICHARD, retired educational association administrator; b. Holden, Mass., Mar. 17, 1932; s. Richard Henry Swallow and Mary Patricia Ryan; m. Virginia Anne Fargione, Oct. 19, 1975; 1 child, Jennifer Mary. BA, St. Mary's U., Balt., 1953, BTh, 1955, ThM, 1957. Cert. educator Md., 1957, adminstr. Commonwealth of Pa., 1973. Educator St. Charles Coll. Soc. of St. Sulpice, Catonsville, Md., 1957—59; assoc. pastor Diocese of Wheeling-Charleston, W.Va., 1959—61, pastor, 1961—63, rector ho. of studies, 1963—65, pastor, 1965—73; adminstr. Early Learning Ctr., Pitts., 1973—89; ret., 1989. Adv. bd. Allegheny County Mental Health, Pitts., 1973—89; mem. Longridge Writer's Group, 2003—. Vol. mother's mar. Mar. of Dimes, Topeka, 1998—; mem. St. Raphael's Cath. Ch., Pitts., 1985—. Mem.: Stroke Club of St. Andrew's Episcopal Ch. (pres. 2000—03). Democrat. Avocations: reading, cards, travel, church volunteer work. Home: 1328 Cordova Rd Pittsburgh PA 15206-1431

SWALM, THOMAS STERLING, aerospace executive, retired military officer; b. San Diego, Sept. 28, 1931; s. Calvin D. and Margaret A. (Rynning) S.; m. Charlene La Vern Garner, June 26, 1954; children: Edward Steven, Lori Ann. BS, U. Oreg., 1954; MS in Pub. Adminstrn., George Washington U., 1964; grad., Air Command and Staff Coll., 1964, Nat. War Coll., 1974. Commd. USAF, 1954, advanced through grades to maj. gen., 1982, instr. fighter-interceptor weapons sch., 1956, pilot 434th Fighter-Day Squadron George AFB, Calif., 1957-58, engrng. test pilot and flight examiner 50th Tactical Fighter Wing, 10th Tactical Fighter Squadron Toul-Rosieres AFB, France, and Hahn AFB, Fed. Republic Germany, 1958-61, hdqrs. 12th Waco, Tex., 1961-64, instr. pilot, flight examiner 4453d Combat Crew Tng. Wing Davis-Monthan AFB, Ariz., 1965-66, flight comdr. 12th Tactical Fighter Wing Cam Ranh Bay AFB, Republic Vietnam, 1966-67; comdr. air-to-air flight, instr. and chief R&D/OT&E sect. Fighter Weapons Sch., Nellis AFB, Nev., 1967-70; comdr., leader Thunderbirds USAF, 1970-73, chief fighter attack directorate, 1974-75, dep. dir. test and evaluation, 1975-76, from vice comdr. to comdr. 8th Tactical Fighter Wing Kunsan AFB, Republic of Korea, 1976-78, comdr. 3d Tactical Fighter Wing Clark AFB, Philippines, 1978-79, comdr. 57th Fighter Weapons Wing, comdt. fighter weapons sch. Nellis AFB, Nev., 1979-80, comdr. 833d air div. Holloman AFB, N.Mex., 1980-81, comdr. tactical air warfare ctr. Eglin AFB, Fla., 1981-86, ret., 1986; pres. T. Swalm and Assocs., Ft. Walton Beach, Fla., 1986-91; v.p. Melbourne Systems Div. Grumman Corp., 1991-95; pres. T. Swalm and Assocs., Melbourne, Fla., 1995—. V.p. Applications Group Internat., Inc., Atlanta, 1986—89; bd. dirs. Nat. Correlation Working Group. Mem. editorial bd. Jour. Electronic Def., 1983-86; contbr. articles to profl. jours. Hon. chmn. Heart Assn., Las Vegas, Nev., 1972; exec. dir. Boy Scouts Am., Las Vegas and Alamagordo, N.Mex., 1970-81; chmn. AFA Scholarship Found., 1989-91; active Fla. Govs. Coun. for TQM, 1992-94; bd. dirs. Jr. Achievement, Ctrl. Fla., 1992-94; mem. USAF scientific adv. bd., 1994-98. Decorated D.S.M., Legion of Merit with two oak leaf clusters, DFC, Air medal with 14 oak leaf clusters, Vietnam Service medal with three service stars, Republic Vietnam Campaign medal; recipient R.V. Jones Trophy Electronic Security Command, 1984, Exceptional Civilian Svc. award USAF, 1999. Mem. Air Force Assn. (exec. advisor, Jerome Waterman award 1985, Jimmy Doolittle fellow 1986), Thunderbirds Pilots Assn., Old Mission Beach Athletic Club (founder), Assn. Old Crows (editl. bd. R.V. Jones trophy 1984), Order of Daedalians (flight capt.), Melbourne C of C. (trustee 1993-95), Sigma Nu. Republican. Presbyterian. Avocations: golf, tennis, sailing.

SWAMIDOSS, STEPHENSON, pathologist, health facility administrator; b. Tanjore, Tamil Nadu, India, Apr. 11, 1946; Came to U.S., 1973; s. Asirwatham and Alice Flora; m. Premila M.K., Jan. 15, 1973; children: Cynthia, Philip. Asst. pathologist Holy Spirit Hosp., Camp Hill, Pa., 1978-82, assoc. pathologist, 1983-96, med. dir. lab. medicine, 1997—; clin. asst. prof. pathology Penn State U. Hershey Med. Ctr., Hershey, Pa., 1995—. Organizer, dir. implementation of thin prep PAP test Holy Spirit Hosp., 1997. Fellow: Internat. Acad. Cytologists, Am. Soc. Clin. Pathologists, Coll. Am. Pathologists; mem.: AMA, Nat. Soc. for Histotechnology, Dauphin County Med. Soc., Pa. Assn. Pathologists, Pa. Med. Soc., Am. Soc. Cytology, Am. Soc. Cytopathologists. Lutheran. Avocations: photography, gardening. Home: 13 Northwatch Ln Mechanicsburg PA 17050-1775 Office: Holy Spirit Hosp-Lab 503 N 21st St Camp Hill PA 17011-2204 Office Phone: 717-763-2209. E-mail: stepswam@msn.com.

SWAMY-MRUTHINTI, SATYANARAYANA, biochemist, developmental biologist; b. Andhra Pradesh, India, Jan. 10, 1955; came to U.S., 1986; s. Anjaneyulu and Kamalamma (Vindamuri) Mruthinti; m. Shyamala Sarvepalli, May 2, 1980; children: Harshita, Navyata, Namrata. MS, M.S. U., Baroda, Gujarat, India, 1977, PhD, 1982. Teaching asst. M.S. U., 1977-78, lectr., 1982-88; Univ. Grants Commn. rsch. fellow New Delhi, 1978-82; travel fellow Internat. Soc. Devel. Biol., L.A., 1985; NIH rsch. grantee Med. Coll. Ga., Augusta, 1988—, asst. prof., 1992-98, assoc. prof., 1998—2001, State U. of West Ga., Carrollton, 2001—. Contbr. articles to Investigative Ophthalmology and Visual Sciences, Exptl. Eye Rsch., Current Eye Rsch., Biochemical and Biophysical Research Communications, Biochemica Biophysica Acta; also to books the Maillard Reaction in Aging, Diabetes and Nutrition, 1989, The Maillard Reaction in Food Processing, Human Nutrition and Physiology, 1990, Nonenzymatic Glycosylation and Browning of Protein Invivo and Invitro, 1992. V.P. Hindu Temple Soc., Augusta, 1989-90, v. chmn., bd. trustees, 1990—. Mem. AAAS, Assn. for Rsch. in Vision and Ophthalmology, Internat. Soc. for Eye Rsch., N.Y. Acad. Scis. Achievements include research in post-translational protein modifications; protein glycation and generation of bruniscence during aging in human lens; switching off of gamma crystallins during aging in lens, glycation of MIP affects lens membrane permeability; discovery that protein glycation contributes to lens opacification in diabetes and aging, that aspirin delays development of cataracts in experimental diabetic animals. Office: Dept Biology State Univ West Ga Carrollton GA 30118

SWAN, GEORGE STEVEN, law educator; b. St. Louis; BA, Ohio State U., 1970; JD, U. Notre Dame, 1974; LLM, U. Toronto, 1976, SJD, 1983. CLU; bar: Ohio 1974, U.S. Dist. Ct. (so. dist.) Ohio 1975, U.S. Supreme Ct. 1987, U.S. Ct. Appeals (6th and 11th cirs.) 1993, U.S. Ct. Appeals (10th cir.) 1994, DC 1997, Ga. 1997, Fla. 1997, U.S. Dist. Ct. (no. dist.) Ga. 1997, Minn. 1998, La. 1999, Mass. 1999; ChFC, CFP. Asst. atty. gen. State of Ohio, Columbus, 1974-75; jud. clk. Supreme Ct. Ohio, Columbus, 1976-78; asst. prof. Del. Law Sch., Wilmington, 1980-83, assoc. prof., 1983-84; prof. law St. Thomas U. Law Sch., Miami, Fla., 1984-88; jud. clk. U.S. Ct. Appeals (7th cir.), Chgo., 1988-89; assoc. prof. N.C. Agrl. & Tech. State U., Greensboro, 1989—. Vis. prof. John Marshall Law Sch., Atlanta, 1996—97, Atlanta, 2000—01. Contbr. articles to profl. jours. Mem.: Am. Polit. Sci. Assn., Fin. Planning Assn., Soc. Fin. Svc. Profls., N.D. State Bar Assn., La. State Bar Assn., Nebr. State Bar Assn., Mass. Bar Assn., Fla. Bar, State Bar Ga., DC Bar, Ohio State Bar Assn., Phi Kappa Phi. Office: Merrick Hall 1601 E Market St Greensboro NC 27411 Office Phone: 336-256-2103 ext. 7022.

SWAN, HENRY, forester, consultant; b. Barre, Mass., Jan. 15, 1935; m. Freda Theopold, June 26, 1960. BS in Forestry, U. Maine, Orono, 1957; MBA, Harvard U., 1963. Registered profl. forester. Asst. dist. ranger U.S. Forest Svc., Laconia, N.H., 1957-61; investment officer John Hancock Ins. Co., Boston, 1963-68; v.p. Keystone Funds Inc., Boston, 1968-76, Legg Mason & Co., Washington, 1976-77; pres. Wagner Woodlands, Inc., Lyme, N.H., 1977-96; chmn. Wagner Forest Investments, Inc., Lyme, 1981-97; gen. ptnr. Wagner Woodlands & Co., Lyme, 1981—99; chmn., pres. Wagner Forest Mgmt. Ltd., Lyme, 1992-98, chmn., 1998—. Mem. adv. com. White Mountain Nat. Forest, Laconia, 1989—; bd. dirs. New Eng. Forestry Cons., Inc., 1994-. Commr. Conn. River Valley Resource Com., Charleston, NH, 1988—; advisor Lake Baikal Watershed Program, Ulan Ude, Buryat, 1991—92, No. Forest Lands, Concord, NH, 1989—91; pres. Friends of Tuckerman Ravine, 2000—; dir. Henry's Fork Found., 2001—04. Mem.: New Eng. Forestry Found. (bd. dirs. 1994—2002), Upper Valley Land Trust, Nature Conservancy N.H. (trustee 1997—), Forest Soc. Maine (bd. dirs. 1984—2000), Soc. for Protection of N.H. Forests (chmn. 1984—86, chmn. emeritus 1986—), Soc. Am. Foresters, Harvard Club Boston, Harvard Club N.Y., Nat. Economists Club, Trout Unltd. Independent. Episcopalian. Avocations: skiing, boating, fly fishing, woodworking, world travel. Home: 133 Breck Hill Rd Lyme NH 03768-3022 Office: Wagner Forest Mgmt Ltd PO Box 160 Lyme NH 03768-0160 Home: 86 Eagle Mountain Rd Jackson NH Office Phone: 603-795-2002. E-mail: hank@wagnerforest.com.

SWAN, KENNETH CARL, surgeon; b. Kansas City, Mo., Jan. 1, 1912; s. Carl E. and Blanche (Peters) S.; m. Virginia Grone, Feb. 5, 1938; children: Steven Carl, Kenneth, Susan. AB, U. Oreg., 1933, MD, 1936. Diplomate: Am. Bd. Ophthalmology (chmn. 1960-61). Intern U. Wis., 1936-37; resident in ophthalmology State U. Iowa, 1937-40, practice medicine specializing in ophthalmology Portland, Oreg., 1945—; staff Good Samaritan Hosp.; asst. prof. ophthalmology State U. Iowa, Iowa City, 1941-44; asso. prof. U. Oreg. Med. Sch., Portland, 1944-45, prof. and head dept. ophthalmology, 1945-78. Chmn. sensory diseases study sect. NIH; mem. adv. council Nat. Eye Inst.; also adv. council Nat. Inst. Neurol. Diseases and Blindness. Contbr. articles on ophthalmic subjects to med. publs. Recipient Proctor Rsch. medal, 1953, Disting. Svc. award U. Oreg., 1963, Meritorious Achievement award U. Oreg. Med. Sch., 1968, Howe Ophthalmology medal, 1977, Aubrey Watzek Pioneer award Lewis and Clark Coll., 1979, Disting. Alumnus award Oreg. Health Scis. U. Alumni Assn., 1988, Disting. Svc. award, 1988, Mentor award Oreg. Health Scis. Found., 1996; named Oreg. Scientist of Yr. Oreg. Mus. Sci. and Industry, 1959. Mem. Assn. Research in Ophthalmology, Am. Acad. Ophthalmology (v.p. 1978, historian), Soc. Exptl. Biology and Medicine, AAAS, AMA, Am. Ophthal. Soc. (Howe medal for distinguished service 1977), Oreg. Med. Soc., Sigma Xi, Sigma Chi (Significant Sig award 1977) Home: 4645 SW Fairview Blvd Portland OR 97221-2624 Office: Oreg Health Scis U Ophthalmology Dept Portland OR 97201

SWAN, PATRICIA BRINTNALL, research administrator; b. Hickory, N.C., Oct. 21, 1937; d. Philip Earle and Mary Lucille (Farmer) Brintnall; m. James Byron Swan, Apr. 23, 1962; children: Kathryn Ann, Deborah Lee. BS, U. N.C., 1959; MS, U. Wis., 1961, PhD, 1964. Rsch. assoc. U. Wis., Madison, 1963-64, U. Minn., St. Paul, 1964-65, asst. prof., 1965-68, assoc. prof., 1968-73, prof., 1973-89; assoc. dean U. Minn. Grad. Sch., Mpls., 1987-89; prof. Iowa State U., Ames, 1989—2001, prof. emeritus, 2002—, vice provost, dean, 1989-91, 92-99, interim provost, 1991-92. Program coord. SEA-USDA, Washington, 1979-80; bd. dirs. Fedn. of Am. Socs. for Exptl. Biology, Bethesda, Md., 1988-91; mem. Bd. Agr., NRC, Washington, 1992-94; mem. Grad. Rsch. Examination Bd., 1996-2002. Contbr. over 80 tech. articles to profl. jours. Pres. U. Minn. Faculty Polit. Action Com., Mpls., 1984-87; bd. dirs. Ames Econ. Devel. Commn., 1991-99. Recipient Disting. Alumni award U. Wis., 1994. Fellow Am. Soc. Nutrition Sci., Am. Inst. Nutrition (sec. 1981-84, historical and biographical editor Jour. Nutrition); mem. Nat. Agrl. Biotech. Coun. (chair 1996-97), Rsch. Coun. of Iowa (pres. 1994-96). Avocation: history of nutrition sci. in U.S. Home: 1301 Crest Ridge Ct Nashville TN 37221-4336 E-mail: pswan@iastate.edu.

SWAN, PEER ALDEN, public utility executive; b. Beverly, Mass., June 16, 1944; s. E.M. and Stella Swan; m. Nancy Carol Mosier, Jan. 24, 1969; children: Michael, Ashley. AA, Orange Coast Coll., Costa Mesa, Calif., 1966; BA, Calif. State U., Fullerton, 1973. Fin. analyst Brunswich, Costa Mesa, 1974-76; asst. treas. Pacific Sci. Co., Newport Beach, Calif., 1977-84, treas., 1984-98. Dir. SC Bancorp, Downey, Calif., 1992-97, Met. Water Dist. of So. Calif., 1999-2002. Dir. Irvine (Calif.) Ranch Water Dist., 1979—, Orange County Sanitation Dist., Fountain Valley, Calif., 1985—2001, So. Calif. Water Com., Irvine, 1984—92, Nat. Water Rsch. Inst., Fountain Valley, 1991—2001. Capt. U.S. Army, 1966—71, Vietnam. Avocations: sailing, hiking. Home: 7 Terraza Dr Newport Coast CA 92657-1510 E-mail: pswan@ix.netcom.com.

SWAN, PHILIP GEORGE, librarian, educator, artist; b. Camp Springs, Md., Feb. 7, 1969; s. Philip George and Diana Morse Swan; m. Jennifer Marguerite Hubert, Sept. 27, 2001. BA, U. Mich., 1991; MA, Coll. William and Mary, 1994; MS in Info., U. Mich., 1996. Libra, asst. mgr. Queensborough Pub. Libr., Jamaica, NY, 1997—99; head libr., asst. prof. Hunter Coll., N.Y.C., 2000—. Chesebrough Pond's Nat. Arts Competition, 1987, juried exhibition, The Haven (Second Pl. Nationally, 1987), Dansforth Gallery, 2000, Longbeach Island Found. Arts, 2002; author: (peer reviewed article) Collection Building (Emerald Publishing's 2003 Highly Commended Award, 2002); contbr. articles to profl. jours. Scholar, Coll. William and Mary and Colonial Williamsburg Found., 1993—94. Mem.: Libr. Assn. CUNY (co-chair 2002—04, co-chair electronic info. svcs. com. 2002—04), Assn. Coll. and Rsch. Libr. (coll. libr. sect. comm. com. 2001—04), ALA, Orgn. Ind. Artists. Office: Hunter Coll 129 E 79th St New York NY 10021

SWAN, RICHARD GORDON, retired mathematics educator; b. N.Y.C., Dec. 21, 1933; s. A. Gordon and Rose (Nespor) S.; m. Erdmuthe J.D.B. Plesch-Ritz, Mar. 18, 1963; children— Adrian Alexander, Irit Alexandra AB, Princeton U., N.J., 1954, PhD, 1957. From instr. to prof. U. Chgo., 1958-96, ret., 1996. Author: Theory of Sheaves, 1964, Algebraic K-Theory, 1968, K-Theory of Finite Groups and Orders, 1970; editor Am. Jour. Math., 1977-83, Jour. Algebra, 1981-95; contbr. articles to profl. jours. Alfred P. Sloan fellow, 1961-65; recipient Cole prize in Algebra Am. Math. Soc., 1970 Fellow AAAS; mem. Nat. Acad. Scis., Am. Math. Soc., Math. Assn. Am., Sigma Xi. Avocation: music. Home: 700 Melrose Ave Apt M3 Winter Park FL 32789-5610

SWAN, ROBERT H. corporate financial executive; BS in Mgmt., MBA, SUNY. V.p. fin. GE Med. Systems; chief fin. officer GE Lighting; v.p. fin., chief fin. officer, chief oper. officer, CEO Webvan, 1999—2001; chief fin. officer TRW, 2001—03; exec. v.p., chief fin. officer Elec. Data Sys., Plano, Tex., 2003—. Office: Elec Data Systems 5400 Legacy Dr Plano TX 75024-3199

SWAN, SHANNA HELEN, epidemiologist, researcher; d. Rudolf Michael and Diana Ray Wittenberg; m. Steven Ravett Brown, Feb. 2, 1996; children: Deborah Ruth Lustig, Joshua Michael Freedman, Christopher Henry. BS in Math., CCNY, 1958; MS in Biostatistics, Columbia U., 1960; PhD in Stats., U. Calif., Berkeley, 1963. Chief reproductive epidemiology program Calif. Dept. Health Svcs., Berkeley, 1981—98; rsch. prof. family and cmty. medicine U. Mo., Columbia, 1998—, adj. prof. stats., 2002—. Recipient Ward Medal in Logic, CCNY, 1958; grantee, Nat. Inst. Environ. Health Scis., 1998—2002, U.S. EPA, 2001—. Mem.: NAS (com. on hormonally related toxicants 1995—99), Am. Statis. Assn., Soc. for Epidemiol. Rsch., Phi Beta Kappa. Democrat. Office: Univ Mo-Columbia Medical Sciences Building (MA306) Columbia MO 65212 Office Phone: 573-884-4534. Personal E-mail: epi@shswan.com. E-mail: swans@health.missouri.edu.

SWAN, SUSAN LINDA, history professor; b. Everett, Wash., May 31, 1943; d. Joseph William Franckevitch and Doris Aline (Doolittle) Berry; m. Victor LaMarr Swan, June 19, 1965 (div. Apr. 1994); 1 child, Kerrigan Aline. BA in History, BA in English, U. Wash., 1965; MA in History, Western Wash. U., 1969; PhD in History, Wash. State U., 1976. Employment interviewer Wash. State Employment Security, Tacoma, 1971-72; asst. prof. history Wash. State U., Pullman, 1977-82, student affairs officer III, 1984-94, assoc. prof. gen. edn. program, 1994—; rsch. assoc. Nat. Coord. Spl. Hist. Projects, Mex., 1991-92. Co-author: Breve Historia de las Sequias en Mexico, 1995; adaptation editor: Study Guide for the Heritage of World Civilizations, vol. I, 2001, vol. II, 2002; contbg. editor: Reading About the World, I, II, 3d edit., 1999; contbr. articles to profl. publs. Mem. student affairs com., mem., chair acad. advising and reinstatement subcom., mus. adv. subcom. Wash. State U., chpt. advisor Alpha Phi Omega, 1995-99; vol. Pullman Meml. Hosp. Aux., 1983-92; group leader Sacajawea coun. Camp Fire, Pullman, 1984-90; adv. Sikh Student Assn.,

2002-04. Recipient Faculty award, Wash. State U. Multicultural Student Svcs., 2002. Mem. AAAS, World History Assn., Am. Mus. Women in the Arts, Seattle Art Mus., Assn. Faculty Women (treas. 1998-99), Phi Alpha Theta (pres. 1974-75), Phi Kappa Phi. Avocations: watercolors, gardening. Home: PO Box 2728 CS Pullman WA 99165-2728 Office: Wash State U Dept History Pullman WA 99164-4030

SWAN, WILLIAM, actor; b. Buffalo, Feb. 6, 1932; s. Earl B. and Irene (Hall) S. Student, Geller Workshop, L.A. Appeared in films including Lady in a Cage, Hotel, The Parallax View, Bombers B-52; over 200 TV guest appearances include Streets of San Francisco, Quincy, Perry Mason, Felony Squad, Twilight Zone, Have Gun Will Travel, Cannon, Barnaby Jones, over 200 others; appeared in off-Broadway plays including Anne of a Thousand Days, Night Fishing in Beverly Hills; appeared in regional theatre prodns. of A Delicate Balance, The Rehearsal, The Cocktail Hour, California Suite, The Middle Ages, Stained Glass, What the Butler Saw, The Price, Golf with Alan Shepard, Moby-Dick-Rehearsed, Medea and Electra, The Miracle Worker, others; actor: (TV) All My Children, 1982-2000. Trustee Berkshire Theatre Festival, Stockbridge, Mass., 1984—. Sgt. U.S. Army, 1948-49, ETO. Mem. Acad. TV, Arts and Scis., The Players, The Yale Club. Democrat. Avocation: tennis. Home: 141 E 55th St Apt 12B New York NY 10022-4034 also: Barberry Close Monterey MA 01245

SWANER-SMOOT, PAULA MARGETTS, clinical psychologist; b. Salt Lake City, Nov. 23, 1927; d. Sumner Gray and Pauline (Moyle) Margetts; m. Leland Scowcroft, May 22, 1951; children: Leland S., Jr., Sumner Margetts, Paula June Swaner-Sargetakis; m. Stephen P. Smoot, Sept. 25, 1997. BA in Eng. Lit., U. Utah, 1949, MA in Eng. Lit., 1972, MS in Ednl. Psychol., 1978, PhD in Clin. Psychology, 1986; postgrad., Washington Sch. Psychiatry, 1991, Mill Valley Calif. Acad., 1990; MA, in Mythological Studies, Pacifica Grad. Inst., 2003. Lic. clin. psychologist, Utah. Psychotherapist Granite Mental Health Ctr., Salt Lake City, 1978-80; intern Mental Health Unit, Juvenile Ct., Salt Lake City, 1984-87; pvt. practice Salt Lake City, 1986—. CEO Evergreen Coalition, 1993—2002; faculty Internat. Psycothotherapy Inst., Chevy Chase, Md., 1996—, dir., Salt Lake City, 1996, founder, 2000; dir. Infant Observation Teleconferencing Satellite Program, 2000; established master tchrs. svcs. IPI Videoconf. Supervision and Clin. Application Program, 2001. Chair Swaner Nature Preserve Found., 1993-2002; established Rock Mountain Psychol. Ctr. for Therapy and Tng., 2003. Mem.: APA, Utah Psychol. Assn. Democrat. Avocations: hiking, cross country skiing, swimming.

SWANGER, DANIEL ANTHONY-IGNATIUS, artist; b. Council Bluffs, Iowa, Aug. 10, 1954; s. Harry LaVerne Swanger and Elisabeth Patermann. BFA in Painting, Sch. of the Art Inst., Chgo., 1982; student, U. Ill., 1972—73, Harper Jr. Coll., 1974—75, No. Ill. U., 1976—77. Instr. Richard J. Daley Coll., Chgo., 1981-82; guest lectr. Sch. Art Inst. Chgo., 1982; curator children's exhibit, co-curator Lithuania: Reflections in Time, Balzekas Mus. Lithuanian Culture, Chgo., 1981-82, children's mus. exhibit and jr. arts program. One man shows include Book Nook, Mt. Prospect, Ill., 1969, Humanities Ctr., Elk Grove (Ill.) HS, 1971, Bird of Paradise, Chgo., 1983-89, Ontario (Wis.) Libr., 1990-96, Unitarian Ch., Chattanooga, Tenn., 2000, 2004, Barnes and Noble, Chattanooga, Tenn., 2001; exhibited in group shows at Gallery 200, DeKalb, Ill., 1976, Neptune Hall, No. Ill. U., 1976, North Wing Sculpture Gallery, Sch. Art Inst. Chgo., 1981, Randolph St. Gallery, Chgo., 1980-81, West Hubbard Gallery, Chgo., 1981, Body Politic Theater Gallery, Chgo., 1982, The Magic Show, Santa Barbara, Calif., 1982, Columbus Dr. Gallery, Sch. Art Inst. Chgo., 1982, Excalibur, Chgo., 1988, Postal Workers' Union, Caspar, Wyo., 1989, Brick City Ctr. for the Arts, Ocala, Fla., 1997, Cooper Seeman Fine Art, N.Y.C., 1988-93 (now Laurie Seeman Fine Art), Willoughby Tower gallery, Chgo., 1980-81, Assn. Visual Artists Mem. Exhibits, Chattanooga, 1997—, Austin-Palmer Galleries, Chattanooga, 1998-2004, Invitational Mail and Book Art Exhibit, Noriguchi City, Japan, 1984, Mail Art, Centre Georges Pompidou, Paris, 1985, Decalomania Gallery, Chgo., 1980, others; mural Euterpe, Muse of Lyric Poetry installed Elk Grove H.S., 1972, Episcopal Found., U. Ill., Champaign, 1973, North Wing Sculpture Gallery, Sch. of Art Inst. Chgo., 1981, others; represented in permenant collections St. Mary of the Lake, Chgo., St. Joseph's Ch., Kendall, Wis., Our Lady of the Springs, Ocala, Fla., Sons of the Revolution, others; author: Classical Sonnets with Lyric Poems, 1971-97, Postmodern Essays on Art, Religion and Society, 1981-2002; continuing art dealers include Linda Woodall Fine Arts, Ooltewah, Tenn, 2004—, Wildwoman's Golden Ceiling, Wilton, Wisc., 1996—, Raintree Fine Arts Gallery, Chattanooga, Tenn., 2003—. Grantee Ill. Arts. Coun., Chgo. Cmty. Trust, 1981-82. Mem. Hunter Mus. (Chattanooga), Blue Army of Fatima (Washington, NJ). Avocations: writing, classical music, French and German languages. Home: 2007 Merlin Dr Chattanooga TN 37421-2600 Office Phone: 423-893-8896.

SWANK, DAMON RAYNARD, lawyer; b. Boulder, Colo., Sept. 14, 1940; s. Raynard Coe and Ethel Louise (Mershon) S.; m. Susan M. Heigl, June 13, 1970; children: Stephen Carl, Lauren Marie. BA, Coll. of Wooster, 1962; JD, U. Calif., Berkeley, 1965. Bar: Calif. 1965, U.S. Dist. Ct. (no. dist.) Calif. 1965, U.S. Ct. Appeals (9th cir.) 1965, U.S. Dist. Ct. (ctrl. dist.) Calif. 1969, Minn. 1977. Dep. pub. defender County of Los Angeles, LA, 1965—84; pvt. practice Long Beach, Calif., 1984—. Judge pro tem L.A. Superior Ct., 1990—. Mem.: Long Beach Bar Assn. (bd. govs. 1993—94). Avocation: offshore sailing. Office: 7 Chaparral Ln Rancho Palos Verdes CA 90275-5167 Personal E-mail: damonswank@cox.net.

SWANK, DARRYL, agricultural products executive; CFO Purina Mills, St. Louis. Office: Purina Mills PO Box 66812 Saint Louis MO 63166-6812

SWANK, HILARY ANN, actress; b. Bellingham, WA, July 30, 1974; m. Chad Lowe, Sept. 28, 1997. Appeared in feature films: Buffy the Vampire Slayer, 1992, The Next Karate Kid, 1994, Sometimes They Come Back...Again, 1996, Kounterfeit, 1996, The Way We Are, 1997, Heartwood, 1998, Boys Don't Cry, 1999 (Golden Globe award for Best Actress, 2000, Oscar award for Best Actress, 2000), Affair of the Necklace, 2000, The Gift, 2000; (tv movies) Cries Unheard: The Donna Yaklich Story, 1994, Terror in the Family, 1996, Dying to Belong, 1997, The Sleepwalker Killing, 1997; (tv series) Camp Wilder, 1992, Beverly Hills, 90210, 1997-98, Leaving L.A., 1997; (tv appearances): Growing Pains, 1985, Evening Shade, Harry and the Hendersons, 1991. Avocations: sky diving, river rafting, skiing, swimming. Office: William Morris Agy 151 S El Camino Dr Beverly Hills CA 90212

SWANK, WILLIAM GEORGE, historian, writer; b. Chgo., June 17, 1940; s. William George and Estelle Jensen Swank; m. Jeri Lynne Bessie; children: William Corey, Eric William, Karen Estelle. BS, San Diego State Coll., 1962. Supervising probation officer County of San Diego, San Diego, 1963—94; historian, lectr., writer San Diego, 1994—. Baseball historian San Diego Hall of Champions, 1988—, San Diego Hist. Soc., 1994—; chmn. Gavy Cravath Hall of Fame Com., Escondido, 1995—; cons. Pacific Coast League, Colorado Springs, 2001—03; editor Whitey Wietelmann Box Score Collection, 1969—. Author: (book) The Lane Field Padres (Two Volumes), 1997, Echoes from Lane Field, 1999 (San Diego Press Club and San Diego Book Awards, 1999), Gold Leather Helmets/Black Hightop Shoes, 2003, Baseball in San Diego: From the Plaza to Petco, 2 vols., 2004, (program) Ted Williams Museum, 2000; editor: (newsletter) Echoes from Lane Field, 1995—; contbr. articles to newspapers, jours. and mags. Coach youth soccer, baseball, basketball, San Diego, 1975—93; judge Greater San Diego Science and Engring. Fair, San Diego, 1992—; Santa Claus, Christmas on the Prado, Balboa Park, San Diego, 2002—; coach House of David Baseball Team, 2003. Officer candidate USMC, 1962. Mem.: Soc. for Am. Baseball Rsch. (dead ball era com. 1998—). Avocations: scale model of Lane Field, baseball scrapbooks. Home: 3474 Via Beltran San Diego CA 92117-5729

SWANKIN, DAVID ARNOLD, lawyer, consumer advocate; b. Boston, Jan. 18, 1934; s. Max and Anne (Rotefsky) S.; m. Jeanne Phyllis Herrick; 1 dau., Sheryl. AB, Brandeis U., 1954; MS, U. Wis., 1957; JD, George Washington U., 1962. Mgmt. intern U.S. Dept. Labor, Washington, 1957-60, spl. asst. to asst. sec. labor, 1961-63, dep. asst. sec. labor, 1967; dir. Bur. Labor Standards, 1967-68; exec. sec. Pres.'s Consumer Adv. Council, Washington, 1964; exec, dir. Pres's Com. on Consumer Interests, Washington, 1965-66; Washington rep. Consumer's Union, 1969-71; exec. dir. Consumer Interests Found., 1971-73; sr. partner Swankin & Turner, 1973—. Pres. Citizen Advocacy Ctr. 1994—; cons. U.S. Dept. Labor; pres. Citizen Advocacy Ctr., 1994—. Mem. president's coun. Brandeis U., 1968-69; mem. PEW Health Profls. Commn., 1997-98. Served with AUS., 1954-56. Recipient Jump award U.S. Govt., 1969 Home: 2305 N Van Buren Ct Arlington VA 22205 Office: 1400 16th St NW Washington DC 20036-2217 Business E-Mail: davidswankin@cacenter.org.

SWANN, BARBARA, lawyer; b. NY, Sept. 15, 1950; d. George Arthur. BA summa cum laude, Montclair State U., 1988; JD, Rutgers Law, 1992. Bar: N.J. 1992, D.C. 1994, N.Y. 1995, Calif. 2000, U.S. Dist. Ct. N.J. 1992, U.S. Ct. Appeals (3rd cir.) 1994, U.S. Dist. Ct. N.Y. 1996, Calif. 2000. Correspondent The Associate Press, Newark, N.J., 1974-80; reporter, bureau chief The Hudson Dispatch, Union City, N.J., 1973-80; editorial page editor The Paterson (N.J.) News, 1980-81; v.p., acct. supr. Gerald Freeman, Inc., Clifton, N.J., 1981-86; pres. LePore Assoc., Inc., West Caldwell, N.J., 1986-89; law clk. to Hon. Robert N. Wilentz N.J. Supreme Ct., 1992-93; law clk. to Hon. Leonard I. Garth U.S. Ct. Appeals (3rd cir.), 1993-94; assoc. Cahill, Gordon & Reindel, N.Y., 1994-97; liaison Republic of Ga. ABA Cen. and East European Law Initiative, 1997-98, media law specialist, 1998-2000; exec. dir. Internat. Sr. Lawyers Project, N.Y.C., 2000—02; mem. adj. faculty U. N.Mex., 2003—. Editor-in-chief: Rutgers Computer & Technology Law Jour., 1991-92. Founding trustee Ctr. for Children's Advocacy, Riverdale, N.J. 1994—. Mem. ABA, Assn. of the Bar of the City of New York, N.J. State Bar Assn., N.Y. County Lawyers' Assn. Am. Inn of Ct., D.C. Bar Assn., State Bar Calif. Home: 205 Greenmount Ave Cliffside Park NJ 07010-2213 Personal E-mail: swann2002@msn.com.

SWANN, ERIC JERROD, professional football player; b. Pinehurst, N.C., Aug. 16, 1970; Student, Wake Tech. Coll. Defensive tackle Ariz. Cardinals, Phoenix, 1991—. Selected to Pro Bowl, 1995. Office: Arizona Cardinals PO Box 888 Phoenix AZ 85001-0888

SWANN, LYNN CURTIS, sportscaster, former professional football player; b. Alcoa, Tenn., Mar. 7, 1952; s. Willie and Mildred (McGarity) Swann; m. Charena Swann; 2 children. BA, U. So. Calif., 1974. Wide receiver Pitts. Steelers Profl. Football Team, 1974-83, leading receiver in team history, 1981; commentator ABC Sports, 1976—; founder, pres. Swann, Inc. Bd. dirs. H.J. Heinz Co., Wyndham Internat. Inc.; chairman President's Coun. Phys. Fitness and Sports, 2002. Entertainment and media apppearances as dancer with Twyla Tharp and Peter Martines Omnibus TV Spl., 1980, guest star Night of 100 Stars I, 1982, 100 Stars II, 1985; host and narrator Britten's Young Person's Guide to Orchestra, Wheeling Symphony Orch., 1982; host of 13 part art edn. spl. Arts Alive, PBS, 1984; major character in episodes Paper Chase, 1984, Hotel, 1984, Love American Style, 1985; other appearances on various TV shows including 20/20, Good Morning America, Merv Griffin, Hollywood Squares, others; intermittent host daily talk show Pittsburgh 2Day, 1985 Spokesman for Big Bros./Big Sisters Assn.; trustee Pitts. Ballet Theatre, creator youth scholarship program; bd. dirs. Scott Newman Juvenile Drug and Alcohol Prevention Found.; bd. dirs. U. So. Calif. Sch. Journalism Alumni Assn. Named All Pro, 1976 77, 78, Most Valuable Player in Super Bowl X, 1976, Pitts. Multiple Sclerosis Athlete of Yr., 1980, NFL Man of Yr., 1981; holder 4 Super Bowl records, 2d in 2 categories; mem. Pitts. Steelers All-Time Team, 50th Anniv.; named to NFL Hall of Fame Team of Decade/1970's, AP, UPI, Kodak All Am. Teams, Pop Warner Hall of Fame; recipient Image award NAACP, 1979, Ebonics Soc. award, Outstanding Alumni award U. So. Calif., 1984, Oleg Cassini Competitors Fashion award, 1985. Mem. Screen Actors Guild, AFTRA. Office: Swann Inc 506 Hegner Way #2 Sewickley PA 15143-1552*

SWANN, NAT HENDERSON, JR., physician; b. Danville, Va, Nov. 2, 1927; s. Nat Henderson, Sr. and Mary Stokes S.; m. Sarah Hayes, Aug. 7, 1952; children: Nat H. III, Wayland Hayes. AB in Chemistry, U. N.C., 1950, MD, 1954. Fellow Royal Soc. Medicine/London. Resident in internal medicine Med. Coll., Va., 1954-56, Boston VA Hosp., 1956-57, Cleve. VA (Crile) Hosp., 1957-58; specialist internal medicine Chattanooga, 1958—. Med. dir. Chattem, Inc., Chattanooga, 1960—; cons. rheumatic heart clin. Children's Hosp., Chattanooga, 1959-63; chief of staff Downtown Gen. Hosp., Chattanooga, 1986-90. Contbr. articles to profl. jours. Dir. Physician's Giving, United Way, Chattanooga, 1980; mem. Chattanooga Met. Coun., 1961; bd. spkr. Air Pollution Control Bd., Chattanooga, 1962; bd. dirs. The Salvation Army. With U.S. Army Med. Corps, 1946-47. Recipient Disting. Achievement award Am. Heart Assn. Fellow: Internat. Coll. Angiology, Royal Soc. Medicine, Am. Coll. Angiology, Am. Coll. Chest Physicians (assoc.); mem.: ACP, AMA, Am. Coll. Cardiology, Athenians Club (Chattanooga), Torch Club (Chattanooga), Mountain City Club (bd. dir.), Rotary (bd. dir.). Avocations: short story and novel writer, golf, tennis. Home: 412 Brady Point Rd Signal Mountain TN 37377-2206 E-mail: natswann@mindspring.com.

SWANSBURG, RUSSELL CHESTER, nursing educator, consultant, health facility administrator; b. Cambridge, Mass., Aug. 6, 1928; s. William W. and Mary A. (Pierce) S.; m. Laurel Clark, Sept. 1951; children: Philip Wayne, Michael Gary, Richard Jeffrey. Diploma, N.S. Hosp. Sch. Nursing, 1950; BSN, Western Res. U., 1952; MA in Nursing Edn., Columbia U., 1961; PhD, U. Miss., 1984. CNAA. Asst. adminstr. U. of S. Ala. Med. Ctr., Mobile; v.p. U. South Ala., Mobile; prof. Auburn U., Montgomery, Ala., Med. Coll. of Ga., Augusta; instr. Univ. of the Incarnate Word, San Antonio, 1998—. Mil. cons. USAF Surgeon Gen., 1972; sr. med. svc. cons., 1973-76; nurse cons. VA Med. Ctr., Tuskegee, Ala., 1987-88; mem. editl. adv. bd. Nursing Adminstrn. Manual. Author: Team Nursing: A Programmed Learning Experience, 1968, Inservice Education, 1968, The Measurement of Vital Signs, 1970, The Team Plan, 1971, Management of Patient Care Services, 1976, Strategic Career Planning and Development, 1984, The Nurse Manager's Guide to Financial Management, 1988, Management and Leadership for Nurse Managers, 1990 (Book of Yr. Selection, Am. Jour. Nursing 1990), 3d edit., 2002 (Book of Yr. Selection, Am. Jour. Nursing 2002), Introductory Management and Leadership for Clinical Nurses, 1993, 2d edit., 1999 (Book of the Yr. Selection, Am. Jour. Nursing 1999), Staff Development: A Component of Human Resource Development, 1994, Budgeting and Financial Management for Nurse Managers, 1997, (audiovisual course) Nurses & Patients: An Introduction to Nursing Management, 1980; contbr. articles to profl. publs. Bd. dirs. Air Force Village Found., Alzheimer's Care and Research Found. Col. USAF, 1956-76. Decorated Air Medal with oak leaf clusters, Legion of Merit; recipient award for outstanding work in hosp. adminstrn. Ala. State Nurses' Assn., 1985, Outstanding Nursing Svc. Adminstrn. award, 1981, Outstanding Nurse Rschr. 1984, Disting. Svc. award Air Force Village Found., 1999. Fellow AONE, Ala. Orgn. Nurse Exec's. (past state pres.); mem. Council Grad. Edn. Adminstrn. in Nursing (sec.), Ala. Acad. Sci., Sigma Xi, Phi Kappa Phi, Sigma Theta Tau. Home and Office: 4917 Ravenswood Dr Apt 1711 San Antonio TX 78227-4356 Office Phone: 210-673-9475.

SWANSEN, DONNA MALONEY, landscape designer, consultant; b. Green Bay, Wis., July 8, 1931; d. Arthur Anthony and Ella Marie Rose (Warner) Maloney; m. Samuel Theodore Swansen, June 27, 1959; children: Jessica Swansen Bonelli, Theodor Arthur Swansen, Christopher Currie Swansen. AS in Integrated Liberal Studies, U. Wis., 1956; AS in Landscape Design, Temple U., 1982. Bridal cons. Richard W. Burnham's, Green Bay, 1951-54, 57-58; asst. buyer Shreve Crump & Low, Boston, 1958-59; buyer Harry S. Manchester, Madison, Wis., 1959-62; ptnr. Corson Borie & Swansen, Ambler, Pa., 1976, Swansen & Borie, Ambler, 1977-82; owner, operator Donna Swansen/Design, Ambler, 1983—. V.p. Energy Islands Internat. Inc., East Troy, Wis., 1963-94. Editor: Internat. Directory Landscape Designers, 1993. Co-founder Friends of Rising Sun, Ambler, Ambler Area Arts Alliance, 1975—76; founder, 1st pres. Plant Ambler, 1973—83, 1997—; chair Do It, Dig It exhibit Temple U., 1987; judge Temple U., 2002, Bucks County Beautiful Flowers Show, 2002, Assn. Profl. Landscape Designers, 2002; Dem. candidate for judge elections, 1988; active Gwynedd (Pa.) Monthly Meeting of Friends, 1974—; judge Del. Valley Coll., Doylestown, Pa., 2002; search com. for chair dept. landscape arch. and horticulture Temple U., 1987, curriculum rev. com., 1993; adv. com. Green Bay Bot. Garden, 1993—, Del. Valley Coll., Doylestown, Pa., 2000—, adv. bd., 2000—. Recipient Key to the Borough, Borough of Ambler, 1972; winner urban beautification project Roadside Coun. Am., Ambler, 1975, Athena award Wissahickon Valley C. of C., 1996. Mem. Assn. Profl. Landscape Designers (cert., co-founder, 1st pres. 1989-91, bd. dirs. 1989-95, 1st pres. Landscape Design Network Phila. 1978-85, Distinction award 1996, judge internat. design competition 2002, 03), Sigma Lambda Alpha (charter mem.). Democrat. Avocations: encouraging women, travel, gardening. Home and Office: 221 Morris Rd Ambler PA 19002-5202 Office Phone: 215-643-3376.

SWANSEN, LARRY, actor, playwright; b. Roosevelt, Okla., Nov. 10, 1932; s. James Leonard Swanson and Ethel Mae. BFA, MFA, U. Okla., 1951. Instr. speech and theater William Woods Coll., Fulton, Mo., 1950—51. Actor: (plays) Dr. Faustus Lights the Lighes, 1952, N.Y. Shakespeare Festival, 1956, Sound of Music, 1961—62, 2003; (Broadway plays) Great White Hope, 1969—71, The King & I, 1977—79; author: (plays) Boston 1721, 1976—77 (grantee Ind. Arts Commn., 1976), Unfamiliar Beds, 1981 (1st prize, 1981), Max, 1993; actor: (plays) The Elephant Man, 1980—81, The Crucible, Much Ado About Nothing, Midwinter Nights Dream; (films) Dueling Accountants, 2004; (TV films) The Prince of Homburg, 1977.

SWANSEN, SAMUEL THEODORE, lawyer; b. Milw., June 6, 1937; s. Theodore Lawrence and Clarinda Dingwall (Crittenden) S.; m. Donna Rae Elizabeth Maloney, June 27, 1959; children: Jessica Swansen Bonelli, Theodor Arthur, Christopher Currie. AB, Dartmouth Coll., 1959; LLB, U. Wis., 1962. Bar: Wis. 1962, Pa. 1964, U.S. Supreme Ct. 1969, accredited estate planner: Nat. Assn. Estate Planners & Couns. 1995. Law clk. to presiding justice Wis. Supreme Ct., Madison, 1962-63; assoc. Dechert, Price & Rhoads, Phila., 1963-68, 70-73, ptnr., 1973-93; asst. dist. atty. City of Phila. Dist. Atty.'s Office, 1968-70, chief frauds div., 1969; pvt. practice Phila., 1963—, Blue Bell, Pa., 1994—. Adj. prof. law Temple U., Phila., 1970-80; lectr. Pa. Bar Inst., Nat. Bus. Inst., Ctr. Profl. Edn., 1985—. Editor, author U. Wis. Law Rev., 1960-62. Corp. mem. Anna T. Jeanes Found., Fox Chase, Phila, 1985—93, Associated Svcs. for the Blind, Phila, 1974—91, Bach Festival of Phila., 1989—, pres., 1993—97; founding dir. Global Bach Cmty., 2000—, pres., 2001—, 2001—; bd. dirs. Friends Rehab. Program, Inc., Phila., 1966—73, 1985—94, Franklin Found., Phila., 1969—; v.p., sec., bd. dirs. Foulkeways at Gwynedd, 1979—97, pres., 1986—97; chmn. bd. dirs. Friends Life Care at Home, Inc., 1990—, bd. dirs., 1990—, Friends Retirement Concepts, Inc., Gwynedd, sec. bd. dirs., 1985—96; hon. bd. dirs. Friends Neighborhood Guild, Greater Phila. Fedn. Settlements; dir., sec. Energy Islands Internat., Inc., 1963—; pres. emeritus Foulkeways at Gwynedd, 1997; mem. Nat. Network of Estate Planning Attys., 1993—, Nat. Acad. Elder Law Attys., 1993—; violinist, trombonist North Penn Symphony Orch., 1977—; mem. Gwynedd Monthly Meeting of Friends, 1974—. Fellow Esperti Peterson Inst. Wealth Strategies Planning, 1996—. Mem. ABA, Pa. Bar Assn., Phila. Bar Assn., Dartmouth Club Phila., Delta Upsilon, Phi Delta Phi. Republican. Mem. Soc. Of Friends. Home: 221 Morris Rd Ambler PA 19002-5202 Office: 660 Sentry Pky Ste 200 Blue Bell PA 19422-2317 E-mail: sam@samswansen.com.

SWANSON, ALFRED BERTIL, orthopaedic and hand surgeon, inventor, educator; b. Kenosha, Wis, Apr. 16, 1923; s. O.P. and Esther (Person) S.; children: Karin Louise, Miles Raymond; m. Genevieve de Groot, MD, Dec. 27, 1969; 1 son, Eric Alfred. BS, U. Ill., 1944, MD, 1947. Diplomate: Am. Bd. Orthop. Surgery. Intern St. Luke's Hosp., Chgo., 1947; spl. tng. orthop. surgery Ill. Crippled Children's Hosp. Sch., Chgo., 1948, St. Luke's Hosp., 1949, Northwestern U. Med. Sch., 1950, Ind. U. Med. Ctr., 1951; practice medicine specializing in orthopaedic/hand surgery Grand Rapids, Mich., 1954—2001; chief hand surgery fellowship, orthopaedic research dir. Blodgett Meml. Hosp.-Spectrum Health East, 1962—; dir. emeritus Grand Rapids Orthopaedic Surgery Residency Tng. Program. Chief of staff Mary Free Bed Children's Hosp. and Orthop. Ctr., Juvenile Amputee Clin., 1963-65, 67-68, 73-78; prof. surgery Mich. State U., Lansing; chmn. Grand Rapids Internat. Symposium on Implant Arthrophasty, 1970-92; nat. and internat. lectr. in field. Author: Implant Resection Arthroplasty in the Hand and Extremities, 1973; Contbr. numerous sci. articles and exhibits in field; producer teaching films. Served with USNR, 1944-45; served to capt. M.C. AUS, 1952-54. Decorated medal of Honor So. Vietnam, 1967; recipient Profl. Medicine award Mich. Internat. Council, 1977; recipient Resolution of Tribute State of Mich., 1986, Order of Merit Orthop. Rsch. Soc., 1982, 89, 91, Disting. Svc. in Health Care award Hosp. Council West Mich., 1984, Nat. Vol. Svc. Citation Arthritis Found., 1984, U. Ill. Alumni Achievement award, 1985, Orthop. Overseas Spl. award for personal svc. and recruitment of orthop. and hand surgery vols. for So. Vietnam and Peru, Disting. Svc. award Arthritis Found., 1990, Cert. of Appreciation, Lifetime Sci. Achievement Award, Nat. Arthritis Found., 2003; Op. Desert Storm, US Dept. VA, 1991; named prof. h.c. Orthop. Alumni of Shriners Hosp. Crippled Children Mexico City; named to Grand Rapids Hall of Fame, 2001. Fellow ACS; mem. Am. Med. Writers Assn., AMA (Disting. Svc. award 1966, 69, Sci. Achievement award 1996), Am. Acad. Orthop. Surgeons (Kappa Delta award 1982), Pan Am. Med. Assn., Pan Pacific Surg. Assn., Assn. Mil. Surgeons, Am. Acad. Cerebral Palsy, Brit. Club Surgery of Hand, Italian Soc. Surgery of Hand, Brazilian, Colombian, South African, Japanese, Argentinian, So. Am., Caribbean Hand soc., Internat. Fedn. Soc. Surgery Hand (sec.-gen. 1978-83, pres. 1983-89, hist. 1989—, Pioneer in Hand Surgery award 1995), Groupe d'Etude de la Main, Am. Assn. Hand Surgeons, Am. Soc. Surgery Hand (pres. 1979-80), Am., Clin., Mich., Lamplighter's orthop. soc., Am. Orthop. Assn., Am. Orthop. Foot Soc., Am. Soc. Plastic and Reconstructive Surgeons, Peruvian Soc. Plastic and Reconstructive Surgeons, Mich. Med. Soc. (Disting. Service award 1966, Nat. Pres. award 1979, 84, Cmty. Svc. award 1993), Assn. Orthop. Chmn., European Rheumatoid Arthritis Surg. Soc., Norwegian Soc. Rheumatoid Surgery, Ga. Orthop. Soc., Fla. Orthop. Soc., Ark. Orthopaedic Soc., Orthop. Letters Club, Brazilian, Latin Am., Chilean, Columbian, Internat., Argentinian, Peruvian, Belgian, Turkish soc. Orthop. Surgery and Traumatology, Internat. Soc. Rehab. Disabled, Rheumatoid Arthritis Surg. Soc., Soc. Am. Inventors, Soc. Biomaterials, Internat. coll. Surgeons, Internat. Soc. Orthop. and Traumatology Rsch., Internat. Soc. Prosthetics and Orthotics Alternative Methods Internat. Stability (founder, chmn. 1983—), Internat. Trees Corps (founder, chmn. 1983—), Airplane Owners and Pilots Assn., World Affairs Coun. Western Mich. (chmn. numerous coms.), Cascade Hills Country Club (Grand Rapids), Rotary Internat. (Paul Harris award), many others. Congregationalist. Achievements include inventing implants for replacement arthritic joints. Office: Spectrum Health Blodgett Campus 1840 Wealthy St SE MC-504 Grand Rapids MI 49506-2969

SWANSON, CELIA, retail executive; BA in Fashion Merchandising, U. Nebr., 1977. Sr. v.p. human resources and adminstrn. PACE Membership Warehouse, Inc., Denver; dr. dir. people group Sam's Club, 1994—95, v.p. people group, 1995—97, sr. v.p. membership, mktg. and adminstrn., 1997—2000, exec. v.p. membership, mktg. adminstrn., 2000—. Bd. govs. Children's Miracle Network, 2000—. Mem.: Nebr. Alumni Assn. (bd. dirs. 1999—). Office: Wal-Mart Stores Inc 702 SW Eighth St Bentonville AR 72716

SWANSON, DAVID HEATH, agricultural company executive; b. Aurora, Ill., Nov. 3, 1942; s. Neil H. and Helen J. (McKendry) S.; m. Carolyn Breitinger; children: Benjamin Heath, Matthew Banford. BA, Harvard U., 1964; MA, U. Chgo., 1969. Account exec. 1st Nat. Bank Chgo., 1967-69; dep. mgr. Brown Bros. Harriman & Co., N.Y.C., 1969-72; treas. Borden, Inc. Internat., N.Y.C., 1972-75; v.p., treas. Continental Grain Co., N.Y.C., 1975-77, v.p., CFO, 1977-79, gen. mgr. European div., 1979-81, exec. v.p. and gen. mgr. World Grain div., 1981-83, corp. sr. v.p., chief fin. and adminstrv. officer, 1983-86, group pres., 1985-86; pres., CEO Cen. Soya, Ft. Wayne, Ind., 1986-93; chmn., CEO Explorer Nutrition Group, N.Y.C., 1994-96; pres., CEO, Countrymark, Inc., Indpls., 1996-98. Mem. adv. bd. U.S. Export-Import Bank, 1985-86; bd. dirs. Fiduciary Trust Internat., Conrail. Founding bd. dirs. Internat. Policy Coun. on Agr. and Trade; mem. adv. bd. Purdue U. Agr. Sch.; mem. Gov.'s Econ. Devel. Ind. Bd.; bd. govs. Exec. Coun. on Fgn. Diplomats and U.S. Agr. Libr.; gov. Found. for U.S. Constn. Mem. Coun. Fgn. Rels., Nat. Assn. Mfrs. (bd. dirs.), Ind. C. of C. (bd. dirs.), Am. Alpine Club (bd. dirs.),

Links Club, Racquet and Tennis Club, Explorers Club (bd. dirs., sec., pres.), Millbrook Golf and Tennis. Republican. Congregationalist. Office: PO Box 609 Bangall NY 12506-0609 also: PO Box 1418 Millbrook NY 12545

SWANSON, DAVID H(ENRY), consultant, retired economist, educator; b. Anoka, Minn., Nov. 1, 1930; s. Henry Otto and Louise Isabell (Holiday) S.; m. Suzanne Nash, Jan. 19, 1952 (dec. Sept. 1990); children: Matthew David, Christopher James; m. Joanne Perkins, Feb. 1, 1991. BA, St. Cloud State U., 1953; MA, U. Minn., 1955; PhD, Iowa State U., 1987. CPCU. Econ. area devel. dept. No. State Power Co., Mpls., 1955-56, staff asst., v.p. sales, 1956-57, economist indsl. devel. dept., 1957-63; dir. area devel. dept. Iowa So. Utilities Co., Centerville, 1963-67, dir. econ. R&D, 1967-70; dir. New Orleans Econ. Devel. Coun., 1970-72; divsn. mgr. Kaiser Aetna Tex., New Orleans, 1972-73; dir. corp. rsch. United Svcs. Automobile Assn., San Antonio, 1973-76; pres. Lantern Corp., San Antonio, 1974-79; adminstr. bus. devel. State of Wis., Madison, 1976-78; dir. Ctr. Indsl. Rsch. and Svc. Iowa State U., Ames, 1978-89, mem. mktg. faculty Coll. Bus. Adminstrn., 1979-85; dir. econ. devel. lab Ga. Inst. Tech., 1989—93; adv. to mfg. extension program Nat. Inst. Stds. U.S Dept. Commerce, 1993—96; prin. rshch assoc., econ devel. Insts. Ga. Insts. Tech., Atlanta, 1996-99, ret., 1999. Cons. Indsl. Modernization and Univ. Ext., Mexico, 1997—2000, Tech. Tng. and Indsl. Ext., Poland, 1998—2000, Mendes England & Assocs. Polish Project, 1998—2000; dir. Iowa Devel. Commn., 1982—83; mem. adv. bd. Iowa Venture Capital Fund, 1985—88; dir. Applied Strategies Internat. Ltd., 1983—88; dir. econ. devel. lab. Ga. Inst. Tech., Atlanta, 1989—93; mem. adv. bd. Nat. Tech. Transfer Ctr, 1992—96; exec. on loan Nat. Inst. Stds. and Tech., 1993—96; chmn. Iowa Curriculum Assistance Sys., 1984—85; cons. Ctr. for Indsl. Rsch., Iowa State U., 1998—2001; award evaluator Fed. Lab. Consortium, 1999—. Mem. Iowa Airport Planning Coun., 1968-70; mem. adv. coun. Office Comprehensive Health Planning, 1967-70; mem. adv. coun. Ctr. Indsl. Rsch. and Svc., 1967-70, New Orleans Met. Area Com., 1972-73; mem. Iowa Dist. Export Coun., 1977-88; mem. Atlanta Dist. Export Coun., 1989-96; mem. region 7 adv. coun. SBA, 1978-88; dir. Mid-Continent R&D Coun., 1980-84; chmn. Iowa del. White House Conf. on Small Bus., 1980; chmn. Gov.'s Task Force on High Tech., 1982-83; chmn. Iowa High Tech. Coun., 1983-86; mem. adv. com. U. New Orleans, 1971-73; county fin. chmn. Rep. Party, 1966-67; bd. dirs. Greater New Orleans Urban League, 1970-73, Indsl. Policy Coun., 1984-88, Suwanee Crossroads Inc., 2001-04; mem. Iowa Gov.'s Export Coun., 1984-89; v.p. Iowa Sister State Friendship Com., 1985-87, pres., 1988; chmn. nat. adv. coun. Fed. Lab. Consortium, 1985-98, chmn., 1993-96, mem., 1985, award reviewer, 1998—; mem. Ga. Tech. Faculty Assembly, 1990-92; pres. Chattahoochee Run Homeowners Assn., 1997-99; mem. planning com. Internat. Tech. Transfer Conf., 1997; mem. adv. com. Ga. Oglethorpe Quality Award, 1997-99, quality examiner, 1998-99, Georgians Mfg., 1997-99; mem. Suwanee Planning and Zoning Bd. Appeals, 1999, chair, 2000-03; vice chmn. econ. devel. com. Suwanee Cmty. Betterment Program, 1999-2000; chmn. transition com. Chattahoochee Run Neighborhood Assn., 2000; chair Suwanee Day Festival, 2001-02. With USAF, 1951-52. Mem. Am. Indsl. Ext. Alliance (pres. 1992-96, editor 1998-2000), Nat. Assn. Mgmt. Tech. Assistance Ctrs. (pres. 1985, bd. dirs. 1982-86), Tech. Transfer Soc. (bd. dirs. 1984-94, v.p. 1987-90, pres.-elect 1991-92, pres. 1992-93), Oak Ridge Assoc. Univs. (tech. transfer adv. coun. 1992-95), Ga. Fin. Developers Assn., Ga. 2000, Profl. Developers Assn., Nat. Univ. Continuing Edn. Assn., Internat. Coun. Small Bus., Rotary (bd. dirs. 1986-88), Toastmasters (past pres.), Marston Club (Iowa State U. Coll. Engring.), Alumni Admissions Coun. (Iowa State U.), Kiwanis (sec. 2004). Episcopalian. Home: 1415 Chattahoochee Run Dr Suwanee GA 30024-3808 Personal E-mail: swansondh@mindspring.com.

SWANSON, DIANE L. business management and economics educator, researcher; b. Manhattan, Kans., Oct. 6, 1950; d. Harold Albin Swanson and Betty Jo Lusby; m. Michael Dale Scott, Aug. 5, 1970 (dec. July 19, 1975); 1 child, Christopher William Scott. BS in Mgmt. and Fin., Avila, Kansas City, Mo., 1980; MA in Econs., U. Mo., Kansas City, 1982; PhD in Bus. Adminstrn., U. Pitts., 1996. Instr. econs., interim dir. Inst. Mgmt. Old Dominion U., Norfolk, Va., 1984—86; asst. prof. fin. Hampton (Va.) U., 1987—88; asst. prof. bus. econs. U. Pitts., 1988—89; assoc. prof. mgmt. Robert Morris Coll., Pitts., 1989—97, Kans. State U., Manhattan, 1997—, von Waaden prof. bus. adminstrn., founder and chair Bus. Ethics Edn. Initiative, 2002—. Mem. Pres.'s Commn. on Women Kans. State U., 2000—01, mentor Developing Scholars Program for Minority Students, 2000—01; presenter confs. and media broadcasts in field; Disting. Spkr. on bus. ethics edn. Book rev. editor, consulting editor: Internat. Jour. Orgnl. Analysis, 1994—2004; contbg. editor: Managing Ego Energy, 1994—; spl. issue editor: Jour. Individual Employment Rights, 2002—03; contbr. articles to profl. jours., chapters to books. Co-founder Nat. Campaign to Improve Bus. Ethics Edn., 2002—; bd. dirs. Women's Intercultural Network, San Francisco, 1994—2002, People's Coop., Manhattan, 1998—2000, All Acad. Task Force on Mentoring, 2002—. Recipient nat. award for tchg. excellence, Bell and Howell, 1982, award for entrepreneurial leadership, Advances in Mgmt. Conf., 1996, Best Article on Bus. and Soc. award, Internat. Assn. for Bus. and Soc. and Calif. Mgmt. Rev., 1999, Outstanding Bus. Ethics Educator award, 2004; fellow, David Berg Family Found. in Bus. Ethics, 1994; grantee, Beard Ctr. for Ethics, Duquesne U., 2000, Australian Grad. Sch. Mgmt., 2000—01; internat. grantee for exec. leadership. Mem.: Nat. Acad. Mgmt. (governing bd. Social Issues in Mgmt. 1998—), Beta Gamma Sigma. Democrat. Avocations: yoga, meditation, travel, gardening, cats. Office: Kans State U 101 Calvin Hall Manhattan KS 66506 Office Phone: 785-532-4352. E-mail: swanson@ksu.edu.

SWANSON, DON RICHARD, university dean; b. L.A., Oct. 10, 1924; s. Harry Windfield and Grace Clara (Sandstrom) S.; m. Patricia Elizabeth Klick, Aug. 22, 1976; children— Douglas Alan, Richard Brian, Judith Ann. BS, Calif. Inst. Tech., 1945; MA, Rice U., 1947; PhD, U. Calif., Berkeley, 1952. Physicist U. Calif. Radiation Lab., Berkeley, 1947-52, Hughes Research and devel. Labs., Culver City, Calif., 1952-55; research scientist TRW, Inc., Canoga Park, Calif., 1955-63; prof. Grad. Library Sch., U. Chgo., 1963-92, dean, 1963-72, 77-79, 86-90, prof. bio-sci. coll. divsn. and divsn. humanities, 1992-96, prof. emeritus, 1996—. Mem. Sci. Info. Council, NSF, 1960-65; mem. toxicology info. panel Pres.'s Sci. Advisory Com., 1964-66; mem. library vis. com. Mass. Inst. Tech., 1966-71; mem. com. on sci. and tech. communication Nat. Acad. Scis., 1966-69 Editor: The Intellectual Founds. of Library Education, 1965, The Role of Libraries in the Growth of Knowledge, 1980; co-editor: Operations Research: Implications for Libraries, 1972, Management Education: Implications for Libraries and Library Schools, 1974; mem. editorial bd.: Library Quarterly, 1963-93; contbr.: chpt. to Ency. Brit, 1968—; sci. articles to profl. jours. Trustee Nat. Opinion Research Center, 1964-73; Research fellow Chgo. Inst. for Psychoanalysis, 1972-76. Served with USNR, 1943-46. Recipient Award of Merit Am. Soc. for Info. Sci. and Tech., 2000. Mem. Am. Soc. for Info. Sci., Am. Assn. Artificial Intelligence. Home: 5468 S Ingleside Ave Chicago IL 60615-5062 Office: U Chgo Divsn Humanities 1010 E 59th St Chicago IL 60637-1512 E-mail: d-swanson@uchicago.edu.

SWANSON, DONALD ALAN, geologist; b. Tacoma, July 25, 1938; s. Leonard Walter and Edith Christine (Bowers) S.; m. Barbara Joan White, May 25, 1974. BS in Geology, Wash. State U., 1960; PhD in Geology, Johns Hopkins U., 1964. Geologist U.S. Geol. Survey, Menlo Park, Calif., 1965-68, 71-80, Hawaii National Park, 1968-71, sr. geologist Cascades Volcano Obs. Vancouver, Wash., 1980-90, rsch. scientist-in-charge, 1986-89, sr. geologist Seattle, 1990-96; assoc. dir. Volcano Systems Ctr. U. Wash., 1993-96; scientist-in-charge Hawaiian Volcano Obs., 1997—. Affiliate prof. U. Wash., 1992—; adj. prof. U. Hawaii, 2002--; cons. U.S. Dept. Energy, Richland, Wash., 1979-83; volcanologist New Zealand Geol. Survey, Taupo, 1984; advisor Colombian Volcano Obs., Manizales, 1986. Assoc. editor Jour. Volcanology and Geothermal Rsch., 1976—, Jour. Geophys. Rsch., 1992-94; editor Bull. of Volcanology, 1985-90, exec. editor, 1995-99; contbr. numerous articles to profl. jours. Recipient Superior Service award U.S. Geol. Survey, 1980, Meritorious Service award U.S. Dept. Interior, 1985; postdoctoral fellow NATO, 1964-65. Fellow Geol. Soc. Am., Am. Geophys. Union, AAAS; mem. Sigma Xi. Avocation: hiking. Home: 417 Linaka St Hilo HI 96720-5927 Office: US Geol Survey Hawaiian Volcano Obs PO Box 51 Hawaii National Park HI 96718-0051 Business E-Mail: donswan@usgs.gov.

SWANSON, DONALD FREDERICK, retired food company executive; b. Mpls., Aug. 6, 1927; s. Clayton A. and Irma (Baiocchi) S.; m. Virginia Clare Hannah, Dec. 17, 1948; children— Donald Frederick, Cynthia Hannah Lindgren, Janet Clare Webster. BA, U. Minn., 1948. With Gen. Mills, Inc., 1949-85, div. v.p., dir. marketing flour, dessert and baking mixes, 1964-65, v.p., gen. mgr. grocery products div., 1965-68, v.p., corporate adminstrn. officer consumer foods group, fashion div., transp. and purchasing depts., advt. and marketing services, 1969, exec. v.p. craft, game and toy group, fashion group, direct marketing group, travel group, dir., 1968-76, sr. exec. v.p. consumer non-foods, 1976-85, chief financial officer, 1977-79, sr. exec. v.p. restaurants and consumer non-foods, 1980-81, vice chmn. restaurants and consumer non-foods, 1981-85. Ret. chmn. bd. Soo Line Corp. Served with AUS, 1946-47. Mem. Lafayette Club, Mpls. Club, Wayzata Country Club, Royal Poinciana Golf Club, Phi Kappa Psi. Home: 2171 Gulf Shore Blvd N Apt 504 Naples FL 34102-4685 Office: 641 Lake St E Wayzata MN 55391-1760

SWANSON, ERIK CHRISTIAN, museum director; b. Breckenridge, Colo., June 17, 1940; s. Glen Leonard and Eveitte Leona (Snell) S.; m. Elizabeth Jane Thompson, Aug. 22, 1976; children: Johannah Elizabeth, Nils Christian. Student, Royal U., Lund, Sweden, 1960-64; BA in History, German Lang., tchg. cert., U. No. Colo. Curator South Pk. City Mus., Fairplay, Colo., 1974-89; dir. Alma (Colo.) Fire House Mus., 1976-82; exec. dir. Cripple Creek (Colo.) Dist. Mus., 1988—. Chief of police Alma, Colo., 1977-80. With U.S. Army, 1966-68. Mem. Odd Fellows (past grand South Park Lodge # 10, Fairplay, Colo.), Masons (sr. warden Cripple Creek chpt. 1995), Elks. Republican. Home: PO Box 27 Alma CO 80420-0027 Office: Cripple Creek Dist Mus PO Box 1210 Cripple Creek CO 80813-1210

SWANSON, FRED A. retired communications designer, councilman; b. Pitts., July 22, 1946; s. Earl F. and Irene F. (McQuaide) S.; m. Leticia Garcia; children: Thomas R., Melissa A., Todd A. Student, Robert Morris Coll., 1964-65, 75-78. Laborer Equitable Gas Co., Pitts., 1965; technician AT&T Long Lines, Pitts., 1970-78; tech. designer AT&T, Pitts., 1978-98, ret., 1998. Baseball coach Brentwood (Pa.) Athletic Assn.; football coach Brentwood Dukes; founding mem. Am. Air Mus. Staff sgt. USAF, 1965-70. Mem. Libr. of Congress (assoc.), Am. Mus. Natural History, Smithsonian Assocs., Non-Commd. Officers Assn., Am. Legion (past vice comdr.). Democrat. Roman Catholic. Avocations: golf, coaching football. Home: 4023 Lawnview Ave Brentwood PA 15227-3235

SWANSON, JACQUELINE V. academic administrator, educator, women's health nurse practitioner; b. Houston, Feb. 12, 1944; d. Ivan Jack and Edith Wilson; m. James Swanson, Aug. 21, 1965; children: Jim, Charlotte, Robert, Guy, Danny. BS, Tex. Woman's U., 1967, MS, 1974; PhD, U. North Tex., Denton, 1989. Cert. clin. nurse specialist, in maternal newborn health, women's health nurse practitioner Planned Parenthood of Rocky Mountains, sexual assault nurse examiner. Various clin. nursing positions, Tex. and Kans., Tex., 1967-73; supr. obstet. and nursery Harris County Hosp. Dist., Houston, 1970-73; instr. Prairie View (Tex.) A&M U., 1973-75; asst. prof. Tex. Woman's U., Denton, 1975-85; labor and delivery nurse Tarrant County Hosp. Dist., Ft. Worth, 1987-89; assoc. prof., chmn. dept. nursing Ft. Hays State U., Hays, Kans., 1989-94; dir. BS nursing program Lamar U., Beaumont, Tex., 1994-95; prof., dean Coll. Nursing, Mont. State U. No., Havre, 1995—98, prof. nursing, 1998-2000; assoc. prof. nursing Tarleton State U., 2000—03; women's health nurse practioner Tarleton Student Health Clinic, 2003—. Contbr. articles to profl. jours.; presenter U.S. and internat. Mem. Denton Area War on Drugs. Mem. AAUP, ANA, Nat. Assn. Nurse Practioners Women's Health, Assn. Women's Health, Obstetric and Neonatal Nurses, Kans. State Nurses Assn., Tex. Nurses Assn., Tex. Nurse Practioner's Assn., Mont. Nurses Assn., Internat. Coun. on Women's Health Issues, Internat. Soc. for Univ. Nurses, Sigma Theta Tau. Home: 614 N Clinton Stephenville TX 76401

SWANSON, KURT, metal fabricating company executive; CFO Tang Industries Inc., Las Vegas. Office: Tang Industries Inc 3773 Howard Hughes PkwySte 350N Las Vegas NV 89109

SWANSON, LARRY, manufacturing executive; CFO Beaulieu Group, Dalton, Ga., 1997-99. Office: Beaulieu Group PO Box 1248 Dalton GA 30722-1248

SWANSON, LAUREN A. consultant, entrepreneur, educator, researcher; b. Apr. 17, 1951; BS, U. Wyo., 1973; MS, 1974; postgrad., Wheaton Coll., 1977; PhD, U. Ga., 1983. Instr. mktg. U. Wyo., Laramie, 1974-76; grad. instr. mktg., mgmt. sci. U. Ga., Athens, 1978-79; vis. prof. mktg. Grad. Sch. Bus. Adminstrn. Atlanta U., 1980-81; asst. prof. mktg. U. Mass., Boston, 1981-86; rsch. cons. Hill-Holliday-Connors-Cosmopulos Inc., Boston, 1983-86; assoc. in rsch. Fairbank Ctr. for East Asian Rsch. Harvard U., Cambridge, Mass., 1986—; fgn. expert, prof. mktg. and econs. U. Internat. Bus. and Econs., Beijing, 1986-87; assoc. prof. mktg. Chinese U. Hong Kong, 1987-98, assoc. dir. MBA programs, 1991-96; v.p. Dalton (Nebr.) Telecom, 1998-99; cons. in mktg. and telecomms. Dalton, 1999—. Cons. to industry; examiner Hong Kong Quality Award, 1991-95. Guest editor: Internat. Jour. Advtsg.; contbr. numerous articles to profl. jours.

SWANSON, LISA TUCKER, human services manager, consultant; b. Bar Harbor, Maine, May 30, 1960; d. Everett and Arletta Ray Tucker; children: Christopher, Matthew, Katie. BS in Nursing, Pensacola Christian Coll., 1983; MS in Bus., Husson Coll., Maine, 1991. Utilization, quality rev. coord. Ea. Maine Med. Ctr., Bangor, Maine, 1987—90, cardiac care coord., 1990—97, staff developer, 1997—2000, change mgmt. specialist, 2000—02, project mgr., 2002—. Parent rep. Children's Miracle Network at Ea. Maine Med. Ctr., Bangor, Maine, 1999—. Author: (booklet) Practical Suggestions for Raising a Child with a Heart Problem. Founder Pediatric Cardiac Support Group, Bangor, Maine, 1990—99; family rep. for Maine Children's Miracle Network, Bangor, Maine, 1999—2002. Mem.: Nursing Leaders of Maine, Sigma Theta Tau Internat. Achievements include first to Develped Project Mgmt. Structure for Healthcare at Ea.Ma. Med. Ctr. Avocations: conference speaker, writing, travel. Office: Ea Maine Med Ctr 489 State St Bangor ME 04401 Office Phone: 207-973-5287. Personal E-mail: lswanson@emh.org. E-mail: lswanson@emh.org.

SWANSON, MARY CATHERINE, educational reform program founder; b. Kingsburg, Calif., Sept. 3, 1944; d. Edwin Elmore and Corrine (Miller) Jacobs; m. Thomas Edward Swanson, Aug. 27, 1966; 1 child, Thomas Jacobs. BA in English and Journalism, Calif. State U., San Francisco, 1966; standard teaching credential in secondary edn., U. Calif., 1966; MA in Edn., U. Redlands, 1977; DHL (hon.), U. San Diego, 2002, U. LaVerne, 2003. Svc. adminstrv. credential, Calif.; specialist learning handicapped, Calif.; gifted cert., Calif. Tchr. English and journalism Woodland (Calif.) High Sch., 1966-67, Armijo High Sch., Fairfield, Calif., 1967-69, Moreno Valley High Sch., Sunnymead, Calif., 1969-70, Clairemont High Sch., San Diego, 1970-86; coord. San Diego County Office Edn., 1986-90, dir. AVID project, 1990-92; founder, exec. dir. AVID Ctr., 1992—. Newspaper and yearbook advisor Moreno Valley High Sch., Moreno Valley Sch. Dist., 1969-70; reading program coord. Clairemont High Sch., 1974-80, project English coord. and site plan coord., 1975-80, English dept. chairperson, 1978-86, coord. Advancement Via Individual Determination and WASC accreditation, 1980-86, in-sch. resource tchr., 1982-86; mem. numerous positions and coms. San Diego City Schs., 1974-91; mem. com. univ. and coll. opportunities commn. Calif. State Dept. Edn., 1981-82; mem. adv. com. tchr. edn. program Pt. Loma Coll., 1982-83, tchr. English methods course for tchrs. secondary edn., 1986-87; mem. accreditation vis. com. WASC, 1983, integration monitoring team Crawford High Sch., 1984, adv. com. San Diego Area Writing Project, 1987—; developer numerous curricular programs, 1967—. Community leader Olivenhain Valley 4-H Club, 1981-90; founder Olivenhain Valley Soccer Club, 1982; coord. Clairemont High Sch./Sea World Adopt-A-Sch., 1982-84. Named Headliner of Yr.-Edn./Creative Tchg., San Diego Press Club, 1991, Headline of Yr. Cmty. Activist, 2002, Woman of Vision, LWV-San Diego, 1992, Nat. Educator of Yr., McGraw Hill, 2001, America's Best Tchr., Time Mag. and CNN, 2001; named to Pres.'s Forum on Tchg. as a Profession, Am. Assn. Higher Edn., 1991; recipient EXCEL award for excellence in tchg., 1985, Exemplary Program award, Nat. Coun. States on Insvc. Edn., 1990, Pioneering Achievement in Edn. award, Charles A. Dana Found., 1991; grantee, BankAmerica Found., 1980, UCSD Acad. Support Svcs., 1980, San Diego Gas and Elec. Found., 1984. Mem. Nat. Coun. Tchrs. English (Nat. Ctr. Excellence award 1985-87), Calif. Coun. Tchrs. English, Calif. Assn. Gifted Edn., Golden Key Nat. Honor Soc. (hon. mem.), Phi Kappa Phi. Office: AVID Ctr 5120 Shoreham Pl Ste 120 San Diego CA 92122 E-mail: mcswanson@avidcenter.org.

SWANSON, NORMA FRANCES, federal agency administrator; b. Blue Island, Ill., Oct. 24, 1923; d. Arnold Raymond and Bessie Oween (Bowley) Brown; m. George Clair Swanson, Mar. 18, 1948; 1 child, Dane Craig. AB, Asbury Coll., 1946; BS cum laude, Eastern Nazarene Coll., Wollaston, Mass., 1970; MA cum laude, Ind. Christian U., 1986. Confidential asst. dep. undersec. interagy. intergovt. affairs U.S. Dept. Edn., Washington, 1981—; pres. Window to the World, Inc., Schroon Lake, N.Y., 1985—; asst. dir. edn. Commn. Bicentennial U.S. Constn., Washington, 1987—; dir. Horizons Plus Values Program Hampton Roads Va. Detention Homes; dir. Project Fresh Start Washington D.C. Pub. Sch., 1993-96. Cons. Conf. Industrialized Nations, Williamsburg, Va., 1982, Nellie Thomas Inst. Learning, Monterey, Calif., 1981-82. Author: Dear Teenager, A Teen's Guide to Correct Social Behavior, 1987, A Constitution is Born, A Teacher's Guide to Resource Materials, 1987, Sunlights and More, Bright Beginnings, 1993, Vols. I, II, 1996, The Ones that Count and Other Stories with Values to Live By, 1994, A Think and Write Journal Sunlights and More Vols. I, II, 1993 (story album) The Ones that Count and Other Stories with Virtues to Live By, 1996, Keeping Christmas: A Family Sampler of Best-Loved Stories and Hymns plus Our Christmas Heritage, Then and Now, 1998; editor: (anthology) Horizons Plus; developer ednl. materials; theorem artist Early Life mag., 1974. Bd. regents Ind. Christian U., 1986—; program dir. Tidewater (Va.) Outreach, 1992; dir. project Fresh Start, Washington Pub. Sch., 1993-94; dir. youth outreach with values program U.S. Dept. Juvenile Justice, 1992-93. Recipient J.C. Penney award for volunteerism, 1993, Precision Tune awrd for svc. tto Washington Inner-City Schs. Republican. Baptist. Avocation: theorem painting. Address: 5501 Woodlyn Rd Frederick MD 21703-6965 Personal E-mail: N.f.swansonF@adelphia.net.

SWANSON, PATRICIA KLICK, foundation administrator; b. St. Louis, May 8, 1940; d. Emil Louis and Patricia (McNair) Klick; 1 child, Ivan Clatanoff. BS in Edn., U. Mo., 1962; postgrad., Cornell U., 1963; MLS, Simmons Coll., 1967. Reference librarian Simmons Coll., Boston, 1967-68, U. Chgo., 1970-79, sr. lectr. Grad. Library Sch., 1974-83, 86-88, head reference service, 1979-83, asst. dir. for sci. libraries, 1983-93, acting asst. dir. for tech. svcs., 1987-88, assoc. provost, 1993-98; program officer MacArthur Found., 1999—. Project dir. Office Mgmt. Svcs., Assn. Rsch. Librs., 1982-83; speaker in field; cons. on libr. mgmt., planning and space. Author: Great is the Gift that Bringeth Knowledge: Highlights from the History of the John Crerar Library, 1989; contbr. articles to profl. jours. Office: John D and Catherine T MacArthur Found 140 S Dearborn St Ste 1100 Chicago IL 60603-5202

SWANSON, PEGGY EUBANKS, finance educator; b. Ivanhoe, Tex., Dec. 29, 1936; d. Leslie Samuel and Mary Lee (Reid) Eubanks; m. B. Marc Sommers, Nov. 10, 1993. BBA, U. North Tex., 1957, M. Bus. Edn., 1965; MA in Econs., So. Meth. U., 1967, PhD in Econs., 1978. Instr. El Centro Coll., Dallas, 1967-69, 71-78, bus. div. chmn., 1969-71; asst. prof. econs. U. Tex., Arlington, 1978-79, asst. prof. fin., 1979-84, assoc. prof., 1984-86, chmn. dept. fin. and real estate, 1986-88, prof. fin., 1987—, interim dean Coll. Bus. Adminstrn., 1999—2000. Expert witness various law firms, primarily Tex. and Calif., 1978—; cons. Internat. Edn. Program, 1992-99; curriculum cons. U. Monterrey, Mexico, 1995, New Saudi Arabia U., 1999. Contbr. articles to acad. profl. jours. Vol. Am. Cancer Soc., Dallas, Arlington, 1981—, Meals on Wheels, Arlington, 1989—; mem. adv. bd. Ryan/Reilly Ctr. for Urban Land Utilization, Arlington, 1986-88. Mem. Fin. Exec. Inst. (chmn. acad. rels. 1987-88), Internat. Bus. Steering Com. (chmn. 1989-91), Am. Fin. Assn., Am. Econ. Assn., Fin. Mgmt. Assn. (hon. faculty mem. Nat. Honor Soc. 1985-86, program com. 1998-99), Southwestern Fin. Assn. (program com. 1987-88, 96), Midwest Fin. Assn. (program com. 1997-98, 98-99), Acad. of Internat. Bus. (program com. 1992-95), Acad. Disting. Tchrs., Phi Beta Delta (membership com. 1987-89). Republican. Episcopalian. Avocations: tennis, gardening. Home: 4921 Bridgewater Dr Arlington TX 76017-2729 Office: U Tex at Arlington PO Box 19449 Arlington TX 76019-0001 Office Phone: 817-272-3841. Business E-Mail: swanson@uta.edu.

SWANSON, PHILLIP DEAN, neurologist; b. Seattle, Oct. 1, 1932; s. William Dean and Kathryn C. (Peterson) S.; m. Sheila N. Joardar, Apr. 20, 1957; children: Stephen, Jennifer, Kathryn, Rebecca, Sara. BS, Yale U., 1954; student, U. Heidelberg, 1952-53; MD, Johns Hopkins U., 1958; PhD in Biochemistry, U. London, 1964. Intern Harvard med. svc. Boston City Hosp., 1958-59; resident in neurology Johns Hopkins Hosp., Balt. City Hosp., 1959-62; asst. prof. U. Wash. Sch. Medicine, Seattle, 1964-68, assoc. prof., 1968-73, prof., 1973—, head divsn. neurology, 1967-95. Mem. med. adv. bd. Puget Sound chpt. Nat. Multiple Sclerosis Soc., 1967-97, chmn., 1970-74; mem. com. to combat Huntington's Disease Nat. Sci. Council, 1975-84. Author: (with others) Introduction to Clinical Neurology, 1976; editor: Signs and Symptoms in Neurology, 1984; contbr. articles to profl. jours. NIH spl. fellow, 1962-64; NIH grantee. Fellow Am. Acad. Neurology; mem. Am. Neurol. Assn., Assn. Univ. Profs. Neurology (pres. 1975-76), Am. Heart Assn., Am. Soc. Neurochemistry, Internat. Soc. Neurochemistry, Biochem. Soc. (London), Am. Soc. Clin. Investigation (emeritus) Home: 6537 29th Ave NE Seattle WA 98115-7234 Office: U Wash Sch Medicine Dept Neurology PO Box 356465 Seattle WA 98195-6465 E-mail: swansonp@u.washington.edu.

SWANSON, RICHARD WILLIAM, retired statistician; b. July 26, 1934; s. Richard () and Erma Marie (Herman) Swanson; m. Laura Yoko Arai, Dec. 30, 1970. BS, Iowa State U., 1958, MS, 1964. Ops. analyst Stanford Rsch. Inst., Monterey, Calif., 1958—62; statistician ARINC Rsch. Corp., Washington, 1964—65; sr. scientist Booz-Allen Applied Rsch., Vietnam, 1965—67, 1967—68; sr. ops. analyst Control Data Corp., Honolulu, 1968—70; mgmt. cons. Honolulu, 1970—73; exec. v.p. SEQUEL Corp., Honolulu, 1973—75; bus. cons. Hawaii Dept. Planning and Econ. Devel., Honlulu, 1975—77; tax rsch. and planning offider Dept. Taxation, 1977—82; ops. rsch. analyst U.S. Govt., 1982—89, shipyard statistician, 1989—97; ret., 1997. Mem.: Hawaiian Acad. Sci., Sigma Xi. Home: 583 Kamoku St Apt 3505 Honolulu HI 96826-5241

SWANSON, ROBERT DRAPER, college president; b. Sioux City, Iowa, Aug. 6, 1915; s. Alfred and Tida Ruth (Draper) S.; m. Roberta B. Clements, May 5, 1941 (dec. Oct. 1975); children: Sara Louise, Mark Robert; m. Dorothy B. Howe, Aug. 4, 1979. AB, Park Coll., 1937; student, U. Iowa, 1937; B.D., McCormick Theol. Sem., 1941; D.D., James Millikin U., 1950; L.H.D., Tusculum Coll., 1966, Olivet Coll., 1971, Central Mich. U., 1979, Alma Coll., 1981; LL.D., Hillsdale Coll., 1968, Hope Coll., 1981. Dir. athletics, phys. edn. Park Coll., 1937-38; ordained to ministry Presbyn. Ch., 1941; pastor Second Presbyn. Ch., Tulsa, 1941-45; dean of students McCormick Sem., 1946-47, v.p., prof. preaching, 1948-56; pres. Alma Coll., 1956-80, pres. emeritus, 1980—. Dir. Gen. Telephone Co. Mich. Served as lt. (j.g.), Chaplain's Corps USNR, 1945-46. Recipient Disting. Alumni award, Pk. Coll., 1971, Disting. Alumnus award, McCormick Theol. Sem., 1981, Higher Edn. Honors award, Presbyn. Ch., 2002. Mem. Phi Beta Kappa. Clubs: Rotary (Alma). Home: 1267 Masonic Ct Alma MI 48801-1167 Business E-Mail: swanson@alma.edu.

SWANSON, ROBERT H. JR. electronics executive; BS Indsl. Engring., Northeastern U. V.p., gen. mgr. Nat. Semiconductor, 1968—81; founder, pres., CEO, dir. Linear Tech. Corp., Milpitas, Calif., 1981, chmn. bd. dirs., CEO, 1999—. Office: Linear Tech Corp 1630 Mccarthy Blvd Milpitas CA 95035-7417

SWANSON, ROBERT KILLEN, management consultant; b. Deadwood, S.D., Aug. 11, 1932; s. Robert Claude and Marie Elizabeth (Kersten) S.; m. Nancy Anne Oyaas, July 19, 1958; children: Cathryn Lynn, Robert Stuart, Bart Killen. BA, U. S.D., 1954; postgrad., U. Melbourne, Australia, 1955. With Gen. Mills, Inc., Mpls., 1955-58, 71-79, v.p., 1971-73, group v.p., 1973-77, exec. v.p., 1977-79; with Marathon Oil Co., Findlay, Ohio, 1958-60; sr. v.p., dir. Needham, Harper & Steers, Inc., Chgo., 1961-69; joint mng. dir. S. H. Benson (Holdings) Ltd., Eng., 1969-71; pres., chief operating officer Greyhound Corp., Phoenix, 1980; chmn., chief exec. officer Del E. Webb Corp., Phoenix, 1981-87; chmn. RKS Inc., Phoenix, 1987—. Bd. dirs. Am. S.W. Concepts Inc., ST Internat. Ltd., Granite Dells LLP, Tri-City LLP, Thurswley Investments World Holdings LLC. 2d lt. U.S. Army, 1955. Fulbright scholar, 1954-55; Woodrow Wilson scholar. Mem. U.K. Dirs. Inst., U.S. Internat. Scholars Assn., English Speaking Union, Phoenix Country Club, Yale Club. Episcopalian. Office: RKS Inc 5600 N Palo Cristi Rd Paradise Valley AZ 85253-7543

SWANSON, ROBERT LAWRENCE, oceanographer, academic program administrator; b. Balt., Oct. 11, 1938; s. Lawrence Wilbur and Hazel Ruth Swanson; m. Dana Lamont, Sept. 12, 1963; children: Lawrence Daniel, Michael Nathan. BSCE, Lehigh U., 1960; MS in Oceanography, Oreg. State U., 1965, PhD in Oceanography, 1971. Cert. hydrographer. Commd. ensign U.S. Coast and Geodetic Survey (now NOAA), 1960, advanced through grades to capt., 1978; ops. officer U.S. Pathfinder, 1965; comdg. officer U.S. Marmer, 1966; chief oceanog. divsn. Nat. Ocean Survey, NOAA, Rockville, Md., 1969-72; mgr. Marine Ecosys. Analysis, NY Bight project, Stony Brook, 1973—78; dir. Office Marine Pollution Assessment NOAA, Rockville, 1978—83, rsch. assoc. Sea Grant Stony Brook, 1983—84; comdg. officer U.S. Researcher, Miami, Fla., 1984—86; chief internat. activities group NOAA, Rockville, 1986, exed. dir. Office Oceanic and Atmospheric Rsch., 1986—87; dir. Waste Reduction and Mgmt. Inst. SUNY, Stony Brook, 1987—, assoc. dean Marine Scis. Rsch. Ctr., 2003—. Adj. prof. Marine Scis. Rsch. Ctr., SUNY, Stony Brook, 1976—; mem. Suffolk County Coun. Environ. Quality, 1988—, vice chair, 1996—; mem. N.Y. State Oversight Com. on Brookhaven Nat. Lab., 1996—, Coastal Mgmt. Commn. Villages Head-of-the-Harbor and Nissequogue, 1994—2002; chmn. Coastal Mgmt. Commn. Villages Head Harbor and Nissequogue, 1995—97, 1999—2001; trustee Three Village Hist. Soc., 1994—2002; co-chair L.I. Environ. Econ. Roundtable, 1995—; adv. bd. Evan L. Lit Meml. Fund, 1998—; trustee Village of Head of the Harbor, 2002—; cons. in field. Co-author, co-editor: Oxygen Depletion and Associated Benthic Mortalities in NY Bight, 1979; co-editor: Floatable Wastes and the Region's Beaches; mem. editl. bd. NY Bight Monograph Series, 1973-81, Chemistry and Ecology, 1995-2003; co-author Images of America, Stony Brook, 2003; co-pub. Waste Mgmt. Rsch. Report, 1988-95; mem. adv. bd. L.I. Hist. Jour., 1995-2003, mem. editl. bd., 2004-. Recipient Karo award Am. Soc. Mil. Engrs., 1972; Silver medal Dept. Commerce, 1973; Program and Adminstrn. Mgmt. award NOAA, 1975, Unit citation, 1981; sr. exec. fellow John F. Kennedy Sch. Govt., Harvard U., 1983, Spl. Achievement award, 1987, NOAA Corps. Commendations, 1987; named Man of Yr. for environment Three Village Times, 1998. Mem. Am. Mil. Engrs., NY Acad. Scis., ASCE (chmn. hydrography and oceanography com. 1972-74), AAAS, Am. Geophys. Union, Marine Tech. Soc. (chmn. marine pollution com. 1982-92), Cosmos Club, Sigma Xi (pres. SUNY SB chpt. 1998—). Presbyterian. Home: 46 Harbor Hill Rd Saint James NY 11780-1217 Office: SUNY Waste Reduction And Mgmt Ins Stony Brook NY 11794-5000 Business E-Mail: lswanson@notes.cc.sunysb.edu.

SWANSON, ROBERT LEE, lawyer; b. Fond du Lac, Wis., July 15, 1942; s. Walfred S. and Edna F. (Kamp) S.; m. Mary Ruth Francis, Aug. 19, 1967; children: Leigh Alexandra, Mitchell Pearson. BS, U. Wis., 1964; JD, Valparaiso U., 1970; LLM, Boston U., 1979. Bar: Wis. 1970, U.S. Dist. Ct. (ea. dist.) Wis. 1970, U.S. Dist. Ct. (we. dist.) Wis. 1974, U.S. Dist. Ct. (we. dist.) Okla. 2002, U.S. Tax Ct. 1981, U.S. Dist. Ct. (cen.) Ill. 1988, Okla. 1999, U.S. Ct. Appeals (7th cir.) 1999. Atty. Kasdorf, Dahl, Lewis & Swietlik, Milw., 1970-73; atty., ptnr. Wartman, Wartman & Swanson, Ashland, Wis., 1973-80; city atty. City of Ashland, Wis., 1976-80; atty., ptnr. DeMark, Kolbe & Brodek, Racine, Wis., 1980-95; ptnr. Hartig, Bjelajac, Swanson & Koenen, Racine, 1995-99, Okla. Indigent Def. Sys., Lincoln County, 2000—02; pvt. practice Robert Lee Swanson Law Office, 2000—. Lectr. civil rights and discrimination laws, 1980—; lectr.bus. law Cardinal Strich U., 1996—99, U. Wis.-Parkside, 1997—99; participating atty. Alliance Def. Fund, 2000—; legal columnist Burlington Std. Press, 1991—95, Wis. Restaurant Assn. Mag., 1986. Bd. dirs. North Ctrl. Regional Airport, Chandler, 2003—; chmn. Ashland County Rep. Party, 1976—79; v.p., bd. dirs. Meml. Med. Ctr., Ashland, 1975—80; bd. trustees Kendrick Mcpl. Authority, Okla., 2001—; vice comdr. USCG Aux. Bayfield (Wis.) Flotilla, 1975—81; vol. atty. ACLU Wis., 1975—90. 1st lt. U.S. Army, 1964—66. Named one of Outstanding Young Men of Am., Jaycees, 1978; recipient Disting. Achievement in Art and Sci. of Advocacy award Internat. Acad. Trial Lawyers, 1970. Mem. Okla. Criminal Def. Lawyers Assn., Racine County Bar Assn. (bd. dirs. 1986-89), Wis. Acad. Trial Lawyers, Def. Rsch. Inst., Am. Hockey Assn. U.S. (coach, referee 1983-90), Am. Legion, Okla. Limousin Assn. (parliamentarian, bd. dirs. 2002—, treas. 2004—). Avocations: softball, volleyball, hockey. Home: RR 1 Box 478 Stroud OK 74079-9723 Office: 109 1/2 W 9th St Chandler OK 74834 Office Phone: 405-258-4850. E-mail: rswanson@brightok.net.

SWANSON, ROGER, architectural firm executive; MArch, U. Calif., Berkeley. Joined Anshen & Allen Archs., Inc., San Francisco, 1990, mng. prin., pres., COO, 2001—. Mem.: Am. Coll. Healthcare Archs. (founder). Office: Anshen & Allen Archs Inc 901 Market St San Francisco CA 94103*

SWANSON, ROY ARTHUR, classicist, educator; b. St. Paul, Apr. 7, 1925; s. Roy Benjamin and Gertrude (Larson) S.; m. Vivian May Vitous, Mar. 30, 1946; children: Lynn Marie (Mrs. Gerald A. Snider), Robin Lillian, Robert Roy (dec.), Dyack Tyler, Dana Miriam (Mrs. Jon Butts). BA, U. Minn., 1948, BS, 1949, MA, 1951; PhD, U. Ill., 1954. Prin. Maplewood Elementary Sch., St. Paul, 1949-51; instr. U. Ill., 1952-53, Ind. U., 1954-57; asst. prof. U. Minn., Mpls., 1957-61, assoc. prof., 1961-64, acting chmn. classics, 1963-64, prof. classics, chmn. comparative lit., 1964-65; prof. English Macalester Coll., St. Paul, 1965-67, coord. humanities program, 1966-67; prof. comparative lit. and classics U. Wis.-Milw., 1967—, prof. English, 1990-96, prof. emeritus, 2003—, chmn. classics dept., 1967-70, 86-89, chmn. comparative lit., 1970-73, 76-83, coord. Scandinavian studies program, 1982-96. Cons. St. Paul Tchrs. Sr. High Sch. English, 1964 Author: Odi et Amo: The Complete Poetry of Catullus, 1959, Heart of Reason: Introductory Essays in Modern-World Humanities, 1963, Pindar's Odes, 1974, Greek and Latin Word Elements, 1981, The Love Songs of the Carmina Burana, 1987, Pär Lagerkvist: Five Early Works, 1989; editor Minn. Rev., 1963-67; Classical Jour., 1966-72; contbr. articles to profl. jours. With AUS, 1944-46. Decorated Bronze Star; recipient Disting. Teaching award U. Minn., 1962, Disting. Teaching award U. Wis.-Milw., 1974, 91, 99. Home: 11618 N Bobolink Ln Mequon WI 53092-2804 Office: U Wis French/Italian/Comp Lit PO Box 413 Milwaukee WI 53201-0413 Office Phone: 414-219-4835. Personal E-mail: rexroy333@aol.com. Business E-Mail: rexcy@uwm.edu.

SWANSON, SHIRLEY JUNE, emergency room nurse, travel nurse, adult education educator; b. Dade City, Fla., Feb. 26, 1942; d. Alan John and Ollie Mae (Jackson) S.; m. James A. Whatley, 1960 (div. 1962); 1 child, Marsha L. Glunt; m. Jerald Ward Steen, Sr., June 7, 1963; children: Linda A. Stanley, Jerald Ward, Jr., Jerald Wagner. AA, Hillsborough C.C., 1974; BA, U. South Fla., 1975; AS, Gupton-Jones Coll., 1992, No. Maine Tech. Coll., 1996; postgrad., St. Joseph's Coll., Windham, Maine, 2001—. RN; cert. in elem. and adult edn. scis., Maine; mortician. Personal life underwriter Home Ins. Co., N.Y.C., 1979-82; with L.L. Bean, Freeport, Maine, 1988-90; tchr. biology Caribou (Maine) Adult Edn., 1994-96. Owner Alan's Dau.'s Place, 1988—, Angel Quilts, 1996—; spkr. in field. Author, editor Coffee Break, 1963-64. Ofcl. spinner Fla. State Fair, Tampa, 1984-85; spinner East Animal Farm/Westshore Mall, Tampa, 1984-85; guest spinner Town of Westfield (Maine) Jubilee Days, 1995; hospice vol. Vis. Nurses of Aroostook County, Caribou, 1995—. Billerica, Mass. O.E.S. scholar, 1975, Am. Bd. Funeral Svc. Edn. scholar, 1992, Caribou Adult Edn. Sys. scholar, 1995. Mem. Phi Theta Kappa, Pi Sigma Eta. Roman Catholic. Avocations: wool spinning, commision quilting, tutoring, weaving, amateur radio w4efm. Home: 1584 Woodland Ctr Rd Perham ME 04766-3314 Office: Caribou Adult Edn Ctr Sweden St Caribou ME 04736

SWANSON, STEPHEN OLNEY, minister, retired English educator; b. Mpls., Aug. 31, 1932; s. Carl R. and Dorothy Olney Swanson; m. Judith Seleen Swanson, June 10, 1956; children: Scott, Shelley, Noel, Kim, Brian. BA, St. Olaf Coll., 1954; grad. in theology, Luther Theol. Sem., St. Paul, 1958, BD, 1960; MA, U. Oreg., 1964, ArtsD, 1970. Ordained to ministry Evang. Luth. Ch. Am., 1958. Instr. theology Augustana Coll., Sioux Falls, SD, 1957; instr. writing U. Oreg., Eugene, 1964—66; asst. prof. English and writing Tex. Luth. Coll., Seguin, 1966—70; assoc. prof. English and writing Camrose (Alta.) Univ. Coll., 1970—73; prof. writing St. Olaf Coll., Northfield, Minn., 1976—99. Parish pastor Luth. congregations, Minn., 1958-61, Oreg., 1962-65, Sask., 1973-74; interim pastor 40 congregations, Minn., Iowa, Wis., Alta., Sask., 1956—; dir. creative writing Tex. Luth. Coll., 1966-70, Camrose Univ. Coll., 1970-73; coach wrestling, football, volleyball, hockey, Tex., Can., Minn.; co-owner Nine-Ten Press, Northfield, 1997—. Author 26 books for adults, teens and children, including Is There Life After High Sch., 1991, The Earthkeeper Mystery Series, 4 vols., 1994, Moving Out on Your Own, 1995, The First Fall: Ytterboe Hall, 1946, 1997; playwright 6 plays; contbr. articles to jours.; columnist Now and Then, 1998-99; metal sculpture exhbns. include Luth. Brotherhood Corp. Gallery, Mpls., 1992, 94, 98, Waldorf Coll., Forest City, Iowa, 1999, Luther Coll., Decorah, Iowa, 2002, Art Ctr. of St. Peter, Minn., 2003, Thrivent Fin. Corp. Gallery, Mpls., 2003, St. Olaf Coll., Northfield, Minn., 2003. Recipient award Minn. Arts Bd., 1987, Blandin Found., Grand Rapids, Minn., 1988-89; fellow NDEA, Washington, 1968-69. Mem.: Am. Swedish Inst. Avocations: metal sculpture, fishing, Volvo repair. Home: 910 St Olaf Ave Northfield MN 55057

SWANSON, VICTORIA CLARE HELDMAN, lawyer; b. Aug. 28, 1949; d. Paul F. and Anne F. (Thomas) Schmitz; m. Louis M. Heldman, Sept. 21, 1971 (div. 1973); m. John Askins, Feb. 28, 1975 (div. 1977); m. Thomas C. Swanson, Feb. 13, 1988 (div. 2004). BA in journalism with distinction, Ohio State U., 1972; JD, U. Detroit, 1975. Bar: Mich. 1975, Colo. 1984, U.S. Dist. Ct. (ea. and we. dists.) Mich. 1975, U.S. Ct. Appeals (6th cir.) 1977, U.S. Ct. Appeals (3d cir.) 1980, U.S. Supreme Ct. 1983, U.S. Ct. Appeals (10th cir.) 1984, U.S. Ct. Appeals (5th cir.) 1989, cert.: NBTA (civil trial advocate) 1994. Assoc. Lopatin, Miller, Bindes & Freedman, Detroit, 1973—76; ptnr. Schaden, Swanson & Lampert, Detroit, 1977—90, Sears, Anderson & Swanson, P.C., Colorado Springs, Colo., 1991—96, Sears & Swanson, Colorado Springs, 1997—. Adj. prof. U. Detroit Sch. Law, 1982. Author (with Richard F. Schaden): (non-fiction) Product Design Liability, 1982; author: (with others) Women Trial Lawyers: How They Succeed in Practice and in the Courtroom, 1986; author: (chpt.) Anatomy of a Personal Injury Lawsuit, 1992; author: (and editor) (handbook) Colorado Auto Litigators Handbook, 1995, Colorado Courtroom Handbook, 1998. Mem.: Mich. Trial Lawyers Assn., Colo. Trial Lawyers Assn. (past pres.), Assn. Trial Lawyers Am., Colo. Bar Assn., Mich. Bar Assn. Office: Sears & Swanson 2 N Cascade Ave Colorado Springs CO 80903-1631 Office Phone: 719-471-1984. Business E-Mail: victoria@searsandswanson.com.

SWANSON, WALLACE MARTIN, lawyer; b. Fergus Falls, Minn., Aug. 22, 1941; s. Marvin Walter and Mary Louise (Lindsey) S.; children: Kristen Lindsey, Eric Munger. BA with honors, U. Minn., 1962; LL.B. with honors, So. Methodist U., 1965. Bar: Tex. 1965. Assoc. Coke & Coke, Dallas, 1965-70; ptnr. firm Johnson & Swanson, Dallas, 1970-88; prin. Wallace M. Swanson, P.C., Ennis, Tex., 1988—; chmn., CEO Ace Cash Express Inc., Irving, Tex., 1987-88, State St. Capital Corp., 1990—. Served with USNR, 1960-65. Mem. Tex. Bar Found., State Bar Tex. (securities com. 1972-86, chmn. 1978-80, coun. bus. law sect. 1980-86), Crescent Club. Methodist. Address: 6234 FM 879 Ennis TX 75119 Office Phone: 214-520-7000.

SWANSON, WILLIAM HENRY, equipment manufacturing company executive; b. Bakersfield, Calif., Feb. 9, 1949; s. William H. and Rosemary O. (Pavicich) S.; B.S.I.E., Calif. Poly. State U., 1972; M.B.A., Golden Gate U., 1977, JD(hon.), Pepperdine U., 2002; m. Cheryl K. Allen, Dec. 21, 1968. Assoc. engr. Raytheon Co., 1972-74, project engr., 1974-75, mfg. program mgr., 1975-77, test engring. mgr., 1977-80, mgr. mfg. group, 1980-81, mfg. mgr. Equipment div., Waltham, Mass., 1981-83, plant mgr., Missile Systems div., Andover, Mass., 1984—1990, asst. gen. mgr., Missle Systems div., 1989-1990, sr. v.p., gen. mgr. Missle Systems div, 1990-95, exec. v.p., Raytheon Co., 1995-2002, gen. mgr. Electronic Systems div., 1995-1997, chmn., CEO, Raytheon Systems Co., 1997-1999, pres., Electronic Systems div., 1999-2002, pres., Raytheon Co., 2002-03, pres., CEO, 2003- . Named Outstanding Indsl. Engring. Grad., Calif. Poly. State U., 1972, Outstanding Indsl. Engring. Alumni, 1981. Mem. Blue Key, Tau Beta Pi, Alpha Pi Mu. Republican. Roman Catholic. Office: Raytheon Co 141 Spring St Lexington MA 02421-7860

SWANSON-PERRELET, DONNA KAY, speech pathology/audiology services professional; b. Holdrege, Nebr., Jan. 28, 1951; d. Irene May and Walter Alvin S.; m. Randal Ross Perrelet, May 1, 1981; children: Guy Philippe Perrelet, Jean-Paul Henri Perrelet. BA in Speech Pathology, U. No. Colo., Greeley, 1974, MA in Speech Pathology, 1976. Cert. clin. rehab. Speech lang. pathologist Ctrl. Nebr. Support Svcs. Program, Grand Island, Nebr., 1976—79, San Diego Unified Sch. Dist., San Diego, 1979—90; lead/dist. bilingual speech lang. pathologist Vista (Calif.) Unified Sch. Dist., 1990—2002, mem. bilingual task force; preschool speech/lang. pathologist Temecula Valley Unified Sch. Dist., Temecula, Calif., 2002—. Presenter Second Lang. Acquisition Conf., Vista, SD county Cross Cultural Conf., San Diego; trainer U. of Tex. Spl. Project in Spl. Edn., Austin, Tex.; mem. Med. Mini Grant Com., Vista, Golden SLPA Adv. Bd., L.A.; adj. faculty child devel. dept. Grossmont Coll., El Cajon, Calif., program devel., dir., instr. SLPA program, 2000—. Mem.: Calif. Speech and Hearing Assn. (Disting. Achievement award 2004). Democrat. Home: 323 Trailview Road Encinitas CA 92024 Office: Grossmont Coll 8800 Grossmont College Dr El Cajon CA 92020-1798 Personal E-mail: perrelet@adelphia.net.

SWANSTROM, THOMAS EVAN, economist; b. Green Bay, Wis., May 17, 1939; s. Alfred Enoch and Elizabeth Nan (Thomas) S.; m. Nancy Anne Roche; children: Amy, Scott. Student, U. Notre Dame, 1957-59; BA, U. Wis., 1962, MA, 1963; postgrad., Am. U., 1963-66. Economist, U.S. Bur. Labor Statistics, Washington, 1963-66. Dir. research Population Ref. Bur., Washington, 1966-68; economist Sears, Roebuck & Co., Chgo., 1968-70, market analyst, 1970-72, mgr. catalog research, 1972-75, asst. mgr. econ. research, 1974-80, chief economist, 1980-90; pres. Consumer Econs., Chgo., 1991—; mem. bus. research adv. council Bur. Labor Stats.; adj. prof. Lake Forest Grad. Sch. Mgmt. Contbr. articles to industry pubs. Mem. Conf. Bus. Economists, The Caxton Club. Personal E-mail: tevanswan@aol.com.

SWANTON, SUSAN IRENE, retired library director; b. Rochester, N.Y., Nov. 29, 1941; d. Walter Frederick and Irene Wray S.; m. Wayne Holman, Apr. 12, 1969 (div. June 1973); 1 child, Michael; ptnr. James Donald Lathrop; children: Kathryn, Kristin. AB, Harvard U., 1963; MLS, Columbia U., 1965. Libr. dir. Warsaw (N.Y.) Pub. Libr., 1963-64, Gates Pub. Libr., Rochester, NY, 1965—2003; ret., 2003. Pres. Drug and Alcohol Coun., Rochester, 1985-91, mem. adv. coun., 1992-94; bd. dirs., co-chair info. svcs. Rochester Freenet, 1995—; sec. Gates Hist. Preservation Commn., 2000-03, Friends of Rochester Pub. Libr., 2004—; chmn. Gates Dem. Com., 2004—; v.p., sec. Friends of Gates Pub. Libr., 2004—; newsletter editor Empire (N.Y.) Friends Roundtable, 2004—. Mem. Gates Hist. Soc. (bd. dirs., pres. 1998—2002, v.p. 2002—03), Gates-Chili C. of C. (pres. 1982, sec. 1990-94, 2004—, bd. dirs. 2003, Citizen Yr. 1994), Harvard Club of Rochester (mem. adv. bd.). Home: 284 Gatewood Ave Rochester NY 14624-1622 E-mail: sswanton@ggw.org.

SWARDENSKI, JAY GORDON, lawyer; b. Peoria, Ill., Sept. 16, 1939; s. Walter and Ruth A. (Lanterbach) S.; m. Susan Hosmer Friedman, June 30, 1961; children— Jay G., Kira H., Kurt B. B.A., U. Wis., 1961; LL.B. cum laude, Harvard U., 1964. Bar: Ill. 1964, N.Y. 1980. Assoc., Seyfarth, Shaw, Fairweather & Geraldsan, Chgo., 1964-67; ptnr. Davis & Morgan, Peoria, Ill., 1968-78; ptnr. Seyfarth, Shaw, Fairweather & Geraldson, N.Y.C., 1979-84; lawyer N.Y. Times, 1984— . Mem. ABA, Ill. State Bar Assn. Club: Harvard (N.Y.C.). Address: NY Times Law Dept 229 W 43rd St New York NY 10036-3913

SWARTHWORTH, SHARON T. military officer; b. Providence, Nov. 8, 1959; Enlisted U.S. Army, 1977; pers. adminstrn. specialist 50th Signal Bn., Ft. Bragg, NC, 304th Signal Bn., Republic of Korea; legal specialist 16th Signal Bn., Ft. Hood, Tex., 1981—82; legal specialist/ct. reporter 110th JAG Detachment, Ft. Carson, Colo., 1st Army, Ft. Meade, Md., sgt. 1st class; legal adminstr. Judge Advocate Gen.'s Corps, 1984; tng., advising and counseling officer Warrant Office Cand. Sch., Ft. McCoy, Wis.; IMA legal adminstr. Spl. Forces Command, Ft. Bragg, NC; legal adminstr. Legal Assistance Task Force/Desert Storm, Office of Judge Advocate Gen., Washington, Legal Svc. Study Group, Office of Gen. Counsel, Washington, Presidio of San Francisco, U.S. Army Litigation Ctr., Arlington, Va., U.S. Army Legal Svcs. Agy.; dir. ops. for legal tech. Office of Judge Advocate, Arlington, Va.; warrant officer Judge Advocate Gen.'s Corps, 1999—. Decorated Meritorious Svc. medal with 3 oak leaf clusters, Army Commendation medal with 6 oak leaf clusters, Army Achievement medal, numerous others. Office: Office of Judge Advocate General US Pentagon Washington DC 20310-1500

SWARTOUT, HANK B. oil and gas industry executive; m. Carol Swartout; 4 children. Grad. in Petroleum Engring., U. Wyo., 1976. Pres. Cypress Drilling, 1985; chmn., pres., CEO Precision Drilling Corp., Calgary, Canada. Office: Precision Drilling Corp 4200 150-6th Ave SW T2P 3Y7 Calgary AB Canada

SWARTOUT, TORIN SHERWIN ROBERTS, logistics executive, transportation consultant; b. Brockport, N.Y., Mar. 14, 1952; s. Sherwin George and Eileen May (Tavenner) S.; m. Anne Elizabeth Washington, July 21, 1978; children: Jesse, Jason, Katherine Lynne, Joseph. BA in Philosophy, Antioch Coll., 1972; cert. custom house broker, World Trade Inst., 1978, cert. of chartering, 1979. Lic. customhouse brokers. European sales mgr. Antioch Bookplate Co., Yellow Springs, Ohio, 1971; pres. Alternative Living, Inc., Brockport, N.Y., 1972-76; import mgr. Spies Shipping Corp., N.Y.C., 1976-77; equipment control mgr. Hansen and Tidemann, N.Y.C., 1977-78; intermodal ops. mgr. Star Shipping of N.Y., Inc., N.Y.C., 1979-81, mgr. container svcs., 1981-85; dist. mgr. midwest Star Shipping, Inc., Des Plaines, Ill., 1985-86, 87-89, v.p. sales Tokyo, 1986-87, trade mgr. U.S. gulf Stamford, Conn., 1989-91; gen. traffic mgr. Atlantic Trades, 1991-96; pres. Viking Homes, Hempstead, N.Y., 1981-85. Bd. dirs. Alternative Living, Inc., Brockport, 1977-91, Viking Homes, Ridgefield, Conn.; custom house broker T. Swartout CHB, Chgo., 1978—; cons. TransNat. Shipping Corp., N.Y.C., 1981-88; owners' rep. Spliethoff's, 1996—; mng. dir. Ocean Transport Svcs., Ridgefield, Conn., 1996—. Vice pres. N.W. Civic Assn., Hempstead, 1983, Georgetown Manor Homeowners Assn., Arlington Heights, 1987; cubmaster pack 74 Cub Scouts, Ridgefield, Conn. Mem. Midwest Fgn. Commerce Club, Ocean Freight Agts. Assn., Norwegian-Am. C. of C., Japanese C. of C. (affiliate), Holland Soc., Sons of Norway (v.p. 1981-82, 90-91, pres. 1983-84), Conn. Maritime Assn., Internat. Forest Products Transport Assn., Railway Industrial Clearance Assn., Project Mgmt. Inst. Congregationalist. Avocations: hiking, farming, travel, coaching, norwegian language. Office: Ocean Transport Svcs 68 Great Hill Rd Ridgefield CT 06877-2629 E-mail: otsusa@aol.com.

SWARTWOUT, JOSEPH RODOLPH, obstetrics and gynecology educator, administrator; b. Pascagoula, Miss., June 17, 1925; s. Thomas Roswell and Marshall (Coleman) S.; m. Brandon C. Leftwich, Jan. 23, 1989. Student, Miss. Coll., 1943-44; MD, Tulane U., 1951. Intern Touro Infirmary, New Orleans, 1951-52; asst. in obstetrics and medicine Tulane U., 1952-53, instr., 1955-60; Nat. Found. fellow Harvard U., 1953-55; asst. in medicine Peter Bent Brigham Hosp., Boston, 1953-55; assoc. in obstetric rsch. Boston Lying-In-Hosp., 1953-55; asst. prof. U. Pitts., 1960-61; assoc. prof. Emory U., Atlanta, 1961-66; assoc. prof. ob-gyn. U. Chgo., 1967-80; chief ob-gyn. at Prime Health, also clin. assoc. prof. U. Kans. Sch. Medicine, 1978-80; prof. dept. ob-gyn. Mercer U. Sch. Medicine, Macon, Ga., 1980-95, prof. emeritus, 1995; dist. health dir. Dist. 5-2, Macon, Ga., 1996—; dist. dir. Ga. Divsn. Pub. Health, Macon, 1996—. Mem. Ga. State Coun. on Maternal and Infant Health. Fellow Am. Coll. Obstetricians and Gynecologists; mem. AMA, APHA, Med. Assn. Ga., Bibb County Med. Soc. Home: 4384 Peach Pkwy Fort Valley GA 31030-8155

SWARTZ, ALLAN JOEL, pharmacist, educator, hospital administrator; b. July 2, 1935; s. Milton and Rosalie Swartz; m. Roslyn Thelma Holt, June 2, 1963. AB, Ctrl. H.S., 1955; PharmD, U. So. Calif., 1958; postgrad., Loyola U. Sch. Law, 1964—66; MA in Edn., Pepperdine U., 1976. Asst. dir. pharmacy City of Hope Nat. Med. Ctr., Duarte, Calif., 1966—69, dir. pharm. svcs., 1969—78, Encino (Calif.) Hosp., 1978—93, quality assurance coord., 1986—93, hazardous materials officer, 1986—93, risk and safety mgr., 1987—93; asst. clin. prof. pharmacy U. So. Calif., 1971—82, 1987—; asst. clin. prof. U. Pacific, 1978—86, regional coord. externship program, 1982—86; dir. pharm. svcs. Century City Hosp., 1994—96, Santa Monica/UCLA Med. Ctr., 1996—98. Chmn. pharm. group purchasing com. Hosp. Coun. So. Calif., 1978—82; mem. prof. edn. com. Am. Cancer Soc., 1970—78. Feature editor: Pharmaceutics Cancer Nursing, 1977—81, mem. editl. bd.; 1983—98, cons. editor: Am. Jour. Hosp. Pharmacy, 1978—83, mem. editl. bd.:, 2001—04. Gold Circle founder Frat. Friends; founder LA Music Ctr.; bd. dirs. Vis. Nurses Assn., LA, 1983—93; chmn. bd. dirs. Vis. Nurse Home Svc., Inc., LA, 1986—88; bd. dirs. H.O.P.E. Unit Found., 1980—83; hon. bd. dirs. West LA Symphony; founder LA County Mus. Art, West Ctr. at UCLA; mem. Royce Ctr. Circle; capital patron Simon Wiesenthal Ctr. With U.S. Army, 1958—59. Recipient Order of Golden Sword award, Calif. divsn. Am. Cancer Soc., 1974, cert. merit, 1978, award of recognition, U. So. Calif. Comprehensive Cancer Ctr., 1983. Mem.: AAAS, Am. Med. Writers Assn., So. Calif. Soc. Health-Systems Pharmacists (pres. 1972), Calif. Soc. Health-Systems Pharmacists (pres. 1976), Am. Soc. Health-Systems Pharmacists (commendation 1976). Address: PO Box 241866 Los Angeles CA 90024

SWARTZ, B(ENJAMIN) K(INSELL), JR., archaeologist, educator; b. LA, June 23, 1931; s. Benjamin Kinsell and Maxine Marietta (Pearce) S.; m. Cyrilla Casillas, Oct. 23, 1966; children: Benjamin Kinsell III, Frank Casillas. AA summa cum laude, L.A. City Coll., 1952; BA, UCLA, 1954, MA, 1958; PhD, U. Ariz., 1964. Curator Klamath County Mus., Oreg., 1959-61, rsch. assoc., 1961-62; asst. prof. anthropology Ball State U., Muncie, Ind., 1964-68, assoc. prof., 1968-72, prof., 1972-2001, prof. emeritus, 2001—. Vis. sr. lectr. U. Ghana, 1970-71; exch. prof. U. Yaounde, Cameroon, 1984-85; field rschr. N.Am. and West Africa; mem. exec. bd., pres. Am. Com. to Advance the Study of Petroglyphs and Pictographs and its rep. to Internat. Fedn. Rock Art Orgns.; mem. adv. bd. Am. Com. for Preservation of Archaeol. Collections. Contbr. revs. and articles to profl. jours.; author books, monographs in field, including: West African Culture Dynamics, 1980, Indiana's Prehistoric Past, 1981, Rock Art and Posterity, 1991, Procs. of Ist Internat. South African Rock Art Assn. Conf., 1991. Klamath County chmn. Oreg. Statehood Centennial, 1959. With USN, 1954-56. Fellow AAAS, Ind. Acad. Sci.; mem. Current Anthropology (assoc.), Soc. Am. Archaeology, Internat. Com. Rock Art, Sigma Xi, Lambda Alpha (nat. coun., exec. sec.). Home: 805 W Charles St Muncie IN 47305-2235 E-mail: 01bkswartz@bsu.edu.

SWARTZ, CONRAD MELTON, psychiatrist; b. Bklyn., Nov. 22, 1946; s. Louis Jules and Frances (Shaw) S.; m. Cynthia Anne Heise, June 22, 1975; children: Meryle, Sandor. B Engring., Cooper Union, 1966; MS, Calif. Inst. Tech., 1968; PhD in Chem. Engring., U. Minn., 1972, MD, 1974. Diplomate Am. Bd. Psychiatry and Neurology. Intern Northwestern Hosp., Mpls., 1974-75; resident in psychiatry U. Iowa Hosps. and Clinics, Iowa City, 1975-78, asst. prof. psychiatry, 1978-82, U. Health Scis./Chgo. Med. Sch., North Chicago, Ill., 1982-83, assoc. prof. psychiatry and pharmacology, 1983-87, prof. psychiatry, 1987-91; assoc. chief of staff for edn. VA Med. Ctr., North Chicago, 1987-91; prof. psychiatry med. sch. U. Okla., Oklahoma City, 1991-92; prof. psychiatry East Carolina U., Greenville, N.C., 1992-96; dir. rsch., prof. psychiatry East Tenn. State U., Johnson City, Tenn., 1996-98; prof. psychiatry St. Louis U., 1998—99; prof. psychiatry, chief psychiat. rsch. So. Ill. U., Springfield, 1999—. Cons. Somatics, Inc., Lake Bluff, Ill., 1984—. Columnist Psychiat. Times, 2002—; editor-in-chief Jour. of Psychiatric Medicine, 2004—; contbr. articles to profl. publs. Recipient clin. rsch. award Am. Acad. Clin. Psychiatrists, 1989, 90. Fellow Am. Psychiat. Assn., Am. Coll. Clin. Pharmacology, Assn. Convulsive Therapy (pres. 1990-92); mem. Soc. Biol. Psychiatry, Tau Beta Pi. Achievements include 11 patents on instrumentation and methods for electroconvulsive therapy; discovery of low levels of male sex hormone testosterone imply substantial risk for myocardial infarction, ECT emergence agitation is induced by the products of muscle metabolism and is thereby similar to chemically-induced panic disorder; rsch. on graphical methods that exactly state drug dose prediction according to 1-compartment pharmacokinetics. Home: PO Box 581 Chatham IL 62629-0581 Office: So Ill U Dept Psychiatry PO Box 19642 Springfield IL 62794-9642 Office Phone: 217-545-4468. Personal E-mail: c_swartz@yahoo.com.

SWARTZ, DONALD PERCY, physician; b. Preston, Ont., Can., Sept. 12, 1921; s. Simon Wingham and Lydia Ethel Swartz; m. Norma Mae Woolner, June 24, 1944 (dec. May 1980); children: Ian Donald, Rhonda Swartz Peterson; m. Isabelle Liz Dales, Apr. 21, 1984. BA, MD cum laude, U. Western Ont., 1951, MSc cum laude, 1953. Intern Victoria Hosp., London, Ont., 1951-52; asst. resident Westminster Hosp., London, 1953-54; resident Johns Hopkins U., Balt., 1954-58; asst. prof. ob-gyn. U. Western Ont., London, 1958-62; prof. Columbia U., N.Y.C., 1962-72; dir. ob-gyn. Harlem Hosp.; prof. dept. ob-gyn. Albany (N.Y.) Med. Coll., 1972-99, prof. emeritus, 2000—, chmn. 1972-79, chief sect. gen. gynecology, 1982-88, head. div. gen. gynecology, 1988—99, acting chmn., 1992. Vis. prof. dept. Ob-Gyn. U. Rochester, N.Y., 1981 Assoc. editor: Advances in Planned Parenthood. Vice pres., pres. Assn. Planned Parenthood Physicians, 1972-74. Served with RCAF, 1942-45. NRC Can. fellow, 1952-53; Am. Cancer Soc. fellow, 1956-57; Markle scholar, 1958-63 Fellow ACOG, Royal Coll. Surgeons Can., Am. Gynecologic Soc., Am. Gyn-Ob Soc., Am. Fertility Soc., Royal Soc. Health, Soc. Gynecologic Surgeons. Home: 24 Devon Rd Delmar NY 12054-3534 Office: Albany Med Coll 47 New Scotland Ave Albany NY 12208-3412 Office Phone: 518-262-5101. E-mail: swartzd@mail.amc.edu. *It has been a privilege and a challenge to participate in the forefront of the revolutionary changes in the health care of women during the past five decades. Acceptance, initiation and implementation of positive change have been guidelines for gratifying action.*

SWARTZ, GORDON, management consultant; BS in Nuclear Engring., MIT, 1979, BS in Polit. Sci., 1980; MBA, Northeastern U., 1986; D in Bus. Adminstrn., Harvard U., 1994. Rsch. assoc. Harvard Bus. Sch., Boston, 1986—89; asst. prof. of mktg. London (Eng.) Bus. Sch., 1993—98, dep. dean MBA program, 1995—98; v.p. MarketBridge Inc., Bethesda, Md., 1998—. Contbr. articles to profl. jours. Achievements include patents pending for market forecasting of IPO pricing. Office: MarketBridge Inc 500 N Tower 4550 Montgomery Ave Bethesda MD 20814

SWARTZ, JACK, chamber of commerce executive; b. Nov. 24, 1932; s. John Ralph and Fern (Cave) S.; m. Nadine Ann Langlois, Aug. 4, 1956; children: Dana, Shawn, Tim, Jay. AA, Dodge City C.C., 1953; student, St. Mary of Plains Coll., 1953-55, 58; BBA, Washburn U., 1973, BA in Econs., 1974. V.p. D.C. Terminal Elevator Co., Dodge City, Kans., 1957-65; exec. v.p. Kans. Jaycees, Hutchinson, 1965-68, Kans. C. of C. and Industry, Topeka, 1968-82; pres. Nebr. C. of C. and Industry, Lincoln, 1982—2000, ret., 2000. Past chmn., bd. regents U.S. C. of C. Inst. U. Colo. With U.S. Army, 1955-57, USAR, 1961. Named Outstanding Local Pres. in State, Kans. Jaycees, 1961, Outstanding Young Man of Yr., Dodge City Jaycees, 1961, Outstanding State V.P., U.S. Jaycees, 1962, Outstanding Nat. Dir., 1963; named to Nebr. Bus. Hall of Fame, 2000, Sublette H.S. Wall of Honor, 2002. Mem. Am. Soc. Assn. Execs. (cert.), Am. C. of C. Execs. (bd. dirs., cert.), Nebr. C.of C. Execs. (sec.-treas.), Nebr. Soc. Assn. Execs. (past pres.), Nebr. Fedn. Bus. Assns. (pres. 1986-88), Nebr. Thoroughbred Breeders Assn. (past bd. dirs.), Washburn U. Alum. (past bd. dirs.), Am. Legion, Rotary. Republican. Roman Catholic. Home: 625 W Gibraltar Ln Phoenix AZ 85023-5243

SWARTZ, JAMES EDWARD, chemistry educator, dean, university administrator; b. Washington, June 12, 1951; s. Donald M. and Geneva R. (Henderson) S.; m. Louanne L. Curtis, June 6, 1980 (dec. 1986); m. Cynthea Mosier, Apr. 1, 1988. BS in Chemistry, Stanislaus State Coll., Turlock, Calif., 1973; PhD in Chemistry, U. Calif., Santa Cruz, 1978. Instr. U. Calif., Santa Cruz, 1978; rsch. fellow Calif. Inst. Tech., Pasadena, 1978-80; asst. prof. Grinnell (Iowa) Coll., 1980-86, assoc. prof. chemistry, 1986-93, prof., 1993—, v.p. acad. affairs, dean, 1998—. Vis. prof. U. Minn., Mpls., 1986—87; mem. adv. coun. Iowa Energy Ctr.; cons.-evaluator Commn. Higher Edn., N. Cent. Assn., 1995—; bd. dirs. Am. Conf. Acad. Deans, 2000—; mem. exec. com. Associated Colls. of the Midwest, 2004—. Contbr. articles to profl. jours. Grantee Petroleum Rsch. Fund, 1981-83, Rsch. Corp., 1981-83, 84-86, 86-88, NSF, 1982-84, 90-93, 91-94. Mem. AAAS, Am. Chem. Soc., Iowa Acad. Scis., Am. Wind Energy Assn. Home: 1233 Summer St Grinnell IA 50112-1547 Office: Grinnell Coll Office of Dean Grinnell IA 50112-1690 Office Phone: 641-269-3100. Business E-Mail: swartz@grinnell.edu.

SWARTZ, JON DAVID, psychologist, educator; b. Houston, Dec. 28, 1934; s. Orville Elmo and Nina June (Baker) S.; m. Carol Joseph Hampton, Oct. 20, 1966; children: Eric Jason McFarland, Sally Katherine Baker, Edward Joseph Bryson. BA, U. Tex., Austin, 1956, MA, 1961, PhD, 1969, postgrad., 1973-74. Rsch. and tng. asst. dept. psychology U. Tex., 1956-62, asst. prof. dept. ednl. psychology, 1969-72; assoc. prof. psychology, chmn. U. Tex.-Permian Basin, 1974-78, chmn. anthropology and sociology, 1975-78, field dir., 1962-65; asst. dir. Austin Longitudinal Rsch. project, 1965-69, co-dir., 1969-74; research scientist Hogg Found. for Mental Health, 1972-74; prof. edn. and psychology Southwestern U., Georgetown, Tex., 1978-90, vis. prof. psychology, 1991, dir. testing and guidance, 1978-81, holder Brown vis. chair, 1978-82, assoc. dean for librs. and learning resources, 1981-90; coord., adminstrv. head Killeen office Cen. Counties Ctr. for MHMR Svcs., Temple, Tex., 1990-91; chief psychol. svcs. Temple, Tex., 1991-99; pvt. practice, 2000—. Lectr. Nat. U., Mexico, 1962, U. Ctrl. Tex., 1994, Temple Coll., 1994. Author: (with W.H. Holtzman) Inkblot Perception and Personality, 1961, (with C.C. Cleland) Mental Retardation: Approaches to Institutional Change, 1969, Administrative Issues in Institutions for the Mentally Retarded, 1972, Exceptionalities Through the Lifespan: An Introduction, 1982, Multihandicapped Mentally Retarded, 1973, (with W.H. Holtzman, R. Diaz-Guerrero) Personality Development in Two Cultures, 1975; editor: (with C.C. Cleland, L.W. Talkington) Profoundly Mentally Retarded, 1976, (with R.K. Eyman, C.C. Cleland) Research with the Profoundly Retarded, 1978, Holtzman Inkblot Technique: An Annotated Bibliography (supplement), 1988, (with R.C. Reinehr, W.H. Holtzman) Holtzman Inkblot Technique: An Annotated Bibliography 1956-1982, 1983, SW U. Bibliographic Series, 1986-90, (with R.C. Reinehr) Handbook of Old-Time Radio, 1993, Holtzman Inkblot Technique: Research Guide and Bibliography, 1999, Southwestern University Bibliographic Series, 1986-1990; contbr.: Handbook of Texas, 1996; editl. assoc. Current Anthropology, 1971-77; assoc. editor: Am. Corrective Therapy Jour., 1971-81, Exceptional Children, 1982-84; mem. editl. bd. Tex. Psychologist, 1979-83, Phi Kappa Phi Jour./Nat. Forum, 1976-80; editl. cons. Mental Retardation, 1972-77; rev. editor Jour. Biol. Psychology, 1972-80, Revista Interamericana de Psicologia, 1983-89, Nat. Fantasy Fan, 2003—; reviewer Sci. Books, Films, 1978—; cons. editor Jour. Personality Assessment, 1981-90; spl. features editor: Scientifiction: The First Fandom Report, 2002—; rev. editor The National Fantasy Fan, 2003—; contbr. over 500 articles to profl. jours. Mem. Mayor's Drug Abuse Panel, Odessa, Tex., 1975-78; chmn. adv. bd. Human Potentials Ctr., Permian Basin Cmty. Ctrs. for Mental Health and Mental Retardation, Odessa and Midland, Tex., 1975-78; bd. govs. Mood-Heritage Mus., 1984-90. U.S. Office Edn. fellow, 1964-66, U. Tex. fellow, 1973-74; recipient Franklin Gilliam prize Humanities Rsch. Ctr. U. Tex., 1965, Spencer Rsch. award Nat. Acad. Edn., 1972, Faculty Fellowship award Southwestern U., 1981 Fellow AAAS, Am. Psychol. Soc., Soc. Personality Assessment (life); mem. Western Rsch. Conf. on Mental Retardation, Am. Acad. Mental Retardation, Southwestern Psychol. Assn., Bell County Psychol. Assn., Sigma Xi, Psi Chi, Mu Alpha Nu, Delta Tau Kappa, Phi Kappa Phi, Phi Delta Kappa. Personal E-mail: jon_swartz@hotmail.com. *All my life I have had teachers, in school and out, who challenged me to do more than I thought I was capable of doing. Any success I have achieved, I owe to them and their efforts in my behalf.*

SWARTZ, JULIANNE, artist; b. Phoenix, Apr. 29, 1967; BA in Photography and Creative Writing, U. Ariz., 1989; postgrad., Skowhegan Sch. for Painting and Sculpture, 1999; MFA, Bard Coll., 2002. One-woman shows include LombardDFreid Fine Arts, N.Y., 1997, The Robert Lehman Gallery at Urban Glass, Bklyn., 1999, Ricco/Maresca Gallery, N.Y.C., 2000, 123 Watts Gallery, 2001, Shroeder-Romero Gallery, Bklyn., 2002, exhibited in group shows at Weatherspoon Art Gallery, U. N.C., Chapel Hill, 1996, Bklyn. Mus. Art, 1997, Robert Lehman Gallery at Urban Glass, Bklyn., 1998, Bronx Mus. for the Arts, 1999, Ellen Kim Murphy Gallery, Santa Monica, Calif., 1999, Tulane U., New Orleans, 1999, Bellevue Art Mus., Seattle, 2000, 123 Watts Gallery, N.Y.C., 2000, U. of the Arts, Phila., 2001, K.S. Art, N.Y.C., 2001, Paul Rogers Gallery, 2001, Space 101, Bklyn., 2001, Sculpture Ctr., N.Y.C., 2001, Palm Beach (Fla.) Inst. Contemporary Art, 2001, Murray Guy Gallery, N.Y.C., 2002, P.S. 1 Inst. for Contemporary Art, Queens, N.Y., 0200, Christinerose/Josee Bienvenu Gallery, N.Y.C., 2003, Artist's Space, Project Room, 2003, Mus. Contemporary Art, Tucson, 2003, Grant Selwyn Fine Art, L.A., 2003, Hosfelt Gallery, San Francisco, 2003, Muller Dechiara Gallery, Berlin, 2004, ARCO, Spain, 2004, Catharine Clark Gallery, San Francisco, 2004, New Mus. Contemporary Art, N.Y.C., 2004. Named Invited Exhibitor, Biennial Exhbn., Whitney Mus. Am. Art, N.Y., 2004.*

SWARTZ, MELVIN JAY, lawyer, writer; b. Boston, July 21, 1930; s. Jack M. and Rose (Rosenberg) S.; children: Julianne, Jonathan Samuel. BA, Syracuse U., 1953; LLB, Boston U., 1957. Bar: N.Y. 1959, Ariz. 1961. Assoc. Alfred S. Julian, N.Y.C., 1957-59; ptnr. Finks & Swartz, Youngtown, Sun City, Phoenix, 1961-70, Swartz & Jeckel, P.C., Sun City, Youngtown, Scottsdale, Ariz., 1971-82. Author: Don't Die Broke, A Guide to Secure Retirement, 1974, rev. edit., 2000, (book and cassettes) Keep What You Own, 1989, rev. edit., 2000, Retire Without Fear, 1995; columnist News-Sun, Sun City, 1979-83; author column Swartz on Aging, If Not Now When, 2004. Bd. dirs. Valley of the Sun Sch. for Retarded Children, 1975-79. Mem. ABA, Ariz. Bar Assn., N.Y. Bar Assn., Maricopa County Bar Assn., Scottsdale Bar Assn., Ctrl. Ariz. Estate Planning Coun., Masons (Phoenix). Jewish. Office: 3416 N 44th St Unit 22 Phoenix AZ 85018-6044 Office Phone: 602-954-6381. E-mail: swartzmj@worldnet.att.net.

SWARTZ, MORTON NORMAN, medical educator; b. Boston, Nov. 11, 1923; s. Jacob H. and Janet (Heller) Swartz; m. Cesia Rosenberg, Sept. 18, 1956; children: Mark David, Caroline Joan. BA, Harvard Coll., 1945; MD, Harvard U., 1947, U. Geneva, Switzerland, 1988. Med. intern and resident Mass. Gen. Hosp., Boston, 1947—50, chief resident in medicine, 1953—54, chief infectious disease unit, 1956—90, chief James Jackson Firm, med. svcs., 1990—; USPHS postdoctoral rsch. fellow Johns Hopkins U., McCollum-Pratt Inst. Enzymology, Balt., 1954—56; assoc. prof. medicine Harvard Med. Sch., Boston, 1967—73, prof., 1973—. Vis. assoc. prof. biochemistry Stanford Med. Sch., Palo Alto, Calif., 1969—70; chmn. Nat. Inst. Child Health and Devel., 1995—97, bd. sci. counselors. Co-author: Osteomyelitis, 1971; editor: Current Clinical Topics in Infectious Diseases, 1980—2002; assoc. editor: New Eng. Jour. Medicine, 1981—2002; contbr. articles to profl. jours. 1st lt. U.S. Army, 1950—52. Mem.: Inst. Medicine, Infectious Diseases Soc. Am. (Bristol award 1984, Feldman award 1989, Soc. Citation award 2003), Assn. Am. Physicians, Am. Soc. for Clin. Investigation, Am. Soc. Biochemistry and Molecular Biology, ACP (Disting. Tchr. award 1989). Jewish. Avocations: biology, birdwatching, cosmology. Home: 54 Shaw Rd Chestnut Hill MA 02467-3122 Office: Mass Gen Hosp Dept Medicine Bulfinch Bldg #127 Boston MA 02114-2696 Office Phone: 617-726-7865. Business E-Mail: mswartz@partners.org.

SWARTZ, RENEE BECKER, civic volunteer; b. Newark, Feb. 25, 1935; d. Sidney David and Adeline (Kleinberg) Becker; m. Harry Mason Swartz, Mar. 8, 1931; children: Stephen, Addi-Lyn, Sidney. Student, Rutgers U., 1950-52, Bryn Mawr Coll., 1952-53; BA, Barnard Coll.-Columbia U., 1955. Planning com. N.J. White Ho. Conf. on Librs. and Info. Sci., 1975-79, del. selection com., mem. programs com., 1978-79; chair del. White Ho. Conf., 1979; re-elected permanent N.J. rep. Nat. Commn. Follow-up Activities White Ho. Conf., 1991, chairperson nat. awards com., 1984-86, chair fundraising com., 1989-90; chmn. N.J. Del. White Ho. Conf. of Librs. and Info. Svcs., 1991—. Pres. Friends of Monmouth County Libr. Assn., 1964-68; founding mem. N.J. Citizens for Better Librs., 1982; chair bldg. com. Dorothy L. Spiwak Meml. Libr., Rumson, N.J., 1971-73, trustee, 1971—; active N.J. Libr. Devel. Com., 1973-84; chair, bd. trustees Grad. Sch. of Comm., Info. and Libr. Studies, Rutgers U., 1980—, chair, 1983—; gov. appointee N.J. State Libr. Adv. Coun., 1975, chair, 1986—, Monmouth County Libr. Commn., 1965—, chair, 1976—; past trustee Barnard Coll.; founder NJ Ctr. in the Book, 2001—, chair, state coord. Recipient Hanna G. Solomon award Greater Red Bank sect. Nat. Coun. Jewish Women, 1979, Pres. medal Barnard Coll.-Columbia U., 1984, Columbia U. medal, 1985, Woman or Achievement award Monmouth County Adv. Com., 1991; named Nat. Trustee of Yr. ALA, 1991. Mem. Nat. Citizens Com. for Pub. Libraries (steering com. 1980-84), Am. Library Trustee Assn. (pres. com. 1983, nat. intellectual freedom com. 1984—), N.J. Library Assn. (centennial com. 1986-89, chairperson N.J. Ednl. Inst. com. 1987-88, N.J. Trustee of Yr. 1980, 99), N.J. Library Trustee Assn. (exec. com. 1976-81, regional rep. 1983-86), Assn. N.J. Library Commrs. (pres. 1973-75), Lotus Club N.Y., Ocean Club N.J. Avocations: tennis, sailing, walking. Home: 136 Rumson Rd Rumson NJ 07760-1238 E-mail: rswartz@shore.co.monmouth.ny.us.*

SWARTZ, ROSLYN HOLT, real estate company executive; b. LA, Dec. 9, 1940; d. Abe Jack and Helen (Canter) Holt; m. Allan Joel Swartz, June 2, 1963. AA, Santa Monica (Calif.) Coll., 1970; BA summa cum laude, UCLA, 1975; MA, Pepperdine U., 1976. Cert. CC instr., student-pers. worker Calif. Mgr. pub. rels. Leader Holdings, Inc., LA, 1968-75, pres., 1991—, sec., treas. North Hollywood, Calif., 1975-81, pres., 1981-91; CEO Beverly Stanley Investments, LA, 1979—. Pres. Leader Properties, Inc., Leader Fairfax, Inc., Leader 358, Inc., Leader 359, Inc., Leader Ventura, Inc., 1996—; condr. Oral History Elderly Jewish Cmty. Venice, Calif. Los Angeles County Planning Dept. Libr., 1974. Founder Pres.'s Cir. L.A. County Mus. Art; founder Gold Circle Music Ctr.; mem. The Blue Ribbon, Club 100; charter mem. Ctr. Dance Assn.; mem. Music Ctr. L.A. County; founder West Alumni Ctr.; chair UCLA Affiliates Sch. of Medicine Scholarship Com., 2004; capital patron Simon Wiesenthal Ctr.; past trustee Odyssey Theatre Ensemble; hon. chmn. bus. adv. coun. Nat. Rep. Congl. Com.; bd. dirs. House Ear Inst.; hon. bd. dirs. West L.A. Symphony. Mem.: NAFE, KCET Womens Coun., Comml. Real Estate Women, Am. Pharm. Assn., Achievement Rewards Coll. Scientists, Fashion Cir. Costume Coun., UCLA Chancellor's Assocs., Nat. Mus. Women in Arts (So. Calif. coun.), UCLA Alumni Assn. (life), Town Hall (life), Santa Monica Coll. Alumni Assn. (life), Friends of Fox, Women's Guild Cedars-Sinai Med. Ctr., Friends of Robinson Gardens, UCLA Las Donas (exec. bd.), UCLA Prytanean Alumnae Assn., Order Eastern Star, Phrateres Internat., Phi Beta Kappa (Bicentennial fellow), Pi Lambda Theta, Pi Gamma Mu, Phi Delta Kappa, Alpha Kappa Delta, Alpha Gamma Sigma, Phi Alpha Theta. Avocation: horticulture. Office: PO Box 241866 Los Angeles CA 90024-9666

SWARTZ, STEVEN R. publishing executive; Grad., Harvard Coll. Report The Wall St. Jour., Phila., 1984-86, N.Y.C., 1986-89, page one editor, 1989-91; editor SmartMoney mag., N.Y.C., 1991-95, pres., CEO, editor-in-chief, 1995—; CEO, editor-in-chief Hearst Newspapers, 1995—2000, exec. v.p., 2001—. Bd. dirs. Dow Jones Profit Sharing Plan; dir. Settlement Housing Fund, N.Y.C. Mem. investment com. Whitney Mus. Am. Art. Office: Hearst Newspapers 8th Ave 3d Fl New York NY 10019

SWARTZ, THOMAS R. economist, educator; b. Phila., Aug. 31, 1937; s. Henry Jr. and Elizabeth (Thomas) S.; m. Jeanne Marie Jourdan, Aug. 12, 1961; children: Mary Butler, Karen Miller, Jennifer, Anne, Rebecca. BA, LaSalle U., 1960; MA, Ohio U., 1962; PhD, Ind. U., 1965. Asst. prof. U. Notre Dame, Ind., 1965-70, assoc. dept. chair, 1968-70, assoc. prof., 1970-78, acting dir. grad. studies, 1977-78, prof. econs., 1978—85, dir. program econ. policy, 1982-85; resident dir. U. Notre Dame London Program, 1990-91, U. Notre Dame Austraulia Program, Fremantle, 1996. Vis. prof. U. Notre Dame London Program 1982, 85, 90-91, 2001—; fellow Inst. for Ednl. Initiatives, 1997—; dir. London Summer Program, 2001—; fiscal cons. Ind. Commn. State Tax, Indpls., 1965-68, also spl. tax cons., 1971-81, City of South Bend, Ind., 1972-75; fiscal cons. Cass County, Mich., 2003—. Co-editor: The Supply Side, 1983, Changing Face of Fiscal Federalism, 1990, Urban Finance Under Siege, 1993, Taking Sides, 11th edit., 2004, America's Working Poor, 1995; contbr. articles to profl. jours. Bd. dirs. Forever Learning Inst., South Bend, Ind., 1988-93; mem. steering com. Mayor's Housing Forum, South Bend, 1989-95; chair Com. Svcs. Block Grant, South Bend, 1985-90, Econ. Devel. Task Force, South Bend, 1985, Rsch. fellow Nat. Ctr. Urban Ethnic Affairs, 1979-85, Found. Bd. S.W. Mihc. Bd., 2004-; recipient Danforth Assoc. award Danforth Found., 1972-86, Tchg. award Kanzajian Found., 1974, numerous tchg. awards Notre Dame; rsch. grantee Mellon Found., 1998-2003. Fellow Inst. Ednl. Initiatives. Democrat. Roman Catholic. Avocations: racquetball, golf. Office: U Notre Dame Dept Econs and Policy Studies 414 Decio Hall Notre Dame IN 46556-5644 Office Phone: 574-631-7737. E-mail: swartz1@nd.edu.

SWARTZ, WILLIAM JOHN, retired transportation resources company executive; b. Hutchinson, Kans., Nov. 6, 1934; s. George Glen and Helen Mae (Prather) S., m. Dorothy Jean Parshall, June 5, 1956; children: John Christopher, Jeffrey Michael. BSME, Duke U., 1956; JD, George Washington U., 1961; MS in Mgmt. (Alfred P. Sloan fellow), MIT, 1967. With AT & SF Ry., 1961-78, 79—, asst. v.p. exec. dept., 1973-77, v.p. adminstrn., 1977-78, exec. v.p., 1979-83, Santa Fe Industries, Chgo., 1978-79, pres., 1983-90; vice chmn. Santa Fe So. Pacific, 1983-90; pres. AT & SF Ry., 1986-89. Past bd. dirs. Chgo. Mus. Sci. and Industry; mem. Dean's Coun. Duke U. Sch. Engring; mem. regent's cir. Mus. N.Mex., 1996—; mem. Coun. on Internat. Rels., 1996—; bd. dirs. U.S. Def. Orientation Conf. Assn., 1998-2003, N.Mex. Mus. Natural History and Sci., 1999-2001, Santa Fe Desert Chorale, 1999-2002; N.Mex. commr. Cubres & Toltec Scenic Rd., 2000-03; bd. dirs. Santa Fe Coun. Internat. Rels., 2001-03. Mem. Assn. Am. R.R. (past bd. dirs.). Methodist. Home: 1201 Ojo Verde Santa Fe NM 87501-8870

SWARTZBAUGH, MARC L. lawyer; b. Urbana, Ohio, Jan. 3, 1937; s. Merrill L. and Lillian K. (Hill) S.; m. Marjory Anne Emhardt, Aug. 16, 1958 (deceased May 20, 2000); children: Marc Charles, Kathleen Marie, Laura Kay. BA magna cum laude, Wittenberg Coll., 1958; LLB magna cum laude, U. Pa., 1961. Bar: Ohio 1961, U.S. Dist. Ct. (no. dist.) Ohio 1962, U.S. Claims Ct. 1991, U.S. Ct. Appeals (6th cir.) 1970, U.S. Ct. Appeals (3d cir.) 1985, U.S. Ct. Appeals (Fed. cir.) 1995, U.S. Supreme Ct. 1973. Law clk. to judge U.S. Ct. Appeals (3d cir.), Phila., 1961-62; assoc. Jones, Day, Reavis & Pogue, Cleve., 1962-69, ptnr., 1970-98; ret., 1998; cons., 1998—. Note editor U. Pa. Law Rev., 1960-61; co-author: Ohio Legal Ethics, 2001. Co-chmn. Suburban Citizens for Open Housing, Shaker Heights, Ohio, 1966; v.p. Lomond Assn., Shaker Heights, 1965-68; trustee The Dance Ctr., Cleve., 1980-83; amb. People to People Internat., 1986; chmn. legal divsn. Cleve. campaign United Negro Coll. Fund, 1989-96; tutor Cleve. Reads, 2003. Mem. ABA (litigation sect., sr. lawyers divsn.), Fed. Bar Assn., Ohio Bar Assn., Cleve. Bar Assn., Rowfant Club, Order of Coif, Beta Theta Pi. Democrat. Avocations: poetry, painting, music, photography, book collecting. Office: Jones Day N Point 901 Lakeside Ave E Cleveland OH 44114-1190

SWARTZLANDER, EARL EUGENE, JR., engineering educator, former electronics company executive; b. San Antonio, Feb. 1, 1945; s. Earl Eugene and Jane (Nicholas) S.; m. Joan Vickery, June 9, 1968. BSEE, Purdue U., 1967; MSEE, U. Colo., 1969; PhD, U. So. Calif., 1972. Registered profl. engr., Ala., Calif., Colo., Tex. Devel. engr. Ball Bros. Rsch. Corp., Boulder, Colo., 1967-69; Hughes fellow, mem. tech. staff Hughes Aircraft Co., Culver City, Calif., 1969-73; mem. rsch. staff Tech. Svc. Co., Santa Monica, Calif., 1973-74; chief engr. Geophys. Systems Corp., Pasadena, Calif., 1974-75, staff engr. to sr. staff engr., 1975-79, project mgr., 1979-84, lab. mgr., 1985-87; dir. ind. R&D TRW Inc., Redondo Beach, Calif., 1987-90; Schlumberger Centennial prof. engring. dept. elec. and computer engring. U. Tex., Austin, 1990—; mem. tech. adv. bd. Automatic Parallel Designs. Gen. chmn. Internat. Conf. Wafer Scale Integration, 1989, Internat. Conf. Application Specific Array Processors, 1990, 94, 11th Internat. Symposium on Computer Arithmetic, 1992, 31st Ann. Asilomar Conf. on Signals, Sys., and Computers, 1997, others; chmn. 3d Internat. Conf. Parallel and Distributed Sys., Taiwan, 1993, 12th Internat. Conf. on Application-Specific Systems, Architectures and Processors, 2000; mem. tech. adv. bd. Automatic Parallel Designs. Author: VLSI Signal Processing Systems, 1986; editor: Computer Design Development, 1976, Systolic Signal Processing Systems, 1987, Wafer Scale Integration, 1989, Computer Arithmetic Vol. 1 and 2, 1990, Application Specific Processors, 1996; editor-in-chief Jour. of VLSI Signal Processing, 1989-95, IEEE Transactions on Computers, 1991-94, IEEE Transactions on Signal Processing, 1995; editor: IEEE Transactions on Computers, 1982-86, IEEE Transactions on Parallel and Distributed Systems, 1989-90; hardware area editor ACM Computing Revs., 1985—; assoc. editor: IEEE Jour. Solid-State Circuits, 1984-88; contbr. more than 300 articles to profl. jours. and tech. conf. procs. Bd. dirs. Casiano Estates Homeowners Assn., Bel Air, Calif., 1976-78, pres., 1978-80; bd. dirs. Benedict Hills Estates Homeowners Assn., Beverly Hills, Calif., 1984—, pres., 1990-95. Recipient Disting. Engring. Alumnus award Purdue U., 1989, U. Colo., 1997, Outstanding Elec. Engr. award Purdue U., 1992, knight Imperial Russian Order St. John of Jerusalem (Knights of Malta), 1993. Fellow: IEEE (hist. com. 1996—, fellows com. 2000—, 3d Millennium medal 2000); mem.: IEEE Solid-State Cirs. Coun. (sec. 1992—93, treas. 1994—97), IEEE Signal Proc. Soc. (bd. govs. 1992—94), IEEE Computer Soc. (bd. govs. 1987—91, Golden Core award 1996), Omicron Delta Kappa, Sigma Tau, Eta Kappa Nu. Office: U Tex Austin Dept Elec Computer Engring Austin TX 78712

SWARZ, JEFFREY ROBERT, investment banker, biotechnologist, neuroscientist; b. Nov. 9, 1949; s. Irvin Brad and Blanche S. (Marcus) S.; m. Kathy Helen Kafer, June 20, 1976. BS with hons., U. Calif., Irvine, 1971; PhD, U. Rochester, 1976. Postdoctoral fellow in neurovirology Johns Hopkins U. Sch. Medicine, Balt., 1976-79; staff fellow infectious diseases NIH, Bethesda, Md., 1979-80; dir. biotech. group Teknekron Rsch. Inc., McLean, Va., 1980-81; pres. AgroBiotics, Inc., Balt., 1981-82; from sr. scientist to dir. mktg. and sales Pall Corp., Glen Cove, N.Y., 1982-85, dir. mktg. and sales, 1985-86; biotech./healthcare analyst Goldman Sachs & Co., Glen Cove, N.Y., 1986-92; dir. CS First Boston, N.Y.C., 1992-99; ptnr. Partner-Eagle Ptnrs., N.Y.C., 1999—; prodr. Shadow Prodns.; mng. dir. Life Sci. Group, 2001—. Cons. U.S. Senate Subcom. on Sci., Tech. and Space, 1979-80; prodr. Shadow Prodns., 1998—. Author: (with others) Genetic Engineering: Issues and Trends, 1982; contbr. articles to profl. jours. Recipient Rsch. award Bank of Am., 1970-71, Nat. Rsch. Svc. award 1976-79; NIH fellow 1975-76. Mem.: N.Y. Acad. Sci., N.Y. Athletic Club, U. Club. Democrat. Jewish. Office: Life Sci Group 1 South Shore Dr Greenwich CT 06830-5449

SWARZ, SAHL, sculptor; b. N.Y.C., May 4, 1912; s. Samuel and Ida (Fass) S.; m. Naoco Kumasaka, May 1978. Student, Clay Club, N.Y.C., 1928-34, Art Students League, 1930-31. Assoc. dir. Clay Club (now Sculpture Center), 1938-54; creative sculpture Italy, 1951-63; residence Am. Acad., Rome, 1955-57; lectr. sculpture Columbia U., N.Y.C., 1966-68, asst. prof., 1969-78.

Instr. Pratt Inst., Bklyn., 1964; instr. New Sch. for Social Rsch., 1965, 66; vis. lectr. art U. Wis., 1966; trustee Mus. Contemporary Sculpture, Tokyo; lectr. art dept. Nippon U., Tokyo, 1997. Author, illustrator: Blueprint for the Future of American Sculpture, 1943, also monograph.; one man exhbn. Sculpture Ctr., 1954, 57, 60, 62, 66, 71, 74, 78, Art Alliance, Phila., 1958, Fairweather-Hardin Gallery, Chgo., 1963, Brandeis U., Waltham, Mass., 1964, (retrospective exhbn.) Fair Lawn (NJ) Pub. Library, 1977, Saikaya Gallery, Fujisawa, Japan, 1983, Mus. Contemporary Sculpture, Tokyo, 1985, Shonan Gallery, Fujisawa, Japan, 1985, 90, 93, 2001 (retrospective exhbn., 2004) Toni de Rossi Gallery, Verona, Italy, 1983, 87, 91, Takashimaya Gallery, Yokohama, Japan, 1984, Atagoyama Gallery, Tokyo, 1988, 91, 94, 99, 1st exhibition of painting Toni de Rossi Gallery, Verona, Italy, 1992, 96, Move Gallery Chigasaki, Japan, 1993; group shows include Fairmont Park Internat., Phila., 1948, Whitney Mus. Am. Art, 1948, 58, 60, 62, 64, Pa. Acad., 1948, 52, 54, 57, 60, 62, 66, Bklyn Mus., 1935, Detroit Inst. Fine Arts, 1957, San Francisco Mus., 1955, U. Ill., 1960, 62, others; represented in permanent collections Norfolk (Va.) Mus., Whitney Mus. Am. Art, Ball State Tchr. Coll., Williams Coll. Mus., Ford Found., Mpl. Inst. Fine Arts, Va. Mus. Fine Arts, Richmond, Newark Mus., NJ State Mus. at Trenton, Vatican Mus. Collection Modern Religious Art, Rose Art Mus., Brandeis U., Stamford (Conn.) Mus., Columbia U., Tokyo Mus. Contemporary Sculpture, others; bronze group The Guardian at Brookgreen (SC), Gardens Mus.; terra cotta wall sculpture, Linden, (NJ), Post Office, sculptural designs, Fed. Courthouse, Statesville, NC; equestrian monument Gen. Bidwell, Buffalo; fountain commn., Spruce Run State Park, NJ; mall sculpture, Pittsfield, Mass.; monument to Demeter in stainless steel, Fujisawa, Japan; subject of biography: Fifty Years of Sculpture by Sahl Swarz. Chmn. sculpture panel N.J. Coun. on Arts. With AUS, 1941-45. Grantee Am. Acad. Arts and Letters, 1955; Guggenheim fellow, 1955, 58 Address: Kumasaka-Swarz Via Strettoia 43 55045 Pietrasanta Italy *The essence of creativity is in the searching after the form. Search leads to revelation, understanding, knowledge. Realization of one's ignorance is the first step to the attainment of wisdom. A wise man makes a work of art out of life itself.*

SWATOS, WILLIAM HENRY, JR., priest, sociologist; b. Paterson, N.J., Sept. 25, 1946; s. William H. Sr. and Lucille (MacNab) S.; children (by previous marriage): Giles S., Eric B.; m. Joanne Longstreet, Oct. 29, 2002. AB, Transylvania U., 1966; MDiv summa cum laude, Episc. Theol. Sem., Lexington, Ky., 1969; MA, U. Ky., 1969, PhD, 1973. Ordained to ministry Episcopal Ch., 1969. Mem. sociology faculty King Coll., Bristol, Tenn., 1973-80; vicar St. Mark's Episc. Ch., Silvis, Ill., 1980-94; mem. sociology faculty No. Ill. U., 1984-88; chair dept. edn. Diocese of Quincy, 1988-90, 93-96. Mem. faculty Black Hawk and Scott Community Coll., Moline, Ill., Bettendorf, Iowa, 1988-96. Editor: Time, Place and Circumstance, 1990, Religious Politics in Global and Comparative Perspective, 1989, Religious Sociology, 1987; editor Sociol. Analysis/Sociology of Religion, 1989-94; editor-in-chief The Encyclopedia of Religion and Society, 1998; contbr. articles to profl. jours. Full grantee World Soc. Found., Zurich, Switzerland, 1987, grantee NEH, 1974, 79, 85, 89, rsch. grantee Soc. for the Sci. Study of Religion, 1984-85, 91-92; named Disting. Alumnus Dept. of Sociology, U. Ky., Lexington, 1990. Fellow Soc. Sci. Study of Religion (program chair 2004—); mem. Assn. for the Sociology of Religion (editor 1989-94, book rev. editor 1986-88, exec. coun. 1984-86, exec. officer 1996—), Religious Rsch. Assn. (sec. 1990-91, bd. dirs. 1986-89, exec. officer 1994—). Home and Office: 618 SW 2nd Ave Galva IL 61434-1912 E-mail: swatos@microd.com.

SWATT, STEPHEN BENTON, communications executive, consultant; b. L.A., June 26, 1944; s. Maurice I. and Lucille E. (Sternberger) S.; m. Susan Ruth Edelstein, Sept. 7, 1968; 1 child, Jeffrey Michael. BSBA, U. Calif., 1966, M in Journalism, 1967. Writer San Francisco Examiner, 1967; reporter United Press Internat., L.A., 1968-69; producer news Sta. KCRA-TV, Sacramento, 1969-70, reporter news, 1970-79, chief polit. and capitol corres., 1979-92; mng. ptnr. NCG Porter Novelli, Sacramento, 1992—2003, sr. counselor, 2003—. Adj. prof., guest lectr. Calif. State U., Sacramento. Contbr. articles to profl. jours. With USCG, 1966. Recipient No. Calif. Emmy NATAS, 1976-77, Pub. Svc. award Calif. State Bar, 1977, Exceptional Achievement Coun. advancement and Support of Edn., 1976, Nat. Health Journalism award Am. Chiropractic Assn., 1978. Mem. Soc. Profl. Journalists (8 awards), Capitol Corres. Assn., U. Calif. Alumni Assn., Sacramento Press Club. Avocations: hiking, jogging, fishing. Office: Porter Novelli 1215 K St # 2100 Sacramento CA 95814 Business E-Mail: steve.swatt@porternovelli.com.

SWAYSLAND, JANET, advertising executive; BA in social sci., edn., Wake Forest U. Pres. Brodeur Worldwide, 2000—, gen. mgr. U.S. ops., 1999; co-dir. pub. rels. group Mullen Advt. & Pub. Rels.; v.p. U.S. divsn. The Body Shop, Inc. Chair U.S. exec. team Brodeur Worldwide. Office: Brodeur Worldwide 855 Boylston St Boston MA 02116

SWAYZE, PATRICK, actor, dancer; b. Houston, Aug. 18, 1952; s. Patsy Swayze. Student, Harkness Sch., Joffrey Ballet Sch. Dancer (Broadway) Goodtime Charley, Grease; film appearances include (debut) Skatetown, U.S.A., 1979, The Outsiders, 1983, Uncommon Valor, 1983, Red Dawn, 1984, Grandview U.S.A., 1984, Youngblood, 1986, Dirty Dancing, 1987, Steel Dawn, 1987, Tiger Warsaw, 1988, Road House, 1989, Next of Kin, 1989, Ghost, 1989, Point Break, 1991, City of Joy, 1992, Father Hood, 1993, Tall Tale, 1994, To Wong Foo, Thanks for Everything, Julie Newmar, 1995, Three Wishes, 1995, Letters From a Killer, 1997, Vanished, 1998, Black Dog, 1998, Letters from a Killer, 1998, Without a Word, 1999, The Winddrinker, 2000, Wakin' Up In Reno, 2000, Forever Lulu, 2000, Green Dragon, 2001, Donnie Darko, 2001, Waking Up in Reno, 2002, One Last Dance, 2003, 11:14, 2003, Dirty Dancing: Havana Nights, 2004; (tv series) Hollywood Squares, 1998; (TV movies) King Solomon's Mines, 2004. Recipient Golden Apple award. Office: William Morris 151 S El Camino Dr Beverly Hills CA 90212-2775*

SWAZEY, JUDITH POUND, academic administrator, sociomedical science educator; b. Bronxville, N.Y., Apr. 21, 1939; d. Robert Earl and Louise Titus (Hanson) Pound; m. Peter Woodman Swazey, Nov. 28, 1964; children: Elizabeth, Peter. AB, Wellesley Coll., 1961; PhD, Harvard U., 1966. Rsch. assoc. Harvard U., 1966-71, lectr., 1969-71, rsch. fellow, 1971-72; cons. com. brain scis. NRC, 1971-73; staff scientist neuroscis. rsch. program MIT, Cambridge, 1973-74; assoc. prof. dept. socio-med. scis. and cmty. medicine Boston U., 1974-77, prof., 1977-80, adj. prof. Schs. Medicine and Pub. Health, 1980—; exec. dir. Medicine in the Pub. Interest, Inc., Boston and Washington, 1979-82, 89-93; pres. Coll. of the Atlantic, Bar Harbor, Maine, 1982-84, Acadia Inst., Bar Harbor, 1984-2001, founding pres., sr. scholar, 2001—. Mem. Army Sci. Bd., 1987-92. Author: Reflexes and Motor Integration, the Development of Sherrington's Integrative Action Concept, 1969, (with others) Human Aspects of Biomedical Innovation, 1971, (with R.C. Fox) The Courage to Fail, a Social View of Organ Transplants and Hemodialysis, 1975, rev. edit., 1978 (hon. mention Am. Med. Writers Assn., C. Wright Mills award Am. Sociol. Assn.), Chlorpromazine in Psychiatry, a Study of Therapeutic Innovation, 1974, (with K. Reeds) Today's Medicine, Tomorrow's Science, Essays on Paths of Discovery in the Biomedical Sciences, 1978; editor: (with C. Wong) Dilemmas of Dying, Policies and Procedures for Decisions Not to Treat, 1981, (with F. Worden and G. Adelman) The Neurosciences: Paths of Discovery, 1975, (with R.C. Fox) Spare Parts, Organ Replacement in American Society, 1992, (with C. Messikomer and A. Glicksman) Society and Medicine. Essays in Honor of Renée Fox, 2002; assoc. editor IRB: A Jour. of Human Subjects Rsch., 1979-2000; mem. editl. bd. Sci. and Engring. Ethics, 1994—; contbr. articles to profl. jours. Mem. Maine Dept. Human Svcs. Bioethics Adv. Com. (chair 1991-94); mem. Commn. on Rsch. Integrity, 1994-95; bd. dirs. Maine Bioethic Network, 1994-99. Wellesley Coll. scholar, 1961; Wellesley Coll. Alumnae fellow Harvard U., 1966, NIH predoctoral fellow, 1966, Radcliffe Coll. Coll. grad. fellow, 1966. Fellow AAAS (sci. freedom and responsibility com. 1986-89, nominations com. 2003-), Inst. Medicine of NAS (mem. health scis. policy bd. 1986-89), Grad. Record Exam. (bd. dirs. 1987-91), Phi Beta Kappa, Sigma Xi (mem. ethics com. 2004-). Office: PO Box 243 Bar Harbor ME 04609-0243

SWEANEY, DONNA, state representative; b. Steubenville, Ohio, June 18, 1943; m. William James Ballantyne. BA, Youngstown State U., 1966; MEd, U. Hartford, 1974. Sch. counselor; rep. Vt. Ho. of Reps., 1996—. Chmn. Windsor Selectboard, 1986-87. Trustee Mt. Ascutney Hosp. Mem. NEA, Am. and Vt. Counseling Assns., Vt. Sch. Counselors. Office: 20 N Main St Windsor VT 05089-1307

SWEARER, WILLIAM BROOKS, lawyer; b. Hays, Kans. Grad., Princeton U., 1951; law degree, U. Kans., 1955. Bar: Kans. 1955. Pvt. practice, Hutchinson, Kans., 1955—; ptnr., now counsel Martindell, Swearer & Shaffer, LLP, Hutchinson, 1955—. Mem. Kans. Bd. Discipline for Attys., 1979-92, chmn., 1987-92; mem. Kans. Commn. on Jud. Qualifications, 2003-. With U.S. Army, 1952-53, Korea. Mem. ABA (ho. of dels. 1995-2000), Am. Bar Found. (state chair 1998-2002), Kans. Bar Assn. (pres. 1992-93, various offices, mem. coms.), Kans. Assn. Sch. Attys. (pres. 1989-90), Reno County Bar Assn. Office: PO Box 1907 Hutchinson KS 67504-1907 Office Phone: 620-662-3331. E-mail: wbs@martindell-law.com.

SWEAT, CARL LEONDUS, JR., minister, educator; b. Virginia Beach, Va., Mar. 14, 1963; s. Carl Leondus Sweat, Sr. and Virginia (Sweat) Murphy, Roy Murphy (Stepfather); m. Janice Belinda Hicks, June 13, 1987; children: Carl Leondus III, April Janiece. BA in Sociology, Va. Union U., 1986; MS in Adminstrv. Sci., Ctrl. Mich. U., 1995; MS in Div., Providence Theol. Sem., 1999, D of Ministry, 2002. Cert. Counselor Am. Assn. Christian Counselors, 2002. Sr. pastor Laurel Hill United Ch. of Christ, Suffolk, Va., 2000—. Bd. dirs. So. Conf. United Ch. Christ, Burlington, NC, 2002—. Author: (theol. book) Why Are Women In The Ministry?. Mem. Holland Civil League, Suffolk, Va., 1993—2004. Mem.: Suffolk Interdenominational Alliance (assoc.; sec. 2003—04). D-Conservative. Avocations: reading, exercising, writing. Home: 9340 New Road Suffolk VA 23437 Office: Laurel Hill United Ch of Christ Suffolk VA 23437 Personal E-mail: minsweat@cs.com.

SWEE, DAVID ETHAN, physician; b. N.Y.C., Sept. 3, 1947; s. Eugene and Joan (Shalit) S.; m. Karen Virginia Hermanson, Dec. 30, 1971; children: Kendra Olivia, Julia Elizabeth. BA, Grinnell Coll., 1969; MD, Dalhousie U., 1975. Diplomate Am. Bd. Family Practice. Dir. premed. programs dept. family medicine U. Medicine and Dentistry N.J.-Robert Wood Johnson Med. Sch., Piscataway, 1977-85, dir. fellowship program, 1985-87, med. dir. family practice ctr., vice chair dept. New Brunswick, 1987-91, prof., chmn. dept. family medicine, 1991—. Chief dept. family medicine Robert Wood Johnson Univ. Hosp., New Brunswick, 1991—; site surveyor Accreditation Coun. Continuing Med. Edn., Chgo., 1993—, site surveyor, Liaison Com. on Med. Edn., 2001—. Editor, main author: Teaching Family Medicine in Medical School: A Companion to Predoctoral Education in Family Medicine, 1991. Grantee Prudential Ins. Co., 1987-89, U.S. Dept. HHS, 1984-87, 91-94, 93-96, 96—99, 99-2002, 02—; Maria Bishop fellow Am. Coun. Edn., 2002-03. Fellow Am. Acad. Family Physicians; mem. Soc. Tchrs. Family Medicine (bd. dirs. 1985-89, group on predocotoral edn. 1984—, group on faculty devel. 1985—). Avocations: music (piano), writing. Home: 259 Lawrence Ave Highland Park NJ 08904-1837 Office: 1 Robert Wood Johnson Pl New Brunswick NJ 08901-1928 Office Phone: 732-235-7655. Business E-Mail: swee@umdnj.edu.

SWEED, ART, social worker, adult education educator; b. Brooklyn, NY, Mar. 1, 1949; s. William Sweed and Mary Hoenig. AA in Pre-Law, Miami-Dade Cmty. Coll., Fla., 1970; Bachelor's in Social Work, Fla. Internat. U., Miami, 1975, Master of Pub. Adminstrn., 1982; MSW, Boston U., 2002. Cert. LCSW Mass., 2003. Ednl. rehab. counselor State of Fla., Div. of Vocat. Rehab., Miami, 1988—90; disability spec. State of Fla., Disability Unit, Miami, 1980—88; adult basic edn. instr. North Miami Beach H.S., North Miami Beach, 1990—91; adult ed. instr. Concord HS, NH, 1993—94; disability claims adjudicator State of N.H., Concord, 1994—2002; case mgr. Genesis Behavioral Health Ctr., Laconia, NH, 2002; vocat. specialist, clinician Tri-City Mental Health Ctr., Lowell, Mass., 2003—. Staff adv. council State of Fla., Miami, 1982—84, Affirmative Action com., 1984—89; newsletter ed., exec. bd. Am. Fed., State, County Mcpl. Employees, Miami, 1985—87; tutor, substitute instr. Second Start Cmty. Edn., Concord, 1995—2001. Contbg. editor: (book) National Poetry Review, 1974; actor(stage mgr.): Spring Players, 1980. Mem.: State Employee Assn. (bd. mem. 1997—2002), Nat. Assn. of Disability Examiners, Nat. Assn. of Social Workers. Independent. Achievements include tchng. developmentally disabled persons to read and write; vol. docent Mus. of N.H. History; being involved in various cmty services. Avocations: walking, cmty. activity. Home: 6 Silver Dr #16 Nashua NH 03060 Office: Tri-City Mental Health Center 391 Varnum Avenue Lowell MA 03184

SWEED, PHYLLIS, publishing executive; b. N.Y.C., Dec. 6, 1931; d. Paul and Frances (Spitzer) S.; m. Leonard Bogdanoff (dec. Oct. 1975); children: Patricia Romano (dec. June 1994), James Alan. BA, NYU, 1950. Asst. buyer Nat. Bellas Hess, N.Y.C., 1950; assoc. editor Fox-Shulman Pub., N.Y.C., 1951-57; significant products and components editor Product Engring. mag. McGraw-Hill Pub., N.Y.C., 1957—61; mng. editor Haire Pub., N.Y.C., 1962-66; editor Gifts & Decorative Accessories Mag., 1966-78; sr. v.p. Geyer-McAllister Pub., N.Y.C., 1978-98, editor-in-chief, co-pub., 1978—98; dir. editl. devel. Gifts & Decorative Accessories, N.Y.C., 1998-99; prin. PS Comms. & Mktg., 1999—; editor-in-chief, pub. Gift Executive, 1999—. Bd. dirs. Frances Hook Scholarship Fund, 1989-96. Recipient Editl. Excellence award Indsl. Mktg., 1964, Nat. Assn. Ltd. Edit. Dealers award, 1993, 96, MagWeek Excellence award, 1992, Dallas Mktg. Ctr. award, 1969, 80, 82. Mem. Nat. Assn. Ltd. Edit. Dealers (assoc.), Internat. Furnishings and Design Assn. Avocations: gardening, collecting antique Belleek. Office: 505 La-Guardia Pl Ste 17D New York NY 10012-2004 Office Phone: 212-533-6174.

SWEEM, BILLY DON, minister; b. Bartlesville, Okla., Aug. 7, 1942; s. Verl D. and Viola J. (Benner) Sweem; m. Roberta Marie Hawthorn, Dec. 26, 1990; children: Mark A. Bradburn. Dipl., Internat. Bible Inst. & Sem., Portsmount, Fla.; ThD magna cum laude, Bethel Full Gospel Sem., Okla. Ordained to ministry Gospel Mins. and Chs. Internat., 1991, Ind. Assemblies Fellowship, 1991. Evangelist Lighthouse Temple, Colorado Springs, Colo., 1977-80, Tulsa, 1980-85; youth pastor Echoes of Faith, Las Vegas, Nev., 1985-89; exec. dir. Billy Sweem Gospel Ministries, Tulsa, 1990—. Evangelist United Meth. Coop. Ministries, Tulsa, 1990—. Special interest in mission works with "Throw Away and Troubled Teens", Pine Meadows Boys Ranch Found. Home: PO Box 2171 Bartlesville OK 74005-2171

SWEENEY, ANNE M. cable television company executive; b. Nov. 4, 1957; m. Philip Miller; 2 children. BA, Coll. of New Rochelle, N.Y., 1979; EdM, Harvard U., 1980. With Nickelodeon/Nick at Nite, 1981-93, sr. v.p. program enterprises; chmn., CEO Fx Networks, N.Y.C., 1993-96; exec. v.p. Disney/ABC Cable Networks, pres. Disney Channel Walt Disney Co., 1996—98, pres. Disney/ABC Cable Networks, Disney Channel, 1998—2000, pres. ABC Cable Networks Group, Disney Channel Worldwide, 2000—04, co-chair Media Networks divsn., pres. Disney/ ABC TV, 2004—. Bd. trustees Coll. of New Rochelle, Harvard U. Ptnrs. Coun.; hon. chair Cable Positive; bd. dirs. Walter Kaitz Found, Spl. Olympics Internat. Recipient Chair Award, Caucus for TV Prodrs., Writers, and Dirs., 2003. Mem. Nat. Acad. Cable Programming (bd. dirs.), Women in Cable (founding mem.) N.Y. Women in Cable (Exec. of Yr. 1994), Am. Women in Radio and TV (Star award 1995), Am. Advt. Fedn. (inducted in Hall of Achievement). Office: The Walt Disney Co 500 S Buena Vista St Burbank CA 91521

SWEENEY, ASHER WILLIAM, state supreme court justice; b. Canfield, Ohio, Dec. 11, 1920; s. Walter William and Jessie Joan (Kidd) S.; m. Bertha M. Englert, May 21, 1945; children: Randall W., Ronald R., Garland A., Karen M. Student, Youngstown U., 1939-42; LL.B., Duke U., 1948. Bar: Ohio 1949. Practiced law, Youngstown, Ohio, 1949-51; judge adv. gen. Dept. Def., Washington, 1951-65; chief Fed. Contracting Agy., Cin., 1965-68; corp. law, 1968-77; justice Ohio Supreme Ct., Columbus, 1977—. Democratic candidate for Sec. of State Ohio, 1958. Served with U.S. Army, 1942-46; col. Res. 1951-68. Decorated Legion of Merit, Bronze Star; named to Army Hall of Fame Ft. Benning, Ga., 1981 Mem. Ohio Bar Assn., Phi Delta Phi. Democrat. Home: 6690 Drake Rd Cincinnati OH 45243-2706 Office: Ohio Supreme Ct 30 E Broad St Fl 3D Columbus OH 43215-3414

SWEENEY, CHRISTOPHER JOHN, psychology educator, consultant; b. Boston, May 22, 1940; s. John James Sweeney and Adelaide Boomhower; m. Nancy Carol Symmes, Aug. 29, 1964; children: Christopher, Daniel, Rachel. AB cum laude, Boston Coll., 1964; MEd, Northeastern U., Boston, 1966; PhD, U. Okla., 1968. Lic. psychologist, Ohio. Assoc. prof. psychology Youngstown (Ohio) State U., 1968-75, prof., 1975—. Contbr. articles to profl. jours. Bd. dirs. Potential Devel. Ctr., Youngstown, 1975-90, Child and Adult Mental health Ctr., Youngstown, 1977-84. Recipient, Disting. Prof. Awd., Youngstown State U., 1979. Mem. Am. Assn. Applied and Preventive Psychology, NDEA fell., U. Oklahoma, 1967-68. Avocations: reading, racquetball. Home: 405 Garden Gate Dr Youngstown OH 44512-5805 Office: Youngstown State U Psychology Dept 1 University Plz Youngstown OH 44555-0002 E-mail: cjsweeney@ysu.edu.

SWEENEY, CLAYTON ANTHONY, lawyer, business executive; b. Pitts., Oct. 20, 1931; s. Denis Regis and Grace Frances (Roche) S.; m. Sally Dimond, Oct. 4, 1958; children: Sharon, Lorrie, Maureen, Clayton Anthony, Tara, Megan. BS, Duquesne U., 1957, LLB, 1962. Bar: Pa. 1962, U.S. Supreme Ct. 1968. Supr. transp. claims H.J. Heinz Co., Pitts., 1955-57; mgr. market research Murray Corp. Am., Pitts., 1957-62; ptnr. Buchanan, Ingersoll, Rodewald, Kyle and Buerger, Pitts., 1962-78; sr. v.p. Allegheny Ludlum Industries, Inc., Pitts., 1978-81; exec. v.p., chief adminstrv. officer Allegheny Internat., Inc., Pitts., 1981-84, vice chmn., 1984-85; ptnr., mng. dir. Dickie, McCamey & Chilcote, Pitts., 1986-98, also bd. dirs.; pres. Sweeney Metz Fox McGrann & Schermer, 1998-2000; with Schnader Harrison Segal & Lewis, LLP, Pitts., 2000—. Bd. dirs. Wilkinson Sword Group Ltd., U.K., Landmark Savs. and Loan Assn., Liquid Air N.Am., Halbouty Energy Co., Koppers Holding Corp., Koppers Industries, Inc., Schaefer Mfg., Inc., Schaefer Marine, Inc., Schaefer Equipment, Inc.; adj. prof. Duquesne U. Sch. Law; lectr. Pa. Bar Inst.; mem. procedural rules com. Supreme Ct. Pa. Named Disting. Alumnus Sch. Law Duquesne U., 1997. Bd. dirs. Met. Pitts. Pub. Broadcasting, Inc., Diocesan Sch. Bd., Roman Cath. Diocese Pitts., Toner Inst., Christian Assocs. of Southwestern Pa., Wesley Inst., Inc., Jr. Achievement S.W. Pa., YMCA Western Pa.; chmn. Seton Hill Coll.; mem. St. Thomas More Sch. Bd., Bethel Park, Pa.; chmn. St. Francis Med. Ctr., St. Francis Health System; chmn. bd. DePaul Inst. With U.S. Army, 1953-55. Named one of 100 Most Disting. Living Alumni Duquesne U. Century Club, 1978 Mem. Acad. Trial Lawyers Allegheny County, ABA, Pa. Bar Assn., St. Thomas More Soc. Home: 232 Thornberry Cir Pittsburgh PA 15234-1025 Office: Schnader Harrison Segal & Lewis LLP Ste 2700 Fifth Ave Pl 120 Fifth Ave Pittsburgh PA 15222-3010 Office Phone: 412-577-5225. Business E-Mail: csweeney@schnader.com.

SWEENEY, DAVID BRIAN, lawyer; b. Seattle, June 23, 1941; s. Hubert Lee and Ann Louise (Harmon) S.; m. Janice Kay Goins, June 18, 1983; children: Stuart, Jennifer, Ann, Katharine. BA Magna cum laude, Yale U., 1963; LLB, Harvard U., 1967. Bar: Wash. 1968, U.S. Dist. Ct. (we. dist.) Wash. 1968, U.S. Ct. Appeals (9th cir.) 1968. Assoc. Roberts, Shefelman, Lawrence, Gay and Moch, Seattle, 1968-75; ptnr. Roberts, Shefelman, Lawrence, Gay & Moch (then Robert & Shefelman, then Foster, Pepper & Shefelman), 1976—2002; of counsel Smith & Zuccarini, P.S., Bellevue, Wash., 2002—. Mem. Seattle-King County Bar Assn., Wash. State Bar Assn., ABA, Estate Planning Council of Seattle. Clubs: College, Harbor. Republican. Presbyterian. Home: 17506 SE 46th St Bellevue WA 98006-6527 Office: Smith & Zuccarini PS 2155 112th Ave NE Bellevue WA 98004 E-mail: D.sweeney@smithzuccarini.com.

SWEENEY, DEIDRE ANN, lawyer; b. Hackensack, NJ, Mar. 17, 1953; d. Thomas Joseph and Robin (Thwaites) Sweeney. AB cum laude, Mt. Holyoke Coll., 1975; JD, Fordham U., 1978. Assoc. Curtis, Mallet-Prevost, Colt & Mosle, N.Y.C., 1978—84, Eaton & Van Winkle, N.Y.C., 1984—86; ptnr. Jacobs, Persinger & Parker, N.Y.C., 1986—2002; of counsel McCanliss and Early, LLP, N.Y.C., 2002—. Hi-five scholarship com. CUNY, 2000—. Mem. Assn. of Bar of City of N.Y. (uniform state laws com. 1982-85).

SWEENEY, FRANCIS E. state supreme court justice; b. Jan. 26, 1934; married; 4 children. BSBA, Xavier U., 1956; JD, Cleve.-Marshall Law Sch., 1963. Profl. football player Ottawa Rough Riders, Ont., Can., 1956-58; mem. legal dept. Allstate Ins. Co., Cleve., 1958-63; asst. prosecuting atty. Cuyahoga County, Cleve., 1963-70; judge Cuyahoga County Ct. of Common Pleas, Cleve., 1970-88; judge (8th cir.) U.S. Ct. Appeals, Cleve., 1988-92; justice Ohio Supreme Ct., Columbus, 1992—. With U.S. Army, 1957-58. Recipient Legion of Honor award Xavier U., 1956, Outstanding Jud. Svc. award Ohio Supreme Ct., 1972-85, Alumnus of Yr. award Xavier U., 1977. Office: Ohio Supreme Ct 30 E Broad St Fl 3 Columbus OH 43215-0001

SWEENEY, GERARD H. real estate company executive; Various positions including fin. v.p., gen. ptnr. The Linpro Co., 1983-94; pres. Brandywine Real Estate Trust, Newtown Square, Pa., 1989—, CEO, 1994—, trustee, 1996—. Bd. dirs. U.S. RealTel, Inc. Bd. dirs. Found. Arch., Pa. Acad. Fine Arst. Mem. AICPAs, N.A.R.E.I.T., Pa. Inst. CPAs., U.L.I.*

SWEENEY, JACK, publishing executive; b. Jersey City; BA in English, King's Coll., Wilkes-Barre, Pa. With adv. dept. Washington Post, 1968—74; adv. dir. Trenton Times, 1974—78, Boston Herald, 1978—80, Houston Chronicle, 1980—83, dir. sales and mktg., 1983—86, v.p. sales and mktg., 1986—91, v.p., gen. mgr., 1991, assoc. pub., 1998—2000, pres., 1998—, pub., 2000—. Leader United Way Tex. Gulf Coast, Greater Houston Partnership, Houston Image Group, Children's Assessment Ctr. Found., Houston Symphony, Houston Internat. Festival, BBB, campaign chair, 2002—03; chmn. Be A Super Host com. Super Bowl 2004, Houston. Mem.: Tex. Daily Newspaper Assn. (Pat Taggart Newspaper Exec. of Yr.), Newspaper Assn. Am. (mem. bd. dirs., mem. exec. com.). Office: Houston Chronicle 801 Texas Ave Houston TX 77002*

SWEENEY, JAMES RAYMOND, lawyer; b. Chgo., Feb. 19, 1928; s. John Francis and Mae J. (McDonald) S.; m. Rhoda W. Davis, May 15, 1987; children from previous marriage: Margaret Elizabeth, John Francis, Thomas Edward. BS, U. Notre Dame, 1950; JD, Northwestern U., 1956. Bar: Ill. 1956. With firm Schroeder, Hofgren, Brady & Wegner, Chgo., 1956-61; ptnr. Hofgren, Wegner, Allen, Stellman & McCord, Chgo., 1962-71, Coffee, Wetzel, Sweeney, Chgo., 1971-72, Coffee & Sweeney, 1972-76, Mason, Kolehmainen, Rathburn & Wyss, Chgo., 1976-82, Mann, McWilliams, 1983-86, Mann McWilliams Zummer and Sweeney, 1986—89, Lee, Mann, Smith, McWilliams & Sweeney, 1989-91, Lee, Mann, Smith, McWilliams, Sweeney & Ohlson, 1991—2002; dir. ctr. intellectual property law John Marshall Law Sch., 1998—2003; ptnr. Barnes & Thornburg, 2003—. Commr. for disbarment matters Ill. Supreme Ct., 1963-73; mem. hearing div. Atty. Registration and Discipline Commn., 1974-77, chmn. commn. 1983-90; chmn. Ctr. for Intellectual Property Law adv. bd. John Marshall Law Sch., 1997-99. Bd. dirs., sec. Highland Park (Ill.) Hosp., 1972-79. Served as lt. (j.g.) USN, 1950-53; lt. comdr. Res. ret. Mem. ABA (coun. patent, trademark and copyright sect., sec. 1978-82), Ill. State Bar (assembly 1990-96), Chgo. Bar Assn. (sec. 1977-79), Bar Assn. 7th Cir., Intellectual Property Law Assn. Chgo., Patent Law Assn. Chgo. (pres. 1974), The Law Club, Skokie (Ill.) Country Club, Union League Club. Home: 505 N Lake Shore Dr Chicago IL 60611-3427 Office: Barnes & Thornburg One N Wacker Dr Chicago IL 60606-2809 Office Phone: 312-357-1313. Business E-Mail: jrsweeney@btlaw.com.

SWEENEY, JOHN E. congressman; b. Troy, N.Y., Aug. 9, 1955; children: Kelly, John, Mary. AAS, Hudson Valley C.C., 1978; BS in Polit. Sci. and Criminal Justice, Russell Sage Coll., 1981; JD, Western New Eng. Coll., 1991. Bar: N.Y. 1990. Dir. Rensselaer County Stop-DWI program, Troy; exec. dir. N.Y. Repub. Party, 1992—95; ptnr. Sweeney, Cholakis & Wollowitz, Troy; commr. of labor State of N.Y., Albany, 1995-97, dep. sec. to Gov. George Pataki, 1997-99; mem. U.S. Congress from 20th N.Y. dist., 1999—, mem.

appropriations com., select com. on homelan security, chmn. subcom. on intelligence and counterterrorism. Chmn. N.Y. Rep. Party, 1992-95. Republican. Office: 416 Cannon Ho Office Bldg Washington DC 20515-3220

SWEENEY, JOHN JOSEPH, labor union administrator; b. Bronx, N.Y., May 5, 1934; m. Maureen Sweeney; children: John, Patricia. Degree in Econs., Iona Coll. With Internat. Ladies' Garment Workers; v.p., chair exec. coun. com. on health care Am. Fedn. Labor and Indsl. Orgns.; pres. Svc. Employees Internat. Union, Am. Fedn. Labor and Indsl. Orgns., 1995—. Author: America Needs a Raise, Fighting for Economic Security and Social Justice, 1996; co-author: Solutions for the New Work Force, 1989; co-editor: Family and Work: Bridging the Gap, 1987. Office: Am Fedn Labor & Indsl Orgns 815 16th St NW Washington DC 20006-4104

SWEENEY, JOSEPH DUDLEY, law educator, political organization worker; b. Omaha, Aug. 5, 1944; s. William Dudley Sweeney and Catherine Teresa Malone. BS in Agrl. Sci. and Animal Sci., U. Ariz., 1972; JD, Alexander Hamilton Evening Law Sch., 1995. Prof., adminstr. Alexander Hamilton Evening Law Sch., Tucson, 1978—, Union Western Sem., Tucson, 1985—. Dem. candidate U.S. Congress Ariz., 1984, 1986, 1991, Rep. candidate U.S. Congress, 1988—. Mem.: KC. Republican. Roman Catholic. Avocations: sports, exercise, reading, video production. Home: 1411 N 3rd Ave Tucson AZ 85705 Office: Alexander Hamilton Law Coll 1411 N 3rd Ave Tucson AZ 85705 Office Phone: 520-617-0656.

SWEENEY, JOYCE C. state representative; b. Colchester, Vt., July 23, 1928; 3 children. Grad., Edmunds H.S., Burlington, Vt. State rep. State of Vt., 2003—. Chairperson Bd. of Authority, 1999—; commr. Cemetery, Colchester; mem. Bd. of Auditors, Colchester, Bd. of Listers, Colchester; assessor Colchester; town clk.; treas.; past treas. United Ch. of Colchester, fin. sec. Mem.: Colchester Cemetery Assn. (clk., treas.). Republican. Protestant. Office: 1228 Main St Colchester VT 05446 E-mail: TheChoiceisJoyce@aol.com.

SWEENEY, JUDITH KIERNAN, secondary school educator; Tchr. science grades 8-12 Lincoln (R.I.) Jr.-Sr. High Sch., 1994; curator of edn. Mus. Natural History, Providence, 1994. Named State Tchr. of Yr. Science award R.I., 1992. Office: Mus Natural History Roger William Park Providence RI 02905

SWEENEY, KEVIN MICHAEL, lawyer; b. Westfield, Mass., May 28, 1965; s. Lawrence Arthur and Maureen Theresa (Cavanaugh) S.; m. Karen Elizabeth Marsian, May 15, 1993. BA, U. Mass., 1987; D Law, U. Wis., 1990. Bar: Mass., Wis.; U.S. Dist. Ct. (we. dist.) Wis., U.S. Dist. Ct. Mass. 2d v.p., assoc. gen. counsel Office Gen. Counsel Mass. Mut. Life Ins. Co., Springfield, Mass., 1993—2002; 2d v.p. law, asst. sec. and chief compliance officer Mass Mutual Internat., Inc., Springfield, 1996—2002, Luxembourg, 1996—2002, also bd. dirs., 1999—2002; chief compliance officer Mass Mutual Internat. Bermuda, Ltd., Hamilton, 1996—2001; counsel, asst. sec. MML Reinsurance Bermuda, Hamilton, 1996-97; corp. sec. Mass Mutual Found. for Hartford, Inc., Hartford, Conn., 1996—2002, also bd. dirs., 2000—; asst. sec. Mass Mutual Holding Co., 1998-2000, C. M. Life Ins. Co., 1998-2000, MML Bay State Life Ins. Co., 1998-2000, Mass. Mutual Benefits Mgmt., Inc., 1998-2000; asst. clk. Mass Mutual Holding MSC, Inc., 1999-2000; corp. sec. MassMutual Trust Co., 2000—01; v.p. recruiting and opers., corp. human resources MassMutual Fin. Group, 2002—. Assoc. Bulkley, Richardson and Gelinas, Springfield, 1990-93; rsch. asst. U. Wis., Madison, 1988-90; law clk. Wis. Dept. Justice, Madison, 1989; project asst. and law clk. Legal Assistance to Institutionalized Persons, Madison, 1988-89, adj. prof. of law, We. New Eng. Coll. Sch. of Law, 2002—. Author: (paper) Restructuring Insurance Companies Through Mergers, Acquisitions and Other Affiliations, ABA Ann. Meeting, 1999; rsch. asst.: (book) Tournament of Lawyers, 1991. Legal counsel, bd. dirs., dir. fin. Mass. Hugh O'Brian Youth Leadership Found., Inc., Boston, 1991-93; atty. advisor Mass. Bar Assn. H.S. Mock Ct. Competition, Springfield, 1990-91; mem. Dem. Town Com., West Springfield, 1990-91. Tech. sgt. ANG, 1983-91. Mem. ABA (young lawyers divsn. in-house counsel com., planning bd. mem. 1994-96), State Bar Wis., Phi Kappa Phi. Democrat. Roman Catholic. Avocations: travel, reading, listening to music. Office: Mass Mut Financial Group 1295 State St Springfield MA 01111-0001

SWEENEY, MICHAEL ANDREW, newspaper editor; b. York, Pa., Nov. 27, 1948; s. Felix William and Deuris C. (Ehehalt) S.; m. Linda Carol Gillam, Nov. 20, 1976; children: Barbara Catherine, Matthew Allan. BA in Communication Art, Seton Hall U., 1972; MA in Polit. Sci., Rutgers U., 1981. Reporter The Courier-News, Bridgwater, N.J., 1972-75, asst. night editor, 1975-77, night editor, 1977-78, nat. editor, 1978-79, asst. news editor, 1980-81; news editor The Advocate Southern Conn. Newspapers Inc., Stamford, Conn., 1981-83, exec. news editor, 1983-85, asst. mng. editor, 1985-88; editorial page editor Greenwich Time/So. Conn. Newspapers, Inc., 1988—, columnist, 1991—. Adviser comms. dept. Norwalk C.C. Contbr. articles to profl. jours. Roman Catholic. Avocations: gardening, computers, Mercedes-Benz automobiles. Office: Greenwich Time 20 E Elm St Greenwich CT 06830-6573

SWEENEY, MIKE, professional baseball player; b. Orange, Calif., July 22, 1973; Baseball player Kansas City (Mo.) Royals, 1995—. Office: Kansas City Royals PO Box 419969 Kansas City MO 64141-6969

SWEENEY, PHILLIP PETER, poet; b. Towanda, Pa., Apr. 3, 1949; s. Robert Gerard and Theresa Alva Sweeney; children: Adam, Seth. BA, SUNY-Binghamton, 1973, MS in Edn., 1993. Cert. tchr., N.Y. Lang. arts instr. St. Michael's Sch., Memphis, 1983-84; tchr. poetry/creative writing alternative lit. programs State of N.Y., 1984-92; arts-in-edn. programs tchr. So. Tier Inst. for the Arts in Edn., 1984-92; tchr. poetry in the schs. program Imagination Celebration, Broome County, N.Y., 1984-92; instr. English and composition Afton (N.Y.) Ctrl. H.S., 1996—. Performance poet/writer Poets & Writers, Inc., 1984—. Author: Dark Shadows for a Thousand Points of Light, 1998; lead singer/songwriter: Truman's Cabin, 1984—. Bd. dirs., sec. So. Tier Ind. Living Ctr., Binghamton, 1995-96; drama dir. Afton Ctrl. H.S., 1997-98; SADD advisor, Afton, 1997—; founder, dir. SADD Care Cmty. Coffeehouse, 1997—; lectr. in field. Recipient Profl. Writing Residency, Blue Mtn. Ctr., 1984; Broome County Arts Coun. Career Enhancement grantee, 1990, United Cultural Fund grantee, 1996. Roman Catholic. Avocations: chess, music and guitar. Home: 137 Shamrock Pl #2 Harpursville NY 13787

SWEENEY, RANDALL W. aerospace transportation executive; BS in Edn., Ohio State U., 1972, MA in Pub. Adminstrn and Orgnl. Develop., 1977. Spl. asst. to regional adminstr. region V U.S. Small Bus. Adminstrn., 1980—81; pres. Def. and Aerospace Internat., Inc., Arlington, Va. Mem. Army Sci. Bd., Va.; dir., co-founder Nat. Ctr. Govt. Contracting, 1982—83; v.p. mktg. and contract adminstrn. Ferrotherm Co., Inc., 1985—. Mem. Ohio Elections Commn., Columbus, 1979—80; chmn. Ohio Bd. Tax Appeals, 1984—99. Mem.: Nat. Small Bus. Govt. Contractors Assn. (v.p. 1984—86, chmn. govt. affairs com. 1984—86). Office: SAAL-ASB Ste 11500 2511 Jefferson Davis Hwy Arlington VA 22202-3911

SWEENEY, RICHARD JAMES, economics educator; b. San Diego, Jan. 13, 1944; s. John Joseph and Catherine Scott (Spahr) S.; m. Joan Long, June 19, 1965; children: Robin Scott, Erin Michaela. BA, UCLA, 1965; PhD, Princeton U., 1972. Acting asst. prof. econs. UCLA, 1968-71; asst. prof. Tex. A&M U., College Station, 1971-73; dep. dir. office of internat. monetary research U.S. Dept. Treasury, Washington, 1973-77; Charles M. Stone prof. econs. and fin. Claremont (Calif.) McKenna Coll., 1977-89, chmn. dept. econs., 1987-89; Bolton Sullivan & Thomas A. Dean chair internat. fin. Georgetown U., Washington, 1989—. Vis. assoc. prof. econs. U. Va., Charlottesville, 1975; vis. prof. bus. adminstrn. Dartmouth Coll., Hanover, N.H., 1979; vis. prof. fin. Gothenburg (Sweden) Sch. Econs., 1991—. Author: A Macro Theory with Micro Foundations, 1974, Principles of Microeconomics, Macroeconomics, 1980, Wealth Effects and Monetary Theory, 1988, Profit-Making Speculation in Foreign Exchange Markets, 1992; author, editor: Capital Control in Emerging Market Economies, 1997, Exchange-Rate Policies for Emerging Market Economies, 1999; contbr. articles to profl. jours. Fellow NSF 1966-68, Woodrow Wilson Found. 1965; grantee Gen. Electric Found., 1980, Mid.-Am. Found., 1987, Earhart Found., 1988. Mem. Western Econ. Assn. (editor Econ. Inquiry jour. 1984-96), Am. Econ. Assn., Am. Fin. Assn., Western Fin. Assn., Phi Beta Kappa. Democrat. Avocations: writing, weightlifting, walking, aerobics. Office: McDonough Sch Bus Georgetown U Washington DC 20057-0001 E-mail: sweeneyr@georgetown.edu.

SWEENEY, ROBERT DAVID, communications engineer; b. Nashville, Aug. 28, 1921; s. John Henry and A. Letty (Bateman) S.; m. Mildred Kathleen Rose, July 14, 1941 (dec. Aug. 1973); children: Robert, Mary, Barbara; m. Marie Ruby Simmons, Dec. 14, 1974; children: Rick, Alan, Robbie. Comm. Engr., Capitol Radio Engring. Inst., Washington, 1942; Elec. Engr., U.S. Mil. Acad., West Point, N.Y., 1950. Commd. U.S. Army, 1951, advanced through grades to col., 1969; comm. and electronic instr. Norwich U., Norfield, Vt., 1948-50; asst. instr. U.S. Army Mil. Acad., West Point, 1950-51; bn. comdr., asst. divsn. signal officer 1st Armored Divsn., Ft. Hood, Tex., 1951-52; commdg. officer 59th Signal Support Co., 1952-53; radio engr. Japan Signal Bn., 1953-56; signal officer 61st Anti Aircraft Artillery Groups, Milw., 1956-60; officer in charge Down Island Comm. Systems, U.S. Comm. Detachment, Taiwan, 1960-61; comm.-electronics officer 28th N.Am. Air Defense Command, Hamilton AFB, Calif., 1961-64; chief Pacific field office U.S. Army Strategic Comm. Command, Okinawa, 1964-67; post signal officer The Infantry Ctr., Ft. Benning, Ga., 1967-68; dep. dir. Comm. Systems Engring. Mgmt. Agy., 1st Signal Brigade, Vietnam, 1968-69; dept. dir. comm.-electronics dept. U.S. Army Infantry Sch., Ft. Benning, 1969-73; congl. aide-dist. rep. Congressman 3rd Dist. Ga., Washington, 1974-83. Counselor Boy Scouts Am., Ft. Riley, Kans., 1950—. Decorated Legion of Merit with oak leaf cross, Bronze Star with 3 oak leaf crosses, Air Medal, Purple Heart. Mem. Assn. Elec. Engrs., Armed Forces Comm.-Elec. Assn. (charter pres. 1968, merit award), Fraternal Order Eagles, Odd Fellows. Democrat. Baptist. Avocations: amateur radio, chess, football, baseball, tennis. Home: 4828 Allegheny Dr Columbus GA 31907-1734 E-mail: sweeneyrd@hotmail.com.

SWEENEY, THOMAS FREDERICK, lawyer; b. Detroit, Feb. 10, 1943; s. Harold Eugene and Marion Genevieve (Lunz) S.; m. Susan Carol Horn, Dec. 27, 1968; children: Sarah Elizabeth, Neal Thomas. AB, U. Mich., 1965, JD, 1968. Bar: Mich. 1968, U.S. Dist. Ct. (ea. dist.) Mich, 1968, U.S. Tax Ct. 1979, U.S. Supreme Ct. 1985. Assoc. Fischer, Franklin, Ford, Simon & Hogg, Detroit, 1969—73, ptnr., 1974—85, Houghton, Potter, Sweeney & Brenner, Detroit, 1986—95; mem. Clark Hill, Birmingham, Mich., 1995—, mem. exec. com., 1999—2002. Spkr. Inst. CLE; guest lectr. U. Mich. Law Sch., 2001-03. Contbr. articles to legal jours. Mem. Birmingham (Mich.) Charter Rev. Commn., 1977; bd. dirs. Cmty. House Assn., 1990—98, pres., 1993—95; trustee Baldwin Pub. Libr., Birmingham, 1981—, pres., 2001—03. Fellow Mich. State Bar Found.; mem. ABA, Oakland County Bar Assn. (chmn. taxation com. 1988-89), Forest Hills Swim Club (pres. 1985-87). Roman Catholic. Home: 1493 Buckingham Ave Birmingham MI 48009-5866 Office: Clark Hill 255 S Old Woodward Ave Ste 301 Birmingham MI 48009-6182 E-mail: tsweeney@clarkhill.com.

SWEENEY, THOMAS JOSEPH, JR., lawyer; b. NYC, Oct. 29, 1923; s. Thomas Joseph and Johanna M. (Flynn) S.; m. Robin Virginia Thwaites, May 30, 1947; children: Thomas Joseph, III, Deidre Ann. BA, N.Y. U., 1947; JD, Columbia U., 1949. Bar: N.Y. 1949. Assoc. in law Columbia U. Law Sch., 1949-50; assoc. Cravath, Swaine & Moore, N.Y.C., 1950-62; with Morgan Guaranty Trust Co. N.Y., 1962-89, v.p., 1965-76, sr. v.p., sr. trust officer, 1976-89, chmn. instl. trust and investment com., 1989-99; ptnr. Decker, Hubbard, Welden & Sweeney, N.Y.C. Bd. dirs. W.R. Kenan Fund. Trustee Pinkerton Found., Jean and Louis Dreyfus Found. 2d lt. USAAF, 1943-45. Mem. N.Y. State Bar Assn. Democrat. Roman Catholic. Home: 525 Teaneck Rd Ridgefield Park NJ 07660-1100 Office: Decker Hubbard Welden & Sweeney 420 Lexington Ave New York NY 10170

SWEENY, ANNE, broadcast executive; m. Philip Miller; 2 children. BA, Coll. New Rochelle; EdM, Harvard U. Sr. v.p. program enterprises Nickelodeon/Nick at Nite; chmn., CEO FX Networks, Inc., 1993; pres. Disney Channel, exec. v.p. Disney/ABC Cable Networks, 1996, pres., 1998—, Disney Channel, 1998—; pres. ABC Cable Networks Group, pres. Disney Channel Worldwide Walt Disney Co., Burbank, Calif., 2000—. Bd. dirs. Spl. Olympics, Walter Kaitz Found. Recipient Advocate Leader award, So. Calif. chpt. Women in Cable and Telecomms., 1998, STAR award, Am. Women in Radio and TV, 1995. Mem.: Women in Cable and Telecomms. (founder, Exec. of Yr. 1994, Woman of Yr. 1997). Office: 3800 W Alameda Ave Burbank CA 91505

SWEENY, ARTHUR, III, realtor; b. N.Y.C., Nov. 11, 1933; BA, Hobart Coll., 1956. V.p. Braisin, Porter & Wheelock, N.Y.C., 1958-82; v.p., dir. William J. Dwyer & Co., N.Y.C., 1982-87, Cross & Brown Co., N.Y.C., 1987-92. Home: 83 Landing Ave Colchester VT 05446-6955

SWEENY, STEPHEN JUDE, academic administrator; b. N.Y.C., Sept. 15, 1943; s. Herbert Vincent and Isabel Mary (Dolan) S.; m. Barbara Mary Stasz, Aug. 7, 1976. BA in Spanish, Cath. U., 1966; MA in Theology, Manhattan Coll., 1971, MA in Counseling Psychology, 1976; PhD, NYU, 1991. Prin. Incarnation Elem. and Jr. High Sch., N.Y.C., 1969-73; dir. campus ministry Manhattan Coll., N.Y.C., 1973-76; asst. to provost Coll. of New Rochelle, N.Y., 1976-78, mem. edn. dept., 1976—, exec. asst. to pres., 1978-80, v.p. for planning, 1980-81, sr. v.p., 1981-97, pres., 1997—. Bd. trustees exec. com., com. on fin. and adminstrn. Commn. Ind. Colls. and Univs.; bd. trustees, chmn. acad. affairs com., chmn., student affairs com. Coll. St. Elizabeth; bd. trustees strategic planning com., mem. com. LaSalle Acad., Network of Sacred Heart Schs.; membership com. Network of Sacred Heart Schs.; bd. dirs. Neylan Commn. Colls. and Univs., Cardinal McCloskey Svcs., Women's Coll. Coalition. Mem.: Soc. Friendly Sons St. Patrick (N.Y.C.), Soc. Friendly Sons of St. Patrick (Westchester), Sovereign Mil. Order of Malta (mem. com.), Knights of the Holy Sepulchre. Roman Catholic. Office: The College of New Rochelle 29 Castle Pl New Rochelle NY 10805-2338

SWEET, ALLAN JAY, lawyer; b. Kansas City, Aug. 11, 1947; s. Phillip and Helen Dorothy (Friedman) S.; m. Bonnie Jean Levin, May 30, 1976; children— Stacy M., Allison K. B.B.A., U. Mich., 1968, J.D., 1973. Bar: Ill. 1973, Fla. 1974. Assoc. McDermott, Will & Emery, Chgo., 1973-77, Miami, Fla., 1977-78; assoc. Schiff, Hardin & Waite, Chgo., 1978-80, ptnr., 1980—; trustee Am. Equity Investment Trust, Cedar Rapids, Iowa, 1981. Editorial advisor Trusts & Estates mag., 1981. Contbr. articles to mags. Served with U.S. Army, 1979-81. Mem. Chgo. Estate Planning Council. Republican. Jewish. Club: Union League (Chgo.). Home: 1327 N Sutton Pl Chicago IL 60610-2007 Office: AMLI Residential 125 S Wacker Dr Ste 3100 Chicago IL 60606*

SWEET, ARNOLD LAWRENCE, industrial engineering educator; b. N.Y.C., Mar. 23, 1935; s. Philip and Jennie (Friedman) S.; m. Janet Ailsa Rae, Aug. 3, 1959; children: David Andrew, Ian Richard. BME, CCNY, 1956; MSME, U. Md., 1959; PhD in Engring. Sci., Purdue U., 1964. Mech. engr. Emerson Rsch. Labs., Washington, 1956-58, U.S. Naval Rsch. Lab., Washington, 1958-60; instr. engring. scis. Purdue U., West Lafayette, Ind., 1960-64, asst. prof. engring. scis., 1964-68, assoc. prof. engring. scis., 1968-73, assoc. prof. indsl. engring., 1973-80, prof. indsl. engring., 1980—. Cons. Midwest Applied Sci. Corp., West Lafayette, 1964-67, Landis and Gyr Metering Co., Lafayette, Ind., 1985, Caterpillar Tractor Co., Morton, Ill., 1986, Autoliv N.A., Inc., Indpls., 1993, 98. Contbg. author: Handbook of Industrial Engineering, 1982, 92; contbr. articles to profl. jours. Dir. 10K race Tippecanoe chpt. Am. Diabetes Assn., Lafayette, 1987-91. Ford Found. fellow, 1960-63; vis. rsch. fellow Dept. of Environment, U.K., 1970-71; univ. resident rsch. assoc. USAF Systems Command, Sch. Aerospace Medicine, San Antonio, 1979-80. Fellow Inst. Indsl. Engrs. (chpt. pres. 1983-84, 99-2001); mem. Am. Soc. Quality, Alpha Pi Mu, Omega Rho, Tau Beta Pi. Democrat. Avocations: jogging, collecting Purdue U. postcards and ephemera. Office: Purdue U Sch Indsl Engring 315 N Grant St West Lafayette IN 47907-2023 Office Phone: 765-494-5424.

SWEET, CHARLES WHEELER, retired executive recruiter; b. Chgo., June 11, 1943; s. Charles Wheeler and Alice Naomi (Grush) Sweet; m. Joy Ann Weidernmiller, Mar. 23, 1968; children: Charles III, Kimberly Ann, Rebecca Townsend. AB, Hamilton Coll., Clinton, N.Y., 1965; MBA, U. Chgo., 1968. Salesman Procter & Gamble, Chgo., 1965-67; with pers. Ford, Dearborn, Mich., 1968-69, R.R. Donnelley, Chgo., 1969-72; exec. recruiter A.T. Kearney Inc. Exec. Search, Chgo., 1972—87, pres., 1987-99, chmn., 2000—01; ret., 2001. Bd. dirs. Gt. Bank Algonquin. Chmn. bd. dirs., exec. advisor No. Ill. U., 1979—88, bd. dirs. Rehab. Inst. Chgo., 1987—. Mem.: Assn. Exec. Search Cons., Barrington Hills Country Club (bd. dirs. 1993—96). Avocations: tennis, bridge. Home: 92 Meadow Hill Rd Barrington IL 60010-9601

SWEET, HARVEY, theatrical set designer, lighting designer; b. Detroit, Oct. 27, 1943; s. Sam and Rose Sweet; m. Susan Perrett, Mar. 16, 1964 (div. Mar. 1975); children: Deborah Anne, Rebecca Lynn, Jason Aaron; m. Patricia Ravn, Sept. 9, 1978 (div. July 1987). BS, Ea. Mich. U., 1965; MS, U. Wis., 1967, PhD, 1974. Instr. U. N.D., Grand Forks, 1967-69; asst. prof. Boise (Idaho) State Coll., 1972-73; instr. U. Wis., Madison, 1973-74; prof. of theater arts U. No. Iowa, Cedar Falls, 1974-89; dir. lighting Landmark Entertainment Group, L.A. and Tokyo, 1989-91; cons. Advanced Tech., Tokyo, 1991; tech. writer Walt Disney Imagineering, Glendale, Calif., 1992; project mgr., sr. designer, sr. estimator, tech. writer Tru Roll, Inc., Glendale, Calif., 1993-99; project mgr. estimator tech. sales LVH Entertainment Sys., Oxnard, Calif., 1999—2002, mgr. theatrical rigging divsn., 2002—03, v.p. rigging systems, 2003—04, v.p. installation sys. and sales, 2004—. Owner, operator Sweet Studios Theatrical Equipment, Cedar Falls, 1981-89; dir. theater tech. and design U. No. Iowa, 1974-87; mem. tech. stds. working group Entertainment, Svcs and Tech. Assn., 2002—, mem. rigging cert. working group, 2002— mem.fire safety curtain standards working group. Author: Graphics for the Performing Arts, 1982, Handbook of Scenery, Properties and Lighting I and II, 1988, 2nd edit., 1995, The Complete Book of Drawing for the Theatre, 1995; scenic designer Summer Repretory Theatre, 1988, Timberlake Playhouse, 1988-89; lighting designer, scenic designer, tech. dir. various coll. theatrical prodns., 1964-89; themed lighting designer Sanrio Puroland, Tokyo, 1989, exec. dir. lighting, 1990. Mem. U.S. Inst. for Theatre Tech. (vice commr. 1979-81, commr. 1981-87, mem. graphic stds. bd. 1979-86, evaluation comm. 1983-88, mem. publs. com. 1986-89, bd. dirs. 1989). Avocations: travel, cooking. Office: LVH Entertainment Sys 300 Irving Dr Oxnard CA 93030 Office Phone: 805-278-4584. E-mail: cre8tivguy@aol.com.

SWEET, HOWARD A. lawyer; b. Madison, Wis., June 6, 1945; s. Harry M. and Esther (Mullin) Sweet. BA, U. Wis., 1967; JD, Harvard U., 1970. Bar: Wis. 1970, U.S. Dist. Ct. (we. dist.) Wis. 1970. Assoc. LaFollette & Sinykin, Madison, 1970—73, ptnr., 1973—97; sr. counsel Hurley, Burish & Milliken SC, Madison, 1998—. Bd. dirs. Kids Fund, Inc., 1973—98, Meriter Found., Inc., Jewish Social Svcs. Madison, 1998. Mem.: Dane County Bar Assn., State Bar Wis. Office: Hurley Burish & Milliken SC 301 N Broom St Madison WI 53703-2010

SWEET, JAMES BROOKS, oral and maxillofacial surgeon; b. Darlington, Pa., Mar. 28, 1934; s. Lufay Anderson and Margaret Jean (Brooks) S.; m. N. Gayle Laird, Oct. 11, 1958; children: James Brooks II, Laird Anderson, Bradley Stephen. BA, Lafayette Coll., 1956; DDS, U. Pitts., 1964, DMD, 1974; MS in Dentistry, NYU, 1975. Aviation flight officer USNR, 1957; advanced through grades to dir. USPHS; rotating intern USPHS Hosp., Staten Island, N.Y., 1964-65, resident oral and maxillofacial surgery, 1970-73; chief dept. dentistry Fed. Correctional Inst. Hosp., Ashland, Ky., 1965-67, Terminal Island, Calif., 1967-70; chief oral and maxillofacial surgery Clin. Ctr. NIH, Bethesda, Md., 1973-80; chief dept. dentistry and oral and maxillofacial surgery USPHS Hosp., Nassau Bay, Tex., 1980-81; ret. USPHS, 1981; assoc. prof. dept. oral and maxillofacial surgery Health Sci. Ctr. U. Tex., Houston, 1981-84, prof., 1984—95, prof. emeritus, 2002—. Asst. clin. prof. med. br. U. Tex., Galveston, 1980-2002, prof. emeritus, 2002–; assoc. attending physicianBen Taub Gen. Hosp., Houston, 1984-95; cons. oral and maxillofacial surgery self study guides, Stoma Press, Seattle, 1983-; cons. VA Hosp., Houston, 1986-. Contbr. articles to profl. jours.; editorial reviewer: Annals of Internal Medicine, 1977-. Coach basketball Olney (Md.) Boys Club, 1975-80; mem. aim rev. Tex. area USCG, 1981-82. Lt. USNR, 1957-64. Fellow Am. Assn. Oral and Maxillofacial Surgeons; mem. Tex. Soc. Oral and Maxillofacial Surgeons, Houston Soc. Oral and Maxillofacial Surgeons, Am. Assn. Dental Schs., USPHS Profl. Assn., NIH Sailing Club, Omicron Kappa Upslion (pres. Mu Mu chpt. 1993-94). Presbyterian. Avocations: sailing, swimming, real estate, travel. Home: 2013 Sweet St Navarre FL 32566-3042 Office: U Tex Health Sci Ctr 6516 John Freeman St Houston TX 77030-3402 E-mail: jbsweet16@msn.com.

SWEET, JERRY JAMES, clinical psychologist; b. East Stroudsburg, Pa., Dec. 1, 1951; s. Waldo Thomas and Betty Jane (Flory) S.; children: Christopher, Jamie. BS with distinction, Pa. State U., 1973; MS, Western Wash. U., 1975; PhD, U. S.D., 1979. Lic. clin. psychologist, Ill.; diplomate Am. Bd. Profl. Psychology in Clin. Neuropsychology and Clin. Psychology. Sr. psychologist pain ctr., neuropsychologist dept. psychiatry Ill. Masonic Med. Ctr., Chgo., 1979-86; dir. psychol. evaluation and testing svc. Evanston (Ill.) Hosp., 1986-89, co-dir. Ctr. Psychol. Evaluation and Learning, 1989-91, dir. neuropsychology svc., 1991—2002, vice chmn. psychiatry, 2002—. Clin. assoc. prof. psychiatry med. sch. Northwestern U., adj. assoc. prof., 1982-2000, prof. psychiatry, 2002—, assoc. dir. clin. tng., 1986—; neuropsychology cons. Cook County Hosp., Chgo., 1983-87, 93—; lectr. psychology Loyola U., Chgo., 1983, 85, 87, 91; neuropsychol. seminar instr. Ill. State Psychiat. Inst., Chgo., 1986. Co-editor Handbook of Clin. Psychology in Med. Settings, 1991; co-author: Psychological Assessment in Medical Settings, 1997; editor: Forensic Neuropsychology, 1999, The Clinical Neuropsychologist, 2003—; founding assoc. editor Jour. Clin. Psychology in Med. Settings, 1993—; contbr. articles to profl. jours. and chpts. to profl. texts. Fellow Nat. Acad. Neuropsychology; mem. APA, Internat. Neuropsychol. Soc., Assn. Postdoctoral Tng. Programs in Clin. Neuropsychology, Am. Acad. Clin. Neuropsychology (bd. dirs.). Avocations: guitar, music. Office: ENH Med Group 909 Davis St Ste 160 Evanston IL 60201

SWEET, LYNN D. journalist; b. Chgo., May 15, 1951; d. Jason and Ione Dover S. AB, U. Calif., Berkeley, 1973; MS in Journalism, Northwestern U., Evanston, Ill., 1975. Reporter Independent-Register, Libertyville, Ill., 1975-76, Chgo. Sun-Times, 1976-93, polit. writer, bur. chief Washington bur., 1993—; bur. chief Wash. bur. Chgo. Sun Times. Bd. dirs. Northwestern Univ.'s Medill Sch. of Journalism Alumni Bd., 1990-93. Office: Chgo Sun Times 1206 National Press Building Washington DC 20045-2200

SWEET, MARGARET ELLEN, writer; b. Elizabethtown, Ky., Dec. 28, 1965; d. Lonnie Walter and Edna Mae Sweet; children: Kenneth Evan, Zachary Lewis Powell. Assoc. Degree, Foley-Belsaw Instn., 2002. Author 1stbooks Libr., Dowagiac, Mich., 1998—; propr. Maggie's Bus. Support, Dowagiac, 2002—03. Propr. Maggie's Bus. Support, Dowagiac, 1999—. Author: Deadly Cries, 2003; contbr. articles to profl. jours. Student Jehovah's Witness, Lawence, Mich., 1991—2003. Office: Maggies Business Support 108 King St Dowagiac MI 49047 Personal E-mail: sweetmaggielogic@verizon.net. E-mail: maggie.sweet@maggiesbusinesssupport.com.

SWEET, NORMAN BYRON, mathematician, educator; b. St. Johnsville, N.Y., Dec. 18, 1920; s. Norman George and Alberta Stiles Sweet; m. Angelyn Mary Bob Sweet; 1 child, Stephen Lee. BS, Albany State Tchrs. Coll., N.Y., 1957; MS, Rensselaer Poly. Inst., Troy, N.Y., 1962. Gen. sci. tchr. Hackett Jr. H.S., Albany, 1956—57; tchr. physics Hudson Valley Tech. Inst., Troy, NY, 1957—59; prof. math. Hudson Valley C.C., Rensselaer, 1957—64, SUNY,

Oneonta, 1964—95; ret., 1995. Tim and motion study rschr. George S. May, N.Y.C., 1940—50; with Watervliet Arsenal, 1950—57. Author: Math for Poets, 1946. Mem.: Math. Assn. Am. Home: 1 Normal Ave Oneonta NY 13820

SWEET, PHILIP W. K., JR., former banker; b. Mt. Vernon, N.Y., Dec. 31, 1927; s. Philip W.K. and Katherine (Buhl) S.; m. Nancy Frederick, July 23, 1950; children— Sandra H., Philip W.K. III, David A.F. AB, Harvard U., 1950; MBA, U. Chgo., 1957. Pres., dir. The No. Trust Co., Chgo., 1975-81; chmn., chief exec. officer No. Trust Corp., 1981-84. Alderman City of Lake Forest, Ill., 1972-74; vis. com. U. Chgo. Grad. Sch. Bus.; trustee Chgo. Zool. Soc., past chmn. 1988-93; life trustee Rush-Presbyn.-St. Luke's Med. Ctr.; vestryman Episc. Ch., 1971-74, 86-89. Mem. Soc. Colonial Wars (gov. Ill. chpt. 1978-80), Chgo. Sunday Evening Club (trustee, chmn. 1997-2000), Econ. Club, Comml. Club, Chgo. Club, Commonwealth Club (past pres.), Old Elm Club (Highwood, Ill.), Onwentsia Club, Shoreacres Club (past pres. Lake Bluff).

SWEET, ROBERT T. humanities educator; PhD, U. Cin., 1988. Assoc. prof. philosophy Clark State CC, Springfield, Ohio, 1993—. Office: Clark State Community Coll PO Box 570 570 E Leffel Ln Springfield OH 45501 Business E-Mail: sweetr@clarkstate.edu.

SWEET, ROBERT WORKMAN, federal judge; b. Yonkers, N.Y., Oct. 15, 1922; s. James Allen and Delia (Workman) S.; m. Adele Hall, May 12, 1973; children by previous marriage— Robert, Deborah, Ames, Eliza. BA, Yale U., 1944, LL.B., 1948. Bar: N.Y. 1949. Asso. firm Simpson, Thacher & Bartlett, 1948-53; asst. U.S. atty. So. Dist. N.Y., 1953-55; asso. firm Casey, Lane & Mittendorf, 1955-65, partner, 1957-65; counsel Interdepartmental Task Force on Youth and Juvenile Delinquency, 1958-78; dep. mayor City of N.Y., 1966-69; partner firm Skadden, Arps, Slate, Meagher & Flom, N.Y.C., 1970-77; mem. hearing office N.Y.C. Transit Authority, 1975-77; U.S. dist. judge So. Dist. N.Y., N.Y.C., 1978—. Participant USIA Rule of Law Program in Albania, 1991; observer Albanian elections, 1992. Pres. Community Service Soc., 1961-78; trustee Sch. Mgmt. Urban Policy, 1970—, Taft Sch.; vestryman St. Georges Epis. Ch., 1958-63. Served to lt. (j.g.) USNR, 1943-46. Recipient Alumni citation of merit Taft Sch., 1985, various other awards, citations for service as dept mayor N.Y.C. Mem. ABA, Assn. of Bar of City of N.Y., N.Y. Law Inst., N.Y. County Lawyers Assn., State Bar Assn., Am. Legion (comdr. Willard Straight Post) Clubs: Quaker Hill Country, Century Assn., Merchants, Indian Harbor Yacht, Mid City Rep.

SWEET, STUART C. pediatrician; BS in Chemistry with highest distinction, U. Mich., 1981, MD with distinction, PhD, U. Mich., 1989. Resident in pediatrics St. Louis Children's Hosp., 1990-93, fellow in pediatric pulmonology, 1993-96; fellow pediatric pulmonology dept. pediatrics Wash. U. Med. Sch. Mem. physicians adv. com. St. Louis Children's Hosp. Contbr. articles to profl. publs. Burton L. Baker Cancer Rsch. fellowship Mich. Cancer Inst., 1986-87. Mem. Phi Beta Kappa. Office: Wash U Sch Medicine Dept Pediatrics One Children's Pl Saint Louis MO 63110-1093

SWEETING, SHARON HOWE, school librarian, editor; b. Erie, Pa., Apr. 11, 1943; d. Earnest Edward and Helen Miller Howe; m. Lester Howe Sweeting, Aug. 27, 1966. BA AB, Syracuse U., 1971; MLS, Cath. U. Am., 1974. Gift & exch. libr. Smithsonian Instn. Libraries, Washington, 1972—81, asst. to dir. pubs. and exhbns., 1981—83; sec. pub. affairs Office of Amb., Am. Embassy, London, 1983—87; program analyst IRS, Washington, 1987—90, legis. libr., 1990—. Libr./editor Prince George's County Hist. Soc., Glenn Dale, Md., 1989—. Editor: Preservation Quarterly and Hysterical Preservationist. Libr./editor Prince George's County Hist. Soc., Glenn Dale, Md., 1989. Mem.: Hyattsville Preservation Assn. (life; pres. 1999), Beta Phi Mu. Avocation: visiting historic sites in u.s. and europe. Office: Internal Revenue Service 1111 Constitution Avenue NW Washington DC 20224 E-mail: sharon.h.sweeting@irs.gov.

SWEETLAND, LORAINE FERN, librarian, educator; b. Morristown Corners, Vt., Aug. 13, 1933; d. William Eric and Sylbil Bedina (Bailey) Bloomfield; m. Ronald David Sweetland, July 1, 1950; children: Kathy L. (dec.), Dale J. Bettis. BS in Elem. Edn., Columbia Union Coll., 1968; MS in LS, Syracuse U., 1973. Tchr. 1st and 2d grade Beltsville (Md.) Seventh-day Adventist Sch., 1960-67; asst. libr., cataloger Vt. Tech. Coll., Randolph Ctr., 1968-69; middle sch. libr. Barre (Vt.) City Schs., 1970-74; tchg. prin. Cen. Vt. Seventh-day Adventist Sch., Barre, 1974-76, Brooklawn Seventh-day Adventist Sch., Bridgeport, Conn., 1976-81; med. libr. Washington Adventist Hosp., Takoma Park, Md., 1981-85; dir. libr. svcs. Seventh-day Adventists World Hdqs., Silver Spring, Md., 1985-95. Med. libr. cons., Balt., 1983-95; pres. Oasis, 1993-94; tchr. Home Study Internat., Silver Spring, Md., 1995-98, IPS-Info. Problem Solvers, Crossville, Tenn., 1998—. Book reviewer Libr. Jour., 1990-98. Trustee Randolph (Vt.) Pub. Library, 1970-71; sec. Nat. Area Hosp. Council, Washington, 1985; treas. Plateau Food Buying Club, 1999-2004. Mem. Laurel Rotary Club (bull. editor 1990-94). Republican. Avocations: gardening, computers, internet. Personal E-mail: lauriefern@charter.net.

SWEETMAN, BEVERLY YARROLL, physical therapist; b. Phila., Apr. 8, 1939; d. Albert Henry and Theresa (Payne) Yarroll; m. Denman John Sweetman, Apr. 1, 1961; children: Denman Eric, John Albert. BA in Biology, Hood Coll., 1961; cert. phys. therapist, Hahnemann U., 1983. Rsch. technician Mass. Gen. Hosp., Boston, 1961-62, Princeton (N.J.) U., 1965-66; part owner, phys. therapist Pain & Stress Control Ctr., Allentown, Pa., 1983-85; pvt. practice Body Ease Phys. Therapy Ctr., Grants Pass, Oreg., 1985, pvt. practice, pres. Staunton and Charlottesville, Va., 1986—. Developer and co-presenter Total Body Concept Seminars, Total Body Concept Aquatic Workshops; v.p. VMG Med., Staunton, 1988—; cons., co-presenter Lossing Orthop., Mpls., 1985—95; lectr. in field. Fellow Am. Back Soc.; mem. Am. Phys. Therapy Assn. Office: Body Ease Phys Therapy Ctr 542 Walnut Hills Rd Staunton VA 24401-6936 also: 901 Preston Ave Charlottesville VA

SWEETSER, GENE GILLMAN, quality assurance professional, state legislator; b. Burlington, Vt., Apr. 24, 1948; s. Archelaus William and Stella Ruth (Brink) S.; m. Elizabeth Ann Hannett, Apr., 1967 (div. May 1972); 1 child, Analei; m. Susan Williams, Aug. 27, 1978 (div. Feb. 1995); 1 child, Virginia Lucretia. BA Polit. Sci. and Environ. Sci., Johnson State Coll., Vt., 1978; MS in Adminstrn., St. Michael's Coll., Vt., 1993. Maintenance machinist Avdel Internat., Inc., Parsippany, N.J., 1982-84; machine shop supr. Mitec Systems, Inc., Williston, Vt., 1984-84; maintenance supr. Fonda, Inc., Albans, Vt., 1985-88; asst. quality control mgr. Chatham Precision, Hinesburg, Vt., 1988-91; state representative Vt. State Ho. of Reps., 1990—; prodn. control IBM, Essex, Vt., 1992—. Mem. Bd. Civil Authority, Essex, Vt., 1988—, Justice of the Peace, 1988—; mem. com. ways and means Vt. State Ho. of Reps., 1991—. Founder, bd. dirs. paper recycling program Worcester Vol. Fire Dept., 1978-82; founder, bd. dirs. Worcester Film Soc., 1978-82, Worcester Views Newsletter, 1978-82; vice chmn. Ctrl. Ct. Regional Planning Commn., 1980-82; vol. The Holiday Project, 1987-89; coach Essex Youth Soccer, 1988, 89; player agt. for minor league Essex Little League Assn., 1990; v.p. Survivors of Crime, Inc. With USMC, 1969-72, Vt. Army nat. Guard, 1978—. Address: 28 Foster Rd Essex Junction VT 05452-3316

SWEETSER, MARIE-ODILE GAUNY, retired foreign language educator; b. Verdun, Meuse, France, Dec. 28, 1925; arrived in US, 1949; d. Eugene Auguste and Madeleine (Schwab) Gauny; m. Franklin Pratt, Dec. 17, 1955; 1 child, Caroline Gauny Sweetser. Grad., U. Nancy, France, 1945; MA, Bryn Mawr Coll., 1950; PhD, U. Pa., 1956. Instr. Mills Coll., Oakland, Calif., 1957-60; from asst. prof. to assoc. prof. French CUNY, 1960-69; from assoc. prof. to prof. French U. Ill., Chgo., 1969-97, ret., 1997. Adv. bd. Papers on French Seventeenth Century Lit., Paris, Seattle, Tübingen, Germany. Author: Les Conceptions dramatiques de Corneille d'après ses écrits théoriques, 1962, La Dramaturgie de Corneille, 1977, La Fontaine, 1987, Parcours Lafontainien D'Adonis Au Livre XII Des Fables, 2004; contbr. articles to profl. jours. Marcelle Pardé scholar, 1949-50, Newberry Libr. Found. fellow, 1980. Mem. Mouvement Corneille (bd. dirs. 1980-1990), Soc. des Amis de la Fontaine (v.p. 1996—), Ctr. Internat. Rencontres sur le 17th Siecle (bd. dirs. 1991—). Avocations: music, theater. Home: 311 Hirst Ct Lake Bluff IL 60044-2754

SWEETSER, SUSAN W. lawyer, advocate, former state legislator; b. Dec. 13, 1958; d. Robert Joseph and Lucretia Rose (Donnelly) Williams. BA in Polit. Sci./Environ. Adminstrn. with high honors, Johnson (Vt.) State Coll., 1982; JD magna cum laude, Vt. Law Sch., 1985; MBA, U. Pa., 2002. Bar: N.Y. 1986, Vt. 1986, U.S. Dist. Ct. Vt. 1989; CLU, ChFC, CFP. Confidential law clk. Appellate div. N.Y. Supreme Ct., Albany, 1985-86; assoc. Gravel & Shea, Burlington, Vt., 1986-90; atty. Nat. Life Ins. Co., Montpelier, Vt., 1990—2002; mem. Vt. State Senate, 1992-96; 2nd v.p. women's markets MassMutual Fin. Group, Springfield, Mass. Victims rights adv. Essex Junction, Vt., 1980—; adj. prof. bus. law St. Michael's Coll., Winooski, Vt., 1991—, Johnson State Coll., 1995-97; justice of peace Town of Essex, 1991-95; chair judiciary com., 1994-96; mem. Health and Welfare Com.; former mem. Appropriations Com.; mem. Housing and Conservation Trust Fund Study Com., Civil Rights Study Com., Adoption Law Reform Study Com. Author articles on victims rights. Trustee Vt. State Colls., Waterbury, 1979-81, Univ. Health Ctr., 1992-94, bd. dirs.; mem. ethics com. Fanny Allen Hosp., Winooski, Vt., 1989-92; v.p. Lyric Theatre, Burlington, 1989-95; mem. Vt. Rep. State Com., Montpelier, chmn. Rep. State Conv., 1988, 92, 96; founder, pres. Survivors of Crime, Inc. Recipient Achievement award Vt. Law Enforcement Coordinating Com., 1990, Vt. Ctr. for Prevention and Treatment of Sexual Abuse and The Safer Soc. Program, 1991, Nat. recognition for victims rights work The Giraffe Project, 1991, award Nat. Found. for Improvement of Justice, 1993; named 754th Point of Light by former Pres. George Bush, 1992, Am. Heroine Ladies Home Jour., 1991, Legislator of Yr. Nat. Rep. Legislators Assn., 1995, Working Mother Mag. Working Mother of Yr., 1998. Fellow AAUW, Life Mgmt. Inst.; mem. Vt. Bar Assn., N.Y. State Bar Assn., Internat. Assn. Fin. Planners (chmn. legis. affairs Greater Vt. chpt. 1988-91). Roman Catholic. Avocations: skiing, flower gardening, running, camping, horseback riding. Office: 15 Cindy Ln Essex Junction VT 05452-3307

SWEEZY, JOHN WILLIAM, political party official; b. Indpls., Nov. 14, 1932; s. William Charles and Zuma Frances (McNew) S.; BS in Mech. Engring., Purdue U., 1956; MBA, Ind. U., 1958; student Butler U., 1953-54, U. Ga., 1954-55, Ind. Cen. Coll., 1959; m. Carole Suzanne Harman, July 14, 1956; children: John William, Bradley E. Design, test engr. Allison div. GM, Indpls., 1953-57; power sales engr. Indpls. Power & Light Co., 1958-69; dir. pub. works City of Indpls., 1970-72; chmn. Marion County Rep. Cen. Com., 1972—; bd. dirs. Lorco Engring., Indpls., Indpls. Industrial Products, Acme Screw & Mfg., Inc., Telnet, Inc., Landmarks Ltd., Innovative Investment Co. Bd. dirs. Indpls. Humane Soc.; chmn. 11th Dist. Rep. Com., 1970, 73—; chmn. Nat. Assn. Urban Rep. County Chmn.; alt. del. Rep. Nat. Conv., 1968, del., 1972, 76, 80, 84, 88, 92, 96, del., mem. credentials com., 1984, 88; mem. credentials com., 1980, spkr. presenter, 1996; mem. Rep. Nat. Com., 1984—, exec. com., 1984—; mem. Warren Schs. Citizens Screening Com., 1958-72; bd. dirs. Warren Devel. Com. With AUS, 1953-55. Mem. AMA, Mensa, Sigma Iota Epsilon. Home: 2089 S German Church Rd Indianapolis IN 46239-9620 Office: 12 N Delaware St Indianapolis IN 46204-3205

SWEIGART, ANNE B. communications company executive; With D&E Comms., Inc., Ephrata, Pa., 1936—, exec. v.p., 1981—85, CEO, 1985—2001, chmn. bd., pres., 1985—. Mem. bd. dirs. D&E Comms., Inc., 1952—. Office: D&E Communications Inc 124 E Main St Ephrata PA 17522

SWEIS MUSSA, RAFIQ, consular general, activist; b. Amman, Jordan, Aug. 8, 1946; came to U.S., 1971; s. Mussa Abdullah Sweis and Rida Ta'amneh; m. Rehab Bajes Shaktah, Jan. 1, 1974; children: Jeannette, Mirdad, Jackie, Violet. MS in Philosophy, U. Lateran, Vatican, Rome, 1967. Dir. fgn. affairs King Hussein, Amman, Jordon, 1967-71; mem. staff Gulf Oil Co., L.A., 1971-73, oil exec., 1973-74; pvt. practice Albuquerque, 1976-79, Chgo., 1979-84; pres. Fuheis Assn., Chgo., 1990-94. Honorary consul Jordan, Amman, 1994-99; pres., editor-in-chief Fuheis Mag., Chgo., 1990-95. Editor-in-chief Fuheis Assn. Fuheis Mag., 1992-94. Democrat. Roman Catholic. Avocations: speak, read and write 5 languages. Office: Super-Fair Foods Inc 6319 S Vernon Ave Chicago IL 60637-3320

SWENKA, ARTHUR JOHN, retired food products executive; b. Lone Tree, Iowa, Oct. 21, 1937; s. Samuel Joseph and Verdis Mary (Weed) S.; m. Elizabeth Simms, July 1956 (div. 1976); children: Lee Arthur, Timothy John; m. Dixie Jo Meade, Feb. 1982. Gen. equivalency diploma, U.S. Army, 1957. Truck driver U.S. Mail, Oelwein, Iowa, 1958-59, Stiles Supermarket, Oelwein, 1959-60; salesman Hoxie Inst. Wholesale Co., Waterloo, Iowa, 1960-68, slaes mgr., 1968-69, br. mgr., 1969-70, Waterloo and Mason City, Iowa, 1970-72, Nobel Inc., Albuquerque, 1972-81; pres. Nobel/Sysco Food Svcs. Co., Albuquerque, 1981-84, Denver, 1985-95; sr. v.p. ops. Sysco Corp., Houston, 1995—2000. Mem. Dirs. Coun., Houston, 1985—2000. Treas., bd. dirs. Albuquerque Conv. and Visitors Bur., 1975-80; v.p., bd. dirs. Albuquerque Internat. Balloon Festival, 1975-82; bd. dirs. New Day Home for Runaway Children, Albuquerque, 1980-89, Found. St. Joseph's Hosp.; pres. Kodak Internat. Balloon Fiesta, Albuquerque, 2001-03, Manzano Morning Assn., Inc., 2001-. Republican. Roman Catholic. Avocation: hot air ballooning. Home: 30 Twin Peaks Dr Estancia NM 87016-9732

SWENSEN, CLIFFORD HENRIK, JR., psychologist, educator; b. Welch, W.Va., Nov. 25, 1926; s. Clifford Henrik and Cora Edith (Clovis) S.; m. Doris Ann Gaines, June 6, 1948; children— Betsy, Susan, Lisa, Timothy, Barbara BS, U. Pitts., 1949, MS, 1950, PhD, 1952. Diplomate Am. Bd. Profl. Psychology. Instr. U. Pitts., 1951-52; clin. psychologist VA, 1952-54; from asst. prof. to assoc. prof. U. Tenn., Knoxville, 1954-62; assoc. prof. psychology Purdue U., West Lafayette, Ind., 1962-65, prof., 1965—, dir. clin. tng., 1975-85; vice chair U. Senate, 1994-95. Vis. prof. U. Fla., 1968-69, U. Bergen, Norway, 1976-77, 83-84; cons. VA, 1981 White House Conf. on Aging, others; Am. Psychol. Assn.-NSF Disting. Sci. lectr., 1968-69; Fulbright-Hays lectr., Norway, 1976-77 Author: An Approach to Case Conceptualization, 1968; Introduction to Interpersonal Relations, 1973; contbr. chpts. to books, articles to profl. jours. Mem. Ind. Gov.'s Task Force Alzheimer's Disease and Related Senile Dementia, 1998—. Served with USN, 1944-46 Recipient Gordon A. Barrows Meml. award for disting. contributions to psychology, 1990; named to Hall of Fame, Brentwood Pa. H.S., 2001. Fellow APA (pres divsn. cons. psychology 1976-77, Presdl. citation 1999, Cert. achievement 2000), Am. Psychol. Soc., Soc. Personality Assessment, Am. Assn. Applied and Preventive Psychology, Acad. of Clin. Psychology; mem. Midwestern Psychol. Assn., Southeastern Psychol. Assn., Ind. Psychol. Assn., Gerontol. Soc., Sigma Xi, Psi Chi. Republican. Mem. Ch. of Christ Home: 1700 Lindberg Rd # 229 West Lafayette IN 47906 Office: Purdue U Dept Psychol Scis West Lafayette IN 47907 E-mail: cswensen@psych.purdue.edu.

SWENSEN, MARY JEAN HAMILTON, graphic artist; b. Laurens, S.C., June 25, 1910; d. Elvin A. and Della (Brown) Hamilton; m. Oliver Severn Swensen, Mar. 3, 1943 (dec.). BS, Columbia U., 1956, MA, 1960; Cert. Notable, U. Madrid, Spain; postgrad., Ariz. State U., 1974-80. Mem. 1st USSA sr. internat. cross-country skiing team. One person shows at Colo. Fed. Savs. and Loan Assn., Denver, 1978, Panoras Gallery, N.Y.C., 1963; exhibited in group shows at Soc. Western Artist, M.H. de Young Mus., San Francisco, 1964, Nat. Art Roundup, Las Vegas, 1965, Fine Arts Bldg., Colo. State Fair, Pueblo, 1965, Duncan Gallery, Paris, 1974, Colo. Fed. Savs. & Loan Assn., Denver, 1978; graphics arts in pub. collections at Met. Mus. Art, N.Y.C., Nat. Graphic Arts Collection, Smithsonian Inst., Laurens (S.C.) Pub. Libr., N.Y.C. Pub. Libr. Assoc. Libr. of Congress, Archael. Inst. Am., Smithsonian Instn., Johns Hopkins. Recipient Duncan Gallery Prix de Paris, 1974, Notable award M.H. de Young Mus., 1964, YWCA of U.S.A. Gold Medal as most admired athlete of yr., 1977, USSA Nat. Vets. X-Country Racing Team Gold, Silver and Bronze medals for downhill, giant slalom, slalom, and cross-country sr. citizen and vet. races, 1963-79. Mem. Internat. Platform Assn., Am. Mensa, Columbia Club N.Y., Delta Phi Delta.

SWENSON, JAMES REED, physician, educator; b. Utah, Nov. 18, 1933; s. Reed K. and Ruth (Freebairn) S.; m. Sharon Coray, Aug. 21, 1953; children— Richard, Karen, Leslie, David, Julie. Student, Weber Coll., 1952-54; MD, U. Utah, 1959. Intern, then resident in phys. medicine and rehab.; mem. faculty div. phys. medicine and rehab. U. Utah Sch. Medicine, Salt Lake City, chmn. div., 1965—2001, asso. prof., 1970-85, prof., 1985—2002. Chmn. bd. trustees U. Utah Sch. Alcoholism and Other Drug Dependencies; founder Miss Wheelchair Utah Pageant. Served to capt. M.C. U.S. Army, 1960-62. Mem. AMA, Utah State Med. Assn., Am. Acad. Phys. Medicine and Rehab., Assn. Acad. Physiatrists, Am. Spinal Injury Assn., Utah Soc. Phys. Medicine & Rehab., Am. Med. Soc. Alcoholism.

SWENSON, MARK GREGORY, architect; b. Mpls., Nov. 29, 1949; s. Stanley S. and Linnea Marie (Anderson) S.; m. Marcy Gayle Stevenson, Apr. 6, 1974; 1 child, Gregory Peter. B in Environ. Design, U. Minn., 1971, MArch, 1973. Registered architect, Minn., Colo., Ariz., Mich., Ohio, Fla., Ill., Iowa, La., Nev., Tex., N.J., Ga., S.D. Project planner Ellerbe, Inc., Bloomington, Minn., 1972-78; prin., pres. BRW Architects, Inc., Mpls., 1978-96, also bd. dirs.; prin., pres., bd. dirs. Elness Swenson Graham Architects Inc., Mpls., 1996—. Lectr. architecture U. Minn., Mpls., 1974-82. Bd. edn. Minnehaha Acad., Mpls., 2000—04. Evans scholar Western Golf Assn., 1967-71. Mem.: AIA (lectr. profl. devel. 1983—87, Minn. bd. dirs. 2001—, pres. Mpls. chpt. 2002), Urban Land Inst., Lambda Alpha. Home: 5501 Dever Dr Edina MN 55424-1641 Office: Elness Swenson Graham Architects Inc 500 Washington Ave S Minneapolis MN 55415-1130 Office Phone: 612-373-4625. E-mail: mark.swenson@esgarch.com.

SWENSON, RICHARD ALLEN, business owner, animal trainer; b. Willmar, Minn., Dec. 1, 1950; s. LeRoy Oswald Boe and Delores G. (Malghist) S.; children: Kristen, Richard Andrew, Kevin. Author: Secrets of Long Distance Sled Dog Racing. Treas. Pride, Alaska, 1993—. Recipient 1st pl. Iditarod, 1977, 79, 80, 81, 91 among others. Office: Denali Sled Dog Tours PO Box 86 Denali National Park AK 99755-0086

SWENSON, SUE, foundation administrator, former health and education administrator; married; 3 children. BA, MA, U. Chgo.; MBA, U. Minn. Mktg. mgr. Barr Engring., Minn. Heart and Lund Inst., U. Minn.; commr. Adminstrn. on Developmental Disabilities, 1998—2001; exec. dir. Joseph P. Kennedy Jr. Foundation, Washington, 2001—. Cons. subcom. on disability policy U.S. Senate, Washington. Fellow Joseph P. Kennedy Jr. Found., 1996. Office: Joseph P Kennedy Jr Found 1325 G St NW Ste 500 Washington DC 20005

SWENSON, TAMI CHARLOTTE, research analyst; b. St. Croix Falls, Wis., Dec. 30, 1969; d. Stuart and Charlotte S. BS, Carroll Coll., 1992; MA, Tex. A&M U., 1996. Rsch. assoc. Ctr. Demographic and Socioecon. Rsch. and Edn., College Station, 1998—2002; data coord. Ctr. for Advanced Study of Child Welfare, Sch. Social Work, U. Minn., Mpls., 2003—. Rsch. paper panelist Midwest Polit. Sci. Annual Meeting, 1995, So. Rural Sociology Annual Meetings, 2001; presenter in field. Author: monographs; editl. asst. Jour. Politics, 1993; contbr. numerous articles to profl. jours. Mem. Our Saviour's Luth. Ch., Bryan, Tex., 1992-2001. Younger scholar rsch. grantee NEH, 1990, Food Assistance Rsch. grantee So. Rural Devel. Ctr. USDA, 1999, travel grantee joint internat. activities Brit. Acad., 1999. Mem. Am. Polit. Sci. Assn. (rsch. paper panelist annual meetings 1999-2000), Am. Sociol. Assn. (rsch. paper panelist annual meetings 1997-2000), Internat. Soc. Advancement of Socioecons. (rsch. paper panelist 1998-99). Avocations: gardening, politics, needlecrafts. Office: U Minn Sch Social Work Saint Paul MN 55108

SWENSSON, EARL SIMCOX, architect; b. Nashville, July 28, 1930; s. Earl Ebenezer and Viola Lazelle (Simcox) Swensson; m. Suzanne Dickenson, June 6, 1953; children: Krista, Lin, Kurt. BS in Bldg. Design, Va. Poly. Inst. and State U., 1952, MSArch, 1953, U. Ill., 1955. Registered 28 states. Founder, prin. Earl Swensson Assocs., Inc., Nashville, 1961—. Adj. prof. Va. Poly. Inst. and State U., Blacksburg, 1971—72, Auburn U., 1976—83; lectr. in field; apptd. chairholder Jennings and Rebecca Jones Chair of Excellence in Urban and Regional Planning, Mid. Tenn. State U., 1999. Contbr. articles to profl. jours.; author (with Richard L. Miller): (books) New Directions in Hospital and Healthcare Facility Design, 1995; author: (book) Hospital and Healthcare Facility Design 2d edit., 2002. Mem. arch. program adv. coun. Auburn U., 1990—94; bd. dirs. Metro Arts Commn., 1979—86; Middle Tenn. Health Systems (pres. 1972) AIA, 1973—78; Leadership Nashville Alumni Groups, 1984—; bd. advisors U. Tenn. Sch. Arch., 1982, chmn., 1985—88. Named Outstanding Nashvillian of Yr., Downtown Kiwanis Club, 1992, One of Top 100 Alumni of Greatest Distinction Throughout 128-yr. History, Va. Poly. Inst. and State U., 2001; recipient Jefferson award, Am. Inst. Pub. Svc. (Nashville chpt.), 1985. Fellow: AIA. Presbyterian. Achievements include patents for on systamodule for pharmacies. Office: Earl Swensson Assocs 2100 W End Ave Ste 1200 Nashville TN 37203-5239

SWENSSON, EVELYN DICKENSON, conductor, composer, librettist; b. Woodstock, Va., Sept. 18, 1928; d. Glenn Gilmer and Evelyn Christine (Ring) Dickenson; m. Sigurd Simcox Swensson, June 9, 1949; children: Lisë, Karen, Erik, Jon. Cert. in piano, Ward-Belmont Coll., 1946; BA in Piano and Voice, Hollins Coll., 1949; MusM, West Chester U., 1972. Condr. Aldersgate Meth. Ch., Wilmington, Del., 1969—2002, Brandywiners Ltd., Kennett Sq., Pa., 1973—2004, Opera Del., Wilmington, 1974—, Bi-Centennial Chorus, Wilmington, 1976; guest condr. Del. Symphony Orch., Wilmington, 1977; condr. Ardensingers, Wilmington, 1978-80; condr. 200th Anniversary Meth. Ch. Am., Balt., 1984. V.p. Opera for Youth Inc.; dir. family opera theater Opera Del., Wilmington, 1974—. Condr.: inaugural concert for Gov. P.S. duPont IV, 1977, Sleeping Beauty (Respighi), 1977, The Zoo (Sullivan and Rowe), 1980, The Lion, the Witch and the Wardrobe (John McCabe), 1980, celebration of Swedes Landing, 1988, The Boy Who Grew Too Fast (Menotti), 1982, Charlotte's Web (Strouse), 1989, A Wrinkle in Time (Larsen), 1992, composer, condr.: The Enormous Egg, 1993, The Adventure of Beatrix Potter, 1994, The Jungle Book, 1995, Anne of Green Gables, 1996, The Homecoming, 1997, The Legend of Redwall Abbey, 1998, All Through the Night, 1999, The Trumpet of the Swan, 2000, The Mixed-Up Files of Mrs. Basil E. Frankweiler, 2002, Billy Lee's Washington, 2003, The Secret of NIMH, 2004. Recipient W. W. Laird Music award, Opera Del., Wilmington, 1987, Internat. Reading Coun. Literacy award, 1989, Disting. Alumna award, West Chester U., 1989, 5 composition awards, Nat. League Am. Pen Women, 2000, Outstanding Svc. award, Nat. Opera Assn., 2004. Mem.: Am. Guild Organists (choir master). Home: 166 Heyburn Rd Chadds Ford PA 19317

SWERDLOVE, DOROTHY LOUISE, librarian, consultant; b. NYC, Jan. 4, 1928; d. Louis and Belle (Cohn) S. BA, Swarthmore Coll., 1948; MSL.S., Columbia U., 1961. Rsch. asst. Fed. Res. Bank N.Y., N.Y.C., 1948—49; social sci. analyst Congl. Ref. Svc. Libr. Congress, Washington, 1949—53; rsch. asst. Princeton U., NJ, 1953—54, Chase Manhattan Bank, N.Y.C., 1954—55; economist Caltex Oil Corp., N.Y.C., 1955—61; libr. Theatre Collection N.Y. Pub. Libr., N.Y.C., 1961—90, 1st asst. Theatre Collection, 1967—80, curator Theatre Collection, 1980—90, ret. Theatre Collection, 1990. Cons. rev. 2d edit. Random House Unabridged Dictionary of English Language, 1987. Asst. editor: abstracts series Pub. Affairs Abstracts, 1950-51; contbr. articles to profl. jours.; author: (with Patterson and Gunn) Survey of U.S. International Finance, 1954. Bd. advisors Night 100 Stars for Actors Fund Am., 1982-90; eligibility com. Tony awards, 1983-84; nominating com. Brendan Gill Prize, Municipal Art Soc. N.Y., 1987-96. Mem. ALA, Am. Soc. Theatre Rsch. (exec. bd. 1979-81, 85-88), Spl. Libraries Assn. (rep. 1971-86), Drama Desk, New Drama Forum Assn. (treas. 1979-82), Theatre Libr. Assn. (exec. bd. 1966-86, 93-95, pres. 1983-85, Disting. Svc. award 1996), Internat. Assn. Performing Arts Libraries and Mus. (v.p. 1991-95), Outer Critics Circle (treas. 1986-96), League of Am. Theatres and Prodrs. (hist. and curators com. 1993-94), Amateur Comedy Club, Snarks. Home: 9225 E Tanque Verde Rd #19204 Tucson AZ 85749-7740

SWERDLOW, MARTIN ABRAHAM, pathologist, educator; b. Chgo., July 7, 1923; s. Sol Hyman and Rose (Lasky) Swerdlow; m. Marion Levin, May 19,*1945; children: Steven Howard, Gary Bruce. Student, Herzl Jr. Coll.,

1941-42; BS, U. Ill., 1945; MD, U. Ill., Chgo., 1947. Diplomate Am Bd Pathology. Intern Michael Reese Hosp. and Med. Center, Chgo., 1947-48, resident, 1948-50, 51-52, mem. staff, 1974—, chmn. dept. pathology, v.p. acad. affairs, 1974-90; pathologist Menorah Med Ctr, Kansas City, Mo., 1954—57. Asst prof, pathologist Univ Ill Col Med, Chicago, 1957—59, assoc prof, 1959—60, clin prof, 1960—64, prof, pathologist, 1966—72, assoc dean, prof pathology, 1970—72; prof pathology, chmn Univ Mo, Kansas City, 1972—74; prof pathology Univ Chicago, 1975—89, Geever prof, head pathology emeritus, 1993—; mem comt standards Chicago Health Sys Agency, 1976—. With MC U.S. Army, 1944—45. Recipient Alumnus of the Yr Award, Univ Ill Col Med, 1973, Instructorship Award, Univ Ill, 1960, 1965, 1968, 1971, 1972. Mem.: Inst Med, Am Soc Dermatopathology, Am Acad Dermatology, Int Acad Pathology, Col Am Pathologists, Am Soc Clin Pathologists, Chicago Pathology Soc (pres 1980—). Jewish. Office: U Ill Coll Medicine Dept Pathology 1819 W Polk St Chicago IL 60612-7331 Business E-Mail: maswerdl@uic.edu. *My credo these years has been to care about patients, students, colleagues, employees, my institution and the many publics I serve. Honesty and thoroughness has been a basic life style, irrespective of the cost. With all, competence is a necessity and ongoing. Continuous responsibility for my education and learning is my way of living.*

SWERDLOW, STEVEN HOWARD, hematopathologist; b. Chgo., Sept. 1, 1950; m. Jennifer Margaret Goodman, May 18, 1975; children: Deborah, Naomi. AB in Biology summa cum laude, Brandeis U., 1971; MD, Harvard U., 1975. Diplomate Am. Bd. Pathology. From asst. to assoc. prof. pathology and lab. medicine U. Cin., 1983-92; dir. divsn. hematopathology, assoc. prof. to prof. pathology U. Pitts., 1992—. Author: Biopsy Interpretation of Lymph Nodes, 1992; mem. editl. bd. jour. Human Pathology, mem. editl. bd., contbr. Am. Jour. Surg. Pathology, contbr. articles to Am. Jour. Pathology, Human Pathology, others. Mem. Am. Soc. Hematology, Am. Soc. Investigative Pathology, U.S. Can. Acad. Pathology (coun. 2001-04), Soc. Hematopathology (pres. 2004—), Europe Assn. Haematopath (exec. com. 2002—), Phi Beta Kappa. Achievements include research in defining centrocytic/mantle cell lymphoma as a distinct clinicopathologic entity. Office: UPMC-Presbyterian Divsn Hematopath PUH C606 200 Lothrop St Pittsburgh PA 15213-2546 E-mail: swerdlowsh@upmc.edu.

SWERLING, JACK BRUCE, lawyer; b. N.Y.C., May 30, 1946; s. Benjamin Fidel and Jeanette (Fidler) S.; m. Erika Andrea Helfer, Jan. 17, 1970; children: Bryan, Stephanie. BA, Clemson U., 1968; JD, U. S.C., 1973. Bar: S.C. 1973, U.S. Dist. Ct. S.C. 1973, U.S. Ct. Appeals (4th cir.) 1974, U.S. Supreme Ct. 1978. Ptnr. Law Firm of Isadore Lourie, Columbia, S.C., 1973-83, Swerling, Harpootlian & McCulloch, Columbia, 1983-92; pvt. practice Columbia, 1992—. Mem. Pre-Trial Intervention Adv. Com., 1980-82; mem. adv. com. Child Victim Ct. Notebook divsn. Pub. Safety Programs, 1987; mem. S.C. Bd. Law Examiners, 1987-92, S.C. Bd. Grievances and Discipline, 1994-97; adj. prof. U. S.C. Sch. Law, Columbia, 1986—; clin. prof. dept. Neuropsychiatry Sch. Medicine, 1988—; mem. S.C. Supreme Ct. com. on model criminal jury instructions, chmn. bule ribbon task force criminal docketing com. Author: South Carolina Criminal Trial Notebook, 1991; co-author: Criminal Trial Advocacy, 1998; contbr. articles to profl. jours. Co-pres. Jewish Cmty. Ctr., Columbia, 1977. Fellow Am. Coll. Trial Lawyers, Am. Acad. Appellate Lawyers, Am. Bd. Criminal Lawyers, S.C. Bar Found.; mem. ABA, ATLA, Am Judicature Soc., Nat. Assn. Criminal Def. Lawyers, S.C. Trial Lawyers Assn. (chmn. criminal law sect. 1979-82), S.C. Bar Assn. (chmn. criminal law sect. 1985-86), Richland County Bar Assn. (chmn. criminal law sect. 1988-89). Democrat. Jewish. Avocation: shooting sporting clays. Office: 1720 Main St Ste 301 Columbia SC 29201-2850

SWETLIK, WILLIAM PHILIP, orthodontist; b. Manitowoc, Wis., Jan. 31, 1950; s. Leonard Alvin and Lillian Julia (Knipp) S.; m. Cheryl Jean Klein, June 30, 1973 (div.); children: Alison Elizabeth, Lindsey Ann, Adam William; m. Joyce M. Caris, Mar. 10, 1995. Student, Luther Coll., Decorah, Iowa, 1968-70; DDS, Marquette U., 1974; MS in Dentistry, St. Louis U., 1977. Diplomate Am. Bd. Orthodontics. Resident in gen. dentistry USPHS, Norfolk, Va., 1974-75; practice dentistry specializing in orthodontics Green Bay, Wis., 1977—. Instr. oral pathology NE Wis. Tech. Coll., Green Bay, 1979-86. Author: (with others) Orthodontic Headgear, 1977. Mem. Prevention Walking Club, Family Crisis Ctr. of Green Bay. Served as lt. USPHS, 1974-75. Fellow Coll. Diplomates Am. Bd. Orthodontics; mem. ADA, Am. Assn. Orthodontists, Wis. Dental Assn. (Continuing Edn. award 1986), Wis. Soc. Orthodontists, Orthodontic Edn. and Research Found., Brown Door Kewaunee Dental Soc. (program chmn. 1985-86, sec., treas. 1986-87, v.p. 1987-88, pres. 1988-89), St. Louis U. Orthodontic Alumni Assn. (pres. 1988-89), Acad. Gen. Dentistry, Violet Club of Am. Roman Catholic. Avocations: racquetball, skiing, jogging, raising violets, recording equipment. Home: 2160 Greenleaf Rd De Pere WI 54115-8621 Office: 115 Alpine Ct Shawano WI 54166-2041 E-mail: jayecars@aol.com.

SWETMAN, GLENN ROBERT, English language educator, poet; b. May 20, 1936; s. Glenn Lyle and June (Read) S.; m. Margarita Ortiz, Feb. 8, 1964 (div. 1979); children: Margarita June, Glenn Lyle Maximilian, Glenda Louise. BS, U. So. Miss., 1957, MA, 1959; PhD, Tulane U., 1966. Instr. U. So. Miss., 1957-58, asst. prof., 1964-66; instr. Ark. State U., 1958-59, McNeese U., 1959-61; instr. English Univ. Coll. Tulane U., 1961-64; spl. asst. dept. elec. engring., 1961-64; assoc. prof. La. Inst. Tech., 1966-67; prof., head dept. langs. Nicholls State Coll., Thibodaux, La., 1967-69, head dept. English, 1969-71, prof., 1971-91; prof. emeritus William Carey Coll., Gulfport, Miss., 1991—. Writer in residence, prof. English William Carey Coll., Gulfport, 1991—; ptnr. Breeland Pl., Biloxi, 1960—; stringer, corr. Shreveport (La.) Times, 1966—; ptnr. Ormuba, Inc., 1975—; cons. tech. writing Union Carbide Corp., Am. Fedn. Tchrs. State v.p. Nat. Com. to Resist Attacks on Tenure, 1974—. Book reviewer Jackson (Miss.) State Times, 1961; contbr. poetry to various publs. including Poet, Prairie Schooner, Trace, Ball State U. Forum, Film Quar., Poetry Australia, numerous others worldwide; author: (books of poems) Tunel de Amor, 1973, Deka #1, 1973, Deka #2, 1979, Shards, 1979, Concerning Carpenters, 1980, Son of Igor, 1982, Poems of the Fantastic, 1990; contbr. numerous articles to encys.; cons. editor (poetry) Paon Press, 1974—, Scott-Foresman, 1975; mem. editl. bd. Scholar and Educator, 1980—. Subdivsn. coord. Rep. Party, Hattiesburg, Miss., 1964. With AUS, 1957. Recipient Poetry awards KQUE Haiku contest, 1964, Coll. Arts contest, L.A., 1966, Black Ship Festival, Yoqosuka, Japan, 1967, Green World Brief Forms award Green World Poetry Editors, 1965. Mem. MLA, S. Cen. MLA, So. Literary Festival Assn. (v.p. 1975-76, 82-83, pres. 1984-85), Coll. Writers Soc. La. (pres. 1971-72, exec. dir. 1983—), IEEE, Am. Assn. Engring. Edn., La. Poetry Soc. (pres. 1971-74, 86—), Internat. Boswellian Inst., Nat. Fedn. State Poetry Socs. (2d v.p., nat. membership chmn. 1972-74, pres. 1976-77), Nat. Soc. Scholars and Educators (bd. dirs. 1982—, sec. exec. bd. 1986—, sec. bd. dirs. 1968—, sec. soc. 1989—, exec. edn. 2001-), Am. Fedn. Tchrs. (chpt. pres. 1973-78), Nat. Fedn. State Poetry Socs. (1st v.p. 1975-76, exec. bd. 1972—), Phi Eta Sigma, Omicron Delta Kappa. Home: PO Box 146 Biloxi MS 39533-0146 Office: William Carey Coll 1856 Beach Dr Gulfport MS 39507-1508

SWETNAM, DANIEL RICHARD, lawyer; b. Columbus, Ohio, Dec. 22, 1957; s. Joseph Neri and Audrey Marguerite (Mason) S.; m. Jeannette Deanna Dean, June 7, 1980; children: Jeremiah Daniel, Laura Janelle, Andrew Michael. BA, Ohio State U., 1979; JD, U. Cin., 1982. Bar: Ohio 1982, U.S. Dist. Ct. (so. dist.) Ohio 1982, U.S. Ct. Appeals (6th cir.) 1986, U.S. Supreme Ct. 1986. Assoc. Schwartz, Warren & Ramirez, Columbus, 1982-88, ptnr., 1989-96; prin. Schottenstein, Zox & Dunn, Columbus, 1997—. Deacon Grace Brethren Ch., Worthington, Ohio, 1989—; mem. Grace Brethren Christian Schs. Commn., 1993-98. Mem. ABA, Ohio State Bar Assn., Columbus Bar Assn., Comml. Law League Am., Order of Coif. Republican. Avocations: golf, tennis. Home: 2178 Stowmont Ct Dublin OH 43016-9563 Office: Schottenstein Zox & Dunn 250 West St Columbus OH 43215 Office Phone: 614-462-2225.

SWETNAM, MONTE NEWTON, petroleum exploration executive; b. Alexandria, La., Oct. 9, 1936; s. Montreville Morris and Margaret Elizabeth (Cullison) S.; m. Elaine Adelia Taylor, Dec. 21, 1957; children: Scott David, Robert Troy. Student, Johns Hopkins, 1955-58; BS in Geology, U. Wyo., 1960, MS in Geology, 1961; MBA in Bus. Adminstrn, Pepperdine U., 1978. Registered geologist, Calif. Exploration geologist Amerada Petroleum Corp., Durango, Colo., 1961-63; exploration geologist Tenneco Oil Co., Durango, 1963-65, dist. project geologist Bakersfield, Calif., 1965-69, div. staff geologist, 1969; partner Argonaut Oil & Gas Cons., Denver, 1969-71; internat. exploration mgr. Tesoro Petroleum Corp., San Antonio, 1971-73, v.p. internat. exploration, 1973-74, sr. v.p. exploration, 1974-82; pres. Tesoro-Bolivia Petroleum Co., 1975-82, Tesoro-Algeria Petroleum Co., 1975-82; sr. v.p. exploration Natural Resource Mgmt. Corp./NRM, Dallas, 1983-86; sr. v.p. exploration and prodn. Harken Energy Corp., 1987-89, exec. v.p., 1991-93; pres. Harken Exploration Co., 1988-91, Harken Bahrain Oil Co., 1989-93; exec. v.p., chief oper. officer Giant Exploration and Prodn. Co., Farmington, N.Mex., 1994-96; v.p. refining ops. Giant Industries, Inc., Scottsdale, Ariz., 1996-97, v.p. corp. affairs, 1997-98, exec. v.p. adminstrn. and corp. affairs, 1998-2000. Contbr. articles to profl. jours. Mem. Am. Assn. Petroleum Geologists, Geol. Soc. Am., Sigma Xi. Clubs: Alamo Yacht, Lake Canyon Yacht. Republican. Home: 420 Marina Dr Port Aransas TX 78373-4907 Office: 420 Marina Dr Port Aransas TX 78373-4907 E-mail: cmcnes@the-i.net.

SWETS, JOHN ARTHUR, psychologist, researcher; b. Grand Rapids, Mich., June 19, 1928; s. John A. and Sara Henrietta (Heyns) Swets; m. Maxine Ruth Crawford, July 16, 1949; children: Stephen Arthur, Joel Brian. BA, U. Mich., 1950, MA, 1953, PhD, 1954. Instr. psychology U. Mich., Ann Arbor, 1954—56; asst. prof. psychology MIT, Cambridge, 1956—60, assoc. prof. psychology, 1960—63; v.p. Bolt Beranek & Newman Inc., 1964—69, sr. v.p., 1969—74, gen. mgr. rsch., devel. and cons., dir., 1971—74; chief scientist BBN Labs., 1975—98, chief scientist emeritus, 1998—; sr. rsch. assoc. dept. radiology Brigham and Women's Hosp., 1997—. Lectr. dept. clin. epidemiology Harvard Med. Sch., 1985—88, dept. health care policy, 1988—; mem. corp. Edn. Devel. Ctr., Newton, Mass., 1971—75; Regent's prof. U. Calif., 1969; advisor vision com., com. on hearing and bioacoustics NAS-NRC, 1960—96; mem. Commn. on Behavioral Social Scis. and Edn., NRC, 1988—92, vice chair, 1992—93, chmn., 1993—96; ex-officio mem. governing bd. NRC, 1994—96, mem. various coms., 1960—. Author: Signal Detection Theory and ROC Analysis in Psychology and Diagnostics, 1996; co-author (with D.M. Green): Signal Detection Theory and Psychophysics, 1966; co-author: (with R.M. Pickett) Evaluation of Diagnostic Systems: Methods From Signal Detection Theory, 1982; editor: Signal Detection and Recognition by Human Observers, 1964; editor: (with L.L. Elliott) Psychology and the Handicapped Child, 1974; editor: (with D. Druckman) Enhancing Human Performance, 1988; mem. editl. bd. Med. Decision Making, 1980—85, Psychol. Sci., 1989—94, 1999—2002, Psychol. Rev., 1995—97, Jour. Exptl. Psychology: Applied, 1995—97, Human Factors, 1997—2001; contbr. articles to profl. jours. Mem. bd. dirs. German-Am. Rsch. Coun. Found., 1999—2001; mem. corp. Winchester Hosp., Mass., 1981—84. Fellow vis. rsch. fellow, Philips Labs., The Netherlands, 1958. Fellow: APA (Disting. Sci. Contbn. award 1990), AAAS (coun. 1986—89), Am. Psychol. Soc., Soc. Exptl. Psychologists (chmn. 1986, exec. com. 1986—89, Howard Crosby Warren medal 1985), Am. Acad. Arts and Scis., Acoustical Soc. Am. (exec. coun. 1968—71); mem.: NAS (chmn., Troland award com. 1991, chair psychology sect. 1998—2001, nominating com. 2001), Soc. Math. Psychology, Psychometric Soc., Psychonomic Soc., Tequesta Country Club, Sigma Alpha Epsilon, Sigma Xi. Congregationalist (Moderator). Home: 10411 SE Terrapin Pl 103-C Tequesta FL 33469-1827 E-mail: swets@bbn.com.

SWETT, ALBERT HERSEY, retired lawyer, business executive, consultant; b. Medina, N.Y., Feb. 18, 1923; s. Raymond Fuller and Marion (Hersey) S.; m. Mary Stewart, Oct. 10, 1944; children: Marion Hersey Swett Robinson, Margaret Stewart Swett Haskell, Albert Louis. Grad., The Hill Sch., 1941; B.Engring., Yale U., 1944; LL.B., Harvard U., 1949. Bar: N.Y. 1949. Assoc. Harris, Beach & Wilcox, Rochester, N.Y., 1949-56, ptnr., 1957-66; v.p., gen. counsel Xerox Corp., Stamford, Conn., 1966-75, Coca-Cola Co., Atlanta, 1975-78, v.p., counsel to chmn., 1978-80; ind. cons., 1980—. Trustee Practising Law Inst., 1977-83. Served with USNR, 1942-46. Mem. Assn. Gen. Counsel (emeritus), Tau Beta Pi. Lodges: Masons. Methodist. Home: Apt 615 1570 East Ave Rochester NY 14610-1640 E-mail: ahs30319@aol.com.

SWETT, RICHARD NELSON (DICK SWETT), diplomat, former congressman; b. Bryn Mawr, Pa., May 1, 1957; s. Philip Eugene Sr. and Ann (Parkhurst) S.; m. Yvonne Katrina Lantos, Aug. 29, 1980; children: Chelsea, Sebastian, Keaton, Chanteclaire, Kismet, Atticus, Sunday. BA in Architecture, Yale U., 1979. Lic. contractor, Calif.; lic. architect, Calif., N.H. Arch. Skidmore Owings & Merrill, San Francisco, 1979-82; pres. Bastion Group, Inc., San Mateo, Calif., 1982-87; project mgr. Grosvenor Properties, San Francisco, 1986-87; pres. Veritas Group Inc., Gilford, N.H., 1987-90; mem. 101st-102d Congresses from 2nd dist. N.H., Washington, 1991—95; mem. pub. works and transp. com. U.S. Ho. of Reps., Washington, 1991-95, mem. sci., space, and tech. com., 1991-95, mem. select com. on aging, 1991-95; amb. to Denmark Am. Embassy, Copenhagen, 1998-2001; pres. Swett Assocs., Bow, NH, 2001—. State chmn. U.S. Olympic Com., 1992—98; founding mem. adv. bd. European Ctr. of Calif., 2001—; sr. counselor APCO Worldwide, 2001—; mem. U.S. Govt. Gen. Svcs. Adminstrn. Archtl. Peer Rev. Bd., 2000—; bd. dirs. Gold Coast Innovation Ctr., Channel Islands Campus of Calif. State U. Sys., 2001—, AeroSat Corp., Amherst, NH. Bd. advisors Hans Christian Andersen Found., Denmark, 2001—, Architects for Humanity, N.Y.C., 2001—, Abildsø Found., Oslo, 2002—, Project for Pub. Spaces, N.Y.C., 2003—. Presented 1st Comdr. Order of Danabrog, Queen Margrethe II of Denmark, 2001; named as one of Top Ten Outstanding Young Ams., U.S. Jr. C. of C., 1993. Fellow AIA; mem. Nat. Hist. Preseervation Soc., Ind. Power Producers N.H. Assn., Yale Club N.H., Sierra Club, Winnipesaukee Yacht Club. Democrat. Avocations: athletics, piano, art, sailing. Office Phone: 603-774-1072.

SWETT, STEPHEN FREDERICK, JR., artist, educator; b. Englewood, N.J., Sept. 14, 1935; s. Stephen Frederick and Frances (Gulotta) S.; m. Annette Palazzolo, Nov. 18, 1961; children: Susan, Kimberly Ann, Stephen Laurence. BA, Montclair State Coll., 1959, MA, 1965; EdD in Edn1. Adminstrn., Rutgers U., 1976; grad., North Light Art Sch., 1995. Tchr. Long Branch (N.J.) H.S., 1961-62, Roselle Park (N.J.) H.S., 1962-73; rsch. asst. Rutgers U., New Brunswick, N.J., 1973-74; instrnl. supr. Elmwood Park (N.J.) Schs., 1974-76, Morris Hills Regional Schs., Denville, N.J., 1976-77; asst. prin. Lawrence H.S., Lawrenceville, N.J., 1977-79; prin. Stafford Intermediate Sch., Manahawkin, N.J., 1979-94; recreation and art cons., 1994—. Participant NSF Inst. in physics, chemistry and math. Seton Hall U., 1964, Newark Coll. Engring., 1965, Stevens Inst. Tech., summers 1966-68; rschr. sch. fin. Exhibited in group shows at Sheldon Meml. Art Gallery, 1998, Period Gallery, Omaha, 1998, 99, Montserrat Gallery, N.Y.C., 2000, The Looking Glass Art Gallery, Hawley, Pa., 2000, Annette Howell Turner Ctr. for the Arts, Valdosta, Ga., 2004. With AUS, 1959-61. Mem. Roselle Park Edn. Assn. (pres. 1971-73), Nat. Sci. Study Edn., Am. Assn. Physics Tchrs., Am. Inst. Physics, Am. Assn. Sch. Adminstrs., N.J. Assn. Sch. Adminstrs., Nat. Assn. Elem. and Mid. Sch. Adminstrs., N.J. Assn. Elem. and Mid. Sch. Adminstrs., Nat. Assn. Secondary Sch. Prins., Phi Delta Kappa (sec. Rutgers chpt. 1977-80, v.p. 1980-82, pres. 1983-84). Home: 306 Tenth Ave Belmar NJ 07719-2313

SWIBEL, STEVEN WARREN, lawyer; b. Chgo., July 18, 1946; s. Morris Howard and Gloria Swibel; m. Leslie Swibel; children: Deborah, Laura. BS, MIT, 1968; JD, Harvard U., 1971. Bar: Ill. 1971, U.S. Dist. Ct. (no. dist.) Ill. 1971, U.S. Tax Ct. 1973, U.S. Ct. Appeals (7th cir.) 1981. Assoc. Sonnenschein Carlin Nath & Rosenthal, Chgo., 1971-78, ptnr., 1978-84, Rudnick & Wolfe, 1984-93, Schwartz, Cooper, Greenberger, Krauss Chartered, Chgo., 1993—. Adj. prof. taxation Ill. Inst. Tech. Kent Coll. Law, Chgo., 1989—2001; lectr. in field. Contbr. articles to profl. jours. Ednl. counselor MIT, 1979—; bd. dirs. MIT Alumni Fund, 1992—95, MIT Enterprise Forum, Chgo., 2002—, Kids in Danger, 1998—, Ragdale Found., 1987—2000, treas., 1987—92. Recipient Lobdell Disting. Svc. award, MIT Alumni Assn., 1989. Mem.: ABA (com. partnerships sect. taxation), Chgo. Bar Assn. (mem. fed. taxation com., mem. exec. subcom. 1984—, chmn. subcom. real estate and partnerships 1986—87, vice-chmn. 1988—89, chmn. 1990), Ill. Bar Assn., MIT Club (dir. Chgo. chpt. 1980—91, 1996—, sec. 1980—87, pres. 1987—89), Met. Club, Sigma Xi, Eta Kappa Nu, Tau Beta Pi. Office: Schwartz Cooper Greenberger & Krauss Chartered 180 N La Salle St Ste 2700 Chicago IL 60601-2757 Office Phone: 312-346-1300. Business E-Mail: swibel@alum.mit.edu.

SWIBINSKI, EDWARD THOMAS, internist, endocrinologist, educator; b. Jersey City, Jan. 26, 1950; s. Stanley Adolph and Celina Frances (Szymanski) S. BA, Rutgers U., 1972; MD, N.Y. Med. Coll., 1975. Diplomate Am. Bd. Internal Medicine, Am. Bd. Endocrinology and Metabolism. Resident in medicine N.Y. Med. Coll., N.Y.C., 1975-78; gen. internist Nat. Health Svcs. Corp., Camden, N.J., 1978-79; fellow in endocrinology Hosp. of U. Pa., Phila., 1979-80; fellow in endocrinology -R.W. Johnson Med. Sch. U. Medicine and Dentistry N.J., Piscataway, NJ, 1980-81, clin. prof. medicine R.W. Johnson Med. Sch.; divsn. chief endocrinology Our Lady of Lourdes Ctr. Mem. ACP, Phila. Endocrinology Soc. (v.p. 1993-94, bd. dirs. 1991-96, pres. 1994-95), Camden County Med. Soc., Phi Beta Kappa, Alpha Omega Alpha. Roman Catholic. Office: 1210 Brace Rd Cherry Hill NJ 08034-3213 Office Phone: 856-795-3597. Personal E-mail: marvoor@aol.com.

SWICEGOOD, STEPHEN, architect; Grad., Auburn U. Prin. Idealspan, 1993—. Spkr. in field. Fellow: AIA (pres., regional dir.). Office: 100 Peachtree St Atlanta GA 30303

SWICK, HERBERT MORRIS, medical educator, humanist, neurologist; b. Baton Rouge, Nov. 22, 1941; s. Edgar Haight and Mary Ellen (Morris) S.; m. Mary Lynne McCluggage, June 29, 1963; children: Kristin Ann, Elizabeth May, Diane Marie. BA with honors, Johns Hopkins U., 1963, MD, 1966. Cert. Am. Bd. Psychiatry and Neurology, Am. Bd. Pediatrics. Resident in pediat. Johns Hopkins U., Balt., 1966-69; resident in neurology U. Ky., Lexington, 1971-74, asst. prof. neurology and pediat., 1974-75; from asst. to prof. neurology and pediat. Med. Coll. Wis., Milw., 1975-94, asst. dean med. edn., interim chmn. dept. neurology, 1987-88, from assoc. to sr. assoc. dean acad. affairs, 1988-93, sr. assoc. dean for acad. programs, 1993-94; prof. neurology U. Kans. Sch. Medicine, Kansas City, 1994-99, sr. assoc. dean acad. affairs, 1994-98; acting chmn. dept. history and philosophy of medicine Sch. Medicine U. Kans., Kansas City, 1995; interim exec. dean U. Kans. Sch. Medicine, Kansas City, 1995-97; scholar-in-residence Assn. Am. Med. Colls., 1998-2000; exec. dir. Inst. Medicine and Humanities, Missoula, Mont., 2000—; prof. U. Mont., 2000—; clin. assoc. prof. medicine U. Wash. Sch. Medicine, 2001—. Chief dept. neurology Children's Hosp. Wis., Milw., 1981-87; vis. prof. Mayo Clinic and Found., Rochester, Minn., 1985, 2002, Univ. S.C., 2001; bd. dirs. Inst. Medicine and Humanities. Contbr. numerous articles to profl. jours. Bd. dirs. Milw. Chamber Music Soc., 1982-88, pres. 1986-88; bd. dirs. Missoula Cultural Coun., 2001—, Mont. Natural History Ctr., 2001-02; A.Murat Willis Lecture, Richmond, 2004. Served to lt. commdr., USN, 1969-71. Fulbright sr. scholar, 1978. Fellow Am. Acad. Neurology (edn. com., undergrad. edn. subcom. 1985-89); mem. Am. Assn. History Medicine, Child Neurology Soc. (archives and history com. 1981-88, exec. com. 1982-86, sci. selection com. 1983, 84), Columbia History of Medicine Club, Internat. Child Neurology Assn., Milw. Acad. Medicine (coun. 1993-94), Profs. of Child Neurology, Wis. Neurol. Soc. (sec.-treas. 1981-82, pres.-elect 1982-84, pres. 1984-85), Assn. Univ. Profs. in Neurology (undergrad. edn. com. 1979-86), Assn. Am. Med. Colls. (coun. deans 1995-97, group on ednl. affairs 1986-98, group on student affairs 1986-94, faculty affairs profl. devel. conf. planning com. 1997-98), Am. Osler Soc. (bd. govs. 2004—), Am. Soc. Bioethics and Humanities. Office: Inst Medicine & Humanities PO Box 4587 Missoula MT 59806-4587 Office Phone: 406-329-5661. Business E-Mail: swick@saintpatrick.org.

SWID, STEPHEN CLAAR, business executive; b. N.Y.C., Oct. 26, 1940; s. David and Selma (Claar) S.; m. Nan Goldman, Mar. 1, 1963; children: Robin, Scott, Jill. BS, Ohio State U., 1962. Mgmt. trainee Alside Aluminum Co., Akron, Ohio, 1962-63; securities analyst Dreyfus Fund, N.Y.C., 1963-66; sr. investment officer Oppenheimer Fund, N.Y.C., 1966-67; gen. ptnr. City Assocs., 1967-69, Swid Investors, N.Y.C., 1970-78; co-chmn. bd. Gen. Felt Industries Inc., Saddle Brook, N.J., 1974-86, Knoll Internat., 1977-86; chmn. bd., CEO SBK Entertainment World, Inc., N.Y.C., 1986-89; chmn., CEO SCS Comm., N.Y.C., 1989—, SESAC, 1992—. Bd. dirs. Bally Fitness Corp. Trustee Solomon Guggenheim Mus.; mem. vis. com. 20th century art Met. Mus. Art; past trustee Horace Mann Sch., N.Y.C.; former exec. vp. bd. dirs. Lenox Sch. N.Y.; dir. Mcpl. Art Soc. Mem.: Coun. Fgn. Rels. Office: SESAC Inc 152 W 57th St New York NY 10019-3310

SWIECICKI, MARTIN, retired neurosurgeon; b. Camden, N.J., June 29, 1934; s. Martin E. and Annetta Swiecicki; m. Gloria J. Whelpley; children: Diane, Annette, Karen, Sheryl, Martin C. BA, Colgate U., 1956; MD, Hahnemann Med. Sch., 1960. Diplomate Am. Bd. Neurol. Surgery. Intern West Jersey Hosp., Camden, 1960—61; resident in neurol. surgery Jefferson U., Phila., 1961—65; mem. staff in neurol. surgery West Jersey Hosp., Camden, Berlin, NJ, 1967—, chief Neurol. Surgery, 1967—89; clin. assoc prof. Neurol. Surgery Hahnemann Med. Coll., Phila., 1977—2004; ret., 2004. Contbr. articles to profl. jours. Recipient N.J. Gov.'s award for Outstanding Svcs., 1970, 71, 72, 73, Award for Support and Svc. Boy Scouts Am., 1992. Fellow ACS; mem. AMA, Camden County Med. Soc. (v.p.1993, pres. 1995), West Jersey Med. Soc., N.J. State Med. Soc., N.J. Neurosurg. Soc.(sec.-treas. 978-79, pres. 1981, chmn. peer rev. com. 1983-89, mem. peer rev. com. 1977—), Camden County Med. Soc. (exec. com. 1977—, v.p. 1993, pres.-elect 1994, pres. 1995), Soc. Air Force Clin. Surgeons, Am. Assn. Neurol. Surgeons. Office Phone: 856-869-0600. Personal E-mail: mswiecicki@aol.com.

SWIENTON, GREGORY T. transportation company executive; BBA in Mktg., Loyola U., Chgo.; MBS in Fin., U. Chgo. Various sales and mktg. positions Ill. Bell and AT&T, Chgo., Mpls., 1971-82; former v.p., gen. mgr. DHL Airways, Inc., Chgo. and Houston; former exec. dir. Europe and Africa DHL Worldwide Express, Brussels; various positions to sr. v.p., growth initiatives Burlington No. Santa Fe Corp., 1994-99; pres., CEO Ryder System, Inc., Miami, 1999—. Office: Ryder System Inc PO Box 20816 Miami FL 33102-0816

SWIERENGA, ROBERT, humanities educator, researcher; b. Chgo., June 10, 1935; s. John R. and Marie Ann (Hoekstra) Swierenga; m. Joan Boomker Swierenga, June 16, 1956. BA in Edn., Calvin Coll., 1953—57; MA in History, Northwestern U., 1957—58; PhD in History, U. of Iowa, 1962—65. Cert. secondary tchr. Mich. State Bd. Edn., 1965. Social studies tchr. Pella Christian H.S., Iowa, 1958—61; history instr. Calvin Coll., Grand Rapids, Mich., 1961—62, asst. prof., 1965—68; prof. Kent State U., Ohio, 1968—96; rsch. prof. Hope Coll., Holland, Mich., 1996—. Bd. trustees Calvin Coll., 1976—82. Author: (books) The Forerunners, 1994, Faith and Family, 2000, Dutch Chgo., 2002; rschr.: Dutch immigration databases, CD #269 Family Tree Maker. Elder Akron Christian Ref. Ch., Ohio, 1970—89; elder/clk. Pillar Christian Ref. Ch., Holland, Mich., 2002—. Named a Knight-Order of Netherlands Lion, Queen Beatrix of Netherlands at Holland, Mich., 2000. Mem.: Agrl. History Soc. (pres. 1996—97), Orgn. of Am. Historians, Assn. for Advancement of Dutch Am. Studies (pres. 2000—02). Republican. Mem. Christian Reformed Ch. Avocations: walking, choral singing. Office: A C Van Raalte Inst Hope Coll 100 E 8th St Holland MI 49422 Office Phone: 616-395-7172.

SWIERINGA, ROBERT JAY, dean, accountant, educator; b. Holland, Mich., July 31, 1942; s. John Gerard and Harriet Julia (Haverdink) S.; m. Pamela Bazett Deane-Butcher, Aug. 5, 1972; children: John William, Elizabeth Bazett. BA in econs., Augustana Coll., 1964; MBA in acctg. and econs., U. Denver, 1965; PhD in acctg. and complex orgns., U. Ill., 1969. Asst. prof. acctg. Grad. Sch. Bus., Stanford U., Calif., 1968-74; assoc. prof. acctg. Johnson Grad. Sch. Mgmt., Cornell U., Ithaca, NY, 1974-81, prof. acctg., 1981-85, Anne and Elmer Lindseth Dean, 1997—; mem. Fin. Acctg. Standards Bd., Norwalk, Conn., 1986—96; prof. in the practice of acctg. Sch. Mgmt., Yale U., 1996—97. Bd. dirs. GE, 2002—; adv. bd. mem. Columbia Bus. Sch.

Ctr. for Excellence in Fin. Reporting and Security Analysis, 2003—; mem. editl. bd. Jour. Acctg. Rsch., 1975—97, Acctg. Jour., 1976—81, Acctg., Orgns., and Soc, 1976—93, Jour. Fin. Statement Analysis, 1995—99, Acctg. Horizons, 1996—, Acctg. Rev., 1973—75, 1976—77, editl. cons., 1977—80, assoc. editor, 1980—84, fin. reporting dept. editor, 1985; mem. editl. panel Abacus, 1976—81; assoc. editor info. systems and acctg. Mgmt. Sci., 1981—86. Co-author: (with R.T. Sprouse) Essentials of Financial Statement Analysis, 1972, (with R.H. Moncur) Some Effects of Participative Budgeting on Managerial Behavior, 1975; (with T.R. Dyckman) Cases in Financial Accounting, 1980, rev. 1981, 3rd edit. 1989; (with H. Bierman Jr.) Financial Accounting: An Introduction, 1987. Grantee Nat. Assn. Accts., 1970, Peat, Marwick, Mitchell & Co. Found., 1976; Recipient Justice Found. Award for Outstanding Teaching, Cornell U., 1976, PhD Alumni of Yr. Award, Accountancy Dept. U. Ill., 1988, Alumni Outstanding Achievement Award, Augustana Coll., 1989, Alumnus of Yr. Award, Sch. Accountancy U. Denver, 1994. Mem. Am. Acctg. Assn. (inducted into Northeast Regional Hall of Fame, 1996), Beta Gamma Sigma, Beta Alpha Psi, Assn. to Advance Collegiate Schs. of Bus. (peer review teams mem., 2001-), Grad. Mgmt. Admissions Coun. (bd. dirs., 2001-, vice chair, 2002-03, chair, 2003-04). Office: Johnson Grad Sch of Management Cornell University 207 Sage Hall Ithaca NY 14853-6201 E-mail: rjs22@cornell.edu.*

SWIFT, CALVIN THOMAS, electrical and computer engineering educator; b. Quantico, Va., Feb. 6, 1937; s. Thomas and Elsie (Hill) S.; m. Joanne Taylor, Sept. 5, 1959; children: Pamela, Janet. BS, MIT, 1959; MS, Va. Poly. Inst., 1965; PhD, William and Mary Coll., 1969. Research engr. N. Am. Aviation Co., Downey, Calif., 1959-62; aerospace technologist NASA, Hampton, Va., 1962-81; prof. elec. and computer engring. U. Mass., Amherst, 1981—2001, prof. emeritus, 2001—. Cons. engring., Amherst, 1981— Editor: Transactions on Geoscience and Remote Sensing, 1980-84; assoc. editor: Jour. Oceanic Engring., 1980-84. F.L. Thompson fellow NASA, 1977; faculty fellow U. Mass., 1997. Fellow IEEE (life); mem. Internat. Union Radio Sci. (chmn. Commn. F 1988-91), Antennas and Propagation Soc. (adminstrv. com. 1974-77, 80-85), Geosci. and Remote Sensing Soc. (adminstrv. com. 1978-86, pres. 1985, Disting. Achievement award 1994). Office: U Mass Dept Elec & Computer Engring Amherst MA 01003

SWIFT, DALE MATTHEW, neurosurgeon; b. Lorain, Ohio, May 26, 1958; m. Denice Swift; 2 children. Degree, Coll. of Wooster, Ohio, 1980; MD, Case Western Res. U., 1984. Diplomate Am. Bd. Neurol. Surgery, Am. Bd. Pediat. Neurol. Surgery. Intern Columbia Presbyn. Hosp., N.Y.C., 1984—85, resident in neurol. surgery, 1985—91; fellow in pediat. neurol. surgery Children's Hosp. Pitts., 1991—92; neurosurgeon Neurosurgeons for Children, Dallas, 1992—. Attending neurosurgeon Children's Med. Ctr. Dallas, 1992—, Med. City Dallas Hosp., 1992—, Tex. Scottish Rite Hosp. for Children, 1992—; assoc. clin. prof. neurosurgery U. Tex. Southwestern Med. Sch., 1992—. Mem.: Alpha Omega Alpha, Phi Beta Kappa. Office: Children's Med Ctr-Neurosurgery 1935 Motor St Dallas TX 75235

SWIFT, EDWARD FOSTER, III, investment banker; b. Chgo., Nov. 1, 1923; s. Theodore Philip I and Elizabeth (Hoyt) S.; m. Joan McKelvy, July 2, 1947; children: Theodore Philip II, Edward McKelvy, Lockhart McKelvy, Elizabeth Hoyt; m. Carol Coffey Whipple, June 21, 1968. Grad., Hotchkiss Sch., 1941; BA, Yale U., 1945. With Esmark, Inc. (formerly Swift & Co.), 1947-75, asst. to v.p. charge meat packing plants, 1958, asst. v.p., 1958-59, v.p. for provisions, fgn., casings and storage, 1959-64, exec. v.p., 1964-75; vice-chmn. Chgo. Corp., 1975-79; vice chmn. Bacon, Whipple & Co., Chgo., 1980-84; mng. dir. A.G. Becker Paribas Inc., Chgo., 1984-85; with E.F. Hutton and Co., Chgo., 1985-87; mng. dir. Shearson Lehman Hutton Inc, Chgo., 1987-92. Bd. dirs. Santa Fe Pacific Pipelines, Inc. Chmn. So. Ind. chpt. United Negro Coll. Fund, 1956; trustee Northwestern U., Evanston, Ill.; bd. dirs. Northwestern Meml. Hosp., Chgo. Served to capt. U.S. Army, 1942-46. Mem. Chgo. Assn. Commerce and Industry (bd. dirs.), Scroll and Key, Chgo. Club, Racquet Club. Econ. Club, Valley Club, Comml. Club, Onwentsia Club, Old Elm ClubBirnam Wood Golf Club, Aurelian Honor Soc. Home: 1500 N Astor St Chicago IL 60610-1635 Office: 70 W Madison St Ste 1400 Chicago IL 60602-4267

SWIFT, FRANK MEADOR, lawyer; b. N.Y.C., Dec. 27, 1911; s. Frank Meador and Alberta (Rankin) S.; m. Harriet Elizabeth Simpson, May 30, 1944 (dec. Jan. 2003); children: Frank Meador (dec.), Thomas Lamar. Student, Emory U., 1930-32; LL.B., U. Ga., 1935. Bar: Ga. 1935. Partner Swift, Currie, McGhee & Hiers, Atlanta, 1965-82, of counsel, 1982—. Served to comdr. USNR, 1942-46. Mem. Am., Ga. bar assns., Lawyers Club Atlanta, Clubs: Piedmont Driving. Republican. Presbyterian. Home: 201 Neptune Rd Apt 455 Saint Simons Island GA 31522-4246 Office: Swift Currie McGhee & Hiers 1355 Peachtree St NE Ste 300 Atlanta GA 30309-3238

SWIFT, JANE MARIA, former governor; b. North Adams, Mass., Feb. 24, 1965; d. John Maynard and Jean Mary (Kent) S.; m. Charles T. Hunt III, Feb. 19, 1994. BA in Am. Studies, Trinity Coll., Hartford, Conn., 1987. Exec. mgmt. trainee G. Fox. & Co., Hartford, 1987-88; adminstrv. aide Sen. Peter C. Webber, Boston, 1988-90; mem. Mass. State Senate, Boston, 1991-96, 3d asst. minority leader, 1993-96; coord. strategic devel. of regional airports Mass. Port Authority, Boston, 1997; dir. consumer affairs and bus. regulation Commonwealth of Mass., lt. gov., 1999-2001, gov., 2001—03. 3d asst. minority leader, 1993-96. Republican. Roman Catholic.

SWIFT, JOHN D. manufacturing executive; CFO Mohawk Industries Inc., Calhoun, Ga. Office: Mohawk Industries Inc 160 S Industrial Blvd Calhoun GA 30701-3030

SWIFT, JOHN FRANCIS, retired health care advertising company executive; b. N.Y.C., June 15, 1935; s. John F. and Mary Veronica (Kehoe) S.; m. Eleanor H. Cunniff, Oct. 10, 1964; children— John Francis, Sharon Ann. BS in Bus. Adminstrn, Seton Hall U., 1960, postgrad., 1960-61. Mktg. research mgr. Lederle Labs. div. Cyanamid Internat., 1960-63; account exec. Robert A. Becker Advt. Agy., N.Y.C., 1963-66; mgr. new products Chesebrough Ponds Co., N.Y.C., 1966-68; v.p. Frohlich Intercon Co., N.Y.C., 1968-72; pres., CEO, Lavey/Wolff/Swift, Inc., N.Y.C., 1972-91, chmn., CEO, 1991-94; pres., CEO, BBDO Health & Med. Comms. Inc., 1977-91; chmn., CEO Health & Med. Comm. Inc., 1991-95, chmn. emeritus, 1995—, ret., 1995; vice-chmn. Lyons Lavey Nickel Swift, Inc., 1995—. Bd. govs. Cathedral Healthcare Systems, 1991—; chmn. Cathedral Healthcare Found., 1994—. Served with USN, 1955-57. Named to, Med. Advt. Hall of Fame, 2004. Mem. Pharm. Advt. Coun. (pres. 1979), Bio-Med. Mktg. Assn., Canoe Brook CC (Summit, N.J.), Manasquan River Golf Club, Skytop Club (Pa.), Royal Palm Yacht and Country Club, Boca Raton Resort and Club, N.Y. Athletic Club. Home: 32 Peppermill Rd Chatham NJ 07928-1312 also: 600 S Ocean Blvd Boca Raton FL 33432-6265 also: 76 Bay Point Harbour Point Pleasant NJ 08742-5509 Office: Health & Med Comm Inc 220 E 42d St New York NY 10017

SWIFT, JONATHAN, educator, television personality; b. Glasgow, Scotland, Apr. 26, 1932; arrived in U.S., 1948, naturalized, 1954; s. John Francis and Catherline Little (McGowan) S. MA, Wayne State U., 1957; postgrad., Ecole Normale Superieure, Paris, 1954-55; studied with Georges Jouatte, 1954-56; cert., Conservatoire Nat. de Musique, France, 1955; postgrad., U. Mich., 1959, Cambridge U., 1981; PhD, Mich. State U., 1983. On-camera tchr. French Sta. WTVS, Detroit, 1955-56, tchr. Am. lit., 1960-62; instr. French Wayne State U., Detroit, 1955-60; tchr. English, French and social studies Detroit Pub. Schs., 1957-64; tchr. English and history Glasgow Corp. Schs., 1967; tchr. English and French Livonia (Mich.) Pub. Schs., 1967; chmn. English dept. Stevenson H.S., Livonia, 1970-78, dir. Sch. Global Edn., 1978-98; dir. Ctr. Internat. Studies Madonna U., Mich., 1998—. Sr. lectr. Mich. State U. Debut in opera as Alfredo in La Traviata, 1961; host PBS TV and cmty. TV series Global Connections, Time Out for Opera, Dining Out With Jonathan Swift; leading tenor with Detroit Piccolo Opera Co., 1981-96, Detroit Grand Opera Assn., 1965, Mich. Opera Co., 1961-64; concert soloist with major symphonies in U.S., Can., Europe, Australia, 1961-81; appeared as tenor soloist in various radio and TV programs, 1961-81; rec. artist with Scotia and Andis, U.K.; contbr. articles and poems to profl. and lit. jours. Mem. adv. bd. Am. Mid.-East Christian Congress, 2003—. Decorated chevalier La Chaine des Rotisseurs; named Fulbright scholar, 1954—55; named to Hall of Fame, Mich. Model UN, 1999; recipient French Govt. medal, 1954, tribute, Mich. State Legislature, 1984, NEA Applegate-Dorros award, 1987, MEA Siddall Internat. award, 1987, Philo Farnsworth award, Alliance Cmty. Media, 1990, 1994, 1995, 1998, 1998, 1999, 2000, Hometown award, Nat. Fedn. Local Cable Programmers, 1994, 1999, 2001, Nat. TV award, Nat. Assn. Telecomm. Officers and Advs., 1995, Human Rels. award, Livonia, 1999, Multi-Cultural award, Birmingham, Mich., 2000, 2004. Mem.: decorated Chevalier de la Confrerie de la Chaine des Rotisseurs, Descs. Knights of Garter, Soc. Friends of St. George. Roman Catholic. also: 4200 Telegraph Rd # 489 Bloomfield Hills MI 48302-2038 E-mail: jswift@madonna.edu.

SWIFT, RICHARD J. engineering company executive; b. 1944; BS in Engring., U.S. Mil. Acad., 1966; MS in Engring., Purdue U., 1972; MBA, Fairleigh Dickinson U., 1972. With TVA, 1970—72, Union Carbide Corp., 1976—77; project mgr., process plants divsn. Foster Wheeler Corp., Clinton, NJ, 1972—81, dir. comml. operations, process plants divsn., 1981—84, pres., COO, power systems group, 1987—89, CEO. group exec., power systems group, 1989—92, group exec., exec. v.p., energy equipment group, 1992, pres., COO, 1992—94, chmn., pres., CEO, 1994—2001; dir. contract ops. Foster Wheeler Corp. (Paris subsidiary), 1984—86; v.p. Foster Wheeler Internat. Corp., 1986—87. Bd. dir. PSE&G, 1994—, mem., audit com. and corp. goverance; bd. dir. Ingersoll-Rand Ltd., 1995—, chmn., audit com, bd. dir. Hubbell, Inc., Kaman Corp.; chmn. Nuclear Com., Fin. Acctg. Standards Adv. Coun., 2002—. Past chmn. Nat. Foreign Trade Coun.; past mem. Bus. Roundtable, mem., trade and investment task force. Commd. officer U.S. Army, 1966—70. Address: Fin Acctg Standards Bd 401 Merritt 7 PO Box 5116 Norwalk CT 06856-5116 Office Phone: 908-730-4000. Fax: 203-849-9714; Office Fax: 908-730-5315.*

SWIFT, STEPHEN CHRISTOPHER, lawyer; b. N.Y.C., Jan. 7, 1954; s. James Stephen and Rhoda Emma Jean (Howd) Swift. AA, Lansing CC, 1980; BA, Mich. State U., 1983; JD, Wayne State U., 1988. Bar: Mich. 1988, Hawaii 1989, U.S. Dist. Ct. Hawaii 1989, U.S. Ct. Fed. Claims 1990, U.S. Ct. Appeals (fed., DC and 9th cirs.) 1990, DC 1991, U.S. Supreme Ct. 1992, Va. 1995, U.S. Dist. Ct. (ea. and we. dists.) Va. 1995, U.S. Bankruptcy Ct. (ea. and we. dists.) Va. 1995, U.S. Ct. Appeals (4th cir.) 1995, U.S. Dist. Ct. DC 1997, U.S. Tax Ct. 1997, Md. 1998, U.S. Dist. Ct. Md. 1998, U.S. Ct. Internat. Trade 2000, U.S. Dist. Ct. (ea. dist.) Mich. 2002, registered: (patent atty.) 1994. Pvt. practice, Honolulu, 1989—94, Arlington, Va., 1995—2003, Alexandria, 2003—. Mem.: ABA, Am. Intellectual Property Law Assn., Fed. Cir. Bar Assn., Fed. Bar Assn. Office: Swift Law Office 1940 Duke St Ste 200 Alexandria VA 22314-3451 Office Phone: 703-418-0000. Business E-Mail: steve@swift.law.pro.

SWIFT, STEPHEN JENSEN, federal judge; b. Salt Lake City, Sept. 7, 1943; s. Edward A. and Maurine (Jensen) S.; m. Lorraine Burnell Facer, Aug. 4, 1972; children: Carter, Stephanie, Spencer, Meredith, Hunter. BS, Brigham Young U., 1967; JD, George Washington U., 1970. Trial atty. U.S. Dept. Justice, Washington, D.C., 1970-74; asst. U.S. atty. U.S. Atty.'s Office, San Francisco, 1974-77; v.p., sr. tax counsel Bank Am. N.T. & S.A., San Francisco, 1977-83; judge U.S. Tax Ct., Washington, 1983—. Adj. prof. Golden Gate U., San Francisco, 1976-83, U. Balt., 1987—. Mem. ABA, Calif. Bar Assn., D.C. Bar Assn. Office: US Tax Ct 400 2nd St NW Washington DC 20217-0002

SWIG, ROSELYNE CHROMAN, community consultant; b. Chgo., June 8, 1930; m. Richard Swig, Feb. 5, 1950 (dec.); children— Richard, Jr., Susan, Marjorie, Carol. Student, U. Calif.-Berkeley, UCLA; MFA (hon.), DHL (hon.), San Francisco Art Inst., 1988. Founder, pres. Roselyne C. Swig Artsource, San Francisco, 1977-94; apptd. by Pres. Clinton as dir. Art in Embassies Program U.S. Dept. of State, 1994-97; founder, pres. Comcon Internat., 1998—. Founder Ptnrs. Ending Domestic Abuse, San Francisco. Trustee San Francisco Mus. Modern Art, U. Art Mus., Berkeley, Calif.; ex officio bd. mem. Jewish Mus. San Francisco; bd. dirs., former treas. Am. Jewish Joint Distbn. Com.; vice chair fine art adv. panel Fed. Res., Washington; past trustee Mills Coll., Oakland, Calif.; past past pres., bd. dirs. Jewish Cmty. Fedn. San Francisco, the Peninsula, Marin and Sonoma Counties; past commr. San Francisco Pub. Libr.; past bd. dirs. San Francisco Opera, Am. Coun. for Arts, KQED Broadcasting Sys.; past. pres. Calif. State Summer Sch. Arts, past chair bd. trustees San Francisco Art Inst.; past pres. San Francisco Arts Commn.; past nat. v.p. Am./Israel Pub. Affairs Com.; past trustee United Jewish Appeal; past chair bd. trustees Univ. Art Mus. Mem. Women's Forum West (bd. dirs.), Internat. Women's Forum. Avocations: skiing, boating, tennis, fishing.

SWIGER, ELINOR PORTER, lawyer; b. Cleve., Aug. 1, 1927; d. Louie Charles and Mary Isabelle (Shank) Porter; m. Quentin Gilbert Swiger, Feb. 5, 1955; children: Andrew Porter, Calvin Gilbert, Charles Robinson. BA, Ohio State U., 1949, JD, 1951. Bar: Ohio 1951, Ill. 1979. Sr. assoc., now of counsel Robbins, Schwartz, Nicholas, Lifton & Taylor, Ltd., Chgo., 1979—. Author: (book) Mexico for Kids, 1971, Europe for Young Travelers, 1972, The Law and You, 1973 (Literary Guild award), Law in Everyday Life, 1977, Careers in the Legal Professions, 1978, Women Lawyers at Work, 1978. Mem. Glenview (Ill.) Fire and Police Commn., 1976—86; chmn. Glenview Zoning Bd. Appeals, 1987—97. Mem.: Chgo. Bar Assn. (chmn. legis. exec. com. 1990—92), Women Bar Assn. Ill., Ill. Coun. Sch. Attys. (past chmn.), Ohio State U. Coll. Law Alumni Coun., Soc. Midland Authors. Republican. Home: 1933 Burr Oak Dr Glenview IL 60025 Office: Robbins Schwartz Nicholas Lifton & Taylor 20 N Clark St Ste 900 Chicago IL 60602-4115

SWIGER, ELIZABETH DAVIS, chemist, educator; b. Morgantown, W Va, June 27, 1926; d. Hannibal Albert and Tyreeca Elizabeth (Stemple) Davis; m. William Eugene Swiger, June 2, 1948 (dec.); children: Susan Elizabeth Swiger Knotts-Case, Wayne William. BS in Chemistry, W.Va. U., 1948, MS in Chemistry, 1952, PhD in Chemistry, 1964. Instr. math. Fairmont State Coll., 1948-49, instr. math. and phys. sci., 1956-57, instr. chemistry, 1957-60, from asst. prof. to assoc. prof., 1960—66, prof., 1966-92, chmn., divsn. sci., math, and health careers, 1991-92; NSF fellow rsch. W.Va. U., Morgantown, 1963-64, prof. emerita, 1992. Advisor Am. Chem. Soc. student affiliates, 1965-88. Author: Morton Family History, 1984-98, Davis-Winters Family History, 1994—, Civil War Letters and Diary of Joshua Winters, 1991, 2d edit., 1996; contbr. articles to profl. jour. Chmn. Blacks Chapel Meml. Found., 1993—; rep. adv. coun. to Bd. Regents Fairmont State Coll., Charleston, W.Va., 1977—78, rep. instl. bd. advisors, 1990—92. NSF grantee, 1963; named Outstanding Prof. W.Va. Legislature, Charleston, 1990. Mem.: Am. Chem. Soc. (advisor student affiliates 1965—88, sec. chmn. North W.Va. 1975—83), W.Va. Acad. Sci. (life; pres. 1978—79, exec. com. edn. chmn. 1990—93), Nature Conservancy (bd. dir. W.Va. chpt. 1970—86, chmn. 1980—82), Marion County Hist. Soc. (life), Prickett's Fort Meml. Found. (life; bd. dir. 1988—2000, chmn. elect 1990—92, chmn. 1992—96, bd. dir 2002—), Morning Gardeners Garden Club (pres. 1999—, 1999—2003). Republican. Methodist. Avocations: local history, local history, genealogy, gardening, computers, quilting. Home: 1599 Hillcrest Rd Fairmont WV 26554-4807 Home (Winter): 242 Laird Dr Freeport FL 32439

SWIGER, L. A. agricultural studies educator; BS in Animal Husbandry, Ohio State U., 1954; MS, Iowa State U., 1957, PhD, 1960. Geneticist USDA, Lincoln, Neb., assoc. prof. animal sci., experiment sta. statistician, 1959—65; grad. chmn. Ohio State U.; prof. animal sci. Va. Tech, Blacksburg, 1965—80, head dept. animal sci., 1980-86, assoc. dean rsch. Coll. Agrl. and Life Scis., 1986-92, interim dean, 1992-93, dean, 1993—. Recipient Rockefeller Prentice Meml. award Am. Soc. Animal Sci., 1984. Office: Va Tech Coll Agrl and Life Sci Blacksburg VA 24061-0402 E-mail: swiger@vt.edu.

SWIGER, MARK, social studies educator; b. Elkins, W.Va., Aug. 3, 1960; s. Arden Leo and Ethel Marie (Welch) S.; m. Dawn Schwertfeger, July 2, 1983; children: Amanda, Shane. BA in History, Bethany Coll., 1982; MA in Curriculum and Instrn., W.Va. U., 1993. Cert. tchr., W.Va. Social studies tchr. Cameron (W.Va.) H.S., 1982-97, cross country coach, 1983-90; social studies tchr. Moundsville (W.Va.) Jr. H.S., 1997—2002; ednl. devel. coord. Acad. Problem-Based Learning, Wheeling, W.Va., 2002—. Track coach John Marshall H.S., Glen Dale, W.Va., 1985-92; cross country coach Wheeling (W.Va.) Jesuit U., 1990—, track & field coach, 1992—; mem. tech. com. Marshall County Schs., Moundsville, 1995-97. Mem. local sch. improvement coun. Cameron H.S., 1995-97; mem. accreditation team North Ctrl. Assn., Wheeling, 1991, 96; mem. rating com. Nat. Assn. Intercollegiate Athletics, 1993-95. Named Cross-Country Coach of Yr. men W.Va. Intercollegiate Athletic Conf., 1992, 93, 2000, 03, women, 1993, 94, 94, 2001, Nat. Assn. Cross-Country Intercollegiate Athletic Conf., 1993, 94; Fulbright-Hayes study abroad fellow U.S. Dept. Edn., 1995; grantee IBM, 1998, 99, Local Unified Sch. Improvement Efforts, 1996-97, Lewis and Clark Rediscovery, 1999—. Mem. NEA, W.Va. Edn. Assn., Marshall County Edn. Assn., Nat. Geog. Soc., Nat. Coun. Social Studies, W.Va. Geog. Alliance, NCAA Coaches Assn., U.S. Track & Field Coaches Assn. (conf. rep.).

SWIGERT, JAMES MACK, lawyer; b. Carthage, Ill., Sept. 25, 1907; s. James Ross and Pearl (Mack) S.; m. Alice Francis Titcomb Harrower, July 7, 1931 (dec. 1990); children: Oliver, David Ladd, Sally Harper (Mrs. Hamilton). Student, Grinnell Coll., 1925-27; SB, Harvard U., 1930, LLB, 1935. Bar: Ill. 1935, Ohio 1937. With Campbell, Clithero & Fischer, Chgo., 1935-36, Taft, Stettinius & Hollister, Cin., 1936—, ptnr., 1948-79, sr. ptnr. and chmn. exec. com., 1979-85, of counsel, 1985—. Dir., mem. exec. com. Union Cen. Life Ins. Co., 1963-79; dir., chmn. audit com. Philips Industries, 1975-82. Author articles on labor rels. and labor law. Bd. dirs. Cin. Symphony Orch., 1976-78; trustee, chmn. exec. com. Am. Music Scholarship Assn., 1987-92. Mem.: Queen City (past dir.), Cincinnati Country (past v.p., dir.), Queen City Optimists (past pres.), Tennis (past pres.), Recess (past pres.), Harvard Law (past pres.) (Cin.). Republican. Presbyterian. Home: 2121 Alpine Pl Cincinnati OH 45206-2690 Office: 1800 US Bank Ctr Cincinnati OH 45202 Office Phone: 513-357-9360. E-mail: swigert@taftlaw.com.

SWIGGER, KEITH, library and information scientist, educator; b. Hutchinson, Kans., Feb. 3, 1943; s. Paul Clarke and Loneta (Miller) S.; children: Jessica, Nathaniel; m. Cindy Johnson Potter, Nov. 29, 1997. BA, U. Chgo., 1965, MA, 1975, Ind. U., 1967; PhD, U. Iowa, 1973. Sketchwriter Marquis Who's Who, Chgo., 1963-67; teaching asst. Ind. U., Bloomington, 1967, U. Iowa, Iowa City, 1968-73, lectr., 1973-74, libr., 1976-77; asst. prof. East Tex. State U., Commerce, 1977-81; asst. prof. libr. scis. Tex. Woman's U., Denton, 1981-85, assoc. prof., 1985-89, prof., 1989—, interim dean Sch. Libr. Sci., 1991-92, dean Sch. Libr. and Info. Studies, 1992-2000, dir. Sch. Libr. and Info. Studies, 2001—02, dir. Ctr. for Consulting and Planning, 1997—, dean Coll. Profl. Edn., 2000—03, dir. Gear Up fed. grant program, 2002—03. Cons. librs., univs., and profl. assns.; mem. adv. com. continuum libr. edn. We. Coun. State Librs., 2003—. Co-editor Jour. of Youth Svcs., 1997-2000; contbr. numerous articles to profl. jours. Bd. dirs. ACLU, Denton, 1990-92, Emily Fowler Pub. Libr., Denton, 1995-97, vice chair, 1997; mem. Tex. Edn. Tech. Coord. Coun., 2000-03; delegate Tex. Dem. Party state convention, 2004. Rsch. grantee OCLC, Inc., 1990-91, Career Tng. grantee U.S. Office Edn., 1990-98; postdoctoral fellow Coun. on Libr. Resources U. Chgo., 1974-75; recipient Svc. award Nat. Storytelling Assn., 1998. Mem. ALA, Tex. Libr. Assn., Libr. and Info. Tech. Assn., Tex. Faculty Assn., Assn. Libr. Info. Sci. Edn. Office: Tex Womans U Sch Libr Info Studies PO Box 425438 Denton TX 76204-5438 E-mail: KeithSwigger@charter.net.

SWIGGETT, HAROLD E. (HAL SWIGGETT), writer, photographer; b. Moline, Kans., July 22, 1921; s. Otho Benjamin and Mildred (Spray) S.; m. Wilma Caroline Turner, Mar. 1, 1942; children: Gerald, Vernon. Grad. h.s. Ordained minister So. Bapt. Ch. Staff photographer San Antonio Express-News, 1947-67, head dept., 1955-67; free-lance writer/photographer San Antonio, 1947—; full-time, 1967—. Contbg. author books on game gunting, gun-oriented paperbacks; author: Hal Swiggett on North American Deer, 1980; sr. editor Harris Publs., Guns/Hunting; editor: Handguns 95; contbg. editor N.Am. Hunter. Minister So. Bapt. Ch. With USAAC, World War II. Recipient 10th ann. Outstanding Am. Handgunner award, 1982, Lifetime Cicero award, 1991, St. Gabriel Possenti medal, 1991; named to Am. Handgunner Hall of Fame, 1987, Anschutz/PSI Gun Writer of Yr., 1990, Handgun Hunter Hall of Fame, 1991. Mem. NRA (life), Wildlife Unltd. (pres. chpt. 1955-58), Outdoor Writers Assn. Am. (dir. 1969-72), Tex. Outdoor Writers Assn. (pres. 1967-68), Ducks Unltd., Tex. Rifle Assn. (life), Internat. Handgun Metallic Silhouette Assn. (life), Game Conservation Internat. Home: 539 Roslyn San Antonio TX 78204-2456

SWIHART, MARK THOMAS, chemical engineer, educator; b. Walsenburg, Colo., Sept. 27, 1969; s. Thomas Donald and Retha Jane Swihart; m. Wendy Kay Good, Jan. 1, 1994; children: Rachel June children: Sarah Katherine, Jacob Carl. BS in Chem. Engring., Rice U., Houston, 1992; PhD in Chem. Engring., U. Minn., Mpls., 1997. Rsch. assoc. U. Minn., Mpls., 1997—98; asst. prof. SUNY, Buffalo, 1998—2004, assoc. prof., 2004—. Mem., sci. adv. bd. Innovalight, Inc., Austin, Tex., 2003—. Contbr. articles to profl. jours. Mem.: AAAS, AIChE, Am. Soc. of Engring. Edn., Materials Rsch. Soc., The Electrochem. Soc. (J.B. Wagner award 2003), Am. Chem. Soc. Achievements include patents for U.S. Patent No. 6, 294, 707, for a fluidized bed chem. reactor; patents pending for Silicon Nanoparticle Production. Home: 311 Countryside Lane Williamsville NY 14221 Office: SUNY 303 Furnas Hall Buffalo NY 14221 Office Phone: 716-645-2911 2205. Business E-Mail: swihart@eng.buffalo.edu.

SWIHART, STEVEN TAYLOR, judge; b. Alexandria, Va., Sept. 7, 1942; s. Albert Taylor and Marian Dorothy (Lille) S.; 1 child, Sarah Ann Rosenbaum. BA, Univ. Nebr., 1966, JD, 1972. Bar: Nebr. 1972. Staff atty. Panhandle Legal Svcs., Scottsbluff, Nebr., 1972-73, Lincoln (Nebr.) Legal Aid Soc., 1974; atty., advisor Health/Human Svcs., Social Security Adminstrn. Office Hearing Appeals, Omaha, 1975-77; ptnr. Christian, Krieg & Swihart, Omaha, 1978-88; adminstrv. law judge SSA, Office Hearing Appeals, Denver, 1989—. 1st lt. U.S. Army, 1966-69, Vietnam. Mem. Nebr. State Bar Assn. Democrat. Avocations: music, reading, chess. Office: Office Hearings Appeals 1244 Speer Blvd Denver CO 80204-3518 E-mail: sswi185037@aol.com.

SWINBURN, CHARLES, rail transportation executive; b. Bowness on Windermere, Cumbria, Eng., Apr. 11, 1942; came to U.S., 1949; s. Joseph and Myra (Sullivan) S.; m. Carol Ann Ditzler, Dec. 16, 1972; children: Ann Elizabeth, Catherine Knowles. BA in Psychology, Princeton U., 1963; MBA, Harvard U., 1971; JD, U. Pa., 1993. Industry analyst U.S. Dept. Transp., Washington, 1971-73, chief Industry Analysis Div., 1973-76, dep. asst. sec., 1979-83; assoc. adminstr. fed. assistance Fed. R.R. Adminstrn., Washington, 1976-79; v.p. FS Rollins Environ. Svcs. Inc., Wilmington, Del., 1983-90; atty. Morgan, Lewis & Bockius, Washington, 1993—2004; CEO RailAmerica, Inc., Boca Raton, Fla., 2004—. Capt. USMC, 1963-69; major USMCR, 1970-75. Decorated DFC (2), Air medal (35); recipient Presdl. Disting. Exec. award, 1980, Dept. Transp. Meritorious Achievement award, 1976, 78, 81 E-mail: charles.swinburn@railamerica.com.

SWINDELL, ARCHIE CALHOUN, JR., research biochemist, statistician; b. Sept. 26, 1936; s. Archie Calhoun and Louise Evelyn (Ellis) S.; m. Dolores Dyer Holland, Dec. 28, 1962; children: Randy Zidick, Matthew Earle. BS in Chemistry, So. Meth. U., 1958; M in Nutritional Sci., Cornell U., 1965, PhD in Biochemistry, 1968. NIH postdoctoral fellow Duke U. Med. Ctr., Durham, NC, 1968-70; rsch. sci. positions in biochemistry, pharmacology, stats. Pfizer, Inc., Groton, Conn., 1970-95; statis. cons., 1995—. Contbr. articles on cholesterol metabolism, hormone action, cell culture, actions of drugs, data analysis, stats. to profl. jours., 1968-2003; patentee several anti-atherosclerosis agts. Mem. Town Coun., Groton, 1991-95, Bd. of Edn., 1997—. With U.S. Army, 1958-61. Mem. AAAS, Am. Statis. Assn., Am. Heart Assn., Am. Assn. Artificial Intelligence, Sigma Xi. Avocations: astronomy, nature photography. Home and Office: 192 Monument St Groton CT 06340-3915 E-mail: swindellac@tvcconnect.net.

SWINDELLS, WILLIAM, JR., lumber and paper company executive; b. Oakland, CA, 1930; married BS, Stanford U., 1953. With Willamette Industries, Inc., Portland, Oreg., 1953—, sr. v.p. prodn., mktg. bldg. materials, until 1978, exec. v.p., 1978-80, pres. forest products div., 1980-82, pres., chief exec. officer, 1982-96, also dir., chmn., 1984-97; chmn., CEO Willamette Industry, Portland, 1997, chmn. bd., 1997—. Dir. Oreg. Bank, Portland Office: Willamette Industries 1300 SW 5th Ave Ste 3800 Portland OR 97201-5671

SWINEHART, DAVID, music educator; s. William and Virginia Swinehart; m. Tammy Kerstetter, Aug. 19, 1989; children: Benjamin, Alicia. BM in Music Edn., Susquehanna U., 1985—89. Music tchr. orch. Del. Valley Sch. Dist., Milford, Pa., 1989—. Drama music dir. DVHS Drama Club, Milford, 1992—2000; assoc. dir. Hemlock Farms Choral Soc., 2002—04. Mem. Ch. at Hemlock Farms, Lords Valley, Pa., 1991—. Mem.: NEA, Nat. Assn. Music Educators, Am. String Tchr.'s Assn. with Nat. Sch. Orch. Assn.

SWINEHART, TIMOTHY E. music educator; b. Coshocton, Ohio, Dec. 12, 1950; s. James Edward and Willanna Fay Swinehart; m. Pauline Sue Toy, July 15, 1972; children: Shad J., Jason E. MusB, Capital U., 1972; MusM, Wichita State U., 1976; PhD, Ohio State U., 1994. Tchr. Berne Union HS, Sugar Grove, Ohio, 1972—75, Wichita State U., Kans., 1975—76, Lexington HS, Ohio, 1976—78, U. Dayton, Ohio, 1978—83, Capital U., Columbus, Ohio, 1983—. Clinician, adjudicator Ohio Music Edn. Assn., Columbus, 1980—; bd. of dir. Bexley Music Assn., Ohio, 1984—. Author: A Parents Guide to Musical Instruments, 1987; composer: (musical score) Fantasies, 1992; author: (articles) various profl. jours., 1998. Fundraiser Bexley Meadow Music Assn., 1984—; series admin. Ctrl. Coll. Concert Series, Westerville, Ohio, 1999—. Recipient Mayor's Cmty. Svc. citation, City of Bexley, 2002. Mem.: Ohio Music Edn. Assn. (conf. chair 1972—, 25 Year award 1998), Phi Beta Mu (Honorary) (pres. 1985—, Golden Baton award 2001). Achievements include founder of the Ohio Music Edn. Assn. Marching Band Competitions; co-founder of "NOW" Music Festival, Ohio. Avocations: woodworking, swimming, automobile detailing, furniture design. Home: 6087 Warbling Ln Westerville OH 43081 E-mail: tswineha@capital.edu.

SWING, MARILYN S. metropolitan clerk; b. Nashville, Tenn., Aug. 21, 1949; BA, St. Mary of the Woods, Terre Haute, Ind., 1976. Adminstr. metro clerks office Govt. City of Nashville, Davidson County, Nashville, 1976—, metro clerk, 1984— Bd. dirs. Municipal Clerks Edn. Found., 1992-99. Mem. Internat. Inst. Municipal Clerks. Office: Metropolitan Government of Nashville and Davidson County Metro Clerk 205 Metro Courthouse Nashville TN 37201-5026

SWING, WILLIAM LACY, ambassador; b. Lexington, N.C., Sept. 11, 1934; s. Baxter Dermot and Mary Frances (Barbee) S.; m. Yuen Fong Cheong; children: Brian Curtis, Gabrielle. AB, Catawba Coll., 1956, LLD (hon.), 1980; BD, Yale U., 1960; postgrad., Oxford (Eng.) U., U. Tuebingen, Germany, 1961, Hofstra U., LLD (hon.), 1994. Vice consul Am. Consulate, Port Elizabeth, Republic of South Africa, 1963-66; internat. economist Bur. Econ. Affairs Dept. State, 1966-68; consul, chief consular sect. Am. Consulate Gen., Hamburg, Germany, 1968-72; internat. rels. officer, desk officer Fed. Republic Germany Dept. State, Washington, 1972-74; dep. chief of mission, counselor Am. Embassy, Bangui, Ctrl. African Republic, 1974-76; fellow Ctr. for Internat. Affairs Harvard U., 1977-79; amb. to People's Republic of Congo, 1979-81; amb. to Republic of Liberia, 1981-85; amb. to South Africa, 1989-92; amb. to Fed. Republic of Nigeria, 1992-93; amb. to Haiti, 1993-98; amb. to Dem. Republic of the Congo (formerly Zaire), Am. Embassy, Kinshasha, 1998—2001; spl. rep. of UN Sec.-Gen. for Western Sahara, 2001—03; spl. rep. of UN sec.-gen. for Democratic Republic of Congo, 2003—. Dir. Fgn. Svc. Career Devel. and Assignments, 1985-87; sr. dep. asst. sec. state for pers., 1987-89. Co-editor: Education for Decision, 1963, U.S. African Policy and the Case of South Africa: Dilemas and Priorities, 1977, Haiti: In Physical Contact with History, 1995. Recipient Meritorious Honor award USIA, 1971, Superior Honor award Dept. State, 1985, Presdl. Disting. Svc. award, 1985, Presdl. Meritorious Svc. award, 1987, 90, 94, Equal Employment Opportunity award Dept. State, 1988, Disting. Honor award, 1994, Valor award, 1995, Disting. Svc. award, 1996, Disting. Pub. Svc. award USCG, 1998, U.S. Presdl. Cert. of Commendation, 1998, Disting. Alumnus award, Yale U. Divinity Sch., 1995. Mem. Army and Navy Club. Yale Club (Washington and N.Y.C.), Harvard Club, Internat. Club, Lions. Mem. United Ch. of Christ. Home: 6002 Paradise Point Dr Miami FL 33157 Office: MONUC-HQ Kinshasa PO Box 4653 Grand Central Sta New York NY 10163-4653 Office Phone: 212-963-0103. E-mail: swing@un.org.

SWINNEY, CAROL JOYCE, secondary school educator; Langs. tchr. Hugoton (Kans.) High Sch., 1972-98; dir. distance learning S.W. Plains Regional Svcs. Ctr., Kans., 1998—. Named Kans. Tchr. of Yr., Disney for Lang. Tchr. of Yr., 1993, Milken Nat. Educator, 1992. Office: PO Drawer 1010 Sublette KS 67877-1010

SWINSON, ANGELA ANTHONY, physician; b. Washington, Nov. 5, 1960; d. Edgar and Phosia Lee (Hanna) Anthony; m. Kevin Lamont Swinson, June 28, 1986; 1 child, Erik Alan. BA, Johns Hopkins U., 1983, MPH, 1991; MD, Georgetown U., 1987. Diplomate Am. Bd. Forensic Examiners, Am. Bd. Forensic Medicine. Phlebotomist Georgetown U. Hosp., Washington, 1984; med. resident Homewood Hosp. Ctr., Balt., 1987-88; clinic physician Ea. Chest Clinic, Balt., 1990-91; resident in preventive medicine Johns Hopkins Sch. Hygiene and Pub. Health, Balt., 1990-92; asst. med. dir. Occupl. Med. Svc., NIH, Bethesda, Md., 1992-97; physician Med-Therapy PA, Balt., 1998—2002; staff physician CHO Meridian Healthcare, Sparrows Point, Md., 2002—03, Multi-Specialty Healthcare, LLC, Balt., 2003—. Mem. workgroup Prince George's County, Cheverly, Md., 1991-92. Contbr. articles to profl. jours. Sr. leader Girl Scouts Ctrl. Md., Balt., 1981—83; mem. Touch of Love Bible Ch., Laurel, Md., 2002—, Faith AME Ch., 1993—2001, mem. inspirational choir, 1993—99, mass choir, 1993—2001, mem. scholarship com., 1995—99, co-chair health and fitness ministry, 1999—2001, instr. vacation Bible sch., 1995; bd. dirs. Nat. Consortium for African Am. Children, Inc., 1995—. Grantee Nat. Med. Fellowships, 1983-85. Mem. Am. Coll. Occupl. and Environ. Medicine, Am. Coll. Forensic Examiners, Md. State Med. Soc., Am. Contact Dermatitis Soc., Nat. Med. Assn., Delta Sigma Theta (Golden Life, co-chair phys. and mental health com. 1996-99, Columbia, Md. alumnae chpt. treas., Mu Psi chpt. 1980-82, pres. Mu Psi chpt. 1982-83, Minerva award 1981, chpt. award 1983). Avocations: music, art, aerobic exercise, religious activities. Office: Multi Specialty Healthcare, LLC 1800 N Charles St Dr, Ste 100 Baltimore MD 21201 Office Phone: 410 234-1600.

SWINTON, DAVID HOLMES, academic administrator; b. New Haven; m. Patricia Lewis; 6 children. BA in Econ. with honors, NYU, 1968; MA in Econ., Harvard U., 1971, PhD in Econ., 1975. Prof. econ. Clark Coll., Atlanta, dir. So. Ctr. of Studies in Pub. Policy; dean Sch. of Bus., Jackson State U. Contbr. articles to profl. jours., including Am. Econ. Rev., Jour. Urban Analysis, others; bd. economists Black Enterprise mag., 1984-90. Chmn. Greater Columbia C. of C.; econ. advisor Nat. Urban League; deacon 1st Calvary Bapt. Ch. Ford Found. fellow. Mem. Phi Beta Kappa, Coat of Arms Soc. Office: Benedict Coll 1600 Harden St Columbia SC 29204-1058 E-mail: swinlond@benedict.edu.

SWINTON, JEFFREY CHEEVER, lawyer; b. Salt Lake City, June 22, 1947; s. Kenneth Perry and Venice (Cheever) S.; m. Heidi Sorensen, Apr. 14, 1972; children: Cameron, Daniel, Jonathan, Ian. BA, U. Utah, 1971, JD, 1974. Bar: Utah 1974, U.S. Ct. Appeals (10th cir.) 1985, U.S. Supreme Ct. 1985. Ptnr. Stringham, Larsen, Mazuran & Sabin, Salt Lake City, 1974-79; sr. v.p. Ruti-Sweetwater, Inc., Salt Lake City, 1979-84; ptnr. Larsen, Mazuran & Verhaaren, Salt Lake City, 1984-85, Jensen & Swinton, Salt Lake City, 1986-87; ptnr., v.p., bd. dirs. Woodbury, Jensen, Kesler & Swinton, Salt Lake City, 1988-91; ptnr. Stoker & Swinton, Salt Lake City, 1991—. Assoc. editor Utah Bar Jour., 1973-74; editor Summation: Jour. Utah Law, 1973. Chmn., v.p., del. Salt Lake City Rep. Com., 1975-88; trustee Bus. Industry Cmty. Edn. Partnership, Salt Lake City, 1979-80; mem. panel judges Utah Pub. Employees Assn., 1980-83, 85-87; bd. dirs., pres. Work Activities Ctr. for Handicapped Adults, Salt Lake City, 1987-93; chair Utah state bd. svcs. People with Disabilities, 1993-99, govs. coun., 1996; dist. chmn. Boy Scouts Am., Salt Lake City, 1987-94, coun. exec. bd., 2004-; bd. dirs. Homeless Youth Resource Ctr., 1998-2000, Cmty. Devel. Corp. Utah, 2002 ; exec. dir. Salt Lake Inner City Project, 1996-2003; chmn. Pioneer Region Welfare Com., 1998-2003; bishop Mormon Ch., 1977-85, stake pres., 1994-2003, Area Authority Seventy, 2002—. Mem. ABA, ATLA, Utah State Bar Assn. (chair franchise law sect. 1997-98, 2003-), Nat. Futures Assn. (arbitrator 1991), U. Utah Law Sch. Alumni Assn. (treas., trustee 1979-83), Young Alumni Assn. U. Utah (pres. 1981-83), Soc. Bar and Gavel (pres. 1976-78), Beehive, Owl and Key, Skull and Bones, Rotary (pres. 1993). Mem. Lds Ch. Avocations: tennis, golf, singing. Home: 1211 East 100 South Salt Lake City UT 84102 Office: 311 S State St Ste 400 Salt Lake City UT 84111-2382 Office Phone: 801-359-4000. Personal E-mail: JCSwinton@aol.com.

SWINWOOD, LAURIE A. writer, educator; b. Malone, N.Y., Feb. 16, 1954; d. Henry Gerald LaVoie and Edith Madeline McGowan; m. Eric John Swinwood, Aug. 16, 1975; children: Corey Thomas, Vanessa Marie Kennedy. BA, SUNY, Potsdam, 1977, MS in Edn., 1987. Cert. tchr. State of N.Y. Tchr. Edwards-Knox Ctrl. Sch., Edwards, NY, 1981—. Editor Walrus and Pelican Press, Canton, NY, 2002—. Author: Rainbows and Other Promises, 1999. Mem.: Adirondack Writers, North Country Writers, Kappa Delta Pi. Avocations: reading, writing, sewing, walking, swimming. Home: 20 Fairlane Dr Canton NY 13617 E-mail: swinwood@usadatanet.net.

SWIRE, JAMES BENNETT, lawyer; b. Bklyn., July 10, 1942; AB, Princeton U., 1963; LLB, Harvard U., 1966. Bar: NY 1967, DC 1976. Assoc. Rogers Hoge & Hills, N.Y.C., 1966-73, ptnr., 1974—82, Townley & Updike, N.Y.C., 1982-95, chmn. mgmt. com., 1990-95; ptnr. Dorsey & Whitney, LLP, N.Y.C., 1995—, office head, 1998—2004, mem. mgmt. com., 1999—2003, mem. exec. com., 2002—03. Guest lectr. food and drug law Seton Hall Law Sch., 1977. Trustee Cancer Care, Inc., 1978—, v.p., 1982-86, chmn. exec. com., 1986-90, pres. 1990-95; trustee N.Y. Bd. Am. Liver Found., 2003—; chmn. cmty. bd. Beth Israel-St. Luke's Roosevelt Cancer Ctr., N.Y.C., 1999-2001. Mem. Assn. Bar City N.Y. (chmn. com. medicine and law 1977-80, sec. com. on trademarks and unfair competition 1985-88), N.Y. State Bar Assn., Internat. Trademark Assn. (assoc.). Office: 250 Park Ave New York NY 10177-0001 E-mail: swire.james@dorseylaw.com.

SWIRNOFF, LOIS, artist, color theorist; b. Bklyn., May 9, 1931; d. Harold and Fannie (Goldstein) Swirnoff; m. Richard Boyce (dec.); 1 child, Dr. Joshua Avram Boyce. Cert. of graduation, Cooper Union Art Sch., N.Y.C., 1951; BFA, Yale U., 1953, MFA summa cum laude, 1956. Instr. art Wellesley (Mass.) Coll., 1954-58; asst. prof. UCLA, 1965-68, vis. lectr., 1981-86, assoc. prof., 1986-90, prof. emerita, 1990—; lectr. Harvard U., Cambridge, Mass., 1968-75; assoc. prof., chmn. art dept. Skidmore Coll., Saratoga Springs, N.Y., 1977-81; guest artist Cooper Union Art Sch., 1990-91, adj. prof., 1991—; Feltman Chair The Cooper Union, N.Y., 2001—02. Author: Dimensional Color, 1989, 2d edit., 2003, Van Nostrand Reinhold, 1992, The Color of Cities, 2000; one-woman shows include Farnsworth Mus., 1958, Swetzoff Gallery, Boston, 1962, Inst. Internat. Edn., N.Y.C., 1978—79, NAS, Washington, 1982—83, The Woman's Bldg., L.A., Bradford Coll. Laura Knott Gallery, 1988, Wellesley Coll., Gallery BAI, N.Y.C., 1996, N.Y. Sch. of Interior Design, 2000—01, exhibited in group shows at City Art Mus., St. Louis, 1951, Bklyn. Mus., 1951, Munson-Williams Proctor Inst., Unica, N.Y., 1956, Swetzoff Gallery, 1963—65, Inst. Contemporary Art, Boston, 1961, LaJolla (Calif.) Mus., 1968, L.A. County Mus., 1968, Represented in permanent collections Addison Gallery Am. Art at Andover, Wellesley Coll., Mary I. Bunting Inst., Radcliffe Coll, UCLA, also pvt.collections. Recipient merit award Art Dirs. Club N.Y., 1979; Fulbright fellow, Florence, Italy, 1951-52, Yale-Norfolk summer fellow, 1953, fellow Mary I. Bunting Inst., Radcliffe Coll., 1961-63, Yaddo fellow, 1985-86; Mellon faculty grantee Skidmore Coll., 1981, grantee Graham Found., 1988, 98. Studio: 80 Monmouth St Brookline MA 02446-5607 Office Phone: 617-731-5071. E-mail: swirnoff@aol.com.

SWIRSKY, JUDITH PERLMAN, arts administrator, consultant, writer; b. Bklyn., Oct. 31, 1928; d. Samuel and Rose (Klein) Perlman; m. Leo Jerome Swirsky, June 26, 1949; 1 child, Marjorie Ann Swirsky Zelner. BA, NYU, 1947; postgrad., Columbia U., 1947-48. Rsch. asst. The Bklyn. Mus., 1947-49, vol. coord., 1983-89; exec. dir. Grand Cen. Art Galleries Edn. Assn., N.Y.C., 1988-90; freelance curator Genest Gallery, Lambertville, N.J., 1990; dir. vol. resources Snug Harbor Cultural Ctr., S.I., 1992-95, dir. spl. events, 1994-95. Dir. art sales and rental Gallery The Bklyn. Mus., 1974-77; del. Vol. Com. of Art Mus., Balt., 1973, panelist, 1979; mem., co-founder Vol. Program Adminstrs., N.Y.C., Cultural Inst., 1984—; ind. curator travelling exhbn. Four Objects, Four Artists, Relatively Speaking: Mothers and Daus. in Art, 1994—, Memory and Desire, Paintings and Watercolors by Harriet Shorr, Charles Parness: A Different View of Life and the World, Together Working, 1999-2002, Series, 2002, American Fractal, 2001-02. Co-author: On Exhibit, 1993-98, author, 1999-2003. Pres. Community Com. for the Bklyn. Mus., 1969-70; bd. dirs. Greater N.Y. Girl Scouts U.S., 1965-71; founder Children's Sch. Time Program and Women's League, Bklyn. Acad. Music, 1961-64; chmn. Bklyn. Guild for Opera, 1966-77; bd. dirs. Arthritis Found. Greater N.Y., 1969-79; trustee Bklyn. Home for Children, 1961-70, Julia Bernstein League of the Free Nurses Inst., 1952-60. Mem. Am. Assn. Mus., Assn. Vol. Adminstrn. (cert., editor region II newsletter), Am. Assn. Mus. Vols., Civitas. Avocations: travel, cooking. Home and Office: 57 Montague St Brooklyn NY 11201-3374

SWISHER, CHARLES FRANCIS, electrical engineer, consultant; b. Schenectady, NY, Mar. 8, 1934; s. Thomas Hyer and Frances Hannan Swisher. BSEE, U. Ill., 1956. Elec. engr. Dukane Corp., St. Charles, 1956—58; product mgr. Ampex Corp., Redwood City, Calif., 1958—65; v.p. Vega Electronics Corp., Cupertino, Calif., 1965—68; sr. cons. Jaffe Holden Acoustics, Inc., Norwalk, Conn., 1968—72; sound designer San Francisco Opera, 1974—79; v.p. Atlantic City Conv. Hall Organ Soc., Inc., Annapolis, Md., 1980—; exec. dir. The Am. Pipe Organ Mus., Lauderhill, Fla., 1994—. Pres. TBG Prodns., Lauderhill, 1971—. Artist, designer (outdoor symphonic sound sys) NY Philharm. Summer Parks Concerts; prodr.: (CD) The Auditorium Organ, John Balka Plays The Great Organ of St. Mary's Cathedral, San Francisco, (cassette recording) A Treasury of Hymns; dir., designer (music edn. and listening ctr.) The Sound Gallery, prodr., designer (opera and symphony audience expansion) Electronic Standing Rm. Chmn. Arts Commn., Springfield, Oreg., 1992—96. Fellow: Audio Engring. Soc. Achievements include discovery of technique to restore master audio tape recordings; first ever to record in a courtroom trial (1960); co-designer and operator of first PLAT (Pilot Landing Aid Television System), now installed on all US aircraft carriers (1961). Home: 3910 Inverrary Blvd B-608 Lauderhill FL 33319 Office Phone: 954-735-0482. Personal E-mail: cswisher@comcast.net.

SWISHER, ROBERT KEIM, JR., writer; b. Logan, Utah, May 8, 1947; s. Robert Keim Swisher and Billie Lee Bailey; m. MIchelle McMahon (div.); children: Deidra, Daphne; m. Sheila Suzett Swisher-Awalt, Aug. 5, 1997; 1 child, Brandon Awalt. Grad., Burgess H.S., 1965. Author: The Man from the Mountain, 1973, Touch Me If You Love Me, 1976, An American Love Story, 1987, Ned, 1987, The Land, 1987, The Last Narrow Gauge Train Robbery, 1988, Love Lies Bleeding, 1989, Fatal Destiny, 1991, Only Magic, 1994, Last Day in Paradise, 2004; contbr. numerous poems, short stories to lit. publs. With U.S. Army, 1965—67, Vietnam. Mem.: Am. PEN Women (hon.). Roman Catholic. Avocations: fishing, golf, reading, gardening. Home: 301 NE 7th Leon IA 50144

SWIT, LORETTA, actress; b. N.J., Nov. 4, 1939; Student, Am. Acad. Dramatic Arts, Gene Frankel Repertoire Theatre, N.Y.C. Broadway appearances include Same Time Next Year, Any Wednesday, Mame, The Mystery of Edwin Drood, Shirley Valentine, Chgo. (winner Sarah Siddons award 1990); films include Stand Up and Be Counted, 1972, Freebie and the Bean, 1974, Race with the Devil, 1975, S.O.B, 1980, Beer, 1985, Whoops Apocalypse (U.K.), 1987, Forest Warrior, 1996, Boardheads, 1999; star TV series M*A*S*H, 1972-83 (Emmy awards 1979, 81); TV movies include Shirts/Skins, 1973, The Last Day, 1975, Mirror, Mirror, 1979, Valentine, 1979, Friendships, Secrets and Lies, 1979, Cagney and Lacey, 1981, Games Mother Never Taught You, 1982, First Affair, 1983, The Execution, 1985, Dreams of Gold: The Mel Fisher Story, 1986, My Dad Can't Be Crazy, Can He?, Hell Hath No Fury, 1992, A Killer Among Friends, 1993, Forest Warrior, 1996; star on major dramatic shows and musical variety shows, including Bob Hope Christmas Special, Perry Como, The Muppets. Mem. AFTRA, Screen Actors Guild, Actors Equity. Address: Artists Group Ltd 10100 Santa Monica Blvd Los Angeles CA 90067-4003

SWITLO, JANICE GEORGINA ALICE E. barrister, solicitor, mediator, legal and business consultant, strategist; b. Vancouver, B.C., Can., Jan. 10, 1959; d. Alexander Donald and Mary (Shutka) Switlo; married; 1 child. LLB, Osgoode Hall, Toronto, 1986, B.Commerce, U. B.C., 1981. Mgmt. cons. Control Data Can. Ltd., Vancouver, 1981-83; articled student Ladner Downs, 1986—87; barrister, solicitor Aydin & Co., Vancouver, 1987-88; legal counsel Dept. Justice of Can., Vancouver, 1989-93; gen. counsel Westbank Indian Band, Westbank, B.C., 1993-94; barrister, solicitor, cons. Switlo & Co., Peachland, B.C., 1993-97; candidate fed. election Okanagan-Coquihalla, 1997; legal advisor Ministry Aboriginal Affairs, Govt. N.W.T., 1999-2000. Mem. adv. coun. on multiculturalism, adv. coun. to Minister of Multiculturalism, B.C., 1996-98; presenter in field. Author: (book/screenplay) Sookinchute, 2001, (treatise) Trick or Treaty?, 1995, Apple Cede: First Nations Land Management Regime, 1999, In a perfect world...Modern day colonialism in Canada, 2001, The River Forks Here: Canada's attempt to execute the 1969 White Paper and Indigenous Peoples, 2002, (book) Gustafsen Lake: Under Seige, 1997. Dir. B.C. Parents in Crisis Soc., Vancouver, 1991—93, Orpheum Kids Club Soc., Vancouver, 1991, Vancouver Youth Theatre, 2001. Scholar, Univ. Mem. Internat. Bar Assn., Internat. Commn. Jurists (Can. sect.), Can. Counsel on Internat. Law, York U. Alumni Assn., U. B.C. Commerce Alumni Assn., Phi Delta Phi. Office: Switlo & Co 141-6200 McKay Ave Ste 955 Burnaby BC V5H 4M9 Canada Office Phone: 800-332-1191. Personal E-mail: janice@switlo.com.

SWITZER, JO YOUNG, academic administrator, dean; b. Huntington, Ind., Mar. 4, 1948; d. John Frederick and Miriam Lucile (Kindy) Young; children: Sarah Kate Keller, John Christian Keller. BA, Manchester Coll., 1969; MA, U. Kans., 1977, PhD, 1980; postdoctoral, Ind. U., 1983, Harvard U., 1995. English tchr., Dearborn Heights, Mich., 1969-70, Fenton High Sch., Bensenville, Ill., 1970-73; asst. instr. U. Kans., Lawrence, 1977-79; asst. prof. Ind. U.-Purdue, Ft. Wayne, Ind., 1979-82; assoc. prof. Manchester Coll., North Manchester, Ind., 1982-87, Ind. U.-Purdue, Ft. Wayne, Ind., 1987-93; v.p., dean for acad. affairs and prof. comm. studies Manchester Coll., 1993—. Recipient E. C. Buehler award U. Kans., 1978; grantee NEH, 1983. Mem. Central States Comm. Assn. (Outstanding Young Educator award 1982), Coun. of Ind. Colls., Am. Coun. on Edn., Am. Assn. Colls. and Univs. Home: 3069 E 1200 N Roanoke IN 46783 Office: Manchester Coll Office Acad Affairs 604 E College Ave North Manchester IN 46962-1276 Fax: 260-982-5042. Office Phone: 260-982-5051. E-mail: jyswitzer@manchester.edu.

SWITZER, JON REX, architect; b. Shelbyville, Ill., Aug. 22, 1937; s. John Woodrow and Ida Marie (Vadalabene) S.; m. Judith Ann Heinlein, July 7, 1962; 1 child, Jeffrey Eric. Student, U. Ill., 1955-58; BS, Millikin U., 1972; MA, U. Ill., Springfield, 1981. Registered architect Ill., Mo., Ohio, Colo.; registered interior designer, Ill. Arch. Warren & Van Praag, Inc., Decatur, Ill., 1970-72; prin. Decatur, 1972-81, Bloomington, Ill., 1981-83; arch. Hilfinger, Asbury, Cufaude, Abels, Bloomington, 1983-84; ptnr. Riddle/Switzer, Ltd., Bloomington, 1984-86; with bldg., design and constrn. divsn. State Farm Ins. Cos., Bloomington, 1986-89; arch. The Riddle Group, Bloomington, 1989-91; prin. J. Rex Switzer, Arch., Bloomington, 1991—. Elder Presbyn. Ch., 1996. With U.S. Army, 1958-61. Mem. AIA (pres. Bloomington chpt. 1983, Decatur chpt. 1976, v.p. Ill. chpt. 1986-87, sec. 1985, treas. 1984), Am. Archtl. Found., Chgo. Architecture Found., Nat. Trust Hist. Preservation, Frank Lloyd Found., Decatur C. of C. (merit citation 1974, merit award 1979), Am. Legion, Masons (32d degree). Republican. Presbyterian. Avocations: swimming, hunting, fishing, reading, drawing. Home: 9 Mary Ellen Way Bloomington IL 61701-2014 Office: 2412 E Washington St Ste 6A Bloomington IL 61704-1613

SWITZER, LINDA THRALL, music educator; b. Dallas, Oct. 16, 1951; m. Dale Glenn Switzer, Mar. 24, 1979; children: Christopher Dale, Kimberly Leigh-Anne. B in Music Edn., East Tex. State U., 1973, MusM, 1975; Bible Sch. advanced cert., Word of Faith, Dallas, 1986. Pvt. brass instr. Greenville (Tex.) Pub. Schs., 1972—74; grad. tchg. asst. music East Tex. State U., Commerce, 1973—74, resident asst. Smith Hall, 1974—75; pvt. brass instr. Commerce Pub. Schs., 1974—75; music instr. Bee County Coll., Beeville, Tex., 1975—91; music dir. Word of Life Ch., Beeville, 1985—; pvt. music instr. Switzer Music, Beeville, 1991—95; music instr. Coastal Bend Coll., Beeville, 1995—. Named Outstanding Young Women Am., 1976. Republican. Avocations: reading, tennis, music. Office: Coastal Bend Coll Performing Arts Divsn 3800 Charco Rd Beeville TX 78102-2110

SWITZER, MAURICE HAROLD, journalist; b. Toronto, Ont., Can., Mar. 28, 1945; s. Harold Switzer and Ruby (Marsden) Hicks; m. Mary Helene Pavlik; children: Andrea Zimperi, Adin, Lisa Doracka. Student, Trent U., Peterborough, Ont., 1964-65. Journalist Belleville (Ont.) Intelligencer, Canada, 1965-67, sports editor, 1967-72, mng. editor, 1972-79, Oshawa (Ont.) Times, 1979-81; pub. Timmins (Ont.) Daily Press, 1981-86, Sudbury (Ont.) Star, 1986-92, Winnipeg (Man.) Free Press, 1992-94; owner Media Help Svcs., 1994—. Mem. faculty Aboriginal Media First Nations Tech. Inst., 1996—97; dir. comm. Assembly of First Nations, Ottawa, 1997—2000, Union Ont. Indians, North Bay, 2000—; mem. faculty Aboriginal Leadership and Mgmt. program Banff Ctr., 1998—; prof. comms. Huntington U., Sudbury, Ont., Canada, 2001—; prof. native studies Canadore Coll., North Bay, Ont. Author: Bruno Cavallo a Conversation, 1991. Mem. elders coun. Mississaugas of Alderville First Nation.

SWITZER, ROBERT LEE, biochemistry educator; b. Clinton, Iowa, Aug. 26, 1940; s. Stephen and Elva Delila (Allison) S.; m. Bonnie George, June 13, 1965; children: Brian, Stephanie. BS, U. Ill., 1961; PhD, U. Calif., Berkeley, 1966. Research fellow Lab. Biochemistry, Nat. Heart Inst., Bethesda, Md., 1966-68; asst. prof. biochemistry U. Ill., Urbana, 1968—73, assoc. prof., 1973—78, prof. biochemistry and basic med. scis., 1978—2002, prof. emeritus, 2002—, dept. head, 1988—93. Mem. biochemistry study sect. NIH, 1985-89, chmn., 1987-89; guest prof. U. Copenhagen, 1995; mem. microbial physiology and genetics study sect., NIH, 1998-2000. Author: (with Liam F. Garrity) Experimental Biochemistry, 3rd rev. edit., 1999; mem. bd. editors Jour. Bacteriology, 1977-82, 1985—2002, Archives Biochemistry and Biophysics, 1977-98, Jour. Biol. Chemistry, 1980-85; contbr. articles to profl. jours. NSF predoctoral fellow, 1961-66; NIH postdoctoral fellow, 1966-68; Guggenheim fellow, 1975 Mem. Am. Soc. for Biochemistry and Molecular Biology, Am. Soc. Microbiology, Am. Chem. Soc., AAAS, Sigma Xi. Home: 404 W Michigan Ave Urbana IL 61801-4948 Office: U Ill Dept Biochemistry 600 S Mathews Ave Urbana IL 61801-3602 E-mail: rswitzer@uiuc.edu.

SWITZER, TOCCOA, artist; b. Clinton, S.C., Dec. 14, 1930; d. Hercules Milledge and Mercer Bailey (Vance) Wise; m. James Layton Switzer, Feb. 20, 1954 (dec.); children: James Layton Jr., Toccoa Bailey, Paul Kent III; m. Paul Kent Switzer, Jr., Oct. 12, 1990. AA, Stephens Coll., Columbia, Mo., 1951; BFA, Ohio State U., Columbus, 1953. Chmn. Switzer/Wise Investment LP, Union, S.C., 1989—. Bd. dirs. M.S. Bailey and Son, Bankers, Clinton, Clinton Investment Co.; mem. adv. bd. Anchor Fin. Corp., Myrtle Beach, S.C. Den mother Cub Scouts Am., Union, 1962-65; vol. ARC, Union, 1968—; Sunday Sch. tchr. Grace United Meth. Ch., Union, 1954-95, chmn. bldg. com., 1976-77, bd. trustees 1985—; bd. dirs. Great Town Program, Union, 1976-82; bd. dirs. Union Main St. Program, 1983-84; mem. bldg. com. Union Carnegie Libr., 1983-85; bd. mem. Union County Health Care Found., Union, 1993—; bd. trustees Wofford Coll., Spartanburg, S.C., 1990—; bd. dir. Bailey Found., Clinton, 1989—; bd. mem. U. S.C.-Union Partnership Bd., 1989—. Recipient Founder Day award U.S.C., Union, 1999. Mem. Friends of the Libr., Union Cotillion Club (pres.), Book and Garden Club (pres. 1989-90), Union County C. of C. (pres. 1981-82). Methodist. Avocations: painting, gardening, reading.

SWOAP, DAVID BRUCE, government affairs consultant; b. Kalamazoo, Mich., Aug. 12, 1937; s. Orlo Frederick and Aileen Esther (Hempy) S. BA in Govt. with honors, Denison U., 1959; MA in Govt, Claremont Grad. Sch., 1961; DSc (hon.), U. Osteo. Medicine and Health Scis., Des Moines, 1981. Asst. sec. Calif. State Pers. Bd., Sacramento, 1972-73; chief dep. dir., acting dir. Calif. State Dept. Social Welfare, 1973, dir., 1973-74, Calif. State Dept. Benefit Payments, 1974-75; sr. rsch. asso. Rep. Study Com., U.S. Ho. of Reps., Washington, 1975-76; profl. staff mem. U.S. Senate Com. on Fin., 1976-79; legis. dir. U.S. Senator William L. Armstrong, 1979-81; dep. sec. HHS, 1981-83; sec. health and welfare State of Calif., Sacramento, 1983-85; ptnr. Franchetti & Swoap, San Francisco, 1985-90; owner Mana Olana Farms, Hakalau, Hawaii, 1989—97; vice chmn. Sacramento Advs., 1991-98; owner The David Bruce Gallery, Carlsbad, Calif., 1995-97. Chmn. bd. Hope Unltd. for Children, San Diego, 1991—96, mem. adv. bd., 1996, chmn. adv. bd., 1996—2003. Elder Presbyn. Ch.; bd. dirs. Friends of SOS Children's Villages, 1989-91; bd. regents John F. Kennedy U., 1990-93; mem. Healthy Families Dorchester adv. bd., 2002-, Md. State Bd. of Physicians, 2003-. Rotary Club Found. fellow, 1961-62 Mem. Wycliffe Assocs., Phi Beta Kappa, Delta Upsilon. Republican.

SWOFFORD, DONALD ANTHONY, architect; b. Houston, Apr. 14, 1947; s. Harry and Henrian (Engbrock) Swofford; 1 child, James McShea. BArch, Tex. A&M U., 1969; MArch, U. Va., 1976. Registered arch., Va., Tex., DC, Nat. Coun. Archtl. Registration Bd.; lic. instrument pilot. Arch., urban designer City of Dallas, 1970-72, Office Milton L. Grigg, FAIA, Archs., 1972-78; prin., owner DASA, PLC, Charlottesville, Va., 1978—. Author: Dallas Historical Landmark Program, 1972; prin. works include Flovanna County Courthouse, Joseph Jarvis residence, 1978, Shrinemont Conf. Ctr., Episcopal Diocese Va., Orkney Springs, 1981, United Coal/Martha Washington Inn, Bristol, Va., 1985, Montpelier, home of James Madison, 1986, restoration Farley, Culpeper, Va., 1987 (Nat. Trust Hist. Preservation Gt. Homes Am., 1985), restoration St. Francis Assisi Cath. Ch., Stanton, Va., 1988, restoration and additions Goochland County (Va.) Courthouse, 1989, George M. McMath residence, Locustville, Va., 1991, restoration of Highlands, home of James Monroe, Charlottesville, 1991, restoration of Clover Hill Tavern, Appomattox, Va., 1994, hist. rehab. of Danville (Va.) Rail Passenger Sta., restoration of Gen. George C. Marshall Home, Leesburg, Va., 1994, Danville City Courthouse, 1995, Danville Cts. and Jails Bldg., 1999, Congl. Cemetery, Washington, 1999, Nottoway County Courthouse, 1999, Ct. Sq. F&M Bank, Winchester, Va. (Nat. Honor award Nat. Trust Hist. Preservation), McGlothlin Family Mus., 2001, Tom McGlothlin residence, 2003, FT Pickett Officer's Club, 2003, James and Cella Rutt residence, 2004. Cub master Pack 119, Stonewall Jackson Coun. Boy Scouts Am., 1994—98. Recipient Design award, Tex.-AIA, 1969—70, Loudoun County award for Jarvis Residence, 1985. Fellow: AIA; mem.: Assn. Preservation Tech., Soc. Archtl. Historians, Nat. Trust Hist. Preservation, Albemarle County Hist. Soc. Office: DASA 812 E High St Charlottesville VA 22902-5126 Office Phone: 434-979-7407. E-mail: dons@dasaonline.com.

SWOFFORD, JOEL DAVID, education educator; b. Okla. City, Okla., Feb. 23, 1963; s. Joel David and Beverly Carlene Swofford. BA, U. Mich., 1986; MA, U. Houston, 1993; PhD, U. Okla., 2001. Instr. The U. Memphis, 2001—. Home: PO Box 11137 Memphis TN 38111 Office: The University of Memphis 375 Dunn Hall Memphis TN 38152 Business E-Mail: jswoffrd@memphis.edu.

SWOFFORD, ROBERT LEE, newspaper editor, journalist; b. Berryville, Ark., Aug. 22, 1949; s. Andrew Madison and Verna Mae (England) S.; m. Karen King, Jan. 24, 1969 (div. 1977); children: Teri, Toby; m. Sandra Dunn, 1978 (div. 1979); m. B. Joanna Rongren, Feb. 14, 1981 (div. 2001); 1 child, Tyler. AA, Coll. of the Sequoias, 1969; student, Calif. State U., 1969-71. Photographer, reporter, news editor The Advance-Register, Tulare, Calif., 1965-78; city editor The Record Searchlight, Redding, Calif., 1978-81; suburban editor, Neighbors editor The Sacramento Bee, 1981-86; assoc. metro. editor, cmty. editor The Orange County Register, Santa Ana, Calif., 1986-89; exec. news editor The Press Democrat, Santa Rosa, Calif., 1989-90, mng. editor, 1990—. Mem. Am. Soc. Newspaper Editors, Assoc. Press Mng. Editors, Calif. Soc. of Newspaper Editors (bd. dirs.). Office: The Press Democrat 427 Mendocino Ave Santa Rosa CA 95401-6385

SWOGER, JAMES WESLEY, magician; b. Wilkinsburg, Pa., Jan. 26, 1918; s. George Edmond and Iva Edna (Heacox) S.; m. Willie Williams, Jan. 8, 1944 (div. 1967); children: Melinda (dec.), James Michael, Andrina; m. Violet Elizabeth Pettit, Oct. 29, 1968. Owner House of Enchantment, Oceanside, Calif., 1937—. Owner, magician Museum of Magic, 1937, Magic Follies of Tomorrow, 1938-41; active numerous war bond drive shows, camp shows, ship entertainment and concert tours in Australia, New Guinea and the Philippines, 1943-46; starred in Magic on Showboat Rhododenron Season, 1965—, Mr. Roger's Neighborhood, Army Hour, 1943; lectr. Magic Castle, 1995; magician Pitts. Children's Theatre, 1941-43, Bascom Prodns., 1941-43, Austin Prodns., 1941-43; bd. dirs. Awesome Balloons, Inc. Magician for more than 80 yrs. Eagle Scout with 3 Palms BSA. Named Magician of Yr. 1960, 50 Yrs Svc. Magic, Internat. Magicians Ring 13 IBM, 1973, Faithful Yr. Svc. Magic, 42d Annual Magicfest, 1973, 60 Yr. Svc. Magic, 1983; named to Order of Arrow Boy Scouts Am.; recipient Internat. Brotherhood of Magician, 80 yrs. in Magic Conv., 2002, Honorary Lifetime Mem. Ring 76, IBM, Sandigo, Calif., 2003. Mem.: Awesome Balloons (bd. mem. 2000), Fellowship Christian Magicians, Acad. Magical Arts Scis., Mystic 52 (pres.), Craftsmen Printers Guild, Internat. Brotherhood Magicians (pres., Order of Merlin Excalibur 1995, Presdl. citation 2001—02, 80 Yrs. in Magic plaque 2002), Soc. Am. Magicians (pres.), San Diego Ring 76 IBM (life). Republican. Avocations: inventing stage effects, model illusions. Home: 3542 Mira Pacific Dr Oceanside CA 92056-3932

SWOOPES, SHERYL DENISE, professional basketball player; b. Brownfield, Tex., Mar. 25, 1971; d. Louise Swoopes; m. Eric Jackson, June 7, 1995 (div. 1999); 1 child, Jordan Eric Jackson. Student, South Plains Jr. Coll., Tex.; grad., Tex. Tech. U., 1993. Basketball player South Plains Jr. Coll., 1989—91, Tex. Tech U., 1991—93; profl. basketball player Houston Comets, WNBA, 1997—. Founder Sheryl Swoopes Found. for Youth. Named Nat. Player of Yr., USA Today, Sports Illustrated, others, 1993, Most Outstanding Player, NCAA Final Four, 1993, Most Valuable Player, WNBA, 2000, 2002, Defensive Player of Yr., 2000, 2002, 2003; named to First Team All-WNBA, 1998—2000, 2002, WNBA All-Star Team, 1999, 2000, 2002, 2003; recipient Coll. Performer of Yr. Award, ESPY, 1994, Women's Pro Basketball Player of Yr. Award, 2001. Achievements include mem., Texas Tech NCAA Championship Team, 1993; mem., US Women's Basketball Gold Medal Team, World Championships, 2002; mem., US Women's Basketball Gold Medal Team, Atlanta Olympics, 1996; mem., US Women's Basketball Gold Medal Team, Sydney Olympics, 2000; mem., US Women's Basketball Team, Athens Olympics, 2004; first woman to have a Nike shoe, the Air Swoopes, named after her. Office: Houston Comets Two Greenway Plz Ste 400 Houston TX 77046 Address: 908 E Felt St Apt 111 Brownfield TX 79316-3703*

SWOPE, ALAN JOSEPH, psychologist, educator; b. Cleve., Apr. 24, 1942; s. Floyd Keene and Leone Louise Swope; children: Alison, Laura. BA, Hiram Coll., 1964; PhD, Columbia U., 1969. Lic. psychologist, Calif. Psychologist City of Berkeley, Calif., 1970-81; pvt. practice as psychotherapist Berkeley, 1971—; prof. Wright Inst., Berkeley, 1978—, Calif. Sch. Profl. Psychology, Alameda, 1982—. Hon. life bd. mem. Calif. Psychology Internship Coun., Berkeley, 1992—. Contbr. articles to profl. jours. Fellow: Am. Bd. Profl. Psychology (diplomate); mem.: APA, No. Calif. Soc. for Psychoanalytic Psychology. Avocations: writing, reading, tennis, piano. Office: 3155 College Ave Berkeley CA 94705-2755 Office Phone: 510-428-1877. E-mail: alanswap@aol.com.

SWOPE, DONALD DOWNEY, retired banker; b. Martinsville, Ill., Feb. 26, 1926; s. Roy V. and Dorothy Irene (Downey) S.; m. Earla Long Markert, Aug. 16, 1960. BS, Ind. State U., 1950. With Ill. Savs. and Loan Commn., Springfield, Ill., 1950-77, chief dept. commr., 1971-77; exec. v.p. Bank for Savs. & Loan Assn., Chgo., 1977-81, pres., 1981-90. Bd. dirs. Country Fair White Elephant, Green Valley, Ariz., 1981—, treas., 1981-84. With USNR, 1944-63. Mem. VFW (life), Nat. Assn. State Savs. and Loan Suprs. (pres. 1972-73), Am. Legion (life), C. C. Green Valley, Kiwanis (pres. Crete, Ill. 1977-78, treas. Green Valley, Ariz. 1994, 95), Elks (treas.).

SWOPE, JEFFREY PEYTON, lawyer; b. Evanston, Ill., June 11, 1945; s. Oliver P. and Elspeth E. (Cahill) S.; m. Linda Lee, Aug. 26, 1967; children: Matthew, Gregory, Timothy. AB, Harvard U., 1967, JD, 1970. Bar: Mass. 1970, U.S. Dist. Ct. Mass. 1971, U.S. Ct. Appeals (1st cir.) 1973, U.S. Ct. Claims 1974, U.S. Supreme Ct. 1979. Assoc. Palmer & Dodge, Boston, 1970-76, ptnr., 1977—. Treas. Social Law Libr., Boston, 1984-2003, pres., 2003-. Treas. Ella Lyman Cabot Trust, Holliston, Mass., 1979-. Home: 54 Hyde St Newton MA 02461-1206 Office: Palmer & Dodge LLP 111 Huntington Ave Boston MA 02199-7613

SWOPE, WILLIAM A. computer company executive; BS in Applied Physics, Tufts Coll.; Master's in Mgmt., MIT. Various positions in mktg., strategic planning, and gen. mgmt. Intel Corp., 1979—, v.p., 1996—2003, v.p. and gen. mgr. Software and Solutions Group, 2003—. Office: 2200 Mission College Blvd Santa Clara CA 95052

SWORT, ARLOWAYNE, retired nursing educator and administrator; b. Bartlesville, Okla., Dec. 9, 1922; d. Arlington L. and Clara E. (Church) S. Diploma, St. Luke's Hosp. Sch. Nursing, Kansas City, Mo., 1944; BSN, U. Colo., 1958; MS in Nursing, Cath. U. Am., 1961; EdD, Columbia U., 1973. Assoc. prof., assoc. dean Sch. Nursing U. Pitts., 1974-77; dean, prof. Sch. Nursing U. Tex. Health Scis. Ctr., Houston, 1977-83, prof. nursing, 1983-85; prof., assoc. in adminstrn. Johns Hopkins U. Sch. Nursing, Balt., 1985-87, prof., assoc. dean for adminstrn. and grad. acad. affairs, 1987-89, sr. assoc. dean, 1990-91. Mem. profl. adv. com. Home Health Care, 1998-2000. Mem. aux. Medina County Cmty. Hosp., Hondo, Tex., 1997-99, charity ball chmn., 1998-99. Recipient numerous rsrch. grants. Mem. Am. Assn. for History of Nursing Inc., Nat. League for Nursing, Sigma Theta Tau, Kappa Delta Pi. Home: 1317 Kollman Dr Hondo TX 78861-1014

SWYERS, DONALD G. information scientist; b. Syracuse, N.Y., Mar. 30, 1958; s. William A. Swyers and Corinne Prall Neville; m. Nancy C. Bargesser, Jan. 2, 1993; 1 child. BS in Mgmt. Sci., SUNY, Geneseo, 1980; MBA in Corp. Investment, U. Hartford, 1991. Cert. computer profl. Inst. Cert. Computing. Database analyst Xerox, Webster, N.Y., 1980-87; computer automated sys. engring. tool cons. Aetna, Hartford, Conn., 1987-94; cons. Hartford, 1994-99; information engr. Citigroup-Travelers Life & Annuity, Hartford, 1999—. Home: 575 Bridge Rd Unit 10-6 Florence MA 01062-1089 Office: Citigroup Travelers Life and Annuity PO Box 990028 Hartford CT 06199-0028

SWYGERT, HAYWOOD PATRICK, academic administrator; b. Phila., Mar. 17, 1943; s. LeRoy and Gustina (Rogers) Huzzy; m. Sonja Branson, Aug. 22, 1969; children: Haywood Patrick, Michael Branson. AB in History, Howard U., 1965, JD cum laude, 1968. Bar: D.C. 1968, Pa. 1970, N.Y. 1970. Law clk. to chief judge U.S. Ct. Appeals (3d cir.), Phila., 1968—69; assoc. Debevoise, Plimpton, Lyons & Gates, N.Y.C., 1969—70; adminstrv. asst. to Congressman Charles B. Rangel NY, 1971—72; spl. asst. dist. atty., 1973; from asst. prof. to prof. law Temple U., 1972—90, v.p. adminstrn., 1982—88, exec. v.p., 1988—90; pres. SUNY, Albany, 1990—95, Howard U., Washington, 1995—. Bd. dirs. United Tech. Corp., Hartford Fin. Svcs. Group, Fannie Mae. Gov.'s rep. Southeastern Pa. Transp. Authority, 1987—90; bd. trustees Inst. Pub. Adminstrn., 1992—99; exec. com. Pub. Law Ctr., Phila., 1980—88; bd. dirs. NY State Coun. on Humanities, 1991—95; chmn. ednl. structure, policies and practices NY State Spl. Commn., 1993—95; co-chmn. joint task force grad. edn. Nat. Assn. State Univs. and Land Grant Colls./Am. Assn. State Coll. and Univs., 1993—95; Bd. dirs. New Community Devel. Corp., HUD, 1980—82; bd. dirs. Nat. Pub. Radio, 1995—96. Mem.: ABA, Victory Funds (trustee 1994—2002), Middle States Assn. Colls. and Schs. (commn. on higher edn. 1992—95). Home: 3119 Arizona Ave NW Washington DC 20016-3420 Office: Howard U Office of Pres 2400 6th St NW Ste 402 Washington DC 20059-0002 Office Phone: 202-806-2500.

SWYGERT, LESLIE ANN, epidemiologist, consultant; b. Griffin, Ga., Mar. 20, 1957; d. James Taylor and JoAnn Bankston Swygert. BS magna cum laude, Emory U., 1979, MD cum laude, 1984, MPH, 1991. Diplomate Nat. Bd. Med. Examiners, Am. Bd. Preventive Medicine, lic. physician and surgeon Med. Bd. of Hawaii, Drug Enforcement Agy., physician and surgeon Med. Bd. of Calif., Composite State Bd. of Med. Examiners, Ga. Internal medicine resident U. of Calif., San Francisco, 1984—85; gen. med. practitioner San Francisco, 1985—87; EIS officer CDC, Atlanta, 1988—90, sr. med. epidemiologist, 1995—99; chronic disease epidemiologist Hawaii State Dept. of Health, Honolulu, 1990—91; owner med. epidemiology consulting firm, Ashburn, Ga., 1991—. Sr. epidemiology cons., advisor South African Nat. Health Care Sys., 1996—97, Hanoi (Vietnam) Sch. of Pub. Health, 1997—98. Contbr. articles to profl. jours. Lt. comdr. USPHS, 1988—99. Fellow: Am. Coll. of Preventive Medicine (life); mem.: Soc. Epidemiologic Rsch., Assn. Tchrs. of Preventive Medicine, Phi Beta Kappa, Alpha Omega Alpha, Phi Sigma, Alpha Epsilon Upsilon. Achievements include research in heat-related deaths in Mo; childhood leukemia near radio towers in Hawaii; Honolulu Aquatic Safety Intervention Project; results of needle exchange services in Hawaii; investigation of cancer clusters around Seattle airport; assessing perinatal periods of risk in southern Georgia. Avocations: photography and videography, scuba diving, travel, naturalist. Office: 751 N Main St Ashburn GA 31714 E-mail: swygert@juno.com.

SY, STANLEY PETER SISON, internist; b. Manila, Philippines, May 4, 1970; s. Danilo Roque and Michaela Sison Sy; 1 child, Sebastian Castillo. MD, U. Santo Tomas, Philippines, 1996. Diplomate Am. Bd. of Internal Medicine, 2001, pulmonary medicine Am. Bd. of Internal Medicine, 2003. Staff physician internal medicine Bronx-Lebanon Hosp. Ctr., NY, 1998—2001, fellow pulmonary medicine, 2001—03; fellow critical care medicine Montefiore Med. Ctr., 2003—. Mem.: Am. Coll. of Chest Physicians (assoc.), Am. Thoracic Soc. (assoc.), Soc. of Critical Care Medicine (assoc.). Roman Catholic. Home: #18-J 3450 Wayne Ave Bronx NY 10467 Office Phone: 718-920-5440. Personal E-mail: stanleysy@aol.com.

SYCHOV, ALYAKSANDR, diplomat; b. Homel, Belarus, Sept. 19, 1951; married; 2 children. Ministry Fgn. Affairs, Belarus, 1979-84; with Belarus permanent mission to UN office, Geneva, 1984-90; head internat. econ. rels. dept. Ministry Fgn. Affairs, Belarus, 1991-92, dep. fgn. min., 1992-94; permanent rep. of Belarus UN, N.Y., 1994-2000, dep. fgn. min., 2000—. Mem. bur., chmn. of session com. Econ. Commn. for Europe, 1988-90; chmn. com. on internat. security and disarmament matters 51st Session UN Gen. Assembly, 1996-97, chmn. 1st com. 19th spl. session UN Gen. Assembly, 1997, vice-chmn. ECOSOC, 1998-99. Office: Ministry Fgn Affairs Belarus 19 Lenin Str Minsk Belarus Office Phone: (375-17)227-29-22.

SYDNOR, EDGAR STARKE, lawyer; b. Lynchburg, Va., Nov. 30, 1943; s. Charles Raine and Louise Allen (Starke) S.; m. Rita Frances Johnson, Dec. 28, 1965; children: Edgar Starke Jr., Elizabeth Sydnor Norris, Carlton Allen. BA in English, Washington and Lee U., 1966, JD, 1973. Bar: Va. 1973. Assoc. Edmunds, Williams, Robertson, Sackett, Baldwin & Graves, Lynchburg, 1973-75, ptnr., 1975-81; atty. Vulcan Materials Co., Birmingham, Ala., 1981-84, gen. atty., 1984-88, asst. gen. counsel, dir. pub. affairs, 1988-95, elected officer of co., 1992-2000, asst. gen. counsel chem. and environ., 1995-2000; ret., 2000. Capt. USAF, 1966-71. Presbyterian.

SYDOW, MICHAEL DAVID, lawyer; b. Dec. 12, 1950; m. Kelli McDonald; children: Kristen, David, Wyatt. BA, Southwestern U., 1973; JD with honors, U. Tex., 1976. Bar: Tex. 1976, U.S. Ct. Claims 1977, U.S. Ct. Appeals (5th cir.) 1977, U.S. Dist. Ct. (so. dist.) Tex. 1977, U.S. Dist. Ct. (ea. dist.) Tex. 1979, U.S. Supreme Ct. 1980, U.S. Dist. Ct. (no. dist.) Tex. 1985, U.S. Dist. Ct. (we. dist.) Tex. 1986; cert. in civil trial law Tex. Bd. Legal Specialization. Trial atty. Office Gen. Counsel USN, Arlington, Va., 1976-77; mem. firm Eastham, Watson, Dale & Forney, Houston, 1977-84, Hagans & Sydow, LLP, Houston, 1985-90, Reynolds & Sydow, LLP, Houston, 1993-94; pvt. practice, 1990-93; with Sydow & McDonald, LLP, 1995-97; shareholder Verner, Liipfert, Bernhard, McPherson & Hand, Houston, 1997—. Fellow Tex. Bar Found., Houston Bar Found.; mem. Houston Bar Assn. (chmn. jud. liaison com. 1988-90, Pres.'s award 1990), Maritime Law Assn. U.S. (mem. com. on gen. average 1977-88, practice and procedures com. 1988—), State Bar Tex., Phi Delta Phi. Address: Verner Liipfert Bernhard McPherson & Hand Chartered 1111 Bagby St Ste 4650 Houston TX 77002-2543 Home: 5773 Woodway Dr Houston TX 77057-1501

SYED, IBRAHIM BIJLI, medical educator and physicist, author, philosopher, theologist, public speaker, writer; b. Bellary, India, Mar. 16, 1939; came to U.S., 1969, naturalized, 1975; s. Ahmed Bijli and Mumtaz Begum (Maniyar) S.; m. Sajida Shariff, Nov. 29, 1964; children: Mubin, Zafrin. BS with honors, Veerasaiva Coll., Bellary U., Mysore, 1960; MS with honors and distinction, Bangalore U., Mysore, 1962; diploma, U. Bombay, 1964; DSc, Johns Hopkins U., 1972; PhD (hon.), Malta, 1985. Cert. hazard control officer, 1980, internat. health care safety profl., 1980; diplomate Am. Bd. Radiology, Am. Bd. Health Physics. Lectr. physics Veerasaiva Coll., Bellary U., Mysore, 1962-63; med. physicist, radiation safety officer Victoria Hosp., India, 1964-67, Bowring and Lady Curz on Hosp. & Postgrad. Med. Rsch. Inst., Bangalore, India, 1964-67; cons. med. physicist, radiation safety officer Ministry of Health, Govt. of Karnataka, India, 1964-67, Bangalore Nursing Home, India, 1964-67; med. physicist, radiation safety officer Baystate Med. Ctr., Springfield, Mass., 1973-79; assoc. prof. Springfield Tech. C.C.; also adj. prof. radiology Holyoke (Mass.) C.C., 1973-79; asst. clin. prof. nuclear medicine U. Conn. Sch. Medicine, Farmington, 1975-79; cons. med. physicist Mercy Hosp., Springfield, 1973-79, Wing Meml. Hosp., Palmer, Mass., 1973-79; med. physicist, radiation safety officer VAMC, Louisville, 1979—, exec. officer radiation safety com., 1979—; prof. medicine U. Louisville Sch. Medicine, 1979—, dir. nuclear med. scis., 1980—; mem. Instl. Review Bd. Veterans Admin. Medical Ctr., Louisville, 2000—. Guest lectr. religious studies program U. Louisville, 1979—; vis. prof. Bangalore U., 1987—88, Gulbarga U., India, 1987—88; vis. scientist Bhabha Atomic Rsch. Ctr., Bombay; invited spkr. Veerasaiva Coll., Bellary, India, 1996, Vijayanagar Coll., Hospet, 1996, Vajayanagar Inst. Med. Scis., Bellary, 1996, Deccan Coll. Med. Scis., Hyderabad, India, Bhabha Atomic Rsch. Ctr., Bombay, 1997, 15th Ann. Islamic Conf. New Eng., Islamic Coun. New Eng., 1999, Coun. for a Parliament of the World's Religions, Cape Town, South Africa, 1999, Garden City Coll. Bangalore, 2000, Veerasaiva Coll., Bellary, 2000, Islamic Rsch. Found., Mumbai, India, 2001, Islamic Assn. of Essex, England, 2001, Assn. Muslim Social Scientists, Detroit, 2001, Islamic Orgn. Med. Scis., Cairo, 2002; PhD thesis examiner Allahabad U., 1996—; course dir. licensing for nuclear cardiologists U. Louisville, 1980—, mem. admissions com. nuclear medicine program, 1980—; guest relief examiner Am. Bd. Radiology, 1991; examiner in radiol physics, 95, 97, 98, 2000; examiner in radiol. physics, 03; mem. panel of examiners Am. Bd. Health Physics; PhD thesis examiner U. Delhi, Internat. Inst. for Advanced Study, Clayton, Mo., 1985—, Allahabad (India) U., 1996—; faculty mem. Med. Physicists of India Ann. Meeting, 1987; IAEA tchr. expert in nuclear medicine on mission to People's Republic of Bangladesh, 86; to Guatemala, 94; founder, pres. Islamic Rsch. Found. Internat., Louisville, 1988—; convener Internat. Conf. on Islamic Renaissance: Action Plan for the 21st Century, Chgo., 1995; cons. Coun. Sci. and Indsl. Rsch., Govt. India, 0809—, Am. Coun. Sci. and Health, 1980—; cons. gastroenterology and urology divsn. FDA, HHS, 1988—, cons. radiopharm. divsn., 1989—; cons. Govt. India in nuclear medicine, diagnostic radiol. physics, therapeutic radiol. physics and radiation safety, 1992; cons. radiol. and med. nuc. physics Govt. India, Un Devel. Program, 1992; convenor Internat. Conf. on Islamic Renaissance, Chgo., 1995; guest spkr. Muslim Cmty. Ctr., Chgo., 1988; invited spkr. objective studies and Islamic voice, Bangalore, 96, Parliament of World Religions, Chgo., 1993, Cape Town, South Africa, 99, Cooper Mosque, Mississauga, Ont., Canada, 2002. Author: Radiation Safety for Allied Health Professionals, Radiation Safety Manual, 1979, Intellectual Achievements of Muslims, 2002; contbg. editor Jour. of Islamic Food and Nutrition Coun. of Am., 1986—, health and sci. column Muslim Jour., 1989—; freelance writer Minaret Biweekly, N.Y.C., 1975—, Islamic Voice, India, 1988—, Al-Balaagh, Lenasia, South Africa, 1989—, AL'FURQAN Internat., Norcross, Ga., 1990, Message Internat., Jamaica, N.Y., 1990, Minaret Monthly Mag., L.A., 1995—, The Message, London, 1998—, The Minaret, Botswana, 1998—; editor: Science and Technology for the Developing World, 1988; mem. editl. bd. Jour. Islamic Med. Assn., 1981—; regular contbr. Pres.'s Page; manuscript reviewer for sci. and med. jours., 1973; assoc. editor AAlim, 1998—; contbr. more than 100 articles to sci. jours.; pub. internat. more than 220 articles on various topics of Islam in jours. and mags. Moderator fgn. policy workshop U.S. Dept. State, Louisville, 2000; spkr. Dayton (Ohio) Islamic Ctr., 2000, Muslim Student Assn. U. Cin., 2000; spkr.. Muslim Cmty. Ctr., Chgo., 2001; invited spkr. Muslim Assn. of Cleveland East, Cleve., 2002; bd. dir. Nur Islamic Sch., Louisville, 2003, Am. Muslim Assn. Louisville, 2003—; bd. dirs. Islamic Ctr. of Louisville, 1992—. Recipient Disting. Cmty. Svc. award India Cmty. Found., 1982, Hind Rattan Jewel of India Title award Govt. India, 1994; WHO fellow, Govt. India scholar Bhabha Atomic Rsch. Ctr., Bombay, 1963-64; USPHS fellow Johns Hopkins U., 1969-72. Fellow Inst. Physics (U.K.), Am. Inst. Chemists, Royal Soc. Health, Am. Coll. Radiology, Internat. Acad. Med. Physics; mem. Am. Assn. Physicists in Medicine, Am. Coll. Nuclear Medicine, Health Physics Soc., Am. Acad. Health Physics, Soc. Nuclear Medicine (faculty mem. ann. meeting 1987, convenor internat. conf. 1995), Nat. Assn. Ams. of Asian Indian Descent (chmn. state pub. rels. com. 1982—), Islamic Med. Assn. N.Am. (life, faculty 1994, 96, 98), Internat. Inst. Islamic Medicine (faculty Orlando, Fla. 1996, 97, Birmingham, U.K. 1998), Islamic Soc. N.Am. (faculty Chgo. 1998), Islamic Soc. Balt. (founding mem.), Islamic Cultural Ctr.(sec. 1999-), Louisville, Islamic Assn. Maritime Provinces Can., Halifax, N.S. (asst. sec. 1967-69), Health Physics Soc. (chmn. med. health physics com. 1989—, affirmative action com. 1984—), Am. Assn. Physicists in Medicine (biol. effects com.), Assn. Muslim Scientists and Engrs. N.Am. (program chmn. ann. conf. 1987, treas. 1987-88, sec. 1988—), AAUP, Soc. Nuclear Medicine India (life, faculty mem. ann. meeting 1987, invited spkr. and faculty ann. meeting 1996), Assn. Med. Physicists India (life, invited spkr. and faculty ann. meeting Madras 1996), Med. and Biol. Physics (divsn. Can.) Assn. Physicists, Hosp. Physicists Assn., N.Y. Acad. Scis., Islamic Assn. Maritime Provinces of Can., Ky. Med. Assn., Jefferson County Med. Soc. (assoc.), Am. Muslim Assn. Louisville (bd. dirs. 2003—), Sigma Xi. Islamic. Home: 7102 W Shefford Ln Louisville KY 40242-6462 Office: 800 Zorn Ave Louisville KY 40206-1433 E-mail: irfi@iname.com.

SYER, FONTAINE, theater director; Degree, Mt. Holyoke Coll., 1969; MFA, U. Del., 2003. Co-founder, artistic dir. Theatre Project Co., 1975—89; various positions, 1989—92; assoc. dir. Oreg. Shakespeare Festival, 1992—96; artistic dir. Del. Theatre Co., Wilimington, Del., 1998—. Office: Delaware Theatre Co 200 Water St Wilmington DE 19801

SYKES, ALAN O'NEIL, lawyer, educator; b. Bethesda, Md., Oct. 10, 1954; s. Alan O'Neil and Emily (Adams) S.; m. Maureen J. Gorman, June 29, 1980; children: Madeleine, Sophie. BA, Coll. William and Mary, 1976; JD, Yale U., 1982, PhD in Econs., 1987. Bar: Mass., D.C. Atty. Office of Arnold & Porter, Washington, 1982-86; asst. prof. law U. Chgo., 1986-90, prof. law, 1990—, Frank and Bernice Greenberg prof., 1996—. Vis. prof. law Harvard U., Cambridge, Mass., 1991, NYU, 1996. Author: Product Standards for International and Integrated Goods Markets, 1995, Legal Problems of International Economic Relations, 2002. NSF fellow, 1976-79. Mem. ABA, Am. Econ. Assn., Am. Law and Econs. Assn. (bd. dirs. 1999—). Office: U Chgo Sch of Law 1111 E 60th St Chicago IL 60637 Business E-Mail: alan_sykes@law.uchicago.edu.

SYKES, BARBARA, state legislator, state representative; b. Holly Grove, Ark., Apr. 12, 1955; married; 2 children. BA in Social Work, MPA, U. Akron. Rep. Ohio State Ho. Reps., Columbus, 2000—. Mem. econ. devel. and tech. com. Ohio State Ho. Reps., mem. pub. utilities com., mem. ways and means com. Mem.: NAACP, Friends of Maple Libr., PTA Firestone HS. Democrat. Office: Ohio State House Reps 77 South High Street 10th Floor Columbus OH 43215-6111

SYKES, DIANE S. federal judge, former state supreme court justice; b. Milw., Dec. 23, 1957; children: Jay, Alexander. B, Northwestern U., 1980; JD, Marquette U., 1984. Reporter Milw. Jour.; law clk. to Hon. Terence T. Evans US Dist. Ct. (ea. dist.) WI, 1984—85; assoc. Whyte & Hirschboeck S.C., 1985—92; judge Milw. County Ct., 1992—99, Wis. Supreme Ct., Madison, 1999—2004, US Ct. Appeals (7th cir.), 2004—. Office: US Ct Appeals Rm 2722 219 S Dearborn St Chicago IL 60604*

SYKES, GREGORY, food products executive; New products mktg. mgr. Hillshire Farms & Kahn's, 1984; pres., CEO Ball Park Brands, 1995, State Fair Foods, Best Kosher, Ball Park and Hillshiar Farm & Kahn's groups; v.p. Sara Lee Corp., Chgo.; pres., CEO Sara Lee Foods Retail, Chgo. Office: Sara Lee Corp 3 First National Plz Chicago IL 60602-4260

SYKES, GREGORY EDWARD, insurance company executive, writer; s. Felix John and Grace Forster Sykes; m. Claudia Lee Gloe, July 28, 1973; children: Gregory E. II, Joshua D., Meridith L., Michael A. BS, Kans. State U., 1974; MS, U. Okla., 1984. Cert. EMT Kans.; police office Okla., Kans. Police officer Plainville (Kans.) Police Dept.; casuality claims examiner Am. Family Ins., Salina, Kans.; police sgt. Lindsborg (Kans.) Police Dept.; claims examiner Columbia Ins. Group, Salina, Am. States Ins., St. Louis; supr. spl. investigations Ohio Casualty Group, Fairfield. Dept. tng. officer Lindsborg Dept. Pub. Safety, 1990—97; radio show host Sta. KJLS-AM, Creve Coeur, Mo., 1998—99. Author: Thou Shalt Not Steal, 2003, Mice in the Pantry, 2003, Grim Corporate Fairy Tales, 2004; contbr. articles to profl. jours.; author: Martin Luther-Private Dectective, Knockout-A Novel of Terrorism, The Fireants-A Novel of Terrorism. Bd. dirs. Parks and Recreation Commn., St. Peters, Mo., 1998—2001; candidate for sheriff Rep. Party, Saline County, Kans., 1996; bd. dirs. Sanford-Fritch (Tex.) Sch., 1983. Capt. USAFA, 1998—2002. Recipient Silver Star for Bravery, Am. Polic Hall of Fame, 1995, Nat. Commendation, Coun. Law Enforcement Accreditation, Kans., 1996. Mem.: Assn. Cert. Fraud Examiners, Internat. Assn. Arson Investigators, Internat. Assn. Spl. Investigation (bd. dirs. 2004—). Office Phone: 303-338-2634. E-mail: gsykes@nfuic.com.

SYKES, GRESHAM M'CREADY, sociologist, educator, artist; b. Plainfield, NJ, May 26, 1922; s. M'Cready and Beatrice (Evans) S.; m. Carla Adelt, July 13, 1946. AB summa cum laude, Princeton U., 1950; PhD (Woodrow Wilson fellow 1950-51, Univ. fellow 1951-52), Northwestern U., 1953; MA (hon.), Dartmouth Coll., 1961. Instr. sociology Princeton U., 1952-54, asst. prof., bicentennial preceptor, 1954-58; assoc. prof. Northwestern U., Evanston, Ill., 1958-60; prof. sociology Dartmouth Coll., Hanover, NH, 1960-63, chmn. dept., 1961-63; exec. officer Am. Sociol. Assn., 1963-65; research prof. law and sociology, dir. adminstrn. of justice program U. Denver, 1965-72; chmn. dept. sociology U. Houston, 1973; prof. sociology U. Va., Charlottesville, 1974-88, chmn. dept., 1978-81, emeritus prof., 1988—. Chmn. Salzburg (Austria) Seminar in Am. Studies, summer 1965; working as artist, with frequent group and one-man exhbn., 1988—. Author: Crime and Society, rev. edit., 1967, The Society of Captives, 1958, Law and the Lawless, 1969, Social Problems in Am., 1971, Criminology, 1978, rev. edit., 1992, The Future of Crime, 1980; criminology editor Jour. Criminal Law, Criminology and Police Sci., 1959-64; assoc. editor Rev. Am. Sociol. Assn., 1960-62, Contemporary Sociology, 1977-80, Criminology, 1980-84; contbr. articles and revs. to Ency. Britannica, profl. jour. Served to capt., C.E. AUS, 1942-46, ETO. Recipient Edwin H. Sutherland award Am. Soc. Criminology, 1980. Home: 2197 Shepherds Ridge Road Charlottesville VA 22901 E-mail: gms6m@virginia.edu.

SYKES, JOHN, communications company executive; BS in Comm., Syracuse U. Staff CBS Records, 1977-80; mem. start-up team to v.p. programming MTV, 1980-86; agt. Creative Artists Agy., 1986-88; pres. Champion Entertainment, 1988—92; exec. v.p. talent acquisition and mktg. EMI Mus. Pub. Worldwide, 1992—94; pres. VH1, N.Y.C., 1994—2004; chmn., CEO Infinity Radio ops. Viacom Inc., 2004—. Bd. mem. The Robin Hood Found., T.J. Martell Cancer Found., The City of Hope, Rock and Roll Hall of Fame; mem. adv. bd. Syracuse U. S.I. Newhouse Sch. Office: VH1 Viacom International 1515 Broadway Fl 20 New York NY 10036-8901*

SYKES, JOLENE, former publishing executive; BS, East Carolina U. Mgr. corp. sales devel. Time Inc., 1990—91, S.E. regional mgr. corp. sales and mktg., 1991—93; S.E. dir. regional sales Sports Illus., 1993—96; pub. Fortune mag. Time, Inc., N.Y.C., 1996—99, pres. Fortune mag., 1999—2001; mem. bd. dirs. Resource Connection, Inc., 2002—. Office: Resources Connection Inc 695 Town Center Dr Ste 600 Costa Mesa CA 92626

SYKES, MELVIN JULIUS, lawyer; b. Balt., Jan. 9, 1924; s. Philip Louis and Sara (Klein) S.; m. Judith Janet Konowitz, Sept. 24, 1950; children: David K., Rachel A. (dec.), Daniel E., Israel J. Grad., Balt. City Coll., 1940, Balt. Hebrew Coll., 1941; AB with honors, Johns Hopkins U., 1943; LLB magna cum laude, Harvard U., 1948. Bar. Md. 1949, U.S. Ct. Appeals (4th cir.) 1949, U.S. Dist. Ct. Md. 1950, U.S. Supreme Ct. 1955. Law clk. to Judge Morris A. Soper U.S. Ct. Appeals (4th cir.), 1948-49; pvt. practice Balt., 1949—. Draftsman Md. Dept. Legislative Reference, 1949—50; rsch. cons. Md. Commn. Adminstrv. Orgn., 1951—52; reporter Md. Commns. to Study Judiciary, 1953, Md. commns. to revise law relating to pub. svc. commn., 1953—55; mem. standing com. on rules of practice, procedure Md. Ct. Appeals, 1954—72, 1978—; mem. legis. coun. Commsn. on Revision Condemnation Laws, 1961—63; mem. Balt. Charter Revision Com., 1962—63; pres. Bar Libr. Balt., 1962—63; mem. Md. Constl. Conv. Commn., 1966—67; cons. Gov. Md. Commn. to Revise Testamentary Laws, 1967—69; mem. Gov. Md. Commns. to study state aid to nonpub. edn., 1969—71, Md. Code Revision Commn., 1970—78. Co-author: West's Maryland Procedural Forms, 1964, Jewish Law (Mishpat Ivri), Cases and Materials, 1999; co-translator Elon, Jewish Law--History, Principles, Sources, 1994. Bd. dirs. Balt. Neighborhoods; mem. governing coun. Am. Assn. Jewish Edn., 1968—81; bd. dirs. Balt. Jewish Coun., 1970—72; bd. dirs. Balt. chpt. Am. Jewish Com.; bd. dirs. Inst. for Christian and Jewish Studies; former mem. and chmn. bd. trustees Balt. Hebrew U. With USAF, 1943—45. Fellow Am. Coll. Trial Lawyers, Am. Acad. of Appellate Lawyers, Am. Coll. Trust and Estate Counsel, Am. Bar Found., Md. Bar Found. (chmn. 1981-83); mem. ABA, Am. Law Inst., Md. Bar Assn., Balt. City Bar Assn. (lectr. continuing edn. programs), Am. Jewish Congress, Balt. Zionist Dist., B'nai B'rith, Phi Beta Kappa Fellows. Democrat. Home: 3811 Fords Ln Baltimore MD 21215-2804 Office: Ste 1701 120 E Baltimore St Baltimore MD 21202-6701 Office Phone: 410-727-3078. E-mail: mjsykes@mjsykes.com.

SYKES, RICHARD NESBIT, history professor, department chairman; b. Charlotte, N.C., Jan. 11, 1942; s. Richard Nesbitt and Sarah Elizabeth (Hovis) Sykes. AB in History and English summa cum laude, So. Wesleyan U., 1964; MA in Social Sci. and Reading Spec., Appalachian State U., 1965; PhD in History, Greenwich U., 2001. Cert. educator S.C., N.C. Instr. history and polit. sci. Gordon Coll., Barnesville, Ga., 1965—67; asst. prof. history and reading Gardner-Webb Coll., Boiling Springs, NC, 1967—69; instr. history and reading Ctrl. Piedmont C.C., Charlotte, 1969—70; coordinator secondary reading Chester County (S.C.) Schs., 1971—73; reading specialist Williamsburg County (S.C.) Schs., 1973—74; reading diagnostician Chesterfield County (S.C.) Schs., 1974—79; tchr., reading specialist Buford H.S., Lancaster, SC, 1979—90; prof. history Aiken (S.C.) Tech. Coll., 1990—, dept. chair, 2001—. Nominee Gov.'s Disting. Prof. award, S.C. Commn. on Higher Edn., 2000; recipient medal, Nat. Inst. Staff and Orgnl. Devel., 2000. Mem.: S.C. State Employees Assn., S.C. Tech. Edn. Assn. (Educator of Yr. 1991—92, Nominee State Educator of Yr. 1991—92), Nat. Geog. Soc., Smithsonian Instn. Avocations: reading, walking, fishing. Home: 838 Osbon Dr Aiken SC 29801-4154 Office: Aiken Tech Coll PO Box 696 Aiken SC 29802-0696 Office Phone: 803-593-9231 ext. 1347. Office Fax: 803-593-6526. Business E-Mail: sykes@atc.edu.

SYKES, SAM JONES, French educator; b. Winston-Salem, Nov. 3, 1946; s. Sam Jones and Margaret Elizabeth Sykes; m. Carol Ann Janda, Aug. 11, 1973 (dec. Aug. 1986). BA in French cum laude, Coll. of William and Mary, 1969; MA in French, Middlebury Coll., Vt., 1972. Cert. gen. ednl. supr. Va., secondary ednl. supr. Va. French tchr. Newport News Pub. Schs., 1969—86, instrnl. specialist, 1986—95; adj. French instr. Christopher Newport U., Newport News, 1995—97; vis. French instr. Coll. of William and Mary, Williamsburg, Va., 1997—98, adj. French instr. H.s. evaluator State Bd. of Edn., Richmond, Va., 1975, state textbook evaluator, 90, h.s. evaluator, 91. Mem.: Fgn. Lang. Assn. of Va. Avocations: reading, running, translating literature.

SYKORA, BARBARA ZWACH, state legislator; b. Tracy, Minn., Mar. 5, 1941; d. John M. and Agnes (Schueller) Zwach; m. Robert G. Sykora, 1965; children: Mona, John, Kara, Mary. BA, St. Catherine Coll., 1963. Tchr. Springfield (Mass.) Sch., 1963-64, Roseville (Minn.) Sch., 1964-66; mem. Minn. Ho. of Reps., St. Paul, 1994—. Bd. dirs. Beacon Bank. Vice chmn. 2d Congl. Dist. Rep. Com., Minn., 1978-82; chmn. 6th Congl. Dist. Rep. Com., 1982-86, 2d congl. dist. Senator Durenberger Campaign, 1980-82, Senator Pillsbury Campaign, Wayzata, Minn., 1980; chair Ind. Rep. State Com., Minn., 1987-93; dist. dir. Office Congressman Rod Grams, 1993-94; bd. dirs. Animal Humane Soc. Hennepin County, Minn. Acad. Excellence Found.; chair Family and Early Childhood Edn. Com., 1999-2002, Edn. Policy, 2003—; chair Legis. Commn. on IEcon. Status of Women, 2001—; asst. majority leader Rep. State Com., Minn. 2003—. Mem. Excelsior C. of C., Minnetonka Rotary. Republican. E-mail: bsykora@uswestmail.net.

SYKORA, HAROLD JAMES, military officer; b. Tripp, S.D., Mar. 10, 1939; s. James J. and Mary (Tucek) S.; m. Patricia Ann Friedrich, Dec. 26, 1962; children: Montgomery James, Gina Marie. BS, U. S.D., 1961, MA in Math., 1965; postgrad., U. Wis., 1971-72, Indsl. Coll. Armed Forces, Ft. McNair, Washington, 1987-88. Math. tchr. Mitchell (S.D.) Sr. H.S., 1961-64, 65-71, 72-74; commd. U.S. Army; advanced through grades to maj. gen.; with U.S. Army Command and Gen. Staff Coll., Ft. Leavenworth, Kans., 1974-75; exec. officer hdqs. 147th F.A. S.D. N.G., Pierre, 1975-80; tng. officer hdqrs. S.D. N.G., Rapid City, 1980-83, chief of staff, 1983-87, adj. gen., 1988-98; pvt. practice def. industry cons. Rapid City, 1998—. Bd. dirs. Am. Sys. Corp., Inc., Am. Sys. Internat. Alumni Achievement award U. S.D., 1996. Mem. N.G. Assn. S.D. (pres. 1979-80), N.G. Assn. U.S. (chmn. fire support task force 1998—), Am. Legion, Assn. U.S. Army, Adjutant's Gen. Assn. U.S. (sec. 1991-97, Army res. forces policy com. 1992-97, chmn. Army res. forces policy com. 1995-97), Rapid City Area C. of C, US Army Field Artillery Ctr. (sr. adv.field artillery, 2004—). Republican. Roman Catholic. Home and Office: 5204 Pinedale Hts Rapid City SD 57702-2079 E-mail: sykorajh@aol.com.

SYKORA, PETR, professional hockey player; b. Plzen, Czechoslovakia, Nov. 19, 1976; Center Cleve. Lumberjacks, 1993—94, Detroit Vipers, 1994—95, AHL, Albany; center, left wing, right wing N.J. Devils, 1995—2002, Anaheim Mighty Ducks, Calif., 2002—. Named to NHL All-Rookie Team, 1995—96. Office: Anaheim Mighty Ducks Arrowhead Pond of Anaheim 2695 East Katella Ave Anaheim CA 92806

SYLER, RENE, newscaster; b. Scott AFB, Belleville, Ill., Feb. 17, 1963; m. Buff Parham; 2 children. BA in Psychology, Calif. State U., Sacramento, 1987. Weekend reporter KTVN-TV, Reno, 1987—89; weekend anchor KOLO-TV, Reno, 1989—90, WVTM-TV, Birmingham, 1990—92; anchor WFAA-TV, Dallas, 1992—97, KTVT-TV, Dallas, 1997—2002; anchor, The Early Show CBS, 2002—. Recipient TV Personality of the Yr., Am. Women in Radio and TV, 1997. Mem.: Nat. Assn. of Black Journalists, Dallas-Ft. Worth Assn. of Black Communicators. Office: c/o CBS News The Early Show 524 W 57th St New York NY 10019

SYLK, LEONARD ALLEN, housing company executive, real estate developer; b. Phila., Feb. 25, 1941; s. Harry S. and Gertrude (Bardy) S.; m. Barbara Ann Lovenduski, Dec. 1, 1975; children: Tristan, Tyler, Galen. BS in Econs., U. Pa., 1963; MBA, Columbia U., 1965. Cert. comml. property builder. Founder, chmn. bd., CEO Shelter Systems Corp., Hainesport, N.J., 1965-99; ret.; prin., CEO Property Mgmt. Svcs., Hainesport, 1996—. Bd. dirs. Home Owners Warranty Corp., N.J., v.p., 1988-95; bd. dirs. Internat. Housing Com., Nat. Comml. Builders Coun., 1986-97; vice chmn. USA Bancshares, Inc., 1998-2000; chmn., bd. govs. Mid. East Forum; trustee Nat. Bldg. Sys. Coun., 1986—; presdl. advisor on housing trade with Soviet Union, 1990; bldg. industry advisor U.S. Dept. Commerce, 1997-99. Contbr. articles to industry publs. Chmn. ann. awards dinner Jewish Nat. Fund, Phila., 1987, v.p., bd. dirs.; bd. dirs. Phila. Orch. Assn., 1990-98, emeritus, 1999—; bd. trustees Roman Catholic H.S., Phila., 2003—; bd. dirs. Pa. Ballet, 1994-99, exec. com., 1996-99, vice-chmn., pres., 1998; bd. dirs. Resources for Childrens' Health, 1993-96, Acad. Music, Phila., 1990-96, Rock Sch. of Pa. Ballet, 1995-98, Young Scholars Charter Sch., 2000—; bd. dirs. Jewish Nat. Fund, 1987—, v.p., 2000—; N.J. chmn. Builders for Bush, 1988; trustee Hahnemann U. and Hosp., 1991-96; vice chmn., trustee St. Christopher's Hosp. for Children, Phila., 1994-2002, chmn. St. Christophers Found. for Children, 1999, v.p., bd. dirs., 1999-2002; chmn. 1999, bd. dirs., vice chmn. St. Peter's Sch, Phila., 1995-03; trustee Allegheny U. Hosps., 1998-2000, Roman Cath. H.S., Plia., 2003—; bd. govs. Young Scholars Charter Sch. Phila., 1999—. Named Man. of Yr., 1988, Man of Yr., N.J. C. of C., 2002; recipient Tree of Life award presented by R. Hon. Margaret Thatcher, 1995. Mem. Nat. Assn. Homebuilders (com. chmn., nat. bd. dirs. 1984—, mem. exec. com. 1990, 97, fundraising chmn. 1991, Man of Yr. in Industrialized Housing 1990), Wood Truss Coun. Am. (bd. dirs. 1983—, pres. 1987, named to Hall of Fame 1990), Builders League South Jersey (v.p., bd. dirs. 1984-94), N.J. Builders Assn. (bd. dirs., com. chmn., exec. com. 1990-96), Merion Civic Assn. (bd. dirs. 1999-2001), Le Club (N.Y.C.), Atlantic City Country Club, Vesper Club, Union League, Capitol Club (Washington), Masons. Republican. Home: 350 N Highland Ave Merion Station PA 19066-1708 Office: Property Mgmt Svcs PO Box 9 Hainesport NJ 08036-0009

SYLLA, RICHARD EUGENE, economics professor; b. Harvey, Ill., Jan. 16, 1940; s. Benedict Andrew and Mary Gladys (Curran) S.; m. Edith Anne Dudley, June 22, 1963; children: Anne Curran, Margaret Dudley. BA, Harvard U., 1962, MA, 1965, PhD, 1969. Prof. econs. and bus. N.C. State U., Raleigh, 1968-90; Henry Kaufman prof. history fin. insts. and markets NYU, N.Y.C., 1990—, prof. econs., 1990—, acting chmn. dept. econs., 2002—03. Cons. Citibank NA, N.Y.C., 1979-82, Chase Manhattan Bank, N.Y.C., 1983-85; vis. prof. U. Pa., Phila., 1983, U. N.C., Chapel Hill, 1988; rsch. assoc. Nat. Bur. of Econ. Rsch., 1983—; trustee Mus. Am. Fin. History, 2002-. Author: The American Capital Market, 1975; co-author: Evolution of the American Economy, 1980, 2d edit., 1993, A History of Interest Rates, 1991, rev. edit., 1996; co-editor: Patterns of European Industrialization, 1991, Anglo-American Financial Systems, 1995, The State, The Financial System, and Economic Modernization, 1999; editor Jour. Econ. History, 1978-84. Study fellow NEH, 1975-76; Rsch. grantee NSF, 1985-94, 98-02, Sloan Found., 1995-97. Mem. Am. Econs. Assn., Econ. History Assn. (v.p. 1987-88, trustee 1977-88, Arthur H. Cole prize 1970, pres. 2000-2001), Bus. History Conf. (trustee 1991-94, 2002—04, pres. elect 2004—), So. Econ. Assn. (v.p. 1981-82), Cliometrics Soc. (trustee 1997-2000, trustee chair 1998-2000). Avocations: golf, hiking, stamp collecting/philately, arts. Home: 110 Bleecker St Apt 23D New York NY 10012-2106 Office: NYU 44 W 4th St New York NY 10012-1106 Office Phone: 212-998-0869. Business E-Mail: rsylla@stern.nyu.edu.

SYLVESTER, JOHN ANDREW, social studies educator; b. Springfield, Mass., Dec. 20, 1935; s. Andrew Armour Sylvester and Stella Elizabeth Davies. AB cum laude, Harvard U., 1957; MA, U. Wis., 1959, PhD, 1967. Assoc. prof. history Okla. State U., Stillwater, 1970—95, asst. prof. history, 1966—70. Contbr. articles to profl. jours. Staff sgt. U.S. Army, 1958—62. Mem.: The Soc. for Historians of Am. Fgn. Rels., Orgn. of Am. Historians. Avocations: classical music, stamp collecting/philately, films. Home: O4 Belden Ct Agawam MA 01001-3803

SYLVESTER, RICHARD RUSSELL, economist, management executive; b. Jan. 10, 1938; s. Leslie Gardner and Effie (Williams) S.; m. Irene Elizabeth Lehman, Apr. 17, 1976; children: Bonnie Ann, Vicky Ellis, Juliesta Elaine. BA, UCLA, 1959; MBA, U. So. Calif., 1962; PhD, UCLA, 1970, postgrad., 1971—74; JD, Loyola U., 1981. Designer corp. offices GM Corp., Warren, Mich., 1958; sr. analyst Lockheed Aircraft Corp., Burbank, Calif., 1962-66; sr. planner corp. offices Hughes Aircraft Co., Culver City, Calif., 1966-68; sr. staff economist, staff mgr. TRW, Inc., Redondo Beach, Calif., 1969-70; pres. Def. Rsch. Co., 1970-81, Sylvester Consulting Group, 1970—, PhD Pub. Co., 1970—, Sylvester Appraisal Co., 1970—, U.S. Electropower Controls Corp., 1970-71. Asst. prof. Calif. State U., 1970-73; mgr. corp. planning Brunswick Def./Celesco, Costa Mesa, Calif., 1973-75; staff specialist strategic planning Gen. Dynamics Corp., 1981-83; strategic analysis specialist Northrop Corp., 1983-89; cons. econs., engring. and fin., L.A., 1970—; lectr. Northrop U., U. Calif., U. So. Calif., Loyola U., La Verne U., 1961-81; asst. prof. Calif. State U., 1970-73, lectr., 1989—; assoc. prof. Pepperdine U., 1975-76, lectr., 1994—; lectr. U. Redlands, 1997—, UCLA, 1999—; co-founder Theta Cable TV, L.A., 1966-67. Author: Management Decisions and Actions, 3d edit., 1988, Investment Strategy, 1982, Tax Planning, 4th edit., 1980, Strategic Planning, 6th edit., 1990, Investment Planning and Tax Planning Software, 1983-93, Strategic Financial Planning, 1993, Future Challenge, Financial Strategy and Tax Planning, 1993, International Transfer Pricing, 1994, Quantitative Methods, 1997, Calculus for Executive Decisions, 1999, 2d edit, 2002, Mathematical Methods for Economics and Law, 1999; contbr. tech. reports to profl. lit. Fellow UCLA, 1970; postdoctoral scholar in engring., UCLA, 1971-74; GM scholar, 1953-57; Ford Found. grantee, 1965, U.S. Fed. Govt. rsch. grantee, 1967-70. Mem. Westwood Hills Christian Ch. (bd. dirs. 1978-81, 91-93), Beta Gamma Sigma, Alpha Kappa Psi. Home: 4253 Beethoven St Los Angeles CA 90066-5705

SYLVESTRE, JEAN GUY, former national librarian; b. Sorel, Que., Can., May 17, 1918; s. Maxime Arthur and Yvonne Marie (Lapierre) S.; m. Francoise Poitevin, Feb. 27, 1943; children: Marie, Jean, Paul. BA, U. Ottawa, 1939, B.Ph., 1940, MA, 1942, D.L.S. (hon.), 1969, D.Litt. (hon.), 1970, LL.D. (hon.), 1974, 75, 82. Translator Dept. Can. Sec. of State, 1942-44; editor Wartime Info. Bd., 1944-45; asst. pvt. sec. to minister of justice, 1945-47; pvt. sec. to sec. of state for external affairs, 1947-48; pvt. sec. to prime minister, 1948-50; adminstrv. officer Dept. Resources and Devel., 1950-53; asst. librarian Library of Parliament, Ottawa, Ont., 1953-56, asso. parliamentary librarian, 1956-68, nat. librarian, 1968-83; pres., chmn. bd. Can. Inst. for Hist. Microprodns., 1983-86; chmn. Ottawa Valley Book Festival, 1988-92; hon. chmn., 1993—. Author: Louis Francoeur, journaliste, 1941, Situation de la poésie canadienne, 1941, Anthologie de la poésie canadienne-française, 1943, 58, 64, 66, 68, 74, Poétes catholiques de la France contemporaine, 1944, Sondages, 1945, Impressions de théâtre, 1950, Amours, délices et orgues, 1953, Panorama des lettres canadiennes-francaises, 1964, Canadian Writers, 1964, Literature in French Canada, 1967, A Century of Canadian Literature, 1967, The Future of the National Library of Canada, 1980, Guidelines for National Libraries, 1987 French, Spanish and Arabic edits., 1988; also articles in profl. jours., encys.; editor: A Canadian Errant (J.P. Manion), 1960; editor: Canadian Universities Today, 1961, Structures sociales du Canada francais, 1967, Chmn. Gov. Gen.'s Lit. Awards, 1960-62; organizer, chmn. World Poetry Conf., Expo 1967; chmn. Can. Council Com. on Aid-to-Publs., 1960-68; lectr. U. Ottawa Library Sch., 1954-71; v.p. Can. Library Week Council, 1965-67; Bd. dirs. Can. Writers Found., pres., 1960-61. Decorated comdr. Ordre International du Bien Public, officer Order of Can.; comdr. Order of Merit of Poland; recipient Centennial medal., Outstanding Pub. Service award, Internat. Fedn. Libr. Assn. medal. Fellow Royal Soc. Can. (hon. sec. 1959-62, pres. sect. I 1963-64, hon. libr. 1969-91, pres. 1973-74); mem. Soc. Ecrivains Canadiens, Can. Libr. Assn. (life), Ont. Libr. Assn. (hon. life), Can. Assn. Info. Sci. (pres. 1971-72), Assn. Scis. et Techniques (life). Home: 2286 Bowman Rd Ottawa ON Canada K1H 6V6

SYMCHOWICZ, SAMSON, retired biochemist; b. Krakow, Poland, Mar. 20, 1923; came to U.S., 1954; s. Chiel and Esther M. S.; m. Sarah R. Nussbaum, May 24, 1953; children: Esther, Beatrice, Caren. Chem. engr., Poly. Inst. Prague, Czechoslovakia, 1950; MS in Chemistry, Bklyn. Poly. Inst., 1956; PhD in Biochemistry, Rutgers U., 1960. Asst. biochemist McGill U., Montreal, Que., Can., 1951-54, SUNY, 1954-56; biochemist Schering-Plough Corp., Bloomfield, N.J., 1956-73, assoc. dir. biol. rsch., 1973-80, dir. drug metabolism, 1980-92; ret. Editorial bd. Drug Metabolism and Disposition; contbr. over 90 sci. papers to profl. publs. Mem. Internat. Soc. Study of Xenobiotics, Am. Chem. Soc., N.Y. Acad. Sci., Soc. Pharmacology and Exptl. Therapeutics.

SYME, DANIEL BAILEY, rabbi, institution executive; b. Sharon, Pa., Feb. 6, 1946; s. Monte Robert and Sonia (Hendin) S.; m. Jill Susan Young; 1 child, Joshua. BA, U. Mich., Ann Arbor, 1967; BHL, MAHL, Hebrew Union Coll.-Jewish Inst. Religion, Cin., 1972; MEd, Columbia U., 1977, EdD, 1980. Ordained rabbi, 1972. Asst. dir. Nat. Fedn. Temple Youth, 1972-73; rabbi Stamford (Conn.) Fellowship for Jewish Learning, 1973-77; asst. nat. dir. edn. Union of Am. Hebrew Congregations, N.Y.C., 1973-77, dir., 1977—; asst. dir. Commn. Jewish Edn. for Reform Movement, N.Y.C., 1973-77, dir., 1977—, Union of Am. Hebrew Congregations TV Inst., N.Y.C., 1982-83, exec. asst. to pres., 1983-85, v.p., 1985-91, sr. v.p., 1991-96; sr. rabbi Temble Beth El, Bloomfield Hills, Mich., 1996—. Chmn. coalition for Alternatives in Jewish Edn., N.Y.C., 1978-80; mem. Nat. Assn. Temple Educators, 1972-91, Commn. on Teaching of Israel and Zionism, World Zionist Orgn., 1980-84; dir.-at-large Jewish Nat. Fund, Jewish Fedn. Met. Detroit, 2000—, internat. bd. Meml. Found. for Jewish Culture; nat. cabinet mem. Am. Zionist Movement, v.p. Am. Zionist Youth Movement; bd. dirs. United Israel Appeal, Ecumenical Inst. Author: 100 Essential Books for Jewish Readers, Finding God, My Body is Something Special, Prayer Is Reaching, I'm Growing, I Learn About God, Books Are Treasures, Jewish Home, What Happens After I Die?, Why I Am a Reform Jew, Drugs, Sex and Integrity, The Jewish Wedding Book, The Book of the Jewish Life; exec. prodr. T.V. programs A Conversation with Menachem Begin, 1981, Choosing Judaism, 1981, To See the World Through Jewish Eyes, 1983, A Conversation with Yitzchak Navon, 1983, You Can Go Home Again, Jewish Youth and Cults, 1984; contbr. articles to religious publs. Mem. Rabbinic Adv. Coun., United Jewish Appeal, Nat. Religious Edn. Assn. (exec. bd.), Nat Coun. Jewish Edn. (exec. bd.), Econ. Club Detroit (bd. dirs.). Office: 7400 Telegraph Rd Bloomfield Hills MI 48301-3876

SYME, SHERMAN LEONARD, epidemiologist, educator; b. Dauphin, Man., Can., July 4, 1932; arrived in U.S., 1950; s. Robert and Rose (Bay) Syme; m. Marilyn Elaine Egenes, July 28, 1932; children: Karen, David, Janet. BA, UCLA, 1953, MA, 1955; PhD, Yale U., 1957. Commd. USPHS, Washington, 1957—68, advanced through grades to chief Tng. Sta. San Francisco, 1962—68, sociologist Washington, 1957—60; exec. sec. NIH, Bethesda, Md., 1960—62; prof. emeritus epidemiology U. Calif., Berkeley, 1968—. Chmn. dept. epidemiology U. Calif., 1975—80; vis. prof. York (Eng.) U., 1975, Teikyo U., Tokyo, 1977, St. Thomas Sch. Medicine, London, 1980, U. London, 1989; expert adv. panels WHO, Geneva, 1975—. Co-editor: Social Stress and Heart Disease, 1967, Social Support and Health, 1985; contbr. over 115 articles to profl. jours. Fellow: Soc. Epidemiol. Rsch., Am. Heart Assn.; mem.: Am. Epidemiol. Soc., Inst. Medicine. Office: U Calif Sch Pub Health Pub Health Biology & Epidemiology 577 University Hall Berkeley CA 94720-1191

SYMENS, MAXINE BRINKERT TANNER, retired marketing professional; b. Primghar, Iowa, June 12, 1930; d. George Herman and Irene Marie (Dahnke) Brinkert; m. Jack Frederiksen Tanner, Dec. 28, 1950 (dec. Oct. 1976); m. Delbert Glenn Symens, Sept. 26, 1981. BS magna cum laude, Westmar Coll., 1970. Cert. tchr., Iowa. Elem. tchr. Rural Sch. O'Brien Co., Primghar, 1949-54, Gaza (Iowa) Com. Sch., 1954-60; secondary tchr. Primghar Com. Sch., 1960-81; fitness salon owner Slim 'N' Trim, George, Rock Rapids, Iowa, 1982-87; restaurant owner George Cafe, 1985-90, Pizza Ranch, 1988-96; with network mktg. divsn. Espial, 1997-99; dir. Coastal Vacations, 2000—03, Delmax Liquidations, Delmax Debt Arbitration; ret., 2003. Advt. sales cons. Internet advt., 1997-99, Antique & Gift Shop, 1998-2000. Pres. Primghar Edn. Assn., 1970-71. Mem. George C. of C., George Kiwanis Club (sec. 1991-95), Delta Kappa Gamma. Lutheran. Home: 307 Dell St NE George IA 51237-1030 E-mail: delmax@siebring.com.

SYMENS, RONALD EDWIN, electrical engineer, consultant; b. Britton, S.D., Jan. 16, 1951; s. Edwin Donald and Dora Marie (Larson) S.; children: Amy Marie, Chad Ronald. BSEE, S.D. Sch. Mines and Tech., 1973. Jr. engr. Firestone Tire Co., Akron, Ohio, 1973-74, engr., 1974-76, sr. engr., 1977-78; systems engr. Hewlett Packard, Cleve., 1977-79; pres. Comml. Timesharing Inc., Akron, 1980—. Inventor defect marker. Deacon Manchester Trinity Chapel, Akron, 1984-88, chmn. deacon bd., 1987-88; mem. Akron Regional Bd. Republican. Avocations: family camping, church, hunting, golf. Office: Comml Timesharing Inc 2740 Cory Ave Akron OH 44314

SYMES, LAWRENCE RICHARD, computer science educator, university dean; s. Oliver Lawrence and Maybell Melita Blanche Symes; m. Evelyn Jean Hewett, Apr. 3, 1964; children: Calvin Richard, Michelle Louise, Erin Kathleen. BA, U. Sask., Saskatoon, Can., 1963, postgrad. in math., 1964; MS, Purdue U., 1966, Phd, 1969. Asst. prof. Purdue U., West Lafayette, Ind., 1969-70; assoc. prof. computer sci. U. Regina, Sask., Can., 1970-74, prof., 1974—, dir. computer ctr., 1970-75, head dept. computer sci., 1972-81, dean of sci., 1982-92, dean grad. studies, assoc. rsch. v.p., 1997-99, dir. info. svcs., 1999—. Dir. tng. Software Tech. Ctr., 1993-94; exec. dir. postsecondary svcs. br. Saskatchewan Edn. Tng. and Employment Govt. of Saskatchewan, 1994-95, exec. dir. multimedia learning, 1995-96; invited lectr. Xian Jiaotong U., 1983; invited lectr., Shandong Acad. Sci., China, 1987, guest prof.; vis. prof. Ednl. Inst. Jilin Province, Shandong U., Jinan, China; co-chair IT cluster Regina Regional Econ. Authority, 2002—. Contbr. articles to profl. jours. Bd. dirs. Hosp. Sys. Study Group, Saskatoon, 1978-94, chmn. bd., 1980-83; dir. SSTA Computer Svcs., Regina, 1972-89; mem. adv. coun. Can./Sask. Advanced Tech. Agreement, 1985-87; mem. Sask. Agrl. Rsch. Found. Bd., 1987-88; mem. steering com. IBM/Sask. Agreement, 1990-92; mem. adv. bd. Plant Biotech. Inst., NRC. Can. Fed. Govt. grantee, 1977-84. Mem. Assn. Computing Machinery, Can. Info. Processing (pres. 1979-80, accreditation com. 1988-94), IEEE Computer Soc., Sask. ADA Assn. (bd. dirs. 1990-93), Software Tech. Ctr. (bd. dirs. 1993-98), Regina Regional Econ. Authority (IT cluster co-chair). Office: U Regina Info Svcs 3737 Wascana Pkwy Regina SK Canada S4S 0A2

SYMINGTON, GAYE R. state representative; b. Boston, Apr. 20, 1954; m. Charles M. Lacey; three children. BA, Williams Coll., 1977; MBA, Cornell U., 1983. V.p. Vt. Cmty. Loan Fund; rep. Vt. Ho. of Reps., 1996—. Treas. Vt. Cmty. Enterprise Fund; bd. dirs. Jericho Ctr. Preservation Assn. Chair Jericho Ctr. Preservation Assn. Mem. Vt. Health and Edn. Fin. Agy. Unitarian Universalist. Office: 324 Browns Trace Rd Jericho VT 05465-9780

SYMLAR, JESSE LEE, executive; b. Cleve., Aug. 4, 1951; s. Jesse Lee and Willa Leeann S. BA in Pub. Adminstrn., Christopher Newport U., 1982; MBA. MS in Tech. Mgmt., U. Md., 2001. Project mgr. VYCOR Corp., Washington, 1986-90; multimedia tng. Multimedia Tng. Inst., Washington, 1987-88; program analyst Det. Vets. Affairs, Washington, 1990; program mgmt. U.S. Dept. Agrl., Washington, 1990-93; program analyst Dept. Vets. Affairs, Washington, 1993-99; bus. process engr. Multimedia, Upper Marlboro, Md., 1998-2000; CEO Kyi Internat., Upper Marlboro, Md., 2000—. Author of poems. Mentor Each-One-Teach-One, Upper Marlboro, 1997-99. Sgt. USAF, 1975-79. Mem. Amherst Soc., Internat. Soc. Poets (disting.). Avocations: art, poetry, music, chess, sports, computers. Home: 3311 Old Largo Rd Upper Marlboro MD 20772-7811 E-mail: jsymlar@msn.com.

SYMMES, DANIEL LESLIE, technology executive, producer, director; b. Los Angeles, June 26, 1949; s. Louis Leslie and Mary (Warkentine) S. Student, Columbia Coll., Hollywood, Calif., 1970-71. Co-founder Stereovision Internat., Inc., North Hollywood, Calif., 1971; cons. Dimension 3e, Beverly Hills, Calif., 1975-87; pres., chmn. Spatial Techs. Inc., 3D Video Corp., Hollywood, Calif., 1987-95; pres., CEO Dimension 3, Woodland Hills, 1995—. Responsible for comml. 3D TV in U.S. and abroad; known worldwide as Mr. 3D. Author: Amazing 3-D; contbr. numerous articles to profl. jours.; dir. photography local 659 IATSE; patentee 3-D TV; inventor 1st reflex widescreen 3D filming system. Mem. SMPTE. Avocations: photography, expert scuba photography.

SYMON, KEITH RANDOLPH, physics educator, consultant; b. Ft. Wayne, Ind., Mar. 25, 1920; s. James Jefferson Keith Symon and Claribel Crego; m. Mary Louise Reinhardt, July 2, 1943; children: Judith Elizabeth, Keith Joseph, James Randolph, Rowena Louise. BSc, Harvard Coll., Cambridge, 1942; MA, Harvard U., Cambridge, 1943, PhD, 1948. Scientist Naval Rsch. Lab., Washington, 1943—46; instr. to assoc. prof. Wayne State U., Detroit, 1947—55; asst. prof. to prof. U. Wis., Madison, 1955—89, prof. emeritus, 1989—. Tech. dir. Midwestern Universities Rsch. Assn., Madison, Wis., 1956—67; acting dir. acad. computing ctr. U. Wis., 1982—83, acting dir. synchrotron radiation ctr., 1983—85. Author: (books) Mechanics, 1953, 1960, 1971; contbr. Handbook of Accelerator Physics and Engring., 1999, articles Ency. Brittannica, 1965, to profl. jours. Scoutmaster Boy Scouts, Madison, Wis.; mem. bd. Friends of the Libr., Spring Green, Wis., 1993—2002, Spring Green Lit. Festival, 1997—, pres., 2000—01. With USNR, 1944—51. Recipient Particle Accelerator Sci. and Tech. award, IEEE, 2003; fellow Ford Found., Geneva, 1962—63. Fellow: Am. Phys. Soc., Am. Assn. Advancement of Sci.; mem.: Am. Assn. of Physics Tchrs. Achievements include invention of fixed field alternating gradient accelerators, distbn. pushing method numerical simulation of plasmas. Avocations: skiing, whitewater canoeing, wilderness camping. Home: 318 S Lexington St Spring Green WI 53588 Office: Physics Dept UW Madison 1150 Univ Ave Madison WI 53706 Business E-Mail: krsymon@wisc.edu.

SYMONDS, PAUL SOUTHWORTH, mechanical engineering educator, researcher; b. Manila, Aug. 20, 1916; came to U.S., 1917; s. George R.B. and Claire Louise (Southworth) S.; m. Ilese Powell, Jan. 23, 1943; children: Alan Powell, Robin Peter. BS, Rensselaer Poly. Inst., 1938; MS, Cornell U., 1941, PhD, 1943; Docteur en Sciences Appliquées (hon.), Faculté Polytechnique de Mons, Belgium, 1988. Instr. mechanics Cornell U., Ithaca, N.Y., 1941-43; physicist Naval Research Lab., Washington, 1943-47; asst. prof. engring. Brown U., Providence, 1947-51, assoc. prof., 1951-54, prof., 1954-83, prof. engring. rsch. emeritus, 1983—, chmn. div. engring., 1959-62. Mem. editl. bd. Quar. Applied Math., 1965—; mem. editl. adv. bd. Internat. Jour. Impact Engring., 1983—; also numerous papers in tech. jours. Recipient Fulbright award 1949-50, 57-58; fellow Imperial Chem. Industries, Cambridge, U.K., 1950-51; Guggenheim fellow Swansea, Wales, 1957-58; NSF sr. postdoctoral fellow Oxford, Eng., 1964-65. Fellow ASME, ASCE, Am. Acad. Mechanics; mem. Internat. Assn. Bridge and Structural Engring. Home: 229 Medway St Apt 110 Providence RI 02906-5300 Office: Brown U Divsn Enging Providence RI 02912-0001 Office Phone: 401-863-2859. E-mail: paul_symonds@brown.edu.

SYMONDS, TERRI LEE, law educator; b. Peoria, Ill., Aug. 25, 1953; d. Robert George and Anna Lee (Offerman) Symonds. BS, Bradley U., Peoria, Ill., 1975, MLS, 1982; MA, U. Minn., 1987; PhD, Ind. U. of Pa., 1997; JD, William Mitchell Coll. of Law, St. Paul, 1999. Instr. St. Cloud (Minn.) State Coll., 1984—95, Normandale C.C., Bloomington, Minn., 2000—. Contbr. articles to profl. jours. Recipient award Excellence, Ctr. Computer Assisted Legal Instr., 1998. Democrat. Avocation: arabian horses. Office: Normandale Community Coll 9700 France Ave S Minneapolis MN 55431

SYMONETTE, LYS, foundation executive, musician, writer; b. Mainz, Germany, Dec. 21, 1920; came to U.S., 1936; d. Max Weinschenk and Gertrude (Metzger) Honheisser; m. Randolph Symonette, Sept. 1, 1949; 1 child, Victor. Student, Curtis Inst., Phila., 1937-39. Piano accompanist to internat. singers, 1940—. Musical asst. to Kurt Weill and L. Lenya, 1945-81; tchr. Curtis Inst., Phila., 1976—; musical exec., v.p. Kurt Weill Found., N.Y.C., 1981—. Translator operas from English to German and German to English, 1945—; co-editor Speak Low, Family Letters, 1996. Mem. Am. Fedn. Musicians, Alumni Assn. Curtis Inst. Music. Home: 160 W 73rd St New York NY 10023-3012 Office: Kurt Weill Found for Music 7 E 20th St New York NY 10003-1106

SYMONS, EDWARD LEONARD, JR., law educator, investment adviser; b. Pitts., Dec. 21, 1941; s. Edward Leonard and Lillian Mae (Daniel) S.; m. Louise Quinn, July 18, 1970; children: Amy, Colin. BA, Cornell U., 1963; JD summa cum laude, U. Pitts., 1969. Assoc., ptnr. Reding, Blackstone, Rea & Sell, Pitts., 1969-72; asst. atty. gen., chief counsel Pa. Dept. Banking, Harrisburg, 1972-74; prof. law U. Pitts. Sch. Law, 1974-98; CEO, Symons Capital Mgmt., Inc., 1983—. Tax cons., Wash., 1987, Del., 95; exec. v.p. investments Smithfield Trust Co., 1996—2000; mem. adv. coun. Conflict Resolution Ctr. Internat., 1994—2004; mem. bd. internat. scholars Ctr. for Comml. Law Studies, Queen Mary and Westfield Coll., U. London, 1993—2004. Co-author: Pennsylvania Professional Corporations, 1974, Banking Law Teaching Materials, 1984, 3d edit., 1991, Regulation of Financial Institutions, 1998; contbr. articles to profl. jours. Commr., Mt. Lebanon, Pa., 1976—80; chmn. St. Clair Hosp. Found., Pitts., 1996—; bd. dirs. Performing Arts for Children, Pitts., 1980—84, Mt. Lebanon Hosp. Authority, 1993—2004, St. Clair Hosp., 1995—. 1st. lt. arty., AUS, 1964—66. Mem. Order of Coif. Office: Symons Capital Mgmt Inc 250 Mount Lebanon Blvd Ste 301 Pittsburgh PA 15234-1248 Office Phone: 412-344-7690.

SYMONS, ROBERT SPENCER, electronic engineer; b. San Francisco, July 3, 1925; s. Spencer W. and Avesia (Atkins) S.; m. Alice Faye Smith, Dec. 21, 1960; children: Julia Ann, Robert Spencer Jr. BS, Stanford U., 1946, MS, 1948. Engr. Eitel-McCullough, Inc., San Bruno, Calif., 1947, Heinz & Kaufman, South San Francisco, 1948, Pacific Electronics Co., Los Gatos, Calif., 1949; sr. engring. mgr. Varian Assocs., Palo Alto, Calif., 1950-83; tech. dir. CTO Litton Sys., Inc., San Carlos, Calif., 1983—. Patentee in field. 1st lt. AUS, 1950-53. Recipient Charles B. Thornton award for Advanced Tech. Achievement, 1991, 99. Fellow IEEE (assoc. editor Transactions on Electron Devices jour. 1980-83); mem. Commonwealth of Calif. Club, Phi Beta Kappa, Tau Beta Pi. Home: 290 Surrey Pl Los Altos CA 94022-2180 Office: Litton Industries 960 Industrial Rd San Carlos CA 94070-4194

SYMOSEK, PETER FRANK, research scientist; b. Lawrence, Mass., Sept. 22, 1953; s. Frank John and Theresa Alice (McTiernan) S. BS, Merrimack Coll., North Andover, Mass., 1978; ScM, Brown U., 1980, PhD, 1985. Sr. prin. scientist Honeywell, Inc., Mpls., 1985—2003; prin. engr. Titan Corp., Waltham, Mass., 2003—. Condr. workshops on computer vision. Contbr. articles to IEEE Jour., Computer Graphics Image Processing, Pattern Recognition; patentee in field. Mem. IEEE (tech. program), Soc. Photo-optical Instrumentation Engrs., Toastmasters. Avocations: golf, scuba diving, swimming, bicycling, reading. Office: Titan Corp Atlantic Aerospace Divsn 470 Totten Pond Rd Waltham MA 02451 E-mail: peter.symosek@titan.com.

SYMS, MARCY, retail executive; MS in Pub. Rels., Boston U.; postgrad., Harvard U.; D (hon.), Bryant Coll. Pres. Syms Corp., Secaucus, N.J., 1983, chief operating officer, 1992-97, CEO, 1998—. Bd. dirs. Stanley Blacker, Inc., Am. Materials, Eau Claire, Wis. Author: Mind Your Own Business, Keep it in the Family; columnist Family Bus. Mag. Founding bd. dirs. Sy Syms Sch. Bus. Yeshiva U., 1985—. Recipient Disting. Bus. Leader of Yr. award Monmouth U., Marvin Feldman award Fashion Inst. Tech., Disting. Alumni award boston U., Good Citizen award Coun. Sr. Ctrs. & Svcs. of N.Y.C., Inc. Mem. Young Pres.' Orgn., Com. of 200, Intenrat. Women's Forum, Econ. Club N.Y. Office: Syms Corp One Syms Way Secaucus NJ 07094

SYNEK, MIROSLAV, physicist, chemist, world affairs independent consultant, researcher; b. Prague, Czechoslovakia, Sept. 18, 1930; came to U.S., 1958, naturalized, 1963; s. Frantisek and Anna (Kokrment) S.; children: Mary Rose, Thomas Robert. Cert., Indsl. Chemistry Tech. Sch., Prague, 1946-50; cert. in liberal arts, Prague, 1951; MS in Physics with distinction, Charles U., Prague, 1956; PhD in Physics, U. Chgo., 1963. Analytical chemist Indsl. Medicine Inst., Prague, 1950-51; rsch. physicist Acad. Scis., Prague, 1956-58; from asst. to assoc. prof. De Paul U., Chgo., 1962-67; prof. Tex. Christian U., Ft. Worth, 1967-71; lectr., rschr. U. Tex., Austin, 1971-75; tenured faculty U. Tex., San Antonio, 1975-95. Sci. advisor Tex. Edn. Agy., Austin, 1971-73, U. Tex., 1971-73; advisor Student Physics Soc., active numerous univ. coms. Contbr. numerous articles to sci. jours., abstracts to presentations. Campaigner United Way, San Antonio, 1975-95; judge Alamo Sci. Fairs and Tex. Acad. of Sci. Fairs, annually; grand award judge Internat. Sci. and Engring. Fairs, 1998, 99. Rsch. grantee Robert A. Welch Found., 1968-71, 76-83, 93-95. Fellow AAAS, Am. Phys. Soc. (life), Tex. Acad. Sci., Am. Inst. Chemists; mem. NEA, Tex. State Tchrs. Assn., AAUP, DAV Comdrs. Club, Am. Assn. Physics Tchrs., Am. Acad. Polit. Sci., Am. Mus. Natural History, Libr. Congress, Smithsonian Instn., Nat. Trust Hist. Preservation, N.Y. Acad. Scis., Am. Chem. Soc. (San Antonio edn. com. chmn.), Czechoslovak Nat. Coun. Am. (dist. sec. Chgo. 1961-63, chmn. 1967), Czechoslovak Soc. Arts and Scis. Am., Internat. Soc. Poets (disting. mem.), Sheriffs' Assn. Tex. (assoc.), San Antonio Astron. Assn., World Affairs Coun. San Antonio (diplomat mem.), Bexar County Czech Heritage Soc. of Tex., Sigma Xi (life), Sigma Pi Sigma (sustaining). Roman Catholic. Achievements include research in atomic structure calculations of laser-active lanthanides, analytical relativistic self-consistent field theory, approximate estimate of the extra-terrestrial intelligence probability, nuclear age requiring free elections, main dangers of our times, suggested priorities for human society. Home and Office: Independent Consultant PO Box 5937 San Antonio TX 78201-0937 Personal E-mail: m.synek@juno.com.

SYNNOTT, MARCIA GRAHAM, history professor; b. Camden, N.J., July 4, 1939; d. Thomas Whitney and Beatrice Adelaide (Colby) S.; m. William Edwin Sharp, June 16, 1979; children: Willard William Sharp, Laurel Beth Sharp. AB, Radcliffe Coll., 1961; MA, Brown U., 1964; PhD, U. Mass., 1974. History tchr. MacDuffie Sch., Springfield, Mass., 1963-68; instr. U. S.C., Columbia, 1972-74, asst. prof., 1974-79, assoc. prof. history, 1979-97, dir. grad. studies history dept., 1990-92, prof. history, 1997—. Author: The Half-Opened Door, 1979; contbr. essays to books. Active university-wide cmty. svc. projects. Fulbright scholar, 1988; Am. Coun. Learned Socs. grantee, 1981. Mem. Am. Hist. Assn., So. Hist. Assn., Orgn. Am. Historians (membership com. 1990-93), S.C. Hist. Assn. (pres. 1994-95), History of Edn. Soc. (mem. editl. bd. 1996, 97, 98, bd. dirs. 2000-02). Avocations: historic sites and museums, skiing, walking. Office: U SC Dept History Columbia SC 29208-0001

SYPHER, BLAKE, medical educator; b. Chgo., Sept. 13, 1961; s. Richard Sypher and Kathlyn Reeves; m. Dunja Saric, Oct. 24, 1998; children: Jelena, Sasha. PhD, CUNY, 1997; BA magna cum laude, NYU, 1989. Assoc. prof. Marshall U. Sch. Medicine, Huntington, W.Va., 1998—. Cons. Cabell-Huntington Hosp., 1999—; presenter in field. Contbr. articles to profl. jours. Adv. com. mem. W.Va. Ctr. for End-of-Life Care, Morgantown, W.Va., 2002—; ethics task force com. mem. Hospice, Huntington; instl. rev. bd. mem. Veterans Adminstrn., Huntington. Mem.: Am. Philos. Assn., Am. Soc. for Bioethics and the Humanities. Avocations: classical dance, photography, homebrewing. Office: Marshall Univ Sch Medicine 1540 Spring Valley Dr Huntington WV 25704 E-mail: sypher@marshall.edu.

SYPHERS, JAMES EDGAR, retired social worker; b. Exeter, NH, Feb. 21, 1933; s. Albion Lionel and Mary Pinkham (Gray) S.; m. Joyce Caswell, June 22, 1952 (div. Mar. 1969); m. Barbara Walters, Dec. 31, 1974; children: Gail N., Dale A., Paul N., Neal A., Dennis L. Walters, Marcia W. Turner. BA in Psychology, U. N.H., 1955; MSW, U. Pitts., 1965; BD, Oberlin Coll., 1968; PhD in Higher Edn., Walden U., 1978. Cmty. peace intern Am. Friends Svc. Com., NY, 1958—61, youth sec., 1961—63; acting. coord., dir. cmty. affairs Hill House Assn., Pitts., 1965-69; instr., acting dir. human svcs. Lincoln U., Pa., 1969-75, assoc. prof., asst. dir. masters human svcs. program, 1977-79; asst. prof., dir. social work and human svcs. Widener U., Chester, Pa., 1975-76; assoc. prof., chair, field coord. dept. social work Saginaw Valley State U., University Center, Mich., 1980-87; asst. prof., field coord. dept. social work Western Carolina U., Cullowhee, NC, 1987-91; dir. social svc. Downingtown (Pa.) Indsl. and Agrl. Sch., 1991-92; asst. prof., acting chair dept. social work and gerontology California U. Pa., 1992—2002; ret., 2002. Evaluator gang control programs City of Phila. and Youth Svc. Inc., 1973-75; cons., evaluator Dauphin Commn. on Drugs and Alcohol, Harrisburg, Pa., 1978; sec. Saginaw County Mental Health/Mental Retardation Adv. Bd., 1982-86; cons. social work program Carlow Coll., Pitts., 1994-99 Author, co-editor: Community Action for Social Change, 1972; contbr. (booklet) The Community is Our Client, 1966. Mem. gen. com., devel. com. Friends Com. on Nat. Legislation, Washington, 1973-79. Recipient grad. fellowship NIMH, 1963-65, rsch. fellowship NIH, 1964, Human Svc. Program grant Social and Rehab. Svcs. of HEW, 1970-76. Mem. NASW (western N.C. unit sec. 1980—, Lifetime Achievement award Pa. 2002), NAACP (student chpt. v.p.), AAUP, Coun. on Social Work Edn. (del. 1980—), Mich. Assn. Baccalaureate Social Work Programs (pres. 1983-85), Pa. Assn. Undergrad. Social Work Edn. (pres. 1997), Phi Alpha. Democrat. Mem. Soc. Of Friends. Avocations: hiking, construction, travel, social justice activities, counseling. Mailing: 110 Martha Ave Hopwood PA 15445 E-mail: jsyphers@juno.com.

SYPOLT, DIANE GILBERT, federal judge; b. Rochester, N.Y., June 14, 1947; d. Myron Birne and Doris Isabell (Robie) Gilbert; m. Dwight Douglas Sypolt; children: Andrew, David Weinstein. BA, Smith Coll., Northampton, Mass., 1969; postgrad., Stanford U., 1977-78, Georgetown U., 1978; JD, Boston U., 1979. Bar: D.C. 1979, Mass. 1979. Law clk. to judge D.C. Ct. Appeals, Washington, 1979-80; assoc. Peabody, Lambert & Meyers, Washington, 1980-83; asst. gen. counsel Office of Mgmt. and Budget, Washington, 1983-86; dep. gen. counsel U.S. Dept. Edn., Washington, 1986-88, acting gen. counsel, 1988-89; legal counselor to V.P. of U.S., White House; counsel Pres.'s Competitiveness Coun., Washington, 1989-90; judge U.S. Ct. Fed. Claims, Washington, 1990—. Bd. dirs. Democracy Devel. Inst. Recipient Young Lawyer's award Boston U. Law Sch., 1989. Mem. Fed. Am. Inn of Ct. (Master), Federalist Soc. Office: US Ct Fed Claims 717 Madison Pl NW Washington DC 20439-0002 Office Phone: 202-219-9655. Business E-Mail: diane_sypolt@ad.uscourts.gov.

SYRON, RICHARD FRANCIS, finance company executive, economist; b. Boston, Oct. 25, 1943; s. Dominick Richard and Elizabeth (McQuire) S.; m. Margaret Mary Garatoni, Oct. 21, 1972; children: Erin Elizabeth, Brendan Paul BS in Econs.-Acctg. with high honors, Boston Coll., 1966; MA in Econs., Tufts U., 1969, PhD in Econs., 1971. Dep. dir. budget Commonwealth of Mass., 1973-74; v.p., economist Fed. Res. Bank of Boston, 1974-82, sr. v.p., econ. advisor, 1982-85; exec. asst. to sec. U.S. Treasury, Washington, 1979-80, dep. sec. for econ. policy, 1980-81; asst. to Chmn. Volcker Fed. Res. Bd., Washington, 1981-82; pres., CEO Fed. Home Loan Bank of Boston, 1986-88; pres., chief exec. officer Fed. Res. Bank of Boston, 1989-94; chmn. Am. Stock Exch., N.Y.C., 1994-99; chmn., CEO Thermo Electron, Waltham, Mass., 1999—2002, exec. chmn., 2002—03; chmn., CEO Fed. Home Loan Mortgage Corp. (Freddie Mac), McLean, Va., 2003—. Past chmn. Boston Coll.; past chmn. Boston Pvt. Industry Coun.; bd. dirs. John Hancock Mut. Life Ins. Co., Boston, McKesson Corp., Nabors Industries, Am. Stock Exch. Author: Urban Fire Insurance, 1972; contbr. articles to profl. jours. Teaching fellow Tufts U., 1966-69. Mem.: Comml. Club Boston, Boston Econ. Club, Wianno Yacht Club, Clover Club Boston. Office: Freddie Mac 8200 Jones Branch Dr Mc Lean VA 22102-3110*

SYTEK, DONNA P. former state legislator; b. Haverhill, Mass., Dec. 14, 1944; m. John Sytek; 1 child. AB, Regis Coll., 1966, MA. Chmn. rules com. N.H. Ho. of Reps., Concord; mem. N.H. Ho. of Reps. (dist. 26), Concord; chmn. Jud. Conduct Commn., Bow, NH, 2001—. Chmn. N.H. Rep. Com., 1982-84; pres. Nat. Rep. Legislators Assn., 1992-93; del. to Rep. Nat. Conv., 1980, 84, 88, 84 Const. Conv., Assembly on the Legislature, chmn., 1991-92; mem. exec. com. NCSL, 1990-94, 97-98, Coun. State Govt., 1989—. Mem. Dist. Nursing Assn. (bd. dirs. 1989—), Boys and Girls Club (bd. dirs. 1989-97). Republican. Roman Catholic. Avocation: travel. Office: Jud Conduct Commn 501 South St Bow NH 03304-3413

SYVERTSON, CLARENCE ALFRED, engineering and research management consultant; b. Mpls., Jan. 12, 1926; s. Alfred and Esther Louise (Goertemiller) S.; m. Helen Hammond Gonnella, May 4, 1953 (dec. May 1981); 1 child, Marguerite Louise.; m. JoAnn Mary Caruso, May 8, 1982. B. Aero. Engring., U. Minn., 1946, MS, 1948, DSc (hon.), 2004; postgrad., Stanford U., 1950-57; grad., Advanced Mgmt. Program, Harvard U., 1977. Research scientist Ames Aero. Lab., NACA, Moffett Field, Calif., 1948-58; exec. dir. Joint Dept. Transp./NASA Civil Aviation Research and Devel. Policy Study, 1970-71; with Ames Research Center, NASA, Moffett Field, 1958-84, dep. dir., 1969-78, dir., 1978-84. Mem. adv. bd. Coll. Engring., U. Calif., Berkeley, 1980-85; cons. prof. Stanford U., 1985-88; hon. prof. Northwestern Poly. U., Xian, China, 1998. Served with U.S. Army, 1946-47. Recipient invention and contbn. award NASA, 1964, Exceptional Service medal, 1971, Disting. Service medal, 1984, Outstanding Achievement award U. Minn., 1982, Comdrs. award for civilian service U.S. Army, 1984 Fellow AIAA (Lawrence Sperry award 1957), Am. Astronautical Soc., Calif. Coun. Sci. and Tech.; mem. Nat. Acad. Engring. Home: 14666 Springer Ave Saratoga CA 95070-5748 Office Phone: 408-867-2663.

SYVERUD, KENT DOUGLAS, dean; b. Rochester, N.Y., Oct. 23, 1956; s. Warren Lukken and Janet (Thatcher) S.l; m. Ruth Chi-Fen Chen, May 22, 1982; children: Steven, Brian, David. BSFS, Georgetown U., 1977; JD, U. Mich., 1981, MA, 1983. Bar: D.C. 1982, Mich. 1993. Law clk. to Judge Oberdorfer U.S. Dist. Ct. D.C., Washington, 1983-84; law clk. Justice O'Connor Supreme Ct. U.S., Washington, 1984-85; assoc. Wilmer, Cutler & Pickering, Washington, 1985-97; exec. sec. Mich. Law Revision Commn., Lansing, 1993-95; prof. U. Mich. Law Sch., Ann Arbor, 1987-97; dean, Garner Anthony prof. Vanderbilt U. Law Sch., Nashville, 1997—. Chair exec. com. Inst. for Continuing Legal Edn., Ann Arbor, 1995-97. Mem. Am. Law Inst., Law and Soc. Assn. Office: Vanderbilt Law Sch 21st Ave S Nashville TN 37240-0001

SZABAN, MARILYN C. small business owner; b. Palmer, Mass., Dec. 24, 1942; d. Joseph J. and Sophie V. (Duda) Martowski; m. Richard J. Szaban, June 9, 1962 (dec. 1993); children: Gregory John, Deborah Ann, Michael John. BFA summa cum laude, U. So. Maine, 1986; student, Notre Dame Coll., 1983. Owner, pres. Automotive Parts and Supply Co., Inc., Ramsdell & Van Dyke, Worcester, Mass., 1977—; co-owner, pres. Plymouth (N.H.) Auto Supply, Inc., 1980-96; owner, pres. Transfigurations, Worcester, 1996—. Bd. dirs. APSCO, Worcester, PASCO, Plymouth; art tchr. Jewish Comm. Ctr., Worcester, 1991, 92. Designer for Transfigurations, 1996; artist Portland Rev. of the Arts, 1986. Bd. dirs., art tchr. gallery com., Art Guild of Farmington, Conn., 1988-90. Recipient hon. mention Manchester Inst. Arts & Scis., 1981, 82, recognition award, 1983, Nat. Competition Juried Art Shows, Northeast and Mid-Atlantic States, 1981—. Mem. Plymouth C. of C. Avocations: fine arts, competition in juried art shows. Address: 116 Village Blvd Ste 200 Princeton NJ 08540-5700

SZABLYA, HELEN MARY, writer, language professional, lecturer; b. Budapest, Hungary, Sept. 6, 1934; came to U.S., 1963; d. Louis and Helen (Bartha) Kovacs; m. John Francis Szablya, June 12, 1951; children: Helen, Janos, Louis, Stephen, Alexandra, Rita, Dominique-Mary. Diploma in Sales, Mktg., U.B.C., 1962; BA in Fgn. Lang., Lit., Wash. State U., 1976. Freelance writer, translator, 1967—; columnist Cath. News, Trinidad, West Indies, 1980-91; adult educator TELOS Bellevue (Wash.) C.C., 1987-89; adult educator Pullman-Spokane (Wash.) C.C., 1976-80; faculty Christian Writers' Conf., Seattle, 1983-88, Pacific N.W. Writers' Conf., Seattle and Tacoma, 1987—92; hon. consul for Wash., Oreg., Idaho Republic of Hungary, 1993—. Lectr. Washington Commn. for Humanities, 1987-89. Author: (with others) Hungary Remembered, 1986 (Guardian of Liberty award, 1986, George Washington Honor medal, Freedoms Found. award 1988), 56-os Cserkèszcsapat, 1986, (with others) The Fall of the Red Star, 1996, Hungarian translation 1999, (1st prize Wash. Press Assn., 1st prize Nat. Fedn. Press Women); pub., editor Hungary Internat. newsletter, 1990-93; columnist Hungarian Bus. Weekly, 1994-95; translator: Emlèkezünk, 1986, Mind Twisters, 1987. Recipient Nat. 1st place editl. Nat. Fedn. Press Women, 1987, Senator Tom Martin Meml. award Pacific N.W. Writers Conf., 1979; grantee Hungarian Am. Assn. Wash., 1986, Wash. Com. for Humanities, 1986; named Cmty. Woman of Yr. Am. Bus. Women Assn., 1990. Mem. AAUW, Wash. Press Assn. (pres. 1987-88, 1st and 2nd place awards, several editl. and profile awards 1983, 87, 89, 90, 91, 92, 96, Communicator of Achievement award 1987), Nat. Fedn. Press Women (Affiliate Pres.' award 1988, bd. dirs. edn.

fund N.W. quadrant, mem. 21st century planning com.), Authors Guild, Am. Translators Assn., Arpad Acad. (Gold medal 1987), Nat. Writers Club, Internat. PEN Club, Sigma Delta Chi (editl. award 1989). Avocations: children, reading, dance, swimming, travel. Home and Office: PO Box 578 Kirkland WA 98083-0578 Office Phone: 425-739-0631. Personal E-mail: szablyahj@aol.com.

SZABLYA, JOHN FRANCIS, electrical engineer, consultant; b. Budapest, Hungary, June 25, 1924; came to U.S., 1963, naturalized, 1979; s. John and Alexandra (Huszar) S.; m. Helen Bartha-Kovacs, June 12, 1951; children: Helen A., Janos L., Louis J., Stephen J.P., Alexandra H.R., Rita H.C., Dominique-Mary H. Diploma engring., Jozsef Nador U., Budapest, 1947, diploma edn., D in Econs., Jozsef Nador U., Budapest, 1948. Registered profl. engr., Wash., Mont., Alaska, Wyo., Oreg., Colo., Idaho, B.C. and Ont., Can. Design engr. Ganz Elec. Works, Budapest, 1947-56; assoc. prof. Tech. U. Budapest, 1951-56, U. B.C., Vancouver, Can., 1957 63; prof. elec. engring. Wash. State U., Pullman, 1963-82, now prof. emeritus; mgr. elec., instrumentation and control engring. EBASCO Svcs., Inc., Bellevue, Wash., 1981-90; ret., 1990; cons. engr., v.p. Szablya Cons., Inc., Kirkland, Wash., 1990—. Vis. prof. Technische Universitat Braunschweig, 1973-74, U. W.I., St. Augustine, Trinidad and Tobago, 1983-2001, U. Wash., Seattle, 1985—, Seattle U., 1987. Contbr. numerous articles to profl. jours. Recipient Zipernowszky medal Hungarian Inst. Elec. Engrs., 1954, diploma of recognition, 1998, Arpad Academia Gold medal, 1990. Fellow IEEE, Instn. Elec. Engrs. (London); mem. Hungarian Acad. Scis., Sigma Xi. Roman Catholic. Home: PO Box 578 Kirkland WA 98083-0578

SZABO, ANDRAS, internist; b. Sopron, Hungary, Nov. 9, 1967; m. Edit Szabo. MD summa cum laude, Debrecen U., 1993. Diplomate Am. Bd. Internal Medicine. Ward physician Hollos Istvan Psychiatry Clinic, Doba, Hungary, 1993-95; resident Meridia Huron Hosp./Cleve. Clin. Health Sys., 1995-98; internist Wagner (S.D.) Cmty. Meml. Hosp. and Clinic, 1998—. Mem. ACP, AMA, Am. Soc. of Internal Medicine, S.D. State Med. Assn., Am. Diabetes Assn. (profl. sect.), Am. Acad. Pain Mgmt. Roman Catholic. Avocations: classical music, history, wildlife. Office: 39 Jane lacey Dr Apt U Endicott NY 13760-3743 E-mail: aszabo@charles-mix.com.

SZABO, BARNA ALADAR, engineering educator; b. Martonvasar, Hungary, Sept. 21, 1935; came to U.S., 1967, naturalized, 1974; s. Jozsef and Gizella (Ivanyi) S.; m. Magdalin Gerstmayer, July 23, 1960; children: Mark, Nicholas. BASc., U. Toronto, Ont., Can., 1962; MS, SUNY, Buffalo, 1966, PhD, 1968; D. honoris causa, U. of Miskolc, Hungary, 1998. Registered profl. engr., Mo. Mining engr. Internat. Nickel Co. Can., 1960-62; engr. Acres Cons. Services Ltd., Niagara Falls, Can., 1962-66; instr. SUNY, Buffalo, 1966-68; mem. faculty Washington U., St. Louis, 1968—, prof. mech. engring., 1974—, Albert P. and Blanche Y. Greensfelder prof., 1975—, dir. Ctr. Computational Mechanics, 1977-92; chmn. engring. software Rsch. and Devel., Inc., St. Louis, 1989—. Author: (with Ivo Babuska) Finite Element Analysis, 1991; contbr. articles to profl. jours. Fellow, St. Louis Acad. Sci. Fellow U.S. Assn. Computational Mechanics (founding mem.); mem. ASME, Hungarian Acad. Sci. Home: 48 Crestwood Dr Clayton MO 63105-3033 Office: PO Box 1129 Saint Louis MO 63188-1129 Office Phone: 314-935-6352. Business E-Mail: szabo@me.wustl.edu.

SZABO, DANIEL, government official; b. Budapest, Hungary, Mar. 23, 1933; came to U.S., 1950, naturalized, 1954; s. Alexander and Maria (Berger) S.; m. Corinne Holiber, July 3, 1955; children— Nancy Beth, Peter Stuart. BA, CCNY, 1957; MA, Johns Hopkins U., 1959. Internat. economist U.S. Tariff Commn., 1959-60; desk officer for Vietnam, Cambodia and Laos U.S. Dept. Commerce, 1960-63; spl. asst. to U.S. Senator Jacob K. Javits, 1963-69; dep. asst. sec. state for Inter-Am. Affairs, Washington, 1969-74; sr. adviser Inter-Am. Devel. Bank, Washington, 1974-95. Bd. dirs. Washington chpt., chmn. Md. legis. task force Am. Jewish Com.; v.p. Md. Interfaith Legis. Com., 1999—. With U.S. Army, 1954—56. Home: 11600 Danville Dr North Bethesda MD 20852-3716 E-mail: ds3693@verizon.net. *In approaching life I want my work to represent a service to our society. I am attracted to new ideas and new ways of solving old problems.*

SZABO, DENIS, criminologist, educator; b. Budapest, Hungary, June 4, 1929; s. Jenö and Catherine (Zsiga) Szabo; m. Sylvie Grotard; children: Catherine, Marianne. D in Social and Polit. Sci., U. Louvain, Belgium, 1956; diploma in Criminology, Sorbonne U., Paris, 1958; Doctorate (hon.), U. Sienna, Italy, 1984, U. Budapest, Hungary, 1985, U. Aix Marseilles, 1992, Panteios U., 1996, U. Bucarest, 2004. Asst. in sociology U. Louvain, 1951—56; lectr. sociology Cath. Univ., Paris, Lyon, 1956—58; mem. rsch. group Ctr. Nat. de la Recherche Scientifique, Paris, 1954—58; asst. prof. to assoc. prof. U. Montreal, Canada, 1958—66, founder, dir. dept. criminology, 1960—70, prof., 1966—95; founder, dir. Internat. Ctr. Comparative Criminology, Canada, 1969—84; prof. emeritus U. Montreal, Canada, 1995—. Emeritus prof. law U. Ecuador, Quito, 1984. Author, editor: book Can. Criminal Justice Sys., 1977, Criminologie et Politique Criminelle, 1978, La Criminologie Empirique au PQ, 1985, Sci. et Crime, 1986, De L' Anthropologie a la Criminologie Comparee, 1993, La Criminologie: Ses Fondements et sa Fondation, 1998; author (with Marc LeBlanc): Le Traité di Criminologie Empirique, 1993, The Criminal Justice Sys., 2001. Decorated officer Order Can.; named Comdr., Nat. Order Merite Hungarian Republic, 1996; recipient Beccaria Award, German Soc. Criminology, 1970, Chevalier Des Arts et des Letters, France, 1996. Fellow: Am. Soc. Criminology (mem. exec. coun., Sutherland award 1968), Am. Sociol. Soc., Royal Soc. Can.; mem.: Medaille de l' Mustitut Basque de Criminology (hon. mem. 2003), Basque Inst. of Criminology San Sebastian (hon. mem. 2003), Can. Soc. Criminology (v.p. 1962—64), Hungarian Acad. Sci., Romanian Soc. Criminology (hon.; elected hon. mem. 2003), Nat. Order Merit (comdr. Ivory Coast 1987), Internat. Assn. Sociology, Order Nat. du Que. (officer 1998—), Soc. de Criminology du Que. (sec.-gen. 1960—70), Soc. Criminology (v.p. 1962—64), Internat. Soc. Criminology (pres. 1978—85, hon. pres.). Roman Catholic. Home: 66 Carré Copp Georgeville QC Canada J0B 1T0 Office: U Montreal Internat Ctr Com Criminology CP 6128 succursale Centre-ville Montreal QC Canada H3C 3J7

SZABO, ISTVAN, music educator; b. Tirgu-Mures, Romania, June 6, 1971; arrived in U.S., 1988, permanent resident, 2003; s. István and Ilona Szabó; BMus, Gheorghe Dima Acad. Music, Cluj, Romania, 1995; M in Musical Arts, U. Ill., 2000, Doctorate, 2004. Chamber music instr. H.S. of Music, Cluj, Romania, 1991—92; artist-violist Transvylvania Philharmonic Orch., Cluj, 1993—95, Tirgu-Mures Philharmonic Orch., 1995—97; faculty Plymouth (Mass.) Chamber Music Festival, 2001; vis. lectr. U. Ill., Champaign, Ill., 2001; prof. music Ea. Ill. U., Charleston, Ill., 2002—. Office: Eastern Ill U 600 Lincoln Ave Charleston IL 61920 E-mail: cfis@eiu.edu.

SZABO, JOSEPH LASZLO, management consultant; b. Darby, Pa. s. Laszlo and Judith S.; m. Stacey Allen, May 31, 1986; children: Brandon, Bradley, Tyler, McKenzie. BSCE, S.D. Sch. Mines Tech., 1986; Exec. MBA, U. Pa., 2000. Owner PC Board Svcs., Ardmore, Pa.; mng. dir. info. tech. Avanta Credit Card, Horsham, Pa., Fleet Credit Card, Horsham; chief info. officer Internet Capital Group, King of Prussia, Pa.; CEO, mng. dir. Szabo Cons. Internat., LLC, King of Prussia. Capt. USAF, 1980-85. Mem. Presdl. Round Table. Republican. Baptist. Avocations: golf, scuba diving, skiing, boating. Home: 43 Washington Ln Coatesville PA 19320 Office: Szabo Consulting Internat LLC 900 E 8th Ave King Of Prussia PA 19406 E-mail: jszabo@szaboconsulting.com.

SZABO, PETER JOHN, investment company executive, financial planner, mining engineer, lawyer; b. Bklyn., Nov. 22, 1946; s. Paul Simon and Marita Ellen (Coughlin) S.; m. Dorothy Anne Steward, Nov. 14, 1970; children: Peter, David, John Paul Steward. BS in Mining Engring., Columbia U., 1968; LLB, LaSalle Law Sch., 1975; MS in Fin. Planning, Coll. Fin. PLanning, 1994. registered profl. engr., CFP. Mining engr. Halecrest Co., Mt. Hope, N.J., 1973-74; mgr. solid fuels & minerals Ford, Bacon & Davis, N.Y.C., 1974-75; asst. v.p. Mfrs. Hanover Trust Co., N.Y.C., 1975-77, Irving Trust Co., N.Y.C., 1977; v.p. Republic Nat. Bank of Dallas, 1977-80; mgr. bus. devel. AMOCO Minerals, Denver, 1980-84; investment broker B.J. Leonard, Denver, 1984-85; investment exec. Wedbush Nobel Cook, Denver, 1985; regional sr. v.p. Alliance Fund Distbrs., N.Y.C., 1985-92, sr. v.p., 1992—. Mining engr. U.S. Bur. Mines, Dallas, 1971-72, IRS, Washington, 1972-73. Treas. Columbia Sch. Engring., 1968—. Lt. USMC, 1969-71, Vietnam, capt. Res. Mem. VFW (post sr. vice comdr. 1993-94, post comdr. 1994-95, all state team post comdrs. 1995, 16th dist. jr. vice comdr. 1995—, 16th dist. sr. vice comdr. 1996—, nat. aide-de-camp 1995-96), Mil. Order of the Cootie (sr. vice comdr. 1994-95). Republican. Roman Catholic. Avocations: sailing, golf, tennis, jogging, scripophily. Home and Office: Alliance Fund Distbrs 810 Oxford Way Benicia CA 94510-3646

SZABO, YURIKA LIN, marketing executive, advertising executive; b. Long Beach, Calif., Mar. 1, 1967; d. Sandor Alex and Taeko (Tsujimura) S. AS in Multimedia, Brooks Coll., 2002. Dir. mktg. Adolphs Food Svc., Lakewood, Calif., 1991—; publicist, cons. L.A. Access Video, 1996—; graphic designer Peepod Prodns., Los Alamitos, Calif., 1996—. Reporter Studio 12, Lakewood, 1997, camera operator, 1997; cons. L.A. Access Video, 1996—. Author of poems. Recipient Editor's Choice award Nat. Libr. Poetry, 1996; Calif. Scholar Fedn. Svc. scholar, 1981-85. Mem. Internat. Soc. Poets (disting.), Alpha Beta Gamma. Avocations: writing, computer graphics, body sculpting, acting, skating.

SZAKAL, ANDRAS KALMAN, immunologist, anatomist, educator; s. Andor Viktor and Maria Szakal; m. Norma Elisabeth Skinner; children: Andras Robert, Tamas Kalman. BA in Zoology, U. Colo., 1961, MA in Biology, 1963; PhD, U. Tenn., 1972. Rsch. biologist for immunology of carcinogenesis group divsn. biology Oak Ridge (Tenn.) Nat. Labs., 1972—74; prin. scientist Meloy Labs., Springfield, Va., 1974—79; assoc. prof. dept. anatomy, divsn. immunobiology Va. Commonwealth Univ./Med Sch., Richmond, 1979—91, prof. dept. anatomy and neurobiology and The Immunology Group, 1991—. Cons. electron microscopist in exptl. biology Oak Ridge Nat. Lab., 1969—70; cons. electron microscopist Lunar Receiving Lab., NASA Manned Spacecraft Ctr., Houston, 1969; cons. on electron micros. autoradiography Nat. Cancer Inst., NIH, Bethesda, Md., 1974. Contbr. articles to profl. jours. Grantee, NIH, NIA, 1985—88, 1991—94, 1999—2004. Mem.: AAAS, Va. Acad. Sci., Am. Assn. Immunologists, Am. Assn. Anatomists. Achievements include discovery of Antigen Transport Cell; ICCOSOMEs. Office: Virginia Commonwealth Univ/Med Sch 1217 East Marshall Str Richmond VA 23298 E-mail: aszakal@hsc.vcu.edu.

SZALKOWSKI, CHARLES CONRAD, lawyer; b. Amarillo, Tex., Apr. 14, 1948; s. Chester Casimer and Virginia Lee Szalkowski; m. Jane Howe, Dec. 28, 1971; children: Jennifer Lee, Stephen Claude. BA, BS in Acctg., Rice U., 1971; MBA, JD, Harvard U., 1975. Bar: Tex. 1975. Assoc. Baker Botts L.L.P., Houston, 1975-82, ptnr., 1983—. Speaker in field. Chmn. ann. fund campaign Rice U., Houston, 1991-93, chmn. Fund Coun., 1995-96; chmn. adminstrv. bd. St. Luke's United Meth. Ch., Houston, 1994, chmn. bd. trustees, 1997, 2003; chmn. DePelchin Children's Ctr., Houston, 2002-2004; bd. dirs. Meth. Children's Home, Waco, 1998-2001, 03—, MIT Enterprise Forum of Tex., Houston. Mem.: ABA (fed. regulation of securities com.), Assn. Corp. Growth (bd. dirs. Houston chpt.), Tex. Bus. Law Found. (mem. exec. com. 1988—, chmn. 1998—2000, bd. dirs.), Harvard Law Sch. Assn. Tex. (pres. 1983—84), Houston Bar Assn. (corp. counsel sect. 1989—90, chmn.), State Bar Tex. (chmn. bus. law sect. 1991—92), Am. Law Inst., Assn. Rice U. Alumni (bd. dirs. 1999—2002). Office: Baker Botts LLP 1 Shell Plz 910 Louisiana St Ste 3000 Houston TX 77002-4991

SZALLER, JAMES FRANCIS, lawyer; b. Cleve., Jan. 22, 1945; s. Frank Paul and Ellen Grace (O'Malley) S.; m. Roberta Mae Curtin, Oct. 23, 1967 (div. Aug. 1975); m. Charlene Nancy Smith, Apr. 28, 1984. AA, Cuyahoga Community Coll., 1967; BA, Cleve. State U., 1970, JD cum laude, 1975. Bar: Ohio 1975, U.S. Dist. Ct. (no. dist.) Ohio 1975, U.S. Supreme Ct. 1982, U.S. Ct. Appeals (6th cir.) 1983, U.S. Ct. Appeals (4th cir.) 1986. Assoc. Metzenbaum, Gaines & Stern, Cleve., 1975-79; sr. ptnr. Brown & Szaller Co., L.P.A., Cleve., 1979—. Lectr. law Cleve. State U., 1977-81. Mem. editorial bd. Cleve. State U. Law Rev., 1973-75.; contbr. articles to profl. jours. Mem. Ohio State Bar Assn., Greater Cleve. Bar Assn., Cleve. Acad. Trial Lawyers, Ohio Acad. Trial Lawyers (trustee, 2002—, Disting. Svc. award 1996), Assn. Trial Lawyers Am., Nat. Coll. Advocacy (advocate, co-chmn. Baycol Litigation Group, 2002—). Democrat. Roman Catholic. Avocations: gourmet cooking, automobile racing. Office: Brown & Szaller Co LPA 14222 Madison Ave Cleveland OH 44107-4510 E-mail: szaller@lawandhelp.com.

SZARA, STEPHEN ISTVAN, pharmacologist, consultant; b. Budapest, Hungary, Mar. 21, 1923; arrived in U.S., 1957; s. János Szára and Mária Katona; m. Madeleine Gadányi, Sept. 5, 1959 (div. June 1980); 1 child, Christopher. D of Natural Scis., Petrus Pázmány U., Budapest, 1950; MD, Med. U. Budapest, 1951. Asst. prof. dept. biochemistry Med. U. Budapest, 1950—53; chief biochemistry lab. State Inst. for Nervous Disorders, Budapest, 1953—56; vis. scientist Clin. Sci. Lab. NIMH, Bethesda, Md., 1957—61, sect. chief Washington, 1961—71; br. chief NIDA NIH, Rockville, Md., 1971—90; sci. cons. Kensington, Md., 1990—. Assoc., clin. prof. psychiatry George Washington U., Washington, 1966—75; mem. adv. bd. Heffter Rsch. Inst., Santa Fe, 1993—. Co-author (with H. Weil-Malherbe): Biochemistry of Functional and Experimental Psychoses, 1971; co-editor (with M. Braude): The Pharmacology of Marihuana, 1976; editor: Neurobiology of Behavioral Control of Drug Abuse, 1986; contbr. articles to profl. jours. Recipient Meritorious Achievement award, ADAMHA/PHS/DHHS, 1984. Fellow: Coll. Internat. Neuro-Psychopharmacology, Am. coll. Neuro-Psychopharmacology; mem.: Am. Soc. Pharmacol. Exptl. Therapy. Achievements include discovery of hallucinogenic effects of NN-Dimethyltryptamine in man. Avocations: sailing, computer programming. Home: 10901 Jolly Way Kensington MD 20895-1111

SZAREK, STANISLAW JERZY, mathematics professor; b. Ladek Zdroj, Poland, Nov. 13, 1953; came to U.S., 1980, naturalized, 1994; s. Mieczyslaw and Bronislawa (Brzezinska) S.; m. Malgorzata Chwascinska, June 22, 1980 (separated 1996, div. 2002); children: Martina, Natalia; 1 stepchild, Olga; m. Margaretmary Daley, May 15, 2004; stepchildren: Blake, Devin. M in Math., Warsaw (Poland) U., 1976; PhD in Math. Scis., Polish Acad. Scis., Warsaw, 1979. Rsch. asst. Math. Inst. Polish Acad. Scis., Warsaw, 1976-79, rsch. fellow, 1979-83; asst. prof. Case Western Res. U., Cleve., 1983-87, prof., 1987—, chair math. dept., 1994-96; prof. U. Paris, 1996—. Vis. positions U. Ill., Urbana, 1980, Ohio State U., Columbus, 1981, U. Tex., Austin, 1981-83, Inst. des Hautes Etudes Scientifiques, Bures-Sur-Yvette, France, 1986-89, U. Paris, 1990, 92, 95, Math. Scis. Rsch. Inst., Berkeley, Calif., 1996. Contbr. articles to profl. jours. Recipient Prize of Sci. Sec., Polish Acad. Scis., 1979; rsch. grantee NSF, 1983—, U.S.-Israel Binat. Sci. Found., 1993-97, 2003-; Sloan fellow Alfred P. Sloan Found., 1986-88. Mem. Am. Math. Soc. Avocations: skiing, sailing, diving, bridge, travel. Office: Case Western Res U Dept of Math Cleveland OH 44106 Office Phone: 216-368-2880. Business E-Mail: szarek@cwru.edu.

SZAREK, WALTER ANTHONY, chemist, educator; b. St. Catharines, Ont., Can., Apr. 19, 1938; s. Anthony and Sophia (Kania) S. BSc, McMaster U., 1960, MSc, 1962; PhD, Queen's U., 1964. Postdoctoral fellow in chemistry Ohio State U., Columbus, 1964-65; asst. prof. biochemistry Rutgers U., New Brunswick, N.J., 1965-67; asst. prof. chemistry Queen's U., Kingston, 1967-71, assoc. prof., 1971-76, prof., 1976—2003, emeritus prof., 2003—, dir. Carbohydrate Research Inst., 1976-85; founding mem., prin. investigator Neurochem, Inc., 1993—. Cons. to govt. and industry; mem. Premier's Coun. Tech. Fund. Mem. editl. adv. bd. Carbohydrate Rsch. jour., 1973-97, Jour. of Carbohydrate Chemistry, 1994-2001; contbr. articles to profl. jours. Recipient Tchg. Excellence award Queen's U. Arts and Sci. Undergrad. Soc., 1988-89, Tchg. Excellence in Chemistry award, 1993, 2000, 2002. Fellow Chem. Inst. Can.; mem. AAAS, Am. Chem. Soc. (chmn. divsn. carbohydrate chemistry 1982-83, councilor 2002—, Claude S. Hudson award in carbohydrate chemistry 1989, Melville L. Wolfrom award 1992), Inst. Theol. Encounter with Sci. and Tech., Royal Soc. Chemistry, N.Y. Acad. Scis., Soc. Glycobiology. Roman Catholic. Office: Dept Chemistry Queens Univ Kingston ON Canada K7L 3N6 Fax: 613-533-6532. E-mail: szarekw@chem.queensu.ca.

SZASZ, FERENC M. historian, educator; b. Davenport, Iowa, Feb. 14, 1940; s. Ferenc Paul Szasz and Mary Ineta Plummer; m. Margaret Connell, Aug. 1, 1969; children: Eric, Chris, Maria. BA, Ohio Wesley U., 1962; PhD, U. Rochester, 1969. Vis. instr. to prof. history U. N.Mex., Albuquerque, 1967—2003. Author: The Day The Sun Rose Twice, 1986, Scots in the North American West, 2000, Religion in the Modern American West, 2000; contbr. articles to profl. jours. Democrat. Mem. United Ch. Of Christ. Avocation: travel. Office: Univ NMex Dept History Albuquerque NM 87131

SZASZ, THOMAS STEPHEN, psychiatrist, educator, writer; b. Budapest, Hungary, Apr. 15, 1920; came to U.S., 1938, naturalized, 1944; s. Julius and Lily (Wellisch) S.; m. Rosine Loshkajian, Oct. 19, 1951 (div. 1970); children: Margot Szasz Peters, Susan Marie Szasz Palmer. AB, U. Cin., 1941, MD, 1944; DSc (hon.), Allegheny Coll., 1975, U. Francisco Marroquin, Guatemala, 1979; LHD (hon.), Towson U., 1999; D Sc(hon.), SUNY, 2001. Diplomate: Nat. Bd. Med. Examiners, Am. Bd. Psychiatry and Neurology. Intern 4th Med. Service Harvard, Boston City Hosp., 1944-45; asst. resident medicine Cin. Gen. Hosp., 1945-46, asst. clinician internal medicine div. out-patient dispensary, 1946; asst. resident psychiatry U. Chgo. Clinics, 1946-47; tng. research fellow Inst. Psychoanalysis, Chgo., 1947-48, rsch. asst., 1949-50, staff mem., 1951-56; practice medicine, specializing in psychiatry, psychoanalysis Chgo., 1949-54, Bethesda, Md., 1954-56, Syracuse, N.Y., 1956—; prof. psychiatry SUNY Health Sci. Ctr., Syracuse, 1956-90, prof. psychiatry emeritus, 1990—. Vis. prof. dept. psychiatry U. Wis., Madison, 1962, Marquette U. Sch. Medicine, Milw., 1968, U. N.Mex., 1981; holder numerous lectureships, including C.P. Snow lectr. Ithaca Coll., 1970; E.S. Meyer Meml. lectr. U. Queensland Med. Sch.; Lambie-Dew orator Sydney U., 1977; Mem. nat. adv. com. bd. Tort and Med. Yearbook; cons. com. mental hygiene N.Y. State Bar Assn.; mem. research adv. panel Inst. Study Drug Addiction; adv. bd. Corp. Econ. Edn., 1977— Author: Pain and Pleasure, 1957, The Myth of Mental Illness, 1961, Law, Liberty and Psychiatry, 1963, Psychiatric Justice, 1965, The Ethics of Psychoanalysis, 1965, Ideology and Insanity, 1970, The Manufacture of Madness, 1970, The Second Sin, 1973, Ceremonial Chemistry, 1974, Heresies, 1976, Karl Kraus and the Soul-Doctors, 1976, Schizophrenia: The Sacred Symbol of Psychiatry, 1976, Psychiatric Slavery, 1977, The Theology of Medicine, 1977, The Myth of Psychotherapy, 1978, Sex by Prescription, 1980, The Therapeutic State, 1984, Insanity: The Idea and its Consequences, 1987, The Untamed Tongue: A Dissenting Dictionary, 1990, Our Right to Drugs: The Case for a Free Market, 1992, A Lexicon of Lunacy, 1993, Cruel Compassion, 1994, The Meaning of Mind, 1996, Fatal Freedom, 1999, Pharmacracy: Medicine and Politics in America, 2001, Liberation By Oppression: A Comparative Study of Slavery and Psychiatry, 2002, Words to the Wise: A Medical-Philosophical Dictionary, 2004, Faith in Freedom: Libertarian Principles and Psychiatric Practices, 2004; editor: The Age of Madness, 1973, cons. editor of psychiatry and psychology: Stedman's Medical Dictionary, 22d edit, 1973; contbg. editor: Reason, 1974—, Libertarian Rev., 1986—; mem. editl. bd. Psychoanalytic Rev, 1965—, Jour. Contemporary Psychotherapy, 1968—, Law and Human Behavior, 1977—, Jour. Libertarian Studies, 1977—, Children and Youth Services Rev, 1978—, Am. Jour. Forensic Psychiatry, 1980—, Free Inquiry, 1980—. Comdr. M.C., USNR, 1954-56. Recipient Stella Feiss Hofheimer award U. Cin., 1944, Holmes-Munsterberg award Internat. Acad. Forensic Psychology, 1969; Wisdom award honor, 1970; Acad. prize Institutum atque Academia Auctorum Internationalis, Andorra, 1972; Distinguished Service award Am. Inst. Pub. Service, 1974; Martin Buber award Midway Counseling Center, 1974, Thomas S. Szasz award Ctr. Ind. Thought, 1990, Alfred R. Lindesmith award for achievement in field of scholarship and writing Drug Policy Found., 1991, Rollo May award APA, 1998; others; named Humanist of Year Am. Humanist Assn., 1973; Hon. fellow Postgrad. Center for Mental Health, 1961, Mencken award, 1981, Humanist Laureate, 1984, Statue of Liberty-Ellis Island Found. Archives Roster, 1986, George Washington award Am. Hungarian Found., 2003. Fellow Am. Psychiat. Assn. (life), Am. Psychoanalytic Assn., Internat. Psychoanalytic Soc., Western N.Y. Psychoanalytic Soc. Home: 4739 Limberlost Ln Manlius NY 13104-1405 Office: 750 E Adams St Syracuse NY 13210-2306 Personal E-mail: tszasz@aol.com.

SZE, MELANIE CHIA-YU, librarian; b. Shanghai, July 1, 1947; arrived in U.S., 1952; d. Palmer Chi-Yuan Sze and Chu-Nien Bien. BA, Skidmore Coll., 1970; MS, NYU, 1973; MLS, Columbia U., 1977. Cert. profl. libr. N.J. Corp. libr. Nabisco Brands, Inc., Wilton, Conn., 1977—83; info. specialist Celanese Splty. Ops., Chatham, NJ, 1984—85, Dresser Pump Co., Harrison, NJ, 1986—89; supr. tech. libr. Internat. Splty. Products, Wayne, NJ, 1989—96; reference libr. Rutherford (N.J.) Pub. Libr., 1999—2000; sr. libr. tech. svcs. West Caldwell (N.J.) Pub. Libr., 2000—. Contbr. articles to profl. jours. and website. Recipient award for excellence, Manhattan Arts Internat., 1998. Mem.: ALA, N.J. Libr. Assn., Am. Chem. Soc. (treas. western Conn. sect. 1982—84). Office: West Caldwell Pub Libr 30 Clinton Rd West Caldwell NJ 07006 Office Phone: 973-226-5441.

SZE, MICHAEL MING-CHIH, actuary, consultant; b. Shanghai, June 1, 1940; came to US, 1968; m. Elsie Sim-Yee Chin, Aug. 19, 1972; children: Benjamin, Samuel, Timothy. BS, U. Hong Kong, 1964; MS, Calif. State U., Hayward, 1969; PhD in Math., Ohio State U., 1975. CFA. Pension cons., ptnr. Hewitt Assocs., Lincolnshire, Ill., 1975-96; pres., fin. planner Sze Assocs., Toronto, Canada, 1996—. Adj. prof. U. Mich., Ann Arbor, 1998—99; tech. panel adv. bd. Social Security Adminstrn., Washington, 1994—96, Washington, 1999; cons. Nat. Social Security Inst. Bulgaria, Sofia, 1997, Sofia, 99; cons. on actuarial profession Kazakhstan Govt., Almaty, 1999—2004; cons. on social security Bhutan Govt., 2000, 02; cons. on pension and ins. reform Egyptian Govt., 2002—03; cons. on ins. laws and regulations Indian Govt., 2003—04; cons. on pension, social security and actuarial profession Serbian Govt., 2004; cons. on private pension regulations Chinese Govt., China. Mem. editl. bd. Jour. Actuarial Practice, 1996—; co-author: Carswell's Benefits Manual, 1999—. Fellow Soc. Actuaries (bd. govs. 1994-97), Can. Inst. Actuaries (com. on investment practice 1994-96); mem. Acad. Social Scis., NY Acad. Scis. Roman Catholic. Avocations: bridge, fitness workouts. Office: Sze Assocs 45 Francine Dr Willowdale ON Canada M2H 2G5 Office Phone: 416-756-2181. Business E-Mail: msze@szeassociates.com.

SZE, SARAH, sculptor; b. Boston; BA magna cum laude, Yale U., 1991; MFA, Sch. of Visual Arts, N.Y., 1997. One-woman shows include, Mus. of Contemporary Art, Chgo, Mus. of Fine Arts, Boston, Inst. of Contemporary Art, London, The Found. Cartier, Paris, The Whitney Mus. Am. Art, N.Y.C., exhibited in group shows, The Whitney Mus. of Am. Art, N.Y.C., The Carnegie Mus. of Art, Pitts., San Francisco (Calif.) Mus. Modern Art, 48th Venice Biennial, The L.A. (Calif.) Mus. Contemporary Art. Fellow John D. and Catherine T. MacArthur Found, 2003.

SZEFLER, STANLEY JAMES, pediatrics and pharmacology educator; b. Buffalo, Aug. 24, 1948; s. Stanley and Bernice Laura (Platt) Szefler; m. Christine M. Drezek, Dec. 26, 1970; children: David, Paul. BS, SUNY, Buffalo, 1971, MD, 1975. Resident pediat. Children's Hosp. Buffalo, 1975—77; postdoctoral fellow in clin. pharmacology and allergy immunology SUNY, Buffalo, 1977—79, asst. prof. pediat. and pharmacology, 1979—82; assoc. prof. pediat. and pharmacology U. Colo., Denver, 1982—90, prof. pediat., pharmacology, 1990—. Dir. clin. pharmacology Children's Hosp., Buffalo, 1979—82, Nat. Jewish Ctr. for Immunology and Respiratory Medicine, Denver, 1982—. Contbr. articles to profl. jours. Mem. steering com., Asthma Camp for Children Am. Lung Assn., Denver, 1987—96. Maj. USAR, 1979—88. Grantee NIH, 1980—84, 1990—, FDA, Denver, 1988—91. Fellow: Am. Acad. Pediat. (liaison mem. com. drugs), Am. Acad. Allergy, Asthma and Immunology (chmn. asthma, rhinitis and respiratory disease interest sect. 1995—97). Avocations: literature, history, reading. Office: Nat Jewish Med & Rsch Ctr Dept Pediat 1400 Jackson St Denver CO 80206-2761

SZEGO, CLARA MARIAN, cell biologist, educator; b. Budapest, Hungary, Mar. 23, 1916; arrived in U.S., 1921, naturalized, 1927; d. Paul S. and Helen (Elek) S.; m. Sidney Roberts, Sept. 14, 1943. AB, Hunter Coll., 1937; MS, U. Minn., 1939, PhD, 1942. Instr. physiology U. Minn., 1942-43; Minn. Cancer Rsch. Found. fellow, 1943—44; rsch. assoc. OSRD, Nat. Bur. Stds., 1944-45, Worcester Found. Exptl. Biology, 1945-47; rsch. instr. physiol. chemistry Yale U. Sch. Medicine, 1947-48; mem. faculty UCLA, 1948—, prof. biology, 1960—. Author (pseudonym Marian Steele) poetry pub. in small lit. presses and anthologies; contbr. articles on steroid protein interactions, mechanisms of hormone action and lysosome participation in normal cell function. Garvan fellow U. Minn., 1939; Guggenheim fellow, 1956; named Woman of Year in Sci. Los Angeles Times, 1957-58; named to Hunter Coll. Hall of Fame, 1987. Fellow AAAS; mem. Am. Physiol. Soc., Am. Soc. Cell Biology, Endocrine Soc. (CIBA award 1953), Soc. for Endocrinology (Gt. Britain), Biochem. Soc. (Gt. Britain), Internat. Soc. Rsch. Reproduction, Phi Beta Kappa (pres. UCLA chpt. 1973-74), Sigma Xi (pres. UCLA chpt. 1976-77). Home: 1371 Marinette Rd Pacific Palisades CA 90272-2627 Office: U Calif Dept Molecular Cell & Devel Biology Los Angeles CA 90095-1606 Office Phone: 310-825-3978. E-mail: cmszego@ucla.edu.

SZENBERG, MICHAEL, economics educator, editor, consultant; b. Sosnowiec, Poland, Apr. 8, 1934; came to US, 1961, naturalized, 1966; s. Henry and Sara (Rosensaft) S.; m. Miriam Silverstein, Sept. 2, 1962; children: Naomi, Avi. Student, Bar Ilan U., Israel, 1959-61; BA summa cum laude, L.I. U., 1963; PhD, CUNY, 1970. Faculty LI U., Bklyn. Ctr., 1965—, prof. econ., 1974-83; disting. prof. econs. Lubin Grad. Sch. Bus. Pace U., 1983—; chmn. fin. and econ., 2000—; dir. Ctr. Applied Rsch., 1994—. Adj. prof. Hunter Coll., 1970-76, Pace U., 1975-83; founder, dir. Lecture Bur. Econ., 1973; chmn. 1st Met. Grad. Conf. Econ., 1973; assoc. Ctr. Tech. Assessment, Newark Coll. Engring., 1973; vis. prof. econ. NYU, 1977-79; cons. in field. Author: Econ. of the Israeli Diamond Industry, 1973, The Welfare Effects of Trade Restrictions: A Case Study of the United States Footwear Industry, 1977, The Economics of the American Footwear Industry, 2d edit., 1984; co-author: Paul A. Samuelson, The Economics wunderkind, 2004; editor: Essays in Economics, The John Commons Meml. Lectures, 1986, Eminent Economists: Their Life Philosophies, 1992, Passion and Craft, Economists at Work, 1999, Cambridge Univ. Press Ency., New Frontiers in Economics, 2004, Reflections of Eminent Economists, 2004; assoc. editor: Am. Economist, 1973-75, editor-in-chief, 1975—; co-editor: contbr. articles to profl. jours., chpt. to books. Served with Israeli Air Force, 1956-59. Recipient Dean Hudson award LI U., 1962, Am. Coll. Abroad award, 1962, Dean Abelson award CUNY, 1963; fellow econs. CUNY, 1963; grantee Israel Diamond Inst., 1970; recipient Irving Fisher Monograph award, 1971; fellow Internat. Honor Soc. in Econ., 1972; grantee Dept. Labor, 1975; recipient Kenan award Pace U., 1983, Schalkenbach Found. Rsch. award, 1987, First Prize Recognition award, 1989, Tchr. of Year Pace U., 1992, Tchg. Excellence award Acad. Bus. Admin., 1993, Achievement award CUNY, 1993, Outstanding Publ. award Pace U., 1993-95, scholarly rsch. award Pace U., 1996, Lubiu Tchr. of Yr. award Pace U., 1999, others. Mem. Atlantic Econ. Soc., Internat. Trade and Fin. Assn., Internat. Fedn. Sci. Editors, Ea. Econ. Assn.(Eugene Lang Rsch. fellowship, 2004), Am. Econ. Assn., Assn. Cultural Econs., Internat. Honor Soc. Econs. (exec. bd. 1975—, regional dir. 1971-74), Optimates Soc. (pres. 1972-80). Home: 1442 E 9th St Brooklyn NY 11230-6405 Business E-Mail: mszenberg@pace.edu.

SZEP, PAUL MICHAEL, editorial cartoonist; b. Hamilton, Ont., Can., July 29, 1941; came to U.S., 1966; s. Paul Joseph and Helen (Langhorne) S.; m. Angela Diane Garton, Feb. 27, 1965 (div. 1976); children: Amy, Jason; m. Lyn Dunlop, June 3, 2003. A.O.C.A., Ont. Coll. Art, 1964; A.O.C.A. hon. degree, 1975, Framingham State Coll., 1975, Worcester State Coll., 1980, William Penn Coll., 1981. Sports cartoonist Hamilton Spectator, 1958-61; graphics designer Financial Post, Toronto, Ont., 1965-66; editorial cartoonist Boston Globe, 1966—2001. Vis. fellow Harvard U., 1981; lectr. various univs. Author: In Search of Sacred Cows, 1967, Keep Your Left Hand High, 1969, At This Point in Time, 1973, The Hader They Fall, 1975, Unvote for a New America, 1976, Them Demaned Pictures, 1977, Warts and All, 1979, To a Different Drummer, 1983, The Gang of Eight, 1985, The Next Szep Book, 1985, Often in Error, Never in Doubt, 1987, And Then Jack Said to Arnie, 1991, And Then Arnie Told Chi Chi and Then Chi Chi Said to Fuzzy, 1993, And Then Fuzzy Told Seve, 1996, Not Just Another Szep Book, 1997, And Then Seve Told Freddy, 1997, Then Freddy Told Tiger, 1998, And Then Tiger Told the Shark, 1999, Talking on Tour, 2001, And Then the Shark Told Justin, 2002; editl. cartoonist: Sta. WNEV-TV, creator comic strip: Mr. Zeep, 1999; contbr. Golf Digest, New Eng. Jour. Golf. Served with F.A. Royal Canadian Army, 1957-58. Recipient Pulitzer prize, 1974, 1977, award, Sigma Delta Chi, 1974, 1977, Toyl award, Boston Jaycees, 1976, Headliners award, 1977, Reuben award for best editl. cartoonist, Nat. Cartoonist Soc., 1979, Thomas Nast award, Internat. Cartoonist award, Best Sports Cartoonist award, Nat. Cartoonists Soc., 1988. Mem. Soc. Illustrators, Kittansett Club, Harvard Club, Weston Golf Club, Belleair Country Club. Home: 552 Pineland Ave Belleair FL 33756-1521 E-mail: paulszep@attbi.com., paulszep@attbi.com.

SZEPESHAZI, KAROLY ISTVAN, pathologist; b. Budapest, Hungary, July 19, 1938; came to U.S., 1989; s. Istvan and Marta (Borszeky) S.; m. Eszter Maria Faluhelyi, Aug. 1, 1984; children: Zsolt, Kinga. MD, U. Med. Sch., Budapest, Hungary, 1963, PhD, 1977. Resident Inst. Traumatology, Budapest, Hungary, 1963-66, asst. prof. dept. pathology, 1966-68; sr. lectr., chief lectr. 1st Inst. Pathology, Cancer Rsch. U. Sch. Medicine, Budapest, Hungary, 1968-80; head dept. pathology Jahn Hosp., Budapest, Hungary, 1980-89; rsch. prof. dept. medicine Tulane U., New Orleans, 1989—. Contbr. articles to profl. jours., chpts. to books. Mem. New Orleans Mus. Art, Smithsonian Inst., 1996-97. Mem. AAAS, N.Y. Acad. Scis. Avocations: travel, hiking, tennis. Office: Tulane U Dep Medicine 1601 Perdido St New Orleans LA 70112-1207 E-mail: karoly@tulane.edu.

SZERBIAK, ROBERT BRUCE, geophysicist, researcher; b. Huntington Station, NY, Sept. 30, 1948; s. Robert and Freya Rosina Szerbiak; m. Beverly Claire Bearden, Feb. 14, 1981. BA in Geology, Mich. State U., 1971; MS in Geophysics, Tex. A&M U., 1982; PhD, U. Tex., Dallas, 2003. Geophysicist Petty Ray Geophysical, Houston, 1971—75, Phillips Petroleum, Bartlesville, Okla., 1979—83, British Petroleum, Houston, 1983—92; prof. geosci. Boise (Idaho) State U., 2003—. Fellow, Shell Oil, 1996—98. Mem.: Am. Geophysics Union, Soc. Exploration Geophysicists. Avocations: woodworking, hiking, bicycling. Home: 930 N Maple Grove E203 Boise ID 83704 Office: Boise State Univ 1910 University Dr Boise ID 83725 Office Phone: 208-426-2759. Business E-Mail: szerbiak@cgiss.boisestate.edu.

SZERLAG, CHESTER THEODORE, health facility administrator; s. Franciszek Szerlag and Anna Blacha; m. Judy Ann Mouilleseaux, July 2, 1982; 1 child, Jessica Anne. MBA, U. Chgo., 1984. Diplomate Am. Coll. Healthcare Executives, 1982. Exec. adminstr. U. Chgo., 1980—. Contbr. articles to profl. jours.; mem. editl. bd.: ADVANCE Jour. for Imaging and Oncology Adminstrs. Bd. trustee Village of Woodridge, Ill., 1997—2005; vice chmn. U. Chgo. Credit Union, Ill., 2001—. Recipient Gold medal, Soc. Radiation Oncology Adminstrs., 1991. Mem.: Assn. Adminstrs Acad. Radiology and Radiation Oncology (bd. dirs., treas.), Healthcare Fin. Mgmt. Assn., Radiol. Soc. N.Am. (chair assoc. sci. consortium), Med. Group Mgmt. Assn. (mem. acad. practice assembly), Soc. Radiation Oncology Adminstrs. (pub. chair, past treas., past. pres., past chmn.), Am. Coll. Med. Practice Exec. (assoc.), Rotary (sec. Woodridge chpt. 2002—). Office: Univ Chgo 5758 S Maryland Ave MC 9006 Chicago IL 60637

SZESCILA, ANDREW J. oil industry executive; BS, Miss. State U. From region engr. Baker Oil Tools to sr. v.p., COO Baker Hughes, Houston, 1973—98, sr. v.p. & COO, Oilfield Ops., 1998—. Office: Baker Hughes 3900 Essex Lane Houston TX 77027-5177

SZETO, GEORGE, mathematician, educator; s. Chok Szeto and America Deng; 1 child, Gene H. BSc, United Coll., Hong Kong, 1963; MSc, Purdue U., 1965, PhD, 1968. Asst. prof. Bradley U., Peoria, Ill., 1968—71, assoc. prof., 1971—76, prof., 1976—. Faculty advisor table tennis club Bradley U., Peoria, 1975. Contbr. articles to profl. jours. Mem.: Am. Math. Soc., Purdue Univ. Alumni Assn., Am. Table Tennis Assn. Avocation: ping pong/table tennis. Office: Math Dept Bradley Univ Peoria IL 61625

SZETO, HUNG, publisher; b. Hoyping, Canton, People's Republic of China, Sept. 8, 1936; s. Cheong Yee and Sau King(Kwan) S.; m. Sau Hing Chow, Jan. 27, 1962; children: Roland, Lisa, Nancy. B in adminstrn., Tsing Hua Coll., Hong Kong, 1969. Mgr. Far East Trade Ctr., Seattle, 1975-81; editor Seattle Chinese Post, 1982; pres. APC Group, Seattle, 1986—; pub. Chinese Bus. Jour., 1989—; pres. Sino-Am. Econ. Devel. Assn., 2002—. Mem. Asian Am. Journalists Assn., Chinese-Lang. Press. Inst., Northwest Minority Pubs. Assn., Sino-Am. Econ. Devel. Assn. (pres. 2000--). Avocations: writing, consulting. Office: APC Group 659 S Weller St Seattle WA 98104-2944 *Personal philosophy: Serving the community by providing information.*

SZETO, PAUL (CHEUK-CHING SZETO), religious mission executive; b. Canton, China, July 28, 1940; came to U.S., 1962; s. Fai and Oi-wan (Wong) S.; m. Dorcas Chow, July 8, 1967; children: Tedd, Christine, Melissa. BA, Seattle Pacific U., 1966, MA, 1968; MDiv, Yale U., 1970; D of Missiology, Fuller Theol. Sem., Pasadena, Calif., 1980. Sr. minister Chinese Bapt. Ch., Seattle, 1971-78; dir. ch. planting ABC Pacific N.W., Seattle, 1978-80; gen. dir. Evangelize China Fellowship, Inc., Monterey Park, Calif., 1980—. Founding dir. N.Am. of Chinese Evangelicals, 1972; participant Internat. Conf. for Itinerant Evangelists 1983, 86; bd. dirs. Chinese Coordination Ctr. of West Hong Kong, 1976-80; Lausanne II, Manila, 1989. Author: Seven Directions of Modern Theology, 1978, Suffering and Hope, 1982, Higher Ground, 1997, My Mentor: J. Edwin Orr, 2002, Ten Heroes Who Changed the World, 2004; translator: Amazing Grace, 1966, Evangelical Awakening in Eastern Asia, 1981; compiler: The Abundant Life, 1987, Committed to Serve, 1985, The Boundless Power of Prayer, 1991. Mem. Greater Seattle Asian Am. Coun., 1972; mem. Royal Brougham Found., Seattle, 1974; mem. Campaign for Yale, L.A., 1977; trustee Azusa (Calif.) Pacific U., 2000. Resident scholar Oxford U., 1991. Mem. Greater L.A. Chinese Ministers Assn., U.S. Chaplains Assn., 1998, Edn. & Culture Found., (pres. 1998). Office: Evangelize China Fellowship 437 S Garfield Ave Monterey Park CA 91754-3328 Fax: 626 288-6727.

SZETO, YVONNE, architectural firm executive; b. Hong Kong, July 4, 1956;, naturalized; BArch, U. Minn., 1977; MArch, Harvard U., 1979. Registered N.Y., cert. Nat. Coun. Archtl. Registration Bds. With I.M. Pei & Ptnrs., 1977—89, Pei Cobb Freed & Ptnrs., 1989—99; ptnr. Pei Cob Freed & Ptnrs., N.Y.C., 1999—. Guest critic Yale U.; panel mem. Bilbao: The Transformation of the City Art Inst. Chgo.; jury Bus. Week/Archtl. Record Awards, 2000. Mem.: AIA (medal and Cert. of Merit 1977). Office: Pei Cobb Freed & Ptnrs LLP 88 Pine St New York NY 10005*

SZILASSY, SANDOR, retired lawyer, library director, educator; b. Magyarbarnag, Hungary, Apr. 9, 1921; came to U.S., 1957; s. Sandor Sr. and Jolan (Fenyves) S.; m. Clara Ida Varkonyi, July 21, 1951; children: Peter S., Thomas S., Paul A.D. LLD, U. Budapest, Hungary, 1944, Lawyer-Judge Dipl., 1949; MA, Ind. U., 1959. Practicing atty., pres. law firm, Veszprém, Hungary, 1944-56; asst. libr. Anderson (Ind.) Coll. Libr., 1959-61; head div. sci. and tech. Auburn (Ala.) U. Libr., 1961-68; head libr., assoc. prof. Ind. State U., Evansville, 1968-69; dir. libr., prof. U. Tampa, Fla., 1969-72; dir. librs. Rowan U. of N.J., 1972-94. V.p. Ala. Acad. Sci., 1963-68; pres. Coun. N.J. Coll. and Univ. Librs., 1978-79, 89-90, Librs. Unltd., N.J., 1981-82, 88-89; cons. numerous orgns; radio commentator, Sta. WTEL, Phila., 1987-91. Author: Revolutionary Hungary, 1971 (Arpad Acad. Gold medal 1972), Ein Amerikanischer Diplomat uber Ungarn, 1974, Hungary's Road to Trianon, 1988, Hungary at the Brink of the Cliff, 1997, From Barnag to Miami, 1999, In The Playing Field of Great Powers, 2002, numerous others; author book chpts.; mem. editorial bd. Ency. Hungarica, 1989—; contbr. essays, studies, articles to profl. jours., newspapers, mags.; former editor Egyesült Amerikai Magyarság. Bd. elders Presbyn. Ch., Lakeland, Fla., 1970-72; 1st Hungarian United Ch. of Christ, Miami, 1996—. Recipient Legion of Honor award Chapel of Three Chaplains, 1981. Mem. N.J. Acad. Libr. Network (exec. bd. 1988—), Tri-State Coll. Libr. Coop. (pres. 1975-76, 88-89, Johanniter Order Knights (Germany), Arpad Acad. (sect. pres. 1979—), Miami Kossuth Club (pres.), Phi Alpha Theta. Mem. Reformed Ch. Avocations: research, writing, reading, swimming, hiking. Home: 133 N Pompano Beach Blvd Pompano Beach FL 33062-5725 E-mail: aracsi@webtv.net.

SZKODY, PAULA, astronomy educator, researcher; b. Detroit, July 17, 1948; d. Julian and Pauline (Wolski) S.; m. Donald E. Brownlee, Mar. 19, 1976; children: Allison, Carson. BS in Astrophysics, Mich. State U., 1970; MS in Astronomy, U. Wash., 1972, PhD in Astronomy, 1975. Rsch. asst. Observatoire de Geneve, 1969, Kitt Peak Nat. Obs., 1970; rsch., teaching asst. U. Wash., Seattle, 1970-75, rsch. assoc., lectr., 1975-82, sr. rsch. assoc., 1982-83, rsch. assoc. prof., 1983-91, rsch. prof., 1991-93, prof., 1993—. Part-time mem. faculty Seattle U., 1974-75, 82, Bellevue Coll., 1975-77; vis. scientist Kitt Peak Nat. Obs., 1976; vis. instr. UCLA, 1977, adj. asst. prof., 1980, 81; vis. asst. prof. U. Hawaii, 1978; vis. assoc. prof. Calif. Inst. Tech., 1978-79, 80, mem. XTE users com., 1996-99; mem. users com. Internat. Ultraviolet Explorer, 1983-85, 93-97; mem. A.J. Cannon adv. com. AAUW, 1986-91, chmn. 1988-90; mem. mgmt. ops. working group on Ultraviolet/Visual/Relativity, NASA, 1988-91. Contbr. numerous articles to profl. jours. Recipient Annie J. Cannon award, 1978. Fellow AAAS (mem. nominating com. 1990-93, chairperson 1993, mem.-at-large 1995-99); mem. Am. Assn. Variable Star Observers, Am. Astron. Soc. (councilor 1996-99), Internat. Astron. Union; mem. commn. 42 organizing com. 1991-97, v.p. 1997-00, pres. 2000—), Astron. Soc. Pacific (bd. dirs. 1988-92), Phi Beta Kappa. Office: U Wash Dept Astronomy PO Box 351580 Seattle WA 98195-1580 E-mail: szkody@astro.washington.edu.

SZKUTAK, TOM, corporate financial executive; married; 2 children. BS in Fin. magna cum laude, Boston U. From exec. v.p. fin. divsn. investments to CFO divsn. lighting GE, 1982—2002; sr. v.p., CFO Amazon.com, Seattle, 2002—. Office: Amazon.com 1200 12th Ave S Seattle WA 98144

SZLAM, ALEKSANDER, manufacturing executive; Founder, chmn., CEO Melita Internat., Norcross, Ga. Office: Eshare Tech 5051 Peachtree Corners Cir Norcross GA 30092

SZLOSEK, ELAINE MARIE (SALOIO), music educator; b. Springfield, Mass., Sept. 2, 1960; d. Arthur and Undina Saloio; m. Frederick Szlosek, Sept. 11, 1987; 1 child, Philip. MusB, Boston Conservatory of Music, 1983; MusM, New England Conservatory of Music, 1987. Flute instr. Cmty. Music Sch. of Springfield, Mass., 1988—99; adj. faculty, prof. of flute Westfield State Coll., Westfield, Mass., 1999—. Exec. bd. Pappoutsakis Flute Competition, Boston, 1998—; bd. dirs. Theatre Project, West Springfield, Mass. Recipient Distinction in Performance, New England Conservatory, 1987, First Prize, Pappoutsakis Flute Competition, 1987. Mem.: Mass. Teachers Assn. Republican. Cath. Home: 435 Holyoke St Ludlow MA 01056 Personal E-mail: laineys@charter.net.

SZOKA, EDMUND CASIMIR CARDINAL, archbishop; b. Grand Rapids, Mich., Sept. 14, 1927; s. Casimir and Mary (Wolgat) Szoka. BA, Sacred Heart Sem., 1950; JCB, Pontifical Lateran U., 1958, JCL, 1959. Ordained priest Roman Catholic Ch., 1954, elevated to cardinal 1988. Asst. pastor St. Francis Parish, Manistique, Mich., 1954—55; sec. to bishop Marquette, 1955—57, 1959—62; chaplain St. Mary's Hosp., Marquette, 1955—57; tribunal, defender of bond Marquette, 1960—71; asst. chancellor Diocese of Marquette, 1962—69, chancellor, 1970—71; pastor St. Pius X Ch., Ishpeming, Mich., 1962—63, St. Christopher Ch., Marquette, 1963—71; bishop Diocese of Gaylord, Mich., 1971—81; archbishop of Detroit, 1981—90. Sec.-treas. Mich. Cath. Conf., Lansing, 1972—77; chmn. region VI Nat. Conf. Cath. Bishops, 1972—77; treas., adminstrv. bd. and adminstrv. com., budget and fin. com. Nat. Conf. Cath. Bishops/U.S. Cath. Conf., 1981—84; pres. Prefecture for Econ. Affairs of the Holy See, 1990—97, Pontifical Commn. For Vatican City State, 1997—2001, Governatorato; mem. Secretariat of State 2d sect. Coun. for Rels. with States; pres. Vatican City State, Roman Curia, 2001—. Trustee Nat. Shrine of the Immaculate Conception, Washington, 1981—90; chmn. bd. trustees Cath. Telecomm. Network Am., 1984—90; trustee, exec. com., chmn. com. for univ. rels. Cath. U. Am, 1981—90. Mem.: Congregation for Clergy, Congregation for Evangelization of Peoples, Congregation for Bishops, Congregation for Causes of Saints, Congregation for Insts. Consecrated Life and Socs. Apostolic Life. Roman Catholic. Address: Governatorato 00120 Vatican City Italy

SZOKODY, ANIKO, pianist, educator; b. Szeged, Hungary, Apr. 24, 1973; arrived in U.S., 1997; d. Fedor Sandor Szokody and Zsuzsanna Szlovak; m. Willis Dee Ottery III, Mar. 1, 2002. MusB, Zoltan Kodaly Spl. Musical Secondary Sch., Kecskemet, Hungary, 1991; Piano Performer Artist Degree, tchrs. diploma, Franz Liszt Acad. Music, Budapest, Hungary, 1997; MusM in Piano Performance, Ind. U., 2000; artist diploma (hon.), Conservatorio Beethoven, Buenos Aires, 1997. Assoc. instr. piano Ind. U., Bloomington, 1998—2000; instrumental accompanist, chamber music coach Chautauqua (N.Y.) Instn., 1999—2002, head instrumental accompanist, chamber music coach, 2002—. Guest instr. piano Conservatorio Beethoven, Buenos Aires, 1996—97; studio pianist for cellist Janos Starker Ind. U., Bloomington, 1998—2000; pvt. piano instr., Albany, NY, 2000—. Musician (pianist): (solo performances) Europe, North and South America. Grantee, Hungarian Nat. Cultural Found., 1996, Conservatorio Beethoven, 1996—97, for profl. career documentary, Hungarian Pub. TV, 2002; scholar, studio of Prof. Gyorgy Sebok, Ind. U., 1998—2000. Mem.: Capitol Chamber Artists, Adirondack Ensemble, N.Y. State Music Tchrs. Assn., Coll. Music Soc., Music Tchrs. Nat. Assn. Home: 819 Woodland Ave Schenectady NY 12309

SZONNTAGH, EUGENE L. chemical engineer, chemist, hygienist, educator, archaeometrist, musicologist, organist, historian; b. Budapest, Hungary, July 31, 1924; s. Jenö Szonntag and Anna Vaisz; m. Nora Jenser, July 27, 1950; children: Desi, Thomas. Diploma in Chem. Engring., Tech. U. Budapest, 1948, DTech, 1975, PhD, 1999. Registered profl. engr., Pa.; profl. indsl. hygienist. Asst. to assoc. prof. Veszprem (Hungary) U., 1950-56; from scientist to sr. scientist Leeds and Northrup Co., North Wales, Pa., 1957-72; prin. engr. Honeywell, Inc., Ft. Washington, Pa., Clearwater, Fla., 1972-86; assoc. prof. U. South Fla., Tampa, 1987-91, prof., 1991—. Contbr. over 100 articles to profl. jours., 8 chpts. to books; 38 patents in field. Dir. music, organist St. Alfred's Ch., Palm Harbor, Fla., 1983—93, Faith Luth. Ch., 1994—95, Holy Spirit Episcopal Ch., Safety Harbor, Fla., 1995—. Recipient Indsl. Rsch. 100 award Chromatography, 1964, Star Inventor award Honeywell, 1982. Mem. Am. Chem. Soc., Am. Inst. Archaeology, Am. Mus. Instrument Soc., Organ Hist. Soc., Instrument Soc. Am. (historian 1978-82), Am. Guild Organists (acad. mem.; cert. choir master, chpt. dean 1970-72, 84-86). Avocations: collecting musical instruments, travel, archaeology, photography. Home: 1161 Cane Mill Ln Bradenton FL 34212 Office: U South Fla MDC-56 13201 Bruce B Downs Blvd Tampa FL 33612 Office Phone: 813-974-6633. Business E-Mail: eszonnta@hsc.usf.edu.

SZOSTAK, JACK WILLIAM, molecular biologist, educator; b. London, Nov. 9, 1952; s. William J. and Viola (Munford) S.; m. Terri-Lynn McCormick, May 29, 1993. BS in Cell Biology, McGill U., 1972; PhD in Biochemistry, Cornell U., 1977. Rsch. assoc. in biochemistry Cornell U., Ithaca, N.Y., 1977-79; asst. prof. dept. biol. chemistry Harvard Med. Sch./Sidney Farber Cancer Inst., Boston, 1979-83; assoc. prof. dept. biol. chemistry Harvard Med. Sch./Dana Farber Cancer Inst., Boston, 1983-84; assoc. prof. dept. genetics Harvard Med. Sch., Boston, 1984-87, prof., 1988—; assoc. molecular biologist Mass. Gen. Hosp., Boston, 1984-87, molecular biologist, 1988—; investigator Howard Hughes Med. Inst., 1998—. Cons. Genetics Inst., 1980-87; mem. sci. adv. bd. Gilead Scis., Inc., 1990-98, Trans-Karyotic Therapies, Inc., 1990—, Cubist, Inc., 1993-97. Contbr. more than 100 articles to sci. jours. Recipient award in molecular biology NAS, 1994, Hans Sigrist prize U. Bern, Switzerland, 1997. Fellow N.Y. Acad. Scis.; mem. NAS. Office: Mass Gen Hosp Dept Molecular Biology Boston MA 02114

SZUCH, CLYDE ANDREW, lawyer; b. Bluefield, W.Va., Nov. 22, 1930; s. Nicholas and Aranka (Rubin) S.; m. Rosalie Hirschman Wulfson, Sept. 5, 1954; children: Peter Alan, Richard Coleman. BA, Rutgers U., 1952; LLB, Harvard U., 1955; LLD (hon.), Kean U., 1998. Bar: N.J. 1955, U.S. Dist. Ct. N.J. 1955, U.S. Ct. Appeals (3rd cir.) 1958, U.S. Supreme Ct. 1962. Law clk. to assoc. justice William J. Brennan Jr. U.S. Supreme Ct., Washington, 1956-57; asst. U.S. atty. U.S. Attys. Office, Newark, 1957-58; assoc. Pitney, Hardin & Kipp, Newark, 1958-62; ptnr. Pitney, Hardin, Kipp & Szuch, Morristown, NJ, 1962—2000, of counsel, 2001—02; coun. Office of Clyde A. Szuch, 2003—. Mem. panel Ctr. for Pub. Resources, N.J.; bd. dirs. J.B. Hanauer & Co., Vt. Ry. Inc., Clarendon & Pittsford R.R. Co., Burlington, Vt., Brennan Ctr. for Justice; panelist AAA Large Complex Cases. Gov. N.J. region Nat. Conf. Cmty. and Justice; bd. dirs. Kean U. Found. Fellow Am. Bar Found.; mem. ABA, Am. Law Inst., N.J. State Bar Assn., Morris County Bar Assn., Essex County Bar Assn., Fed. Bar Assn. (N.J. chpt.), N.J. C. of C. (bd. dirs.), Nat. Legal Aid Defender Assn., Hist. Soc. U.S. Ct. Appeals for 3d Cir.

SZUCS, ANDREW ERIC, freelance/self-employed writer; b. Cleve., Apr. 25, 1946; s. Andrew Elmer and Katherine (Krizsak) S.; m. Laura Jean Nyhan, June 4, 1971; children: Andrew Edward, Eric Stephen. BA, U. Dayton, 1968; Diploma, Cleve. Inst. Electronics, 1972; MBA, Wright State U., 1984. Pub. affairs specialist USAF, Laughlin AFB, Tex., 1968-70; exhibit rschr., writer USAF Orientation Group, Wright-Patterson AFB, Ohio, 1970-73; cmty. rels. dir. Wright-Patterson AFB, 1973-77; publ. mgr. Air Force Logistics Command, Wright-Patterson AFB, 1977-85, chief pub. officer, 1985-90; civilian command tng. mgr./adminstrn. Air Force Materiel Command, Wright-Patterson AFB, 1990-2001; program mgr. Materiel Sys. Group Supply Logistics Wright-Patterson AFB, 2001—04; freelance writer The Arts & Sci. of Commn., 2004—. Contbr. articles to profl. jours. (AWA Jour. award 1986). Staff sgt. USAF, 1968—73. Named Disting. Alumnus, St. Ignatius High Sch., Cleve., 1994. Mem. Soc. Aerospace Communicators, Nat. Press Club (Silver Owl), Am. Radio Relay League, Amateur Satellite Corp., U.S. Soccer Fedn. (referee), Ohio High Sch. Athletic Assn. (referee), Wright State U. Bus. Alumni Assn. (rec. sec. 1985-89), Nat. Assn. Sports Ofcls. Roman Catholic. Avocations: ham radio operator, creative writing, trainer for pvt. soccer team. Home: 1135 Mint Springs Dr Fairborn OH 45324-5728 Office: 1135 Mint Springs Dr Fairborn OH 45324-5728

SZUCS, LORETTO DENNIS, internet publishing executive, editor; b. Bklyn., Apr. 14, 1941; d. Joseph Raymond and Muriel Dennis; m. Robert John Szucs, May 27, 1961; children: Juliana Smith, Diana Sullivan, Patricia Stitz, Laura Pfeiffer. BA in History, St. Joseph's Coll., Rensselaer, Ind., 1990. Archives specialist Nat. Archives & Records Adminstrn., Great Lakes Region, Chgo., 1990-92; acquisitions editor Ancestry Pub., Salt Lake City, 1992-97; v.p. Ancestry.com, Provo, Utah, 1997—. Author: They Became Americans, 1998, Chicago & Cook County Sources, 1996; co-editor: The Source: A Guidebook of American Genealogy, 1997, The Archives: A Guide to National Archives, 1988 (ALA Choice 1988). Mem. history adv. com., Statue of Liberty-Ellis Island Found., 1991. Recipient award of merit, Nat. Geneal. Soc., 1997, award of excellence in geneal. methods and sources, 1991. Mem. ALA (genealogy com.), Fedn. Geneal. Socs. (v.p., David S. Vogels Jr. award 1990), Polish Geneaological Soc. Am. (Wigilia award 2003). Roman Catholic. Office: Ancestry.com 360 W 4800 Provo UT 84604

SZULIK, MATTHEW J. information technology executive; With Sapiens Internat., MapInfo Corp.; pres. Relativity Technologies, 1997—98; COO Red Hat, Inc., Raleigh, NC, 1998—99, CEO, 1999—, pres., 1999—, dir., 1999—, chmn., 2002—. Office: Red Hat Inc 1801 Varsity Dr Raleigh NC 27606-2072 Office Phone: 919-754-3700. Office Fax: 919-754-3701.*

SZWALBENEST, BENEDYKT JAN, lawyer; b. Poland, June 13, 1955; s. Sidney and Janina (Bleishtif) S.; m. Shelley Joy Leibel, Nov. 8, 1981. BBA, Temple U., 1978, JD, 1981. Law clk. Fed. Deposit Ins. Corp., Washington, 1980; law clk. to presiding justice U.S. Dist. Ct. (ea. dist.) Pa., Phila., 1980-81;

staff atty., regulatory specialist Fidelcor, Inc. and Fidelity Bank, Phila., 1981-86; regulations specialist sr. regulatory staff Fed. Res. Bank of N.Y., N.Y.C., 1986-89; s.v.p. regulatory compliance, sec. Custodial Trust Co. subs. Bear Stearns, Princeton, 1990—2001, pres., CEO, 2001—; mng. dir. Bear Stearns & Co., Inc., 1998—. Author: Federal Bank Regulation, 1980. Mem. Commonwealth of Pa. Post-secondary Edn. Planning Commn., Harrisburg, 1977-79, trustee Pop Warners Little Scholars, Phila., 1981-86. Recipient E. Gerald Corrigan Pres.'s Award for Excellence, 1988. Mem.: ABA (nat. sec., treas. law student divsn. 1980—81, Silver Key award 1980, Gold Key award 1981), N.J. Bankers Assn. (legis. and compliance com. 1992—), Securities Industry Assn. (anti-money laundering com. 2001—), Temple U. Sch. Bus. Alumni Assn. (sec. 1982—84, v.p. 1984—86, pres. 1986—88, bd. dirs. gen. alumni assn. 1986—88), Am. Bankers Assn. (cert. compliance specialist, lectr. 1984—), Am. Judicature Soc., Omicron Delta Epsilon. Avocations: baseball, tennis, skiing. Home: 1504 Brookfield Rd Yardley PA 19067-3930 Office: Custodial Trust Co 101 Carnegie Ctr Princeton NJ 08540-6231

SZYBALSKI, WACLAW, geneticist, educator; b. Lwów, Poland, Sept. 9, 1921; arrived in U.S., 1950, naturalized, 1957; s. Stefan and Michalina (Rakowska) Szybalski; m. Elizabeth Hunter, Feb. 5, 1955; children: Barbara A. Szybalski Sandor, Stefan H. BSChemE, Politechnika Lwów, 1944; MSChemE, Politechnika Slaska, Gliwice, Poland, 1945; DSc, Inst. Tech., Gdansk, Poland, 1949, PhD (hon.), 2001, U. Marie Curie, Lublin, Poland, 1980, U. Gdansk, 1989, Med. Acad. Gdansk, 2000. Asst. prof. Inst. Tech., Gdansk, 1945—50; staff Cold Spring Harbor (N.Y.) Biol. Labs., 1951—55; asst. prof. Inst. Microbiology, Rutgers U., New Brunswick, NJ, 1955-60; prof. oncology McArdle Lab., U. Wis., Madison, 1960—. Mem. recombinant DNA adv. com. NIH, 1974—78; Wendel H. Griffith meml. lectr. St. Louis U., 1975; Raine vis. prof. U. Western Australia, Perth, 1997. Author: numerous papers, revs., abstracts and books in field; editor-in-chief: Gene, 1976—96, hon., founding editor-in-chief:, 1996—; mem. editl. bd. other jours. Recipient Karl A. Forster lectr. award, U. Mainz, 1970, A. Jurzykowski Found. award in biology, 1988, Hilldale award in biology, U. Wis., 1994, G. J. Mendel Hon. Gold medal for merit in biol. scis., Acad. Scis. Czech Republic, 1995, Cogene lectr. Internat. Union Biochemistry, Nairobi, 1987, Cairo, 1988, Harare, Zimbabwe, 1989. Mem.: AAAS, Polish Inst. Arts and Scis. Am. (C. Funk Natural Sci. award 2003), Polish Acad. Scis., European Molecular Biology Orgns. (lectr. 1971, 1976), Am. Soc. Microbiologists (chmn. virology divsn. 1972—74, chmn. divsn. IV 1974—75), Genetic Soc. Am., Am. Soc. Biochemists, Polish Med. Alliance (hon.), Italian Soc. Exptl. Biology (hon.), Polish Soc. Microbiologists (hon.). Home: 1124 Merrill Springs Rd Madison WI 53705-1317 Office: U Wis McArdle Lab Madison WI 53706 E-mail: szybalski@oncology.wisc.edu. *The profession should also be the hobby and a constant source of enjoyment and satisfaction.*

SZYBIST, MARY, poet; Grad., U. Va., U. Iowa. Author: (poetry collection) Granted, 2002 (Beatrice Hawley award, 2002); contbr. poetry to jours. Recipient prize, Acad. Am. Poets, Writing award, Rona Jaffe Found. Office: c/o Alice James Books Univ Maine Farmington 98 Main St Farmington ME 04938*

SZYDLOWSKI, RALPH, retired die maker, formability consultant; b. Alpena, Mich., Nov. 14, 1942; s. Chester and Bridget (Romel) Sedloske; m. Geraldine Bryson, Oct. 8, 1971; children: Denise E., George S., Ruth A., Regina M. Assoc. in Indsl. Tech. summa cum laude, Baker Coll., Flint, Mich., 1991, B of Indsl. Mgmt. summa cum laude, 1994. With Flint Metal Ctr., Draw Die Tryout, 1972-96; die maker Flint Metal Ctr., 1996—2001, formability cons., 1995—2001; die engr. tech. staffing divsn. Trialon Corp., GM Metal Fabricating divsn., 2003—. Served with U.S. Army, 1962-69. Decorated Silver Star, Purple Heart. Mem. VFW, DAV, Am. Legion, Mil. Order of the Purple Heart, 26th Inf. Regt. Assn., Soc. 1st Inf. Divsn., Eagles. Roman Catholic. Avocations: woodworking, travel, books. E-mail: rsgs42@aol.com.

SZYGENDA, RALPH J. automotive executive; b. McKeesport, Pa., Sept. 6, 1948; BS in Computer Sci., U. Mo., 1970; MEE, U. Tex., 1975; ED (hon.), U. Mo. With Tex. Instruments Inc., 1972—93; v.p., chief info. officer Bell Atlantic Corp., Arlington, Va., 1993—96, GM Corp., 1996—2000, group v.p., chief info. officer, 2000—. Mem.: Sodalia Corp. (bd. dirs.), Covisint L.L.C. (bd.mem.), GM Automotive Stratey Bd., U. Mo. Sch. Mgmt. Info. Sys. (chmn. advisory bd.), InformationWeek Mag. (editl. bd.), Rsch. Bd. Office: GM Corp 300 Renaissance Ctr PO Box 300 Detroit MI 48265-3000

SZYGENDA, STEPHEN A. electrical and computer engineering educator, researcher; b. McKeesport, Pa., Oct. 5, 1938; s. Stephen A. Sr. and Elizabeth B. (Zolczer) S.; m. Marie A. Deli, Apr. 2, 1960; children: Stepahnie Burden, Diana Easton, Mark. BS, Fairleigh Dickinson U., 1965; MS, Northwestern U., 1967, PhD, 1968. Registered profl. engr., Tex. Engr. Comprehensive Design, NJ, 1959-62; mem. tech. staff Bell Tel. Labs., NJ, Ill., 1962-68; assoc. prof. elec. engring. and computer engring. U. Mo., Rolla, 1968-70; prof. elec. engring. and computer engring. So. Meth. U., Dallas, 1970-73, U. Tex., Austin, 1973-86, dir. Ctr. for Tech. Tng., 1986-89, Clint Murchison Sr. Chair of Free Enterprise prof., 1986-96, chmn. elec. and computer engring. dept., 1993-96; dean Sch. Engring. U. Ala., Birmingham, 1996-2000, So. Meth. U., Dallas, 2000—. Pres. CCSS, Austin, 1972-81, Comsat Gen. Internat. Sys., Austin, 1981-83, SBI, Inc., Austin, 1985—; pres., CEO Rubicon Group, Austin, 1983-85; active Tex. Gov. Coun. for Sci. and Tech., 1984-87. Contbr. articles to profl. jours. Dir. Laguna Gloria Mus., Austin, 1981-83; pres. bd. Austin Ballet, 1983. With USN, 1956-59. Fellow IEEE (bd. dirs. 1973-75 Svc. awards 1977, 79, 83, 87, 96), IC2, Soc. for Design and Process Sci.; mem. Assn. Computing Machinery (Svc. award 1975, 79, 87, 88, Disting. lectr. 1991-95). Roman Catholic. Achievements include pioneering in CAD, simulation, fault tolerant computing, telecommunications, entrepreneurship, and software engineering. Home: 5227 Beckington Ln Dallas TX 75287 Office: Southern Methodist Univ Sch of Engring Dallas TX 75275 E-mail: szygenda@msn.com.

SZYMANCZYK, MICHAEL, tobacco products executive; BS in Finance, Indiana U., 1972. Various sales and gen. mgmt. positions Procter & Gamble, 1971-87; v.p. sales Kraft Inc., Glenview, Ill., 1987-88, v.p retail ops., 1988; sr. v.p. Swift-Eckrich Inc., 1989; sr. v.p. sales Philip Morris USA (now div. of Altria Group, Inc.), N.Y.C., 1990-97, pres., CEO, 1997—, chmn., 2002—. Mem.: Indiana U. Kelley Sch. of Bus. Dean's Adv. Council (chmn.), bd. trustees Va. Found. for Independent Coll. Office: Philip Morris USA 120 Park Ave New York NY 10017-5592

SZYMANSKI, BOLESLAW KAROL, computer scientist, educator, entrepreneur; b. Paslek, Poland, Apr. 22, 1950; came to U.S., 1982; s. Kazimierz and Aniela Marta (Langer) S.; m. Emilia Haraf, Dec. 15, 1973; children: Peter Rafal, Witold Andrew. M in Engring. Electronics, Warsaw Poly. Inst., Poland, 1973; PhD in Computer Sci., Nat. Acad. Scis., Warsaw, 1976. Asst. prof. Warsaw Poly. Inst., 1973-75; rschr. Inst. Sci. Technol. and Econ. Info., Warsaw, 1975-78; divsn. head Inst. STEI, Warsaw, 1979-82; postdoctoral fellow Aberdeen U., England, 1978; vis. asst. prof. U. Pa., Phila., 1982-85, assoc. prof. computer sci., 1985-89; prof. computer sci. CSCI, 1990—, acting chmn., 1993-94; assoc. dean info. tech. Rensselaer Poly. Inst., Troy, NY, 1997—2001, dir. Ctr. for Pervasive Computing and Networking, 2003—; founder/chmn. bd. dirs. Premonitia, Inc., Boston, 2000. Cons. Cardiomag, Inc., Schenectady, NY, 2001—. Internat. Med. Programs, Albany, 2003-, IBM Corp., Poughkeepsie, NY, 1992-96, GE Rsch. and Devel. Ctr., Schenectady, 1987-90; expert UN Indsl. Devel. Office, Vienna, Austria, 1990-96; chief sci. officer CCCC, Phila., 1984-87; editor-in-chief Sci. Computing IOS Press, Amsterdam, 2000—. Author: Parallel Functional Languages and Compilers, 1993; editor: Languages, Compilers & RT Systems, 1996, Advances in Pervasive Computing and Networking, 2004; developer Tempest parallel sys. for ecol. simulations, EPL parallel computer lang. Expert witness U.S. Congress, Washington, 1987. Rsch. grantee IBM, Lucent, CISCO, DARPA, ARO, NSF, ONR, 1986—; recipient Wiley Disting. Faculty award, 2003; Tech. Innovation award NASA, 1998, SuPaCup '93 German Computer Soc., Mannheim, 1993. Fellow IEEE; mem. Assn. for Computing Machinery (nat. lectr. 1987-88). Avocations: tennis, history. Home: 6 Hollow Rd Newtonville NY 12110-5100 Office: Rensselaer Poly Inst 110 8th St Troy NY 12180-3590 Office Phone: 518-276-2714. Personal E-mail: bkszym@yahoo.com. Business E-Mail: szymab@rpi.edu.

SZYMANSKI, EDNA MORA, dean; b. Caracas, Venezuela, Mar. 19, 1952; came to U.S., 1952; d. José Angel and Helen Adele (McHugh) Mora; m. Michael Bernard, Mar. 30, 1973. BS, Rensselaer Poly. Inst., 1972; MS, U. Scranton, 1974; PhD, U. Tex., 1988. Cert. rehab. counselor. Vocat. evaluator Mohawk Valley Workshop, Utica, N.Y., 1974-75; vocat. rehab. counselor N.Y. State Office Vocat. Rehab., Utica, 1975-80, sr. vocat. rehab. counselor, 1980-87; rsch. assoc. U. Tex., Austin, 1988-89; asst. prof. U. Wis., Madison, 1989-91, assoc. prof., 1991-93, assoc. dean sch. edn., 1993-97, dir. rehab. rsch. and tng. ctr., 1993-96, prof. rehab. psychology and spl. edn., 1997—99, chair dept. rehab. psychology and spl. edn., 1997-99, fellow tchg. acad., 1997; dean Coll. Edn. U. Md., College Park, 1999—. Cons. Rsch. Assocs. Syracuse, N.Y., 1988-90. Co-author various book chpts.; co-editor: Rehabilitation Counseling Basics and Beyond, 1992, 98; co-editor Work and Disability, 1996, 2003, Rehabilitation Counseling Bull., 1994-2000; contbr. articles to profl. jours. Mem. Pres.'s Com. on Employment of People with Disabilities, Washington, 1987-97. Recipient Rsch. award Am. Assn. Counselor Edn. and Supr., 1991. Mem. ACA (chair rsch. com. 1992-94, Rsch. awards 1990, 93, 95), Am. Rehab. Counseling Assn. (pres. 1985-86, rsch. award 1989, 94, Disting. Profl. award 1997, James F. Garrett award for disting. career in rehab. rsch. 1999), Coun. Rehab. Edn. (chair rsch. com. 1990-95, v.p. 1993-95, 97), Nat. Coun. Rehab. Edn. (chair rsch. com. 1992-99, Rehab. Edn. Rschr. of Yr. 1993, New Career in Rehab. Edn. award 1990). Office: U Md Coll Edn 3119 Benjamin Bldg College Park MD 20742-1100 Business E-Mail: ednas@umd.edu.

SZYMANSKI, JOHN MATTHEW, investment officer; b. N.J., July 18, 1958; s. Edward and Mary F., m. Helen Louise Sisler, April 20th, 1985; 3 children. BS, Columbia U., N.Y.C, 1980. Cert. fin. planner, chartered retirement planning counselor. Cons. Arthur Anderson, N.Y.C, 1980-82, Bankers Trust, N.Y.C., 1982-83; fin. adv., Smith Barney, Paramus, N.J., 1983-86; fin. adv. Shearson Lehman Hutton, Paramus, N.J., 1986-90; assoc. v.p. Prudential Securities, Paramus, N.J., 1990-96; sr. v.p. Wachovia Securities, Paramus, NJ, 1996—. Author: Five Secrets to Successful Investing, 1996. Avocations: swimming, golf, travel, politics, rowing. Office: Wachovia Securities 45 Eisenhower Dr Paramus NJ 07652

SZYMCZAK, EDWARD JOSEPH, mechanical engineer; b. Anderson, Tex., Sept. 28, 1938; s. Harold and Verna (Walkoviak) S.; m. Lorena Jane Sharp, Sept. 26, 1964; children: Denise, Lisa, Brian. Student, U. St. Thomas, 1958; BSME, Tex. A&M, 1961; MBA, U. Houston, 1970. Registered profl. engr., Tex. Engr. trainee to engring. mgr. Cameron Iron Works, Houston, 1961-90; dir. engring. ea. hemisphere Cooper Oil Tool Div./Cooper Industries, London, 1990-91, dir. engring. Houston, 1991-95, Cameron div. Cooper Cameron Corp., Houston, 1995-97; mgr. design process tech. ABB Vetco Gray, Houston, 1998—. Mem., past chmn. indsl. adv. bd. U. La., Lafayette (formerly U. Southwestern La.), 1991—; trustee Tex. A&M U. Rsch. Found., College Station, 1994—; mem. mech. engring. adv. bd. U. Tenn., Knoxville, 1996-2000. Patentee (8) on oil tool equipment. Mem. ASME, Tex. A&M Former Students Assn., Tex. A&M 12th Man Found., Tex. A&M Mech. Engring. Acad. Disting. Grads., Soc. Petroleum Engrs., Nat. Assn. Corrosion Engrs., Tau Beta Pi. Republican. Roman Catholic. Avocations: ranching, farming, mechanic, investing, technical and personnel recruiting. Home: 4002 Cypress Hill Dr Spring TX 77388-5717

SZYMONIAK, ELAINE EISFELDER, retired state senator; b. Boscobel, Wis., May 24, 1920; d. Hugo Adolph and Pauline (Vig) Eisfelder; Casimir Donald Szymoniak, Dec. 7, 1943; children: Kathryn, Peter, John, Mary, Thomas. BS, U. Wis., 1941; MS, Iowa State U., 1977. Speech clinician Waukesha (Wis.) Pub. Sch., 1941-43, Rochester (N.Y.) Pub. Sch., 1943-44; rehab. aide U.S. Army, Chickasha, Okla., 1944-46; audiologist U. Wis., Madison, 1946-48; speech clinician Buffalo Pub. Sch., 1948-49, Sch. for Handicapped, Salina, Kans., 1951-52; speech pathologist, audiologist, counselor, resource mgr. Vocat. Rehab. State Iowa, Des Moines, 1956-85; mem. Iowa Senate, Des Moines, 1989—2000; ret., 2000. Bd. dir. On With Life, Terrace Hill Found. Adv. bd. Iowa State Inst. for Social and Behavioral Health; mem. Child Care Resource and Referral Cmty. Empowerment Bd., Greater Des Moines Coun. for Internat. Understanding, United Way, 1987—88, Urban Dreams, Iowa Maternal and Child Health com.; pres. Chrysalis Found., 1997; mem. City-County Study Commn.; Mem. Des Moines City coun., 1978—88; bd. dirs. Nat. League Cities, Washington, 1982—84, Civic Ctr., House of Mercy, Westminster House, Iowa Leadership Consortium, Iowa Comprehensive Health Assn. Named Woman of Achievement, YWCA, 1982, Visionary Woman, 1993, Young Women's Resource Ctr., 1989; named to Iowa Women's Hall of Fame, 1999; named Des Moines Woman of Influence, Bus. Record, 2000. Mem. Am. Speech Lang. and Hearing Assn., Iowa Speech Lang. and Hearing Assn. (pres. 1977-78), Nat. Conf. State Legislators (fed. state com. on health, adv. com. on child protection), Women's Polit. Caucus, Nexus (pres. 1981-82, mem. Supreme Ct. Select Com.), Wellmark Found. (adv. bd.), Des Moines (Iowa) Women's Club (bd. dir. 2003—). Avocations: reading, travel, swimming, whitewater rafting. Home: 2116 44th St Des Moines IA 50310-3011 E-mail: ElaineSzy@aol.com.

SZYPULSKI, WAYNE R. controller, food products executive; b. 1951; BS in Acctg., MS in Acctg., No. Ill. U., DeKalb. Acctg mgr. Sara Lee Corp., Chgo., 1983, asst. corp. controller, 1991—93, controller, 1993—, corp. v.p., 1994—2001, sr. v.p., 2001—, chief acctg. officer. Office: Sara Lee Corp 3 First Nat Plaza Chicago IL 60602-4260

SZYSZKA, ROSWITA EVELYN, artist; b. Chgo., Apr. 5, 1955; d. John and Regina (Rizinger) Schilli; m. Michael C. Szyszka, Jan. 29, 1977; children: David M., Eric S. AA, Am. Acad. Art, 1976. Illustrator The World Healing Book; artist: Looking Out, Looking In; featured Woodstock Colony of Arts Web Site (Top 100 artists of the 20th Century). Mem. Woodstock Artist Assn., The Woodstock Guild. E-mail: RoswitaSzyszka@hotmail.com.

TA, TAI VAN, lawyer, researcher; b. Ninh Binh, Vietnam, Apr. 16, 1938; came to U.S., 1975; s. Duong Van and Loan thi (Pham) T.; m. Lien-Nhu Tran, Oct. 26, 1967; children: Becky, John, Khuong Virginia, Dora. LLB, U. Saigon, Vietnam, 1960; MA, U. Va., 1964, PhD, 1965; LLM, Harvard U., 1985. Bar: Mass. 1986, U.S. Dist. Ct. Mass. 1987. Prof. U. Saigon Law Sch., 1965-75, Nat. Sch. Adminstrn., 1965-75; ptnr. Tang thi Thanh Trai & Ta Van Tai, 1968-75; legal rschr. Reed Smith Shaw & McClay, Pitts., 1975; rsch. assoc. Harvard U. Law Sch., Cambridge, Mass., 1975—, adj. lectr., 1998—; pvt. practice, Brookline, Mass., 1986—; rsch. scholar NYU Law Sch., N.Y.C., 1990-94. Cons. Milbank Tweed Hadley & McCloy, N.Y.C., 1979, Shearman & Sterling, N.Y.C., 1979, Paul Weiss Rifkind Wharton and Garrison, N.Y.C., 1989, 90. Co-author: The Laws of Southeast Asia, 1986, The Le Code: Law in Traditional Vietnam, 1987, Investment Law in Vietnam, 1990, Histoire de La codification Juridique au Vietnam, 2001; author: Vietnamese Tradition of Human Rights, 1988; contbr. articles to profl. jours. Commr. Mass. Govs. Asian-Am. Coun., 1992—. Fulbright scholar 1960-62; grantee Asia Found., 1972, Ford Found., 1975-76, Aspen Inst. 1993. Avocations: piano, swimming, foreign languages. Home: 145 Naples Rd Brookline MA 02446-5748 Office: Harvard U Law Sch Pound 423 1563 Massachusetts Ave Cambridge MA 02138-2903

TAAFFE, PAUL, utilities company executive; Pres. Hill & Knowlton, Inc.; mng. dir. Shandwick Cons.; developer comm. programs. Office: Hill & Knowlton 466 Lexington Ave 3rd Fl New York NY 10017-

TABACHNICK, NORMAN DONALD, psychiatrist, educator; b. Toronto, Ont., Can., Feb. 21, 1927; BS, U. Ill., 1947, MD, 1949; PhD in Psychoanalysis, So. Calif. Psychoanalytic Inst., 1977. Diplomate Am. Bd. Med. Examiners, Am. Bd. Psychiatry and Neurology. Intern Michael Reese Hosp., 1949-50; resident in psychiatry U.S. VA Hosp., Bedford, Mass., 1950-51, U.S. AFB, Biloxi, Miss., 1951-52, L.A. County Gen. Hosp., 1953-54; staff psychiatrist Sepulveda VA Hosp., 1976-78; pvt. practice L.A.; mem. staff Resthaven Sanitarium, U. So. Calif. Med. Ctr., L.A. County, Westwood Hosp., Edgemont Hosp., Cedars-Sinai Med. Ctr.; mem. staff Neuropsychiatric Inst. UCLA; clin. prof. psychiatry U. So. Calif., L.A., 1970-75, UCLA, 1975—. Hon. mem. med. staf. Resthaven Cmty. Med. Health Ctr., 1973; guest lectr. Cedars-Sinai Med. Ctr., 1985; mem. adv. bd. divsn. psychoanalysis Nassau County Med. Ctr.; mem. faculty Calif. Sch. Profl. Psychology, L.A. Ctr. Group Psychotherapy, Grad. Ctr. Child Devel. and Psychotherapy; cons. L.A. County Coroner's Office, 1963-70, Bur. Vocat. Rehab., Jewish Family Svc., profl. adv. bd. Resthaven Sanitarium, Marianne Frostig Sch. Ednl. Therapy, W. Valley Ctr. Edl. Therapy. Author: Accident or Suicide?, 1973; mem. edtl. bd. Jour. Acad. Psychoanalysis, book rev. editor, 1978; mem. edtl. bd. Internat. Jour. Psycho-analytic Psychotherapy, 1979-83; reviewer Am. Jour. Psychiatry, 1983 , Jour. Neuropsychiatry and Clin. Neuro Scis., 1988-90; contbr. articles to profl. jours.; cons. (film) Suicide Prevention: The Physician's Role, 1967, Highlights of the 1964 American Psychiatric Association; cons., participant The Thin Edge--Guilt., 1975; author book revs. Assoc. chief psychiatrist L.A. Suicide Prevention Ctr., 1968-76, prin. investigator; adv. com. Walter Briehl Human Rights Found., 1984; v.p., bd. dirs. Suicide Prevention Ctr., Inc.; bd. dirs. Inst. Suicide Prevention, L.A., 1996, chmn. funding a crisis line com., 1997; bd. dirs. We. divsn. Am. Found. Suicide Prevention, 1998, chair program com., 1999-2002. Recipient award for disting. creativity and leadership, Am. Found. for Suicide Prevention, 2003; rsch. grantee, Founds. Fund Rsch. Psychiatry, 1963, NIMH, 1970. Fellow Am. Psychiatric Assn. (life), Am. Acad. Psychoanalysis (pres. 1974, chmn. nominating com, 1975, trustee, chmn. com. on rsch., mem. editl. bd. The Acad., presdl. citation 1975), mem. Internat. Psychoanalytic Assn., Internat. Assn. Suicide Prevention, Am. Psychoanalytic Assn. (cert., mem. com. liason with AAAS 1977-80), Am. Assn. Suicidology, (founder, mem. editl. bd. Life-Threatening Behavior, cert. recognition 1996) Inst. Contemporary Psychoanalysis (founding mem., trustee 1990-93), So. Calif. Psychoanalytic Inst. (pres., tng. and supervising analyst, selection rsch. clin. assocs. com., dir. rsch. divsn. 1970-81, chief investigator 1976-88, chmn. com. rsch. award stds. 1979, pres.-elect 1980, 86, pres. 1981, 87-90), Am. Coll. Psychiatrists, Med. Rsch. Assn. So. Calif., So. Calif. Psychiat. Soc. (consultation and violence panel), L.A. County Med. Assn. Office: 505 N Bonhill Rd Los Angeles CA 90049-2325 E-mail: ndtund@aol.com.

TABACKMAN, STEVEN CARL, lawyer; b. Balt., Apr. 2, 1950; s. Nathan and Evelyn (Caplan) T.; m. Leslie Adele Stout, Dec. 27, 1986; children: Alexa, Robert, Julia, Lia. BA with distinction, U. Va., 1971, JD, 1976. Bar: Va. Supreme Ct. 1976, D.C. Ct. Appeals 1977, U.S. Dist. Ct. D.C. 1978, U.S. Dist. Ct. Md. 1990, U.S. Dist. Ct. (ea. dist.) Va. 1992, U.S. Ct. Appeals (D.C. cir.) 1978. Law clk. to Hon. Leonard Braman D.C. Superior Ct., Washington, 1976-77; law clk. to Hon. Theodore R. Newman, Jr. D.C. Ct. Appeals, Washington, 1977-78; asst. U.S. atty. U.S. Atty.'s Office D.C., Washington, 1978-88; assoc., ptnr. Perkins Coie, Washington, 1988-94; ptnr. Tighe, Patton, Tabackman & Babbin, Washington, 1994-99, Oblon Spivak McClelland Maier & Neustadt, Arlington, Va., 1999—2002, Tighe Patton Armstrong Teasdale, Washington, 2002—. Mem. editorial bd. Money Laundering Law Reporter, 1990-2000; contbr. articles to profl. jours. Gen. counsel Duke Ellington Fund, Washington, 1988—. Fellow Am. Bd. Criminal Lawyers; mem. ABA, Nat. Assn. Criminal Def. Lawyers. Home: 1458 Highwood Dr Mc Lean VA 22101-2517 Office: Tighe Patton Armstrong Teasdale 1747 Pennsylvania Ave NW Washington DC 20006

TABAK, LAWRENCE, federal agency administrator, dentist; b. Bklyn., N.Y. BS, City Coll. of City U. of N.Y.; DDS, Columbia U., 1977; PhD, SUNY at Buffalo, 1981. Certificate of Proficiency in Endodontics SUNY at Buffalo. Sr. assoc. dean for rsch., Sch. Medicine and Dentistry U. Rochester, prof., dentistry, biochemistry and biophysics, dir., Ctr. Oral Biology, AAB Inst. Biomedical Scis.; dir. Nat. Inst. Dental and Craniofacial Rsch., 2000—. Vis. scientist Nat. Inst. Dentistry and Craniofacial Rsch., prin. investigator for tng. grants, co-chair planning com. for workshop on saliva and other fluid-based diagnostics, ad hoc reviewer, intramural rsch. program. Fellow: AAAS; mem.: Soc. Glycobiology, Am. Assn. for Dental Rsch., Internat. Assn. for Dental Rsch. Office: Nat Inst of Dental and Craniofacial Research Bldg 31 Rm 2C39 31 Center Dr MSC 2290 Bethesda MD 20892*

TABAKIN, SCOTT M. healthcare executive; CFO, exec. v.p. Beverly Enterprises Inc., Fort Smith, Ark. Office: Beverly Enterprises Inc 1000 Bevery Way Fort Smith AR 72919-9007

TABATABAI, M. ALI, chemist, biochemist; b. Karbala, Iraq, Feb. 25, 1934; BS, U. Baghdad, 1958; MS, Okla. State U., 1960; PhD in Soil Chemistry, Iowa State U., 1965. Rsch. assoc. soil biochemistry Iowa State U., Ames, 1966-72, from asst. prof. to assoc. prof., 1972-78, prof. soil chemistry and biochemistry, 1978—. Cons. Electric Power Rsch. Inst., Palo Alto, 1978-83. Fellow AAAS, Am. Inst. Chemists, Am. Soc. Agronomy (Soil Sci. rsch. award 1992), Soil Sci. Soc. Am., Iowa Acad. Sci. (Disting. scientist, Disting. fellow); mem. Coun. Agrl. Sci. and Tech., Am. Chem. Soc., Am. Soc. Microbiology, Am. Soc. Agronomy, Soil Sci. Soc. Am., Assn. Univ. Profs., Iowa Acad. Sci., Gamma Sigma Delta (Alumni award of merit Iowa Beta chpt. 1993), Sigma Xi, Phi Kappa Phi. Achievements include research in soil enzymology and chemistry of sulfur, nitrogen and phosphorus in soils, nutrient cycling in the environment. Office: Iowa State U Sci & Tech Dept Agronomy Ames IA 50011-0001 E-mail: malit@iastate.edu.

TABATSKY, DAVID, theater educator, director; b. McKeesport, Pa., Jan. 6, 1954; s. Israel and Irene Helen Tabatsky; children: Max, Stella. BA, Adelphi U., 1976, MA, 1989. Cert. tchr. NY, 2002. Clowning instr. Gene Frankel Theatre, New York, 2001—; theatre/circus instr. UN Internat. Sch., New York, 2001—; family arts dir. The Calhoun Sch., New York, 2001—; theatre dir. Adelphi U., Garden City, NY, 2002—03; teen theatre acting tchr. Jewish Cmty. Ctr., New York, 2002—; acting tchr. City Lights Youth Theatre, New York, 2002—; performing arts camp dir. ACT Program-Cathedral of St. John the Divine, New York, 2003—. Author (actor): (solo theatre productions) The Man with Three Balls (Outstanding Solo Performance-Moers Internat. Theatre Festival, 1994), (solo theatre production) How I Survived My Jewish Mother, Help! I Married a German, Meschugge in Paradise; author: (comedy travel guide) What's Cool Berlin, (memoir) American Misfit; dir.: (theatre) Working, (circus) Taborka. Vol. Amnesty Internat., New York, 1987—2003, Habitat for Humanity, New York, 1997—2003. Individual Artist grant, Conn. Commn. on the Arts, 1979, 1980. Mem.: Internat. Jugglers Assn., SAG, Actors Equity Assn. Avocations: basketball, photography, carpentry. Home and Office: 162 W80 St Apt F New York NY 10024 Office Phone: 917-689-8778. Personal E-mail: tabatsky@aol.com.

TABATZNIK, BERNARD, retired cardiologist; b. Mir, Poland, Jan. 8, 1927; came to U.S., 1959, naturalized, 1966; s. Max and Fay (Ginsberg) T.; m. Marjorie Turner, Jan. 8, 1956; children: Darron Mark, Keith Donald, Ilana Wendy; m. Charline Edwards Harmon, Aug. 7, 1992. BSc, U. Witwatersrand, South Africa, 1945, MB, BChir, U. Witwatersrand, South Africa, 1949. Intern Baragwanath Hosp., Johannesburg, 1950-51, Hillingdon Hosp., Ashford Hosp., also rsch. unit Can. Red Cross Meml. Hosp., Taplow, England, 1951-54; med. registrar Ashford Hosp., 1954-56, Johannesburg Gen. Hosp., 1956-58; physician Baragwanath Hosp., 1958-59; fellow in medicine Sch. Medicine Johns Hopkins U., Balt., 1959-60, fellow in cardiology, 1960-61, asst. prof. medicine, 1966-97, ret., 1997; head cardiopulmonary divsn. Sinai Hosp., Balt., 1961-72, assoc. chief medicine, 1964-72; chief cardiology dept. North Charles Gen. Hosp., Balt., 1972; also dir. med. edn., dir. Postgrad. Inst., coord. ambulatory svcs.; med. dir. Nurse Practitioner-Physician Asst. Program Ch. Hosp., Balt., 1987-90. Contbr. articles to profl. jours. Recipient Save-A-Heart Humanitarian award, 1977, Maimonides award, 1983, Shaarei Zion Humanitarian award, 1987. Fellow Royal Coll. Physicians (London); mem. South African Cardiac Soc., Am. Heart Assn., Md. Heart Assn. (chmn. health careers 1964-66), Laennec Cardiovasc. Sound Group. Home: HC 3 Box 180 Monterey VA 24465-9313 Personal E-mail: btabatznik@aol.com.

TABB, WALLER CROCKETT, retired allergist, retired immunologist; b. Richmond, Va., 1935; MD, U. Va., 1959. Diplomate Am. Bd. Internal Medicine, Am. Bd. Allergy and Immunology. Intern U. Va. Hosp., Charlottesville, 1959-60, resident in internal medicine, 1964-66, fellow in allergy/immunology and pulmonary medicine, 1966-67; mem. staff Lakeland (Fla.) Regional Med. Ctr., 1967—; pvt. practice Watson Clinic, Lakeland, ret., 1997. Fellow ACP, Am. Acad. Allergy and Immunology, Am. Coll. Chest Physicians; mem. Alpha Omega Alpha. Address: PO Box 178 Ware Neck VA 23178-0178 Home: 6102 WAre Neck Rd Ware Neck VA 23178

TABBAL, NICOLAS G. plastic surgeon; b. Beirut, 1946; MD, Am. U., Beirut, 1972. Diplomate Am. Bd. Plastic Surgery, Am. Bd. Surgery. Intern Am. U. Med. Ctr., Beirut, 1971—72, resident in surgery, 1972—76; resident in plastic surgery Akron City Hosp., Ohio, 1977—79; fellow in gen. surgery Upstate Med. Ctr., Syracuse, NY, 1976—77; fellow in plastic reconstructive surgery NYU, 1979—80; pvt. practice plastic surgery N.Y.C., 1980—; attending plastic surgeon Manhattan EET Hosp. Clin. instr. plastic surgery NYU Med. Ctr. Office: 521 Park Ave New York NY 10021-1840 Office Phone: 212-644-5800. E-mail: mail@tabbal.us.

TABER, DAVID O. urological surgeon; b. Panama City, Panama, June 30, 1938; s. Alden Pugh and Virginia (Kresler) Taber; m. Rebecca M.; children: Sharon Taber Silverman, Jeffrey, Andrew, Richard; m. Rebecca M. Taber, Dec. 20, 1987. BA, Syracuse U., 1959; MD, George Washington U., 1963. Diplomate Am. Bd. Urology. Urologic surgeon in pvt. practice, El Paso, Tex., 1972—. Chief med. staff Columbia West Hosp., El Paso, 1975-76, chief of urology, 1998-99; chief of surgery Sierra Med. Ctr., El Paso, 1977-78, chief of urology, 1995-97; prof. urology Tex. Tech Sch. Medicine, El Paso, 1998-99. Mem. state com. on prostate cancer Am. Cancer Soc., Austin, 1998-99; bd. dirs. El Paso unit Am. Cancer Soc., 1999; mem. Tex. Rangers Found., Waco, 1998-99. Served to lt. U.S. Army, 1963-72, judge Santa Fe Indian Market; founder Am. Mus. Fellow ACS; mem. AMA, Tex. Urol. Soc., Am. Urol. Assn., Tex. Med. Assn., Am. Fertility Soc., Am. Lithotripsy Soc., Alpha Epsilon Delta, Pi Sigma, 32nd Degree Mason of Scottish Rite, Elmaida Shrine, Rotary Club. Episcopalian. Avocation: photography. Office: 125 W Hague Rd Ste 170 El Paso TX 79902-5811

TABER, MARGARET RUTH, engineering educator; b. St. Louis, Apr. 29, 1935; d. Wynn Orr and Margaret Ruth (Feldman) Gould Stevens; m. William James Taber, Sept. 6, 1958 B of Engring. Sci., BEE, Cleve. State U., 1958; MS in Engring., U. Akron, 1967; EdD, Nova Southeastern U., 1976; postgrad., Western Res. U., 1959-64. Registered profl. engr., Ohio; cert. engring. technologist. From engring. trainee to tng. dir. Ohio Crankshaft Co., Cleve., 1954-64; from instr. elec.-electronic engring. tech. to prof. Cuyahoga C.C., Cleve., 1964-79, chmn. engring. tech., 1977-79; assoc. prof. elec. engring. tech. Purdue U., West Lafayette, Ind., 1979-83, prof., 1983-2000, prof. emeritus, 2000—. Lectr. Cleve. State U., 1963-64; mem. acad. adv. bd. Cleve. Inst. Electronics, 1981—; cons. in field. Author: (with Frank P. Tedeschi) Solid State Electronics, 1976; (with Eugene M. Silgalis) Electric Circuit Analysis, 1980; (with Jerry L. Casebeer) Registers, 1980; (with Kenneth Rosenow) Arithmetic Logic Units, 1980, Timing and Control, 1980, Memory Units, 1980; 6809 Architecture and Operation, 1984, Programming I: Straight Line, 1984; contbr. articles to profl. jours. Bd. dirs. West Blvd. Christian Ch., deaconess, 1974-77, elder, 1977-79; deacon Federated Ch., 1981-84, 86-89, Stephen Leader, 1988—; mem. Cancer Support Group; vol. Lafayette Reading Acad., 1992—; ednl. resource vol., vol. tchr. Sunburst Farm Rainbow Acres, Inc., Ariz., 1988—. Recipient Helen B. Schleman Gold Medallion award Purdue U., 1991, The Greater Lafayette Cmty. Survivorship award, 1994, Outstanding Alumni award U. Akron Coll. Engring., 1994, Disting. Alumni award, Cleve. State U., 2002; Margaret R. Taber Microcomputer Lab. named in her honor Purdue U., 1991; NSF grant, 1970-73, 78; Rainbow Acres Computer Lab named The Marge Taber Computer Lab., 2002. Fellow Soc. Women Engrs. (counselor Purdue chpt. 1983-94, Disting. Engring. Educator award 1987); mem. IEEE (life sr.), Am. Cancer Soc. (co-chair svc. and rehab com. 1992-94, vol. coord. CanSurmount 1993-98, chair Cmty. Connections, mem. Resource, Info. and Guidance CoreTeam, 1994-98, v.p. Tippecanoe bd. dirs. 1996-98, relay for life hon. chair 1999), Am. Bus. Women's Assn. (ednl. chmn. 1964-66), Am. Soc. Engring. Edn., Am. Tech. Edn. Assn., Tau Beta Pi (hon.), Phi Kappa Phi. Avocations: robotics, computers. Home: 3036 State Rd 26 W West Lafayette IN 47906-4743 Office: Purdue U Elec Engring Tech Dept Knoy Hall Tech West Lafayette IN 47907

TABIN, CLIFFORD S. geneticist, educator; Prof. dept. genetics Harvard Med. Sch., Boston. Recipient award in molecular biology NAS, 1999. Office: Harvard Med Sch Warren Alpert Bldg 4th Fl 240 Longwood Ave Boston MA 02115

TABIN, JULIUS, patent lawyer, physicist; b. Chgo., Nov. 8, 1919; s. Sol and Lillian (Klingman) T.; m. Johanna Krout, Sept. 7, 1952; children: Clifford James, Geoffrey Craig. BS, U. Chgo., 1940, PhD in Physics, 1946; LLB, Harvard U., 1949. Bar: Calif., D.C. 1949, Ill. 1950. Jr. physicist metall. lab. U. Chgo., 1943-44; physicist Los Alamos Sci. Lab. (U. Calif.), N.Mex., 1944-45, Argonne Nat. Lab., AEC, Chgo., 1946; staff mem., group supr. Inst. Nuc. Studies, MIT, 1946-49; patent examiner U.S. Patent Office, Washington, 1949-50; assoc. firm Fitch, Even, Tabin & Flannery, Chgo., 1950-52; mem. firm Fich, Even, Tabin & Flannery, Chgo., 1952—. Lectr. U. Chgo., 1959. Mem. Am., D.C., Calif., Ill., Chgo. bar assns., Sigma Xi. Home: 162 Park Ave Glencoe IL 60022-1352 Office: 120 S La Salle St Chicago IL 60603-3403 E-mail: cgtabin@aol.com.

TABLER, SUSAN BEIDLER, lawyer; b. Quakertown, Pa., Nov. 13, 1943; d. Henry Landis and Pauline Henrietta Beidler; m. Bryan Grant Tabler, Dec. 28, 1968 (div. July 1987); children: Justin Elizabeth, Gillian Gardner. BA, Wellesley Coll., 1965; JD summa cum laude, Ind. U., Indpls., 1975. Intern BBC, London, 1965-67; examiner Ednl. Testing Svc., Princeton, N.J., 1967-69; adminstrv. assoc. Long Wharf Theatre, New Haven, 1969-72; assoc. Ice Miller Donadio & Ryan, Indpls., 1975-81, ptnr., 1982—. Bd. dirs. Ind. Sports Corp., Indpls. Pres. bd. dirs. Julian Ctr., Indpls., 1975-80; bd. dirs. Cathedral Arts, Indpls., 1975-79. Fellow Ind. Bar Found.; mem. ABA (chmn. standing com. on Gavel awards 1985-88, labor law div. vice chair gen. practice sect. 1988-91), Ind. State Bar Assn., Indpls. Bar Assn., Ind. U. Alumni Assn. (bd. dirs. 1989—). Office: Ice Miller Donadio & Ryan 1 American Sq Indianapolis IN 46282-0020

TABOADA, JAVIER GUSTAVO, neurologist; b. Trujillo, Peru, Feb. 20, 1940; came to U.S., 1966; s. Manuel and Esperanza (Vives) T.; m. Martha Rivas-Plata, June 25, 1966; children: Lucia, Martha, Suzanne, Tina. BS, Nat. U. Trujillo, Peru, 1960, MD, 1966. Diplomate Am. Bd. Psychiatry, Am. Bd. Neurology. Neurology residency Georgetown U., Washington, 1968-72; capt. U.S. Army, 1969, advanced through grades to col., 2000; psychiatry residency N.Y. Hosp.-Cornell, White Plains, N.Y., 1972-75, chief geriatric unit; chief neurology svc. USPHS Hosp., S.I., N.Y., 1975-78; pvt. practice Assoc. Neurologists of N.J., PA, Trenton, 1978—, pres., 1990—; clin. asst. prof. SUNY Downstate, Bklyn., 1975-78; clin. asst. prof. neurology Hahneman U., Phila., 1980—; chief neurology svc. H. Fuld Med. Ctr., Trenton, N.J., 1994—. Fellow ACP, Am. Acad. Neurology, Royal Med. Soc.; mem. Mercer County Med. Soc. (exec. coun. 1990—, v.p. 1995-96, pres. 1997-98), KC. Roman Catholic. Avocation: soccer. Office: Assoc Neurologists of NJ PA 1245 Whitehorse Ave Trenton NJ 08619 E-mail: kapoed24@aol.com.

TABOR, CURTIS HAROLD, JR., librarian, minister; b. Atlanta, July 3, 1936; s. Curtis Harold and Gerturde Olive (Casey) Tabor; m. Dorothy May Corbin, June 30, 1957 (dec. June 1996); m. Paulene C Pennington, July 12, 1997; children: Timothy M, John M. AA, Fla. Coll., Temple Terrace, 1957; BA, Harding Coll., 1960; MA, Butler U., 1969; MDiv, Bapt. Missionary Assn. Theol. Sem., Jacksonville, Tex., 1974; MLS, Tex. Woman's U., 1977. Min. Ch. of Christ, Bowling Green, Ky., 1960-61, Hamilton, Ont., Can., 1961-64, Indpls., 1964-67, Nacogdoches, Tex., 1967-75, Dallas, 1976-77, Columbus, Miss., 1977-79, Tampa, Fla., 1993-97, Maryville, Tenn., 1997—; reference libr. Blount County Pub. Libr., 1998—. Teacher Great Lakes Christian Col, Beamville, Ont, Canada, 1961—64; bible chair dir Stephen F Austin State Univ, Nacogdoches, 1967—75; participated archeological excavations, Tell Gezer, Israel, 1969, Tell Lachish, Israel, 80; profl libr sci Fla Col, Temple Terrace, 1979—85, libr dir, 1985—97. Author (with others): (book) Resurrection, 1973, Biblical Authority, 1974, The Lord of Glory, 1980, Making A Difference: Florida College, the First Fifty Years, 1996. Cub master Boy Scouts Am, Nacogdoches, 1970—75; pres Nacogdoches Baseball Asn, 1974—75; vol driving instr 55 Alive AARP, 1998—2001. Recipient Scouters Key, Cub Scouts Ams, 1975. Mem.: SAR, Tampa Bay Libr. Consortium (treas 1986—89), Beta Phi Mu, Eta Beta Rho. Republican. Mem. Ch. Of Christ. Avocations: amateur radio (KC4XS), locksmithing. Home: 1906 Raulston View Dr Maryville TN 37803-2868 E-mail: haltabor@yahoo.com.

TABOR, HERBERT, biochemist; b. N.Y.C., Nov. 28, 1918; s. Edward and Henrietta (Tally) T.; m. Celia White, Apr. 8, 1946; children: Edward, Marilyn, Richard, Stanley. AB, Harvard U., 1937, MD, 1941. Intern Yale U. and New Haven Hosp., 1942; with Lab. Biochem. Pharmacology Nat. Inst. Diabetes, Digestive and Kidney Disease, Bethesda, Md., 1943. Editor in chief Jour. Biol. Chemistry; contbr. articles to profl. jours. Mem. NAS, Am. Soc. Pharm. and Exptl. Therapeutics, Am. Chem. Soc., Am. Soc. for Biochemistry and Molecular Biology, Am. Acad. Arts and Scis. Office: NIH 8 Center Dr Bldg 8 Rm 223 Bethesda MD 20892-0830 E-mail: tabor@helix.nih.gov.

TABREZ, SHAMS S.M. gastroenterologist; b. Rawahindi, Pakistan, June 10, 1962; arrived in U.S., 1993; s. Sayeed S.M. Akhter and Sabira Khatoon; m. Salma Ali Tabrez, Aug. 5, 1993; children: Elsa, Mariam, Sana Shams. MB BS, Rawal Pindi Med. Coll., 1986. Diplomate Am. Bd. Internal Medicine. Emergency med. officer Dist. Hdqs. Hosp., Chakwal, Pakistan, 1986—87; lectr. pharmacology dept. Rawal Pindi Med. Coll., 1987—93; extern dept. pulmonary medicine VA Med. Ctr., Bklyn., 1993—95; intern in internal medicine NYU Med. Ctr., 1995—96, resident in internal medicine, 1996—98; fellow in gastroenterology Yale U. Affiliated Hosp., Bridgeport, Conn., 1998—2001; attending physician gastroenterology and hepatology So. N.Mex. Med. Assn., Eastern N.Mex. Med. Ctr., Roswell, 2001—; cons. gastroenterologist So. N.Mex. Assocs., Roswell, 2001—. Contbr. articles to profl. jours., chapters to books. Recipient Physician award, AMA, 2001. Mem.: ACP, Am. Gastroent. Assn., Am. Coll. Gastroenterology. Avocations: literature review, travel. Home: 12 Berrendo Meadows Roswell NM 88201 Office: So NMex Med Assn 303 W Country Club Rd Roswell NM 88201

TABRON, WENDY, paper company executive; Pres. Document Enterprise Inc., Atlanta, 1997—. Office: Document Enterprises 3200 Highland Dr SE #108 Smyrna GA 30080-3736

TABUSSI, STEPHEN JOHN, banker; b. Bklyn., July 21, 1949; s. Angelo G. and Eileen (Pryce) T. BA, Bklyn. Coll., 1971; MA, U. So. Calif., 1978. Mgr. media ops. Mfrs. Hanover Trust, N.Y.C., 1973-75; supr. ops. Union Bank, Los Angeles, 1975-77; media specialist Los Angeles Community Coll. Cist., 1977-78; asst. v.p. communications Western Bancorp, Los Angeles, 1978-81; v.p., advt. mgr. First Interstate Bancorp, Los Angeles, 1981—. With U.S. Army, 1971-73.

TACAL, JOSE VEGA, JR., retired public health official, veterinarian; b. Ilocos Sur, Philippines, Sept. 5, 1933; arrived in US, 1969; s. Jose Sr. and Cristina (Vega) T.; m. Lilia Caccam, 1959; children: Joyce, Jasmin, Jose III. DVM, U. Philippines, Quezon City, 1956; diploma, U. Toronto, 1964. Diplomate Am. Coll. Vet. Preventive Medicine; lic. vet., Calif. Provincial veterinarian Philippine Bur. Animal Industry, Manila, 1956-57; instr. vet. medicine U. Philippines, Quezon City, 1957-64, asst. prof., chmn. dept. vet. microbiology, pathology and pub. health, 1965-69; pub. health veterinarian San Bernardino (Calif.) County Dept. Pub. Health, 1970-83, sr. pub. health veterinarian, program mgr., sect. chief, 1984-2000. Zoonotic diseases lectr. Calif. State U., San Bernardino, 1984; lectr. U. Calif. Ext., Riverside, 1985; vis. prof. vet. pub. health U. Philippines at Los Banos, Laguna, 1988; participant 1st Internat. Conf. on Emerging Zoonoses, Jerusalem, 1996; presenter Internat. Symposium on Ectoparasites of Pets, U. Calif., Riverside, 1997; presenter Rabies in the Ams. Conf., Kingston, Ont., Can., 1997; rabies and ferret adv. group Calif. Dept. Health Svcs., 1998; presenter Western Poultry Disease Conf., Vancouver, B.C., Can., 1999, Rabies in Ams. Meeting, San Diego, 1999. Columnist LA Free Press, 1991, Pilipinas Times, 1993, Mabuhay Times, 1994-95; contbr. more than 50 articles to profl. jours. Pres. Filipino Assn. of San Bernardino County, Highland, Calif., 1979; charter mem. Greater Inland Empire Filipino Assn., Highland, 1986—; del. First Filipino Media Conf. N.Am., LA, 1993; mem. San Bernardino County Africanized Honey Bee Task Force, 1993-2000; participant 1st Internat. Conf. on Emerging Zoonoses, Jerusalem, 1996. Recipient Donald T. Fraser Meml. medal U. Toronto, 1964, Hon. fellow, Philippine Coll. Vet. Pub. Health, 2002, Cert. of Merit Philippine Vet. Med. Assn., 1965, Cert. of Appreciation Calif. State Bd. Examiners in Vet. Medicine, 1979, 84, Cert. of Recognition, Congressman George E. Brown Jr., 42d Congl. Dist. Calif., 1994, Assemblyman Joe Baca, 62d Assembly Dist., Calif. State Legis., 1994, Vet. Medicine/Journalism award Greater Inland Empire Filipino Assn., 1999; Colombo Plan Study fellow Can./Philippine Govts., 1963-64; hon. fellow Philippine Coll. Vet. Pub. Health, 2002. Mem.: ACLU, AVMA, AAAS, Highland Area Hist. Soc., Calif. Rare Fruit Growers (Inland Empire chpt.), Soc. for Advancement of Rsch., Western Poultry Disease Conf., Am. Vet. Med. History Soc., Friends of the Highland Libr. (bd. dirs.), Phi Sigma, Phi Kappa Phi. Office: PO Box 1023 Highland CA 92346-1023

TACHA, ATHENA, sculptor, artist, educator; b. Larissa, Greece, Apr. 23, 1936; came to U.S., 1963; MA, Nat. Acad. Fine Arts, Athens, Greece, 1959; MA in Art History, Oberlin Coll., 1961; PHD, U. Paris, 1963. Curator modern art Allen Art Mus., Oberlin, Ohio, 1963-73; prof. art Oberlin Coll., 1973-2000; adj. prof. art U. Md., College Park, 1999—. One-woman shows include Zabriskie Gallery, N.Y., 1979, 81, Max Hutchinson Gallery, N.Y., 1984, High Mus. Art, Atlanta, 1989, Franklin Furnace, N.Y., 1994, Beck Ctr., Cleve., 1998-99, Found. for Hellenic Culture, N.Y., 2001, also numerous other exhibits throughout the world, 1966—; prin. pub. commns. include sculptures at Am. Airlines Ctr., Dallas., City of Phila., Dept. Environ. Protection, Trenton, N.J., Case-Western Res. U., Cleve., Low Water Dam Riverfront Pk., Tulsa, Dept. of Transp., Hartford, Conn., City of Sarasota, Fla., Ecology Dept. U. Minn., St. Paul; collections include Hirshhorn Mus., Washington, Albright-Knox Art Gallery, Buffalo, Mus. Fine Arts, Houston, Nat. Coll. Fine Arts, Washington, Cleve. Mus. Art, Munson-Williams-Proctor Inst., Uttica, Nelson-Atkins Mus. Art, Kansas City, Allen Art Mus., Oberlin, Speed Art Mus., Louisville; author: (as A. T. Spear) Rodin Sculpture in the Cleveland Museum of Art, 1967, Brancusi's Birds, 1969; contbr. articles to profl. jours.; subject of book Cosmic Rhythms: Athena Tacha's Public Sculpture (E. McClelland), 1998, Dancing in the Landscape: The Sculpture of Athena Tacha, 2000. Recipient 1st prize May Show, Cleve. Mus. Art, 1968, 71, 79; NEA grantee, 1975; Bogliasco Found./Liguria Study Ctr. fellow, 2003. Home: 3721 Huntington St NW Washington DC 20015-1817 E-mail: atacha@umd.edu.

TACHA, DEANELL REECE, federal judge; b. Jan. 26, 1946; BA, U. Kans., 1968; JD, U. Mich., 1971. Spl. asst. to U.S. Sec. of Labor, Washington, 1971—72; assoc. Hogan & Hartson, Washington, 1973, Thomas J. Pitner, Concordia, Kans., 1973—74; dir. Douglas County Legal Aid Clinic, Lawrence, Kans., 1974—77; assoc. prof. law U. Kans., Lawrence, 1974—77, prof., 1977—85, assoc. dean, 1977—79, assoc. vice chancellor, 1979—81, vice chancellor, 1981—85; judge U.S. Ct. Appeals (10th cir.), Denver, 1985—; U.S. sentencing commr., 1994—98; chief judge U.S. Ct. Appeals (10th cir.), Denver, 2001—; nat. pres. Am. Inns. of Ct., 2004—.

TACHE, YVETTE FRANCE, neurogastroenterologist; b. Feb. 1, 1945; d. Lucien Joseph Laurant and Jeanne Marthe Fouillat; m. Jean Arthur Tache, June 20, 1970 (dec. Apr. 1979); children: Stephanie, Veronique. Master's degree, U. Claude Bernard, Lyon, France, 1968, DEA, 1969; PhD, U. Montreal, Can., 1974; Dr. Honoris Causa, U. Pecs, Hungary, 1994. Asst. rsch. U. Montreal, 1977-78; vis. scientist Salk Inst., La Jolla, Calif., 1978-80; from asst. rsch. prof. to assoc. rsch. prof. U. Montreal, 1980-82; assoc. prof. in rsch. UCLA, 1982-85, prof. medicine, 1985—. External referee Specialized Sci. Jour., 1977—, Med. Rsch. Coun., Que., Can., 1981—; mem. selection com. Med. Rsch. Coun., Que., 1982. Contbr. articles to profl. jours. Recipient Merit award, NIH, 1996—, Janssen award in gastroenterology, 1998, Dist. Rsch. award in Gastrointes, APA, 2003—08, Rsch. Career Scientist's award, Dept. VA. Mem. Am. Physiol. Soc., Am. Gastroenterol. Soc., Soc. Neurosci., Hans Selye Found. (v.p. 1984—). Democrat. Roman Catholic. Avocations: tennis, travel, skiing. Office: CURE: DDRC West La VA Med Ctr 11301 Wilshire Blvd Los Angeles CA 90073-1003 E-mail: ytache@ucla.edu.

TACHER, ROBERT FREDERICK, lawyer; b. Bklyn., Jan. 24, 1951; s. Abraham and Ilona Tacher; m. Roberta Caplowaith, Aug. 12, 1984. BA, U. Miami, 1972, JD, 1977. Bar: Fla. 1977, U.S. Dist. Ct. (so. dist.) Fla. 1977, U.S. Ct. Appeals (5th cir.) 1978, Fed. Trial Bar 1986. Assoc. Law Office Arnold Levy, Miami, Fla., 1977-78, Law Office David Willing, Miami, 1978-80, Law Office Lawrence Friedman, Miami, 1980-82; sr. litigation atty. Nelson & Tacher, Miami, 1982-94; mng. atty. Law Office of Robert F. Tacher, Miami-Ft. Lauderdale, 1994—, Law Office of Tacher and Fee, Miami-Ft. Lauderdale, 1995-96; atty. Law Office Robert F. Tacher, Ft. Lauderdale, 1996—. Mem. City of Lauderhill (Fla.) Planning and Zoning Bd., 1987-88. Mem. Fla. Bar Assn. (chmn. code and rules of evidence com. 2002—). Office: Ste 120 1700 NW 49th St Fort Lauderdale FL 33309

TACHI, DOUGLAS PAUL, architect, interior designer; b. Chgo., Mar. 1, 1945; s. Sadayoshi and Ruth Nobuko (Shikami) T.; m. Fleta Ross Collins, Dec. 27, 1987; children: Erin Paige, Brett Spencer. BS in Arch., Wash. U., St. Louis, 1968, MArch, 1974. Apprentice in arch. Mies van der Rohe, Chgo., 1961-63; designer Anselevicius & Rupe, St. Louis, 1974-76; project designer Harry Weese & Assocs., Washington, 1976-77, chief designer, v.p. in charge of design Miami, Fla., 1977-83; ptnr., v.p. Tilden, Tachi and Pales, Miami, 1983-87; ptnr., pres. Loggia Arch., Orlando, Fla., 1987—. Master plan cons. Rollins Coll., Winter Park, Fla., 1996-97; chief designer Miami Metrorail, 1977-83; project mgr. stas. L.A. Rapid Transit Dist., 1981. Exec. prodr. documentary: Bruyeres: The Courage of Our Fathers, 2000. Mem. master plan com./architect Miami Downtown Govt. Ctr., 1979-84; architect Art in Transit Screening Com., Miami, 1979-82. With U.S. Army, 1969-71. Recipient Master Plan award U. Miami, 1985, Architecture award Downtown Devel. Assn., Orlando, 1989. Mem. AIA (assoc., Henry Adams Cert. for Excellence in Arch. 1972). Avocations: biblical archaeology, fly fishing, yacht design.

TACHNER, LEONARD, lawyer; b. Bklyn., Jan. 18, 1944; BEE, CCNY, 1965; MSEE, Calif. State U., Long Beach, 1969; JD, Western State U., Fullerton, Calif., 1973. Bar: Calif. 1973, US Patent Office 1972. Supr. electronic counter measures sect. Ford Aerospace Corp., Newport Beach, Calif., 1969—73; patent atty. Reed C. Lawlor, LA, 1973—76, Rockwell Internat. Corp., Anaheim, Calif., 1976—78; ptnr. Fischer, Tachner & Strauss, Newport Beach, 1978—84; pvt. practice Irvine, Calif., 1984—. Instr. intellectual property Calif. State U., Long Beach, 1979—; com. maintenance profl. competence Calif. State Bar, 1978—. Mem. editl. bd. Western State U. Law Rev., 1972—73, columnist Interface Age mag., 1979—, Bus.-to-Bus. mag., 1983—. Mem.: Orange County Patent Law Assn., Calif. Bar Assn., Greater Irvine Indsl. League, Phi Kappa Phi. Office: 17961 Sky Park Cir Ste 38-E Irvine CA 92614 Office Phone: 949-752-8525. Personal E-mail: ltachner@aol.com. Business E-Mail: ltachner@pacbell.net.

TACHOVSKY, THOMAS G. medical company executive; BS in biology, Gonzaga U.; MS in Mgmt., Lesley Coll.; PhD in Microbiology, U. Rochester. R&D mgr. Johnson & Johnson; with Creative Biomolecules, Cytogen Corp.; gen. ptnr. MATCO & Assocs., 1991—98; dir., exec. v.p. Protyde Pharms., Inc., 1995—97; with Redox Pharms. Corp., Novavax, Inc., Paracelsian, Inc.; pres., CEO, dir. Entropin, Inc., Indio, Calif., 1999—. Office: Entropin Inc 45926 Oasis St Ste 810 Indio CA 92211

TACK, THERESA ROSE, women's health nurse; b. Lunenburg, Vt., Nov. 10, 1940; d. Gustave L. and Blanche Rose Fournier; m. Dennis M. Tack, Sept. 2, 1961; children: Lynelle Scullard, Karyn Terry, LeAnn Gomez. Diploma, Cen. Maine Gen. Hosp., 1961. Cert. ACLS, neonatal resuscitation Am. Heart Assn. Staff nurse neurosurgery unit Hillcrest Med. Ctr., Tulsa, 1961-62; staff nurse cardiovascular unit Meth. Hosp., Houston, 1962-65; staff nurse St. John's Hosp., Red Wing, Minn., 1979-85, Wasatch County Hosp., Heber City, Utah, 1985-97. Columnist, Nurses Notes in Wasatch Wave, Heber City, Utah, 1990-97.

TACKET, HALL SANFORD, retired internist; b. Dyer, Tenn., Apr. 12, 1921; s. John Otis and Lucile (Sanford) T.; m. Jeanne Snedecor, Apr. 17, 1925; children: Lynn, Carol, Hall Sanford Jr. BS, U. Tenn., 1943, MD, 1944. Diplomate Am. Bd. Internal Medicine, 1952. Instr. to assoc. prof. medicine U. Tenn. Coll. Medicine, Memphis, 1950-64, clin. prof., 1964-87, prof., 1987-96, emeritus prof., 1996—; internist pvt. practice, Memphis, 1950-86. Chief gen. internal med. Baptist Meml. Hosp., Memphis, 1979-91, dir. med. edn., 1979-91. Contbr. articles to profl. jours. Cpt. U.S. Army, 1945-47. Master ACP (gov. Tenn.); fellow Am. Coll. Cardiology. Home: 8100 Connecticut Ave Apt 1609 Chevy Chase MD 20815-2821

TACKETT, VITI LEE, writer; d. Clarence James and America Jane (Mason) Hunt; m. Floyd Vernon Tackett, July 2, 1953; children: Floyd Randall, Terry Lynn, Lucinda Gail Tackett/Hines. Diploma, Inst. Children's Lit., West Redding, Conn. Author: (novel series) Roseanna, Belle's Restless Heart, Beyond the Tempest, Rainbow's End, Girl on the Run, Two Roads. Personal E-mail: goviti@hotmail.com.

TADA, HIROSHI, manufacturing executive; Degree in Mining Engring., Kyoto (Japan) U., 1968; grad. Advanced Mgmt. Program, Harvard U., 1993. Joined Mitsui & Co., 1968—, sr. mng. officer, COO Iron & Steel Raw Materials Unit, 2000—03; pres., CEO, chmn. for the Ams. Mitsui & Co. (U.S.A.), Inc., N.Y.C., 2003—; exec. mng. officer Mitsui & Co., Ltd., Tokyo, 2003—. Mem.: Japan Soc., Japanese C. of C. and Industry, The Nippon Club. Office: Mitsui & Co Inc Corp Hdqrs 200 Park Ave New York NY 10166

TADDEI, LOIS ANNETTE MAGOWAN, artist, decorator; b. Phila., Sept. 17, 1935; d. Frank Rue Magowan and Grace Gloria (Valentino) Weinstein; m. Robert Matthew Taddei, May 21, 1960; 1 child, Robyn Grace. Degree, Pierce Coll. Represented by Phila. Mus. of Art. Watercolor botanicals shown at Phila. Mus. Art; one-woman shows include Pa. Hort. Soc., Phila, La Grande Gallery, Moorestown, N.J., Camden County Libr.; group shows include Art at Armory, Phila, Great Galleries, New Hope, Pa., Hardcastle Gallery, Wilmington, Del., Hockessin, Del., Gallery I, Chadds Ford, Pa., Rhoads Gallery, Gwynedd Valley, Pa., Festival Arts, Cape May, N.J., Ocean City (N.J.) Arts Festival; designer Vassar Designers Showcase House, 1991-92, Haddonfield Design Showcase House, 1992, Barry Decorators Haddonfield & Cherry Hill, Interiors by Marilouise, West Chester, Pa., Rocco Marianni & Assoc. Interior Design, Haddonfield. Mem. Graphic Artist Guild, United Visual Artists, Burlington County Art Guild. Avocations: gardening, needlepoint, ballet, museums.

TADDESSE, SAMUEL, economist, consultant; b. Addis Ababa, Shoa, Ethiopia, Oct. 16, 1944; came to U.S., 1968; s. Altaye and Askale (Yitabarek) T.; children: Tsehay, Samson, David. BSc, Haile Selassie 1st U., 1968; MBA, Fairleigh Dickinson U., 1970; PhD in Fin. and Applied Econs., U. Pa., 1975. Asst. prof. fin. and econs. Bernard Baruch Coll. CUNY, N.Y.C., 1973-77; sr. economist Fed. Res. Bank of N.Y., N.Y.C., 1977-80; dist. mgr. AT&T, Morristown, N.J., 1980-87; v.p. Debo Enterprises, Inc., Washington, 1987—. Sr. cons. Mgmt. Systems Internat., Washington, 1992—. Founder World Class Schs., Inc. Mem. Am. Bus. Assn. of Kenya, Internat. Soc. for African Devel., Soc. for Internat. Devel., Am. Econ. Assn., Washington Assn. Ethiopian Jews (pres.). Republican. Jewish. Avocation: camping. Home: Apt 701 5300 Columbia Pike Arlington VA 22204-5816 Office: Apt 701 5300 Columbia Pike Arlington VA 22204-5816

TADDIKEN, MARK, state legislator; b. Clay Center, Kans., Jan. 27, 1950; m. Debra Taddiken; children: Tawnya, Bria, Shawn. BS, Ft. Hays State U., 1972. Mem. Kans. State Senate, 2000, vice chair natural resources com., mem. agr. com., assessment and taxation com., utilities com. Sec., treas. Riverdale Cemetery Dist., 1993—; mem. Clay County Ext. Coun., 1997—. Mem. Farmers Coop Shipping Assn. (pres. 1980's), Lower Rep Water Users Assn. (v.p. 1991—), Kans. Soybean Assn. (v.p. 1994—), Bluestem Rural Electric Cooperative (pres. 1994—). Republican. Episcopalian. Office: 2614 Hackberry Rd Clifton KS 66937 Fax: 785-926-3210. E-mail: taddiken@senate.state.ks.us.

TADEO, ELVIA, artist; b. Ensenada, B.C., Mex., Nov. 21, 1970; d. Austreberto and Consuelo (Tadeo) T. Student art, Rafael Contreras, Ensenada, 1986-89, Lorraine M. Rowley, San Diego, 1990-96, Silvia Moonier, 1997-98, Edward Mores, 1998-99. Represented by The Gallery on Broadway, San Diego. Juror La Jolla Art Assn., 1999-2001, Del Mar Fair, Calif., 2001—. Contbg. artist pastel painting: Baja 4 You, 1999; poetry pub. in Art Venues Mag., Newsletter of Pastel Soc. San Diego, Pastel Soc. West Coast; exhibited at LaJolla (Calif.) Art Assn. Gallery, 1997-2001, Galerias Internacionales of Hotel Hyatt Regency, Guadalajara, Mex., 1996-98, Gallery of Pastel Soc. of West Coast, Camino, Calif., 1997, Ceudonium de la Mujer, Ensenada, 1999-2001, Galeria de la Ciudad de Ensenada, B.C., Mex., 2000, Giorgio Santini's Gallery of Fine Arts, Rosarito, Mex., 2000-2001, El Centro Cultural San Angel, Mexico City, 2000, Centro Cultural Riviera, Ensenada, 2000, Centro Cultural Siglo 21, Mexico City, 2001, Hosp. Tembre, Mexico, 2001, Teatro la Cjuda-deia, Mexico, 2001, Hosp. of Pemex City, 2002, House of Reps., Mexico City, 2002, The Gallery on Broadway, San Diego; rep. Gallery on Broadway, San Diego, Gallery Giorgio Santini, Rosarito, San Diego Mus. of Art, Artist Guild, 2002-03. Art cons. Cultural Ctr. of Ensenada, 2000—; nat dir. Mexican Rep. in the Art Miles project, United Nations U.S.A. rep., 2002-03. Recipient 1st place Del Mar Fair, 1996, Spl. award, 1996. Mem. LaJolla Art Assn. (publicity chair 1999-2001), Pastel Soc. of West Coast, Degas Pastel Soc., Pastel Soc. San Diego, Carlsbad and Oceanside Art League, Internat. Assn. Pastels, Directorio Enciclopedico de las Artes Plasticas, Directorio of Artistas Plasticos de la Cordinacion Nacional de Artes Plasticas de Bellas Artes. Roman Catholic. Avocations: horseback riding, hiking. Office: PO Box 2229 Vista CA 92085 E-mail: elviatadeo@aol.com.

TAESCH, RICHARD EDMOND, music educator; b. San Diego, Calif., Dec. 17, 1942; s. Edmond Thomas Taesch and Ann Marcella Simeone; m. Sandra Aiken, June 15, 1968 (div. Jan. 0, 1980). Cert. lit. Braille Libr. of Congress, 1988, music Braille Libr. of Congress, 1992. Tchr. Adler Music Acad., Van Nuys, Calif., 1961—71; tchr. pvt. studio Van Nuys Music, 1971—94; tchr., chair dept. guitar So. Calif. Conservatory of Music, Sun Valley, 1976—, tchr., founder Braille music divsn., 1992—; tchr. L.A.City Coll., 1983—90. Br. pres. Music Tchrs. Assn. Calif, San Fernando East Valley, 1971—79; music specialist Calif. Transcribers and Educators of Visually Handicapped, LA, 1996—. Author: An Introduction to Music for the Blind Student Parts I & II; contbr. articles to profl. jours. Founder Music Edn. Network for The Visually Impaired, 1996. Recipient Ptnr. Sch. Award, Blend School-LAUSD, 1999. Mem.: Nat. Assn. of Schools of Music, Nat. Braille Assn. Roman Catholic. Achievements include development of Cal Transcribers and Educators of the Visually Handicapped music committee; developed curriculum for teaching of braille music. Avocations: hiking, amateur radio, flying. Office: SCCM Braille Music Divsn 8711 Sunland Blvd Sun Valley CA 91352

TAFANELLI, LEE, state representative; m. Tammy Tafanelli; children: Nicholas, Francesca. M in Environ. Planning and Mgmt., Kans. State U., 1999; student, Pitts. State U. Commd. 2d lt. Kans. Army Nat. Guard, 1982; mil. asst. to asst. sec. Army Pentagon; commdr., lt. col. Kans. Army Nat. Guard, 2001. Decorated Meritorious Svc. medal with oak leaf cluster, Army Commendation medal with two oak leaf clusters, Army Achievement medal with oak leaf cluster. Office: 175-W State Capitol 300 SW 10th Ave Topeka KS 66612 also: 800 SW Jackson # 1000 66612

TAFEL, EDGAR, architect; b. N.Y.C., Mar. 4, 1912; s. Samuel and Rose (Chary) T. Student, NYU, 1930-32; DFA (hon.), SUNY, Geneseo, 2001. Sr. fellow Frank Lloyd Wright's Taliesin Fellowship, Spring Green, Wis., 1932-41; practice architecture N.Y.C., 1946—. Lectr. USIS, Eng., Israel, India, Netherlands, 1972-73, New Sch. for Social Rsch., N.Y.C., 1974; faculty Smithsonian Instn., 1978; co-producer, actor (video) The Frank Lloyd Wright Way. Author: Years with Frank Lloyd Wright, 1993, Frank Lloyd Wright, 1993; contbr. articles to profl. jours.; Prin. works include: Protestant Chapel at Kennedy Airport, 1964, First Presbyn. Ch. Addition, 1959, De Witt Ch., all N.Y.C., Fine Arts Bldg., State U. N.Y. at Geneseo, 1967, Fulton-Montgomery Community Coll, Johnstown, N.Y., 1969, Grace Ch, White Plains, 1970, Allentown (Pa.) Art Mus. addition, 1975, Columbia-Greene Community Coll, Hudson, N.Y., 1974, Salvation Army Corps Community Centers; master plans for: State Coll. at Geneseo, York Coll., N.Y.C., Cadet Corps Hdqrs., Bronx, N.Y.; designed over 100 residences. Bd. dirs. N.Y.C. Mission Soc. Served with AUS, World War II, CBI. Recipient award of merit for Presbyn. Ch. Fifth Ave. Assn., N.Y.C., service citation State U. N.Y. Coll. at Geneseo, 1970 Fellow AIA; mem. Nat. Acad. Arts (assoc.), Taliesin Fellowship (coun.), Fallingwater (adv. com.). Home (Summer): 624 Granada Ave Venice FL 34285 Office Phone: 212-673-6000.

TAFLOVE, ALLEN, electrical engineer, educator, researcher, consultant; b. Chgo., June 14, 1949; s. Harry and Leah T.; m. Sylvia Hinda Friedman, Nov. 6, 1977; children: Michael Lee, Nathan Brent. BS with highest distinction, Northwestern U., 1971, MS, 1972, PhD, 1975. Assoc. engr. IIT Rsch. Inst., Chgo., 1975-78, rsch. engr., 1978-81, sr. engr., 1981-84; assoc. prof. Northwestern U., Evanston, Ill., 1984-88, prof., 1988—, Charles Deering McCormick prof., 2000—03; master Lindgren/Slivka Residential Coll. Sci. & Engring., 2000—. Author: Computational Electrodynamics: The Finite Difference Time-Domain Method, 1995; co-author: Computational Electromagnetics: Integral Equation Approach, 1993, Computational Electrodynamics: The Finite-Difference Time-Domain Method, 2d edit., 2000; editor: Advances in Computational Electrodynamics: The Finite-Difference Time-Domain Method, 1998; contbr. 14 chpts. to books, more than 90 articles to profl. jours.and mags. Fellow: IEEE. Achievements include pioneer of finite-difference time-domain method in computational electrodynamics. Office: Northwestern U Dept Elec and Comp Engring 2145 Sheridan Rd Evanston IL 60208-0834 Office Phone: 847-491-4127. Business E-Mail: taflove@ece.northwestern.edu.

TAFOYA, MICHELE, sports reporter; Talk show host Minn. Vikings Talk Radio, KFAN, 1993—94; reporter CBS Sports, 1994—2000, ESPN, 2000—, NBA on ABC, 2003; sideline reporter Sunday Night NFL, ESPN, 2002—04, Monday Night Football, ABC, 2004—. Office: 77 W 66th St New York NY 10023

TAFRATE, POLLY HARE, retired elementary school educator; b. N.Y.C., Apr. 9, 1941; d. Clarence Clifton Hare and Margaret Elizabeth McGeary; m. Raymond John Tafrate, Sr., Aug. 17, 1963; children: Raymond Chip, Jill Susan, Karla Partilla. BS, U. Vt., 1963; MS, Western Conn. State U., 1988. Tchr. Katonah (N.Y.)-Lewisboro Sch. Dist., 1976—2000; ret. Pvt. tutor, South Salem, NY, 1970—2004; presenter in field. Author ednl. lit., newspapers, mags. Vol. Norwalk (Conn.) Hosp. Emergency Rm., 2000—04. Mem.: Soc. Children's Book Writers and Illustrators, Conn. Press Club. Avocations: travel, writing, cooking, literature, child advocacy. Home: 54 Lockwood Rd South Salem NY 10590

TAFT, BOB, governor; b. Jan. 8, 1942; m. Hope Taft; 1 child, Anna. BA, Yale U., 1963; MA, Princeton U., 1967; JD, U. Cin., 1976. Pvt. practice; mem. Ohio Ho. of Reps., Columbus, 1976-80; commr. Hamilton County, Ohio, 1981-90; sec. of state State of Ohio, Columbus, 1991-99, gov., 1999—. Vol. Peace Corps., E. Africa. Republican. Office: Governor's Office 30th Fl 77 S High St Fl 30 Columbus OH 43215-6117

TAFT, EARL JAY, mathematics professor; b. N.Y.C., Aug. 27, 1931; s. David and Terry (Gordon) T.; m. Hessy Levinsons, Jan. 18, 1959; children: Nina, Alexander. BA, Amherst Coll., 1952; MA, Yale U., 1953, PhD, 1956. Instr. Columbia U., N.Y.C., 1956-59; asst. prof. Rutgers U., New Brunswick, N.J., 1959-62, assoc. prof., 1962 66, prof. math., 1966—. Exec. editor: Communications in Algebra, 1974-99, math. series Marcel Dekker Inc., 1974—; contbr. numerous articles to profl. jours. NSF grantee. Mem. Am. Math. Soc., Math. Assn. Am., Phi Beta Kappa, Sigma Xi. Home: 65 Central Park W Apt 8A New York NY 10023-6009 Office: Rutgers U Dept Math Piscataway NJ 08854-8019 Office Phone: 723-445-2467.

TAFT, NELLIE LEAMAN, artist; b. Cin., May 22, 1937; d. Hulbert and Elizabeth (Brady) Sutphin; m. A.M. Gammell, Dec. 1, 1973 (div. Apr. 1981). AB, Briarcliff Jr. Coll., 1957; BA, Columbia U., 1968; MA, Tchrs. Coll., 1970. Counselor Oreg. State Sch. for Deaf, Salem, 1960; asst. tchr. art Brearley Sch., N.Y.C., 1961; tchr. pottery Greenwich House Pottery, N.Y.C., 1965-66; tchr. Lexington Children's Ctr., N.Y.C., 1965-66; intern New World Sch., Hackensack, N.J., 1969-70; tchr. The Caedmon Sch., N.Y.C., 1970-73; founder, prin. The Learning Ctr., East Greenwich, R.I., 1978-81. Cons. in field. One-woman shows include Carnegie Art Ctr., Ky., 1984, Closson's Gallery, Cin., 1986, 1989, 1993, Wooden Tent Gallery, Mass., 1990, Gallery 68, Belfast, Maine, 1992, Between the Muse Gallery, Rockland, Maine, 1996, St. Botolph Club Odysseys, Boston, 2002, Round Top, Damariscotta, Maine, 2002, exhibited in group shows at John S. Ames Gallery, Belfast, Ireland, 1994, Contemporary Art Ctr., Cin., 1994, Nielsen Gallery, Boston, 1998—99, 2001, Muse Gallery, 1998—99, Maine Coast Artist Gallery, 1999, Represented in permanent collections Cin. Art Mus., Cin. Bell Tel. Bd. dirs. Cambridge Art Assn.; nat. com. mem. Whitney Mus. Fellow, Va. Ctr. for Creative Arts, 2002; Clarissa Bartlett Traveling scholar, 1991, Albert H. Whitin Traveling scholar, 1991. Mem. St. Botolph Club (art com.), Camargo Club. Avocations: tennis, golf, kayaking, flying, dance.

TAFT, PERRY HAZARD, retired lawyer; b. L.A., Jan. 23, 1915; s. Milton and Sarah Taft; m. Callie S. Taft, Aug. 15, 1968; children by previous marriage: Stephen D., Sally L., Sheila R. Student, U. Calif., Berkeley, 1932-35; AB, UCLA, 1936; LLB, George Washington U., 1940. Bar: Calif. 1940. Spl. atty. Antitrust Divsn. U.S. Dept. Justice, L.A., 1941-42; dep. atty. gen. State of Calif., San Francisco, 1943-44; regional rep. Coun. State Govts., San Francisco, 1944-45; regional dir. govt. affairs Trans World Airlines, L.A., 1945—47; Pacific coast mgr. Am. Ins. Assn., San Francisco, 1948-66; gen. counsel Assn. Calif. Ins. Cos., Sacramento, 1967-73; asst. city atty. City of Stockton, Calif., 1973-79; pres. Perry H. Taft, P.C., Stockton, 1979-85; arbitrator Surps Line Assn., Calif., 1965-98. Contbr. articles to profl. jours. Bd. dirs. Stockton East Water Dist., 1979-83, pres., 1981-83; mem. San Joaquin County Water Adv. Com., 1982-85. Mem. State Bar of Calif., Elkhorn Country Club, Psi Upsilon. Home: 7254 Southfield Way Stockton CA 95207-1137

TAFT, SETH CHASE, retired lawyer; b. Cin., Dec. 31, 1922; s. Charles Phelps and Eleanor K. (Chase) T.; m. Frances Prindle, June 19, 1943; children: Frederick, Thomas, Cynthia, Tucker. BA, Yale U., 1943, LL.B., 1948. Bar: Ohio 1948. Assoc. Jones, Day, Reavis & Pogue, Cleve., 1948-59, ptnr., 1959-88. Mem. Cuyahoga County (Ohio) Bd. Commrs., 1971—78, pres., 1977—78; mem. Cuyahoga County Charter Commn., 1958—59; pres. Fedn. for Cmty. Planning, Cleve., 1986—89, Cleve. Internat. Program, 1990—94; chmn. Substance Abuse Initiative Greater Cleve., 1989—, Coun. Internat. Programs USA, 1999—2002, Cleve. Coun. World Affairs, 2000—02; Rep. candidate for mayor of Cleve., 1967; for gov. of Ohio, 1982. With USNR, 1943—46. Mem.: City Club of Cleveland (Hall of Fame 2004). Home: 6 Pepper Ridge Rd Cleveland OH 44124-4904 Office: Jones Day 901 Lakeside Ave E Cleveland OH 44114-1190 E-mail: sethtaft@aol.com.

TAFT, SHELDON ASHLEY, lawyer; b. Cleve., Mar. 2, 1937; s. Kingsley Arter and Louise Parsons (Dakin) T.; m. Rebecca Sue Rinehart, Dec. 26, 1962; children: Mariner R., Ashley A., Curtis N. BA, Amherst Coll., 1959; LLB, Harvard U., 1962. Bar: Ohio 1962. Assoc. Vorys, Sater, Seymour & Pease, Columbus, Ohio, 1965-69, 71-73, ptnr., 1974—2001, of counsel, 2002—; chief legal counsel Pub. Utilities Commn. Ohio, Columbus, 1969-71. Ohio bd. advisors Chgo. Title Ins. Co., 1967-98. Rep. candidate for justice Ohio Supreme Ct., 1974; trustee Opera Columbus, 1989—, pres., 1991-93, life trustee, 1995—; trustee Columbus Bach Ensemble 2002—, pres. 2002—; 1st lt. USAF, 1963-65. Mem. ABA (pub. utilities sect.), Ohio State Bar Assn. (pres. pub. utilities com. 1984-87), Columbus Bar Assn. (pub. utilities com.), Ohio Camera Collectors Soc. (pres. 1985-87), Rocky Fork Hunt and Country Club, Hillsboro Club, 41 Club, Review Club. Congregationalist. Avocation: camera collecting. Home: 27 Sessions Dr Columbus OH 43209-1440 Office: Vorys Sater Seymour & Pease PO Box 1008 52 E Gay St Columbus OH 43216-1008

TAFT, WILLIAM HOWARD, IV, federal agency administrator; b. Washington, Sept. 13, 1945; s. William Howard and Barbara Hoult (Bradfield) T.; m. Julia Vadala, May 4, 1974; Maria Consetta, William Howard V, Julia Harris. BA, Yale U., 1966; JD, Harvard U., 1969. Bar: D.C. 1969. Assoc. Winthrop, Stimson, Putnam & Roberts, N.Y.C., 1969-70; atty.-advisor to chmn. FTC, Washington, 1970; prin. asst. to dep. dir. Office of Mgmt. and Budget, Washington, 1970-72, exec. asst. to dir., 1972-73; exec. asst. to sec. HEW, Washington, 1973-76, gen. counsel, 1976-77; ptnr. Leva, Hawes, Symington, Martin & Oppenheimer, Washington, 1977-81; gen. counsel The Pentagon, Washington, 1981-84; dep. sec. def. Dept. Def., Washington, 1984—89; perm. rep. U.S. Mission to NATO, 1989—92; ptnr. Fried Frank Harris Shriver & Jacobson, Washington, 1992—2001; legal adviser U.S. Dept. State, Washington, 2001—. Recipient Disting. Service award HEW, 1975 Mem. D.C. Bar Assn., Lit. Soc. (Washington) Clubs: Cosmos (Washington), Leo (Washington). Republican. Office: US Dept State Legal Adviser 2201 C St NW Washington DC 20520 Business E-Mail: taftwh@state.gov.

TAGATZ, GEORGE ELMO, retired obstetrician, gynecologist, educator; b. Milw., Sept. 21, 1935; s. George Herman and Beth Elinore (Blain) T.; m. Susan Trunnell, Oct. 28, 1967; children: Jennifer Lynn, Kirsten Susan, Kathryn Elizabeth. AB, Oberlin Coll., 1957; MD, U. Chgo., 1961. Diplomate Am. Bd. Obstetricians and Gynecologists, Am. Bd. Reproductive Endocrinology (examiner, bd. reproductive endocrinology 1976-79). Rotating intern Univ. Hosps. of Cleve., 1961-62, resident in internal medicine, 1962-63; resident in ob-gyn U. Iowa, 1965-68; sr. research fellow in endocrinology U. Wash. dept. obstetrics and gynecology, 1968-70; from asst. prof. ob-gyn to prof. emeritus Med. Sch. U. Minn., 1970—2000, prof. emeritus Med. Sch., 2000—. Mem. fertility and maternal health adv. com. FDA, USPHS, HHS, 1982-86; cons. in field, 1986-87. Ad hoc editor: Am. Jour. Ob-Gyn, Fertility and Sterility; contbr. articles to profl. publs. Served with M.C. U.S. Army, 1963-65. Mem. AMA, Minn., Hennepin County med. socs., Minn. Obstet. and Gynecol. Soc., Am. Coll. Ob-Gyn (subcom. on reproductive endocrinology 1979-82), Endocrine Soc., Am. Fertility Soc., Central Assn. Obstetricians and Gynecologists, U. Iowa Ob-Gyn Alumni Soc. Home: 5828 Long Brake Trl Edina MN 55439-2622

TAGAYEV, LEV C. art director; b. Tehran, Iran, Feb. 13, 1952; s. Constantine Stephanovich Tagayev and Knarik Shahijanian; m. Susane F. Bryant, Aug. 20, 1994. AA, Queensborough C.C., 1974; BA, Queens Coll., 1976; M of English and History, NYU, 1980. Video and Computer Graphics Ctr. for the Media Arts, 1986; cert. tchr. Nev., 1992, Calif., 1993. Asst. to Ruben Ter Arturian NYC Ballet, 1972—79; tech. dir. summer concerts N.Y. Philharm., N.Y.C., 1976—84; pub. InStep in N.Y., N.Y.C., 1979—82; computer graphics artist U. of Medicine and Dentistry, Newark, 1986—90; mgr. Scandia Down Gift Store, Tahoe City, Calif., 1988—2003. Author: (book of poetry and prose) My Lev Life; tech. dir.: Festival Orch., 1976—86; (Jekyll and Hyde) Tahoe Arts, P.T.R., 2002—; dir.: (A Funny Thing Happened on the Way to the Forum), 2000—; actor: Tahoe Players, 1993—94, Tahoe Arts, P.T.R., 1999—, Western Nev. Mus. Theatre Co., 2004. Sgt. spl. forces, 1969—71, Vietnam. Republican. Achievements include design of logos for Into the Woods and Les Miserable. Avocations: acting, directing, lighting design, writing, bass guitar. Home: PO Box 3302 Incline Village NV 89450 Personal E-mail: tahoearts@charter.net.

TAGER, LOUISE ARLENE, high court advocate; b. Johannesburg, Nov. 4, 1935; d. Abe Harold and Fanny (Stein) Cohen; m. Harris Hirsch Joseph Tager, July 5, 1955; children: Erle, Beverley, Saul. BA, U. Witwatersrand, 1965, LLB, 1970, diploma in Tax Law, 1975; ML, Harvard Law Sch., 1978. cert. advocate high ct. South Africa. Tutor Sch. Law U. Witwatersrand, 1969, sr. bursar Sch. Law, 1970, lectr. Sch. Law, 1971-74, sr. lectr. Sch. Law, 1975-78, prof. Sch. Law, 1978-89, hon. prof. Sch. Law, 1990-94; exec. dir. The Law Review Project, 1985-96, dean faculty law, 1980-85; prof. extraordinarius, dept. mercantile law U. South Africa, 1995—97; prof. extraordinary dept. mercantile law U. Orange Free State, 1999-2001. Dir. Zakhelizwe, 1988-97, Progress Through Employment, 1989-97, Alexandra TREK Recration Edn. Ctr., 1990-97, ABT Diamond Cutting Works, Ltd., 1997; bd. dirs. TRANSNET Ltd., 1990-2001, chmn. 1996-2001; chmn U.S. S. Africa Leadership Devel. Exchg. Program USSALEP, 1990-96, Rural and Urban Devel. Corp., 1991—, ORT Science and Tech. Edn. Project, 1992, The Law Review Project, 1985-96, Barloworld Ltd., 1992—, Legal Assist Ltd., 1993-96, Women's Devel. Bus., 1993-2000, Wooltru Ltd., 1993—, chmn., 2001-04; bd. dirs Theta Securities Ltd, 1996, Ind Bus. Enrichment Ctr., 1993-98, Ind. Bus. Finance Ctr., 1993-98, Truworths Internat. Ltd., 1998-2003, South African Inst. Bus. Ethics Ltd., 1991-2000, Nat. Indsl. Chamber, 1991—99, Coun. Free Market Found., 1992—; trustee Internat. Assn. Students Interested in Econ. and the Mgmt. Process (AIESEC), 1995-98. Author: Negotiable Instruments Lawsa Student Texts, 1984; contbr. chpts. to books. Chmn. VATWATCH, South Africa, 1990-91, Bus. Practices Com., 1988-99; mem. standing com. Sml. Claims Ct. Johannesberg, 1985-2000, Coord. Consumer Coun. of South Africa, 1988-95; mem. deregulation com. Competition Bd. of South Africa, 1987-94; mem. Land Affairs Adv. Com., 1989-92, mem. Nat. Manpower Commn., 1993-94, Nat. Health Legislation Rev. Com., 1995-96, mem. standing adv. commn. on company law, 1996-99; mem. S.A. Diamond Bd., 1999-2002. Recipient Paul Harris award Rotary Internat. Mem. Soc. Advs. South Africa. Jewish. Avocations: gardening, pilates, bridge. Home: 48 8th Ave Lower Houghton Johannesburg 2198 South Africa

TAGGART, HELEN M. adult education educator, nurse; b. Savannah, Ga., Dec. 6, 1946; d. Thomas Anthony and Ruth Elizabeth (Sisson) McKenzie; m. Thomas Robert Taggart, Mar. 9, 1968; children: Kathleen Taggart Swanner, Thomas Robert Jr. BSN, Armstrong State Coll., 1978; MSN, Ga. So. U., 1992; postgrad., U. Ala., Birmingham, 1995—. Staff nurse St. Joseph's Hosp., Savannah, 1967-68, 77-89, head nurse, 1971-74, St. Mary's Hosp., Athens, Ga., 1968-71; instr. Armstrong State Coll., Savannah, 1989-92; asst. prof. Armstrong Atlantic State U., Savannah, 1992—. Profl. adv. com. Nat. Multiple Sclerosis Soc., Atlanta, 1992-96; bd. mem. Ga. Bd. Nursing, Atlanta, 1994—; mem. Clin. Simulation Task Force Nat. Coun. State Bds. Nursing, Chgo., 1996-99. Editor, contbr.: Adult Nursing in Acute Community, 1998; contbr. articles to profl. jours. and chpts. to books. Counselor Multiple Sclerosis Support Group, Savannah, 1989-97. Nat. Assn. Orthop. Nurses rsch. grantee, 1996, U. Ala. (Birmingham) traineeship grantee, 1997, Armstrong Atlantic State U. rsch. grantee, 1997-98. Mem. Nat. League Nurses (exec. bd. 1996-98), Assn. Bus. Women Am. (exec. bd. 1994-96), Nat. Assn. Orthop. Nurses (rsch. com. 1995-99), Ga. Nurses Assn. (exec. bd. 1992-96). Avocations: gardening, swimming, skiing. Home: 6 Mulberry Bluff Dr Savannah GA 31406-3226 Office: Armstrong Atlantic State Univ 11935 Abercorn St Savannah GA 31419-1989

TAGGART, LINDA DIANE, women's health nurse; b. Balt., June 14, 1940; d. Louis and Annie Helena (Heertje) Glick; divorced; 1 child, Keri Anne. AS in Nursing, Pensacola Jr. Coll., 1967; BA, U. West Fla., 1970; postgrad., St. Joseph's Coll., 1976-78. RN, Fla., Ala. Staff nurse Bapt. Hosp., Pensacola, Fla., 1967-70, head nurse, 1970-72; dir. in-svc. edn. Baycrest, Inc. Extended Care Facility, Pensacola, 1973, DON, 1973-74, Medica Media, Pensacola, 1974; clinic adminstr. Cmty. Healthcare Ctr. (formerly Medica Media), Pensacola, 1974—. Dir. sex and health edn. Cmty. Healthcare Ctr., Pensacola, 1974—; regional dir. Medica Media, ea. U.S., 1990; testified before Jud. com. U.S. Ho. of Reps., 1994. Contbr. project The Gideon Project, 1993, project Wrath of Angels, 1998, articles to profl. jours.; appeared on (documentaries) Dateline NBC, 48 Hours, Nightline, Turning Point, ABC, CNN, (HBO documentaries) Soldiers in the Army of God, 2000, Keeping It Real, Program of RCRC, South Africa, 2002; contbr. documentary I, Witness, 1998, documentary AGB "I Witness" Addy & Goldwater, 1999. Bd. dirs. Rape Crisis Ctr., Pensacola, 1976-91, chair, 1980, 84, 89 (Addie Brooks award 1984); mem. exec. com. Lakeview Community Mental Health Ctr., Pensacola, 1989 (Expression of Appreciation award 1980-91). Recipient Pioneer/Heroe award Fla. Abortion Coun., 1989, Woman of Yr. award NOW, 1995, Women's Equity Day award 1986. Mem. ACLU, Am. Assn. Sex Educators, Counselors and Therapists (cert. sex educator), Feminist Majority Found., Religious Coalition for Reproductive Choice (bd. dirs. 2000—), People for Am. Way, So. Poverty Law Ctr., Internat. Platform Assn., Planned Parenthood Fedn. Am. Democrat. Presbyterian. Avocations: skiing, jewelry design, cross-stitch, reading, ballroom dancing. Office: Cmty Healthcare Ctr 6770 N 9th Ave Pensacola FL 32504-7346 Office Phone: 850-478-9660. E-mail: ldtagg@aol.com.

TAGGART, RICHARD J. corporate financial executive; BS, U. Wyo., 1967, MS in Agrl. Econs., 1970; grad. exec. mgmt. program, U. Wash. CPA. With ops. rsch. and systems devel. depts. Ford Motor Co., 1970—74; with Weyerhaeuser Co., Federal Way, Wash., 1974—, dir. investor rels., 1994—96, v.p. investor rels., 1996—98, v.p., treas., 1998—2001, v.p. fin., 2001—03, exec. v.p., CFO, 2003—. Office: Weyerhaeuser Co 33663 Weyerhaeuser Way S Federal Way WA 98063-9777

TAGGART, THOMAS MICHAEL, lawyer; b. Sioux City, Iowa, Feb. 22, 1937; s. Palmer Robert and Lois Allette (Sedgwick) T.; m. Dolores Cecilia Baroway Renfro, Jan. 4, 1963; children: Thomas Michael Jr., Theodore Christopher; m. Mary Ann Gribben, Feb. 7, 1976. BA, Dartmouth Coll., 1959; JD, Harvard U., 1965. Bar: Ohio 1965, U.S. Dist. Ct. (so. dist.) Ohio 1967, U.S. Dist. Ct. (no. dist.) Ohio 1981, U.S. Supreme Ct. 1997. Ptnr. Vorys, Sater, Seymour & Pease, Columbus, Ohio, 1965—, now of counsel. Lectr. Ohio Legal Ctr. Inst., Ohio Mfrs. Assn., Capital U. Ctr. for Spl. and Continuing Legal Edn. Capt. USMC, 1959-63. Mem. ABA, Ohio Bar Assn. (bd. govs. 1991-99, liability ins. com. 1996-, pres. 1997-98, trustee Found. 1996-98, 2000—, chair commn. on jud. evaluations 2000, Ohio Bar medal 1999), Columbus Bar Assn. (bd. govs., pres. 1989-90), Ohio Assn. Civil Trial Attys., Am. Bd. Trial Advocates, Columbus Area C. of C. Methodist. Home: 145 Stanbery Ave Columbus OH 43209-1465 Office: Vorys Sater Seymour & Pease 52 E Gay St Columbus OH 43215-3161

TAGIURI, CONSUELO KELLER, child psychiatrist, educator; b. San Francisco; d. Cornelius H. and Adela (Rios) Keller; m. Renato Tagiuri; children: Robert, Peter, John. BA, U. Calif.-Berkeley; MD, U. Calif.-San Francisco. Diplomate Am. Bd. Psychiatry and Neurology. Resident psychiatry Mass. Gen. Hosp., Boston; staff psychiatrist Children's Hosp., Boston, 1951-59; med. dir. Gifford Sch., Weston, Mass., 1965-85; chief psychiatrist Cambridge (Mass.) Guidance Ctr., 1961-84; mem. faculty dept. psychiatry Harvard Med. Sch., 1965—2002; cons. early childhood program Children's Hosp., 1985—. Contbr. articles in field to books. Fellow Am. Orth. Psychiat. Assn., Mass. Med. Soc., New Eng. Coun. Child Psychiatry.

TAGLE, HILDA GLORIA, former judge; b. Corpus Christi, Dec. 18, 1946; d. Manuel Cisneros and Dolores (Cipriano) T.; 1 child, Santiago. AA, Del Mar Coll., Corpus Christi, 1968; BA, East Tex. State U., 1969; MLS, North Tex. State U., 1971; JD, U. Tex., 1977. Bar: Tex. 1977, U.S. Dist. Ct. (so. dist.) Tex. 1989, U.S. Supreme Ct. 1985. Asst. city atty. City of Corpus Christi, 1977-78; asst. county atty. Nueces County, 1978-79; asst. dist. atty. Nueces County Dist. Atty., 1979-81; pvt. practice law Corpus Christi, 1981-85; judge Nueces County Ct. at Law No. 3, Corpus Christi, 1985—. Mem. State Commn. on Jud. Conduct, Austin, Tex., 1989—; mem. Gov.'s Commn. for Women; mem. jud. edn. exec. com. Supreme Ct. Tex., Austin, 1987-89. Recipient Good Gals award Tex. Women's Polit. Caucus, 1990. Mem. Corpus Christi Bar Assn. (chmn. lawyers for literacy com. 1989-90, Women Lawyers of Coastal Bend, State Bar Tex. (co-chmn. ann. meeting planning com. 1991), Alpha Lambda Sigma. Mem. Christian Ch. (Disciples Of Christ). Office: Nueces County Ct at Law 3 901 Leopard Ste 703 Corpus Christi TX 78401

TAGLIABUE, PAUL JOHN, national football league commissioner; b. Jersey City, Nov. 24, 1940; s. Charles and Mary Tagliabue; m. Chandler M. Minter, Aug. 28, 1965; children: Drew, Emily. BA, Georgetown U., 1962; JD, NYU, 1965; PhD. Humane Letters (hon.), Northeastern Univ., 1990; PhD. of Laws (hon.), Colgate Univ., 2001. Bar: N.J. 1965, D.C. 1969. Atty. to sec. def. Dept. Def., Washington, 1966—69; assoc. Covington & Burling, Washington, 1969—74, ptnr., 1969—89; commr. NFL, N.Y.C., 1989—. Bd. dir. Pro Football Hall of Fame; chairman United Way of Am., 1998—99. Contbr. articles to profl. jours. Named Sports Industrialist of the Yr., Sports Business Daily, 2000, Sports Executive of the Yr., Sports Business Journal, 2001, Most Powerful Person in Sports, The Sporting News, 2001. Mem.: ABA (chmn. sports and entertainment industry com. antitrust sect. 1986), D.C. Bar Assn. Office: NFL Commr's Office 280 Park Ave New York NY 10017-1216*

TAGLIAFERRI, LEE GENE, investment banker; b. Mahanoy City, Pa., Aug. 14, 1931; s. Charles and Adele (Cirilli) T.; B.S., U. Pa., 1957; M.B.A., U. Chgo., 1958; m. Maryellen Stanton, Apr. 29, 1962; children— Mark, John, Maryann. Div. comptroller Campbell Soup Co., Camden, N.J., 1958-60; securities analyst Merrill, Lynch, Pierce, Fenner & Smith, Inc., N.Y.C., 1960-62; asst. v.p. U.S. Trust Co. of N.Y., 1962-71; v.p. corporate finance div. Laidlaw & Co., Inc., N.Y.C., 1972-73; pres. Everest Corp., N.Y.C., 1973—; dir. Fairfield Communities Inc., UEC, Inc., LRA, Inc., Industrialized Bldg. Systems, Inc. Past pres. West Windsor Community Assn. Trustee Schuyler Hall, Columbia, Madison Sq. Boys Club. Served with AUS, 1953-55. K.C. Clubs: University of Pa., Princeton (N.Y.C.). Home: 77 Lillie St Princeton Junction NJ 08550-1307 Office: 1 Penn Plz New York NY 10119-0002

TAGLIARINO, SALVATORE, set designer, educator; b. Buffalo, Aug. 16, 1946; s. Frank Vincent Tagliarino and Phyllis Izzo; m. Sonia Ragir; 1 child, Ulysses. B Indsl. Design, Pratt Inst., Bklyn., 1971; MFA in Set Design, NYU, 1974. Theatrical designer; faculty, design dept. NYU Sch. of the Arts; faculty NYU Tisch Sch. of the Arts. Artistic dir. Byrdcliffe Festival, Woodstock, NY; mem. bd. governors, NY chpt. NATAS. Theatrical designer (Houston Grand Opera Operas), (Nevada Opera Assn. Operas), (NY Lyric Opera Operas), (Alvin Ailey's tribute to Duke Ellington), costume design (Larry Richardson Dance Co.), theatrical designer with Rouben TerArutunian (NYC Ballet), (Joffrey Ballet), theatrical designer (several Broadway, Las Vegas, and internat. shows) including Lou Rawls, Natalie Cole, Neil Diamond, Demis Roussos (at the London Palladium), set designer (HBO specials for Alan King and Helen Reddy), (spl. for PBS, Dance in Am., CBS Cable, Outdoor Life Channel), (Fleetwood Mac and Ben Vereen), (decor for Liza Minnelli and Frank Sinatra), theatrical designer (numerous commercials/indsl. shows). With U.S. Army, Vietnam. Democrat. Home: 172 W 79th St Ste 19F New York NY 10024-6419 Office Phone: 212-580-2811. E-mail: st2@nyu.edu.

TAGLIENTE, JOSEPHINE MARLENE, artist; b. Chisholm, Minn., Nov. 23, 1939; d. Joseph and Carmela (DeLuca) T.; m. Wayne W. Brown, May 28, 1960 (div. 1972); children: Michael Anthony, Troy Tagliente, Roben Tagliente, Angela Monique, Ninon Terese, Anina Maria (dec.). Student, Mpls. Coll. Art and Design, 1957-59, Mankato State Coll., 1966, Kansas City Art Inst., 1972; MFA, U. Guanajuato, Mex., 1974. Artist-in-residence Jewish Cmty. Ctr., Wilmington, 1969; illustration chairperson, mem. faculty Ray Coll. of Design, Chgo., 1980-87; adj. faculty Paradise Valley C.C., Phoenix; spkr. in field. One-woman exhbn. Natalini Gallery, Chgo., 1986; group exhbns. include Windbell Gallery, Wilmington, Del., Newark (Del.) Gallery, Galeria San Miguel, Mex., Galeria Osman, Mex., Galeria Condor, Mex., Torres Gallery, Albuquerque, Dartmouth Gallery, Albuquerque, Edith Lampert Gallery, Santa Fe, La Luna Nueva, Santa Fe, Herberger Theatre, Phoenix Little Theatre, Artesimo Gallery, Scottsdale, Ariz., Del. Art Mus., Wilmington, Sky Harbor Airport, 1994, Westaff, UK-Ariz., Canticles: Sight and Sound, 2002, others; represented in corp. collections Collins, Miller & Hutchins, Chgo., Mt. Sinai Hosp., N.Y.C.; also pvt. and pub. permanent collections; represented by Artisimo Gallery, Scottsdale; illustrations published in books; poetry published in anthologies; inventor garden products, office implements. Vol. art educator St. Anne's Intercity, Wilmington, 1967-68, Recreation Intercity, Chgo., 1978-79; cultural advocate for homeless Cultural Labor Party, Chgo., 1980-87, cultural advocate for minority concerns, 1985-88. Recipient Fine Art award Artist's Guild of Chgo., 1977, Print Drawing award, 1978, Educator/Svcs. award Sauk Area Career Ctr., 1984. Mem. Nat. Mus. Women in Arts, The Drawing Soc., Soc. Children's Book Writers and Illustrators, Statue of Liberty-Ellis Island Found. Social Democrat. Avocations: writing, digital painting, raising turtles and studying their habitat. E-mail: joyfulsunrise@qwest.net.

TAGUE, CHARLES FRANCIS, retired engineering, construction and real estate development company executive; b. N.Y.C., Aug. 16, 1924; s. Charles and Isabelle (Carey) T.; m. Alicia Patricia Murtha, Aug. 6, 1949; children: Patrick, Charles, Thomas, Mary Alicia Haberman, James, Beth Anne Giuliano BS, Fordham U., 1952. Auditor Scovell, Wellington & Co., N.Y.C., 1951-57; comptroller Chem. Constrn. Corp., N.Y.C., 1957-75; contr. Burns and Roe, Inc., Oradell, N.J., 1975-81; fin. dir. Alfred Sanzari Enterprises, Hasbrouck Heights, N.J., 1981-84; v.p. fin. Alexander Summer Co., 1984-93; ret., 1993. Fin. advisor Cath. Cmty. at Seabrook Village. Mem. Colts Neck (N.J.) Sports Found.; active Boy scouts Am.; mem. Lacawac Sanctuary Steering Com.; pres. parish coun. Ch. of Presentation; mem. pastoral coun. St. Thomas More Cath. Ch. With USNR, 1943-46, PTO, ETO, NATOUSA. Mem. Controllers Inst., Nat. Contract Mgmt. Assn., Assn. Govt. Accts., Scranton Club. Democrat. Roman Catholic. Address: Seabrook Village 521 North Shore Tinton Falls NJ 07753

TAGUE, JOHN P, air transportation executive; married; 2 children. Dir., then v.p. Midway Airlines, 1985—91; with ATA Holdings, 1991—95; co-chmn., CEO The Pointe Group, 1995—97; pres., CEO ATA Holdings, 1993—2002; exec. v.p., customer United Airlines Corp., 2003—04, exec. v.p. mktg., sales and revenue, 2004—. Bd. mem. Pacer Internat.

TAHA, ASSAD M. surgeon; b. Nabatieh, Lebanon, Dec. 12, 1955; came to U.S. 1980; s. Muhyddin S. and Hind (Jaber) T. BS, Am. U. Beirut, 1976, MD, 1980; PhD, Med. Coll. Ohio, Toledo, 1992. Diplomate Am. Bd. Surgery, Am. Bd. Surg. Critical Care. Surgery resident Good Samaritan Hosp., Cin., 1980-82, Med. Coll. Ohio, Toledo, 1982-85, attending surgeon, 1985-94, Am. U. of Beirut, 1994—, assoc. prof. surgery and physiology, 1994—. Dir. hyperbaric medicine Med. Coll. Hosp., Toledo, 1987—94, dir. surg. intensive care, 1988—94, assoc. prof. surgery; vis. surgeon surg. critical care Brigham & Women's Hosp., Harvard Med. Sch., Boston, 2000—01; vis. assoc. prof. Harvard U., 2000—01. Mem. editl. bd. European Jour. Emergency Surgery and Intensive Care; contbr. articles to profl. jours. Recipient AMA Physician Recognition award, 1987, 1991, 1997, 2000; grantee, Ohio Lions, 1987—92, Am. U.- Beirut U. Rsch. Bd., 1993—2000. Fellow ACS, AMA, Am. Heart Assn., Am. Physiologic Soc., Am. Soc. Gastrointestinal Endoscopy, European Assn. Trauma and Emergency Surgery, Royal Coll. Surgeons Can., Soc. Critical Care Medicine, Undersea and Hyperbaric Med. Soc., Am. Soc. Laser Medicine and Surgery, Am. Coll. Nutrition, Internat. Coll. Surgeons, Assn. Acad. Surgery, Shock Soc., European Soc. Intensive Care Medicine, World Assn. Disaster and Emergency Medicine, Soc. Am. GI Endoscopic Surgeons, World Med. Assn., Laser Inst. Am., Royal Soc. Medicine, Am. U. Beirut Alumni Assn., Am. Trauma Soc., Crit. Care Club, Disaster Med. Asst. Team; mem. AMA, AAUP. Avocations: chess, bridge. Office: Am U Beirut 3 Dag Hammarskjold Plz 8th Fl New York NY 10017-2303 Fax: 212-583-7650, 011-961-1363291. E-mail: at03@aub.edu.lb.

TAHERI, ABBAS ALI, economist, educator; s. Mahmood Taheri and Azam Sadat Shabari; m. Flora Ravanfar; children: Sharlin M, Shyli. BS, Iranian Nat. U., Tehran, 1972—77; MBA, Roosevelt U., Chgo., 1980; PhD, U. Ill., 1980—87. Vis. rsch. scholar U. Wis., Madison, 1996—, vis. prof. Oshkosh, 2000—, prof. Fox Valley, 1989—; instr. U. Ill., Chgo., 1983—85, Haper Rainy Coll., Paletine, Ill., 1985—89, Roosevelt U., Ill., 1983—89. Author (referee/book reviewer): (articles/book) The Energy Journal (UN TOKTEN Award, 1996). Mem. U. Found., Menasha, Wis., 1993—2003. Recipient Tchg. Excellence Award, Appleton Rotary Cutting Edge Award, 1999; grantee Rsch. Collaboration Grant, U. of Wis.-Madison 1996, 1998, 2001. Mem.: Internat. Assn. for Energy Econ., Western Econ. Assn. (assoc.), Am. Econ. Assn. (assoc.), Econometric Soc. (assoc.; mem. 1995—2003). Achievements include research in Environmental Regulation Impact on Productivity. Office: Univ of Wis at Fox Valley 1478 Midwar Rd Menasha WI 54952 Home: 3525 S Bob-o-Link Ln Appleton WI 54915 Personal E-mail: ataheri@uwc.edu. E-mail: ataheri@uwc.edu.

TAHERI, MARSHALL M. lawyer, educator; b. Iran, Dec. 29, 1934; came to U.S., 1963; children: Tara, Sara, Dara Jon. BBA, U. Houston, 1968; JD, So. Tex. Coll. Law, 1973; PhD in Law, Ministry Scis. and Higher Edn., Iran, 1974. Bar: Tex. 1974, N.Y. 1999, U.S. Supreme Ct. 1981, D.C. 1982, U.S. Ct. Internat. Trade 1989, U.S. Dist. Ct. (so. dist.) 1975, U.S. Ct. Appeals (5th cir.) 1975, U.S. Ct. Appeals (11th cir.) 1981, U.S. Ct. Appeals (9th cir.) 1986, U.S. Ct. Appeals (fed. cir.) 1991. Pvt. practice, Houston, 1974—. Adj. prof. internat. civil litig. South Tex. Coll. Law, Houston, 1980—; participant internat. bus. litig. and arbitration conf., N.Y.C., 2002. Fellow Houston Bar Found.; mem. ABA, ATLA, Tex. Bar Assn., State Bar Tex. (coll., vice chmn. com. on laws relating to immigration and nationality), Houston Bar Assn., Tex. Trial Lawyers Assn., Houston C. of C. (internat. bus. com., ad hoc mem. immigration task force 1982, 87), World Trade Assn., Inst. Internat. Edn., Internat. Lawyers Assn., South Tex. Coll. Law Alumni Assn. (past pres.), Iran-Am. C. of C. (founder), Forum Club. Office: PO Box 460165 Houston TX 77056-8165 Office Phone: 713-871-0000. E-mail: taheri@marshalltaheri.com.

TAHIR, MARY ELIZABETH (LIZ TAHIR), marketing professional, consultant, speaker, writer; b. Greenwood, Miss., Dec. 14, 1933; d. Mahmoud Ibrahim and Mary Constance Tahir. Student, U. Miss., 1951-53. Cert. Profl. Cons., Acad, Profl. Cons. and Advisors. Mgmt. trainee Neiman-Marcus Co., Dallas, 1954-56; asst. buyer D.H. Holmes Co. Ltd., New Orleans, 1956-58, buyer, 1958-65, assoc. divisional mdse. mgr., 1965-67, divisional v.p., 1969-79, corp. v.p., gen. mdse. mgr., 1979-89; pres. Liz Tahir & Assocs., New Orleans, 1990—. Author: Mexico's Cosmetic and Fragrance Market: Past, Present and Future Opportunities, 1991, The Changing World of Mexican Retail Opportunities, 1991, Mexico: Window of Opportunity, 1991, Art of Negotiating, 1993, Negotiating More Profitable with Your Suppliers, Customers and Employees, 1994, Sizzling Customer Service, 1998. Bd. dirs. Vieux Carre Property Owners Assn., New Orleans, 1990, 2002, YWCA, 1996-2002. Recipient Role Model award YWCA, 1990, Woman Bus. Owner of the Yr. award, 1996. Mem. Women's Profl. Coun. (pres. 1998, chmn. New Choices 1989), Fashion Group Internat. (Alpha award 1987-88, Lifetime Achievement award 1993), Nat. Spkrs. Assn., Am. Mktg. Assn. (bd. dirs. 1996—, pres. 1997), Am. Assn. Profl. Cons., Am. Mgmt. Assn., Fgn. Rels. Assn. (bd. dirs. 1992—, pres. bd. dirs. 1994-96), Nat. Retail Fedn. Avocations: art collecting, textiles collecting. Home: 817 Esplanade Ave New Orleans LA 70116-1940 Office: Liz Tahir & Assocs 201 Saint Charles Ave Ste 2500 New Orleans LA 70170-2500 Office Phone: 504-569-1670. Personal E-mail: liz@liztahir.com.

TAI, CHONG-SOO STEPHEN, political scientist, educator; b. Seoul, Oct. 15, 1940; came to U.S., 1969, naturalized, 1983; s. Hyung-Kyoon and Ock-Hee (Park) T.; m. Susan Gillja Kang, Aug. 28, 1965; children: Audrey, Elizabeth, Michael. BA, Yonsei U., Seoul, 1963; MA, Ill. State U., 1972, Northwestern U., 1972, PhD, 1974. Lectr. Northwestern U., Evanston, Ill., 1974-75; asst. prof. U. Ark., Pine Bluff, 1976-80, assoc. prof. polit. sci., 1980-86, prof. polit. sci., 1986—, dir. polit. sci. program, 1980—. Fulbright program adviser, 1986—; great decisions coordinator Fgn. Policy Assn., Pine Bluff, 1977-84; cons. S.E. Ark. Planning Commn., Pine Bluff, 1979-80; active Southwestern Internat. Studies Consortium, Mex., 1986; pres. Internat. Faculty Club, U. Ark., Pine Bluff, 1986-91; vis. prof. polit. sci., Kyung Hee U., Korea, 1992-93; faculty adviser Pine Bluff chpt. Nat. Polit. Sci. Hon. Soc. U. Ark., 2000—. Contbr. articles to profl. jours. Bd. dirs. Korean Cmty. Assn. Little Rock, 1996—. Served with Korean AF, 1963-67. Grantee KOTN radio sta., 1978, Ark. Endowment for Humanities, 1979-80, NEH, 1980; Fulbright-Hays scholar, China, 1985. Fellow Internat. Ctr. for Asian Studies; mem. Am. Polit. Sci. Assn., Ark. Polit. Sci. Assn., Assn. for Asian Studies, Assn. Korean Polit. Studies N.Am. Roman Catholic. Avocations: golf, swimming, collecting jazz albums, samurai films, and chinese and japanese paintings and calligraphy. Home: 11324 Hickory Hill Rd Little Rock AR 72211-4368 Office: U Ark Pine Bluff 1200 University Dr Pine Bluff AR 71601-2799 Office Phone: 870-575-8189. E-mail: tai_c@vx4500.uapb.edu.

TAI, ELIZABETH SHI-JUE LEE, library director; b. Si-Ann, China, Aug. 12, 1942; came to the U.S., 1965; d. Jun-Yee Lee and Fang-Yee Liu; m. Hsiang Tai, Dec. 29, 1969; children: Alan C., Victoria C., Brian C. BA in English Lang. and Lit., Nat. Cheng Kung U., Taiwan, 1965; M in Libr. and Info. Sci., Tex. Woman's U., 1967. Sr. libr. Queens (N.Y.) Borough Pub. Libr., 1967-73; asst. regional libr. Cin. Pub. Libr., Libr. for Blind and Physically Handicapped, 1973-75; libr. Ga. State Libr., Atlanta, 1975-78; dir. Poquoson (Va.) Pub. Libr., 1979—. Vol. Va. chpt. ARC-York County, 1980—; vice-chair Peninsula Ret. Sr. Vol. Program Coun., Newport News, Va., 1994—99, chair, 2000; mem. York County (Va.) Sch. Sys. Extend Program Coun., 1997; mem. Va. social svcs. bd. York County/City of Poquoson, 2002—; bd. dirs. Peninsula Ret. Sr. Vol. Program Coun., Newport News, Va., 2001—. Named City Employee of Yr., City of Poquoson, Va., 1989; recipient Letter of Commendation, Va. Gov. James Gilmore III, 2001, Unsung Hero/Heroine award Nat. Cheng Kung U. N.Am. Alumni and Found., 2003. Mem. ALA, Va. Libr. Assn., Va. Pub. Libr. Dirs. Assn. (region 3 rep. 2003—, Outstanding Pub. Rels. award 1998, 2001, 02, 04, Outstanding Facility award 1998, Outstanding Young Adult Program award 1999, Outstanding Children's Program award 1999, Outstanding Libr. Staff award 2003, Outstanding Va. Pub. Libr. Dir. award 2004), Tidewater Area Libr. Dirs. Coun., Peninsula Chinese Am. Assn. (bd. mem., 2004—), Kiwanis Club of Tabb (charter mem.). Avocations: reading, gardening, swimming, tennis. Home: 129 Loblolly Dr Yorktown VA 23692-4254 Office: 500 City Hall Ave Poquoson VA 23662-1996 Office Phone: 757-868-3066. Business E-Mail: etai@ci.poquoson.va.us.

TAI, KWOK-KEUNG, biologist, researcher; b. Hong Kong, China, May 8, 1962; s. Hon-Ying Tai and Yee-Nui Chu. BSc(hon.), U. Leeds, 1988; PhD, U. Hong Kong, 1993. Assoc. dir. The Parkinson's and Movement Disorder Inst., Long Beach, Calif., 2001—; postgrad. rsch. biologist U. of Calif., San Diego, La Jolla, Calif., 1998—2001; postdoctoral fellow Yale U. Sch. of Medicine, New Haven, 1993—97. Asst. clin. prof. U. Calif., 2002—. Contbr. articles to profl. jours.; exec. guest editor Current Pharm.Design, 2003—. Recipient Oral Presentation Winner, Soc. for the Study of Endocrinology, Metabolism, and Reproduction, 1992; fellow Sir Edward Youde Meml. Fellowship, Sir Edward Youde Coun., 1992—93; scholar Wong Ching Yee Med. Scholarships, Mary Sun Med. Scholarship, U. of Hong Kong, 1992—93. Mem.: Soc. for Neuroscience. Achievements include patents for Novel neuroprotectant with unique chemical structure. Office: Parkinson's and Movement Disorder Inst 2625 Pasadena Ave Long Beach CA 90806 E-mail: kktai@yahoo.com.

TAIMUTY, SAMUEL ISAAC, physicist; b. West Newton, Pa., Dec. 20, 1917; s. Elias and Samia (Hawatt) Taimuty; m. Betty Jo Travis, Sept. 12, 1953 (dec.); children: Matthew, Martha; m. Rosalie Richards, Apr. 3, 1976; stepchildren: Charles Scott Holman, Martha Ruth Holman, Elizabeth Ann Holman. BS, Carnegie Inst. Tech., 1940; PhD, U. So. Calif., 1951. Physicist U.S. Naval Shipyard, Phila. and Long Beach, Calif., 1942—46; rsch. asst. U. So. Calif., 1947—51; sr. physicist U.S. Naval. Radiol. Def. Lab., 1950—52, SRI Internat., Menlo Park, Calif., 1952—72; sr. staff engr. Lockheed Missiles & Space Co., Sunnyvale, Calif., 1972—89; cons. Sci. Applications Internat. Corp., 1990—. Cons. physicist, 1971—. Contbr. articles to sci. publs.; patentee in field. Mem.: Am. Phys. Soc., Sigma Xi. Episcopalian. Home: 3346 Kenneth Dr Palo Alto CA 94303-4217 E-mail: staimuty@sigmaxi.org.

TAINATONGA, ROSIE R. former director of education; b. Guam; BS in Bus. Adminstrn., U. Guam. Dir. of edn. Coun. of Chief State Sch. Officers, Washington, 1999—2003.

TAIRA, DARRYL M. lawyer; b. L.A., July 1, 1959; s. Lorrin Toshiro and Shirley (Sakata) T.; m. Stephanie Koto Kometani, Aug. 18, 1984; children: Sean Katsumi, Lindsay Kaleo'onalani, Jessica Lynn Na'aualii. BS, U. So. Calif., 1981, MBT, JD, U. So. Calif., 1984. Bar: Hawaii 1985, U.S. Dist. Ct. Hawaii 1985, U.S. Tax Ct. 1985, D.C. 1989. Assoc. Case & Lynch, Honolulu, 1984-87; shareholder, dir. Tam, O'Connor, Henderson, Taira & Yamauchi, Honolulu, 1987—2000; of counsel Pacific Law Group, 2000—. Speaker Law Seminars, Inc., Honolulu, 1988—, Nat. Bus. Inst., Sterling Edn. Sys. Named U. So. Calif. Alumni Merit scholar, 1977. Mem. ABA (sect. taxation, real property, probate, trust law and bus.), Hawaii Bar Assn. (sect. taxation, probate and estate planning), Hawaii Assn. Pub. Accts., Beta Gamma Sigma, Alpha Kappa Psi, Beta Alpha Psi, Phi Alpha Delta. Avocations: golf, running. Office: The Pacific Law Group 700 Bishop St Ste 2000 Honolulu HI 96813 Office Phone: 808-523-2999. E-mail: trojanhawaii@yahoo.com.

TAISHOFF, LAWRENCE BRUCE, publishing company executive; b. Washington, Aug. 30, 1933; s. Sol Joseph and Betty (Tash) T.; m. Nancy Lee Stuckey, Sept. 17, 1962 (div. 1979); children: Robert Paul, Randall Lawrence, Jonathan Bradford. AB, Duke U., 1955. Asst. dir. Sta. WTOP-TV, Washington, 1955-56; with Broadcasting Publs., Inc., Washington, 1958—91, pres., pub., 1971-91, chmn., 1991—95, also dir.; adviser Cahners Consumer/Entertainment Pub. divsn. Cahners Pub. Co., Washington, 1991—95; v.p. Jolar Corp., Washington, 1952-72, dir., 1958-72. Gen. ptnr. Jolar Assocs., Washington, 1972—; chmn. bd., pres. Graphictype, Inc., 1976-86, also dir.; chmn., pres. Solar Corp., 1982-86; chmn. Broadcasting-Taishoff Found., 1982-2001; chmn., CEO Chuckie Broadcasting, Ardmore, Okla., 1993—, Trustco, Washington, 1988—; CEO Solar Investments, Naples, Fla., 1996—. Co-author radio and TV segment Britannica Book of the Yr., 1983—. Trustee Washington Journalism Ctr., 1982-93, Nat. Press Found., 1993—, mem. adv. bd., 1993—; bd. dirs. Nat. Press Found., 1982—, mem. exec. com., 1990-94; mem. journalism and comms. exec. com. Capital Campaign for Arts and Scis., Duke U., 1984—, mem. athletic adv. bd., 1999—; bd. advisors Am. Journalism Ctr., Budapest, 1991-95; mem. White House Press Corps, 1983—; mem. Met. Washington Bd. Trade, 1970—; team capt. pubs. divsn. United Givers Fund drive, 1965; mem. admissiosn adv. com. Duke Alumni Assn,. 1968-70; mem. U.S. Senate and Ho. of Reps. Periodical Press Gallery, 1958-95; trustee Broadcast Pioneers Ednl. Fund Inc., 1985; judge VFW Voice of Democracy contest, 1978—; mem. bd. judges Peabody awards, 1985-91; mem. Am. U. Sch. Comms. Disting. Adv. Commn., 1985—; mem. Founders Soc. Duke U., 1985—, Duke Athletic Adv. Bd., The Mus. of TV and Radio Roundtable, 1988-89; bd. dirs. Ardissone, Naples, Fla., 1994-99; chmn., trustee Taishoff Family Found. With AUS, 1956-58. Mem. IEEE (sr.), Internat. Radio & TV Soc., Broadcast Pioneers (life, bd. dirs., exec. com. Broadcast Pioneers Libr.), Am. Sportscasters Assn. (exec. com. 1990—), White House Corrs. Assn., Nat. Press Club, Woodmont Country Club (Rockville, Md.), Cosmos Club (Washington), Sigma Delta Chi, Zeta Beta Tau. Jewish. Office Phone: 239-261-2660. E-mail: solarlc@earthlink.net.

TAIT, C(OLUMBUS) DOWNING, JR., physician, medical educator; b. Valdosta, Ga., Sept. 3, 1923; s. C. Downing Sr. and Mary Lucretia (Jacobs) T.; m. Nancy Reep, Aug. 25, 1956; children: Carl, Jennifer. BA in Philosophy, U. Va., 1943, MD, 1947; cert. in psychoanalytic medicine, Columbia U., 1957. Diplomate Am. Bd. Psychiatry and Neurology; cert. in adult psychoanalysis. Intern Bellevue Hosp., N.Y.C., 1947-48; resident in psychiatry Compton (Calif.) Sanitarium, 1948-49, N.Y. State Hosp., Orangeburg, 1950-51; psychoanalytic trainee Columbia U., N.Y.C., 1950-51, 53-57; pvt. practice N.Y.C., 1953-64; assoc. prof. Emory U. Sch. of Medicine, Atlanta, 1964-67, prof. psychiatry, 1967-81; pvt. practice N.Y.C., 1953-64, Atlanta, 1977—. Geographical tng. and supervising psychoanalyst Emory Columbia U. Psychoanalytic Tng., Atlanta, 1966-78; dir. rsch. Ga. Mental Health Inst. Emory U. and State, Atlanta, 1965-71. Co-author: Delinquents, Their Families, and the Community, 1962; contbr. articles to profl. jours. Cons. to juvenile ct. judges Atlanta, 1966-71; Lt. USNR, 1951-53. Rsch. fellowship Atomic Energy Commn., Duke U., 1949, Yale U., 1950. Fellow Ga. Psychiat. Assn., Am. Psychiat. Assn.; mem. AMA, Atlanta Med. Assn., Ga. Med. Assn., Internat. Psychoanalytic Assn., Am. Psychoanalytic Assn., Atlanta Psychoanalytic Assn. (pres. 1979-81). Avocations: travel, music. Home and Office: 3895 Chaucer Wood NE Atlanta GA 30319-1687

TAIT, JOHN REID, lawyer; b. Toledo, Apr. 7, 1946; s. Paul Reid and Lucy Richardson (Rudderow) T.; m. Christina Ruth Bjornstad, Mar. 12, 1972; children: Gretchen, Mary. BA, Columbia U., 1968; JD, Vanderbilt U., 1974. Bar: Idaho 1974, U.S. Dist. Ct. Idaho 1974, U.S. Ct. Appeals (9th cir.) U.S. Supreme Ct., Nez Perce Tribal Ct. Assoc. Keeton & Tait, Lewiston, Idaho, 1974-76, ptnr., 1976-86, 89—, Keeton, Tait & Petrie, Lewiston, 1986-88. Chmn. bd. No. Rockies Action Group, Helena, Mont., 1985-86, bd. dirs., 1981-88; active Lewiston Hist. Preservation Commn., 1975-94, chmn., 1988-94; bd. dirs. Idaho Legal Aid Svcs., Boise, 1975-99, Idaho Housing Agy., Boise, 1984-91, St. Joseph Regional Med. Ctr. Found., Inc., 1989-94, Lewiston Ind. Found. for Edn., Inc., 1996—; Dem. precinct committeeman, 1976-86, state committeeman, 1977-94, 2000—; del. Dem. Nat. Conv., 1980, 84; regional coord. Idaho State Dem. Party, 1996-99; treas. Larry LaRocco for Congress, 1990, 92. With U.S. Army, 1968-71. Recipient Pro Bono Svc. award Idaho State Bar, 1988, Cmty. Recognition award Lewiston Intergovtl. Coun., 1992, Spl. Recognition award Idaho Legal Aid Svcs., 1993. Mem. ABA, ATLA, Idaho Trial Lawyers Assn. (regional dir. 1976-77, 86-88, 97-03), Idaho State Bar (bd. dirs. worker's compensation sect. 2002—, chmn. 2004—), Clearwater Bar Assn. (sec. 1974-76, pres. 1984-86), Consumer Attys. Calif., Workplace Injury Litigation Group (bd. dirs. 2002-). Office: Keeton & Tait PO Drawer E 312 Miller St Lewiston ID 83501-1944 Office Phone: 208-743-6231. Office Fax: 208-746-0962. Business E-Mail: lewlawus@lewiston.com.

TAIT, ROBERT E. lawyer; b. Lima, Ohio, Sept. 3, 1946; s. Robert and Helen (Smith) T.; m. Donna G. Dome, June 22, 1968; children: Heather, Jennifer, Robert. BA, Kenyon Coll., 1968; JD, U. Mich., 1973. Bar: Ohio 1973, U.S. Dist. Ct. (so. dist.) Ohio. 1976, U.S. Dist. Ct. (no. dist.) Ohio 1976, U.S. Dist. Ct. Md. 1980, U.S. Ct. Appeals (6th cir.) 1981, U.S. Supreme Ct. 1982. Ptnr. Vorys, Sater, Seymour & Pease, LLP, Columbus, Ohio, 1973—. Staff counsel Govs. Select Com. on Prevention Indsl. Accidents, Columbus, 1977-78. Served with U.S. Army, 1969-70. Fellow Columbus Bar Found.; mem. ABA (litigation sect., products liability com.), Ohio Bar Assn. (worker's compensation com.), Columbus Bar Assn. (workers compensation and professionalism coms.), Def. Rsch. Inst. (workers compensation com.), Am. Bd. Trial Advocates, Assn. Def. Trial Attys. (exec. com. 1991-94, treas., 2002-), Fedn. Def. and Corp. Counsel (toxic torts com). Home: 2045 Wickford Rd Columbus OH 43221-4223 Office: Vorys Sater Seymour & Pease PO Box 1008 52 E Gay St Columbus OH 43215-3161 Office Phone: 614-464-6341. Business E-Mail: retait@vssp.com.

TAITT, EARL PAUL, psychiatrist, army officer; b. L.A., Nov. 6, 1956; s. Earl and Mary (Freitas) T.; m. Puruca Estepa, May 11, 1985; children: Anamaria, Earl. AA, East L.A. Coll., 1976; BS, U. Calif., Irvine, 1978; MD, Northwestern U., Chgo., 1984. Commd. capt. U.S. Army, 1984, advanced through grades to maj., 1991; intern in psychiatry Tripler Army Med. Ctr., Honolulu, 1984-85; resident in psychiatry Eisenhower Army Med. Ctr., Ft. Gordon, Ga., 1985-88; staff psychiatrist Community Mental Health Ctr., Ft. Gordon, Ga., 1988; div. psychiatrist, chief mental health 10th Mountain Div., Ft. Drum, N.Y., 1988-90; staff psychiatrist Community Mental Health Ctr., Ft. Meade, Md., 1990—; chief resident in psychiatry U.S. Army Hosp., Ft. Gordon, Ga., 1988. Cons. Army Drug and Alcohol Program, Ft. Drum, 1988-90, Installation Detention Facility, Ft. Meade, 1990—. Mem. San Gabriel (Calif.) Mission Parish Coun., 1975-76; pres. Medicai Soc., L.A., 1976. Mem. Assn. U.S. Army, Order of Green Key. Republican. Roman Catholic. Home: 14403 Altamaha Ct Orlando FL 32837-5425 Office Phone: 407-931-3001.

TAKABE, KAZUAKI, gastroenterology surgeon, research scientist; b. Nishinomiya City, Hyougo, Japan, Aug. 12, 1966; s. Tokuji and Ayako T. MD, Niigata U., 1992; PhD, Yokohama City U., 1999. Rsch. trainee dept. legal medicine Niigata (Japan) U. Sch. of Medicine, 1992-93; surg. resident Niigata U. Hosp., 1993-94, Akita (Japan) Red Cross Hosp., 1994-95; surg. fellow Yokohama (Japan) U. Hosp., 1995-97; rsch. assoc. The Salk Inst., PBL, La Jolla, Calif., 1997—. Prof., chmn. gene diagnosis and therapy Internet Med. Coll., 2000—; com. mem. Soc. of Rsch. Fellows The Salk Inst., 1999—.

Contbr. articles to profl. jours. Yoshida scholarship found. fellowship, 1997-2000. Mem. The Endocrine Soc., Internat. Liver Transplantation Soc., Internat. Assn. of Surgeons and Gastroenterologists, Japan Surg. Soc., Japanese Soc. of Gastroenterology, Japan Hepatology Soc. Office: The Salk Inst PBL 10010 N Torrey Pines Rd La Jolla CA 92037 Fax: 858-552-1546; Office Fax: 858-657-0925. E-mail: ktakabe@aim.salk.edu

TAKACS, LASZLO, physicist, educator; PhD, Loránd Eötvös U., Budapest, 1969—78. Rsch. assoc. Ctrl. Rsch. Inst. for Physics, Budapest, 1975—84; post-doctoral fellow Northeastern U., 1984—86; vis. asst. prof. Clark U., 1987—89; assoc. prof. U. of Md., Balt., 1989—. Author: (review article) Self-sustaining reactions induced by ball milling. Grantee Combustion reactions induced by ball milling, Nat. Sci. Foundations, 1998-2002. Mem.: The Minerals, Metals & Materials Soc., Materials Rsch. Soc., Am. Phys. Soc. Achievements include research in Magnetic nanocomposites by mechanical alloying; Mechanochemistry of highly exothermic reactions. Office: U Md Balt County 1000 Hilltop Cir Baltimore MD 21250 Business E-Mail: takacs@umbc.edu.

TAKACS, MICHAEL JOSEPH, secondary school educator; b. N.Y.C., July 28, 1940; s. Michael and Elizabeth Agnes (Scharschmidt) T. AB in Sociology, Fordham U., 1964; MA in Sociology, St. John's U., 1968. Tchr. Bklyn. Prep. Sch., 1964-67, Turtle Hook Sch., Uniondale, N.Y., 1968-73, 74-95, Nairobi U., 1971, Colegio San Ignacio, Rio Piedras, P.R., 1973-74. Vis. scholar Robert Black Coll., Hong Kong U., 1975, Ramkamhang U., Bangkok, 1975. Vol., Pub. Benefits Resource Ctr., cmty. outreach program Our Holy Redeemer Ch., Freeport, N.Y., L.I. Assn. for AIDS Care, L.I. People with AIDS Coalition, Advocacy Counseling Entitlements Svcs. of Ret. and Sr. Vol. Program, Safe Horizon 9/11 Disaster Assistance Program, advisor Nat. Jr. Honor Soc.; mem. Sr. Action in Gay Environment, L.I. bears. Mem. Nat. Coun. for Social Studies, Md. States Coun. for Social Studies, L.I. Coun. for Social Studies, N.Y. State Coun. for Social Studies, West Fla. Growlers. Episcopalian. Home: 13915 83rd Ave Briarwood NY 11435-1561

TAKAHASHI, MASATO, pediatric cardiologist, educator; b. Tokyo, Feb. 10, 1933; came to U.S., 1952; s. Noboru and Fujiko (Tarumoto) T.; m. Marcia Parnell, Jan. 16, 1966; children: Rumi Anne, Yuki Lynn. AB, Wabash U., 1956; MD, Ind. U., 1960. Attending physician Children's Hosp., L.A., 1968—; prof. pediatrics U. So. Calif., L.A., 1986—. Chmn. 4th Internat. Kawasaki Disease Symposium, 1991. Vol. Habitat for Humanity, San Fernando Valley, Calif., 1993-94, Am. Heart Assn. L.A., 1982-85, com. mem. 1991-93 (Disting. Achievement award 1983). Mem. Am. Acad. Pediatrics, Am. Coll. Cardiology, Methodist. Avocations: long distance running, wood working. Office: Keck Sch Medicine 4650 Sunset Blvd MS #71 Los Angeles CA 90027 Office Phone: 213-669-4634. Business E-Mail: mtakahashi@chla.usc.edu.

TAKAKURA, TAMIO, bank official; BS, Kobe U., Japan; MBA, U. Ill. Various mgmt. positions Sanwa Bank Calif., Golden State Sanwa Bank, Bus. Credit Corp, San Francisco/L.A./Chgo., 1968-88; sr. mgr. Sanwa Bank, Ltd. Internat. Divsn., Japan, 1988-91; sr. exec. v.p., CEO Sanwa Bank Calif., 1991-96, pres., CEO, 1996—. Office: Sanwa Bank Calif 601 S Figueroa St Los Angeles CA 90017

TAKAMURA, JEANETTE CHIYOKO, dean; b. Honolulu, Aug. 1, 1947; d. Jiro and Jane Chiseko (Ishida) Chikamoto; m. Carl Takeshi Takamura, May 17, 1974; 1 child, Mari Leigh. BA, U. Hawaii, 1969, MSW, 1972; PhD, Brandeis U., 1985. Program dir. Moiliili Community Ctr., Honolulu, 1972-74; instr. sch. medicine and social work U. Hawaii, Honolulu, 1975-78, asst. prof., 1982-86; dir. exec. office on aging Office of Gov., Honolulu, 1987-94; dep. dir. State Dept. of Health, Honolulu, 1995-97; asst. sec. for aging U.S. Dept. HHS, Washington, 1997—2002; endowed chair in applied gerontology and pub. svc. Calif. State U., L.A., 2001—02; dean, Sch. Social Work Columbia U., N.Y.C., 2002—. Ptnr. Browne/Takamura, Honolulu, 1985-86. Contbr. articles to profl. jours. and chpts. to books; editorial bd.: Aging Today, 1991—. Adv. com. long term care Milbank Meml. Fund; adv. com. on aging issues World Econ. Forum. Grantee NIMH, 1982-84, U.S. Dept. HHS, 1985, 86, 89-90, 91. Mem. Nat. Assn. State Units on Aging (2d v.p. 1991-92, bd. officer), Am. Soc. on Aging (program planning com. 1992-93, exec. com. 1996-, nat. adv. bd. White House Conf. on Aging, 1995), Gerontology Soc. Am., Futurist Soc. Congregationalist. Avocations: travel, reading, walking. Office: Columbia U Sch Social Work 1255 Amsterdam Rm 614 New York NY 10027 Personal E-mail: jctakamura@aol.com.

TAKANISHI, RUBY N. foundation administrator, researcher; d. Kazuo and Misae Takanishi; m. Louis L. Knowles, Aug. 23, 1969; 1 child. AB in Psychology with honors, Stanford U., 1968; AM, U. Mich., 1969; postgrad., U. Chgo., 1969-70; PhD, Stanford U., 1973; postgrad., Harvard U., 1978-79. Teaching asst. Bing Nursery Sch. Stanford U., 1968, teaching asst. Sch. Edn., 1972, 73; asst. prof. dept. edn. Grad. Sch. Edn. UCLA, 1973-80, acting head early childhood devel. specialization, 1974, faculty Bush Tng. Program in Child Devel. and Social Policy, 1978-80, assoc. prof., 1980-86; exec. dir. Carnegie Coun on Adolescent Devel Carnegie Corp., N.Y., 1986—. Vis. asst. prof. dept. psychology Yale U., 1980; adj. assoc. prof. Tchrs. Coll., Columbia U., 1981-82; exec. dir. Fedn. Behavioral, Psychol. and Cognitive Scis., Washington, 1982; co-investigator Asian-Am. Edn. Project, 1973-76; bd. dirs. Grantmakers for Children, Coun. Founds.; rsch. assoc. Stanford Ctr. for Rsch. and Devel. in Teaching, Stanford U., 1973; adv. bd. Ms. Found. for Women, 1992, divsn. biobehavioral scis. and mental disorders Inst. Medicine, 1992; U.S. rep. UNESCO Mexico Conf., 1972; Harvard-Henry A Murray Ctr., Cambrige, Mass., 1997, Agy. Health Care Rsch. and Quality/U.S. Dept. Health and Human Svcs., Washington, 1997—; cons. to numerous insts. Assoc. editor: Am. Psychologist; consulting editor: Rehab. Psychology, Young Children; mem. editorial bd. Early Childhood Rsch. Quar.; mem. bd. reviewing editors: Ednl. Researcher; reviewer Am. Ednl. Rsch. Journ., Child Devel., Health Psychology, Psychology of Women Quar., Rev. Ednl. Rsch.; contbr. articles to profl. jours., chpts. to books; co-author: Preparing Adolescents for the 21st Century, 1997. Bd. trustees St. Augustine-by-the-Sea Sch., Santa Monica, Calif., 1976-77; mem. child care com. Calif. LWV, 1975-77; legis. asst. Office of Senator Daniel K. Inouye, Washington, 1980-81. Named one of Outstanding Young Women of Am., 1978. Mem. AAAS, APA (fellow, dir. office sci. affairs 1984-86, adminstrv. officer for children, youth and family policy office of nat. policy studies 1982-83, pub. interest, ethnic minority), APHA, Am. Ednl. Rsch. Assn. (program chair learning and devel. 1978, program chair spl. interest group in early edn. 1980), Nat. Assn. Edn. Young Children (chair com. orgnl. history and archives 1976-78), Soc. Rsch. in Child Devel. (program com. 1985-89, governing coun. 1989-95), Soc. Rsch. in Adolescence, Phi Beta Kappa. Avocation: volunteering for community service.

TAKANISHI, JR. DANNY M. medical educator, department chairman; MD, U. of Hawaii, John A. Burns Sch. of Medicine, 1983—87; BS, U. of Hawaii, 1977—81; Cert. of Completion (Gen. Surgery Residency), U. of Hawaii Surg. Residency Program, 1987—92, Cert. of Completion (Surg. Critical Care Fellowship), 1992—93; Cert. of Completion (Surg. Oncology Fellowship), The U. of Chgo., 1993—96. Clin. Lab. Scientist Nat. Certification Agy. for Med. Lab. Pers., 1982, Medical Technologist Am. Soc. of Clin. Pathologists, 1982, diplomate The Nat. Bd. of Med. Examiners, 1988, The Am. Bd. of Surgery, 1993, Qualification in Surg. Critical Care The Am. Bd. of Surgery, 1993, MD Hawaii Bd. of Med. Examiners, 2001. Instr. of surgery The U. of Chgo., 1996—98, asst. prof. of surgery, 1998—2001; assoc. prof. and chmn. of surgery U. of Hawaii, 2001—. Dir., surg. ICU Louis A. Weiss Meml. Hosp./The U. of Chgo., 1998—2000; dir., the u. of chgo. breast ctr. The U. of Chgo., 2000—01, dir., breast surg. oncology program, 2000—01, cancer rsch. ctr. mem./investigator, 2000—01, assoc. program dir., surg. residency tng. program, 2000—01; dir., surg. residency tng. program U. of Hawaii, 2001—; dir., surg. clin. rsch. The Queen's Med. Ctr., Honolulu, 2001—; bd. of directors U. Clin. Ednl. and Rsch. Associates, Honolulu, 2001—. Sect. editor (jour.) Jour. of Intensive Care Medicine; author: (book chapters) Operative Strategies in Inflammatory Bowel Disease, Mgmt. of Benign and Malignant Small Bowel Tumors, Chassin's Operative Strategy in Gen. Surgery; invited discussant (rsch. presentation) Differential Expression of Vascular Endothelial Growth Factor Isoforms at Different Stages of Melanoma Progression; author: (jour. articles) Surgery, Critical Care Medicine, Archives of Surgery, Jour. of the Am. Coll. of Surgeons, Molecular Diagnostics, Archives of Surgery, Critical Care Medicine, (jour. invited commentary) Oncology. Expert external adv. panel for 2 for life women's health outreach initiative CBS 2 TV, Chgo., 2000—01; unit bd. mem. and state del. Am. Cancer Soc., Chgo., 2000—01; cancer rsch. advocacy bd. Cancer Rsch. Ctr. of Hawaii, Honolulu, 2002; 2003 breast cancer symposium planning com. Straub Found., Honolulu, 2002—03; 2003 sci. symposium moderator and planning com. Hawaii Med. Assn., Honolulu, 2003—03. Recipient Alpha Omega Alpha Nat. Med. Honor Soc., Alpha Omega Alpha, 1986, Merit Award for Outstanding Rsch., Am. Soc. of Clin. Oncology, 1995, Nat. Collegiate Honor Soc., Alpha Lambda Delta, 1978, Unit Leadership Citation, Am. Cancer Soc., Ill. Divsn., 2001, Nat. Collegiate Honor Soc., Phi Eta Sigma, 1978, Outstanding Musical Performance, Morning Music Club of Hawaii, 1978, Merit Citation for Outstanding Music Performance, U. of Hawaii Dept. of Music, 1978, Nat. Collegiate Honor Soc., Phi Kappa Phi, 1980, Forrest J. Pinkerton Award for Outstanding Med. Tech. Intern, Blood Bank of Hawaii, 1982; scholar E. Palmer Payne Meml. Scholarship for Outstanding Achievement, Achievement Rewards for Coll. Scientists (ARCS, Inc.), 1986 Fellow: ACS (exec. com., hawaii chpt. and com. on applicants 2003); mem.: Hawaii Soc. of Clin. Oncology, Assn. for Program Directors in Surgery, Soc. of Surg. Chairmen, Assn. for Surg. Edn., The Am. Soc. of Breast Surgeons, Am. Soc. of Clin. Oncology, Soc. of Critical Care Medicine, Soc. of Surg. Oncology, Soc. of U. Surgeons, Pan Pacific Surg. Assn. (bd. of directors 2002). Achievements include research in Determination and identification of Surrogate markers of prognosis in stomach and colon cancers. Avocations: travel, cooking, classical music and opera, swimming. Office: U of Hawaii 1356 Lusitana St 6th Fl Honolulu HI 96813

TAKAO, MOTOHARU, physiologist; b. Takatsuki, Japan, Feb. 27, 1968; s. Takashi and Haruko Takao; m. Fusako Yagi; 1 child, Cay Raymond. PhD, Osaka U. Rsch. engr. Matsushita Refrigeration Co., Japan, 1993—96; post-doctoral rsch. assoc. Brown U., 2000—. Postdoctoral Rsch. Fellowship on Abroad, Japan Soc. for the Promotion of Sci., 2002. Achievements include research in discovery of the intrinsic photosensitive retinal ganglion cell in mammalian retina. Office: Brown University 190 Thayer St Providence RI 02912 E-mail: takao@phys2.med.osaka-u.ac.jp.

TAKASUGI, NAO, state official, business developer; b. Oxnard, Calif., Apr. 5, 1922; s. Shingoro and Yasuye (Hayashi) T.; m. Judith Shigeko Mayeda, Mar. 23, 1952; children— Scott, Russell, Ronald, Tricia, Lea. BS, Temple U., 1945; MBA, U. Pa. Wharton Sch., 1946. Mem. city council City of Oxnard, Calif., 1976-82, mayor, 1982-92; mem. Calif. State Assembly, 1992-98, chmn. revenue and taxation com. Bus. developer, cons.; commr. Oxnard Harbor Dist., 2000—. bd. of trustees, Pacific Commr. Bank, 2002-. Profiled in Tom Brokaw's The Greatest Generation, 1999. Mem. Oxnard Planning Commn., 1974-76; pres. World Trade Ctr. Assn., Oxnard; apptd. (by Calif. gov.) chmn. UN Anniversary; assemblyman Calif. State Assembly 37th Dist.; bd. govs. Japanese Am. Nat. Mus. Decorated Order of Sacred Treasure with Gold Rayette medal Japanese Gov., 1992. Mem. Ventura County Japanese Am. Citizens League, World Trade Ctr. Assn. (pres. Oxnard chpt.), U.S. Conf. Mayors (mem. nat. adv. bd.), Nat. League of Cities (nat. bd. dirs.), Ventura County Transp. Com., League Calif. Cities (bd. dirs.), South Coast Area Bd. Dirs. (chmn. transp. com.), Assn. Ventura County Cities, Oxnard Housing Authoritry (chmn.), Oxnard Redevel. Agy. (chmn.), Optimists Club (Oxnard). Republican. Methodist. Home: 1221 El Portal Way Oxnard CA 93035-2511

TAKASUGI, ROBERT MITSUHIRO, federal judge; b. Tacoma, Sept. 12, 1930; s. Hidesaburo and Kayo (Otsuki) T.; m. Dorothy O. Takasugi; children: Jon Robert, Lesli Mari. BS, UCLA, 1953; LLB, JD, U. So. Calif., 1959. Bar: Calif. bar 1960. Practiced law, Los Angeles, 1960-73; judge East Los Angeles Municipal Ct., 1973-75, adminstrv. judge, 1974, presiding judge, 1975; judge Superior Ct., County of Los Angeles, 1975-76; U.S. dist. judge U.S. Dist. Ct. (cen. dist.) Calif., 1976—. Nat. legal counsel Japanese Am. Citizens League; guest lectr. law seminars Harvard U. Law Sch. Careers Symposium; commencement spkr.; mem. Legion Lex U. So. Calif. Law Ctr.; mem. Civil Justice Reform Act and Alt. Dispute Resolution Com., mem. Adv. Com. on Codes of Conduct of the Jud. Conf. of the U.S., 1987-92, Code of Conduct of Judges. Mem. editorial bd. U. So. Calif. Law Rev., 1959; contbr. articles to profl. jours. Calif. adv. com. Western Regional Office, U.S. Commn. on Civil Rights, 1983-85; chmn. blue ribbon com. for selection of chancellor L.A. C.C. With U.S. Army, 1953-55. Harry J. Bauer scholar, 1959; recipient U.S. Mil. Man of Yr. award for Far East Theater U.S. Army, 1954, Jud. Excellence award Criminal Cts. Bar Assn., Disting. Svc. award Asian Pacific Ctr. and Pacific Clinics, 1994, Freedom award Sertoma, 1995, Pub. Svc. award Asian Pacific Am. Legal Ctr. So. Calif., 1995, cert. of merit Japanese-Am. Bar Assn., Lifetime Achievement award, 2000, Trailblazer award So. Calif. region NAPABA, 1995, Spl. award Mex.-Am. Bar Assn., 1996, Spirit of Excellence award ABA, 1998, Pub. Svc. award Japanese Am. Citizens League, 1999, lifetime achievement award Japanese-Am. Bar Assn., 2000, Judicial Excellence award Criminal Cts. Bar Assn., 2002, Judicial Courage award, 2003, PACE-Setter award Pacific Asian Consort. in Employment, 2003; named Judge of Yr. Century City Bar Assn., 1995, Mem. U. So. Calif. Law Alumni Assn. (dir.), Criminal Ct. Bar Assn. (Jud. Courage award 2003). Office: US Dist Ct 312 N Spring St Los Angeles CA 90012-4701

TAKATA, LISA D. city manager, artist; BS, UCLA, L.A., 1985; MA, Harvard, Cambridge, Mass., 1987. Mgmt. intern City of Phoenix, Phoenix, 1987—88; project mgr. Econ Devel. Phoenix, Phoenix, 1988—90; mgmt. asst. III City Coun. Office, Phoenix, 1990—94, Inter Gov. Programs, Phoenix, 1994—99; asst. to city mgr. City of Phoenix, 2000—. Prin. works include Yosemite Nat. Pk., 2004, Rocky Mtn. Nat. Pk., 2002. Bd. dirs. Japanese Am. Citizens, Glendale, Ariz., 1999—2004, Herberger Theater Ctr., Phoenix, 2002—04, Pueblo Grand Mus., 2003—04, Ariz. Arts. Commn., 2004. Grantee Bromoil Workshop, Ariz. Com. on Arts, 2001. Avocations: photography, pottery, art, creative writing. Office: City Mgr Office City of Phoenix 200 Washington 12 Flr Phoenix AZ 85003

TAKATSU, KO, automotive executive; married; 3 children. JD, Tokyo U.; MBA, U. Chgo. Joined Toyota Motor Corp., 1980; exec. coord. Toyota Motor Sales, Washington, 1992; mgr. strategic planning dept. Ams. divsn. Toyota Motor Corp., Japan; v.p. corp. planning and adminstrn. Toyota Motor N.Am., N.Y.C., 2002—. Avocations: Go, golf. Office: Toyota Motor N Am Ste 4900 Nine West 57th St New York NY 10019

TAKEDA, YASUHIKO, pathologist; b. Iiyama, Nagano, Japan, Mar. 16, 1927; arrived in U.S., 1953; s. Hideyoshi and Hanna Takeda; m. Tamako Kawai Takeda, May 5, 1958; children: James, Mary, Clara, Basil. MD, Chiba Sch. Medicine, Japan, 1952. Lic. physician Colo., 1969, diplomate Am. Bd. Pathology 1970. Intern Bethesda Hosp., Cin., 1953—54; resident in anatomic pathology Sacred Heart Hosp., Spokane, Wash., 1954—56; resident in clin. pathology U. Colo. Hosp., Denver, 1956—58; resident fellow in dept. medicine U. Colo. Sch. Medicine, 1958—60; rsch. fellow Can. Rsch. Coun. McGill U. Med. Clinic, Montreal, 1960—63; instr. dept. medicine U. Colo., Denver, 1963—64, asst. prof., 1965—69, assoc. prof., 1969—78, prof., 1978—88, prof. emeritus medicine, 1988—, dir. immunoassay lab., 1972—86, dir. hematology lab., 1986—88, dir. Medicine 501 course, 1970—82. Reviewer manuscripts. Contbr. more than 60 articles to profl. jours. Recipient Career Devel. award, NIH, 1967—72; Rsch. fellow, Am. Heart Assn., 1964—66, Rsch. grantee, NIH, 1969—78. Fellow: Am. Soc. Clin. Pathologists, Coll. Am. Pathologists; mem.: Internat. Soc. Thrombosis and Hemostasis, Am. Physiol. Soc. Avocations: Go, gardening, ballroom dancing, fishing. Home: 635 Dexter St Denver CO 80220-5037 Office: Univ Colo Sch Medicine 4200 E 9th Ave Denver CO 80262

TAKEI, GEORGE HOSATO, actor; b. L.A., Apr. 20, 1937; s. Takekuma Norman and Fumiko Emily (Nakamura) T. BA, UCLA, 1960, MA, 1964. Dir., chmn. Golden Security Bancorp, Alhambra, Calif., 1981--. Appeared in films, including Green Beret, 1967, Star Trek I-VI, 1979-91, Return from the River Kwai, 1989, Blood Oath, 1990, Prisoners of the Sun, 1990, Live by the Fist, 1993, Oblivion, 1994, Chongbal, 1994, Oblivion 2: Backlash, 1996, Trekkies, 1997, Bug Buster, 1998, Mulan, 1998, Who Gets the House, 1999; plays include The Wash, 1990, Undertow, 1988, Year of the Dragon, 1974, Macbeth, 1972; TV shows include, Star Trek, 1966-69, Playhouse '90, 1959, Hercules, 1998; (TV movie) Kissinger and Nixon, 1995, The Best Bad Thing, 1997. Trustee, Japanese Am. Nat. Mus., L.A. Theatre Ctr., 1984—; dir., v.p. So. Calif. Rapid Transit Dist., L.A., 1973-84. Mem. Nat. Japanese-Am. Citizens League (cultural affairs chmn. 1970-73), SAG, Assn. of Asian Pacific Am. Artists, Am. Pub. Transit Assn. (v.p. 1978-80). Democrat. Buddhist. Avocations: running, architecture, historic preservation. Mailing: 419 N Larchmont Blvd # 41 Los Angeles CA 90004-3013

TAKETOMI, SUSAMU, physicist, researcher; b. Chiba City, Japan, Sept. 25, 1950; s. Manjiro and Kimie (Kida) T. B of Engring., U. Tokyo, 1975; DSc, Keio U., Yokohama, Japan, 1989. Rschr. Ctrl. Rsch. Lab. Fuji Elec. Co. Ltd., Yokosuka City, Japan, 1975-85; rschr. Matsumotoyushi Seiyaku Co. Ltd., Yao City, Japan, 1985—; vis. rschr. Keio U., Yokohama, Japan, 1985-89, Seikei U., Tokyo, 1990-95, U. Ctrl. Fla., 1995-96, U. Wash., Seattle, 1996-98, Kans. State U., Manhattan, 1998-2000, Nat. Inst. Stds. and Tech., Gaithersburg, Md., 2001—03, Matsumoto Yeshi-Seiyaku Co. Ltd., Yao City, Japan, 2004—. Lectr. in field. Author: (book) Magnetic Fluids: Principle and Application, 1988, Magnetic Fluid Handbook, 1995. Mem. Am. Phys. Soc., Japan Phys. Soc., Japan Applied Phys. Soc. Avocation: playing violin. Office: Matsumoto Yushi-Seiyaku Co Ltd Shibukawa-Cho 581-0075 Japan Home: 710 6th Ave S #1042 Seattle WA 98104-3819 also: 1-1-4 # 201 Osakabe Yao City Osaka 581-0015 Japan Office Phone: 81 729 91 1006 Business E-Mail: staketomi@hotmail.com.

TAKEUCHI, TETSUYA, materials engineer; b. Okazaki, Aichi, Japan, Oct. 13, 1967; BS, Nagoya U., Japan, 1990; MS, Nagoya U., 1992; PhD, Meijo U., Japan, 1999. Tech. staff Hewlett Packard Lab., Kawasaki, Japan, 1992—99; hardware engr. Agilent Technologies, Palo Alto, Calif., 1999—2003; sr. scientist Lumileds Lighting, San Jose, Calif., 2003—. Co-author: Properties, processing and applications of gallium nitride and related semiconductors, 1999, III-V Nitride Semiconductors: Applications and Devices, 2002. Recipient Young Rschrs. award, Japan Applied Physics Soc., 1999. Achievements include patents for group III-V semiconductor light emitting devices with reduced piezoelectric fields and increased efficiency, and method for obtaining high quality InGaAsn semiconductor devices. Avocation: guitar. Office: Lumileds Lighting 370 W Trimble Rd MS 91UE San Jose CA 95131 Office Phone: 408-435-6207. Business E-Mail: tetsuya.takeuchi@lumileds.com.

TAKEYAMA, EIZO, company executive; CEO Toyota Tsusho, Nagoya, Japan; chmn. Office: Toyota Tsusho 4-7-23 Meieki Nakamura-ku Nagoya 450-8575 Japan

TAKIS, STEPHANIE, state senator; Ret.; Dem. rep. dist. 36 Colo. Ho. of Reps., 1996-2000; Dem. senator dist. 25 Colo. State Senate, 2000—; fin. specialist FEMA, Denver, 1992—94; rep. AtLarge City Coun., Aurora, Colo., 1989—93; mgmt. analyst U.S. Army, Aurora, Colo., 1983—92; congl. rels. Dept. Commerce, Washington, 1980—82; asst. to sen. Housing & Urban Devel. Com., Washington, 1979—80. Mem. bus. affairs and labor and fin. coms. Colo. Ho. of Reps.; mem. govt., vets. and mil. rels. and transp. and legis. audit coms. Colo. State Senate, bus., labor and fin. com. Office: Colo State Senate State Capitol 200 E Colfax Denver CO 80203

TAKUMI, ROY MITSUO, state legislator; b. Honolulu, Oct. 13, 1952; m. Wanda A. Kutaka; children: Aisha, Jaron. BA, Friends World Coll., 1991; MPA, U. Hawaii, 1993. Cmty. organizer, Osaka, Japan, 1977-83; program dir. Am. Friends Svc. Com., Honolulu, 1984-90; polit. dir. Hawaii State AFL-CIO, Honolulu, 1990-92, comms. dir., 1992—. Rep. Ho. of Reps., Honolulu, 1992—. Office: State Ho Reps State Capitol Honolulu HI 96813 E-mail: reptakumi@capitol.hawaii.gov.

TAL, JACOB, electronics executive; b. Tiberias, Israel, Nov. 29, 1940; s. Refael and Seniora Tboul; 1 child, Tomer; m. Rivka Barlev. BS, Technion, Haifa, Israel, 1966; MS, U. Minn., 1968, PhD, 1970. Research fellow U. Minn., Mpls., 1970-71; elec. engring. prof. U. Utah, Salt Lake City, 1971-78; research engr. Hewlett Packard, Palo Alto, Calif., 1978-81; founder, owner Motion Control Seminar, Mountain View, Calif., 1981—; founder, pres. Galil Motion Control, Mountain View, 1983—. Cons. Control Data, Mpls., 1970-75, Electro Craft, Mpls., 1970-78, Ford Motor Corp., Detroit, 1976-78, Burroughs Corp., Westlake, Calif., 1981-82. Author: Motion Control by Microprocessors, 1984, (with others) Incremental Motion Control, 1978, Motion Control Applications, 1989; contbr. articles to profl. jours. Mem. IEEE, Electronic Motion Control Assn. Avocations: folk dancing, hiking, windsurfing. Office: Galil Motion Control 3750 Atherton Rd Rocklin CA 95765 Office Phone: 916-626-0101. E-mail: jacobt@galilmc.com.

TALACHIAN, REZA, filmmaker; b. Isfahan, Iran, Dec. 1, 1944; arrived in U.S., 1972; s. Ramezan Talachian and Taybeh Ajalouiean. BS in Motion Picture Prodn., So. Ill. U., 1977, MA in Pub. Visual Communication, 1981. Bank mgr. Bank Saderat, Shaikh-Bahiee, 1969—72; sales mgr. Southwestern Co., Franklin, Tenn., 1975—76; instr. Sch. Cinema and TV, Tehran, Iran, 1977—79; creative arts project coord. Sta. WSIU-TV, Carbondale, Ill., 1979—81; owner, prodr., editor Megatrend Visual Prodns., Hollywood, Calif., 1981—82. Screenwriter: (films) Darraab, 1977; Ashura, 1979; animator, editor: Graphic and Edn. Tech., 1978; co-prodr., writer: (films) How to count from 1 to 5, 1978; prodr., dir., editor Bazzar, 1979; author: (book) Brief Critical History and Survey Catalogue of Iranian Films from 1896 to 1975, 1981, Discover Your Mind, 1987, The Hidden Path, 1997. Home: 1831 8th Ave Apt 406 Seattle WA 98101

TALALAY, PAUL, pharmacologist, educator; b. Berlin, Mar. 31, 1923; arrived in U.S., 1940, naturalized, 1946; s. Joseph Anton and Sophie (Brosterman) Talalay; m. Pamela Judith Samuels, Jan. 11, 1953; children: Antony, Susan, Rachel, Sarah. SB, Mass. Inst. Tech., 1944; student, U. Chgo. Sch. Medicine, 1944—46; MD, Yale U., 1948; DSc (hon.), Acadia U., 1974. House officer, asst. resident surg. services Mass. Gen. Hosp., Boston, 1948—50; asst. prof. surgery U. Chgo., 1950—51, asst. prof. biochemistry, 1955—57, assoc. prof., then prof., 1957—63; asst. prof. Ben May Lab. Cancer Research, 1951—57, assoc. prof., then prof., 1957—63; John Jacob Abel prof., dir. dept., pharmacology and exptl. therapeutics Johns Hopkins Sch. Medicine, 1963—75, John Jacob Abel Distinguished Service prof., 1975—, Am. Cancer Soc. prof., 1958—63, 1977—. Sr. asst. surgeon USPHS, 1951—53; vis. prof. Guy's Hosp. Med. Sch., London, 1970, London, 1974—76; nat. adv. cancer coun. USPHS, 1967—71; vis. com. dept. biology MIT, 1964—67; bd. sci. advisers Jane Coffin Childs Meml. Fund for Cancer Rsch., 1971—80; bd. sci. consultants Sloan-Kettering Inst. Cancer Rsch., 1971—81. Hon. editl. adv. bd. Biochem. Pharmacology, 1963—68, editl. bd. Jour. Biol. Chemistry, 1961—66, Molecular Pharmacology, 1965—68, 1971—80, editor-in-chief, 1968—71. Recipient Premio Internationale la Madonnina Milan, 1978, Med. Alumni Disting. Svc. award, U. Chgo., 1978; fellow Guggenheim Meml., 1973—74; scholar Am. Cancer Soc., 1954—58. Fellow: Am. Acad. Arts and Scis.; mem.: NAS, AAAS (Theobald Smith award med. scis. 1957), Am. Soc. Pharm. and Exptl. Therpeutics, Am. Chem. Soc., Biochem. Soc., Am. Soc. Clin. Investigation, Am. Soc. Biochem. Molecular Biology, Am. Philos. Soc., Alpha Omega Alpha, Sigma Xi, Phi Beta Kappa. Home: 5512 Boxhill Ln Baltimore MD 21210-2039 Office: Johns Hopkins U Sch Medicine 725 N Wolfe St Baltimore MD 21205 Fax: 410-502-6818. Business E-Mail: ptalalay@jhmi.edu.

TALAPATRA, DIPAK CHANDRA, aerospace engineer; b. Laur, Bangladesh, Jan. 20, 1942; s. Upendra Chandra and Jalada Sundari Talapatra; m. Brigitte Hildegard Fischer; children: Indrani, Anika. B with honors, Indian Inst. Tech., Kharagpur, 1963; M in Engring., McGill U., 1968; PhD, U. BC, Vancouver, Can., 1972. Sr. scientist ENSCO Inc., Springfield, Va., 1972—77; sr. rsch. engr. Gen. Tire, Akron, Ohio, 1977—80; mech. engr. Naval Ordinance Sta., Indian Head, Md., 1980; aerospace engr. NASA, Goddard Space Flight Ctr., Greenbelt, Md., 1982—83, mgr. flight support sys., 1983—85, structural dynamics mgr., 1985—87; mgr. Can. programs NASA, Space Sta. Program

Office, Reston, Va., 1987—92; mgr. NASA liaison in Can. Internat. Space Sta. Program, Montreal, 1992—. Patentee light weight arch type structures for large reflective mirrors for space and ground based telescopes (U.S. Patent #406634, 1977); contbr. articles to profl. jours. Presenter HS-Space Awareness Presentation, Montreal, 2000, Internat. Tng. Environ. Leadership Group, Brazil Environ. Observations from Space, Montreal, 1995—. Recipient NRC of Can. Rsch. Assistantship, McGill U., 1966—68, U. BC, 1968—72, Exceptional Svc. medal, NASA, 2000. Mem.: ASME. Avocations: tennis, swimming, badminton, reading, art. Office: NASA International Space Station Program 2101 NASA Road 1 Houston TX 77058-3963 Office Phone: 450-926-4570. Office Fax: 450-926-4948. Business E-Mail: dipak.talapatra@space.gc.ca.

TALBERT, ARTHUR THOMAS, music educator; b. Jackson, Miss., Aug. 29, 1925; s. Arthur William Talbert and Lucy Esther McIntosh. BA, Miss. Coll., 1948; MusM, La. State U., 1950; M of Sacred Music, Southwestern Bapt. Sem., 1954. Assoc. prof. Calif. Bapt. Coll., Riverside, 1960—69; organist 1st Congrl. Ch., Corona, 1975—80, March Air Force Base, Riverside, 1980—82, St. Albans Episcopal Ch., Houston, 1992—94, Salem Luth. Ch., 1994—2000, 1st Ch. Christ Scientist, Bellaire, 2000—02, Spring, 2002—. Organist 9th Ch. of Christ Scientists, 2002—. Mem.: Am. Guild of Organists (assoc.). Home: 791 Bateswood Dr #121 Houston TX 77079

TALBERT, CHARLES HAROLD, religion educator; b. Jackson, Miss., Mar. 19, 1934; s. Carl E. and Audrey (Hale) T.; m. Betty O'Neal Weaver, June 30, 1961; children: Caroline O'Neil, Charles Richard. BA, Samford U., 1956, LittD (hon.), 1990; BD, So. Bapt. Theol. Sem., Louisville, 1959; PhD, Vanderbilt U., 1963. Asst. prof. Wake Forest U., Winston-Salem, N.C., 1963-68, assoc. prof., 1968-74, prof., 1974-89, Wake Forest prof., 1989-96; disting. prof. religion Baylor U., Waco, Tex., 1996—. Author: Reading Luke, 1982, Reading Corinthians, 1987, Learning Through Suffering, 1991, Reading John, 1992, The Apocalypse, 1994, Reading Acts, 1997, Romans, 2002, Reading Luke-Acts in its Mediterranean Milieu, 2003, Reading the Sermon on the Mount, 2004. Postdoctoral fellow U. N.C., 1968-69, Soc. for Values in Higher Edn., 1971-72. Mem. Soc. Bibl. Lit. (editor SBL Dissertation Series, N.T. 1984-86, 87-89, editorial bd. jour. 1984-89), Cath. Bibl. Assn. (assoc. editor Cath. Bibl. Quar. 1991-98, pres. 1999-00), Nat. Assn. Bapt. Profs. Religion (pres. 1985), Studiorum Novi Testamenti Societas. Independent. Baptist. Home: 9602 Old Farm Rd Waco TX 76712-6402 Office: Baylor Univ Dept Religion PO Box 97284 Waco TX 76798-7284 Business E-Mail: charles_talbert@baylor.edu.

TALBERT, DOROTHY GEORGIE BURKETT, social worker; b. Rison, Ark.; d. Booker T. and Dorothy (Ragan) Burkett; m. Ernest Talbert, May 14, 1949; children— Ernest George, Dorothy Ernette. A.B., Ark. State A. M. and N. Coll., 1946; M.S.W., Atlanta U., 1948; postgrad. U. Pa., 1962, Tulane U., 1965. Caseworker child welfare services Miss. Dept. Pub. Welfare, 1948-49, Ill. Pub. Aid Commn., Chgo., 1951-53; probation counselor Family Ct. Del., 1956-58; with Del. State Dept. Pub. Welfare, Dover, 1958-71, unit supr., 1962-64, supr. licensing and day care services, 1964-67, chief program devel. Child Welfare Services, 1967-68, chief services to families and children, 1968-71; asst. dir. family services, div. social services Del. Dept. Health and Social Services, 1971-78, dep. dir. adult and spl. services, 1978-82, adult crisis intervention coordinator, Newark, 1982—, staff tng./resource developer, 1985—; instr. continuing edn. program U. Del., part time 1968—, ret. 1989—; mem. social services adv. com. Del. Adolescent Program, 1969-75, bd. dirs., 1969-75; mem. State Adv. Council on Alcoholism, 1972-76; mem. Del. Devel. Disabilities Planning Council, Del. Adv. Council for Coordination of Services to Handicapped; social work edn. adv. com. Del. State Coll., 1978— . Bd. dirs. United Way of Del., 1979. Mem. Nat. Assn. Social Workers, Am. Pub. Welfare Assn., Nat. Council Pub. Welfare Adminstrs., Black Profl. Forum (sec. 1979), Nat. Caucus Black Aged, NAACP, Delta Sigma Theta. Home: 3007 W 3rd St Wilmington DE 19805-1703 Office: Div State Service Ctrs 501 Ogletown Rd Newark DE 19711-5403

TALBERT, HUGH MATHIS, lawyer; b. Kennett, Mo., Dec. 3, 1937; s. Clifford Roscoe and Katharyn (Hoy) T.; m. Carol Sullivan, June 1, 1962 (div. Feb. 1968); m. Carol Ann Frederick, July 18, 1973; children: Katharyn Hoy, William Hugh, Geoffrey Richard. AB, Washington U., St. Louis, 1959, LIB, 1962. Bar: Mo. 1962, Ill. 1965, Ky. 2001, U.S. Dist. Ct. (ea. dist.) Mo. 1965, U.S. Dist. Ct. (so. dist.) Ill. 1966, U.S. Dist. Ct. (we. dist.) Ky. 2001, U.S. Dist. Ct. (ctrl. dist.) Ill. 2001, U.S. Ct. Appeals (7th cir.) 1971. Assoc. Strubinger, Tudor, Tombrink and Wion, St. Louis, 1962-65, Wiseman, Hallett, Mosele and Shaikewitz, Alton, Ill., 1965-67; ptnr. Chapman and Talbert, Granite City, Ill., 1967-73; pres. Talbert & Assocs., PC, Alton, 1974—. Asst. adj. prof. Trial Advocacy St. Louis U. Law Sch., 1992—2000. Mem. ABA, ATLA, Ill. State Bar Assn., Ill. Trial Lawyers Assn. (bd. mgrs. 1978-87), The Mo. Bar Assn., Ky. Bar Assn., Mo. Assn. Trial Lawyers, Madison County Bar Assn., Maritime Law Assn. of the U.S., Acad. of Rail Labor Attys., Internat. Acad. Litigators, Am. Coll. Barristers. Acad. Trial Lawyers, Million Dollar Advs. Forum, Coll. Masters Advs. and Barristers, Ky. Acad. Tr. Lawyers. Democrat. Methodist. Avocations: landscaping, hiking and mountaineering. Home: 1750 Liberty St Alton IL 62002-4514 Office: Talbert & Assocs PC PO Box 800 630 E Broadway Alton IL 62002-6308 Office Phone: 618-465-1000. E-mail: hughtalbert@charter.net.

TALBERT, JAMES LEWIS, pediatric surgeon, educator; b. Cassville, Mo., Sept. 26, 1931; s. William David and Frances (Lewis) T.; m. Alice Quintavell, July 25, 1958; children: William David, Alison Whitney. BA, Vanderbilt U., 1953, MD, 1956. Diplomate: Am. Bd. Surgery (with cert. of spl. competence in pediatric surgery), Am. Bd. Thoracic Surgery. Intern, then resident in surgery Johns Hopkins Hosp., 1956-64, resident in pediatric surgery, 1964-65, Harvey Cushing fellow, 1958-59; instr. surgery, Garrett scholar pediatric surgery Johns Hopkins U. Med. Sch., 1965-66, asst. prof., 1966-67; mem. faculty U. Fla. Med. Sch., Gainesville, 1967—, prof. pediatric surgery, chmn. div., chief children's surgery, 1970-98, prof. emeritus, 1998—. Mem. affiliated faculty VA Hosp., Gainesville; med. dir. Fla. Regional Med. Program for Diagnosis and Treatment Cancer in Children, 1970-73, N. Referral Center Children's Med. Service Program Fla., 1970-80; chmn. Alachua County Emergency Med. Services Adv. Council, 1973-75; chmn. emergency med. services com. N. Central Fla. Health Planning Council, 1972-73; mem. Fla. Emergency Med. Services Adv. Council, 1973-75, 76-79 Author numerous articles in field; contbr. 16 chpts. to books. Served with USPHS, 1960-62. Recipient Founders medal, Roche award Vanderbilt U. Med. Sch., 1956 Fellow ACS (chmn. Fla. trauma com. 1969-77, gov.-at-large 1979-85, sec. bd. govs. 1982-85, rep. to Coun. of Med. Spl. Socs. 1988-89), Am. Acad. Pediatrics (exec. com. sect. oncology and hematology 1978-85); mem. AMA, Am. Pediatric Surg. Assn. (founding mem., chmn. trauma com. 1976-79), Pediatric Oncology Group (chmn. group retreat 1980), Am. Fedn. Clin. Rsch., Assn. Acad. Surgery, Soc. U. Surgeons, Soc. Pediatric Rsch., Am. Coll. Emergency Physicians, Am. Surg. Assn., Halsted Soc., Am. Assn. Surgery Trauma, Am. Burn Assn., Am. Pediatric Soc., Brit. Assn. Pediatric Surgeons, Soc. Internat. Chirurgie, So. Soc. Pediatric Rsch., So. Surg. Assn., Fla. Med. Assn., Fla. Heart Assn. (chmn. cardio-pulmonary resuscitation com. 1972-76), Fla. Assn. Pediatric Surgeons (pres. 1976-78), Fla. Assn. Pediatric Tumor Programs (pres. 1973—), Alachua County Med. Soc. (chmn. emergency med. svcs. adv. com. 1973-75), Phi Beta Kappa, Alpha Omega Alpha, Phi Eta Sigma. Office: J Hillis Miller Health Ctr PO Box 100286 Gainesville FL 32610-0286

TALBOT, BERNARD, government medical research facility official, physician; b. N.Y.C., Oct. 6, 1937; s. Harry and Gertrude (Salkin) T.; m. Ane Katrine Larsen, June 2, 1963; children: Akia, Kamilla. BA, Columbia U., 1958, MD, 1962; PhD, MIT, 1967. NIH postdoctoral fellow MIT, 1962-69; NSF postdoctoral fellow U. Rome, 1969-70; commd. USPHS, 1975—, advanced through grades to med. dir.; med. officer Nat. Cancer Inst., Bethesda, Md., 1971-75; spl. asst. intramural affairs NIH, Bethesda, 1975-78, spl. asst. to dir., 1978-81; dep. dir. Nat. Inst. Allergy and Infectious Diseases, Bethesda, 1981-87, med. officer nat. ctr. for rsch. resources, 1987—. Contbr. articles on protein chemistry to profl. jours., chpts. on recombinant DNA guidelines to books. Recipient Commendation medal USPHS, 1977, Meritorious Service medal, 1984 Mem. Phi Beta Kappa Office: NIH 9000 Rockville Pike Bethesda MD 20892-0003

TALBOT, DONALD ROY, consulting services executive; b. Bridgeport, Conn., Jan. 23, 1931; s. Grant Edward and Elvera (Gilbert) T.; m. Beverly Rinebold, Aug. 15, 1953; children: Donna, Randall, Theodore, Timothy, Thomas. B in Marine Engring., N.Y. State Maritime Coll. Project engr. atomic power equipment div. GE, San Jose, Calif., 1952-58; mgr. nuclear labs., nuclear div. Martin Marietta Corp., Balt., 1958-62, project dir. nuclear div., 1962-67, dir. spl. studies Friendship, Md., 1967-71, project dir. environ. programs Balt., 1971-74, dir. environ. tech. ctr. Relay, Md., 1974-83, gen. mgr. environ. systems div. Columbia, Md., 1984-87; corp. v.p. Versar, Inc., Springfield, Va., 1987-89; pres. R.E. Mgmt. Svc., Inc., Towson, Md., 1989—. Recipient Antarctica Svc. medal Civil Engrs. Corps USN, 1965, Cert. of Appreciation Sec. Dept. Commerce, 1975 Avocation: outdoor activities. Home: 712 Hickory Lot Rd Baltimore MD 21286-1427 Office: R E Mgmt Svcs Inc PO Box 10614 Baltimore MD 21285-0614 Office Phone: 410-583-1334. Personal E-mail: remsdrt@comcast.net.

TALBOT, EMILE JOSEPH, French language educator; b. Brunswick, Maine, Apr. 12, 1941; s. Joseph Emile and Flora Talbot; m. Elizabeth Mullen, Aug. 6, 1966; children: Marc, Paul. BA, St. Francis Coll., Biddeford, Maine, 1963; MA, Brown U., 1965, PhD, 1968. From instr. French to prof. U. Ill., Urbana, 1967—86, prof., 1986—2004, prof. emeritus, 2004—, head dept. French, 1988-94. Author: (book) Stendhal and Romantic Esthetics, 1985, Stendhal Revisited, 1993, Reading Nelligan, 2002; editor: La Critique Stendhalienne, 1979; rev. editor: The French Rev., 1979—82, Quebec Studies, 1988—93, mem. editl. bd.: Nineteenth-Century French Studies, 1986—2003, La Revue Francophone, 1990—96, Quebec Studies, 1993—96; mem. editl. bd. Quebec Studies, 2003—; mem. editl. bd.: Etudes Francophones, 1996—. Decorated chevalier Ordre des Palmes Académiques (France); fellow, Ctr. Advanced Study U. Ill., 1973, Assoc., 1988, NEH, 1973—74, Camargo Found., France, 1976. Mem.: MLA, Am. Coun. Que. Studies (v.p. 1995—97, pres. 1997—99), Assn. Can. Studies in U.S., Am. Assn. Tchrs. French. Roman Catholic. Office: U Ill Dept French 707 S Mathews Ave Urbana IL 61801-3625 Office Phone: 217-333-9628. E-mail: ejtalbot@uiuc.edu.

TALBOT, LEE MERRIAM, ecologist, educator, foundation administrator; b. New Bedford, Mass., Aug. 2, 1930; s. Murrell Williams and Zenaida (Merriam) T.; m. Martha Walcott Hayne, May 16, 1959; children: Lawrence Hayne, Russell Merriam. BA, U. Calif., Berkeley, 1953, MA, PhD, U. Calif., Berkeley, 1963. Biologist Arctic Research Lab., Point Barrow, Alaska, 1951; staff ecologist Internat. Union for Conservation, Brussels, 1954-56; ecologist, dir. East African ecol. research project Nat. Acad. Scis., Govts. of Kenya and Tanzania, 1959-63; wildlife advisor UN Spl. Fund, Africa, 1963-64; dir. S.E. Asia project Internat. Union for Conservation, 1964-65; resident ecologist, field rep. for internat. affairs Smithsonian Instn., Washington, 1966-70; sr. scientist, dir. internat. activities Pres.'s Council on Environ. Quality, Washington, 1970-78; sr. sci. advisor Internat. Council Sci. Unions, Paris, 1978-83; dir. conservation, spl. sci. advisor World Wildlife Fund Internat., Switzerland, 1978-80; dir. gen. Internat. Union for Conservation of Nature and Natural Resources, Gland, Switzerland, 1980-83; research fellow Environ. and Policy Inst., East West Ctr., 1983-87; vis. fellow World Resources Inst., Washington, 1984-89; sr. environ. advisor World Bank, 1984—; pres. Lee Talbot Assocs. Internat., 1991—; sr. prof. environ. scis., internat. affairs and pub. policy George Mason U., Va., 1994—. Cons. UNESCO, World Bank, Asian Devel. Bank, Nat. Geog. Soc., Inter-Am. Devel. Bank, The Nature Conservancy, U.S. Govt., U. Calif., UN Spl. Fund, WHO, UN Environment Program, UN Univ., UN Devel. Programme, African and Asian Govts.; conservation coord. Internat. Biol. Program, 1965-70; bd. dirs. Defenders of Wildlife, Inst. Ecosys. Studies, World Found. for Environment and Devel.; mem. corp. NY Bot. Gardens. Author 17 books and monographs; contbr. more than 270 articles to profl. jours. Active Boy Scouts Am., Geneva, 1980-82, Washington, 1987-95. With USMC, 1953-54. Decorated officer Order of Lion (Senegal); recipient Regents Lectureship award U. Calif., Santa Barbara, 1986, Pierre Chaleur prize for lit. French Acad. Scis., 1993; Centenary Symposium named in his honor Bombay Natural History Soc., 2003. Fellow Royal Geog. Soc., Royal Soc. Arts, AAAS, N.Y. Zool. Soc.; mem. Am. Inst. Biol. Scis. (Disting. Svc. award 1979), Acad. Medicine, World Conservation Union (hon.), Am. Assn. for Club of Rome, Am. Soc. Mammalogists, Ecol. Soc., Wildlife Soc. (Outstanding Publ. award 1963), Soc. for Conservation Biology, Internat. Soc. for Ecol. Econs., Boone and Crockett Club (N.Y.C.), Explorers Club (N.Y.C.), Cosmos Club (Washington), Sigma Xi, Phi Kappa Sigma. Achievements include incorporation of ecological principles in international development; development of new principles for management of wild resources; biodiversity conservation; definition of ecosystem dynamics of tropical savannahs including role of fire, feeding habits and migrations of wild herbivores; development and negotiation of national legislation and international agreements for environmental protection. Home: 6656 Chilton Ct Mc Lean VA 22101-4422 *My career is based on two premises: first, that our most important challenges are environmental issues which determine the earth's carrying capacity for human life and, equally important, the quality of that life; and second, that it is important to obtain direct experience in as much of the world as possible to understand the human ecological setting as a basis for action to improve it.*

TALBOT, MARTHA HAYNE, conservationist, biologist; b. San Francisco, Aug. 3, 1932; d. Francis Bourn and Anna (Walcott) Hayne; m. Lee Merriam Talbot, May 16, 1959; children: Lawrence Hayne, Russell Merriam. BA, Vassar Coll., 1954. Co-founder, asst. dir. student conservation program U.S. Nat. Parks, 1955-59; co-dir. East African Ecol. Rsch. Project, Kenya and Tanzania, 1959-63; asst. dir. S.E. Asia Project, Internat. Union for Conservation of Nature/Natural Resources, 1964-65; asst. coord. Internat. Biol. Programme, London, 1966; rsch. assoc. Smithsonian Instn., Washington, 1966-75; mem., treas. Fairfax County Park Authority, Fairfax, Va., 1973-77; sec.-treas. Talbot Racing Assocs., McLean, Va., 1983—; owner, dir. Talbot Hayne Vineyard, St. Helena, Calif., 1988—; sec.-treas. Lee Talbot Assocs. Internat., McLean, 1991—. Bd. dirs. Student Conservation Assn., 1966-78, 83-87, hon. dir., 1987— (Svc. Honor award), Defenders of Wildlife, 1974-77, Audubon Naturalist Soc., 1975-78, Rachel Carson Coun., 1975-94, treas., 1994-98, v.p., 1998—. Co-author: Introduction to the Landscape, East Africa, 1961, (monograph) The Wildebeest in Western Masailand East Africa, 1963, Renewable Natural Resources in the Philippines, 1964, Conservation of the Hong Kong Countryside, 1966; co-editor: Conservation in Tropical South East Asia, 1968; contbr. numerous articles to sci. jours. Cub Scout troop leader Boy Scouts Am., Geneva, 1978-83, transp. coord., McLean, 1989-95. Recipient Outstanding Pub. award The Wildlife Soc., 1963, Cinema Golden Eagle award Documentary Film, 1968, Disting. Alumna award Katharine Branson Sch., 1981, Conservation Svc. award U.S. Dept. Interior, 1986, Bd. Tribute to co-founder, Student Conservation Assn., 1984, Resolution of Honor, 1999; N.Y. Zool. Soc. grantee, 1961. Mem. Soc. Women Geographers (bd. dirs. 1972-75, treas. 1984-89, treas. Washington group 1990-96), Napa Valley Grape Growers Assn. Avocations: hiking, backpacking, bicycling, skiing, travel. Home: 6656 Chilton Ct Mc Lean VA 22101-4422

TALBOT, MARY LEE, minister; b. Cleve., Apr. 18, 1953; d. Richard William and Mary Helen (Jacobs) T. BA, Coll. Wooster, 1975; MDiv, Andover-Newton Theol. Sch., 1979; MPhil, Tchrs. Coll. Columbia U., 1990; PhD, Columbia U., 1997. Ordained to ministry Presbyterian Ch. (U.S.A.), 1981. Asst. in ministry Grace Congl. Ch., Framingham, Mass., 1975-78; resources coord. Women's Theol. Coalition, Boston, 1977-79; assoc. editor Youth Mag., Phila., 1979-80; co-dir. youth and young adult program Presbyn. Ch. U.S.A., N.Y.C., 1981-88; cons. in religious edn. N.Y.C., 1988-90; dir. continuing edn. Pitts. Theol. Sem., Pitts., 1990—2001; interim pastor Hebron U.P. Ch., Clinton, 2002—. Bd. dirs. Christian Assn., U. Pa., 1979-81; mem. religion com. Chautauqua Inst., 1988-91. Author, editor: (program resource) Suicide and Youth, 1981, (newsletter) Trackings, 1986-88; editor: Racism and Anti-Racism, 1982, One Fantastic Book, 1982, My Identity: A Gift from God, 1987, A Guidebook for Presbyterian Youth Ministry, 1988, God's Gift of Sexuality, 1989, Celebrate Bible Study, 1990; contbr. articles to Youth Mag., Alert, Chautauquan Daily, others. Bd. dirs. Christian Assn., U. Pa., 1979-81. Recipient English award Bus. and Profl. Women, 1971. Mem. Assn. Presbyn. Ch. Educators, Assn. Presbyn. Clergywomen, Religious Edn. Assn. (bd. dirs. 1986-91), History of Edn. Soc., Kappa Delta Pi. Democrat. Office: 1767 Rte 30 Clinton PA 15026 Office Phone: 724-899-2620.

TALBOT, NINA ISADORA, artist, educator; b. N.Y.C., Mar. 19, 1954; d. Daniel and Toby Talbot; m. Mark J. Rand, Nov. 1, 1987; children: Joshua, Sophie. Student, N.Y. Studio Sch. Drawing, Painting and Sculpture, 1974—76; BA, SUNY, N.Y.C., 1995. Tchg. artist Arts for Edn., N.Y.C., 1995—, Bklyn. Coll., N.Y.C., 1998—2000, Mercy Coll., N.Y.C., 1998—2000; staff developer Bd. Edn. Dist. 22, N.Y.C., 1997—2001. Visual arts advisor Bklyn. Arts Coun., 2003. Exhibitions include The Smithsonian, 1983, Bklyn. Mus., 1985, Bronx Mus., 2001, Williamsburg Art and Hist. Ctr., 2002, Bklyn. Pub. Libr., 2002, Gallery 1199, 2002, one-woman shows include Shelter Rock Gallery, 2003. Cmty. artist Crown Heights Youth Coalition, Bklyn., 1995, Coun. Pakistan Orgn., Midwood, Bklyn., 2002—. Recipient 25th Ann. Poster award, Empire State Coll., 1995. Mem.: Bklyn. Arts Coun., Bread and Roses Cultural Project (Visual Arts grant 2002). Avocations: reading, writing. Office Phone: 718-434-4953.

TALBOT, PAMELA, public relations executive; b. Chgo., Aug. 10, 1946; BA in English, Vassar Coll., 1968. Reporter Worcester, Mass. Telegram and Gazette, 1970—72; account exec. Daniel J. Edelman, Inc., Chgo., 1972—74, account supr., 1974—76, v.p., 1976—78, sr. v.p., 1978—84, exec. v.p., gen. mgr., 1984—90; pres. Edelman West, Chgo., 1990—95; pres., COO Edelman U.S., 1995—. Office: Edelman Pub Rels 200 E Randolph Dr Ste 6300 Chicago IL 60601-6436 E-mail: pam.talbot@edelman.com.

TALBOT, PHILLIPS, Asian affairs specialist; b. Pitts., June 7, 1915; s. Kenneth Hammet and Gertrude (Phillips) T.; m. Mildred Aleen Fisher, Aug. 18, 1943; children: Susan Talbot Jacox, Nancy, Bruce Kenneth. BA, BS in Journalism, U. Ill., 1936; student, London Sch. Oriental Studies, 1938—39, Aligarh Muslim U., India, 1939—40; PhD, U. Chgo., 1954; LLD (hon.), Mills Coll., 1963. Reporter Chgo. Daily News, 1936-38, corr. India and Pakistan, 1946-48, 49-50; assoc. Inst. Current World Affairs, 1938-41, 46-51; instr. U. Chgo., 1948-50, Columbia U., NYC, 1951; exec. dir. Am. Univs. Field Staff, 1951-61; asst. sec. Near Eastern and S. Asian affairs Dept. State, 1961-65; U.S. amb. to Greece, 1965-69; pres. Asia Soc., NYC, 1970-81, pres. emeritus, 1981—. Phi Beta Kappa vis. scholar, 1973-74. Author: (with S.L. Poplai) India and America, 1958, India in the 1980s, 1983; editor: South Asia in the World Today, 1950. Trustee emeritus Aspen Inst., U.S.-Japan Found.; counselor United Bd. for Christian Higher Edn. in Asia; elder Presbyn. Ch. 2d lt. cav. Officers Res. Corps, 1936; 1st lt. N.G., 1937-38; lt. comdr. USNR, 1941-46. Recipient Padma Shri honors, India, 2002. Mem. Am. Acad. Diplomacy, Coun. Am. Ambs., Coun. Fgn. Rels., Century Assn., Cosmos Club. Address: 200 E 66th St New York NY 10021-9175 E-mail: talbotp@pipeline.com.

TALBOT, PIERRE JOSEPH, microbiologist, researcher; b. Quebec City, Que., Can., July 11, 1956; s. Arthur and Suzanne (Hudon) T.; m. France Ouellet, July 29, 1977; children: Natalie, Benoit, Dominic. BSc in Biochemistry, Laval U., Ste-Foy, Que., 1977; PhD in Biochemistry, U. B.C., Vancouver, 1981. Rsch. assoc. Scripps Clinic and Rsch. Found., La Jolla, Calif., 1981-84; asst. prof. Inst. Armand-Frappier U. Que., Laval, 1984-89; assoc. prof. Inst. Armand-Frappier, Laval, Que., 1989-92, prof., 1992—, dir. Human Health Rsch. Ctr., 1998—2001; dir. INRS Inst. Armand-Frappier, 2002—. Com. reviewer Med. Rsch. Coun., Ottawa, Ont., Can., 1989-96, 98-2000, Multiple Sclerosis Soc., Toronto, Ont., 1993-96, Nat. Sci. Engring. Res. Coun., Ottawa, 1999-2002, Can. Inst. Health Rsch., 1998—. Mem. editl. bd. Viral Immunology, San Antonio, 1990-99; contbr. articles to Virology, Jour. Virology, Annals Neurology, Jour. Immunology. Fonds de la Recherche en Santé du Que. scholar of exceptional merit, 1992-97. Mem. AAAS, Am. Soc. Virology, Am. Soc. Microbiology, Can. Soc. Microbiologists (Fisher Sci. award 1987, Roche Diagnostics award 2002), Can. Soc. Immunology, Assn. Can.-Francaise Pour L'Avancement des Scis., Internat. Soc. Neuroimmunology, Internat. Soc. Neurovirology. Achievements include research in immuno and molecular biology of neurotropic coronaviruses and possible involvement in neurologic disease. Home: 38 59th Ave Laval QC Canada H7V 2A9 Office: INRS Inst Armand-Frappier 531 Boul Des Prairies Laval QC Canada H7V 1B7 Office Phone: 450-686-5515. E-mail: pierre.talbot@inrs-iaf.uquebec.ca.

TALBOT, STEPHEN HENDERSON, television producer, documentary filmmaker, writer; b. Hollywood, Calif., Feb. 28, 1949; s. Lyle and Margaret (Epple) T.; m. Pippa Gordon; children: Dashiell, Caitlin. BA, Wesleyan U., 1970. Asst. to pres., lectr. Am. studies SUNY, Old Westbury, 1970-73; reporter Internews, Berkeley, Calif., 1973-79; producer, reporter KQED-TV, San Francisco, 1980-89; producer, writer Frontline (PBS), San Francisco, 1992—; series editor Frontline World, 2002—. Appeared in Leave It To Beaver as Gilbert, 1958-63, also Twilight Zone, Perry Mason, Lassie, others; correspondent Front Line Diet Wars, 2004; prodr., co-writer for Frontline: The Best Campaign Money Can Buy (Columbia U. Dupont award), 1992, Rush Limbaugh's America, 1995, The Long March of Newt Gingrich, 1996, Justice for Sale, 1999 (Gold medal Houston Internat. Film Festival 2000); writer, co-prodr.: (PBS-TV) Beryl Markham, 1986, Ken Kesey, 1987, Carlos Fuentes, 1989, Maxine Hong Kingston, 1990, John Dos Passos, 1994, Frontline: Spying on Saddam, 1999; prodr., writer: The Case of Dashiell Hammett, 1982 (Peabody award, Edgar Allan Poe award), 1968: The Year That Shaped a Generation, 1998, Frontline: The Battle Over School Choice, 2000 (First prize Edn. Writers Assn.); co-prodr., reporter: Broken Arrow, 1980 (George Peabody & George Polk award), others; contbr. articles to mags. including Salon, Washington Post Mag., San Francisco Chronicle. Recipient Thomas Storke Internat. Journalism award World Affairs Coun. No. Calif., San Francisco, 1983, 86, Golden Gate award San Francisco Film Festival, 1986, 89, Emmy award NATAS, 1980-83, 87-88, 90-91, Online Journalism award Columbia U. Mem. Writer's Guild Am. West, Am. Fedn. TV and Radio Artists. Office: Frontline World Care Grad Sch Journalism 121 North Gate Hall Berkeley CA 94720-5860 Office Phone: 510-643-3065.

TALBOTT, BEN JOHNSON, JR., lawyer; b. Louisville, May 2, 1940; s. Ben Johnson and Elizabeth (Farnsley) T.; m. Sandra Riehl, Oct. 19, 1963; children: Elizabeth, Betty, John, Ben, Sandra. AB magna cum laude, Xavier U., Cin., 1961; LLB, Harvard U., 1964. Bar: Ky. 1965, U.S. Ct. Appeals (6th cir.) 1967. Law clk. to presiding justice U.S. Dist. Ct. Ky., Louisville, 1964-65; assoc. Middleton, Reutlinger & Baird, Louisville, 1965-68, ptnr., 1968-80, Westfall, Talbott & Woods, Louisville, 1980-2000, Talbott & Talbott, PLLC, Louisville, 2000—. Atty. Stitzel-Weller Distillery, 1970—72, Louisville Gen. Hosp., 1974—83, Louisville and Jefferson County Bd. Health, 1974—80, U. Louisville, 1980—95. Mem. adv. bd. Louisville 15, Sta. WKPC-TV, bd. dirs., 1972-74, pres. 1974; past bd. dirs. U. Louisville Found., U. Louisville Med. Sch. Fund Orgn.; bd. dirs. Louisville Theatrical Assn., 1971—; pres., 1975-76, chmn., 1977-78; bd. dirs. Def. Enterprise Fund, 1994—; bd. dirs. Macauley Theatre, 1975, TARC Adv. Com., 1971, Jefferson County Capital Constrn. Com., 1971, Louisville Orch., 1976-86, pres., 1979-81; trustee U. Louisville, 1970-79, sec., 1974, vice chmn., 1975, chmn. fin. com., 1976; bd. dirs. Ky. Ctr. for the Arts, 1983—, Louisville Lung Assn., 1974-75, treas., 1975; bd. dirs. Hist. Homes Found., 1972-78, 95-97, 2000-01, 02—, v.p. 1978, 2002—, advisor, atty. 1978-98; bd. regents Whitehall, 1993-2001. Named Outstanding Young Man of Louisville, Louisville Jaycees, 1976. Mem.: SAR, ABA, Louisville Bar Assn. (past mem. exec. com.), The Def. Rsch. and Trial Lawyers Assn., Ky. Bar Assn. (chmn. 1989, Gen. Practice Session of CLE), Gulf Stream Bath and Tennis Club, Louisville Boat Club, Pendennis Club, Soc. Colonial Wars, Harvard Law Sch. Assn. Ky. (sec. 1965, pres. 1989—), Mayflower Soc., Filson Club, Louisville Country Club, U. Louisville Club, Big Sand Lake Club, Phi Kappa Phi (bd. dirs., treas. Louisville chpt. 1990—). Avocations: golf, tennis, skiing, fishing. Home: 566 Blankenbaker Ln Louisville KY 40207-1167 Office: Talbott & Talbott 501 S 2nd St Louisville KY 40202-1864 E-mail: lynn@talbottandtalbottlaw.com.

TALBOTT, FRANK, III, lawyer; b. Danville, Va., Mar. 26, 1929; s. Frank and Margaret (Jordan) T.; m. Mary Beverley Chewning, July 11, 1952; children: Beverley, Frank IV. BA, U. Va., 1951, LLB, 1953. Bar: Va. 1952. With firm Meade, Talbott & Tate, Danville, 1956—59, Talbott, Wheatley & Talbott, Danville, 1959—66; with Dan River Inc., 1966-76, v.p., gen. counsel, 1968-76; ptnr. firm Clement, Wheatley, Winston, Talbott & Majors, Danville, 1977-78; individual practice law Danville, 1979-92; gen. counsel Va. Mfrs. Assn. Inc., 1983-92; of counsel Woods, Rogers & Hazlegrove, Danville, Va., 1992—. Chmn. adv. bd. NationsBank, Danville, 1984-94. Vice-chmn. Danville Sch. Bd., 1964-70; trustee Va. Student Aid Found., 1963-68; bd. dirs. United Fund Danville, 1959-63, Meml. Hosp., Danville, 1977-90. Served with AUS, 1953-56. Decorated Commendation medal. Fellow Am. Bar Found. (life); mem. Va. Bar Assn. (v.p. 1965-66, exec. com. 1967-70), Danville Bar Assn. (pres. 1965-66), Am. Judicature Soc., Newcomen Soc., U. Va. Alumni Assn. (bd. mgrs.), Danville Golf Club, Farmington Country Club, Country Club Va., Country Club of North Carolina, Delta Psi, Phi Alpha Delta. Methodist. Home: 221 Salisbury Cir Danville VA 24541-5571 Office: 530 Main St Danville VA 24541

TALBOTT, GEORGE ROBERT, physicist, mathematician, educator; b. San Diego, Oct. 1, 1925; s. George Fletcher and Mary (Lanz) T. BA with honors, UCLA, 1960; DSc, Ind. No. U., 1973. Physicist, tech. staff Rockwell Internat. Co., Anaheim, Calif., 1960-85; lectr. computer sci. Calif. State U., Fullerton, 1979—. Cons. physics, computer sci.; disting. guest lectr. Brunel U., London, 1974, 76; spl. guest Forschungsbibliothek, Hannover, W. Ger., 1979; assoc. editor KRONOS jour., Glassboro (N.J.) U., 1978—; chief computer scientist and ednl. videotape dir. Specialized Software, Wilmot, Wis., 1982—; phys. scientist and rsch. assoc. San Diego Mus. Man, 1993—. Author: Electronic Thermodynamics, 1973, Philosophy and Unified Science, 1977, Computer Applications, 1989, Sir Arthur and Gravity, 1990, Fermat's Last Theorem, 1991, The Signal Processing Library, 1995, Etwas Von Nichts, 2000, A Twelfth Dynasty Egyptian Mathematical Papyrus, 2001, Finding Molecular Weight By Light Scatter, 2001, Mostowski's Theorem In Digital Signal Processing, 2001, Lecomte Du Nouy and The Beauty of Precision, 2001, A New Equation for Orbital Velocities, 2001, Derivatives in Cardinal Arithmetic, 2002; mem editl. bd.: KRONOS jour., 1978—; co-inventor burner, —. With M.C., U.S. Army, 1956. Recipient Vis. Scholars award Western Mich. U., 1979; named to Herbert Hoover H.S. Hall of Fame, San Diego, 1998. Mem. Am. Soc. Med. Technologists, Am. Math. Soc., Math. Assn. Am., Am. Soc. clin. Pathologists (lic. med. lab. technologist), Sigma Xi. Buddhist. Home: 4031 E Charter Oak Dr Orange CA 92869-2611 E-mail: ptahseti@aol.com.

TALBOTT, JOHN, mayor; m. Claudia Field; 2 children. BA in Soc. Sci., Coll. Great Falls, 1976; MA in Polit. Sci., Ctrl. Mich. U., 1978. Enlisted USAF, advanced through grades to col., ret., 1982, served in various assignments including Joint Svc. Commands, past comdr. commn. squadron; with Jet Propulsion Lab, to 1989; former mayor City of Spokane. Active cmty. devel. and politics, Spokane, 1989—.

TALBOTT, STROBE, think-tank executive; b. Dayton, Ohio, Apr. 25, 1946; s. Nelson S. and Josephine (Large) T.; m. Brooke Lloyd Shearer, Nov. 14, 1971; children: Devin Lloyd, Adrian Nelson. BA, Yale U., 1968, MA (hon.), 1976; MLitt, Oxford U., Eng., 1971. East european corr. Time Mag., 1971-73, U.S. state dept. corr., 1973-75, white house corr., 1975-77, diplomatic corr., 1977-84, chief Washington bur. & fgn. affairs columnist, 1984-89, editor at large, 1989-94; amb. at large & spl. advisor to the Sec. of State on the new independent states U.S. Dept. State, Washington, 1993—94, dep. sec. state, 1994—2001; pres. Brookings Instn., Washington, 2002—. Editor, translator: Khrushchev Remembers, 1970, (with Edward Crankshaw) Khrushchev Remembers: The Last Testament, 1974, The Age of Terror: America & The World After September 11, 2001; author: Endgame: Inside Story of SALT II, 1979, Deadly Gambits: Reagan Administration & Arms Controls, 1984, The Russians and Reagan, 1984, Reagan and Gorbachev, 1987, The Master of the Game: Paul Nitze and the Nuclear Peace, 1988, (with Michael Beschloss) At the Highest Levels: The Inside Story of the End of the Cold War, 1993, The Russia Hand: A Memoir of Presidential Diplomacy, 2002, (with Robert L. Suettinger) Beyond Tiananmen: The Politics of U.S.-China Relations 1989-2000, 2003, Engaging India: Diplomacy, Democracy, and the Bomb, 2004 . Trustee Yale U. 1976-82, Hotchkiss Sch., 1982-87; bd. dirs. Carnegie Endowment Internat. Peace; Council on Fgn. Relations. Recipient Edward Weintal Prize for Disting. Diplomatic Reporting Georgetown U., Overseas Press Club award, Stanley Hillman award. Office: The Brookings Instn 1775 Massachusetts Ave NW Washington DC 20036*

TALCOTT, ROBERT MARC, lawyer; b. New Haven, Conn., Sept. 18, 1932; s. Samuel L. and Gertrude (Rosenbaum) T.; m. Sandra L. Weinstein, Feb. 4, 1973. BA, U. Conn., 1954; LLB, Georgetown U., 1959, LLM, 1961. Bar: Calif., D.C. Asst. U.S. atty. U.S. Dept. of Justice, L.A., 1959, trial atty. Washington, 1962-64; sr. ptnr. Talcott, Lightfoot et al, L.A., 1967—. Adj. faculty Loyola Law Sch., 1975-85; lectr. in field. Chairperson L.A. World Cup Bid Com.; lawyer's adv. com. Nat. Ctr. on Instns. and Alternatives, Found. for People, Constitutional Rights Found.; citizen's adv. com. L.A. Olympic Com.; founder L.A. Mus. of Contemporary Art; bd. dirs. L.A. Theatre Works, L.A. Police Meml. Found.; pres. L.A. Bd. of Police Commrs., 1984-90. Capt. USAF, 1954-56. Fellow Am. Coll. of Trial Lawyers; mem. State Bar of Calif. (gov. 1988-91), L.A. County Bar Assn. (trustee 1980-82), Fed. Bar Assn. (pres. L.A. chpt. 1975-76), Chancery Club, U.S. Dist. Ct. for the Ctrl. Dist. of Calif. (mem. standing com. on discipline 1982—, mem. fed. indigent def. panel 1968-80, chmn. fed. indigent def. panel 1974-77). Avocations: golf, boating. Office: Talcott Lightfoot et al 13th Fl 655 S Hope St Fl 13 Los Angeles CA 90017-3211

TALEN, WILLIAM CLAIRE, bank executive, financial consultant; b. Ogilvie, Minn., Dec. 28, 1924; s. Clare and Anna (Minnema) T.; m. June Sieswerda (dec.); children: Deborah Ann, William Claire Jr., Julie, Ruth Elizabeth, Mary June; m. Caroline Sarah Hall, July 31, 1982; children: Caroline Rich, Robert Lassiter. BA, Calvin Coll., 1948; student in Banking, U. Wis., 1950; student in Fin. Pub. Rels., Northwestern U., 1955; cert., Am. Inst. Banking, 1961. Pres., bd. dirs. Farmers & Merchants Bank, Watertown, S.D., 1960-62, Univ. State Bank, Green Bay, Wis., 1962-70, New Franken (Wis.) Bank, 1963-71, Algoma (Wis.) Bank, 1964-71; exec. v.p., bd. dirs. Bankers Trust Co., Des Moines, 1970-73; bd. dirs., chair exec. com. First Bank & Trust, Menomonie, Wis., 1973-81; chmn., pres. First State Bank, Edgerton, Wis., 1973-88; pres., bd. dirs. Farmers Savings Bank & Trust, Traer, Iowa, 1974—; pres., chair Talen, Inc.-Bank Holding Co., Traer, Iowa, 1976—, Farmers Savings Bank & Trust, Vinton, Iowa, 1988—. Bank cons., Northfield, Minn., 1973—; v.p. Iowa, Am. Bankers Assn., Washington, 1974-76; pres., owner Farmers & Merchant Bank, Greenwood, Wis., 1992-94. Pres. Menomonie (Wis.) C. of C., 1954-55, Green Bay Symphony, 1968-70, Des Moines Symphony, 1972-73; dir. Green Bay YMCA, Jr. Achievement. 1st lt. U.S. Army, 1943-46. Mem. Am. Mgmt. Assn., Am. Consulting League, Nat. Cert. Profl. Mgmt. Cons., Iowa Ind. Bankers, Iowa Bankers Assn., Bank Mktg. Assn., Am. Bankers Assn., Am. Legion, VFW, Toastmasters (pres. 1953-54), Internat. Fellowship Flying Rotarians, Des Moines C. of C. (dir.), Rotary (Paul Harris fellow 1978, 94), 50 Year Club, Wis. Bankers Assn., 50th Yr. Club, Iowa Bankers Assn. Republican. Presbyterian. Avocations: flying (commercial pilot), amateur radio. Office: PO Box 535 Northfield MN 55057-0535

TALENT, JAMES M. senator, former congressman, lawyer; b. Des Peres, Mo., Oct. 18, 1956; m. Brenda Lyons, 1984; children: Michael, Kathleen Marie, Christine. BA in Polit. Sci., Washington U., 1978; JD, U. Chgo. Law Sch., 1981. Law clk. 7th Ct. Appeals, 1981-82; adj. prof. law, 1982-84; mem. Mo. State Ho. Reps., 1984-93; minority leader, 1989-93; mem. 103rd-106th Congresses from 2nd Mo. Dist., 1993—2001, mem. edn. and the workforce com., armed svcs. com., chmn. small bus. com., 1993—2001; U.S. senator from Mo., 2002—. Legislative Achievement award Mo. Hosp. Assn., 1989. Mem. Mo. Bar Assn. (Award for significant contbns. to adminstrv. justice 1989), Mo. C. of C. (Spirit of Enterprise award 1990), Order of the Coif. Republican. Office: 493 Russell Senate Office Building Washington DC 20510

TALERMAN, ALEKSANDER, pathologist, educator; b. Warsaw, Jan. 8, 1932; came to U.S., 1979; s. Nattali and Stanislawa (Naiman) T.; m. Karin Margaretha Barkland, Feb. 28, 1962; children: Robert Alexander, Edward Mark Olof. MB, BChir, U. Sheffield, Eng., 1957, MD, 1968. Lectr. pathology U. London, 1965-70; sr. lectr. pathology, head dept. pathology Rotterdam (The Netherlands) Cancer Inst., 1970-79; prof. pathology and ob-gyn. U. Chgo., 1979—90; Peter A. Herbut prof. pathology and cell biology Thomas Jefferson U., Phila., 1990—. U. and rsch. inst. cons. Co-author: Atlas of Germ Cell Tumors, 1989; editor: Pathology of the Testis and its Adnexa, 1985; contbr. articles to profl. jours. With Royal Air Force, 1960-63. Recipient Silver medal German Cancer Soc., 1979. Fellow Royal Coll. Pathologists; mem. Internat. Soc. Gynecol. Pathologists (exec. coun. 1976-82, sec. 1982-86, pres. 1990-92), Internat. Acad. Pathology, European Soc. Pathology, Path. Soc. Great Britain and Ireland. Home: 243 S 4th St Philadelphia PA 19106-3803 Office: Thomas Jefferson Univ Dept Pathology Main Bldg 11th & Walnut Sts Rm 285Q Philadelphia PA 19107-5244 Fax: 215-923-1969. Office Phone: 215-955-2433. E-mail: mtaleman@aol.com.

TALESE, GAY, writer; b. Ocean City, N.J., Feb. 7, 1932; s. Joseph Francis and Catherine (DiPaola) T.; m. Nan Ahearn, June 10, 1959; children—Pamela, Catherine. BA in Journalism, U. Ala., 1953. Staff writer N.Y. Times, N.Y.C., 1955-65; writer Esquire mag., N.Y.C., 1960. Author: New York - A Serendipiter's Journey, 1961, The Bridge, 1964, The Overreachers, 1965, The Kingdom and the Power, 1969, Fame and Obscurity, 1970, Honor Thy Father, 1971, Thy Neighbor's Wife, 1980, Unto the Sons, 1992; co-author: (with Barbara Lounsberry) The Literature of Reality, 1995; editor: Italians in America: A Celebration, 2001, The Gay Talese Reader, 2003; contbr. articles to Esquire mag., The New Yorker, others. Served to 1st lt. AUS, 1954-56. Mem. P.E.N. (v.p. 1984-87, bd. dirs. 1980—), Phi Sigma Kappa. Home: 109 E 61st St New York NY 10021-8101 also: 154 E Atlantic Blvd Ocean City NJ 08226-4511

TALESE, NAN AHEARN, publishing company executive; b. N.Y.C., Dec. 19, 1933; d. Thomas James and Suzanne Sherman (Russell) Ahearn; m. Gay Talese, June 10, 1959; children: Pamela Frances, Catherine Gay. BA, Manhattanville Coll. of Sacred Heart, 1955; LHD (hon.), Manhattanville, 2003. Fgn. exchange student 1st Nat. City Bank, London and Paris, 1956; editorial asst. Am. Eugenics Soc., N.Y.C., 1957-58, Vogue mag., N.Y.C., 1958-59; copy editor Random House Pub., N.Y.C., 1959-64, assoc. editor, 1964-67, sr. editor, 1967-73, Simon & Schuster Pubs., N.Y.C., 1974-81, v.p., 1979-81; exec. editor, v.p. Houghton Mifflin Co., N.Y.C., 1981-83, v.p., editor-in-chief, 1984-86, v.p., pub., editor-in-chief, 1986-88; sr. v.p. Doubleday & Co., N.Y.C., 1988-90; pres., pub., editorial dir. Nan A. Talese Books, 1990—. Home: 109 E 61st St New York NY 10021-8101

TALGO, HARRISON, chief administrator tribal government; b. Bylas, Ariz., Feb. 7, 1950; s. Oliver B. Sr. and Eunice Talgo; m. Elouise Talgo, Oct. 13, 1972; children: Geron Randall, Elina Louise, Harrison Jr., Randall Lee. AA, Ea. Ariz. Coll., 1976; student, U. Ariz., 1992. Livestock mgr. Slaughter Mt. Livestock, San Carlos, Ariz., 1980-2000; with early childhood/head start Human Health Svc., San Carlos, 1980-2000; tribal councilman San Carlos Tribal Govt., 1986-2000, tribal govt. chief adminstr., 1993-96; tribal coun. chmn. San Carlos Apache Tribe; cons. U. Ariz., Tucson, U.S. Dept. Agrl., Billings, Mont., 1996-98. Housing bd. commr. San Carlos Housing Authority, 1998-2000; bd. commr. Bur. of Land Mgmt., Safford, Ariz., 1998-2000. Active Bylas Luth. Ch. Coun., 1976-86, Ft. Thomas Sch. Bd., 1984-98; bd. dirs. Migrant Head Start, Phoenix, 1986-90; chmn. strategic planning San Carlos Apache, 1994-99; mem. Rep. Party Tax Reform, 1998-99. With USMC, Vietnam, 1970-73. Recipient recognition Inter Tribal Coun. Ariz., 2000. Mem. Nat. Congress Am. Indian, Nat. Indian Gaming Assn., VFW, Am. Legion (post #36), Marine Corps League. Home: PO Box 47 Bylas AZ 85530-0047 Office: Tribal Govt Box O Tonto Ave San Carlos AZ 85550

TALIAFERRO, ELLEN, medical educator; Grad., U. Okla. Sr. rsch. scientist dept. advanced biotech. and power McDonnel Douglas Astronautics Co.; staff emergency physician, dir. emergency svcs. Santa Monica Hosp. Med. Ctr.; dir. ambulatory care and emergency svcs. St. Joseph Hosp., Denver; assoc. clin. prof. medicine, chmn. dept. emergency medicine Kern Med. Ctr./UCLA, Bakersfield; faculty physician emergency medicine Parkland Meml. Hosp.; assoc. clin. prof. dept. surgery U. Calif., San Francisco; assoc. prof. surgery U. Tex. Southwestern Med. Sch.; faculty physician emergency svcs. San Francisco Gen. Hosp.; med. dir. Violence Intervention and Prevention Ctr. Co-founder Physicians for a Violence-free Soc. Recipient James D. Mills award for outstanding contbn. to emergency medicine. Office: Univ Tex Southwestern Med Sch # 106 5323 Harry Hines Blvd Dallas TX 75390

TALIAFERRO, ROBERT See BROOKE, TAL

TALIAFERRO, THERESA LYNN, reporter, educator, artist; b. Southfield, Mich., Aug. 18, 1967; BA in polit. sci., U. Calif., 1990; MA in journalism, U. Mich., 1992. NABJ scholarship intern WBAL-TV, Balt., 1988; undergrad. student intern KPIX-TV, San Francisco, 1989—90; grad student intern WDIV-TV, Detroit, 1991—92; sideline reporter ESPN at U. Mich., 1991; morning news anchor/reporter/overnight prodr. WMC-TV, Memphis, 1992—93; gen. assignment reporter KOMO-TV, Seattle, 1993—95; freelance reporter/newsroom anchor KNTV-TV, San Jose, 1995—96; weekend anchor/reporter KCBA-TV, 1996; freelance creative cons. Trans World Internat., 1997; sub. tchr. Santa Clara Unified Sch. Dist., 2002—, Woodside Unified Sch. Dist., 2002—. Voice over (instructional video) Federal Express, Memphis, Tenn., 1993—94, on-camera talent Dobbs Internat., Memphis, 1993—94, Lockheed Missiles & Space Co., Sunnydale, Calif., 1991; dir.: (theatre) Magic To Do Chorus, 2000—01; company mem. Theatre Works, Palo Alto, Calif., 1977—86. Fund raising coord./mistress of ceremonies An Evening with Ben Vereen-Mt. Zion Ethnic Sch. Save the Children Program Fundraiser, Mt. Zion Bapt. Ch., Seattle, 1995; mistress of ceremonies Installation Ceremony - 100 Black Women of Silicon Valley, San Jose, 1995; choir mem. St. Francis of Assisi, 2001, St. Joseph Cathedral Basilica, 2000; music ministry Plymouth United Meth. Ch., Detroit, 1999. Recipient Mid-Peninsula Ret. Tcrs. Assn. Scholarship, 1985, First Place Solo, Spring Sing Competition, 1987, UCLA scholarship intern, 1988; grantee U. Mich. Rackham Minority Merit fellowship, 1990—92; Readers Digest scholarship, 1990—92. Avocations: singing, writing, swimming.

TALKINGTON, WILLIAM ALE, retired publishing company executive; b. Seymour, Ind., Apr. 14, 1948; s. Robert James and Margaret (Ale) T.; m. Marilyn Kay Huffman, Aug. 30, 1969; children— Matthew A., Bradley AB in English, Ind. U., 1970. Mktg. mgr. McGraw-Hill, N.Y.C., 1974-75, dist. mgr., 1975-78, editor, 1978-80, regional mgr., 1980-82, editorial dir., 1982-84, dir. mktg. services, 1984-92; v.p. sales and mktg. Merrill Pub., 1984-92; pres. Holt, Rinehart & Winston, Austin, 1992-99; ret., 1999. Mem. Am. Mgmt. Assn., Assn. Am. Pubs.

TALL, CRAIG E. finance company executive; B in Econs., U. Pa.; postgrad., U. Calif., Berkeley. Former pres. Compensation Programs, Inc.; exec. v.p. WM Fin. Washington Mut., Inc., 1985—87, exec. v.p. corp. devel., 1987—99, mem. exec. team, 1990—, vice chair corp. devel., 1999—2002, vice chair for corp. devel. and strategic planning, 2002—. Founder, past pres. bd. trustees Seattle Acad. Arts and Scis.; former pres. bd. trustees Wash. chpt. Leukemia Soc. Am.; mem. program adv. coun. Puget Sound Blood Ctr. Office: Washington Mut Inc 1201 3d Ave Seattle WA 98101

TALL, SONIA TERRY, humanities educator, researcher; arrived in U.S., 1993; m. Abasse Tall; children: Amadou, Mouhamadou, Oumar, Billy. BA, U. Paris IV, PhD, 1991. Asst. prof. Roosevelt U., Chgo., 1995—2003, Kennedy-King Coll., Chgo., 2003—. Author: (literary criticism) Collective creation in Soyinka's Dance of the Forests, The New Negro Movement and the African Heritage, (film criticism) African Cinema as a Tool for Development. Recipient Peace Edn. award for St Mary Sch., Senegal, UNESCO, 1990. Mem.: Coll. Lang. Assn.

TALLACKSON, HARVEY DEAN, state legislator, real estate and insurance salesman; b. Grafton, N.D., May 15, 1925; s. Arthur J. and Mabel R (McDougald) T.; m. Glenna M. Walstad, Aug. 4, 1946; children: Lynda, Thomas, Debra, Amy, Laura. Grad. h.s., Park River, N.D. Grain and potato farmer, Grafton, 1946-68; ins. agt. Tallackson Ins., Grafton, 1968—; mem. N.D. Senate, Bismark, 1976—; real estate salesman Johnson Real Estate, Grafton, 1982—. Chmn. appropriation com. N.D. Senate, 1987-93. Bd. dirs. Nodak Rural Electric Coop., Grand Forks, N.D., 1965—; bd. dirs. Minnkota Power Coop., Grand Forks, 1979—, pres., 1990—. Recipient Pub. Svc. award N.D. Lignite Coun., 1989; named Outstanding Young Farmer by Area Chamber of Walsh & Pembina Counties, 1951-52. Mem. Nat. Coun. Ins. Legislatures (mem. exec. com. 1985—, pres. 1996-97), Lions (pres. 1977-79), Masons. Democrat. Lutheran. Avocations: golf, curling, travel, reading. Office: Tallackson Ins & Real Estate 53 W 5th St Grafton ND 58237-1468

TALLCHIEF, MARIA, ballerina; b. Fairfax, Okla., Jan. 24, 1925; d. Alexander Joseph and Ruth Mary (Porter) Tallchief; m. Henry Paschen, Jr., June 3, 1956; 1 child, Elise Paschen. DFA (hon.), Lake Forest (Ill.) Coll., Colby Coll., Waterville, Maine, 1968, Ripon Coll., 1973, Boston Coll., Smith Coll., 1981, Northwestern U., Evanston, Ill., 1982, Yale U., 1984, St. Mary-of-the-Woods (Ind.) Coll., 1984, Dartmouth Coll., 1985, St. Xavier Coll., 1989, U. Ill., 1997. Ballerina Ballet Russe de Monte Carlo, 1942-47; with N.Y.C. Ballet Co., 1947-65, prima ballerina, 1947-60; founder Chgo. City Ballet, 1979; now ballet dir. Lyric Opera Chgo., 1979—. Ballerina Ballet Russe de Monte Carlo, 1942—47, N.Y.C. Ballet Co., 1947—65, prima ballerina, 1947—60; founder Chgo. City Ballet, 1979; dir. ballet Lyric Opera Chgo., 1979. Performer: (films) Presenting Lily Mais, 1943, Million Dollar Mermaid, 1953. Named Hon. Princess, Osage Indian Tribe, 1953; named to Nat. Women's Hall of Fame, 1996, Internat. Women's Forum Hall of Fame, 1997; recipient Disting. Svc. award, U. Okla., 1972, Dance Mag. award, 1960, Jane Addams Humanitarian award, Rockford Coll., 1973, Order of Lincoln award, 1974, Bravo award, Rosary Coll., 1983, award, Dance Educators Am., 1956, Achievement award, Women's Nat. Press Club, 1953, Capezio award, 1965, Nat. Medal of Arts, Pres. Clinton, 1999. Mem.: Nat. Soc. Arts and Letters. Office: Lyric Opera Ballet 20 N Wacker Dr Ste 860 Chicago IL 60606-2874

TALLEDO, OSCAR EDUARDO, medical educator; b. Sullana, Piura, Peru, Aug. 1, 1929; s. Jorge Antonio and Flora Natividad (Cordova) T.; m. Jeanette McCarley, June 8, 1959; children: Roy Anthony, Paul Frederick, Linda Jeanette. BS, San Marcos U., 1948, MD, 1955. Diplomate Am. Bd. Ob-Gyn., Am. Bd. Laser Surgery. Intern Crawford W. Long Hosp., Atlanta, 1956-57, resident, 1957-58, Med. Coll. Ga., Augusta, 1958-60, fellow in gynecology, 1960-61, chief gynecologic oncology, 1961—, prof. ob-gyn, 1970—, instr., 1961-63, asst. prof., 1963-68, assoc. prof., 1968-71, prof., 1971—, acting chmn., 1981-82. Nat. Heart Inst. grantee, 1965 Fellow Am. Coll. Ob-Gyn, ACS, Gynecologic Oncology Soc.; mem. Soc. Gynecologic Investigation, AMA, Am. Fertility Soc., Richmond County Med. Soc., Ga. Ob-Gyn Soc., So. Med. Assn., S. Atlantic Assn. Ob-Gyn, Gyn-Urology Soc., Ga. Med. Assn. Clubs; Augusta Country. Lodges: Rotary (chmn. world community service com., Augusta 1983). Presbyterian. Home: 817 Aumond Pl W Augusta GA 30909-3106 Office: Med Coll Ga Dept Gyn Oncology Dept Ob Gyn Augusta GA 30912

TALLENT, STEPHEN EDISON, lawyer; b. Columbus, Nebr., Aug. 10, 1937; s. William E. and Helen Tallent; m. Martha Sutcliffe, Apr. 6, 1971; 1 child, Jennifer Diane. BA, Stanford U.; JD, U. Chgo.; LLD (hon.), Lincoln U. Bar: Calif. 1963, U.S. Dist. Ct. (so. and cen. dists.) Calif. 1965, U.S. Dist. Ct. (so. and ea. dists.) N.Y. 1989, U.S. Ct. Appeals (D.C. cir. 1981), U.S. Ct. Appeals (2d cir.) 1987, U.S. Ct. Appeals (3d. cir.) 1980, U.S. Ct. Appeals (4th cir.) 1982, U.S. Ct. Appeals (9th cir.) 1968, U.S. Ct. Mil. Appeals 1965, U.S. Supreme Ct. 1973. Ptnr. Gibson, Dunn & Crutcher, L.A., 1962-96; pvt. practice Washington, 1997—. Former adj. prof. Loyola Law Sch., L.A.; mem. vis. com. U. Chgo. Law Sch.; former mem. Calif. Atty. Gen.'s adv. com. for Evaluation of Anti-Organized Crime Programs; mem. L.A. Town Hall, L.A. World Affairs Council; mem. bd. visitors Stanford Law Sch.; founding dir. Am. Employment Law Coun., 1993—. Fellow Coll. Labor and Employment Lawyers (founding, pres. and gov. 1995—); mem. ABA (chair labor and employment law sect. 1998-99), Indsl. Rels. Rsch. Assn. Home: PO Box 512 Reedville VA 22539-0512 Office: 1050 Connecticut Ave NW Ste 900 Washington DC 20036-5320 Office Phone: 202-955-8552.

TALLERICO, DELMA DOLORES, elementary school educator; b. Pricedale, Pa., May 2, 1952; d. Thomas Delmar Hepple and Elizabeth Theresa (Katchmark) Ambler; m. Samuel Joseph Tallerico, Aug. 9, 1975; children: Robert Peter, Michael James, Patrick Joseph. BA, Seton Hill Coll., 1974; MA in Tchg., U. Pitts., 1975; diploma, Inst. Children's Lit., 1994. Lic. real estate broker, Pa. Counselor Youth Corps, Greensburg, Pa., 1972-74; intern Greensburg (Pa.)-Salem, 1974-75; tchr. St. James Elem., Pitts., 1975-80; real estate agt. Metro Realty, Pitts., 1989-92; mus. tchr. Frick Art and Hist. Ctr., Pitts., 1993—99; computer tchr. St. Sebastian Sch., 2002—. Mem. St. Mary's Choir. Mem.: Cath. Bus. and Women's Profl. Assn. Republican. Roman Catholic. Avocation: piano.

TALLET, JORGE ANTONIO, philosopher, writer; b. Havana, Cuba, Feb. 3, 1928; came to the U.S., 1956; s. José Zacarías Tallet and Judith Martínez; m. Elena Villazón, Oct. 13, 1958; children: Julio, Lourdes María. PhD, U. Havana, 1953; grad., Havana Inst. Secondary Edn., 1945. Columnist Newspaper El Mundo, Havana, 1950-55; writer, editor AP, N.Y.C., 1956-59, Fgn. News Svc., N.Y.C., 1961-64, UPI, N.Y.C., 1964-71, Editl. Am., Miami, Fla., 1971-76, The Miami Herald, 1976-90. Lectr. philosophy SUNY, Purchase and Mount Vernon, 1970-71. Author: Perspectivas Actuales de la Filosofía, 1954, The Absolute Being, 1955, 58, The Possible Universe, 1990, 97; author of essays. Avocations: reading, music listening, meditating, walking, travel.

TALLET, MARGARET ANNE, theatre executive; b. Binghamton, N.Y., Feb. 14, 1953; d. George Francis and Wilma Ann (Wagner) T.; m. Peter A., Myks, July 6, 1991. BA, St. Mary's Coll./U. Notre Dame, 1975; MBA, SUNY, 1979. Asst. dir. Parrish Art Mus., Southampton, N.Y., 1979-81; assoc. dir. devel. Detroit Inst. Arts Founders Soc., 1981-92; v.p. Franco Pub. Rels. Group, Detroit, 1992-96; pres. Music Hall Ctr. for the Performing Arts, 1996—. Bd. dirs. Aid for AIDS Rsch., 1987-92, Detroiters at Heart, 1992—; mktg. com. Mich. Cancer Found., Detroit, 1992—, Cultural adv. comm. city of Detroit, Adv. bd.:Arts Serve MI. Mem. Pub. Rels. Soc. Am. Roman Catholic. Office: Music Hall Ctr for Performing Arts 350 Madison St Detroit MI 48226-2290

TALLETT, ELIZABETH EDITH, biopharmaceutical company executive; b. London, Apr. 2, 1949; d. Edward and Edith May (Vickers) Symons; m. James Edward Wavle Jr.; children: James Edward Tallett, Alexander Martin Tallett, Christopher Andrew Wavle. BS with honors, U. Nottingham (Eng.), 1970. Ops. rsch. analyst So. Gas Bd., 1970-73; mgmt. svcs. mgr. Warner-Lamber (UK), Eastleigh, Eng., 1973-77, strategic planning mgr., 1977-81; internat. dir. strategic planning Warner-Lambert, Morris Plains, N.J., 1981-82, corp. dir. strategic planning, 1982-84; dir. mktg. ops. Parke-Davis, Morris Plains, 1984-87; exec. v.p. therapeutic products Centocor, Malvern, Pa., 1987-89, pres. pharms. div., 1989-92; pres., CEO Transcell Techs., Inc., Monmouth Junction, N.J., 1992-96, Dioscor, Inc., Stockton, 1996—2003; prin. Hunter Ptnrs. LLC, 2002—. Bd. dirs. Prin. Fin. Group, Inc., Varian, Inc., Coventry Health Care, Inc., IntegraMed Am. Inc., Immunicon Inc., Varian Semi Conductor Equipment Assoc. Inc.; dir. Biotech. Coun. N.J., NJ Ctr. Life Sci. Contbr. articles to profl. jours. Avocations: acting, badminton, travel, skiing.

TALLEY, CAROL LEE, newspaper editor; b. Bklyn., Sept. 10, 1937; d. George Joseph and Viola (Kovash) T.; children— Sherry, Jill, Scott. Student, U. Ky., 1955-57, Ohio U., 1957-58. Reporter Easton (Pa.) Daily Express, 1958-60; reporter N.J. Herald, 1962-64, edn. editor, 1964-66; reporter Daily Advance, Dover, N.J., 1966-68, polit. editor, investigative reporter, from 1969, mng. editor, 1974-81; editor Evening Sentinel, Carlisle, Pa., 1982—. Mem. A.P. Task Force N.J., 1970, Pa. Associated Press Mng. Editor's Bd. Dirs. Past

bd. dirs. Helen Stevens Cmty. Mental Health Ctr. (chair), Carlisle; past pres. bd. dirs. Stevens Mental Health Ctr., Carlisle. Recipient pub. service awards Nat. Headliners, 1971, Sigma Delta Chi, 1971, George Polk Meml. award for local reporting, 1974, Dew Meml. award Pa. Newspaper Pub.'s Assn., 1985. Mem. Pa. Newspaper Editors Soc., Kiwanis Club. Office: 457 E North St Carlisle PA 17013-2655

TALLEY, CHARLES RICHMOND, commercial banking executive; b. Richmond, Va., Dec. 23, 1925; s. Charles Edward and Marie (Thorckmorton) Talley; m. Anne Marie Smith, June 4, 1948; children: Laurie Anne, Charles Richmond Jr. BA in Econs, U. Richmond, 1949; postgrad., Sch. Banking Rutgers U., 1959-61, Sch. Fin. Pub. Relations, Northwestern U., 1954-55; grad. exec. program, U. Va., 1974. Asst. cashier 1st & Mchts. Nat. Bank, Richmond, 1955-57, asst. v.p., 1957-63, v.p., 1963-69, sr. v.p., 1969-73, exec. v.p., 1973-84; corp. exec. officer Sovran Bank N.A., 1984-86, ret., 1986, 1986. Bd dirs Security Atlantic Life Ins Co; vpres. bd dirs Security Atlantic Ins Agency; bd dirs Sovran Properties Inc; vice chmn bd dirs Va Educ Loan Authority, 1983—87, chmn, 1988—91; vpres, mem exec comt Richmond Eye and Ear Hosp, pres, 1988—91. Pres Richmond Jr Cof C, 1960—61; treas Richmond chpt Nat Found, 1956—; pres Baptist Extension Bd Va, 1973—75; bd dirs Commonwealth Eye and Ear, 1986—89, Richmond Symphony Orchestra, Richmond Better Bus Bur. With USNR, 1944—46. Mem.: Richmond Clearing House Asn (pres 1977), Richmond Metropolitan CofC (bd dirs 1979—89), Tides Lodge Golf and Country Club (Irvington, Va), Bull and Bear Club, Willow Oaks Country Club Richmond (pres 1971), Rotary (bd dirs Richmond 1981—83). Home: 4301 Stratford Rd Richmond VA 23225-1060 also: Bldg 2 Unit 2 The Green At Tides Lodge Irvington VA 22480

TALLEY, DOUGLAS ERIC, music educator; b. Louisiana, Mo., Sept. 10, 1959; s. Joseph B. and Norine K. Talley; m. Elena M Lence, May 22, 1993; 1 child, Cecilia Ann. MusB in Edn., U. Kans., 1982; MusM in Edn., U. North Tex., 1984. Cert. tchr. Kans. Musician Gaslight Gang, Lawrence, Kans., 1981—82; showroom musician Dunes Hotel and Country Club, Las Vegas, 1982—82; music instr. Shawnee Mission (Kans.) USD 512, 1984—; musician Vista Orch., Kansas City, Mo., 1985—87, Blvd. Big Band, Kansas City, Mo., 1987—98, Trilogy Big Band, Kansas City, Mo., 1990—, Trinity Jazz Ensemble, Kansas City, Mo., 1991—97, New Kans. City Seven, Kansas City, Mo., 1991—98, Doug Talley Quartet, Lenexa, Kans., 1995—. Kans. City Jazz Orch., Kansas City, Mo., 2003—; music instr. Baker U., Baldwin City, Kans., 1998—99, Mid Am. Nazarene U., Olathe, Kans., 2000—01. Music dir. Rotary Youth Jazz Band, Overland Pk., Kans., 1992—; saxophone artist Selmer Co., Elkhart, Ind., 1995—; clinician Internat. Assn. of Jazz Assn. Tchr. Tng. Inst., Kansas City, Mo., 2003. Musician: (albums) Town Topic, 1996, Night and Day: musings on the Cole Porter Songbook, 1998, Kansas City Suite, 2001. Fellow, Mid-America Arts Alliance, 1995, 1997, Kans. Arts Commn., 1997; grantee, Shawnee Mission Found., 1995, 1998. Mem.: Music Educators Nat. Conf., Internat. Assn. of Jazz Edn., Am. Fedn. of Musicians, Kans. Music Educators Assn. (festival chmn. 2001—03), Pi Kappa Lambda, Phi Kappa Phi (life). Independent. Home: 7807 Caenen Lake Dr Lenexa KS 66216 Office: Shawnee Mission USD 512 7500 Quivira Shawnee Mission KS 66216 Office Phone: 913-993-1031. E-mail: trtalley@smsd.org.

TALLEY, HAYWARD LEROY, communications executive; b. Nov. 3, 1923; s. Roy and Reta (Hayward) T.; m. Emma Mae Chandler, Sept. 2, 1950; children: Brian, Kevin. BS, U. Ill., 1948. Chief engr. Sta. WOKZ-AM-FM, Alton, Ill., 1948-50; pres., gen. mgr. Talley Broadcasting Corp. (sta. WSMI AM and FM), Litchfield, Ill., 1950—; pres. Talley Broadcasting Co. (sta. KBKB AM and FM), Ft. Madison, Iowa, 1960-99, North Cen. Iowa Broadcasting Co. (stas. KLSS, KSMN), Mason City, 1963-83, Talley Broadcasting Corp. (sta. WAOX), Staunton, Ill., 1999—. Chmn. ofcl. bd. Meth. Ch., 1961-63, 65-66, 2003-, chmn. ch. coun., 2003—; adv. bd. Lewis & Clark Coll., 1978—. With Signal Corps, U.S. Army. Recipient Vincent T. Wasilewski Broadcaster of Yr. award, Ill. Broadcasters Assn., 2002. Mem.: Ill. Broadcasters Assn., Nat. Assn. Broadcasters, Am. Legion, Masons, Rotary (pres. Litchfield Club 1989—90). Home: 1414 N Harrison St Litchfield IL 62056-1209 Office: Sta WSMI PO Box 10 Litchfield IL 62056-0010

TALLEY, JOSEPH EUGENE, psychologist; b. Springfield, Mass., May 27, 1949; s. Joseph Addison and Miriam Louise (Ayers) T.; m. Vibeke Absalon, Jan. 3, 1981; children: Kirsten, David, Jonathan. BA, U. Richmond, 1971; MA, Radford Coll., 1973; PhD, U. Va., 1978. Diplomate Am. Bd. Profl. Psychology; lic. psychologist, N.C.; cert. health svc. provider, N.C. Assoc. clin. prof. dept. psychiatry and behavioral scis. Duke U. Med. Ctr., Durham, N.C., 1977—, coord. rsch., program evaluation and testing svcs., 1979—; gen. practice psychotherapy Durham, N.C., 1980—. Author: Study Skills, 1981, Performance Prediciton of Law Enforcement Personnel, 1990, The Predictors of Successful Very Brief Psychotherapy, 1992, Seeking Something Sacred: Managing Our Frustrations, Losses and Fears, 2001; author, editor: Counseling and Psychotherapy Services, 1985, Counseling and Psychotherapy with College Students: A Guide to Treatment, 1986, Multicultural Needs Assessment with College and University Populations, 1995; contbr. articles to profl. jours. Bd. deacons Hillsborough Presbyn. Ch., N.C., 1983-85, chmn., 1985, bd. elders, 1987-94, 2002—, v.p. bd. trustees, 1992-94; bd. dirs. Orange County Mental Health Assn., Chapel Hill, N.C., 1982-83, mem. legis. com., 1983, site visitor for accreditation. Fellow APA, Am. Acad. Clin. Psychology, Am. Acad. Counseling Psychology, Am. Acad. Counseling Psychology (pres. 1995-97, Disting. Svc. award 2002); mem. Am. Bd. Profl. Psychology (sec./treas. coun. of pres.'s psychology splty. acads. 1997-98, chmn./CEO 2000-03, spl. liaison to related groups 2003—, past chmn., CEO 2003—, Disting. Contbns. award 2002), N.C. Psychol. Assn., Nat. Soc. Clin. Hypnosis (cert. and approved cons., supr. and practitioner, ethics com. 1995-97), Phi Kappa Phi, Omicron Delta Kappa, Psi Chi, Phi Kappa Sigma. Democrat. Presbyterian. Home: 134 E Tryon St Hillsborough NC 27278-2550 Office: Duke U Counseling & Psychol Svcs PO Box 90955 214 Page Bldg Durham NC 27708-0955 Business E-Mail: jtalley@acpub.duke.edu.

TALLEY, NICHOLAS JOSEPH, educator, physician, scientist; b. Perth, Australia, Jan. 9, 1956; s. Nicholas Alexander and Irene Mary Talley; children: Nicholas Stephen, Matthew Jonathon, Nicole Sarah. MB, BS, U. NSW, Sydney, Australia, 1979; PhD, U. Sydney, 1987; MD, U. NSW, Sydney, Australia, 1993; M in Med. Sci., 2003. Resident med. officer/registrar Prince of Wales Hosp., Sydney, 1979-83; rsch. fellow, prof. registrar Royal North Shore Hosp., Sydney, 1983-87; rsch. fellow Mayo Clinic, Rochester, Minn., 1987-88, asst. prof. medicine, 1988-91, assoc. prof., 1991-93; found. prof. Nepean Hosp., U. Sydney, 1993—2002; prof. medicine, cons. Mayo Clinic Coll. Med., 2002—. Author: (textbooks) Examination Medicine, 1985, 4th edit., 2000, Clinical Examination, 1988, 4th edit., 2001, Internal Medicine, 1990, 2d edit., 2000, Clinical Gastroenterology, 1996, Multiple Choice Questions in Clinical Examination, 1996, Pocket Clinical Examination, 1998, 2nd. edit., 2002; asst. editor Am. Jour. Gastroenterology, 1992-97; co- editor - in chief, Am. Jour. of Gastroenterology, 2004-; mem. editl. bd. Gastroenterology, 1993-98, Jour. Clin. Gstroenterology, 1994—, Alimentary Pharmacology and Therapeutics, 1995-2003; mem. editl. bd. Jour. Gastroenterology and Hepatology, 1994-98, editor, 1998-2003; contbr. articles and revs. to prof., jours., chpts. to books. Pres. Miranda br. Young Liberals, Sydney, 1976; wing comdr. Royal Australia Air Force, 2000. Postgrad. rsch. scholar Nat. Health and Med. Rsch. Coun., Australia, 1984-85. Fellow ACP, Royal Australasian Coll. Physicians, Am. Coll. Gastroenterology, Australian Faculty Pub. Health Medicine (founding mem.), Royal Coll. Physicians; mem. Am. Gastroent. Assn., Gastroent. Soc. Australia, Brit. Soc. Gastroenterology, Functional Brain Gut Rsch. Group (pres.). Avocations: tennis, writing, travel, jogging, martial arts. Office: Mayo Clinic 200 First St SW Rochester MN 55905 Office Phone: 507-266-1989.

TALLEY, RICHARD WOODROW, accountant; b. Birmingham, Ala., Sept. 10, 1941; s. Alton Woodrow and Alta O. (Tittle) T.; m. Anita Marcell Moses, Jan. 14, 1966; children: Richard Woodrow Jr., Leah Michelle. BS in Commerce and Bus. Adminstrn., U. Ala., 1964. CPA Ala. Pres. Smither, Talley & Mauldin, P.C., Decatur, Ala., 1964—. Officer Boy Scouts Am., Decatur, Austin Band Boosters, Decatur, PTA, Decatur; mgr., coach Dixie Youth Baseball, Decatur; deacon Ch. of Christ. Served as sgt. USAR, 1964-70. Named Boss of Yr. Decatur Jaycees, 1980. Mem. AICPA, Tenn. Soc. CPAs, Ala. Soc. CPAs, Commerce Execs. Soc. U. Ala., Lions (sec. 1982-83, treas. 1985-86, sec.-treas. 1994-95). Avocations: genealogy, photography. Home: 1266 Brandywine Ln SE Decatur AL 35601-4582 Office: Smither Talley & Mauldin PC PO Box 2067 Decatur AL 35602-2067 Office Phone: 256-353-1421. Business E-Mail: rtalley@stm.cpa.com.

TALLEY, ROBERT COCHRAN, medical school dean and administrator, cardiologist; b. May 26, 1936; m. Katherine Ann Plocar; children: Andrew, Katherine, David. BS, U. Mich., 1958; MD, U. Chgo., 1962. Diplomate Nat. Bd. Med. Examiners (mem. medicine com. 1984-88, com. chair 1988-93). Asst. prof., dept. physiology and medicine U. Tex. Med. Sch., San Antonio, 1969—71, head, sect. cardiovascular diseases, 1971—75, assoc. prof., dept. medicine, 1971—75; acting chief medicine VA Hosp., San Antonio, 1974, chief cardiology svc., 1973—75; chmn. dept. internal medicine U. S.D. Sch. Medicine, Sioux Falls, 1975—87, Freeman prof. medicine, 1984—87, interim v.p., dean, 1986—87, v.p., dean, 1987—. Mem. Liaison Com. on Med. Edn., 1998—; mem. adminstrn. bd., coun. of deans Assn. Am. Med. Colls., 1999—2000. Contbr. articles to med. jours. Surgeon USPHS, 1966—68. Tchg. scholar, Am. Heart Assn. U. Chgo., 1972—75. Fellow: ACP, Am. Coll. Cardiology; mem.: AMA, Liasion Commt. on Med. Edu., Assoc. of Amer. Med. Coll. Council of Deans New Dean Mentoring Prog., 1998-, Am. Fedn. Clin. Rsch., Am. Heart Assn. (bd. dirs. Dakota affiliate). Home: 1305 Cedar Ln Sioux Falls SD 57103-4512 Office: U SD Sch Medicine 1400 W 22nd St Sioux Falls SD 57105-1505

TALLEY, ROBERT MORRELL, aerospace company executive; b. Erwin, Tenn., Mar. 13, 1924; s. Robert Taylor and Anna Laura (Morrell) T.; m. Mary Sue Williams, June 5, 1948; children: David, Carol. Student, East Tenn. State Coll., 1942-43, U. Va., 1943-44; BS U. S.C., 1945; MS, U. Tenn., 1948, PhD, 1950. Chief infrared br., chief solid state div. U.S. Naval Ordnance Lab., White Oak, Md., 1951-58; mgr. lab. Santa Barbara Rsch. Ctr. subs. Hughes Aircraft, Calif., 1958-69, v.p., 1969-76, pres., 1976-89, ret. Contbr. articles to profl. jours.; patentee in field. Trustee, hon. alumnus U. Calif.-Santa Barbara Found.; bd. dirs. Ptnrs. in Edn., Santa Barbara. With USN, 1943-46. Fellow Am. Phys. Soc.; mem. Optical Soc. Am., LaCumbre Club, Sigma Xi

TALLEY, SUSAN ANN, physical therapist, educator; b. Highland Park, Mich., Apr. 7, 1955; d. Archibald Lee Talley and Barbara E. Burns; m. Joseph F. Olesnavage, Aug. 30, 1986; children: Jason N. Olesnavage, Kathryn M. Olesnavage. BS in Phys. Therapy, Wayne State U., 1976, MA in Human Devel., 1982. Cert. phys. therapist Mich., 1976, clin. instr. Am. Phys. Therapy Assn., 1997. Phys. therapist Met. Soc. Crippled Children and Adults, Detroit, 1976—79; asst. prof., phys. therapy Wayne State U., 1980—; phys. therapist Macomb Hosp. Ctr., Warren, 1990—93; academic coord. clin. edn., phys. therapy Wayne State U., 1996—, phys. therapy program dir., 2003—. Clin. rsch. evaluator Henry Ford Hosp., Detroit, 1992—96, U. Mich., Dept Neurology, Ann Arbor, 2000—; adj. faculty, clin. rsch. evaluator Wayne State U., Dept. Neurology, 1995—. Citizens rev. com. facility utilization Ferndale Pub. Schools, Mich., 1998—2000, long term strategic planning com., 1999—2000, dist. transition team, 2000—03. Mem.: Am. Phys. Therapists Assn. (edn., neurology and pediatric sects.), Mich. Phys. Therapy Assn. (ea. dist. chair, vice chair, com. chair 1982—2000, dir. 1989—92, President's Recognition award 1990), Am. Phys. Therapy Assn. (del. ho. del.), Pi Lambda Theta, Phi Beta Kappa. Office: Wayne State University Physical Therapy 259 Mack Ave 2248 EACPHS Detroit MI 48201

TALLEY, TRUMAN MACDONALD, publisher; b. N.Y.C., Feb. 3, 1925; s. Truman Hughes and Helen Nicholson (Macdonald) T.; m. Madelon DeVoe, Oct. 17, 1953 (dec. 1997); children: Melanie, Macdonald, Marina. Student, Buckley Sch., Deerfield Acad., Sorbonne, 1945—46; grad. cum laude, Princeton U., 1949. Assoc. editor New Am. Libr. of World Lit., N.Y.C., 1949-59, editl. v.p., 1959-64; pres., editl. dir. Weybright & Talley, N.Y.C., 1966-78; pub. Truman Talley Books with Times Books, 1978-82; with E.P. Dutton, 1983-98, St. Martin's Press, N.Y.C., 1998—. Mem. grad. bd. Princeton Tiger, 1950—. Trustee Clinton Hall Assn. Merc. Libr., N.Y.C. With AUS, 1943-46, ETO. Decorated Purple Heart. Mem. PEN, Anglers Club, Brook Club, Maidstone Club, Southampton Beach Club. Office: Truman Talley Books St Martin's Press 175 5th Ave New York NY 10010-7703 Office Phone: 212-674-5151 x 461.

TALLEY, WILLIAM GILES, JR., manufacturing executive; b. Adel, Ga., Sept. 25, 1939; s. William Giles and Mary (McGlamry) Talley; m. Jacqueline Vickery, Apr. 14, 1962; children: William Giles, John Lindsey, Bronwyn Ashley. BSBA, U. S.C., 1961. Mgmt. trainee Talley Veneer & Crate Co., Inc., Adel, 1961-62; with Talley's Box Co., Leesburg, Fla., 1962-69, plant mgr., ptnr., 1967-69; gen. mgr. Growers Container Coop., Inc., Leesburg, 1969-96; pres. Talley Acres, Inc., Leesburg, 1979—, Talley Ent., Inc., Leesburg, 1997—. Bd. dirs. Sun Trust Bank Ctrl. Fla., N.A. Past chmn. bd. dirs. Leesburg Hosp. Assn.; bd. dirs. Hospice of Lake Sumter, Inc., 1997—, pres., 1999; bd. dirs., treas., mem. exec. com. Ctrl. Fla. Healthcare Devel. Found., Inc.; trustee Bethune-Cookman Coll., Daytona Beach, Fla., 1999—. Mem.: Leesburg C. of C., Sigma Alpha Epsilon. Republican. Methodist. Home: 2206 Talley Court Rd Leesburg FL 34748-3177 Office: Po Box 49817 Leesburg FL 34749-0817 E-mail: jtalley@aol.com.

TALLMAN, DENNIS EARL, chemistry professor, research scientist; b. Bellefontaine, Ohio, Apr. 23, 1942; s. Maurice Earl and Mary Elizabeth Tallman. PhD, Ohio State U., Columbus, 1968. Postdoctoral rsch. assoc. Cornell U., Ithaca, NY, 1968—70; asst. prof. of chemistry N.D. State U., Fargo, 1970—73, assoc. prof. of chemistry, 1973—78, prof. of chemistry, 1978—. Co-dir. Corrosion/Coatings Rsch. Ctr. N.D. State U., Fargo, 2000—. Contbr. articles to profl. jours. (Fred Waldren Award for Outstanding Rsch., 2000); N.Am. editor: Jour. Solid State Electrochemistry, 1997—. Recipient postdoctoral fellowship, NIH, 1968—70, numerous rsch. grants, NSF, Dept. of Def., NIH, and EPA, 1970—. Mem.: Nat. Assn. of Corrosion Engrs., Electrochem. Soc., Am. Chem. Soc. (lobbied Congress for increases in fed. rsch. funding 2000—03), Soc. for Electroanalytical Chemistry (life; bd. dirs. 1998—2002), Phi Kappa Phi, Sigma Xi, Phi Lambda Upsilon. Achievements include patents pending for Direct Electrodeposition of Conducting Polymers on Active Metals. Avocations: four-wall handball, skiing, canoeing, biking, backpacking. Office: ND State U Dept Chemistry Fargo ND 58105-5516 E-mail: dennis.tallman@ndsu.nodak.edu.

TALLMAN, MARTIN STUART, hematologist, oncologist; b. Chgo., July 6, 1954; m. Wendy S. Tallman; children: Sarah Chaya, Miriam Leah, Samuel Joseph, Jacob Ezra. BS, U. Mich., Ann Arbor, 1976; MD, Chgo. Med. Sch., 1980. Cert. Am. Bd. Internal Medicine, 1983, in Hematology 1987, in Med. Oncology 1988. Intern, internal medicine McGaw Med. Ctr., Evanston, Ill., 1980—81, resident, internal medicine, 1981—83, chief resident, dept. medicine, 1983—84; asst. attending physician Evanston Hosp., Ill., 1983—84, adj. attending physician, divsn. hematology and oncology, 1989—93; fellow, hematology and oncology U. Wash., Fred Hutchinson Cancer Rsch. Ctr., Seattle, 1984—87; attending physician, divsn. oncology VA Med. Ctr., Seattle, 1987—88; attending physician Rehab. Inst. of Chgo., 1988—; attending physician, divsn. hematology & oncology Northwestern Meml. Hosp., Chgo., 1988—; adj. attending physician, divsn. hematology & oncology Lakeside VA Med. Ctr., Chgo., 1988—; mem. Robert H. Lurie Cancer Ctr., Northwestern U., Evanston, Ill., 1988—, co-chmn., edn. com., 1989—, dir., clin. leukemia rsch. program, 1990—, asst. dir., bone marrow transplant program, 1991—2000, dir., hematologic malignancy program, 2001—; asst. prof., divsn. hematology & oncology Northwestern U. Feinberg Sch. Medicine, Evanston, Ill., 1988—96, assoc. prof., divsn. hematology & oncology, 1996—2002, prof., divsn. hematology & oncology, 2002—. Med. adv. bd. mem. Leukemia Rsch. Found., 1992—97, chmn., med. adv. bd., 1997—99; mem., leustatin adv. bd. Pharms. Rsch. Inst., Raritan, NJ, 1993—; mem., internat. adv. group Pharmacia, 1995—; mem., autologous bone marrow transplant adv. group U.S. Gen. Acctg. Office, Dept. Health and Human Svcs., 1995—; mem., med. adv. bd. Earl J. Goldberg Aplastic Anemia Found., 1995—; mem., hematology adv. bd. Chiron Therapeutics, Emerville, Calif., 1996—; mem., med. adv. bd. Hairy Cell Leukemia Rsch. Found., 1996—; mem., adv. bd. Supergen, 1997—; mem., safety bd. Can. Leukemia Study Group, 1999—; mem., adv. bd. Searle/Monsanto, 1999—, Wyeth-Ayerst Pharm., 1999—. Recipient John T. O'Connell award, Chgo. Med. Soc., 1992. Fellow: ACP; mem.: AAAS, Am. Soc. for Blood and Marrow Transplantation, Eastern Cooperative Oncology Group (mem., leukemia com. 1989—, mem., myeloma com. 1989—, mem., bone marrow transplant com. 1989—, mem., cytogenetics subcom. 1991—, co-chmn., leukemia com. 1993—97, mem., bone marrow transplant instl. rev. com. 1993—, mem., audit team 1995—, chair, leukemia com. 1997—), Am. Soc. Clin. Oncology, Ill. Med. Oncology Soc., Ill. Cancer Ctr., Am. Fedn. Clin. Rsch., Am. Cancer Soc., Am. Assn. Cancer Rsch., Internat. Soc. Exptl. Hematology, Internat. Soc. Hematology (mem., internat. sci. com. 1999—), Am. Soc. Hematology (mem., subcom. on neoplasia 1998—, mem., subcom. on publs. 2000—), Internat. Soc. Thrombosis and Haemostasis (mem., haemostasis and malignancy subcom. 1992—, chair, Ea. Coop. Oncology Group Leukemia Com., assoc. editor Blood Jour.). Office: Northwestern Univ Feinberg Sch Medicine Divsn Hematology/Oncology 676 N St Clair St #850 Chicago IL 60611 Office Phone: 312-695-6180. E-mail: m-tallman@northwestern.edu.

TALLMAN, RICHARD C. federal judge, lawyer; b. Oakland, Calif., Mar. 3, 1953; s. Kenneth A. and Jean M. Tallman; m. Cynthia Ostolaza, Nov. 14, 1981. BSC, U. Santa Clara, 1975; JD, Northwestern U., 1978. Bar: Calif. 1978, Wash. 1979, U.S. Dist. Ct. (no. dist.) Calif. 1979, U.S. Dist. Ct. (we. dist.) Wash. 1979, U.S. Dist. Ct. Hawaii 1986, U.S. Dist. Ct. (fed. cir.) Wash. 1999, U.S. Ct. Appeals (9th cir.) 1979, U.S. Dist. Ct. (ea. dist.) Wash. 1998, U.S. Supreme Ct. 1997. Law clk. to Hon. Morrell E. Sharp U.S. Dist. Ct. (we. dist.) Wash., Seattle, 1978—79; trial atty. U.S. Dept. Justice, Washington, 1979—80; asst. U.S. atty. (we. dist.) Wash., Seattle, 1980—83; assoc., then ptnr. Schweppe, Krug & Tausend, PS, Seattle, 1983—89; mem. Bogle & Gates, PLLC, Seattle, 1990—99; ptnr. Tallman & Severin, LLP, Seattle, 1999—2000; apptd. U.S. cir. judge U.S. Ct. Appeals (9th cir.), 2000—. Chmn. western dist. Wash. Lawyer Reps. to Ninth Cir. Jud. Conf., 1996—97. Instr. Nat. Pk. Svc. Seasonal Ranger Acad., Everett and Mt. Vernon, Wash., 1983—93; chmn. Edmonds C.C. Found., Lynnwood, Wash., 1990—92; gen. counsel Seattle-King County Crime Stoppers, 1987—99; mem. exec. bd. Chief Seattle coun. Boy Scouts Am., 1997—. Mem.: ABA, Fed. Judges Assn. (bd. dirs. 2002—), King County Bar Assn., Fed. Bar Assn. (we. dist. trustee 1992—93, v.p. 1994, pres. 1995), Wash. Athletic Club, Rainier Club. Avocations: hunting, hiking, fishing. Office: Park Place Bldg 1200 Sixth Avenue 21st FL Seattle WA 98101-3123

TALLMAN, ROBERT HALL, investment company executive; b. Creston, Iowa, Aug. 10, 1915; s. Ralph H. and Hazel Verne (Hall) T.; m. Elizabeth Childs, Sept. 19, 1938; children: Susan, Mary, Timothy. BS, U. Nebr., 1937. Trainee to dist. mgr. Firestone Tire & Rubber Co., Akron, Ohio, 1937-50; pres. Tallman Oil Co., Fargo, N.D., 1950-80; chmn. bd. State Bank of Hawley, Minn., 1966-70, 1st Nat. Bank of Barnesville, Minn., 1965-88; pres. Tallman Investment Ent., Fargo, 1980—; pres., dir. Dak Tech. Inc. Dir. Bell Farms. Past pres. Fargo Bd. Edn., N.D. Petroleum Coun.; past pres. St. Lukes Hosp. Assn.; past chmn. trustees 1st Congl. Ch. of Fargo; trustee U. Nebr. Found., 1987—. Mem. Fargo C. of C. (past pres.), Am. Assn. Ret. Persons, Nat. Rifle Assn., N.D. State U. Teammakers Club (past pres.), Fargo Country Club, Kiwanis (past pres.), Masons, Shriners, Elks. Republican. Congregationalist. Avocations: golf, hunting, fishing, travel, photography. Office: Box 9886 2108 S University Dr Fargo ND 58103-5342 Home: 1200 Harwood Dr Apt 332 Fargo ND 58104-6294

TALLMER, MARGOT SALLOP, psychologist, psychoanalyst, gerontologist; b. N.Y.C., NY, Sept. 8, 1925; d. Harry and Mildred (Schifrin) Sallop; m. Jonathan Tallmer, Apr. 12, 1949 (dec.); children: Mary, Megan, Jill, Andrew. MS, NYU, 1948; MA, Yeshiva U., 1962, PhD, 1967; postgrad., NYU, 1976. Faculty dept. psychol. founds. Hunter Coll., NYC, 1969-76, assoc. prof., 1976-79, prof., 1979—94, prof. emeritus; staff psychologist Mt. Sinai Hosp., NY, 1967-68; pvt. practice NYC, 1969—2004; faculty NY Ctr. for Psychoanalytic Tng., NY. Lectr. N.Y. Ctr. Psychoanalytic Tng. Author: Sex in Later Life, 1996; editor: Sex and Life Threatening Illness, HIV Testing Positive, The Child and Death, Sexuality and the Older Adult; co-author: Suicide in the Elderly; mem. editl. bd. Current Issues in Psychoanalysis, Psychoanalytic Rev.; contbr. chpts. to textbooks, articles to profl jours. Mem. APA, Boston Soc. Gerontologic Psychiatry, N.Y. State Psychol. Assn. (past pres. divsn. adult devel. and aging), Nat. Psychol. Assn. for Psychoanalysis (trustee 1972—, bd. dir. 1972—). Address: 515 E 85th St New York NY 10028-0246 Personal E-mail: mamadoc4@nyc.rr.com.

TALLY, LURA SELF, state legislator; b. Statesville, NC, Dec. 9, 1921; d. Robert Ottis and Sara (Cowles) Self; m. J.O. Tally Jr., Jan. 30, 1943 (div. 1970); children: Robert Taylor, John Cowles. AB, Duke U., 1942; MA, NC State U., 1970. Tchr., former guidance counselor Fayetteville (NC) city schs.; mem. NC Ho. of Reps. from 20th Dist., 1971—83, chmn. com. higher edn., 1975, 1980—83, vice-chmn. com. appropriations for edn., 1973—86; state senator from 12th Dist. NC, 1983—95; chmn. NC Senate Com. of Natural Resources, Cmty. Devel. and Wildlife, 1987, Environment and Natural Resources, 1989—94. Past pres. Cumberland County Mental Health Assn., NC Historic Preservation Soc.; trustee Fayetteville Tech. Inst., 1981—94; active Legis. Rsch. Com. Mem.: Am. Pers. and Guidance Assn., Fayetteville Woman's Club (past pres.), Fayetteville Bus. and Profl. Women's Club, Kappa Delta, Delta Kappa Gamma. Methodist. Office: W Jones St Raleigh NC 27601

TALMADGE, PHILIP ALBERT, former state supreme court justice, former state senator; b. Seattle, Apr. 23, 1952; s. Judson H., Jr. and Jeanne C. Talmadge; m. Darlene L. Nelson, Sept. 6, 1970; children: Adam, Matthew, Jessica, Jonathan, Annemarie. BA magna cum laude, Yale U., 1973; JD, U. Wash., 1976. Bar: Wash. 1976. Atty. Karr Tuttle Campbell, 1976—89; pres. Talmadge & Cutler, P.S., 1989—95; senator State of Wash., 1979—94; justice Supreme Ct. Wash., 1995—2001; ptnr. Talmadge Law Group PLLC, 2001—. Author: The Nixon Doctrine and the Reaction of Three Asian Nations, 1973; editor: Law Rev., 1975—76; contbr. articles to profl. jours. Chair Senate Judiciary Com., 1981, 1983—87, Senate Health and Human Svcs. Com., 1992—95, Wash. Senate, 1978—94, ways and means com., children and family svcs. com., edn. com. Fellow: Am. Assn. Appellate Lawyers; mem.: King County Bar Assn., Wash. State Bar Assn. Office: Talmadge Law Group PLLC 18010 Southcenter Pkwy Tukwila WA 98188

TALMAGE, DAVID WILSON, microbiology and medical educator, physician, former university administrator; b. Kwangju, Korea, Sept. 15, 1919; s. John Van Talmage and Eliza (Emerson) Talmage; m. LaVeryn Marie Hunicke, June 23, 1944; children: Janet, Marilyn, David, Mark, Carol. Student, Maryville (Tenn.) Coll., 1937—38; BS, Davidson (N.C.) Coll., 1941; MD, Washington U., St. Louis, 1944. Intern Ga. Baptist Hosp., 1944—45; resident medicine Barnes Hosp., St. Louis, 1948—50, fellow medicine, 1950—51; asst. prof. pathology U. Pitts., 1951—52; asst. prof., then assoc. prof. medicine U. Chgo., 1952—59; prof. medicine U. Colo., 1959—, prof. microbiology, 1960—86, disting. prof., 1986—, chmn. dept., 1963—65, assoc. dean, 1966—68, dean, 1969—71; dir. Webb-Waring Lung Inst., 1973—83, assoc. dean for research, 1983—86. Mem. nat. council Nat. Inst. Allergy and Infectious Diseases, NIH, 1963—66, 1973—77. Author (with John Cann): Chemistry of Immunity in Health and Disease; editor: Jour. Allergy, 1963—67; editor: (with M. Samter) Immunological Diseases. Served with M.C. AUS, 1945—48. Scholar Markle, 1955—60. Mem.: Am. Assn. Immunologists, Am. Acad. Allergy, Inst. Medicine, NAS, Alpha Omega Alpha, Phi Beta Kappa. Fax: 303-388-6955.

TALMAGE, EDWARD ARTHUR, anesthesiologist; b. East Orange, N.J., 1927; AA, Princeton U., 1948; MD, N.Y. Med. Coll., 1952. Diplomate Am. Bd. Anesthesiology, Am. Bd. Pain Medicine. Intern St. Luke's Hosp., Bethlehem, Pa., 1952-53; pvt. practice Newton, N.J., 1953-56; resident in anesthesiology Robert Packer Hosp., Sayre, Pa., 1956-57, Jackson Meml. Hosp., Miami, Fla., 1957-58; instr. anesthesiology U. Miami (Fla.) Med. Sch., 1958-60; chief anesthesiologist No. Miami Gen. Hosp., 1960-63, Robert Packer Hosp., Sayre, Pa., 1963-65; with Meml. Bapt. Hosp., Houston, 1965-70; chief anesthesiology Guthrie Clinic, Robert Packer Hosp., Sayre,

1970-78; with S.W. Meml. Hosp., Houston, 1978-85; physician in interventional pain medicine West Houston Med. Ctr., 1985—. Assoc. clin. prof. Tex. U. Med. Sch. Fellow Am. Coll. Pain Medicine, Am. Coll. Chest Physicians; mem. AMA, Internat. Soc. Study Pain, World Soc. Pain Clinicians, So. Med. Assn., Am. Soc. Regional Anesthesiologists, Soc. Critical Care Medicine, Am. Acad. Pain Medicine, Am. Pain Soc., Tex. Pain Soc., Am. Neuromodulation Soc., Internat. Spine Injection Soc. Office: West Houston Doctors Ctr 12121 Richmond Ave Ste 403 Houston TX 77082-2439

TALMAGE, KENNETH KELLOGG, business executive; b. Morristown, NJ, Jan. 16, 1946; s. Edward Taylor Hunt Jr. and Dorothy Rogers Talmage. BA, Claremont Men's Coll., 1968; MBA, Boston U., Brussels, 1976. Aide to U.S. ambassador to Austria, Vienna, 1969-72; asst. to chmn. Fin. Com. to Re-elect Pres. Nixon, 1972-73; assoc. Hon. Leonard K. Firestone, L.A., 1973-74; attaché Am. Embassy, Brussels, 1974-77; pres. Sprague Corp., Cape Elizabeth, Maine, 1978—79; mgmt. cons. strategic planning and fin. Arthur D. Little, Inc., Cambridge, Mass., 1977-80; pres. Boston Co. of New Orleans, 1980—81; sr. v.p. Boston Safe Deposit & Trust Co., 1980-87; pres. Lloyd's, Inc., Denver, 1987-92. Bd. dirs. Monterey Water Co., pres., 1995-97, chmn., CEO, 1997—; bd. dirs. Pure West Industries, Inc., vice-chmn., 1993-95. Mem. exec. com. Outward Bound, U.S.A., 1980—85; dir. Vols. for Outdoor Colo., 1988—94, Breckenridge Outdoor Edn. Ctr., 1989—92; advisor Hurricane Island Outward Bound Sch., Maine, 1987—, bd. trustee, 1979—87, chmn. bd. trustees, 1980—83; bd. trustee Colo. Outward Bound Sch., 1990—96, vice chmn., 1995—96, bd. govs., 1996—. With USNR, 1968—69. Mem. The Country Club (Mass.), Denver Country Club, The Spanish Bay Club (Pebble Beach). Home: PO Box 1526 Carmel CA 93921-1526 Office: Monterey Water Co 1158 S Main St Manteca CA 95337-9505 E-mail: kktalm@aol.com.

TALMAGE, LANCE ALLEN, obstetrician/gynecologist, career military officer; b. Vandergrift, Pa., Feb. 23, 1938; s. Guy Wesley and Martha Lois (Bradstock) T.; m. Diana Elizabeth Heywood, June 23, 1962; children: Tamara, Lance Jr., Tenley. BS in Chem. Engring., U. Toledo, 1960; MD, U. Mich., 1964. Flight surgeon 24th Infantry Divsn. U.S. Army, Europe, 1966-69; resident U. Mich. Med. Ctr., Ann Arbor, 1969-73; clin. prof. Med. Coll. Ohio, Toledo, 1987—2000; med. dir. Ctr. for Women's Health, Toledo, 1987—. Brigadier gen. 112th Med. Brigage Ohio Army Nat. Guard, Columbus, 1995-97; pres. med. staff Toledo Hosp., 1989-91, chair dept. Ob-gyn., 1979-86; pres. Toledo Lucas County Acad. Medicine, 1994-95; mem. Toledo Hosp. Found. Bd., 2000—, Ohio State Med. Bd., 1999—, supervising sec., 2003—. Cabinet mem. United Way, Toledo, 1994-96; hon. chmn. March of Dimes Mothers-March, Toledo, 1989; pres. Ottawa Hills (Ohio) Athletic Boosters, 1986-88, team physician, 1981—; bd. trustees U. Toledo Found., 2003—. Decorated Legion of Merit; named to, Ohio Vets. Hall Fame, 2001; recipient Garde Nationale Trophy, N.G. Assn. U.S., 1998, Outstanding Team Physician, Ohio H.S. Athletic Assn., 2002, Blue T award, U. Toledo, 2002, Outstanding Chem. Engr. Grad. award, 2002—03. Fellow ACS, Am. Coll. Obstetricians and Gynecologists (dist. chair 1996-99, v.p. 2000-01, Disting. Dist. Svc. award, 2004); mem. AMA (mem. ho. of dels.), Ohio State Med. Assn. (pres. 1998-99), Kiwanis, Pi Kappa Phi Alumni Assn., U. Toledo Alumni Assn. (trustee 1996-2002, pres. 2000-01), Lucas County Domestic Violence Task Force, Res. Officers Assn., Soc. Med. Cons. to Armed Forces. Republican. Lutheran. Office: The Toledo Hosp 2150 W Ctrl Ave Toledo OH 43606 Office Phone: 419-291-2193. Personal E-mail: latalmage@voyager.net.

TALMAN, LOUIS A. mathematician; b. San Diego, Oct. 24, 1944; s. S. Arthur and Elizabeth A. Talman; m. Jean S. Stevenson, July 3, 1981; 1 child, Anna S. BA, Coll. Wooster, 1966; MA, PhD, U. Kans., 1976. Temp. asst. prof. math. Pittsburg (Kans.) State U., 1976—77; vis. asst. prof. math. So. Ill. U., Carbondale, 1977—80; asst. prof. math. U. Ctrl. Ark., Conway, 1980—81; assoc. prof. math. Coll. Ganado, Ariz., 1981—83; asst. prof. math. scis. Met. State Coll. Denver, 1983—90, assoc. prof. math. scis., 1990—. Presenter in field. Editor: (anthology) Readings in Mathematics. Mem.: Am. Math. Soc., Math. Assn. Am. (chair Rocky Mountain sect. 2002—04). Office: Met State Coll Denver Campus Box 38 PO Box 173362 Denver CO 80217-3362 Office Phone: 303-556-8438. E-mail: talmanl@mscd.edu.

TALMI, YOAV, conductor, composer; b. Kibbutz Merhavia, Israel, Apr. 28, 1943; m. Erella Gottesmann; 2 children. Diploma, Rubin Acad. Music, Tel Aviv; postgrad., Julliard Sch. Music; D (hon.), Laval U., 2001. Artistic dir., condr. Gelders Symphony Orch., Arnhem, 1974-80; prin. guest condr. Munich Philham. Orch., 1979-80; artistic dir. Israel Chamber Orch., 1984-88; music dir. New Israeli Opera, 1985-89, San Diego Symphony Orch., 1990-96, Waterloo Festival, N.J., 1994-95, Que. Symphony, Can., 1999—, Hamburg (Germany) Symphony, 2000—04. Guest condr. Berlin Philharm., Munich Philharm., London Philharm., Philharmonia, Royal Philharm., Concertgebouw, Paris Orch. Nat., Israel Philharm., NHK Symphony, Tokyo, New Japan Philharm., Vienna Symphony, St. Petersburg Philharm., Pitts. Symphony, Detroit Symphony, St. Louis Symphony, Houston Symphony, Dallas Symphony, Montreal Symphony, N.Y. Chamber Symphony, LA Chamber Orch., Oslo Philharm., Tonhalle Orch., Zurich, others. Composer: Dreams for choir a capella, Music for Flute and Strings; Overture on Mexican Themes (recorded), 3 Monologues for Flute Solo (pub.), Inauguration Fanfare, Elegy for Strings, Timpani, and Accordion, 1997, Suite on Israeli Songs; recs. include: Bruckner 9th Symphony (Oslo Philharm.), Tchaikovsky 1st Symphony (Quebec Symphony), Gliere 3d Symphony, Brahms Sextet/4 Serious Songs, Rachmaninov's Isle of the Dead, Berlioz: Symphonie Fantastique, Overtures, Harold in Italy, Romeo and Juliette, (San Diego Symphony), Tchaikowsky/Schoenberg, Bloch/Barber/Grieg/Puccini (Israel Chamber Orch.); (with Erella Talmi) works for flute and piano. Recipient Boskovitch prize for composition, Israel, 1965, Koussevitzky Meml. Conducting prize, Tanglewood, 1969, Ruppert Found. Condr. competition award, London, 1973, Ahad Ha'am award L.A. Ctr. Jewish Culture and the Am.-Israel Cultural Found., 1997. Home: PO Box 1384 Kfar Sava 44113 Israel Office: ICM Artists 40 W 57th St Fl 16 New York NY 10019-4098 Fax: 972-9-765-6553. E-mail: talmi@netvision.net.il.

TALTY, KATHRYN MELENE, women's health nurse, artist; b. Cleve., Aug. 6, 1960; d. Thomas Peter Talty and Eva Melene Hirsch; m. Robert L. Venorsky, Sept. 1997; children: Hanna, Elizabeth Lena, Danny. ADN, Cuahoga C.C., 1989. Staff nurse St. Luke's Hosp., Cleve., 1989—97; edn. dir. Diabetes Assn. Greater Cleve., 1998—2000; postpartum nurse Hillcrest Hosp., Cleve., 2002—. Author: (children's book) Babba's Day Out, 1997; prodr., composer: children's video The Babba Show, 1997; exhibitions include plesiglass and glass art various galleries, Ohio. V.p. Western Res. Rep. Com., Bratehahl, Ohio, 1999— 2000. Mem.: MOCA, Cleve. Opera League, Bratehahl Book Club. Avocations: skiing, swimming, travel.

TALTY, LORRAINE CAGUIOA, accountant; b. Makati, Manila, The Philippines, July 3, 1957; arrived in U.S., 1973, naturalized, 1983; d. Leon Perez and Asuncion (Rodriguez) Caguioa; m. Kevin Michael Talty, Jan. 23, 1982; 1 child, Leah Marie. BBA in Acctg. magna cum laude, Chaminade U., 1979. Office mgr., comptr. Caro of Honolulu, 1976-82; acct. David Schenkein, CPA, Latham, NY, 1984-86; sales rep. Caromat Corp., Torrance, Calif., 1985-86; owner Kevlor Internat., Fairport, NY, 1985—; acct. Cortland L. Brovitz & Co., CPA's, Rochester, NY, 1986-87; pvt. practice acctg. Fairport, 1986—. Comptr. Tal-Tee Assocs., Inc., Webster, NY, 1995—. Newsletter editor Country Knolls West Civic Assn., Clifton Park, 1984—85, civic com. rep., 1985—86; bd. dirs., vol. coord. Rochester Children's Theatre, 1994—96; treas. adv. com. St. Joseph's Sch., Penfield, NY, 1995—99, chair, 1999—2000; treas. Fil-Am. Assn., Rochester, 1998—99; Class of 2006 parents' bd. rep. Our Lady Mercy HS, 2000—, treas. parents assn., 2002—. Home: 8 Silver Fox Dr Fairport NY 14450-8665 Office Phone: 585-872-1981. Business E-Mail: ktalty1@rochester.rr.com.

TALUCCI, SAMUEL JAMES, retired chemical company executive; b. Newark, Del., Feb. 13, 1929; s. Anthony and Josephine (Valocchi) T.; m. Charlotte Sisofo, Sept. 22, 1951 (dec. Oct. 1985); children: Samuel J., Charlene, Anthony, Catherine, Christina, Louisa; m. Louise Coulter, Oct. 1987. BS, U. Del., 1951. Resident mgr. Italian Subs. Rohm & Haas Co., Milan, 1956-58, gen. mgr. Italian Subs., 1958-66, mng. dir. Brit. Subs., 1966-68, dir. European ops. Phila., 1968, asst. gen. mgr. Internat. div., 1971, v.p. gen. mgr. Plastics div., 1974, v.p. corporate bus., group dir. agrl. and indsl. chems. Plastics div., 1975-83, regional dir. N.Am. region, 1983-89, ret., 1989. Bd. dirs. Rosemont Coll. Mem. Nat. Agrl. Chems. Assn. (bd. dirs.), Pa. Chamber Bus. & Industry (bd dirs.), Middle States Assn. Colls. and Secondary Schs. (mem. commn. on secondary schs.) Address: 9 Thatcher Ct 251 Montgomery Ave Haverford PA 19041

TALUKDAR, ANUP KUMAR, computer engineer, researcher; arrived in U.S., 1991; BE, Jadavpur U., Calcutta, India, 1987; ME, Indian Inst. of Sci., Bangalore, 1990; PhD, Rutgers U., N.J., 1999. Engr. R & D WIPRO Infotech Ltd., Bangalore, India, 1990—91; sr. rsch. staff engr. Motorola Labs, Schaumburg, Ill., 1999—2003, prin. rsch. staff engr., 2003—. Author sci. conf. papers IEEE, INFOCOM, MOBICOM, VTC. Contbr. scientific papers to profl. jours. Achievements include patents pending for traffic dependent channel quality feedback; research in wireless networks. Home: Ste 743 1310 Valley Lake Dr Schaumburg IL 60195 Office: Motorola Labs 1301 E Algonquin Rd Schaumburg IL 60195 E-mail: anup.talukdar@motorola.com.

TALVI, ILKKA ILARI, violinist; b. Kuusankoski, Finland, Oct. 22, 1948; came to U.S., 1977; s. Veikko Tuomo and Irja Margareta (Saajos) T.; m. Judith Frances Aller, Sept. 4, 1969 (div. Aug. 1982); children: Silja Joanna, Sonja Louisa; m. Marjorie Jill Kransberg, Aug. 29, 1984; children: Anna Mirjam, Sarah Lilian. Diploma in violin, Sibelius Acad., Helsinki, Finland, 1966; student Heifetz master class, U. So. Calif., 1967-68; student, Curtis Inst., Phila., 1968-69; pvt. studies, Bouillon, Odnoposoff, Paris, Vienna, 1965-67. Lectr. Sibelius Acad., Helsinki, 1969-75, Porin Musiikkiopisto, Pori, Finland, 1970-76; concertmaster Malmö (Sweden) Symphony, 1976-77; prin. Los Angeles Chamber Orch., Pasadena, Calif., 1979-85; concertmaster Seattle Symphony, 1985—, Seattle Opera, 1985—, Waterloo Festival, N.J., 1988—. Guest concertmaster Seattle Symphony, 1983-85; freelance violinist, film, TV, and recording industries, Los Angeles, 1977-85. Performed as soloist and in recital in Europe, U.S., 1965—; appeared in Finland, U.S., 1972—; played Klami Violin Concerto, Albert "In Concordian," Diamond 2, violin concerto and numerous other recordings Recipient Kuusankoski (Finland) award, 1967, numerous grants, Finland, 1965-75. Lutheran. Avocations: dogs, computers, science. Home: 3456 10th Ave W Seattle WA 98119-1413 Office: Seattle Symphony Seattle Center House PO Box 21906 Seattle WA 98111-3906

TALWANI, MANIK, geophysicist, educator; b. Patiala, India, Aug. 22, 1933; came to U.S., 1954; s. Bir Sain and Saraswati (Khosla) T.; m. Anni Fittler, Apr. 3, 1958; children: Rajeev Manik, Indira, Sanjay. BSc with honors, Delhi U., India, 1951, MSc, 1953; PhD, Columbia U., 1959; PhD (hon.), Oslo U., 1981. From rsch. scientist to assoc. prof. Lamont-Doherty Geol. Obs., Columbia U., N.Y.C., 1959-70, dir. obs., 1972-81; prof. Columbia U., N.Y.C., 1970-82; dir. Ctr. for Crustal Studies Gulf R & D Co., Pitts., 1981-83, chief scientist exploration div. Houston, 1983-85; Schlumberger prof. geophysics Rice U., Houston, 1985—; pres. Integrated Ocean Drilling Program-Mgmt. Internat., 2004—. Cons. Govt. of Iceland, 1982-92, Lockheed Martin, 1998-2000, dir. Geotech. Rsch. Inst., Houston Advanced Rsch. Ctr., Woodlands, 1985-98; Sackler disting. lectr. U. Tel Aviv, 1987; prin. investigator Apollo 17 first gravity measurements on moon. Co-author: Geophysical Atlas of the Norwegian Sea; editor 12 books on earth sci., Maurice Ewing Meml. Symposium; co-editor: Geophysical Atlases of Indian, Atlantic and Pacific Oceans; contbr. over 150 papers to profl. jours. Recipient Krishnan award Indian Geophys. Union, 1964, Exceptional Sci. Achievement award NASA, 1973, Guggenheim award, 1974, Alfred Wegener medal European Union Geoscis., 1993; Fulbright-Hays fellow, 1974. Fellow: AAAS, Geol. Soc. Am. (George P. Woollard award 1984), Am. Geophys. Union (James B. Macelwane award 1964, Maurice Ewing award 1981), Geol. Soc. India (hon.); mem.: Houston Philos. Soc., Acad. Nat. Scis. Russian Fedn., Petroleum Club, Houston Geophys. Soc. (hon.), Norwegian Acad. Scis., Am. Assn. Petroleum Geologists, Soc. Exptl. Geophysicists, Sigma Xi. Home: 1111 Hermann Dr Apt 10 D Houston TX 77004-6929 Office: Rice U PO Box 1892 Houston TX 77251-1892 Office Phone: 713-348-6067. Business E-Mail: mtalwani@iudp.org.

TAMARELLI, ALAN WAYNE, venture captial executive; b. Wilkinsburg, Pa., Aug. 13, 1941; s. John Adam Tammarelli and Florence Eleanor (Heacock) T.; m. Carol Ann Crawford, Aug. 3, 1963; children: Robin Carol, Alan Wayne. BS, Carnegie Mellon U., 1963, MS, 1965, PhD, 1966; MBA, NYU, 1972. Engr. Exxon Corp., Linden, N.J., 1966, project leader, 1968-70; corp. planner Engelhard Minerals & Chem. Corp., Newark, 1970-71, asst. to exec. v.p., 1971-74, gen. mgr., 1974-77, v.p., 1977-79, group v.p., 1979-81; sr. v.p. Engelhard Corp., Iselin, N.J., 1981-83; chmn., chief exec. officer Dock Resins Corp, Linden, NJ, 1983—2000; pres. AWT Private Investments, 2000—. Mem. exec. com. nat. adv. coun. for environ. policy and tech. U.S. Dept. Environment Protection, Gov's. Econ. Task Force, N.J.; mem. exec. com. Alliance for Union County; chmn. Jumpstart N.J., Joseph Priestley Soc. Capt. U.S. Army, 1966-68. NSF fellow, 1963-66 Mem. Synthetic Organic Chems. Mfrs. Assn. (chmn., vice chmn., bd. govs.), Am. Chem. Soc., N.Y. Paint and Coatings Assn. (chmn., pres., v.p., sec., treas., bd. dirs.), Chem. Industry Coun. (chmn., bd. dirs., exec. com.), N.J. Energy Rsch. Inst. (founding trustee), Am. Mgmt. Assn., N.Y. Acad. Scis., Scabbard and Blade, Rotary (pres., v.p., sec. Linden Club), Linden Indsl. Assn. (pres.), Joseph Priestley Soc. (chmn.), Shakespeare Theater of N.J. (bd. dirs.), Sigma Xi, Tau Beta Pi, Phi Kappa Phi, Omicron Delta Kappa. Home: 49 Wexford Way Basking Ridge NJ 07920-2432 Office: 49 Wexford Way Basking Ridge NJ 07920-6385 Office Phone: 908-766-2207.

TAMAREN, MICHELE CAROL, coach, educational consultant, writer, retired special education educator; b. Hartford, Conn., Aug. 2, 1947; d. Herman Harold and Betty (Leavitt) Liss; m. David Stephen Tamaren, June 8, 1968; 1 child, Scott. BS in Elem. Edn., U. Conn., 1969; MA in Spl. Edn., St. Joseph Coll., West Hartford, Conn., 1976. Cert. elem. and spl. edn. tchr. Conn., Mass. Tchr. N.Y. Inst. Spl. Edn., Bronx, 1971-74; ednl. cons. Renbrook Sch., West Hartford, 1975-78; grad. instr. St. Joseph Coll., 1978; elem. tchr. Acton (Mass.) Pub. Schs., 1969-70, tchr. spl. edn., 1978-94, inclusion and behavioral specialist, 1996-2000; learning specialist and writer Educators Pub. Svc., Cambridge, Mass., 1994-96. Ednl. cons. to schs., parents, orgns., pubs., 1980—2000; personal coach; presenter in field. Author: (book) I Make a Difference, 1992; contbr. articles to profl. jours. Bd. dirs. United Way, Acton-Boxborough, 1996—99. Grantee, Mass. Gov.'s Alliance Against Drugs, 1992; Horace Mann grantee, Mass. Dept. Edn., 1987, 1988. Mem.: Kappa Delta Pi, Phi Kappa Phi. Avocations: travel, writing, reading, yoga, swimming. Home and Office: 34 Constitution Way Apt D Marblehead MA 01945-4652 E-mail: to_life@earthlink.net.

TAMARGO, MAURICIO J. federal agency administrator; b. Cuba; m. Tara Tamargo; children: Greg, Erin. BA in History, U. Miami, 1985; JD, Samford U., 1989. Bar: Fla., D.C., U.S. Supreme Ct. Adminstrv. asst. Fla. State Rep. Ileana Ros-Lehtinen; legis. dir. Congresswoman Ileana Ros-Lehtinen; staff dir., counsel subcom. on internat. econ. policy and trade House Internat. Rels. Com., staff dir., counsel subcom. on Africa, staff dir. internat. ops. and human rights subcom.; chief of staff, legal counsel Congresswoman Ileana Ros-Lehtinen; chmn. Fgn. Claims Settlement Commn. U.S. Dept. Justice, Washington, 2002—. Republican. Office: US Dept Justice Fgn Claims Settlement Commn 600 E St NW Rm 6002 Washington DC 20579

TAMARGO, RAFAEL J. neurological surgeon, educator; b. Havana, Cuba, Mar. 22, 1958; AB magna cum laude, Princeton U., 1980; MD, Columbia U., 1984. Diplomate Am. Bd. Neurol. Surgery. Intern Columbia Coll. Physicians and Surgeons, N.Y.C., 1984-85; resident in neurosurgery Johns Hopkins Hosp., Balt., 1985-92, active staff, 1992—, assoc. prof. neurosurgery, 1998—, assoc. prof. of otolaryngology, 2002—. Fellow ACS; mem. Am. Assn. Neurol. Surgeons, Am. Heart Assn. Office: Johns Hopkins Hosp 600 N Wolfe St Meyer 8-181 Baltimore MD 21287-0001 Business E-Mail: rtamarg@jhmi.edu.

TAMARKIN, KATE, conductor; b. Newport Beach, Calif. Student, Academia Musicale Chigiana, Siena, Italy; MusB magna cum laude, Chapman U.; MusM, Northwestern U., MusD, Peabody Conservatory. Conducting fellow Tanglewood Music Festival, 1987, L.A. Philharm. Inst., 1988-89; music dir. Fox Valley Symphony, Appleton, Wis., 1982-90, Vt. Symphony Orch. Assn., Inc., Burlington. Music dir. E. Tex. Symphony Orch.; guest condr. Okla. City Philharm., Riverside Symphony N.J., Okla. Sinfonia, Tulsa Philharm., Grant Pk. Festival Orch., Chgo., others; vis. assoc. prof. orchestral studies U. Minn.; assoc. condr. Dallas Symphony, 1989-94; vis. condr. U. Minn. Sch. Music, 1997-98. Appeared in numerous TV prodns. including Christmas concerts, 1993, 94, CNN-TV, (CBS-TV) Today Show. Recipient Alunni Merit award Northwestern U., Alumni of Yr. award Chapman U., 1997. Office: Vt Symphony Orch Assn Inc 2 Church St Burlington VT 05401-4445

TAMARO, GEORGE JOHN, consulting engineer; b. Weehawken, N.J., Mar. 16, 1937; s. Giorgio Angelo and Giacomina T.; m. Rosemary Ann Volta, June 24, 1961; children: Peter Louis, Jean Marie, Paul Anthony, Mark Joseph. B of Civil Engring., Manhattan Coll., 1959; M of Civil Engring., Lehigh U., 1961; M of Archtl. Tech., Columbia U., 1969. Profl. engr., N.Y., N.J., D.C., Md., Pa., Calif., Ill., Tex., La., Wis., Wash., R.I., Ark., Mo., Miss., Idaho; structural engr., Ill., Mass.; geotech. engr., Calif.; chartered engr., U.K.; registered European engr. Staff engr. Port Authority of N.Y. & N.J., N.Y.C., 1961-71; v.p., chief engr. ICOS Corp. Am., N.Y.C., 1971-80; sr. ptnr. Mueser Rutledge Cons. Engrs., N.Y.C., 1980—. Patentee in field; author tech. papers. Chmn. Bergen County Planning Bd., N.J., 1978-82; vice-chair Leonia (N.J.) Planning Bd., 1971-89; mem. Bd. Adjustment, Leonia, 1974-76; councilman Borough Governing Body, Leonia, 1972. Mem. ASCE (hon., Martin S. Kapp Found. Engr. award 1987, Homer Gage Balcom award 2002, Ralph B. Peck medal 2003, Friedman Profl. Recognition award 2003, OPAL award for engrng. design 2004), Instn. Civil Engrs. U.K., Instn. Structural Engrs. U.K., Nat. Acad. Engring., Internat. Soc. Soil Mechs. and Found. Engrs., Post-Tensioning Inst. (com. on rock and soil anchors), Deep Found. Inst. (Disting. Svc. award), The Moles (past pres., Outstanding Achievement in Constrn. award 2003, The Beavers' award for outstanding achievement in heavy engrng. constrn. 2004), Coun. on Tall Bldgs. and Urban Habitat, Chi Epsilon (hon. mem. award 1990), Tau Beta Pi. Avocations: sailing, photography. Office: Mueser Rutledge Cons Engrs 225 W 34th St New York NY 10122-0002

TAMBAKERAS, MARKOS I. machine tool manufacturer; BA, U. Witwatersrand, Johannesburg, South Africa. Various positions Honeywell Inc., 1984-92, v.p. mktg. and bus. ops., pres. indsl. automation and control bus., 1995-99; pres. Honeywell Asia Pacific, 1992-94; pres., CEO Kennametal Inc., Latrobe, Pa., 1999—. Office: Kennametal Inc PO Box 231 1600 Technology Way Latrobe PA 15650-0231

TAMBLYN, AMBER ROSE, actress; b. Santa Monica, Calif., May 14, 1983; d. Russ and Bonnie Tamblyn. Actor: (TV series) General Hospital, 1995—2001; (TV miniseries) Joan of Arcadia, 2003—; (films) Live Nude Girls, 1995, Rebellious, 1995, Johnny Mysto: Boy Wizard, 1996, The Ring, 2002, (guest appearances): Buffy the Vampire Slayer, 2001, Boston Public, 2002, Twilight Zone, 2002, CSI: Miami, 2002, Without a Trace, 2003, Punk'd, 2003, Late Show with David Letterman, 2004, Sharon Osbourne Show, 2004, Wayne Brady Show, 2004. Office: 8383 Wilshire Blvd Ste 530 Beverly Hills CA 90211

TAMBOLI, AKBAR RASUL, consulting engineer; b. Babhulgon, India, July 20, 1942; s. Rasul M. and Chandbi T.; m. Rounkbi A. Tamboli, May 21, 1969; children: Tahira, Ajim, Alamgir. BS, U. Poona, India, 1965; MS, Stanford U., 1967. Sr. engr. Miller Assocs., Pottsville, Pa., 1967-69; assoc. Edwards & Hjorth, N.Y.C., 1970-76; sr. project engr. Engrs. Inc., East Orange, N.J., 1977-80; v.p. Office of Irwin G. Cantor PC, N.Y.C., 1981-91; cons. engr. CUH2A Inc., Princeton, N.J., 1992-98; sr. v.p. Thornton-Tomasetti Group, N.Y.C., 1999—. Editor: Steel Design LFRD Method Handbook, 1996, Handbook of Structural Steel Connection Design and Details. Vol. Cancer Fund Drive, N.J., 1986. Fellow ASCE; mem. Am. Steel Constrn., Am. Soc. Welding. Avocations: golf, boating. Home: 10 Davenport Dr Princeton Junction NJ 08550-3001 Office: Thornton-Tomasetti Group 641 Ave of the Americas New York NY 10011-2014

TAMBOR, JEFFREY, actor, theatre director, educator; b. San Francisco, July 8, 1944; m. Kasia Ostlun, Oct. 6, 2001. BA, San Francisco State; MFA, Wayne State U. Acting tchr. Milton Katselas' Acting Workshops, Beverly Hills, Calif. Actor (theatre) Sly Fox, 1976 (Broadway and L.A.), Measure for Measure, The Hands of the Enemy, Flea in Her Ear, American Mosaic; (films) ...And Justice For All, 1979, Saturday the 14th, 1981, Dreamchasers, 1982, The Man Who Wasn't There, 1983, Mr. Mom, 1983, No Small Affair, 1984, Desert Hearts, 1985, Three O'Clock High, 1987, Brenda Starr, 1989, Lisa, 1990, City Slickers, 1991, Life Stinks, 1991, Pastime, 1991, Article 99, 1992, Crossing the Bridge, 1992, The Webbers, 1993, A House in the Hills, 1993, Radioland Murders, 1994, Heavyweights, 1995, My Teacher's Wife, 1995, Big Bully, 1996, Dr. Dolittle, 1998, There's Something About Mary, 1998, Meet Joe Black, 1998, Muppets From Space, 1999, Teaching Mrs. Tingle, 1999, Girl Interrupted, 1999, Pollock, 2000, How the Grinch Stole Christmas, 2000, Never Again, 2001, Get Well Soon, 2001, Scorched, 2002, The Freshman, 2002, Malibu's Most Wanted, 2003, My Boss's Daughter, 2003, Nobody's Perfect, 2003, Hellboy, 2004; (TV series) The Ropers, 1979-80, Hill Street Blues, 1981-87, 9 to 5, 1982, Mr. Sunshine, 1986, Jonny Quest (voice), 1986, Max Headroom, 1987-88, Studio 5-B, 1989, American Dreamer, 1990, The Larry Sanders Show, 1992-98 (Emmy award nominee 1993), Me & George, 1998, The Lionhearts (voice), 1998, Everything's Relative, 1999, The Lot, 1999, Sammy (voice), 2000, That Was Then, 2002, 3-South, 2002, Hollywood Squares (announcer), 2002-03, Arrested Development, 2003—; (TV episodes) M*A*S*H, Barney Miller, L.A. Law, The Golden Girls, Empty Nest, Who's The Boss, Doogie Houser, M.D., Equal Justice, Murder She Wrote, Tales From The Crypt (Dead Right) (TV movies) Eddie and Herbert, 1977, Alcatraz: The Whole Shocking Story, 1980, A Gun in the House, 1981, The Star Maker, 1981, Pals, 1981, The Awakening of Candra, 1981, Take Your Best Shot, 1982, The Zertigo Diamond Caper, 1982, Cocaine: One Man's Seduction, 1983, Sadat, 1983, The Three Wishes of Billy Grier, 1984, Wildfire, 1986, A Quiet Little Neighborhood, a Perfect Little Murder, 1990, The Burden of Proof, 1992, 1775, 1992, Jonny's Golden Quest (voice), 1993, Another Midnight Run, 1994, Jonny Quest vs. the Cyber Insects (voice), 1995, The Man Who Captured Eichmann, 1996, Weapons of Mass Distraction, 1997, Eloise at the Plaza, 2003, Eloise at Christmastime, 2003; (TV spls.) Living and Working in Space: The Countdown Has Begun; (TV miniseries) Robert Kennedy and His Times, 1985; dir. for numerous theatre companies including Seattle Repertory Theatre, Actors Theatre of Louisville, Milw. Repertory Theatre, Acad. Festival Theatre, Chgo., San Diego Shakespeare Festival, South Coast Repertory Theatre, Loeb Drama Ctr., Cambridge, Mass., Sky Light Theatre, L.A. Office: Care The Gersh Agency c/o Leslie Siebert 232 N Canon Dr Beverly Hills CA 90210-5302

TAMBS, LEWIS ARTHUR, diplomat, historian, educator; b. San Diego, July 7, 1927; s. Fred B. and Marguerite Johanna (Tambs) Jones; m. Phyllis Ann Greer, 1982. BS, U. Calif., Berkeley, 1953; MA, U. Calif., Santa Barbara, 1962, PhD, 1967. Plant engr. Std. Brands, San Francisco, 1953—54; pipeline engr. Creole Petroleum Co., Caracas, Maracaibo, Venezuela, 1954—57; gen. mgr. Cacyp, Maracaibo, 1957—59; instr. Creighton U., 1965—67, asst. prof., 1967—69; prof. history Ariz. State U., Tempe, 1969—82, 1987—2002, dir. Ctr. L.-Am. Studies, 1972—76; cons. NSC, 1982—83; U.S. amb. to Colombia, 1983—85; U.S. amb. to Costa Rica, 1985—87; ret., 2002. Author: East European and Soviet Economic Affairs, 1975, Historiography, Method and History Teaching, 1975, Hitler's Spanish Legion, 1979; editor: United States Policy Toward Latin America, 1976, Inter-American Policy for the 80's; co-editor: Santa Fe IV, 2000, English translation of Karl Haushofer's Geopolitics of the Pacific, 2002; co-author periodical guides; contbr. articles to profl. jours. Bd. dirs. Ariz.-Mex. Commn., 1974-82, Coun. Inter-Am. Security, 1979-90. With U.S. Army, 1945-47, 50-51. Faculty grantee, Ariz. State U., 1970, 1971, 1974, 1978, 1979. Roman Catholic.

TAMBURRO, PETER JAMES, JR., secondary school educator; b. Hoboken, N.J., Jan. 20, 1947; s. Peter James and Rose Catherine (Verta) Tamburro; m. Andrea Everitt Huber, Aug. 21, 1976 (div. 1998); children: Peter James III, Christopher Harding, Matthew Everitt. BA in Polit. Sci, Dickinson Coll., 1969; MAT in Social Studies, Trenton State Coll., 1973. Cert. secondary sch. tchr., social studies N.J. Tchr. Morris Sch. Dist., Morristown, N.J., 1973-76, Hanover Park Regional H.S. Dist., East Hanover, NJ, 1976—. Cross country coach Hanover Park H.S., East Hanover, 1983—2003, volleyball coach, 1990—98, asst. basketball coach, 1994—2001; judge Bicentennial Comn., NJ; asst. basketball coach Caldwell (N.J.) Coll., 1989—93; cons. Hist. Commn., East Hanover, 1989—92; cons. for developing Advanced Placement history programs, reader Advanced Placement exams ETS; mem. hist. com. Washington Twp., 1994—97, curriculum adv. com., 1996—97; adj. prof. William Paterson U., NJ, 1999—; spkr. in field. Author: (book) Gateway to Morris, 1993, Learn Chess from the Greats, 2000; editor (with Dale Brandreth): The Chess Diary of Rudolph Spielmann; editor: Atlantic Chess News, 1973—76, 2000—02; contbr. articles to chess mags.; nationally syndicated columnist: U.S. Chess Fedn., 1994—2001, columnist: Chessmates, Newark Star Ledger, 1997—; host internet radio show Openings for Amateurs, www.chess.fm. Mem. Hist. Commn., Washington Twp., NJ, 1994—96; scoutmaster Boy Scouts Am., 1994—97; team capt. Rep. Nat. Conv., 2000; Rep. County Committeeman Hanover Twp., NJ, 1984—88; legis. aide Assemblyman Robert Martin, Trenton, 1985—89; Rep. County Committeeman Morristown, NJ, 2002—03. Named N.J.'s Outstanding Tchr. History, DAR, 1990, Cross Country State Section Champions, 1987, 2000, 2001, 2002, Morris County Coach of the Yr., Cross Country, 2000; fellow Taft Inst. Two Party Govt., Fairleigh Dickinson U., 1984, Woodrow Wilson Found., 1991, Nat., Coun. Basic Edn., Washington, 1993; grantee, NSF, 1978, Dodge Found., Madison, N.J., 1987. Mem.: Chess Journalists Am. (v.p. 1990—99, pres. 1999—2003, awards 1995, 1996, 1997, 2002, 2003), U.S. Chess Fedn. (nat. chmn. hist. com. 1994—99), N.J. Edn. Assn., Hanover Park Regional Ednl. Assn. (v.p. 1994—95, pres. 1995—2001, chief negotiator 2003—), Morris County Hist. Soc., Nat. Coun. Social Studies. Avocations: rare books, chess. Home: 22 Budd St Morristown NJ 07960-5304 Office: Hanover Park High Sch 63 Mount Pleasant Ave East Hanover NJ 07936-2601 Office Phone: 201-887-0300.

TAMEZ GUERRA, REYES S. secretary of public education for Mexico; b. Monterrey, Nuevo León, Mex., Apr. 18, 1953; BS in Parasitological Bacteriological Chemistry, U. Nuevo León; MS, DS, Nat.Sch. Biol. Scis., Nat. Polytech. Inst. Asst. prof. Nat. Polytech Inst.; assoc. prof. Zaragosa Nat. Sch. Profl. Studies of UNAM; prof. Immunology and Chemoimmunity Autonomous U. Nueva León, Mexico, pres.; sec. of public edn. México, Mex. City, 2000—. Mem. appraisal com. for scholarships and rsch. projects Asst. Directorate of Sci. Devel. CONACyT; lectr. to sci. groups Various world wide.; mem. com. coop. and study Univs. of Latin Am.; chmn. of northeastern regional coun., mem. nat coun. ANUIES; alt v.p. Am. Univ. Orgn. Author: books; contbr. articles. Office: Office Pub Edn de Orgentina de Gonzalez Obregon # 28 06029 Mexico City Mexico

TAMIMI, MAHER M. language educator; b. Hebron, Palestine, Sept. 4, 1963; arrived in U.S., 1995; s. Muhammed Ahmad and Ezeya Abdulhameed Tamimi; m. Konul Gabulzade; 1 child, Aziza. Diploma in Edn., diploma in Transl., BA in English Lang., Bethlehem U., Palestine, 1986; MA in Arabic Lang., Ohio State U., 1998. Instr. English Hebron H.S., Pa., 1986—95; lectr. Ohio State U., Columbus, 1998; asst. prof. Def. Lang. Inst., Monterey, Calif., 1999—; instr. Monterey Peninsula Coll., Calif., 2001—. Prof. Islamic culture course Calif. State U. Monterey Bay, 2004.

TAMINIAUX, PIERRE SIMON, writer, educator; b. Brussels, Brabant, Belgium, Mar. 19, 1958; s. Jacques and Francoise Taminiaux; m. Maria Cristina De Sampaio, May 29, 1999. PhD, U. Calif., Berkeley, 1990. Prof. Georgetown U., Washington, 1991—2003; vis. prof. U. of Strasbourg, Strasbourg, France, 1999—2000. Dir. of internat. program Georgetown U., Tours, France (incl. Monaco), 2003—04. Author: (novel) Le Matin d'un voleur, (collection of critical essays) Surmodernites: entre reve et technique, Poetique de la negation; works on paper, Excavations, photographs, The colors of memory; author: (poetry) L'oeil a cote; photomontages, Inner Crossings, Lasting spaces. Donor Cmty. Coun. for the Homeless, Washington, 2003—04. Fellow Fellow of the Belgian Am. Ednl. Found., BAEF, 1983; grantee Academic Summer Grants, Faculty of Languages and Linguistics-Georgetown U., 1995, Faculty of Languages and Linguistics, 1999. Mem.: ALA (assoc.). Home: 3825 Davis Pl NW #101 Washington DC 20007 Office: Georgetown Univ 37th and O Stt Washington DC 20057 Personal E-mail: taminiap@georgetown.edu.

TAMIR, THEODOR, electrophysics researcher, educator; b. Bucharest, Romania, Sept. 17, 1927; came to U.S., 1958, naturalized, 1968; s. Martin and Helena (Hart) Berman; m. Hadassah Cohen, Oct. 5, 1949; children: Jonathan, Yael. BS Technion, Israel Inst. Tech., 1953, Dipl. Ingenieur, 1954, MS, 1958; PhD, Poly. Inst. Bklyn., 1962. Instr. Technion Israel Inst. Tech., Haifa, 1956-58; mem. rsch. staff Poly. Inst., Bklyn., 1958-62; mem. faculty Poly. Univ., Bklyn., N.Y., 1962—; prof. electrophysics Poly. Inst. N.Y., 1969-92, Univ. prof., 1992—, head dept. elec. engring., 1974-79. Sci. and engring. cons. to indsl. and govtl. labs. Editor, author: Integrated Optics, 1975 (transl. into Russian and Chinese), Guided Wave Optoelectronics, 1988 (transl. into Russian); co-editor: Springer Series in Optical Sciences, 1979-96; contbr. chpts. to books, articles to profl. jours. Served with Israeli Army, 1947-49. Awarded Instn. Premium, 1964, Electronics Premium, 1967, Instn. Elec. Engrs., London; citation for disting. research Polytechnic chpt. Sigma Xi, 1978 Fellow IEEE, Optical Soc. Am.; mem. Internat. Union Radio Sci., Sigma Xi. Home: 981 E Lawn Dr Teaneck NJ 07666-6604 Office: Polytechnic Univ Elec & Comp Engring Dept 5 MetroTech Ctr Brooklyn NY 11201 Office Phone: 718-260-3320. Business E-Mail: ttamir@duke.poly.edu.

TAMKE, GEORGE WILLIAM, printing/copying company executive; b. Beacon, N.Y., May 16, 1947; s. George William and Josephine Edna (Carbone) Tamke; m. Christine Barbara MacLeod, June 28, 1969; children: Kara Lee, Shannon. BSChemE, Vanderbilt U., 1969; MS in Mgmt. Sci., Stanford U., 1979. With IBM, N.Y., Fla., Calif., Ga., Minn., 1969—86, dir. orgn. planning and sec. to corp. mgmt. com. White Plains, NY, 1981—82, v.p. mfg. Communication Products div., 1982—83, v.p. display products Communication Products div., 1983—84, asst. group exec. Info Systems, Products Group, 1984—86; pres. Cullinet Software, Inc., Westwood, Mass., 1986—87, COO, 1987—88; exec. v.p. Emerson Electric Co., St. Louis, 1989—; CEO Kinkos, 2001—. CEO Astec (BSR) Plc, Hong Kong, 1989—. Contbr. articles to profl. jours. Avocations: tennis, golf. Home: 9915 Litzsinger Rd Saint Louis MO 63124-1129 Office: 255 W Stanley Ave Ventura CA 93001-1348

TAMKIN, CURTIS SLOANE, real estate development company executive; b. Boston, Sept. 21, 1936; s. Hayward and Etta (Goldfarb) T.; m. Priscilla Martin, Oct. 18, 1975; 1 child, Curtis Sloane. BA in Econs., Stanford U., 1958. V.p., treas., dir. Hayward Tamkin & Co., Inc., mortgage bankers, L.A., 1963-70; mng. ptnr. Property Devel. Co., L.A., 1970-82; pres. The Tamkin Co., 1982—2000; chmn. Tamkin Capital Group L.L.C., 1999—. Mem. bd. govs. Music Ctr. L.A., 1974—98; pres. L.A. Master Chorale Assn., 1974—78; mem. vis. com. Stanford U. Librs., 1982—86; vice-chmn. bd. dirs., mem. exec. com. L.A. Philharm. Assn., 1985—, vice chmn. bd., 2004, chmn. bd. overseers, 2001—. Lt. (j.g.) USNR, 1960—63. Mem.: Pacific Council Internat. Policy, L.A. Jr. C. of C. (dir. 1968—69), Founders League L.A. Music Ctr. (pres. 1988—98, chmn. emeritus 1998—), Hillcrest Country Club, Burlingame Country Club. Home: 1230 Stone Canyon Rd Los Angeles CA 90077-2920 Office: 9460 Wilshire Blvd Beverly Hills CA 90212-2732

TAMKIN, S. JEROME, business executive, consultant; b. L.A., Apr. 19, 1926; s. William W. and Thelma (Brandel) T.; m. Judith Deborah, Mar. 23, 1963; children: Steven Marc, Windy Lynn, Gary William, Sherry Dawn. BS, U. So. Calif., 1950; MA, Fremont Coll., 1951, PhD, 1952; LL.D., St. Andrews U., London, 1954. Mem. rsch. staff chemistry dept. U. Calif. at Los Angeles, 1943; rsch. chemist, analyst supr. synthetic rubber div. U.S. Rubber Co., 1943-44; rsch. engr. Coll. Engring., U. So. Calif., 1946-48; gen. mgr. Pan Pacific Oil Co., Long Beach, Calif., 1948-55; plant mgr. indsl. sales and mfg., 1953-55; v.p., sales mgr. Wilco Co., Los Angeles, 1948-55, v.p. charge indsl. sales and mfg., 1953-55; v.p., sales mgr. Unit Chem. Corp., Los Angeles, 1955-56; pres. Phillips Mfg. Co. (merger Instl. Food Equipment Corp.), Los Angeles, 1957-62, Waste King Corp. (subs. Instl. Food Equipment Corp.), 1962-67; also dir.; v.p., dir. Dyna Mfg. Co., Los Angeles, 1962-68; pres., dir. Profl. Rsch. Inc., Los Angeles, 1965-73; exec. v.p. Am. Med. Internat., Inc., Beverly Hills, Calif., 1966-71, dir., 1966-89; sec., dir. Rodger Young, Inc., L.A., 1971-77; pres., chmn. bd. TGT Petroleum Corp., Wichita, 1972—; pres., dir. Tamkin Cons. Corp., 1978—; owner, operator Tamkin Securities Co., 1979-86; vice chair bd., dir. Integrated Voice Solutions Inc., Chattanooga, 1991-96; bd. dirs. CAPP Care Inc., Newport Beach, Calif., 1991-99. Tech. cons. Daylin Inc., Beverly Hills, 1973-75; bd. dirs. Healthcare Decisions, Inc., Newport Beach, Calif., 1996-99. Contbr. articles to profl. jours.; patentee electronic gas detector, circuits for automatic control hazardous vapors. Cmty. warden W. Adams-Baldwin Hills Cmty. CD, 1950—52; bd. govs. West Los Angeles County coun. Boy Scouts Am., 1977—, Technion-Israel Inst. of Tech., 2001—; dep. sheriff L.A. County, 1949; bd. dirs. Sunair Home Asthmatic Children; city commr. L.A. Bd. Environ. Quality, 1972—73; bd. dirs. Recovery Found., Fund for Higher Edn.; mem. exec. com. adv. coun. crime prevention L.A. Police, 1985—; trustee, bd. visitors U. Calif.-Irvine Coll. Medicine, 1989—; bd. visitors UCLA Sch. Medicine, 1990—; trustee Scripps Found. for Medicine and Sci., 1996—; bd. dirs. U. of Judaism, 1999—, UCLA Brain Mapping Found., 1999—; trustee Morehouse Sch. Medicine, 1995—. Officer USNR, 1944—46. Mem. AIM, Am. Mgmt. Assn., Inst. Aero. Scis., Am. Soc. Naval Engrs., Soc. Am. Mil. Engrs., Am. Chem. Soc., IEEE, Soc. Motion Picture and TV Engrs., Am. Inst. Chem. Engrs., Soc. Advancement Mgmt., U.S. Naval Inst., Calif. Scholarship Fedn. (life), Nat. Eagle Scout Assn., Sunrise Country Club, The Springs Country Club, Malibu Riding and Tennis Club, Alpha Eta Rho. Office: 2100 Sawtelle Blvd Ste 201 Los Angeles CA 90025-6264 Office Phone: 310-479-2555.

TAMMEN, RONALD, international politics educator; b. Portland, Oreg., Nov. 30, 1943; s. Clement William and Wanda Wave (Hamner) T.; m. Susan Smith, May 20, 1970. BA in Polit. Sci., Pacific U., 1965; cert., Reed Coll., 1966; MA in Polit. Sci., U. Mich., 1966, PhD in Polit. Sci., 1975. Def. analyst CIA, 1966-69; staff cons. Arms Control and Fgn. Policy Caucus, 1969-72; legis. asst. to Senator William Proxmire, 1972-82, chief of staff to, 1982-89; pres. The Tammen Group, Washington, 1989-91; mng. ptnr. Potomac Ptnrs., Washington, 1989-91; prof. nat. strategy Nat. War Coll., Washington, 1991-94, assoc. dean of faculty, 1994-98, dept. chair, 1998-2000; dir. Mark O. Hatfield Sch. Govt., Portland State U., 2000—. Editor: The Economics of Defense Spending, 1971; author: MIRV and the Arms Race, 1973; co-author: Power Transitions, 2000; contbr. articles to profl. publs. Home: 15855 Oswego Shore Ct Lake Oswego OR 97034-3601 Office Phone: 503-725-8443. E-mail: tammen@pdx.edu.

TAMMEUS, WILLIAM DAVID, journalist, columnist; b. Woodstock, Ill., Jan. 18, 1945; s. W. H. and Bertha H. (Helander) T.; m. Marcia Bibens, Nov. 29, 1996; children: Lisen Tammeus Mann, Kate Tammeus Willaredt; stepchildren: Christopher L. Johnston, Daniel Bednarczyk, Kathryn B. Dandino, David Bednarczyk. BJ, U. Mo., Columbia, 1967; postgrad., U. Rochester, 1967-69. Reporter Rochester (N.Y.) Times-Union, 1967-70; reporter Kansas City (Mo.) Star, 1970-77, columnist, 1977—; syndicated columnist N.Y. Times News Svc., 1989-99, Knight Ridder/Tribune Info. Svcs., 2000—. Author: A Gift of Meaning, 2001; editor-at-large Presbyn. Outlook, 1993; contbg. editor Mo. Life mag., 1980-81; commentator Sta. KCPT-TV, 1979-90. Co-recipient Pulitzer prize for gen. local reporting of Hyatt Regency Hotel disaster, 1982; recipient 1st pl. opinion-editl. divsn. Heart of Am. award Kansas City Press Club, 1991, 93, 1st pl. column divsn., 1994, 1st pl. award best column/humor divsn. Mo. Press Assn., 1997, 2002, Best In-Depth Reporting on Religion award Am. Acad. Religion, 2001, David Steele Disting. Writer award Presbyn. Writers Guild, 2003, 1sr pl. religion coverage Kans. Press Assn., 2004. Mem. Nat. Soc. Newspaper Columnists (v.p. 1990-92, pres. 1992-94, 1st pl. items divsn. Writing award 1992, 3d place humor writing, 1999, 2000), Soc. Profl. Journalists. Presbyterian. Office: 1729 Grand Blvd Kansas City MO 64108-1413 Office Phone: 816-234-4437. Business E-Mail: tammeus@kcstar.com.

TAMMINGA, CAROL ANN, neuroscientist; b. Grand Rapids, Mich., Jan. 26, 1946; d. Samuel William and Freda (Hekman) T.; children: Cristan Fredericka, Bonnie Michael. BS, Calvin Coll., 1966; student, U. Tubingen, Fed. Republic of Germany, 1966-67; MD, Vanderbilt U., 1971. Lic. physician, Ill., Md. Vivian Allen fellow Vanderbilt Med. Sch., 1968-71; intern in medicine Blodgett Meml. Hosp., Grand Rapids, Mich., 1971-72; resident in psychiatry U. Chgo., 1972-74, chief resident in psychiatry, 1974-75, instr. dept. psychiatry, 1975-77, asst. prof. psychiatry, 1978-79; assoc. prof. psychiatry U. Md., Balt., 1979-85, chief inpatient rsch. program, 1979—, prof. psychiatry, 1985—. Chief clin. investigator Manteno (Ill.) State Hosp., 1975-79; chief clin. biochemsitry unit Nat. Inst. Neurologic & Communicative Diseases & Stroke NIH, Bethesda, Md., 1979-85; mem. treatment devel. and assessment rsch. rev. com. NIMH, 1981-85, 90-94, 96-99; mem. FDA Psychopharm Adv. Com., 1990-92, 97—, chair, 1991-92, 98—; mem. Inst. Medicine, NAS, 1998—; cons. in field. Author: Schizophrenia: Scientific Progress, 1988, Schizophrenia Research, 1989; editorial bd. Am. Jour. Psychiatry, Biol. Psychiatry, Jour. Nervous and Mental Diseases, Schizophrenia Bull., Schizophrenia Rsch., Functional Neurology, Progress in Neuroendocrinimmunology, Progress in Neuro-Psychopharmacology and Biol. Psychiatry; contbr. articles to Archive Gen. Psychiatry Sci., Am. Jour. Psychiatry, Jour. Neural Transmission, Lancet, Physiol. Behavior, and other. Recipient McAlpin award Nat. Assn. Mental Health, 1979, Dean award, 1995; Beauchamp scholar, 1971; Found. for Rsch. in Psychiatry fellow, 1975-76, NIMH fellow, 1978-79. Mem. AAAS, Am. Psychiatric Assn., Am. Coll. Neuropharmacology, Internat. Psychoneuroendocrine Soc., Soc. Neurosci., Biol. Psychiatry. Achievements include research in schizophrenia. Office: U Md PO Box 21247 Baltimore MD 21228-0747 E-mail: ctamming@MPRC.umaryland.edu.

TAMONY, KATIE, editor-in-chief; m. Patrick Tamony; children: Sara, Caitlin. BA in History, U. Calif., Berkeley, 1989. Mng. editor No. Calif. Home and Garden mag.; copy editor Sunset mag., N.Y.C., 1994—97, editl. dir., 1997—98, dir. custom pub., 1998, v.p., 1998, editor in chief, 2001—. Author: Your Second Pregnancy: What to Expect This Time, 1995. Office: Sunset Time and Life Bldg 20th Fl 1271 Avenue of the Americas New York NY 10020

TAMPAS, JOHN P. radiologist; married; children: Jessica, Peter, Andrea, Christiana. BS, U. Vt., 1951, MD, 1954. Diplomate Am. Bd. Radiology. Radiology resident U. Vt., Burlington, 1957—60; teaching fellow pediat. radiology L.A. Children's Hosp., 1960—61; NIH Nat. Heart Inst. resident fellow cardiovascular radiology U. Ind., Indpls., 1961—62; attending radiology Med. Ctr. Hosp. Vt., Burlington, 1962—; asst. prof. radiology Coll. Medicine U. Vt., 1962—70; prof. & chmn. dept. radiology Med. Ctr. Hosp. Vt., Burlington, 1970—96. Contbr. articles to profl. jours. Recipient Karl Jefferson Thompson Meml. Excellence in Tchg. award, 1969, 1975; scholar, James Picker Found./NRC, 1962—65. Fellow: Am. Coll. Radiology (pres. 1987—88, bd. chancellors, emergency radiology com., accreditation com., chmn. mem. ins. com., adminstrv. affairs commn., radiologic practice commn., Gold medal 1996); mem.: AMA, Vt. Med. Soc., Vt. Radiol. Soc., Assn. Univ. Radiologists, Soc. Chmn. Acad. Radiology Depts., New Eng. Roentgen Ray Soc., Radiol. Soc. N.Am., Am. Roentgen-Ray Soc. (pres. 1982—83, Gold medal 1992), Soc. Pediat. Radiology, Alpha Omega Alpha. Office: Fletcher Allen Health Ctr 111 Colchester Ave Burlington VT 05401-1416 also: Hosp Vt Med Ctr Dept Radiology Burlington VT 05401

TAMURA, CARY KAORU, consultant; b. Honolulu, Jan. 9, 1944; s. Akira and Harue T.; m. Denise Jeanne Mitts, Oct. 17, 1987; children: Jennifer Joy, Matthew D. Student, U. Hawaii, 1961-63; BA in Philosophy, Nyack Coll., 1966; MA in Theology, Fuller Sem., 1986. Dir. svc. tng. ops. Fin. Adv. Clinic of Hawaii, Honolulu, 1972-76; dir. planned giving The Salvation Army, Honolulu, 1976-78, Portland, Oreg., 1981—85; planned giving cons. Inter-Varsity Christian Fellowship, Portland, Oreg., 1978-80; account exec. Am. Income Life, Portland, Oreg., 1980-81; dir. devel., planned giving U. So. Calif., 1985-90; dir. gift planning UniHealth America, Burbank, Calif., 1990-94; pvt. practice Brea, Calif., 1995—. Adv. com., adj. faculty UCLA Extension; lectr. in field. Bd. dirs. Nat. Com. on Planned Giving, Indpls., 1991-93, sec. exec. com., 1993; bd. dirs. Japanese Evang. Missionary Soc., 1990-95, 2003—, Simpson Coll., 1998—; deacons Evang. Free Ch., 1992-95. With U.S. Army, 1969-72. Mem. Planned Giving Round Table So. Calif. (pres. 1989-91, Pres.'s award 1992), Assn. of Fundraising Profls. (bd. dirs. Greater L.A. chpt. 1990-97, v.p. 1993, 95, treas. 1996-97, Profl. Fund Raiser of Yr. award 1995). Republican. Avocations: photography, golf, travel. Office: PO Box 908 Brea CA 92822

TAMURA, ROBERT, economics professor, consultant; b. Oak Ridge, Tenn., Nov. 28, 1959; s. Tsuneo and Amy Fumiyo Tamura; m. Sarah Hewett, Sept. 9, 1966; children: Alexandra Akemi, Elizabeth Emiko. SB, Coll. William and Mary, 1981; AM, PhD, U. Chgo., 1988. Asst. prof. econs. U. Iowa, Dept. of Econs., Iowa City, 1988—96; assoc. prof. econs. Clemson U. John E. Walker Dept. of Econs., Clemson, SC, 1996—. Cons. Fed. Res. Bank f Atlanta, Atlanta, 1997—2004. Contbr. articles to prof. jours. Fin. coun. St Mary Magdalene Cath. Ch., Simpsonville, SC, 2002—04. Fellow John Stauffer Nat. Pub. Policy, Staford U., Hoover Inst., 1994. Mem.: Soc. Labor Economists, Soc. Econ. Dynamics, Am. Economics Assn., Econometric Soc. Office: John E Walker Dept Econs Clemson U Clemson SC 29634-1309 E-mail: rtamura@clemson.edu.

TAN, AMY RUTH, writer; b. Oakland, Calif., Feb. 19, 1952; d. John Yueh-han and Daisy Ching (Tu) T.; m. Louis M. DeMattei, Apr. 6, 1974. BA in Linguistics and English, San Jose (Calif.) State U., 1973, MA in Linguistics, 1974; LHD (hon.), Dominican Coll. San Rafael, 1991. Specialist lang. devel. Alameda County Assn. for Mentally Retarded, Oakland, 1976-80; project dir. M.O.R.E. Project, San Francisco, 1980-81; free-lance writer, 1981-88. Author: The Joy Luck Club, 1989 (Nat. Book Critics Circle award for best novel nomination 1989, L.A. Times Book award nomination 1989, Gold award for fiction Commonwealth Club 1990, Bay Area Book Reviewers award for best fiction 1990), The Kitchen God's Wife, 1991, The Moon Lady, 1992, The Chinese Siamese Cat, 1994, The Hundred Secret Senses, 1995, The Bonesetter's Daughter, 2001, The Opposite of Fate: A Book of Musing, 2003; also numerous short stories and essays; screenwriter, prodr.: (film) The Joy Luck Club, 1993. Recipient Best Am. Essays award, 1991. Office: care Ballantine Publ Publicity 201 E 50th St New York NY 10022-7703

TAN, ENG MENG, immunologist, biomedical researcher; b. Seremban, Malaysia, Aug. 26, 1926; came to U.S., 1950; s. Ming Kee and Chooi Eng (Ang) T.; m. Liselotte Filippi, June 30, 1962; children: Philip, Peter. BA, Johns Hopkins U., 1952, MD, 1956. Intern Duke U., Durham, N.C., 1956-57; resident, fellow Case-We. Res. U., Cleve., 1957-62; rsch. assoc. Rockefeller U., N.Y.C., Calif., 1962-65; asst. prof. Washington U. Sch. Medicine, St. Louis, Calif., 1965-67; assoc. mem. and mem. Scipps Rsch. Inst., LaJolla, Calif., 1967—77; prof. Scripps Rsch. Inst., LaJolla, Calif., 1982—, U. Colo. Sch. Medicine, Denver, 1977-82. Chmn. allergy & immunology rsch. com. NIH, Bethesda, Md., 1982-84; mem. nat. arthritis adv. bd. HHS, Washington, 1981-85. Contbr. chpts. in books, articles to profl. jours. Named an hon. prof., Shanghai 2d Med. U.; named to Nat. Lupus Hall Fame, 1984; recipient US Sr. Scientist award, Humboldt Found., Germany, 1986, Ciba-Giegy-Internat. League against Rheumatism award, 1989, Carol Nachman award, Wiesbaden, Germany, 1989, Lee Howley Sr. award, Arthritis Found., 1989, Paul Klemperer award and medal, NY Acad. Medicine, 1993, City Medicine award, Durham, NC, 1996, Disting. Med. Alumnus award, Duke U., 2000, Mayo Soley award, Western Soc. Clin. Investigation, 2002, Japan Rheumatism Found. Internat. prize, 2003. Fellow AAAS; mem. Am. Coll. Rheumatology (pres. 1984-85, chmn. Blue Ribbon com. Future Acad. Rheumatology 1997-98, Disting. Investigator award 1991, Gold medal award 1998), Assn. Am. Physicians, Am. Soc. Clin. Investigation, Western Assn. Physicians (v.p. 1980-81), Am. Assn. Immunologists, Brazilian Soc. Rheumatology (hon.), Australian Rheumatism Assn. (hon.), Brit. Soc. Rheumatology (hon.), Mex. Nat. Acad. Medicine (hon.). Achievements include research on antibodies and antigens in cancer and in autoimmune diseases, systemic lupus erythematosus, scleroderma, Sjogren's syndrome, myositis and mixed connective tissue disease; relationship of autoantibodies to pathogenesis. Home: 8303 Sugarman Dr La Jolla CA 92037-2224 Office: Scripps Rsch Inst 10550 N Torrey Pines Rd La Jolla CA 92037-1000 Office Phone: 858-784-8686. Business E-Mail: emtan@scripps.edu.

TAN, GUOLONG, research scientist; s. YunSheng Tan and AiLian Zheng; m. Hongyan Sun, Nov. 8, 1994; children: Jiaqi Emily, Edward Jiazhen. BS, Jingdezheng Ceramic Inst., China, 1983—87; MS, Zhejiang U., China, 1990—93, PhD, 1998. Rsch. asst. prof. Hampton U., Hampton, Va., 2001—02; post doctorate rschr. U. Pa., Phila., 2002—. Vis. scientist Max-Planck Inst. of Microstructure Physics, Halle (Saale), Saxan Anhalt, Germany, 1999—2001. Author: (novel nanotechnology) Novel route for CdTe, CdSe nanocrystals (Scripta Materialia, 2003). Coord. Chinese Baptista Ch., Newport News, Va., 2001—02. Fellow GuangHua fellowships, Zhejiang U., 1996, 1997. Mem.: Am. Ceramic Soc. Achievements include research in mechanical alloying process to prepare long term stable dispersion of CdTe, CdSe nanocrystals in much larger scale; process of fabricate Nanostrucutred WC-Co Alloys in high hardness. Avocations: ping pong/table tennis, basketball, swimming.

TAN, HUI QIAN, computer science and civil engineering educator; b. Tsingtao, China, June 12, 1948; s. Dumen Tan and Ruifan Rao; m. Ren Zhong, June 16, 1994; children: William W., Danny D. BA, Oberlin Coll., 1982; MS, Kent State U., 1984, PhD, 1986. Asst. prof. computer sci. and civil engring. U. Akron, Ohio, 1986-89, assoc., 1990—; rsch. prof. Kent (Ohio) State U., 1987. Contbr. articles to profl. jours. Grantee NASA, 1987—, 91—, NSF, 1988-92. Mem. IEEE Computer Soc., Assn. for Computing Machinery, SIGSAM Assn. for Computing Machinery, Phi Beta Kappa. Avocations: classical music, history, literature, swimming, bicycling.

TAN, KEAH-CHOON, finance educator; s. Keah-Soon Chien and Yoke-Mui Sui; m. Shaw-Yun Chiu, Dec. 27, 1986; children: Wen-Hui, Wen-Jay. PhD, Mich. State U., East Lansing, 1989—95. Cert. Production and Inventory Management Am. Prodn. and Inventory Control Soc., 1996, Purchasing Manager Inst. Supply Mgmt., 1996, Accredited Purchasing Practitioner Inst. Supply Mgmt., 1996. Assoc. prof. ops. mgmt. U. Nev., Las Vegas, 1998—. Recipient Person Yr., Inst. Supply Mgmt., 1997, UNLV Coll. Bus. Rschr. Yr., U. Nev., 2001; grantee Mng. Supply Chain Bus. Enterprise Rsch. grant, Am. Prodn. and Inventory Control Soc., Supply Chain Coun., 1999, New Investigator Rsch. award grant, U. Nev., 1999. Mem.: Inst. Supply Mgmt., Am. Prodn. and Inventory Control Soc., Decision Scis. Inst. (co-track chair 2003—03). Office: U Nev Las Vegas Box 456009 4505 Maryland Pkwy Las Vegas NV 89154-6009

TAN, LI-SU LIN, accountant, insurance executive, investment consultant; b. Keelung, Taiwan, Republic of China, Mar. 7, 1956; came to U.S., 1985; d. I-Chang and Sung-Mei (Chen) Lin; m. Bert T. Tan, Aug. 19, 1985; children: Patricia Tan, Peter Puwen Tan, Lotus Tan. BBA, Nat. Taiwan U., 1978; MBA, Ill. Inst. Tech., 1991. CPA, Ill., Taiwan; lic. ins. agt., Ill.; registered investment advisor. Asst. mgr. T.N. Soong & Co. (mem. firm Arthur Anderson & Co., SC), Taipei, 1978—85; practitioner Li-Su Lin, CPA, Taipei, 1981—85, Li-Su Lin Tan, CPA, Naperville, Ill., 1988—90; pres. Lisu L. Tan & Co., Ltd., CPAs, Naperville, 1990—; agt. Mut. Omaha Co., Lombard, Ill., 1991—94, Met. Life and Affiliated Cos., Bloomingdale, Ill., 1993—98, GE Fin. Assurance, Schaumburg, Ill., 1999—. Chair family Naperville Chinese Assn., 1990; bd. dirs. Amitabha Buddhist Libr. in Chgo., 2003-, pres., 2003-. Mem.: AICPA (tax divsn., quality control program), Ill. Soc. CPA, Amitabha Buddhist Libr. Chgo. (pres. 2003—, bd. dirs.), Buddha's Light Internat. Assn. (Chgo. chpt. pres. 2002—, bd. dirs.), Chinese Am. Culture Found. (bd. dirs., pres. 2001—), Nat. Taiwan U. Alumni Assn. Greater Chgo. (bd. dirs. 1999—2003), World Taiwanese C. of C. (dep. treas. 1998—99), Taiwanese C. of C. N.Am. (treas. 1998—99, bd. dirs.), Greater Chgo. Area Taiwanese Am. C. of C. (bd. dirs.),

Taipei First Girls High Alumni Assn. (treas. 1990—94). Buddhist. Avocations: travel, art collecting, photography. Office: Lisu L Tan & Co Ltd CPAs 6S235 Steeple Run Dr #200 Naperville IL 60540-3754 Office Phone: 630-416-9422. E-mail: lisu@lisutancpas.com.

TAN, LI-ZHE, engineering educator, researcher; b. Huainan, Anhui, China, Apr. 30, 1963; came to U.S., 1985; s. Zhi-neng and Wan-shun (Yu) T.; m. Jean Qian Jiang, June 29, 1989; children: Ava, Alexander, Amber. BS, Southeast U., Nanjing, China, 1984; MS in Structural Engring., U. N.Mex., 1987, MS in Elec. Engring., 1989, PhD in Elec. Engring., 1992. Tchg. and rsch. asst. U. N.Mex., Albuquerque, 1986-91, rsch. assoc., 1992-93; sr. software/rsch. engr. Am. Laser Games Inc., Albuquerque, 1993-94; prin. scientist Iterated Systems Inc., Atlanta, 1994-97; prof. DeVry U., Decatur, Ga., 1997—. Patentee in field. Mem. IEEE (sr.; advisor Atlanta sect.), IEEE Circuits and Systems Soc., IEEE Signal Processing Soc., IEEE Comm. Soc. Avocations: music, travel. Home: 375 Victorian Ln Duluth GA 30097-5769 Office: DeVry U 250 N Arcadia Ave Decatur GA 30030-2198 E-mail: ltan@faculty.atl.devry.edu.

TAN, LUCAS G. anesthesiologist; b. Maasin, Leyte, Philippines, Oct. 18, 1932; s. Yu Chin and Nga sio (Go) Tan; m. Victoria A. Ong, Oct. 18, 1967; children: Lowell, Vivian, Verna, Violeta. MD, U. Santo Tomas, 1960. Diplomate Am. Bd. Anesthesiology. Intern Pitts. Mercy Hosp., 1962-63; resident in surgery Lebanon Hosp., Bronx, N.Y, 1963-67; resident in anesthesiology U. Toronto, 1969-70; fellow in anesthesiology St. Luke's Hosp., Cleve., 1971-72; chmn. dept. anesthesiology Alexian Bros. Hosp., San Jose, Calif., 1978-83, vice-chmn. dept. anesthesiology, 1984-85, chmn. dept. anesthesiologist, 1991-1992; active staff mem. Alexian Bros. Hosp. (now Regional Med Ctr. San Jose), 1992—. Com. mem. surg. care Alexian Bros. Hosp., 1979-80, respiratory care, 1984-85, continuing edn. and libr., 1990-91, continuing med. evaluation, 1992-93. Fellow Am. Coll. Anesthesiology; mem. Am. Soc. Anesthesiologists, Calif. Soc. Anesthesiologists. Office: 10165 Dougherty Ave Morgan Hill CA 95037-9212 E-mail: lucvic@aol.com.

TAN, MARIANNE MEE-RYUNG, pharmacist, medical liaison, consulant; d. Hee-Kyoo and Ill-Bae Park; m. Mark Tan, Sept. 20, 1986; children: Sarah Jennifer, Lisa Jin-Joo. PhD, Albany Coll. of Pharmacy, New York, 1999—2002. Registered Pharmacist NY, Md., 2003. Clin. oncology pharmacist Johns Hopkins U., Balt., 1987—93; oncology clin. pharmacist Stony Brook U. Hosp., Stony Brook, NY, 1995—2003; regional med. liaison Amgen Pharm., Thousand Oaks, Calif., 2003—. Cons. Roche Pharm., Nutley, NJ, 2002—03. Author: (rev. and rsch. articles) Role of Kytril as an Antiemetic. Recipient Ortho-McNeil Profl. Award, McNeil Pharm., 2002. Mem.: Ea. Coop. Oncology Group (corr.), Am. Soc. of Health Systems Pharmacist (assoc.), Am. Soc. of Clin. Oncologist (assoc.).

TAN, TJIAUW-LING, psychiatrist, educator; b. Pemalang, Java, Indonesia, June 2, 1935; came to U.S., 1967; naturalized, 1972; s. Ping-Hoey and Liep-Nio (Liem) T.; m. Esther Joyce Kho, June 2, 1961; children: Paul Budiman, Robert Yuling, Alice Ayling. BS, U. Indonesia Faculty Medicine, 1957, MD, 1961; postgrad., U. Indonesia, Jakarta, 1961-65, UCLA, 1967-71, Pa. State U., 1971-72. Diplomate Am. Bd. Psychiatry and Neurology, Am. Bd. Gen. Psychiatry, Am. Bd. Geriat. Psychiatry. Lectr. psychiatry U. Indonesia, Jakarta, 1965-67; psychiat. cons. Ctrl. Gen. Hosp., Jakarta, 1965-67; postdoctoral fellow UCLA Brain Rsch. Inst., 1967-69; asst. rsch. psychiatrist, dept. psychiatry Neuropsychiat. Inst., UCLA, 1969-70; asst. prof. psychiatry Pa. State U., 1972-87, assoc. prof. psychiatry, 1987-99, prof. psychiatry, 1999—. Chief inpatient psychiatry Univ. Hosp. Milton S. Hershey Med. Ctr., 1972—, dir. Behavioral Medicine Clinic, co-dir. Biofeedback Lab., 1975—; cons. psychiatry Family and Children's Svc. Lebanon County, Lebanon, Pa., 1971-79. Contbr. articles to profl. jours. Bd. dirs. Retarded Children's Assn. Dauphin County, Inc., 1971—73. Fellow Am. Psychiat. Assn. (disting. life); mem. Pa. Psychiat. Soc., Ctrl. Pa. Psychiat. Soc., Assn. Advancement Behavior Therapy, Assn. Applied Psychophysiology and Biofeedback, Soc. Behavioral Medicine, Assn. Psychophysiol. Study of Sleep, Am. Acad. Sleep Disorder Medicine, Am. Assn. for Geriat. Psychiatry, Am. Geriat. Soc. Home: 1478 Bradley Ave Hummelstown PA 17036-9143 Office: Pa State U Coll Medicine Dept Psychiatry 500 University Dr Hershey PA 17033-2390 Office Phone: 717-531-8207. Business E-Mail: lingtan@psu.edu.

TANABE, CHARLES Y. lawyer; b. Denver, Nov. 27, 1951; BA, U. Colo., 1973; JD, U. Calif., Berkeley, 1976. Bar: Colo. 1976. Mem. Sherman & Howard, L.L.C., Denver. Mem. ABA, Phi Beta Kappa. Office: Sherman & Howard LLC 633 17th St Ste 3000 Denver CO 80202-3665

TANAKA, J(EANNIE) E. lawyer; b. L.A., Jan. 21, 1942; d. Togo William and Jean M. Tanaka. BA, Internat. Christian U., Tokyo, 1966; MSW, UCLA, 1968; JD, Washington Coll., 1984. Bar: Calif. 1984, U.S. Dist. Ct. (cen., no. dists.) Calif. 1985, U.S. Ct. Appeals (9th cir.) 1985, D.C. 1987. Instr. Aoyama Gakuin, Meiji Gakuin, Sophia U., Tokyo, 1968-75; with program devel. Encyclopedia Britannica Inst., Tokyo, 1976-78; instr. Honda, Mitsubishi, Ricoh Corps., Tokyo, 1975-80; with editorial dept. Simul Internat., Tokyo; assoc. Seki and Jarvis, L.A., 1984-86, Jones, Day, Reavis & Pogue, L.A., 1986-87, Fulbright, Jaworsky and Reavis, McGrath, L.A., 1987-89; asst. counsel Unocal, L.A., 1989-91; pvt. practice L.A., 1991—; counsel Calif. Dept. Corps., L.A., 1993—. Active Japan-Am. Soc., L.A., 1984-95, Japanese-Am. Citizens League, L.A., 1981, 92—, Japanese Am. Cultural and Cmty. Ctr., 1986-89; vol. Asian Pacific Am. Legal Ctr. So. Calif., 1985-86. Mem. Japanese-Am. Bar Assn., Mensa. Democrat. Mem. Foursquare Meth. Ch. Avocations: Japanese language, Chinese language, U.S.-Far East relations, martial arts.

TANAKA, KAY, genetics educator; b. Osaka, Japan, Mar. 2, 1929; came to U.S., 1969; d. Kumaji and Fusa (Nakamae) T.; m. Tomoko Hasegawa, Nov. 5, 1954; children: Atau, Elly Margaret. MD, U. Tokyo, 1956, Dr. Med. Sci., 1961; MA (hon.), Yale U., 1983. Asst. prof. medicine Harvard Med. Sch., Boston, 1969-73; sr. rsch. scientist Yale U., New Haven, Conn., 1973-82, prof. genetics, 1983-94, prof. emeritus, 1995—. Mem. biochemistry study sect. NIH, Bethesda, Md., 1983-84. Contbr. numerous articles to sci. jours., chpts. to books. Grantee NIH, 1971-95, March of Dimes, 1974-92. Mem. Am. Soc. Biol. Chemistry, Am. Soc. Human Genetics, Soc. Inborn Metabolic Disorders.

TANAKA, KOUICHI ROBERT, hematologist, educator; b. Fresno, Calif., Dec. 15, 1926; s. Kenjiro and Teru (Arai) T.; m. Grace Mutsuko Sakaguchi, Oct. 23, 1965; children: Anne M., Nancy K., David K. BS, Wayne State U., 1949, MD, 1952. Intern Los Angeles County Gen. Hosp., 1952—53; resident, fellow Detroit Receiving Hosp., 1953—57; instr. Sch. Medicine UCLA, 1957—59, asst. prof. medicine, 1959—61, assoc. prof. medicine, 1961—68, prof. Sch. Medicine, 1968—97, prof. emeritus, 1998—. Chief hematology divsn. Harbor-UCLA, Torrance, Calif., 1961—97, chief hematology, 1998—2000. Served with AUS, 1946-48. Master ACP (gov. So. Calif. region I 1993-97); mem. Am. Fedn. Med. Rsch., We. Soc. Clin. Investigation, L.A. Soc. Internal Medicine (pres. 1971), Am. Soc. Hematology, Internat. Soc. Hematology, We. Assn. Physicians, Am. Soc. Clin. Investigation, Assn. Am. Physicians, Sigma Xi, Alpha Omega Alpha. Achievements include research on red cell metabolism. Home: 4 Cayuse Ln Rancho Palos Verdes CA 90275-5172 Office: Dept Med Box 400 Harbor-UCLA Med Ctr Torrance CA 90509 Office Phone: 310-222-3695.

TANAKA, PATRICE AIKO, public relations executive; b. Hawaii; BA, U. Hawaii, 1974. Editor Hawaii Press Newspapers, 1974-77; dir. pub. rels. Hotel Inter-Continental Maui, 1977-79; from acct. exec. to sr. v.p. and creative dir. Jessica Dee Comm., N.Y.C., 1979-87, exec. v.p., gen. mgr., 1987-90; CEO, creative dir. PT&Co., N.Y.C., 1990—. Featured in books: American Dreamers, Visionaries and Entrepreneurs, 1995, The Art of Public Relations, 2002. Bd. dirs. Greater N.Y. coun. Girl Scouts U.S., U.S. Fund for UNICEF, Family Violence Prevention Fund. Named one of nation's 500 Most Influential Asian Ams., Avenue mag., 1996; recipient Mothering That Works award, Working Mother mag., 1994, Women Mean Bus. award, Bus. and Profl. Women USA, 1999, Paul M. Lund award for pub. svc., Pub. Rels. Soc. Am., 2002. Mem.: Asian Women in Bus. (bd. dirs.), Coun. Pub. Rels. Firms (founding bd. dirs.), Women Execs. in Pub. Rels., N.Y. Women in Comm. (pres. 2001—02, 2002—03, Matrix award for pub. rels. 1996), Asian Pacific Am. Women's Leadership Inst. (founding bd. dirs.), Women's Forum N.Y., U. Hawaii Alumni Assn. (bd. dirs. N.Y. chpt.). Home: One River Pl #2610 New York NY 10036 Office: Patrice Tanaka & Co Inc 320 W 13th St Fl 7 New York NY 10014-1200

TANAKA, RICHARD I. computer products company executive; b. Sacramento, Dec. 17, 1928; s. G. and Kei Tanaka; m. Edith M. Arita, Aug. 18, 1951; children: Steven Richard, Jean Elizabeth, John Richard, Anne Mariko. BS with highest honors, U. Calif., Berkeley, 1950, MS, 1951; PhD, Calif. Inst. Tech., 1958. Sr. rsch. engr. N.Am. Aviation, Inc., 1951-54; mem. tech. staff Hughes Aircraft Co., 1954-57; dept. mgr., sr. mem. comuter rsch. Lockheed Missiles & Space Co., Palo Alto, Calif., 1957-65; sr. v.p. Cal Comp (Calif. Computer Products, Inc.), Anaheim, 1966-77; pres. Internat. Tech. Resources Co., Tustin, Calif., 1977-80; pres., CEO Systonetics, Inc., Fullerton, Calif., 1980-86; pres. Lundy Electronics & Sys., Inc., Glen Head, N.Y., 1986-89; chmn., CEO, pres. Scan-Optics, Inc., Manchester, Conn., 1989-97; chmn., CEO V-Sys., Inc., San Juan Capistrano, Calif., 1999-2000; pres. ITR Co., Santa Ana, Calif., 2000—. Vis. prof. U. Calif., Berkeley, 1962 Author: Residue Arithmetic and Its Applications to Computer Technology, 1967. Hughes fellow Calif. Inst. Tech., 1955-57 Fellow IEEE (pres. computer soc. 1965-66, centennial medal, Golden Core award 1996); mem. Internat. Fedn. Info. Processing (pres. 1974-77, hon. life mem., U.S. del.), Am. Fedn. Info. Processing Socs. (pres. 1969-71, disting. service award 1983), Phi Beta Kappa, Tau Beta Pi, Eta Kappa Nu. Home: 10321 Shadyridge Dr Santa Ana CA 92705-1568 Office Phone: 714-838-7450.

TANAKA, RICHARD KOICHI, JR., architect, planner; b. San Jose, Calif., Oct. 16, 1931; s. Richard Inoru and Mae Yoshiko (Koga) T.; m. Barbara Hisako Kumagai, Oct. 7, 1961; children: Craig, Todd, Sandra, Trent. BArch, U. Mich., 1954; M in Urban Planning, Calif. State U., San Jose, 1978. Arch., planner Steinberg Group, San Jose, L.A., 1954. Chair. bd. dirs. Happi House Restaurants, Inc., 1972—. Author: American on Trial, 1988. Dir. Human Rels. Com., San Jose, 1969-73; dir., pres. Bicentennial Com., San Jose, 1974-77; bd. dirs. Santa Clara County Sch. Bd. Assn., 1980—; pres. Internment of Local Japanese Ams., San Jose, 1984—; past pres., trustee East Side H.S. Dist., San Jose, 1971-92, Japanese Am. Citizens League, San Jose; mem. bd. govs. Boy Scouts Am., San Jose, 1978—, NCCJ, San Jose, 1976—; past pres. Tapestry and Talent, 1976-80; trustee San Jose/Evergreen C.C., 1992—, pres., 1993-94, 97-98; bd. dirs. Calif. C.C. Trustees, 1993-2002, pres., 1997-98. Mem. AIA, Am. Planning Inst., Constrn. Specification Inst., Rotary. Avocations: golf, painting. Home: 14811 Whipple Ct San Jose CA 95127-2570 Office: 60 Pierce Ave San Jose CA 95110-2819 Personal E-mail: rktanaka@sbcglobal.net.

TANANBAUM, JAMES, medical engineering company executive; b. N.Y.C., May 5, 1963; s. David J. and Elizebeth Zelda (Belfer) T. BS cum laude, Yale U., 1985; postgrad. health scis., tech. program, Harvard U. and MIT (joint), Boston, 1985-89; postgrad., Harvard Bus. Sch., Boston, 1989—. Rsch. asst. MIT, Cambridge, 1986—; chmn. Med. Engring. Devices, Inc., Boston, 1987—. Computer cons. Nat. Retirement Programs, Inc., N.Y.C., 1981—, Software Engring., Inc., N.Y.C., 1985, Clin. Computing Ctr., Inc., Boston, 1985—; student pres. Health, Scis., and Tech. Program, Harvard U. and MIT, 1986—. Mem. Sigma Xi. Home: 107 Avenue Louis Pasteur Rm 215 Boston MA 02115-5750 Office: Advanced Medical Inc 901Gateway Blvd South San Francisco CA 94080

TANCREDI, JAMES J. lawyer; b. Hartford, Conn., Apr. 1, 1954; s. Joseph I. and Angelina C. (Lanza) T.; children: Lauren, Jamie, Brian. BA in Urban Studies and Polit. Sci., Coll. Holy Cross, 1976; JD, U. Conn., 1979. Bar: Conn. 1979, U.S. Dist. Ct. Conn. 1979, U.S. Ct. Appeals (2d cir.) 1982, U.S. Dist. (so. dist.) N.Y. 1988, U.S. Supreme Ct., 1991. From assoc. to ptnr. Day, Berry & Howard, Hartford, Conn., 1979—, ptnr., chmn fin. restructuring group, 1996—. Editor: CT Bankruptcy Desk Book. Bd. dirs. Conn. Mental Health Assn., Hartford, 1986-89, 2001—. Mem. ABA (bus. sect.), Am. Bankruptcy Inst., Conn. Bar Assn. (exec. com. mem. bankruptcy section), Hartford County Bar Assn. (dir., chair cmty. comml. law 1997—). Congregationalist. Office: Day Berry & Howard LLP CityPlace I Hartford CT 06103 E-mail: jjtancredi@dbh.com.

TANCREDI, LAURENCE RICHARD, law and psychiatry educator, physician; b. Hershey, Pa., Oct. 15, 1940; s. Samuel N. and Alvesta (Pera) T. AB in English, Franklin and Marshall Coll., 1962; MD, U. Pa., 1966; JD, Yale U., 1972. Diplomate Am. Bd. Neurology and Psychiatry; Bar: N.Y. 1982. Sr. profl. assoc. Inst. Medicine, NAS, Washington, 1972-74; fellow in psychiatry Columbia U. Coll. Physicians and Surgeons, N.Y.C., 1974-75; postdoctoral fellow in psychiatry Yale U. Med. Sch., New Haven, 1975-77, assoc. prof. psychiatry, 1977-84; Kraft Eidman prof. medicine and law U. Tex. Health Sci. Ctr., Houston, 1984-92, dir. health law program, 1983-92; clin. prof. psychiatry NYU, 1992—; clin. prof. health care scis. U. Calif., San Diego, 1993—2003; mem. staff Brookhaven nat. Labs. Clin. Ctr., 1994-96; pvt. practice N.Y.C., 1994—. V.p., bd. dirs. Internat. Acad. Law and Mental Health, 1987—95, bd. dirs., 2002—, v.p., 2003—; mem. adv. com. on transplantations Health Care Fin. Adminstrn., Dept. Health and Human Svcs., 1981—84; mem. nat. adv. bd. NIMH Ctr. Study of Pub. Mental Health N.Y. State Office Mental Health, 1994—99; cmty. svcs. bd. Dept. Mental Health, Mental Retardation and Alcohol Svcs., City of N.Y., 1995—2001; mem. sci. adv. com. Am. Suicide Found., 1995—; cons. Commn. on Med. Profl. Liability; co-prin., investigator study ABA, 1978—80; cons. in field. Fellow: Am. Coll. Psychiatry, N.Y. Acad. Med. Office: 129B E 71st St New York NY 10021-4201 Office Phone: 212-288-5197.

TANCREDO, THOMAS G. congressman; b. North Denver, Colo., Dec. 20, 1945; m. Jackie Tancredo; 2 children. BA, U. No. Colo., 1968. Mem. Colo. State Ho. Reps., 1977-81; regional rep. U.S. Dept. Edn., 1981-93; mem. U.S. Congress from 6th Colo. dist., 1999—; mem. edn. and workforce, internat. rels., and resources coms.; mem. Ho. Budget Com. Republican. Office: US Ho Reps 1130 Longworth Ho Office Bldgce Bldg Washington DC 20515-2701 also: 6099 S Quebec St Ste 200 Centennial CO 80111-4547

TANDLER, BERNARD, cell biology educator; b. Bklyn., Feb. 18, 1933; s. Arthur and Pauline (Solomon) T.; m. Helen Weisman, Dec. 25, 1955 (dec. Aug. 14, 1986); children: Janice Dena, Evan Charles. BS, Bklyn. Coll., 1955; AM, Columbia U., 1957; PhD, Cornell U., 1961; DMD (hon.), U. Cagliari, 1997. Instr. anatomy NYU, N.Y.C., 1962-63; assoc. Sloan Kettering Inst., 1963-67; asst. prof. cell biology Cornell U., N.Y.C., 1965-67; assoc. prof. Case Western Res. U., Cleve., 1967-72, prof. oral biology, 1972-91, acting chmn. dept. oral biology, 1987-89. Affiliate prof. oral biology U. Wash., Seattle, 1993—; vis. prof. U. Copenhagen, 1973, U. Cagliari, 1983, Kyushu Dental Coll., 1994-98, bio. sci. Case We. Res. U., 2003—; sr. rsch. scientist Tex. Tech U., Lubbock, 1999-01; cons. NIH, NSF, VA. Author: (with C.L. Hoppel) Mitochondria, 1972; assoc. editor: Anatomical Record, 1974-98; guest editor: Microscopy Rsch. and Technique, 1993-94, European Jour. Morphology, 1995-2000, 02—; contbr. chpts. to books, articles to profl. jours. Recipient Disting. Alumnus award Bklyn. Coll., 1981, Robert E. Kennedy award for Acad. Freedom, Ohio chpt. AAUP, 1992, Disting. Scientist award Am. Assn. Dental Rsch., 1999; USPHS fellow, 1957-62. Mem. Am. Assn. Anatomists, Am. Soc. Cell Biology, Electron Microscopy Soc. Am., Japanese Soc. Oral Biology, Japanese Assn. Anatomists, Internat. Assn. Dental Rsch. (Disting. Scientist award 1999) Am. Soc. Mammalogists, Italian Soc. Anatomy (hon.), Sigma Xi. Office Phone: 216-368-0563. Business E-Mail: bernard.tandler@case.edu.

TANDON, RAJIV, psychiatrist, educator; b. Kanpur, India, Aug. 3, 1956; came to U.S., 1984; s. Bhagwan Sarup and Usha (Mehrotra) T.; m. Chanchal Nammi Vohra; children: Neeraj, Anisha, Gitanjali. Student, St. Xavier's Coll., Bombay, India, 1974; BS, All India Inst., New Delhi, 1980; MD, Nat. Inst. of MH, India, 1983. Sr. resident Mental Health and Neuro-Scis., India, 1983-84; resident U. Mich. Hosps., Ann Arbor, 1984-87, attending psychiatrist, 1987-2000. Dir. schizophrenia program, dir. hosp. svcs. divsn. U. Mich., Ann Arbor, 1987—2000, assoc. prof., 1993—99, prof., 1999—; cons. Lenawee County Cmty. Mental Health, Adrian, Mich., 1985—99. Author: Biochemical Parameters of Mixed Affective States; Negative Schizophrenic Symptoms: Pathophysiology and Clinical Implications; contbr. over 120 articles to profl. jours. Recipient Young Scientist's award Biennial Winter workshop on Schizophrenia, 1990, 92, Travel award Am. Coll. Neuropsychopharmacology/Mead, 1990, Rsch. Excellence award Am. Assn. Psychiatrists from India, 1993, Sci. award, Best Drs. in Am. award, 1994-98, Gerald Klerman award for outstanding rsch. by a Nat. Alliance for Rsch. in Schizophrenia and Depression young investigator, 1995, FuturPsych award CINP, 1997. Mem. Am. Psychiat. Assn. (Wisniewski Young Psychiatrist Rschr. award 1993), World Fedn. Mental Health, Soc. for Neurosci., N.Y. Acad. Scis., Soc. Biol. Psychiatry, Mich. Psychiat. Soc. Democrat. Hindu. Office: U Mich Med Ctr Dept Psychiatry Box 0120 1500 E Medical Center Dr # 9C Ann Arbor MI 48109-0005 Office Phone: 734-936-4960. Business E-Mail: rtandon@umich.edu.

TANDON, RAJIV, training company executive; b. Allahabad, India, May 9, 1944; came to U.S., 1969; s. Jagdish Bihari and Vimla Devi (Mehrotra) T.; m. Priti Khanna, Sept. 1969; children: Ribhu Dev, Veeti. BTech with honors, Indian Inst. of Tech., 1966, MS in Ops. Rsch., 1972; MBA, U. Minn., 1972, PhD, 1987. Trainee Kumardhubi (India) Engring. Works, 1966-67, prodn. control officer, 1967-69; ops. rsch. analyst Nat. Car Rental, Mpls., 1971-72, mgr. ops. rsch., 1972-75, dir. fin. analysis, 1975-77, corp. v.p., MIS, 1977-81, corp. v.p., gen. mgr. car rental, 1981-86; dir. venture mgmt. U. St. Thomas, Mpls., 1988-93, dir. corp. venturing, 1993-95; pres., CEO Learning Byte Internat. (formerly Inst. for Advanced Tech.), Mpls., 1995—2001, Adayana, Inc., Mpls., 2001—. Mgmt. cons., 1986-95. Exec. editor New Venture Rev., 1985-90; contbr. articles to profl. jours. Pres. Planners League, 1978. Mem. Am. Mgmt. Assn., Inst. of Noetic Sci., Inst. of Mgmt. Scis. (sec. upper Midwest chpt. 1975-76, v.p. 1976-77, pres. 1977-78). Avocations: reading, news. Home: 8109 Rhode Island Ave S Bloomington MN 55438-1146 Office: 4444 W 76th St Minneapolis MN 55435 E-mail: rtandon@adayana.com.

TANDY, KAREN P. government agency administrator; b. Ft. Worth, Tex. married; 2 children. Grad., Tex. Tech. U., Tex. Tech. Law Sch., 1977. Asst. U.S. atty. ea. dist., Va., 1979—90; asst. U.S. atty. western dist., 1979—90; supr. dept. drug and forfeiture litig. Criminal Divsn. of Dept. Justice, 1990—99; assoc. dep. atty. gen., dir. Organized Crime Drug Enforcement Task Forces, 1999—2003, mgr., 2001—03; adminstr. Drug Enforcement Adminstrn., 2003—. Chief asset forfeiture unit U.S. Attys. Office Western Dist., Wash., 1988—90; clk. Chief Judge of No. Dist., Tex.; dep. chief Narcotics and Dangerous Drug Sect. Recipient Atty. Gens. award for disting. svc., Award for Extraordinary Achievement, Dept. Justice, Award for Superior Svc., U.S. Atty. Dir. Office: Drug Enforcement Adminstrn 2401 Jefferson Davis Hwy Alexandria VA 22301

TANE, SUSAN JAFFE, retired manufacturing company executive; b. N.Y.C. d. Irving and Beatrice (Albert) J.; m. Irwin R. Tane; children by previous marriage: Robert Wayne, Stephen Mark. BS, Boston U., 1964; postgrad., Hofstra U., C.W. Post U. Elem. sch. tchr., Long Beach, N.Y., 1964-67; pres. Fashions by Appointment, Glen Cove, N.Y., 1967-71; adminstrv. asst. Peerless Sales Corp., Elmont, N.Y., 1967-71; from sales mgr. to mktg. dir. United Utensils Co., Inc., Port Washington, N.Y., 1973-78; v.p. ops. and control United Molded Products divsn. United Utensils Co., Inc., Port Washington, 1978-80; v.p. mktg. Utensco, Port Washington, 1980-88. Bd. dirs. Peerless Aerospace Corp. Co-inventor plastic container and handling assembly. Life mem. Ronald McDonald House; mem. Friends of the Arts-L.I. U.; friend N.Y. Pub. Libr.; pres. Susan Jaffe Tane Found.; fellow Morgan Libr.; trustee, sr. v.p. Am. Jewish Congress; life mem. Hadassah; chair Commn. for Women's Equality/Am. Jewish Congress; bd. dirs. Poe Found. Mem. Boston U. Alumni Assn., Lotos Club (mem. libr. com.).

TANENBAUM, ALLAN JAY, lawyer; b. Savannah, Ga., Aug. 9, 1946; s. Nathan and Gertrude Sadie (Palefsky) T.; m. Elaine Kruger, Aug. 8, 1971; children: Louis, Sharon, Stephen, Eric. BS in Econs., U. Pa., 1967; JD, U. Va., 1971. Bar: Ga. 1972. Ptnr. Frankel, Hardwick, Tanenbaum, Fink, P.C., Atlanta, 1972-96, Cohen Pollock Merlin Axelrod & Tanenbaum, 1996-2001; gen. counsel AFC Enterprises, Inc., 2001—; mng. dir. Lawyer Reference Svc. of Atlanta, 1977-87. Trustee Congregation B'nai Torah; sec., exec. com., bd. dirs. Jewish Family and Career Svcs., Inc. With USAR, 1968-74. Fellow Am. Bar Found.; mem. ABA (ho. of dels., chair gen. practice sect., spkr. young lawyers divsn., lawyer referral and info. svc., chair pub. edn. divsn., chair com. on scope and correlation of work, chair fellows young lawyers divsn., chair coun. fund for justice and edn. 2003—), Atlanta Bar Assn. (past sec., del.), Lawyers Club Atlanta, Atlanta Council Younger Lawyers (past pres.). Office: AFC Enterprises Inc Office of General Counsel Six Concourse Pkwy Ste 1700 Atlanta GA 30328 E-mail: atanenbaum@afce.com.

TANENBAUM, BASIL SAMUEL, engineering educator; b. Providence, Dec. 1, 1934; s. Harry Milton and Rena Ada (Herr) Tanenbaum; m. Carol Binder, Aug. 26, 1956; children: Laurie, Stephen, David. BS summa cum laude, Brown U., 1956; MS, Yale U., 1957, PhD in Physics, 1960. Staff physicist Raytheon Co., Waltham, Mass., 1960-63; prof. engring. Case Western Res. U., Cleve., 1963-75; prof. Harvey Mudd Coll., Claremont, Calif., 1975—, Norman F. Sprague, Jr. prof. life scis., 1996—, dean faculty, 1975-93. Vis. scientist Arecibo (P.R.) Obs. Cornell U., 1968—69; vis. assoc. prof. Northwestern U., Evanston, Ill., 1970; mem. sci. adv. com. Nat. Astronomy and Ionosphere Ctr., 1972—77; dir. Minority Engrs. Indsl. Opportunity Program, 1973—75; mem. sci. adv. com. Calif. Poly. Inst., Pomona, 1976—87; mem. engring. and sci. adv. com. Calif. State U., Fullerton, 1976—87; dir. summer sci. program Thacher Sch., Ojai, Calif., 1977—82; vis. scholar Beckman Laser Inst. U. Calif., Irvine, Calif., 1993—94, 1998, 2000—, mem. biomed. engring. adv. com., 2000—; mem. nat. adv. com. Rowan Coll., Glassboro, NJ, 1993—2000; mem. Eisenhower adv. com. Calif. Postsecondary Edn. Com., 1993—97; pres.'s adv. coun. Olin Coll. Engring., Needham, Mass., 2001—, vice chmn., 2001, chmn., 02; interim assoc. dean joint sci. dept. The Claremont Colls., 2003—; cons. in field. Author: (book) Plasma Physics, 1967. Trustee Western U. Health Scis., Pomona, 1997—2004. Recipient Wiitke Tchg. award, Case Western Res. U., 1973; Woods Hole Oceanog. Inst. fellow, 1959, NSF fellow, Yale U., 1956—60, Sr. Sterling fellow, 1959. Mem.: AAUP, IEEE, AAAS, Am. Soc. Engring. Edn., Am. Phys. Soc., Sigma Xi (Rsch. award 1969). Home: 611 W Delaware Dr Claremont CA 91711-3458 Office: Harvey Mudd Coll 301 E 12th St Claremont CA 91711-5901 Office Phone: 909-621-8864. Business E-Mail: sam_tanenbaum@hmc.edu.

TANENBAUM, JAY HARVEY, lawyer; b. N.Y.C., Nov. 17, 1933; s. Leo Aaron and Regina (Stein) T.; m. Linda Goldman, May 28, 1961; children: Susan Hillary, Steven Eric. BA, Hobart and William Smith Colls., 1954; LLB, Union U., 1957, JD, 1961. Bar: N.Y. 1957, U.S. Dist. Ct. (so. dist.) N.Y. 1961, U.S. Supreme Ct. 1967. Internat. trader Associated Metals and Minerals Corp., N.Y.C., 1960-64; pvt. practice, N.Y.C., 1964—. Corp. counsel Internat. Gate Corp., Gen. Gate Corp. Mem. N.Y. State Bar Assn., N.Y. Trial Lawyers Assn., Bronx County Bar Assn. Clubs: St. James (London), Le Club (N.Y.).

TANENHAUS, DAVID SPINOZA, historian, educator; b. Iowa City, Iowa, Jan. 8, 1968; s. Joseph and Gussie Tanenhaus; m. Virginia Louise Pitts, Oct. 25, 2001; m. Jenifer Lee Stenfors, July 27, 1997 (dec. Sept. 9, 1999). BA, Grinnell Coll., Iowa, 1990; MA, U. of Chgo., 1991, PhD, 1997. Asst. prof. history U. of Nev., 1997—; asst. prof. law William S. Boyd Sch. of Law, Las Vegas, 2002—03, assoc. prof., 2003—. Author: Juvenile Justice in the Making, 2004; editor: A Century of Juvenile Justice; contbr. chpt. to book. Adv. Juvenile Ct. Centennial Com., Washington, 1999, Children and Family Justice Ctr., Northwestern U. Sch. of Law, Chgo., 2001. Mellon Postdoctoral Long Term Fellowship, The Newberry Libr., 2000—01. Mem.: Am. Soc. for Legal History, Orgn. of Am. Historians, Am. Hist. Assn. Office: U of Nevada 4505 Maryland Pkwy Las Vegas NV 89123

TANENHAUS, SAM, editor; m. Kathryn Bonomi; 1 child. BA in English, Grinnell Coll., 1977; MA in English Lit., Yale U., 1978. With publicity Farrar, Straus and Giroux; with trade, acad., and crossover books Oxford Univ. Press,

Chelsea House; asst. editor op-ed page N.Y. Times, 1997—99, editor book rev., 2004—; contbg. editor Vanity Fair, 1999—2004. Juror on biography Pulitzer Prize Com., 2000; affiliated writer Sch. Journalism NYU, 2002—03. Author: Literature Unbound: A Guide for the Common Reader, 1984, Louis Armstrong: Biography of a Musician, 1989, Whittaker Chambers: A Biography, 1997 (L.A. Times Book prize for biography, 1997, finalist Nat. Book award for nonfiction, 1997, finalist Pulitzer prize for biography, 1998); contbg. author: Wall St. Jour., Washington Post; contbg. author Boston Globe, LA Times, N.Y. Times Mag., Nat. Rev., New Criterion, N.Y. Rev. Books, New Republic, Am. Scholar, Commentary. Recipient award, John M. Olin Found., Bradley Found.; grantee, NEH, 1997; Media fellow Hoover Instn., Stanford U., 2000, 2002. Mem.: Soc. Am. Historians (mem. exec. bd.). Office: The NY Times 229 W 43rd St New York NY 10036

TANG, C. MARK, investment banker, venture capitalist, writer; b. Jiangyin, China, June 21, 1964; s. J.H. Tang and R.F. Kong; m. S. Sharon Guo, Jan. 20, 1994; children: Alexander, Gloria. BS in Biochemistry, Nanjing (China) U., 1985; PhD in Biochemistry and Molecular Biol., U. Calif., 1993; MBA in Fin., NYU, 2000. Postdoctoral rsch. assoc. Rockefeller U., N.Y.C., 1993-96; assoc. v.p. biotech., merchant banking and venture capital DH Blair Investment Banking Corp., N.Y.C., 1996-98; co-founder, CFO, vice chmn. Aegisoft Corp. (acquired by RealNetwork Inc.), Rockville, Md., 1998-2000; investment advisor UBS PaineWebber, Inc., N.Y.C., 1998-2000, Morgan Stanley, Jersey City, 2001—02; pres. World Tech. Ventures, LLC, 2002—. Author: The Essential Biotech Investment Guide, 2002; founding mng. editor, biotech. analyst Bio/Med. Tech. Stock Newsletter, 1994—98; contbr. articles to profl. jours. Mem.: Soc. Chinese Bioscientists in Am. Avocations: tennis, golf, volleyball, reading, writing. Home: PO Box 212 Jersey City NJ 07303 Office: World Tech Ventures One Exchange Pl # 1000 Jersey City NJ 07302 E-mail: cmtang21@ureach.com.

TANG, CHENXI, literature educator; b. Jiyuan, Henan, China, Jan. 20, 1968; Ph.D, Columbia U., NY, 1993—2000. Asst. prof. U. Chgo., 2000. Office: Dept of German The Univ of Chicago 1050 East 59th Street Chicago IL 60615

TANG, ESTHER DON, development consultant, retired social worker; b. Tucson, Mar. 5, 1917; d. Don Wah and Yut (Gnan) Fok; m. David W. Tang, June 14, 1942; children: Patricia Karen Tang Crowley, Diana Cheryl Tang Simoes, David. Jr., Elizabeth Carol. Student, Draughn's Bus. Sch., San Antonio, 1936, U. Ariz., 1938-41, DHL (hon.), LHD (hon.), U. Ariz., 1992. Owner, operator supermarket, Tucson, 1940-66; exec. dir. Pio Decimo Ctr., Cath. Diocese, Tucson, 1966-85; cons., ptnr., vice chmn. bd. Netwest Devel. Corp., Tucson, 1985—. Mem. Tucson Airport Authority, 1975—, Pima County Crime and Pub. Safety Coun., 1999; chmn. Tucson-Taichung Sister Cities, 1979-91; chmn. Tucson Sister Cities Steering Com., 1984—, Sister Cities Assn. Tucson, 1990, Ariz. Pers. Bd.; chmn. bd. dirs. Pima Community Coll., 1975-85; pres. bd. dirs. Pima Coun. on Aging, 1986-90; coord. U.S. Bicentennial, Tucson; mem. adv. bd. Ariz. Dept. Econ. Security; master of ceremonies to welcome Pres. Clinton, City of Tuscon, 1999. Named Woman of Yr., City of Tucson, 1955, Woman of Yr. in Adminstrn., 1968, Lady Comdr. the Holy Sepluchre Jerusalem; recipient Disting. Friend of the Humanities award Nat. Adv. Bd., 1989, Jefferson award Ariz. Daily Star, 1987, Svc. award Pima Coun. on Aging, 1987-89, Disting. Svc. award U. Pima C.C. Found., 1988, Roots and Wings Comty. award, 1988, Rosie award So. Ariz. Ctr. Against Sexual Assault, 1990, Lifetime Achievement award YWCA, 1992, 93, La Doña de los Descendientes del Precido de Tucson, 1997-98, centennial alumni award U. Ariz., 1998, Pan-Asian Cmty. Leadership award, 1999, Arthritis Humanitarian award, 1999, Altrusa Women in Svc. award, 2000, Asia Am. Times Devel. Mgmt. Excellence award, 2000, Voices into the Millennium award Ariz. Border Patrol, Dynamic Duo—Pointing Lives in New Directions award Compass Health Care, Congl. Recognition, 2002, Lulac Nat. Presdl. citation, 2002, award Agave Ariz. Hist. Tape TV, 2002, Lifetime award U. Ariz. Coll. Agr. and Life Sci., 2002; Learning Svc. Bldg. and Gallery named in her honor, U. Ariz., 2001; named Ariz. History Maker State of Ariz. Hist. League, 2003, 15th annual cath. Found. Honoring Ester Don Tang, 2004. Mem. Soroptimist (hon., Women Who Helped Build Tucson award), Rotary Club Tucson (4 way test award 1998) Cath. Found. Diocese of Tucson (honorable mention, honoree Corner Stone Gala, 2004). Roman Catholic. Avocations: travel, cooking, golf. Home: 701 E Camino De Los Padres Tucson AZ 85718-1921

TANG, FENG, research scientist; b. Zhengzhou, Henan, China, Mar. 11, 1963; arrived in U.S., 2002; s. Qiuhua Tang and Lingcheng Shen; m. Yayun Zhang; 1 child, Luming. B Engring., Huazhong U. Sci. and Tech., Wuhan, China, 1984; PhD, U. Tsukuba, Japan, 1995. Rsch. scientist Nat. Inst. Materials Sci., Tsukuba, Japan, 1997—2002, U. Calif., Davis, 2002—. Contbr. articles to profl. publs. Mem.: Minerals, Metals and Materials Soc. (licentiate). Achievements include patents for lightweight and high strength titanium alloys for application at high temperature. Avocations: travel, mountain-climbing, badminton, movies, reading. Home: 1527 El Capitan St Davis CA 95616 Office: U Calif One Shields Ave Davis CA 95616 Office Phone: 530-752-9819. Personal E-mail: tangf80@hotmail.com. E-mail: ftang@ucdavis.edu.

TANG, GUOQING, mathematics professor; b. Anqing, Anhui, China, Oct. 1, 1959; s. Senbao Tang and Daidi Hu; m. Wenning Yan, Apr. 21, 1987; 1 child, Jeffrey Yong. BS in Applied Math., Anhui U., 1982; MS in Applied Math. & Stats., Nanjing U. Sci. and Tech., 1984; PhD in Math., Rutgers U., 1992. Instr. math., stats. Nanjing U. of Sci. and Tech., Applied Math. Dept., China, 1984—87; instr. Rutgers U., Math. Dept., New Brunswick, NJ, 1987—92; asst. prof. math. N.C. A&T State U., Greensboro, NC, 1994—99, assoc. prof. math., 1999—2002, dir. rsch. Coll. Arts and Scis., 2001—, rsch. assoc. prof. physics, 2002—03, prof. math., 2003—. Mng. dir. Transpacific Computer Cons., Greensboro, 2000—02; vis. asst. prof. math. N.C. A&T State U., 1992—94. Contbr. articles to profl. jours. V.p. IYXLSTA, Greensboro, 1999; treas. Greensboro Chinese Assn., 1996—99. Nominee Millennium awards, N.C. A&T State U. Coll. Arts and Scis., 2003; recipient Academic Site Lic. award, Universal Tech. Systems, 1999, Citation award, N.C. A&T State U. Coll. Arts and Scis., 2000; grantee, NSF, 1997, 1999, 2001, 2002, 2003, U.S. Dept. Edn., 2002, Sloan Found., 2002, N.C. A&T State U., 2003, U. N.C. Systems, 2003. Mem.: Soc. Exploration Geophysicists, Nat. Assn. Math., Am. Soc. Engring. Edn., Soc. Indsl. and Applied Math., Am. Math. Soc. Office: North Carolina A&T State University 1601 East Market Street Greensboro NC 27411 Office Phone: 336-334-7822. E-mail: gtang@ncat.edu.

TANG, JINSHAN, computer scientist, researcher; BS in Math., Xiangtan Normal U.; PhD in Engring., Beijing U., 1998. Invited rschr. ATR Media Integration and Comm. Rsch. Labs., Kyoto, 1998—2000; rsch. assoc. Harvard Med. Sch., Boston, 2000—01; rsch. sci. U. Va., Charlottesville, 2001—. Mem.: IEEE. Office: Dept ECE U Va Thornton Hall 351 McCormick Rd Charlottesville VA 22903

TANG, JOE, electronics executive; b. 1950; With Gen. Instruments; bus. mgr. Intel, 1980—90; from mng. dir. to corp. v.p. Solectron Corp., Milpitas, Calif., 1990—2000, corp. v.p., 2000—, mng. dir. S.E. Asia Sub-region, 2000—. Office: Solectron Corp 777 Gibraltar Dr Milpitas CA 95035

TANG, JOHN, network technician, information scientist, educator; b. Hong Kong, Oct. 21, 1959; s. Chew Sang and Miu King Tang; m. Juana Teresita Enriquez, Mar. 15, 1990; 1 child, Jonathan Alexander. BA, San Francisco State U., 1981; MA, San Francisco State Univeristy, 1983; PhD, U. of Va., 1991. MIS mgr. Oakland Pvt. Industry Coun., Oakland, Calif., 1991—95; IT mgr. Western Human Nutrition Rsch. Ctr., San Francisco, 1995—98; network analyst Shaman Pharms., South San Francisco, Calif., 1995—98; instr. The Computer Learning Ctr., San Francisco, 1997—2001; adj. prof. City Coll. of San Francisco, 2000—; prof. DeVry U., Fremont, Calif., 2002—. Founder/pres. easyRE.net, Fremont, Calif., 2003—; founder, CEO Home Opportunities Inc., Oakland, Calif., 2003—. Contbr. articles to profl. jours., chpts. to books. Pres. Dance for Power, Oakland, 1993—98; mem. of bd. of advisors American-Viet League, Oakland, 1991—2003. Recipient Dupont fellow, U. of Va., 1984—88, Grad. Achievement award, San Francisco State U., 1983. Roman Catholic. Avocations: creative writing, travel. Home: 6651 Gunn Dr Oakland CA 94611 Office: DeVry Univ 6600 Dumbarton Cir Fremont CA Personal E-mail: jltang@sbcglobal.net. Business E-Mail: jtang@fre.devry.edu.

TANG, PAUL C. lawyer; b. Hong Kong, Oct. 4, 1952; m. Shirley Tang; children: Elizabeth, Margaret. BA, Harvard U., 1974; JD, Columbia U., 1977, MBA, 1978. Bar: (N.Y.) 1981, N.J. 1994. Tax acct. Deloitte & Touche, 1978—80; mem. Phillips Nizer, 1980—85, ptnr., 1985—87; co-founder law firm, 1987—89; ptnr. Reid & Priest, 1989—93; exec. v.p., gen. counsel, sec. Burlington (N.J.) Coat Factory Warehouse Corp., 1993—. Office: Burlington Coat Factory 1830 Rt 130 Burlington NJ 08016-3020*

TANG, PAUL CHI LUNG, philosophy educator; b. Vancouver, B.C., Can., Jan. 23, 1944; came to U.S., 1971; s. Pei-sung and Violet (Wong) T. BSc with high distinction, U. B.C., 1966; MA in Edn., Simon Fraser U., Vancouver, 1971; MA, Washington U., St. Louis, 1975, PhD, 1982; cert. in bioethics, Kennedy Inst. Ethics, 1983; diploma in piano, Royal Conservatory Music, Toronto, 1962. Teaching asst. philosophy of edn. Simon Fraser U., 1969-71; instr. philosophy St. Louis C.C. at Meramec, Kirkwood, Mo., 1975-82; instr., lectr. philosophy Washington U., 1972-76; adj. asst. prof. Harris-Stowe State Coll., St. Louis, 1980-82; asst. prof. philosophy Grinnell (Iowa) Coll., 1982-85; asst. prof. to assoc. prof. to prof. dept. philosophy Calif. State U., Long Beach, 1985—, chmn. dept. philosophy, 1988-94, acting chmn., 1998. Vis. lectr. philosophy So. Ill. U., Edwardsville, 1978-79. Editor: Philosophy of Sci. Assn. Newsletter, 1985—90; asst. editor: Philosophy of Sci. acad. jour., 1972—75, dep. editor: The Social Sci. Jour., 1999—; contbr. articles to profl. publs., revs. to profl. publs. Senator Internat. Parliament for Safety and Peace, Palermo, Italy. Decorated knight Templar Order of Jerusalem, knight Order Holy Cross of Jerusalem, knight comdr. Lofsenic Ursinius Order, chevalier Grand Croix de Milice du St. Sepulcre; recipient cert. of merit Student Philosophy Assn., 1988-90, 93-94, spl. award, 1992, Calif. State Senate Recognition award for commitment to edn., 1997; named faculty advisor of yr. Assoc. Students, 1987, 90, 91, 95, Highland Lord of Camster, Scotland, 1995; Paul Tang prize in philosophy named in his honor, 1996-99; fellow Washington U., 1971, summer rsch. fellow Calif. State U., 1988, 96, NEH fellow Harvard U., 1988, NEH Summer Seminar fellow, 1988; internat. scholar Phi Beta Delta, interdisciplinary scholar Phi Kappa Phi, 1993, Phi Beta Kappa, 2000, Phi Sigma Tau; grantee vis. philosophers program Coun. for Philos. Studies, 1987, 91, 92; Disting. Vis. Scholars and Artists Fund, Calif. State U., 1988, 89, rsch. grantee, 1995, 97, 99. Fellow: World Lit. Acad.; mem.: Maison Internat. des Intellectuels de l'Acad. Francaise, Soc. Philosophy and Psychology, Brit. Soc. Philosophy of Sci., Iowa Philos. Soc. (pres. 1985—86), Hastings Ctr., Kennedy Inst. Ethics, History of Sci. Soc., Philosophy of Sci. Assn., Am. Philos. Assn. (Excellence in Tchg. award 1995, 1997), numerous others, Order Internat. Fellowship (Eng.), Companion of Honour (Eng.), Golden Key Internat. Hon. Soc. (Internat. Man of Yr. 1995—96), Internat. Order Merit (Eng.). Avocations: hiking, tennis, chess, music, travel. Home: 5050 E Garford St Apt 228 Long Beach CA 90815-2859 Office: Calif State U Dept Philosophy 1250 N Bellflower Blvd Long Beach CA 90840-0006 E-mail: pcltang@csulb.edu.

TANG, ROGER YIN WU, accounting educator; b. Fuhai, Yunan, People's Republic of China, Feb. 19, 1947; came to U.S., 1973; s. Van How and Yu Hwa (Liu) T.; m. Ann Sun, Dec. 24, 1974; children: Sherri, Kevin. B in Commerce, Nat. Taiwan U., Taipei, Republic of China, 1968; MBA, Ea. N.Mex. U., 1974; PhD, U. Nebr., 1977. Cert. mgmt. acct., cert. internal auditor. Instr. acctg. U. Nebr., Lincoln, 1975-77; asst. prof. acctg. McGill U., Montreal, Can., 1977-80; assoc. prof. acctg. U. Calgary (Can.), 1980-86, chmn. acctg. area. faculty of mgmt., 1987-88; prof. acctg., Upjohn chair bus. adminstrn. Western Mich. U., Kalamazoo, 1988—. Cons. Centre for Trasnat. Corps., UN, N.Y.C., 1985-87; sr. mgmt. cons. Taiwan Computer Cons. Corp., Taipei, 1974; cons. Mgmt. Cons. Corp., Taipei, 1971-72. Author: Multinational Transfer Pricing, 1981, Transfer Pricing Practices in the U.S. and Japan, 1979, Intracorporate Transfer Pricing, Management and Tax Implications, 1983, Transfer Pricing in the 1990s, 1993; contbr. articles to profl. jours. Mem. Am. Acctg. Assn., Acad. Internat. Bus., Inst. Internal Auditors, Nat. Assn. Accts. (cert. of merit 1979), Inst. Mgmt. Acctg., Assn. Asian Studies. Office: Western Mich U 1201 Oliver St Kalamazoo MI 49008-3804 Office Phone: 269-387-5247.

TANG, YI, radiologist, researcher; b. Yichang, Hubei, China, Dec. 20, 1963; s. Zhongni and deying (Liu) T.; m. Xuling Huang, Oct. 2, 1988; 1 child, Zhicao. MD, Sun Yat-Sen U. of Med. Scis., Guangzhou, China, 1987; PhDd., Kumamoto (Japan) U., 2000. Resident Guangdong Provincial People's Hosp., Guangzhou, 1987-93, attending physician, 1993-95; guest rschr. Kumamoto U., 1995-96; postdoctoral fellow MD Anderson Cancer Ctr., 2000-2001; rsch. fellow Mass. Gen. Hosp., 2001—. Reviewer Jour. of Magnetic resonance Imaging, 1999; contbr. articles to profl. jours. Higo Yiyoku Seshikai scholar, 1998, Konan Asia Internat. Found. scholar, 1999. Mem. Radiol. Soc. N.Am., Japanese Soc. of Magnetic Resonance Imaging. Avocations: ping pong/table tennis, swimming, driving. Office: Mass Gen Hosp CMIR/Radiology 13th St # 5420 Bldg 149 Boston MA 02129 E-mail: tangyiradiology@hotmail.com.

TANGORA, MARTIN CHARLES, mathematician, educator; b. N.Y.C., June 21, 1936; s. Albert and Virginia T.; m. Linda Perry, June 17, 1973; children: Charles, Elizabeth. *Father Albert Tangora (1903-1978), was a professional speed typist, who won the professional contest seven times between 1925 and 1941, and whose record of 142 net 5-stroke words per minute for an hour (from unfamiliar copy on a manual typewriter) remains unequalled.* BS, Calif. Inst. Tech., 1957; MS, Northwestern U., 1958, PhD, 1966. Instr. Northwestern U., Evanston, 1966-67, U. Chgo., 1967-69; asst. prof. U. Ill., Chgo., 1970-72, assoc. prof., 1972—2002, assoc. prof. emeritus, 2002—. Temp. lectr. U. Manchester, Eng., 1969-70; sr. vis. fellow U. Oxford, Eng., 1973-74. Author: Computing the Homology of the Lambda Algebra, 1985; co-author: Cohomology Operations and Applications in Homotopy Theory, 1968; editor: Computers in Algebra, 1988, Computers in Geometry and Topology, 1989, Algebraic Topology Oaxtepec 1991 (conf. proc.), 1993. Bd. dirs. Landmarks Preservation Coun. Ill., Chgo., 1971—, pres., 1976, v.p. 1997-99; bd. dirs. Uptown Theatre and Ctr. for the Arts, 2002—, chmn. bd., 2003—. Mem. Math. Assn. Am., Am. Math. Soc. Office: U Ill Chgo Math M/C 249 851 S Morgan St Chicago IL 60607-7045

TANGUAY, PETER EUGENE, child and adolescent psychiatry educator; b. Quebec City, Que., Can., Nov. 6, 1935; came to U.S., 1960, naturalized, 1971; s. Oscar E. and Marion L. (Grady) T.; m. Margaret Fife, Dec. 22, 1960; children: Heather Louise, Gretchen Marie. BA, U. Ottawa, Ont., Can., 1956, MD, 1960. Diplomate Am. Bd. Psychiatry and Neurology (com. for cert. in child and adolescent psychiatry 1981-87, written exam. com. for child and adolescent psychiatry 1981-87, chmn. 1985-87, dir. 1990—). Intern Harper Hosp., Detroit, 1960-61; resident in psychiatry UCLA Med. Ctr.-Harbor Gen. Hosp., 1961-64; registrar in psychiatry Kingsway Hosp., Derby, Eng., 1966-68; fellow in child psychiatry UCLA Ctr. for Health Scis., 1968-70, from asst. prof. to assoc. prof., 1970-8076, prof., 1980-94, dir. child psychiatry clin. rsch. ctr., 1977-87, assoc. chief div., 1984-91, acting chief, 1992-94; Ackerly prof. child psychiatry U. Louisville Sch. Medicine, 1994—. Tech. advisor Rainman, 1988; vis. prof. U. Tours, France, 1982, U. Hawaii, 1987, 90; Roy Grinker vis. prof. Michael Reese Hosp., Chgo., 1984; mem. gen. assembly Am. Bd. Med. Specialists, 1990—, rep. to Accreditation Coun. on Continuing Med. Edn., 1993—, mem. exec. com., 1994-96; bd. advisors Rieger Found., Santa Barbara, Calif., 1992—; mem. psychol. scis. rev. com. NIMH, 1976-80; lectr., presenter in field; edit. cons. EEG and Clin. Neurophysiology, 1979-85; numerous others. Author: (with Margaret Tanguay) Travel Adventure in Europe with Tent, Van or Motorhome, 1970; contbr. over 60 articles, abstracts and book revs. to sci. jours., over 20 chpts. to books. Mem. Clinton-Gore Nat. Leadership Coun., 1991-93. Recipient career sci. devel. award NIMH, 1970-75; grantee USPHS, 1977-87, 84-89, NIMH, 1980-95, MacArthur Found., 1983-88. Fellow Am. Psychiat. Assn. (coun. on rsch. 1980-95, vice chmn. 1981-94, mem. com. on chronically ill-emotionally handicapped child 1990-94), Am. Acad. Child and Adolescent Psychiatry (assoc. editor Jour. 1988—, co-chmn. task force on universal access to health care 1991—), Am. Coll. Psychiatry; mem. AMA, AAAS, Group for Advancement Psychiatry (chmn. child com. 1988—), Soc. for Rsch. in Child and Adolescent Psychopathology, Royal Coll. Psychiatry (Gt. Britain, affiliate). Democrat. Avocations: microcomputers, vegetable gardening, travel. Home: 1129 Cardinal Dr Louisville KY 40213-1363 Office: U Louisville Bingham Child Guidance Ctr 200 E Chestnut St Louisville KY 40202-1822

TANHAM, GEORGE KILPATRICK, retired research company executive; b. Englewood, N.J., Feb. 23, 1922; s. Francis Thomas and Irene (Kilpatrick) T.; m. Mary Finch, 1958 (div. 1962); m. Barbara Hunt, May 27, 1966 (div. 1989); children: George K., Gerald Francis, Helen Tanham Woods, Barbara Tanham Stampora, Maedi Carney, Ruth Tanham Marshall, Ramsey; m. Kathleen Van Wyck, Oct. 27, 1989. BA, Princeton U., 1943; MA, Stanford U., 1947, PhD, 1951. Assoc. prof., master student houses Calif. Inst. Tech., Pasadena, 1947-55; research staff Rand Corp., Santa Monica, Calif., 1955-58, dep. to v.p. Washington, 1958-64, 65-68, v.p., trustee, 1971-82, sr. researcher, 1982-87, cons., 1987—; assoc. dir. AID, Saigon, Vietnam, 1964-65; minister counsellor U.S. Embassy, Bangkok, Thailand, 1968-70. Cons. SAIC, McLean, Va.; lectr. in field. Author: Communist Revolutionary Warfare: The Vietminh in Indochina, 1961, 67, 85, War Without Guns: American Civilians in Rural Vietnam, 1966, Contribution a l'Histoire de la Resistance Belge, 1971, Trial in Thailand, 1974; co-author: (with Douglas S. Blaufarb) Who Will Win a Key: An Answer to the Puzzle of Revolutionary War, 1989, (with Marcy Agmon) The Indian Air Force: Trends and Prospects, 1996, (with K. Bhapal and A. Mattoo) Securing India, (with Ralph Salmi and Cesar Majul) Conflict Resolution in Islam, 1997. Bd. visitors Patterson Sch. of Diplomacy and Internat. Commerce, U. Ky., 1985-95, U. Pitts., 1982-92; bd. dirs. Ethics and Pub. Policy Ctr., 1988-98; adv. trustee Rand Corp., 1988—. Served with U.S. Army, World War II Decorated Purple Heart, Silver Star with oak leaf cluster, Air medal; Croix de Guerre avec etoile d'argent (Republic of France); Most Exalted Order of White Elephant (Thailand); Belgian-Am. Edn. Found. grantee, 1950; Ford Found. fellow, 1952-53; Social Scis. Research Council grantee, 1955-57; grantee U.S. Inst. Peace and Rockefeller Found., 1989-91, Alton Jones Found. 1996-98; Rajiv Gandhi Found. vis. fellow, New Delhi, 1995. Mem. Coun. Fgn. Rels., Cosmos Club, Spl. Forces Club (London). India Internat. Ctr. (New Delhi). Avocations: music, travel, gardening, sports. Home: PO Box 373 Strasburg VA 22657-0373 Office: Rand 1333 H St NW Washington DC 20005-4707

TANI, DANIEL M. astronaut; b. Ridley Park, Pa., Feb. 1, 1961; m. Jane Egan. BS in Mech. Engring., MIT, 1984, MS in Mech. Engring., 1988. Design engr. Hughes Aircraft Corp., El Segundo, Calif.; dept. exptl. psychology Bolt Beranek and Newman, Cambridge, Mass.; sr. structures engr. Orbital Scis. Corp., Dulles, Va., mission ops. mgr., launch ops. mgr.; astronaut NASA, Redmond, Wash., 1996, with Astronaut Office Computer Support Br. Recipient Outstanding Tech. Achievement award, Orbital Scis. Corp., 1993. Mem.: Aircraft Owners and Pilots Assn., Japanese Am. Citizens League, Alpha Delta Phi. Achievements include logged over 11 days in space; mission specialist STS-108 Endeavour (2001). Avocations: golf, flying, running, tennis, music. Office: Astronaut Office/CB NASA Johnson Space Ctr Houston TX 77058

TANIS, JAMES ROBERT, library director, history educator, clergyman; b. Phillipsburg, N.J., June 26, 1928; s. John Christian and Bertha Marie (Tobiasson) T.; m. Florence Borgmann, June 26, 1963; children— Marjorie Martha, James Tobiasson. BA, Yale, 1951; B.D., Union Theol. Sem., N.Y.C., 1954; Dr. Theol., U. Utrecht, Netherlands, 1967; LittD (hon.), Dickinson Coll., Carlisle, Pa., 1994. Ordained to ministry Presbyn. Ch., 1954. Co-pastor Greystone Presbyn. Ch., Elizabeth, N.J., 1954-55; librarian, mem. faculty Harvard Div. Sch., 1956-65; univ. librarian Yale U., 1965-68; mem. faculty Yale Div. Sch., 1968-69; dir. libraries, prof. history Bryn Mawr (Pa.) Coll., 1969-97; guest curator Phila. Mus. Art, 1997—2002; parish assoc. Valley Forge Presbyn. Ch., King of Prussia, Pa., 1973—. Author: Calvinistic Pietism in the Middle Colonies, 1967; co-author: Bookbinding in America, 1983, Images of Discord/De Tweedracht Verbeeld, 1993, Fantasy and Fashion, 1996, Leaves of Gold: Manuscript Illumination from Philadelphia Collections, 2001. Decorated officer Order Orange-Nassau. Home: 11302 Shannondell Dr Audubon PA 19403 E-mail: jrtanis@sdlifestyle.com.

TANK, GERHARD WILLI, obstetrician and gynecologist; b. Jan. 26, 1926; s. Frederick Karl and Martha Marie (Lade) T. BSc in Med. Sci., U. Wis., 1951, MD, 1953. Diplomate Am. Bd. Ob-Gyn. Rsch. asst. dept. physiology U. Wis. Med. Sch., Madison, 1949-51; intern Swedish Hosp., Seattle, 1953—54, resident in ob-gyn., 1954—56, Calif. Hosp./Orange County Hosp., 1956-57; practice medicine specializing in ob-gyn. Grants Pass, Oreg., 1957-90; ptnr. Grants Pass Clin., 1957-90, ptnr. emeritus, 1990; med. staff Josephine Gen. Hosp., 1957—90, chief of staff, 1968, bd. dirs., 1984-94; ret., 1990. Pres. Rogue Valley Physicians Svc., Medford, Oreg., 1972; former bd. dirs. Our Valley Clinic, So. Oreg. Regional Area Health Edn. Ctr., Siskiyou Cmty. Health Ctr. Contbr. articles to profl. jours. Vol. Project Hope, 1967, 72. Fellow Am. Coll. Ob-Gyn.; mem. Pacific N.W. Soc. Ob-Gyn. (emeritus), Oreg. Med. Assn. (past trustee). Personal E-mail: badger1gt@charter.net.

TANKERSLEY, MICHAEL LEONARD (MUJAHIDE ABDULLAH RAFI RASHID), computer systems administrator; b. Oct. 14, 1941; m. Doris M. Tankersley, 1967; children: Troas, Kevin, Roy, Karamoko Owusu, Sussie, Kim, Kokaiya Nkenge, Ayoka Ayanna. AA in Libr. Scis., L.A. Trade Tech. Coll., 1967; PhD (hon.), Calcutta (India) U., 1998. Libr. L.A. City Libr., 1961—62; with USN, 1962—63; systems adminstr. Dept. Social Svcs. County of Los Angeles, Compton, Calif., 1967—; assoc. chemist Datta Metal Inc. Chem. Rsch. Labs., L.A., 1987—97; exec. v.p. Micro-Rom Computers, Inc., Clearwater, Fla., 1996—98. Founder, pres. Afrikan Acad. Scis. Corp., 1965—. Mem.: AAAS, Internat. Chem. Soc., Am. Chem. Soc. (VIP medal of excellence 1994), N.Y. Acad. Scis. Avocations: astronomy, computers, automation, robotics. Mailing: 706 Poinsettia Pl Perris CA 92571 E-mail: michaeltankersley@yahoo.com.

TANKOOS, SANDRA MAXINE, court reporting services executive; b. Bklyn., Nov. 12, 1936; d. Samuel J. and Ethel (Seltzer) Rich; m. Kenneth Robert Tankoos, Mar. 17, 1957; children: Robert Ian, Gary Russell, Jenine Sheryl. AA, Stenotype Inst., 1957; BA, Queens Coll., 1969; MA, C.W. Post Coll., 1973. Cert. stenotype reporter, 1959. Ct. reporter free lance, N.Y.C., 1957-70; tchr. Spanish various high schs., L.I., 1970-76; pres. Tankoos Reporting, N.Y.C., 1976—, Ar-Ti Recording, Mineola, N.Y., 1977—, Sterling Reporting Svc., 2000—. Author: (children's book) Ettie and the Evil Eye; contbr. articles to profl. jours. Past pres., bd. dirs. Temple Sinai, Roslyn Hts., N.Y., 1989-91, Am. Jewish Acad., West Hempstead, 1984-94, LWV, Roslyn, 1969-75, NOW, Nassau County, 1975-77, bd. dirs. Religious Action Ctr., Washington, 1995—, ARZA, 1997—. Avocations: writing, piano. Home: 77 Shepherd Ln Roslyn Heights NY 11577-2508 Office: Ar-Ti Recording Inc 142 Willis Ave Mineola NY 11501-2613 also: Tankoos Reporting Co 305 Madison Ave New York NY 10165 Office Phone: 516-741-5235. E-mail: sandra@tankoos.com.

TANNEBAUM, SAMUEL HUGO, accountant; b. Aug. 15, 1933; s. Simon L. and Eva (Kapp) T.; m. Nita Mae Levy, June 12, 1955; children: Joel L., Marilyn J. BBA with spl. distinction, U. Okla., 1955. CPA, Tex., Okla. Staff acct. Alford, Meroney & Co., Dallas, 1955—61; pvt. practice acctg. Dallas, 1961—63; ptnr. Tannebaum & Bindler CPAs, Dallas, 1963—67; mng. ptnr. Tannebaum, Bindler & Lewis, Dallas, 1967—80, Tannebaum Bindler & Co. CPAs, Dallas, 1980—84; pres. Tannebaum Bindler & Co., PC, Dallas, 1984—94; sr. exec. ptnr. Weaver & Tidwell LLP, Dallas, 1995—99; cons. Dallas, 1999—; mng. dir. Weaver and Tidwell Fin. Advisors, 2000—03; registered investment advisor Dallas, 2003—. Mem. adv. coun. Cmtys. Found. Tex., 1987—; bd. dirs. Dallas Home for Jewish Aged, 1973-76, Mental Health Assn. Greater Dallas, treas. 1998-2000; trustee Temple Emanu-El, Dallas, 1976-83, treas., 1980-82, v.p., 1982-83; trustee Found. Jewish Fedn. Greater Dallas, 1987-96, 2001—; dir. Tex. Mental Health Assn., 2001—. Mem. AICPA (coun. 1979-82, 95-97, personal fin. specialist), Tex. Soc. CPAs (dir., past v.p., past chpt. pres., CPA of Yr. Dallas chpt. 1976), Nat. Assn. Estate Planners (accredited estate planner), Nat. Assn. Estate Planning Couns. (dir. 1978-82,

treas. 1982-83, v.p. 1983-84, pres. 1984-85), Dallas Estate Planning Coun. (past pres.), Brookhaven Country Club. Home: 5820 Meletio Ln Dallas TX 75230-2108 Office: Ste 1300 12221 Merit Dr Dallas TX 75251-2280

TANNEN, DEBORAH FRANCES, writer; b. Bklyn., June 7, 1945; d. Eli S. and Dorothy (Rosen) T. BA, SUNY, Binghamton, 1966; MA, Wayne State U., 1970, U. Calif., Berkeley, 1976; PhD, U. Calif., 1979. English instr. Mercer County C.C., Trenton, N.J., 1970-71; lectr. in acad. skills CUNY, Bronx, N.Y., 1971-74; asst. prof. Georgetown U., Washington, 1979-85, assoc. prof. linguistics, 1985-90, prof. linguistics, 1989-91, univ. prof., 1991—. McGraw disting. lectr. in writing Coun. for Humanities and dept. anthropology Princeton U., fall 1991; visitor Inst. for Advanced Study, Princeton, spring 1992; fellow Ctr. for Advanced Study in Behavioral Scis., Stanford, Calif., 1992-93. Author: Lilika Nakos, 1983, Conversational Style: Analyzing Talk Among Friends, 1984, That's Not What I Meant!: How Conversational Style Makes or Breaks Your Relations With Others, 1986, Talking Voices: Repetition, Dialogue and Imagery in Conversational Discourse, 1989, You Just Don't Understand: Women and Men in Conversation, 1990, Gender and Discourse, 1994, Talking From 9 to 5: Women and Men in the Workplace: Language, Sex and Power, 1994, The Argument Culture: Moving from Debate to Dialogue, 1998, The Argument Culture: Stopping America's War of Words, 1999; editor: Analyzing Discourse: Text and Talk, 1982, Spoken and Written Language: Exploring Orality and Literacy, 1982, Coherence in Spoken and Written Discourse, 1984, Perspectives on Silence, 1985, Linguistics in Context: Connecting Observation and Understanding, 1988, Gender and Conversational Interaction, 1993, Framing In Discourse, 1993, (play) An Act of Devotion, 1994. Rockefeller Humanities fellow, 1982-83; grantee NEH, 1980, 85, 86; recipient Elizabeth Mills Crothers prize U. Calif., 1976, Dorothy Rosenberg Meml. prize U. Calif., 1977, Joan Lee Yang Meml. Poetry prize U. Calif., 1977, Shrout Short Story prize, 1978, Emily Chamberlain Cook prize, 1978. Office: Georgetown U Lang & Linguistics ICC Bldg Rm 471 37th & O St NW Washington DC 20057-0001

TANNEN, RICHARD LAURENCE, medical educator, nephrologist; b. N.Y.C., Aug. 31, 1937; s. Harold and Fannie (Rosenberg) T.; m. Elizabeth Whitney Harriman, Aug. 8, 1964 (div. Apr. 1990); m. Vivien Baraban, Nov. 17, 1990; children: Bradford, Whitney, Jennifer, Alison, Julie. Student, Vanderbilt U., 1957; MD, U. Tenn., Memphis, 1960. Rsch. internist Walter Reed Inst. Rsch., Washington, 1966-69; assoc. prof., co-dir. nephrology unit U. Vt., Burlington, 1969-78; prof., chief nephrology divsn. U. Mich., Ann Arbor, 1978-88; prof., chmn. dept. medicine U. So. Calif., L.A., 1988-95; vice dean for rsch. U. Pa., Phila., 1995-97, prof. medicine, 1995—, sr. vice-dean, 1997—2002. Established investigator Am. Heart Assn., 1971-76. Co-editor: Fluids and Electrolytes, 1986, 3d edit., 1996; contbr. more than 130 sci. articles to profl. jours. Maj. U.S. Army, 1966-69. Recipient Merit award NIH, 1986-94, Disting. Alumnus award U. Tenn., 1991. Fellow ACP; mem. Am. Soc. Nephrology (pres. 1991-92), Am. Soc. Clin. Investigation, Assn. Am. Physicians, Nat. Kidney Found. (regional v.p. 1984-87, Pres.'s award 1986). Jewish. Avocations: tennis, travel. Office: U Pa Sch of Med 295 John Morgan Bldg Philadelphia PA 19104 Office Phone: 215-898-2270. Business E-Mail: tannen@mail.med.upenn.edu.

TANNEN, RICKI LEWIS, lawyer, psychologist, educator; b. N.Y.C., Apr. 29, 1952; d. Paul and Lillian (Singer) Lewis; m. Marc Jay Tannen, Aug. 25, 1972; children: Laine Amy, Adam Jesse. BA in Social Scis., U. Fla., 1975, MEd in Psycholinguistics, JD with honors, U. Fla., 1981; LLM, Harvard U., 1991; PhD, Pacifica Grad. Inst., 2002. Bar: Fla. 1982. Tchr., guidance counselor Oak Hall Pvt. Sch., Gainesville, Fla., 1976-79; atty., jud. clk. U.S. Dist. Cts., Miami, Fla., 1981-82; rep. assoc. Ft. Lauderdale (Fla.) News, Sun-Sentinel newspaper, Ferrero, Middlebrooks, Strickland & Fischer, 1982-88; of counsel Klein & Tannen, Hollywood, Fla., 1990-91; mem., 1992—. Mem. gender bias study commn. Fla. Supreme Ct., 1986, apptd. commr., reporter, 1987—; adj. prof. women and the law, media law, rhetoric, comm. law Fla. Atlantic U., 1984-88, 1995—; mem. faculty Chautauqua Instn., 1995-98; co-chmn. Fla. Bar Media Law Conf., 1996; rsch. coord. Ctr. for Govtl. Responsibility, Gainesville, 1979-81. Editor: Elderly Law in Florida, 1982; author: Report of the Florida Supreme Court Gender Bias Commn.; contbr. articles to profl. jours. Pres. Ctr. for Jungian Studies, 2002--; dir. Inner Work Studies Program, 1995—; dir. Communitas. Mem. APA, ABA, AAUW, NOW, Nat. Coun. Jewish Women, Fla. Bar Assn. (com. on equal opportunity 1988—), Fla. Assn. women Lawyers, Assn. Psychol. Type, Assn. Transpersonal Psychology. Office: 1007 S North Lake Dr Hollywood FL 33019-1314 E-mail: rtannen@gate.net.

TANNENBAUM, BERNARD, lawyer; b. N.Y.C., July 14, 1928; s. Jacob and Lillian (Jupiter) T.; m. Elinor Fried, June 3, 1950; children: Jody, Ilene, Carol, Jeffrey. BA in Edn., NYU, 1950, JD, 1953; MA (hon.), Internat. U. Comm., 1974. Bar: N.Y. 1954, D.C. 1980, U.s. Dist. Ct. (so. and ea. dists.) N.Y. 1961, U.S. Ct. Claims 1964, U.S. Supreme Ct. 1964. Assoc. Halperin, Natanson, Shivitz & Scholar, N.Y.C., 1952-54; sole practice Mineola, N.Y., 1954-60, N.Y.C., 1969-87; mng. ptnr. Fried, Beck, Tannenbaum & Field, N.Y.C., 1960-69; counsel Meltzer, Lippe & Goldstein, Mineola, 1987—. Spl. counsel U.S. Senate Subcom. on Juvenile Delinquency, Washington, 1965-70, subcom. on Panama Canal U.S. Ho. of Reps., Washington, 1970-71, com. on mcht. marine and fisheries U.S. Ho. of Reps., 1977-80; arbitrator Small Claims Divsn. Civil Ct., N.Y.C., 1975—. Contbr. NYU Law Rev., editor, pub., The Democratic Forum, 1960-73; bd. dirs., trstee, chmn. Daytop Village Inc., N.Y.C., 1983—; bd. advisors Assn. Children with Retarded Mental Devel., N.Y.C., 1984-86. Office: 190 Willis Ave Mineola NY 11501-2693 E-mail: Tanbern@aol.com.

TANNENBAUM, BERNICE SALPETER, national religious organization executive; b. N.Y.C. d. Isidore and May Franklin; 1 child, Richard Salpeter. BA, Bklyn. coll. Chmn. Commn. on the Status of Women of the World Jewish Congress; mem. exec. bd. Am. sect. World Jewish Congress; chmn. internat. affairs com.; mem. Zionist Gen. Coun.; active Exec. World Zionist Orgn. Bd. dirs., mem. gen. assembly Jewish Agy.; bd. dirs., v.p. United Israel Appeal; mem. exec. com. Am. Zionist Movement; former chair Hadassah mag.; nat. pres. Hadassah, 1976-80; nat. chmn. Hadassah Internat., 1984-95; liaison Hadassah Found.; sec. Jewish Telegraphic Agy.; bd. govs. Hebrew U. Office: Hadassah 50 W 58th St New York NY 10019-2590

TANNENBAUM, HARVEY, defense technology consultant; b. NYC, June 26, 1923; s. Alfred and Ida (Kolbe) T.; m. Mildred Cohen, July 4, 1946; children: David Bruce, Mark Scott, Lynne Ellen. BS, NYU, 1946; postgrad., George Washington U., 1963-64. Chemist U.S. Army Chem. R & D Ctr., Aberdeen Proving Ground, Md., 1949-62, chief remote sensing, 1962-79; prin. staff engr. Honeywell, Inc., Clearwater, Fla., 1979-84; cons. Reistertown, Md., 1984-86; sr. program dir. SRI, Internat., 1986-88. Cons. EPA, CIA, Arms Control and Disarmament Agy., USAF, 1962-79; group chmn. NATO panel of experts on laser monitoring of atmosphere, Norway, 1976. Contbr. articles to profl. jours.; patentee in field. Served to cpl. USAF, 1942-45, ETO. Mem. Optical Soc. Am., Internat. Soc. Optical Engring., Infrared Symposia, Sigma Xi. Jewish. Avocations: bridge, photography. Home and Office: 12611 Mt Laurel Ct Reisterstown MD 21136-1801

TANNENBAUM, MICHAEL J(AY), physicist; b. N.Y.C., Mar. 10, 1939; s. Morris and Ann Tannenbaum; m. Barbara C. Moshinsky, July 15, 1973; children: Nina Fay, Lisa Marie. AB magna cum laude, Columbia U., 1959, MA, 1960, PhD, 1965. Vis. scientist CERN, Geneva, 1965-66, 91, attache scientifique, 1973-84; from asst. prof. to assoc. prof. Harvard U., Cambridge, Mass., 1966-71; assoc. prof. Rockefeller U., N.Y.C., 1971-80; physicist Brookhaven Nat. Lab., Upton, NY, 1980-87, sr. physicist, 1987—, group leader, 2001—. Mem. sci. coun. Lab. Leprince-Ringuet, Ecole Polytechnique, France, 2002—. Contbr. articles to profl. jours. Ernest Kempton Adams fellow, 1965, NSF fellow, 1959-63, 66, Alfred P. Sloan Found. fellow, 1967-69. Fellow: AAAS, Am. Phys. Soc.; mem.: NY Acad. Scis., Sigma Xi, Phi Beta Kappa. Home: 245 E 93rd St Apt 10F New York NY 10128-3965 Office: Physics Dept Brookhaven Nat Lab Bldg # 510C Upton NY 11973-5000 Office Phone: 631-344-3722. E-mail: mjt@bnl.gov.

TANNENBAUM, STEVEN ROBERT, toxicologist, chemist; b. N.Y.C., Feb. 23, 1937; m. Carol Eigen, Sept. 6, 1959; children: Lisa, Mark. BS in Food Tech, MIT, 1958, PhD in Food Sci. and Tech, 1962. From asst. prof. to co-dir. Biol. Engring. Divsn. MIT, Cambridge, Mass., 1964—2002, co-dir. Biol. Engring. Divsn., 2002—03. Vis. prof. Hebrew U. of Jerusalem, 1973-74; BASF vis. prof. U. Kaiserslautern, 1994; mem. adv. com. on biochemistry and chem. carcinogenesis Am. Cancer Soc., 1977-81, Inst. Medicine, Nat. Acad. Sci., 1996; bd. sci. advisors divsn. cancer etiology, NCI, 1994-95, Frederick Cancer Rsch. Facility, 1989—94, Nat. Cancer Inst., 1989-93; mem. cancer spl. program adv. com., 1979-82; mem. peer rev. com. Nat. Toxicology Program, 1983-85; founder, bd. dirs. Vicam, Ltd., Partnership; chmn. rev. homeland security safe bldg. program EPA, 2003; mem. sci. adv. bd. USAF, 1999. Editor: (with R.I. Mateles) Single-Cell Protein, 1968, (with D.I.C. Wang) Single-Cell Protein II, 1975, (with others) The Economics, Marketing and Technology of Fish Protein Concentrate, 1974, (with J.R. Whitaker) Food Proteins, 1977, Nutritional Safety Aspects of Food Processing, 1979, (with others) Gastrointestinal Cancer: Endogenous Factors, 1981, (with R.A. Scanlan) N-Nitroso Compounds, 1981; mem. editl. bd. Japanese Jour. Cancer Rsch., 1986—, Chem. Rsch. Toxicology, 1988 91, 95-98, Cancer Epidemiology, Prevention and Biomarkers, 1990—, Cancer Rsch., 1993-2001; contbr. over 350 articles to profl. jours. Fellow Japan Soc. Promotions Cancer Rsch.; mem. AAAS, Nat. Acad. Scis., Inst. Medicine, Am. Chem. Soc., Inst. Food Technologists (sect. councillor N.E. chpt. 1966-69, Samuel Cate Prescott Rsch. award 1970, Babcock Hart award 1980), editorial bd. sci. jour. 1970-73, Am. Inst. Nutrition, Am. Assn. Cancer Rsch., Soc. Toxicology, Oxygen Soc., Sigma Xi. Achievements include 11 U.S. patents. E-mail: srtcmit.edu. Office: MIT Div Biol Engring 77 Mass Ave Rm 56-731A Cambridge MA 02139-4307 *Motto: Crisis equals danger plus opportunity.*

TANNENBERG, DIETER E. A. retired manufacturing company executive; b. Chevy Chase, Md., Nov. 24, 1932; s. E.A. Wilhelm and Margarete Elizabeth (Mundhenk) T.; m. Ruth Hansen, Feb. 6, 1956; 1 child, Diana Sylvia Tannenberg. BSME, Northwestern U., 1959. Registered profl. engr., N.Y., Ohio, Ill., Ind., Wis., N.J. Supervising engr. Flexonics div. Calumet & Hecla, Inc., Chgo., 1959-61, chief engr., 1961-63, program mgr. advanced space systems, 1963-65, dir. mfg. services, 1965-67; dir. mfg. engring. SCM Corp., Cortland, N.Y., 1967-69; tech. dir. internat. Singer Co., N.Y.C., 1969-71; v.p. ops. internat. div. Addressograph-Multigraph Corp., Cleve., 1971-74; mng. dir. Addressograph Multigraph GmbH, Frankfurt/Main, W. Ger., 1974-78; v.p., gen. mgr. Europe, Middle East, Africa AM Internat. Inc., Chgo., 1978-79; pres. AM Bruning div., 1979-82, AM Multigraphics Div., Mt. Prospect, Ill., 1982-86; corp. v.p. AM Internat., Inc., 1981-83, corp. sr. v.p., 1983-86; chmn. bd. dirs., pres., chief exec. officer Sargent-Welch Sci. Co., Skokie, Ill., 1986-89; pres., CEO ExhibitGroup, Inc., Elk Grove Village, Ill., 1990-91, Bell & Howell Document Mgmt. Products Co., Chgo., 1991-94, Bell & Howell Postal Sys. Inc., Chgo., 1994-97; corp. v.p. Bell & Howell Co., Skokie, Ill., 1991-97. Chmn. AM Internat. GmbH, Frankfurt, 1977-86; bd. dirs. Gerard Daniel Worldwide INc. Contbr. chpts. to handbooks, articles to tech., trade mags.; patentee in machinery field. Served with M.I., U.S. Army, 1953-56. Named Man of Yr. Quick Print Mag., 1985. Mem. NSPE, ASME, Assn. Reprodn. Materials Mfrs. (bd. dirs. 1979-82, v.p. 1980 82), Nat. Assn. Quick Printers (bd. dirs. 1982-84), Nat. Printing Equipment and Supplies Mfg. Assn. (bd. dirs. 1983-86, chmn. govt. affairs com. 1985-86), Computer and Bus. Equipment Mfg. Assn. (bd. dirs. 1983-86, 91-93), Soc. Am. Value Engrs. (hon. v.p. 1985—), Value Found. (trustee 1985—), Barrington Hills Country Club, Pi Tau Sigma.

TANNENWALD, LESLIE KEITER, rabbi, justice of peace, educational administrator, chaplain; b. Boston, May 5, 1949; d. Irving Jules and Barbara June (Caplan) Keiter; m. Robert Tannenwald. BA, Brandeis U., 1971, MA, 1976; MA in Edn. and Counseling, Simmons Coll., Boston, 1972. Cert. social worker, tchr., Mass.; justice of the peace. Sr. assoc. Combined Jewish Philanthropies of Greater Boston, 1977-84; ednl. cons. Bur. Jewish Edn., Boston, 1985-87; ednl. dir. Congregation Shalom Emeth, Burlington, Mass., 1987-92; religious sch. dir. Falmouth (Mass.) Jewish Congregation, 1993-99; pres. Jewish Life Svcs., Newton, Mass., 1993—; rabbi Temple Emmanuel, Chelsea, 2001—. Cons. Selected Ednl. Orgns., Boston, 1972; chaplain, rabbi to local nursing home facilities. Author: Curriculum, Male and Female, 1979 (Honors award 1971), Understanding the Holocaust, 1990, Awakening: Alternative Creative Learning Techniques, 1995. Officer, bd. dirs. Combined Jewish Philantropies of Greater Boston, 1972—; mem. Am. Jewish Congress, Boston, 1976—; rabbi, religious leader Sherborn Congregation, 1995—97, Congregation Agudath Achim (Medway), 1999—2001; title of damsel Imperial Order St. John Ecumenical Found. Recipient Leadership award Inst. Leadership Devel. and Fund Raising Mem. Nat. Alliance Profl. & Exec. Women, Alumni Assn. Benjamin S. Hornstein Program of Jewish Communal Svc., Assn. Jewish Community Personnel. Democrat. Avocations: swimming, watercolor painting, music. Home: 6 Clifton Rd Newton MA 02459-3147 Office Phone: 617-559-9746. E-mail: rabbiles18@aol.com.

TANNENWALD, PETER, lawyer; b. Washington, Apr. 8, 1943; s. Judge Theodore and Selma (Peterfreund) T.; m. Carol B. Baum, May 25, 1969; 1 child, Jonathan Mark. AB, Brown U., 1964; LLB, Harvard U., 1967. Bar: U.S. Dist. Ct. D.C. 1968, U.S. Ct. Appeals (D.C. cir.) 1968, U.S. Supreme Ct. 1972. Assoc. Arent, Fox, Kintner, Plotkin & Kahn, Washington, 1967-74, ptnr., 1975-94; v.p. Irwin, Campbell & Tannenwald, P.C., Washington, 1995—. Columnist The LPTV Report, 1988-92. Mem. cmty. coun. Sta. WAMU-FM, Washington, 1986-93, 94-97, 2003—; dir. Brown Broadcasting Svc., Inc., Providence, 1970—; chmn. maj. law firms divsn. Nat. Capital Area affiliate United Way, 1977-79. Mem. Harvard Law Sch. Assn. D.C. (pres. 1979-80), Harvard Law Sch. Assn. (sec. 1982-84). Avocations: electronics, photography. Office: Irwin Campbell Tannenwald PC 1730 Rhode Island Ave NW Washington DC 20036-3101 Office Phone: 202-728-0400.

TANNER, ANTHONY J. healthcare services corporation executive; grad., degree in biomed. engring., Poly. Inst. Bklyn. Dir. clin. & profl. programs shared svcs. divsn. LifeMark Corp.; prof., chmn. health scis. dept. L.I. Univ., Bklyn.; exec. v.p., adminstrn. HealthSouth Corp., Birmingham, 1984—. Bd. dirs. Fedn. Am. Health Sys. Chmn. bd. trustees Ala. chpt. Nat. Multiple Sclerosis Soc., bd. nat. Soc. Office: HealthSouth Corp 1 Healthsouth Pkwy S Birmingham AL 35243-2358

TANNER, DANIEL, curriculum theory educator; b. N.Y.C., Sept. 22, 1926; s. Jack and Lillian (Jupiter) T.; m. Laurel Nan Jacobson, July 11, 1948 (div. 1988). BS with honors, Mich. State U., 1949, MS, 1952; PhD, Ohio State U., 1955. Asst. prof. edn. San Francisco State Coll., 1955-60; assoc. prof. edn., coord. Midwest program on airborne TV instrn. Purdue U., 1960-62; assoc. prof. edn., assoc. dir. internat. program for edn. leaders Northwestern U., 1962-64; assoc. prof. rsch. divsn. tchr. edn. CUNY, 1964-66; prof. edn., dir. Ctr. for Urban Edn., U. Wis.-Milw. Sch. Edn., 1966-67; prof. edn., dir. grad. programs in curriculum theory and devel. Grad. Sch. Edn., Rutgers U., New Brunswick, N.J., 1967—, chmn. dept. curriculum and instrn., 1969-72, faculty rsch. fellow, 1974-75, 88-89. Vis. lectr. U. Kansas City, summer 1956, Tchrs. Coll. Columbia, summer 1966; vis. prof. Emory U., summer 1968, SUNY, Binghamton, winter 1968, U. London, 1975, King Abdulaziz U., Saudi Arabia, winter 1992, U. Iowa, summer 1996; disting. lectr. ASCD, 1985, 86, Dewey Meml. lectr., 1984, Raths Meml. lectr., SUNY, 1984; Leadership Inst. lectr. U. Del., summer 1990; disting. lectr. Rider U., 1996; vis. scholar U. London Inst. Edn., 1974-75; mem. rev. bd. coll. work-study program U.S. Office Edn., 1965; mem. symposium on comparative curriculum history Inst. Sci. Edn. Kiel U., Fed. Republic Germany, 1989; del. leader Citizen Amb. Program, People-to-People Internat., Republic of South Africa, 1996, China, 1997, Dem. Citizenship Project Czech Republic, USIA, 1996-98; cons. U. Tex. Med. Ctr., 1961-62, Chgo. Sch. Survey, 1964-65, ctr. Urban Edn., N.Y.C., 1964-65, West Chgo. Sch. Survey, 1963-64, Nat. Ednl. TV Ctr., N.Y.C., 1963, Campbell County (Va.) Sch. Survey, 1970, Memphis Schs., 1977-78, Perth Amboy (NJ) Schs., 1996-97; ASCD Commn. on Gen. Edn., 1980-81, West Orange, N.J., Curriculum Study, 1984, ASCD Commn. on Secondary Sch. Practices, 1985, ASCD Ednl. Policy Task Force, 1985, NASSP Curriculum Coun., 1985-95; SUNY Buffalo External Evaluation, 1988; dir. Nat. Curriculum Inst., Washington, 1987; delivered Founder's Day address Delaware Valley Coll., 1985' keynote address Nat. Conf. Citizen Edn., Palacky U., Czech Rep., 1998. Author: Schools for Youth: Change and Challenge in Secondary Education, 1965, Secondary Curriculum: Theory and Development, 1971, Secondary Education: Perspectives and Prospects, 1972, Using Behavioral Objectives in the Classroom, 1972, Curriculum Development: Theory into Practice, 3rd edit., 1995, Supervision in Education, 1987, History of the School Curriculum, 1991, Crusade for Democracy: Progressive Education at the Crossroads, 1991, 2002; founding editor, contbg. author: Rsch. Rev. for Sch. Leaders, 1996, 98, 00, Philosophy of Edn. Ency., 1996, Ency. of Education, 2d edit., 2003, Curriculum Issues, 87th Yearbook NSSE, 1988, 98th Yearbook, 1999, Ency. of Ednl. Rsch., 5th edit., 1982, Readings in Education Psychology, 1965, Yearbook of the Association for Student Teaching, 1962, The Great Debate, Our Schools in Crisis, 1959, Educational Issues in a Changing Society, 1964, Programs, Teachers and Machines, 1964, Views on American Schooling, 1964, The Training of America's Teachers, 1975, Curriculum and Instruction, 1981; co-author: Teen Talk: Curriculum Materials in Communications, 1971; co-editor: Improving the School Curriculum, 1988, Restructuring for an Interdisciplinary Curriculum, 1992, Curriculum Issues and the New Century, 1995; contbg. editor: Ednl. Leadership, 1969-74; mem. editl. bd. Tex. Tech. Jour. Edn., 1984-89, Tchg. Edn., 1986-90, Jour. Curriculum Supervision; editorial cons.: Ency. of Ednl. Rsch., 5th edit., 1982, Ency. of Edn., 2d edit., 2003, Jour. Ednl. Psychology; founding editor Rev. of Rsch. for Sch. Leaders; contbr. Atlantic Monthly, Bull. of Atomic Scientists and other nat. mags., ednl. jours. Trustee Delaware Valley Coll., Doylestown, Pa., 1981-95; bd. dirs. Ohio State Alumni Assn. N.J., 1990-96. Recipient Excellence award Edn. Press Am., 1989, Distinguished Educator award Rider U., 1996; Univ. scholar Ohio State U., 1955. Fellow AAAS, John Dewey Soc. (bd. dirs. 1985-88, archivist 1989-, chmn. lectrs. commn. 1999-, pres. 2001-03); mem. AAUP, Am. Ednl. Rsch. Assn., N.Y. Acad. Scis., Am. Polit. Sci. Assn., Am. Ednl. Studies Assn., Nat. Soc. Study Edn., Phi Kappa Phi, Phi Delta Kappa (Svc. award 1957). Home: Highwood Rd Somerset NJ 08873 Office: Grad Sch Edn Rutgers U New Brunswick NJ 08901-1183 Fax: 732-732-6803. E-mail: mbunnyk@aol.com. *The essential quality of education and life is growth. Hence problems must be seen as opportunities and not as limitations if solutions are to be found and progress is to be made.*

TANNER, DEE BOSHARD, retired lawyer; b. Provo, Utah, Jan. 16, 1913; s. Myron Clark and Marie (Boshard) T.; m. Jane Barwick, Dec. 26, 1936 (div. Aug. 1962); children: Barry, Diane McDowell; m. Reeta Walker, Dec. 6, 1981. BA, U. Utah, 1935; LLB, Pacific Coast U., 1940; postgrad., Harvard U., 1936, Loyola U., L.A., 1937. Bar: Calif. 1943, U.S. Dist. Ct. (so. dist.) Calif. 1944, U.S. Ct. Appeals (9th cir.) 1947, ICC 1964, U.S. Dist. Ct. (ea. dist.) Calif. 1969, U.S. Supreme Ct. 1971. Assoc. Spray, Davis & Gould, L.A., 1943-44; pvt. practice L.A., 1944; assoc. Tanner and Sievers, L.A., 1944-47, Tanner and Thornton, L.A., 1947-54, Tanner, Hanson, Meyers, L.A., 1954-64; ptnr. Tanner and Van Dyke, L.A., 1964-65, Gallagher and Tanner, L.A., 1965-70; pvt. practice Pasadena, Calif., 1970-95; retired, 1995. Mem. L.A. Bar Assn., World Affairs Assn., Harvard Law Sch. Assn., Lawyers' Club L.A. Home and Office: 1720 Lombardy Rd Pasadena CA 91106-4127 E-mail: rpltd@aol.com.

TANNER, DOUGLAS ALAN, lawyer; b. Palo Alto, Calif., Aug. 30, 1953; s. Bernard R. and Caroline (Orris) Tanner; m. Carol Scilacci, May 28, 1977; children: Lauren Elizabeth, Wynn Ann, Leigh Caroline. AB in History, Stanford U., 1974, MBA, JD, Stanford U., 1978. Bar: Calif. 1978, U.S. Dist. ct. (no. dist.) Calif. 1978, U.S. Ct. Appeals (9th cir.) 1979, N.Y. 1987. Law clk. to judge U.S. Ct. Appeals (9th cir.), San Francisco, 1978-79; assoc. Orrick, Herrington & Sutcliffe, San Francisco, 1979-83, ptnr. San Jose, Calif., 1984-86, N.Y.C., 1986-89, Milbank, Tweed, Hadley & McCloy, L.A., 1989-92, Hong Kong, 1992-2001, Palo Alto, Calif., 2001—. Mem.: San Francisco Barristers (chmn. corps. com. 1981—82), Order of Coif, Phi Beta Kappa. Republican. Episcopalian. Office: 5 Palo Alto Sq 3000 El Camino Rd Palo Alto CA 94306-2109 E-mail: dtanner@milbank.com.

TANNER, ERIC BENSON, lawyer; b. St. Louis, Aug. 27, 1949; s. Robert H. and Delores (Benson) T.; m. Rosalind Grace Tanner, June 23, 1978; children: Jacob, Adam. BA, U. Mo., Columbia, 1971; JD, U. Mo., Kansas City, 1975; cert., Coll. Fin. Planning, Denver, 1988. Bar: Mo. 1975. Instr. paralegal program Avila Coll., Kansas City, 1982-84; staff atty. Legal Aid Western Mo., Kansas City, 1975-83; pvt. practice, Kansas City, 1983-86; of counsel Stafford & Assoc. LLC, Kansas City, 2004—, Spencer Fane Britt & Browne, LLP, Kansas City, 2002—03; asst. v.p. trust dept. United Mo. Bank, NA, Kansas City, 1986-90; staff atty. Shook, Hardy & Bacon, Kansas City, 1990-93; v.p., trust counsel Commerce Bank, N.A., Kansas City, 1993—2002; of counsel Staffor & Assoc., LLC, Kansas City. CLE lectr. on estate planning topics to various bar assns. and univs., 1975—. Contbr. articles to law jours. Mem. planned giving com. Nat. Kidney Found., Kans. and Kansas City met. area, 1995-97; vol. Habitat for Humanity, 1997, 99, 2002, 2004; bd. dirs. Prime Health, 1980-86, Marillac, 2003—. Mem. ABA, Mo. Bar Assn., Kansas City Met. Bar Assn., Nat. Acad. Elder Law Attys., Kansas City Corp. Fiduciaries Assn. (pres. 1997), Estate Planning Soc. Kansas City.

TANNER, GLORIA TRAVIS, state legislator; b. Atlanta, Ga., July 16, 1935; d. Marcellus and Blanche Arnold Travis; m. Theodore Ralph Tanner, 1955 (dec.); children: Terrance Ralph, Tanvis Renee, Tracey Lynne. BA, Met. State Coll., 1974; MUA, U. Colo., 1976. Office mgr. Great Western Mfg. Co., Denver, 1965-67; writer Rage mag., 1969-70; reporter, feature writer Denver Weekly News, 1970-75; dir. East Denver Cmty. Office, 1974—; also real estate agt.; mem. Colo. Ho. of Reps., 1985-94; mem. from dist. 33 Colo. Senate, 1994—. Minority caucus chairwoman; mem. appropriations, bus. affairs, labor coms. Dist. capt. Denver Dem. Com., Colo., 1973-75; chairwoman Senatorial Dist. 3 Dem. Com., 1974-82; adminstrv. aide Colo. State Senator Regis Groff, Denver, 1974-82; alt. del. Dem. Nat. Conv., 1976, del., 1980; commr. Colo. Status of Women, 1977—; chairwoman Colo. Black Women for Polit. Action, 1977—; exec. asst. to Lt. Gov., 1978-79; mem. adv. bd. United Negro Coll. Fund, Colo. State Treas. Served USAF, 1952-55. Recipient Outstanding Cmty. Leadership award Scott's Meth. Ch., 1974, Tribute to Black Women award, 1980; named Woman of Yr., Colo. Black Women Caucus, 1974. Mem. Colo. Black Media Assn. (pub. dir. 1972—), Reginas' Civic Club (founder, first pres. 1959—, Outstanding Woman of Yr. 1975), Nat. Assn. Real Estate Brokers. Roman Catholic. Democrat. Home: 2841 Colorado Blvd Denver CO 80207-3015 Office: State Senate 200 E Colfax Ave Ste 274 Denver CO 80203-1716

TANNER, HAROLD, investment banker; b. N.Y.C., May 7, 1932; s. Irving and Pauline (Steinlauf) T.; m. Estelle Newman, July 6, 1957; children: David, James, Karen. BS, Cornell U., 1952; MBA, Harvard U., 1956. V.p., dir. Blyth & Co. Inc., N.Y.C., 1956-69; exec. v.p. New Court Securities Corp., N.Y.C., 1969-76, Blyth Eastman Dillon & Co., Inc., N.Y.C., 1977-80; ptnr. Salomon Bros. Inc., 1980-81, mng. dir., 1981-87; pres. Tanner & Co., Inc., N.Y.C., 1987—. Co-founder Vol. Urban Cons. Group. Pres. Am. Jewish Com.; chmn. bd. trustees Cornell U., Russell Sage Found., Revson Found., Classroom Inc. Lt. (j.g.) USNR, 1952—54. Mem. Coun. on Fgn. Rels., Century Country Club, Harmonie Club. Home: 2 Morris Ln Scarsdale NY 10583-6053 Office: Tanner & Co 650 Madison Ave New York NY 10022-1029

TANNER, HAROLD MILES, education educator, researcher; b. Princeton, NJ, June 14, 1959; s. Earl Chapin and Mary Cobb (Nelson) Tanner; m. Yiyun Jiang; children: Sophia, William. BA, New Eng. Coll., Henniker, N.H., 1982, Beijing Lang. Inst., Beijing, China, 1987; MA, Sch. of Orential & African Studies, London, Eng., 1985; PhD, Columbia Univ., N.,Y.C., 1994. Asst. prof. dept. history Univ. N. Tex., Denton, Tex., 1994—2000, assoc. prof., 2000—01, assoc. prof. & dept. chair, 2001—. Author: Strike Hard, 1999; contbr. articles pub. ti profl. jour. Mem.: Am. Hist. Assn., Southwest Conf. on Asian Studies. Office: Univ North Tex Dept History PO Box 310650 Denton TX 76203-0650

TANNER, HELEN HORNBECK, historian, consultant; b. Northfield, Minn., July 5, 1916; d. John Wesley and Frances Cornelia (Wolfe) Hornbeck; m. Wilson P. Tanner, Jr., Nov. 22, 1940 (dec. 1977); children: Frances, Margaret Tanner Tewson, Wilson P., Robert (dec. 1983) AB with honors, Swarthmore Coll., 1937; MA, U. Fla., 1949; PhD, U. Mich., 1961. Asst. to dir. pub. rels. Kalamazoo Pub. Schs., 1937-39; with sales dept. Am. Airlines Inc.,

N.Y.C., 1940-43; tchg. fellow, then tchg. asst. U. Mich., Ann Arbor, 1949-53, 57-60, lectr. ext. svc., 1961-74, asst. dir. Ctr. Continuing Edn. for Women, 1964-68; project dir. Newberry Libr., Chgo., 1976-81, rsch. assoc., 1981-95, sr. rsch. fellow, 1995—. Expert witness in Indian treaty litig., 1963—; dir. D'Arcy McNickle Ctr. for Indian History, 1984-85; cons., expert witness mus. exhibits, documentary films; mem. Mich. Commn. Indian Affairs, 1966-70. Author: Zespedes in East Florida 1784-1790, 1963, 89, General Green Visits St. Augustine, 1964, The Greeneville Treaty, 1974, The Territory of the Caddo Tribe of Oklahoma, 1974, The Ojibwas, 1992; editor: Atlas of Great Lakes Indian History, 1987, The Settling of North America: An Atlas, 1995. NEH grantee, 1976, fellow, 1989; ACLS grantee, 1990. Mem. Am. Soc. Ethnohistory (pres. 1982-83), St. Augustine Hist. Soc., Conf. L.Am. History, Soc. History Discoveries, Chgo. Map Soc., Hist. Soc. Mich. Home: 5178 Crystal Dr Beulah MI 49617-9618 Personal E-mail: hhtanner@charter.net.

TANNER, JIMMIE EUGENE, retired dean; b. Hartford, Ark., Sept. 27, 1933; s. Alford C. and Hazel Ame (Anthony) Tanner; m. Carole Joy Yant, Aug. 28, 1958; children: Leslie Allison, Kevin Don. BA, Okla. Baptist U., 1955; MA, U. Okla., 1957, PhD, 1964. Prof. English Okla. Bapt. U., Shawnee, 1958—64, 1965—72; assoc. prof. Franklin Coll., Ind., 1964—65; v.p. acad. affairs Hardin-Simmons U., Abilene, Tex., 1972—78, La. Coll., Pineville, 1978—80; dean William Jewel Coll., Liberty, Mo., 1980—97, prof., 1997—2003, interm pres., 1993—94; ret. Contbg. author: The Annotated Bibliography of D. H. Lawrence, Vol. 1, 1982, Vol. 2, 1985. Mem. Shawnee Sch. Bd., 1966—72; mem. edn. commn. So. Bapt. Conv., 1967—72; bd. dirs. Mo. Coun. for Humanities, 2003—. So. Fellowships Fund fellow, 1960—61, Danforth fellow, 1962—63. Mem.: SAR. Democrat. Baptist. Avocations: tennis, photography. Home: 609 Lancelot Dr Liberty MO 64068-1023 *As I reflect on my life, the thought that presses on me is my incredible luck at having been born in America in the 20th century, my good fortune in having the opportunity for education, for a satisfying career, for supportive family, friends, mentors at every stage of my life. I must recognize any accomplishment as communal as well as individual.*

TANNER, JOHN DOUGLAS, JR., retired history educator, writer; b. Quantico, Va., Oct. 2, 1943; s. John Douglas and Dorothy Lucille (Walker) T.; m. Jo Ann Boyd, Jan. 1964 (div. Aug. 1966); 1 child, Lorena Desiree; m. Laurel Jean Selfridge, Dec. 19, 1967 (div. Oct. 1987); children: John DouglasIII, Stephen Douglas, Elizabeth Jane; m. Karen H. Olson, Apr. 16, 1988. BA, Pomona Coll., 1966; MA, Claremont Grad. U., 1968; postgrad., U. Calif., Riverside, 1976, 84-86, U. Calif., San Diego, 1984-87, U. Pacific, 1993. Cert. tchr. Calif. Asst. swimming, water polo coach Pomona Coll., 1966-69; rsch. asst. history dept. Claremont Grad. U., 1967-69; prof. history Palomar Coll., San Marcos, Calif., 1969—2004, pres. faculty, 1970-71, v.p. faculty senate, 1971-72. Author: Olaf Swenson and his Siberian Imports jour., 1978 (Dog Writers Assn. Am. Best Series award, 1979), Campaign for Los Angeles, 1846-47, 1969, Alaskan Trails, Siberian Dogs, 1998; co-author: Last of the Old-Time Outlaws: The George West Musgrave Story, 2002; co-editor: Don Juan Forster, 1970; contbr. articles to profl. jours. Citizens com. Fallbrook (Calif.) San. Dist., 1980; merit badge counselor Boy Scouts Am., 1975-85; Fallbrook Hist. Soc., San Diego Opera Guild. Chautauqua fellow NSF, 1979. Mem. Nat. Assn. for Outlaw and Lawman History, Inc., Western Outlaw-Lawman History Assn. (adv. bd., editl. bd.), Custer Battlefield Hist. and Mus. Assn. (life), Western Writers Am., Old Trail Drivers Assn. Tex., The Westerners, So. Calif. Siberian Husky Assn. (pres. 1972-79), U.S. Shooting Team (Inner Circle), Sons of the Rep. of Tex., Western History Assn., Ariz. Hist. Soc., Siberian Husky Club Am. (bd. dirs. 1974-78, 1st v.p. 1978-79). Republican. Episcopalian. Avocations: collecting S.W. Indian art, backpacking, wine making, writing, opera. Home: 2308 Willow Glen Rd Fallbrook CA 92028-8605 Office Phone: 760-744-1150 x2422. E-mail: jtanner@palomar.edu.

TANNER, JOHN S. congressman, lawyer; b. Halls, Tenn., Sept. 22, 1944; s. E.B. and Edith (Sumners) T.; m. Betty Ann Portis, Sept. 2, 1967; children: Elizabeth Tanner Atkins, John Portis. BS, U. Tenn., 1966, JD, 1968. Bar: Tenn. 1968. Mem. Tenn. Ho. of Reps., 1976-88, 101st-108th Congresses from 8th Tenn. dist., Washington, 1989—. Mem. Ways and Means, Cong. Sportsmen's Caucus (founding mem. The Blue Dog Coalition). Active Obion County Cancer Soc.; former mem. bd. visitors USAF Acad.; bd. visitors U.S. Naval Acad.' former mem. bd. visitors U.S. Mil. Acad. Lt. USN, 1968-72; col. Tenn. Army N.G., 1974- 2000. Mem. Obion County C. of C., Obion County Bar Assn., Rotary. Democrat. Mem. Christian Ch. (Disciples Of Christ). Avocations: golf, hunting. Office: US House of Reps 1226 Longworth Hob Washington DC 20515-4208

TANNER, JOSEPH RICHARD, astronaut; b. Ill., 1950; married; 2 children. BSc in Mech. Engring., BS, U. Ill., 1973. Commd. ensign USNR, 1973, advanced through grades to comdr., 1988, pilot, 1975—89; astronaut NASA, Houston, 1992—. Astronaut Space Shuttle Atlantis, 1994, svc. to Hubble Space Telescope, Discovery, 1997, ISS Assembly Flt 4A Endeavour, 2000. Recipient Outstanding Alumnus award, U. Ill. Avocations: swimming, camping, mountain climbing, time with family. Office: Astronaut Office CB NASA Johnson Space Ctr Houston TX 77058

TANNER, LAUREL NAN, education educator; b. Detroit, Feb. 16, 1929; d. Howard Nicholas and Celia (Solovich) Jacobson; m. Daniel Tanner, July 11, 1948; m. Kenneth J. Rehage, Nov. 25, 1989. BS in Social Sci, Mich. State U., 1949, MA in Edn., 1953; EdD, Columbia U., 1967. Pub. sch. tchr., 1950-64; instr. tchr. edn. Hunter Coll., 1964-66, asst. prof., 1967-69; supr. Milw. Pub. Schs., 1966-67; mem. faculty Temple U., Phila., 1969—, prof. edn., 1974-89, prof. emerita, 1993—; prof. edn. U. Houston, 1989-96. Vis. professorial scholar U. London Inst. Edn., 1974-75; vis. scholar Stanford U., 1984-85, U. Chgo., 1988-89; curriculum cons., 1969—; disting. vis. prof. San Francisco State U., 1987. Author: Classroom Discipline for Effective Teaching and Learning, 1978, La Disciplina en la enseñanza y el Aprendizaje, 1980, Dewey's Laboratory School: Lessons for Today, 1997; co-author: Classroom Teaching and Learning, 1971, Curriculum Development: Theory into Practice, 1975, 3d edit., 1995, Supervision in Education: Problems and Practices, 1987, (with Daniel Tanner) History of the School Curriculum, 1990; editor Nat. Soc. Study Edn. Critical Issues in Curriculum, 87th yearbook, part 1, 1988. Faculty rsch. fellow Temple U., 1970, 80, 81; recipient John Dewey Rsch. award, 1981-82, Rsch. Excellence award U. Houston, 1992, Outstanding Writing award Am. Assn. Colls. Tchr. Edn., 1998; Spencer Found. rsch. grantee, 1992. Mem. ASCD (dir. 1982-84), Soc. Study Curriculum History (founder, 1st pres. 1978-79), Am. Edn. Rsch. Assn. (com. on role and status of women in ednl. R & D 1994-97), Profs. Curriculum Assn. (Factotum 1983-84, chair membership com. 1994-95), Am. Ednl. Studies Assn., John Dewey Soc. (bd. dirs. 1989-91, pres. 2000-01), Alumni Coun. Tchrs. Coll. Columbia U. *In my view, America has progressed over the years, and the best days are still to come. We have the single necessary resource to solve our most urgent problems and achieve our deepest moral values — human intelligence.*

TANNER, LEE E. retired materials scientist, photographer, writer, curator; b. Bklyn., May 28, 1931; s. Vladimir and Pearl Enid (Tanner) Chenkoff; m. Lucia Antonioli, Mar. 25, 1956 (div. Aug. 1978); children: Lisa Esther, Dina Beth; m. Linda Brandt Boam, Dec. 1983. BS in Mech. Engring., NYU, 1953; MS in Metall. Engring., U. Pa., 1956. Metall. rsch. assoc. Armour Rsch. Found., Chgo., 1953, 1956—59; sr. metallurgist Manlabs, Inc., Cambridge, Mass., 1959—63, 1978—80, Kennecott Copper Corp., Lexington, Mass., 1963—73, Allied Chem. Corp., Morristown, NJ, 1973—78; materials scientist U. Calif., Lawrence Nat. Labs., Livermore and Berkeley, 1980—93; ret.; pres., proprietor The Jazz Image, 1990—. Editor First Order Displacive Phase Transformation Symposia, 1981, 88, 90; category editor of beryllium Am. Soc. Metals-Nat. Bur. Stds. Phase Diagram Program, 1981—87. Contbr. articles to profl. jours.; author: Dizzy; John Birks Gillespie in his 75th Yr., 1993, Images of Jazz, 1996, Images of the Blues, 1998. Cpl. U.S. Army, 1953—55. Recipient Outstanding Accomplishment in Metallurgy and Ceramics award, U.S. Dept. of Energy, 1988; Barium Steel Found. fellow, U. Pa., 1956—57. Achievements include research in and publication of work on metallic alloys, phase transformations and electron microscopy. Avocations: photography, painting, sculpting, tennis, basketball. Home: 769 Vincente Ave Berkeley CA 94707 Mailing: 1563 Solano Ave Berkeley CA 94707 Office Phone: 510-524-3661. E-mail: www.jazzimage@aol.com.

TANNER, LOIS, magazine editor; BA in English, Buffalo State U., 1977. Prodn. asstn. Harcourt Brace Jovanovich, N.Y.C., 1980-86; assoc. editor Rolling Stone Mag., N.Y.C., 1980-86; contract rsch. editor N.Y. Times, N.Y.C., 1986-92; assoc. editor, staff writer Working Woman Mag., N.Y.C., 1992-93; editor Her New York, N.Y.C., 1993-94; editor-in-chief Where Mag., N.Y.C., 1994—. Free-lance rschr., reporter Health, Self, Premiere, Entertainment Weekly, Seventeen mags., 1986-92. Mem. Am. Soc. Mag. Editors. Office: Where Mag 475 Park Ave S Ste 200 New York NY 10016-6901

TANNER, LYNN, actress; b. NYC, Mar. 22, 1953; d. Harry J. and Barbara Sylvia (Hirschman) Maurer; m. Allen Barry Witz, Aug. 31, 1975. BS, NYU, 1975; JD, DePaul U., 1980. Bar: Ill. 1980. Actress, various, 1980—. Actor: (films) Human Error, 1987, Another Time, Another Place, 1988, Twisted, 1995; (TV series, pilot) Hollywood Flat; (plays) Pack of Lies, Back at the Blue Dolphin Saloon, Toyer, Burying Rose, Dolores and Her Loved Ones, Final Placement, Facing the Dragon, The Workroom, Sign in Sidney Brusteins Window, Summer and Smoke, The Maids, Under Milkwood, Dark at the Top of the Stairs, Rosa; co-author: (screenplays) Wrong Turn, Tessa Deare, Reasons; co-prodr.: Hollywood Flat; dir.: (plays) Dickens, A Christmas Story, 2003. Mem. SAG, AFTRA, Actors Equity Assn., Women in Film, Women in Theatre, Ill. Bar Assn. E-mail: lynnjettstar@adelphia.net.

TANNER, MARTIN ABBA, statistics and human oncology educator; b. Highland Park, Ill., Oct. 19, 1957; s. Meir and Esther Rose (Bauer) T.; m. Anat Talitman, Aug. 14, 1984; 1 child, Noam Ben. BA, U. Chgo., 1978, PhD, 1982. Asst. prof. stats. and human oncology U. Wis., Madison, 1982-87, assoc. prof., 1987-90; dir. lab., prof. and dept. chair biostatistics U. Rochester, 1990-94; prof. dept. statistics Northwestern U., 1994—. Cons. Kirkland & Ellis, 1980-82; mem. Nat. Inst. Allergy and Infectious diseases study sect., 1994-98; reviewer NIH, NSF, VA. Assoc. editor Jour. Am. Stat. Assn., 1987-99; editor Jour. Am. Statis. Assn., 1999-2003; contbr. articles to profl. jours. Recipient New Investigator Rsch. award NIH, 1984, Mortimer Spiegelman award Am. Pub. Health Assn., 1993; NSF grantee, 1983, 95, NIH grantee, 1986—. Fellow Royal Statis. Soc., Am. Statis. Assn. (Continuing Edn. Excellence award); mem. AAAS, Mensa, Sigma Xi. Avocations: classical guitar, medieval poetry. Office: Northwestern U 2006 Sheridan Rd Evanston IL 60208-0852 E-mail: mat132@northwestern.edu.

TANNER, PEGGY, retired nurse; b. N.Y.C., N.Y., Sept. 9, 1929; d. Denis Michael Hegarty and Minnie Daly; m. Henry V. Tanner, Sept. 5, 1959; children: Denise Fontenelli, James. Student, Iona Coll., 1974. RN N.Y. Staff nurse Queen Mary's Hosp., Sidcup, England, 1950—53, Jewish Meml. Hosp., New York, NY, 1955—59; med. asst. Dr. Arthur Antenucci, N.Y.C., 1960—62; claimes examiner Am. Prog. Ins., Mount Vernon, NY, 1962—65; interviewer N.Y. State Unemployment Office, New Rochelle, NY, 1973—76; staff nurse New Rochelle Hosp., New Rochelle, 1977—92, ret., 1992. Author: Tales of Two Countries, 1997, The Joy of the Journey, 1999. Adv. com. Parks & Recreation, New Rochelle, 1971—75; oral history recorder Bicentennial Com., New Rochelle, 1975—76; dist. leader Rep. Party, New Rochelle, 1970—74. Mem.: Jersey Shore Writers Guild, Irish History Roundtable. Personal E-mail: pegoty4@aol.com.

TANNER, R. MARSHALL, lawyer; b. Santa Monica, Calif., Dec. 4, 1946; s. Stanley Robert and Kathryn (Lau) Tanner; m. Colleen Bonner, Sept. 3, 1969; children: David, Brent, Julie, Glenn, Scott, Holly. BA, Brigham Young U., 1970; JD, UCLA, 1977. Ptnr. Lawler, Felix & Hall, L.A., 1977-86, Pettit & Martin, Newport Beach, Calif., 1986-95, Sheppard, Mullin, Richter & Hampton, 1995—. Lt. USNR, 1970-74. Mem. Calif. State Bar Assn., Orange County Bar Assn. Mem. Lds Ch. Office: Sheppard Mullin Richter & Hampton 650 Town Center Dr Fl 4 Costa Mesa CA 92626-1993 Office Phone: 714-513-5100. Business E-Mail: mtanner@smrh.com.

TANNER, TRAVIS, travel executive; b. 1951; With So. Airways, Inc., Gulfport, Miss., Chgo., Ft. Lauderdale, Fla., 1972-79, Republic Airlines Inc., Mpls., 1984-88; pres., exec. v.p. resorts Walt Disney Co. Inc., Orlando, Fla., 1989-93; pres., CEO Mr. Foster Travel Svc., Carlson Travel Group, Inc., Mpls., 1993-98; founder, CEO Grand Expeditions, Boca Raton, Fla., 1998—. Office: Grand Expeditions 4800 N Federal Hwy Ste 307D Boca Raton FL 33431-5188

TANNER, W(ALTER) RHETT, lawyer; b. Athens, Ga., May 16, 1938; s. Johnnie Bryson and Walterette (Arwood) T.; m. Carolyn Laverne Watson, Nov. 11, 1967; 1 child, Walter Rhett (dec. 1989). AB cum laude, U. Ga., 1960, JD cum laude, 1962. Bar: Ga. 1961; cert. neutral Ga. Office of Dispute Resolution. Assoc. Hansell, Post, Bandon & Dorsey, Atlanta, 1963-66, ptnr., 1966-89, Jones, Day, Reavis & Pogue, Atlanta, 1989-95, of counsel, 1995-99, retired, 1999; mediator Resolution Resources, Atlanta, 1999—. Panelist Am. Arbitration Assn., 1995—. Bd. dirs. Atlanta Symphony Orch., 1975—95, mem. exec. com., 1977—86, v.p., 1978, chmn. maj. gifts campaign, 1980, bd. counsellors, 1996—; mem. Leadership Atlanta, 1980, Leadership Ga., 1982; mem. bd. visitors Grady Meml. Hosp., 1983—92; trustee Ga. Legal History Found., 1986—, pres., 1996—; hon. chmn. Atlanta Decorators Show House, 2002; trustee, vice chmn. Sr. Citizens Svc. Met. Atlanta, Inc., 2000—; bd. dirs. Highlands/Cashiers Chamber Music Festival, 2003—. Lt. comdr. USNR, 1964—72. Mem. Atlanta Bar Assn. (bd. dirs. 1982-87, exec. com. 1983-87), State Bar Ga. (vice chmn. bar and media com. 1979-82), Atlanta Bar Found. (trustee 1985-91), U. Ga. Alumni (pres. chpt. 1973-74, chmn. Atlanta/Met. coun. 1975, mem. state bd. mgrs., v.p. 1976-78), Rotary Club, Gridiron, Capital City Club, Peachtree Racket Club, Phi Beta Kappa, Omicron Delta Kappa, Phi Kappa Phi, Phi Delta Phi, Delta Tau Delta. Home: 2097 Bohler Rd NW Atlanta GA 30318-1515 Office: Jones Day Reavis & Pogue 3500 Suntrust Plz 303 Peachtree St NE Ste 3500 Atlanta GA 30308-3263 E-mail: wtanner516@aol.com.

TANNIAN, FRANCIS XAVIER, economist, educator; b. Boston, Dec. 5, 1933; s. John Joseph and Marie (Killian) T.; m. Beatrix Laube, May 19, 1962; children— Monica, Margaret Joyce, Mark, Michele BA, Boston Coll., 1955, MA, 1959; PhD, U. Va., 1965. Bus trainee Gen. Electric Co., Schenectady, 1955-56; asst. prof. econs. Duquesne U., Pitts., 1962-66; assoc. prof. econs. U. Del., Newark, 1967-72, prof. urban econs., 1972—91, assoc. dean, 1978-79, prof. emeritus, 1991—. Vis. prof. U. Stuttgart, Fed. Republic Germany, 1972-73, U. Karlsruhe, Fed. Republic Germany, 1982, San Diego State U., 1989, U. Nitra, Czechoslovakia, 1990, 96, 2001; cons. Fed. Water Pollution and Control Adminstrn., 1965-68, Deutsche Gesellschaft, Frankfurt, Fed. Republic Germany, 1982-83; lectr. urban studies U.S. Dept. State, Budapest, Bucharest, Belgrade, 1975; guest lectr. Czechoslovakian Acad. Scis., 1975. Editor: Externalities, 1972; contbr. articles to profl. jours. Mem. Del. Gov.'s Econ. Adv. Council, 1969-72; bd. dirs. Del. OIC, Wilmington, 1970-78; bd. dirs. Parity Econ. Devel. Corp., Wilmington, 1978-84; mem. Wilmington Mayor's Econ. Devel. Com., 1976-82. Served with U.S. Army, 1957-58 Mem. Am. Econ. Assn., So. Econs. Assn., Am. Real Estate and Urban Econs. Assn. Democrat. Roman Catholic. Home: 910 Baylor Dr Newark DE 19711-3128 Office: U Del Coll Urban Affairs Newark DE 19711

TANNO, JANICE POLAND, financial consultant, investment advisor; b. Kearny, N.J., Oct. 7, 1941; d. Cornelius Van Rancelar Poland and Lida Steel Spencer; m. Nicholas A. Tanno (div.); children: Nicholas, Alexander, Chiare. M in Fin. Sci., Am. Coll., 1979, M in Mgmt. Sci., 1982; MS in Theology Pastoral Studies, Loyola U., 1997. CLU Am. Coll., Bryn Mawr, Pa., 1969, ChFC Am. Coll., Bryn Mawr, Pa., 1982. Pres. Legacy Group, Wall Township, NJ, Las Vegas, Profl. Planners, Las Vegas; gen. agt. Guardian Life Ins. Co., Las Vegas, gen. agt., agt. Clifton. Mem. Freed Adv. Bd. Security Life Denver, 1991—94; mem. Pres.'s Cir. Am. Coll., Bryn Mawr. Author articles to profl. jours. including Chu Jour., Life Ins. Selling, Best'o Rev. Spkr. Million Dollar Roundtable, Boston, 1976; mem. Las Vegas Leadership C. of C., 1990; mem., bd. regents Bishop Gomon H.S., Las Vegas, 1995—98; founder Landmark Sch., Prides Crossing, Mass.; mem. bd. dirs. So. Nev. Cath. Charities, 1990—93; chmn. bd. dirs. Las Vegas Ctr. Children, 1993—95, Nev. Symphony Orch., 1995—2000. Recipient Agt. of Yr., Gen. Agts. and Mgrs. Assn. Nev., 1978. Republican. Roman Catholic. Avocations: writing, painting. Office: Legacy Group PO Box 1346 2333 Hwy 34 Wall NJ 07719 E-mail: thelegacygroup@aol.com.

TANNOUS, ROBERT JOSEPH, lawyer; b. Amman, Jordan, June 4, 1962; came to U.S., 1968; s. Jerry J. and Nadia Tannous; m. Marlo B. Tannous, Apr. 22, 1989; children: Mallory E., Alexander B. BSBA, Ohio State U., 1984, JD, 1987. Bar: Ohio 1987, U.S. Dist. Ct. (so. dist.) Ohio 1987. Ptnr. Porter, Wright, Morris & Arthur LLP, Columbus, Ohio, 1987—. Trustee Children First Inc., Columbus, 1996-00, Ohio Hist. Found., Columbus, 1999-02, Ohio Historical Soc. Devel. counsel, 2002-; fundraiser, com. various charitable orgns., Columbus, 1987—; team walk coord. March of Dimes, 1988-90; mem. Columbus Mus. of Art, Columbus Zoo. Recipient Forty Under 40 award Bus. First, 1997; named one of Ten Outstanding Young Citizens U.S. Jr. C. of C., 1997. Mem. ABA (bus. law sect.), Columbus Bar Assn. (corps. law com., securities law com.), Capital Club, Columbus Venture Network, Columbus Coun. on World Affairs, Columbus Area C. of C. (capt. club 1991-92), Alpha Lambda Delta, Phi Eta Sigma, Phi Alpha Kappa, Beta Gamma Sigma (past pres.), Pace Setters. Republican. Episcopalian. Avocations: golf, travel, reading, ohio state buckeyes. Office: Porter Wright Morris & Arthur LLP 41 S High St Ste 2800 Columbus OH 43215-6194 Office Phone: 614-227-1953. E-mail: rtannous@porterwright.com.

TANOUE, DONNA A. bank executive, former federal agency administrator; BA, U. Hawaii, 1977; JD, Georgetown U., 1981. Spl. dep. atty. gen. Dept. Commerce and Consumer Affairs, Hawaii, 1981-83; commr. financial inst. State of Hawaii, 1983-87; ptnr. Goodsill Anderson Quinn & Stifel, Hawaii, 1987-98; chmn. FDIC, Washington, 1998—2002; vice chmn. Bank of Hawaii Investment Svcs. Group, 2002—. Office: PO Box 2900 Honolulu HI 96846-6000

TANOUS, HELENE MARY, radiologist, educator; b. Zanesville, Ohio, Oct. 22, 1939; d. Joseph and Rose Marie (Mokarzel) T.; m. John Camp, 1986 (dec. 1990). BA, Marymount Coll., 1961; MD, U. Tex., 1967. Diplomate Am. Bd. Radiology. Intern County Hosp., L.A., 1967-68; resident in radiology Cedars-Sinai Med. Ctr., L.A., 1968-69, U. So. Calif. Hosp., L.A., 1969-71; pvt. practice medicine specializing in radiology L.A., 1972-73; instr. radiology U. So. Calif. Med. Sch., L.A., 1971-72; asst. prof. diagnostic radiology Baylor Med. Sch., Houston, 1973-75; dir. med. student elective in diagnostic radiology Ben Taub Hosp., Houston, 1973-75; pvt. practice diagnostic radiology Largo, Fla., 1975—. Chief Radiology Diagnostic Clinic, Largo, Fla.; asst. prof. diagnostic radiology U. South Fla. Med. Sch., 1980—; asst. prof., dir. med. student edn. in diagnostic radiology U. Tex., Galveston, 1988-91. Pres., founder Children's Advs., Inc., 1977-85; bd. dirs. Fla. Endowment for Humanities, 1979-83. Decorated Chevalier des Palmes Academiques Govt. of France, 1988. Mem. AMA, So. Med. Assn., L'Alliance Francaise of Tampa (bd. dirs. 1984—, pres. 1985-87), Fedn. Alliances Francaises U.S.A. (bd. dirs. 1987-89), Houston Com. Fgn. Rels. Home: 661 Bering Dr Unit 108 Houston TX 77057-2137 Office Phone: 713-785-3975.

TANOUS, PETER JOSEPH, investment advisor; b. NYC, May 21, 1938; s. Joseph Carrington and Rose Marie (Mokarzel) T.; m. Barbara Ann MacConnell, Aug. 18, 1962; children: Christopher, Helene, William. BA in Econs., Georgetown U., 1960. With Smith Barney & Co., Inc. (now Salomon Smith Barney, Inc.), N.Y.C., 1963-78, 2d v.p., mgr. Paris office, 1967, v.p., 1968-78; resident European sales mgr. in Paris Smith Barney & Co., Inc. (now Salom0n Smith Barney, Inc.), N.Y.C., 1969-71; internat. sales mgr. Smith Barney & Co., Inc. (now Salomon Smith Barney, Inc.), N.Y.C., 1971-78, 1st v.p., 1975-78; chmn. bd. Petra Capital Corp., N.Y.C., 1978-81; pres. Lynx Investment Advisory Inc., Washington, 1992—. Exec. v.p. Bank Audi (USA), N.Y.C., 1984—92; del. U.S.-Saudi Arabian Joint Econ. Commn. Bus. Dialogue; bd. dirs. Cedars Bank, L.A., MPS Group, Inc. (formerly Modis Profl. Svcs., Inc.), Jacksonville, Fla., Christian Children's Fund. Author: Investment Gurus, 1997, The Wealth Equation, 1999, Investment Visionaries, 2003. Trustee Browning Sch., N.Y.C., 1987—93. Recipient Nat. Order of Cedar, Govt. of Lebanon, 2002. Office: 1100 Connecticut Ave NW Washington DC 20036-4101

TANOV, ROMIL RAYKOV, mechanical engineer, researcher; b. Rousse, Bulgaria, July 10, 1962; arrived in U.S.A., 96; s. Rayko Ivanov Tanov and Ekaterina Yordanova Tanova; m. Nadya Tsvetanova Georgieva, June 23, 1988; children: Radostin Romilov, Srebrina Romilova Tanova. MSc, U. for Architecture, Civil Enging. and Geodesy, Sofia, Bulgaria, 1988; PhD, U. Cin., 2000. Asst. prof. U Rousse, Bulgaria, 1989—96; rsch. asst. U. Cin., 1996—2000; applied mechanics engr. Ctr. Advanced Product Evaluation divsn. Ind. Mills & Mfg. Inc., Westfield, Ind., 2000—. Reviewer Finite Elements in Analysis and Design, Internat. Jour. of Solids and Structures, AIAA Jour.; contbr. articles to sci. jours. R.T. Davis scholarship, U. of Cin., 2000. Mem.: ASME, Internat. Assn. for Computational Mechanics, U.S. Assn. for Computational Mechanics, Am. Soc. for Composites, Soc. Automative Engr. Home: 3814 Rolling Springs Dr Carmel IN 46033 Office: CAPE A Divsn of IMMI 18881 US 31 North Westfield IN 46074-1020 Office Phone: 317-867-8407.

TANPHAICHITR, KONGSAK, rheumatologist, allergist, immunologist, internist; b. Bangkok, Feb. 22, 1946; came to U.S., 1971; s. Boonchoo and Hong (Nayakovit) T.; m. Sirirat Tareesung, June 17, 1973; children: Saksiri Marc, Marisa. Student, Mahidol U., Bangkok, Thailand, 1964-66, MD cum laude, 1970. Diplomate Am. Bd. Internal Medicine, Am. Bd. Rheumatology, Am. Bd. Allergy and Immunology; cert. Rheumatology Royal Coll. Physicians Can. Straight med. intern Detroit Gen. Hosp.-Wayne State U., 1971-72; resident Barnes Hosp.-Washington U., St. Louis, 1972-74, fellow in rheumatology and immunology, 1974-76; instr. in medicine Washington U., St. Louis, 1976-77, asst. prof. medicine, 1977-97, assoc. prof. medicine, 1997—; attending physician Barnes Hosp., St. Louis, 1976—, Jewish Hosp. of St. Louis, 1981—. Dir. Allergy, Rheumatology & Immunology Specialists, St. Louis; cons. rheumatology Washington U., St. Louis, 1976—. Author: Amyloid Fibrils in Joint Fluid, 1976, Studies of Tolerance in NZB/NZW Mice, 1977, Vasculitis and Multiple Sclerosis, 1980, Buddhism and Science, 1987, Buddhism: Answers to Common Questions, 1990, Buddhism Answers Life, 1995, Mindfulness: The Key to Perfect One's Life, 1997, Mind and Universe, Mindfulness and Stress Management, 1998, Awakened Life for the New Millennium, 2000, Ethics and Morality, 2000, Parenting, 2000, Buddhism Beyond Non-Violence, 2001, Mom, 2001, The Best, the Worst and the Horrible of 9/11, 2001, Miracle of the Buddha's Wisdom, 2002, Mindfulness Amidst the Evolving World, 2003, Self-Awareness: The Neglected Essence of Life, 2003, Universal Language, Laws, and Community, 2004; editor: Vipassana 101, 2004. Dharma tchr., bd. dirs., sec. Wat Phrasriratanaram Buddhist Temple, St. Louis, 1983—; co-dir. Buddhist Coun., St. Louis, 1985-90; chmn. Buddhist Coun. Greater St. Louis, 1999—. Named Am.'s Top Physician, Consumers' Rsch. Coun. Am., 2003—. Fellow: ACP, Royal Coll. Physicians Can., Am. Coll. Rheumatology, Am. Acad. Allergy, Asthma, and Immunology; mem.: Thai-Am. Physicians Found. (treas., bd. dirs. 2000—), Thai Physicians Assn. Am. (treas. Midwest chpt. 1994, sec. Midwest chpt. 1997, nat. treas. 1998, nat. bd. dirs. 1999—2001, nat. treas. 2000), UN Assn. Greater St. Louis (bd. dirs. 2004—), UN Assn. U.S.A., Thai Assn. Greater St. Louis (pres.), Thai Temple Karate Shorinryu Club (Black Belt). Avocations: Karate, karaoke, insight meditation. Home: 12413 Ladue Rd Saint Louis MO 63141-8100 Office: Allergy Rheum & Immun Specs 11115 New Halls Ferry Rd Florissant MO 63033-7613

TANSELLE, GEORGE THOMAS, English language educator, foundation executive; b. Lebanon, Ind., Jan. 29, 1934; s. K. Edwin and Madge R. (Miller) T. BA magna cum laude, Yale U., 1955; MA, Northwestern U., 1956, PhD, 1959. Instr. Chgo. City Jr. Coll., 1958-60, U. Wis., Madison, 1960-61, asst. prof., 1961-63, assoc. prof., 1963-68, prof. English, 1968-78; v.p. John Simon Guggenheim Meml. Found., 1978—; adj. prof. English and comparative lit. Columbia U., 1980—. Mem. Planning Inst. Commn. on English, 1961; mem.

exec. com. Ctr. for Edits. Am. Authors, 1970-73; mem. adv. com. for drama for bicentennial Kennedy Ctr., 1974-76; mem. Soviet-Am. symposium on editing Ind. U., 1976; mem. adv. com. Howells Meml., Kittery Point, 1976-78; exec. com. Ctr. for Scholarly Edits., 1976-81; mem. nat. adv. bd. Ctr. for Book, Libr. of Congress, 1978—; mem. adv. bd. Burton's Anatomy of Melancholy, 1978—, Pub. and Printing History, A Guide to Manuscript Resources in the U.S., 1980—; bd. dirs. Lit. Classics of U.S., Inc., 1979—, chmn. editl. standards com., 1979—, corp. sec., 1989—; mem. adv. com. N.Am. imprints program, 1980-92; Hanes lectr. U. N.C., 1981; mem. adv. coun. Rosenbach Mus. and Libr., 1980—; mem. adv. coun. Ind. U. Inst. Adv. Study, 1983—; mem. faculty Summer Rare Book Sch., Columbia U., 1984-87; mem. adv. bd. Ctr. for Am. Culture Studies, Columbia U., 1985-94; mem. adv. coun. Am. Trust for the Brit. Libr., 1987—; Rosenbach lectr. U. Pa., 1987; mem. adv. coun. Am. Literary Manuscripts project, 1988—; bd. dirs. 18th Century Short-Title Catalogue/N.Am., Inc., 1988—, chmn., 1994—, Mark Twain Edition Project, 1991—; mem. vis. com. Lilly Libr., 1988-92; mem. adv. bd. Ctr. for Renaissance and Baroque Studies, U. Md., 1990—; mem. adv. com. Writings of J.F. Cooper, 1990—; Sandars lectr. Cambridge U., 1997; mem. adv. bd. Blake Archive, 1998—; bd. dirs. Am. Newspaper Repository, 1999—; mem. faculty Beineke Libr. Master Classes, 1999—; mem. adv. bd. Cambridge edit. of Jonathan Swift, 2002—. Author: Royall Tyler, 1967, Guide to the Study of United States Imprints, 1971, A Checklist of Editions of Moby-Dick, 1976, Selected Studies in Bibliography, 1979, The History of Books as a Field of Study, 1981, Textual Criticism since Greg, 1987, A Rationale of Textual Criticism, 1989, Parkman Dexter Howe Library, Hawthorne and Melville, 1989, Textual Criticism and Scholarly Editing, 1990, Libraries, Museums, and Reading, 1991, A Description of Descriptive Bibliography, 1992, The Life and Work of Fredson Bowers, 1993, Literature and Artifacts, 1998; co-editor: The Writings of Herman Melville, 1968—, Samuel Johnson's Translation of Sallust, 1993; editor: Library of Am. Melville, 1982-83, Books as a Way of Life: Essays by Gordon N. Ray, 1988; mem. editorial bd. Contemporary Literature, 1962-91, Abstracts of English Studies, 1964-78, Papers of Bibliog. Soc. Am, 1968-80, Resources for American Literary Study, 1971—, Analytical and Enumerative Bibliography, 1977—, Review, 1978—, Am. Literature, 1979-82, Literary Research, 1986-90, Common Knowledge, 1991—, Book History, 1996—, Leviathan, 1998—; contbr. articles to books and profl. jours. Mem. coun. Friends of Columbia U. Librs., 1990-94; bd. dirs. Friends of Lilly Libr., 1990-92. Recipient Kiekhofer Teaching award U. Wis., 1963, Jenkins award for bibliography, 1973; Guggenheim fellow, 1969-70; Am. Council Learned Socs. fellow, 1973-74; Nat. Endowment for the Humanities fellow, 1977-78, Laureate award Am. Printing History Assn., 1987. Mem.: MLA (mem. exec. com. bibliog. evidence group 1974-75, methods of lit. rsch. div. 1979-83, chmn. 1982, mem. Hubbell award Com. Am. lit. sect. 1978-82, chmn. 1982, mem. com. on prize for ind. scholars 1983-87, chmn. 1985-87, chmn. ad hoc com. on future of print record 1993-95), Modern Humanities Rsch. Assn., Bibliog. Soc. London (pres. Am. Friends 1992—), Bibliog. Soc. Australia, Bibliog. Soc. Am. (mem. council 1970-94, vice chmn. publs. com. 1974-76, chmn. 1981-84, sec. 1976-78, chmn. com. on regional groups, 1978-80, 2d v.p. 1978-80, 1st v.p. 1980-82, pres. 1984-88), Bibliog. Soc. U. Va. (pres. 1992—), Oxford, Cambridge, Edinburgh, Birmingham, No. Ill., Can. bibliog. socs. (mem. coun. 1996—), Soc. for Bibliography of Natural History, Printing Hist. Soc. (Am. corr. 1970-84), Am. Printing Hist. Assn. (trustee N.Y. chpt. 1979-85), Pvt. Librs. Assn., Ind. Rsch. Librs. Assn. (com. on standards for rare book cataloging in machine-readable form 1978-79), Fellows Morgan Libr., Manuscript Soc. (bd. dirs. 1974-79), Am. Pub. Libr. Film Project (bd. advisors 1993—), Am. Antiquarian Soc. (mem. publs. com. 1972-81, chmn. com. 1978-81, mem. coun. 1974-92, hon. councillor, 1992—, del. to Am. Coun. Learned Socs. 1978-93, exec. com. dels., 1987-89, chmn. exec. com. program on book in Am. culture 1983-89, com. on edn., 1982-85, chmn., 1983-85, chmn. com. on libr. 1988-91), Soc. Textual Scholarship (adv. bd. 1979—, pres. 1981-83), The Johnsonians (chmn. 1993), Melville Soc. (pres. 1982, Electronic Melville Com. 1997—), Book Club Calif., Typophiles, Guild Book Workers, Wis. Acad. Scis., Arts and Letters, Renaissance Soc. Am., Am. Soc. 18th-Century Studies, Renaissance English Text Soc., Assn. Documentary Editing (chmn. Julian Boyd award com. 1986, Boydston award com. 1995), Soc. Scholarly Pub., Assn. internationale de bibliophilie, Soc. History of Authorship, Reading and Pub. (bd. dirs. 1993—), Century Club, Yale Club, Caxton Club, Grolier Club (publs. com. 1979-82, 83-87, 97—, coun. 1980—, small exhbns. com. 1979-87, chmn. 1980-82, sec. 1982-86, chmn. libr. com. 1985-86, 90-2002, pres. 1986-90), Odd Volumes, Phi Beta Kappa. Office: John Simon Guggenheim Meml Found 90 Park Ave Fl 33 New York NY 10016-1301

TANSEY, ROBERT PAUL, SR., pharmaceutical chemist; b. Newark, Apr. 27, 1914; s. William Austin and Charlotte E. (Endler) T.; m. Natalie C. McMahon, Feb.22, 1941; children— Barbara, Carol, Robert, David. B.S., Rutgers U., 1938, M.S. in Pharm. Organic Chemistry, 1950. Sect. head Schering Corp., Bloomfield, N.J., 1953-58; mgr. research Strong Cobb Arner, Inc., Cleve., 1958-63; tech. dir., v.p. Vet. Labs., Inc., Lenexa, Kans., 1963-84, cons., 1984— . Registered pharmacist, N.J., Mo., Ohio. Contbr. articles to profl. jours. Patentee in field (5). Mem. Am. Pharm. Assn., Rho Chi, Kappa Psi. Club: Toastmasters (cert.). Home: 61 Pier 7 Charlestown MA 02129-4227

TANSILL, FREDERICK JOSEPH, lawyer; b. Washington, Feb. 27, 1948; s. Frederick Riker and Mary Eileen (Loftus) T.; m. Joan Louise Trefsgar, July 10, 1971; children: Brendan Frederick, Brooke Charlotte, Charlotte Trefsgar. BA with honors, Brown U., 1970; JD, Georgetown U., 1974, LLM in Taxation, 1982. Bar: D.C. 1974, U.S. Tax Ct. 1976, Va. 1983. Assoc. Cross, Murphy & Smith, Washington, 1974-77; ptnr. Bird & Tansill, Washington, 1977-79; assoc. Ober, Grimes & Shriver, Washington, 1979-81; ptnr. Lewis, Mitchell & Moore, Vienna, Va., 1981-86; counsel Boothe, Prichard & Dudley, McLean, Va., 1986-87; ptnr. McGuire, Woods, Battle & Boothe, McLean, 1987-90; shareholder Verner, Liipfert, Bernhard, McPherson & Hand, Chartered, McLean, 1990-97; owner-mgr. Frederick J. Tansill & Assocs., LLC, McLean, 1997—. Gen. counsel No. Va. Cmty. Found., 1995-98, 1st v.p., 1998-99, pres., 1999-2000. Fellow Am. Coll. Trust and Estate Counsel; mem. ABA, Va. Bar Assn. (exec. coun. taxation sect. 1989-92, coun. and legis. com. wills sect. 1993-99—, trusts and estate sect. 1983-99, bd. govs. 1988-96, chmn. bd. govs. 1991-92, co-chmn. spl. task force lawyers as fiduciaries 1993-95), D.C. Bar Assn. (steering com. estates, trusts and probate law sects. 1995-97, co-chair 1997-99), Fairfax County Bar Assn. (will sect. 1986, chmn. tax sect. 1987-88, CLE com. 1988-89), No. Va. Estate Planning Coun. (exec. com. 1987-92, pres. 1990-91), Tower Club (bd. dirs. 1988—). Office: Frederick J Tansill & Assocs 1355 Beverly Rd Ste 215 Mc Lean VA 22102-3654 Fax: 703-847-1357. Office Phone: 703-847-1359. Business E-Mail: fred@fredtansill.com.

TANSKY, BURTON, department store executive; b. 1938; married BA, U. Pitts., 1960. With Kaufmann's, 1961-67; from asst. store mgr. to mgr. Filenes, Boston, 1967-71; mdse. mgr. Rikes, Dayton, Ohio, 1971-74; v.p. Forbes and Wallace, Springfield, Ohio, 1974, I. Magnin, San Francisco, 1974-77; from sr. v.p. to exec. v.p. Saks and Co., N.Y.C., 1977-80, pres., 1980—94; chmn., CEO Saks & Co., N.Y.C., 1990—94, Neiman Marcus Stores, Dallas, 1994—98; exec. v.p. Neiman Marcus Group, Dallas, 1998, pres., COO, 1998—2001, pres., CEO, 2001—; interim CEO Bergdorf Goodman, 2004—. Office: Neiman Marcus Group One Marcus Sq 1618 Main St Dallas TX 75201-2581*

TANSY, MARTIN F. dean; m. Margaret Tansy; children: Martin Jr., Margaret, Matthew. BS, Wilkes Coll.; MS, Thomas Jefferson Med. Coll., PhD, 1964. From asst. to assoc. prof. physiology Temple U., Phila., 1964—72, prof., 1972—86, chmn. dept. physiology and biophysics in basic sciences, acting dean Sch. Dentistry, 1986, dean Sch. Dentistry, 1987—. Bd. dirs. Friends of the Nat. Inst. Dental and Craniofacial Rsch. Recipient Alumni Excellence Award in Edn. and Adminstrn., Wilkes U., 2000. Fellow: Internat. Coll. Dentists (hon.), Am. Coll. Dentists (hon.). Office: Temple U Sch Dentistry 3223 N Broad St Philadelphia PA 19140*

TANTILLO ELTON, NINA, artist, graphics designer, educator; d. John Anthony Tantillo and Linda Egidi; m. Bruce Elton, July 23, 1978; children: Alexis Elton, Mara Elton. BA in Design, Adelphi U., 1970; MA in Art History, Am. U., 1973. Cert. in arts, fine arts, N.Y. Designer Vogue Mag., Condé Naste, NY, 1973, Seventeen Mag., 1973—76; designer, pres. Elton Assoc., Garrison, 1975—76; tchg. artist Doing Art Together, 1995—99; developer art staff PS7: NYC Bd. Edn., Bronx, 1999—2002; tchr. art edn. Byram Hills Elem. Sch., Armonk, 2002—03, Byram Hills H.S., 2003—04; adj. prof. Coll. Mt. St Vincent, Riverdale, NY, 2003—. Adj. prof. Purchase Coll., SUNY, 2000—. Designer (art direction) Seventeen Mag., 1973 (Soc. Pub. Designers award, 1973), 1974 (Soc. Pub. Designers award, 1974). Achievements include integration of the arts into the school's curriculum in the tri-state working with teachers and children; designed art direction of ads, publications, brochures, and other graphic materials. Office: Byram Hills High Sch Armonk NY 10504

TANTRA, MULJADI, corporate marketing professional; b. Selatpanjang, Riau, Indonesia, July 1, 1971; came to U.S., 1988; s. Pingardi and Lesmina Tantra; m. Vivi Effendy, Nov. 24, 1996; children: Vincent, Grace. BS, Iowa State U., 1992; MBA, San Diego State U., 1996. Ops. rsch. engr. Cymer, Inc., San Diego, 1996-98, mktg. analysis mgr., 1998-2000; dir. corp. mktg. Lam Rsch., Fremont, Calif., 2000—. Inventor, patentee in field. Mem. Sigma Xi (rsch. grantee 1995), Beta Gamma Sigma, Phi Beta Delta. Buddhist. Avocations: music, tennis, scuba diving, travel. Home: 2667 Torrey Ct Pleasanton CA 94588 Office: Lam Rsch 4650 Cushing Pky Fremont CA 94538 E-mail: muljadi.tantra@lamrc.com.

TANUR, JUDITH MARK, sociologist, educator; b. Jersey City, Aug. 12, 1935; d. Edward Mark and Libbie (Berman) Mark; m. Michael Isaac Tanur, June 2, 1957; children: Rachel Dorothy, Marcia Valerie. BS, Columbia U., 1957, MA, 1963; PhD, SUNY, Stony Brook, 1972. Analyst Biometrics Rsch., N.Y.C., 1955-67; lectr. SUNY, Stony Brook, 1967-71, from asst. prof. to prof. sociology, 1971-94, disting. teaching prof., 1994—. Cons. NBC, N.Y.C., 1976—89, Lang. of Data Project, Los Altos, Calif., 1980—89, Inst. for Rsch. on Learning, 1994—95; mem. com. on nat. stats. NAS, 1980—87, com. on applied and theoretical stats., 1997—2000; trustee NORC, U. Chgo., 1987—; bd. dirs. Social Sci. Rsch. Coun., 2000—; mem. adv. com. SBE, NSF, 2000—. Author: The Subjectivity of Scientists and the Bayesian Approach, 2001; editor: Statistics: A Guide to the Unknown, 1972, Internat. Encyclopedia of Statistics, 1978, Cognitive Aspects of Survey Methodology, 1984, Questions About Questions, 1991, Cognition and Survey Research, 1999, Internat. Ency. of Social Scis., 1963—67; contbr. articles to sci., stats., and social sci. jours. Bd. dirs. Vis. Nurse Svc., Great Neck, N.Y., 1970-2000; bd. govs. Gen. Soc. Survey, Chgo., 1989-92. Sr. rsch. fellow, Am. Statis. Assn./NSF/Bur. Labor Statistics, 1988-89. Fellow AAAS, Am. Statis. Assn. (Founders award 1997); mem. Internat. Statis. Inst., Phi Beta Kappa. Home: PO Box 280 Montauk NY 11954 Office: SUNY Dept Sociology Stony Brook NY 11794-4356 Office Phone: 631-632-7738. E-mail: jtanur@ntes.cc.sunysb.edu.

TAN-WANG, GRACE, aeronautical engineer; married; children: Kelly, Marisa. Grad., MIT. Champollion mission engr. NASA; dep. system engring. mgr. Mars Exploration, Jet Propulsion Laboratory, La Canada, Calif.; dep. mgr. spacecraft system engring. Mars Exploration Rover Mission, 2003. Avocations: travel, bicycling, volleyball. Office: NASA Jet Propulsion Lab 4800 Oak Grove Dr M/S T1723 Pasadena CA 91109 8099

TANZER, JED SAMUEL, lawyer, financial consultant; b. Arverne, N.Y., Nov. 16, 1947; s. David and Mildred (Bondy) T.; m. Sally Jane Ketcham, July 10, 1971. BS with honors in Social Sci., SUNY, Oneonta, 1970; JD cum laude, MBA, Syracuse U., 1978. Bar: N.Y. 1979, Fed. Dist. Ct. 1979, U.S. Tax. Ct. 1979; permanent tchg. cert. N.Y. State. Tchr., union grievance chmn. Ctrl. Sch. Dist., Windsor, NY, 1970-75; rsch. asst. Sch. Mgmt. Syracuse (N.Y.) U., 1977-78; sr. atty. Ayco/Am. Express Corp., Albany, NY, 1978-82, assoc. regional mgr., 1982-85, v.p., regional mgr., 1986-92, regional v.p., 1988-91, v.p. counseling, 1992-93, fin. cons., 1978-93; v.p. Sanford Bernstein Co., Palm Beach, Fla., 1993-99; dir. Newberger & Berman, LLC, Palm Beach, Fla., 1999, regional v.p., 1999—2002; with Hillsborough County Cts., 2003—. Bd. trustees Tampa Mus. of Art, 2002—. Bd. dirs. Cobb Youth Chorus, 1988-93, treas. 1988-93; bd. dirs. Martin County Coun. for Arts, 1998-2000, Neuberger Berman Trust Co. of Fla., 2001; mediator/regional v.p., Hillsborough County Ct., 1999—. Mem. ABA (com. state and local taxation 1981-82), N.Y. State Bar Assn., Justinian Law Soc., Beta Gamma Sigma, Kappa Delta Pi. Home: 1116 Abbeys Way Tampa FL 33602-5957 Business E-Mail: jsjtanzer@alum.syracuse.edu.

TANZER, LESTER, editor; b. N.Y.C., Aug. 3, 1929; s. Charles and Clara (Ente) T.; m. Marlene June Luckton, June 29, 1949; children— Stephen Drew, Jeffrey Marc, Andrew Wayne, M. David. AB, Columbia U., 1951, MS, Sch. Journalism, 1952. Reporter, Washington bur. Wall St. Jour., 1952-59; assoc. editor Changing Times mag., Washington, 1959-64, U.S. News & World Report, Washington, 1964-76, mng. editor, 1976-85; editor Cosmos Jour., 1990-93. Author: (with Stefan Ilok) Brotherhood of Silence, 1962; editor: The Kennedy Circle, 1961. Mem.: Cosmos. Home: 4859 30th St N Arlington VA 22207-2715

TANZI, DAVID E. military officer; BS in Edn., SUNY, Cortland, 1965; MEd, Ohio State U., 1967; postgrad., Squadron Officer Sch., Air Command and Staff Coll. Commd. 2d lt. USAF, 1969, advanced through grades to maj. gen., 2000; F-100 fighter pilot 166th Tactical Fighter Squadron, Lockbourne AFB, Ohio, 1970—72; F-105 pilot 465th Tactical Fighter Squadron, Tinker AFB, Okla., 1972—73; F-100 instr. pilot, flighter exainer 128th Tactical Fighter Squadron, Dobbins AFB, Ga., 1973—77; F-104 and F-4 flight examiner 457th Tactical Fighter Squadron, Carswell AFB, Tex., 1977—81; comdr. 89th Tactical Fighter Squadron, Wright-Patterson AFB, Ohio, 1981—85; dep. comdr. ops. 906th Tactical Fighter Group, Wright-Patterson AFB, Ohio, 1985; dep. comdr. ops., comdr. 917th Tactical Fighter Group, Barksdale AFB, La., 1985—87; comdr. 906th Fighter Group, Wright-Patterson AFB, Ohio, 1987—93, 419th Fighter Wing, Hill AFB, Utah, 1993—99; dir. plans and programs Hdqrs. AF Res. Command, Robins AFB, Ga., 1999—2002; comdr. 10th Air Force Naval Air Sta. Joint Res. Base, Ft. Worth, 2002—. Decorated Legion of Merit with oak leaf cluster, Air medal. Mem.: Air Force Assn., Res. Officer Assn., Order of Sword, Order of Daedalians. Office: Naval Air Sta Joint Res Base Carswell Field Fort Worth TX 76127-6200

TAO, LIXIN, computer scientist, computer science educator; arrived in USA, 1984; s. Xinhua Tao and Jinqian Zhang; m. Weilan Jiang, July 22, 1966; children: Michael Wenhan, Victor Wenhao. MSE in Computer Sci., East China Normal U., Shanghai, 1981, U. Pa., 1985, PhD in Computer Sci., 1988. Asst. prof. computer sci. Concordia U., Montreal, Canada, 1988—93, assoc. prof. computer sci., 1993—2001; full prof.,computer sci. Pace U., Pleasantville, NY, 2001—. Contbr. articles to profl. jours. Grantee, Natural Sci. and Engring. Rsch. Coun./Can., 1989—91, 1991—94, Fonds pur la formation de chereheurs et l'aide á la recherche (FCAR)/ Que., Can., 1991—94, Strategic Tech. Program of Industry, Sci. and Tech. Can., 1993—95, Natural Sci. and Engring. Rsch. Coun. (NSERC)/Can., 1994—97, 1997—2001, 2001—. Mem.: IEEE (sr. mem. 2003), ACM. Achievements include research in parallel and distributed computing, Internet computing, and operations research. Office: Pace University CSIS 861 Bedford Rd Pleasantville NY 10570 E-mail: lixin@ieee.org.

TAO, WEI-KUO, meteorologist, researcher; b. Taipei, Taiwan, Dec. 18, 1951; s. Chu-Chien and Fung-Ming Li Tao; m. Lanshing Hwang, July 16, 1984; children: Robert D., Michael A. BS in Atmospheric Physics, Nat. Ctrl. U., Chung-Li, Taiwan, 1974; MS in Atmospheric Sci., U. Ill., 1978; MS in Computer Sci., Johns Hopkins U., 1987; PhD in Atmospheric Sci., U. Ill., 1982. Rsch. asst. U. Ill., Urbana-Champaign, 1976—82; postdoctoral rsch. fellow NRC/ NAS, Washington D.C., DC, 1982—84; sr. rsch. scientist Gen. Scis. Corp., Laurel, Md., 1984—89, Lab. for Atmospheres, NASA, Greenbelt, Md., 1989—. Affiliate faculty, dept. atmospheric Sci. Colo. State U., Ft. Collins, Colo., 2000—; lectr. Monash U., Australia, 1989—89. Contbr. articles to profl. jours. Staff sgt. Taiwan Air Force Weather Wing, 1974—76. Fellow: Am. Meteorol. Soc.; mem.: Am. Geophys. Union (chair com. on precipitation and cloud 2001—). Avocations: basketball, recreational historical research, movies. Office: NASA Goddard Space Flight Ctr Greenbelt MD 20771

TAPE, GERALD FREDERICK, former association executive; b. Ann Arbor, Mich., May 29, 1915; s. Henry A. and Flora (Simmons) T.; m. Josephine Waffen, June 18, 1939; children: Walter Richard, James William, Thomas Gerald. AB, Eastern Mich. U., 1935, Sc.D. (hon.), 1964; MS, U. Mich., 1936, PhD, 1940. Asst. physics Eastern Mich. U., 1933-35, U. Mich., 1936-39; instr. physics Cornell U., 1939-42; staff mem. radiation lab. Mass. Inst. Tech., 1942-46; asst., then assoc. prof. physics U. Ill., 1946-50; asst. to dir., then dep. dir. Brookhaven Nat. Lab., 1950-62; v.p., then pres. Associated Univs., Inc., 1962-63, pres., 1969-80, spl. asst. to pres., 1980-82; commr. AEC, 1963-69; U.S. rep. to IAEA with rank of amb., 1973-77; former pres., cons. Associated Univs., Inc. Dir. Sci. Svc. Inc., 1971—2002, Atomic Indsl. Forum, 1970-73; mem. Pres.'s Sci. Adv. Com., 1969-73, Def. Sci. Bd., 1970-73, chmn., 1970-72; mem. sci. adv. com. IAEA, 1972-73; mem. gen. adv. com. ERDA, 1975-77; mem. adv. council Electric Power Rsch. Inst., 1978-85; mem. U. Chgo. bd. govs. for Argonne Nat. Lab., 1982-85; cons. Def. Nuclear Facilities Safety Bd., 1991-2000. Author: (with L.J. Haworth) Relay Radar Chapter of MIT Radiation Laboratory Technical Series, 1947, also papers, reports. Recipient Army-Navy Certificate of Appreciation, 1947, Meritorious Civilian Service medal Sec. Def., 1969, Dept. State Tribute Appreciation, 1969, Dept. Def. medal for pub. service, 1973; Henry DeWolf Smyth Nuclear Statesman award Atomic Indsl. Forum/Am. Nuclear Soc., 1978; Disting. Pub. Service award NSF, 1980; Disting. Assoc. award Dept. Energy, 1980; Enrico Fermi award U.S. Energy Dept., 1987; decorated comdr. Order Leopold II, Belgium. Fellow Am. Phys. Soc., Am. Nuclear Soc., AAAS; mem. Nat. Acad. Engring., Am. Astron. Soc., Phi Beta Kappa, Sigma Xi, Phi Kappa Phi, Kappa Delta Pi. Home: 9707 Old Georgetown Rd 2518 Bethesda MD 20814

TAPELLA, GARY LOUIS, manufacturing executive; b. Antioch, Calif., Sept. 1, 1943; s. Anthony M. and Mary (Lopez) T.; m. Karen Kent, June 24, 1967; children: Robert, Michael. BA in Internat. Rels., San Francisco State U., 1969. Staff asst. Rheem Mfg. Co., N.Y.C., 1969-71; plant mgr. Rheem Can., Vancouver, 1971-73, mktg. mgr. Toronto, 1973-79; regional sales mgr. Rheem Mfg. Co., New Orleans, 1979-80; mng. dir. Rheem Far East, Singapore, 1980-85; gen. mgr. Rheem Can., Toronto, 1985-89; corp. v.p. internat. Rheem Mfg. Co., N.Y.C., 1989-90, chief oper. officer, 1990-91, pres., chief exec. officer, 1991—. Dir. various Rheem Cos. With USN, 1961-63. Avocation: scuba diving. Office: Rheem Mfg Co 405 Lexington Ave Fl 22 New York NY 10174-0112

TAPHORN, JOSEPH BERNARD, lawyer; b. Beckemeyer, Ill., Oct. 9, 1921; s. Herman Henry and Marie (Gasser) T.; m. Anna Marie Klinge, June 25, 1944 (dec. Dec. 1991); children: Robert J., Joanne M., John F.; m. Joan Campen Klemmer, July 13, 1996. BS in Agr., U. Ill., 1943; BS in Engring., George Washington U., 1949, LLB, 1950. Bar: N.Y. 1952, D.C. 1952, U.S. Dist. Ct. (so. and ea. dists.) N.Y. 1952, U.S. Dist. Ct. (no. dist.) N.Y. 1991, U.S. Dist. Ct. D.C., 1952, U.S. Ct. Appeals (D.C. cir.) 1961, U.S. Ct. Appeals (fed. cir.) 1996, U.S. Supreme Ct. 1961. Patent examiner U.S. Patent Office, Washington, 1946-49, patent classifier, 1949-50; patent agt. Pollard and Johnston, N.Y.C., 1950-52; patent atty. IBM Corp., N.Y.C., 1952-59, patent mgr., counsel various locations, 1959-70, copyright counsel Armonk, N.Y., 1970-78, copyright and trademark counsel, 1978-88; pvt. practice Poughkeepsie, N.Y., 1989—. Chmn. bd. U.S. Dynamics, Yonkers, N.Y. 1975-77. Contbr. articles to profl. jours. Pres. Huntley Civic Assn., Eastchester, N.Y., 1958-59; trustee Copyright Soc. USA, N.Y.C., 1985-88. Capt. U.S. Army, 1943-46, ETO. Mem. ABA (com. chmn. 1983-87), N.Y. State Bar Assn., Dutchess County Bar Assn., Am. Intellectual Property Law Assn., N.Y. Intellectual Property Law Assn. (com. chmn. 1987-89), Ea. N.Y. Intellectual Property Law Assn., Dutchess Golf and Country Club, Americana Tennis Club. Republican. Roman Catholic. Avocations: golf, hunting, fishing, tennis, skiing. Home and Office: 8 Scenic Dr Poughkeepsie NY 12603-5521 E-mail: jbtaphorn@prodigy.net.

TAPIA, MARIO EDUARDO, cultural organization administrator; b. San Felipe, Chile, Sept. 11, 1947; came to U.S., 1973; s. Viterbo Topia and Maria Ernstina Guerrero; m. Cecilia C., July 11, 1970 (div. Oct. 1985); 1 child, Susana C. MA in Edn., Cath. U., Valparaiso, Chile, 1971. Pres., CEO Centro Gerontologio Latino, N.Y.C., 1991—. Pres. Chilean Civic Ctr., N.Y.C., 1995—. Recipient Illustrious Son award Mcpl. of San Reude, Chile, 1994. Office: Centro Gerontologico Latino 75 Maiden Ln #208 New York NY 10038-4810

TAPIA, MARTHA LUISA, mathematics professor; b. Havana, Cuba, Apr. 1, 1949; arrived in U.S., 1961; d. Enrique José Tapia and Luisa María Fernández-Puente; children: Martha Silvia Euresti, David Evelio Euresti. BS, U. of P.R., Rio Piedras, 1968; MS, U. of P.R., Mayagüez, 1970; MA, Pa. State U., University Park, 1972; PhD, U. of Ala., 1998. Sys. analyst IBM, Mexico City, 1973—74; math. tchr. Peterson Sch., Mexico City, 1978—86, Am. Sch. Found., Mexico City, 1986—99; instr. Interamerican U. of P.R., Rio Piedras, PR, 1986—91; asst. prof. of math. edn. Berry Coll., Mt. Berry, Ga., 1999—. Reviewer Austrian Sci. Fund, Vienna, 2002—, Psychol. Reports, 2003. Contbr. articles to profl. jours. ESOL instr. Hispanic Initiative, Rome, Ga., 2000. Mem.: S.W. Ednl. Rsch. Assn., Am. Math. Soc., Mid-South Ednl. Rsch. Assn., Assn. of Math. Tchr. Educators, Nat. Coun. of Tchrs. of Math., Ga. Coun. of Tchrs. of Math., Phi Delta Kappa. Roman Catholic. Avocation: travel. Home: # 9 2 Robin St Rome GA 30165-1558 Office: Berry Coll PO Box 495014 Rome GA 30165-5014 Personal E-mail: mtapia29@usa.net. E-mail: mtapia@berry.edu.

TAPLETT, LLOYD MELVIN, human resources specialist, consultant; b. Tyndalll, SD, July 25, 1924; s. Herman Leopold and Emiley (Nedvidek) T.; m. Patricia Ann Sweeney, Aug. 21, 1958; children: Virginia Ann, Sharon Lorraine, Carla Jo, Carolyn Patricia, Catherne Marie, Colleen Elizabeth. BA, Augustana Coll., 1949; MA, U. Nebr., 1958; postgrad., S.D. State U., U. S.D., U. Iowa, Colo. State U. Accredited personnel dir.; prof. human resources; cert. tchr. & counselor. Tchr. Sioux Falls (S.D.) pub. schs., 1952-69; with All-Am. Transport co., Sioux Falls, 1969-78, Am. Freight System, Inc., Overland Park, Kans., 1978-79; dir. human resources & pub. rels., corp. affirmative action Chippewa Motor Freight, Inc., Sioux Falls, 1979-80; human resources & mgmt. cons., 1980-81; mgr. Sioux Falls Job Svcs., 1981-85, Pioneer Enterprises, Inc., 1985-86; ops. mgr. ATE Environ., Inc., 1986-88; cons. Royal River Casino, 1988-90; acad. dean Huron U., Sioux Falls, 1990-97; instr. econs. Coll. Bus., 1992—. Chmn. Chippewa Credit Union; mem. adv. bd. dirs. Nelson Labs., Sioux Falls, 1981-82; evening mgmt. instr. Nat. Coll., Sioux Falls, 1981-90, chmn. adv. com., 1984-90, Huron U., 1990-97, S.F. Washington H.S. Sports Heritage 1889-98; spkr. in field. Contbr. articles to popular mags. Past bd. dirs. Jr. Achievement, United Way, Sioux Vocat. Sch. Handicapped; past mem. Gov.'s Adv. Bd. Cmty. Adult Manpower Planning; chmn. bus. edn. adv. com. Sioux Falls Pub. Schs., 1982-85; chmn. adv. com. South East Area Vocat. Sch., 1982-85; mem. alumnae bd. Augustana Coll., 1985-88. Capt. USMC, 1943-46, 50-52, WWII, Korea. Recipient USMC Letter of Commendation award, 1944, Liberty Bell award S.D. Bar Assn., 1967, Sch. Bd. award NEA/Thom McAn Shoe Corp., 1966, S.D. Unsung Heroes Edn. Recognition award Sta. KSFV-TV, 1998; named Boss of Yr., Sioux Falls, 1977. Mem. NEA (life, Pacemaker award), Am. Soc. Pers. Adminstrn. (accredited pers. mgr., profl. human resources, life, S.D. dist. dir. 1980-84), Am. Trucking Assn. (mem. pub. rels. coun.), S.D. Edn. Assn. (life), Sioux Falls Pers. Assn. (past pres.), Sales and Mktg. Club Sioux Falls, Sioux Falls Traffic Club, VFW (life, Nat. Polit. Action Recognition award 1990), Am. Legion, Toastmasters (past gov. dist. 41, Disting. Toastmaster award, Outstanding Toastmaster award dist. 41, Hall of Fame 1977), Elks. Republican. Roman Catholic.

TAPLEY, JAMES LEROY, retired lawyer, railway corporation executive; b. Greenville, Miss., July 10, 1923; s. Lester Leroy and Lillian (Clark) T.; m. Priscilla Moore, Sept. 9, 1950. AB, U. N.C., 1947, JD with honors, 1950. Bar: N.C. 1951, D.C. 1962. With So. Ry. Co., Washington, 1953-83, gen. solicitor, 1967-74, asst. v.p. law, 1974-75, v.p. law, 1975-83; v.p. Washington counsel Norfolk So. Corp., Washington, 1983-87; ret., 1987. Mem. Phi Beta Kappa, Kappa Sigma. Clubs: Chevy Chase.

TAPLIN, WINN LOWELL, historian, retired senior intelligence operations officer; b. Saint Albans, Vt., Oct. 3, 1925; s. Winn Lowell and Elinor (Cunningham) T.; m. Ellajean Allard, July 16, 1949; children: Leslie Taplin Baumann, Mark Allard. BSCE, U. Mich., 1946, AB, 1948, AM, 1950, PhD, 1956. Oper. officer CIA, Washington, Saigon, Bucharest, Geneva, Bangkok, 1955-81; cons. Stowe, Vt., 1981-94, Sarasota, Fla., 1994—. Author: Secret New England: Spies of the American Revolution, 1991, We Vermonters, 1992. Mem. U.S. del. to UN Commn. on Human Rights, 1969; pres. Vt. Hist. Soc., 1989-93, trustee, 1983-96; mem. Sarasota Geneal. Soc., v.p., 1999-2001, pres., 2001—03; pres. Mansfield View Water Corp., Stowe, 1989-92. 1st lt. USMC, 1943-46, 50-52, Korea. Decorated Bronze Star, Intelligence Medal of Merit. Mem. DAV, Central Intelligence Retirees Assn., Assn. Former Intelligence Officers, First Day Cover Soc., Am. Philatelic Assn., Soc. Mayflower Descendants, Am. Legion, U. Mich. Club Sarasota (dir. 1994—), Sigma Chi. Avocations: historical research, genealogy, classical music, stamp collecting/philately. Home: 4468 Calle Serena Sarasota FL 34238-5641

TAPP, GARY L. state senator; b. Louisville, Dec. 29, 1953; m. Beverly Tapp; 4 children. Rep. K.Y. State House of Reps., 1998—2002; senator K.Y. State Senate, 2002—. V.p., co-owner WT's Electric City, Inc., 1987—. Former mem. Parents & Profls. Involved in Edn.; mem. Shelby County C. of C., Farm Bur. Site Base Coun., Shelby Co. HS, 1997—98, U.S. C. of C., Nat. Fedn. of Ind. Bus., K.Y. Retail Fedn., Shelby Christian Ch. Office: Capitol Annex Rm 424B Frankfort KY 40601 E-mail: gary.tapp@lrc.state.ky.us.

TAPP, MAMIE PEARL, educational association administration; b. Aiken, SC, July 20, 1955; d. Willie Lee and Nancy (Madison) Garrett; m. Anthony Karl Tapp, Aug. 13, 1983; children: Anthony K. II, Barry Garrett, Myles Jarvis. BA, CUNY, 1977; MA, New Sch. for Social Rsch., 1984; postgrad., Nova Southeastern U., 1994—. Flight attendant Capitol Airlines, Jamaica, N.Y., 1976-81; pers. assoc. Cmty. Svc. Soc., N.Y.C., 1982-83; pers. specialist Marriott Hotel, Tampa, Fla., 1983-84; dir. placement Tampa Coll., 1984-86, facility coord., 1986-87, compliance officer, 1987-88; career counselor Alpha House, Tampa, 1988-91; career specialist U. Tampa, 1991-96, adj. prof., 1992-93; career specialist Jr. Achievement Greater Tampa, Inc., Tampa, 1996—, tchr. asst. program adv. com. mem., 1996-98. Tchr. asst. program adv. com. Hillsborough H.S., 1996-97; sr. edn. svc. mgr. Jr. Achievement, 1997—. Author: (novels) Resumes, 1992, Cover Letters, 1991, Thank You Letters, 1992, (poetry) Inner Peace, 1999; co-editor: I Cried, 2001, Life, 2002. Bd. dirs. Children's Mus. Tampa, 1992-94; com. mem. United Way, Tampa, 1994-95; mem. bd. St. Peter Claver Cath. Sch., Tampa, 1995-99, exec. com. Glee Club, 1995; vol. Scout troop leader, 1997-98. Recipient Outstanding Bus. Woman award Am. Bus. Women's Assn., Tampa, 1987, Cmty. Svc. award Tampa Connections, 1993, Editor's Choice award Internat. Libr. of Poetry, 1999. Mem.: AAUW, Fla. Assn. Women in Edn., Am. Vocat. Assn. Roman Catholic. Avocations: reading, sewing. Office: Jr Achievement Central Maryland Inc 10711 Red Run Blvd Ste 110 Owings Mills MD 21117 E-mail: tapptbjpt@earthlink.net.

TAPP, PAUL WAYNE, music educator; b. Kans. City, Mo., July 14, 1946; s. Edmund Pendleton and Lucile (Tomason) Tapp; m. Sharon Joan Berry, Sept. 18, 1970; children: Stephen Koy, Marcia Kate Stutes. MusB, East Tex. Bapt. U., 1969; MusM, Southwestern Bapt. Theol. Seminary, 1989. Art dir. Fisher Mid. Sch., Lafitte, La., 1970—72; min. of music and youth Oak Pk. Bapt. Ch., New Orleans, 1969—70, 1972—75; min. music and youth discipleship Daniel Meml. Bapt. Ch., Jackson, Miss., 1975—80; christian svc. corps SBC- No. Am. Mission Bd., Ruidoso, N.Mex., 1980—85; assoc. pastor First Bapt. ch., Ruidoso, N.Mex., 1981—85; min. of music Richland Hills Bapt. Ch., Ft. Worth, 1986—92, Henderson St. Bapt. Ch., Cleburne, Tex., 1993—2001; music tchr. Arlington Classics Acad., 1999—2001; dir. alumni rels ETBU, Marshall, Tex., 2001—. Oil paintings; mem. editl. staff U. Mag., 2001—; author: (short stories) The Scarborough/Linebery Legacy, 2003. Nat. adv. counsel ring Camps Farthest Out, St. Paul, 1970—72; bd. mem. Ruidoso Lodgers Assn., 1980—85; mem. sch. bd. Ruidos Christian Sch., 1981—85. Avocations: music, piano, painting. Home: 4606 Jeff Davis Marshall TX 75672 Office: East Tex Bapt U 1209 No Grove St Marshall TX 75670

TAPPÉ, ALBERT ANTHONY, architect; b. Pitts., Aug. 12, 1928; s. Albert Anthony and Martha Ann (McKee) T.; m. Jean Bates, June 27, 1963; children: Eliza Bruce, Albert Anthony III. Student, William and Mary Coll., 1947-48, Fontainebleau Fine Art and Music Sch., 1951; BS, U. Va., 1952; M.Arch., MIT, 1958, M.City Planning. Designer McLeod & Ferrara (Architects), Washington, 1954-55; planner Boston City Planning Bd., 1957-58; architect, planner Architects Collaborative, Cambridge, Mass., 1958-61; ptnr. Huygens & Tappé, Inc. (architects and planners), Boston, 1962-80; pres. A. Anthony Tappé & Assocs., Inc., Boston, 1980—. Instr. dept. city planning MIT, 1959-60; instr. office exec. edn. Harvard U., 1989—; cons. architect Mass. Bur. Library Extension, 1965-76; chmn. bldg. commn., Brookline, Mass., 1977, mem. bd. examiners, Brookline; v.p. Guild Religious Architecture; mem. Back Bay Archtl. Commn.; bd. dirs. Boston Archtl. Center, 1980, bd. overseers, 2001-; vis. architect Am. Acad. Rome, 1997. mem. bd. trustees Fountain BCEA Assn., 2003-. Author: Guide to Planning a Library Building, 1967; important works include: Longy Concert Hall, Cambridge, Mass., Campus NH Coll., Franklin Park Zoo, Boston, Lynn Inst. for Savs., Interfaith Religious Ctr., Columbia, Md., student housing W.Va. Wesleyan Coll., Hotel, Costa Smeralda, Sardinia, Newton Pub. Libr., Beverly Pub. Libr., Am. Coll., Athens, Greece, Morse Inst. Library, Natick, Mass., Newton Public Library, Mass., Ctrl. Sch., Longmeadow, MA.; also residences in US, France, Switzerland, housing projects in New Eng. Served with AUS, 1946-47, 52-54. Recipient Prog. Architecture Design award, 1966, 1st place single family category Plywood Design Awards Program, 1973, award Merit, 1974 Fellow AIA (mem. nat. urban planning design com. 1975, citation, hon. mentions 1969, 1st honor award 1970, honor award New Eng. Regional Council 1976); mem. Mass. Assn. Architects (exec. com.), Boston Soc. Architects (dir., v.p. 1981-82, pres. 1982-83, award 1998), Am. Inst. Planners, Am. Planning Assn., Am. Inst. Cons. Planners, Ecoles D'Art Americanes Fontainebleau (trustee 2003), Harvard Travelers Club. Clubs: Union Boat (Boston), Eastern Point Yacht (Gloucester, Mass.), Harvard Club (Boston), Bass Rocks Golf Club (Gloucester, Mass.). Home: 58 Euston St Brookline MA 02446-4045 Office: Tappe Assocs Inc 6 Edgerly Pl Boston MA 02116-5327 E-mail: aatappe@tappe.com.

TAPPER, JOAN JUDITH, magazine editor; b. Chgo., June 12, 1947; d. Samuel Jack and Anna (Swoiskin) T.; m. Steven Richard Siegel, Oct. 15, 1971. BA, U. Chgo., 1968; MA, Harvard U., 1969. Editor manuscripts Chelsea House, N.Y.C., 1969-71, Scribners, N.Y.C., 1971; editor books Nat. Acad. Scis., Washington, 1972-73; assoc. editor Praeger Pubs., Washington, 1973-74; editor New Rep. Books, Washington, 1974-79; mng. editor spl. pubs. Nat. Geog. Soc., Washington, 1979-83; editor Nat. Geog. Traveler, Washington, 1984-88; editor-in-chief Islands, internat. mag., Santa Barbara, Calif., 1989—; editl. dir. Islands Pub. Co., Santa Barbara, 1996—. Recipient Pacific Asia Travel Assn. Journalist of the Yr. award, 1995. Mem. Am. Soc. Mag. Editors, Soc. Am. Travel Writers (editors' coun.), Channel City Club. Democrat. Jewish. Avocations: travel, reading, tennis. Home: 603 Island View Dr Santa Barbara CA 93109-1508 Address: 6309 Carpinteria Ave Carpinteria CA 93013-2901

TAPPER, LEONA (LEELA) SIFF, artist; b. Akron, Ohio, Jan. 27, 1918; d. David M. and Dorothea (Rossen) Siff; m. William Tapper, Aug. 1942 (dec.); children: Bruce Elliot, Devore Tapper Treewater; m. Paul Revivi, Aug. 1984 (dec.). BA, U. Mich., 1938; postgrad., U. Wis., 1938—40; art student, Cleve. Inst. Art, 1944—48, Art Students League, N.Y.C., 1949—51, Han Hoffman, Provincetown, Mass., 1951—53; MA NYU, 1965. Pvt. art tchr., N.Y.C., 1952—58; art tchr. j.r. h.s., N.Y.C., 1958; pvt. art tchr. N.Y.C., 1959—62, Jaffa, Israel, 1962—93, Balt., 1993—99. Pvt. art therapist, N.Y.C., 1955—58. Exhibitions include Cleve. Art Mus., 1944, Denver Art Mus., Chappel Ho., 1948—49, Petrantonio Gallery, N.Y.C., 1956—61, Old City of Jaffa, Israel, 1965—93. Mem. mental health exec. com. Riverdale, N.Y.C., 1961—; mem. exec. com. Hosp. Joint Diseases, N.Y.C., 1956—58; UPA rep. New Lincoln Sch., N.Y.C., 1954—62, H.S. Music and Art, N.Y.C., 1954—62; mem. Denver Civic Symphony, 1942—45, Fla. String Quartet, 1949—51. Mem.: Artists Equity Assn. N.Y. Avocations: yoga, music, horseback riding, travel. Home and Studio: 725 Mount Wilson Ln # 600 Baltimore MD 21208

TAQUEY, ANTONY, accountant; b. Albert, Somme, France, Aug. 13, 1953; arrived in U.S., 1955; s. Charles Henri and Ruth McVitty Taquey; m. Karen Elizabeth Anderson, June 17, 2001. BA in Econs., New Eng. Coll., 1976; MS in Acctg. and Fin., Johns Hopkins U., 1997. Editor: War is Personal, 2001. Republican. Episcopalian. Home: PO Box 1751 Clemmons NC 27012

TAR, LASZLO, artist; b. Szabolcs, Hungary, June 9, 1922; arrived in U.S., 1956; s. Laszlo Tar; m. Olga Vida; children: Julia LaScalere, Leslie, Julius. BA, Royal Acad. Fine Arts, Budapest, 1948; apprentice, Italian master Giorgio Morandi, 1946; postgrad., New Sch., N.Y.C.; student, Art Students League, N.Y., 1971—77. Artist, 1927—; with WestPoint Pepperell, F. Schumacher & Co. Exhibitions include Washington Sq. Park Outdoor Art Show, maj. personal art works projects, Eng., France, Italy and Holland, 1977, 1995, exhibitions include Budapest Galeria, 1989, one-man shows include various locations throughout Hungary, Art Expo, N.Y.C., 1996, 1997, 1999, exhibitions include N.Y. Consulate of Republic of Hungary, 2000, Huntington Arts Counsel Art in the Atrium, 2001, Represented in permanent collections Budapest Mus. of Fine Art, Mcpl. Mus., Rome. Home: 3 Cliftwood Dr Huntington NY 11743 Office Phone: 631-223-2700. Personal E-mail: ltar@tarart.com.

TARAKJI, AHMAD HOUSSAM, research scientist, electrical engineer; s. Mohamad Tarakji. PhD in Elec. Engring., U. S.C., 2003. Rsch. asst. Photonics and Microelectronics Lab., Columbia, SC, 1999—2000; rsch. scientist, test engr. Sensor Electronic Tech., Inc., Columbia, 2001—. Consulting Photonics and Microelectronics Lab., Columbia, 2001—. Grantee, Missile Def. Agy., Def. Advanced Rsch. Projects Agy., Office of Naval rsch., 2002—03. Mem.: IEEE. Achievements include first to 1st GaN-based submicron MOSHFET, 1st AlGaN/InGaN/GaN operating transistor device, some novel system level models for analog integrated circuits. Office: Sensor Electronic 1195 Atlas Rd Columbia SC 29209

TARAN, LEONARDO, classicist, educator; b. Galarza, Argentina, Feb. 22, 1933; came to U.S., 1958, naturalized, 1976; s. Miguel and Liuba Taran; m. Judit Sofia Lida, Dec. 10, 1971; 1 child, Gabriel Andrew. Legal degree, U. Buenos Aires, 1958; PhD in Classics, Princeton U., 1962. Jr. fellow Inst. Rsch. in Humanities, U. Wis., 1962-63, Ctr. Hellenic Studies, Washington, 1963-64; asst. prof. classics U. Calif., L.A., 1964-67; mem. faculty Columbia U., N.Y.C., 1967—, prof. Greek and Latin, 1971—, Jay prof. Greek and Latin, 1987—, chmn. dept., 1976-79; emeritus, 2004. Mem. Inst. Advanced Study, Princeton, N.J., 1966-67, 78-79; trustee Assn. Mems. Inst. Advanced Study, 1974-79; mem. mng. com. Am. Sch. Classical Studies, 1976-. Author: Parmenides, 1965, Asclepius of Tralles, Commentary to Nicomachus' Introduction to Arithmetic, 1969, Plato, Philip of Opus and the Pseudo-Platonic Epinomis, 1975, Anonymous Commentary on Aristotle's De Interpretatione, 1978, Speusippus of Athens, 1981, Collected Papers (1962-1999), 2001; co-author: Eraclito: Testimonianze e imitazioni, 1972; mem. editl. bd.: Columbia Studies in the Classical Tradition, 1976-80. Am. Coun. Learned Socs. fellow, 1966-67, 71-72, Guggenheim Found. fellow, 1975, NEH fellow, 1986-87; grantee Am. Philos. Soc., 1963, 71, 75, Am. Coun. Learned Socs., 1968, 72, NEH, 1985-87, 88-89. Mem. Am. Philol. Assn., Classical Assn. Atlantic States, Soc. Ancient Greek Philosophy, Assn. Guillaume Budé. Home: 39 Claremont Ave New York NY 10027-6802 Office: Columbia U 615 Hamilton Hall New York NY 10027 E-mail: lt1@columbia.edu.

TARANIK, JAMES VLADIMIR, geologist, educator; b. Los Angeles, Apr. 23, 1940; s. Vladimir James and Jeanette Downing (Smith) T.; m. Colleen Sue Glessner, Dec. 4, 1971; children: Debra Lynn, Danny Lee. BSc in Geology, Stanford U., 1964; PhD, Colo. Sch. Mines, 1974. Chief remote sensing Iowa Geol. Survey, Iowa City, 1971-74; prin. remote sensing scientist Earth Resources Observation Systems Data Ctr., U.S. Geol. Survey, Sioux Falls, S.D., 1975-79; chief non-renewable resources br., resource observation div. Office of Space and Terrestrial Applications, NASA Hdqrs., Washington, 1979-82; dean mines Mackay Sch. Mines U. Nev., Reno, 1982-87, prof. of geology and geophysics, 1982—, Arthur Brant chair of geophysics, 1996—; pres. Desert Research Inst., Univ. and C.C. Sys. Nev., 1987-98; Regent's prof. and pres. emeritus Desert Rsch. Inst., Univ. and C.C. Sys. Nev., 1998—; adj. prof. geology U. Iowa, 1971-79; vis. prof. civil engring. Iowa State U., 1972-74; adj. prof. earth sci. U. S.D., 1976-79; program scientist for space shuttle large format camera expt. for heat capacity mapping mission, liaison Geol. Scis. Bd., Nat. Acad. Scis., 1981-82; dir. NOAA Coop. Inst. Aerospace Sci. & Terrestrial Applications, 1986-94; program dir. NASA Space Grant consortium Univ. and C.C. Sys. Nev., Reno, 1991—, dir. NASA EPSCOR program, 1998—; dir. Great Basin Ctr. Geothermal Energy, 2000—03; acting dean Mackay Sch. Mines, 2003; dir. Mackay Sch. Earth Sci. and Engring. U. Nevada, 2004—. Team mem. Shuttle Imaging Radar-B Sci. Team NASA, 1983-88, mem. space applications adv. com., 1986-88; chmn. remote sensing subcom. SAAC, 1986-88; chmn. working group on civil space commercialization Dept. Commerce, 1982-84, mem. civil operational remote sensing satellite com., 1983-84; bd. dirs. Earth Satellite Corp., 1994-2002, Newmont Mining Corp., Spectir Corp., e-Quake, Inc.; mem. adv. com. NASA Space Sci. and Applications Com., 1988-90, Nat. Def. Exec. Res., 1986-94, AF studies bd., com. on strategic relocatable targets, 1989-91; mem. pre-launch rev. bd., NASA, Space Radar Lab., 1993-94; mem. fed. lab. rev. task force, NASA, 1994-96; prin. investigator Japanese Earth Resources Satellite, 1991-94; mem. environ. task force MEDEA, Mitre Corp., McLean, Va., 1993-98; mem. mapping scis. com. Nat. Rsch. Coun., 2001-04; cons. Jet Propulsion Lab., Calif., Hughes Aircraft Corp., Lockheed-Marietta Corp., Mitre Corp., TRW; developer remote sensing program and remote sensing lab. for State of Iowa, ednl. program in remote sensing for Iowa univs. and U. Nev., Reno; program scientist for 2d space shuttle flight Office Space and Terrestrial Applications Program; mem. terrestrial geol. applications program NASA, 1981-82; co-investigator Can. Radarsat Program, 1995—; program dir. NASA Space Grant, 2001-, NASA EPSCOR, Nev., 1998-. Contbr. to profl. jours. Bd. dirs. Mountain States Legal Found., 2000-. Served with C.E. U.S. Army, 1965-67; mil. intelligence officer Res. Decorated Bronze Star medal; recipient Spl. Achievement award U.S. Geol. Survey, 1978, Exceptional Sci. Achievement medal NASA, 1982, NASA Group Achievement award Shuttle imaging radar, 1990, NASA Johnson Space Ctr. Group Achievement award for large format camera, 1985; NASA prin. investigator, 1973, 83-88, prin. investigator French Spot-1 Program to Evaluate Spot 1986-88; NDEA fellow, 1968-71. Fellow: AAAS, Am. Soc. Photogrammetry Remote Sensing, Explorers Club, Geol. Soc. Am.; mem.: AIAA (sr.), IEEE (sr.), Soc. Econ. Geologists, Am. Geol. Inst. Found. (trustee 1999—), Am. Inst. Metall. Engrs., Am. Astron. Soc. (sr.), Soc. Mining Engrs. Am., Am. Assn. Petroleum Geologists (chmn. rsch. com. 2000—), Am. Geophys. Union, Soc. Exploration Geophysicists, Internat. Acad. Astronautics, Bohemian Club San Francisco. Home: PO Box 7175 Reno NV 89510-7175 Office Phone: 775-784-6987. Business E-Mail: jtaranik@mines.unr.edu. *I have always been in awe of the universe in which we live and the little time we have on earth to perceive and understand it.*

TARANTINO, DAVID A., JR., military officer, emergency physician; b. Dec. 17, 1965; MD, Georgetown U., 1992. Surgeon Office Peace Keeping and Humanitarian Affairs, US Dept. Def., Washington. Lt. comdr. USN. Decorated medal Navy/Marine Corps; named regional finalist, White House Fellows Program, 2003—04; recipient Washingtonian Yr. award, Washingtonian Mag., 2001, Humanitarian Svc. medal, 2001, Medal Valor, AMA, 2003.

TARANTINO, DOMINIC A. A. retired professional services firm executive; b. San Francisco, Aug. 1, 1932; m. Leona Lazzareschi, July 24, 1954; children: John Robert, Stephen, Leanne. BS, U. San Francisco, 1954. With Price Waterhouse, 1957-98, mem. policy bd. and mgmt. com., 1979-93, vice chmn. tax svcs., 1982-88, co-chmn. bd., mng. ptnr., 1988-93; chmn. Price Waterhouse World Firm, 1995-98; ret., 1998. Mem. IRS Commr.'s Adv. Group, 1978. Trustee U. San Francisco, 1996—, chair bd. trustees, 1999-2003; treas., bd. dirs. Bus. Opportunities for Leadership Diversity, 1988-. Recipient Delta Sigma Pi Career Achievement award, 1997. Mem. AICPA (bd. dirs. 1988-95, vice chair 1992-3, chmn. 1993-94, Dixon Meml. award 1990, Gold medal for disting. svc. 2000). Address: Mead Point Nipowin Ln Greenwich CT 06830

TARANTINO, LOUIS GERALD, business executive, consultant, lawyer; b. Bridgeport, Conn., Sept. 7, 1934; s. Louis Gerald and Mary Louise (Boyle) T. BA, U. Pa., 1955, LLB, 1958. Bar: Conn. 1958, N.Y. 1960. Assoc. Beekman & Bogue, 1959-67, ptnr., 1968-76; pres., bd. dirs. Berkeley Mgmt. Assocs., Inc., Boston, 1984—. Mem. enterprise adv. bd. Photonics Ctr., Boston U.; ptnr. Berkeley Investment Ptnrs., N.Y.C., Wintzen Pharms, L.P., The Netherlands, Early Stage Advisors., Boston; bd. dirs. SiteLab Corp., Newbury Port, Mass., Anyparty.com.Inc., Boston, Midnight Trader, Inc., Boston. Mem. Bar Assn. City N.Y., N.Y. Bar Assn., Conn. Bar Assn., Huguenot Soc. Pa., St. Anthony Hall, Knickerbocker Club, India House (N.Y.C.), St. Anthony Club (Phila.). Home: One Devonshire Pl Apt 3409 Boston MA 02109

TARANTINO, QUENTIN, film director, screenwriter; b. Knoxville, Tenn., Mar. 27, 1963; s. Tony and Connie T. Screenwriter, dir., actor: Reservoir Dogs, 1992, Pulp Fiction, 1994 (Palme d'Or,Cannes Internat. Film Festival, 1994, Academy award best original screenplay 1994); screenwriter: True Romance, 1993; story: Natural Born Killers, 1994; producer: Killing Zoe, 1994; film appearances include Sleep With Me, 1994, Destiny Turns On the Radio, 1995; TV appearances include The Golden Girls, All-American Girl; actor: Desperado, 1995, Girl 6, 1996, From Dusk Till Dawn, 1996, Full Tilt Boogie, 1997; producer: Red Rain, 1995, Four Rooms, 1995, From Dusk Till Dawn, 1996, Curdled, 1996, Little Nicky, 2000; dir., writer, prodr. Jackie Brown, 1997, Kill Bill: Vol. 2, 2004; dir., writer Kill Bill: Vol. 1, 2003; dir. (TV series) ER, 1994. Address: 6201 W Sunset Blvd Ste 35 Los Angeles CA 90028-8704 also: WMA 151 S El Camino Dr Beverly Hills CA 90212-2704

TARANTO, MARIA ANTOINETTE, psychology researcher and educator; b. Framingham, Mass., Dec. 28, 1941; d. Gaetano (Tom) Peter and Rose Marie (Busceme) T.; m. John Curtis Mahon, June 5, 1988. BA in Psychology, Bennington Coll., 1965; MA in Psychology, George Peabody Coll., 1968; M Philosophy in Psychology, Columbia U., 1981, PhD, 1985. Tchr. Head Start Pub Sch. System, Pitts., 1966-67; rsch. assoc. Hofstra U., Hempstead, N.Y., 1968-69, instr., 1969-72; co-dir. Inst. for Piagetian Studies, Hempstead, 1972-76; instr. Nassau C.C., Garden City, N.Y., 1976-78, asst. prof., 1978-85, assoc. prof. psychology, 1985-95, prof. emeritus, 1996—. Jour. reviewer Baywood Pub. Co., Long Island, N.Y., 1989, Karger, Basel, Switzerland, 1989. Co-author: (monographs) A Study of Number..., 1972, Liquid Conservation, 1976; contbr. articles to profl. jours and govt. pubs. Mem. Union of Concerned Scientists, 1981—, Amnesty Internat., 1987—; sponsor Pearl S. Buck Found., 1984—. Recipient Mellon fellowship CUNY, N.Y.C., 1987. Mem. Am. Psychol. Assn., Jean Piaget Soc., Gerontol. Soc., New Eng. Psychol. Assn., Filicudi Assn. (pres. 2002-04). Avocations: hiking, gardening, picniking.

TARAS, PAUL, physicist, researcher; b. Tunis, Tunisia, May 12, 1941; emigrated to Can., 1957, naturalized, 1962; s. Wladimir and Benita (Koort) T.; m. Marja-Leena Malinen, Aug. 3, 1963; children— Lisa Helene, Michele Anne. BASc., U. Toronto, 1962, MA, 1963, PhD, 1965. Asst. prof. physics U. Montreal, Que., Can., 1965-70, assoc. prof., 1970-76, prof., 1976—. Spokesman U. Montreal in rsch. projects. Helios, SDC, Babar. Rsch. on nuclear and particle physics; co-managed conception and constrn. of 8pi Spectrometer, Chalk River Nuclear Labs, 1984-86; contbr. articles to profl. jours.; presenter papers to profl. confs. U. Toronto, Province of Ont., U.K. Atomic Energy Authority fellowships; France-Que., NRC, Natural Scis. and Engring. Research Council Can. grantee. Mem. Am. Phys. Soc., Can. Assn. Physicists, Soc. Galilée (mem. exec. bd.), Babar Collaboration (bd. dirs.). Home: 1639 Norway Rd Montreal QC Canada H4P 1Y3 Office: Univ de Montreal Lab Physique Nucleaire Montreal QC Canada H3C 3J7 Office Phone: 514-343-7683. E-mail: taras@lps.umontreal.ca.

TARASI, LOUIS MICHAEL, JR., lawyer; b. Cheswick, Pa., Sept. 9, 1931; s. Louis Michael and Ruth Elizabeth (Records) T.; m. Patricia Ruth Finley, June 19, 1954; children: Susan, Louis Michael III, Elizabeth, Brian, Patricia, Matthew. BA, Miami U., Ohio, 1954; JD, U. Pa., 1959. Bar: Pa. 1960, U.S. Dist. Ct. (we. dist.) Pa. 1960, U.S. Ct. Appeals (3d cir.) 1964, U.S. Supreme Ct. 1969, U.S. Dist. Ct. (we. dist.) Tex. 1988, U.S. Ct. Appeals (5th cir.) 1989, U.S. Ct. Appeals (4th cir.) 1994, U.S. Ct. Fed. Claims 1987, U.S. Dist. Ct. Colo. 1998; cert. civil trial adv. Nat. Bd. Trial Advocacy. Assoc., owner Burgwin, Ruffin, Perry & Pohl, Pitts., 1960-68; ptnr. Conte, Courtney & Tarasi, Beaver County, Pa., 1968-78, Tarasi & Tighe, Pitts., 1978-82, Tarasi & Johnson, P.C., Pitts., 1982-95, Tarasi & Assocs., P.C., Pitts., 1995-99, The Tarasi Lawfirm, P.C., Pitts., 1997-2001, Tarasi, Tarasi & Fishman, P.C., Pitts., 2001—. Mem. parish coun. St. James Ch., Sewickley, Pa.; mem. Sewickley Borough Allegheny Coun., 1978-1982. With U.S. Army, 1954-56. Fellow: Internat. Soc. Barristers; mem.: Am. Coll. Barristers (sr. counsel), Am. Bd. Trial Advs., Melvin Belli Soc., St. Thomas More Soc. (award 1991), West Pa. Trial Lawyers Assn. (pres. 1975), Pa. Bar Assn., Allegheny County Bar Assn., Acad. Trial Lawyers Allegheny County, Pa. Trial Lawyers Assn. (pres. 1979—80), Assn. Trial Lawyers Am. (gov., rep.). Democrat. Roman Catholic. Avocations: reading, golf, lecturing. Home: 1 Way Hollow Rd Sewickley PA 15143-1192 Office: Tarasi Tarasi & Fishman 510 3d Ave Pittsburgh PA 15219-2107

TARAVELLA, ROSIE, actress; b. Mt. Morris, N.Y., July 8, 1962; d. Charles James and Carrie (Sardinia) T.; m. Michael Anthony Valerio, May 27, 1994. BA in Dramatic Arts, San Diego State U., 1985. Entertainment dir., staff trainer Johnny Rockets, Inc., L.A., 1986-98; staff writer, voice talent The Rick Dees Weekly Top 40, L.A., 1990-93; freelance writer, voice talent The Premiere Comedy Radio Network, L.A., 1992-98; actress L.A., 1992—; writer L.A. Times Calendar Live! Website, 1999—. Theatrical prodr., cons. The Tamarind Theater, L.A., 1993-94. Author (plays) Rose's Bowl-O-Rama, 1992, The Wives, 1994, Pa's Funeral, 1995; (with Diane Kelber) Blue Grass, 1999; screenwriter: Carlo's Wake, 1997; actress (commls.) AT&T, Dial, Radio Shack and others, 1992—, (TV) Who's the Boss, Ellen, Full House, Married with Children, The Client, Almost Perfect, Brooklyn South, Sinatra, Norma Jean and Marilyn, George and Leo, Roswell; actress, co-writer (film) Carlo's Wake, 1999. Pres. Boards and Boards Prodns., North Hollywood, Calif., 1994-98. Recipient Am.'s Best Sitcom Writing Competition award, 1999. Mem. Mus. TV and Radio, KCRW-Nat. Pub. Radio, Am. Soc. Prevention Cruelty Animals, Nat. Geog. Soc. Democrat. Roman Catholic. Avocations: cooking, genealogy, internet, film and tv history. Office: Broads and Boards 12828 Victory Blvd Ste 334 North Hollywood CA 91606-3013

TARAZA, DINU, engineering educator, researcher; b. Bucharest, Romania, Oct. 10, 1936; s. Petre and Melania Valeria Taraza; m. Octaviana Croitoru, July 21, 1961; 1 child, Carmen Marina Mihai. BS in Mech. Engring., Poly. Inst. Bucharest, 1954—59, PhD in Mech. Engring., 1965—75. Mech. engr., Ministry Edn./Romania, 1959. Product engr. 23 Aug. Heavy Industry Plant, Bucharest, Romania, 1959—60; product devel. engr. Tech. Inst. of the Ministry of Transp., Bucharest, 1960—65; asst. Poly. Inst. of Bucharest, 1965—69, lectr., 1969—75, assoc. prof., 1975—90, prof., 1990—95; vis. prof. Darmstadt U. of Tech., Germany, 1992—92, Wayne State U., Detroit, 1995—97, prof. (tenure 2003), 1997—. Cons. Ministry Machine Bldg., Bucharest, 1977—95. Recipient Arch. T. Colwell Merit award, Soc. of Automotive Engineers (SAE), 1998. Fellow: Soc. Automotive Engineers; mem.: ASME, Am. Soc. for Engring. Edn. Christian Orthodox. Achievements include research and original contributions in the field of internal combustion engines, especially in engine dynamics. Avocations: travel, photography, skiing. Home: 415 Calvin Grosse Pointe Farms MI 48236 Office: Wayne State Univ 5050 Anthony Wayne Dr Detroit MI 48202 Office Phone: 313-577-3701. Business E-Mail: taraza@eng.wayne.edu.

TARBOX, GURDON LUCIUS, JR., retired museum executive; b. Plainfield, N.J., Dec. 25, 1927; s. Gurdon Ludius and Lillie (Hodgson) T.; m. Milver Ann Johnson, Sept. 25, 1952; children: Janet Ellen LeGrand, Joyce Elaine Schumacher, Paul Edward, Lucia Ann Raatma. BS, Mich. State U., 1952; MS,

Purdue U., 1954; D Pub. Svc., U. S.C., 1993. Asst. dir. Brookgreen Gardens, Murrells Inlet, S.C., 1954-59, trustee, 1959-94, dir., 1963-94, pres., 1990-94, pres. emeritus, 1994—. Bd. dirs. Bartlett Tree Expert Co. Chmn. Georgetown County Mental Health Commn., 1964-66; mem. exec. coun. Confedn. S.C. Local Hist. Socs., 1976-80; trustee S.C. Hall Fame, 1976, S.C. Heritage Trust, 1981-86, S.C. Mansion Commn., 1986-99. Served with AUS, 1946-48. Recipient Order of Palmetto, State of S.C., 1999, Francis K. Hutchinson medal for svc. to conservation The Garden Club of Am., 1995. Mem. Soc. Am. Foresters, Am. Assn. Bot. Gardens and Arboreta (dir. 1971-74, sec.-treas. 1982, v.p. 1983, pres. 1985-86), Georgetown County Hist. Soc. (pres. 1970-74), Am. Hort. Soc., Royal Hort. Soc., Am. Assn. Mus. (coun. 1983), Southeastern Mus. Conf. (dir. 1977-80), S.C. Fedn. Museums (pres. 1974-76), Am. Assn. State and Local History, S.C. Confedn. Local Hist. Socs., Rotary (pres. 1979-80). Episcopalian. Home: 641 Crooked Oak Dr Pawleys Island SC 29585-8104

TARBUCK, BARBARA JOAN, actress; b. Detroit, Jan. 15, 1942; d. George and Ruth Erma (Fillmore) T.; m. James Denis Connolly, May 17, 1980; 1 child, Jennifer Lane. B of Philosophy, Wayne State U., 1963; MA, U. Mich., 1965; postgrad., Ind. U., 1965-66. Author: (children's play) Who Am I?, 1972; Author/actor: They Call Me Dr. Greer, 1994; Actress:(TV movies) The Cracker Factory, 1979, Mrs. R's Daughter, 1979, A Christmas Without Snow, 1980, Between Two Loves, 1982, Victims for Victims: The Theresa Saldana Story, 1984, Out of Time, 1988, David, 1988, I Know My First Name is Steven, 1989, Death of the Incredible Hulk, 1990, A House of Secrets and Lies, 1992, A Child Lost Forever: The Jerry Sherwood Story, 1992, Jack Reed: Badge of Honor, 1993, Moment of Truth: Eye of the Stalker, 1995, Seduced by Madness: The Diane Borchardt Story, 1996, Before He Wakes, 1998, Mr. Murder, 1998, Just Ask My Children, 2001, (films) Short Circuit, 1986, Big Trouble, 1986, Curly Sue, 1991, Midnight Witness, 1993, Scanner Cop II, 1995, Tie That Binds, 1995, Legend of Razorback, 2002, Tulse Luper Suitcases: The Moab Story, 2003, Walking Tall, 2004; guest appearances: (TV shows) include M*A*S*H*, 1982, Cagney & Lacey, 1983-84, Falcon Crest, 1986-87, The Golden Girls, 1997, Knots Landing, 1979, Quantum Leap, 1992, Picket Fences, 1992, The Practice, 1997 ER, 1999, CSI, 2000, Judging Amy, 2001, Crossing Jordan, 2001, Six Feet Under, 2002, Without a Trace, 2003, Cold Case, 2003; Broadway shows include Brighton Beach Memoirs, Water Engine, Landscape and Silence; nat. tours: Broadway Bound, America Hurrah!. Fulbright grantee, 1966-67; recipient L.A. Drama Critics award, 1985. Mem. Zeta Phi Eta. Democrat. E-mail: btarbuck@futurewest.ca.

TARBUTTON, LLOYD T. franchise consultant; b. Easton, Md., Jan. 3, 1932; s. William Lloyd and Ethel Ford T.; m. Virginia Rachael Johnson, 1952 (div. 1977); children: Gregory Alan, Kenton Lyle.; m. Layne E. Johnson, 1981; 1 stepchild, C. Todd Woolston. Dr Comml. Sci. in Mktg., Pacific Western U. Grad. Realtors Inst.; cert. franchise exec., La. State U., cert. hotel adminstr. Divsn. sales mgr. Reuben H. Donnelley Corp. (advt. agy.), Norfolk, Va., 1953-58; chmn. bd., dir. Tarbutton Assocs., Inc., Norfolk, 1962—; founder, dir., pres., chmn. bd. Econo Lodges of Am., Norfolk, 1967-83; chmn. bd. emeritus Econo Lodges of Am. (formerly Econ-Travel Motor Hotel Corp.), Norfolk, 1983—. Co-founder, chief judge Franchising Hall of Fame, Washington, 1979-82; co-founder, chmn. Coun. Franchise Suppliers, Washington, 1986-88. Author: Franchising–The How To Book, 1986. Trustee Edn. Found. Old Dominion U., 1979-86, chmn. bd. trustees Ctr. Econ. Edn., Old Dominion U., 1983-84. Recipient Hon. Tchr. award Maury High Sch., Norfolk, 1959. Mem. Internat. Franchise Assn. (hon. life, chmn. bd. dirs., chmn. 1st Asian Symposium on Franchising, Tokyo 1978, 1st European Symposium on Franchising, Amsterdam 1978, 1st So. Pacific Symposium on Franchising, Jakarta 1991), 1st Ea. Europe Franchise Symposiums (Varna, Bulgaria, 2000, inducted into Franchise Hall of Fame 2000), Internat. Coun. Hotel/Motel Mgmt., Realtor's Inst. Norfolk (chmn. 1965), Internat. Sales Execs. Club (Distinguished Sales award 1957), Internat. Platform Assn., Airplane Owners and Pilots Assn., Cavalier Golf and Yacht Club, Town Point Club, Registry Resort Tennis Club, The Club at Pelican Bay. Presbyterian. Home: 7911 Grand Bay Dr Naples FL 34108-7556 Office: 700 Orlole Dr Ste 116A Virginia Beach VA 23451-4960 E-mail: ltarbutton@aol.com. *I believe the greatest assist to my progress in business and personal life came when I became more aware of the "value of self" and thus others.*

TARDE, GERARD (JERRY), magazine executive; Editor-in-chief Golf Digest; chmn., editl. dir. The Golf Digest Co., Wilton, Conn., 2000—. Office: Golf Digest 20 Westport Rd Box 850 Wilton CT 06897

TARDIFF, JILL ALEXANDRIA, publishing executive; b. Morristown, NJ, Apr. 8, 1953; d. Howard James Tardiff and Jean Elizabeth Cook; m. Paul Edward Kozlowski, Feb. 11, 1984. BA in liberal arts, Coll. of St. Elizabeth, 1971—75. Cert. teacher, K-12 NJ, 1975. Retail mgr. Hallmark Cards Inc./Flagship, NYC, 1976—81; mgr./gen. mgr. Doubleday Book Shops/Flagship, NYC, 1981—91; sales mgr./dir. of sales Tiffany & Co., NYC, 1991—93; entrepreneur, self-proprietor Bamboo River Associates, Hoboken, NJ, 1993—; mng. editor/sr. rschr. Lintel Press, NYC, 1993—94; assoc. editor BookWire Online, NYC, 1995—98; contbg. editor/project mgr. Publishers Weekly, NYC, 1996—; advt. mgr. Persimmon, Asian Lit., Arts, and Culture Mag., NYC, 1999—2002. Profl. spkr./tour facilitator Bamboo River Associates, Hoboken, NJ, 1991—; sec./bd. of directors Contemporary Asian Culture Inc., NYC, 1999—; adv. bd. mem. Women's Ink., NYC, 1999—2004. Contbr. book Bob Vila's Guide to Historic Homes Series; reporter Shinbunka Weekly, Tokyo, 1995—2000. Mem.: Internat. Women's Writing Guild (hon.), Am. Women in Enterprise (assoc.), Am. Assn. of U. Women (assoc.), Women's Nat. Book Assn. (assoc.; main rep. UN DPI/NGO 2000—), Women's Nat. Book Assn./NYC Chpt. (assoc.; newsletter editor/v.p. 1997—2000), Women's Nat. Book Assn./NYC Chpt. (assoc.; pres. 2000—), Women's Nat. Book Assn. (assoc.; nat. v.p., pres. elect 2002—04, nat. pres. 2004—), Editl. Freelancers Assn. (assoc.), Japan Soc. (assoc.), Asia Soc./NY (assoc.). Avocations: travel, photography, gardening, architecture, cooking. Office: Bamboo River Associates 625 Madison StSte 2 Hoboken NJ 07030-6305 Personal E-mail: jat-bambooriver@worldnet.att.net.

TARDIO, THOMAS A. public relations executive; V.p. strategic planning and other positions Columbia Pictures Industries, 1979-88; CFO, v.p. adminstrn. Rogers & Cowan, Inc., L.A., 1988-89, exec. v.p. entertainment sect., 1989-91, pres., CEO, 1991-95, co-chmn., mng. dir., 1996—2000; pres. Shandwick, United States, L.A., 1998—2000; pres., COO, Weber Shandwick, Western Region, 2001—; CEO Shandwick Convergence, L.A., 2001—. Mem. IBM mobile computing mktg. adv. bd. Mem. bd. visitors adv. bd. Loyola Law Sch. Mem. Pub. Rels. Soc. Am., Nat. Acad. Recording Arts and Scis., Pub. Communicators L.A., Contry Music Assn. Office: Rogers & Cowan 1888 Century Park E Ste 500 Los Angeles CA 90067-1709

TARDY, MEDNEY EUGENE, JR., retired otolaryngologist, facial plastic surgeon; b. Scottsburg, Ind., Dec. 3, 1934; MD, Ind. U., 1960. Diplomate Am. Bd. Otolaryngology (v.p. 1993, pres. 1994). Intern Tampa Gen. Hosp., 1960—61; resident in otolaryngology U. Ill. Hosp., 1963—67, fellow head, neck and plastic surgery, 1967—68; otolaryngologist St. Joseph Hosp., Chgo.; prof. clin. otolaryngology U. Ill.; pvt. practice Chgo.; dir. divsn. facial plastic and reconstructive surgery U. Ill.; prof. clin. otolaryngology Ind. U. Med. Ctr., Indpls.; pvt. practice Chgo.; ret. Bd. govs. Chgo. Symphony Orch., Hubbard St. Dance Co., Chgo. Mem.: Soc. Univ. Otolaryngologists, Am. Rhinol. Soc., Am. Laryngol. Soc., Am. Acad. Otolaryngology-Head and Neck Surgery (past pres.), Am. Acad. Facial Plastic and Reconstructive Surgery (past pres.), ACS. Office: 2913 N Commonwealth Ave Ste 430 Chicago IL 60657-6238

TAREN, JAMES ARTHUR, neurosurgeon, educator; b. Toledo, Nov. 10, 1924; s. Joseph Clarence and Mary Frances (Walker) T. BS, U. Toledo, 1948; MD, U. Mich., 1952. Diplomate Am. Bd. Neurosurgery. Intern U. Mich. Hosp., Ann Arbor, 1952-53, resident in surgery, 1953-54, resident neurosurgery, 1955-57; clin. instr. U. Mich. Med. Sch., Ann Arbor, 1955-57, instr. neurosurgery, 1957-58, asst. prof., 1958-63, assoc. prof., 1963-67, prof. neurosurgery, 1967—, dir. neurobehavioral sci. program, 1975-78, assoc. dean acad. programs, 1978-87, dir. Brain Tumor Lab., 1985-88; dir. Integrated Acad. Info. Mgmt., 1988-89; dir. neuromodulation program U. Mich. Med. Sch., Ann Arbor, 1994-97. Neurosurgeon Wayne County Gen. Hosp., Eloise, Mich., 1957-71, VA Hosp., Ann Arbor, 1957-73, U.S.S. Hope (Project Hope), Peru, 1962, Ecuador, 1963, Guinea, 1965; vis. prof. Hosp. Foch, Paris, 1966-67, St. Anne Hosp., Paris, 1981, Karolinski Inst., Stockholm, 1981, Haukland Sykehus, Bergen, Norway, 1984, Gumma U., Japan, 1989, Nihon U. Sch. Medicine, Tokyo, 1990. Author, co-editor: Correlative Neurosurgery, 1969, 3rd edit., 1982; contbr. articles to profl. jours. Dep. med. examiner Washtenaw County Dept. Health, Ann Arbor, 1962-90; pres. Hawaii Youth New Leadership Forum, 2000. Active U.S. Armed Forces, 1943-46, PTO. Fellow NIH, 1953; rsch. fellow in neurosurgery Boston Children's Hosp., Peter Bent Brigham Hosp., Boston, 1955. Fellow ACS; mem. AMA, Congress of Neuro. Surgeons, Am. Assn. Neuro. Surgery, Am. Assn. Med. Colls., Am. Soc. for Stereotactic and Functional Neurosurgery, Am. Neuromodulation Soc. (treas. 1994-98, v.p. 1998-99), Royal Soc. Medicine (affiliate), Brit. Med. Soc., Internat. Assn. Study of Pain, Ferrari Club Am. E-mail: jtaren@ilhawaii.net.

TAREN, JEFFREY LYNN, lawyer; b. Wilkes Barre, Pa., Sept. 20, 1952; s. Arnold and Ruth Taren; m. Carolyn Therese Bieszat, May 26, 1985; children: Jordan, Mariel. BA in Polit. Sci., Rutgers Coll., 1974; JD, Boston Coll., 1977. Staff atty. Legal Assistance of Chgo., 1977-80; ptnr. Kinoy, Taren, Gerraghty & Potter, Chgo., 1980-98; hearing officer Chgo. Human Rels. Commn., 1991—. Adv. bd. employment, Chgo., 1995—. Author: (with others) Civil Rights Annual Review, 1995. Bd. dirs. Chgo. Lawyers Com. for Civil Rights, 1996—; chmn. Oak Park Parking Traffic Commn., 1993—, commr. Oak Park Housing Athority. Recipient Award Hope Fair Housing Ctr., 1987, Pro Bono award Lawyers Com. for Civil Rights, 1996. Avocations: basketball, playing banjo. Office: Kinoy Taren & Geraghty PC 224 S Michigan Ave Ste 300 Chicago IL 60604-2505

TARGAN, HOLLI HART, lawyer; b. Detroit, Jan. 3, 1960; m. Anthony Andrew Targan, Aug. 11, 1985. BA, Mich. State U., 1982; JD cum laude, Wayne State U., 1985. Bar: Md. 1985, D.C. 1988, Mich. 1990. Staff atty. Office of Comptroller of the Currency, Washington, 1985-89; assoc. Dykema Gossett, Bloomfield Hills, Mich., 1989-91; staff counsel Mich. Nat. Corp., Farmington Hills, Mich., 1991-95; prin. Law Offices of H.H. Targan, Farmington Hills, 1995-96; ptnr. Jaffe, Raitt, Heuer & Weiss, P.C., Detroit, 1996—. Spkr. in field. Co-author: Guide to Smart Cards and Stored Value, 1999; contbr. articles to profl. jours. Sec., vice chair B'nai B'rith Youth Orgn., Mich., 1991-99. Mem. ABA (cyberspace law com.), Md. State Bar, State Bar Mich., DC Bar Assn., Nat. Assn. Women Bus. Owners, Electronic Transactions Assn. (bd. dirs., chair govt. rels. com.). Office: Jaffe Raitt Heuer & Weiss 27777 Franklin Rd #2500 Southfield MI 48034 E-mail: htargan@jafferaitt.com.

TARGOVNIK, SELMA E. KAPLAN, physician; b. N.Y.C., Apr. 22, 1936; d. Harry A. and Helen (Goodstein) Kaplan; m. Jerome H. Targovnik, Dec. 2, 1961; children: Nina Rebecca, Labe Eric (dec.), Diane Michelle. BA, NYU, 1957; MD, Albert Einstein Col. Medicine, 1961. Diplomate Am. Bd. Dermatology. Intern Kaiser Found. Hosp., San Francisco, 1961-62; resident in internal medicine Bellevue Hosp., NYU Med. Ctr., 1962 63, U. Colo. Med. Ctr., Denver, 1963-64; rsch. fellow, resident in dermatology Boston U. Med. Ctr., 1964-66, mem. staff, 1968-69, NYU Med. Ctr., 1966-68, St. Joseph's Hosp., Columbia Hosp., Phoenix, 1969—98, Good Samaritan Hosp., Phoenix, 1969—; practice medicine specializing in dermatology Phoenix, 1969-98; ret. Part-time staff Carl Hayden VA Hosp., Phoenix, 1998—; mem. staff St. Joseph's Hosp., Phoenix, St. Luke's Hosp., Phoenix, Columbia Hosp., Phoenix; mem. staff Good Samaritan Hosp., Phoenix, chief divsn. dermatology, 1985-90; adj. assoc. prof. Midwestern U. Coll. Medicine, Glendale, Ariz., 1998—; clin. asst. prof. dermatology Kirksville Coll. Osteopathic Medicine, 2000–. Bd. dirs. ACLU, Ariz., 1973-78, 83-94, Congregation Beth El, Phoenix, 1971-75, Flagstaff Festival of the Arts, 1984-86; active Jewish Nat. Fund. Fellow Am. Acad. Dermatology, Assocs. for the Weizmann Inst. Sci., Assocs. for the Technion Inst.; mem. Am. Technion Soc. (bd. dirs. 1988-92, pres. Ariz. divsn. 1990-92), Dermatology Found., Sonoran Dermatologic Soc., Southwestern Dermatologic Soc., Pacific Dermatologic Soc., Noah Worcester Dermatologic Soc., Phi Beta Kappa, Mu Chi Sigma, Pi Delta Phi, Beta Lambda Sigma. Democrat. Jewish. Home: 3706 E Rancho Dr Paradise Valley AZ 85253 Office Phone: 602-954-8335. Personal E-mail: selmaderm@cox.net.

TARIN, DAVID, oncologist, researcher; b. U.K., Aug. 28, 1939; BSc Honors Class I, Leeds (Eng.) U., 1961; BM, BChir, Oxford (Eng.) U., 1963, DM, MA, 1969. House surgeon/physician Radcliffe Infirmary, Oxford, 1964-65; MC Smith lectr. pathology Brimingham (Eng.) U., 1965-67; lectr. anatomy Leeds (Eng.) U., 1967-73; sr. registrar neuropathology Gen. Infirmary, Leeds, 1973-74; sr. lectr. histopathology, hon. cons. pathologist Royal Postgrad. Med. Sch., London, 1975-79; clin. reader pathology John Radcliffe Hosp., Oxford, 1979-80, Nuffield reader pathology, 1980-97; dir. cancer ctr., prof. pathology U. Calif. San Diego, La Jolla, 1997—. Professorial fellow Green Coll. Oxford, 1984—. Author: Tissue Interactions in Carcinogenesis, 1972; contbr. articles on cancer diagnosis and tumor invasion and metastasis to sci. and med. jours. Mem. Royal Coll. Pathologists, Path. Soc., Internat. Soc. Differentiation (bd. dirs., mem. exec. com., pres. 1987-90), Brit. Assn. Cancer Rsch., Am. Assn. Cancer Rsch. Avocations: literature, poetry, music, art, cinema. Office: Rebecca and John Moores UCSD Cancer Center 0658 9500 Gilman Drive La Jolla CA 92093-0658

TARINO, GARY EDWARD, lawyer; b. Jersey City, Oct. 3, 1951; s. Edward G. and Veronica Tarino; m. Maureen Fitzpatrick, May 9, 1987. BA summa cum laude, Rutgers U., 1973, JD, 1976. Bar: N.J. 1976, U.S. Dist. Ct. N.J. 1976, D.C. Ct. Appeals 1978, U.S. Supreme Ct. 1980, N.Y. 1982, U.S. Dist. Ct. (so. dist.) N.Y. 1988, U.S. Dist. Ct. (ea. dist.) N.Y. 1990. Assoc. Winne, Banta, Rizzi & Harrington, Hackensack, N.J., 1976-79; asst. pros. Bergen County Pros. Office, Hackensack, 1979-83, chief organized crime squad, 1981-83; atty. Automatic Data Processing, Inc., Roseland, N.J., 1983—, assoc. gen. counsel, staff v.p., 1994—. Pub. defender Borough of Maywood, N.J., 1987, 20. bd. dirs. N.J. Coun. Econ. Edn., 1990-2000; master Sidney Reitman Employment Law Am. Inn Ct., 1995-2000. Bd. dirs. Am. Heart Assn., N.J., 1976-81, Middlesex County (N.J.) chpt., 1973-81; trustee Integrity, Inc., 1991-97; grad. Leadership N.J., 1989; cubmaster pack III Boy Scouts Am., 2000-04; mem. oper. coun. N.J. Bus. Force, 2003—. Recipient cert. of appreciation U.S. Treasury Dept., 1983, letter of commondation PBA, 1983, Alumni Vol. Leadership award 1st Ann. Leadership N.J., 1991. Office: Automatic Data Processing 1 A D P Blvd Roseland NJ 07068-1786

TARJAN, ROBERT WEGG, retired information services executive, part-time math teacher; b. Evanston, Ill., July 28, 1943; s. Robert David and Constance Rita (Wegg) T.; m. Elizabeth Lindner; children: Robert J., Anne Marie, Katie, Michael, Eileen. BS in Math., Loyola U., Chgo., 1965. Programmer Kemper Nat. Ins. Cos., Long Grove, Ill., 1965-67, supr., 1967-79, teleprocessing mgr., 1969-78, tech. systems mgr., 1978-81, ops. and system support mgr., 1981-85, asst. mgr. info. svcs., 1985-96, v.p. info. svcs., 1986-97. Bd. dirs. Acord, Pearl River, N.Y., chmn., 1996; math. tchr. Loyola Acad., Wilmette, Ill., 1998-2001. Roman Catholic. Avocations: golf, travel, bridge.

TARLETON, LARRY WILSON, editor; b. Wadesboro, N.C., July 19, 1943; s. Harold Wilson and Martha (Roberson) T.; m. Judith Elaine Huntley, Sept. 8, 1963; children: Laurie Leigh, Larry Huntley. BA in Journalism, U. N.C., 1965. Reporter The Charlotte (N.C.) Observer, 1965-73; sports writer The Miami (Fla.) Herald, 1973-74; sports editor The Charlotte Observer, 1974-76; exec. sports editor, mng. editor, exec. editor The Dallas Times Herald, 1976-88, exec. editor, 1988—98; asst. pub. The Post and Courier, Charleston, SC, 1998—2000, pub., 2000—. Mem. Am. Soc. Newspaper Editors, S.C. Press Assn. (former pres.), Dallas Press Club (pres. 1988). AP Mng. editors, AP Sports Editors. Avocations: golf, travel. Home: 27 New St Charleston SC 29401-2405 Office: The Post and Courier 134 Columbus St Charleston SC 29403-4800 E-mail: Harleton@postandcourier.com.

TARLETON, ROBERT STEPHEN, producer and distributor fine arts videos; b. N.Y.C., Feb. 27, 1946; s. Rollin and Helen (Boyle) Tarleton. BA, Wesleyan U., Middletown, Conn, 1968; postgrad. studies, U. Pa., Columbia, N.Y.U. V.p., exec. dir. Intercollegiate Broadcasting System, Vails Gate, N.Y., 1973-74; adjudicator U.S. VA, N.Y.C., 1974-88; prin. Applause Prodns., Inc., Port Washington, N.Y., 1989—. Author: (book) The Spirit of Kappa Alpha, 1994; (booklet) Always...Everywhere. Mem. operating com. John Philip Sousa Meml. Band Shell, Port Washington, 1985—. Staff sgt. U.S. Air Force, 1969-73. Recipient several svc.-wide awards for journalism while in air force. Mem. Broadcast Found. of Coll., Univ. Students (bd. dirs. 1977), Black and Gold Found. (chmn. organizing com. 1998—), Omega Gamma Delta (nat. pres. 1970-82, 96—, nat. sec. 1989-2000), Kappa Alpha Soc. (internat. sec. 1993—), Kappa Alpha Soc. Found. Inc. (sec. 1993—). Avocations: amateur radio, stamp collecting/philately. Home and Office: 89 Longview Rd Port Washington NY 11050-3039 Office Phone: 516-883-0159. Personal E-mail: rstarleton@aol.com.

TARLOV, ALVIN RICHARD, former philanthropic foundation administrator, physician, educator, researcher; b. Norwalk, Conn., July 11, 1929; s. Charles and Mae (Shelinsky) T.; m. Joan Hylton, June 12, 1956 (div. 1976); children: Richard, Elizabeth, Jane, Suzanne, David. BA, Dartmouth Coll., 1951; MD, U. Chgo., 1956. Intern Phila. Gen. Hosp., 1956-57; resident in medicine U. Chgo. Hosps., 1957-58, 62-63, research assoc., 1958-61; asst. prof. medicine U. Chgo., 1963-68, assoc. prof., 1968-70, prof., 1970-84, chmn. dept. medicine, 1969-81, chmn. grad. med. edn. nat. adv. com. HHS, Washington, 1980; pres. Henry J. Kaiser Family Found., Menlo Park, Calif., 1984-90; sr. scientist New Eng. Med. Ctr., Boston, 1990-99, exec. dir. The Health Inst., 1995-99; prof. of Pub. Health Harvard U., Boston, 1990-99; prof. of medicine Tufts U., 1990-99; dir. Tex. Inst. for Soc. and Health Rice U., Tex., 1999—. Dir. Tex. Program for Soc. and Health, James Baker III Inst. for Pub. Policy, Rice U. Pres. Med. Outcomes Trust, Inc., 1993-2000; chmn. bd., pres. Mass. Health Data Consortium, 1994-98. Served to capt. U.S. Army, 1958-61. Recipient Research Career Devel. award NIH, 1962-67; John and Mary Markle Found. scholar, 1966-71. Mem. ACP (master), Inst. Medicine of Nat. Acad. Scis. Office: Tex Program Soc & Health Rice U Baker Inst Pub Policy 6100 Main St Houston TX 77005 Home: 1111 Caroline St Apt 2504 Houston TX 77010-3059 E-mail: atarlov@rice.edu.

TARN, NATHANIEL, poet, translator, educator; b. Paris, June 30, 1928; s. Marcel and Yvonne (Suchar) T.; children: Andrea, Marc. BA with honors, Cambridge (Eng.) U., 1948, MA, 1952; postgrad., U. Sorbonne, U. Paris, 1949-51; MA, U. Chgo., 1952, PhD, 1957; postgrad., London Sch. Econs., 1953-58. Anthropologist, Guatemala, Burma, Alaska, and other locations, 1952—; prof. comparative lit. Rutgers U., 1970-85, prof. emeritus modern poetry, comparative lit, anthropology, 1985. Vis. prof. SUNY, Buffalo and Princeton, 1969-70. Author: Old Savage/Young City, 1964, Where Babylon Ends, 1968, The Beautiful Contradictions, 1969, October, 1969, A Nowhere for Vallejo, 1971, Lyrics for the Bride of God: Section: The Artemision, 1972, The Persephones, 1974, Lyrics for the Bride of God, 1975, The House of Leaves, 1976, Birdscapes, with Seaside, 1978, The Desert Mothers, 1985, At the Western Gates, 1985, Palenque, 1986, Seeing America First, 1989, Flying the Body, 1993, Multitude of One, 1995, Views from the Weaving Mountain: Selected Essays in Poetics and Anthropology, 1991, Scandals in the House of Birds: Shamans & Priests on Lake Atitlan, 1997, The Architextures, 2000, Three Letters From The City: The St. Petersburg Poems 1968-1998, 2000, Selected Poems 1950-2000, 2002, Dying Trees, 2003, Recollections of Being, 2004; co-author: (with Janet Rodney) The Forest, 1978, Atitlan/Alashka, 1979, The Ground of Our Great Admiration of Nature, 1978; contbg. author: Penguin Modern Poets No. Seven: Richard Murphy, Jon Silkin, Nathaniel Tarn, 1965, A.P.E.N. Anthology of Contemporary Poetry, 1966, The Penguin Book of Modern Verse Translation, 1966, Poems Addressed to Hugh MacDiarmid, 1967, Music and Sweet Poetry: A Verse Anthology, 1968, Frontier of Going: Anthology of Space Poetry, 1969, Shaking the Pumpkin, 1972, America: A Prophecy, 1973, Open Poetry, 1973, Active Anthology, 1974, Symposium of the Whole, 1983, Random House Book of Twentieth Century French Poetry, 1983, Beneath a Single Moon: Buddhism in American Poetry, 1991, American Poetry since 1950: Innovators and Outsiders, 1993; translator: The Heights of Macchu Picchu (Pablo Neruda), 1966, Stelae (Victor Segalen), 1969, Zapotec Struggles, 1993; editor, co-translator: Con Cuba: An Anthology of Cuban Poetry of the Last Sixty Years, 1969, Selected Poems (Pablo Neruda), 1970; editor Cape Edits. and founder-dir. Cape Goliard Press, J. Cape Ltd., 1967-69. Recipient Guinness prize for poetry, 1963. Office: PO Box 8187 Santa Fe NM 87504-8187

TARNACKI, DUANE L. lawyer; b. Detroit, Dec. 21, 1953; s. Leo A. and Dorothy O. (Roginski) T.; m. Sheila Rimmel, July 28, 1994. BA in Psychology with high distinction and high honors, U. Mich., 1976; MBA with honors, JD cum laude, U. Notre Dame, 1980. Bar: Mich. 1980, U.S. Dist. Ct. (so. dist.) Mich., 1980. Ptnr., mem. Clark Hill P.L.C., Detroit, 1980—. Sec. Ctr. for Creative Studies, 1991-96; bd. dirs. Stratford Shakespearean Festival of Am., sec., 1991—; bd. dirs. Detroit Hist. Soc., Juvenile Diabetes Found. Met. Detroit chpt., 1990-95, Acct. Aid Soc., 1990-96; gen. counsel Econ. Club of Detroit, 1995—; vice chmn., exec. com. Planned Giving Roundtable of S.E. Mich., 1992-98. Author: Establishing a Charitable Foundation in Michigan, 1986, 3d edit., 1999, The Responsibilities of Service: A Guide for Directors of Nonprofit Organizations in Michigan, 1997, 99; co-author: The Michigan Community Foundation Legal Reference, 1993, 2d edit., 1996; assoc. editor Notre Dame Lawyer, 1977-80. Mem. increasing philanthropy and govt. rels. coms., Coun. Mich. Founds., planned giving com., Karmanos Cancer Inst., 1991-94; bd. dirs. Mich Supreme Court Hist. Soc. Inc., 1988-96; mem. legal adv. subcom. to comty. found. com. Coun. on Founds., IRS Exempt Orgns. Liaison Group; trustee Thompson-McCully Found., 1999-2003, The Futures Found. Fellow: Mich. State Bar Found.; mem.: ABA (nonprofit corps. com., bus. law sect., real property, probate and trust law and tax sects., Outstanding Nonprofit Atty. award bus. law sect. 2003), Mich. Bar Assn. (nonprofit corp. com., bus. law sect., probate and estate planning law and tax sects.), Detroit Regional C. of C. (bus. contbns. com.), Detroit Athletic Club, Econ. Club. Roman Catholic. Home: 39824 Woodside Dr N Northville MI 48167-3429 Office: 500 Woodward Ave Ste 3500 Detroit MI 48226-3435

TARNAY, THOMAS N. lawyer; b. Morgantown, W.Va., Oct. 19, 1960; s. Thomas J. and Marie H. Tarnay; m. Barbara G. Osmalov, Apr. 8, 1989; children: Alexandra M., Kathryn M., Joseph M. BS, Cornell U., 1982; MBA, Northeastern U., 1984; JD, So. Meth. U., 1997. Registered profl. engr., Tex., 1995; bar: Tex. 1997, U.S. Patent and Trademark Office 1997. Program mgr. Tex. Instruments, Dallas, 1984—97; atty. Sidley Austin Brown & Wood LLP, Dallas, 1997—. Mem.: ASME, Am. Intellectual Property Law Assn., Licensing Exec. Soc. Achievements include patents in field. Avocations: swimming, bicycling. Home: 2920 Cherry Spring Ct Plano TX 75025 Office: Sidley Austin Brown & Wood LLP Ste 3400 717 North Harwood St Dallas TX 75201

TARNOFF, JEROME, lawyer; b. June 22, 1931; s. Meyer and Anne (Soshnick) T.; chldrn: Marcy Jane, Margery Lynne; m. Nancy Radin, 1990. AB, Syracuse U., 1952; JD, Columbia U., 1957. Bar: NY 1957, U.S. Dist. Ct. (so. and ea. dists.) NY 1960, U.S. Ct. Appeals (2d cir.) 1961. Ptnr. Sheldon and Tarnoff, NYC, 1957-78, Feldesman, D'Atri, Tarnoff & Lubitz, NYC, 1978, Baskin and Sears, P.C., NYC, 1979-84, Baskin & Steingut P.C., 1984-85, Berger & Steingut, 1986-92, Morrison, Cohen, Singer & Weinstein, LLP, 1993—. Contbr. articles to legal jours. Chmn. policy com. NY Dem. Party, 1975-78, vice chmn. NY County, 1978—, mem. nat. com., 1980-88; mem. Cmty. Planning Bd. #8, 1966-75; bd. dirs. Grand St. Settlement, 1973—1981, Assoc. Y's of NY, 1972-80. With U.S. Army, 1952-54. Recipient Disting. Svc. award NAACP, 1975, Cert. Achievement, El Diario-La Prensa, 1977. Mem. ABA, NY State Bar Assn., Assn. Bar City of NY, N.Y. County Lawyers, Am. Arbitration Assn. (nat. panel arbitrators), Phi Alpha Delta, Sunningdale Country Club (Scarsdale, NY), Harmonie Club (NYC), Audubon, Masons. Jewish. Office: Morrison Cohen Singer & Weinstein 750 Lexington Ave New York NY 10022-1200 Office Phone: 212-735-8632. E-mail: jtarnoff@mcsw.com.

TARNOFF, PETER, former federal agency administrator, business consultant; b. N.Y.C., Apr. 19, 1937; s. Norman Tarnoff and Henrietta (Goldfarb) Laing; m. Daniele Oudinot, Jan. 13, 1962 (div. Oct. 1981); children: Nicholas, Alexander; m. Mathea Falco, Dec. 24, 1981; 1 child, Benjamin. Student, U. Paris, 1956-57, postgrad., 60-61; BA, Colgate U., 1958; postgrad., U. Chgo., 1958-60. Joined Fgn. Svc., Dept. State, 1961; spl. asst. to amb. Am. Embassy, Bonn, Fed. Republic Germany, 1969; trainee Nat. Sch. Adminstrn., Paris, 1970; prin. officer Am. Consulate Gen., Lyon, France, 1971-73; dep. chief of mission Am. Embassy, Luxembourg, 1973-75; dir. Office Rsch. and Analysis for Western Europe Dept. State, Washington, 1975-76, exec. sec. Dept. State, 1977-81, fgn. affairs fellow San Francisco, 1981-82; exec. dir. World Affairs Coun. No. Calif., San Francisco, 1983-86; pres., dir. Coun. on Fgn. Rels., N.Y.C., 1986-93; under sec. state for polit. affairs Dept. State, Washington, 1993-97; pres. Internat. Adv. Corp., San Francisco, 1997—. Office: Internat Adv Corp 2028 Green St San Francisco CA 94123-4813 E-mail: iacmail@aol.com.

TARNOFSKY-OSTROFF, DAWN, broadcast executive; V.p. dev. Kushner-Locke Co., 1984-89; pres. Michael Jacobs Prodns.; sr. v.p. creative affairs 20th Century Fox TV, 1989-96; sr. v.p. programming, prodn. Lifetime TV, N.Y.C., 1996-99, exec. v.p. entertainment, 1999—. Office: Lifetime TV 309 W 49th St Fl 16 New York NY 10019-7316

TARNOPOL, MICHAEL LAZAR, bank executive; b. 1936; s. Irving and Charlotte (Weber) T.; m. Lynne Lichtenstein, June 29, 1958; children: Lisa Silverman, Lori Moore. Gen. ptrn., sr. mng. dir., also bd. dirs. Lehman Bros. Inc., 1959-75; with Bear Stearns & Co. Inc., 1975—, vice-chmn., bd. dirs.; chmn. investment banking divsn., bd. dirs. Bear Stearns Internat. Mem. pres.'s coun. Solomon R. Guggenheim Found.; vice chmn. bd. trustees U. Pa., bd. overseers Wharton Sch.; bd. overseers, bd. mgrs. Meml. Sloan Kettering Cancer Ctr.; Bd. dirs. Cap Cure Found., U.S. Polo Tng. Found., Robert Steel Found., Inc. Mem. Palm Beach Country Club, Harmonie Club, East Hampton Tennis Club, Atlantic Golf Club, Quaker Ridge Golf Club, Trump Internat. Golf Club. Office: 245 Park Ave New York NY 10167-0002

TARNOVE, LORRAINE, medical association executive; b. Atlantic City, July 26, 1947; d. Leonard Robert Tarnove and Jeanne Tarnove Yudkin; m. Steven B. Friedman, June 1, 1969; children: K. Brooke, Ari-Benjamin. BA, U. Md., 1969. Pres. Lorraine Tarnove Consulting, Columbia, Md., 1985-93; exec. dir. Am. Med. Dirs. Assn., Columbia. Contbr. chpt. to book. Office: AMDA 10840 Little Patuxent #760 Columbia MO 21044*

TARONJI, JAIME, JR., lawyer; b. NYC, Nov. 20, 1944; s. Jaime and Ruth T.; m. Mary Taronji, May 16, 1970; children: Ian A., Mark N., Nicole V. BA, George Washington U., 1972; JD, Georgetown U., 1976. Bar: Va. 1977, DC 1978, Ohio (corp. counsel) 1996. Asst. to dep. staff dir. U.S. Commn. on Civil Rights, Washington, 1972-76; trial atty. FTC, Washington, 1976-79; antitrust counsel Westinghouse Electric Corp., Pitts., 1979-81; group legal counsel Dana Corp., Toledo, 1982-88; v.p., gen. counsel Packaging Corp. Am. subs. Tenneco, Evanston, Ill., 1988-95; law v.p. NCR Corp., Dayton, 1996-99; v.p., gen. counsel, sec. Dayton Superior Corp., Dayton, 1999—. Adv. bd. mem. Corp. Counsel Inst., Georgetown U. Law Ctr. Author: The 1970 Census Undercount of Spanish Speaking Persons, 1974; editor: Puerto Ricans in the U.S., 1976. Capt. M.I., U.S. Army, 1965-70, Vietnam. Mem. ABA (antitrust sect.), Am. Corp. Counsel Assn., Minority Corp. Counsel Assn., Hispanic Nat. Bar Assn. Democrat. Roman Catholic. Home: 5 Grandon Rd Dayton OH 45419-2548 Office: Ste 130 7777 Washington Village Dr Dayton OH 45459-3976 E-mail: jtaronjijr@woh.rr.com.

TARPEH-DOE, LINDA DIANE, controller; b. Laramie, Wyo., Mar. 19, 1957; d. Leland Dean and Marilyn Lee (McClurg) Wheeler; m. Nyenpan Tarpeh-Doe, Jan. 16, 1982 (div. Nov. 1985); 1 child, Nyenpan Tarpeh-Doe II. BS in Acctg., U. Colo., 1979. CPA, Cert. Govt. Fin. Mgr. Asst. auditor First Bank Holding Co., Lakewood, Colo., 1979-80; internat. devel. intern USAID, Monrovia, Liberia, 1981-82, sys. acct. Washington, 1982-84, fin. analyst Kingston, Jamaica, 1984-88, macs coord. Washington, 1988-93, contr. Colombo, Sri Lanka, 1993-97, REDSO, Nairobi, Kenya, 1997-2000, USAID/Ethiopia, Addis Ababa, 2000—02, USAID, Jakarta, Indonesia, 2002—. Mem.: AICPA, Assn. Govt. Accts. Democrat. Methodist. Avocations: music, reading. Home: 3851 Paseo Del Prado Boulder CO 80301-1527 Office: Am Embassy Jakarta Unit 8135 USAID Fpo AP 96520-8135 E-mail: ltarpeh-doe@usaid.gov.

TARPGAARD, PETER THORVALD, naval architect; b. Knoxville, Tenn., Sept. 25, 1937; s. Peter Thorvald and Edith Margurite (Mees) T.; m. Judith Ann Burgess; 1 child, Andrew Christian. BS, U.S. Naval Acad.; SM mech. engr., naval engr., MIT, 1968, PhD, 1970. Spl. project asst. Office of the Chief of Naval Devel., Washington, 1970-73; profl. staff U.S. Arms Control & Disarmament Agy., Washington, 1973-76; design supr. Portsmouth Naval Shipyard, Portsmouth, N.H., 1976-79; prin. analyst Congressional Budget Office, Washington, 1979-85; mgr. submarine programs Draper Lab., Cambridge, Mass., 1985-92; prof. U.S. Naval War Coll., Newport, R.I., 1992-97; mgr. Noesis Inc., Arlington, Va., 1997—. Cons. Congressional Office of Tech. Assessment, Washington, 1991-92. Contbr. articles to profl. jours. With U.S. Navy, 1959-79. Mem. Soc. Naval Architects & Marine Engrs., Assn. for Public Policy Analysis & Mgmts., U.S. Naval Inst. Episcopalian. Home: 5 Longmeadow Ave Middletown RI 02842-5225 Office: Noesis Inc 4100 N Fairfax Dr Ste 800 Arlington VA 22203-1663 Office Phone: 401-846-2200., 703-741-0300. Personal E-mail: ptarpgaard@alum.mit.edu.

TARPLEY, JAMES DOUGLAS, journalism educator, magazine editor; b. Los Angeles, May 2, 1946; Cert. tchr., Mo. BS in Edn., S.W. Mo. U., 1968, MA in English, 1972; MA in Mass Comm., Ctrl. Mo. U., 1976; PhD in Journalism, So. Ill. U., 1983. Prof. journalism Evangel Coll., Springfield, Mo., 1976-87; chmn. Sch. of Journalism Regent U. (formerly Christian Broadcasting Network U.), Virginia Beach, Va., 1987—; dir. The Wash. Grad. Journalism Ctr. Guest lectr. Cen. Mo. U., S.W. Mo. U., So. Ill. U., U. Ohio summer journalism workshops, 1976—. Youth page editor Eldon Advertiser, 1972-76, mng. editor Home Free, 1988-90, High Adventure, 1983-87, Criminal Justice Management, 1978-81, editor Ranger News, 1979-81, design and layout editor Vision Mag., 1984-87; free-lance writer, contbr. biog. entries to profl. publs.; free-lance photographer; graphic artist, copywriter Disco-Fair advt. dept., 1964-68. Exec. com. Eldon PTA, 1971-74; youth dir. Eldon Assembly of God, 1968-75; Sunday sch. supt. Cen. Assembly of God, Springfield, Mo., 1978-82; mem. Sch. Effectiveness Evaluation Team Springfield Pub. Schs., 1985-86, 86-87. Recipient Mo. Journalism Tchr. Yr. award, 1976, Cert. of Merit Columbia U., 1984, Gold Medal of Merit Columbia U. Scholastic Press Assn., 1984, Ruritan Gov.'s award, 1997, Ruritan of Yr. award Great Bridge Ruritans, 1998, 99; named Outstanding Grad., Dept. Mass Communication Cen. Mo. U. 1976; fellow U. Pa. and Freedom Found. project on press freedom, 1984, Nat. Newspaper Fund Fellow Dow Jones and U. Mo., 1975; named fellow of Scripps-Howard CCCU Washington D.C. Capstone proj., 1995, 2002, Am. Press Inst. fellow, 1995, 2002. Mem. Assn. Christian Collegiate Media (nat. exec. dir. 1995—), Coll. Media Advisers (bd. dirs., chmn. various coms., pres. citation 1981, 84-89), Soc. Coll. Journalists (pres. 1992—, exec. dir. 1983-92, pres. citation 1981, 85, 87, 90), Assn. Christian Collegiate Media (exec. dir. 1995—), Assn. Edn. in Journalism and Mass Comm., Nat. Conf. Editl. Writers (com. scholarly rsch. 1985), Soc. Newspaper Design (edn. com. 1986-88), Broadcast Edn. Assn. (intern. com. 1984), Assn. Journalism Historials, Inst. Cert. Photographers, Mo. Tchrs. Assn., Evang. Press Assn., Ruritan Outstanding Club Pres. award Holland dist. 1999), Pi Delta Kappa. Republican. Avocations: writing, photography, painting. Office: Washington Grad Journ Ctr Regent U No Va 1650 Diagonal Rd Alexandria VA 22314 Home: 42843 Shaler St Chantilly VA 20152-3921 E-mail: Doc44685@aol.com., dougtar@regent.edu.

TARPLEY, JOHN R. lawyer; b. Lebanon, Tenn., Aug. 18, 1954; BS, U. Tenn., 1976, JD, 1980. Bar: Tenn. 1981. Law ckl. to Hon. Lewis H. Conner, Jr., Assoc. Judge, Tenn. Ct. Appeals, Mid. Divsn., 1981—82; asst. atty. gen. State of Tenn., 1982—89; atty. Lewis, King, Krieg & Waldrop, P.C., Nashville. Mem.: ABA (Young Lawyers divsn. long range planning com. 1986—89, editor Barrister 1987—89, Young Lawyers divsn. assembly clk. 1989—90, Young Lawyers exec. coun. 1989—91, standing com. on assn. comm. 1989—92, Young Lawyers divsn. assembly spkr. 1990—91, coun. mem. 1991—93, Ho. of Dels. 1997—2001, coun. mem. 1999—2002, revenue officer 1999—2002, torts and ins. practuce sect.), Nashville Bar Assn. (pres. Young Lawyers divsn. 1985, bd. dirs. Young Lawyers divsn. 1985—86, sec. 1989, bd. dirs. 1991—94, 1st v.p. 1994), Tenn. Bar Assn. (editor Young Lawyers Quar. 1984—86, bd. govs. 1984—90, moving v.p. 1986—87, pres.-elect 1987—88, bd. govs. 1987—89, pres. 1988—89, 1988—89, treas. 1997—2000, v.p. 2001—02, Young Lawyers Conf., pres.-elect 2002—03, chairperson-elect 1989—90, chairperson 1990—91, litigation coun.). Office: Lewis King Krieg and Waldrop Suntrust Bank Bldg 201 Fourth Ave N Ste 1500 Nashville TN 37219

TARPY, THOMAS MICHAEL, lawyer; b. Columbus, Ohio, Jan. 4, 1945; s. Thomas Michael and Catherine G. (Sharshal) T.; m. Mary Patricia Canna, Sept. 9, 1967; children: Joshua Michael, Megan Patricia, Thomas Canna, John Patrick. AB, John Carroll U., 1966; JD, Ohio State U., 1969. Bar: Ohio 1969, U.S. Dist. Ct. (so. dist.) Ohio 1972, U.S. Dist. Ct. (no. dist.) Ohio 1974, U.S. Ct. Appeals (6th cir.) 1982, U.S. Supreme Ct. 1997. Assoc. Vorys, Sater, Seymour & Pease LLP, Columbus, 1969-76, ptnr., 1977-85, 87—; v.p. Liebert Corp., Columbus, 1985-87. Chmn. Columbus Graphics Commn., 1980; mem. Columbus Area Leadership Program, 1975. With U.S. Army, 1969-75. Fellow Coll. Labor and Employment Lawyers; mem. ABA, Ohio Bar Assn., Columbus Bar Assn. Office: Vorys Sater Seymour & Pease LLP PO Box 1008 52 E Gay St Columbus OH 43215-3161 E-mail: tmtarpy@vssp.com.

TARR, CURTIS W. business executive; b. Stockton, Calif., Sept. 18, 1924; s. F.W. and Esther (Reed) T.; m. Elizabeth May Myers, 1955 (div. 1978); children: Pamela Elizabeth, Cynthia Leigh; m. Marilyn Van Stralen, 1979 (div. 1991); m. Mary Katherine Stegmiller, 1992. BA, Stanford U., 1948, PhD, 1962; MBA, Harvard U., 1950; L.H.D., Ripon Coll., 1965, Grinnell Coll., 1969, Lincoln Coll., 1980; LL.D., Lawrence U., 1974, Ill. Wesleyan U., 1980. Rsch. asst., instr. Harvard U., 1950-52; v.p. Sierra Tractor & Equipment Co., Chico, Calif., 1952-58; staff mem. 2d Hoover Commn., 1954-55; asst. dir. summer session Stanford U., 1961-62, dir., 1962-63, asst. dean humanities and scis., 1962-63, lectr. bus. sch., 1962-63; pres. Lawrence U., Appleton, Wis., 1963-69; asst. sec. for manpower and res. affairs Air Force, 1969-70; dir. SSS, Washington, 1970-72; under sec. state for security assistance, 1972-73; acting dep. under sec. state for mgmt., 1973; from v.p. overseas devel. to v.p. mgmt. devel. Deere & Co., Moline, Ill., 1973—83; dean, prof. Johnson Sch. Mgmt., Cornell U., 1984—89, prof. mgmt., 1989-90, dean emeritus, 1990—; vice chmn. Intermet Corp., 1992-95. Bd. dirs. Phyton Corp., Ithaca, N.Y., 1985-2002, State Farm Ins. Companies, 1985-98, Banta Corp, 1976-95, Intermet Corp., 1984-98; mem. Internat. Rsch. Coun. Ctr. for Strategic and Internat. Studies, Washington, 1989-92; adj. prof. mgmt. Emory U., 1991-93. Author: Private Soldier, 1976, By the Numbers, 1981, Youth, 1994. Trustee Inst. Paper Chemistry, 1963-69, Morehouse Sch. Medicine, Atlanta, 1994—2004; chmn. Task Force on Govt. Orgn., Fin. and Tax Distbn. for State Wis., 1967-69; chmn. Def. Manpower Commn., 1974-76, Ill. State Scholarship Commn., 1978-79, Quad Cities Grad. Study Ctr., 1982-84, Rep. candidate for Congress 2d Dist., Calif., 1958; trustee Am. Coll., Bryn Mawr, Pa., 1989-92; dir. Bethesda Home, Savannah, Ga., The Mighty 8th Air Force Mus., Savannah. With AUS, 1943-46, ETO. Recipient Exceptional Civilian Service medal Air Force Dept., 1970; Distinguished Service award SSS, 1975 Mem. Univ. Club (Chgo.), Cosmos Club (Washington). Methodist.

TARR, GREGORY L. health and medical products company executive; With Alpha Beta Co., McKesson Corp., 1986-99, v.p., mgr. distbn. ctr., v.p. sales and ops. Everett, until 1997, sr. v.p. customer ops. group western region, 1997—; pres., CEO, URM Stores, Inc., Spokane, Wash., 1999—. Office: URM Stores Inc 7511 N Freya St Spokane WA 99217-8043

TARR, JOEL ARTHUR, history and public policy educator; b. Jersey City, May 8, 1934; s. Max Alfred and Florence (Levin) Tartalsky; m. Arlene Green, Sept. 2, 1956 (dec. June 1969); children: Michael Jay, Joanna Sue; m. Tova Brafman, Aug. 11, 1978; children: Maya Leah, Ilana Ariel. BS, Rutgers U., 1956, MA, 1957; PhD, Northwestern U., 1963. Asst. prof. Calif. State U., Long Beach, 1961-66; vis. prof. U. Calif., Santa Barbara, 1966-67; asst. prof. Carnegie Mellon U., Pitts., 1967-70, assoc. prof., 1969-72, prof. history and pub. policy, 1973-90, Richard S. Caliguiri prof. urban and environ. history and policy, 1990—, dir. program in tech. and soc., 1975-87, co-dir. program in applied history and social sci., 1978-86, acting dean Sch. Urban and Pub. Affairs, 1986, assoc. dean Coll. Humanities and Social Sci., 1988-91, acting dean Coll. Humanities and Social Sci., 1991-92, acting head dept. history, 1992-93, Univ. prof., 2004—. Author: A Study in Boss Politics, 1971; editor: Patterns of City Growth, 1974, Retrospective Technology Assessment, 1977, Transportation Innovation and Spatial Change in Pittsburgh, 1850-1934, 1978, Pittsburgh-Sheffield: Sister Cities, 1986, Technology and the Rise of the Networked City in Europe and America, 1988, The Search for the Ultimate Sink: Urban Pollution in Historic Perspective, 1996, Devastation and Renewal: An Environmental History of Pittsburgh and Its Region, 2003. Bd. dirs. Action Housing, Pitts., 1983; trustee Hist. Soc. Western Pa., 1993-2000. NEH fellow, 1969-70; grantee NSF, 1975-79, 78-80, 83-85, 95-98, NOAA, 1982-84; recipient Robert Doherty Prize for contbns. to excellence in edn., 1992, Choice Outstanding Acad. Book award, 1997. Mem. AAAS, Pub. Works Hist. Soc. (pres. 1982-83, Abel Wolman prize 1989), Orgn. Am. Historians, Pub. History Assn., Am. Soc. Environ. History, Soc. for the History of Tech., Urban History Assn. (pres. 1999). Democrat. Jewish. Home: 5418 Normlee Pl Pittsburgh PA 15217-1116 Office: Carnegie-Mellon U Schenley Pk Pittsburgh PA 15213 Office Phone: 412-268-2609. E-mail: jt03@andrew.cmu.edu.

TARR, RALPH WILLIAM, lawyer, former federal government official; b. Bakersfield, Calif., Sept. 29, 1948; BA, Dartmouth Coll., 1970; MPA, Calif. State U., 1973; JD, U. Calif., Hastings, 1976. Extern to assoc. justice Calif. Supreme Ct., 1976; rsch. atty. to presiding justice Ct. Appeal (5th dist.) Calif., 1976-77; assoc. Baker, Manock & Jensen, Fresno, Calif., 1977-81, dir., mem. exec. com., 1981-82; mem. adminstrv. com. Fed. Register, Washington, 1982-85; dep. asst. atty. gen. U.S. Dept. Justice, Washington, 1982-84, acting asst. atty. gen., 1984-85; solicitor U.S. Dept. Interior, Washington, 1985-89, counselor, 1989-90; pvt. practice L.A., 1990—. Home: 24011 Alder Pl Calabasas CA 91302-2394 Office: Andrews & Kurth LLP 601 S Figueroa St Ste 1725 Los Angeles CA 90017-5747 E-mail: rtarr@andrewskurth.com.

TARR, ROBERT JOSEPH, JR., publishing executive, retail executive; b. Freeport, NY, Dec. 7, 1943; s. Robert Joseph and Janet Christman (Laughton) T.; m. Molly Worthington Upton, Feb. 28, 1970; children: William Upton, Robert Joseph, III, David Worthington. BS, U.S. Naval Acad., 1966; MBA, Harvard U., 1973; MA, Fletcher Sch. Law & Diplomacy, 1976. Asst. v.p. corp. fin. Paine Webber Jackson Curtis, Boston, 1973-75; dir. corp. planning, then v.p., treas. Gen. Cinema Corp., Chestnut Hill, Mass., 1976-78, sr. v.p., 1978-83, exec. v.p., COO, 1983-85, pres., COO, 1985-91; pres., CEO, COO Harcourt Gen., Inc. (Gen. Cinema Corp., 1993), Chestnut Hill, Mass., 1991-97; pres., spl. ptnr. Chartwell Investments, NYC, 2002—. Pres., CEO, COO The Neiman Marcus Group, Inc., 1987—91, pres., bd. dirs., CEO, COO, 1991—97; bd. dirs. John Hancock Fin. Svcs., Inc., Barneys, NY, WESCO Intenrat., Inc.; chmn., pres., CEO HomeRuns.com, Inc., 1999—2001. Lt. USN, 1966-71. Mem. Kiawah Island Club., Wianno Yacht Club, The Oyster Harbors Club, Briar's Creek Club. Home: 3 Commonwealth Ave Unit 2 Boston MA 02116- Office: Chartwell Investments LLC 717 Fifth Ave Fl 23 New York NY 10022

TARRANCE, VERNON LANCE, JR., public opinion research executive; b. Harlingen, Tex., Dec. 4, 1940; s. Vernon Lance Sr. and Mary Gilmore (Rea) T.; m. Eugenia Aline McCuistion, July 2, 1966; children: Vernon Lance III, Haloway McCuistion, Kyle Rea. BA, Washington & Lee U., 1962; postgrad., U. Mich., 1971; MA, Am. U., 1973; postgrad., Harvard U., 1973-74. Dir. rsch. Tex. Rep. Com., Austin, 1964-67, Rep. Nat. Com., Washington, 1969-70; spl. asst. to dir. U.S. Census Bur., Washington, 1970-73; v.p. Decision Making Info. Inc., Santa Ana, Calif., 1974-77; pres., founder Tarrance, Hill, Newport & Ryan, Houston, 1977-92; pres., mng. dir. Gallup China Ltd., Beijing, 1993-95; vis. prof. polit. sci. Tex. A&M U., College Station, 1995-96; scholar in residence Washington and Lee U., Va., 1996; mng. dir. Burson-Marsteller, Washington, 1997-99. Bd. dirs. Gallup Orgn., 1987-92; cons. Gallup Internat. Rsch. Ctr., Lincoln, Nebr.; co-chmn. adv. adjustment panel U.S. Census, 1990. Co-author: The Ticket Splitter, 1972, Checked and Balanced, 1998; editor: Texas Precinct Votes '66, '68, '70. Fellow John F. Kennedy Inst. Politics Harvard U., 1973-74; named one of 150 People Who Influence Fed. Govt. Nat. Jour. Mag., 1986. Mem.: Raleigh Tavern Philos. Soc. (founder), Am. Polit. Sci. Assn., Kappa Sigma. Avocations: mountain trekking, golf, aviculture, travel.

TARRANT, R(ICHARD) J(OHN), classicist, educator; b. Bklyn., Apr. 4, 1945; s. John Joseph and Bertha (Slaney) T.; m. Jacqueline Brown, Sept. 14, 1968. BA, Fordham U., 1966; DPhil, Oxford U., 1972; AM (hon.), Harvard U., 1982. P.S. Allen jr. research fellow Corpus Christi Coll., Oxford, Eng., 1968-70; lectr. Univ. Coll., Toronto, Ont., Can., 1970-71, asst. prof., 1971-74, assoc. prof., 1974-79; prof. U. Toronto, 1979-82; prof. Greek and Latin Harvard U., Cambridge, Mass., 1982-87, Carl A. Pescosolido prof. Roman civilization, 1987-93, Pope prof. Latin language and Literature, 1993—, Harvard Coll. prof., 1999—2004, chmn. dept., 1988-94, acting dean Grad. Sch. Arts and Scis., 1995-96. Vis. Mellon prof. Inst. for Advanced Study, Princeton, 1991-92; vis. fellow Corpus Christi Coll. U. Oxford, 1992. Author: Greek and Latin Lyric Poetry in Translation: A Bibliographical Survey, 1972, Seneca, Agamemnon, 1976, (with others) Texts and Transmission: A Survey of the Latin Classics, 1983, Seneca's Thyestes, 1985, Ovid's Metamorphoses, 2004; editor Phoenix: Jour. Classical Assn. Can., 1978-82, Harvard Studies in Classical Philology, 1985-88, 93-94; editorial bd. Toronto Medieval Latin Texts, 1977—, Cambridge Classical Texts and Commentaries, 1992—; advisory bd. Text: Transactions of the Soc. for Textual Scholarship, 1994—, Materiali e discussioni comitato scientifico, 2002--; contbr. articles to profl. jours. Cabot fellow, 1993-94; Marshall scholar, 1966-69. Mem. Am. Philol. Assn. (bd. dirs. 1987-89, v.p. publs. 1992-95), Cambridge Philol. Assn., Classical Assn. Can., Classical Assn. New Eng., Phi Beta Kappa. Office: Harvard U Dept Classics Boylston Hall 204 Cambridge MA 02138 Office Phone: 617-496-3611. Business E-Mail: tarrant@fas.harvard.edu.

TARRANTS, WILLIAM EUGENE, federal official; b. Liberty, Mo., Dec. 9, 1927; s. Joseph Eugene and Mildred Jane (Wright) Tarrants; m. Mary Jo Edman, Jan. 19, 1952 (div. 1981); children: James Timothy, Jennifer Lynn; m. Loma D. Lundberg, Sept. 24, 1988; stepchildren: David Murphy, Christine Walls, Janelle McCrea. B in Indsl. Engring., Ohio State U., 1951; MS in Indsl. Engring., 1959; PhD, NYU, 1963. Instr. indsl. engring. Ohio State U., Columbus, 1958-59; asst. prof., research asso. N.Y. U., 1959-64; chief accident research div. Bur. Labor Stats., Dept. Labor, Washington, 1964-67; dir. manpower devel. div. Nat. Hwy. Traffic Safety Adminstrn., Dept. Transp., 1967-80; chief scientist Office of Program and Demonstration Evaluation, 1980-84; program analyst Office of Occupant Protection, 1984-87, program analyst evaluation staff, 1987-90, also chmn. sci. and tech. info. adv. bd., 1984-91. Cons. safety program evaluation Indsl. Commn. Ohio, 1959; instr. Johns Hopkins U., 1984—91, U. Md., 1991—92; planning and adminstrn. transp. safety mem. Transp. Rsch. Bd., NAS; mem. exec. com. Related Accreditation Commn., 1994—; accreditation bd. Engring. and Tech., Inc., 1994—. Co-author: A Selected Bibliography of Reference Materials in Safety Engineering and Related Fields, 1967, Selected Readings in Safety, 1973, Readings in Industrial Accident Prevention, 1980, Dictionary of Terms Used in the Safety Profession, 1971, Measurement of Safety Performance, 1980, Handbook of Occupational Safety and Health, 1987; contbr. articles to profl. jours.; mem. editl. bd. Jour. Safety Rsch., Accident Analysis and Prevention; editor-in-chief: Traffic Safety Evaluation Rsch. Rev. Region 8 rep. to bd. trustees E. Coast Conf., 1986—92; trustee, ch. chmn. Evang. Covent Ch., 1976—80, 1984—88. Capt. USAF, 1951—57. Named to Safety and Health Hall of Fame Internat., 1990; recipient Founder's Day award, NYU, 1963, 1st pl., Nat. Tech. Paper Awards, 1961, 1963, 1967, cert. for outstanding performance, Nat. Hwy. Traffic Safety Adminstrn., 1973, 1986, Disting. Svc. to Safety award, Nat. Safety Coun., 1989, Disting. Career Svc. award, U.S. Dept. or Transp., 1990. Fellow: Am. Soc. Safety Engrs. (dir., v.p. rsch. and tech. devel., pres. 1977—78, chmn. acad. accreditation coun. 1978—97, chmn. profl. and ednl. stds. com. 1997—, fellow rev. bd. 1980—88, Pres.'s award 1996); mem.: AAAS, Nat. Safety Coun. (chmn. rsch. proejcts com. 1973—78, mem. exec. com. indsl. conf. 1977—78, Disting. Svc. award 1989), Soc. Risk Analysis, Am. Nat. Stds. Inst. (mem. stds. com.), Vets. Safety, Evaluation Rsch. Soc., Sys. Safety Soc., Human Factors Soc., Am. Inst. Indsl. Engrs., Am. Soc. Safety Rsch. (trsutee), Kappa Delta Pi, Alpha Pi Mu. Home: 606 Woodsmans Way Crownsville MD 21032-2317 Office: 400 7th St SW Washington DC 20590-0001 *We often look with awe at the successful person, much as we admire a well designed structure or a beautiful painting. Behind the finished product usually lies exhaustive effort, frustration, disappointment, and even failure which is obscured by the glow of accomplishment. Success is achieved by some ability, lots of hard work, perserverance, courage of convictions, help and support from others, a desire to reach a goal, self-discipline, and considerable personal sacrifice as we make choices concerning the use of our limited resources. The ability to bounce back from adversity is crucial. Most important of all is the strength and insight gained through prayer and the willingness to permit your life to be guided by Christian faith.*

TARRO, GIULIO, virologist; b. Messina, Italy, July 9, 1938; s. Emanuele and Emanuela (Iannello) Tarro. MD, U. Naples, 1962, postgrad. in Nervous Diseases, 1968, PhD in Virology, 1971; postgrad. in Med. and Biol. Scis., Roman Acad., 1979; hon. degree in Medicine, U. Pro Deo, Albany, N.Y., 1989; hon. degree in immunology, St. Theodora Acad., N.Y., 1991; hon. degree in bioethics, Constantinian U., Cranston, R.I., 1996. Asst. in med. pathology Naples U., Italy, 1964-66; rsch. assoc. divsn. virology and cancer rsch. Children's Hosp., Cin., 1965-68; asst. prof. rsch. pediat. U. Cin. Coll. Medicine, 1968-69; rsch. fellow Nat. Rsch. Coun., Naples, 1966-74, rsch. chief, 1974; prof. oncologic virology Coll. Medicine U. Naples, 1971-85, prof. microbiology and immunology Sch. Specialization, 1972—; chief divsn. virology D. Cotugno Hosp. for Infectious Diseases, Naples, 1973—, pres. ethic com., 1998—, head dept. diagnostic labs., 2003—; dean faculty natural and phys. scis. Nobile Accademia di Santa Teodora Imperatrice, Capua, Italy, 1993—; head dept. medicine Naples People U., 2000—. Sr. scientist Nat. Cancer Inst. Frederick (Md.) Ctr., 1973; project dir. Nat. Cancer Inst., Bethesda, Md., 1971-75; edn. min. rep. Zool. Sta., Naples, 1975-79; cons. Italian Pharmacotherapic Inst., Rome, 1980-98; mem. nat. com. on bioethics, 1995-98; pres. De Beaumont Bonelli Found. for Cancer Rsch., Naples, 1978—, ethic com. D. Cotugno Hosp. for Infectious Diseases, 1998-, European Group Econ. Interest, Rsch. and Devel., Naples, 2003-, Campania Tech. and Ecology Ctr., 2004—; sci. coord. extracorporeal hyperthermia in HCV patients First Circle Med., Mpls., 2000—; sci. adv. bd. Unihart Biotech Pharm., London, 2003-. Author: Virologia Oncologica, 1979, Patologia dell'AIDS, 1991, Con il Cancro si PuÒ Vivere, 1992, AIDS Cosa Possiamo Fare Cosa Dobbiamo Sapere, 1994, Pocket File Research Collection, 1997, 6th edit., 2003, To Prevent Is To Win, 1998, Bioethics and Culture of Prevention, 2001; editor-in-chief: Internat. Jour. Clin. Investigation, 2000—; contbr. over 360 articles to profl. jours. Pres. Sci. Cultural Com., Torre Annunziata, Italy, 1984, Tumor Prevention Assn., Rome, 1984; mem. acad. senate Constantinian U., Providence, 1990, U. Pro Deo, NY, 1994; hon. acad. U. Sancti Cyrilli, Valletta, Malta, 2001; mem. UNESCO-Hebrew U. Jerusalem Internat. Sch. Molecular Biology and Microbiology; hon. rector Ruggero II U., Fla., 2003. Maj. Italian Navy, 1982-84, lt. col., 1993-95. Decorated comdr. Nat. Order of Merit, Star of Europe, knight grand cross Sovereign Constantinian Order St. George, gt. officer Italian Republic; recipient Internat. Lenghi award Lincei Acad., 1969, Gold Microscope award Italian Health Min., 1973, Knights of Humanity award Internat. Register of Chivalry, Malta, 1978, gold medal of Culture, Pres. of Italian Republic, 1975, Culture award, 1985, 1st prize in Biomed. Rsch., Italian Acad. Arts and Scis., 1987, Castello di Pietrarossa award, Italy, 1991, gold Cesare award Padova, 1991, 20th Century award in Medicine, 1994, Gold Little Horse, Transnat. European Fedn., Rome 1996, Man of Yr. award Am. Biog. Inst., 1998, 2000, King Manfredi award Manfredonia, 1999, Equestris Ordinis S. Sepulcri of Jerusalem, Rome, 1999, Gold medal of Health Pres. of Italian Republic, 1999, Saint Catherin award, Siena, 2003. Fellow: AAAS; mem.: European Soc. Clin. Virology, Internat.

Sch. for Molecular Biology and Microbiology, N.Y. Acad. Scis., Nat. Order Journalists, AIDS Soc. Asia and the Pacific, Assn. Res. Prevention of Cancer (sci. com. 1995), Italian Assn. Viral Study and Rsch. (pres. 1995—), Italian Soc. Immuno-Oncology (v.p. 1975—, pres. 1990—), Internat. League Drs. for Abolition of Vivisection (pres. 1992—), Internat. Assn. Leukemias, Am. Assn. Cancer Rsch., Am. Soc. Microbiology, Rotary, Lions (pres. Pompei chpt. 1987—89, vice gov. dist. 1991—92, pres. com. fight cancer 1992—94, pres. com. sci. and life 1994—95, pres. com. fight drug addiction and AIDS 1995—97, pres. com. transplant and donations 1998—99, pres. com. oncology 2000—02, pres. com.on stem cells 2002—, dist. dir. operative area health and rsch. 2003, pres. Pompei chpt. 2004—05, Melvin Jones fellow 1993). Roman Catholic. Achievements include patents in field; discovery of RSV virus in infant deaths in Naples and of tumor liberated protein as a tumor associated antigen, 100 kilodalton protein overexpressed in lung tumors and other epithelial adenocarcinomas. Home: 286 Posillipo 80123 Naples Italy Office: A O D Cotugno Hosp 54 Quagliariello 80131 Naples Italy Office Phone: +39 081 5463222. E-mail: gitarro@tin.it.

TARR-WHELAN, LINDA, policy center executive; b. Springfield, Mass., May 24, 1940; d. Albert and Jane Zack; m. Keith Tarr-Whelan; children: Scott, Melinda. BSN, Johns Hopkins U., 1963; MS, U. Md., 1967. Program dir. AFSCME AFL-CIO, Washington, 1968-74, union area dir., 1974-76; adminstr. dir. N.Y. State Labor Dept., Albany, N.Y., 1976-79; dep. asst. to pres. Carter White House, Washington, 1979-80; dir. govt. rels. NEA, Washington, 1980-86; CEO, pres. Ctr. for Policy Alternatives, Washington, 1986—, bd. dirs., 1985—. Apptd. U.S. rep. UN Commn. on Status of Women, 1996—. Bd. dirs. Benton Found., Adv. Inst., Ind. Sector; pres. State Issues Forum; mem. Freddie Mac Affordable Housing Adv. Bd. Recipient Disting. Grad. award Johns Hopkins U., 1981, Breaking the Glass Ceiling award, 1996; leadership fellow Japan Soc., 1987-88. Democrat. Avocations: walking, travel. Home: 3466 Roberts Ln Arlington VA 22207-5335

TARSES, JAMIE, television producer, former television network executive; b. Pitts., Pa., 1964; s. Jay and Rachel Tarses; m. Dan McDermott (div.). BA in Theater, Williams Coll., 1985. Casting dir. Lorimar Prodns.; mgr. creative affairs NBC, 1987, mgr. current comedy programs, 1987-88, mgr. comedy devel., 1988-89, dir. comedy devel., 1989-94, supr. programming team, 1994-95, sr. v.p. primetime series, 1995-96; pres. ABC Entertainment, 1996—99; founder, owner Untitled Burke-Tarses Project, 2003—. Consulting prodr. (TV films) Imagine That, 2002; exec. prodr.: (TV films) Crazy Love, 2003.*

TARTAGLIA, RICHARD V. priest; b. White Plains, N.Y., Nov. 6, 1946; s. Valentine Tartaglia and Louise M. DiPopolo. BA, St. Mary's Coll., St. Mary, Ky., 1968; MDiv, Mt. St. Mary's Seminary, Emmitsburg, Md., 1972. Ordained priest St. John the Bapt. Cathedral, 1972. Deacon St. Clement Ch., Dover, NJ, 1971—72; assoc. pastor St. Andrew Ch., Clifton, NJ, 1972—73, Holy Family Ch., Forham Park, NJ, 1973—74, St. Mary Ch., Denville, NJ, 1974—. Advisor Juvenile Conf. Com., Denville, 1977—87. Mem.: KC (chaplain 1975—). Roman Catholic. Avocations: photography, tennis, baseball, electronics, military history. Home: 15 Myers Ave Denville NJ 07834 Office: St Marys Ch 15 Myers Ave Denville NJ 07834

TARTAGLIONE, CHRISTINE M. state legislator; b. Phila., Sept. 21, 1960; Grad., Pierce Coll., 1980. Legal asst. to City Councilwoman Joan Krajewski, 1986—89; sr. exec. asst. to state treas., 1989—92; bus. rep. United Food and Comml. Workers Union, Phila., 1992—94; mem. from Dist. 2 Pa. Senate, Harrisburg, 1994—, Dem. chair labor and industry com. Democrat. Office: State Legislature Rm 458 Main Capitol Bldg Harrisburg PA 17120 also: 1061 Bridge St Philadelphia PA 19124-1824

TARTAKOVSKY, ALEXANDER G. mathematician, educator; b. Moscow, Nov. 19, 1955; s. Georgiy P and Elena F Tartakovsky; m. Marina Blanco, Aug. 4, 1993; children: Kirill A, Alejo Blanco, Daniel. PhD, Moscow Inst. Physics and Tech., 1981, Dr. Scis. (hon.), 1990. Sr. scientist Inst. Radio Tech., Moscow, 1982—89; dept. head Inst. Radio Tech., Moscow, 1990—94; adj. prof./rsch. scientist USC Dept. Math., Los Angeles, 1997—. Assoc. dir. Ctr. for Applied Math. Scis., USC, Los Angeles, 1997—. Mem.: SPIE, Info. Fusion Soc., IMS, IEEE. Achievements include research in Sequential Hypothesis tests and change-point detection. Office: Univ Southern Calif 3620 S Vermont Ave KAP-108 Los Angeles CA 90089-2532 Personal E-mail: tartakov@math.usc.edu. E-mail: tartakov@math.usc.edu.

TARTARO, CHRISTINE, criminologist, educator; d. Angelo Anthony and Sylvia Maria Tartaro. BS, Trenton State Coll., New Jersey, 1996; MS, Rutgers U., N.J., 2000; PhD, Rutgers U., New Jersey, 2000. Rsch. scientist NJ. Dept. Corrections, Trenton, 1999—2000; asst. prof. of criminal justice Richard Stockton Coll. of NJ., Pomona, 2000—. Rsch. cons. Juvenile Justice Commn., Jamesburg, NJ, 2002—. Contbr. articles to profl. jours. Mem.: NJ. Am. Correctional Assn., Am. Jail Assn., Am. Correctional Assn., Acad. of Criminal Justice Sciences, Am. Soc. of Criminology.

TARTER, CURTIS BRUCE, physicist, science administrator; b. Louisville, Sept. 26, 1939; s. Curtis B. and Marian Turner (Cundiff) T.; divorced; 1 child, Shana Lee; m. Gabriela Odell, 2003. BS, MIT, 1961; PhD, Cornell U., 1967. Tchg. asst. Cornell U., Ithaca, NY, 1961—63, rsch. asst., 1964—67; physicist, summers Lawrence Radiation Lab., Livermore, Calif., 1962—63; staff mem. theoretical physics divsn. U. Calif., Lawrence Livermore Nat. Lab., 1967—69, group leader macroscopic properties of matter, 1969—71, assoc. divsn. leader, 1971—74, group leader opacities, 1972—78, divsn. leader, 1974—84; dep. assoc. dir. for physics Lawrence Livermore Nat. Lab., 1984—88, assoc. dir. for physics, 1988—94, dep. dir., 1994, dir., 1994—2002, assoc. dir. at large, 2002—04, dir. emeritus, 2004—. Sr. scientist Applied Rsch. Labs. Aeronutronic divsn. Philco-Ford Corp.; cons. Hertz Found., field com. study on astronomy in the 80's, NRC, 1980; mem. Army Sci. Bd., Washington, 1989-96; adj. prof. dept. applied sci., U. Calif., Davis, 1999-; mem. Calif. Coun. on Sci. and Tech., 1996-2002, Pacific Coun. on Internat. Policy, 1998—, lab. opers. bd. DOE, 1998-2002, Nuc. Energy Rsch. Adv. Bd., 1999-2002, Coun. Fgn. Rels., 1999—; bd. dirs. Draper Lab. Contbr. numerous articles to profl. jours. Recipient Roosevelts Gold Medal award for sci., NNSA Gold medal for disting. svc., U.S. Dept. Energy Exceptional Pub. Svc. award. Fellow AAAS, Calif. Coun. Sci. and Tech., Am. Phys. Soc. (phys. policy com. 2002—); mem. Am. Astron. Soc., Internat. Astron. Union. Republican. Avocations: golf, running, music. Office: Lawrence Livermore Nat Lab PO Box 808 Livermore CA 94551-0808 Office Phone: 925-422-4169. E-mail: tarter1@llnl.gov.

TARTER, FRED BARRY, advertising executive; b. Bklyn, Aug. 16, 1943; s. Irving and Edna (Kupferberg) T.; m. Lois; children: Scott Andrew, Heather Michelle, Megan Elizabeth. BS, CCNY, 1966. Pres. Jamie Publ. Hootenanny Enterprises, Inc., 1962-65; mdse. dir. Longines Symphonette Soc., 1965-67; with Universal Comm., Inc., NYC, 1967—, pres., CEO, 1969-74; exec. v.p. Deerfield Comm., Inc., NYC, 1974-87, pres., CEO, 1977-88; pres. Deerfield Books, Inc., NYC, 1988-89; pub. S.E.W. mag., NYC, 1977-88; pres. The Rainbow Group Ltd., NYC, 1988—; chmn. Stagebill Mag., 1997-2001; pres., CEO The Lakeside Group of Co., 2001—. Bd. dirs. Caribbean Internat. News Corp., Lakeside Group, Inc., Boardwalk Entertainment, Ltd.; chmn. Stagebill Enterprises, LLC, 1997—2001; vice chmn. Affinity Comm., Inc., 1997—2001; pres., CEO The Telephone Co. LLC, 1999—2003; CEO Affinity Settlements, LLC, Epic Assocs., LLC; exec. prodr. Joanne Carson's VIP's Miss Am. Teenager Pageant, 1972—73; pres. The Programme Exch., U.K. Ltd.; prodr. Spenser Judas Goat, 1995, Ceremony, 1996, Wounded Heart, 1996, Lover's Leap, 1996, Hearts Adrift, 1995, Marriage Counselor, 1994, Spenser: Pale Kings & Princes, 1995, Spenser: A Savage Place, 1995, Reasons of the Heart, 1996. Home: 578 Westport Tpke Fairfield CT 06430-1670 Office: The Lakeside Group Ltd 210 E 39th St New York NY 10016-2754 Office Phone: 212-679-3800. E-mail: ftarter@lakesideglobal.com. *An integral part of success is the capacity for failure. Persistence, combined with responsibility, has proven to be the winning combination time and again.*

TARTER, JILL CORNELL, science foundation director, astronomer, researcher; BEP, Cornell U. Sch. of Engring., 1966; attended, Cornell U. Grad. Sch. Theoretical Physics, 1965—67; MA in Astronomy, U. Calif., Berkeley, 1971, PhD in Astronomy, 1975. Teaching & rsch. asst. U. Calif., Berkeley, Calif., 1965—75; NRC resident rsch. assoc. postdoctoral fellow NASA Ames Rsch. Ctr., Moffett Field, Calif., 1975—77; asst. rsch. astronomer II-IV U. Calif. Space Sciences Lab, Berkeley, Calif., 1977—83, assoc. rsch. astronomer I, 1983—85; assoc. rsch. astronomer dept. of astronomony U. Calif., Berkeley, Calif., 1983—93; co-founder SETI Inst., Mountain View, Calif., 1984—, principal investigator, 1984—89, project scientist NASA SETI Microwave Observing Project & High Resolution Microwave Survey, 1989—93, dir. Project Phoenix, 1993—99, Bernard M. Oliver chair, 1997—; dir. SETI Research, Mountain View, Calif., 1999—2000, Ctr. for SETI Research, Mountain View, Calif., 2000—. Chair Internat. Acad. of Astronautics SETI Com., 1997—, Internat. Square Kilometer Arry Steering Com., 2002—; adv. bd. mem. Odyssey Mag., 1997—, Space.com, 2000—. Recipient Public Service medals, NASA, 1993, HRMS Group Achievement award, 1993, Chabot Observatory Person of Yr. award, 1997, Women's Fund Women of Achievement award, San Jose Mercury News, 1998. Fellow: Com. for Scientific Investigation of Claims of the Paranormal, Calif. Acad. Sci., Explorer's Club; mem.: AAAS (fellow 2002), World Tech. Network, Women in Aerospace (Lifetime Achievement award 1989), Internat. Soc. for Study of Origin of Life, Internat. Acad. of Astronautics, Internat. Radio Sci. Union (URSI Commn.), Internat. Astronomical Union, Am. Astronomical Soc. Office: SETI Inst 2035 Landings Dr Mountain View CA 94043*

TARTT, BLAKE, lawyer; b. Houston, Mar. 16, 1929; s. Herbert Blake and Bernice (Schwalm) T.; m. Barbara Jean Moore, Jan. 30, 1960; children: Blake III, Courtnay Elias. BBA, So. Methodist U., 1949, JD cum laude, 1959. Bar: Tex. 1959. Assoc. Fulbright & Jaworski, Houston, 1959-70, ptnr., 1970-2000, Beirne, Maynard & Parsons, LLP, Houston, 2000—. Mem. Tex. Commn. on Jud. Conduct, 1996-2001. Bd. dirs. Mus. Fine Arts, Houston. Served to 1st lt. USAF, 1951-55, Korea. Decorated Air medal. Fellow Am. Bar Found. (chmn. fellows 1987, life), Tex. Bar Found. (chmn. bd. 1974-75, chmn. fellows 1978-79, life), Am. Coll. Trial Lawyers; mem. ABA (ho. of dels. 1976-99, state del. 1990-99, standing com. fed. jud. 1996-99, chair 1997, bd. govs. 2001—), Am. Bd. Trial Advocates (advocate), Houston Bar Found. (life., chmn., bd. dirs. 1992), Fed. Bar Assn., Internat. Assn. Def. Counsel, Am. Judicature Soc. (bd. dirs. 1984-88), So. Conf. Bar Pres. (pres. 1984), State Bar Tex. (dir. 1972-75, exec. com. 1975-76, pres. elect 1982-83, pres. 1983-84), Houston Bar Assn., Dallas Bar Assn., Am. Law Inst., Tex. Jud. Council, Citizens Commn. on the Tex. Judiciary, Houston Philosophical Soc., Coronado Club, Forest Club, Argyle Club (San Antonio), Reform Club (London), Delta Theta Phi, Alpha Tau Omega. Episcopalian. Office: Beirne Maynard & Parsons 1300 Post Oak Blvd Houston TX 77056-3028 Office Phone: 713-960-7331.

TARUN, ROBERT WALTER, lawyer; b. Lake Forest, Ill., Sept. 1, 1949; s. Donald Walter and Bonnie Jean (Cruickshank) T.; m. Helen J. McSweeney, May 1, 1987; children: Abigail Esch, Tyler Vincent, Parker Donald, Aimée Dakota. AB, Stanford U., 1971; JD, DePaul U., 1974; MBA, U. Chgo., 1982. Bar: Ill. 1974, Calif. 1975, U.S. Dist. Ct. (no. dist.) Ill. 1974, U.S. Dist. Ct. (we. dist.) Ark. 1986, U.S. Dist. Ct. (so. dist.) Ind. 1995, U.S. Dist. Ct. (no. dist.) Calif. 1995, U.S. Dist. Ct. (ea. dist.) Mich. 1996, U.S. Dist. Ct. (ea. dist.) Wis. 2000, U.S. Dist. Ct. (ctrl. dist.) Ill. 2001, U.S. Ct. Appeals (7th cir.) 1975, U.S. Ct. Appeals (5th cir.) 1992, U.S. Ct. Appeals (3d cir.) 1993, U.S. Ct. Appeals (Fed. cir.) 1995, U.S. Ct. Appeals (9th and 11th cirs.) 1996, U.S. Supreme Ct. 1978. Asst. atty. gen. State of Ill., Chgo., 1974-76; asst. U.S. atty. U.S. Dept. Justice, Chgo., 1976-79, dep. chief criminal div., 1979-82, exec. asst. U.S. atty. no. dist. Ill., 1982-85; ptnr. Reuben & Proctor, Chgo., 1985-86, Isham, Lincoln & Beale, Chgo., 1986-88, Winston & Strawn, Chgo., 1988—2003, Latham & Watkins LLP, Chgo., 2003—. Lectr. in law white collar criminal and bus. litig. U. Chgo. Law Sch., 2001—; adj. prof. Northwestern U. Sch. Law, 1999—2001; instr. Atty. Gen.'s Advocacy Inst., Washington, 1980—85, Nat. Inst. Trial Advs., 1990. Author (with Dan K. Webb): Corporate Internal Investigations, 1993—2003. Bd. dirs. Chgo. Ctrl. Area Com., 1994—. Named one of Best Lawyers in Am., Euroguide's Guide to World's Leading Litigators, Chambers USA Leading Bus. Lawyers. Fellow Am. Coll. Trial Lawyers (chair. fed. criminal procedure com. 2003-2004, admission to fellowship com. 1997-2000), bd. of regents, 2004-; mem. ABA (white collar crime inst. 1997—, planning com.), Bar Assn. San Francisco, Chgo. Bar Assn., U. Chgo. Grad. Sch. Bus. Alumni Assn. (bd. dirs. 1986), Racquet Club, Wong Sun Soc. (San Francisco), Kenilworth Club, H.O.G. (Black Hills chpt.), Chgo. Stanford Assn. Presbyterian. Avocations: architecture, screenplays, motorcycling. Office: Latham & Watkins Sears Tower 5800 233 S Wacker Dr Chicago IL 60606 Home: 219 Leicester Rd Kenilworth IL 60043-1244 Office Phone: 312-876-7605.

TARVER, MARGARET LEGGETT, retired lawyer, forensic scientist; b. Birmingham, Ala., Mar. 7, 1942; d. Booker Thomas and Ernestine Williametta (Rutland) Leggett; divorced; children: James, Derrick. BS, Talladega (Ala.) Coll., 1962; MS, Howard U., 1966; JD, Seton Hall U., 1982. Bar: Pa., 1982, N.J., 1982, U.S. Dist. Ct. (ea. dist.) Pa., 1983, U.S. Dist. Ct. N.J., 1982, U.S. Supreme Ct. 2000. Rsch. asst.med. sch. Howard U., Washington, 1962-64; sci. cons. Bd. Edn., Washington, 1966-68; instr. Tech. Tng. Project, Newark, 1970-71; sr. learning ptnr. SUNY, Albany, 1972-74; forensic scientist N.J. State Police Lab., Hammonton, 1976—82, tech. dir., 1983—2001, acting lab. dir., 2001—02; ret., 2002. Cons., EMT, U. Medicine and Dentistry N.J., 1975, adj. faculty, 2002—04, adj. asst. prof., 2004—. Vol. atty. Phila. Lawyers Vol. Indigent Program, 1983-2001; bd. dirs. YWCA, Paterson, N.J., 1976-81, Women's Haven Battered Women's Program, Paterson, 1976-81. Fellow Am. Acad. Forensic Scis. (jurisprudence sect. 1997, program co-chair ann. meeting 2000, chmn. annual mtg. poster sessions 2003—, sect. sec. 2004—); mem. ABA, N.J. State Bar Assn. (bd. dirs. minorities in the profession sect. 1990-96, jud. adminstrn. com. 1999—, by-laws com. 1999—, by-laws com. co-chair 2003-04, editor-in-chief minorities in the profession sect. newsletter 1990-95), Pa. Bar Assn., Burlington County Bar Assn., Phila. Bar Assn., Northeastern Assn. Forensic Scientists, Mid-Atlantic Assn. Forensic Scientists, N.J. Assn. Forensic Scientists (bd. dirs. 1998-2002), Assn. Black Women Lawyers-South Jersey (mem.-at-large 1999-2001, pres. 2001—03), Talladega Coll. Alumni Assn. (pres. Phila. chpt. 1983-85). Avocations: pianist, organist, painting, tennis, bicycling. Home: 42 Garland Ln Willingboro NJ 08046-3012

TARVESTAD, ANTHONY M. psychiatrist; BA magna cum laude, Winona State U., 1973; JD, William Mitchell Coll. of Law, 1977. Exec. dir. Am. Bd. Physical Medicine and Rehab. Named Super Lawyer Minn. Jour. Law and Politics, 1994. Mem. Am. Coll. Healthcare Execs., Am. Health Laywers Assn., ABA, Am. Arbitration Assn. (arbitrator), Minn. State Bar. Assn. Office: Am Bd PM&R 21 1st St SW Ste 674 Rochester MN 55902-3007

TASA, KEN, college dean; b. Greenville, Tex., Apr. 29, 1947; s. Kenneth A. and Juanita (Holley) T.; m. Patricia Ann Langford, Mar. 28, 1969; children: Laura Ann, Heather Denise. BS, East Tex. State U., 1967, MS, 1969, EdD, 1973. Tchr. Lone Oak (Tex.) High Sch., 1969-72; prof. chemistry Brazosport Coll., Lake Jackson, Tex., 1973-97, pres. faculty assembly, 1990-91, chmn. div. Math. and Sci., 1991-97, dean ednl. programs and svcs., 1998—. Contbr. articles to sci. jours. Mem. adminstrv. coun. 1st United Meth. Ch., Angleton, Tex. Mem.: Nat. Coun. Instrnl. Adminstrs., Rotary. Republican. Avocations: golf, upland bird hunting, astronomy. Office: Brazosport Coll 500 College Dr Lake Jackson TX 77566-3136

TASH, BILL, state senator; b. Dillon, Mont., Aug. 21, 1932; m. Marlene Tash. Student, Western Mont. Coll., Mont. State U. Rancher; Rep. rep. dist. 34 Mont. Ho. of Reps., 1992-2000; Rep. senator dist. 17 Mont. State Senate, 2000—. Mem. state adminstrn. com. Mont. State Senate, chair natural resources. With USN. Office: 240 Vista Dr Dillon MT 59725-3100 also: Mont State Senate Capitol Station Helena MT 59620

TASH, PAUL CLIFFORD, editor, publishing executive; b. South Bend, Ind., July 17, 1954; s. Robert N. and Barbara R. (Eller) T.; m. Karyn E. Krayer, Aug. 19, 1983; children: Kaley Marie, Kendyl Barbara. BA, Ind. U., 1976; LLB, Edinburgh (Scotland) U., 1978. Reporter St. Petersburg Times, 1978-83, city editor, 1983-86, metro editor, 1986-89, editor, pub. Fla. Trend Mag., 1990 91, Washington bur. chief, 1991-92, exec. editor, dep. chmn., 1992-2000, pres., editor, dep. chmn., 2000—. Bd. dirs. Times Pub. Co., Newspaper Assn. Am., Com. to Protect Journalists, Mich. Journalism Fellows, Fla. Trend Mag., Congressional Quar., Poynter Inst. Media Studies. Chmn. Fla. First Amendment Found.; mem. adv. bd. Ind. U. Sch. Journalism; bd. govs. Fla. C. of C. Marshall Aid Commemoration Commn. scholar, 1976-78. Mem.: Fla. First Amendment Found., Tampa Bay Area Com. on Fgn. Rels., Am. Soc. Newspaper Editors, Fla. C. of C. Home: 111 Bay Point Dr NE Saint Petersburg FL 33704-3805 Office: St Petersburg Times 490 1st Ave S Saint Petersburg FL 33701-4204 also: PO Box 1121 Saint Petersburg FL 33731-1121

TASHIMA, ATSUSHI WALLACE, federal judge; b. Santa Maria, Calif., June 24, 1934; s. Yasutaro and Aya (Sasaki) Tashima; m. Nora Kiyo Inadomi, Jan. 27, 1957; children: Catherine Y., Christopher I., Jonathan I. AB in Polit. Sci., UCLA, 1958; LLB, Harvard U., 1961. Bar: Calif. 1962. Dep. atty. gen. State of Calif., 1961—67; atty. Spreckels Sugar divsn. Amstar Corp., 1968—72, v.p., gen. atty. Spreckels Sugar divsn., 1972—77; ptnr. Morrison & Foerster, L.A., 1977—80; judge U.S. Dist. Ct. (ctrl. dist.), L.A., Calif., 1980—96, U.S. Ct. Appeals (9th cir.), Pasadena, Calif., 1996—2003, sr. judge, 2003—. Mem. Calif. Com. Bar Examiners, 1978—80. With USMC, 1953—56. Mem.: ABA, LA County Bar Assn. Democrat. Office: Richard A Chambers US Ct Appeals PO Box 91510 125 S Grand Ave Pasadena CA 91109-1510

TASHJIAN, ARMEN H., JR., medical educator; MD, Harvard U., 1957. Prof. toxicology Sch. Pub. Health Harvard U., Boston, prof. biol. chemistry and molecular pharmacology Med. Sch. Contbr. articles to profl. jours. Office: Harvard Med Sch Bldg I, Rm 111 Dept Cancer Cell Biology Boston MA 02115 Fax: 617-432-1177. E-mail: tashjian@hsph.harvard.edu.

TASKER, JOHN BAKER, veterinary medical educator, college dean; b. Concord, NH, Aug. 28, 1933; s. John Baker and Catherine Mabel (Baker) T.; m. Grace Ellen Elliott, June 17, 1961; children: Sybil Alice, Sarah Catherine, Sophia Ethel DVM, Cornell U., 1957, PhD, 1963. Instr. Cornell U., Ithaca, N.Y., 1960-61, from assoc. prof. to prof., 1967-78; from asst. prof. to assoc. prof. Colo. State U., Fort Collins, 1963-67; prof. vet. clin. pathology, assoc. dean La. State U., 1978-84; dean Coll. Vet. Medicine Mich. State U., East Lansing, 1984-94; prof. vet. pathology Coll. Vet. Medicine/Mich. State U., East Lansing, 1984-95; dean, prof. emeritus Mich. State U., East Lansing, 1995. Cons. Ralston-Purina Co., St. Louis, 1978, Universidad Nacional P. Urena, Dominican Republic, 1980, U. Nebr., Lincoln, 1982-83 Editor: Veterinary Clinics of North America, 1976 Served to 1st lt. U.S. Army, 1958-60 Recipient Outstanding Instr. award Colo. State U. Vet. Coll., 1967; Norden Teaching award Cornell U. Vet. Coll., 1977 Mem. AVMA, Am. Coll. Vet. Pathologists (diplomate; examiner 1972-74), Am. Soc. Vet. Clin. Pathology (pres. 1971-72), Assn. Am. Vet. Med. Colls. (exec. com. 1986-91, pres. 1989-90). Avocations: reading, travel. Home: 200 Leslie Dr #626 Hallandale FL 33009 Personal E-mail: jtasker8@comcast.net.

TASKER, MOLLY JEAN, lawyer; b. Cumberland, Md., Feb. 13, 1945; d. Samuel Paul Tasker and Peggy Evelyn Purinton; m. Richard Mark Curtis, June 7, 1985. AA, Santa Fe Jr. Coll., 1968; BA, Fla. Atlantic U., 1970; JD, Fla. State U., 1973. Bar: Fla. 1973, U.S. Supreme Ct. 1992, U.S. Dist. Ct. (mid. dist.) Fla. 1997. Atty., advisor CIA, Washington, 1974-82, asst. gen. counsel, 1983-95, chair publs. rev. bd., 1993-95; ptnr. Tasker & Stephens, PA, Indian Harbour Beach, Fla., 1996—. Bd. dirs. Brevard County Emergency Med. Svc. Found., Melbourne, Fla., Cmty. Housing Initiative, Melbourne; guest lectr. Fla. So. Coll., Lakeland, 1997-01. Exec. sec. Brevard County (Fla.) Juvenile Justice Coun., 1997—; vice-chair Brevard County Dem. Exec. Com., 1997-98; chair govtl. affairs com. C. of C., Melbourne, 1998-99. Recipient Spl. Recognition award Brevard County Legal Aid, Inc., Fla., 1997, 2000; Fulbright Travel grant Fla. State U. Ctr. for Slavic and East European Studies, 1972. Mem. AAUW, LWV, Phi Alpha Delta, Phi Gamma Nu. Lutheran. Avocations: photography, reading, tennis, boating. Home: 4050 Carolwood Dr Melbourne FL 32934-7179 Office: 244 E Eau Gallie Blvd Indian Harbor Beach FL 32937-4874

TASMAN, ALLAN, psychiatry educator; b. Louisville, Feb. 8, 1947; s. Goodman and Zelda Tasman; m. Cathy Faye Goldstein, May 24, 1970. BA in Chemistry, Franklin and Marshall Coll., 1969; MD, U. Ky., 1973. Diplomate Am. Bd. Psychiatry and Neurology. Resident in psychiatry U. Ky. Med. Sch., Lexington, 1973-74, U. Cin. Med. Ctr., 1974-76; asst. prof. psychiatry U. Conn. Med. Sch., Farmington, 1976-82, assoc. prof. psychiatry, 1982-88, prof. psychiatry, 1988-91; prof. psychiatry and behavioral scis., tenure and chmn. U. Louisville Sch. Medicine, 1991—. Editor: Annual Review of Psychiatry, Vol. ll, 1992, Clinical Challenges in Psychiatry, 1993, Less Time to Do More, 1993; sr. editor: Textbook of Psychiatry, 1997, 2d edit., 2003; assoc. editor Am. Jour. Psychotherapy. Recipient Alpha Omega Alpha Faculty award, 2002, Pres.'s Disting. Faculty award for svc. to the profession, U. Louisville, 2003. Fellow Am. Psychiat. Assn. (v.p. 1996-98, pres.-elect 1998-99, pres. 1999-00, Nancy Roeske award for excellence in med. student edn. 1991); mem. Am. Assn. Dirs. of Psychiat. Residency Tng. (pres. 1993-94), Assn. Acad. Psychiatry (pres. 1993-94, Educator of Yr. award 2000), Am. Assn. Chmn. Depts. Psychiatry (pres. 1996-97, 97-98), World Psychiat. Assn. (bd. dirs. 2002-), Royal Coll. Psychiatrists. Office: U Louisville Sch Medicine Dept Psychiatry & Behavioral Louisville KY 40292-0001

TASMAN, WILLIAM SAMUEL, ophthalmologist, educator; b. Phila., 1929; MD, Temple U., 1955. Intern Phila. Gen. Hosp., 1955-56; resident in ophthalmology Wills Eye Hosp., Phila., 1959-61; fellow Mass. Eye and Ear Infirmary, Boston, 1961-62; prof., chmn. dept. ophthalmology Jefferson Med. Coll., Phila., 1985—; attending surgeon Wills Eye Hosp., Phila., 1974—, ophthalmologist-in-chief, 1985—. Mem. AMA, Am. Acad. Ophthalmologists (sec. ann. meeting 1992-97, pres. elect. 1998, pres. 1999), Pa. Acad. Ophthalmologists, Am. Ophthal. Soc. (pres. 1999). Office: Wills Eye Hosp 840 Walnut St Ste 1510 Philadelphia PA 19107-5109

TASOOJI, MICHAEL B. retail executive; m. Linda Tasooji; 3 children. BS in internat. trade and quantitative bus. analysis, MBA in internat. fin. and bus. econ., U. So. Calif. With Getty Oil Co., Columbia Pictures Studio; v.p., application systems Bergen Brunswig Corp.; v.p., info. svcs. Disneyland, 1995—2000; sr. v.p., CIO Walt Disney Attractions, 2000, Walt Disney Co., 2000—03; exec. v.p., CIO Gap, Inc., 2003—. Office: Gap Inc 2 Folsom St San Francisco CA 94105

TASSÉ, ROGER, lawyer, former Canadian government official; b. Montreal, Que., Can., 1931; BA, Coll. St. Marie, Montreal, 1952; Lic. in Law, U. Montreal, 1955; diploma d'Etudes Superieures, U. Ottawa, Ont., Can., 1957. Bar: Que. 1956, Ont. 1986; called to Queens Counsel 1971. Joined Dept. Justice, 1956, civil law counsel for Can. govt., from 1957, supt. bankruptcy, 1965-68, asst. dep. min. consumer and corp. affairs, 1968-72; dep. min. Dept. of Solicitor Gen., 1972-77; dep. min. of justice, atty. gen. of Can., 1977-85; ptnr. Land Michener Lash Johnston, Toronto and Ottawa, Noel Décary Aubry & Assocs., Hull, Que., 1985-88; exec. v.p. legal and environ. affairs Bell Can., 1988-91; of counsel Fraser & Beatty, Toronto, 1992-95, Gowling, Lafleur & Henderson, Ottawa, 1995—. Prin. constl. advisor to Spl. Joint Com. of the Senate and the House of Commons on a Renewed Can., 1991-92. Mem. Citizens' Forum on Canada's Future, 1990; co-chair task force Can. Mags., 1993; mem. DTH Panel, 1995. Decorated officer Order of Can. Avocations: skiing, tennis. Office: Gowling Lafleur Henderson LLP 160 Elgin St Ste 2600 Ottawa ON Canada K1P 1C3 Fax: (613) 563-9869. Office Phone: 813-786-0208. E-mail: roger.tasse@gowlings.com.

TASSINARI, MELISSA SHERMAN, toxicologist; b. Lawrence, Mass., Sept. 26, 1953; m. R. Peter Tassinari; children: Michael, Emily, Sara. AB, Mt. Holyoke Coll., 1975; postgrad., U. St. Andrews, Scotland, 1973-74; PhD, Med. Coll. Wis., 1979. Diplomate Am. Bd. Toxicology. Rsch. asst. in orthopedic surgery., Lab. Human Biochemistry Children's Hosp. Med. Ctr.,

Boston, 1981-83; rsch. affiliate in toxicology Forsyth Dental Ctr., Boston, 1983-86, staff assoc. dept. toxicology, 1986-89; asst. prof. cell biology U. Mass. Med. Ctr., Worcester, 1989-91; head reproductive and developmental toxicology Pfizer Global R&D, Groton/New London, Conn., 1991—99, group dir. worldwide safety scis., 2001—02, group dir. sr. tech. advisors, 2002—04, sr. dir. regulatory policy and intelligence, 2004—. Rsch. fellow oral biology Harvard Sch. Dental Medicine, Boston, 1978-81, instr. oral biology and pathophysiology, 1981-83; asst. prof. biol. scis. Wellesley Coll., Mass., 1985-91, biology Simmons Coll., Boston, 1986-87. Contbr. abstracts, articles to profl. jours. Mem. Teratology Soc. (coun. 2000—, v.p. 2004), Neurobehavioral Teratology Soc., Mid. Atlantic Reprodn. and Teratology Assn. (steering com. 1994), Midwest Teratology Assn., Soc. Toxicology. Office: Pfizer Inc 50 Pequot Ave New London CT 06320

TASSONE, GELSOMINA (GESSIE TASSONE), metal processing executive; b. N.Y.C., July 8, 1944; d. Enrico and A. Cira (Petriccione) Gargiulo; children: Ann Marie, Margaret, Theresa, Christine; m. Armando Tassone, Mar. 20, 1978. Student, Orange County Community Coll., 1975-79, Iona Coll., 1980—. Head bookkeeper Gargiulo Bros. Builders, N.Y.C., 1968-72; pres., owner A&T Iron Works, Inc., New Rochelle, N.Y., 1973—. Recipient Profl. Image award Contractors Coun. Greater N.Y.C., 1986; named Businesswoman of Yr., Contractors Coun. Greater N.Y.C., 1985, N.Y. State Small Bus. Person of Yr., 1988, Entrepreneur of Yr. Inc. mag., 1990; company named a Successful Small Bus. Co. Westchester County C. of C./BSBA, 1986-88. Mem. Nat. Ornamental and Miscellaneous Metal Assn., Builders Inst. Westchester and Putnam County, Westchester Assn. Women Bus. Owners, Profl. Women in Constrn., Westchester C. of C. Office: A&T Iron Works Inc 25 Cliff St New Rochelle NY 10801-6803 Office Phone: 914-632-8992.

TASSOS, ALICE CROWLEY, writer; b. Dallas, June 19, 1925; d. Thomas Francis and Geneiva Edna (Lee) Crowley; m. John Tassos, Mar. 4, 1950 (div. June 1960); 1 child, Penelope Geneiva Tassos Grima. BA in English, French, BS in Journalism, So. Meth. U., 1945, BA in Psychology, 1960; MA in French, Columbia U., 1947. Solo pilot cert. Sec. to fashion editor Vogue Mag., N.Y.C., 1945-46; airline stewardess Trans-Caribbean Airline, N.Y.C., 1946; embassy libr. U.S. Info. Svc. Fgn. Svc. Dept. State, Athens, Greece, 1947-49; jr. exec. J. Walter Thompson Co., N.Y.C., 1950-51; city side reporter Miami Daily News, 1952; pub. rels. exec. Boca Raton (Fla.) Hotel & Club, 1953; pvt. practice writer, linguist Dallas, 1960—. Author poems. Canvasser Am. Heart Assn., New Canaan, Conn., 1959; office sec. Easter Seals, Dallas, 1960-61; vol. recreational therapy asst. Timberlawn Psychiat. Hosp., Dallas, 1961-64; vol. March of Dimes, Dallas, 1997. Sr. scholar So. Meth. U., Dallas Woman's Club, 1944-45; consumer price index pub. svc. commendation Dept. Commerce, Dallas, 1999. Mem. AAUW, NAFE, Cmty. of the Holy Spirit (assoc.), Daus. of the King, Alpha Theta Phi, Theta Sigma Phi, Psi Chi. Episcopalian. Avocations: skin diving, swimming, bicycling, walking.

TATA, GIOVANNI, publishing executive; b. Taranto, Italy, Apr. 26, 1954; came to U.S., 1974, naturalized, 1982; s. Vito and Angela (Colucci) T.; m. Brenda Susan Smith, Feb. 14, 1978; children: Elizabeth Ariana, Katherine Allison, Margaret Anne, Michael Anthony, Hanna Amelia. BS cum laude, Brigham Young U., 1977, MA, 1980; grad. cert. area studies, U. Utah, 1980, PhD, 1986; postgrad., U. Turin, Italy, 1980-81. Archaeologist Utah State Hist. Soc., Salt Lake City, 1979; instr. dept. langs. U. Utah, Salt Lake City, 1983-85; Mediterranean specialist Soc. Early Hist. Archaeology, Provo, Utah, 1978-91; rsch. fellow Direzione Gen. Cooperazione Sci. Culturale e Technica, Rome, 1980-81; mus. curator Pioneer Trail State Park, Salt Lake City, 1982-83; instr. dept. art Brigham Young U., Provo, 1982-84, dir. creative works, 1996—; rsch. curator Utah Mus. Fine Arts, Salt Lake City, 1985-87; pres. Mus. Info. Sys., 1987-93, Transoft Internat., Inc., 1988—. Chmn. 35th Ann. Symposium on the Archaeology of the Scriptures, 1986, Taras Devel. Corp., 1994—97, MuseMedia, Inc., 1995—2000. Patentee method and system for computerized learning, response, and evaluation. Brigham Young U. scholar. Mem.: Intellectual Property Owners Assn., Assn. Univ. Tech. Mgrs., Nat. Coun. Museums, Am. Assn. Museums. Republican. Mem. Ch. Jesus Christ of Latter-day Saints. Home: PO Box 2194 Provo UT 84603-2194 Office: Transoft Internat 3325 N University Ave Ste 300 Provo UT 84604-7412 Office Phone: 801-422-3724. E-mail: tata@lexinet.com., giovanni_tata@byu.edu.

TATA, ROBERT JOSEPH, retired geographer, educator; b. New Britain, Conn., Mar. 3, 1935; s. Rosario and Anna Marie Tata; m. Maryann Hanson; children: Virginia Tata-Phillips, Amy Tata-Winslow, Steven. AB in Geography, Syracuse U., 1957, MA in Geography, 1961, PhD in Geography, 1968; MA in Econs., Fla. Atlantic U., 1975. Asst. prof. Fla. Atlantic U., Boca Raton, 1964—67, assoc. prof., 1968—80, chair geography, 1970—76, prof., 1980—99, prof. emeritus, 1999—. Cons. faculty U.S. Army Command & Gen. Staff, Ft. Leavenworth, Kans., 1967—80; cons. Pan Am Inst. Geography & History, 1974—75; reviewer NSF, Washington, 1982—98. Author: (book) Structural Changes in Puerto Rico's Economy, 1980, Haiti: Land of Poverty, 1982; editl. bd.: The Southeastern Geographer, 1968—72; contbr. articles to profl. jours. Col. U.S. Army, 1957—86. Rsch. grantee, U.S. Army Engr. Rsch. Inst. Mem.: Assn. Am. Geographers, Fla. Soc. Geographers (past. v.p., past pres. 1977—79, Profl. Cartography award 1966), Mil. Officers' Assn., Sigma Xi. Avocations: reading, travel, fishing, baseball, wine. Home: 2637 SW Cranbrook Ct Boynton Beach FL 33436 Office: Fla Atlantic Univ 500 NW 20th St Boca Raton FL Office Phone: 561-297-2101. Home Fax: 561-738-7519. Personal E-mail: b33bacchus@earthlink.net.

TATAR, ARNOLD MARSHALL, internal medicine physician, educator; b. Chgo., June 26, 1933; s. Louis and Rose Goldberg Tatar; m. Marina Deull-Wirszup, Aug. 30, 1959; children: Carolyn Beth, Audrey Michelle, Lauren D. W. BA in Chemistry, U. Ill., 1954; BS in Medicine, U. Ill., Chgo., 1955, MD cum laude, 1957. Lic. physician, Ill.; cert., recert. Am. Bd. Internal Medicine. Resident in internal medicine Michael Reese Hosp. and Med. Ctr., Chgo., 1957-60, chief med. resident, 1960-61, attending physician, 1961—2001; pres. Drs. Tatar, Tatar, Buchanan and Hunt, Chgo., 1961—; attending physician Northwestern Meml. Hosp., Chgo., 1991—. Assoc. prof. internal medicine U. Chgo., 1973-91; asst. prof. internal medicine Northwestern U., Evanston/Chgo., 1991—; dir. med. intensive care Michael Reese Hosp., Chgo., 1969-76, dir. investigative hypertension clinic, 1964-76, pres. med. staff, 1988-90, hosp. trustee, 1982-91. Contbr. rsch. articles to profl. jours. Pres. Parent-Tchr. Orgn., John F. Kennedy Sch., Highland Park, Ill., 1970-72. Lt. col. U.S. Army, 1967-69. Named one of Chgo.'s Top Drs., Chgo. Mag., 1997, 2001, 2004, Outstanding Primary Care Physicians in U.S., Town and Country Mag., 1999. Fellow Am. Coll. Chest Physicians, Am. Coll. Angiology, Am. Heart Assn. (coun. on hypertension, coun. on clin. cardiology), Am. Soc. Internal Medicine. Avocations: music, theater, dance, bicycling, skiing. Home: Apt 5-East 189 E Lake Shore Dr Chicago IL 60611 Office: Drs Tatar Tatar Buchanan Hunt and Suh Ste 1919 111 N Wabash Chicago IL 60602

TATAR, JEROME F. business products executive; V.p., operating officer Mead Corp., Dayton, Ohio, 1994—96, pres., COO, 1996—97, chmn., CEO, 1997—2002; chmn. MeadWestvaco Corp., 2002. Bd. mem. Robbins & Myers Inc., Nat. City Corp., Bartech Group Inc. Office: Mead Corp Courthouse Plz NE Dayton OH 45463-0001*

TATARINOV, KIRILL, computer software industry expert; b. Moscow, Sept. 17, 1964; came to U.S., 1994; s. Lev Gorinshteyn and Inna Tatarinova; m. Osksana Grekina Tatarinov, Jan. 18m 1986; children: Katherine, Konstantin. MS in Elec. Engring., Moscow U. Railroad Engring., 1986; MBA, Houston Bapt. U., 1997. Tech. lead Fibronics Ltd., Haifa, Israel, 1990-91; dir. R&D Patrol Software Pty. Ltd., Sydney, Australia, 1991-94; v.p. R&D BMC Software, Inc., Houston, 1994-98, v.p. strategic planning, 1998-2000, sr. v.p., chief tech. officer, 2000—02; chmn. Kontora, LLC, Houston, 2002—. Inventor: System for monitoring and managing computer resources, 1997, 99. Office: PO Box 550412 Houston TX 77255 Address: 110 Carnarvon Dr Houston TX 77024 E-mail: kirill@tatarinov.com.

TATARSKII, VALERIAN IL'ICH, physics researcher; b. Kharkov, USSR, Oct. 13, 1929; s. Il'ya A. and Elizabeth A. (Lapis) T.; m. Maia S. Granovskaia, Dec. 22, 1955; 1 child, Viatcheslav V. MS, Moscow State U., 1952; PhD, Acoustical Inst. Acad. Scis., 1957; DSc, Gorky State U., 1962. Scientific rschr. Geophys. Inst. Acad. Sci. USSR, Moscow, 1953-56, Inst. Atmospheric Physics, Acad. Sci. USSR, Moscow, 1956-59, sr. scientific rschr., 1959-78, head lab., 1978-90; head dept. Lebedev. Phys. Inst. Acad. Sci., Moscow, 1990-91; sr. rsch. assoc. U. Colo. Coop. Inst. for Rsch. in Environ. Sci., Boulder, 1991—2001; sr. rsch. scientist Zel Technologies and NOAA/ERL, Boulder, 2001—. Author: Wave Propagation in a Turbulent Medium, 1961, 67, The Effect of the Turbulent Atmosphere on Wave Propagation, 1971, Principles of Statistical Radiophysics, 1989; contbr. articles to profl. jours. Recipient of Max Born award, 1994, Optical Soc. of Am., USSR State prize, 1990. Fellow Optical Soc. Am. (Max Born award 1994), Inst. of Physics; mem. Russian Acad. Sci., U.S.A. Nat. Acad. Engring., N.Y. Acad. Sci. Avocations: classical music, kayaking. Office: NOAA ERL ETL 325 Broadway St Boulder CO 80305-3337 E-mail: vtatarskii@hotmail.com.

TATE, ANTOINETTE COOPER, marriage and family therapist; b. Rochester, N.Y., July 13, 1975; d. William Charles and Margot Steele Tate. BA cum laude in Psychology and History, Kenyon Coll., Gambier, Ohio, 1997; MA in Psychology, Am. U., 2002, PhD in Clin. Psychology, 2003—. Residential counselor The Renfrew Ctr., Phila., 1997—99, rsch. asst., 1998—2000, group therapist, case mgr., intensive outpatient program, 1999—2000; rsch. intern APA, Washington, 2000—03; crisis intervention counselor Greenbelt CARES Youth and Family Svcs. Bur., Greenbelt, Md., 2002—; clin. psychology extern U. Md. Parent Cons. and Child Evaluation Svcs., Coll. Pk., Md., 2003—. Cons. APA Grad. Students Com. on Students with Disabilities, Washington, 2002—03; phone friend vol. Prevent Child Abuse of Met. Wash., Washington, 2002—03; family counseling student trainee Greenbelt CARES Youth and Family Services Bur., Greenbelt, Md., 2001—02. Presenter (poster presentation) 15th Ann. Conv., Atlanta; contbr. scientific papers, articles to profl. jour. Mem.: Am. Psychol. Soc., APA (Soc. for the Study of Women, Soc. of Clin. Psychology), Acad. of Eating Disorders. Office: Greenbelt CARES 25 Crescent Rd Greenbelt MD 20770

TATE, FRAN M. small business owner; b. Auburn, Wash., Oct. 5, 1929; d. Frank Joseph and Theresa Mary (Bingesar) Pfulg; m. Rory Tate, Sept. 30, 1970 (div.); children: Michael C., Joseph M.; m. Juan Ramon Ramirez, Sept. 6, 1981 (div. May 1986). Student, U. Wash. Gen. mgr. Sorensen Heating Co., Auburn, 1952-70; cons. Success Motivation Inst., Bellevue, Wash., 1970-72; field engr., draftsman J. Dalton and Assocs., Point Barrow, Alaska, 1973-75; pres., owner Inupiat Water Delivery Co., Point Barrow, 1977—, Elephant Pot Sewage Haulers, Point Barrow, 1977—; pres., owner, operator Pepe's North of the Border Restaurant, Point Barrow, 1978—; pres., owner Tate Enterprises, Inc., Burger Barn, Point Barrow, 1984—. Disc jockey, Sta. KBRW, Barrow. Guest of Johnny Carson Show, 1984; featured on Carson Comedy Classics and Stephen Cox book Here's Johnny. Mem. Barrow Zoning Commn.; mem. citizens adv. bd. Barrow Mus. and Cultural Ctr., 1989-91; regional coord. Gov.'s Conf. for Small Bus., 1989-90. Recipient Boss of Yr. award Credit Women Internat., 1969, Outstanding Svc. award Barrow PTA; named Alaska's Outstanding Women, State Commn. for Status of Women, 1984, Outstanding Radio Vol. of Yr., State of Alaska, 1991; Paul Harris fellow for cmty. svc. Rotary Found. Rotary Internat. Mem. NAFE, Barrow C. of C. (pres. 1989—, bd. dirs.), Blues Alley Music Soc., Nat. Geog. Soc., Smithsonian Instn., Jazz Heritage Found., Arctic Slope Scholarship Found., Las Vegas Jazz Club. Roman Catholic.

TATE, HAROLD SIMMONS, JR., lawyer; b. Taylors, S.C., Sept. 19, 1930; s. Harold Simmons and Cleone (Clayton) T.; m. Elizabeth Anne Coker, Dec. 22, 1952; children— Mary Elizabeth Anne, Martha Coker, Virginia Clayton. Grad. cum laude, Harvard U., 1951, JD, 1956, postgrad., 1954. Bar: S.C. 1956. Ptnr. Haynsworth Sinkler Boyd, PA, Columbia, SC, 1962—. Chmn. U.S. Dist. Ct. (S.C.) Adv. Com., 1984—; lectr. Am. Law Inst.-ABA seminars; adv. com. on rules and procedures U.S. Ct. Appeals (4th cir.), 1990-95. Co-author: South Carolina Appellate Practice, 1985; bd. editors Federal Litigation Guide Reporter, 1985—; co-draftsman S.C. Rules of Evidence, 1995; contbr. articles and book revs. to profl. jours. Chmn. Richland County Mental Health Ctr., 1965-66; co-chmn. Columbia Hearing and Speech Ctr., 1962-64; mem. admission and scholarship com. Harvard U., 1961—; chmn. subcom. on legislation, legislation and fin. study commn. Gov.'s Adv. Group on Mental Health Planning, 1963-65; chmn. Columbia Bd. Supervisory of Registration, 1961-70; pres. Columbia Philharm. Orch., 1966-67, Town Theatre, 1967-70; bd. trustee Richland County Pub. Libr., 1973-78, Hist. Columbia Found., 1971-75, Caroliniana Soc., 1978—, Bostick Charitable Trust, 1968—, Archaeol. Rsch. Trust, 2000—; bd. mgrs. S.C. Hist. Soc., 1993-99, 2002—; commr. S.C. Commn. of Archives and History, 1995—. Capt. U.S. Army, 1951-53. Recipient DuRant award Disting Pub. Svc., 2001. Fellow Am. Coll. Trial Lawyers; mem. ABA, Am. Law Inst., Am. Judicature Soc., S.C. Bar Assn., Assn. Bar City N.Y., Richland County Bar Assn., Harvard Law Sch. Assn. S.C. (sec.-treas. 1968-70, pres. 1988—), Forest Lake Country Club, Columbia Drama Club (pres. 1963-64), Palmetto Club (sec. 1963-70, pres. 1973-76), The Forum Club, Harvard Club (N.Y.C.), Harvard Club S.C., Carolina Yacht Club. Episcopalian. Home: 15 Gibbes Ct Columbia SC 29201-3923 Office: Haynsworth Sinkler Boyd PA Fl 22 1201 Main St Ste 2200 Columbia SC 29201-3232 Office Phone: 803-779-3080. Business E-Mail: state@hsblawfirm.com.

TATE, HORENCENA, state legislator, software company executive; BS in Edn., U. Ga., 1977; M Ednl. Adminstrn., Atlanta U., 1988; PhD in Ednl. Adminstrn., Clark-Atlanta U., 1992. With Ga. Dept. Labor, Atlanta, from 1977, United Airlines, Atlanta, Apollo Travel Svcs., Atlanta; pres. Tate, Marsh and Assocs., Inc., software-mgmt. tng., Atlanta; mem. Ga. Senate, Atlanta, 1999—. Sec. state and local govtl. ops. com., mem. health and human svcs. com., retirement com., transp. com. Former del. Ga. Dem. Conf.; former computer literacy advisor Butler St. YMCA, Atlanta; vol. software instr. for local chs.; Clark-Atlanta U. del. to Internat. Cmty. Edn. Conf., Trinidad; spkr. to Atlanta pub. schs.; v.p. Rosalie Wright Cmty. Coun.; active Cascade United Meth. Ch., Atlanta. Mem. United Meth. Women. Office: Ga Senate Legislative Office Bldg 18 Capitol Sq SW Ste 320B Atlanta GA 30334-2000

TATE, JOHN WILLIAM, food products executive; BA in Econs., U. Tex., 1972. Various fin. and gen. mgmt. positions Dole Food Co. Inc., Westlake Village, Calif.; CFO fresh vegetables divsn. Dole Food Co., 1993-96, CFO Dole Europe, CFO Westlake Village, Calif., 1998—2000, Krispy Kreme, 2000—02, COO, 2002—. With USAF, 1973-79. Office: Krispy Kreme Doughnut Corp PO Box 83 Winston Salem NC 27103

TATE, PENFIELD, state senator; b. Phila., May 19; m. Valencia Tate. BA, Colo. State U., 1978; JD, Antioch U., 1981. Atty. FTC, 1981-84, 1984—; Dem. rep. dist. 8 Colo. Ho. of Reps., 1996-2000; Dem. senator dist. 33 Colo. State Senate, 2000—. Mem. bus. affairs and labor and fin. coms. Colo. Ho. of Reps.; mem. joint budget com. Colo. State Senate, vice chmn. appropriations com. Mem. bd. dirs. Metro State Coll. Found., Colo. Housing and Fin. Authority; adminstr. asst. to Mayor of Denver, 1990-91; exec. dir. Colo. Dept. Adminstrn., 1993-94; 2d vice chair Colo. Dem. Party, 1995-97. Mem. Denver Metro C. of C. (bd. dirs.). Office: Colo State Senate 200 E Colfax Rm 263 Denver CO 80203 also: 2520 Ash St Denver CO 80207-3118 E-mail: ptate@csn.net., ptate@sni.net.

TATE, RANDALL J. (RANDY TATE), former congressman; b. Puyallup, Wash., Nov. 23, 1965; m. Julie; 2 children. AA, Tacoma C. C., Wash.; BA in Econs. and Polit. Sci., We. Wash. U. Mem. Wash. Ho. of Reps., 1988-94, 104th Congress from 9th Wash. dist., 1994-96; exec. dir. Christian Coalition, Chesapeake, Va., 1997-99; dir. Rep. affairs voter.com, Inc., Boston, 2000—. Former mem. com. rules, com. fin. instns. and ins., judiciary com., Wash. Ho. Reps.; mem. Congrl. com. transp. and infrastructure, com. govt. reform. Address: Voter com Inc 54 Canal St Boston MA 02114-2011

TATE, ROBERT HALE, academic administrator; b. Radford, Va., Sept. 24, 1958; s. Robert Dewitt and Phyllis Hale T. BA, Va. Tech., 1980, MA, 1983; PhD, Fla. State U., 1997. Instr. Fla. So. Coll., Lakeland, 1982-85, asst. prof., 1986-97, assoc. prof., 1997—, sr. devel. officer, 1998-99, exec. dir. devel., 1999, v.p. for advancement, 2000—. Cons. Cohen & Assocs., Tampa, 1986-98. Mem. Lakeland Yacht and Country Club (bd. govs.), Rotary, Omicron Delta Kappa (Tchr. of Yr. award/Fla. So. Coll. 1986, faculty sec. 1992-2000, province vice-dir. 1998-2000), Phi Eta Sigma (Lover of Wisdom award 1987), Phi Kappa Phi, Sigma Tau Delta. Methodist. Office: Fla So Coll 111 Lake Hollingsworth Dr Lakeland FL 33801-5607 E-mail: rtate@flsouthern.edu.

TATE, SHEILA BURKE, public relations executive; b. Washington, Mar. 3, 1942; d. Eugene L. and Mary J. (Doherty) Burke; m. William J. Tate, May 2, 1981 (dec. Aug. 1998); children: Hager Burke Patton, Courtney Paige Patton Manzel. BA in Journalism, Duquesne U., 1964; postgrad. in mass comm., U. Denver, 1975—76. Rsch. asst. Westinghouse Air Brake Co.; asst. account exec. Fahlgren and Assocs.; copywriter Ketchum, MacLeod and Grove, 1964—66; account exec. Burson-Marsteller Assocs., Pitts., 1967, sr. v.p. Washington, 1985—87; pub. rels. mgr. Colo. Nat. Bank, Denver, 1967—70; account exec. Hill and Knowlton, Inc., Houston, 1977—78, v.p. Washington, 1978—81; dep. to the chmn. Hill and Knowlton Inc., Washington, 1987—88; press sec. to First Lady White House, Washington, 1981—85; press sec. George Bush for Pres. Campaign, 1988; press sec. to Pres.-elect George Bush, 1988—89; vice chmn. Cassidy and Assocs. Pub. Affairs, Washington, 1989—91; pres. Powell Tate, Washington, 1991—99, vice-chmn., 1999—. Bd. dirs., former mem. Corp. for Pub. Broadcasting, vice chmn., 1990—92, chmn., 1992—94; bd. dirs. Ethics Resource Ctr., Washington, Guest Svcs. Corp., Fairfax, Va. Chmn. pub. affairs adv. bd. U.S. Mil. Acad.; mem. adv. bd. Ronald Reagan Inst. Emergency Med., George Washington Univ. Hosp., Washington; mem. nat. adv. bd. The Salvation Army; bd. dirs. First Tee of Greater Washington; adv. bd. Am. Acad. Family Physicians, Kansas City, Kans. Mem.: Nat. Press Club, Belfair Club, Farmington Country Club, Washington Golf and Country Club, Duquesne U. Century Club. Office: Powell Tate 700 13th St NW Ste 1000 Washington DC 20005-5926 Business E-Mail: state@webershandwick.com.

TATE, SONSYREA, journalist, writer; d. Joseph and Meauvelle Tate. Masters, Regents U., Va. Beach, 2000—03. Mng. editor Wash. Informer, 2000—02; polit. reporter Post-Newsweek Media, Inc., Gaithersburg, Md., 2003—04. Arts com. U.S. Rep. Eleanor Holmes Norton, Washington, 2001—02. Author: (memoir) Little X: Growing Up in the Nation of Islam (ALA Best Books for Young Adults, 1998). Congl. aide U.S. Rep. Eleanor Holmes Norton, Washington, DC, 1993—95. Recipient Echoes of Excellence award, Nat. Assn. Black Journalists, 1992, 1993, 1994. Mem.: Hurston/Wright Found. Avocations: reading, golf, walking, dancing.

TATE, STANLEY G. diversified business executive, expert witness; b. N.Y., Apr. 25, 1928; s. Jack A. and Anna B. Tatelman; m. Joanne Marilyn Greenwood, Sept. 10, 1949; children: J. Kenneth, James David, Linda Sue Tate Best. BA, U. Fla., 1946, BS, 1948, postgrad., 1949, Columbia U., NYU. Nat. cert. appraiser; lic. gen. contractor, Fla.; cert. in forensic documentaton Am. Bd. Forensic Examiners. Founder Stanley Tate Builders, Inc., North Miami, Fla., 1954—, Investment Diversified Ltd., North Miami, 1964—, High Point of Delray Builders, Inc., North Miami, 1969—, Tate Enterprises, North Miami, 1986—. Chmn. bd. Envirocivil Engring. Corp.; receiver for real estate devels. and other bus. entitites throughout U.S.; expert witness in fed. and state cts. on real estate matters in litigation, before U.S. Ho. of Reps. and Senate coms. on fed. legis. in housing and banking areas; pres., COO, King Internat. Corp., 1985-86, CEO Assoc. Mortgage Investors, 1971-81; past dir., chmn. region I adv. bd. Nat. Bd. Resolution Trust Corp.; past mem. adv. bd. BlueStone Capital Ptnrs., N.Y.C., BlueStone Capital Online, Inc.; bd. dirs. KFx, Inc.; charter mem. adv. coun. U. Fla. Sch. Bldg. Constrn.; hon. mem. adv. staff Apt. and Constrn. News; guest lectr. U.Miami Bus. Sch.; guest spkr., lectr., participant numerous industry-related seminars and programs; dir. Team Fla./Free Trade Ams. Contbr. numerous articles on gen. real estate and condominium develing, mktg. and Property devel. to profl. publs. Past bd. dirs. Miami Heart Inst., Fla. League Cities; past trustee pub. health trust Met. Dade County, Fla., also past mem. exec. com.; past mem. Performing Arts Ctr. Trust, Inc., Dade County; past mem. and vice chmn. bd. Fla. Endowment Fund for Higher Edn.; past pres. Temple Israel, Miami, now trustee; past bd. dirs. and mem. exec. com. Miami City Ballet; past chmn. Metro Dade County Housing Oversight Com.; past bd. dirs. and vice chmn. Magnet Edn1. Choice Assn., Inc.; past chmn. Dade County Housing and Urban Devel. Adv. Bd.; past mem. adv. exec. com. YWCA Miami; mem. campaign cabinet United Way Dade County; trustee Fla. Taxwatch, Inc., James E. Scott Cmty. Assn., Mt. Sinai Med. Ctr.; bd. dirs. Miami Jewish Home and Hosp. for Aged, Keep Dade Beautiful, Dade County unit Am. Cancer Soc., Miami-Dade C.C. Found., Fla. Coun. of 100, Fla. Coun. on Econ. Edn., Easter Seals Dade County; trustee Thomas U., Kids Voting U.S.A., United Way Dade County; mem. family counseling svcs. adv. bd. Family Svc. Found., Inc.; mem., chmn. Fla. Prepaid Postsecondary Edn. Expense Bd., 1st chmn., 1987-; mem., chmn. Fla. Prepaid Coll. Found.; mem. cmty. adv. bd. Jr. League Miami; mem. exec. com. Fla. Guardian Ad Litem Program for 11th Jud. Cir.; hon. trustee Miami Children's Mus.; mem. program coordinating com. Dade County Family Self Sufficiency Program; mem. adv. coun. Voices for Children; past asst. mayor and mayor City of Bay Harbor Islands, Fla.; endowed tchg. chair Miami-Dade C.C. Med. Campus; pres. bd. dirs. Elephant Forum; mem. Ptnrs. in Productivity Task Force; mem. Fannie Mae's Nat. Housing Impact Adv. Coun.; mem. Miami-Dade adv. bd. Gulf Coast Jewish Family Svcs. (non-custodial parent employment program); mem. Assn. Governing Bds. of Univs., Am. Nurses Credentialing Ctr.; mem. adv. coun. Fla. Bd. Edn.; bd. govs. Rep. Jewish Coalition. Recipient Shalom award State of Israel, 1971, Ben Gurion award, spl. honoree Israel Bonds Campaign and Greater Miami Jewish Fedn., Cmty. Star award Family Counslng Svcs. Greater Miami, 1991, award for devoted outstanding cmty. svc. B'nai B'rith, 1992, Dorothy Shula award United Way, 1996, Unsung Hero award Youth Law Ctr., 1996, Most Valuable Protector Vol. award Voices for Children, 1999, Disting. Svc. award Coll. Savs. Plan-USA Network, 1999, Eagle award for Outstanding Cmty. Svc., Miami-Dade County Rep. Party, 2001, Disting. Svc. award Fla. Student Assn., 2002, Arete award, Vol. Adv. of Yr., Miami-Dade County Commn. on Ethics and Pub. Trust, 2003; recipient Outstanding Citizen award and named hon. Dade County Mayor, 1998; named Bus. Assoc. of Yr., Hurricane chpt. Am. Bus. Women's Assn., 1988, hon. treas. State of Ala., 1989; named one of Twelve Good Men, Ronald McDonald House, 2004. Fellow Am. Coll. Forensic Examiners; mem. Nat. Assn. Home Builders, Nat. Assn. Real Estate Appraisers (cert.), Nat. Assn. Rev. Appraisers and Mortgage Underwriters (cert.), Internat. Real Estate Inst., Latin Builders Assn., Hispanic-Am. Builders Assn. (dir. dirs.), Home Builders Assn. South Fla. (past dir., named to Hall of Fame 1994), Am. Israel Pub. Affairs (nat. exec. com.), Jewish Nat. Fund (investment com.), U.S. Senatorial Trust, Westview Country Club (past 1st v.p. and dir.), Bankers Club, Hound Ears Lodge and Club, Jockey Club. Republican. Jewish. Avocations: golf, tennis. Office: Tate Enterprises 1175 NE 125th St Ste 102 North Miami FL 33161 Business E-Mail: stanley@Tateenterprises.com.

TATE, STONEWALL SHEPHERD, lawyer; b. Memphis, Dec. 19, 1917; m. Janet Graf; children: Adele Shepherd, Shepherd Davis, Janet Reid Walker. BA, Southwestern at Memphis (now Rhodes Coll.), 1939; JD, U. Va., 1942; LLD (hon.), Samford U., 1979, Suffolk U., 1982, Capital U., 1989, Rhodes Coll., 1993. Bar: Va. 1941, Tenn. 1942. Chmn. bd. Martin, Tate, Morrow & Marston, P.C. (and predecessor firms), Memphis, 1947—. Chmn. pres.'s coun. Rhodes Coll., 1995-96, sec. bd. trustees, 1967-77, 80-84. Pres. Episcopal Churchmen of Tenn., 1961-62; sec. standing com. Episcopal Diocese of Tenn., 1969-71; pres. Chickasaw Coun. Boy Scouts Am., 1967-78. With USNR, 1942-46; comdr. USNR; ret. Decorated Order of Cloud Banner (China); recipient Silver Beaver award Boy Scouts Am., 1963, Disting. Eagle Scout award, 1980, Disting. Svc. medal Rhodes Coll., 1978, Disting. Alumni award, 1991, Lawyers' Lawyer award Memphis Bar Assn., 1990; Memphis Rotary Club Civic Recognition award, 1983, Benjamin L. Hooks award, Memphis Bar Found., 2003; Paul Harris fellow, 1985. Fellow Am. Bar Found., Am. Coll. Trust and Estate Counsel, Internat. Acad. Estate and Trust Law, Coll. Law

Practice Mgmt. (hon.), Tenn. Bar Found., Memphis Bar Found. (Benjamin L. Hooks award 2003), Shelby County Bar Found.; mem. ABA (chmn. standing com. on profl. discipline 1973-76, chmn. standing com. on scope and correlation of work 1977, chmn. task force on lawyer advt. 1977, pres. ABA 1978-79, chmn. standing com. on lawyer competence 1986 92, mem. coun. sr. lawyers divsn. 1997-2001), Am. Judicature Soc. (past bd. dirs.), Am. Law Inst., Lawyer-Pilots Bar Assn., Tenn. Bar Assn. (pres. 1963-64), Memphis and Shelby County Bar Assn. (pres. 1959-60), Nat. Conf. Bar Pres. (pres. 1972-73, Alumnus of Yr. 1996), U.S. 6th Cir. Jud. Conf. (life), U. Va. Law Sch. Alumni Assn. (mem. exec. coun. 1974-77), Rhodes Coll. Alumni Assn. (pres. 1951-53), Rotary (pres. 1982-83, bd. dirs. 1974, 80-84, 89-90), Raven Soc., Order of Coif, Phi Beta Kappa, Omicron Delta Kappa, Phi Delta Phi, Sigma Alpha Epsilon (highest effort award N.Y.C. Alumni Assn. 1979). Office: Martin Tate Morrow & Marston PC Falls Bldg 22 N Front St Ste 1100 Memphis TN 38103-1182 E-mail: sstate@martintate.com.

TATEL, DAVID STEPHEN, federal judge; b. Washington, Mar. 16, 1942; s. Howard Edwin and Molly (Abramowitz) Tatel; m. Edith Sara Bassichis, Aug. 29, 1965; children: Rebecca, Stephanie, Joshua, Emily. BA, U. Mich., 1963; JD, U. Chgo., 1966. Bar: Ill. 1966. Instr. U. Mich., Ann Arbor, 1966—67, assoc. Sidley & Austin, Chgo. and Washington, 1967—69, 1970—72; dir. Chgo. Lawyer's Com., 1969—70, Nat. Lawyers Commn. for Civil Rights Under Law, Washington, 1972—74; dir. Office for Civil Rights HEW, Washington, 1977—79; assoc., ptnr. Hogan & Hartson, Washington, 1974—77, ptnr., 1979—94; cir. judge U.S. Ct. Appeals (D.C. cir.), Washington, 1994—. Lectr. Stanford U. Law Sch., 1991—92; co-chmn. Nat. Lawyers Com. for Civil Rights Under Law, Washington, 1989—91; chmn., bd. dirs. Spencer Found., Chgo., 1990—97. Bd. dirs. Carnegie Found. for Advancement in Tchg., Stanford, Calif., 1997—. Office: US Ct Appeals 333 Constitution Ave NW US Courthouse Washington DC 20001-2866

TATERA, JAMES FRANK, chemist, process analysis specialist; b. Milw., June 27, 1946; s. Harry Frank and Agnes Rose (Szymanowski) T.; m. Kaaren Marie Piekarski, Sept. 9, 1972; children: Patrick, Monica, David. BS in Chemistry, Math., U. Wis., Oshkosh, 1968; postgrad., U. Minn., 1968, 71-73; MBA, Cen. Mich. U., 1982. Cert. specialist in analytical tech. Tchg. rsch. assoc. chemistry dept. U. Minn., Mpls., 1968, 71-73; analytical chemist Dow Corning Corp., Midland, Mich., 1973-76, scale up engr. new products commercialization, 1976-78, prodn. bldg. supt. prodn. dept., 1978-80, analytical systems specialist project and plant engring. Dow Corning Ltd., Barry, Wales, 1981-84; analytical systems supr. plant engring. & maintenance Dow Corning Corp., Carrollton, Ky., 1984-85, analytical systems specialist plant engring. and maintenance, 1985-87, sr. analytical and control specialist project engring., 1988-90, sr. analytical systems specialist strategic change program, 1991-98, sr. analytical sys. specialist Process Analysis Expertise Ctr., 1998-2000; ret., 2000; sr. process analysis cons. Tatera & Assocs. Inc., Madison, Ind., 2001—. Conf. program. chmn., symposium chmn.; session developer, panelist, course instr., presenter in field; U.S. nat. com. Internat. Electrotech. Commn., Paris, 1993, Milan, 94, Montreal, 96, Houston, 98, Beijing, 2002, Madrid, 03; U.S. nat. com. tech. advisor subcom. 65D, 1993—. Editl. adv. bd.: novels; contbr. articles to profl. jours., chpts. to books; author, presenter: internat. process analysis courses. 1st lt. U.S. Army, 1969-71. Decorated Bronze Star, Bronze Star with oak leaf cluster. Fellow: Instrumentation Sys. and Automation Soc. (formerly Instrument Soc. Am.) (various sect. offices 1976—79, pres. N.E. Mich. sect. 1979—80, chmn. SP 76 stds. com. 1991—96, dir.-elect, sec.-treas. analysis divsn. 1994—96, Louisville sect. del. 1995—, dir. 1996—98, com. mem. 1998—, various divsn. and dept. positions 1998—); mem.: Air and Waste Mgmt. Assn. (optical sensing divsn. indsl. issues and applications, com. on enhanced monitoring 1993—99), Am. Chem. Soc. (sect. careers program and nat. chemistry week com. 1992—99, Louisville sect. chmn.-elect 1998—99, Louisville sect. chair 1999—2001, sect. careers program and nat. chemistry week com. 2001—, soc. councilor 2003—, soc. com. mem. 2004—, rep. vol. in pub. outreach program), KC, VFW, Elks, Am. Legion, Sigma Iota Epsilon, Phi Lambda Upsilon, Delta Sigma Phi. Roman Catholic. Home and Office: 2038 Ridgewood Dr Madison IN 47250-2729 E-mail: jtatera@seidata.com.

TATGENHORST, ROBERT (CHARLES TATGENHORST), lawyer, educator; b. Cin., Apr. 21, 1918; s. Charles and Clara (Strebel) T.; m. Louise Thompson, Sept. 6, 1951; children: David, John, James, Richard. AB, Dartmouth Coll., 1940; LL.B., U. Cin., 1947. Bar: Ohio 1947. Asst. atty. gen., State of Ohio, 1947-49; asso. firm Taft, Stettinius & Hollister, Cin., 1951-58; ptnr. firm Tatgenhorst & Tatgenhorst, Cin., 1958-61; prin. firm Robert Tatgenhorst & Assos., Cin., 1961-85; ptnr. Tatgenhorst & Bruestle, Cin., 1986—, 1986-95. Adj. prof. law Chase Coll. Law, No. Ky. U., 1962-86. Pres. Westwood Civic Assn., Cin., 1959, Meth. Union, 1960; chmn. dist. Boy Scouts Am., 1970; trustee Twin Towers Retirement Ctr., 1968-93, Westwood United Meth. Ch., bd. trustees 1985-88, pres., 1990-92, trustee, 1992. With CIC U.S. Army, 1942-46. Mem. Ohio State Bar Assn., Cin. Bar Assn. (sec. 1973-75), Ryland Lakes Country Club, Optimists (pres. Cin. club 1962), Dartmouth of Cin. Club (pres. 1965), Masons (33 deg.), Sigma Alpha Epsilon, Phi Alpha Delta (pres. 1946). Republican.

TATHAM, DAVID FREDERIC, art historian, educator; b. Wellesley, Mass., Nov. 29, 1932; s. Richard Merton and Florence Elizabeth (Mallette) T.; m. Cleota Reed, Dec. 12, 1979. AB, U. Mass., 1954; MA, Syracuse U., 1960, PhD, 1970. Dean students Syracuse (N.Y.) U., 1966-71, assoc. prof. fine arts, 1972-78, chmn. dept. fine arts, 1980-86, prof., 1978—2002, prof. emeritus, 2002—. Author: The Lure of the Striped Pig, 1973, Prints and Printmakers of New York State, 1986, Winslow Homer and the Art of the Book, 1990, Winslow Homer and the Illustrated Book, 1992, Fishing in the North Woods, 1995, Winslow Homer in the Adirondacks, 1996, Winslow Homer and the Pictorial Press, 2002, (exhbn. catalogs) Winslow Homer Drawings, 1979, Art, Artists and Museums, 1980, Bolton Brown, 1981, Abraham Tuthill, 1983, Winslow Homer: Masterworks from the Adirondacks; contbr. articles to profl. jours. Served with U.S. Army, 1956. Daniels research fellow, 1974; Am. Philos. Soc. grantee, 1980, 86, 98; Am. Art Jour. award for outstanding scholarship, 1984; NEH grantee, 1987-88, Newman Prize, 2004. Fellow Athenaeum of Phila., Royal Soc. Arts; mem. Am. Antiquarian Soc. (rec. sec. 1988-93), Coll. Art Assn. Home: 329 Westcott St Syracuse NY 13210-2107 Office: Syracuse U Dept Fine Arts Bowne Hall Syracuse NY 13244-1200 E-mail: dftatham@syr.edu.

TATHAM, ROBERT HAINES, geophysicist, educator; b. Merced, Calif., Dec. 10, 1943; s. Robert and Dorothy (Fitzgerald) T.; m. Henna E. Solomin, Aug. 29, 1970; children: Sarah, Rachel, Benjamin. BS in Physics, Calif. State U., Northridge, 1967; MS in Applied Geophysics, U. Houston, 1970; PhD in Geophysics, Columbia U., 1975. Geophysicist Texaco Inc., Houston, 1967-71, spl. projects geophysicist, 1975-81; rsch. geophysicist Geosource, Houston, 1981-86; mgr. geophys.rsch. Texaco Inc., 1986-99; prof., Shell Centennial chair U. Tex., Austin, 1999—. Adj. prof. U. Houston, 1988-99. Co-author: Multicomponent Seismology in Petroleum Exploration; contbr. articles to tech. jours. and books. Mem. IEEE, Soc. Exploration Geophysicists (Disting. Lectr. 2001), European Assn. Exploration Geophysicists, Am. Assn. Petroleum Geologists, Am. Geophys. Union, Seismol. Soc. Am., Geophys. Soc. Houston (life, pres. 1998-99). Democrat. Jewish. Avocation: gardening. Home: 3807 Laurel Ledge Ln Austin TX 78731-4051 Office Phone: 512-471-9129. Business E-Mail: tatham@mail.utexas.edu.

TATIBOUET, ANDRE STEPHAN, condominium and resort management firm executive; b. Honolulu, Mar. 10, 1941; s. Joseph J. F. and Annalie (Knaack) T.; m. Jane Inez Barrows, Apr. 19, 1968; children: Cartier, Cecily. BA in Russian and Am. History, U. Hawaii, 1964. Cert. Hotel Adminstr. Owner, developer Pacific Beach Hotel, Honolulu, 1968—71; founder, pres. Aston Hotels & Resorts (formerly Hotel Corp. of Pacific), Honolulu, 1969; chmn., CEO Aston Hotels & Resorts, 2002; bd. dirs. ResortQuest Internat. Inc., 1998-2000, AFM Hospitality Corp., 2000—. Life mem. founders circle Punahou Sch., 1981—; mem. Hebrew U., 1982—; emeritus mem. U. Hawaii Pres. Club, 1983—; state chmn. U.S. Commn. on Civil Rights, 1985-95; 2d v.p. Waikiki Improvement Assn., 1985-90; mem. travel industry mgmt. adv. com. U. Hawaii, 1986—; mem. Honolulu Symphony Soc., 1986-2000, vice chmn. bd. dirs., 1988-89; mem. travel industry mgmt. adv. coun. Hawaii Pacific Coll., 1988—; mem. Hawaii Coun. Econ. Edn., 1988—; trustee Honolulu Chamber Music Soc., 1975-85, Jewish Fedn. Hawaii, 1982-86; bd. dirs. Hawaii Performing Arts Co., 1982 87, Hawaii Visitors and Convention Bureau, 1987—, Filipino Cmty. Ctr., 1996—; regent Chaminade U., 1986-90; mem. Ctrl. Union Congregational Ch., 1968—, deacon, 1996-99, investment com., 1998-2000. Recipient Gov.'s award for svc. as mem. of Commn. on Yr. 2000, 1978, Man of Yr. award Temple Emanu-El, 1986, Beautification award Hawaii Outdoor Circle, 1987, Judah L. Magnes Gold Medal award Am. Friends Hebrew U., 1988, Exec. of Yr. award Hawaii chpt. Profl. Secs. Internat., 1988, Disting. Alumni Outstanding Svc. award U. Hawaii, 1990, Hope Award Nat. Multiple Sclerosis Soc., 1997, Enterpreneur of Yr. in Hawaii-Hospitality Ernst & Young, 1997, Junior Achievement Hawaii award Bus. Hall of Fame, 1998. Mem. Hawaii Execs. Coun., Hawaii Hotel Assn. (dir. 1967—, chmn. 1986-87, pres. 1987 88, treas. polit. action com. 1985-90), Am. Hotel and Motel Assn. (nat. bd. dirs. 1985-2003, Lawson A. Odde award 1997), Am. Lodging Assn. (dir. 1995—), Waikiki Beach Operators Assn. (founding charter mem., exec. dir. 1984—), Soc. of Family Hoteliers of Am. Hotel and Motel Assn., Hawaii ParkConv. Coun. (founding dir., sustaining mem.), Young Pres.' Orgn., Skal Club Hawaii, Plaza Club, Beverly Hills Country Club, Honolulu Club, Oahu Country Club, Outrigger Canoe Club, Lambda Alpha Internat. Congregationalist. Avocations: tennis, music, history, literature. Office: Aston Hotels Internat 3075 La Pietra Cir Honolulu HI 96815-4514

TATIPAMULA, MALLIKARJUN, telecommunications and networking engineer; b. Warangal, India, Dec. 20, 1968; BTech, Regional Engring Coll., Warangal, 1988; MTech in Electrical Engring., Indian Inst. Tech., Madras, India, 1990. Rsch. scholar, tchg. asst. Indian Inst. Tech., Madras, 1989, sr. project officer, sys. designer electrical engring. dept., 1990-92; asst. exec. engr. R&D transmission labs. Indian Telephone Industries, Bangalore, 1990; rsch. asst. electrical engring. dept. Queen's U., Kingston, Canada, 1993; sr. mem. sci. staff, team leader Northern Telecom Broadband Networks & Wireless Network Divsn, Ottawa, Canada, 1993-97; prin. staff engr. ground sys. divsn. Motorola Cellular Infrastructure Group, Chandler, Ariz., 1997-98; sr. sys. architect Cisco Sys., Inc., San Jose, Calif., 1998—. Spkr. in field; tech. cons. GTE, MCI, Pacific Bell, Bell Canada. Lead editor: Multimedia Communication Networks: Technologies and Services, 1998. Mem. IEEE (sr. mem., mem. tech. com. on computers and comms., others), Software Project Mgrs. Network (register mem.). Achievements include development of bringing together the telecommunications and networking communities, integration of legacy networks and new networks, existing and emerging technologies, and new architectures and revamped/extended architectures, and others. Office: Cisco Sys Inc MS SJ-9/2 170 W Tasman Dr San Jose CA 95134-1706 Fax: 408-527-1221.

TATLOCK, ANNE M. trust company executive; b. White Plains, NY, July 1, 1939; d. John and Kathleen (McGrath) McNiff; m. William Tatlock, Apr. 29, 1967; children: Julina, Kerry, Christopher. BA, Vassar Coll., 1961; MA in Econs., NYU, 1968. 1st v.p. Smith Barney Harris Upham, N.Y.C., 1962-84; exec. v.p. Fiduciary Trust Internat., N.Y.C., 1984-94, pres. NYC, 1994 -99, pres., CEO, 1999—2000, chmn., CEO, 2000—. Bd. dirs. Fortune Brands, Lincolnshire, Ill., 1996—, Franklin Resources, San Mateo, Calif., 2001—, Merck, NJ, 2000—. Trustee Am. Ballet Theatre, NYC, 1994-, (pres., 1999-2001), Vassar Coll., 1994—, The Teagle Found., NYC, 1995—, Andrew W. Mellon Found., N.Y.C., 1995—, chmn., 2003—, Cultural Instns. Retirement Sys., NYC, 1989—, (chmn., 1995-99), Howard Hughes Med. Inst., Md., 2000—, The Conf. Bd., NYC, 2001—, Mayo Found., Minn., 2002—.

TATUM, BEVERLY DANIEL, psychology and education educator; b. Tallahaassee, Sept. 27, 1954; d. Robert Alphonse and Catherine Faith (Maxwell) Daniel; m. Travis James Tatum, July 28, 1979; children: Travis Jonathan Daniel, David Alexander Daniel. BA, Wesleyan U., Middletown, Conn., 1975; MA in Psychology, U. Mich., 1976, PhD, 1984. Lic. clin. psychologist. From asst. prof. to assoc. prof. dept. psychology Westfield (Mass.) State Coll., 1983-89; assoc. prof. dept. psychology and edn. Mt. Holyoke Coll., South Hadley, Mass., 1989—; pvt. practice Northampton, Mass., 1989—. Lectr. dept. black studies U. Calif., Santa Barbara, 1980-83, counseling psychologist, 1979-83; vis. scholar Stone Ctr., Wellesley (Mass.) Coll., 1991-92; chair, bd. dirs. Equity Inst., Emeryville, Calif., 1987-89. Author: Assimilation Blues, 1987. Predoctoral fellow APA Minority Program, 1976-79, dissertation fellow U. Calif., 1980-81, postdoctoral fellow Ford Found., 1991. Mem. APA, Am. Psychol. Soc., Ea. Psychol. Assn., Mass. Psychol. Assn., Assn. Women in Psychology, Assn. Black Psychologists. Office: Mount Holyoke College Dept Psychology And Ed South Hadley MA 01075

TATUM, JACKIE, former parks and recreation manager, municipal official; b. Kansas City, Mo., June 11, 1932; 2 children. BS in Phys. Edn., U. So. Calif. Tchr., Calif. With Ctrl. Recreation Ctr. Parks and Recreation Ctr. City of L.A., 1955; recreation dir. various recreation ctrs.; prin. recreation supr.; asst. gen. mgr. Valley Region, 1989-92; gen. mgr., 1992-98; cons. City of L.A., Dept. Recreation and Parks, 1998—. Chair nat. exec. com., creator, developer Wonderful Outdoor World (WOW); presenter in field. Contbr. articles to profl. jours.; appearances in tv, radio shows. Recipient Ticket to Life award Inner City Games; named Woman of the Yr. World Ops. Internat., 1976, City Employee of Yr. All City Employees Benefits Svc. Assn., 1992., One of Ten Most Powerful Black Women in L.A. Mem. Nat. Recreation and Parks Assn. (Disting. Svc. award 1997, tchr. Pacific Mktg. and Revenue Sources Mgmt. Sch.), Chi Kappa Rho (v.p., pres., past pres. Helen I. Pontius Nat. award of merit). Office: City of Los Angeles Recreation 200 N Main St Rm 1330 Los Angeles CA 90012-4110

TATUM, STEPHEN LYLE, lawyer; b. New Orleans, Apr. 3, 1954; s. Gail Douglas and Barbara (Lyle) T.; m. Nenetta Carter, July 5, 1977; children: Carter Ann, Stephen Lyle Jr. BS in Anthropology, So. Meth. U., 1976; JD, U. Tex., 1979. Bar: Tex. 1979, U.S. Dist. Ct. (no. dist.) Tex. 1980, U.S. Dist. Ct. (ea. dist.) Tex. 1986, U.S. Dist. Ct. (we. dist.) Tex. 1991, U.S. Ct. Appeals (5th and 11th cirs.) 1981, U.S. Ct. Appeals (10th cir.) 1986, U.S. Supreme Ct. 1993; cert. in civil appellate law Tex. Bd. Legal Specialization. Law clk. Judge David O. Belew Jr. U.S. Dist. Ct., Ft. Worth, 1979-80; assoc. Cantey & Hanger, Ft. Worth, 1980-85, ptnr., 1985-90; sr. ptnr. Thompson & Knight, P.C., Ft. Worth, 1990-93; ptnr. Brown, Herman, Dean, Wiseman, Liser & Hart LLP, Ft. Worth, 1993—. Bd. dirs. Tex. Dept. Health, Austin, 1992-95, Trinity River Authority, Arlington, Tex., 1990-92; trustee Southwestern U., Georgetown, Tex., 1997—, Ft. Worth Country Day Sch., 1993—; chair bd. trustees YMCA of Tarrant County, Ft. Worth, 1987-91. Named Outstanding Young Leader of Tarrant County, Tarrant County Jaycees, Ft. Worth, 1988. Mem. Fedn. Ins. and Corp. Counsel, Internat. Assn. Def. Counsel, State Bar of Tex. (adminstrn. of justice com. 1987-91). Methodist. Avocations: soccer, golf, reading, drumming. Office: Brown Herman Dean Wiseman Liser & Hart LLP 306 W 7th St Ste 200 Fort Worth TX 76102-4905

TATUM, VALORIE, elementary school educator, pharmacist; d. Louis Joe and Ruth (Gary) Tatum. Cert. in pharmacology, Kennedy King Coll., 1990; BA in Elem. Edn., Nat. Lewis U., 1994. Lic. pharmacist tech. Ill.; cert. tchr. Ill. Pharmacist technician Watson Pharmacies, Chgo., 1987—94; tchr. Chgo. Bd. Edn., Chgo., 1995—. Spl. edn. head tchr. McAuliffe Elem., Chgo., 1997—99. Adminstrv. coun. Rust Meml. United Meth. Ch., Chgo., 2000—03, Sunday sch. tchr., 2002—, pastor parish rels. com., 2003—. Nominee Golden Apple award, 2003; recipient Wall of Tolerance award, 2004, Poet of the Year, Internat. Library of Poetry, 2004, Who's Who in Poetry, 2004; Bilingual Mini grant, Chgo. Bd. Edn., 2003. Democrat. Methodist. Avocations: reading, writing, movies. Office Phone: 773-875-1032., 773-534-4400.

TATYREK, ALFRED FRANK, consultant, materials and environmental engineer, analytical and research chemist; b. Hillside, N.J., Jan. 23, 1930; s. Frank Peter and Frances (Luxa) T. BS, Seton Hall U., 1954; postgrad., Rutgers U., 1956—57. Rsch. chemist Bakelite div. Union Carbide, Bloomfield, NJ, 1953-58; rsch. chemist Bakelite divsn. U.S. Radium Corp., Morristown, NJ, 1959-62; analytical chemist insp. Chem. Procurement Dist. U.S. Army, N.Y.C., 1962-64, rsch. chemist Picatinny Arsenal Dover, NJ, 1964-73; chem. materials engr. U.S. Army Armament Rsch., Devel. and Engring. Ctr., NJ, 1973-95. Cons. polymer materials, environ. chemistry. Patentee pyrotechnic compositions, chemiluminescent compounds and processes, crank case oil vacuum purification sys. for internal combustion engines, method for the removal of thermoset potting compound from the electronics package of a munitions item; lectr., contbr. articles on mountaineering expdns. and adventures in the great mountain ranges of N.Am., S.Am., Europe and Africa to mags.; contbr. more than 50 sci. and tech. reports to profl. publs. 1st aid instr. ARC, Essex County, N.J., 1969-82; chief 1st aid Maplewood (N.J.) CD, 1971-91; patrol dir. Nat. Ski Patrol, Phoenicia, N.Y., 1978-84, sr. status, 1979-, lifetime Nat. Ski patroller So. N.Y. region, 1993-. Staff sgt. N.J. Air N.G., 1948-57. Recipient comdr.'s award for pub. svc. Dept. of Army, 1996. Mem. Nat. Soc. Inventors, Nat. Assn. Underwater Instrs. (cert. basic and advanced diver and underwater photographer 1971-, cert. for Nitrox diving 1999), Magician's Roundtable, Internat. Magicians Soc. (life), Alpine Club of Can. (life mem.), Appalachian Mountain Club (life mem., hiking leader), Sierra Club, Sigma Xi, The Sci. Rsch. Soc. (pres. Picatinny chpt. 1974-75, 79-80, 85-86). Roman Catholic. Climbed 15,771 feet Mt. Blanc, highest mountain peak in Europe; climbed to highest summit on Point Uruhu on 19,730 feet on Mt. Kilimanjaro, highest mountain peak in Africa, 1972; leader of climb on Matterhorn and Monte Rosa, Switzerland's highest peak; participant in numerous mountain expdns. in U.S. and Can., including 3 first ascents in No. Cascades of Wash. (S.E. ridge of Mt. Goode, Aug. 1963, Peak 7732 via the Snow Chute, Aug. 1964, East ridge of Bear Mountain Aug. 1964); numerous undersea photography expeditions to Caribbean and South Pacific coral reefs. Home: 27 Orchard Rd Maplewood NJ 07040-1919 Personal E-mail: atatyrek@worldnet.att.net. *"God has given us a world rich in physical and intellectual beauty as well as intriguing scientific discovery. To earn these rewards we must seek out and meet the challanges of life, not as distasteful burdens, but as true opportunities upon which to build where others have failed or left off, using all the infinite resources that God has given to all of us".*

TAUB, AARON MYRON, retired healthcare administrator, consultant; b. Jersey City, Dec. 21, 1935; s. Isadore and Beatrice (Grotsky) T.; m. Rosemary Elizabeth Dessel, July 24, 1967; children: Michael David, Deborah Anne. BS, Wagner Coll., 1960; PhD, SUNY, Buffalo, 1965. Mgr. med. svcs. Fisons Can., Toronto, 1969-72; mgr., dir. quality control Fisons Corp., Bedford, Mass., 1972-82, dir. regulatory affairs, 1982-84, sr. scientist, 1984, dir. project mgmt., 1985-88, dir. new product coord. Rochester, N.Y., 1988-96; ret. Mem., chmn. Bd. of Health, Stow, Mass., 1977-82. With USNR, 1953-55. Predoctoral fellow NIH, SUNY, 1962-64. Mem. Sigma Xi. Avocation: reading. Home: 5 Glen Cannon Trl Pittsford NY 14534-2346

TAUB, ALEX A.G. writer, educator; b. Seattle, Wash., July 23, 1968; s. Jack H and Frieda B Taub; m. Amanda Harriett Stephenson, June 24, 1995. BS in anthropology, Ctr. Wash. U.; MA in anthropology, Western Wash. U., 1992. Prof. asst. Ctrl. Wash. U., Ellensburg, Wash., 1987—90, Western Wash. U., Bellingham, Wash., 1990—92; juvenile detention counselor King County, Seattle, 1994—95; social worker Child Protection Services, Yakime, Wash., 1995—96; ct. case load mgr. Kittias County, Ellensburg, Wash., 1996—2001; tchr. Cashmere E. Wenatchee, Wash., 2001—. Vol. Youth Services of Kittitas County, Ellensburg, Wash., 1988—90, bd. dirs., 1995—2001; adj. faculty Wenatchee Valley Coll., 2003. Author: (book) Blindflight, 1998, Death of Curtis Jones, 2001. Pres. and bd. mem. Temple Shalom, 1998—2001. Mem.: Leavenworth Coffee House (bd. mem. housing coord. 2002—). Jewish. Avocations: woodworking, art, hiking, sewing. Home: 203 W Benton Leavenworth WA 98826 E-mail: ataub@urx.com.

TAUB, AMY F. dermatologist; b. Chgo. d. Max and Martha Forman; m. Jeff M. Taub, Sept. 6, 1992; 1 child, Zachary. MD, Northwestern U., 1985. Diplomate Am. Bd. Dermatology. Med. dir. div. dermatology Northwestern Meml. Physicians Group, Chgo., 1998—2003; founder, CEO Skinfo, LLC, Buffalo Grove, Ill., 1999—; founder, med. dir. Advanced Dermatology, LLC, Lincolnshire, Ill., 2003—. Founder skin care website Skinfo.com, 2000. Fellow Am. Acad. Dermatology, Am. Soc. Dermatologic Soc., Am. Soc. Laser Medicine and Surgery, Chgo. Dermatol. Soc., Ill. State Dermatol. Soc. (chair laser subcom. 2000-01). Jewish. Office: Advanced Dermatology 275 Parkway Dr Ste 521 Lincolnshire IL 60069 E-mail: drtaub@skinfo.com.

TAUB, EDWARD, psychology researcher; b. Bklyn., Oct. 22, 1931; s. Samuel Hart and Ida Pearl (Kimmel) T.; m. Mildred Allen Taub, Aug. 13, 1959. BA, Bklyn. Coll., 1953; MA, Columbia U., 1959; PhD, NYU, 1969. Rsch. asst. Columbia U., N.Y.C., 1956, Dept. Exptl. Neurology, Jewish Chronic Disease Hosp., N.Y.C., 1957-60, rsch. assoc., 1960-68; dir. Behavioral Biology Ctr., Inst. for Behavioral Rsch., 1968-83; assoc. dir. Inst. for Behavioral Rsch., 1978-83; univ. prof. psychology U. Ala., Birmingham, 1986—2000, univ. prof., 2000—; standing guest prof. U. Konstanz, Germany, 1995—; guest prof. U. Jena, Germany, 1996—. Asst. prof. dept. psychiatry Johns Hopkins U., Balt., 1972-82; vis. prof. grad. program dept. psychology CUNY, 1984-85; vis. prof. U. Tuebingen, U. Muenster, Humboldt U., Germany, 1993—. Contbr. articles to profl. jours. Recipient Pioneering Rsch. Contbn. award, 1989, Disting. Scientist of 1998 award Assn. of Applied Psychophysiol. and Biofeedback, Ireland Prize for Scholarly Distinction U. Ala., Birmingham, 1997, Humboldt Rsch. award, 2000; Guggenheim Found. fellow, 1983-84. Fellow AAAS, APA (exec. com. divsn. 6, Disting. Sci. award for the applications of psychology 2004), Soc. for Behavioral Medicine, Am. Psychol. Soc. (charter, William James Fellow award 1997); mem. Soc. for Neurosci., Biofeedback Soc. Am. (pres. 1978-79, Outstanding Rsch. Contbn. award 1988), Am. Physiol. Soc. (exec. com. neurosci. sect. 1988-91). Achievements include invention of technique of thermal biofeedback, 1970-71; inventor Constraint-Induced Movement therapy for stroke rehabilitation. Office: U Ala at Birmingham 712 CPM 1530 3d Ave S Birmingham AL 35294-0018 Office Phone: 205-934-2471. Business E-Mail: etaub@uab.edu.

TAUB, HENRY, retired computer services company executive; b. Paterson, N.J., Sept. 20, 1927; s. Morris and Sylvia (Sievitz) T.; m. Marilyn Adler, Sept. 13, 1958; children: Judith, Steven, Ira. BS, N.Y. U., 1947. Pres. Automatic Data Processing, Inc., Roseland, N.J., 1949-69, chmn. bd., 1970-77, 82-86, chmn. exec. com., 1977—, hon. chmn. bd., 1986—; ptnr. N.J. Nets, 1998—. Dir. Leumi Bank & Trust Co., N.Y.C., Rite Aid Corp., Hasbro, Inc.; past pres., hon. chmn. Joint Distbn. Com. Chmn., hon. pres. N.Y. chpt. Hemophilia Found., 1970-76; past vice chmn. Nat. Hemophilia Found.; bd. dirs. Am. Friends Hebrew U., Interfaith Hunger Appeal, 1979—, N.Y. Shakespeare Festival, 1981—, Ch. United Israel Appeal, 1986-90; trustee NYU, Avi Chai Found.; mem. bd. govs. Jewish Agy., 1981-90; pres. Jewish Community Ctr. of Palisades, 1980-84; chmn. Bus. Employment Found., Inc., 1980-90. Mem. Am. Technion Soc. (chmn., internat. bd. govs. 1990—), Paterson Alumni Assn. (chmn. 1987-94). Office: ADP Inc 1 A D P Blvd Roseland NJ 07068-1786 also: NJ Nets Meadowlands Arena East Rutherford NJ 07073

TAUB, JESSE J. electrical engineering researcher; b. N.Y.C., Apr. 27, 1927; s. Julius and Ida (Orlansky) T.; m. Eva Pollack, Dec. 24, 1955 (dec. Nov. 1973); children: Richard Lawrence, Jocelyn Cara, Suzanne Mara; m. Naomi Etta Trachtenberg, June 30, 1974. BEE, CCNY, 1948; MEE, Poly. U., 1949. Group leader microwave electronics, Material Lab. USN, Bklyn., 1949-55; engr. Airborne Instruments Lab., Mineola, N.Y., 1955-58, sect. leader, 1958-61, engring. cons., 1961-75; chief scientist AIL Systems Inc., Melville, N.Y., 1975-93; cons., 1993—. Mem. engring. adv. bd. N.Y. Tech., Hofstra U. Author: (with others) Microwave Measurements, 1963; contbr. numerous papers to profl. publs.; patentee microwave techniques With USN, 1945-46. Fellow IEEE (Centennial medal 1984, 3rd Millenium medal 2000, C.A. Fowler award 1993, Region 1 William Terry award 2001, adminstrv. com. 1972-74, program chmn. microwave symposium, steering com., chmn. L.I. sect. awards, USAB Divsn. award 2002); mem. Archaeology Inst. Am. Democrat. Jewish. Avocations: classical musician, contract bridge, archaeology. Home and Office: 115 Northgate Cir Melville NY 11747-3045 E-mail: jjtaub@aol.com.

TAUB, RICHARD PAUL, social sciences educator; b. Bklyn., Apr. 16, 1937; s. Martin Glynn and Frances (Israel) T.; m. Doris Susan Leventhal, Aug. 14, 1961 (dec. Feb. 1996); children: Neela Robin, Zachariah Jacob; m. Betty G. Farrell, June 21, 2000. BA, U. Mich., 1959; MA, Harvard U., 1962, PhD in Social Relations, 1966. Asst. prof. sociology Brown U., Providence, 1965-69; from asst. prof. to Paul Klapper prof. of social scis. U. Chgo., 1969—, assoc. dean Coll. of Univ., 1982-86, chmn. com. on human devel., 2000—. Adv. bd. Neighborhood Preservation Initiative, 1993-2000; chair adv. bd. Nat. Comty. Devel. Initiative, 1991-95; dir. South Ark. Rural Devel. Study, 1988-96; Disting. visitor Mac Arthur Found., 1998. Author: Community Capitalism, Bureaucrats Under Stress, (with D. Garth Taylor and Jan Dunham) Paths of Neighborhood Change, (with Doris L. Taub) Entrepreneurship in India's Small Scale Industries; editor: (with Doris L. Taub) American Society in Tocqueville's Time and Today; co-editor Studies of Urban Soc., 1978—; contbr. articles to profl. jours. Chmn. bd. St. Thomas the Apostle Sch., Chgo., 1983-86; bd. dirs. Hyde Park Kenwood Cmty. Conf., Chgo., 1972-75; bd. seminary Coop Bookstore, Chgo., 1994—. Angell scholar U. Mich., 1956; Woodrow Wilson fellow Harvard U., 1959-60, W.E.B. DuBois Inst. fellow, 1997-98; grantee Am. Inst. Indian Studies, Ford Found., MacArthur Found., NSF, Wieboldt Found., Nat. Inst. Justice. Mem. Am. Sociol. Assn., Midwest Sociol. Soc., Assn. for Asian Studies. Avocations: bicycling, music. Office: Univ Chgo 5730 S Woodlawn Ave Chicago IL 60637 Office Phone: 773-834-8907. E-mail: rpt2@uchicago.edu.

TAUB, ROBERT ALLAN, lawyer; b. Denver, Nov. 25, 1923; s. Clarence Arthur and Mary Frances (Jones) T.; m. Doris Irene Schroeder, Dec. 22, 1945; children: Amanda, Jonathan, Barbara. BA, U. Chgo., 1944, JD, 1947. Bar: Ill. 1947. Legal staff Marshall Field & Co., Chgo., 1947-50; mgr. exec. compensation Ford Motor Co., Dearborn, Mich., 1950-63, asst. sect., 1963-74, dir. corp. affairs planning, 1974-98. Pres. Dearborn Community Arts Council, 1971-72; trustee Internat. Mus. Photography, George Eastman House, Rochester, N.Y., 1976—, chmn., 1979-82; mem. adv. bd. U. Mich. Dearborn, 1980—, Met. Mus. Art, N.Y.C., 1987—; trustee Henry Ford Hosp., Detroit, 1983—; chmn. Dearborn Pub. Libr., 1986—; bd. dirs., mem. exec. com., chmn. fin. com., Health Alliance Plan, 1992—. Mem. ABA, Ill. Bar Assn, Art Inst. Chicago, 1998—. Presbyterian. Home: 1824 Hawthorne St Dearborn MI 48128-1448 E-mail: robert@rataab.org.

TAUBE, HENRY, chemistry professor; b. Sask., Can., Nov. 30, 1915; arrived in U.S., 1937, naturalized, 1942; s. Samuel and Albertina (Tiledetski) Taube; m. Mary Alice Wesche, Nov. 27, 1952; children: Linda, Marianna, Heinrich, Karl. BS, U. Sask., 1935, MS, 1937, LLD, 1973; PhD, U. Calif., 1940; PhD (hon.), Hebrew U. of Jerusalem, 1979; DSc (hon.), U. Chgo., 1983, Poly. Inst., N.Y., 1984, SUNY, 1985, U. Guelph, 1987, Seton Hall U., 1988, Lajos Kossuth U. Debrecen, Hungary, 1988; DSc, Northwestern U., 1990, U. Athens, 1993. Instr. U. Calif., 1940—41; instr., asst. prof. Cornell U., 1941—46; faculty U. Chgo., 1946—62, prof., 1952—62, chmn. dept. chemistry, 1955—59; prof. chemistry Stanford U., 1962—90; prof. emeritus Stanford U, 1990—; Marguerite Blake Wilbur prof. Stanford U., 1976, chmn. dept., 1971—74. Baker lectr. Cornell U., 1965. Recipient Harrison Howe award, 1961, Chandler medal, Columbia U., 1964, F. P. Dwyer medal, U. NSW, 1973, Nat. medal of sci., 1976—77, Excellence in Grad. Tchg. and Innovative Sci. award, Allied Chem., 1979, Nobel prize in chemistry, 1983, Bailar medal, U. Ill., 1983, award in chemistry, Robert A. Welch Found., 1983, Disting. Achievement award, Internat. Precious Metals Inst., 1986, Merit award, Brazilian Order of Sci., 1994; fellow, Guggenheim, 1949, 1955. Fellow: Royal Soc. Can. (hon.), Indian Chem. Soc. (hon.), Royal Soc. Chemistry (hon.); mem.: NAS (award in chem. scis. 1983), Royal Soc., Royal Danish Acad. Scis. and Letters, Finnish Acad. Sci. and Letters, Am. Philos. Soc., Royal Physiographical Soc. of Lund, Am. Chem. Soc. (award for nuclear applications in chemistry 1955, Kirkwood award 1965, Disting. Svc. in Advancement Inorganic Chemistry award 1967, Nichols medal 1971, Willard Gibbs medal 1971, T.W. Richards medal 1980—81, Monsanto Co. award in inorganic chemistry 1981, Linus Pauling award 1981, Priestley medal 1985, Oesper award 1986, G.M. Kosolapoff award 1990), Engring. Acad. Japan (assoc.), Am. Acad. Arts and Scis., Australian Acad. Scis. (corr.), Brazilian Acad. Scis. (corr.), Chem. Soc. Japan (hon.), Hungarian Acad. Scis. (hon.), Can. Soc. Chemistry (hon.), Coll. Chemists of Catalonia and Beleares (hon.), Sigma Xi, Phi Beta Kappa, Phi Lambda Upsilon (hon.). Office: Stanford U Dept Chemistry Stanford CA 94305-5080 E-mail: cdpiercy@stanford.edu.

TAUBENFELD, HARRY SAMUEL, lawyer; b. Bklyn., June 27, 1929; s. Marcus Isaac and Anna (Engelhard) T.; m. Florence Spatz, June 17, 1956; children: Anne Gail Weisbrod, Stephen Marshall. BA, Bklyn. Coll., 1951; JD, Columbia U., 1954. Bar: NY 1955, U.S. Supreme Ct. 1965, U.S. Dist. Ct. (so. and ea. dists.) NY 1976. Assoc. Benjamin H. Schor, Bklyn., 1955-58; ptnr. Zuckerbrod & Taubenfeld, Cedarhurst and N.Y.C., 1958—; bd. dir. Cornerstone Real Estate Income Trust, 1993—. Bd. dir. Cornerstone Real Estate Income Trust; village atty. Village of Cedarhurst, 1977-88, trustee, 1989-2001; mem. bd. Downtown Cedarhurst Bus. Improvement Dist., 1993; legis. chmn., counsel Nassau County Village Ofcls., 1979-86, v.p., 1991-93, pres., 1993-94, mem. exec. com., 1989-99, chmn. intergovtl. liaison com., 1991-93; mem. legis. com. NY State Conf. Mayors, 1979-87, 92-93; mem. exec. bd. Tri-County Village Ofcls., 1991-95, pres., 1993-94; arbitrator Am. Arbitration Assn. Dist. Ct. Nassau County, 1980—, Assessment Rev. Panel, Supreme Ct., Nassau County, 1981—; mem. Constl. Bicentennial Com., 1987-89; adv. bd. First Am. Title Ins. Co. of N.Y., 2004-. Del. World Zionist Congress, 1977, 82, 87; mem. Zionist Gen. Coun., 1977-83; assoc. chmn. Am. Zionist Fedn., 1985-87; pres. Herut Zionists Am., 1977-79; v.p. Hartman YMHA, 1983-87; hon. trustee Cong. Beth Shalom, Lawrence, N.Y., 1990-2001; nat. bd. dir. Zionist Orgn. Am.; bd. govs. Jewish Agy., 1983-92; mem. exec. com. World Zionist Orgn., 1983-92; trustee United Jewish Appeal, 1986-91; bd. dir. United Israel Appeal, 1986-91; hon. vice chmn., bd. dir. Jewish Nat. Fund, 1987-89; nat. bd. dir. Am. for a Safe Israel; hon. pres. World Coun. Herut Hatzoa, Jerusalem, Internat. Bd. Youthtown of Israel. Recipient Centenial award Jabotinsky Found. 1981, Betar Youth award World Betar 1982, award Internat. League for Repatriation of Russian Jews 1977, Youth Towns of Israel Leadership award 1973, Israel Bonds Leadership award 1976, Life Time Achievement award Israel Bonds 1991, Defender of Jerusalem award 1991, Israel Bonds Menachem Begin Leadership award, 1999. Mem.: Internat. Assn. Jewish Lawyers and Jurists, Beth El (New Rochelle, NY), Zionist Orgn. Am., Jewish War Vets., B'nai B'rith, Nordau Circle Club. Home: 21 N Chatsworth Ave Larchmont NY 10538 Office: PO Box 488 575 Chestnut St Cedarhurst NY 11516-2223 E-mail: handfzin@verizon.net.

TAUBER, MARK J. lawyer; b. Detroit, Mar. 25, 1949; s. Max M. and Beatrice R. (Roth) T.; m. Anita L. Tilben, June 23, 1970; children: Melissa A., Benjamin M., Allison B. BA, U. Mich., 1970; JD, George Washington U., 1973. Bar: D.C. 1973, Md. 1974, U.S. Supreme Ct. 1980. From assoc. to ptnr. Pierson, Ball & Dowd, Washington, 1973—82; ptnr. Piper & Marbury, Washington, 1982-99, Piper, Marbury, Rudnick & Wolfe, Washington, 1999—2002; ptnr., chair comm. practice group Piper Rudnick LLP, Washington, 2002—. Home: 110 St Martin Dr Palm Beach Gardens FL 33418 Office: Piper Rudnick LLP 1200 19th St NW Washington DC 20036-2430 Office Phone: 202-861-3913.

TAUBIN, DAWN, film company executive; Staff prodr., cable television programming Warner Amex Cable Comms., Ohio; dir., publicity and promotion Nat. Amusements Inc., Boston, 1983—85; west coast regional publicity/promotion rep. to v.p., publicity MGM, 1985—89; v.p., publicity Warner Bros. Pictures, 1989—93, v.p., advt. and publicity, 1993—96, sr. v.p., advt. and publicity, 1996—99, exec. v.p., mktg., 1999—2001, pres., domestic mktg., 2001—. Office: Warner Bros Pictures 4000 Warner Blvd Burbank CA 91522-0001*

TAUBMAN, A. ALFRED, real estate developer; b. Pontiac, Mich., Jan. 31, 1924; s. Philip and Fannie Ester (Blustin) T.; m. Reva Kolodney, Dec. 1, 1949 (div. July 1977); children: Gayle Kalisman, Robert S., William S.; m. Judith Mazor, June 17, 1982. Student, U. Mich., 1945-48, LLD (hon.), 1991; student, Lawrence Inst. Tech., 1948-49, DArch (hon.), 1985; D in Bus. (hon.), Eastern Mich. U., 1984; D in Edn. (hon.), Mich. State U., 1993; HHD (hon.), No. Mich. U., 1995. Chmn. The Taubman Co., Bloomfield Hills, Mich., 1950—, Taubman Ctrs., Inc., Bloomfield Hills, Mich., 1992—. Prin. shareholder Sotheby's Holdings, Inc., N.Y.C., 1983-2001. Trustee Ctr. for Creative Studies, Detroit, Harper-Grace Hosps., Detroit; chmn. emeritus Archives Am. Art Smithsonian Inst., Washington, U. Pa. Wharton Real Estate Ctr., Phila.; pres. Arts Commn. of Detroit; mem. nat. bd. Smithsonian Assocs.; established Taubman Ctr. for State and Local Govt. Harvard U., Cambridge, Mass., chmn. Mich. Partnership for New Edn., Program in Am. Instns., U. Mich., Brown U.'s Pub. Policy and Am. Instns. Program; prin. benefactor A. Alfred Taubman Health Care Ctr. and A. Alfred Taubman Med. Libr., U. Mich.; bd. dirs. Detroit Renaissance, Inc., Friends of Art and Preservation in Embassies, Washington; active State of Mich. Gaming Commn. Recipient Bus. Statesman award Harvard Bus. Sch. Club of Detroit, 1983, Sportsman of Yr. award United Found. Detroit, SE Mich. Chpt. March of Dimes Birth Defects, 1983; named Michiganian of Yr. The Detroit News, 1983. Mem. Urban Land Inst. (trustee), Nat. Realty Com. (bd. dirs.).

TAUBMAN, JANE ANDELMAN, Russian literature educator; b. Boston, Oct. 23, 1942; d. Hyman M. and Esther (Rosenthal) Andelman; m. William Chase Taubman; children: Alexander, Phoebe. BA, Radcliffe Coll., 1964; MA, Yale U., 1968, PhD, 1972. Instr. Russian Smith Coll., Northampton, Mass., 1968-72; asst. prof. Russian Amherst (Mass.) Coll., 1973-83, assoc. prof. Russian, 1983-89, prof. Russian, 1989—. Author: A Life Through Poetry: Marina Tsvetaeva's Lyric Diary, 1989, (Russian transl. 2001), Cinetek: Asthenic Syndrome, 2000, Kira Muratova, 2004; co-author: Moscow Spring, 1989; co-editor: Marina Tsvetaeva: One Hundred Years, 1994; contbr. articles to profl. jours. Woodrow Wilson Found. fellow, 1964—, Am. Coun. Learned Socs.-SSRC, 1974, trustee-faculty fellow Amherst Coll., 1978, fellow Nat. Def. Title VI, 1965-68; grantee Am. Philos. Soc., 1975, Amherst Coll., 1991, 94, IREX grantee USSR, 1988. Mem. AAUP, Modern Langs. Assn., Am. Assn. Tchrs. Slavic and East European Langs., Am. Assn. Slavic Studies, Am. Coun. Tchrs. of Russian, Am. Assn. Tchrs. of Slavic and East European Langs. Office: Amherst Coll Dept Russian Amherst MA 01002

TAUBMAN, JENNY, museum program director; b. Sofia, Bulgaria; m. Nicholas F. Taubman; children: Marc, Lara. Pres. Personal Image Consulting, 1981—97; chmn. capital campaign Art Mus. Western Va., Roanoke. Va. Israel adv. bd. Commonwealth of Va.; chmn. Brotherhood Week; coord. Bravo Arts, Inc.; bd. dirs. Temple Emmanuel; past pres. Hadassah and Temple Emanuel Sisterhood; bd. dirs. Va. Mus. Fine Arts, Richmond, Art Mus. Western Va., Western Va. Found. for Arts and Scis., Roanoke Symphony Aux., Roanoke City Arts Commn. Non-commd. officer Israeli Army. Avocations: art, tennis, design. Office: Art Mus Western Va Ctr in the Sq One Market Sq Roanoke VA 24011-1436

TAUBMAN, MARTIN ARNOLD, immunologist, educator; b. N.Y.C., July 10, 1940; s. Herman and Betty (Berger) T.; m. Joan Petra Mikelbank, May 30, 1965; children: Benjamin Abby, Joel David. BS, Bklyn. Coll., 1961; DDS, Columbia U., 1965; PhD, SUNY, Buffalo, 1970; MA (hon.), Harvard U., 1997. Asst. mem. staff Forsyth Dental Ctr., Boston, 1970—, head immunology dept., 1972—, assoc. mem. staff, 1974-80; sr. staff mem. The Forsyth Inst., 1980—; asst. clin. prof. oral biology and pathophysiology Harvard U. Sch. Dental Medicine, 1976-79, assoc. clin. prof., 1979-97, prof. oral biology, 1997—. Mem. oral biology and medicine study sect. NIH, 1980-84. Editor: (with J. Slots) Contemporary Microbiology and Immunology; contbr. articles to profl. jours, chpts. to books. Recipient Rsch. Career Devel. award, 1971-76, Fred Birnberg Alumni award for disting. dental rsch. Columbia U. Assn. Dental Alumni, Disting. Faculty award Harvard Sch. Dental Medicine, 1990, MERIT award NIH, 1991-2000; USPHS fellow, 1962-63; postdoctoral fellow, 1966-70. Mem. Am. Soc. Microbiology, Soc. Mucosal Immunology, Internat. Assn. Dental Rsch. (Oral Biology award 1991), Am. Assn. Immunologists, Am. Assn. Dental Rsch. (v.p. 1987—, pres.-elect 1988, pres. 1989). Office: The Forsyth Inst 140 Fenway Boston MA 02115-3799

TAUBMAN, ROBERT S. real estate developer; b. Detroit, Dec. 27, 1953; s. A. Alfred and Reva (Kolodney) T.; m. Julie Reyes, Aug. 27, 1999; 1 child, Alexander Alfred. BS in Econs., MA, Boston U. With Taubman Co. Inc., Bloomfield Hills, Mich., 1976—, exec. v.p., 1984—, exec. v.p., chief oper. officer, 1988-90; pres. chief exec. officer, 1990—. Bd. dirs. Taubman Ctrs. Inc., Comerica, Inc., Sotheby's Holdings, Inc., fashionmall.com. Chmn. Mich. campaign drive UNCF; bd. dirs. Beaumont Hosp.; trustee Cranbrook Ednl. Cmty. Mem. Nat. Sssn. Real Estate Investment Trusts (bd. govs.), Real Estate Roundtable (bd. dirs.), Urban Land Inst. (trustee, chmn. Detroit regional dist. coun.). Office: Taubman Co Inc 200 E Long Lake Rd Bloomfield Hills MI 48304-2360*

TAUBMAN, WILLIAM CHASE, political science educator, writer; b. N.Y.C., Nov. 13, 1941; s. Howard and Nora (Stern) T.; m. Jane Dea Andelman, May 18, 1969; children: Alexander, Phoebe. AB, Harvard U., 1962; MA, cert. of Russian Inst., Columbia U., 1965, PhD, 1969; MA (hon.), Amherst (Mass.) Coll., 1978. Instr. Amherst Coll., 1967-69, asst. prof., 1969-73, assoc. prof., 1973-78, prof. dept. polit. sci., 1978-83, Bertrand Snell prof., 1983—. Mem. planning staff U.S. Dept. State, Washington, 1970-71; mem. bd. Internat. Rsch. and Exch. Bd., N.Y.C., 1971-74, mem. selection com., 1984-85; vis. assoc. prof. Yale U., New Haven, spring 1975; chmn. adv. com. Cold War Internat. History Project, Woodrow Wilson Ctr., Washington, 1993—; mem. Internat. Acad. Adv. Group, Russian Fgn. Ministry Archives, 1992-97; assoc. Davis Ctr. for Russian Studies, Harvard U. Author: The View from Lenin Hills, 1967; Governing Soviet Cities, 1973; Stalin's American Policy, 1982, Khrushchev: The Man and His Era, 2003 (Nat. Book Critics Circle award, 2004, Pulitzer Prize for biography, 2004); co-author: (with Jane Taubman) Moscow Spring, 1989; editor, translator: Khrushchev on Khrushchev (Sergei N. Khrushchev), 1990; editor: Globalism and Its Critics, 1973; co-editor: Nikita Khrushchev, 2000. Recipient Robert H. Ferrell Book prize for disting. scholarship in Am. fgn. rels., 2003; named Alumnus of Yr., Harriman Inst., Columbia U., 2003; Woodrow Wilson Nat. Found. fellow, 1962; Ford Found. fellow, 1963-67; Coun. Fgn. Rels. fellow, 1970-71; Rockefeller Found. fellow, 1983; Columbia U. Harriman Inst. sr. fellow, 1987; grantee Nat. Coun. Soviet and East European Rsch., 1984; Fulbright-Hays Faculty Rsch. fellow, 1988, NEH fellow, 1992, Woodrow Wilson Internat. Ctr. for Scholars fellow, 2000. Mem. Coun. Fgn. Rels., Authors Guild. Home: 43 Hitchcock Rd Amherst MA 01002 Office: Amherst Coll Dept Polit Sci Amherst MA 01002 Office Phone: 413-542-2420. E-mail: wctaubman@amherst.edu.

TAUC, JAN, physics educator; b. Pardubice, Czechoslovakia, Apr. 15, 1922; came to U.S., 1969, naturalized, 1978; s. Jan and Josefa (Semonska) T.; m. Vera Koubelova, Oct. 18, 1947; children: Elena (Mrs. Milan Kokta), Jan. Ing.Dr. in Elec. Engring., Tech. U. Prague, 1949; RNDr., Charles U., 1956; Dr.Sc. in Physics, Czechoslovak Acad. Scis., 1956. Scientist microwave research Sci. and Tech. Research Inst., Tanvald and Prague, 1949-52; head semiconductor dept. Inst. Solid State Physics, Czechoslovak Acad. Scis., 1953-69; prof. exptl. physics Charles U., 1964-69, dir. Inst. Physics, 1968-69; mem. tech. staff Bell Telephone Labs., Murray Hill, N.J., 1969-70; prof. engring. and physics Brown U., 1970-83, L. Herbert Ballou prof. engring. and physics, 1983-92, L. Herbert Ballou prof. emeritus, 1992—, dir. material research lab., 1983-88. Dir. E. Fermi Summer Sch., Varenna, Italy, 1965; vis. prof. U. Paris, 1969, Stanford U., 1977, Max Planck Inst. Solid State Research, Stuttgart, Germany, 1982; UNESCO fellow, Harvard, 1961-62 Author: Photo and Thermoelectric Effects in Semiconductors, 1962, also numerous articles; editor: The Optical Properties of Solids, 1966, Amorphous and Liquid Semiconductors, 1974; co-editor: Solid State Communications, 1963-92. Recipient Nat. prize Czechoslovak Govt., 1955, 69; Sr. U.S. Scientist award Humboldt Found., 1981, Silver medal Union of Czechoslovak Mathematicians and Physicists, 1992; Jan Tauc Grad. Fellowship in Engring. at Brown U. in his honor, 2003. Fellow AAAS, Am. Phys. Soc. (Frank Isakson prize 1982, David Adler award 1988); mem. NAS, European Phys. Soc. (founding), Czechoslovak Acad. Scis. (corr. 1963-71, 90-91, fgn. 1991-92, Hlavka medal 1992, de Scientia et Humanitate Optime Meritis medal 2003), Czech Learned Soc. (hon.). Office: Brown U Divsn Engring Providence RI 02912-0001

TAUER, PAUL E. mayor, educator; b. 1935; m. Katherine Eldredge, Sept. 1, 1956; children: Paul E. Jr., Edward, Roch, Eugene, Kathryn, Tammie, Andrew, Timothy. BA in History and Edn., Regis Coll., 1961; MA in Edn. Adminstrn., U. No. Colo., 1964. Tchr. Denver Pub. Schs., 1961-92; ret., 1992. Mayor City of Aurora, Colo., 1987—, mem. Aurora City Coun., 1979-1987; mem. Adams County Coordinating Com., Gov.'s Met. Transp. Roundtable; active Aurora airport coms. Mem. N.O.I.S.E. Office: Office of Mayor 1470 S Havana St Aurora CO 80012-4014 E-mail: ptauer@ci.aurora.co.us.

TAUKE, THOMAS JOSEPH, telecommunications company executive, former congressman; b. Dubuque, Iowa, Oct. 11, 1950; s. Joseph A. and Esther M. (Reicher) T.m. Beverly Tauke, 2 children. BA magna cum laude, Loras Coll., 1972; JD, U. Iowa, 1974. Bar: Iowa 1974. Mem. firm Curnan, Fitzsimmons, Schilling and Tauke, Dubuque, 1976-79; mem. Iowa Gen. Assembly, 1975-79, 96th-101st Congresses from Iowa 2d Dist., 1979—91; v.p., govt. affairs Nynex Corp., Washington, 1991—97; exec. v.p. Nynex Govt. Affairs Co., 1991—97; sr. v.p., govt. relations Bell Atlantic Corp., 1997—2000; sr. v.p, pub. policy & external affairs Verizon Communications Inc., 2000—. Del. Republican Nat. Conv., 1976; chmn. 2d Congl. Dist. of Iowa Rep. Party, 1974-77; mem. Iowa Rep. Central Com., 1974-77; chmn. Dubuque County Rep. Party, 1972-74 Mem. pastoral council Roman Catholic Archdiocese of Dubuque, 1971-73; trustee Mt. Mercy Coll., Cedar Rapids, Iowa. Mem. Am. Bar Assn., Iowa Bar Assn., Dubuque County Bar Assn., Dubuque C. of C., Cedar Rapids Area C. of C. Clubs: Rotary, Junipera Serra. Office: Verizon Communications Inc 1095 Ave Americas New York NY 10036

TAULBEE, THOMAS LESTER, psychotherapist, educator; b. Normal, Ill., June 12, 1947; s. Marion L. and Marjorie S. T. BS, Ill. State U., 1970; MS, Tex. A&M U., 1971, EdD, 1973. Cert. marriage and family therapist; cert. sports counselor; ordained min. Psychotherapist Human Resource Devel. Ctr., Dallas, 1974-76; prof. psychology Richland Coll., Dallas, 1976—, prof. history, 1994—. North Tex. regl. dir. Nat. Inst. Sports, 2000-2003, nat. coord. of divsn. chmn., 2002-03; bd. advisors Revival Fires Ministries, Branson West, Mo., 1997-99, bd. dirs. Sports Sys. Internat., 2001-2003, mem. sports chaplaincy adv. com. U.S. Coun. for Sports Chaplaincy, 2002-2003, exec. dir., exec. v.p., chief orgnl. officer, 2003—. Co-author: Psychology from a Personal Perspective, 1992, rev. edit., 1997; editor, co -author: Personal Applications of Psychology, 1997. Dir. Superior Student Roundtable, Parker, Tex., 1993, 1996—; bd. dirs. U.S. Coun. for Sports Chaplaincy, 2003—. Recipient Nat. Inst. for Staff and Orgnl. Devel. excellence award U. Tex., 2004; Ctr. for Behavioral Studies U. North Tex., Denton, 1973-74; named Basketball All-Am., Ill. State U., 1969; named to Ill. State U. Athletic Hall of Fame. Mem. Tex. Jr. Coll. Teachers Assn., Nat. Assn. Scholars, Assn. Behavior Analysis. Avocations: world travel, scuba diving, cooking. Office: Richland Coll 12800 Abrams Rd Dallas TX 75243-2173 E-mail: taulbee@flash.net.

TAURASI, DIANA, college basketball player; Grad, U. Conn., 2004—. Guard women's basketball U. Conn., 2000—04; profl. basketball player Phoenix Mercury, WNBA, 2004—. Player USA Senior Nat. Team, 2004. Named Big East Preseason Rookie of the Yr., 2000—01, Most Outstanding Player of the NCAA East Region, 2000—01, Big East Championship Most Outstanding Player, 2000—01, Kodak All-Am. and AP Second Team All Am., 2001—02, Naismith Player of the Yr., 2001—02, 2003, NCAA Final Four and East Regional Most Outstanding Player, 2003, USBWA Nat. Player of the Yr., 2003, Big East First Team Performer, 2002—03, Preseason All-Am., 2003; named to Big East All-Rookie Team, 2000—01, NCAA Mideast Region All-Tournament Team, 2001—02, All Big-East First Team, 2002, Big East All Tournament Team, 2002, Big East All-Tournament Team, 2003; recipient Honda award for Women's Basketball Finalist, 2001—02, Honda Trophy Award, 2003, Wade Trophy, 2003, Espy Award for Best Female College Athlete, ESPN, 2003, 2004, Espy Award for Best Female Athlete, 2004. Achievements include #1 overall in WNBA draft, 2004; mem. U. Conn. NCAA Championship Teams, 2002, 03, 04; mem. US Women's Basketball Team, Athens Olympics, 2004. Office: c/o Phoenix Mercury 201 East Jefferson St Phoenix AZ 85004*

TAUREL, SIDNEY, pharmaceutical executive; b. Casablanca, Morocco, Feb. 9, 1949; came to U.S., 1986; US citizen, 1995; s. Jose and Marjorie (Afriat) T.; m. Kathryn H. Fleischmann, Mar. 22, 1977; children: Alexis, Patrick, Olivia. BSBA, Ecole des Hautes Etudes Commerciales, Paris, 1969; MBA, Columbia U., 1971. Mktg. assoc. Eli Lilly Internat. Corp., Indpls., 1971-72; mktg. planning mgr. Eli Lilly Do Brasil Limitada, Sao Paulo, Brazil, 1972-75, gen. mgr., 1981—83; mgr. pharm. ops. Eastern Europe Eli Lilly und Elanco Gesmbh, Vienna, 1976; sales mgr. pharm. Eli Lilly France SA, Paris, 1977-79, mktg. dir. pharm., 1980-81; v.p. Europe Lilly European ops., London, 1983—85; pres. Eli Lilly Internat. Corp., Indpls., 1986-91, exec. v.p. pharm. divsn., 1991; bd. dirs. Eli Lilly and Co., 1991—, exec. v.p., 1993—98, pres. pharm. divsn., 1993, pres., COO, 1996—, CEO, 1998—, chmn., 1999—. Bd. dirs. McGraw-Hill, Cies, IBM, ITT Industries; bd. overseers Columbia Bus. Sch. Bd. dirs. RCA Tennis Championships. Recipient Ellis Island medal of honor, 2000; named a chevalier (Knight) of the French Legion of Honor, 2001. Mem. Pharm. Rsch. and Mfrs. Assn.(PhRMA), Bus. Coun., Bus. Roundtable, President's Homeland Security Adv. Coun., 2002, President's Export Coun., 2003; trustee, Indpls. Mus. Art Avocations: tennis, music. Office: Eli Lilly and Co Lilly Corporate Ctr Indianapolis IN 46285 E-mail: staurel@lilly.com.*

TAURMAN, JOHN DAVID, lawyer; b. Charleston, W.Va., May 22, 1946; s. Ralph and Mikanna Elizabeth (Clark) T.; m. Donna Jill Naroff, June 13, 1981; children: Devon Elliott, Kyra Justine, Quinn Juliet. BA magna cum laude, Duke U., 1968; JD cum laude, Harvard U., 1971. Bar: D.C. 1971, U.S. Supreme Ct. 1981, Tex. 1984, U.S. Ct. Appeals (D.C., fed., 3d, 5th, 9th and 10th cirs.), U.S. Dist. Ct. (D.C.), U.S. Dist. Ct. (so., no. and ea. dists.) Tex., U.S. Ct. Fed. Claims. Assoc. Covington & Burling, Washington, 1971-78, Vinson & Elkins, Washington, 1979-82, ptnr. Houston, 1982-90, Washington, 1990—. Lectr. State Bar Inst. Tex., 1983. Editor Harvard Law Rev., 1969-71. Mem. ABA, State Bar Tex., D.C. Bar Assn., Phi Beta Kappa. Office: Vinson & Elkins Willard Office Bldg 1455 Pennsylvania Ave NW Fl 7 Washington DC 20004-1013 E-mail: jtaurman@velaw.com. *Notable cases include: ETSI vs. Burlington No., Ea. Dist. Tex., antitrust jury trial; Bank United v. U.S., Ct. Fed. Claims, breach of contract trial; First Nationwide Bank v. U.S., Ct. Fed. Claims, breach of contract; United Investors v. Waddell & Reed, Ala. state ct., tortious interference jury trial; David's Supermarkets v. Fleming, Tex. state ct., fraud jury trial.*

TAURO, JOSEPH LOUIS, federal judge; b. Winchester, Mass., Sept. 26, 1931; s. G. Joseph and Helen Maria (Petrossi) T.; m. Elizabeth Mary Quinlan, Feb. 7, 1959 (dec. 1978); children— Joseph L., Elizabeth H., Christopher M.; m. Ann Lefavour Jones, July 12, 1980. AB, Brown U., 1953; LLB, Cornell U., 1956; JD (hon.), U. Mass., 1985, Suffolk U., 1986, Northeastern U., 1990, New Eng. Sch. Law, 1992, Boston U., 1997, Brown U., 1998. Bar: Mass. 1956, D.C. 1960. Assoc. Tauro & Tauro, Lynn, Mass., 1958-59; asst. U.S. atty. Dept. Justice, Boston, 1959-60; ptnr. Jaffee & Tauro, Boston and Lynn, Mass., 1960-71; chief legal counsel Gov. of Mass., Boston, 1965-68; U.S. atty. Dept. Justice, Boston, 1972; judge U.S. Dist. Ct., Boston, 1972—; chief judge U.S. Dist. Ct., Mass., 1992-99. Mem. exec. com. Cornell Law Assn., Ithaca, N.Y., 1968-71; mem. adv. coun. Cornell Law Sch., Ithaca, 1975-80; vis. prof. law Boston U. Law Sch., 1977—; mem. Jud. Conf. U.S., 1994-97, mem. com. on operation of jury sys., 1979-86, mem. adv. com. on codes of conduct, 1988-94. Trustee Brown U., 1978—, Mass. Gen. Hosp., Boston, 1968-72, Children's Hosp. Med. Ctr., Boston, 1979-94. 1st lt. U.S. Army, 1956-58. Recipient Disting. Alumnus award Cornell U. Law Sch., 1992, Brown Bear award Brown U., 1993; named one of 10 Outstanding Young Men, Greater Boston Jaycees, 1966. Fellow Am. Bar Found.; mem. Mass. Bar Assn., Boston Bar Assn. (coun. 1968-71), D.C. Bar Assn., Boston Yacht Club (Marblehead, Mass.). Republican. Roman Catholic. Avocations: sports; reading; music; films; theater. Office: 1 Courthouse Way Ste 7110 Boston MA 02210-3009 Office Phone: 617-748-9288.

TAUSAN, CAROL A. music educator; b. Holyoke, Mass., Mar. 14, 1958; d. Eugene A. and Margaret M. Miller; m. Jon Criss Tausan, June 20, 1994. MA, Chapman U., Colorado Springs, Colo., 1994; MusB, Nebr. Wesleyan U., 1980.

Cert. tchr. Fla., 1996. Music tchr. Mary Our Queen Sch., Omaha, 1980—86, Panorama Mid. Sch., Colorado Springs, 1987—94, Turman Elem. Sch., Colorado Springs, 1994—96, Garden Elem. Sch., Venice, Fla., 1996—. Choir dir. Panorama Mid. Sch., Colorado Springs, Colo., 1987—94, gifted and talented coord., 1988—92; mem. authentic assessment com. Harrison Sch. Dist. #2, Colorado Springs, Colo., 1989—90; mem. coun. Curriculum, Instrn. and Assessment Coun., Colorado Springs, Colo., 1990—92; choir dir. Turman Elem. Sch., Colorado Springs, Colo., 1994—96, Garden Elem. Sch., Venice, Fla., 1996—, mem. faculty leadership com., 1996—; team leader Garden Elem., Venice, Fla., 1999—; mem. lang. arts com. Garden Elem. Sch., Venice, Fla., 1999—2002, bldg. rep. Sarasota Classified/Tchrs. Assn., 2001—02, sr. bldg. rep., 2002—; mem. com. Cmty./Schs. Partnership for Arts, Sarasota, Fla., 1997—, Renaissance Com., Venice, Fla., 2001—03; mem.music textbook adoption com. Sch. Bd. of Sarasota County, Fla., 2002—03. Choir dir. (performance) St. Mary's Cath. Ch., Bellevue, Nebr., 1982—84, All-City Eighth Grade Chorus, Sun Fiesta Parade (Best Edn. Entry, 1997), Venetian Holiday Festival. Grantee Sing out for Am., The Edn. Found. of Sarasota, 1997—98, The Magnificent 7, Edn. Found. of Sarasota, 1998—99, Hooray for the Red, White and Blue, 1998—99, All Am. Celebration, 1999—2000, Rockin' and Readin', 2000—01, Young Americans and Proud of It, 2000—01, True to the Red, White, and Blue, 2002—03, Rockin' and Readin', Cmty. Found. of Sarasota County, 2000-2001, The Merry Minstrel, 2002-2003, Recorders - An instrumental Opportunity, 2002-2003, Create and Communicate with Recorders, 2003-2004, You Can BEAT This!, 2003-2004; African Artist-in-Residence, Arts for a Complete Edn./Fla. Alliance for Arts Edn., 1998—99. Mem.: Colo. Music Educators Assn., Sarasota Area Music Educators, Fla. Music Educators Assn., Music Educators Nat. Conf. Home: 427 Pebble Creek Ct Venice FL 34285 Office: Garden Elem Sch 700 Center Rd Venice FL 34285

TAUSCHER, ELLEN O. congresswoman; b. Newark, N.J., 1951; m. William Y. Tauscher; 1 child, Katherine. BS in early Childhood Edn., Seton Hall U., 1974. With Bache Securities, N.Y.C., N.Y. Stock Exchange; dir. Tauscher Found.; mem. U.S. Congress from 10th Calif. dist., 1997—; mem. house armed svcs. com., house transp. com. U.S. Ho. Reps. Founder The ChildCare Registry; bd. regents Seton Hall U.; co-chair Delaine Eastin's State Supt. Pub. Instrn. Campaign, 1994; transp. and infrastructure com., surface transp. and water resources and environ. Author: The ChildCare Sourcebook, 1996. Active The Coalition, New Dem. Coalition, Bipartisan Freshman Campaign Fin. Reform Task Force, House Cancer Awareness Working Group, Congl. Caucus on the Arts; vice-chair Calif. Dem. Del. Democrat. Roman Catholic.

TAUSSIG, LYNN MAX, healthcare administrator, pulmonologist, pediatrician, educator; b. Milw., July 19, 1942; m. Lisa Peter; children: Heather, Jennifer. AB cum laude, Harvard U., 1964; MD, Washington U., St. Louis, 1968. Diplomate Am. Bd. Pediat., Nat. Bd. Med. Examiners, Am. Bd. Pediat. Pulmonary. Rsch. asst. dept. neuroanatomy Marquette U., Milw., 1965; intern in pediat. St. Louis Children's Hosp., 1968-69; resident in pediat. U. Colo. Med. Ctr., Denver, 1969-70; clin. assoc. pediat. metabolism br. Nat. Inst. Arthritis, Metabolism, and Digestive Diseases, NIH, Bethesda, Md., 1970-72; pulmonary fellow Montreal (Que., Can.) Children's Hosp., 1972-74; asst. prof. pediat. Ariz. Health Scis. Ctr., Tucson, 1974-77, cystic fibrosis ctr. dir., 1974-85, assoc. chief pulmonary function labs., 1974-85, dir. pulmonary sect., 1974-85, asst. dir. divsn. respiratory scis., 1976-92, assoc. prof. pediat., 1977-81, assoc. head dept. pediat., 1979-84, prof., 1981-93, head dept. pediat., 1985-93, dir. Steele Meml. Children's Rsch. Ctr., 1986-93; prof. pediats. U. Colo. Health Scis. Ctr., Denver, 1993—; pres., CEO Nat. Jewish Med. and Rsch. Ctr., Denver, 1993—. Frank Stevenson vis. prof. U. Con., 1977, 82; Robert Chinnock Meml. lectr. Loma Linda U., Calif., 1983; Jour. Pediats. vis. prof. U. Chgo., 1984; Brennenman lectr. L.A. Pediat. Soc., 1988, 94; Danis Meml. lectr. St. Louis U., 1989; Talamo Meml. lectr. Johns Hopkins U., Balt., 1989; Anna Zager vis. lectr. in pediats. Technion U., Haifa, Israel, 1990; Sir Clavering Fison vis. prof. Inst. Child Health, U. London, 1992; Benjamin Meaker vis. prof. U. Bristol, Eng., 1992; Ben Kagan vis. lectr. Cedars-Sinai Hosp., L.A., 1993. Mem. editl. bd. Chest, 1983-88, Am. Rev. Respiratory Diseases, 1983-89; contbr. articles to profl. jours. Trustee Congregation Anshei Israel, 1978-80; bd. dirs. Jerwish Cmty. Ctr., 1982-90, sec., 1984-86, v.p., 1987-89; mem. allocations com. Jewish Fedn. So. Ariz., 1985, 88, Allied Jewish Fedn. Denver, 1996—; bd. dirs. Colo. Biomed. Venture Ctr., 1994—, Congregation Rodef Shalom, 1996—; active Martin Luther King Jr. Minority Scholarship Program, 1994—, Colo. Concern, 1995—. Cystic Fibrosis Found. Clin. fellow, 1972-74, Sr. Internat. fellow Fogarty Internat. Ctr., 1980-81; Young Investigator Pulmonary Rsch. grantee Nat. Heart and Lung Inst., 1974-76, and numerous other med. grants; Pfizer Labs. Med. scholar, 1966; recipient Lange Med. Book award, 1966 Mem. Am. Acad. Pediat. (mem. exec. com. sect. on diseases of chest 1978-80, mem. ad hoc com. for pediat. pulmonary bds., sect. on diseases of chest 1978-85), Am. Pediat. Soc., Am. Thoracic Soc. (mem. com. to advise pres. 1975-76, sec. sci. assembly for pediats. 1975-77, mem. respiratory care com. 1976-78, mem. nominating com. 1977, 84-85, chmn. prograom com. 1979-81, mem. ann. meeting com. 1979-81, mem. rsch. rev. com. 1981-82, chmn. publs. policy com. 1988-89, 90-92, mem. exec. com. 1989-90, sec.-treas. 1989-90, active many other coms.), Am. Coll. Chest Physicians (mem. steering group for com. on cardiopulmonary diseases in children 1977-79), Ariz. Pediat. Soc., Ariz. Lung Assn., Pima County Pediat. Soc., Soc. Pediat. Rsch. (founder Lung Club 1985), Western Soc. Pediat. Rsch. (mem. nominating com. 1979-80, elected to coun. 1994—), Rotary, Harvard Club of So. Ariz. (schs. com. 1982-93, sec.-treas. 1989-93), Harvard Club of Colo., Alpha Omega Alpha. Office: Nat Jewish Med & Rsch Ctr 1400 Jackson St Denver CO 80206-2761

TAUSSIG, MARGARET C. artist; b. Boston, Jan. 11, 1922; d. George Herbert Crocker, Jr. and Elsie Tyler Goodhue; m. William M. Taussig, Apr. 7, 1945 (dec. July 1980); children: Margo Pinkerton Zann, William Murray Taussig, Jr. Cert. secretarial course, Copley Secretarial Inst., Boston, 1941; cert. mech. drawing, Newton Trade Sch., 1943. Sec. rsch. Dr. Burton Hamilton, Boston, 1941; sec., lab. technician Dr. Irving and Dr. Winsor, Boston, 1942; draftsman ink lettering Reece Buttonhole Machine Co., Boston, 1942—45; painter Pigsty Studio, Canaan, NH, 1979—. Mem.: N.H. Art Assn., Ava Gallery, Chaffee Ctr. for the Arts, Sharon Art Ctr., N.H. Art Assn. (asst. to exec. dir. for office work 1997—2002, 1st prize watercolor 1988), So. Vt. Art Ctr., The Copley Soc. Boston. Episcopalian. Avocations: cross country skiing, hiking, sewing, interior decorating. Home and Office: Margaret Taussig Studio 543 Canaan St Canaan NH 03741

TAUTZ, BIRGIT, education educator, researcher; d. Wilfried and Gudrun Tautz. Diploma, U. of Leipzig, 1991; MA U. of Wis., 1992; PhD, U. of Minn., 1998. Vis. asst. prof. St. Olaf Coll., Northfield, Minn., 1997—98; asst. prof. Lawrence U., Appleton, Wis., 1998—2002, Bowdoin Coll., Brunswick, Maine, 2002—. Editor: Colors 1800, 1900, 2000: Signs of Ethnic Difference, 2004; contbr. chapters to books, articles to profl. jours. Mem.: Am. Assn. of Tchrs. of German, Modern Lang. Assn., German Studies Assn. Office: Bowdoin Coll 77 College Station Brunswick ME 04011 Office Phone: 207-798-7079.

TAUZIN, W. J. BILLY, II, (WILBERT J. TAUZIN), congressman; b. Chackbay, La., June 14, 1943; s. Wilbert Joseph and Enola (Martinez) T.; m. Cecile Bergeron, May 29, 1993; children: Kristie René, Wilbert J. III, John Ashton, Thomas Nicholas, Michael James. BA, Nicholls State U., 1964; JD, La. State U., 1967. Bar: La. 1967. Practice, Houma and Thibodaux, La., 1967-80; mem. firm Marcel Fanguy & Tauzin, 1967-72, Tauzin-Sonnier, 1972-80; mem. La. Ho. of Reps., 1971-80, house floor leader, 1974-79, chmn. Teche Clearinghouse Rev. Bd., 1975-78, chmn. house natural resources com., 1975-80; mem. U.S. Congress from 3d La. Dist., 1980—; mem. commerce com., mem. resources com.; chmn. energy and commerce com., 2001—04; dep. whip Ho. of Reps., 1995—. Mem. Thibodaux Playhouse, 1967-75; mem. Criminal Justice Inst. Recipient Thibodaux Outstanding Young Man award, 1971 Mem. ABA, La. State Bar Assn., Lafourche Parish Bar Assn. (past pres.), Chackbay-Choupic Jr. C. of C. (past pres.), Nicholls Alumni Council (v.p.) Lodges: Kiwanis; K.C. Republican. Home: Rienzi B-5 PO Box 1407 Thibodaux LA 70302-1407 Office: US House of Reps 2183 Rayburn House Office Bldg Washington DC 20515-1803

TAVALIN, FERN, educational consultant; b. Plainfield, N.J., Feb. 10, 1953; d. Marian Dorothy Higgins and Lester Amos Pagano; m. Peter Robert Tavalin, Apr. 11, 1981; children: Kuna Leya, Julian Zoe. BA, Franklin and Marshall Coll., Lancaster, Pa., 1976; EdD, U. Mass, Amherst, 1994. Tchr. English and social studies Putney Ctrl. Sch., Vt., 1987—93; grad. asst. U. Mass., Amherst, 1992—93; dir. Vt. Arts Assessment Initiative, Montpelier, 1993—96; exec. dir. The WEB Project, Vt., 1995—; project dir. The Flow of History, Vt., 2002—. Steering com. mem. framework of stds. Vt. Dept. of Edn., Montpelier, Vt., 1993—96; adv. coun. IDM Reinventing Edn. Software Devel., Essex Junction, Vt., 1995—99; cons. Spaulding Cmty. Svc. Learning, Barre, Vt., 2002—; program presenter Tech. Innovation in Edn.; dir. The WEB Exch.: Using Multimedia and Telecomm. to Improve Student Learning; spkr. at profl. confs. Contbg. writer: Putney: World's Best Known Small Town; author: (learning guide) Collaborative Learning: A Guide to Inquiry-Based Study Groups; co-author: Improving Student Learning through Multimedia Projects (ASCD book pick, 2002); prodr.(and dir.): (videos) Vt. MIDI Project, Art Responding through Tech., From Inside Out: Creating Dance in a Pub. Sch., We Can Work It Out: Using Students as Mediators, Taking a Stand in Cyberspace; dir.: Artifacts, History, and the World Wide Web; contbr. chapters to books, articles to profl. jours. Founding bd. mem. Strolling of the Heifers, Brattleboro, Vt., 2000—; com. chair Strolling of the Heifers Ednl. Grants Com.; pres. Putney (Vt.) Hist. Soc., 1998—; chair Putney Econ Devel. Com., Putney, Vt., 2004—. Named Promising Tech. Program, U.S. Dept. Edn., Putney Person of Yr., 2004; recipient Gov. and Commr. award Contrbn. to Tech. Avocations: photography, videography, international travel, house building, gardening.

TAVARES, CHARLETA B. former state legislator; Student, Spelman Coll., Ohio State U. Mem. Ohio Ho. of Reps., Columbus, 1993-98; council mem. City of Columbus, OH. Mem. Met. Human Svc. Commn. Vol. Huckleberry House, Literacy Initiative. Recipient award Black Students in Comm. Ohio State U., 1992, Ctrl. Comty House award, 1992, Pub. Children's Svc. Assn. award, 1993; named Franklin County Dem. Women's Club Sweetheart, 1993. Mem. LWV, Far East Dem. Women's Club, Columbus Area Women's Polit. Caucus, Coalition of 100 Black Women.

TAVARES, CLARA, writer; b. Caracas, Venezuela, July 24, 1963; arrived in U.S., 1995; d. Oscar Tavares de Almeida and Angeles Sanchez de la Cuesta; widowed; 1 child, Luis Jose. Degree in computer engring., U. Ctrl. Venezuela, Caracas, 1986. Author: Los Hombres, Mi Fuente de Inspiracion, 2001, Inteligentemente Brutas, 2002. Named Spotlight Woman of Yr., Miami-Dade Pub. Libr., Fla., 2002. Avocations: basketball, weightlifting, exercise.

TAVARES, JOS(É) ANTONIO, finance executive; b. Apr. 1, 1955; BA, Lehman Coll., 1978; MBA, NYU, 1991. Gannet Corp. Westchester-Rockland Newspapers, 1978-80; mgmt. assoc. Citibank, N.Y.C., 1980-82, mgr. Brazil region, 1982-84; asst. v.p. Brazil region Citibank, N.A., N.Y.C., 1984-85, v.p. S.Am. region, 1985-89, v.p. Latin Am. region, 1989-92; v.p. Latin Am. Pvt. Bank Bankers Trust Co., N.Y.C., 1993-94; v.p. Western Hemisphere Pvt. Bank Chase Manhattan Bank, N.A., N.Y.C., 1994-96; sr. v.p. Latin Am. ops. Sumitomo Corp. of Am., N.Y.C., 1997—. Trustee, chmn. fin. com. Berkeley Coll.; trustee The Havens Relief Fund Soc., chmn. audit com. Office: Sumitomo Corp Am 600 3rd Ave New York NY 10016-1901

TAVARES, TONY, professional hockey and baseball leagues executive; b. Fall River, Mass., Oct. 17, 1949; m. Elizabeth Tavares; children: Sheila, Kristen, Mark. BS in Acctg., Roger Williams Coll. Comptroller, acting dir. Providence Civic Ctr.; with Centrum, Worcester, Mass., New Haven Vets. Meml. Coliseum, Nassau Vets. Meml. Coliseum, Uniondale, N.Y., Spectacor Mgmt. Group, pres., CEO; cons. Walt Disney Co.; pres. Anaheim Sports Inc., Anaheim, Calif., 1992—2002; chmn., gov. Mighty Ducks of Anaheim, 1993—2002; pres. Anaheim Angels, 1996—2002, Montreal Expos,, 2002—. Mem. Internat. Assn. Auditorium Mgrs. Office: Montreal Expos Olympic Stadium 4549 Pierre-de-Coubertin Ave Montreal QC H1V 3N7 Canada

TAVEGGIA, THOMAS CHARLES, business educator; b. Oak Lawn, Ill., June 15, 1943; s. Thomas Angelo and Eunice Louise (Harris) T.; m. Brigitte I. Adams, Jan. 23, 1965; children: Michaela, Francesca. BS, Ill. Inst. Technology, 1965; MA, U. Oreg., 1968, PhD, 1971. Prof. U. Oreg., Eugene, 1970, U. B.C., Vancouver, Can., 1970-73, U. Calif., Irvine, 1973-74, Ill. Inst. Technology, Chgo., 1974-77; mgmt. cons. Towers, Perrin, Forster, & Crosby, Chgo., 1977-80; ptnr. Manplan Cons., Chgo., 1980-81, Coopers & Lybrand, San Francisco, 1981-86, Touche Ross, San Francisco, 1986-88; prof. Calif. Sch. Profl. Psychology, Berkeley, 1988-98, U. Ariz., Tucson, 2000—. Author: (with Dubin and Arends) From Family and School to Work, 1967; (with Dubin) The Teaching-Learning Paradox: A Comparative Analysis of College Teaching Methods, 1968; (with Dubin and Hedley) The Medium May Be Related to the Message: College Instruction by TV, 1969; contbr. articles to profl. jours. NDEA Title IV fellow, 1967-71; U. B.C. faculty rsch. grantee, 1970, 71, 73; grantee Calif. Sch. Profl. Psychology, 1993-98. Home: 1506 W Canada Hills Dr Tucson AZ 85737-9052 Office Phone: 520-575-0590.

TAVEL, JORGE ALBERTO, internist, researcher; b. Havana, Cuba, June 6, 1965; s. Jose Amable and Mary Antonieta Tavel. MD, Johns Hopkins U., Balt., 1991. Diplomate Internal Medicine Bd. of Internal Medicine, 1996. Clin. investigator NIH, Bethesda, Md., 1994—2003; sr. advisor for medicine Office of the Vice Pres., Washington, 2003—04; clin. rsch. NIH, Bethesda, Md., 2004—. Office: Nat Inst Health Bldg 10 Rm 11C 9000 Rockville Pike Bethesda MD 20892-0002 Office Phone: 301-402-0564. Personal E-mail: jtavel@nih.gov.

TAVEL, MARK KIVEY, money management company executive, economist; b. Cambridge, Mass., May 9, 1945; s. Bernard Benjamin and Elizabeth (Rogers) T.; m. Susana Sara Doño, Dec. 14, 1980; children: Sarah Emily, Rachel Florence, Amanda Victoria, Nathaniel Benjamin, Roberto Aaron Doño. BA cum laude, Harvard U., 1967; MBA, Columbia U., 1968. Sr. mng. dir. Rothschild Asset Mgmt., Inc., N.Y.C. Trustee, treas. Trevor Day Sch., N.Y.C. Mem. Harvard Club (N.Y.C.). Home: 110 Riverside Dr New York NY 10024-3715 Office: Rothschild Inc 44th Fl 1251 Ave of the Americas New York NY 10020-1193

TAVERNER, PAMELA JOHNSON, secondary school educator; b. Benton, Ill., July 3, 1948; d. Elmer Ellsworth and Ruth Elizabeth (Claybourn) Johnson; m. Clyde K. Taverner, June 29, 1990. AB, Friends U., Wichita, Kans., 1971; M in Comm., Wichita State U., 1981. Cert. tchr. Kans., Mo. Tchr. Elk Valley High Sch., Longton, Kans., 1971-72, Summersville (Mo.) High Sch., 1972-75, Clearwater (Kans.) High Sch., 1975—. Comm. cons. Fourth fin. Corp., Wichita, 1989—93. Named Outstanding Tchr./Dir., Assn. Kans. Theatre, 1993. Mem.: NEA (bd. dirs. Kans. chpt. 1989—95, mem. exec. com. 1991—92, dir. Kans. 2001—, treas., pres. s. ctrl. Kans., nat. bd. dirs. Kans. chpt. 2001—, mem. exec. com. 2001—), Kans. Exemplary Educators Network, Clearwater Tchrs. Assn. (pres. 1977—78, 2001, Oustanding Mem. 1990), Nat. Coun. Tchrs. English, Paretns-FLAG (bd. dirs. Wichita chpt. 1993—95). Democrat. Mem. Soc. Of Friends. Avocations: victorian restoration, needlecrafts, gourmet cooking. Home: 1551 Fairview St Wichita KS 67203-2635 Office: Clearwater High Sch 801 E Ross St Clearwater KS 67026-9176 Office Phone: 620-584-2361.

TAVOSSI, HASSON M. physics and engineering educator, consultant; b. Kermanshah, Iran, Oct. 22, 1948; s. Mohammad and Ashraf-el-Sadat Tavossi. BSc, U. Essex, Colchester, Eng., 1973; MS, U. Paris, 1981, PhD, 1984. Cert. process engr., French Ministry Higher Edn. and Rsch., Commn. Energy and Process Engring. Instr. Telecom France, Paris, 1985; postdoctoral and instr. U. Paris XII and VII, 1986-94; instr. Pa. Coll. Tech., Williamsport, 1994; prof. Lycoming Coll., Williamsport, 1995; instr. Pa. State U., State College, 1995—2000; prof. Mesa State Coll., 2000—. Rschr. France Atomic Energy Commn., Val-de-Marne Lab., 1982-86; cons. Lockheed Martin Tactical Def., University Park, 1996—. Contbr. chpt. to book, articles to profl. jours. and conf. procs., including Atmospheric Pollution Jour., Chem. Soc. Am. Jour., Ultrasonics and Acoustics. Instr. Continuing and Distance Edn., Pa. State U., 1996-97. Recipient Northampton (Eng.) County Coun. scholarship, 1970-73, Assn. Contamination Prevention prize, Paris, 1984. Mem. IEEE, AAAS, ASME, Am. Phys. Soc., Acoustical Soc. Am., Sigma Xi. Achievements include development of new technique for air pollution control of submicron particles using high-intensity acoustic waves; contribution to advancement of theory of wave propagation in porous and granular materials. Office: Mesa State Coll 1100 North Ave Grand Junction CO 81501-3122 Home: 463 Margi Ct Grand Junction CO 81504-2611 Business E-Mail: htavossi@mesastate.edu.

TAVROW, RICHARD LAWRENCE, lawyer, corporate executive; b. Syracuse, NY, Feb. 3, 1935; s. Harry and Ida Mary (Hodess) T.; m. Barbara J. Silver, Mar. 22, 1972; children— Joshua Michael, Sara Hallie. AB magna cum laude, Harvard U., 1957, LL.B., 1960, LL.M., 1961; postgrad., U. Copenhagen, 1961-62, U. Luxembourg, 1962. Bar: N.Y. bar 1961, U.S. Supreme Ct. bar 1969, Calif. bar 1978. Atty. W.R. Grace & Co., NYC, 1962-66; asst. chief counsel Gen. Dynamics Corp., NYC, 1966-68; chief counsel office of fgn. direct investments U.S. Dept. Commerce, Washington, 1969-71; ptnr. Schaeffer, Dale, Vogel & Tavrow, NYC, 1971-75; v.p., sec., gen. counsel Prudential Lines, Inc., NYC, 1975-78, also bd. dirs.; v.p., sec., gen. counsel Am. Pres. Lines, Ltd., Oakland, Calif., 1978-80, sr. v.p., sec., gen. counsel, 1980-91, also bd. dirs.; sr. v.p., sec., gen. counsel Am. Pres. Cos., Ltd., Oakland, Calif., 1983-91, also bd. dirs.; sr. ptnr. Law Offices of R.L. Tavrow, 1991—; chmn., pres., CEO Diabetes Healthcare & Life Enhancement Ltd., 2000—. Instr. Harvard Coll., 1959-61; lectr. Am. Mgmt. Assn., Practising Law Inst., other assns. Recipient Silver Medal award Dept. Commerce, 1970; Fulbright scholar, 1961-62 Mem. ABA, State Bar Calif., Internat. Bar Assn., Am. Soc. Internat. Law, Am. Corp. Counsel Assn., Am. Soc. Corp. Secs. Inc., Harvard Law Sch. Assn., Navy League, Harvard Club (N.Y.C.). Home: 172 Newtown Turnpike Weston CT 06883-1616

TAW, DUDLEY JOSEPH, sales executive, director; b. Cleve., Mar. 11, 1916; s. William C. and Ella (Gedeon) T.; m. Louise E. Forshey, Sept. 10, 1938; children: Judith (Mrs. William W. Beck, Jr.), Dudley Joseph. Student, Hiram Coll., 1938. With McKesson & Robbins, Inc. (pharm. co.), after 1937, sales mgr., 1947, v.p. sales N.Y.C., 1953-60; v.p. Revlon, Inc., N.Y.C., 1960-64; v.p. mktg. East Ohio Gas Co., Cleve., 1964-74, pres., 1975-81, chmn., 1981-82, Middtaw, Ltd., Inc., 1982. Bd. dirs. No. New England Gas Corp., First Union Mgmt. Co., Biskind Devel. Co., Vt. Gas Systems Inc. Mem. Better Bus. Bur., Cleve., chmn., 1973; trustee Lakewood Hosp.; treas. Salvation Army, Cleve. With USNR, 1946-47. Named Sales Exec. of Year Sales and Mktg. Execs. Cleve., 1966, Man of Year, 1977 Mem. Sales and Mktg. Execs. Cleve. (pres. 1969-70), Westwood Country Club, Union Club, Pepper Pike Club, Rotary (pres. Cleve. 1972-73). Methodist. Home: Apt 302 22500 Lake Rd Cleveland OH 44116 1025

TAYLER, IRENE, English literature educator; b. Abilene, Tex., July 13, 1934; d. B. Brown Smith and Madeline (Bowron); m. Edward W. Tayler, June 3, 1961 (div. 1971); children: Edward Jr., Jesse; m. Saul Touster, Jan. 14, 1978. BA in Philosophy, Stanford U., 1956, MA in Am. Lit., 1961, PhD in English Lit., 1968. Tchr. Breadloaf Sch. of Eng., Middlebury, Vt., 1970, 71, 75, 76; teaching asst. Stanford U., Calif., 1958-60; lectr. Columbia U., N.Y., 1961-71; asst. prof. CUNY, 1971-73, assoc. prof., 1973-76, MIT, Cambridge, 1976-82, prof., 1982-96, sec. of the faculty, 1993-95, retired, 1996. Chair gov. com. The English Inst., 1981. Author: Blake's Illustrations to the Poems of Gray, 1971, Holy Ghosts: The Male Muses of Emily and Charlotte Bronte, 1990, Samuel Bak: Between Worlds, Paintings and Drawings from 1946 to 2001, 2002; contbr. articles to profl. jours. Internat. Inst. Edn. fellow U. Munich, 1957-58; Wilson fellow Stanford U., 1961-62; ACLS study grantee, 1968-69; Faculty Rsch. Found. grantee CUNY, 1972-73; NEH sr. scholar fellow, 1980; Mac Vicar faculty fellow MIT, 1993-2003. Mem.: St. Botolph Club (Boston) (pres. 2000—03). E-mail: itayler@mit.edu.

TAYLOR, A. JEFFRY, lawyer; b. L.A., Nov. 29, 1943; s. Henry Allen and Jane Clara (Bosco) T.; m. Kate Colemen Hanrahan, Apr. 10, 1965; children: Jennifer, Stefanie, Bryce, Zachary. BA, UCLA, 1965; JD, Loyola U., L.A., 1969. Bar: Calif. 1970, Vt. 1972, U.S. Supreme Ct. 1976, U.S. Tax Ct. 1985, U.S. Claims Ct. 1988, U.S. Ct. Appeals (D.C. cir.) 1990, U.S. Dist. Ct. (ctrl. dist.) Calif. 1970, U.S. Dist. Ct. Vt. 1972. Law clk. U.S. Dist. Judge 9th Cir. Ct. Appeals, L.A., 1969-70; trial atty. U.S. Dept. Justice Antitrust Divsn., L.A., 1970-72; corp. counsel Vt. Elec. Power Co., Rutland, 1972-79; hearing officer Vt. Dept. Edn., Montpelier, 1979-88; bar counsel Vt. Profl. Conduct Bd., Montpelier, 1979-88; adj. prof. law Vt. Law Sch., South Royalton, 1978—88, 1995—96; pvt. practice Rutland, 1979—. Contbr. articles Vt. Law Rev., 1997—. Vt. state counsel Clinton/Gore '92 and '96; Vt. rep. Nat. Lawyers Coun./Dem. Nat. Com., State Counsel, Gore 2000; Vt. bd. mem. UN Assn. U.S.; presdl. elector for State of Vt., 2000. Mem. Am. Soc. Internat. Law. Democrat. Unitarian Universalist. Avocations: opera, trout fishing. Home: 1415 East St Clarendon VT 05759-9765 Office: One Justice Sq Rutland VT 05701 E-mail: jeffreyT905@yahoo.com.

TAYLOR, ALAN CHARLES, chaplain, counselor, researcher; b. Saratoga Springs, NY, Dec. 30, 1958; s. Alfred Tobias and Mary Catherine (Gunn) T.; m. Susan Laurence McCall, Sept. 20, 1997. BA cum laude in Art, SUNY, Plattsburgh, 1980; MS in Ednl. Psychology and Stats., SUNY, Albany, NY, 1988; post grad., Russell Sage Coll., Albany, NY, 1990-91; MS in Rehab. Counseling, SUNY, Albany, NY, 1992; MA in Ministry (hon.), Bibl. Theol. Sem., Hatfield, Pa., 2000; postgrad., Bibl. Theol. Sem., 2000—. Cert. rehab. counselor; credentialed alcoholism and substance abuse counselor; lic. min. Grad. asst., evaluator intern Evaluation Consortium SUNY, Albany, NY, 1988-89, grad. asst. dept. ednl. psychology and stats., 1989-90; rsch. asst. Regents Coll., Albany, NY, 1990-91, vocat. rehab., alcohol and drug counselor, 1993-97; residence dir. Bibl. Theol. Sem., 1999—; dir. care min. E. Swamp Ch. Cons. tchg. asst. Sch. Edn. Computing Facility U. Albany, 1987—88, summers, 1989, 90; adj. faculty Coll. St. Rose, spring, 1991; pastoral counseling and tng. Albany Area Bibl. Counseling, 1995—98; chaplain asst. Frederick Mennonite Cmty., 1999—2000; residence dir. Bibl. Theol. Sem., 2000; chaplain Ruidoso (N.Mex.) Downs Race Track, 2001; pray ministry, devel. Messianic Jewish Alliance Am., 2001—. Editor software Inst. for Internat. Rsch., Washington, 1989; contbg. editor: Commitment e-jour., 1999; contbr. presentations to profl. mtgs.; co-editor: (tng. manual) Improving the Efficiency of Educational Systems, Volume 1: DOS, Enable, SPSS/PC, Lotus, Introduction to Statistics, Volume 2: Manpower Education and Planning Model, Volume 3: Manpower Education and Planning Model, 1989; photographs exhibited in various shows. Mem.: AACD, Internat. Ministerial Fellowship, Soc. Biblical Lit., Race Track Chaplaincy Am. (bd. dirs.), Evang. Theol. Soc., Grad. Network Edn. (co-founder 1987, pres. 1990—92), New Eng. Ednl. Rsch. Orgn. (program com. ann. mtg. 1991), Am. Assn. Christian Counselors, Ea. Ednl. Rsch. Assn. (assoc. Disting. Paper award 1988), Mensa. Avocations: reading, travel, photography, writing. Address: Apt 104 2748 Cobb Rd Hatfield PA 19440-2601

TAYLOR, ALLAN BERT, lawyer; b. Cin., June 28, 1948; s. H Ralph and Henrietta Irene (Medalia) Taylor; m. Sally Ann Silverstein, June 6, 1971; children: Rachel Elizabeth, Karen Ruth. AB, Harvard U., 1970, M in Pub. Policy, JD, Harvard U., 1975. Bar: Conn 1975, US Ct Appeals (DC cir) 1977, US Dist Ct (so dist) NY 1979, US Ct Appeals (2d cir) 1979, US Supreme Ct 1979, US Ct Appeals (1st and 10th cirs) 1991. Law clk. to J. Skelly Wright D.C. Cir., Washington, 1975-76; law clk. to Thurgood Marshall U.S. Supreme Ct., Washington, 1976-77; assoc. Day, Berry & Howard, Hartford, Conn., 1977-83, ptnr., 1983—. Overseer Bushnell Meml Hall Corp, Hartford, 1992—. Bd dirs Hartford Infant Action Project, 1990—, pres, 1999; elected mem Hartford City Coun, 1981—87; mem. Hartford Bd. Edn., 1989—93, v.p., 1991—93; mem. Conn .State Bd. Edn., Hartford, 1994—; chmn. charter revision comns. City of Hartford, 1999—2002; bd dirs Conn Asn Bds Educ, Hartford, 1989—93, Hartford Stage Co, 1993—2001. Mem.: ABA, Hartford

Bar Asn, Conn Bar Asn, Phi Beta Kappa. Democrat. Jewish. Avocations: astronomy, reading. Home: 238 Whitney St Hartford CT 06105-2270 Office: Day Berry & Howard City Place Hartford CT 06103 Office Phone: 860-275-0225. E-mail: abtaylor@dbh.com.

TAYLOR, ALLAN RICHARD, retired banker; b. Prince Albert, Sask., Can., Sept. 14, 1932; s. Norman and Anna Lydia (Norbeck) T.; m. Shirley Irene Ruston, Oct. 5, 1957; children: Rodney Allan, Leslie Ann. LLD(hon.), U. Regina, Sask., 1987, Concordia U., Montreal, Can., 1988; DBA (hon.), Laval U., Quebec City, Can., 1990; LLD (hon.), Queen's U., Kingston, Ont., 1991; Doctorate of Univ. (hon.), U. Ottawa, 1992. With Royal Bank of Can., Toronto, 1949-95, pres., COO, dir., 1983-86, chmn., CEO, dir., 1986-94, chmn., 1994-95, ret., 1995. Bd. dirs. Can. Inst. Advanced Rsch., Toronto, Max Bell Found., Calgary, NeuroScience Can. Found., Montreal; mem. adv. coun. Can. Exec. Svc. Overseas; former chmn. Can. Bankers Assn.; past pres. Internat. Monetary Conf. Former chmn. corp. program IMAGINE; mem. adv. bd. Can. Found. AIDS Rsch.; chmn. hon. adv. bd. Can. Assn. for Cmty. Living. Decorated officer Order of Can. Address: 200 Bay St 18th Fl North Tower Toronto ON Canada M5J 2J5 E-mail: allan.taylor@rbc.com.

TAYLOR, ANDREW C. rental and leasing company executive; b. 1947; BSBA, Denver U., 1970. With RLM Leasing Co., San Francisco, 1970—73, Enterprise Rent-A-Car, St. Louis, 1973—, pres., COO, 1980—91, CEO, 1991—, chmn., 2001—. Dir. Anheuser Busch Co., Commerce Bancshares; pres., CEO Crawford Group. Trustee Nation Urban League, Washington U., St. Louis Symphony Orch.; bd. dirs. United Way Greater St. Louis; life trustee Mo. Bot. Garden. Office: Enterprise Rent-A-Car 600 Corporate Park Dr Saint Louis MO 63105-4204*

TAYLOR, ANDREW T., JR., radiologist, educator; b. Jackson, Tenn., Jan. 14, 1942; MD, Duke U., 1968. Cert. nuclear medicine Splty. Bd. 1, internal medicine Splty. Bd. 2. Resident U. Hosp.-U.C.S.D., San Diego, 1970, 1972—74, intern, 1969; co-dir. nuc. medicine Emory U. Sch. Med., prof. radiology, 2002—. Mem.: Am. Bd. of Nuclear Medicine. Office: Emory U Sch of Medicine Radiology 1440 Clifton Rd Atlanta GA 30322*

TAYLOR, ANGELO, Olympic athlete; b. Albany, Ga., Dec. 29, 1978; Student, Ga. Tech. Champion 400 meter hurdles NCAA Championship, 1998; 2nd place U.S. Championships, 1998; winner 1st nat. title; co-winner Gold Medal 4X400 relay World Championships, 1999; winner Gold Medal 400 meter hurdles and gold medal 4x400m relay Sydney, 2000; IAAF Grand Prix overall and GP final champion, 2000; Jesse Owens award winner for top U.S. male track and field athlete, 2001; world outdoor champs gold medalist in 4x400m relay, 1999; 3 time US champion, 1999—2001; US indoor 400m champion, 1999; NCAA 400H champion, 1998. Named Collegiate Athlete of the Yr., T&FN, 1998. ranked no. 3 400 meter hurdles. Office: USA Track and Field Team One RCA Dome Ste 140 Indianapolis IN 46225

TAYLOR, ANN, human resources specialist, educator; b. Gordonville, Pa., Feb. 28, 1940; d. Gideon S. and Elizabeth L. Stoltzfus; m. James R. Taylor III, Feb. 18, 1983 (dec. Sept. 1995). BA, Ea. Mennonite U., 1966; MEd, Millersville (Pa.) U., 1979; EdD, Temple U., 1995. Caseworker Lancaster (Pa.) Welfare Dept., 1969-72, Rockingham County Welfare Dept., 1966—67, Lancaster County Probation Parole Dept., 1967-69; parole agent Pa. Bd. Probation, Parole, Harrisburg, 1972-85; human resource cons., trainer Taylor Assocs., Lancaster, 1985—. Adj. prof. bus. mgmt. Pa. State U., Lancaster, 1979-2000; spkr. in field; free lance trainer Hamilton Bank, Lancaster, 1985-91, Armstrong World Industries, Lancaster, 1987, 91; adv. com. staff trainer Vantage Drug and Alcohol Facility, Lancaster, 1983-85. Co-author: Fire Up Your Brilliance; co-author articles to profl. jours. Vol. Lancaster County Mental Health Ctr., 1983-94; seminar leader Fulton County (Pa.) C. of C., 1985-86, York County (Pa.) C. of C., 1985-86, Lancaster County C. of C., 1985-88. Mem. Am. Counseling Assn. Democrat. Episcopalian. Avocations: travel, reading, gardening, hiking. Office: 214 E King St Lancaster PA 17602 Office Phone: 717-394-6859. Personal E-mail: brilliance@comcast.net.

TAYLOR, ANNA DIGGS, federal judge; b. Washington, Dec. 9, 1932; d. Virginius Douglass and Hazel (Bramlette) Johnston; m. S. Martin Taylor, May 22, 1976; children: Douglass Johnston Diggs, Carla Cecile Diggs. BA, Barnard Coll., 1954; LLB, Yale U., 1957. Bar: D.C. 1957, Mich. 1961. Atty. Office Solicitor, Dept. Labor, W, 1957-60; asst. prosecutor Wayne County, Mich., 1961-62; asst. U.S. atty. Eastern Dist. of Mich., 1966; ptnr. Zwerdling, Maurer, Diggs & Papp, Detroit, 1970-75; asst. corp. counsel City of Detroit, 1975-79; U.S. dist. judge Eastern Dist. Mich. Detroit, 1979—. Hon. chair United Way, Cmty. Found., S.E. Mich.; trustee emeritus Detroit Inst. Arts; co-chair, vol. Leadership Coun.; vice-chair Henry Ford Health Sys. Mem. Fed. Bar Assn., State Bar Mich., Wolverine Bar Assn. (v.p.), Yale Law Assn. Episcopalian. Office: US Dist Ct 740 US Courthouse 231 W Lafayette Blvd Detroit MI 48226-2700

TAYLOR, ANTHONY BALDWIN, civil engineer; b. Nassau, Bahamas, Nov. 25, 1971; came to U.S., 1990; s. Anthony Baldwin Sr. and Ruth Inez (McKenzie) T.; m. Kaaryn Wilaine Rogers, July 2, 1994; children: Anthony Baldwin III, Andrew Benjamin. BSCE, N.C. State U., 1994; PhD, Columbia State U., 1997. Owner/engr. TNT Constn., Nassau, 1992-94; constrn. engr. Greenman Pedersen Inc., Durham, N.C., 1994-96; resident engr. Parsons, Butner, 1996—2000, dir. of engring. Newport, 2000—. Mem. ASCE, Assn. for Advancement of Cost Engring. Avocations: reading, writing, basketball, sport shooting, fishing.

TAYLOR, AUBREY ELMO, physiologist, educator; b. El Paso, Tex., June 4, 1933; s. Virgil T. and Mildred (Maher) Taylor; m. Mary Jane Davis, Apr. 4, 1953; children: Audrey Jane Hildebrand, Lenda Sue Taylor Brown, Mary Ann. BA in Math. and Psychology, Tex. Christian U., 1960; PhD in Physiology, U. Miss., 1964. Fellow biophysics lab. Harvard U. Med. Sch., Boston, 1965-67; from asst. prof. to prof. dept. physiology U. Miss. Coll. Medicine, Jackson, 1967-77; prof., chmn. dept. physiology U. South Ala. Coll. Medicine, Mobile, 1977—2002, Louise Lenoir Locke eminent scholar disting. prof. emeritus, 2002—. Pulmonary score com. mem. Nat. Heart, Lung and Blood Inst., 1976; with Surgery and Anesthesiology, 1979—82, Manpower Com., 1985—95; chmn. RAP, 1983; spl. lectr. Wu-Ho-Su Meml. Symposium. Mem. editl. bd.: Jour. Applied Physiology, 1994—, Critical Care Medicine, 1991—97, Circulation Rsch., Am. Jour. Physiology, Internat. Pathophysiology, Microcirculatory and Lymphatic Rsch., Chinese Jour. Physiology, Microcirculation, Jour. Biomed. Sci., Am. Rev. Resp. and Critical Care Jour., Internat. Soc. Pathology, author 9 books:; contbr. chapters to books, over 730 articles to profl. jours.; N.Am. editor: Clin. Scis., 1998—. With U.S. Army, 1953—55. Named Disting. Physiologist, Am. Coll. Chest Physicians, 1994; recipient Lederle Faculty award, 1967—70, Philip Dow award, U. Ga., 1984, NIH Merit award, 1987—97, Lucian award, McGill U., 1988, John Whitney award, U. Ark., 1990, Gelen award, Intestinal Shock Soc., 1991, Arthur C. Guyton award, U. Miss Coll. Medicine, 1993, Myerson-De Luzio Lectr., Tulane Sch. Medicine, 1997, Disting. Lectr., La State U., Shreveport, 1997, Med. Student Rsch. Conf., U. Tex. Sch. Medicine, Galveston, 1998, Abreu Meml. Keynote Spkr., 1998, Disting. Alumnus award, Tex. Christian U., 1998, 1998, Disting Svc. award, USA med. Alumni Assn., 2000, Disting. Graduate award, Paschal H.S., 2002; grantee NIH, 1964—. Fellow: Royal Soc. Medicine (bd. dirs.), Am. Heart Assn. (So. regional rev. com. 1977—81, cardiopulmonary, critical care coun. 1977—, chmn. 1979—81, EIA Rev. Com. 1986—95, pulmonary and devel. rev. com. 1987—95, nat. rsch. com. 1990—95, del. assembly 1990—99, chmn. 1993—98, chmn. grant/rev.com 1994—95, coun. affairs com. 1994—98, nominating com. 1998—99, basic sci. com. 1998—, circulation coun., chmn., AALAC bd. trustees rep., Bronze award Miss. AHA 1976, Dickinson W. Richards award 1988, Outstanding Ala. AHA program 1993, Sci. Coun. Achievement award 1995, Disting. Svc. award 1995, Rsch. Achievement award 1997, So. Ala. Dist. Achievement award 2000, Gala honoree 2000, Hall of Fame Spring Hill Hosp. Heart Assn. 2001), AAAS; mem.: European Respiratory Soc. (sec. lung injury group), Am. Thoracic Soc., Fedn. Am. Socs. for Exptl. Biology (bd. dirs. 1988—90, reorganizing com.), Biophys. Soc., N.Y. Acad. Scis., Internat. Pathophysiology Soc. (v.p. 1991—99), N. Am. Soc. Lymphology (pres. 1988—90, Cecil Drinker Rsch. award 1988), Internat. Lymphology Soc., Ala. Acad. Scis. (Ann. State Rsch. award 1988), Micro Circulatory Soc. (coun. 1977—81, pres. 1981—83, Eugene Landis Rsch. award 1985), Assn. Dept. Chairs of Physiology (exec. com. 1996—2001, sec. treas. 1998—2002), Am. Physiol. Soc. (coun. 1984—87, chmn. mem. com. 1985—87, pres. 1987—90, hon. com., chmn. 1993—96, chmn. Perkins fellow com. 1996—98, Cannon lectr. 1999, Wiggers award 1987, Achievement award 2002), NAS (com. for Internat. Union Physiol. Sci.), Sigma Xi, Alpha Omega Alpha. Democrat. Presbyterian. Achievements include research in in cardio-pulmonary physiology, fluid balance, edema, microcirculation and capillary exchange of solute and water and inflammatory processes in the lung. Home: 11 Audubon Pl Mobile AL 36606-1907

TAYLOR, BARBARA ALDEN, public relations executive; b. Dallas, Aug. 21, 1943; d. Harold Earl and Sally Alden (Howard) T. BA, Smith Coll., 1965; MA, Antioch Coll., 1971. Vol. Peace Corps., India, 1966-68; tchr. Upper Merion Sch. Dist., King of Prussia, Pa., 1969-70, Cheltenham Sch. Dist., Elkins Park, Pa., 1970-74; pub. rels. dir. Princess Hotels Internat., N.Y.C., 1974-75; chmn. Taylor & Hammond Ltd., N.Y.C., 1975-84; pres. Doremus/Marketshare, 1984-86; exec. v.p. Porter/Novelli, N.Y.C., 1986-90; sr. v.p. Hill and Knowlton, Inc., N.Y.C., 1990-93; sr. v.p. corp. comm. Lancaster Group Worldwide, 1993-95; sr. v.p. Coty Inc. and Benckiser Group, 1995-97; exec. v.p. Edelman Pub. Rels. Worldwide, N.Y.C., 1997—. Bd. dirs. Madison Square Boys' and Girls' Club N.Y., 1978—, also mem. women's bd. Boys' Club N.Y. Named to Acad. of Women Achievers YWCA, 1985; bd. dirs. Up With People, Tucson, 1990—; trustee Smith Coll., 1999—. Mem. Women in Comms., Pub. Rels. Soc. Am. (counselors acad.), Internat. Women's Forum, Advt. Women N.Y., Cosmetic Exec. Women, Fashio Group, Doubles Internat., Smith Coll. Alumnae Assn. (bd. dirs. 1993-96), Club N.Y., Lyford Cay Club, Jr. League City N.Y. Avocations: tennis, walking. Office: Edelman Pub Rels Worldwide 1500 Broadway Ste 504 New York NY 10036-4048

TAYLOR, BARBARA ANN OLIN, writer, educational consultant; b. St. Louis, Feb. 8, 1933; d. Spencer Truman and Ann Amelia (Whitney) Olin; m. F. Morgan Taylor Jr., Apr. 5, 1954; children: Frederick M. III, Spencer O., James W., John F. AB, Smith Coll., 1954; M in Mgmt., Northwestern U., 1978, PhD, 1984; LHD, U. New Haven, 1995. Mem. faculty Hamden (Conn.) Hall Country Day Sch., 1972-74; cons. Booz, Allen & Hamilton, Inc., Chgo., 1979; program assoc. Northwestern U., Evanston, Ill., 1982; co-founder, exec. dir. Nat. Ctr. Effective Schs. R&D, Okemos, Mich., 1986-89, rsch. assoc., 1987; chmn. Nat. Ctr. for Effective Schs. Resource and Devel. Found., 2002—03; cons. on effective schs. rsch. and reform Nat. Ctr. Effective Schs. R&D U. Wis., Madison, 1990-96; pres. Excelsior! Found., Chgo., 1994—. Mem. exec. com. Hudson Inst., New Am. Schs. Devel. Corp. Design Team, 1990-94; Danforth Disting. lectr. U. Nebr., Omaha, 1993. Co-author: Making School Reform Happen, 1993, Keepers of the Dream, 1994, The Revolution Revisited: Effective Schools and Systemic Reform, 1995; editor: Case Studies in Effective Schools Research, 1990; contbr. articles to profl. jours. Pres. Jr. League of New Haven, 1967-69; pres. NCCJ, New Haven, 1971-73; co-chair Coalition Housing and Human Resources, Hartford-New Haven, 1970-73; co-chair steering com. Day Care Conn., Hartford, 1971-73; trustee U. New Haven, 1961-71, Smith Coll., Northampton, Mass., 1984-90, Choate Rosemary Hall Sch., 1973-78, Lake Forest Coll., 1996—, Hudson Inst., 1989-97, Northwestern U., 1998-2002, Lake Forest Coll., 1996-2004 (life). Recipient Humanitarian award Mt. Calvary Bapt. Ch., 1988, Outstanding Alumna award John Burroughs Sch., 1994, Pres.'s award U. New Haven, Alumni Merit award N.W. U., 2004. Mem. ASCD, Nat. Commn. Citizens Edn. (bd. dirs. 1980-86), Nat. Staff Devel. Coun., Phi Delta Kappa (Internat. award for Outstanding Svc. 2000). Episcopalian. Office: Nat Ctr Effective Schs Rsch & Devel 1124 Lake Rd Lake Forest IL 60045-1723

TAYLOR, BARRY LLEWELLYN, microbiologist, educator; b. Sydney, Australia, May 7, 1937; came to U.S., 1967; s. Fredrick Llewelyn and Vera Lavina (Clarke) T.; m. Desmyrna Ruth Tolhurst, Jan. 4, 1961; children: Lyndon, Nerida, Darrin. BA, Avondale Coll., Cooranbong, New South Wales, 1959; BSc with honors, U. New South Wales, Sydney, 1966; PhD, Case Western Res. U., 1973; postgrad., U. Calif., Berkeley, 1973-75. Vis. postdoctoral fellow Australian Nat. U., Canberra, 1975-76; asst. prof. biochemistry Loma Linda (Calif.) U., 1976-78, assoc. prof. biochemistry, 1978-83, prof. biochemistry, 1983—, prof., chmn. dept. microbiology and molecular genetics, 1988-2000, interim dir. Ctr. for Molecular Biology, 1989-94, 96-98, v.p. for rsch. affairs, 2000—. Contbr. articles to profl. publs. Rsch. grantee Am. Heart Assn., 1978-85, NIH, 1981—. Mem. Am. Soc. Microbiology, Am. Soc. Biochemistry and Molecular Biology. Office: Loma Linda U VP Rsch Affairs Loma Linda CA 92350-0001

TAYLOR, BARRY NORMAN, physicist; b. Phila., Mar. 27, 1936; s. Morris and Sarah (Weiss) T.; m. Sheila Anne Cohen, Dec. 28, 1958; children: Deborah Susan, David Joel, Denise Beth. AB, Temple U., Phila., 1957; MS, U. Pa., 1960, PhD, 1963. Instr., then asst. prof. physics U. Pa., 1963-66; mem. tech. staff RCA Rsch. Labs., 1966-70; chief absolute elec. measurements sect. Nat. Bur. Standards (name changed to Nat. Inst. of Standards and Tech. 1988), Gaithersburg, Md., 1970-74, adminstr. NIST Precision Measurement Grants Program, 1974-2000, chief electricity divsn., 1974-89; mgr. Fundamental Cons. Data Ctr., Gaithersburg, Md., 1989-2001, scientist emeritus, 2001—. Instr. Rider Coll., Trenton, N.J., 1969-70; mem., chairperson nat. and internat. tech. coms. Co-author: Fundamental Constants and Quantum Electrodynamics, 1969; co-editor: Precision Measurement and Fundamental Constants, 1971; Co-editor: Precision Measurement and Fundamental Constants II, 1984; contbr. articles to sci. jours. Recipient Silver medal U.S. Dept. Commerce, 1975, Gold medal, 1989, John Price Wetherill medal Franklin Inst., 1975, Codata prize, 2000, Disting. Exec. award Sr. Exec. Svc. of USA U.S. Pres., 2000. Fellow IEEE, Am. Phys. Soc. (chair topical group on fundamental constants and precise tests of phys. laws 1990-92); mem. Sigma Xi. Office: Nat Inst of Stds and Tech 100 Bureau Dr Stop 8401 Gaithersburg MD 20899-8401 E-mail: barry.taylor@nist.gov.

TAYLOR, BERNARD J., II, banker, director; b. Phila., Nov. 10, 1925; s. Bernard and Marie (Pearce) T.; m. Barbara Silverstein; children: Dorothy Taylor Tomlinson, Lawrence Dean, David Stewart. BS, U. Pa., 1949. Asst. mgr. McCrory Stores Corp., Phila., 1949-51; fin. analyst Fidelity Bank, Phila., 1951-57, asst. to v.p. investments, 1957-59, asst. to pres., 1959-60, corp. sec., 1960-63, v.p., sec., 1963-66, sr. v.p. in charge adminstrn. dept., 1966-72, exec. v.p., 1972-74; v.p. Fidelcor, Inc. (parent co. Fidelity Bank), 1969-72, exec. v.p., 1973-76; sr. exec. v.p., 1976-79; pres., dir. Fidelity Bldg. Corp., 1970-79; pres., CEO Wilmington (Del.) Trust Co., Del., 1979-92, dir., 1979-98, chmn., 1980-92. Ptnr. Golf Ptnrs. (Hartefield Nat. Golf Course), 1993-99. Pres. Savoy Opera Co., Phila., 1961-63, prodn. mgr., dir., 1970-75; pres., bd. dirs. Pa. Opera Theatre, 1975-80, treas., bd. dirs., 1980-93; mem. adv. bd. mgrs. Inglis House Phila., 1967-70; mem. Del. Round Table, 1980-92; bd. dirs. Greater Wilmington Devel. Coun., 1980-84, Sta. WHYY, PBS-TV, Phila., 1980-92; bd. dirs., 1986-91; bd. dirs. Del. Theatre Co., 1987-91. With AUS, 1944-46, PTO. Inducted to State of Del. Bus. Leaders Hall of Fame, 1999. Mem.: Orpheus (Phila); Wilmington Country; Jonathan's Landing Golf. Home: 8 Oak Tree Hollow Rd West Chester PA 19382-8341

TAYLOR, BILLY (WILLIAM EDWARD TAYLOR), jazz musician; b. Greenville, N.C., July 24, 1921; s. William Edward and Antoinette (Bacon) Taylor; m. Theodora Castion, June 22, 1946; children: Duane, Kim. BS in Music, Va. State Coll., 1942; D. Mus. Edn., U. Mass.; L.H.D., Fairfield U.; D. Mus., Va. State Coll.; PhD, Clark Coll.; Mus.D. (hon.), Berklee Coll. Mus., 1981. Lectr. Music Educators Nat. Conf., 1957, New Eng. Music Tchrs. Assn., 1958, New Jazz Soc., Phila., 1967; owner Sta. WSOK, Savannah, Ga., WLIB, also WBLS-FM, N.Y.C; pres. Billy Taylor Productions, Duane Music Co., N.Y.C.; spl. cons. to chmn. Nat. Endowment Arts; chmn. bd. Creative Arts Pub. Svc. Jazz pianist, 1937—; prodr.(staff): (TV series, jazz TV program) Billy Taylor Show, 1965—; performer (narrator): (TV series) The Pop Explosion, 1966, Dial M for Music, 1965; pres., founder (TV series) Jazz Mobile, 1967; performer (host, narrator): (TV series) Black, White and Blue, 1966; dir.(music, cons., leader orch.): (TV series) Subject was Jazz, 1957, (program): WLIB-FM, 1965-69, 1965—69, (mus.): David Frost Show, 1969; mus. cons. (TV series), 1964—, host Jazz Alive, Nat. Public Radio, guest soloist numerous symphonies; composer: (ballets) (mus.) Your Arms Too Short to Box with God, Suite for Jazz Piano and Orch., Make a Joyful Noise, Peaceful Warrior, For Rachel, numerous other works; dir.(mus.): PBS variety show. Black Jour. Tonight; rec. Jazz Alive, 1977, Where've You Been, 1980, Dr. T, 1993, Custom Taylored, It's A Matter of Pride, 1994; author: Jazz Piano. Trustee Rockefeller Found, 1978—; mem. Nat. Council Arts, 1972—78; Bd. dirs. Harlem Cultural Council. Named to Nat. Assn. Jazz Educators Hall of Fame, 1979; recipient Mayor's award for arts and culture, 1981, Edward E. Elson Disting. Service award, Nat. Public Radio, 1981, George Foster Peabody award, 1981, Emmy award, 1984, Lifetime Achievement award, Down Beat mag., 1984, Tiffany award, Internat. Soc. Performing Arts, 1991, Nat. Medal of Arts, 1992. Mem.: Arts and Bus. Council N.Y. (pres.), Acad. TV Arts and Scis., ASCAP (dir. 1976—78), Nat. Acad. Rec. Arts and Scis. (v.p. 1964—).

TAYLOR, BRIAN STEVON, music educator; b. Cullman, Ala., Apr. 22, 1968; s. James Stevon Taylor and Charlotte Bentley Graham; life ptnr. Antonio Jesus Baena. BS in Edn., Jacksonville State U., 1991; MusM, U. of So. Miss., 1999. Dir. of bands Cold Springs Sch., Bremen, Ala., 1992—94; band dir. Cobb County Schs., Marietta, Ga., 1994—98; grad. asst. U. of So. Miss., Hattiesburg, 1998—2001; asst. dir. of bands, athletic band dir. U. of La., Lafayette, 2001—. Music dir., condr. Iberia Cmty. Band, New Iberia, La., 2003—. Democrat. Avocations: travel, performing arts. Home: # 371 655 Marie Antoinette St Lafayette LA 70506 Office: U La PO Box 41207 Lafayette LA 70504 Office Phone: 337-482-5157. E-mail: btaylor@ull.edu.

TAYLOR, BRUCE STEVENSON, architect, planner; b. N.Y.C., Sept. 3, 1946; s. James Stevenson and Linnea Sarrah (Hendrickson) T.; m. Sandra Dee Butzman, Oct. 9, 1970; 1 child, Eric Stevenson. BArch, Miami U., Oxford, Ohio, 1969. Registered architect, Mass., Conn., N.H., Maine, N.Y. Design draftsman Architects Collaborative, Cambridge, Mass., 1969-73; project architect W.M. Design Group, Nahant, Mass., 1973-76; pvt. practice architecture West Newbury, Mass., 1976-78; corp. dir. Claude Miquelle Assocs., Inc., Melrose, Mass., 1978-85; architect, planner Bruce S. Taylor, Architect, West Newbury, 1985—. Vis. critic Boston Archtl. Ctr., 1976-77; student counselor Students from Boston Archtl. Ctr., 1980-85. Archtl. projects featured in mags. Bd. dirs. Bd. Health, West Newbury, 1981-83, chmn., 1984-85. Recipient Merit award Builder Mag., 1984, 1st Honor award Soc. Am. Registered Architects, 1984, Grand award Nat. Assn. Home Builders and Better Homes and Gardens, 1984. Mem. Nat. Council Archtl. Registration Bds., AIA, Boston Soc. Architects. Lutheran. Avocations: skiing, fishing, model railroading, historical architecture. Home and Office: 248 Main St West Newbury MA 01985-1414 Office Phone: 978-363-5433.

TAYLOR, BRYCE B, music educator, consultant; b. Edinburg, Tex., Feb. 12, 1925; s. Charles B and Cecile B Taylor; m. Diana Olivia Rodriguez, Apr. 4, 1946; children: Scott Lee, David Kim, Cynthia Diane, Richard Kerry. MusB, Tex. A&I, 1951, M of music edn., 1955. Music band instr. 3 Rivers Tex. Pub. Schools, 1951—61; music supr./band dir. Alice Ind. Sch. Dist., Alice, Tex., 1961—91, music cons., 1991—; music edn. prof. Tex. A&M, Kingsville, 1993—; condr./music dir. Corpus Christi Wind Symphony, 1986—. Music cons. U. Interscholastic League, 1960—; adjudicator Tex. Music Adjudicators Assn., 1958—. Cpl. USMC, 1942—46, Pearl Harbor. Recipient Outstanding Music Educator, Nat. Fedn. Music Assn., 1991, Tchr. of the Yr., 1982, Bandmaster of the Yr., Tex. Bandmasters Assn., 1983. Mem.: Am. Concert Band Assn., Am. Bandmasters Assn. (past pres., bd. mem. 1999—2000), Tex. Music Educators Assn. (past. pres., divsn. chair 1962—64), Phi Beta Mu Nat. Band Assn. Independent. Cath. Avocations: golf, auto restoration, guest conducting. Home: 1001 Lincoln Alice TX 78332 Office Phone: 361-660-2127.

TAYLOR, CARL ERNEST, preventive medicine physician, epidemiologist, educator; b. Landour, Mussoorie, India, July 26, 1916; s. John C. and Elizabeth (Siehl) Taylor; m. Mary Daniels, Feb. 14, 1943; children: Daniel, Elizabeth, Henry. BS, Muskingum Coll., 1937, DSc, 1962; MD, Harvard, 1941, MPH, 1951, DPH, 1953; LHD (hon.), Towson U., 1974. Diplomate Am. Bd. Preventive Medicine. Intern, resident pathology, surg. staff, tropical disease rsch. Gorgas Hosp., Panama, 1941—44; charge med. service Marine Hosp., Pitts., 1944—46; supt. Meml. Hosp., Fategarh, India, 1947—50; rsch. assoc. Harvard Sch. Pub. Health, Boston, 1950—52, asst. prof. epidemiology, 1957—59, assoc. prof., 1959-61; prof. preventive and social medicine Christian Med. Coll., Ludhiana, India, 1953—56; prof. internat. health, chmn. dept. internat. health Johns Hopkins Sch. Hygiene and Pub. Health, Balt., 1961—83, prof. emeritus, 1984—. Cons. AID, 1959—; UNICEF country rep. in China, 1984—87; expert com. WHO, 1963, 1966—67, 1970—73, 1975; mem. Nat. Adv. Commn. Health Manpower; chmn. Nat. Council for Internat. Health. Contbr. articles to profl. jours. Fellow: Am. Pub. Health Assn., Royal Soc. Tropical Medicine and Hygiene, Royal Coll. Physicians; mem.: Nat. Acad. Medicine, Inst. Medicine, Indian Assn. for Advancement Med. Edn., Am. Soc. Tropical Medicine and Hygiene, Assn. Tchrs. Preventive Medicine. Achievements include research in rural health, population dynamics, nutrition, epidemiology of leprosy. Home: Bittersweet Acres 1201 Hollins Ln Baltimore MD 21209-2209 Office: Johns Hopkins Sch Hygiene and Pub Health 615 N Wolfe St Baltimore MD 21205-2103 *The growing complexity of human relationships around this increasingly crowded world presents new challenges to concerned scientists. Solutions to our problems must come from new collaborative styles of work bridging the usual boundaries between people, since the problems we face are mutual.*

TAYLOR, CARSON WILLIAM, electrical engineer; b. Superior, Wis., May 24, 1942; s. William Stanley and Elizabeth Marie (Christophersen) T.; m. Gudrun Renate Leistner, Dec. 28, 1966; 1 child, Natasha Marie. BSEE, U. Wis., 1965; M in Engring., Rensselaer Poly. Inst., 1969. Elec. engr. U.S. Bur. Reclamation, Billings, Mont., 1967-68, Bonneville Power Adminstrn., Portland, Oreg., 1969-89, prin. engr., 1989—. Prin. Carson Taylor Seminars, Portland, 1986—. Author: Power System Voltage Stability, 1994; contbr. papers to profl. publs.; patentee in field. Lt. U.S. Army, 1965-67. Lt. U.S. Army, 1965-67. Fellow IEEE (chmn. subcom. 1982—); mem. Conférence Internationale des Grands Réseaux Électriques a Haute Tension (CIGRE, disting. mem.), Eta Kappa Nu. Lutheran. Avocations: fishing, hunting, woodworking, reading, computers. Office: Bonneville Power Adminstrn PO Box 491 Vancouver WA 98666-0491

TAYLOR, CARTER W. aviation educator, consultant, lecturer; b. St. Louis, Oct. 10, 1937; s. George Wellford and Carola Whitman T.; children by a previous marriage: Carter W. Jr., Patricia L.; m. Judy Hall Taylor, Nov. 16, 1991; children: G. Scott Moore, Tamara Moore Polson. BS, N.Mex. State U., 1961. Cert. flight instr. FAA; cert. airline transport pilot FAA. Tchr. El Paso Pub. Sch., 1962-63; air traffic controller FAA, Jacksonville, Fla., 1963-64; pilot Eastern Airlines, Inc., Miami-N.Y.C., 1964, Am. Airlines, Inc., N.Y.C.-Dallas, 1964-67, capt., 1967-97, flight instr. Dallas, 1983-95, sr. flight instr., 1995-97. Recipient World Speed Record Dallas to London Fedn. Aeronautique Internat., 1997, World Speed Record London to Dallas Fedn. Aeronautique Internat., 1997, Nat. Speed Record Chgo. to Dallas Nat. Aeronautic Assn., 1997. Mem. Antique Automobile Club Am. (nat. dir. 1991-94), Antique Automobile Libr. and Rsch. Ctr. (bd. dirs. 1985-86). Avocations: antique automobiles, antique aircraft, photography. Home: 1228 Old Spartanburg Rd Greer SC 29650-3266 Fax: 864-244-9511. E-mail: captcwt@bellsouth.net.

TAYLOR, CELIANNA ISLEY, information systems specialist; b. Youngstown, Ohio; d. Paul Thornton and Florence (Jacobs) Isley; divorced; children: Polly, Jerry, Jim. BA in Philosophy, Denison U., 1939; MLS, Western Res. U., 1942. Worked in several pub. libraries and univ. librs., 1939-50; head Libr. Cataloging Dept. Battelle Mem. Inst., Columbus, Ohio, 1951-53; head pers. office, assoc. prof. libr. adminstrn. Ohio State U. Librs., Columbus, 1954-65; coord. info. svcs., assoc. prof. libr. adminstrn. Nat. Ctr. for Rsch. in Vocat. Edn., Ohio State U., Columbus, 1966-70; sr. rsch. assoc., adminstrv. assoc., assoc. prof. libr. adminstrn. dept. computer and info. sci. Ohio State U., Columbus, 1970-86, assoc. prof. emeritus Univ. Librs., 1986—. Mem. Task

Force on a Spl. Collections Database, Ohio State U. Librs., Columbus, 1988-89, comm. systems and recs. coord. Ohio State U. Retirees Assn., Columbus, 1992-93, info. specialist, MacForum, Ohio State U., Columbus, 2001—; cons. for several profl. orgns. including Ernst & Ernst CPA's and Oreg. State Sys. of Higher Edn., 1961 82. Author. (with J. Magisos) Guide for State Voc-Tech Edn. Dissemination Systems 1971, (with A.E. Petrarca, and R.S. Kohn) Info. Interaction 1982; editor Highlights-Coun. for Ethics in Econs., 1997—; contbr. several articles to profl. jours.; designer info. sys.: CALL Sys., 1977-82, Channel 2000 Proj. Home Info. Svc., 1980-81, Continuing Education Info. Ctr., 1989-90, Human Resources (HUR) Sys., 1976-77,1979-82, DECOS, 1975-86, Computer-asst. libr. Sys., Optical Scan Sys., 1972-73, ERIC Clearinghouse for vocat. edn., 1966-70. Bd. dirs. Columbus Reg. Info. Svc., 1974-78, Cmty. Info. Referral Svc., Inc. 1975-81; chmn. subcom. on design, info. and ref. com. Columbus United Cmty. Coun., 1972-73; dir. Computer Utility for Pub. Info. Columbus, 1975-81; acct. coord. Greater Columbus Free-net, 1994-98; info. specialist, coord. LWV Met. Columbus Website Com., 2001-02. Mem. ALA, Assn. Computing Machinery (Ctrl. Ohio chpt.), Am. Soc. Info. Sci. and Tech., Assn. Faculty and Profl. Women Ohio State U., Columbus Metro Club, Coun. for Ethics in Econs., World Future Soc., Olympic Indoor Tennis Club. Avocations: bicycling, bird watching, gourmet cooking, tennis, water aerobics. Home and Office: 3471 Greenbank Ct Columbus OH 43221-4724 Office Phone: 614-876-0069.

TAYLOR, CHARLES ELLETT, biologist, educator; b. Chgo., Sept. 9, 1945; s. Stewart Ferguson and Barbara (Ellett) Taylor; m. Minna Glushien, June 22, 1969. AB, U. Calif., 1968; PhD, SUNY, Stony Brook, 1973. Prof. U. Calif., Riverside, 1974-80, UCLA, 1980 . Cons. artificial life and population genetics; dir. UCLA Cognitive Sci. Rsch. Program, 1990—99; mem. adv. bd Computer Mus. Fishtank. Co-author: Artifical Life II, 1992, Artifical Life VI, 1998; editor: Artificial Life, 1997—2002; assoc. editor: IEEE Transactions on Evolutionary Computing, 1997—99; assoc. editor Artifical Life and Robotics, 1999—2200, Artificial Life, 2002—03; contbr. articles to profl. publs. Office: Dept Organismic Biology Ecology and Evolution UCLA Box 951606 Los Angeles CA 90095-1606 E-mail: ctaylor@ucla.edu.

TAYLOR, CHARLES H. congressman; b. Brevard, N.C., Jan. 3, 1941; m. Elizabeth Owen; 3 children. BA, Wake Forest U., 1963, JD, 1966. Tree farmer, N.C.; mem. N.C. Ho. of Reps., Raleigh, 1967-73, minority leader, 1969-73; mem. N.C. Senate, Raleigh, 1973-75, minority leader, 1973-75; mem. U.S. Congress from 11th N.C. dist., Washington, 1991—; mem. appropriations com., commerce, justice, state jud. subcom., subcom. on interior. chmn. subcom. on legis. branch. Republican. Baptist. Office: US Ho of Reps 231 Cannon Ho Office Bldg Washington DC 20515-3311 also: 22 S Pack Sq Ste 330 Asheville NC 28801-3503

TAYLOR, CHARLES HENRY, psychoanalyst, educator; b. Boston, Oct. 2, 1928; s. Charles Henry and Rosamond (Stewardson) T.; m. Diana Burgess, 1950; children: Stephen, Diana Beth, Charles S., Eleanor; m. Patricia Finley, 1988. BA, Yale U., 1950, MA, 1952, PhD, 1955; postgrad., Cambridge (Eng.) U., 1950-51. From instr. to asst. prof. English Ind. U., 1955-61; from asst. dean to assoc. dean, also assoc. prof. English Yale U., 1961-63, acting provost, 1963-64, provost, prof. English, 1964-72, pres. rep., 1972-76; grad. C.G. Jung Inst., N.Y., 1979; pvt. practice, 1976—. Bd. dirs. Meridian Audio, Ltd. Author: The Early Collected Editions of Shelley's Poems, 1958, (with Patricia Finley) Images of the Journey in Dante's Divine Comedy, 1997; editor: Essays on the Odyssey, 1963; contbr. articles to profl. jours. Mem. com. on libr. Yale U. Coun., 1990-95; trustee Hampshire Coll., 1988-93, 99—, chair, 2000—. Mem. Internat. Assn. Analytical Psychology, Archive for Rsch. in Archetypal Symbolism (pres. 1987-93, treas. 1993—), N.Y. Assn. Analytical Psychology, Nat. Assn. for Advancement Psychoanalysis, Phi Beta Kappa.

TAYLOR, CHARLES LEWIS, political science educator; b. Ware Shoals, SC, Nov. 8, 1935; s. Humphrus Lee and Sue (Brissey) Taylor; m. Mary Frances Taylor, June 1, 1958; children: Susan, James. BA, Carson-Newman Coll., Jefferson City, Tenn., 1957; MA, Yale U., 1959, PhD, 1963. Asst. prof. Coll. William & Mary, Williamsburg, Va., 1962-66; rsch. assoc. Yale U., New Haven, Conn., 1966-70; prof. Va. Tech., Blacksburg, Va., 1970—. John Marshall profl Budapest (Hungary) U. Econ. Scis., 1991-92; recurring vis. rsch. prof. Berlin Sci. Ctr., 1993—. Author: World Handbook of Political and Social Indicators, 1972, 83. Pastor Roanoke Valley Presbyn. Ch., Blacksburg, 1985-2002. Democrat. Avocations: hiking, travel. Office: Va Tech Mailcode 0130 Blacksburg VA 24061 Office Phone: 540-231-5555.

TAYLOR, CHRIS R. architect; BArch, Calif. State Polytechnic U., Pomona, Calif. From arch. to prin. Ontario Office HMC Group, Ontario, Calif., 1984—98, prin. Ontario Office, 1998—. Office: HMC Group Ontario East 3270 Inland Empire Blvd Ontario CA 91764-4854 also: HMC Group Pasadena 766 E Colorado Blvd Ste 200 Pasadena CA 91101-4129*

TAYLOR, CHRISTINE, actress; b. Allentown, Pa., July 30, 1971; d. Skip and Joan Taylor; m. Ben Stiller, May 13, 2000; 1 child, Ella Olivia Stiller. Actor: (films) Calendar Girl, 1993, Showdown, 1993, The Brady Bunch Movie, 1995, Breaking Free, 1995, The Craft, 1996, A Very Brady Sequel, 1996, Cat Swallows Parakeet and Speaks, 1996, Campfire Tales, 1997, The Wedding Singer, 1998, Overnight Delivery, 1998, Denial, 1998, Kiss Toledo Goodbye, 1999, Desperate But Not Serious, 1999, Zoolander, 2001, Dodgeball: A True Underdog Story, 2004; (TV films) Here Come the Munsters, 1995, To the Ends of Time, 1996, Heat Vision and Jack, 1999. Office: United Talent Agy 9560 Wilshire Blvd Ste 500 Beverly Hills CA 90212*

TAYLOR, CLAYBORNE DUDLEY, engineering educator; b. Kokomo, Miss., July 15, 1938; s. Dudley Clayborne and Winnie Lee ((Holmes)) Taylor; m. Mary Jean Blue, June 23, 1963; children: Clayborne Dudley, Jr., David Edward, Rebecca Lynn Taylor Burg. BS in Physics, Miss. State U., 1961; MS in Physics, N.Mex. State U., 1964, PhD in Physics, 1965. Registered Miss. Tech. staff mem. Sandia Labs., Albuquerque, 1965—67; assoc. prof. Miss. State U., Starkville, 1967—69, 1969—71, prof. elec. engring., 1972-86, 88-91, assoc. dean. engring., 1991—98, interim dean continuing edn., 1998—; prof. elec. engring. U. Miss., Oxford, 1971—72; vis. Stocker prof. Ohio U., Athens, 1986—88. Cons. Phillips Lab., Albuquerque, 1972—. Author: (novels) High-Power Microwave Systems and Effects, 1994; contbr. articles to tech. jours. Recipient cert. of Recognition, NASA, 1986; fellow Electromagnetic Pulse Tech., Summa Found., 1988. Mem.: Am. Soc. Engring. Edn., Internat. Union of Radio Scientists, IEEE (sr.). Presbyterian. Home: 517 Greensboro St Starkville MS 39759-2861 Office: Miss State U Divsn Continuing Edn PO Box 5247 Mississippi State MS 39762-5247 E-mail: ctaylor@ce.msstate.edu., cdtaylor517@yahoo.com.

TAYLOR, CLIFFORD OTIS, retired principal; b. Ft. Pierce, Fla., Jan. 4, 1926; s. Thomas Archie and Margaret Emeline (Tyler) T.; m. Dorothy Ann Pearce, Dec. 27, 1952. BA, Fla. State U., 1950; MEd, U. Ill., Urbana, 1954; postgrad., U. Miami, Appalachian State U. Cert. tchr., prin. Tchr. Fairlawn Sch., St. Lucie County, Ft. Pierce, North Grade Sch., Palm Beach County Bd. Edn., West Palm Beach, Fla.; prin. South Grade Sch., Palm Beach County Bd. Edn., West Palm Beach, Fla., Kirklane Elem. Sch., Palm Beach County Bd. Edn., West Palm Beach, Fla., ret., 1991. Hon. mem. state and nat. PTA. With USN, 1944-46. Kirklane Elem. Sch. renamed Clifford O. Taylor/ Kirklane Elem. Sch. in his honor. Mem. ASCD, NAESP, Palm Beach County Prins. Assn., So. Assn. Schs. and Colls., Fla. Assn. Sch. Adminstrs., Retired Educators Assn., Lions, Phi Delta Kappa. Episcopalian. Home: 1811 N J Ter Lake Worth FL 33460-6523

TAYLOR, CLIFFORD WOODWORTH, state supreme court justice; b. Delaware, Ohio, Nov. 9, 1942; s. Alexander E. and Carolyn (Clifford) T.; m. Lucille Taylor; 2 children. BA, U. Mich., 1964; JD, George Washington U., 1967. Asst. prosecuting atty. Ingham County, 1971-72; ptnr. Denfield, Timmer & Taylor, 1972-92; judge Mich. Ct. of Appeals, 1992-97, Supreme Ct. Justice, 1997—. Mem. standing com. on professionalism Mich. State Bar, 1992. Bd. dirs. Mich. Dyslexia Inst., 1991—, Friends of the Gov.'s Residence, 1991—; mem. St. Thomas Aquinas Ch. With USN, 1967-71. Fellow Mich. State Bar Found.; mem. Mich. Supreme Ct. Hist. Soc., Federalist Soc., Cath. Lawyers Guild, State Bar. Home: 9760 Sunny Point Dr Laingsburg MI 48848 Office: Mich Supreme Ct PO Box 30052 Lansing MI 48909

TAYLOR, COLLETTE, public relations executive; Sr. v.p. human resources Golin/Harris Internat., Chgo., 1998, chief adminstrv. officer, 1998—. Office: Golin/Harris Internat 111 E Wacker Dr Chicago IL 60601-3713

TAYLOR, CORA HODGE, social worker; b. Fayetteville, N.C., Nov. 25, 1942; d. John Marlin and Cora Louise (Mitchell) Hodge; m. Charles L. Taylor, June 26, 1965; children: Charles L., John M. BS, N.C. Coll., Durham, 1963; MSW, U. N.C., Chapel Hill, 1965. Clin. social worker VA Hosp., Bedford, Mass., 1965-68, 73-79; chief social worker Regional Health Center, Wilmington, Mass., 1978-79; clin. social worker VA Hosp., Bedford, Mass., 1979-91, supervisory social worker geriatrics and long term care, 1991—2000, coord. contract programs, 1993—. Field instr. Boston U. Sch. Social Work, 1979-87, Smith Coll. Sch. of Social Work, 1986-89; instr., cons. primary care residents Tufts U. Med. Sch., Regional Health Center, Wilmington, Mass., 1978-79. Mem. Town Meeting, Billerica, Mass., 1981-2000; precinct clk., 1981, 82, 89, precinct chmn., 1984, 85, 86; deacon first Congl. Ch., 1986—; women vets. coord. VA Bedford; Social Work Leadership Tng. program, 1998; mem. bd. commrs. Housing Authority Atlantic Beach, CS, 2003-04. Mem. LWC (dir. 1970-73), Acad. Cert. Social Workers, Nat. Assn. Social Workers. Office: 200 Springs Rd Bedford MA 01730-1114

TAYLOR, CRAIG C. biotechnology company executive; With Asset Mgmt. Co.; gen. ptnr. AMC Ptnrs. 89 L.P.; acting CFO Lynx Therapeutics, Inc., Hayward, Calif., 1994—97, dir., 1994—, chmn. bd. dirs., 2000—. Dir. Pharmacyclics, Inc. Office: Lynx Therapeutics Inc 25861 Industrial Blvd Hayward CA 94545

TAYLOR, D. LANSING, cell biology educator; b. Balt., Dec. 26, 1946; BS, U. Md., 1968; PhD in Biology, SUNY, Albany, 1973. Fellow biophysics Marine Biol. Labs., 1973-74; asst. prof. biology Harvard U., 1974-78, assoc. prof., 1978-82; prof. biol. scis. Carnegie-Mellon U., Pitts., 1982-99, vice dean Mellon Coll. Sci., 1998-99, dir. ctr. light microscope imaging biotechnology, 1998-99, adj. prof., 1999—; pres., CFO Cellomics, Pitts., 1999—. Editor Jour. Cell Biology, 1981—, Jour. Cell Motility, 1981—. Mem. Am. Soc. Cell Biology, Biophys. Soc., N.Y. Acad. Sci. Achievements include research in molecular basis of amoeboid movements, utilizing biochemical, cell biological and biophysical approaches and fluorescence spectroscopy. Address: Cellomics Inc 100 Technology Dr Pittsburgh PA 15219-3130

TAYLOR, DAVID, clergy member, religious administrator; Fgn. missionary, Venezuela, 1978-90; dir. World Witness Dept. of the Pentecostal Free Will Baptist Ch., Dunn, N.C., 1990-97; pastor Oak Grove Pentecostal Free Will Ch., 1997—. Instr. Heritage Bible Coll., 1992—. Office: Oak Grove Pentacostal Free Will Bapt Ch 6535 Oak Grove Church Rd Stedman NC 28391-9716 E-mail: davidt@intrstar.net.

TAYLOR, DAVID BROOKE, lawyer, banker; b. Salt Lake City, Oct. 14, 1942; s. Lee Neff and June Taylor; m. Carolyn Kaufholz, May 29, 1965; children: Stewart, Allison. BA, U. Utah, 1964; JD, Columbia U., 1967. Bar: N.Y. 1967, N.C. 1995. Ptnr. Wickes, Riddell, Bloomer, Jacobi & McGuire, N.Y.C., 1967-79, Morgan, Lewis & Bockius, N.Y.C., 1979-89; banker, lawyer Chase Manhattan Bank, N.A., N.Y.C., 1989-92; pres. Geoenertec Corp., N.Y.C., 1992-93; ptnr. Fennebresque, Clark, Swindall & Hay, Charlotte, N.C., 1994-98, McGuire & Woods, LLP, Charlotte, N.C., 1999—. Mem. ABA, N.Y. State Bar Assn., N.C. Bar Assn. Home: 3815 Beresford Rd Charlotte NC 28211-3713 Office: McGuire & Woods LLP 100 N Tryon St Ste 2900 Charlotte NC 28202-4022

TAYLOR, DAVID GEORGE, retired banker; b. Charlevoix, Mich., July 29, 1929; s. Frank Flagg and Bessie (Strayer) Taylor; m. Robyne T. McCarthy, July 28, 1990; children from previous marriage: David, Amy, Jeanine. BS, Denison U., 1951; MBA, Northwestern U., 1953. With Continental Ill. Nat. Bank and Trust Co. Chgo., 1958—86, asst. cashier, 1961—64, 2d v.p., 1964—66, v.p., 1966—72, sr. v.p., 1972—74, exec. v.p., 1974—80, exec. v.p., treas., 1980—83, vice chmn., 1983—84, chmn., CEO, 1984; vice chmn. Irving Trust Co., N.Y.C., 1986—89; group exec. Chem. Bank, N.Y.C., 1989—94; ret., 1994. Mem. Dealer Bank Assn. Com. on Glass-Steagall Reform, 1985—86; bd. dirs. CNA Income Shares. Bd. dirs. Evanston Hosp., Glenbrook Hosp.; trustee Art Inst. Chgo., 1981—86; advisor J.L. Kellogg Grad. Sch. Mgmt., Northwestern U., 1984—. Served to 1t. USN, 1953—56. Mem.: Assn. Ret. City Bankers (asset/liability com., govt. rels. com. 1983—), Govt. and Fed. Agys. Securities Com. (chmn. bd. dirs. 1982—83), Pub. Securities Assn. (chmn. 1977, bd. dirs. 1977—78, treas. 1978). Republican. Presbyterian.

TAYLOR, DAVID KERR, international business educator, consultant; b. Oxford, N.C., Oct. 11, 1928; s. David Kerr and Myrtle Norman (Shamburger) T.; m. Isabel de Sousa Botelho de Albuquerque, Apr. 23, 1960; children: Anne de Albuquerque Taylor Grave, Katherine Rowena Taylor. BA, Duke U., 1947, JD, 1949. Bar: N.Y., N.C. Atty. Ins. Co. N.Am., N.Y.C., 1949-51, Milbank, Tweed, Hadley & McCloy, N.Y.C., 1954-55; internat. exec. Mobil Corp., N.Y.C., Washington, Can., Portugal, Nigeria, France, others, 1955-86; adj. prof. internat. affairs, sr. fellow intrnat. bus. Georgetown U. Sch. Fgn. Svc., Washington, 1987-2000. Pres. Luso-Am. Bus. Coun., 1987-89; bd. visitors Duke U. Law Sch. 1st lt. U.S. Army, 1951-54, Germany. Mem. Am. Portuguese Soc. (bd. dirs., pres. 1968-70, 76-80), Washington Export Coun., Washington Inst. Fgn. Affairs, Dacor Bacon House, Cosmos Club, Phi Beta Kappa. Avocation: singing. Home: 2737 Devonshire Pl NW Washington DC 20008-3479

TAYLOR, DAVID WYATT AIKEN, retired clergyman; b. Tsingkiangpu, Kiangsu, China, Dec. 13, 1925; s. Hugh Kerr and Fanny Bland (Graham) T.; m. Lillian Ross McCulloch, Aug. 25, 1951; children: Frances Bland, David Wyatt. BA, Vanderbilt U., 1949; B.D. cum laude, Union Theol. Sem. Va., 1952; Th.M., Princeton Theol. Sem., 1953; D.D. (hon.), King Coll., Bristol, Tenn., 1959. Ordained to ministry Presbyn. Ch. U.S., 1952. Pastor chs., Elkton, Va., 1953-55, Bristol, Va., 1955-62; ednl. sec. bd. world missions Presbyn. Ch. U.S., 1962-68, program div. dir., 1968-73, ecumenical officer gen. assembly mission bd., 1973-82; pastor Orange Park Presbyn. Ch., Orange Park, Fla., 1982-86; gen. sec. for strategy and interpretation Consultation on Ch. Union, Princeton, N.J., 1986-88, gen. sec., 1988-93; ret., 1993. Instr. Bible Presbyn. Jr. Coll., Maxton, N.C., 1951; mem. program bd., div. Christian edn. Nat. Council Chs., 1965-69, bd. mgrs., dept. edn. for mission, 1962-68, mem. program bd., div. overseas ministries, 1968-78, mem. governing bd., 1976-80, chmn. governing bd. credentials com., 1978; chmn. Church World Service, Inc., 1973-75; mem. adminstrn. and fin. com. Nat. Council Chs., 1973-75, mem. commn. on faith and order, 1978-93; mem. commn. on interchurch aid World Council Chs., 1973-75; mem. 5th Assembly, 1975; rep. Presbyn. Ch. U.S. to World Alliance Ref. Chs., 1976-82; bd. dirs. Presbyn. Survey mag., 1963-68; mem. Consultation on Ch. Union, 1974-93; chmn. Nat. Ecumenical Officers Assn., 1978-81; exec. coun. NC Coun. Chs., 2003—. Bd. dirs. Abingdon Presbytery's Children's Home, Wytheville, Va., 1958-62. Served with AUS, 1944-46, PTO. Mem. Sigma Chi. Presbyterian. Home: 3113 Glenhope Ct Cary NC 27511

TAYLOR, DIANA LANCASTER, school system administrator; b. Summit, N.J., Feb. 6, 1955; d. Edwin Douglas and Lois Johnston (O'Neill) T. AB, Dartmouth Coll., 1977; MBA, Columbia U., 1979-81. Analyst N.Y. State Dept. Soc. Service, N.Y.C., 1977-79; assoc. Smith, Barney, Harris, Upham, N.Y.C., 1981-82, Lehman Brothers Kuhn Loeb, N.Y.C., 1982-83, v.p., 1983-84, Donaldson, Lufkin & Jenrette, N.Y.C., 1984-86, sr. v.p., mgr. short-term banking, 1987-88, sr. v.p., mgr. edn. fin. group, 1987-88; founding ptnr. M.R. Beal & Co., 1988—90, pres., 1990—93; exec. v.p., head capital markets Muriel Siebert & Co., 1993—95; sr. v.p. pub. fin. Smith Mitchell Investment Group Inc., 1996—99; asst. sec. for pub. authorities NY, 1999; v.p. governmental and regulatory affairs KeySpan Energy, N.Y.C., 2000—; CFO LI Power Authority, NY, 2001—02; dep. sec. for state authorities NY; dep. sec. for fin. and housing, 2003; NY State Supt. of Banks, 2003—. Bd. dirs. YMCA Greater NYC, Hudson River Park Trust, The After Sch. Corp., NYC Transit Mus., Bklyn. Acad. Music. Mem., Yale, (N.Y.C.). Office: Supt Banks NY State Banking Dept One State St New York NY 10004-1417 Office Phone: 212-709-3501.

TAYLOR, DONALD, retired manufacturing company executive; b. Worcester, Mass., June 2, 1927; s. John A. B. and Alice M. (Weaver) T.; m. Ruth L. Partridge, June 24, 1950; children: Linda Taylor Robertson, Donald, Mark, John. BSME, Worcester Poly. Inst., 1949; grad., Northeastern U. Mgmt. Devel. Program, 1962, Harvard Bus. Sch. Advanced Mgmt. Program, 1979. Registered profl. engr., Mass. With George J. Meyer Mfg. Co., Milw., 1954-69; pres. mfg. div. A-T-O, Inc., 1969; exec. v.p. Nordberg div. Rex Chainbelt, Inc., Milw., 1969-73; v.p. ops. Rexnord Inc., Brookfield, Wis., pres., chief operating officer, 1978-85, chief exec. officer, from 1985, chmn., 1985-88; pres. Nordberg Machinery Group, Milw., 1973-78. Served with USNR, 1951—54. Mem. ASME. Clubs: Milw. Country, Milw. Town, Univ., Masons. Office: 1 Runnymede Dr North Hampton NH 03862-2328

TAYLOR, DOUGLAS HOWARD, translator; b. Washington, Apr. 4, 1961; s. Richard Powell and Barbara Jo Anne (Harris) T. BA, Amherst Coll., 1984; MA, Am. U., 1990. Freelance Russian and French translator, Germantown, Md., 1988—. Editor-in-chief Landon News, 1979-80; editor mag. Nat. Soc. for Children of Am. Revolution, 1979-80; contbr. articles to profl. jours. Vol. Reagan/Bush Campaign, Potomac, 1980; asst. to chmn. Md. Bush/Quayle Campaign, Bethesda, 1988. Mem.: Phi Beta Kappa. Republican. Episcopalian. Avocations: coin collecting/numismatics, bowling, tennis, running, reading. Home and Office: 14914 Spring Meadows Dr Germantown MD 20874-3444

TAYLOR, DOUGLAS JOHN, materials scientist, researcher, materials engineer; s. William Harry Douglas and Diane Taylor; m. Karen Rasinski, May 18, 2001. BS in materials engring., N.Mex Inst. of Mining and Tech., 1985—89; PhD in materials sci. and engring., U. of Ariz., 1989—95. Rsch. assoc. U. Ariz., Tucson, 1989—95; sr. scientist TPL, Inc., Albuquerque, 1995—. Adv. bd. Dept. of Materials and Metall. Engring., N.Mex Inst. of Mining and Tech., Socorro, N.Mex., 2001—. Contbr. articles to profl. jours. Dept. of Energy Grad. Student fellow, Oak Ridge Nat. Lab., 1993—95. Mem.: ASM Internat. (albuquerque chpt. pres. 1999—2000), Tau Beta Pi (life). Roman Catholic. Achievements include patents pending for laser direct writing of erbium doped coatings for optical devices using the same. Office: TPL Incorporated 3921 Academy Pkwy NNE Albuquerque NM 87109-4416 E-mail: dtaylor@tplinc.com.

TAYLOR, DUNCAN PAUL, research neuropharmacologist; b. Bremerton, Wash., Feb. 4, 1949; s. Alan Earl and Barbara Eleanor (Thiel) T.; m. Jeanne Louise Damgaard, Apr. 8, 1972; 1 child, Aubrey Elizabeth. BS in Chemistry, Calif. Inst. Tech., 1971; PhD in Biochemistry, Oreg. State U., 1977. Technician analytical svcs. Carnation Co. Rsch. Labs., Van Nuys, Calif., 1967-70; Peace Corps vol. Princess Margaret Secondary Sch., St. Johns, Antigua and Barbuda, 1971-73; grad. tchg. and rsch. asst. biochemistry and biophysics Oreg. State U., Corvallis, 1973-77; rsch. assoc. sect. biochemistry and pharmacology NIMH, Bethesda, Md., 1977-79; scientist, neuropharmacologist, rsch. assoc. Pharm. divsn. Mead Johnson & Co., Evansville, Ind., 1979-80; sr. scientist, group leader Pharm. div. Mead Johnson & Co., Evansville, Ind., 1980-82; sr. scientist, group leader, neuropharmacologist Pharm. R & D divsn. Bristol-Myers Co., Evansville, 1982-83, sr. rsch. scientist, mgr., 1983-85, rsch. fellow preclin. ctrl. nervous sys. rsch., 1985-89; sr. rsch. fellow preclin. ctrl. nervous sys. rsch. Pharm. Rsch. Inst. Bristol-Myers Squibb Co., Wallingford, Conn., 1989-94; dir. pharmacology Symphony Pharms., Malvern, Pa., 1994-95; cons., 1995-96; analyst bus. devel. Pharmacia & Upjohn, Kalamazoo, 1996-98, dir. strategic rsch. assessment, 1998—2003; prin. MT Enterprises, Kalamazoo, 2003—04; dir. strategic rsch. assessment Biovail Techs., Ltd., Bridgewater, NJ, 2004—. Mem. external adv. bd. dept. chemistry U. So. Miss.; grant reviewer NSF, 1981, 82, Med. Rsch. Coun. Can., 1987, 88; frequent presenter to profl. confs.; cons. in field. Contbr. numerous articles and abstracts to profl. jours. Bd. dirs. Posey County chpt. Am. Cancer Soc., 1983—85; mem. Tri-State Cursillo Cmty.; mentor Horizons Leadership Acad., Evansville-Vanderburgh Sch. Corp., 1985; cons. Project Bus. Jr. Achievement, 1988; mem. chancel choir 1st United Meth. Ch., Mt. Vernon, Ind., 1976—86; mem. adult choir South Congl. Ch., Middletown, Conn., 1986—96, deacon, 1987—90, 1995—96, co-chmn., 1989—90, 1996, mem. coun., 1989—90, mem. task force on long-range planning, 1989—90; mem. adult choir 2d Reformed Ch., Kalamazoo, 1997—2004, mem. handbell choir, 1997—2004, mem. worship coun., 1997—99, elder, 1998—2001, consistory mem., 1998—2001, ch. outreach coun., 2000—01. Scholar Carnation Co., 1967-70, Calif. State scholar, 1967-68, 70; rsch. fellow NSF, 1970, Cold Spring Harbor Labs., 1974. Fellow: Am. Inst. Chemists; mem.: AAAS, Soc. Competitive Intelligence Profls., Internat. Brain Rsch. Orgn.-World Fedn. Neuroscientists, Fedn. Am. Socs. for Exptl. Biology, European Brain and Behavior Soc., Brit. Brain Rsch. Assn, Soc. for Neurosci. (v.p. Conn. chpt. 1989—93), Am. Soc. for Pharmacology and Exptl. Therapeutics, Am. Chem. Soc., Phi Lambda Upsilon, Sigma Xi. Democrat. Achievements include patent for method and treatment of ischemia in the brain; made significant efforts in identification and development of new antipsychotics and antidepressants; identification of potential mechanism of action of the antipsychotic BMY14802; research in receptors, in etiology, expression and pharmacotherapy of psychiatric disorders. Home: 11 Jockey Ln Flemington NJ 08822-1599 Office: Biovail Techs Ltd 700 Route 202/206 North PO Box 6935 Bridgewater NJ 08807 Office Phone: 908-927-1797. Personal E-mail: duncan.taylor@patmedia.net. Business E-Mail: duncan.taylor@biovail.com.

TAYLOR, E. DENNIS, English language educator, editor; b. Balt., Md., Feb. 26, 1940; s. Frank Edmund and Mary Chester Taylor; m. Mary Barber Brown, Aug. 28, 1966; children: John Edmund, Frank Matthew, Kathryn Elizabeth Wall, MaryRebecca Hayden. PhD, Yale U., 1965. Editor Religion and the Arts, Boston Coll., Chestnut Hill, 1996—; prof. English dept. Boston Coll., Chestnut Hill, Mass., 1971—. Author: (scholarly work) Hardy's Metres and Victorian Prosody, 1988, Hardy's Literary Language and Victorian Philology, 1998, Hardy's Poetry 1860-1928, 1998 (Macmillan/Hardy Soc. prize, 1990), Jude the Obscure, 1998, Shakespeare and the Culture of Christianity in Early Modern England, 2003. Democrat. Roman Catholic. Achievements include research in Victorian scholarship, Poetry, Shakespeare. Avocation: handball. Office: Boston Coll 25 Lawrence Ave Chestnut Hill MA 02467 E-mail: taylor@bc.edu.

TAYLOR, EDNA JANE, retired employment program counselor; b. Flint, Mich., May 16, 1934; d. Leonard Lee and Wynona Ruth (Davis) Harvey; children: Wynona Jane MacDonald, Cynthia Lee Zellmer. BS, No. Ariz. U., 1963; MEd, U. Ariz., 1967. Tchr. high sch. Sunnyside Sch. Dist., Tucson, 1963-68; employment program counselor employment devel. State of Calif., Canoga Park, 1968-98, ret., 1998. Mem. adv. coun. Van Nuys Cmty. Adult Sch., Calif., 1983-96, steering com., 1989-91, leadership coun., 1991-92; mem. adv. coun. Pierce C.C., Woodland Hills, Calif., 1979-81; first aid instr., recreational leader ARC. Mem. NAFE, Internat. Assn. of Pers. in Employment Security, Calif. Employment Counselors Assn. (state treas. 1978-79, state sec. 1980), Delta Psi Kappa (life). Avocations: writing, tennis, health and fitness, gardening. E-mail: tauchi2@mindspring.com.

TAYLOR, EDWARD CURTIS, chemistry professor; b. Springfield, Mass., Aug. 3, 1923; s. Edward Curtis and Margaret Louise (Anderson) T.; m. Virginia Dion Crouse, June 29, 1946; children: Edward Newton, Susan Raines. Student, Hamilton Coll., 1942-44, DSc (hon.), 1969; AB, Cornell U., 1946, PhD, 1949. Postdoctoral fellow Nat. Acad. Scis., Zurich, Switzerland, 1949-50; DuPont postdoctoral fellow chemistry U. Ill., 1950-51, faculty, 1951-54, asst. prof. organic chemistry, 1952-54; faculty Princeton U., 1954—, prof. chemistry, 1964—, A. Barton Hepburn prof. organic chemistry, 1966—, A. Barton Hepburn prof. organic chemistry emeritus, 1997—, chmn. dept. chemistry, 1974-79, sr. rsch. scientist, 1997—. Vis. prof. Technische Hochschule, Stuttgart, Fed. Republic Germany, 1960, U. East Anglia, 1969, 71; Disting. vis. prof. U. Buffalo, 1968, U. Wyo., 1977; Backer lectr. U. Groningen, Holland, 1969; mem. chemistry adv. com. Office Sci. Research,

USAF, 1962-73, Cancer Chemotherapy Nat. Service Ctr., 1958-62; mem. internat. adv. bd. Ctr. Medicinal Chemistry, Bar-Ilan U., Israel, 1994—; cons. rsch. divs. Parke-Davis Co., 1951-56, Procter & Gamble, 1953-80, Smith Kline & French, 1956-62, Eastman Kodak Co., 1965-83, Tenn. Eastman Co., 1968-83, Eli Lilly & Co., 1962-2002, Burroughs Wellcome Co., 1983-95, E.I. duPont de Nemours & Co., 1986-90, Polaroid Corp., 1986-2001, Dow Elanco Co., 1989-96, DuPont Merck Pharm. Co., 1990-97, Dow AgroScis., 1997-2003, DuPont Pharms. Co., 1997-2001. Author: (with McKillop) Chemistry of Cyclic Enaminonitriles and o-Aminonitriles, 1970, Principles of Heterocyclic Chemistry: film and audio courses, 1974; editor (with Raphael and Wynberg) Advances in Organic Chemistry, vols I-V, 1960-65, (with Wynberg) Vol VI, 1969, vols. VII-IX, 1970-79 (with W. Pfleiderer) Pteridine Chemistry, 1964, The Chemistry of Heterocyclic Compounds, 1968—, General Heterocyclic Chemistry, 1968—; organic chemistry editl. advisor John Wiley & Sons, Inc., 1968—; mem. editl. adv. bd. Jour. Medicinal Chemistry, 1962-66, Jour. Organic Chemistry, 1971-75, Synthetic Communications, 1971—, Heterocycles, 1973—, Chm. Substructure Index, 1971—, Advances in Heterocyclic Chemistry, 1983—, Pteridines, 1989—. Recipient rsch. awards SmithKline and French Found., 1955, Hoffmann-LaRoche Foun., 1964-65, Ciba Found., 1971, Disting. Hamilton award, 1977, U.S. Sr. Scientist prize Alexander von Humboldt Found., 1983, Disting. Alumni medal Hamilton Coll., 1990, F. Gowland Hopkins medal, 1993; sr. faculty fellow Harvard U., 1959; Guggenheim fellow, 1979-80. Fellow N.Y. Acad. Scis., Am. Inst. Chemists; mem. Am. Chem. Soc. (award for creative work in synthetic organic chemistry, 1974, chmn. organic chemistry div. 1976-77, Arthur C. Cope scholar award 1994), German Chem. Soc., Royal Soc. London, Internat. Soc. Heterocyclic Chemistry (5th Internat. award 1989), Phi Beta Kappa, Sigma Xi, Phi Kappa Phi. Home: 288 Western Way Princeton NJ 08540-5337 Office Phone: 609-258-3914. Business E-Mail: etaylor@princeton.edu.

TAYLOR, EDWARD MICHAEL, insurance, enterprise risk management consultant; b. Cambridge, Mass., June 26, 1947; s. Edward D. and Rita P. (Collins) T.; children from previous marriage: Philip A., Donandrea M.; m. Leslie Foxen, 1996; children: Erica Arruda, Lindsay Ingraham. BSA, Bentley Coll., Waltham, Mass., 1970; MBA, Almeda Coll. and U., Boise, Idaho, 2002; ThD, Trinity Seminary & Bible Coll. Ordained to ministry United Christian Ministries Internat., 2002. V.p. J.H. Albert Internat. Ins. Advisors, Needham, Mass., 1974-80; prin., exec. v.p. Pine Ins. Agy., Melrose, Mass., 1980-83; pres., chief exec. officer, founder Taylor Risk Mgmt. Assocs., New Bedford, Mass., 1983-92; sr. v.p., prin. cons. Kevin F. Donoghue and Assocs., Boston, 1992-97; dir. ins. risk mgmt. solutions PriceWaterhouseCoopers, LLP, Boston, 1997—. Capt. NG U.S. Army, 1971—76. Decorated Internat. Order of Merit; recipient Leadership award for contbns. to risk mgmt. profession. Mem. Internat. Ins. Soc., Soc. Risk Mgmt. Cons., Risk and Ins. Soc. Am., Am. Biog. Inst. (Disting. Leadership award 1988, apptd. hon. mem. rsch. bd. advisors 1988), Am. Arbitration Assn. (appointed to nat. panel of arbitrators), Am. Soc. Safety Engrs., KC (dep. grand knight), Assn. of Contingency Planners, Global Assn. of Risk Profls. Office: PricewaterhouseCoopers LLP 125 High St Boston MA 02110-1707 also: PO Box 90 Middleboro MA 02346-0090 Office Phone: 617-530-7605. E-mail: edward.m.taylor@us.pwc.com.

TAYLOR, EDWARD STEWART, physician, educator; b. Hecla, S.D., Aug. 20, 1911; s. Robert Stewart and Sylvia Frances (Dewey) T.; m. Ruth Fatherson, June 15, 1940; children: Edward Stewart, Elizabeth Dewey Taylor Bryant, Catherine Wells Taylor. BA, U. Iowa, 1933, MD, 1936. Diplomate Am. Bd. Ob-Gyn (dir. 1962-69). Intern, Hurley Hosp., Flint, Mich., 1936-37; splty. tng. ob-gyn L.I. Coll. Hosp., 1937-41; prof. ob-gyn, chmn. dept. Sch. Medicine, U. Colo., 1947-76, clin. prof., 1976-81, prof., chmn. emeritus, 1981—. Nat. cons. ob-gyn to surg. gen. USAF, 1958-62. Author: Manual of Gynecology, 1952, Essentials of Gynecology, 4th edit.; editor: Beck's Obstetrical Practice, 10th edit.; editor-in-chief for obstetrics: Obstetrical and Gynecol. Survey, 1967-92. Trustee Denver Symphony Orch., 1979-85. Served to lt. col. AUS, 1942-45. Endowed ob-gyn. chair U. Colo., 1999. Fellow ACS, Am. Coll. Obstetricians and Gynecologists (Disting. Svc. award 1984); mem. AMA, Am. Gynecol. Soc. (v.p. 1974-75), Am. Assn. Obstetricians and Gynecologists (pres. 1970-71), Ctrl. Assn. Obstetricians and Gynecologists, S.W. Obstet. and Gynecol. Soc. (hon.), Am. Gynecol. and Obstet. Soc., Assn. Profs. Ob-Gyn (pres. 1974-75), Western Surg. Soc., Finnish Gynecol. Soc. (hon.), University Club (Denver), Alpha Omega Alpha. Clubs: University (Denver). Congregationalist. Home: 80 S Dexter St Denver CO 80246-1051

TAYLOR, ELINOR ZIMMERMAN, state legislator; b. Norristown, Pa., Apr. 18, 1921; d. Harold I. and Ruth A. (Rahn) Zimmerman; m. William M. Taylor, 1947; 1 child, Barbara. BS, West Chester State Tchrs. Coll., 1943; student, Columbia U., 1944, U. Del., 1955; MEd, Temple U., 1958. Tchr. Ridley Park (Pa.) H.S., 1943-46, West Chester (Pa.) H.S., 1946-50; prof. West Chester State Coll., 1955-68, adminstr., 1968-76, now. prof. emeritus; mem. Pa. Ho. of Reps., 1977—. Chmn. subcom. on higher edn.; sec. Rep. Caucus; bd. dirs. Pa. Higher Edn. Assistance Agy.; active Gov. Commn. on Funding Higher Edn., Women; in Politics and Polit. Action Com.; Rep. chmn. Health and Welfare Com.; trustee Charles S. Swope Found.; founding trustee Bd. Chester County Edn. Found. Councilwoman Borough of West Chester, Pa., 1974-77, mem. recreation com., 1974-77. Named West Chester Citizen of Yr., 1985, Legislator of Yr. Pa. Assn. Home Health Agys., 1993; recipent Hon. award Pa. State Assn. for Health, Phys. Edn. and Recreation, 1962, Hon. Umpires award U.S. Field Hockey Assn., 1967, Disting. Alumni award West Chester State Coll., 1977, alumni award Temple U., 1982, Love of Children of Greater West Chester Golden Heart award, Achievement cert. Pa. Fedn. of Bus. and Profl. Women's Club, George Washington Honor award Valley Forge Freedom Found., Guardian of Small Bus. award, 1993-94, cert. of appreciation Am. Legion, 1995, Margaret Hoover Brigham award Chester County Emergency Med. Svc., 1995, Police Athletic League award, 1995; named to Henderson H.S. Hall of Fame, 1994. Mem. AAUW (former pres.), Nat. Assn. Women Legislators, Chester County Art Assn., Pa. Paramedice Assn. (hon.). Republican. Presbyterian. Office: Pa Ho of Reps 315-G Main Capitol Bldg House Box 20202 Harrisburg PA 17120-2020

TAYLOR, ELISABETH COLER, retired secondary school educator; b. N.Y.C., Jan. 24, 1942; d. Gerhard Helmut and Judith Coler; m. Billie Wesley Taylor II, Jan. 27, 1960; children: Letitia Rose, Billie Albert. Student, Wilmington Coll., 1959-60; BS, Wayne State U., Detroit, 1969; MS, The Ohio State U., 1980; postgrad., Wright State U., Dayton, Ohio, 1989—. Cert. home economist. H.s. tchr. home econs., computer sci., lang. arts Dayton (Ohio) City Schs., 1972-99. Bd. dirs. Camp Fire Girls, 1970-71, vol. Detroit Mus. of Art, 1970-71, group leader Camp Fire Girls, Boy Scouts, Dayton, 1968-74. Mem. AAUW (life), Am. Mensa Ltd. (life). Avocations: birding, travel, needlecrafts. Home: 131 Snow Hill Ave Dayton OH 45429-1705

TAYLOR, ELIZABETH, elementary school educator; m. Wendell Taylor, June 10, 1950 (dec. Mar. 1980); 1 child, James Wendell. BA, Georgetown Coll., 1949; MA, U. Ky., 1953; edn. specialist, Ea. Ky. U., 1956. Lic. real estate Ky. Bd. Realtors. Tchr. Russell County Bd. Edn., Jamestown, Ky., 1947—48; acct. Fayette Crutcher Clothing Bus., Frankfort, 1957—63; tchr. Ky. State U., Frankfort, 1958—64, Franklin County Bd. Edn., Frankfort, 1949—89; banker Farmers Bank and Trust Co., Frankfort, 1980—90; realtor Rector Hayden, Lexington, Ky., 1990—91; tchr. Woodford County Bd. Edn., Versailles, Ky., 1992—. Rep. Internat. Mission Bd., 1992—; worker Ky. Disaster Relief, 2000—. Author: Prayer-A Link to God's Power, 2001; writer: lyrics Trust the Invisible God, 2002. Mem.: NEA, Ky. Edn. Assn. Baptist. Avocations: travel, music, sports, walking, hiking. Home: 115 S Hill Versailles KY 40383

TAYLOR, ELIZABETH JANE, investment consultant, real estate and international marketing executive; b. Tiffin, Ohio, Oct. 27, 1941; d. Albert Joseph Lucas and Mary Jane Siebenaller-Swander; m. Gaylen Lloyd Taylor, July 11, 1977. Student, Heidelberg Coll., 1961, Austin (Tex.) C.C., 1983-84; grad., Real Estate Edn. Ctr., 1984, Inst. Real Estate, 1988, Real Estate Inst., 1989; Tex. Realtors Inst., 1989; student, Rockhurst Coll., 1991-92. Dir. regional mktg. Sibrow, Inc., Ottawa, Can., 1981-83; realtor assoc. Alliance Sales, Austin, 1985-88; assoc. Broadway Comml. Investments, 1988-91; prin. Taylor & Assocs. Internat. Mktg. & Bus. Devel., 1980-98. Cons. Hypnosis Conn., Ohio, Tex. and Ariz., 1967—; tchr. mktg. and bus. devel., 1980-96. Author: (poetry) Letters from Home, 1986, Best New Poets of 1986, American Poetry Anthology, vol. VI, #3, 1986, Unfinished Business and the Tapestry, 2001, Reflections and Dreams, 2002, Southwest Celebration, 2003, A Dark and Stormy Night, 2003, Soul's Music, 2003, A Christmas Collection, 2003, (novel) Unfinished Business, 2002, (cookbook) Sourdough & More, 2003; columnist Austin Women Mag., 1984-86. V.p. Am. Congress on Real Estate, 1982-83; arbitrator Better Bus. Bur., 1984-89, sr. arbitrator, Austin, 1989-95; spkrs. bur. Austin Womans Ctr., 1985-88; v.p. Austin World Affairs Coun., 1984-94; adv. panel Austin Woman Mag., 1984-86. Nominee to Tex. Womens Hall of Fame, 1984. Mem. NAFE (network dir. 1980-88), Am. Biog. Inst. Rsch. (hon., bd. advisors 1988). Avocations: writing, behavior research. Home: 3926 E Cherokee St Phoenix AZ 85044-3827

TAYLOR, ELIZABETH R. counselor, educator; b. Houston, Aug. 19, 1953; d. L. G. and Edna Taylor. BS psychology, Abilene Christian Univ., 1975; M. Ed., Sul Russ State Univ., 1979; PhD, St. Mary's Univ., San Antonio, Tex., 1994. Lic. profl. counselor Tex., 1990, marriage and family therapist Tex., cert. elem. edn. Tex., 1976, visual impairment Tex., emotional disturbance Tex., lang. and learning disabilities Tex., spl. edn. counselor Tex., sch. counselor Tex. Spl. edn. tchr., diagnostician San Felipe Del Rio Ind. Consol. Sch. Dist., Del Rio, Tex., 1979—89; asst. prof. U. Tex. Health Sci. Ctr., San Antonio, 1993—98, Tex. Christian U., Ft. Worth, 1998—. Editor: Tex. Counseling Assn. Jour. Crown group leader Richland Hills Ch. of Christ, Ft. Worth, 1992—93. Mem.: Am. Sch. Counseling Assn., Tex. Counseling Assn. (Disting. Svc. award 1999), Internat. Assn. for Personal Meaning. Office: Texas Christian Univ TCU Box 297900 Fort Worth TX 76129 Office Phone: 817-257-6768. Personal E-mail: e.taylor@tcu.edu. E-mail: e.taylor@tcu.edu.

TAYLOR, ELIZABETH ROSEMOND, actress; b. London, Feb. 27, 1932; d. Francis and Sara (Sothern) Taylor. Student, Byron House, Hawthorne Sch., Metro-Goldwyn-Mayer Sch. Actress: (films) There's One Born Every Minute, 1942; Lassie Come Home, 1943; The White Cliffs of Dover, 1944; Jane Eyre, 1944; National Velvet, 1944; Courage of Lassie, 1946; Cynthia, 1947; Life with Father, 1947; A Date with Judy, 1948; Julia Misbehaves, 1948; Little Women, 1950; Conspirator, 1950; The Big Hangover, 1950; Father of the Bride, 1950; Father's Little Dividend, 1951; A Place in the Sun, 1951; Callaway Went Thataway, 1951; Lover is Better Than Ever, 1952; Ivanhoe, 1952; The Girl Who Had Everything, 1953; Elephant Walk, 1954; Rhapsody, 1954; Beau Brummel, 1954; The Last Time I Saw Paris, 1954; Giant, 1956; Raintree County, 1957; Cat on a Hot Tin Roof, 1958; Suddenly Last Summer, 1959; Scent of Mystery, 1960; Butterfield 8, 1960 (Acad. award Best Actress, 1960); Cleopatra, 1963; The V.I.P.'s, 1963; The Sandpiper, 1965; Who's Afraid of Virginia Woolf?, 1966 (Acad. award Best Actress, 1966); The Taming of the Shrew, 1967; The Comedians, 1967; Reflections in a Golden Eye, 1967; Dr. Faustus, 1967; Boom!, 1968; Secret Ceremony, 1968; The Only Game in Town, 1970; Under Milkwood, 1971; X, Y and Zee, 1972; Hammersmith is Out, 1972; Night Watch, 1973; Ash Wednesday, 1973; That's Entertainment, 1974; The Driver's Seat, 1974; Blue Bird, 1975; Winter Kills, 1977; A Little Night Music, 1977; The Mirror Crack'd, 1980; Young Toscanini, 1988; The Flintstones, 1994; The Visit, 1999; appearances include: (TV films) Divorce His/Divorce Hers, 1973; Victory at Entebbe, 1977; Return Engagement, 1979; Between Friends, 1982; (TV series) Hotel (series), 1984; (TV films) Malice in Wonderland, 1986; (TV miniseries) North and South, 1986; (TV films) There Must Be a Pony, 1986; Poker Alice, 1987; Sweet Bird of Youth, 1989; theatre appearances include: (Broadway plays) The Little Foxes, 1981; Private Lives, 1983; narrator: (documentaries) Genocide, 1981; co-author (with Richard Burton): (novels) World Enough and Time, 1964; author Elizabeth Taylor, 1965, Elizabeth Taylor Takes Off: On Weight Gain, Weight Loss, Self Esteem and Self Image, 1988; lic. (fragrances) Elizabeth Taylor's Passion, Passion for Men, White Diamonds/Elizabeth Taylor, Elizabeth Taylor's Diamonds & Emeralds, Diamonds and Rubies, Diamonds & Sapphires, Elizabeth Taylor Black Pearls. Active philanthropic, relief, charitable causes internationally, including Israeli War Victums Fund for the Chaim Sheba Hosp., 1976, UNICEF, various children's hosps., med. clinics, Botswana; initiated Ben Gurion U. - Elizabeth Taylor Fund for Children of the Negev, 1982; supporter AIDS Project, L.A., 1985; founder, nat. chmn. Am. Found. for AIDS Rsch. (AmFAR), 1985—, internat. fund, 1985—; founder Elizabeth Taylor AIDS Found., 1991—. Named Comdr. Arts Letters, France, 1985, an honoree with dedication of Elizabeth Taylor Med. Ctr. Whitman - Walker Clinic, Washington, 1993; recipient Legion of Honor (for work with AmFAR), France, 1987, Aristotle S. Onassis Found., 1988, Jean Hersholt Humanitarian Acad. award (for work as AIDS advocate), 1993, Life Achievement award, Am. Film Inst., 1993.*

TAYLOR, ESTELLE WORMLEY, English educator, dean; b. Washington, Jan. 12, 1924; d. Luther Charles and Wilhelmina Wormley; m. Ivan Earle Taylor, Dec. 26, 1953. BS magna cum laude, Miner Tchrs. Coll., 1945; MA, Howard U., 1947; PhD, Cath. U. Am., 1969. Instr. English Howard U., 1947-52; tchr. Langley Jr. H.S., Washington, 1952-55, Eastern Sr. H.S., Washington, 1955-63; from instr. to prof. D.C. Tchrs. Coll., 1963-91, prof. English emerita, 1991—, acad. dean, 1975-76; assoc. provost Fed. City Coll., Washington, 1974-75; prof. Howard U., 1976-91, chmn. dept. English, 1976-85; assoc. dean Howard U. Coll. Liberal Arts, 1985-86; dir. expository writing program Grad. Sch. Arts and Scis., 1988-91. Mem., sec. Edn. Licensure Commn. of D.C., 1993—; mem. Commn. on Higher Edn., Mid. States Assn. Colls. and Schs., 1984-87, 88-90, co-chair steering com. to revise Characteristics of Excellence, 1992-93; mem. ctrl. exec. com. Folger Inst. Renaissance and 18th Century Studies, 1982-91; adv. bd. Humanities Inst. Montgomery Coll., 1997—. Contbg. editor A Howard Reader, 1997. 1st v.p. Order Daus. of King Episc. Ch. Diocese, Washington, 1994-98; commr. Edn. Licensure Com. of D.C., 1993—, also sec., vice chmn., 1995—; trustee U. D.C., 1979-83, vice chmn., 1983; mem. D.C. Cmty. Humanities Coun., 1990-91; co-chmn. planning com. Centennial Celebration of the Andrew Rankin Chapel Howard U., 1994; adv. bd. Coll. Arts and Svcs., Howard U., 2002—; mem. selection bd. Fgn. Agrl. Svc., 2002. Named Disting. Alumni, Howard U., 1995, Alumni award for Disting. Postgrad. Achievement in Edn. and Lit., 1997; So. fellow, 1968-69; Rockefeller/Aspen Inst. fellow, 1978-79. Mem. MLA (del. assembly 1994—), Nat. Assn. for Equal Opportunity in Higher Edn., Coll. Lang. Assn., Shakespeare Assn. Am., Pub. Mems. Assn. Fgn. Svc. Dept. of State, Links (v.p. Capital City chpt. 1979-81, corr. sec. 1989, rec. sec. 1991-93, 95—). Democrat. Home: 3221 20th St NE Washington DC 20018-2421 *Throughout my career I have been climbing a giant ladder, invisible to all but me. The challenging but humbling feature of this ladder is that whenever I get the feeling that I have almost reached the top, several additional rungs attach themselves to my Jacob's Ladder. Thus, that thing called success is for me forever a goal to be reached. As long as I continue to feel a restlessness and a yearning to climb another rung, I shall know that I am alive.*

TAYLOR, FANNIE TURNBULL, social education and arts administration educator; b. Kansas City, Mo., Sept. 11, 1913; d. Henry King and Fannie Elizabeth (Sills) Turnbull; m. Robert Taylor, Dec. 2, 1938 (div. 1974); children: Kathleen Muir Taylor Isaacs, Anne Kingston Taylor Wadsack. BA, U. Wis., 1938; LHD (hon.), Buena Vista Coll., Storm Lake, Iowa, 1975. Mem. faculty U. Wis., Madison, 1941—, prof. social edn., 1949—, emerita, 1979—. Dir. Wis. Union Theater, 1946-66, coord. univ. systems arts coun., 1967-70, assoc. dir. Ctr. Arts Adminstrn., 1970-72, coord. Consortium for Arts, 1976-84; cons. in field. Author: The Arts at a New Frontier: The National Endowment for the Arts, Wisconsin Union Theater: Fifty Golden Years (Book award of Merit, State Hist. Soc. Wis. 1990); contbr. articles to profl. jours. Program dir. music Nat. Endowment Arts, 1966-67, program info. dir., 1972-76; bd. dirs. Wis. Arts Coun., 1964-72, Wis. Found. Arts, 1976-91, Madison Civic Music Assn., 1976-84, Madison Children's Mus., 1983-96, Elvehjem Mus. Art Coun., 1976—, chair 1983-86; Madison Civic Ctr. Found., 1981-94; hon. chair Wis. Union Theater Program Endowment Fund, 1985—; bd. dirs. Wis. chpt. Nature Conservancy, 1963-84, chmn. 1976-77; bd. dirs. Shorewood Hills Found., 1976-2002, pres., 1976-81. Recipient Oak Leaf award Nature Conservancy, 1981, Wis. Gov.'s award in Support of the Arts, 1992, Madison Cmty. Found. Asset Builders Leadership award, 2002; named Woman of Distinction, Madison YWCA, 1994. Fellow Wis. Acad. Scis., Arts and Letters; mem. Assn. Performing Arts Presenters (founder, exec. dir. 1957-72, 1st recipient Fannie Taylor award 1972), Am. Assn. Dance Cos. (bd. dirs. 1967-72), Nat. Assn. Regional Ballet (bd. dirs. 1975-77), Nat. Guild Cmty. Music Schs. Arts (bd. dirs. 1977-80), Women in Comm. (Writers' Cup 1980), U. Wis. Found., U. Wis. Alumni Assn. (Disting. Svc. award 1979), Madison Civics Club (pres. 1969-70), Univ. Club (pres. 1982-85), Blackhawk Club. Home: 8301 Old Sauk Rd Apt 303 Middleton WI 53562-4393 Business E-Mail: ftaylor@facstaff.wisc.edu.

TAYLOR, FELICIA, newscaster; BS in Comm., Northwestern U. Prodr., field reporter WLS-TV, Chgo.; anchor, prodr., writer Fin. News Network; anchor bus. shows Fin. Times; London corr. CNBC, Ft. Lee, N.J., 1992-93, co-anchor Today's Bus., anchor This Morning's Bus., 1993—98, co-anchor MarketWatch; co-anchor Weekend Today in New York NewsChannel4, N.Y.C., NY, 1998—2003, co-anchor NewsChannel 4 at 6 and 11, 2003—. Office: NBC News 30 Rockefeller Plaza New York NY 10112

TAYLOR, FOSTER JAY, retired university president; b. Gibsland, La., Aug. 9, 1923; s. Lawrence Foster and Marcia Aline (Jay) T.; m. Lou Kavanaugh; 1 son, Terry Jay. Student, La. Poly. Inst., 1940-42; BA, U. Calif., Santa Barbara, 1948; MA, Claremont (Calif.) Grad. Sch., 1949; PhD, Tulane U., 1952. Assoc. prof. history, dean men. La. Coll., Pineville, 1952-56, prof., 1956-62, dean coll., 1960-62; pres. La. Tech. U., Ruston, 1962-87, pres. emeritus, 1987—. Past chmn. La. Labor Mediation Bd.; arbitrator Am. Arbitration Assn., Fed. Mediation and Conciliation Svc.; former mem. La. Adv. Coun. on Vocat.-Tecy. Edn.; bd. dirs. First Guaranty Bank, Pizza Inn, Inc. Author: The United States and the Spanish Civil War, 1936-39, 1956, Reluctant Rebel, The Secret Diary of Robert Patrick, 1861-1865, 1959. Served to lt. comdr., aviator USNR, 1942-46. Mem. Am. Hist. Assn., Miss. Valley Hist. Assn., So. Hist. Assn., Nat. Acad. Arbitrators., Phi Alpha Theta. Clubs: Rotary. Home: 500 Audubon Dr Ruston LA 71270-7800 Office Phone: 318-251-1790.

TAYLOR, FRANCIS MICHAEL, auditor, municipal official; b. Munich, 1960; came to the U.S., 1961; BS, Va. Tech., 1982. CPA Va., cert. internal auditor. Pub. acct., Roanoke, Va., 1982-84; controller ARC Roanoke, Inc., Roanoke, 1984-87; audit supr. City of Roanoke, 1987-94; city auditor City of Stockton (Calif.), 1994—. Mem. AICPA, Nat. Assn. Local Govt. Auditors (past pres.), Calif. Soc. CPAs, Inst. Internal Auditors, Govt. Fin. Officers Assn., Info. Sys. Audit and Control Assn., Bay Area Local Govt. Auditors. Office: 22 E Weber Ave Ste 325 Stockton CA 95202-1951

TAYLOR, FRED, professional football player; b. June 27, 1976; Student, U. Fla. Running back Jacksonville Jaguars, Fla., 1998—. Achievements include ranks fourth on U. Fla. all-time rushing list; played in 3 college bowl games; team was 14-0 in games in which he had over 100 yards rushing. Office: Jacksonville Jaguars 1 Alltel Stadium Pl Jacksonville FL 32202-1917

TAYLOR, FREDERICK JEROME, music educator, consultant; b. Albany, Ga., Mar. 13, 1944; s. Frederick Hilyard Taylor, Jr. and Parmel Duhart Taylor; m. Gloria Ann Jones-Taylor, Feb. 26, 1966; children: Frederick Jerome, Derrick Bernard. BS in Music, Ky. State U., 1965; MusM, U. Ill., 1965; D in Musical Arts, Temple U., 1981. Tchr. Chgo. Pub. Schs., 1966—70; prof. music Cheyney U. Pa., 1970—87; assoc. prof. music Ga. State U., Atlanta, 1987—. Pub. adv. bd. ASCAP, N.Y.C., 1983—89; bd. mem. Music Entertainment Industry Educators Assn., Nashville, Rehab. Exposure, Inc., Atlanta. Co-author: Marketing in the Music Industry, 2003; freelance musician:. Chmn. North Atlanta United Negro Coll. Fund, Atlanta, 1997—2001. Recipient Svc. award, United Negro Coll. Fund, Atlanta, 1999. Mem.: Nat. Assn. for the Study/Performance African Am. Music (pres. 1999—2001, v.p. 2001—03), Music Educators Nat. Conf. (affiliate mem. pres. 1999—2001). Democrat. Baptist. Avocation: popular and jazz pianist. Home: 1140 Charlton Trace Marietta GA 30064

TAYLOR, FREDERICK WILLIAM, JR., (FRITZ TAYLOR), lawyer; b. Cleve., Oct. 21, 1933; s. Frederick William Sr. and Marguerite Elizabeth (Kistler) T.; m. Mary Phyllis Osborne, June 1, 1985; children: Frederick III, Ellen, Christopher, Stephanie, Andrew, Susan, Sarah Beth, Derek, Douglas. BA in History, U. Fla., 1957; MA in Near East Studies, U. Mich., 1959; JD cum laude, NYU, 1967. Bar: N.Y. 1968, Calif. 1969, U.S. Dist. Ct. (cen. dist.) Calif. 1969. Govt. rels. rep. Arabian Am. Oil Co., Dhahran, Saudi Arabia, 1959-63, oil supply coord. N.Y.C., 1963-68, sr. counsel Dhahran, 1969-71, gen. mgr. govt. rels. orgn., 1971-74, v.p. indsl. rels., 1974-78; assoc. O'Melveny & Myers, L.A., 1968-69; ptnr. Burt & Taylor, Marblehead, Mass., 1978-80; pres., chief exec. officer Nat. Med. Enterprises Internat. Group, L.A., 1980-82; counsel Chadbourne, Parke & Afridi, United Arab Emirates, 1982-84; ptnr. Sidley & Austin, Cairo, 1984-87, 1987-93; spl. counsel Heller Ehrman White & McAuliffe, L.A. and Singapore, 1993-95; legal advisor, corp. counsel law divsn. Lucent Techs. Internat. Inc., Riyadh, Saudi Arabia, 1995—2003; dir. MEA strategy and bus. ops., 2003—04; corp. counsel labor, litigation and employment Lucent Law Divsn., Murray Hill, NJ, 2004—. Contbr. articles to profl. jours. Mem. ABA, Calif. Bar Assn., Order of Coif, Singapore Cricket Club, Tanglin Club, Changi Sailing Club, Singapore Am. Club, Dirab Golf Club. Home: 9875 E Shadowlake Ct Claremore OK 74017-1444 Office: Lucent Techs Int Inc PO Box 44770 Abu Dhabi United Arab Emirates Office Phone: 908-582-4323. Business E-Mail: taylorf@lucent.com.

TAYLOR, GARY B. music educator; s. Junior E and Jean M Taylor; m. Kay E. Bailey, June 24, 1978; children: Lori A, Kevin S, Brian P. MA, Pa. State U., 1980; B Music Edn., Clarion U., 1974. Instrumental music St. Marys (Pa.) Area Sch. Dist, 1974—80, Wilmington (Pa.) Area Sch. Dist, 1980—. Office: Wilmington Area School District 350 Wood St New Wilmington PA 16142

TAYLOR, GAVIN HALL, music educator; s. Mary Elizabeth and LeRoy Gerald Taylor. MusB, Jacksonville U., 1981—84; MusM, Hartt Sch. Music, U. Hartford, 1984—86. Adj. asst. prof. music Jacksonville U., Jacksonville, Fla., 1989—; piano dept. chmn. Douglas Anderson Sch. Arts, Jacksonville, 1998—99; dir. music/organist Ft. Caroline Presbyn. Ch., Jacksonville, 1990—2000; asst. min. music Arlington United Meth. Ch., Jacksonville, 2000—. Accompanist Bel Canto Nat. Opera Auditions, Jacksonville, Fla., 1994—94; accompanist for masterclasses, auditions, Delius festivals, faculty and student recitals Jacksonville U., Jacksonville, Fla.; guest recitalist Edwards Waters Coll., Jacksonville, Fla., 1991—91; pvt. piano studio tchr., Jacksonville, Fla., 1989—; pub. radio broadcasts/ wjct stereo 90 Jacksonville U. Faculty Recital Series, Jacksonville, Fla., 1990—2000. Recipient Omicron Delta Kappa Hon. Frat., Pi Kappa Lambda Hon. Music Frat. Mem.: Fla. Fedn. Music Clubs/St. Johns Dist. (dir. comm. 1998—2003), Nat. Guild Piano Teachers, Fla. Music Teachers Assn. Office: Jacksonville U 2800 University Blvd N Jacksonville FL 32211

TAYLOR, GENE, congressman; b. New Orleans, La., Sept. 17, 1953; m. Margaret Gordon; children: Sarah, Emily, Gary. BA, Tulane U., 1974; grad., U. So. Miss. Sales rep. Stone Container Corp.; city councilman Bay St. Louis, 1981—83; dist. 46 sen. Miss. State Sen., 1984-89; mem. U.S. Congress from 4th Miss. dist. (formerly 5th), 1989—; ranking mem. house armed svcs. com., mem. transp. and infrastructure com. With USCGR, 1971-1984. Mem. Lions, Rotary, Kappa Sigma. Democrat. Roman Catholic. Office: US House of Reps 2311 Rayburn Hob Washington DC 20515-2405

TAYLOR, GEORGE ALLEN, advertising agency executive; b. Lake City, Iowa, Oct. 26, 1906; s. Bertrand Franklin and Mabel (Minard) T.; m. Regina Helen Wickland, July 3, 1938 (div. 1956). PhB in Fine Arts, Northwestern U., 1947, MEd, 1951, postgrad., 1951-54; art edn. diploma, U. No. Iowa, 1926. Art supr. pub. schs., Indianola, Iowa, 1926-29; instr. art Simpson Coll., Indianola, 1926-29; designer Modern Art Studios, Chgo., 1929-30; display designer W.J. Rankin Corp., Chgo., 1930-35; creative dir. Arthur Meyerhoff Assocs., Inc., Milw., 1935-38, br. mgr. L.A., 1938-42, account exec. Chgo., 1942-59, account supr., 1959-61, v.p. adminstrn., 1961-65, vice chmn., 1965-80. Pres. GATA Ltd.; lectr. semantics Ill. Inst. Tech., Chgo., 1947-50, Northwestern U. Sch. Commerce, 1948. Lyricist popular songs. Reader Recs.

for Blind, Inc., 1956-94, CRIS Radio, 1981-85. Recipient 1st place awards in copy and layout L.A. Advt. Club, 1940. Mem.: AAAS (life; emeritus), Art Inst. Chgo. (life). Office: Ste 1910 8515 Costa Verde Blvd San Diego CA 92122-1150

TAYLOR, GEORGE FREDERICK, newspaper publisher, editor; b. Portland, Oreg., Feb. 28, 1928; s. George Noble and Ida Louise (Dixon) T.; m. Georga Bray, Oct. 6, 1951; children— Amelia Ruth, Ross Noble. BS, U. Oreg., 1950. Reporter Astoria (Oreg.) Budget, 1950-52, Portland Oregonian, 1952-54; copy reader Wall St. Jour., 1955-57, reporter, 1957-59, Detroit Bur. chief, 1959-64, Washington corr., 1964-68, asst. mng. editor, 1968-69, mng. editor N.Y.C., 1970-77, exec. editor, 1977-86; pub. North Bend (Oreg.) News, 1981-86, Prime Time, 1987—, Coquille Valley Sentinel, 1989-2000. Lt. USAF, 1955-57. Mem. Oregon Newspaper Publishers Assn. (bd. dirs. 1997-2000). E-mail: Ftaylor@harborside.com.

TAYLOR, GEORGE KIMBROUGH, JR., lawyer; b. Atlanta, Aug. 28, 1939; s. George Kimbrough and Helen Whiteside (Shepard) T.; m. Carol Ann McKinney, July 1, 1961 (div. 1976); children: George Kimbrough III, Thomas Haynes; m. Triska Ashley Drake, Oct. 2, 1981. BA, Emory U., 1961; LLB, U. Va., 1964. Bar: Ga. 1964, U.S. Dist. Ct. (no. dist.) Ga. 1964, U.S. Ct. Appeals (11th cir.) 1964. Assoc. Kilpatrick & Cody, Atlanta, 1964-70, ptnr., 1970-96, Kilpatrick Stockton LLP (formerly Kilpatrick & Cody), 1997—. Bd. dirs. Ont. Reins. Co. Ltd., Atlanta; chmn., bd. dirs. MFI Am., Inc., Atlanta. Chmn. bd. dirs. Spl. Audiences, Inc., Atlanta, 1985-87; bd. dirs. Atlanta Symphony Orch., 1986—, treas., 1995-97; trustee Woodruff Arts Ctr., Atlanta, 1997—; bd. dirs. Atlanta Opera, 1995—, Ga. Humanities Coun., Atlanta, 1986-93, Ga. Conservancy, 1979-85, Ga. Trust for Hist. Preservation, 2002—; bd. dirs. Ga. Coun. Internat. Visitors, Atlanta, 1987-94, pres., 1993; bd. dirs. Brit.-Am. Bus. Group, 1989-95, pres., 1994; bd. visitors Emory U., Atlanta, 1993-96, Brit.-Am. Bus. Coun., 1997—, chmn. 1997-98; mem. alumni coun. U. Va. Law Sch., 1995-98; active Leadership Atlanta. Woodrow Wilson fellow, 1961. Mem. ABA, Internat. Bar Assn., Atlanta Bar Assn., Order of Coif, Soc. Internat. Bus. Fellows, Capital City Club, Phi Beta Kappa, Omicron Delta Kappa. Democrat. Avocations: sailing, skiing. Office: Kilpatrick Stockton LLP 1100 Peachtree St NE Ste 2800 Atlanta GA 30309-4530 Business E-Mail: ktaylor@kilpatrickstockton.com.

TAYLOR, GERALD H. telecommunications company executive; b. 1941; married. BS in Physics, San Francisco State U., 1969. With MCI Telecom. Corp., 1969-98, COO, 1993-96, pres., 1994-96; CEO MCI Comm. Corp., 1996-98, also bd. dirs., 1998; bd. dirs. Ciena Corp., 2000—. Bd. dirs. Ciena Corp., LaFarge Corp., E2Enet. Inc., Voyager.net With USAF, 1961-65

TAYLOR, GLEN A. printing, direct mail and technology company executive, professional sports team executive; Grad., Minn. State U., 1962. State sen. Minn. Senate, 1980—90; chmn., CEO Taylor Corp., Mankato, Minn., 1975—2001, chmn. only, 2001—; owner Minn. Timberwolves and Minn. Lynx, Mpls., 1994—. Office: Taylor Corp 1725 Roe Crest Dr Mankato MN 56003-1807 also: Minnesota Timberwolves Target Ctr 600 1st Ave N Minneapolis MN 55403-1416

TAYLOR, GREGORY ALWIN, coast guard officer, engineer; b. Jan. 9, 1952; USCG grad., Oreg. Inst. Tech., 1990; BS in Computer Sci., U. Md., 1993; MS in Telecomms., Golden Gate U., 1996, MBA, 1998. Commd. chief warrant officer USCG, 1980, advanced through grades to lt. comdr., 1993, comdg. officer, 1987—88; chief electronics engring. divsn. U.S. Coast Guard, Tokyo, 1990—93, chief electronics programs support Alameda, Calif., 1993—98; ret. lt. comdr. USCG, 1998; COO, gen. mgr. Attitude Aviation, Livermore, Calif., 1998—2001; instr. bus. mgmt. and computer sys. Klamath (Oreg.) C.C., 2001—. Office: PO Box 997 Klamath Falls OR 97601-0053

TAYLOR, HAROLD ALLEN, JR., industrial mineral-speciality metals marketing consultant; b. San Jose, Calif., June 27, 1936; s. Harold Allen and Marie Anna (Briody) T.; m. Theresa Josephine Kustritz, Aug. 29, 1963; children: Harold Allen III, Ruth F. Cook, Jonathan L.E. BA, Brown U., 1958; MA, U. Minn., 1968. Project leader Office Mineral Supply, U.S. Bur. Mines, Mpls., 1968-70, commodity specialist divsn. ferrous metals Washington, 1970-74; commodity analyst U.S. internat. Trade Commn., Washington, 1974-80; sr. commodity specialist br. indsl. minerals U.S. Bur. Mines, Washington, 1980-95; pres. Basics Mines, Summit Point, W.Va., 1995—. Pub., editor Dimension Stone Advocate News, Graphite Advocate News, Bismuth Advocate News, Indium Advocate News, 2000—; contbr. articles to profl. jours. and encys. Pres. Arlington (Va.) Interfaith Coun., 1994, 95. Mem. AIME (sec 1983-84, 1st vice chmn. 1984-85, chmn. 1985-86, mem. exec. adv. bd. mineral econs. subsect. 1981-83, 87-91), ASTM (chmn. subcom. nomenclature of com. on dimension stone 1987—, sec. of com. 1990-95), Soc. Govt. Economists (chmn. materials policy panels, 1979-84), Capitol Metals Forum (steering com. 1979-85), Toastmasters (pres. 1978, 81, 87, 91, asst. area gov. 1978-79, area gov. 1979-80, dep. divsn. lt. gov. 1989-90), Sigma Gamma Epsilon. Address: PO Box 185 Summit Point WV 25446-0185

TAYLOR, HARRIS C. consultant endocrinologist, diabetologist; b. Bklyn., N.Y., Apr. 30, 1940; s. William and Florence Ruth T.; m. Diana Kahn, Sept. 3, 1962; children: Brian David, Rebecca Lynn. BS, Queens Coll., 1961; MD, U. Chgo., 1965. Diplomate Am. Bd. Internal Medicine, Am. Bd. Endocrinology and Metabolism. Cons. endocrinologist Kaiser Found., Cleve., 1972-86; chief divsn. endocrinology Luth. Med. Ctr., Cleve., 1977-96, dir. endocrinology & radioimmunoassay lab., 1978-96, dir. internal medicine residency, 1985-94, dir. rsch., internal medicine residency program Fairview Health Sys., 1996—. Sr. clin. instr. Case We. Res. U. Sch. Medicine, Cleve., 1977-81, clin. asst. prof., 1981-88, clin. assoc. prof. medicine (endocrinology), 1988-2003, clin. prof., 2003—. Contbr. articles to profl. jours. Chmn. program com. Diabetes Assn. Cleve., 1976-81, exec. com. mem., 1978-85, pres.-elect, 1981-82, pres., 1982-84. Sr. asst. surgeon USPHS, 1966-68. Named One of Best Drs. in Cleve., Cleve. Mag., 1998, 2002, 2004. Fellow: ACP (reviewer Annals of Internal Medicine 1986—, Master Tchr. award 2001), Am. Coll. Endocrinology (editl. bd. Endocrine Practice 1997—2004); mem.: Endocrine Soc., Am. Thyroid Assn., Am. Assn. Clin. Endocrinologists, Phi Beta Kappa. Jewish. Avocations: stamp collecting/philately, classical music. Office: Case Western Reserve Univ Sch of Medicine-Div of Endocrinology 2109 Adelbert Rd Cleveland OH 44106 Office Phone: 216-368-6129.

TAYLOR, HENRY SPLAWN, literature educator, poet, writer; b. Loudoun County, Va., June 21, 1942; s. Thomas Edward and Mary Marshall (Splawn) Taylor; m. Mooshe Taylor, 2002. BA, U. Va., 1965; MA, Hollins (Va.) Coll., 1966. Instr. English Roanoke Coll., Va., 1966—68; asst. prof. U. Utah, 1968—71; faculty Am. U., Washington, 1971—2003, prof. lit., 1976—2003, co-dir. MFA program in creative writing, 1982—2003, dir. Am. studies program, 1983—84. Dir. writer's conf. U. Utah, 1970—72; writer-in-residence Hollins Coll., 1978; poet-in-residence Wichita State U., 1994, Randolph-Macon Woman's Coll., 1997; prof. poetry U. Cin., 2002. Author: (poetry) The Horse Show at Midnight, 1966, Breakings, 1971, An Afternoon of Pocket Billiards, 1975, Desperado, 1979, The Flying Change, 1985 (Pulitzer prize, 86), Understanding Fiction: Poems 1986-96, 1996, Brief Candles: 101 Clerihews, 2000, Compulsory Figures: Essays on Recent American Poets, 1992, Poetry: Points of Departure, 1974; editor: The Water of Light: A Miscellany in Honor of Brewster Ghiselin, 1976; author: (cassette) Landscape with Tractor, 1985; translator (with others): The Children of Herakles, 1981; contbg. editor: Hollins Critic, 1971—78, 1997—; editl. cons.: Magill's Literary Annual, 1972—90, adv. editor: Bellingham Rev., New Va. Rev., 2000—, cons. editor: Poet Lore, 1977—84; translator: Plautus' The Weevil, 1995, Sophocles' Electra, 1998. Recipient Pulitzer Prize, Poetry, 1986, Michael Braude award for light verse, Am. Acad. Arts and Letters, 2002; fellow, Nat. Endowment Arts, 1978, 1986; grantee, NEH, 1980—81. Mem.: PEN, Am. Lit. Translators Assn. Democrat. Mem.Soc.Of Friends. Office: Am U Dept Lit Washington DC 20016-8047 E-mail: htaylor@american.edu.

TAYLOR, HUMPHREY JOHN FAUSITT, information services executive; b. Meshed, Iran, Sept. 6, 1934; came to U.S., 1976; s. Geoffrey Fausitt and Frances Margaret (Kenyon) T.; m. Penelope Helen Taylor, Dec. 19, 1970; children: Zanthe, Helena. BA with honors, Cambridge (Eng.) U., 1958. Dist. officer Govt. of Tanganyika, 1959-62; mktg. and opinion researcher Nat. Opinion Poll, Eng., 1963-66; mng. dir. Opinion Rsch. Ctr., Eng., 1966-76; with Louis Harris and Assocs., N.Y.C., 1976-81; pres. Harris Interactive Inc., N.Y.C., 1981-98, CEO, 1992-98; chmn. The Harris Poll, N.Y.C., 1997—. Trustee U.S. com. UNICEF, N.Y.C., 1981—87; trustee Overseas Devel. Coun., Washington, 1987—2001; trustee, chmn. Am. Health Found., 1988—91; trustee Royal Soc. Medicine Found., 1992—; mem. Coun. on Grad. Med. Edn., 2000—. 2d lt. Brit. Army, 1953—55. Fellow: Am. Acad. Ophthalmology (hon.; trustee); mem.: Nat. Coun. Pub. Polls (chmn.). Avocations: history, biographies, skiing, tennis, travel. Address: Harris Interactive 111 5th Ave Fl 8 New York NY 10003-1005

TAYLOR, IAN LOGAN, dean; b. Eng. MD, PhD, Liverpool Med. Sch. Fellow in gastrointestinal rsch. UCLA, mem. Wadsworth V.A. Tng. Program, various positions, prof. medicine; chief of gastroenterology Duke U., 1986—89, dir. Sarah W. Stedman Ctr. for Nutritional Studies, 1989—90, prof. physiology, dept. cell biology, 1990—93; prof. and chmn. dept. medicine Med. U. S.C., 1993—2001, pres. U. Med. Assocs., 1999—2001; dean Sch. Medicine Tulane U., 2001—. Office: Tulane Health Scis Ctr 1430 Tulane Ave New Orleans LA 70112

TAYLOR, JACK, state senator; b. Chgo., Nov. 22, 1935; m. Geneva Taylor. BS, Iowa State U. Businessman; Rep. rep. dist. 56 Colo. Ho. of Reps., 1992-2000; Rep. senator dist. 8 Colo. State Senate, 2000—. Mem. agr., livestock and natural resources comms. Colo. Ho. of Reps., chair bus. affairs and labor, vice chair legis. audit; mem. bus. affairs and labor and fin. and legis. audit coms. Colo. State Senate. Mem. bd. dirs. Irrigation Water Co.; former mem. Steamboat Springs Home Rule Charter Commn.; mem. Naval ROTC; chmn. Routt County Reps., 1989-92; mem. dist. bd. West Steamboat Water and Sanitation; past pres. Steamboat Springs Kiwanis Club. With USN. Mem. Steamboat Springs Chamber/Resort Assn. (former bd. dirs.). Office: PO Box 772867 Steamboat Springs CO 80477 also: Colo State Senate State Capitol 200 E Colfax Rm 274 Denver CO 80203

TAYLOR, JACK C. rental and leasing company executive; b. 1922; With Lindburg Cadillac, St. Louis, 1944-50, Forrest Cadillac, St. Louis, 1951-56; chmn. bd. Enterprise Rent-A-Car, St. Louis, 1980—2001, chmn. emeritus, 2001—. With USN, ret. Office: Enterprise Rent-A-Car 600 Corporate Park Dr Saint Louis MO 63105-4204*

TAYLOR, JACK P. lumber company executive; BS in Biology, U. Wash., 1966. With Weyerhaeuser Co., 1969—, Far East forester, raw materials ops. mgr., 1975—78, raw materials ops. mgr., 1978—83, woods and raw materials mgr., 1983—87, Coos Bay ops. mgr., 1987—92, gen. mgr. S.W. Oreg. ops., 1992—96, v.p., dir. ops. Western Timberlands, 1996—2003, sr. v.p. Timberlands, 2003—. Bd. dirs. Keep Oreg. Green; past pres., former bd. dirs. Pacific Lumber Inspection Bur.; former bd. dirs. Oreg. Forest Industries Coun.; former mem. S.W. Oreg. Region Forest Practices Com. Office: Weyerhaeuser Co 33663 Weyerhaeuser Way S Federal Way WA 98063-9777

TAYLOR, JAMES, JR., lawyer; b. Florence, S.C., Dec. 6, 1942; s. James and Thelma (Baker) T.; m. Jayne S.C. Bridge, May 19, 1974; children: James Robson, Ashley Baker. BA cum laude, U. of the South, 1965; JD, Georgetown U., 1973. Bar: D.C. 1973, U.S. Ct. Internat. Trade 1977, U.S. Ct. Appeals (fed. cir.) 1982, U.S. Supreme Ct. 1978. Assoc. Busby Rivkin Sherman Levy and Rehm, Washington, 1973-76, Busby and Rehm, Washington, 1977-78; ptnr. Busby Rehm and Leonard, Washington, 1979-87, Dorsey & Whitney, Washington, 1988-92, Stroock & Stroock & Lavan, Washington, 1992-95, Ablondi, Foster, Sobin & Davidow, P.C., Washington, 1996—2001, Adduci, Mastriani & Schaumberg LLP, Washington, 2001—. Lt. USN, 1967-70; Vietnam. Mem. ABA, D.C. Bar Assn., Club Interallié (Paris). Episcopalian. Avocations: sailing, fishing, languages. Home: PO Box 101 4153 School Rd Broomes Island MD 20615 Office: Adduci Mastriani & Schaumberg LLP 1200 17th St NW Washington DC 20036

TAYLOR, J(AMES) BENNETT, management consultant; b. Sarasota, Fla., June 15, 1943; s. Thurman Ralph and Lucille (Bennett) Taylor; 1 child, Kelly Christine. BS in Advt., U. Fla., 1965. Dist. mgr. Coca-Cola Co., Shreveport, La., 1966-68, allied product splst. Dallas, 1968-70, dist. mgr. Cin. and Indpls., 1970-75; v.p. Ott R&D, Miami, Fla., 1975-78; pres., CEO Exec Group, Inc., Tampa, Fla., 1978-98, Think Track Inc., Miami, 1998—. Career Mgmt. fellow, Inst. Career Cert. Internat., 1996. Home: 3001 SW 1st Ave #201 Miami FL 33129-2743 Office: 2000 S Dixie Hwy Ste 104 Coconut Grove FL 33133-2441 E-mail: jbtaylor@thinktrack.com.

TAYLOR, JAMES C. writer; b. Nashville, Oct. 17, 1924; s. James Custer Taylor and Winnie Olive Duncan. AB in Journalism and Psychology, U. Ky., 1941; postgrad., Vanderbilt U., 1941, Notre Dame U., Ind., 1942, Kans. U., 1942. Sports writer Topeka State Jour., Kans., 1950—52; reporter, editor Kansas City Star, Mo., 1953—57; sr. editor TV Guide Mag., 1957—82; fgn. corr. Internat. Am., various locations, 1982—2000; ret., 2000. Guest columnist CDL Report, World Intelligence Rev.; lectr. in field. Author: (book) Dubious Duty, 1976, Pearl Harbor II, 1978, Khadafy, Man or Myth, 1984. Lt. comdr. USNR, 1941—61. Recipient Outstanding Book award, Mark Twain Soc., St. Louis, 1958, Del Oro award, Fria Ord, Stockholm, 1982. Republican. Roman Catholic. Avocation: teaching tennis to under-privileged children. Home: 5519 N 77th Pl Scottsdale AZ 85250

TAYLOR, JAMES FRANCIS, marketing professional; b. Detroit, Sept. 5, 1951; s. Harold James and Mary Frances (Law) T.; m. Janet Elizabeth Joss, May 21, 1977; children: Jonathan Harold, Jessica Frances, Jenna Leigh, Jeanette Mary. BA in Polit. Sci., Mich. State U., 1976; postgrad., Thomas Cooley Law Sch., 1979. Product mgr. Gen. Aluminum Products, Charlotte, Mich., 1975-77; sales mgr. Empire Metal Products, Columbus, Ohio, 1978; bus. mgr. Law Offices of Paul Martin, Lansing, Mich., 1978-79; dir. mktg. and sales Feather-Lite Mfg. Co., Troy, Mich., 1979-81; v.p. mktg. and sales Innovative Products Corp., Madison Heights, Mich., 1981-82; pres. J.F. Taylor Assocs., Inc., Durham, N.C., 1982—, Meadowcrest Group, Inc., 1989—; pres., bd. dirs. The Taylor-Grant-Joss Found., Durham, N.C.; COO C.J. Woodmaster, Inc., Durham, 1998—. Corp. sec., bd. dirs., CFO of All Corps. Unifinished Furniture Express, Inc., 1997—, Durham, N.C., C.J. Woodmaster of Raleigh, Inc.; CFO C.J. Woodmaster of Cary, Inc., 1999—; CFO, corp. sec. C.J. Woodmaster Devel., Inc., Durham, N.C., C.J. Woodmaster of Fayetteville, Inc. Mem.: Hope Valley Country Club, Rotary. Republican. Roman Catholic. Home: 4 Roswell Ct Durham NC 27707-5070 Office: 102C Commonwealth Ct Cary NC 27511 Office Phone: 919-460-0400. Personal E-mail: cjwoodmaster@aol.com.

TAYLOR, JAMES JOHN, academic administrator; b. Mpls., July 26, 1940; s. James John and Mary Elizabeth (Mason) T.; m. Margaret Claire Zacha, Dec. 28, 1976; children: Jerry William, John Allen. BA, Oblate Coll. of S.W., 1966; MEd, St. Louis U., 1969, MBA in Fin., 1972; cert. of advanced studies, Harvard U., 1977; PhD in Adminstrn., Curriculum and Instrn, U. Nebr., 2002. Dept. head, tchr. Althoff High Sch., Belleville, Ill., 1966-71; asst. to controller U. of South Fla., Tampa, 1972-79; project mgr. W.Va. Bd. of Regents, Morgantown, 1979-83; prin., project dir. Am. Mgmt. Systems, Arlington, Va., 1983-90; mng. cons. Taylor Mgmt. Group, Arlington, 1990-91; v.p. bus. and finance Guam Community Coll., 1991—. Founder, treas. Guam Ednl. Radio Found., KPRG-FM, 1992-99; organizer Chief Bus. Officers of the Pacific, 1997, 98, 99; elected mem. Govt. Guam Retirement Bd., 2004—. Member adv. com. on spl. edn. Arlington Sch. Bd., 1981-83; founder, producer St. Louis High Sch. Film Makers Festival, 1968-72; contbr. articles to profl. jours. Bd. trustees Govt. Guam Retirement Fund, 2004. Founding mem. Harvard Club at Nat. Press Club; mem. Rotary. Avocations: photography, duplicate bridge, scuba diving. Home: 29 Cruz Hts Talofofo GU 96915-3736

TAYLOR, JAMES L. naval officer; Grad., U.S. Naval Acad., 1965; M in Computer Systems, Naval Post Grad. Sch., Monterey, Calif., 1977, M in Mech. Engring., 1979. Commd. ensign USN, 1965, advanced through grades to rear adm., 1996; various assignments to dep. dir. for shipyard mgmt. Naval Sea Systems Command Hdqtrs., 1989-90; dir. Supportability, Maintenance and Modernization Divsn. Chief of Naval Opers., 1994-96; fleet maintenance officer, dep. chief of staff U.S. Pacific Fleet, 1996-99; sr. v.p., group mgr. SAIC AMSEC LLC, 1999—. Decorated Legion of Merit, Meritorious Svc. medal, Disting. Svc. medal. E-mail: james_taylor@amsec.com.

TAYLOR, JAMES SHEPPARD, communications educator; b. Montgomery, Ala., Dec. 15, 1943; s. Elbert Ruppert and Mary Pinckard (Bryan) T.; m. Mary Ann Luck, Mar. 30, 1972; children: John Brinson Overstreet, Laura Luck Biering. BA in Speech, Auburn U., 1965, MA in Speech, 1966; PhD in Rhetoric and Pub. Address, Fla. State U., 1968. Grad. asst. Auburn (Ala.) U., 1965-66, asst. prof. speech, 1969-73; grad. asst. Fla. State U., Tallahassee, 1966-68; asst. prof. speech N.C. State U., Raleigh, 1968-69, assoc. prof., chair comms. Houston Bapt. U., 1973-94, prof., chair comms., assoc. dean arts and humanities, 1994-98, dean arts and humanities, 1998—. Editl. assoc. So. Speech Jour., 1967-68; mem. editl. bd. N.C. Jour. Speech, 1966-69; news and notions editor So. Speech Comm. Jour., 1972-75. Recipient Tchg. Excellence and Campus Leadership award Sears-Roebuck Found., 1989-90. Mem. Tex. Speech Comm. Assn., So. States Comm. Assn., Speech Comm. Assn. (ERIC evaluator 1973-76), Phi Kappa Phi, Phi Delta Kappa, Kappa Delta Pi, Omicron Delta Kappa. Democrat. Methodist. Avocations: golf, running, tennis, hiking, reading. Office: Houston Bapt U 7502 Fondren Rd Houston TX 77074-3298 Office Phone: 281-649-3337. E-mail: jtaylor@hbu.edu., sheptaylor@msn.com.

TAYLOR, JAMES WALTER, business and management educator; b. St. Cloud, Minn., Feb. 15, 1933; s. James T. and Nina C. Taylor; m. Joanne Syktte, Feb. 3, 1956; children: Theodore James, Samuel Bennett, Christopher John. BBA, U. Minn., 1957; MBA, NYU, 1960; DBA, U. So. Calif., 1975. Mgr. rsch. divsn. Atlantic Refining, Phila., 1960-65; dir. new product devel. Hunt-Wesson Foods, Fullerton, Calif., 1965-72; mng. dir. Digital Workbook Internat., LLC, Laguna Beach, Calif., 1975—. Vis. prof. U. Calif., Irvine; cons. Smithkline Beecham Corp., Tokyo, Govt. of Portugal, Lisbon, Austrade, Govt. of Australia, Hagenfeldt-Affarerna AB, Stockholm. Author: Profitable New Product Strategies, 1984, How to Create a Winning Business Plan, 1986, Competitive Marketing Strategies, 1986, The 101 Best Performing Companies in America, 1987, The Complete Manual for Developing Winning Strategic Plans, 1988, Every Manager's Survival Guide, 1989, Developing Winning Strategic Plans, 1990, How to Develop Successful Advertising Plans, 1993, Marketing Planning: A Step by Step Guide, 1997, The Marketing Strategy and Planning Workbook, 2004. Fulbright scholar Ministry of Industry, Lisbon, Portugal, 1986-87, U. We. Sydney, Australia, 1989-90; recipient Merit award Calif. State U., 1986-90. Home: 3190 Mountain View Dr Laguna Beach CA 92651-2056

TAYLOR, JANET R. mayor; b. 1942; m. Duane Taylor; 5 children. Student, Chemeketa C.C. Lic. pvt. pilot. Co-founder, exec. Taylor Metal Products, Salem, Oreg. Mayor City of Salem, Oreg., 2003—; past chairwoman Salem Econ. Devel. Corp., S.E. Mill Creek Neighborhood Assn.; mem. Willamette River Bridge Task Force; sponsor A.C. Gilbert Discovery Village. Mem.: Salem Area C. of C. (v.p.), Salem Futures, Salem City Club, Salem Downtown Rotary. Office: Taylor Metal Products 3796 Turner Rd SE Salem OR 97302-2047

TAYLOR, JEFF, reporter, editor; Reporter Kansas City Star; asst. mng. editor Detroit Free Press. Recipient Pulitzer prize for nat. reporting, 1992, Sigma Delta Chi award, George Polk award. Office: Detroit Free Press 600 W Lafayette Blvd Detroit MI 48226-2703

TAYLOR, JILL OLSEN, lawyer, artist; b. Logan, Utah, June 1, 1955; d. Keith Conrad and Norma Elveda (Correll) Olsen; m. Bruce T. Taylor, July 3, 1979; children: Jenny, Benjamin, Christina. BA summa cum laude, Brigham Young U., 1977, JD, 1980. Bar: Utah 1980. Dep. county atty. Emery County, Utah, 1980-81; corp. atty. Physicians Emergency Svc., Price, Utah, 1981-88; pvt. practice Provo, Utah, 1986—. Bd. dirs., pres. Covered Bridge Canyon Homeowners Assn., 1983-89; mem. Utah County Planning Commn., 1993-2002, chair planning comm., 1993-2000. Mem.: ABA, Meridian Sch. Found., Meridian Sch. Bd., Order of Barristers (headmaster Meridian Sch. 2001—02), Utah State Bar Assn., Am. Immigration Lawyers Assn. (chair Utah chpt. 1996, bd. govs.), Phi Kappa Phi. Republican. Mem. Lds Ch.

TAYLOR, JIMMY LYNN, retired family practice physician, administrator; b. Franklin County, N.C., May 11, 1936; s. Herman Benjaman and Ruby Lynn (Perry) T.; m. Dorothy Keenum, Sept. 4, 1960; children: Gregory Scott, Sonya Lynn Taylor Loper. AA, Mars Hill Coll., 1956; BS, Wake Forest U., 1958; MD, Bowman Gray Med. Sch., 1962. Postdoctoral fellow Greenville (S.C.) Gen. Hosp., 1962-63; staff physician USPHS Indian Hosp., Pine Ridge, SD, 1963-65, chief of obstetrics, 1964-65; family physician, co-founder Monroe (N.C.) Family Med. Ctr., 1965, family physician, ptnr., 1965-95; student physician Wingate (N.C.) U., 1987-94; med. dir. Brian Ctr. Nursing Facility, Monroe, 1992-95. H.s. team physician1965 1995. Lt. commdr. USPHS, 1963-65. Recipient Head Start Child Care Achievement award N.C. Head Start Assn., 1990. Fellow Am. Acad. Family Physicians; mem. Am. Bd. Family Practice (diplomate), N.C. Acad. Family Physicians, N.C. Med. Soc., Union County Med. Soc. (pres. 1976-77). Republican. Baptist. Avocations: golf, fishing, gardening, bridge, collecting autographed first edition books. Home: 1657 Pageland Hwy Monroe NC 28112-8737 Office: Monroe Family Med Ctr PA 1420 E Franklin St Monroe NC 28112-5160 E-mail: jtaylor6@carolina.rr.com.

TAYLOR, JOB, III, lawyer; b. N.Y.C., Feb. 18, 1942; s. Job II and Anne Harrison (Flinchbaugh) T.; m. Mary C. August, Oct. 24, 1964 (div. 1978); children: Whitney August, Job IV; m. Sally Lawson, May 31, 1980; 1 child, Alexandra Anne. BA, Washington & Jefferson Coll., 1964; JD, Coll. William and Mary, 1971. Bar: N.Y. 1972, Mass. 2003, U.S. Dist. Ct. (no., so. ea. and we. dists.) N.Y. 1973, U.S. Ct. Appeals (2d cir.) 1973, U.S. Ct. Claims 1974, U.S. Tax Ct. 1974, U.S. Supreme Ct. 1975, U.S. Ct. Appeals (9th cir.) 1976, U.S. Ct. Mil. Appeals 1977, U.S. Ct. Appeals (D.C. and 10th cirs.) 1977, D.C. 1981, U.S. Ct. Internat. Trade 1981, U.S. Ct. Appeals (fed. cir.) 1982, U.S. Dist. Ct. (no. dist.) Calif. 1983, U.S. Ct. Appeals (6th cir.) U.S. Dist. Ct., 1987, U.S. Ct. Appeals (3d cir.) 1990, U.S. Dist. Ct. Conn. 1996. Ptnr. Olwine, Connelly, Chase, O'Donnell & Weyher, N.Y.C., 1971-85, Latham & Watkins, N.Y.C., 1985—. Served to lt. USN, 1964-68. Mem. ABA, Assn. Bar City N.Y., La Confrerie des Chevaliers du Tastevin, Racquet and Tennis Club, Wee Burn Country Club (Darien, Conn.). Republican. Episcopalian. Avocations: squash, tennis, golf, reading. Office Phone: 508-240-3069.

TAYLOR, J(OCELYN) MARY, museum administrator, zoologist, educator; b. Portland, Oreg., May 30, 1931; d. Arnold Llewellyn and Kathleen Mary (Yorke) T.; m. Joseph William Kamp, Mar. 18, 1972 (dec.); m. Wesley Kingston Whitten, Mar. 20, 2001. BA, Smith Coll., 1952; MA, U. Calif., Berkeley, 1953, PhD, 1959. Instr. zoology Wellesley Coll., 1959-61, asst. prof. zoology, 1961-65; assoc. prof. zoology U. B.C., 1965-74; dir. Cowan Vertebrate Mus., 1965-82, prof. dept. zoology, 1974-82; collaborative scientist Oreg. Regional Primate Research Ctr., 1983-87; prof. (courtesy) dept. fisheries and wildlife Oreg. State U., 1984-95; dir. Cleve. Mus. Nat. History, 1987-96, dir. emerita, 1996—. Adj. prof. dept. biology Case Western Res. U., 1987-96. Assoc. editor Jour. Mammalogy, 1981-82. Contbr. numerous articles to sci. jours. Trustee Benjamin Rose Inst., 1988-93, Western Res. Acad., 1989-94, U. Circle, Inc., 1987-96, The Cleve. Aquarium, 1990-93, Cleve. Access to the Arts, 1992-96; corp. bd. Holden Arboretum, 1988-98, The Cleve. Mus. Natural History, 1996—, The Catlin Gabel Sch., 1998-2000, The Inst. for the Northwest, 1999—2001. Recipient Lake County Environ. award, Lake county metro parks.; Fulbright scholar, 1954-55; Lalor Found. grantee, 1962-63; NSF grantee, 1963-71; NRC Can. grantee, 1966-84; Killam Sr. Rsch. fellow, 1978-79 Mem. Soc. Women Geographers, Am. Soc. Mammalogists (1st v.p.

1978-82, pres. 1982-84, Hartley T. Jackson award 1993, hon. mem. 2001), Australian Mammal Soc., Cooper Ornithol., Assn. Sci. Mus. Dirs. (v.p. 1990-93), Rodent Specialist Group of Species Survival Commn. (chmn. 1989-93), Sigma Xi. Home: 2718 SW Old Orchard Rd Portland OR 97201-1637 E-mail: taylorjm@teleport.com.

TAYLOR, JOE CLINTON, judge; b. Durant, Okla., Mar. 28, 1942; s. Luther Clinton and Virena (Parker) T.; m. Margaret Pearl Byers, June 8, 1963; children: Marna Joanne, Leah Alison, Jocelyn Camille. Student, Southeastern State Coll., 1960—62; BA, Okla. State U., 1965; JD, U. Okla., 1968. Bar: Okla. 1968. Pvt. practice, Norman, Okla., 1968-69; apptd. spl. dist. judge Durant, 1969-72; assoc. dist. judge Bryan County, Okla., 1972-76; dist. judge, chief judge 19th Dist. Ct., Bryan County, Okla., 1976-93; presiding judge Southeastern Okla. Jud. Adminstrv. Dist., 1984-92, Choctaw Tribal Ct., 1979-83; pres. Okla. Jud. Conf., 1987-88; chmn. Assembly Presiding Judges, 1989-90; presiding judge trial divsn. Okla. Ct. on the Judiciary, 1991-93, Okla. Ct. of Tax Rev., 1992—; judge Okla. Ct. of Civil Appeals, Tulsa, 1993—. Chmn. bd. dirs. Durant Youth Svcs., 1976-93; bd. dirs. Bryan County Youth Svcs., Inc., 1971-93. Lt. Col. USAR. Mem. Lions, Phi Sigma Epsilon, Delta Theta Phi. Mem. Ch. of Christ. Home: PO Box 329 Durant OK 74702-0329 Office: Ct Civil Appeals 601 State Bldg 440 S Houston Ave Tulsa OK 74127-8922 E-mail: joe.taylor@oscn.net.

TAYLOR, JOEL SANFORD, retired lawyer; b. Hazleton, Pa., Oct. 8, 1942; s. Robert Joseph and Alice Josephine (Sanford) T.; m. Donna Rae Caron, Mar. 26, 1967; children: Jason, Adam, Jeremy. BA, Swarthmore Coll., 1965; LLB, Columbia U., 1968. Bar: N.Y. 1969, U.S. Ct. Appeals (2d cir.) 1970, U.S. Dist. Ct. (no. dist.) Ohio 1974, U.S. Supreme Ct. 1974, U.S. Dist. Ct. (so. dist.) Ohio 1975, U.S. Ct. Appeals (6th cir.) 1975, U.S. Dist. Ct. (ea. dist.) Ky. 1979. Law clk. hon. Constance B. Motley U.S. Dist. Ct., N.Y.C., 1968-69; assoc. Paul, Weiss, Rifkind, Wharton & Garrison, N.Y.C., 1969-72; exec. asst. Ohio Office of Budget & Mgmt., Columbus, Ohio, 1972-74; asst. atty. gen. Ohio Atty. Gen., Columbus, 1974-83, chief counsel, 1983-91; ptnr. Dinsmore & Shohl, Columbus, 1991-2000; fin. dir. City of Columbus, 2000—. Pres. Ohio Sundry Claims Bd., Columbus, 1972-74, Ohio State Controlling Bd., Columbus, 1973-74; mem., bd. trustees Ohio State Tchrs. Retirement Sys., Columbus, 1986-91, Solid Waste Authority Ctrl. Ohio, 2001—. Mem. Govt. Fin. Officers Assn., Columbia Law Alumni Assn., Ohio Sierra Club, Nat. Wildlife Fedn., Nature Conservany. Office: City Hall 90 W Broad St Columbus OH 43215-9000 E-mail: jstaylor@columbus.gov.

TAYLOR, JOHN BRIAN, federal agency administrator; b. Yonkers, N.Y., Dec. 8, 1946; s. John Joseph and Lorraine (Crowley) T.; m. Raye Allyn Price, Dec. 30, 1972; children: Jennifer Lynn, John Andrew. AB in Econs. summa cum laude, Princeton U., 1968; PhD, Stanford U., 1973. Asst. prof. econs. Columbia U., N.Y.C., 1973-77, assoc. prof., 1977-79, prof., 1979-80; prof. econs. and pub. affairs Princeton U., 1980-84; prof. econs. Stanford U., 1984—, dir. Ctr. for Econ. Policy Rsch., 1994-97, dir. Introductory Econs. Ctr., 1997-2001; under sec. treasury for internat. affairs U.S. Treasury, Washington, 2001—. Vis. prof. econs. Yale U., 1980; sr. staff economist Pres.'s Coun. Econ. Advisers, 1976—77, mem., 1989—91; econometric cons. Townsend-Greenspan and Co., NY, 1978—81; rsch. advisor Fed. Res. Bank, Phila., 1981—84; rsch. assoc. Nat. Bur. Econ. Rsch., 1980—2001; rsch. economist Bank of Japan, Tokyo, 1987, hon. adviser, 1994—2001; panel of econ. advisers Congl. Budget Office, 1995—2001. Author: (non-fiction) Macroeconomics, 1986, Macroeconomic Policy in the World Economy, 1993, Economics, 1995, Unemployment, Inflation, and Monetary Policy, 1998, Monetary Policy Rules, 1999, Handbook of Macroeconomics, 2000; co-editor: Am. Econ. Rev., 1985—89; editor (assoc.): Econometrica, 1981—85, (jour.) Jour. Econ. Dynamics and Control, 1978—85, Jour. Monetary Econs., 1978—83, Jour. Econ. Perspectives, 1997—2001; contbr. articles to profl. jours. NSF grantee, 1979-81, 81-83, 83-86, 86-89, 92-95; Guggenheim Found. fellow, 1983-84; sr. fellow Hoover Instn., 1996—. Fellow Econometric Soc., Am. Acad. of Arts and Sci.; mem. Am. Econ. Assn. (exec. com. 1991-94, v.p. 2000-01). Office: US Dept Treasury 1500 Pennsylvania Ave NW Washington DC 20220

TAYLOR, JOHN CALVIN, dentist, missionary; b. Cin., July 22, 1914; s. John Calvin Taylor V and Magdala Elizabeth Siehl; m. Adah Packard Boggs, Mar. 7, 1941; children: Sarah, Margaret, Virginia, John, Frederick, Alison, Carla. BS, Muskingum Coll., 1937; BD, Cedarville Sem., 1939; DDS, U. Pitts., 1949; cert. excellence in Hindi and Urdu, Lang. Sch., Landour, India, 1940, 41. Diploma Acad. Gen. Dentistry. Missionary Reformed Presbyn. Synod, Roorkee, India, 1939-46; moderator, pastor Reformed Presbyn., Pitts., Fairview, Pa., 1946-47; nat. missions missionary Presbyn. Bd. Home Missions, Pitts., Tyre, Pa., 1947-52; missionary dentist United Presbyn., Pitts., Seattle, 1953-59; dir. Meth. Mission Hosp. Dental Clinic, Bariely, India, 1954—55; founder Dental Clinic Landour Cmty. Hosp., Mussoorie, India, 1955-59; pres. Rotary Club Internat., Mount Union, Pa., 1964-65; pastor 3 chs. Mt. Union, Johnsonburg and St. Mary areas, 1964-68; founder Shanta Bhawan Hosp. Dental Clinic, Katmandu, Nepal, 1968, Missionary Dentist, Inc., 1977; dental missionary svc. E.L.W.A. Hosp., Liberia, 1977, Tank Hosp., Pakistan, 1980—81, Sakowal Hosp., Pakistan, 1981, Shell Clinics, Ecuador, 1983; provider free dental care India, 1984—; founder Oral Clinic Ctr., Dera Dun, India, 1981—. Tchr. emergency dentistry Vellore (India) Med. Coll., 1958; dentist Youth With a Mission, Mercy Ship, Hawaii, 1985. Author: Wildlife in India's Tiger Kingdom, 1980, Face the Devil's Roar, 1995, God's Kingdom helps Animal Kingdoms, 2004. Co-founder, life mem. Wildlife Preservation Soc., Dehra-Dun, India, 1954—, organizer, founder Rajpur Wildlife Park, 1954—. Recipient Cert. of Honor for 50 Yrs. of Dedicated Svc. to Dentistry, ADA, 1999. Mem. Herminie Lions Club (fgn. chmn. 1988—, Lions Hat award 1993), N.Am. Hunting Club, NRA. Republican. Presbyterian. Avocations: zoology, hunting, taxidermy, photography, music. Home: 110 Highland Ave Herminie PA 15637-1310 E-mail: tgrtlr@juno.com.

TAYLOR, JOHN D. pharmacist, health services executive; b. Apr. 8, 1949; m. Kay Taylor; children: Michael, Kelli. BS in Pharmacy with high honors, U. Fla., 1972. Store mgr., pharmacy mgr. Cook's Pharmacy, Chipley, Fla., 1973-78; staff pharmacist Jackson Drugs, Panama City, Fla., 1978-79; pharmacist, asst. store mgr. Revco Store 2616, Panama City, 1979-81; sr. pharmacist Fla. Dept. of Profl. Regulation, 1988-90; exec. dir., bd. of pharmacy Fla. Dept. of Health, 1990—. Presenter in field. Mem. Am. Pharm. Assn., Nat. Assn. of Bds. of Pharmacy, Fla. Pharmacy Assn., Fla. Soc. Health System Pharmacists, Leon County Pharmacy Assn., Capital Soc. Health System Pharmacists, Rho Chi, Kappa Psi. Office: Bin #C04 2020 Capital Cir SE Tallahassee FL 32399-6539

TAYLOR, JOHN JACKSON (JAY TAYLOR), writer, documentarist, retired foreign service officer; b. Little Rock, Dec. 4, 1931; s. Alfred Wesley and Annie Laurie (Cain) T.; m. Elizabeth Rose, July 9, 1954; children: John Jr., Laurie, Amy, Cynthia. BA, Vanderbilt U., 1952; MA, U. Mich., 1968. 3d sec. U.S. Fgn. Svc., Accra, Ghana, 1957-59, 2d sec. Taichung and Taipei, China, 1960-65; Chinese affairs analyst Dept. State, Washington, 1966-67; staff assoc. Ctr. for Chinese Studies, U. Mich., Ann Arbor, 1967-68; U.S. consul Sarawak, Sabah and Brunei, Kuching, Malaysia, 1968-70; chief external affairs reporting U.S. Consulate Gen., Hong Kong, 1970-74; officer-in-charge Chinese affairs Dept. State, Washington, 1974-75; staff mem. E. Asian affairs Nat. Security Coun., Washington, 1975-77; polit. counselor U.S. Embassy, Pretoria/Capetown, 1977-80, polit. cons. Peking, 1980-82; rsch. fellow Fairbank Ctr. for East Asian Studies Harvard U., Cambridge, Mass., 1982-83; dir. East Asian analysis Dept. State, Washington, 1983-85; dep. asst. sec. state Bur. Intelligence and Rsch., Dept. State, Washington, 1986-87; chief of mission U.S. Interests Sect., Havana, Cuba, 1987-90; diplomat in residence Carter Presdl. Ctr., Emory U., 1990-92; sr. mem. State Task Force 2000, 1992-93; sr. assoc. Global Bus. Access; assoc. in rsch. Fairbank Ctr. for East Asian Studies, Harvard U.; prodr., writer, dir. ?Why Prodns. Guest faculty Emory U. and Spelman Coll. Author: China and Southeast Asia, 1974, 1976, The Dragon and the Wild Goose, 1987, 1990, The Rise and Fall of Totalitarianism, 1993, The Generalissimo's Son, 2000, (documentaries) Ubuntu, African and Afrikaner, 2000; contbr. China and National Security, 1985, columns in newspapers Washington Post, L.A. Times, N.Y. Times. Served as Naval Aviator with USMC, 1953-57. Mem.: Wash. Inst. Fgn. Affairs, Fgn. Svc. Assn. E-mail: jaytaylor888@sprintmail.com.

TAYLOR, JOHN JOSEPH, nuclear engineer, researcher; b. Hackensack, N.J., Feb. 27, 1922; s. John J.D. and Johanna F. (Thibideau) T.; m. Lorraine Crowley, Feb. 5, 1943; children: John B., Nancy M., Susan M. BA, St. John's U., Jamaica, NY, 1942, DSc (hon.), 1975; MS, U. Notre Dame, 1947. Mathematician Bendix Aviation Corp., Teterboro, NJ, 1946-47; engr. Kellex Corp., N.Y.C., 1947-50; v.p. water reactor divsn. Westinghouse Electric Corp., Pitts., 1950-81; v.p. nuc. power Electric Power Rsch. Inst., Palo Alto, Calif., 1981-95; energy cons., 1995—. Mem. adv. com. Oak Ridge (Tenn.) Nat. Lab., 1973-83, Brookhaven Nat. Lab., Upton, N.Y., 1986-92, Inst. for Nuc. Power Ops., 1988-95; mem. adv. com. Argonne (Ill.), Nat. Lab., 1980-86, bd. dirs.; cons. Office Tech. Assessment, Washington, 1975-93; mem. internat. adv. group IAEA, Vienna, Austria, 1992-95; mem. nuc. rsch. rev. com. NRC, 1995-97; mem. U.S.-Russian Commn. on Weapons Plutonium Disposition, 1996-2001, Nat. Acad. Bd. Radioactive Waste Mgmt., 1998-2001, DOE Nuc. Energy Rsch. Adv. Bd., 1998-2002; co-chair Atoms for Peace Study, Livermore Lab., 2003-04. Co-author: Reactor Shielding Manual, 1953, Naval Reactor Physics Manual, 1956, Nuclear Power, Policy and Prospects, 1987, Management and Disposition of Excess Weapons Plutonium; contbr. articles to profl. jours. Bd. regents emeritus St. Mary's Coll., Moraga, Calif. Lt. (j.g.) USN, 1942-45. Lt. j.g. USN, 1942—45. Recipient Order of Merit Westinghouse Electric Corp., 1957, George Westinghouse Gold medal ASME, 1990. Fellow AAAS, Am. Phys. Soc., Am. Nuc. Soc. (bd. dirs., Walter Zinn award 1993); mem. NAE, Cosmos Club (Washington). Republican. Roman Catholic. Home: 15 Oliver Ct Menlo Park CA 94025-6685 Office: Electric Power Rsch Inst PO Box 10412 3412 Hillview Ave Palo Alto CA 94304-1344

TAYLOR, JOHN LOCKHART, former city official; b. N.Y.C., Nov. 4, 1927; s. Floyd and Marian (Lockhart) T.; m. Barbara Becker, July 19, 1952; children: Catherine Fair, Robert, William, Susan. AB, Middlebury Coll., 1952; M.Govtl. Adminstrn., U. Pa., 1956. Reporter Providence Jour.-Bull., 1952-54; adminstrv. intern City of Xenia, Ohio, 1955-56; mcpl. mgr. Borough of Narberth, Pa., 1956-60, Twp. of Lakewood, N.J., 1960-64; asst. city mgr. Fresno, Calif., 1964-65; city mgr., 1965-68, Kansas City, Mo., 1968-74, Berkeley, Calif., 1974-76; lectr. U. Pa., 1957-58, Golden Gate U., 1977; sr. urban mgmt. specialist Stanford Research Inst., 1977-80; dir. Internat. Devel. Center, 1980-82; clk. of bd. suprs. City of San Francisco, 1982-98, spl. asst., 1998—. Pres. Calif. Clks. Bd. Suprs. Assn., 1988-89. Served with USN, 1945-48. Mem. Internat. City Mgrs. Assn., Mcpl. Execs. Assn. (pres. 1991-93, 98). Address: 1005 Creston Rd Berkeley CA 94708-1503 E-mail: misterclerk@msn.com.

TAYLOR, JOHN MCKOWEN, lawyer; b. Baton Rouge, Jan. 20, 1924; s. Benjamin Brown and May (McKowen) T.; 1 child, John McKowen. BA, La. State U., 1948, JD, 1950. Bar: La. 1950, U.S. Supreme Ct. 1960. Assoc. Taylor, Porter, Brooks, Fuller & Phillips, Baton Rouge, 1950-55, Huckaby, Seale, Kelton & Hayes, Baton Rouge, 1955-58; ptnr. Kelton & Taylor, Baton Rouge, 1958-61; pvt. practice, Baton Rouge, 1961—. With AUS, 1943-46; maj. USAR, 1946—, ATO, ETO, PTO. Mem. ABA, AAAS, La. State Bar Assn., Baton Rouge Bar Assn., Mil. Order of World Wars, Am. Radio Relay League, Baton Rouge Country Club, City Club of Baton Rouge, Baton Rouge Amateur Radio Club, Camelot Club, SAR, Sigma Chi, Pi Gamma Mu, Phi Delta Phi. Republican. Presbyterian. Home and Office: 2150 Kleinert Ave Baton Rouge LA 70806-6712 Office Phone: 225-343-1928. E-mail: jmcktaylor@cox.net.

TAYLOR, JOSEPH HOOTON, JR., radio astronomer; b. Phila., Mar. 29, 1941; s. Joseph Hooton and Sylvia Hathaway (Evans) T.; m. Marietta Bisson, Jan. 3, 1976. BA in Physics, Haverford Coll., 1963; PhD in Astronomy, Harvard U., 1968; DSc (hon., U. Chgo., 1985, U. Mass., 1994. Research fellow, lectr. Harvard U., 1968-69; asst. prof. astronomy U. Mass., Amherst, 1969-72, assoc. prof., 1973-77, prof., 1977-81; prof. physics Princeton U., 1980—, James McDonnell Disting. prof. physics, 1986—, dean of faculty, 1997—. Author: Pulsars, 1977. Recipient Dannie Heineman prize in astrophysics, Am. Inst. Physics/Am. Astron. Soc., 1980, prize in gravitation and cosmology, Tomalla Found., 1985, Magellanic Premium award, Am. Philos. Soc., 1990, Einstein prize laureate, Albert Einstein Found., 1993, Wolf Prize in Physics, Wolf Found., 1992, Nobel Prize in Physics, Nobel Found., 1993; fellow MacArthur fellow, 1981. Fellow: Am. Phys. Soc., Am. Acad. Arts and Scis.; mem.: Internat. Astron. Union, Internat. Sci. Radio Union, Am. Astron. Soc., Am. Philos. Soc., NAS. Mem. Soc. Of Friends. Home: 272 Hartley Ave Princeton NJ 08540-5656 Office: Princeton U Dept Physics 215 Jadwin Hall PO Box 708 Princeton NJ 08544-0001

TAYLOR, JULIA FISHER, communications executive; d. James Washington Fisher, Jr. and Hannelore Enke Fisher; children: Alexander, Benjamin. BA in humanities magna cum laude, U. Colo., 1989. Pub. rels. specialist Smithsonian Inst., Washington, 1989—92; pub. rels and comty. rels. dir. Weld Libr. Dist., Greeley, Colo., 1992—99; dep. press sec. Nat. Audubon Soc., Washington and Boulder, 1999—2000; sr. pub. rels. mgr. Denver Mus. Nature and Sci., 2000—03, comm. dir., 2003—. Guest spkr. U. Colo., Boulder, Colo., 2002, Metro State U., Denver, 2003. Contbr. articles on parenting and education, 1992—88. Campaign vol., 1995—. Mem.: PRSA. Avocations: skiing, hiking, running, creative writing. Office: Denver Mus Nature & Sci 2001 Colorado Blvd Denver CO 80205 Office Phone: 303-370-6384. Business E-Mail: jtaylor@dmns.org.

TAYLOR, KATHLEEN (CHRISTINE TAYLOR), physical chemist, researcher; b. Cambridge, Mass., Mar. 16, 1942; d. John F. and Anna M. (Maloney) T. BA in Chemistry, Douglass Coll., New Brunswick, N.J., 1964; PhD in Phys. Chemistry, Northwestern U., 1968. Postdoctoral fellow U. Edinburgh, Scotland, 1968-70; assoc. sr. rsch. chemist Gen. Motors Rsch. Labs., Warren, Mich., 1970-74, sr. rsch. chemist, 1974-75, asst. phys. chemistry dept. head, 1975-83, environ. sci. dept. head, 1983-85, phys. chemistry dept. head, 1985-96; physics and phys. chemistry dept. head Gen. Motors Global Rsch. & Devel. Operations, Warren, Mich., 1995-98, materials and protesses dir., 1998—2002. Recipient Mich. Sci. Trailblazer award Detroit Sci. Ctr., 1986. Fellow AAAS, mem. NAE, Am. Chem. Soc. (Garvan medal 1989), Materials Rsch. Soc. (treas. 1984, 2d v.p. 1985, 1st v.p. 1986, pres. 1987), Soc. Automotive Engrs., The Catalysis Soc., Sigma Xi.

TAYLOR, KATHLEEN N. state legislator; b. Nyack, N.Y., May 28, 1942; 6 children. Student, U. N.H. Mem. N.H. Ho. of Reps. (dist. 11), Concord, 1996—; mem. mcpl. and county govt. com. N.H. Ho. of Reps., Concord, 1996—. Mem. Dover City Coun., 1996-98, mayor pro tem, 1997. Roman Catholic.

TAYLOR, KATHY DEANNE, marketing executive, consultant; b. Peoria, Ill., Sept. 20, 1951; d. Chas S. and Carol A. (McDonough) Guynn; m. Harold N. Taylor Jr. (dec. Nov. 1982); 1 child, Shawn. AA in Bus., Ill. Cen. Coll., Peoria; student in mktg. mgmt., Sangamon State, Springfield. Mgr. sales Credit Bur. Accounts, Inc., Peoria, 1986-87; sales exec. Rsch. Inst. Am., N.Y.C., 1987-93, mem. adv. coun., 1989, pres. bd., 1990-91; sales exec. Paramount Comm., Waterford, Conn., 1993-95; govt. sales cons. West Group Thompson Legal Pub., 1995—2001; pres. bd. Million Dollar Club, 1998, 2 Million Dollar Club, 2000; owner A Sweet Arrangement, 1999—; sales exec. Lexis-Nexis, 2001; propr. A Sweet Arrangement, 2000—. Dir. cardiac ctr. Proctor Community Hosp., 1972-81, risk mgmt. coord., 1981-83; pres. Cen. Ill. Risk Mgmt., Inc., 1983-86. Chmn. bd. Tri-County Heart Assn., Peoria, 1987-88, pres., 1986-87; div. and regional mgr. Am. Heart Assn., Ill. affiliate, Springfield, 1985-89, mem. speakers bur., risk factor com., 1972-81; bd. dirs. Dept. Rehab. Svcs., 1989-91; active ARC hospice tng. Meth. Med. Ctr. Vol. Svcs.; asst. CE dir. Springfield Rd. Bapt. Ch., 2001-02. Mem. NAFE, Am. Inst. Banking, Peoria Jaycee Women (v.p. 1984), Ill. Jaycee Women (state chaplain, mgr. family life program 1984-85), Morton Jaycettes (pres. 1980). Republican. Home and Office: 4709 N Prospect Rd Peoria Heights IL 61616-6439

TAYLOR, KENNETH DOUGLAS, stockbroker, finance and computer consultant, educator; b. Topeka, Nov. 21, 1942; s. Olin Orlando and Lola Louise (Conley) T.; AB, George Washington U., 1964, MS in Stats., 1966; MS in Computer Sci. SUNY, 1990, PhD in Math. Eurotech, 1992, (univ. fellow); student of Peter Hilton; postgrad., McGill U., 1974, Bowdoin Coll., U. Montreal; m. Joy Ellen Rice, May 25, 1973 (div. Nov. 1981); m. Elizabeth Flanagan Brunner, May 6, 1995. Registered rep./stockbroker, options principal. Sr. programmer C-E-I-R, Inc., 1963, 69; instr. Army Map Svc., 1964-65; student instr. McGill U., 1966-71; rsch. assoc. U. Va. Med. Sch., 1972; fin. and computer cons., Plymouth, N.Y., 1973-87; computer scientist USAF, 1989-90; broker Russell Hawkes Assoc./Linsco/Pvt. Ledger, 1993-94, LESKO Fin Svcs, 1994—; sec. Richmond (Va.) Computer Club, 1977. Contbr. articles to profl. jours. Summer grantee NSF, Can. Research Council. Mem. ASTM, Am. Math. Soc. Home: PO Box 288 Montrose PA 18801-0288 Office: LESKO Fin Svcs Centre Plz 53 Chenango St Binghamton NY 13901-2820

TAYLOR, KENNETH NATHANIEL, publishing executive, writer; b. Portland, Oreg., May 8, 1917; s. George Nathaniel and Charlotte Bodwell (Huff) T.; m. Margaret Louise West, Sept. 13, 1940; children: Becky, John, Martha, Peter, Janet, Mark, Cynthia, Gretchen, Mary Lee, Alison. BA, Wheaton Coll., 1938, DLitt (hon.), 1965; student, Dallas Theol. Sem., 1940-43; ThM, No. Bapt. Theol. Sem., 1944; DLitt (hon.), Trinity Evang. Div. Sch., 1972; LHD (hon.), Huntington Coll., 1974, Taylor U., 1989. With Moody Press (pub. protestant religious lit.), Chgo., 1947-63, dir., 1948-62, Moody Lit. Mission (prodn. and distbn. lit.), 1948-62; pres. Tyndale House Publishers, 1963-84, chmn. bd., 1984—, Coverdale House Pubs., London, Eng., 1969-79. Pres. Tyndale House Found., 1964-79, bd. dirs., 1964—; dir. Inter-Varsity Christian Fellowship, 1956-59, Evang. Lit. Overseas, 1951-70, Short Terms Abroad, 1963-77; pres. Living Bibles Internat., Wheaton, Ill., 1968-77, internat. pres., 1977-90, internat. chmn. emeritus, 1990-92; chmn. Unilit., Inc., Portland, 1972-73 Author: Is Christianity Credible, 1946, Living Letters: The Paraphrased Epistles, 1962; juveniles Stories for the Children's Hour, 1953, Devotions for the Children's Hour, 1954, I See, 1958 (reprinted as Small Talks About God, 1995), Bible in Pictures for Little Eyes, 1956, Lost on the Trail, 1959, Romans for the Children's Hour, 1959; Living Prophecies - The Minor Prophets Paraphrased, 1965, Living Gospels, 1966, Living Psalms and Proverbs With the Major Prophets Paraphrased, 1967, The Living New Testament, 1967, Almost 12, 1968, revised, 1995, Living Lessons of Life and Love, 1968, Living Books of Moses, 1969, Living History of Israel, 1970, The Living Bible, 1971, Taylor's Bible Story Book, 1970, The Lord Is My Strength, 1975; juveniles What High School Students Should Know About Creation, 1983, What High School Students Should Know About Evolution, 1983, Big Thoughts for Little People, 1983, Giant Steps for Little People, 1985, Wise Words for Little People, 1987, Next Steps for New Christians (originally How To Grow), 1989, My First Bible in Pictures, 1989 (ann. Angel award 1990, Platinum Book award 1990), The Good Samaritan, 1989, Jesus Feeds A Crowd, 1989, The Lost Sheep, 1989, The Prodigal Son, 1989; Good News for Little People, 1991 (ann. Angel award 1992), My Life, A Guided Tour, 1991, Daniel and the Lions' Den, 1992, Noah's Ark, 1992, Family-Time Bible in Pictures, 1992, A Boy Helps Jesus, 1994, The Good Neighbor, 1994, Noah Builds a Boat, 1994, A Very Special Baby, 1994, The Story of Noah's Ark, 1994, Small Talks About God, 1995, Everything a Child Should Know About God, 1996; co-editor: The Bible for Children, 1990 (ann. Angel award 1991); pub. The Christian Reader, 1964-92, Have a Good Day, 68—; co-author: My First Bible Words: A Kid's Devotional, 1998, Right Choices, 1999, Family Devotions With Children, 1999, A Child's First Bible, 2000, The New Bible in Pictures for Little Eyes, 2002 (ECPA Gold Medallion Book award 2003), God Cares for Me Listen and Learn Bible Storybook, 2003, God Helps Me Lift and Look Bible Storybook, 2003, God Knows Me Scratch and Sniff Bible Storybook, 2003, God Loves Me Touch and Feel Bible Storybook, 2003, Family Time Bible, 2003, Jesus in Pictures for Little Eyes, 2003; contbr. to numerous publications. Bd. dirs. Christian Libr. Svc., 1972-75, InterSkrift forlage Aktiebolag, Sweden, Internat. Bible Soc., 1992-94; trustee Living Bible Found., Fuller Theol. Sem.; mem. adv. bd. Internat. Bible Reading Assn. Recipient citation Layman's Nat. Bible Com., 1971; award Religious Heritage Am., 1972; disting. svc. citation Internat. Soc. Christian Endeavor, 1973; Nelson Bible award, 1973; Better World award VFW Aux., 1974; disting. pub. svc. award 1974; Recognition award Urban Ministries, Inc., 1977; Svc. award Wheaton Coll. Alumni Assn., 1977; Crusader award Wheaton Coll., 1979; Gutenberg award Chgo. Bible Soc., 1981; Internat. Christian Edn. Assn. award, 1983, Disting. Svc. to Family award Wheaton Coll. Alumni Assn.; Inducted into DuPage County Heritage Gallery, 1983; named Man of Yr. Com. Internat. Goodwill, 1983; recipient 1st Ann. Lit. award Evang. Lit. Overseas, 1983; Svc. award YFC/USA, 1984; Gold Medallion Achievement award Evang. Pubs. Assn., 1984; recipient Ann. James DeForest Murch award Nat. Assn. Evangelicals, 1995, Annual Golden Word award Internat. Bible Soc., 1996, award Evangelical Christian Publ. Assn., 1997, Charles V. Hogren award The Cabrini Green Legal Aid Clinic, 2003; named to Christian Booksellers Hall of Fame, 1989. Mem.: Internat. Soc. Bible Collectors (William Tyndale award 2003), Wheaton Coll. Alumni Assn. (Disting. Svc. to Family award 2000), Wheaton Coll. Scholastic Honor Soc. (Retailer's Choice Award for Visionary Industry Pioneer, Christian Booksellers Assn. Expo 2001). Home: 1515 E Forest Ave Wheaton IL 60187-4469 Office: 351 Executive Dr Carol Stream IL 60188-2420 *Who but God could make an unending universe, sized by billions of light years? And who could dream of knowing such a God personally? I am one who believes this, and have based my life on the Bible as God's message to mankind, and to you and me. But how to manage Bible reading when it is in such an ancient language? How to crack the shell of the coconut and find the milk and meat? That is why I spent 16 years translating the Bible into living English, with 40 million copies now in print.*

TAYLOR, KENNETH RICHARD, information technology executive, consultant; b. Boston, Mass., July 24, 1976; s. William Archibald and Roberta Lee Taylor; m. Angela Marie Lefebvre, Sept. 6, 1997; children: Veronica Lee, Henry Joseph. BA, Maranatha Coll., 1996. Pres. AS&ST, New Hampton, NH, 1999—. Republican. Baptist. Avocations: model railroading, simulation gaming. Home and Office: As&St 41 Ridge Rd New Hampton NH 03256

TAYLOR, KOKO, singer; Albums include The Earthshaker, from the Heart of a Woman, I Got What It Takes, Queen of the Blues, 1985, Koko Taylor, 1987, Live From Chicago: An Audience with the Queen, 1987, Teaches Old Standard New Tricks, Jump for Joy, 1990, What It Takes: The Chess Years, 1991, Force of Nature, 1994. Office: Alligator Records care Nora Kinnally PO Box 60234 Chicago IL 60660-0234

TAYLOR, LANCE JEROME, economics professor; b. Montpelier, Idaho, May 25, 1940; s. Walter Jerome and Ruth (Robinson) T.; m. Yvonne S.M. Johnsson, May 31, 1963; children: Ian Lance, Signe Marguerite. BS with honors, Calif. Inst. Tech., 1962; PhD, Harvard U., 1968. Instr. econs. Harvard U., Cambridge, Mass., 1967-68, asst. prof., assoc. prof., 1970-74; research assoc. MIT, Cambridge, 1968-70, prof. econs., 1974-93, New Sch. for Social Rsch., N.Y.C., 1993—. Vis. prof. U. Brasilia, 1974, Pontifical Cath. U. Rio de Janeiro, 1981, U. Delhi, 1987-88, Stockholm Sch. Econs., 1990; Marshall lectr. Cambridge U., 1986-87; cons. World Bank, UN, various fgn. govts. Author: Macro Models for Developing Countries, 1979, Models of Growth and Distribution for Brazil, 1980, Structuralist Macroeconomics, 1983, Varieties of Stabilization Experience, 1988, Income Distribution, Inflation, and Growth, 1991, The Market Meets its Match: Restructuring the Economies of Eastern Europe, 1994, Global Finance at Risk, 2000, Restructuring Macroeconomics: Structuralist Proposals and Critiques of the Mainstream, 2004. Fulbright fellow, 1962-63 Mem. Am. Econ. Assn., Royal Econ. Soc. Home: PO Box 378 Washington ME 04574-0378 Office: New School for Social Rsch Grad Faculty 65 5th Ave New York NY 10003-3089 E-mail: lance@blacklocust.com.

TAYLOR, LAWRENCE DOW, geologist, educator; b. Boston, Oct. 6, 1932; s. Theodore and Dorothea Mae (Dow) T.; m. Jean Ann Ryland, Sept. 24, 1955; children: Charles, Keith. AB, Dartmouth Coll., 1954, MA, 1958; PhD, Ohio State U., 1962. Geologist geophysics br. U.S. Geol. Survey, Boston, and Greenland, 1954-55, geologist fuels br. Denver, 1958; rsch. assoc. Dartmouth

Coll., Hanover, N.H., and Greenland, 1957-58, Ohio State U. Inst. Polar Studies, Columbus, Ohio, and Antarctica, 1962-63, Glacier Bay, Alaska, 1959-60; asst. prof. Coll. of Wooster, Ohio, 1963-64, Albion (Mich.) Coll., 1964-68, assoc. prof., 1968-77, prof., 1977-98, prof. emeritus, 1998—, chair dept. geol. scis., 1968-85. Chief glaciologist Trans-Antarctic Traverse, NSF, U.S. Antarctic Rsch. Program, 1962-63. Contbr. articles to profl. jours. With U.S. Army, 1955-57. Grantee NSF, 1960, 62-63, 65, 69, Hewlett Melon Found., 1981, Pew Sci. Program, 1991, Albion Coll., 1992-97; recipient Exemplary Tchr. award United Meth. Ch., 1997, Mich. Campus Compact Cmty. Svc. award, 1998, Antarctic Svc. Congl. medal; Taylor Hills, Antarctica, named in his honor. Fellow Geol. Soc. Am., Am. Quaternary Assn., Am. Geophys. Union, Nat. Assn. Geology Tchrs. (pres. East Ctrl. sect. 1984-85), Explorers Club, Rotary, Sigma Xi. Avocations: mountain climbing, backpacking, cross country skiing, tennis. Office: Albion Coll Dept Geol Scis Albion MI 49224

TAYLOR, LELAND BARIDON, lawyer; b. Poughkeepsie, N.Y., July 5, 1920; s. Alexander J. and Elsie Jane (Van Wyck) T.; m. Rosemary Olcott Coon, June 24, 1945; children: Barry Eugene, Craig Cameron, Mark Alexander, Meg Olcott Taylor Casey. BS, Syracuse U., 1942, JD, 1948. Bar: N.Y. 1948, U.S. Dist. Ct. (no. dist.) N.Y. 1954, U.S. Supreme Ct. 1958. Ptnr. Fitzgerald, Taylor, Pomeroy & Armstrong and predecessor, Cortland, N.Y., 1948-2000; of counsel Pomeroy, Armstrong, Baranello & Casullo, Cortland, N.Y., 2000—. Judge City of Cortland, 1952-57; bd. dirs. First Nat. Bank of Dryden, Monroe Abstract & Title Corp. Trustee Cortland Free Libr., 1950—. With Supply Corps, USNR, 1942-45. Named Cortland County Jr. C. of C. Young Man of Yr., 1952, N.Y. State Young Man of Yr., N.Y. State Jaycees, 1953, Syracuse U. Letterman of Distinction, 1977. Fellow N.Y. Bar Found., Am. Bar Found., mem. ABA, N.Y. State Bar Assn. (v.p. 1974-76, sec. 1976-79, chmn. fin. com. 1979-84), Cortland County Bar Assn., Rotary (Paul Harris fellow), Masons. Presbyterian. Address: 16 Tompkins St Cortland NY 13045-2541

TAYLOR, LEONARD STUART, engineering educator, consultant; b. N.Y.C., Dec. 28, 1928; m. Lillian Rachel Schlang, Apr. 12, 1954; children: Robin Jolie, Allyn Lise. AB, Harvard Coll., 1951; MSc, N.Mex. State U., 1955, PhD, 1960. Microwave engr. Raytheon Mfg. Co., Bedford, Mass., 1950-55; research physicist Gen. Electric Co., Phila., 1960-63; assoc. prof. Case Western Res. U., Cleve., 1964-67; prof. U. Md., College Park, Md., 1967-96, prof. emeritus, 1996—. Cons. USN, Silver Spring, Md., 1967-96. Contbr. articles to profl. jours; inventor Microwave Scalpel, Implantable Microwave Hyperthermia Applicator and numerous others. Recipient Disting. Alumni award, N.Mex. State U., 1975, Outstanding Contbn. award, U. Md. Coll. Engring., 2002. Fellow IEEE (life), Am. Soc. for Laser Medicine and Surgery; mem. Am. Phys. Soc., Optical Soc. of Am., Bioelectromagnetics Soc. Avocations: tennis, music. Office: U Md Dept Ee College Park MD 20742-0001 Office Phone: 301-405-3741. Business E-Mail: taylor@umd.edu.

TAYLOR, LEWIS JEROME, JR., retired priest; b. Norfolk, Va., Feb. 22, 1923; s. Lewis Jerome and Roberta Page (Newton) T.; m. Pauline Rector Green, Nov. 24, 1945; children: Lewis J. III, Michael R., John B., Mary F., Joan E. BS in Engring., U.S. Naval Acad., 1944; MDiv, Seabury-Western Theol. Sem., Evanston, Ill., 1961; PhD in Religion, Duke U., 1972. Ordained priest Episcopal Ch., 1962. With George R. Green, Inc., White Post, Va., 1949-52, Travelers Ins. Co., Norfolk, 1956-58; chaplain Coll. William and Mary, Williamsburg, Va., 1961-63; curate Bruton Parish Ch., Williamsburg, Va., 1961—63; rector St. Aidan's Episc. Ch., Virginia Beach, Va., 1963-68; prof. theology St. Andrews Sem., Manila, 1971-76; rector Ch. of the Messiah, Chester, N.J., 1978-86; interim rector of various parishes Diocese of Southern Va., 1986-93; instnl. chaplain Indian Creek Correctional Ctr., Chesapeake, Va., 1993-98. Mem. Dept. Missions Diocese of Newark, 1965-68, Commn. on Ministry, Newark, 1979-82; dean Lay Sch. of Christian Studies, Newark, 1977-82; chmn. Commn. on Racism, Southern Va., 1992-95. Author: In Search of Self: Life, Death, and Walker Percy, 1985; contbr. articles to profl. jours. Bd. dirs. Samaritan House, Virginia Beach, 1995—. Comdr. USN, 1944—49, active duty USNR, 1952—56, PTO. Trinity Inst. grantee, 1986. Mem.: Rotary (pres. 1985—86). Democrat. Avocations: tennis, camping, reading, writing. Home: 701 San Remo Ct Virginia Beach VA 23454-7343

TAYLOR, LILI, actress; b. Chgo., Feb. 20, 1967; Appeared in films Mystic Pizza, Say Anything, Born on the Fourth of July, Bright Angel, Dogfight, Watch It, Household Saints, Short Cuts, Rudy, Arizona Dream, Mrs. Parker and the Vicious Circle, Ready to Wear, The Addiction, Cold Fever, I Shot Andy Warthol, Girls Town, Ransom, Cosas Que Nunca te Deve, 1996, Letters Not About Love, 1997, Kicked in the Head, 1997, O.K. Garage, 1998, Pecker, 1998, The Impostors, 1998, Spring Forward, 1999, A Life Slipping Down, 1999, Janis, 1999, The Haunting, 1999, High Fidelity, 2000, Julie Johnson, 2001, Gaudi Afternoon, 2001; broadway plays include What Did He See, Aven U Boys; regional plays include Mud, The Love Talker, Fun.; TV appearance in (films) Subway Stories: Tales from the Underground, 1997, Deadline, 2000, Anne Frank: The Whole Story, 2001, Live From Baghdad, 2002, (TV series) Six Feet Under, 2002-2003. Office: c/o William Morris Agy 151 S El Camino Dr Beverly Hills CA 90212-2704*

TAYLOR, LINDA RATHBUN, investment manager; b. Rochester, N.Y., May 25, 1946; d. Lewis Standish and Elizabeth Florence (Hunt) Rathbun; m. Donald Gordon Taylor, Mar. 1, 1975; children: Alexander Standish, Abigail Elizabeth, Elizabeth Downing. BA, Vassar Coll., 1968; MBA, Harvard U., 1973. Cert. CFA Cert. Fin. Analyst Inst., 1981. Assoc. corp. fin. Donaldson, Lufkin & Jenrette, N.Y.C., 1973-75; cons. IBRD, Washington, 1975; fin. analyst U.S. Treas. Dept., Washington, 1976-78; chief investment officer United Mine Workers Fund, 1978-85; investment mgr. Cen. Pension Fund Internat. Union Oper. Engrs., Washington, 1985-86; investment banker Sarasota Co., 1986-89; pvt. investor, 1990—; mng. ptnr. Sakonnet Mgmt., LLC, 1998-2000. Pres. Boundary Farm Inc.; CEO CMAC, LLC, 2001—03; bd. dirs. J.P. Morgan Venture Capital Investors, J.P. Morgan Corp. Fin. Investors, 1998—; dir. Legg Mason Instnl. Funds, 1999—2002; bd. dirs. Fauquier Hosp. Found. Devel. Coun., 2002—. Contbr. articles to profl. jours. Trustee Montgomery County (Md.) Employees' Retirement Sys., 1987-93; bd. dirs. Washington Internat. Horse Show, 1995-2003; com. mem. Vassar Coll. Endowment Fund, 1992—; elder Bradley Hills Presbyn. Ch., 1992-95; dir. bd. pensions Presbyn. Ch. U.S.A., 1996-99; dir. Va. Horse Shows Assn. Found., 1998—. Recipient Disting. Alumni award Carolina Day Sch., 1996. Mem. Jr. League Washington, Washington Soc. Investment Analysts (bd. dirs. 1984-85), Cert. Fin. Analyst Inst. Republican. E-mail: lrtaylorcfa@aol.com.

TAYLOR, LINDSAY DAVID, JR., health care executive; b. Balt., Dec. 15, 1945; s. Lindsay David Sr. and Lillian Helen (Wagner) T.; children: Sarah Ruth, John David, Margaret Katherine. B in Mech. Engring., Rensselaer Poly. Inst., 1967; MBA, Dartmouth Coll., 1969. Bus. assoc. U.S. Steel Corp., Pitts., 1968-70; spl. asst. to asst. sec. for health HEW, Washington, 1970-71, mgr. operational planning, 1971-74, dep. asst. sec. mgmt., 1977-79; programming officer World Bank, Washington, 1974-76; dir. exams. and supervision Fed. Home Loan Bank Bd., Washington, 1979-81; exec. v.p. Perpetual Bank, Alexandria, Va., 1981-89; pres., CEO Columbia (Md.)-FreeState Health Sys., 1989-91, Preferred Health Network, 1992-96; CEO Alpha Health Plan, 1997-99; COO NPD, LLC, Bethesda, Md., 1999—, Nat. Assn. Cmty. Health Ctrs., Washington, 2001—. Cons. Nat. Acad. Pub. Adminstrn., Washington, 1985—86, Ctr. for Advancement of Health, Washington, 1988—89, Diabetex Corp., Balt., 1996—2003, Latin Am. Youth Ctr., 2003—04; trustee Md. Sci. Ctr., 1996—2000; co-chair Greater Balt. Health Care Coun., 1996—2001, Leadership Md., 1996; mem. bd. advisors Found. for Island Health, 2001—04; mem. adv. bd. WAMU Pub. Radio, 1985—88; bd. dirs. Hospice No. Va., 1984—88; chmn. Washington Employers Coalition on Day Care, 1983—90; chair CHC Funding, LLP, 2002—04; bd. dirs. Capital Link, 2003—04. Recipient Mgmt. Improvement award Pres. U.S., 1973, 77; Edward Tuck scholar. Mem. Ctr. for Excellence in Govt. (prin. 1986-2004), Washington Coun. Govts. (devel. policy com. 1986-89, mem. editl. adv. bd. Managed Care 1989-94), Tau Beta Pi, Pi Tau Sigma. Avocations: photography, folk music instruments, travel, wilderness, coaching youth baseball and basketball. Office: 4800 Montgomery Ln Ste 1000 Bethesda MD 20814-3472 also: Ste 210 7200 Wisconsin Ave Bethesda MD 20814 E-mail: LDavidTaylor@yahoo.com.

TAYLOR, LYN ANN, principal; b. N.Y.C., Dec. 27, 1942; d. Edward H. and Ann G. McGuire; m. Turner Worthington Taylor, Feb. 1, 1975; children: Christopher Edward, Adam Worthington. BS in Elem. Edn., St. John's U., Jamaica, N.Y., 1964; MA in Edn. Adminstrn., LaSalle U., 2000. Tchr. grade 2 St. Mary's Sch., Manhasset, N.Y., 1964-65; tchr. grades 2, 4, 5 and 6 Wantagh (N.Y.) Sch. Sys., 1965-69; tchr.-prin. grades K, 1, 2 and 4 Dept. Def. Overseas Sch., Japan, Philippines, Cuba, 1969-74; substitute tchr. Health, Edn. and Welfare, P.R., 1975-77, various schs., R.I., 1980-89; pres. sch. bd. St. Lucy's Sch., Middletown, R.I., 1982-86; prin. St. Joseph's Sch., Beverly, N.J., 1995—. Team leader Dept. Def., Japan, Philippines, Bahamas, Cuba, 1969-74; pres. sch. bd. St. Lucy's Sch., Middletown, R.I., 1982-84. Mem. ASCD, NAFE, Nat. Cath. Educators Assn. (chairperson conv. New Orleans 1999), Pvt. Sch. Mgmt. Roman Catholic. Avocations: painting, dance, travel, raising great danes. Office: St Josephs Sch 805 Warren St Beverly NJ 08010 Home: 15608 SW 16thCt Pembroke Pines FL 33027-2348

TAYLOR, L(YNN) FRANKLIN, lawyer; b. Hutchinson, Kans., Sept. 25, 1945; s. Lynn Franklin and Rebecca Ellen (Jones) T.; m. Kathryn Ruth Achterberg, May 31, 1968; children: Laura Jeanne, Deborah Lynne. BA, Doane Coll., 1967; JD, U. Kans., 1975. Bar: Kans. 1975, U.S. Tax Ct. 1975, U.S. Supreme Ct. 1978, Mo. 1990. Pvt. practice Payne & Jones, Chartered, Overland Park, Kans., 1975-86, Speer, Austin, Holliday, Ruddick & Taylor, Olathe, Kans., 1986-89, Armstrong, Teasdale, Schlafly & Davis, Overland Park, 1989-92, Watson & Marshall L.C., Olathe, 1992-96, Norton, Hubbard, Ruzicka & Kreamer L.C., Olathe, 1996—; pres., CEO Olathe C. of C., 1999—. City atty. City of DeSoto, Kans., 1979-92; mcpl. judge City of Olathe, 1980-85. Contbr. to Kans. Estate Adminstrn. Handbook, 1980, 86, 93, Kans. Corp. Law Handbook, 1997. Active Kans. Commn. on Edn. Restructuring and Accountability, Topeka, 1992; edn. adv. com. Kans. City Partnership for Children, 1992-96; mem. bd. edn. Unified Sch. Dist. 233, Olathe, 1987-2003; vice chmn., then chmn. bd. dirs. Hidden Glen Arts Festival, 1992-94; bd. dirs. Olathe Region United Way, 1979-2000; vice chancellor Episcopal Diocese Kans., Topeka, 1981-94, chancellor, 1994—. Fellow Am. Coll. Trust and Estate Counsel; mem. Olathe C. of C. (Citizen of Yr. 1994), Rotary (Paul Harris fellow Olathe club 1994), Order of Coif. Republican. Avocations: skiing, boating, gardening, sports. Home: 26391 W Cedar Niles Cir Olathe KS 66061 Office: Norton Hubbard Ruzicka & Kreamer LC 130 N Cherry St Olathe KS 66061-3401 Office Phone: 913-782-2350. E-mail: ftaylor@nhrk.com.

TAYLOR, MARETTA MITCHELL, state legislator; b. Columbus, Ga., Jan. 25, 1935; BS, Albany State, 1957; MS, Ind. U., 1966. Mem. Ga. Ho. of Reps., 1991-92, 93—; mem. edn., retirement, state planning and cmty. affairs coms.; co-owner, mgr. Designers Ltd., 1987—. Democrat. Baptist. Home: 1203 Bunker Hill Rd Columbus GA 31907-6718 Office: Ga House of Reps State Capitol Atlanta GA 30334

TAYLOR, MARGARET TURNER, clothing designer, architectural designer, economist, writer, planner; b. Wilmington, N.C., May 7, 1944. A.B. in Econs., Smith Coll., 1966; M.A. in Econ. History, U. Pa., 1970, now Ph.D. candidate in City and Regional Planning. Tchr. Jefferson Jr. High Sch., New Orleans, 1966-69; instr. econs. U. Tex.-El Paso, 1974-75; adj. prof. econs., Salisbury State U., Md., 1976-78; prin. mgr., designer Margaret Norriss, women's clothing, Salisbury, Md., 1980-95; owner Functional Design Ideas, Inc., 1995—; planner at Wharton Ctr. Applied Research, Phila., 1985-86; planning cons., writer.

TAYLOR, MARGARET UHRICH, educational administrator; b. Lebanon, Pa., Nov. 27, 1952; d. William Murray and Anne (Schultz) Uhrich; m. Timothy Norman Taylor, Sept. 29, 1979; 1 child, Walter Marshall. BA, Shippensburg U., 1974. Adminstrv. asst. Patriot-News Co., Harrisburg, Pa., 1974; reporter Pub. Opinion sect., Chambersburg, Pa., 1975-78; assoc. editor, Miami bur. chief OAG, Inc., N.Y.C., 1978-79; dir. mktg., pub. affairs Wilson Coll., Chambersburg, 1980-90, co-founder women in transition program, 1985; pres. Margaret Taylor's Mktg. Comms., 1989; sr. rschr. Brizius & Foster, McConnellsburg, Pa., 1990, pvt. practice cons., 1990—; exec. dir. Fulton County Econ. Devel. Corp., 1993-96, Fulton Indsl. Devel. Assn., McConnellsburg, 1997-2000; comm. chair Pa. Econ. Devel. Assn., 1997-2000; owner McConnellsburg Inn, 1992-2000; dir. instnl. advancement Pa. State U. Mont Alto Campus, 2000—04; dir. devel. and univ. rels. Pa. State U. The Behrend Coll., 2004—. Adj. faculty Shippensburg U., Pa., 1981-90; lectr. comms. Wilson Coll. Founding mem. Commonwealth Assn. Students, 1972; charter mem. Friends of Fulton County Libr., McConnellsburg, 1975; founder Unforgettable Charity Ball, Chambersburg, 1983-86; active Gotemba Sister-City Com., Borough of Chambersburg, 1981-90; pub. rels. counsel Greater Chambersburg Area United Way, 1985-90; cons. dir. Straight Love Franklin County, Chambersburg, 1982-83; founder Women's Network Franklin County, 1982-90; bd. dirs. Fulton County Med. Ctr. Corp., 1987-93, sec. 1989-90, vice-chmn. 1990-91, chmn. 1992-93; bd. dirs. Pa. Downtown Ctr. Assn., 1998-2000, Fulton County Tourist Promotion Agy., 1995-2000, Pa. Rural Devel. Coun., 1999-2001; bd. dirs. Inst. for Caregiver Edn., 2003—. Mem. Soc. Profl. Journalists (treas. Central Pa. chpt. 1981-82, v.p. 1982-83, pres. 1983-84, chmn. freedom of info. com. 1980-81, chpt. del. nat. conv. 1977). Rotary (chair ambassadorial scholarship com.). Kitochtinny Hist. Soc. (bd. dirs. 2002—04). Home: 110 Fischer DR Erie PA 16511

TAYLOR, MARGARET WISCHMEYER, retired language educator; b. Terre Haute, Ind., Aug. 5, 1920; d. Carl and Grace (Riehle) Wischmeyer; m. John Edward Taylor, Sept. 5, 1942 (dec. 1988); children: Deborah Ann, Tobin Edward (dec. 2002), Mary Leesa. BA magna cum laude, Duke U., 1941; MA, John Carroll U., Cleve., 1973. Feature writer Dayton (Ohio) Daily News, 1945-53; freelance writer Cleve., 1953—; asst. to Dr. Joseph B. Rhine Duke U. Parapsychology Lab., Durham, NC, 1941; asst. prof. English and journalism Ea. Campus, Cuyahoga CC, Cleve., 1973-92, prof. emeritus, 1992—, advisor campus newspaper, 1973-84, dir. Writers Conf., 1975-90. Writing cons., editor various cos. and pubs., Cleve., 1973—; founder, operator Grammar Hot Line, 1987-92. Author: Crystal Lake Reflections, 1985, English 101 Can Be Fun, 1991, The Basic English Handbook, 1995. Recipient top state honors Ohio Newspaper Women's Assn., 1947, award for best edn., best overall stories Am. Heart Assn., 1970, Besse award for tchg. excellence, 1980, Profl. Excellence award, 1985, Provost's Pride award, 1987, Nat. Tchg. Excellence award Coun. for Advancement and Support of Edn., 1989; named Ohio Outstanding Citizen, Ohio Ho. Reps., 1987, 89, Innovator of Yr., League for Innovations in C.C.s, 1988, Pres.'s award Cuyahoga C.C., 1992. Mem. Mensa, Phi Beta Kappa, Pi Beta Phi. Presbyterian. Avocations: grammar consulting, reading, writing. Home: 27900 Fairmount Blvd Cleveland OH 44124-4616 E-mail: taylorstock@ameritech.net.

TAYLOR, MARILYN HORTON, secondary school educator; b. Memphis, Tenn., Feb. 9, 1956; d. Claude E. and Lois Drewry Horton; m. Jimmy Taylor, Aug. 6, 1982; children: Jamie Alexis, Michael Harrison. MA, U. Memphis, Memphis, Tenn., 2000. Acct. Rhodes Coll., Memphis, 1988—94; tchr. Trezevant H.S., Memphis, 1994—. Adv. bd. Tchg. Am. History Grant, Memphis, 2002—. Contbr. journal. Grantee Tchg. Japan in Mid-South Schools, U.S.-Japan Found., 2002, Tchg. Am. History, 2002-2004, Tchg. the Cold War Inst., Nat. History Day, 2001, Colonial Williamsburg Inst., 1996; scholar Study in China, Fulbright, 2004. Mem.: Nat. Coun. for History Edn. (assoc.), Orgn. of Am. Historians (assoc.), Phi Kappa Phi (assoc.). Home: 5704 Ashbriar Memphis TN 38120 Office: Trezevant H S 3350 North Trezevant Memphis TN 38127 Personal E-mail: mtaylorsis@hotmail.com. Business E-Mail: mtaylorsis@hotmail.com.

TAYLOR, MARILYN JORDAN, architectural firm executive; m. Brainerd O. Taylor; children: Brainerd I., Alexis. Degree in govt. and urban affairs, Harvard Coll., 1969; MArch, U. Calif., Berkeley; postgrad., MIT. Joined Skidmore, Owings and Merrill LLP, Washington, 1971, urban designer, dir. design stations program of N.E. Corridor Improvement Project, 1978—85, chief urban design and planning practice N.Y.C., 1985—2001, chmn., 2001—. Past pres. N.Y.C. chpt. AIA; chmn. Nat. AIA Regional and Urban Design Com.; vis. prof. Harvard Grad. Sch. Design; David Rockefeller fellow N.Y.C. Partnership, fellows adv. com. Key projects include N.J. Performing Arts Ctr., Newark, Riverside South, Manhattan, NYNEX Hdqs., Battery Park City, Penn Sta. Redevelopment Project, various airports, many others. Bd. dirs. N.Y.C. Bldg. Congress (chmn. 2002-04), Comml. Real Estate Women N.Y., Inst. for Urban Design. Named Woman of Yr., Comml. Real Estate Women N.Y., 1998; named one of Most Influential Women in Am. Real Estate, GRID mag., 2001; named to List of Most Influential Women, Crain's N.Y., 1996, 2000; recipient Profl. Leadership award, Profl. Women in Constrn., 2001. Office: Skidmore Owings and Merrill LLP 14 Wall St New York NY 10005*

TAYLOR, MARK, lieutenant governor; b. Atlanta, May 7, 1957; m. Sacha Taylor; 1 child. Degree in polit. sci., Emory U., degree in law, U. Ga. Exec. Fred Taylor Co., Albany; mem. Ga. Senate, Atlanta, 1987—; asst. adminstrn. floor leader then adminstrn. floor leader Gov. Zell Miller; sec. transp. com.; mem. appropriations, ethics, ins. and labor, rules coms.; also reapportionment com.; lt. gov. State of Ga., Atlanta, 1999—. Mem. bd. dirs. March of Dimes, Albany/Dougherty 2000 Partnership, Thronateeska Heritage Found. Mem. Ga. Bar Assn., Dougherty County Bar Assn., Leadership Albany (charter), Artesian City Sertoma Club (past pres.), Rotary. Democrat. Office: Rm 240 State Capitol Atlanta GA 30334 E-mail: mtaylorx@legis.state.ga.us.

TAYLOR, MARK CHANDLEE, choreographer; b. Wichita Falls, Tex., Apr. 26, 1953; s. William Mottu and Vonna (Gigoux) Taylor; m. Barbara Winfield Sieck, Mar. 1, 1980. BA in Medieval Studies, Swarthmore (Pa.) Coll., 1975. Artistic dir. Mark Taylor & Friends, N.Y.C., 1981-91, Dance Alloy/Mark Taylor, Pitts., 1991—. Lectr. dance Princeton U., Princeton, NJ, 1984—91; movement cons. CSC Repertory Theater, N.Y.C., 1989—90. Choreographer Paris Opera Ballet, 1986. Fellow, N.Y. Found., 1985, Nat. Endowment for Arts, 1988, Gulkentian Found., Ireland, 1986. Mem.: Dance Theater Workshop. Mem. Soc. Of Friends. Office: Dance Alloy/Mark Taylor 5530 Penn Ave Pittsburgh PA 15206-3562

TAYLOR, MARK DOUGLAS, publishing executive; b. Geneva, Ill., Jan. 16, 1951; s. Kenneth Nathaniel and Margaret Louise (West) T.; m. Carol E. Rogers, May 28, 1973; children: Jeremy Peter, Kristen Elizabeth, Margaret Louise, Rebecca Cynthia, Stephen Rogers. BA, Duke U., 1973. Exec. dir. Tyndale House Found., Wheaton, Ill., 1973-78; v.p. Tyndale House Pubs., Wheaton, Ill., 1978-84, pres., chief exec. officer, 1984—. Dir. Living Bibles Internat., Naperville, Ill., 1972-92; trustee Taylor U., 1998—. Author The Complete Book of Bible Literacy, 1992. Mem. Wheaton Liquor Control Commn., 1986—, chmn., 1994—; chmn. bd. dirs. Outreach Cmty. Ctr., 1986-93. Mem. Internat. Bible Soc. (bd. dirs. 1992-96). Office: Tyndale House Publishers Inc PO Box 80 Wheaton IL 60189-0080 *What we accomplish in life is soon forgotten. Our best legacy is to pass on to our children and grandchildren our positive values.*

TAYLOR, MARK LYMAN, music educator; b. Longmont, Colo., Oct. 26, 1955; s. Gaylord Lyman and Florence Stratton Taylor; m. Sandra Lynn Curneal, Nov. 15, 1958. MusB, Cornerstone U., 1978; MusM, Mich. State U., 1981; PhD, Case Western Res. U., 1995. Music tchr. First Bapt. Christian Sch., Elyria, Ohio, 1982—85; dir. of bands Mansfield (Ohio) Christian Sch., 1985—91; dir. of music Parma (Ohio) South Presbyn. Ch., 1991—94; asst. prof. of music Northwestern Coll., Orange City, Iowa, 1994—95; assoc. prof. of music Houghton (N.Y.) Coll., 1995—2001, Cornerstone U., Grand Rapids, Mich., 2002—; dir. Met. Choir of Praise, Grand Rapids. Com. mem. N.Y. State Tchr. Certification Examination-Content Adv. Com. for Music, Albany, NY, 2001—02; music dir. Wellsville (N.Y.) Performing Arts Orch., 1999—2002; founder & dir. Allegany Youth Wind Symphony, Houghton, NY, 1999—2001; headmaster's adv. coun. mem. Houghton (N.Y.) Acad., 1998—2002; spkr. in field. Mem.: ASCD, Mich. Sch. Band and Orch. Assn., Mich. Sch. Vocal Music Assn., N.Y. State Coun. of Music Tchr. Edn. Programs (sec. 1998—2002), Coll. Music Soc., Music Educators Nat. Conf., Phi Delta Kappa. Avocations: basketball, reading. Office: Cornerstone University 1001 East Beltline Avenue NE Grand Rapids MI 49525 E-mail: mark_l_taylor@cornerstone.edu.

TAYLOR, MARTHA ELIZABETH (BETSY TAYLOR), investment company executive; b. Phila., Dec. 30, 1950; d. Harry Colvin and Jeannette M. (Hartwell) Taylor; 1 child, Jeannette E. Student, Phila. Coll. of Textiles & Science, Phila., 1990—. Telecommunications mgr. Miller Anderson & Sherrerd, West Conshohocken, Pa., 1985-89; asst. treas./sec., mgr. gen. affairs LTCB-MAS Investment Mgmt., Inc., West Conshohocken, Pa., 1989—. Office: LTCB-MAS Investment Mgmt Inc 1 Tower Brg Ste 950 West Conshohocken PA 19428

TAYLOR, MARY, state representative; M in Taxation, U. Akron. CPA. Sr. mgr. Bober, Markey, Fedorovich & Co.; state rep. dist. 43 Ohio Ho. of Reps., Columbus, 2002—, vice chair, homeland security, engring. and archtl. design com., mem. econ. devel. and tech., edn. and ways and means comms., fed. grant rev. and edn. oversight subcom. Councilwoman, fin. com. chair, mem. rules & pers. and intergovtl. and utilities coms. Green (Ohio) City Coun., 2001—. Republican. Office: 77 High St llth fl Columbus OH 43215-6111

TAYLOR, MILDRED D. author; b. Jackson, Miss., Sept. 13, 1943; d. Wilbert Lee and Deletha Marie (Davis) Taylor. BA in Edn., U Toledo, 1965; MA, U Colo., 1969. Vol., tchr. English and history Peace Corps, Ethiopia, 1965-67, then recruiter, 1967-68; study skills coord. black edn. program U. Colo., 1969-71. Author: (children's fiction) Song of the Trees, 1975, Roll of Thunder, Hear My Cry, 1976, Let the Circle Be Unbroken, 1981, The Gold Cadillac, 1987, The Friendship and Other Stories, 1987, Mississippi Bridge, 1990, The Road to Memphis, 1990, The Well, 1995 (winner Jane Addams book award, 1996), The Land, 2001. Address: care Dial Books For Young Readers 375 Hudson St New York NY 10014-3658

TAYLOR, MILDRED LOIS, nursing home administrator; b. Conroe, Tex., July 23, 1927; d. George Carl and Bertha Elizabeth (Swift) Ferguson; student Hunter Coll., 1944, U.S. Navy Hosp. Corps Sch., Bethesda, Md., 1944, corr course Am. Sch., Chgo., 1971, Central Tex. Coll., 1971, U. Tex., Austin, 1975; m. Thomas Nielsen Taylor, Dec. 1, 1945; children— Linda Sue, Thomas Grant, Charles Nielsen. Nurse aide St. David's Hosp., Austin, Tex., 1965-67; adminstr.-in-tng. North Lamar Nursing Home, Austin, 1971-72, adminstr., 1973-75; adminstr. Austin Nursing & Convalescent Center, 1976—, sec., treas., 1976— . Pres. Episcopal Women of the Ch., Austin, 1966; mem. Tex. Nursing Home Adminstrs. Polit. Action Com., 1976— . Served with WAVE, USNR, 1944-45. Lic. nursing home adminstr., Tex. Mem. Tex. Nursing Home Assn., Am. Health Care Assn., Austin C. of C., U.S. C. of C. Clubs: Lost Creek Country, Order Eastern Star, St. David's Hosp. Women's Aux. (Austin). Office: 110 E Live Oak St Austin TX 78704-4355 Home: 301 Nicole Way Bastrop TX 78602-6629

TAYLOR, MILLICENT RUTH, elementary school educator; b. Kingston, Jamaica, Nov. 18, 1944; came to U.S., 1981; m. Henry Taylor; children: T'ousant, Howard, Annette, Kerry-Ann. BE, U. West Indies, 1981; MS, U. Miami, 1991. Cert. elem. edn. tchr., secondary social sci. tchr., Fla. Chairperson dept. history Mays Middle Sch., Miami, Fla., 1987—, peer tchr., 1987—; clin. tchr., 1990—; seminar presenter Mays Middle Sch., Miami, Fla., 1987-88, clin. tchr., 1990—. Leader, trainer Global Edn., Miami, Fla. 1989, sponsor History Bee, Miami, 1988-90, Geography Bee, 1988-90, 2003. Recipient State award for tchg. econs. Dade County Sch., 1992, Nat. award for tchg. econs. Joint Coun. Econ. Edn., 1991, State award for Gov. Awards for Excellence, 1995, Nat. award for tchg. econs. Nat. Coun. Econ. Edn., 1995. Mem. ASCD, Seventh Day Adventist. Avocations: reading, travel, sewing, photography. Home: 19834 SW 118th Ave Miami FL 33177-4435 Office: Mays Middle Sch Goulds FL 33170

TAYLOR, MINNA, lawyer; b. Washington, Jan. 25, 1947; d. Morris P. and Anne (Williams) Glushien; m. Charles Ellett Taylor, June 22, 1969; 1 child, Amy Caroline. BA, SUNY, Stony Brook, 1969; MA, SUNY, 1973; JD, U. So. Calif., 1977. Bar: Calif. 1977, U.S. Dist. Ct. (cen. dist.) Calif. 1978. Extern to presiding justice Calif. Supreme Ct., 1977; field atty. NLRB, L.A., 1977-82; dir. employee rels., legal svcs. Paramount Pictures Corp., L.A., 1982-85, v.p. employee rels. legal svcs., 1985-89; dir. bus. and legal affairs Wilshire Ct. Prodns., L.A., 1989-91; sr. counsel Fox Broadcasting Co., L.A., 1991-92, v.p. legal affairs, 1992-97, sr. v.p. legal affairs, 1997—. Webmaster www.ifcome-.com, 2001—. Editor notes and articles: U. So. Calif. Law Rev., 1976-77. Mentor MOSTE, L.A., 1986-87, 88-89; pres. Beverly Hills chpt. ACLU, L.A., 1985. Fellow ABA, Calif. State Bar (mem. copyright subcom. 1994-95), L.A. County Bar Assn.; mem. Beverly Hills Bar Assn., L.A. Bead Soc. (membership sec. 1992-94, mem. bd. dirs. 1994-95), Order of Coif. Office: Fox Broadcasting Co 10201 W Pico Blvd Los Angeles CA 90064-2606

TAYLOR, NELLIE RUBY, artist, poet; b. Lundale, W.Va., Apr. 18, 1946; d. John Otis and Blanche L. (Wright) Taylor; m. Ivan Lee Hurt, July 31, 1965 (div. Nov. 1982); children: Ivan Lee Hurt Jr., Bradley Allen Hurt. MA, 1995. Adminstr. Cleve. Sch., Cleve., 1987—; nursing Mary Farmers Nurses, Cleve. Heights, Ohio, 1987—2002; agent A.L. Williams Ins., Athens, Ohio, 1984—87; tchr. Manor-Care, Mayfield Heights, Ohio, 2002—. Author: (book) Mental Education; inventor Hopter-Copter; prodr., dir., host: (television) In Time Like These; founder & pres. (corporation) The Mean Corporation; Represented in permanent collections Portrait of Bill Clinton, Presdl. Libr., Ark. Recipient Award of Excellence, Ohio Sch. Bd. Assn, 1985—87, Lifetime Congl. award, U.S. Congress 11th Dist., 1998. Mem.: Am. Fedration of Teachers. Achievements include represented as permanent leader, justice, tolerance new civil rights mem. ctr. with Rosa Parks, Montgomery, Ala. Avocations: writing, travel, poetry, drama. Home: 2826 E 130th Unit # 102 Shaker Heights Cleveland OH 44120 Office Phone: 216-324-2887.

TAYLOR, NICHOLAS C. lawyer, state agency administrator, energy executive; b. Washington, Sept. 18, 1937; s. James Spear Taylor and Helen Livingston MacGregor Strauss; m. Catherine Blaffer, d. Jan. 1,1999; children: Nicholas Van Campen, Katherine C., Christie. AB, Harvard U., 1959; JD, Georgetown U., 1963. Bar: DC 64, NY 66, Tex. 71. Assoc. Wilson, Woods & Villalon, Washington, 1964-65, Shearman & Sterling, N.Y.C., 1965-70, Locke, Liddell, Sapp, Dallas, 1970-74; shareholder Stubbeman, McRae, Sealy, Laughlin & Browder, Inc., Midland, Tex., 1974-93; atty. Midland, 1993—; pres. Mexco Energy Corp., Midland, 1983—; chmn., mem. State Securities Bd. of Tex., 1995—2003. Pres. Mexco Energy Corp., 1983—2003. Mem. Tex. Jud. Coun., 1990-95. Recipient Am. Jurisprudence prizes for constnl. law, oil, and gas taxation So. Meth. U. Law Sch. Mem. Natural Gas Prodrs. Assn., Permian Basin Petroleum Assn. (bds. dirs. 2002-03). Episcopalian. Office: 214 W Texas Ave Ste 1101 Midland TX 79701-4616 E-mail: mexco@msn.com.

TAYLOR, NICOLE RENÉE (NIKI TAYLOR), model; b. Miami, Fla., Mar. 5, 1975; d. Ken and Barbara Taylor; m. Matt Martinez (div.); 2 children. With Irene Marie, Miami, 1989. Contracts with L'Oreal, 1990-92, Cover Girl Makeup; appeared in Seventeen (cover girl) 1989, Vogue, Elle, Mademoiselle, Harper's Bazaar; modeled for Yves Saint Laurent, Karl Lagerfeld; modeled swimsuit Sports Illus., 1997, cover Sports Illus. Calendar, 1998. Achievements include appeared on over 320 mag. covers worldwide; youngest model to appear on the cover of Vogue. Office: TriStar Entertainment Group Suite 200 215 Ward Circle Brentwood TN 37027

TAYLOR, PALMER W. pharmacology educator; b. Oct. 3, 1938; m. Susan Serota; three children. BS in Pharmacy, U. Wis., 1960, PhD in Phys. Pharmacy, 1964. Rsch. assoc. pharmacology-toxicology assoc. program Lab. Chem. Pharmacology, 1965-68; NIH fellow molecular pharmacology unit Med. Rsch. Coun., Cambridge, Eng., 1968-70; NIH fellow Max Planck Inst. for Phys. Chemistry, Gottingen, Germany, 1970; asst. prof. divsn. pharmacology dept. medicine U. Calif., San Diego, 1971-74, assoc. prof. divsn. pharmacology dept. medicine, 1974-78, prof. divsn. pharmacology dept. medicine, 1978-87, head divsn. pharmacology dept. medicine, 1979-87, prof., chair dept. pharmacology, 1987—, Sandra & Monroe Trout endowed chair pharmacology, 1994—. Mem. pharmacology study sect. NIH, 1974-78; mem. study sect. on chemotherapeutic agts. Multiple Sclerosis Soc., 1974-86; co-chmn. conf. on membrane receptors and diseases NIH-NIGMS, Bethesda, Md., 1978; participant Nat. Acad. Scis. Pharmacology Symposium, 1979; co-chair ASPET Symposium on Application of Molecular Pharmacology to Therapeutic Considerations, 1980; mem. pharmacol. scis. rev. com. NIH, 1980-85; vis. fellow Darwin Coll., U. Cambridge, 1980-81; Sterling Drug Co. vis. prof. U. Mich., 1985, U. Oreg., 1990; nat. adv. coun. mem. Nat. Inst. Gen. Med. Scis., 1988-92; vice chair, chair Gordon Conf. on Molecular Pharmacology, 1987-89; Krantz Meml. lectr. U. Md., 1989; Harold C. Hodge lectr. U. Rochester Med. Ctr., 1992; vis. prof., lectr. series Coll. de France, 1999, Tyler lectr. series Purdue U.; bd. trustees Gordon Rsch. Confs., 1999—. Co-editor: (with W.B. Pratt) Principles of Drug Action, 3d edit., 1990, (with A.G. Gilman, T.W. Rall and A.S. Nies) Godoman and Gilman's Pharmacological Basis of Therapeutics, 8th edit., 1990; assoc. editor Molecular Pharmacology, 1971-75; mem. editl. bd. Jour. Biol. Chemistry, 1981-86, 92-98, Molecular Pharmacology, 1983—, Trends in Pharmacol. Scis., 1983-90, Jour. Molecular Medicine, 1992-98, Pharm. News, 1997—; cons. editor Jour. Clin. Investigation, 1992-98; contbr. articles to profl. jours. Recipient Borden award, Phi Lambda Upsilon award in pharm. chemistry; Fogarty fellow U. Cambridge, 1980-81. Mem. NAS-Inst. Medicine, Internat. Union Pharmacology (del. 1995—), Am. Soc. for Clin. Investigation (hon.), Am. Soc. for Pharmacology and Exptl. Therapeutics (councillor 1987-90, pres.-elect 1994-95, pres. 1995-96), Am. Soc. for Biochemistry and Molecular Biology, Am. Assn. for Med. Sch. Pharmacology, Fedn. Exptl. Biologists (bd. mem. 1995-99). Office: Dept Pharmacology Basic Sci Bldg 9500 Gilman Dr La Jolla CA 92093-0636 E-mail: pwtaylor@ucsd.edu.

TAYLOR, PAUL B. choreographer; b. Allegheny County, Pa., July 29, 1930; s. Paul B. and Elizabeth (Rust) Taylor. Student, Syracuse U., 1949-52, Juilliard Sch. Music, 1952-53; hon. doctoral degrees include, Duke U., 1983, Conn. Coll., 1983, Syracuse U., Juilliard, SUNY at Purchase, Cal. Inst. Arts, Skidmore U., 1995. Artistic dir. Paul Taylor Dance Co., 1957—. Dancer Merce Cunningham Co., 1954, Martha Graham, 1955—60, Paul Taylor Dance Co., 1957—75. Dancer Paul Taylor Dance Co. has performed in over 400 U.S. cities and made 34 overseas tours, numerous arts festivals in 36 nations, PBS TV Dance in Am., Live From the Am. Dance Festival, Two Landmark Dances, Three Modern Classics, The Wrecker's Ball, The Taylor Co.: Recent Dances, Am. Masters, Paul Taylor, Dancemaker, choreographer (partial list) Aureole, 1962, Private Domain, 1969, Esplanade, 1975, Cloven Kingdom, 1976, Airs, 1978, Le Sacre du Printemps (the Rehearsal), 1980, Arden Court, 1981, Mercuric Tidings, 1982, Sunset, 1983, Roses, 1985, Last Look, 1985, Musical Offering, 1986, Ab Ovo Usque ad Mala, 1986, Syzygy, 1987, Kith and Kin, 1987, Minikin Fair, 1989, Speaking in Tongues, 1989, Company B, 1991, Spindrift, 1993, A Field of Grass, 1993, Oz, 1991, Moonbine, 1994, Funny Papers, 1994, Offenbach Overtures, 1995, Eventide, 1996, Piazzolla Caldera, 1997, The Word, 1998, Oh, You Kid!, 1999, Cascade, 1999, Arabesque, 1999; author (autobiography): Private Domain, 1987 (Nat. Book Critics Cir. award for biography, 1987). Decorated Chevalier des Arts et Lettres, elevated to Officier France, Comdr. Legion of Honor; named Dancer of Yr., London's Dance and Dancers, 1965; named to Nat. Mus. Dance Hall of Fame, 1995; recipient Internat. Cir. of Criticism for Artistic Rsch. and Cultural Exch. award, Festival Nations, Paris, 1962, Best Fgn. Attraction prize, Critics of Chile, 1966, Capezio Dance award, 1967, Creative Arts award, Brandeis U., 1978, Dance Mag. award, 1980, Samuel H. Scripps Am. Dance Festival award, 1983, Arts award, State N.Y., 1987, Lions of Performing Arts award, N.Y. Pub. Libr., 1989, Emmy award, Speaking in Tongues, 1992, Kennedy Ctr. Honors award, 1992; Guggenheim fellow, 1961, 1966, 1983, MacArthur Found. fellow, 1985. Office: Paul Taylor Dance Co 552 Broadway New York NY 10012-3922

TAYLOR, PAUL PEAK, pediatric dentist, educator; b. Childress, Tex., May 11, 1921; s. Noah Peak and Lois C. (Vinson) T.; m. LaVerne Countryman, Aug. 11, 1945; chi dren: Scott, Peri Ann. Student, W. Tex. State Coll., 1938-40; DDS, Baylor U., 1944; MS, U. Mich., 1951. Diplomate Am. Bd. Pediatric Dentistry (examining mem. 1977-84, chair 1983). Prof. Baylor U. Coll. Dentistry, Dallas, 1958-86, chmn. grad. pediatric dentistry, 1960-69, chmn. dept. pediatric dentistry, 1969-86, prof. emeritus, 1986—; dir. dental svcs. Children's Med. Ctr., Dallas, 1965-86, dir. emeritus dental svcs., 1986—; dir. dental svcs. Tex. Scottish Rite Hosp. for Children, Dallas, 1965-86, dir. emeritus dental svcs., 1986—. Contbr. articles to Jour. of Dentistry for Children, 1960-82; author (with others) Pediatric Dentistry, 1986, Current Therapy in Pediatric Infectious Disease, 1989; mem. edtl. and publs. com. Jour. Dentistry for Children. Capt. U.S. Army, 1951-53. Named to Baylor Coll. Dentistry Hall of Fame, 1999; Mott Found. fellow, 1949-51. Fellow Am. Coll. of Dentists (life); mem. ADA (life), Tex. Dental Assn., Dallas County Dental Assn. (Dentist of Yr. 1999, Lifetime Achievement award 2002), Masons (life, 32d degree, KCCH), Shriners. Episcopalian. Avocation: golf. Home: 2615 Briarcove Dr Plano TX 75074-4905

TAYLOR, PETER VAN VOORHEES, advertising and public relations consultant; b. Montclair, N.J., Aug. 25, 1934; s. John Coard and Mildred (McLaughlin) T.; m. Janet Kristine Kirkebo, Nov. 4, 1978; 1 child, John Coard III. BA in English, Duke U., 1956. Announcer Sta. WQAM, Miami, Fla., 1956; announcer, music dir. Sta. KHVH, Honolulu, 1959-61; promotion mgr. Sta. KPEN, San Francisco, 1962; with Kaiser Broadcasting, 1962-74, GE Broadcasting Co., 1974-78; program and ops. mgr. Sta. KFOG, San Francisco, 1962-66; mgr. Sta. WXHR-AM-FM, Cambridge, Mass., 1966-67; gen. mgr. Sta. WJIB, Boston, 1967-70; v.p., mgr. FM divsn. Kaiser Broadcasting, 1969-72; v.p., gen. mgr. Sta. KFOG, San Francisco, 1970-78; pres. Taylor Comm., 1978-90, 97—, Baggott & Taylor, Inc., 1990-91, Taylor Advt. & Pub. Rels., 1991-96, No. Calif. Broadcasters Assn., 1974-76, Broadcast Skills Bank, 1975-76. Pres. Roast Host, 1993—96. Trustee WDBS, Inc., Duke U., 1974-80; bd. dirs. San Francisco BBB, 1976-78, 89-94, Calif. Broadcasters Assn., 1982-84, KCRH Chabot Coll., 1982-83, San Francisco Boys and Girls Club, 1991-93, Coast Guard Found., 1991-2000, Leukemia Soc., San Francisco, 1992-93, Duke Devel. Coun., 1992-96; bd. dirs. Commencement Bay Rowing Club, sec., 1997-98, v.p. 1998-99, pres., 1999-2000; mem. exec. bd., sec. Scandinavian Culture Coun., 2001—, v.p., 2002-03, pres., 2003-; bd. dirs. Lindquist Children's Dental Clinic, 2004—. Lt. USCGR, 1957—63. Mem. Nat. Radio Club, Internat. Radio Club, Long Wave Radio Club, Worldwide TV-FM Dx Assn., Golden Gate Breakfast Club (bd. dirs. 1995-96, v.p. 1995-96), Rotary (bd. dirs. San Francisco, 1988-93, 1st v.p. 1990-91, pres. 1991-92, chmn. pub. rels. dist. 5150 1986-89, conf. chmn. 1990, area rep. 1992-93, dist. gov. nominee 1995-96, pub. rels. chair Tacoma 2002-03, auction chair 2004-, bd. dirs. 2004-). Home and Office: 6002 Bayview Dr NE Tacoma WA 98422-1227 E-mail: taytac@comcast.net.

TAYLOR, PEYTON TROY, JR., gynecologic oncologist, educator; b. Tuscaloosa, Ala., July 21, 1941; s. Peyton Troy Sr. and Frances (Sutter) T.; m. Helena Ström, Sept. 23, 1967; children: Annika, Karin, Sarah. BS, U. Ala., 1963, MS, 1968; MD, Med. Coll. Ala., 1968. Intern U. Va. Hosp., Charlottesville, 1968-69, resident, 1969-70, 72-75; asst. prof. ob-gyn. U. Va., Charlottesville, 1976-79, assoc. prof., dir. divsn. ob-gyn., 1981-87, Richard N. and Louise R. Crockett prof., 1987—; prof. ob-gyn., dir. divsn. ob-gyn. U. Va. Health Scis. Ctr., Charlottesville, 1981-97; med. dir. Cancer Ctr. U. Va., 1996—; clin. assoc. surgery Nat. Cancer Inst., Bethesda, Md., 1970-72. Assoc. prof. U. Ala., Birmingham, 1979-81. Contbr. articles to profl. jours. Served with USPHS, 1970-72. Fellow ACS, Am. Coll. Obstetricians and Gynecologists; mem. Assn. Acad. Surgeons, Soc. Gynecol. Oncologists, Soc. Surg. Oncology, Am. Soc. of Clin. Oncology, Am. Assn. for Cancer Rsch., Internat. Gynecol. Cancer Soc., So. Surg. Assn. Episcopalian. Office Phone: 434-924-9933.

TAYLOR, PHILIP CRAIG, physics educator; b. Paterson, N.J., Mar. 17, 1942; s. Philip D. and Elizabeth (Erdman) T.; m. Muriel Allison Taylor, Dec. 20, 1969; children: Allison L., Heather M. AB, Carleton Coll., 1964; PhD, Brown U., 1969. Research physicist Naval Research Lab., Washington, 1971-80, supervisory research physicist, 1980-82; prof. physics U. Utah, Salt Lake City, 1982—2001, dist. prof. physics, 2001—, chmn. dept. physics, 1989-98, assoc. dir. laser inst., 1987-98, dir. laser inst., 1998—. Fellow Am. Phys. Soc.; mem. AAAS, Materials Rsch. Soc., Am. Assn. Physics Tchrs. Office: U Utah Dept Physics Salt Lake City UT 84112 Office Phone: 801-581-8751. Business E-Mail: craig@physics.utah.edu.

TAYLOR, R. ERVIN, JR., archaeologist; b. Los Angeles, Jan. 15, 1938; s. Royal Ervin and Francys Ellen (McMurtry) T.; m. Marilynn Julia Lampley, Aug. 30, 1959; children: Gregory Michael, Karen Louane. BA, Pacific Union Coll., 1960; MA, UCLA, 1965, PhD, 1969. Asst. prof. Calif. State U., Northridge, 1967-70; from assoc. prof. to prof. anthropology U. Calif., Riverside, 1970—, chmn. dept. anthropology, 1994-2000. Author: Radiocarbon Dating, 1987; editor: Chronologies in New World Archaeology, 1978, Advances in Obsidian Glass Studies, 1980; co-editor: Radiocarbon After Four Decades, 1992, Chronometric Dating in Archaeology, 1997. Grantee NSF, 1978—. Fellow AAAS, Am. Anthropol. Assn.; mem. Southwestern Anthropol. Assn. (pres. 1975-76), Soc. Archaeol. Scis. (pres. 1982, gen. sec. 1982-2002). Home: 25155 Crestview Dr Loma Linda CA 92354-3508 Office: U Calif Riverside CA 92521-0001 E-mail: retaylor@ucr.edu.

TAYLOR, R. EUGENE, bank executive; B in fin., Fla. State U. Credit analyst Bank of Am. Corp., 1969—86, pres. Fla. bank, 1986—93; pres. NationsBank Mid Atlantic, 1993—97; pres. cons. and comml. banking Bank of Am. Corp., 2000—. Office: Bank of America Corp 100 N Tryon St Charlotte NC 28255

TAYLOR, RALPH ARTHUR, JR., lawyer; b. Washington, Jan. 19, 1948; s. Ralph Arthur Sr. and Mary Florence Taylor; m. Joanna Lamb Moorhead, Jan. 30, 1988; children: Alison M., John Duncan. BS in Engring. with honors, Princeton, 1970; JD, U. Va., 1975. Bar: Va. 1975, D.C. 1976, Md. 1989, U.S. Dist. Ct. D.C. 1977, U.S. Dist. Cts. (ea. and we. dists.) Va. 1986, U.S. Dist. Ct. Md. 1988, U.S. Dist. Ct. Colo. 1998, U.S. Ct. Appeals (4th cir.) 1991, U.S. Ct. Appeals (D.C. cir.) 1977, U.S. Ct. Appeals (6th cir.) 1991, U.S. Ct. Claims 1985, U.S. Supreme Ct. 1980. Program advisor U.S. EPA, Boston, 1970-72; assoc. Steptoe & Johnson, Washington, 1975-84, Shaw, Pittman, Potts, & Trowbridge, Washington, 1984-86, ptnr., 1986-2001, leader tech. and intellectual property litigation group, co-leader Yr. 2000 practice group; ptnr. Dorsey & Whitney, LLP, 2000—, co-chair intellectual property litigation group, 2000—03, chair intellectual property litigation group, 2003—. Assoc. editor Litigation News, 1985-99, exec. editor, 1999-2004; notes editor Va. Law Rev., 1974-75; contbg. author: International Technology Transfers, 1995; co-chair com. newsletters com. ABA Litigation Sect., 2004—. Pres. Cloisters West Homeowners Assn., Washington, 1989, 90; pres. 1625 Q St. Condominium Assn., Washington, 1982-86; mem. grad. bd trustees Princeton Quadrangle Club; mem. bd. dirs. Am. Liver Found., Greater D.C. Chpt. Lt. USPHS, 1970-72. Mem. Order of the Coif, Met. Club (Washington), Barristers, Princeton Club (Washington), Chevy Chase Club. Protestant. Avocations: sailing, skiing, tennis, squash, amateur radio. Office: Dorsey & Whitney LLP Ste 400 South 1001 Pennsylvania Ave NW Washington DC 20004

TAYLOR, RALPH ORIEN, JR., real estate developer, investor; b. Kansas City, Mo., Jan. 6, 1919; s. Ralph Orien Sr. and Genevieve (Sturgeon) T.; m. Betty Boswell, Dec. 7, 1940 (dec. Oct. 1959); children: Ralph Bradley, Nancy Virginia Stevens; m. Deborah Rosemary Berger, Oct. 10, 1982. BS in Bus. and Pub. Adminstrn., U. Mo., 1940. Ptnr. Sturgeon & Taylor, Kansas City, Mo., 1940-42; chmn., pres. Sturgeon & Taylor, Inc., Kansas City, Prairie Village (Kans.), 1946, Sturgeon & Taylor Devel. Co., Inc., Prarie Village, Kans., 1949—, Sturgeon & Taylor, Co., Prarie Village, Kans., 1955-90; ptnr., co-founder ScripTpro LLC, Pharmacy Robotics & Automation, Mission, Kans., 1994, Orien Rose, LLC. Lt. comdr. USNR, 1942-46, PTO, ETO. Decorated Bronze Star with combat V; recipient Alumnus of Yr. award, Phi Delta Theta Fraternity, 2000, Ralph and Debbie Taylor Phi Delta Theta Baseball Stadium dedicated in his honor, U. Mo., 2000. Charter mem. Nat. Assn. Home Builders (life bd. dirs.), Home Builders Assn. Greater Kansas City (pres. 1951-52, life bd. dirs., Builder of Yr. award 1979); mem., Ft. Lauderdale Country Clu b, Phi Delta Theta (Raymond L. Gardner Alumnus of Yr. award 2000). Republican. Mem. Christian Ch. Avocations: golf, boating. Home: 1050 Seminole Dr PHB Fort Lauderdale FL 33304-3225 Office Phone: 954-648-1064. E-mail: ralphotaylor@aol.com.

TAYLOR, RAYMOND MASON, lawyer, former government official, educator; b. Washington, N.C., Jan. 1, 1933; s. Thaddeus Raymond and Mary Ada (Mason) T.; m. Rachel High; 1 dau., Elizabeth Lee Taylor Garber (Mrs. Kenneth Richard Garber). AB, U. N.C.-Chapel Hill, 1955, JD, 1960. Cert. law librarian Am. Assn. Law Libraries, 1968. Bar: N.C. 1960, U.S. Dist. Ct. (ea. dist.) N.C. 1960, U.S. Supreme Ct. 1970, U.S. Ct. Appeals (4th, 5th, 6th, 7th, 8th and 9th cirs.) 1977, U.S. Ct. Internat. Trade 1978, U.S. Ct. Appeals (11th cir.) 1981, U.S. Ct. Appeals (D.C. cir.) 1983, U.S. Ct. Mil. Appeals 1983. Staff reporter Washington (N.C.) Daily News, 1952, 54; adminstrv. asst. CD, Winston-Salem and Forsyth County, N.C., 1955; adminstrv. intern City of Winston-Salem, 1958; research asst. Assoc. Justice N.C. Supreme Ct., Raleigh, 1960-61; assoc. Gardner, Connor & Lee, Wilson, N.C., 1961-64; adj. instr. bus. law Atlantic Christian Coll. (now Barton Coll.), Wilson, 1962-63, adj. prof., 1963-64; marshal, librarian N.C. Supreme Ct., 1964-77; sole practice Raleigh, NC, 1977—81, 1983—84, 1988—. Asst. U.S. atty., chief of appellate sect. Eastern Dist. N.C., 1981-82; supt. documents of US, asst. pub. printer of U.S., assoc. gen. counsel U.S. GPO, Washington, D.C., 1982-83; ptnr. Hall, Hill, O'Donnell, Taylor, Manning & Shearon, 1985-87; vis. lectr. econs. and bus. law N.C. State U., Raleigh, 1967-85; project dir. Fed. Jud. Ctr. Study of Fed. Ct. Libraries, 1976-77; dir. N.C. Law Research Facilities Study, 1970; chmn. State and Ct. Law Libraries of the U.S. and Can., 1973-74; mem. Info. Industry Council to Pub. Printer of U.S., 1981-83. Author: Federal Court Libraries, 1981; mem. editl. bd.: N.C. Law Rev. Chmn. Parents' Day Campbell U., 1979, chmn. Parents Fund, 1981-82; mem. Wake County Libr. Commn., 1979-81. Served with CIC, U.S. Army, 1955-57. Recipient N.C. Soc. County and Local Historians award, 1955, U. N.C. Press Club Awards Editorial Writing and News Writing, 1955, Tar Heel of Week, 1971, award of Excellence Soc. Tech. Communication, 1976. Mem. N.C. Bar Assn. (chmn. Legislative Com. Elder Law Section N.C. Bar Assn, 2002-2003), Nat. Acad. Elder Law Attys. (state coord. 1991-95), Sons of Confederate Vets., Order Golden Fleece (pres. 1958-59), West Raleigh Rotary (pres. 1992-93, Paul Harris fellow 1992, Holoman Disting. Svc. award 1997), Pi Sigma Alpha, Phi Delta Phi, Omicron Delta Kappa, N.C. Supreme Ct. Hist. Soc. (trustee, 1999-). Home: 3073 Granville Dr Raleigh NC 27609-6917 Office: 503 Oberlin Rd Ste 203 Raleigh NC 27605-1327

TAYLOR, RENEE, actress, writer; m. Joseph Bologna; 1 child, Gabriel. Grad., Acad. Dramatic Arts. Actress (films) The Errand Boy, Last of the Red Hot Lovers, A New Leaf, The Detective, Lovesick, White Palace, Delirious, End of Innocence, (stage) Three Sisters, Machinal, Annie Get Your Gun, Li'l Abner, Wish Your Were Here; writer (film) Lovers and Other Strangers (Academy award nomination), (TV) Paradise, (HBO spl.) Bedrooms (Writers Guild award); author: My Life On A Diet. Address: 16830 Ventura Blvd Ste 326 Encino CA 91436-1725

TAYLOR, RICHARD EDWARD, physicist, researcher; b. Medicine Hat, Alta., Can., Nov. 2, 1929; arrived in U.S., 1952; s. Clarence Richard and Delia Alena (Brunsdale) Taylor; m. Rita Jean Bonneau, Aug. 25, 1951; 1 child, Norman Edward. BS, U. Alta., 1950, MS, 1952; PhD, Stanford U., 1962; DHC (hon.), U. Paris-Sud, 1980; DSc, U. Alta., 1991; LLD (hon.), U. Calgary, Alta., 1993; DSc (hon.), U. Lethbridge, Alta., 1993, U. Victoria, B.C., Can., 1995; DHC (hon.), U. Blaise Pascal, 1997; DSc (hon.), Carleton U., Ottawa, Ont., 1999, U. Liverpool, U.K., 1999, Queen's U., Kingston, Ont., 2000. Boursier Lab. de l'Accelerateur Lineaire, Orsay, France, 1958—61; physicist Lawrence Berkeley Lab., Berkeley, Calif., 1961—62; staff mem. Stanford (Calif.) Linear Accelerator Ctr., 1962—68, assoc. dir., 1982—86, prof., 1968—. Recipient Nobel prize in Physics, 1990; fellow Guggenheim Found., 1971—72, von Humboldt Found., 1982. Fellow: AAAS, Royal Soc. London, Royal Soc. Can., Am. Acad. Arts and Scis.; mem.: NAS (fgn. assoc.), Can. Assn. Physicists, Am. Phys. Soc. (W.K.H. Panofsky prize divsn. particles and fields 1989). Office: Stanford Linear Accelerator Ctr M/S 96 2575 Sand Hill Rd Menlo Park CA 94025-7015 E-mail: retaylor@slac.stanford.edu.

TAYLOR, RICHARD JAMES, lawyer; b. Merrill, Wis., Jan. 19, 1939; s. M.N. and Billie (Mead) T.; m. Nancy Hildebrand, Nov. 25, 1966. BA, U. Wis., 1962; DEF, U. Orleans, France, 1963; JD, U. Mich., 1966; postgrad., U. Paris II, 1971-72. Bar: N.Y. 1968. Assoc. Langner Parry Card & Langer, N.Y.C., 1966—68, Conboy Hewitt O'Brien & Boardman, N.Y.C., 1968—71; asst. prof. U. Paris I Law Sch., 1973—78; trademark and copyright counsel Colgate-Palmolive Co., N.Y.C., 1978—2001. Seminar leader Am. Law and Lang., N.Y.C., 1987—; pro bono counsel Hearts and Voices, N.Y.C., 1992—95; mem. com. of experts World Intellectual Property Orgn. Trademark Law Treaty, Geneva, 1993—94; lectr. intellectual property symposia. Co-author: Doing Business in France, 1973, Worldwide Trademark Transfers, 1992; contbr. chpt. to book, articles to Nat. Law Jour., Trademark Reporter, Jour. Japan Trademark Assn., Bus. Latin Am., others. Mem. ABA (chair com. on internat. trademark treaties and laws 1990-91, del. to World Trademark Symposium 1992), Internat. Trademark Assn. (chair internat. com. 1987-89, mem. internat. task force 1989-90, bd. dirs. 1992-95, mem. task force on trademark law treaty 1991-95, publ. bd. 1995—).

TAYLOR, RICHARD L., JR., engineer, consultant; b. Greensboro, N.C., Feb. 25, 1955; s. Richard L. and Norma J. Taylor; m. Rachelle L. Stelzer, Sept. 12, 1997; 1 child, James T. AA, Johnson County C.C., Overland Park, Kans., 1987; BA, Ottawa U., 1996; M in Liberal Arts, Baker U., 1998; MBA, Park U., 2001. Constrn. engr. Babcock & Wilcox Constrn., Barberton, Ohio, 1999—2000; cost and schedule engr. Panda Energy Mgmt. Internat., Dallas, 2001—03; owner So. Design, Goodyear, Ariz., 1997—. Active Johnson County Recreation Commn., Overland Park, Kans., 1995—96. Named Vol. of the Yr., Johnson County Ct.-Appointed Spl. Advocate, 1999. Mem.: ASME. Republican. Mem. Unity Ch. Avocations: sailing, travel, tennis, running. Home and Office: 2741 North 137 Ave Goodyear AZ 85338 Office Phone: 623-640-7757. Personal E-mail: rtdelta@netzero.net.

TAYLOR, RICHARD POWELL, lawyer; b. Phila., Sept. 13, 1928; s. Earl Howard and Helen Moore (Martin) Taylor; m. Barbara Jo Anne Harris, Dec. 19, 1959 (dec. Oct. 29, 2002); 1 child, Douglas Howard. BA, U. Va., 1950, JD, 1952. Bar: Va. 1952, D.C. 1956. Law clk. U.S. Ct. Appeals for 4th Circuit, 1951-52; assoc. Steptoe & Johnson LLP, Washington, 1956-61, ptnr., 1962—, chmn. transp. dept., 1978—; sec., corp. counsel Slick Corp., 1963-69, asst. sec., 1969-72, also bd. dirs., 1965-68; sec., corp. counsel Slick Indsl. Co., 1963-72; sec., bd. dirs. Slick Indsl. Co. Can. Ltd, 1966-72. Bd. dirs. Intercontinental Forwarders, Inc., 1969-72. Mem. Save the Children 50th Anniversary Com., 1982; gen. counsel Am. Opera Scholarship Soc., 1974—; mem. lawyer's com. Washington Performing Arts Soc., 1982—; mem. adv. com. Rock Creek Found. Mental Health, 1982—; mem. nat. adv. bd. DAR, 1980-83, chmn., 1983—; mem. men's com. Project Hope Ball, 1980—; nat. vice chmn. for fin. Reagan for Pres., 1979-80; mem. exec. fin. com. 1981 Presdl. Inauguration; mem. President's Adv. Com. for Arts, 1982—, Rep. Nat. Com., 1983—; Md. fin. chmn. Reagan-Bush '84, Bush-Quayle '88. Served to lt (j.g.), Air Intelligence USNR, 1952-56. Mem. ABA (co-chmn. aviation com. 1964-76, chmn. 1976-77), Fed. Bar Assn., D.C. Bar Assn., Va. Bar Assn., Fed. Energy Bar Assn., Am. Judicature Soc., Assn. Transp. Practitioners, Internat. Platform Assn., Raven Soc., Order of Coif, Univ. Club, Capital Hill Club, Nat. Aviation Club, Aero Club, Congl. Country Club (Washington), Potomac (Md.) Polo Club. Episcopalian. Home: 14914 Spring Meadows Dr Germantown MD 20874-3444 Office: 1330 Connecticut Ave NW Washington DC 20036-1704 Personal E-mail: rtaylor@steptoe.com. *Everyone should devote a portion of his or her life to efforts which help ensure that our country remains free and strong and that its concept of government under law is maintained and expanded throughout the world.*

TAYLOR, RICHARD WILLIAM, investment banker, securities broker; b. Toledo, Sept. 16, 1926; s. Everett Ellsworth and Hazel (Broer) T.; m. Lyn Westerlund, Sept. 11, 1954; children: Julie Everett, Richard William, Alison Nichols, Jennifer Broer, Liane Westerlund. BS, U.S. Naval Acad., 1949; postgrad., U. Calif., 1952. Mem. Ohio Ho. of Reps. (100th gen. assembly from

9th Dist.); asst. mgr. Navy sales Martin Aircraft, Balt., 1953-56; with McKinsey & Co. (mgmt. cons.), N.Y.C., 1956-60; asst. to v.p. Cerro Corp., N.Y.C., 1960-62, spl. asst. to pres., 1965; pres. Cerro Aluminum Co., N.Y.C., 1962-65; successively v.p., exec. v.p., pres. and CEO Carter, Walker & Co., Inc., 1967-69; pres., CEO Burton, Dana, Westerlund, Inc., N.Y.C., 1969—; v.p. Sterling, Grace & Co., Inc., 1971-74, sr. v.p. corp. fin., 1980-81; v.p. corp. fin. Moseley, Hallgarten, Estabrook & Weeden Inc., 1975-80; v.p. Kidder, Peabody & Co. Inc., 1981-93; dir. investments, pvt. client divsn. Oppenheimer & Co., 1993—. Bd. dirs., pres., chmn. fin. com. YWCA Retirement Fund, Inc. With USN, 1944-52. Decorated Air medal, Navy Commendation medal. Mem. U.S. Naval Acad. Alumni Assn., U.S. Naval Inst. Home: Apt D 132 Heritage Hill Rd New Canaan CT 06840-4631 Office: Oppenheimer & Co Inc 200 Park Ave New York NY 10166 Office Phone: 212-667-4022. E-mail: richard.taylor@opco.com.

TAYLOR, RICHARD WIRTH, political science educator; b. Cleve., Jan. 15, 1923; s. Robert and Irmgard (Wirth) T.; m. Sadie White, Sept. 19, 1946; children: Peter, Karla, Mark, Stephen. BA, U. Ill., 1947, MA, 1948, PhD, 1950. Instr. polit. sci. U. Minn., Mpls., 1950-52; asst. prof. polit. sci. Lehigh U., Bethlehem, Pa., 1952-55, Wis. State U., Stevens Point, 1955-56; vis. asst. prof. Northwestern U., Evanston, Ill., 1956-57; assoc. prof. Coe Coll., Cedar Rapids, Iowa, 1957-60, chmn., prof., 1960-67; prof. polit. sci. Kent State U., Ohio, 1967-92, prof. emeritus, 1992—, chmn., 1974-82. Vis. prof. Karl-Marx-Universität, Leipzig, Fed. Republic Germany, 1990. Co-exec. editor Peace and Change, 1986-87. Policy com. Friends Com. Nat. Legis., Washington, 1964-85, exec. com., 1986-87; acad. adv. com., ombudsman com. Internat. Bar Assn., Edmonton Alta., Can., 1980—; active Friends World Com. on Consultation, 1991-98, Am. Friends Svc. Com., 2000—, clk. Lake Erie Yearly Meeting, 1977-79. Home: 115 Kendal Dr Oberlin OH 44074-1905

TAYLOR, ROBERT BROWN, medical educator, physician, writer; b. Elmira, N.Y., May 31, 1936; s. Olaf C. Taylor and Elizabeth (Place) Brown; m. Anita Dopico; children: Diana Taylor Root, Sharon Taylor Oliverio. Student, Bucknell U., 1954-57; MD, Temple U., 1961. Diplomate Am. Bd. Family Practice. Gen. practice medicine, New Paltz, N.Y., 1964-78; faculty physician Sch. Medicine Wake Forest U., Winston-Salem, N.C., 1978-84; prof. dept. family medicine Oreg. Health Scis. U. Sch. Medicine, Portland, 1984—, chmn., 1984-98. Mem. comprehensive part II com. Nat. Bd. Med. Examiners, Phila., 1986-91. Author: Common Problems in Office Practice, 1972, The Practical Art of Medicine, 1974; editor: Family Medicine: Principles and Practice, 1978, 6th edit., 2003, Health Promotion: Principles and Clinical Applications, 1982, Difficult Diagnosis, 1985, Difficult Medical Management, 1991, Difficult Diagnosis II, 1992, Fundamentals of Family Medicine, 1996, 3rd edit, 2003, Manual of Family Practice, 1997, 2d edit., 2002, Taylor's Review of Family Medicine, 1998, Manual of Ten-Minute Diagnosis, 2000, The Clinician's Guide to Medical Writing, 2004; contbg. editor Physicians Mgmt. Mag., 1972-99; editl. bd. The Family Practice Rsch. Jour., 1980-90, The Female Patient, 1984—, Am. Family Physician, 1990-98, Jour. of Family Practice, 1990-93, Med. Tribune, 1993-99. Served as surgeon USPHS, 1961-64. Fellow Am. Acad. Family Physicians (sci. program com., Thomas Johnson award, bd. curators found. archives, John G. Walsh Lifetime Achievement award), Am. Coll. Preventive Medicine; mem. Soc. Tchrs. Family Medicine (bd. dirs., cert. of excellence), Assn. Am. Med. Colls., Am. Assn. for Study Headache, World Orgn. Family Doctors (chmn. sci. program com.), Portland City Club, Multnomah Athletic Club, Phi Beta Kappa, Alpha Omega Alpha. Home: 1414 SW 3rd Ave Apt 2904 Portland OR 97201-6629 Office: Oreg Health Sci U Sch Medicine Mail Code FM 3181 SW Sam Jackson Park Rd Portland OR 97239-3098

TAYLOR, ROBERT EDWARD, foreign language educator; b. Portland, Oreg., Nov. 22, 1919; s. Dolph J. and Lula May (Nicholas) T.; m. Naomi Ellen Klatt, Feb. 13, 1943 (div. 1962); 1 child, Thomas Robert; m. Olga Zazuliak, May 19, 1962; 1 child, Anne-Marie. BA, Reed Coll., 1943; MA, Columbia U., 1947, PhD, 1951. Instr. french Columbia Univ., N.Y.C., 1947-50; instr. to prof. french NYU, N.Y.C., 1950-62, prof. french, 1962-63; prof. French U. Mass., Amherst, 1963-90, dept. head, 1963-70, prof. emeritus, 1990—. Seminar assoc. Columbia Univ., 1959-80; chair Nat. Fulbrigt Com. for France, N.Y.C., 1963-65; dir. programs in France, Univ. Mass., 1971, 1990-91, 1997-98. Cons. editor Merriam-Webster's 3rd Internat. Dictionary, 1961; contbg. editor: Bibliographie Internat. de l'Humanisme et de la Renaissance; contbr. articles to Renaissance Soc. of Am., Modern Lang. Assn. 1st lt. USAAF, 1942-46. Decorated Chevalier dans l'Ordre des Palmes Académiques. Mem. Am. Assn. Tchrs. French, Assn. des Prof. de Lang. Modernes. Avocations: music, theater. Home: 154 Lincoln Ave Amherst MA 01002-2011

TAYLOR, ROBERT HOMER, quality assurance professional, pilot; b. Rochester, N.Y., Mar. 18, 1922; s. C. Gilbert and Josephine Mary (Woodward) T.; m. Mignon Jane Beight, Aug. 1945; children: Robert Jr., Douglas Beight, Scott Woodward, Sondra Lee. BSME, Case Western Res. U., 1947. Commd. 2d lt. USAF, 1944, advanced through grades to lt. col., 1975; v.p., gen. mgr. Taylor Corp., 1947-53; mgr. quality assurance Spectra Physics Laserplane, Dayton, Ohio, 1976-89; pres., gen. mgr. CON-AV Corp., Tipp City, Ohio, 1989—, pres., sec., 1990—. Chief quality assurance staff on NASA Mercury Booster for USAF, Cape Canaveral, Fla., 1961-63; mgr. nuc. tng. weapons devel. USAF Weapons Lab., 1964-67; CAT I test mgr. F-111, 1967-68; instr. pilot C-7, tng. officer, Vietnam, 1969; project element monitor T-43, attache, A-37, C-130 aircraft, Pentagon, 1970-74; br. chief WPAFB, 1974-75. Advisor Aero Scis. Alternatives, Tipp City, 1990—. Lt. col. CAP, Vietnam. Decorated Air medal with three oak leaf clusters, DFC; named to Aviation Hall of Fame, 1986. Mem. VFW, Exptl. Aircraft Assn., Flying Angels, Inc. (pres. 1991), Vets. Am., Masons, Beta Theta Pi (Case chpt. pres. 1942), Theta Tau, Early Birds. Episcopalian. Avocations: boating, flying, fishing, refurbishing antique aircraft. Office: CON-AV Corp 5855 Us Route 40 Tipp City OH 45371-9419 Home: 809 N Medway Carlisle Rd New Carlisle OH 45344-8223

TAYLOR, ROBERT LARRY, author, freelance writer; b. Abilene, Tex., July 22, 1940; s. Larry Thornton and Virginia (Kerby) T.; life ptnr. Theodore Thomas Nowick, June 22, 1975. BA in Journalism, Tex. Tech U., 1962. Editor NHSC Newsletter, Nat. Home Study Coun., Washington, 1968-72; asst. editor Music Educators Jour., Music Educators Nat. Conf., Washington, 1972-76; editor Transp. USA mag. U.S. Dept. Transp., Washington, 1976-80; dep. text editor Am. Illustrated mag. USIA, Washington, 1980-86; freelance writer and author, 1986—. Author: (novels) The Innocent, 1997, All We Have Is Now, 2002, Whose Eye Is On Which Sparrow?, 2004, (short stories) Revelation and Other Stories, 2002; contbg. author: Gay Pride: Photographs from Stonewall to Today, 1994; contbg. author I Do / I Don't: Queers on Marriage, 2004; contbr. short stories to publs. Mem. nat. coun. Am. Speaks Out, 2001—; trustee Pierre Monteux Meml. Found., treas., 1994—97, exec. com., 1997—2002, v.p., 2002—; bd. dirs. Down East AIDS Network, 2003—04. With U.S. Army, 1962—67. Decorated Bronze Star; recipient Blue Pencil award as 1st place for best mag. Nat. Assn. Govt. Communicators, 1980, Outstanding Alumnus award Tex. Tech U. Sch. Mass Comm., 1986. Mem.: Authors Guild. Democrat. Avocations: singing, making handmade books. Home: Kendal at Oberlin Oberlin OH 44074 E-mail: kailuum@oberlin.net.

TAYLOR, ROBERT LEWIS, management educator; b. Pitts., Dec. 10, 1939; s. Robert William and Elinor (Miller) T.; m. Linda Taylor Shapiro, Oct. 28, 1988; 1 child, Kara; children by previous marriage: Rob, Mike. AB in Am. Studies, cum laude, Allegheny Coll., 1961; MBA, Ohio State U., 1966; D in Bus. Adminstrn., Mgmt., Ind. U., 1972. Asst. prof., dir. rsch. USAF Acad., Colorado Springs, Colo., 1971-77, assoc. prof., dir. instrn. dept. econ., geography, mgmt., 1977-79, prof. mgmt., head dept. econs., geography, mgmt., 1980-81; assoc. dean Coll. Letters and Sci., head div. Bus. and Econs., Carl N. Jacobs Prof. of Bus. U. Wis., Stevens Point, 1981-84; dean Coll. Bus. Pub. Adminstrn. U. Louisville, 1984—2003, dean emeritus and prof. of mgmt., 2003—. Chmn. bd. dirs. Ky. Wood Floors, Louisville, 1988-98; bd. advisors Rawlings Co., Louisville; bd. dirs. Logan Aluminum, AACSB: Internat., St. Louis, chmn. 1999-2000, Stock Yards Bancorp, 2003—; cons., advisor Kellogg Nat. Fellowship program Kellogg Found., Battle Creek, Mich., 1985-89. Co-editor: Contemporary Issues in Leadership, 1984, 5th edit., 2001, Leadership Challenges for Today's Manager, 1988, Military Leadership: In Pursuit of Excellence, 4th edit., 2000; contbr. articles to profl. jours. Chmn. Mayor's Strategic Planning Group, Louisville, 1986—; mem. Gov.'s Econ. Devel. Com., Frankfort, Ky., 1987-89, exec. com. Bus. Advs., 1988-92, task force on econ. devel. Ky. Legis. Rsch. Coun., 1991, Leadership Louisville, 1986, Leadership Ky., 1987; bd. trustees Jewish Hosp. Healthcare Svcs., Louisville, 2000—. Mem. Acad. Mgmt. (proceedings editor 1976-77, newsletter editor 1983-86), Louisville C. of C. (bd. dirs., exec. com 1990-94), Sigma Xi, Beta Gamma Sigma, Pi Gamma Mu. Mem. Eastern Orthodox Ch. Avocations: travel, walking, stamp collecting/philately, reading. Home: 1516 Sylvan Way Louisville KY 40205-2408 Office: U Louisville Coll Bus & Pub Adminstrn Louisville KY 40292-0001 Office Phone: 502-852-4786. Business E-Mail: rltayl01e@wise.louisville.edu.

TAYLOR, ROBERT M, minister; b. Englewood, N.J., Mar. 5, 1932; s. Robert M. and Irene Maude T.; m. Anna Elizabeth Taylor, Dec. 27, 1953 (dec. Sept. 1970); m. Beverly Ann Taylor, Nov. 7, 1971; children: Robert M., William Harrison, Joanne Elizabeth, Susan Ruth. BA cum laude, Lafayette Coll., 1953; MDiv, Princeton Seminary, 1956. Ordained min. Presbyn. Ch., 1956. Pastor Mahoning Presbyn. Ch., Danville, Pa., 1956-59; asst. pastor Harundale Presbyn. Ch., Glen Burnie, Md., 1959-62; pastor Cen. Presbyn. Ch., Downingtown, Pa., 1962-69; sr. pastor The Presbyn. Ch., New Brunswick, N.J., 1969-75, Rosedale Gardens Presbyn. Ch., Livonia, Mich., 1975-79, Immanuel Presbyn. Ch., Albuquerque, 1979-85; interim pastor Community Presbyn. Ch., Mountainside, N.J., 1985-86; interim sr. pastor First Presbyn. Ch., Matawan, N.J., 1986-88; pastor Christ Ch. on Quaker Hill, Pawling, N.Y., 1988-94, Hope Presbyn. Ch., Lakewood, N.J., 1994-97; retired, 1997. Commr. Gen. Assembly/Presbyn. Ch., Mpls., 1968; supt. Princeton Sem. Tchg. Ch., New Brunswick, N.J., 1969-75; v.p. Inter-Ch. Coalition on Mission in Southwest, Phoenix, 1984; mem. Monmouth Presbytery, 1994—; mem. ethics com. Harlem Valley Psychiat. Ctr.; mem. Interfaith Clergy Coun.; bd. dirs., v.p. Cmty. Resource Ctr. Pawling, 1988-94. Mem. bd. govs. United Fund, Downingtown, 1969, Citizen's Adv. Com., 1969, Mayor's Youth Adv. Com., East Brunswick, 1973; sec. Coll. Scholarship Found., 1975. Fellow in Pastoral Leadership Devel., Princeton Theol. Seminary, 1973. Mem. Rotary, Alpha Chi Rho (pres. 1952-53). Home: 1500 Bishop Estates Rd Villa 13B Jacksonville FL 32259 *Life is a marvelous journey of caring and sharing with continual opportunities for growth. The challenge is to remain open to God's leading, even when the necessary hurdles are many.*

TAYLOR, ROBERT MORGAN, electronics executive; b. Orange, N.J., May 13, 1941; s. Morgan H. M. Taylor and Grace Anna (Bonynge) Loding; m. Sandra Ruth Cox, Sept. 11, 1965; children: Scott Joseph, Karen Lynne. BA in Chemistry, Williams Coll., 1963; PhD in Chemistry, Pa. State U., 1968; MBA, Drexel U., 1973. Scientist Leeds & Northrup Co., North Wales, Pa., 1968-70, sr. scientist, 1970-72, prin. scientist, 1972-84, corp. scientist, 1984-85, dir. R&D, 1985-92, dir. analytical mktg., 1990-93; v.p. The Capital Controls Group, Colmar, Pa., 1993-99; pres. RMT Cons., Lansdale, Pa., 1999—. Contbr. articles to profl. jours. Chmn. indsl. com. Montgomery County (Pa.) Sci. Rsch. Competition, 1987-99. Mem. IEEE, Electrochem. Soc. (fin. com. 1971-73, controlling mems. com. 1977), Am. Chem. Soc., Instrument Soc. Am. (sr.), Indsl. Rsch. Inst. (rep.). Achievements include patents for for water analysis (5). Personal E-mail: rmtconsulting@comcast.net.

TAYLOR, ROBERT P. lawyer; b. Douglas, Ariz., May 6, 1939; s. Paul Burton and Mary Ruth (Hart) T.; m. Sybil Ann Cappelletti, May 30, 1963 (div. Apr. 1974); children: David Scott, Nicole; m. Anne Dale Kaiser, Sept. 21, 1991. BSEE, U. Ariz., 1961; JD, Georgetown U., 1969. Bar: U.S. Ct. Appeals (9th circ.) 1969, U.S. Ct. Appeals (1st, 2d, 3d, 6th, and Fed. circs.), U.S. Supreme Ct., 1975. Elec. engr. Motorola Corp., Phoenix, 1961, Bell & Howell, Pasadena, Calif., 1964-65; examiner U.S. Patent Office, Washington, 1966-69; atty. Pillsbury Madison & Sutro, San Francisco, 1969-96, Howrey, Simon, Arnold & White, LLP, Menlo Park, Calif., 1996—. Mem. adv. commn. Patent Law Reform, Washington, 1990-92; mem. adv. bd. Litigation Risk Analysis, Palo Alto, Calif., 1985—. Contbr. articles to profl. jours. Dir. Ind. Colls. of No. Calif., San Francisco, 1982-96, officer, 1988-96. Fellow Am. Coll. Trial Lawyers; mem. ABA (chair sect. antitrust 1991-92), Am. Law Inst. Avocations: bicycling, cooking, hiking. Office: Howrey Simon Arnold & White LLP 301 Ravenswood Ave Menlo Park CA 94025-3434

TAYLOR, ROBERT WILSON, military officer, publishing executive; b. Cambridge, Mass., Sept. 7, 1926; s. Walter Denzelo and Lucy Goudie Taylor; m. Shirley Hosmer, Apr. 3, 1948; children: Tobey Lee, David Alan, Stephen Hosmer. AA in Polit. Sci., Syracuse U., 1959. With U.S. Army and USAF, 1945; advanced through grades to Sgt. Maj. USAF, 1965; asst. v.p. Skaneateles (NY) Savs. Bank, 1965—78; land and residential appraiser Pomeroy Appraisal Assoc., Syracuse, NY, 1978—88; co-owner Family Rm. Miniatures, Skaneateles, 1980—95; owner Romance Lives Publ. Co., Marcellus, NY, 2004—. Pres. consortium of NY savs. banks NY State Savs. Banks Study Group, NYC, 1977—78; instr. Syracuse U. Coll. Liberal Arts, 1954—59. Author: The Secret Life of William Roberts. Fund originator, bd. mgmt. United Ch. of Change Islands, Newfoundland, 2000—; charter pres. Kiwanis Club Western Onondaga County, Skaneateles, 1974—77. Mem.: Small Publishers Assn. N.Am., Syracuse U. Alumni Club Ctrl. NY, Am. Legion. Republican. Presbyterian. Avocations: writing, gardening, literature. Home: 2474 Roman Ave Marcellus NY 13108 Office: Romance Lives Publ Co PO Box 134 Marcellus NY 13108 Office Phone: 315-673-0788. Office Fax: 315-673-0788. Personal E-mail: bobtaylor@mailstation.com.

TAYLOR, ROGER DALE, lawyer; b. Booneville, Ark., Apr. 6, 1950; s. Carl Edward and Amanda (Wilkins) T.; m. Elizabeth Payne, Feb. 20, 1988; children: Zachary, Grace, Greta, Wilkins. BSEE, U. Ark., 1972; JD with honors, George Washington U., 1980. Bar: D.C. 1980, Tex., 1981, Ga., 1996. Assoc. Vinson & Elkins, Houston, 1981-83, Busby, Rehm & Leonard, Washington, 1983-85, Finnegan, Henderson, Washington, 1985-90, ptnr. Tokyo, 1990-92, Washington, 1992-96, Atlanta, 1997—, Alston & Bird, Atlanta, 1996-97. Adj. prof. Law Sch. Cath. U. Am., Washington, 1992-95. Mem. Am. Intellectual Property Assn., Atlanta Soc. Clubs, Licensing Execs. Soc. (chmn. Japan com. 1994—), World Trade Ctr. Atlanta, Order of the Coif, Tau Beta Phi, Etta Kappa Nu. Office: Finnegan Henderson 3200 Suntrust Plz 303 Peachtree St NE Atlanta GA 30308-3201 Home: 552 Wood Valley Dr SW Marietta GA 30064-3359

TAYLOR, ROGER LEE, academic administrator, lawyer; b. Canton, Ill., Apr. 6, 1941; s. Ivan and Pauline Helen (Mahr) T.; m. E. Anne Zweifel, June 13, 1964. BA, Knox Coll., 1963; JD cum laude, Northwestern U., 1971. Bar: Ill. 1971, U.S. Dist. Ct. (no. dist.) Ill. 1971, U.S. Dist. Ct. (no. dist.) Tex. 1975, U.S. Ct. Appeals (7th cir.) 1972, U.S. Ct. Appeals (5th and 11th cirs.) 1981, U.S. Supreme Ct. 1975. Assoc. Kirkland & Ellis, Chgo., 1971-78, ptnr., 1978—; pres. Knox Coll., Galesburg, Ill., 2002—. Trustee Knox Coll., interim pres. 2002; trustee Ill. Hist. Preservation Agy., dir. Assoc. Coll. of Midwest, dir. Assoc. Coll. of Ill. Mem. Friends of the Parks (bd. dirs.), Order of Coif, Univ. Club, Soangetaha Country Club (Galesburg, Ill.). Office: Knox College Galesburg IL 61401

TAYLOR, RONALD CHARLES, retired meteorologist; b. Port Huron, Mich., Nov. 28, 1932; BA, U. Calif., 1959; PhD in Meteorology, U. Hawaii, 1968. Asst. prof. meterology St. Louis U., 1968-69, U. Hawaii, 1969-74, SUNY, Brockport, 1975; assoc. prof. meteorology Inst. Fluid Dynamics U. Md., 1975-76; program dir. meteorology NSF, Arlington, Va., 1976-97; meteorologist U.S. Weather Bur. at Little America IV, Antarctica, during IGY, 1956—58. Recipient Cleveland Abbe Disting. Svc. to Atmospheric Scis. award Am. Meteorol. Soc., 1996. Mem. Am. Geophys. Union, Am. Meteorology Soc.

TAYLOR, RONALD LEE, academic administrator; b. Urbana, Ill., Nov. 11, 1943; s. Lee R. and Katherine L. (Becker) Taylor; m. Patricia D. Fitzimmons, Mar. 10, 1973; children: Jamie, Lara, Meredith, Dana. AB, Harvard U., 1966; MBA, Stanford U., 1971. Asst. contr. Bell & Howell, Chgo., 1971-73; pres., co-CEO DeVry Inc., Chgo., 1973—2004, CEO, 2004—. Bd. dirs. La Petite Acad., Inc.; trustee Higher Learning Commn., North Ctrl. Assn. Colls. and Schs., 2003—. Com. chmn. Ill. Bd. Higher Edn., Springfield, 1985—; mem. mgmt. bd. Stanford U. Sch. Bus. Office: DeVry Inc 1 Tower Ln Ste 1000 Hinsdale IL 60181-4663 Business E-Mail: rtaylor@devry.com.

TAYLOR, RONALD LOUIS, lawyer; b. Memphis, July 18, 1942; s. George Festus and Ina Dell (Sanderson) T.; m. Elsa Juanita Parker, Dec. 28, 1969; children: Anna-Kathryn, Benjamin Louis. BA magna cum laude, Miss. State U., 1964; JD, U. Miss., 1970. Bar: Miss. 1970, U.S. Ct. Appeals (5th cir.) 1976, U.S. Supreme Ct. 1976. Assoc. B.G. Perry, Southaven, Miss., 1970-71; ptnr. Perry & Taylor, Southaven, 1971-73, Perry, Taylor & Whitwell, Southaven, 1973-75, Taylor & Whitwell, Southaven, 1976-85, Taylor, Jones, Alexander, Seale & Ryan, Ltd., Southaven, 1985-89, Taylor, Jones Alexander & Sorrell Ltd., Southaven, 1991 2003, Taylor, Jones & Alexander Ltd., Southaven, 2003—. Mcpl. judge City of Horn Lake, Miss., 1975-77; city atty. City of Southaven, 1982—. Vice chmn. Southaven Libr. Bd., 1973-76. Lt. col. USAR, 1964-2002. Fellow Miss. Bar Found.; mem. ATLA, Miss. Trial Lawyers (bd. govs. 1980), DeSoto County Bar Assn. (pres. 1978, 86), Exch. Club (pres. 1973), Lions, Masons (32d degree), Shriner (Al Chymia Shrine Temple), Rotary (chmn. Southhaven Spring Fest). Republican. Baptist. Home: 5872 Rolling Hill Dr Olive Branch MS 38654-9583 Office: Taylor Jones & Alexander Ltd PO Box 188 961 Main St Southaven MS 38671-0188 Office Phone: 662-342-1300.

TAYLOR, ROSEMARY, artist; b. Joseph, Oreg. d. Theodore and Sarah A. (Lambright) Resch; m. Robert Hull Taylor; children: Barbara Taylor Ryalls, Robert H. Student, Clevc. Inst. Art, 1937-40, NYU, 1947. Tchr. pottery Rahway (N.J.) Art Ctr., 1950-55. Pottery cons. McCalls Mag., 1962-72. One woman shows include Paterson (N.J.) Coll., 1964, Westchester (Pa.) Coll., 1970, Gallery 100, Princeton, N.J., 1967, George Jensen's, N.Y.C., 1972, Artisan Gallery, Princeton, 1974, Am. Crafts (Ohio), 1979-99, Guild Gallery, 1986-91, Little Art Gallery, N.C., 1985-99, Olde Queens Gallery (N.J.), 1987, N.J. Designer Craftsmen, 1990, 97, 98, 99 (bd. dirs. 1986-87, std. chmn. 1994), Creative Hands, 1995, 97, 98, 99, Princeton, 1994; group shows include Mus. Natural History, N.Y.C., Newark Mus., Trenton (N.J.) Mus., Montclair (N.J.) Mus., Phila. Art Alliance, Pa. Horticulture Soc., 1988, Nat. Design Center, N.Y.C., Michener Mus., Pa., 1996; represented in permanent collection Westchester Coll. Bd. dirs. Solebury Cmty. Sch.; mem. Fulbright award com., 1982, 83. Mem. LWV (pres. Plainfield, N.J. chpt.), Am. Craft Coun., N.J. Designer-Craftsmen, Phila. Craft Group, Bucks County (Pa.) C. of C., Visual Artists and Galleries Assn., Nat. Assn. Am. Penwoman, Michener Mus., Doylestown, Pa., Women in the Arts (charter). Democrat. Unitarian Universalist. Home: 10 Ingham Way New Hope PA 18938 Office: PO Box 282 Stockton NJ 08559-0282 E-mail: romy282@nni.com.

TAYLOR, ROSLYN DONNY, family physician; b. Columbia, S.C., Feb. 14, 1941; d. Otto G. and Roslyn Elizabeth (Alfriend) Donny; divorced; children: Cynthia Gambill Taylor Veal, Kevin Emory. BA, Emory U., 1963, MD, 1967. Diplomate Am. Bd. Family Practice. Rotating intern Jacksonville (Fla). Naval Regional Med. Ctr., 1967-68; pvt. practice, Green Cove Springs, Fla., 1968-70; resident in family practice Spartanburg (S.C.) Regional Med. Ctr., 1974-76; pvt. practice, Imman, S.C., 1976-78; staff physician student health svc. U. S.C., Columbia, 1978-82, mem. faculty dept. family medicine, 1979-87, med. dir. Woodrow Intermediate Care Facility, 1983-86; attending physician Pain Therapy Ctr., Richland Meml. Hosp., Columbia, 1986—87; vis. prof. dept. family and preventive medicine U. Utah, Salt Lake City, 1987-88, dir. family practice residency, 1988-94; assoc. dir. family practice residency Meml. Med. Ctr., Savannah, Ga., 1994—2001; interim program dir., chair dept. family medicine Mercer U. Sch. Medicine, Savannah, 2002; assoc. dir. family practice residency Meml. Health U. Med. Ctr., Savannah, 2002—. Contbg. author: Saunders Manual of Medical Practicd, 1996, 98, The Primary Care Patient's Teaching Guide, 1998; mem. editl. bd. Family Practice News, 1990—; also articles. Vol. physician Homeless Shelter Clinic, Salt Lake City, 1990-94; chmn. rural physician loan assistance program com. State of Utah, 1990-94; mem. Chatham County Bd. Health, Savannah, 1998—. Lt. comdr. M.C., USNR, 1967-73. Named Physician of Yr., Columbia Mayor's Com. on Employment Handicapped, 1984, Outstanding Clin. Faculty in Family Medicine, Mercer U. Sch. Medicine, 1998. Fellow Am. Acad. Family Physicians (editl. bd. Home Study and Self Assessment program 1994-96, congress del., credentials com. 2004); mem. AMA, Soc. Tchrs. Family Medicine, Ga. Med. Soc., Ga. Acad. Family Physicians, Med. Assn. Ga., Phi Beta Kappa, Alpha Omega Alpha. Presbyterian. Avocations: photography, reading, beach combing. Office: Meml Med Ctr Family Practice 1107 E 66th St Savannah GA 31404-5701

TAYLOR, ROY LEWIS, botanist, educator; b. Olds, Alta., Can., Apr. 12, 1932; s. Martin Gilbert and Crystal (Thomas) T. B.Sc., Sir George Williams U., Montreal, Que., Can., 1957; PhD, U. Calif. at Berkeley, 1962; DSc (hon.), U. B.C., Vancouver, Can., 1997. Pub. sch. tchr. Olds Sch. Div., 1949-52; jr. high sch. tchr. Calgary Sch. Bd., Alta., 1953-55; chief taxonomy sect., research br. Can. Agrl. Dept., Ottawa, Ont., 1962-68; dir. Bot. Garden, prof. botany, prof. plant scis. U. B.C., Vancouver, 1968-85; pres., CEO Chgo. Hort. Soc., 1985-94; dir. Chgo. Bot. Garden, Glencoe, Ill., 1985-94; exec. dir. Rancho Santa Ana Bot. Garden, Claremont, Calif., 1994-99; prof. botany, chmn. botany program Claremont Grad. U., 1994-99, dir. emeritus, 1999. Pres. Western Bot. Svcs. Ltd. Author: The Evolution of Canada's Flora, 1966, Flora of the Queen Charlotte Islands, Vols. I and II, 1968, Vascular Plants of British Columbia: A Descriptive Resource Inventory, 1977; The Rare Plants of British Columbia, 1985; assoc. editor Pacific Horticulture, 2001—. Mem. State of Ill. Bd. Natural Resources and Conservation, 1987-94; trustee Nature Ill. Found., 1990-94, Elisabeth C. Miller Bot. Garden Trust, Seattle, 1994—, Elisabeth C. Miller Bot. Garden Endowment, 2001—, The Arbor Fund, Seattle, 1997—, chmn., 2002—; bd. dirs. Milner Gardens and Woodland Soc., Qualicum Beach, B.C., Can., 2000—, chmn., 2002—. Fellow Linnean Soc. London (hon.); mem. Can. Bot. Assn. (pres. 1967-68), Biol. Coun. Can. (pres. 1973-74), Am. Assn. Mus. (accreditation com. 1980-85, chmn. 1985-91, chmn. ethics commn. 1991-93), Am. Assn. Bot. Gardens and Arboreta (hon. life; pres. 1976, 77, award of merit 1987), Am. Soc. Bot. Artists (bd. dirs. 1997—), Claremont C. of C. (bd. dirs. 1995-98), Ottawa Valley Curling Assn. (pres. 1968-69), Miner Gardens and Woodland Soc. (bd. dirs. 2000—, chmn. 2002—), B.C. Soc. Landscape Archs. (hon.), U. B.C. Bot. Garden (hon.), Chgo. Hort Soc. (life, medal 1994), Gov. Gen.'s Curling Club Can. (life). E-mail: taylor.rl@shaw.ca.

TAYLOR, RUSSELL BENTON, mining executive; b. Eskridge, Kans., May 16, 1925; s. Bayard Charles and Eva May (Russell) T.; m. Arlene Marie Krehbiel, Aug. 14, 1959; 1 child, Bruce Charles. BSBA, U. Kans., 1949; JD, U. Kans, 1951. Asst. cashier Eskridge (Kans.) State Bank, 1951-57, cashier, 1957, pres., 1958-69, chmn., 1969-78; v.p., dir South Standard Mining Co., Salt Lake City, 1978-96. Mayor City of Eskridge, Kans., 1959. Decorated Purple Heart. Mem. Kans. Bar Assn., Kiwanis, Masonic, Arab Shrine. Republican. Methodist. Avocations: travel, ranching. Home and Office: 18213 Sanford Rd Eskridge KS 66423 E-mail: rbt@kansas.net.

TAYLOR, RUTH ANNE, lawyer; b. Honolulu, Feb. 18, 1961; d. Gerald Lou and Charlotte Anne (Nelson) Allison; m. Thomas Scott Taylor, Dec. 28, 1985; children: Kyle Thomas, Kelly Gerald, Kory Scott. BA in Journalism, U. So. Calif., 1984; JD, N.Y. Law Sch., 1987. Bar: Calif. 1987, U.S. Dist. Ct. (so. dist.) Calif., U.S. Ct. Appeals (9th cir.). Assoc. Carlsmith, Wichman, Case Mukai & Ichiki, L.A., L.A., 1987-89, Christensen, White, Miller, Fink & Jacobs, L.A., 1989-93; assoc. gen. counsel Warner Bros. Records, Inc., 1993-98, v.p. legal and bus. affairs, 1998—. Mem. Los Angeles County Bar Assn., Beverly Hills Bar Assn. Republican. Avocations: scuba diving, skiing, photography, cooking.

TAYLOR, RUTH ARLEEN LESHER, marketing educator; b. Riverton, Iowa, Mar. 7, 1941; d. Clyde Almond and Bernice Emogene (Graves) Lesher; m. Leslie (Milburn) Taylor, Aug. 10, 1963; children: Treg Anthony, John Leslie II. BS in Home Econs. Edn. magna cum laude, U. Houston, 1975; MEd, Tex. Christian U., 1977; PhD, U. N. Tex., 1981. Prof. mktg. Tarrant County C.C., Ft. Worth, 1977-78, North Tex. State U., Denton, 1978-81, Southwestern U., Georgetown, Tex., 1982-87, S.W. Tex. State U., San Marcos, 1981-82,

87—. Dir. travel to China, Japan, Hong Kong, Costa Rica, Morocco, Europe, Eng., Mex., Dominican Republic, Venezuela, Chile, Peru; faculty intern Tex. Dept. Econ. Devel. and Tex. Sec. of State Office; collaborator STAT-USA and Internat. Catalog Exhbn. U.S. Dept. Commerce. Author: Text Maps Study Guides, 1994—; contbg. author: The Psychology of Fashion, 1985, Ethics in Accounting, 1994; contbr. articles to profl. jours. Mem. Lost Creek Garden Club, Austin, Tex., 1985—, v.p.; vol. Bob Bullock State Hist. Mus. Grantee Merrick Found., 1991. Mem.: DAR, Am. Soc. for Competitiveness, Winthrop Soc., French Huguenot Soc., Colonial Dames, Internat. Hospitality Coun. (bd. dirs.), Mayflower Soc., Mktg. Mgmt. Assn., Western Mktg. Educators Assn., Am. Mktg. Assn., Alpha Mu Alpha, Alpha Kappa Psi, Phi Delta Kappa, Phi Epsilon Omicron, Beta Gamma Sigma. Avocations: travel, gardening, reading, entertaining. Office: Texas State University 601 University Dr San Marcos TX 78666-4685

TAYLOR, SANDRA E. public relations executive; BA in French, JD, Boston U.; grad., Colo. Women's Coll. Atty., Colo., 1975-77; internat. economist overseas and State Dept. U.S. Fgn. Svc., 1978; legis. asst. internat. trade and fin. staff Sen. John H. Chafee, 1984; v.p. pub. affairs govt. rels., media rels., crisis comms., comty. rels. Imperial Chem. Industries PLC Britain, 1988; v.p., dir. comms., pub. affairs fed., state, local, internat. govt. rels. Eastman Kodak Co., Washington, N.Y., 1996. Mem. Meridian Internat. Ctr. (bd, trustees, exec. com.), Martha's Table, Keystone Ctr., Atlantic Coun., Bus.-Govt. Rels. Coun., The Choral Arts Soc., Nat. Coun. UN Assn., U.S. South Africa Bus. Devel. Com., Internat. Women's Forum. Office: Eastman Kodak Co 1250 H St NW Ste 800 Washington DC 20005-5936

TAYLOR, SCOTT, real estate company executive; b. Atlanta; B in Fin., U. Ga. With Holder, 1991—2003; exec. v.p., COO Carter & Assocs., Atlanta, 2003—. Active Atlanta Zoning Rev. Bd., 2002—; chmn. bd. Buckhead YMCA. Avocations: golf, exercise, reading. Office: Carter 1275 Peachtree St NE Atlanta GA 30309*

TAYLOR, SCOTT MAXFIELD, business educator; b. Evanston, Ill., Aug. 13, 1953; s. Brett Maxfield and Gretchen Pauline (Porter) T. Jr. BA, Coe Coll., 1975; M in Mgmt., Northwestern U., 1977; MSc, New Sem., 1985; EdD, U. St. Thomas, 2001. Sales mgr. Daytons, Mpls., 1977-78, asst. buyer, 1978-79; store mgr. Brett's Dept. Store, Mankato, Minn., 1979-80, buyer jr. dept., 1981-83, v.p., 1981-87, divsn. mdse. mgr., 1984-85, gen. mdse. mgr., 1985-89, pres., 1988-92, also bd. dirs.; v.p. sales and mktg. Phenix Biocomposites, Inc., 1993-95; founder Expanded Awareness Inst., 1985—. Adj. faculty Minn. State U., Mankato, 1996-98, Metro State U., 2004; bd. dirs. New Music Network; prof. small bus. mgmt. South Ctrl. Tech. Coll., 1999—. Bd. dirs. Blue Earth County Hist. Soc., Mankato, 1984-87, Mankato Area Conv. and Vis. Bur., 1986-89, chmn., 1987-88; Presbyn. deacon, 1986-88, moderator, 1987-88. George F. Baker scholar, 1975. Mem. Minn. Assn. Small Bus. Mgmt. Instrs. (pres. 2002-2004), Small Bus. Mgmt. Cons. and Educators Orgn. (pres., 2002—), Nat. Retail Fedn. (bd. dirs. 1991-92), Kiwanis (bd. dirs. 1984-90, pres. 1988-89, named Disting. Club Pres. 1988-89), Rotary, Omicron Delta Epsilon. Avocation: curling. Home: 4528 Casco Ave Edina MN 55424-1125 also: S Ctrl Tech Coll PO Box 608 New Ulm MN 56073 Office Phone: 507-354-5858.

TAYLOR, SHANNON, lawyer, not-for-profit developer; b. Passaic, NJ, June 14, 1955; s. Michael and Rita Taylor; m. Judith Ann Bernz. BA magna cum laude, Tufts U., 1976; attended, Hebrew U. Law, 1977; JD, Temple U., 1979. Bar: NJ 1979, NY 1980, So. Dist. 1980, US Dist. Ct. 1980, Ea. Dist. 1981. Ct. atty. to Hon. David Follender, Supreme Ct.-Civil Term, Hackensack, NJ, 1979—80; assoc. comml. litigation Goetz & Fitzpatrick, NYC, 1981—85; assoc. Nathan Cyperstein & Paul Gerstner, Bklyn., 1985—90; pvt. practice NJ, 1991—92, 1991—92; ct. atty. to Hon. Jerome Hornblass, Supreme Ct.-Criminal Term, NYC, 1993—96, NY State Criminal Ct., 1997—. Exec. dir. Blacks and Jews in Conversation, Inc., NYC, 1993—; pub. rels. and press coord., photographer, chronicler Not Just Blacks and Jews in Conversation, 1994—, stand-up comic, 1998—; adminstrv. law judge NYC Taxi and Limousine Commn., 1997; radio show co-host, NYC, 1983—88; guest news commentator radio and TV news, NYC, 1990—; panelist for TV and radio. Photographer (for TV, newspapers, films, and mag.), contbr. columnist. Prodr., promoter comedy-celebrity workshops fundraiser Not-for-Profit Religious and Health Instn., 1990—; fundraiser Orchestra for Animal Rights, NYC, 2004. Recipient Most Productive Cmty. Assistance Orgn., YWCA, 1999. Mem.: NYC Bar Animal Rights Divsn., NY Jewish Lawyers Guild, NY Players Club. Avocations: ping pong/table tennis, percussionist. Home: 225 W 83rd St 5 L New York NY 10024 Office: NYC Criminal Ct Law Dept 120 Schermerhorn St Brooklyn NY 11201

TAYLOR, SHELLEY E. psychology researcher and educator; b. Mt. Kisco, N.Y., Sept. 10, 1946; d. Charles Fox and Pearl May (Harvey) T.; m. Mervyn Francis Fernandes, May 1, 1972; children: Sara F., Charles F. AB magna cum laude in Psychology, Conn. Coll., 1968; PhD in Social Psychology, Yale U., 1972. Asst. prof. psychology and social rels. Harvard U., Cambridge, Mass., 1972-77, assoc. prof., 1977-79; assoc. prof. psychology UCLA, 1979-81, prof., 1981—. Mem. vis. faculty dept. adminstrv. scis. Yale U., New Haven, 1971-72, vis. Sloane fellow, 1978; mem. basic sociocultural rsch. rev. com. NIH, 1979-83; Katz-Newcomb lectr. U. Mich., 1982; cons. to pub. houses and TV producers. Author: Social Cognition, 1986, 2d edit., 1991, Health Psychology, 1986, 3d edit., 1995, 5th edit., 2002. Positive Illusions: Creative Self-Deception and the Healthy Mind, 1989, The Tending Instinct: How Nurturing is Essential to Who We Are and How We Live, 2002; contbr. numerous articles to sci. publs. Active numerous charitable and fund-raising orgns. including Curtis Sch. PTA and U. So. Calif./Norris Cancer Ctr. Recipient Rsch. Scientist Devel. award NIMH, 1981-86, 86-91, MERIT award, 1987, Donald Campbell award for disting. sci. contbn. to sociology, 1995; numerous rsch. grants in field; Winthrop scholar, 1967; Woodrow Wilson fellow, 1968, NIMH fellow, 1968-72. Fellow APA (Sci. Weekend lectr. 1988, Disting. Sci. award 1980, Outstanding Sci.Contbn. award Divsn. 38, 1994), Brit. Psychol. Soc. (flying fellow), Acad. Behavioral Medicine Rsch., Soc. Psychol. Study Social Issues, Soc. Behavioral Medicine; mem. AAAS, Soc. Exptl. Social Psychology, Western Psychol. Assn. (pres. 1993-94), Inst. Medicine, 2004. Office: UCLA Dept Psychology Franz 4611 Box 951563 Los Angeles CA 90095-1563

TAYLOR, SHERRIL WIGHTMAN, broadcasting company executive; b. Salt Lake City, Jan. 4, 1924; s. Kenneth E. and Florence May (Wightman) T.; m. Josephine Vermillion, May 2, 1970; 1 child by previous marriage, Sarah. Student, U. Utah, 1943-46; BJ, U. Mo., 1947; postgrad., Yale U. Promotion mgr. KSL Radio, Salt Lake City, 1947-51; sales promotion mgr. CBS, Hollywood, Calif., 1951-53, CBS radio sales N.Y.C., 1953-56; dir. sales promotion and advt. CBS Radio, N.Y.C.; also v.p. Radio Advt. Bur., N.Y.C., 1956-58; sr. group head J. Walter Thompson, Chgo., 1958-61; ind. TV producer Kukla, Fran, and Ollie Show, N.Y.C., 1961-64; v.p. Nat. Assn. Broadcasters, Washington, 1964-67, dir., 1969-78; v.p. affiliate relations CBS, 1967-79. Cons. Bonneville Internat. Corp., 1979-85; pres. Taylor Co., 1985-91; vice chmn. Coltrin & Assoc., 1991—; pvt. sector coordinator USIA, Washington, 1982, cons., 1982—; chmn. adv. com. Voice of Am., Washington, 1989—; vis. lectr. Brigham Young U., Provo, Utah, 1980—, Emerson Coll., Boston, Mich. Central U., Southern Vt. Coll.; adv. faculty-industry seminar, 1980, 81; bd. dirs. Am. Communications Inc., Utica-Rome TV Svcs. Inc., 1988—. Author: Radio Programming in Action, 1967. Mem. Carnegie Hall com. for Utah Symphony, Park Avenue Preservation Com.; past trustee The Helene Toolen Inst. Med. Rsch., Bennington, Vt., 1985—; mem. futures com. Bennington Mus., 1985—; bd. dirs. Nautical Ventures Inc., N.Y.C., 1987—; chmn. bd. Cmty. Action Network-N.Y., 2000-01. Recipient Nat. Assn. Broadcasters Ann. Conv. Am. Broadcast Pioneer award, 1998. Mem. So. Calif. Broadcasters Assn. (dir.), Internat. Radio and TV Soc. (v.p., bd. dirs., pres., chmn., bd. dirs. found.), Broadcasters' Found. (dir.), Food and Wine Soc. (N.Y. chpt.), Belleair (Fla.) Country Club, Yale Club of N.Y., Sigma Chi (Significant Sig award 2000). Episcopalian. Home: PO Box 4004 Bennington VT 05201 Office: 1212 Ave of the Americas 10th Fl New York NY 10036

TAYLOR, STEPHEN EMLYN, publishing executive; b. Cambridge, Eng., Apr. 28, 1951; s. Charles Henry and Diana (Burgess) T.; m. M. E. Malone, May 24, 1987; children: Maxwell, Conrad. BA in Psychology, Yale U., 1973. U.S. sales mgr., tech. advisor Snapir Ltd., Conn., 1973-74; mgr., sail designer North Sails, Boston, 1974-80; mgmt. trainee Boston Globe, 1980-82, asst. to bus. mgr., 1980-82, dir. info. svcs., 1982-86, asst. bus. mgr., 1986-88, bus. mgr., 1988-91, v.p., 1991-93, exec. v.p., 1993—; pres. Boston Globe Electronic Pub., 1996—. Bd. dirs. Greater Boston Food Bank, 1991—; mem. corp. Woods Hole (Mass.) Oceanographic Inst., 1993—; mem. U.S. Olympic Yachting Com., 1980-84. Mem. Am. Press Inst. (bd. dirs. 1996—), New Eng. Newspaper Assn. (bd. dirs.), Yale Sailing Assocs. (treas., trustee), Cruising Club Am., N.Y. Yacht Club, New Bedford Yacht Club. Home: 18 Webster Rd Milton MA 02186-5318 Office: Globe Newspaper Co PO Box 2378 Boston MA 02107-2378

TAYLOR, STEPHEN H. state commissioner; m. Gretchen Taylor; 3 children. Grad., U. N.H. Reporter and editor daily newspaper; owner, operator dairy and maple, Meriden Village, N.H.; commr. N.H. Dept. Agr., Markets and Food. Active numerous charitable and civic orgns. Served with U.S. Army. Office: NH Dept Agr Markets and Food PO Box 2042 Concord NH 03302-2042 E-mail: staylor@agr.state.nh.us.

TAYLOR, STEPHEN LLOYD, food toxicologist, educator, food scientist; b. Portland, Oreg., July 19, 1946; s. Lloyd Emerson and Frances Hattie (Hanson) T.; m. Susan Annette Kerns, June 23, 1973; children: Amanda, Andrew. BS in Food Sci. Tech., Oreg. State U., 1968, MS in Food Sci. Tech., 1969; PhD in Biochemistry, U. Calif., Davis, 1973. Research assoc. U. Calif., Davis, 1973-74, research fellow, 1974-75; chief food toxicology Letterman Army Inst., San Francisco, 1975-78; asst. prof. food toxicology U. Wis., Madison, 1978-83, assoc. prof., 1983-87; head dept. food sci. technology, dir. Food Processing Ctr. U. Nebr., Lincoln, 1987—. Cons. in field. Contbr. articles to profl. jours. Fellow: Inst. Food Technologists (divsn. chmn. 1981—82, sect. chmn. 1984—85, exec. com. 1988—91), Nat. Acad. Scis. (bd. food and nutrition), Nat. Inst. Environ. Health Sco.; mem.: Soc. Toxicology, Am. Chem. Soc., Am. Acad. Allergy, Asthma and Immunology. Democrat. Presbyterian. Home: 941 Evergreen Dr Lincoln NE 68510-4131 Office: U Nebr Dept Food Sci Tech Lincoln NE 68583-0919 Office Phone: 402-472-2831. Business E-Mail: staylor2@unl.edu.

TAYLOR, STEVE HENRY, zoologist; b. Inglewood, Calif., Mar. 18, 1947; s. Raymond Marten and Ardath (Metz) T.; 1 child, Michael Travis; m. Sarah Margaret Young, May 14, 1993. BA in Biology, U. Calif.-Irvine, 1969. Animal keeper Los Angeles Zoo, 1972-75, assoc. curator, 1975-76; children's zoo mgr. San Francisco Zoo, 1976-81; zoo dir. Sacramento Zoo, 1981-88; dir. Cleve. Met. Zoo, 1989—. Bd. dirs. Sacramento Soc. Prevention Cruelty to Animals, 1983-87, Sacramento Red Cross, 1988-89, Conv. and Visitor Bur. of Greater Cleve., 1995—2003, Leadership Cleveland Class 1997; mem. admissions com. United Way, 1999. Recipient Robert P. Bergman Impact award Convention & Visitors Bur. Greater Cleve., 2000. Fellow Am. Assn. Zool. Parks and Aquariums (infant care diet advisor 1979, 85, bd. dirs. 1987-93, pres. 1991-92, chmn. pub. edn. com. 1987-89, bd. regents, mgmt. sch., chmn. accreditation com. 1998, 99, Outstanding Svc. award 1979, 85, 88, 89, 91, 95, 98, 99, 2001); mem. Conservation Breeding Specialist Group, World Assn. Zoos and Aquariums, Sierra Club, Audubon Soc. Democrat. Home: 1265 Elmwood Rd Rocky River OH 44116-2236 Office: Cleveland Metroparks Zoo 3900 Wildlife Way Cleveland OH 44109-3132 E-mail: sht@clevelandmetroparks.com.

TAYLOR, STEVEN BRUCE, agriculture company executive; b. Salinas, Calif., Dec. 29, 1954; s. Edward Horton and Joanne (Church) T.; m. Kathryn Hagler, Dec. 17, 1978; children: Meghan Jean, Kyle Hagler, Christian Steven. BA, U. Calif., Berkeley, 1978; MBA, Harvard U., 1985. Pres. Fresh Concepts, San Marino, Calif., 1985-87; mktg. staff Bruce Church, Inc., Salinas, Calif., 1987-91; pres. Fresh Express Retail Mktg., Salinas, 1991-93, Fresh Internat., Salinas, 1991-93; CEO, chmn. Fresh Express Fresh Foods (formerly Fresh Internat.), Salinas, 1993—. V.p. Salinas Valley Lettuce Co-op, Salinas, 1990—; bd. dirs. Produce for Better Health, Del., 1991—. Bd. Elders First Presbyn. Ch., Salinas, 1989-92, personnel com. 1989-94, bldg. com. 1990—; founding mem. Lincoln Club of Monterey County, Salinas, 1990. Avocations: basketball, skiing, soccer coach, bible study, board games. Home: 515 Santa Paula Dr Salinas CA 93901-1517 Office: Fresh Express Fresh Foods 1020 Merrill St Salinas CA 93901-4409

TAYLOR, STRATTON, state legislator, lawyer; b. Sallisaw, Okla., Jan. 25, 1956; s. Owen and Velma T. AA, Claremore (Okla.) Jr. Coll., 1976; BSE with hons., U. Tulsa, 1978, JD, 1983. Bar: Okla. 1983. State rep. State of Okla., 1978-82, state senator, 1982—; ptnr. Taylor, Burrage, Foster & Singhal, Claremore, 1985—; commr. Uniform Commrs. on State Laws, 1985—; pres. of Okla.Sen., 1995—2002. Chmn. Okla. Senate Jud. com., 1985-88, appropriations chmn., 1988-94; bd. dirs. State Legis. Found., Oklahoma City, 1988—. Acypl Tour of Japan. Mem. Okla. Bar Assn. Democrat. Baptist. Home: PO Box 309 Claremore OK 74018-0309 Office: Oklahoma State Senate 2300 N Lincoln Blvd Oklahoma City OK 73105

TAYLOR, STUART ROSS, geochemist, author; b. Ashburton, New Zealand, Nov. 26, 1925; s. Thomas Stuart and Anne Grace (Lloyd) T.; m. Noel Elvie White, May 21, 1958; children: Susanna, Judith, Helen. BSc, U. New Zealand, 1948, MSc, 1951; PhD, Ind. U., 1954; DSc, Oxford U., 1978. Lectr. U. Oxford, Eng., 1954-58; sr. lectr. U. Cape Town, South Africa, 1958-60; professorial fellow Australian Nat. U., Canberra, 1961-90, vis. fellow, 1990-99, prof. emeritus, 1997; prof. U. Vienna, 1992, 96. Vis. scientist Lunar and Planetary Inst., Houston, 1969-90. Author: Lunar Science: Post-Apollo View, 1975, Planetary Science, 1982, Solar System Evolution, 1992, (with others) Continental Crust, 1985, Destiny or Chance: Our Solar System and Its Place in the Cosmos, 1998, Solar System Evolution, 2d edit., 2001; contbr. more than 220 articles to profl. jours. Recipient Goldschmidt medal Geochem. Soc., 1993, Gilbert award Geol. Soc. Am., 1994, Bucher medal Am. Geophys. Union, 2002; Asteroid 5670 named Rosstaylor, 1997. Fellow Royal Soc. New Zealand (hon.), Australian Acad. Sci., Geol. Soc. London (hon.), Geol. Soc. India (hon.); mem. NAS (fgn. assoc.), Meteoritical Soc. (pres. 1989-90, Leonard medal 1998). Office: Australian Nat U Dept Geology Canberra 0200 Australia E-mail: ross.taylor@anu.edu.au.

TAYLOR, SUSAN SEROTA, biochemistry researcher; b. Racine, Wis., June 20, 1942; d. Rudolph M. and Helen L. (Vohs) S.; m. Palmer William Taylor, July 3, 1965; children: Tasha Katherine, Ashton David, Palmer Andrew. BS, U. Wis., 1964; PhD, Johns Hopkins U., 1968. Postdoctoral fellow MRC Lab. Molecular Biology, Cambridge, England, 1969—71, U. Calif. San Diego, La Jolla, 1971-72, asst. prof. chemistry, 1972-79, assoc. prof., 1979-85, prof. chemistry, biochemistry, 1985—. Investigator Howard Hughes Med. Inst., 1997; mem. adv. coun. GM Cancer Rsch. Found. Recipient Career Devel. award NIH; postdoctoral fellow NIH 1969-72, Fogarty Internat. Fellow NIH, 1981-82. Mem. Am. Chem. Soc., AAAS, NAS, Inst. Medicine, Am.Soc. Biochemistry and Molecular Biology (mem. coun. 1989-92, pres. 1995-96). Office: U Calif San Diego Dept Chemistry D-006 La Jolla CA 92093*

TAYLOR, SUZONNE BERRY STEWART, real estate broker; b. Memphis, Sept. 27, 1926; d. Andrew Cleveland and Sue Hodge (Berry) Stewart; m. Robert Allen Taylor, Sr., June 15, 1946; children: Robert A. Jr., Suzonne Stewart Taylor Davids. Student, Rhodes Coll., 1948, U. S.C., 1969. Cert. residential specialist CRS Coun., 1996; grad. Realtors Inst.; cert. real estate broker; accredited buyer's rep. Am. Bd. Realtors. Sales agt. E. Roy Stone Realtors, Greenville, S.C., 1967-69; real estate broker Aven Assoc. Realtors, Dover, Del., 1970-80, Emerson & Co. Realtors, Dover, 1980—2000; realtor ERA Harrington Realty, 1998—. Active Cresent Music Club, Greenville, 1955, Wildwood Garden Club, Greenville, 1960; mem., costume chmn. Greenville Little Theater, Jr. League Greenville, 1956-66, sustaining mem., 1966—, Jr. League Wilmington, Del., 1999—, dir., 1999. Mem. Nat. Bd. Realtors, Del. Bd. Realtors, Kent County Bd. Realtors, Del. Hist. Soc., Biggs Mus., Alpha Omicron Pi. Republican. Episcopalian. Home: 517 Greenhill Rd Dover DE 19901-3766 Office: Emerson ERA Harrington 1404 Forest Ave Dover DE 19904 E-mail: suetaylor@doverhouses.com.

TAYLOR, TERESA, communications executive; BS, U. Wis., LaCrosse. Joined US West (now Qwest), 1988; exec. v.p. wholesale markets group Qwest Comm. Internat., Inc., 2003—, exec. v.p. products and pricing group, 2000—03. Bd. dirs. Colo. Inst. Tech., Colo. Children's Campaign. Office: Qwest Comm Internat Inc 1801 California St Denver CO 80202

TAYLOR, TERRY R. editor, educator; b. Valley Forge, Pa., Oct. 4, 1952; d. Thomas R. and Anna P. (Bystrek) T. BA in Journalism, Temple U., 1974. Reporter gen. assignments, sch. news Charlotte (N.C.) News, 1974-77; supr., writer AP, Phila., 1977-81, supr., writer sports desk N.Y.C., 1981-85, asst. editor sports, 1985-87, dep. editor sports, 1987-91, asst. chief bur., 1991-92, editor sports, 1992—; asst. editor sports N.Y. Times, 1991. Assoc. in journalism Columbia U., N.Y.C., 1991-95; adv. bd. Honda Awards, 1996—. Recipient John A. Domino Meml. award St. Bonaventure U., 1996, Founder's award Temple U., 1999; inductee Delaware County Sports Hall of Fame, 1998. Roman Catholic. Achievements include first woman sports editor at the AP. Office: AP Sports 50 Rockefeller Plz New York NY 10020-1605

TAYLOR, THEODORE LANGHANS, author; b. Statesville, N.C., June 23, 1921; s. Edward Riley and Elnora Alma (Langhans) T.; m. Gweneth Ann Goodwin, Oct. 25, 1946; children: Mark, Wendy, Michael; m. Flora Gray Schoenleber, Apr. 18, 1981. Student, Fork Union Mil. Acad., 1939-40, U.S. Mcht. Marine Acad., 1942-44. Reporter Portsmouth (Va.) Star, 1941-42, Bluefield (W.Va.) News, 1946-47; sportswriter NBC-Radio, N.Y.C., 1942; asst. dir. pub. relations N.Y. U., 1947-48; dir. pub. relations YMCA Schs. and Colls., N.Y.C., 1948-50; publicist Paramount Pictures, Hollywood, Calif., 1955-56; assoc. producer Perlberg-Seaton Prodns., Hollywood, 1956-61. Free lance writer 1961—; author: The Magnificent Mitscher, 1954, Fire on the Beaches, 1957, People Who Make Movies, 1968, The Cay, 1969 (Jane Addam's Children's Book award 1970), The Children's War, 1971, Air Raid: Pearl Harbor, 1971, The Maldonado Miracle, 1973, Rebellion Town, 1973, Showdown, 1973, Teetoncey, 1974, Teetoncey and Ben O'Neal, 1975, Battle in the Arctic Seas, 1976, The Odyssey of Ben O'Neal, 1977, A Shepherd Watches, A Shepherd Sings, 1977, Jule, 1979, Battle of Midway Island, 1981, The Trouble with Tuck, 1981, Sweet Friday Island, 1981, HMS Hood vs Bismarck, 1982, Battle in the English Channel, 1983, The Cats of Shambala, Rocket Island, 1985, Walking Up a Rainbow, 1986, The Stalker, 1987, The Hostage, 1988, Monocolo, 1989, Sniper, 1989, Tuck Triumphant, 1991, The Wierdo, 1991, Maria, 1992, To Kill the Leopard, 1993, Timothy of the Cay, 1993, The Bomb, 1995, Rogue Wave, 1996, The Flight of Jesse Leroy Brown, 1998, A Sailor Returns, 2000, The Boy Who Could Fly Without A Motor, 2002, Lord of The Kill, 2002, Hello, Artic, 2002, Ice Drift, 2005. Served with USNR, 1945-46, 50-55. Recipient Lewis Carroll Shelf award, 1970, Silver medal Commonwealth Club, 1970, Best Book award So. Calif. Coun. on Children's Lit., 1970, Best Book award U. Calif. at Irvine, 1970, 74, Best Non-Fiction award Western Writers Am., 1977, Young Reader's Medal Calif. Reading Assn., 1984, 92, Edgar Allan Poe award, 1992, Utah Young Adult Book award, 1993, Md. Children's Book award, 1994, Scott O'Dell Best Hist. Fiction award, 1995, The Kerlan Body of Work award, 1997. Mem. Calif. Writers Guild, Acad. Motion Picture Arts and Scis., Screen Writers Guild. Republican. Lutheran. Address: 1856 Catalina Laguna Beach CA 92651-3340

TAYLOR, T(HOMAS) ROGER, educational consultant, educator; b. Urbana, Ill., May 31, 1945; s. Thomas and Ora Wilma Taylor; m. Beverly Milam, Dec. 19, 1981; 1 child, Whitney Brinson. BS, U. Ill., 1967; MA, So. Ill. U., 1972, PhD, 1980. Tchr. Mt. Vernon (Ill.) Schs., 1967-71; cons. Ill. Dept. State, 1971-74; dir. Area Svc. Ctr. for Gifted Children, South Cook County, Ill., 1975-79; prof. urban edn. Govs. State U., 1975-79; cons. Ednl. Cons. Assocs., Denver, 1977-82, also dir. Pres. Curriculum Design for Excellence, Oak Brook, Ill.; former sr. ptnr. T & H Investments, Hinsdale, Ill. V.p. Mt. Vernon C.C. Orch. Named Ky. Col., 1979, Outstanding Young Men of Am., YMCA, 1980, Best of the Best, IDEA Fellows Program, 1992, 93. Mem. NRA, NEA, Ill. Edn. Assn. (bd. dirs.), Nat. Assn. Gifted Children, World Coun. for Gifted, Assn. Childhood Edn. Internat., U. Ill. Alumni Assn. (dir. 1967-71), Profl. Assn. Diving Instrs., Demolay Club, Phi Delta Kappa. Home: 1907 Midwest Club Pkwy Oak Brook IL 60523-2525 Office: PO Box 4505 Hinsdale IL 60522-4505

TAYLOR, THOMAS S. diversified financial services company executive; BS in Acctg., Miami U. Ohio, 1980; MBA, U. Notre Dame, 1990. Audit mgr. Price Waterhouse, 1980—87; v.p., controller Ctrl. Soya Co., 1988—90; v.p., fin. and strategy Kraft Foods, 1990—95; v.p., CFO Colo. Prime Corp., 1996—98; exec. v.p., CFO Epix Holdings Corp., Tampa, 1998—99, co-pres., co-CEO, vice chmn., 1999—2001, pres., CEO, 2001—. Office: Epix Holdings 3710 Corporex Park Dr Tampa FL 33619

TAYLOR, THOMAS WILLIAM, lawyer; b. Columbus, Ind., Feb. 11, 1943; s. Virgil W. and Margaret Emma (Voiles) T.; m. Linda Kay Followell, Jan. 1, 1964; children: Pamela Kay, William Lansing. AB with honors, Ind. U., 1965; LLB cum laude, Harvard U., 1968. Bar: Mass. 1968, U.S. Dist. Ct. Mass. 1969. Assoc. Ropes & Gray, Boston, 1968-78, ptnr., 1978-98, of counsel, 1999—. Lectr. Pres.'s urban policy program seminars U.S. Coun. of Mayors, 1982; chmn. tax panel nat. workshop Coun. of Infrastructure Financing Authorities, 1993; vol. astronomer Chaco Obs., Chaco Culture Nat. Hist. Park, 2000, prin. astronomer, 2001; Wilderness First Responder, 2002—. Snowboard instr. Nashoba Valley Ski Area, 1999—. Mem. Nat. Assn. Bond Lawyers (opinions com., chmn. securities law panel Washington workshop 1992, lectr. atty.'s workshop Chgo. 1983-97), Am. Coll. Bond Counsel (founding fellow), Appalachian Mountain Club Stewardship Soc. Avocations: rock climbing, orienteering, trumpet playing. Office: Ropes & Gray 1 International Pl Fl 4 Boston MA 02110-2624

TAYLOR, TIMOTHY DEAN, music educator; b. Lansing, Mich., Mar. 17, 1961; s. James Lee Taylor and Margaret Jane Lundeen; m. Sherry Beth Ortner, July 25, 1994. BA, Middlebury Coll., 1983; MusM, Yale Sch. Music, 1985; MA, U. Mich., 1990, PhD, 1993; MA, Queens U. Belfast, 1990. Asst. prof. Denison U., Granville, Ohio, 1993—94, U. Calif. Berkeley, 1994—96; asst. prof., assoc. prof. Columbia U., N.Y.C., 1996—2004; assoc. prof. UCLA, 2004—. Author: Global Pop: World Music, World Markets, 1997, Strange Sounds: Music, Technology and Culture, 2001. Fellow, Am. Coun. Learned Socs., 1999—2000, Nat. Humanities Ctr., 1999—2000. Mem.: Internat. Assn. for Study of Popular Music, Soc. Ethnomusicology, Am. Musciol. Soc. Avocations: gardening, yoga, Irish music-playing flute. Office: UCLA Dept Ethnomusicology Box 951657 Los Angeles CA 90095 E-mail: tdtaylor@ucla.edu.

TAYLOR, VICTORIA, sculptor; b. Toronto, Ont., Can., Oct. 18, 1935; arrived in U.S., 1978; d. Alberto A. Equable and Evelyn McLaughlin; children: James R., Joseph J., Sherry L., Vincent A. AA, Fla. Keys C.C., 1989. Owner, operator Spring Dale Nursing Home, Peterborough, Canada, 1973—78, Sun & Surf Motel, Key West, Fla., 1978—79, Dairy Queen, Key West, 1979—82; real estate salesman/broker Key West, 1983—96. Mem.: Nat. Sculpture Soc. Home: 158 E Circle Dr Key West FL 33040-4013

TAYLOR, VIRGINIA S. lawyer; b. Quitman, Ga. d. Allen Candler and Anne (Sanderson) Smith; divorced; children: Anne Taylor Hendry, Thomas Fielding. AB, Smith Coll., 1961; JD with distinction, Emory U., 1977. Bar: Ga. 1977, U.S. Dist. Ct. (no. dist.) Ga. 1977, U.S. Dist. Ct. (mid. dist.) Ga. 1979, U.S. Dist. Ct. (ea. dist.) Mich. 1988, U.S. Ct. Appeals (fed. cir.) 1982, U.S. Supreme Ct. 1981. Assoc. Kilpatrick & Cody, Atlanta, 1977-83, ptnr., 1983—, Kilpatrick & Stockton, L.L.P., Atlanta. V.p. Olmstead Parks Soc., Atlanta, 1985-93; bd. dirs. Piedmont Park Conservancy, Atlanta, 1991—, YWCA Metro. Atlanta, 1989-92, Leadership Atlanta, 1990. Mem. Ga. State Bar (chair patent, trademark and copyright sect. 1985-86), Order of Coif, Lawyer's Club Atlanta, Internat. Trademark Assn. (mem. publs. bd. 1995—, chair internat.

forums subcom. 1992-95, bd. dirs. 1991-93, chair pub. com. 1988-90). Democrat. Methodist. Avocations: gardening, travel, reading, fly fishing. Office: Kilpatrick & Stockton LLP 1100 Peachtree St NE Ste 2800 Atlanta GA 30309-4530

TAYLOR, VOLNEY, retired information company executive; b. Portsmouth, Ohio, Dec. 6, 1939; s. Lafayette and Martha Louise (Frederick) T.; m. Kathleen Ann MacMahon, May 17, 1969; children: Lafayette, Lloyd MacMahon, Kerry Erin, Frederick Daly. BS in Indsl. Engring, Ohio State U., 1962; MBA, Harvard U., 1966. Assoc. mem. McKinsey & Co., Inc. (mgmt. cons.), N.Y.C., 1966-72; exec. v.p., dir. Funk & Wagnalls, Inc., N.Y.C., 1972-74; v.p. fin. Reuben H. Donnelley Co., N.Y.C., 1974-76; dir. corp. planning Dun & Bradstreet Corp., N.Y.C., 1976-77, v.p. corp. planning, 1977-78, corp. v.p., 1979-80, sr. v.p., 1980-82, exec. v.p., 1982-96; gen. mgr. Official Airline Guides, Oak Brook, Ill., 1978-79; chmn. bd. dirs. Dun & Bradstreet Info. Svcs., Murray Hill, N.J., 1991-2000; chmn. bd., CEO Dun & Bradstreet Corp., Murray Hill, 1996-2000; ret., 2000. Bd. dirs. Dun & Bradstreet, Inc., Dun & Bradstreet Europe, Dun & Bradstreet Internat., Dun's Mktg. Svcs., Inc., Moody's Investors Svc.; bd. dirs. Reuben H. Donnelley Corp., pres., 1988-90. Served to lt. (j.g.) USNR, 1962-64. Mem. Harvard Bus. Sch. (N.Y.C.) Club, Beta Theta Pi.

TAYLOR, WALTER WALLACE, retired lawyer; b. Newton, Iowa, Sept. 18, 1925; s. Carrol W. and Eva (Greenly) T.; m. Mavis A. Harvey, Oct. 9, 1948; children: Joshua Michael (dec. 1980), Kevin Eileen, Kristin Lisa, Jeremy Walter, Margaret Jane, Melissa E., Amy M. AA, Yuba Coll., 1948, AB, 1950; MA, U. Calif., 1955; JD, McGeorge Coll. Law, 1962. Adminstrv. analyst USAF, Sacramento, 1951-53; personnel, research analyst Calif. Personnel Bd., Sacramento, 1954-56; civil svc., personnel analyst, chief counsel, gen. mgr. Calif. Employees Assn., Sacramento, 1956-75; staff counsel, chief profl. standards Calif. Commn. Tchr. Credentialing, 1975-88, ret., 1988. Staff counsel State Office Real Estate appraiser Licensing and Certification, 1992-94, ret.; tchr. discipline civil service, personnel cons. Author: Know Your Rights, 1963-64. Served USCGR, 1943-46. Mem. Calif. State Bar, Am., Sacramento County Bar Assns. Democrat. Home: 4572 Fair Oaks Blvd Sacramento CA 95864-5336 E-mail: walt_taylor@surewest.net.

TAYLOR, WATSON ROBBINS, construction company executive; b. Wetumpka, Ala., Sept. 7, 1925; s. Henry Watson and Helen Robbins Taylor; m. Ernestine Jenkins, Sept. 10, 1949; children: Jane Albright, W. Robbins Jr., George Lewis. BS, U. Ala., 1948; DSc (hon.), Auburn (Ala.) U., 1986. Estimator Std. Roofing Co., Montgomery, Ala., 1948-52, v.p., 1952-66, pres., CEO, 1966-97, CEO, chmn. bd., 1997—; chmn., pres. Std.-Taylor Industries Inc., Montgomery, 1979—. Chmn. bd. Union Bank and Trust Co., Montgomery, 1980-94. Chmn. bd., founding chmn. Auburn U., Montgomery, 1967-80; dir. Ala. Shakespeare Festival, 1995—, Ala. State Docks, Mobile, 1992—. Lt. j.g. USN, 1943-45. Named Contractor of Yr. RSI mag., 1999; named univ. ctr. in his honor Watson Robbins Taylor Ctr. Auburn U., 1999. Republican. Episcopalian. Avocations: golf, hunting. Home: PO Box 1 Letohatchee AL 36047-0001 Office: Std Roofing Co 516 N Mcdonough St Montgomery AL 36104-2645 Office Phone: 334-265-1262.

TAYLOR, WATSON ROBBINS, JR., investment banker; b. Montgomery, Ala., Mar. 16, 1956; s. Watson Robbins and Ernestine (Jenkins) T.; m. Davis Anne Denson, July 12, 1980; children: Watson Robbins III, Caroline Davis, Davis Denson. BS, Auburn U., 1979, MBA, 1982. Ranch foreman Johnston & Sons, Letohatchee, Ala., 1975-76; estimator Standard Roofing Co., Montgomery, Ala., 1976-78, v.p., 1978-84; pres. Standard Roofing USA, Inc., Montgomery, 1984-93, Standard-Taylor Industries, 1990-93; ptnr. First Commerce Capital, Inc., Montgomery, 1993-98; mgr. agribus. and middle market fin. group Morgan Keegan, Montgomery, 1998-99; pres. W.R. Taylor & Co., LLC, Montgomery, 1999—. Bd. dirs. Auburn U. Sch. Bus., Montgomery, Montgomery Acad. Fin. chmn. Ala. Rep. Com., Birmingham, 1989; trustee YMCA Endowment Found., Montgomery, 1989; bd. dirs. ARC, 1989, Montgomery coun. Boy Scouts Am., 1989. Mem. Montgomery Area C. of C. (bd. dirs. 1989-92), Ala. Alliance Bus. and Industry (bd. dirs. 1989-92), Rotary (past dir.), Young Pres.'s Assn. (Rebel chpt.), Montgomery Country Club, Ocean Reef Club. Methodist. Avocations: tennis, hunting, fishing, travel. Home: 9415 Dunleith Dr Montgomery AL 36117-5106 E-mail: rtaylor@wrtayco.com.

TAYLOR, WELTON IVAN, microbiologist, consultant, food scientist; b. Birmingham, Ala., Nov. 12, 1919; s. Frederick Enslen and Cora Lee (Brewer) Taylor; m. Jayne Rowena Kemp, Nov. 21, 1945; children: Karyn Jayne, Shelley Patrice. AB in Bacteriology, U. Ill., Urbana, 1941, MS in Bacteriology, 1947, PhD in Bacteriology, 1948. With U.S. Army, 1941, advanced through grades to maj., ret., 1952; rsch. microbiologist Swift and Co., Chgo., 1954—59; microbiologist-in-chief The Children's Meml. Hosp., Chgo., 1959—64; freelance cons., 1964—; microbiologist-in-chief West Suburban Hosp., Oak Pk., Ill., 1964—69; cons. microbiologist Mason-Barron Labs. Grant Hosp., Chgo., 1969—75; cons. microbiologist St. Mary of Nazareth Hosp. Ctr., Chgo., 1973—80. From instr. to asst. prof. Dept. Bacteriology U. Ill., Chgo., 1948—52, asst. prof., 1952—54; assoc. Dept. Pathology Northwestern U., Chgo., 1961—67; from asst. prof. to assoc. prof. Dept. Microbiology U. Ill., 1965—69, assoc. prof. Dept. Microbiology, 1969—87; cons. Resurrection Hosp. Ctr., 1967—93. Contbr. over 40 articles to profl. jours. Pres. Chatham Avalon Pk., Chgo., 1960—61, Episc. Soc. Cult-Race Unity, Chgo., 1960—61. Recipient James M. Yard Brotherhood award, Nat. Conf. Christians and Jews, 1961, Alumni Achievement award, U. Ill., 1996, Award for scientific leadership and dedicated service to ASM, Minority Microbiologists of ASM, 2002, Enterobacter taylorae named in his honor, Ctrs. for Disease Control, 1985; fellow, USPHS, 1961—62, WHO, Pasteur Inst., Lille, France, Ctrl. Pub. Health Lab. London. Fellow: Am. Acad. Microbiology; mem.: Ill. Soc. Microbiology (Pasteur award 1996), Am. Bd. Med. Microbiology, Am. Soc. Microbiology (chmn. jour. com. 1966—75, bd. editors Applied Microbiology 1968—70, subcom. on Enterobacteriaceae 1972—75, bd. editors Jour. Clin. Microbiology 1975—83, archives com. 1984—86, pres.-elect 1985—86, pres.'s fellowship awards com. 1985—87, pres. 1986—87, honoree 1984, 1998, 1999, 2002), Am. Bd. Bioanalysts (bd. dirs. 1973—82), Am. Assn. Bioanalysis (bd. sci. advisors 1970—82, referee 1970—2001, bd. editors Test of the Month 1971—82, Archives, History-Makers 2001), Druids Club, Kappa Alpha Psi, Sigma Xi. Achievements include patents in field. Avocations: fishing, camping, travel, photography.

TAYLOR, WENDY, magazine editor; Editor PC Computing, San Francisco. Office: Smart Business 50 Beale St Fl 13 San Francisco CA 94105-1813

TAYLOR, WESLEY BAYARD, JR., retired army officer; b. Covington, Ky., June 5, 1944; s. Wesley B. Sr. and Varina Martha (Morgan) T.; m. Linda L. Taylor, June 2, 1967; children: Kathleen C., Clint C. BS, U.S. Mil. Acad., 1965; MA in Internat. Rels., U. Calif., Santa Barbara, 1973; student, U.S. Army War Coll., 1985-86. Commd. 2d lt. U.S. Army, 1965, advanced through grades to brig. gen., 1990; asst. bn. advisor, sr. bn. advisor Airborne Divsn. Adv. Detachment, U.S. Mil. Assitance Command, Vietnam, 1967-68; staff officer Dept. of Army, Washington, 1980-81; bn. comdr. 3rd Bn., 5th Inf. U.S. Army, Republic of Panama, 1981-83; bn. comdr. 1st Ranger Bn. Hunter Army Airfield, Ga., 1983-85; strategic fellow U.S. Army War Coll., Carlisle Barracks, Pa., 1986-87; regimental comdr. 75th Ranger Regiment, Ft. Benning, Ga., 1987-89; asst. divsn. comdr. 1st Armored Divsn., Germany, 1989-91; dep. dir. ops, readiness and mobilization Dept. of Army, Washington, 1991-92; dep. asst. sec. of def. for policy and missions Office Sec. of Def., Washington, 1992-94; pres., CEO Cal Farley's Boys Ranch & Affiliates, U.S.A., Amarillo, Tex., 1995-99, Family & Childrens Ctr, Mishawaka, Ind., 2000—. Dist. commr. Boy Scouts Am., Germany, 1989-91. Decorated DSM, Def. Superior Svc. medal, Silver Star, Legion of Merit, Def. Meritorious Svc. medal, Bronze Star medal with oak leaf cluster, Air medals. Mem. Assn. U.S. Army, U.S. Army Ranger Assn., 75th Ranger Regiment Assn., Soc. Vietnamese Airborne Advisors, Soc. 173rd Airborne Brigade. Methodist. Avocations: fishing, hunting.

TAYLOR, WILLARD B. lawyer; b. N.Y.C., 1940; BA, Yale U., 1962, LLB, 1965. Bar: N.Y. 1966. With firm Sullivan & Cromwell, N.Y.C. Adj. faculty NYU Law Sch. Trustee North European Oil Royalty Trust. Mem. N.Y. State Bar Assn. (chair tax sect. 1983-84), Am. Law Inst. Office: Sullivan & Cromwell 125 Broad St Fl 28 New York NY 10004-2489

TAYLOR, WILLIAM AL, church administrator; b. Danville, Va., Sept. 26, 1938; s. Preston Floyd and Helen Elizabeth (Doss) T.; m. Brenda Flo Owen, June 4, 1961 (dec. 1996); children: Fawnia Rae Ricks, Albert Todd, Athena Dawn Jarman; m. Norma S. Pierce, June 28, 1997. AA, Lee Coll., 1957; postgrad., U. Calif., Santa Barbara, 1980. Br. mgr. Ency. Britannica, Greensboro, N.C., 1960-62, divsn. trainer Mpls., 1963, dist. mgr. Omaha, 1964-72; adminstrv. asst. Forward in Faith Internat. Broadcast, Cleveland, Tenn., 1972-80; gen. mgr. Sta. WQNE-FM, Cleveland, 1980—; dir. stewardship Ch. of God Internat. Offices, Cleveland, 1980—. Pres. Pathway Credit Union, Cleveland, 1985—, Vision Found., Cleveland, 1985—, exec. dir., 1979-80; chmn. Internat. Commn. on Prayer, Cleveland, 1986—. Author: Proving God, 1991, Days of Heaven on Earth, 1993, Stewardship Masterplanning, 1993, The Power of Vision, 2003. Pres. Clean Water Soc., Gastonia, N.C., 1974-75; speaker Citizens Against Legalized Liquor, Bradley County, Tenn., 1973, 75; advisor Mothers on March, Cleveland, 1976; active Nat. Conf. on Drug Abuse, Washington, 1978; master of ceremonies Nat. Religious Leaders Conf. on Alcohol and Drug Abuse, Indpls., 1979; pres. Ch. of God Found., 2002. Recipient Mass Communications award Ch. of God Media Ministries, 1980, Stephen award Ch. of God Lay Ministries, 1990. Mem. Nat. Assn. Evangelicals (bd. adminstrs. 1985-98, chmn. stewardship commn. 1985-89), Christian Stewardship Assn. (bd. dirs. 1990-96, nat. prayer com. 1999—, Best of the Best Faculty award 1999, Outstanding Stewardship Profl. award 2000). Mem. Ch. Of God. Avocations: flying, travel, racquetball. Office: Ch of God Dept Stewardship 2490 Keith St NW Cleveland TN 37311-1309 E-mail: stewardcog@mindspring.com. *We are all spending the precious gift of life, and we have been given the privilege to decide upon what we shall spend it. I have found the most worthy and fulfilling investment of life is God's stated purpose, "that we be conformed to the image of His son Jesus Christ".*

TAYLOR, WILLIAM B., JR., ambassador; married; 2 children. Grad., U.S. Mil. Acad., 1969; MA in Pub. Policy, Harvard U., 1977. Dir. Office Emergency Preparedness Dept. Energy; mem. staff Senator Bill Bradley; dir. Def. Dept., Washington; spl. dep. def. adv. U.S. Ambassador to NATO, Brussels, 1987—92; corrd. U.S. Assistance to Europe and Eurasia U.S. Dept. State, Washington, 1992—2002; spl. rep. Donor Assistance to Afghanistan U.S. State Dept., Washington, 2002—03, Afghanistan coord., 2003—. With U.S. Army, 1969—75, Vietnam. Office: US Dept State 2201 C St NW Washington DC 20520*

TAYLOR, WILLIAM C. physician, medical educator; b. Boston, Jan. 25, 1948; s. Manuel S. and Marjorie Tina Taylor; m. Julia Katherine Landau, Dec. 3, 1983; children: Rachel, Hannah, Daniel, Ben, Jessica. BA, Yale U., 1970; MD, U. Pa., 1974. Resident, intern Boston City Hosp., 1974—77; assoc. prof. internal medicine Harvard U. Med. Sch., Boston, 1977; sr. physician, internal medicine Beth Israel Deaconess Med. Ctr., Boston, 1977—. Office: BIDMC 330 Brookline Ave Boston MA 02215

TAYLOR, WILLIAM JAMES (ZAK TAYLOR), lawyer; b. Milw., Jan. 26, 1948; s. William Elmer and Elizabeth Emily (Lupinski) T.; m. Marlou Belyea, Sept. 20, 1975; children: Danielle Belyea, James Zachary Belyea. BA in Econs., Yale U., 1970; JD, Harvard U., 1976. Bar: Calif. 1976, U.S. Dist. Ct. (cen. dist.) Calif. 1976, U.S. Dist. Ct. (no. dist.) Calif. 1977, U.S. Ct. Appeals (9th cir.) 1977, U.S. Dist. Ct. (ea. dist.) Calif. 1980, U.S. Supreme Ct. 1980, U.S. Tax Ct. 1988. Law clk. to hon. Shirley M. Hufstedler U.S. Ct. Appeals (9th cir.), L.A., 1976-77; assoc. Broebeck, Phleger & Harrison, San Francisco, 1977-83; ptnr. Broebeck, Phleger and Harrison, San Francisco, 1983-95; shareholder Taylor & Jenkins, P.C., Oakland, Calif., 1995-96, Chilvers & Taylor, P.C., Oakland, 1996-99; of counsel Brobeck, Phleger & Harrison, LLP, San Francisco, 2000—03, Morgan Lewis & Bockius, LLP, San Francisco, 2003—. Bd. dirs. Berkeley (Calif.) Law Found., 1988-91, Legal Svcs. for Children (recipient Jean Waldman Child Advocacy award, San Francisco 1988), 1983-89; co-chmn. Attys. Task Force for Children, San Francisco, 1983-89. Editor-in-chief Harvard Civil Rights, Civil Liberties Law Rev., 1976; bd. editors No. Dist. Calif. Digest, 1978-83; co-author: California Antitrust Law, 1991; contbg. editor: Calif. Bus. Law Reporter, 1995—, Antitrust Law Developments, 1997, 4th edit., 2002. With U.S. Army, 1970-73. Mem. ABA, Bar Assn. San Francisco (bd. dirs. 1986-87, chair antitrust sect. 1987, chair fed. cts. sect. 1995-97), Am. Bus. Trial Lawyers Assn., Am. Health Lawyers Assn., Calif. Soc. Healthcare Attys., Barristers of San Francisco (bd. dirs. 1980-82, v.p. 1982-83). Democrat. Office: Morgan Lewis & Bockius LLP 1 Market Spear Tower San Francisco CA 94105-1420 E-mail: wtaylor@morganlewis.com., william.taylor@sbcglobal.net.

TAYLOR, WILLIAM JAPE, physician; b. Booneville, Miss., Sept. 5, 1924; s. William Melton and Cora Leona (Smith) T.; m. Audrey Y. Dennison, Jan. 31, 1948; children: J. Holley, Andrew D., Richard M., D. Lee. BS, Yale U., 1944; MD, Harvard U., 1947. Intern in internal medicine Boston City Hosp., 1947-48; resident in internal medicine Duke U. Hosp., 1948-50, fellow in cardiology, 1950-52, 54-55; instr. Duke U. Med. Sch., 1954-55, U. Pitts. Med. Sch., 1955-58; mem. faculty U. Fla. Coll. Medicine, Gainesville, 1958-95, prof. medicine, 1964-74, chief cardiology, 1958-74, disting. service prof. medicine, 1974-95; emeritus, 1995—. Vis. prof. U. Ife (Nigeria) Med. Sch., 1974-75; bd. dirs. PSRO, Fla. Area II, 1977-81 Author papers on human rights and health, human rights and peace, chpts. in books. Mem. human rights advocacy com. mentally retarded Fla. Dist. III, 1977-81; bd. dirs. Gainesville-Matagalpa Sister City, 1988—, Gainesville UNA, 1999—; mem. adv. coun. for Ctr. for African Studies, U. Fla., 1981-96. Fellow ACP (rsch. fellow 1950-51), Am. Coll. Cardiology; mem. Assn. U. Cardiologists, Am. Heart Assn. (fellow coun. clin. cardiology), Am. Fedn. Clin. Rsch., So. Soc. Clin. Investigation (pres. 1972-73), Fla. Heart Assn. (Disting. Svc. award 1975), Am. Soc. Tropical Medicine and Hygiene, Physicians for Social Responsibility (ho. of dels. 1985-90). Democrat. Home: 500 NW 80th Blvd Gainesville FL 32607-1531 Office: U Fla Med Sch Dept Medicine Gainesville FL 32610

TAYLOR, WILLIAM JESSE, JR., international studies educator, research corporation president; b. Florence, S.C., Dec. 28, 1933; s. William J. and Dorothy (Byrd) T.; m. Louise Inger Haegerstrom, Apr. 9, 1977; 1 child, Nicolaus; children by previous marriage: Juliana C., William J. III, L. Scott, Christopher B., Helen B. BS, U. Md., 1962; MA, Am. U., 1964, PhD, 1967. Enlisted U.S. Army, commd. 2d lt., 1955, advanced through grades to col., 1976; prof. U.S. Mil. Acad., West Point, N.Y., 1970-81; vis. prof. U.S. Nat. War Coll., 1975-76; ret. col. U.S. Army, 1981; sr. exec. Ctr. for Strategic and Internat. Studies, Washington, 1981—2001, v.p. internat. security programs, 1987-92; pres. Taylor Assocs. Inc., 1984—. Internat. lectr., debater, T.V. and radio mil. analyst, 1970—. Author: Future of Conflict: U.S. Interests, 1982, Future of Conflict into the 21st Century, 1987; co-author: American National Security: Policy and Process, 1981, 83, 89, 93, 99; co-editor: Defense Manpower Planning, 1980, The Future of Conflict in the 1980's, 1982, Strategic Requirements for the Army to the Year 2000, 1983, Strategic Responses to Conflict in the 1980's, 1984, Nordic Defense: Comparative Decisionmaking, 1985, Strategic Dimensions of Military Manpower, 1987, The Future of U.S.-Republic of Korea Security Ties, 1989, The Korean Peninsula: Prospects for Arms Control, 1990, Korea 1991: The Road to Peace, 1991, Elvis in The Army, 1995, 97. Mem. Presiding Bishop's Nat. Episc. Roundtable, 1983-86. Decorated Bronze Star with oak leaf cluster, Legion of Merit (2), Air Medal (3), Air medal for valor, Vietnam Cross of Gallantry, Combat Infantry Badge; recipient Pitman Potter Medal Am. U., 1964; named to Infantry Officer Hall of Fame, 1976; named Disting. Alumnus, Episcopal Acad., 1995, Disting. Alumnus, CSIS, 2001. Mem. St. Anthony Club. Republican. Episcopalian. Home: 6010 Maiden Ln Bethesda MD 20817-6261 Office Phone: 202-775-3203. E-mail: wjtaylor44@aol.com.

TAYLOR, WILLIAM OSGOOD, newspaper executive; b. Boston, July 19, 1932; s. William Davis and Mary (Hammond) Taylor; m. Sally Coxe, June 20, 1959; children: William Davis II, Edmund C., Augustus R. BA, Harvard U., 1954. With Globe Newspaper Co., Boston, 1956—, treas., 1963, bus. mgr., 1965—69, gen. mgr., 1969—; chmn. emeritus The Boston Globe, 1998—; chmn. Fed. Res. Bank of Boston. Trustee Boston Pub. Libr., Boston Pub. Libr. Found.; chmn. emeritus The Freedom Trail Found.; dir. Internat. Crisis Group; chmn. founder's com. Boston Mus. Project. With U.S. Army, 1954—56. Address: Globe Newspaper Co Three School St Boston MA 02108-4317

TAYLOR, WILSON H. retired diversified financial company executive; Grad., Trinity Coll., 1964. With Conn. Gen., 1964—82; v.p. Aetna Ins. Co., 1975; exec. v.p., CFO Cigna Corp., Phila., 1982-88, pres. property casualty group, 1983-88, COO, 1988, pres., chief exec. officer, 1988—2000; ret., 2000. Phi Beta Kappa.

TAYLOR CLAUD, ANDREA, educational consultant; b. Warrenton, Va., Nov. 5, 1952; d. Andrew Earl and Catherine (Dennis) Taylor; m. Maurice J. Claud. BS, Norfolk State U., 1974, MA, 1983; postgrad., Old Dominion U., 1975-76, 89; MA in Cmty. Counseling, Regent U., 2000. Profl. collegiate cert. in learning disabilities, mentally handicapped and emotionally handicapped. Classrm. tchr. Facquier County Sch. System, Warrenton, Va., 1974-75; child devel. specialist, team leader Norfolk Pub. Schs., Norfolk, Va., 1976-82, ednl. diagnostician, 1982-87; ednl. cons. Va. State Dept. Edn., Norfolk, 1987—; v.p. M.A. Trucking, Inc. and MAC Leasing, Inc. V.p. DECAA Enterprises, Norfolk, 1983—. Mem. Nat. Kidney Found. of Va., Hampton Rds., Lindenwood Civic League, Norfolk, Pleasant Grovet Bapt. Ch., Va. Beach; troop leader Girl Scouts U.S.A., Norfolk, 1977-79. Named Dubutante, Norfolk Med. Soc. Aux., 1969, Outstanding Young Women of Am., 1983; recipient Apple for Tchr. award, 1997, Outstanding Renal Healthcare Profl. Yr. award, 1998. Mem. NAFE, NEA, Va. Edn. Assn., Norfolk Edn. Assn., Coun. Exceptional Children, Assn. Supervision and Curriculum Devel., Delta Sigma Theta. Democrat. Avocations: travel, reading, listening to music, fishing. Office: Children's Hosp of King's Daus Hosp Edn Program 601 Childrens Ln Norfolk VA 23507-1910

TAYLOR-WILLIAMS, BONNIE JEAN, cosmetics executive; b. Chgo., Oct. 26, 1959; d. William Crawford and Juanita J. (Parker) Dunbar; m. Paxton G. Williams, Aug. 30, 1987. Grad., Pivot Point Beauty Sch. Lic. cosmetologist, Ill. Mgr., cosmetologist Selena's House of Beauty and Sch. HairWeev Tech., Chgo., 1978—. Technician, instr. Sch. Hair Weev Tech., Chgo.; pres. Beautee, Inc., Chgo., 1989—, E-Z Beautee Extraordinary Maintenance Sys. & Hairgasm; instr. First Internat. Indep. Hair Weevers Assn., Chgo., 1974—. Choir mem. First Ch. Deliverance, 1978-88, Christ Universal Temple, 1996—. Avocations: professional writing, dance, writing, travel. Office: Beautee Inc 444 E 83rd St Chicago IL 60619-5726

TAYMOR, JULIE, theater, film and opera director and designer; b. Newton, Mass., 1952; d. Melvin L. and Betty Taymor. BA in folklore and mythology, Oberlin Coll., 1974; attended, L'Ecole Mimet Theatre in Paris, France, Herbert Berghof Studio, N.Y.C. Founder Teatr Loh. Dir. Way of Snow, The Transposed Heads, 1984, The Tempest, 1986, Liberty's Taken, 1985, Juan Darién, 1988, Fool's Fire, 1992, Titus Andronicus, 1994, Oedipus Rex, 1992, The Magic Flute, Salomé, The Flying Dutchman, The Lion King, 1997, (Tony awards for best director and costume design 1998), operas, classical plays and exptl. theater projects; prodr. Shakespeare plays and operas; designer puppets, masks, imaginative costumes and other visual elements. MacArthur grantee, Watson fellow, 1974-79, Obie awards, 1988. Office: Internat Creative Mgmt 40 W 57th St New York NY 10019-4001*

TBRESLOW, ESTHER MAY GREENBERG, biochemistry educator, researcher; b. N.Y.C., Dec. 23, 1931; d. Harry Daniel and Lillian (Solomon) Greenberg; m. Ronald Charles David Breslow, Sept. 4, 1955; children: Stephanie Ruth, Karen Ann. BS with distinction, Cornell U., 1953; MS in Biochemistry, NYU, 1955, PhD in Biochemistry, 1959; postgrad., Radcliffe Coll., 1954-55. Postdoctoral fellow Cornell U. Med. Coll., N.Y.C., 1959-61, rsch. assoc., 1961-64, asst. prof., 1964-72, assoc. prof., 1972-78, prof. biochemistry, 1978—, acting chmn. dept. biochemistry, 1992-95. Mem. rev. panels NIH, Bethesda, Md., 1973—77, Bethesda, 1994—97, NSF, Bethesda, 1981—84. Mem. editorial bd. Jour. Biol. Chemistry, 1982-87, Internat. Jour. Peptide and Protein Rsch., 1981-97; contbr. articles to profl. jours. Mem. Englewood (N.J.) Bd. Health, 1986-94; mem. Dem. Mcpl. Com., Englewood, 1985-91. Eli Lilly fellow, 1954-55; USPHS fellow, 1959-61; NIH grantee, 1961—. Fellow AAAS; mem. Am. Soc. for Biochemistry and Molecular Biology, Am. Chem. Soc. (sec. div. biol. chemistry 1972-76), Harvey Soc., Sigma Xi. Home: 44 W 77th St New York NY 10024 Office: Joan and Sanford I Weill Med Coll Cornell U 1300 York Ave New York NY 10021-4805 Business E-Mail: ebreslow@med.cornell.edu.

TCHAICHA, JANE DAVAGIAN, education educator, consultant; b. Waltham, Mass., May 27, 1949; d. John Sarkes Davagian and Vehanush Hachadorian; m. Josef Vaclav Pavlic, Nov. 24, 1984; m. Mohamed Tchaicha, Jan. 3, 1974 (div. May 14, 1982); children: Khaled, Jeremy Hatem. AB, Goucher Coll., 1967—71; EdM, Harvard U., 1988—89; EdD, Harvard U., Cambridge, MA, 1990—96. English instr. Université de Droit, d'Economie, et de Sciences Sociales, Paris, 1977—79; lang. tng. specialist Citicorp, N.A., Paris, 1978—80; dir. of spl. projects, Esl and French instr. Babson Coll./ALA, Wellesley, Mass., 1981—90; asst. prof., computers and tech. in edn. Bunsai Gakuen (Boston Inst. of Intercultural Comm.), Lincoln, Mass.; dir., ctr. for languages and internat. collaboration Bentley Coll., Waltham, Mass., 1993—. Contbr. articles to profl. jours. Cmty. prodr. Cmty. TV, Needham, Mass., 1986—89. Recipient Gregory H. Adamian award for Excellence in Tchg., Bentley Coll., 2002—03, The Alpha Delta/David M. Levine award for Innovation in Tchg., NE Decision Sci. Inst., 2002, Davis Found. Scholar, Davis Ednl. Found. and Bentley Coll., 2000—01. Mem.: Internat. Assn. for Lang. Learnings Technologies, Assn. for Bus. Edn., Phi Beta Delta Internat. Scholars. Achievements include development of mutlimedia software, the multilingual jukebox, an online, real-time dissemination of instructional language materials. Avocations: sports, gardening, travel. Office: Bentley College 175 Forest St Waltham MA 02452

TCHAIKOVSKY, LESLIE J. federal judge; b. 1943; BA, Calif. State Univ., Hayward, 1967; JD, Univ. of Calif., Berkeley, 1976. Law clk. to Hon. John Mowbray Nev. Supreme Ct., 1976-77; with Dinkelspiel, Steefel, Leavitt & Weiss, 1977-80, Gordon, Peitzman & Lopes, 1981, Dinkelspiel, Donovan & Reder, 1981-88; bankruptcy judge U.S. Bankruptcy Ct. (Calif. no. dist.), 9th circuit, Oakland, 1988—. Office: US Courthouse 1300 Clay St Oakland CA 94612-1425

TCHAMENGO, MATHIAS NGOUFI, energy executive, mathematician; b. Douala, Cameroon, Jan. 1, 1971; s. Joseph Ndjoumngwe and Marthe Kamkwe; m. Nicole Martin, Sept. 23, 1995; 1 child, Landry Ngoufi. Ingenieur Civil des Mines, Ecole des Mines de St-Etienne, France, 1994; PhD in Math., U. Bourgogne, Dijon, France, 1998. Quantitative analyst Dresdner Kleinwort Benson, Paris, 1995—97, Schroders Structured Products, London, 1997—98; sr. quantitative analyst Koch Energy Trading, Houston, 1998—2000, Shell Trading, Houston, 2000—. Recipient Leopold Vigneron award, U. of Rennes, France, 1992. Mem.: Bachelier Fin. Soc., Internat. Assn. Fin. Engrs., Soc. for Indsl. and Applied Math. Achievements include research in Static strategies in finance: Provide means to reduce the risk induced by a liability through discrete transactions on other financial vehicle; patents pending for Means to describe prices of future contracts on seasonal commodities: electricity, natural gas, cocoa. Home: 2226 Blue Rose Dr Missouri City TX 77459 Personal E-mail: mtchamengo@yahoo.com. E-mail: mtchamengo@equiva.com.

TCHERNEV, VELIZAR TZVETANOV, physician and biomedical scientist; b. Sofia, Bulgaria, Oct. 29, 1969; arrived in US, 1994; s. Lilia Zaharieva Jeleva and Tzvetan Vasilev Tchernev; m. Ralitza Vladislavova Gueorguieva; children: Alexander Velizar, Liliana Velizar. Cert. in tropical medicine, Higher Med. Inst., Sofia, Bulgaria, 1992, MD, 1993; cert. in biotechnology, U. Fla., 1994, PhD, 1998. Rsch. asst. dept. pathology, immunology and lab. medicine U. Fla., Gainesville, 1994—98; rsch. scientist discovery dept. CuraGen Corp.,

Alachua Fla. and Branford, Conn., 1998—2001; rsch. scientist Molecular Staging Inc., New Haven, 2001—03, sr. rsch. scientist, 2003—; scientist Molecular Stating, Inc., New Haven. Contbr. articles to profl. jours. Recipient award, Am. Fedn. for Clin. Rsch., 1996; Scholarship, Internat. Mammalian Genome Soc., 1998, Fellowship for Excellent Academic Performance, Higher Med. Inst. Sofia, Bulgaria, 1988—93. Mem.: AAAS. Achievements include diplomas for translations of med. lit. to Eng. lang. and German lang; more than 50 patents pending in field. Home: 45 Jefferson Rd #3-12 Branford CT 06405 Office Phone: 203-772-5097. Personal E-mail: vtchernev@hotmail.com.

TCHIVZHEL, EDVARD, music director; b. Leningrad, Russia, Jan. 29, 1944; Music dir. Fort Wayne Philharm Orch., Ft. Wayne, Tex., 1993-98, Greenville Symphony Orch., Greenville, S.C., 1999—. Office: Greenville Symphony Orch 200 S Main St Greenville SC 29601-2832

TCHOBANOGLOUS, GEORGE, civil engineering educator; b. Patterson, Calif., May 24, 1935; s. Christo and Penelope (Megdani) T.; m. Rosemary Ash, June 16, 1957; children: Kathryn, Lynn, Julianne. B.C.E., U. Pacific, 1958; M.C.E., U. Calif., Berkley, 1960; PhD, Stanford U., 1969. Registered profl. engr., Calif. Research engr. U. Calif.-Berkeley, 1960-62; cons. Metcalf & Eddy Engrs., Palo Alto, Calif., 1963-81, Nolte & Assocs., Sacramento, 1981—, Calif. Water Resources Control Bd., 1972-80; assoc. prof. U. Calif.-Davis, 1970-76, prof. engring., 1976—. Prin. author: Wastewater Engineering: Collection, Treatment, Disposal, 1972; author: (with R. Smith and R. Crites) Wastewater Management: A Guide to Information Sources, 1976, (with H. Theisen and R. Eliassen) Solid Wastes: Engineering Principles and Management Issues, 1977, (with Schroeder) Water Quality: Characteristics, Modeling, Modification, 1985, (with Peavy and Rowe) Environmental Engineering, 1985, (with H. Theisen, S.A. Vigil) Integrated Solid Waste Management: Engineering Principles and Management Issues, 1993, (with R. Crites) Small and Decentralized Wastewater Management Systems, 1998; co-author: Wastewater Engineering: Treatment, Disposal, Reuse, 1991, 4th edit., 2002; author, editor: Wastewater Engineering: Collection and Pumping of Wastewater, 1981; co-editor: Pumping Station Design, 1989 (with F. Burton and D. Stensel) Wastewater Engineering: Treatment and Reuse, 4th ed., 2002, co-editor: (with F Kreith) Solid Waste Handbook, 2d edit., 2002; contbr. numerous articles to profl. jours. Mem. bd. Calif. Integrated Waste Mgmt.; lectr. T.R. Camp, 1990. Mem. AAAS, ASCE, Assn. Environ. Engring. Profs. (bd. dirs., past pres.), Am. Acad. Environ. Engrs., Water Environ. Fedn. (Gordon Maskew Fair medal 1985, Jack Edward McKee medal 1999), Am. Water Works Assn. (Thomas R. Camp lectr. 1991), Nat. Water Rsch. Inst. (Clarke prize 2003), Nat. Acad. Engring. Home: 662 Diego Pl Davis CA 95616-0123

TCHOSHANOV, MOURAT ASHIROVICH, mathematician, educator; b. Dashoguz, Turkmenistan, July 11, 1959; arrived in U.S., 1998; s. Ashir Tchoshanov and Amangul Tchoshanova; m. Natalia Ivanovna Tchoshanova, Mar. 17, 1989; 1 child, Aina Mouratovna Tchoshanova. Specialist degree, Turkmen State Pedagogical Inst., Chardjou, Turkmenistan, 1980; Candidate of Sci., Kazan State Pedagogical Inst., Russia, 1987; DSc, postgrad., Kazan State Pedagogical U., Russia, 1996. Prof. math. Tatar-Am. Inst., Kazan, 1992—97, Kostroma State Tech. U., Russia, 1997—98; prof. tchr. edn. U. Tex., El Paso, 2000—. Vis. scholar Case Western Res. U., Cleve., 1994—95; vis. prof. Ohio State U., Columbus, 1998—2000; adv. bd. mem. Supporting and Strengthening Stds.-based Math. Tchr. Preparation State Dept. Edn., Austin, Tex., 2001—, mem. screening bd. math. and sci. partnership, El Paso, Tex., 2003—. Author: Flexible Technology of Problem-based Modular Instruction, 1996, Visual Mathematics, 1997, America Learns to Count, 2001. Recipient Fulbright award, U.S. Info. Agy., Washington, 1994. Fellow: Fulbright Assn.; mem.: N.Y. Acad. Sci., Internat. Group on Psychology Math. Edn. Office: U Tex El Paso EDU 603 500 W University Ave El Paso TX 79968

TCHOUNWOU, PAUL BERNARD, environmental health specialist, toxicologist, educator; b. Bangou, Cameroon, Aug. 14, 1960; came to U.S., 1985; s. Maurice and Christine (Kouanang) Seumo; m. Martha Namondo Mondoa, Aug. 3, 1990; children: Christine K., Hervey M., Solange S. BSc, U. Yaounde, Cameroon, 1983, MSc, 1984; MS in Pub. Health, Tulane U., 1986, ScD, 1990. Cert. toxicologist Nat. Environ. Health Assn.; registered sanitarian La. State Bd. Examiners for Sanitarians. Tchg. asst. Tulane Sch. Pub. Health, New Orleans, 1988—90; med. rschr. Inst. Med. Rsch., Yaounde, 1991—94; asst. prof. Faculty Medicine, Yaounde, 1992—94; rsch. assoc. Xavier & Tulane Univs., New Orleans, 1994—96; assoc. prof., dir. environ. sci. PhD program Jackson State U., 1996—; adj. assoc. prof. sch. pub. health Tulane U., 1999—; prof., dir. environ. sci. doctoral program Jackson State U., 2001—; dep. dir. Ctr. for Environ. Health, Jackson State U., 2003—. Adj. assoc. prof. Tulane U. Sch. Pub. Health, 1999—; environ. health cons. Orstom & UNICEF, Yaounde, 1992-93, U.S. AID, Kaele, 1991-93; rsch. supr. Tulane Sch. Pub. Health, New Orleans, 1994—; tng. and rsch. fellow U.S. AID, Washington, 1985-90; adj. assoc. prof. environ. health scis. Tulane U. Sch. Pub. Health and Tropical Medicine, 1999—; dep. dir. Ctr. Environ. Health Jackson State U., 2003—. Editor-in-chief: Internat. Jour. of Environ. Rsch. and Pub. Health, 2003—, mem. editl. bd.: Internat. Jour. Environ. Toxicology and Water Quality, 1994—, guest editor: Internat. Jour. Molecular Scis., 2002—, regional editor: USA-Environ. Toxicology, 2002—, mem. overseas editl. bd.: Jour. Environ. Biology, 2002—; contbr. articles to profl. jours. Grantee, Internat. Devel. Rsch. Ctr., 1992—93, Nat. Aeronautics and Space Adminstrn., 1977—99, NIH, 1998—, Nat. Oceanic and Atmospheric Adminstrn., 2001—, Dept. Army, 2002—03. Mem. APHA, AAUP, AAAS, Am. Assn. Cancer Rsch., Water Environ. Fedn., Cameroon Bioscis. Soc., Cameroon Assn. Epidemiology, Nat. Environ. Health Assn., N.Y. Acad. Scis., Soc. Environ. Toxicology and Chemistry, Soc. Toxicology, Delta Omega. Roman Catholic. Avocations: travel, playing tennis, watching tv sport programs. Home: 230 Clark Farms Rd Madison MS 39110-8112 Office: Jackson State U Sch Sci & Tech PO Box 18540 Jackson MS 39217

TEAGAN, JOHN GERARD, newspaper executive; b. Detroit, Sept. 23, 1947; s. Stanley John and Margaret Suzanne (Sullivan) T.; m. Carla Kay Eurich, Sept. 13, 1975; 1 child, Elizabeth Margaret. BBA, U. Notre Dame, 1969. C.P.A., Mich. Audit supr. Ernst & Whinney (C.P.A.s), Detroit, 1969-73; acctg. mgr. Detroit Free Press, 1973-77, treas., controller, 1977-83, v.p. fin., treas., 1983-89, v.p., bus. mgr., 1989—. Adv. bd. Providence Hosp., Southfield, Mich., 1984-93, sec., 1989, vice chmn. 1990, chmn., 1991; trustee Grosse Pointe (Mich.) Acad., 1990-96, Children's Home Detroit, Grosse Pointe, 1997—; bd. dirs., treas. Free Press Charities, Inc.; bd. dirs. Providence Hosp. and Med. Ctrs., Southfield, 1998—; Metro Detroit bd. dirs. Am. Heart Assn., 1999—; bd. dirs. Holy Cross Children's Svcs., 2001—; mem. cmty. adv. bd. Knight Found., 2002—. Mem. AICPA, Internat. Newspaper Fin. Execs., Mich. Assn. CPAs, Grosse Pointe Yacht Club. Roman Catholic. Office: Detroit Free Press Inc 600 W Fort St Detroit MI 48226-2706 E-mail: teagan@freepress.com.

TEAGLE, DAVID BRYAN, manufacturing executive; b. Abilene, Tex., Nov. 18, 1956; s. Ollie Bryan Teagle and Carolyn Ann Dorr; m. Colinda Jean Torrez, Sept. 17, 1999; 1 child from previous marriage, Kezia Anne. BBA, Abilene Christian U., 1979, MBA, 1980. With energy sys. divsn. NCR Corp., 1980—81; landman ARCO Exploration/ARCO Oil, 1981—84; with Burroughs Sys., 1985—86, Continental Airlines, 1986—92; actor, 1992—2002; pres. Am. Ventilation Equipment Co., 2002—03; freelance photographer Cowboy mag., 1992—2002, Tex. State Troopers Assn. mag., Denver Post. Author: Fallen Angels of Sans Espair, 1997. Finalist Ernest Hemingway 1st Book award. Mem.: Bldg. Engineers Assn., Nat. Def. Industry Assn., Indsl. Hygienists Assn., Nat. Press Photographer Assn. Achievements include patents for Enviroblower, emergency portable ventilation and capture equipment for chemical and biological containment. Home: 403 W Cherry St Kaufman TX 75142

TEAGUE, BRUCE WILLIAMS, chiropractor; b. Dayton, Ohio, Sept. 6, 1947; s. Bige Barnett and Lena Teague; m. Germaine Lee Mullican, Oct. 15, 1977; children: Deanna, Katrina, Bret, Travis, Krystal. BBA, Ea. Ky. U., 1970; D.Chiropractic, Palmer Coll. Chiropractic, 1977. Chiropractor, pres., dir. Teague Chiropractic Ctr., Anchorage, 1980—. Mem. L.A. Coll. Chiropractic Orthopedics, 1988—. Mem. Am. Chiropractic Assn. (mem. nutrition coun., coun. on sports injuries and phys. fitness), Coun. Diagnostic Imaging, Am. Coll. Chiropractic Edn. and Rsch., Alaska Chiropractic Soc., Internat. Chiropractors Assn., Palmer Coll. Alumni Assn., Moose, Rotary. Office: Teague Chiropractic Ctr 11435 Old Seward Hwy Anchorage AK 99515-3041

TEAGUE, DEBORAH GANT, elementary school educator; b. Mankato, Minn., Jan. 23, 1952; d. Dorsett H. and Gwynlyn (Himmelman) Gant; m. William Lial Teague, June 7, 1991. AA, Meramec C.C., Kirkwood, Mo., 1972; BS, U. Mo., 1974, Edn. Specialist, 1989; MS, U. Minn., 1982. Tchr. Mexico (Mo.) Pub. Sch., 1977—. Recipient Presdl. Award in Excellence in Math. and Sci., NSF and Nat. Sci. Tchr. Assn., 1993; Fulbright Exch. fellow, 1985; Mo. State Incentive grantee Mo. State Dept. Edn., 1987, 88. Mem. Nat. Sci. Tchrs. Assn., Coun. of Elem. Sci. Teaching Internat., Assn. Presdl. Awardee Sci. Tchrs., Mo. Sci. Tchrs. Assn., N.E. Mo. State Tchrs. Assn. (exec. com. 1992-94), Phi Delta Kappa. Avocations: walking, swimming, travel. Home: 701 Ringo St Mexico MO 65265-1220 Office: Mexico Public Sch 1250 W Curtis St Mexico MO 65265-1855

TEAGUE, LAVETTE COX, JR., systems educator, consultant; b. Birmingham, Ala., Oct. 8, 1934; s. Lavette Cox and Caroline Green (Stokes) T. Student, Auburn U., 1951-54; BArch, MIT, 1957, MSCE, 1965, PhD, 1968; MDiv with distinction, Ch. Div. Sch. Pacific, 1979. Cert. computer profl. Inst. Cert. Computer Profls. Archtl. designer Carroll C. Harmon, Birmingham, 1957, Fred Renneker, Jr., Birmingham, 1958-59; architect Rust Engring. Co., Birmingham, 1959-62, Synergetics, Inc., Raleigh, N.C., 1962-64, Rust Engring. Co., Birmingham, 1964-68; rsch. asst., instr., rsch. assoc. MIT, Cambridge, 1964-68; dir. computer svcs. Skidmore Owings & Merrill, San Francisco, Chgo., 1968-74; postdoctoral fellow UCLA, 1972; adj. assoc. prof. arch. and civil engring. Carnegie-Mellon U., Pitts., 1973-74; archtl. systems cons. Chgo., 1974-75, Berkeley, Calif., 1975-80, Pasadena, 1980-82, Altadena, Calif., 1982—. Lectr. info. systems Calif. State Poly. U., Pomona, 1980-81, prof., 1981-98, prof. emeritus, 1998—, asst. chair, 1990-91, chair, 1991-93, 96-98; Fulbright lectr., Uruguay, 1985; lectr. Peking U., 2004. Author: Event-Based Analysis and Design: An Introduction to Structured Methods, 2000; co-author: Structured Analysis Methods for Computer Information Systems, 1985, Object-Oriented Analysis and Design with UML, 2005. Mem. adv. bd. Ch. Div. Sch. of the Pacific. Recipient Tucker-Voss award MIT, 1967; Fulbright scholar, 1985. Mem. AIA (Arnold W. Brunner scholar 1966), Assn. Computing Machinery, Sigma Xi, Phi Eta Sigma, Scarab, Scabbard and Blade, Tau Beta Pi, Chi Epsilon, Beta Gamma Sigma. Episcopalian. Home: 1696 N Altadena Dr Altadena CA 91001-3623 Office: 3801 W Temple Ave Pomona CA 91768-2557 Business E-Mail: lcteague@csupomona.edu.

TEAGUE, LIAM RICHARD, musician, researcher; b. San Fernando, Trinidad, Jan. 13, 1974; s. Russell and Pearl Teague. MusB, No. Ill. U., 1996, MusM, 1999. Rsch. scholar No. Ill. U., Dekalb, 2000, co-dir. No. Ill. U. Steelband. Musician: Hands Like Lightning, Emotions of Steel, Impressions, T'NT, For Lack of Better Words, A Christmas Gift. Office: Sch Music No Ill Univ Dekalb IL 60115

TEAGUE, MARY ELIZABETH, small business owner; b. Mt. Vernon, Tex., Aug. 18, 1928; d. Jodie Felter and Martha Willie (Crafts) T. AAS, C.C. of Air Force, 1987. Advanced through grades to chief master sgt. USAF, 1950, retired, 1988. Editor, publ.: (cmty. newsletter) Waterwood News, 1990—. Lutheran. Avocations: travel, handicrafts, writing. Home: 4027 Waterwood Pass Dr Elmendorf TX 78112-6024

TEAGUE, RANDAL CORNELL, SR., lawyer; b. Durham, N.C., May 19, 1944; s. Roy M. Sr. and Lottie (Rhew) T.; children: R. Cornell, R. Townsend, Mary Robb Durham, James K.B. BA, Am. U., 1967; JD, George Washington U., 1971, LLM with highest honors, 1972; LLD (hon.), Allen U., 1973. Bar: Fla. 1972, D.C. 1972, U.S. Dist. Ct. D.C. 1972, U.S. Tax Ct. 1972, U.S. Ct. Mil. Appeals 1972, U.S. Ct. Appeals (D.C. and fed. cirs.) 1972, U.S. Ct. Appeals (5th cir.) 1973, U.S. Supreme Ct. 1975, Mass. 1979, U.S. Ct. Appeals (1st cir.) 1979, U.S. Dist. Ct. Mass. 1979, U.S. Ct. Internat. Trade. Coord. policy devel. Exec. Office of Pre. of U.S., Washington, 1971-73; chief of staff, legis. counsel to Rep. Jack F. Kemp Ho. of Reps., Washington, 1973-79; div. counsel Cabot Corp., 1979-81; counsel Vorys, Sater, Seymour & Pease LLP, Washington, 1981-83, ptnr., 1984—. Pres. Internat. Exch. Coun., 1984—; trustee Fund Am. Studies, Washington, 1976—, chmn., 1998—; trustee, dir. Air Force Acad. Found., Colorado Springs, Colo., 1983—; chmn. adv. com. voluntary aid U.S. AID, 1987-91; trustee Earth U., Costa Rica, 1987—; councillor Atlantic Coun. of U.S., 1990—; co-founder Am. Inst. on Polit. and Econ. Sys., Charles U., Prague, 1993—; founder Internat. Inst. Polit. and Econ. Studies, Athens, Greece, 1996—; dir. Salzburg Seminar, 1997—. Named one of Outstanding Young Men Am., 1973; recipient George Washington medal Freedoms Found., 1978. Mem. Fla. Bar Assn., Mass. Bar Assn., D.C. Bar Assn., Univ. Club (Washington). Republican. Episcopalian. Office: Vorys Sater Seymour & Pease LLP 1828 L St NW Fl 11 Washington DC 20036-5109 E-mail: rcteague@vssp.com.

TEAGUE, ROBERT COLE, physician; b. Waxahachie, Tex., June 13, 1930; s. Isaac Lawson and Frances (Cole) T.; m. Virginia M. Teague, Nov. 11, 1960; children: Patrick, Michael. BA in Chemistry, Baylor U., Waco, Tex., 1951; MD, U. Tex., Galveston, 1955. Intern McLaren Hosp., Flint, Mich., 1955-56; med. officer USNR, 1956-58; physician family practice LaJolla, Calif., 1958-63, Phoenix, 1963—. Med. dir. Vis. Nurse Svc., Phoenix; chmn. Family Practice Humana Hosp., 1984-86, past chmn.; chmn. Family Practice Good Samaritan Hosp., 1990-91. Fellow Am. Acad. Family Physicians (charter); mem. Ariz. Acad. Family Physicians (pres. 1988). Republican. Episcopalian. Avocations: golf, travel. Office: 5501 N 19th Ave Ste 106 Phoenix AZ 85015-2451

TEAGUE, SHARON BEASLEY, state legislator; b. Feb. 15, 1952; married. AA, Ind. Coll. Bus. and Tech. Mem. Ga. Ho. of Reps., 1992—, mem. motor vehicles com., regulated beverages and state inst. and property com.; realtor. Cmty. activist. Baptist. Democrat. Home: PO Box 988 Red Oak GA 30272 Office: Ga House of Reps 504 Legis Office Bldg Atlanta GA 30334

TEAHAN, KATHLEEN M. state legislator, educator; b. Brockton, Mass., June 11, 1947; d. Joseph and Florence (Mahoney) Keras; m. Robert S. Teahan, 1971; children: Anne Teahan Berry, Jean, Robert J., John. BA, Bridgewater State Coll., 1969. Mem. Mass. Ho. of Reps., Boston, 1997—, mem. health care com., mem. state adminstrn. com.; tchr. Whitman Sch. Mem. Plymouth County Dem. League, Whitman Dem. Town Com., Whitman Sch. Com., Whitman-Hanson Regional H.S. Com.; mem. coun. Holy Ghost Parish Coun., 1993-97; pres. Whitman-Hanson Citizens Scholarship Found., 1979; mem. family selection com. Whitman Habitat for Humanity, 1994-95. Mem. Nat. Coun. Tchrs. English, Mass. Tchrs. Assn. Democrat. Office: Mass State Legis Rm 540 State House Boston MA 02133

TEAL, ARABELLA W. lawyer, former state attorney general; b. N.Y.C., Jan. 1961; m. Gary Teal; 2 children. BA, Harvard Coll., 1984; JD, Georgetown U. Law Ctr., 1987. Law clerk for sr. judges D.C. Superior Court, 1987—88; section chief General Litigation Section I, 1996—99; acting prin. dep. corp. counsel D.C., 1999—2000, prin. dep. corp. counsel, 2000—02, interim corp. counsel, 2002—03; atty. McCabe & Mack LLP, Poughkeepsie, 2003—. Office: McCabe & Mack LLP 63 Washington St PO Box 509 Poughkeepsie NY 12602-0509*

TEARE, RICHARD WALLACE, retired foreign service officer; b. Cleve., Feb. 21, 1937; m. Jeanie Walter; 3 children. BA, Harvard U., 1958; diploma, Nat. War Coll., 1977-78. Joined Fgn. Svc., 1959; vice consul U.S. Consulate, Bridgetown, Barbados, 1960-62; consular officer U.S. Embassy, Manila, 1962-64, polit. officer Saigon, Vietnam, 1965-67, Mexico City, 1971-74, counselor for polit. affairs Vientiane, Laos, 1974-76, dep. chief mission Wellington, New Zealand, 1983-86, Canberra, Australia, 1986-89; dep. and acting prin. officer U.S. Consulate Gen., Nha Trang, Vietnam, 1973; intelligence and rsch. specialist Dept. State, 1967-69, desk officer Vietnam Working Group, 1969-71, spl. asst. to asst. sec. for East Asian and Pacific Affairs, 1976-77, dep. dir. Office Philippine Affairs, 1978-80, dep. and acting U.S. rep. for Micronesian Status Negotiations, 1980-83, dir. Office of Indonesia, Malaysia, Brunei and Singapore Affairs, 1989-92, spl. projects officer Office of Dir. Gen., 1992-93, U.S. amb. to Papua New Guinea, Solomon Islands and Vanuatu, 1993-96; fgn. policy advisor to the Commander in Chief U.S. Pacific Command, Camp Smith, Hawaii, 1996-98; dir. Ctr. Australian and New Zealand studies Sch. Fgn. Svc., Georgetown U., 1998—2004, sr. fellow, 2004—. Mem.: Australian and New Zealand Studies Assn. N.Am. (pres. 2003—), U.S.-New Zealand Coun. (bd. dirs.), Am. Fgn. Svc. Assn. Address: 3111 Oliver St NW Washington DC 20015-1654

TEARPOCK, DANIEL J. geologist; b. Mocanaqua, Pa. s. John G. and Laura (Tiberi) T.; m. Silvia Cantu; children: Nicole, Danielle. BS, Bloomsburg Univ., 1970; MA, Temple Univ., 1977. Cert. petroleum geologist. Mgr. tech. svcs. Cert. Ctr., King of Prussia, Pa., 1970-72; pres., ptnr. Altantic Computer Svcs., Pennsauken, N.J., 1972-74; geothermal devel. specialist Sperry Rand, Jackson, Miss., 1977-79; petroleum cons. Atwater Cons., New Orleans, La., 1979-85; proj. geologic engr. Tenneco, Lafayette, La., 1985-87, sr. geologic engr., 1987-88; CEO/pres. Subsurface Cons. & Assocs., Lafayette, La., 1988—. CEO, pres. SPX Oil & Gas Co., 1996—; tech. adv. PDVSA Venezuela, 1996—; geology instr. Montgomery Coll., Blue Bell, Pa., 1974-75, instr. Hinds Jr. Coll., Jackson, Miss., 1979-80, adj. asst. prof. Tulane U., 1984-85; guest lectr. U. S.W. La., 1993-95. Author: Applied Subsurface Geological Mapping, 1990, Quick Look Techniques for Prospect Evaluation, 1994; contbr. numerous articles to profl. jours. Mem. Rep. Nat. Com. Recipient Best Paper award New Orleans Geological Soc., 1990, 91. Mem. Am. Assn. Petroleum Geologists, Gulf Coast Am. Geol. Soc., Lafayette Geol. Soc., Geol. Soc. Am., Indonesian Petroleum Soc., Houston Geol. Soc., New Orleans Geol. Soc. Office: Subsurface Cons & Assocs LLC 400 E Kaliste Saloom Rd Lafayette LA 70508-8508

TEASDALE, KENNETH FULBRIGHT, lawyer; b. St. Louis, Nov. 8, 1934; s. Kenneth and Ann (Fulbright) T.; m. Elizabeth Driscol Langdon, June 13, 1964; children: Caroline, Doug, Cindy. AB, Amherst Coll., 1956; LLB, Washington U., St. Louis, 1961. Bar: Mo. 1961. Atty. antitrust div. U.S. Dept. Justice, Washington, 1961-62; asst. counsel Dem. Policy Com. U.S. Senate, Washington, 1962-63, gen. counsel Dem. Policy Com., asst. to majority leader, 1963-64; assoc. Armstrong, Teasdale, Kramer & Vaughan, St. Louis, 1964-67, ptnr., 1967-86; mng. ptnr. Armstrong, Teasdale, Schlafly & Davis, St. Louis, 1986-93, chmn. of firm, 1993—. Trustee United Way Greater St. Louis, Sci. Ctr. St. Louis, St. Louis Art Mus.; trustee, chmn. bd. regents St. Louis U.; mem. nat. coun. Washington U. Law Sch., 1988—. Mem. ABA, Bar Assn. Mo., Bar Assn. St. Louis, St. Louis Coalition for Plant and Life Scis., Racquet Club, Noonday Club, Old Warson Country Club. Episcopalian. Office: Armstrong Teasdale LLP Metropolitan Sq Saint Louis MO 63102-2733

TEASLEY, JOHN RAY SANDERS, JR., writer; b. Charleston, SC, Mar. 8, 1962; s. John Ray Sanders Teasley and Regenia McQueen; m. Sheila Renee Fegan, May 4, 1985 (div. 2001); children: Raphael, Jamila, William. Cert. security mgmt. Cin. Tech. Coll., 1985, legal asst./paralegal Blackstone Sch. Law, Dallas, 2000. Child care worker Cin. Children Home, 1993—94; unit leader/trainer Hamilton Juvenile Ct., Cin., 1994—96; guardian ad litem Pub. Defenders Office, 1996; counselor Hamilton County Juvenile Ct., Cin., 1996—98. Author: (book) All it took was a Rumor, 2002, (books) The World's Largest Unsettled Estate, 2004. Avocations: genealogy, chess, fishing, travel, electronics projects. Home: 118 Promontary Dr Covington KY 41015 Mailing: PO Box 141018 Cincinnati OH 45250

TEAT, HERBERT LEROY, retired music educator; b. El Paso, Tex., May 14, 1923; s. Herbert Leroy Teat and Martha Motee Shannon; m. Angelien Francis, Aug. 4, 1951 (div. Jan. 1975); children: Herbert L. III, James Stephen, Adonna Mary; m. Sue Ellen French, Dec. 17, 1976 (div.); 1 child, Timothy Shannon. MusB, North Tex. State Tchrs. Coll., 1948; MusM, Westminster Choir Coll., 1954. Cert. music tchr., Tex., Ala. Band dir., music dir. Rusk (Tex.) Sch. Dist., 1948-52; choral dir., music dir. Longview (Tex.) Sch. Dist., 1954-69, Tarleton State U., Stephenville, Tex., 1969-83, U. North Ala., Florence, 1984-86; ret. Cons. choral music edn. Contbr. articles to profl. jours.; mem. editl. bd. Southwestern Musician mag., 1958-62; author workbook: EEV Music Reader, 1968. Chmn. campaign March of Dimes, Cherokee County, Tex., 1950; charter mem., v.p. Tex. Choral Dirs. Assn., 1955; state v.p. Music Educators Assn., 1958-60, state pres., 1960-62, mem. state pres. assembly nat. conf., Washington, 1962. Mem. San Gabriel Writers League, Tex. Music Educators (hon. life mem.), Congress of Parent-Tchrs. (hon. life mem.). Methodist. Home: 1105 Church Georgetown TX 78626 E-mail: herble@thegateway.net.

TEATER, DOROTHY SEATH, retired county official; b. Manhattan, Kans., Feb. 11, 1931; d. Dwight Moody and Martha (Stahnke) Seath; m. Robert Woodson Teater, May 24, 1952; children: David Dwight, James Stanley, Donald Robert, Andrew Scott. BS, U. Ky., 1951; MS, Ohio State U., 1954. Home econs. tchr. Georgetown (Ky.) City Schs., 1951-53; extension specialist Ohio Coop. Extension, Columbus, 1967-73; consumer affairs adminstr. City of Columbus, 1974-79, Bank One Columbus NA, 1980-85; councilmember Columbus City Coun., 1980-85; commr. Franklin County, Columbus, Ohio, 1985-2000; ret. Mem. Columbus Met. Area Cmty. Action Orgn.; mem. adv. bd. Ohio Housing Trust; chairwoman Franklin County Children's Cabinet; pub. mem. Ohio Bd. Pharmacy, 2000—. Bd. dirs. BBB; Silesian Boys and Girls Club, Rickenbacker-Woods Mus.; mem. hon. adv. bd. Girl Scouts. Recipient Outstanding Alumnus award U. Ky., 1989, Women of Achievement award YWCA, 1995, Disting. Svc. award Ohio State U., 1997; named Disting. Alumni, Ohio State U., 1977. Mem. County Commrs. Assn. Ohio (pres. 1994), Columbus Met. Club, Greater Columbus C. of C. (Columbus award 1997). Republican. Methodist. Avocations: gardening, sewing.

TEATES, CHARLES DAVID, radiologist, educator; b. Luray, Va., July 1, 1936; s. Gilbert Grove and Mae Frankie (Pierce) T.; m. Mary Bruce Bucher, June 6, 1958; children— Elizabeth Susan, David Bruce, Mary Catherine BS, Lebanon Valley Coll., Annville, Pa., 1958; MS, MD, U. Va., Charlottesville, 1963. Diplomate Am. Bd. Radiology, Am. Bd. Nuclear Medicine. Intern U. Kans. Med. Ctr., 1963-64; resident in radiology U. Va. Med. Ctr., 1964-67; Asst. prof. radiology U. Va., Charlottesville, 1969-73, assoc. prof., 1973-79, prof., 1979-2000, emeritus prof., 2000—. Contbg. author books on radiology and nuclear medicine Served to maj. M.C., U.S. Army, 1967-69, Vietnam Mem. Am. Coll. Radiology (pres. Va. chpt. 1984-85), Soc. Nuclear Medicine (pres. Mid-Eastern chpt. 1984-86), AMA, Alpha Omega Alpha Home: 4635 Watts Passage Charlottesville VA 22911-5932 Office: U Va Med Ctr PO Box 170 Charlottesville VA 22908-0001

TEBBE, JAY, publishing executive; b. Belleville, Ill. m. Diane Tebbe; children: Nathan, Jessica. A in Archtl. Tech., Bailey Tech. Sch.; BS in Bus. Mgmt., Empire State Coll., 1990. Truck driver Belleville News-Dem., 1976, circulation dir., 1990—96, circulation dir./post-press mgr., 1996—99, advt. dir./post-press mgr., 2000—01, v.p. and dir. advt., 2001—, pres. and pub., 2004—. Active Belle-Scott Com.; mem. fin. coun. St. Peter's Cathedral; mem. adv. bd. St. Elizabeth's Hosp.; bd. dirs. Dist. 118 Found. Recipient James K. Batton Knight Ridder Gen. Excellent award, 2002. Mem.: Downtown Belleville Optimists Club, Greater Belleville C. of C. (bd. dirs.). Office: Belleville News-Democrat PO Box 427 120 S Illinois St Belleville IL 62222-0427*

TEBBEN, JOSEPH RICHARD, ancient language educator; b. Columbus, Nov. 26, 1943; s. Leroy Joseph and Janet May Tebben; m. Mary Virginia Welsh, June 22, 1968; children: Andrew Joseph, Mary Ann, Monica Ellen Wong, Patrick Alexander, Susan Diane, Janet Theresa Okoben. BA, Duquesne U., Pitts., 1965; MA, U. of Pitts., 1966; PhD, Ohio State U., 1971. Prof. Greek and Latin Ohio State U., Newark. Author: (book) A Computer Concordance to Hesiod, A Computer Concordance to the Homeric Hymns, Concordantia Homerica: Odyssea, Concordantia Homerica: Ilias, A Course in Medical and Technical Terminology; editor: (newsletter) Computing and the Classics. Dir.

St. Vincent de Paul Food Pantry, Newark, Ohio; sec., bd. dirs. Heartbeats of Licking County, Newark, Ohio. Home: 896 Dietrich Ct Newark OH 43055 Office: Ohio State University 1179 University Dr Newark OH 43055 Office Phone: 740-366-9338. Personal E-mail: tebben@alltel.net. E-mail: tebben.1@osu.edu.

TEBBEN, SHARON LEE, education educator; b. Fairfield, Iowa, Oct. 15, 1943; d. Richard Paul and Arline Marie (Sires) Brandt; m. E. Marvin Tebben, Sept. 7, 1963; children: Laurel Ann, Leslie Kay, Paul Marvin. BS, Mankato State U., 1965; MS, U. Wyo., 1973; EdD, U. St. Thomas, 1992. Tchr. chemistry San Diego City Schs., 1965-68, Alhambra City Schs., Calif., 1968-70; tchg. asst. U. Wyo., Laramie, 1970-73; mem. faculty Presentation Coll., Aberdeen, S.D., 1974-92, chmn. dept. chemistry, 1975-92; asst. prof. edn. Northern State U., Aberdeen, 1992-95, assoc. prof., 1995—, assoc. dean sch. of edn., dir. grad. studies, 1995, dean of edn., 1999—; NCA cons./evaluator, 1990—. NDEA fellow, 1971-73. Mem. AAUW, ASCD, Higher Learning Commn. (cons., evaluator, mem. accreditation review coun.), Phi Kappa Phi, Alpha Lambda Delta, Phi Delta Kappa. Office: Northern State U 1200 S Jay St Aberdeen SD 57401-7155

TEBBS, CAROL ANN, secondary school educator, academic administrator; b. Columbus, Ohio, Sept. 9, 1939; d. John Arthur and Ann Laurie (Wickham) Williams; m. Ronald Daniel Tebbs, Mar. 31, 1957; children: Kimberly Ann, Ronald Dan. BA in English, Whittier Coll., 1963, MA in English and Edn., 1972. Cert. tchr. K-adult Calif. Tchr. art and English Hacienda La Puente Unified Sch. Dist., Hacienda Heights, Calif., 1963-84; tchr. advanced placement English, acad. decathlon advisor, yearbook advisor Glen A. Wilson H.S., Hacienda Heights, 1984—2000, Mentor tchr. Hacienda La Puente Sch. Dist., Hacienda Heights, 1988—2000; reader, tchr. trainer advanced placement English Coll. Bd., 2000—; bd. dirs. Kepler Coll., Lynnwood, Wash., pres., 2003—; bd. dirs., tchr. Online Coll., 2000—. Author (e-books): Beyond Basics: Moving the Chart in Time, Beyond Basics: Tools for the Consulting Astrologer; writer (jour.) Kosmos, Mountain Astrologer, 1995—. Named Tchr. of the Yr., Nat. Walmart Stores Found., 1998; recipient D. Fedderson Cmty. Svc. award, PTA, 1970, Teacher of the Year, 1971, Glen A. Wilson Faculty Tchr. of Yr. award, 1999—2000. Mem.: United Astrology Congress (program chair 1986, 1989, 1992, coord. 1995, bd. chmn. 1995—99, co-founder), Internat. Soc. Astrol. Rsch. (pres. 1988—95, bd. dirs. 1995—2004), Delta Kappa Gamma. Methodist. Home and Office: 56870 Jack Nicklaus Blvd La Quinta CA 92253-5074 Office Phone: 425-673-4292. Personal E-mail: Caroltebbs@aol.com.

TEBEDO, MARYANNE, state legislator; b. Denver, Oct. 30, 1936; m. Don Tebedo; children: Kevin, Ronald, Linda, Thomas, Christine. Mem. Colo. Ho. of Reps., Denver, 1982-88, Colo. Senate, Denver, 1988—2001. Profl. parliamentarian; profl. mediator. Republican.

TECCO, ROMUALD GILBERT LOUIS JOSEPH, violinist, concertmaster; b. Toulon, Var, France, May 1, 1941; came to U.S., 1960; s. Raymond Charles and Angele (Cornille) T. Student, Paris Conservatoire, 1954-60; diploma, postgrad. diploma, Juilliard Sch. Music, 1967-68. Mem. N.Y. String Quartet, 1969-72; concertmaster Juilliard Ensemble, N.Y.C., 1969-72, St. Paul Chamber Orch., 1972-98; soloist Chgo. Symphony, Bavarian Radio Orch., Orch. of Mex., Orchestre Colonne, Paris, Rotterdam Philharm.; performer numerous festivals, Sweden. Recs. with Aaron Copland and Lou Harrison Chamber Music. Served with French Navy, 1964-65, NATO hdqrs. Recipient first prize in violin Conservatoire Paris; recipient first prize chamber music Conservatoire Paris Mem. St. Paul Univ. Club.

TECHAR, FRANK J. bank executive; b. Minn. BS in engring., Princeton U., 1978; MBA, U. Denver, 1983; exec. program, USC, 1992. Various banking positions First Interstate Bank, Denver; various engring. positions USG Corp., Oakfield, NY; sr. v.p., gen. mgr. BMO Fin. Group, London; acct. officer, corp. banking Bk. of Montreal, Denver, 1984, mgr. dir., corp. banking Houston, 1993—95, exec. v.p., small bus. banking; pres., CEO Harris Bankcorp, BMO Fin. corp., Toronto, Canada, 2002—. Mem.: Northwestern U. Bus. Sch. Adv. Coun., Chicagoland C.of.C. (bd. mem.), Exec. Club Chgo. (bd. mem.), U. Club, Chgo. Club, Econ. Club, Comml. Club of Chgo. Office: 111 W Monroe St Chicago IL 60603

TECTOR, ALFRED J. cardiothoracic surgeon; s. Alfred J. Tector and Mariea Francis Ogden; m. Joy Ann Kelly, Apr. 20, 1963; children: Alfred, Matthew, Leslie, Kelly. BA in Biology, Utica Coll., 1959; MD, St. Louis U. Sch. Medicine, 1963; MS in surgery, U. Iowa, 1970; PhD (hon.), Utica Coll., 1997, Milw. Sch. Engrs., 2004. Cardio thoracic surgeon St. Lukes Med. Ctr., Milw., 1970—75, Cleve. Clin. Found., 1975—. Office: Midwest Heart Surgery Inst 2901 W KK River Pkwy Milwaukee WI 53215

TEDDER, THOMAS FLETCHER, immunology educator, researcher; b. Chateauroux, France, May 14, 1956; came to U.S. 1959; s. Raymond Percy and Barbara (Hagemann) T. AA, Okaloosa-Walton C.C., Niceville, Fla., 1976; BS with honors, U. Fla., 1978, MS, 1980; PhD, U. Ala., Birmingham, 1984. Rsch. fellow in pathology Harvard Med. Sch., Boston, 1984-85, instr. pathology, 1986-88, asst. prof. pathology, 1988-93; assoc. prof. pathology Harvard U. Med. Sch., Boston, 1993; prof. immunology Duke U. Med. Ctr., Durham, NC, 1993—, chmn. dept. immunology, 1993—. Alter Geller prof. rsch. in immunology Duke U. Med. Ctr., 1997—. Assoc. editor Jour. Immunology, 1989-93, sect. editor, 1993-98; contbr. numerous articles to med. jours., including Jour. Immunology, Nature, Lancet, Immunity. Recipient LeRoy Collins Disting. Alumnus award Fla. Assn. C.C.'s; named 25th Anniversary Disting. Alumnus, Okaloosa-Walton C.C., 1989; Damon Runyon-Walter Winchell rsch. fellow, 1985-87; scholar Leukemia Soc. Am., 1991-96, Stohlman scholar, 1995-96. Mem. Am. Soc. for Microbiology (Pres. fellow 1982), Am. Assn. Immunologists, Sigma Xi, Phi Kappa Phi. Achievements include identification and determination of structure and function of many human B lymphocyte cell-surface molecules. Office: Duke U Med Ctr Dept Immunology PO Box 3010 Durham NC 27710-0001 Office Phone: 919-684-3578. E-mail: thomas.tedder@duke.edu.

TEDESCHI, GEORGE, labor union administrator; Journeyman newspaper pressman Newsday, Long Island, NY; pres. Nassau County 406C Graphic Comm. Internat. Union, 1972—2000, Graphic Comm. Internat. Union, 2000—. Mem. gen. bd. Graphic Comm. Internat. Union, 1988—2000, pres. N.A. Newspaper Conf., 1979—2000; exec. bd. Long Island Fedn. Labor, AFL-CIO. Dir. and sec. United Way of Long Island. Office: Graphic Comm Internat Union 1900 L St NW Washington DC 20036 Office Phone: 202-462-1400.

TEDESCHI, JOHN ALFRED, historian, librarian; b. Modena, Italy, July 17, 1931; came to U.S., 1939, naturalized, 1944; s. Caesar George and Piera (Forti) T.; m. Anne Wood Christian, Sept. 8, 1956; children: Martha, Philip, Sara. BA, Harvard U., 1954, MA, 1960, PhD, 1966. Bibliographer European history and lit. Newberry Library, Chgo., 1965-84, curator rare books and manuscripts, head dept. spl. collections, 1970-82, dir. Ctr. Renaissance Studies, 1979-84; curator rare books and spl. collections Meml. Library U. Wis.-Madison, 1984-96. Lectr. history U. Chgo., 1969-71; vis. prof. U. Ill.-Chgo., 1972-73, adj. prof., 1979-84 Co-editor: (series) Corpus Reformatorum Italicorum, 1968-96; editor-in-chief: Bibliographie Internat. de L'Humanisme et de la Renaissance, 1977-82; editor: Italian Reformation Studies in Honor of Laelius Socinus, 1965, (with Anthony Molho) Renaissance Studies in Honor of Hans Baron, 1971, (with Gustav Henningsen) The Inquisition in Early Modern Europe: Studies on Sources and Methods, 1986, The Prosecution of Heresy: Collected Studies on the Inquisition in Early Modern Italy, 1991 (transl. into Italian 1997), Tomasso Sassetti, Il Massacro di San Bartolomeo, 1995, The Italian Reformation of the Sixteenth Century and the Diffusion of Renaissance Culture: A Bibliography of the Secondary Literature (c. 1750-1997), 2000, The correspondence of Roland H. Bainton and Delio Cantimori, 1932-66, 2002; translator: (with Anne Tedeschi) The Cheese and the Worms. The Cosmos of a Sixteenth-Century Miller (Carlo Ginzburg), 1980 (named an Outstanding Acad. Book by Choice mag.), The Night Battles. Witchcraft and Agrarian Cults in the Sixteenth and Seventeenth Centuries (Carlo Ginzburg), 1983, Clues, Myths, and the Historical Method (Carlo Ginzburg), 1989, Hans Urs von Balthasar: A Theological Style (Angelo Scola), 1995, Domenico Scandella Known as Menocchio: His Trials Before the Inquisition (1583-1599) (Andrea Del Col), 1996, The Protestant Reformation in Sixteenth-Century Italy (Salvatore Caponetto), 1999, Books of the Body: Anatomical Ritual and Renaissance Learning (Andrea Carlino), 1999; mem. editl. com.: Index des Livres Interdits (Sherbrooke), Collected Works of Erasmus (Toronto); mem. editl. bd.: Studi e Testi per la Storia Religiosa Italiana del '500 (Florence), The Peter Martyr Libr. (Kirksville, Mo.); contbr. articles to profl. jours. Served with U.S. Army, 1954-56. Grantee Am. Philos. Soc., 1961; grantee NEH, 1967; Old Dominion fellow Harvard U. Ctr. Renaissance Studies, Florence, Italy, 1967-68; fellow Inst. Research in Humanities, U. Wis.-Madison, 1976-77; Huntington Library fellow, 1984. Mem. Am. Soc. Reformation Research (pres. 1972), Renaissance Soc. Am. (exec. bd. 1971-96), 16th Century Studies Conf. (pres. 1987), Archive of Congregation for the Doctrine of the Faith (Vatican City; pres. 1999-2002, scholarly adv. com.), Am. Hist. Assn., Am. Cath. Hist. Assn. Home: 57211 Rush Creek Rd Ferryville WI 54628 E-mail: tede@frontiernet.net.

TEDESCO, FRANCIS JOSEPH, retired academic administrator, medical educator; b. Derby, Conn., Mar. 8, 1944; s. Lena (Tufano) Tedesco; m. Luann Lee Ekern, Aug. 1, 1970; 1 child, Jennifer Nicole. BS cum laude, Fairfield U., 1965; MD cum laude, St. Louis U., 1969. Asst. instr. Hosp. of U. Pa., Phila., 1971-72; asst. prof. Washington U. Sch. Medicine, St. Louis, 1974-75, U. Miami (Fla.) Sch. Medicine, 1975-77, co-dir. clin. research, 1976-78, assoc. prof., 1977-78, Med. Coll. Ga., Augusta, 1978-81, chief of gastroenterology dept., 1978-88, prof., 1981—, acting v.p. clin. activities, 1984, v.p. for clin. activities, 1984-88, Interim dean Sch. of Medicine, 1986-88, pres., 1988—2001, pres. emeritus, 2001—. Cons. Med.-Letter/AMA divsn. drugs, Dwight D. Eisenhower Army Med. Ctr., Ft. Gordon, Ga., VA Med. Ctr., Augusta, Walter Reed Army Med. Ctr., Washington; mem. gastroenterology spl. study sect. NIH, Washington, 1982—, mem. nat. digestive disease adv. bd., 1985-88, vice chmn., 1986-87, chmn., 1987-88; mem. Ty Cobb Found. Scholarship Bd., 1998—. Contbr. numerous articles to profl. jours. Bd. dirs. Augusta Country Day Sch., 1981-83, Am. Cancer Soc., Augusta, 1985—, v.p., 1986—; bd. dirs., exec. com. Ga. Coalition for Health, 1995-2002; chmn. Gov.'s Health Strategies Coun., 1992-2002; bd. visitors CDC, 1998—; nat. adv. bd. Ga. Acad. Sci., Math. and Engring., 1998—; mem. Ty Cobb Fedn. Bd., 1998—. Recipient Eddie Palmer award for gastrointestinal endoscopy, 1983, cert. of appreciation Am. Cancer Soc., 1986, Outstanding Faculty award Med. Coll. Ga. Sch. Medicine, 1988, Profl. Achievement award Fairfield U., 1993, alumni merit award St. Louis U. Sch. Medicine, 1996; Avalon Found. scholar St. Louis U., 1968-69, Paul Harris fellow Rotary, 1990, Spirit of Ga. award Ga. Econ. Devel. Assn., 1998. Fellow ACP, Am. Fedn. Clin. Investigation, Am. Gastroent. Assn., Am. Soc. Gastrointestinal Endoscopy (treas. 1981-84, pres.-elect 1984-85, pres. 1985-86, Rudolph Schindler award 1993); mem. Am. Coll. Gastroenterology, So. Soc. Clin. Investigation, Richmond County Med. Soc., Med. Assn. Ga. Roman Catholic. Avocations: reading, swimming. Home: 2810 Peachtree Pl Augusta GA 30909 Office: Med Coll Ga Office Pres 1120 15th St Augusta GA 30912-0006

TEDESCO, KRISTI, newscaster; married; 1 child. Degree in Comms., U. Ariz. Reporter, Topeka; anchor, reporter Sta. KWCH-TV, Wichita, Kans., Sta. WRTV-TV, Indpls., 2000—. Recipient First Pl. award, Kans. Assn. Broadcasters, 1995. Office: WRTV TV 1330 N Meridian St Indianapolis IN 46202*

TEDESCO, PAUL HERBERT, humanities educator; b. Nashua, N.H., Dec. 28, 1928; s. Steven R. and Ruth (Weaver) T.; m. Eleanor Martha Hollis, Jan. 24, 1953; children: Steven Anthony, Sara Adams Tagget, James Beattie. AB in History, Harvard Coll., 1952; AM in History, Boston U., 1955, PhD in History, 1970; CAGS in Adminstrn., Northeastern U., Boston, 1974. Instr. humanities Mich. State U., East Lansing, 1955—60; tchr. history Great Neck North H.S., NY, 1960—62; chmn. dept. social studies Canton H.S., Mass., 1962—65; prof., chmn. edn. Northeastern U., Boston, 1965—87; Fulbright prof. history Peking U., Beijing, 1988—89; historian-in-residence City of Haverhill, Mass., 1989—90; lectr. bus., history, govt. edn. Asian divsn. U. Md., Korea, Japan, Guam, 1990—94; team leader, lectr. Joint Siberian-Am. Faculty Irkutsk State U., Russia, 1994—95; edn. coord. Asian divsn. U. Md., 1995—97, lectr. European divsn., 1997—. Nat. dir. BHelp (Bus., History and Econ. Life Program), Boston, 1968—; cons. in field. Author: Teaching with Case Studies, 1978, A New England City: Haverhill Massachusetts, 1987, Attleboro, Massachusetts: The Hub of the Jewelry Industry, 1979, Protection, Patriotism and Prosperity: James M. Swank, the AISA, and the Tariff, 1872-1913, 1985; author, editor: The Creative Social Science Teacher, 1970, The Thunder of the Mills, 1981, Dover, Mass., 2000. Mem. Town Fin. Com., Canton, Mass., 1966-68. With U.S. Army, 1952-54. Recipient FEI Nat. collegiate award, 1985, Freedoms Found. George Washington medal for econ. edn., 1984. Mem. New Eng. History Tchrs. Assn. (past pres., Kidger award 1975), Dover Hist. Soc. (pres.).

TEDFORD, CHARLES FRANKLIN, biophysicist; b. Lawton, Okla., June 26, 1928; s. Charles E. and Loula B. (Waters) T.; m. Julie Reme Sauret, Sept. 15, 1951; children: Gary Franklin, Mark Charles, Philip John. BS with distinction in Chemistry, S.W. Tex. State U., 1950, MS, 1954; postgrad. in radiobiology Reed Coll., 1957, in biophysics U. Calif., Berkeley, 1961-63. Enlisted USN, 1945-47, commd. ensign, 1950, advanced through grades to capt., 1968; biochemist U.S. Naval Hosp., San Diego, 1953-54, U.S. Naval Biol. Lab., Oakland, Calif., 1954-56; sr. instr., radiation safety officer Nuclear, Biol. and Chem. Warfare Def. Sch., Treasure Island, Calif., 1956-61; asst. chief nuclear medicine div. Navy Med. Sch., Bethesda, Md., 1963-66; adminstrv. program mgr. radiation safety br. Bur. Medicine and Surgery, Washington, 1966-72; dir. radiation safety and health physics program Navy Regional Med. Center, San Diego, 1972-74; mgr. Navy Regional Med. Clinic, Seattle, 1974-78, ret., 1978; dir. radiation health unit Ga. Dept. Human Resources, Atlanta, 1978-79; dir. Ariz. Radiation Regulatory Agy., Tempe, 1979-91; chief, Radiological Health Prog., Juneau, Alaska, 1991-93, ret. 1993; cons. 1993—. elected chmn. Conf. Radiation Program Dirs., 1987; named Ariz. Southwestern Low Level Radioactive Waste Compact Commr., 1990. Recipient Ariz. Adminstr. of Yr. award Ariz. Adminstrs. Assn., 1988; decorated Legion of Merit, Meritorious Service medal. Mem. Health Physics Soc., Am. Nuclear Soc. Contbr. articles on radiation safety to profl. publs.

TEDFORD, DEBORAH J. lawyer; b. Dec. 1950; Grad. cum laude, Yale U., 1972; grad., Boston U., 1976. Ptnr. Tedford, Gianni & Jensen, P.C., Mystic, Conn. Bd. dirs. Hospice Southeastern Conn. Fellow: Conn. Bar Found., Am. Coll. Trust and Estate Counsel; mem.: Southeastern Conn. Estate and Tax Planning Coun. (past pres.), Conn. Bar Assn. (chair legal problems of the elderly 1990—92, chair estates and probate sect. 1997—, sec. 1999—2000, pres. 2002—03, founding editor Estates and Probate Newsletter), Mystic Rotary Club (past pres.). Office: PO Box 350 30 Bank St New Britain CT 06050

TEDFORD, JACK NOWLAN, III, construction executive, small business owner; b. Reno, Jan. 1, 1943; s. Jack Nowlan Jr. and Elizabeth (Kolhoss) T.; m. Nancy Joanne Stiles, Feb. 27, 1971; children: Jack Nowlan IV, James Nathan. BS, U. Nev., 1966, MBA, 1969. Bus. mgr. Los Angeles Bapt. Coll., Newhall, Calif., 1969-71; v.p. Jack N. Tedford, Inc., Fallon, Nev., 1971-98; owner/broker Tedford Realty, Fallon, 1974-94; owner/mgr. Tedford Bus. Systems, Fallon, 1978-94; pres. JNT, Inc., Fallon, 1994—. Pres., Jack N. Tedford, Inc., 1998—. Author numerous computer programs. Member Selective Svc. Local Bd., Fallon, 1971-76; chmn. City of Fallon Bd. Adjustment, 1972-95, chmn. Churchill Co. Reps., Fallon, 1976-80; mem. ctrl. com. Nev. Reps., 1976-2002; del. Nat. Conv., Detroit, 1980, Dallas, 1984; former coun. ofcls. Western Nev. Devel. Dist.; former treas. Lahontan Valley Environ. Alliance. Mem. Assn. Gen. Contractors (past pres., former v.p., treas. Nev. chpt., dir.), Nat. Bd. Realtors, State Bd. Realtors, Incline Village Bd. Realtors, CEDA Bus. Coun. (bd. dirs. 1991-97), Rotary (bd. dirs. 1980-81), Master's Coll. (bd. dirs. 1971-95), Slavic Gospel Assn. (bd. dirs.), Nat. Assn. Gen. Contractors (bd. dirs. open shop com., closely held bus. com.), Fellowship of Cos. for Christ Internat. Republican. Baptist. Avocations: computers, family activities, golf. Home and Office: PO Box 7937 Incline Village NV 89452 Business E-Mail: jnt@jntinc.com.

TEDLOCK, BARBARA HELEN, anthropologist, educator, academic administrator; b. Battle Creek, Mich., Sept. 9, 1942; d. Byron Taylor and Mona Gerteresse (O'Connor) McGrath; m. Dennis E. Tedlock, July 19, 1968. BA in Rhetoric, U. Calif., Berkeley, 1967; MA in Anthropology, Wesleyan U., 1973; PhD in Anthropology, SUNY, Albany, 1978. Lectr. in music Tufts U., Medford, Mass., 1977-78, asst. prof. anthropology, 1978-82, assoc. prof., 1982-87; assoc. prof. anthropology SUNY, Buffalo, 1987-89, prof. anthropology, 1989—, disting. prof., 2003, chair dept. anthropology, 1998—2000, 2002—03, assoc. dean undergrad. edn., 2000—01. Vis. mem. Inst. for Advanced Study, Princeton, 1986. Author: Time and the Highland Maya, 1982, The Beautiful and the Dangerous Encounters with Zuni Indians, 1992, The Woman in the Shaman's Body: Reclaiming the Feminine in Religion and Medicine, 2003, editor: Dreaming: Anthropological and Psychological Interpretations, 1987; co-editor: Teaching From the American Earth, 1975; assoc. editor Jour. of Anthropol. Rsch., 1987-93; sr. editor Dreaming, 1990-95; assoc. editor Latin Am. Rsch. Rev., 1992—; mem. editl. adv. bd. Encyc. Cultural Anthropology, 1993-95, Handbook of Qualitative Research, 1998—. Adv. bd. Mus. of Indian Arts, Santa Fe, 1991-95; mem. Roycrofters-at-large East Aurura, N.Y., 1989—; mem. Cultural Survival, 1980—; mem. humanities panel WGBH, Boston, 1983-84; judge pottery Southwestern Assn. on Indian Affairs, Santa Fe, 1981-83. Fellowships NEH, 1986, 93, sr. fellowship Am. Coun. of Learned Socs., 1994, Weatherhead fellowship Sch. of Am. Rsch., 1980, sr. fellowship Ctr. for the Study of World Religions/Harvard U., 1998; Sabbatical fellow Am. Philos. Soc., 2002-03; recipient Charles Bordon, Geoffrey Bushnell Juan Cosmos prize in linguistics Internat. Congress of Americanists, 1979. Fellow Am. Anthropol. Assn. (bd. dirs. 1991-93, editor-in-chief Am. Anthropologist 1994-98, Pres.'s award for leadership 1997), Soc. for Cultural Anthropology, Am. Philosophical Soc.; mem. AAUW, PEN (elected), Soc. for Humanistic Anthropology (pres. 1991-93, Writing prize 1986), Soc. for Psychol. Anthropology (bd. dirs. 1993-96), Assn. for Study of Dreams (bd. dirs. 1990-95), Soc. for Ethnohistory (exec. bd. 1980-82), Am. Studies Assn. (exec. bd. 1983-85), Assn. on Am. Indian Affairs. Avocations: skiing, running, swimming, dancing, videoing. E-mial. Office: SUNY Buffalo Dept Anthropology Buffalo NY 14261-0001 E-mail: tedlockb@acsu.buffalo.edu.

TEDOLDI, ROBERT LOUIS, JR., financial planner, consultant; b. Meriden, Conn., Jan. 4, 1967; s. Robert Louis and Carol (Amesbury) T. BA in Journalism, U. S.C., 1989. Assoc. Coordinated Fin. Planning, Farmington, Conn., 1990-92; jr. ptnr. Benefit Plans Design & Adminstrn., Inc., Vernon, Conn., 1992-96; pres., CEO Tedoldi Fin., South Windsor, Conn., 1996—; pres., ptnr. DiSanto Bertoline Fin. Svcs. LLC, Glastonbury, Conn., 1999—. Team capt. March of Dimes, Hartford, Conn., 1992, 93; bd. dirs. Plum Ridge Condo Assn., South Windsor, Conn., 1994—, pres., 1997—; mem. Greater Hartford Jaycees, 1991—. Recipient Conn. Ofcl. citation Gov. of Conn./House and Senate, 1992-93. Mem. Internat. Assn. Fin. Planning, Nat. Assn. Life Underwriters (voting del. 1990), U.S. Golf Assn., Conn. State Assn. Life Underwriters, Hartford Life Underwriters Assn. (bd. dirs. 1991—, cmty. svc. chmn. 1991, 92, Pres.'s award 1993, 96, golf com. chmn. 1996-97, Pres.'s award 1996), Tolland County C. of C. (bd. dirs., mem. golf com. 1995—), Ellington Ridge Country Club (green com. 1990—), Pi Kappa Phi. Republican. Roman Catholic. Avocations: golf, hockey, boating, water and snow skiing, mountain hiking. Office: Tedoldi Fin 409 Sand Stone Dr South Windsor CT 06074-2867

TEDROS, THEODORE ZAKI, real estate broker, appraiser, educator; b. Cairo, June 25, 1910; Naturalized, 1966; s. Zaki and Faika (Lotfi) T.; married 1962; 1 child, Samuel N. BA in Math., Tex. Christian U., 1957, MEd with honors, 1958; postgrad., Fla. State U., 1961. Tchr. pub. schs., Addis Ababa, Ethiopia, 1947-56, The American Inst., Addis Ababa, Ethiopia, 1952-56; instr. math. Fla. State U., Tallahassee, 1958-59; tchr. math. Fla. Mil. Sch. and Coll., Deland, Fla., 1961-64; tchr. Volusia County Bd. Instrn., Deland, 1964-75; real estate broker Daytona Beach, Fla., 1975-98; appraiser, 1978-92. Prof. ednl. sociology U. Man., Winnipeg, Can., summers 1962-64. Sunday sch. tchr., Fla.; mem. Nat. Coun. Math. Tchrs., 1959-75, Phi Delta Kappa, 1960-80. Mem. Nat. Assn. Master Appraisers (v.p. 1985-86), Fla. Assn. Realtors, Daytona Beach Area Bd. Realtors, Nat. Assn. Realtors (cert. 1978-90). Democrat. Home: 611 E Tall Pine Ter Deland FL 32724-7122

TEDROW, JOHN CHARLES FREMONT, soils educator; b. Rockwood, Pa., Apr. 21, 1917; s. John Wesley and Emma Grace (Younkin) T.; m. Mary Jane Lough, Mar. 20, 1943 (dec. Mar. 1991); children: John Charles Fremont, Thomas Lough (dec.). BS, Pa. State U., 1939; MS, Mich. State U., 1940; PhD, Rutgers U., 1950. Jr. soil technologist Dept. Agr., 1941-42, soil scientist, 1946-47; instr. Rutgers U., New Brunswick, N.J., 1947-50, asst. prof., 1950-53, assoc. prof., 1953-57, prof. soils, 1957—73, prof. II, soils, 1973—84, prof. emeritus, 1984—. Cons. N.S. Research Found., 1949—; sr. pedologist Boston U., 1953—; prin. investigator Arctic Inst. N.Am., Washington, 1955-68, NSF, 1961-62, Atomic Energy Commn., Washington, 1961-63; cons. to govt. and industry. Author: (with R.C. Murray) Forensic Geology: Earth Sciences and Criminal Investigation, 1974, Soils of the Polar Landscapes, 1977, (with K.A. Linell) Soil and Permafrost Surveys in the Arctic, 1981, Soils of New Jersey, 1986, (with R.C. Murray) Forensic Geology, 1991; editor in chief Soil Science, 1968-79; editor: Antarctic Soils and Soil Forming Processes, 1966. Served to lt. USNR, 1942-46. Recipient Lindback Research award Rutgers U., 1978, Antarctic Service medal. Fellow Am. Soc. Agronomy, Soil Sci. Soc. Am., Arctic Inst. N.Am.; mem. Internat. Soc. Soil Sci., Am. Geophys. Union, Sigma Xi, Alpha Zeta (hon.), Phi Mu Delta. Achievements include investigation of polar soils in Alaska, Can., Greenland, Scandinavia, Siberia and Antarctica. Home: 5 Bluebird Ct Edison NJ 08820-3677 Office: Rutgers U Ecology Evolution and Natural Resources PO Box 231 New Brunswick NJ 08903-0231

TEEGARDEN, KENNETH LEROY, clergyman; b. Cushing, Okla., Dec. 22, 1921; s. Roy Albert and Eva B. (Swiggart) T.; m. Wanda Jean Strong, May 28, 1944; children: David Kent, Marshall Kirk. Student, Okla. State U., 1938-40; AB, Phillips U., 1942, MA, 1945, D.D., 1963; B.D., Tex. Christian U., 1949, D.D., 1976, Bethany Coll., 1974; LL.D., Lynchburg Coll., 1975; L.H.D., Culver-Stockton Coll., 1975. Ordained to ministry Christian Ch. (Disciples of Christ), 1940; pastor in Kaw City, Okla., 1941-43, Chandler, Okla., 1944-47, Texas City, Tex., 1947-48, Healdton, Okla., 1948-49, Vernon, Tex., 1949-55, Fort Smith, Ark., 1955-58; exec. minister Christian Ch. in Ark., 1958-65; asst. to pres. Christian Ch. in U.S. and Can., Indpls., 1965-69; exec. minister Christian Ch. in Tex., 1969-73; gen. minister, pres. Christian Ch. in U.S. and Can., 1973-85; faculty Brite Div. Sch., Tex. Christian U., 1985-89. Mem. governing bd. Nat. Council Chs., 1973-85; del. 5th Assembly of World Council Chs., Nairobi, Kenya, 1975, 6th Assembly, Vancouver, B.C., Can, 1983; rep. Nat. Council Chs. in Exchange of Ch. Leadership with Soviet Union, 1974 Author: We Call Ourselves Disciples, 1975. Named Disting. Alumnus Tex. Christian U., 1973, Phillips U., 1975; Outstanding Citizen Vernon, Tex., 1954 Mem. Christian Ch. Home: 7013 Serrano Dr Fort Worth TX 76126-2317 E-mail: kltfwt@msn.com.

TEEGAVARAPU, RAMESH SATYA, engineering educator, researcher; s. Prabakarara Rao and Leela Teegavarapu; m. Sreelatha Vinnakota Teegavarapu. PhD, U. Manitoba, Winnipeg, 2000. PE, Ky., 2003. Rsch. engr. U. Calif., Davis, 2000—01. Contbr. articles various profl. jours. Fellow NSERC fellowship, Nat. Scis. Engring. Rsch. Coun., Can., 2. Office: U Ky 161 Oliver Raymond Hall Lexington KY 40506 E-mail: ramesh@engr.uky.edu.

TEEGUARDEN, DENNIS EARL, forest economist, educator; b. Gary, Ind., Aug. 21, 1931; s. Gary Leon and Mary Dessa (Purciful) T.; m. Sally Annette Gleason, Dec. 23, 1954; children: Jason Earl, Julie Annette, Justin Gary. BS in Forestry with honors, Mich. Tech. U., Houghton, 1953; M.Forestry, U. Calif., Berkeley, 1958, PhD in Agrl. Econs. (Bidwell research fellow 1962-63), 1964. Rsch. aid U.S. Forest Service, 1957; asst. rsch. specialist U. Calif., Berkeley,

1958-63, mem. faculty, 1963-91, prof. forestry econs. Sch. Forestry, 1963-91, S.J. Hall prof. forest econs., 1989-91, prof. emeritus, 1991—, chmn. dept. forestry and resource mgmt., 1978-86, acting dir. forest products lab., 1987-88, assoc. dean for acad. affairs, 1990-92, assoc. dean rsch. and extension, 1992-93. Mem. Calif. Commn. on Agr. and Higher Edn., 1993-95, com. scientists Dept. Agr., 1977-80; cons. in field; mem. adv. bd. U. Calif. Forest Products Lab., 1994-98; mem. adv. coun. Alberta Heritage Found. for Sci. and Engring. Rsch., 2001-03. Co-author: Forest Resource Management: Decision-Making Principles and Cases, 1979; contbr. articles to profl. jours. Trustee Mich. Tech. Fund, Mich. Tech. U., Houghton, 1994-2004, life trustee, 2004—. Lt. USNR, 1953-57, Korea. Recipient Outstanding Alumnus award Mich. Tech. U., 1993, Berkeley citation U. Calif., Berkeley, 1994; grantee U.S. Forest Svc., Bur. Land Mgmt.; named to Honor Acad. Sch. Forestry and Wood Products, Mich. Tech. U., 1995. Fellow Soc. Am. Foresters; mem. Western Forest Economists, Calif. Water Fowl Assn. Home: 4732 Westwood Ct Richmond CA 94803-2441 Office: U Calif Coll Natural Resources Berkeley CA 94720-0001

TEEL, JAMES E. supermarket and drug store retail executive; b. 1930; V.p. Raley's, West Sacramento, 1950-1991; co-chmn., dir., 1991—. Office: Raleys Inc 500 W Capitol Ave West Sacramento CA 95605-2696

TEEL, JOYCE RALEY, retail executive; b. 1930; m. James Teel. Dir. Raley's, West Sacramento, 1950—; co-chmn. bd. dirs. Raley's, Bel Air Markets, Food Source, Nob Hill Foods, No. Calif., Nev., NMex., 1991—. Dir. non-profit Food for Families. Office: Raleys & Belaire 500 W Capitol Ave West Sacramento CA 95605-2696

TEELE, CYNTHIA LOMBARD, lawyer; b. Boston, Oct. 11, 1961; d. John Hughes and Patricia Jeanne (Linder) T. AB in Urban Studies magna cum laude, Brown U., 1983; JD, U. Va., 1986. Bar: Calif. 1986. Assoc. Lillick McHose & Charles, L.A., 1986-87, Wyman Bautzer Kuchel & Silbert, L.A., 1987-91; sr. atty. Paramount Pictures Corp.-TV Divsn., Hollywood, Calif., 1991-92, dir., legal, 1992-94, v.p., legal, 1994—. Home: 3644 Berryman Ave Los Angeles CA 90066-3306

TEEM, CLAYTON L(AVERNE), II, education educator, psychologist; s. Clayton LaVerne and Dorothy Elizabeth Teem. PhD Clin. Psychology, Calif. Sch. Profl. Psychology, Berkeley, Calif., 1980. Lic. Psychologist Ga. State Bd. of Examiners of Psychology, 1989, cert. Treatment of Alcohol & Other Psychoactive Substance Use Disorders APA, 1996. Staff clin. psychologist U.S. Air Force, Scott, AFT, Ill., 1982—86; neuropsychologist Learning Svcs. Corp., Lawrenceville, Ga., 1986—96; asst. prof. psychology Gainesville Coll., Ga., 2000—. Cons. psychologist In-House Med. Resources, Inc., Atlanta, 1998—98, in field, 1996—98; chairperson, judging com. Regional Sci. & Engring. Fair, Gainesville, Ga., 2002—; chairperson, tech. com. Div of Soc Sci & Educ, Gainesville Coll., Ga., 2002—; chairperson, instl. rev. bd. devel. com. Gainesville Coll., Ga., 2001—03. Contbr. scientific papers (pub. in 30th Ann. Conf. of Air Force Behavioral Scientists), articles (Publ. in re-Learning Times, 1994). Mem. Nat. Alliance for Mental Illness, Gainesville, Ga., 2003. Capt. USAF, 1981—86, Scott AFB, IL. Decorated Air Force Tng. Ribbon U.S. Air Force, Air Force Longevity Svc. Award Ribbon; recipient Director's Choice - Clinician of the Yr., Learning Svcs. - Peachtree campus, 1993; fellow Psychology internship, U.S. Air Force, 1981-1982. Mem.: APA, APA Divsn. 50 - Psychology of Addictions, APA Divsn. 40 - Neuropsychology, APA Divsn. 38 - Health Psychology, APA Dividion 28 - Psychopharmacology & Substance Abuse, APA Divsn. 27 - Cmty. Psychology, APA Divsn. 22 - Rehab. Psychology, APA Divsn. 20 - Adult Devel., APA Divsn. 2 - Tchg. Psychology, Nat. Acad. of Neuropsychology, Internat. Neuropsychological Soc., Am. Psychol. Soc., Psychology Club (faculty advisor 2003), Phi Kappa Phi, Phi Beta Kappa. Libertarian. Catholic. Avocations: reading, nature, computers, music. Home: 3404-B Water Vistas Pkwy Lawrenceville GA 30044 Office: Gainesville Coll Divsn Social Sci and Edn 3820 Mundy Mill Rd Gainesville Georgia GA 30503 Business E-Mail: cteem@gc.peachnet.edu.

TEEM, PAUL LLOYD, JR., bank executive; b. Gastonia, N.C., Mar. 10, 1948; s. Paul Lloyd Sr. and Ruth Elaine (Bennett) T. BA, U. N.C., 1970; Cert., Inst. Fin. Edn., Chgo., 1984, Diploma, 1985, Degree of Distinction, 1989. Cert. tchr. N.C., cert. consumer credit exec.; lic. real estate broker; lic. lay Eucharistic minister. Exec. v.p., sec. Citizens South Bank, Gastonia, NC, 1983—; exec. v.p., sec., bd. dirs. Citizens South Fin. Svcs. Inc., Gastonia, 1988—; exec. v.p., sec. Citizens South Holdings, Mut. Holding Co., Gastonia, 1998—2002, Citizens South Banking Corp., Gastonia, 1998—. Bd. dirs. Gastonia Mchts. Assn., Inc., 1981-83; lay reader, lay eucharistic min. Episcopal Ch. Decorated Order Purple Cross, Legion of Honor. Fellow Soc. Cert. Credit Execs.; mem. Nat. Soc. Sons and Daus. of Pilgrims, SAR, Sons of Confederate Vets., Mil. Order of Stars and Bars, Masons (32d degree, bd. dirs., Disting. Svc. award 1987, Gold Honor award 1988, Active Legion of Honor 1989, Order of the Purple Cross of York 1990), Shriners, KT, Royal Order of Scotland, Hon. Order Ky. Cols., Phi Alpha Theta. Democrat. Avocation: genealogy. Home: 1208 Poston Cir Gastonia NC 28054-4634 Office: Citizens South Bank PO Box 2249 Gastonia NC 28053-2249 Office Phone: 704-884-2262. E-mail: paul.teem@citizenssouth.com.

TEEPEN, THOMAS HENRY, newspaper editor, journalist; b. Nashville, Jan. 19, 1935; s. Albert George and Elizabeth Blanche (Winfree) T.; m. Nancy Irene Roux, Feb. 2, 1957 (div. 1974); children— Kristina Lynn, Jeremy Roux; m. Sandra Jean Richards, May 14, 1975; 1 stepchild, Jennifer Koerlin BS in Journalism, Ohio U., 1957. Reporter Urbana (Ohio) Daily Citizen, 1957-58; asst. editor Kettering-Oakwood Times, Dayton, Ohio, 1958-59; from reporter to editorial writer Dayton Daily News, 1959-68, editorial page editor, 1968-82, Atlanta Constitution, 1982-92; nat. corr. Cox Newspapers, Atlanta, 1992-2000, columnist, 2000—. Contbg. columnist Liberal Opinion Week. Former pres. Joel Chandler Harris Assn., Atlanta; mem. Atlanta Opera, 1985—, Joint Internat. Observer Group, Ethiopian Elections, 1992; mem. internat. adv. com. The African-Am. Inst., N.Y.C., 1985-97; bd. trustees Freedom to Read Found., Chgo. Profl. journalism fellow Stanford Univ., 1967 Home and Office: 900 Charles Allen Dr NE Atlanta GA 30308-1722 Office Phone: 404-874-1421. E-mail: tteepen@earthlink.net., teepencolumn@coxnews.com.

TEEPLE, FIONA DIANE, librarian, lawyer; b. St. Thomas, Ont., Can., Jan. 9, 1943; d. William Lloyd and Grace (Hathaway) T. BA, U. Western Ont., London, 1964; BLS, U. B.C., Vancouver, 1965; MLS, U. Toronto, Ont., 1976; LLB, York U., Toronto, 1980. Bar: Ont., 1985. Asst. law librarian U. Western Ont., London, 1965-70; reference librarian York U. Law Library, Toronto, 1971-77; adminstrv. asst. Ont. Legis. Library, Toronto, 1980, exec. asst., 1981-83; chief librarian Supreme Ct. of Can., Ottawa, 1983-90, dir. libr., 1990—2003, spl. advisor libr. and info. svcs., 2004—. Editor: Practitioner's Desk Book, 1976-80; mng. editor CALL Newsletter, 1973-75; features editor Canadian Law Libraries, 2001—; chair Supreme Ct. of Can. 125th Ann. commemorative Book com., 1999-2000; contbr. articles, revs., book chpts. in field. Mem. Can. Assn. Law Librs., Law Soc. Upper Can., Assn. Can. Ct. Adminstrs. Mem. United Ch. Can. Mem. United Ch. Can.

TEEPLE, SCOTT D. conductor, music educator, director; B Music Edn, U. Mich., 1993, MusM, 2000. Music tchr. Port Huron (Mich.) Northern H.S., 1994—98; asst. dir. bands U. Mich., Ann Arbor, 2001—02; dir. bands U. Wis.-Stevens Point, 2002—. Music dir. Little Theater, Port Huron, 1996—97. Music dir. First United Bapt. Ch., Port Huron, 1996—98. William D. Revelli scholar, U. Mich. Sch. Music, 1999—2000. Mem.: Wis. Sch. Music Assn. (North Ctrl. v.p.), Kappa Kappa Psi, Phi Kappa Lambda, Phi Mu Alpha. Avocations: golf, tennis, running. Office: U Wis Stevens Point 140 College of Fine Arts Stevens Point WI 54481

TEERLINK, J(OSEPH) LELAND, real estate developer; b. Salt Lake City, July 16, 1935; s. Nicholas John and Mary Luella (Love) T.; m. Leslie Dowdle, Nov. 5, 1975; children: Steven, David, Andrew, Suzanne, Benjamin. Student, U. Utah, 1953-55. Sales rep. Eastman Kodak Co., Salt Lake City, 1960-69; founder Graphic Systems, Inc., Salt Lake City, 1969-82, pres., 1969-79, chmn. bd., 1979-82; founder Graphic Ink Co., Salt Lake City, 1973, pres., 1975-79, chmn. bd., 1979-82; founder G.S.I. Leasing Co., Salt Lake City, 1975, pres., 1975-82; chmn. bd. Graphic Sys. Holding Co., Inc., Salt Lake City, 1978-82; dir. leasing and acquisitions Terra Industries, Inc., real estate developers, 1982-86, ptnr., 1986—. Bd. dirs. ARC, Salt Lake City, 1979-82; co-founder, dir. Hope Living Ctr. Found. for Mothers and Children, 1993-99; vice consulate of the Netherlands for Utah, 1977-92; mem. active corps of execs., SBA, 1979-83; adv. bd. House of Hope Mothers and Children Utah Alcoholism Found., 1992-94. Recipient Masters award Salt Lake Bd. Realtors, 1993; named Small Businessman of Yr. for Utah, SBA, 1978. Mem. Graphic Arts Equipment and Supply Dealers of Am. (dir. 1978-82), Printing Industry of Am., Nat. Assn. Indsl. and Office Parks (pres. Utah chpt. 1986-87), Nat. Fedn. Ind. Businessman, Million Dollar Club (life). Republican. Mem. Lds Ch. Home: 2984 Thackeray Pl Salt Lake City UT 84108-2517 Office: 6925 Union Park Ctr Midvale UT 84047-4135 Business E-Mail: receptionist@terrautah.com.

TEES, RICHARD CHISHOLM, psychology educator, researcher; b. Montreal, Que., Can., Oct. 31, 1940; s. Ralph Charles and Helen Winnifred (Chisholm) T.; m. Kathleen F. Coleman, Sept. 1, 1962; children: Susan M., Carolyn V. BA, McGill U., 1961; PhD, U. Chgo., 1965. Asst. prof. U. B.C., Vancouver, Canada, 1965-67, assoc. prof., 1969-75, prof. psychology, 1975—, head dept. psychology, 1984—94, 1999—. Rsch. prof. U. Sussex, Brighton, Eng., 1972-73, 77-78; chmn. grant selection panel Nat. Scis. and Engring. Rsch. Coun. Can., Ottawa, 1993-96, B.C. Health Care Rsch. Found., Vancouver, 1984-87; chmn. studentship com. Med. Rsch. Coun., Ottawa, 1985-92; chmn. Can. Coun. Dept. Psychology, 1987-93. Author: (with Kolb) Cerebral Cortex of the Rat, 1990; mem. editl. bd. Can. Jour. Exptl. Psychology, 1975-84, 87—; contbr. articles to profl. jours., chpts. to books. Rsch. fellow Killam Found., 1972-73, 77-78; Rsch. fellow Can. Coun., 1972-73. Fellow APA, Am. Psychol. Soc., Can. Psychol. Assn.; mem. Soc. for Neurosci., Psychonomic Soc., Can. Soc. Brain, Behaviour, and Cognitive Sci. (pres. 1997-98), U. B.C. Senate, Nat. Ctr. Excellence Can. Stroke Network. Home: 1856 Acadia Rd Vancouver BC Canada V6T 1R3 Office: U BC Dept Psychology Vancouver BC Canada V6T 1Z4 Office Phone: 604-822-3245. Business E-Mail: rtees@psych.ubc.ca.

TEETER, DWIGHT LELAND, JR., journalism educator; b. L.A., Jan. 6, 1935; s. Dwight Leland and Ruth Elizabeth (Sauer) T.; m. Letitia Ruth Thoreson, July 7, 1956; children: Susan Letitia Hall, John Thoreson, William Weston. AB in Journalism, U. Calif.-Berkeley, 1956, M.J., 1959; PhD in Mass Communications, U. Wis., 1966. Reporter Waterloo Daily Courier, Iowa, 1957-60; asst. prof. Iowa State U., Ames, 1964-66; asst. to assoc. prof. U. Wis., Madison, 1966-72; assoc.prof. to prof. U. Ky., Lexington, 1972-77, dir. journalism dept., 1975-77; prof. journalism, chmn. dept. journalism U. Tex., Austin, 1977-84, William P. Hobby Centennial prof. communication, 1983-87; prof., dept. mass communications U. Wis., Milw., 1987-91; dean Coll. Communications U. Tenn., Knoxville, 1991—2002; prof. journalism, 2002—. Vis. assoc. prof. U. Wash., Seattle, 1969-70; treas. Journalism Council, Inc., N.Y.C., 1972-81 Author: (with Bill Loving) Law of Mass Communications, 10th edit., 2001, (with Jean L. Folkerts) Voices of a Nation: A History of Media in the United States, 4th edit., 2002, (with Lorman A. Ratner) Fanatics and Fire-Eaters: Newspaper Publications Leading to Civil War, 2003; contbr. articles to legal, hist., comm. jours. Chair Headliners Club of Tex. Media Contest, 1979-83; judge Tex. Bar Assn. Media Contest, 1981-85; mem. pub. affairs com. Tex. State Bar, 1985-87. Recipient Tex. Excellence in Teaching award Tex. Ex-Students' Assn., 1983, Harold L. Nelson award U. Wis., 1985. Mem. Assn. for Edn. in Journalism and Mass Comm. (chmn. prof. freedom and responsibility com. 1971-73, pres. 1985-86, Disting. Svc. award 2001), Soc. Profl. Journalists (Disting. Tchr. award 1991), Phi Kappa Phi, Kappa Tau Alpha. Office: U Tenn 430 Communication Knoxville TN 37996-0330 E-mail: teeter@utk.edu.

TEETERS, NANCY HAYS, economist, director; b. Marion, Ind., July 29, 1930; d. S. Edgar and Mabel (Drake) Hays; m. Robert Duane Teeters, June 7, 1952; children: Ann, James, John. AB in Econs., Oberlin Coll., 1952, LLD, 1979; MA in Econs., U. Mich., 1954, postgrad., 1956-57, LLD, 1983, Bates Coll., 1981, Mt. Holyoke Coll., 1983. Tchg. fellow U. Mich., 1954-55, instr., 1956-57, U. Md. Overseas, Germany, 1955-56; staff economist govt. fin. sect. Bd. Govs. of FRS, Washington, 1957-66, mem. bd., 1978-84; economist (on loan) Coun. Econ. Advs., 1962-63; economist Bur. Budget, 1966-70; sr. fellow Brookings Instn., 1970-73; sr. specialist Congl. Rsch. Svc., Library of Congress, Washington, 1973-74; asst. dir., chief economist Ho. of Reps. Com. on the Budget, 1974-78; v.p., chief economist IBM, Armonk, N.Y., 1984-90. Bd. dirs., trustee Prudential Mut. Funds, 1985—2003. Author: (with others) Setting National Priorities: The 1972 Budget, 1971, Setting National Priorities: The 1973 Budget, 1972, Setting National Priorities: The 1974 Budget, 1973; contbr. articles to profl. publs. Recipient Comfort Starr award in econs. Oberlin Coll., 1952; Disting. Alumnus award U. Mich., 1980 Mem. Nat. Economists Club (v.p. 1973-74, pres. 1974-75, chmn. bd. 1975-76, gov. 1976-79), Am. Econ. Assn. (com. on status of women 1975-78), Am. Fin. Assn. (dir. 1969-71) Democrat. Home: 243 Willowbrook Ave Stamford CT 06902-7020

TEETS, JOHN WILLIAM, retired diversified company executive; b. Elgin, Ill., Sept. 15, 1933; s. John William and Maudie Teets; m. Nancy Kerchenfaut, June 25, 1965; children: Jerri, Valerie Sue, Heidi Jayne, Suzanne. Student, U. Ill.; LLD (hon.), Trinity Coll., 1982; DBA in Foodsvc. Mgmt. (hon.), Johnson and Wales U., 1991; D in Comml. Sci. (hon.), Western Internat. U., 1992. Pres., ptnr. Winter Garden Restaurant, Inc., Carpenterville, Ill., 1957-63; v.p. Greyhound Food Mgmt. Co.; pres. Post Houses, Inc., and Horne's Enterprises, Chgo., 1964-68; pres., chief operating officer John R. Thompson Co., Chgo., 1968-71; pres., corp. v.p. pub. restaurant divsn. Canteen Corp., Chgo., 1971-75; divsn. pres. Jacques Restaurant Group, 1975; exec. v.p., CEO Bonanza Internat. Co., Dallas, 1975; group v.p. food svcs., pres. Greyhound Food Mgmt., Inc. (now named Restaura), Phoenix, 1975; vice chmn. The Greyhound Corp., Phoenix, 1980; chmn., CEO Greyhound Corp. (now The Dial Corp), Phoenix, 1981-96; chmn., pres., CEO The Dial Corp, Phoenix, 1996-97; chmn., CEO JW Teets Enterprises LLC, Phoenix; chmn. The FINOVA Group, Inc., Scottsdale, AZ, 2001; ret., 2001. Vice chmn. Pres.' Conf. on Foodservice Industry. Recipient Silver Plate award, Golden Plate award Internat. Foodsvc. Mgrs. Assn., 1980, Bus. Leadership award Harvard Bus. Sch. Club Ariz., 1985, Order of the Crown, Kingdom of Belgium, 1990, Ellis Island medal of honor Nat. Ethnic Coalition of Orgns. Found., 1995; named Top Bus. Spkr. of Yr., Forbes Mag., 1990, Capt. of Achievement, Acad. of Achievement, 1992, CEO of Yr., Leaders Mag., 1986. Mem. Nat. Inst. Foodsvc. Industry (trustee), Am. Mgmt. Assn., Christian Businessmen's Assn. (chmn. steering com. 1977). Office: JW Teets Enterprises LLC 1850 N Central Ave Phoenix AZ 85077-0001

TEETS, PETER B. federal agency administrator; b. 1942; BS, U. Colo., 1963, MS, 1965, PhD. Sciences (hon.), 1990; M.A., MIT, 1978. V.p. Martin Marietta Denver Aerospace, Colo., 1980—82, v.p. aerospace strategic launch sys., 1982—85, pres., 1985—93, Martin Marietta Space Grp, Md., 1993—95; pres., CEO Lockheed Martin Info. and Services, Md., 1995—97, Lockheed Martin Corp., Md., 1997—99; under secy. of air force U.S. Dept. Defense, Washington, 2001—. Recipient Sloan Fellow Award. Fellow: Am. Astronautical Society, Am. Institute of Aeronautics and Astronautics. Office: US Dept Defense Under Secy Air Force 1670 Air Force Pentagon Washington DC 20330-1670

TEETSELL, JANICE MARIE NEWMAN, business owner, lawyer; b. N.Y.C., Aug. 11, 1951; d. Robert and Clara (White) Swindler; m. Roger Kevin Newman, Jan. 20, 1972 (div. 1980); 1 child, Germaine M. Swindler-Newman (dec.); m. Robert Charles Teetsell, Dec. 29, 1998. BA, Smith Coll., 1973; JD, Rutgers U., 1980. Bar: N.J. 1983, U.S. Supreme Ct. 1987. Adminstrv. asst. Corp. Ann. Reports, N.Y.C., 1972-73; pub. rels. asst. Lippincott & Margulies, N.Y.C., 1973; journalist Essex Forum Newspaper, East Orange, N.J., 1973; pub. info. officer City of Newark, 1974-82; producer, host Newark and Reality TV show, Newark, 1974-85; asst. communications dir. Mayor's Office, Newark, 1982-86; legis. liaison, publ. info. officer N.J. Div. on Women, Trenton, 1988-90, acting dir., 1990, women svcs. coord., 1990-91; environ. issues specialist N.J. Dept. Environ. Protection and Energy, Trenton, 1991-92; comm. specialist Dept. Environ. Protection, Lawrenceville, N.J., 1992-95; pvt. practice South Orange, N.J., 1994—; host, prodr. New Jersey Issues TV Show, 1995-98. Mem. working group N.J. Supreme Ct. Domestic Violence, 1994-96; pres. JM Newman & Assocs.; chair Interest on Lawyers Trust Accounts, 1995-96, mem., 1986-96; dir. Legal Consultation Svc. Resource Ctr. Women, 1997-99. Mem. editl. bd. N.J. Lawyer mag., 1987-96, The Voice, Episcopal Diocese of Newark, 1999—; design editor: The Voice, 1993-94; contbr. articles to mags. Bd. dirs. Instrns. Exposures Experiences, 1983-87, Greater Newark Conservancy; 2d v.p. Women's Polit. Caucus, N.J., 1991-92, 1st v.p., 1992-93; appt. to N.J. Supreme Ct. Com. on Women in the Cts., 1990-94, Com. on Character, 1992—, N.J. Women Vets. Adv. Com., 1993-94; lay reader, Episc. Diocese of Newark, 1980—, eucharistic lay min., 1993—, parliamentarian, 1992-94; sr. warden, House of Prayer Espisc. Ch., Newark, 1992; vestry clk. St. Andrew Holy Communion Episcopal Ch., 1997-99, warden, 2001-02, sr. warden, 2002—. Recipient Pub. Svc. award N.J. Voice Newspaper, 1977, Achievement award Minority Contractors and Craftsmen Trade Assn., 1982, award Nat. Council Negro Bus. and Profl. Women Legal Achievement, 1987, award N.J. Unit Nat. Assn. Negro Bus. and Profl. Women's Clubs, 1987; named to Outstanding Young Women Am. U.S. Jaycees, 1984. Mem. Nat. Assn. Media Women (rec. sec. 1985-87, Media Woman of Yr. award 1985, pres. N.J. chpt. 1986-88), N.J. Bar Assn. (pub. rels. com. 1987—, 2d vice chmn. women's rights sect., 1990-92, 1st vice chmn. women's rights sect., 1992-93, chmn., 1993-95, trustee minorities in the profession sect., Cmty. Svc. award young lawyers divsn. 1989), N.J. State Bar Found. (trustee 1994-95), N.J. Women Lawyers Assn. (pres. 1986-88, trustee pub. rels. com., entertainment and arts com., Essex County Bar Assn., Nat. Coun. Negro Women, Garden State Bar Assn., Essex County Women Lawyers (trustee 1991-94, v.p. 1997-99), Rotary (pres. South Orange 1999-2000, Paul Harris fellow 2000, dist. 7470 youth exchange program comms. chair 2000-01, asst. gov. 2001-02, dist. pub. rels. chair 2002—). Democrat. Episcopalian. Home: 40 Woodland Ave East Orange NJ 07017 also: 76 S Orange Ave Ste 308 South Orange NJ 07079-1923 E-mail: Jteetsell@aol.com.

TEFFT, JOHN, ambassador; b. Madison, Wis. BA, Marquette Univ.; MA in History, Georgetown Univ. Various positions to rank of min./counselor U.S. Sr. Fgn. Svc., 1972—; U.S. amb. to Lithuania, 2000—. Recipient Disting. Honor award, U.S. Dept. of State. Office: DOS Amb 4510 Vilnius Pl Washington DC 20521

TEGENU, MESFIN, health services administrator, consultant; b. Addis Ababa, Ethiopia, Mar. 24, 1956; s. Tegenu Tekil-Agaist and Adanch Habtemariam; m. Nina Minale, Feb. 22, 1996; children: Sephanit, Mahalet. BPharm, Addis Ababa U., 1980; MS, St. John's U., 1988. Registered pharmacist. Coord. injectable and ctrl. supplies program HIP of N.Y., N.Y.C., 1991-94, mgr. corp. pharmacy programs, 1994-96, mgr. pharm. contracting/materials mgmt., 1996-98; assoc. v.p. pharmacy svcs. Keystone Mercy Health Plan, Phila., 1998-2001, v.p. pharmacy affairs, 2001—. Mem. Am. Managed Care Pharmacy. Home: 15 N Koewing Pl West Orange NJ 07052-4014 Office: Keystone Mercy Health Plan 200 Stevens Dr Philadelphia PA 19113-1522 E-mail: MTegenu@aol.com.

TEGTMEIER, RONALD EUGENE, physician, surgeon; b. Omaha, Jan. 16, 1943; s. Harvey and Edna T.; children: Anne, Amy; m. Victoria Susan, June 28, 1985; children: Justina Becerra, Gregory Galvan, Mark Tegtmeier. AB, Dartmouth Coll., 1965; BMS, Dartmouth Med. Sch., 1966; MD, Harvard Med. Sch., 1968. Diplomate Am. Bd. Plastic Surgery. Internship in surgery U. Colo. Med. Ctr., Denver, 1968-69, residency in gen. surgery, 1969-70; plastic surgery preceptorship Kingston-upon-Hull, England, 1973; residency in plastic surgery U. Mexico, Albuquerque, 1974-76, fellowship, 1976; plastic surgeon pvt. practice Arvada, Colo., 1977—, Artistic Ctr. for Cosmetic Surgery, Golden, Colo., 1988—. Pres. Clear Creek Valley Med. Soc., Lakewood, Colo., 1983-84; speaker of ho. Colo. Med. Soc., denver, 1985-87. Author: Aesthetica Tapes, 1988—; contbr. numerous papers and publs. to profl. jours. Named Outstanding Bus. Person, Arvada Jaycees, 1978; recipient Arvada Image award, 1981, Denver Post Gallery of Fame award, 1979. Mem. Am. Soc. Plastic and Reconstructive Surgeons, Am. Soc. for Aesthetic Plastic Surgery, Am. Soc. Laser Medicine and Surgery, Am. Acad. of Anti-Aging Medicine. Avocations: scuba, music, skiing, tennis, model trains, flying, aquariums.

TEGUH, COLLIN, physician, educator; b. Medan, Indonesia, Aug. 25, 1957; s. Tonga and Tsit Wati (Salim) T.; m. Lisa Hom; children: Justen W., Branden C., Brittany Lisa. BA, U. Calif. San Diego, 1983; DO, U. Osteo. Medicine Des Moines, 1991. Diplomate Am. Acad. Family Physicians, Am. Acad. Ambulatoory Care. Rsch. asst. Scripp Meml. and Whittier Inst. for Endocrinology & Diabetes, LaJolla, Calif., 1983-87, U. Osteo. Medicine and Health Scis., Des Moines, 1988-90; intern, resident San Bernardino (Calif.) County Med. Ctr., 1991-93; clin. rsch. investigator, pvt. practice San Diego, 1999—. Asst. clin. prof. U. Calif. San Diego, LaJolla, 1995—, Coll. Osteo. Medicine, Pomona, Calif., 1995—; mem. pharmacy and therapeutic com. Cmty. Health Care Group, San Diego. Contbr. articles to profl. jours. Pharmacy and therapeutic com. mem. for Cmty. Health Group. Fellow: Am. Acad. Family Physician (diplomate); mem.: Am. Tropical Medicine and Hygiene, San Diego Acad. Family Physicians, San Diego Osteo. Med. Assn. (exec. bd.), Am. Acad. Ambulatory Care (diplomate), U. Osteo Medicine and Health Scis. Alumni Assn., U. Calif. San Diego Alumni Assn. Avocations: snorkeling, hiking, reading, horticulture, travel. Office: North Park Med Ctr 3780 El Cajon Blvd San Diego CA 92105-1033 Office Phone: 619-281-8988.

TEHAN, JOHN BASHIR, lawyer; b. Utica, NY, May 13, 1948; s. Louis Bashir and Frances Mary (Argenzia) Tehan; m. Regina Anne Callahan, Aug. 1, 1970; children: Aaron J., Lauren R., Eileen L. BA, LeMoyne Coll., 1970; JD, Catholic U., Washington, DC, 1973. Bar: NY 1974, US Dist. Ct. (so. and ea. dists.) NY 1975, US Ct. Appeals (2d cir.) 1975. Assoc. Sullivan & Cromwell, NYC, 1973—81; ptnr. Simpson Thacher & Bartlett, NYC, 1981. Roman Catholic. Home: 33 Arrowhead Ct Manhasset NY 11030-4413 Office: Simpson Thacher & Bartlett 425 Lexington Ave Fl 15 New York NY 10017-3954 E-mail: jtehan@stblaw.com.

TEHRANI, FLEUR TAHER, electrical engineer, educator, researcher; b. Tehran, Iran, Feb. 16, 1956; came to U.S., 1984; d. Hassan and Pourandokht (Monfared) T.; m. Akbar E. Torbat, June 16, 1997. BS in Elec. Engring., Arya-Mehr U. of Tech., Tehran, 1975; DIC in Comm. Engring., Imperial Coll. Sci. and Tech., London, 1977; MSc in Comm. Engring., U. London, 1977, PhD in Elec. Engring., 1981. Registered profl. engr., Calif. Comm. engr. Planning Orgn. of Iran, Tehran, 1977-78; lectr. A elec. engring. Robert Gordon's Inst. Tech., Aberdeen, U.K., 1982-83; lectr. II elec. engring. South Bank U., London, England, 1983—84; asst. prof. elec. engring. Calif. State U., Fullerton, 1985-91, assoc. prof. elec. engring., 1991-94, prof. elec. engring., 1994—, dir. pharm. engring. program, 1999-2001. Vis. assoc. prof. elec. engring. Drexel U., Phila., 1987-88; sys. cons. Telebit Corp., Cupertino. Calif., 1985; engring. cons. PRD, Inc., Dresher, Pa., 1989-92; mem. NASA/Am. Soc. Engring. Edn. summer faculty Jet Propulsion Lab., Calif. Inst. Tech., Pasadena, 1995, 96. Contbr. articles to profl. jours.; patentee in field. Recipient Best Rsch. Manuscript award Assn. for the Advancement of Med. Instrumentation, 1993, NASA/Am. Soc. Engring. Edn. Recognition award for rsch. contbns., 1995, 96. Fellow Inst. for Advancement of Engring.; mem. IEEE, Women in Sci. and Engring. (chair Calif. State U. chpt. 1990-91), Assn. Profs. and Scholars of Iranian Heritage (pres. 1991-92), Sigma Delta Epsilon. Avocations: music, literature, poetry, stamp collecting/philately. Office: Calif State U Coll Engring & Computer Sci 800 N State College Blvd Fullerton CA 92831-3547 E-mail: ftehrani@fullerton.edu.

TEHRANIAN, MAJID, political economy and communications educator; b. Iran, Mar. 22, 1937; m. Katharine Kia; children: Terrence, Yalda, John, Maryam. BA in Govt., Dartmouth Coll., 1959; MA in Middle Eastern Studies, Harvard U., 1961, PhD in Polit. Economy and Govt., 1969. Asst. prof. econs. Lesley Coll., 1964-69; assoc. prof. polit. sci. New Coll. U. South Fla., 1969-71; dir. social planning Plan Orgn. of Iran, 1971-72; sr. analyst, dir. rsch.

Indsl. Mgmt. Inst., 1972-74; dir. prospective planning project Nat. Iranian Radio & TV, 1974-75; prof., founding dir. Iran Communications & Devel. Inst., 1976-78; program specialist communication planning and studies Div. Devel. of Communication Systems UNESCO, Paris, 1979-80; fellow Communication Inst., East West Ctr., 1981-82; chair dept. communication U. Hawaii, Manoa, 1986-88, prof. dept. communication, 1981—, dir. Matsunaga Inst. Peace, 1990-92, dir. Toda Inst. Global Peace Policy Rsch., 1996—. Vis. scholar Inst. for Communication Rsch., Stanford U., 1977; vis. fellow St. Anthony's Coll., Oxford U., 1978-79; vis. scholar Ctr. for Internat. Affairs MIT, 1980-81, Can., U.S. and USSR universities, 1988; rsch. affiliate Ctr. for Middle Eastern Studies, Harvard U., 1980-81; vis. prof. dept. govt. Harvard Summer Sch., 1989-90; dir.-elect and dir. Inst. for Peace, U. Hawaii, coun. and exec. com., 1986—; rsch. fellow Social Sci. Rsch. Inst., U. Hawaii, Manoa, 1982-83, 84-86; lectr. in field. Author: Towards a Systematic Theory of National Development, 1974, Socio-Economic and Communications Indicators in Development Planning, 1981, Technologies of Power, 1990; co-author: The Middle East: Its Government and Politics, 1972, The Global Context of the Formation of Domestic Communications Policies, 1975, Policy Towards Social Sciences in Asia and Oceania, 1978, Worlds Apart: Human Securityand Global Goverance, 1999, Asia Peace: Security and Goverance in the Asia Pacific Region, 1999, Global Communication and World Politics, 1999, Global Civilization (in Japanese, English, Persian), 2000-2003, Dialogue of Civilizations, 2002; editor: Communications Policy for Development, 1977, Letters from Jerusalem, 1990, Deconstructing Paradise: Dependency, Development and Discourse in Hawaii, 1990, Peace and Policy, Bridging a Gulf: Peacebuilding in West Asia, 2003; co-editor: Restructuring for World Peace: On the Threshold of the 21st Century, 1992, Toward Democratic Governance 2000, Choose Dialogue, 2000 (in Japanese), (with David W. Chappell) Dialogue of Civilizations. A New Peace Agenda for the New Millenium, 2002, (with Michael Intriligator and Alexander Nikitin) Eurasia: A New Peace Agenda, 2003; contbr. articles to profl. jours.; reviewer in field. Scholar Dartmouth Coll., 1955-59, Fujio Matsuda scholar, 1990-91; Jane Addams Peace Found. fellow, 1961, Ford Found. fellow Harvard U., 1959-61, fellow St. Anthony's Coll., Oxford, 1978-79, fellow East West Ctr. Communication Isnt., 1977, 81, 82; rsch. grantee Social Sci. Rsch. Inst., U. Hawaii, Manoa, 1982-85, UNESCO rsch. grantee, 1983-84, Can. Studies Faculty Enrichment grantee, 1988, Hawaii Interactive TV System Curriculum Devel. grantee, 1989; recipient Dartmouth Colby & Grimez Prizes, 1959, Excellence in Teaching award 1989, Soka U. award of highest honor, Disting. Svc. award Assn. Edn. in Journalism and Mass Communication, 1998. Fellow World Acad. Art & Sci.; mem. Internat. Inst. Comm. (bd. trustees 1979-81), Internat. Comm. Assn. (conf. theme chair for Asia 1989), Pacific Telecomm. Coun., Middle East Studies Assn. N.Am., Middle East Econs. Assn. (nat. adv. bd.), Soc. for Iranian Studies (founding exec. sec. 1967-71), Worldview Internat. Found. Avocations: swimming, tennis, chess, poetry. Home: 2627 Manoa Rd Honolulu HI 96822-1767 Office: U Hawaii Sch of Communication Honolulu HI 96822 also: Toda Inst 1600 Kapiolani Blvd Ste 1111 Honolulu HI 96814-3806 Fax: 808 955-6476.

TEI, TAKURI, accountant; b. Korea, Feb. 25, 1924; s. Gangen and Isun (Song) T.; came to U.S., 1952, naturalized, 1972; diploma Concordia Theol. Sem., 1959; B.D., Eden Theol. Sem., 1965; M.Ed., U. Mo., 1972; m. Maria M. Ottwaska, Dec. 1, 1969; 1 dau., Sun Kyung Lee. Partner, Madeleine Ottwaska & Assos., St. Louis, 1968—; pres. TMS Tei Enterprises Inc., Webster Groves, Mo., 1969—; instr. Forest Park Community Coll. Mem. Am. Coll. Enrolled Agts. (pres. 1976—), Am. Accounting Assn., Am. Taxation Assn., Assn. Asian Studies, NAACP. Republican. Lutheran. Home and Office: 7529 Big Bend Blvd Saint Louis MO 63119-2103

TEICH, ALBERT HARRIS, professional society administrator; b. Chgo., Dec. 17, 1942; s. Maurice and Ina (Szuldiner) T.; m. Carolyn R. Richmond, June 3, 1965 (div. 1987); children: Mitchell Craig, Kenneth David; m. Jill H. Pace, Jan. 29, 1989; 1 child, Samantha Lynne. BS, MIT, 1964, PhD, 1969. Rsch. fellow Syracuse (N.Y.) U. Rsch. Corp., 1969-71, dir., sci. and tech. studies, 1971-73; coord. rsch. SUNY, Binghamton, 1973-74; dir. rsch. SUNY Inst. for Pub. Policy Alternatives, Albany, 1974-76; assoc. prof. pub. affairs and dep. dir., grad. program sci. tech. and pub. policy George Washington U., 1976-79; mgr., sci. policy studies AAAS, Washington, 1980-84, head, office of pub. sector programs, 1984-89, dir. sci. and policy programs, 1989—. Cons. Nat. Acad. Scis., Office of Tech. Assessment, Washington, 1976-95, Orgn. for Econ. Cooperation and Devel., Paris, 1994—96, Hertz Found., 2003; chmn. SRS adv. com. NSF, Washington, 1988-90; pres. Technosci. Assocs., Inc., Silver Spring, Md., 1977-82; chair Ga. Inst. Tech., Sch. Pub. Adv. Bd., 2001-; mem. bd. govs. US-Israel Binational Sci Found., 2001—, vice chmn., 2004—; mem. rsch. adv. bd. U. Calif., Davis, 2003—; mem. rsch. and tech. coord. com. Nat. Rsch. Coun., 2003—. Editor: Science and Technology in the U.S.A., 1986, Technology and the Future, 9th edit., 2002; editor, author: Scientists and Public Affairs, 1974; mem. editl. bd. Science Communication, 1991—, Science, Technology and Human Values, 1994—, Prometheus, 1999—. Recipient Sci. Achievement award, Wash. Acad. Scis., 2004. Fellow AAAS (chmn. sect. X 1988); mem. Tech. Transfer Soc. (v.p. 1985-91), Soc. for Social Studies of Scis., Nat. Press Club, Sigma Xi. Avocations: swimming, photography, travel writing. Office: AAAS 1200 New York Ave NW Washington DC 20005-3941 Office Phone: 202-326-6600. Business E-Mail: ateich@aaas.org.

TEICH, HOWARD BERNARD, lawyer, activist, public affairs specialist; b. Huntington, N.Y., Nov. 1, 1946; s. Samuel and Beatrice Ann (Kay) T. AB, U. Pa., 1967; JD, Boston U., 1970. Bar: N.Y., 1971, U.S. Dist. Ct. (so. dist.) N.Y. 1984. Counsel N.Y. State Senator Emanuel Gold, N.Y.C., 1971-72; law sec. N.Y. State Supreme Ct. Justin Martin Evans, N.Y.C., 1972-75; assoc. pub. Firehouse mag., N.Y.C., 1975-79; pub. Midtown South Bus., N.Y.C., 1985-87; prin. Law Offices Howard B. Teich, N.Y.C., 1980—; sr. cons. The Kamber Group, Washington, 1995—; sr. counsel McLaughlin & Stein, P.C., N.Y.C., 1997—. Founder, chair New Dem. Dimensions, N.Y.C., 1981-91, Nat. Task Force on Life Safety for Handicapped, Washington, 1979-81; bd. dirs. Boys Choir of Harlem, N.Y.C., 1983-85, Assn. on Am. Indian Affairs, 1990-97, adv. bd., 1997—; chmn. New Leadership of Israel Bonds, N.Y.C., 1977-79; pres. Am. Jewish Congress Met. Region N.Y.C., 1992—, past nat. v.p.; bd. dirs. Jewish Comty. Rels. Coun., N.Y., 1995—, past v.p., 1995-98; co-chair Jewish Heritage, N.Y.C., 1997—;dep. dir. N.Y. state citizens com. McGovern for Pres., 1972, Samuels for Gov., 1974, Carey for Gov., 1974; dep. dir. N.Y. state primary campaign Carter for Pres., 1980; co-chair N.Y. state citizens com. Glenn for Pres., 1984, Mondale/Ferraro '84, 1984; bd. dirs. Manhattan Playhouse. Recipient Robert Briscoe award Emerald Isle Immigration Soc., 1996, Israel Leadership award Israel Bonds, 1979, Martin Luther King Jr. Living-the-Dream award, Gov. George Pataki, N.Y., 1999. Mem. AJ Congress Met Region (pres. 1992—), U. Pa. Club, Assn. on Am. Indian Affairs (bd. dirs., nat. adv. bd.). Democrat. Jewish. Avocations: N.Y.C. marathon, softball, tennis, reading, theatre, dance. Home: 185 E 85th St New York NY 10028-2140 Office: 260 Madison Ave New York NY 10016-2401

TEICH, JONATHAN MARC, emergency medicine physician, internist, medical informatics specialist; b. New Brunswick, N.J., Oct. 23, 1955; MD, Harvard U., 1983. Diplomate Am. Bd. Internal Medicine, Am. Bd. Emergency Medicine. Resident in internal medicine Brigham and Women's Hosp., Boston, 1983-86, fellow in emergency medicine, 1986-88, mem. staff; asst. prof. medicine Harvard Med. Sch., Boston; co-founder, chief med. officer Healthvision, Boston, 1999—. Recipient Nicholas Davies award, 1997; fellow Am. Coll. Med. Informatics. Mem. Am. Med. Informatics Assn, (bd. dirs. 1999-2002), eHealth Initiative Found., Health Info. and Mgmt. Sys. Soc. (chair patient safety). Office: Brigham and Women's Hosp Dept Emergency Medicine 75 Francis St Boston MA 02115-2402 Office Phone: 781-906-8437. E-mail: jteich@harvard.edu.

TEICH, MALVIN CARL, electrical engineering educator; b. N.Y.C., May 4, 1939; s. Sidney R. and Loretta K. Teich SB in Physics, MIT, 1961; MSEE, Stanford U., 1962; PhD in Quantum Electronics, Cornell U., 1966. Research scientist MIT Lincoln Lab., Lexington, Mass., 1966-67; prof. engring. sci. Columbia U., N.Y.C., 1967-96, prof. emeritus, 1996—, chmn. dept. elec. engring., 1978-80, mem. Columbia Radiation Lab., faculty applied physics dept.; prof. elec. computer engring., biomed. engring., physics Boston U., 1995—. Mem. Photonics Ctr., Boston U., also Ctr. Adaptive Sys., Hearing Rsch. Ctr.; mem. sci. bd. Inst. Physics, Czech Acad. Scis., Prague. Author: (with B.E.A. Saleh) Fundamentals of Photonics, 1991; dep. editor Quantum Optics, 1988-92, bd. editors Jour. Visual Comm. and Image Representation, 1989-92, Jemná Mechanika a Optika, 1994—; contbr. articles to profl. jours.; patentee in field. Recipient Citation Classic award Inst. for Sci. Info., 1981; Meml. Gold medal of Palacky U., Czech Republic, 1992; Guggenheim Meml. Found. fellow, 1973. Fellow AAAS, IEEE (Browder J. Thompson Meml. prize 1969, Morris E. Leeds award 1997), Optical Soc. Am. (editl. adv. panel Optics Letters 1977-79), Am. Phys. Soc., Acoustical Soc. Am.; mem. Sigma Xi, Tau Beta Pi. Office: Boston U Dept Elec and Computer Engr 8 Saint Mary's St Boston MA 02215-2421 Office Phone: 617-353-1236. Business E-Mail: teich@bu.edu.

TEICHER, HENRY EARL, retired education educator; b. Jersey City, July 9, 1922; s. Leo and Anna Binn Teicher; m. Anne Severin, Aug. 14, 1962; 1 child, Rikke Jordahn. BA, State U. Iowa, 1946; MA, Columbia U., 1947, PhD, 1950. From asst. prof. to prof. Purdue U., West Lafayette, Ind., 1951—67; asst. prof. Stanford U., Palo Alto, Calif., 1955—56; assoc. prof. NYU, NYC, 1960—62; prof. Columbia U., NYC, 1967—68, Rutgers U., New Brunswick, NJ, 1968—93; ret., 1993. Cons. Radio Corp. Am., Indpls., 1967. Author: Probability Theory: Independence, 1977, Interchangeability, 1987, Martingales, 1997; contbr. articles to profl. jours. With U.S. Army, 1943—46. Fellow: Inst. Math. Statis.; mem.: Phi Beta Kappa. Avocations: reading, music. Home: 14 Rue De Sevigne 75004 Paris France

TEICHMAN, RUTH, state senator; m. Dennis Teichman; 4 children. Student, Kans. State U. Farmer; banker; mem. Kans. Senate, 2001—. Mem. Stafford Edn. Found.; founding mem. Sout Ctrl. Cmty. Found.; mem. Stafford Bd. Edn. Mem.: Stafford Drama Guild, Stafford Booster Club. Republican.

TEICHNER, BRUCE A. lawyer; b. Chgo. BA, U. Iowa, 1981; JD, De Paul U., 1985; MBA, U. Chgo., 1997. Legal writing tchg. asst. Coll. Law De Paul U., Chgo., 1982-83; assoc. coun. Allstate Ins. Co., Northbrook, Ill. Mem. writing staff De Paul Law Rev., 1983-85; contbr. articles to profl. jours. Mem. ABA, Chgo. Bar Assn. (corp. law coms.), Am. Corp. Counsel Assn. (assoc. counsel), Phi Beta Kappa. Office: Allstate Ins Co 3075 Sanders Rd Ste G5A Northbrook IL 60062-7127 E-mail: bteichner@allstate.com.

TEICHNER, LESTER, management consulting executive; b. Chgo., Apr. 21, 1944; s. Ben Bernard and Eva Bertha (Weinberg) T.; m. Barbara Rae Bush, Jan. 30, 1966 (div. Aug. 1969); m. Doris Jean Ayres, Jan. 31, 1980; children: Lauren Ayres, Caroline Ayres. BSEE, U. Ill., 1965; MBA in Mktg. and Fin., U. Chgo., 1969. Sales engr. Westinghouse Electric Corp., Chgo., 1965-69; v.p. ops. Intec Inc., Chgo., 1969-74; pres., CEO The Chgo. Group Inc., 1974—, also bd. dirs., 1974—. Bd. dirs. Strategic Processing Inc., N.Y.C., Dees Communications Ltd., Vancouver, B.C., Maxcor Mfg. Co., Colorado Springs; CEO, bd. dirs. Axcess Worldwide Ltd., Coal Gasification, Inc., Chgo.; guest lectr. U. Chgo. Grad. Sch. Bus., 1982-95. Co-inventor U.S. patent electronic marketplace; contbr. articles to profl. publs. Mem. The Chgo. Forum, 1976—; bd. dirs. Am. Israeli C. of C. Mem. Am. Mgmt. Assn., Am. Mktg. Assn., Midwest Planning Assn. (bd. dirs. 1981). Republican. Jewish. Avocations: comml. renovation, astronomy, skiing, venture capital investment. Home: 2230 N Seminary Ave Chicago IL 60614-3507 Office: The Chicago Group Inc 2230 N Seminary Ave Chicago IL 60614-3507

TEIG, MARLOWE GILMAN, investment banker; b. Fargo, N.D., Sept. 13, 1938; s. Julius Berner Teig and Inez (Hedlund) Teig-Erickson; m. Carole Lynne Werner, Nov. 25, 1961; children: Jennifer Lynne, Alan Gilman. BA, U. Mich., 1961; postgrad., CCNY, 1962-64. With Harcourt Brace Jovanovich, 1964-80, Houghton Mifflin Co., 1980-87, Macmillan, Inc., 1987-88; mng. dir. Berkery, Noyes & Co., Newton, Mass., 1990—. Home: 40 Kirkstall Rd Newton MA 02460-2218 Office Phone: 617-969-7935. Business E-Mail: marlowe.teig@berkerynoyes.com.

TEILLON, LOUIS PIERRE, JR., lawyer; b. N.Y.C., Nov. 15, 1943; AB, Yale U., 1965; LLB, Columbia U., 1968. Bar: Pa. 1968. Mem. Heckscher, Teillon, Terrill & Sager, P.C., West Conshohocken, Pa. Mem. Am. Coll. Trust and Estate Counsel, Pa. Bar Assn. (real property, probate and trust sects.), Phila. Bar Assn. (past chmn. probate sect.). Office: Heckscher Teillon Terrill & Sager 100 Four Falls Corp Ctr Ste 300 West Conshohocken PA 19428 Fax: 610 940-6042. E-mail: perry@htts.com.

TEIMAN, RICHARD B. lawyer; b. Bklyn., May 19, 1938; AB, Princeton U., 1959; LLB, Harvard U., 1962. Bar: N.Y. 1963. Ptnr. Winston & Strawn LLP and predecessor Cole & Deitz, N.Y.C., 1968—. Trustee Citizens Budget Commn., 1993—. Mem. Assn. Bar City N.Y. (com. Admiralty 1975-78, 87, chair 1988-91, 2003—), Maritime Law Assn. (com. Maritime Financing 1980—, chmn. subcom. Recodification U.S. Ship Mortgage Act 1986-91, chmn. subcom. U.S. Coastguard, Citizenship and Related Matters 1988-94), Phi Beta Kappa. Home: 5 Pryer Ln Larchmont NY 10538-4012 Office: Winston & Strawn LLP 200 Park Ave Rm 4100 New York NY 10166-0005 Office Phone: 212-294-6730. E-mail: rteiman@winston.com.

TEISCH, MORTON, management consultant; b. NYC, May 9, 1935; s. Herman and Jean Teisch; m. Janice Rita Persofsky, Oct. 15, 1960; children: Jeffrey, Steven, Andrea. BS in Acctg., NYU, 1958; MBA in Mgmt., Fairleigh Dickinson U., 1978. Pub. acct. various CPA firms, NYC, 1959—66; mgr. adminstrn. Am. Broadcasting Co., NYC, 1966—80; pres. Clearwater Assoc., NYC, 1980—. Presenter, cons. in field. Author: The Manager's Indispensable Guide, 2002. Past chancellor Ramapo Lodge K of P, Pomona, NY, 1985. With U.S. Army, 1958—64. Home: 13771 Flora Pl Apt D Delray Beach FL 33484-1696

TEISON (BASS-TEITELBAUM), HERBERT J. editor, publisher; b. NYC, Nov. 22, 1927; s. Irving and Celia (Wolkowisky) Teitelbaum. BS, CCNY, 1949. Writer Mexico City News, 1950-51; announcer, prodr. Sta. XELA, Mexico City, 1950-51; pub. rels. dir. Schwerin Rsch., NYC, 1952-53; asst. rsch. dir. Dumont TV Network, NYC, 1954-55; advt. mgr. St. Regis Publs., NYC, 1956-59; assoc. pub. programs Saturday Rev., NYC, 1960-73; adj. prof. New Sch. Social Rsch., NYC, 1961-75; editor, pub., pres. Comm. House/Travel Smart, Dobbs Ferry, NY, 1973—. Co-author: Travel Smarts, 1996; author: Daniel, Molly & Me, 1997. Mem. Soc. Am. Travel Writers, Music Therapy Soc. (v.p. 1965—). Avocations: gardening, collecting, language tutoring.

TEITEL, SIMON, economist, educator; b. Buenos Aires, Dec. 5, 1928; came to U.S., 1961; s. Gregorio and Regina (Tarnorudzka) T.; m. Raquel Schenkolewski, June 20, 1954; children: Rut Gabriela, Ariel Dan. BS in Indsl. Engring., U. Buenos Aires, 1956, MS in Indsl. Engring., 1963; PhD in Econs., Columbia U., 1969. Econ. affairs officer Ctr. for Indsl. Devel., UN, N.Y.C., 1963-67; sr. indsl. devel. officer policies and programming div. UN Indsl. Devel. Orgn., Vienna, 1967-68; sr. cons. Office Program Advisor to Pres., Inter-Am. Devel. Bank, Washington, 1968-76, sr. econ. advisor econ. and social devel. dept., 1976-89; sr. rsch. adv., 1989-92; rsch. cons. World Bank, Washington, 1992-94; econ. cons. UN, 1994—2004; rsch. fellow ICER, Turin, Italy, 2001—02. Adj. assoc. prof. econs. Cath. U. Am., Washington, 1971-77, adj. prof., 1977-81, prof., 1981-88; adj. prof. Am. U., 1992; professorial lectr. Georgetown U., Washington, 1996-98; vis. lectr. internat. econs. Yale U., New Haven, 1977-78; lectr. to numerous profl. assns. and univs.; occasional referee Econ. Devel. and Cultural Change, Jour. Devel. Econs., World Devel., L.Am. Rsch. Rev., Jour. Internat. Manpower; mem. spl. internat. panel on appropriate techs. for developing countries Bd. on Sci. and Tech. for Internat. Devel., NAS-NAE, 1974-77. Author: Politica Economica en Centro y Periferia, 1976, Integracion Economica, 1977, Trade, Stability, Technology and Equity in Latin America, 1982, Symposium on Technological Change and Industrial Development, 1984, Growth, Reform and Adjustment: Latin America's Trade and Macroeconomic Policies in the 1970s and 1980s, 1986, Handbook of Latin American Studies, Library of Congress, Economics: Argentina, 1989, Towards a New Development Strategy for Latin America, 1992, Industrial and Technological Development, 1993, Technology and Enterprise Development, 1994, Resources, Industrialization and Exports in Latin America, 1998, Technology and Skills in Zimbabwe's Manufacturing. From Autarky to Competition, 2000; contbr. articles to profl. jours. Fellow: Internat. Ctr. for Econ. Rsch.; mem.: Am. Econ. Assn. Jewish. Home: 5610 Wisconsin Ave Apt 606 Chevy Chase MD 20815-4432 E-mail: steitel@starpower.net.

TEITELBAUM, HARRY, English educator; b. Leipzig, Germany, Sept. 23, 1930; came to U.S., 1939; s. Simon and Rencia (Spindel) T.; m. Marilyn L. Nober, Nov. 7, 1953; children: Mark, David, Deborah. BA, Bkyn. Coll., 1952, MA, 1953; ABD, NYU, 1968. Cert. tchr. English, math., supr. secondary edn., N.Y.; cmty. coll. instr. liberal arts, Calif. Teaching fellow Bklyn. Coll., 1953; instr. U.S. Armed Forces Inst., Germany, 1954-55; substitute tchr. N.Y.C. High Schs., Bklyn., 1955; tchr. English Elmont (N.Y.) Meml. High Sch., 1955-60; tutor SAT Plainview, N.Y., 1963-68; English tchr. Plainview-Old Bethpage Sch. Dist., 1960-85; dept. chmn. John F. Kennedy High Sch., Plainview, 1966-70; adj. prof. Hofstra U., Hempstead, N.Y., 1958-74, Suffolk County C.C., Selden, N.Y., 1974-87, Saddleback Coll., Mission Viejo, Calif., 1988—2001; ret., 2001. Judge various writing and speaking contests, L.I., N.Y., 1964-85; scholar-lectr. Orange County Calif. Librs., 1989. Author: How to Write a Thesis, 1964, 75, 94, 98, How to Write Book Reports, 1975, 89, 95, 98; co-author: How to Write Themes and Essays, rev. edit., 1994; contbr. articles to profl. jours. and newspapers. Cpl. U.S. Army, 1953-55. Recipient Disting. Tchr. award Alpha Sigma Lambda Hofstra U., 1969, John F. Kennedy High Sch., 1979. Avocations: skiing, tennis, woodworking, jogging. Home: 29562 Avante Laguna Niguel CA 92677-7949

TEITELBAUM, HOWARD S. academic administrator; BA in mathematics, Calif. State Polytech. Coll., Pomona; MA in curriculum devel., PhD in philosophy and statistics, MD, Mich. State U.; MPH, Harvard Sch. Pub. Health. Cert. preventive medicine, diplomate Nat. Bd. Examiners for Osteo. Physicians and Surgeons. Intern Mount Clemens (Mich.) Gen. Hosp.; chief resident in preventive medicine Yale U. Sch. Medicine, Dept. Epidemiology and Pub. Health; prof. Coll. Osteo. Medicine, Mich. State U.; dean Coll. Osteo. Medicine and Surgery, Des Moines U., 2000—. Pres. Am. Osteo. Coll. Occupl. and Preventive Medicine, 1996—98. Named Prof. of Yr., Yale Sch. Medicine, 1988; recipient Spl. Golden Apple award for Tchg., 1992, Outstanding Golden Apple award for Tchg., 1996. Fellow: Am. Osteo. Coll. Preventive Medicine. Office: Coll Osteo Medicine and Surgery 3200 Grand Ave Des Moines IA 50312

TEITELBAUM, LEONARD H. state legislator; b. Bklyn., Feb. 27, 1931; married; 1 child. BME, Rensselaer Poly. Inst., 1953. Pres. Terminal Data Corp., Rockville, Md.; mem. dist. 19 Md. Ho. of Dels., Annapolis, 1987-95; environ. matters com.; vice-chmn. com. on bi-county agencies; mem. dist. 19 Md. Senate, Annapolis, 1995—, mem. fin. com., 1997—. Sen. fin. com., chair health sub-com., jt. com. on health care delivery and fin., sen. chmn., jt. adv. com. on legis. data sys., joint com. on children, youth and families, task force to conquer cancer, task force on quality of care in nursing homes. Bd. dirs. Montgomery County unit Am. Cancer Soc.; mem. Md. Dem. Ctrl. Com., Montgomery County, 1978-81; mem. Washington Suburban Sanitary Commn., 1981-87, vice chmn., 1982-83, 86-87, chmn., 1983-84. Recipient Outstanding Svc. award Jewish Cmty. Coun. of Greater Washington, 1985. Mem. B'nai B'rith. Address: 214 James Senate Office Bldg Annapolis MD 21401

TEITELBAUM, MARILYN LEAH, retired special education educator; b. Bklyn., June 12, 1930; d. Abraham and Fay (Ingis) Nober; m. Harry Teitelbaum, Nov. 7, 1953; children: Mark, David, Deborah. BA, Bklyn. Coll., 1953; MS, Queens Coll., 1968, L.I. U., 1982. Cert. tchr., N.Y. Elem. and spl. edn. tchr., Franklin Square, N.Y., 1955-57; elem. tchr. Manetto Hill Sch., Plainview, N.Y., 1968-70, Northport (N.Y.) Sch. Dist., 1970-78, spl. edn. tchr., 1978-87; pvt. spl. edn. tchr. Laguana Niguel, Calif., 1988—2002; ret., 2002. Author: Teachers as Consumers-What They Should Know About the Hearing Impaired Child, 1981. V.p. Friends of Libr., Laguna Niguel Pub. Libr., 1988—. Recipient outstanding tchr. award Northport PTA, 1987. Mem. NEA, Coun. Exceptional Children, United Tchrs. Northport, Orange County Dyslexic Soc. Avocations: reading, travel, painting, piano. Home: 29562 Avante Laguna Niguel CA 92677-7949

TEITELBAUM, STEVEN LAZARUS, pathology educator; b. Bklyn., June 29, 1938; s. Hyman and Rose Leah (Harnick) T.; m. Marilyn Ruth Schaffner; children: Caren Beth, Aaron Michael, Rebecca Lee. BA, Columbia U., 1960; MD, Washington U., St. Louis, 1964. Intern Washington U. Sch. Medicine, St. Louis, 1964-65, 3d. yr. asst. resident, ACS clin. fellow, 1967-68; intern NYU, 1965-66, 2d yr. resident, 1966-67; assoc. pathologist Jewish Hosp. at Washington U. Med. Ctr., St. Louis, 1969-89, pathologist-in-chief, 1987-96; assoc. pathologist Barnes-Jewish Hosp., St. Louis, 1986—; pathologist St. Louis Shriners Hosp. for Crippled Children, 1986—; Wilma and Roswell Messing prof. pathology Washington U. Sch. Medicine, St. Louis, 1987—. Mem. Othopedics and Musculoskeletal Study Sect. NIH, 1983-87; adv. counsel NIH, 2003—. Contbr. numerous sci. articles to med. jours., 1965—, 12 chpts. to med. books and texts, 1976—; mem. editorial bd. Calcified Tissue Internat., 1980-85, 89-91, Human Pathology; mem. bd. assoc. editors Jour. Orthopaedic Rsch., Jour. Cellular Biochemistry. Mem. Am. Soc. Clin. Investigation, Assn. Am. Physicians, Am. Acad. Orthopaedic Surgeons (Ann Doner Vaughan Kappa Delta award 1988), Paget's Disease Found. (adv. panel), Am. Soc. for Bone and Mineral Rsch. (pres. 1993, William F. Neuman award 1998), Fed. Am. Soc. Expl. Biology (bd. dirs. 1997—, pres. 2002--). Office: Washington U Sch Medicine 216 S Kingshighway Blvd Saint Louis MO 63110-1026 E-mail: teitelbs@medicine.wustl.edu.

TEITELL, CONRAD LAURENCE, lawyer, author; b. N.Y.C., Nov. 8, 1932; s. Benson and Belle (Altman) T.; m. Adele Mary Crummins, May 26, 1957; children: Beth Mary, Mark Lewis. AB, U. Mich., 1954; LL.B., Columbia U., 1957; LL.M., N.Y. U., 1968. Bar: N.Y. 1958, D.C., 1968. Mem. Prerau & Teitell, N.Y.C. and White Plains, N.Y., 1964-96, Cummings & Lockwood, Stamford, Conn., 1996—. Dir. Philanthropy Tax Inst., Old Greenwich, Conn., 1964—; adj. prof. U. Miami Law Sch., 1980—. Author: Philanthropy and Taxation, 5 vols., 1993-2004; editor, pub. Taxwise Giving, 1964—; contbr. articles to legal jours. Served with U.S. Army, 1957. Recipient Disting. Svc. to Higher Edn. award Am. Coll. Pub. Relations Assn., 1970, Disting. Svc. award Nat. Com. on Planned Giving, 1990, Harrison Tweed Spl. Merit award Am. Law Inst./ABA, 1992. Fellow Am. Coll. Trust and Estate Counsel; mem. ABA (former co-chmn. com. charitable giving, trusts, founds.), Assn. of Bar of City of N.Y. Home: 16 Marlow Ct Riverside CT 06878-2614 Office: Cummings & Lockwood 4 Stamford Plz Stamford CT 06902-3834 also: PO Box 299 Old Greenwich CT 06870-0299 Office Phone: 203-351-4164. Business E-Mail: cteitell@cl-law.com.

TEITELMAN, RICHARD B. state supreme court judge; b. Phila., Sept. 25, 1947; s. Nathan and May B. (Schreibman) T. BA in Math., U. Pa., 1969; JD, Washington U., St. Louis, 1973. Bar: Mo. 1974. Pvt. practice, St. Louis, 1974-75; staff atty. Legal Svcs. Ea. Mo., St. Louis, 1975-76, mng. atty., 1976-80, exec. dir., gen. counsel, 1980—; judge Mo. Ct. Appeals (ea. dist.), 1997—2000, Mo. Supreme Ct., 2002—. Bd. dirs. Citizens for Mo.'s Children, St. Louis, 1988—. Recipient Durward K. McDaniel award Am. Coun. of Blind, 1986. Mem. ABA (chair commn. on mental and disability law), Mo. Bar Assn (v.p. 2000-01, pres.lect 2001-02), Kansas City Met. Bar Assn., Met. St. Louis (pres. 1989-90; award of merit Young Lawyers sect., 1985), Mound City Bar Assn., Lawyers Assn., St. Louis, Women Lawyers' Assn. Greater St. Louis, St. Louis County Bar Assn., Am. Blind Lawyers Assn., St. Louis Bar Found., Am. Judicature Soc. (bd. dirs. 1986—), Leadership St. Louis. Office: Mo Supreme Court PO Box 150 Jefferson City MO 65102 Office Phone: 573-751-1004. Business E-Mail: rteitelm@courts.mo.gov.

TEITZ, CAROL, orthopedist, surgeon, educator; BS, U. of Cin., 1970; MD, Yale U., 1974. Diplomate in orthopaedic surgery Am. Bd. of Orthopaedic Surgery, 1981. Intern in orthop. U. Wash., Seattle, 1974—75, resident in

orhtop., 1975—80; prof. orthopaedics and sports medicine U. of Wash., Seattle, 2000—. Contbr. articles to profl. jours. Team physician Goodwill Games, Seattle, 1990, Jr. Maccabi Games, Seattle. Recipient Guidon award, U. of Cin., 1968, Mortar Bd. award, 1969, Trauma award, Am. Orthop. Internat., 1980. Fellow: Am. Orthopaedic Soc. for Sports Medicine (chmn. membership 1996, chmn. travelling fellowship 1998, bd. dir., fellow 2003, 1993), Am. Acad. of Orthopaedic Surgeons (travelling fellow 1993); mem.: ISAKOS, Western Orthopaedic Assn., Wash. State Orthopaedic Assn., King County Med. Soc., Magellan Soc. (sci. program chmn. 1998), Ruth Jackson Soc., Pi Delta Epsilon, Phi Beta Kappa. Office: University of Washington Box 354060 Seattle WA 98195-4060

TEIXEIRA, ARTHUR ALVES, food engineer, educator, consultant; b. Fall River, Mass., Jan. 30, 1944; s. Arthur Araujo and Emelia (Alves) T.; m. Jean E. Lamb, Dec. 26, 1966 (dec. Dec. 1983); children: A. Allan, Scott C.; m. Marjorie St. John, June 28, 1986; 1 stepchild, Craig St. John. PhD, U. Mass., 1971. Registered profl. engr., Fla., Mass. Rsch. engr. Ross Labs., Columbus, Ohio, 1971-73, R&D group leader, 1973-77; sr. cons. Arthur D. Little, Inc., Cambridge, Mass., 1977-82; assoc. prof. U. Fla., Gainesville, 1982-89, prof., 1989—. Sci. advisor Escola Superior de Biotecnologia, Porto, Portugal, 1991-96, FMC Corp., Santa Clara, Calif., 1989-92; internat. cons., Australia, Belgium, Brazil, Bulgaria, Chile, Cuba, Eng., France, Hungary, Indonesia, Israel, Ireland, Kenya, Netherlands, Poland, Portugal, Peru, Romania; reviewer USDA, Washington, 1991—. Author: Computerized Food Processing Operations, 1989; contbr. 10 chpts. to books, 60 articles to profl. jours. Judge Internat. Sci. Fair, Orlando, Fla., 1991. Recipient Golden Retort Award of Merit (IFTPS), 1994, Fulbright scholar award, Portugal, 1990—91, Peru, 2000, Disting. Food Engr. award, IAFIS/FPEI/ASAE, 2001, Sr. Faculty award, U. Fla. chpt. Gamma Sigma Delta, 1996, Tchr. of Yr. award, U. Fla. Coll. Engring., 1996; fellow, NATO, 1988—89. Fellow Am. Soc. Agrl. Engrs. (dir. 1988-90, Paper awards 1988-89, 2001, assoc. editor Transactions of ASAE 1985—); mem. AIChE, ASEE, Inst. Food Technologists (mem. editl. bd. 1980-83, 2003—), Am. Soc. Engring. Edn., Inst. Thermal Process Specialists, Coun. on Agrl. Sci. and Tech., R & D Assocs., Gamma Sigma Delta (chpt. pres. U. Fla. 1999-2000), Sigma Xi, Alpha Epsilon, Tau Beta Pi. Roman Catholic. Achievements include design of on-line process control system to assure safety of sterilized canned foods; tech. and economic feasiblity for radiation sterilization of disposable feeding devices; research in computer optimization and control of food sterilization processes, mathematical modelling of bacterial spore population dynamics in processed foods, and anaerobic composting for solid waste management on long-term NASA space missions. Office: U Fla Rogers Hall Gainesville FL 32611-0570 Office Phone: 352-392-1864. E-mail: aateixeira@mail.ifas.ufl.edu.

TEJADA, FRANCISCO, physician, educator; b. Moyobamba, San Martin, Peru, July 25, 1942; s. Francisco Tejada and Semiramis Reatequi; m. Barbara Ann Kotowski, Feb. 1, 1970; children: Anamaria, Semiramis, Barbara Lee, Francisco, James. BS, U. Nacional Mayor de San Marcos, Lima, Peru, 1961; MD, U. Peruana Cayetano Heredia, Lima, 1967. Diplomate Am. Bd. Internal Medicine, Am. Bd. Oncology. Resident in medicine Johns Hopkins U., Balt., 1969-72; sr. cancer rschr. Nat. Cancer Inst., NIH, Bethesda, Md., 1972-75; asst. clin. dir. Comprehensive Cancer Ctr. Fla., Miami, Fla., 1975-80; asst. prof. U. Miami, 1975-79, assoc. prof., 1979-85, prof., 1985—; vis. prof. U. Peruana Cayetano Heredia, Lima, 1994—; sr. ptnr. Oncology Assocs., Miami, 1980-85; chief cancer control Papanicolaou Cancer Ctr., Miami, 1984-86; assoc. dir. AMC Cancer Rsch. Ctr., Denver, 1986-87; pres. Am. Oncology Ctrs., Miami, 1985—; prof. U. San Agustin, Arequipa, Peru, 1992—, U. Peruana Cayetano Heredia, Lima, Peru, 1994—; clin. rsch. scientist UM/Sylvester Comprehensive Cancer Ctr., 2001—; investigator Lovelace Rsch. Svcs., Inc., 2002—. Oncology expert Pan Am. Health Orgn., Washington, 1975-85, Nat. Cancer Inst., Bethesda, Md., 1984-86; dir. Miami Cancer Inst., 1980—; dir. Peruvian-Am. Endowment Inc., 1993-99, v.p., 1995-97; bd. dirs. Integrated Med. Svcs. Fla. Keys, Key West, 1997-2000; dir. oncology dept. Clinica Ricardo Palma, Lima, Peru, 1991-99; med. dir. Fla. Comprehensive Cancer Control Initiative, 2000-03; dir. CureMeDoctor Inc., 2002-2002. Editor Miami Health Letter, 1986—; inventor cancer risk assessment. Mem. Beacon Coun., Miami, 1984, Latin Am. Cancer Info., Washington, 1976, Hispanic Cancer Rsch. Network, Washington, 1990; chpt. pres. Peruvian Am. Med. Soc., Miami, 1986; trustee Miami-Dade County Pub. Health Trust, 2002—; bd. dirs. Miami-Dade County Policy Health Authority, 2002-03. Lt. Peruvian Army, 1966-67. Decorated comendador Orden Sociedad, Peruvian U. Cayetano Heredia; recipient Gold Medal Merit award Ministry of Edn., Lima, 1959, Hipolito Unanue award Hipolito Unanue Inst., Lima, 1968. Fellow ACP, Johns Hopkins U., Nat. Cancer Inst.; mem. Colegio Medico del Perú, Am. Assn. Cancer Rsch., Am. Soc. Clin. Oncology, Am. Soc. Hematology, Bolivian Cancer Soc. (hon. mem.), Peruvian Cancer Soc. (hon. mem.), Chilean Soc. Cancer (hon. mem.), Argentinian Soc. Head and Neck Pathology (hon. mem.). Roman Catholic. Avocations: hiking, photography, reading. Office: 1801 NW 9th Ave Rm 200F Miami FL 33136 Office Phone: 305-251-4540. E-mail: f.tejeda-poc@att.net.

TEJADA, MIGUEL, professional baseball player; b. Bani, Dominican Republic, May 25, 1976; Shortstop Oakland (Calif.) Athletics, 1997—2003, Balt. (Md.) Orioles, 2004—. Named Most Valuable Player, Am. League, 2002; named to Am. League All-Star Team, 2002, 2004. Achievements include won All-Star home run derby, 2004. Office: 333 West Camden St Baltimore MD 21201*

TE KANAWA, KIRI, opera and concert singer; b. Gisborne, N.Z., Mar. 6, 1944; d. Thomas and Eleanor Te Kanawa; m. Desmond Park, Aug. 30, 1967 (div. 1997); children— Antonia Aroha, Thomas Desmond. Student, St. Mary's Coll., Auckland, N.Z., 1957-60, London Opera Centre, 1966-69; DMus (hon.), Oxford U., Dundee U., 1983, Warwick U., Auckland U., Waikato U., Nottingham U., Chgo. U., Durham U., Cambridge U. Joined Royal Opera House, London, 1971; appeared in role of Countess in Le Nozze di Figaro, 1971; U.S. debut in Santa Fe Festival, 1971; Met. Opera debut as Desdemona in Otello, 1974; appearances with all major European and Am. opera houses, including Australian opera cos., Royal Opera House, Covent Garden, London, Paris Opera, Munich Opera, La Scala, others; opera appearences include Boris Gudonov, Carmen, Don Giovanni, the Magic Flute, Eugene Onegin, La Boheme, Manon Lescaut, many others; appeared in film Don Giovanni as Elvira, 1979; recs. include Blue Skies, 1986, Kiri Sings Gershwin, 1987, Kiri Te Kanawa: Italian Opera Arias, 1991, Kiri Her Greatest Hits, Ave Maria, Kiri on Broadway, The Kiri Selection, Kiri Side Tracks, My Fair Lady, Maori Songs; PBS appearance: Great Performances: West Side Story, 1985; author: Land of the Long White Cloud, 1989, Opera for Lovers, 1996. Decorated comdr. Order Brit. Empire, 1973, Dame Comdr. Brit. Empire, 1983, Order of Australia, 1990, Order of New Zealand, 1995. Mem.: Royal Acad. Music (hon.). Address: care Nick Grace Mgmt Ltd 69 Sheen Rd Richmond TW9 1YJ England

TEKLITS, JOSEPH ANTHONY, lawyer; b. Belleville, Ill., July 18, 1952; s. Frank Anthony and Mary (Bodish) T.; m. Deborah Ann Keevill, June 1, 1974; children: Jessica, Joseph, Michael. BA, Coll. St. Francis de Sales, Allentown, Pa., 1974; JD, U. Notre Dame, 1977. Bar: Ind. 1977, U.S. Dist. Ct. (so. and no. dists.) Ind. 1977, Pa. 1988, Pa. 1988, U.S. Dist. Ct. (ea. dist.) Pa. 1988, U.S. Ct. Appeals (3d cir.) 1988, U.S. Dist. Ct. (ea. dist.) Mich. 1989, U.S. Ct. Appeals (6th cir.) 1990, U.S. Ct. Appeals (11th cir.) 1993, U.S. Supreme Ct. 1995, U.S. Dist. Ct. Colo. 1999. Legal counsel CTS Corp., Elkhart, Ind., 1977-80; mng. labor counsel Sperry Corp. (name now Unisys Corp.), Blue Bell, Pa., 1980-87; asst. gen. counsel Unisys Corp., Blue Bell, 1987-95, assoc. gen. counsel, 1995—. Mem. mgmt. com. Equal Employment Opportunity Law. Mem. ABA (EEO com. labor and employment law and litigation sects.), Delta Epsilon Sigma. Republican. Roman Catholic. Office: Unisys Corp Hdqrs Unisys Way Blue Bell PA 19424-0001

TEKLU, DAWIT, researcher; s. Teklu Dilnesahu and Nafekech Berhane; m. Abenet Tilahun Teklu, Sept. 2, 1989; children: Teklu Moti Dawit, Maya Gelila Dawit. Cert. of Adv. Grad. Studies, Va. Poly. State U., Madison, 1991—96. Dir. rsch. William Rainey Harper Coll., Palatine, Ill., 1997—2001; dir. planning, rsch., instl. assessment Anne Arundel CC, Arnold, Md., 2001—. Dir. instl. rsch. Va. CC, Annandale, Va., 1984—97. Sec. Ethiopian Human Rights Coun., Washington, 1998; chair Ethiopian Cmty. Ctr., Washington, 2001. Adv. Opportunity fellow, U. Wis., 1980-1982. Mem.: Md. Assn. Instl. Rsch., Nat. Coun. Rsch. Planning, Soc. Coll. and U. Planning, Assn. Instl. Rsch. Avocations: travel, hiking, camping, bicycling, reading. Home: 8596 Dark Hawk Cir Columbia MD 21045 Office: Anne Arundel CC 101 College Pkwy Arnold MD 21012 Office Phone: 410-777-2766. Business E-Mail: dteklu@aacc.edu.

TELEGDI, ANDREW, member of parliament; b. Budapest, Hungary, May 28, 1946; arrived in Can., 1957; s. Alexander Sandor and Elenora Maria (Friedrich) T.; m. Nancy Curtin; 1 child, Erin., U. Waterloo. Mem. Waterloo City Coun., 1985-93, Waterloo Regional Coun., 1988-93; M.P. for Waterloo Ho.of Commons., 1993-97, vice chair standing com. on human rights and disabled, 1994-95, vice chair pub. accounts standing com., 1995-96; mem. justice com. Ho. of Commons, 1997-98, mem. caucus com. on postsecondary edn., 1996—, vice chair, regional licensing com.; assoc. mem. fin., environ., and industry coms. Ho. of Commons, 1993—2002; M.P. for Kitchener-Waterloo Ho. of Commons. Exec. dir. Youth in Conflict with the Law, 1976-93; coord. Justice Week, Waterloo, 1979-; pres. Fedn. of Students, U. Waterloo, 1973-75; councillor City of Waterloo, 1985-93; advisor to Prime Min., Budapest Conf. on Security and Coop. in Europe, 1994; mem. standing com. on citizenship and immigration, Ho. of Commons, Ottawa, 1998-2000; parliamentary sec. to Minister of Citizenship and Immigration, 1998-2000; parliamentary sec. to Prime Min. with spl. emphasis on aboriginal affairs, 2004-; mem. standing com. on aboriginal affaris, no. devel. and natural resources, 2004-; mem. standing com. on citizenship and immigration, 2004-. Bd. dirs. The Working Centre and St. John's Soup Kitchen, 1986—, Kitchener House, 1979—; pres. K.W. Multicultural Centre, 1987-89; chair Conestoga Coll. Basic Job Readiness Tng. Adv. Group, 1980-84; mem. clin. adv. com. Cath. Family Counseling Centre, 1986-87, family violence com.; chair People, Working and Learning Inc., 1984-86. Mem. Waterloo Uptown Bus. Assn., Kitchener-Waterloo C. of C. (bus. edn. com.). Libr. Com. Mem. Office: House of Commons 285 Confederation Bldg Ottawa ON Canada K1A 0A6 E-mail: telega@parl.gc.ca.

TELEMAN, SILVIU, mathematician, educator; b. Corbeni, Romania, Aug. 21, 1931; arrived in U.S., 1986; m. Ecaterina Cioranescu, May 15, 1962; children: Calin Nicolae Stefan, Constantin. *My father's name Aurel Teleman, my mother's name Adele Maria Pia Dinorah Ida Elda Gemma Teleman, nee Della Torre. Son Constantin Teleman, brothers Kostake Teleman and Nicolae Teleman, nephew Andrei Teleman and niece Ana Maria Teleman are mathematicians. Son Stefan Teleman is a pianist and is active in Computer Science. Wife Ecaterina Teleman earned her Ph.D. in Theoretical Physics. My brother, Petrache Teleman, who is a construction engineer, and my sister Ruxandra Teleman. Elizabeth Gasparim, wife of Constantin Teleman, is also a mathematician.* BS, M. Eminescu H.S., 1950; MS in Math., U. Bucharest, 1957, PhD of Math., 1968. Editor Inst. Romanian-Soviet Studies Romanian Acad. Sci., Bucharest, 1960—62; reader, chmn., lectr., dean Pedagogical Inst., Pitesti, Romania, 1962—68; rschr. Inst. Math. Romanian Acad. Scis., Bucharest, 1968—86; vis. prof. Dept. Math. Ind. U., Bloomington, 1986—87, U. Cin., 1987—88; Otto Szasz vis. prof. dept. math. U. Mich., Ann Arbor, 1988—89; assoc. prof. Dept. Math. U. P.R., San Juan, 1989—95, prof. Dept. Math., 1995—. Author: Theory of Harmonic Algebras, with Applications to Von Neumann Algebras and Cohomology of Locally Compact Spaces (de Rham's Theorem), 1971 (Gh. Tzitzeica award, 1971), An Introduction to Choquet Theory, with Applications to Reduction Theory, 1980; contbr. articles to profl. jours. Recipient Order of Work 3d Class, Pres. Romania, 1967, Rep. Presdl. Legion of Merit, Rep. Presdl. Legion Exec. Bd., 1997, Rep. Sen. Medal of Freedom, Rep. mems. of U.S. Senate, 1999. Mem.: AAAS, N.Y. Acad. Scis., Math. Assn. Am., Am. Math. Soc. Avocation: music. Home: 221 Calle Emmanuelli #2 Hato Rey San Juan PR 00917-4103 Office: Univ Puerto Rico Dept Math Rio Piedras Campus PO Box 23355 San Juan PR 00931 Office Phone: 787-764-0000 4699. E-mail: silviu1@bigplanet.com.

TELESCA, MICHAEL ANTHONY, federal judge; b. Rochester, N.Y., Nov. 25, 1929; s. Michael Angelo and Agatha (Locurcio) T.; m. Ethel E. Hibbard, June 5, 1953; children: Michele, Stephen. AB, U. Rochester, 1952; JD, U. Buffalo, 1955. Bar: N.Y. 1957, U.S. Dist. Ct. (we. dist.) N.Y. 1958, U.S. Ct. Appeals (2nd cir.) 1960, U.S. Supreme Ct. 1967. Ptnr. Lamb, Webster, Walz, Telesca, Rochester, N.Y., 1957-73; surrogate ct. judge Monroe County, N.Y., 1973-82; judge U.S. Dist. Ct. (we. dist.) N.Y., Rochester, 1982—, chief judge, 1989-95. Apptd. to Alien Terrorist Removal Ct. by Chief Justice Rehnquist, U.S. Supreme Ct., 1996; bd. dirs. Fed. Jud. Ctr. Bd. govs. Genesee Hosp., Rochester; mem. adv. bd. Assn. for Retarded Citizens, Al Sigl Ctr., Rochester. Served to 1st lt. USMC, 1955-57. Recipient Civic medal Rochester C. of C., 1983, Hutchinson medal U. Rochester, 1990. Mem. ABA, Am. Judicature Soc., Am. Inns. of Ct. (founder, pres. Rochester chpt.), Justinian Soc. Jurists, N.Y. State Bar Assn., Monroe County Bar Assn. Republican. Roman Catholic. Office: US Dist Ct 272 US Courthouse 100 State St Ste 212 Rochester NY 14614-1309

TELESETSKY, WALTER, government official; b. Boston, Jan. 22, 1938; s. Keril and Nellie (Krelka) T.; m. Sharron-Dawn Lamp, July 15, 1961; children: Stephanie Ann, Anastasia Marie. BS in Mech. Engring., Northeastern U., 1960; MBA, U. Chgo., 1961; postgrad., Harvard U., 1977. Engr. trainee Chrysler Corp., Detroit, 1956-59; rsch. asst. Microtech Rsch. Co., Cambridge, Mass., 1959-60; engr. Allis Chalmers Mfg. Co., Milw., 1960-61; mem. tech. staff The Mitre Corp., Bedford, Mass., 1962-68; sr. mem. tech. staff Data Dynamics, Inc., Washington, 1969; phys. scientist NOAA, Rockville, Md., 1970-71, U.S. Gate Project coord., 1972-74, dir. U.S. Global Weather Experiment Project Office, 1974, dir. Program Integration Office, 1975-77, dir. Programs and Tech. Devel. Office, 1977-79, dir. Programs and Internat. Activities Office, 1979-81; dep. assoc. dir. for tech. svcs., chief AFOS ops. div. Nat. Weather Svc., Silver Spring, Md., 1981-86, dir. Office of Systems Ops., 1986-2000, dir. Office Operational Sys., 2000—02. Liaison to NAS coms. on atmospheric scis., geophysics studies and internat. environ. programs, 1975-81; U.S. coord. U.S./Japan Coop. Program in Natural Resources, 1980-88; chmn. U.S.-Japan Marine Resources and Engring. Coordination Com., 1980-88; U.S. del. governing coun. UN Environ. Program and World Meteorol. Orgn.; mem. commn. for Basic Systems World Meteorol. Orgn., 1988—; speaker in field. Contbr. articles to profl. publs. Recipient Silver medal Dept. Commerce, 1975, Gold medal Dept. Commerce, 1998. Mem. AAAS, Am. Geophys. Union, Am. Meteorol. Soc., Am. Soc. Mech. Engrs., Marine Tech. Soc. Home: 16 Eton Overlook Rockville MD 20850-3003 Office: 1325 E West Hwy Silver Spring MD 20910-3280

TELFER, MARGARET CLARE, internist, hematologist, oncologist; b. Manila, Apr. 9, 1939; came to U.S., 1941; d. James Gavin and Margaret Adele (Baldwin) T. BA, Stanford U., 1961; MD, Washington U., St. Louis, 1965. Diplomate Am. Bd. Internal Medicine, Am. Bd. Hematology, Am. Bd. Oncology; lic. Ill., Mo. Resident in medicine Michael Reese Hosp., Chgo., 1968, fellow in hematology and oncology, 1970, assoc. attending physician, 1970-72, dir. Hemophilia Ctr., 1971—, interim dir. div. hematology and oncology, 1971-74, 81-84, 89—, attending physician, 1972—, Rush-Presbyn. St. Luke's Hosp., 1999—, Olympia Fields (Ill.) Hosp., 1999—, Cook County Hosp., Chgo., 2000—; asst. prof. medicine U. Chgo., 1975-80, assoc. prof. medicine, 1980-85, assoc. prof. clin. medicine, 1985-89; assoc. prof. medicine U. Ill., Chgo., 1990-2001, Rush U., Chgo., 2001—. Mem. med. adv. bd. Hemophilia Found. Ill., 1971, chmn., 1972—83, lectr. annual symposium, 1978—84; mem. med. adv. bd. State of Ill. Hemophilia Program; dir. hematology-oncology fellowship program Michael Reese Hosp., 1971—75, 1981—84, 1989—2000, lectr. and mem. numerous coms.; lectr. Cook County Grad. Sch. Medicine, 1980—85, U. Chgo., ARC. Contbr. articles to profl. jours. Fellow ACP; mem. Am. Soc. Clin. Oncology, Am. Assn. Med. Colls., Am. Soc. Hematology, World Fedn. Hemophilia, Blood Club (Chgo.), Thrombosis Club (Chgo.). Office: Florsheim Bldg 29th & Ellis Chicago IL 60616 Office Phone: 312-864-7250. E-mail: mtelfer@ameritech.net.

TELFORD, GORDON LAING, surgeon, educator; b. Warrington, Eng., Dec. 3, 1944; came to U.S., 1946; s. Wayne M. and Helen Telford. BA, Drake U., Des Moines, 1967; MD, U. Chgo., 1971. Intern U. Fla., 1971-72; resident in surgery U. Iowa, 1972-74, U. Md., 1976-80; rsch. fellow in GI physiology Mayo Clinic, 1980-82; prof. surgery Med. Coll. Wis., Milw., 1982—, chmn. GI and minimally invasive surgery, 1998—. Mem. adv. commn. med. ethics Archdiocese Milw., 1987-92; bd. dirs. Ranch Cmty. Svcs., Menomonee Falls, Wis., 1994-98. Mem. ACS, Am. Surg. Assn. Ctrl. Surg. Assn., Phi Beta Kappa. Avocations: hiking, fishing, canoeing, biking, history, farming. Office: Med Coll Wis 9200 W Wisconsin Ave Milwaukee WI 53226-3522

TELFORD, KENNETH ALDERMAN, philosopher, humanities educator; b. Springfield, Mass., Apr. 13, 1922; s. Harold George Telford Sr. and Edna Clara Alderman; m. Nancy Jo Taylor, 1948 (div. 1968); children: Clinton, Cassie, Laurie. BA, Denison U., 1948; MA, U. Chgo., 1954, PhD, 1961. From instr. to full prof. and chmn. humanities divsn. Chgo. City Coll., 1953—78; prof. New Sch. for Social Rsch., N.Y.C., 1968—69. Author: Aristotle's Poetics, Translation and Analysis, 1961, The Origins of the Modern Morgan, 1988, The Lippitt Register, 1990, Selected Poems, by Kenneth A. Telford, 1992, Collected Writings on Equine Topics, 1993, What Ever Happened to the Pacer?, 1995, Aristotle's Nicomachean Ethics, Translation, 1997, Aristotle's Nicomachean Ethics, Commentary, 1997, Aristotle's Organon, Vol. I, Categories and On Interpretation, with Commentaries, 1998, Aristotle's Organon, Vol. II, Prior Analytics, with Commentary, 1998, Aristotle's Organon, Vol. III, Posterior Analytics, with Commentary, 1998, Aristotle's Organon, Vol. IV, On Topics and On Sophistical Refutations, with Commentary, 1999, Aristotle's Physics, Translation, 1999, Aristotle's Physics, Commentary, 1999, Aristotle's On the Heaven, with Commentary, 2000, Aristotle's On Genesis and Destruction, with Commentary, 2000, Aristotle's On the Soul, with Commentary, 2000, Aristotle's Metaphysics, Translation, 2000, Aristotle's Metaphysics, Commentary, 2000, Aristotle's Politics, Translation, 2001, Aristotle's Politics, Commentary, 2001, Aristotle's Poetics, with Commentary, 2001, Plato's Republic, Book I, with Commentary, 2001, Plato's Phaedo, with Commentary, 2001. Sgt. maj. U.S. Army, 1942—47, ETO. Home: 220 Vine St Northfield VT 05663-6751

TELGENHOF, ALLEN RAY, lawyer; b. Flint, Mich., Jan. 31, 1964; s. Gerald H. and Bernice Kay Telgenhof; m. Judy Michele Campbell, Sept. 5, 1986; children: Tyler, Allyson, Will, Luke. BA, Mich. State U., 1987; JD cum laude, 1989. Bar: Mich. 1989, U.S. Dist. Ct. (ea. dist.) Mich. 1992, U.S. Ct. Appeals (6th cir.) 1992, U.S. Dist. Ct. (we. dist.) Mich. 1997. Legis. analyst Mich. Ho. of Reps., Lansing, 1989; assoc. Hicks & Schmidlin, P.C., Flint, 1990-93; pvt. practice law Clio, Mich., 1993-94; ptnr. Pointner, Joseph, Corcoran & Telgenhof, P.C., Charlevoix, Mich., 1994-98, Joseph, Corcoran & Telgenhof, P.C., Charlevoix, 1998-2000, Joseph, Corcoran, Telgenhof & Snyder, P.C., Charlevoix, 2000—. Advisor Clio H.S. Law Club, 1992-94; founder, pres. Clio Area Edn. Found., 1992-94; presenter in field. Trustee Clio Bd. Edn., 1992-94, Charlevoix Bd. Edn., 1995-2003, pres., 1997-2003; commr. City of Charlevoix Planning Commn., 1995-96. Named Alumnus of Yr. Clio H.S., 1999. Mem. ABA, Charlevoix-Emmet Bar Assn. Avocations: sports, sailing, family activities. Office: Joseph Corcoran Et Al PO Box 490 203 Mason St Charlevoix MI 49720-1337 Office Phone: 231-547-8990. Office Fax: 231-547-3014. Personal E-mail: atelgenhof@chartermi.net.

TELL, WILLIAM KIRN, JR., retired oil company executive, lawyer; b. Evanston, Ill., Feb. 27, 1934; s. William Kirn and Virginia (Snook) T.; m. Karen Nelson, July 16, 1960; children— Catherine, Caroline, William F. BA in Govt., Dartmouth Coll., 1956; JD, U. Mich., 1959. Bar: Ohio, 1960, D.C., 1979. V.p. Texaco Inc., Washington, 1973—79, sr. v.p. N.Y.C., 1979—98; ret., 1998. Adj. fellow Am. Enterprise Inst., 1997—. Mem. adv. bd. dirs. Met. Opera, N.Y.C., 1983-98; trustee Am. Coun. Trustees and Alumni, 1992—. Mem.: Inst. for Am. Values (mem. bd. 2001—), Am. Hwy. Users Assn. (chmn. 1991, 1995, 1996, chmn. emeritus 1997—2003), Manhattan Inst. (trustee 1997—), Fgn. Policy Assn. (bd. govs. 1991—), Sankaty Head Golf and Beach Club, Everglades Club, Met. Club, Congl. Country Club, Greenwich Country Club. Home: 633 Steamboat Rd Greenwich CT 06830-7145 Office: 660 Steamboat Rd Greenwich CT 06830-7150

TELLEEN, JUDY, counselor; b. Chgo., Dec. 13, 1942; d. Kurt Theodore and Gertrude Lillian Lockwood Johnson; m. David Roger Telleen, June 15, 1964; children: Karin, Kirstin, Erik. BA, Lawrence U., 1964; MA, U. Mich., 1967, PhD, 1970. Program dir. counseling svcs. Asian Human Svcs., Chgo., 1994-95, coord. of counseling svcs., 1995-96, coord. of case mgmt., 1997-98; adj. prof. Gov.'s State Univ., University Park, Ill., 1995-99; counselor Arlington Heights, Ill., 1999—. Adv. com. mem. Bd. Suprs. and Sch. Bd., Va., 1993; mem. Pub. Policy and Legis. com. Ill. Counseling Assn., 1994, mem. governing coun., 2000—. Author: (book) A Predictive Model of the Cumulative Academic Achievement of Indian Students, 1970, (monograph) Gridance Factors Influencing Indian Students to Attend the University of Michigan, 1971; mem. editl. bd. (periodical) Ill. Counseling Assn. Quarterly, 1995—98. Youth adv. Bridge Youth & Family Svcs., Palatine, Ill., 1994—96; chairperson learning com. All Saints Luth. Ch., Palatine, 1993—2001. Mem. Am. Counselor's Assn., Ill. Counselor's Assn., Ill. Assn. of Couples & Family Couns. (pres.), Ill. Assn. for Multicultural Counseling, Ill. Assn. Mental Health Counselors, Assn. for Multicultural Counseling Develop., Internat. Assn. Marriage & Family Counselors, Internat. Assn. Addictions & Offender Counselors, Pi Lambda Theta, Phi Kappa Phi. Lutheran. Office: Ste 102 1040 S Arlington Heights Rd Arlington Heights IL 60005-3162

TELLEM, NANCY REISS, broadcast executive; b. Dec. 1952; m. Arn Tellem. Joined Warner Bros. TV, 1987, exec. v.p. bus. and fin. affairs; exec. v.p. bus. affairs CBS Entertainment, exec. v.p. CBS Prodns. CBS, 1997—98, pres. CBS Entertainment, 1998—; mem. bd. of dir. ThirdAge Media, 2000—. Office: CBS Entertainment 7800 Beverly Blvd Los Angeles CA 90036

TELLEM, SUSAN MARY, public relations executive; b. N.Y.C, May 23, 1945; d. John F. and Rita C. (Lietz) Cain; m. Marshall R.B. Thompson; children: Tori, John, Daniel. BS, Mt. St. Mary's Coll., L.A., 1967. Cert. pub. health nurse; RN. Pres. Tellem Pub. Rels. Agy., Marina del Rey, Calif., 1977-80, Rowland Grody Tellem, L.A., 1980-90; chmn. The Rowland Co., L.A., 1990—; pres., CEO Tellem, Inc., L.A., 1992-93. Instr. UCLA Extension, 1983-97; adj. prof. Pepperdine U., 1999—; speaker numerous seminars and confs. on pub. rels. Editor: Sports Medicine for the '80's, Sports Medicine Digest, 1982-84. Bd. dirs. Marymount High Sch., 1984-87, pres., 1984-86; bd. dirs. L.A. Police Dept. Booster Assn., 1984-87; mem. Cath. Press Coun.; mem. pres.'s coun. Mus. Sci. and Industry. Mem. Am. Soc. Hosp. Mktg. and Pub. Rels., Healthcare Mktg. and Pub. Rels. Assn., Pub. Rels. Soc. Am. (bd. dirs. 1994—), L.A. Counselors, PETA, Am. Lung Assn. (chair comm. com. L.A. chpt.) Soc. for Prevention of Cruelty to Animals (chair PetSet), Sports Club (L.A.). Roman Catholic. Avocations: reading, tennis, aerobic dance. Office: 23852 Pacific Coast Hwy # 928 Malibu CA 90265-4879 Fax: 310-589-6101. Office Phone: 310-479-6111 x16. E-mail: stellem@tellem.com.

TELLEP, DANIEL MICHAEL, aerospace executive, mechanical engineer; b. Forest City, Pa., Nov. 20, 1931; m. Pat. Tellep; 6 children. BS in Mech. Engrng. with highest honors, U. Calif., Berkeley, 1954, MS, 1955; grad. Advanced Mgmt. Program, Harvard U., 1971. Prin. scientist Lockheed Missiles & Space Co., 1955-69, chief engr. missile systems div., 1969-75, v.p., asst. gen. mgr. advanced systems div., 1975-83, exec. v.p., 1983-84, pres., 1984—, Lockheed Missiles & Space Systems Group, 1986—; chmn., chief exec. officer Lockheed Corp., 1989-95; chmn. bd. Lockheed Martin Corp., Bethesda, Md., 1996, retired chm., 1997. Cons. in field; bd. dirs. Wells Fargo, SCE Corp. Contbr. article to profl. jours. Bd. govs. Music Ctr. L.A. County, 1991-95; mem. adv. bd. U. Calif. Berkeley Sch. Engring.; mem. Calif. Bus. Roundtable, 1992—; nat. chmn. vol. com. U.S. Savs. Bond Campaign, 1993. Recipient Tower award San Jose State U., 1985, Aeronautics and Propulsion Laurels award Aviation Week and Space Tech., 1993, John R. Alison award, 1993, James V. Forrestal award, 1996, award Calif. Mfrs., 1996, Nat. Engring. award Am. Assn. Engring. Socs., 1996, award Internat. Acad. Astronautics, 1996, John W. Dixon medal Assn. U.S. Army, 1996, David Packard Leadership award Silicon Valley Def. Space Consortium, 1997, Tech.'s Hall of Fame,

Aviation Week and Space Tech., 1997, Internat. von Karman Wings award Calif. Mus. Sci. and Industry, 1997; named Exec. of Yr., Nat. Mgmt. Assn., 1993. Fellow AIAA (hon., Lawrence Sperry award 1964, Missile Sys. award, 1986), Am. Astronautical Soc. (Indsl. Leadership award 1992); mem. NAE, Nat. Aero. Assn., Soc. Mfg. Engrs., Sigma Xi, Pi Tau Sigma. Office: Lockheed Martin Corp 6801 Rockledge Dr Bethesda MD 20817-1877

TELLEZ, CORA, healthcare company executive; BA, Mills Coll.; MPA, Calif. State U. Various exec. positions to v.p., regional mgr. Hawaii Region Kaiser Found. Health Plan, 1978-94; sr. v.p., regional CEO Blue Shield, Calif., 1994-97; pres., chairwoman Prudential Health Care Plan of Calif., Inc., 1997-98; pres. CEO Health Net Foundation Health Systems, Inc., 1998—. Bd. mem. Golden State Bancorp Ince., Inst. Med. Quality, Calif. Assn. Health Plans, Holy Names Coll., Asian Cmty. Mental Health Svcs., Inst. for the Future. Mem. Phi Beta Kappa. Office: Health Net 21600 Oxnard St Ste 2000 Woodland Hills CA 91367-4969

TELLEZ KUENZLER, LUIS, government official; b. Mexico City, Mex., 1958; Grad., Inst. Tech.; PhD in Econs., MIT. Gen. dir. fin. & planning Sec. Fin. & Pub. Credit, 1988; undersec. planning Sec. Agrl. & Hydraulic Resources, chief staff to pres., 1994; sec. Energy, Mines & Parastatal Industry, Mex., 1997—. Office: Sec Energy Mines Industry Avenida Insuirgentes 552 Piso 06769 Mexico

TELLIER, HENRI, retired Canadian military officer; b. Montreal, Que., Can., Sept. 1, 1918; s. Henry Joseph and Jeanne (St. Cyr) T.; m. Virginia Wright, July 23, 1945; children: Pierre, Michele, Suzanne, John, Nicole. Student, U. Montreal, 1935-40, U. Ottawa, 1946-47, Canadian Army Staff Coll., 1942-43, Imperial Def. Coll., London, Eng., 1966, Dept. Def. Computer Inst., Washington, 1968; PhD in mil. sci., H.C. With Robert Howard & Co. (ins. brokers), Montreal, 1937-40; commd. 2d lt. Canadian Army, 1940, advanced through grades to lt. gen., 1973; asst. sec. to minister (Nat. Def.), 1945-48; comdg. officer (Royal 22d Regt.), 1948-51; instr. (Canadian Army Staff Coll.), 1951-54; army mem. (Joint Intelligence Staff), 1954-57; mil. adviser Vietnam, 1957-58; chief of staff (Que. Mil. Dist.), 1958-60; mil attache Rome, 1960- 63; dir. mil. ops. and plans Army, 1963-64, dir. internat. plans, 1964-65; comdr. (Canadian Contingent), Cyprus, 1965 66; dir. gen. plans (Forces Hdqrs.), Ottawa, Ont., 1967-70, chief plans, 1970-71; Canadian mil. rep. to mil. com. (NATO Hdqrs.), Brussels, 1971-73; ret., 1973. Assoc. nat. commr. Canadian Red Cross Soc., Toronto, Ont., 1973-75, nat. commr., 1975, sec.-gen., 1981-83, hon. v.p.; pvt. mem. Refugee Bd., 1984-89; chmn. Canadian sect. Mil. Coop. Com. Can.-U.S., Joint Permanent Bd. Def. Can.-U.S.; commr. Commn. for Strategic and Internat. Studies; mem. adv. council Can. Exec. Services Orgn. Decorated Mem. Order of Canada; Disting. Service Order (Canada); Queens medal Netherlands; comdr. Order of Merit (Italy), officer Order of Red Cross. Mem. Canadian Inst. Internat. Affairs., Can. Exec. Svc. Orgn., Inst. Assn. Execs., The Empire Club of Can., Royal 22 Regiment Assn., UN Assn. Office: 19 Bay Hill Ridge Stittsville ON Canada K2S 1B9

TELLIER, PAUL M. railroad transportation executive; b. Joliette, Que., Can., May 8, 1939; s. Maurice J. and Eva M. (Bouvier) T.; m. Andree Poirier, June 6, 1959; children: Claude, Marc. BA, U. Ottawa, 1959, LLL, 1962; BLitt, Oxford U., 1966; LLD (hon.), U. Alta., Can., 1996, U. Ottawa, 2000; DCommerce (hon.), St. Mary's U., 2001. Bar: Que. 1963. Sr. gov. official, Can., 1967-92; dep. minister Indian affairs and no. devel., 1979-82; dep. minister energy, mines and resources, 1982-85; chmn. governing bd. Internat. Energy Agy., 1985-92; clk. of Privy Council and sec. to Cabinet Govt. of Can., Ottawa, 1985-92; dir. Petro Can., 1985-92; pres., CEO Canadian Nat. Railway Co., 1992—2002, Bombardier Inc., Montreal, Canada, 2003—. Bd. dirs. Alcan Aluminum Ltd., Montreal, Can., BCE/Bell Can., Montreal, McCain Foods Ltd., Florenceville, Can., Bombardier Inc., Montreal, Can. Coun. of Chief Execs., Assoc. Am. R.R.; vice chair Can. Coun. Chief Execs., co-chair N.Am. policy com.; chair Conf. Bd. Can. Decorated companion Order of Can., 1993; recipient Pub. Policy Forum Outstanding Achievement award, 1988; recipient Gov. Gen.'s Outstanding Achievement award, 1990, Right Hand Man award Greenbrier, 1996, B'nai Brith Can. award of merit, 2000, McCullough Logistics Exec. of Yr. award, 2001, Partnership award Am. Short Line and Regional R.R. Assn., 2001, Fellowship award, Inst. of Corp. Dirs., 2003; named to Queen's Privy Counsel, Her Majesty Queen Elizabeth, 1992, Queen's counsel, 1981, Transp. Person of Yr., 1997, Railroader of Yr., 1997, Grand Montréalais, 1998; named Canada's Outstanding CEO of Yr., 1998, Personality of Yr., Les Affaires jour., 2000, McCullough Logistics Exec. of Yr., 2001, Most Respected CEO of the Year, Globe and Mail (ROB Mag.), 2003, 2004. Mem. Que. Bar Roman Catholic. Office: Bombardier Inc 800 Rene-Levesque Blvd W H3B 1Y8 Montreal QC Canada E-mail: paul.tellier@bombardier.com.

TELLIER, RICHARD DAVIS, management educator; b. Darby, Pa., Feb. 18, 1942; s. Joseph Campbell and Jane Grace (Davis) T.; m. Susan Gammon, June 10, 1974; children: John-Jo and Tiekka (twins). BSEE, Drexel U., 1967; MBA, Fla. State U., 1971, DBA, 1973. Elec. engr. Philco-Ford Corp., Phila., 1960-67; aerospace sys. engr. GE, Cape Canaveral, Fla., 1967-70; lectr. Fla. State U., Tallahassee, 1970-73; prof. mgmt. Calif. State U., Fresno, 1973-2000, chmn. dept. mgmt. and mktg., 1979-84, assoc. dean Sch. Bus., 1984-85, asst. dean, 1990-92, assoc. provost acad. resources, 1995-99, prof. emeritus, 2000—. Cons. ops. mgmt., market rsch. orgnl. behavior. Author: Operations Management: Fundamental Concepts and Methods, 1978, Production and Operations Management Test Bank, 1990; contbr. articles to profl. jours. Grantee 1975; recipient Meritorious Performance award, 1987, 88, 90. Mem. Ops. Research Soc. Am., Phi Kappa Phi. Home: 8294 N Academy Ave Clovis CA 93619-9454 Office: Calif State U Shaw and Maple Ave Fresno CA 93740-0001 Business E-Mail: rickt@csufresno.edu.

TELLIS, GERARD J. business educator; b. Bombay, Mar. 27, 1950; came to U.S., 1979; s. Aloysius Louis and Lucy Tellis; m. Cheryl Anne Evelyn, Mar. 5, 1980; children: Neil, Viren, Kethan, Sonia. BS, U. Bombay, 1975; PGDBM, Xavier Inst. Mgmt., Jamshedpur, India, 1977; PhD, U. Mich., 1983. Sales devel. mgr. Johnson & Johnson, Bombay, 1977-79; assoc. prof. mktg. U. Iowa, Iowa City, 1983-88; prof. mktg. U. So. Calif., L.A., 1989-95, Neely chair in Am. Enterprise LA, 1996—. Author: Advertising and Sales Promotion Strategy, 1998, Will & Vision, 2001. Dir. coaches Am. Youth Soccer Assn., Hacienda Heights, Calif., 1996-2002, tournament dir., 1998-2002. Recipient Frank M. Bass award Mktg. Sci., 1998, William F. Odell award Jour. Mktg. Rsch., 1998, Harold D. Maynard award, Jour. Mktg., 2001. Mem. Am. Mktg. Assn., Inst. Ops. Rsch. and Mgmt. Sci. (Ama-Berry award 2003), Assn. Consumer Rsch. Avocations: soccer, hiking, gardening. Office: U So Calif Dept Bus Los Angeles CA 90089-0001 Office Phone: 213-740-5031.

TELNAES, ANN, cartoonist; b. Stockholm, 1960; m. David Lloyd. BFA, Calif. Inst. Arts. Animator and layout designer for various animation studios in London, L.A., Taiwan and N.Y.C., Warner Bros., Walt Disney Imagineering; editorial cartoonist. Bd. dirs. Cartoonists Rights Network. Named Best Cartoonist, Population Inst. XVIIth Global Media awards, 1996, Best Editl. Cartoonist, 6th Ann. Environ. Media Awards, 1996; recipient Nat. Headliner award for Editl. Cartoons, 1997, Pulitzer prize, 2001, Berryman award, Nat. Press. Found., 2003. Mem.: Assn. Am. Editl. Cartoonists (past v.p.).

TELSER, LESTER GREENSPAN, educator, economist; b. Chgo., Jan. 3, 1931; s. Asher and Edith (Greenspan) T.; m. Sylvia R. Trossman, June 24, 1956; children— Joshua, Tamar. AB, Roosevelt U., 1951; student, Harvard, 1951-52; A.M., U. Chgo., 1953, PhD in Econs, 1956. Asst. prof. econs. Iowa State U., 1956; mem. faculty Grad. Sch. Bus., U. Chgo., 1958-64; prof. econs. U. Chgo., 1965—98, prof. emeritus, 1998—. Cons. to industry, 1964— Author: Competition, Collusion and Game Theory, 1972, Functional Analysis in Mathematical Economics, 1972, Economic Theory and the Core, 1978, A Theory of Efficient Cooperation and Competition, 1987, Theories of Competition, 1988, Joint Ventures of Labor and Capital, 1997, Classic Futures, 2000. Served with AUS, 1956-58. Fellow Am. Statis. Assn. (asso. editor jour. 1966-69), Econometric Soc.; mem. Am. Econs. Assn. Home: 1456 E 56th St Chicago IL 60637-1866

TELSEY, SUZANNE LISA, lawyer; b. N.Y.C., Mar. 18, 1958; d. Daubert and Jacqueline (Messite) T.; m. Steven C. Bennett, July 26, 1986; children: Danielle, Nicole. AB, Brown U., 1980; JD with honors, NYU, 1984. Bar: N.Y. 1985, U.S. Dist. Ct. (so. dist.) N.Y. 1985. Law clk. Hon. Pierre N. Leval U.S. Dist. Ct. (so. dist.) N.Y., N.Y.C., 1984-86; litig. assoc. Kramer, Levin, Naftalis & Frankel, N.Y.C., 1986-89; assoc. gen. counsel Bantam Doubleday Dell Pub. Group, Inc., N.Y.C., 1989-96; gen. counsel Atlas Editions, Inc., N.Y.C., 1996—2000; assoc. gen. counsel McGraw Hill Cos., Inc., N.Y.C., 2000—. Contbr. articles to profl. jours. Mem. Assn. of the Bar of the City of N.Y. (copyright law com. 1990-94, comms. and media law sect. 1994-97, 2000—), N.Y. State Bar Assn. (media law sect. 1998-2002), Order of the Coif. Jewish. Avocations: tennis, gardening, hiking, horseback riding, photography. Office: McGraw Hill Cos Inc 1221 Avenue of the Americas New York NY 10020

TEMAM, ROGER M. mathematician, educator; b. Tunis, Tunisia, May 19, 1940; s. Ange M. and Elise (Ganem) T.; m. Claudette Cukorja, Aug. 21, 1962; children: David, Olivier, Emmanuel. M in Math., U. Paris, 1962, DSc, 1967. Asst. prof. math. U. Paris, 1960-67, prof., 1967—2003, Ind. U., 1986—2004, dir. Inst. for Sci. Computing and Applied Math., 2003—, prof. emeritus, 2004—. Prof. Ecole Polytechnique, Paris, 1968-85. Author: Numerical Analysis, 1969, Navier-Stokes Equations, 1977, rev. edit., 2001, Mathematical Problems in Plasticity, 1983, Infinite Dimensional Dynamical Systems in Mechanics and Physics, 1988, 2nd edit., 1997; co-author: Convex Analysis and Variational Problems, 1976, rev. edit., 1999, Dynamic Multilevel Methods and the Numerical Simulation of Turbulence, 1999, Navier-Stokes Equations and Turbulence, 2001; assoc. editor: profl. jours.; contbr. articles to profl. jours. Recipient several prizes. Mem. AAAS, Am. Math. Soc., Am. Phys. Soc., Soc. Indsl. and Applied Math. (first pres. French chpt. 1983-87), NY Acad. Scis. Office: Ind U Dept Math Rawles Hall Bloomington IN 47405

TEMARES, STEVEN H. retail executive; BA, Rutgers U., 1980, JD, U. Pa., 1983. Assoc. Real Estate Group Schulte Roth & Zabel LLP, N.Y.C., 1983—85; counsel Universal Maritime Svc. Corp., N.Y.C., 1986—88; atty. Real Estate Group Riker Danzig Scheler Hyland & Perretti, Morristown, NJ, 1988—92; from dir. real estate, gen. counsel to CEO Bed Bath & Beyond Inc, Union, NJ, 1992—2003, CEO, 1903—. Office: Bed Bath & Beyond Inc 650 Liberty Ave Union NJ 07083

TEMBREULL, MICHAEL A. automotive executive; Gen. mgr. PACCAR, Inc., 1985—, sr. v.p., 1990-92, exec. v.p., 1992-95, dir., 1994—. Office: PACCAR Inc Paccar Bldg 777 106th Ave NE PO Box 1518 Bellevue WA 98009

TEMERLIN, LIENER, advertising agency executive, b. Ardmore, Okla., Mar. 27, 1928; s. Pincus and Julie (Kahn) T.; m. Karla Samuelsohn, July 23, 1950; children: Dana Temerlin Crawford, Lisa Temerlin Gottesman, Hayden Crawford, Sandy Gottesman. BFA, U. Okla., 1950. Assoc. editor Sponsor Mag., N.Y.C., 1950-51; from copywriter to COO Glenn Advt. Inc., Dallas, 1952—74; pres. Glenn, Bozell & Jacobs, Inc., 1974-79; chmn. bd. dirs. Bozell & Jacobs Inc., 1979-86, Bozell, Jacobs, Kenyon & Eckhardt, Dallas, 1986-89; chmn. Bozell, 1989-92, Temerlin McClain, Irving, Tex., 1992—2001; pres. Temerlin Cons., 2001—. Bd. dirs. East/West Inst. Chmn. Winston Churchill Found. award dinner, 1986; chmn. Dallas Symphony Assn., 1986-88, pres., 1984-86, bd. govs., 1982-84, pres. coun., 1989—; mem. Blair House Restoration Com., 1987-88; vice-chmn. Am. Film Inst., 1992-93, bd. trustees, 1992-2000; bd. dirs. United Way of Met. Dallas Exec. Com., 1986-89, Dallas Bus. Com. for Arts, 1989, Dallas Citizen's Coun., 1984-86, 92; trustee Southwestern Med. Found., 1988—, bd. trustees, 1992-96, adv. com., 2003—, So. Meth. U., trustee com. Univ. devel., 1988, exec. bd., 1990-91, bd. dirs. Tate lectr. series, 2002—; trustee and chmn. of devel. com. Dallas Mus. Art, 1993-96; steering com. Susan G. Komen Found., 1989-91, art acquisition com. Meyerson Symphony Ctr., 1989-92, exec. coun. Daytop/Dallas, 1989—; chmn. grand opening fortnight Morton H. Meyerson Symphony Ctr., 1989; active Madison Coun. Libr. Congress, Washington, 1991-2002; hon. chair rsch. dinner Am. Lung Assn. Tex., 1996; corp. chmn. Sr. Citizens Greater Dallas for Spirit of Generations Award to Stanley Marcus, 1997; fundraising campaign chmn. Lieberman Rsch. Bldg., Baylor Med. Ctr., 1997; hon. chmn. ann. dinner Make A Wish Found., 1998; exec. bd. Meadows Sch. Arts, So. Meth. U., 2001; co-chair ann. fundraising event Vogel Alcove Child Care Ctr. for the Homeless, 2001; fund devel. adv. com. Jr. League of Dallas, 2001-02; adv. develop. com. Dallas Ctr. Performing Arts, 2003-. Recipient Bill D. Kerss award Dallas Advt. League, 1983, Brotherhood award NCCJ, 1984, Susan G. Komen Found. for Breast Cancer Rsch. Cmty. award, 1989, Neiman Marcus (formerly James K. Wilson) Silver Cup award, 1990, Linz award 1990, Silver Medal award Dallas Advt. League, 1991, Vol. Fundraiser of Yr. award Nat. Soc. Fundraising Execs., 1991, Inst. Human Rels. award Am. Jewish Commn., Dallas, 2003; named Dallas Father of Yr., 1991, Best Man in Advt. award McCall's Mag., 1992; named Temerlin Advt. Inst. for Edn. and Rsch. in his honor So. Meth. U. Sch. Advt., 2001; inducted into Am. Advt. Hall Fame, 2004.

TEMES, GABOR CHARLES, electrical engineering educator; b. Budapest, Hungary, Oct. 14, 1929; s. Erno and Rozsa (Angyal) Wohl-Temes; m. Ibi Kutasi-Temes, Feb. 6, 1954; children: Roy Thomas, Carla Andrea. Dipl.Ing., Tech. U. Budapest, 1952, DSc (hon.), 1991; Dipl. Phys., Eotvos U., Budapest, 1954; PhD, U. Ottawa, Ont., Can., 1961. Asst. prof. Tech. U. Budapest, 1952-56; project engr. Measurement Engring. Ltd., 1956-59; dept. head No. Electric Co. Ltd., 1959-64; group leader Stanford Linear Accelerator Center, 1964-66; corp. cons. Ampex Corp., 1966-69; prof. elec. engring. UCLA, 1969-90, chmn. dept., 1975-80; dept. head Oreg. State U., Corvallis, 1990—. Cons. Xerox Corp., ANT GmbH Author: (with others) Introduction to Circuit Synthesis and Design, 1977, Analog MOS Integrated Circuits for Signal Processing, 1986; assoc. editor: (with others) Jour. Franklin Inst, 1971-82; co-editor, contbg. author: (with others) Modern Filter Theory and Design, 1973, Oversampling Delta-Sigma Data Converters, 1991. Recipient Western Electric Fund award Am. Soc. Engring. Edn., 1982, Humboldt Sr. Rsch. award, 1991; NSF grantee, 1970— Fellow IEEE (life, editor Transactions on Circuit Theory 1969-71 Best Paper award 1969, 81, 85, Centennial medal 1984, Edn. award 1987, Tech. Achievement award 1989, Grad. Tchg. award 1998, Millenium medal 2000, CAS Golden Jubilee medal 2000). Home: 7100 NW Grandview Dr Corvallis OR 97330-2708 Office: Oreg State U Dept Elec Engring Corvallis OR 97331 E-mail: temes@ece.orst.edu., temes@ieee.org.

TEMIN, DAVIA B. marketing executive; b. Cleve., June 5, 1952; d. J.T. and Sylvia (Black) T.; m. Walter T. Kicinski, Aug. 10, 1991. BA, Swarthmore Pa./Coll., 1974; MA, Columbia U., 1976. Cmty. svcs. specialist Commonwealth Mass., Boston, 1975; editor-in-chief, founder Hermes mag. Columbia U. Bus. Sch., N.Y.C., 1976-79, dir. publ. affairs, 1979-83; v.p., dir. mktg. Citicorp Global Investment Bank, N.Y.C., 1983-86; v.p., dir. corp. mktg. Scudder, Stevens & Clark, N.Y.C., 1986-89; pres. The Temin Group, N.Y.C., 1989-90; v.p., dir. mktg. Schroder Wertheim & Co., Inc., N.Y.C., 1990-96; corp. v.p., head corp. mktg. GE Capital, N.Y.C., 1996-98; pres. Temin and Co., Inc., N.Y.C., 1998—. Exec. prodr. The Night & The Music Prodns., 1994—; bd. dirs. Soma Found.; chmn., bd. dirs. Mark Taylor Dance Co.; advisor to pres. Swarthmore Coll., 1994—, trustee, 1995—99, chair long range planning task force on ednl. leadership and visibility, devel. com., 1995—; bd. advisors Knight-Bagelot Fellowship Journalism Sch. Columbia U., 1995—; pres. bd. dirs., exec. com. Pub. Rels. Soc., N.Y.; bd. advisors Office.com, 2000—; trustee The Women's Leadership Fund; bd. dirs. The White House Project, Women's E-News; adv. bd. Goldman Sachs Investment Mgmt. Fin. Rsch. Initiative, Breakthrough TV. Chair Women's Counseling Project, 1978-81, Beth Cachet Dance Co., 1980-90; bd. trustees The Elaine Kaufman Cultural Ctr., 2000—. Recipient Meritorious Svc. award Commonwealth of Mass., 1976. Mem. Fgn. Policy Assn., Fin. Women's Assn., Women Pres.'s Orgn., Nat. Investor Rels. Inst., Women Inc., Nat. Arts Club, Strategic Adv. Bd., Devel. Com., Comm. Com., Columbia Bus. Sch. Club, Swarthmore Club, Princeton Club. Home: 530 E 90th St Apt 5K New York NY 10128-7860 Office: Temin and Co Inc Ste 1700 136 E 57th St New York NY 10022-2707

TEMIN, MICHAEL LEHMAN, lawyer; b. Phila., July 18, 1933; s. Henry and Annette (Lehman) T.; children: Aaron Lehman, Seth Lehman; m. Anne L. Hearn, 2000. BA magna cum laude, Yale U., 1954; LL.B. cum laude, U. Pa., 1957. Bar: Pa. 1958, Del. 2000, U.S. Ct. Appeals (3d cir.) 1958, U.S. Supreme Ct. 1969, U.S. Ct. Appeals (2d cir.) 1986, U.S. Ct. Appeals (9th cir.) 1992, U.S. Ct. Appeals (11th cir.) 2002. Asst. U.S. atty. U.S. Atty.'s Office, Phila., 1958-59; assoc. Wolf, Block, Schorr and Solis-Cohen, Phila., 1959-66, ptnr., 1966—. Lectr. Law Sch., U. Pa., Phila., 1982-90, adj. prof., 1990-93, 94-95, 2002—; Thomas A. O'Boyle vis. disting. practitioner, 1985, I. Grant Irey lectr., 1988, 2003-04. Editor U. Pa. Law Rev., 1955-57 Vice chmn. Ednl. Nominating Panel, Phila., 1981-83; bd. dirs. Citizens Com. in Pub. Edn., Phila., 1970-96, pres. 1980-82. Fellow: Am. Coll. Bankruptcy (regent 1997—2003); mem.: ABA (chmn. rules subcom. 1985 92, bus. bankruptcy com. on sect. corp. banking and bus. law), Pa. Bar Assn. (ho. of dels. 1985—89, 1990—, vice chmn. Chpt. 11 subcom. 1992—96, vice chmn. ea. dist. Pa. bankruptcy conf. 1994—95, chmn. ea. dist. Pa. bankruptcy conf. 1995—96, co-chmn. legal ethics and profl. responsibility com. 2004—). Phila. Bar Assn. (banking and bus. law 1979—86, chmn. profl. guidance com. 1985, sec. sect. corp. banking and bus. law 1985, treas. sect. corp. banking and bus. law 1986, vice chmn. sect. corp. banking and bus. law 1987, chmn. sect. corp. banking and bus. law 1988, chmn. bankruptcy com., sect. corp.), Order of Coif. Jewish. Office: Wolf Block Schorr & Solis-Cohen LLP 22d Fl 1650 Arch St Philadelphia PA 19103-2097 Office Phone: 215-977-2256. E-mail: mtemin@wolfblock.com.

TEMIN, PETER, economist, educator; b. Phila., Dec. 17, 1937; s. Henry and Annette T.; m. Charlotte Brucar Fox, Aug. 21, 1966; children: Elizabeth Sara, Melanie Wynn. BA, Swarthmore Coll., 1959; PhD, MIT, 1964. Mem. faculty MIT, 1965—, prof. econs., 1970—. Author: Iron and Steel in Nineteenth Century America, 1964, The Jacksonian Economy, 1969, Causal Factors in American Economic Growth in the 19th Century, 1975, Did Monetary Forces Cause the Great Depression?, 1976, Taking Your Medicine: Drug Regulation in the United States, 1980, The Fall of the Bell System, 1987, Lessons from the Great Depression, 1989, Inside the Business Enterprise, 1991, (with C. Feinstein and G. Toniolo) The European Economy Between The Wars, 1997, Engines of Enterprise: An Economic History of New England, 2000. Mem. Am. Econ. Assn., Econ. History Assn., Econ. History Soc., Phi Beta Kappa. Home: 15 Channing St Cambridge MA 02138-4713 Office: MIT Dept Econs Cambridge MA 02139

TEMIRKANOV, YURI, music director; b. Nal'chik, 1938; Grad., Leningrad (Russia) Conservatoy, postgrad., 1965. Condr. Maly Opera and Ballet Theatre, Leningrad, 1966, Moscow Philharm. Orch., 1967; prin. condr. Leningrad Symphony Orch., 1968-76; music dir. Kirov Opera and Ballet, 1976; condr. Balt. Symphony, 1992, 95, 98-00; musical dir. Baltimore Symphony Orchestra, Baltimore, MD, 2000—; musical dir., chief condr. St. Petersburg's Philharmonic, Russia. Guest condr. Berlin Philharm., Vienna Philharm., l'Orch. Paris, Dresden Staatskapelle, Amsterdam's Royal Concertgebouw, N.Y. Symphony Orch., Phila. Symphony Orch., Boston Symphony Orch., Chgo. Symphony Orch., Cleve. Symphony Orch., San Francisco Symphony Orch., L.A. Symphony Orch., Danish Nat. Radio Symphony; condr. laureate Royal Philharm., London. Recipient prize, Moscow Nat. Competition, 1967. Office: Balt Symphony Orch 1212 Cathedral St Baltimore MD 21201-5517

TEMKIN, HARVEY L. lawyer; b. Madison, Wis., Jan. 1, 1952; s. Joe L. and Sylvia (Libanoff) T.; m. Barbara Jean Myers, June 13, 1976; children: James, Daniel, Eli. BA, U. Wis., 1974; JD, U. Ill., 1978. Bar: Wis. 1978. Assoc. Foley & Lardner, Madison, 1978—83; prof. Tulane Law Sch., New Orleans, 1983-87; ptnr. Foley & Lardner, Madison, 1987—2002; shareholder Reinhart Boerner Van Deuren, s.c., Madison, 2002—. Lectr. U. Wis. Law Sch., 1990-93; mem. U.S. Senator Feingold's Bus. Adv. Group. 1st v.p. Hillel Found., Madison, 1982-83, bd. dirs., 1987-95; chmn. edn. com. Beth Israel Synagogue, Madison, 1980-82; chmn. Jewish edn. panel Madison Jewish Cmty. Coun., 1993-98, bd. dirs., 1998-2003. Fellow Am. Coll. Real Estate Lawyers; mem. ABA (real property probate and trust sect., reporter significant legis. panel 1983-85, significant lit. panel 1985-87), Downtown Madison, Inc. (chmn. 1989-91), Friends of Overture Ctr. Office: Reinhart Boerner Van Deuren 22 East Mifflin St PO Box 2018 Madison WI 53701-2018 E-mail: htemkin@reinhartlaw.com.

TEMKIN, ROBERT HARVEY, accountant; b. Boston, Oct. 21, 1943; s. Max and Lillian (Giller) T.; m. Ellen Phyllis Band, Sept. 25, 1966; 1 child, Aron; m. Debra Gottlieb, Oct. 3, 1998; 1 child, Rachel; m. Douglas Moore, Feb. 29, 1999; 1 child, Joshua. BBA, U. Mass., 1964. CPA, Mass. With Ernst & Young LLP, 1964—72, 1973—2002, ptnr., 1976—2002, nat. dir. auditing standards, 1980-88; prin. Robert H. Temkin, CPA, 2002—. Assoc. prof. NYU, 1982. Bd. dirs. Jewish Home for Elderly of Fairfield County, 1979—, pres., 1985-87; mem. Bd. Edn., Weston, Conn., 1983-87; dir. United Synagogue of Conservative Judaism, 1984-99, 2004—; mem. bus. adv. coun. U. Mass.; bd. dirs., chmn. bd. dirs. Jewish Cmty. Ctrs. of Greater Boston; mem. exec. com. Combined Jewish Philanthropies of Greater Boston, 1995-99, 2000—, bd. dirs. 1993—; treas. Synagogue Coun., Mass., 1988-93; dir. Hillel Found., U. Mass., 1992-99. Recipient Acctg. Alumni award U. Mass., 1978, Alumnus Award Sch. Mgmt. U. Mass., 1986; Cmtys. of Excellence award Combined Jewish Philanthropies, 2003. Mem. AICPA (staff dir. commn. on auditors responsibilities 1976-78, peer rev. com. 1982-84, auditing stds. bd. 1984-88, chmn. internat. auditing task force 1988-90), Mass. Soc. CPAs (Silver medal 1964), N.Y. State Soc. CPAs, Mass. Bd. Pub. Accountancy (sec. 1996, 2001, chmn. 1997, 2002). Assoc. mem., Hyannis Yacht Club. Home and Office: 1611 Commonwealth Ave Newton MA 02465-2800 Office Phone: 617-527-7705. E-mail: bobtemkin@rcn.com.

TEMKO, ALLAN BERNARD, writer; b. N.Y.C., Feb. 4, 1924; s. Emanuel and Betty (Alderman) T.; m. Elizabeth Ostroff, July 1, 1950 (dec. Aug. 1996); children: Susannah, Alexander. AB, Columbia U., 1947; postgrad. U. Calif., Berkeley, 1949-51, Sorbonne, 1948-49, 51-52. Lectr. Sorbonne, 1953-54, Ecole des Arts et Metiers, Paris, 1954-55; asst. prof. journalism U. Calif., Berkeley, 1956-62, lectr. in city planning and social scis., 1966-70, lectr. Grad. Sch. Journalism, 1991; lectr. art Stanford U., 1981, 82; architecture critic San Francisco Chronicle, 1961-93, art editor, 1979-82. Archtl. planning cons.; chmn. Yosemite Falls Design Workshop, 1992; Pulitzer Prize juror, 1991-92; architecture advisor Roman Cath. Cathedral, Oakland, Calif., 2000—. Author: Notre Dame of Paris, 1955, Eero Saarinen, 1962, No Way To Build a Ballpark and Other Irreverent Essays on Architecture, 1993; contbr. articles to U.S. and fgn. mags. and newspapers; West Coast editor, Archtl. Forum, 1959-62. Served with USNR, 1943-46. Recipient Gold medal Commonwealth Club Calif., 1956, Silver medal, 1994, Journalism award AIA, 1961, Silver Spur award San Francisco Planning and Urban Renewal Assn., 1985, AIA Inst. Honor award, 1991, Nathaniel A. Owings award AIA Calif. Coun., 1995, 1st prize in archtl. criticism Mfrs. Hanover/Art World, 1986, Critic's award Mfrs. Hanover/Art World, 1987, Profl. Achievement award Soc. Profl. Journalists, 1988, Pulitzer Prize for criticism, 1990; grantee Rockefeller Found., 1962-63, 20th Century Fund, 1963-66, NEA, 1988, Graham Found., 1990; Guggenheim fellow, 1956-57. Home: 1015 Fresno Ave Berkeley CA 94707-2517 *My chief intellectual and professional goal has always been to create excellence in a democratic America, and, where possible, in the world at large. This Jeffersonian aim, which came to me directly from Lewis Mumford, naturally includes architecture, environmental planning, the fine arts, and literature. Through education, in which history, criticism, and serious journalism play important roles, I think it is still possible to attain such excellence despite the complex problems of technological civilization.*

TEMKO, STANLEY LEONARD, lawyer; b. N.Y.C., Jan. 4, 1920; s. Emanuel and Betty (Alderman) T.; m. Francine Marie Salzman, Mar. 4, 1944 (dec. Dec. 1998); children: Richard J., Edward J., William D. AB, Columbia U., 1940, LLB, 1943. Bar: N.Y. 1943, D.C. 1951. Practice in, N.Y.C., 1943, 46-47; law clk. Mr. Justice Wiley Rutledge, U.S. Supreme Ct., Washington,

1947-48; legal counsel Econ. Coop. Adminstrn., 1948-49; assoc. Covington & Burling, Washington, 1949-55, ptnr., 1955-90, sr. counsel, 1990—. Editor-in-chief: Columbia Law Rev, 1942-43. Trustee Beauvoir Sch., 1963-69; trustee Columbia U., 1980-91, trustee emeritus, 1991—, mem. bd. visitors Sch. Law, 1961-98, mem. emeritus, 1999—; mem. bd. govs. St. Albans Sch., 1967-73, chmn., 1971-73. 2nd lt. U.S. Army, 1943-46. Decorated Bronze Star; recipient medal for conspicuous alumni svc. Columbia U., 1979, Excellence medal Columbia U. Law Sch., 2004. Fellow Am. Bar Found. (chmn. rsch. com. 1970-72); mem. ABA, Am. Law Inst., D.C. Bar Assn., Columbia U. Sch. Law Alumni Assn. (pres. 1982-84), Met. Club, Nat. Press Club, Phi Beta Kappa. Home: 4811 Dexter Ter NW Washington DC 20007-1020 Office: Covington & Burling 1201 Pennsylvania Ave NW Washington DC 20004-2401 Office Phone: 202-662-5514. Business E-Mail: stemko@cov.com.

TEMMER, JAMES DONALD, museum director; BA, U. Wis., 1987; MA, Marquette U., 1991; postgrad., Pa. State U., 2002—. Dir. Stonefield, Wis., 1996—99, H.H. Bennett & History Ctr., Wisconsin Dells, Wis., 1999—2002, Charles Allis/Villa Terr. Art Mus., Milw., 2002—. Recipient Nancy Hanks award for Profl. Excellence, Am. Assn. Mus., 2001. Mem.: State Hist. Soc. Wis. Office: Charles Allis Art Museum 1801 N Prospect Ave Milwaukee WI 53202

TEMPEL, JEAN CURTIN, venture capitalist; b. Hartford, Conn., Mar. 23, 1943; d. John J. and Sally (Miller) Curtin Jr.; m. Louis J. Tempel, Nov. 23, 1968 (div. 1978); m. Peter A. Wilson, May 10, 1980. BA in Math., Conn. Coll., 1965; MS in Computer Sci., Rensselaer Poly. Inst., 1972; advanced mgmt. program cert., Harvard U., 1979. Various sr. mgmt. positions Conn. Bank and Trust Co., 1965-80; mgr. strategic planning and mktg. Bank New Eng., 1980-82; sr. v.p., mgr. of custody The Boston Co., 1983, pres. Boston Safe Clearing Corp., 1984-90, exec. v.p., chief ops., info. officer, 1985, exec. v.p., COO, 1988-90; prin. Tempel Ptnrs. Inc., Boston, 1991; pres., COO Safeguard Scientifics Inc., Wayne, 1992-93, bd. dirs.; gen. ptnr. TL Ventures LP, Boston, 1994-96, spl. ltd. ptnr., 1997-99; founder, mng. ptnr. First Light Capital Inc., 2000—. Bd. dirs. Cambridge (Mass.) Tech. Ptnrs., Cambridge, Mass., 1991-98, Centocor, Malvern, Pa., Sonesta Internat. Hotels, Inc., Boston; trustee Scudder Funds, Boston, Northeastern U., Conn. Coll. Trustee Northeastern U., Conn. Coll. Mem. Internat. Women's Forum (dir.). Avocations: skiing, bicycling, sailing. Office: First Light Capital Inc 60 State St Fl 11 Boston MA 02109

TEMPELIS, CONSTANTINE HARRY, immunologist, educator; b. Superior, Wis., Aug. 27, 1927; s. Harry and Thelma Marie (Hoff) T.; m. Nancy Louise Foster, Aug. 27, 1955; children: William H., Daniel S. BS, U. Wis.-Superior, 1950; MS, U. Wis.-Madison, 1953, PhD, 1955. Project assoc. immunology U. Wis., Madison, 1955-57; instr. immunology U. W.Va., Morgantown, 1957-58; asst. rsch. immunologist U. Calif., Berkeley, 1958-66, assoc. prof. immunology, 1966-72, prof., 1972-95, prof. emeritus, 1995—, prof. grad. sch., 1996—. Vis. scientist Wellcome Rsch. Labs., Beckenham, Kent, Eng., 1977-78, U. Innsbruck, Austria, 1985, 90, 91; cons. in field. Contbr. articles to profl. jours. Served with USNR, 1945-46. Recipient Rsch. Career Devel. award, 1965-70; Fogarty sr. internat. fellow NIH, 1977-78 Mem. AAAS, Am. Assn. Immunologists, Fedn. Am. Soc. Exptl. Biology, Sigma Xi. Office: U Calif Sch Pub Health Berkeley CA 94720-0001 Office Phone: 510-642-3744. Business E-Mail: chtemp@uclink4.berkeley.edu.

TEMPELMAN, JERRY HENRY, investment funds trader, financial analyst; b. Nijmegen, Gelderland, The Netherlands, Aug. 4, 1962; s. Franciscus Andreas Maria and Catherina Petronella (Classen) T. Gymnasium Beta, Maurick Coll., Vught, Netherlands, 1980; candidaats, Erasmus U., Rotterdam, Netherlands, 1983; cert. in theol. studies, Bethel Theol. Sem., San Diego, 1988; MBA with hons., Boston U., 1991. Chartered fin. analyst. Mktg. dir. Quinsept, Inc., Lexington, Mass., 1984-86; portfolio acct. State St. Bank & Trust. Co., Boston, 1987-88, account adminstr., 1989, money market trader, 1989-90, sr. money market trader, 1990-94; high yield bond trader Putnam Investment Mgmt., Boston, 1994-99; sr. fixed income desk mgr. Bank Hapoalim, N.Y.C., 1999-2000; trading supr. BondBook, LLC, N.Y.C., 2000—01; v.p. high yield portfolio mgr. Intrepid Capital Mgmt., Inc., Jacksonville Beach, Fla., 2002—. Mem.: Met. Rep. Club of NY, The Cornell Club. Office: Intrepid Capital Management Inc 3652 South Third St 200 Jacksonville Beach FL 32250 Home: 201-25th Ave S, #N-1 Jacksonville Beach FL 32250

TEMPELMEYER, TERESA CATLIN, psychologist, social sciences educator, researcher; b. Houston, Tex., June 5, 1961; d. Lois Lavonne Fuquay; m. Patrick Earl Tempelmeyer, June 1, 1983; children: Sarah Gui, Matthew Earl, Rebekah Elizabeth. PhD, U. Houston, Tex., 1990—96. Cert. Psychologist State Com. Psychologists of Mo., 1996. Assoc. prof. Forest Inst. Profl. Psychology, Springfield, Mo., 2000—. Mem.: APA. Office: Forest Inst of Profl Psychologists 2885 W Battlefield Road Springfield MO 65807 Personal E-mail: ttempelmeyer@forest.edu. Business E-Mail: ttempelmeyer@forest.edu.

TEMPERLEY, NICHOLAS, music educator, writer; b. Beaconsfield, Bucks, England, Aug. 7, 1932; s. Arthur Cecil and Joyce Van Oss Temperley; m. Mary Dorothea Sleator, Sept. 17, 1960; children: Lucy, David, Sylvia. Assoc., Royal Coll. Music, 1952; BA, Cambridge U., 1955, MusB, 1956, PhD, 1959. Cert. ARCO, Assoc. royal Coll. Organists. Postdoctoral fellow U. Ill., Urbana, 1959—61; asst. lectr. music Cambridge U., Cambridge, England, 1961—66; fellow Clare Coll., Cambridge, 1961—66; asst. prof. music Yale U., New Haven, 1966—67; assoc. prof. music U. Ill., 1967—72, prof. music, 1972—96, chair, musicology divsn., 1972—75, 1992—96. Editl. bd. mem. 19th Century Music, Berkeley, Calif., 1973—, Victorian Studies, Bloomington, Ind., 1978—2000; editor-in-chief Am. Musicological Soc., 1980—82. Author: (book) The Music of the English Parish Church, 1979, Bound for America: Three British Composers, 2003; compiler (books and databases) The Hymn Tune Index, 1998. Pres. Baroque Artists of Champaign-Urbana, 2001—04. Recipient Otto Kinkeldey award, Am. Musicological Soc., 1980; hon. fellow, Guild Church Musicians, London, 1990. Mem.: Hymn Soc. U.S. and Can. (rsch. chair 1983—87), Soc. Am. Music, Royal Musical Assn. (life). Achievements include revived the music of neglected British composers, including George F. Pinto and Edward J. Loder; completed an unfinished Mozart opera, "L'Oca del Cairo", Act I, and revived it on stage. Home: 805 W Indiana St Urbana IL 61801 Office Phone: 217-333-6205. Business E-Mail: ntemp@uiuc.edu.

TEMPEST, RICK, state representative; m. Donna Tempest; 2 children. Grad. U. Wyo. Mem. Wyo. Ho. of Reps., 1986—, former chmn. appropriations com., former majority floor leader, speaker, 2000—. Active Am. Legis. Exchange Coun.; mem. Energy Coun. Dir. Wyo. Cmty. Devel. Authority; founder Wyo. Bus. Coun.; bd. dirs. Casper Econ. Devel. Alliance. Republican. Avocations: golf, travel, the arts. Office: Speaker of the House 111 W Second # 508 Casper WY 82601

TEMPLE, DONALD, retired allergist and dermatologist; b. Chgo., May 21, 1933; s. Samuel Leonard and Matilda Eve (Riff) T.; m. Sarah Rachel Katz, Sept. 29, 1957; children: Michael A., Matthew D., Madeline B. AB in Biology cum laude, Harvard U., 1954; MD, U. Chgo., 1958. Diplomate Am. Bd. Allergy and Immunology, Am. Bd. Dermatology, Nat. Bd. Med. Examiners; lic. Intern Michael Reese Hosp., Chgo., 1958-59; resident in dermatology U. Chgo. Hosps., 1959-62; clin. asst., dept. dermatology Boston U. Sch. Medicine, 1963-64; clin. instr. dermatology Stanford U. Sch. Medicine, 1965; preceptee in allergy Offices of Leon Unger, M.D., and Donald Unger, M.D., Chgo., 1965-69; pvt. practice Des Plaines, Ill., 1969-76; with allergy dept. Glen Ellyn (Ill.) Clinic, 1972-97; ret., 1997. Dermatology and allergy staff Louis A. Weiss Hosp., Chgo., 1965-73, allergy sect. Loyola U. Med. Ctr., Maywood, Ill., 1977-80, exec. and contract medicine coms. Glen Ellyn; clin. asst. prof. dermatology Abraham Lincoln Sch. Medicine, U. Ill., 1972-75; clin. asst. prof. medicine sect. allergy and dermatology, Loyola U., 1977-85; mem. staff Cen. DuPage Hosp., Winfield, Ill., 1973-97, Glen Oaks Med. Ctr., Glendale Heights, Ill., Glendale Heights Cmty. Hosp., 1980-92. Contbr. articles to profl. jours. Bd. dirs. Am. Lung Assn., DuPage, McHenry counties, 1980-91; chmn. Contract Medicine, HMO Com., Glen Ellyn Clinic, 1985, mem. exec. com., 1988-92. Fellow Am. Coll. Chest Physicians, Am. Assn. Cert. Allergists, Am. Coll. Allergists, Am. Acad. Allergy, Ill. Soc. Allergy and Clin. Immunology, Chgo. Dermatol. Soc.; mem. AMA, Ill. State Med. Soc., DuPage County Med. Soc., Chgo. Med. Soc., Fla. Med. Assn. Collier County Med. Soc. Jewish. Avocations: sailing, investing. Home: 6585 Nicholas Blvd Ph 3 Naples FL 34108-7210 Also: 110 E Delaware Pl Apt 2004 Chicago IL 60611-4904 E-mail: don.temple@postharvard.edu.

TEMPLE, DONALD EDWARD, medical association administrator; b. N.Y.C., Nov. 28, 1946; s. James Edward and Helen Louise (Gannon) Temple; m. Lucy Chirinos de Lorentzen, Feb. 23, 1974 (div. 1989); 1 child, Gail Marie. BBA, St. Francis Coll., Bklyn., 1968. Vol. U.S. Peace Corps, Lima, Peru, 1968-72; asst. to pres., gen. mgr. Barrons Ednl. Series, Inc., Hauppauge, NY, 1973-78; dir. supply svc. Am. Lung Assn., N.Y.C., 1978-84; bus. mgr. Am. Jour. Respiratory and Critical Care Medicine, N.Y.C., 1985—, Am. Jour. Respiratory Cell and Molecular Biology, N.Y.C., 1989—; dir. bus. affairs Am. Lung Assn., N.Y.C., 1985-89, dep. mng. dir. bus. affairs, 1990-94; dir. bus. affairs Am. Thoracic Soc., 1994—. Mem. mailers tech. adv. com. U.S. Postal Svc., Washington, 1987—93. Vol. L.I. Assn. AIDS Care, 1994—98. Recipient Merit award, Soc. Tech. Communication, 1990. Mem.: N.Y. Soc. Assn. Execs., Healthcare Mktg. Comm. Coun., Am. Soc. Assn. Execs., Alliance Non-Profit Mailers (bd. dirs., chmn. tech. com. 1986—94, v.p. 1990—94), Soc. Scholarly Pub. Home: 63 Vanderwater St Farmingdale NY 11735-5235 Office: Am Thoracic Soc 61 Broadway New York NY 10006-2755 Business E-Mail: dtemple@thoracic.org.

TEMPLE, JACK DONALD, JR., physician, medical educator; b. Miami, July 30, 1952; s. Jack Donald and Helen (Underhill) T.; m. Regina Ann Kramer, Jan. 14, 1984; children: Laura, Kathleen, Elizabeth. AA, Miami-Dade C.C., 1972; BS in Chemistry, U. Miami, 1974, MD, 1978. Diplomate Nat. Bd. Med. Examiners. Med. intern Jackson Meml. Hosp., Miami, 1978-79, med. resident, 1978-81, clin. fellow, 1981-85, attending physician, 1985—, dir. hematology clinic, 1985-92; clin. instr. U. Miami, 1981-82, asst. prof., 1985-91, assoc. prof., 1991—. Chief med. svc. U. Miami Hosp., 1993—; dir. Harrington Lat. Am. Tng. Programs, Miami, 1992—. Contbr. chpt. to book, articles to med. jours. Named Dr. of Yr. S. Fla. Mag., 1991. Mem. AAAS, Leukemia Soc. Am. (bd. trustees S. Fla. 1992—), U. Miami Alumni Assn. (pres. medicine 1991-94). Achievements include development of new treatments for sickle cell anemia and lymphomatoid granulomatosis. Office: U Miami Sch Medicine Sylvester Cancer Ctr 1475 NW 12th Ave Miami FL 33136-1002 Business E-Mail: jtemple@med.miami.edu.

TEMPLE, JOHN R. publishing executive; b. Apr. 12, 1953; Mng. editor Rocky Mountain News, Denver, 1995—98, editor, 1998—, pres., 2001—, pub., 2001—. Bd. dir. Father's Day Coun. Office: Rocky Mountain News 100 Gene Amole Way Denver CO 80204

TEMPLE, JOSEPH GEORGE, JR., retired pharmaceutical executive, retired chemicals executive; b. Bklyn., Aug. 29, 1929; s. Joseph George and Helen Frances (Beney) T.; m. Ann Elizabeth McFerran, June 21, 1952; children: Linda Jo, James, John. BSChemE, Purdue U., 1951, DEng (hon.), 1988. With Dow Chem. Co., Midland, Mich., 1951-89, v.p. mktg., 1976-78, dir., 1979-94; pres. Dow Chem. Latin Am., Coral Gables, Fla., 1978-80; group v.p. human health Dow Chem. Co., Cin., 1980-83; chief exec. officer, pres. Merrell Dow Pharms. Inc., Cin., 1983-87; exec. v.p. Dow Chem. Co., 1983-89; chief exec. officer, chmn. bd. dirs. Merrell Dow Pharms. Inc., Cin., 1988-89; chmn., chief exec. officer Marion Merrell Dow, Inc., Kansas City, Mo., 1989-92, also bd. dirs., chmn., 1992-94, vice chmn., 1994-95; ret., 1995. Former trustee Com. for Economic Devel. Mem. pres.'s coun. Purdue U., 1978—; bd. fellows Saginaw Valley State U., 1987-89. Recipient Disting. Engr. Alumni award Purdue U., 1978, Outstanding Chem. Engr. award Purdue U., 1993. Mem. Am. Inst. Chem. Engrs., Soc. Plastics Industry (bd. dirs. 1980-82), Pharm. Mfrs. Assn. (bd. dirs. 1981-83), Mgmt. Assn. (Silver Knight award 1976, Gold Knight award 1982). Episcopalian.

TEMPLE, LARRY EUGENE, lawyer; b. Plainview, Tex., Dec. 26, 1935; s. Herman Edward and Grace Eileen (Ivey) T.; m. Laura Louann Atkins, Feb. 23, 1963; children: Laura Allison, John Lawrence. BBA, U. Tex., 1957, LLB with honors, 1959; LLD (hon.), Lamar U., 1985. Bar: Tex., U.S. Dist. Ct. (we. dist.) Tex., U.S. Ct. Appeals (5th cir.), U.S. Supreme Ct. Law clk. to justice Tom Clark U.S. Supreme Ct., Washington, 1959-60; assoc. Powell, Rauhut, McGinnis, Reavley & Lochridge, Austin, Tex., 1960-63; legal adminstrn. asst., exec. asst. (chief of staff) Tex. Gov. John B. Connally, Austin, 1963-67; spl. counsel to pres. Lyndon Baines Johnson, Washington, 1967-69; pvt. practice Austin, 1969—. Bd. dirs. Temple-Inland, Inc., Guaranty Fed. Bank. Mem. U. Tex. Cancer Found., Houston, 1978-84, U. Tex. Devel. Bd., Austin, 1980-85, 90—, chmn., 1993-95; pres. U. Tex. Ex-Students Assn., 1997-98; mem. Tex. Higher Edn. Coordinating Bd., Austin, 1983-89, chmn., 1983-87; chmn. Select Com. for Higher Edn., Austin, 1985-87; bd. dirs. Lyndon B. Johnson Found., 1986—, vice chmn., 1989-2000, pres., 2000—; trustee U. Tex. Law Sch. Found., 1989—. Recipient Faculty award U. Tex. Law Sch., 1987, Humanitarian award Austin region NCCJ, 1988, Santa Rita award U. Tex. System, 1989, Disting. Alumnus award U. Tex., Austin, 1990, Outstanding Alumnus award U. Tex. Law Sch., 1999, Leon Green award Tex. Law Rev., 2003, Disting. Lawyer award Travis County Bar Assn., 2004. Fellow Tex. Bar Found.; mem. ABA, Tex. Bar Assn. (chmn. legis. com. 1980, 83-86), Tex. Jr. Bar Assn. (chmn. bd. dirs. 1967), Austin Jr. Bar Assn. (pres. 1962-63). Democrat. Episcopalian. Home: 2606 Escondido Cv Austin TX 78703-1610 Office: 400 W 15th St Ste 1510 Austin TX 78701-1648 Office Phone: 512-477-4467.

TEMPLE, LEE BRETT, architect, songwriter, writer; b. Balt., June 7, 1956; BArch, Cornell U., 1979. Cert. Nat. Coun. Archtl. Registration Bds. Gen. ptnr. Temple Gebelein Partnership, Ithaca, N.Y., 1981-91; prin. and sole propr. Lee Temple Architect AIA, Ithaca and Crestone, Colo., 1985-98. Vis. critic dept. architecture Cornell U., Ithaca, 1981; vis. prof. architecture Hobart Coll., 1981-82, prof., 1992-93; asst. prof. architecture Syracuse (N.Y.) U., 1982-87; owner Shining Golden Suns, LLC, 2004—. Author (screenplay) Last Eagle, songwriter; prin. works include Athena Residence, Chapelle Frontenac; author: Medieval Town Study, 1981; songwriter (CDs) Thunderstormin', Reel Whirl. Chmn. social justice com. Cornell Cath. Cmty., Ithaca, 1989-92, trustee parish coun., 1989-90; mem. founding bd. dirs. Eco Village at Ithaca, 1991-93; mem. steering com. Tibetan Resettlement Project at Ithaca, 1991-92; founder Sustainable Resource Ctr., Crestone, 1993; founder Temple Mountain Music, 1996. Recipient 1st prize Storey Com. Compact House Competition, 1983; Eidlitz fellow dept. arch. Cornell U., 1979, 81, Design Excellence award AIA, 1987, Residential Design award N.Y. chpt. AIA, 1985-86. Mem. ASCAP, Coustean Soc. Home and Office: PO Box 220 Crestone CO 81131 E-mail: windstallion@ctelco.net.

TEMPLE, MARK ALLEN, adult education educator, consultant; b. West Monroe, La., Oct. 18, 1962; s. Floyd Aaron and Doris Burdeaux Temple; m. Adrian Renae Na, June 25, 1974. BS, N.E. La. U., 1980—85, MS in Edn., 1985—87; PhD, So. Ill. U. Carbondale, 1992—96. Asst. prof. Ill. State U., 1997—, Tex. Tech U., 1996—98; hiv, aids edn. coord. Jackson County Health Dept., Murphysboro, Ill., 1992—94; tchr., coach West Ouachita H.S., Calhoun, La., 1987—90. Co-director Ill. HIV Prevention Edn. Project, Normal, Ill., 1999—2002. Author: (journal article) Opinions of Ill. Voters About Coordinated Sch. Health Programs (Am. Sch. Health Assn. Disting. Svc. Award, 2002); contbr. numerous articles in profl. jours. Advocacy chair Am. Sch. Health Assn., Kent, Ohio, 2001—; mem., Ill .Sch. Health Adv Bd. Ill. Dept. of Human Services, Springfield, 2000—03; Am. Sch. Health Assn. rep. Coalition of Nat. Health Edn. Organizations, Washington, 1998—2003; pres. Ill. Sch. Health Assn., Chgo., 2000—01. Grantee Nat. Sch. Health Coord. Leadership Inst., Am. Cancer Soc., 2002. Mem.: APHA (sect. counselor 2002—03), Am. Assn. for Health Edn., Am. Sch. Health Assn. (advocacy chair, exec. com. 1999—, Disting. Svc. Award 2002), Eta Sigma Gamma. Democrat. Avocations: endurance sports, martial arts, reading contemporary philosophy. Office: Illinois State University Campus Mail 5220 Normal IL 61790-5220 Home: 49 Whites Place Bloomington IL 61701 E-mail: matempl@ilstu.edu.

TEMPLE, ROBERT, physician, federal agency administrator; b. N.Y.C., July 18, 1941; s. Samuel A. and Judith (Coslow) T.; m. Bonnie Streifer, Oct. 27, 1963; 1 child, James. BA magna cum laude, Harvard U., 1963; MD, NYU, 1967. Diplomate Am. Bd. Internal Medicine, Am. Bd. Clin. Pharmacology. Intern Columbia-Presbyn. Med. Ctr., N.Y.C., 1967-68, resident, 1968-69; clin. assoc. Nat. Inst. Arthritis and Metabolic Disease, NIH, Bethesda, Md., 1969-72; med. officer FDA, Rockville, Md., 1972-74, asst. to dir., bur. of drugs, 1974-76, dir. div. cardio-renal drug products, 1976-82, dir. office drug research and rev., 1982-84, dir. office of drug evaluation I, 1984—. Mem. coop. studies rev. com. VA, 1977-80. Contbr. articles to profl. jours. Served with USPHS, 1969-72. Recipient Disting. Alumni award NYU Sch. Medicine, N.Y. 1987; Pub. HealthSuperior Svc. award HHS, 1986, Disting. Svc. award, 1991; NORD Ann. Tribute, 2001; Outstanding Svc. award Drug Info. Assn., 2001, Disting. Svc. and Leadership award FDLI, 2002. Fellow Am. Coll. Clin. Pharmacology (hon.); mem. Soc. Clin. Trials (bd. dirs. 1983, v.p. 1986, pres. 1987), Am. Soc. Clin. Phrmacology and Therapeutics (bd. dirs. 1987-90, 92—, Rawls-Palmer Progress in Medicine lecture and award 2001), Alpha Omega Alpha. Democrat. Jewish. Avocations: model trains, tennis, gardening, cooking. Home: 3325 Rowland Pl NW Washington DC 20008-3226 Office: FDA 5600 Fishers Ln Rockville MD 20857 Office Phone: 301-594-6758. Business E-Mail: temple@cder.fda.gov.

TEMPLE, ROBERT WINFIELD, chemical company executive; b. New Albany, Ind., Feb. 25, 1934; s. Edgar Winfield and Kathryn (Rady) T.; m. Katrina Voorhis, Jan. 4, 1954 (div. Oct. 1970); children: James V., Robert K., Jennifer Anne; m. Katharine Ann Stobbs, Apr. 29, 1977 (div. June 1985); children: Andrew, Philip; m. Angela J. Temple, Aug. 5, 1986; 1 child, Sarah Louise. BSChemE, BS in Indsl. Mgmt., postgrad., MIT, 1955, NYU, 1955—58, Columbia U., 1966. Dist. sales mgr. ACF Industries, 1955-59; sr. staff cons. Arthur D. Little, Inc., 1959-64; dir. planning and devel. Am. Cryogenics, Inc., Atlanta, 1964-69; v.p. Williams Bros. Co., Atlanta, 1969; pres. Lang Engring., Coral Gables, Fla., 1970-74; CEO Western Process Co., Geneva and Houston, 1974—87; head agribus and biotechnology Brit.-Am. Tobacco Co., London, 1988—91; pres. TMR-Viterra Interant., Ltd., 1989-92; CEO Gulfcrest Internat., 1987—, Newco Internat., 1999—2001; sr. advisor Bacteria Bar Codes Inc., 1998—2001, Synthecon, 1999—2001; CEO Surface BioSolutions Inc., 2001—02; sr. adv. dir. Telerad Inc., 2002—03; ptnr. Roteva Advisors, 2002—03. Dir. World Congress on Super Conductivity, Global Econ. Action Inst. Conf. on African Devel.; dir. MIT Enterprise Forum (former chmn.); spkr. on mgmt. and mktg. various seminars. Contbr. articles to profl. jours. Fellow Am. Inst. Chemists and Chem. Engrs.; mem. Am. Chem. Soc., Am. Mgmt. Assn., Chem. Mktg. Rsch. Assn., Internat. Food Technologists (chmn. seminars on food irradiation 1995, 99), MIT Alumni Assn. (past regional pres., adv. bd.), Houston Fresh Fruit and Vegetable Assn. (dir., past pres.), Sigma Chi Alumni Assn. Presbyterian. Home: 14134 Bluebird Ln Houston TX 77079-6836 Office: Gulfcrest Internat PO Box 19435 Houston TX 77224-9435

TEMPLE, THOMAS C. oil company executive; V.p. supply and distbn. U.S. Oil & Refining Co., L.A., 1981-86, pres., CEO Tacoma, 1984—; exec. v.p. MacMillan Ring-Free Oil Co. Inc., N.Y.C., 1986—. Office: US Oil & Refining Co 3001 E Marshall Ave Tacoma WA 98421-3116

TEMPLE, WAYNE CALHOUN, historian, writer; b. nr. Richwood, Ohio, Feb. 5, 1924; s. Howard M. and Ruby March (Calhoun) T.; m. Lois Marjorie Bridges, Sept. 22, 1956 (dec. Apr. 1978); m. Sunderine Wilson, Apr. 9, 1979; stepson, James C. Mohn. AB cum laude, U. Ill., 1949, AM, 1951, PhD, 1956. Rsch. asst. history U. Ill., 1949-53, tchg. asst., 1953-54; curator ethnohistory Ill. State Mus., 1954-58; editor-in-chief Lincoln Herald, Lincoln Meml. U., 1958-73, assoc. editor, 1973—, also dir. dept. Lincolniana, dir. univ. press, John Wingate Weeks prof. history, 1958-64; with Ill. State Archives, 1964—, now chief dep. dir. Lectr. U.S. Mil. Acad., 1975; sec.-treas. Nat. Lincoln-Civil War Council, 1958-64; mem. bibliography com. Lincoln Lore, 1958—; hon. mem. Lincoln Sesquicentennial Commn., 1959-60; advisory council U.S. Civil War Centennial Commn., 1960-66; maj. Civil War Press Corps, 1962—; pres. Midwest Conf. Masonic Edn., 1985. Author: Indian Villages of the Illinois Country: Historic Tribes, 1958, rev. edits., 1966, 77, 87, Lincoln the Railsplitter, 1961, Abraham Lincoln and Others at the St. Nicholas, 1968, Alexander Williamson-Tutor to the Lincoln Boys, 1971, (with others) First Steps to Victory: Grant's March to Naples, 1977, Lincoln and Grant: Illinois Militiamen, 1981, Stephen A. Douglas: Freemason, 1982, Lincoln as a Lecturer, 1982, By Square and Compasses: The Building of Lincoln's Home and Its Saga, 1984, Lincoln's Connections with the Illinois and Michigan Canal, 1986, Dr. Anson G. Henry: Personal Physician to the Lincolns, 1988, Abraham Lincoln: From Skeptic to Prophet, 1995, Thomas and Abraham Lincoln as Farmers, 1996, Alexander Williamson: Friend of the Lincolns, 1998, By Square and Compass: Saga of the Lincoln Home, 2002, The Taste Is In My Mouth a Little...Lincoln's Victuals and Potables, 2004; co-author: Illinois's Fifth Capitol: The House that Lincoln Built, 1988; contbg. author: Capitol Centennial Papers, 1988; editor: Campaigning with Grant, 1961, 72, The Civil War Letters of Henry C. Bear, 1961; 71 radio scripts A. Lincoln 1809-1959, Indian Villages of the Illinois Country: Atlas Supplement, 1975; editorial advisory bd. Am. Biog. Inst., 1971—, Ency. Indians of Ams., 1973—; contbr. articles to profl. jours., encys. Sponsor Abraham Lincoln Bay, Washington Nat. Cathedral; mem. adv. com. Abraham Lincoln Bicentennial Commn.; mem. Ill. State Flag Commn., 1969—; trustee, regent Lincoln Acad. Ill., 1970-82; bd. govs. St. Louis unit Shriners Hosps. for Crippled Children, 1975-81; mem. commissioning com., hon. crew mem. and plank owner USS Springfield submarine, 1990—; hon. crew mem. USS Abraham Lincoln aircraft carrier, 1989—. With U.S. Army, 1943-46, gen. Res. (ret.). Decorated Bronze Star Medal, Silver Citizenship medal SAR, 1993, Literary Merit Gold medal Ill. Lodge of Rsch., 1993; recipient Order of Arrow Boy Scouts Am., 1957, Scouters award, 1960, Scouter's Key, also medallion, 1967, Lincoln medallion Lincoln Sesquicentennial Commn., 1960, award of Achievement U.S. Civil War Centennial Commn., 1965, Algernon Sydney Sullivan medallion, 1969, Distinguished Service award Ill. State Hist. Library, 1969, 77, I.H. Duval Distinguished Service award, 1971, legion of honor Internat. Supreme Council, Order of De Molay, 1972, Disting. Service award Civil War Round Table of Chgo., 1983, 91, Cert. Excellence Ill. State Hist. Soc., 1985, Archbishop Richard Chenevix Trench award, 1999;Lincoln Diploma Honor, Lincoln Meml. U., Harrogate, Tenn., 1963, Lifetime Achievement award 2001; named Hon. Ky. Col., Marshal of Okla. Territory. Fellow Royal Soc. Arts (life); mem. NRA, KT (Red Cross Constantine), Lincoln Group D.C. (hon.), U. Ill. Alumni Assn., Ill. State Hist. Soc., Board of Advisors, The Lincoln Forum, Ill. Profl. Land Surveyors Assn., Ill. State Dental Soc. (citation plague 1966), Res. Officers Assn., Lincoln Fellowship of Wis., Iron Brigade Assn. (hon. life), Mil. Order Loyal Legion U.S. (hon. companion), Mil. Order Fgn. Wars U.S., Army and Navy Union, Masons (33 degree, Meritorious Svc. award, grand rep. from Grand Lodge of Colo.), Shriners, Kappa Delta Pi, Phi Alpha, Phi Alpha Theta (Scholarship Key award), Chi Gamma Iota, Phi Beta Kappa, Tau Kappa Alpha, Alpha Psi Omega, Sigma Pi Beta (Headmaster), Sigma Tau Delta (Gold Honor Key award for editorial writing), Zeta Psi. Presbyterian (elder). Home: 1121 S 4th Street Ct Springfield IL 62703-2200 Office: Ill State Archives Springfield IL 62756-0001 *Only in America could a poor farm boy from Ohio work his way through a great university, like the University of Illinois, and receive a doctor's degree. Life has been kind to me, and I have tried hard and worked hard. I am proud to be an American.*

TEMPLETON, ALAN ROBERT, biology professor; b. Litchfield, Ill., Feb. 28, 1947; s. John Smith and Lois Arlene (McCormick) T.; m. Bonnie A. Altman, Dec. 20, 1969; children: Jeremy Alan, Jeffrey Alan. BA, Washington U., 1969; MS in Stats., PhD in Genetics, U. Mich., 1972. Jr. fellow Mich. Soc. Fellows, Ann Arbor, 1972-74; asst. prof. U. Tex., Austin, 1974-77; assoc. prof. Washington U., St. Louis, 1977-81, prof., 1981—, Charles Rebstock prof. biology, 2001—. Cons. St. Louis Zool. Park, 1979—; founding mem., dir. Soc. for Conservation Biology, 1985—. Editor: Theoretical Population Biology,

1981-91; mem. editl. bd. Molecular Phylogenetics & Evolution, 1991—, Brazilian Jour. Genetics, 1991-97, Genetics and Molecular Biology, 1998-2001, Animal Conservation, 2004—; assoc. editor Am. Naturalist, 2002—; contbr. numerous article to profl. jours. Grantee NSF, 1974-80, 90—, NIH, 1980—, Nixon Griffis Fund for Zool. Rsch., 1986-87, Burroughs Welcome Fund for Functional Genomics, 2000—04. Fellow AAAS; mem. Soc. for Study Evolution (v.p. 1982, pres. 1996-97), Soc. Conservation Biology (bd. dirs. 1985-88), Nature Conservancy (trustee Mo. chpt. 1988—, v.p. 1996-2000). Avocations: hiking, caving, music, ethnomusicology, scuba diving. Office: Washington U Dept Biology Saint Louis MO 63130-4899

TEMPLETON, DENNIE, III, educational administrator, consultant; b. San Antonio, Tex., Dec. 12, 1948; s. Dennie E. and Helen (Gamble) T.; m. Debra Roberts, July 17, 1992. BA in Bus., U. Hawaii, 1987; BA in Vocat. Edn., So. Ill. U., 1991; M of Tech. Edn., U. Ga., 1995, EdD, 1998. Master chief petty officer/LTJG (lieutenant JG) U.S. Navy, 1971, served, 1971-92; retired USN, 1992; rsch., tng. U. Ga., Athens, 1993-97; dir. instrnl. devel. and distance edn. Patrick Henry C.C., Martinsville, Va., 1997-99; dir. distance edn. Radford Univ., 1999—. Cons. U. Ga., 1996. Rschr. in field. Mem. Internat. Tech. Edn. Assn., Tng. Devel. Assn., USS Nevada Assn. Avocations: music, golf, tennis. Office: Radford U PO Box 6719 Radford VA 24142-6719 Home: 189 Fairway Dr Radford VA 24141-3905

TEMPLETON, HILDA B. psychiatrist, educator; BA in Biology, Rutgers U., Newark, 1962, MS in Biol. Scis., 1965; MD, U. Medicine and Dentistry N.J., 1978. Diplomate Am. Bd. Psychiatry and Neurology. Tchg. asst. in physiology Rutgers U., 1963-65; field dir. state of La. Med. Com. for Human Rights, 1965, dir. health and welfare The Urban League of Essex County, N.J., 1965-67; rsch. asst. dept. anatomy U. Medicine and Dentistry N.J., 1970-71; tchr. Ctrl. Mid. Sch., Orange, N.J., 1971-74; intern N.J. Med. Sch., 1978-79; resident Med. Sch. Rutgers U., 1978—81, chief resident Med. Sch., 1981; sr. resident Princeton (N.J.) Med. Ctr., 1982; pvt. practice Livingston, 1982—; clin. asst. prof. psychiatry and behavioral medicine N.Y. Coll. Osteo. Medicine, 1998—2001. Attending physician dept. psychiatry, dept. ob-gyn. St. Barnabas Med. Ctr., Livingston, 1982—, chair dept. psychiatry, 1997-2000, clin. chief dept. psychiatry, 1986-90, 91-93, 95-97, assoc. clin. chief dept. psychiatry, 1985-86, acting chair dept. psychiatry, 1986-87, mem. various hosp. coms.; clin. instr. dept. psychiatry U. Medicine and Dentistry of N.J., 1987-97; cons. Kessler Inst. for Rehab., 1982-91, Cmty. Psychiat. Inst., 1982-85, Jewish Vocat. Svcs., 1982-88; med. dir. interim out-patient program East Orange (N.J.) Gen. Hosp., 1982-83; mem. assoc. med. staff Fair Oaks Hosp., Summit, N.J., 1980-82; lectr. in field. Chair Newark Arts and Scis. Devel. Coun. Rutgers U. Found., 1995—98; mem. leadership com. Campaign for Cmty., Diversity and Ednl. Excellence, 1994—96; nat. bd. dirs. Down Syndrome Soc., 2001—; mem. med. adv. bd. No. N.J. chpt. Nat. Multiple Sclerosis Soc., 1982—86; mem. governing bd. The Cmty. Mental Health Ctr. of the Oranges, Maplewood and Millburn, 1983—84. Mem. AMA, Am. Soc. Psychosomatic Ob-Gyn., Am. Psychiat. Assn., Med. Women's Assn., Post Partum Internat., Depression After Delivery, N.J. Acad. Medicine, N.J. Psychiat. Assn., Tri-County Med. Soc., Essex County Med. Soc. (chmn. com. mental health 1998—). Office: 22 Old Short Hills Rd Ste 217 Livingston NJ 07039-5605 E-mail: hbtmdl@msn.com.

TEMPLETON, JACK KENNETH, headmaster; b. Statesville, N.C., June 16, 1944; s. Jack Kenneth and Margaret Rebecca Templeton; m. Diane Cornelia Palmer; children: Joey Rebecca, Amy Theresa. BA, Catawba Coll., 1968; MEd, U. N.C., Charlotte, 1975. Head of upper sch. Gaston Day Sch., Gastonia, NC, 1968—78, headmaster, 1985—90; tchr. Teheran (Iran) Am. Sch., 1978—79; h.s. prin. Collegio Nueva Granada, Bogota, Colombia, 1980—85; head of upper sch. Charlotte Latin Sch., 1991—2000; headmaster Union Acad., Monroe, NC, 2000—. Mem.: Rotary.

TEMPLETON, JOHN MARKS, JR., retired pediatric surgeon, foundation executive; b. N.Y.C., Feb. 19, 1940; s. John Marks and Judith Dudley (Folk) T.; m. Josephine J. Gargiulo, Aug. 2, 1970; children: Heather Erin, Jennifer Ann. *Earliest documented ancestor in America in 1750 is John Templeton of Iredell County, North Carolina. Other family lines include the Folks and Handlys from Tennessee. Mother was Judith Dudley Folk, an Advertising Executive for McCann Erickson in New York City. Father is Sir John Templeton of Lyford Cay, Bahama Islands, Founder of the Templeton Group of Mutual Funds and of the Management Company, Templeton, Galbraith & Hansberger.* BA, Yale Coll., 1962; MD, Harvard U., 1968; hon. degree, Beaver Coll., Buena Vista U., Va. Commonwealth U., Alvernia Coll. Intern Med. Coll. Va., Richmond, 1968-69, resident, 1969-73; prof. pediat. surgery U. Pa. and Children's Hosp. Phila., 1995, dir. trauma program, 1989-95. Chmn. bd. Templeton Growth Fund, Ltd. *Twenty-two years' experience as Pediatric Surgeon at Children's Hospital of Philadelphia and Portsmouth Regional Naval Hospital in Virginia. Professional interests included newborn pediatric surgery such as esophageal atresia and ano-rectal anomalies, bioethics in medicine, pediatric surgical emergencies, and pediatric trauma. In his role as President of the John Templeton Foundation, John M. Templeton, Jr.'s present interests include spirituality and healing in medicine; character development in youth; free enterprise education; the impact of culture on political, social, and economic development; religious liberty; the religious foundations of liberty; trauma prevention; and the health costs of behavior and lifestyle.* Assoc. editor: Textbook of Pediatric Emergencies, 1993; pub. 6000 Name Geneology, 1997, A Searcher's Life, 1999. Chmn. health and safety, exec. bd. Coll. of Physicians of Phila., Cradle of Liberty coun. Boy Scouts Am.; mem. exec. bd. Eastern U., Fgn. Policy Rsch. Inst., Nat. Recreation Found., Melmark Charitable Found.; nat. bd. dirs., pres. Pa. divsn. Am. Trauma Soc.; bd. dirs. Nat. Bible Assn., Nat. Liberty Mus., Phila.; elder Proclamation Presbyn. Ch.; pres. John Templeton Found. With M.C., USNR, 1975-77. Barclay fellow Templeton Coll., Oxford U., Eisenhower Exch. fellow, fellow George H. Gallup Internat. Inst.; mem. Order of Charlemagne. Mem. ACS, AMA, Am. Pediat. Surg. Assn., Am. Acad. Pediats., Am. Assn. Surgery Trauma, Ea. Assn. Surgery Trauma, Phila. Coll. Physicians, Union League, Lyford Cay Club, Merion Cricket Club, Athenaeum Club London, Rotary Internat., White's London, United Oxford and Cambridge U. Club (London). Republican. Evangelical. Office: 5 Radnor Corp Ctr Ste 100 Radnor PA 19087-4534 Office Phone: 610-525-1961. Business E-Mail: bmcgraw@templeton.org.

TEMPLETON, RICHARD K. electronics company executive; BSEE, Union Coll., 1980. Various positions Tex. Instruments, Inc., Dallas, 1980—91, v.p., semiconductor group, 1991—94, mgr., worldwide application specific prods., 1993—96, sr. v.p., semiconductor group, 1994—96, exec. v.p., semiconductor group, 1996—2000, COO, 2000—04, pres., CEO, 2004—. Mem. bd. dirs. Tex. Instruments, 2003—, Semiconductor Industry Assn. Office: Texas Instruments Inc 12500 TI Blvd Dallas TX 75266-4136

TEMPLIN, JOHN LEON, JR., healthcare consulting executive; b. New Brunswick, N.Y., Aug. 5, 1940; s. John Leon and Theresa Veronica (Revolinski) T.; m. Barbara Maria Ribley, Sept. 12, 1970; children: John, Joseph, Kevin, Nan, Danielle, Christopher. BS in Mgmt. Engring., Rensselaer Poly. Inst., 1962, MS in Mgmt., 1969. Cert. healthcare cons. Am. Assn. Healthcare Cons. Mgr. customer svc. Norton Abrasives, Troy, N.Y., 1968-70; cons., sr. cons. Hosp. Assn. N.Y. State, Albany, 1970-79, dir. mgmt. svcs., 1979-80, sr. dir. mgmt. svc., 1981-83; dir. productivity improvement Applied Leadership Technologies, Inc., Greenfield Center, N.Y., 1983-84, v.p., productivity improvement div., 1984-85, pres., 1985-86, Templin Mgmt. Assocs., Inc., Greenfield Center, 1987—, The Northeastern Cons. Alliance, Albany, N.Y., 1995-98. Editor quar. jour. Healthcare Supr., 1983—; mem. editorial com. ann. Manual for Workload Recording, 1978-91. Mem. budget com. Greater Saratoga Sch. Dist., Saratoga Springs, N.Y., 1978-79; mem. energy com. Blue Cross Assn., Chgo., 1978-81; mem. Gov.'s Task Force on Nursing, Albany, 1980; mem. parish coun. St. Joseph's Ch., Greenfield Center, 1981-87. Capt. U.S. Army, 1962-64. Fellow Am. Coll. Healthcare Execs., Healthcare Info. and Mgmt. Sys. Soc. (liaison Coll. Am. Pathologists 1978-91, chair edn. com. 1995-96, 97-98); mem. Am. Hosp. Assn. (seminar spkr. 1980-93), Clin. Lab. Mgmt. Assn. (bd. dirs. 1980-84), KC. Republican. Roman Catholic. Avocations: golf, computers, gardening, fishing. Home and Office: Templin Mgmt Assocs Inc 265 Locust Grove Rd Greenfield Center NY 12833-1501

TEMPLIN, KENNETH ELWOOD, paper company executive; b. Mason City, Nebr., Jan. 26, 1927; s. Otto Rudolph and Marianna (Graf) T.; m. Harriet Elaine Ressel, Aug. 24, 1951; children: Steven, David, Daniel, Benjamin, Elizabeth. BS in Bus. Adminstrn, U. Nebr., 1950; MBA, Wayne State U., 1961. Fin. analyst Ford Motor Co., 1950-54; fin. analyst, corp. staff Chrysler Corp., 1955-60, div. controller marine engine div., 1961-63, gen. sales mgr., 1964-65; v.p. Marsh and Templin, N.Y.C., 1966-69; v.p., gen. mgr. operating group Saxon Industries, N.Y.C., 1970-79, group v.p., 1979-82, sr. v.p., c.o.o., 1982-85; v.p.-converting Paper Corp. Am., Wayne, Pa., 1985-86; exec. v.p. Quality Park Products Inc., St. Paul, 1986-88, 1986-88, pres., 1988-96, ret., 1996. Mem. exec. com. Single Service Inst., 1971-79 Regional chmn. Minn. devel. com. Nat. Multiple Sclerosis Soc., 1970-71; co-pres. Home and Sch. Assn., Bernardsville, N.J., 1975-76; bd. dirs. West Hennepin Counseling Svcs., Inc., 1996-2000, Brain Injury Assn. Minn., 1997-2001; mem. Svc. Corps Ret. Execs. (SCORE), 1996—, chmn. Mpls. chpt., 1999-2000; bd. dirs. Hennepin History Mus., 2000—. With U.S. Army, 1945-47, 50-51. Mem. Envelope Mfrs. Assn. Am. (postal affairs com. 1989-96, fin. com. chmn. 1994-95, bd. dirs. 1990-91, 93-95). Presbyterian. Office Phone: 612-339-5200. E-mail: templink@aol.com.

TENBOSCH, GERALD JOHN, fundraising executive; b. Cin., Dec. 22, 1950; s. Karl Alfred and Gertrude (Lowenbeg) T.; m. Betsy Ann Tenbosch, Jan. 16, 1976; children: David, Gabe, Abby. AA, U. Cin., 1971, BS, 1973, MS, 1981. Youth supr., career mgr. Citizen's Com. on Youth, Cin., 1973-78; project mgr. Cin. Bd. Edn./Pub. Schs., Cin., 1978-81; project dir. Workshop for Retarded Citizens, Cin., 1981-82; asst. dir. regional office City of Hope Med. and Rsch. Ctr., Cin., 1982-84; resource devel. dir. Cin. Speech and Hearing Ctr., 1984-96; exec. dir. Invest in Neighborhoods Inc., Cin., 1996—. Mem. adv. bd. Ret. Sr. Vol. Program, Cin., 1983-89. Bd. dirs. Finneytown Elem. PTA, Cin., 1988-95. Mem. Nat. Soc. Fundraising Execs. (treas., officer 1984-90), Assn. Vol. Adminstrn., Finneytown Athletic Assn. Jewish. Avocations: sports, coaching, golf, family activities. Home: 1009 Pinehollow Ln Cincinnati OH 45231-5732 Office: Invest in Neighborhoods Inc 927 Mcpherson Ave Cincinnati OH 45205-1814

TENDLER, DAVID, international trade company executive; b. N.Y.C., Jan. 15, 1938; s. Philip and Pearl (Berman) T.; m. Beatrice Weisberg, Oct. 11, 1958; children: Pearl, Karen. BBA in Internat. Econs., CCNY, 1959. With Philipp Bros. Co., 1960—, mgr. Far Eastern ops., 1968-75, pres., 1975—; dir. parent corp. Engelhard Minerals & Chems. Corp. (name changed to Phibro Corp. 1981), N.Y.C., 1975-85, vice chmn. bd., 1979-81, chmn. bd., CEO, 1981—; co-chmn., co-CEO Phibro-Salomon Inc., N.Y.C., 1983-84; ptnr. Tendler Beretz, L.L.C. Ltd., N.Y.C., 1985—. Chmn. subcom. trade U.S.-German Dem. Rep. Trade and Econ. Coun., 1978—84; bd. dirs., mem. exec. com. U.S./USSR Trade and Econ. Coun., 1979—85, U.S.-China Bus. Coun., 1983—94; chmn. exec. com., bd. dirs. V.I. Technologies, Inc., Watertown, Mass., 1994—; bd. dirs. Savient Pharm., East Brunswick, NJ, Agrifos Fertilizer Inc., Pasadena, Tex. Mem. bd. overseers NYU Grad. Sch. Bus., 1981-85; trustee Lenox Hill Hosp., 1981-94; trustee, mem. exec. com. N.Y. Blood Ctr., 1987—; bd. dirs., mem. exec. com. Fgn. Policy Assn., 1983-96; bd. dirs. Ctr. for Advancement of Women, N.Y.C., 1999—; mem. adv. coun. Weissman Ctr. for Internat. Bus., Baruch Coll., 2001. Recipient Torch of Liberty award metals and metal products divsn. Anti-Defamation League, 1976, Edith and Herbert Lehman award Henry St. Settlement, 1982; named Man of Yr., Fgn. Trade Soc., Baruch Coll., CUNY, 1985. Office: Tendler Beretz LLC 150 E 52nd St New York NY 10022-6017 Office Phone: 212-593-0550. E-mail: tenchan@aol.com.

TENENBAUM, INEZ MOORE, superintendent of education; b. Hawkinsville, GA; m. Samuel J. Tenenbaum. Bsc, U. Ga., 1972, MEd, 1974; JD, U. S.C., 1986. Tchr. Elementary Sch.; dir. rsch. S.C. House Reps., 1977-83; attorney Sinkler & Boye, P.A., 1986-92; supt. edn. S.C. Dept. Edn., Columbia, 1999—. Founder S.C. Ctr. Family Policy. Office: South Carolina Dept Edn Rutledge Bldg 1429 Senate St Columbia SC 29201-3730

TENER, CAROL JOAN, retired secondary school educator; b. Cleve., Feb. 10, 1935; d. Peter Paul and Mamie Christine (Dombrowski) Manusack; m. Dale Keith Tener, Feb. 13, 1958 (div. Aug. 1991); children: Dean Robert, Susan Dawn Tener Belair. Student, Cleve. Mus. Art, 1948-53, Cleve. Art Inst., 1953-54; BS in Edn. cum laude, Kent State U., 1957; MS in Supervision, Akron U., 1974; postgrad., Kent State U., 1964, 81, 88-90, Akron U., 1975, 79, John Carroll U., 1982, 83, 85-86, Ohio U., 1987, Baldwin Wallace Coll., 1989. Cert. permanent K-12 tchr., Ohio; cert. vol. counselor for Ohio sr. health ins. Ohio Dept. Ins. Stenographer Equitable Life Iowa, Cleve., 1953-54; tchr. elem. art Cuyahoga Falls (Ohio) Bd. Edn., 1957-58, 62-63, 65-68, tchr. jr. high sch., 1968-69; tchr. high sch. Brecksville (Ohio)-Broadview Heights Sch. Dist., 1969-94; chmn. dept. art Brecksville-Broadview Heights (Ohio) H.S., 1979-94, chmn. curriculum devel., 1982, 89; ret., 1994. Instr. for children Kent State U., 1956; advisor, prodr. cmty. svc. in art Brecksville Broadview Heights Bd. of Edn., 1969-94; former tchr. recreation and adult art edn. City of Cuyahoga Falls, 1967-68; com. mem. North Ctrl. evaluation com. Nordonia H.S., Nordonia City, Ohio, 1978, Solon H.S., Solon City, Ohio, 1989; chmn. north ctrl. evaluation com. Garfield Heights H.S., 1991; chair pilot program curriculum devel. com. in art/econs. Brecksville-Broadview Heights H.S., 1985-86, 86-87. Contbr. articles to newspapers, brochures, mags.; commd. artist for mural Brecksville City's Kids Quarters, 1994, Christopher Columbus/John Glen portraits in relief commemorating Columbus Day, 1961, Wooster (Ohio) Products Co.; editor Greater Cleve. chpt. Ohio Ret. Tchrs. Assn., 1998-2002; contbr. to Resources for You, 2003, Ohio Sr. Health Ins. Info. Program, Ohio Dept. Ins., 2001—. Chmn. Artmart Invitational Exhibit PTA, 1982-94; active Meals on Wheels program in Brecksville and Broadview Hts., 1995-98, Heart Disease collection, 1995, Stow-Glen Assisted Living Visitations, 1994-95, NCR Assisted Living transp. provision to hosps. and dr. in neighboring county; trustee, sec. Gettysburg Devel. Block Group Parma, 1995-96, Kids Quarters, 1994; Med Save fraud vol. Cuyahoga County Dept. Sr. and Adult Svcs., 2000-2002, spkrs. bur.; sr. health ins. info. program, cert. vol. counselor of OSHIIP under the Dept. of Insurance, Ohio Dept. Ins., 2001-04—, vol. coord., 2004-. Recipient Ohio Coun. on Econ. Edn. award, 1985-86, award for significant svc. to cmty. Ret. and Sr. Vol. Program of USA, 1996, Svc. award Greater Cleve. Chpt./Ohio Ret. Tchrs. Assn., 1998, Outstanding Svc. award Sr. Medicare Patrol Projects, Cert. of Appreciation, U.S. Dept. Health and Human Svcs. Adminstrn. on Aging, 2002; Pres.'s scholar Kent State U., 1954-57; Resolution to thank a Med-Save Project Vol. signed by Cuyahoga County Commrs. Tim McCormack, pres., Jimmy Dimora, v.p., and Peter Lawson Jones, commr. Mem.: NAFE, ASCD, NEA (life), AAUW, S.W. Area Ret. Educators (co-chair 1996—98, program chair 1996—98, program coord. 1999—2000), Nat. Mus. Women in Arts, Cleve. Mus. Art, Acad. Econ. Edn., Brecksville Edn. Assn., Internat. Platform Assn., Nat. Art Edn. Assn., Ohio Ret. Tchrs. Assn. (life; registration chair 1997—98, pres.-elect Cleve. chpt. 1998, program chair 1998, interim editor 1998, circulation mgr. 1998—2002, chpt. pres. 1999, editor 1999—2002, trustee 2000, guest spkr. on newsletter writing and pub. 2000, nominating chair 2000—01, by-law chair 2000—01, Pub. Rels. awards 1999—2002), Phi Delta Kappa Pi. Roman Catholic. Avocations: photography, collecting books on architecture, painting. Home: 7301 Sagamore Rd Parma OH 44134-5732

TENET, GEORGE JOHN, former CIA Director; b. Flushing, N.Y., Jan. 5, 1953; m. A. Stephanie Glakas; 1 child. BS in Fgn. Svc., Georgetown U., 1976; MIA, Columbia U., 1978. Legis. asst. to Sen. H. John Heinz III Senate Select Com. on Intelligence, Washington, 1985-86, designee to vice chair Sen. Patrick J. Leahy, 1986-89, dir. oversight of arms control negotiations Soviet Union/US, 1989-93, staff dir., 1993; mem. presdl. transition team Nat. Security Coun., Washington, 1993-95, spl. asst. to pres., sr. dir. intelligence programs, 1995-97; dep. dir. CIA, Washington, 1995-96, acting dir., 1996-97, dir., 1997—2004. Author: The Ability of U.S. Intelligence to Monitor the Intermediate Nuclear Force Treaty.

TENG, BING-SHENG, finance educator, researcher; s. Yongkang Teng and Lizhi Yuan; m. Suen Li; 1 child, Joanne Yifei. BS, Troy (Ala.) State U., 1993; MBA, CUNY, 1995, PhD, 1998. Instr. Baruch Coll., CUNY, N.Y.C., 1995—98; asst. prof. strategic mgmt. and pub. policy George Washington U., Washington, 1998—. Contbr. articles to profl. jours. Mem.: Strategic Mgmt. Soc., Acad. Mgmt. Office: George Washington U 2115 G St NW Washington DC 20052 E-mail: teng@gwu.edu.

TENG, CHEN, import/export company executive, wholesale distribution executive; b. Beijing, Nov. 22, 1952; arrived in U.S., 1987; s. Yu-Jie Kang and Wei Shi; m. Shan Wang (div.); 1 child, Elaine. BA, Jilin (China) U., 1982; MA, China U. Polit. Sci. and Law, Beijing, 1986; postgrad., U. Utah, 1987—89, UCLA, 1996—97. Farmer Two Family People's Commune, Jilin, 1969—72; worker No. 1 Motor Plant, Chang Chun, China, 1972—78; h.s. tchr. Nan Kou Locomotive Factory, Beijing, 1982—83; asst. prof. China U. Polit. Sci. and Law, 1986—87; importer, wholesaler L.A., 1997—. Author: Historical Materialism and China's Great Cultural Revolution, 2003. Avocations: reading, writing. Home and Office: 2635 Pointe Coupee Chino Hills CA 91709 Personal E-mail: cteng2635@aol.com.

TENG, XIAOLIN, education educator, researcher; s. Wenchun Teng and Anna Yan. B, Beijing U. Aeronautics and Astronautics, 1991; M in Engring., Tsinghua U., China, 1994; PhD in Indsl. Engring., MS in Comp. Sci., Rutgers U., 2001, MS in Stats., 2004. Adj. prof. Rutgers U., Newark, 2002—; chief tech. specialist Chiron Tech., Inc, Holmdel, NJ, 2002—03. Author (with others): Handbook of Reliability Engineering; contbr. articles to profl. jours. Mailing list coord. Rutgers Chinese Scholar and Student Assn., Piscataway, NJ, 1998—2001. Rutgers Grad. Excellence fellowhip, Rutgers U., 1996—97, 1997—98. Mem.: IEEE, Inst. of Indsl. Engineers, Inst. for Ops. Rsch. and the Mgmt. Sciences. Achievements include development of the first software reliability growth model for N-version programming fault-tolerance systems based on Non-homogeneous Poisson Process.

TENGEN, THOMAS L. financial planner, finance educator; b. Lafayette, Ind., June 4, 1938; s. William E. and Marie C. (Faustich) T.; m. Rebecca R. Hawtin, Jan. 27, 1962 (div. Jan. 1978); 1 child, Scott A.; m. Judith Laurence, May 25, 1994; step children: Michael B. Laurence, Valerie Laurence. BS, Ind. State U., 1957. CFP; chartered fin. cons.; CLU. Gen. agent Lafayette Life, Ft. Wayne, Ind., 1960-63; supr. Mass Mutual Life, Ft. Wayne, 1963-66, gen. agent, 1966-80, Penn Mutual Life, Cin., 1980-85; pres. Mercantile Fin. Group, Cin., 1985—. Chmn. Lucas County fund Rep. Party, Toledo, Ohio, 1974. Mem. Gean. Agents and Mgrs. Assn. (dir. Toledo, Ohio 1974-80, pres. Toledo, 1977-78, dir. Cin. 1981-83), Queen City Assn. (bd. dirs. 1988-94, pres. 1991), Cin. Estate Planning Coun., Hyde Park Golf and Country Club, Cincinnatus. Republican. Avocations: golf, hiking, horticulture. Office: Mercantile Fin Group 4755 Cornell Rd Cincinnati OH 45241-2432

TENHOEVE, THOMAS, academic administrator; b. Bklyn., Oct. 1, 1935; s. Thomas and Adeline Ruth (Vander Hill) T.; m. Suzanne Underwood, June 7, 1957; children: Thomas III, Carol, Timothy. AB, Hope Coll., 1956; MA, U. Mich., 1957; PhD, U. Toledo, 1965; postgrad., U. Western Mich.; EdD (hon.), Northwestern Coll., 1995. Biology tchr. South Haven. Mich. Pub. Schs., 1957-58; biology instr. Northwestern Coll., Orange City, Iowa, 1958-63; supr. biology student tchrs. U. Toledo, Ohio, 1963-65; acad. dean, acting pres. Northwestern Coll., Orange City, 1965-70; pres. Butler (Pa.) County Community Coll., 1970-84, Oakton Community Coll., Des Plaines, Ill., 1984-95. Dir. CoVest Banc, 1987—99. Bd. dirs. Sister Cities Internat., 1986-95, 1998-2004, nat. v.p., treas., 2001-04; trustee Northwestern Coll., 1988-95; mem. Ill. C.C. State Found. Bd., 1993-95, Ill. Math. and Sci. Acad. Selection Bd., 1986, 87, Cook County Sheriff's Scholarship Panel; exec. com. Golden Corridor, 1986-92. Recipient Pacesetter award Nat. Coun. for Community Rels., 1986, Orchard Village award. Mem. Am. Coun. on Internat. Intercultural Edn. (chmn. 1992-95), Coun. North Ctrl. Two-Yr. Colls. (state rep. 1988-92, exec. bd. 1989-95, 2d v.p. 1990-91, 1st v.p. 1991-92, pres. 1992-93).

TENHOLDER, EDWARD J. pharmaceutical executive; Sr. v.p. client svcs. and ops. Right Choice Managed Care, Inc., 1994—97; exec. v.p., COO Blue Cross and Blue Shield Mo., 1997—2000; sr. v.p., chief info. officer Express Scripts, Inc., Maryland Heights, Mo., 2000—. Office: Express Scripts Inc 13900 Riverport Dr Maryland Heights MO 63043

TENNANT, DIANE P. editor; m. Tom Tennant; 2 children. BA in English, Syracuse U.; MA in English Edn., SUNY, Binghamton. With Sarasota (Fla.) Herald-Tribune, 1982, part-time advt. clk., various positions features dept., asst. mng. editor, 1999—2002, interim mng. editor, 2002, mng. editor, 2003—. Office: Sarasota Herald-Tribune 801 S Tamiami Tr PO Box 1719 Sarasota FL 34230*

TENNANT, JOHN RANDALL, management advisory company executive; b. North Bend, Wash., Aug. 23, 1940; s. Maurice Andrew and Jane Downing (Vinnedge) T.; m. Nikki Mae Priem, July 17, 1965 (div.); children: Ann Elizabeth, Randall Warren; m. Deborah Ann Francis, Oct. 25, 1986 (div.); 1 child, Alyssa Jane. BS in Indsl. Engring., Stanford U., 1962; MBA, U. Wash., 1966. Registered profl. engr., Wash. Sr. rsch. engr. Boeing Co., Seattle, 1962-68; mgr. Price Waterhouse, Seattle, 1968-73, ptnr. Tokyo, 1973-79, Los Angeles, 1979-89; founder, CEO, Manex, Inc., Newport Beach, Calif., 1989—; dir. subs. Price Waterhouse Assocs., Pacific region, 1975-79. Mem. John Tracy Clinic Men's Com., Santa Catalina Island Conservancy, pres., 1985-87; capt. Long Beach Mounted Police. Mem. NSPE, Japan Computer Assn. (founder, pres. 1976-77), Japan Modapts Assn. (founder), Japan Am. Soc., Inst. Mgmt. Cons., Am. Inst. Indsl. Engrs. (pres. Seattle chpt. 1970-71), Data Processing Mgmt. Assn., Tokyo Lawn and Tennis Club, L.A. Country Club, Jonathan Club, Empty Saddle Club, Los Rancheros Visitadores Club, Los Caballeros Club. Home: 13 Village Park Way Santa Monica CA 90405 Office Phone: 310-581-0678. Personal E-mail: tennantrjohn@aol.com.

TENNANT, WILLIAM J. consumer products company executive; Sr. v.p., CFO Duane Reade Inc., N.Y.C. Office: Duane Reade Inc 440 9th Ave New York NY 10001

TENNEN, LESLIE IRWIN, lawyer, consultant, inventor; b. Toronto, Aug. 26, 1952; came to U.S., 1961; s. Edward and Elsie (Liberbaum) T. BA with distinction, U. Ariz., 1973, JD, 1976; Mount Scopus, Hebrew U., Jerusalem, 1975. Bar: Ariz. 1977, U.S. Dist. Ct. Ariz. 1979. Sole practice, Tucson, 1977—79; ptnr. Sterns and Tennen, Phoenix, 1979—. Cons. internat. law and aerospace activities; lectr. univs., colls. and law schs.; mem. Ariz. Space Commn., 1994-2000, also profl. aviation and aerospace congresses and seminars in N.Am., Europe, Asia, S.Am., Australia; judge Jessup Internat. Moot Court Competition, 1982, 83, 85, 92; dir., treas. Assn. U.S. Mems. Internat. Inst. Space Law; com. mem. U. Belarusian Culture Internat. Orgn. Mem. editl bd. Space Regulations Libr.; contbr. Ariz. Law Rev., 1975-76; contbr. articles to profl. jours. Precinct committeeman State Dem. Conv., 1972-73. Received highest score Ariz. Bar Exam., Feb. 1977. Mem. AIAA (sr.), Ariz. Bar Found., Internat. Eurasian Acad. Scis., Internat. Inst. Space Law (Appreciation award (with Patricia Margaret Sterns) 1998), Internat. Acad. Astronautics, Am. Soc. Internat. Law, Soc. Aerospace Communicators Inc., Internat. Law Assn., Planetary Soc., Fedn. Aerospace Socs. in Tucson (exec. bd.). Office: 849 N 3rd Ave Phoenix AZ 85003-1408 E-mail: LTennen@astrolaw.com.

TENNENT, VALENTINE LESLIE, accountant; b. Apia, Western Samoa, Apr. 5, 1919; came to U.S., 1922; s. Hugh Cowper and Madge Grace (Cook) T.; m. Jeanne Marie Elder, Dec. 10, 1941; children: Madeline Jeanne Walls, Hugh Cowper II, Michael Waller, Val Leslie, Paul Anthony. Student, U. Calif., Berkeley, 1938-40. CPA, Hawaii, La. Mgr. Tennent & Greaney, CPAs, Hilo, Hawaii, 1945-50; ptnr. Cameron, Tennent & Dunn, CPAs, Honolulu, 1950-56, KPMG LLP, Honolulu, 1956-79, cons., 1979-84. Ind. rschr. pub. fin. and banking, polit. economy, moral philosophy, San Diego, 1984-2000. Founding trustee, pres., treas. Tennent Art Found., Honolulu, 1955-77; trustee, treas. Watumull Found., Honolulu, 1963-90; bd. dirs. Iolani Sch., Inst. for Human

Svcs., Honolulu, Lyman Mus., Hilo. Capt. USAF, 1941-45. Recipient Bishop's Cross for disting. svc. Protestant Episcopal Ch., Dist. Hawaii, 1965, G.J. Watumull award for disting. achievement Watumull Found., Honolulu, 1982. Mem. AICPA (governing coun. 1961-64), Hawaii Soc. CPAs (pres. 1960). Episcopalian. Avocations: swimming, fine arts, music, literature. Home and Office: 4365 Executive Dr Fl 18 San Diego CA 92121-2194 *Joy in life comes from knowing the things you want to accomplish within God's overall purpose, pursuing them to the end regardless of difficulties, and accepting full responsibility for inevitable failures.*

TENNER, EDWARD, publishing executive, writer; b. Chgo., Aug. 1, 1944; s. Irving and Evelyn (Talmadge) T. AB, Princeton U., 1965; AM, U. Chgo., 1968, PhD, 1972. Jr. fellow Harvard Soc. Fellows, Cambridge, Mass., 1969-72; instr. Chgo. City Colls., 1972-73; research assoc. U. Chgo., 1973-74; editor Ctr. for Ill. Studies, Inc., Chgo., 1974-75; sci. editor Princeton (N.J.) U. Press, 1975-88, exec. editor phys. sci., 1988-91; visitor Sch. of Social Sci. Inst. for Advanced Study, Princeton, N.J., 1991-92; vis. fellow dept. geoscis. Princeton U., 1992—98; sr. rsch. assoc. Lemelson Ctr., Nat. Mus. Am. History, 2003—; vis. scholar dept. history and social sci. U. Pa., 2003—. Cons. Exxon Edn. Found., N.Y.C., 1975-82, Charles A. Dana Found., N.Y.C., 1982-84, Nat. Mus. Am. History, 1995—; vis. lectr. Coun. of Humanities, Princeton U., 1990. Author: Tech Speak, 1986, Why Things Bite Back, 1996, Our Own Devices, 2003; contbg. editor Harvard Mag., 1988—, Wilson Quar., 1997—; contbr. articles to periodicals. Mem. friends of Princeton Pub. Libr., Bucks County Hist. Soc. John Simon Guggenheim fellow, 1991, Woodrow Wilson Internat. Ctr. for Scholars fellow, 1995-96; recipient Wadsworth prize Harvard mag., 1985. Mem. Am. Hist. Assn., History Sci. Soc., Soc. for History Tech., Soc. for Social Studies of Sci., Cosmos Club (Washington, D.C.). Avocations: tennis, swimming, music, birdwatching. Home: 4316 Hunters Glen Dr Plainsboro NJ 08536-3911

TENNEY, BARBARA ANN, librarian, director; b. Morristown, N.J., Feb. 15, 1946; d. Robert Edward Mojor and Ann May Booth; m. Richard C. Tenney, Apr. 23, 2001. BE, Coll. of St. Elizabeth, N.J., 1968; M in Libr. Sci., Pratt Inst., Bklyn., 1973. Cert. pub. libr. N.J. Libr. intern Newark Pub. Libr., 1968—73, children's libr., 1973—75, in charge schs. divsn., 1975—90, br. mgr., 1990—. Sunday Sch. tchr. Brookside (N.J.) Cmty. Ch., 1966—68, ch. libr., 1968—69. Mem.: Am. Libr. Assn., Pratt Inst. to Alumni Assn., Alumni Assn. Coll. of St. Elizabeth. Republican. Mem. Ch. Of Christ. Avocations: reading, writing, travel. Home: 2904 Vantage Ct Danville NJ 07834 Office: Newark Pub Libr 235 Clifton Ave Newark NJ 07104 Office Phone: 973-773-7760. E-mail: bsullivan@npl.org.

TENNEY, FRANK PUTNAM, marketing executive; b. Orono, Maine, Oct. 6, 1937; s. Carl Bither and Velma May (Williamson) T.; m. Margaret Anne Seymour, Apr. 23, 1960; children: Jane Dossiere, Carl B., Janet M., Alan F., Janice M. Lovell. Cert. notary public, Maine. Nat. sales mgr. Shaw & Tenney Oar & Paddle Co., Orono, 1958—68; sales mgr. George D. Wetherill, Phila., 1968—69; with R.M. Flagg, Veazie, Maine, 1968—69; salesman DuBois Chem., Cin., 1969—76; Maine sales mgr. Rochester Midland Co., NY, 1976—82; with H.A. Manning Co., Bellows Falls, Vt., 1982—86; dist. sales mgr. U.S. West Mktg. Resources, Loveland, Colo., 1986—90; sales mgr. City Directory, Inc., Belmond, Iowa, 1990—92; with RAK Industries, 1993; v.p. Maine Mktg. Resources, Brewer, Maine, 1994—. Adv. bd. Salvation Army. Tech. sgt. Maine ANG, 1955-87, ret. Mem.: KC (past grand knight Pine Cone coun., 4th degree, past faithful navigator Pine Cone assembly), VFW (pub. chmn.), Greater Bangor C. of C., Golden Cir. (Averill plaque), 40/8, Profl. Sales Club Bangor, Am. Legion (Americanism officer 1997, post comdr. 1999—2000, adj. 2001—04, past vice comdr. II). Republican. Roman Catholic. E-mail: mten@midmaine.com.

TENNEY, ROBERT CARL, lawyer; b. Walla Walla, Wash., Aug. 12, 1950; s. Robert DeMar and Mary (Schreiner) T.; m. Rhodi Elizabeth Nygaard, Dec. 23, 1977; children: Robert David, Christopher James. Student, Whitman Coll., 1968-70; BA, U. Wash., 1972; JD, U. Puget Sound, 1979. Bar: Wash. 1979, U.S. Dist. Ct. (ea. dist.) Wash. 1979, U.S. Dist. Ct. (we. dist.) Wash. 1983, U.S. Ct. Appeals (9th cir.) 1987. Ptnr., shareholder Halverson & Applegate, Yakima, Wash., 1979-87; atty., shareholder Meyer, Fluegge & Tenney, Yakima, 1987—. Bd. dirs. ARC, Yakima, 1985-91, United Way, Yakima, 1991—; mem. planning commn. Yakima City. 1981-84. Mem. Fed. Bar Assn., Wash. State Bar Assn., Yakima County Bar Assn., Def. Rsch. Inst., Wash. Def. Trial Lawyers Assn. (former trustee), Am. Bd. Trial Advocates. Republican. Presbyterian. Avocations: family, tennis. Office: Meyer Fluegge & Tenney PO Box 22680 Yakima WA 98907-2680

TENNEY, SARAH G. music educator; b. N.Y.C., Apr. 30, 1948; d. John Wool Griswold and Margaret Brett Tenney. BA, Bennington Coll., 1971; MusM, New Eng. Conservatory, 1976. Founder Spectrum Young Audiences Trio, Boston, 1976-80; marimba, percussion tchr. Rivers Music Sch., Weston, Mass., 1976-80, 85—, St. Ann's Sch., Bklyn., 1980-85; founder, dir. Marimba Magic, Weston, 1987—; tchr. improvisation Northeastern U., Boston, 1991-95. Percussionist on 6 Revel records; percussionist/timpanist in Christmas Revels, 1980—; presenter in field; concert performer Clarimba, 2002—. Composer: (composition/musical) Gamelon Dream, 1989, Mysterious Waltz, 1991, Whole Tone Dream, 1996, Adventures, 1999, Machines, 2000, Jaja Mani Dreams, 2001, Drum Circle, 2002, 3 Canons, 2003, Moving Music, 2004. Concert performer Concerts for Children, 1976-80, Cambridge World's Fair, 1997, 98, Clarimba Duo, 2002—. Recipient Am. Composers Forum grant. Mem. Music Tchrs. Nat. Assn. (conf. presenter 1991), Musicians Union, Music Educators Nat. Conf. (presenter ea. conf. 1992, 96), Percussive Arts Soc. (presenter internat. conv. 1989, 97), Orff Schulwerk Assn. (presenter nat. conf. 1996) presenter European Piano Tchrs. Assn., Internat. Conf., Budapest, 2000, Internat. Marimba Conf., Belgium, 1992. Office: The Rivers Music Sch 337 Winter St Weston MA 02493-1072 Office Phone: 781-235-6840.

TENNEY, TOM FRED, bishop; b. DeRidder, La., Dec. 6, 1933; s. Fred and Jenny Veve (Nichols) T.; m. Thetus Pearl Caughron, Dec. 27, 1952; children: Tom Gregory, Teri Denise Tenney Spears. Student, Apostolic Bible Inst., St. Paul, 1952; DD (hon.), 1992. Ordained to ministry United Pentecostal Ch., 1954. Pastor United Pentecostal Ch., Monroe, La., 1953-56, DeRidder, 1976-78, youth pres. La. dist., 1953-60, dist. supt. for La., 1978—; youth pres. United Pentecostal Ch., Internat., St. Louis, 1960-69, dir. fgn. missions, mem. exec. bd., 1969-76, mem. gen. bd., 1978—. Internat. radio speaker Harvestime, St. Louis, 1976-78. Author: Pentecost: What's That?, 1975, The Flame Still Burns, 1989, The Main Thing, 1993, Advice to Pastors and Other Saints, 1995, Beyond Sunrise, 1996, Some Things I've Learned, 1998, Secret Sources of Power, 2000, More Power To You, 2003. Trustee Tupelo (Miss.) Children's Mansion, Spirit of Freedom, Metairie, La., Lighthouse Ranch for Boys, Hammond, La. Democrat. Mem. United Pentecostal Ch. Home and Office: PO Box 248 Tioga LA 71477-0248

TENNIES, ROBERT HUNTER, headmaster; b. Bogotá, Colombia, Aug. 19, 1952; s. Leo C. and Ruth (Winston) T.; m. Ruth Ellen Fischer, June 14, 1975; children: Debbie, Julie. BS, Wheaton (Ill.) Coll., 1973; MA, U. South Fla., 1975; EdS, Fla. Atlantic U., 1978, EdD, 1982. Sci. tchr. Cypress Lake Middle Sch., Ft. Myers, Fla., 1973-77, Boca Raton (Fla.) Christian Sch., 1977-78, asst. adminstr., 1978-84, headmaster, 1984—, min. of children, 1984-90; interim. min. of edn., 1991-93. Spkr. Internat. Conf. Religious Edn., Petrozavodsk, Russia; mem. Nat. Rev. Panel Blue Ribbon Schs., 1999. Recipient Excellence in Edn. award Nat. Assn. Elem. Prins., 1990, 97. Mem. Nat. Sci. Tchrs. Assn., Assn. of Christian Schs. Internat. (accreditation commn.), Nat. Assn. Elem. Sch. Prins. Avocation: camping. Home: 2415 NW 30th Rd Boca Raton FL 33431-6214 Office: Boca Raton Christian Sch 315 NW 4th St Boca Raton FL 33432-3739 E-mail: Tennies_r@popmail.firn.edu., bocachristian@bocachristian.org.

TENNYSON, JOSEPH ALAN, engineering executive; b. St. Paul, May 28, 1958; s. Walter Arnold and Carol Jean (Hauenstein) T.; m. Patricia Ann Jordan, Aug. 29, 1981; children: Alexa Jordan, Ryley Joseph. BSBA, AA in Lib. Arts, U. Minn., 1981. Fin. planner K.A. Richard & Assocs., St. Paul, 1981-83; reporting analyst Control Data Corp., Mpls., 1983-84, systems analyst, 1984-85, fin. analyst, 1985-86; dir. ops. Michaud, Cooley, Erickson, Mpls., 1986-89, corp. sec., 1986—, v.p. fin. and adminstrn., 1989-93, prin., 1993—. Bd. dirs. Compas. Mem. Leadership Mpls., 1988-89; bd. dirs. United Arts Partnership Fund, 1996-98, Wolf Ridge Environ. Learning Ctr., 1999-2000; mem. assembly com. on intercollegiate athletics U. Minn., 1994-97; trustee Minnetonka Pub. Schs. Found., 2000—. Mem. Mpls. Club, U. Minn. Alumni Assn. (nat. bd. dirs. 1995-97), Sigma Chi (Grand Consul citation 1983, L.G. Balfour award 1981), Omicron Delta Kappa, Order of Omega. Avocations: computers, fly fishing, golf. Office: Michaud Cooley Erickson 333 S 7th St Ste 1200 Minneapolis MN 55402-2422 Home: 20260 Excelsior Blvd Excelsior MN 55331-8731

TENNYSON, PETER JOSEPH, lawyer; b. Winona, Minn., Mar. 18, 1946; s. Richard Harvey and Sylvia Josephine (Jadrich) T.; m. Mary Eileen Fay, Jan. 3, 1970; children: Mark Christian, Rachel Christine, Matthew Patrick, Erica Ruth. BA, Purdue U., 1968; JD, U. Va., 1975. Bar: Calif. Assoc. atty. O'Melveny & Myers, LA, 1975-82; v.p., gen. counsel Cannon Mills Co., Kannapolis, NC, 1982-84; ptnr. Stradling, Yocca, Newport Beach, Calif., 1984-89, Jones, Day, Reavis & Pogue, Irvine, Calif., 1990-95, Paul, Hastings, Janofsky & Walker, Costa Mesa, Calif., 1995—. Mem. Calif. Commn. on Future of Legal Profession and State Bar, 1994; lectr. in field. Mem. adv. com. St. Joseph Hosp., Orange, Calif., 1987-93; bd. dirs. Lincoln Club Orange County, 1991-93, South Coast Symphony, 1989-92; mem. found. bd. Orange County H.S. Arts. Capt. U.S. Army, 1968—72. Recipient Attys. of Yr. award, Calif. Lawyer, 2003. Mem. Orange County Bar Assn., Performing Arts Bus. Alliance, South Coast Repertory Silver Circle. Roman Catholic. Avocations: downhill skiing, swimming. Home: 19 Monaco Newport Beach CA 92660 Office: Paul Hastings Janofsky & Walker LLP 695 Town Center Dr Fl 17 Costa Mesa CA 92626-1924 Office Phone: 714-668-6237. E-mail: petertennyson@paulhastings.com.

TENOPIR, CAROL, information science educator; Grad. with highest honors, Whittier Coll., 1974; MS in Libr. Sci., Calif. State U., Fullerton, 1975; D in Libr. and Info. Scis., U. Ill., 1984. Supervisory libr. Cibbarelli and Assocs., Huntington Beach, Calif., 1976—77, v.p. ops., 1978—79; systems libr. U. Hawaii, Manoa, 1979—81; asst. prof. U. Hawaii Sch. Libr. and Info. Studies, Manoa, 1983—88, assoc. prof., 1988—93, prof., 1993—94; 1prof. U. Tenn. Sch. Info. Scis., Knoxville, 1994—. Grad. rsch. asst. Info. Retrieval Rsch. Lab. U. Ill., Urbana-Champaign, 1981—83; mem. grad. faculty U. Hawaii, Manoa, 1987—94, adj. prof. dept. comm., 1988—94, chair doctoral dissertation coms., mem. various coms.; adj. prof. coll. comm. U. Tenn., Knoxville, 1995—. Mem. editl. bd.: Online, 1986—; editor: Database Searching Series, Librs. Unltd., 1988—. Named one of Leaders of the Online Industry, Online Mag., 1987; recipient Doris Banks Pubs. award, Calif. State U. Libr. Sci. Alumni Assn., 1983; fellow Univ. fellow, U. Ill., 1981—82, Josie B. Houchens fellow, 1982—83. Mem.: Assn. Records Mgrs. and Adminstrs., Spl. Librs. Assn., Hawaii Libr. Assn. (Disting. Libr. 1994), Am. Soc. Info. Scis. (Doctoral Dissertation Scholarship award 1983, Outstanding Info. Sci. Tchr. award 1993), Beta Phi Mu, Phi Kappa Phi. Office: U Tenn Sch Info Scis 804 Volunteer Blvd Knoxville TN 37996-0001

TENOPYR, MARY LOUISE WELSH (MRS. JOSEPH TENOPYR), psychologist; b. Youngstown, Ohio, Oct. 18, 1929; d. Roy Henry and Olive (Donegan) Welsh; m. Joseph Tenopyr, Oct. 30, 1955. AB, MA, Ohio U., 1951; PhD, U. So. Calif., 1966. Psychometrist Ohio U., Athens, 1951—52, also house mother Sigma Kappa; personnel technician to rsch. psychologist USAF, 1953—55, 1952—53, Hempstead, NY; indsl. rsch. analyst to mgr. employee evaluation N.Am. Rockwell Corp., El Segundo, Calif., 1956—70; assoc. prof. Calif. State Coll., L.A., 1966—70; assoc. rsch. educationalist UCLA, 1970—71; program dir. U.S. CSC, 1971—72; dir. selection and testing AT&T, N.Y.C., 1972—98. Lectr. U. So. Calif., L.A., 1967—70; vice chmn. rsch. com. Tech. Adv. Com. on Testing, Fair Employment Practice Commn. Calif., 1966—70; adviser on testing Office Fed. Contract Compliance, U.S. Dept. Labor, Washington, 1967—73; mem. tech. adv. bd. ePredix, Inc. Mem. editl. bd.: Jour. Applied Psychology, 1972—87, Jour. Vocat. Behavior, 1992—2000, cons. editor: Jour. Applied Psychology, 2000—, Jour. Personal Social Psychology, 2002—; contbr. chpts. to books, articles to profl. jours. Pres. ASPA Found., 1985—87; mem. Army Sci. Bd.; trustee NJ Psychol. Found., 1995—97, Am. Bd. Assessment Psychology. Mem.: NAS (coms. on ability testing, math. and sci. edn., panel on secondary edn.), APA (pres. divsn. evaluation, measurement and stats. 1994—95, bd. profl. affairs, edn. and tng. bd., mem. coun. reps., pres. divsn. indsl. orgnl. psychology, Outstanding Profl. Psychology award Divsn. Indsl. Orgn., Disting. Svc. award, Karl F. Heiser award), Am. Ednl. Rsch. Assn., NJ Psychol. Assn. (bd. trustees 1995—98), Met. NY Assn. Applied Psychology, Psychometric Soc., Nat. Coun. Measurement in Edn., Soc. Indsl. and Orgnl. Psychology (pres. 1979—80, Profl. Practices award 1984), Am. Soc. Pers. Adminstrn. (bd. dirs. 1984—87), Ea. Psychol. Assn., Am. Bd. Assessment Psychology (trustee 1997—), Kappa Phi, Alpha Lambda Delta, Psi Chi, Sigma Kappa, Sigma Xi.

TENORIO, PEDRO A. resident representative; b. Saipan; BA in Geology, MS in Hydrology, U. Hawaii. Sen. for Northern Marianas Congress of Micronesia, 1972—74; mem. Northern Marianas Polit. Status Commn., 1973—76; exec. dir. Northern Marianas Office Transition Studies and Planning, 1975—77, Marianas Pub. Land Corp., 1977—81; legis. adv. 1st Commonwealth of Northern Mariana Islands (CNMI) Legislature, 1977—81; lt. gov. CNMI, 1981—89; resident rep. CNMI U.S. Ho. of Reps., Washington, 2001—. Mem. Rep. Nat. Com. and Presdl. Victory Team. Mem.: Nat. Rep. Club Capitol Hill, Lions Club East Manoa. Republican. Office: Resident Rep US Ho of Reps 2121 R St NW Washington DC 20008 also: PO Box 504959 Saipan MP MP 96950

TENOSO, HAROLD J. consumer products company executive; Various positions including CEO and cons. UNIMED Inc., 1984-93; pres., CEO Serologicals Corp., Atlanta, 1993—, also bd. dirs. Office: Serologicals Corp 5655 Spalding Dr Norcross GA 30092-2504

TENPAS, RONALD J. federal agency administrator, lawyer; m. Kathryn Dunn; children: Nathaniel, William. BA with hons., Mich. State U., 1985; degree in Philosophy, Politics and Econs., Oxford (Eng.) U., 1987; JD, U. Va., 1990. Law clk. U.S. Dist. Ct. (ea. dist.) Pa., 1990—91, U.S. Supreme Ct., 1991—92; law clk. Iran-U.S. Claims Tribunal The Hague, Netherlands, 1992—93; assoc. Carlton, Fields Law Firm, Tampa, Fla., 1993—97; asst. U.S. atty. U.S. Atty.'s Office, Fairview Heights, Ill., 1997—2003, branch chief Dist. Md. So. Divsn., 2001—03, U.S. atty. So. Dist. Ill., 2003—. Editor: Va. Law Rev. Rhodes scholarship, 1985—87, Hardy Cross Dillard scholarship, 1987—90. Office: US Attorneys Office So Dist Ill Nine Executive Dr Ste 300 Fairview Heights IL 62208 Office Phone: 618-628-3700.

TENT, JAMES FOSTER, historian; b. Ridgewood, N.J., Jan. 15, 1944; s. James Robert and Virginia June (Foster) T.;m. Margaret Bunting Wyman, Aug. 17, 1968; children: John Fleming, Virginia Foster. AB, Dartmouth Coll., 1966; MA, U. Wis., 1969, PhD, 1973. Vis. asst. prof. Cornell Coll., Mt. Vernon, Iowa, 1973-74; from asst. prof. to dept. chmn. U. Ala., Birmingham, 1974—2002, dept. chmn., 2002—. Guest prof. U. Hanover, Germany, 1982-83, Free Univ. Berlin, 1985-88. Author: Mission on the Rhine: Denazification & Reeducation in Germany, 1982, The Free University of Berlin: A Political History, 1988, E-Boat Alert: Defending the Normandy Invasion Fleet, 1996, In the Shadow of the Holocaust: Nazi Persecution of Jewish-Christian Germans, 2003; author, editor: Academic Proconsul: E.Y. Hartshorne and Reopening German Universities, 1998. Den Deutschen Freund Sein: Das American Friends Service Community und die humantiare Hilfe im Deutschland nach 1945, 1996. Ford Found. grantee, 1969-72. Mem. Am. Hist. Assn., German Studies Assn., So. Hist. Assn., Birmingham Soc. Piping, Phi Kappa Phi. Avocations: reading, hiking, gardening, model aircraft building, drumming. Office: U Ala Dept History 1212 University Blvd Birmingham AL 35294-3350 E-mail: jtent@uab.edu.

TENTZERIS, EMMANOUIL MANOS, engineering educator, researcher; b. Athens, Greece, Mar. 20, 1970; came to U.S., 1992; s. Markos E. Tentzeris and Irene M. Tentzeri. Diploma summa cum laude, Nat. Tech. U. Athens, 1992; MSc, U. Mich., 1993, PhD, 1998. Assoc. prof. Ga. Inst. Tech., Atlanta, 1998—2004. Invited prof. Tech. U. Munich, Germany, 2002; assoc. dir. for RF rsch. and RF Alliance Leader NSF-GT-Packaging Rsch. Ctr., 1998; broadband tech. hardware, subthrust leader Ga. Electronics Design Ctr. Initiative of State of Ga., 2000; tech. program co-chair Automatic Radio Frequency Techniques Group, Atlanta, 1999; vice-chair IEEE-Components Packaging and Mfg. Tech. Tech. Com. 16 Radio Frequency/Wireless. Author: (with others) Advances Computational FM, 1998, Electronic Packaging, 2000, The RF and Microwave Handbook, 2001, Microwave and RF Product Applications, 2003, Encyclopedia of RF Microwave, 2004; reviewer in field. Recipient Best Paper award, Internat. Microelectronics and Packaging Soc. Symposium, 1997, Applied Computational Electromagnetics Soc. Symposium, 2001, 2002, Career award NSF, 2000, Ga. Tech.-ECE Outstanding Jr. Faculty award 2002; Greek Acad. Excellence fellow Greek Dept. Edn., 1988-92; Papastavridios Greek Math Excellence fellow Greek Govt., 1989. Mem. IEEE (sr., Outstanding Young Engr. award 2003, MTT-AP Atlanta chpt., chmn. bd. com. 2002, tech. session chair 1996, 2000, 2001, 2002, chair steering com.1998), Ga. Tech. Wireless Inst., Tech. Chamber of Greece. Avocations: sports, history books, travel. Home: 5121 Lenox Park Cir Atlanta GA 30319 Office: Ga Inst Tech Sch ECE 777 Atlantic Dr Atlanta GA 30332-0250 Office Phone: 404-385-0378.

TENUTA, LUIGIA, lawyer; b. Madison, Wis., June 4, 1954; d. Eugene P. and Nancy (Gardner) T. AB in Internat. Studies with honors, Miami U., Oxford, Ohio, 1976; JD, Capital U., 1981; postgrad., Pontifical Coll. Josephinum, 1987-88. Bar: Ohio 1981. With internat. mktg. dept. Dresser Industries, Columbus, Ohio, 1976-80, analyst strategic planning, 1980, mgr. internat bus. planning Stratford, Conn., 1981; pvt. practice law Columbus, 1981—. Former mem. devel. com. Miami U. Mem. Ohio Bar Assn., Columbus Bar Assn. Roman Catholic. Office: 6400 Riverside Dr Dublin OH 43017-5197

TENZELDAM, JUSTINE CUBBAGE, publishing executive, editor-in-chief; b. Mountain View, Calif., Nov. 20, 1964; d. Paul Vernon and Florette Anne Cubbage; m. Michael Allen tenZeldam, Aug. 3, 1991; children: Faye Audra, Gerrit Paul; 1 child, Beau Dustin Carpenter. Student, West Valley, Saratoga, CA, 1981—82. Pub., editor in chief Calaveras Times, West Point, Calif., 2001—. Pres. Mountain Maniacs, West Point, Calif., 2003—. Mem.: Calaveras County C of C. Home and Office: Calaveras Times PO Box 1075 West Point CA 95255 Office Phone: 209-293-6090. Personal E-mail: jtenzeldam@yahoo.com. Business E-Mail: editor@calaverastimes.com.

TEOLI-PHELPS, BROOK ELAINE, advocate, dance educator; b. Kissimmee, Fla., Feb. 24, 1977; d. Daniel Joseph and Catherine (Green) Teoli; m. Charles Lee Phelps, Dec. 9, 1999; children: Dylan John Daniel Phelps, Austin Charles Phelps stepchildren: Kayla Leslie Ann Phelps, Taylor Rae Phelps. Profl. dancer Walt Disney Co., Singapore, 1997—98, Taipei, Taiwan, 1998—98; listing clk. Michaelson, Connor, Boul, Huntington Beach, Calif., 1999—2000; personal asst. to the project mgr. Showpower/Gen. Electric Energy Rentals, Sydney, Australia, 2000—00; adminstrv. asst. to the exec. dir. Workforce Investment Bd. of Solano County, Fairfield, Calif., 2001—01; rental coord., adminstrv. asst., sales asst., web designer Gen. Electric Energy Rentals, Benicia, Calif., 2001—01; dance tchr., dir. of performance dance Fairfield, 2002—; child adv. Ct. Apptd. Spl. Advocates, Fairfield, 2003—. Designer, author, editor, and publisher (christian newsletter) The Messenger. Avocations: golf, travel.

TEPHLY, THOMAS ROBERT, pharmacologist, educator, toxicologist; b. Norwich, Conn., Feb. 1, 1936; m. Joan Bernice Clifcorn, Dec. 17, 1960; children: Susan Lynn, Linda Ann, Annette Michele. BS, U. Conn., 1957; PhD, U. Wis., 1962; MD, U. Minn., 1965. Research asst. U. Wis., Madison, 1957-62, instr., 1962; asst. prof. U. Mich., Ann Arbor, 1965-69, assoc. prof., 1969-71; prof. pharmacology U. Iowa, Iowa City, 1971—2003, prof. emeritus, 2003. Contbr. articles to profl. jours. Rsch. scholar Am. Cancer Soc., 1962-65; recipient John Jacob Abel award, 1971, Kenneth P. Dubois award, 1992; Fogarty sr. internat. fellow NIH, 1978; rsch. grantee NIH, 1966—. Mem. Am. Soc. Pharmacology and Exptl. Therapeutics, Soc. Toxicology, AAAS, Am. Soc. Biochem. Molecular Biologists. Home: 6 Lakeview Dr NE Iowa City IA 52240-9142 Office: U Iowa Dept Pharmacology 2-452 BSB Iowa City IA 52242

TEPLEN, PHILIP H. lawyer; b. N.Y.C., Apr. 26, 1957; s. Martin Joseph and Pearl Faye Teplen; m. Patti Anne Teplen, Sept. 22, 1984; children: William, Amanda. BSBA in Fin., Georgetown U., 1979, Oxford U., 1979; JD, Bklyn. Law Sch., 1982. Prin. Teplen & Assocs. PLLC, N.Y.C., 1984—; founder, pres. Tepco Fin., N.Y.C., 1986—88; gen. counsel, v.p. Baron Devel., N.Y.C., 1988—91; founder, pres. Intelligent Solutions, N.Y.C., 1994—96. Guest lectr. Fla. Internat. U. Miami, 1999. Avocations: boating, tennis, golf. Office: 350 Fifth Ave New York NY 10118 E-mail: pteplen@teplenlaw.com.

TEPLOW, THEODORE HERZL, retired valve company executive; b. Brockton, Mass., Apr. 14, 1928; s. Edward Abraham and Evelyn (Stone) T.; m. Charlotte Leah Savitz, June 14, 1953; children: Rachel P., David I., Deborah R., Evan S., Jonathan P. BS, U.S. Mcht. Marine Acd., 1950; MBA, Harvard U., 1953; DHL honoris causa, Hebrew Coll., 1999; PhD honoris causa, Weizmann Inst. Sci., 2002. Mgmt. trainee to pres. Crosby Valve Inc. a Tyco Internat. Ltd. Co., Wrentham, Mass., 1953-82, cons., 1982—2001; dir. Emerson Investment Mgmt., Inc., Boston, 1985—. Cons. Firesafe Products Corp., N.Y.C., 1982-96. Trustee Am. Mcht. Marine Mus. Found., Kings Point, N.Y., 1988-98, Rofeh Internat., Boston, 1990—, Hebrew Coll., Newton Center, Mass., 1971—, chmn., 1992-99; chmn. Hebrew Coll. Bd. Mgrs. of Trust Property, 1999—; trustee Kings Point Challenge, 1997—, U.S. Mcht. Marine Acad., Kings Point, N.Y., 2002—; v.p., bd. dirs. Internat. Catacomb Soc., Boston, 1982-99; bd. dirs. Cong. Beth El-Atereth Israel, Newton Center, Mass., 1975-85, Beth El Cmty. Hebrew Sch., Newton Center, 1965-85, USMMA Alumni Found., Kings Point, 1988—; asst. treas., dir. Am. Com. for Weizmann Inst. Sci., N.Y., 1987—; gov. Weizmann Inst. Sci., Rehovoth, Israel, 1991-2002, vice chair fin. and adminstrn., dir., 2002—; bd. dirs. Wilstein Inst. Jewish Policy Studies, L.A., Boston, 1993—, Stone Charitable Found., 1982-99; dir. Archives for Hist. Documentation, Boston, 1994—. Comdr. USNR, ret. Recipient Outstanding Profl. Achievement award U.S. Mcht. Marine Acad. Alumni Assn., 1970, Meritorious Alumni Svc. award, 1990, Disting. Svc. award, 1995. Democrat. Office Phone: 617-492-9552.

TEPLY, MARK LAWRENCE, mathematics professor; b. Lincoln, Nebr., Jan. 11, 1942; s. Lawrence Joseph and Gertrude M. (Kupfer) T.; m. Kathleen K. McGrayel, Aug. 1968 (div. 1978); 1 child, David; m. Nancy Lee Wilkowske, Mar. 12, 1983; children: Stephanie, Andrew, Grant. BA, U. Nebr., 1963, MA, 1965, PhD, 1968. Instr. U. So. Calif., L.A., 1967-68; asst. prof. U. Fla., Gainesville, 1968-73, assoc. prof., 1973-81, prof., 1981-85, U. Wis., Milw., 1985—. Editor: Communications in Algebra, 1982—; editor 2 book series by Marcel Dekker, 1983—; author: Finiteness Conditions on Torsion Theories, 1984, A History of the Singular Splitting Problem, 1984, Semicocritical Modules, 1987; contbr. 70 articles to profl. jours. NSF grantee U. Fla., 1973, 77-78, U.S. Dept. Edn. grantee U. Wis., Milw., 1990—. Mem. Am. Math. Soc., Math. Assn. Am. Lutheran. Office: U Wis Dept Math Milwaukee WI 53201-0413 Office Phone: 414-229-5110. Business E-Mail: mlteply@uwm.edu.

TEPPER, CLIFFORD, allergist, immunologist, educator; b. Schenectady, N.Y., Oct. 26, 1922; s. Solomon B. and Annette (Lifset) T.; m. Cynthia S. Tepper; children: Stewart, Nancy, Henry, Audrey. Chief allergy dept. Ellis Hosp., Schenectady, 1990—; allergist allergy asthma immunology ctr. Albany (N.Y.) Med. Coll., 1992—, prof. pediats., 1973—. Co-dir. Schenectady Vol. Physicians Free Clinic; cons. in field. Trustee Schenectady Mus., 1987-99, Schenectady Pub. Libr., 1985—; pres. Antismoking Acad. Schenectady County; co-dir. Vol. Physician Clinic, Shcenectady County. Mem. Coll. Allergy and Immunology, Am. Acad. Pediatrics, Am. Acad. Allergy and

Immunology, New Eng. Soc. Allergy (pres. 1990-92), N.Y. State Allergy Soc. (treas. 1993-95), Eastern Allergy Soc. (exec. com.), Physicians for Social Responsibility. Avocations: bird watching, art history. Home: 2216 Stoneridge Rd Niskayuna NY 12309-5524 Office: Allergy Asthma Immunology Ctr Albany Med Coll 1201 Washington Ave Ext Albany NY 12205 Fax: 518 452 2683. E-mail: CTEPPER804@aol.com.

TEPPER, LLOYD BARTON, preventive medicine physician, educator; b. L.A., Dec. 21, 1931; m. Lamonte Leverage; children: Jeffrey Hamilton, Evan Clothier. AB, Dartmouth Coll., 1954; MD, Harvard U., 1957, MIH, 1960, ScD in Hygiene, 1962. Diplomate Am. Bd. Preventive Medicine (trustee, vice chair, 1986-94), Am. Bd. Occupl. Medicine. Intern U. Calif., San Francisco, 1957—58; resident Harvard Sch. Pub. Health, 1959—62; rsch. fellow Harvard Med. Sch., Boston, 1958-59; clin. fellow Mass. Gen. Hosp., Boston, 1958-60; rsch. assoc. MIT, Cambridge, 1959-61; physician U.S. AEC, Washington, 1962-65; prof. environ. health U. Cin., 1965-72; assoc. dir. Kettering Lab., Cin., 1965-72; assoc. commr. U.S. FDA, Washington, 1972-76; corp. med. dir. Air Products and Chems., Inc., Allentown, Pa., 1976-97; adj. prof. medicine Jefferson Med. Coll., 1998—2001. Adj. prof. emergency medicine occupl. and environ. medicine U. Pa., 2000—. Editor: Jour. Occupl. Medicine, 1979—91. Fellow: Am. Acad. Occupl. Medicine (pres. 1980—81), Am. Coll. Occupl. and Environ. Medicine. Office Phone: 610-527-8918. E-mail: lbtepper@icdc.com.

TEPPER, LYNN MARSHA, gerontology educator; b. N.Y.C., Mar. 16, 1946; m. William Chester Tepper, Aug. 27, 1967; children: Sharon Joy, Michelle Dawn. BS, SUNY, Buffalo, 1967; MA, Wayne State U., 1971; MS, Columbia U., 1977, EdM, 1978, EdD, 1980. Instr. John F. Kennedy Sch., Berlin, 1967-68, adnl. counselor, 1968-69; ednl. coordinator Army Edn. Ctr., Berlin, 1969-71; psychologist U.S. Dept. Def., Berlin, 1971-73; prof. Gerontology L.I. U., 1979-99, Columbia U., N.Y.C., 1982—. Cons. NATO, Naples, Italy, 1969-71, SHAPE, Brussels, 1969-71, also numerous nursing homes, N.Y., 1978—. Found. for Long Term Care, 1992—; prof. gerontology Mercy Coll., Dobbs Ferry, 1979—; dir. Gerontology Resource Ctr., Ctr. for Geriatrics and Gerontology, Columbia U., N.Y.C., 1980-85, dir. Behavioral Sci. Program, 1982—; del. White House Conf. on Aging, 1980. Author: (textbooks) Long Term Care, 1993, Respite Care, 1993, Multidisciplinary Perspectives on Aging, 2004; contbr. articles to profl. jours., chpts. to books. Advisor Office on Aging, State of N.Y., Albany, 1980-90, dir. Mercy Coll., Inst. Gerontology, 1990—; trustee, St. Cabrini Nursing Home, 1988-98, Morningside Nursing Home, 1998—; bd. dirs. Found. Long Term Care. Brookdale Inst. on Aging fellow, 1983; rsch. grantee NIH, Nat. Inst. on Aging, Nat. Inst. Gen. Med. Sci., U.S. Dept. Edn., U.S. Bur. Health Professions, interdisciplinary geriat. tng. U.S. Dept. Health Resources Svcs. Adminstrn. Fellow Gerontol. Soc. Am.; mem. Am. Psychol. Assn. Avocations: physical fitness, hiking. Office: Columbia U Med Campus Box 20 630 W 168th St New York NY 10032-3702

TEPPER, MARCY ELIZABETH, drug education director; b. Salt Lake City, Aug. 22, 1949; d. Warren Roswell and Rosemary Tepper. PhD, U. Ariz., Tucson, Ariz., 1983; MEd, U. Utah, Salt Lake City, Utah, 1972; Filosfia Y Letras, U. Valencia, Valencia, Spain, 1971; BA, San Francisco Coll. for Women, San Francisco, Calif., 1971. Cert. principal, mathematics, spanish tchr. 1990. Adjunct asst. prof. U. Arizona, Tucson, 1983—86; dir., owner 1.2.1 Tutoring, Tucson, 1984—90; counselor Teton County Sch. Dist., Jackson, Wyo., 1990—94; lectr. Ariz. State U., Tempe, Ariz., 1995—98; tchr. Santa Fe Public Schools, Santa Fe, 1998—99; coun. Safe Sch. Healthy Students Grant, Ethete, Wyo., 1999—2001; mid. sch. coord. Fremont County Schools #14, Ethete, Wyo., 2001—. Bd. mem. Ariz. Women Mathematics Sci., Tempe, 1997—98. Recipient Nat. Outdoor Leadership Sch. (NOLS) scholarship, 2003. Mem.: Interagy. Coord. Coalition (v.p. 2000—01, pres. 2001—03), Teton County Task Force (bd. 1992—94). Office: Wyoming Indian Sch 638 Blue Sky Highway Ethete WY 82520 Personal E-mail: marcyet@mail.trib.com. Business E-Mail: marcyt@fremont14.k12.wy.us.

TEPPER, MICHAEL HOWARD, publishing company executive; b. Balt., Sept. 4, 1941; s. Jack and Betty Lee (Chodak) T.; m. Veronica Ann Schofield, Nov. 15, 1972; children: Alex, Megan, Sarah. BA, U. Md., 1963; MA, NYU, 1965, PhD, 1970. Pres., mng. editor Geneal. Pub. Co., Inc., Balt., 1971—. Author: American Passenger Arrival Records, 1988; editor: The Famine Immigrants (7 vols.), 1983-86, Passenger Arrivals at the Port of Baltimore 1820-1834, 1982, New World Immigrants (2 vols.), 1979, Immigrants to the Middle Colonies, 1978, Passengers to America, 1977, Emigrants to Pennsylvania, 1975. Recipient Founders' Day award NYU, 1970. Office: Geneal Pub Co Inc 1001 N Calvert St Baltimore MD 21202-3823

TEPPER, R(OBERT) BRUCE, JR., lawyer; b. Long Branch, N.J., Apr. 1, 1949; s. Robert Bruce and Elaine (Ogus) T.; m. Belinda Wilkins, Nov. 26, 1971; children: Laura Katherine, Jacob Wilkins. AB in HIstory, Dartmouth Coll., 1971; JD cum laude, MA in Urban Affairs, St. Louis U., 1976. Bar: Mo. 1976, Calif. 1977, Ill. 1978, U.S. Ct. Appeals (7th cir.) 1978, (8th cir.) 1976, (9th cir.) 1978, U.S. Dist. Ct. (ctrl., no., so. and east dists.) Calif. 1978, U.S. Supreme Ct. 1991. Asst. gen. counsel St. Louis Redevel. Authority, 1976-77; assoc. Goldstein & Price, St. Louis, 1977-78, Loo, Merideth & McMillan, L.A., 1978-82; sole practice L.A., 1982-84; sr. prin., CFO Kane, Ballmer and Berkman, L.A., 1984—2001; with R. Bruce Tepper, ALC, 2002—. Litigation counsel to San Diego, Santa Barbara, Huntington Beach, Anaheim, Culver City, L.A., Lynwood, Norwalk, Redondo Beach, Oceanside, Ontario, Oxnard, Pasadena, Moreno Valley, Grover Beach, Glendale, Hawthorne,and Calif. City Calif.; spl. counsel Castaic Lake Water Agy., 1993—; judge pro tempore Los Angeles County Mcpl. Ct., 1983—95; grader State Bar Calif., 1980-84; lectr. in land use and environ. issues. Assoc. editor St. Louis U. Law Jour., 1974-76; mem. editl. bd. L.A. Lawyer; contbr. articles to legal jours. Mem. ABA, Los Angeles County Bar Assn. (com. on jud. evaluations), Assn. Bus. Trial Lawyers., So. Calif. Dartmouth Club (bd. dirs. 1980-83), L.A. Athletic. Republican. Jewish. Home: 10966 Wrightwood Ln Studio City CA 91604-3957 Office: 1880 Century Park East Ste 200 Los Angeles CA 90067-1602 Office Phone: 310-551-9700. E-mail: TAPatRBT@aol.com., tap@rbtlaw.com.

TEPPER, SCOTT M. mining executive; Bd. dirs. Horizon Natural Resources (formerly AEI Resources), Ashland, Ky., 2002—, chief restructuring officer, 2002—, acting CEO, 2003—. Vice chmn., bd. dirs. Bio-Plexus Inc. Office: Horizon Natural Resources 2000 Ashland Dr Ashland KY 41161

TERADA, ALICE MASAE, retired elementary school educator; b. Hilo, Hawaii, Nov. 13, 1928; d. David Matsuo and Mitsuko (Sekido) Marutani; m. Harry T. Terada, Aug. 25, 1951; children: Suzanne T. Henderson, Keith Y., Lance S. Diploma, Queen's Hosp. Sch. Nursing, 1950; BS, We. Res. U., 1953; MEd, U. Hawaii, 1971. Cert. tchr., Hawaii. Registered nurse County Meml. Hosp., Hilo, Hawaii, 1950-51, U. Hosps., Cleve., 1952-53; lang. arts tchr. Dept. Edn., Honolulu, 1967-68; reading tchr. Reading Ctr., Honolulu, Hawaii, 1968-82; ret. Author: Under the Starfruit Tree, 1989, The Magic Crocodile, 1994. Mem. AAUW, Internat. Reading Assn., Zonta Club Internat., Zonta Club Honolulu (bd. dirs. 1996-97). Avocations: art, art history, porcelain antiques, yoga, swimming.

TERANES, PAUL S. county judge, mediator; b. Milw., June 25, 1935; s. Stephen Raymond and Anne Teresa Teranes; m. Barbara J. Teranes, Dec. 28, 1966; children: Richard, Jane, Daniel, Amy. AB, Coll. Holy Cross, Worcester, Mass., 1958; JD, U. Mich., 1961. Bar: Mich. 1961. Asst. prosecuting atty. Wayne County, Detroit, 1962-82; cir. ct. judge Wayne County Circuit Ct., Detroit, 1982—. Trustee Upshaw Inst. for Blind, Detroit, 1982-2001, pres., 1995; trustee Great Lakes Ctr. Ind. Living, Detroit, 1988-94; chmn. disabilities com., Mich. Open Justice Commn., 1998—; bd. trustees Leader Dog Sch. for Blind, Rochester, Mich., 1998—, sec., 2000—. Voted in top 5 most respected Mich. judges, Lawyers Weekly newspaper poll, 1991; named Outstanding Profl. Alumnus, U. Detroit H.S., 1985. Mem. Cath. Lawyers Assn. (bd. trustees), Mich. Judges Assn., Mich. Bar Assn., Detroit Met. Bar Assn., Witenagamode Soc. Avocation: bicycling. Office: Wayne County Circuit Ct 2 Woodward Ave CYMB Detroit MI 48226

TERAUDS, JURIS, retired science educator, research scientist; b. Jelgava, Latvia, Oct. 15, 1936; s. Janis Hermanis and Tatijana (Odins) Terauds; m. Shirley Jean Henry, Apr. 1, 1961 (div. Oct. 15, 1986); children: Jeffry Juris, Dana Kelly, Kimberly Kirsten. BS, Univ. Dubuque, Dubuque, IA, 1961; MS, Biomechanics, LA State Univ., Lost Angeles, CA, 1965; PhD (hon.), Univ. Md., College Park, MD, 1972. Instr. Univ. Md., College Park, Md., 1968—72; assoc. prof. Univ. Tex., Odessa, 1972—75; prof. Univ. Alta., Edmonton, Canada, 1975—80; adj. prof. San Diego State Univ., San Diego, 1981—86; prof./dept. head Colo. State Univ., Fort Collins, 1986—90, prof. emeritus, 1991—. Pres. Internat. Soc. of Biomechanics Sports, San Diego, 1978—85, Rsch. Ctr. for Sports, San Diego and Fort Collins, Colo., 1978—; ceo X-Iser Industries, Fort Collins, Colo., 1991—. Author: 13 books on biomechanics, over 80 articles. Editor IAF Internat. Olympic Com., London, England, 1978—90, IAAF Internat. Olympic Cmte., London, England, 1978—90; rsch. dir. Olympics of Montreal, Montreal, Canada, 1976; chmn. SPIE Photooptical Instruments, 1982; chmn. photooptical instruments SPIE, 1982. Recipient Superior Contbn., Internat. Olympic Cmte., 1976, Profl. Achievement, Univ. Dubuque, IA, 1999; fellow, Internat. Soc. of Biomechanics in Sports, 1998. Fellow: Internat. Soc. of Biomechanics in Sports (dir. 1978—2002); mem.: Internat. High Speed Cinematography & Videography (chmn. 1982—88). Achievements include invention of Stepping Exercise Machine, 1977-2002. Avocations: reading, digital motion analysis, photography, videography. Home: 3319 Lone Jack Rd Encinitas CA 92024-7014 Office: X-Iser Industries RCS 1501 West Lake Fort Collins CO 80521

TEREN, MARC, publishing executive; Former gen. mgr. interactive entertainment Walt Disney Co.; former CEO Washingtonpost.Newsweek Interactive subs. Washington Post Co.; CEO Cahners Bus. Info., 2000—. Office: Cahners Bus Info 350 Hudson St Fl 4 New York NY 10014 E-mail: mteren@cahners.com.

TERESHCHENKO, ALEXANDER PAVLOVICH, research scientist, educator; b. Simferopol, Ukraine, Sept. 2, 1954; s. Pavel Kirillovich and Ludmila Fedorovna Tereshchenko; m. Lena Vasilyevna Kononova, July 31, 1976; children: Paul Aleksandrovich, Sergey Aleksandrovich. BS, Crimean Agrl. U., Ukraine, 1975, MS, 1980; PhD in Agrl. Scis., All-Union Rsch. Inst. of Vine and Wine, Ukraine, 1991. Sr. Rschr. Supreme Com. at Coun. of Ministers of USSR, 1989. Rschr. Crimean Agrl. U., Simferopol, Russia, 1981—84; dir. plant propagation dept. All-Union Rsch. Inst. of Vine and Wine, Yalta, Russia, 1984—94; rsch. dir. Duarte Nursery, Inc., Hughson, Calif., 1995—2002; pres. Torg GP, Turlock, Calif., 2002—. Author 65 profl. articles and 3 books. Active mem. N.Y. Acad. of Scis., N.Y.C., 2000—03. Recipient Golden medal for rsch. in viticulture, 1991. Mem.: Farm Bur. Achievements include patents for 9 Russian patents and 2 U.S. patents; research in New tech. of plant propagation. Avocations: martial arts, making pictures on the metal, writing songs, guitar, computer games. Office: Torg GP 4364 Bellevue Ct Turlock CA 95382 E-mail: torggp@concentric.net.

TERESI, JOSEPH, publishing executive; b. Mpls., Mar. 13, 1941; s. Cliff I.A. and Helen Ione (Leslie) (dec.); 1 child, Nicholas (dec.). CEO Jammer Cycle Products Inc., Burbank, Calif., 1968—80, Paisano Pubs. LLC, Agoura Hills, Calif., 1970—; chmn. bd., CEO V-Twin Expo, Agoura Hills, Calif., 1998—. Promoter motorcycle events; prodr. Easyriders Video mag.; owner Teresi Dyno Drags. Pub. (mags.) Easyriders, 1971—, In the Wind, 1974—, Biker, 1986—, Tattoo, 1986—, Am. Rodder, 1987-2001, Womens Enterprise, 1987-89, V-Twin News, 1989—, V-Twin, 1989, Tattoo Flash, 1993—, Tattoo Savage, 1993—, VQ, 1994—, Early-Riders, 1994-96, Quick Throttle, 1995-99, Roadware, 1995—, Tailgate, 2000, Tattoo Industry, 2000, Highbeams, 2003, Street Customs, 2004, Am. Choppers, 2004, Cable TV Prodr., 2004. Achievements include holding the world speed record for motorcycles set at 322 miles per hour, 1990. Office: Paisano Pubs LLC PO Box 3000 Agoura Hills CA 91376-3000

TEREY-SMITH, MARY, music educator, conductor; b. Budapest, Hungary, Dec. 4, 1933; arrived in U.S., 1967; m. Charles Anthony Smith, June 21, 1958 (dec. Dec. 1995). MusB in Conducting and Composition, Liszt Acad. Music, 1951; MA in Music Lit., U. Vt., 1964; PhD in Musicology, Eastman Sch. Music, U. Rochester, 1971. Vocal coach Hungarian Opera Co., Budapest, 1952—56; resident conductor Tatabanya Symphony, 1952—56; music specialist Prot. Sch. Bd. Montreal, 1957—64; vocal coord., asst. conductor Toronto Opera Sch., 1958—64; prof. music history Western Wash. U., Bellingham, 1967—72, dir. opera, prof. musicology, dir. Collegium Music, 1976—2001, prof. emeritus, 2001—. Contbr. articles to profl. jours. Mem.: Internat. Musicological Soc., Am. Musicological Soc. Avocations: tapestry, sailing. Office: Western Wash U Dept Music Bellingham WA 98225-9107

TERHAAR, JOYCE, editor; b. Minn. m. Geoff Long; 2 children. Grad. magna cum laude, U. St. Thomas, 1981. Reporter Herald, Grand Forks, ND; reporter, bus. editor Santa Rosa (Calif.) Press Dem., 1984—88; bus. reporter Sacramento Bee, 1988—91, asst. met. editor, 1991—93, city editor, 1993—99, mng. editor, 1999—. Office: Sacramento Bee 2100 Q St PO Box 15779 Sacramento CA 95852*

TER HORST, JERALD FRANKLIN, public affairs counsel; b. Grand Rapids, Mich., July 11, 1922; s. John Henry and Maude (Van Strien) ter H.; m. Louise Jeffers Roth, Jan. 20, 1945; children: Karen Bayens Morris, Margaret Fulton Robinson, Peter Roth, Martha Morgan Lubin. Student, Mich. State U., 1941-42; AB, U. Mich., 1947. Reporter Grand Rapids Press, 1946-51; mem. staff Detroit News, 1953-74, city and state polit. writer, 1953-57, Washington corr., 1958-60; chief Detroit News (Washington bur.), 1961-74; White House press sec. to Pres., 1974; columnist Detroit News/Universal Press Syndicate, 1974-81; dir. nat. pub. affairs Ford Motor Co., 1981-91; fgn. assignments include Berlin crisis Geneva Fgn. Ministers Conf., Yugoslavia, 1959, 70, 1960, 1963, 69, 1966, 70, 1972, 1974, 1978. Writer N.Am. Newspaper Alliance, 1958-74 Author: Gerald Ford and Future of the Presidency, 1974, The Flying White House: The Story of Air Force One, 1979; contbr. to mags. and TV documentaries. Bd. dirs. Nat. Press Found., 1982-98, Gridiron Found., WETA-TV (Channel 26), 1988-99, Grad. Sch. Polit. Mgmt., George Washington U., 1985-96, Washington, Brady Campaign to Prevent Gun Violence, 1992-2002. Officer USMCR, 1943-46, 51-52. Mem. Pub. Rels. Soc. Am., Soc. Profl. Journalists, Psi Upsilon. Presbyterian (elder). Clubs: Gridiron, Nat. Press. Overseas Writers.

TERHUNE, KAREN MARIE, mathematician, secondary school educator; b. Chgo., Nov. 8, 1949; d. Kenneth E. and Lorraine Anderson; m. Douglas S. Terhune, Oct. 10, 1948; children: Cindy L., Jackie M., Sandy L. BS, Carroll Coll., 1971; MA in Interdisciplinary Curriculum, Nat. Louis U., 2000. 9-12 math. tchr. Sun Prairie (Wis.) HS, Sun Prairie, Wis., 1971—. 9-12 math. coord. Sun Prairie (Wis.) HS, 1997—. Home: 2834 Northwynde Psg Sun Prairie WI 53590 Office: Sun Prairie High School 220 Kroncke Dr Sun Prairie WI 53590

TERILLI, JOSEPH ANTHONY, secondary school educator; b. Winthrop, Mass., June 14, 1948; s. Joseph Anthony and Mary Grace (Colontuoni) T.; m. Carol Ann Saccardo, Oct. 8, 1971; 1 child, Joseph Anthony III. BS, Boston Coll., 1970, MEd, 1973. Tchr., adminstr. Boston Pub. Schs., 1972-77; tchr. Coolidge Jr. H.S., Reading, Mass., 1977-84, Reading Meml. H.S., 1984—, mentor tchr., 1988—. Pres., CEO Terilli Enterprises Devel. Corp., Aruba, 1986—; mem. Profl. Devel. Com., Reading, 1988-92. Author: Blood on the Chalkboard, How Children Succeed, also newspaper articles, booklets, monographs and mock trial; pub. (newsletter) Political Action Network (PAN). Mem. exec. bd., Mass. state chair Dem. Party (New Dems.). Mem. C. of C., Kiwanis (past sec.). Roman Catholic. Avocations: politics, travel, writing, collecing comic books. Home: 27 Lawndale Rd Stoneham MA 02180-1014 Office: Reading Meml HS 62 Oakland Rd Reading MA 01867-1613

TERILLI, SAMUEL A., JR., newspaper publishing executive; Gen. Coun. The Miami Herald, Fla.; of cousel Ford Harrison LLP, Fla., 2000—. Office: Ford Harrison LLP 25 SE 2nd St Ste 516 Miami FL 33131-2102

TERK, GLENN THOMAS, lawyer; b. Feb. 27, 1949; s. Raymond Arthur and Marguerite Ida (Nichols) T.; m. Mary Ann Michaud, Sept. 25, 1982. BSME, Clarkson Coll. Tech., 1971; JD, U. Conn., 1976. Bar: Conn. 1976, U.S. Dist. Ct. Conn. 1976, U.S. Ct. Appeals (2d cir.) 2002. Engr. Combustion Engrng. Co., Windsor, Conn., 1971-76; assoc. Francis, Kroopnick & O'Neil, Hartford, Conn., 1976-78; ptnr. Brignole & Terk, Hartford, Conn., 1993-95; pvt. practice Hartford, Conn., 1995—. Mem. Dem. Town Com., Windsor, 1978-79, Windsor Inland Wetlands Commn., 1978-79, Rep. Town com., Wethersfield, 1997—; chmn. Trinity United Meth. Ch. adminstrv. bd., Windsor, 1982-83, finance chmn. 1997-99. Mem. Conn. Bar Assn. (cmty. subcom. 1981-85, real property exec. com. 1994—, comml. law com. 1994—). Home: 445 Old Reservoir Rd Wethersfield CT 06109-3956 Office: 81 Wolcott Hill Rd Wethersfield CT 06109-1242 E-mail: Gterk@cs.com.

TERKEL, STUDS (LOUIS TERKEL), writer, interviewer; b. N.Y.C., May 16, 1912; s. Samuel and Anna (Finkel) T.; m. Ida Goldberg, July 2, 1939; 1 son, Dan. PhB, U. Chgo., 1932, JD, 1934. Disting. Scholar in Residence, Chgo. Hist. Soc., 1998—. Stage appearances include Detective Story, 1950, A View From the Bridge, 1958, Light Up the Sky, 1959, The Cave Dwellers, 1960; moderator: (TV program) Studs Place, 1950-53, (radio programs) Wax Museum, 1945— (Ohio State Univ. award 1959, UNESCO Prix Italia award 1962), Studs Terkel Almanac, 1952—, Studs Terkel Show, Sta. WFMT-FM, Chgo.; master of ceremonies Newport Folk Festival, 1959, 60, Ravinia Music Festival, 1959, U. Chgo. Folk Festival, 1961, others; panel moderator, lectr., narrator films; author: (books) Giants of Jazz, 1957, Division Street: America, 1967, Hard Times. An Oral History of the Great Depression, 1970, Working: People Talk about What They Do All Day and How They Feel about What They Do, 1974 (Nat. Book award nomination 1975), Talking to Myself: A Memoir of My Times, 1977, American Dreams: Lost and Found, 1980, The Good War: An Oral History of World War II (Pulitzer prize in nonfiction 1985), Chicago, 1986, The Great Divide: Second Thoughts On The American Dream, 1988, Race: How Blacks and Whites Think and Feel About the American Obsession, 1992, Coming of Age, 1995, My American Century, 1997, Spectator, 1999, Will the Circle Be Unbroken, 2001; (play) Amazing Grace, 1959; also short stories. Named Communicator of Yr. U. Chgo. Alumni Assn., 1969; recipient Nat. Humanities Medal, 1997, Nat. Book Critics Circle lifetime achievement award, 2004. Office: Chgo Hist Soc Clark St at North Ave Chicago IL 60614*

TERMAN, DONNA LEA, lawyer, foundation administrator; b. Columbia City, Ind., Jan. 8, 1954; d. Don and Sheran Terman; m. William Reid Brown; children: Russell Ward Brown, Rachel Sierra Brown. BA, Purdue U., 1976; JD, Stanford Law Sch., 1979. Bar: Calif. 1979. Exec. dir. Walter S. Johnson Found., Palo Alto, Calif., 1981—92; policy analyst and editor David and Lucile Packard Found., Los Altos, Calif., 1992—98; trust adminstr. William R. Hewlett Revocable Trust, Palo Alto, Calif., 1998—2000; cons. Poizner Family Found., 2000—, Calif. Charter Sch. Assn., 2004—. Co-chair No. Calif. Grantmakers Com. to Examine the Impact of the Buck Trust Dispute on Philanthropy, San Francisco, 1984—87; chair Coun. on Foundations Pre-College Edn. Group, Washington, 1985—86. Editor: (policy journal) The Future of Children. Pres. Geokids Day Care Ctr., Palo Alto, 1991—93. Home: 1043 Berkeley Ave Menlo Park CA 94025 Personal E-mail: dtwebstuff@yahoo.com.

TERMAN, LEWIS MADISON, electrical engineer, researcher; b. San Francisco, Aug. 26, 1935; s. Frederick Emmons and Sibyl (Walcott) T.; m. Barbara Chertok, Aug. 28, 1958. BS in Physics, Stanford U., 1956, MSEE, 1958, PhD, 1961. Mem. rsch. staff T.J. Watson Rsch. Ctr., IBM, Yorktown Heights, N.Y., 1961-89, sr. mgr., 1989-91, sr. mem. tech. planning staff, 1991-93; mgr. VLSI processor design IBM Rsch. Ctr., Yorktown Heights, NY, 1993-94, pres. Acad. Tech., 1994—2001, rsch. staff T.J. Watson Rsch. Ctr., 2001—, assoc. dir. Sys. Dept., 2001—. Co-chmn. Symposium on Very Large Scale Integrated Technology, Systems and Application, Taiwan, 1989, 91, 93, 95, 97, 99, 2001, 03, tech. program co-chmn., 1985, 87; tech. program chmn. Internat. Solid State Cirs. Conf., N.Y.C., 1983; chmn. Symposium on Very Large-Scale Integrated Tech., Kobe, Japan, 1985, San Diego, 1986, Symposium on Very Large-Scale Integrated Cirs., Karuizawa, Japan, 1988, Kyoto, Japan, 1989, Symposium on Low Power Electronics, San Diego, 1994. Contbr. articles to profl. jours. Pres. Twin Lakes Water Works Corp., S. Salem, N.Y., 1980—. Recipient IEEE Solid-State Cirs. Tech. Field award, 1995. Fellow: IEEE (chmn. tech. mtgs. coun. 1993—94, tech. activites bd. treas. 1995—98, chair strategic planning and rev. com. 1999—2000, v.p. elect tech. activities bd. 2000, v.p. tech. activities bd. 2001, treas. publs., svcs. and products bd. 2003, divsn. 1 dir., bd. dirs. 2004—), AAAS; mem.: Nat. Acad. Engring., Circuits and Sys. Soc. of IEEE (adminstrv. com. 1981—83), IEEE Solid-State Circuits Soc. (editor jour. 1974—77, treas. 1988—89, v.p. 1996—97, pres. 1998—99), IEEE Electron Devices Soc. (v.p. 1988—89, pres. 1990—91, Disting. Svc. award 1995), IBM Acad. Tech. (co-chair tech. program com. 1996, chair components and processes com., tech. coun. 1996—98, pres. 2001—03, past pres. 2003—). Achievements include patents in field. Avocations: music, theater, opera, hiking. Home: 61 Twin Lakes Rd South Salem NY 10590-1012 Office: IBM TJ Watson Rsch Ctr 1101 Kitchawan Rd PO Box 218 Yorktown Heights NY 10598 Office Phone: 914-945-2060.

TERMEER, HENRICUS ADRIANUS, biotechnology company executive; b. Tilburg, Holland, Feb. 28, 1946; came to U.S., 1971, naturalized, 1999; s. Jacques and Mary (Van Gorp) T. Student, Economisch Hogeschool, Rotterdam, The Netherlands, 1969; MBA, U. Va., 1973. Mgr. mgmt. svcs. Norvic Co., Norwich, England, 1969-71; mgr. internat. product planning Baxter Travenol, Inc., Deerfield, Ill., 1973-74, internat. mktg. mgr., 1975-76; gen. mgr. Travenol GMBH, Munich, 1976-79; v.p. Hyland Therapeutics divsn. Baxter Travenol, Glendale, Calif., 1979-81, exec. v.p., 1981-83; pres. Genzyme Corp., Inc., Boston, 1983—, COO, 1983-85, CEO, 1986—, chmn., 1988—. Dir. Abiomed, Mass. Cystic Fibrosis Found., Biotech. Industry Orgn., PHRMA, Mass. High Tech.; trustee H&Q Lifescis. Fund, Hambrecht & Quist Healthcare Investors Fund. Trustee Mus. Sci., Boston, Darden Bus. Sch. U. Va; mem. bd. fellows Harvard Med. Sch. Served to 1st lt. Netherlands Royal Air Force, 1966-67. Fellow AAAS. Office: Genzyme Corp 500 Kendall St Cambridge MA 02139-1562

TERMINI, OLGA ASCHER, music educator; b. Hamburg, Germany, May 19, 1930; came to U.S., 1952; d. Viktor and Martha M. (Schuett) Ascher; married, Nov. 20, 1955 (dec. July 1979). MusB, U. So. Calif., 1954, MusM, 1957, PhD, 1970. Instr. music Stevenson Jr. H.S., L.A., 1954-57, Fairfax H.S., L.A., 1957-72; asst. prof. music Calif. State U., L.A., 1972-76, assoc.prof. music, 1976-81, prof. music, 1981-96, part-time prof. music, 1996—, prof. emeritus, 1997—. Instr. voice classes L.A. City Coll., 1957-64; instr. music history and theory Pasadena (Calif.) City Coll., 1973-76; vis. prof. musicology Claremont (Calif.) Grad. Sch., 1986, 95, 98, 2002, Pomona Coll., 2003. Contbr. articles to music revs. and profl. publs.; translator various German-English articles for profl. jours. Mem. edit. bd. Jour. of the Arnold Schoenberg Inst., 1974-81; bd. dirs. Glendale (Calif.) Chamber Orch., 1985-89, CSULA Friends of Music, pres., 1997—; vp. bd. dirs. Pacific Contemporary Music Ctr., 1987-96, newsletter editor, 1988-96; substitute soloist 1st Ch. Christian Scientist, Alhambra, Calif., 1990-2001; bd. dirs. Neighborhood Music Sch. Music scholar Ebell Club, 1953-54, Fulbright grantee, Venice, Italy, 1966-67, Calif. State U. Instnl. grantee, 1974-75, 75-76; recipient Trustees' Outstanding Prof. award Calif. State U. Sys., 1990. Mem. NEA, Am. Musicol. Soc. (Pacific S.W. chpt. sec. 1981-83, v.p. 1984-86, pres. 1986-88, elective counselor 1990-92), Coll. Music Soc. (life), Calif. Music Tchrs. Assn., Am. Handel Soc., Music Tchrs. Assn. Calif. (Glendale br.), Friends of Music Calif. State U. L.A. (pres. 1997—), Phi Kappa Phi, Phi Kappa Lambda. Democrat. Avocations: concerts, operas, museums. Home: 4278 Sea View Ln Los Angeles CA 90065-3350 Office: Calif State U dept Music 5151 State University Dr Los Angeles CA 90032-4226

TERMINI, ROSEANN BRIDGET, law educator; b. Phila., Feb. 2, 1953; d. Vincent James and Bridget (Marano) Termini. BS magna cum laude, Drexel U., 1975; MEd, Temple U., 1979, JD, 1985; grad. in food and pharmacy law, 1998. Bar: Pa. 1985, U.S. Dist. Ct. (ea. dist.) Pa. 1985, DC 1986. Jud. clk. Superior Ct. Pa., Allentown, 1985-86; atty. Pa. Power & Light Co., Allentown,

1986-87; corp. counsel food and drug law Lemmon Co., Sellersville, Pa., 1987-88; sr. dep. atty. bur. consumer protection plain lang. law (Notable cases include: Waste Conversion case, 1990, violation of Pa. Solid Waste Mgmt. Act.) Office of Atty. Gen., Harrisburg, Pa., 1988-96; prof. Villanova U. Sch. Law, 1996-2000; prof. food and drug law Temple U. Sch. Pharmacy, Phila., 1998—, St. Joseph U., 2000—. Adj. prof. Widener U. Sch. Law, 1993—, Dickinson Sch. Law; specialized food, drug, cosmetic and med. device law course dir. pres.'s coun. Immaculata Coll.; on-line distance learning legal issues pharmacy promotion and legal environ. bus. St. Joseph U., 2002—; instr. online exec. MBA program Drexel U., 2002—; spkr. in field. Author: Food, Drug and Medical Device Law: Topics and Cases, 2001, Health Law: Federal Regulation of Drugs, 2003, Biologics, 2003, Medical Devices, 2003, Foods and Dietary Supplements, 2003, Statutory Supplement and Teacher's Manual, 2003; contbr. articles to profl. jours.;: 2d edit., 2004. Active Sr. Citizens Project Outreach, Hospice, 1986—; mem. St. Thomas More Law Bd. Mem.: ABA (mem. various coms.), Pa. Bar Assn. (ethics, exceptional children and environ. sects., Plain English award 1999), Bar Assn. DC, Drexel U. Alumni Assn., Temple U. Law Alumni Assn., Phi Alpha Delta, Omicron Nu. Avocations: tap dancing, hiking, cross country skiing. E-mail: rtermini@attorney.com., info@fortipublications.com.

TERNBERG, JESSIE LAMOIN, pediatric surgeon; b. Corning, Calif., May 28, 1924; d. Eric G. and Alta M. (Jones) T. AB, Grinnell Coll., 1946, Sc.D. (hon.), 1970; PhD, U. Tex., 1950; MD, Washington U., St. Louis, 1953; Sc.D. (hon.), U. Mo., St. Louis, 1981. Diplomate: Am. Bd. Surgery. Asst. resident in surgery Barnes Hosp., St. Louis, 1954-57, resident in surgery, 1958-59; rsch. fellow Washington U. Sch. Medicine, 1957-58; practice medicine specializing in pediatric surgery St. Louis, 1966—; intern Boston City Hosp., 1963—64; instr., trainee in surgery Washington U., 1959-62, asst. prof. surgery, 1962-65, assoc. prof. surgery, prof., 1965-71, prof. surgery, 1971-96, chief divsn. pediatric surgery, 1972-90, prof. emeritus, 1996—; mem. staff Barnes Hosp., 1959—90; gen. surgeon in chief Children's Hosp. of St. Louis, 1974-90. Mem. staff Children's Hosp., dir. pediatric surgery, 1972-90. Contbr. numerous articles on pediatric surgery to profl. jours. Trustee Grinnell Coll., 1984—. Recipient Alumni award Grinnell Coll., 1966, Faculty/Alumni award Washington U. Sch. Medicine, 1991, 1st Aphrodite Jannopaulo Hofsommer award, 1993, Local Legend Changing the Face of Medicine award AMWA. Fellow AAAS; mem. SIOP, Am. Pediatric Surg. Assn., We. Surg. Assn. (2d v.p. 1984-85), St. Louis Med. Soc., Soc. Surgery of the Alimentary Tract, Am. Acad. Pediatrics, Soc. Pelvic Surgeons (v.p. 1991-92), Brit. Assn. Paediatric Surgeons, Assn. Women Surgeons (disting. mem. 1995), Mo. State Surg. Soc., St. Louis Surg. Soc. (pres. 1980-81), St. Louis Pediatric Soc., Soc. Surg. Oncology, Pediatric Oncology Group (chmn. surg. discipline 1983-96), St. Louis Childrens Hosp. Soc. (pres. 1979-80), Acad. Sci. St. Louis (Trustees award 2002), St. Louis Met. Med. Soc. (hon., councilor, trustee), Barnes Hosp. Soc., Phi Beta Kappa, Sigma Xi, Iota Sigma Pi, Alpha Omega Alpha. Office: St Louis Childrens Hosp 1 Childrens Pl Saint Louis MO 63110-1002 E-mail: ternbergj@msnotes.wustl.edu.

TERNUS, MARSHA K. state supreme court justice; b. Vinton, Iowa, May 30, 1951; BA, U. Iowa, 1972; JD, Drake U., 1977. Bar: Iowa 1977, Ariz. 1984. With Bradshaw, Fowler, Proctor & Fairgrave, Des Moines, 1977—93; justice Iowa Supreme Ct., Des Moines, 1993—. Editor-in-chief: Drake Law Rev., 1976—77. Mem.: Polk County Bar Assn. (pres. 1984—85), Order of Coif, Phi Beta Kappa. Office: Iowa Supreme Ct Jud Br Bldg 1111 E Court Ave Des Moines IA 50319-0001*

TERP, THOMAS THOMSEN, lawyer; b. Fountain Hill, Pa., Aug. 12, 1947; s. Norman T. and Josephine (Uhran) T.; m. Pamela Robinson; children: Stephanie, Brian, Adam; step-children: Taylor Mefford, Grace Mefford. BA, Albion (Mich.) Coll., 1969; JD, Coll. of William and Mary, 1973. Bar: Ohio 1973, U.S. Dist. Ct. (so. dist.) Ohio 1973, U.S. Ct. Appeals (6th cir.) 1973, U.S. Supreme Ct. 1979. Assoc. Taft, Stettinius & Hollister, Cin., 1973-80, ptnr., 1981—. Bd. dirs. Starflo Corp., Orangeburg, S.C., Attorneys' Liability Assurance Soc., Ltd., Hamilton, Bermuda, ALAS, Inc., Chgo. Editor-in-chief William & Mary Law Rev., 1972-73; mem. bd. editors Jour. of Environ. Hazards, 1988—, Environ. Law Jour. of Ohio, 1989—. Mem. Cin. Athletic Club, Camargo Club, Epworth Assembly (Ludington, Mich.), Lincoln Hills Golf Club (Ludington), Queen City Club. Avocations: tennis, golf, travel. E-mail: terp@taftlaw.com.

TERPELUK, PETER, JR., ambassador; b. Pa., Feb. 1948; Bachelors Degree, LaSalle Coll.; MPA, Rider Coll. Founder Terpeluk and Assocs., 1986—93; prin. Wojdak and Assocs., Washington, 1989—93; mng. dir. Am. Continental Group, 1994—2002; U.S. amb. to Luxembourg Dept. of State, Washington, 2002—. Active U.S. SBA, 1981—84; bd. dirs. Pa. Ave. Devel. Commn.; town mgr. Pa., 1972. Office: Am Embassy Luxembourg 5380 Luxembourg Pl Washington DC 20521

TERPENING, DONALD LESTER, science educator, medical technologist; b. Poughkeepsie, N.Y., Nov. 13, 1949; s. Kenneth B. and Marion A. T.; m. Barbara Hale, Nov. 23, 1974; children: Ethan Kenneth, Nathaniel Albert. BA in Biology, Marist Coll., 1973; MS in Med. Biology, C.W. Post Col. Long Island U., 1975. Lab tech. Vassar Bros. Hosp., Poughkeepsie, N.Y., 1969-71, med. tech., 1971-73, supervisor hematology dept., 1973-74; prog. dir. med. lab. tech. prog. Ulster County C.C., Stone Ridge, N.Y., 1976-81, biology prof., 1975—. Dir. tchg. ctr. Ulster County C.C., Stone Ridge, N.Y., 1997-2000; mem. exec. com. Ulster County C.C. Faculty Senate, 2000—, chmn., 2000-2002. Pres. Ulster Adv. Council, Kingston, N.Y., 1978-83; chmn. Recreation Com., Town of Olive, West Shoken, N.Y., 1992-99. Recipient SUNY Chancellor's award for excellence in tchg., 2003. Mem. Am. Soc. Clinical Pathologists, Empire State Assn. Two Year Coll. Biologists (treas. 2000—). Avocations: muzzle-loading sports, archery, woodworking, revolutionary war reenactor. Office: Ulster County CC Cottekill Rd Stone Ridge NY 12484 E-mail: terpenid@sunyulster.edu.

TERPENING, VIRGINIA ANN, artist; b. Lewistown, Mo., July 17, 1917; d. Floyd Raymond and Bertha Edda (Rodifer) Shoup; m. Charles W. Terpening, July 5, 1951; 1 child by previous marriage, V'Ann Baltzelle Deatrick. Student, William Woods Coll., Fulton, Mo., 1936-37, Washington U. Sch. Fine Arts, St. Louis, 1937-40. Lectr. on art; jurist for selection of art for exhibits Labelle (Mo.) Centennial, 1972; chmn. Centennial Art Show, Lewistown, 1971, Bicentennial, 1976; dir. exhibit high sch. student for N.E. Mo. State U., 1974; supt. ann. art show Lewis County (Mo.) Fair, 1975-90. One-woman shows include Culver-Stockton Coll., Canton, Mo., 1956, Creative Gallery, N.Y.C., 1968, The Breakers, Palm Beach, Fla., 1976, others; group shows include Mo. Ann. Show, City Art Mus., St. Louis, 1956, 65, Madison Gallery, N.Y.C., 1960, Ligoa Duncan Gallery, N.Y.C., 1964, 78, Two Flags Festival of Art, Douglas, Ariz., 1975, 78-79, Internat. Art Exhibit, El Centro, Calif., 1977, 78, Salon des Nations, Paris, 1985, UN World Conf. of Women, Narobi, Kenya, 1985, William Woods Coll., Fulton, Mo., 1992-95, La Junta Coll. Art League Internat., 1992, 94, Coffret Musée, Paris, 1995; represented in permanent collection Nat. Mus. of Women in Art, 1990; executed Mississippi RiverBoat oil painting presented to Pres. Carter by Lewis County Dem. Com., Canton, 1979. Mem. Lewistown Bicentennial Hist. Soc.; charter mem. Canton Area Arts Coun. of N.E. Mo. Recipient Cert. of Merit Latham Found., 1960-63, Mo. Women's Festival of Art, 1974, Bertrand Russell Peace Found., 1973, Gold Medallion award Two flags Festival of Art, 1975, Safeco purchase award El Centro (Calif.) Internat. Art Exhibit, 1977, 1st Pl. award LaJunta (Colo.) Fine Arts League, 1981, diploma Univ. Delle Arti, Parma, Italy, 1981, Purchase award Two Flags Art Festival, 1981, award Assn. Conservation and Mo. Dept. Conservation Art Exhibit, 1982, Purchase award Canton Area Arts Coun., 1988, Colorado Springs Art Festival, 1989; paintings selected for Competition '84 Guide by Nat. Art Appreciation Soc., 1984, 1st Pl. award New Orleans Internat. Art Exhibit, 1984, Two Flags Festival of Art, 1986, Sunflower Judges award Harlin Mus., West Plains, Mo., 1994, Key to City, Lifetime award, 1998; named artist laureate, Nepenthe Mondi Soc., 1984. Mem. Artist Equity Assn., Internat. Soc. Artists, Internat. Platform Assn., Nat. Mus. Women in Art (charter), Animal Protection Inst. Mem. Christian Ch. (Disciples Of Christ). Address: 105 S Vine St PO Box 117 Lewistown MO 63452-0117

TERPENNY, JANIS P. engineering educator, researcher; d. Herbert W. and Betty C. Pinchefsky; m. Walter E. Terpenny, June 10, 1979; children: Jonathan L., Jason W. BS in Math. Sciences with honors, Va. Commonwealth U., 1979; MS in Indsl. Engring. & Ops. Rsch., Va. Poly. Inst. & State U., 1981, PhD in Indsl. & Systems Engring., 1996. Info. systems mgmt. program GE - Dr. Systems, Salem, Va., 1982—84; systems analyst GE - Consumer Electronics, Portsmouth, 1984—87; tchg. asst. Va. Tech., Blacksburg, 1990—96, instr., 1996—97; asst. prof. U. Mass., Amherst, 1999—2004; assoc. prof. Va. Tech., Blacksburg, 2004—. Dir. Systems Modeling and Realization Technologies Lab., U. Mass., Amherst, 1999—2004; faculty advisor Inst. Indsl. Engring., U. Mass., 1999—; vis. asst. prof. Va. Tech., Blacksburg, 1997—98; co-dir. NSF Ctr. for e-Design. Contbr. articles to profl. jours. Team capt. for ann. relay for life event Am. Cancer Soc., Roanoke, Va., 1996—98; vol. in fundraising activities for numerous organizations (leukemia soc., am. cancer soc., mar. of dimes, bone marrow registry) Roanoke, VA and Amherst, MA, 1992—2003; chair of cmty. concerns com., edn. programs Unitarian Universalist Ch., Roanoke, 1996—98. Recipient Outstanding Faculty Advisor award, IIE Student Chpt., U. of Mass., 1999, Nat. Best Paper award, ASEE, 2002; fellow Charles Minor fellow, Va. Tech. Coll. Engring., 1991—96. Mem.: ASME, Math. Assn. of Am., Soc. Women Engrs., Am. Soc. Engring. Edn. (sec.-treas. engring. economy divsn. 2002—03, program chair 2003—04), Inst. Indsl. Engrs. (Bronze Recognition award 2002—03), Alpha Pi Mu. Achievements include research in engineering design and design automation; development of internet-based systems for engring. design and engring. edn. Office: U Mass Mech & Indsl Engring Amherst MA 01003-9265 Business E-Mail: terpenny@vt.edu.

TERR, ABBA ISRAEL, allergist, immunologist; b. Cleve., 1930; MD, Case Western Res. U., 1956. Diplomate Am. Bd. Allergy and Immunology. Intern U. Wis. Hosps., Madison, 1956-57; resident in internal medicine U. Mich. Med. Ctr., Ann Arbor, 1957-60, fellow in allergy, 1960-62; physician Stanford (Calif.) U. Med. Ctr. and U. Calif. SF Med. Ctr.; clin. prof. medicine U. Calif. Med. Ctr., San Francisco. Fellow ACP, Am. Acad. Allergy, Asthma, and Immunology; mem. Am. Thoracic Soc. Address: 450 Sutter St Rm 2534 San Francisco CA 94108-4204 E-mail: abbaterrmed@attglobal.net.

TERR, LENORE CAGEN, psychiatrist, writer; b. N.Y.C., Mar. 27, 1936; d. Samuel Lawrence and Esther (Hirsch) Cagen; m. Abba I. Terr; children: David, Julia. AB magna cum laude, Case Western Res. U., 1957; MD with honors, U. Mich., 1961. Diplomate Am. Bd. Psychiatry and Neurology, Subspecialty Bd. Child and Adolescent Psychiatry. Intern U. Mich. Med. Ctr., Ann Arbor, 1961-62; resident Neuropsychiat. Inst. U. Mich., Ann Arbor, 1962-64, fellow Children's Psychiat. Hosp., 1964-66; from instr. to asst. prof. Case Western Res. U. Med. Sch., Cleve., 1966-71; pvt. practice Terr Med. Corp., San Francisco, 1971—; from asst. clin. prof. to clin. prof. psychiatry Sch. Medicine U. Calif., San Francisco, 1971—. Lectr. law, psychiatry U. Calif., Berkeley, 1971—90, Davis, 1974—88; dir. Am. Bd. Psychiatry and Neurology, 1988—96, chair psychiatry coun., 1996. Author: Too Scared to Cry, 1990, Unchained Memories, 1994, Beyond Love and Work, 1999; contbr. articles to profl. jours.; exhibited works in art show at Canessa Gallery, San Francisco, 2002. Named to Cleveland Heights H.S. Disting Alumni Hall of Fame, 2003; recipient Career Tchr. award, NIMH, 1967—69, Child Advocacy award, APA, 1994; grantee, William T. Grant Found., 1986—87, Leon Lowenstein Found., 2002; scholar-in-residence, Rockefeller Found., Italy, 1981, 1988, project grantee, Rosenberg Found., 1977. Fellow: Am. Acad. Child and Adolescent Psychiatry (coun. 1984—87), Am. Coll. Psychiatrists (program chair 1991—92, Bowis award 1993), Am. Psychiat. Assn. (Child Psychiatry Rsch. award 1984, Clin. Rsch. award 1987, Marmor Sci. award 2002); mem.: Phi Bet Kappa, Alpha Omega Alpha. Avocations: piano, walking, travel, gardening, needlepoint. Office: Terr Med Corp 450 Sutter St Rm 2534 San Francisco CA 94108-4204 Office Phone: 415-433-7800.

TERRAGNO, PAUL JAMES, information industry executive; b. Ogden, Utah, May 17, 1938; s. Charles L. and Florence E. (Gabardi) T.; m. Nancy Robinson, Aug. 26, 1961; children— Thomas C., Paul A., Teresa A. BA, U. Utah, 1960; MS, U. Wyo., 1962. Vice pres. Westat, Inc., Rockville, Md., 1962-70; vice pres. Remac Information, Gaithersburg, Md., 1970-76; dir. U.S. Patent Office, Washington, 1976-80; v.p. Pergamon Internat., McLean, Va., 1980-84; pres. Pergamon InfoLine, McLean, Va., 1984-87, Pergamon ORBIT InfoLine, McLean, 1987-89, Maxwell Online, Inc., 1989-92. Pres. Pergamon Orbit InfoLine, Ltd., London, 1984-89, Pergabase, Inc., Gainesville, Fla., 1985-92, pres. Topate Info. Svcs. Inc., 1992-97; dir. Eagle Design and Mgmt., Inc., Bethesda, Md. Contbr. articles to various publs. Mem. Am. Soc. Info. Sci. Roman Catholic. Office: 7830 Old Georgetown Rd Bethesda MD 20814-2432 Home: Apt 8108 306 Prettyman Dr Rockville MD 20850-7706 E-mail: terragno@comcast.net.

TERRAS, AUDREY ANNE, mathematics professor; b. Washington, Sept. 10, 1942; d. Stephen Decatur and Maude Mae Bowdoin. BS with high honors in Math., U. Md., 1964; MA, Yale U., 1966, PhD, 1970. Instr. U. Ill., Urbana, 1968-70; asst. prof. U. P.R., Mayaguez, 1970-71, Bklyn. Coll., CUNY, 1971-72; asst. prof. math. U. Calif.-San Diego, La Jolla, 1972-76, assoc. prof., 1976-83, prof., 1983—. Prin. investigator NSF, 1974-88; vis. positions U. Aachen, Germany, 1998, Tsuda Coll., Tokyo, 1999, MIT, fall 1977, 83, U. Bonn (W.Ger.), spring 1977, Inst. Mittag-Leffler, Stockholm, winter, 1978, Inst. Advanced Study, spring 1984, Math. Scis. Rsch. Inst., Berkeley, Calif., winter 1992, spring 1995, CRM, U. Montreal, 1999, others; dir. West Coast Number Theory Conf., U. Calif.-San Diego, 1976, AMS joint summer rsch. conf., 1984; lectr. in field. Author: Harmonic Analysis on Symmetric Spaces and Applications, Vol. I, 1985, Vol. II, 1988, Fourier Analysis on Finite Groups and Applications, 1999; editor: The Selberg Trace Formula and Related Topics, 1986; contbr. chapters to books, articles to profl. jours. Woodrow Wilson fellow, 1964, NSF fellow, 1964-68; NSF grantee Summer Inst. in Number Theory, Ann Arbor, Mich., 1973. Fellow: AAAS (nominating com. math. sect. project 2061); mem.: Assn. for Women in Sci., Assn. for Women in Math. (travel grants com. 1996), Soc. Indsl. and Applied Math., Math. Assn. Am. (program com. for nat. meeting 1988—90, chair joint program com. Am. Math. Soc. and Math. Assn. Am. 1991), Am. Math. Soc. (com. employment and ednl. policy com. on coms., coun., trans. editor, com. for the yr. 2000, western sect. program com., assoc. editor book revs. Bull., assoc. editor Notices). Achievements include research in harmonic analysis on symmetric spaces and number theory. Office: U Calif San Diego Dept Math La Jolla CA 92093-0112

TERREAULT, CHARLES, engineer, management educator, researcher; b. Montreal, Que., Can., Mar. 21, 1935; s. Charles Terreault and Antonia Clark; m. Marie Rolland, Sept. 10, 1960; children: Genevieve, François, Patrick, Olivier-Hugues. BA, Coll. Stanislas, Montreal, 1954; BA in Sci., Ecole Poly., Montreal, 1959; hon. doctorate, U. Que., 1986. Engr. Bell Can., Montreal, 1959-65, staff engr., 1967-69, chief engr., 1971-73, asst. v.p. rsch., 1978-91, v.p. tech. devel., 1979—96; rschr. Bell Telephone Labs., Holmdel, NJ, 1965-67; dir. planning Bell No. Rsch., Ottawa, Ont., Can., 1969-71, v.p. systems engring. Montreal, 1973-78; Jvr Cyr prof. mgmt. tech. Ecole Poly., Montreal, 1991-96. Bd. dirs. Natural Scis. and Engring. Rsch. Coun. Can., Ottawa; treas., Dr. Clown; chmn. Can. Inst. Telecomm. Rsch. Contbr. articles to profl. jours. Fellow IEEE (Armstrong award 1984), Canadian Acad. Engring., Ordre Ingénieurs de Que., Que. Assn. Indsl. Rsch. (Annual award 1992). Avocations: computers, classical music, skiing. Home and Office: 1665 Victoria Ave # 804 Saint-Lambert QC Canada J4R 2T6 E-mail: cterreault@sympatico.ca.

TERREL, JAMES E. controller; b. Elyria, Ohio, June 28, 1949; BS in Acctg., Miami U., 1971, MBA in Fin. & Acctg., 1972. CPA 1972. Sr. acct. Ernst & Whinney, 1972—76; fin. acct. Internat. Harvester Co., 1976—77, sr. ops. analyst, 1977—78, mgr. fin. components group, 1978—81, mgr. spl. fin. projects, 1981, mgr. mfg. analysis, 1981—83; dir. external reporting Ga. Pacific, Atlanta, 1983—84, controller fin. reporting, 1984—87, group controller, 1987—89, v.p., controller, 1989—91, 1991—. Mem.: AICPA, Inst. Mgmt. Accts., Ga. Soc. CPA's, Fin. Execs. Internat. (mem. nat. com. corp. reporting). Office: GA Pacific 133 Peachtree St NE Atlanta GA 30303

TERREL, RONALD LEE, civil engineer, business executive, educator; b. Klamath Falls, Oreg., Sept. 2, 1936; s. Theodore Thomas and Ruth Margaret (Fausset) T.; m. Susan Laura Harrower, Feb. 28, 1959 (div. July 1981); children: Douglas Scott, Nancy Dawn, Janet Lynn; m. 2d Alice Marie Blanchard, July 23, 1981. BSC.E., Purdue U., 1960, MS, 1961; PhD, U. Calif.-Berkeley, 1967. Estimator J.H. Pomeroy & Co., San Francisco, 1955; lab. asst. Purdue U., 1956-60; asst. field geologist Bear Creek Mining Co., Mpls., 1957-58; materials engr. U.S. Bur. Reclamation, Denver, 1960-64; project engr. J.H. Pomeroy & Co., Antigua, B.W.I. and, Calif., 1964-65; rsch. asst. U. Calif.-Berkeley, 1965-67; asst. prof. civil engr. U. Wash., Seattle, 1967-70, assoc. prof., 1970-75, prof., 1975-85, prof. emeritus, 1985—, head Transp. Constrn. and Geometronics divsn., 1976-79; prof., sr. rschr. Oreg. State U., 1989-94; pres. Pavement Systems Inc., 1970-82; exec. v.p. Seattle Engring. Internat., Inc., 1979-81; pres. Terrel Assocs., Inc., 1981-85; owner Terrel Rsch. LLC, 1986—; v.p. Pavement Techs. Inc., 1985-86; chmn., CEO RL Techs. LLC, 1996—. Bd. dirs., v.p. Hydrogenesis, Inc.; cons. in field. Patentee in field. Co-founder, dir. Wash. State Transp. Ctr., 1981-84. Nominated Constrn. Man of Yr. Engring. News-Record, 1972; Recipient Disting. Svc. award The Asphalt Inst., 2004; Ford fellow, 1965-67; Purdue Alumni scholar, 1959-60. Mem. ASTM, ASCE, Tranps. Rsch. Bd., Assn. Asphalt Paving Technologists (bd. dirs. 1979-83, Emmons award 1983, 95, award of merit 1990), Triaxial Inst. (chmn. 1971-73), Can. Tech. Asphalt Assn., Internat. Soc. for Asphalt Pavements (founding mem. 1987), Sigma Xi, Tau Beta Pi, Chi Epsilon, Sigma Gamma Epsilon. Office: 9703 241st Pl SW Edmonds WA 98020-6512 Office Phone: 206-542-9223. Personal E-mail: rterrel@comcast.net.

TERRELL, A. JOHN, retired university telecommunications director; b. Pasadena, Calif., Dec. 27, 1927; s. Harry Evans and Elizabeth (Eaton) T.; m. Elizabeth Schalk, June 6, 1949; children: Patricia Elyse, Marilee Diane, John Scott. Student, Chaffey Coll., 1947-48; BBA, U. N.Mex., 1952. Communications cons. Mountain States Tel. & Tel., Albuquerque, 1951-56; mgr. office and communications services A.C.F. Industries, Inc., Albuquerque, 1956-62; mgr. communications and services Norton Simon Industries, Inc., Fullerton, Calif., 1962-68; v.p. gen. mgr. Wells Fargo Security Guard Service div. Baker Industries, Fullerton, 1968-71; adminstrv. mgr., budget adminstr. Hyland div. Baxter-Travenol Labs. Inc., Costa Mesa, Calif., 1971-77; exec. v.p. Am. Tel. Mgmt. Inst. Inc., Newport Beach, Calif., 1977-78; telecommunications dir. UCLA, 1978-89; ret., 1989. Contbr. articles to profl. jours. Rep. candidate for state rep., Albuquerque, 1960; precinct chmn. and mem. Barnalillo County Rep. Central Com., 1961-62; Rep. candidate for N.Mex. State Bd. Edn., 2d Jud. Dist., 1962; colonial aide-de-camp Gov. N.Mex., Santa Fe, 1968. Served with U.S. Mct. Marine, 1944-45, U.S. Army, 1946-47, USAR, 1947-50. Mem. Nat. Assn. Accts. (dir. 1967-77, Most Valuable Mem. 1974-75), Am. Legion, VFW. Lodges: Greater Irvine Lions (charter pres. 1975-76), U.S. Merchant Marines Vets. of WWII, 82nd Airborne Div. Assn., Albuquerque Jaycees (v.p., treas. 1956-62). Episcopalian. Home: 2727 Island View Dr Corona Del Mar CA 92625-1309 E-mail: ajterrell@uclalumni.net.

TERRELL, G. IRVIN, lawyer; b. Houston, Sept. 28, 1946; s. George I. and Adella (Weichert) T.; m. Karen Steenberg, Jan. 8, 1984; 1 child, Katharine. BA, U. Tex., 1968, JD, 1972. Bar: Tex., U.S. Supreme Ct., U.S. Ct. Appeals (3d and 5th cirs.), U.S. Dist. Ct. (so., no. and ea. dists.) Tex., U.S. Dist. Ct. (we. dist.) Pa. Assoc. Baker & Botts, Houston, 1972-79, ptnr., 1980—. Mem. ABA, Houston Bar Assn., Internat. Soc. Barristers. E-mail: irv.terrell@bakerbotts.com.

TERRELL, HOWARD BRUCE, psychiatrist; b. Feb. 19, 1952; BS magna cum laude, Calif. State U., Hayward, 1974; MD, U. Calif., San Diego, 1980. Diplomate in psychiatry and in forensic psychiatry Am. Bd. Psychiatry and Neurology. Intern. Kaiser Found. Hosp., Oakland, Calif., 1980-81; resident in psychiatry U. Calif., San Francisco/Fresno, 1982-85; staff psychiatrist Kings View Corp., Reedley, Calif., 1985-87, sr. staff psychiatrist, 1987-88, dir. outpatient psychiatry, 1988-89; dir. dual diagnosis and affective disorders programs Sierra Gateway Hosp., Clovis, Calif., 1989-91. Asst. clin. prof. psychiatry U. Calif. Sch. Medicine, San Francisco; lectr. in field. Contbr. articles to profl. jours. Fellow Am. Coll. Forensic Psychiatry, Am. Psychiat. Assn.; mem. Am. Acad. Psychiatry and the Law, Ctrl. Calif. Psychiat. Soc. (pres. Sierra chpt. 1996-98). Avocations: golf, computers, photography, enology, music. Office: 3100 Willow Ave Ste 102 Clovis CA 93612-4741

TERRELL, J. ANTHONY, lawyer; b. N.Y.C., Sept. 20, 1943; s. Claude M. and Kathleen L. (Prevost) T.; m. Karen E. Terrell, Aug. 8, 1969; 1 child, Elizabeth S. BA, NYU, 1965, LLM in Taxation, 1975; JD, Villanova U., 1968. Bar: N.Y. With Frueauff, Farrell, Sullivan & Bryan, N.Y.C., 1970-74, ptnr., 1974; assoc. Thelen Reid & Priest LLP, N.Y.C., 1974-76, ptnr., 1977—. Mem. ABA (sect. bus. law, sect. pub. utility, comm. and transp. law, vice chmn. corp. finance com.), Internat. Bar Assn. (bus. law sect.), Nat. Assn. Bond Lawyers, Belle Haven Club, Met. Club, Coral Beach and Tennis Club. Home: Indian Harbor Greenwich CT 06830 Office: Thelen Reid & Priest LLP 40 W 57th St New York NY 10019-4097 also: Dewey Ballantine LLP 1301 Avenue of the Americas New York NY 10019 Address: 101 Oneida Dr Greenwich CT 06830

TERRELL, JAMES DANIEL, lawyer; b. Kansas City, Oct. 22, 1956; s. D. Ronald and Bobbie L. (Graham) T.; m. Lori J. McAlister, May 31, 1980; children: Justin Daniel, Christopher James, Alexander Graham. BS, Ctrl. Mo. State U., 1979; JD, U. Mo., 1982. Bar: Mo. 1982, U.S. Dist. Ct. (we. dist.) 1982, U.S. Dist. Ct. (ea. dist.) Mo. 1984. Assoc. Wasinger, Parham & Morthland, Hannibal, Mo., 1982-87; ptnr. Wasinger, Parham, Morthland Terrell & Wasinger, Hannibal, 1987—. Bd. dirs. Marion County Svcs. for the Developmentally Disabled, Hannibal, 1989—. Mem.: 10th Jud. Cir. Bar Assn. (pres. 2001—), Mo. Bar Assn. (family law sect.), U. Mo. Alumni Assn. (life), Phi Delta Phi. Office: Wasinger Parham Morthland Terrell & Wasinger 2801 Saint Marys Ave Hannibal MO 63401-3775

TERRELL, W(ILLIAM) GLENN, university president emeritus; b. Tallahassee, May 24, 1920; s. William Glenn and Esther (Collins) T.; m. Gail Strandberg Terrell; children by previous marriage: Francine Elizabeth, William Glenn III. BA, Davidson Coll., 1942, LLD (hon.), 1969; MS, Fla. State U., 1948; PhD, State U. Iowa, 1952; LLD (hon.), Gonzaga U., 1984, Seattle U., 1985. Instr., then asst. prof. Fla. State U., Tallahassee, 1948-55; assoc. prof., then assoc. prof., chmn. dept. psychology U. Colo., Boulder, 1955—63, acting dean Coll Arts and Scis., 1963-65; prof. psychology, dean Coll. Liberal Arts and Scis., U. Ill. at Chgo., 1963-65, dean faculties, 1965-67; pres. Wash. State U., Pullman, 1967-85, pres. emeritus, 1985—. Pres. Nat. Assn. State Univs. and Land-Grant Colls., 1977-78; cons. The Pacific Inst., Seattle, 1987—. Author The Ministry of Leadership, 2002; Contbr. articles to profl. jours. Served to capt. inf. U.S. Army, 1942-46, ETO. Recipient Disting. Alumnus award U. Iowa, 1985; Disting. Grad. Dept. Psychology, U. Iowa, 1996. Fellow APA, Soc. Rsch. in Child Devel.; mem. AAAS, Sigma Xi, Phi Kappa Phi. Avocations: golf, reading, travel. Home: 2438 36th Ave W Seattle WA 98199-3704 Office: The Pacific Inst 1709 Harbor Ave SW Seattle WA 98126-2073 Office Phone: 206-628-4800. E-mail: gterrell@pac-inst.com.

TERRILL, KAREN STAPLETON, retired medical planning consultant; b. Milw., Mar. 21, 1939; d. Thomas John and Olive Patrea (Thorbjornsen) Stapleton; m. Max Kurt Winkler, Dec. 18, 1965 (dec. June 1976); m. Richard Terrill, Jan. 23, 1991 (dec. May 1991). BS in Nursing, U. Mich., 1961; MBA, U. Nev., 1974. RN, Calif. Project nurse Langley Porter N.P.I., San Francisco, 1962-64; asst. dir. nursing Milw. County Mental Health Ctr., 1964-66; instr. Fond du Lac (Wis.) Sch. Dist., 1966-67; sch. nurse Inglewood (Calif.) Sch. Dist., 1968-69; instr. nursing U. Nev., Reno, 1969-74; health planner manpower State of Nev. Comp B. Agy., Carson City, 1974-75; planning analyst St. Mary's Hosp., Reno, 1974-76; sr. system analyst U. Calif., San Francisco, 1976-79; med. planning cons. Stone Marraccini & Patterson, San Francisco, 1979-93. Mem. citizen's adv. group City of Richmond, Calif., 1987-88; founding dir. of B.O.A.T. non-profit corp. to promote ferry transit on San Francisco Bay. Mountain State Regional Planning Commn. grantee, 1973-74. Home: 1308 Mallard Dr Richmond CA 94801-4113 E-mail: ktturkish@aol.com.

TERRILL, ROBERT CARL, hospital administrator; b. Oklahoma City, Dec. 10, 1927; s. D. Willard and Velma (Mitchell) T.; m. Jessica Doe, Dec. 14, 1957; children: Thane Bennett, Sarah Haven. BA, U. Okla., 1948, MA in History, 1961; MA in Hosp. Adminstrn., State U. Iowa, 1954; EdD in Edn1. Adminstrn., Ind. U., 1978. Adminstrv. resident Mary Fletcher Hosp., Burlington, Vt., 1953-55, asst. adminstr., pers. dir., 1955-57, assoc. adminstr., 1957-65; adminstr. Hosps. of U. Okla., Okla. City, 1965-72; dir. Ind. Univ. Hosps., Indpls., 1972-77; assoc. prof. Coll. Mgmt. U. Mass., Boston, 1977-87; preceptor in hosp. adminstrn. Washington U., St. Louis, Trinity U., San Antonio; asst. prof. U. Okla. Health Scis. Center. Pub. edn. planning svcs. corp., 1987—. Fellow Am. Coll. Hosp. Adminstrs.; mem. Mass. Hosp. Assn., Am. Hosp. Assn., Assn. Programs Hosp. Adminstrn., Pub. Health Assn., New Eng. Hosp. Assembly, Nat. League Nursing, State U. Iowa. Alumni Assn., Ind. U. Alumni Assn. Clubs: Rotarian. Home: 30 N Sandyside Ln Yarmouth Port MA 02675-1749 Office: 923 Old Kings Hwy Yarmouth Port MA 02675 E-mail: robertterrill@comcast.net.

TERRILL, ROSS GLADWIN, writer, educator; b. Melbourne, Australia; arrived in U.S., 1965, naturalized, 1979; s. Frank and Miriel (Lloyd) Terrill. BA with honors, U. Melbourne; PhD, Harvard U., 1970. Tutor in polit. sci. U. Melbourne, 1962-63; staff sec. Australian Student Christian Movement, 1964-65; tchg. fellow Harvard U., 1968-70, lectr. govt., 1970-73, assoc. prof., 1974-78, rsch. assoc. E. Asian studies, 1970—, dir. student programs Ctr. Internat. Affairs, 1974-78; contbg. editor Atlantic Monthly, 1970-84; rsch. fellow Asia Soc., 1977—79. Vis. prof. U. Tex., Austin, 1999—. Author: China Profile, 1969, China and Ourselves, 1971, 800,000,000: The Real China, 1972, R. H. Tawney and His Times, 1973, Flowers on an Iron Tree, 1975, The Future of China, 1978, The China Difference, 1979, Mao: A Biography, 1980, rev., 2000, White-Boned Demon, 1984, The Australians, 1987, Madam Mao, 1992, rev., 1999, China in Our Time, 1992, The Australians: How We Live Now, 2000, The New Chinese Empire, 2003; contbr. articles to profl. jours. Recipient Sumner prize, 1970, Nat. Mag. award, 1972, George Polk Meml. award outstanding mag. reporting, 1972, Book prize, L.A. Times, 2003. Mem.: PEN, Authors Guild, Harvard Club (N.Y.C.). Home: PO Box 230772 Astor Station Boston MA 02123-0772 Office Phone: 617-445-2542. E-mail: terr@compuserve.com.

TERRILL, THOMAS EDWARD, health facility administrator; b. Mpls., Oct. 4, 1939; BS, U. Minn., 1961; M in Health Care Adminstrn., U. Pitts., 1963, DS, 1970. Adminstrv. resident Homestead (Pa.) Hosp., 1962-63; adminstrv. asst. Truman Med. Ctr.-West, Kanasas City, Mo., 1963-65, asst. adminstr., 1965-67; asst. prof. U. Pitts., 1967-73, assoc. prof., 1973-74; dir. mktg. and planning Mountain States Regional Med. Program, Boise, Idaho, 1974-76, divsn. dir., 1976-77; v.p. Hollywood Presbyn. Med. Ctr., L.A., 1977; assoc. dir. Akron (Ohio) City Hosp., 1978-81, v.p. med. affairs, 1981-83; sr. mgr. Peat Marwick Mitchell, Phila., 1983-87; v.p. Network Inc., Randolph, N.J., 1987-90; exec. v.p. Univ. Health Sys., New Brunswick, N.J., 1990-93, pres., 1994—. Contbr. articles to profl. publs. Office: Univ Health Sys 154 W State St Trenton NJ 08608-1102 Home: 154 W State St Trenton NJ 08608-1102 E-mail: terrillphd@erols.com.

TERRIS, ALBERT, metal sculptor; b. N.Y.C., Nov. 10, 1916; s. Aaron and Fania (Rosenthal) Teraspulsky; children: Susan, Abby, David, Enoch. BSS, CCNY, 1939; postgrad., NYU Inst. Fine Arts, 1939-42. Lectr. Met. Mus. Art, 1941-42; tchr. fine arts N.Y.C. High Sch. System, 1947-54; prof. emeritus Bklyn. Coll., 1947-86. Steel sculptures include Non-Fixed Relationship, 1948, Homely Cosmology, 1948, Anti-Gravity, 1950, Giraffes, 1953, Short Art, 1953, Pro-Gravity Chains, 1956, Tools, 1956, Crushed Sculpture, 1956, Words, 1957, Discursive-Illegible-Boustrophedon, 1975, Plates of Charlemagne, 1975, Fireharps, 1975, Cycle of Life, 1977, Wipes, 1996, Quantum Photography, 1995, Meals, 1998, Visitors, 1998, Twigs Door Music, 2001; one-man shows: Saidenberg, 1955, Duveen-Graham, 1958, Carnegie Internats., 1958, 62, Bklyn. L.I. Artists Bklyn. Mus. (awarded first prize), 1960, Allan Stone, 1962, Critics Choice, 1972, Artists Space, 1975, Gloria Cortella, 1977, (retrospective) The Artist in the Civil Service Bklyn. Coll. Gallery, 1985; exhibited in group shows at Tanager Gallery, 1952-61, Stable Anns., 1952-60, Mus. Modern Art, N.Y.C., 1962, others; represented in permanent collections: Stephen Paine, Boston, Arnold Maremont, Evanston, G. David Thompson Estate, NBC-TV, others. Served with 1st Allied Airborne, 1942-45. Home: 25 Coleman Place Red Bank NJ 07701

TERRIS, LILLIAN DICK, psychologist, association executive; b. Bloomfield, N.J., May 5, 1914; d. Alexander Blaikie and Herminia (Doscher) Dick; m. Louis Long, Apr. 22, 1935 (dec. Sept. 1968); 1 son, Alexander Blaikie Long; m. Milton Terris, Feb. 6, 1971 (dec. Oct. 2002). BA, Barnard Coll., 1935; PhD, Columbia U., 1941. Diplomate Am. Bd. Examiners in Profl. Psychology. Instr. psychology Sarah Lawrence Coll., Bronxville, N.Y., 1937-40; jr. pers. tech. SSA, Washington, 1941; sr. pers. clk. OWI, N.Y.C., 1941-43; dir. profl. examination svc. Am. Pub. Health assn., N.Y.C., 1943-70; pres., 1970-79; pres. emeritus, 1979—. Assoc. editor: Jour. Pub. Health Policy, 1979—; contbr. articles to profl. jours. Recipient Nat. Environ. Health assn. award, 1976, Cert. Svc. award Bd. Preventive Medicine, 1979. Fellow Am. Psychol. Assn., Am. Coll. Hosp. Adminstrs. (hon.); mem. Am. Pub. Health Assn., N.Y. State Psychol. Assn., Phi Beta Kappa, Sigma Xi. Home: 1450 Post St 506 San Francisco CA 94109 Office: 475 Riverside Dr New York NY 10115-0122 E-mail: jphpterris@aol.com.

TERRITO, MARY C. health facility administrator, oncologist, educator; BS in Biology, Wayne State U., 1965, MD, 1968. Intern/resident in internal medicine Parkland Hosp., Dallas, 1971-73; fellow in hematology/oncology Harbor-U. Calif., L.A., 1973-74, UCLA, 1974-75; rsch. assoc. Wadsworth VA Hosp., L.A., 1975-81; asst. prof. dept. medicine UCLA, 1981-86, assoc. prof., 1981-96, prof., 1996—, dir. bone marrow transplant program Ctr. Health Scis., 1981—. Contbr. articles to profl. jours. Office: UCLA Bone Marrow Transplantation Program Ctr 42-121 CHS 10833 Le Conte Ave Los Angeles CA 90095-3075

TERRY, CLIFFORD LEWIS, journalist; b. Highland Park, Ill., Jan. 19, 1937; s. Clifford Lewis and Isabelle (Marlow) T.; m. Patricia West Dickelman, Sept. 1, 1966; children: Christopher West, Scott Marlow. Student, Carleton Coll., Northfield, Minn., 1954-55; BA, Trinity Coll., Hartford, Conn., 1958; postgrad., Columbia U., 1962-63. Tchr., English and history Mt. Hermon (Mass.) Sch., 1958-59; police reporter City News Bur. Chgo., 1959-60; mem. staff Chgo. Tribune, 1960-94, movie critic, 1965-70; assoc. editor Chgo. Tribune (Sunday mag.), 1970-82, feature writer, 1982-85, TV critic, 1985-89, arts feature writer, 1989-94; ind. writer, 1994—. Author: Chicago: Off the Beaten Path, 2001. Served with AUS, 1960. Nieman fellow Harvard U., 1969-70 Mem. Phi Beta Kappa.

TERRY, ELIZABETH HAYS, needlepoint designer; b. Bryn Mawr, Pa., July 29, 1935; d. James Franklin and Mary Ellen (Carmichael) Hays; m. Charles L. Terry, III, Feb. 8, 1958; children: Elizabeth Harllee Carmichael Terry Moran, Charles L. IV. AB, Smith Coll., 1957. Asst. to profs. Harvard U., Cambridge, Mass., 1957-58; art tchr. Exeter (N.H.) Day Sch., 1968-72; asst. editor Phillips Exeter Acad. Alumni Quarterly, 1972-75, dir. alumni records, 1975-85; owner Elizabeth Terry, Needlepoint Design, Exeter, N.H., 1980—. Tchr. needlepoint Guild of Strawbery Banke, Portsmouth, N.H. Dir. for Town of Exeter-Save Our Shores, 1972. Mem. Smith Coll. Class of 1957 (class fund agt. 1972-77, alumnae fund com. 1977-80, class bequest chair 1982—, com. on deferred giving 1990—), N.H. Colonial Dames (pres. 1989-92, nat. historian 1992-94, nat. v.p. 1994-2000). Episcopalian. Avocations: tennis, needlepoint, historic preservation. Home and Office: 77 Brookside Dr Stratham NH 03885-2128 Office Phone: 603-772-8942. E-mail: ceterry@rcn.com.

TERRY, ELIZABETH HUDSON, personal care industry executive, realtor; d. Otis Hudson and (Russell) Evelena; m. Lester Terry; 1 child, Darric. Student, Clark Coll., Atlanta, 1966; BA business, Atlanta Sch. Bus., 1968; student, Dekalb Perimeter Coll., Decatur, Ga., 1978—83; cert. entrepreneurship program, U. Ga., 1993; cert., Speak Easy Sch., Atlanta, 1993. Lic. real estate salesperson Ga., 1996. Asst. dir. Count Jackson Studio, Atlanta, 1968—72; mgr. BellSouth Corp., Atlanta, 1970—97, Bank of Am., Atlanta, 1998—; wedding dir., cons. Weddings by Liz, Decatur, Ga., 1980—, realtor, sales assoc. Coldwell Banker Buckhead Brokers, Tucker, 1996—2000, Quest Realty Inc., Decatur, 2000—. Notary, Decatur; featured in numerous newspapers and mags.; guest appearances on several t.v. and radio shows. Author: Just Think About It, 1993. Mem. Veracruz Homeowners Assn., Decatur, 2001—, Nat. Coalition of 100 Black Women's Assn., NAACP, United Negro Coll. Fund; pub. rels. advisor Uptown Social Club, Decatur; vol. Habitat for Humanity, Atlanta; asst. dir. The Colored People Prodn., Atlanta; program dir. Azusa St. Revival Prodn., 1995; asst. dir., program dir. Fix Me Jesus Prodn., Atlanta; mem. Beulah Bapt. Ch., Decatur; adv. bd., bd. dirs. Suncrest Resources, Inc., Stone Mountain, Ga. Recipient Pearl award, Diamond award, Ruby award, Emerald award, Gold award. Mem.: Chamber of Commerce, Rainbow Internat. chpt. (Am. Bus. Women's Assn.) (founder 1985—86, v.p. 1985—86, pres. 1986—87, chmn. Program Com., Woman of the Year 1985—86), Sphnix chpt. (Am. Bus. Women's Assn.) (exec. bd. secy. 1984, chmn. Extension Com., Woman of the Year 1984—85, Woman of Quarter 1985, Hand of Friendship award), St. Peter and Paul Parent-Teacher Assn., United Coun. for Negro Women Assn., Am. Bus. Women's Assn. (chpt. chmn. adminstrv. bd. 1986—88, chmn. mem. com., chmn. bus. assn. com., chmn. edn./scholarship com.), Sharwood Vacation Assn., Toastmasters (v.p. edn. 2003—04, pres. Bank of Am. 2004—, Competent Toastmaster award 2004). Avocation: writing. Office Phone: 770-374-4900.

TERRY, FREDERICK ARTHUR, JR., lawyer; b. Buffalo, May 24, 1932; s. Frederick Arthur and Agnes Elizabeth (Tranter) T.; m. Barbara (Anderson). BA, Williams Coll., 1953; LLB, Columbia U., 1956. Bar: N.Y. 1957, U.S. Dist Ct. (so., no., and ea. dist.), N.Y., U.S. Tax Ct., U.S. Supreme Ct. Law clk. to Hon. Sterry R. Waterman U.S. Ct. Appeals (2d cir.), N.Y.C., 1956—57; assoc. Sullivan and Cromwell, N.Y.C., 1957—64, ptnr., 1965—99, sr. counsel, 2000—. Trustee Harold K. Hochschild Found.; chmn. Flagler Found.; bd. dir. Eisenhower Fellowships, Natural Resources Def. Coun., Rockefeller U., McIntosh Found., Weinman Found. Mem. ABA, N.Y. State Bar Assn., Assn. Bar City of N.Y., River Club, Union Club, India House, Maidstone Club, The Bathing Corp., Lyford Cay Club. Office: Sullivan and Cromwell 125 Broad St Fl 25 New York NY 10004-2400 Office Phone: 212-558-3923.

TERRY, GARY A. lawyer, former trade association executive; b. Ogden, Utah, Apr. 2, 1935; s. Hyrum Aceal and Viola (Sorenson) T.; m. Carole Ann Eitel, June 23, 1962; children— Stephanie Ann, Brendan Gary BA in Polit. Sci., UCLA, 1964; JD, George Washington U., 1968. Bars: Va. 1969 D.C. 1969. Mem. staff U.S. Ho. of Reps., Washington, 1964-65; Washington staff Bethlehem Steel Corp., 1965-69; atty. HUD, Washington, 1969; exec. v.p. Am. Land Devel. Assn. (now Am. Resort Devel. Assn.), Washington, 1969-82, pres., 1982-91, also dir.; with Jones, Waldo, Holbrook & McDonough, Washington, 1991-95, St. George, 1995-97. Dir. Internat. Found. for Timesharing, Washington, 1981-91, mem. consultative council Nat. Inst. Bldg. Scis., Washington, 1982-85; U.S. rep. land use and town planning com. Internat. Real Estate Fedn., Brussels, 1984-91; mem. Found. for Internat. Meetings, Washington, 1984-92; del. Lincoln Inst. Land Policy, Harvard U., 1984, 85 Contbr. articles to profl. jours. Asst. to exec. dir. Presdl. Inaugural Com., 1969-70; mem. adv. bd. NOAA, Washington, 1972; bd. dirs. Zacchaeus Free Med. and Legal Clinics, Washington, 1991-95, co-chair lawyers com., 1992-95; bd. dirs. Celebrity Concert Series, St. George, 1999—, pres., 2004—; chmn. Pioneer Ctr. for the Arts Found., St. George, 2000-02, bd. trustees, 1998-2003. Served with USN, 1953-56. Decorated Am. Spirit of Honor medal. Mem. Va. Bar Assn., D.C. Bar Assn. Mem. Lds Ch. Avocations: music, literature, flying, art, travel. Home: 952 Lizzie Ln Saint George UT 84790-2255 E-mail: gaterry@earthlink.net.

TERRY, JAMES JOSEPH, JR., lawyer; b. Yonkers, N.Y., July 2, 1952; s. James Joseph Sr. and Marie Catherine (O'Boyle) T.; m. Marguerite Mary O'Connor, Sept. 29, 1985; 1 child, James Daniel. BA, NYU, 1974; JD, Columbia U., 1977. Bar: N.Y. 1978, U.S. Dist. Ct. (so. and ea. dists.) N.Y. 1978, U.S. Ct. Appeals (2d cir.) 1981, U.S. Ct. Appeals (3d cir.) 1989, U.S. Supreme Ct. 2000. Assoc. Cole & Deitz, N.Y.C., 1977-89; ptnr. Winston & Strawn (formerly Cole & Deitz), N.Y.C., 1989—2002; v.p., gen. counsel F.J. Sciame Constrn. Co., Inc., N.Y.C., 2002—. Mem. ABA, N.Y. State Bar Assn., Def. Rsch. Inst., N.Y. County Lawyers Assn. Democrat. Roman Catholic. Avocations: fishing, reading. Home: 190 Kneeland Ave Yonkers NY 10705-2713 Office: Sciame Constrn Co Inc 80 South St New York NY 10038 E-mail: jterry@fjsciame.com.

TERRY, JOHN ALFRED, state supreme court judge; b. Utica, N.Y., May 6, 1933; s. Robert Samuel and Julia Berenice (Collins) T. BA magna cum laude, Yale U., 1954; JD, Georgetown U., 1960. Bar: D.C. 1960. Asst. U.S. atty. for D.C., 1962-67; staff atty. Nat. Commn. Reform of Fed. Criminal Laws, Washington, 1967-68; pvt. practice law Washington, 1968-69; chief appellate div. U.S. Atty.'s Office for D.C., 1969-82; judge D.C. Ct. Appeals, 1982—. Mem. D.C. Bar (bd. govs. 1977-82), ABA, Phi Beta Kappa Office: DC Ct Appeals 500 Indiana Ave NW Washington DC 20001-2138

TERRY, JOHN JOSEPH, transportation investor; b. Chgo., July 29, 1937; s. Michael Parnell and Honore (Ryan) T.; m. Terese Rose Mulkern, Dec. 31, 1960; children: Michael P., Gregory, Deirdre BS, Loyola U., Chgo., 1959; postgrad., U. So. Fla., 1967. C.P.A., Ill. With Touche, Ross & Co., 1959-65; v.p. Nat. City Lines, Denver, 1965-71; v.p. fin. Pepsico Transp., Inc., Tulsa, 1971-74; v.p. U.S. Rwy. Assn., Washington, 1974-76; chmn. P.I.E. Transport Europe, 1976-79; exec. v.p. IU Internat. Corp., Wilmington, Del., 1976-85; pres. Transp. Mgmt. Investment Group, Inc., Phila., 1985—. V.p.-at-large Am. Trucking Assn., Washington, 1984-85, chmn., internat. competitiveness task force, 1991, tax policy com., 1987—; bd. dirs. Caldwell Freight Lines, Lenoir, N.C., Basin Western, Inc., Roosevelt; cons. freight transp. World Bank and European Bank for Reconstrn. and Devel., 1986—. Served with U.S. Army, 1960-63 Recipient Best Motor Carrier Rsch. award Transp. Rsch. Forum, 1991. Office: Transp Mgmt Investment Group Inc 210 Locust St Apt 11B Philadelphia PA 19106-3923

TERRY, JOSEPH H. lawyer; b. Louisville, July 9, 1945; s. Wilbur H. and Reba Mae Terry; m. Donna Lynn Hogg, Apr. 21, 1967; children: Anne Griffin, Alexandra E. BA, U. Louisville, 1968; JD with distinction, U. Ky., 1971. Bar: Ky. 1971, U.S. Dist. Ct. (we. dist.) Ky. 1971, U.S. Ct. Appeals (6th cir.) 1975, U.S. Dist. Ct. (ea. dist.) Ky. 1983. Assoc., then ptnr. Middleton Reutlinger & Baird, Louisville, 1971-75; ptnr. Eldred Paxton & Terry, Princeton, Ky., 1975-79; spl. counsel Ligon Specialized Hauler Inc., Madisonville, Ky., 1979-80, pres., 1980-82; ptnr. Wyatt, Tarrant & Combs, Lexington, Ky., 1983-97, Dinsmore & Shohl, LLP, Lexington, 1997—. Contbr. articles to profl. jours. Vice chmn. Lexington Transit Authority, 1984-91; chmn. Lexington Area Sports Authority, 1998-2001, Ky. Registry of Elections, Frankfort, 1988-95. Fellow ABA (life); mem. Ky. Bar Assn., Sports Lawyers Assn. Democrat. Presbyterian. Avocation: golf. Home: 1805 St Ives Cir Lexington KY 40502-7714 Office: Dinsmore & Shohl LLP 250 W Main St Ste 1400 Lexington KY 40507-1735 Office Phone: 859-425-1005.

TERRY, KAY ADELL, marketing executive; b. Portland, Oreg., July 11, 1939; d. Langdon Alcott and Emma Francis (Meyer) Howard; m. Frank F. Terry, Aug. 31, 1963 (div. Mar. 1988); 1 child, Kimberly Sue. CPC, CIPC. Office mgr. Merck Sharp & Dohme, Portland, 1959—63; asst. dir. admissions Seattle Pacific U., Seattle, 1963-66; owner United Personnel Svc., Seattle, 1966-86; pres., CEO Ram Force Cos., Seattle, 1986-91; pres. N.W. region Robert Half Internat., Seattle, 1991-93; pres., CEO Terry & Assocs., Seattle, 1993—; CEO Key Staff, LLC, 1996—2003. Bd. dirs. Ram Force Cos., Seattle Acctg. Force, Inc., Office Force, Inc., Data Force, Inc. Contbr. articles to profl. jours. Vol. Spl. Olympics, Seattle. Named 16th Fastest Growing Co. in Wash. State, 1999, 2000; recipient Best Co. to Work for award, Wash. CEO mag., 1996—2000; fellow, Seattle Pacific U., 1989. Mem.: Nat. Tech. Svcs. Assn., Wash. Software Assn., Nat. Staffing Pers. Svcs. Assn. (vice-chmn. 1993), Nat. Assn. Accts. (bd. dirs. 1985—87, Mem. Achievement award 1987, Disting. Svc. award 1987), Women Bus. Owners, Columbia Tower Club, Desert Falls Country Club, Wash. Athletic Club. Republican. Avocations: travel, tennis, swimming, golf. E-mail: KTerry1010@aol.com., Kay@Keystaff.com.

TERRY, LEE R. congressman, lawyer; b. Omaha, Jan. 29, 1962; s. Leland R. Terry; m. Robyn L. Terry, Feb. 14, 1992; children: Nolan E., Ryan, Jack. BS, U. Nebr., 1984; JD, Creighton U., Omaha, 1987. Bar: Nebr. 1987, U.S. Dist. Ct. Nebr. 1987. Staff atty. Schrempp & Salerno, Omaha, 1987-92; ptnr. Schrempp, Salerno & Terry, Omaha, 1992-93, Terry & Kratville, Omaha, 1993-98; mem. U.S. Congress from 2d Nebr. dist., 1999—; former mem. banking and fin. svcs. com.; former mem. govt. reform and oversight com.; former mem. transport and infrastructure com.; mem. Energy & Commerce Com., Omaha City Coun., 1991—98. Co-author: Trying the Soft Tissue Case in Nebraska, 1995. Mem. Omaha City Coun., 1991—, pres., 1995-97; chair elect Am. Diabetes Assn., Great Plains, 1996-97, chair Nebr. area, 1997-99. Named One of Ten Outstanding Young Omahans, Omaha Jaycees-C. of C., 1994. Mem. Nebr. Assn. Trial Attys. (dir. 1995—), Suburban Rotary. Republican. Methodist. Avocations: travel, playing, spending time with family. Office: Ho Reps 1524 Longworth House Office Bldg Washington DC 20515-0001 Home: 35 Spyglass Pt Valley NE 68064-9325 Office: Dist Office 11640 Arbor St Omaha NE 68144

TERRY, LEON CASS, neurologist, educator; b. Dec. 22, 1940; s. Leon Herbert and Zella Irene (Boyd) T.; m. Suzanne Martinson, June 27, 1964; children: Kristin, Sean. Pharm. D., U. Mich., 1964; MD, Marquette U., 1969; PhD, McGill U., 1982; MBA, U. So. Fla., 1994. Diplomate Am. Bd. Psychiatry and Neurology, Am. Bd. Med. Mgmt. Intern U. Rochester, N.Y., 1969-70; staff assoc. NIH, 1970-72; resident in neurology McGill U., Montreal, Que., Can., 1972-75; MRC fellow, 1975-78; assoc. prof. U. Tenn., Memphis, 1978-81; prof. neurology U. Mich., Ann Arbor, 1981-89; assoc. prof. physiology, 1982-89; asst. chief neurology VA Med. Ctr., Ann Arbor, 1982-89; chmn. dept. neurology Med. Coll. of Wis., Milw., 1989—2000, prof. neurology and physiology, 1989—2003; chief med. officer Nexostherapeuticals, 2003—; pres., CEO Neurologic Cons., LLP, 2004—, Longevitech, 2004—. Dir. clin neurosci. ctr. and multiple sclerosis clinic, Med. Coll. Wis.; assoc. dean for amb. care, 1996-98; vice chief of staff Froedtert Hosp., 1994-97; chief of staff, 1997-98; chief med. officer cenegenics, 1997-98. Contbr. articles to profl. jours, chpts. to books. Served to lt. comdr. USPHS, 1970-72. NIH grantee, 1981-92; VA grantee, 1980-92; VA Clin. Investigator award, 1980-81. Mem. AMA, Am. Soc. Clin. Investigation, Cen. Soc. Clin. Investigation, Am. Neurol. Assn., Am. Coll. Physician Execs. (vice chmn. academic health ctr. soc. 1994-95, chair, 1995-98, leader forum health care delivery 1995-98), Am. Coll. Healthcare Execs., Endocrine Soc., Am. Acad. Neurology, Internat. Soc. Neuroendocrinology, Internat. Soc. Psychoeuroendocrinology, Soc. Neurosci., Soc. Rsch. Biol. Rhythms, Milw. Acad. Physicians, Wis. Neurol. Assn., Wis. State Med. Soc. (del.-elect 1995-96), Med. Soc. Milw. County, Milw. Neuropsychiatric Soc. (pres.-elect.). Avocations: pilot, skiing, scuba diving, computers. Office: Neurologic Consultnats LLP Suite 209 1009 W Glen Oaks Lane Mequon WI 53092 Office Phone: 262-241-8512. E-mail: cass@cass-terry.com, drcassterry@wi.rr.com.

TERRY, MARSHALL NORTHWAY, JR., English language educator, author; b. Cleve., Feb. 7, 1931; s. Marshall Northway and Margaret Louise (Carpenter) T.; m. Antoinette Barksdale, Sept. 5, 1953; children: Antoinette Terry Bryant, Mary Marshall Terry Benton. Student, Amherst Coll., 1949-50, Kenyon Coll., 1950-51; BA, So. Meth. U., 1953, MA, 1954. Teaching fellow English So. Meth. U., Dallas, 1954, dir. pub. relations, lectr. English, 1957-64, instr. English, 1956, 65-67, asst. dir., 1968, assoc. prof., 1969-71, prof. English, 1972—, chmn. dept., 1971-75, 79-82, dir. creative writing program. Book critic Dallas News, 1970-75; pres. faculty senate So. Meth. U., 1993-94, assoc. provost, 1994-98, E.A. Lilly prof. Eng., 1998—. Author: Old Liberty, 1961, Tom Northway, 1968, Dallas Stories, 1986, Ringer, 1987, My Father's Hands, 1993, Land of Hope and Glory, 1996, Angels Prostate Fall, 2001, Tex Rex, 2003; contbr. short stories to various jours. and mags.; editor Prize Stories, 1986. Past trustee Incarnate Word Coll., San Antonio; sec. bd. trustees Fort Burgwin Research Ctr., Ranchos de Taos, N.Mex. Recipient Jesse H. Jones fiction award Tex. Inst. Letters, 1968, Best Short Story award S.W. Rev., 1973, S.W. Writer of Yr. award, 1988, Willis M. Tate award So. Meth. U., 1990, 94, Lon Tinkle award for continuing excellence in Letters, Tex. Inst. Letters, 1991, Disting. Alumnus award, So. Meth. U., 2003. Mem. AAUP (chpt. pres. 1971), Coll. Conf. Tchrs. English, South Central MLA, Tex. Inst. Letters (pres. 1977-79, councilor 1980—) Democrat. Methodist. Home: 2717 Lovers Ln Dallas TX 75225-7905 Office: So Meth Univ Dept English Dallas TX 75275-0001 Business E-Mail: mterry@mail.smu.edu.

TERRY, PAMELA MAYS, psychology educator; b. Macon, Ga., Oct. 20, 1949; d. Thomas Littleton and Nancy Valyne Smith M.; m. Stephen Wesley Terry, Feb. 4, 1984; 1 child, Valyne Kathryne. AB, U. Ga., 1971, MS, 1974, PhD, 1975. Rsch. psychologist U.S. Army Rsch. Inst., Fort Benning, Ga., 1976-92; asst. prof. psychology Gordon Coll., Barnesville, Ga., 1999—. Tech. cons. U.S. Army Infantry Sch., Ft. Benning, 1986-92, U.S. Army Basic Tng. Task Force, Ft. Benning, 1983-85; spl. equal employment opportunity officer Fort Benning, 1985. Mem. Forsyth Womens Club, 1996-98. Fellowship NSF, U. Ga., 1972-75. Mem. Am. Psychol. Soc., Ga. Sociol. Assn., Phi Beta Kappa, Sigma Xi, Phi Kappa Phi. Southern Baptist. Avocations: playing piano, genealogy. Home: 22 Brooklyn Ave Forsyth GA 31029 Office: Gordon Coll Divsn Bus and Social Sci 419 College Dr Barnesville GA 30204

TERRY, RALPH BRUCE, education educator; s. Ralph and Hazel Terry; m. Barbara L Knapp, Dec. 21, 1968; children: Brina D. Snyder, Breta H. Sandifer, Becka H. Jameson. BA, Abilene Christian Coll., Tex., 1969; MA, Abilene Christian Coll., 1971, Abilene Christian U., 1987, MDiv, 1988; PhD, U. Tex., Arlington, 1993. Missionary Montezuma Creek Ch. of Christ, Utah, 1979—85; grad. tchg. asst. U. Tex., Tex., 1990—93, part-time instr., 1993—94, Tarrant County Jr. Coll., Hurst, 1994; missionary in residence Abilene Christian U., 1994—98; prof. Ohio Valley Coll., Vienna, W.Va., 1998—. Webmaster Ohio Valley Coll., Vienna, 1998—2002. Author: A Discourse Analysis of First Corinthians; contbr. articles to profl. jours. Officer Lion's Club, Montezuma Creek, Utah, 1978—85. Office: Ohio Valley College 1 Campus View Dr Vienna WV 26105 Office Phone: 304-865-6120. E-mail: terry@ovc.edu.

TERRY, REESE, JR., engineering executive; Pres. Engring. Co., Webster, Tex.; exec. v.p., chmn. (engring.) Cyberonics, Houston, 1998—.

TERRY, RICHARD EDWARD, public utility holding company executive; b. Green Bay, Wis., July 7, 1937; s. Joseph Edward and Arleen (Agamet) T.; m. Catherine Lombardo, Nov. 19, 1966; children— Angela, Edward BA, St. Norbert's Coll., West DePere, Wis., 1959; LLB, U. Wis., 1964; postgrad., Harvard U., 1986. Assoc. Ross & Hardies, Chgo., 1964-72; atty. Peoples Energy Corp., Chgo., 1972-79, asst. gen. counsel, 1979-81, v.p., gen. counsel, 1981-84; exec. v.p. People's Energy Corp., Peoples Gas Light & Coke Co. and North Shore Gas Co., 1984-87, pres., COO, 1987-90, chair, CEO, 1990—. Bd. dirs. Peoples Energy Corp., Peoples Gas Light, North Shore Gas Co., Harris Bankcorp, Harris Trust & Savs., Amsted Industries. Bd. dirs. Mus. Sci. & Ind., 1991—, Inst. Gas Tech., 1987—, Ill. Coun. on Econ. Edn., 1987—, Big Shoulders, 1991—; mem. Chgo. Area Ctrl. Com., 1991—; mem. bus. adv. coun. Chgo. Urban League, 1991—; prin. Chgo. United, 1991—; trustee St. Xavier U., 1989—, St. Norbert Coll., 1982—, DePaul U., 1992—. 1st lt. U.S. Army, 1959-61. Mem. Am. Gas Assn. (bd. dirs. 1991—), Nat. Petroleum Coun., Chgo. C. of C. (bd. dirs. 1988—), Univ. Club, Mid-Am. Club, Chgo. Club, Econ. Club, Comml. Club Chgo. (mem. civic com. 1991—). Avocations: golf, fishing, reading. Office: Peoples Energy Corp 130 E Randolph St Chicago IL 60601-6207

TERRY, ROBERT BROOKS, food products executive, lawyer; b. Kansas City, Mo., July 7, 1956; s. Frank R. and Susan S. (Smart) T.; m. Penny Susan Kanterman, July 2, 1987; children: Ryan, Kevin, Erin. Student, Vanderbilt U., 1974-75; BS in Acctg., U. Mo., 1978, JD, 1981. Bar: Mo. 1981, U.S. Dist. ct. (we. dist.) Mo. 1981, U.S. ct. Appeals (8th and 10th cirs.) 1983. Assoc.

Spencer, Fane, Britt & Browne, Kansas City, Mo., 1981—89; v.p., gen. counsel Farmland Industries, Inc., Kansas City, 1993—, pres., CEO, 2002—. Mem. ABA, Kansas City Mo. Bar Assn., Lawyers' Assn. Kansas City, Order of Coif. Avocation: baseball. Home: 4952 W 132nd Ter Leawood KS 66209-3460 Office: Farmland Industries Inc PO Box 7305 3315 N Oak Trfy Kansas City MO 64116-2798

TERRY, ROBERT DAVIS, neuropathologist, educator; b. Hartford, Conn., Jan. 13, 1924; m. Patricia Ann Blech, June 27, 1952; 1 son, Nicolas Saul. AB, Williams Coll., 1946, DSc (hon.), 1991; MD, Albany (N.Y.) Med. Coll., 1950. Diplomate: Am. Bd. Pathology, Am. Bd. Neuropathology. Postdoctoral tng. St. Francis Hosp., Hartford, 1950, Bellevue Hosp., N.Y.C., 1951, Montefiore Hosp., N.Y.C., 1952-53, 54-55, Inst. Recherches sur le Cancer, Paris, France, 1953-54, sr. postdoctoral fellow, 1965-66; asst. pathologist Montefiore Hosp., 1955-59; assoc. prof. dept. pathology Einstein Coll. Medicine, Bronx, N.Y., 1959-64, prof., 1964-84, acting chmn. dept. pathology, 1969-70, chmn., 1970-84; prof. depts. neuroscis. and pathology U. Calif.-San Diego, 1984-94, prof. emeritus, 1994—. Mem. study sect. pathology NIH, 1964-68; study sects. Nat. Multiple Sclerosis Soc., 1964-72, 74-78; mem. bd. sci. counselors Nat. Inst. Neurol. and Communicative Disorders and Stroke, NIH, 1976-80, chmn., 1977-80; mem. nat. sci. coun. Huntington's Disease Assn., 1978-81; mem. med. and sci. adv. bd. Alzheimer Assn., 1978-88; mem. sci. adv. bd. Max Planck Inst., Martinsried, 1990-96. Mem. editorial adv. bd. Jour. Neuropathology and Exptl. Neurology, 1963-83, 85-88, Lab. Investigation, 1967-77, Revue Neurologique, 1977-87, Annals of Neurology, 1978-82, Ultrastructural Pathology, 1978-86, Am. Jour. Pathology, 1985-89. Served with U.S. Army, 1943-46, ETO. Recipient Potamkin prize for Alzheimer Rsch., 1988, Met. Life Found. award, 1991. Fellow AAAS, Am. Acad. Arts and Sci.; mem. Am. Assn. Neuropathologists (pres. 1969-70, Meritorious Contbn. award 1989), N.Y. Path. Soc. (v.p. 1969-70, pres. 1971-73), Am. Assn. Pathologists, Am. Neurol. Assn., Am. Acad. Neurology. Achievements include research and publications on Alzheimer disease and Tay Sachs disease. Office: U Calif San Diego Dept Neuroscis La Jolla CA 92093 Office Phone: 858-534-6208.

TERRY, ROGER, retired pathologist, consultant; b. Waterville, N.Y., May 8, 1917; s. Orrin and Mary Isabelle (Kennedy) T.; m. Eleanor Virginia Wallace, Dec. 13, 1942; children: Robin, Orrin. AB magna cum laude, Colgate U., 1939; MD, U. Rochester, 1944. Cert. anatomic pathologist. Intern then resident Strong Meml. Hosp., Rochester, N.Y., 1944-51; asst. prof. U. Rochester Sch. Medicine, 1951-56, assoc. prof., 1956-61, prof. pathology, 1961-69, U. So. Calif. Sch. Medicine, Los Angeles, 1969-82; pathologist San Gabriel (Calif.) Valley Med. Ctr., 1982—2003; ret., 2003. Exec. dir. Calif. Tumor Tissue Registry, Los Angeles, 1969-84. Contbr. articles to profl. jours. Served to capt. USAF, 1954-56. Fellow Am. Soc. Clin. Pathologists, Coll. Am. Pathologists; mem. AMA, Internat. Acad. Pathology (councilor 1973-76), Am. Soc. Investigative Pathology, LA Soc. Pathologists (pres. 1974), Am. Soc. Cytopathology, Internat. Soc. Dermatopathology, Phi Beta Kappa, Sigma Xi, Alpha Omega Alpha. Republican. Episcopalian. Avocations: ballroom dancing, snorkeling, bike riding. Home: 2841 Shakespeare Dr San Marino CA 91108-2230

TERRY, ROY D. apparel manufacturing company executive; b. Dayton, Ohio, Dec. 27, 1944; s. Jesse A. and Velma G. Terry; m. Willo Terry; children: Corey, Cotina. BA, Morehouse Coll., 1966. Pres., CEO Terry Mfg. Co., Inc., Roanoke, Ala., 1972—. Chmn. bd. dirs. Birmingham (Ala.) br. Fed. Res. Bank, 1985-92. Author: Shared Production Concept, 1992. Founding bd. dirs. Minority Bus. Enterprise Legal Def. and Edn. Fund., 1980—; voting rights coord. Ala. Dem. Conf., 1980—; mem. Operation PUSH, World Trade Coun., 1986—. Recipient initial Shared Prodn. award U.S. Dept. Def., 1992, Bennie award Morehouse Coll., 1992, Minority Mfr. of Yr. award U.S. Dept. Commerce, 1989, Black Enterprise Mag., 1974, AG Gaston award Ala. Dem. Conf., 1980. Mem. NAACP, Am. Apparel Mfrs. Assn. Office: 924 South St PO Box 648 Roanoke AL 36274-0648

TERRY, W. BURKS, science administrator; b. Balt., Dec. 12, 1950; BA in Econ. and Philosophy, U. Calif., Berkeley, 1973; JD, U. Notre Dame, 1976. Bar: Calif. From program counsel and contracts mgr. to v.p. dep. gen. counsel Northrop Grumman Corp., LA, 1976—99, corp. v.p., gen. counsel, 2000—. Mem.: ABA, Ill. Bar Assn. Office: Northrop Grumman Corp 1840 Century Park E Los Angeles CA 90067-2199

TERRY, WAYNE GILBERT, healthcare executive, hospital administrator, mediator; b. Plymouth, Mass., Oct. 2, 1932; s. Lawrence Arthur and Betty Frances (Boutemain) Terry; m. Barbara Bromwell, Sept. 20, 1980; children: Karleton Wayne, Dale Duane, Kendrick Shane, Kristen Alayne, Tammye Van Clief, Wade Bromwell Delk. AA, Allan Hancock Coll., Santa Maria, Calif., 1960; BBA, U. Hawaii, 1966; M in Hosp. Adminstrn., Med. Coll. Va., 1973; PhD in Health Svcs. Mgmt., LaSalle U., 1999. Commd. 2d lt. USAF Med. Svc. Corps, 1967, advanced through grades to maj., 1976; asst. adminstr. for registrar activities USAF Hosp., Orlando AFB, Fla., 1966-67; assoc. adminstr. aeromed. evacuation activities USAF, Hickam AFB, Hawaii, 1967-71; adminstrv. resident USAF Regional Hosp., Langley AFB, Va., 1972-73; CEO USAF Hosp., Columbus AFB, Miss., 1973-75; nat. health edn. and tng. program advisor Office of Surgeon Gen., Dept. of Air Force, Washington, 1975-78; dir. health professions pers. planning and policy divsn. Office of Asst. Sec. Def. for Health Affairs, The Pentagon, Washington, 1978-80; dep. project mgr./adminstrv. dir. King Faisal U. Teaching Hosp., Al-Khobar, Saudi Arabia, 1980-82; dep. project mgr., hosp. dir. North Yemen Healthcare Project, As-Salem Hosp., Sadah, Yemen Arab Republic, 1982-83; hosp. dir., CEO western area Armed Forces Hosps., Khamis Mushayt, Saudi Arabia, 1983-84; chief adminstr./commissioning team chief Orbit Summit Health, Ltd., Riyadh, Saudi Arabia, 1984-85; hosp. dir., adminstrv. dir. Truk State Dept. Health Svcs., Moen, Federated States of Micronesia, 1985-87; assoc. adminstr. support svcs. King Fahad Hosp., Saudi Arabian N.G., Riyadh, 1987-90; project mgr., CEO N.W. Armed Forces Hosps. Program, Tabuk, Saudi Arabia, 1990-98, cons. in health svcs. mgmt., 1998-99; cons., mediator in health svcs. mgmt. Crozet, Va., 1999-2000; exec. dir., CEO Southside Area Health Edn. Ctr. Longwood U., Farmville, Va., 2000—. Apptd. cons. in healthcare planning Air Force Surgeon Gen., 1979; apptd. preceptor program in healthcare adminstrn. to U. Mich. for adminstrv. residents at N.W. Armed Forces Hosps. Programs, Tabuk, Saudi Arabia, 1993; lectr. in field; cons. in field; mem. supervisory bd. Royal Coll. Surgeons in Ireland, Dublin, 1990-98; active various symposium organizing coms.; cert. sr. grant specialist, grants reviewer, grants cons. Author books and monographs in field; contbr. articles to profl. jours. Warden to Am. Cmty. N.W. Region of Yemen Arab Republic to Am. Embassy in Sanaa, 1982-83, warden to Am. Cmty. N.W. Region of Saudi Arabia to Am. Embassy in Riyadh, 1990-99; mem. Internat. Sch. Sys. Coord. Com., Tabuk, 1990-99; mem. bd. dirs. Taif Sch. Dist. Sys., Saudi Arabia, 1981-82; mem., chmn. nominating com., bd. dirs. Ctrl. Va. Health Planning Agy., Richmond, Va., 2001—; bd. dirs. Va. Tobacco Settlement Found., Regional Adv. Bd., Richmond, Va., 2001—, Southside Area Health Edn. Ctr., Longwood U., Farmville, 2001—; mem. leadership and planning group Nat. Area Health Edn. Ctr. Assn., Balt., 2003-04. Decorated Def. Meritorious Svc. medal, Air Force Meritorious Svc. medal with 3 oak leaf clusters, Air medal with 2 oak leaf clusters, Air Force Commendation medal with 2 oak leaf clusters, Republic of Vietnam Gallantry Cross with palm, Republic of Vietnam Svc. medal with 11 battle stars, Sec. of Def. Svc. medal/badge, Air Force Chief Med. Svc. Corps badge; recipient Citation of Appreciation Nat. Coun. Social Welfare, Seoul, Republic of Korea, 1963, Citation of Appreciation award Suchan Province Gov., Choong Nam, Republic of Korea, 1963, award of merit Pacific Air Forces Command, Hickam AFB, Hawaii, 1965, Outstanding Rsch. award Med. Coll. Va., 1973, Personality of the South award, 1975, Men of Achievement award, Cambridge, Eng., 1982, Citation of Appreciation Gov. Truk State, Federated States of Micronesia, 1987, Citation of Merit Internat. Red Cross Commn., Bern, Switzerland, 1991, N.W. Armed Forces Hosps., Ministry of Def. and Aviation, Tabuk, 1991, Citation of Appreciation Presidency of Gen. Staff Hdqs., Ministry of Def. and Aviation, Tabuk, 1992, 93, 95, 96, 97, 98, 99, Disting. Alumni award Allan Hancock Coll., Santa Maria, 2000. Fellow Am. Coll. Healthcare Execs., Royal Soc. Health; mem. Am. Hosp. Assn., Am. Mgmt. Assn., Air Force Med. Svc. Corps Assn., Air Force Assn. (membership and awards com. 2003-), Assn. Mil. Surgeons of U.S. Republican. Baptist. Avocations: tennis, coin collecting/numismatics, hiking. Office: Southside Area Health Edn Ctr Longwood Univ 201 High St Farmville VA 23909 Office Phone: 434-395-2862.

TERSCHAN, FRANK ROBERT, lawyer; b. Dec. 25, 1949; s. Frank Joseph and Margaret Anna (Heidt) T.; m. Barbara Elizabeth Keily, Dec. 28, 1974; 1 child, Frank Martin. BA, Syracuse U., 1972; JD, U. Wis., 1975. Bar: Wis. 1976, U.S. Dist. Ct. (ea. and we. dists.) Wis. 1976, U.S. Ct. Appeals (7th cir.) 1979, U.S. Ct. Appeals (10th cir.) 1989, U.S. Supreme Ct. 1992. From assoc. to ptnr. Frisch, Dudek & Slattery Ltd., Milw., 1975-88; ptnr. Slattery and Hausman Ltd., Milw., 1988-94, Terschan & Steinle Ltd., Milw., 1994-96, Terschan, Steinle & Ness, Milw., 1996—. Chmn. MBA Fee Adminstrn. Com., 2000—; mem. Wis. Jud. Conduct Adv. Com., 2002—. Treas., sec. Ville du Park Homeowners Assn., Mequon, Wis., 1985-86; cub scout packmaster pack 3844 Boy Scouts Am., 1989-90, asst. scoutmaster Troop 865, 1991-93. Mem. ABA, Am. Bd. Trial Advocates, Wis. Bar Assn., Milw. Bar Assn., Assn. Trial Lawyers Am., Wis. Acad. Trial Lawyers (bd. dirs. 1996—), 7th Cir. Bar Assn., Order of Coif. Republican. Lutheran. Avocations: swimming, coin collecting/numismatics, reading, outdoor activities. Home: 10143 N Lake Shore Dr Mequon WI 53092-6109 Office: 2600 N Mayfair Rd Ste 700 Milwaukee WI 53226-1314 Office Phone: 414-258-1010. Business E-Mail: frt@tsn-law.com.

TERSOFF, JERRY DAVID, physicist; b. Washington, June 12, 1955; s. Abraham and Karen Tersoff; m. Deborah Franzblau. BA in Physics, Swarthmore Coll., 1977; PhD in Physics, U. Calif., Berkeley, 1982. Postdoctoral fellow Bell Labs., Murray Hill, N.J., 1982-84; mem. rsch. staff IBM T.J. Watson Rsch. Ctr., Yorktown Heights, N.Y., 1984—. Contbr. numerous articles on solid state physics to scholarly and profl. jours. Fellow Am. Physical Soc. (Davisson Germer prize 1997); mem. Materials Rsch. Soc. (MRS medal 1996), Am. Vacuum Soc. (Peter Mark award 1988). Achievements include first to scan tunneling microscopy; research in theory of heterojunction band offsets and Schottky barriers, theory of epitaxial growth. Office: IBM TJ Watson Rsch Ctr PO Box 218 Yorktown Heights NY 10598-0218

TERWILLEGAR, JANE CUSACK, librarian, educator; b. Warsaw, N.Y., Nov. 7, 1935; d. James Scott and Estella B. (Ackerman) Cusack; m. Gordon H. Terwillegar, July 26, 1958 (div. Mar. 1989); children: Sarah Ann Terwillegar Smedley, Arne Matthew. BA, Elmira (N.Y.) Coll., 1957; MLS, SUNY, Geneseo, 1960; EdS, U. Ga., 1977. Cert. tchr., Fla. Instr. U. Ga., Athens, 1975-81; libr. Palm beach County Libr., West Palm Beach, Fla., 1981-83, Palm Beach County Schs., Royal Palm Beach, Fla., 1983-94, dist. libr. media svcs. mgr. West Palm Beach, 1994—2000; dir. Lake Park Public Libr., 2000—. Lectr. Sch. Libr. and Info. Sci., U. South Fla., Tampa, 1987—, Nova U., Ft. Lauderdale, Fla., 1995—; task force mem. SUNLINK project Fla. Dept. Edn., 1995-2000; mem. adv. coun. Fla. Libr. Svcs. and Tech. Act., 1999—. Co-author: Commonsense Cataloging, 3d edit. 1983, 4th edit. 1990; reviewer Sch. Libr. Jour., 1986—; contbr. articles to profl. jours. Pres. Staff Assn. Palm Beach Sch. Dist., 1997-99. Mem. ALA, AAUW (pres. No. Palm Beach br. 2001-), Am. Assn. Sch. Librs. (exec. bd. 1990-94), Assn. for Libr. Svc. to Children (Newbery com. 1988-89), Fla. Assn. Media in Edn. (sec. 1988-89, bd. dirs. 1997—, pres. 1999-2001), Ednl. Media Assn. Fla. (pres. 1988), Kiwanis Club of Lake Park, Delta Kappa Gamma, Phi Beta Kappa, Delta Kappa Phi, Phi Delta Kappa. Avocations: scuba diving, sports cars. Home: 911 Oak Harbour Dr Juno Beach FL 33408-2173 Office: Lake Park Public Libr 529 Park Ave West Palm Beach FL 33403-

TERWILLIGER, J. RONALD, real estate company executive; Honor grad., U.S. Naval Acad.; MBA with high distinction, Harvard U. Pres., COO Sea Pines Plantation Co., Hilton Head (S.C.) Plantation Co.; chmn., CEO Trammell Crow Residential, Atlanta, 1986—. Chmn. emeritus Wharton Real Estate Ctr.; mem. Fannie Mae Adv. Coun. Mem. internat. bd. dirs. Habitat for Humanity; vice chmn. Atlanta Neighborhood Devel. Partnership; dir. Naval Acad. Found. Baker scholar, Harvard Grad. Sch. Bus. Mem.: Real Estate Roundtable, Urban Land Inst. (immediate past chmn.). Office: Trammell Crow Residential Ste 1100 2859 Paces Ferry Rd Atlanta GA 30339*

TERZIAN, GRACE PAINE, publisher; b. Boston, Oct. 19, 1952; d. Thomas Fite and Grace Hillman (Benedict) Paine; m. Philip Henry Terzian, Oct. 20, 1979; children: William Thomas Hillman, Grace Benedict Paine. BA in Art History, Williams Coll., 1974. Art dir. The New Republic, Washington, 1976-78; asst. editor The Chronicle of Higher Edn., Washington, 1978-79; rsch. editor Archtl. Digest, L.A., 1982-85; pub. The Women's Quar., Arlington, Va., 1994—. Editor Ex Femina, 1996—; sr. v.p. Ind. Women's Forum. Mem. Soc. Colonial Dames in Am., Phi Beta Kappa. Episcopalian. Home: 10505 Adel Rd Oakton VA 22124-1605 Personal E-mail: gterzian@cox.net.

TERZIAN, KARNIG YERVANT, retired civil engineer; b. July 4, 1928; came to U.S. s. Yeznig and Marie Terzian; m. Helen S., Dec. 21, 1958. BCE, Am. U. Beirut, Lebanon, 1949; MCE, U. Pa., 1954. Assoc. L. T. Beck & Assocs., 1956-60; prin. Urban Engrs., Inc., Phila., 1960-93, sr. v.p., sec.-treas., 1960-93, co-founder, ptnr., 1993-99; ret., 1999. Cons. major transp. projects in Pa., N.Y., N.J., Nigeria, Zaire; cons., exec. Urban Engrs., 1993—. Bd. dirs. Armenian Sisters Acad., 1970-74. Mem. ASCE (Life Membership award 1993), ASTM, Prestressed Concrete Inst. Armenian Apostolic. Office: Urban Engrs Inc 530 Walnut St Fl 14 Philadelphia PA 19106-3685

TERZIAN, PHILIP HENRY, journalist; b. Kensington, Md., July 5, 1950; s. L. A. and Louise (Anderson) Terzian; m. Grace Barrett Paine, Oct. 20, 1979; children: William Thomas Hillman, Grace Benedict Paine. BA in English, Villanova U., 1973; DTS, Episcopal Theol. Sem., Va., 1995; postgrad., Oxford (Eng.) U., 1976. Desk editor Reuters, Washington, 1973, U.S. News & World Report, Washington, 1973-74; asst. editor The New Republic, Washington, 1974-78; mem. policy planning staff Dept. State, Washington, 1978-79; asst. editor Anniston (Ala.) Star, 1979-80; assoc. editor Lexington (Ky.) Herald, 1980-82; asst. editor of editl. pages L.A. Times, 1982-86; editor of editl. pages Providence Jour. Scripps Howard News Svc., 1986-92, assoc. editor, syndicated columnist Providence Jour., 1992—. Panelist Washington Wk. in Rev., C-SPAN, Fox News, Nat. PUb. Radio. Contbr. articles to newspapers and jours. Pres. Providence Com. Fgn. Rels., 1989—92. Named finalist Disting. Commentary, Pulitzer Prize, 1991; recipient Edn. Writers award, Edn. Writers Am., 1981, Svc. to Preservation award, Ida Lee Willis Found., 1982, juror, Pulitzer Prize, 1994—95; Media fellow Hoover Instn., Stanford U., 2002, 2004. Fellow: Am. Journalism Found.; mem.: Va. Hist. Soc., Am. Coun. on Germany, Order Hosp. St. John of Jerusalem, Wolver Beagles (hon. whip), Soc. King Charles the Martyr, St. Andrew's Soc. Washington, Sons of Union Vets. of Civil War, Univ. Club, Nat. Beagle Club, Nat. Press Club. Republican. Episcopalian. Home: 10505 Adel Rd Oakton VA 22124-1605 Office: Providence Jour 1325 G St NW Ste 250 Washington DC 20005-3124 Office Phone: 202-661-8424. E-mail: pterzian@belo-dc.com.

TERZIAN, YERVANT, astronomy and astrophysics educator; b. Alexandria, Egypt, Feb. 9, 1939; came to the U.S., 1960, naturalized, 1971; s. Bedros and Maria (Kiriakaki) T.; children: Sevan, Tamar. BS, Am. U., Cairo, 1960; MS, Ind. U., 1963, PhD, 1965, DSc (hon.), 1989, Yerevan State U., 1994, Aristotle U. Thessaloniki, Greece, 1997, Union Coll., N.Y., 1999. Rsch. assoc. Arecibo Obs., P.R., 1965-67; asst. prof. astronomy and astrophysics Cornell U., Ithaca, N.Y., 1967-72, assoc. prof., 1972-77, prof., 1977—, chmn. dept. astronomy, 1979-99, dir. Pew Program in Sci. Edn., 1988-99, James A. Weeks prof. in phys. scis., 1990-99, David C. Duncan prof. in phys. scis., 1999—. Editor: Interstellar Ionized Hydrogen, 1968, Planetary Nebulae, 1978; co-editor: Cosmology and Astrophysics, 1982, Carl Sagan's Universe, 1997; sci. editor The Astrophys. Jour., 1989-99; contbr. over 200 articles to tech. jours. Recipient Clark Disting. Tchg. award Cornell U., 1984. Fellow AAAS; mem. Internat. Astron. Union, Internat. Sci. Radio Union, Am. Astron. Soc., Armenian Acad. Sci. Office: Cornell U Astronomy Dept Space Scis Bldg Ithaca NY 14853 E-mail: yt28@cornell.edu.

TERZIC, PETAR, mathematician, educator; b. Podgorica, Montenegro, Serbia-Monteneg (Yugoslavia), July 9, 1944; arrived in U.S., 1994; s. Vojin and Koviljka Terzic; m. Slavka Kaludjerovic, Jan. 28, 1950; children: Balsa, Katarina Terzic Conrad. BS, U. of Montenegro, Podgorica, 1974; MS, U. of Belgrade, Yugoslavia, 1985; MA, Liberty Theol. Sem., Lynchburg, Va., 2001; Bible cert., Liberty Bible Inst., Lynchburg, Va., 1996. Math. tchr. Dusan Vlahovic Agrl. H.S., Bar, 1973—74; instr. elec. engring. E. T. C. Nikola Tesla, Belgrade, 1974—80; comm. adminstr. City of Belgrade, 1980—90; prof. of elec. engring. Mil. Acad., Belgrade, Yugoslavia, 1990—94; instr. of math. Liberty U., Lynchburg, 1997—. Author: (book) Einstein's Picture of the World, 1996, Philosophy of Nature, 1996, (5-vol. book) Famous Military Leaders of the World, 1992—93 (2nd Pl. award Internat. Book Fair, Belgrade, 1993). Recipient Recognition for excellence in tchg., State of Montengro, 1974, 2nd Pl. award at the European Vet.'s Athletic Competition, European Recreation Assn., 1989, 3rd Pl. award at the amateur chess competition in Belgrade, Chess Assn. of Belgrade, 1977, 1st Pl. award in shot put in the jr. competition, Athletic Assn. of Montenegro, 1961. Mem.: Am. Math. Assn., Nikola Tesla Amateur Radio Club (bd. dirs. 1980—90). Avocation: recreation. Home: 412 Wildflower Ln Blacksburg VA 24060 Office: Liberty U 1971 University Blvd Lynchburg VA 24506 Office Phone: 434-582-2199. Personal E-mail: pterzic@liberty.edu.

TERZIS, JULIA KALLIPOLITOU, plastic surgeon; b. Salonica, Greece, Feb. 28, 1943; MD, Thomas Jefferson U., Phila., 1970; PhD in Neurophysiology, McGill U., Montreal. Cert. plastic surgery 1983, hand surgery 1990. Intern Royal Victoria Hosp., Montreal, Canada, 1970—71, resident, surgery, 1971—74; resident, plastic surgery Dalhousie U., Halifax, Canada, 1974—76, rsch. fellow, 1976—77; staff mem. Royal Victoria Hosp., Montreal, Canada; prof., dept. surgery, divsn. plastic surgery Ea. Va. Med. Sch., Norfolk, dir., microsurg. program. Contbr. articles to profl. jours.; author: 4 textbooks. Recipient James Barrett Brown award, Am. Assn. Plastic Surgeons, 1976, 2000, Gold medal, Royal Coll. Physicians and Surgeons of Can., 1981, Achievement in the field of Natural Scis., AHEPA Ednl. Found., 1987. Mem.: Internat. Soc. for Reconstructive Microsurgery, Plastic Surgery Rsch. Coun. (past chmn.), Internat. Microsurg. Soc. (past pres.), Am. Soc. Peripheral Nerve (founding pres.), World Soc. for Reconstructive Microsurgery (bd. mem., New Orleans, pres.-elect), Am. Soc. Reconstructive Microsurgery (founding mem., past pres.). Office: Eastern Va Med Sch PO Box 1980 Norfolk VA 23501-1980*

TESAR, DELBERT, machine systems and robotics educator, researcher, manufacturing consultant; b. Beaver Crossing, Nebr., Sept. 2, 1935; s. Louis and Clara (Capek) T.; m. Rogene Kresak, Feb. 1, 1957; children: Vim Lee, Aleta Anne, Landon Grady, Allison Jeanne B.Sc. in Mech. Engring., U. Nebr., 1958, M.Sc., 1959; PhD, Ga. Tech. U., 1964. Assoc. prof. U. Fla., Gainesville, 1965-71, prof., 1972-83, grad. research prof., 1983-84, dir., founder Ctr. Intelligent Machines and Robotics, 1978-84; Curran chair in engring. U. Tex., Austin, 1985—, dir. robotic rsch. Lectr. in field; mem. rev. panel Nat. Bur. Stds., Gaithersburg, Md., 1982-88; mem. sci. adv. bd. to Air Force, 1982-86; mem. standing com. NRC for Space Sta. (ISSA), 1992-95; mem. panel to rev. sci. for nuclear facilities dismantlement NRC, 2000—; interactor with Russian Acad. Sci. on sci. and tech. Author: (with others) Cam System Design, 1975. Patentee in field; contbr. articles to profl. jours.; assoc. editor 3 computer and mfg. jours. Expert witness house sci. and tech. com. U.S. Ho. of Reps., 1978-84 Fellow AAAS; mem. Fla. Engring. Soc. (Outstanding Tech. Achievement award 1982), ASME (machine design award 1987). Avocations: antiques, art, travel. Home: 8005 Two Cove Dr Austin TX 78730-3125 Office: U Tex R9925 Dept Mechanical Engineering Austin TX 78712-1063

TESAREK, DENNIS GEORGE, retired business consultant, writer, educator; b. Chgo., Jan. 2, 1935; s. George Joseph and Mary (Basl) T.; m. Caroline Arrena Myers, Jan. 1956 (div. Oct. 1968); children: William Paul, Dianne, Peter Bond; m. Kathleen Leigh Holm, Nov. 26, 1969; children: Philip Shawn, Leigh-Anne. BA in Math., U. Mo., 1956; postgrad., Systems Rsch. Inst., 1966, UCLA, 1984, Harvard U., 1985, MIT, 1986. Saleman Conn. Mut. Life Ins. Co., Dallas, 1959-61; systems engr. IBM, Phoenix, 1961-66, instr. L.A., 1966-68, mgr. Houston, 1968-74, industry mgr. White Plains, N.Y., 1974-76, project mgr. L.A., 1976-78, planning cons. Houston, 1978-84, cons. in bus. transformation, planning and gen. mgmt., 1984-97; owner Tesarek Enterprises (Consulting and Investments), 1997—. Adj. prof. Ariz. State U., 1963-65; guest lectr. U. Houston, 1980, 81, 83, 87. Author: Distributed Information Systems Planning Methodology, 1982, Information Systems Management Effectiveness Assessment, 1983, Business Systems Planning for Competitive Advantage Methodology, 1986, Executive Strategy Session Methodology, 1987, Management Planning Session Methodology, 1987, Steps in Strategic Investment Methodology, 1989. Tutor Vols. in Pub. Schs., Houston Ind. Sch. Dist., 1972-74, 80-82. 1st lt. USMC, 1956-59. Republican. Mem. Christian Sci. Ch. Avocations: color photography and printing, wood working, reading, jogging. E-mail: dtesarek@earthlink.net.

TESCHER, DONALD R. lawyer; b. Brooklyn, N.Y., Sept. 26, 1944; s. Harry A. and Irma (Gordon) T.; m. SuAnn Leiken; children: Jennifer L., Jonathan M. BSBA in Acctg., U. Fla., 1966, JD, 1969; LLM, NYU, 1973. Bar: Fla., 1969, U.S. Dist. Ct. (so. dist.) Fla., U.S. Tax Ct. Sr. shareholder Schwartz Nash Heckerling & Tescher, Miami, 1973-84, Fine Jacobson Schwartz Nash Block & England P.A., Miami, 1984-86, Tescher & Milstein, P.A., 1986-90, Tescher Gutter Chaves Josepher Rubin Ruffin and Foreman, P.A., Miami, 1990—. Adj. prof. grad. tax programs Sch. Law U. Miami, 1974-80, 92-95; spkr. in field. Contbr. articles to profl. jours., chpts. to books. Bd. trustees Found. Jewish Philanthropies of The Gtr. Miami Jewish Fedn., 1985—, chmn. profl. adv. com., 1989-91; mem. profl. adv. com. Dade Cmty. Found., 1989—; bd. dirs. Switchboard of Miami, 1986-90, bd. trustees, 1990—95 pres. Beth David Congragation, 1981-83. Fellow Am. Coll. Trust and Estate Counsel (mem. bus. planning com. 1994—, spkr.), Am. Coll. Tax Counsel; mem. ABA (sect. taxation mem. com. fgn. tax problems 1973-74, com. partnerships 1974-75, com. income taxation estates and trusts 1975-77, estate and gift tax com. 1977—, charitable transfers subcom. 1990—, bus. planning-chpt. 14 subcom., chmn. subcom. internat. estate and gift taxation 1987-89), Fla. Bar (tax sect. chmn. 1984-85, del. tax sect. s.e. region liaison conf., bd. dirs. tax sect. exec. coun., spkr., real property, probate and trust law sect., mem. estate and trust tax planning com. 1986—, chmn. probate and trust problems study com. 1995-98, chair trust law com. 1998—), Gtr. Miami Tax Inst., Estate Planning Coun. Gtr. Miami, Dade County Planned Giving Coun., Boca Raton Tax Inst., South Palm Beach County Jewish Fed. (adv. com.), Planned Giving Coun. of Miami-Dade County. Avocations: skiing, tennis, reading. Office: Tescher Gutter Chaves Josepher Rubin Ruffin & Forman PA 2101 NW Corporate Blvd Boca Raton FL 33431-7306 Office Phone: 561-998-7847. E-mail: dtescher@floridatax.com.

TESCHNER, DOUGLASS PAUL, project administrator; b. Cambridge, Mass., Oct. 29, 1949; s. Douglass P. Teschner and Mary Elizabeth (Bernt) Teschner Zeller; m. Martha Weaver, Sept. 26, 1981. BS in Forestry, U. Mass., 1971, EdD in Adminstrn., 1985; MS in Botany, U. Vt., 1978. Land surveyor Lincoln Engring. and Burnell Land Surveying, 1974, 78; tchr. White Mountain Sch., 1976; dir. Inst. Exptl. Studies, various locations, 1984-87; fin. officer Becket Acad., East Haddam, Conn., 1984-85; devel. dir. Riverbend Cmty. Mental Health, Concord, 1987—2002; state rep. N.H. Ho. of Reps., Concord, 1988—98, 2000—02; project dir. Rwanda Parliament Support Project, Kigali, 2002—. Co-editor: Wilderness Challenge: Outdoor Education Alternatives for Youth in Need, 1984; contbr. articles to profl. jours. Mem. Haverhill Hist. Soc.; vol. Peace Corps, 1971-73, Haverhill Congl. Ch. Mem.: Appalachian Mountain Club. Avocations: mountain climbing, hiking, rock and ice climbing, skiing. Home: 2100 Brushwood Rd Pike NH 03780-9706

TESELLE, EUGENE ARTHUR, JR., religion educator; b. Ames, Iowa, Aug. 8, 1931; s. Eugene Arthur and Hildegarde (Flynn) TeS.; m. Sallie McFague, Sept. 12, 1959 (div. Oct. 1976); children: Elizabeth, John; m. Penelope Saunders, Mar. 4, 1978; children: William, James, Thomas. BA, U. Colo., 1952; BD, Princeton Theol. Sem., 1955; MA, Yale U., 1960, PhD, 1963. Commr. to gen. assembly Presbyn. Ch. in U.S.A., 1993. Issues analyst Witherspoon Soc., 1987-93, 99—, pres., 1996-99; chmn. global missions com.

Presbytery Mid. Tenn., 1989-93, mem. nominating com., 2002—. Author: Augustine, the Theologian, 1970, Augustine's Strategy as an Apologist, 1974, Christ in Context, 1975, Thomas Aquinas: Faith and Reason, 1988, Living in Two Cities: Augustinian Trajectories in Political Thought, 1998. Incorporator Belmont-Hillsboro Neighbors, Nashville, 1971, Consumer Coalition for Health, Nashville, 1980, Nashville Local, Dem. Socialists Am., 1983, Cen. Am. Solidarity Assn., Nashville, 1986. Presbyn. Grad. fellow, 1958, Rockefeller doctoral fellow, 1960, Kent fellow, 1961; recipient Thomas Jefferson award Vanderbilt U., 1996. Mem. Am. Acad. Religion, Am. Soc. Ch. History, Soc. for Values in Higher Edn., Workgroup on Constructive Christian Theology, Witherspoon Soc. (pres. 1995—99), Phi Beta Kappa. Home: 2007 Linden Ave Nashville TN 37212-5021

TESFATSION, LEIGH S. economics educator, consultant; d. Morton F. and Dorothy Hess Spears. PhD, U. Minn., Mpls., 1975. From asst. to prof. econs. U. So. Calif., L.A., 1975—90; prof. econs. and math. Iowa State U., Ames, 1990—. Cons. Los Alamos Nat. Lab., N.Mex., 2002—. Mem.: Econometric Soc., Soc. for Computational Econs. (adv. coun. mem. 1997—2002). Achievements include research in Http:/Www.Econ.Iastate.Edu/Tesfatsi/Bio.Htm. Office: Iowa State Univ Dept Econs/Heady 260 Ames IA 50011-1070

TESHIROGI, JERRY TAKAHIDE, aerospace engineer; s. Tsuyoshi and Wakako Teshirogi. ME, Tohoku U., Sendai, Japan, 1998; BS, U. Calif., L.A., 1996. Cert. spacecraft design & operation proficiency, Stanford U., 2002. Sys. engr. Lockheed Martin Space Sys. Co., Sunnyvale, Calif., 1999—2002, Northrop Grumman Space Tech., Redondo Beach, Calif., 2003—. Contbr. articles to profl. jours. Mem.: AIAA. Achievements include design of small satelite. Home: 322 31st St Hermosa Beach CA 90254-2320 Personal E-mail: jtteshirogi@netscape.net.

TESK, JOHN ALOYSIUS, materials scientist; b. Chgo., Oct. 19, 1934; s. John August and Theresa Mary (Mattea) T.; m. Regina Sophia Budzyn, Dec. 10, 1966; 1 child, John A.W. BS in Engring. Sci., Northwestern U., 1957, MS in Metallurgy, 1960, PhD in Materials Sci., 1963. Asst. prof. U. Ill., Chgo., 1964-67; cons. Argonne (Ill.) Nat. Lab., 1964-67, asst. metallurgist, 1967-70; dir. rsch. Dental, Howmedica Inc., Chgo., 1970-77; dir. edn. svcs. Inst. Gas. Tech., Chgo., 1977-78; gen. phys. scientist, group leader, biomaterials coord. polymers divsn., sr. tech. advisor, indsl. liaison dir.'s office Nat. Inst. Stds. & Tech., Gaithersburg, Md., 1978—. Mem. bioengineered materials applications bd. Nat. Acads.; cons. Dentsply Internat., York, Pa., 1977-78; mem. review bd. Dental Sch. Case Western Res. U., Cleve., 1987-88, Biomaterials Program, Clemson U., 1972-74, Dental Sch., Tokushima U., Japan, 1997; mem. orthopaedic adv. bd. Clemson U., 1999-2001; mem. adv. bd. Industry/Univ. Ctr. of NSF, U. Buffalo, 2002—; chmn. dental stds. ADA, Chgo., 1980-86; leader U.S. Del. Internat. Stds. Orgn., 1980-86; organizer confs. Holder 8 patents; mem. editl. bd. Jour. Dental Materials, 1988-91, Jour. Oral Implantology, 1984-2000, Biomaterials Forum, 1996—, Applied Biomaterials, 1998—; mem. editl. rev. bd. Nat. Inst. Stds. and Tech., 1996-2001; contbr. chpts. to books, articles to profl. jours. Mem. bldg. com. Divine Savior Parish, Downers Grove, Ill., 1971-72; chmn. troop 737 Cub Scouts, Highland, Md., 1980; adult supr. youth group Saint Louis Parish, Highland, 1982-83. Fellow Acad. Dental Materials (exec. com. 1987-94); mem. ASTM (exec. com. 2000—), Am. Phys. Soc., Am. Soc. Metals (exec. com. Chgo. chpt. 1964-67, 78), Biomaterials Soc. (charter, nominating com. 1987, 96, editl. bd. Applied Biomaterials 1998—, stds. com. 1995—, contbg. editor Biomaterials Forum, co-chmn. reference materials/reference data com. coun. 1996-2003, liaison com. 1996-98, program com. 1999), Internat. Assn. Dental Rsch. (treas. dental materials group 1987-94), Tech. Materials Soc. (exec. com. Chgo chpt. 1965), Japanese Soc. for Dental Materials (hon.). Roman Catholic. Avocations: gardening, boating, travel, walking. Home: 6759 Cortina Dr Highland MD 20777-9501 Office: Nat Inst Stds & Tech Rm A143 Bldg 224 Gaithersburg MD 20899-0001 Office Phone: 301-975-6799. Business E-Mail: john.tesk@nist.gov.

TESMER, NANCY ANN STUTLER, retired librarian; b. Aug. 25, 1934; d. Ernest Lynn and Sophrona Rebecca (Pepper) Stutler; m. John A. Tesmer, Sept. 10, 1980. Student, U. Akron, 1952—54; BA, Kent State U., 1956. Jr. asst. libr. E. Br. Libr., Akron, 1956—59; hosp. libr. VA Hosp., Northampton, Mass., 1959—61, med. libr. Brecksville, Ohio, 1961—65, chief libr., 1965—73, assoc. chief libr. Cleve., 1973—75, chief libr., 1975—. Chief Regional Libr. Svc., 1986—90. Mem.: N.E. Ohio Med. Libr. Assn., Med. Libr. Assn., Zeta Tau Alpha. Home: 8537 SW 90th Pl Unit G Ocala FL 34481-7516 E-mail: nst0825@aol.com.

TESON, FERNANDO ROBERTO, law educator, consultant; b. Buenos Aires, Aug. 3, 1950; s. Roberto Julio and Marta (Grun) T.; m. Maria Teresa Martinez, Nov. 11, 1976 (div. Feb. 1992); children: Fernando, Marcelo; m. Bettina C. Rauleder, Oct. 11, 1996; 1 child, Carolina. Grad., U. Buenos Aires, 1975; lic. internat. law, U. Libre de Bruxelles, Brussels, 1982; SJD, Northwestern U., 1987. Assoc. prof. law Ariz. State U., Tempe, 1984-88, prof. law, 1988—2002; prof. Fla. State U. Sch. Law, Tallahassee, 2002—. Vis. prof. San Diego Summer Program, Mex., 1987, Dublin, Ireland, 1988, Paris, 1990, 93, Hastings Law Sch., San Francisco, Spring 1990, Cardozo Law Sch., N.Y.C., Fall 1992, Ind. U., Bloomington, Spring 1993, Cornell U., Ithaca, N.Y., 1994-95; permanent vis. prof. Di Tella U., Buenos Aires, 1996—; career diplomate Argentina Govt., Buenos Aires, 1977-81; prof. George Washington/Oxford U. Internat. Human Rights Program, New College, Oxford, 1999, 2001. Author: A Philosophy of International Law, Humanitarian Intervention: An Inquiry into Law and Morality, 2d edit.; contbr. articles to profl. jours. James N. Raymond fellow Northwestern U., 1982-83; Tobias Simon Eminent scholar Fla. State U. Sch. Law, 2002. Mem. Am. Soc. Internat. Law, Am. Soc. Social and Polit. Philosophy. Avocations: music, bridge, food. Office: Fla State U Coll of Law Tallahassee FL 32306-1601 Home: 1001 Gardenia Dr Tallahassee FL 32312-3003

TESORI, JEANINE, composer; b. 1961; m. Michael Rafter; 1 child. Composer: (Broadway plays) How to Succeed in Business Without Really Trying, 1995, Violet, 1997, Dream, 1997, Twelfth Night, 1998 (Tony nom. best original musical score, 1999), Swing!, 1999, Thoroughly Modern Millie, 2002 (Tony nom. best original musical score, 2002), Caroline, or Change, 2004 (Tony nom. best original musical score, 2004, Drama Desk award best musical score, 2004, Obie award, 2004). Office: Eugene O'Neill Theatre 230 W 49th St New York NY 10019

TESSENEER-STREET, SUSAN, photographer, artist, writer; b. Murray, Ky., Dec. 14, 1939; d. Ralph Athen and Susan Geneva (Kirkland) Tesseneer; m. Robert Beni Street Sr., Jan. 16, 1939 (div.); children: Robert Beni II, Ralph Calvin Sr. Student, Blue Mountain Coll. for Women, 1959—61, Memphis State U., 1963—66; BA, S.E. Mo. U., 1974; student, Harvard U., 2002. Tchr., 1974-79; bus. owner, 1977-85; writer, 1984-86; photographer, 1990—; artist, 1998—. Author: (book) Gift in Celebration of Women. Mem. Sikeston Art League, 1980—, pres., 1990-94; sec., treas., organizer Cmty. Concert, Sikeston, 1989. Mem. AAUW (charter), Profl. Photographers Am., Am. Soc. Portrait Artists, Hemingway Soc., Nat. Writers Club, Women in the Arts (charter), Am. Soc. Portrait Painters, Impressionist Soc., Nat. Writers Assn., Hemingway Soc., Nat. Assn. Women Writers, Nat. Women's History Mus. (charter). Office: Susan Tesseneer-Street Studio Gallery 1003 Allen Blvd Sikeston MO 63801-4711

TESSER, ABRAHAM, social psychologist; b. N.Y.C., May 24, 1941; s. Louis and Ruth (Buchholz) T.; m. Marsha Richman Rosenthal, June 4, 1967 (div. Feb. 22, 1983); children: Louis J., Rachel A.; m. Carmen Chaves, Dec. 15, 1990. BA, L.I. U., 1962; MS, Purdue U., 1965, PhD, 1967. Rsch. assoc. Inst. for Behavioral Rsch., U. Ga., 1971-78, assoc. dir., 1978-84, acting dir. Ctr. for Rsch. on Deviance, 1984-86, dir., 1984-94; from asst. prof. to assoc. prof. social psychology U. Ga., 1967-74, prof., 1974-89, rsch. prof. psychology, 1989-99, prof. emeritus, 2000—, sr. affiliate Inst. for Behavioral Rsch., 2001—. Vis. fellow Yale U., 1976-77, Princeton U., spring 1983; fellow Ctr. for Advanced Studies in the Behavioral Scis., Stanford, Calif., 1992-93, Ohio State U., 1999-2000. Editor Jour. Personality and Social Psychology, 1991-94; contbr. numerous articles to profl. jours. Pres. Congregation Children of Israel, Athens, 2002. Mem. APA, Am. Psychol. Soc., Soc. for Personality and Social Psychology (pres. 2000), Soc. Exptl. Social Psychology, So. Soc. for Social Psychology. Office: Inst Behavioral Rsch Barrow Hall U Ga Athens GA 30602

TESSER, DOROTHY, artist; b. Bklyn., Mar. 11, 1926; d. Max and Ethel Weber; m. Jack Tesser, Oct. 12, 1947; children: Clifford Charles(dec.), Jean Karasic, Barbara Campbell. Degree in graphic art, Pratt Inst.; cert. art therapist, New Sch. U., 1983. Artist Famous Studios, N.Y.C.; owner, artist and prodr. D&J Films Animation, N.Y.C.; freelance artist All Animation Studios, N.Y.C.; art dir. D&R Animation, N.Y.C., Storyboard, N.Y.C. N.J. Ctr. Healing Arts, Freehold Area Hosp. Pediat. Ward; author: (biography) Darkness to Light (subtitle) Drawing from Pain, 2002. Mem.: Ladies Aux. War Vets. (pres. 2001—03, v.p., Pres. of Yr. award 2001—02). Mailing: 525 Ocean Blvd Apt 307 Long Branch NJ 07740-8910

TESSING, LOUISE SCIRE, graphic designer; b. Chgo., May 13, 1946; d. Rocco Roy and Ruth Louise (Knueppel) Scire; m. Arvid Victor Tessing, Jan. 18, 1975. BS in Visual Design, Ill. Inst. Tech., Chgo., 1968; MBA in Mktg., Loyola U., Chgo., 1986. Jr. designer Field Mus. of Natural History, Chgo., 1968-69, Charles MacMurray & Assocs., Chgo., 1969-74; designer, art dir. Grant-Jacoby Inc., Chgo., 1974-76, Playboy Enterprises Inc., Chgo., 1976-78, Stevens Biondi Decicco Inc., Chgo., 1978-80; prin., owner Tessing Design Inc., Chgo., 1980—. Lobby treas. Ill. Women's Agenda, Chgo., 1990-92. Mem.: Soc. Typographic Arts (v.p. 2000—), Internat. Assn. Bus. Communicators (v.p. comm. and design 1998—2002), Am. Ctr. for Design (bd. dirs. 1971—77, pres. 1976—77), Women in Design Chgo. (founder 1977, pres. 1977—78, 1991—93, Friend award 1990, Founder award 1997). Home and Office: Tessing Design Inc 3822 N Seeley Ave Chicago IL 60618-3912 Office Phone: 773-525-7704. E-mail: tess46@comcast.net.

TESSLER, STEVEN, ecologist, data processing executive; b. Phila., July 8, 1954; s. Harry Tessler and Ella Mae (DeHaas) Barry; m. Karen DiNenno, Oct. 16, 1987; 1 child, Julia. AS, Del. County C.C., Pa., 1974; BS, Pa. State U., 1976, PhD, 1991; MS, Purdue U., Ind., 1979. Rsch. technician Biology Dept., Bryn Mawr Coll., Pa., 1979—80, Allergy and Immunology Sect., U. of Pa, Sch. of Medicine, Phila., 1980—81; edn. specialist Sea World, Inc, San Diego, 1981—83; rsch. asst. Temple U. Sch. of Medicine, Phila., 1983—84; rsch. assoc. Sch. of Forest Resources, Penn State U., Univ. Pk., Pa., 1990; asst. prof. biology Lock Haven U., Pa., 1990—92; ecologist, data mgr. Shenandoah Nat. Pk., Luray, Va., 1993—95, U.S. Geol. Survey, West Trenton, NJ, 1995—. Database cons. Clean Data Sys., Upper Darby, Pa., 1998—. Contbr. articles to profl. jours. Recipient Outstanding Student award, Entomol. Soc. Pa., 1990. Mem.: DAMA Internat., Sigma Xi, Internat. Soc. Arachnology, Brit. Arachnological Soc., Am. Inst. Biol. Scis., Am. Arachnological Soc., Xerces Soc. (Invertebrate Conservation). Achievements include research in structure of terrestrial and aquatic invertebrate communities, graphic representation of multivariate data; water use data systems. Avocations: fishing, mountain dulcimer. Office: US Geological Survey 810 Bear Tavern Rd Ste 206 West Trenton NJ 08628 E-mail: stessler@usgs.gov.

TESTA, MICHAEL HAROLD, lawyer; b. N.Y.C., 1939; m. Carol Waldenberg, 1962; 2 children. BS summa cum laude, NYU, 1958, LLB cum laude, 1961, LLM in Taxation, 1967. Bar: N.Y. 1961. Assoc. White & Case, N.Y.C., 1962-71, Skadden, Arps, Slate, Meagher & Flom, N.Y.C., 1971-72, ptnr., 1972-91; conservation lawyer N.Y.C., 1992—. Advisor U.S. del. to UN Conf. on Straddling Fish Stocks and Highly Migratory Fish Stocks, 1994-95, U.S. del. to Kyoto Internat. Conf. on Sustainable Contribution of Fisheries to Food Security, 1995, to N.W. Atlantic Fisheries Orgn., 1996, 98, to 22d Session of FAO Com. on Fisheries, 1997, to Western and Ctrl. Pacific Fisheries Conf., 1998-2001; adj. assoc. prof. law NYU Law Sch., 1986; mem. consultative com. to secs. state and commerce N.W. Atlantic Fisheries Conv., 1996-2002. Assoc. editor, contbr.: NYU Law Rev., 1960-61; contbr. articles to legal jours. Mem. planning bd. Town of Tuxedo (N.Y.), 1971-76. Served to capt. USAFR, 1961-72. Root-Tilden-Snow scholar, 1958-61. Mem. Order of Coif. Home: 860 UN Plz New York NY 10017 Office: Ste 28-424 4 Times Square New York NY 10036-6522

TESTAVERDE, VINCENT FRANK (VINNY TESTAVERDE), professional football player; b. Bklyn., Nov. 13, 1963; Student, U. Miami, Fla. Quarterback Tampa Bay (Fla.) Buccaneers, 1987—92, Cleve. Browns, 1993—95, Balt. Ravens, 1996—98, N.Y. Jets, Hempstead, NY, 1998—2004, Dallas Cowboys, 2004—. Named Coll. Football Player of Yr., The Sporting News, 1986; named to NFL Pro-Bowl, 1996, 1998; recipient Heisman trophy, 1986. Achievements include Passing for over 40,000 yards. Office: c/o Dallas Cowboys 1 Cowboys Pkwy Irving TX 75063*

TESTER, LEONARD WAYNE, psychology educator; b. Nampa, Idaho, Aug. 21, 1933; s. Walter Vernon and Dora Dorothy (Peters) T. BTh, Kansas City Coll., Overland, Kansas, 1957; MA, Abilene Christian Coll. (now Abilene Christian U.), 1961; STB, Harvard U., 1969; EdM, Columbia U., 1971, EdD, 1976, MPhil, 1979, PhD, 1981. Lic. psychologist, N.Y. 1983. Pers. mgr. Boston Safe Deposit & Trust Co., 1966-69; adj. instr. clin. counseling N.Y. Inst. Tech., Westbury, 1971-80, adj. asst. prof., 1980-84, sr. counselor, 1980-92, assoc. prof., 1984-92, dir., 1992-95, prof., 1992—, prof., chmn., 1992-93, prof., dir., 1993-95. Cons., grad. asst. Bus. Sch. and Tchrs. Coll. Columbia U., 1977-81. Contbr. articles to profl. jours.; presenter workshops in field. Exec. dir. Ho. of the Carpenter, Boston, 1967-68; bd. dirs. Pierre (S.D.) Coun. of Arts, Counseling Ctr. Episcopal Ch., Great Neck, N.Y., Tech. Sch. in N.Y.C. William Wayne Jackson honors scholar Harvard Div. Sch. Fellow Am. Orthopsychiat. Assn.; mem. APA, N.Y. Soc. Clin. Psychologists, N.Y. Soc. Hypnosis and Psychotherapy, others. Home: PO Box 20107 New York NY 10023-1477 Office: NY Inst Tech 1855 Broadway New York NY 10023-7692

TETEF, MERRY LYNN, internist, oncologist; b. Burbank, Calif., May 9, 1961; MD, Harvard U., 1987. Diplomate Am. Bd. Internal Medicine, Am. Bd. Oncology. Resident in internal medicine UCLA Med. Ctr., L.A., 1987-90; fellow in hematology, oncology City of Home Med. Ctr., Duarte, Calif., 1990-93, mem. staff dept. med. oncology and therpeutic rsch., 1993-99; oncologist South Orange County Hematology Oncology Assocs., Laguna Hills, Calif., 1999—2001, Oncology Ctr. of Orange County, Irvine, Calif., 2001—. Mem ACP, Am. Soc. Clin. Oncology, Orange County Med. Assn. Office: Ste 300 33 Creek Rd Irvine CA 92604-7705 also: Oncology Ctr Orange County 33 Creek Rd Ste 300 Irvine CA 92604

TETELMAN, ALICE FRAN, small business owner; b. N.Y.C., Apr. 15, 1941; d. Harry and Leah (Markovitz) T.; m. Martin A. Wenick, Dec. 7, 1980. BA, Mt. Holyoke Coll., South Hadley, Mass., 1962. Rsch. and info. asst. Edn. and World Affairs, N.Y.C., 1963-67; legis. asst. U.S. Sen. Charles Goodell, Washington, 1968-70; land use and energy specialist Citizens Adv. Com. on Environ. Quality, Washington, 1973-74; sr. assoc. prog. mgr. Linton & Co., Washington, 1971-73, 75-76; pub policy cons. Washington, 1977-78; adminstrv. asst. U.S. Congressman Bill Green (N.Y.), Washington, 1978-81; cons. The Precious Legacy Project, Prague, Czechoslovakia, 1982-83; Rep. staff dir. Select Com. on Hunger, U.S. Ho. of Reps., Washington, 1984-85; dir. State of N.J. Washington Office, 1986-90; exec. dir. Coun. of Gov.'s Policy Advisors, Washington, 1991-94; dir. Washington Office, The City of N.Y., 1994-98. Pres. Italian Vacation Villas, Washington. Bd. dirs. Republican Women's Task Force, Nat. Women's Polit. Caucus, 1976-80, Women in Senate and House (WISH) List, 1998-2001. European Community grantee, 1975. Mem. Ripon Soc. (nat. exec. com. 1971-73). Office: Italian Vacation Villas PO Box 9586 Washington DC 20016-9586

TETHER, ANTHONY J. government agency administrator; BEE, Rensselaer Poly. Inst., 1964; MS, Stanford U., 1965, PhD in Elec. Engring., 1969. Exec. v.p. Systems Control Inc., 1969—78; dir. nat. intelligence office Office of the Sec. of Def., 1978—82; dir. strategic tech. office Dept. Def., 1982—86; v.p. tech. and advanced devel. Ford Aerospace Corp., 1986—92; v.p. advanced tech. sector, then v.p., gen. mgr. range systems Sci. Applications Internat. Corp., 1992—99; CEO Dynamics Tech., Inc.; CEO, pres., founder The Sequoia Group, 1996—2001; dir. Def. Advanced Rsch. Projects Agy., Washington, 2001—. Mem. Army Sci. Bd., Def. Sci. Bd.; mem. control policy R&D com. Office of Nat. Drug Control. Recipient Nat. Intelligence Medal, Civilian Meritorious Svc. medal, Dept. of Def. Mem.: IEEE. Office: DARPA 1400 Defense Pentagon Rm 34 750 Washington DC 20301-1400

TETHER, ANTHONY JOHN, aerospace executive; b. Middletown, N.Y., Nov. 28, 1941; s. John Arthur and Antoinette Rose (Gesualdo) T.; m. Nancy Engle Pierson, Dec. 27, 1963 (div. July 1971); 1 child, Jennifer; m. Carol Suzanne Dunbar, Mar. 3, 1973; 1 child, Michael. AAS, Orange County C.C., N.Y., 1961; BS, Rensselaer Poly Inst., 1963; MSEE, Stanford (Calif.) U., 1965, PhD, 1969. V.p., gen. mgr. Sys. Control Inc., Palo Alto, Calif., 1968-78; dir. nat. intelligence Office Sec. of Def., Washington, 1978-82; dir. strategic tech. DARPA, Washington, 1982-86; corp. v.p. Ford Aerospace, Newport Beach, Calif., 1986-90, LORAL, Newport Beach, 1990-92; corp. v.p., gen. mgr. Sci. Application Internat., Inc., San Diego, 1992-94; CEO Dynamics Tech. Inc., Torrance, Calif., 1994-96; CEO, pres. Sequoia Group, Newport Beach, Calif., 1996-2001; dir. def. advanced rsch. project agy. Office of Sec. of Def., Washington, 2001—. Bd. dirs. Condyne Tech., Inc., Orlando, Fla., 1990—92, chmn., 1990—92; dir. Orincon, La Jolla, Calif., 1996—99, Evans & Sutherland, Salt Lake City, 2001; mem. def. sci. bd. Army Sci. Bd. Task Forces, 1998—2002; cons. Army Sci. Bd., Def. Sci. Bd. Contbr. articles to profl. jours. Recipient Nat. Intelligence medal DCI, 1986, Civilian Meritorious medal U.S. Sec. Def., 1986. Mem. IEEE, Cosmos Club, Sigma Xi, Eta Kappa Nu, Tau Beta Pi. Avocations: amateur radio, skiing, golf. Home: 6400 Lyric Ln Falls Church VA 22044 Personal E-mail: ttether@aol.com.

TETI, LOUIS N. lawyer; b. Bryn Mawr, Pa., May 29, 1950; BA, Dickinson Coll., 1972; JD, Temple U., 1976, LLM in Taxation, 1981. Bar: Pa. 1976. Ptnr. MacElree Harvey, Ltd., West Chester and Exton, Pa. Mem. disciplinary bd. Supreme Ct. Pa., 2000—, chair, 2004. Fellow Am. Coll. Trust and Estate Counsel; mem. ABA (ho. dels. 1985-91, 99-2001), Pa. Bar Assn. (chmn. young lawyers divsn. 1982-83, bd. govs. 1982-85, 91-94, 97-2001, pres. 1999-2000), Chester County Bar Assn. (sec. 1979-82, 86-88, v.p. 1989, pres.-elect 1990, pres. 1991, chair young lawyers sect. 1977, bd. dirs. 1977-92), Chester County Estate Planning Coun. (pres. 1988-89). Office: MacElree Harvey Ltd 740 Springdale Dr Ste 110 Exton PA 19341-2865 Fax: 610-524-9857 610 524 9857. Office Phone: 610-524-7575. E-mail: lteti@macelree.com.

TETLEY, GLEN, choreographer; b. Cleve., Feb. 3, 1926; s. Glenford and Eleanor (Byrne) T. Student, Franklin and Marshall Coll., 1944-46, DFA (hon.), 2001; BS, NYU, 1948; student contemporary dance with, Hanya Holm, Martha Graham, 1946; student classical ballet with, Margaret Craske, Anthony Tudor at Met. Opera Ballet Sch., 1949; Doctor of Fine Arts (hon.), Franklin and Marshall Coll., 2001. Choreographer Major Ballet Co., 1948—. Guest instr. Yale Dramatic Workshop, 1947-48, Colo. Coll., 1946-49, Hanya Holm Sch. Contemporary Dance, 1946-52, Ballet Rambert, 1966-68, Netherlands Dance Theatre, 1962-65, B. De Rothschild Found., Israel, 1965-67 Featured dancer in Broadway musical Kiss Me Kate, 1949, Out of This World, 1950, Juno, 1958; premiered in Broadway musical Menotti's Amahl and the Night Visitors, NBC Opera, 1951; soloist with Broadway musical, N.Y.C. Opera, 1951-54, John Butler's Am. Dance Theatre, 1951-55, Robert Joffrey Ballet, 1955-56, Martha Graham Dance Co., 1957-59, Am. Ballet Theatre, 1959-61, Jerome Robbins: Ballets USA, 1961-62, Netherlands Dance Theater, 1962-65, own co., 1962-69; made govt.-sponsored tour of Europe, 1969, appearances at Spoleto Festival, all maj. Am. dance festivals; guest choreographer, Netherlands Dance Theatre; artistic dir.: Netherlands Dance Theatre, 1969-71; guest choreographer, Am. Ballet Theatre, Ballet Rambert, Batsheva Co. Israel, Robert Joffrey Ballet, Alvin Alley Co., U. Utah Repertory Dance Theatre, Vancouver Festival, Royal Danish Ballet, 1969, Royal Ballet Covent Garden, Royal Swedish Ballet, Den Norske Opera, Hamburg State Opera, Stuttgart Ballet; former artistic dir., Stuttgart Ballet Co., 1973-1976; artistic assoc., Nat. Ballet of Canada, Toronto, 1987-89; ballets include Pierrot Lunaire, 1962, Birds of Sorrow, 1962, The Anatomy Lesson, 1964, Sargasso, 1964, Field Mass, 1965, Mythical Hunters, 1965, Ricercare, 1966, Chronochromie, 1966, Tehilim, 1966, Freefall, 1967, The Seven Deadly Sins, 1967, Dithyramb, 1967, Ziggurat, 1967, Circles, 1968, Embrace Tiger and Return to Mountain, 1968, Arena, 1968, Imaginary Film, 1970, Mutations, 1970, Field Figures, 1971, Rag Dances, 1971, Small Parades, 1972, Threshold, 1972, Laborintus, 1972, Strophe-Antistrophe, 1972, The Moveable Garden, 1973, Gemini, 1973, Voluntaries, 1973, Sacre du Printemps, 1974, Tristan, 1974, Strender, 1974, Daphnis and Chloe, 1975, Greening, 1975, Alegrias, 1975, Poeme Nocturne, 1977, Sphinx, 1978, Praeludium, 1979, The Tempest, 1979, Contredances, 1979, Summer's End, 1980, Dances of Albion-Dark Night: Glad Day, 1980, Firebird, 1981, Murderer Hope of Women, 1983, Revelation and Fall, 1984, Pulcinella, 1984, Dream Walk of the Shaman, 1985, Alice, 1986, Orpheus, 1987, La Ronde, 1987, Tagore, 1989, Dialogues, 1991, Oracle, 1994, Amores, 1997, Lux in Tenebris, 1999; off-Broadway choreographer-dir. ballets including Fortuna, 1961, Ballet Ballads, 1961. Patron Benesh Inst. Choreology; bd. dirs. Tag Found., N.Y.C. Served with USNR, 1944-46. Recipient German critics award for Die Feder; Queen Elizabeth II Coronation award Royal Acad. Dancing, 1981; recipient Prix Italia Rai prize, 1982, Tennant Caledonia award Edinburgh Festival, 1983, Ohioana Career Medal, 1986, achievement award N.Y.U., 1988; named knight Order Merit, 1997.

TETLIE, HAROLD, priest; b. Madison, Minn., Aug. 24, 1926; s. H. Ben and Anna (Mauland) T. BA cum laude, St. Olaf Coll., Northfield, Minn., 1951; MBA, U. Denver, 1956; postgrad., Cornell U., 1959—60; MDiv, Luther Sem., St. Paul, 1965. Ordained to ministry Am. Luth. Ch., 1965. Pastor Christ the King Chs. (True Caths.), Alice, Tex., 1965—, congregation supr., 1969—. Cir. parish priest, Nuevo Leon, Tamaulipas, Hidalgo, San Luis Potosi, Mex. Author numerous poems. Coord. Joint Action in Cmty. Svc., Inc., Alice, 1970—. Sgt. U.S. Army, 1945-46, PTO. Recipient Svc. to Mankind award Sertoma Club, Corpus Christi, Regional Vol. of Yr. award Joint Action in Cmty. Svc., 1991, Michael Madhusudan award for poem, Calcutta, 1996; Ky. Col., 1992. Mem. NEA (life), VFW (life), Am. Legion (life), 40 et 8 (life), Family Motor Coach Assn., Sons of Norway, Order of Ky. Col., Internat. Platform Assn., Thousand Trails, WWII Tank Destroyer Soc. (chaplain). Home and Office: Christ the King Chs PO Box 1607 Alice TX 78333-1607 Office Phone: 361-664-3316. *It is by the Power of Jesus Christ: He tells us in John 13:34: "Love one another, even as I loved you."*

TETOR, DAVID R. agriculturist, consultant; b. Montour Falls, N.Y., Dec. 16, 1943; s. Donald Booth and Margaret Eva (Howell) Tetor; m. Louise Anne Weeks, Apr. 23, 1966; children: Brian David, Michael James, Eric John. BS, Cornell U., 1965. Cert. pesticide applicator/trainer N.Y. Dept. Environ. Conservation. Student trainee USDA Soil Conservation Svc., summers, 1962—64, soil scientist Rochester, NY, 1965; systems analyst Cornell Coop. Ext., Ithaca, NY, 1970; agr. program leader Herkimer (N.Y.) County Cornell Coop. Ext., 1970—72, Dutchess County Cornell Coop. Ext., Millbrook, NY, 1972—2000. Agr. cons.; pres. N.Y. State Assn. County Agrl. Agts., NY, 1972—, Cornell Coll. Agr. Alumni, Ithaca, NY, 1990—2000; co-chair Dutchess County Tourism Bd., Poughkeepsie, NY, 1998—2000. Treas. adv. bd. Pine Plains Future Farmers Am., 1976—; supr. Town of Stanford, NY, 1992—95; pres. Pine Plains (N.Y.) Sch. Bd., 1982—87; bd. dirs. Dutchess County Indsl. Devel. Agy., Poughkeepsie, 1990—, Stanford Town Bd., 2002—; mem. coun. Cornell U., 2002—. Capt. U.S. Army, 1965—69. Named Outstanding Young Agt., Nat. Assn. County Agrl. Agts., 1979; named to Alumni Honor Roll, SUNY, 2000; recipient Disting. Svc. award, Nat. Assn. County Agrl. Agts., 1984, Outstanding Alumni award, Coll. of Agr. and Life Scis., Cornell U., 2002. Mem.: Dutchess County Farm Bur. (bd. dirs. 1990—), Dutchess County Agrl. Soc., N.Y. State Agrl. Soc. (bd. dirs. 2002—), Grange. Republican. Avocations: attending NASCAR races, coin collecting/numismatics, stamp collecting/philately, camping. Home: 5626 Rt 82 Clinton Corners NY 12514 Office: Dave Tetor Agr Cons PO Box 46 Stanfordville NY 12581

TETRAULT, JEANNE L. building inspector; b. St. Petersburg, Fla., Dec. 10, 1944; d. Edgar N. and Irene C. Tetrault; life ptnr. Jan Zaitlin. Attended, Vassar Coll., 1963—65; student, Laney Coll., Oakland, Calif., 1999—2001. Cert. bldg. inspector, mech. inspector, combination residential inspector. Farmer,

Albion, Calif., 1970—75; writer, 1975—82, 1970—75; carpenter, bldg. contractor 7 Sisters Constn., Berkeley, Calif., 1980—94; self-employed carpenter, designer Berkeley, 1994—96; carpenter, supr. U. Calif., Berkeley, 1996—97; bldg. inspector level 2 Contra Costa Bldg. Dept., Martinez, Calif., 2001—. Mem. adv. bd. Spinsters Inc.-Aunt Lute, San Francisco, 1984—85; workshop tchr. in field. Author: (books) Countrywomen: A Handbook for the New Farmer, 1976, A Woman's Carpentry Book, 1980; founding editor Countrywomen Mag., 1975—80, Tradeswomen Mag., 1980—81. Vol., designer accessible residential projects Rebuilding Together/Christmas in April. Mem.: Internat. Conf. Bldg. Officials. Green Party. Avocations: writing, horseback riding. Office: Contra Costa Bldg Dept 651 Pine St Martinez CA 94553 E-mail: savsarah@ix.netcom.com.

TETTEH, EMMANUEL, director; 3 children. B of Profl. Studies, Met. Coll. N.Y., 2000, MS in Adminstrn., 2001; Phd, Sch. of Mgmt. Kladen Univ., 2004—. Ordination Mt. Calvary Holy Ch. of Am., N.Y., 1995, Internat. Evangelism Crusades, 1993, Internat. Ever-Living Praise Tabernacle of CGEM, Ghana, 1988; School Certificate and General Certificate of Education West African Exam. Coun., Ghana, 1986. Assoc. min. Mt. Calvary Holy Ch. of Am., Staten Island, NY, 1994—; learning ctr. tutor Met. Coll. NY, 1999—2000, adminstrv. asst., 1999—2000, asst. to v.p. for student fin., 2000—. Ch. missions Internat. Evangelism Crusaders/Internat. Coun. of Cmty. Churches, Bklyn., 1991—94; ch. devel. Praise Tabernacle Ch./Ever-Prevailing Word Ch., Osu-Accra, Ghana, 1988—91; pastoral services Christian Growth Ch., 1986—88; adj. prof. Met. Coll. NY, N.Y.C., 2001—. Author: (instructional outlines/study guide) Classes (Purpose) I, V, VII, & A (Constructive Action) Lesson Outlines, (instructional computer lesson manual) 4) How to Create Labels and to Build a Database, (instruc. computer literacy lesson manual) 3) How to Construct an Eco-Map and to Build a Database, (biblical studies:) 1) The Importance of Christian Fellowship, (biblical studies) 2) The Principles of Obtaining the Exaltation of God, Theories of Democratioc Governance in the Institution of Higher Education, 2004. Rsch. svc. learning Service-Learning in Higher Edn., Staten Island, 2000; min. religion Mt. Calvary Holy Ch., 1996. Recipient Disting. recognition as mem. of the Honor and Crystal Societies, Met. Coll. NY, 1998—2001, Dean's List, 1998—2001; College's Presdl. scholar, 1998—2001, Juanita Blake Meml. scholar, 1999, 2000. Mem.: ASPA (life), Soc. Human Ecology (corr.), Am. Ednl. Rsch. Assn. (corr.), Am. Assn. Christian Counselors (life), Nat. Orgn. Human Svc. Edn. (life). Democrat. Achievements include discovery of At the epilogue of my Masters' degree research project, I emerged with the discovery of a metaphorical concept that I called Communal Photosynthesis based on this discovery and; commitment to scientific rsch., I have estblished The Ctr. for Communal Photosynthesis Rsch. which is located at the website www.cfcpr.org. Avocation: travel.

TETTLEBAUM, HARVEY M. lawyer; m. Ann Safier; children: Marianne, Benjamin. AB, Dartmouth Coll., 1964; JD, AM in History, Washington U. Sch. Law, 1968. Asst. dean Washington U. Sch. Law, 1969-77; asst. atty. gne., chief counsel Consumer Protection and Anti-Trust Div., 1970-77; pvt. practice Jefferson City, Mo., 1977-90; former mem., chmn. health law practice group Husch & Eppenberger, LLC, Jefferson City, Mo., 1990—. Contbr. articles to profl. jours. Rep. Mo. Rep. State Com., 1976—; v.p. Moniteau County R-1 Sch. Dist. Bd., 1991-95, pres., 1995-96; mem. Calif. R-1 Sch. Bd., 1990-96, v.p., 1993-95, pres., 1995-96. Mem. Am. Health Lawyers Assn. (bd. dirs. 1993-99, co-chair long-term care and the law program 1993-2001, chair 2001—, chair long-term care and law program 2001—, former chair long term care substantive law com. 1997-2001), Mo. Bar Assn. (health and hosp. law com., chmn. adminstrv. law com., vice chair delivery of legal svc. com., Mo. statewide legal svc. com.),Best Lawyers in Am., 2003-2004, Am. Health Care Assn. (legal subcom. 1994—, chair 2004-), Rep. Nat. Lawyers Assn. (bd. dirs. 1988—, 1st v.p. 2002—, pres. 2003). Home: 56295 Little Moniteau Rd California MO 65018-3069 Office: Husch & Eppenberger LLC Monroe House Ste 300 235 E High St PO Box 1251 Jefferson City MO 65102-1251 Office Phone: 573-761-1107.

TETZELI, RICK, editor; With FORTUNE Mag., 1990—93, assoc. editor, 1993—93, editor, 1996—97, sr. editor, 1997—99, asst. mng. editor, 1999, exec. dir., 2000, asst. mng. editor, 2001; mng. editor Entertainment Weekly, N.Y.C., 2002—. Office: Entertainment Weekly 111 8th Ave New York NY 10011

TETZLAFF, CHARLES ROBERT, lawyer; b. Oct. 15, 1938; s. Donald H. and Harriet (Ranney) T.; m. Joan Seugling, July 1, 1962; children: Julie Lynn Mulrow, Carl Lawrence. BA, U. Vt., 1960; LLB, Boston U., 1963; LLM, NYU, 1964. Bar: Vt. 1964, U.S. Supreme Ct. 1970. Judge advocate USAF, 1965-68; dep. state's atty. Chittenden County, Vt., 1968-70; ptnr. Latham, Eastman, Schweyer and Tetzlaff, 1969-93; U.S. atty. dist. Vt. Office U.S. Atty., Burlington, 1993—; gen. counsel U.S. Sentencing Commn., Washington, 2002—. Trustee Vt. Legal Aid, 1976-78; chair Dist. 4 Environ. Commn., 1979-83, Gov. Sentencing Study Commn., 1985-86; active Vt. Bd. Bar Examiners, 1980-84, State Police Adv. Commn., 1985-86, Gov. Bail Amendment Task Force. Capt. USAF, 1965-68. Mem. ABA, Vt. Bar Assn., Chittenden County Bar Assn. Office: US Sentencing Commn One Columbus Circle NE Washington DC 20002-8002

TETZLAFF, JOHN EDWIN, physician; b. N.Y.C., N.Y., Feb. 26, 1953; m. Susan Joan Harrison, May 21, 1982; children: Roger, John, Glen, Laura, James, Christopher, Emily. MD, St. Louis U., 1979. Anesthesiologist Cleve. Clinic, 1988—2003; prof. anesthesiology Cleve. Clinic Lerner Coll. of Medicine of Case Western Reserve U. Author: (text book) Orthopedic Anesthesiology, 1995, Clinical Pharmacology of Local Anesthetics, 1999. Lcdr NAVY, 1975—88. Office: The Cleve Clin Found E-30 9500 Euclid Ave Cleveland OH 44195

TETZLAFF, THEODORE R. lawyer; b. Saukville, Wis., Feb. 27, 1944; AB magna cum laude, Princeton U., 1966; LLB, Yale U., 1969. Bar: Ind. 1969, D.C. 1969, Ill. 1974. Legis. asst. to Congressman John Brademas, 1970; exec. dir. Nat. Conf. Police Community Rels., 1970-71; acting dir. U.S. Office Legal Svcs., Office Econ. Opportunity, Washington, 1972-73; counsel, Com. Judiciary U.S. Ho. of Reps., Washington, 1974; v.p., legal and external affairs Cummins Engine Co., 1980-82; gen. coun. Tenneco, Inc., Greenwich, Conn., 1992-99; ptnr. Jenner & Block, Chgo., 1976—80, 1982—2001; mng. ptnr. Chgo. office McGuireWoods LLP, Chgo., 2002—; gen. coun. Peoples Energy, 2003—. Bd. dirs. Continental Materials Corp., Chgo. Pres. Chgo. area Found. Legal Svcs., 1983—; commr. Pub. Bldg. Commn. Chgo., 1990—. Reginald Heber Smith fellow, 1969-70. Mem. ABA (chair sect. litigation 1991-92), Ill. State Bar Assn., Ind. State Bar Assn., D.C. Bar. Office: McGuireWoods LLP Suite 4400 77 West Wacker Dr Chicago IL 60601

TEUBER, WILLIAM J, JR., corporate financial executive; B, Coll. of the Holy Cross; MBA, Babson Coll.; MS in taxation, Bentley Coll. V.p., contr. EMC, 1995—97, v.p., CFO, 1997—2000, sr. v.p., CFO, 2000—01, exec. v.p., CFO, 2001—. Ptnr. Coopers & Lybrand. Office: EMC 171 South St Hopkinton MA 01748-9103

TEUBNER, FERDINAND CARY, JR., retired publishing company executive; b. Phila., Sept. 22, 1921; s. Ferdinand Cary Teubner and Esther Roslyn (Test) Alperstein; m. Ruth May Hazen, Nov. 1, 1953; 1 child, Janell Caron Teubner Crispyn. Student, U. Pa., 1940-41; grad., Charles Morris Price Sch. Advt. and Journalism, 1949. Rep. W.H. Hoedt Studios, Inc., Phila., 1945-52; account exec. Patterson Prodns., Inc., Phila., 1955-56, v.p., 1956-57; staff exec. Am. Assn. Advt. Agys., N.Y.C., 1957-59; rep. W.H. Martin & Co., Inc., N.Y.C., 1959-62; advt. salesman Editor & Pub. Co., Inc., N.Y.C., 1962-65, advt. mgr., 1965-76, gen. mgr., treas., 1976-78, treas., pub., 1978-95, dir., 1969-95; sec.-treas., dir. E & P Research, Inc., N.Y.C., 1985-95, ret., 1995. Served with USAAF, 1942-45, ETO; served with U.S. Army, 1952-55, Korea, ret. maj. AUS, 1981. Decorated Purple Heart; recipient Silver Shovel award Internat. Newspaper Mktg. Assn., 1993, David Paul Hegg II Lifetime Achievement award Episcopal Diocese Newark, 2003. Mem. Sales Execs. Club N.Y.C., Res. Officer Assn. Clubs: Union League, Lake Valhalla Country. Episcopalian. Home: 18 Lenape Dr Montville NJ 07045-9795

TEUFEL, ROBERT J. publishing executive; Pres., chief opers. officer Rodale Press, Inc., Emmaus, Pa. Office: Rodale Press Inc 33 E Minor St Emmaus PA 18098-0001

TEUFEL, WILLIAM LOCKWOOD, emergency physician; b. Cleve., Ohio, Mar. 21, 1941; s. William John and Dorothy Margaret (Lockwood) T.; m. Margaret Ong, June 28, 1969 (div. Sept. 1980); 1 child, Drew William; m. Zoe Ann Zimmerman (dec. Oct. 1999); children: Thea Anna, Kallie Abra. BS in Chemistry, Denison U., 1963; MD, U. Cin., 1967. Resident in gen. surgery Highland Hosp., Oakland, Calif., 1968-69; resident in emergency medicine U. Cin., 1971-73; from asst. dir. to dir. emergency svc. Highland Gen. Hosp., Oakland, 1973-76, San Francisco Gen. Hosp., 1976-80; ptnr. Calif. Emergency Physicians Med. Group, Oakland, Calif., 1980—90; med. dir. emergency svc Marin Gen. Hosp., Greenbrae, Calif., 1986-99; sr. ptnr. Calif. Emergency Physicians Med. Group, 1990—; med. dir. Coastal Valleys Emergency Med. Svc. Agy., Santa Rosa, Calif., 1999—. Oral examiner Am. Bd. Emergency Medicine, Lansing, Mich., 1981—; health coun. County of Marin, San Rafael, Calif., 1997-2002. Lt. comdr. USNR, 1964—74. Fellow Am. Acad. Emergency Medicine (bd. dir. Calif. chpt. 1998—2002). Avocations: motorcycling, native plant gardening. Office: Calif Emergency Physicians 2101 Webster St Ste 1770 Oakland CA 94612-9700 Home: PO Box 471 437 Meadow Way San Geronimo CA 94963-0471 E-mail: WLTEUFEL@comcast.net.

TEUKOLSKY, SAUL, physicist, educator; BS in Physics with honors, BS in Applied Math. with honors, U. Witwatersrand, S. Africa, 1970; PhD in Theoretical Physics, Calif. Inst. Tech., 1973. Richard Chace Tolman Rsch. fellow Calif. Inst. Tech., 1973—74; from asst. prof. to assoc. prof. physics and astronomy Cornell U., Ithaca, NY, 1974—83, prof. physics and astronomy, 1983—99, Hans A. Bethe prof. physics and astrophysics, 1999—. Vis. prof. dept. applied math. and theoretical physics Cambridge U.; vis. prof. dept. astronomy Harvard U.; vis. prof. Inst. Theoretical Physics, Santa Barbara, Calif. Recipient Forefronts of Large-Scale Computing award, 1990; Alfred P. Sloan fellow, 1973, John Simon Guggenheim fellow, 1981. Fellow: Am. Astron. Soc., Am. Phys. Soc.; mem.: AAAS, NAS. Office: Cornell U 608 Space Sciences Bldg Ithaca NY 14853

TEUTSCH, CLIFFORD L. publishing executive; Mng. editor Hartford (Conn.) Courant. Office: Hartford Courant 285 Broad St Hartford CT 06115-3785

TE VELDE, REBECCA GROOM, organist, music educator, composer; b. Decatur, Ga., Sept. 20, 1956; d. Lester Herbert and Myrtle Vera (Jacobson) Groom; m. John Raymond te Velde, Aug. 21, 1981; children: Vera Louise, Brent Arthur. MusM Organ Lit. & Performance, Univ. of W. Ontario, London, Ont., Can., 1978—82; MusB Organ Performance, Seattle Pacific Univ., Seattle, Wash., 1974—78. Cert. Music Assoc. of Am. Guild of Organists, 1989. Organist Denny Pk. Luth. Ch., Seattle, 1983—87, choir dir., 1984—87; organist, choir dir. St. Mark's Luth. Ch., Fargo, ND, 1987—91; organist First Pres. Ch., Stillwater, Okla., 1991—; adj. instr. of music Okla. State Univ., Stillwater, Okla., 1999—. Dean Am. Guild of Organists (Cimarron Chpt.), Stillwater, Okla., 1999—2001; Dist. convenor for Okla. Am. guild of Organists, Stillwater, Okla., 1997—98. Composer: (songs) (2-part with piano) "A Thought", 2000, (SATB a cappella) "Super Flumina Babylonis", 2002, (2-part with piano or organ) "Two German Chorales", 2003. Recipient Internat. Flor Peeters Masterclass Participant, Belgian Govt./ Mechelen, Begium, 1980; grantee one yr. full grant for study with Michael Schneider, DAAD (German Acad. Exch. Svc.)/Staatliche Hochschule fur Musik, Köln, 1980—81. Mem.: Am.Guild of Organists (Profl. concerns and competition chairperson 2002—03, mem. com. for ednl. resources 2003). Avocations: reading, hiking, travel, watercoloring. Home: 716 S Gray St Stillwater OK 74074-4331 Office: First Presbyterian Ch 524 S Duncan Stillwater OK 74074

TEVRIZIAN, DICKRAN M., JR., judge; b. LA, Aug. 4, 1940; s. Dickran and Rose Tevrizian; m. Geraldine Tevrizian, Aug. 22, 1964; children: Allyson Tracy, Leslie Sara. BS, U. So. Calif., 1962, JD, 1965. Tax acct. Arthur Andersen and Co., LA, 1965-66; atty., ptnr. Kirtland and Packard, LA, 1966-72; judge LA Mcpl. Ct., 1972-78, State of Calif. Superior Ct., LA, 1978-82; ptnr. Manatt, Phelps, Rothenberg & Tunney, LA, 1982-85, Lewis, D'Amato, Brisbois & Bisgaard, LA, 1985-86; judge U.S. Dist. Ct., LA, 1986—. Adv. dir. UCLA Sch. Pub. Policy. Recipient Peter the Great Gold Medal of Honor Russian Acad. Natural Scis., 1998, Ellis Island Medal of Honor award, 1999, Disting. Pub. Svc. award Orange County Fed. Bar Assn., 2003. Mem. Calif. Trial Lawyers Assn. (Trial Judge of Yr. 1987), LA County Bar Assn. (Trial Judge of Yr. 1994-95), Malibu Bar Assn. (fed. ct. trial judge of yr. 1998, Maynard Toll award 2002). Office: US Dist Ct Royal Federal Bldg 255 E Temple St Los Angeles CA 90012-3332

TEW, E. JAMES, JR., management services company executive; b. Dallas, July 7, 1933; s. Elmer James and Bessie Fay (Bennett) T.; children: Teresa Annette, Linda Diane, Brian James. Student, Arlington State Jr. Coll., 1955-57; BBA in Indsl. Mgmt., So. Meth. U., 1969; MS in Quality Systems, U. Dallas, 1972, MBA in Mgmt., 1975; EdD in Adult Edn., Nova U., 1986. Registered profl. engr., Calif. Mgr. quality assurance ops. Tex. Instruments Inc., Dallas, 1957-98; chmn. corp. metric implementation com. Texins Credit Union, co-chmn. credit com. Adj. faculty Richland Coll. Mountain View Coll., LeTourneau U.; precinct chmn., election judge, del. several county and state convs.; bus. computer info. systems adv. bd. U. North Tex., bd. dirs. ctr. for quality and productivity U. North Tex.; bd. examiners Malcolm Baldridge Nat. Quality award, U.S. Dept. Commerce, Nat. Inst. Standard and Tech., 1988, 89, 90, 91, 95, 96; chmn. panel judges, fellow Tex. Quality Award, 1993-2001; cons. nat. quality award Govt. Singapore, 1994; spkr. in field; bd. examiners Presdl. Quality Award, 1994-96, judge 1997-2000; quality examiner U.S. Army, 1996—; sr. quality examiner USAF, 1995-98, postdoctoral edn. in mediation and arbitration edn., 1998, 99; vol. mediator for dispute mediation svc., 1998—. Spkr. in field. Contbr. articles to profl jours. Decorated Army Commendation medal with oak leaf cluster, Meritorious Svc. medal, Legion of Merit. Fellow Am. Soc. Quality Control (cert. quality auditor, cert. quality mgr., cert. as quality and reliability engr., chmn. Dallas-Ft. Worth sect. 1974-75). Fellow U.S. Metric Assn. (cert., chmn. cert. bd. 1986-87); mem. U.S. Res. Officers Assn., Dallas C. of C. (chmn. world mfg. com. 1974-77, chmn. spl. tasl force career edn. adv. bd. 1973-74), Mensa (mem. air force blue ribbon commn. on assesments and evaluations 1996-98), Sigma Iota Epsilon, Phi Delta Kappa. Baptist. Clubs: Texins Rod and Gun (pres. 1969-70), Texins Flying, Masons (32 degree). Fax: 214-349-3686. E-mail: ejtew@swbell.net.

TEWARSON, REGINALD PRABHAKAR, retired mathematics educator, consultant; b. Pauri, Garhwal, India, Nov. 17, 1939; came to U.S., 1957; s. Seth Narottam and Chand (Mani) Tewarson; m. Hedi Thomann, July 1, 1960 (div. Nov. 1990); children: Anita Jasmine, Monique Shanti; m. Ghenwah Albarazi, Apr. 16, 2003. MA, Agra (Ind.) U., 1952; PhD, Boston U., 1961. Lectr. Lucknow (Ind.) U., 1951-57; sr. mathematicisn Honeywell EDP, Wellesley Hills, Mass., 1960-64; leading prof. applied math. and stats. SUNY, Stony Brook, 1964-2000, leading prof. physiology and biophysics dept., 1964-2000, leading prof. emeritus, 2001—. Cons. NIH, Washington, 1971-74. Author: Sparse Matrices, 1973; mem. editorial bd. Applied Math. Letters, 1986—, Math. Computer Modeling, 1991—, Pan. Am. Math. Jour., 1991—; contbr. articles to profl. jours. Centenary scholar Govt. of India, 1946-50, Crusade scholar U.S. Coun. Chs., 1957-59; rsch. grantee NIH, 1973-97, Air Force Office Sch. Rsch. Math. and Info. Scis., 1983-85, NSF, 1993-95. Mem. Am. Math. Soc., Soc. Indsl. and Applied Math., Soc. for Math. Biology. Democrat. Achievements include pioneering research on sparse matrices based largely on own research; co-development of mathematical model of kidney concentrating mechanism, of computer model of neuronal function. Home: 22 Night Heron Dr Stony Brook NY 11790-1108 Office: SUNY Dept Applied Math And Stats Stony Brook NY 11794-0001 E-mail: tewarson@ams.sunysb.edu.

TEWELL, JOSEPH ROBERT, JR., electrical engineer; b. Albany, N.Y., May 19, 1934; s. Joseph Robert and Florence Edna Tewell; m. Barbara Ann Johnson, Nov. 20, 1960; children— Patricia Ann, Donna Lynn, Joseph Robert, III. B.E.E., Rensselaer Poly. Inst., 1955, M.E.E., 1958. Rsch. engr. N.Am. Aviation, Inc., Downey, Calif., 1955; assoc. rsch. engr. Lockheed Aircraft Corp., Burbank, Calif., 1956; instr. Rensselaer Poly. Inst., 1957-64; sr. rsch. scientist Martin Marietta Corp., Denver, 1964-79, mgr. advanced programs Michoud, La., 1979-87, mgr. shuttle-C project, 1988-90, mgr. computer-aided productivity, 1991-93, mgr. sys. engring., 1994-96; ret., 1996; pvt. cons., 1996—. Founding sponsor Challenger Ctr.; cons. Redford Corp., Scotia, N.Y., 1961. Contbr. articles to profl. jours.; inventor dual action single drive actuator, spacecraft docking and retrieval mechanism. Founding sponsor Challenger Ctr. Served with Army Security Agy., 1957. Recipient NASA Manned Awareness citation, 1970, NASA Skylab Achievement award, 1974, NASA New Tech. award, 1976, Tech. Achievement award Martin Marietta Corp., 1977, Sustained Performance award Martin Marietta Corp., 1981, NASA cert. of recognition, 1977, Author of Yr. award, 1986, also 38 publ. awards, 1965— Fellow Explorers Club; mem. AIAA, Smithsonian Assocs., Air and Space Mus., Unmanned Vehicle Sys., Nat. Audubon Soc., Sigma Xi, Eta Kappa Nu, Tau Beta Pi, Theta Chi. Home and Office: 619 Legendre Dr Slidell LA 70460-3427

TEWES, R. SCOTT, lawyer; b. Chgo., Mar. 23, 1956; s. Raymond Henry and Vivian Marie Tewes; m. Marcia Anne King, June 5, 1981; children: Benjamin Scott, Matthew Philip, Madeline Anne Marie, Carrie Elizabeth, Aimee Marie. BS, Bob Jones U., 1978, MS, 1980; JD, U. S.C., 1983. Bar: S.C. 1983, D.C. 1985, Ga. 1987, U.S. Supreme Ct. Assoc. Brown & Hagins, Greenville, S.C., 1983-86; law clk. to Hon. Jean Galloway Bissell U.S. Ct. Appeals Fed. Cir., Washington, 1986-87; assoc., ptnr. Kilpatrick Stockton, Atlanta, 1987—2002; with Tewes Law Group, 2002—. Articles editor S.C. Law Rev., 1982-83; contbr. articles to profl. jours. Active Greenville (S.C.) County Alcohol and Drug Abuse Commn., 1985-86; trustee Killian Hill Baptist Ch., Lilburn, Ga., 1994-2000. Mem. S.C. Bar (practice and procedure com., bar ethics adv. com. 1985-86), Am. Intellectual Property Law Assn., Christian Legal Soc., Federalist Soc., Order of Barristers. Avocations: tennis, biking, skiing. Office: 2180 Satellite Blvd Ste 400 Duluth GA 30097-4927 Office Phone: 678-382-0388. E-mail: STewes@TewesLaw.com.

TEWFIK, DIANE BURAK, occupational therapist, educator; b. Detroit, Mich., May 14, 1949; d. Genevieve Burak; m. Zaki Tewfik, Sept. 24, 1950; children: Shereen, Omar. BA, Wayne State U., 1968—72; MA, NYU, 1981—83. Occupational Therapist Registered (OTR) N.Y., 1983, lic. Occupational Therapist N.Y. State Dept. Edn., 1983. Sr. occupl. therapist Met. Hosp., N.Y.C., 1983—92, Mt Sinai Med. Ctr., N.Y.C., 1992—94; asst. prof., assoc. prof. York Coll. of the CUNY, 1994—. Mem., mental health partnership program AOTA; founding mem., mental health task force, mental health spec. interest group MNYD of NYSOTA; mem. strategic objective AD Hoc group AOTA. Co-author: (jour. article) Occupl. Therapy as a Means to Wellness with the Elderly, (profl. newsletter) Counseling Enrichment in an Occupl. Therapy Program, (chapter in book) 'The New York Experience: The Remodeling of Mental Health Practice, (jour. article - ot practice) Cultural Context Competency and Children; co- presenter (aota preconference inst.) Cultural Competency-Are You Sure You're Competent?, 2002, co-presenter (aota conf. presentation) Occupl. Therapy On Bd. at the Airport, Two Models: Job Opportunities in Mental Health, 2001; author: (occupl. therapy jour.) Collaboration in Community: A Capstone Experience; co-author: (book chpt.) Surviving 9/11 (ed. Pat Precin). Recipient Merit of Practice in Mental Health Award, NY State Occupl. Therapy Assn., 1997, Recognition Achievement award, AOTA, 2003; grantee Co - Author of A Clearinghouse for Consumer Centered Cmty. Occupl. Therapy Models in Mental Health and Phys. Disabilities, NYSOTA & NJOTA CSAP Grant, 1997, Co -Author of Collaboration Survey, MNYD's Rsch. Spl. Interest Group Grant, 2000. Mem.: World Fedn. of Occupl. Therapy, N.Y. State Occupl. Therapy Assn. (Recognition award 2003), Met. N.Y. Dist. of the N.Y. State Occupl. Therapy Assn. (co -chair of the mental health spl. interest group 1995—2003), Am. Occupl. Therapy Assn.

TEWS, LEONARD L. retired science educator, poet; b. Rush Lake, WI, May 28, 1934; s. Lawrence Franklin and Jeannette Starr Tews; m. Violet Lucille Herring, Dec. 17, 1960 (div. Sept. 27, 1983); children: Matthew, Heather, Charles, Edith. BS, U. Wis., Oshkosh, 1956; MA, Ind. U., Bloomington, 1958; PhD, Univ. Wis., Madison, 1964. Prof. of biology U. Wis., Oshkosh, 1964—96, chmn. biology dept., 1974—80. Poet: Family Poems, Dance Steps in Brass; author: Poets Table Anthology, 2002; contbr. scientific papers, poems to literary jours. Recipient, Nat. League Women Pen Women, 2000, Hon. Mention, Peninsula Pulse, 2001. Mem.: Wash. Poets Assn. Democrat. Avocations: poetry, music, nature. Home: No 2 710 Belmont Pl E Seattle WA 98102 Personal E-mail: ltews@earthlink.net.

TEXAS, SAM FAYAD, small business owner, political activist; b. Monrovia, Liberia, Oct. 20, 1958; came to U.S., 1979; naturalized; s. Moufid and Elizabeth (Mowad) Fayad. Student, U. Houston, 1977-80. Handler pub. complaints against govt. agencies, 1980-90; owner, mgr. Texas Sam Import/Export, Houston, 1990—. Contbr. articles to jours. and newspapers. Vol. Bib Brothers, Houston, 1990—, Human Rights Watch, Houston, 1990—, Amnesty Internat., Houston, 1990—, Habitat for Humanity, Houston, 1990—, ARC; precinct judge, Houston, 1990, 91; del. to state and nat. Rep. and Dem. convs., 1992; mgr. local polit. campaigns, 1990; investigator genicide in Bosnia, 1996; Dem. nominee for Tex. Ho. of Reps., 1992. Named Outstanding Citizen, Mayor of Tex. and Gov. of Tex., 1988, 90, 92, 93; recipient outstanding vol. award Amnesty Internat., 1994. Republican. Roman Catholic. Avocations: prison ministry, councillor for needy, teaching sunday school, counseling youth. Home: PO Box 55707 Houston TX 77255-5707 Office: Texas Sam Import/Export 6510 Sivley St Houston TX 77055-5362 E-mail: samtexas@samtexas.simplenet.com.

TEXTOR, ROBERT BAYARD, cultural anthropology writer, consultant, educator; b. Cloquet, Minn., Mar. 13, 1923; s. Clinton Kenney and Lillian (Nickles) T.; divorced; children: Alexander Robertson, Marisa Elizabeth. Student, Lafayette Coll., 1940-41, Antioch Coll., 1941-43; BA in Asian Studies, U. Mich., 1945; PhD in Cultural Anthropology, Cornell U., 1960. Civil info. and edn. officer Mil. Govt., Kyoto-Wakayama, Japan, 1946-48; rsch. fellow anthropology and S.E. Asia studies Yale U., 1959-60, assoc., 1960-61; rsch. fellow in stats. Harvard U., 1962-64; assoc. prof. edn. and anthropology Stanford U., 1964-68, prof. edn. and anthropology, 1968-86, prof. anthropology, 1986-90, prof. anthropology emeritus, 1990—; courtesy prof. internat. studies U. Oreg., 1991—. Vis. prof. U. Saar, Saarbrücken, Germany, 1984-85; cons. Motorola, Inc., 1991-2001, Ministry of Planning, Kuwait, 1999; mem. S.E. Asia Coun., 1974-77; cons. cultural anthropology to govt. agys., 1957-58, 61-62. Author: Roster of the Gods: An Ethnography of The Supernatural in a Thai Village, 6 vols., 1973, Austria 2005: Projected Sociocultural Effects of the Microelectronic Revolution, 1983, Anticipatory Anthropology, 1985, (with Sippanondha Ketudat) The Middle Path for the Future of Thailand, 1990, (with others) Uncompromising Integrity: Motorola's Global Challenge, 1998; editor: Margaret Mead and the World Ahead, 2004; editor, commentator: Margaret Mead and Anticipating the Future, 2004; assoc. editor Jour. Conflict Resolution, 1965-70; mem. editl. bd. Human Orgn., 1966-71, Jour. Cultural Futures, 1979-87; adv. editor Behavior Sci. Rsch., 1974-86. Bd. dirs. Vols. in Asia, Stanford, Calif., 1968-73; mem. Metro Portland Future Vision Commn., 1993-95; mem. Portland, Oreg., Organizing Com. for Lewis and Clark Bicentennial, 1996-97. Served with U.S. Army, 1943-46. Fellow Rockefeller Found., 1951-52, fgn. area tng. fellow Ford Found., Thailand 1955-58, Carnegie fellow, 1959-71, Fulbright West Europe rsch. fellow, 1984-85, East-West Ctr. fellow, 1988-90; NSF grantee, Thailand, U.S., 1969-73, Volkswagen Found. grantee, Thailand and Germany, 1984.

Fellow Am. Anthrop. Assn. (life, chair resource devel. com. 2003—), Soc. Applied Anthropology; mem. Siam Soc. (life), Assn. Asian Studies (life), Council on Anthropology and Edn. (pres. 1974-75), AAUP (pres. Stanford chpt. 1975-76), Phi Kappa Phi

TEYAN, FREDERICK GENE, pediatrician; b. N.Y.C., Sept. 16, 1938; s. Jack H. and Pearl A. (Chernesky) T.; m. Dec. 18, 1965; children: Frederick II, Julie, Jonathan. AB, St. Peter's Coll., 1960; MD, Seton Hall, 1964. Diplomate Am. Bd. Pediatrics. Intern Kings County Hosp., Bklyn., 1964-65, resident in pediat., 1969-70, L.I. Jewish Hosp., New Hyde Park, N.Y., 1970-71; pvt. practice, Rockville Centre, N.Y., 1971—. Major U.S. Army, 1966-69. Fellow Am. Acad. Pediatrics; mem. Nassau Pediatric Soc. Roman Catholic. Office: 36 Lincoln Ave Rockville Centre NY 11570-5768 Office Phone: 516-766-2602. Personal E-mail: fgjteyan@ix.netcom.com.

TEYKL, JAMES STEPHEN, lawyer; b. Houston, Dec. 21, 1954; s. Irvin Frank and Marjorie Doris (Johnston) T.; m. Mary Beth Crowson, Apr. 30, 1983. BA, U. Ill., 1977; JD, Northwestern U., 1980. Bar: Ill. 1980, U.S. Dist. Ct. (no. dist.) Ill. 1980, U.S. Ct. Appeals (7th cir.) 1981. Assoc. Anthony Scariano & Assocs., P.C., Chicago Heights, Ill., 1980-81; ptnr. Greenberg & Teykl, P.C., Homewood, Ill., 1981-91; sole practice Crete, Ill., 1991—. Guest lectr. law Thornton C.C., South Holland, Ill., 1982—. Trustee, Ill. C.C. Dist. 515, Chicago Heights, 1983-89; mem. Taxpayers Adv. Bd., Chgo, 1983. Mem. Ill. Bar Assn. Episcopalian. Home: 3417 Huntley Ter Crete IL 60417-1393 Office: Law Offices James S Teykl PC PO Box 283 Crete IL 60417-0283 Office Phone: 708-367-0730.

TEZAK, EDWARD GEORGE, mechanics educator; b. Steelton, Pa., Oct. 16, 1940; s. John Frank and Mary Cecilia (Shiprak) T.; m. Martha Katherine Leyko, Sept. 10, 1966; children: Christine Louise, Edward Scott. BS, U.S. Mil. Acad., 1963; MS in Astrodynamics, UCLA, 1967; PhD in Engring. Mechanics, Va. Poly. Inst. and State U., 1979. Commd. 2d lt. U.S. Army, 1963, advanced through grades to col., 1985; co. comdr., exec. officer B Co. 13th Engr. Bn., Camp Casey, Republic of Korea, 1964-65; engr. bn. advisor 6th ARVN Engr. Group, QuiNhon and DaNang, Vietnam, 1967-68; instr., then asst. prof. dept. mechanics U.S. Mil. Acad., West Point, NY, 1969-72, group dir. dept. mechanics, 1976-88, dep. head dept. mechanics, 1988, assoc. dean, 1989-93; plans officer U.S. Army Engr. Group, Saigon, Vietnam, 1972-73; USMA fellow Army War Coll., Carlisle, Pa., 1982-83; ret. U.S. Army, 1993; dean Sch. Info. Sys. and Engring. Tech. SUNY, Utica, 1993-97, dean Coll. Tech. Alfred State, 1998-99; assoc. prof. Alfred State Coll., 1999-2000, prof. mechanics, 2000—; sec., treas. Coun. for Engring. Tech. NY State (CETNYS), 2000—. Mem. adv. bd. dept. math. U.S. Mil. Acad., 1993-97, mem. adv. bd. dept. civil and mech. engring., 2002-. Mem. Cmty. Counsel, Utica, 1994-97. Decorated Legion of Merit. Mem. ASME, Am. Soc. Engring. Edn. (bd. dirs., chair PIC III 1993-95, exec. com. mech. divsn., program chair, divsn. chair 1989-93, vice program chair engring. tech. divsn. 2001-02, program chair 2002-03, Outstanding Campus Liaison Rep. award Mid. Atlantic sect. 1991, Outstanding Tchr./Educator of Yr award St. Lawrence sect. 2001), NY State Engring. Tech. Assn. (exec. com. 2000—), Phi Kappa Phi. Roman Catholic. Avocations: bowling, golf, skiing. Home: 450 N Main St Wellsville NY 14895-1042 Business E-Mail: tezakeg@alfredstate.edu.

TEZANOS-PINTO, ROSA, Hispanic American literature educator; d. Alfredo Tezanos Pinto and Enriqueta Otiniano Tezanos Pinto; m. Jose L. Vargas Vila, Aug. 6, 1993; children: Sebastian Martin Valverde, Isabel Maria Valverde. BA, U. of Miami, 1975—79, MA, 1992—94, PhD, 1996—2002. Cons. and test evaluator U. Fla., Tampa, 1985—99; pres. Sigma Delta Pi, Miami, 1988—91; symposia coord. The Michel de Certeau Ctr. for Critical Studies, Coral Gables, Fla., 1990—92; lectr. U. Miami, 1992—99; dir. The John Adams Pub. Co., Coral Gables, Fla., 1994—97; prof. of hispanic am. lit. Lebanon Valley Coll., Annville, Pa., 1999—; dir. Alroquema Publishers, Miami, 1999—; coord. youth scholars program in spanish Lebanon Valley Coll., Annville, Pa., 2000—, advisor, spanish club, 2001—, advisor, spanish majors and minors, open majors, 2001—; dir. Asociación de Poetas de América, Buenos Aires, 2000—; coord., meeting hispanic authors program Lebanon Valley Coll., Annville, Pa., 2001—; advisor Nat. Assn. of Fellowships Advisors, Ark., 2002—. Rschr. Alroquema Pub. Co., Miami, 2003—. Recipient Jayanca Disting. Visitor Diploma, Chiclayo, Peru, 2002, Comodoro Rivadavia Book Fair Plaque, Comodoro Rivadavia Book Fair (Argentina), 2001; Profl. grant, Lebanon Valley Coll., 2001—03. Mem.: Assn. Cervantister, Colloquium Com., Diversity Adv. Com., Círculo Panamericano, Instituto Literario y Cultural Hispánico, Casa del Poeta del Perú, Am. Assn. of Teachers of Spanish and Portuguese, Nat. Assn. of Fellowships Advisors, Grad. Fellowship Com., Sigma Delta Pi, Phi Sigma Iota. Achievements include research in the relationship in form and practice of poetic language and the Freudian psychoanalytic language; the hidden text of Infancy in the Poetic works of Ester de Izaguirre and Loreina Santos Silva and testimonial literature; publications in the USA, France, Spain, Argentina, Peru, Paraguay, Brazil, Puerto Rico, India, etc; presented papers at USA, Chile, Venezuela, Guatemala, Puerto Rico, Australia, Peru, Colombia, Paraguay, Argentina, Spain, France, India, Mexico and Brazil. Office: Lebanon Valley College 101 North College Ave Annville PA 17003 E-mail: tezanos@lvc.edu.

TEZDUYAR, TAYFUN ERSIN, engineering educator; b. Elazig, Turkey, Aug. 6, 1954; s. Kamil and Esma Tezduyar; m. Tomoko Sasaki, Oct. 15, 1988. MS in Mech. Engring., Calif. Inst. Tech., 1978, PhD in Mech. Engring., 1982; Hon. Doctorate, Slovak Republic, 2001. Postdoctoral rsch. engr. in mech. engring. Stanford U., Palo Alto, Calif., 1982-83; asst. prof. in mech. engring. U. Houston, 1983-87; assoc. prof. in aerospace engring. and mechanics U. Minn., Mnpls., 1987-91, prof. in aerospace engring. and mechanics, 1991-97, disting. McKnight Univ. prof., 1997-98; James F. Barbour prof. engring. Rice U., Houston, 1998—, chmn. dept. mech. engring. and materials sci., 1999—2004. Dir. Army High Performance Computing Rsch. Ctr., Mpls., 1994-98. Authored over 110 jour. papers, 30 book chpts., 130 conf. papers; editor 12 jour. vols. various internat. jours. Recipient Presdl. Young Investigator award NSF, 1986, Comdr.'s Edn]. award for excellence U.S. Army Soldier Sys. Command, Natick, Mass., 1996, Computational Mechanics award Japan Soc. Mech. Engrs., Tokyo, 1997. Fellow ASME, U.S. Assn. Computational Mechanics (Computational Fluid Dynamics award 1997), Internat. Assn. Computational Mechanics (Computational Mechanics award 1998). Office: Rice Univ Mech Engr MS 321 6100 Main St Houston TX 77005 E-mail: tezduyar@rice.edu.

TEZLA, ALBERT, English educator; b. S. Bend, Ind., Dec. 13, 1915; s. Mihály and Lucza (Szénási) Tezla; m. Olive Anna Fox, July 26, 1941; children: Michael William, Kathy Elaine. BA, U. Chgo., 1941, MA, 1947, PhD, 1952. Instr. Ind. U. Ext., S. Bend, 1946-48; from instr. to assoc. prof. U. Minn., Duluth, 1949-61, prof., 1961-82, prof. emeritus, 1982—. Vis. prof. Hungarian lit. Columbia U., N.Y.C., 1966, cons., 1967-71, 77-81, vis. scholar, 1975; cons. U. Minn., Mpls., 1968-83; project reviewer NEH, Washington, 1979-82; vis. prof. Hungarian lit. U. Minn., Duluth, 1998. Author: An Introductory Bibliography to the Study of Hungarian Literature, 1964, Hungarian Authors: A Bibliographical Handbook, 1970, The Hazardous Quest: Hungarian Immigrants in the United States, 1895-1920, 1993; co-author: Academic American Encyclopedia, 1980, World Authors, 1975-80, 1985, Benét's Readers Encyclopedia, 1987, World Authors, 1980-85, 1991; editor, contbg. translator: Ocean at the Window: Hungarian Prose and Poetry since 1945, 1980, Three Contemporary Hungarian Plays, 1992; contbg. translator: Hungarian Short Stories, 1983, The Kiss: 20th Century Hungarian Short Stories, 1993; translator: God in the Wagon: Ten Short Stories (Ferenc Sánta), 1985 (Hungarian Pubs. award 1985), The Fifth Seal (Ferenc Sánta), 1986 (Hungarian Pubs. award 1986), Somewhere in a Distant Fabled Land: American Hungarians, 1895-1920, 1987, On the Balcony: Selected Short Stories (Iván Mándy), 1988 (Hungarian Pubs. award 1988), Hungary: A Brief History (István Lázár), 1990, An Illustrated History of Hungary (István Lázár), 1992, Memoir of Hungary, 1944-48 (Sándor Márai), 1996, Once There Was a Central Europe: Selected Short Stories and Other Writings (Miklós Mészoly), 1997, A Wartime Memoir, Hungary, 1944-45 (Alaine Polcz), 1998, Authoring, Barbering and Other Occupations, 2002; editl. cons. Holmes and Meier Pubs., 1998. Lt. (s.g.) USN, 1942-46, PTO. Recipient Diplome d'honeur, Inst. Cultural Rels., Hungary, 1970, Commemorative medal, 1970, Endre Ady Medallion, Presidium Hungarian PEN Ctr., 1986, Pro Cultura Hungarica award, Rep. Hungary, 1996, Abraham Lincoln award, Am. Hungarian Found., 1998; fellow Fulbright Rsch. fellow, Associated Bd. Rsch. Coun., 1959—60, Rsch. fellow, Internat. Co. Traveling Grants, 1963—64, Internat. Rsch. and Exchs. Bd., 1978; grantee Rsch. grantee, Am. Coun. Learned Socs., 1961, 1968, NEH, 1978—82. Mem. Internat. Assn. Hungarian Studies (mem. exec. com. 1978-83, John Lotz Meml. award 1986), Am. Hungarian Educators' Assn., Fulbright Assn. Democrat. Avocations: gardening, physical fitness, reading, classical films. Home: 5412 London Rd Duluth MN 55804-2511 E-mail: atezla@d.umn.edu.

THACH, WILLIAM THOMAS, JR., neurobiology and neurology educator; b. Okla. City, Jan. 3, 1937; s. William Thomas and Mary Elizabeth T.; m. Emily Ransom Otis, June 30, 1963 (div. 1979); children: Sarah Brill, James Otis, William Thomas III. AB in Biology magna cum laude, Princeton U., 1959; MD cum laude, Harvard U., 1964. Diplomate Am. Bd. Psychiatry and Neurology (in Neurology). Intern Mass. Gen. Hosp., Boston, 1964-65, asst. residency, 1965-66; staff assoc. physiology sect. lab. clin. sci. NIMH, Bethesda, Md., 1966-69; neurology resident, clin. and rsch. fellow Mass. Gen. Hosp., 1969-71; from asst. prof. neurology to assoc. prof. neurology Yale U. Sch. Medicine, New Haven, Conn., 1971-75; assoc. prof. neurobiology and neurology dept. anatomy and neurobiology Washington U. Sch. Medicine, St. Louis, 1975-80, prof. neurobiology and neurology dept. anatomy and neurobiology, 1980—, chief divsn. neurorehab. dept. neurology, 1992—. Acting dir. Irene Walter Johnson Rehab. Inst. Washington U. Sch. Medicine, 1989-91, dir., 1991-92; attending neurologist Barnes Hosp., med. dir. dept. rehab.; attending neurologist Jewish Hosp., St. Louis Regional Hosp.; bd. sci. counselors NINCDS, 1988-92; mem. NIH Study Sect. Neurology A, 1981-85. Assoc. editor Somatosenory and Motor Research; contbr. numerous articles to profl. jours. Fulbright grantee U. Melbourne, Australia, 1959-60; NIH grantee, 1971— Mem. Physiol. Soc., Am. Acad. Neurology, Soc. Neurosci., Am. Neurol. Assn., Am. Soc. Neurorehab., Phi Beta Kappa, Sigma Xi, Alpha Omega Alpha. Achievements include research on brain control of movement and motor learning, roles of the basal ganglia and the cerebellum in health and disease. Home: 7520 Clayton Rd Saint Louis MO 63117-1418 Office: Washington Univ Dept Anatomy & Neurobiol 600 S Euclid Ave Dept Anatomy& Saint Louis MO 63110-1010

THACHER, BARBARA AUCHINCLOSS, history educator; b. Oyster Bay, N.Y., July 27, 1918; d. Hugh and Frances Coverdale (Newlands) Auchincloss; m. Thomas Thacher, Aug. 4, 1942; children: Barbara Burrall Thacher Plimpton, Elizabeth Coverdale Thacher Hawn, Thomas Day II, Hugh Auchincloss, Peter Anthony, Andrew. BA cum laude, Bryn Mawr Coll., 1940; MA in History, Columbia U., 1965. Editl. rschr. Newsweek, N.Y.C., 1940-41, 44; writer N.Y. Times Sunday Mag., News of Week Rev., N.Y.C., 1941-43; co-editor Christmas Booklist for Children Harper's Mag., N.Y.C., 1957-59; asst. history dept. Barnard Coll., N.Y.C., 1964-65; rsch. asst. Ctr. Urban Edn., N.Y.C., 1966. Bd. dirs. Bryn Mawr Coll., 1966-88, chair bd. trustees, 1980-87, emeritus, 1988—, City Univ. of N.Y, trustee, 1970-73, WNET-TV-Channel 13, trustee, 1978-88; active Sheltering Arms Children's Svc., Istanbul Women's Coll., Leake & Watts Children's Home Svcs., Yonkers and N.Y.C., 1961-83, emeritus, 1983—, N.Y.C. Park Assn., Riverdale Girls Sch.; trustee Tchrs. Coll. Columbia U. Mem. Cosmopolitan Club (gov.), North Haven Casino. Democrat. Presbyterian. Office: 289 Adelphi St Brooklyn NY 11205-4602

THACKER, CATHERINE A. music educator; b. Salt Lake City, Aug. 23, 1971; d. Joseph Arthur Gale and Cheryl Eva Eldredge; m. A. Kent Thacker, Mar. 14, 1991; children: Ashley, Rebecca, Amy, Nathan, James. MusB, U. Utah, 1994, postgrad., 1994—95. Pvt. piano instr., 1984—. Accompanist Intermountain Suzuki String Inst., 2001—04. Ward organist LDS Ch., Utah, 1987—, pianist for ward choir, 1991—. Presdl. scholar, U. Utah, 1989. Mem.: Nat. Fedn. Music Club, Utah Music Tchrs. Assn. (state aim chmn. 1991—2004, v.p. Sandy chpt. 1995—96, regional aim chmn. 1997—2000), Music Tchrs. Nat. Assn. Republican. Avocations: running, reading, piano, gardening. Home: 798 Molasses Mill Dr Draper UT 84020

THACKER, STEPHEN BRADY, medical association administrator, epidemiologist; b. Independence, Mo., Dec. 30, 1947; m. 1976; 2 children. AB, Princeton U., 1969; MD, Mt. Sinai Sch. Medicine, 1973; MSc, London Sch. Hygiene and Tropical Medicine, 1984. Chief consolidated surveillance and commn. activity epidemiol. program office Ctrs. Disease Control and Prevention, Atlanta, 1978-83, dir. surveillance and epidemiol. studies, 1983-86, dir. epidemiol. program office, 1989—2004, acting dep. dir., 1998, acting dir. Nat. Ctr. Injury Prevention and Control, 1999-2000, acting dir. Nat. Ctr. Environ. Health, 1993-95, dir. Office of Workforce and Career Devel., 2004—; asst. dir. sci. Ctr. Environ. Health and Injury Control, Atlanta, 1986-89. Mem. steering com. Assn. Behavioral Sci. Med. Edn., 1971-74; assoc. Dept. Cmty. Medicine, Med. Ctr. Duke U., Durham, N.C., 1975-76; lectr. Cmty. Ctr. Mt. Sinai Sch. Medicine, N.Y.C., 1978—, Sch. Medicine Emory U., Atlanta, 1985-86; cons. epidemiology Arab Republic Egypt, 1979-91; clin. asst. prof. cmty. health Sch. Medicine Emory U., 1986-91; adj. prof. Emory U. Sch. Pub. Health, 1992—. Editor: Epidemiologic Revs., 1990-2003. Clin. scholar Robert Wood Johnson Found., 1974-75; recipient Mosby Book award for excellence, 1973, Pub. Health Svc. Outstanding Svc. medal, 1987, Pub. Health Svc. Meritorious Svc. medal, 1988, 2002, Saul Horowitz Jr. Meml. award, 1990, Supervisory award for contbr. advantage of women, 1991, Pub. Health Svc. Commendation medal, 1991, Pub. Health Svc. Disting. Svc. medal, 1993, Pub. Health Svc. Surgeon Gen.'s Exemplary Svc. medal, 1993, Pub. Health Svc. Disting. Svc. medal, 1997, Medal of Excellence William C. Watson, Jr., 1996, Ray E. Brown award Assn. Mil. Surgeons of U.S., 2003. Achievements include rsch. public health surveillance, infectious disease, environ. health, injury prevention, alcohol abuse, health care delivery, meta-analysis, technology assessment. Office: Ctrs for Disease Control and Prevention MS C08 1600 Clifton Rd NE Atlanta GA 30333 Business E-Mail: sbt1@cdc.gov.

THACKERAY, JONATHAN E. lawyer; b. Athens, Ohio, July 30, 1936; s. Joseph Eugene and Betty Rutherford (Boright) T.; m. Sandra Ann McMahon; children: Jennifer, Sara, Amy, Jonathan. AB cum laude, Harvard U., 1958, JD, 1961. Bar: Ohio 1961, U.S. Dist. Ct. (no. dist.) Ohio 1961, U.S. Supreme Ct. 1972, U.S. Ct. Appeals (6th cir.) 1973, U.S. Ct. Appeals (9th cir.) 1982, N.Y. 1993. Assoc. Vorys, Sater, Seymour & Pease, Columbus, Ohio, 1961, Baker & Hostetler, Cleve., 1965-72, ptnr., 1973-93; v.p., gen. counsel The Hearst Corp., N.Y.C., 1993—2003; ret., 2003. Served to lt. USNR, 1961-65. Mem. ABA, Ohio Bar Assn., Cleve. Bar Assn., Am. Law Inst. Office: The Hearst Corp 959 8th Ave New York NY 10019-3795 *Notable cases include: administrative proceedings leading to approval of joint newspaper operating agreements in Cincinnati, Seattle and Las Vegas; litigation of newspaper antitrust cases in Memphis, Trenton and Dallas.*

THACKRAY, ARNOLD WILFRID, historian, foundation executive; b. Eng., July 30, 1939; came to U.S., 1967, naturalized, 1982; s. Wilfrid Cecil and Mary (Clarke) T.; m. Barbara Hughes, 1964 (div. 1990); children: Helen Mary, Gillian Winifrid, Timothy Arnold; m. Diana Schueler, 1994; 1 stepchild, Gregory Jordan. B.Sc., Bristol (Eng.) U., 1960; MA, Cambridge (Eng.) U., 1965, PhD, 1966. Research chemist Robert Dempster and Co., Yorkshire, Eng., 1960-61; research fellow Churchill Coll., Cambridge U., 1965-68; prof. history and sociology of sci. U. Pa., Phila., 1968-96, Joseph Priestley prof. emeritus history/sociology of sci., 1996—, chmn. dept., 1970-77, dir. Beckman Ctr. for History of Chemistry, 1982-96; prof. history, prof. chemistry, dean grad. studies and research U. Md., 1985-86. Exec. dir., libr. Chem. Heritage Found., 1987-96, pres., 1996—; vis. lectr. Harvard U., 1967-68; vis. fellow All Souls Coll., Oxford, Eng., 1977-78; mem. Inst. Advanced Study, 1980. Editor: Isis, an Internat. Rev. of History of Science and its Cultural Influences, 1978-85, Osiris, 1985-94, Science After '40, 1992, Constructing Knowledge in the History of Science, 1995, Private Science, 1998, (with others) Science and Values, 1974, Toward a Metric of Science, 1978; author: Atoms and Powers, 1970, John Dalton, 1972, (with others) Gentlemen of Science, 1981-82, Chemistry in America, 1985, (with others) Arnold O. Beckman, 2000; contbr. articles to profl. jours. Recipient Gladstone Essay prize, also pub. speaking prize Churchill Coll., Cambridge U.; Guggenheim fellow, 1971-72, 85-86; Ctr. for Advanced Study in Behavioral Scis. fellow, 1973-74, 83-84 Fellow AAAS, Am. Acad. Arts and Scis., Royal Hist. Soc., Royal Chem. Soc.; mem. Am. Chem. Soc. (Dexter award 1983), Am. Hist. Assn., Manchester Lit. and Philos. Soc. (corr.), History of Sci. Soc., Am. Coun. Learned Socs. (bd. dirs., treas. 1985-96), Soc. for Social Studies of Sci. (pres. 1981-83), Am. Coun. on Edn. (bd. dirs. 1987), Société Chimie (bd. dirs. 1997—), Cosmos Club (Washington); trustee U. Pa. Press, Chem. Edn. Found. Episcopalian. E-mail: athackray@chemheritage.org.

THACKSTON, EDWARD LEE, engineer, educator; b. Nashville, Apr. 29, 1937; s. Guy Carleton and Sydney Virginia (Adams) T.; m. Betty Tucker, Mar. 19, 1961; children: Carol Elizabeth Thackston Nixon, Leah Virginia Thackston Hawkins. BE summa cum laude, Vanderbilt U., 1961; MS, U. Ill., 1963; PhD, Vanderbilt U., 1966. Registered profl. engr., Tenn. City engr. City of Lebanon, Tenn., 1959; design engr. City of Nashville, 1961-62; instr. Vanderbilt U., Nashville, 1965-66, asst. prof., 1966-69, assoc. prof., 1969-75, prof. engring., 1975-2000, chmn. dept. civil and environ. engring., 1980-99. Asst. to gov. for environ. affairs, State of Tenn., 1972-74; cons. in field. Author book, tech. reports; contbr. to profl. publs. Bd. dirs. Tenn. Environ. Coun., Nashville, 1971-76; bd. dirs. Tenn. Conservation League, Nashville, 1974-2003, v.p., 1977, pres., 1978-80; trustee Cumberland Mus., Nashville, 1986-92; trustee Cumberland U., Lebanon, 1996—, mem. exec. com., 1996-2002, 04—, sec.-treas., 2000-02, 04—. Recipient Tenn. Lifetime Environ./Conservation Stewardship award State Tenn. 1996, Engr. of Yr. Mid. Tenn. Tenn. Soc. Prof. Engring., 2001, Landmark Paper award Assn. Environ. Engring. and Sci. Profs., 2001; named Tenn. Conservationist of Yr., 1974. Fellow ASCE; mem. Am. Water Works Assn. (life), Water Environ. Fedn. (life), Assn. Environ. Engring. Profs. (emeritus; Landmark Paper award 2001), Tenn. Hist. Soc., Tau Beta Pi, Chi Epsilon. Republican. Episcopalian. Avocations: genealogy, history, photography.

THADANI, UDHO, physician, cardiologist; b. Hyderabad, India, Apr. 1, 1941; came to U.S., 1980; s. Vensimal Mulchand and Gopi Thadani; m. Dorothy Ann Thadani, 1974; 1 child, Emma Sarala. MBBS, All India Inst. Med. Scis., New Delhi, 1964. Lic. physician, Okla., Ont., Can., Eng., India; cert. internal medicine, U.K., Can.; cert. cardiology, Can.; diplomate in internal medicine and cardiovasc. diseases Am. Bd. Internal Medicine. Intern All India Inst. Med. Scis., New Delhi, 1964-65, house physician, surgeon, 1965-66; house physician in medicine Joyce Green Hosp., Dartford, Kent, England, 1966-67; sr. house physician in medicine Kingston Gen. Hosp., Hull, England, 1967-69, registrar, rsch. fellow in medicine and cardiology, 1969-71, U. Leeds (Eng.), The Gen. Infirmary at Leeds, 1971-75; sr. rsch. fellow, clin. asst. medicine Queen's U., Kingston Gen. Hosp., Ont., Canada, 1975-78; asst. prof. medicine Queen's U., Kingston, 1978-80; staff physician Kingston Gen. Hosp., 1978-80; assoc. prof. medicine U. Okla. Health Scis. Ctr., Oklahoma City, 1980-83; prof. medicine Okla. U. Health Scis. Ctr., Oklahoma City, 1983—2001, prof. emeritus medicine, 2001, mem. cardiology fellowship com., 1980 82; dir. clin. cardiology Okla. U. Health Scis. Ctr. and VA Med. Ctr., Oklahoma City, 1980-87, cons., 1980—, vice chief cardiovasc. sect., 1981-99, dir. clin. rsch., 1987-99. Vice-chmn. rsch. and devel. com. VA Med. Ctr., Oklahoma City, 1989-92, chmn. physiology-pharmacology categorical rev. com., 1989-94, chmn. rsch. and devel. com., VA Med. Ctr. Oklahoma City, 1992-94, 2003—; sr. rsch. fellow Ont. Heart Found., 1978-80, rsch. fellow, 1976-78; rsch. fellow dept. medicine Queen's U., Kingston, Ont., 1975-76; rsch. fellow U. Leeds, Pub. Health and Ciba Found., dept. medicine and cardiovasc. sect. Leeds Gen. Infirmary, 1971-75. Editor: Medical Therapy of Ischemic Heart Disease, 1992, Nitrates Updated, 1996; mem. editl. bd. panel Cardiology Drug Facts and Comparison, 1989; contbg. rev. panel Drug Facts and Comparisons, 1989—; mem. editl. bd. Internat. Jour. Cardiology, 1987-93, Cardiovascular Drugs and Therapy, 1987—, Heart Diseases, 1999-2004, Am. Jour. Pharmacology, 2000-; reviewer Circulation, Jour. Am. Coll. Cardiology, Am. Jour. Cardiology, Brit. Heart Jour., Internat. Jour. Cardiology, Can. Jour. Cardiology, European Heart Jour., Annals of Internal Medicine, New Eng. Jour. Medicine, Archives of Internal Medicine, Cardiovasc. Drugs and Therapy, Drugs, European Jour. Pharmacology, Clin. Pharmacology and Therapeutics; contbr. over 200 articles to profl. jours., chpts. to books. Recipient Provost Rsch. award, OUHSC, 1995, James F. Hamerstein award for physicians of excellence award, VA Med. Ctr., Okla., Best Dr. in Am. (Okla.) cardiovascular diseases, 1997, 1999, 2000, 2001, 2004. Fellow: Royal Coll. Physicians and Surgeons Can., Coun. Clin. Cardiology Am. Heart Assn. (coun. rep. Okla. 1989—2000), Am. Coll. Cardiology (mem. cardiovasc. drug com. 1990—94), Royal Soc. Medicine London; mem.: Can. Cardiovasc. Soc., Royal Coll. Phycisians U.K., Phi Kappa Phi (mem. FDA cardiovasc. and renal drugs adv. com. 1995—99). Avocations: gardening, tennis, travel. Office: Okla U Health Sci Ctr Cardiology Sect 920 SL Young WP 3120 Oklahoma City OK 73104 Office Phone: 405-271-4742. Business E-Mail: udho-thadani@ouhsc.edu.

THADDEUS, PATRICK, physicist, researcher; b. Wilmington, Del., June 6, 1932; s. Victor and Elizabeth (Ross) T.; m. Janice Petherbridge Farrar, Apr. 6, 1963 (dec. Dec. 2001); children: Eva, Michael; m. Valerie McCollom, Nov. 1, 2003. B.Sc., U. Del., 1953; MA, Oxford (Eng.) U., 1955; PhD, Columbia U., 1960; DSc (hon.), U. Chgo., 2003. Research assoc. Columbia Radiation Lab., 1960-61; research assoc. Goddard Inst. Space Studies, N.Y.C., 1961-63, mem. sci. staff, 1963-86; mem. faculty Columbia U., 1965-86, adj. prof. physics, 1971-86; prof. astronomy and applied physics Harvard U., 1986-2000, Robert Wheeler Willson prof. applied astronomy, 2000—; mem. sci. staff Smithsonian Astrophys. Obs., 1986—. Vis. com. Nat. Radio Astronomy Obs., 1973-76, 91-94; mem. Astronomy Survey Com., 1978-80, 89-90; chair task group on Space Astronomy and Astrophysics, 1996-97; Fairchild Disting. Scholar Calif. Inst. Tech., 1994; Russell Marker lectr. Pa. State U., 1989; vis. fellow Inst. Astronomy, Cambridge, Eng., 1983. Author papers on microwave spectroscopy, optical and radio astronomy. Recipient Exceptional Sci. Achievement medal NASA, 1970, 85; John C. Lindsay Meml. award Goddard Space Flight Center, 1976; Alexander von Humboldt award, 1983; Herschel medal Royal Astron. Soc., 2001; Fulbright fellow, 1953-55. Fellow Am. Phys. Soc.; mem. Am. Astron. Soc., Am. Acad. Arts and Scis., Nat. Acad. Scis., Internat. Astronomical Union, Saturday Club, Sigma Xi. Address: 58 Garfield St Cambridge MA 02138-1802

THADEN, EDWARD CARL, history professor; b. Seattle, Apr. 24, 1922; s. Edward Carl and Astrid (Engvik) T.; m. Marianna Theresia Forster, Aug. 7, 1952. BA, U. Wash., 1944; student, U. Zurich, Switzerland, 1948; PhD, U. Paris, 1950. Instr. Russian history Pa. State U., 1952-55, asst. prof., 1955-58, assoc. prof., 1958-64, prof., 1964-68, U. Ill., Chgo., 1968—92, chmn. dept. history, 1971—73, prof. emeritus, 1992—. Vis. prof. Ind. U., 1957, U. Marburg, 1965, U. Ill., Urbana, 1980, U. Halle, Germany, 1988, U. Helsinki, Finland, 1990; editl. cons. Can. Rev. Studies in Nationalism, 1973—78; vis. rsch. scholar USSR Acad. Scis., 1975, 88, 90; project prin. rschr. Ford Found., 1975—78; U.S. rep. Internat. Congress of Hist. Scis., 1980; project dir. NEH grant, 1980—82. Author: Conservative Nationalism in Nineteenth-Century Russia, 1964, Russia and the Balken Alliance of 1912, 1965, Russia Since 1801: The Making of a New Society, 1971, Russia's Western Borderlands, 1710-1870, 1984, Interpreting History: collected Essays on Russia's Relations with Europe, 1990, Essays in Russian and East European History: Festschrift in Honor of Edward C. Thaden, 1995, The Rise of Historicism in Russia, 1999; co-author, editor: Russification in the Baltic Provinces and Finland, 1855-1914, 1981; co-author, co-editor: Finland and the Baltic Provinces in the Russian Empire, 1984; mem. editorial bd. Jour Baltic Studies, 1984-93, assoc. editor, 1987-93, East European Quarterly, 1998—. Served to lt. (j.g.) USNR, 1943-46. Carnegie Inter-Univ. Com. travel grantee to USSR, 1956; Fulbright rsch. grantee Finland, 1957-58, Germany, 1965, Poland and Finland, 1968; Soc. Sci. Rsch. Coun. grantee, 1957; Am. Coun. Learned Socs. grantee, 1963, 65-66; fellow Woodrow Wilson Internat. Ctr. for Scholars, 1980 Mem. Am. Hist. Assn. (life), Am. Assn. for Advancement Slavic Studies (pres. Midwest br. 1975-76, exec. sec. 1980-82), Chgo. Consortium for Slavic and Ea. European Studies (pres. 1982-84), Baltische Historische Kommission, Göttingen (corr. mem. 1985—), Commn. Internat. des Etudes Historiques Slaves (v.p. 1985-95, pres. 1995-2000, pres.d'honneur 2000—). Office: U Ill Dept History 913 UH (M/C 198) 601 S Morgan St Chicago IL 60607-7100

THAGARD, NORMAN E. astronaut, physician, engineer, educator; b. Marianna, Fla., July 3, 1943; s. James E. Thagard and Mary F. Nicholson; m. Rex Kirby Johnson; children: Norman Gordon, James Robert, Daniel Cary. BS, Florida State U., 1965, MS, 1966; MD, U. Texas S.W. Med. Sch., 1977; LHD (hon.), Fla. Atlantic U. Intern, internal medicine Medical U. South Carolina, 1977-78; astronaut NASA, 1978-96, ret., 1996; mission specialist NASA Space Shuttle Challenger Flight STS-7, deployed satellites (ANIK C-2, PALAPA B-1), operated Remote Manipulator Sys., conducted experiments, 1983, NASA Spacelab-3 Mission STS-51 B, 1985, NASA Space Shuttle Atlantis Flight STS-30, deployed Magellan Venus exploration spacecraft, 1989; payload comdr. NASA Space Shuttle Discovery Flight STS-42, International Microgravity Lab.-1 module experiments, 1992; cosmonaut-rschr. Space Station MIR-18, 1995; prof. elec. engring., assoc. dean coll. rels. Coll. Engring. Fla. A&M U.-Fla. State U., Tallahassee, 1996—. Contbr. articles to profl. jours. With USMC, 1966-71. Capt. 1967-71, in Vietnam flew 163 combat missions. Decorated 11 Air medals, Navy Commendation medal with Combat V, Marine Corps E award, Vietnam Svc. medal, Vietnamese Cross of Gallantry with Palm. Fellow AIAA (assoc.); mem. IEEE, Assn. Space Explorers, Aerospace Med. Assn., Soc. for Human Performance in Extreme Environments, Phi Kappa Phi. Achievements include breaking U.S. space endurance record of 84 continuous days aboard the Russian space station Mir. Avocations: classical music, electronic design. Office: Fla A&M U-Fla State U Coll Engring 2525 Pottsdamer St Tallahassee FL 32310-6046 Fax: 850-487-6486. E-mail: nthagard@fsu.edu.

THAIN, JOHN A. stock exchange executive; b. Antioch, Ill. m. Carmen Thain; 4 children. BS, MIT, 1977; MBA, Harvard U., 1979. CFO, head of ops., tech. & fin. The Goldman Sachs Group, L.P., 1994—99, pres., COO, 1999, co-chief exec., European ops., 1995—97; dir. Goldman, Sachs, & Co., 1998—2004; pres., co-COO Goldman, Sachs & Co., N.Y.C., 1999—2003, pres., COO, 2003—04; CEO N.Y. Stock Exchange, 2004—. Mem., dean's adv. coun. MIT Sloan Sch. Mgmt.; mem. MIT Corp., INSEAD, U.S. Nat. Adv. Bd., Fed. Reserve Bank N.Y. Internat. Capital Mkts. Adv. Com. Mem. James Madison Coun. Library of Congress, French-Am. Found., Trilateral Commn.; bd. trustees Nat. Urban League; bd. trustee N.Y. Presbyn. Hosp.; gov. N.Y. Presbyn. Found., Inc.; trustee Howard U. Office: NY Stock Exchange c/o Ray Pellecchia 11 Wall St New York NY 10005*

THAL, LEON JOEL, neuroscientist; b. N.Y.C., June 17, 1944; s. Bernard and Esther (Beller) T.; m. Donna Jean Norbo, June 25, 1967. MD, Downstate Med. Ctr., N.Y.C., 1969. Diplomate Am. Bd. Psychiatry and Neurology. Instr., asst. prof., assoc. prof. neurology Albert Einstein Coll. Medicine, Bronx, N.Y., 1975-85; assoc. prof. neuroscis. U. Calif. San Diego, 1985-89; prof. neuroscis. U. Calif., San Diego, 1989—, chmn. dept. neuroscis., 1993—. Editor: Cognitive Disorders, 1992; contbr. chpts. in books and articles to profl. jours. Lt. comdr. USPHS, 1970-72. Office: U Calif San Diego Dept Neuroscience 9500 Gilman Dr La Jolla CA 92093-5004

THALACKER, ARBIE ROBERT, lawyer, director; b. Marquette, Mich., Apr. 17, 1935; s. Arbie Otto and Jeanne (Emmett) T.; m. Rita Annette Skaaren, Sept. 11, 1956 (div. July 1992); children: Marc Emmett, Christopher Paul, Robert Skaaren; m. Deborah B. Garrett, Jan. 10, 1998. AB, Princeton U., 1957; JD, U. Mich., 1960. Bar: NY 1961, U.S. Ct. Appeals (2d cir.) 1962. Assoc. Shearman & Sterling, N.Y.C., 1960—68, ptnr., 1968—2000, of counsel, 2001—. Dir. Detrex Corp., Detroit, 1981—, chmn. bd., 1993-96. Leader Rep. Dist. Com., 1966-68; v.p., trustee Greenwich Village Soc. for Hist. Preservation; trustee Naropa Univ.; bd. dirs. Meredith Monk House Found., Shambhala Internat. Mem. ABA, N.Y. Bar Assn., Assn. Bar City N.Y. (securities regulatory comm. 1975-78), Wine and Food Soc. (bd. dirs. 1976-78, 85-93, 94—), Chevaliers du Tastevin, Commanderie de Bordeaux, Siwanoy Country Club (bd. govs. 1976-79), Derby Club, Links Club, Verbank Hunting and Fishing Club. Home: 17 Commerce St New York NY 10014-3763 Office: Shearman & Sterling 599 Lexington Ave Fl C2 New York NY 10022-6069

THALDEN, BARRY R. architect; b. Chgo., July 5, 1942; s. Joseph and Sibyl (Goodwin) Hechtenthal; m. Irene L. Mittleman, June 23, 1966 (div. 1989); 1 child, Stacey; m. Kathyn McKnight, Sept. 1996. BArch, U. Ill., 1965; M in Land Architecture, U. Mich., 1969. Landscape architect Hellmuth, Obata, Kassebaum, St. Louis, 1969-70; dir. landscape architecture PGAV Architects, St. Louis, 1970-71; pres. Thalden Corp. Architects, St. Louis, 1971—; ptnr. Thalden-Boyd Architects. Prin. works include Rock Hill Park, 1975 (AIA award, 1977), Wilson Residence, 1983 (AIA award), Nat. Bowling Hall of Fame, 1983 (St. Louis RCGA award, 1984), Village Bogey Hills (Home Builders award, 1985, St. Louis ASLA award, 1994), St. Louis U. Campus Mall (St. Louis ASLA award, 1989), Horizon Casino Resort, Lake Tahoe, Nev., St. Louis Airport's Radisson Hotel, Lady Luck, Treasure Bay, Palace Casinos, Biloxi, Miss., Boomtown Casino, New Orleans, Pres. Casino on the Admiral, St. Louis, Plaza of Champions, Busch Stadium, Ho Chunk Casino, Wisconsin Dells (ABC award Best Bldg. in Wis., 2000), Potowatomi Casino, Milw., Terrible's Casino, Las Vegas, Chumash Casino Resort, Santa Ynez, Calif. Bd. dirs. St. Louis Open Space Coun., 1973—83, St. Louis Art., Ednl. Coun.; bd. trustees Las Vegas Art Mus.; apptd. Mo. Lands Architect Coun., 1990—94. Named Architect of Yr. Builder Architect mag., 1986. Fellow Am. Soc. Landscape Architects (nat. v.p. 1979-81, pres. St. Louis chpt. 1975, trustee 1976-79, nat. conv. chair 1991); mem. AIA, World Future Soc. (pres. St. Louis chpt. 1984-94, keynote conf. spkr. 1995). Avocations: painting, gardening, tennis, guitar. Home: 2204 Chatsworth Ct Henderson NV 89074-5307 Office: Thalden Corp 7777 Bonhomme Ave Ste 2200 Saint Louis MO 63105-1911

THALER, LINDA KAPLAN, communications executive; m. Fred Thaler; children: Michael, Emily. BA magna cum laude, MA in music, CCNY. Former music instr. CCNY; with J. Walter Thompson, most recently as exec. v.p., exec. group creative dir.; exec. v.p., exec. creative dir. Wells Rich Greene BDDP, 1994—97; founder, CEO, chief creative officer Kaplan Thaler Group Ltd., N.Y.C., 1997—. Former mem. comedy improv troupe. Author: (jingle) I Don't Want to Grow Up, I'm a Toys 'R' Us Kid, Eastman Kodak-Because Time Goes By, (book) BANG! Getting Your Message Head in a Noisy World, 2003. Named Advertising Women of Yr., Advertising Women of N.Y., 2001; recipient 13 Clio awards. Office: Kaplan Thaler Group Ltd 58 W 40th St New York NY 10018*

THALER, PAUL SANDERS, lawyer, arbitrator, mediator; b. Washington, May 4, 1961; s. Martin S. Thaler and Barbara (Friedman) Mishkin; m. Melinda Ann Frostic, Oct. 12, 1991; children: Rachel Leigh, Daniel Martin. AB, Vassar Coll., 1983; JD, Georgetown U., 1987. Bar: Md. 1987, D.C. 1988, U.S. Ct. Appeals (D.C. and 4th cirs.) 1988, U.S. Dist. Ct. Md. 1988, U.S. Ct. Appeals (fed. cir.) 1989, U.S. Dist. Ct. D.C. 1989, U.S. Ct. Internat. Trade 1990, U.S. Supreme Ct. 1992. Assoc. Cooter & Gell, Washington, 1987-93; ptnr. The Robinson Law Firm, Washington, 1993-96, Thaler, Liebeler LLP, 1996—; guest lectr. negotiations mediation George Washington U. Law Sch., 1996—. Adj. prof. Kogod Sch. Bus., Am. U. Bus. Ethics, Bus. Law, 1999—. Treas. Montgomery Highlands Estates Homeowners Assn., Silver Spring, Md., 1990-99; mediator Superior Ct. of D.C., 1991—; mem. adv. com. Vassar Coll. Fund, 1996-99; trustee Nat. Child Rsch. Ctr., Washington, 1998-2001. Mem. ABA (sect. dispute resolution, vice chmn. ethics 1994-98), D.C. Bar Assn., Md. Bar Assn., Soc. Profls. in Dispute Resolution, Acad. Family Mediators. Home: 9429 Locust Hill Rd Bethesda MD 20814-3939 Office: Thaler Liebeler LLP Ste 200 1919 Pennsylvania Ave NW Washington DC 20006 Office Phone: 202-466-4110. Business E-Mail: PThaler@ThalerLiebeler.com.

THALER, RICHARD WINSTON, JR., investment banker; b. Boston, Apr. 9, 1951; s. Richard Winston and Victoria Louise (Sears) T.; m. Mary Alice Gast, June 28, 1980; children: Julia Davis, Sarah Sears, Hannah Warren. BA in Am. Polit. History cum laude, Princeton U., 1973; MBA, Harvard U., 1978. Salesman Media Networks, N.Y.C., 1973-74; banker Bank of Boston, Rio de Janeiro, 1975-77, Boston, 1978-80; mng. dir. investment banking Lehman Bros., N.Y.C., 1980-96, Deutsche Banc, N.Y.C., 1996—. Spl. gifts solicitor Princeton U. Ann. Giving, N.Y.C., 1987-88, 97-98, class agt., 1988-93; del. Dem. Nat. Conv., 1996; trustee Daily Princetonian, 1989—, pres. bd. dirs., 2004—; trustee Episc. Divinity Sch., Cambridge, Mass., 1995—; mem. vestry Chapel of St. James the Fisherman, Wellfleet, Mass.; trustee at large Plimouth Plantation, Plymouth, Mass., 1995—; active Dem. Leadership Coun. Mem. Mass. Soc. Mayflower Descendants, Harvard Club, Siwanoy Country Club, University Cottage Club. Democrat. Episcopalian. Avocations: gardening, sailing, American political history, travel.

THALL, BURNETT MURRAY, retired newspaper executive; b. Toronto, Ont., Can., Sept. 27, 1922; s. Henry and Selina (Harris) Rosenthal; m. Eleanor Langbord, Sept. 23, 1945; children: Nelson Spencer, Martin Evan. BASc., U. Toronto, 1945, MASc., 1947, PhD, 1949. Registered profl. engr., Ont. Spl. lectr. applied sci. and engring. U. Toronto, 1947; cons. engr., then prodn. engr. Toronto Star, 1947-50, v.p., 1958-68, sr. v.p., 1968-96, also dir. Chmn. Toronto Star Newspapers Ltd., elected chmn. bd., 1996-99. Trustee Atkinson Charitable Found.; hon. trustee Women's Coll. Hosp. Urgent Care Ctr.; founding trustee Princess Margaret Hosp. Urgent Care Centre named in his honour Women's Coll. Hosp., 1989. Mem. Assn. Profl. Engrs. Ont. (Citizenship medal 1991). Home: 15 Rosemary Ln Toronto ON Canada M5P 3E7 Office: The Toronto Star 1 Yonge ST Toronto ON Canada M5E 1E6

THALL, ROBERT, photographer, educator; b. Chgo., Dec. 6, 1948; BA in Design, U. Ill., 1972, MFA in Photography, 1986. Prof. photography Columbia Coll., Chgo., 1976—, chmn. Photography Dept. Vis. artist U. Ill., Chgo., 1975, adj. asst. prof. art, 80; lectr. in field. One-man shows include Evanston (Ill.) Art Ctr., 1980, Morning Art and Dance Ctr., Chgo., 1980, Edwynn Houk Gallery, 1984, Art Inst. Chgo., 1994, Ehlers Caudill Gallery, Chgo., 1995, City of Chgo. Photography Gallery at Water Tower, 1999, Mus. Contemporary Photography, 1999, exhibited in group shows at Hodges Taylor Gallery, Charlotte, N.C., 1996, Mus. Contemporary Art, Chgo., 1996, Mus. Van Bommel-Van Dam, Venlo, The Netherlands, 1997, Milw. Art Mus., 1999, others; curated exhbns. include Truman Coll., 1980, Chgo. Ctr. Contemporary Photography, Columbia Coll., 1983; commns. include, Historic Bldgs. Iowa, 1976, Ctrl. Mfg. Dist., 1983, Midway Airport Pub. Art Competition, 1999, others, Represented in permanent collections Art Inst. Chgo., Calif. Mus. Photography, Riverside, Calif., Can. Ctr. Arch., Montreal, Chgo. Hist. Soc., Getty Ctr. History Art and Humanities, Santa Monica, Calif., Hallmark Collection, Kansas City, Mo., Milw. Art Mus., Mus. Fine Art, Houston, Mus. Folkwang, Essen, Germany, Mus. Modern Art, N.Y.C., Seagram Collection, Victoria and Albert Mus., London, others; book and exhbn. reviewer Exposure and New Art Examiner, 1980—83; author: The Perfect City, 1994; The New American Village, 1999, City Spaces, 2002. Grantee Project Completion grantee, Ill. Arts Coun., 1980; Graham Found. grantee, 1998, John Simon Guggenheim Meml. Found. fellow, 1998. Office: Columbia Coll Dept Photography 600 S Michigan Ave Chicago IL 60605-1900

THALLER, GREGG P. music educator; s. Frank and Jane Thaller. BM, Boston U., 1985; MME, U. Hartford, 1989; DME, U. Cin. Coll.-Conservatory Music, 1993. Cert. music tchr. Conn. Music tchr. Norwich Free Acad., Norwich, Conn., 1985—90; music min. Grace Bapt. Ch., Loveland, Ohio, 1990—93; chair dept. music Salem State Coll., Mass., 1993—2002; assoc. prof. music, band/orch. condr. S.W. Bapt. U., Bolivar, Mo., 2002—. Percussionist Springfield Symphony Orch., 2003—; timpanist various orchs., Mass., 1985—2001; adj. instr. Boston U., 1994—95. Music condr. Grace Chapel, Lexington, Mass., 2000—01. Mem.: Coll. Band Dirs. Nat. Assn. Christian-Evangelical. Achievements include research in music edn.-adult music-making. Avocations: motorcycle riding, travel, recreational airplane flying. Office: SW Bapt U Music Dept 1600 University Ave Bolivar MO 65613

THALOS, MARIAM G, philosopher, educator; d. Grant Samuel and Angel Morcos Thalos; m. Robert D Richardson, Mar. 28, 1991; children: Oliver Ethan Richardson, Elijah Graham. PhD, U. Ill., 1993. Author: Degrees of Freedom in the Social World (Kavka prize, 2001). Mem. Tanner Humanities Ctr., Salt Lake City, Utah, 2002—. Fellow fellowship for U. Professors, NEH, 2000-2001. Mem.: Am. Philos. Assn. (com. mem. 2000—04). Achievements include research in causation, explanation and control. Avocations: swimming, painting, hiking. Office: U Utah 260 S Ctrl Campus Dr 341 OSH Salt Lake City UT 84103 Personal E-mail: mthalos@philosophy.utah.edu. E-mail: mthalos@philosophy.utah.edu.

THAMAN, MICHAEL H. building material systems executive; BSEE, BS in Computer Sci., Princeton U. V.p. Mercer Mgmt. Cons., N.Y.C.; dir. corp. devel. Owens Corning, 1992-94, plant mgr. Toronto insulation facility, 1994-96, gen. mgr. OEM solutions group, 1996-97, v.p., pres. engineered pipe systems bus. Brussels, 1997-99, v.p., pres. exterior systems bus., 1999-2000, CFO, 2000—. Office: Owens Corning Dept 2-D One Owens Corning Pkwy Toledo OH 43659

THAMES, RICK, publishing executive, editor; b. Laurinburg, NC; m. Debbie Thames; children: Nathan, Hunter, Lucy. AB in English, Pfeiffer Coll., Misenheimer, NC; MS in Comm., U. Tenn., Knoxville. Reporter The Fayetteville Observer, NC, 1978—80; various positions including mng. editor Miami News, 1980—88; various positions including govt. editor, city editor, assist. mng. editor, public editor The Charlotte Observer, 1988—96; editor The Wichita Eagle, Kans., 1997—2004; v.p., editor The Charlotte Observer, 2004—. Chmn. adv. bd. Elliot Sch. of Comm., Wichita State U. Mem.: Am. Soc. of Newspaper Editors (mem. Freedom of Info. Com.), Kansas Press Assn. (bd. dirs.). Office: The Charlotte Observer PO Box 32188 600 S Tryon St Charlotte NC 28232*

THAMHAIN, HANS JURGEN, management educator; b. Dresden, Saxony, Germany, Oct. 1, 1936; s. Hans Florenz Thamhain, Martha Thamhain; m. Ingrid Katharina Schwoch; children: Petra Lively, Thilo. BSEE, Ingenieurschule Koblenz, Germany, 1961; MSEE, U. Waterloo, Can., 1967; MBA, Syracuse U., 1972, PhD in Bus. Adminstrn., 1974. Elec. engr. Standard Electric Co.,ITT, Pforzheim, Germany, 1961—64, Westinghouse Corp., Hamilton, Canada, 1964—67; project mgr. Gen. Electric Co., Syracuse, NY, 1967—75; bus. mgr. GTE/Verizon, Needham, Mass., 1975—81; assoc. prof. mgmt. Worcester Polytech. Inst., Worchester, Mass., 1981—87; prof. mgmt. Bentley Coll., Waltham, Mass., 1987—, dir. project mgmt. programs, 1987—. Cons. tech. and project mgmt. with numerous worldwide cos., 1981—; vis. prof., guest lectr. numerous univs. and insts., 1981—. Author: Project Management for Small and Medium-Size Businesses, 1984, Engineering Program Management, 1985, Project Management Operating Guidelines, 1986 (Nat. Book award, AAP, 1993), Engineering Management, 1993, Management of Technology, 2004; contbr. articles to numerous profl. jours.; seven patents, Germany, Can, and U.S. Scholar, Fulbright, 1998. Mem.: IEEE (life; Editorial Board 1985—date, Engring. Mgr. of Year 2000), Project Mgmt. Inst. (Publications Advisory Board 1990—93, Dist. Contbn. award for Mgmt. Rsch. 1998, cert. project mgmt. profl. 1988), Am. Soc. Engring. Mgmt. (Editorial Board 1987—date), Product Develop. Mgmt. Assn. (Publications Review Board 1990—date, cert. new product develop. profl. 2001), Phi Beta Delta. Avocations: ironman triathlete, marathons. Home: 25 Lanewood Ave Framingham MA 01701-3660 Office: Bentley Coll Forest St Waltham MA Office Phone: 781-891-2189. Office Fax: (781) 891-2896. Personal E-mail: hthamhain@bentley.edu. Business E-Mail: hthamhain@bentley.edu.

THAMPI, MOHAN VARGHESE, environmental health and civil engineer; b. Kuching, Sarawak, Malaysia, Mar. 25, 1960; s. Padmanabha Ramachandran and Sosamma (Varghese) T. Gen. Cert. Edn., Cambridge U., 1976; B in Tech. with honors, Indian Inst. Tech., Kharagpur, India, 1983; MS in Engring., U. Tex., 1985; DSc (hon.), London Inst. Applied Rsch., 1992. Registered profl. engr., Tex., Fla., registered environ. mgr.; cert. safety tng. OSHA; cert. Nat. Coun. Examiners for Engrs. and Surveyors. Assoc. engr. Brown & Caldwell, Dallas, 1985-87, project mgr. Orlando, 1987-88, Stottler Stagg & Assocs., Cape Canaveral, Fla., 1988-91; sr. project engr. Chastain-Skillman, Inc., Lakeland, Fla., 1991-93; project mgr. Glace & Radcliffe, Inc., Winter Park, Fla., 1993-94; mgr. FDEP, West Palm Beach, Fla., 1995-96; project mgr. Office of Capital Projects Mgmt., Naples, Fla., 1996—2004; projects engring. mgr. Project Mgmt., Bradenton, Fla., 2004—. Author: Ultraviolet Disinfection Studies in a Teflon-Tube Reactor, 1985; contbr. articles to profl. jours. Active Rep. Pres.'s Citizens Adv. Commn., 1992. Recipient Cert. of Cont. Profl. Devel. award Fla. Engring. Soc., 1992. Mem. NRA, NSPE, ASCE (assoc.), Project Mgmt. Inst., Internat. Assn. Water Pollution Rsch. and Control, Am. Mensa, Am. Water Works Assn., Water Pollution Control Fedn. (com. for preparing design practice manuals 1989—), Internat. Freelance Photographers Assn., Internat. Platform Assn., Internat. Assn. Air Travel Couriers, Am. Mgmt. Assn., Am. Smokers Alliance, Am. Gunsmithing Assn., Smithsonian Instn., Nat. Geog. Soc., Nat. Registry Environ. Professionals, U. Tex. Ex-Students Assn., Wine Soc. Am., Nat. Family Opinion, Internat. Deep Purple Appreciation Soc., Wilson Ctr. Assocs., I.I.T. Kharagpur Tech. Found., NASA Tech Briefs Reader Opinion Panel, Chemical Engring. Jour. Product Rsch. Panel, Nat. Rifle Assn., Plant Engring. Editl. Quality Panel, Kharagpur Tech. Alumni Found., N.Am. Hunting Club, Knight Order of Templars (Jerusalem), PC Bug Computer Club. Mar Thoma Syrian Christian. Avocations: photography, music, travel, sports. Home: PO Box 11954 Naples FL 34101-2954 Personal E-mail: thampimv@juno.com.

THAPA, KHAGENDRA, survey engineering educator; b. Murtidhunga, Dhankuta, Nepal, Oct. 16, 1950; came to U.S., 1982; s. Ranadhoj and Krishna (Basnet) T.; m. Rajani Basnet, July 7, 1981; children: Samrat, Birat, Charisma. BSc, Tribhuran U., Kathmandu, Nepal, 1973, U. East London, 1978; MSCE, U. N.B., Fredericton, Can., 1980; MS, Ohio State U., 1985, PhD, 1987. Rsch. asst. U. N.B., Fredericton, 1978-80; researcher Geodetic Survey Can., Ottawa, 1980; lectr. Engring. Inst. Tribhuvan U., Kathmandu, 1980-82; teaching/rsch. assoc. Ohio State U., Columbus, 1982-87; assoc. prof. Ferris State U., Big Rapids, Mich., 1987-91, prof., program coord. Coll. Tech., 1991—. Rschr. Ctr. for Mapping, Columbus, Ohio, 1990; cons. Techs., Archs. and Engrs. Consultancy, Kathmandu, 1980-82; chairperson Engring. Topographic Mapping Com. Am. Soc. Photogrammetry and Remote Sensing, Washington, 1991—; evaluator accreditation bd. for engring. and tech. Engring. Accreditation Commn. Recipient Disting. Prof. award Mich. Assn. Governing Bd., 1996, Provost award for excellence; grantee NSF, Washington, 1989, 91. Mem. Royal Instn. Chartered Surveyors (rsch. grant 1988-89), Am. Congress on Surveying and Mapping, Am. Soc. Photogrammetry, Inst. Navigation, Geodetic Sci. Club (v.p. 1985-86). Achievements include devising a new technique to find inconsistent observations and constraints in horizontal networks, using linear programming in optimal design of leveling networks, devising a new method of line generalization in computer cartography and digital mapping; worked on critical points detection and data compression using zero-crossings; analysed the accuracy of spatial data used in geographic information system. Home: 20796 Edgewood Dr Big Rapids MI 49307-9024 Office: Ferris State U Coll Tech Surveying Engring Program 915 Campus Dr Rm 312 Big Rapids MI 49307-2291

THARALDSON, GARY DEAN, hotel developer and owner; b. Valley City, N.D., Oct. 17, 1945; BA in Phys. Edn., Valley City State U.; postgrad., N.D. State U. Tchr., Leonard, N.D.; ins. agt., agy. owner, 1969-89; owner of 350 hotels, Valley City, 1982; pres. Tharaldson Enterprises, Fargo, N.D., 1982—. Office: Tharaldson Enterprises 1202 Westrac Dr Fargo ND 58103-2344

THARNEY, LEONARD JOHN, education educator, consultant; b. New Haven, Nov. 6, 1929; s. Lillian A. Batey; m. Denise A. Gauvin, June 20, 1981; children: Karen L., Linda L. BS, Trenton (N.J.) State Coll., 1954; MEd, Rutgers U., 1959; postgrad., Lehigh U., Bethlehem, Pa., 1963-70, Columbia U.; grad., Command & Gen. Staff Coll., Ft. Leavenworth, Kans., 1972. Cert. secondary math. and sci. tchr., elem. tchr. Tchr. (elem. demonstration) Trenton State Coll., NJ, 1954-60; tchr. (jr. high demonstration) Ewing Twp. Sch., NJ, 1960-63; cons., evaluator Am. Coun. on Edn., Washington, 1975-95, field coord., 1995—2003; cons., evaluator Mid. States Assn., Phila., 1987; prof. Trenton State Coll., 1963-92, dept. chmn., 1988-92, prof. emeritus, 1993—; cons., evaluator Nat. Assn. Indsl. Tech., 2003. Cons. to internat. sch. for curriculum or sci. edn., Monrovia, Accra, Athens, Mogadishu, Cairo, Alexandria, Aleppo, Damascus, 1975—; tchr. grad. courses in curriculum and ednl. rsch. at overseas sites, Spain, Cyprus, Saudi Arabia, Syria, 1981—; exch. prof. Worcester Coll. Higher Edn., Eng., 1984-85; presenter sci. edn. workshops, AISA Internat. Conf., Nairobi, 1987; rep. from Coll. to Prins. Tng. Ctr., London, 1994; bd. dir. Trenton, NJ chpt. People to People Internat., 1995-98, chpt. pres., 1998—; NJ del. Worldwide Conf. of People to People Internat., Chester, Eng., 1998, Hong Kong, 2000, Aalborg, Denmark, 2001, Kansas City, Mo., 2002, Stockholm, 2002, Roman, Romania, 2003; internat. trustee, 2000; 15th World Wide Conf. del., Kansas City, Mo., 2002, 16th World Wide Conf. del., Milan, 2004; mem. Accrediting Commn. of the Distance Education and training Council, Wash., DC, 2000—. Co-author 7 manuals for uniform constrn. codes. Col. AUS, 1947-81. Recipient ACE award for outstanding svc. in mil. evaluations, 1987, cert. of appreciation, presdl. citation, 1989, spl. plaque award, others, Outstanding Svc. and Support award 112th FA Assn., 1998; decorated meritorious svc. medal U.S. Army, 1981. Mem.: ASCD, Nat. Coun. Social Studies, Assn. for Edn. Tchrs. in Sci., Assn. Tchr. Educators, Am. Air Mus. in Britain (founding mem.), Trenton Club (pres. 2002—03), Torch Club Internat. (bd. dir. 1998—2001, v.p. 2001—02). Home: 20 Lawrenceville-Penning Rd Lawrenceville NJ 08648-1648 Office: Nat Assn Indsl Tech 3300 Washtenaw Ave Ste 220 Ann Arbor MI 48104-4200

THARP, BENJAMIN CARROLL, JR., retired architect; b. Austin, Tex., Sept. 3, 1919; s. Benjamin Carroll Tharp and Norris (Ophelia) Wallis; m. Mae Sibley; children: Ronald Emery, Carolyn Jeanine Tharp Love. BArch, U. Tex., 1943. Registered architect, Tex. Draftsman Wurdeman & Beckett, L.A., 1944, Richard Neutra, L.A., 1945, Merrill Baird, L.A., 1946, Golemon & Rolfe, Houston, 1947, Milton Foy Martin, Houston, 1948; prin. Koetter & Tharp, Houston, 1949-64, Koetter, Tharp & Cowell, Houston, 1964-78; architect Koetter, Tharp, Cowell and Lockwood, Andrews, Newnam, Houston, 1978-81; ret. Lockwood, Andrews, Newnam, 1981. Bd. dirs. Harris County Soil and Water Conservation Dist., Houston, 1972-82; pres. Constrn. Industry Coun., Houston, 1970; major contbr. real estate to Sam Houston State U., Huntsville, Tex. Recipient 1st Restoration award Red Cedar Shingle and Handsplit Shake Bur./AIA, Seattle, 1975 Fellow AIA, Tex. Soc. Architects (chmn. hist. resources com. 1986); mem. Montgomery (Tex.) Hist. Soc., Optimist Club (pres. Houston chpt. 1970). Republican. Baptist.

THARP, ROLAND GEORGE, psychology professor; b. Galveston, Tex., June 6, 1930; s. Oswald Roland and Berma Lucille (Keefer) T.; m. Stephanie Dalton; children: Donald Martin, Thomas Roland, David Michael, Julie. Student, Middlebury Coll., 1956, 60; BA cum laude, U. Houston, 1957; MA, U. Mich., 1958, PhD, 1961. Cert. Am. Bd. Examiners in Profl. Psychology. Reporter Tex. City Sun, 1946-47; mgr. Tharp Lumber Co., LaMarque, Tex., 1949-54; intern VA Hosp., Menlo Park, Calif., 1960; asst. prof. U. Ariz., Tucson, 1961-65, assoc. prof., 1965-68; prof., dir. clin. studies, dir. multicultural ctr. for higher edn. U. Hawaii, Honolulu, 1968-87; provost and v.p. for acad. affairs U.S. Internat. U., San Diego, 1987-89; prof. edn., psychology U. Calif., Santa Cruz, 1990—; dir. Nat. Rsch. Ctr. for Diversity, 1995—. Dir. Ctr. for Rsch. on Edn., Diversity and Excellence, 1996—; prin. investigator Kamehameha Early Edn. Program, Honolulu, 1969-89; field selection officer Peace Corps, Washington, 1965-67. Author: (poetry) Highland Station, 1978; co-author: Behavior Modification in the Natural Environment, 1969, Self-Directed Behavior, 1980, Rousing Minds to Life, 1988, Teaching Transformed, 2000; writer, producer, dir. film Scenes from the Life, 1981 (Purchase prize The Contemporary Mus. 1981). Mem. Bd. Psychologist Examiners, Ariz., 1964-67; pres. Hawaii Literary Arts Coun., Honolulu, 1982. Robert Frost fellow Middlebury Coll., 1960; recipient Am. Film Mag. award for filmmaking Hawaii Internat. Film Festival, 1990, Grawemeyer award edn., 1993. Mem. Am. Ednl. Rsch. Assn., Am. Anthropol. Assn. Episcopalian. Avocations: tennis, painting. Office: U Calif CREDE 1156 High St Santa Cruz CA 95064-1077

THARP, TWYLA, dancer; b. Portland, Ind., July 1, 1941; m. Peter Young (div.); m. Robert Huot (div.); 1 child, Jesse Huot. Student, Pomona Coll.; BA in Art History, Barnard Coll., 1963; D of Performing Arts (hon.), Calif. Inst. Arts, 1978, Brown U., 1981, Bard Coll., 1981; LHD, Ind. U., 1987; DFA, Pomona Coll., 1987; studied with Richard Thomas, Merce Cunningham, Igor Schwezoff, Louis Mattox, Paul Taylor, Margaet Craske, Erick Hawkins.

Dancer Paul Taylor Dance Co., 1963-65; freelance choreographer with own modern dance troupe and various other cos. including Joffrey Ballet and Am. Ballet Theatre, 1965-87; founder, choreographer Twyla Tharp Dance Found., N.Y.C., 1965-87; artistic assoc., resident choreographer Am. Ballet Theatre, N.Y.C., 1987-91; teaching residencies various colls. and univs. including U. Mass., Oberlin Coll., Walker Art Ctr., Boston U. Choreographer White Oak Dance Project. Choreographer Tank Dive, 1965, Re-Moves, 1966, One Two Three, 1966, Forevermore, 1967, Generation, 1968, Medley, 1969, After Suite, 1969, Dancing in the Streets of London and Paris, 1969, The One Hundreds, 1970, The Fugue, 1970, The Bix Pieces, 1971, Eight Jelly Rolls, 1971, The Raggedy Dances, 1972, Deuce Coupe, 1973, As Time Goes By, 1974, Sue's Leg, 1975, Ocean's Motion, 1975, Push Comes to Shove, 1976, Once More Frank, 1976, Mud, 1977, Baker's Dozen, 1979, When We Were Very Young, 1980, Nine Sinatra Songs, 1982, The Catherine Wheel, 1982, Bach Partita, 1984, The Little Ballet, 1984, with Jerome Robbins Brahms Handel, 1988, At the Supermarket, 1984, In the Upper Room, 1987, Ballare, 1987, Stations of the Crossed, 1988, Everlast, 1989, Quartet, 1989, Bum's Rush, 1989, The Rules of the Game, 1990, Brief Fling, 1990, Grand Pas: Rhythm of the Saints, 1991, Deuce Coupe II, 1992, The Men's Piece, 1992, with Mikhail Baryshnikov Cutting Up, 1992—93, Demeter and Persephone, 1993, Waterbaby Bagatelles, 1994, Demeter and Persephone, 1994, Red, White & Blues, 1995, How Near Heaven, 1995, I Remember Clifford, 1995, Jump Start, 1995, Americans We, 1995, (films) Hair, 1979, Ragtime, 1981, Amadeus, 1984, White Nights, 1985, Valmont, 1989, I'll Do Anything, 1994, video spls. Making Television Dance, 1977, CBS Cable Confessions of a Corner Maker, 1980, (Broadway plays) Sorrow Floats, 1985, Singin' in the Rain, 1985, TV Baryshnikov by Tharp, 1985 (Emmy award for Outstanding Choreography, 1985, Emmy award for Outstanding Writing of Classical Music/Dance Programming, 1985), The Catherine Wheel, 1982 (Emmy award nomination for Outstanding Choreography, 1982); author (autobiography): When Push Comes to Shove, 1982. Recipient Creative Arts award, Brandeis U., 1972, Dance Mag. award, 1981, Univ. Excellence medal, Columbia U., 1987, Lions of the Performing Arts award, N.Y. Pub. Libr., 1989, Samuel M. Scripps award, Am. Dance Festival, 1990; MacArthur Found. fellow, 1992.

THATCHER, GEORGE ROBERT, banker, author, journalist, columnist; b. Austin, Pa., Sept. 18, 1922; S. Walter Robert and Roberta Estelle (Bernard) T.; widowed; children: Georgia Anne Thatcher Faneca, Janie Estelle Thatcher Holmes, Walter Wimberly. BA, U. Miss., 1948. Pvt. U.S. Army, 1942, infantry maj., 1948, ret., 1952; ptnr. Rand-Thatcher Advt. Agy., Gulfport, Miss., 1948—67; pres. coast divsn. Magnolia Fed. Bank, Gulfport, 1981-92; councilman City of Gulfport, 1989; hon. canon St. Peter's Cathedral, Likoma Island, Malawi, 1997—; daily columnist The Sun Herald, Biloxi, Miss., 1997—; commentator Pub. Radio Miss., 2004. Author: Misrepresentation in MS, 1954, Beach Walks, 1998, 2d edit., 1999, Beach Walks II, 2000, Scenes From the Beach, 2003. Chmn. Miss. Arts Commn., 1991-2000; past chmn. United Way, Harrison County Libr., Harrison County Libr.; past pres. Episcopal Laymen of Miss., Miss. Hist. Assn. Decorated Bronze Star; named Outstanding Citizen Miss. Coast C. of C., 1998. Mem. Gulfport Rotary Club (pres. 1995-96, Citizen of Yr. 1993, Paul Harris fellow), Century Club (pres.), Gulfport Yacht Club, Bayou Bluff Tennis Club, Great So. Club. Republican. Roman Catholic. Avocations: tennis, chess, reading, classical music. Home: 1302 2nd St Gulfport MS 39501-2219 Office: Union Planters Bank 2200 14th St Gulfport MS 39501-2005 E-mail: fishcrow@aol.com.

THATSNEYAKUL, YAOVARES, physician, consultant; b. Bangkok; m. Michael Pulaski, 1975. MD, Siriraj Med. Sch., Bangkok. Diplomate Am. Bd. Pediatrics. Cons. Dept. Human Svcs., State of N.J., 1985—. Office: Divsn Med Assistance and Health Svcs PO Box 712 Trenton NJ 08625-0712 E-mail: yaovares.thatsneyakul@dhs.state.nj.us.

THAW, ANDREW KURT, psychologist, educator, research scientist; b. Salisbury, Md., Apr. 1, 1965; s. Bonnie L. Weiss and Clifton B. Thaw; m. Melanie Suzanne Cudlipp, Sept. 29, 1990; children: Chelsea A., Carley J., Zoe L. PhD, Fla. State U., Tallahassee, 1994. Postdoctoral fellow Cornell Med. Coll., White Plains, NY, 1997—98; prof. psychology Millsaps Coll., Jackson, Miss., 1998—. Tchr. St. Mark's United Meth. Ch., Brandon, Miss., 2000—03. AREA Grant, NIH, 2001 - 2003. Achievements include research in endogenous factors that regulate appetite. Office: Millsaps Coll 1701 N State St Jackson MS 39210 E-mail: thawak@millsaps.edu.

THAWLEY, MICHAEL, diplomat; b. Eng., 1950; arrived in Australia, 1960; m. Deborah Wilkins; children: Samuel, Thomas, Cosimo. BA with honors, Australian Nat. U., 1971; postgrad. diploma in Russian, Surrey (Eng.) U., 1980. Joined Australian Fgn. Svc., 1972, first asst. sec. Prime Mins. Dept., 1993-96; nat. security advisor Prime Min. Australia, 1996; dep. sec. dept. fgn. affairs and trade; Australian amb. to the U.S., 2000—. Avocations: reading, music, gardening. Office: Embassy of Australia 1601 Massachusetts Ave NW Washington DC 20036-2273 Fax: 202-797-3209.

THAYER, BRUCE ALLEN, automotive executive, artist; b. Eaton Rapids, Mich., Feb. 7, 1952; s. Alfred James and Beatrice Thayer; m. Ilene Alice Thayer, May 26, 1986. BS, Ctrl. Mich. U., 1974, BFA in Painting, 1975; MFA in Painting, Sch. Art Inst. Chgo., 1980. Sub. tchr. Lansing (Mich.) Schs., 1978-79; art instr. Kresge Art Mus. Mich. State U., East Lansing, 1998-2001; test driver GMC, Milford, Mich., 1988—. Vis. artist Aquinas Coll., Grand Rapids, Mich., 1998, G.M.I. Engring. Inst., Flitn, 1995; spkr., artist Aesthetic and Ideologies Conf., Mich. State U., East Lansing, 1999, Cranbrook Art Mus., Bloomfield Hills, Mich., 1995. Exhbns. include 15th Biennial Mich. Arts Exhbn., 1987 (Best of Show award 1987), Rutgers Nat. Works on Paper, 1986 (Purchase award 1986), 5th Ann. Mich. Fine Arts, 1983 (Best of Show award 1983), 20th Biennial Regional Arts Exhbn., 1999 (Purchase award 1999). Head juror San Jane Venable Scholarship, Lansing, 1993, 94; juror h.s. art Rep. U.S. Congress, East Lansing, 1998, 99. Fellow Art Matters, 1994; Visual Arts fellow Arts Midwest/NEA Regional, 1990; art grantee Mich. Coun. for the Arts, 1987. Mem. Soc. Am. Graphic Artists (Purchase award 1993), Cen. Mich. U. Art Alumni (adv. bd. dirs. 1999—). Avocations: horticulture, collecting arts and crafts, pottery. Home: 1515 Kelly Mason MI 48854 E-mail: brucellenethayer@aol.com.

THAYER, CHARLES J. investment banker; b. Abilene, Kans., Feb. 28, 1944; s. Bruce V. and Neoma (Obermeyer) T.; 1 child, Travis J. Grad., U. Kans., 1967. Exec. v.p., CFO Citizens Fidelity Bank, Louisville, 1977-87; exec. v.p. fin. PNC Bank Corp., Pitts., 1987-89; chmn., mng. dir. Chartwell Capital Ltd., Ft. Lauderdale, Fla., 1989—; interim chmn. Sunbeam-Oster, Providence, 1993. Adv. dir. Louisville Cmty. Devel. Bank, 1997—, Keefe Mgrs., Inc., N.Y.C., 1990-2002; bd. dirs. CogenAmerica, Mpls., Republic Bank, St. Petersburg, Fla.; mem. adv. bd. Am. Assn. Bank Dirs. Trustee Cystic Fibrosis Found., Washington, 1980—; chmn. Cystic Fibrosis Svcs., Washington, 1994—. Avocation: sailing. Office: Chartwell Capital Ltd 420 Isle Of Capri Dr Fort Lauderdale FL 33301-2438 E-mail: CJT@chartwellCapital.com.

THAYER, EDNA LOUISE, medical facility and nursing administrator; b. Madelia, Minn., May 21, 1936; d. Walter William Arthur and Hilda Engel Emily Ann (Geistfeld) Wilke; m. David LeRoy Thayer, Aug. 30, 1958; children: Scott, Tamara, Brenda. Diploma in nursing, Bethesda Luth., 1956; BS in Nursing Edn., U. Minn., 1960; MSN, Washington U., St. Louis, 1966; MS in Counseling, Mankato (Minn.) State U., 1972. Cert. nursing adminstr. advanced ANA. Nurse Bethesda Luth. Hosp., St. Paul, 1956-58, U. Minn. Hosp., Mpls., 1958; from nurse to asst. head nurse supr., edn. dir. Fairmont (Minn.) Community Hosp., 1959-63; instr. Alton (Ill.) Meml. Hosp., 1963-66; from nursing instr. to assoc. prof. and dean Sch. Nursing Mankato State U., 1966-77; asst. adminstr. Rice County Dist. One Hosp., Faribault, Minn., 1977-89; RN, adminstrv. supr. St. Peter (Minn.) Regional Treatment Ctr., 1990-96; spkr., 1996—. Nurse surveyor Minn. Dept. Tech. Edn., St. Paul, 1980-93; mem. adv. co. LPN and MA programs Tech. Inst., Faribault, 1977-2001. Mem. Rice County Ext. Bd., Faribault, 1986-91, adult leader 4-H Club, Rice County and St. Paul, 1971-97; advisor Med. Explorers, Faribault, 1977-89; mem. Rep. Rodosovich Health Com., Faribault, 1984-94; coun. mem. Our Savior's Luth. Ch., Faribault, 1984-87; mem. Rep. Boudreau Health Care Adv. Com., 1996-2001. Recipient alumni award Nat. 4-H Club, 1983, Disting. Friend of Nursing award Mankato State U., 1995. Mem. Minn. Orgn. Nurse Execs. (bd. dirs. 1987-89), Dist. F Nursing Svc. Adminstrs. (pres. 1980-82), Minn. Nurses Assn. (bd. dirs. 1982-87, Pres.'s award 1983, pres. 5th dist. 1974, 75, pres. 13th dist. 1984-86), AAUW, Sigma Theta Tau, Delta Kappa Gamma (pres. Pi chptr. 1982-84, Woman of Achievement award 1985), Hosp. Aux. Republican. Avocations: crafts, volunteer work, theater, plays. Home: 7 Roots Beach Ln Elysian MN 56028-9731 Personal E-mail: dethayer@myclearwave.net.

THAYER, FREDERICK CLIFTON, public policy educator; b. Sept. 6, 1924; m. Carolyn Conn Easley, 1952; children: Jeffrey Lee, Sarah Diane. BS, U.S. Mil. Acad., 1945; MA, Ohio State U., 1954; PhD, U. Denver, 1963. Commd. 2d lt. USAF, 1945, advanced through grades to col., 1965, ret., 1969; assoc. prof. U. Pitts., 1969-83, prof., 1983-91; prof. European div. Troy State U., 1991-94, George Washington U., Washington, 1995-96; prof. public policy, dir. doctoral program So. U., Baton Rouge, 1997-99; vis. prof. U. of the Incarnate Word, San Antonio, 1999-2000, Ctrl. Mich. U., Mt. Pleasant, 2000—. Author: Air Transport Policy and National Security, 1965, An End to Hierarchy and Competition, 1973, 2d edit., 1981, Rebuilding America: The Case for Economic Regulation, 1984; contbr. articles to prof. jours. Office: Coll Extended Learning Ctrl Mich Univ Mount Pleasant MI 48859 E-mail: fthayer@yahoo.com.

THAYER, GAYLORD BERTRAM, JR., retired electronics executive; b. Jamestown, NY, July 2, 1944; s. Gaylord Bertram and Marion Brown (Klock) T. BSME, U. Rochester, 1966; MBA, Harvard U., 1968. Asst. to contr. Teradyne, Inc., Boston, 1968-70, mgr. MIS, 1970-72, sales engr., 1972-76, product mgr., 1976-84, divsn. mgr., 1984-91, mktg. dir., 1991-98; pvt. investor, 1998—. Exec.-in-residence entrepreneurship program Babson Coll., 2003—; bd. dirs. Erickson Materials, Inc.; adv. bd. Lexent Techs., Lexington, Mass., 1999—, Simply Media Inc., Lincoln, Mass.; gubernatorial appt. to Mass. Pub. Health Coun. Policy Bd. State Dept. of Pub. Health, 2003. Bd. dirs. New Eng. divsn. Am. Cancer Soc., Boston; elected town meeting mem., 2003—; bd. trustees South Boston Harbor Acad. Charter Sch. Mem.: Nat. Assembly Am. Cancer Soc. Avocations: cooking, reading, travel, flying. Home: 52 Royalston Rd Wellesley MA 02481-1244

THAYER, JANE See WOOLLEY, CATHERINE

THAYER, MARILYN, political organization executive, civic worker; married; 2 children. Fellow Inst. Politics, Loyola U., New Orleans. Former pres. women's aux. Vols. of Am.; past mem. bd. dirs. Sophie Gumble Guild; past v.p. and program chmn. Women for Better La.; pres. La. Fedn. Rep. Women, 1987-91; former nat. treas., mem.-at-large exec. com., and chmn. membership com. Nat. Fedn. Rep. Women, Alexandria, Va., pres., 1996-97, immediate past pres., 1997-98; immediate past nat. committeewoman for La., Rep. Nat. Com., also past mem. various coms.; co-chmn. vol. com., mem. host com. Rep. Nat. Com., 1988, mem. platform com., chmn. com. on human resources, 1984, 88; co-chmn. parish campaign, then co-chmn. state campaign Reagan-Bush Campaign. Office: Nat Fedn Rep Women 124 N Alfred St Alexandria VA 22314-3011 Fax: 703-548-9836.

THAYER, RUSSELL, III, airlines executive; b. Phila., Dec. 5, 1922; s. Russell and Shelby Wentworth (Johnson) T.; m. Elizabeth Wright Mifflin, June 12, 1947; children: Elizabeth, Dixon, Shelby, Samuel, David. Student, St. George's Sch., 1937-42; AB, Princeton U., 1949. Mgmt. trainee Eastern Air Lines, 1949-52; mgr. cargo sales and service Am. Airlines, Los Angeles, 1952-63; v.p. mktg. Seaboard World Airlines, N.Y.C., 1963-70; sr. v.p. Braniff Airways, Inc., Dallas, 1970-72, exec. v.p., 1972-77, pres., chief oper. officer, 1977-80, vice chmn., 1981-82; dir. (Braniff Airways, Inc.), 1971-82; v.p. Pan Am. World Airways, Inc., N.Y.C., 1982-84, sr. v.p., 1984-88, Airline Econs., Inc., Washington, 1988—, also bd. dirs., 1988—. Dir. Ft. Worth Nat. Bank, 1977-82; vice chmn. Airline Capital Assn; bd. dirs. Kiwi Internat. Airlines, Inc., World Aux. Power Corp. Mem. Trinity Ch. Ushers Guild, Princeton, N.J., 1968—; Trustee Aviation Hall of Fame N.J. Served with USAAF, 1942-45, ETO. Decorated D.F.C., Air medal with 11 oak leaf clusters. Mem. Am. Aviation Hist. Assn., Air Force Assn., Exptl. Aircraft Assn., Nat. Aeros. Assn., Ivy Club (Princeton), Pretty Brook Tennis Club (Princeton), Bay Head (N.J.) Yacht Club, Nassau Club (Princeton), Princeton Club (N.Y.C.), Phila. Club, Delta Psi. Home: Hulfish St Apt 17-I Princeton NJ 08542-3706 Office: Airline Capital Assocs Inc 535 5th Ave Rm 905 New York NY 10017-3610

THAYER, THOMAS MANOR, JR., artist; b. Lansing, Mich., Apr. 8, 1958; BFA, U. Mich., 1981. Owner, lead artist Alexander Raymond Thomas Quality Fine Art, Camano Island, Wash., 1996—. Instr. Art Workshop, 1999—. One-man shows include Mountlake Terrace Civic Ctr. Gallery, Mountlake Terrace, Wash., 1999, Edmonds C.C., Edmonds, Wash., 1996, PACCAR Corp., Bellevue, Wash., 1995, Mountlake Terrace Libr., 1995, Cascade Estates Winery, Seattle, 1992, exhibited in group shows at The Artist's Mag. Competition, 2001, 2002, Statements DC 207 Exhbn., Seattle, 2001, The Colored Pencil Soc. of Am., 2d Ann. Internat. Exhbn., Portland, 1994, 4th Ann. Internat. Exhbn., San Diego, 1996, 8th Ann. Internat. Exhbn., Birmingham, Mich., 2000, 9th Ann. Internat. Exhbn., San Francisco, 2001 (Cippy Best of Show award), 10th Ann. Internat. Exhbn., Dallas, 2002, numerous others, including the Points of Color DC 207 Exhbn., Bothell, Wash., 2000; contbr. artwork and articles to mags.; contbr. (books) Best of Colored Pencil, 1994, 1997, Creative Colored Pencil, 1995, Creative Colored Pencil Portraits, 1996, Exploring Colored Pencil, 1999; Exhibited in group shows at Edmonds Art Festival, 2002 (1st pl. award, 2002), 2003 (1st pl. award, 2003). Mem.: Am. Soc. of Classical Realism, Colored Pencil Soc. of Am. Avocation: collecting and restoring classic cars of the 1960s and 1970s, snow skiing. Home: 1633 Hemlock Dr Camano Island WA 98282

THEALL, DONALD FRANCIS, retired university president; b. Mt. Vernon, N.Y., Oct. 13, 1928; s. Harold A. and Helen (Donaldson) T.; m. Joan Ada Benedict, June 14, 1950; children: Thomas, Margaret, John, Harold, Lawrence, Michael. BA with honors, Yale U., 1950; MA with 1st class honors, U. Toronto, 1951, PhD with 1st class honors, 1954. Teaching fellow U. Toronto, 1950-52, mem. faculty, 1952-65, prof. English, chmn. joint depts. English, 1964-65; dir. communication studies York U., also prof. English and communications, 1965-66; dir. English Atkinson Coll., 1965-66; mem. faculty McGill U., Montreal, Que., Can., 1966-79, prof. English, 1966-79, chmn. dept., 1966-74, Molson prof., 1972-79, dir. grad. program in communications, 1976-79, adj. prof. grad. comm., 1989-91; pres., vice chancellor, prof. English and cultural studies Trent U., Peterborough, Ont., 1980-87, univ. prof., 1987-94, univ. prof. emeritus, 1994—. Cultural exch. prof. Govt. of Can. and China, 1974; mem. adv. bd. Semiotic Inquiry, 1982—; cons. in field. Author: (with Robinson and Wevers) Let's Speak English, 4 vols., 1960-61, The Medium Is the Rear View Mirror: Understanding McLuhan, 1971, (with G.J. Robinson) Studies in Canadian Communications, 1975, Beyond the Word: Reconstructing Sense in the Joyce Era of Technology, Culture, and Communication, 1995 (short-listed Harold Adams Innis prize 1997), James Joyce's Techno-Poetics, 1997, The Virtual Marshall McLuhan, 2001; mem. editl. bd. Sci. Fiction Studies, 1976—, Can. Jour. Comm., 1979—, Jour. Can. Studies, 1980-87. Mem. Greater Peterborough Econ. Council, 1982-87; mem. fed. adv. council to minister employment and immigration for Peterborough area, 1986-87. Recipient awards Social Sci. and Humanities Rsch. Coun., 1991-94, 94-97, 97-2000, 2000—, Can. Fedn. Humanities-Aid to Scholarly Publs., 1994, 96, 2000; grantee Humanities Rsch. Coun. Can., 1954-56, 73-76, Ont. Dept. Edn., 1956-59, 91, Atkinson Found., 1960, CBC, 1961, Can. Coun., 1966-68, 73-76, Eastman Kodak Corp., Nat. Film Bd. Can., Can. Dept. Industry, Can. Dept. Trade and Commerce, Can. Ctrl. Mortgage and Housing, 1967-69, Que. Ministry Comm., 1977; sr. leave fellow Can. Coun., 1975. Corr. fellow Acad. Medicine (Toronto); mem. Internat. Communications Assn. (dir. 1978-81), Can. Communications Assn. (chmn. com. to investigate formation 1978, pres. 1979-80), MLA, Philol. Soc. Gt. Britain, Can. Assn. Chmn. English (founding chmn. 1971-74), Assn. Can. Univ. Tchrs. English, Internat. Inst. Communications, Soc. Arts Publs. (v.p. 1967-68), Sci. Fiction Research Assn., University Club of Toronto, Yale Club (Toronto), McGill Faculty Club, Elizabethan Club (Yale). Office: Trent Univ Grad Methodologies Program Peterborough ON Canada K9J 7B8 E-mail: dtheall@trentu.ca., dtheall@cogeco.ca.

THEALL, SUSAN LORNA, lawyer; b. Jennings, La., Mar. 10, 1957; d. Francis Avery and Doris (Landry) T. BA in English, U. So. La., 1980; JD, Loyola U., 1985. Bar: La. 1985. Pvt. practice, Opelousas and Lafayette, La., 1985—. Counsel La. Sch. Bus Operators, Alexandria, 1992-97. Chmn. Lafayette Vol. Lawyers, Lafayette, 1997. Mem. La. Bar Assn. (Pro Bono publico 1996, bd. cert. family law specialist 1995, family law sec. treas. 2001-2003, family courts com. 1999-2003), Lafayette Parish Bar Assn. (bd. dirs. 1996-97, 2001, family law sec. pres., v.p., treas. 1999, 2000, 2001), Am. Inns of Ct. (Acadiana chpt. 1991). Republican. Roman Catholic. Avocation: reading. Office: 1304 Lafayette St Lafayette LA 70501-6842

THEIS, PETER GEORGE, retired classics educator; b. Milw., Dec. 18, 1930; s. Peter Joseph and Laura Gertrude (Kornely) T.; m. Jane Elizabeth Grattan, Aug. 12, 1961; children: Peter Leo, Paul Joseph, Mary Ellen Brune, Thomas George. BA magna cum laude, Marquette U., 1952; AM, U. Chgo., 1957. Part-time instr. U. Wis., Milw., 1956; instr. Rockhurst U., Kansas City, Mo., 1960-61; instr., then asst. prof. classics Marquette U., Milw., 1961-90; ret., 1990. Mem. edn. bd. Holy Family Cath. Ch., Whitefish Bay, Wis., 1974-75; troop fundraising chmn. Boy Scouts Am., Whitefish Bay, 1976-77; pres. Post-Polio Resource Group of Southeastern Wis., Wauwatosa, 1987, Milw. Area Latin Tchrs. Assn., 1963-64, Fox River Valley Classical Assn., Milw., 1970-71, Wis. Latin Tchrs. Assn., Milw., 1976-78. Cpl. U.S. Army, 1953-55. NEH grantee, 1973. Mem. AAUP, Am. Classical League, Am. Philological Assn., Classical Assn. of the Mid. West and South, Wis. Assn. Fgn. Lang. Tchrs. (pres. 1980-82, Recognition award 1989), Paralyzed Vets. Am. (life), Disabled Am. Vets. (life), Wis. Latin Tchrs. Assn., Marquette U. Retirees Assn. Avocations: reading, videotaping movies and documentaries. Home: 2328 W Apple Tree Rd Milwaukee WI 53209-3312

THEIS, STEVEN THOMAS, safety engineer; b. Trenton, N.J., June 16, 1959; s. Thomas Donald and Pauline (Ciko) T.; m. Mary L. Crane; children: Christopher William, Nicholas Thomas. BS, U. So. Calif., L.A., 1981; Cert. German Lang., Johann Wolfgang Goethe U., Frankfurt am Main, Germany, 1983; postgrad., Friedrich Alexander U., Erlangen, Germany, 1983-84; MS, U. Pa., 1999, MPhil, 2002. Cert. safety profl., cert. hazardous materials mgr., EMT, N.J. With Henkels & McCoy, Inc., various locations, 1978—, constrn. coord. Phoenix, 1982, project mgr. Burlington, N.J., 1985-87, safety dir. N.J. div., 1987-92; staff support coord. corp. office Henkels & McCoy, Blue Bell, Pa., 1992—, corp. dir. safety, 1992—; v.p. safety Myr Group Inc., Rolling Meadows, Ill., 2002—. Safety and health instr. ARC, Woodbury, N.J., 1984—, safety and health instr., trainer, 1990—; basic instr. OSHA constrn. ind. stds. U.S. Dept. Labor, Chgo., 1987—; chairperson safety and health com. Gloucester County ARC, Woodbury, 1991—. Patentee in field. 1st lt. West Deptford Emergency Squad, Thorofare, N.J., 1987-88, capt., 1989-90, hon. mem. 1991—; vice chmn. West Deptford Twp. Bd. Health, 1989-90, v.p. West Deptford Vol. Fire and Ambulance Assn., 1989-90; emergency med. spl. coord. West Deptford Office Emergency Mtmg., 1989-90. Named Mem. of the Yr., West Deptford Emergency Squad, 1988, Ditch Digger of Yr., Nat. Utility Contractors Assn., 2001; recipient Cameron award Nat. Safety Coun., 1992—93, 1993—94, Safety Dir. of Yr. award Distribution Contractors Assn., 2000, V.P. Safety award, Liberty Mut. Mem.: IEEE, APA, ASTM (membership sec. 1994, 1st vice-chmn. 2000—, rec. sec. 1998—99), Nat. Utility Contractors Assn., Nat. Electric Safety Code, Nat. Safety Coun., Am. Nat. Stds. Inst., Nat. Safety Coun., Am. Soc. Safety Engrs., Common Ground Alliance. Republican. Roman Catholic. Avocations: antiques, classical music, model building, fishing. Office: Myr Group Inc 1701 West Golf Rd Ste 1012 Rolling Meadows IL 60008

THEIS, WILLIAM HAROLD, lawyer, educator; b. Chgo., Nov. 8, 1945; s. Clarence M. and Marion K. (McLendon) T.; m. Maria Luisa Belfiore, Dec. 5, 1973; children: Catherine, Elizabeth. AB, Loyola U., Chgo., 1967; JD, Northwestern U., 1970; LLM, Columbia U., 1977, JSD, 1982. Bar: Ill. 1970, D.C. 1971, Wis. 1998, U.S. Ct. Appeals (7th cir.) 1971, U.S. Supreme Ct. 1974, Wis. 1998. Assoc. prof. La. State U. Law Ctr., 1972-78, Loyola U. Law Sch., Chgo., 1978-81; practiced in Chgo., 1981-99; pvt. practice, 1999-2000; chief appellate atty. Fed. Defender Program, Chgo., 2000—. Part-time lectr. admiralty Northwestern Sch. Law, Chgo. Contbr. articles to legal jours. Lt. USNR, 1970-72. Mem. Am. Law Inst. Office: 55 E Monroe St Ste 2800 Chicago IL 60603

THEISMANN, JOSEPH ROBERT, former professional football player, announcer; b. New Brunswick, N.J., Sept. 9, 1949; s. Joseph James and Olga (Tobias) T.; m. Robin Smith, Dec. 5, 1970 (div.); children: Joseph Winton, Amy Lynn, Patrick James. BA in Sociology, U. Notre Dame, 1971. With Toronto Argonauts, CFL, 1971-74, Washington Redskins, 1974-86, punt returner, 1974-79, starting quarterback, 1979-86; analyst CBS Nat. Football League broadcasts, 1987-88, ESPN Nat. Football League broadcasts, 1988—. Pres., CEO JRT Assocs.; tchr. Offense-Def. Football Camp; Superstar participant, 1979-80, played in Pro-Bowl, 1983-84; mem. Pres.'s Athletic Adv. Com., 1975; active Pres. Nat. Svc. Adv. Com., 1993. Author: Quarter Backing. Mem. corp. bd. Children's Hosp. Nat. Med. Center, Washington; participant benefits for Multiple Sclerosis children's hosps., Armed Forces Christmas benefits. High sch. All-Am. Football, 1967; All-Am. Coll., 1971; Acad.-All-Am.; All-Pro UPI; recipient Brian Picollo award; played in Pro Bowl, 1982, 83; mem. Super Bowl XVII Championship Team, 1982; cable Ace award, Best Sports Commentator-Analyst, 1994. Mem. Nat. Football Players Assn. Republican. Methodist. Office: JRT Assocs 5661 Columbia Pike # 100B Falls Church VA 22041-2868

THEISS, GENA LEE, genealogist, researcher; b. Caneyville, Ky., May 16, 1925; d. Clarence Harbon Johnson and Gracie Higdon; m. Robert Maple Hunt, Nov. 9, 1946 (div. May 1948); 1 child, Nancy Jane; m. George William Theiss, July 15, 1949; children: Patricia Sue, Donna Lee, Martha Rhea. Grad. h.s., Caneyville, Ky., 1943. Bookkeeper Lincoln Bank & Trust Co., Louisville, 1944-47, Citizens Nat. Bank, Louisville, 1948-56, First Nat. Bank, Louisville, 1957-84. Author, editor: Christian Weedman and his Descendants 1735-1986, 1986, revised edit., 1989, Descendants of John Higdon and Millicent, 1998, Update on Christian Weedman and his Descendants, 2002, Possible Update on John Higdon and Millicent, 2002. Active Hillview Cumberland Presbyn. Ch. Mem. Ky. Hist. Soc., DAR, Ea. Star Chpt. 154. Republican. Avocations: genealogy, quilting, photography, stamp collecting/philately, travel. Home: 8417 Burlingame Rd Louisville KY 40219-5205

THEISS, PATRICIA KELLEY, public health researcher, educator; b. Atlanta, Dec. 12, 1934; d. Charles Henry and Susie Carlota (Tate) Kelley; m. Erich Albert Theiss (div. Aug. 1996). BA, Wellesley Coll., 1956; MS, Howard U., 1958, Cert. in Secondary Edn., 1959. Rsch. asst. Armed Forces Inst. Pathology, Washington, 1959-61; heath edn. phone coord. Howard U. Cancer Ctr., Washington, 1977-81; program assoc. D.C. Lung Assn., Washington, 1981-85; co-project dir. Know Your Body Evaluation Project Georgetown U. Sch. Medicine, Washington, 1985-87; coord. minority health grant for cancer coalition Commn. Pub. Health, Washington, 1988-89, coord. data-based intervention rsch., 1989-93, protocol coord. immunization protocol NIH-DC initiative, 1994-97; pub. health advisor Dept. Health State Ctr. Health Stats. Inst. Minority Health Statistics Initiative, Washington, 1997—; coord. D.C. Healthy People 2010 Plan Initiative, 1998—; state contact U.S. Office Minority Health, Washington, 1999—. Mem. task force for substance abuse use Abuse Edn. for D.C. Pub. Schs., 1984-85; mem. Health Mothers/Health Babies Coalition, 1985-89. Contbr. articles to profl. jours. Chair health and welfare com. D.C. PTA, 1986-89; coord. AIDS awareness edn. State PTA, D.C., 1987-89. Recipient Cmty. Svc. award D.C. Assn. Health, Recreation and Dance, 1987. Mem. APHA, Met. Washington Pub. Health Assn. (pres. 1987-88). Democrat. Congregationalist. Avocations: painting, horseback riding. Home: 2501 Calvert St NW #902 Washington DC 20008 Office: DC Dept Health SCHS 825 N Capitol St NE Washington DC 20002-4210 E-mail: patricia.theiss@dc.gov.

THELANDER, BEVERLY, oil company executive; BS, MBA in Fin., UCLA. Variuos fin. positions ARCO, 1981-98, v.p. comm. pub. affairs & investor rels., 1998—. Office: ARCO 4 Centerpointe Dr La Palma CA 90623-2502

THELEN, BRUCE CYRIL, lawyer; b. St. Johns, Mich., Nov. 24, 1951; BA, Mich. State U., 1973; JD, U. Mich., 1977. Bar: N.Y. 1978, Mich. 1980, Ill. 1992. Assoc. Dewey, Ballantine, Bushby, Palmer & Wood, N.Y.C., 1977-80; ptnr. Dickinson, Wright, Moon, Van Dusen & Freeman, Detroit, 1981-83, Dickinson Wright PLLC, Detroit, 1984—. Mem. U.S. Dept. Commerce-Mich. Dist. Export Coun., 1995—. Contbr. articles to profl. jours. Mem. allocation panel, mem. spkrs. bur., chmn. rsch. and info. svcs. com., mem. strategic planning com. and comty. leaders coun. United Way Cmty. Svcs., 1987—; mem. state of Mich. Task Force on Internat. Trade, Lansing, 1990; mem. Detroit Com. on Fgn. Rels., Greater Detroit-Windsor Japan Am. Soc. Decorated Order of Merit (Fed. Rep. Germany). Mem. N.Y. Bar Assn. (mem. internat. law sect.), State Bar Mich. (chmn. internat. law sect. 1990-91), Internat. Bar Assn. (chmn. fin. aspects internat. sales subcom.), Am. Soc. Internat. Law, Ill. Bar Assn. (internat. law sect.), Internat. Inst. Detroit (bd. dirs. 1997-99, v.p. 1999-2000), French-Am. C. of C. of Detroit, German Am. C. of C. of Midwest (bd. dirs. 1992—, pres. Mich. chpt. 1994—), Mich. Israel C. of C. (bd. dirs. 1997-01), Greater Detroit C. of C. (chmn. European mission com. 1991-92, 95, export com. 1992-95, Leadership Detroit VIII program 1986-87), World Trade Club and Internat. Bus. Coun. (exec. com. 1992—), Internat. Bridge, Coun. Mentors, Wayne State U., Econ. Club Detroit, Detroit Athletic Club. Office: Dickinson Wright PLLC 500 Woodward Ave Ste 4000 Detroit MI 48226-3416 Office Phone: 313-223-3624.

THELEN, EDMUND, research executive; b. Berkeley, Calif, May 8, 1913; s. Paul and Alice (Arnold) T.; m. Helen Naomi Betton, Oct. 30, 1965; children: Nancy Anne, Joan Arnold Thelen Hanson. BS, U. Calif., Berkeley, 1934. Asst. chemist Certain-Teed Products Corp., Richmond, Calif., 1934-35; chemist O. C. Field Gasoline Corp., Santa Maria, Calif., 1936-41; asst. mgr. Eclipse Pioneer divsn. Bendix Corp., Teterboro, N.J., 1946-47; sr. rsch. chemist Franklin Inst. Rsch. Labs., Phila., 1947-51, mgr. colloids and polymers br., 1951-74, v.p., dir. phys. and life scis. dept., 1974-76, Inst. fellow, sec. com. on sci. and the arts, 1976-82, mem., 1982-2001, emeritus, 2001—. Pres. Safety Surface Corp., 1983-88; mem. Coun. for Delivery of Dental Care, 1970-85; bd. govs. Franklin-Hahnemann Inst. Occupl. and Environ. Health, 1975-80, Mayor's Sci. and Tech. Adv. Com. on Environment, 1973-80; instr. dental medicine Hahnemann Med. Coll. and Hosp., 1964-74; v.p., dir. Pa. Environ. Coun., 1974-85; treas. Home Health Svcs. of Chester County and Vicinity, 1981-86. Co-author: (book) Porous Pavement for Runoff Control, 1978; editor Am. Assn. Ret. Persons, Eastern Chester County newsletter, 1994-97; contbr. papers to tech. publs. Bd. dir. Neighborhood Vis. Nurse Assn., 1987-93. With USN, 1941-45; comdr. USNR, 1941-66. Recipient spl. recognition award Am. Soc. Landscape Archs., 1974. Mem. Franklin Inst., Sierra Club (ea. Pa. group chmn. 1968, Atlantic chpt. vice-chmn. 1971-73, founding chmn. Pa. chpt. 1974), Ret. Officers Assn. (treas. Valley Forge chpt. 1980-85, v.p. 1987, pres. 1988-89, sec. 1994-97), Toastmasters Internat. (dist. gov. 1960-61), Sunday Breakfast Spkr. Club (pres. 1960-61), Sigma Xi, mem., Nat. Resources Defense Coun., Southern Poverty Law Ctr. Home: 658 Davis Ln Wayne PA 19087-5418

THELEN, GIL, newspaper publisher; b. Chgo. s. Gilbert Carl and Violet (Okonn) T.; m. Carol Abernathy, July 1966 (div. Apr. 1978); children: Deborah Brooke, Todd Foster; m. Cynthia Jane Struby, Sept. 2, 1979; children: Matthew David, Jonathan Whitfield. BA, Duke U., 1960. Reporter Milw. Jour., 1960-61, AP, Washington, 1965-72; writer Consumer Reports, Mt. Vernon, N.Y., 1972-77; reporter Chgo. Daily News, 1977-78; asst. met. editor Charlotte (N.C.) Observer, 1978-82, met. editor, 1982-83, asst. mng. editor, 1983-87; editor The Sun News, Myrtle Beach, S.C., 1987-90; exec. editor The State, 1990-97; cons. editor Knight-Ridder, Inc., Columbia, S.C., 1997-98; exec. editor The Tampa Tribune, 1998—2003, pub., 2003—. Adj. prof. U. S.C., Aiken, 1989-98. Pres. Montgomery County Big Bros., Bethesda, Md., 1967-69; co-founder Alpha Group, Myrtle Beach, S.C., 1989. Mem. Am. Soc. Newspaper Editors, Fla. Soc. Newspaper Editors, Leadership S.C., Leadership Columbia, Leadership Tampa, Phi Beta Kappa, Omicron Delta Kappa. Methodist. Avocations: golf, reading, classical music. Office: 200 S Parker St Tampa FL 33606-2308 also: Tampa Tribune PO Box 191 Tampa FL 33601 E-mail: gtheien@tampatrib.com.

THELIN, JOHN ROBERT, academic administrator, education educator, historian; b. West Newton, Mass., Oct. 15, 1947; s. George Willard and Rozalija Katherine (Komarec) T.; m. Anna Sharon Blackburn, June 24, 1978. AB cum laude, Brown U., 1969; MA, U. Calif., Berkeley, 1972, PhD, 1973. Rsch. asst. Brown U., Providence, 1968-69; rschr., lectr. U. Calif., Berkeley, 1972-74; asst. prof. U. Ky., Lexington, 1974-77; asst. dean Pomona Coll., Claremont, Calif., 1977-79; from asst. dir. to rsch. dir. Assn. Ind. Calif. Colls. and Univs., Santa Ana, 1979-81; chancellor prof. Coll. William and Mary, Williamsburg, Va., 1981-93, pres. faculty assembly, 1990-91; prof. higher edn. & philanthropy Ind. U., Bloomington, 1993-96; prof. ednl. policy and history U. Ky., Lexington, 1996—, disting. univ. rsch. prof., 2001—. Vis. prof. grad. sch. Claremont U., 1978—81; vis. scholar U. Calif., Berkeley, 1995; curator Marquandia Soc., 1971—2003; essay rev. editor Rev. of Higher Edn., 1979—91; rsch. cons. NSF, Washington, 1991; mem. faculty senate U. Ky., 1997—; guest faculty Coll. Bus. Mgmt. Inst., summer, 1998, 99, 2000, 01, 02, 03; mem., chair social sci. com. Grad. Coun., U.K., 1998—2001; keynote spkr. Sesquicentennial of Harvard Athletics Assn., Harvard U., 2002. Author: Higher Education and Its Useful Past, 1982, The Cultivation of Ivy, 1976, Higher Education and Public Policy, 1991, Games Colleges Play, 1994, A History of American Higher Education, 2004; author: (with others) The Old College Try, 1989, One Hundred Classic Books About Higher Education, 2001; assoc. editor (jour.) Higher Edn.: Theory and Rsch., 1983—91, guest columnist Lexington Herald-Leader, 2001. Pres., bd. dirs. United Way, Williamsburg, 1987-89; pres. Friends of Williamsburg Libr., 1989. Rsch. grantee Spencer Found., 1989-91, 99-2001; Regents fellow U. Calif., 1972; named to Order of Ky. Cols., 1998; recipient Outstanding Faculty Rsch. award Coll. of Edn., U. Ky., 2000, Great Tchrs. award U. Ky., 2004. Mem. Assn. for Study of Higher Edn. (bd. dirs. 1988-90, keynote spkr. 1994, pres. 1999-2000), History of Edn. Soc. (editl. bd. 1988-91), Lexington Club, Phi Beta Kappa (Faculty award for advancement of scholarship Alpha of Va. 1986, Alpha of R.I. 1969), Omicron Delta Kappa. Avocations: long-distance running, history of Los Angeles and California, sports history. Home: 1745 Richmond Rd Lexington KY 40502 Office: U Ky Edn Policy Studies Lexington KY 40506-1 Office Phone: 859-257-4996. E-mail: JThelin@uky.edu.

THELLMANN, EDWARD L. mayor; m. Catherine Thellmann; children: Mark, Leah, Kenn, Kim. BS in chemistry and Math., Cleve. State U., 1959; Cert. of Metallurgy, Fenn Inst., 1963. With Clevite/Gould, Inc., sr. staff engr., mgr. applied materials; councilman Village of Walton Hills, 1982—87, mayor, 1987—2000; ret., 2000. Contbr. articlels to profl. jours. Mem. Walton Hills Planning Commn.; chmn. Chagrin/S.E. Coun. Govts. for Hazmat Svc.; mem. governing bd. N.E. Ohio Areawide Coord. Agy.; v.p. Greater Cleve. Regional Transit Authority Bd. Trustees; chmn. hazardous materials planning adv. task force N.E. Ohio Areawide Coord. Agy., mem. water quality subcom., mem. commuter rail adv. task force, mem. environ. adv. bd. With USN, 1945—46. Named to Alumni Hall of Fame, West Tech H.S., 1988; recipient Civic Leadership award, Cleve. State U. Alumni Assn., 2000. Mem.: Cuyahoga County Mayors and City Mgrs. Assn. (past pres., v.p., treas. and sec.), Walton Hills Lake Club, Walton Hills Men's Club (past chmn.). Achievements include patents for in field. Home: 18307 Orchard Hill Rd Walton Hills OH 44146

THEOBALD, EDWARD ROBERT, lawyer; b. Chgo., Feb. 10, 1947; BA, So. Ill. U., 1969; JD, Ill. Inst. Tech., 1974. Bar: Ill. 1974, U.S. Dist. Ct. (no. dist.) Ill. 1974. Asst. state's atty. Cook County, Chgo., 1974-79, supr. felony trial divsn., 1980-81; assoc. Conklin, Leahy & Eisenberg, Chgo., 1977; ptnr. Boharic & Theobald, Chgo., 1981-83, owner, ptnr., 1983—. Legal adv. Sheriff of Cook County, Ill., 1986-89; spl. state's atty. U.S. Dist. Ct. no. dist. Ill., 1989-91, Cook County, Ill., 2002—; apptd. spl. corp. counsel City of Chgo., 1994. Mem. Parent adv. bd. Downers Grove (Ill.) South H.S., 1992-94. Named Number One Trial Atty. in Felony Trial Divsn. of Office of Cook County State's Atty., Felony Trial Divsn. Suprs., 1979. Mem. ABA (sect. on tort and ins. law, sect. on labor and employment law, chmn. com. on sentencing alternatives young lawyers sect. 1982-83, tort and ins. practice sect., labor and employment law sect.), ATLA, Chgo. Bar Assn. (mem. bd. mgrs. 1985-87, mem. labor and employment law com. 1983—2002, mem. com. on coms. 1990-94, mem. membership com. 1990-95, vice chair judicial evaluation com. 1999-2000), Ill. Bar Assn. Roman Catholic. Office: 111 W Washington St Ste 759 Chicago IL 60602-2705

THEOBALD, THOMAS CHARLES, banker; b. Cin., May 5, 1937; m. Gigi Mahon, Jan. 1987 AB in Econs., Coll. Holy Cross, 1958; MBA in Fin. with high distinction, Harvard U., 1960. With Citibank, N.A. div. Citicorp, 1960-87; vice-chmn. Citicorp, N.Y.C., 1982-87; CEO, chmn. Continental Bank Corp., Chgo., 1987-94; chmn. bd. dirs. Continental Bank N.A., Chgo., 1987-94; mng. dir. Blair Capital Ptnrs., Chgo., 1994—. Bd. dir. Jones, Lang LaSalle US Realty Income & Growth Fund, Anixter Internat., Liberty Funds, Mac Arthur Found., MONY Group. Trustee Northwestern U. Office: William Blair Capital Partners 227 N Monroe Ste 3500 Chicago IL 60606-5307

THEODOLI, KATRIN, manufacturing executive; m. Filippo Theodoli. Mng. dir. Magnum Marine Motor Yachts, Aventura, Fla., until 1990, CEO, pres., 1990—. Office: Magnum Marine 2900 NE 188th St Miami FL 33180-2998 Fax: 305-931-0088.

THEODORE, ARES NICHOLAS, research chemist; b. Kalamata, Greece, Oct. 28, 1933; came to U.S., 1954; s. Nicholas A. and Angeliki (Myseros) Theodoracopulos; m. Peggy Salvarakis, Sept. 3, 1961; children: Nicholas A., Angie A. BA cum laude, Westminster Coll., Salt Lake City, 1958; MS, U. Utah, 1961; postgrad., Case Western Res. U., 1967-68. Asst. prof. chemistry Westminster Coll., 1961-64; sr. rsch. chemist Diamond Shamrock Corp., Cleve., 1964-69; rsch. scientist Ford Motor Co., Detroit, 1969-73, sr. rsch. scientist, 1973-84, prin. rsch. scientist, 1984—2000. Contbr. articles to profl. jours.; patentee in field (59). Mem. ch. bd. Holy Cross Greek Orthodox Ch., Farmington Hills, Mich., 1986-88; campaigner Farmington Hills Dem. Com., 1986-88; mem. bus. coun. Boston Dem. Com., 1988—. Nat. Dem. Com., 1988—. U. Utah fellow, 1958-61, NSF fellow, 1964. Mem. Am. Chem. Soc. (treas. 1967), Ahepa (bd. govs. Dearborn, Mich. 1985-86). Avocations: swimming, golf, photography. Home: 34974 Valley Forge Dr Farmington Hills MI 48331-3210

THEODORE, CRYSTAL, artist, retired educator; b. Greenville, S.C., July 27, 1917; d. James Voutsas and Florence Gertrude (Bell) T. AB magna cum laude, Winthrop Coll., 1938; MA, Columbia U., 1942, EdD, 1953; postgrad., U. Ga., 1947. Instr. art Winthrop Coll., 1938-43; prof. art, head dept. Huntingdon (Ala.) Coll., 1946-52, E. Tenn. State U., 1953-57, Madison Coll., 1967—68; vis. prof. art World Campus Afloat Chapman Coll., Calif., 1967; prof. art James Madison U., Harrisonburg, Va., 1968-83, prof. emeritus, 1983—. Contbr. articles to profl. jours.; paintings in regional and nat. art exhbns. Bd. dirs. Rockingham Fine Arts Assn., 1980—85, 1989, Citizens for the Downtown, 1989, Women's Coop. Coun. Harrisonburg and Rockingham County, 1976—79, Valley Coun. of the Arts, 1998—99, Shenandoah Coun. of the Arts, 1996—, pres., 1996—2002; founder OASIS Co-op Gallery, 2000. Served with USMC, 1944—46. Gen. Edn. Bd. of Rockefeller Found. fellow, 1952-53; recipient award Carnegie Found. Advancement of Tchg., 1947, 48, 49, 50; Ednl. Found. Program grantee AAUW, 1981-82; rsch. grantee Ednl. Radio and TV Ctr., 1956. Mem.: AAUW (cultural interests rep., nat. dir. 1980—82), Va. Mus., Va. Watercolor Soc., Mensa, Pi Lambda Theta, Eta Sigma Phi, Kappa Pi. Democrat. Lutheran. Home: 150 Bear Wallow Ln Harrisonburg VA 22802-0153

THEODORE, DAVID, research scientist; MS in Materials Sci. and Engring., Northwestern U., 1986; PhD in Materials Sci. and Engring., Cornell U., 1991. Sun Certified Programmer For Java 2 Platform Sun Microsystems, Inc., 2003. Staff scientist Advanced Custom Technologies Motorola Inc., Mesa, Ariz., 1990—91, sr. staff scientist Advanced Custom Technologies, 1991—92, prin. staff scientist Materials Rsch. & Strategic Technologies, 1992—96, mem. tech. staff, rsch. scientist and tech. mgr. Ctr. for Integrated Systems Devel., 1997—99, mem. tech. staff, tech. mgr. and rsch. scientist Materials Rsch. & Strategic Technologies, 1999—2001, disting. mem. tech. staff, tech. mgr. and rsch. scientist Advanced Products R&D Labs. Tempe, Ariz., 2001—. Contbr. articles to profl. jours. Vol. tchr. 5th-6th grade kids, Mesa, 1995—2004. Mem.: Materials Rsch. Soc. Achievements include patents in field; patents pending in field. Office: Freescale Semiconductor Inc Advanced Products R&D Lab 2100 East Elliot Rd Tempe AZ 85284 Personal E-mail: femtophysicist@yahoo.com.

THEODORE, EUSTACE D. educational advancement consultant, management consultant; b. Marietta, Ohio, Aug. 4, 1941; s. Demetrios E. and Nicoletta D. T.; m. Carol Nagy, June 13, 1964; children: Kyle James, Graham Clark. BA, Yale U., 1963; MA, Cornell U., 1965, PhD, 1967. Mem. faculty Hollins Coll., Roanoke, Va., 1967-71, Mt. Holyoke Coll., South Hadley, Mass., 1971-72; dean Calhoun Coll., Yale U., New Haven, 1972-81; exec. dir. Assn. Yale Alumni, 1981-97; pres. Coun. for Advancement and Support of Edn., Washington, 1997-2000; prin. eAdvancement.org, 2000—. Mgmt. and ednl. cons., 1965—. Contbr. articles to jours. Office: eAdvancement 1301 21st St NW Washington DC 20036-1503 Office Phone: 202-463-7310. E-mail: theodore@eAdvancement.org.

THEODORE, JOSE, professional hockey player; b. Sept. 13, 1976; Hockey player Montreal Canadiens, 1995—. Player NHL All-star game, 2002, 04; mem. Team Can., World Cup of Hockey, 2004. Named Player of Week, Nat. Hockey League, 1999, Fredericton's Player of Yr., Am. Hockey League; named to World Hockey Championship 2nd All-Star team, 2000; recipient Vezina Trophy, 2002, Hart Meml. Trophy, 2002. Achievements include mem. World Cup Champion Team Can., 2004. Office: Molson Ctr 1260 d La Gauchetiere Street W Montreal QC H3B 5E8 Canada

THEODORE, NICHOLAS, neurosurgeon, researcher; b. San Diego, Oct. 3, 1963; s. Charles and Pauline Stamatopoulos Theodore; m. Eyphemia Stamos Theodore, Oct. 22, 1994; children: Constantine Nicholas, John Nicholas. AB, Cornell U., 1985; MS, Georgetown U., 1987, MD, 1991. Chief divsn. neurosurgery Naval Med. Ctr., San Diego, 2001—03; chief neurotrauma sect. Barrow Neurol. Inst., Phoenix, 2003—. Contbr. articles to profl. jours. Comdr. USN. Mem.: Congress Neurol. Surgeons, N.Am. Spine Soc. (Nass Rsch. award 1999), Am. Assn. Neurol. Surgeons (Mayfield award 2000, Pain Sect. award 2000). Achievements include patents in field. Avocations: hiking, music. Office: Barrow Neurosurg Assocs Ltd 2910 N 3rd Ave Phoenix AZ 85013

THEODORESCU, RADU AMZA SERBAN, mathematician, educator; b. Bucharest, Romania, Apr. 12, 1933; emigrated to Can., 1968, naturalized, 1975; s. Dan and Ortensia Maria (Butoianu) T.; children: Dan, Paul, Anne. BSc, U. Bucharest, 1954, DSc, 1967; PhD, Acad. Romania, 1958. Asst. prof. Inst. Math. of Acad., 1954-57, sr. asst. prof., 1957-60, assoc. prof., sci. sec., 1960-64; prof., head dept. Center Math. Statistics, 1964-68; prof. U. Bucharest, 1968-69, Laval U., Quebec, Canada, 1969-2000, prof. emeritus, 2000—; guest prof., lectr. univs. in Europe, N.Am. and Australia. Author: (with G. Ciucu) Processes with Complete Connections, 1960, (with S. Guiasu) Mathematical Information Theory, 1968, Uncertainty and Information, 1971, (with M. Iosifescu) Random Processes and Learning, 1969, (with W. Hengartner) Concentration Functions, 1973, 2d edit., 1980, Monte-Carlo Methods, 1978, (with E. Bertin and I. Cuculescu) Unimodality of Probability Measures, 1997; mem. editl. bd. Annales des Sciences Mathématiques du Québec, 1976-99, Optimization, 1970-2000, Statistics and Decisions, 1981-2003, Revstat, 2002—; contbr. articles to profl. jours. Mem. bd. European Orgn. Quality Control, 1966-69. Recipient prize Acad. Romania, 1960 Fellow Inst. Math. Stats., Am. Soc. Quality; mem. Statis. Soc. Can. (hon.), Statis. Soc. Romania (hon.), Am. Math. Soc., Internat. Statis. Historians. Home: Apt 1603 9 Jardins Mérici Quebec City QC Canada G1S 4S8 Office: Laval U Dept Math and Stats Quebec City QC Canada G1K 7P4 Office Phone: 418-656-3057. E-mail: radutheo@mat.ulaval.ca.

THEODORIDIS, GEORGE CONSTANTIN, biomedical engineering educator, researcher; b. Braila, Romania, Dec. 3, 1935; came to U.S., 1959; s. Constantin George and Anastasia (Haritopoulos) T.; m. Lilly Kate Hyman, Sept. 20, 1975; 1 child, Alexander. BS in Mechanical and Elec. Engring., Nat. Tech. U. Athens, 1959; DSc, MIT, Cambridge, Mass., 1964. Rsch. assoc. MIT, Cambridge, Mass., 1964; sr. scientist Am. Sci. Engring., Cambridge, Mass., 1964-68; assoc. prof. in residence U. Calif., Berkeley, 1968-70; biomedical engring. U. Va., Charlottesville, 1970—; prof. elec. engring. U. Patras, Greece, 1976-83. Cons. Food and Drug Adminstrn., Washington, 1975-76, Applied Physics Lab, Columbia, Md., 1978-79. Author: Applied Math, 1983; contbr. articles to profl. jours. Den leader Boy Scouts Am., Charlottesville, Va., 1984-85. Fulbright fellow U.S. Govt., MIT, 1959-60; Nato fellow NATO, MIT, 1961-64; Spl. fellow NIH, U. Calif., 1968-70; recipient teaching award GE, MIT, 1963. Mem. Inst. Elec. and Electronics Engrs., Sigma Xi. Greek Orthodox. Avocations: history, travel. Home: 1817 Fendall Ave Charlottesville VA 22903-1613 Office: U Va Dept Biomed Engring PO Box 377 Charlottesville VA 22902-0377

THEODOROPOULOS, CHRISTINE O. architecture educator; BS in Civil Engring., Princeton U., 1979; MArch, Yale U., 1982. Registered arch., Calif., 1997; civil engr., Calif. Assoc. prof., dept. head dept. arch. U. Oreg., Eugene. Office: Dept Arch 210 Lawrence Hall 1206 Univ Oreg Eugene OR 97403-1206*

THEODOROU, ANDREAS A. pediatrician, educator; b. Detroit, Nov. 15, 1957; s. Theodore A. and Evangelia Theodorou; m. Maria Spirtos, July 19, 1979; children: Theodore, Penelope, Evangelia. BS in Biology, Wayne State U., 1979, MD, 1983. Lic. Nat. Bd. Med. Examiners, Mich., 1984, Am. Bd. Pediatrics, Mich., 1987, cert. PALS instr. Mich., 1990, lic. Am. Bd. Pediatrics, Ariz., 1996. Staff pediatrician Samaritan Health Ctr., Detroit, 1987—89, Children's Hosp. Mich., 1987—89; asst. prof. dept. pediat. U. Ariz. Health Sci. Ctr., Tucson, 1992—96, asst. prof. clin. pediat., 1996—97, assoc. prof. clin. pediat., 1997—; med. dir. pediatric ICU Tucson Med. Ctr., 1997—. U. Med. Ctr., U. Ariz. Health Scis. Ctr., 1998—; chief staff elect U. Med. Ctr., 2000—03, chief staff, 2003—04, porf. of clinical pediatrics, 2004—. Spkr. in field. Contbr. chapters to books, articles to profl. jours. Named Father of Yr., St. Demetrios Greek Orthodox Ch., 2003; recipient Anna Rutzky Meml. award, 1983, Student Senate award, Wayne State U., 1983, Aesculapian award, Svc. Honors Soc., 1983, Governor's award excellence, Dept. Econ. Security, Dept. Health Scis., 2000. Mem.: Am. Thoracic Soc., Pima County Pediatric Soc., Soc. Critical Care Medicine, Am. Acad. Pediat. Greek Orthodox. Avocations: piano, drawing, running, church youth group advisor. Office: Arizona Health Sciences Center 1501 N Campbell Avenue Tucson AZ 85724-5073 Office Phone: 520-626-5485. E-mail: aat@peds.arizona.edu.

THEODOSIUS, HIS BEATITUDE METROPOLITAN See LAZOR, THEODOSIUS

THEODOSIUS, retired leader of the Orthodox Church in America; b. Canonsburg, P.A., 1933; Grad., Washington and Jefferson Coll., Washington, PA; Master of Divinity, Saint Vladimir Orthodox Theological Seminary, 1960. Ordained to the diaconate & priesthood Orthodox Church in Amer., 1961; bishop Diocese of Sitka and Alaska, 1967—72, Diocese of Pittsburgh, Pa., 1972—77; metropolitan of Amer., Canada Orthodox Church of Amer., 1977—2002; archbishop of Washington, 1977—2002. Office: Orthodox Ch in Am PO Box 675 Syosset NY 11791-0675

THEOFANOUS, THEO G. engineering educator, consultant; b. Athens, Greece, May 21, 1942; s. George T. and Smaro (Voudouris) T.; m. Danae P. Kembe, May 15, 1969; children: George, Lydia. BS in Chem. Engring., Nat. Tech. U., Athens, Greece, 1965; PhD in Chem. Engring., U. Minn., 1969; D in Laaperanta (hon.), U. Finland, 1999. Instr. in chem. engring. U. Minn., Mpls., 1968-69; asst. prof. chem. engring. Purdue U., West Lafayette, Ind., 1969-73, assoc. prof. chem. engring., 1973-74, assoc. prof. nuc. engring., 1974-76, prof. nuc. engring., 1976-85; prof. chem. and nuc. engring. U. Calif., Santa Barbara, 1985—, dir. Ctr. for Risk Studies and Safety, 1985—, prof. mech. and environ. engring., 1994—. V.p. Fauske, Grolmes, Henry & Theofanous, Ltd., Hinsdale, Ill., 1979-81; pres. Theofanous & Co., Inc., Santa Barbara, 1981—; cons. in field. Recipient Ernest Orlando Lawrence Meml. award U.S. Dept. of Energy, 1996. Fellow Am. Nuc. Soc.; mem. AIChE, AAAS, NAE. Achievements include finding the mechanism that caused the Sevesco accident; invented a methodology for risk assessment and mgmt. of high-consequence hazzards; contbr. in risk analyses of nuc. reactors and in mitigating the consequence of severe accidents. Office: U Calif Dept Chem Engring Santa Barbara CA 93106-5080 E-mail: theo@theo.ucsb.edu.

THEOHARIDES, THEOHARIS CONSTANTIN, pharmacologist, physician, educator; b. Thessaloniki, Macedonia, Greece, Feb. 11, 1950; s. Constantin A. and Marika (Krava) T.; m. Efthalia I. Triarhou, July 10, 1981; children: Niove, Konstantinos. Diploma with honors, Anatolia Coll., 1968; BA in Biology, History of Sci. and Med., Yale U., 1972, MS in Immunology, MPhil in Endocrinology, Yale U., 1975, PhD in Pharmacology, 1978; postgrad., Tufts U., Harvard U. Asst. in rsch. biology Yale U., New Haven, 1968—71, asst. in rsch. pharmacology, 1973—78, spl. instr. modern Greek, 1974, 77, exec. sec. univ. senate, 1976—78, rsch. assoc. faculty clin. immunology, 1978—83; asst. prof. biochemistry and pharmacology Tufts U., Boston, 1983—88, co-dir. med. pharmacology curriculum, 1983—85, 1983—85, dir. med. pharmacology, 1985—93, assoc. prof. pharmacology, biochemistry and psychiatry, 1989—94, dir. grad. pharmacology, 1994—2000, prof. pharmacology and internal medicine, 1995—, prof. biochemistry, 2002—. Vis. faculty Aristotelian U. Sch. Medicine, Thessaloniki, 1979; trustee Anatolia Coll., 1984-85; clin. pharmacologist Commonwealth Mass. Drug Formulary Commn., 1985—; co-chmn. neuro-immunology 2d and 3d World Conf. on Inflammation, Monte Carlo, 1986, 89; mem. internat. adv. bd. 4th, 5th, 6th and 7th World Conf. on Inflammation, Geneva, 1991, 93, 95, 97; spl. cons. Min. of Health, Greece, 1993-95; mem. supreme spl. sci. health coun. Hellenic Republic, 1998—; chmn. Internat. Com. to Upgrade Med. Edn. in Greece, 1994; bd. dirs., spl. cons. Inst. Pharm. Rsch. & Tech., Athens, 1994—; mem. supreme health bd. Hellenic Inst. Social Welfare, 1999—. Author books on pharmacology; mem. editorial bd. numerous jours.; contbr. articles to profl. jours.; patentee in field. Bd. dirs., v.p. for rels. with Greece, Krikos, 1978-79; sec. Assn. Greeks to Yale, 1974-79, pres., 1982-83; mem. supreme sci. health coun. Hellenic Republic, 1997-2000, mem. supreme health care bd. Ministry of Labor, 1999-2002; bd. trustees, exec. bd. Hellenic Coll., 2000-02. Recipient Theodore Buyler award, Yale U., 1972, George Papanicoalou Grad. award, 1977, Med. award, Hellenic Med. Soc. N.Y., 1979, 1983, M.C. Winternitz prize in pathology, Yale U., 1980, Disting Svc. award, Tufts U. Alumni Assn., 1986, Spl. Faculty Recognition award, Tufts U. Med. Sch., 1987, 1988, Boston Mayor Menino Cmty. Svc. award, 1998, Oliver Smith award, 1999, Archon of Ecunemical Patriarchate of Christian Orthodox Ch., 2000. Mem. AMA, AAUP, AAAS, Hellenic Biochem. and Biophys. Soc., N.Y. Acad. Scis., Am. Inst. History Pharmacy, Soc. Health and Human Values, Am. Assn. History Medicine, Am. Soc. Cell Biology, Soc. Neurosci., Am. Fedn. Clin. Rsch., Conn. Acad. Arts and Scis., Am. Soc. Pharmacology and Exptl. Therapeutics, Hellenic Soc. Cancer Rsch., Hellenic Soc. Med. Chemistry, Internat. Soc. Immunopharmacology, Am. Soc. Microbiology, Am. Assn. Immunologists, Internat. Soc. History of Medicine, Mass. Med. Soc., N.E. Hellenic Med. Soc. (sec. 1984-85, v.p. 1985-86, 94-96, pres. 1986-87), Hellenic Sci. Assn. Boston (bd. dirs. 1985), Internat. Anatolia Alumni Assn. (sec. 1984-85), Alpha Omega Alpha, Sigma Xi. Achievements include research on mechanisms of release of secretory products: immunopharmacology membrane functions of polyamines; pathophysiology of mast cells in neuroimmunoendocrine diseases exacerbated by stress such as irritable bowel syndrome, interstitial cystitis, migraines and multiple sclerosis. Home: 14 Parkman St Apt 2 Brookline MA 02446-3802 Office: Tufts U Sch Med 136 Harrison Ave Boston MA 02111-1817

THEOHARIS, ATHAN GEORGE, history educator; b. Milw., Aug. 3, 1936; s. George A. and Adeline M. (Konop) T.; m. Nancy Artinian, Aug. 21, 1966; children: Jeanne, George, Elizabeth. AB, U. Chgo., 1956, AM, 1959, PhD, 1965. Instr. Tex. A&M U., College Station, 1962-64, asst. prof. Wayne State U., Detroit, 1964-68; assoc. prof. CUNY, S.I., 1968-69; assoc. prof. history Marquette U., Milw., 1969—76, prof., 1976—. Cons. select com. on intelligence activities U.S. Senate, Washington, 1975-76; cons. Nat. Archives FBI Records Task Force, Washington, 1980-81. Author: Seeds of Repression, 1972, Spying on Americans, 1978, The Boss, 1988, Chasing Spies, 2002, The FBI and American Democracy, also authored 13 other books. Mem. bd. dirs. ACLU-Wis., Milw., 1975—. Recipient hon. mention Gavel award ABA, 1972, Outstanding Reference Source award database user sect. ALA, 1998, Haggerty award for rsch. excellence, 2002; 18 rsch. grants. Fellow Wis. Acad. Scis., Arts. and Letters; mem. Am. Hist. Assn. (nat. com. 1990-92), Orgn. Am. Historians (chmn. nat. com. 1980-82, Binkley-Stephenson award 1979), Am. Polit. Sci. Assn. Democrat. Greek Orthodox. Avocations: playing basketball, fan of professional and college sports. Home: 8527 N Manor Ln Fox Point WI 53217 Office: Marquette U PO Box 1881 Milwaukee WI 53201-1881

THEON, JOHN SPERIDON, meteorologist, researcher; b. Washington, Dec. 12, 1934; s. Lewis and Merope Theon; m. Joanne Edens, July 31, 1965; children: Christopher James, Catherine. BS in Aero. Engring, U. Md., 1957; BS in Meteorology, Pa. State U., 1959, MS, 1962; PhD in Engring. Sci. and Mechanics, U. Tenn., 1985. Aero. engr. Douglas Aircraft Co., Santa Monica, Calif., 1957-58; engr. U.S. Naval Ordnance Lab., White Oak, Md., 1962; rsch. meteorologist, 1962-74; head meterology br. NASA Goddard Space Flight Center, Greenbelt, Md., 1974-77; asst. chief lab. Atmospheric Scis., 1977-78, Nimbus project scientist, 1972—78; chief atmospheric dynamics and radiation program, scientist Spacelab 3 program NASA Hdqrs., Washington, 1982—87, program scientist tropical rainfall measuring mission, 1984—95, chief climate process rsch. program, 1987—94, exec. sec. task force on observations and data mgmt., 1994—95. Cons. Inst. Global Environ. Strategies, 1995—, Orbital Scis. Corp., 1995—96, Cal Tech Jet Propulsion Lab., 1997—99. Contbr. articles to profl. jours. With USAF, 1958—60. Named Disting. Alumnus, U. Tenn., 1989; recipient Goddard Exceptional Performance award, 1978, Exceptional Performance award, NASA, 1986, Radio Wave award, Ministry of Posts & Telecom. Japan, 1995. Fellow: Am. Meterol. Soc. Presbyterian. Home and Office: 6801 Lupine Ln Mc Lean VA 22101-1518

THEOPOLD, KLAUS HELLMUT, chemistry professor; b. Berlin, Apr. 18, 1954; arrived in U.S., 1978; s. Arnold and Gudula (Henjes) T.; children: Beatine Elise, Jessica Gudula, Nikolas McGeary, Karl Arnold. Vordiplom, U. Hamburg, Germany, 1977; PhD in Inorganic Chemistry, U. Calif.-Berkeley, 1982. Postdoctoral assoc. MIT, Cambridge, 1982-83; asst. prof. inorganic chem. Cornell U., Ithaca, NY, 1983-90; assoc. prof. inorganic chemistry U. Del., 1990-95, prof. inorganic chemistry, 1995—, joint appointment in chem. engring., 1993. Vis. scientist inorganic chem., Oxford U., 1994; cons. Chevron Chem. Co., Kingwood, Tex., 1991-2001, Chevron Phillips Chem. Co., Bartlesville, Okla., 2001—; vis. prof. U. B.C., 2001—. Contbr. articles to profl. jours. Served with German Army, 1974—75. Recipient Newly Appointed Young Faculty in Chemistry award Camille and Henry Dreyfus Fund, 1983, Presdl. Young Investigator award NSF, 1985; Alfred P. Sloan Rsch. fellow, 1992. Fellow AAAS; mem. Am. Chem. Soc., Gesellschaft Deutscher Chemiker, Sigma Xi. Office: U Del Dept Chemistry Biochem Newark DE 19716 E-mail: theopold@udel.edu.

THERIOT, EDWARD C. museum director; BS in Zoology, La. State U., Baton Rouge, 1975, MS in Fisheries Biology, 1978; PhD, U. Mich. Sch. Natural Resources, 1983. V.p. biodiversity and evolution Acad. Natural Scis., Phila.; dir. Tex. Meml. Mus., Austin; prof. molecular evolution U. Tex., Austin. Nat. bd. dirs. Assn Systematics Collections, 1995—97, past pres. nat. bd. dirs., 1997—99; com. mem. Species Concepts, Systematics Agenda, 2000; adv. panel Nat. Sci. Found. Biol. Databases and Informatics, 2000. Editl. bd. Phycological Soc. Am., 1988—90, assoc. editor, 1991—93, editl. bd. Molecular Phylogenetics and Evolution, 1992—2000. Office: Tex Meml Mus 2400 Trinity St Austin TX 78705-5730*

THERNSTROM, STEPHAN, historian, educator; b. Port Huron, Mich., Nov. 5, 1934; s. Albert George and Bernadene (Robbins) T.; m. Abigail Mann, Jan. 3, 1959; children— Melanie Rachel, Samuel Altgeld. BS, Northwestern U., 1956; A.M., Harvard, 1958, PhD, 1962. Instr. history Harvard U., Cambridge, Mass., 1962-66, asst. prof., 1966-67, prof., 1973-81, Winthrop prof., 1981—, chmn. com. on higher degrees in history of Am. civilization, 1985-92; prof. Brandeis U., 1967-69, UCLA, 1969-73; Pitt. prof. Am. history and instns. Cambridge U., 1978-79; dir. Charles Warren Ctr. for Research in Am. History, 1980-83. Author: Poverty and Progress, 1964, Poverty, Planning and Politics in the New Boston, 1969, The Other Bostonians, 1973, History of the American People, 1984, 88; co-author: America in Black and White, 1997, Reflections on The Shape of the River, 1999, No Excuses: Closing the Racial Gap in Learning, 2003; editor: Harvard Ency. Am. Ethnic Groups; co-editor: Harvard Studies in Urban History; Cambridge Interdisciplinary Perspectives on Modern History Series, Beyond the Color Line, 2001. Recipient Bancroft prize, R.R. Hawkins award, Faculty prize Harvard U. Press, Waldo G. Leland prize; Guggenheim fellow, John M. Olin fellow, ACLS fellow, sr. fellow Manhattan inst., 1998—, Nat. Humanities Coun., 2003—, Nat. Coun. for the Humanities, 2003—. Office: Harvard U Robinson Hall Cambridge MA 02138 Office Phone: 617-495-3035.

THERON, CHARLIZE, actress; b. Benoni, South Africa, Aug. 7, 1975; d. Charles and Gerda Theron. Studied dance, Joffrey Ballet, N.Y.C. TV and print ad representative for J'Adore perfume Christian Dior, 2004—. Actor: (films) Children of the Corn III, 1995, 2 Days in the Valley, 1996, That Thing You Do!, 1996, The Devil's Advocate, 1997, Trial and Error, 1997, Celebrity, 1998, Mighty Joe Young, 1998, The Astronaut's Wife, 1999, The Cider House Rules, 1999, Reindeer Games, 2000, The Yards, 2000, Men of Honor, 2000, The Legend of Bagger Vance, 2000, Sweet November, 2001, 15 Minutes, 2001, The Curse of the Jade Scorpion, 2001, Trapped, 2002, Waking Up in Reno, 2002, The Italian Job, 2003, Monster, 2003 (Golden Globe for best dramatic actress, 2004, Screen Actors Guild Award for best actress, 2004, Acad. Award for best actress, 2004); (TV films) Hollywood Confidential, 1997. Address: United Talent Agy Ste 500 9560 Wilshire Blvd Beverly Hills CA 90212*

THEROUX, DAVID JON, economist, educator, research and development company executive; b. Lansing, Mich., May 25, 1949; s. Paul Richard and Marjorie Erma (Withrow) Theroux; m. Elaine Laconia Shipp, 1976 (div. 1991); children: Paul Jacques, Drake Emeri; m. Mary Lyn Garvey, 1991. AB in Applied Math., BSME, U. Calif., Berkeley, 1973, MSME, 1974; MBA, U. Chgo., 1977. Rsch. asst. Richmond Field Sta., U. Calif., Berkeley, 1974, U. Chgo., 1976; project engr. Exxon Co. U.S.A., 1975—76; dir. vis. lectr. program in econ. sci. U. Chgo., 1977; v.p., dir. acad. affairs, dir. pub. policy studies Cato Inst., San Francisco, 1977—79; pres., dir. Pacific Rsch. Inst. Pub. Policy, San Francisco, 1979—86, Ind. Inst., Oakland, Calif., 1986—90; pres., gen. ptnr. LTN Ptnrs., 1986—90; pub., editor LibertyTree Network, 1986—; pub. Independent Review: A Journal of Political Economy. Adv. bd. No. Calif. Econ. Seminars, 1981—; bd. dirs. Grocery Express, Ltd., 1986—; mem. Coun. for Monetary Reform. Sr. editor Policy Report, 1978—79; editor: Cato Papers, 1978—79, The Energy Crisis: Government Policy and the Economy, 1978; editor (with P. Truluck) Private Rights and Public Lands, 1983; editor: Politics and Tyranny: Lessons in Pursuit of Freedom, 1985. Trustee William Koch Found., 1978—79; mem. Mencken award book com. Free Press Assn., 1990—; exec. com. Templeton Honor Roll for Higher Edn. in a Free Soc. With USAF, 1967—72. Recipient George Washington Honor medal for excellence, Freedoms Found., 1983, Mencken award for Best Book, Free Press Assn., 1988. Mem.: Pub. Choice Soc., Nat. Assn. Bus. Economists, So. Econ. Assn., Western Econ. Assn., Royal Econ. Soc., Am. Econ. Assn., John Randolph Club, Omicron Delta Epsilon, Pi Tau Sigma. Home: 11990 Skyline Blvd Oakland CA 94619-2421 Office: 100 Swan Way Oakland CA 94621-1428

THEROUX, PAUL EDWARD, author; b. Medford, Mass., Apr. 10, 1941; s. Albert Eugene and Anne (Dittami) T.; m. Anne Castle, Dec. 4, 1967 (div. 1993); children: Marcel, Louis; m. Sheila Donnelly, Nov. 18, 1995. BA, U. Mass., Amherst, DLitt, 1988, Trinity Coll., Washington, 1980, Tufts U., 1980. Lectr. U. Urbino, Italy, 1963, Soche Hill Coll., Malawi, 1963-65; faculty English dept. Makerere U., Uganda, 1965-68, U. Singapore, 1968-71; vis. lectr. U. Va., 1972-73. Author: (fiction) Waldo, 1967, Fong and the Indians, 1968, Girls at Play, 1969, Murder in Mt. Holly, 1969, Jungle Lovers, 1971, Sinning with Annie, 1972, Saint Jack, 1973, The Black House, 1974, The Family Arsenal, 1976, The Consul's File, 1977, Picture Palace, 1978 (Whitbread prize for fiction), A Christmas Card, 1978, London Snow, 1980, World's End, 1980, The Mosquito Coast, 1981, The London Embassy, 1982, Half Moon Street, 1984, O-Zone, 1986, My Secret History, 1988, Chicago Loop, 1990, Millroy and the Magician, 1993, My Other Life, 1996, Kowloon Tong, 1997, Collected Stories, 1997, Collected Short Novels, 1998, Hotel Honolulu, 2001, The Stranger at the Palazzo d'Oro, 2003; (nonfiction) V.S. Naipaul, 1973, The Great Railway Bazaar, 1975, The Old Patagonian Express, 1979, The Kingdom by the Sea, 1983, Sailing Through China, 1983, Sunrise with Sea Monsters, 1985, The White Man's Burden, 1987, Riding the Iron Rooster, 1988, The Happy Isles of Oceania, 1992, The Pillars of Hercules, 1995, Sir Vidia's Shadow, 1998, Fresh Air Fiend, 2000, Nurse Wolf and Dr. Sacks, 2001, Dark Star Safari, 2002; (film script) Saint Jack, 1979, Chinese Box, 1998. Recipient Editorial award Playboy mag., 1972, 76, 77, 79, Lit. award AAAL, 1977, James Tait Black award, 1982, Yorkshire Post Best Novel award, 1982, Thomas Cook Travel Book prize, 1989. Fellow Royal Soc. Lit., Royal Geog. Soc.; mem. AAAL.

THEROUX, WILLIAM GERARD, lawyer; b. Morristown, N.J., May 6, 1959; s. William E. and Mary T. (Conroy) T. BA magna cum laude, Montclair State Coll., 1981; JD cum laude, Seton Hall Law Sch., 1984. Bar: N.J. 1984, U.S. Dist. Ct. (N.J.) 1984; cert. civil trial atty. Corp. atty. Hannoch Weisman, Roseland, N.J., 1984-86; litigation atty. Francis & Berry, Morristown, 1986—96, Jackson & Buckley, PC, 1996—98, Buckley & Theroux, LLC, 1998—. Mem. N.J. State Bar Assn. Roman Catholic. Avocation: reading. Office: Buckley & Theroux LLC 932 State Rd Princeton NJ 08540 Office Phone: 609-924-9099. Business E-Mail: bill@buckleytheroux.com.

THERRIAULT, GENE, state senator; b. Fairbanks, Alaska, Jan. 31, 1960; m. Jo Therriault; children: Justin, Jordyn. AA in Computer Info. Systems, BBA, U. Alaska, 1983. Ptnr. Hector's Welding Inc., T.H.E. Co.; Rep. senator dist. F, Alaska State Senate, 1992—. Mem. St. Nicholas Parish. Office: Alaska State Senate State Capitol Rm 111 Juneau AK 99801-1182 also: 119 N Cushman St Ste 226 Fairbanks AK 99701 Fax: 907 465 3884; 907 488 4271. E-mail: Senator_Gene_Therriault@legis.state.ak.us.

THERRIEN, FRANCOIS XAVIER, JR., business and tax consultant; b. Amesbury, Mass. June 6, 1928; s. Francis Xavier and Doris Alma (Cote) T.; BS, U.S. Mil. Acad., 1950; MS, U. Ariz., 1962; Cert. tax profl., tax advisor, enrolled agt., environ. inspector, bd. cert. bus. appraiser; m. Yoshiko Kashima, July 22, 1969; children: Francois Xavier, Norman, Sakura, Izumi. Commd. 2d lt., U.S. Army, 1950, advanced through grades to lt. col., 1965, ret., 1970; dist. dir. R. J. Carroll Assoc., Inc., Atlanta, 1970-71; with Treasure Lake, Atlanta, 1971, pres. Identiseal of Fla., Orlando, 1972-74; owner Yoshiko Enterprises, Winter Park, Fla., 1974-87, bd. dirs., pres., 1988—; instr. Seminole Community Coll., 1974-79; regional rep. H.D. Vest Investment Securities, Inc., Irving, Tex., 1989—. Decorated Army Commendation medals (2), Air medal, Bronze Star medal, Silver Star, Croix DeGuerre with palm. Mem. Nat. Assn. Enrolled Agts. Roman Catholic. Office: 2265 Lee Rd Ste 223 Winter Park FL 32789-1858

THERRIEN, MICHEL, former professional hockey coach; b. Nov. 4, 1963; m. Genevieve Therrien; children: Elizabeth, Charles. Coach Lvaal Titan, Granby Predateurs; 1st head coach Quebec Citadelles, 1999—2000; head coach Montreal Canadiens, 2000—03.

THESEN, ARNE, industrial engineering educator; b. Oslo, May 6, 1943; came to U.S., 1963; s. Gudbrand and Astrid (Siggerud) T.; m. Maria Tan, Jan. 25, 1969 (div. Dec. 1987); children: Anita Mei-Ling, Britt Wei-Ling; m. Sharon W. Foster, June 21, 1991 (div. Mar. 1994). Student, Schous Tekniske Inst., Oslo, 1961-63; BS, U. Ill., 1965, MS, 1968, PhD, 1972. Systems analyst Bell Telephone Labs., Piscataway, N.J., 1970-72; prof. dept. indsl. engring. U. Wis.-Madison, 1972—; chmn. dept. indsl. engring., 1978-81, 91-95; prof. dept. computer sci., 1981-93; ptnr. Troll Assocs., Madison, 1976-84; prin. Troll Software, Madison, 1984—. Author: Computer Methods in O.R., 1976; co-author: Systems Tools for Planning, 1976, Simulation for Decision Making, 1992; contbr. articles to profl. jours. With Royal Norwegian Air Force, 1965-66. Mem. INFORMS, Inst. for Indsl. Engring. Home: 4310 Fawn Ct Cross Plains WI 53528-9780 Office: Univ Wis Dept Indsl Engring 1513 University Ave Madison WI 53706-1539

THEURER, BYRON W. aerospace engineer, business owner; b. Glendale, Calif., July 1, 1939; s. William Louis and Roberta Cecelia (Sturgiss) T.; m. Sue Ann McKay, Sept. 15, 1962 (div. 1980); children: Karen Marie, William Thomas, Alison Lee; m. Patricia Anne Pilcher, Nov. 2, 2002. BS in Engring. Sci., USAF Acad., 1961; MS in Aero. Sci., U. Calif., Berkeley, 1965; MBA, U. Redlands, 1991. Commd. USAF, 1961, advanced through grades to lt. col., ret., 1978; project officer Space Shuttle Devel. Prog., Houston, 1971-76; chief of test F-15 Systems Prog. Office Wright Patterson AFB, Ohio, 1976-78; sr. engr. Veda, Inc., Dayton, Ohio, 1979-81, Logicon Inc., Dayton, 1981-83; project mgr. Support Systems Assocs., Inc., Dayton, 1983-84, CTA Inc., Ridgecrest, Calif., 1985-89; owner, operator The Princeton Rev. of Ctrl. Calif., Ridgecrest, 1989-92, San Luis Obispo, 1993—2002; counselor Svc. Corps. Ret. Execs., 2002—. Cons. in field. Counselor SCORE. Decorated Silver Star, D.F.C., Air Medals (16); named Officer of the Yr., Air Force Flight Test Ctr., Edwards AFB, 1970. Mem. Air Force Assn., Assn. Old Crows, USAF Acad. Assn. Grads. (nat. bd. dirs. 1972-75, chpt. pres. 1981-83), Svc. Corps Ret. Execs. Republican. Episcopalian. Avocation: walking. Home: PO Box 697 Cayucos CA 93430-0697

THEVENET, PATRICIA CONFREY, social studies educator; b. Norwich, Conn., Apr. 16, 1924; d. John George and Gertrude Pauline (Doolittle) Confrey; m. Rubén Thevenet, Dec. 15, 1945 (dec. Mar. 1983); chldren: Susanne, Gregory, Richard, R. James. BS, U. Conn., 1944; AM, U. Chgo., 1945; EdM, Columbia U., 1992, EdD, 1994. Cert. elem. tchr., N.J. Counselor testing and guidance U. Chgo., 1945; home economist Western Mass. Electric Co., Pittsfield, 1946; tchr. Unquowa Sch., Fairfield, Conn., 1950-53, Alpine (N.J.) Sch., 1968-86; program asst. soc. studies Tchrs. Coll. Columbia U., N.Y.C., 1987-93; ret., 1993. Historian Borough Northvale, N.J., 1987-94; participant summer seminar Smithsonian Instn., Washington, 1984. Del. 2d dist. rep. Town Mtg., Trumbull, Conn., 1954-56; pres., trustee Northvale Pub. Libr. Assn., 1957-63; trustee Northvale Bd. Edn., 1963-72, pres. Northvale Bd. Edn., 1969-70; exec. bd. dirs. Bergen County (N.J.) County Bds. Edn., 1965-72; mem. Evening Sch. Comm. No. Valley Regional Dist., Bergen County, 1976-83; trustee Voluntown Libr., 1997-2001. Mem. AAUW, Voluntown Hist. Soc., Friends of Slater Mus., DAR. Home: 88 N Shore Rd # B Voluntown CT 06384-1719

THEVENOT, MAUDE TRAVIS, retired home economist; b. Many, La., Dec. 31, 1914; d. Rennie L. and Fairy D. (Minter) Travis; m. Aubrey J. Thevenot, July 4, 1952 (dec. Sept. 1981); 1 stepchild, Peter A. BA, Northwestern State U., 1939; MS, La. State U., 1963. Tchr. home econs. Bienville Parish High Sch., Jamestown, La., 1940-41; parish home mgmt. supr. Farmers Home Adminstrn., USDA, Natchitoches, Oak Grove, Winnefield, La., 1942-47, state home mgmt. supr. Alexandria, La., 1948-52; social worker La. Dept. Pub. Welfare, New Roads, Alexandria, Marksville, La., 1952-56; home economist La. State U.-La. Coop. Extension Svc., Makrsville, Alexandria, 1957-74, specialist expanded food & nutrition edn. program Baton Rouge, 1975-79. Co-advisor in home econs. Ptnrs. of Am. La./El Savador and La. Home Econs., 1975. Author: Central District Louisiana Home Economics Association, 1984 Louisiana Federation of Chapters of the National Association of Retired Federal Workers, 1989; co-author: A Taste of Yesterday, 1988. Mem. Kent Plantation House, Inc., Alexandria, 1970—, com. mem. for orgn., 1970, exec. bd., 1985-88, cookbook chmn., 1985-90; mem. Friendship House-Adult Day Care Ctr., Alexandria, 1982-90, exec. bd., 1982-88, organizer, pres. vol. orgn., 1978-90; advisor Anchors as Pilot Club of Alexandria Outreach Com., Anchor Club of Pineville (La.) High Sch., 1978-90; mem. La. Avoyelles & Rapides Parish Farm Bur., Marksville, Alexandria, 1967-90, Avoyelles & Rapides Cowbelles, Alexandria, Marksville, 1967-70; mem. Calvary Bapt. Ch., leader Sunday Sch. class, mem. sr. group decoration com. for monthly luncheons, leader Dottie Hayes Bible Study Group. Recipient Plaque for Svc. Rapides Parish Coun. on Aging, Alexandria, 1971, Plaque for Outstanding Leadership & Svc., Rapides Parish Homemakers Coun., Alexandria, 1974, Plaque of Appreciation as Coord., Expanded Food and Nutrition Ednl. Program La. State U., Baton Rouge, 1978, 11 Certs. of Appreciation, Anchor Club of Pineville High Sch., 1980-90, Cert. of Recognition (3) Friendship House-Day Care for Adults, 1983, 84, 85, Plaque for Outstanding Svc., Rapides Coun. on Aging 20th Ann., 1967-87. Mem. Internat. Fedn. Home Econs., Am. Assn. Family and Consumer Sci., La. Home Econs. Assn. (v.p. 1972-73, Disting. Home Economist 1979-80), Am. Assn. Family and Consumer Svcs. (Wiley-Berger award 1995), Cen. Dist. Home Econs. (pres. 1972-73, Disting. Svc. award 1967, hon. mem. 1985), Nat. Assn. Extension Home Economist, La. Assn. Extension Home Economist, AAUW, La. Assn. Nat. Assn. Retired Fed. Employees (past pres., v.p. region VI, Meritorious Svc. plaque and cert. of citation 1988-89, Meritorious Svc. award 1992-93, life), CENLA (past pres.), Am. Assn. Retired Persons, La. State U. Alumni, La. State U. Home Econs. Retiree, Northwestern State U. Alumni, La. Retired Tchrs. Assn. (life), Pilot Club Internat., Epsilon Sigma Phi (life), Gamma Sigma Delta (Extension award of merit 1978). Democrat. Avocations: travel, voluntary activities. Home: 507 Tanglewood Dr Alexandria LA 71303-3354

THIBADEAU, EUGENE FRANCIS, education educator, consultant; b. N.Y.C., May 18, 1933; s. Eugene Servanis and Lillian (Archer) T.; 1 child, Christine. BA, N.Y. U., 1959, MA, 1967, MA, 1968, PhD, 1973. Instr. N.Y. U., N.Y.C., 1968; lectr. in philosophy Dowling Coll., Oakdale, 1968-70; prof. edn. Indiana U. of Pa., 1970—. Vis. assoc. prof. Adelphi U., Garden City, N.Y., 1974-75; vis. scholar N.Y. U., N.Y.C., 1984-85; vis. prof. Hofstra U., Hempstead, 1974-75, 84, 86, Fudan U., Shanghai, China, 2000; cons. Central Bur. of Ednl. Visits, London, 1980-81, Commonwealth Speakers Bur., Harrisburg, Pa., 1983-85, U.S. Dept. Edn., Washington, 1983-85, Pa. Dept. Edn., Harrisburg, 1988—. Author: Opening Up Edn.-In Theory and Practice, 1976, Curriculum Theory, 1988, Existentialism in the Classroom, 1994; rev. editor: Focus on Learning, 1973-77, editor, 1977-84; contbg. editor: Internat. Ency. of Edn., 2d edit., Internat. Ency.of Teaching and Tchr. Edn., 2nd edit., Internat. Ency. of Social and Behavioral Scis.; contbr. articles to profl. jours. Active United Way, Indiana, Pa., 1980—, NAACP, Indiana, 1985—, Red Cross, Indiana, 1985—. Fulbright sr. lectr. Thames Polytechnic, London, 1978-79, Fulbright sr. scholar Janus Pannonius U., Peces, Hungary, 1990-91; foreign expert Shanghai (China) Tchrs. U., 1988; designated faculty rsch. assoc. Inst. for Applied Rsch. and Pub. Policy, Indiana U. Pa., 1989; named Commonwealth Teaching fellow and Cert. Excellence in Teaching, Pa. State Colls. and Univ. Disting. Faculty Awards Com., 1976; recipient Founder's Day award, NYU, 1973, Outstanding Prof. award Ind. U. Pa.-Pa. State Edn. Assn., 1993. Fellow Am. Philosophy Edn. Soc.; mem. AAUP, ASCD, Am. Ednl. Studies Assn., The S.W. Philosophy Edn. Soc. Avocations: travel, skiing, tennis, reading, chess. Home: 534 Chestnut Ridge Rd Penn Run PA 15765 Office: Indiana Univ Pa 131 Stouffer Hall Indiana PA 15705 Office Phone: 724-357-4543. E-mail: eftt@iup.edu.

THIBAUDEAU, MARY FRANCES, cultural organization administrator; b. Anaconda, Mont., Dec. 6, 1943; d. Frank Albert and Mary (May) T.; m. Alex W. Wells, Jr.; 1 child, Christopher. BA magna cum laude, U. Wash., Seattle, 1969. Therapist, counselor Thibaudeau and Assocs., Atlanta, 1976-88; chmn. Vietnam Reconciliation Bus. Group, Atlanta, 1988—. Cons. Ga. Vets. Leadership Program, Atlanta, 1994. Exec. prodr. (documentaries) Vietnam: POWs Return—The Final Healing, 2000, TET '68: Healing Wounds of War. . .30 Years After, 1998, TET Vietnam Reconciliation Documentary; co-author, editor (feature film screenplay) Perfume River, 2002. Exch. dir. Friendship Force Internat., Atlanta, 1993-94; co-founder, chmn. Tet Vietnam Reconciliation Found. for Internat. Healing/Friendship Ctr., 2002. Named Ga. Outstanding Citizen, Ga. Sec. State, 1994. Mem. Atlanta Vets. Assn. (hon.). Avocations: travel, reading, languages, hiking, photography. Home and Office: 800 Marshview Close Roswell GA 30076-3285

THIBAUDEAU, PATRICIA, state legislator; BA, Whitman Coll.; MSW, Smith Coll. Mem. Wash. Senate, Dist. 43, Olympia, 1995—; chair legis. and long term care com. Wash. Legislature, Olympia, 1999, Dem. caucus vice chair, 1997, Dem. asst. whip, 1994, mem. jud. com., mem. ways and means com. Mem. King's County Women's Polit. Caucus; mem. adv. com. Youth Care Bd.; mem. Wash. Ceasefire. Recipient award N.W. Women's Law Ctr., Bailey Boushay Citizen's award Youth Care Outstanding Cmty. Advocate, 1995, Cert. Recognition Wash. Alliance for Mentally Ill. Mem. AAUW. Democrat. Office: 414 John Cherberg Bldg Olympia WA 98504-0001

THIBAULT, GEORGE EDWIN, medical educator, non-profit healthcare organization administrator; b. 1943; Degree, Georgetown U., 1965; MD, Harvard Med. Sch., 1969. Resident internal med. Mass. Gen. Hosp., 1971, 1974, chief med. resident, 1975, fellow cardiology, 1976, dir. med. practices evaluation unit, dept. med., 1977, dir. ICU/CCU, 1977, dir. tng. program internal med., 1978, assoc. chief; fellow cardiology Nat. Heart & Lung Inst., Bethesda, Md., 1973; chief med. svcs. Brockton/West Roxbury VA Med. Ctr., Mass., 1988; vice chmn. med. Brigham and Women's Hosp., 1988—95, chief med. officer, 1995—99; v.p. clin. affairs Partners HealthCare System Inc., Boston, 1999—; prof. med. Harvard Med. Sch., dir. The Academy, 2001—. Chmn. special med. adv. group Dept. Vet. Affairs, Boston. Office: Partners HealthCare Sys Inc Prudential Tower 800 Boylston St Ste 1150 Boston MA 02199-8001

THIBAULT, J(OSEPH) LAURENT, service company executive; b. Sturgeon Falls, Ont., Can., Dec. 31, 1944; s. J. Rene and Leone (Doucet) T.; m. Paulette Patricia Lalonde, June 4, 1966; children— Alain, Andre BA in Econs., Laurentian U., Sudbury, 1966; MA in Econs., U. Toronto, Ont., 1968. Cons. Kates, Peat & Marwick Co., Toronto, 1968-72; dir. econs. and communications Can. Mfrs. Assn., Toronto, 1972-76, v.p., 1976-81, sr. exec. v.p., 1981-84, pres., exec. dir., 1985-91; co-chair Can. Labour Force Devel. Bd., Ottawa, Ont., Can., 1991-95; fin. advisor Assante Capital Mgmt. Ltd., Mississauga, Ont., 1995—. Treas. World Skills; bd. dirs. William Osler Health Ctr. Found., Skills Can., Ontario. Mem. Can. Assn. Bus. Econs. (hon.). Home: 24 Cindebarke Terr Georgetown ON Canada L7G 4S5 Office: City Ctr Plz 1 City Centre Dr Ste 1520 Mississauga ON Canada L5B 1M2 E-mail: lthibault@assante.com.

THIBEAULT, GEORGE WALTER, lawyer; b. Cambridge, Mass., Sept. 21, 1941; s. George Walter and Josephine (Maraggia) T.; m. Antoinette Miller, June 30, 1963; children: Robin M., Holly Ann. BS, Northeastern U., 1964; MBA, Boston Coll., 1966, JD, 1969. Bar: Mass. 1969. Assoc. Gaston & Snow, Boston, 1969-73; ptnr. Testa, Hurwitz & Thibeault, Boston, 1973—. Mem. ABA, Mass. Bar Assn., Am. Arbitration Assn. Home: 181 Caterina Hts Concord MA 01742-4773 Office: Testa Hurwitz & Thibeault High St Tower 125 High St 22d Fl Boston MA 02110-2704 Office Phone: 617-248-7520. Business E-Mail: thibeault@tht.com.

THIBERT, ROGER JOSEPH, clinical chemist, educator; b. Tecumseh, Ont., Can., Aug. 29, 1929; s. Charles and Violet (Hebert) T.; m. Audrey M. Wissler, July 10, 1954; children: Mark Roger, Robert Francis. BA, U. Western Ont., 1951; MS, U. Detroit, 1954; PhD, Wayne State U., 1958; DSc, U. Windsor, 2004. Diplomate: Am. Bd. Clin. Chemistry (past bd. dirs.). Mem. faculty U. Windsor, Canada, 1953—, prof. chemistry, 1967-94, dir. clin. chemistry, 1972-94, prof. emeritus, 1994—; prof. pathology Med. Sch. Wayne State U., Detroit, 1972-94; assoc. divsn. head, clin. chemistry Detroit Receiving Hosp., Univ. Health Ctr., 1973-94, mem. med. staff, 1973-94. Cons. med. biochemistry Med. Labs. Windsor, Ont., Can., 1995-2000; sci. dir. Med. Labs., Windsor, 2000—. Contbr. articles on chemistry, biochemistry, analytical chemistry, clin. chemistry to profl. jours. Recipient Smith Kline award Am.

Assn. Clin. Chemistry, 1980, Tchg. award Ont. Confederation U. Faculty Assns., 1990, Beckman Edn. Excellence award Canadian Soc. Clin. Chemists, 1992; Chem. Inst. Can. fellow, 1968—; Nat. Acad. Clin. Biochemistry fellow, 1978—; recipient grants Natural Scis. and Engring. Rsch. Coun., Can., award Union Carbide, Chem. Inst., Can., 1978. Fellow AAAS, Can. Acad. Clin. Biochemistry; mem. Am. Chem. Soc., Chem. Inst. Can., Assn. Chem. Profession Ont., Am. Assn. Clin. Chemistry, Nat. Acad. Clin. Biochemistry, Can. Soc. Clin. Chemists (Ames award 1988), Ont. Soc. Clin. Chemists, Am. Soc. for Biochemistry and Molecular Biology, Fedn. Am. Socs. Exptl. Biology, Can. Soc. Biochemistry and Molecular Biology, Can. Fedn. Biol. Scis., Can. Soc. for Chemistry, Sigma Xi. Roman Catholic. Home: 4612 Dali Ct Windsor ON Canada N9G 2M8 Office: U Windsor Dept Chemistry/Biochemistry Windsor ON Canada N9B 3P4

THIBODEAU, GARY A. academic administrator; b. Sioux City, Iowa, Sept. 26, 1938; m. Emogene J. McCarville, Aug. 1, 1964; children: Douglas James (dec.), Beth Ann. BS, Creighton U., 1962; MS, S.D. State U., 1967, MS, 1970, PhD, 1971. Profl. service rep. Baxter Lab., Inc., Deerfield, Ill., 1963-65; tchr., researcher dept. biology S.D. State U., Brookings, 1965-76, asst. to v.p. for acad. affairs, 1976-80, v.p. for adminstrn., 1980-85; chancellor U. Wis., River Falls, 1985-2000; sr. v.p. acad. affairs U. Wis. Sys., 2000—01. Mem. investment com. U. Wis., River Falls Found.; trustee W. Cen. Wis. Consortium U. Wis. System; bd. dirs. U. Wis. at River Falls Found.; mem. Phi Kappa Phi nat. budget rev. and adv. comm., Phi Kappa Phi Found. investment comm., comm. on Agrl. and Rural Devel., steering commn. Coun. of Rural Colls. and Univs., Joint Coun. on Food and Agrl. Scis., USDA. Author: Basic Concepts in Anatomy and Physiology, 1983, Athletic Injury Assessment, 1994, The Human Body in Health and Disease, 2003, Textbook of Anatomy and Physiology, 2004, Structure and Function of the Body, 2004. Mem. AAAS, Am. Assn. Anatomists, Human Anatomy and Physiology Soc., Sigma Xi, Phi Kappa Phi, Gamma Sigma Delta, Gamma Alpha. Office: U Wis 116 N Hall River Falls WI 54022

THIEBAUD, WAYNE, artist; b. Mesa, Ariz., Nov. 15, 1920; s. Morton J. and Alice Eugenia (LeBaro) T.; m. Betty Jean Carr, Dec. 11, 1959; children: Twinka, Mallary Ann, Paul LeBaron. BA, Sacramento State Coll., 1951, MA, 1952; MFA (hon.), Calif. Coll. Arts and Crafts, 1975. Art dir., N.Y.C.; also Hollywood, 1946-49; chmn. art dept. Sacramento City Coll., 1951; design cons. Calif. State Fair and Expn.; guest instr. San Francisco Art Inst., 1958; assoc. prof. art U. Calif. at Davis, now prof., Faculty Research lectr., from 1973. Vis. artist Cornell U., U. Hawaii, U. Wis., U. Utah, U. Ill., Yale U., U. Va., Bradley U. Author: Etching Delights, 1965, Prints, 1970-71, Seven Still Lifes and a Rabbit; one-man shows include Crocker Art Gallery, Sacramento, Calfif., 1952, Artists Coop. Gallery, 1954, DeYoung Mus., San Francisco, 1962, Allan Stone Gallery, N.Y.C., 1962—70, Stanford, 1965, Sao Paulo Biennale, 1966, Galleria Schwarz, Milan, 1963, San Francisco Mus., 1967, Pasadena Mus. Art, 1967—68, Whitney Mus., 1972, Indocumenta, 1972, Boston Inst. Contemporary Art, 1976, Walker Art Ctr., Mpls., 1981, Ft. Worth Art Mus., 1981, Mus. Fine Arts, St. Petersburg, Fla., 1981, museums, U.S., Toronto, The Hague, Vienna, Berlin, Hong Kong, S.Am., Oakland Mus., Phoenix Mus., U. So. Calif., Des Moines Mus., one-man shows include organized by Mus. Modern Art for 50th Ann. Wayne Thiebaud exhibn., Newport, R.I., 1985, Milw., 1985, Columbus, 1985, Kansas City, 1985, exhibited in group shows at Santa Barbara (Calif.) Mus. Art, 1980, Bklyn. Mus., 1980, 1981, Whitney Mus. Am. Art, 1981, San Antonio Mus. Art, 1981, Indpls. Mus. Art, 1981, Inst. Contemporary Art, U. Pa., Phila., 1981, Carnegie Inst., Pitts., 1981, Allan Stone Gallery, N.Y.C., 1982, Represented in permanent collections Mus. Modern Art, Whitney Mus. Am. Art, Albright Knox Mus., Wadsworth Athenaeum, Libr. Congress, Woodward Found., Rose Art Mus., Brandeis U., Stanford, Sheldon Meml. Art Gallery U. Nebr., Fines Arts Mus., San Francisco, Utah Mus. Fine Arts U. Utah, Kemper Mus. Contemporary Art, U. Maine Mus. Art, Spencer Mus. Art U. Kans., Nat. Mus. Am. Art, Washington, Crown Point Press, also numerous pvt. collections, commns. include fountain mobile sculpture Calif. State Fair, 1952, paintings Wimbledon Tennis Tournament, 1968, woodblock prints Crown Point Press, Kyoto, Japan, 1987, Yosemite Ridge Line for Bicentennial Exhibn., 1976, 42 works on paper Arts Club Chgo., 1987; prodr., dir.: 12 ednl. motion pictures (1st prize Art Film Festival, 1956, award for Space Golden Reel Film Festival Calif. State Fair, 1956, named Univ. Art Studio Tchr. of Yr. Coll. Art Assn. Am., 1981, Faculty Rsch. medal U. Calif., Davis., 1984, Award of Distinction Nat. Art Schs. Assn., 1984, Spl. Citation Nat. Assn. Schs. Art and Design, 1984). Recipient Cyril Magnin award, San Francisco, 1987, Golden Plate award, Am. Acad. Achievement, 1987, Nat. Medal Arts, 1994. Mem.: Nat. Acad. Design (academician), Am. Acad. and Inst. Arts and Letters. Office: Paul Thiebaud Gallery 631 Union St San Francisco CA 94133

THIEL, DAVID BRIAN, physician assistant; b. Cin., July 2, 1956; s. Joseph Lee and Mary Jane (Otting) T. BA, Wabash Coll., Crawfordsville, Ind., 1978; AS with honors, Kettering Coll. Med. Arts, 1980. Cert. physician asst. Resident Los Angeles County-U. So. Calif. Med. Ctr., L.A., 1985-86; physician asst. in orthopedic surgery Ketchikan, Alaska, 1980-85; physician asst. in phys. medicine and electrodiagnostic medicine New Orleans, 1987—. In-svc. lectr. HealthSouth Rehab., Harahan, La., 1990—. Tannenbaum scholar, 1974-78; recipient Orchid award Paphiopedilum Mystic Jewel, David's Dream, Highly Commended Cert. Am. Orchid Soc., 2003. Fellow: Sigma Xi (numerous Orchid awards); mem.: Internat. High IQ Soc. Republican. Avocations: swimming, skiing, sailing, orchid growing, bicycling. E-mail: cynicno@hotmail.com.

THIEL, PHILIP, design educator; b. Bklyn., Dec. 20, 1920; s. Philip and Alma Theone (Meyer) T.; m. Midori Kono, 1955; children: Philip Kenji, Nancy Tamiko, Susan Akiko, Peter Akira (dec.). BSc, Webb Inst. Naval Architecture, 1943; MSc, U. Mich., 1948; BArch, MIT, 1952. Registered arch., Wash. Instr. naval architecture MIT, Cambridge, 1949-50; instr. architecture U. Calif., Berkeley, 1954-56, asst. prof., 1956-60; assoc. prof. U. Wash., Seattle, 1961-66, prof. visual design and experiential notation, 1966-91; guest prof. Tokyo Inst. Tech., 1976-78; vis. prof. Sapporo (Japan) Sch. of Arts, 1992-98. Lectr., U.S., Can. Japan, Norway, Denmark, Sweden, Eng., Austria, Switzerland, Peru, Bolivia, Korea; cons. FAO, Rome, 1952; co-founder Environment and Behavior, 1969; founder Ctr. for Exptl. Notation, Seattle, 1981. Author: Freehand Drawing, 1965, Visual Awareness and Design, 1981, People, Paths and Purposes, 1997; patentee in field. Soc. Naval Architects and Marine Engrs. scholar, 1947; Rehmann scholar AIA, 1960; NIMH grantee, 1967, Nat. Endowment for Arts, 1969, Graham Found., 1995. Mem. Soc. Naval Archs. and Marine Engrs. (assoc.), Phi Beta Kappa, Sigma Xi.

THIELE, GLORIA DAY, retired librarian, small business owner; b. L.A., Sept. 4, 1931; d. Russell Day Plummer and Dorothy Ruby (Day) Plummer Thi; m. Donald Edward Cools, June 13, 1953 (div.); children: Michael, Ramona, Naomi, Lawrence, Nancy, Rebecca, Eugene, Maria, Charles. MusB, Mt. St. Mary's Coll., L.A., 1953. Libr. asst. Anaheim (Calif.) Pub. Libr., 1970-73, head Biblioteca de la Comunidad, 1973-74, children's libr. asst., 1974-76, childre's br. specialist, 1976-78, children's libr., 1978-81; head children's svcs. SantaM Maria (Calif.) Pub. Libr., 1981-85; cons. Organizationsl Ch.-Sch. Libr., L.A., 1980; owner, founder Discovery Garden, Grass Valley, Calif., 1989-93. Guest lectr. children's lit. Allan Hancock Coll., Santa Maria, 1981-85; cons. children's libr. programs, 1986—; profl. storyteller, 1989—. Contbr. poems to Amherst Soc.'s Am. Poetry Ann., 1988. Libr. liaison Casa Amistad Cmty. Svc. Group, Anaheim, 1973-74; mem. outreach com. Santiago Libr. System, Orange County, 1973-74, mem. children's svcs. com., 1971-81; mem. Cmty. Svcs. Coord. Coun., Santa Maria, 1982-85; chair children's svcs. com. Black Gold Libr. System, 1983-84; Allegro Alliance vol. for music in mountains, 1994-98; vol. Oasis Sr. Ctr., 1998-2002; mem. steering com. Cmty. Svcs. Dist. Status, Orcutt, 1999-2002; rep. 4th supervisorial dist. adv. com. Santa Barbara County Libr., 1999-2002. Mem. So. Calif. Coun. Lit. for Children and Young People, Kiwanis (sec., publicity chair, newsletter editor 1996-98, sec. Orcutt 1999-2000, Central Coast Winds & Waves, 2000—, bd. dirs. 2000-2001), Orcutt Friends of Libr. (v.p. 1999-2000, pres. 2000), P.E.O. Sisterhood (rec. sec. chpt. VZ 2002-03), Delta Epsilon Sigma. Republican. Roman Catholic.

THIELE, HOWARD NELLIS, JR., lawyer; b. Dayton, Ohio, June 22, 1930; s. Howard Nellis and Irma Laura (Scheibe) T.; m. Alma Kuhn, Oct. 14, 1995; children: Leslie, Howard III, Craig. AB, Miami U., Oxford, Ohio, 1952; JD with distinction, U. Mich., 1955. Bar: Ohio 1955. Assoc., ptnr. Smith & Schnacke, LPA, Dayton, Ohio, 1957-89; ptnr. Thompson, Hine & Flory, Dayton, 1989-95; ret., 1995. Pres. Dayton Art Inst., 1981-85; bd. dirs. Dayton Area chpt. ARC, 1983—, 1st vice chmn., 1990-91, chmn., 1992-94. Capt. USAF, 1955-57. Mem.: Phi Beta Kappa, Order of the Coif. Republican. Lutheran.

THIELE, LESLIE PAUL, political science educator; b. Moose Jaw, Sask., Can., Jan. 27, 1959; s. Jacob Zach and Wilfrida Maria Thiele; m. Susan Wapner, June 30, 1991; children: Jacob, Jonah. PhD, Princeton U., 1989. Asst. prof. Swarthmore (Pa.) Coll., 1989-91; asst. prof. polit. sci. U. Fla., Gainesville, 1991-95, assoc. prof., 1995-97, prof., 1998—, mem. affiliate faculty Coll. Natural Resources and Environ., 1996—, U. Fla. Rsch. Found. prof., 1997-99, chmn. dept., 1997—2002. Author: Friedrich Nietzsche and the Politics of the Soul, 1990, Timely Meditations: Martin Heidegger and Postmodern Politics, 1995, Thinking Politics, 1997, 2nd edit., 2003, Environmentalism for a New Millennium, 1999. Summer inst. grantee NEH, 1990; postdoctoral fellow Social Sci. and Humanities Rsch. Coun. Can., 1991-93; fellow Social Sci. Rsch. Coun.-MacArthur Found., 1994-96. Mem. Am. Polit. Sci. Assn. Democrat. Avocations: ultimate frisbee, hiking, canoeing. Office: U Fla Dept Polit Sci Anderson Hall Gainesville FL 32611-7325 Fax: 352-392-8127. E-mail: thiele@polisci.ufl.edu.

THIEMAN, FREDERICK W. lawyer; b. Pitts., July 16, 1951; m. Christine Thieman; 4 children. BA in English and Journalism with distinction, Pa. State U., 1973; JD magna cum laude, U. Pitts., 1977. Bar: Pa. 1979, U.S. Dist. Ct. (we. dist.) Pa. 1985, U.S. Ct. Appeals (3d cir.) 1985, U.S. Supreme Ct. 1985. Law clk. Supreme Ct. of Pa., Pitts., 1977—78; asst. U.S. Atty., chief white collar crime unit We. Dist. Pa., Pitts., 1979—83, U.S. Atty., 1993—97; ptnr. Hilner, Thieman & Fraas, Pitts., 1983—93; counsel Titus & McConomy LLP, Pitts., 1997—99, Thieman & Ward, Pitts., 1999—. Mem. spl. master program Allegheny County, Pa., 1991—; mem. magistrate judge merit selection panel We. Dist. Pa., 1993—, sspl. arbitrator fed. ct., 1993—, spl. mediator, 1994—; mem. Civil Justice Adv. Act Panel, 1993—. Contbr. articles to profl. jours.; asst. editor U. Pitts. Law Rev., 1976—77. Dir. Neighborhood Legal Svcs. Assn., 1987—93, officer, 1990; chair Youth Crime Prevention Coun. of Allegheny County, 1994—, Law Enforcement Agy. Dirs.; mem. Allegheny County Drug Task Force, 1994—97; co-chair steering com. Youth Works, 1994—97, emeritus bd. mem., 2002—; mem. adv. coun. Youth Places, 1996—97, chair adv. bd., 2000—; action leader Working Together Consortium, 1994—2001; advisor Criminal Justice Program in the Pks., 1993—97; mem. coun. Edgewood Cmty. Club, 1993—98, pres., 1997—98; mem. adv. bd. Youth Crime Prevention Systems Group Carnegie Mellon U., 1998—99; vol. atty. Exec. Svc. Corps, 1998—; chair Allegheny County Chief Exec. Pub. Safety Transition Com., 2000; Sunday sch. tchr., mem. fin. com., vestry, sr. warden Ch. of the Ascension, 1995—99; Blue Ribbon panel appointee, mem. fin. policies rev. com. Diocese of Pitts., 1998; bd. dirs. Howard Heinz Endowments, 1997—, United Way of Allegheny County, 1997—2002, Boy Scouts Am., 1994—97, Mentoring Partnership of Southwestern Pa., 1994—2002, emeritus bd. mem., 2002—. Named Disting. Alumnus of Yr., U. Pitts. Law Alumni Assn., 1997; recipient spl. commendation for outstanding svc., Dept. of Justice, 1982, Ronald R. Brown Civic Leadership award, Urban League, 1997, spl. award for outstanding performance, Law Enforcement Agy. Dirs., 1998, Spl. Recognition award, The Mentoring Partnership of Southwestern Pa., 1999, Western Pa. Cmty. Leadership award, Dept. Justice, 1999. Master: Inns of Ct.; fellow: Allegheny County Bar Found. (fellows com. 1999—); mem.: Nat. Assn. Former U.S. Attys. (bd. dirs. 2000—), Acad. Trial Lawyers of Allegheny County (fed. jud. com. 1991—, chair 1992, bd. govs. 1992—94, fed. program com. 1996—, chair 1999, bd. govs. 2000—), Allegheny County Bar Assn. (young lawyers coun. 1984—86, officer young lawyers sect. 1986, pub. svc. com. 1987—92, rules com. 1987—93, CLE com. 1987—93, fed. ct. sect., coun. 1991—97, chair 1992, fed. sect. criminal law practice com. 1992—, nominating com. 2002, fed. ct. sect. nominating com. 2002), Order of Coif. Avocations: fishing, cross country skiing, hiking, golf. Office: Thieman & Ward Ste 2312 Koppers Bldg 436 7th Ave Pittsburgh PA 15219 Office Phone: 412-395-1245. Office Fax: 412-395-1246. Business E-Mail: fwt@thiemanward.com.

THIEMANN, CHARLES LEE, banker; b. Louisville, Nov. 21, 1937; s. Paul and Helen (Kern) T.; m. Donna Timperman, June 18, 1960; children: Laura Gerette, Charles Lee, Rodney Gerard, Jeffrey Michael, Matthew Joseph. BA in Chemistry, Bellarmine Coll., 1959; MBA, Ind. U., 1961, DBA, 1963. Mem. rsch. dept. Fed. Res. Bank, St. Louis, 1963-64; with Fed. Home Loan Bank, Cin., 1964—, sr. v.p., then exec. v.p., 1974, pres., 1976—. Past chmn. bd. dirs. Office Fin.; trustee Fin. Instns. Retirement Fund; past mem. First Step Home. Bd. dirs. Habitat for Humanity Internat., Bellarmine U. Named Bellarmine Coll. Alumnus of Yr., 1999. Mem. Rotary Club, Queen City Club. Roman Catholic. Office: Fed Home Loan Bank 221 E 4th St Ste 1000 Cincinnati OH 45202-5139

THIEMANN, RONALD FRANK, dean, religion educator; b. St. Louis, Oct. 4, 1946; s. Frank Joseph and Marie Magdalene (Graeser) T.; m. Beth Arlene Barkow, June 15, 1968; children: Sarah Elizabeth, Laura Kristen. BA magna cum laude, Concordia Sr. Coll., Fort Wayne, Ind., 1968; MDiv, Concordia Sem., St. Louis, 1972; MA, Yale U., 1973, MPhil, 1974, PhD, 1976; postgrad., Eberhard-Karls Universitat, Tubingen, W.Ger., 1974-75. Asst. prof. dept. religion Haverford Coll., Pa., 1976-82, assoc. prof. dept. religion, 1982-85, prof. dept. religion, 1985-86, acting provost, 1985, acting pres., 1986; dean Div. Sch. Harvard U., Cambridge, Mass., 1986-98, John Lord O'Brian prof. divinity, 1986-98, prof. theology, religion & soc., 1998—, faculty fellow Hauser Ctr., JFK Sch. Govt. Vis. prof. honors program Villanova U., 1981; vis. asst. prof. Luth. Theol. Sem., Phila., 1977; mem. Ctr. Theol. Inquiry, Princeton, N.J., 1982-83; mem. consultation on Christianity and Marxism, U.S.A. nat. com. Luth. World Fedn., 1979-83, mem. consultation on civil religion, 1983-86, mem. consultation on problem of common good, 1985-88; bd. dirs. Trinity Press Internat.; mem. exec. com. Assn. Theol. Schs., 1994-2000; faculty mem. Hanser Ctr. JFK Sch. Govt. Harvard U., 1998—. Author: Revelation and Theology, 1985, Constructing a Public Theology: The Church in a Pluralistic Culture, 1991, Religion in Public Life: A Dilemma for Democracy, 1995, Who Will Provide? The Changing Role of Religion in American Social Welfare, 2001; editor: The Legacy of H. Richard Niebuhr, 1991, Why Are We Here? Everyday Questions and the Christian Life, 1998, Where Shall My Wandering Soul Begin: The Landscape of Evangelical Piety and Thought, 2000; mem. editl. bd.: Dialog, 1987—; contbr. numerous articles to profl. jours. Mem. bd. trustees Buckingham Browne & Nichols Schs., 1988-90; mem. task force on theol. education, Evang. Luth. Ch. in Am., 1989-91, task force on Luth.-Reformed Conversations, Evang. Luth. Ch. Am., 1988-92. Recipient Disting. Teaching award Lindback Found., 1982, Lilly Scholars award, 1998-99; Mellon Found. fellow, 1982-83; Deutscher Akademischer Austauschdienst fellow, 1974-75. Mem. Am. Acad. Religion, (chmn. narrative interpretation and theology group 1982-86), Soc. Christian Ethics, Am. Theol. Soc. Avocations: tennis; squash; piano. Home: 186 Shadyside Ave Concord MA 01742-2740 Office: Harvard Div Sch 45 Francis Ave Cambridge MA 02138-1911

THIEMENS, MARK H. chemistry professor; b. St. Louis, Jan. 6, 1950; BS, U. Miami, 1972; MS, Old Dominion U., 1974; postgrad., Fla. Inst. Technology, 1974-75; PhD, U. Chgo., 1980. Grad. rsch. asst. dept. oceanography Old Dominion U., Norfolk, Va., 1972-74; grad. rsch. asst. dept. physics Fla. Inst. Technology, Melbourne, 1974-75; participant trace element aerosol rsch. program Fla. State U., Tallahassee, 1975-76; researcher dept. atmospheric chemistry Brookhaven Nat. Labs., Upton, N.Y., 1976-77; rsch. assoc. Enrico Fermi Inst. U. Chgo., 1977-80; vis. prof. dept. chemistry U. Calif., San Diego, La Jolla, 1980-81, asst. prof. step II dept. chemistry, 1981-83, asst. prof. step IV dept. chemistry, 1983-85, assoc. prof. step I dept. chemistry, 1985-87, assoc. prof. dept. chemistry step II, 1987-88, assoc. prof. step III dept. chemistry, 1988-89, prof. step I dept. chemistry, 1989-91, prof. step II dept. chemistry, 1991-93, prof. step III dept. chemistry, 1993-95, prof. step VII dept. chemistry, 1996-2000, prof. step IX dept. chemistry, 2000—, chair dept. chemistry, 1996-99, dean divsn. phys. sci., 1999—. Dir. Cr. Environ Rsch. and Tng. U. Calif., San Diego, 1996—, mem. Ctr. Astrophysicis and Space Sci., 1980—, Scripps Inst. Oceanography, 1996—; mem. workshop panel Origins of Solar Sys. NASA, 1989, mem. panel cosmochemistry divsn. group b isotope geochemistry, 1996—, cosmochemistry rev. panel Johnson Space Ctr., 1997; organizer, convenor 1997 Informal Symposium on Kinetic and Photochemical Processes in the Atmosphere, 1997. Contbr. numerous articles to profl. jours. Alexander von Humboldt fellow Inst. Phys. Chemistry U. Göttingen (Germany), 1990-91, 93; Camille and Henry Dreyfus tchg. scholar, 1983-88; recipient Ernest Orlando Lawrence Meml. award U.S. Dept. of Energy, 1998. Fellow Meteoritical Soc. Achievements include development of analytical capability to measure stable isotope variations at ultra-high precision in sulfur, oxygen, carbon and nitrogen to use in development of experimental programs in varying research fields including atmospheric chemistry, physical chemistry of gas phase photochemical eractions, electrical plasmas, early solar system history, and gas-solid conversion mechanisms; development of the ability to measure sulfur isotopic in meteoritic and lunr material to a precision greater than an order-of-magnitude over previous laboratory determination to determine the nature of pre-solar sulfur chemistry, cosmic-ray-spallation, and nucleosynthetic inputs; development of rocket borne atmospheric sampling and analysis. Office: U Calif Chem & Biochem Dept Urey Hall 9500 Gilman Dr La Jolla CA 92093-5004 E-mail: mht@checfs2.ucsd.edu.

THIENEMAN, MICHAEL D. manufacturing executive; b. Louisville; BA in Physics, Bellarmine Coll., 1970; MS, PhD in Physics, U. Ky., 1977; MBA, U. Evansville, 1981. Former project engr. Whirlpool Corp., former pres., CEO Inglis Ltd. subs., former pres. Whirlpool Compressor Ops., former corp. v.p. global procurement ops., exec. v.p. N.Am. region, 1997—, chief tech. officer, 2000—. Chair fund devel. com. Harbor Habitat for Humanity; trustee Whirlpool Found., 1997—. Office: Whirlpool Corp 2000 N M-63 Benton Harbor MI 49022 Business E-Mail: michael_d_thieneman@whirlpool.com.

THIEN-STASKO, VICKI LYNN, civil engineer; b. Scott Air Force Base, Ill., Apr. 22, 1953; d. Cordell Albert Knepper and Erna Rose (Studnicka) Knepper; m. Michael Lee Stasko, Nov. 19, 1988; stepchildren: Julie Stasko, Elliott Stasko; m. William Frederick Thien, Mar. 12, 1971 (div.); 1 child, Kyle Thien. Associates of Arch., Belleville Area Coll., 1982, Associates of Applied Sci., 1988; BSC cum laude, Greenville Coll., 1998. Civil engr. tech. St. Clair County Hwy. Dept., Belleville, Ill., 1982—2002; part-time real estate agent Better Homes & Gardens /Strano, Belleville, Ill., 1993—94; part-time cosmetic cons. Christian Dior, Belleville, Ill., 1995—97; part-time census enumerator U.S. Dept. Commerce-Census Dept., Belleville, Ill., 2000—01. Co-chmn. "Operation Bag-It", Belleville, 1998—2002. Exhibitions include gingerbread creations/gingerbread scene Not a Creature was Stirring, 1996 (Best of Show, 1996), exhibitions include gingerbread creation/3'tall gingerbread Nutcracker Nuts Anyone?, 1997 (Merchant's award, 1997), exhibitions include gingerbread creation Frosty the Gingerbread Snowman, 1998 (Downtown Merchant's award, 1998), Mr. G. Shops Downtown Belleville, 2000 (Best of Show, 2000), exhibitions include gingerbread Crayola Factory, 2002 (first place profl. divsn.). Precinct committeewoman Dem. Party, Belleville, 1978—91; sec. Belleville Dem. Orgn., Belleville, 1979—91; mayoral appointment/mem. Belleville Re-develop. Com., Belleville, 1982—84; member St. Clair County Hist. Soc., Belleville, 2000—02; ch. sch. bd. mem., tchr. Christ United Ch. of Christ, Belleville, 1987—91. Recipient Ill. Gov.'s Hometown award, State of Ill., 1999. Protestant. Avocations: gardening, remodeling, travel. Office: St Clair County Hwy Dept 1415 N Belt W Belleville IL 62226

THIER, SAMUEL OSIAH, physician, educator; b. Bklyn., June 23, 1937; s. Sidney and May Henrietta Thier; m. Paula Dell Finkelstein, June 28, 1958; children: Audrey Lauren, Stephanie Ellen, Sara Leslie. Student, Cornell U., 1953—56; MD, SUNY, Syracuse, 1960, DSc (hon.), 1987, Tufts U., 1988, George Washington U., 1988, Mt. Sinai Sch. Med., 1989, Hahnemann U., 1989; DSc (hon.), U. Pa., 1994, Dartmouth Coll., 1996; LHD (hon.), Rush U., 1988, Va. Commonwealth U., 1992, Med. Coll. Pa., 1992; LHD (hon.), Brandeis U., 1994. Diplomate Am. Bd. Internal Medicine. Intern Mass. Gen. Hosp., Boston, 1960—61, asst. resident, 1961—62, sr. resident, 1964—65, clin. and research fellow, 1965, chief resident, 1966; clin. asso. Nat. Inst. Arthritis and Metabolic Diseases, 1962—64; from instr. to asst. prof. medicine Harvard U. Med. Sch., 1967—69; prof. medicine, health care policy Harvard Med. Sch., 1994—; asst. in medicine, chief renal unit Mass. Gen. Hosp., Boston, 1967—69; asso. prof., then prof. medicine U. Pa. Med. Sch., 1969—72, vice chmn. dept., 1971—74; assoc. dir. med. svcs. Hosp. U. Pa., 1969—71; David Paige Smith prof. medicine Yale U. Sch. Medicine, 1978—81, Sterling prof. medicine, 1981—85, chmn. dept., 1975—85; pres. Inst. Medicine NAS, Washington, 1985—91; pres., Univ. prof. Brandeis U., Waltham, Mass., 1991—94; pres. Mass. Gen. Hosp., Boston, 1994—97, Ptnrs. HealthCare Sys., Inc., Boston, 1994—96, 1997—2002, CEO, 1996—2002. Chief medicine Yale-New Haven Hosp., 1975—85, trustee, 1978—85; bd. dirs. Conn. Hospice, Inc., 1976—82; dir. Am. Bd. Internal Medicine, 1977—85, exec. com., 1981—85, chmn., 1984—85. Mem. editl. bd.: New Eng. Jour. Medicine, 1978—81; contbr. articles to med. jours. Mem. adv. com. to the dir. NIH, 1980—85. With USPHS, 1962—64. Recipient Christian R. and Mary F. Lindback Found. Disting. Tchg. award, 1971. Mem.: ACP (bd. regents 1982—85), Interurban Clin. Club, Assn. Am. Physicians, Assn. Profs. Medicine, Internat. Soc. Nephrology, Am. Physiol. Soc., Am. Soc. Nephrology, Am. Fedn. Clin. Rsch. (pres. 1976—77), John Morgan Soc., Assn. Am. Med. Colls. (adminstrv. bd. coun. acad. socs.), Alpha Omega Alpha. Home: 99-20 Florence St # 8 Chestnut Hill MA 02467-1927

THIERRY, LAUREN, anchor; Grad. in English, Sarah Lawrence Coll.; MS in Journalism, Columbia U. Writer South China Morning Post, Hong Kong, 1984; writer, field prodr. Sta. WTNH-TV, New Haven, Conn., 1984-86; anchor, gen. assignment reporter Sta. WKRN-TV, Nashville, 1987-89, Sta. WBZ-TV, Boston, 1989-91, Sta. KCAL-TV, L.A., 1991-92; corr. King World T.V., N.Y.C., 1993-95, CNBC, Ft. Lee, N.J., 1995-96; anchor CNN Fin. News, N.Y.C., 1996—. Recipient H.W. Sackett award for Excellence in 1st Amendment Law. Office: CNN 5 Penn Plz Fl 20 New York NY 10001-1810

THIERSTEIN, GERALD E. (GERRY THIERSTEIN), retired agricultural engineer; b. Newton, Kans., Apr. 30, 1931; s. C.B. and Ella (Regier) T.; m. Samia Shehade, Apr. 2, 1973. BS, Kans. State U., 1957, MS, 1963. Lic. prof. engr., Fla. Rsch. engr. engines dept. Caterpillar Tractor Co., Peoria, Ill., 1957-58; agrl. engr. Internat. Voluntary Svcs., Washington, 1958-60; asst. prof. agrl. engring. dept. W.Va. U., Morgantown, 1962-67; rsch. assoc. Brace Rsch. Inst. McGill U., Montreal, Que., Can., 1967-71; sr. lectr. agrl. engring. dept. Makerere U., Kampala, Uganda, 1971-73; prin. sci. agrl. engring. farming syss. dept. Internat. Crops Rsch. Inst. Semi-Arid Tropics, Patancheru, India, 1976-84; assoc. prof., rsch. engr. dept. agrl. engring. Kans. State U., Manhattan, 1984-93; ret., 1993. Dept. head agrl. engring. dept. Egerton Coll., Kenya, 1962-67; vis. assoc. prof. agrl. mechanization Am. U. Beirut, 1973-76; adj. prof. agrl. engring. dept. U. Fla., Gainesville, 1984. Recipient Jyoti award Indian Soc. Agrl. Engrs. Mem. Am. Soc. Agrl. Engrs. (Kishida Internat. award 1994), Sigma Xi. Home: 2525 Baxter Pl Fort Collins CO 80526-5360 E-mail: thierstn@frii.com.

THIERSTEIN, HANS, biotechnology company executive; Chmn. bd. dirs. Ribapharm Inc., Costa Mesa, Calif., 1999—; CFO Ares-Serono, 1980—96, chmn. bd., 1992—99. Office: Ribapharm Inc 3300 Hyland Ave Costa Mesa CA 92626

THIES, RICHARD LEON, lawyer, director; b. Nov. 7, 1931; s. Arnold C. Thies and Wilma J. (Pattison) Player; m. Marilyn Lucille Webber, June 15, 1954; children: David, Nancy, Susan, John, Anne. BA, U. Ill., 1953; JD, 1955. Bar: Ill. 1955, U.S. Dist. Ct. (ea. dist.) Ill. 1958, U.S. Supreme Ct. 1986. Instr. engring. law U. Ill., Urbana, 1955-56; ptnr. Webber & Thies, P.C., Urbana, 1958—. Past mem. Urbana Park Dist. Bd.; bd. dirs., past mem. Nat. Acad. Arts, Champaign-Urbana Urban League; past bd. dirs., past pres. Salvation Army, Champaign County. Served as 1st lt. USAF, 1956-58. Fellow Am. Bar

Found (chair 1993-94), Ill. State Bar Found.; mem. ABA (ho. of dels. 1984-2005, bd. govs. 1988-91, exec. com. 1990-91, state del. 1993—), Am. Bar Retirement Assn. (bd. 1992-2000, chair 1997-99), Am. Law Inst. Ill. Bar Assn. (various offices, pres. 1986-87), Bar Assn. Ctrl. and So. Fed. Dists. Ill. (pres., co-founder, bd. dirs. 2001—), Champaign County Bar Assn. (v.p.), Urbana C. of C. (pres.), Urbana Country Club, Kiwanis (pres. Champaign-Urbana). Democrat. Presbyterian. Office: Webber & Thies PC 202 Lincoln Sq PO Box 189 Urbana IL 61803-0189 E-mail: rthies@webberthies.com.

THIESENHUSEN, WILLIAM CHARLES, agricultural economist, educator; b. Waukesha, Wis., Feb. 12, 1936; s. Arthur Henry and Myrtle O. (Honeyager) Thiesenhusen; children: James Waring(dec.), Kathryn Hague, Gail Ann. BS, U. Wis., 1958, MS, 1960, PhD, 1965; MPA (Danforth Found. fellow), Harvard U., 1962, postgrad., 1968-69. Instr. agrl. ext. U. Wis., Madison, 1959-61; exec. asst. rsch. team Land Tenure Ctr. and Instituto de Economia Universidad de Chile, Santiago, 1963-65, asst. prof. agrl. econs., 1965-68, assoc. prof., 1971-72, assoc. prof. agrl. journalism, 1968-72, prof. agrl. journalism and agrl. econs., 1972—98, prof. emeritus, 1998—, dir., 1971—75, 1994—98. Under AID contract, 1965; Fulbright-Hays lectr., 65, 72; asst. prof. econs. U. Wis., Milw., 1966—67; prof. agrl. econs. Escuela Nacional de Agricultura, Chapingo, Mexico; vis. prof. Universidad Autonoma de Madrid, 1977; cons., condr. seminars in field. Author: (book) Chile's Experiment in Agrarian Reform, 1966, Reforma Agraria en Chile: Experimentos en Cuatro Fundos de la Iglesia, 1968, Broken Promises: Agrarian Reform and the Latin American Campesino, 1995; editor: Searching for Agrarian Reform in Latin America, 1989; mem. editl. bd. Latin Am. Rsch. Rev., Pakistan Devel. Rev.; contbr. articles to profl. jours With USAR, 1960. Recipient award for best article, Am. Jour. Agrl. Econs., 1969; fellow, U. Wis., 1956; Adminstrn. fellow, Harvard U., 1962. Mem.: Wis. Acad. Scis., Arts and Letters, Coun. Internat. Exch. Scholars (chmn. com. econs. selection 1979—80), Latin Am. Studies Assn., Am. Econ. Assn., Am. Agrl. Econs. Assn., Inter-Am. Found. (selection bd.), Sigma Delta Chi, Alpha Zeta (nat. fellow 1957), Phi Kappa Phi. Unitarian Universalist. Office: U Wis Land Tenure Ctr 1357 University Ave Madison WI 53715-1054 E-mail: wthiesen@wisc.edu.

THIESSEN, DELBERT DUANE, psychologist; b. Julesberg, Colo., Aug. 13, 1932; s. David and Eva Peters (Wetherby) T.; children: Trevor, Theron, Kendell Courtney. BA in Psychology with distinction, San Jose (Calif.) State Coll., 1958; PhD, U. Calif., Berkeley, 1963. Extension instr. U. Calif., La Jolla, fall 1964; asst. sect. med. psychology, divsn. psychiatry and neurology Scripps Clinic and Research Found., La Jolla, 1962-65; faculty U. Tex., Austin, 1965-2000, prof. psychology, 1971-2000, prof. emeritus, 2000—. Rsch. cons. NIMH. Author: Gene Organization and Behavior, 1972, The Evolution and Biochemistry of Aggression, 1976, Bitter-Sweet Destiny: The Stormy Evolution of Human Behavior, 1996, Universal Desires and Fears: The Deep History of Sociobiology, 1997, Survival of the Fittest: The Darwinian Diet and Exercise Program, 1998; contbr. articles and chpts. to books. With AUS, 1952-54, Korea. Fellow USPHS, 1960-61; recipient Career Devel. award NIMH, 1967-72, grantee, 1967-78; grantee Russel Sage Found., NSF, U. Tex. Rsch. Inst. Fellow AAAS, APA; mem. Alumni Assn. Roscoe B. Jackson Meml. Lab., Am. Genetic Assn., Psychonomic Soc., Animal Behavior Soc., Southwestern Psychol. Assn., Behavior Genetics Assn., Sigma Xi, Phi Kappa Phi, Psi Chi. Business E-Mail: wolf@delthiessen.com.

THIGPEN, ALTON HILL, motor transportation company executive; b. Kinston, N.C., Feb. 3, 1927; s. Kirby Alton and Alice (Hill) T.; m. Rebecca Ann Braswell, May 16, 1953; children: David Alton, Jennifer Ann, Steven Roy. BS in Indsl. Engring., N.C. State U., 1950. With Assoc. Transport, Inc., Burlington, NC, 1950-71, engr., 1950-57, asst. terminal mgr. Phila., 1957-58, terminal mgr. Knoxville, Tenn., 1959, regional mgr. Valley region, 1960-62, South region, 1962-68, v.p.,dir. So. divsn., 1968-71; v.p. R.S. Braswell Co. Inc., Kannapolis, NC, 1971-80, pres., 1980—, Hartford Motor Inn Inc., North Myrtle Beach, SC, 1982—, A.T. Developers, Inc., North Myrtle Beach, 1983-97. Pres. Cherokee 2 Inc., Shelby, N.C., 1986-95, bd. dirs.; bd. dirs. First Union Nat. Bank, Earl Ownsby Studios Inc., Shelby. Bd. regents Berkshire Christian Coll., Lenox, Mass., 1975—; mem. adv. bd. Salvation Army, chmn. adv. bd., 1997-99. Served with USNR, 1945-46. Mem. Motor Carriers Va. (pres. 1967-68), N.C. Motor Carriers Assn. (dir. 1968-), Masons (32d degree), Lions, Sigma Chi, Tau Beta Pi. Mem. Advent Christian Ch. Home: 5395 Mooresville Rd Kannapolis NC 28081-8726 Office: PO Box 1197 Kannapolis NC 28082-1197 Office Phone: 704-933-2269.

THIGPEN, JAMES TATE, physician, oncology educator; b. Columbia, Miss., June 6, 1944; m. Louisa Berdie Kessler, June 14, 1969; children: Monroe Tate, James Howard, Samuel Calvin, Richard Allen, David Albert. BS, U. Miss., 1964, MD, 1969. Intern Strong Meml. Hosp., U. Rochester, N.Y., 1969-70; resident U. Miss. Sch. Medicine, 1970-71, prof., dir. divsn. med. oncology dept. internal medicine, 1973—; also prof. ob-gyn. Nat. med. del. from Miss. Am. Cancer Soc., 1983-85, mem. nat. pub. issues com., 1983-85; mem. cancer clin. investigations rev. com. Nat. Cancer Inst., 1990-95, chmn., 1993-95. Nat. bd. govs. ARC, 1981-87. Fellow divsn. hematology/oncology dept. medicine, 1971-73. Fellow ACP; mem. AMA, Miss. Med. Assn., Ctrl. Med. Soc., Jackson Acad. Medicine, Miss. Acad. Scis., SW Oncology Group, Gynecologic Oncology Group (group vice chmn. sci. 1988—), Am. Fedn. Clin. Rsch., Am. Assn. Cancer Edn., Am. Soc. Clin. Oncology, Am. Assn. cancer Rsch., Am. Soc. Hematology, Soc. Gynecologic Oncologists, Soc. Assn. Oncology (pres. 1988-90), Am. Radium Soc., (diplomists (internat. v.p. 1983-84, internat. pres. 1990-91). Baptist. (deacon 1978—, Sunday sch. tchr. 1979-85). Home: 3601 Kings Hwy Jackson MS 39216-3322 Office: Miss Oncology Assocs 2500 N State St Jackson MS 39216-4500 Office Phone: 601-984-5590. E-mail: jtthigpen@att.net.

THIGPEN, MARY CECELIA, city official, consultant; b. L.A., Jan. 27, 1949; d. Tom Allen and Inell Theresa (Evans) Johnson; m. Willie Edward Thigpen, Apr. 30, 1971; children: Sonna Aminata, Monifa Ayodele. BA, Xavier U., New Orleans, 1971; MS in Urban Planning, U. New Orleans, 1979. Planner Urban Systems, Inc., New Orleans, 1977-79, Grimball/Garrandon/Savoy Engrs. and Architects, New Orleans, 1979-80; planner, cons. Mayor's Office, City of New Orleans, 1979; grants program evaluator Pinellas County Manpower Council, Clearwater, Fla., 1980-81; personnel mgmt. specialist Pinellas County Personnel Dept., Clearwater, 1981-83; adminstrv. analyst U. Calif., San Diego, 1983-85; sr. and personnel analyst City of Chula Vista, Calif., 1985—. Planning cons. Mayor's office, New Orleans, 1979; b.p. bd. dirs. Cajon Valley Ednl. Found., El Cajon, Calif., 1988—; v.p. personnel commn. City of El Cajon, 2000—. Writer poetry. Named Woman of Distinction, San Diego County Women, Inc., 1990; named Mother of Yr., Delta Sigma Theta of San Diego County, 1996. Mem. Nat. Med. Assn. Aux. (v.p. 1986—), Jack and Jill Am, Calif. Women in Govt., Internat. Pers. Mgmt. Assn., Altrusa Club of Chula Vista, Nat. Coalition of 100 Black Women, Inc. Roman Catholic. Avocations: fashion design, arts promotion, handcrafts, writing poetry and plays, photography. Home: 1551 Heron Ave El Cajon CA 92020-8810 Office Phone: 619-585-5663.

THIGPEN, RICHARD ELTON, JR., lawyer; b. Washington, Dec. 29, 1930; s. Richard Elton and Dorathy (Dotger) T.; m. Nancy H. Shand, Dec. 15, 1951; children: Susan B., Richard M. AB, Duke U., 1951; LLB, U. N.C., 1956. Bar: NC 1956, U.S. Ct. Appeals (4th cir.) 1960, U.S. Ct. Appeals (5th cir.) 1960, U.S. Ct. Appeals (10th cir.) 1974, U.S. Tax Ct. 1958, U.S. Ct. Claims 1978, U.S. Supreme Ct. 2003. Lawyer FTC, Washington, 1956-58, Thigpen & Hines, Charlotte, NC, 1958-84, Moore & Van Allen, Charlotte, 1984-88, Poyner & Spruill, Charlotte, 1988-93; gen. counsel Richardson Sports, 1994-98. Bd. dirs. O.L. Miller Rsch. Inst. Bd. dirs. Charlotte-Mecklenburg YMCA, 1964—88, Heineman Med. Rsch. Ctr., Charlotte, 1970—, Charlotte (N.C.) C. of C., 1982—85. Lt. USNR, 1951—53. Fellow Am. Bar Found., Am. Coll. Tax Counsel (regent 1989-95, vice chmn. 1992, chmn. 1993-94); mem. ABA, N.C. State Bar, N.C. Bar Assn. (pres. 1988-89, chmn. tax sect. 1976-80), Sports Lawyers Assn. (bd. dirs. 1995—, pres. 2003—). Avocations: golf, travel. Office: 1045 Providence Rd Ste 200 Charlotte NC 28207-2568

THILL, JOHN VAL, communications professional, writer, consultant; b. Milw., Dec. 27, 1953; s. Lewis Dominic and Carol Jean (Werner) T. BS, San Diego State U., 1977; MBA, U. San Diego, 1982. Mgr. Pacific Bell, San Diego, 1979-82; CEO Comm. Specialists of Am., Las Vegas, 1982—; pres. Bovee & Thill LLC, Las Vegas, 1997—. Bd. dirs. Comm. Rsch. Inst., L.A. Author: Business in Action, 2003, Business Communication Today, 2004, Excellence in Business Communication, 2004, Business Today, 2004. Named Outstanding Bus. Communicator Am. Soc. Journalists, 1982, Nat. Cmty. Leadership award, 1997. Mem. Assn. Bus. Communication, 1985, Text and Acad. Authors Assn. Avocations: swimming, travel. Office: Bovee & Thill LLC 2950 E Flamingo Rd Ste B Las Vegas NV 89121-5208

THIMMIG, DIANA M. lawyer; b. Germany, May 5, 1959; BA cum laude, John Carroll U., 1980; JD, Cleve. State U., 1982. Bar: Ohio 1983, U.S. Dist. Ct. (no. dist.) Ohio 1983, U.S. Ct. Appeals (6th cir.) 1983, U.S. Supreme Ct. 1983, U.S. Ct. Appeals (3d cir. 1996); cert. Am. Bankruptcy Bd. for Consumer and Bus. Bankruptcy. Ptnr. Roetzel & Andress, Cleve. Contbr. articles to profl. jours. Hon. consul of Germany, 1988—; trustee Geauga United Way Svcs. Coun., 1992-96, Altenheim, 1992-97, Internat. Svcs. Ctr., 1998—2004; trustee Cuyahoga County Bar Assn., 1995—2004, pres.-elect, 2004—; trustee Legal Aid Soc., 1998—, pres., 2003—. Mem. Women's City Club Cleve. (pres. 1995-97). Office: Roetzel & Andress 1375 East Ninth St One Cleveland Ctr Ninth Floor Cleveland OH 44114 Office Phone: 216-696-7078.

THIMOTHEOSE, KADAKAMPALLIL GEORGE, psychologist; b. Karipuza, India, Feb. 11, 1938, came to the U.S., 1976; s. K.G. and Mariamma Varghese; m. Mariamma Thimotheose, May 20, 1968 (div.); children: Geebee, Sonia T. Andrews. MA in Psychology, ME.D 1st class & rank, Kerala U., India, 1967, B in Edn., 1960, MA in Sociology, 1969; MA in History, PhD in Psychology, Kerala U., 1975; D Therapeutic Philosophy (hon.), World U., 1989. Lic. psychologist, marriage and family therapist, Mich.; diplomate Am. Bd. Med. Psychotherapists, Am. Bd. Psychotherapy, Am. Bd. Sexology, Am. Bd. Forensic Examiners, Am. Bd. Forensic Medicine, Am. Bd. Psychol. Specialities. Lectr., head dept. ednl. psychology S.N. Tchrs. Coll., Trivandrum, India; clin./adminstrv. dir. Alexandrine House, Inc., Detroit, 1976-81; chief exec. officer Cen. Therapeutic Svcs., Inc., Southfield, Mich., 1981—. Adv. bd. Trivandrum Med. Coll. Hosps., 1969-75; edn. faculty mem. U. Calicut, Kerala, India, 1969-75; v.p. forum ednl. rsch. and studies Kerala U., 1969-73. Author: Educational Psychology for B.Ed. Students, 1970; editor: Kerala University Journal of Education, 1969-73. Fellow Am. Bd. Med. Psychotherapists, Am. Acad. Clin. Sexologists. Am. Coll. Forensic Examiners, Am. Coll. Advanced Practice Psychologists; mem. APA, Am. Coll. Sexologists (sexologist), Am. Bd. Sexology (clin. supr.), World U. Round Table (hon. cultural doctorate in therapeutic philosophy), diplomate Am. Bd. Psychological Specialities. Republican. Avocations: photography, travel, reading, sightseeing. Home: 3048 Brewster West Bloomfield MI 48322-2471 Office: Cen Therapeutic Svcs Inc 17600 W 8 Mile Rd Ste 7 Southfield MI 48075-4316

THIRSK, ROBERT BRENT, astronaut; b. New Westminster, Brit. Columbia, Aug. 17, 1953; m. Brenda Biasutti; 3 children. BSc in Mech. Engring., U. Calgary, 1976; MSc in Mech. Engring., MIT, 1978; MD, McGill U., 1982; MBA, MIT, 1998. Resident Queen Elizabeth Hosp., Montreal, Canada, 1982—83; astronaut Can. Astronaut Program, 1984—; sabbatical yr. Victoria, Canada, 1994—95; chief astronaut Can. Space Agy., 1996—98; astronaut NASA, Houston, 1998—. Dir. Can. Found. Internat. Space U., 1992—; crew comdr. CAPSULS mission, 1994; astronaut Space Shuttle mission STS-78, 1996. Recipient Disting. Alumni award, U. Calgary, 1985. Mem.: Coll. Physicians and Surgeons B.C., Coll. Physicians & Surgeons Ontario, Aerospace Med. Assn., Can. Aeronautics & Space Inst., Can. Coll. Family Physicians, Assn. Profl. Engrs. Ontario (Gold Medal award 1997). Avocations: flying, hockey, squash, playing the piano. Office: Astronaut Office CB NASA Johnson Space Center Houston TX 77058

THIRUVAIYARU, DHARMA S. mathematics and statistics educator, consultant, researcher; d. Sivadattan S. and Saraswaty Thiruvaiyaru; m. Sankar N. Sethuraman, Mar. 16, 1989. B, U. Madras, 1983; M, Madras Christian Coll., 1985, U. Ga., 1987, PhD, 1991. Tchg. asst. U. Ga., Athens, 1985—91; asst. prof. Augusta (Ga.) State U., 1991—99, assoc. prof. stats., 1999—. Contbr. articles to profl. jours. Cultural program organizer Hindu Temple of Augusta, 1992—2003. Mem.: Am. Statis. Assn. (corr.), Joseph Still Burn Rsch. Consortium (corr.; statis. cons. 1995—2003). Avocations: reading, music, debating. Office: Augusta State U 2500 Walton Way Augusta GA 30904 E-mail: dthiruvi@aug.edu.

THIRY, KENT J. health facility administrator; BA in Polit. Sci., Stanford U., 1978; MBA with honors, Harvard U., 1983. Sr. cons. Andersen Consulting, 1978-81; ptnr. Bain & Co.; pres., COO Vivra, Inc., San Francisco, 1991-92, pres., CEO, 1992-97; CEO, chmn. bd. dirs. Total Renal Care, Inc., Torrance, Calif., 1999—. Bd. dirs. Oxford Healthcare, Vol. Ctr. San Mateo County. Mem. Phi Beta Kappa. Office: 601 Hawaii St El Segundo CA 90245-4814

THISTED, RONALD AARON, statistician, educator, consultant; b. L.A., Mar. 2, 1951; s. Dale Owen and Barbara Jean (Walker) T.; m. Linda Jeane Soder, Dec. 30, 1972; 1 child, Walker. BA, Pomona Coll., 1972; PhD, Stanford U., 1977. Asst. prof. statistics U. Chgo., 1976-82, assoc. prof. statistics, 1982-92, assoc. prof. anesthesia and critical care, 1989-92, prof. stats. and anesthesia and critical care, 1992—, prof. health studies, 1996—, chmn. health studies, 1999—. Co-dir. Clin. Rsch. Training Program, 1999—. Author: Elements of Statistical Computing, 1988; contbr. over 80 articles to profl. jours. Fellow AAAS, Am. Statis. Assn.; mem. Assn. for Computing Machinery, Inst. for Math. Stats. Office: U Chgo MC 2007 5841 S Maryland Ave Chicago IL 60637-1463 Office Phone: 773-834-1242.

THISTLETHWAITE, DAVID RICHARD, architect; b. Burlington, Iowa, Aug. 24, 1947; s. Robert and Nona (Binder) T.; m. Carol Anne Armstrong, Aug. 22, 1970. BArch, Iowa State U., 1971. Registered arch., Calif., 1979, Minn., 1975; registered Nat. Coun. Archtl. Registration Bds., 1978; cert. Health Care arch., Am. Coll. Healthcare Archs., 2000. Designer Morrison Architects, St. Paul, 1971-73, Times Architects, Mpls., 1973-74; project architect Bentz/Thompson Assocs., Mpls., 1974-77; project mgr. Setter Leach Lindstrom, Mpls., 1977-78; project architect Wurster Bernardi Emmons, San Francisco, 1978-79, Strotz & Assocs., Tiburon, Calif., 1979-81, Hood Miller Assoc., San Francisco, 1981-84; prin., ptnr. R S T Architects, San Francisco, 1984-88; prin. Thistlethwaite Archtl. Group, San Francisco, 1988—. Contbr. articles to profl. jours. Mem. AIA (nat. profl. devel. com. 1983-86, treas. San Francisco chpt. 1985-86, chmn. Calif. coun. health facilities com. 1994-96, chmn. design com. Acad. Architecture for Health, 1994-96, Calif. coun. ins. bd. trustees 1988-2002, Calif. coun. legis. com. 1996-98), Am. Soc. Healthcare Engring., Design Profls. Safety Assn. (bd. dirs.). Office: 355 Bryant St Ste 210 San Francisco CA 94107 Business E-Mail: dthistlethwaite@tagarchitects.com.

THOBURN, CRAWFORD RANDALL, music educator, composer; b. Cleve., Ohio, Oct. 23, 1933; s. Crawford Bennett and Mary Hinds Thoburn; m. Karen A Hindenlang; m. Ingrid S Thoburn (div.); children: Matthew, Sarah, Laura, Martha. BA, Allegheny Coll., 1954; MusM, Boston U., 1960. Cert. tchg. sec. music and english Ohio, 1955. Choir dir. Saegertown Meth. Ch., 1951—55, St. Paul Luth. Ch., Arlington, Mass., 1957—60, United Min., Aurora, NY, 1960—92, S.S.Peter John Episc. Ch., Auburn, 1992—96; prof. music/dir. choral activities Wells Coll., Aurora, NY, 1960—. Chair, music dept. arts divsn. and major faculty coms. Wells Coll., Aurora, 1964—. Choral rev. The Choral Jour., 1975—80; composer: of over 100 pub. titles. First lt. USAF, 1955—58, Fla. and Mass. Recipient Campbell Prof. of Arts, Wells Coll., 1992—98, Alumni Assn. Gold Citation, Allegheny Coll., 1999. Mem.: Am. Assn. Univ. Profs., Am. Guild Organists, Am. Choral Dir. Assn. Avocations: travel, antiques. Home: 290 Main St Aurora NY 13026

THOERING, ROBERT CHARLES, elementary school educator; s. Robert Theodore and Mary Agnes Thoering. BA, St. John's U., 1986, MEd, 1991; prof. diploma, Fordham U., 2003. Cert. tchr. reading, social studies, N.Y. Assoc. tchr. Holy Cross H.S., Flushing, N.Y., 1985; tchr. English, reading Our Lady of Refuge Sch., Bklyn., 1986—2002, prin., 2002—. Editor: Hope's Treasure, 1991—2000. Founder, dir. St. Anne's Mission Bd., Middle Village, 1997-2002; mem. Greater Ridgewood (N.Y.) Hist. Soc., Queens Genealogy Workshop, Ridgewood, Irish Family History Forum, Hempstead, N.Y. Mem. ASCD, Nat. Cath. Edn. Assn., Nat. Assn. Student Activity Advisers, Nat. Coun. Tchrs. English, Internat. Reading Assn., N.Y. State English Coun. Republican. Roman Catholic. Avocations: gardening, travel, literature. Home: 7207 66th Rd Middle Village NY 11379-2115 Office: Our Lady of Refuge Sch 1087 Ocean Ave Brooklyn NY 11230

THOM, RICHARD DAVID, retired aerospace executive; b. St. Louis, Oct. 4, 1944; s. Reginald James and Vlasta (Koukl) T.; m. Linda Marie Hunt, Sept. 9, 1967; children: Elizabeth Marie, Robert James. BS in Physics, U. Mo., Rolla, 1967; MSEE, UCLA, 1971. Co-op engr. McDonnell Aircraft Corp., St. Louis, 1962-67; head advanced tech. group IR systems dept., aerospace group Hughes Aircraft Co., Culver City, Calif., 1967-72; mem. tech. staff Santa Barbara Rsch. Ctr., Hughes Aircraft Co., Goleta, Calif., 1972-76, asst. mgr. R&D Lab., 1976-80, mgr. advanced applications, 1980-83, chief engr., 1984-86, chief scientist, 1986-90, dir. tech., 1990-95; tech. program exec. Hughes Aircraft Co., Goleta, Calif., 1995-98; asst. mgr. Raytheon Santa Barbara Rsch. Ctr., Goleta, Calif., 1998-99; ret. Contbr. articles to profl. jours.; patentee in field. Recipient Hughes Group Patent award for pioneering contbns. in infrared detector tech., 1990. Mem. IEEE, Tau Beta Pi, Sigma Pi Sigma, Delta Sigma Phi. Republican. Avocations: freelance travel writing and photography, specializing in railway travel around the world. Home: 38 Fawn Run Pl PO Box 326 Coupeville WA 98239-0326 Personal E-mail: Richthommail@aol.com.

THOMA, AUGUST JOHN, music educator; b. Bronx, May 16, 1953; s. August Carl and Evelyn Eberhardt Thoma; m. Maureen Therese Wiegers, Aug. 4, 1978; children: Matthew August, Christopher August, Megan Maureen. BA, Mich. State U., 1971—75, MusB, 1971—76; MusM, Oakland U., 1991—99. Continuing Tchng. Cert. Mich. State Bd. Edn., 1977. Day camp program dir. North Oakland YMCA, Rochester, 1977—78, elem. instrumental music tchr. Lake Orion Cmty. Schools, Mich., 1977—79; dir. of music ministry St. John Fisher Parish U. Chapel, 1978—; dir. of bands Van Hoosen Jr. H.S., 1979—83, Rochester H.S., 1983—; adj. instr., music Rochester Coll., 2000—; lectr., music Oakland U., 2001—. Adjudicator Mich. Sch. Band and Orch. Assn., Ann Arbor, 2000—. Recipient Eagle Scout, Boy Scouts of Am., 1971, State Tchr. of the Yr. Nominee, Mich. Alliance for Gifted Edn., 1991, Founders Day Award, Rochester PTSA, 2000, Excellence in Edn. Award, Rochester Cmty. Schools Found., 2002; scholar Nat. Merit Scholarship, Nat. Merit Scholarship Corp., 1971-1975, Music Scholarship, Mich. State U., 1972-1976. Mem.: Mich. Sch. Band and Orch. Assn. (dist. 16 4th v.p. 2002—04), Am. Sch. Band Directors Assn., Music Educators Nat. Conf., Internat. Clarinet Assn., Mich. State U. Alumni Band. Roman Catholic. Avocations: travel, reading, camping, sports. Home: 2685 Munster Dr Rochester Hills MI 48309 Office. Rochester High School 180 South Livernois Rochester Hills MI 48307 Personal E-mail: athoma@rochester.k12.mi.us.

THOMA, KURT MICHAEL, business owner; b. Boston, Aug. 9, 1946; s. Kurt Richard and Janet (Holdsworth) T.; divorced; children by previous marriage: Heather Anne, Heidi. Student, U. N.H., 1964-68. Clk., supr., asst. divsn. EDP coord., EDP coord. mutual funds divsn. 1st Nat. Bank, Boston, 1968-69; v.p. ctrl. N.H. bldg. corp. Barry Dashner, Inc., Sunapee, N.H., 1969-72; field rep. Acorn Structures, Inc., New London, N.H., Vt., 1972-75; v.p., treas. Design Structures Group, Inc., Quechee, Vt., 1975-76; pres. Witthom Assocs., Inc., New London, 1976-79; v.p. Confetti, Inc., Newport, R.I., 1978-89; pres., treas., propr. dessin batir Newport, 1979-89; Christian Sci. practitioner Warner, N.H., 1990-93; ops. mgr. Arctic Dreams, New London, 1993—. With U.S. Army N.G., 1966-72. Avocations: writing, tennis, skiing, residential and furniture design, photography. Home and Office: PO Box 2064 New London NH 03257-2064 Office Phone: 603-526-9477. E-mail: kmthoma@tds.net. *"Prior" to the Knowledge or Science of Christ, I was an atheist. In King James Bible demonstrations, I Kings 17, II Kings 4, Daniel 3, Matthew, Mark, Luke, John, Acts 9, 14 and 20 all express the Christ Fact that there is no "death". In medical science "near death experience" is unfolding the same truth, which converges as One. "Death" is only in the "eye of the beholder". You will never see "death" for yourself.*

THOMA, RICHARD WILLIAM, chemical safety and waste management consultant; b. Milw., Dec. 7, 1921; s. Joseph Donath and Margaret Mary (Murphy) T.; m. Ida Mary Scharfschwerdt, Mar. 15, 1952; children: Adele, Richard W., Joseph O., John C. AA, U. Chgo., 1941; BS, U. Wis., Madison, 1947, MS in Biochemistry, 1949, PhD, 1951. R&D fermentation E.R. Squibb & Sons, Inc., New Brunswick, NJ, 1951-82; dir. process devel. New Brunswick Sci. Co., Inc., Edison, 1982-84, cons., 1984—. Safety officer Harbor br. Oceanographic Inst. St. Lucie County, Fla., 1988—96. Contbr. articles to profl. jours.; patentee microbiol. transformation of steroids. Commr. Somerset County Bd. Elections, 1981-84; mem. Bridgewater Town Coun., 1975-81, Environ. Commn., 1974-75, Sewerage Authority, 1975-76, Police Commn., 1977-81; chmn. Birdgewater Dem. Mcpl. Com., 1980-87; alderman St. Lucie Village, 1996-98. With AUS, 1942-46. Mem. VFW, Am. Chem. Soc., Am. Soc. Microbiology, Am. Acad. Microbiology, Phi Beta Kappa, Sigma Xi, Phi Lambda Upsilon. Home and Office: 3772 Outrigger Ct Fort Pierce FL 34946-1911 E-mail: rthoma3772@aol.com.

THOMAJAN, ROBERT, lawyer, management consultant; b. N.Y.C., May 4, 1941; s. Leon and Fay T. BS, NYU, 1962; JD, St. John's U., 1965. Bar: N.Y. 1965, Tex. 1987, U.S. Ct. Internat. Trade 1975, U.S. Supreme Ct. 1975, U.S. Ct. Appeals (9th cir.) 1976, U.S. Dist. Ct. (we. dist.) Tex. 1979. Atty. Nixon, Mudge, Rose, Guthrie, Alexander & Mitchell, N.Y.C., 1965—68; ptnr. Milgrim, Thomajan & Lee, N.Y.C., 1968-90; exec. dir. Richco, Inc., 1990—93; pres. Eterna Investments, Austin, Tex., 1995—. Arbitrator Civil Ct., N.Y., 1981-86; mem. adv. bd. Ronald McDonald House, 1988-90; bd. dirs. Big Bros./Big Sisters, 1988-90; mem. World Econ. Forum, 1990-93. Mem. Am. Soc. Internat. Law, Internat. Law Assn.

THOMAN, DAVID SCOTT, surgeon; b. Haverford, Pa., Mar. 14, 1968; s. Richard Aaron and Elizabeth Jane Thoman. BS, U. Notre Dame, 1990; MD, Jefferson Med., Phila., 1994. Bd. cert. Am. Bd. Surgery. Dir. minimally invasive surgery Navel Med. Ctr., San Diego, 2001—. Author: (book) Laparoscopic Ventical Hernia Repair, 2002. Fellow: Am. Coll. Surgeons. Office: Navel Med Ctr 34800 Bob Wilson Dr San Diego CA 92134-1098

THOMAN, G. RICHARD, corporate and financial executive; b. Tuscaloosa, Ala., June 25, 1944; s. Richard S. and Evelyn (Zumwalt) Thoman; m. Wenke Helina Brier, Aug. 25, 1966 (div. Dec. 1987); children: Camille, Alexis; m. Lynn Susan Bendheim, Sept. 16, 1989; children: Kylie, Max, Amy, Eric. BA with honors, McGill U., 1966; MA, Grad. Inst. Internat. Studies, Geneva, 1968; MA in Internat. Econs., Tufts U., 1967, MA in Law and Diplomacy, 1969, PhD in Internat. Econs., 1971. Exec. trainee Citicorp, N.Y.C., 1968-69; sr. fin. analyst Exxon Corp., N.Y.C., 1970-72; sr. assoc. McKinsey and Co., N.Y.C. and Paris, 1972-79; exec. v.p., CFO Am. Express Travel Related Svcs., N.Y.C., 1979-85, pres., Travel Related Svcs. Internat., 1985-89, chmn., CEO, 1989-92; pres., CEO Nabisco Internat. RJR Nabisco, Inc., N.Y.C., 1992-94; sr. v.p., group exec. IBM Corp., Somers, N.Y., 1994-95, sr. v.p., CFO Armonk, N.Y., 1995-97; pres., COO Xerox Corp., 1997-99, pres., CEO, 1999-2000, also bd. dirs.; pvt. investor; sr. advisor Evercore Ptnrs., N.Y.C., 2001—02; mng. ptnr. Corporate Perspectives, N.Y.C., 2002—; adj. prof. Columbia U., 2003—. Bd. dirs. Union Bancaire Privee, Geneva; mem. U.S. adv. bd. INSEAD; mem. adv. bd. Mid Oceanic Capital Ptnrs. Bd. dirs. Americas Soc., N.Y.C., 1990—. French-Am. Found.; bd. advisors Fletcher Sch. Law and Diplomacy, Tufts U., Medford, Mass., 1990—; mem. adv. bd. Sch. Mgmt. McGill U., Montreal, Bus. Coun.; U.S. chair TransAtlantic Bus. Dialogue. Recipient Legion of Honors, Govt. of France, 1992. Mem.: Trilateral Commn., Coun. on Fgn. Rels., River Club, Links Club. Avocations: tennis, reading, jogging, travel. Office: Corp Perspectives 126 E 56th St Fl 9 New York NY 10022 Office Phone: 212-813-0323.

THOMAN, HENRY NIXON, lawyer; b. Cin., May 5, 1957; s. Richard B. and Barbara (Lutz) Thoman; m. Anne Davies, May 25, 2002; children: Victoria E., Nicholas B. BA, Duke U., 1979; JD, U. Chgo., 1982. Bar: Ohio 1982, U.S. Dist. Ct. (so. dist.) Ohio, 1982. With Taft, Stettinius & Hollister, Cin., 1982-88; sr. atty. John Morrell & Co., Cin., 1988-90; sr. counsel Chiquita Brands Internat. Inc., Cin., 1990-91, corp. planner, 1991-92; sr. dir. CTP ops. Chiquita Brands, Inc., Cin., 1993-94, chief adminstrv. officer Armuelles divsn., 1994-95; corp. counsel The Loewen Group, Covington, Ky., 1995-97; asst. chief counsel, asst. v.p. The Midland Co., Amelia, Ohio, 1997-99; v.p. orgnl. devel. Kendle Internat. Inc., 1999-2000, v.p. complementary ops., 2000—02; pvt. atty., 2002—; exec. dir. Madisonville Edn. and Assistance Ctr., 2004—. Mem. counselors com. U.S. Swimming, Colo., 1983-89; bd. dirs. Friends of Cin. Parks, 1990-93, 96-98, Starshine Children's Hospice, 1996-99, Cinci. Aquatic Club, 1997-2002, Kids Helping Kids, 2000-2001, Mariemont Aquatic Club, v.p., 1992-93; pres. Club Atletico Y Socialde Chiriqui, 1994-95. Mem. ABA, Ohio State Bar, Cin. Bar Assn. E-mail: thoman.henry@fuse.net.

THOMAN, MARK EDWARD, pediatrician; b. Chgo., Feb. 15, 1936; s. John Charles and Tasula Mark (Petrakis) T.; m. Theresa Thompson, 1984; children: Marlisa Rae, Susan Kay, Edward Kim, Nancy Lynn, Janet Lea, David Mark. AA, Graceland Coll., 1956; BA, U. Mo., 1958, MD, 1962. Diplomate Am. Bd. Pediat., Am. Coll. Toxicology (examiner), 1975-90. Intern U. Mo. at Columbia, 1962—63; resident in pediat. Blank Meml. Children's Hosp., Des Moines, 1963—65; cons. in toxicology USPHS, Washington, 1965—66; chief dept. pediat. Shiprock (N.Mex.) Navajo Indian Hosp., 1966—67; dir. N.D. Poison Info. Ctr.; also practice medicine specializing in pediat. Quain & Ramstad Clinic, Bismarck, ND, 1967—69; dir. Iowa Poison Info. Ctr., Des Moines, 1969—99; mem. pediat. exec. com. Broadlawns Med. Ctr., Des Moines, 1969—2000, pres. med. staff, 2000—01. Accident investigator FAA, 1976—, sr. aviation examiner, 1977—2000; sr. cons. in field; lectr. aviation seminars, 1977—; mem. faculty Des Moines U., 1969—, dir. cystic fibrosis clin., 1973—82; dir. Mid-Iowa Drug Abuse Program, 1972—76; mem. med. adv. bd. La Leche League Internat., 1965—; pres. Medic-Air Ltd., 1976—; chief med. officer Broadlawns Med. Ctr., Des Moines, 2000—02; sci. rev. panel Nat. Libr. Medicine, 2003—; med. cons., expert witness Office Hearings and Appeals Social Security Adminstrn., 2003—. Editor-in-chief AACTION, 1975-90. Bd. dirs. Polk County Pub. Health Nurses Assn., 1969-77, Des Moines Speech and Hearing Ctr., 1974-79, Ecumenical Coun. Iowa, 1990-99; bd. govs. Mo. U. Sch. Medicine Alumni, 1988—, pres., 1997-99; elder mem. Cmty. of Christ Ch. With USMCR, 1954-59; lt. comdr. USPHS, 1965-66; capt. USNR, 1988-96, ret. 1996; dir. Dept. Health Svcs. USNR. Recipient N.D. Gov.'s award of merit, 1969, Cystic Fibrosis Rsch. Found. award, 1975, Am. Psychiat. Assn. Thesis award, 1962. Fellow Am. Coll. Med. Toxicology (diplomate 1996); mem. AMA (del. 1970-88), APHA, NRA (life), Assn. Am. Physicians & Surgeons (chief of staff, pres. Broadlawns Polk County Med. Ctr. 2000-02), Polk County Med. Soc., Iowa State Med. Assn., Aerospace Med. Assn., Res. Officers Assn., Civil Aviation Med. Assn., Soc. Adolescent Medicine, Inst. Clin. Toxicology, Internat. Soc. Pediat., Am. Acad. Pediat. (chmn. accident prevention com. Iowa chpt. 1975-2000), Cystic Fibrosis Club, Am. Acad. Clin. Toxicology (trustee 1969-90, pres. 1982-84), Am. Assn. Poison Control Ctrs., Am. Coll. Physician Execs., U.S. Naval Inst., Flying Physicians Club, Aircraft Owners and Pilots Assn, Nat. Pilots Assn. (Safe Pilot award), Hyperion Field and Country Club. Republican. Home: 6896 NW Trail Ridge Dr Johnston IA 50131-1322 Office: PO Box 349 Johnston IA 50131-0349 Office Phone: 515-270-2364. Personal E-mail: paro1795@aol.com.

THOMAN, ROY EDWARD, political scientist, educator; b. Evansville, Ind., Mar. 11, 1938; s. Joseph Henry and Nell Yates Thoman; m. Judith Ann Schiff, May 20, 1967 (div. Apr. 18, 1985); 1 child, Mark. BA magna cum laude, U. Evansville, 1960; MA, Ind. U., 1964; PhD, U. Ky., 1967. Asst. prof. West Tex. A&M U., Canyon, 1968—70, assoc. prof., 1970—76, prof., 1976—. Contbr. articles to profl. jours.; consulting editor World Affairs, 1979—82. Recipient scholarship medal, Pi Gamma Mu, 2000, endowed scholarship in his name, Phi Eta Sigma, 2000; grantee, Tex. Ednl. Assn., 1972—75. Mem.: KC, Am. Polit. Sci. Assn. Republican. Roman Catholic. Home: 4404 Bell Apt 311A Amarillo TX 79109 Office: West Tex A&M U WT Box 725 Canyon TX 79016 Business E-Mail: rthoman@mail.wtamu.edu.

THOMAS, ADRIAN WESLEY, research scientist, director, retired science educator; b. Edgefield, S.C., June 23, 1939; s. Hasting Adrian and Nancy Azalena (Bridges) T.; m. Martha Elizabeth McAllister, July 12, 1964; children: Wesley Adrian, Andrea Elizabeth. BS in Agrl. Engring., Clemson U., 1962, MS in Agrl. Engring., 1965; PhD, Colo. State U., 1972. Rsch. scientist USDA-Agrl. Rsch. Svc., Tifton, Ga., 1965-69, Fort Collins, Colo., 1969-72, rsch. leader Walkinsville, Ga., 1972-89, lab. dir. Tifton, 1989-98, retired, 1998. Mem. acad. faculty Colo. State U., Ft. Collins, 1969—72; adj. faculty U. Ga., Athens, 1973—, grad. faculty, 1988—2002. Contbr. agrl. rsch. articles to profl. jours. With U.S. Army, 1962-63. Mem. Am. Soc. Agrl. Engrs., Am. Soc. Agronomy, Soil and Water Conservation Soc. Am., Soil Sci. Soc. Am., Sigma Xi, Alpha Epsilon, Gamma Sigma Delta, Phi Kappa Phi. Lutheran. Avocations: reading, gardening, yard care, remodeling home, sports. Personal E-mail: awthomas39@hotmail.com.

THOMAS, ALAN, candy company executive; b. Evansburg, Pa., Jan. 1, 1923; s. William Roberts and Letta (Garrett) T.; m. Marguerite Atria, July 1, 1972; children: Garrett Lee, Michael Alan, Randall Stephen, Brett Eliot. BS, Pa. State U., 1949; MS, U. Minn., 1950, PhD, 1954. Instr. Temple U., Phila., 1950-51, U. Minn., St. Paul, 1951-54; rsch. asst. Bowman Dairy Co., Chgo., 1954-56; rsch. project mgr. M&M Candies divsn. Mars, Inc., Hackettstown, N.J., 1956-60, product devel. mgr., 1961-64, chocolate rsch. dir., 1964; v.p. rsch. & devel. Mars Candies, Chgo., 1964-67, v.p. rsch. & devel. M&M/Mars divsn. Hackettstown, 1967-77, v.p. sci. affairs, 1977-78; gen. mgr. Ethel M, Las Vegas, 1978-83; cons., 1985; sr. cons. Knechtel Rsch. Scis., Inc., Skokie, Ill., 1984; v.p. tech. Ferrara Pan Candy Co., Forest Park, Ill., 1986-92; cons., 1993—. Mem. coun. industry liaison panel Food and Nutrition Bd., Nat. Acad. Scis./NRC, 1968-78, chmn., 1972-73; adv. U.S. del. Codex Alimentarius Com. on Cocoa and Chocolate Products, 1967-78. Served to 1st lt. inf. AUS, 1942-46. Recipient Rsch. award, Nat. Confectioners Assn. U.S., 1971. Mem. Chocolate Mfrs. Assn. (chmn. FDA liaison com. 1975-77, tech. com. 1974-78), Inst. Food Technologists, Am. Assn. Candy Technologists, Gamma Sigma Delta, Phi Kappa Phi. Home: 2005 Sedona Morning Dr Las Vegas NV 89128-8484 Office: Ferrara Pan Candy Co 7301 Harrison St Forest Park IL 60130-2016

THOMAS, ALLEN LLOYD, lawyer, private investor; b. Orange, NJ, Sept. 15, 1939; s. Richard Lloyd and Dorothy (Carr) Thomas; m. Virginia Dehnert, June 24, 1961 (div. 1974); children: Sarah Ann, Anne Marjorie; m. Barbara Singer, Mar. 12, 1978 (div. 2001); 1 child, Allen Lloyd. BA, Wesleyan U., 1961; LLB, Yale U., 1964. Bar: N.Y. 1965, U.S. Ct. Appeals (D.C. cir.) 1981; solicitor, Eng. and Wales, 1996. Ptnr. Paul Weiss Rifkind Wharton & Garrison, N.Y.C., 1973—92; resident ptnr. Hong Kong, 1983-87; dir., gen. counsel Gerard Atkins & Co. Ltd., 1992-94; gen. counsel Gen. Atlantic Group Ltd, 1992-94. Bd. dirs. Penna Cons PLC, Eidos PLC, Moves Ltd., Highway Insurance Holdings, PLC. Chmn. Urban Bus. Assis. Corp., N.Y.C., 1971-82; chmn. Hong Kong Ballet, 1985-87; co-chmn. Internat. Com., N.Y.C. Ballet, 1986-91; pres. Internat. Salzburg Assn. Am., 1987-92; dir., mem. exec. com., gen. counsel Child Care Action Campaign, 1990-92. Mem. River Club (NY), Boodle's, Met. Club of Washington, Hong Kong Club, Hong Kong Jockey Club, Lenox Club, Buck's Club. Home: 3 Chester St London SW1X 7BB England E-mail: allenlloydthomas@hotmail.com.

THOMAS, ANDREW S.W. astronaut; b. Adelaide, S. Australia, Dec. 18, 1951; s. Adrian C. and Mary E. Thomas. B with hon. in Mech. Engring., U. Adelaide, 1973, PhD in Mech. Engring., 1978. Rsch. scientist to divsn. mgr. Lockheed Aero. Sys. Co., Marietta, Ga., 1977—87, mgr. flight sci. divsn., 1987—89; with Jet Propulsion Lab., Pasadena, Calif., 1989—92, NASA, Houston, 1992—93, astronaut, 1993—. Payload comdr. Endeavour Space Shuttle, 1996; bd. engr. 2 Russian Space Sta. Mir, 1998; with space flight STS-102, 2001; dep. chief astronaut office NASA. Mem.: Am. Inst. Aeronautics & Astronautics. Avocations: horseback riding, mountain biking, running, wind surfing, playing classical guitar. Office: Astronaut Office CB NASA Johnson Space Ctr Houston TX 77058

THOMAS, ANN VAN WYNEN, law educator; b. The Netherlands, May 27, 1919; came to U.S., 1921, naturalized, 1926; d. Cornelius and Cora Jacoba (Daansen) Van Wynen; m. A.J. Thomas Jr., Sept. 10, 1948. AB with distinction, U. Rochester, 1940; JD, U. Tex., 1943; post doctoral degree, So. Meth. U., 1952. U.S. fgn. svc. officer, Johannesburg, South Africa, London, The Hague, The Netherlands, 1943-47; rsch. atty. Southwestern Legal Found., Sch. Law So. Meth. U., Dallas, 1952-67; asst. prof. polit. sci. So. Meth. U. Sch. Law, Dallas, 1968-73, assoc. prof., 1973-76, prof., 1976-85, prof. emeritus, 1985—. Author: Communism versus International Law, 1953, (with A.J. Thomas Jr.) International Treaties, 1950, Non-Intervention—The Law and its Import in the Americas, 1956, OAS: The Organization of American States, 1962, International Legal Aspects of Civil War in Spain, 1936-1939, 1967, Legal Limitations on Chemical and Biological Weapons, 1970, The Concept of Aggression, 1972, Presidential War Making Power: Constitutional and International Law Aspects, 1981, An International Rule of Law—Problems and Prospects, 1974. Chmn. time capsule com. Grayson County Commn. on Tex. Sesquicentennial, 1986-88; co-chmn. Grayson County Commn. on Bicentennial U.S. Constn., 1988-93; co-chmn. com. Grayson County Sesquicentennial, 1994-97; co-chmn. Grayson County Commn. on the Millenium, 1997—. Recipient Am. medal Nat. DAR Soc., 1992. Mem. Tex. Bar Assn., Am. Soc. Internat. Law, Grayson County Bar Assn. Home: Spaniel Hall 374 Coffee Cir Pottsboro TX 75076-3164

THOMAS, ANNE MOREAU, former newspaper owner; b. Trenton, N.J., May 23, 1930; d. Daniel Howard and Lillis Dale (Simmonds) Moreau; m. Henry Seely Thomas, Jr., June 14, 1952 (dec. Aug. 1994); children: Catherine, John Martin II, Howard Moreau. BA, Middlebury Coll., 1951; DHL, Rutgers U., 1999; AA (hon.), Raritan Valley C.C. Tchr. North Hunterdon H.S., Annandale, N.J., 1951-52, Hunterdon Adult Sch., Flemington, N.J., 1953-70; home and food editor Hunterdon County Democrat, Flemington, 1954-99, owner, bd. sec., 1985-94, owner, chmn. bd., 1994—2001. Trustee Rutgers U., New Brunswick, N.J., 1985—, bd. govs., 1991—, chmn. bd. govs., 1995-98; mem. N.J. Commn. Higher Edn., Trenton, 1995-98; trustee Hunterdon Healthcare Sys. Recipient N.J. Food Communicator of Yr. award N.J. Dept. Agr., 1981, Golden award for cmty. svc. Hunterdon County C. of C., 1990, Eagle Leadership award Ctr./Urban cmty. Leadership, 1996, Hunterdon Disting. Citizen award Ctrl. N.J. Coun. Boy Scouts Am., 1999-2000; named Woman of Yr., Hunterdon County YMCA, 1997. Mem. N.J. Press Assn. (bd. dirs. 1977-85, pres. 1984, chmn. 1985), DAR, Copper Hill Country Club, N.J. Mus. Agr. (trustee). Republican. Presbyterian. Avocations: restoration of circa 1750 cape cod family homestead, gardening, cooking. Home: 38 Pennsylvania Ave Flemington NJ 08822-1222

THOMAS, ARCHIBALD JOHNS, III, lawyer; b. Jacksonville, Fla., Apr. 27, 1952; s. Archibald Johns and Jean (Snodgrass) T.; m. Martha Ann Marconi, Sept. 1, 1973. BA, U. So. Fla., 1973; JD, Stetson U., 1977. Bar: Fla. 1977, U.S. Dist. Ct. (mid. dist.) Fla. 1977, U.S. Ct. Appeals (11th cir.) 1981, U.S. Supreme Ct. 1981, U.S. Claims Ct. 1990; cert. labor and employment law, Fla. Law clk. to U.S. magistrate U.S. Dist. Ct., Tampa, Fla., 1977-78; 1st asst. fed. pub. defender U.S. dist. Ct., Jacksonville, 1978-84; sr. ptnr. Thomas & Skinner, P.A., Jacksonville, 1984-89; pvt. practice Jacksonville, 1990—. Faculty mem. Stetson U. Coll. Law, 1999—; mem. labor and employment law cert. com. Fla. Bar, 2002—. Mem.: NACDL, ATLA (employment rights sect.), Jacksonville Bar Assn., Fla. Nat. Employment Lawyers Assn. (pres. 2002), Nat. Employment Lawyers Assn. (co-chmn. Fla. chpt. 1992), Fed. Bar Assn., Fla. Bar Assn. (co-chmn. individual rights com. 2001). Democrat. Avocation: sailing. Home: 708 Mccollum Cir Neptune Beach FL 32266-3789 Office: Riverplace Tower Ste 1640 Jacksonville FL 32207 Office Phone: 904-396-2322. E-mail: archibald@job-rights.com.

THOMAS, BERTRAM DAVID, retired chemical engineer; b. Renton, Wash., May 5, 1903; s. David and Minnie Belle (Custer) T.; m. Dorothy Glorian Butler, Dec. 21, 1928 (dec. 1986); children: Preston David, Nancy Glorian, Lawrence Eldon. BS, U. Wash., 1929, PhD in Chemistry, 1933. Registered profl. engr., Ohio. Rsch. engr. Battelle Meml. Inst., Columbus, Ohio, 1934-40, asst. dir., 1940-56, pres., 1956-68; ret. Mem. adv. com. on environment, Santa Barbara, Calif., 1970-73. Patentee ore dressing and coal preparation methods; contbr. articles to sci. publs. Trustee Columbus Mus. Art, 1962-67, Ohio State U., Columbus, 1965-68, Santa Barbara Mus. Art, 1973—; trustee, pres. Santa Barbara Botanic Garden, 1974-82. Recipient Order Civil Merit 1st Class, Republic of Korea, 1965; DEng. (hon.), Mich. Coll. Mining and Tech., 1957; DSci (hon.) Ohio State U., 1963, Otterbein Coll., Westerville, Ohio, 1965, Cleve. State U., 1968. Fellow AAAS; mem. Chemists Club N.Y., Am. Che. Soc., Sigma Xi. Home: 300 Hot Springs Rd Apt 312 Santa Barbara CA 93108-2043

THOMAS, BETTY, director, actress; b. St. Louis, July 24, 1948; BFA, Ohio U. Former sch. tchr.; co-star Hill St. Blues, from 1981. Joined Second City Workshop, Chgo.; appeared on Second City TV, 1984; appeared in after sch. spl. The Gift of Love, 1985, Prison of Children, 1986. Appeared in The Fun Factory game show, 1976; (TV film) Outside Chance, 1978, Nashville Grab, 1981, When Your Lover Leaves, 1983, The Late Shift, 1996 (Dirs. Guild Am. dramatic spl. award 1996); star TV series Hill Street Blues, 1981-87 (Emmy nominations 1981, 82, 83), (Emmy award, 1985); dir.: (TV) Dream On: "For Peter's Sake" (Emmy award, Outstanding Individual Achievement in Directing in a Comedy Series, 1993), 1993, Male Pattern Baldness, 1998; (films) Troop Beverly Hills, 1989, The Brady Bunch Movie, 1995, Private Parts, 1997, Doctor Dolittle, 1998, 28 Days, 1999, I Spy, 2002; prodr.: Can't Hardly Wait, 1998. Recipient Women in Film Crystal award, 2001.*

THOMAS, BEVERLY IRENE, special education educator, educational diagnostician, substance abuse counselor; b. Del Rio, Tex., Nov. 12, 1939; d. Clyde and Eve Whistler; m. James Thomas, Jan. 28, 1972; children: Kenneth (dec.), Wade, Robert, Darcy, Betty Kay, James III, Debra, Brenda, Michael. BM summa cum laude, Sul Ross State U., 1972, MEd, 1976, MEd in Counseling, 1992, MEd in Mid. Mgmt., 1996. Cert. music, elem. edn., music edn., learning disabilities, spl. edn. generic, ednl. diagnosis, ednl. counseling, spl. edn. counseling and mid. mgmt. Tchr. Pecos-Barstow-Toyah Ind. Sch. Dist., 1974—92, 1999—2000; edn. diagnostician West Tex. State Sch., Tex. Youth Commn., ret., 1999; tchr. spl. edn. and enhanced 5th grade Pecos-Barstow-Toyah Ind. Sch. Dist., 1999-2000; youth counselor Tex. Workforce Ctr., Pecos, 2000; substance abuse counselor Reeves County Detention Ctr., 2001—. Gifted-talented coordinator 5th grade, Pecos-Barstow-Toyah Ind. Sch. Dist., 1999-2000. Mem. AAUW, ASCD, NEA, MENSA, Assn. for Children with Learning Disabilities (local sec. 1974), Tex. State Tchrs. Assn. (treas. 1991-94), Tex. Ednl. Diagnosticians Assn., Tex. Profl. Ednl. Diagnosticians, Reeves County Assn. of Children with Learning Disabilities, Nat. Coun. Tchrs. of Maths., Nat. Coun. Tchrs. English, Learning Disabilities Assn., Nat. Coun. for Geog. Edn., Learning Disabilities Assoc., Tex., Coun. for Exceptional Children, Tex. Counseling Assn., Am. Correctional Assn., Alpha Chi, Kappa Delta Pi, Chi Sigma Iota.

THOMAS, BROOKS, publishing company executive; b. Phila., Nov. 28, 1931; s. Walter Horstman and Ruth Sterling (Boomer) T.; m. Galen Pinckard Clark, Apr. 15, 1969 (div. 1973). BA, Yale U., 1953, LLB, 1956; grad. Advanced Mgmt. Program, Harvard U., 1973. Bar: Pa. 1957, N.Y. 1960. With law firm Winthrop, Stimson, Putnam & Roberts, N.Y.C., 1960—68; sec., gen. counsel Harper & Row, Pubs., Inc., N.Y.C., 1968—69, v.p., gen. counsel, 1969—73, exec. v.p., 1973—79, CEO, 1977—81, pres., 1979—87, CEO, 1981—87, chmn. bd., 1986—87. Chmn. bd. Harper & Row, Ltd., London, 1973-87; dir. Harper & Row, Pty. Ltd., Australia, Harla S.A. de C.V., Mex., Harper & Row Pubs. Asia, Pte. Ltd., Singapore. Pres., bd. dirs. Butterfield House, 1968-72, 90-93; trustee, dir. RADG, Inc., 1987-89; dir. Thompson Island Outward Bound Edn. Ctr., 1987-95, Colo. Outward Bound Sch., 1990-96, bd. govs., 1996—; bd. dirs. Young Audiences, Inc., 1977—, chmn., 1985—; trustee Outward Bound USA, 1980—, vice chmn., 1983-84, chmn., 1984-87; chmn. Nat. Book Awards, 1984-85, dir., 1985-87; mem. devel. bd. Yale U., 1985-89; adv. bd. Yale Sch. Orgn. and Mgmt., 1987-96; chmn. Vail Valley Inst., 1989—; dir. Outward Bound Internat., 1997-2003, dir. Outward Bound Expeditionary Learning, 2000—; trustee Episcopal Acad., 2000—, sec., 2002—. Lt. (j.g.) USNR, 1956-59. Mem. Am. Bar Assn., Assn. Bar City of N.Y., Assn. Am. Pubs. (bd. dirs. 1980-85, chmn. 1983-85), Council Fgn. Relations, Yale U. Alumni Assn. (law sch. rep. 1980-83) Clubs: Merion Cricket (Phila.); Century (N.Y.C.), Yale (N.Y.C.), University (N.Y.C.), N.Y. Yacht (N.Y.C.); Essex Yacht (Conn.). Home: 5 Tudor City Pl New York NY 10017-6853 also: 141 Saybrook Rd Essex CT 06426-1412 also: 63 Willow Pl Vail CO 81657-5304

THOMAS, BRUCE LARRY, counselor; b. Longview, Tex., Apr. 6, 1949; s. Darnell D. Thomas and Myrtle Elizabeth Williams; m. Martha Cruz DeAmores, July 29, 1995; children: Mark Shawn, Stephanie Elizabeth. BS, Ariz. State U., 1975, M Counseling, 1988. Chmn. counseling dept. Glendale (Ariz.) C.C., 1997—2000, counselor, mem. faculty, 2000—; faculty assoc. Ariz. State U. West, Phoenix, 1998—2003. Pvt. practice Bell & Thomas Counseling Svcs., Phoenix, 1995—97; cons. Tempe Elem. Sch. Dist., 1995—96, Sports Assist, Scottsdale, Ariz., 1997—98, Omega Charter Schs., Phoenix, 2001—03. Mem. Ariz. State Selective Svc. Bd., Phoenix, 2002—03; mem. sch. bd. St. Caterine Elem. Sch., Phoenix, 1995—96. Finalist Innovation of the Yr., Maricopa County C.C. Dist., 1999; named Mentor of the Yr., Spl. Friends Project, 1992. Mem.: Ariz. Coalition Against Domestic Violence (assoc.), Nat. Coun. on Black Am. Affairs, Assn. Cmty. Colleges (assoc.). Methodist. Avocations: travel, public speaking, tennis, community service. Office: Glendale CC 6000 W Olive Ave Glendale AZ Office Phone: 623-845-3061. E-mail: bruce.thomas@gcmail.maricopa.edu.

THOMAS, CAROL F. educational association administrator; MA in Ednl. Psychology, San Francisco State U.; PhD in Edn., U. Calif., Berkeley. Sr. program dir. S.W. Regional Lab., Los Alamitos, Calif., 1989—95; assoc. exec. dir. N.W. Regional Edn. Lab., Portland, Oreg., 1995—2001, CEO, 2001—. Office: NW Regional Ednl Lab Ste 500 101 SW Main St Portland OR 97204

THOMAS, CAROL LOUISE JOSEPH, community planning company executive; b. Poughkeepsie, N.Y., Aug. 29, 1923; d. Harold Kritzman and Charlotte Carolyn (Freiberg) Joseph; m. Charles Raymond Thomas, Mar. 21, 1943; children: Charles Joseph, Katharine Louise Thomas Noer. Student, Vassar Coll., 1941-43, Boston U., 1943, 49; AB cum laude, Syracuse U., 1948; MA, U. Conn., 1950; postgrad., MIT, 1950. Dir. Thomas Assocs. divsn. Universal Engring. Corp., Boston, 1969-78; pres. Thomas Planning Svcs., Inc., 1978—, TPS/China, Inc., 1995—. Mem. faculty U. R.I. Grad. Curriculum in Cmty. Planning and Area Devel., 1964-98; guest lectr. various colls., 1987-97, Harvard U., 1975-85; cons., author articles land use planning. Mem. parish com., 1958-60, mem. standing com. 1st and 2d ch. Unitarian Ch., 1958-60, 99-2002, chmn. 2001-02. Named Hon. Citizen of Guangzhou, China. Fellow Am. Inst. Cert. Planners (chmn. 1984-86, pres. New Eng. chpt. 1965-67); mem. Am. Planning Assn. (pres. chpt. 1979-82, pres. pvt. practice divsn. 1988-92), Mass. Assn. Planning Dirs., Mass. Fedn. Planning Bds., Mass. Cons. Planners (vice chmn. 1984-88). Home: 151 Tremont St Apt 23P Boston MA 02111-1121 Office: 60 Temple Pl Boston MA 02111

THOMAS, CHARLES ALLEN, JR., molecular biologist, educator; b. Dayton, Ohio, July 7, 1927; s. Charles Allen and Margaret Stoddard (Talbott) T.; m. Margaret M. Gay, July 7, 1951; children: Linda Carrick, Stephen Gay. AB, Princeton (N.J.) U., 1950; PhD, Harvard U., 1954. Rsch. scientist Eli Lilly Co., Indpls., 1954-55; NCR fellow U. Mich., Ann Arbor, 1955-57; prof. biophysics Johns Hopkins U., Balt., 1957-67; prof. biol. chemistry Med. Sch. Harvard U., Boston, 1967-78; chmn. dept. cellular biology Scripps Clinic & Rsch. Found., La Jolla, Calif., 1978-81; pres., dir. Helicon Found., San Diego, 1981—; founder, CEO The Syntro Corp., San Diego, 1981-82; founder, CEO, now dir. of R & D Pantox Corp., San Diego, 1989—. Mem. genetics study sect. NIH, 1968-72; mem. rsch. grants com. Am. Cancer Soc., 1972-76, 79-85. Mem. editl. bd. Virology, 1967-73, Jour. Molecular Biology, 1968-72, Bio-Physics Jour., 1965-68, Chromosoma, 1969-79, Analytic Biochemistry, 1970-79, Biochim Biophys. ACTA, 1973-79, Plasmid, 1977—. With USNR, 1945-46. NRC fellow, 1965-66. Mem. AAAS, Am. Acad. Arts and Scis., Am. Fedn. Biol. Chemists, Genetics Soc. Am., Am. Chem. Soc. Achievements include research in genetic and structural organization of chromosomes and development of a practical assessment of independent antioxidant defense system by analytical biochemistry. Home: 1640 El Paso Real La Jolla CA 92037-6304 E-mail: cathomas@pantox.com.

THOMAS, CHARLES CARROLL, retired investment management executive; b. Feb. 15, 1930; s. Charles Carroll and Miriam (Smith) T.; m. Carolyn Rose Hirchert, June 16, 1951; children: Charles Carroll, Anne Hatheway, Megan Lloyd. Grad., Deerfield Acad., 1947; BA, Yale U., 1951. Divsn. retail programs mgr. Mobil Oil Corp., Boston, 1953-63; exec. v.p. Lionel D. Edie & Co., N.Y.C., 1963-72, Bank New Eng., Boston, 1972-76; v.p., dir. mktg. Loomis, Sayles & Co., Boston, 1976-85; pres. Concord Mgmt. Co., 1985-99; ret., 1999. Co-pub. Cons. Compendium Inc., 1985-95. Trustee Deerfield Acad., 1975-78, Babson Coll., 1976-82, 83-89; Cambridge Sch. of Weston, Mass., 1976-82, New Eng. Home for Little Wanderers, 1983-86, Maine Coll. of Art, 1993—, chair, 1999-2001. With USAF, 1951-53. Mem. Assn. of Investment Mgmt. Sales Execs. (pres. 1980-81, dir. 1980-84), Air Force Assn., Yale Club N.Y.C., Downtown Club Boston, Cumberland Club Portland. Republican. Home: 24 Hillside Ave Cumberland Center ME 04021-9333

THOMAS, CHARLES COLUMBUS, dance educator, artist; b. McAlester, Okla., Sept. 10, 1940; s. Claude Morris Thomas and Wilhelmina Rebecca Threat. BA in Music, Langston (Okla.) Coll., 1962; MFA in Speech, Theater, Bklyn. Coll., 1973; PhD in Equivalency, City U., 1980. Chmn. music Ben Franklin Jr. High, San Francisco, 1963-65; chmn. music and dance Lefferts Jr. High, Bklyn., 1965-70; asst. prof. Richmond Coll., S.I., N.Y., 1970-96, dir. african am. studies, 1972-73; assoc. prof., chmn. dance Coll. Staten Island, N.Y., 1997—. Adj. asst. prof. N.Y. Tech. Coll., Bklyn., 1971—74; vis. prof. U. Ghana, 1972; cons. Sandy Ground Hist. Soc., S.I., NY, 1985—, Nuyorican Poets Cafe, N.Y.C., 1990—, N.Y. Housing Authority, S.I., 1999; vocalist-in-residence M. Eliot's Jazz Parlor, N.Y.C., 2001. Designer in field; actor: (Operas) Gethsemane Park, 2001. Adv. Richmond Historical Soc., S.I., 1994—; com. mem. Grammy Awards in the Schs., N.Y.C., 1995; lectr., performer Mayor's Counc. Youth & Physical Fitness, N.Y.C., 1969-73; mem. Urban League, S.I., 1998. Recipient Pres. citation, Nat. Assn. Equal Opportunity Higher Edn., Washington, 1995, Xi Phi Achievement award, Columbia U., 2000. Mem.: SAG, NATAS, NARAS, Omega Psi Phi (Man of Yr. 1982). Avocations: collecting african artifacts, dance, memorabilia. Home: 1245 Park Ave New York NY 10128-1735 Office: College of Staten Island CUNY 2800 Victory Blvd Staten Island NY 10314-6600

THOMAS, CHERRYL T. former federal agency administrator; b. Oct. 31, 1946; BS Biology & Chem., Marquette U.; MS Physiology, U. Illinois, Chicago. Dir., mgmt. services Dept. Aviation, 1983—89; dir., personnel policy & utilization Dept. Water, 1989—92; deputy chief of staff Mayor Richard M. Daley City of Chgo., 1992—94, commr. Dept. Bldgs., 1994-98, chmn. U.S. Railroad Retirement Bd., 1998—2003. Mem., bd. trustees U. Chgo., 2000—. Home: 5020 S Lake Shore Dr Apt 2716N Chicago IL 60615-3220

THOMAS, CHRISTOPHER YANCEY, III, surgeon, educator; b. Kansas City, Mo., Oct. 27, 1923; s. Christopher Yancey and Dorothea Louise (Engel) T.; m. Barbara Ann Barcroft, June 27, 1946; children— Christopher, Gregg, Jeffrey, Anne Student, U. Colo., 1942-44; MD, U. Kans., 1948. Diplomate Am. Bd. Surgery. Intern U. Utah Hosp., Salt Lake City, 1948-49; resident in surgery Cleve. Clinic Found., 1949-52; pvt. practice specializing in surgery Kansas City, Mo., 1954-89. Mem. staff St. Luke's Hosp., chief surgery, 1969-70; mem. staff Children's Mercy Hosp.; clin. prof. surgery U. Mo., Kansas City Med. Sch.; pres. St. Luke's Hosp. Edn. Found., 1977-83, Med. Plaza Corp., 1977-79; pres. Midwest Organ Bank, 1977-82. Editor IMTRAC investment adv. letter, 1978-2000. Served to capt. M.C., U.S. Army, 1952-54 Fellow ACS; mem. AMA, Southwestern Surg. Congress, Central Surg. Assn., Mo. State

Med. Soc., Kansas City Surg. Soc. (pres. 1968), Jackson County Med. Soc. (pres. 1971) Clubs: Kansas City Country. Republican. Methodist. Home: 50 Coventry Ct Shawnee Mission KS 66208-5225 Personal E-mail: christhomas5452@sbcglobal.net.

THOMAS, CLARA MCCANDLESS, retired English language educator, biographer; b. Strathroy, Ont., Can., May 22, 1919; d. Basil and Mabel (Sullivan) McCandless; m. Morley Keith Thomas, May 23, 1942; children: Stephen, John. BA, U. Western Ont., London, 1941, MA, 1944; PhD, U. Toronto, 1962; DLitt (hon.), York U., 1986, Trent U., 1991; LLD (hon.), Brock U., 1992. Instr. English U. Western Ont., London, 1947-61, U. Toronto, 1958-61; asst. prof. English York U., Toronto, 1961-68, prof., 1969-84, prof. emeritus, Librs. Can. Studies Rsch. fellow, 1984—; acad. adv. panel Social Scis. and Humanities Research Council, 1981-84; mem. Killam Awards Selection Bd., 1978-81; rsch. fellow York U. Librs. Can. Studies, 1984—. Author biography of Anna Jameson, 1967, of Egerton Ryerson, 1969, of Margaret Laurence, 1969, 75, (with John Lennox) of William Arthur Deacon, 1982; Literary criticism (Can.), 1946, 72, 94, Memoir, 1999; mem. editl. bd. Literary History of Can., 1980—, Collected Works of Northrop Frye, 1993-. Recipient Internat. Coun. of Can. Studies prize No. Telecom, 1989; grantee Can. Coun., 1967, 73, Social Sci. and Humanities Rsch. Coun. Can., 1978-80 Fellow Royal Soc. Can.; mem. Assn. Can. Univs., Tchrs. English (pres. 1971-72), Assn. Can. and Que. Lit., Bus. and Profl. Women's Club, Assn. for Can. Studies. New Democratic. Office: York U 305 Scott Libr 4700 Keele St North York ON Canada M3J 1P3

THOMAS, CLARENCE, United States supreme court justice; b. Savannah, Ga., June 23, 1948; BA, Holy Cross Coll., 1971; JD, Yale U., 1974. Bar: Mo. Asst. atty. gen. State of Mo., Jefferson City, 1974—77; atty. Monsanto Co., St. Louis, 1977—79; legis. asst. to Sen. John C. Danforth, Washington, 1979—81; asst. sec. for civil rights Dept. Edn., Washington, 1981—82; chmn. U.S. EEOC, Washington, 1982—90; judge U.S. Ct. Appeals, Washington, 1990—91; assoc. justice U.S. Supreme Ct., Washington, 1991—. Office: US Supreme Court Supreme Ct Bldg 1 First St NE Washington DC 20543-0001

THOMAS, CLAUDEWELL SIDNEY, psychiatry educator; b. N.Y.C., Oct. 5, 1932; s. Humphrey Sidney and Frances Elizabeth (Collins) T.; m. Carolyn Pauline Rozansky, Sept. 6, 1958; children: Jeffrey Evan, Julie-Anne Elizabeth, Jessica Edith. BA, Columbia U., 1952; MD, SUNY, Downstate Med. Ctr., 1956; MPH, Yale U., 1964. Diplomate Nat. Bd. Med. Examiners, Am. Bd. Psychiatry, Am. Bd. Forensic Medicine, Am. Bd. Psychol. Specialties. From instr. to assoc. prof. Yale U., New Haven, 1963-68, dir. Yale tng. program in social community psychiatry, 1967-70; dir. div. mental health service programs NIMH, Washington, 1970-73; chmn. dept. psychiatry U.M.D.N.J., Newark, 1973-83; prof. dept. psychiatry Drew Med. Sch., 1983—, chmn. dept. psychiatry, 1983-93; prof. dept. psychiatry UCLA, 1983-94, vice chmn. dept. psychiatry, 1983-93, prof. emeritus dept. psychiatry, 1994—; med. dir. Tokanui Hosp., TeAwamutu, N.Z., 1996. Cons. A.K. Rice Inst., Washington, 1978—80, SAMSA/PHS Cons., 1991—99, L.A. County Homeless Outreach Program, 2001—04; mem. LA County Superior Ct. Psychol. Panel, 1991—97; cons. psychiatrist L.A. County AB2034 Homeless Outreach Program (Skid Row Dual Diagnoses), 2001—04. Author: (with B. Bergen) Issues and Problems in Social Psychiatry, 1966; editor (with R. Bryce LaPorte) Alienation in Contemporary Society, 1976, (with J. Lindenthal) Psychiatry and Mental Health Science Handbook; mem. editl. bd. Internat. Jour. Mental Health, Adminstrn. In Mental Health. Bd. dirs. Bay Area Found., 1987—. Served to capt. USAF, 1959-61. Fellow APHA, Am. Psychoanalytic Assn. (hon.), Am. Psychiat. Assn. (disting. life), Royal Soc. Health, N.Y. Acad. Sci., N.Y. Acad. Medicine; mem. Am. Sociol. Assn., Am. Coll. Mental Health Adminstrs., Am. Coll. Forensic Examiners, Am. Coll. Psychiatrists, Sigma Xi. Avocations: tennis, racquetball, violin, piano. Office: 30676 Palos Verdes Dr E Palos Verdes Peninsula CA 90275-6354 also: 500 Pacific Coast Hwy Ste 208 Seal Beach CA 90740 Business E-Mail: cysid32@ucla.edu. *Personal philosophy: Integrity sooner or later calls upon courage. If courage is not home integrity goes away.*

THOMAS, CLAUDIA LYNN, orthopedic surgeon; b. N.Y.C., Feb. 28, 1950; d. Charles Mitchell and Daisy Mae T; m. Maxwell Delaine Carty, Aug. 24, 1985. BA, Vassar Coll., 1971; MD, Johns Hopkins U., 1975. Diplomate Am. Bd. Orthopedic Surgery. Intern Yale-New Haven Hosp., 1975-76, resident in surgery, 1976-77, resident in orthopaedic surgery, 1977-80; orthopaedic trauma fellow Md. Inst. Emergency Med. Services Systems, Balt., 1980; asst. prof. orthopaedic surgery Johns Hopkins Hosp., 1981-85, Balt. City Hosp., 1981-85; mem. staff Children's Hosp., Provident Hosp. (both Balt.). Mem. AMA, Eastern Orthopaedic Assn., Yale Orthopaedic Assn., Newington Alumni Assn., Nat. Med. Assn., Monumental Med. Assn. (v.p. 1983-85), Johns Hopkins Minority Faculty Assn. (pres. 1983-85). Author: (with A.A. White, M.M. Panjabi) Clinical Biomechanics of the Spine, 1978; (with P. Leppert, E. Siff, C. Thomas) Being a Woman: Your Body and Birth Control, 1979. First black female orthopedic surgeon; contbr. articles to profl. jours. Democrat. Office: Orthopaedic Surgery Johns Hopkins Sch Med 601 North Caroline St Baltimore MD 21287-0765

THOMAS, COLIN GORDON, JR., surgeon, medical educator; b. Iowa City, July 25, 1918; s. Colin Gordon and Eloise Kinzer (Brainerd) T.; m. Shirley Forbes, Sept. 14, 1946; children: Karen, Barbara, James G., John F. BS, U. Chgo., 1940, MD, 1943. Diplomate Am. Bd. Surgery. Intern U. Iowa Hosp., 1943-44, resident surgery, 1944-45, 47-50; assoc. in surgery U. Iowa Med. Sch., 1950-51, asst. prof., 1951-52; mem. faculty U. N.C. Med. Sch., Chapel Hill, 1952—, prof. surgery, 1961—, Byah Thomason Doxey-Sanford Doxey prof. surgery, 1982—, chmn. dept., 1966-84, chief div. gen. surg., 1984-89, part-time prof., 1991—. Contbr. surg. texts, numerous articles to med. jours. Served to capt., M.C. AUS, 1945-47. Recipient Prof. award U. N.C. Sch. Medicine, 1964, Disting. Svc. award U. Chgo., 1982, Med. Alumni Disting. faculty award U. N.C., 1984; Berryhill lectr. U. N.C., 1989; recipient Fleming Fuller award U. N.C. Hosps., 1994. Mem. AMA, ACS (Disting. Leadership award N.C. chpt. 1990), AAUP, Am. Thyroid Assn., Am. Assn. Cancer Research, Am. Assn. Endocrine Surgeons (pres. 1989-90), Soc. Univ. Surgeons, So. Surg. Assn. (v.p. 1989-90), N.Y. Acad. Scis., Halsted Soc., Ga. Surg. Soc., Soc. Exptl. Biology and Medicine, Am. Surg. Assn., Womack Surg. Soc. (pres. 1981-83), Soc. Internationale de Chirurgie, Soc. Surgery Alimentary Tract, N.C. Surg. Assn., Internat. Assn. Endocrine Surgeons, Kiwanis (pres.-elect Tarheel Golden Kiwanis 2003), Alpha Omega Alpha. Episcopalian (warden 1961-62). Home: 408 Morgan Creek Rd Chapel Hill NC 27517-4934 Office Phone: 919-843-8230. E-mail: cqt@med.unc.edu.

THOMAS, CRAIG, senator; m. Susan Roberts; children: Peter, Paul, Patrick, Alexis. BS, U. Wyo., 1955; LLB, La Salle U., 1963. V.p. Wyo. Farm Bur., Laramie, 1959-66; with Am. Farm Bur., 1966-75; gen. mgr. Wyo. Rural Elec. Assn., 1975-89; mem. Wyo. Ho. of Reps., 1985—88; rep. from Wyo. U.S. Ho. of Reps., Washington, 1989—95; senator from Wyo. U.S. Senate, Washington, 1995—. Mem. energy and natural resources com., environment and pub. works com., fin. com., Indian affairs com. Former chmn. Natrona County (Wyo.) Rep. Com.; state rep. Natrona County Dist.; del. Rep. Nat. Conv., 1980. Capt. USMC. Mem. Am. Soc. Trade Execs., Masons. Republican. Methodist. Office: US Senate 307 Dirksen Senate Office Bldg Washington DC 20510-0001

THOMAS, DANIEL FOLEY, retired financial services company executive; b. Washington, Aug. 24, 1950; s. Richard Kenneth and Margaret (Foley) T.; m. Barbara Jane Clark, June 30, 1973; 1 child, Alison Clark. BS in Acctg., Mt. St. Mary's Coll., 1972. CPA, Va. Auditor Deloitte & Touche, Washington, 1972-74; various fin. positions Comm. Satellite Corp., Washington, 1974-78, asst. treas., 1984-85, treas., 1986-87, contr., 1987-89, Comsat Telesystems, Washington, 1978-79; mgr. acctg. and taxes Satellite Bus. Systems, McLean, Va., 1979-81, treas., 1981-84; v.p. fin. Comsat Tech. Products, Inc., Washington, 1985-86, Comsat Video Enterprises, Inc., Washington, 1989-90; exec. v.p. Leasetec Corp., Boulder, Colo., 1990—2002; ret., 2002. Active cmty. svc. activities. Mem. AICPA, Va. Jaycees (life), Great Falls Jaycees (pres. 1978). Roman Catholic. Avocations: running, golf. Home: 1299 S Teal Ct Boulder CO 80303-1480 Office Phone: 303-473-9611. E-mail: dfthomas@aol.com.

THOMAS, DANIEL J. health services executive; BS, U. No. Iowa. Cert. public acct. Various positions Med. Care Internat., Inc.; exec. v.p. and COO OccuSystems, 1993—96, dir., pres. and COO, 1997, exec. v.p. and pres. practice mgmt. svcs., 1997—98; pres. and COO Concentra, 1998, CEO and dir., 1998—. Office: Concentra 3200 Highland Ave Downers Grove IL 60515

THOMAS, DAVID LLEWELLYN, physician; b. Clinton, Iowa, June 11, 1948; s. Marvin Llewellyn and Marjorie Emma (Mayer) Thomas; m. Sheryl L. Miller, 2002; children: Tana, Paige, Drew, Aleksandr. BA in Zoology, U. Iowa, 1970, MD, 1974. Diplomate Am. Bd. Family Practice, Am. Bd. Geriatric Medicine. Resident in family medicine U. Ill., Rockford, 1977; pvt. practice Marshalltown, Iowa, 1977—; family physician McFarland Clinic, PC, Marshalltown, 1994—, also bd. dirs., v.p., 1995-98, treas., 1999—. Clin. lectr. U. Iowa Coll. Medicine, Iowa City, 1981—. Bd. dirs. Iowa Found. Med. Care, Des Moines, 1986—2001, Iowa Ctrl. Agrl. Safety and Health, 1995—97; trustee Marshalltown Med. and Surg. Ctr., 1998—2003. Mem.: Am. Health Quality Assn. (bd. dirs. 1995, v.p. 1997—2000, pres. 2000—03). Republican. Episcopalian. Office: McFarland Clinic 303 Nicholas Dr Ste 1 Marshalltown IA 50158-4443 Office Phone: 641-752-0099. E-mail: dthomas@mcfarlandclinic.com.

THOMAS, DAVID LLOYD, accountant, consultant; b. Atlanta, May 10, 1942; s. Elbert and Evelyn Thomas; m. Mary Jo Ann Matney, June 25, 1966; children: Christine, Michael. BSBA, U. N.C., 1964. CPA, N.C. Auditor Price Waterhouse, N.Y.C., 1964, Atlanta, 1969-70; divsn. contr. Dart Industries, Atlanta, 1971; contr. Ithaca Industries, Inc., Wilkesboro, N.C., 1971-82, sec.-treas., 1982-91, CFO, bd. dirs., 1983-91; prin. David L. Thomas, CPA, 1991—. CFO Wilkes Regional Med. Ctr., 1993-2000, v.p., 1996-2000; sec. N.W. Health Care, 1994-95. Bd. dirs., mem. Wilkes Art Gallery, 1985-91; bd. dirs. Wilkes Edn. Found., 1988-91, N.C. Citizens for Bus. and Industry, 1989-92, John A. Walker Cmty. Ctr., 1996-02, mem. exec. com., 1999-02, v.p., 2000-01, pres., 2001-02; mem. adv. bd. Wilkes C.C., 1989-97, vice chair, 1994-96, chmn., 1996-97, mem. vision 2010 cultural and quality of life com., 2001; mem. maj. firms calling com. Wilkes United Way, 1994-02. Capt. MSC, U.S. Army, 1965-68. Fellow: N.C. Assn. CPAs (sec. Catawba Valley chpt. 1982—83); mem.: AICPA, Healthcare Fin. Mgrs. Assn., Inst. Mgmt. Accts., U. N.C. Alumni Assn. (reunion vice chmn. 2004), Wilkes C. of C. (bd. dirs. 1979—81, v.p. 1982, trustee found. 1983—90, v.p. 1986, bd. dirs. 1990—92, v.p. 1991), Kiwanis (co-chmn. interclub visitation com. 2003—, dir. 2004—, treas. 2004—). Republican. Methodist. Home and Office: 172 Walnut Pl Wilkesboro NC 28697-8775

THOMAS, DAVID P. telecommunications industry executive; B in History and Edn., CCNY; MBA, U. Mo. Regional dir. human resources Am. Express; v.p. human resources Citibank; from dir. nat. staffing long distance divsn. to asst. v.p. corp. rels. Sprint Corp., Overland Park, Kans., 1989—2003, v.p., chief diversity officer, 2003—. Bd. dirs. Ctr. for Corp. Citizenship. Past chmn. Kans. Workforce Investment Partnership Coun.; past chmn. drugs don't work program Greater Kansas City C. of C.; past. chmn. Kansas City Consensus Promise Project, Kansas City, bd. dirs. Kansas City Area Devel. Coun., Mo. Repertory Theatre, Urban League Greater Kansas City. Recipient Up and Comers award, 1994, Black Achievers in Industry award, 1994, Disting. Leadership award, Nat. Assn. for Cmty. Leadership, 1998, Kansas City Tomorrow Disting. Alum award, 1998, Henry and Marion Bloch Cmty. Svc. award, 2000, Pres. award, Southern Christian Leadership Conf., 2000. Office: Sprint Corp 6200 Sprint Pkwy Overland Park KS 66251

THOMAS, DAVID SNOW, plastic surgeon; b. Chgo., Feb. 7, 1951; s. Allan Perry and Verna Bea (Snow) T.; m. Becky Williams Thomas, Aug. 25, 1973; children: Nathan David, Abigail, Elizabeth. BA, U. Utah, 1974, MD, 1978. Diplomate Am. Bd. Plastic Surgery, Am. Bd. Surgery. Resident surgery UCLA, 1978-83, resident plastic surgery, 1983-85, fellow craniofacial surgery, 1985; pvt. practice Salt Lake City, 1986—; chief plastic surgery Primary Childrens Med. Ctr., Salt Lake City, 1988-90, LDS Hosp., 1993-99. Clin. asst. prof. U. Utah Plastic Surgeons, Salt Lake City, 1986-89, assoc. prof. surgery, 1990-93, clin. assoc. prof., 1993—. Bd. Dirs. AMICUS, Salt Lake City, Utah, 1990-92. Fellow ACS; mem. Am. Soc. Plastic and Reconstructive Surgery, Am. Soc. Maxillofacial Surgery, Am. Cleft Palate Craniofacial Assn., Am. Soc. Aesthetic Plastic Surgery, Interplast (pres. Salt Lake City, 1992—, bd. dirs. Palo Alto, Calif., 1992—), The Country Club (Salt Lake City), Alta Club (sec.). Office: 370 9th Ave Ste 200 Salt Lake City UT 84103-3185 Office Phone: 801-355-0731. Business E-Mail: dst@davidsthomasmd.com.

THOMAS, DEBI (DEBRA J. THOMAS), ice skater; b. Poughkeepsie, N.Y., Mar. 25, 1967; d. McKinley and Janice Thomas; m. Christopher Bequette, Nov. 1996; children: Christopher Jules II, Luc. BS, Stanford U.; MD, Northwestern U., 1997. Competitive figure skater, 1976-88. Winner U.S. Figure Skating Championship, 1986, 88, World Figure Skating Championship, 1986, World Profl. Figure Skating Championship, 1988, 89, 91. Recipient Am. Black Achievement Award, Ebony mag., named Women Athlete of Yr., 1986; winner Bronze medal Olympic Games, 1988; named to U.S. Figure Skating Hall of Fame, San Jose Sports Hall of Fame. Address: Mentor Mgmt 5610 Town Center Dr # 5 Granger IN 46530-

THOMAS, DENE, academic administrator, educator; 3 children. B Lit., S.W. State U., cert. in secondary edn., 1978; PhD English, U. Minn., 1984; course, Bryn Mawr's Women in Higher Edn. Adminstrn. program, 1990. Vice provost acad. affairs to tchr., dept. chmn., dean U. Idaho; pres. Lewis-Clark State Coll., 2001—. Office: Lewis-Clark State Coll 500 8th Ave Lewiston ID 83501

THOMAS, DENNIS, paper company executive, former government official; b. Balt., Dec. 8, 1943; s. George Crosby and Justa Mae (Witherspoon) T.; m. Dawn Frances Haines, 1965; 1 son, William David. BS, Frostburg State Coll., 1965; MSW., U. Md., 1967. Asst. to Hon. J. Glenn Beall, Jr. U.S. Ho. of Reps., Washington, 1969-71, spl. asst., 1971-73, 1973-77, adminstrv. asst. to Hon. William V. Roth, Jr., 1977-81; asst. sec. legis. affairs Dept. Treasury, Washington, 1981-83; dep. asst. to Pres. for legis. affairs White House, Washington, 1983-85; ptnr. Touche Ross and Co., Inc., 1985; asst. to Pres., The White House, 1985-87; sr. v.p. pub. affairs and comm. Internat. Paper Co., Stamford, Conn., 1987—. Republican. Office: Internat Paper 400 Atlantic St Stamford CT 06921

THOMAS, DONALD A. astronaut; b. Cleve., Ohio, May 6, 1955; s. Irene M. Thomas; m. Simone Lehmann Thomas; 1 child. BSc with hon. in Physics, Case We. Reserve U., 1977; MSc in Materials Sci., Cornell U., 1980, PhD in Materials Sci., 1982. Sr. mem. tech. staff AT&T Bell Lab., Princeton, NJ, 1982—87; with Lockheed Engrng. & Sci. Co., Houston, 1987—88; materials engr. NASA, Houston, 1988—90, astronaut, 1990—. Astronaut Space Shuttle Columbia STS-65, 1994, Space Shuttle Discovery STS-70, 1995, Space Shuttle Columbia STS-83, 1997, Space Shuttle Columbia STS-94, 1997; adj. prof. in physics Trenton State Coll., Trenton, NJ. Mem.: Assn. Space Explorers, Tau Beta Pi. Avocations: swimming, bicycling, camping, flying. Office: Astronaut Office CB NASA Johnson Space Center Houston TX 77058

THOMAS, DONALD LEE, construction technology educator; b. Hampton, Va., Jan. 28, 1964; s. Lloyd Jene Thomas Sr. and Elsie Marie Thomas, Senior. Cert. in project planning and cost estimating, Old Dominion U., 1989, cert. in purchasing and supply chain mgmt., 2002; B in Mgmt., Calif. Coast U., Santa Ana, 2004; Cert. in Bus. Info. Tech., No. Va. C.C., Woodbridge, Virginia, 2000—00; Cert. in Paralegal Studies, Old Dominion U., Ctr. for Global Bus. & Exec. Edn., Norfolk, Virginia, 1993—93. Cert. quality assurance sys. Def. Logistics Agy. Quality assurance specialist Def. Logistics Agy., Richmond, Va., 2001—; instr. constrn. tech. No. Va. C.C., Woodbridge, Va., 2000—, Germanna C.C., Fredericksburg, Va., 2002—; bldg. inspector nat. office IRS, Washington. *A noted authority in development and instruction of workforce development courses for the Northern Virginia/Washington D.C. metropolitan area. Courses taught and developed include architectural drafting, construction print reading, and mathematics. Author of "Reading Construction Prints, Student Supplement," a comprehensive supplemental text including Spanish translations. Over 19 years experience in the area of Quality Assurance and Control. Specialization areas include machinery failure analysis, ship hull design, and weld testing. Over five years experience in federal contracting with a primary focus on contract quality assurance, including federal contract oversight of small business awards. Newly accomplished inventor of patented building insulating equipment.* Author: (instr. manual) Reading Construction Prints, Student Supplement. Mem.: Am. Soc. Mil. Comptrs., Intellectual Property Owners Assn. (corr.; apptd. com. mem. small bus. affairs 2004—). Achievements include invention of Building Energy Saving Equipment.

THOMAS, DUKE WINSTON, lawyer; b. Scuddy, Ky., Jan. 25, 1937; s. William E. and Grace T. Thomas; m. Jill Staples, Oct. 24, 1964; children: Deborah L., William E. II, Judith A. BSBA, Ohio State U., 1959, JD, 1964. Bar: Ohio 1964, U.S. Dist. Ct. Ohio 1966, U.S. Ct. Appeals (3d cir.) 1971, U.S. Ct. Appeals (6th cir.) 1972, U.S. Supreme Ct. 1973, U.S. Ct. Appeals (7th cir.) 1979. Ptnr. Vorys, Sater, Seymour and Pease, LLP, Columbus, Ohio, 1964—. Chmn. bd. dirs. Ohio Bar Liability Ins. Co. Fellow: Columbus Bar Found., Ohio Bar Found., Am. Coll. Trial Lawyers (chmn. Ohio joint select com. jud. compensation 1987), Internat. Soc. Barristers, Am. Bar Found. (life); mem.: ABA (ho. of dels. 1985—, state del. 1989—95, bd. govs. 1995—98), Columbus Bar Assn. (pres. 1978), Ohio Bar Assn. (pres. 1985), Columbus Athletic Club, Pres.'s Club Ohio State U. Home: 2090 Sheringham Rd Columbus OH 43220-4358 Office: Vorys Sater Seymour & Pease LLP PO Box 1008 52 E Gay St Columbus OH 43215-3161 Office Phone: 614-464-6263. Business E-Mail: dwthomas@vssp.com.

THOMAS, DWIGHT REMBERT, writer; b. Savannah, Ga., Dec. 8, 1944; s. Huguenin and Alma (Sanders) Thomas. BA in English with honors, Emory U., 1967; PhD in Am. Lit., U. Pa., 1978. Fellow English dept. U. Pa., Phila., 1971-78; writer Savannah, 1979—. Cons. Film Odyssey, Washington, 1988—89. Author: (book) The Poe Log: A Documentary Life of Edgar Allan Poe, 1987. Dir. Edgar Allan Poe Mus., Richmond, 1988—96. With U.S. Army, 1969—71. Mem.: MLA, Am. Med. Writers Assn., Mensa (treas. Savannah area 1985—88, local sec. 1989—90), Phi Beta Kappa. Roman Catholic. Avocations: German language, current cinema, bicycling. Home: 7 E Gordon St Savannah GA 31401-4925

THOMAS, EDWARD DONNALL, internist, hematologist, retired medical educator; b. Mart, Tex., Mar. 15, 1920; married; 3 children. BA, U. Tex., 1941, MA, 1943; MD, Harvard U., 1946, U. Cagliari, Sardinia, 1981, U. Verona, Italy, 1991, U. Parma, 1992, U. Barcelona, Spain, 1994, U. Warsaw, Poland, 1996, U. Jagiellonski, Cracow, Poland, 1996. Lic. physician Mass., N.Y., Wash., diplomate Am. Bd. Internal Medicine. Intern in medicine Peter Bent Brigham Hosp., Boston, 1946—47, rsch. fellow hematology, 1947—48; NRC postdoctoral fellow in medicine dept. biology MIT, Cambridge, 1950—51; chief med. resident, sr. asst. resident Peter Bent Brigham Hosp., 1951—53, hematologist, 1953—55; instr. medicine Harvard Med. Sch., Boston, 1953—55; rsch. assoc. Cancer Rsch. Found. Children's Med. Ctr., Boston, 1953—55; physician-in-chief Mary Imogene Bassett Hosp., Cooperstown, NY, 1955—63; assoc. clin. prof. medicine Coll. Physicians and Surgeons Columbia U., N.Y.C., 1955—63; attending physician U. Wash. Hosp., Seattle, 1963—90; prof. medicine Sch. Medicine U. Wash., Seattle, 1963—90, head divsn. oncology Sch. Medicine, 1963—85, prof. emeritus medicine Sch. Medicine, 1990—; dir. med. oncology Fred Hutchinson Cancer Rsch. Ctr., Seattle, 1974—89, assoc. dir. clin. rsch. programs, 1982—89, mem., 1974—. Mem. hematology study sect. NIH, 1965—69; mem. bd. trustees and med. sci. adv. com. Leukemia Soc. Am., Inc., 1969—73; mem. clin. cancer investigation rev. com. NCI, 1970—74; 1st ann. Eugene C. Eppinger lectr. Peter Bent Brigham Hosp. and Harvard Med. Sch., 1974; Lilly lectr. RCP, London, 1977; Stratton lectr. Internat. Soc. Hematology, 1982; Paul Aggeler lectr. U. Calif., San Francisco, 1982; 65th Mellon lectr. U. Pitts. Sch. Medicine, 1984; Stanley Wright Meml. lectr. Western Soc. Pediat. Rsch., 1985; Adolfo Ferrata lectr. Italian Soc. Hematology, Verona, Italy, 1991. Mem. editl. bd. Blood, 1962—75, 1977—82, Transplantation, 1970—76, Proc. of Soc. for Exptl. Biology and Medicine, 1974—81, Leukemia Rsch., 1977—87, Hematological Oncology, 1982—87, Jour. Clin. Immunology, 1982—87, Am. Jour. Hematology, 1985—, Bone Marrow Transplantation, 1986—. With U.S. Army, 1948—50. Recipient A. Ross McIntyre award, U. Nebr. Med. Ctr., 1975, Philip Levine award, Am. Soc. Clin. Pathologists, 1979, Disting. Svc. in Basic Rsch. award, Am. Cancer Soc., 1980, Kettering prize, GM Cancer Rsch. Found., 1981, Spl. Keynote Address award, Am. Soc. Therapeutic Radiologists, 1981, Robert Roesler de Villiers award, Leukemia Soc. Am., 1983, Karl Landsteiner Meml. award, Am. Assn. Blood Banks, 1987, Terry Fox award, Can., 1990, Internat. award, Gairdner Found., 1990, Hong Kong prize, N.Am. Med. Assn., 1990, Nobel Prize in Medicine, 1990, Presdl. medal of sci., NSF, 1990, Lifetime Achievement award, Am. Soc. Blood and Marrow Transplantation, 2004. Mem.: NAS, Soc. Exptl. Biology and Medicine, Western Assn. Physicians, Swiss Soc. Hematology, Internat. Soc. Hematology, Internat. Soc. Exptl. Hematology, Am. Soc. Hematology (pres. 1987—88, Henry M. Stratton lectr. 1975), Am. Soc. Clin. Investigation, Am. Soc. Clin. Oncology (David A. Karnoksky Meml. lectr. 1983), Am. Fedn. Clin. Rsch., Assn. Am. Physicians (Kober medal 1992), Am. Assn. Cancer Rsch., Academie Royale de Medicine de Belgique (corr.), Nat. Acad. Medicine Mex. (hon.), Royal Coll. Physicians and Surgeons Can. (hon.), Swedish Soc. Hematology (hon.). Office: Fred Hutchinson Cancer Ctr 1100 Fairview Ave N D5-100 PO Box 19024 Seattle WA 98109-1024

THOMAS, ELIZABETH MARSHALL, writer; b. Boston, Sept. 13, 1931; d. Laurence K. and Lorna (McLean) Marshall; m. Stephen Thomas, 1956; children: Stephanie, Ramsay. Student, Smith Coll.; BA in English, Radliffe Coll., 1954. Writer, 1954—. Author: The Harmless People, 1959, Warrior Herdsmen, 1965, Reindeer Moon, 1987, The Animal Wife, 1990, The Hidden Life of Dogs, 1993, The Tribe of Tiger, 1994, Certain Poor Shepherds, 1998, The Social Lives of Dogs, 2000. Office: 80 E Mountain Rd Peterborough NH 03458-2318

THOMAS, ELLA COOPER, lawyer; b. Ft. Totten, N.Y. d. Avery John and Ona Caroline (Gibson) C.; m. Robert Edward Lee Thomas, Nov. 22, 1938 (dec. Jan. 1985); 1 child, Robert Edward Lee Jr. Student, Vassar Coll., 1932-34, U. Hawaii, 1934-35, George Washington U., 1935-36, JD, 1940. Bar: U.S. Dist. Ct. D.C. 1942, U.S. Ct. Appeals (D.C. cir.) 1943, U.S. Supreme Ct. 1947, U.S. Tax Ct. 1973. Secret maps custodian U.S. Dist. Engrs., Honolulu, 1941-42; contbg. editor Labor Rels. Reporter, Washington, 1942; assoc. Smith, Ristig & Smith, Washington, 1942-45; law libr. George Washington Law Sch., Washington, 1946-53; reporter of decisions U.S. Tax Ct., Washington, 1953-75. Computer vol. Mote Marine Lab., 1992—98. Author: Law of Libel and Slander, 1949. Mem. Inter-Am. Bar Assn. (coun. mem. 1973-99), D.C. Bar Assn. Avocations: physical fitness, crostics. Home: 1700 3rd Ave W Apt 118 Bradenton FL 34205

THOMAS, EMORY M. history professor; b. Richmond, Va., Nov. 3, 1939; s. W. Lynn and Mary Morton Thomas; m. Frances Taliaferro Thomas, Aug. 25, 1962; children: Emory M. Jr., John Taliaferro. BA with honors, U. Va., 1962; PhD, Rice U., 1966. Asst., assoc. prof. U. Ga., Athens, Ga., 1967—2002; vis. prof. The Citadel, Charleston, SC, 2003—. Author: The Confederate State of Richmond: A Biography of the Capital, 1971, The Confederacy as a Revolutionary Experience, 1971, The American War and Peace: 1860-1877, 1973, The Confederate Nation, 1861-1865, 1979, Bold Dragoon: The Life of J.E.B. Stuart, 1986, Travels to Hallowed Grounf, 1987, Robert E. Lee: A Biography, 1995, Robert E. Lee: An Album, 2000. Capt. U.S. Army, 1965—67. Democrat. Episcopalian. Avocations: reading, running, sailing. Home: 595 Hill St Athens GA 30606

THOMAS, ESTHER MERLENE, elementary and adult education educator; b. San Diego, Oct. 16, 1945; d. Merton Alfred and Nellie Lida (Von Pilz) T. *The Thomas family came from Wales. Esther's great-great grandfather James Thomas was born in Tennessee in 1807, married Jane Walker, and died at age 106 in Missouri. Great-grandfather Calvin Thomas married Melissa Mattingly who was one quarter Cherokee. Great-great-grandfather John Dabbs from Tennessee married Margaret Jones. Great-great-grandfather Dr. Logan Wallace (a.k.a. Wallis) was born in North Carolina in 1803. He founded Milton, Iowa in 1851. He married Anna Chiles. Great-grandfather Bernhart Von Pilz*

was born in Germany. He married Minna Handle, daughter of Godeif Handel. Minna came to America in 1902. Great-grandparents Friedrick Ziegler and Henrietta Yunge came to America from Germany in 1887. AA with honors, Grossmont Coll., 1966; BA with honors, San Diego State U., 1969; MA, U. Redlands, 1977. Cert. elem. and adult edn. tchr. Tchr. Cajon Valley Union Sch. Dist., El Cajon, 1969—; sci. fair coord. Flying Hills Sch. Tchr. Hopi and Navajo Native Americans, Ariz., Utah, 1964-74, Goose and Gander Nursery Sch., Lakeside, Calif., 1964-66; dir., supt. Bible and Sunday schs. various chs., Lakeside, 1961-87; mem. sci. com., math. coun. Cajon Valley Union Sch. Dist., 1990-91, libr. com., 1997-98. Author: Individualized Curriculum in the Affective Domain; co-author: Campbell County, The Treasured Years, 1990, Legends of the Lakeside (Four Star award, 2003); songwriter: songs Never Trouble Trouble, Old Glory, Jesus Is Our Lord, Daniel's Prayer, There Lay Jesus, God's Hands, Washing Machine Charlie, Playmates, The Kid in the Hall, Spring Time on the Blue Ridge, Christ's DNA, If You Need Me, Chances, Blame, The Star of Bethlehem, Where the Eagle Flies, Born to Win, Happy Birthday Dear Jesus, Christmas Lights, Walk the Line, You Don't Know What Repentance Is, I'm Asking You, Clear the Path Lord, Aqua Forte, In the Volume of the Book, Home is Where the Heart Is, You Don't Even Know Who I Am, No Place to Cry, To Walk With God, Ixnay, If You Never Loved Me, for Columbine Records Corp., Life of A Single Woman, Take This Pain Away, We Can Keep In Touch, Let Me Know, A Letter Is A Letter, The Battle, 2004; contbr. articles to profl. jours., newspapers, chpts. to books. Tem. U.S. Senatorial Club, Washington, 1984—, Conservative Caucus, Inc., Washington, 1988—, Ronald Reagan Presdl. Found., Ronald Reagan Rep. Ctr., 1988, Rep. Presdl. Citizen's Adv. Commn., 1989—, Rep. Platform Planning Com., Calif., 1992, at-large del. representing dist. #45, Lakeside, Calif., 1992, 1995—, Am. Security Coun., Washington, 1994, Congressman Hunter's Off Road Adv. Coun., El Cajon, Calif., 1994, Century Club, San Diego Rep. Century Club, 1995; mem. health articulation com. project AIDS, Cajon Valley Union Sch. Dist., 1988—, Recruit Depot Hist. Mus., San Diego, 1989, Citizen's Drug Free Am., Calif., 1989—, The Heritage Found., 1988—; charter mem. Marine Corps Mus.; life mem. San Diego Aerispace Mus.; mem. Lakeside Centennial Com., 1985-86; hon. mem. Rep. Presdl. Task Force, Washington, 1986; del. Calif. Rep. Senatorial Mid-Term Conv., Washington, 1994; mus. curator Lakeside Hist. Soc., 1992-93, life mem.; mem. Rep. Nat. Com., Washington, 2003 Recipient Outstanding Svc. award PTA, 1972-74, Outstanding Tchr. award KYXY Radio, San Diego, 1999; recognized for various contbns. Commdg. Post Gen., San Diego Bd. Edn., 1989. Mem. NRA, Tchrs. Assn., Calif. Tchrs. Assn., Cajon Valley Educators Assn. (faculty advisor, rep. 1980-82, 84-86, 87-88), Nat. Trust for Hist. Preservation, Christian Bus. and Profl. Women, Trust for Hist. Preservation, Nat. WWII Memml. (life, charter), Ridgecrest Golden Terrace Park Assn. (pres. 1998-99), Nashville Songwriters Assn., Capitol Hill Women's Club, Am. Ctr. for Law and Justice, Internat. Christian Women's Club (Christian amb. to Taiwan, Korea, 1974), Paul Revere Soc. Republican. Avocations: travel, vocal music, piano, guitar. Home: 13594 Hwy 8 # 3 Lakeside CA 92040-5235 Office: Flying Hills Elem Sch 1251 Finch St El Cajon CA 92020-1433

THOMAS, EUGENE C. lawyer; b. Idaho Falls, Idaho, Feb. 8, 1931; s. C. E. Thomas; m. Jody Raber; children: Michael E., Stephen R. BA, Columbia U., 1952; JD, 1954; LLD (hon.), Univ. Idaho, 1986, Coll. of Idaho, 1987. Bar: Idaho 1954, US Dist. Ct./Idaho 1957, US Ct. Appeals (9th cir.) 1958, US Supreme Ct. 1970. Pros. atty. Ada County, Boise, Idaho, 1955—57; founding ptnr. Moffatt, Thomas, Barrett, Rock & Fields, Boise, 1957—58; bd. dir. Shore Lodge, Inc., McCall, Idaho, McCall, Idaho, Nelson-Ball Paper Products, Inc., Longview, Wash., Peregrine Industries, Inc., Boise; bd. editors ABA Jour., 1980—87. Named Exec. of Yr., Boise chpt. Nat. Sec. Assn., 1978; recipient Disting. Lawyer award, 1980, Disting. Svc. award, Idaho Pros. Atty., 1985, Chgo. Vol. Legal Svc. Found., 1986, Disting. Lawyer award, 1986; fellow Internat. Acad. Trial Lawyers. Mem.: Rocky Mountain Oil and Gas Assn. (dir. 1977—79), Nat. Conf. Bar Pres. (trustee 1974—76), Conference of Pres. Union Internat. des Avocats (pres.), Internat. Bar Assoc. (chmn. biennial conf., governing coun. 1985—86), Fourth Dist. Bar Assn. (pres. 1962—63), Am. Bd. Trial Advocates, Internat. Assn. Ins. Counsel, Idaho Assn. Def. Counsel (trustee 1966—69, pres. 1967—68), Def. Rsch. Inst. (state chmn. Pacific region 1978—), Idaho State Bar, ABA, Am. Law Inst., Am. Bar Found., Nat. Coll. Dist. Atty., Boise Chpt. Nat. Sec. Assn., Mayor's Select Com. on Downtown Develop. (chmn. 1982—83), Univ./Cmty. Health Sci. Assn. (bd. dir. 1981—), Boise Futures Found. (trustee 1973—, bd. dir. 1981), Assoc. Taxpayers of Idaho (trustee 1983—, chmn. 1988—90), Integrated Bar of the Philippines (hon.), Can. Bar Assn. (hon.), New Zealand Law Soc. (hon.), La Barra Mexicana (hon.), Law Soc. Eng. and Wales (hon.), Mountain States Tumor Inst. (pres., chmn. bd 1972—79, mem. exec. com. 1982—, trustee 1983—), St. Luke's Regional Med. Ctr. (bd. dir. 1963—), Hillcrest Country (bd. dir., (Boise) 1969—72), Arid. Office: Moffatt Thomas Barrett Rock & Fields PO Box 829 Boise ID 83701-0829

THOMAS, EVELYN B. agricultural products supplier; Sec., treas., bookkeeper Brandt Fertilizer, Pleasant Plains, Ill., 1953—; co-owner Har Brand, 1963-67, Brandt Chemical, 1967; sec./treas. Brandt Consolidated, Pleasant Plains, Ill. Office: Brandt Consolidated PO Box 277 Pleasant Plains IL 62677-0277 Fax: 217-626-1927. E-mail: bcadmin@brandtconsolidated.com.

THOMAS, FAYE EVELYN J. elementary and secondary school educator; b. Summerfield, La., Aug. 3, 1933; d. Reginald Felton and Atlee (Hunter) Johnson; m. Archie Taylor Thomas, Sept. 8, 1960; 1 child, Dwayne Andre. BA, So. U., 1954; student, Tuskegee Inst., 1958, student, 1969, U. Detroit, 1961, student, 1962, student, 1963, Ctrl. Mich. U., 1965; MS, U. Ctrl. Ark., 1971, Cleve. State U., 1979. Tchr. Cullen (La.) Elem. Sch., 1957; tchr. English and social studies Charles Brown H.S., Springhill, La., 1957—70; tchr. English, Upward Bound Program, Grambling State U., 1968; tchr. English, Springhill H.S., 1970; elem. intermediate tchr. Riveredge Elem. Sch., Berea, Ohio, 1971—93; tchr. 7th grade English, Ford Mid. Sch., 1993—94; program dir. Teen Pregnancy Prevention Program, 2003—04. Tchr. asst. elem. coun. curriculum and instrn. Berea Sch. Dist., 1984—85. Author: When the Time Is Right, Move On, A Journey to the Mountain Top, 2003. Dir. teen pregnancy prevention program First Bapt. Ch., Cullen, La., 2003—04. Grantee, EDPA, 1970—71, Internat. Paper Found., 1958, 1960, NDEA, 1965; scholar Martha Holden Jennings scholar, 1984—85. Mem.: NEA, Assn. Supervision and Curriculum Devel., N.E. Ohio Tchrs. Assn., Berea Edn. Assn., Ohio Edn. Assn., Ohio Motorists Assn., Charles Brown Soc. Orgn. (trustee 1984—), Black Caucus NEA, People United to Save Humanity, Toastmasters, Order Eastern Star. Democrat. Baptist. Office: 311 Henrietta White Blvd Springhill LA 71075-8407

THOMAS, FRANK EDWARD, professional baseball player; b. Columbus, Ga., May 27, 1968; Student, Auburn U. With Chgo. White Sox, 1990—. Named Maj. League Player of Yr., Sporting News, 1993; named to All-Star Coll. All Am. team, 1989, All-Star Team, 1991, 1993—94, Am. League, 1993—95; recipient Silver Slugger award, 1991, 1993, 1994, Most Valuable Player award, Am. League, 1994. Office: Chgo White Sox Comiskey Park 333 W 35th St Chicago IL 60616-3651

THOMAS, FRANKLIN A., III, lawyer; b. Charleston, W.Va., Oct. 17, 1948; BA, U. Va., 1970, MA, 1971. Bar: Va. 1974, U.S. Tax Ct. 1974, U.S. Ct. Appeals (4th cir.) 1974. Atty. Shackelford, Thomas & Gregg, PLC, Orange, Va. Fellow: Am. Bar Found., Am. Coll. Trust and Estate Counsel; mem.: ABA, Order of Coif, Va. State Bar (bd. govs. trust and estates sect. 1983—90, chmn. 1988—89), Va. Bar Assn. (chair sect. wills, trusts and estates 1997—98, pres.-elect 2002). Office: Shackelford Thomas and Gregg PO Box 871 149 W Main St Orange VA 22960

THOMAS, FRANKLIN AUGUSTINE, lawyer, consultant; b. Bklyn., May 27, 1934; s. James and Viola (Atherley) T.; div.; children: Keith, Hillary, Kerrie, Kevin. BA, Columbia U., 1956, LL.B., 1963; LL.D. (hon.), Yale U., 1970, Fordham U., 1972, Pratt Inst., 1974, Pace U., 1977, Columbia U., 1979, New School U., 2002. Bar: N.Y. 1964. Atty. Fed. Housing and Home Finance Agy., N.Y.C., 1963-64; asst. U.S. atty. for So. Dist. N.Y., 1964-65; dep. police commr. charge legal matters N.Y.C., 1965-67; pres., chief exec. officer Bedford Stuyvesant Restoration Corp., Bklyn., 1967-77; pres. The Ford Found., 1979-96; atty., cons., 1996—. Bd. dirs. ALCOA, Citigroup, Lucent Techs., PepsiCo, Inc. Trustee Columbia U., 1969-75. Served with USAF, 1956-60. Recipient LBJ Found. award for contbn. to betterment of urban life, 1974, medal of excellence Columbia U., 1976, Alexander Hamilton award Columbia U., 1983

THOMAS, FREDERICK BRADLEY, lawyer; b. Evanston, Ill., Aug. 13, 1949; s. Frederick Bradley and Katherine Kidder (Bingham) T.; m. Elizabeth Maxwell, Oct. 25, 1975; children: Bradley Bingham, Stephens Maxwell, Rosa Macaulay. AB, Dartmouth Coll., 1971; JD, U. Chgo., 1974. Bar: Ill. 1974. Law clk. to hon. judge John C. Godbold U.S. Ct. Appeals (5th cir.), Montgomery, Ala., 1974-75; assoc. Mayer, Brown, Rowe & Maw, Chgo., 1975—80, ptnr., 1981—. Bd. dirs. St. Gregory Episcopal Sch., 1989—; bd. trustees La Rabida Children's Hosp., 1990—; bd. mgrs. YMCA Met. Chgo., 2002--. Mem.: ABA, Chgo. Coun. Lawyers. Republican. Episcopalian. Office: Mayer Brown Rowe & Maw 190 S La Salle St Ste 3100 Chicago IL 60603-3441

THOMAS, FREYDA, playwright, actress; d. Edward Spiegel and Natalie Elayne Truitt. BA, Penn State U., 1961—65, MA, 1965—67; MFA, Calif. Inst. of the Arts, 2000—01. Translator (adapter): (plays) The Learned Ladies, Tartuffe: Born Again; author The Heir Transparent, The Gamester. Recipient Women's Playwriting award Finalist, Susan Smith Blackburn Internat. Playwriting award, 2000, The Heidemann award (Finalist), Actor's Theatre of Louisville, 2001, Anna Zornio Children's Playwriting award, U. of NH., Dramafest, Lodi Arts Festival, 1996. Mem.: Actor's Equity Assn., Screen Actors' Guild, Dramatists' Guild. Avocations: big band singing, travel, swimming. Office Phone: 310-288-1575.

THOMAS, GARNETT JETT, accountant; b. Farmington, Ky., July 27, 1920; s. Pinkney Madison and Ethel (Drinkard) T.; m. Katherine Gardner, Mary. 26, 1948 (dec. Sept. 1979); m. Nell Penton, May 23, 1981; stepchldren: Vernon Bice, Michael Bice, Gina Black. BS, Lambuth U., 1947; MS, Miss. State U., 1949. Clk., acct. Ill. Cen. R.R., Paducah, Ky., 1941-42; mgr. Coll. Bookstore Lambuth U., Jackson, Tenn., 1946-47; acct. Miss. Agrl. and Forestry Expt. Sta., Mississippi State, 1948-60, chief acct., 1960-75, administrv. officer and chief acct., 1975-85; administrv. officer emeritus, 1985—; pres. PBR Corp., Starksville, Miss., 1974-84. Fin. adminstr. seed tech., rsch. internat. programs Brazil, India, Guatemala, Columbia, Thailand, Kenya, 1958-85; pres. Govt. Employees Credit Union. Mem. adv. bd. Nat. Bank of Commerce of Miss., 1974—; fin. administr. seed tech, research internat. programs Brazil, India, Guatemala, Columbia, Thailand, Kenya, 1958-85; bd. dirs. Govt. Employees Credit Union, 1967-86, pres., 1969-73. With USN, 1942-46. Decorated Bronze Star with oak leaf cluster. Mem. Nat. Assn. Accts., Asn. Govt. Accts., Am. Assn Accts., Acad. Acctg. Historians, So. Assn. Agrl. Scientists, Rotary (pres., 1959-90, dist. 682 gov. 1977-78, adv. com. to pres. 1979-80, dist. chmn. Poloplus, 1987-90). Republican. Methodist. Home: 114 Grand Ridge Rd Starkville MS 39759-4112

THOMAS, GARY L. academic administrator; b. Willows, Calif., May 12, 1937; s. Leonel Richard and Myrtle Blanch (Moncur) T.; m. Margaret Anderson, Aug. 11, 1960 (div. 1975); children: Katelin, Elizabeth Ann, Derek Alan. AA, Modesto Jr. Coll., 1958; BS in Elec. Engring., U. Calif., Berkeley, 1960, MA in Physics, 1962, PhD in Elec. and Computer Engring., 1967. Acting asst. prof. U. Calif., Berkeley, 1967; asst. prof. elec. engring. SUNY, Stony Brook, 1967-70, assoc. prof. elec. engring., 1970-73, assoc. dean grad. sch., 1973-74, chairperson, prof. elec. engring., 1975-79; congl. fellow A.A.A.S., Washington, 1974-75; provost, v.p. acad. affairs N.J. Inst. Tech., Newark, 1980-98, prof. elec. and computer engring., 1980—2000; chancellor U. Missouri-Rolla, Rolla, Mo., 2000—. Student asst. bd. Dept. Higher Edn., N.J., 1980-97; chairperson rsch. adv. bd. PSE & G, Newark, 1986-90, Regional Transp. Rsch. Bd., N.Y. and N.J., 1987-90; bd. dirs. Kessler Inst. for Rehab., West Orange, N.J., 1988—; chair bd. dirs. Kessler Med. Rehab. Rsch. & Edn. Corp., 1997-2002. Author, editor: Fundamentals of Electrical and Computer Engineering, 1983. State of Calif. scholar, 1960, Schumberger scholar, 1961; NSF grantee, 1973-79. Home: 506 W 11th St Rolla MO 65401-3959 Office: U Missouri-Rolla 206 Parker Hall 1870 Miner Cir Rolla MO 65409-0910

THOMAS, GARY LYNN, financial executive; b. Port Vue, Pa., May 15, 1942; s. Willis L. and Luella M. (Rorabaugh) T.; m. Sharen A. Gibbons, May 13, 1967; children— Gregory Scott, Tara Elizabeth. BS in Bus. Adminstrn, Pa. State U., 1964; grad., Sch. Bank Adminstrn., U. Wis., 1973. CPA, Pa. Sr. auditor Arthur Andersen & Co., Los Angeles and Pitts., 1964-69; v.p. and dep. comptroller Pitts. Nat. Bank, 1969-77; v.p. and treas. Md. Nat. Corp., Balt., 1977-80; v.p., mgr. corp. fin. div. Md. Nat. Bank, Balt.; exec. v.p. adminstrn. Peterson, Howell & Heather, Hunt Valley, Md., 1980-82; v.p. fin. Am. TeleServices, Inc, a Metromedia co., Balt., 1983-85; chief fin. officer First Cellular Group, Inc., Balt., 1985-88, Schelle, Warner, Murray & Thomas, Inc., Balt., 1988—95. Mng. dir. Schelle Cellular Group, Inc., 1989—; pres. Ruxton Capital Group, Inc., 1989-95; chief fin. officer Am. Personal Communications, Inc., Balt. and D.C., 1990-98; adj. instr. Sch. Bank Adminstrn., U. Wis., 1975-80; speaker 14th ann. Bank Tax Inst., 1978. Mem. adv. bd., fin. com. St. Joseph Hosp., Balt., 1979-1982; bd. dirs. industry luncheon club Towson State U., 1980-1985. Served with USAR, 1965-1971. Inducted into McKeesport H.S. Hall of Fame, 1994. Mem. AICPA, Pa. Inst. CPAs, Md. Assn. CPAs (prior chmn. mems. in industry com.), Greater Naples Leadership Program, Conservancy of SW Fla.(bd. dirs.). Republican. Methodist. Home: 575 18th Ave S Naples FL 34102-7536

THOMAS, GARY WAYNE, actor; b. Oklahoma City, Dec. 28, 1953; s. Wayne Saxon and Thelma (Hitchcock) T. BBA, U. Okla., 1976. Actor films including Dark Before Dawn, 1988, Rain Man, 1988, Born on the Fourth of July, 1989, JFK, 1991, Robin Hood-Men in Tights, 1993, The Flintstones, 1994, Wild Bill, 1994, Mel Brooks Dracula, 1995, Pulp Fiction, 1995, Independence Day, 1996, L.A. Confidential, 1997, Outskirts, 1998, (TV shows) The Nearly Quiet Orb, 1990, Winchester, 1989, A House of Shadows and Lies, 1992, Melrose Place, 1992, 96, Long Shadows, 1994, Tracy Takes On..., 1995, (plays) Feiffer's People, 1988, Strip! Barely Legal, 1996. Mem. Actor's Fund Am. (life), Am. Film Inst., Screen Actors Guild. Democrat. Avocations: body building, movies, rappeling, dance, piano. Home: 1208 SW 78th Ter Oklahoma City OK 73139-2420 E-mail: imgarythomas@worldnet.att.net.

THOMAS, GEORGIE A. state official; BA, Cornell U., 1965; MBA, Columbia U., 1973. Asst. portfolio mgr. Money Mgmt. dept. R.W. Pressprich & Co. Inc., N.Y.C., 1968-71; portfolio analyst Bache & Co., N.Y.C., 1971-72; with Exxon Corp., N.Y.C., 1973-76, consolidation analyst Treas. dept., 1975-76; treas. Penntech Papers Inc., N.Y.C., 1976-79; budget dir. Yankee Publishing Inc., Dublin, N.H., 1982-85; treas. State of N.H., Concord, 1985—. Mem. econ. growth and productivity and tech. coms. Bus. Research Adv. Council of Bur. Labor Statistics, 1978-79; mem. alumni counseling bd. Columbia U. Bus. Sch., 1973-79 Editor: Jour. World Bus., Columbia Bus. Sch. Mem. Fin. Women's Assn. N.Y. (mem. exec. bd. 1977-78), Womens Econ. Roundtable Clubs: Cornell of Fairfield County (Conn.). Home: PO Box 1317 Campton NH 03223-1317 Office: State NH State House Annex Rm 121 Concord NH 03301

THOMAS, GERALD E. ambassador; b. Natick, Mass., June 23, 1929; s. Walter W. T. and Lelia L. (Jacob) T.; m. Rhoda H. Henderson, Oct. 3, 1954; children: Kenneth, Steven, Lisa. BS, Harvard U., 1951; MS, George Washington U., 1966; PhD, Yale U., 1973; grad., Naval War Coll., 1965-66. Commd. ensign U.S. Navy, 1951, advanced through grades to rear adm., 1975, comdr. Cruiser Destroyer Group, 1974-76; dir. Near East and South Asia region Office Asst. Sec. Def., 1976-78; comdr. tng. command Pacific Fleet U.S. Navy, 1978-81, ret., 1981; ambassador to Guyana, Georgetown, 1981-83; ambassador to Kenya Nairobi, 1983-86. Decorated Meritorious Service medal; decorated Navy Commendation medal with combat V Mem. Alpha Phi Alpha Office: US Ambassador to Kenya Care Dept Ofstate Washington DC 20520-0001

THOMAS, GREGG DARROW, lawyer; b. Jacksonville, Fla., July 31, 1951; BA magna cum laude, Vanderbilt U., 1972; JD with honors, U. Fla., 1976. Bar: Fla. 1976, D.C. 1978. Law clk. U.S. Dist. Ct. (mid. dist.) Fla., 1976-79; mem. Holland & Knight, Tampa, Fla., 1979—; ptnr., 1983—. Exec. editor U. Fla. Law Rev., 1975-76. Bd. dirs. Vol. Lawyer's Resource Ctr., 1990-95; trustee Tampa Mus. of Art, 1993—, vice chmn., 1998, chair, 1999-2001. Mem. ABA (mem. forum com. comm. law 1983—), Am. Judicature Soc., Fla. Bar (co-chair Fla. bar media and comm. com. 1987-88, mem. grievance com. 1988, chmn. 1989-91), Fla. Bar Found. (mem. legal assistance to poor com. 1988-91), Hillsborough Bar Assn., D.C. Bar, Phi Beta Kappa. Office: Holland & Knight 100 N Tampa St Ste 4100 Tampa FL 33602-3644 E-mail: gthomas@khlaw.com.

THOMAS, GREGORY HALL, psychology professor; b. Ocala, Fla., May 17, 1957; s. Karon William and Virginia Mae Thomas; BA, U. Ctrl. Okla., 1979; MA, Angelo State U., 1994; PhD, U. Okla., Oklahoma City, 2000. Adj. instr. Cameron U., Lawton, Okla., 1995—96, instr., 1997—98; psychol. intern U. Fla. Counseling Ctr., Gainesville, Fla., 1996—97; psychometrist Mental Health Ctr., Newport News, Va., 1998—99; counselor Garden City (Kans.) C.C., Kans., 1999—2000, instr. psychology and sociology, 2000—. Faculty senate mem. Garden City C.C., 2001—. Contbr. articles to profl. jours. Grant writer Habitat for the Humanities, Garden City, 2001; Sunday sch. tchr. Bible Christian Ch., Garden City, 2002; active Garden Valley Ch., 2003—; bd. mem. Big Bros./Big Sisters, Garden City, 2001—02. Mem.: Assn. for Pro Basketball Rsch., Pro Football Rschrs. Assn. Home: 909 Amy St Garden City KS 67846 Office: Garden City CC 801 Campus Dr Garden City KS 67846

THOMAS, HARRY K., JR., ambassador; m. Ericka O. Smith-Thomas; 1 child, Casey Merie Eunice. Grad., Coll. Holy Cross; postgrad., Columbia U. With U.S. Fgn. Svc., New Delhi, Harare, Kaduna, and Lima, 1984; staff asst. Asst. U.S. Sec. for African Affairs; spl. asst. Under Sec. Polit. Affairs; dep. dir. to dir. Ops. Ctr. U.S. State Dept., sr. watch officer; dir. for South Asia Nat. Security Coun., White HOuse, Washington, 2001—02; U.S. amb. to Bangladesh, 2003—. Office: 6120 Dhaka Pl Washington DC 20521-6120 also: Madani Ave Baridhara Dhaka 1212 Bangladesh

THOMAS, HAYWARD, manufacturing executive; b. LA, Aug. 9, 1921; s. Charles Sparks and Julia (Hayward) T.; m. Phyllis Mary Wilson, July 1, 1943; children: H. David, Steven T. BS, U. Calif., Berkeley, 1943. Registered profl. engr. Staff engr. Joshua Hendy Corp., Los Angeles, 1946-50; prodn. mgr. Byron Jackson Co., Los Angeles, 1950-55; mgr. mfg. Frigidaire div. Gen. Motors Corp., Dayton, Ohio, 1955-70; group v.p. White Motor Corp., Cleve., 1971-73; sr. v.p. Broan Mfg. Co., Hartford, Wis., 1973-85; pres. Jensen Industries, Los Angeles, 1985-87; retired, 1987. Served to lt. USNR, 1943-46. Mem. Soc. Mfg. Engrs. (chmn. mfg. mgmt. council 1984-86). Republican. Episcopalian. Avocations: tennis, fishing. Home: 1320 Granvia Altamira Palos Verdes Peninsula CA 90274-2006

THOMAS, HAZEL BEATRICE, state official; b. Franklin, Tenn. d. William Henry Fuller and Mattie Betty (Covington) Fuller Young; m. Charles B. Thomas (dec. 1969); children; Charles Bradford Jr., Deborah Carlotta (dec.). BA, Fisk U., 1946; MA, Tenn. State U., 1972. Cert. elem. and secondary tchr., Tenn. Tchr. elem. Met.-Nashville Sch., 1954—87; rsch. assoc. Johns Hopkins U., Balt., 1978—79, Marquette U., Milw., 1979—86; exec. asst. to commr. edn. Tenn. Dept. Edn., Nashville, 1987—. Cons. Peer Mediated Learning System, Nashville, 1980-82; instr. Met. Sch. Tchr. Ctr., Nasvhville, 1985-87; mem. tech. assistance team for high sch. that work, So. Regional Edn. Bd., 1998-99; nat. disseminator student team learning rsch. project, Johns Hopkins U., 1978-1979. Author training modules Substitute Teaching, Tchr. Aides. Pres. Davidson County Dem. Women, Nashville, 1985-87; v.p. Tenn. Fedn. Dem. Women, 1989-91, pres., 2001—; pres. elect Nashville Women's Polit. Caucus, 1991—; pres. Tenn. Women's Polit. Caucus, 1994-95; mem. adminstrv. com. of bd. Nat. Women's Polit. Caucus, 1993-95, v.p., 1995—, v.p. edn. and tng., 2001—; mem. Tenn. Leadership, Inc., 1992—; spkr., polit. trainer US Info. Agy., Nairobi, Kenya, 1997; mem. exec. bd. Citizen's Com. for Ann. Gov.'s Prayer Breakfast, 1992—; mem. exec. com. Tenn. Dem. Party, 2001—; chmn. edn. com. Bellevue C. of C.; pres. Tenn. Fedn. Dem. Women, 2001-03; v.p. Nat. Fedn. Dem. Women, 2002—; mem. pub. edn. and govt. com. Metro. Govt. Nashville, Tenn., 2002-03. Recipient Svc. to Edn. and Teaching Profession award Nat. Coun. Negro Women, 1988; Nat. Def. Edn. Act scholar, 1965, 67. Mem. Am. Bus. Womens Assn. (charter), Tenn. Edn. Assn. (pres. dept. classroom tchr. 1974-75, state dept. affiliate, pres. 1988-Ed. c90), Bellevue C. of C. (bd. govs. 1990-91, edn. chair 2002-03), Assn. Classroom Tchr. (pres. S.E. region 1975-76), Met. Nashville Edn. Assn. (exec. bd. 1971-77), Bellevue Sertoma Club (life, pres. 1990-91), Nat. Women's Polit. Caucus (v.p. 1995—), Nat. Assn. Dem. Women (v.p., 2003-05, named Woman of Distinction for Tenn., 2002, 03), Nat. Fedn. Dem. Women (v.p. 2003). Democrat. Baptist. Avocations: reading, bridge. Office: Tenn Dept Edn Andrew Johnson Tower 710 James Robertson Pkwy Nashville TN 37243-1219 Office Phone: 615-532-5740. E-mail: hazel.thomas@state.tn.us.

THOMAS, HELEN A. (MRS. DOUGLAS B. CORNELL), columnist, former White House correspondent; b. Winchester, Ky., Aug. 4, 1920; d. George and Mary (Thomas) T.; m. Douglas B. Cornell. BA, Wayne State U., 1942; LLD, Ea. Mich. State U., 1972; LHD, Wayne State U., 1974; LLD, Ferris State Coll., 1978; LHD, U. Detroit, 1979; LLD (hon.), Brown U., 1986, St. Bonaventure U., 1988, Franklin Marshall U., 1989, No. Mich. U., 1989, Skidmore Coll., 1992, Susquehanna U., 1993, Sage Coll., 1994, U. Mo., 1994, Northwestern U., 1995, Franklin Coll., 1995, Mich. State U., 1996, Potsdam U., 1998, A. Willenberg Univ., 1999; BA in Law, Mount Vernon Coll., 1999; LLD (hon.), Milliken U., 2002, Am. U. Beirut, 2003; LittD, Ohio Dominican U., 2004. With United Press Radio, UPI, 1943-2000, wire svc. reporter, 1943-74; White House corr. Washington, 1970; White House bur. chief UPI, Washington, 1974-2000; columnist Hearst Newspapers, 2000—. Author: Dateline White House, Front Row at the White House: My Life and Times, Thanks for the Memories Mr. President: Wit and Wisdom from the Front Row at the White House. Named one of the 25 Most Influential Women in Am., World Almanac; recipient Woman of Yr. in Comm. award, Ladies Home Jour., 1975, 4th Estate award, Nat. Press Club, 1984, Journalism award, U. Mo., Al Newharth award, 1990, Ralph McGill award, 1995, Lifetime award, Internat. Media Found., Internat. Women's Press Found., 1996, Lowell Thomas award, Marist Coll., 2001, Kahlil Gibran award, 2003, NOW award, 2003, Torch Bearer award, Planned Parenthood award, Physician Social Responsibility award, Utah Am. Women of Yr., 2004, Eleanor Roosevelt Legacy award, 2004. Mem. Women's Nat. Press Club (pres. 1959-60, William Allen White Journalism award), Am. Newspaper Women's Club (past v.p.), White House Corrs. Assn. (pres. 1976, Helen Thomas Lifetime Achievement award 1998), Nat. Newspaper Assn. (Lifetime award 2002), Gridiron Club (pres. 1993), Sigma Delta Chi (fellow, Hall of Fame), Delta Sigma Phi (hon.). Achievements include fighting hard for women's representation in the fields of journalism and politics, and in clubs and organizations where they had been excluded; the first women officer of the National Press Club, the White House Correspondents Association, and first women member of the Gridiron Club; entered into political reporting in 1961, when she began filing stories about the Kennedy administration. She has covered eight presidents; the only print journalist to go on President Nixon's historic trip to China. Traveled with presidents Ford, Carter, Reagan, Bush, Sr., Clinton, & Bush and covered every presidential economic summit; first female White House chief of a wire service in 1974; considered the "dean of Washington press corps" and she was allowed to ask the first question at the presdl. conferences; referred to as "The First Lady of the Press"; at the end of her first presidential press conference in 1961, she said "Thank you, Mr. President", establishing a tradition, which recently ended in 2003. Office: Hearst Corp 959 8th Ave New York NY 10019 Office Phone: 202-263-6437. E-mail: helent@hearstdc.com.

THOMAS, HOWARD, business educator; b. Jan. 31, 1943; BSc, London U., 1964, MSc, 1965; MBA, U. Chgo., 1966; PhD, Edinburgh U., 1970. From prof. dept. bus. adminstrn. to dean emeritus U. Ill., Urbana-Champaign, 1981—2001, dean emeritus Commerce and Bus. Adminstrn., 2001—; dean

Warwick Bus. Sch. U. Warwick, Coventry, U.K., 2000—. Vis. prof. MIT, 1986-87, Northwestern U., 1990. Office: Warwick Bus Sch U Warwick Coventry CV4 7AL England Office Phone: 44-2476-524534. E-mail: Howard.Thomas@wbs.ac.uk.

THOMAS, HOWARD LAMAR, chef, consultant, writer; b. Tucker, Ga., Jan. 30, 1956; s. William Lyle Thomas and Dorthea Mary (England) Whitelaw; (div. 1989). BA in Philosophy, West Ga. Coll., 1975; postgrad. in philosophy, U. Ga., 1989-91. Chef St. Orres, Gualala, Calif., 1980-83; owner, chef Olde Town Inn, Conyers, Ga., 1986-88; exec. chef GRO Enterprises: The Mansion, Atlanta, 1984-85, Windchimes, Point Arena, Calif., 1991-93, East-West Bistro, Athens, Ga., 1994—. Cons. Athens Coffee House, Cappi-Davis Corp., Athens, 1993; lectr. Rolling Pin Kitchens, Athens, 1996-2001; spkr. in field. Author: (poetry chapbook) Coyote and Other Poems; contbr. poetry to lit. jours. Parnassus, Nimrod, Wis. Rev., Poetry Motel, Am. Writing, Lummox Rev., Hidden Oak, Nanny Fanny, Clark St. Rev., others; contbr. recipes to Atlanta Jour. Constn., monthly columnist Ga. Good Life Mag., So. Distractions Mag. Lectr. Athens-Clarke County Pub. Libr., 1996, 97, 98, 99, 2000; mem. Democratic Nat. Party, Ga., 1994—. Recipient 3d place award Circumference Lit. Jour., N.J. Coun. of Arts, 1994; finalist Pablo Neruda award 1999. Mem. ACLU, Am. Acad. Poets. Democrat. Baptist. Avocations: writing cookbooks, piano, modern literature, fly fishing, poetry. Office: East West Bistro 351 East Broad St Athens GA 30601 E-mail: hlamar@hlamarthomas.net.

THOMAS, HOWARD PAUL, civil engineer, consultant; b. Cambridge, Mass., Aug. 20, 1942; s. Charles Calvin and Helen Elizabeth (Hook) T.; m. Ingrid Nybo, Jan. 4, 1969; children: Kent Michael, Lisa Karen, Karina Michelle. BS in Engring., U. Mich., 1965, MS in Engring., 1966. Registered profl. engr., Alaska, Calif. Engr. Ove Arup & Ptnrs., London, 1966-67; project engr. Woodward-Clyde Cons., San Francisco, 1967-73, assoc. Anchorage, 1975-89; spl. cons. Cowiconsult Cons., Copenhagen, 1973-75; prin. engr. Harding-Lawson Assocs., Anchorage, 1989-90; v.p., chief engr. EMCON Alaska, Inc., Anchorage, 1991-94; gen. mgr. Internat. Tech. Corp., Anchorage, 1994-96; assoc. GeoEngrs., Inc., Anchorage, 1996—2002; prin. engr. CH2M Hill, Anchorage, 2001—; mem. Anchorage Mayor's Geotech. Adv. Commn., 1997—2003. Chmn. Nat. Tech. Coun. Cold Regions Engring., 1988-89, chmn. com. program and publs., 1982-84; chmn. 4th Internat. Conf. Cold Regions Engring., Anchorage, 1986; liaison NAS/Nat. Rsch. Coun. Polar Rsch. Bd., 1989-99. Contbr. articles to profl. jours. Fellow ASCE (pres. Anchorage chpt. 1985-86, chair mgmt. group A. 1996-97, pres. Alaska sect. 1998-99, named Alaskan Engr. of Yr. 1986, Harold R. Peyton award 2001); mem. Internat. Soc. for Soil Mechanics and Geotech. Engring., Cons. Engrs. Coun. Alaska (pres. 1989-90), Am. Cons. Engrs. Coun. (nat. dir. 1990-91), Project Mgmt. Inst. (v.p. Alaska chpt. 1991-95), Toastmasters (pres. Anchorage club 1984), Sons of Norway (pres. Anchorage lodge 2000-02). Lutheran. Avocations: playing french horn in Anchorage Civic Orchestra, travel, skiing, sailing. Home: 2611 Brittany Dr Anchorage AK 99504-3332 Personal E-mail: hthomas@ch2m.com.

THOMAS, HUW FRANCIS, dental educator, dean; BDS, U. London, Guy's Hosp., 1975; MS in Dental Rsch., U. Rochester, 1978; PhD in Biomedical Sci., U. Conn., 1986. Cert. pediatric dentistry Eastman Dental Ctr., U. Rochester, 1978. Postdoctoral fellow. NIH, 1980—84; asst. prof. pediatric dentistry U. Tex. Health Sci. Ctr., San Antonio, 1978—80; assoc. prof. pediatric dentistry dept. U. Conn. Health Ctr., Conn., 1980—92; prof., chmn. dept. pediatric dentistry U. Tex. Health Sci. Ctr., San Antonio, 1992—2003, prof. dept. pediat. & cellular and structural biology; prof., dean Sch. Dentistry, U. Ala., Birmingham, 2004—. Sci. cons. ADA Commn. on Dental Accreditation. Reviewer: American Journal of Anatomy, Archives of Oral Biology, Journal of Dental Education. Recipient New Investigator Research award, NIH, 1985. Fellow: Internat. Coll. Dentists, Am. Coll. Dentists, Am. Acad. Pediat. Dentistry; mem.: AAAS (mem. at large sec. on dentistry and oral health sci.), Am. Assn. Dental Rsch. (mem. nominating com.), Am. Acad. Pediat. (mem. exec. com. pediat. dentistry sect.), Omicron Kappa Upsilon. Office: U Ala Birmingham Sch Dentistry SDB 406 1530 3rd Ave S Birmingham AL 35294-0007

THOMAS, IRV, journalist, publisher; b. San Francisco, Apr. 14, 1927; s. David Goldstein and Minnie Resnick; m. Vivian Laure Allen, Nov. 30, 1956; life ptnr.: Alice Joy. BA, U. Wash., 1990. Pub./editor Black Bart Brigade/Yin Times, Canyon, Calif., 1971-83; editor Earthstewards jour./newsletter, Bainbridge Island, Wash., 1985-89; pub./editor Ripening Seasons Jour., Seattle, 1995—2003. Tchr., workshop organizer Finding a Way Out, San Francisco, 1971-75; presenter World Futurist Conf., Toronto, Ont., 1980, Assn. for Humanistic Psychology Conv., Estes Park, Colo., 1976, Calif. Libr. Assn. Conv., Disneyland, 1972. Author, illustrator: Innocence Abroad, 1994, rev. edit., 2001, Derelict Days..., 2004; contbr. anthology: Alternative Papers, 1982; contbr. articles to profl. jours. Housing activist Seattle Sr. Housing Program Advocates, 1996-99; co-founder Afterlife.org, 2001. Avocation: hitchhiking. Home: 6545 Ravenna Ave NE #307 Seattle WA 98115 E-mail: irvthom1@comcast.net.

THOMAS, ISIAH LORD, III, professional sports team executive, former professional basketball coach; b. Chgo., Apr. 30, 1961; m. Lynn Thomas; children: Joshua, Lauren. Grad. in Criminal Justice, Ind. U., 1987. With Detroit Pistons, 1981—94; v.p. Toronto Raptors, 1994—97, now v.p. basketball ops., owner, exec. v.p., 1996—97; sportscaster N.B.C. Sports, N.Y.C., 1997—2000; head coach Ind. Pacers, Indpls., 2000—03; founder Enlighten Sports, Inc.; pres., basketball ops. N.Y. Knicks, 2003—. Named to NBA All-Rookie team, 1982, All-Star Team, 1982—93, All NBA First Team, 1984, 1985, 1986; recipient All-Star Team MVP award, 1984, 1986, NBA Playoff MVP award, 1990, NBA Finals MVP, 1990. Achievements include being a mem. of U.S. Olympic Basketball Team, 1980; being in NBA Championship Teams, 1989-90. Office: NY Knicks Two Pennsylvania Plz New York NY 10121-0091

THOMAS, J. MARK, sociology educator, research fellow, minister; b. Ft. Worth, Dec. 20, 1947; s. Jacob Gillespie and Eleanor Rose (Geivett) T.; m. Jacquelyn Higby, Sept. 2, 1978; children: Megan Lane, Drew Martin. BA, Tex. Christian U., 1971, MDiv, 1974; PhD, U. Chgo., 1983. Ordained to ministry United Ch. of Christ, 1974. Asst. prof. philosophy and religion, chaplain Drury Coll., Springfield, Mo., 1983-85; adj. asst. prof. religion, chaplain Ripon (Wis.) Coll., 1985-87; vis. asst. prof. philosophy and religion Beloit (Wis.) Coll., 1987-89; sr. rsch. fellow Au Sable Inst. Environ. Studies, Mancelona, Mich., 1989—. Sociology instr., chair dept. social sci. Madison Area Tech. Coll. Author: Ethics and Technoculture, 1987, (with others) Being and Doing, 1987, Philosophy and Technology, Vol. 10, 1990, Religion in the New Millennium, 2001; editor: Paul Tillich, The Spiritual Situation in Our Technical Society, 1988, God and Capitalism, 1991, Religion in the New Millennium, 2001. Chmn. planning com. Congress of Sci., Tech. and Religion for the Parliament of World Religion, 1993. Recipient Disting. Tchr. Yr., Madison Area Tech. Coll., 1999. Mem. Midwest Sociol. Soc., Communitarian Network. Democrat. Mem. United Ch. of Christ. Home: 816 Lincoln St Madison WI 53711-2163 Office: Madison Area Tech Coll Downtown Edn Ctr 211 N Carroll St Madison WI 53703-2211

THOMAS, J. MIKESELL, bank executive; b. Grand Rapids, Mich., Jan. 19, 1951; s. Joseph Alexander and Betty Jane (Mikesell) T.; m. Phyllis Scholl, Aug. 3, 1973. AB, Duke U., 1973; MBA, U. Chgo., 1976. Treas. First Chgo. Corp., 1981-86, chief fin. officer, 1986-89; exec. v.p., co-head corp. instl. banking First Nat. Bank Chgo., 1989—94; mng. dir. Lazard Freres & Co. LLC, 1995—2001; ind. fin. advisor, 2001—04; pres., CEO Fed. Home Loan Bank Chgo., 2004—. Bd. dirs. Jr. Achievement Chgo., 1986, Evanston Hosp., Ill., 1991, Leadership Greater Chgo., 1991. Office: Fed Home Loan Bank of Chgo 111 E Wacker Dr Ste 800 Chicago IL 60601*

THOMAS, JACK WARD, wildlife biologist; b. Ft. Worth, Sept. 7, 1934; s. Scranton Boulware and Lillian Louise (List) T.; m. Farrar Margaret Schindler, June 29, 1957 (dec. Feb. 1994); children: Britt Ward, Scranton Gregory; m. Kathleen Connelly, Feb. 11, 1997. BS, Tex. A&M U., 1957; MS, W.Va. U., 1969; PhD, U. Mass., 1972; PhD (hon.), Lewis & Clark Coll., 1994, Lakehead U., 2001. Biologist Tex. Game & Fish Commn., Sonora, 1957-60; rsch. biologist Tex. Parks & Wildlife Dept., Plano, 1962—67; wildlife rsch. biologist, forestry sci. lab., Northeastern Forest Exptl. Sta. U.S. Forest Svc., Morgantown, W.Va., 1967-71; project dir. environ. forestry rsch. Pinchot Inst. Environ. Forestry, 1971-73; project leader range & wildlife habitat rsch. Pacific Northwest Forest Exptl. Sta. U.S. Forest Svc., LaGrande, Oreg., 1973-93; chief U.S. Dept. Agr.- Forest Svc., Washington, 1993-96; Boone & Crockett prof. wildlife conservation U. Mont., Missoula, 1996—. Author, editor: Wildlife Habitats in Managed Forests, 1979 (award The Wildlife Soc. 1980), Elk of North America, 1984 (award The Wildlife Soc. 1985), North American Elk: Ecology and Management, 2002; contbr. over 500 articles to profl. jours. Served to lt. USAF, 1957, USNR. Recipient Conservation award Gulf Oil Corp., 1983, Earle A. Childs award Childs Found., 1984, Disting. Svc. award USDA, Disting. Citizen's award, E. Oreg. State Coll., Nat Wildlife Fedn. award for Sci., 1990, Disting. Achievement award Soc. for Cons. Biology, 1990, Giraffe award The Giraffe Project, 1990, Scientist of Yr. award Oreg. Acad. Sci., 1990, Disting. Svc. award Soc. Conservation Biology, 1991, Sci. Conservation award Nat. Wildlife Fedn., 1991, Disting. Achievement award Soc. Conservative Biology, 1991, Chuck Yeager award Nat. Fish and Wildlife Found., 1992, Conservationist of Yr. award Oreg. Rivers Coun., 1992, Chief's Tech. Transfer award USDA, 1992, Tech. Transfer award Fed. Lab. Consortium, 1993, named Outstanding Scientist N.W. Sci. Assn., 1995, Disting. Alumni award Coll. Agr., Tex. A&M U., 1995, Disting. Svc. award Oreg. State U., 1996, Fed. Statesman award Found. N.Am. Wild Sheep, 1997, Claus J. Murie award Rocky Mountain Elk Found., 1999, Sustained Achievement award Renewable Natural Resources Found., 1999. Fellow Soc. Am. Foresters; mem. NAS (bd. agr. and natural resources 2001-2003), The Wildlife Soc. (cert., hon., pres. 1977-78, Oreg. Chpt. award 1980, Arthur Einarsen award 1981, spl. svcs. award 1984, Aldo Leopold Meml. medal 1991, group achievement award 1990), Am. Ornithologists Union, Am. Soc. Mammalogists, W.Va. U. Alumni Assn. (Disting. Alumni award 1996), U. Mass.-Amherst Alumni Assn. (Disting. Alumni award 1995), Rocky Mountain Elk Fouind. (bd. dirs. 1997-2003, chmn. 2003—), Bear Trust Internat., Forest Trust (adv. bd. gen. acctg. office 1999-2003), Lions, Elks. Avocations: hunting, fishing, white-water rafting, shooting, carpentry. Office: U Mont Sch Forestry Missoula MT 59812-0001

THOMAS, JACQUELINE MARIE, journalist, editor; b. Nashville, Aug. 31, 1952; d. John James and Dorothy Jacqueline (Phillips) T. BA, Briarcliff Coll., 1972; M.Internat. Affairs, Columbia U., 1974. Reporter Chgo Sun-Times, 1974-85; assoc. editor Courier-Jour. and Louisville Times, 1985-86, Detroit Free Press, 1986-93; deputy bureau chief, news editor Detroit News, Washington Bureau, 1993-94, bur. chief, 1994-97; editl. page editor The Balt. Sun, 1997—. Instr. Roosevelt U., Chgo., 1983 Nieman fellow Harvard U., 1983 Mem. Chgo. Assn. Black Journalists (Print Journalist of Yr. 1982), Nat. Assn. Black Journalists, Nat. Press Found. (bd. mem., vice chair), Am. Soc. Newspaper Editors, Nat. Assn. Minority Media Execs., Nat. Conf. Editl. Writers. Office: Balt Sun 501 N Calvert PO Box 1377 Baltimore MD 21278-0001

THOMAS, JACQUELYN MAY, librarian; b. Mechanicsburg, Pa., Jan. 26, 1932; d. William John and Gladys Elizabeth (Warren) Harvey; m. David Edward Thomas, Aug. 28, 1954; children: Lesley J., Courtenay J., Hilary A. BA summa cum laude, Gettysburg Coll., 1954; student, U. N.C., 1969; MEd, U. N.H., 1971. Libr. Phillips Exeter Acad., Exeter, N.H., 1971-77, acad. libr., 1977—. Chair governing bd. Child Care Ctr., 1987-91; chair Com. to Enhance Status of Women, Exeter, 1981-84; chair Loewenstein Com., Exeter, 1982—; pres. Cum Laude Soc., Exeter, 1984-86; James H. Ottaway Jr. prof., 1990—; mem. bldg. com. Exeter Pub. Libr., 1986-88; chair No. New Eng., Coun. for Women in Ind. Schs., 1985-87; chmn. Lamont Poetry Program, Exeter, 1984-86. Editor: The Design of the Library: A Guide to Sources of Information, 1981, Rarities of Our Time: The Special Collections of the Phillips Exeter Academy Library; pub.: Memorial Minutes, Phillips Exeter Academy, 1936-2002. Libr. trustee, treas. Exeter Day Sch., 1965-69; bd. Exeter Hosp. Vols., 1954-59; mem. Exeter Hosp. Corp., 1978—; bd. dirs. Greater Portsmouth Cmty. Found., 1990—; active AAC&U, On Campus with Women, Wellesley Coll. Ctr. for Rsch. on Women; mem. People to People Amb. Program, sch. and youth svcs. libr. del. to People's Rep. China, 1998. Grantee N.H. Coun. for Humanties, 1981-82, NEH, 1982; recipient Lillian Radford trust award, 1989. Mem. ALA, Internat. Assn. Sch. Librs., New Eng. Libr. Assn., N.J., Ednl. Media Assn., New Eng. Assn. Ind. Sch. Librs., Am. Assn. Sch. Librs. (chmn. non-pub. sch. sect.), Phi Beta Kappa. Home: 17 Eagle Dr Newmarket NH 03857 Office: Class of 1945 Libr Phillips Exeter Acad 20 Main St Exeter NH 03833-2460 Fax: 603-777-4389. Office Phone: 603-777-3328. E-mail: jthomas@exeter.edu.

THOMAS, JAMES A. pediatrician; BA in romance lang. and lit, L. Am. fiction, Princeton U., 1981; MD, Stanford U., 1989. Cert. Nat. Bd. Med. Examiners, Am. Bd. Pediat., sub-bd. pediat. critical care medicine. Resident, gen. pediat. Children's Hosp. Los Angeles, 1989—92; fellowship, pediat. critical care medicine U. Tex. SW, Dallas, 1992—95; assoc. prof. U. Tex. SW Med. Ctr. at Dallas; dir, divsn. critical care medicine Children's med. Ctr. at Dallas. Recipient Circulo Hispano-Americano award, 1981, Rsch. Honors award for Disting. Rsch. in Pediatrics, 1989, Victor E. Stork award, 1992, Jaws award for Outstanding Fellow, 1995. Mem.: AAAS, Internat. Endotoxin Soc., Shock Soc., Soc. for Critical Care Medicine, Am. Acad. Pediat. Office: Childrens Med Ctr U Tex SW 5323 Harry Hines Blvd Dallas TX 75390

THOMAS, JAMES BERT, JR., government official; b. Tallahassee, Mar. 16, 1935; s. James Bert and Stella E. (Lewis) T.; m. Sharon Mae Kelly, June 16, 1962; children: James Bert III, Mary Elizabeth, John Christopher. BS, Fla. State U., 1957. C.P.A., Fla. Spl. auditor Office State Comptr., Jacksonville, Fla., 1958; jr. auditor J.D.A. Holley & Co., C.P.A.'s, Tallahassee, 1959; sr. auditor Office of the State Auditor, Tallahassee, 1959-60; trainee, audit dir. HUD audit divsn., Washington, 1960-71; asst. dir. Bur. Accounts ICC, Washington, 1972-75, dir. Bur. Accounts, 1977-80; insp. gen. U.S. Dept. HUD, Washington, 1975-77, U.S. Dept. Edn., Washington, 1980-95; dir. auditing Office of the Gov., State of Fla., Tallahassee, 1995—. Mem. Pres.'s Coun. Integrity and Efficiency, chmn. audit stds. subcom., 1984-95, chmn. audit com., 1989-90. Mem. AICPA (strategic planning com. 1987-90, chmn. govt. auditing stds. adv. coun. 1991—), Inst. Internal Auditors (trustee Rsch. Found. 1991-92), Assn. Govt. Accts. (chmn. fin. mgmt. stds. bd. 1985-86), Accts. Roundtable. Roman Catholic. Home: 4737 Tory Sound Ln Unit 601 Tallahassee FL 32309-2266 Office: Exec Office of Governor Rm 2107 The Capitol Tallahassee FL 32399-0001

THOMAS, JAMES EDWARD, accountant; b. Darlington, S.C., Oct. 18, 1944; s. Willie Thomas and Cleola (Sawyer) T.; m. Joan Yvette Grant, Mar. 15, 1945; 1 child, James E. II. BS in Acctg., Johnson C. Smith Coll., Charlotte, N.C., 1966; MA in Fin., C.W. Post Coll., Greenvale, N.Y., 1980; PhD in Edn., Fordham U., 1996; MBA, Pace U., 1976. Cert. paralegal. Asst. mgr. Mfrs. Hanover Trust, N.Y.C., 1970-78, Met. Savs. Bank, N.Y.C., 1978-81; auditor N.Y. State Dept. Social Svcs., N.Y.C., 1981-83; acct. N.Y.C. Bd. Edn., 1983-86; acct., agt. IRS, N.Y.C., 1987-99; dir. fin. N.Y.C. Dept. Design and Constrn., Long Island City, 1999—. Instr. Katherine L. Gibbs, Inc., N.Y.C., 1987-89. Mem.: Internat. Platform Assn., Nat. Soc. Pub. Accts., Nat. Assn. Sch. Bus. Ofcls., Am. Mgmt. Assn., Assn. MBA Execs., Sigma Rho Sigma. Avocations: woodworking, basketball, baseball, track, reading. Home: 99-72 66th Rd# 3R Rego Park NY 11374

THOMAS, JAMES EDWARD, JR., brokerage house executive; b. Atlanta, Apr. 23, 1950; s. James Edward and Dortha Jean (White) Thomas; m. Leslie Ann Stagmaier, Sept. 6, 1975; children: Steele Stagmaier, Katherine Mills. BA magna cum laude, U. Ga., 1972, JD cum laude, 1975. Mgr. Genuine Parts Co., Atlanta, 1975-77; v.p. Robinson Humphrey Co., Atlanta, 1977-94; ptnr. J.C. Bradford and Co., Atlanta, 1994—2000; mng. dir. Wachovia Securities, Ga., 2000—02; chmn., CEO Stillpoint Advisors, Inc., 2003—. Bd. dirs. Enstar Comm. Corp., The Kinston Group, Inc., Atlanta, Tophat Soccer Club, Atlanta, Hall's Boathouse, Inc., Lakemont, Ga., Vista Environ. Info., Inc., San Diego. Pres. Castlewood Civic Orgn., Inc., Atlanta; mem. Lake Rabun Homeowners Assn., Lakemont, Ga.; mem. bd. advisors U. Ga., Habitat for Humanity. Mem. Internat. Platform Assn., Ga. Bar Assn., La Societe des Tetes Grandes, Capital City Club, U. Ga. LEADS Adv. Bd., Ga Tennis Found. (treas., trustee). Republican. Episcopalian. Avocations: boating, tennis, golf.

THOMAS, JAMES PATRICK, special education educator; b. Chgo., Sept. 24, 1946; s. Jacque Anthony and Dorothy Lucille (Brown) T.; m. Cathy E. Hanks, Sept. 29, 1979 (div. Aug. 1990); 1 child, Nicholas Jacque. BA in History and Polit. Sci., Drake U., 1973; MS in Pub. Adminstrn., Troy State U., 1983; MS in Spl. Edn., cert. advanced grad. studies, Johns Hopkins U., 1994. cert. spl. educator. Commd. 2nd lt. USAF, 1973, advanced through grades to maj., 1985; missile launch officer, instr., crew comdr., contr. 91st Strategic Missile Wing, Minot, N.D., 1974-78; exec. officer, asst. ops. officer, resource advisor 6916th Electronic Security Squadron, Hellenikon Air Base, Greece, 1978-81; chief programs br. 6940th Electronic Security Wing, Ft. Meade, Md., 1981-82; program mgr. USAF Ops. Security Hq USAF/XOEO Directorate of Electronic Combat, Washington, 1982-85; intelligence collection activities mgr./chief Hdqrs. U.S. European Command, Stuttgart, Germany, 1986-88; signals intelligence planning staff officer Nat. Security Agy., Ft. Meade, 1988-90; cons. spl. edn. Balt., 1991—. Adj. faculty mem. Catonsville (Md.) C.C., 1991—; spl. educator Howard County Sch. System, Columbia, 1992-94, Boonsboro (Md.) Middle Sch., 1994-96, Hiatt Mid. Sch., Des Moines, 1996-98, Johnston (Iowa) Mid. Sch., 1998-99, Johnston High Sch., 1999 2000, Variety Sch., Las Vegas, Nev., 2000—. Author: (pamphlet) Your Rights to Legal Advice, 1994; co-author: The Outcome of a Services Evaluation for Families of Vietnam Vets. with Children with Disabilities in the Balt. Met. Area, 1995. Pres. Cath. Men Parish Athens, Greece, 1979—81, 1975—78. With USN, 1964—73. Decorated Purple Heart, 2 Def. Meritorious Svc. medals, Meritorious Svc. medals, Air Force Commendation medal, Air medal, Air Force Achievement medal, Navy Combat Action Ribbon, Vietnam Gallantry Cross. Mem.: KC, VFW (life), Swiftboat Sailors Assn. Inc. (pres. 1995—2002), Am. Legion China Post 1, Assn. Air Force Missileers (life), Vets. Vietnam War (life), Navy League (life), Mil. Order Purple Heart (life), Ret. Officers Assn. (life), Air Force Assn. (life), Disabled Am. Vets. (life), Phoenix Soc., Soaring Assn. Am., Phi Delta Gamma. Roman Catholic. Avocations: pilot of sailplanes, sailing, snorkeling, golf, running. Home: 1929 High Mesa Dr Henderson NV 89012-6182

THOMAS, JAMES WILLIAM, lawyer; b. N.Y.C., May 12, 1949; s. Howard and Alice (Brennan) T.; m. Cecilia Coleman Goad, July 7, 1973; children: James William, Brennan McKinney. BS, U. Dayton, 1971; JD, Ohio No. U., 1974. Bar: Ohio 1974, U.S. Dist. Ct. Ohio 1976. Ptnr. Earley & Thomas, Eaton, Ohio, 1974-89; pvt. practice Eaton, 1989—. Village solicitor Village of Lewisburg (Ohio), 1977-81, Village of Verona (Ohio), 1979-81; asst. pros. atty. Preble County (Ohio), 1980-81. Mem. Preble County Cmty. Corrections Planing Bd. Fellow Ohio State Bar Found.; mem. ABA, Ohio State Bar Assn., Ohio State Bar Coll., Ohio Acad. Trial Lawyers, Ohio Assn. Criminal Def. Lawyers, Preble county Bar Assn. (pres. 1982-84), Comm. Improvement Corp., Eaton Country Club, Rotary (dir. 1980-87, pres. 1987-88). Republican. Roman Catholic. Avocations: boating, tennis. Home: 761 Vinland Cv Eaton OH 45320-2536 Office: 112 N Barron St Eaton OH 45320-1702

THOMAS, JANEY SUE, elementary school principal; b. Clarksville, Tenn., Feb. 10, 1949; d. James Ernest and Ethel Mae (Evans) Kirkland; m. Tony Lee Thomas, Oct. 9, 1965; children: Jeff, Kelli. BS in Elem. Edn., Austin Peay State U., 1979, MA in Elem. Edn. Adminstrn., 1982, postgrad., 1987-89. Tchr. Charlotte (Tenn.) Jr. High Sch., 1979-86; prin. Vanleer (Tenn.) Elem. Sch., 1986-91, Oakmont Elem. Sch., Dickson, Tenn., 1991—. Ednl. rep. Concerned Citizens for Edn., Dickson County, 1988; mem. com. United Way Med. Tenn., Dickson County, 1990-91, bd. dirs., 1992-93. Recipient Nat. Sch. of Recognition award U.S. Dept. Edn., 1990. Mem. NAESP (Excellence in Edn. award 1989-90), Tenn. Assn. Elem. Sch. Prins. (Nat. Exemplary Sch. award 1989-90), Dickson County Edn. Assn. (pres. 1989-90). Baptist. Avocations: reading, travel, shopping. Home: 226 Druid Hills Dr Dickson TN 37055-3331 Office: Oakmont Elem Sch 630 Highway 46 S Dickson TN 37055-2552

THOMAS, JASON SELIG, lawyer; b. Lansing, Mich., Jan. 23, 1954; s. William Ellsworth and Esta (Berg) T.; m. Edith Madeline Gettes, Oct. 28, 1995; children: Monica, Sophia, Hannah. BMus, Oberlin Coll., 1976; MMus, SUNY, Stony Brook, 1978; JD, U. N.C., 1991; D of Mus. Arts, U. Wis., 1991. Bar: N.C. 1991, U.S. Dist. Ct. (ea. dist.) N.C. 1992, U.S. Dist. Ct. (mid. and we. dists.) N.C. 1995, U.S. Ct. Appeals (4th cir.) 1994. Prin. cellist Ark. Symphony Orch., Little Rock, 1978-81; asst. prof. U. Ky., Lexington, 1981-82; freelance cellist Ludwigshafen, West Germany, 1986-87; assoc. Moore & Van Allen, Raleigh, N.C., 1991-92, Hunton & Williams, Raleigh, 1992—. Contbg. author: Toxic Tort and Hazardous Substance Litigation, 1985. Recipient Outstanding Vol. Atty. award Wake County, N.C., 1995, 97. Mem. ABA, N.C. Bar Assn. (pro bono com. 1998). Office: Hunton & Williams 1 Hannover Sq Ste 1400 Raleigh NC 27601-2947 E-mail: jsthomas@hunton.com.

THOMAS, JEFFREY CONE, financial executive, consultant; b. New Orleans, Oct. 10, 1941; s. Eads Poitevent and Virginia Lee (King) T.; m. Brenda Gayle Ballard, June 7, 1969 (div. Mar. 1972). BA, La. State U., 1965. CLU; ChFC; CFP; CFS. Mgmt. trainee Am. Bank and Trust Co., Baton Rouge, 1965-68; supr. Travelers Ins. Co., Baton Rouge, 1968-71; dist. dir. Conn. Gen. Life Ins. Co., Baton Rouge, 1971-74; pres., CEO Pension & Profit Sharing Cons., Baton Rouge, 1974-77; pres. Fin. Advisor & Cons., Baton Rouge, 1977—. Adj. instr. adult eve. classes Coll. Fin. Planning, 1987-92; cons. Ethyl Corp., Baton Rouge, 1982, Dow Chem., Plaquemine, La., 1986. Vol. ARC, Baton Rouge, 1965-69; mem. adminstrv. bd. First Meth. Ch., Baton Rouge, 1987-89. Avocations: golf, tennis, fishing, gardening. Office: Fin Advisor & Cons PO Box 65238 Baton Rouge LA 70896-5238 Office Phone: 225-293-1035.

THOMAS, JEREMIAH LINDSAY, III, lawyer; b. Wilmington, Del., June 20, 1946; s. Jeremiah Lindsay Jr. and Dorothy Eleanor (Conway) T.; m. Clara Ewing Ruthrauff, Oct. 17, 1981; children: Catherine Ewing, Lindsay Barlow. BA, U. Va., 1968, JD, 1972. Bar: N.Y. 1973. Assoc. Simpson Thacher & Bartlett, N.Y.C., 1972-79, ptnr., 1979—. Mem.: ABA, Met. Golf Assn. (legal counsel 1984—, exec. com. 1992—98, dir. Found. 1992—98), Assn. Bar of City of N.Y., N.Y. State Bar Assn. Office: Simpson Thacher & Bartlett 425 Lexington Ave Fl 15 New York NY 10017-3954 E-mail: jthomas@stblaw.com.

THOMAS, JIM GUS, music educator; b. El Paso, Tex., July 10, 1945; s. Gus Demetrios Thomopoulos and Antigone Mourgelas; m. Evi Deligianni Thomas, Aug. 15, 1970 (div. May 18, 1998); children: Gus James, Georgianna. Bachelor Music Edn., Ariz. State U., Tempe, AZ, 1969, MA, 1975. Music educator Creighton Sch. Dist., Phoenix, Ariz., 1970—; choral, gen. music educator Isaac Sch. Dist., Phoenix, Ariz., 1972—76; founder, orchestral strings educator Paradise Valley Dist., Phoenix, Ariz., 1976—79; music educator Cartwright Sch. Dist., Phoenix, Ariz., 1979—. Dir., educator Summer Music Camp, Prescott, Ariz., 1993—; instr. Honors String Orch., 2002—, The Funky Fiddlers, 2002—; music curriculum coord. Cartwright Sch. Dist., Phoenix, 2002—, adminstrv. asst. to dist. music cons., 2002—. Composer: (greek folk dance for clarinet trio) Pentozalis. Mem.: Ariz. Music Educators Assn. (O.M. Hartsell Excellence Tchg. Music award 2002), Am. String Teachers Assn., Music Educators Nat. Conf. D-Liberal. Greek Orthodox. Achievements include two tours to Europe with music students. Avocations: biking, travel, learning and performing multicultural music and instruments. Home: 4905 E Robin Lane Phoenix AZ 85054 Office: Peracta Elementary School 7125 West Encanto Phoenix AZ 85033

THOMAS, JIMMY LYNN, financial executive; b. Mayfield, Ky., Aug. 3, 1941; s. Alben Stanley and Emma Laura (Alexander) T.; m. Kristin H. Kent, Oct. 1986; children: James Nelson, Carter Danforth. BS, U. Ky., 1963; MBA, Columbia U., 1964. Fin. analyst Ford Motor Co., Detroit, 1964-66; asst. treas. Joel Dean Assocs., N.Y.C., 1966-67; asst. contr. Trans World Airlines, N.Y.C.,

1967-73; sr. v.p. fin. svcs., treas. Gannett Co., Inc., Arlington, Va., 1973-98. Bd. dirs. HSBC, Rochester, Tremont Ptnrs. Fundraiser United Negro Coll. Fund; bd. trustees, treas. Harley Sch., Rochester, N.Y.; bd. overseers Strong Meml. Hosp., Rochester; bd. govs. Genesee Hosp., Rochester; bd. dirs. Arlington Cmty. Found., Nat. Press Club Bldg., Washington. With U.S. Army, 1966-72. Ashland Oil Co. scholar, 1959-63, McKinsey scholar 1964; Samuel Bronfman fellow, 1963-64. Mem. Nat. Assn. Corp. Treas., U. Ky. Alumni Assn., Columbia U. Alumni Assn., Country Club of Rochester, Genessee Valley Club, Beta Gamma Sigma, Omicron Delta Kappa, Sigma Alpha Epsilon. Democrat. Mem. Christian Ch. (Disciples Of Christ). Home: 9700 Jennings Rd Eden NY 14057-9518 Office Phone: 716-992-9935.

THOMAS, JO, journalist, educator; b. Long Beach, Calif., Dec. 7, 1943; d. Guy O'Neil DeYoung, Jr. and Josephine (Bradley) DeYoung; m. William L. Thomas III, June 12, 1965 (div. Sept. 1969); m. William F. Kelleher Jr., Dec. 19, 1985; children: Susan Elizabeth Kelleher, Kathleen DeYoung Kelleher. BA summa cum laude, Wake Forest U., 1965; MA, U. N.C., 1967. Reporter Cin. Post and Times-Star, 1966—70, Detroit Free Press, 1971—77; from Washington corr. to writer N.Y. Times, 1977—2001, writer, 2001—02; assoc. prof. U. Ill., Urbana, 1987—94, asst. chancellor, 2003—04; assoc. chancellor Syracuse U., NY, 2004—, prof. journalism, 2004—. Contbr. articles to newspapers and mags. Recipient Outstanding Reporting award Detroit Press Club, 1974-75, Robert F. Kennedy award, 1973; Nieman fellow Harvard U., 1970-71. Mem. Phi Beta Kappa, Kappa Tau Alpha. Office Phone: 315-443-3793.

THOMAS, JOAB LANGSTON, retired university president, biology educator; b. Holt, Ala., Feb. 14, 1933; s. Ralph Cage and Chamintney Elizabeth (Stovall) Thomas; m. Marly A. Dukes, Dec. 22, 1954; children: Catherine, David, Jennifer, Frances. AB, Harvard U., 1955, MA, 1957, PhD, 1959; DSc (hon.), U. Ala., 1981; LLD (hon.), Stillman Coll., 1987; LHD (hon.), Tri-State U., 1994; LHD (hon.), N.C. State U., 1998. Cytotaxonomist Arnold Aboretum, Harvard, 1959—61; prof. biology U. Ala., University, 1966—76, 1988—91, asst. dean Coll. Arts and Scis., 1964—65, 1969, dean for student devel., 1969—74, v.p., 1974—76, dir. Herbarium, 1961—76, dir. Arboretum, 1964—69, pres. Tuscaloosa, 1981—88; chancellor N.C. State U., Raleigh, 1976—81; pres. Pa. State U., University Park, 1990—95, pres. emeritus, 1995. Intern acad. adminstrn. Am. Coun. on Edn., 1971. Author: A Monographic Study of the Cyrillaceae, 1960, Wildflowers of Alabama and Adjoining States, 1973, The Rising South, 1976, Poisonous Plants and Venomous Animals of Alabama and Adjoining States, 1990. Bd. dirs. Internat. Potato Ctr., 1977—83, chmn., 1982—83; bd. dirs. Internat. Svc. for Nat. Agrl. Rsch., 1985—91. Named Citizen of Yr., City of Tuscaloosa, 1987; recipient Ala. Acad. Honor, 1983, Palmer Mus. Art medal, Coll. Pres.'s award, All-Am. Football Found., 1997, Spl. Recognition award, Assn. for Continuing Higher Edn., 1998. Mem.: Golden Key, Phi Kappa Phi, Omicron Delta Kappa (Laurel Crowned Circle award 2001), Sigma Xi, Phi Beta Kappa. Office: Univ Ala 413 Sci Collections Bldg Tuscaloosa AL 35487-0001 Business E-Mail: jlthomas@dbtech.net.

THOMAS, JOE CARROLL, retired human resources director; b. Belmont, N.C., Nov. 2, 1931; m. Ruth Stone, June 17, 1951; children: Joe (dec.), Jerry, Angela. BA, Belmont Abbey Coll., 1954; MS, Cornell U., 1961; postgrad., U. N.C., 1985. Diplomate in profl. counseling; cert. Sr. Profl. in Human Resources. Terr. salesman Gen. Foods Corp., Charlotte, NC, 1954—59, adminstrv. asst. to dist. mgr. Atlanta, 1960, mgr. terr. sales San Antonio, 1962; asst. dir. personnel textiles divsn. Kendall Co., Charlotte, N.C., 1962-64; dir. personnel S.E. region Gifford Hill & Co., Charlotte, 1964-71; dir. mgmt. svcs. Ervin Industries, Charlotte, 1971-75; v.p. indsl. rels. Crompton & Knowles, Charlotte, 1975-76; exec. v.p., dir. human resources Barclays Group Inc. (USA), Charlotte, 1976-97; ret., 1997. Mem. adv. coun. Sch. Bus., Western Carolina U., Cullowhee, N.C., 1980-84; mem. bd. arbitrators NASD Dispute Resolution, Inc., 2001. Vice chmn. bd. trustees Belmont Abbey Coll., 1982-88; chmn. fundraising campaign Charlotte chpt. Am. Heart Assn., 1984; mem. bd. visitors mercy Hosp., Charlotte, 1984-87; bd. dirs. mercy Health Svcs., Charlotte, 1988-96; bd. dirs. Jr. Achievement Charlotte, 1985-88; chmn. bd. dirs. INROADS divsn. Charlotte, Inc., 1987-88; bd. visitors Johnson C. Smith Univ., 1989-92. Mem. Soc. Human Resource Mgmt., Employers Assn. (bd. dirs. 1993-99, exec. com. 1995-99), Charlotte Athletic Club (pres. 1982-83), Charlotte Rotary, Charlotte C. of C. (bd. advisors 1992-97, aldersgate bd. advisors 2000-, aldersgate bd. dirs. 2003-). Republican.

THOMAS, JOHN, mechanical engineer; b. Tiruvalla, Kerala, India, Jan. 2, 1946; came to U.S., 1974; s. Munnencheril Varghese and Rachel (Mathai) T.; m. Mary Parapat Varghese, Apr. 28, 1975; children: Joel George, Sayana Rachel. BSMechE, Birla Inst. Tech., Ranchi, India, 1969; MSMechE, U. Waterloo, Ont., Can., 1974. Registered profl. engr., Wis. Lectr. mech. engring. U. Kerala, India, 1970-71; design engr. Combustion Engring., Inc., Springfield, Ohio, 1974-76; mech. engr. Ingersoll-Rand Co., Painted Post, N.Y., 1977-80; engr. Allis-Chalmers Corp., Milw., 1980-82; pvt. practice engring. cons. Milw., 1982-84; sr. tech. devel. engr. Cross & Trecker divsn. Kearney & Trecker Corp., Milw., 1984-87; prin. John Thomas & Assocs., Brookfield, Wis., 1988-90; sr. product engr. N.W. Water Group, Pub. Ltd. Corp., Waukesha, Wis., 1989-94; pres. Thomas Products Co., Brookfield, Wis., 1995—; staff engr. Milsco Mfg. Co. unit of Jason Inc., Milw., 1997—2003. Patentee in field. Mem. ASME, U. Waterloo Alumni Assn. Mem. Mar Thoma Syrian Ch. of Malabar. Avocations: photography, golf. Home: 18330 Benington Brookfield WI 53045-5419 Office: Thomas Products Co PO Box 401 Brookfield WI 53008-0401

THOMAS, JOHN ARLEN, pharmacology educator, health science administrator; b. LaCrosse, Wis., Apr. 6, 1933; s. John M. and Eva Hazel (Nelson) T.; m. Barbara A. Fisler, June 22, 1957; children: Michael J., Jane L. BS in Sci. Edn., U. Wis., 1956; MA in Physiology, U. Iowa, 1958, PhD in Physiology, 1961. Diplomate Am. Acad. Toxicologic Sci. Instr. U. Iowa, Iowa City, 1961; asst. prof. U. Va., Charlottesville, 1961-64; assoc. prof. Creighton U., Omaha, 1964-67, W.Va. U., Morgantown, 1968-69, prof. pharmacology, 1970-80; asst. dean W.Va. Sch. Medicine, Morgantown, 1973-75, assoc. dean, 1973-80; v.p. corp. rsch. Baxter Internat. Travenol Labs., Round Lake, Ill., 1980-87; v.p. acad. svcs. U. Tex. Health Sci. Ctr., San Antonio, 1988-99, prof. emeritus pharmacology dept. toxicology, 1988—. Cons. NIH, Bethesda, Md., 1975, Nat. Libr. Medicine, Bethesda, 1994; bd. dirs. ILSI, Washington, NAS Com., Washington, 1998-2003; bd. dirs. Tex. Soc. Biomed. Rsch., Austin, v.p., 1996; chmn. expert adv. com. Can. Network Toxicol. Ctr., 1999-2002; mem. sci. adv. bd. USAF, 2002-, FDA, 2003-, Nat. Toxicol. Program, Repro. Toxicol. Panels (chmn. 2004), EPA Rev. Panel. Author (with M.G. Mawhinney): Synopsis of Endocrine Pharmacology, 1978; author: (with E.J. Keenan) Principles of Endocrine Pharmacology, 1986; editor (with others): Basic and Clinical Toxicology of Lead, 1985; editor: Endocrine Toxicology, 1985, 1996, Drugs Athletes & Physical Performance, 1988, Biotechnicology and Safety Assessment, 1993; editor: (with Laurie A. Myers) Biotechnicology and Safety Assessment 2d edit., 1981; editor: (with Roy L. Fuchs) Biotechnicology and Safety Assessment, 3d edit., 2002; editor: Endocrine Methods, 1996, Toxic Substances Mechanism Jour.; contbr. articles to profl. jours. Sgt. U.S. Army, 1951-53. Recipient Cert. Svc. U.S. EPA, 1977; named Outstanding Tchr., W.Va. U., 1971, 73, 79, Outstanding alumnus U. Wis.-La Crosse, 1978, Disting. Alumni, U. Iowa, 1997; named to Hall of Excellence-LaCrosse, 2002. Fellow Acad. Toxicol. Sci. (pres. 2001); mem. Endocrine Soc., Soc. Toxicology (councilor, Merit award 1998), Am. soc. Pharmacology and Exptl. Therapeutics, Am. Coll. Toxicology (councilor, pres., disting. fellow 2004, Disting. Svc. award), Teratology Soc., Am. Acad. Vet. Pharmacology, Am. Chem. Soc. (pres. chem. toxicology pathology), Tex. Soc. Biomed. Rsch. (bd. sci. advisors 1989-99, Disting. Svc. award 1996), Russian Acad. Med. Sci. (fgn.fellow-elect 1995). Home: 219 Wood Shadow St San Antonio TX 78216-1633 Personal E-mail: jat-tox@swbell.net.

THOMAS, JOHN CHARLES, lawyer, former state supreme court justice; b. Norfolk, Va., Sept. 18, 1950; s. John and Floretta V. (Sears) T.; m. Pearl Walden, Oct. 9, 1982; children: John Charles Jr., Ruby Virginia, Lewis LeGrant. BA in Am. Govt. with distinction, U. Va., 1972, JD, 1975. Bar: Va. 1975, U.S. Dist. Ct. (ea. and we. dists.) 1976, U.S. Ct. Appeals (4th cir.) 1976, U.S. Supreme Ct. 1979, U.S. Ct. Appeals (D.C. cir.) 1980, U.S. Ct. Appeals (10th cir.) 1991, U.S. Ct. Appeals (11th cir.) 1992. Assoc. Hunton & Williams, Richmond, Va., 1975-82, ptnr., 1982-83, 89—; justice Supreme Ct. of Va., Richmond, 1983-89. Former mem. adv. con. on appellate rules U.S. Jud. Conf., permanent mem. 4th cir. Hon. dir. U. Va. Law Sch. Found. Master John Marshall Inn of Ct. (exec. com.); fellow Am. Bar Found., Va. Bar Found.; mem. ABA (former co-chair nat. conf. of lawyers and reps. of media, mem. coun. appellate lawyers), Am. Arbitration Assn. (bd. dirs., exec. com., law com.), Am. Acad. Appellate Lawyers, Va. State Bar, Va. Bar Assn., Bar Assn. City of Richmond, Old Dominion Bar Assn., Omega Psi Phi, Sigma Pi Phi. Office: Hunton & Williams Riverfront Plz East Tower PO Box 1535 Richmond VA 23218-1535 Office Phone: 804-788-8522.

THOMAS, JOHN DAVID, musician, composer, arranger, graphic designer, recording engineer, producer, photographer; b. Muncie, Ind., Mar. 30, 1951; s. John Charles and Phyllis Lorraine (Wear) T.; m. Rosalie Faith Baldwin, July 27, 1974 (div. 1991); children: Bethany Carol, Mark David. Student, Purdue U., 1969-71, Jordan Coll. of Music, Indpls., 1961-65; BS in Music Theory and Composition, Ball State U., 1976. Musician, composer, 1955—; cellist The Howe String Quartet (with Ann Pinney, Mary Ann Tilford, Anne Wuster), Indpls., 1967-68; keyboardist, vocalist, cellist Fire and The Rebel Kind rock bands, Indpls., 1967-69, Good Conduct rock band, Muncie, Ind., 1972-73; pianist The Pavillion at Olde Towne, Los Gatos, Calif., 1969; radio announcer John David's Late Night Rock Show WCCR-AM, West Lafayette, Ind., 1969-70; photographer Indpls., 1964—84, 1991—2000; budget analyst Office of Comptr. USAFAC, Indpls., 1976-84; co-leader, keyboardist, composer, arranger, vocalist, sound technician Jetstream band, Carmel, Indpls., Kokomo, Columbus, Bloomington, Ind., 1979-83; co-leader, keyboardist, vocalist, sound technician The Thomas Bros., King's Crown Inn, Kokomo, 1979; sound/audio visual technician Valley Cathedral Ch., Phoenix, 1987; CEO/owner, digital and film photographer, graphic designer Have Camera Will Travel, 2003—. Pianist, synthesist Paul Thomas and Night and Day, The Tim Barnett Band, Indpls. Mus. Art, 1992, Radisson Hotel and Broadmoor Country Club, Indpls., 1991, Highland Country Club, Indpls., The Ritz Charles Hotel and Summertrace, Carmel, Ind., Stonehenge Resort, Bedford, Ind., 1991; solo pianist Terranova Mansion, Paradise Valley, Ariz., 1987, Wrigley Mansion, Phoenix, 1988, Boulders Resort, Carefree, Ariz., 1987, Clarion Inn/McCormick's Ranch Resort, Scottsdale, Ariz., 1986, China Gate, Phoenix, 1988, Victor's, Phoenix, 1988, Cascade Club, Everett, Wash., 1990; keyboardist, synthesist, key bassist, The Gulch Gang, Pinnacle Peak Patio, Scottsdale, 1984, Dee Dee Ryan, The Longhorn Saloon, Apache Junction, Ariz., 1984-86, The Last Straw Band, Country City saloon, Mesa, Ariz., 1986; keyboardist, pianist, vocalist with Peter, Paul and John, Anderson (Ind.) Coll., 1977; CEO, owner, composer, photographer, arranger, prodr., musician, engr., graphic designer, computer operator, John David Thomas Prodns., Indpls., 1993—; CEO, owner JD Thomas Music Co., 1999—, Monolith Records, 1999-2001, JDT Records, 2001—, Serious Bizness Music Co., 2002—, Global Concept Music Co., 2002—, Silky Rd. Music Co., 2002—, Spirit Realm Music Co., 2002—, Mega Modern Music Co., 2002—; rec. artist CD label mp3.com., 2000-2004, CD label besonic.com, Europe, 2002-, JDT Records, 2001-. Composer, lyricist of over 350 classical, religious, comml., rock, jazz, popular and avante garde/futuristic compositions, including Infinity, 1970-71, Death of Rock and Roll, 1970, Night Visions, 1972, First Things First, 1972, Two Nudes and a Fire Hydrant, 1972-73, Chant for Orchestra, 1972, 2001, Love Theme in D, 1972, 98, Zeitgeist: The Spirit of the Time, 1974, The Little Prince, 1973, 2001, When We Dead Awaken, 1973, Pray, 1972, Apogee, 1974, Chinese Baby, 1973, Alabama DA (Top Forty recording), 1973, Angel, 1974, Music for French Horn, Cello, and Piano, 1976, Cruising Beyond, 1979, Jetstream Theme, 1979, Chrissy, 1979, Love Theme in B Minor, 1979, In Your Heart, 1983, Future Music, 1987, The Recurrent New Millenium Orchestral Olympic Disco Festival Dance, 1989, Jubilee in F, 1989, Praise Him, The King Liveth, 1989, Love Flowers: Reflections and Meditations on Beauty and Truth, 1990, Sheena's Theme, 1992, I Want You Forever You're My Miracle, 1992, My Pseudo-Erotic, Sensual, Exotic Musical Fantasy and Romance for Our Heavenly Nocturnal Starry-Skied Carpet Ride to Paradise in Istanbul and Constantinople, 1992, I'm in Love with Someone Beautiful, 1992, Improvisations for Sheena, 1992, Musical Essences, 1994, 2002, Mystery World #1, 1994, Mystery World #2, 1994, Orient, 1994, Orchestral #17, 1994, Drums and Percussion Music, 1994, My Renaissance Brass Music, 1994, Postlude, 1994, Music for Baritone Vocal and String Orch., 1995, Meditations for Pipe Organ and Male Choir, 1996, Trumpet Voluntary in F, 1996, Pathway to Love, 1996, Majestic Brass Music in F#, 1997, J.D.'s Theme, 1998, The Road to Tomorrow, 1999, Let Me Be the One, 2000, God and the Everlasting, 2000, Sunshine, 2000, Love Theme, 2000, Dreaming, 2000, Together, 2000, Love You, 2000, The Road of Life, 2000, Desires of the Heart, 2000, The Open Sky, 2000, Just Me and You, 2000, In the Spirit of Mozart, 2001, God and the Everlasting, 2001, From Me to You, 2001, Ostinato for Double Reeds, 2001, God 1, 2001, God 2, 2001, Randy's Theme, 2002, Music for Suzy, 2003, Music for Beautiful Women, 2003, over 140 short piano compositions, 1999-2003; (albums) The Journey of Life, Destiny's Calling: Improvisations, 1994, 2002; (cd's) The Journey of Life, 1994, 2002, Musical Essences, 1994, 2002, Music for Bethany, 2002, The Avant-Garde of John David Thomas, 2002, From Me to You, 2002, Desires of the Heart, 2002, Spirit Music, 2002, The Seen and the Unseen, 2000, Potpourri: Music for the World, 2000, Music for the World, vol. 2, 2000, (broadcast) Hometown Hour, Sta. WFBQ-FM, Indpls., 1979-80, Music for Kelly, Judy, Karyn, and Stacey, 2003; performed orginal composition, Someday, WFBM-TV, Indpls., 1969; designer automotive concepts and popular fashions; recordings of over 120 original songs and compositions including Love Theme in D, 1972, 98, Majestic Brass Music in F# for Bethany and Mark, 1997, J.D.'s Theme, 1998; plus over 90 recordings on CD's; author numerous poems. Musician, vocalist, composer Downey Ave. Christian Ch., Indpls., 1961-69, Univ. Presbyn. Ch., West Lafayette, Ind., 1969-71, Castleview Bapt. Ch., Indpls., 1974-84, Valley Cathedral Ch., Phoenix, 1986-87, Edmonds (Wash.) Christian Ch., 1988-90, Edmonds United Meth. Ch., 1989-90; page to speaker Ho. of Reps. Ind. State Legislature, 1963; active All Souls Unitarian Ch., Indpls., 1994-96. GM scholar Purdue U., 1969-70, Hoosier scholar, 1969, Palmer Meml. Music scholar Ball State U., 1971-74; named to Ind. All-State Orch. (cellist), 1968; recipient 1st place award (cellist) Ind. State Music Contest, 1968, God and Country award, 1965, Outstanding Musician award Irvington Music Club, Indpls., 1969, Purdue U. Symphonette, 1970, Hometown Hour award WFBQ-FM Radio Sta., Indpls., 1979. Mem. ASCAP, NARAS, Audio Engring. Soc., Mensa. Avocations: reading, computers, listening to music, dining, photography. Mailing: PO Box 3593 Carmel IN 46082 Home and Office: 2704 Central Ct Indianapolis IN 46280-1930 Office Phone: 317-844-3161. E-mail: johndavidthomas1@yahoo.com., moderncomposer@hotmail.com., johndavidthomas@hotmail.com.

THOMAS, JOHN HOWARD, astrophysicist, engineer, educator; b. Chgo., Apr. 9, 1941; s. William Whitney and Dorothy Loretta (Derris) T.; m. Lois Ruth Moffit, Aug. 11, 1962; children: Jeffrey, Laura. BS in Engring. Sci., Purdue U., 1962, MS in Engring. Sci., 1964, PhD in Engring. Sci., 1966. Lic. profl. engr., NY. NATO postdoctoral fellow U. Cambridge, Eng., 1966-67; asst. prof. mech. and aerospace sci. U. Rochester, 1967-73, assoc. prof., 1973-81, prof., 1981—, prof. astronomy, 1986—, assoc. dean for grad. studies Coll. Engring. and Applied Sci., 1981-83, univ. dean grad. studies, 1983-91. Vis. astronomer Nat. Solar Obs., Sunspot, N.Mex., 1971, 81; vis. scientist Max-Planck Inst. for Physics and Astrophysics, Munich, 1973—74, High Altitude Obs., Boulder, Colo., 1985; vis. fellow Worcester Coll., vis. prof. dept. theoretical physics U. Oxford, England, 1987—88; affiliate scientist Nat. Ctr. for Atmospheric Rsch., Boulder, 1989—; vis. prof. Rsch. Ctr. for Theoretical Astrophysics U. Sydney, Australia, 1991, Sch. Math. and Stats., 1993; vis. fellow Clare Hall, vis. prof. dept. applied math. and theoretical physics U. Cambridge, England, 2002, sr. fellow Isaac Newton Inst., 04; prin. investigator NASA, NSF, USAF, Office Naval Rsch. Editor: Physics of Sunspots, 1981, Sunspots: Theory and Observations, 1992; assoc. editor Astrophys. Jour., 1993—96, sci. editor, 1996—2002, author articles on astrophysics, solar physics and fluid dynamics. NSF fellow, 1963-66; Guggenheim fellow, 1993-94. Fellow Am. Phys. Soc.; mem. AAAS, Am. Astron. Soc. (chair solar physics divsn. 1995-97), Internat. Astron. Union, Am. Geophys. Union, Royal Astron. Soc. (UK), Sigma Xi, Tau Beta Pi, Sigma Delta Chi. Office: U Rochester 223 Hopeman Bldg Rochester NY 14627

THOMAS, JOHN MELVIN, retired surgeon; b. Carmarthen, U.K., Apr. 26, 1933;, U.S. 1958; s. Morgan and Margaret (Morgan) T.; m. Betty Ann Mayo, Nov. 3, 1958; children: James, Hugh, Pamela. MB, BChir, U. Coll. Wales, U. Edinburgh, 1958. Intern Robert Packer Hosp., Sayre, Pa., 1958-59, chief surg. resident, 1963, pres. med. staff, 1968; assoc. surgeon Guthrie Clinic Ltd., Sayre, 1963-69, chmn. dept. surgery, 1969-91; vice chmn. Guthrie Healthcare System, 1995—99. Pres. bd. dirs. Guthrie Clinic Ltd., 1972-89; pres. bd. dirs. Donald Guthrie Found., 1983-95; chmn. Chemung Springwater Co.; trustee Robert Packer Hosp.; chmn. exec. com. Guthrie Healthcare Sys., 1990-92, dir., 1994-2001; guest examiner Am. Bd. Surgery, 1979, 81, 85; bd. dirs. Measurement Innovations Corp., Mansfield, Pa., Trianalytics Corp., First Citizens Nat Bank; cons. The Hunter Group, 1993-96; bd. dirs. Citizen Fin. Bank, interim pres., 2003—. Bd. dirs. Donald Guthrie Found. for Rsch., pres., 1983-94; bd. dirs. Pa. Trauma Sys. Found., 1984-90, pres., 1988, 89; chmn. licensure and accountability Gov.'s Conf., 1974; bd. dirs. Vol. Hosps. Am., 1993-95; trustee Mansfield (Pa.) U. Found., 1991-98; trustee Mansfield Univ. Found., 1991-95. Fellow ACS (gov. 1985-91); mem. AMA, Am. Group Practice Assn., Soc. for Surgery Alimentary Tract, Pa. Med. Soc., Bradford County Med. Soc., Cen. N.Y. Surg. Soc., Internat. Soc. Surgery, Soc. Surgery Alimentary Tract, Ea. Vascular Soc., Ithaca Country Club, Moselem Springs Golf Club, Ft. Lauderdale Country Club, Tower Club (Ft. Lauderdale). Presbyterian. Home: L'Hermitage I Apt 908 3100 N Ocean Blvd Fort Lauderdale FL 33308 E-mail: jthoma8422@aol.com.

THOMAS, JOHN THIEME, management consultant; b. Detroit, Aug. 21, 1935; s. John Shepherd and Florence Leona (Thieme) T.; m. Ellen Linden Taylor, June 27, 1959; children: Johnson Taylor, Evan Thurston. BBA, U. Mich., 1957, MBA, 1958. Mfg. dept. mgr. Procter & Gamble Co., Cin., 1958-60, brand mgr., 1960-63; sr. cons. Glendinning Cos. Inc., Westport, Conn., 1964-66, v.p. London, 1967-69, exec. v.p. Westport, 1970-74, also bd. dirs.; exec. v.p., chief operating officer Ero Industries, Chgo., 1974-76; v.p. Lamalie Assocs. Inc., Chgo., 1977-81; pres. Wilkins & Thomas Inc., Chgo., 1981-87; ptnr. Ward Howell Internat., Chgo., 1987—, mng. dir., cons. practice, 1992-98, chief of staff, 1995-98; also bd. dirs.; cons. ret. LAI Ward Howell, Chgo., 1999—, El Jefe, Thomas Ent. Inc., 1989—. Exec. dir. Procter & Gamble Alumni Assn., Chgo., 1981—. Pub. Procter & Gamble Mktg. Alumni directory, 1981—; author articles in profl. jours. Chmn. bd. dirs. Winnetka (Ill.) Youth Orgn., 1986—; bd. dirs. No. Ill. Girl Scouts Coun., 2002—, United Way of Winnetka, 2001—, United Way North Shore; mem. planning commn. City Winnetka, 2003—; selector Winnetka Town Coun., 1978, 1980, 1984, Winnetka Caucus Exec. Com., 1997—2001, Winnetka Zoning Bd., 2002—. Mem. Nat. Assn. Corp. & Profl. Recruiters, Assn. Exec. Search Cons., Am. Soc. Pers. Adminstrn. Clubs: Fairfield (Conn.) Hunt (treas. 1971-74). Avocations: gardening, music, playing tuba. Home and Office: 525 Ash St Winnetka IL 60093-2601 Office Phone: 847-446-5401. E-mail: enjthomas@aol.com.

THOMAS, JOHN VAL FAIA, architect; Grad arch., Rice Univ., Houston; MArch, MCP, U. Pa. Prin. Val Thomas, Inc., Seattle, 1985—; devel. mgr. Pike Pl. Market Preservation and Devel. Authority, Seattle, 1974. Cons. ptnr. Cardwell/Thomas & Assoc., Seattle. Conversion, W. Queen Anne Sch. (Award for Excellence, Nat. Endowment for the Arts). Fellow: Am. Inst. Arch.; mem.: Housing Comm. of the Greater Seattle Chamber of Commerce, Univ. of Wash. Profl. Coun. for the Sch. of Urban Planning, Planning Commission (chrmn.). The Val Thomas Inc. firm is currently completing two projects. Klee Lofts, a 156-unit condominium project with ground level commercial and 19th Ave. Lofts, a 47-unit condominium. Office: Thomas Inc 1221 2nd Ave Ste 480 Seattle WA 98101

THOMAS, JOSEPH ERUMAPPETTICAL, psychologist; b. Piravom, Kerala, India, Feb. 11, 1937; came to U.S., 1971; s. Iype Erumappettiyil and Kunjamma M. (Padiyil) T.; m. Chinnamma Kavatt, Nov. 23, 1964; children: Joseph Jr., Kurian, Elizabeth. BA, Kerala U., India, 1957, MA, 1960, PhD, 1969. Diplomate Internat. Acad. Behavioral Medicine, Counseling, and Psychotherapy; lic. psychologist; bd. cert. neurotherapist. Lectr. psychology U. Kerala, Trivandrum, India, 1967-70; postdoctoral fellow in psychology Northwestern U. Med. Sch., Chgo., 1971-72; psychologist U. Chgo., 1972-74; instr. psychiatry Northwestern U. Med. Sch., Chgo., 1972-76, asst. prof. dept. psychiatry, 1977-97; psychologist Northwestern Meml. Hosp., Chgo., 1974-80; pvt. practice psychology Chgo., 1980—. Cons. Michael Reese Hosp., Chgo., 1980-86; founding mem. Inst. Psychiatry, Northwestern U., Chgo.; dir. psycho-oncology program Integrative Cancer Care, Evanston, 1995-2004. Contbr. articles to profl. jours. Mem. Dupage County Health Planning Com., Wheaton, Ill., 1984; founding mem., trustee St. Thomas Ch. Chgo., St. Gregorios Orthodox Ch., Oak Park, Ill. Commonwealth fellow Govt. U.K., U. Glasgow, 1970; sr. fellow Biofeedback Certification Inst. Am. Mem. Am. Psychological Assn., Mental Health Assn. DuPage County (bd. dirs. 1982-84), Biofeedback Soc. Ill. (pres. 1984-85). Home: 16w731 89th Pl Burr Ridge IL 60527-6087 Office: Sallas Ctr 401 N Michigan Ave Ste 818 Chicago IL 60611-4277 E-mail: josefthomas@msn.com.

THOMAS, JOSEPH FLESHMAN, retired architect; b. Oak Hill, W.Va., Mar. 23, 1915; s. Robert Russel and Effie (Fleshman) T.; m. Margaret Ruth Lively, Feb. 28, 1939 (dec.); children: Anita Carol, Joseph Stephen; m. Dorothy Francene Root, Apr. 29, 1967 (div.); m. Bonnie Abbott Buckley, June 15, 1991 (dec.). Student, Duke U., 1931—32; BArch, Carnegie-Mellon U., 1938. Practice architecture various firms, W.Va., 1938-49; staff arch. Calif. Divsn. Architecture, L.A., 1949-52; prin. Joseph F. Thomas, Arch., Pasadena, Calif., 1952-53; pres. Neptune & Thomas (archs.-engrs.), Pasadena and San Diego, 1953-78. Mem. Pasadena Planning Commn., 1956-64, chmn., 1963-64; pres. Citizens Coun. for Planning, Pasadena, 1966-67; mem. steering com. Pasadena NOW, 1970-74; mem. Pasadena Design Com., 1979-86; mem. adv. bd. Calif. Office Architecture and Constrn., 1970-72; mem. archtl. adv. com. Calif. State U. Sys., 1981-84; mem. adv. coun. Sch. Environ. Design Calif. Poly. Inst., 1983-2002; mem. outreach for architecture com. Carnegie Mellon U., 1989-95, pres.'s devel. com., 1991-95. Prin. works include Meth. Hosp., Arcadia, Calif., Foothill Presbyn. Hosp., Glendora, Calif., master plans and bldgs., Citrus Coll., Azusa, Calif., Riverside (Calif.) Coll., Westmont Coll., Monticeto, Calif., Northrop Inst. Tech., Inglewood, Calif, Indian Valley Coll., Marin County, Calif., Pepperdine U., Malibu, Calif., UCLA, U. Calif., San Diego, Long Beach (Calif.) State U., Calif. Inst. Tech., Pasadena, other coll. bldgs. Pacific Tel. Co., Pasadena, L.A. County Superior Ct. Bldg., U.S. Naval Hosp., San Diego. Trustee Almansor Edn. Ctr., 1986-92; bd. dirs., co-founder Syncor Internat., 1973-83; founding dir. Bank of Pasadena, 1962-65. Lt. (j.g.) USNR, 1943-46. Recipient Svc. award City of Pasadena, 1964, Disting. Svc. award Calif. Dept. Gen. Svcs., 1972, Gold Crown award Pasadena Arts Coun., 1981. Fellow AIA (4 awards honor, 13 awards merit 1957-78, dir. Calif. coun. 1966-68, exec. com. 1974-77, pres. Pasadena chpt. 1967, chmn. Calif. sch. facilities com. 1970-72, mem. nat. jud. bd. 1973-74, nat. dir. 1974-77, treas. 1977-79, exec. com., planning com., chmn. finance com.); mem. Breakfast Forum (chmn. 1983), Annandale Golf Club, Pi Kappa Alpha. Republican. Methodist. Home: 330 San Miguel Rd Pasadena CA 91105-1446

THOMAS, JOSEPH WINAND, lawyer; b. New Orleans, Aug. 2, 1940; s. Gerald Henry and Edith Louise (Winand) T.; m. Claudette Condoll, Aug. 2, 1960 (div. Nov. 1985); children: Jeffery J., Anthony W.; m. Shawn B. Watkins, May 26, 1986 (div. June 1989); children: Adelle, Anne; m. Sandra J. Green, May 17, 1992; children: Winand, Elizabeth, Alice, Shepard, Julia. BS, Loyola U., Chgo., 1967; JD, Loyola U., New Orleans, 1973; MBA, Tulane U., 1984. Bar: La. 1973, U.S. Dist. Ct. (ea. dist.) La. 1973, U.S. Ct. Appeals (5th cir.) 1973, U.S. Supreme Ct. 1976, D.C. 1980. Staff atty. New Orleans Legal Assistance Corp., 1973-74; asst. atty. gen. State of La., 1974-80; pvt. practice New Orleans, 1980—. Pres., bd. dirs. New Orleans Legal Assistance Corp. Active NAACP, New Orleans, 1987-89; bd. dirs. Urban League, New Orleans. Mem. ABA, Louis Martinet Legal Soc., New Orleans Bar Assn., La. Bar Assn. Democrat. Roman Catholic. Office: Ste 1295 1615 Poydras St New Orleans LA 70112 E-mail: jthomas@bellsouth.net.

THOMAS, JUDY JANET, reporter, health services professional; b. Detroit, Mich., Feb. 28, 1964; d. J.W. and Geneva Anna Thomas; children: Robert A., Arrelle R. BA, U. of D Mercy, Detroit, MI; Associates, Wayne County Coll., Detroit, MI. Job developer U. D Mercy, Detroit, 1999—2000; mgr. Alstate

Glass Co., Detroit, 2000; reporter Metroplex Newspaper, Detroit, 2002—; cmty. svc. Doctors Ho. Svc., Detroit, 2002—. Dir. sr. organ Consortium, Detroit. Mem. Voice Writers Orgn., Detroit, 2001—01. Liberal. Avocations: reading, writing, banking, art. Home: 19144 Robson Detroit MI 48235 Office: Doctors House Call Service 17117 W 9 Mile Road Southfield MI Office Phone: (313) 864-7062.

THOMAS, KAREN P. composer, conductor; b. Seattle, Sept. 17, 1957; BA in Composition, Cornish Inst., 1979; MusM in Composition and Conducting, U. Wash., 1985. Condr. The Contemporary Group, 1981-85; condr., music dir. Wash. Composers Forum, 1984-86; artistic dir., condr. Seattle Pro Musica, 1987—. Conducting debut Seattle, 1987; composer: Four Delineations of Curtmantle for Trombone or Cello, 1982, Metamorphoses on a Machaut Kyrie for Strong Orch. or Quartet, 1983, Cowboy Songs for Voice and Piano, 1983, There Must Be a Lone Range for Soprano and Chamber Ensemble, 1987, Brass Quintet, 1987, Four Lewis Carroll Songs for Choir, 1989, (music/dance/theater) Boxiana, 1990, Elementi for Clarinet and Percussion, 1991, (one-act children's opera) Coyote's Tail, 1991, Clarion Dances for Brass Ensemble, 1993, Roundup for Sax Quartet, 1993, Three Medieval Lyrics for Choir, 1992, Sopravvento for Wind Quartet and Percussion, 1994, When Night Came for Clarinet and Chamber Orch. or Clarinet and Piano, 1994, Over the City for Choir, 1995, also numerous others. Recipient Composers Forum award N.W. Chamber Orch., 1984, King County Arts Commn., 1987, 90, Artist Trust, 1988, 93, 96, Seattle Arts Commn., 1988, 91, 93, New Langton Arts, 1988, Delius Festival, 1993, Melodious Accord award 1993; fellow Wash. State Arts Commn., 1991; Charles E. Ives scholar AAAL. Mem. Am. Choral Dirs. Assn., Broadcast Music, Am. Music Ctr., Internat. Alliance for Women in Music, Soc. Composers, Chorus Am., Conductors Guild. Office: 4426 1st Ave NW Seattle WA 98107-4306 E-mail: kpthomas1@aol.com.

THOMAS, KATHERINE JANE, magazine and newspaper columnist; b. Bryan, Tex., Mar. 22, 1942; d. William Holt Jr. and Mary Anne (McCasland) Oliver; m. Robert Wayne Thomas, June 1, 1968; children: Jennifer Ann, Michael Frederick. BA, U. Tex., 1964. News reporter Abilene Reporter, Tex., 1964-67; with Ralston Purina Co., 1967-68; journalist The Eagle, Bryan, Tex., 1969-72, Wall St. Jour., Houston Bus. Jour., 1976-80; bus. columnist Houston Post, 1980-95. Sr. bus. columnist; features editor Hart's Energy Markets; electric power editor Oil & Gas Jour. Online. Judge Houston Area Inc. Mag. Entrepreneur of Yr., 1995; vol. judge out-of-state journalism competitions. Recipient Writing awards Tex. Press Assn., 1978-79, AP, 1966, 88, 91, Dallas Press Club Katie Finalist, 1990, 94, Matrix, 1989-90, Press Club of Houston, 1987, 89, 90, 91, 95, 96, Sierra Club of Houston, 1989, St. Louis United Fund, 1968, Abilene C. of C., 1965. Mem. Press Club of Houston (bd. dirs., sec. 1991), Press Club of Houston Ednl. Found. (treas. 1991, bd. dirs.). Episcopalian. Avocations: sailing, entertaining, walking, reading. Office: 1700 West Loop S Ste 1000 Houston TX 77027-3007 E-mail: katet@ogjonline.com.

THOMAS, KENNETH EUGENE, auditor; b. Meridian, Miss., Dec. 27, 1943; s. John and Winnie Adline (White) T. AA, East Miss. Jr. Coll., 1962; BS in Acctg., Miss. State U., 1967. CPA, Miss.; cert. pub. mgr., Miss. Asst. contr. So. Pipe & Supply Co., Meridian, 1967-69, 70-75; plant acct. Quitman (Miss.) Knitting Mills, Inc., 1969-70; corp. contr. Acme Bldg. Supply Co., Meridian, 1977-78; corp. controller Reliable Trucks of Meridian, 1979-80; operating acct. Dept. Housing and Urban Devel., Atlanta, 1980-81; supervisory operating acct. Dept. of Def.-Army, Hinesville, Ga., 1981, sr. auditor Atlanta, 1981-83; fin. planner Miss. Band of Choctaw Indians, Phila., Miss., 1984; sr. auditor Dept. of Def.-Army, Lexington, Ky., 1985-87; supervisory operating acct. Dept. of Def. USAF, Blytheville, Ark., 1987-88; comptroller Dept. Corrections, Parchman, Miss., 1989; internal auditor Dept. Mental Health, Meridian, Miss., 1989—. Editor: (poetry) The Comforter. MSgt. Miss. Air Nat. Guard, 1967-91. Mem. AICPAs, Miss. Soc. CPAs, Phi Kappa Phi, Phi Theta Kappa. Republican. Methodist. Home: 6826 Valley Rd Meridian MS 39307-9429 E-mail: kenthomascpa@excite.com.

THOMAS, KENNETH GLYNDWR, mining executive; b. Llanelli, Wales, June 25, 1944; arrived in Can., 1980; m. Elizabeth June Hickman, Sept. 25, 1976; children: Louise June, Kelly Jane. BSc in Metallurgy, U. Wales, Cardiff, 1970; MSc in Mgmt. Sci., U. London, 1971; PhD in Tech. Sci., U. of Delft, The Netherlands, 1994. Chartered engr., U.K.; registered profl. engr., Ont., Can. Metallurgist Brit. Steel Corp., Wales, 1959-67, Anglo Am. Corp., Kitwe, Zambia, 1971-75, plant supt. Klerksdorp, South Africa, 1975-80; design metallurgist Kilborn Engring., Toronto, Ont., 1980-85; mill supt. Giant Yellowknife (Can.) Mines Ltd., N.W.T., 1985-87; sr. v.p. metallurgy and constrn. Barrick Gold Corp., Toronto, 1987-95, sr. v.p. tech. svcs., 1995-2001; mng. dir. mining and mineral processing Hatch, Mississauga, 2001—02; mng. dir. We. Australia Hotel, 2002—03; COO, Crystallex Internat. Corp., Toronto, 2003—. Contbr. articles to tech. jours.; co-patentee in field. Fellow Inst. Materials, Minerals & Mining (U.K.), Can. Inst. Mining, Metallurgy and Petroleum (Mill Man of Yr. award 1990, Airey award 1999, Selwyn G. Blaylock medal 2001). Office Phone: 416-777-7237. E-mail: kthomas@crystallex.com.

THOMAS, LAURA MARLENE, artist, retired private antique dealer; b. Chico, Calif., Apr. 29, 1936; d. Boyd Stanley Beck and Lois Velma (Behnke) Lyons; m. Charles Rex Thomas (div.); children: Tracy Loraine, Jeffory Norris. AA in Fine Arts, Sacramento City Coll., 1978; BA in Fine Arts, Calif. State U., 1981. Tchrs. asst. Hanford Elem. Sch., Hanford, Calif., 1963-68; asst. dir. RSVP: Retired Sr. Vol. Program, Hanford, 1971-74; dir. of Art Bank Sacramento City Coll., Sacramento, 1976-78; pub. asst. Student Activities Calif. State Univ., Sacramento, 1978-81; antique dealer pvt. practice, Sacramento, 1981—, arts and crafts bus., 1976-99; ret., 1999; social worker Cath. Social Svcs., Sacramento, 1985-93. Vol. worker Sr. Ctr., 1999—. Artist: weaving, Double Image, 1977, 2nd Place 1977. Charter mem. YWCA, Sacramento, 1972, Folsum Hist. Soc., 1988; vol. Hart Sr. Ctr., Sacramento, Friends for Survival Inc., Sacramento. Cert. of appreciation, Carmellia City Ctr. Adv. Council, Sacramento, 1986. Mem. Internat. New Thought Alliance, Statue of Liberty-Ellis Island Found., 1985, North Shore Animal League (Benefactors award 1985), Calif. State U. Alumni Assn., Hanford Sportsman Club (v.p. 1963-68). Republican. Protestant. Avocations: tennis, needlepoint, gourmet cooking. Home: 2714 E Street #14 Sacramento CA 95816

THOMAS, LEE MULLER, former government offical; b. Ridgeway, S.C., June 13, 1944; s. Robert Walton and Laura (Muller) T.; m. Dixie Gay Smily, June 20, 1981; children: Jordan, Braden; children by previous marriage— Lee, Elliott BA, U. of South, 1967; M.Ed., U. S.C., 1971. Exec. dir. criminal justice program Office Gov., Columbia, S.C., 1972-77, dir. pub. safety programs, 1979-81; ind. cons. Criminal Justice Planning, 1977-79; assoc. dir. state and local programs and support FEMA, Washington, 1981-82, dep. dir., 1982-83; asst. adminstr. EPA, Washington, 1983-85, adminstr., 1985-89; chmn., chief exec. officer Law Environmental Inc., Atlanta. Mem. Ridgeway (S.C.) Town Council. Mem. Nat. Criminal Justice Assn. (chmn. 1979-81), S.C. Corrections Assn., S.C. Law Enforcement Officers Assn., Sigma Nu. Office: Law Environmental Inc 7295 Chattahoochee Bluff Dr Atlanta GA 30350-1071

THOMAS, LEONA MARLENE, health information educator; b. Rock Springs, Wyo., Jan. 15, 1933; d. Leonard H. and Opal (Wright) Francis; children: Peter, Paul, Patrick, Alexis. BA, Govs. State U., 1982, MHS, 1986; cert. med. records adminstrn., U. Colo., 1954. Asst. prof. Chgo. State U., 1984—, acting dir. health info. adminstrn. program, 1991-92; acting dir. health info. Internat. Coll., Naples, Fla., 1994; dir. Chgo. State U., 1994—. Chairperson dept. health info. adminstrn. Chgo. State U., 1994—. Mem. adv. com. Wellness Ctr., mem. adv. com. occupl. therapy program Chgo. State U. Mem. Assembly on Edn., Am. Health Info. Mgmt. Assn., APHA, Chgo. and Vicinity Med. Records Assn., Ill. Assn. Allied Health Profls., Gov.'s State Alumni Assn. Democrat. Methodist. Home: 6340 Americana Dr Apt 1101 Willowbrook IL 60527 Office: Chgo State U Coll Health Scis 95th at King Dr Chicago IL 60628

THOMAS, LESTENE, nurse; b. Hampton, Ark., May 1, 1956; d. James Earnest Moore and Alma Lee Moore-Penny; m. Emile Garth Thomas; children: Learie D., Stephen J.R. AAS in Nursing, U. Ark. Little Rock, 1978. RN; notary public, Ark. Nurse U. Hosp., Little Rock, 1978-82, Vets. Hosp., Little Rock, 1982-86, Ctrl. Ark. Home Health Agy., Little Rock, 1986-89, St. Vincent Infirmary, Little Rock, 1989-90, Jefferson Regional Med. Ctr., Pine Bluff, Ark., 1990-94, Ark. Convalescent Nursing Home, Pine Bluff, 1996-97, Pulaski County Regional Detention Facility, Little Rock, 1998—2002, Maxim Health Svcs., 2002—, Parkview Rehab. and Health Care, 2003—. Mem. Angel Flight, UAM, Monticello, Ark., 1975—76. 2d lt. Ark. NG, 1984—86. Mem. Nat. Alliance for Mentally Ill, Zeta Phi Beta. Baptist. Avocations: calligraphy, photography, music, international pen-friends. Home: 8501 Dreher Ln Apt 25 Little Rock AR 72209

THOMAS, LEWIS, physicist, researcher; b. Kingston, Pa., Mar. 16, 1924; s. Lewis Clatyon and Marion Hay Thomas; m. Jean Bartle; children: Bart, James, Dwight. BEE, Cornell U., 1949; BSEE, Newark Coll. Engring., 1958; PhD in Physics, MIT, 1960; PhD in Astronomy, London U., 1999. Radar engr. Philco Radio Corp., Phila., 1947-49; mem. tech. staff elec. transmission divsn. Bell Labs., Murray Hill, N.J., 1950-89; cons. in physics Lucent Techs., Murray Hills, 1989—; lectr., tchr. Am. Mus. Natural History, Hayden Planetarium, N.Y.C., 1950-86. Pres. Astrosoft Co., North Plainfield, N.J., 1980—; trustee Amateur Astronomers Inc., Cranford, N.J. Author: Celestial Mechanics, 1992, 2d rev. edit., 1999, Astronomy of Solar System, 1997, Astronomy Beyond Solar System, 2000, Vistas in Astronomy, 2002; patentee in field. Pres. North Plainfield City Coun., 1969-71. Sgt. U.S. Army. Decorated Bronze star; named Ark. Traveler, Gov. of Ark., 1972. Avocations: astronomy, computer science, camping. Home: 236 Watchung Ave North Plainfield NJ 07060

THOMAS, LINDSEY KAY, JR., research ecology biologist, educator, consultant; b. Salt Lake City, Apr. 16, 1931; s. Lindsey Kay and Naomi Lurie (Biesinger) T.; m. Nancy Ruth Van Dyke, Aug. 24, 1956; children: Elizabeth Nan Thomas Cardinale, David Lindsey, Wayne Hal, Dorothy Ann Thomas Brown. BS, Utah State Agrl. Coll., 1953; MS, Brigham Young U., 1958; PhD, Duke U., 1974. Park naturalist Nat. Capital Pks., Nat. Pk. Svc., Washington, 1957—62, pk. naturalist (rschr.) Region 6, 1962—63, rsch. pk. naturalist Nat. Capital Region, 1963—66; rsch. biologist S.E. Temperate Forest Pk. Areas, Washington, 1966, Durham, NC, 1966—67, Great Falls, Md., 1967—71, Nat. Capital Pks., Great Falls, 1971—74, Nat. Capital Region, Triangle, Va., 1974—93, Washington, 1985—93, Nat. Biol. Svc., Washington, Triangle, 1993—96; resource mgmt. specialist Balt.-Washington Pkwy., Greenbelt, Md., 1996, Nat. Capital Parks-East, 1996—98; rsch. ecologist emeritus and cons. Nat. Capital Region, Nat. Park Svc., 1998—. Bd. dirs. Prince William County (Va.) Svc. Authority, 1996-2004; adj. prof. George Mason U., Fairfax, Va., 1988—, George Washington U., Washington, 1992-98; instr. Dept. Agr. Grad. Sch., 1964-66; aquatic ecol. cons. Fairfax County (Va.) Fedn. Citizens Assns., 1970-71; guest lectr. Washington Tech. Inst. (now U. D.C.), 1976. Contbr. articles to profl. jours. Wildlife mgmt. cons. Girl Scouts Am., Loudoun County, Va., 1958; asst. scoutmaster, scoutmaster, merit badges counselor Boy Scouts Am., 1958—, Scouters Tng. award, 1961. Recipient incentive awards Nat. Park Svc., 1962, Superior Performance award, 1989; rsch. grantee Washington Biologists' Field Club, 1977, 82. Mem.: AAAS, Nat. Trust for Historic Preservation, Washington Biologists' Field Club, So. Appalachian Bot. Soc., Soc. for Early Hist. Archaeology, The Nature Conservancy, George Wright Soc., Ecol. Soc. Am., Bot. Soc. Washington, Sigma Xi. Mem. Lds Ch. Home: 13854 Delaney Rd Woodbridge VA 22193-4654 Office: Balt-Washingtn Pky 6565 Greenbelt Rd Greenbelt MD 20770-3207 also: Prince William Forest Park 18100 Park Hdqs Rd Triangle VA 22172

THOMAS, LISA, food service executive; Co-founder Kali's Sweets and Savories (now Clif Bar, Inc.), 1986—, CEO, 1996—. Office: Clif Bar Inc 1610 5th St Berkeley CA 94710-1715

THOMAS, LLOYD BREWSTER, economics professor; b. Columbia, Mo., Oct. 22, 1941; s. Lloyd B. and Marianne (Moon) T.; m. Sally Leach, Aug. 11, 1963; 1 child, Elizabeth. AB, U. Mo., 1963, AM, 1964; PhD, Northwestern U., 1970. Instr. Northwestern U., Evanston, Ill., 1966-68; asst. prof. econs. Kan. State U., Manhattan, 1968-72, assoc. prof., 1974-81, prof., 1983—; asst. prof. Fla. State U., Tallahassee, 1973-74, head of dept., 2004—. Vis. prof. U. Calif., Berkeley, 1981-82, U. Del., 1993, U. Ind., Bloomington, 1997-98, Adelaide U., 2002; prof., chair dept. econs. U. Idaho, 1989. Author: Money, Banking and Economic Activity, 3d edit., 1986, Principles of Economics, 2d edit, 1993, Principles of Macroeconomics, 2d edit, 1993, Principles of Microeconomics, 2d edit, 1993, Money, Banking and Financial Markets, 1997; contbr. articles to profl. jours. Mem. Am. Econs. Assn., Midwest Econs. Assn., So. Econs. Assn., Western Econs. Assn., Phi Kappa Phi. Avocations: tennis, classical music. Home: 1501 N 10th St Manhattan KS 66502-4607 Office Phone: 785-532-4584. Business E-Mail: lbt@ksu.edu.

THOMAS, LOIS C. musician, educator, religious organization administrator; b. Ft. Worth, Oct. 15, 1932; d. Walter Scott and Margaret Alice Dawn Cook; m. Richard Wallace Thomas, Nov. 5, 1988. BA in Organ Performance, Tex. Christian U., 1986; postgrad., SWBT Sem. Organist Western Hills Bapt. Ch., Ft. Worth, 1959-69, 1st Ch. of Christ, Scientist, Ft. Worth, 1969-84, First Congl. Ch., Ft. Worth, 1985-87; organist, dir. Anglican Ch. St. Charles the Martyr, Grand Prairie, Tex., 1989—99; organist, dir., assoc. rector Agnlican Ch. St. Raphael, the Archangel, Grand Prairie, 2002—. Deacon United Cath. Ch., 1996; priest Communion Evang. Episcopal Chs., 1997; fin. officer US Coast Guar Aux., Grapevine, Tex., 1989—95; sec. US Coast Guard Aux., Grand Prairie, Tex., 1995. Commd.: hymnal Diocese St. Paul, the Apostle, 2000. Fin. officer USCG Aux., 1989—95, sec. USCG Aux., 1995. Mem.: Music Tchr.'s Nat. Assn. (mem. tel. com.), Tex. Music Tchr.'s Assn., Arlington Music Tchr.'s Assn., Am. Guild Organists (mem. phone com., mem. tel. com., svc. playing cert.). Home: 1501 Connally Ter Arlington TX 76010-4514

THOMAS, LOWELL, JR., writer, lecturer, former lieutenant governor, former state senator; b. London, Oct. 6, 1923; s. Lowell Jackson and Frances (Ryan) T.; m. Mary Taylor Pryor, May 20, 1950; children: Anne Frazier, David Lowell. Student, Taft Sch., 1942; BA, Dartmouth Coll., 1948; postgrad., Princeton Sch. Pub. and Internat. Affairs, 1952. Asst. cameraman Fox Movietone News, S.Am., 1939, Bradford Washburn Alaskan mountaineering expdn., 1940; illustrated lecturer, 1946—; asst. economist, photographer with Max Weston Thornburg, Turkey, 1947, 1948; film prodn. Iran, 1949; Tibet expdn. with Lowell Thomas, Sr., 1949; field work Cinerama, S.Am., 1951-52; travels by small airplane with wife, writing and filming Europe, Africa, Middle East, 1954-55; mem. Rockwell Polar Flight, first flight around the world over both poles, Nov., 1965; mem. Alaska State Senate, 1967-74; lt. gov. State of Alaska, 1974-79; owner Talkeetna Air Taxi, Inc., air contract carrier, Anchorage, Alaska, 1980-94. Producer series of films Flight to Adventure, NBC-TV, 1956; producer, writer TV series High Adventure, 1957-59; producer documentary film Adaq, King of Alaskan Seas, 1960; producer two films on Alaska, 1962, 63, film on U. Alaska, 1964, South Pacific travel documentary, 1965, film on Arctic oil exploration, Atlantic-Richfield Co., 1969. Author: Out of this World, A Journey to Tibet, 1950, (with Mrs. Lowell Thomas, Jr.) Our Flight to Adventure, 1956, The Silent War in Tibet, 1959, The Dalai Lama, 1961, The Trail of Ninety-Eight, 1962, (with Lowell Thomas Sr.) More Great True Adventures, 1963, Famous First Flights that Changed History, 1968. Past pres. Western Alaska coun. Boys Scouts Am.; bd. dirs. Anchorage unit Salvation Army, Alaska Conservation Found. 1st lt. USAAF, 1943-45. Mem. Nat. Parks and Conservation Assn. (bd. dirs.), Alaska C. of C., Aircraft Owners and Pilots Assn. Clubs: Explorers, Marco Polo, Dutch Treat (N.Y.C.); Rotary, (Anchorage), Press (Anchorage); Dartmouth Outing; American Alpine. Address: 10800 Hideaway Lake Dr Anchorage AK 99507-6139

THOMAS, LOWELL SHUMWAY, JR., lawyer; b. Phila., Aug. 9, 1931; s. Lowell Shumway and Josephine (McVey) T.; m. Judith Evans, Aug. 27, 1955; children: Megan E., Heather McVey, Lowell S., Taylor G. BA, Dartmouth Coll., 1953; JD, U. Pa., 1960. Bar: Pa. 1961, U.S. Tax Ct. 1961, U.S. Dist. Ct. (ea. dist.) Pa. 1961, U.S. Ct. Appeals (3d cir.) 1961. Assoc. Duane, Morris & Heckscher, Phila., 1960-64, Saul, Ewing LLP, Phila., 1965-68, ptnr., 1968-96, of counsel, 1997—. Bd. dirs. Boardwalk Securities Corp., Peter Lumber Co., Chestnut Hill Acad., Phila., 1978-86; bd. dirs. Southeastern Pa. ARC, 1975-82, chmn., 1983-86, bd. govs., 1989-95; trustee Arcadia U., 1987-2000, emeritus trustee, 2001—, chmn., 1989-903. Author: Taxation of Marriage, Separation and Divorce, 1986. Trustee Barra Found., 1999—. Lt. USN, 1953-57. Fellow Am. Coll. Tax Counsel; mem. ABA, Pa. Bar Assn., Phila. Bar Assn., Phila. Bar Found. (trustee 1980-83), Am. Law Inst., Sunnybrook Golf Club. Republican. Episcopalian. Office: Saul Ewing LLP 3800 Centre Sq W Philadelphia PA 19102 E-mail: LST8012@acadia.net.

THOMAS, LYDIA WATERS, research and development executive; b. Norfolk, Va., Oct. 13, 1944; d. William Emerson and Lillie Ruth (Roberts) Waters; m. James Carter Thomas (div. 1970); 1 child, Denee Marrielle. BS in Zoology, Howard U., 1965, PhD in Cytology, 1973; MS in Microbiology, Am. U., 1971. Pres., CEO Mitretek Sys., McLean, Va., 1996—. Appointee Strategic Environ. R&D Sci. Adv. Bd., 1995-98; bd. dirs. Cabot Corp., George Washington U., U.S. Energy Assocs.; mem. Labs., Inc. Author: Automation Impacts on Industry, 1983; contbr. First World Energy Demand, 1996. Mem. Environ. Adv. Bd., U.S. C.E., 1980-82; expert witness, Senate. U.S. govt. pub. hearings, Washington, 1985; House of Reps., 1994; mem. adv. bd. George Wash. U. Va. campus; mem. Supt.'s Bus./Industry Adv. Coun. Fairfax County Pub. Schs.; mem. Va. Rsch. and Tech. Adv. Commn. Recipient Tribute to Women in Internat. Industry YMCA, 1986, EBONE Image award Coalition of 100 Black Women, 1990, Dean's award Black Engineer of Yr., 1991. Mem. AAAS, AIAA, Am. Soc. Toxicology, Nat. Def. Indsl. Assn., Teratology Soc., U.S. Energy Assn., Conf. Bd., Alpha Kappa Alpha. Office: Mitretek Systems 3150 Fairview Park Dr Falls Church VA 22042-4504

THOMAS, M. ANN, bank executive; m. Tony Singer, Aug. 31, 2001. JD, Ohio No. U., 1985. Atty. Bracewell & Patterson; exec. v.p. Woodforest Nat. Bank, Houston, 1995—99, COO, 1999—2001, pres., COO, 2001—. Named one of 25 Women to Watch, US Banker Mag., 2003. Office: Woodforest Nat Bank 13301 E Fwy Houston TX 77015

THOMAS, MARGARET ANN, not-for-profit developer; b. Milw., Sept. 12, 1946; m. John Thomas. Bachelor's Degree, U. Wis., 1973; Master's Degree, DePaul U., 1979. Pers. dir. Goodwill Rehab. Ctr., Milw., 1974—80; exec. dir. Hagerstown Goodwill Industries, 1980—84; pres. Goodwill Industries of Southeastern Pa., Inc., 1984—91, Goodwill Industries of the Gulf Coast, Inc., 1991—94, Goodwill Industries of the Chesapeake, Inc., 1994—. Chair leadership devel. task team Goodwill Industries INternat., mem. exec. coun., bd. mem.; mem. workforce investment bd. City of Balt.; mem. adv. bd. Schaefer Ctr., U. Balt. Trustee, chair planning com. Anne Arundel County Cultural Art Found.; co-chair Opera Gala Annapolis Opera Co.; bd. mem. Scholarships for Scholars. Recipient Mayor's Bus. Recognition award, 1998, Bus. 2000 award, Network 2000 and The Daily Record, 1999, Svc. Above Self award/Outstanding Non-Profit Agy., Rotary Club Woodlawn-Westview, 1999. Mem.: Md. Works (sec.), Md. Assn. Non-Profits (treas.). Office: Goodwill INdustries Chesapeake Inc 222 E Redwood St Baltimore MD 21202

THOMAS, MARGARET JEAN, clergywoman, religious research consultant; b. Detroit, Dec. 24, 1943; d. Robert Elcana and Purcella Margaret (Hartness) T. BS, Mich. State U., 1964; MDiv, Union Theol. Sem., Va., 1971; DMin, San Francisco Theol. Sem., 1991. Ordained to ministry United Presbyn. Ch., 1971. Dir. rsch. bd. Christian edn. Presbyn. Ch. U.S., Richmond, Va., 1965-71, dir. rsch. gen. coun. Atlanta, 1972-73; mng. dir. rsch. div. support agy. United Presbyn. Ch. U.S.A., N.Y.C., 1974-76, dep. exec. dir. gen. assembly mission coun., 1977-83; dir. N.Y. coordination Presbyn. Ch. (U.S.A.), 1983-85; exec. dir. Minn. Coun. Chs., Mpls., 1985-95; synod exec. Synod of Lakes and Prairies Presbyn. Ch. (U.S.A.), Bloomington, Minn., 1995—. Mem. Permanent Jud. Commn., Presbyn. Ch. (U.S.A.), 1985-91, moderator, 1989-91, mem. adv. com. on constn., 1992-98, moderator, 1997-98, mem. synod exec. forum, 1995—, mem. coop. com. on partnership funding, 1997-98, chair, 1998, gen. assembly coun., 2000—; sec. com Contbr. articles to profl. jours. Active alumni bd. Union Theol. Seminary Va., 1980-85; mem. adv. panel crime victims svcs. Hennepin County Atty.'s Office, 1985-86, Police and Cmty. Rels. Task Force, St. Paul, 1986; mem. adv. panel Hennepin County Crime Victim Coun., 1990-93, chair 1990-93; bd. dirs. Minn. Foodshare, 1985-95, Minn. Coalition on Health, 1986-92, Minn. Black-on-Black Crime Task Force, 1988, Twin Cities Coalition Affordable Health Care, 1986-87, Presbyn. Homes of Minn., 1995—, Clearwater Forest, Deerwood, Minn., 1995-96; co-chmn. Minn. Interreligious Com., 1988-95; bd. dirs. Abbott Northwestern Pastoral Counseling Ctr., 1988-91, chair 1990-91; chaplains adv. panel, Immortal Chaplains Found., 1999—. Recipient Human Rels. award Jewish Community Rels. Coun./Anti-Defamation League, 1989, Gov.'s Cert. of Commendation for Women's Leadership, 1993. Mem. NOW (Outstanding Woman of Minn. 1986). Mem. Democrat-Farm-Labor Party. Office: Synod of Lakes and Prairies Presbyn Ch USA 8012 Cedar Ave S Bloomington MN 55425-1204

THOMAS, MARIANNA, volunteer community activist, writer, speaker; b. Greenville, Ohio, Dec. 9, 1927; d. John Darl and Eva Jane (Hill) Munn; m. Harold D. Krickenbarger, Aug. 31, 1947 (div.); children: Harold Jr., Jane, Maryln, John; m. Lowell J. Thomas, Jan. 5, 1977 (dec.); 1 stepchild Lowell J. Student, Dayton (Ohio) Art Inst.; MA (hon.), Union (Ky.) Coll., 1978. Farmer Holstein Show Herd, Arcanum, Ohio, 1947-68; advt., broadcasting sta. work and writing positions Arcanum Times; sales and decorating positions Lowe Bros., Greenville, Ohio; exec. dir./fundraising Help for Children in the Holy Land/Spafford Children's Ctr., N.Y.C., 1969-76. Author: Catitudes, 1987, The Second Mrs. Lowell Thomas, 2002; mem. bd. contbrs. Dayton Daily News. Founder Citizens for Moral War peace orgn., 1967-70; mem. coun. Freedoms Found. at Valley Forge, 1982-84; nat. bd. dirs. Family Svc. Assocs. Am., N.Y.C., 1979-85, Am. Judicature Soc., 1978-80; founder, chmn. U.S. Civil Responsibilities, Dayton, 1988-93. Mem. Dayton Engrs. Club (hon.). Avocations: painting, poetry, swimming, cooking. Home: PO Box 626 Dayton OH 45405-0626 E-mail: MARIANNAMUNN@aol.com.

THOMAS, MARLIN ULUESS, industrial engineer, educator, academic administrator; b. Middlesboro, Ky., June 28, 1942; s. Elmer Vernon and Helen Lavada (Banks) T.; m. Susan Kay Stoner, Jan. 18, 1963; children: Pamela Claire Thomas Davis, Martin Phillip. BSE, U. Mich., Dearborn, 1967; MSE, U. Mich., Ann Arbor, 1968, PhD, 1971. Registered profl. engr., Mich. Asst. and assoc. prof. dept. ops. rsch. Naval Postgrad. Sch., Monterey, Calif., 1971-76; assoc. prof. systems design dept. U. Wis., Milw., 1976-78; mgr. tech. planning and analysis vehicle quality-reliability Chrysler Corp., Detroit, 1978-79; prof. dept. indsl. engring. U. Mo., Columbia, 1979-82; prof. indsl. engring., chmn. dept. Cleve State U., 1982-88, acting dir. Advanced Mfg. Ctr., 1984-85; prof., chmn. indsl. engring. Lehigh U., Bethlehem, Pa., 1988-93; prof., head Sch. Indsl. Engring. Purdue U., West Lafayette, Ind., 1993-98; dir. Inst. Interdisciplinary Engring. Studies, West Lafayette, 1998—. Program dir. NSF, Washington, 1987-88. Contbr. numerous articles on indsl. engring. and ops. rsch. to profl. jours. With USN, 1958-62; capt. USNR, 1971—. Named Outstanding Tchr., U. Mo. Coll. Engring., 1980, Coll. Man of Yr, Cleve. State U. Coll. Engring., 1985, Disting. Alumnus of Yr., U. Mich.-Dearborn, 1996. Fellow Inst. Indsl. Engrs. (past pres.), Am. Soc. for Quality, Inst. for Ops. Rsch. and Mgmt. Scis.; mem. Am. Soc. for Engring. Edn., VFW. Office: Sch Indsl Engring Purdue Univ 315 N Grant St West Lafayette IN 47907-2023 Fax: 765-494-1299. Business E-Mail: muthomas@ecn.purdue.edu.

THOMAS, MARLO (MARGARET JULIA THOMAS), actress; b. Detroit, Nov. 21, 1943; d. Danny and Rose Marie (Cassanti) T.; m. Phil Donahue, May 21, 1980. Ed., U. So. Calif. Theatrical appearances in Thieves, Broadway, 1974, Barefoot in the Park, London, Social Security, Broadway, 1986, The Shadow Box, Broadway, 1994, Two Goldsteins on Acid, 1999; star: TV series That Girl, 1966-71 (Golden Globe award Best TV actress, 1967); appeared in TV films: The Body Human: Facts for Girls (Emmy award Best Performer Children's Program), 1981, The Last Honor of Kathryn Beck, 1984 (also exec. prodr.), Consenting Adults, 1985, Nobody's Child, 1986 (Emmy Best Dramatic Actress), Held Hostage: The Sis and Jerry Levin Story, 1991, Ultimate Betrayal, 1994, Reunion, 1994, A Century of Women, 1994, Playing Mona Lisa, 2000; TV movies: Two Against Time, 2002, Our Heroes, Ourselves, 2002, Deceit, 2004; TV appearances include Friends, 1996, 2002, Roseanne,

1996, Ally McBeal, 2000, Law & Order: Special Victims Unit, 2004; conceived book and record, starred in TV spl. Free to Be. . . You and Me, 1974 (Emmy for best children's show); films include Jenny, 1963, Thieves, 1977, In the Spirit, 1991, The Real Blonde, 1997, Startucker, 1998; conceived book, record and TV spl. Free to Be A Family (Emmy Best Children's Show). Recipient 4 Emmys, Golden Globe award, George Foster Peabody award, Tom Paine award Nat. Emergency Civil Liberties Com.; inducted into Broadcasting & Cable Hall of Fame. Mem. Ms. Found., Nat. Women's Polit. Caucus. Address: William Morris Agy 151 El Camino Dr Beverly Hills CA 90212 also: Creative Artists Agy 9830 Wilshire Blvd Beverly Hills CA 90211 also: Bayonne Entertainment 3815 Hughes Ave Culver City CA 90232*

THOMAS, MARY ANN MCCRARY, counselor, school system administrator; b. Washington, Feb. 11, 1935; d. Frank Robert and Mary (Davison) McCrary; m. John Ralph Thomas, Sept. 30, 1961; children: Robert Davison, John Shannon, Kristen Aldridge. BA, U. Calif., Berkley, 1956; MA, UCLA, 1959. Cert. tchr., Calif. Supr. Pacific Bell, San Francisco, 1962-67; advisor gifted, talented San Rafael (Calif.) City Schs., 1973—, counselor, 1973—, dir. student affairs, 1982—. Pres. San Rafael PTA Coun., 1981-84, outstanding svc. award, 1983, 86, 89, San Rafael High Sch. Site Coun., 1985; pres. bd. dirs. Marin Wildlife Ctr., 1979-85. Recipient Golden Bell award, Marin Community Found., 1987, Outstanding Student Activities program state award, 1992; named Pub. Schoolmaster of Yr., 1993. Mem. Calif. Assn. Gifted, Calif. Assn. Tchrs. English. Republican. Episcopalian. Avocations: reading, gardening. Home: 70 Windsor Ave San Rafael CA 94901-1068 Office: Davidson Mid Sch 280 Woodland Ave San Rafael CA 94901-5097

THOMAS, MARY AUGUSTA, library administrator; b. Washington, Mar. 15, 1951; d. Abram Henry and Mary Agnes Rosenfeld; m. George D. Thomas Jr., Nov. 9, 1991. AB cum laude, Mt. Holyoke Coll., 1973; MSLS, Cath. U., Washington, 1978. From rare book libr. to mgr. planning and adminstrn. Smithsonian Libr., Washington, 1976-91, asst. dir., 1991—2002, assoc. dir., 2002—. Author: An Odyssey in Print: Adventures in the Smithsonian Libraries/ Smithsonian Press, 2002; editor: Information Imagineering, 1998; contbr. mags. to librs. Recipient Smithsonian Inst. Sec.'s award for Excellence in Equal Employment Opportunity, 2000. Mem. ALA (chair editl. adv. bd. LA & M, 1998-2002, councilor 1999-2003, chair com. on resolutions), DC Libr. Assn. (pres. 1999, Disting. Svc. award 2001), Fed. Librs. and Info. Ctrs. (adv. bd. 1997-99), Libr. Adminstrn. and Mgmt. Assn. (chair bus. and fiscal officer discussion group 1998-2000, chair, editl. adv. bd. 1999-2002), Beta Phi Mu. Avocations: cooking, writing. Office: Smithsonian Librs Nhb 22 Washington DC 20560-0001 Business E-Mail: thomasm@si.edu.

THOMAS, MATTHEW SHAWN, civil engineer; b. Marion, Va., Dec. 3, 1969; s. Charles Alan Thomas and Rebecca Sturgill Goble, David Eugene Goble (Stepfather) and Patricia Haulsee Thomas(Stepmother). BS in Physics, Longwood Coll., Va., 1993; BS in Civil Engring., U. of Ctrl. Fla., 1996; M in Pub. Health, Nova Southeastern U., Ft. Lauderdale, 2000—, Dr. of Osteo. Medicine, 2001—. EIT State Bd. of Engring., Fla., 1996; EMT Va., 2000. Physics tchr. Lake Highland Prep. Sch., Orlando, 1993—95; geotechnical engr. Antillian Engring., Orlando, 1996—97; civil engr. Froehling & Robertson, Inc., Chesapeake, Va., 1997—98; field engr. VMS, Inc., Wytheville, Va., 1998—2000. Author: (short stories) The Three Legged Cat (Writer's Jour. Short Story award, 2nd Pl., 1999), (short story) The Botanical Incident (Tenn. Mountain Writer's Short Story Contest, Second Pl., 1997). Bd. mem. Smyth County Hist. & Mus. Soc., Marion, Va., 1997—2000; pres. NSU COM Class of 2005, Davie, Fla., 2001—. 2d lt. Health Professions Scholarship U.S. Army, 2002. Master: Masonic Blue Lodge 31; mem.: NSU Docare, NSU COM Pediat. Club, Pub. Health Student Assn. Achievements include Med. Missionary to Guatemala; Founder Mountain Follies Old Time Music Show (Fundraiser for Smyth County, Va. Hist. Soc.).

THOMAS, MICHAEL A. endocrinologist, gynecologist; b. Harvey, Ill., Dec. 5, 1958; s. Rudolph and Margaret Ann Thomas; m. Megan L. Kessler; m. Kimberly Hilderbrand, Sept. 1, 1984 (div. Jan. 1986); children: Langston, Maya. BS, Northwestern U., 1980; MD, U. Ill., Chgo., 1984. Resident Wayne State U., Detroit, 1984—88; fellow U. Cin., 1988—90, dir. reproductive endocrinology. Fellow: ACOG, Am. Soc. Reproductive Medicine. Home: 4048 Clifton Ridge Cincinnati OH 45220 Office: Ctr for Reproductive Health Univ of Cin 2123 Auburn #A44 Cincinnati OH 45219 Office Phone: 513-558-6560. E-mail: mthomas867@aol.com.

THOMAS, MICHAEL S. software engineer; b. Ft. Benning, Ga., Dec. 11, 1977; s. Timothy Lee and Christine Marie Thomas. Student, Kans. State U., 1996—. Sys. engr. Logicon RDA, Leavenworth, Kans., 1998; sys. software specialist Logican LAT, Grafenwoehr, Germany, 1999; automation intern Motorola Corp., Austin, Tex., 2000; software engr. Lockheed Martin, 2002—. Mem. NSPE, N.Y. Acad. Scis. Lutheran. Avocations: running, basketball, skiing. Home: 2803 Riverside Pkw Grand Prairie TX 75050 E-mail: Michael_S_Thomas@lycos.com.

THOMAS, NADINE, state senator, nurse; b. Fort Myers, Fla., May 14, 1952; d. Marvin Lee and Carrie Lee (North) Dixon; m. Jolivet Aurelious Thomas, Jan. 15, 1977 (div. 1982); children: Nadia Joli, Doris Silas, Dorothy Silas. A, Edison Community Coll., 1974; student, Ga. State U., 1978-82. RN, Ga. Nursing unit coord. Crawford Long Hosp., Atlanta, 1977-90; nursing supr. S.W. Hosp. and Med. Ctr., Atlanta, 1990-92; mem. Ga. Senate from 10th dist., Atlanta, 1992—. Chmn. Changed Living Recovery, Decatur, Ga., 1991-92; bd. dirs. Ctr. for Drug Rehab. Mem. DeKalb Dem. Party Exec. Com., Decatur, 1988-90; pres. Brookwood and Knollwood Community Assn., Atlanta, 1988-92; state rep. Ga. Ho. Reps., Atlanta, 1990-92; co-pres. Sky Haven Pres. PTA, Atlanta, 1991-92. Mem. ANA, Ga. Nurses Assn. (Nurse Excellence award 1991). Avocations: golf, walking, music and dancing. Home: 3679 Talonega Trl Ellenwood GA 30294-1158 Office: Ga State Senate Rm 304 121H State Capitol Atlanta GA 30334

THOMAS, ORVILLE C. retired physician, consultant; b. Haynesville, La., Aug. 23, 1915; children— David, Diane, Cody Pre-med. Student, Marian Mil. Inst., 1932-33, Tulane U., 1933, MD, 1939. Diplomate Am. Bd. Pediatrics. Diplomate Am. Bd. Allergy and Immunology. Intern Shreveport Charity Hosp., La., 1939-40; asst. resident in pediatrics Children's Meml. Hosp., Chgo., 1946-47, resident in pediatrics, 1947, chief resident in pediatrics, 1948; active staff Tex. Children's Hosp., Houston, 1962—, fellow pediatric allergy, 1963-65, chief allergy sect., 1973-78; fellow in pediatric allergy Baylor Coll. Medicine, Houston, 1963-65; chief pediatrics Schumpert Meml. Hosp., Shreveport, La, 1958-61, chief of staff, 1958; sr. staff pediatrics Confederate Meml. Hosp., Shreveport, La, 1948-61; active staff Highland Hosp., Shreveport, La, 1948-61, North La. Hosp., Shreveport, La, 1948-61, Physicians and Surgeons Hosp., Shreveport, La, 1948-61, Ben Taub Gen. Hosp., Houston, 1962—, Hermann Hosp., Houston, 1966-69; hon. staff St. Luke's Hosp., Houston, 1962—; cons. staff Meth. Hosp., Houston, 1962—, St. Joseph Hosp., Houston, 1966—, Bellaire (Tex.) Gen. Hosp., 1966-86, Rosewood Gen. Hosp., Houston, 1967—, Meml. Bapt. Hosp., Houston, 1968—, Pasadena Bayshore Hosp., Pasadena, Tex., 1970—; instr. pediatrics Northwestern U. Sch. Medicine, Chgo., 1948; assoc. prof. pediatrics La. State U. Postgrad. Sch. Medicine, 1956-61; clin. instr. pediatrics Baylor Coll. Medicine, Houston, 1961-66, asst. clin. prof. pediatrics, 1966-76, assoc. clin. prof. pediatrics, 1977—. Assoc. clin. prof. allergy and immunology U. Tex. Grad. Sch. Biomed. Scis., Houston, 1970—. Book reviewer: Venom Diseases; Aspects of Allergy and Applied Immunology. Contbr. articles to profl. jours. Served to maj. USMC AUS, 1942-46. Fellow Am. Coll. Allergy and Immunology (pediatrics com. 1964—, pres. 1978), Am. Acad. Allergy and Immunology, Am. Assn. Cert. Allergists (bd. govs. 1974, pres. 1979); mem. AMA, Am. Acad. Pediatrics, So. Med. Assn. (chmn. allergy sect. 1970-71), Tex. Allergy Research Found. Houston-(research and edn. com. 1966-86, chmn. sci. adv. council 1973—), Tex. Pediatric Soc., Harris County Med. Soc., Tex. Med. Assn. (chmn. allergy sect. 1976-77), Am. Assn. for Inhalation Therapy (awards com. 1969-72, spl. edn. com. 1969-72), Greater Houston Allergy Soc. (pres. 1977), Joint Council of Allergy and Immunology, Internat. Assn. of Allergology and Clin. Immunology (U.S. rep. 1981-85). Home: 1111 Bering Dr Apt 704 Houston TX 77057-2320

THOMAS, PAMELLA DELORES, medical director, physician, educator; b. Wetmoreland, Jamaica, May 11, 1947; came to U.S., 1976; d. Wellesley Johnston and Hyacinth Ida Muir; m. Earl A. Thomas, Apr. 9, 1977; children: Ramogi O., Monifa J. MD, U. W.I., 1974; MPH, Med. Coll. Wis., 1990. Diplomate Am. Bd. Preventive Medicine in Occupational Medicine, Am. Bd. Managed Care Medicine. Intern in surgery Brookdale Hosp., Bklyn., 1976-77, attending physician, 1979-83; resident in surgery Cath. Med. Ctr., Queens, N.Y., 1978-79; staff physician N.Y.C. Transit, Bklyn., 1983-86, asst. med. dir., 1986-89; med. dir. Lockheed Aeronautics, Marietta, Ga., 1989—2002; dir. Wellness & Health Promotion, Marietta, Ga., 2002—. Adj. asst. prof. Emory Sch. Pub. Health, 1992-2002, adj. assoc. prof., 2002—, chair residency adv. com. occupl. medicine program, 1995-2002; chair bd. dirs. Lockheed Ga. Employees Fed. Credit Union, 1997—2001, sec., 1996-97, bd. dirs., 1993—. Bd. dirs. Am. Cancer Soc., 1989-2003, Cobb County, Ga., 1989—; mem. Promina N.W. Hosp. Found., 1993-2002; dir. pub. rels. Cobb Med. Soc., 1993-96; v.p. bd. govs. Atlanta Wellness Alliance, 1993-95; active Mentor Ga. 100, 1997-2001; mem. employers adv. coun. Inst. Health and Productivity Mgmt., 1998-. Fellow Am. Coll. Preventive Medicine, Am. Coll. Occupl. and Environ. Medicine (pres. Ga. chpt. 1996-97); mem. AMA, APHA, Am. Occupl. Medicine Assn., Am. Coll. Physicians Execs. (cert. physician exec.), Tchrs. Pub. Health Med. Assn. Ga. Avocations: reading, baking, gardening, music. Office: Lockheed Aeronautics 86 S Cobb Dr # 0454 Marietta GA 30063-0001 Office Phone: 770-494-4134. E-mail: pamella.thomas@lmco.com.

THOMAS, PATRICIA ANNE, retired law librarian; b. Cleve., Aug. 21, 1927; d. Richard Joseph and Marietta Bernadette (Teevans) T. BA, Case Western Res. U., 1949, JD, 1951. Bar: Ohio, 1951, U.S. Supreme Ct., 1980. Libr. Arter & Hadden, Cleve., 1951-62; asst. libr., libr. IRS, Washington, 1962-78; libr. dir. Adminstrv. Office U.S. Cts., 1978-93; ret., 1993. Mem. Am. Assn. Law Librs., Soc. D.C. (pres. 1967-69), Soc. Benchers (Case Western Res. Law Sch.)

THOMAS, PATRICIA GOODNOW, journalist; b. Framingham, Mass., Dec. 28, 1924; d. Charles Frederick and Dorothy (Eaton) G.; m. Roy Condit Thomas, Oct. 7, 1961. BS, Simmons Coll., 1946; MAT, Rollins Coll., 1971. News reporter-writer Radio Station WCOP, Boston, 1946-52; editorial specialist Central Intelligence Agy., Washington, 1952-54; asst. editor Hood Milk Corp., Boston, 1954-55; sr. writer/editor Voice of America, Washington, 1955-61; writer Orlando Mag., Orlando, Fla., 1964-72; tchr. French, Eng. Oviedo (Fla.) H.S., 1965-66; prof. of journalism Seminole Cmty. Coll., Sanford, Fla., 1972-88; freelance writer Blairsville, Ga., 1988—. Editor: From Sky to Sea, 1993; contbr. articles to profl. jours. Mem. Fla. Freelance Writers Assn., Kappa Delta Pi. E-mail: rpthomas@alltel.net.

THOMAS, PATRICIA JOANNE, journalist, writer; b. Kenosha, Wis., July 17, 1948; d. Leatrice Shuman Magic and Russell Morton Maxwell(Stepfather); life ptnr. Meriwether Burruss Rhodes. BA, U. of Calif., Berkeley, 1967—69; MA, Stanford U., 1969—70. Vis. scholar, knight ctr. for sci. and med. journalism Boston U., Boston, 2002—03; editor, harvard health letter Harvard Med. Sch., Boston, 1991—97. Mem., bd. of advisors Am. Bd. of Internal Medicine, Philadelphia, Pa., 1992—98. Author: (non-fiction book) Big Shot: Passion, Politics, and the Struggle for an AIDS Vaccine (Leonard Silk Journalism fellowship, 1998). Elected mem. Town Meeting, Arlington, Mass., 1992—2002. Fellow Knight Sci. Journalism Fellowship, MIT, 1986-1987. Mem.: Nat. Assn. of Sci. Writers. Avocations: tennis, standard poodles. Home: 176 Mount Vernon Street Arlington MA 02476 Personal E-mail: pthomasauthor@yahoo.com.

THOMAS, PATRICK ROBERT MAXWELL, oncology educator, academic administrator; b. Exmouth, Devon, Eng., Feb. 23, 1943; came to U.S., 1976; s. Christopher Codrington and Aileen Daphne (Gordon) T.; m. Linda Sharon Rich, June 23, 1986 (dec. 1987), m. Geraldine M. Jacobson, Mar. 2, 1996 (div. 1999). Diploma in biochemistry, London U., 1965, MB, BS, 1968. Lectr. Inst. Cancer Rsch., London, 1974-76; assoc. chief clinician Roswell Park Meml. Inst., Buffalo, 1976-79; asst. prof. Washington U., St. Louis, 1979-83, assoc. prof., 1983-89, prof., 1989-90; prof., chmn. Temple U., Phila., 1991-98; radiation oncologist Pinellas (Fla.) Radiation Oncology Assocs., 1998—. Extramural bd. PDQ, Bethesda, Md., 1989—; mem. in-svc. exam. com. Am. Coll. Radiology, Reston, Va., 1990-97; examiner Am. Bd. Radiology, Louisville, 1990—. Mem. editl. adv. bd.: Med. and Pediatric Oncology, 2002—. Fellow Am. Coll. Radiologists, Royal Coll. Physicians of London; mem. Internat. Soc. Pediatric Oncology (sci. com. 2000—). Home: 100 Beach Dr NE Saint Petersburg FL 33701-3965 Office: 3155 N McMullen Booth Rd Clearwater FL 33761

THOMAS, PAUL LINDSLEY, composer, organist, music director; b. N.Y.C., Mar. 18, 1929; s. Richard Banks and Virginia Bartholomew (Carrington) T.; m. Joyce Robertshaw, Sept. 3, 1955; 1 child, Craig Carrington. BA, Trinity Coll., Hartford, Conn., 1950; diploma, Am. Conservatory, Fontainbleau, France, 1954; MusB, Yale U., 1957, MusM, 1958; D of Musical Arts, U. North Tex., 1979. Organist, choirmaster St. George's-by-the-River, Rumson, N.J., 1950-55, St. James Episcopal Ch., West Hartford, Conn., 1955-60; organist Wesleyan U., Middletown, Conn., 1958-60; dir. Apollo Glee Club, Yale U., New Haven, 1958-60; instr. in organ So. Meth. U., Dallas, 1960-65; music dir., organist St. Michael and All Angels Ch., Dallas, 1960-97, composer in residence, music dir. emeritus, 1997—; music dir. Trinity Epis. Ch., Dallas, 1998—. Chmn. liturgy and music commn. Episcopal Diocese of Dallas, 1995—. Composer (opera) Everyman, 1986; composer ch. anthems and organ music. Named Canon of Ch. Music, Episcopal Diocese of Dallas, 1980; recording grantee Stemmons Found., Dallas, 1995; Joyce and Paul Thomas Music Wing named in his honor St. Michael and All Angels, Dallas, 1994. Fellow Am. Guild Organists (dean Dallas chpt. 1967-69, gen. chmn. nat. conv. 1972, nat. coun. 1972-75); mem. Assn. Anglican Musicians, Am. Choral Dirs. Assn. Republican. Episcopalian. Home: 6822 Northwood Rd Dallas TX 75225-2538 Office: Trinity Episcopal Ch 12727 Hillcrest Rd Dallas TX 75230-2007

THOMAS, PAUL MILTON, retired science educator; b. Sligo, Pa., Dec. 1, 1929; s. Milton Ivan and Maude Hazel Thomas; m. Dorothy Marie McGinnett; 1 child, Mona Lee Callahan. BA, Allegheny Coll., 1958; MEd, U. Mich., 1959, MA, 1962, D of Philosophy, 1964; DMin, Drew U., 1980. Instr., biol. Houghton Coll., Houghton, NY, 1959—62; asst. prof. Point Loma Coll., San Diego, 1964—66; rsch. fellow Calif. Inst. of Tech., Pasadena, 1967—68; vis. prof. Johns Hopkins Univ., Baltimore, 1968; prof., biol./chmn. Edinboro Univ., Edinboro, 1968—90; pastor United Ch. of Christ, Greensburg, 1995—2002. Vis. scholar Harvard U., Cambridge, Mass., 1993. Contbr. articles to profl. jours.; author: (books) W. Edwards Deming: Improving Quality in Colleges and Universities, Easter Urges Us to Look at Death, A Christian Looks at Death, Pennsylvania Fish Commission, Fishes of Erie County, Fishes of Pymatuning. Mem. Sch. Bd., Union City, Pa., 1969—75. Mem.: Audubon Soc., Sigma Xi (Caltech), Phi Kappa Phi (Univ. Mich.). R-Consevative. United Church Of Christ. Avocations: hiking, world traveling. Home: 87 West High Street Union City PA 16438-1239 Office: Edinboro University of Pennsylvania Edinboro PA 16444 Personal E-mail: pthomas@velocity.net.

THOMAS, PAULETTE SUZANNE, holistic health practitioner, physician assistant; b. Lowell, Mass., Aug. 29, 1948; d. Armand Avila and Lucienne Adrienne (Lanseigne) Sawyer; Philip Edward Thomas Jr., June 9, 1979. AN, No. Essex C.C., Haverhill, Mass., 1972; cert. cardiac care nurse, Merrimack Coll., 1975; student, Boston Coll., 1976, Northeastern U., 1976-78, John A. Burns Sch. Medicine, 1981; D of Naturology, PhD in Naturology, Am. Inst. Holistic Theology, 1997. RN, Mass., Maine, Hawaii, Fla.; registered hypnotherapist; cert. hypnotherapist; diplomate naturopathic physician Am. Naturopathic Med. Cert. & Accreditation Bd. Head nurse insvc. and daycare Solomon Mental Health Ctr., Lowell, 1972-73; charge nurse ICU Las Olas Gen. Hosp., Ft. Lauderdale, Fla., 1973-74, Lemuel Shattuck Hosp., Jamaica Plain, Mass., 1975-76; charge nurse cardiac care unit Bon Secours Hosp., Methuen, Mass., 1974-75; supr., medicare coord. Oxford Manor, Haverhill, 1978-79, 84; physician asst. to chief internal medicine Straub Clinic and Hosp., Honolulu, 1980-82; owner managed elderly housing, Haverhill, 1982-87; physician asst. employee/occupl. health Lawrence (Mass.) Gen. Hosp., 1984-87; owner Tuckaway Shores Cabins and Restaurant, Jackman, Maine, 1987—; nursing educator cert. nursing asst. course Kennebec Valley Vocat. Tech. Inst., Fairfield, Maine, 1990-94; asst. program dir., dir. nursing svcs., adminstr. Northland Living Ctr., Jackman, Maine, 2000—. Mem. profl. policies com., mem. safefy com. Northland Living Ctr., Jackman, 1990-92. Author, editor, pub. Hawaiian Acad. Physician Assts. Newsletter, 1980-82; contbr. biweekly health column to Jackman/Moose River Chronicle, 1988-89. Bd. dirs. Tuckaway Assn., Nottingham, N.H., 1985-87; mem. Conservation Commn., Jackman, 1989; chmn. Main St. '90, Jackman and Moose River, 1989-90; originator, coord. Wellcome Wagon, Jackman and Moose River, 1990-92; mem. Town of Jackman Budget Com., 1991—. Mem. Am. Acad. Physician Assts. (pres. Hawaii chpt. 1980-82), First Nations Coun., Am. Naturopathic Med. Assn., Inst. Holistic Studies, Jackman/Moose River C. of C. Avocations: hiking, dance, hand-crafts, music, boating. Home and Office: PO Box 44 Jackman ME 04945-9602

THOMAS, PHILIP ROBINSON, management consulting company executive; b. Torquay, Devon, Eng., Dec. 9, 1934; came to U.S., 1963, naturalized, 1969. s. Leslie Robinson and Margaret (Burridge) T.; m. Wayne Laverne Heirtzler, Apr. 6, 1973; children by previous marriage: Martin N.R., Stephen D.R. BSc, U. London, 1959, MSc, 1961, PhD, 1964. With Tex. Instruments Corp., 1961-72, ops. mgr., 1963-72, Bedford, Eng., 1961-63; v.p., gen. mgr. MOS/LSI divsn. Gen. Instruments Co., N.Y.C., 1972-73; gen. mgr. MOS Products divsn. Fairchild Camera and Instrument Corp., Mountainview, Calif., 1973-75; v.p. Integrated Circuits divsn. RCA, Somerville, N.J., 1975-78; chmn. bd. dirs., CEO Thomas Group Inc., Dallas, 1978-98. CEO, chmn. bd. dirs. Woodland Lakes LLC, PRT Global; gen. ptnr. Celerity Investment Fund; spkr. industry confs. Author: Competitiveness Through Total Cycle Time: An Overview for CEOs, 1989, Getting Competitive, 1990, Time Warrior, 1992, Quality Alone is Not Enough, 1993, Survival at Nodulex, 1994; contbr. articles to profl. jours.; patentee semicondrs. Office: 15851 N Dallas Pkwy Ste 654 Addison TX 75001-6030 Home: 3104 Highway 956 Ethel LA 70730-4521

THOMAS, PHILIP STANLEY, economist, educator; b. Hinsdale, Ill., Oct. 23, 1928; s. Roy Kehl and Pauline (Grafton) Thomas; m. Carol Morris, Dec. 27, 1950; children: Lindsey Carol, Daniel Kyle, Lauren Louise, Gay Richardson. BA, Oberlin Coll., 1950; MA, U. Mich., 1951, PhD, 1961; postgrad., Delhi U., 1953-54. Instr. U. Mich., 1956-57; asst. prof. Grinnell (Iowa) Coll., 1957-63, assoc. prof., 1963-65; assoc. prof. econs. Kalamazoo Coll., 1965-68, prof. econs., 1968-94, prof. emeritus, 1994—. Econ. advisor Pakistan Inst. Devel. Econs., 1963—64, USAID, 1965—68, 1971, Planning Commn., Pakistan, 1969—70, Ctrl. Bank Swaziland, 1974—75, Ministry Planning, Kenya, 1980—81, 1983—85, 1986—88, Ministry Fin., Swaziland, 1990, Kenya, 91, 92, Ministry Indsl. Devel., Sri Lanka, 1997, Res. Bank Malawi, 1998—99, Jordan-U.S. Bus. Partnership, 2000—01. Contbr. articles to profl. jours. Mem. alumni coun. Oberlin Coll., 1961—63, 1974—76, 1983—86, 1995—2001, 2004—. With AUS, 1954—56. Fellow Overseas, Ford Found., 1953—54; scholar Fulbright. Mem.: Am. Econs. Assn., Phi Beta Kappa. Home and Office: 313A S Shabwasung St Northport MI 49670-9604 E-mail: pcthomas@traverse.net.

THOMAS, R. DAVID, food services company executive; b. Atlantic City, July 2, 1932; s. R. and Olivia (Sinclair) T.; m. I. Lorraine Buskirk, May 21, 1954; 5 children. Student pub. schs. Past owner, mgr. Ky. Fried Chicken Franchise; founder, chmn. bd. Wendy's Internat., Inc. (parent co. Wendy's Old Fashioned Hamburgers restaurants), Columbus, Ohio, from 1969, also Dublin, Ohio., now sr. chmn. bd., founder, 1981—. Bd. dirs. Children's Hosp., Columbus, Ohio, St. Jude Children's Research Hosp., Memphis; founder Dave Thomas Found. for Adoption. Served with U.S. Army. Recipient Horatio Alger award, 1979 Mem. Ohio Restaurant Assn., Nat. Restaurant Assn. (dir.) Clubs: Ohio Commodores. Office: Wendy's Internat Inc PO Box 256 4288 W Dublin Granville Rd Dublin OH 43017-1442

THOMAS, RALPH CHARLES, III, federal official; b. Roanoke, Va., Apr. 10, 1949; s. Ralph C. Jr. and Dorothy (Easley) T. BA, U. Calif., Berkeley, 1975; JD, Harvard U., 1978. Assoc. Bergson, Borkland, Margolis & Adler, Washington, 1978-80; sr. ptnr. Thomas, John & Everett, Washington, 1980-85; clin. instr. in Law Sch. George Washington U., Washington, 1982-83; exec. dir. Nat. Assn. Minority Contractors, Washington, 1985-92; assoc. adminstr. for small/disadvantaged bus. utilization NASA, Washington, 1992—. Adj. instr. U. Va., Charlottesville, 1989—91; chmn. Fed. Small Bus. Dirs. Interagy. Coun., 2001—03. Author: Extreme Flashbacks, 1997; contbr. articles to profl. jours. Mem. Pres.'s Interagy. Working Group on Minority Bus. Devel., 1995. Staff sgt. USAF, 1967-71, Vietnam. Recipient Presdl. Rank for Disting. Exec. award, 2001, Spl. Honor award, World Assn. Small and Medium Enterprises, 1999, Minority Bus. Entrepreneur Adv. of Yr. award, Asian Enterprise mag., 2004. Mem. Fed. Bar Assn. (chair govt. contracts sect. 2002--). Office: NASA Small & Disadvantaged Bus Utilization 300 E St SW Code K Washington DC 20546-0005

THOMAS, RAMONIA, political organization executive, civic worker; Former mgr. customer svc. dept. Ariz. Pub. Svc. Co., Phoenix; now program adminstr. Ariz. Dept. Econ. Security, Phoenix. Ariz. del. Rep. Nat. Conv., 1992; past pres. Cactus Wren Rep. Women; past chmn. Ariz. African Am. Rep. Com.; precinct committeewoman dist. 25 Phoenix Rep. Com.; vol. numerous state and county level campaigns; pres. Ariz. Fedn. Rep. Women, 1996-97; mem.-at-large exec. com. Nat. Fedn. Rep. Women, Alexandria, Va., 1997—, also regent and dir. region 8; bd. dirs. Phoenix Parks and Recreation Dept.; mem. Ariz. State Arts Commn.; grad. Valley Leadership; former mem. Ariz. Gov.'s Coun. for Non-traditional Employment Women, Ariz. Women's Town Hall; past chmn. and mem. bd. dirs. Metro Youth Ctr.; past mem. bd. dirs. League United L.Am. Citizens, Ariz. NAACP. Mem. Maryvale C. of C. (past bd. dirs.), Soroptimists (past pres. Camelback chpt.). Office: Nat Fedn Exec Women 124 N Alfred St Alexandria VA 22314-3011 Fax: 703-548-9836.

THOMAS, RANDALL STUART, lawyer, educator; b. Princeton, N.J., Nov. 25, 1955; s. John Bowman and Eleanor (Graefe) T.; m. Cheri D. Ferrari; children: Cameron Stuart, Cortland Andrew, Colin Duncan, Carson F. Thomas. BA, Haverford Coll., 1977; MA, U. Mich., 1979, PhD, 1983, JD, 1985. Bar: Del. 1987, U.S. Dist. Ct. Del. 1987. Economist U. Mich., Ann Arbor, 1979-83; law clk. Fed. Dist. Ct. (ea. dist.) Mich., Ann Arbor, 1985; assoc. Potter, Anderson & Corroon, Wilmington, Del., 1986, Skadden, Arps, Slate, Meagher & Flom, Wilmington, 1987-90; assoc. prof. law U. Iowa, 1990-94, prof. law, 1994—, Vanderbilt Univ., 2000—, John Beasley prof. law and bus., 2003—. Vis. prof. Boston U. Law Sch., 1995, U. Mich. Law Sch., 1996, Duke U. Sch. Law, 1999. Rackham fellow U. Mich., 1982-83. Mem.: Order of Coif. Democrat. Methodist. Office: Vanderbilt Univ Sch Law 131 21st Ave S Nashville TN 37203-1120

THOMAS, REGENA L. secretary of state; BA in U. Studies, Morehead State U. Cons. Dem. Gov.'s Assn.; legislative analyst Legislative Research Commn., KY State Legislature, 1980—85; ptnr. IEM Mesage mgmt., Inc.; served Torricelli for Senate, 1996, McGreevey for Gov., 1997, Corzine for Senate, 2000; Sec. of State State of N.J., 2002—. Prin. liaison non-govtl. orgns., key Dem. constituencies; dep., dir. Constituent Svcs. Govt. Dist. Columbia; legis. analyst Legis. Rsch. Commn. Ky. State Legislature; with Nat. Rainbow Coalition and its founder, Rev. Jesse L. Jackson. Office: PO Box 300 Trenton NJ 08625-0300

THOMAS, REGINA D. state legislator; m. Ervin J. Thomas Sr.; four children. Student, C.C. Balt. Mem. Ga. Ho. of Reps., 1995-98, asst. majority whip, 1997-98; mem. Ga. State Senate, Atlanta, 2000—, sec. def., sci. and tech. com., sec. vets. and consumer affairs com., mem. appropriations com., edn. com., reapportionment com.; tax assoc. H&R Block. Mem. com. for pathway to tchg. Savannah State U.; vol. Ralph Mark Gilbert Civil Rights

Mus., Chatham-Savannah Citizen Adv.; active Liberty City Ch. of Christ, Savannah. Office: 1406 E 35th St Savannah GA 31404 also: 323-A Legislative Office Atlanta GA 30334 Office Fax: 404-463-7783. E-mail: rthomas@legis.state.ga.us.

THOMAS, RICHARD, actor; b. N.Y.C., June 13, 1951; s. Richard and Barbara (Fallis) T.; m. Alma Gonzalez, Feb. 14, 1975 (div. 1993); children: Richard F., Barbara, Gwyneth and Pilar (triplets); m. Georgiana Bischoff, Nov. 20, 1995; 1 child, Montana; children from previous marriage: Brooke, Kendra. Student, Columbia U. Owner, prin. Melpomene Prodns. (broadway debut at age 7 in) Sunrise at Campobello, 1958, (regular on children's series) One, Two, Three-Go!, 1961-62, regular (TV series) The Waltons, 1972—77 (Emmy award, 1973, Golden Globe nominee); dir.: (TV series) The Waltons, 1972; actor: (films) Strange Interlude, 1962, The Playroom, 1965, Winning, 1969, Last Summer, 1969, You Can't Have Everything, 1970, Red Sky at Morning, 1971, The Todd Killings, 1971, Cactus in the Snow, 1971, You'll Like My Mother, 1972, 9/30/55, 1977, Battle Beyond the Star, 1980, Wonder Boys, 2000, Fortune Hunters, 2000; (stage appearances) Sunrise at Campobello, 1958, Whose Life Is It Anyway?, 1980, The Fifth of July, 1981, The Sea Gull, 1984, The Count of Monte Cristo, 1985, Citizen Tom Paine, 1986, The Front Page, 1986, Hamlet, 1987, Peer Gynt, 1989, Love Letters, 1989-90, Square One, 1990, Lisbon Traviata, 1990, Danton's Death, 1992, Richard II, 1993, Richard III, 1994, Tiny Alice, 1998, 2000, Measure for Measure, 1999, A Midsummer's Night's Dream, 1999, ART (West End), 2000, 2001, A Distant Country Called Youth, 2002; author: (poems) Poems by Richard Thomas, Vols. I and 2, 1974; actor: (TV dramatic spl. and movies) The Homecoming-A Christmas Story, 1971, The Red Badge of Courage, 1974, The Silence, 1975, All Quiet on the Eastern Front, 1979, The Hank Williams Jr Story, 1983, Hobson's Choice, 1984, The Master of Ballantrae, 1984, Getting Married, No Other Love, 5th of July, 1981, Common Ground, Glory!, Glory!, 1990, Andre's Mother, 1990, It, 1990, Mission of the Shark, 1991, Yes, Virginia There Is a Santa Claus, 1991, A Walton's Thanksgiving Reunion, 1993, Death in Small Doses, 1993, Linda, 1993, A Walton Wedding, 1995, A Christmas Box, 1995, What Love Sees, 1996, A Walton Easter, 1998, Swiss Family Robinson, 1997, 1,000 Men and a Baby, 1997, Swiss Family Robinson, 1997, 1,000 Men and a Baby, 1997, Flood: A River's Rampage, 1997, Down Out and Dangerous, 1997, Big and Hairy, 1998, Beyond the Prairie, 2000, In the Name of the People, 2000, It's a Miracle, 1999-2000, The Christmas Secret, 2000, Miracle of the Cards, 2001, Beyond the Grave II, 2002; (TV dramatic spl. and movies) Anna's Dream, 2002, (host children's spl.) H.M.S. Pinafore, 1973; actor: (TV series) Touched By an Angel, 1994, Promised Land, 1996, The Practice, 1997, Law & Order: Special Victims Unit, 1999, Just Cause, 2002—03; host: It's a Miracle. Nat. chmn. Better Hearing Inst., 1987—. Office: care Springer Assoc 1501 Broadway Ste 1314 A New York NY 10036-5601

THOMAS, RICHARD IRWIN, lawyer; b. Pitts., Jan. 28, 1944; s. Donald Martin and Mary Jane (Smith) T.; m. Karen Sorg (dec. Aug. 1979); children: Amy, Joe, Mike, Jim, Mauri, Mark, John; m. Jacalyn Silagyi, Feb. 1, 1992. Student, Georgetown U., 1961-62; BA, W.Va. Wesleyan Coll., 1965; JD, Duquesne U., 1972. Bar: Pa. 1972, U.S. Dist. Ct. (we. dist.) Pa. 1972, U.S. Ct. Appeals (3d cir.) 1974, U.S. Dist. Ct. (ea. dist.) Pa. 1976, U.S. Supreme Ct. 1977, U.S. Ct. Appeals (6th cir.) 1981, W.Va. 1999. Asst. personnel mgr. Continental Can Co., Pitts., 1966; mgr. labor relations U.S. Steel Corp., Pitts., 1966-72; ptnr. Thorp, Reed & Armstrong, Pitts., 1972-97; exec. mem. Burns White & Hickton, Pitts., 1997—. Adj. prof. Duquesne U., Pitts., 1974-76; jud. mgr. Allegheny County Common Pleas Ct., Pitts., 1985; pres. Four North Shore Assocs., Pitts., 1997—; bd. dirs. Gen. Roofing Co., Bridgeville, Pa. Coach Upper St. Clair (Pa.) Athletic Assn., 1977-85; firefighter Upper St. Clair (Pa.) Vol. Fire Co., 1977-84. Named one of Outstanding Young Men in Am., 1973. Mem. ABA, Pa. Bar Assn., Allegheny Bar Assn. Republican. Roman Catholic. Avocations: skiing, white water rafting, golf, athletics. Home: 283 Mcmurray Rd Pittsburgh PA 15241-1613 E-mail: rithomas@bwhllc.com.

THOMAS, RICHARD LEE, banker; b. Marion, Ohio, Jan. 11, 1931; s. Marvin C. and Irene (Harruff) Thomas; m. Helen Moore, June 17, 1953; children: Richard L., David Paul, Laura Sue. BA, Kenyon Coll., 1953; postgrad. (Fulbright scholar), U. Copenhagen, Denmark, 1954; MBA (George F. Baker scholar), Harvard U., 1958. With First Nat. Bank Chgo., 1958—, asst. v.p., 1962-63, v.p., 1963-65; v.p., gen. mgr. First Nat. Bank Chgo. (London br.), 1965-66; v.p. term loan divsn. First Nat. Bank, Chgo., 1968; sr. v.p., gen. mgr. First Chgo. Corp., 1969-72, exec. v.p., 1972-73, vice chmn. bd., 1973-75, pres., 1975-92, chmn., pres., CEO, 1992-95; chmn. First Chgo. NBD Corp., 1995-96, ret. chmn., 1996. Bd. dirs. Sara Lee Corp., Sabre Holdings Corp, IMC Global Inc., PMI Group Inc., EXELON Corp. Trustee, past chmn. bd. trustees Kenyon Coll., Chgo. Symphony Orch.; life trustee Kenyon Coll., Chgo. Symphony Orch., Northwestern U.; trustee Rush-Presbyn.-St. Luke's Med. Ctr., Northwestern U. With AUS, 1954—56. Mem.: Chgo. Coun. Fgn. Rels., Old Elm Club Highland Park, Ill., Indian Hill Club Winnetka, Ill., Mid-Am. Club, Chgo. Club, Econ. Club (past pres.), Sunningdale Golf Club London, Comml. Club (past chmn.), Casino Club, Beta Theta Pi, Phi Beta Kappa. Office: First Chgo NBD Corp 1 Bank One Plz Ste IL1-0518 Chicago IL 60670-0001 E-mail: richard_l_thomas@bankone.com.

THOMAS, RIEDEL, education educator; s. Gottfried Riedel; m. Donna Riedel, Nov. 12, 1988; children: Albert Riedel Mishaan, Abraham Riedel-Mishaan. PhD, U. Mass., 1990. Prof. math. U. Louisville, 1990—. Co-author (with p. k. sahoo): (book) Mean Value Theorems and Functional Equations. Scholar Stipend, Studienstiftung des Deutschen Volkes, 1985—87; Travel Grant, Fulbright, 1985. Mem.: Math. Assn. of Am., Am. Math. Soc. Office: Dept of Math Univ Louisville Louisville KY 40292 Office Phone: 502-852-6826. Office Fax: 502-852-7132. E-mail: t0ried01@louisville.edu.

THOMAS, RITCHIE TUCKER, lawyer; b. Cleve., Aug. 12, 1936; s. Myron F. and Marjorie (Ritchie) T.; m. Elizabeth Blackwell Hanes Main, Jan. 1, 1994. BA, Cornell U., 1959; JD, Case-Western Res. U., 1964. Bar: Ohio 1964, U.S. Dist. Ct. (no. dist.) Ohio 1964, U.S. Ct. Appeals (D.C. cir.) 1971, U.S. Ct. Appeals (fed. cir.) 1973, U.S. Ct. Fed. Claims 1973, U.S. Ct. Internat. Trade 1976, U.S. Ct. Appeals (9th cir.) 1985. Assoc. office of gen. counsel U.S. Tariff Commn., Washington, 1964-67; assoc. Squire, Sanders & Dempsey, Cleve., 1967-69, Cox, Langford & Brown, Washington, 1969-74; ptnr. Squire, Sanders & Dempsey, Washington, 1974—. Mem. exec. com. Meridian House Internat., Washington, 1977-94. Assoc. editor Western Res. U. Law Rev., 1964; columnist Commerce Germany; contbr. articles to profl. jours. Mem. Waring Prize Com., Western Res. Acad., 1996—. Recipient various book award West Pub. Co., 1964. Mem. Fed. Bar Assn., D.C. Bar Assn., Belgian American Assn. (v.p. bd. dirs. 1989—, Bretton Woods com. 2003—), Am. C. of C. (Washington rep. 1984—), Order of Coif. Home: 6700 Bradley Blvd Bethesda MD 20817-3045 Office: Squire Sanders & Dempsey 1201 Pennsylvania Ave NW PO Box 407 Washington DC 20044-0407 Business E-Mail: rtthomas@ssd.com.

THOMAS, ROB, singer, songwriter; b. Landstuhl, Germany, Feb. 14, 1972; m. Marisol Maldonado, 1999; 1 child from previous relationship, Maison Avery William. Co-founder, band mem. Tabitha's Secret, 1993—95; lead singer, pianist Matchbox Twenty, 1996—. Singer: (albums) Yourself or Someone Like You, 1996, Mad Season, 2000, More Than You Think You Are, 2002, (songs) Smooth (with Carlos Santana), 1999 (Grammy awards: Record of the Year, 1999, Song of the Year, 1999, Best Pop Collaboration with Vocals, 1999); vocals: (albums) The Great Divide (with Willie Nelson), 2002, background vocals: (albums) Goddess in the Doorway (with Mick Jagger), 2001, Broken Promises (with Rusty Truck), 2003. Office: Atlantic Records 9229 W Sunset Blvd #900 West Hollywood CA 90069

THOMAS, ROBERT EGGLESTON, retired corporate executive; b. Cuyahoga Falls, Ohio, July 28, 1914; s. Talbott E. and Jane S. (Eggleston) T.; children: Robert Eggleston, Barbara Ann. BS in Econs, U. Pa., 1936. Asst. to gen. mgr., sec., mgr. r.r. investments Keystone Custodian Funds, Boston, 1936-53; v.p. Pennroad Corp., N.Y.C., 1953-59; chmn. exec. com., dir. M.-K.-T. R.R., 1956-65; mem. exec. com. MAPCO Inc., 1960-84, dir., chief exec. officer, 1960-80, pres., 1960-76, chmn. bd., 1973-84. Adv. bd. BancOkla. Corp. Mem.: Newcomen Soc., Nat. Mining Assn. (hon. dir.), Am. Petroleum Inst. (hon. dir.), Desert Horizons Country Club (Indian Wells, Calif.), San Diego Yacht Club, Summit Club (Tulsa), So. Hills Country Club (Tulsa), Chgo. Club. Episcopalian. Office: Williams Cos PO Box 4679 Tulsa OK 74159-0679

THOMAS, ROBERT L. retired manufacturing company executive; b. Atlanta, Aug. 1, 1941; s. Orville Kermit Smith and Ina Evelyn (Farris) Peterson; m. Karen Degenhardt, Dec. 4, 1960 (div. Apr. 1978); children: John Harding, Gregory James, Kristen Ann; m. Mary Ellen Seaman, May 2, 1981; children: Lindsey Marian, Mark Gordon. BA in History, Queens Coll., 1968. Buyer J.C. Penney Co. Inc., N.Y.C., 1964-70; sales mgr. Avon Products Inc., Atlanta, 1970-72; pres. Saul Bros. & Co. Inc., Atlanta, 1973—2002; ret., 2002. Bd. dirs. Murphey Candler Little League, Atlanta, 1972, also bd. trustees; bd. dirs. Leukemia Soc., Atlanta, 1988—; mem. Dekalb County Exec. Com. Rep. Party, Atlanta, 1970-74; del. State Convention Rep. Party, Atlanta, 1972. Established scholarship Michael Daniel and Alexander Tyler Smith Scholarship Found., U.S.C., 1995. Mem. South East Textile and Apparel Mfrs., U.S. Polo Assn., Atlanta Polo Club, Gulfstream Polo Club (West Palm Beach), N.Y. Athletic Club (N.Y.C.), Country Club of the South (Alpharetta, Ga.). Republican. Roman Catholic. Home: 4095 Big Creek Overlook Alpharetta GA 30005-4213

THOMAS, ROBERT MCGUFFEY, automotive executive, educator; b. Newcastle, Pa., Jan. 7, 1917; s. Trevor Thomas and Clara Belle Speer; m. Millie Reddy, Jan. 7, 1945 (div. Apr. 11, 1962); children: Trevor, Diane, Robert; m. Natalie Khoranoff, Apr. 10, 1964. Degree in Music(hon.), Music Master, Sharon, Pa., 1938. Exec. stalist Ford Motor Co., Dearborn, Mich., 1965—74. Author: How To Play Piano, 1984, War Is Hell, 1985, Life Is Life, 1995. With U.S. Army, 1940—45, Europe. Mem.: Piano Club. Avocation: piano. Home: 10539 Caminito Pollo San Diego CA 92126

THOMAS, ROBERT MORTON, JR., lawyer; b. Kansas City, Kans., Jan. 1, 1941; s. Robert Morton Sr. and Arlowyne Edith (Arganbright) T.; m. Rebecca Ann Myers, Aug. 21, 1965; children: Brooke J., Austin B. BA, U. Kans., 1962; LLB, Harvard U., 1966. Bar: N.Y., U.S. Dist. Ct. (so. dist.) N.Y., U.S. Ct. Appeals (2d cir.). Local govt. advisor Republic of Botswana, Gaborone, 1966, dist. officer Serowe, 1967, dist. commr. Maun, 1968; assoc. Sullivan & Cromwell, N.Y.C., 1969-75, ptnr., 1975—, ptnr.-in-charge London, 1979-82, mng. ptnr. gen. practice group N.Y.C., 1986-91. Mem. exec. bd. Manhattan coun. Boy Scouts Am.; trustee U. Kans. Endowment Assn., Helen Keller Internat. Mem. ABA, N.Y. State Bar Assn., Assn. Bar City of N.Y., Internat. Bar Assn., India House, Buck's Club, Harvard Club, Mill Reef Club, Verbank Hunting and Fishing Club (dir., pres.), Knickerbocker Club, Confrerie des Chevaliers de Tastevin, Bentley Drivers Club, Vintage Sports Car Club Am. Republican. Presbyterian. Office: Sullivan & Cromwell 125 Broad St New York NY 10004-2498

THOMAS, ROBERT PAIGE, lawyer; b. Columbus, Ohio, July 31, 1941; s. Charles Marion and Elsie (Cavanaugh) T.; children: Paige Cason, Park Cavanaugh. B.A., Vanderbilt U., 1963, M.A., 1965, J.D., 1970. Bar: Tenn. 1970, U.S. Dist. Ct. (mid. dist.) Tenn. 1970, U.S. Ct. Appeals (6th cir.) 1977. Assoc. Boult, Cummings, Conners & Berry, Nashville, 1970-74, ptnr., 1974—, mng. ptnr., 1977-84. chmn. Tenn. Dem. Party; Mem. Bill Clinton's Nat. Fin. Com.; fin. chmn. Sen. Jim Sasser. Mem. ABA, Tenn. Bar Assn., Nashville Bar Assn. Democrat. Episcopalian. Clubs: Yale of N.Y.C.; Belle Meade Country, Cumberland. Office: PO Box 198062 Nashville TN 37219-8062 Office Phone: 615-252-2314. Business E-Mail: bthomas@boultcummings.com.

THOMAS, ROBERT R. state supreme court justice; b. Rochester, N.Y., Aug. 7, 1952; m. Maggie Thomas; 3 children. BA in govt., U. Notre Dame, 1974; JD, Loyola U., 1981. Cir. ct. judge DuPage County, 1988, acting chief judge, 1989—94; judge Appellate Ct. Second Dist., 1994—2000; Supreme Ct. justice Ill. State Supreme Ct., 2000—. Mem.: DuPage County Bar Assn., Acad. All-Am. Hall of Fame (life NCAA Silver Ann. Award 1999). Office: Bldg A Rm 207A 1776 S Naperville Rd Wheaton IL 60187

THOMAS, ROBERT RENE, physician assistant, athletic trainer; b. Santa Monica, Calif., July 19, 1955; s. Erving Robert Thomas and Vertis Lee Sample; adopted parents: Terry and Ann Corrigan. BE, Gonzaga U., 1980; MS in Physician Asst., U. Detroit, 1998. Cert. physician asst. Tchr., Spokane, Wash., 1981-82, Fed. Way (Wash.) Sch. Dist., 1983-90; summer intern Phila. Eagles, 1988, 89; asst. athletic trainer Detroit Lions, 1990-97; physician asst. Henry Ford Hosp., W. Bloomfield, Mich., 1998-2000, Ctr. for Spine and Orthopedic Surgery, Cheyenne, Wyo., 2000-01, Sportsmedicine Fairbanks, Alaska, 2001—03; physician asst. in orthopedics Elmendorf AFB, Alaska, 2003—. Athletic trainer Goodwill Games, Seattle, 1990, U.S. Womens Soccer, Pontiac, Mich., 1994. Treas. Alaska Com. of Sportsmedicine. Grantee NSF, 1984. Fellow Am. Assn. Physician Assts. (diversity coun.); mem. Nat. Athletic Trainers Assn., Alaska Assn. Physician Assts. (pub. edn. chair). Democrat. Roman Catholic. Avocations: hunting, fishing, golf.

THOMAS, ROGER MERIWETHER, lawyer; b. Hartford, Conn., Feb. 28, 1930; s. Frederick Metcalf and Helen Meriwether (Lewis) T.; m. Mary Dorothea Wyman, Dec. 4, 1965; children— Donald Wyman, Helen Dorothea AB, Princeton U., 1952; LL.B., Va. U., 1957; LL.M., Boston U., 1964. Bar: N.Y. 1958, Mass. 1960, U.S. Dist. Ct. (Mass) 1965, U.S. Tax Ct. 1965, U.S. Supreme Ct. 1967. Assoc. Angulo, Cooney, Marsh & Ouchterloney, N.Y.C., 1957-60; assoc., then ptnr. Gaston & Snow, Boston, 1960-91; counsel Condit & Assocs., P.C., Boston, 1992-94. Outline author and lectr. Mass. Continuing Legal Edn., Inc., Boston; past panelist New Eng. Law Inst. Estate Planning Forums, Boston. Trustee Buckingham Browne & Nichols Sch., Cambridge, Mass., 1967-69. Served to 1st lt. U.S. Army, 1952-54, Korea. Mem. Am. Coll. Trust and Estate Counsel, Boston Bar Assn., Mass. Bar Assn. Avocations: reading; sports; old movies. Home: 40 Byron Rd Weston MA 02493-2229

THOMAS, RUSSELL JOSEPH, JR., lawyer; b. Cambridge, Mass., Dec. 19, 1942; s. Russell Joseph and Gertrude Ann (Clancy) T.; m. June Thomas, June 2, 1979; children— Dagian Clancy, Russell Joseph III. A.B., Harvard U., 1964, LL.B., 1967. Bar: Mass. 1967, D.C. 1972, Mich. 1972, Calif. 1979, U.S. Supreme Ct. 1977, U.S. Ct. Appeals (4th, 6th, 9th cirs.) 1970, U.S. Dist. Cts. (ea., we. dists.) Mich. 1972, U.S. Dist. Ct. (cen., no. dists.) Calif. 1980. Atty. Appellate Ct. Br. Office Gen. Counsel, NLRB, Washington, 1967-71; atty.-in-charge office gen. counsel, labor and personnel, adminstrv. agencies Gen. Motors Corp., Detroit, 1971-77; asst. gen. counsel Digital Equipment Corp., Maynard, Mass., 1977-78; assoc. Pepper, Hamilton & Scheetz, Detroit, 1978-82, ptnr., 1982— . Mem. ABA (labor law sect. coms. content editor Treatise on Occupational Safety and Health Law, 1981—). Club: Dodger Stadium (Los Angeles). Contbr. articles to profl. jours. Home: 864 Barclay Ct Troy MI 48085-4806 Office: 100 Renaissance Ctr Fl 36 Detroit MI 48243-1001

THOMAS, SARA R. state legislator; b. Indianola, Miss., Apr. 21, 1941; m. Arthur Lee Thomas. Student, Miss. Valley State U., Delta State U. State legislator Miss. Ho. of Reps., Jackson, 1996—. Mem. edn., municipalities, penitentiary, pub. bldgs., state libr. coms. Miss. Ho. of Reps. Mem. NEA, Miss. Assn. of Educators, Miss. Ret. Tchrs., Miss. Valley State U. Alumni Assn., Regulette Civic and Social, Crepe Myrtle Garden Club, Delta Uniserv Region, Phi Delta Kappa, Alpha Kappa Alpha. Democrat. Baptist. Home: 512 B King Rd Indianola MS 39367 Office: State Capitol Bldg PO Box 1018 Jackson MS 39215-1018 E-mail: sthomas@mail.house.state.ms.us.

THOMAS, SCOTT E. federal government executive, lawyer; b. Buffalo, Wyo., Mar. 5, 1953; s. Ralph E. and Bonnie E. Thomas; m. Elena W. King, Apr. 28, 1984. BA, Stanford U., 1974; JD, Georgetown U., 1977. Bar: D.C. 1977, U.S. Ct. Appeals (9th cir.) 1980, U.S. Supreme Ct. 1981. Atty. Office of Gen. Counsel, Fed. Election Commn., Washington, 1977-80, asst. gen. counsel, 1980-83; exec. asst. to commr. Fed. Election Commn., Washington, 1983-86, commr., 1986—. Mem. D.C. Bar Assn. Office: Fed Election Commn 999 E St NW Washington DC 20463-0002

THOMAS, SHIRLEY, author, educator, business executive; b. Glendale, Calif. d. Oscar Miller and Ruby (Thomas) Annis; m. W. White, Feb. 22, 1949 (div. June 1952); m. William C. Perkins, Oct. 24, 1969. BA in Modern Lit., U. Sussex, Eng., 1960, PhD in Comm., 1967; diploma, Russian Fedn. Cosmonautics, 1995. Actress, writer, producer, dir. numerous radio and TV stas., 1942-46; v.p. Commodore Prodns., Hollywood, Calif., 1946-52; pres. Annis & Thomas, Inc., Hollywood, 1952—; prof. technical writing U. So. Calif., L.A., 1975—. Hollywood corr. NBC, 1952-56; editor motion pictures CBS, Hollywood, 1956-58; corr. Voice of Am., 1958-59; now free lance writer; cons. biol. scis. communication project George Washington U., 1965-66; cons. Stanford Rsch. Inst., 1967-68, Jet Propulsion Lab., 1969-70. Author: Men of Space vols. 1-8, 1960-68, Spanish trans., 1961, Italian, 1962; Space Tracking Facilities, 1963, Computers: Their History, Present Applications and Future, 1965; The Book of Diets, 1974. Organizer, chmn. City of L.A. Space Adv. Com., 1964-73, Women's Space Symposia, 1962-73; founder, chmn. Aerospace Hist. Soc. Inc.; chmn. Theodore von Karman Postage Stamp Com., 1965—, stamp issued 1992; bd. dirs. World Children's Transplant Fund, 1993—, Achievement Rewards for Coll. Scients. Recipient Aerospace Excellence award Calif. Mus. Found. 1991, Nat. Medal Honor DAR, 1992, Yuri Gagarin Medal Honor, 1995. Fellow Brit. Interplanetary Soc.; mem. AIAA, AAAS, Internat. Acad. Astronautics, Internat. Soc. Aviation Writers, Air Force Assn. (Airpower Arts and Letters award 1961), Internat. Acad. Astronautics, Nat. Aero. Assn., Nat. Asn. Sci. Writers, Soc. for Tech. Communications, Am. Astronautical Soc., Nat. Geog. Soc., Am. Soc. Pub. Adminstrn. (sci. and tech. in govt. com. 1972—), Achievement Awards for Coll. Scientists, Theta Sigma Phi, Phi Beta. Home: 8027 Hollywood Blvd West Hollywood CA 90046 Office: U So Calif Profl Writing Program University Park Waite Phillips Hall 404 Los Angeles CA 90089-0001 Office Phone: 213-740-3250. E-mail: snowtech@pacbell.net.

THOMAS, SIDNEY, fine arts educator, researcher; b. N.Y.C., Dec. 21, 1915; s. Hyman and Rose (Samilowitz) T.; m. Rae Dinkowitz, May 26, 1940; children: David Phillip, Deborah Rose. BA, CCNY, 1935; MA, Columbia U., 1938, PhD, 1943. Tutor in English CCNY, N.Y.C., 1939-43; instr. English Queens Coll., N.Y.C., 1946-54; self-employed as editor, 1954-58; asst. editor Merriam-Webster, Springfield, Mass., 1958-61; assoc. prof. fine arts Syracuse U. (N.Y.), 1961-66, prof., 1966-85, prof. emeritus, 1985—, dir. humanities doctoral program, 1964-72, chmn. dept. fine arts, 1969-73. Bibliographer Shakespeare Assn., N.Y.C., 1949-54 Author: The Antic Hamlet, 1943; co-editor: The Nature of Art, 1964; editor: Images of Man, 1972. Served to sgt., inf. U.S. Army, 1943-45, ETO. Research fellow Folger Shakespeare Library, Washington, 1947-48 Fellow Royal Soc. Arts (London); mem. MLA (life), Shakespeare Assn. Am., AAUP (pres. Syracuse U. chpt. 1974), ACLU, Phi Beta Kappa Office: Syracuse U Dept Fine Arts Syracuse NY 13210

THOMAS, SIDNEY R. federal judge; b. Bozeman, Mont., Aug. 14, 1953; m. Martha Sheehy. BA in Speech-Comm., Mont. State U., 1975, JD cum laude, 1978; D (hon.), Rocky Mountain Coll., 1998. Bar: Mont. 1978, U.S. Dist. Ct. Mont. 1978, U.S. Ct. Appeals (9th cir.) 1980, U.S. Dist. Ct. (9th cir.) 1980, U.S. Ct. Fed. Claims 1986, U.S. Supreme Ct. 1994. Shareholder Moulton, Bellingham, Longo and Mather, P.C., Billings, Mont., 1978—96; judge U.S. Ct. Appeals 9th Cir., Billings, 1996—. Adj. instr. Rocky Mountain Coll., Billings, 1982—95. Contbr. articles to profl. jours. Recipient Gov.'s award for Pub. Svc., 1978, Outstanding Faculty award, Rocky Mountain Coll., 1988. Mem.: ABA, Yellowstone County Bar Assn., State Bar Mont. Office: US Ct Appeals Ninth Circuit PO Box 31478 Billings MT 59107-1478

THOMAS, STEPHEN, retired industrial engineer; b. NYC, Aug. 29, 1923; s. Peter and Amelia Thomas; m. Jane Anne Broderick, July 3, 1948; children: Barbara Gail, Jessica Lynne, Susan Amelia. BS in Indsl. Mech. Engring., U. Mich., 1951. From foreman to personnel supr. EI du Pont, Buffalo, Wilmington, Del. and Brevard, NC, 1951—84, personnel supr., 1970—84, ret., 1984. Asst. chem. lab. U. Mich., Ann Arbor, 1948, asst. metalurgical lab., 1948—51; instr. Blue Ridge C.C., Hendersonville, NC, 1970—75; cons. human rels. EI du Pont, Brevard, NC, 1984—91. Chmn. Mayor's Com. for Handicapped, Henderson County, 1980; bd. dirs. Cmty Found. Henderson County, 1986—88; mem. bd. dirs. Laurel Park (NC) Alcohol Beverage Control Bd., 1983—99; mediator Dispute Settlement Ctr. Henderson County, 1984—2002; arbitrator BBB, Asheville, NC, 1986—2002; mem. bd. dirs. Dispute Settlement Ctr. Henderson County, 2001—02; treas. Rep. Party, Henderson County, NC; mem. bd. dirs. Western Carolina Cmty. Action, Henderson County, 1970, Western NC Tomorrow, 1986—94, Margaret R. Pardee Meml. Hosp., Henderson County, 1981—94. 2d lt. transp. corp. U.S. Army, 1945—46. Home: 555 Walnut Loop Rd Hendersonville NC 28739

THOMAS, STEPHEN CRAWFORD, social worker; b. Columbus, June 14, 1954; s. William Lawrence and Annabel Crawford Thomas; m. Patricia Dalasta Thomas, Mar. 21, 1981; 1 child, Marian M. BA, Kenyon Coll., 1976. Tchr. English Waverly High Sch., Ohio, 1983—88; income maintenance worker III Pike County Dept. Job & Family Svcs., 1989—. Avocations: reading, music, running.

THOMAS, STEPHEN JAY, anesthesiologist; b. Washington, 1943; Intern San Francisco Gen. Hosp., 1968-69; resident in anesthesiology Mass. Gen. Hosp., Boston, 1971-73, fellow, 1973-74; assoc. prof. NYU Med. Ctr.; vice chmn., Topkins-Van Poznak prof. dept. anesthesiology N.Y. Presbyn. Weill Cornell Ctr., 1989—; pres. Am. Bd. Anesthesiology, 2001—. Office: NY Presbyn Weill Cornell Ctr Dept Anesthesiology 525 E 68th St New York NY 10021-4870

THOMAS, STEPHEN PAUL, lawyer; b. Bloomington, Ill., July 30, 1938; s. Owen Wilson and Mary Katherine (Paulsen) T.; m. Marieanne Sauer, Dec. 7, 1963 (dec. June 1984); 1 child, Catherine Marie; m. Marcia Aldrich Toomey, May 28, 1988; 1 child, Ellen Antonia. BA, U. Ill., 1959; LLB, Harvard U., 1962. Bar: Ill. 1962; cert. naturalist Morton Arboretum, 2001. Vol. Peace Corps, Malawi, Africa, 1963-65; assoc. Sidley, Austin, Brown & Wood, Chgo., 1965-70, ptnr., 1970-2000. Lectr. on law Malawi Inst. Pub. Adminstrn., 1963-65. Pres. Hyde Park-Kenwood Cmty. Conf., Chgo., 1988-90; life trustee Chgo. Acad. for Arts, chmn., 1992-97; bd. dirs. Union League Civic and Arts Found., Chgo., 1999—. Recipient Paul Cornell award Hyde Park Hist. Soc., 1981. Mem. ABA, Chgo. Bar Assn., Chgo. Fedn. of Musicians, Lawyers Club of Chgo., Union League Club Chgo., Chgo. Literary Club. Democrat. Roman Catholic. Avocations: jazz piano playing, naturalist studies. Home: 9756 S Longwood Dr Chicago IL 60643-1610 Office: Sidley Austin Brown & Wood 55 W Monroe St Chicago IL 60603-5001 E-mail: sthomas@sidley.com.

THOMAS, STEPHEN S. health facility administrator; BBA and Econs., Ind. Ctrl. U., 1977. Various mgmt. positions Burroughs Corp., 1978—83, Digital Equipment Corp., 1978—83; pres. Datapro Info. Svcs. Group divsn. McGraw-Hill Cos., 1993—97; exec. v.p., pres. Cardinal's Pyxis Corp.; exec. v.p. Cardinal Health, Inc., 1999—, group pres. automation and info. svcs., 1999—. Bd. dirs. SupplyPro, San Diego. Mem.: Honor Soc. Nursing Indpls., Sigma Theta Tau (mem. adv. group). Office: Cardinal Health Inc 7000 Cardinal Pl Dublin OH 43017

THOMAS, STEVE, professional hockey player; b. Stockport, Eng., July 15, 1963; m. Lori Thomas; children: Lauren, Christian. Left wing Toronto Mapleleafs, 1984—87, 1998—, Chgo. Black Hawks, 1987—92, N.Y. Islanders, 1992—95, N.J. Devils, 1995—98. Capt. Team Can. World Hockey Championships, Vienna. Recipient MVP award, SportsChannel, Nystrom award, 1992—93.

THOMAS, STEVEN ALLEN, lawyer; b. Birmingham, Ala., Mar. 19, 1951; s. Reginald Allen and Billie Ruth (Brewer) T.; m. Rebecca Phillips, Aug. 1972; children: Jennifer Ruth, Matthew Allen. AS, Walker Coll., Jasper, Ala., 1971; BA, U. Ala., Tuscaloosa, 1973; JD, Samford U., Birmingham, Ala., 1976. Bar:

Ala. 1977, U.S. Dist. Ct. (no. dist.) Ala. 1986. Law clk. Circuit Ct. Walker Co., Jasper, 1978-83; lawyer Beaird, Thomas, Higgins, Jasper, 1983-91; ptv. practice, Jasper, 1991—. Judge Mcpl. Ct., Carbon Hill, Ala., 1983—, Nauvoo, Ala., 1985-88, Arley, Ala., 1991—, Oakman, Ala., 1997—; prosecutor, Addison, Ala., 2001—03; atty. City of Jasper Civil Svc. Bd., 2001-03. Legal counsel Ala. Jaycees, 1986-88; pres. Ala. Mining Mus., Dora, 1989—; treas. Jasper Band Boosters, 1993-95; advisor Explorers, 1991-98; bd. dirs. Assn. Ala. Fairs, Inc., 1998-2003, 1st v.p. 2000, pres. 2001-02. Named Jaycee of Yr., Jasper Jaycees, 1983-84, Officer of Yr., 1984, 88, Blue Ribbon Club (Hall of Fame), 2004. Mem. ABA, Ala. Bar Assn. (elder law section, family law section), Walker County Bar Assn. (pres. 1990-91), Ala. Mcpl. Judges Assn., Ala. Assn. Mcpl. Attys., East Walker C. of C. (pres. 1992-94), Phi Alpha Delta. Methodist. Avocations: fishing, reading, swimming, boating, spectator sports. Home: 1401 9th Ave W Jasper AL 35501-4538 Office: PO Box 1951 Jasper AL 35502-1951 Office Phone: 205-221-3100. E-mail: stevenjd76@aol.com.

THOMAS, TARQUIN CRAIG, computer scientist, writer; b. Haslemere, Surrey, Eng., May 7, 1966; s. Leicester Craig and Margaret Lina T. Systems analyst Multisoft Systems Ltd., Alton, Eng., 1984-85; cons. Migration Techs. Ltd., Windsor, Eng., 1987; prin. tech. mgr. TIS Ltd., Bourne End, Eng., 1988-94; cons. Barclays Global Investors, San Francisco, 1995—. Cons. MISYS P.L.C., Eng., 1994. Author: (CD-Rom) EJW-CDR, 1994; contr. articles to profl. jours. Recipient Barclays Chmn.'s award for Cmty. Involvement. Mem. Inst. Data Processing Mgmt., Brit. Mensa. Avocations: art, advocacy child rights and welfare.

THOMAS, TERESA ANN, microbiologist, educator; b. Wilkes-Barre, Pa., Oct. 17, 1939; d. Sam Charles and Edna Grace T. BS cum laude, Coll. Misericordia, 1961; MS in Biology, Am. U., Beirut, 1965; MS in Microbiology, U. So. Calif., 1973; cert. in ednl. tech., U. Calif., San Diego, 1998. Tchr., sci. supr., curriculum coord. Meyers H.S., Wilkes-Barre, 1962-64, Wilkes-Barre Area Pub. Schs., 1961-66; rsch. assoc. Proctor Found. Rsch. in Ophthalmology U. Calif. Med. Ctr., San Francisco, 1966-68; instr. Robert Coll. of Istanbul, Turkey, 1968-71, Am. Edn. in Luxembourg, 1971-72, Bosco Tech. Inst., Rosemead, Calif., 1973-74, San Diego C.C. Dist., 1974-80; prof. microbiology and ecology Sch. Math Sci. and Engring. Southwestern Coll., Chula Vista, Calif., 1980—; mem. Vecinos Baja Studies EcoMundo team internat. program Southwestern Coll., mem. staff devel. com., 2001—. Pres. acad. senate, 1984-85, del., 1986-89; chmn., coord., steering com. project Cultural Rsch. Ednl. and Trade Exch., 1991-2000, Southwestern Coll.-Shanghai Inst. Fgn. Trade; coord. Southwestern Coll. Great Tchg. Seminar, 1987, 88, 89, coord. scholars program, 1988-90; steering com. Southwestern Coll.; exec. com. Acad. Senate for Calif. C.C.s, 1985-86, Chancellor of Calif. C.C.s Adv. and Rev. Coun. Fund for Instrnl. Improvement, 1984-86; co-project dir. statewide, coord. So. Calif. Biotech. Edn. Consortium, 1993-95, steering com., 1993-98; adj. asst. prof. Chapman Coll., San Diego, 1974-83, San Diego State U., 1977-79; chmn. Am. Colls. Istanbul Sci. Week, 1969-71; adv. bd. Chapman Coll. Cmty. Ctr., 1979-80; cons. sci. curriculum Calif. Dept. Edn., 1986-89; pres. Internat. Rels. Club, 1959-61; mem. San Francisco World Affairs Coun., 1966-68, San Diego World Affairs Coun., 1992—; v.p. Palomar Palace Estates Home Owners Assn., 1983-85, pres., 1994-99, 2003-, v.p., 1999-2003; mem. Rsch. Conf. on Undergraduate Microbiology Edn., Conn. Coll., 1999; bd. dir. US Orgn. Med. Ednl. Needs, US Internat. Boundary and Water Commn. Citizens Forum; presenter in field. Emeritus mem. edlt. rev. bd.: Jour. of Coll. Sci. Tchg. Life mem. Chula Vista Nature Ctr.; mem. Internat. Friendship Commn., Chula Vista, 1985-95, vice chmn., 1989-90, chmn., 1990-92; mem. US-Mex. Sister Cities Assn., nat. bd. dir., 1992-94, gen. chair 30th nat. conv., 1993; active City of Chula Vista Resource Conservation Commn., 1996—, chmn. 2002—; active Chula Vista Bd. Ethics, 1999-2000; co-organizer Chula Vista People-to-People Sister City Dels. to Odawara City, Japan, 1991, 94, 99; cmty. adv. com. San Diego Mus. Man, 2000-03; mem. County San Diego Solid Waste Hearing Panel, 2000—; citizens forum bd. US Internat. Boundary and Water Comm., 2002-; steering com. Chula Vista Gen. Plan Update, 2002-; hon. coach SWC Jaguars Basketball Team, 2003; com. mem. Chula Vista Environ., Open Space and Sustainable Devel., 2002—. Rsch. grantee Pa. Heart Assn., 1962; NSF fellow, 1965, USPHS fellow, 1972-73; recipient Nat. Tchg. Excellence award Nat. Inst. Staff and Orgnl. Devel., 1989; named Southwestern Coll. Woman of Distinction, 1987, Hon. Coach Southwestern Coll. Ladies Basketball Apaches, 2001. Mem.: NEA, NIH (mentor Bridges to the Future program Southwestern Coll. and San Diego 1993—98, steering com.), NSTA (life; coord. internat. honors exch. lectr. competition 1986, internat. com.), Faculty Assn. Calif. C.C.s (state policy com. 2003—), Am. Assn. Cmty. and Jr. Colls., Calif. Tchrs. Assn., Am. Soc. Microbiology (So. Calif. Microbe Discovery Team 1995—99), Calif. Sci. Tchrs. Assn. (life), Nat. Assn. Biology Tchrs. (life), Chula Vista-Odawara (Japan) Sister Cities Assn. (founding pres. 1994—), Am. U. Beirut Alumni and Friends of San Diego (1st v.p. 1984—91), San Diego Zool. Soc., Japan Soc. San Diego and Tijuana (life), Japanese Hist. Soc. San Diego (life), Chula Vista Nature Ctr. (life), Am.-Lebanese Assn. San Diego (1st v.p. 1984—91, pres. 1988—93, chmn. scholarship com.), Am. Lebanese Syrian Ladies Club (pres. 1982—83), Lions Internat. (bull. editor 1991—93, 2d v.p. 1992—93, 1st v.p. 1993—94, editor Roaring Times Newsletter 1993—94, chmn. dist. internat. rels. and cooperations com. 1993—95, pres. S.W. San Diego County chpt. 1994—95, Sweetwater Zone chmn. dist. 4-L6 1996—97, pub. rels. 1997—98, Best Bull. award 1992—93, named S.W. San Diego County Lion of Yr. 2000), Delta Kappa Gamma (Outstanding Pub. Svc. award Gamma Omicron chpt. 2003), Phi Theta Kappa, Sigma Phi Sigma, Kappa Gamma Pi (pres. Wilkes-Barre chpt. 1963—64, pres. San Francisco chpt. 1967—68), Alpha Pi Epsilon (life; advisor Southwestern Coll. chpt. 1989—90, founder). Office Phone: 619-421-6700 ext. 5517. E-mail: tthomas@swc.cc.ca.us.

THOMAS, THORP, retired lawyer; b. Alexander, Ark., Sept. 15, 1923; s. Howard Norman and Letitia Helen (Miller) T.; m. Kermit Maurice Toombs (dec. Feb. 1998); children: Victoria, Helen, Deborah, Thorp Jr., Terry; m. Marie Elaine Underwood, July 22, 1999. Student, Little Rock Jr. Coll., 1945; JD, U. Ark., 1950. Bar: Ark. 1951, U.S. Dist. Ct. 1951, U.S. Ct. Appeals (8th cir.) Ark. 1953, U.S. Supreme Ct. 1954. Claims trainee Fidelity & Casualty Co. N.Y., Little Rock, 1950-53; asst. atty. gen. Atty. Gen.'s Office, Little Rock, 1953-63; pvt. practice law Little Rock, 1963—. Chmn. planning commn., Alexander, Ark., 1980—. Mem. ABA, Ark. Bar Assn., Masons. Democrat. Methodist. Avocations: music, art, aviation. Home: 8310 Louwanda Dr Little Rock AR 72205-1666 E-mail: tmthomas@arkansas.net.

THOMAS, THURMAN LEE, professional football player; b. Houston, May 16, 1966; m. Patti Thomas; children: Olivia, Angelica, Annika Lee. Student, Okla. State U., 1984—87. Running back Buffalo Bills, 1988—99, Miami Dolphins, 2000—. Named AP MVP, 1991, AP Offensive Player of Yr., 1991, The Sporting News Player of Yr., 1991, Football News Player of Yr., 1991, Buffalo Bills/Edge 1993 Man of Yr., 1993; named to Pro Bowl, 1989—93, UPI All-AFC squad, Pro Football Weekly's All-AFC team, AP Second Team All-Pro, Coll. and Pro Football Newsweekly All-Pro Second Team and Sports Illustrated's All-Pro Team, Tex. H.S. Hall of Fame, 1992, numerous others. Office: Miami Dolphins Tng Facility 7500 SW 30th St Davie FL 33314

THOMAS, TOM, retired plastics company executive; b. Malang, Java, Indonesia, Feb. 15, 1932; arrived in Can., 1954; s. Ferdinand and Elfrieda Emma (Macht) T.; m. Jannie Chine Sneep, Jan. 19, 1956; children: Gregory John, Renée Sonja Elfrieda, Michael Grant, Thomas. Grad. high sch., The Hague, Holland. Jr. mgr. Lever Bros. Ltd., Toronto, Ont., Can., 1954-60; sr. mgr. Impac & Somerville Plastics, Toronto, Ont., Can., 1960-64; founder, C.E.O. Can. Cup Inc., Toronto, Ont., Can., 1964—, also bd. dirs., 1964-93; ret., 1993. Inventor in field. Trustee Frazer Inst., Vancouver, B.C., Can., 1977-93; gov. Massey and Roy Thomson Hall, Toronto, 1991-92; bd. dirs. Toronto Symphony, 1986-92, mem. Maestro's Club, 1984, mem. pres.'s coun. Can. Opera Co., 1980, adv. coun. Toronto Symphony, 1995-2000, pres. Coun. Can. Opera, 1980-95. Avocations: sailing, history, classical music, chess.

THOMAS, TONY, producer; Prodr., ptnr. Witt-Thomas Prodns., L.A., 1976-81; ptnr. Witt-Thomas-Harris Prodns., 1981—. Exec. prodr. (with others) (TV series) Fay, 1975-76, Loves Me, Loves Me Not, 1977, Soap (Emmy award nominations best nighttime and primetime comedy series, 1978, 80, Emmy award best primetime comedy series 1981), Benson, 1979, It's a Living, 1980-81, Making a Living, 1982, It Takes Two, 1982-83, Condo, 1983; exec. prodr. (TV series), The Golden Girls, 1985-92 (Emmy awards best primetime comedy series 1986, 87), Beauty and the Beast, 1987, Empty Nest, 1988-95, Nurses, 1991, Herman's Head, 1991, Blossom, 1991-95, The John Larroquette Show, 1993-97; prod. (TV movies) Bloodsport, 1973, Snatched, 1973, Griffin and Phoenix: A Love Story, 1976; co-exec. prodr. (TV movies) Satan's Triangle, 1975; assoc. prodr. (TV movies) Brian's Song, 1971, No Place to Run, 1972, Home for the Holidays, 1972, The Letters, 1973, A Cold Night's Death, 1973, Remember When, 1974, The Gun and the Pulpit, 1974, High Risk, 1993; co-prodr. (films) Firstborn, 1984, Dead Poets Society, 1989, Final Analysis, 1992. Office: Danny Thomas Productions 11240 Magnolia Blvd Ste 201 North Hollywood CA 91601-3790

THOMAS, TRACEY WILLIAMS, researcher; b. Birmingham, Ala., Nov. 14, 1971; d. Donald Randolph and Mary Hunter Williams; m. Stephen Wesley Thomas, Feb. 18, 1971. BA, Hampton U., 1994; PhD, Howard U., 2000. Postdoctoral rsch. fellow Johns Hopkins Sch. of Medicine, Balt., 2000—03; aaas sci. policy fellow U.S. EPA, Washington, 2003—. Founder, CEO TWThomas Solutions, LLC, Wash., DC; officer Postdoctoral Assn., Johns Hopkins Sch. of Medicine, Balt., 2001—03; rsch. supr. BioTechnical Inst. of Md., Balt., 2002—. Contbr. articles various profl. jours. Team leader Greater DC Cares, Youth Impact, Wash., DC, 1995—98; mem. Joint Steering Com. for Pub. Policy, Bethesda, Md., 2002—04. Recipient Predoctoral and Postdoctoral Travel awards, Am. Soc. of Cell Biology, 1998-2000, XIV Internat. Conf. on AIDS Young Sci. Investigator award, Conf. Com., 2002; Postdoctoral fellowship Funding, NIH, 2001-2003, Sci. Policy fellowship, AAAS, 2003-2004. Mem.: AAAS, Am. Soc. of Cell Biology, Assn. of Women in Sci. (assoc.). Democrat. Roman Catholic. Achievements include research in calcium release mechanism in eggs of a protostome; posttranslational modification mutation of a G-Protein coupled receptor involved in HIV. Avocations: travel, reading. Home: 200 K St NW #308 Washington DC 20001 Office: US Environ Protection Agcy 1200 Pa Ave NW MC 8601D Washington DC 20460 Office Fax: 202-565-0090. Personal E-mail: tracey.thomas@twtsolutions.com. E-mail: thomas.tracey@epa.gov.

THOMAS, VIOLETA DE LOS ANGELES, real estate broker; b. Buenos Aires, Dec. 21, 1949; came to U.S., 1967; d. Angel and Lola (Andino) de Rios; m. Jess Thomas, Dec. 23, 1974; 1 child, Victor Justin. Student, Harvard U. and U. Buenos Aires, 1967—73. Mgr. book div. Time-Life, N.Y.C., 1985-94; real estate broker First Marin Realty, Inc., Mill Valley, Calif., 1996-97; assoc. broker Trump Corp., N.Y.C., 1997—, Brown Harris Stevens, N.Y.C., 1997—. Rep. N.Y.C. Bd. dirs. Alliance Francaise, St. Louis, 1995-96, City of Tiburon, Calif., 1987-93, Art and Heritage Commn., Tiburon. Named Woman of Yr., City of Buenos Aires, 1977, Broker of Yr., Marin County and San Francisco, 1987-92. Mem. Principia Coll. Club (pres. 1997—). Office: Brown Harris Stevens 655 Madison Ave Fl 3 New York NY 10021-8056 E-mail: violetathomas@aol.com.

THOMAS, WALTER DILL, JR., retired forest pathologist, consultant; b. St. Louis, July 3, 1918; s. Walter D. and Helen (Gardner) T.; m. Dolores B. Thomas, Dec. 31, 1939 (div. May 1984); children: Sandra Thomas Bosworth, Arthur D; m. Nancy McCarthy, Feb. 15, 1985. BS, Colo. State U., 1939; MS, U. Minn., 1943, PhD, 1947. Diplomate Am. Bd. Forensics Examiners. Prof. plant pathology Colo. State U., Ft. Collins, 1947-55; supr. biol. research Chevron Chem. Co., Richmond, Calif., 1955-70; v.p. rsch. Nat. Resource Mgmt., Eureka, Calif., 1970-72; pres. Forest Ag Corp., Lafayette, Calif., 1972-86; ret., 1999. Coord. bd. forest stewardship Calif. Dept. Forestry and Fire Control, 1990-94; cons. in field, 1986-97. Author: Field Manual of Forest and Shade Tree Diseases, 1947, Not Long Apart, 1965, Mauget Field Manual: Insects and Diseases of Shade Trees, 1995. Commr. Park and Recreation Com., Ft. Collins, 1949-54, Concord, Calif., 1959-65; city forester, Ft. Collins, 1950-55. Comdr. USNR, 1944-80. Fellow AAAS (life); mem. Am. Phytopathol. Soc., Soc. Am. Foresters, Foresters Assn. (Calif. lic.), Pesticide Applicators Profl. Assn., Internat. Soc. Arboriculture, Nat. Forensic Soc., Bd. Forensics Examiners, Assn. Cons. Foresters, Am. Soc. Cons. Arborists, Soc. Tech. Comms. (sr. mem.), VFW, Lions. Democrat. Avocations: swimming, writing, music. Home: 2435 Heatherleaf Ln Martinez CA 94553-4337 *It is better to fail humbly while trying to succeed than to never even try.*

THOMAS, WAYNE LEE, lawyer; b. Sept. 22, 1945; s. W. M. and June F. Thomas; m. Patricia H. Thomas, Mar. 16, 1968; children: Brigitte Elisabeth Williams, Kate Adelaide Culpepper. BA, U. Fla., 1967, JD cum laude, 1971. Bar: Fla. 1971, U.S. Supreme Ct. 1975, U.S. Ct. Appeals (5th cir.) 1975, U.S. Ct. Appeals (11th cir.) 1981, U.S. Ct. Claims 1976, U.S. Dist. Ct. (mid. dist.) Fla. 1973, U.S. Dist. Ct. (so. dist. trial bar) Fla. 1975; cert. mediator and arbitrator. Law clk. U.S. Dist. Ct. (mid. dist.) Fla., 1971-73; assoc. Trenam, Simmons, Kemker, Scharf, Barkin, Frye & O'Neill, PA, Tampa, 1973-77, ptnr., 1978-81; founder, pres. McKay & Thomas, PA, Tampa, 1981-89; ptnr. Carlton, Fields, Ward, Emmanuel, Smith & Cutler, PA, 1989-95; pvt. practice Tampa, 1995—. Mem. ABA, Fla. Bar (chmn. sect. gen. practice 1981-83, mem. ethics com., vice chmn. unauthorized practice law com. 1994-98, 2000-04, chmn. 2004—, vice chmn. fed. practice com. 1995-96, chmn. 1996-97, mem. bd. bar examiners 1986-91, chmn. 1990-91, chmn. unauthorized practice law com. 13A 1998-2001), Nat. Conf. Bar Examiners (multistate profl. responsibility exam. policy com. 1994-2004), Hillsborough County Bar Assn. (chmn. grievance com. 1985-86), Order of Coif, Wm. Glenn Terrell Am. Inn of Ct., Fla. Blue Key, Phi Kappa Phi, Omicron Delta Kappa. Democrat. Office: 707 N Franklin St Fl 10 Tampa FL 33602-4430

THOMAS, W(ILLIAM) BRUCE, retired steel, oil, gas company executive; b. Ripley, Mich., Oct. 25, 1926; s. William and Ethel (Collins) T.; m. Phyllis Jeanne Smith, June 25, 1950; 1 son, Robert William. BA magna cum laude, Western Mich. U., 1950; JD with distinction, U. Mich., 1952; postgrad., Law Sch., NYU, 1953. Bar: Mich. 1952. With USX Corp. (formerly U.S. Steel) and subs., various locations, 1952-91; tax atty. Oliver Iron Mining Div., Duluth, Minn., 1952-53; tax atty., tax supr., comptroller Orinoco Mining Co., N.Y.C. and Venezuela, 1953-64, dir., v.p. taxes, 1967-70, v.p., asst. treas., 1970-71, v.p., treas., 1971-75; exec. v.p., CFO, dir. USX Corp., Pitts., 1975-82, vice chmn., CFO, dir., 1982-91. Bd. dirs. Mfrs. Hanover Bank, Chem. Bank, Chase Manhattan Bank, Nat. Distillers Corp., Quantum Chem. Corp., Discount Corp. of N.Y. Bd. dirs. Duquesne U.; trustee Kenyon Coll. With USAAF, 1943-45. Mem. ABA, Mich. Bar Assn., Fin. Execs. Inst., Order of Coif, Duquesne Club, Pitts. Club, Laurel Valley Golf Club, Rolling Rock Club, Allegheny Country Club, Sky Club, Links, Belleair Country Club, Phi Alpha Delta. Methodist. Home: Blackburn Rd Rte 4 Sewickley PA 15143 Office: USX Corp 600 Grant Building Ste 6200 Pittsburgh PA 15219-2203 Office Phone: 412-433-1135.

THOMAS, WILLIAM GRIFFITH, lawyer; b. Washington, Nov. 1, 1939; s. Henry Phineas and Margaret Wilson (Carr) T.; m. Suzanne Campbell Foster, June 7, 1960. Student, Williams Coll., 1957-59, Richmond Coll., 1960; JD, U. Richmond, 1963. Bar: Va. 1963. Ptnr. Reed Smith LLP, Falls Church, Va., 1999—. Dir. Va. Electric and Power Co., Richmond, 1987-2000. Sec. Va. Dem. Com., 1968-70, chmn., 1970-72. Mem. ABA, Va. State Bar Assn., Alexandria Bar Assn., Am. Law Inst., Am. Coll. Real Estate Lawyers. Home: 4783 Herring Creek Rd Aylett VA 23009 Office: Reed Smith LLP 3110 Fairview Park Dr Ste 1400 Falls Church VA 22042-4503 Office Phone: 703-641-4238. E-mail: wthomas@reedsmith.com.

THOMAS, WILLIAM JOSEPH, secondary school educator, administrator; b. Orange, N.J., June 1, 1966; s. Willie Thomas and Sandra Thomas; m. Lisa, Dec. 30, 1990; children: William, Sydney, Jordan. BA, Jersey City State Coll., 1993; EdM, St. Peters Coll., 1998; postgrad., Seton Hall U., 1998—. Cert. elem. and secondary tchr., N.J. Dir. summer inst. Roselle (N.J.) Pub. Schs.; math. and sci. staff developer Newark (N.J.) Pub. Schs.; adj. prof. Rutgers U.; vice-prin. Plainfield (N.J.) H.S. Mem. AAUP, Orgn. of African Am. Adminstrs., Plainfield Assn. Supers. and Adminstrs. (pres.), N.J. Prins. and Supers. Assn. Avocations: sailing, gardening, singing. Office: Cedarbrook Elem Sch 1049 Central Ave Plainfield NJ 07060 Home: 920 Cedarbrook Rd Plainfield NJ 07060-2647

THOMAS, WILLIAM MARSHALL (BILL THOMAS), congressman; b. Wallace, Idaho, Dec. 6, 1941; s. Virgil and Gertrude Thomas; m. Sharon Lynn Hamilton, Jan. 1968; children: Christopher, Amelia. BA, San Francisco State U., 1963, MA, 1965. Mem. faculty dept. Am. govt. Bakersfield (Calif.) Coll., 1965-74, prof., 1965-74; mem. Calif. State Assembly, 1974-78, U.S. Congress from 22nd Calif. dist. (formerly 21st), 1979—; chmn. ways and means com., 2001—; chmn. Com. on House Oversight, 1995-2001. Mem. del. to Soviet Union, by Am. Council Young Polit. Leaders, 1977; chmn. Kern County Republican Central Com., 1972-74; mem. Calif. Rep. Com., 1972-80; del. Republican Party Nat. Conv., 1980, 84, 88; mem. Rep. Leader's Task Force on Health Care Reform. Republican. Office: House Reps 2208 Rayburn Ho Office Bldg Washington DC 20515-0001

THOMAS, WILLIAM SCOTT, lawyer; b. Joliet, Ill., Aug. 16, 1949; AB, Stanford U., 1971; JD, U. Calif., Hastings, 1974; LLM in Taxation, Golden Gate U., 1981. Bar: Calif. 1975, U.S. Dist. Ct. (no. dist.) Calif. 1975, U.S. Tax Ct. 1982. Tax editor Internat. Bur. Fiscal Documentation, Amsterdam, Holland, 1974-75; tax atty. Chevron Corp., San Francisco, 1975-77; from assoc. to ptnr. Brobeck, Phleger & Harrison, San Francisco, 1978—2003; ptnr. Morgan Lewis & Bockius, San Francisco, 2003. Mem. ABA (taxation sect.), Calif. Bar Assn. (exec. com. taxation sect. 1984-89, chmn. 1987-88). Office: Morgan Lewis & Bockius 1 Market Plz Ste 2700 San Francisco CA 94105 Office Phone: 415-442-1000. Business E-Mail: wthomas@morganlewis.com.

THOMAS, ZACH MICHAEL, professional football player; b. Pampa, Tex., Sept. 1, 1973; B.S. in Exercise Science, Tex. Tech, 1996. Linebacker Miami Dolphins, 1996—. Opened health and fitness club Zach's Club 54, Amarillo, Tex. Mem. Crunch on Paralysis team. Named First Team All-American, 1995; named to NFL Pro-Bowl, 1999—2003. Avocations: weightlifting, basketball. Office: Miami Dolphins Tng Facility 7500 SW 30th St Davie FL 33314

THOMASCH, ROGER PAUL, lawyer; b. N.Y.C., Nov. 7, 1942; s. Gordon J. and Margaret (Molloy) T.; children: Laura Leigh, Paul Butler. BA, Coll. William and Mary, 1964; LLB, Duke U., 1967. Bar: Conn. 1967, Colo. 1974. Assoc. atty. Cummings & Lockwood, Stamford, Conn., 1967-70; trial atty. U.S. Dept. Justice, Washington, 1970-73; ptnr. Roath & Brega, Denver, 1975-87; mng. ptnr. Denver office of Ballard, Spahr, Andrews & Ingersoll LLP, 1987—. Vis. assoc. prof. of law Drake U. Sch. Law, Des Moines, 1973-74; frequent lectr. in field, U.S. and Can.; adj. faculty mem. U. Denver Coll. Law, 1976-80. Recipient Leland Forrest Outstanding Prof. award, Drake U. Sch. Law, 1973. Fellow Am. Coll. of Trial Lawyers, Colo. Bar Found.; mem. ABA, Colo. Bar Assn., Denver Country Club, Univ. Club. Office: Ballard Spahr Andrews & Ingersoll LLP 1225 17th St Ste 2300 Denver CO 80202-5535 Office Phone: 303-299-7301. E-mail: Thomasch@BallardSpahr.com.

THOMAS-GRAHAM, PAMELA, communications executive; m. Lawrence Otis Graham; 1 child. grad., JD, Harvard Coll. Ptnr. McKinsey & Co., 1989—99; pres., CEO CNBC.com, 1999—2001; pres., COO CNBC, Burbank, Calif., 2001, pres., CEO, 2001—. Author: Ivy League Mystery Series, (novels) A Darker Shade of Crimson, Blue Blood; editor: Harvard Law Rev. Bd. dirs. N.Y. Opera, Am. Red Cross, NY, Inner-City Scholarship Fund. Named Woman of Yr., Finl. Women's Assn.; named one of Forty Under Forty Rising Young Bus. Leaders, Crain's N.Y. Bus., Top 20 Women in Fin., Global Fin. Mag., Top 10 Cons. in Am., Cons. Mag.; recipient Matrix award, N.Y. Women Comm., 2001. Mem.: Phi Beta Kappa. Office: CNBC 3000 W Alameda Ave #C296 Burbank CA 91523*

THOMASHOW, LINDA SUZANNE, microbiologist; b. Norwood, Mass. d. John Michael and E. Jean (Cole) Ravinski. BS, U. Mass., 1968; PhD, UCLA, 1979. Asst. prof. Wash. State U., Pullman, 1983-84; rsch. geneticist USDA Agrl. Rsch. Svc., Pullman, 1985—. Adj. prof. dept. plant pathology Wash. State U. Editorial bd. Applied & Environ. Microbiology, Washington, 1990—; contbr. articles to profl. jours. Mem. Am. Soc. Microbiology, Am. Phytopathol. Soc. (Ruth Allen award 1997), Internat. Soc. for Molecular Plant-Microbe Interactions. Achievements include research in production of antibiotics by beneficial bacteria that live in association with the roots of plants, structure, function and regulation of genes involved in antibiotic synthesis by bacteria, the ecological significance of antibiotic production in natural environments. Office: Wash State Univ PO Box 646430 Dept Plant Pathology Pullman WA 99164-6430

THOMASHOW, MICHAEL F. microbiologist, educator; AB in Bacteriology, UCLA, 1972, PhD in Bacteriology, 1978. Damon Runyon-Walter Winchell Cancer Fund Rsch. fellow dept. microbiology and immunology U. Wash., Seattle, 1978—81; asst. prof. dept. microbiology Wash. State U., Pullman, 1981—86, assoc. prof. dept. microbiology, 1986; assoc. prof. dept. crop and soil scis. and dept. microbiology Mich. State U., E. Lansing, 1986—91, prof. dept. crop and soil scis. and dept. microbiology, 1991—; vis. scholar dept. microbiology U. Wash., Seattle, 1996. Vice chair Gordon Rsch. Conf. on Plant Temperature Stress, 1992—93, chair, 1994—95; chair 6th conf. planning com. Nat. Agrl. Biotechnology Coun., 1992—94; mem. grant rev. panel plant responses to environ. stress USDA/NRICGP, 1993, 97; mem. grant rev. panel eukaryotic genetics NSF, 1990; cons. DNA Plant Tech. Corp., Oakland, Calif., 1994, Mendel Biotechnology, Inc., 1998—. Contbr. articles to profl. jours.; patents in field, mem. editl. bd. Plant Physiology, 1988—92, Planta, 1990—94, Cryo-Letters, 1995—, monitoring editor Plant Physiology, 1999—. Mem.: NAS, Am. Soc. Microbiology, Am. Soc. Plant Physiologists. Office: MSU-DOE Plant Rsch Lab Mich State Univ East Lansing MI 48824-1312

THOMASHOW, STEVEN ROY, military officer, intelligence officer; b. Bronx, Jan. 27, 1957; s. Isaac Tom and Dorothy (Cuillino Bodsky) T. Accredited, U.S. Mil. Acad. Commd. United States of the World, adm., with spl. ops., 1988—; served with Israeli War USN, served with Gulf War. Recipient Pres. Nat. Medal of Patriotism, Am. Police Hall of Fame, 1996. Fellow Nat. Law Enforcement Acad. (hon.); mem. Am. Fedn. Police. Avocations: Karate (black belt), torah studies, boxing, reading. Home and Office: US of the World Recon One 4644 Myrtle Ln West Palm Beach FL 33417-5316 Fax: 561 640-4359.

THOMASON, DUSTIN, writer; b. 1976; BS in Anthropology & Medicine, Harvard U., 1998; MD, MBA, Columbia U., 2003. Co-author: (novels) (with Ian Caldwell) The Rule of Four, 2004 (Publishers Weekly bestseller list, 2004, NY Times bestseller list, 2004, San Francisco Chronicle bestseller list, 2004, Boston Globe bestseller list, 2004, NY Post bestseller list, 2004). Office: c/o Dial Books 375 Hudson St New York NY 10014*

THOMASON, NOLA FAYE, critical care-emergency supervisor; b. East St. Louis, Ill., May 23, 1957; d. Noel Noble and Dorothy Bernice (Burkett) Manring; m. Paul David Thomason, Mar. 23, 1979; children: Paula Faye, Rachel Elisabeth. ADN, Frontier C.C., Fairfield, Ill., 1986; Mobile Intensive Care Nurse/Emergency Care RN, Good Samaritan Hosp., Mt. Vernon, 1992; Trauma Nurse Specialist, Carbondale Meml. Hosp., 1996; EMT Basic, Frontier C.C., 1997. Cert. mobile intensive care nurse, mobile intensive care instr., emergency nursing care pediatric core curriculum, 1997. Charge nurse Rest Haven Manor, Albion, Ill., 1986—; staff nurse Kimberly Quality Care, Belleville, 1986—87; staff nurse emergency room Clay County Hosp., Flora, 1987—88; RN, supr. Good Samaritan Hosp., Mt. Vernon, 1990—92, Crossroads Cmty. Hosp., 1988—91; night supr. Fairfield (Ill.) Meml. Hosp., 1993—. Home: RR 3 Box 86 Fairfield IL 62837

THOMASON, SCOTT, automobile executive; b. 1953; BS, U of Oreg., Portland. Prin. Thomason Toyota, Gladstone; pres. Dee A. Thomason Ford Co., Gladstone, 1974—2002, Thomason Nissan Inc., Gladstone, 1990—2002, Heritage Auto Ctr. Inc., Kirkland, Wash., 1991—2002, Thomason Auto Group, Portland, Oreg., Barber Auto Group, Bakersfield, Calif., 2003—. Office: Barber Auto Group 4600 Wible Rd Bakersfield CA 93313

THOMASOS, DENYSE, artist; b. Trinidad, 1964; BA in Painting and Art History, U. Toronto, 1987; student, Skowhegan Sch., 1988; MFA in Painting and Sculpture, Yale U., 1989. Asst. prof. painting Tyler Sch. Art Temple U., Phila., 1990—95; asst. prof. painting visual and performing arts Rutgers U., Newark, 1995—. One-woman shows include Fleisher Art Meml. Gallery, Phila., 1993, Olga Korper Gallery, Toronto, Ont., Can., 1994, 1998, Queens (N.Y.) Mus. Art, Bulova Corp. Ctr., 1997, Lennon, Weinberg Gallery, N.Y.C., 1997, 1999, exhibited in group shows at Alpha Gallery, Boston, 1989, A Space, Toronto, 1992, Vox Populi, Phila., 1993, Mercer Union, Toronto, 1994, Ottawa (Ont.) Art Gallery, 1994, Lennon, Weinberg Gallery, N.Y.C., 1996, 1998, Newhouse Ctr. Contemporary Art, Snug Harbor Cultural Ctr., S.I., 1997, Art Gallery North York, N.Y., 1997, Fine Arts Ctr. Galleries, U. R.I., Kingston, 1999, others; curator (exhibitions) Art in Gen., Gallery 6, N.Y., 1998. Recipient Joan Mitchell Found. award, 1998; grantee Exploration grantee, Can. Coun., 1990, "B" Nat. grantee, 1994, Visual Arts fellow in painting, Pa. Coun. on Arts, Phila., 1994, Mid-Atlantic Regional grantee, NEA, 1994; Pew fellow in Arts, Phila., 1995, Guggenheim Found. fellow, 1997. Office: care Lennon Weinberg Inc 560 Broadway Rm 308 New York NY 10012-3945 Fax: 212 941-0098.

THOMAS-WILLIAMS, PAMELA RAE, publishing executive, writer; b. La Crosse, Wis., July 30, 1955; d. Dale Richard and Betty Jean (Clark) Thomas; m. Richard G. Williams, Oct. 30, 1987. BA in Journalism, Marquette U., 1977. Pres. Visual Concepts, ltd., La Crosse, 1979-85, Books By Pamela, Ltd., La Crosse, 1985—. Dir. developmental resources Cath. Cmty. Svcs., Las Vegas, Nev., 1990-91; cons., fundraiser Cath. Charities, La Crosse, 1985-91, U.S. Dept. Commerce-Census Bur., 1999—; co-owner Williams Properties. Author: From My Pallet of Winter, Let Me Paint Your Spring, 1978, The Bride's Guide-A Complete Guide on How to Plan Your Wedding, 7th edit., 2000, (Spanish translation Bridal Guide) Guía Nupcial, 1994, Wedding Showers for Couples, 2nd edit., 2000, Elvis Lives--The Business of Being Elvis, 2003. Mem. area VFW aux., 1992—. Mem. Pub. Rels. Soc. Am., Sigma Delta Chi. Republican. Lutheran. Avocations: reading, collecting antiques and handguns. Office: Books By Pamela Ltd 2820 Leonard St La Crosse WI 54601-

THOME, JAVIER, medical/surgical nurse; s. Josefina Pina; married; m. Yolanda Thome, children: Victor Thomas, Stephanie. ADN, El Paso C.C., 1986. RN, lic. nurse, Tex. RN, El Paso, 1986—; stationed in 101 airborne div. USARMY, Vietnam, stationed in, 2/33rd field artillery battalion, stationed in, 44th evacuation hosp.; served in Operation Dessert Storm. Author: (textbook) Nursing as a Function of Time, 17th Ann. Clinical Symposium Skin and Wound Care, 2002; contbr. 400 published works. 1st lt. U.S. Army, 1967—91. Decorated Bronze Star Medal, Army Commendation.

THOME, JIM, professional baseball player; b. Peoria, Ill., Aug. 27, 1970; m. Andrea Pacione; 1 child. Student Illinois Central College. Player Cleve. Indians, 1991—2002, Philadelphia Phillies, 2003—. Honorary Co-Chmn. United Way Home Run Derby. Named to Am. League All-Star Team, 1997—99, Nat. League All-Star Team, 2004. Achievements include led Nat. League in Home Runs (47), 2003; hit 400th career Home Run, June 13, 2004. Office: Cleve Indians 2401 Ontario St Cleveland OH 44115*

THOMFORDE, CHRISTOPHER MEREDITH, minister; b. Cleve., Jan. 25, 1947; s. Fredrich Henry and Marie (Meredith) T.; m. Christine Elizabeth Stone Huber, June 10, 1972; children: Christopher, Rebecca, Sarah, Jonathan. BA, Princeton U., 1969; MDiv, Yale U., 1974. Ordained to ministry Luth. Ch. in Am., 1976. Asst. chaplain Colgate U., Hamilton, N.Y., 1974-78; pastor St. Paul's Luth. Ch., Dansville, N.Y., 1978-86; chaplain Susquehanna U., Selinsgrove, Pa., 1986—. Pres. Dansville Ministerim, 1979-81. Sec. ARC, Danville, 1983-86. Named Citizen of Yr., Dansville, 1986. Office: Susquehanna U Chaplain's Office Selinsgrove PA 17870 Home: 1215 Saint Olaf Ave Northfield MN 55057-1534

THOMLINSON, RALPH, demographer, educator; b. St. Louis, Feb. 12, 1925; s. Ralph and Ora Lee (Barr) T.; m. Margaret Mary Willits, Dec. 21, 1946; children: Elizabeth Barr, William Lockwood. BA, Oberlin Coll., 1948; postgrad., U. Pitts., 1943-44, Harvard U., 1948; MA, Yale U., 1949; PhD, Columbia U., 1960. Asst. town planner, Montclair, N.J., 1949-50; asst. city planner Paterson, N.J., 1950; research asst. Bur. Applied Social Research, N.Y.C., 1952; med. statistics asst. actuarial dept. Met. Life Ins. Co., N.Y.C., 1952-53; instr. statistics and population U. Wis., 1953-56; instr. sociology and anthropology Denison U., Granville, Ohio, 1956-59; asst. prof. sociology Calif. State U., L.A., 1959-62, assoc. prof., 1962-65, prof., 1965-88, prof. emeritus, 1988—, chmn. dept. sociology, 1967-69; vis. prof. sociology U. Alta., Can., 1966; vis. prof. biostatistics U. N.C., Chapel Hill, 1972-73; demographic adviser Inst. Population Studies, Chulalongkorn U., Bangkok, Thailand, 1969-71; cons. Nat. Family Planning Program, Thailand, Census of Thailand, 1970-71, Population/Food Fund, 1977-79, also various research centers abroad, 1969-73. Cons. to fourteen book pubs., 1965—; field assoc. Population Coun., N.Y.C., 1969-71; rsch. adviser Ctr. for Rsch. and Demographic Studies, Rabat, Morocco, 1972-73; acad. visitor Population Investigation Com., London Sch. Econs., 1973; vis. scholar Nat. Inst. Demographic Studies, Paris, 1973-74 Author: A Mathematical Model for Migration, 1960, Population Dynamics, 2d edit., 1976, Sociological Concepts and Research, 1965, Demographic Problems, 2d edit, 1975, Urban Structure, 1969, Thailand's Population, 1971, (with others) The Methodology of the Longitudinal Study of Social, Economic and Demographic Change, 1971; editor: (with Visid Prachuabmoh) The Potharam Study, 1971; adv. editor: Sociol. Abstracts, 1963-67, Sociology Quar, 1978-84; cons. editor: As-Soukan, 1972-73; assoc. editor: Pacific Sociol. Rev, 1976-83; Sociol. Perspective, 1983-85; chmn. editorial bd. Calif. Sociologist, 1981-84; cons.: Dictionary of Modern Sociology, 1969; contbr. to: Dictionary of Demography, 5 vols., 1985-86; books, profl. jours. Served with AUS, 1943-45, ETO. Mem. Population Assn. Am., Internat. Union for Sci. Study Population, Am. Sociol. Assn., Internat. Assn. Survey Statisticians, Assn. Asian Studies. Home: 712 Coronado Ln Foster City CA 94404-2925

THOMOPOULOS, MICHAEL, music educator; b. Lowell, Mass., Apr. 24, 1953; s. George and Doris Thomopoulos. MusB, The New Eng. Conservatory of Music, Boston, 1975; MusM, The Juilliard Sch., N.Y.C., 1977. Founder, music dir. Palisades Chamber Players, Ft. Lee, NJ, 1979—. Founder, dir., tchr. Palisades Sch. Music. Recipient Morris Loeb Meml. prize, Internat. Concert Artist Guild, 1977. Avocations: private piloting, scuba diving, politics, travel. Home: 30 West 63d St Apt 30-U New York NY Office: The Palisades Sch of Music 196 Washington Ave Fort Lee NJ 07024 Office Phone: 201-944-1311. Office Fax: 201-944-1311. E-mail: mthomopoulos@yahoo.com.

THOMOPULOS, GREGS G. consulting engineering company executive; b. Benin City, Nigeria, May 16, 1942; s. Aristoteles and Christiana E. (Ogiamien) T.; m. Patricia Walker, Sept. 4, 1966 (div. 1974); 1 child, Lisa; m. Mettie L. Williams, May 28, 1976; children: Nicole, Euphemia. BSCE with highest distinction, U. Kans., 1965; MS in Structural Engring., U. Calif., Berkeley, 1966; PhD (hon.), Teikyo Marycrest U., 1996. Sr. v.p. internat. div. Stanley Cons., Inc., Muscatine, Iowa, 1978-84, sr. v.p. project divsn., 1984-87; pres., CEO Stanley Consultants, Inc., Muscatine, Iowa, 1987—; exec. v.p. SC Co., Inc., Muscatine, 1992-98; pres., COO, 1998-99; pres., CEO, 2000—; also bd. dirs. SC Co., Inc., Muscatine; chmn., CEO Stanley Environ., Inc., Chgo., 1991—, also bd. dirs.; chmn., CEO SC Power Devel., Inc., 1992—. Chmn., CEO Stanley Design-Build, Inc., 1995—; bd. dirs. Stanley Cons., Inc., Muscatine, Wellmark, Inc., Blue Cross Blue Shield Iowa and S.D., 1999—; mem. adv. bd. U. Kans. Sch. Engring., 2002—. Mem. adv. bd. Coll. Engring. U. Iowa, 1992-2000, Hydraulics Inst., 2000—. Fellow ASCE, Am. Coun. Engring. Cos.; mem. NSPE, Internat. Fedn. Cons. Engrs. (exec. com.), 33 Club (pres. 1987), Rotary. Presbyterian. Avocations: tennis, computers, music. Home: 75 Shagbark Ct Iowa City IA 52246-2786 Office: Stanley Cons Inc 225 Iowa Ave Muscatine IA 52761-3765 E-mail: thomopulos@home.com., thomopulosg@stanleygroup.com.

THOMPSON, ADRIENNE, secondary school educator; Tchr. advanced placement art history Sch. for Creative and Performing Arts, Cin. Mem. arts assessment steering com. Ohio Art Coun. Named Music Educator of the Yr., Ohio Art Edn. Assn. Mus. Divsn., 2000; recipient Ohio Govs. award for excellence in tchg., 1998, Outstanding Excellence award, Cin. Pub. Schs., 1999. Mem.: Nat. Bd. for Profl. Tchg. Stds. (bd. mem.). Office: Sch for Creative and Performing Arts 1310 Sycamore St Cincinnati OH 45202

THOMPSON, ALAN ERIC, economics professor; b. Sept. 16, 1924; s. Eric Joseph and Florence Thompson; m. Mary Heather Long, 1960; 4 children. MA, U. Edinburgh, 1949, MA with 1st class honors, 1951, PhD, 1953. Asst. in polit. econ. U. Edinburgh, 1952-53, lectr. econs., 1953-59, 64-71; prof. econs. of govt. Heriot-Watt U., Edinburgh, 1972—. Adviser to Scottish TV, 1966-76; Scottish gov. BBC, 1976-79; vis. prof. Grad. Sch. Bus., Stanford U. (Calif.), 1966, 68; chmn. adv. bd. econs. edn. Esmee Fairbairn Rsch. Project, 1970-76. Author: (with others) Development of Economic Doctrine, 1980; contbr. articles to profl. jours. M.P. Labour Party, Dunfermline, 1959-64; mem. Scottish Com. Pub. Schs. Commn., 1969-70; mem. Joint Mil. Edn. Com. Edinburgh and Heriot-Watt Univs., 1975—, local govt. boundary commn. for Scotland, 1975-82; chmn. No. Offshore Resources Study, 1974-84; chmn. bd. govs. Newbattle Abbey Coll., 1980-82; bd. govs. Leigh Nautical Coll., 1981-87; trustee Bell's Nautical Trust, 1981-87; parliamentary adviser Pharm. Gen. Coun., 1985-2000; bd. dirs. Scottish AIDS Rsch. Found., 1992; adv. Robert Burns Meml. Trust, 1995—; advisor Robert Burns Meml. Trust, 1995-2000. With Brit. Army, WWII. Carnegie Rsch. scholar, 1951-52. Fellow Royal Soc. Arts, Soc. Antiquaries (Scotland); mem. Assn. Nazi War Camp Survivors (v.p. 1960—), Edinburgh Amenity and Transport Assn. (pres. 1970-75), New Club, Edinburgh Univ. Staff Club, Loch Earn Sailing Club.

THOMPSON, ALVIN W. judge; b. 1953; BA, Princeton U., 1975; JD, Yale U., 1978. With Robinson & Cole, Hartford, Conn., 1978-94; dist. judge U.S. Dist. Ct., Conn., 1994—. Mem. ABA, Conn. Bar Assn., Hartford County Bar Assn. Office: US Dist Ct 450 Main St Rm 240 Hartford CT 06103-3022

THOMPSON, ANDREA, TV host, former newscaster, actress; b. Dayton, Ohio, 1959; m. David Guc, 1987 (div. 1990); m. Jerry Doyle, 1995 (div. 1997); 1 child, Alec. Correspondent KRQE-TV, Albuquerque, 2000—01; news anchor, Headline News CNN, 2001—02. Films include Wall Street, 1987, Doin' Time on Planet Earth, 1988, Delirious, 1991, Lost Valley, 1998, A Gun, A Car, A Blonde, 1998, Rocket's Red Glare, 2000; TV series include Falcon Crest, 1989-90, Babylon 5, 1994-95, JAG, 1995-96, NYPD Blue, 1996-2000; host: Court TV, Saturday Night Line Up, 2002.

THOMPSON, ANDREW, medical products executive; MA in Prodn. Engring., Cambridge (Eng.) U.; MA in Edn., MBA, Stanford U. Cons. Booz Allen & Hamilton; ptnr., cons. Savage-Thompson Mgmt.; co-founder Medtronic CardioRhythm; pres., CEO, co-founder FemRx, Sunnyvale, Calif. Office: FemRx 1221 Innsbruck Dr Sunnyvale CA 94089-1317

THOMPSON, ANNE ELISE, federal judge; b. Phila., July 8, 1934; d. Leroy Henry and Mary Elise (Jackson) Jenkins; m. William H. Thompson, June 19, 1965; children: William H., Sharon A. BA, Howard U., 1955, LLB, 1964; MA, Temple U., 1957. Bar: D.C. bar 1964, N.J. bar 1966. Staff atty. Office of Solicitor, Dept. Labor, Chgo., 1964-65; asst. dep. public defender Trenton, N.J., 1967-70; mcpl. prosecutor Lawrence Twp., Lawrenceville, N.J., 1970-72; mcpl. ct. judge Trenton, 1972-75; prosecutor Mercer County, Mercer County, Trenton, 1975-79; judge U.S. Dist. Ct. N.J., Trenton, 1979—. Vice chmn. Mercer County Criminal Justice Planning Com., 1972; mem. com. criminal practice N.J. Supreme Ct., 1975-79, mem. com. mcpl. cts., 1972-75; v.p. N.J. County Prosecutors Assn., 1978-79; chmn. juvenile justice com. Nat. Dist. Attys. Assn., 1978-79 Del. Democratic Nat. Conv., 1972. Recipient Assn. Black Women Lawyers award, 1976, Disting. Service award Nat. Dist. Attys. Assn., 1979, Gene Carte Meml. award Am. Criminal Justice Assn., 1980, Outstanding Leadership award N.J. County Prosecutors Assn., 1980, John Mercer Langston Outstanding Alumnus award Howard U. Law Sch., 1981; also various service awards; certs. of appreciation. Mem. Am. Bar Assn., Fed. Bar Assn., N.J. Bar Assn., Mercer County Bar Assn. Democrat. Office: US Dist Ct US Courthouse-4000 402 E State St Trenton NJ 08608-1507

THOMPSON, ANNE KATHLEEN, entertainment journalist; b. N.Y.C., Aug. 10, 1954; d. Charles Torrington Thompson and Eleanor Josephine (Callahan) Dekins; m. David Christopher Chute, Oct. 23, 1983; 1 child, Nora Thompson Chute. BA in Cinema Studies, NYU, 1976. Assoc. editor Film Comment, N.Y.C., 1981-82; West Coast editor Film Comment Mag., N.Y.C., 1982-96; publicity dir. Twentieth Century Fox Pictures, 1983-85; columnist Risky Bus., L.A. Weekly, L.A. Times Syndicate, 1985-93, Inside Film, 1988-90; U.S. editor Empire Mag., London, 1989-91; sr. writer Entertainment Weekly, 1993-96; west coast editor Premier Mag., 1996—. Account exec. P/M/K Pub. Rels., N.Y.C., 1979-81; publicist United Artists, N.Y.C., 1976-79; asst. mgr. Bleecker St. Cinema, N.Y.C., 1975-76. Unit publicist Terms of Endearment, The Adventures of Buckaroo Banzai, 1983; contbr. Entertainment Weekly, 1991—, (weekly variety) 7 Days mag., 1990, N.Y. Times, 1992—. Mem. Nat. Writer's Union, Women in Film. Office: Premiere 1990 S Bundy Dr Ste 250 Los Angeles CA 90025-5244

THOMPSON, ANNIE FIGUEROA, retired academic director, educator; b. Río Piedras, P.R., June 7, 1941; d. Antonio Figueroa-Colón and Ana Isabel Laugier; m. Donald P. Thompson, Jan. 23, 1972; 1 child, John Anthony. BA, Baylor U., 1962; MSLS, U. So. Calif., 1965; AMD, Fla. State U., 1978, PhD, 1980. Educator Mayan Sch., Guatemala City, Guatemala, 1962-63; cataloger libr. sys. U. P.R., Río Piedras, 1965-67, head music libr., 1967-81, assoc. prof. librarianship, 1981-85, dir. grad. sch. libr. info. sci. Rio Piedras, 1986-93, prof., 1986-96; ret., 1996. Author: An Annotated Bibliography About Music in Puerto Rico, 1975; co-author: Music and Dance in Puerto Rico from the Age of Columbus to Modern Times, An Annotated Bibliography, 1991; contbr. articles to profl. jours.; performed song recitals Inst. of P.R. Culture and U. P.R. Artist Series, 1974-78; soloist with P.R. Symphony Orch., San Juan, 1978; performed in opera, on radio and TV, San Juan, 1968-81. Sec. P.R. Symphony Orch League, San Juan, 1982-84; mem. pub. libr. adv. com. Adminstrn. for Devel. of Arts and Culture, P.R., 1982-84, Pub. Libr. Adv. Bd., 1989-94. Recipient Lauro a la Instrucción Bibliotecaria Sociedad de Bibliotecarios de P.R., 1985, Lauro a la Bibliografía Puertorriqueña, 1993. Mem. Sarasota Rotary (bd. dirs. 2000-02), Sociedad de Bibliotecarios de P.R. (pres. 1994-96), Music Libr. Assn. (bd. dirs. 1982-84, asst. conv. mgr. 2002-04, conv. mgr. 2004-), Sarasota Rotary Found. (bd. dirs.), Sigma Delta Kappa, Mu Phi Epsilon, Beta Phi Mu. Episcopalian. Home: 435 S Gulfstream Ave Sarasota FL 34236-6736 E-mail: annietmla@aol.com.

THOMPSON, ANNIE LAURA (ANNE), foreign language educator; b. Henderson, Tenn., July 8, 1937; d. Wesley Sylvester and Letha Irene (Jones) T.; m. Edward L. Patterson, June 7, 1980. BA, U. Ala., 1959; MA, Duke U., 1961; PhD, Tulane U., 1973. Instr. Spanish lang. U. Miss., Oxford, 1960-64; instr. Auburn (Ala.) U., 1964-66; tchg. asst. Tulane U., New Orleans, 1966-70; prof. Spanish lang. Delgado C.C., New Orleans, 1970—. Instr. Spanish for Physicians and Med. Persons Tulane U., La. State U. Med. Eye Ctr., Ochsner Clinic and Hosp. Author: Religious Elements in the Quijote, 1960, The Attempt of Spanish Intellectuals to Create a New Spain, 1930-36, 1973, The Generation of 1898: Intellectual Politicians; asst. editor The Crusader, 1961-64. Rep. candidate for gov. State of La., 1991, 95, for 1st Dist. U.S. Congress, 1992; alt. mem. La. Coastal Commn., 1984—; del. Women's State Rep. Conv., 1987, La. State Rep. Conv., 1990, 93, La. Coastal Adv. Coun., 1988, Pan Am. Commn., 1992-95; v.p. pub. rels. Alliance for Good Govt., 1990; candidate State Senate La., 1994; mem. DAR (Vieux Carré chpt.), 2000. Recipient Outstanding Tchr. award Delgado Coll. Student Govt. Assn., 1974; Woodrow Wilson fellow, 1959-60, NDEA fellow, 1968-69. Mem. AAUP, DAR, Pachyderm Club, Women's Rep. Club, Phi Beta Kappa, Phi Alpha Theta, Sigma Delta Pi. Republican. Mem. Ch. of Christ. Home: PO Box 24399 New Orleans LA 70184-4399 Office Phone: 504-288-1796. E-mail: pilgrim70124@yahoo.com.

THOMPSON, ANTHONY WAYNE, metallurgist, educator, consultant; b. Burbank, Calif., Mar. 6, 1940; s. William Lyman and Mary Adelaide (Nisbet) T.; m. Mary Ruth Cummings, Aug. 24, 1963; children: Campbell Lyman, Michael Anthony. BS, Stanford U., 1962; MS, U. Wash., 1965; PhD, MIT, 1970. Research engr. Jet Propulsion Lab., Pasadena, Calif., 1962-63; mem. tech. staff Sandia Labs., Livermore, Calif., 1970-73, Rockwell Sci. Ctr., Thousand Oaks, Calif., 1973-77; assoc. prof. Carnegie Mellon U., Pitts., 1977-79, prof., 1980-94, dept. head, 1987-90; staff scientist Lawrence Berkeley Lab., Berkeley, Calif., 1994-99; rsch. engr. U. Calif., Berkeley, Calif., 1995—. Vis. scientist U. Cambridge, Eng., 1983, Risø, Denmark, 1987, U. Calif., 1991; cons. Sandia Labs., 1977—, GE, 1988-2000. Editor: Work Hardening, 1976, Metall. Transactions, 1983-88; co-editor: Hydrogen in Metals, 1974, Hydrogen Conf. Proc., 1976, 81, 89, 94, 2002; mem. editl. bd. Internat. Metals Revs., 1980-88; contbr. articles to profl. jours. Overseas fellow Churchill Coll. Cambridge U., 1982 Fellow Am. Soc. Metals; mem. AIME, Sigma Xi Clubs: Sierra, Nat. Model R.R. Assn. Democrat. Home: 2942 Linden Ave Berkeley CA 94705 2328 Office: Lawrence Berkeley Lab Material Sci Divsn Berkeley CA 94720-0001

THOMPSON, BARBARA STORCK, state official; b. McFarland, Wis., Oct. 15, 1924; d. John Casper and Marie Ann (Kassabaum) Storck; m. Glenn T. Thompson, July 1, 1944; children— David C., James T. BS, Wis. State U., 1956; MS, U. Wis., 1959, PhD, 1969; L.H.D. (hon.), Carroll Coll., 1974. Tchr. pub. schs., West Dane County, Mt. Horeb, Wis., 1944-56; instr. Green County Tchrs. Coll., Monroe, Wis., 1956-57; coordinator curriculum Monroe Pub. Schs., 1957-60; instr. U. Wis., Platteville, 1960; supr. schs. Waukesha County Schs., Wis., 1960-63, supt. schs., 1963-65; prin. Fairview Elem. Schs., Brookfield, Wis., 1962-64; adminstrv. cons. Wis. Dept. Pub. Instrn., Madison, 1964-72, state coordinator, 1971-72; instr. U. Wis., Madison and Green Bay, 1972; supt. pub. instrn. Madison, Wis., 1973—81. Mem. Wis. State Bd. Vocat. Edn., 1973-81, Wis. Edn. Comm. Bd., 1973-81, Univ. Wis. Sys. Bd. Regents, 1973-1981. Author: A Candid Discussion of Critical Issues, 1975; Mem. editorial bd.: The Education Digest, 1975—; Contbr. articles to profl. jours. Mem. White House Conf. Children, 1970, Gov.'s Com. State Conf. Children and Youth, 1969-70, Manpower Council, 1973-81; bd. dirs. Vocational, Tech. and Adult Edn., 1973-81, Ednl. Communications, 1973-81, Higher Edn. Aids, 1973-81, Agy. Instructional TV, 1975-81; mem. nat. panel on SAT score decline; bd. regents U. Wis., 1973-81, U.S. office f Edn. Visiting Sch. Team - England, GErmany, Sweden, Poland, Iran, Syria, India, and Japan. Recipient State Conservation award Madison Lions CLub, 1956; Waukesha Freeman award, 1961 Mem. Nat. Coun. Adminstrv. Women in Edn. (named Woman of Year 1974), Nat. Coun. State Cons. in Elem. Edn. (pres. 1974-75), Wis. Assn. Sch. Dist. Adminstrs., Assn. Supervision and Curriculum Devel., Wis. Assn. Supervision and Curriculum Devel., Southwestern Wis. Assn. Supervision and Curriculum Devel., Southeastern Wis. Assn. Supervision and Curriculum Devel. (mem. exec. council 1972-73), Dept. Elem. Sch. Prins., Wis. Elementary Sch. Prins. Assn., NEA, Wis. Edn. Assn. (pres. local chpt. 1970-71); life mem. So. Wis. Edn. Assn., Wis. Ednl. Rsch. Assn., Dept. Elem.-Kindergarten-Nursery Edn., Assn. Childhood Edn. Internat., Assn. Childhood Edn., Coun. Chief State Sch. Officers, Edn. Commn. of States, Nat. Coun. State Cons. in Elem. Edn. (pres. 1974-75), Am. Assn. Sch. Dist. Adminstrs. (chmn. policy com. 1963-81), Madison Ctrl. Internat. Lions Club, U. Wis. Alumni Orgn. (Sarasota, Fla. and Madison), U. Wis. League (Madison chpt.), Delta Kappa Gamma, Pi Lambda Theta. Office: Apt 123 325 S Yellowstone Dr Madison WI 53705-4301

THOMPSON, BASIL F. ballet master; b. Newcastle-on-Tyne, Eng., 1937;, U.S., 1958; Grad., Royal Acad. Dance; studies with, David Lichine, Tania Riabouchinska; student, Sch. Classical. Ballet, 1958-60. Dancer Covent Garden Opera Co., Sadler Wells Opera Co., London, 1954-55, Royal Ballet Eng., London, 1955-58; instr. ballet and character Eugene Loring Sch. Ballet, L.A., 1958-60, Al Gilber Sch. Ballet, L.A., 1958-60; instr. ballet Michael Panaieff Sch. Ballet, L.A., 1958-60; soloist Am. Ballet Theatre, N.Y.C., 1960-67; ballet master Joffrey Ballet Co., N.Y.C., 1967-79; ballet master, choreographer N.J. Ballet Co., West Orange, 1979-80; mem. faculty ballet and character N.J. Ballet Sch., Morristown/West Orange, 1979-80; ballet master Milw. Ballet, 1981-86, also artistic head; ballet master Pa. and Milw. Ballet; apptd. artistic dir. Milw. Ballet, spring 1995; now prof. dance U. Iowa, Iowa City. Guest ballet instr. Internat. Ballet Inst., Aux-en-Provence, France, 1980; guest instr. character Am. Ballet Co. Sch., 1981. Dancer Roles include (prin.) Billy the Kid, Sleeping Beauty, Graduation Ball, La Sylphide, Moon Reindeer, Peter and The Wolf, Three Cornered Hat, others; guest appearances include for Dame Margo Fontayne Royal Acad. Gala, Pres. John F. Kennedy, Pres. Lyndon B. Johnson, L.A. Civic Light Opera, Michael Panaieff Ballet Theatre; choreographer La Traviata; soloist Rodeo, Fall River Legend, Fire Bird, Coppelia, Swan Lake, Cinderella, La Boutique Fantastic, Undertow, others, guest appearances Dame Margo Fontayne Royal Acad. Gala, Pres. John F. Kennedy, Pres. Lyndon B. Johnson, L.A. Civic Light Opera, Michael Panaieff Ballet Theatre, TV appearances Bell Telephone Hour Spectacular prodn. Graduation Ball, NBC prodn. Sleeping Beauty and Cinderella; Broadway prodns. On a Clear Day You Can See Forever, Tavarich, Happiest Girl in the World. Office: Univ of Iowa Dept Dance 107 W Halsey Hall Iowa City IA 52242 E-mail: basil-thompson@uiowa.edu.

THOMPSON, BENNIE G. congressman; b. Bolton, Miss., Jan. 28, 1948; m. London Johnson; 1 child, Benda Lonne. BA Polit. Sci., Tougaloo Coll., 1968; MS Ednl. Adminstrn., Jackson State U., Miss., 1972; grad., U. So. Miss. Alderman, Bolton, Miss., 1969—73; mayor, 1973—79; supr. dist. 2 Hinds County Bd., Miss., 1980-93; mem. U.S. Congress from 2d dist. Miss., 1993—; mem. agr. com., homeland sec. com., former mem. budget com. Presdl. appointee Nat. Coun. Health Planning and Devel. Bd. trustees Tougaloo Coll.; bd. dirs. So. Regional Coun., Housing Assistance Coun. Mem.: Miss. Assn. Black Suprs. (founding mem.), Miss. Assn. Black Mayors (founding mem.). Democrat. Methodist. Original plaintiff in 1975 Ayers case. Office: 2432 Rayburn House Office Bldg Washington DC 20515-0001

THOMPSON, BERNADETTE MARIA, poet; b. Oakland, Calif., June 15, 1952; Cert. key punch operator, Healds Coll., 1984. Poet, Calif., 1985—. Composer numerous songs including Guide My Hand; author: (poems) Love, 2001, Oh Faithful Blue Eyes, 2000. Named to Internat. Hall of Fame for Poetry, 1996. Mem. Internation Soc. Poets, Famous Poets Soc. (Muse of Fire trophy 2000). Avocations: reading, tennis, writing, bowling. Home: # 126 2124 Kittredge St Berkeley CA 94704-1436

THOMPSON, BERNIDA LAMERLE, principal, consultant, educator; b. Tuskegee, Ala., July 5, 1946; d. Berry James Sr. and Doris LaMerle (Askey) T.; m. Rolando Amerson, June 15, 1968 (div. Aug. 1988); children: Afriye Amerson, Mwando Amerson. BS in Elem. Edn., Cen. State U., 1968; MEd in Adminstrn. and Curriculum, Miami U., Oxford, Ohio, 1971; EdD in Early and Mid. Childhood Edn., Nova U., 1992. Classroom elem. sch. tchr. Dayton Pub. Schs.; asst. prin., intern St. James Cath. Sch., Dayton, Ohio; tchr. St. Augustine Cath. Sch., Washington; sci. resource tchr. D.C. Pub. Schs., Washington; founding tchr., prin. Roots Activity Learning Ctr., Washington, 1977—, Roots Pub. Charter Sch., 1999—. Multicultural advisor HBJ 1992 Reading Textbook. Author: Black Madonnas and Young Lions a Rite of Passage for African American Adolescents, 1992, rev. edit., 1998, Africentric Interdisciplinary Multi-Level Hands On Science, 1994, rev. edit., 2001; contbr. articles to profl. jours. Mem. Nat. Assn. Edn. Young Children, World Coun. Curriculum Instrn., Coun. Ind. Black Inst., Inst. Ind. Edn., Nat. Black Child Devel. Inst. Office: Roots Pub Charter Sch 15 Kennedy St NW Washington DC 20011-5201 Office Phone: 202-882-8073. Business E-Mail: bthompson@rootspcs.org.

THOMPSON, BERT ALLEN, retired librarian; b. Bloomington, Ind., Dec. 13, 1930; s. James Albert and Dorothy Fern (Myers) T.; m. Martha Ellen Palmer; children— John Carter II, Anne Palmer, Paul Julian. BS, Ball State Tchrs. Coll., 1953; AM, Ind. U., 1960; certificate in archival adm., U. Denver, 1967. Tchr., libr. Ind. pub. schs., 1953-55; ref. asst. Indpls. Pub. Libr., 1956-59; head ref. svc. Mankato (Minn.) State U., 1959-61; instr. Grad. Libr. Sch. No. Ill. U., Dekalb, 1961-63; dir. libs., asst. prof. ednl. media U. Nebr. at Kearney, 1963-69; dir. libr. svc. Benedictine U., Lisle, Ill., 1969-90, spl. collections libr., 1990-92. Mem. exec. bd. Ill. regional Libr. Coun., 1976-79.

Recipient 1st Melvin R. George LIBRAS award for Outstanding Svc. to Libr. Cooperation, 1993. Mem. Ill. (de Lafayette Reid Research scholar 1976), Cath. Libr. Assn. (treas. Ill. chpt. 1973-75, nat. sec.-treas. coll./univ. sect. 1981-85, nat. bd. dirs. 1987-93), Nebr. Libr. Assn. chmn. coll. and univ. sect. 1963-64) Episcopalian. Home: 1808 Caxton Dr Wheaton IL 60187-6140

THOMPSON, BERTHA BOYA, retired education educator, antique dealer and appraiser; b. New Castle, Pa., Jan. 31, 1917; d. Frank L. and Kathryn Belle (Park) Boya; m. John L. Thompson, Mar. 27, 1942; children: Kay Lynn Thompson Koolage, Scott McClain. BS in Elem. & Secondary Edn., Slippery Rock State Coll., 1940; MA in Geography and History, Miami U., 1954; EdD, Ind. U., 1961. Cert. elem. and secondary edn. tchr. Elem. tchr., reading specialist New Castle (Pa.) Sch. System, 1940-45; tchr., chmn. social studies Talawanda Sch. System, Oxford, Ohio, 1954-63; assoc. prof. psychology and geography, chair edn. dept. Western Coll. for Women, Oxford, 1963-74; assoc. prof. edn., reading clinic Miami U., Oxford, 1974-78, prof. emeritus, 1978—; pvt. antique dealer, appraiser Oxford, 1978—. Contbr. articles to profl. jours. Folk art com. Miami U. Art Mus., Oxford, 1974-76; adv. com. Smith libr., Oxford Pub. Libr., 1978-81. Mem. AAUP, Nat. Coun. Geographic Edn. (exec. bd. dirs. 1966-69), Nat. Soc. for Study Edn., Assn. Am. Geographers, Soc. Women Geographers, Nat. Coun. for the Social Studies, Pi Lambda Theta, Zeta Tau Alpha, Pi Gamma Mu, Gamma Theta Upsilon, Kappa Delta Pi. Avocations: antique collecting, reading, travel, tennis. Home: 6073 Contreras Rd Oxford OH 45056-9708

THOMPSON, BRIAN JOHN, university administrator, optics educator; b. Glossop, Eng., June 10, 1932; came to U.S., 1962; s. Alexander William and Edna May (Gould) T.; m. Joyce Emily Cheshire, Mar. 31, 1956; children: Karen Joyce, Andrew Derrick. B of Sci. Tech., U. Manchester, Eng., 1955, PhD, 1959. Demonstrator in physics dept. tech. U. Manchester, 1955-56, asst. lectr. dept. tech., 1957-59; lectr. physics U. Leeds, Eng., 1959-62; sr. physicist Tech. Optics, Inc., Burlington, Mass., 1963-65, dir. dept. optics, 1966-67; mgr. tech. ops. west, tech. dir. Beckman and Whitley, Mountainview, Calif., 1967-68; prof. Inst. Optics U. Rochester, N.Y., 1968-94, dir. Inst. Optics, 1968-75, dean Coll. Engring. and Applied Scis., 1975-84, Wm. F. May prof. engring., 1982-85, provost, 1984-94, provost emeritus, prof. of optics emeritus, Disting. U. prof., 1994—. Editor Optics and Laser Tech., 1969-96; assoc. editor: Optical Engring., 1972-76, Optics Comm., 1978-86; editor Optica Acta, 1981-85, Optical Engring. Series, vols. 1-84, 1980—; mem. editl. bd. Laser Focus, 1970-84, Particle Characterization, 1984-95, Optics and Lasers in Engring., 1985, Milestone Series of Selected Papers, vols. 1-167, 1984—, Optical Engring., 1991-98; chmn. adv. bd. Marquis Who's Who Directory Optical Scientists and Engrs., 1983-86; contbr. articles to profl. jours. With Brit. Army, 1950-52. Fellow: Inst. Physics and Phys. Soc. (Gt. Britain), Optical Soc. Am. (bd. dirs. 1969—72, exec. com. 1970—73, assoc. editor jour. 1966—77), Soc. Photo-Optical Instrumentation Engrs. (life; pres. 1974—76, editor jour. 1991—98, Pres.'s award 1967, Pezzuto award 1978, Kingslake medal 1978, Gold medal 1986, Dir. award 1998); mem.: AAAS, Am. Phys. Soc. Home and Office: 9 Esternay Ln Pittsford NY 14534-1014

THOMPSON, C. MICHAEL, congressman; b. St. Helene, Calif., Jan. 24, 1951; s. Charles Thompson and Beverly (Forni) Powell; m. Janet Thompson, Mar. 8, 1982; children: Christopher, Jon. BA in Political Sci., Calif. State U., Chico, 1982, MA in Public Admin., 1996. Owner, maintenance supr. Beringer Winery; mem. Calif. State Senate, 1991—98, U.S. Congress from 1st Calif. dist., 1999—; mem. armed svcs. com., agr. com. Former chair select com. on Calif.'s Wine Industry; former chair Calif. Senate budget com.; former vice chair Calif. Senate natural resources com; lectr. San Francisco State U., Calif. State U., Chico. Staff sgt. U.S. Army, Vietnam. Staff sgt. U.S. Army, Vietnam. Decorated Purple Heart. Named Freshman Legislator of the Yr. Calif. Sch. Bds. Assn., 1990, Legislatorof the Yr. Calif. Abortion Rights Action League, Legislator of the Yr. Calif. Assn. Persons with Handicaps, Legislator of the Yr. Police Officers Rsch. Assn. Calif., Legislator of the Yr. Disabled in State Svc., 1994, Senator of the Yr. Calif. Assn. Homes and Svcs. for Aging, 1995; Recipient Disting. Svc. award Calif. State Assn. Counties, Disting. Svc. award Calif. Assn. Hosps., Legis. Leadership award Calif. Assn. Health Svcs. Home, 1994, Disting. Svc. award Aids Project L.A., 1995, Outstanding Senator award Planned Parenthood Affiliates Calif., 1996, Outstanding Senator of the Yr. award Calif. Sch. Bds. Assn., 1996, Outstanding Senator of the Yr. award Calif. Profl. Firefighters, 1996 Democrat. Roman Catholic. Office: 119 Cannon House Office Bldg Washington DC 20515-0001

THOMPSON, CARLTON FREDERICK, lawyer; b. Syracuse, N.Y., Aug. 18, 1924; s. Fredrick and Dorothy (Nielsen) T.; m. Betty Sue, June 18, 1949; children: C. Kendall, Gail. AB magna cum laude, Syracuse U., 1948, JD cum laude, 1950. Bar: N.Y. 1950, U.S. Dist. Ct. (no. dist.) N.Y., U.S. Dist. Ct. (we. dist.) N.Y., U.S. Dist. Ct. Vt. Assoc. Levene and Gouldin, Binghamton, N.Y., 1950-53; ptnr. Levene, Gouldin & Thompson, Binghamton, N.Y., 1953—. 1st lt. U.S. Army, 1943-46. Fellow Am. Coll. Trial Lawyers; mem. N.Y. State Bar Assn. (chmn. trial lawyers sect. 1982-83), Broome County Bar Assn. (pres. 1966-67), Phi Beta Kappa. Home: 30 Clifton Blvd Binghamton NY 13903-1420 Office: PO Box F1706 Binghamton NY 13902-0106

THOMPSON, CAROLINE WARNER, film director, screenwriter; b. Washington, Apr. 23, 1956; d. Thomas Carlton Jr. and Bettie Marshall (Warner) T.; m. Alfred Henry Bromell, Aug. 28, 1982 (div. 1985). BA summa cum laude, Amherst Coll., 1978. Film dir., screenwriter William Morris Agy., Inc., Beverly Hills, Calif. Author: First Born, 1983; screenwriter: (films) Edward Scissorhands, 1990, The Addams Family, 1991, Homeward Bound: The Incredible Journey, 1993, The Secret Garden, 1993, Tim Burton's The Nightmare Before Christmas, 1993; screenwriter, dir.: Black Beauty, 1994, Buddy, 1997. Mem. Phi Beta Kappa. Avocation: horseback riding. Office: William Morris Agency Inc 151 S El Camino Dr Beverly Hills CA 90212-2775

THOMPSON, CARSON R. retail and manufacturing company executive; b. Feb. 10, 1939; s. Silas and Della (Woods) T.; m. Charlotte Arwine, Dec. 26, 1959; children: Shelley Elaine, Susan Denise. BS, Tex. Wesleyan U., 1962, D Bus. and Fin. (hon.). Leather buyer, mdse. mgr. Tandy Leather Co., Ft. Worth, 1970-74, 74-77; pres. Tex Tan Welhausen Corp., Yoakum, Tex., 1978; v.p. Tandy Brands Corp., Ft. Worth, 1981—, chmn., CEO. Pres., CEO Bombay Co., Inc. (formerly Tandy Brands, Inc.), 1996—; chmn. bd., pres., CEO CRT Group, Inc., 1991—; chmn., CEO PawnMart, Inc., Tony Jeary High Performance Resources; pres. Concept Keys, Inc.; mng. ptnr. Resource Optimization Group. Home: 1801 Sanguinet St Fort Worth TX 76107-3765

THOMPSON, CATHY JOANNE, nursing educator, consultant, acute care nurse practitioner; b. NYC, Feb. 17, 1959; AS in Nursing, Mesa Coll., 1984; BS in Nursing, U. of Tex., Houston, Tex., 1990; MSN, U. of Tex., Houston, Texas, 1991; PhD, Tex. Woman's U., Denton, Texas, 1997. Cert. critical care nurse, Am. Assn. Critical Care Nursing, 1986. Staff nurse Tex. Heart Inst. St. Luke's Episcopal Hosp., Houston, 1984—94; asst. prof. Health Sci. Ctr., Sch. of Nursing U. of Tex., Houston, 1994—96; asst. prof. Sch. for Health Care Professions Dept. of Nursing Regis U., Denver, 1996—98; asst. prof. Health Sciences Ctr. Sch. of Nursing U. of Colo., Denver, 1998—. Instr. clin. nursing Houston Health Sci. Ctr. Sch. Nursing U. Tex., Houston, 1991—94. Mem. editl. bd.: The Internet Jour. of Advanced Nursing Practice, 1996, Critical Care Nursing Clinics of N.Am., 1999; contbr. articles to profl. jours. Mem.: AACN Certification Corp. (bd. mem. 1997—99), Nat. Orgn. of Nurse Practitioner (faculty), Am. Heart Assn. (nat. adv. coun. Mended Heart Orgn. 1996—2000), Western Inst. of Nursing Rsch., Soc. of Critical Care Medicine, Am. Assn. of Critical-Care Nurses (mem. various coms. 1986—, bd. mem. 1996—99, AACN Svc. Appreciation award 1999), Sigma Theta Tau Internat. Lutheran. Achievements include research in the area of research utilization, critical care, pain, and end-of-life care. Office: University of Colorado School of Nursing 4200 E Ninth Ave Box C288 Denver CO 80262 E-mail: cathy.thompson@uchsc.edu.

THOMPSON, CHARLES MURRAY, lawyer; b. Childress, Tex., Oct. 13, 1942; s. Walter Lee and Lois S. (Sheehan) T.; children: Murray McKay, McLean Ann. BS with honors, Colo. State U., 1965; JD cum laude, U. S.D., 1969, LLD (hon.), 1995. Bar: S.D. 1969, U.S. Dist. Ct. S.D. 1969, U.S. Ct. Claims 1989, U.S. Ct. Appeals (8th cir.) 1972, U.S. Supreme Ct. 1973. Ptnr. May, Adam, Gerdes & Thompson, Pierre, S.D., 1969—. Bd. dirs. Bank West, Pierre, SD; past pres. Delta Trust, Pierre; spkr. in field. Editor S.D. Law Rev., 1969 Pres. S.D. Council Sch. Attys., 1984-86. Fellow Am. Bar Found. (chmn. 1991-92, bd. dirs. 1989-92), Coll. Law Practice Mgmt., Am. Coll. Trial Lawyers; mem. ABA (ho. of dels. 1978-2002, bd. govs. 1983-86, standing com. on fed. judiciary 2004—), ATLA, Am. Bd. Trial Advs., Am. Counsel Assn., Am. Judicature Soc. (bd. dirs. 1981-85), Am. Bar Endowment (bd. dirs. 1991—, pres. 2000-02), Nat. Conf. Bar Pres.'s (exec. coun. 1986-94, pres. 1992-93), State Bar S.D. (pres. young lawyers sect. 1974-75, pres. 1986-87), S.D. Bar Found. (pres. 1991), S.D. Trial Lawyers Assn. (pres. 1980-81), Jackrabbit Bar Assn. (chancellor 1981-82), S.D. Cmty. Found., Kiwanis (pres. local club 1977). Democrat. Avocations: flying, ranching. Home and Office: PO Box 160 Pierre SD 57501-0160 Office Phone: 605-224-8803.

THOMPSON, CHARLES WILLIAM SYDNOR See THOMPSON, SYDNOR JR.

THOMPSON, CLIFTON C. retired chemistry educator, university administrator; b. Franklin, Tenn., Aug. 16, 1939; s. Clifton C. and Ruby M. (Moore) T.; m. Sarah Ellen Gaunt, Dec. 1, 1978; children: Brenda Kay, Victoria Lea. BS, Middle Tenn. State U., 1961; PhD, U. Miss., 1964. Asst. prof. Rutgers U., New Brunswick, N.J., 1965, Marshall U., Huntington, W.Va., 1965-66; assoc. prof. Middle Tenn. State U., Murfreesboro, 1966-68, Memphis State U., 1968-74; prof. chemistry, dept. head, dean Coll. Sci. and Math., dir. Ctr. for Sci. Rsch., assoc. v.p. for grad. studies and rsch. S.W. Mo. State U., Springfield, 1974-96, prof. emeritus, 1996—; prof. chemistry Cen. Mich. U., Mt. Pleasant, 1996-98. Rsch. assoc. U. Tex., Austin, 1964-65; rschr. Oak Ridge Nat. Lab., 1968; cons. Mid-South Research Assocs., Memphis, 1969-71; mem. med. tech. rev. com. Nat. Accrediting Agy. for Clin. Lab. Sci., Chgo., 1974-80; vis. prof. So. Ill. U., Carbondale, 1995. Author: Ultraviolet-Visible Absorption Spectroscopy, 1974; contbr. articles to profl. jours. Mem. health care com. Springfield C. of C., 1978-79, mem. econ. devel. com., 1983-89; bd. dirs. United Hebrew Congregation, Springfield, 1983-86, United Hebrew Found., Inc., 1994-96. NSF fellow, 1961-64; Sigma Xi grantee-in-aide, 1970; NSF sr. fgn. scientist grantee, 1971; NSF coop-coll. sch. sci. grantee, 1972; Higher Edn. Applied Projects grantee, 1987-90. Mem. Am. Chem. Soc., Royal Soc. Chemistry, Sigma Xi, Phi Kappa Phi. Jewish. Office: SW Mo State U Dept Chemistry Springfield MO 65804

THOMPSON, CRAIG SNOVER, corporate communications executive; b. Bklyn., May 24, 1932; s. Craig F. and Edith (Williams) T.; m. Masae Sugizaki, Feb. 21, 1957; children: Lee Anne, Jane Laura. Grad., Valley Forge Mil. Acad., 1951; BA, Johns Hopkins U., 1954. Newspaper and radio reporter Easton (Pa.) Express, 1954-55, 57-59, Wall St. Jour., 1959-60; account exec. Moore, Meldrum & Assocs., 1960; mgr. pub. relations Cen. Nat. Bank of Cleve., 1961-62; account exec. Edward Howard & Co., Cleve., 1962-67, v.p., 1967-69, sr. v.p., 1969-71; dir. pub. relations White Motor Corp., Cleve., 1971-76; v.p. pub. relations No. Telecom Inc., Nashville, 1976-77, White Motor Corp., Farmington Hills, Mich., 1977-80, v.p. corp. communications, 1980-81; dir. exec. communications Rockwell Internat. Corp., Pitts., 1981-86, El Segundo, Calif., 1986-91, Seal Beach, Calif., 1992-97, sr. communications exec., 1997; pres. Craig S. Thompson. Inc., 1997—. Bd. dirs. Shaker Lakes Regional Nature Center, 1970-73. Served to 1st lt., inf. U.S. Army, 1955-57. Mem. Pub. Rels. Soc. Am. (accredited), Alumni Assn. Valley Forge Mil. Acad. (bd. dirs. 1988-94).

THOMPSON, DANIEL EMERSON, vending machine service company executive; b. Fairbanks, Alaska, Jan. 24, 1947; s. George Edmond and Emma Jean (Burns) T.; m. Yvette Clarice Brazeau, Aug. 16, 1980. Student, U. Notre Dame, 1965-67. Vice-pres. Music Inc., Fairbanks, 1965-67; pres. Music Inc. (doing bus. as Alaska Music Co.), Fairbanks, 1967-81; sec. Music Inc. (doing bus. as Vend Alaska-Fairbanks), Fairbanks, 1984-87; pres. Vend Inc. (doing bus. as Vend Alaska-Anchorage), Anchorage, 1987—. Bd. dirs. Music Inc., Fairbanks, Vend Inc., Anchorage, Denali State Bank, Fairbanks, Alaska First Bank & Trust, N.A., Anchorage; ptnr. Thompson Investment Co., Fairbanks, 1976—. Trustee Hi Pow, Fairbanks, 1972—; pres. Fairbanks Downtown Assn., 1987-88, bd. dirs., 1984-94; bd. dirs. Alaska State Devel. Corp., Juneau, 1971-82, Monroe Found., Fairbanks, 1991-2000, North Star Dance Found., 2002—; vocatonal edn. adv. com. Fairbanks North Star Borough Sch. Dist., 1993—. Mem. Amusement Music Operators Am., Nat. Automatic Merchandising Assn., N.W. Automatic Vending Assn. (bd. govs. 1983—), Rotary, Fairbanks C. of C. (co-chmn. local govt. com. 1988-90). Roman Catholic. Office: 1810 Burgess Ave Fairbanks AK 99709-5516

THOMPSON, DARLENE BENNETT, realtor, musician; b. Simpson, La., June 28, 1931; d. Odis Pharon and Carrie Josephine (Knight) Blackwell; m. Elmo Bennett (dec.); children: Debra Kathleen Bennett, Eric Blane Bennett, Denise Darlene Bennett; m. Mitchell Glenn Thompson, Dec. 28, 1990. BS, Northwestern State U., Natchitoches, La., 1952, EdM, 1959, MusM, 1963, EdD, 1981. Tchr. K-12 Vernon Parish Sch. Bd., Leesville, La., 1952—82; dir. alternative sch. Vidor (Tex.) Ind. Sch. Dist., 1982—85; reading specialist Burkville (Tex.) Ind. Sch. Dist., 1986—2000; realtor ERA Broker, Leesville, 2003—. Dir. music Simpson Ch. of God, Simpson Assembly of God; organist Pok Episcopal Ch., St. Michael's Cath. Ch. Mem.: Ret. Tchrs. La., Piano Tchrs. La., Music Educators La., Pilot Club Leesville, Phi Delta Kappa. Home: 554 Alexandria Hwy Leesville LA 71446

THOMPSON, DAVID, publishing executive; m. Jane Thompson; 3 children. Grad., U. Ctrl. Okla., 1973. Mem. retail adv. sales staff Oklahoman, 1974, asst. adv. dir., 1986, dir. adv., 1987—2001, mgr. phone room classified adv. dept.; mgr. adv. Colo. Springs Sun, 1977; v.p. adv. Charlotte Observer, 2001—03; pres., pub. Daily Oklahoman, 2003—. Mem. bd. Carolina Regional Partnership; mem. Mecklenburg Coun., exec. bd. dirs. Last Frontier Coun. Boy Scouts Am.; with Charlotte C. of C.; chmn. elect YMCA, Oklahoma City; mem. bd. Ind. Coll. Found.; chmn. econ. develop. dept. C. of C. Mem.: So. Newspaper Pubs. Assn., Newspaper Assn. Am., Kiwanis (pres.). Office: Daily Oklahoman 9000 Broadway Ext Oklahoma City OK 73114

THOMPSON, DAVID, economist, researcher; PhD, U. Mass. Sr. health economist Policy Analysis Inc., Brookline, Mass., 1988—99; mng. dir., US ops. Innovus Rsch. Inc., Medford, Mass., 2000—. Office: Innovus Rsch Inc 10 Cabot Rd Ste 102 Medford MA 01944

THOMPSON, DAVID ALFRED, industrial engineer; b. Chgo., Sept. 9, 1929; s. Clifford James and Christobel Eliza (Sawin) T.; children: Nancy, Brooke, Lynda, Diane, Kristy. B.M.E., U. Va., 1951; BS in Indsl. Engring, U. Fla., 1955, MS in Engring, 1956; PhD, Stanford U., 1961. Registered profl. engr., Calif; cert. profl. ergonomist; bd. cert. diplomate in forensic engring. Research asst. U. Fla. Engring. and Industries Exptl. Sta., Gainesville, 1955-56; instr. indsl. engring. Stanford U., 1956-58, acting asst. prof., 1958-61, asst. prof., 1961-64, asso. prof., 1964-72, prof., 1972-83, prof., asso. chmn. dept. indsl. engring., 1972-73, prof. emeritus, 1983—; clin. faculty occupational medicine U. Calif. Med. Sch., San Francisco, 1985—; pres., chief scientist Portola Assocs., Palo Alto, Calif., 1962—97, Incline Village, Nev., 1997—; prin. investigator NASA Ames Rsch. Ctr., Moffatt Field, Calif., 1974-77. Cons. Dept. State, Fed. EEO Commn., maj. U.S. and fgn. cos.; cons. emergency commn. ctr. design Santa Clara County Criminal Justice Bd., 1974, Bay Area Rapid Transit Control Ctr., 1977, Govt. of Mex., 1978, Amadahl Corp., 1978-79, Kerr-McGee Corp., 1979, Chase Manhattan Bank, 1980, St. Regis Paper Co., 1980-82, Pacific Gas & Electric, 1983-85, Pacific Bell, 1984-86, 89-93, IBM, 1988-91, Hewlett-Packard, 1990-91, 98-99, Reuter's News Svc., 1990-92, Safeway Corp., 1992-94, New United Motors Mfg., 1993-95, Sun Microsys., 1993-94, Microsoft, 1995-00; mem. com. for office computers Calif. OSHA. Dir., editor: documentary film Rapid Answers for Rapid Transit, Dept. Transp., 1974; mem. editorial adv. bd. Computers and Graphics, 1970-85; reviewer Indsl. Engring. and IEEE Transactions, 1972-86; contbr. articles to profl. jours. Served to lt. USNR, 1951-58. HEW grantee, 1967-70 Fellow Nat. Assn. Forensic Engrs.; mem. IEEE, Am. Inst. Indsl. Engrs., Human Factors and Ergonomics Soc., Am. Soc. Safety Engrs., Soc. Forensic Engrs. and Scientists, Am. Assn. Forensic Scientists. Home: PO Box 6685 Incline Village NV 89450-6685 Address: PO Box 6088 Incline Village NV 89450-6088 Office Phone: 775-833-3304. E-mail: davidthompson@human-factors.org.

THOMPSON, DAVID RENWICK, federal judge; b. 1930; BS in Bus., U. So. Calif., 1952, LLB, 1955. Pvt. practice Thompson & Thompson (and predecessor firms), 1957—85; judge U.S. Ct. Appeals (9th cir.), 1985—98, sr. judge, 1998—. With USN, 1955—57. Mem.: ABA, Am. Bd. Trial Lawyers (sec. San Diego chpt. 1983, v.p. 1984, Pres. 1985), San Diego County Bar Assn. Office: US Ct Appeals 940 Front St Rm 2193 San Diego CA 92101-8919

THOMPSON, DAVID RUSSELL, engineering educator, academic dean; b. Cleve., Apr. 4, 1944; s. Dwight L. and Ella Caroline (Wolff) T.; m. Janet Ann Schall, Aug. 27, 1966; children: Devin Mathew, Colleen Michelle, Darin Michael. BS in Agrl. Engring., Purdue U., 1966, MS in Agrl. Engring., 1967; PhD in Agrl. Engring., Mich. State U., 1970. Asst. prof. agrl. engring., food sci. and nutrition depts. U. Minn., St. Paul, 1970-75, assoc. prof., 1975-81, prof., 1981-85; prof. agrl. engring., head dept. Okla. State U., Stillwater, 1985-91, assoc. dean Coll. Engring., Architecture and Tech., 1991—. Engr. ops. dept. Green Giant Co., La Sueur, Minn., 1978-79; reviewer Colo. State U., Cooperative State Rsch. Svc., USDA, Ft. Collins, 1989, foods, feeds and prodn. cluster U. Mo., Columbia, 1989, 93, dept. agrl. engring. Pa. State U., University Park, 1990, Tex. A&M U., College Station, 1992, Utah State U., Logan, 1993, USAF, Tyndall, Fla. and San Angelo, Tex., 1994-95, 97, Wash. State U., Pullman, 1995, U. Ga., Athens, 1996, S.D. State U., 1997, U. Fla., 1998, U. Del., 1998, U. Neb., 1999, U. Wis., 2000, U. Idaho, 2001, Rutgers U., 2003, Lake Superior State U., Sault St. Marie, 2003, others; reviewer USDA, 1983; vis. scholar Va. Poly. Inst. and State U., Blacksburg. Author: The Influence of Materials Properties on the Freezing of Sweet Corn, 1984, Mathematical Model for Predicting Lysine and Methionine Losses During Thermal Processing of Fortified Foods; contbr. over 50 articles to profl. jours. including Jour. Food Sci. Fellow Am. Soc. Agrl. Engrs. (div. chmn. 1976-77, bd. dirs. 1981-84, 87-89, v.p. 1994-98, stds. coun. chmn. 1997-98, Farm and Indsl. Equip. Inst., Young Rschr. award 1983, Pres.'s citation 1989, 98); mem. ASHRAE, NSPE (chair Okla. mid-north sect. 1994-95), Okla. Soc. Profl. Engrs. (v.p. 2000-2001), Inst. Food Technologists (program com. 1982-85, state officer 1987-89), Am. Soc. Engring. Edn. (chair Midwest sect. 1994-95), Sigma Xi, Phi Kappa Phi, Tau Beta Pi, Alpha Epsilon, Phi Eta Sigma, Gamma Sigma Delta. Office: Okla State U Coll Engring Arch & Tech 201 Adv Tech Rsch Ctr Stillwater OK 74078-5010 Office Phone: 405-744-5140. Business E-Mail: dthomps@okstate.edu.

THOMPSON, DAVID W. retail executive; V.p. Value City Furniture, Columbus, Ohio, 0198—1993, pres., 1993—. Bd. dirs. Am. Eagle Outfitters, Inc. Office: Value City Furniture 1800 Moler Rd Columbus OH 43207*

THOMPSON, DAVID WALKER, astronautics company executive; b. Phila., Mar. 21, 1954; s. Robert H. and Nancy S. (Walker) T.; m. Catherine K. Ahulii, April 16, 1983. BS in Aeronautics and Astronautics, MIT, 1976; MS, Calif. Inst. Tech., 1977; MBA, Harvard U., 1981. Project engr. Jet Propulsion Lab., Pasadena, Calif., 1976; aerospace engr. NASA, Houston, 1977, project mgr. Huntsville, Ala., 1977-79; spl. asst. to pres. Hughes Aircraft Co., Los Angeles, 1981-82; pres., chief exec. officer Orbital Scis. Corp., Dulles, Va., 1982—. Cons. Rockwell Internat., Thousand Oaks, Calif., 1980-81, Rand Corp., Santa Monica, Calif., 1982. Recipient Nat. award Space Found., Houston, 1981, Nat. Medal Tech. U.S Dept. Commerce Tech. Adminstrn., 1991; Nat. Air and Space Mus. Trophy, 1990; fellow Hertz Found., 1976, NSF fellow, 1976, Rockwell Internat. fellow, Harvard U. fellow, 1979; named Va. Industrial of Yr., 1991, Satellite Exec. of Yr., 1990, George M. Low Space Transportation award, Am. Inst. of Aeronautics and Astronautics, 1994 Fellow AIAA (assoc., Young Engr./Scientist Yr. award 1984, George M. Low Space Trans. award 1994), mem. Nat. Space Club. Office: Orbital Sciences Corp 21839 Atlantic Blvd Sterling VA 20166-6850

THOMPSON, DAVID WILLIAM, business educator; b. Ft. Wayne, Ind., Sept. 3, 1914; s. William Byron and Georgia Louise (Davis) T.; m. M. Miriam Vollmer, Dec. 21, 1956 (dec.); m. Shirley Carr, June 15, 1989. BS, Ind. U., 1938, MS, 1940. C.P.A., N.Y., Ill., Ind., Va., N.C., N. Mex., La. Prof. Samford U., Birmingham, Butler U., Indpls., 1941-42, Ind. U., Bloomington, 1942-54; cons. Gen. Electric Co., N.Y.C., 1954-56; ptnr. KPMG Peat Marwick, N.Y.C., 1956-76; Frank S. Kaulback Jr. prof. commerce McIntire Sch. Commerce U. Va., Charlottesville, 1976—. Chmn. State Bd. Examiners C.P.A.s, N.Y.C., 1966-70, State Bd. Pub. Accountancy, N.Y.C., 1974-76 Dir. Univ. of the Ams., Mexico City, U. of the Ams. Found., San Antonio. Mem. AICPA, Ind. U. Acad. Alumni Fellows, Indpls. Athletic Club, India House Club N.Y.C., Univ. Club N.Y.C., Farmington Country Club Charlottesville Va., Beta Gamma Sigma (dirs. table). Home: Ednam Forest 425 Wellington Dr Charlottesville VA 22903-4746 Office: U Va Monroe Hall McIntire Sch Commerce Charlottesville VA 22903

THOMPSON, DEAN ALLAN, cattleman; b. Peru, Ind., Jan. 29, 1934; s. Paul Franklin and Pauline St. Clair (Thrush) T. Student Purdue U., 1952-54. Mgr. Thompson Farms, breeders registered Hereford cattle, Peru, 1956-69; owner Thompson Farms, Wartrace, Tenn. and Peru, 1970-87, Dean Thompson Prodns., Wartrace, Wartrace Records; chmn. bd. Instant Copy and Printing, Inc., Monterrey, Calif., 1976-86, Trenton Energy Inc., 1977-83, Bloomfield, Ind.; v.p., dir. 5B Cattle Co., Twin Bridges, Mont., 1986-87; ptnr., Brann-Thompson Ltd.; internat. beef cattle judge; dir. Maine Manna, Gorham. Bd. dirs. Thrush-Thompson Found. (formerly H.A. Thrush Found.), Peru; trustee Middle Tenn. State U. Found., 1981-83, 85-89, chmn. fin. com., 1982-83, 85-87, exec. com., 1983-89, sec. 1988, pres.-elect, 1989; precinct committeeman, chmn. Miami County (Ind.) Young Republican Com., 1962-67; elder Presbyn. Ch., 1986-88. With U.S. Army, 1955-56. Mem. Nat. Western (dir.), Ind. (dir. 1958-68, pres. 1960) Polled Hereford Assns., Ind. Cattleman's Assn. (founding dir.), Ind. Livestock Breeders Assn., Am. Hereford Assn. (v.p. pres.'s coun. 1981, pres. 1982), Tenn. Hereford Assn. (dir. 1977-81, 93-97, v.p. 1979, pres. 1980-81, 97), Toastmasters (pres., area gov.), Columbia Club. Home and Office: 900 19th Ave S Apt 1201 Nashville TN 37212-2155

THOMPSON, DENNIS PETERS, plastic surgeon; b. Chgo., Mar. 18, 1937; s. David John and Ruth Dorothy (Peters) T.; m. Virginia Louise Williams, June 17, 1961; children: Laura Faye, Victoria Ruth, Elizabeth Jan. BS, U. Ill., 1957, BS in Medicine, 1959, MS in Physiology, MD, U. Ill., 1961. Diplomate Am. Bd. Surgery, Am. Bd. Plastic Surgery. Intern Presbyn.-St. Lukes Hosp., Chgo., 1961—62; resident in gen. surgery Mayo Clinic, Rochester, Minn., 1964—66, fellow in gen. surgery, 1964—66; resident in gen. surgery Harbor Gen. Hosp., L.A., 1968—70; resident in plastic surgery UCLA, 1971—73, clin. instr. plastic surgery, 1975—82, asst. clin. prof. surgery, 1982—97, assoc. clin. prof. surgery, 1998—. Practice medicine specializing in plastic and reconstructive surgery, L.A., 1974-78, Santa Monica, Calif., 1978—; chmn. plastic surgery sect. St. John's Hosp., 1986-91; mem. staff Santa Monica Hosp./UCLA Med. Ctr.; chmn. dept. surgery Beverly Glen Hosp., 1978-79; pres. Coop. of Am. Physicians Credit Union, 1978-80, bd. dirs., 1980-97, chmn. membership devel. com., 1983-97, treas., 1985-97. Contbr. articles to med. jours. Moderator Congl. Ch. of Northridge (Calif.), 1975-76, chmn. bd. trustees, 1973-74, 80-82; bd. dirs. L.A. Bus. Coun., 1987-90. Am. Tobacco Inst. rsch. grantee, 1959-60. Fellow ACS; mem. AMA (Physicians Recognition award 1971, 74, 77, 81, 84, 87, 90, 93, 96, 99, 2002), Calif. Med. Assn., L.A. County Med. Assn. (chmn. bylaws com. 1979-80, chmn. ethics com. 1980-81, 2000-01, sec.-treas. dist. 5 1982-83, program chmn. 1983-84, pres. 1985-86, councilor 1988-96, 2001-03, councilor-at-large 2004—, v.p. 1999-2000), Pan-Pacific Surg. Assn., Am. Soc. Plastic Surgeons, Calif. Soc. Plastic Surgeons (chmn. bylaws com. 1982-83, chmn. liability com. 1983-85, councilor 1988-91, sec. 1993-95, v.p. 1995-96, pres.-elect 1996-97, pres. 1997-98), L.A. Soc. Plastic Surgeons (sec. 1980-82, pres. 1982-97), Lipoplasty Soc. N.Am., UCLA Plastic Surgery Soc. (treas. 1983-84, v.p. 1996-98, pres. 1998—), Am. Soc. Aesthetic

Plastic Surgery, Internat. Soc. Clin. Plastic Surgeons (bd. dirs. 1999—), Am. Assn. Accreditation of Ambulatory Surg. Facilities (bd. dirs. 1995-97, 2002-, ofcl. observer to AMA ho. of dels. 1999—), Western L.A. Regional C. of C. (bd. dirs. 1981-84, 86-89, chmn. legis. action com. 1978-80), Phi Beta Kappa, Alpha Omega Alpha, Nu Sigma Nu, Phi Kappa Phi, Delta Sigma Delta, Omega Beta Pi, Phi Eta Sigma. Republican. Office: 1301 20th St # 460 Santa Monica CA 90404-2102 E-mail: dthompso@ucla.edu.

THOMPSON, DIANA ROSEBUD, poet, educator, history exhibit coordinator, marketing consultant, playwright; b. NYC, Dec. 25, 1957; d. Samuel Joseph Daniels and Anna Louise Thompson. BA in Psychology, Columbia U., 1979; AAS in cosmetics mktg. cum laude, Fashion Inst. Tech., 1979—81; MS in early childhood edn., Bklyn Coll., CUNY, 1987—89; JD, Fordham U. Sch. Law, 1990—93. Cert. victim relief training NY Evang. Sem., 2001. Prin. coll. instr. and coord. of retention D.R. Thompson Enterprises, NYC, 1980; mktg. cons. 127th Street Repertory Ensemble, 1982—83, 20 West Theatre, NYC, 1983, Art Against Apartheid, NYC, 1984. Judge math. NAACP Acad., Cultural, Technol. and Sci. Olympics Competition II, Queens, NY, 1980, adj. prof. Touro Coll., NYC, 2002—. Author: (plays) Who Needs Earthlings?; co-host: Educators of Digital Media Network; contbr. articles to magazines; host (forum) Writers, Actors of Digital Media and Artists Network (www.d-mnforums.com), 2003. Host, writers, actors & artists www.dmnforums.com, 2003; ho. builder Habitat for Humanity, 2000; vol. Ctrl. Pk. Conservancy, NYC, 1998—2003; soloist and song leader NYC Marathon Worship Svc., 2001—. Recipient cert. merit, Nat. Council Negro Women, N.Y.C., 1981, Centrum Creative Residency, Centrum Creative Edn., Port Townsend, WA, 2003, Ann. Poetry Slam, Exoterica, 1995, NY Regional Winner of Singing/Songwriting Contest, Lever Bros., 1996, Cert. Appreciation, FDIC - NY, 1998, 1999. Mem.: NARAS, AAUW (publicity chmn. Queens br. 1980—81), MLA, Am. Soc. Composers, Authors and Publs., Metamorphosis Writers Collective, Dramatists Guild Am., Am. Indian Comty. House, NY Rd. Runners, Zeta Phi Beta (fin. sec. L.I. br. 1980—81). Office Phone: 212-368-8293. Personal E-mail: dianapoet@aol.com.

THOMPSON, DIANE E. lawyer; married; 2 children. Grad., Vassar Coll.; JD, George Washington U., 1976. Ptnr. Rogers, Joseph, O'Donnell and Quinn, 1981-83; counsel San Francisco Human Rights Commn., 1981-83; mem. Mondale for Pres. Compaign, 1984; gen. counsel NOW, 1985; adminstrv. asst., legis. dir. to Barbara Mikulski of Md., U.S. Ho. of Reps., Washington, 1986; chief to staff to Senator Mikulski of Md., U.S. Senate, Washington, 1987-89; ptnr. Foreman and Heidepriem, 1992-93; assoc. commr. for legis. affairs FDA, HHS, Rockville, Md., 1994—. Mem. adj. faculty Hastings Coll. Law, U. Calif. Office: US EPA 1200 Pennsylvania Ave NW Washington DC 20460-0001

THOMPSON, DIDI CASTLE (MARY BENNETT), writer, editor; b. Terre Haute, Ind., Feb. 7, 1918; d. Robert Langley Bennett and Marjorie Rose (Tyler) Castle; student U. Ill., Champaign, 1935-36, U. Ky., 1936-39; m. Jamie Campbell Thompson, Jr., June 24, 1939; children— Jamie III, Julia King Balko, Langley Stewart Ruede. News editor Glen-Echoes, Glencoe, Ill., 1930; columnist Ky. Kernel, U. Ky., Lexington, 1937-39; radio script writer Modern Am. Music, 1940-42; asst. pub. relations dir. Salem Coll., Winston-Salem, N.C., 1945; pub. relations chmn. Barrington (Ill.) Horse Show, 1959-67; staff writer, columnist Barrington Press Newspapers, 1958-84; editor ECHO, Defenders of the Fox River, Inc. newsletter, 1970-80; travel editor Barrington Press Newspapers, 1973-84; columnist The Daily Herald, Paddock Publs., 1984-86; columnist Rapid City (S.D.) Journal, 1990-95; freelance writer, 1943— . Past bd. mem. Barrington chpt. Lyric Opera Guild Chgo., Barrington Sr. Center, Infant Welfare Soc. Chgo., Art Inst. Chgo., Barrington Assos.; elected trustee Village of Barrington Hills, 1969-73, health, pub. relations chmn., 1969-73; mem. Barrington Hills Plan Commn., 1986. Mem. DAR, Women in Communications (past dir.), Citizens for Conservation (past dir.), Barrington Countryside Assn. (past dir.), Barrington Hist. Soc., Spring Creek Basset Hounds Club, Barrington Hills Riding Club (past dir.), Pan Hellenic Coun., Gulf Shore Lit. Soc., Conservancy S.W. Fla. (Naples), Chgo. Press Club, Chi Omega. Episcopalian. Address: 1827 Princess Ct Naples FL 34110-1001

THOMPSON, DON, food products executive; m. Elizabeth Thompson; children: Xavier, Maya. BSc in elec. engring., Purdue U. Engr. specialist, def. systems divsn. Northrop Corp., Rolling Meadows, Ill.; restaurant systems engr. McDonald's Corp., 1990—91, project mgr., 1991—93, staff dir., then dir. ops. for Denver region, 1993, regional v.p., San Diego region, 1998, sr. v.p., restaurant support officer, Midwest divsn., 1998—2000; pres., Midwest divsn. McDonald's USA, 2000—01; pres., West divsn. McDonald's Corp., 2001—. Office: McDonald's Corp McDonald's Plaza Oak Brook IL 60523

THOMPSON, DONALD CHARLES, electronics company executive, former coast guard officer; b. Hollis, N.Y., Nov. 9, 1930; s. Arthur I. and Gertrude M. (Hauck) T.; m. Jeannie Germaine Kline, Oct. 4, 1952; children: Dennis C., Mitchell L., Sandra J., Janice M., Theresa A., Patrick J. BS, U.S. Coast Guard Acad., 1952; MS (Krannert scholar), Krannert Grad. Sch., Purdue U., 1966. Commd. ensign USCG, 1952, advanced through grades to vice adm., 1986; shipboard navigator and engr., 1952-54; naval flight tng., 1954-55; search and rescue aviator and aircraft maintenance officer, 1955-65; chief computer-based mgmt. info. div., 1966-70; chief aero. engring. div. USCG Hdqrs., 1970-74; capt. of the port, group comdr., air sta. comdr. San Diego, 1974-76; chief ops. 11th USCG Dist., Long Beach, Calif., 1976-78, chief of staff, 1979; chief office of engring. USCG Hdqrs., Washington, 1979-81, chief office of ops., 1981-82, chief staff, 1984-86, comdr. Atlantic area, 1986-88; comdr. 7th Coast Guard Dist., Miami, Fla., 1982-84; math. instr. Coll. Albermarle, N.C., 1967-70, Nat. U., San Diego, 1975-76; chmn. Interagy. Com. Search and Rescue, 1981-82; ret. USCG, 1988; v.p. strategic devel. R&E Electronics, Inc., Wilmington, N.C., 1990-93; pres. D.C. Thompson Consulting, Wilmington, 1994—. V.p.'s coordinator for S.E. region Nat. Narcotics Border Interdiction System, 1983-84 Contbr. articles to profl. jours. Coordinator White House South Fla. Task Force on Crime, 1983-84. Decorated DSM with two gold stars, Coast Guard Meritorious Service medal, Def. Superior Service medal, Commendation medal with three gold stars, Legion of Merit with gold star Mem. Soc. Am. Mil. Engrs. (dir. 1979-81), Am. Soc. Naval Engrs., Am. Helicopter Soc. (dir. 1981-82), Air Force Assn., Naval Inst. Clubs: Propeller, Nat. Aviation. Roman Catholic. Home and Office: 2213 Tattersall Dr Wilmington NC 28403 E-mail: deeset@earthlink.net.

THOMPSON, DOREEN, public relations executive; b. Somerville, Mass., Mar. 26, 1955; 2 children. BA in Mass. Comm., U. N.H., 1977; MA in Speech Comm., Emerson Coll., 1982. Account exec. Arnold Pub. Rels., Boston, 1984-85; account exec., account supr., v.p. Ingalls, Quinn & Johnson Pub. Rels., Boston, 1985-88; v.p., then sr. v.p. The Weber Group, Cambridge, Mass., 1988-98, exec. v.p., 1998—. Trustee Lasell Coll., Newton, Mass., 1990—; pro bono work Gang Peace, Boston, 1994. Recipient Regional award CIPPRA, 1993, Bellringer award Publicity Club, 1994. Office: The Weber Group 101 Main St Ste 3 Cambridge MA 02142-1527

THOMPSON, DOROTHY BARNARD, elementary school educator; b. Flushing, NY, Aug. 14, 1933; d. Henry Clay and Cecelia Minnie Theresa (La Pardo) Barnard; m. Norman Earl Thompson, Aug. 12, 1956 (dec.); children: Greg, Scot, Henry, Marc (dec.), Matthew. BSEd, SUNY, New Paltz, 1953; MS, Hofstra U., 1984. Cert. elem. tchr. K-6th grades, reading specialist K-12th grades, NY. Adjunct prof. Suffolk Community Coll., Brentwood, NY, 1987—; adj. prof. Nassau Cmty. Coll., Uniondale, NY, 1986—; adj. prof., instr. Ctr. for Acad. Achievement Long Isl. U., Greenvale, NY, 1984-92; tchr. reading, 1st and 2nd grades Long Beach Pub. Sch., NY, 1988—. Mem. founding group Parent/Tchr., The Learning Tree, Garden City, NY, 1971; founder parent coop. Happy Day Nursery Sch., Bellmore, NY, 1975; parent-tchr. Commonwealth Sch., Bay Shore, Oakdale, 1976-82. Office: 456 Neptune Blvd Long Beach NY 11561-2400 Office Phone: 516-897-2184. E-mail: anetco01@aol.com.

THOMPSON, EDWARD OTIS, mathematician, educator; b. Madison County, Mont., Feb. 8, 1944; s. Orvil Ward and Eva Maxine (Bogue) Thompson; m. Darylene Jo Stroud, Aug. 13, 1963; children: David Lance, Shelley Lynn. BS, Western Mont. Coll., 1966; MS, Mont. State U., 1968, EdD, 1992. Math. prof. Flathead Valley Community Coll., Kalispell, Mont., 1969-79, Western Mont. Coll., Dillon, Mont., 1979—. Mem. Am. Fed. Tchrs., Nat. Coun. Tchrs. Math., Mont. Coun. Tchrs. Math. (sec. 1974-75, v.p. 1976-78, pres. 1978-79), Math. Assn. Am., Mont. Coun. for Computers in Edn. Avocations: fly fishing, hunting, computers. Home: 1025 Fox Farm Rd Dillon MT 59725-9415 Office: Western Mont Coll Math Dept Dillon MT 59725-3598

THOMPSON, EMMA, actress; b. London, Apr. 15, 1959; d. Eric Thompson and Phyllida Law; m. Kenneth Branagh, Aug. 1989 (div.). Student of English, Cambridge U., Eng. Performances include: (films) Henry V, 1989, The Tall Guy, 1989, Dead Again, 1991, Impromptu, 1991, Howard's End, 1992 (Acad. award for best actress 1993), Peter's Friends, 1992, Much Ado About Nothing, 1993, The Remains of the Day, 1993 (Acad. award nominee for best actress 1993), In the Name of the Father, 1993 (Acad. award nominee for best supporting actress 1993), My Father, the Hero, 1994, Junior, 1994, Carrington, 1995 (Best Actress award Nat. Bd. Rev. 1995), Sense and Sensibility, 1995 (Golden Globe award nominee for best actress in film 1996, Acad. award nominee for best actress 1996), Winter Guest, 1996, Primary Colors, 1998, Judas Kiss, 1998, Maybe Baby, 2000, Treasure Planet (voice), 2002, Love Actually, 2003, Imagining Argentina, 2003, Harry Potter and the Prisoner of Azbakan, 2004; (TV in Eng.) Al Fresco, Up For Grabs (a.k.a. Sexually Transmitted), Tutti Frutti, (miniseries) Fortunes of War, Thompson; (TV in Am.) Fortunes of War, 1987, Cheers, 1991, Wit, 2001, (miniseries) Angels in America, 2003;(London stage) Me and My Girl, Look Back in Anger; also writer screen adaptation: Sense and Sensibility (Jane Austin), 1995 (Best Screenplay award N.Y. Film Critics 1995, L.A. Film Critics 1995, Boston Film Critics 1995, Golden Globe award for best adapted screenplay 1996, Acad. award for best adapted screenplay 1996, BAFTA Best Actress award 1996). Active in Footlights Theatrical Group, Cambridge, Eng. Office: William Morris Agy 151 S El Camino Dr Beverly Hills CA 90212-2775

THOMPSON, ERMIS ARMENTER, retired education educator; b. Brilliant, Ala., July 18, 1914; s. Malta Armenter and Elizabeth Jane (Doss) Thompson; m. Nathlene Ingle Thompson, Dec. 3, 1945; children: David Errol, James Milton. BS, Florence State Tchrs. Coll., 1949; MA, U. Ala., 1952, PhD, 1963. Author: Memoirs of a Naive Unprofitable Soldier, 2004, Here and There and This and That, 2004. With Corps. of Engrs. U.S. Army, 1942—45, Iran, Europe. Avocations: reading, volleyball, restoring antique radios, cryptograms. Home: 2322 Sheraton Ln Florence AL 35630

THOMPSON, EUGENE MAYNE, retired minister; b. Oxford, N.S., Can., Jan. 5, 1931; s. Curry Allison and Hortense Essie (Mayne) T.; m. Rhoda Mitchell, May 21, 1955; children: Adrian Calvin, Nancy Lynn, Howard Allison. BA, Acadia U., 1954, BD, 1956, DD, 2000, MDiv, 1976; D of Ministry, So. Bapt. Theol. Sem., 1979. Pastor South End United Bapt. Ch., Dartmouth, N.S., 1954-58; assoc. sec. of Christian Edn. United Bapt. Conv. of Atlantic Provinces, St. John, N.B., 1958-61, exec. min., 1984-96, area min. for West N.S. Middleton, N.S., 1974-84; pastor Immanuel Bapt. Ch., Truro, N.S., 1961-65, Hillcrest Bapt. Ch., St. John, N.B., 1965-68; area min. for Man. Bapt. Union of Western Can., 1968-74; ret., 1996. Coun., exec. mem. Can. Bapt. Ministries, Mississauga, Ont.; bd. dirs. Atlantic Bapt. Sr. Citizen Homes, Inc., Moncton, N.B.; bd. govs Atlantic Bapt. Coll., Moncton; trustee Acadia Div. Coll.; mem. Bapt. Found. Author: Baptist Youth Fellowship Handbook, 1958, New Design for a Dynamic Church, 1973. Dir. St. John, N.B., Habitat for Humanity. Avocations: music, gardening, painting. E-mail: emtrt@nbnet.nb.ca.

THOMPSON, EWA M. foreign language educator; b. Kaunas, Lithuania; came to U.S., 1963; d. Jozef and Maria Majewski; m. James R. Thompson. BA in English and Russian, U. Warsaw, Poland, 1963; MFA in Piano, Sopot Conservatory Music, 1963; MA in English, Ohio U., 1964; PhD in Comparative Lit., Vanderbilt U., 1967. Instr. Vanderbilt U., Nashville, Tenn., 1964-67; asst. prof. Ind. State U., Terre Haute, 1967-68, Ind. U., 1968-70, Rice U., Houston, 1967-73, assoc. prof., 1974-79, prof., 1979—, chair, 1987-90; assoc. prof. U. Va., Charlottesville, 1973-74. Cons. NEH, 1973—, The John D. and Catherine T. MacArthur Found., The John Simon Guggenheim Found., U.S. Dept. Edn.; vis. cons. Tex. A&M U.; seminar dir. NEH Summer Inst., Southeastern La. U., 1990; chair Russian lit. conf. Rice U., 1989; lectr. various colls. and univs. Author: Russian Formalism and Anglo-American New Criticism: A Comparative Study, 1971, Witold Gombrowicz, 1979, Polish transl., 2002, Understanding Russia: The Holy Fool in Russian Culture, 1987 (Chinese transl. 1995, 2nd Chinese edit. 1998), The Search for Self-Definition in Russian Literature, 1991, Imperial Knowledge: Russian Literature and Colonialism, 2000, Polish transl., 2000; editor the Sarmatian Rev., 1988—; contbr. articles to profl. jours., chpts. to books. Mellon grant, 1990, Rice U. grant 1990, Internat. Rsch. and Exchanges Sr. Scholar grant, 1991; Hoover Inst. fellow, 1988; scholar Vanderbilt U., 1964-67; recipient Silver Thistle award Houston's Scottish Heritage Found., 1988. Roman Catholic. Home: 142 Stoney Creek Houston TX 77024 Office: Rice Univ 6100 S Main St MS 32 Houston TX 77005-1892 Business E-Mail: ethomp@rice.edu.

THOMPSON, FRANK JOSEPH, political science educator; b. New Ulm, Minn., Mar. 21, 1944; s. Joseph Mariem and Alice Louise (Lindquist) T.; m. Benna Miriam, June 15, 1944; children: Samuel, Aliza, Elizabeth. BA in Polit. Sci., U. Chgo., 1966; MA in Polit. Sci., U. Calif., Berkeley, 1967, PhD in Polit. Sci., 1973. Asst. prof. polit. sci. Calif. State U., Long Beach, 1971-72; asst. prof. U. Ga., Athens, 1972-78, assoc. prof., 1978-83, prof., 1983-88, head dept., 1982-87; prof. pub. adminstrn., policy, polit. sci. and pub. health SUNY, Albany, 1987—, dean Grad. Sch. of Pub. Affairs, 1988—97, assoc. provost, 1990-97, interim provost, 1998—2000; dean Rockefeller Coll., 2000—. Analyst HEW, Washington, 1968, City Govt. Oakland, Calif., 1968-71; cons. USPHS, 1976-79, 82, U.S. Pres.'s Commn. for Nat. Agenda for 80's, 1980, Am. Pub. Welfare Assn., 1981-83; publ. cons. U.S. Adv. Commn. on Intergovtl. Rels., 1983; mem. task force on exec. and mgmt. devel. U.S. Office Pers. Mgmt., 1990; exec. dir. Nat. Commn. on the State and Local Pub. Svc., 1991-97. Author: Personnel Policy in the City, 1975, Health Policy and the Bureaucracy, 1981, Public Administration: Challenges, Choices, Consequences, 1990; editor: Classics of Public Personnel Policy, 1979, 3d edit., 2003, Revitalizing State and Local Public Service, 1993, Medicaid and Devolution: A View from the States, 1998; contbr. articles to profl. jours. Bd. dirs. Upper Hudson Planned Parenthood, 1990-96, Albany-Tula Alliance, 1998-2003. Pub. adminstrn. fellow U.S. Pub. Health Service, 1975-76, NSF fellow, 1970-71; recipient Simon award Internat. Jour. Pub. Adminstrn., 1981. Fellow Nat. Acad. Pub. Adminstrn.; mem. Am. Pub. Health Assn., Assn. for Pub. Policy Analysis and Mgmt., Am. Soc. for Pub. Adminstrn. (publs. com. 1982-84, William E. Mosher award 1983), Am. Polit. Sci. Assn. (chmn. departmental services com. 1985-87, exec. com. sect. pub. adminstrn. 1985-87, 89, 91, 96—98, chair sect. pub. adminstrn. 1990-91, chair Gaus award com. 1991-92), Nat. Assn. Schs. Pub. Affairs and Adminstrn. (peer rev. com. 1984-86, 1st chmn. commn. on peer rev. and accreditation 1986-87, chmn. task force on revitalizing the pub. svc., v.p. 1990-91, pres. 1991-92, chmn. com. advancement of pub. adminstrn. 1996-98), N.Y. State Acad. Pub. Adminstrn. (bd. dirs. 1994—98). Home: 9 Harvard Ave Albany NY 12208-2019 Office: SUNY Rockefeller Coll Milne 102 Albany NY 12222-0001 E-mail: thompson@albany.edu.

THOMPSON, FRED DALTON, former senator; b. Sheffield, Ala., Aug. 19, 1942; m. Sarah Lindsey, 1959; children: Tony, Daniel, Elizabeth Betsy Panici(dec.); m. Jeri Kehn, 2002. BS, Memphis State U., 1964; JD, Vanderbilt U., 1967. Asst. U.S. atty. Mid. Tenn., 1969-72; min. counsel Senate Watergate Com., 1973-74; pvt. practice, 1975-94; spl. counsel U.S. Senate Fgn. Rels. Coms., 1980, Senate Intelligence Com., 1982; atty. Arent, Fox, Kintner, Plotkin & Kahn, 1991-94; U.S. senator from Tenn., 1994—2002. Chmn. senate govtl. affairs com., 1997-2001. Appeared in 18 films including Marie: A True Story, 1985, No Way Out, 1987, Feds, 1988, Fat Man and Little Boy, 1989, The Hunt for Red October, 1990, Days of Thunder,1990, Die Hard 2: Die Harder,1990, Flight of the Intruder,1991, Class Action, 1991, Necessary Roughness, 1991, Curly Sue, 1991, Cape Fear, 1991, Aces: Iron Eagle III, 1992, Thunderheart, 1992, White Sands, 1992, Born Yesterday, 1993, In the Line of Fire, 1993, Baby's Day Out, 1994, Download This, 2002; TV movies include: Unholy Matrimony, 1988, Bed of Lies, 1992, Stay the Night, 1992, Keep the Change, 1992, Barbarians at the Gate, 1993; TV guest appearances: Wiseguy, 1988, China Beach, 1989, Roseanne, 1989, Matlock, 1989, Law & Order: Special Victims Unit, 2003; TV series: Law and Order, 2002-; author: At That Point In Time, 1975. Republican. Address: PO Box 143 Hermitage TN 37076-0143

THOMPSON, G. GAYE, lawyer; b. Greensboro, N.C., Sept. 15, 1945; d. O.C. and Jean T.; m. Alvis Layton Barrier, Jr., Aug. 28, 1965 (div. 1988); children: Breton Foster, Amé Rebecca. BA, Southwestern U., 1967; JD, St. mary's U., 1987. Bar: 1987, U.S. Ct. Appeals (5th cir.) 1991, U.S. Supreme Ct. 1991. Psychiat. caseworker Austin (Tex.) State Hosp., 1967-68; counselor, acting dir. counseling Meth. Mission Home Tex., San Antonio, 1968-70; assoc. Irvine & Dial, P.C., Attys. at Law, Seguin, 1987; 1st asst. county atty. Guadalupe County, Seguin, 1987-90; ptnr. Thompson & Tiemann LLP, Attys. and Counselors at Law, Austin, 1991—. Pres., bd. dirs. Marywood Child and Family Svcs., 1995-97,; pres bd. dirs. Family Eldercare, 1996-97. Mem. AAUW, Nat. Acad. Elder Law Attys. (bd. dirs. Tex. chpt.), Travis County Bar Assn. (bd. dirs. probate and estate planning sect.), Tex. Dist. and County Attys. Assn., Delta Delta Delta. Episcopalian. Avocations: orchids, fly fishing, photography. Home: PO Box 201988 Austin TX 78720-1988 Office: Thompson & Tiemann LLP Attys and Counselors at Law PO Box 201988 Austin TX 78720-1988 E-mail: ggt@elderlawline.com.

THOMPSON, G. KENNEDY (KEN THOMPSON), bank executive; b. Rocky Mount, N.C., Nov. 25, 1950; BA in Am. Studies, U. N.C.; MBA, Wake Forest Fu. With 1st Union Corp., Charlotte, NC, 1976—, head S.E. divsn., mgr. mid. market dept., 1999—, mgr. N.Y. loan prodn. office, pres. 1st Union-Ga., sr. v.p., head human resources, pres. 1st Union-Fla., vice chmn. corp., head global capital markets, until 1999, pres., CEO, 1999—2001, Wachovia Corp. (merger of 1st Union and Wachovia Corp.), 2001—, chmn., 2003—. Bd. dirs. Fla. Rock Industries, Inc., N.Y. Clearing House; mem. fin. svcs. roundtable Fin. Svcs. Forum. Bd. visitors U. N.C., Chapel Hill, Babcock Grad. Sch. Mgmt., Wake Forest U.; bd. dirs. N.C. Blumenthal Performing Arts Ctr., Charlotte Latin Sch., so. region Boy Scouts Am., United Way, Charlotte, Teach for Am.; mem. met. bd. YMCA, Charlotte. Morehead scholar U. N.C. Office: 301 S College St Charlotte NC 28288

THOMPSON, G. NANETTE, state agency administrator; m. Bill Cooke; 5 children. BA in Internat. Rels., Stanford U., 1978; JD, U. Washington, 1982. Bar: Washington 1982, Alaska 1983. Pvt. practice, 1982—99; chmn. Regulatory Commn. Alaska, Anchorage, 1999—; asst. atty. gen. State of Alaska. Mem. fed.-state joint conf. on delivery advanced svc. FCC, 1999, state chmn. fed.-state joint conf. on delivery advanced svc., 1999—2001, mem. universal svc. joint bd., 2000—01, chmn. universal svc. joint bd., 2001 . Booth home adv. bd. Salvation Army, 1989—94, pres. booth home adv. bd., 1994; bd. dir. Campfire Boys & Girls, 1995—2000. Office: RCA 701 West 8th Ave Ste 300 Anchorage AK 99501

THOMPSON, GARY W. public relations executive; b. Berkeley, Calif., July 15, 1947; BA, Northwestern U., England, 1969—. Acct. exec. Allen & Doward Advt., 1971-74, Hoefer-Amedei Assocs., 1978-81, acct. supr., 1978, v.p., 1978-81; v.p., assoc. dir. Ketchum, 1981-82, sr. v.p., dir., 1982-84, exec. v.p., 1984-87, exec. v.p., dir. we. region, 1987-89, exec. v.p., dir. U.S.A., 1989-90; pres., CEO Hi-Tech Comm., 1990-95, Golin/Harris Techs., 1995—; pres. Shandwick Internat., N.Y.C., 1995—. Mem. Pub. Rels. Soc. Am. (counselors acad., membership chmn. San Francisco chpt. 1983, placement, newsletter chmn. 1985), Internat. Assn. Bus. Communicators, Office: Shandwick Intl 387 Park Ave S Fl 4 New York NY 10016-8818

THOMPSON, GEORGE ALBERT, geophysics educator; b. Swissvale, Pa., June 5, 1919; s. George Albert Sr. and Maude Alice (Harkness) T.; m. Anita Kimmell, July 20, 1944; children: Albert J., Dan A., David C. BS, Pa. State U., 1941; MS, MIT, 1942; PhD, Stanford U., 1949. Geologist, geophysicist U.S. Geol. Survey, Menlo Park, Calif., 1942-49; asst. prof. Stanford (Calif.) U., 1949-55, assoc. prof., 1955-60, prof. geophysics, 1960—, chmn. geophysics dept., 1967-86, chmn. geology dept., 1979-82, Otto N. Miller prof. earth scis., 1980-89, dean sch. earth scis., 1987-89. Part-time geologist U.S. Geol. Survey, Menlo Park, 1949-76; cons. adv. com. on reactor safeguards Nuclear Regulation Commn., Washington, 1974-94; mem. bd. earth sci. NRC, 1986-88, vice chmn. Yucca Mountain Hydrology-tectonics panel NRC, 1990-92; mem. exec. com. Inc. Rsch. Inst. for Seismology, Washington, 1990-92; mem. sr. external events rev. com. Lawrence Livermore Nat. Lab., 1989-93; mem. Coun. on Continental Sci. Drilling, 1990-94; cons. Los Alamos Nat. Lab. on volcano-tectonic processes, 1993-96, S.W. Rsch. Inst., 1993; chair com. to review sci. issues NRC, Ward Valley, Calif., 1994-95; mem. panel on probabalistic volcanic hazard analysis Geomatrix Cons., Inc., 1995-96. Author over 100 research papers. With USNR, 1944-46. Recipient G.K. Gilbert award in seismic geology, 1964, John Wesley Powell award U.S. Geol. Survey, 1999; NSF postdoctoral fellow, 1956-57; Guggenheim Found. fellow, 1963-64 Fellow AAAS, Geol. Soc. Am. (coun. mem. 1983-86, George P. Woollard award 1983, v.p. 1995, pres. 1996), Am. Geophys. Union; mem. NAS (chair geology sect. 2000-03), Seismol. Soc. Am., Soc. Exploration Geophysicists. Avocation: forestry. Home: 421 Adobe Pl Palo Alto CA 94306-4501 Office: Stanford U Geophysics Dept Stanford CA 94305-2215 Office Phone: 650-723-3714. Business E-Mail: thompson@pangea.stanford.edu.

THOMPSON, GEORGE FREDERICK, JR., public management educator; b. Anderson, Ind., Oct. 29, 1942; s. George Frederick and Ellen Leah (Reuter) T.; m. Sharon O'Rand, Sept. 8, 1968 (div. Nov. 1978); children: MacKendree and Kyrie' O'Rand; m. Ruth Ann Crowley, June 20, 1980; 1 child, Jonathan Crowley. BA, Pomona Coll., 1964; PhD, Claremont Grad. Sch., 1972. Asst. to sr. analyst Dept. Fin. State of Calif., Sacramento, 1972-75; asoc. dep. dir. for fin. and capital outlay planning Calif. Postsecondary Edn. Commn., Sacramento, 1975-76; vis. asst./assoc. prof. U. British Columbia faculty commerce and bus. adminstrn., 1976-77; sr. rsch economist Econ. Coun. Can., Ottawa, Ont., 1978-79; vis. assoc. prof., acting chmn. Grad. Sch. Mgmt. Pub. and Not for Profit Mgmt. Group UCLA, 1981; assoc. prof. Columbia U. Sch. Internat. and Pub. Affairs MPA Program, N.Y.C., 1980-85; Grace and Elmer Goudy Prof. Pub. Mgmt. and Policy Analysis Atkinson Grad. Sch. Mgmt. Willamette U., Salem, Oreg., 1985—. Bd. dirs. Fin. Pub., Inc.; mem. task force on state budgeting Nat. Ctr. for Higher edn. Mgmt. Systems, Boulder, Colo., 1975-76, adv. com. Calif. State Senate Judiciary Com. subcom. on Consumr Affairs, 1980-81, Gov.'s Task Force on Sch. Fin. Reform, Oreg., 1988-89, adv. com. on Tax Reform, Oreg., 1990, Govt. Standards and Practices Commn., Oreg., 1995—; cons. House of Commons Can., on Regulatory Reform, Pub. Svcs. Commn. N.Y. Atty. Gen.'s Office of Consumer Affairs, Defense Sec.'s Commn. on Base Realignment and Closure, Senate Armed Svcs. subcom. on mil. constrn., others Co-author: (with W.T. Stanbury) Regulatory Reform in Canada, 1982, (with L.R. Jones) Regulatory Policy and Practices: Regulating Better and Regulating Less, 1982, Reinventing the Pentagon, 1994, Public Management: Institutional Renewal for the 21st Century, 1999; translator (with Ruth Crowley) F. Scharpf's Crisis and Choice in European Social Democracy, 1991; editor: Regulatory Regimes in Conflict, 1984; co-editor: (with LeRoy Gramer) Reforming Social Regulation, 1982, (with W.T. Stanbury) Managing Public Enterprises, 1982; editor Internat. Pub. Mgmt. Jour.; contbr. numerous articles, notes, essays, book revs. to profl. jours. Mem. acad. adv. bd. Cascade Policy Inst. Recipient Clara Ihrig Linhardt Traveling fellowship, Mexico, Cen. Am., 1970-71, Mayr Found. Essay award, Lincoln Inst. Pub. Fin., Claremont Grad. Sch., 1973; nominated for Koopman prize of ORSA spl. interest group of defense analysis, 1987. Mem. Assn. for Pub. Policy and Mgmt., ASPA (exec. coun. sect. on pub. budgeting and fin. 1991-97, pres. 1998, sect. on rsch. and theory 1996—, Mosher award 1994, NASPAA/ASPA Disting Rsch. award 2000), Am. Soc. Mil. Controllers (Gold medal 1994), Oreg. Acad. Scis. Home: 540 Tillman Ave SE Salem OR 97302-3786 Office: Willamette Univ Atkinson Grad Sch Mgmt Salem OR 97301 E-mail: fthompso@willamette.edu.

THOMPSON, GEORGE LEE, consulting and retailing company executive; b. Denver, June 12, 1933; s. George H. and Frances M. (Murphy) T.; m. Patricia M. Mackenzie, Sept. 25, 1993; children: Shannon, Tracy, Bradley. BS in Bus., U. Colo., 1957; degree in Advanced Mgmt., NYU, 1969. With GTE Sylvania, Danvers, Mass., 1957-65, nat. sales mgr., 1965-67, mktg. mgr., 1967-68; v.p. sales entertainment products Batavia, N.Y., 1968-73; dir. corp. mktg. Stamford, Conn., 1973-74; v.p. mktg. Servomation Corp., N.Y.C., 1974-76, exec. v.p., 1976-78, Singer Co., Edison, N.J., 1978-81, pres., 1981-83; pres. consumer products SCM Corp., N.Y.C., 1983-86; pres., CEO Smith-Corona Corp., New Canaan, Conn., 1986-89, chmn., CEO, 1989-95; chmn. Mackenzie-Thompson Assocs., Essex, Conn., 1995—. Bd. dirs. Vol. Products, Inc.; chair Sweet P's, Essex, Conn., 1998—; mem. Conn. State Tourism Coun., 2003-. Chmn. Standards Com. U.S. Dept. Commerce; mem. bus. alumni adv. coun. U. Colo., 1989—94; mem. bd. overseers Sch. Bus. U. Conn., 1993—96; mem. Pres.'s Export Coun., 1991—93; mem. bd. advisors Jr. League; mem. Essex Econ. Devel. Commn., Conn., 2003—; bd. dirs. Internat. Tennis Hall of Fame, Am. Jr. Golf Found., 1986—89, Am. Jr. Golf Assn., 1986—2000, United Way of New Canaan, 1989—93. Recipient Disting. Bus. Alumni award, U. Colo., 1990. Mem. Computer and Bus. Equipment Mfg. Assn. (bd. dirs. 1992-94), Sales and Mktg. Execs. Internat. (trustee), Am. Mgmt. Assn. (trustee, exec. com. chmn., gen. mgmt. coun. 1989-99), St. John Assn. (bd. dirs., pres. 1983-93), Woodway Country Club, Club at Seabrook Island, Wilton Riding Club (bd. govs. 1980-83), Navesink Country Club (bd. govs. 1983-86), Harbour Ridge Yacht and Country Club, Essex Yacht Club, Old Lyme Country Club, Chi Psi. Episcopalian. Office: Mackenzie Thompson Assocs 51 Main St Essex CT 06426-1150 also: Sweet P's LLC Griswold Sq Essex CT 06426 Office Phone: 860-767-7805. E-mail: leethompson51@sbcglobal.net.

THOMPSON, GEORGE RALPH, church administrator; b. Connell Town, Saint Lucy, Barbados, Mar. 20, 1929; s. George Gilbert and Edna (Griffith) T.; m. Imogene Clotilde Barker, July 19, 1959; children: Carol Jean, Linda Mae, Gerald Randolph. BA, Atlantic Union Coll., 1956; MA, Andrews U., 1958, BD, 1962, DDiv (hon.), 1983. Ordained to ministry Seventh-day Adventists, 1959. Evangelist South Caribbean conf. Seventh-day Adventists, Trinidad and Tobago, 1950-53; tchr., ch. pastor, chmn. dept. theology Caribbean Union Coll., Trinidad and Tobago, 1953-54, 59-64; pres. East Caribbean conf. Seventh-day Adventists, Barbados, 1964-70, pres. Caribbean Union conf., 1970-75; v.p. Gen. Conf. Seventh-day Adventists, Washington, 1975-80, sec. Silver Spring, Md., 1980-2000; field rep. Ellen G. White Estate, Gen. Conf. Seventh-day Adventists, Silver Spring, Md., 2000—. Host radio shows, Barbados. Seventh-Day Adventist. Office: Gen Conf Seventh-day Adventists Ch 12501 Old Columbia Pike Silver Spring MD 20904-6601 E-mail: ThompsonR@gc.adventist.org.

THOMPSON, GORDON, JR., federal judge; b. San Diego, Dec. 28, 1929; s. Gordon and Garnet (Meese) T.; m. Jean Peters, Mar. 17, 1951; children—John M., Peter Renwick, Gordon III. Grad., U. So. Calif., 1951, Southwestern U. Sch. Law, Los Angeles, 1956. Bar: Calif. 1956. With Dist. Atty.'s Office, County of San Diego, 1957-60; partner firm Thompson & Thompson, San Diego, 1960-70; U.S. dist. judge So. Dist. Calif., San Diego, 1970—, chief judge, 1984-91, sr. judge, 1994—. Mem. ABA, Am. Bd. Trial Advocates, San Diego County Bar Assn. (v.p. 1970), San Diego Yacht Club, Delta Chi. Office: US Dist Ct 940 Front St San Diego CA 92101-8994

THOMPSON, HERBERT ERNEST, tool and die company executive; b. Jamaica, N.Y., Sept. 8, 1923; s. Walter and Louise (Joly) T.; m. Patricia Elaine Osborn, Aug. 2, 1968; children: Robert Steven, Debra Lynn. Student, Stevens Inst. Tech., 1949-51. Foreman Conner Tool Co., 1961-62, Eason & Waller GrindingCorp., 1962-63; owner Endco Machined Products, 1966-67, Thompson Enterprises, 1974—. Pres. Method Machined Products, Phoenix, 1967; pres., owner Quality Tool, Inc., 1967-96. Served to capt. USAAF, 1942-46. Decorated DFC, Air medal with cluster. Home: 14009 N 42nd Ave Phoenix AZ 85053-5306

THOMPSON, HERBERT STANLEY, neuro-ophthalmologist; b. Shansi, China, June 12, 1932; arrived in U.S., 1949, naturalized, 1955; s. Robert Ernest and Ellen Thompson; m. Delores Lucille Johnson, June 27, 1953; children: Geoffrey, Peter, Kenneth, Philip, Susan. Student, Methodist Coll., Belfast, No. Ireland, 1947—49; BA, U. Minn., 1953, MD, 1961; MS, U. Iowa, 1966. Diplomate Am. Bd. Ophthalmology (assoc. examiner 1972-88, bd. dirs. 1989-96, chmn. ABO 1996). Intern U. Iowa, Iowa City, 1961—62, resident in ophthalmology, 1962—66; fellow in pupillography Columbia Coll. Physicians and Surgeons, 1962; fellow in clin. neuro-ophthalmology U. Calif., San Francisco, 1966—67; prof. ophthalmology U. Iowa, Iowa City, 1976—97, emeritus prof., 1997—, dir. neuro-ophthalmology unit, 1967—97; practice medicine specializing in neuro-ophthalmology Iowa City, 1967—97. Editor: Topics in Neuro-ophthalmology, 1979; assoc. editor: Am. Jour. Ophthalmology, 1981—84, book rev. editor:, 1984—91, cons.: Stedman's Med. Dictionary, 26th edit. Served with AUS, 1954-55. Recipient rsch. career devel. award, NIH, 1968—72; fellow spl. fellow, 1966—67. Fellow: N.Am. Neuro-ophthalmol. Soc., Am. Acad. Ophthalmology; mem.: Cogan Ophthalmic History Soc. (Charles Snyder lectr. 1995), Am. Ophthalmol. Soc. Avocation: research on movements of the pupil of human eye. Office: U Iowa Dept Ophthalmology Iowa City IA 52242

THOMPSON, HOLLEY MARKER, lawyer, marketing professional; b. Jamestown, NY, Jan. 30, 1947; d. Burdette James and Mary (Novitske) Marker; m. Lawrence D. Thompson; children: Jennifer Kristen Simos, Kendra Elise Blair, Jennifer Lynn, Stephanie Lynn. AAS, Jamestown C.C., 1966; BS, Ohio U., 1969; MA, W.Va. U., 1974, JD, 1980. Bar: W.Va. 1980, U.S. Dist. Ct. (so. dist.) W.Va. 1980, Pa. 1982, U.S. Dist. Ct. (we. dist.) Pa. 1982. Tchr. math. various pub. schs., Santa Ana (Calif.), Lakewood (N.Y.) and Morgantown (W.Va.), 1970-77; atty. for students W.Va. U., Morgantown, 1980; assoc. libr., lectr. W.Va. U. Coll. Law, Morgantown, 1980-83; assoc., libr. Jackson, Kelly, Holt & O'Farrell, Charleston, W.Va., 1983-86; cons. Hildebrandt, Inc., Somerville, NJ, 1986-94; sr. v.p. mktg. LexisNexis, Dayton, Ohio, 1994—. Spkr. in field. Contbr. articles to profl. jours. Mem.: ABA, Legal Mktg. Assn., N.J. Assn. Law Librs., Am. Assn. Law Librs., Spl. Libr. Assn., Phi Delta Phi. Office: LexisNexis 9443 Springboro Pike Miamisburg OH 45342 E-mail: holley.thompson@lexisnexis.com.

THOMPSON, HUGH LEE, academic administrator; b. Martinsburg, W.Va., Mar. 25, 1934; s. Frank Leslie and Althea T.; m. Patricia Smith; children: Cheri, Linda, Tempe, Vicki. BS, BA in English and Secondary Edn, Shepherd Coll., Shepherdstown, W.Va., 1956; MS, Pa. State U., 1958; PhD in Higher Edn. Adminstrn, Case Western Res. U., 1969. Mem. faculty Pa. State U., 1957-60, Akron (Ohio) U., 1960-62, Baldwin-Wallace Coll., Berea, Ohio, 1962-70, asst. to pres., 1966-69, dir. instl. planning, asst. to pres., 1969-70; coord. Associated Colls., Cleve., 1970-71; pres. Siena Heights U., Adrian, Mich., 1971-77, Detroit Inst. Tech., 1977-80; chancellor Ind. U., Kokomo, 1980-90; pres. Washburn U., Topeka, 1990-97, Higher Edn. Assocs., Cape Canaveral, Fla., 1997—; interim v.p. for acad. affairs Clarke Coll., 1999-2000. Former mem. pres.'s adv. coun. Assn. Governing Bds. Univs. and Colls.; Fulbright scholar to China, 1998, to Bulgaria, 2001, to Cyprus, 2002, to Trinidad, 2003. Mem. Am. Assn. State Colls. and Univs. (coun. of state reps., steering com. urban and met. univs. coun.), North Ctrl. Assn. (evaluator, cons.). Home and Office: 2728 Newfound Harbor Dr Merritt Island FL 32952-2866 E-mail: hughthompson@worldnet.att.net. *I have found that to be successful in any field of endeavor an individual must work very diligently at finding solutions to problems, should be highly goal oriented, honest and forthright, and adhere to the teachings of Christ.*

THOMPSON, HUGH P. state supreme court justice; b. Montezuma, Ga., July 7, 1943; married; 2 children. JD, Mercer U., 1969. Bar: Ga. 1970. Pvt. practice, Milledgeville, Ga., 1970—71; judge Recorder's Ct. of Milledgeville, 1971—79, Baldwin County Ct., 1973—78, Superior Ct. of Ga., 1979—94; chief judge Ocmulgee Jud. Cir., 1987—94; assoc. justice Supreme Ct. of Ga., Atlanta, 1994—. Instr. bus. law Ga. Coll., 1971—72; pres. Coun. Superior Ct. Judges, 1993—94. Communicant St. Stephen's Episcopal Ch. Named Outstanding Young Man of Baldwin County, 1972; recipient Disting. Svc. award, Baldwin County Jaycees, 1972, Outstanding Alumnus award, Mercer U. Law Sch., 1994, Disting. Svc. award, Ga. Coll. and State U., 2002. Mem.: ABA, Ga. Bar Found., State Bar Ga., Charles Longstreet Weltner Family Law Inn of Ct., Old War Horse Lawyers Club, Lawyers Club Atlanta. Avocations: hunting, gardening, golf, fishing. Office: Supreme Ct Ga State Judicial Bldg 244 Washington St SW Rm 572 Atlanta GA 30334-9007

THOMPSON, HUNTER STOCKTON, author, political analyst, journalist; b. Louisville, July 18, 1937; s. Jack R. and Virginia (Ray) T.; m. Anita Thompson; 1 child, Juan. Carribean corr. N.Y. Herald Tribune, 1959—60; South Am. corr. Nat. Observer, 1961—63; West Coast corr. The Nation, 1964—66; columnist Ramparts, 1967—68, Scanlan's, 1969—70; nat. affairs editor Rolling Stone, 1970—99; global affairs corr. High Times, 1977—82; political columnist San Francisco Examiner, 1985—89; polit. analyst European mags. London Observer, Tempo, Time Out, Das Magazine, Nieuwe Revu, Die Woche, 1988—; "Hey Rube!" columnist ESPN.com, 2000—. Conbr. U.S. pubs. including Time, New Yorker, Esquire, Vanity Fair, men's Health, GQ, Cycle World, Smart, Lexis.com; creative cons. CBS-TV series "Nash Bridges", 1996—2000; screenplay adaptation cons. Where the Buffalo Roam, 1980, Fear & Loathing in Las Vegas, 1998, The Rum Diary; song lyricist music by Warren Zevon, Paul Oakenfold, 2001; judge Nat. Book Awards, 1975. Author: Prince Jellyfish, 1960, Hell's Angels, 1966, Fear and Loathing in Las Vegas, 1972, Fear and Loathing On the Campaign Trail '72, 1973, The Great Shark Hunt, 1979, (with Ralph Steadman) The Curse of Lono, 1983, Generation of Swine, 1988, Songs of the Doomed, 1990, Screwjack, 1991, Better Than Sex, 1993, The Proud Highway, 1997, The Rum Diary, 1998, Fear and Loathing in America, 2000, Kingdom of Fear, 2002; creator Gonzo journalism. Mem. pres.'s task force; mem. nat. adv. bd. Nat. Orgn. for the Reform of Marijuana Laws, 1976—; founder 4th Amendment Found. Recipient Literary Lion award, N.Y. Pub. Libr., 1989. Mem. NRA, ACLU, Athenaeum Lit. Assn., U.S. Naval Inst., Air Force Assn., Hong Kong Fgn. Corrs., Kona Coast Marlin Fisherman's Assn., Vincent Black Shadow Soc., Woody Creek Rod and Gun Club (exec. dir.), Overseas Press Club, Nat. Press Club, Bengal Snow Leopard Breeders, Castlewood A.C. Club, Key West Mako Club.

THOMPSON, JACK EDWARD, mining company executive; b. Central City, Nebr., Nov. 17, 1924; s. Ray Elbert and Bessie Fay (Davis) T.; m. Maria del Carmen Larrea, May 8, 1948; children: Jack Edward, Ray Anthony, Robert Davis. Student, Northwestern U., 1942-43, Colo. Sch. Mines, 1943-45, D of Engring. (hon.), 1993. V.p. Cía. Química Comercial de Cuba S.A., 1946-60, Cía. de Fomento Químico S.A., 1946-60; with Newmont Mining Corp., N.Y.C., 1960-86, asst. to pres., 1964-67, v.p., 1967-71, dir., 1969-86, exec. v.p., 1971-74, pres., 1974-85, vice chmn., 1985-86, cons., 1986-90. Chmn. bd. trustees Minerals Industry Ednl. Found. Recipient Distinguished Achievement medal Colo. Sch. Mines, 1974 Mem. AIME, Mining and Metall. Soc. Am., Mining Found. of S.W. (past pres., bd. govs.), Tucson Country Club. E-mail: rayonera@aol.com.

THOMPSON, JAMES CHARLES, surgeon; b. San Antonio, Aug. 16, 1928; s. Oscar Augustus and Vera Marie (Powell) T.; children: Patricia A., Jan L. Thompson Brown, Gayle A. Thompson Crocker, James Charles, John W.; 1 stepchild, Laura V. Fargas. BS, A&M Coll. Tex., 1948; MD, U. Tex. Med. Br., Galveston, 1951, MA in Anatomy and Endocrinology, 1952; MD (hon.), U. Lund, Sweden, 2000. Diplomate Am. Bd. Surgery (examiner 1978—93). Intern U. Tex. Med. Br. Hosps., Galveston, 1951-52, chief of surgery, 1970-95, prof., chmn. dept. surgery, 1970-87, prof. physiology and biophysics, 1975—, John Woods Harris prof., chmn., 1987-95, Ashbel Smith prof. surgery, 1995—; resident in surgery U. Pa. Hosp., Phila., 1952-54, 56-59; assoc. in surgery Sch. Medicine U. Pa., Phila., 1959-61, asst. prof. surgery Sch. Medicine, 1961-63; surgeon Pa. Hosp., Phila., 1959-63, Harbor Gen. Hosp., Torrance, Calif., 1963-67, chief of surgery, 1967-70; assoc. prof. UCLA, 1963-67, prof., 1967-70. U.S.-USSR health exchange prof., 1973; vis. prof. China Acad. Medicine, 1980, 82, 86, 90; cons. FDA, 1983-86; hon. prof. for life U. Beijing, 1991; elected mem., Inst. Medicine, 2000. Author: Atlas of Surgery and the Stomach, Duodenum and Small Bowel, 1991; also numerous articles on gastrointestinal physiology and clin. surgery in profl. jours.; editor: Gastrointestinal Hormones, 1975; sr. editor: Gastrointestinal Endocrinology, 1987, Gastrointestinal Hormones: Receptors and Post-Receptor Mechanism, 1990. Served with M.C. U.S. Army, 1954-56. Recipient Career Devel. award NIH, 1961-62, Merit award, 1986; Outstanding Clin. Prof. award U. Tex. Med. Br., 1973, Herman Barnett award, 1975, Ashbel Smith Disting. Alumnus award, 1979; NIH grantee, 1960—97, program-project grantee, 1985—97, John A. Hartford Found. grantee, 1963-73, 77-81. Fellow ACS (chmn. surg. forum com. 1977-78, bd. govs. 1985-91, exec. com. of program com. 1985-94, scholarship com. 1988-94, chmn. com. on rsch. and edn. 1989-94, pres. 1999-2000, Disting. Svc. award 1996), Royal Coll. Surgeons (hon.); mem. AAAS, Am. Philos. Soc., Am. Assn. Surgery of Trauma, Am. Fedn. Clin. Rsch., Am. Gastroenterol. Assn., Am. Physiol. Soc., Am. Surg. Assn. (treas. 1985-90, pres. 1991-92), Endocrine Soc., Pacific Coast Surg. Assn., Soc. for Surgery Alimentary Tract (pres. 1982-83, Founder's medal 1990), Soc. Univ. Surgeons (chmn. com. on edn., mem. exec. coun. 1967-71), So. Surg. Assn. (pres. 1995), Tex. Surg. Soc. (pres. 1993), Surg. Biology Club, Soc. Surg. Chmn. (pres. 1993-94), Transplantation Soc., Soc. Gastroenterology Chile (hon.), Hungarian Soc. Gastroenterology (hon.), Japan Surg Soc. (hon.), German Surg. Soc. (hon.), Cosmos Club, Alpha Omega Alpha. Office: U Tex Med Br Dept Surgery Galveston TX 77555-0001

THOMPSON, JAMES HOWARD, historian, library administrator; b. Memphis, Aug. 20, 1934; s. Curtis Barnabas and Clara (Terry) T.; m. Margareta Ortenblad, Nov. 24, 1961; children— Ralph, Anna, Howard. BA in History, Rhodes Coll., Memphis, 1955; MA, U. N.C., Chapel Hill, 1957, PhD in History, 1961; MS in LS, U. Ill., 1963. Teaching fellow U. N.C., Chapel Hill, 1955-56, departmental asst., 1956-57, reference asst., 1959-61, dir. undergrad. library, lectr. in history, 1968-70; circulation asst. U. Ill., 1961-63; asst. Center for Russian Area and Lang. Studies, 1962-63; cataloger Duke U., 1963-65; asst. prof. history U. S.W. La., 1965-66; asst. prof. U. Colo., 1966-68; dir. libraries, prof. history U. N.C., Greensboro, 1970-94; ret., 1994. Bd. dirs. Southeastern Library Network, 1979-82, treas., 1981-82 Contbr. articles, revs. to profl. jours. Ford Found. research fellow, 1957-58; U. Colo. grantee, 1967; U. N.C. at Greensboro grantee, 1977-78, 89. Mem. Phi Beta Kappa (chpt. pres. 1979-80), Beta Phi Mu, Phi Alpha Theta, Chi Beta Phi. Episcopalian. Home: 4020 Crown Hill Dr Durham NC 27707-5393

THOMPSON, JAMES LEE, lawyer; b. L.I., N.Y., Sept. 9, 1941; s. Robert Luther and Marjorie Emma (Jones) T.; m. Diana Dill Stevenson, June 29, 1963; children: James C., Thomas J. BA, Yale U., 1963; JD, U. Va., 1966. Bar: Va. 1966, Md. 1966, U.S. Ct. Mil. Appeals 1968, U.S. Dist. Ct. Md. 1972, U.S. Supreme Ct. 1978. Ptnr. Miller & Canby, Rockville, Md., 1970—, head litigation, 1975—. Mem. jud. conf. U.S. Ct. Appeals (4th cir.). Mem. Thousand Acres Assn., Deep Creek Lake, Md., 1985-87. Capt. JAGC, USMC, 1966-70. Decorated D.S.M. Fellow Am. Coll. Trial Lawyers; mem. ABA, Md. State Bar Assn. (bd. govs. 1975, 78, 79, 83, 89, 94, sec. 1995, pres. 1999-00), Montgomery County Bar Assn. (pres. 1987-88, Cert. of Merit 1985), Nat. Conf. Bar Pres., Md. Bar Found., Montgomery County Bar Found. (pres. 1988-89), Loophole Club (pres. 1978-79), Phi Delta Phi. Democrat. Episcopalian. Avocations: sailing, skiing, tennis, golf, gardening. Home: 419 Russell Ave Apt 110 Gaithersburg MD 20877-2836 Office: Miller & Canby 200 Monroe St Ste B Rockville MD 20850-4423

THOMPSON, JAMES NICHOLAS, medical association administrator; b. Cin., Oct. 20, 1944; m. Carol Washburn; children: Carrie, David, Victoria, Deborah. BA, DePauw U., 1966; MD, Ohio State U., 1971. Lic. otolaryngologist NC, diplomate Am. Bd. Otolaryngology. Intern Mercy Hosp., Pitts., 1971—72, resident in gen. surgery, 1972—73, resident in otolaryngology, 1973—76; fellow in otolaryngology U. Calif., Irvine, 1976—77; asst. prof. surg. scis., otolaryngology Bowman Gray Sch Medicine, Winston-Salem, NC, 1979—81, assoc. prof. surg. scis., otolaryngology, 1981—88, dep. assoc. dean, 1986—87, assoc. dean, 1987—94, prof. surg. scis., otolaryngology, 1988—2002, assoc. sports medicine, 1989—2002, assoc. pediat., 1991—2002, dean, 1994—97; v.p., dean Wake Forest U. Sch. Medicine, 1997—2001, spl. adv. to exec. v.p. for health affairs, 2001—02, dean emeritus, 2002—, prof. emeritus, 2002—; pres., CEO Fedn. of State Med. Bds. of U.S., Inc., Dallas, 2002—. Libr. and learning resources com. Wake Forest U. Sch. Medicine, 1981—82, clin. skills workshops and rev., 1982, 84, admissions and pre-med. rels. com., 1984—86, clin. faculty adv. coun., 1985—2001, chair dept. clinics computer adv. com., 1985—87, faculty exec. coun., 1986—2002, vice chair, 1993—94, chair, 1994—2001, clin. svcs. coord. com., 1988—89, chair clin. scis. bldg. com., 1988; profl. ins. com. Risk and Ins. Mgmt. Adv. Coun., 1989—2001, affirmative action com., 1990—2001, 50th anniversary com., 1990—91, compliance com., 1999—2001; acad. coun. Wake Forest U., 1987, adminstrv. coun., 87, affirmative action com., 90, long range planning standing com., 93, intra-univ. ops. com., 2001, exec. coun., 1994, univ. ofcl. for animal care, 97, audit and compliance com., 99; clin. prof. otolaryngology U. Tex. S.W. Med. Ctr., Dallas, 2002; composite com. U.S. Med. Licensing Exam., 2002—, budget com., 2002—. Contbr. chapters to books, articles to profl. jours. Chair med. adv. com. Wake Forest U. Sch. Medicine/VA Med. Ctr., Salisbury, NC, 1995—2001; med. audit/utilization rev. com. NC Bapt. Hosp., 1982—84, capital equipment com., 1984—92, chiefs of profl. svcs. com., 1984—2001; bd. trustees The Med. Found., 1984—2001, Wake Forest Sch. Medicine, 1984—2001, NC Bapt. Hosp., 1984—2001, Arts Coun. Winston-Salem and Forsyth County, 1992; bd. visitors Wake Forest U. Bapt. Med. Ctr., 1997—2001; internat. med. edn. cons. to China China Med. Bd. N.Y., Inc., 2000; bd. govs. Bermuda Run Country Club, 1982—84; disting. citizens dinner steering com. Old Hickory Coun. Boy Scouts Am., 1994, 1997, 2000; indsl. devel. and econ. authority City of Winston-Salem, 1998—99; mem. planning com. Crosby Golf Classic, Bermuda Run, NC, 1987; bd. advisors Here's Life Winston-Salem, 1985—87; corp. recruitment chair Juvenile Diabetes Found. Winston-Salem, 2000; mem. Leadship Winston-Salem, 1987—88, health and human svc. day com., 1988—89, co-chair health and human svc. day com., 1991—92; dinner of champions com. Nat. Multiple Sclerosis Soc., Ctrl. NC chpt., 1999; campaign coord. surgery dept., otolaryngology sect. United Way Forsyth County, 1983—84, mem. med. ctr. com., 1987, health care campaign divsn. chair, 1989, vice chmn. divsn. III, 1992, mem. campaign cabinet, 1997—99, cmty. chair Forsyth County Cmty. Campaign, 2001—02, bd. dirs. Forsyth County, 2001—02; bd. dirs. Forsyth County Day Sch., 1987—90, Greater Winston-Salem C. of C., 1995—97. Served with USAR, 1972—78. Mem.: Tex. Med. Assn., Dallas County Med. Soc., Am. Acad. Med. Ethics, Am. Coll. Physician Execs., Am. Acad. Med. Dirs., Am. Laryngological, Rhinological and Otological Soc., Am. Acad. Otolaryngology, Head and Neck Surgery, So. Med. Assn., Christian Soc. Otolaryngology, Head and Neck Surgeons, Christian Med. and Dental Assns., Bapt. Med./Dental Fellowship. Office: Fedn State Med Bds of the US Inc PO Box 619850 Dallas TX 75261-9850 Office Phone: 817-868-4000. E-mail: jthompson@fsmb.org.

THOMPSON, JAMES ROBERT, JR., lawyer, former governor; b. Chgo., May 8, 1936; s. James Robert and Agnes Josephine (Swanson) T.; m. Jayne Carr, 1976; 1 child, Samantha Jayne. Student, U. Ill., Chgo., 1953-55, Washington U., St. Louis, 1955-56; JD, Northwestern U., 1959. Bar: Ill. 1959, U.S. Supreme Ct. 1964. Asst. state's atty., Cook County, Ill., 1959-64; assoc. prof. law Northwestern U. Law Sch., 1964-69; asst. atty. gen. State of Ill., 1969-70; chief criminal div., 1969; chief dept. law enforcement and pub. protection, 1969-70; 1st asst. U.S. atty. No. Dist. Ill., 1970-71, U.S. atty., 1971-75; counsel firm Winston & Strawn, Chgo., 1975-77, ptnr., chmn., 1991—; gov. Ill., 1977-91. Chmn. Pres.' Intelligence Oversight Bd., 1989—93; adv. bd. Fed. Emergency Mgmt. Agy., 1991—93; bd. govs. Chgo. Bd. Trade; bd. dirs. FMC Corp., FMC Techs., Inc., Hollinger Internat., Inc., Navigant Cons. Inc., Maximus, Inc., Chgo. Mus. Contemporary Art, Lyric Opera Chgo., Econ. Club Chgo., Civic Com., Comml. Club Chgo. Co-author: Cases and Comments on Criminal Justice, 1974, Criminal Law and Its Adminstration. Chmn. Rep. Govs. Assn., 1982, Nat. Govs. Assn., Midwest Govs. Assn., Coun. Gt. Lakes Govs., 1985; mem. Nat. Commn. on Terrorist Attacks Upon the U.S., 2002—; mem. Abraham Lincoln Bicentennial Commn., 2000—. Mem. ABA, Ill. Bar Assn., Chgo. Bar Assn. Republican. Office: Winston & Strawn 35 W Wacker Dr Ste 4200 Chicago IL 60601-1695

THOMPSON, JAMES W., JR., state official; b. Sidney, Ohio, Feb. 7, 1948; s. James and Margret Louise (Mote) T.; m. Virginia Ann Wilcoxen, June 11, 1976; 1 child, James W. AAS, Lima (Ohio) Tech. Coll., 1978; student, Wittenberg U., Springfield, Ohio, 1973; grad., FBI Nat. Acad., 1981. Dep. sheriff Shelby County Sheriff's Dept., Sidney, Ohio, 1972-75, chief dep., 1976-83; chief of police Botkins (Ohio) Police Dept., 1975-76; chief criminal investigations Ohio Dept. Agr., Columbus, 1983-88; chief investigator Ohio Vet. Med. Bd., Columbus, 1988—2000; exec. dir. Shelby Co. ARC, 2000—02; mgr. No. Miami Valley ARC, 2002—. Disaster svcs. coordinator Ohio Dept. Agr., 1983-88. Charter, mem., v.p., co-founder Ohio Coun. on Welfare Fraud, Columbus, 1988-89; pres. Botkins Village Coun., 1989, 94, 95; councilman, 1986-90, 92-96; pres. Botkins Pub. Libr., 1989-93; mem. Shelby County Regional Planning Commn., 1988-93; bd. dirs. Shelby County Red Cross. With USN, 1968-72. Recipient Combat Action ribbon USN, 1969, Legion of Valor award, Buckeye State Sheriff's Assn., 1977; Disting. Pub. Svc. Hon., Am. Police Officers Hall of Fame, 1980. Mem. FBI Assn., Masons. Democrat. Avocations: reading, photography, bird watching, antiques, book plate collecting. Home: PO Box 474 Botkins OH 45306-0474 Office: 207 W Water Sidney OH 45365

THOMPSON, JAMES WILLIAM, lawyer; b. Dallas, Oct. 22, 1936; s. John Charles and Frances (Van Slyke) Thompson; m. Marie Hertz, June 26, 1965 (dec. 1965); children: Elizabeth, Margaret, John; m. Linda Ball Dozier, May 2, 1998. BS, U. Mont., 1958, JD, 1962. Bar: Mont. 1962; CPA, Mont. Acct. Arthur Young & Co., NYC, 1959; instr. bus. adminstrn. Ea. Mont. Coll., Billings, 1959-60, U. Mont., Missoula, 1960-61; assoc. Cooke, Moulton, Bellingham & Longo, Billings, 1962-64, James R. Felt, Billings, 1964-65; asst. atty. City of Billings, 1963-64, atty., 1964-66; ptnr. Felt, Speare & Thompson, Billings, 1966-72, McNamer, Thompson & Cashmore, 1973-86, McNamer & Thompson Law Firm PC, 1986-89, McNamer, Thompson, Werner & Stanley, P.C., 1990-93, McNamer Thompson Law Firm PC, 1993-98, Wright Tolliver Guthals Law Firm PC, Billings, Mont., 1999—2003, Guthals Hunnes Reuss Thompson PC, Billings, 2004—. Bd. dirs. Associated Employers of Mont., Inc., 1989—98; mem. adv. coun. Sch. Fine Arts, U. Mont., 1997—2001. Mem. Billings Zoning Commn., 1966—69; v.p. Billings Cmty. Action Program (now Dist. 7 Human Resources Devel. Coun.), 1968—70, pres., 1970—75, bd. trustees, 1975—; mem. Yellowstone County Legal Svcs. Bd., 1969—70, City-County Air Pollution Control Bd., 1969—70; pres. Billings Symphony Soc., 1970—71; bd. dirs. Billings Studio Theater, 1967—73, United Way Billings, 1973—81, Mont. Inst. Arts Found., 1986—89, Downtown Billings Assn., 1986—90, Billings Area Bus. Incubator, Inc., 1991—94, Found. of Mont. State U, Billings, 1992—98, Our Mont., Inc., 1997—, pres., 2000—; bd. dirs. Rimrock Opera Co., 1998—2004, treas., 1998—2002; mem. Billings Transit Commn., 1971—73, City Devel. Agy., 1972—73; Diocesan Exec. Coun., 1972—75. Mem. ABA, Am. Acad. Estate Planning Attys., Nat. Acad. Elder Law Attys., State Bar Mont., Yellowstone Area Bar Assn. (bd. dirs. 1983-87, pres. 1985-86), Elks, Kiwanis (pres. Yellowstone chpt. 1974-75), Sigma Chi (pres. Billings alumni assn. 1963-65). Episcopalian. Home: 123 Lewis Ave Billings MT 59101-6034 Office: 10 N 27th St PO Box 1977 Billings MT 59103-1977 Office Phone: 406-245-3071. Personal E-mail: jwtldt@aol.com.

THOMPSON, JAYNE CARR, public relations and communications executive, lawyer; b. Oak Park, Ill., Apr. 7, 1946; d. Robert Edward and Laurette (Rentner) Carr; m. James R. Thompson, June 19, 1976; 1 child, Samantha Jayne. BA, U. Ill., Chgo., 1967; JD, Northwestern U., 1970; degree (hon.), Lincoln (Ill.) Coll., 1990, St. Xavier U., Chgo., 1995, Ill. Coll., 1995. Assoc. in litigation McDermott, Will & Emery, Chgo., 1970; asst. atty. gen. State of Ill., Chgo., 1970-77, chief of criminal appeals divsn., 1972-77, dep. chief prosecution assistance bur., 1975-76, dep. chief criminal divsn., 1976-77, acting chief criminal divsn., 1977; of counsel Brown, Hay & Stephens, Springfield, Ill., 1977-78, Silets & Martin, Chgo., 1983-84; house counsel and v.p. devel. Nat. Coll. Edn., Evanston, Ill., 1984-85; atty. Lydon & Griffin, Chgo., 1989-91; prin. Dilenschneider Group Inc., Chgo., 1999-2000, mng. prin., 2000—02; CEO, pres. Jayne Thompson and Assocs. Ltd., 2002—.

Contbr. chpt. to book, articles to profl. jours. First Lady of Ill., Springfield, 1977-91; mem. Ill. Commn. on Status of Women, 1997-2001; pres. bd. dirs. Chgo. Pub. Libr., 1998—; mem. women's bd. Northwestern U., 1978—; bd. dirs. Chgo. Pub. Libr. Found., 1998—; mem. adv. bd. for Ill. Treas. for Women's Issues, 2002—; mem. chmn.'s adv. coun. Lincoln Pk. Zoo, 2002—; mem. Met. Planning Coun., 2002--. Mem. Ill. State Bar Assn., Execs. Club (Chgo.), Coun. on Fgn. Rels. (Chgo. com.), Econ. Club (Chgo.). Avocations: reading, cooking, tennis. Office: Jayne Thompson & Assocs Ltd 33 N Dearborn St Ste 2200 Chicago IL 60602 E-mail: jthompson@jaynethompson.com.

THOMPSON, JEAN TANNER, retired librarian; b. San Luis Obispo, Calif., June 15, 1929; d. Chester Corey and Mildred (Orr) T.; 1 child, Anne Marie Miller Student, Whitworth Coll., Spokane, Wash., 1946-49; AB, Boston U., 1951; postgrad., U. Wis., Eau Claire, 1964-67; MSL.S., Columbia U., 1973; Ed.M., U. Va., Charlottesville, 1978. Asst. social sci. librarian Univ. Libraries Va. Polytechnic Inst. and State U., Blacksburg, 1973-77, head social sci. dept. Univ. Libraries, 1977-83; head reference dept. Meml. Library U. Wis., Madison, 1983-86, asst. dir. reference and info. svcs., 1986-91, ret. Contbg. editor: ALA Guide to Information Access, 1994; mem. editorial bd. RQ, 1984-89. Mem. ALA, Assn. Coll. and Research Libraries (edn. and behavioral sci. sect. vice chmn. 1985-86, chmn. 1986-87), Wis. Library Assn., Wis. Assn. of Acad. Librarians. Presbyterian. Home: 4929 High Grove Rd Tallahassee FL 32309-2957

THOMPSON, JENNIFER B. Olympic swimmer; b. Dover, N.H., Feb. 26, 1973; B.S. in Human Bio., Stanford Univ., 1995; student in Med. Sch., Columbia U. Mem. U.S. Olympic Swim Team, Barcelona, 1992, Atlanta, 1996, Sydney, 2000, Athens, 2004. Active Swim Across Am. Named Sportswoman of Yr., Women's Sports Found., 2000, Swimmer of Yr., USA Swimming, 1993, 1998, 10-time USA Swimming All-Star; recipient Spring Nationals Kiphuth award, 1993, Performance of Yr. award, USA Swimming, 1999. Achievements include being the most decorated olympic female athlete in U.S. history; Gold Medal, 4x100m medley relay, 4x100m free relay, Olympic Games, 1992, 1996, 2000, 4x200m free relay, 1996, 2000; 8 career Olympic Gold medals, 3 Silver, 1 Bronze; World Champion, 4x100m free relay, World Championships, 1991, 1998, 2003, 4x100m medley relay, 1991, 1998, 100m butterfly, 1998, 2003, 100m free, 1998; 36 career Pan Pacific titles; 26 U.S. National titles.*

THOMPSON, JEREMIAH BEISEKER, international medical business executive, sinologist; b. Harvey, ND, July 20, 1927; s. Linden Brown and Ferne Althea (Beiseker) T.; m. Paula Maria Ketchum, Feb. 5, 1960; children: Cole, Per, Gover, Susannah. BS, U. Minn., 1949, MD, 1966. Rsch. assoc. U. Colo. Med. Sch., Denver, 1955-56, U. Calif. Med. Sch., San Francisco, 1956-57, Stanford U., 1957-59; applications rsch. scientist Beckman/Spinco Co., Palo Alto, Calif., 1959-61; mgr. Asia and Africa Hewlett Packard Co., Palo Alto, 1966-72; med. cons. Alyeska Co., Anchorage, 1973-76; mgr. Asia, Africa, Australasia Corometrics Med. Systems, Wallingford, Conn., 1976-82; dir. internat. ops. Oximetrix (Abbott), Mountain View, Calif., 1982-84, Novametrix Med. Systems, Wallingford, 1984-88; ptnr. TMC Internat., Tokyo and Concord, Calif., 1988—. Advisor, cons. Yokogawa-Hewlett Packard, Tokyo, 1966—70; cons. Kupat Holim, Tel Aviv, 1967—92, Itochu, Tokyo, 1984—2002, Nat. Heart-Lung Inst., Beijing, 1984—2002. Project dir. Comparative Study of Western and Japanese Medicine in Taisho and Showa Eras, 1991—. With USN, 1945-46; PTO. Officer Legion of Honor, France, 1998. Founding fellow Brit. Interplanetary Soc.; assoc. Japan Found., Assn. Asian Studies; mem. Kokusai Bunka Kaikan, Tokyo, World Affairs Coun., Mechanics Inst. Achievements include cancer research, joint Japan/U.S. project screening and evaluation for anti-cancer activity of halogenated methane derivatives, augmentation of irradiation effects by chemotherapy. Home and Office: TMC Internat 3718 Barrington Dr Concord CA 94518-1614 E-mail: tjbeiseker@astound.net.

THOMPSON, JESSE ELDON, vascular surgeon; b. Laredo, Tex., Apr. 7, 1919; s. Jesse Eathel and Sara Gail (Bolton) T.; m. Madeleine Jane Curtis, Sept. 18, 1944; children: Sally C., Jesse E., Janet E., Diane B. BA, U. Tex., 1939; MD, Harvard U., 1943; Rhodes scholar, Oxford U., 1949-50. Intern Mass. Gen. Hosp., Boston, 1943, resident in surgery, 1944-48; practice medicine specializing in surgery, tchr. surgery Boston U., 1949-54; practice medicine specializing in surgery, tchr. vascular surgery Baylor Hosp., Dallas, 1954—, chief vascular surgery, 1980-86. Clin. prof. surgery U. Tex. Southwestern Med. Sch., Dallas; attending surgeon Baylor Hosp., 1954-92, hon. surgeon, 1992—, chief surgery Baylor Hosp., Dallas, 1982-86; Mem Ark. and Dist. Rhodes Scholar Selection Coms. Author: Surgery for Cerebrovascular Insufficiency, 1968; mem. editl. bd. Surgery, 1975-89, Jour. Cardiovasc. Surgery, 1975—; sr. editor Jour. Vascular Surgery, 1984-86; contbr. over 200 articles to profl. jours. Served to capt. M.C. AUS, 1945-47. Fulbright sr. fellow, 1949-50 Fellow ACS (treas., pres. N. Tex. chpt. 1961); mem. Am. Surg. Assn., So. Surg. Assn., Tex. Surg. Soc. (pres. 1972), Soc. Vascular Surgery (pres. 1977), Internat. Cardiovascular Soc. (pres. N.Am. chpt. 1973), Internat. Soc. Surgery, So. Assn. for Vascular Surgery (pres. 1986-87), Dallas Country Club, Dallas Petroleum Club. Methodist. Home: 3705 Stanford Ave Dallas TX 75225-7204

THOMPSON, JILL LYNETTE LONG, federal agency administrator, former congresswoman; b. Warsaw, Ind., July 15, 1952; BS, Valparaiso U., 1974; MBA, Ind. U., 1978, PhD, 1984. Mgmt. cons. Campbell and Pryor, 1985-86; mem. 101st-103rd Congresses from 4th Ind. dist., 1989-95; mem. agrl. com.; mem. vets. affairs com.; under sec. for rural development USDA, 1995—. Asst. instr., lectr. Indiana U., Bloomington; adj. prof. Indiana U.-Purdue U. Ft. Wayne,; asst. prof. Valparaiso U. Councilwoman City of Valparaiso, Ind., 1984; chair Congrl. Rural Congress. Democrat. Methodist. Office: FSA State Office 101 SW Main St Stee 1300 Portland OR 97204-3221

THOMPSON, JOE D. physicist; BS in Physics, 1969, PhD in Physics, 1975. Postdoctoral Cryogenics Group Los Alamos Nat. Lab., N.Mex., 1975—77, tech. staff mem. Condensed Matter and Thermal Physics Group, 1977—2001, dep. group leader, 1989—92, group leader, 1992—2001, Lab. fellow, 2001—. Office: Los Alamos Nat Lab PO Box 1663 Los Alamos NM 87545

THOMPSON, JOE FLOYD, aerospace engineer, researcher; b. Grenada, Miss., Apr. 13, 1939; s. Joe Floyd and Bernice Thompson; m. Emilie Kay Wilson, June 1, 1974; children: Mardi, Douglass. BS, Miss. State U., 1961, MS, 1963; PhD, Ga. Tech., 1971. Aerospace engr. NASA Marshall, Huntsville, Ala., 1963-64; prof. Miss. State U., Starkville, 1964—. Disting. prof. aerospace engring., 1995—. Mem. tech. rev. bd. Army Rsch. Lab., Adelphi, Md., 1993-95; dir. computer code Nat. Grid Project 1993-96; dir. NSF Engring. Rsch. Ctr. for Computational Field Simulation, 1990-95; dir. acad. team Dept. of Def. Cewes Major Shared Resource Ctr., 1996—; mem. Pres.'s Info. Tech. Adv. Com., 1997—. Author: Numerical Grid Generation, 1985, (computer code) Eagle Grid System, 1987; sr. assoc. editor Applied Math. and Computation, 1985-94; assoc. editor Numerical Heat Transfer, 1989—; mem. edit. bd. Computational Fluid Dynamics Jour., 1993—, Jour. Computational Physics, 1995—. Recipient Commdr.'s award Army Waterways Exp. Sta., Vicksburg, Miss., 1992. Mem. IEEE Computer Soc., AIAA (Aerodynamics award 1992), Assn. for Computing Machinery. Presbyterian. Achievements include establishment of NSF Engineering Research Center; pioneering work in field of numerical grid generation; led academic team in winning competition for programming environment and training support at three of the four Dept. of Defense Major Shared Resource Center. Home: Miss State U PO Box 255 Mississippi State MS 39762-0255 Office: Miss State U PO Box 9627 Mississippi State MS 39762

THOMPSON, JOEL ERIK, lawyer; b. Summit, NJ, Sept. 15, 1940; s. Maurice Eugene and Charlotte Ruth (Harrington) T.; m. Bonnie Gay Ransa, June 15, 1963 (div. Dec. 1980); m. Deborah Ann Korp, Dec. 24, 1980 (div. Jan. 1987); children: Janice Santiesteban, Amber; m. Shandae EmLaw, Apr. 21, 2002. Student, Va. Poly. Inst., 1958, Carnegie Inst. Tech., 1960-61; BSME cum laude, Newark Coll. Engring., 1966; JD, Seton Hall, 1970. Bar: N.J. 1970, Ariz. 1975, U.S. Tax Ct. 1972, U.S. Ct. Claims 1972, U.S. Customs Ct., 1972, U.S. Ct. Mil. Appeals, 1972, U.S. Ct. Customs and Patent Appeals 1972, U.S. Dist. Ct. N.J. 1970, Ariz. 1975, U.S. Ct. Appeals (9th cir.) 1975, U.S. Supreme Ct. 1975; cert. specialist criminal law Ariz. Bd. Legal Specialization; lic. profl. engr., N.J. Sr. technician Bell Tel. Labs., Inc., Murray Hill, N.J., 1965-67, patent agent, 1967-70, staff atty., 1970-73; sr. trial atty. N.J. Pub. Defender's Office, Elizabeth, N.J., 1973-74; assoc. Cahill, Sutton and Thomas, Phoenix, 1974-76; trial lawyer Maricopa County Pub. Defender's Office, Phoenix, 1976-80; trial lawyer, criminal law specialist Henry J. Florence, Ltd., Phoenix, 1980-86; pvt. practice Phoenix, 1987—. Judge Superior Ct. Ariz., Phoenix, 1987-95; instr. Phoenix Regional Police Acad., 1976-80, Glendale C.C., 1977, Ariz. State U. Sch. Law, 1978, Am. Inst., 1990; pres., CEO Eagle Master Corp., Phoenix, 1995—; pres. Joel Erik Thompson, Ltd., Phoenix, 1987—; bd. dirs. Am. Loans, Inc., San Diego; presenter in field. Contbr. articles to profl. jours. Mem. planning com. Camelback East Village, Phoenix, 1992-98, chmn., 1993-96; mayor's select com., Phoenix, 1997, blue ribbon com. Maricopa Assn. Govs., 1996-97. Mem. Ariz. Bar Assn., Nat. Assn. Criminal Def. Lawyers, Ariz. Attys. Criminal Justice (charter), Ariz. Assn. Pvt. Investigators (hon.), Internat. Assn. Identification (hon.), Tau Beta Pi, Pi Tau Sigma. Office: 3104 E Camelback Rd # 521 Phoenix AZ 85016-4502 E-mail: joel.thompson@azbar.org.

THOMPSON, JOHN ALBERT, JR., dermatologist; b. Austin, Tex., June 5, 1942; s. J. Albert Sr. and Elizabeth (Brady) T. BA, Georgetown U., 1963; MD, Bowman Gray Sch. Medicine, 1967; Dermatology Fellowship, U. N.C., 1971-73. Diplomate Am. Bd. Dermatology. Resident in internal medicine N.C. Baptist Hosp., Winston-Salem, N.C., 1967-69; resident in dermatology N.C. Meml. Hosp., Chapel Hill, N.C., 1971-73; pvt. practice Charlotte, N.C., 1974—; clin. prof. dermatology Dept. Dermatology, U. N.C. Sch. Medicine, Chapel Hill, 1974—. Author profl. papers. Lt. comdr. USNR, 1969-71, Vietnam. Mem. Am. Acad. Dermatology (chmn. subcom. for sch. health edn. 1976-79, task force--nat. health ins.), Carolinas-Va. Dermatology Assn. (adv. bd. council rep. 1976-79), Charlotte Dermatology Assn., Mecklenburg County Med. Soc., N.C. Med. Soc., North Am. Clin. Dermatology Soc. Southern Med. Assn., Southeastern Consortium for Continuing Dermatol. Edn. (steering com. 1983—), South Cen. Dermatol. Congress (organizing com. 1982-86), Am. Soc. Dermatol. Surgery, Am. Dermatol. Soc. Allergy and Immunology, Am. Soc. Laser Medicine and Surgery, Inc. Democrat. Episcopalian. Home: 2633 Richardson Dr Apt 8A Charlotte NC 28211-3346 Office: Dermatol Laser Ctr Dermatologic Laser Ctr 2310 Randolph Rd Charlotte NC 28207-1526 Office Phone: 704-376-9849.

THOMPSON, JOHN DOUGLAS, financier; b. Montreal, Quebec, Canada, Sept. 28, 1934; s. William Douglas and Anne F. (Whebby) T.; children: Jacqueline, Catherine, Peter, Anne Marie, Francois. B, McGill U., 1957; MBA, U. Western Ont., Can., 1960. Dep. chmn. bd. Montreal Trustco Inc. Past chmn. bd. dirs. Trust Cos. Assn. of Can.; bd. dir. Air Transat, Shermag Inc., Nat. Trust Co., Scotia Mortgage Corp., Scotia Life Ins. Co., Scotia Gen. Ins. Co., The Bank of N.S. Trust Co., The Mortgage Ins. Co. of Can, Victoria and Grey Corp. Bd. dirs. MacDonald Stewart Found., Windsor Found., mem. audit com. McGill U.; past pres. St. Mary's Hosp. Found.; gov., past pres. St. Mary's Hosp. Ctr. Mt. Royal Club, Montreal, Royal Montreal Golf Club, Mt. Bruno Country Club, Inc., The Forest and Stream Club. Roman Catholic. Office: Montreal Trust 4th Fl 1002 Sherbrooke West Montreal QC Canada H3A 3L6 Office Phone: 514-499-5517.

THOMPSON, JOHN H. social science research executive; b. Washington, June 9, 1951; s. Edwin Hubert and Edna Claire Thompson; m. Bonnie Jean Horrigan, June 30, 1973; children: Lowell, Meredith, John. BS in math, Va. Tech., 1973, MS in math, 1975. Rsch. U.S. Bur. Census, Washington, 1975—97, assoc. dir., 1997—2001, prin. assoc. dir., 2001—02; exec. vice pres. Nat. Opinion Rsch. Ctr., Chgo., 2002—. Recipient Gold medal, Dept. of Commerce, 2000, Disting. Exec. award, The White House, 2001. Fellow: Am. Statis. Assn.; mem.: Sr. Exec. Svc., Am. Statis. Assn. Achievements include directed the 2000 Decennial Census on time and on budget. Office: Nat Opinion Rsch Ctr 55 E Monroe St Chicago IL 60603

THOMPSON, JOHN HERD, history professor; b. Winnipeg, Man., Can., Sept. 18, 1946; came to U.S. 1989; s. Joseph Whyte and Gladys Kate T.; m. Katrin Ann Partelpoeg, Jan. 15, 1977 (div. Sept. 2001); children: Anne Marie, Mark Thomas; m. Janet J. Ewald, May 2002. BA with honors, U. Winnipeg, 1968; MA, U. Man., 1969; PhD, Queens U., Kingston, Ont., 1975. Faculty Duke U., Durham, N.C., 1989—, chair dept. history, 2000—. Author: Harvests of War, 1978, Decades of Discord: Canada 1922-1939, 1985, Canada and the United States: Ambivalent Allies, 1994, 2d edit., 1997, 3d edit., 2002, Forging the Prairie West, 1998. Mem. Am. Hist. Assn., Can. Hist. Assn., Soc. for Am. Baseball Rsch., Assn. for Can. Studies in the U.S. Avocation: baseball. Home: Duke Univ Dept History Durham NC 27708 Office Phone: 919-684-8102.

THOMPSON, JOHN TILYNN, ophthalmologist, medical educator; b. Ann Arbor, Mich., June 8, 1956; s. John Morgan and Dorothy Georgene (Kinne) T.; m. Mary Ann Serpi; children: Lauren Alexis, John Michael. Student, Oberlin Coll., 1973-75; BA cum laude, Johns Hopkins U., 1977, MD, 1980. Diplomate Am. Bd. Ophthalmology, 1985. Intern Cedars-Sinai Med. Ctr., L.A., 1980-81; resident Wilmer Ophthalmologic Inst., Balt., 1981-84, asst. chief svc., 1986; asst. prof. Yale U., New Haven, 1986-90, assoc. prof., 1990-91; assoc. clin. prof. U. Md., Balt., 1993—; ptnr. The Retina Inst. Md., Balt., 1991-96, Retina Specialists, Balt., 1996—; asst. prof. The Wilmer Inst., Johns Hopkins U. Dir. retina sect. Yale U., 1986-91. Contbr. articles to profl. jours. Grantee Conn. Lions Eye Found., 1986-91, The Hearst Found., 1989-90; Wilmer Ophthalmologic Inst. fellow, 1984-85, Heed Found. fellow, 1984; recipient Lamport award Biomed. Rsch. Johns Hopkins U., 1978. Fellow Am. Acad. Ophthalmology (honor award 1988); mem. AMA, Assn. Rsch. in Vision & Ophthalmology, The Retina Soc., The Macula Soc., The Vitreous Soc., Phi Beta Kappa. Avocations: tennis, classical piano, computer programming. Office: Retina Specialists 6569 N Charles St Ste 605 Towson MD 21204-6833

THOMPSON, JOHN W. information technology executive; BBA, Fla. A&M U.; M in Mgmt. Sci., MIT's Sloan School of Mngmt. Sr. exec. pos. in sales, mktg. and software devel. IBM, 1971—99; gen. mgr. IBM Ams.; chmn., pres., CEO The Antivirus Guardian Co., Symantec Corp., Cupertino, Calif., 1999—. Bd. dirs. UPS, 2000—, NiSource, Inc., Seagate Tech., 2004—, Crystal Decisions; appt. mem. Nat. Infrastructure Adv. Com., Washington, 2002—; chair Silicon Valley Blue Ribbon Task Force on Aviation Security & Tech.; mem., Worldwide Mgmt. Coun. IBM. Chmn. Fla. A&M U. Cluster; Ill. Gov's human resource adv. coun. Office: Symantec Corp 20330 Stevens Creek Blvd Cupertino CA 95014*

THOMPSON, JON L. oil industry executive; BS in geology, MS in geology,, U. Fla. Geologist Exxon Co. U.S.A., New Orleans, 1962; v.p. Exxon Corp., 1992—99; pres. Exxon Exploration Co., 1992—99; v.p. ExxonMobil Corp., 2000—; pres. ExxonMobil Exploration Co., 2000—. Office: ExxonMobil Exploration Co Ste 1241 233 Benmar St Houston TX 77066-3105

THOMPSON, JOSEPH PAUL, retired systems administrator; b. Denver, Colo., Apr. 11, 1949; s. James Paul Thompson and Emma Lucinda Neal; m. Nola Ann Schlorholtz (div.). Planner data analyst Colo. Dept. of Transp., Denver, 1974—2001. Adv. bd. mem. Nat. Ctr. for Voice and Speech, Denver. Mem.: Toastmasters Internat. (lt. gov. edn. and tng. 2002—03, dist gov-elect 2003—). Libertarian. Avocations: reading, bicycling. Home: 7474 E Arkansas Ave #3010 Denver CO 80231

THOMPSON, JOSEPH T., JR., health facility administrator; b. Cranston, R.I., Jan. 13, 1946; s. Joseph T. Thompson Sr. and Frances R. (Marshall); m. Sidney Carla Lopez, June 22, 1986; children: Endre J., Paige Nicole. BS, La Salle U., 1999. Cert. CCFC, LADAC, S.A.P. Case mgr. San Juan Youth Shelter, Aztec, N.Mex., 1998—99; DWI counselor San Juan County DWI Detention/Treatment Facility, Farmington, N.Mex., 1999—2001; intake coord. Four Winds Recovery Ctr., Farmington, N.Mex., 2001—; dir., owner White Eagle Counseling & Edn. Svc., Farmington, N.Mex., 2001—; with dept. behavioral health svcs. Navajo Nation, 2001. Adj. faculty San Juan Coll., Farmington, N.Mex., 1999 ; prin. substance abuse counselor Dept. Behavioral Health Navajo Nation, 2001—. Chief petty officer USN, 1964—86. Mem.: Am. Coll. Cert. Forensic Counselors, NAADAC. Avocations: fishing, hunting, camping. Home: 2011 Troy King Rd # 428 Farmington NM 87401 Office: White Eagle Counseling 605 N Butler Ave Farmington NM 87401

THOMPSON, JUDITH KASTRUP, nursing researcher; b. Marstal, Denmark, Oct. 1, 1933; came to the U.S., 1951; d. Edward Kastrup and Anna Hansa (Knudsen) Pedersen; m. Richard Frederick Thompson, May 22, 1960; children: Kathryn Marr, Elizabeth Kastrup, Virginia St. Claire. BS, RN, U. Oreg., 1958, MSN, 1963. RN, Calif., Oreg. Staff nurse U. Oreg. Med. Sch., Eugene, 1957-58, Portland, 1958-61, head staff nurse, 1960-61; instr. psychiat. nursing U. Oreg. Sch. Nursing, Portland, 1963-64; rsch. asst. U. Oreg. Med. Sch., Portland, 1964-65, U. Calif., Irvine, 1971-72; rsch. assoc. Stanford (Calif.) U., 1982-87; rsch. asst. Harvard U., Cambridge, Mass., 1973-74; rsch. assoc. U. So. Calif., L.A., 1987—. Contbg. author: Behavioral Control and Role of Sensory Biofeedback, 1976; contbr. articles to profl. jours. Treas. LWV, Newport Beach, Calif., 1970-74; scout leader Girl Scouts Am., Newport Beach, 1970-78. Named Citizen of Yr. State of Oreg., 1966. Mem. Soc. for Neurosci., Am. Psychol. Soc. (charter), ANA, Oreg. Nurses Assn. Republican. Lutheran. Avocations: art collecting, travel, tennis. Home: 28 Sky Sail Dr Corona Del Mar CA 92625-1436 Office: U So Calif University Park Los Angeles CA 90089-0001 E-mail: judith@neuro.usc.edu.

THOMPSON, KATHLEEN SHAMBAUGH, marriage and family counselor; b. Bakersfield, Calif., Oct. 22, 1945; d. Stephen W. and Marilyn L. Shambaugh; m. John W. Thompson, June 10, 1967 (dec. Mar. 1971); children: Stephen, Charles. *Parents moved to Canada-1956. Father was VP of an oil company. The family benefited from experiences there; the two daughters went through late childhood and teens. Father then started a capital business in Spokane, Washington; then a law practice in Denver, Colorado (thirty years); was also in military reserves. Sister was editor/publisher of Silver Lining/Golden Edge international cat magazine. She died, 1998. Mother died, 1996. Husband received his PhD (Physics) but died soon after, of cancer. Biographee was in a car accident (1996), had surgery, and transitioned to writing. Most writings relate to experiences, are non-fiction, and involve research. Biographee is family focused.* Student, Colo. Women's Coll., 1964; BA in English, U. Colo., 1968; MA in Counseling, U. Denver, 1976. Tchg. credential U. Colo., 1971, lic. marriage and family counselor. Tchr., Denver, 1971—76; marriage, family and child counselor, 1982—. Editor, proofreader, 1977—80. Author: Going Through Life-A Collection of Poems, 2000, An American Girl in Canada, 2002, Coping with Grief and the Death of Loved Ones, 2003, A Life Filled With Poetry, 2003, Professional Guides: The Case Study, Human Sexuality in Marriage, Crime and Rehabilitation, Introducing the Gap Theory, 2003, Counseling Helps, 2004, A Car Accident, Different Kinds of Pain, and Surgery 5 Years Later, 2004, Writers and Writing, 2004. Named one of Best Poets of 2000, Internat. Libr. Poetry, 2001. Mem.: Internat. Soc. Poets (Internat. Poet Merit 2000), Delta Delta Delta. Presbyterian. Avocations: stamp collecting/philately, doll collecting, art, gardening, animal rights. Home and Office: 1655 W Ajo Way # 170 Tucson AZ 85713 Office Phone: 520-741-1731.

THOMPSON, KATHY C. bank executive; From. sr. v.p. to exec. v.p. Stock Yards Bancorp Inc, Louisville, 1992—96, exec. v.p., 1996—. Named No. 3 Fast Tracker in the Industry, U.S. Bankers Mag., 2003. Office: Stock Yards Bancorp Inc 1040 East Main St Louisville KY 40206

THOMPSON, KATHY SELF, secondary school educator; b. Birmingham, Ala., Nov. 3, 1961; d. Lawrence Thomas and Paula June (Adams) Self; m. Mark Thomas Thompson, July 14, 1994; children: Jacob Thomas, Sarah Kathryn. BA in English and Music, U. Montevallo, 1984; MA in Tchg., U. Louisville, 1995. Cert. tchr. Ky. Tchr. Central Hardin HS, Cecilia, Ky., 1991—. Home: 1921 Mud Splash Rd Glendale KY 42740 Office: Central Hardin HS 3040 Leitchfield Rd Cecilia KY 42724

THOMPSON, KEITH J. medical services company executive; Ops. dir. Bioscot, 1992-94, mng. dir., 1995-97; v.p. diagnostic ops. Serologics Corp., Atlanta, 1998—. Office: Serologicals Corp 5655 Spalding Dr Norcross GA 30092-2504

THOMPSON, KEN See THOMPSON, G. KENNEDY

THOMPSON, KENNETH, software engineer; b. 1943; MSEE, U. Calif., Berkeley, 1966. With Computer Scis. Rsch. Ctr. Bell Labs/Lucent Techs, Murray Hill, NJ, 1966—2000, disting. mem. tech. staff. Recipient Japan's C&C prize, Emmanuel R. Piore award, IEEE, Richard Hamming medal, Turing award, ACM, 1983, U.S. Nat. Medal of Tech., 1999. Mem.: Assn. Computing Machinery (Turing award and software sys. award), Nat. Acad. Engring., Nat. Acad. Scis., IEEE Computer Soc. (Tsutomu Kanai award 1999). Achievements include patents for computer technology; research in operating systems, programming languages, software for voice and data communications, security, computer games and digital music distribution; development of UNIX operating system in 1969.

THOMPSON, KENNETH W(INIFRED), educational association administrator, writer, editor, social sciences educator; b. Des Moines, Aug. 29, 1921; s. Thor Carlyle and Agnes (Rorbeck) T.; m. Betty Bergquist (dec.); m. Beverly Bourret (dec.); children: Kenneth Caryle, Paul Andrew, James David, Carolyn Cordry. AB, Augustana Coll., 1943, LHD (hon.), LLD, Augustana Coll., 1986; MA, U. Chgo., 1948, PhD, 1950; LLD, U. Notre Dame, 1964, Bowdoin Coll., 1972, St. Michael's Coll., 1973, St. Olaf Coll., 1974, U. Denver, 1983; L.H.D., W.Va. Wesleyan U., 1970; LHD, Nebr. Wesleyan Coll., 1971. Lectr. social scis. U. Chgo., 1948, asst. prof. polit. sci., 1951-53; from asst. prof. to assoc. prof. polit. sci. Northwestern U., 1949-55, chmn. internat. relations com., 1951-55; asst. dir. social scis Rockefeller Found., 1955-57, from assoc. dir. social scis. to v.p., 1957-73; dir. higher edn. for devel. Internat. Council for Ednl. Devel., 1974-76; Commonwealth prof. govt. and fgn. affairs U. Va., 1975-78, White Burkett Miller prof. govt. and fgn. affairs, 1979-86; J. Wilson Newman prof. govt. and fgn. affairs, 1986—; dir. White Burkett Miller Ctr. Pub. Affairs, 1978-98; dir. emeritus Miller Ctr., 1999—. Riverside Meml. lectr. Riverside Ch., N.Y.C., 1958; Lilly lectr. Duke, 1959; James Stokes lectr. N.Y.U., 1962; Rockwell lectr. Rice U., 1965; Ernest Griffith lectr. Am. U.; Andrew Cecil lectr. U. Tex., 1983; Stuber lectr. U. Rochester, 1984; Morgenthau Meml. lectr., N.Y.C., Mike Mansfield Ctr. lectr., U. Mont.; dir. Inst. Study World Politics, N.Y.C., 1975-01; cons. in field. Author, editor: Principles and Problems of International Politics, 1951, 82, Man and Modern Society, 1953, Christian Ethics and the Dilemmas of Foreign Policy, 1959, 81, Conflict and Cooperation Among Nations, 1960, Political Realism and the Crisis of World Politics, 1960, 82, American Diplomacy and Emergent Problems, 1962, 82, Foreign Policies in a World of Change, 1964, The Moral Issue in Statecraft, 1966, Reconstituting the Human Community, 1972, Foreign Assistance: A View From Private Sector, 1972, 82, Higher Education for National Development, 1972, Understanding World Politics, 1975, Higher Edn. and Social Change, 1976, World Politics, 1976, Truth and Tragedy, 1977, Ethics and Foreign Policy, 1978, Interpreters and Critics of the Cold War, 1978, Foreign Policy and the Democratic Process, 1978, Ethics, Functionalism and Power, 1979, Morality and Foreign Policy, 1980, Masters of International Thought, 1980, The Virginia Papers, vols. 1-30, 1979-96, The President and the Public Philosophy, 1981, Cold War Theories: World Polarization, 1944-53, Vol. I, 1981,91. Winston S. Churchill's World View, 1983, 89, Toynbees's World Politics and History, 1985, Moralism and Morality, 1985, Ethics and International Relations, 1985, Theory and Practice of International Relations, 1987, Arms Control and Foreign Policy, 1990, Traditions and Values in Politics and Diplomacy, 1992, Fathers of International Thought, 1994, Schools of Thought in International Relations, 1996; editor: Am. Values Series, Vols. I-XX, Presdl. Nominating Process, Vols. I-IV, Portraits of American Presidents, Vols. I-IX, Herbert Butterfield: The Ethics of History; The American Presidency, Vols. I-XVI, 1982-83, Ethics and International Relations, 1985, Moral Dimensions of American Foreign Policy, 1985, 94, The Credibility of

Leadership and Institutions, Vols. I-XX, 1983-86, Rhetoric and Political Discourse, Vols.I-XX, Governance, Vols. I-VII, 1990-97, Constitutionalism, Vols. I-VII, 1989-91, Presidency and Science Advising, Vols. I-VIII, 1986-90, Political Transitions and Foreign Policy, Vols. I-IX, 1985-91, A World in Change, Vols. I-XI, 1989-96, Presidential Disability, Vols. I-IV, 1989-96, A New World Order, Vols. I-VI, 1991-97, Great American Presidents, 1994, Defeated Presidential Candidates, 1994, Statesmen Who Were Never President, 1996; bd. editors Society, Ethics and International Affairs, Interpretation, The Rev. of Politics; contbr. articles to profl. jours. Pres. Dist. of Scarsdale and Mamaroneck (N.Y.) Bd. Edn., 1965-68; trustee Union Theol. Sem., 1967-71, Dillard U., 1975-96, Social Sci. Found., U. Denver, 1974-94, Compton Found., 1975-98. 1st lt. AUS, 1943-46. Named Va. laureate, 1981; recipient Phi Beta Kappa and Va. Coll. Stores prizes, Va. Social Sci. Assn. ann. award, English Speaking Union award.Spl. Edward Weintal prize Georgetown U. Acad. Diplomacy, 1999. Fellow Soc. Religion Higher Edn., Am. Acad. Arts and Scis.; mem. Century Club, Scarsdale Town Club, Raven Soc. (ann. award U. Va.), Phi Beta Kappa (pres.), Omicron Delta Phi. Office: Univ Va Miller Ctr PO Box 400406 Charlottesville VA 22904-4406 Office Phone: 434-924-6049.

THOMPSON, KIRK, transportation executive; CPA, Ark. With J.B. Hunt Transport Svcs., Inc., Lowell, Ark., 1973-78, v.p. fin., 1979-84, exec. v.p., CFO, 1984-85, pres., CEO, 1986-87, pres., CEO, 1987—. Office: JB Hunt Transport Svcs Inc 615 JB Hunt Corporate Dr Lowell AR 72745

THOMPSON, KURT B. healthcare provider executive; Various fin. positions F & M Distributors, Inc., Arthur Andersen & Co.; fin. exec. Kmart Corp., Troy, Mich., 1997-2000; exec. v.p., CFO Oxford Health Plans, Inc., Trumbull, Conn., 2000—. Office: Oxford Health Plans Inc 48 Monroe Turnpike Trumbull CT 06611

THOMPSON, LARRY ANGELO, motion picture and TV producer, lawyer, personal manager, author, lecturer; b. Clarksdale, Miss., Aug. 1, 1944; s. Angelo and Ann (Tuminello) T.; m. Kelly Ann LeBlanc, 1999; children: Taylor Ann. BBA, U. Miss., 1966, JD, 1968. Bar: Miss. 1968, Calif. 1970. In-house counsel Capitol Records, Hollywood, Calif., 1969-71; sr. ptnr. in entertainment law Thompson, Shankman and Bond, Beverly Hills, Calif., 1971-77; pres. Larry A. Thompson Orgn., Inc., 1977—. Co-owner New World Pictures, 1983-85; lectr. in entertainment bus. UCLA, U. So. Calif., Southwestern U. Law Sch.; founder Project Rise and Shine, 2004. Author: How to Make a Record Deal and Have Your Songs Recorded, 1975, Prime Time Crime, 1982, Shine: A Powerful Four Step Plan to Becoma a Star in Anything You Do, 2004; prodr.: (TV) Jim Nabors Show, 1977 (Emmy nominee), Mickey Spillane's Margin for Murder, 1981, Bring 'Em Back Alive, 1982, Mickey Spillane's Murder Me, Murder You, 1982, The Other Lover, 1985, Convicted, 1986, Intimate Encounters, 1986, Eagle and My Bear, 1987, The Woman He Loved, 1988 (Emmy nominee, Golden Globe nominee), Original Sin, 1989, Class Cruise, 1989, Little White Lies, 1989, Mann in the Middle, 1989, Lucy and Desi: Before The Laughter, 1990 (Emmy nominee), Broken Promises, 1993, Separated By Murder, 1994, Face of Evil, 1996, Replacing Dad, 1998, Tonight @ House of Blues, 1998, The Beat Goes On: The Sonny and Cher Story, 1999 (Emmy nominee), Murder in the Mirror, 2000, Iron Chef USA: Showdown in Las Vegas, 2001, Iron Chef USA: Holiday Showdown, 2001, Celebrity Home Video, 2003, A Date with Darkness: The Trial of Andrew Luster, 2003, Little Girl Lost: The Delimar Vera Story, 2004; (film) Crimes of Passion, 1984, Fraternity Vacation, 1985, Quiet Cool, 1987, My Demon Lover, 1987, Breaking the Rules, 1992. Co-chmn. Rep. Nat. Entertainment Com.; apptd. by Gov. of Calif. to Calif. Entertainment Commn.; mem. Inauguration of Thompson Ctr. for Fine Arts in Clarksdale, 1986. Served with JAGC, U.S. Army, 1966-72. Recipient Show Bus. Atty. of Yr. award Capitol Records, 1971, Vision award, 1993; named Showman of Yr., U.S. TV Fan Assn., 1997. Mem. ABA, Miss. Bar Assn., Calif. Bar Assn., Inter-Am. Bar Assn., Hon. Order Ky. Cols., Am. Film Inst., Nat. Acad. Rec. Arts and Scis., Acad. TV Arts and Scis. Republican. Roman Catholic. Office: Larry A Thompson Orgn 9663 Santa Monica Blvd Ste 801 Beverly Hills CA 90210-4303 Home: 1348 Club View Dr Los Angeles CA 90024-5304 Office Phone: 310-288-0700. E-mail: ltbeverlyhills@aol.com.

THOMPSON, LARRY DEAN, former federal agency administrator, lawyer; b. Hannibal, Mo., Nov. 15, 1945; s. Ezra W. and Ruth L. (Robinson) T.; m. Brenda Anne Taggart, June 26, 1970; children: Larry Dean, Gary E. BA cum laude, Culver-Stockton Coll., Canton, Mo., 1967; MA, Mich. State U., 1969; JD, U. Mich., 1974. Bar: Mo. 1974, Ga. 1978. Indsl. rels. rep. Ford Motor Co., Birmingham, Mich., 1969-71; atty. Monsanto Co., St. Louis, 1974-77, King & Spalding, Atlanta, 1977-82; U.S. atty. U.S. Dist. Ct. (no. dist.) Ga., 1982-86; ptnr. King & Spalding, Atlanta, 1986—2001; dep. atty. gen. U.S. Dept Justice, Washington, 2001—03; sr. fellow Brookings Instn., Washington, 2003—04. Mem. 11th Cir. Commn. on Lawyer Qualifications and Conduct; ind. counsel HUD investigation, 1995, visiting prof., U. Ga Sch. of Law, 2004; mem. Ga. Bd. Bar Examiners. Editor: Jury Instructions in Criminal Antitrust Cases 1976-80, 1982. Chmn. Atlanta Urban League; mem. Ga. Bd. Edn., 1997; bd. dirs. Ga. Rep. Found. Recipient Outstanding Achievement award FBA, 1992. Mem. ABA, Nat. Bar Assn; bd. dirs. Delta Air Lines Inc., 2003-. Republican. Presbyterian.

THOMPSON, LARRY FLACK, nanotechnology and semiconductor process company executive; b. Union City, Tenn., Aug. 31, 1944; s. Rufus Russell and Polly (Flack) T.; m. Frank O. Wilson, Mar. 1, 1991; children: Anthony Scott, Russell Allen. BS, Tenn. Tech. U., Cookeville, 1966; MS, Tenn. Tech. U., 1968; PhD, U. Mo., Rolla, 1970. Mem. tech. staff Bell Labs., Murray Hill, N.J., 1971-80; dept. head AT&T Bell Labs., Murray Hill, N.J., 1981-94; v.p. product devel., chief tech. officer Integrated Solutions, Inc., Austin, Tex., 1994-97; pres. Ultrabeam Lithography, 1997—2002, Ultrabeam Lithography Inc. (divsn. of Ultratech Stepper), 1999—; CEO, N.J. Nanotech. Consortium, 2002—. Mem. adv. coun. dept. chem. engring. Cornell U., Princeton U.; chmn. adv. com. to divsn. of chem., biochem. and thermal engring. NSF. Author: Introduction to Microlithography, 1993, 98; patentee in field. Recipient SEMI award for N. Am., 1997. Mem. NAE, Am. Chem. Soc. (bd. dirs. 1993-96, Indsl. Chemistry award 1993, Roy W. Tess award 1993), Am. Inst. Chem. Engring. Avocations: gardening, hunting. Home: 309 Comet St Austin TX 78734 E-mail: larry@ipsslp.com.

THOMPSON, LARRY JAMES, retired gifted and social studies education educator; b. Savannah, Ga., May 14, 1948; s. James Howell and Dorothy (Hendley) T. BA, Armstrong Atlantic State U., 1970; MAT, Tulane U., 1974; EdD, U. Ga., 1986. Cert. tchr., instrnl. supr., adminstr., Ga. Tchr. social studies Chatham County Bd. Edn., Savannah, 1970-71, 75-87, adminstrv. coord. social studies, 1987-97, gifted, talented educator, 1997-2001; ret., 2001. With USNR, 1971-73. Mem. Nat. Coun. Social Studies, Ga. Coun. Social Studies, Profl. Assn. Ga. Educators, Ga. Hist. Soc. Home: 18 E Deerwood Rd Savannah GA 31410-3171

THOMPSON, LAWRENCE HYDE, federal agency official; b. Hamilton, Ohio, Oct. 6, 1943; s. William Hayton and Evelyn (Covault) T.; m. Catherine Crosby, Feb. 3, 1973; children: Bradford Stephen, Sarah Catherine. BS, Iowa State U., 1964; MBA, U. Pa., 1966; PhD, U. Mich., 1971. Economist Office Sec. Health, Edn. and Welfare, Washington, 1974-77, dir. Soc. Security Planning, 1977-79; assoc. commr. Social Security Adminstrn., Washington, 1979-81, dir. rsch., 1981-83; chief economist Gen. Acctg. Office, Washington, 1983-89, asst. comptroller gen., 1989-93; prin. dep. commr. Social Security Adminstrn., 1993-95; sr. fellow The Urban Inst., Washington, 1996—. Contbr. articles to pubs., books. Mem. Am. Economic Assn., Nat. Acad. Social Ins. (dir. 1985-96, sec. 1997-99, pres. 1999-2003). Avocations: racquetball, choral singing. Office: The Urban Inst 2100 M St NW Ste 401 Washington DC 20037-1264

THOMPSON, LEA, actress; b. Rochester, Minn., May 31, 1961; m. Howard Deutch. Actress: (films) Jaws 3-D, 1983, All the Right Moves, 1983, The Wild Life, 1984, Red Dawn, 1984, Back to the Future, 1985, Howard the Duck, 1986, Space Camp, 1986, Some Kind of Wonderful, 1987, Casual Sex, 1988, The Wizard of Loneliness, 1988, Going Undercover, 1988, Back to the Future II, 1989, Back to the Future III, 1990, Article 99, 1991, Dennis the Menace, 1993, The Beverly Hillbillies, 1993, The Little Rascals, 1994, The Right to Remain Silent, 1996 (TV movies) Nightbreaker, 1989, Montana, 1990, Stolen Babies, 1993, The Substitute Wife, 1994, The Unspoken Truth, 1995, The Unknown Ciclist, 1997, (TV series) Tales from the Crypt, 1989, Robert Wuhl's World Tour, 1990, Caroline in the City, 1995—, (TV miniseries) A Will of Their Own, 1998. Pa. Ballet Co. scholar, Am. Ballet Theatre scholar, San Francisco Ballet scholar. Office: care NBC PO Box 5617 Burbank CA 91523-0001

THOMPSON, LOHREN MATTHEW, oil company executive; b. Sutherland, Nebr., Jan. 21, 1926; s. John M. and Anna (Ecklund) T.; children: Terence M., Sheila M., Clark M. Ed., U. Denver. Spl. rep. Standard Oil Co., Omaha, 1948-56; sales mgr. Frontier REF. Co., 1956-67, v.p. mktg., 1967-68; mgr. mktg. U.S. region Husky Oil Co., Denver, 1968-72; v.p. Westar Stas., Inc., Denver, 1967-70; chmn. bd. Colo. Petroleum, Denver, 1971—. Served with USAAF, 1944-46 Mem. Colo. Petroleum Council, Am. Petroleum Inst., Am. Legion Clubs: Denver Petroleum, Denver Oilman's,. Lodges: Lions. Lutheran. Home: 2410 Spruce Ave Estes Park CO 80517-7146 Office: Colo Petroleum 4080 Globeville Rd Denver CO 80216-4906

THOMPSON, LOIS JEAN HEIDKE ORE, psychologist; b. Chgo., Feb. 22, 1933; d. Harold William and Ethel Rose (Neumann) Heidke; m. Henry Thomas Ore, Aug. 28, 1954 (div. May 1972); children: Christopher, Douglas; m. Joseph Lippard Thompson, Aug. 3, 1972; children: Scott, Les, Melanie. BA, Cornell Coll., Mt. Vernon, Iowa, 1955; MA, Idaho State U., 1964, EdD, 1981. Lic. psychologist, N.Mex. Tchr. pub. schs. various locations, 1956-67; tchr., instr. Idaho State U., Pocatello, 1967-72; employee/orgn. devel. specialist Los Alamos (N.Mex.) Nat. Lab., 1981-84, tng. specialist, 1984-89, sect. leader, 1989-93; pvt. practice indsl. psychology and healthcare, Los Alamos, 1988—. Sec. Cornell Coll. Alumni Office, 1954-55, also other orgns.; bd. dirs. Parent Edn. Ctr., Idaho State U., 1980; counselor, Los Alamos, 1981-88. Editor newsletter LWV, Laramie, Wyo., 1957; contbr. articles to profl. jours. Pres. Newcomers Club, Pocatello, 1967, Faculty Womens Club, Pocatello, 1968; chmn. edn. com. AAUW, Pocatello, 1969. Mem.: APA, N.Mex. Soc. Adlerian Psychology (pres. 1990, treas. 1991—97, bd. dirs. 1996—), N.Mex. Psychol. Assn. (bd. dirs. divsn. II 1990, 1999, sec. 1988—90, chmn. 1990, 1999—2000). Mem. Lds Ch. Avocations: racewalking, backpacking, skiing, tennis, biking. Home and Office: 340 Aragon Ave Los Alamos NM 87544-3505 *Honesty, dependability, spiritual inspiration, and always doing our best are ingredients that lead to a successful and happy life.*

THOMPSON, LORAN TYSON, lawyer; b. N.Y.C., Dec. 23, 1947; s. Kenneth Webster and Mary (Tyson) T.; m. Meera Eleanora Agarwal, Apr. 2, 1976. BA magna cum laude, Amherst Coll., 1969; MA, Harvard U., 1970, JD, 1976. Bar: N.Y. 1977, U.S. Tax Ct. 1977. Assoc. Breed, Abbott & Morgan, N.Y.C., 1976-83, ptnr., 1983-93, Whitman Breed Abbott & Morgan LLP, N.Y.C., 1993-2000, Winston & Strawn, N.Y.C., 2000—. Mem. ABA, N.Y. State Bar Assn. (exec. com., tax sect. 1991-98, co-chmn. com. on nonqualified employee benefits 1991-95, co-chmn. com. on qualified plans 1995-98), Assn. Bar of City of N.Y., Phi Beta Kappa. Home: 79 W 12th St Apt 12G New York NY 10011-8510 Office: Winston & Strawn LLP 200 Park Ave New York NY 10166-4193 E-mail: lthompson@winston.com.

THOMPSON, LORING MOORE, retired college administrator, writer; b. Newton, Mass., Feb. 17, 1918; s. Henry E. and Ella (Gould) T.; m. Pearl E. Judiesch, Dec. 30, 1949 (dec. May 2002); children— Bruce C., Douglas P. (dec.). BS in Indsl. Engring, Northeastern U., 1940; MS, U. R.I., 1947; PhD, U. Chgo., 1956. Instr. U. R.I., 1946; asst. to pres. Assn. Colls. Upper N.Y., 1947-49; assoc. prof. U. Toledo, 1952-59, asst. dean acad. adminstrn., 1958-59; dir. univ. planning Northeastern U., Boston, 1959-63, dean adult programs, 1964-66, v.p. planning, 1967-80, emeritus, 1980—; faculty assoc. continuing edn. Ariz. State U., 1982-84. Cons. in field. Author: (with others) Business Communication, 1949; contbr. articles to profl. jours. Bd. dirs. Back Bay Assn., Boston, 1961-63, v.p., 1963; trustee Huntington Gen. Hosp., Boston, 1970-80; mem. Fenway Project Area Com., 1973-76; mem. Mass. conf. ch. and edn. com. United Ch. of Christ, 1972-78, chairperson, 1973-74, mem. task force on ch. growth, 1978-80; mem. Chandler Area Coun., 1988-89; sec. Interfaith Coun. Greater Sun Lakes, 1993-96. Lt. USNR, 1942-45. Mem. Inst. Noetic Scis., Tau Beta Pi. Home: 25408 S Sedona Dr Sun Lakes AZ 85248-6636

THOMPSON, LOUIS MILTON, agronomy educator, scientist; b. Throckmorton, Tex., May 15, 1914; s. Aubrey Lafayette and Lola Terry (Frazier) T.; m. Margaret Stromberg, July 10, 1937 (dec. Nov. 1972); children: Louis Milton, Margaret Ann, Glenda Ray (dec.), Carolyn Terry, Jerome Lafayette; m. Ruth Hiatt Phipps, July 7, 1990. BS, Tex. A&M U., 1935; MS, Iowa State U., 1947, PhD, 1950. Soil surveyor, Tex., 1935-36, 39-40; instr. Tex. A&M U., 1936-39, 40-42; asst. prof. soils Iowa State U., Ames, 1947-50, prof. soils, head farm operation curriculum, 1950-58, assoc. dean agr. charge resident instrn., 1958-83, emeritus prof. agronomy, 1983—, assoc. dean emeritus, 1984—. Author: Soils and Soil Fertility, rev. edit., 1957; co-author: rev. edit., 1978, 1983; contbr. articles on weather-crop yield models and climate change to profl. jours. Elder Presbyn. Ch. With AUS, 1942-46; col. Res. (ret.). Recipient Henry A. Wallace award for Disting. Svc. to Agr., 1982, Faculty citation Iowa State U. Alumni Assn., 1990, Disting. Achievement citation, 1993, Alumni Recognition medal, 1996, Disting. Iowa Scientist award Iowa Acad. Sci., 1991, Agr. Innovator award Iowa State U. Agr. Alumni Soc., 1992, Friends of Agrl. award Iowa Dept. Agr. and Nat. Agrl. Mktg. Assn., 1993, Disting. Svc. to Iowa Agr. award Iowa Farm Bur., 1995, Disting. Svc. to Agr. award Iowa chpt. Am Soc. Farm Mgrs. and Rural Appraisers, 2000; named one of 150 Iowans Who Made a Difference, Iowa Farm Bur., 1996. Fellow AAAS, Am. Soc. Agronomy, Soil Sci. Soc. Am., Soil and Water Conservation Soc. (pres.'s citation); mem. Farm House (hon.), Rotary (past local pres., Paul Harris fellow), Sigma Xi, Alpha Zeta (Tall Corn award 1957), Gamma Sigma Delta (nat. pres. 1956-58), Phi Kappa Phi (chpt. pres. 1961, Centennial medal 1997). Home: 2214 Hamilton Dr Ames IA 50014-8287 *To succeed in an academic community one must become an authority on a subject and be able to communicate it.*

THOMPSON, LOUIS MILTON, JR., association executive, horse breeder; b. Bryan, Tex., Sept. 21, 1938; s. Louis Milton and Margaret (Stromberg) T.; m. Anne Strand, Aug. 5, 1961 (div. Feb. 1992); children: Louis Milton III, Eric Norman, Christopher Scott, Mary Margaret, Mary Elizabeth; m. Laura Russell, Nov. 28, 1992; children: Emily Allan, Helen Aubrey. BS, Iowa State U., 1961, MS with honors, 1969. News editor, anchor Sta. WOI-TV-AM-FM, Ames, Iowa, 1960-61; commd. 2d lt. U.S. Army, 1961, resigned, 1974; advanced through grades to lt. col. USAR, 1981; asst. press sec. The White House, Washington, 1974-75; asst. to pres. Am. Enterprise Inst., Washington, 1975-76; dir. pub. affairs Nonprescription Drug Mfrs. Assn., Washington, 1976-78; sr. v.p. Nat. Assn. Home Builders, Washington, 1978-82; pres., CEO, Nat. Investor Rels. Inst., Vienna, Va., 1982—. Mem. individual investor adv. com. N.Y. Stock Exch., N.Y.C., 1990—92; mem. new founds. working group Harvard U. John F. Kennedy Sch., Cambridge, Mass., 1992—94; mem. consumer affairs adv. com. SEC, Washington, 1996—; mem. adv. bd. Greenlee Sch. Journalism and Comm., Iowa State U., Ames, 1998—, mem. liberal arts and scis. dean's coun., 2001—; mem. Conf. Bd., 1995—96. Contbg. author: The Handbook of Investor Relations, 1989; contbr. articles to profl. jours. Va. chmn. U.S. Equestrian Team, Gladstone, NJ, 1978—82; dressage judge Am. Horse Shows Assn., Lexington, Ky., 1979—86; bd. dirs. Nat. Coun. Econ. Edn., 2001—. Recipient Disting. Svc. award, Investment Edn. Inst., 1987, Investor Rels. Mag. and Barron's lifetime achievement award in investor rels., 2000, J.W. Schwartz award for disting. svc. in journalism, Iowa State U., 2001. Mem. Investor Rels. Assn., Internat. Investor Rels. Fedn., Am. Hanoverian Soc. (disting. mem., pres. 1988-94), Univ. Club, Phi Kappa Phi. Avocations: equestrian sports, golf, wine collecting. Home: Wanderland Farm 11539 Spicers Mill Rd Orange VA 22960-2103 Office: Nat Investor Rels Inst 8045 Leesburg Pike Ste 600 Vienna VA 22182-2797

THOMPSON, LYLE EUGENE, electrical engineer; b. Pocatello, Idaho, May 16, 1956; s. Clyde Eugene and Doris (Pratt) T.; m. Barbara Mae Dickerson, Dec. 31, 1986. Grad. high sch. Sr. diagnostic engr. Calma/GE, Santa Clara, Calif., 1978-83; mem. tech. staff Telecommunications Tech., Inc., Milpitas, Calif., 1983-84; proprietor/cons. Lyle Thompson Cons., Fremont, Calif., 1984-87; sys. analyst Raynet Corp., Menlo Park, Calif., 1987-88; proprietor/cons. Lyle Thompson Cons., Hayward, Calif., 1988-89; mgr. sys. design Raylan Corp., Menlo Park, Calif., 1989-90, dir. system design, 1990-91; pvt. practice cons. San Lorenzo, Calif., 1991-96; pres., CEO HelioSoft, Inc., San Lorenzo, Calif., 1996—; instr. U. Calif., Berkeley, 1999—2003. Cons. in field. Mem.: IEEE, ACM. Achievements include patents in field. Avocations: music, role playing, golf. Home: 664 Paseo Grande San Lorenzo CA 94580-2364 E-mail: lyle@heliosoft.com.

THOMPSON, MACK EUGENE, history educator; b. Burley, Idaho, Feb. 24, 1921; s. Eugene and Nora (McFate) T.; m. Helen Goldhamer, Oct. 30, 1945. AB, Queen's Coll., CUNY, 1948; MA, Brown U., 1951, PhD, 1955. Instr. history Brown U., 1954-55; asst. prof. Calif. Inst. Tech., 1955-56, U. Calif. at Riverside, 1956-62, asso. prof., 1962-66, prof., 1966-77; emeritus prof., 1977—; chmn. div. humanities U. Calif. at Riverside, 1961-63, asso. univ. dean acad. planning, 1965-66, dean, div. undergrad. studies, 1971-74; exec dir. Am. Hist. Assn., Washington, 1974-81. Chmn. editorial bd. Experiment and Innovation: New Directions in Edn., U. Calif., 1966-68 Author: The Ward-Hopkins Controversy and the American Revolution in Rhode Island: An Interpretation, 1959, Moses Brown, Reluctant Reformer, 1962, Causes and Circumstances of the Du Pont Family's Emigration, 1969. Bd. dirs. Harry S. Truman Libr. Inst., 1974-81. With AUS, 1942-45. Home: 1378 River Oaks Ct Oldsmar FL 34677-4828

THOMPSON, MARGARET M. physical education educator; b. Merrifield, Va., Aug. 1, 1921; d. Lesley L. and Madeline (Shawen) T. BS, Mary Washington Coll., 1941; MA, George Washington U., 1947; PhD, U. Iowa, 1961. Tchr., supr. phys. edn. Staunton (Va.) City Schs., 1941-44; tchr. jr. high sch. phys. edn. Arlington County, Va., 1944-47; instr. women's phys. edn. Fla. State U., Tallahassee, 1947-51; instr., asst. prof., assoc. prof. phys. edn. Purdue U., Lafayette, Ind., 1951-65, dir. gross motor therapy lab., 1963-65; assoc. prof. phys. edn. U. Mo., Columbia, 1965-68, prof., 1968-71, dir. Cinematography and Motor Learning Lab. Dept. Health and Phys. Edn., 1965-71; prof. phys. edn. U. Ill., Champaign-Urbana, 1971-87, prof. emeritus, 1987—. Vis. prof. Escola de Educacão Fisica, U. de São Paulo, Brazil, 1985; vis. prof. phy. edn. Inst. Bioscis. de Rio Claro, U. Estadual Paulista, Brazil, 1991. Author: (with Barbara B. Godfrey) Movement Pattern Checklists, 1966, (with Chappelle Arnett) Perceptual Motor and Motor Test Battery for Children, 1968, (with Barbara Mann) An Holistic Approach to Physical Education Curriculum: Objectives Classification System for Elementary Schools, 1977, Gross Motor Inventory, 1976, revised edit., 1980, Developing the Curriculum, 1980, Setting the Learning Environment, 1980, Sex Stereotyping and Human Development, 1980; also film strips, articles. Mem.: AAHPER. Home and Office: 1311 Wildwood Ln Mahomet IL 61853-9770

THOMPSON, MARIAN NELL, poetry, historical, non-fiction and fiction writer, educator, poet; b. Birmingham, Ala., Aug. 30, 1938; d. Euclid Derring and Gena Grace Meadows; m. Claude Thompson, Jr., Aug. 2, 1962; children: Steven Claude, Shirley Nell. BS, Samford U., Homewood, AL, 1959. Salesperson Darling Shoppe, Birmingham, Ala., 1955—56; student asst. Samford Libr., East Lake, Ala., 1956—59; youth dir. various churches, Birmingham, Ala., Ocilla, Ga., and Flint, Mich.; educator Atherton Elem. Sch., Flint, Mich., 1959—61; writer, student libr. asst. New Orleans Seminary Libr., New Orleans, 1961—62; educator Chalmette El. Sch., Chalmette, La., 1962—63; preschool dir. Golden Acres Bapt. Ch., Pasadena, Tex., 1979—88; educator St. Pias Parochial Sch., Pasadena, Tex., 1988—89, Richey E & South Shaver Elem. Schools, Pasadena, 1989—98. Substitute tchr. Pasadena Schools, Pasadena, Tex., 1970—74; vol. Golden Acres Sch. Libraries, Pasadena, Tex., 1970—79. Author short stories, (chapbook) Thank God For His Creations, (poetry) Wheels of Thoughts, Strong Foundations Building for a Proud Future, 2003, Wonderful But Troublesome Times, The James Family Moving to Texas, Transforming in the Firm Foundation, 2003. Sustaining and life membership Rep. Party, 2001, 2002. Recipient Life Membership, Internat. Libr. of Photography, 2001. Mem.: AARP, Golden Vista Ext. for Home Edn. R-Conservative. Baptist. Avocations: music, reading, writing, photography. Office: Read Writing of MYNE 2722 Randolph Road Pasadena TX 77503-4244 E-mail: Marian_Tho@msn.com.

THOMPSON, MARIE ANGELA, computer engineer, consultant; b. Sheffield, Yorkshire, Eng., Aug. 8, 1951; came to U.S., 1979. d. Leslie Arthur and Gloria Mabel (Sheldon) Findley; m. Stephen J. Thompson, Feb. 10, 1990. BS with honors, U. Leeds, 1973; MS, U. Reading, 1975. Software engr. ITT, London, 1975-79, GTE, Northlake, Ill., 1979-80, St. Petersberg, Fla., 1980-82, Reston, Va., 1982-83; dir. rsch. Northcor, Hamden, Conn., 1985-90; mgr. spl. projects SAC of Am., Ridgefield, Conn., 1990-98; cons. Universal Solutions 2000, Ridgefield, Conn., 1998, Thompson, Findley & Co., Hampton Bays, N.Y., 1998—. Cons. Ivy League Corp., Ridgefield, Conn., 1995—98, Digital Network 1, Ridgefield, 1995—98. Dir. concessions Pop Warner Football, Ridgefield, 1993, 94, dir. registration, 1994, 95, 96, 97, dir. fundraising, 1996-98. Recipient Bob Scalzo Meml. award Ridgefield Pop Warner Football, 1997. Mem. AAUW, AAAS, Am. Inst. Chem. Engrs., Conn. Assn. for the Gifted, N.Y. Acad. Scis., Conn. Business and Industry Assn., Ridgefield C. of C., Mensa. Avocations: tennis, Go, computing, skiing, reading. Office: Thompson Findley & Co 14 Rutland Plz 301 Rutland VT 05701

THOMPSON, MARSHA, newscaster; married; 4 children. News dir. WLBT, Jackson, Miss., health reporter. Bd. dirs. Miss. Leukemia Soc., Madison County Cultural Ctr. Named Investigative Reporter of Yr., Miss. AP, 1998; recipient Fannie Lou Hamer award, NAACP, Sple. Svc. award, Miss. Commn. for Prevention of Child Abuse. Mem.: Miss. AP Broadcasters Assn., Ctrl. Miss. Med. Alliance Aux., Miss. Women's Club (past pres.). Avocation: sailing. Office: WLBT 715 S Jefferson St Jackson MS 39201

THOMPSON, MARTIN CHRISTIAN, news service executive; b. Council Bluffs, Iowa, Oct. 25, 1938; s. Ross Kenneth and Mary Ellen (Pierce) T.; m. Janet Ann Morrow, Aug. 4, 1962; children: Chris Michael, Sean Martin. BA in Communications, U. Wash., 1960. Newsman Sta. KEDO, Longview, Wash., 1960-61; news dir. Sta. KREW, Sunnyside, Wash., 1961-66; newsman AP, Seattle, 1966-68, corr. Reno, Nev., 1968-70, newsman San Francisco, 1970-72, news editor, 1972-75, chief of bur., 1975-86, Los Angeles, 1986-88, mng. editor N.Y.C., 1989-92, dir. state news, 1992—. Mem. Beta Rho Tau, Sigma Delta Chi. Methodist. Office: 50 Rockefeller Plz New York NY 10020-1605

THOMPSON, MARTYN PHILIP, political and literary studies educator, translator; b. Hitchin, Gt. Britain and No. Ireland, Nov. 13, 1945; arrived in U.S., 1991; s. Philip John and Doris Primrose Thompson; m. Penelope Ann Burden, Jan. 15, 1972; 1 child, Daniel. BS in Econs., London Sch. Econs., 1967; PhD, London U., 1974; Dr. phil. habil., Tübingen (Germany) U., 1984. Lectr. in polit. studies London U., 1971-74; lectr. Tübingen, 1974-76, asst. prof., 1976-85, assoc. prof., 1985-87, prof. lit. and intellectual history, 1987-91; prof. polit. theory Tulane U., 1991—. Founder, mem. exec. com. German Soc. Study of Polit. Thought, Münster, 1989; vice chmn. Conf. for Study of Polit. Thought, 1991-96, chmn., 1996; mem. nat. screening com. for Fulbright Awards, Inst. Internat. Edn., N.Y.C., 2000—. Author: Ideas of Contract in the Age of John Locke, 1987; editor: Locke and Kant: Historical Reception and Contemporary Relevance, 1991, co-editor Yearbook of German Political Thought, 11 vols., 1991—; contbr. articles to profl. jours. Huntington Libr. and Art Gallery fellow, 1980; fellow commoner Churchill Coll., Cambridge U., Eng., 1985—; recipient Mellon fellowship William Andrews Clark Meml. Libr., UCLA, 1981. Mem. Am. Polit. Sci. Assn., Polit. Studies Assn. Gt. Britain, Inst. Hist. Rsch. U.K., Collingwood Soc. UK (hon. life), Deutsche Gesellschaft zur Erforschung des politischen Denkens (exec. com. 1989-2001). Avocations: travel, chess, non-pedigree dogs. Office: Tulane Univ Dept Polit Sci St Charles Ave New Orleans LA 70118-5698 E-mail: martynpt@aol.com., mpt@tulane.edu.

THOMPSON, MARY EILEEN, chemistry professor; b. Mpls., Dec. 21, 1928; d. Albert C. and Blanche (McAvoy) T. BA, Coll. St. Catherine, 1953; MS, U. Minn., 1958; PhD, U. Calif., Berkeley, 1964. Tchr. math. and sci. Derham Hall H.S., St. Paul, 1953-58; mem. faculty Coll. of St. Catherine, St. Paul, 1964-69, prof. chemistry, 1969-2000, chmn. dept., 1969-90, prof. emeritus, 2000—. Project dir. Women in Chemistry, 1984-98. Contbr. articles to profl. jours. Mem. AAAS, Am. Chem. Soc. (chmn. women chemists com. 1992-94, award for encouraging women into chem. scis. careers 1997), Coun. Undergrad. Rsch. (councillor 1991-96), N.Y. Acad. Scis., Chem. Soc. London, Sigma Xi, Phi Beta Kappa (senator 1997-2003). Democrat. Roman Catholic. Achievements include research interests in Cr(III) hydrolytic polymers, kinetics of inorganic complexes, Co(III) peroxo/superoxo complexes. E-mail: MTHOM17349@aol.com.

THOMPSON, MARY KOLETA, sculptor, non-profit organization management consultant; b. Portsmouth, Va., Dec. 27, 1938; m. James Burton Thompson, May 5, 1957; children: Burt, Suzan, Kate, Jon. BFA, U. Tex., 1982; postgrad., Boston U.; MA in Philanthropy and Devel., St. Mary's U. Minn., 1999. Cert. non-profit mgmt. Pres., CEO The Planning Resource People, Lampasas, Tex., 1990—; Tex. fin. devel. specialist ARC Tex., 1994-98; devel. dir. Very Spl. Arts Tex., 1991-92; dir. devel. ARC, Austin, 1992-94; pub. affairs adminstr. Pink Palace Mus. and Memphis Mus. Inc., Memphis, 1998; CEO Lamapasas C. of C., Lampasas, TX, 1998-99; pres., CEO Assn. Non-Profit Orgns., 1998—, Tex. Assn. Bed and Breakfast Innkeepers, 1998; pres. A Little Cottage B&B, 1999—2004; owner Heritage Sta. Antiques, 1999—. Dir. Tex. Children's Mus., Fredericksburg, 1987-88, Internat. Hdqrs. SHAPE Command Arts and Crafts Ctr., 1985-86; com. chmn. Symposium for Encouragement Women in Math. and Natural Sci., U. Tex., Austin, 1990; instr. nonprofit mgmt., fin. devel., bd. leadership, grant proposal writing Ctrl. Tex. Coll., 2002—. Sculptor portrait busts. Bd. dirs. Teenage Parent Coun., Austin, 1990-92, ARC. Named U.S. Vol. of Yr., Belgium, 1986; grantee, NEA, 1988. Mem.: AAUW (life; pres. 1990—92), Women in Comm. (co-chmn. SW regional conf.), Lometa Lions Club (pub. rels. com. 1999—), Heritage Station Antique Vehicle Show (founder), Heritage Station Antiques Show and Sale (founder), Leadership Tex. (life), U. Tex. Ex-Student Assn. (life), Heritage Station Antiques Forum (founder), Raleigh Tavern Soc. (founder), Leadership Tex. Alumnae Assn. (bd. dir.), Tex. Hist. Found (life). Avocations: writing, lecturing, meeting and strategic planning. Office: 100 W 190 PO Box 10 Lometa TX 76853-0010

THOMPSON, MARY LOU, elementary school educator; b. Cambridge, Mass., Dec. 29, 1933; BS in edn., Framingham (Mass.) State Tchrs. Coll., 1956; MEd, Boston U., 1962; postgrad., Simmons Coll., Boston, Lesley Coll., Cambridge, Mass., Fitchburg (Mass.) State Coll. Elem. tchr. Burlington (Mass.) Pub. Sch., 1956—61, Sudbury (Mass.) Pub. Sch., 1961—2001; substitute tchr. Maynard Pub. Schs. Tutored learning disabled adult, 1997—99. Author curr. materials. Edn. liaison state senate campaign, Sudbury, Mass., 2002. Recipient sculpture placed in Sudbury Libr. in honor, by staff and parents of Israel Loring Sch., 2001. Mem.: NEA, Mass. Tchr. Assn. Avocations: art hist., reading, gardening, home maintenance, photography. Home: 4 DeMarco Rd Sudbury MA 01776-2036

THOMPSON, MICHAEL, lawyer; b. Des Moines, Aug. 2, 1951; s. Harold L. and Carolyn Annette (Yacinich) T.; m. Barbara Ann Haafke, Oct. 29, 1977 (div. Oct. 1984). BA, U. No. Iowa, 1973; JD, U. Iowa, 1976, MA, 1977. Bar: Iowa 1976, N.Y. 1979, Mo. 1980, Tex. 1994, Ill. 1999, U.S. Ct. Appeals (2d cir.) 1980, U.S. Ct. Appeals (7th cir.) 1982, U.S. Ct. Appeals (D.C. cir.) 1981, U.S. Ct. Appeals (fed. cir.) 1988, U.S. Ct. Internat. Trade 1988, U.S. Supreme Ct. 1984. Asst. atty. gen. Iowa Dept. Justice, Des Moines, 1976; economist Iowa Commerce Commn., Des Moines, 1976-77; spl. asst. N.Y. Pub. Svc. Commn., Albany, 1977-80; commerce counsel Mo. Pacific R.R., St. Louis, 1980-83; atty. Southwestern Bell Corp., St. Louis, 1983—86; exec. v.p., gen. counsel SBC Internat. Devel. Corp., 1986—2000; pvt. practice Chgo., 2000—. Adj. instr. corp. fin. Drake U., Des Moines, 1977. Mem.: ABA, Caxton Club, Union League Club, Arts Club Chgo., Grolier Club, Houston Yacht Club, Chgo. Yacht Club. Republican. Office: 401 N Michigan Ave Ste 1200 Chicago IL 60611 E-mail: michaelthompsonlaw@earthlink.net.

THOMPSON, MICK, state commissioner; BA, S.E. Okla. State U., Durant; MEd, Northeastern State U., Tahlequah; grad. degree in banking, U. Colo., Boulder. Exec. v.p. Ctrl. Nat. Bank, Poteau, Okla., 1977—90; dir. legis. and govtl. rels. Okla. Gov.'s Office; commr. Okla. State Banking Dept., Okla. City, 1992—. Dem. state rep. State of Okla., Poteau, 1976—84; chmn. House banking and fin. com.; mem. appropriations and budget Com.; majority floor leader, 1983—84; pres. Okla. Cmty. Banker's Assn., 1988—90; bd. dirs. UICI, North Richland Hills, Tex., 2004—. Adv. Coun. S.E. Okla. State U. Bus. Sch., Durant; Advisor to the bd. trustees U. Colo. Grad. Sch. Banking, Boulder. Mem.: Conf. State Bank Suprs. (chmn. 2003—). Office: Okla Banking Dept 4545 N Lincoln Blvd Ste 164 Oklahoma City OK 73105-3403*

THOMPSON, MORLEY PUNSHON, textile company executive; b. San Francisco, Jan. 2, 1927; s. Morley Punshon and Ruth (Wetmore) T.; m. Patricia Ann Smith, Jan. 31, 1953 (dec.); children: Page Elizabeth Tredennick, Morley Punshon; m. Katharine Shaw Wallace. AB, Stanford U., 1948; MBA, Harvard U., 1950; JD, Chase Law Sch., 1969; LLD, Xavier U., 1981. CPA, Ohio. Chmn. Stearns Tech. Textiles Co., Cin., 1985—, Stearns Can., Inc., Cin., 1985—. Bd. dirs. Cin. Inst. Fine Arts. Lt. Supply Corps USNR, 1952-54. Mem. Beta Theta Pi. Office: 100 Williams St Cincinnati OH 45215-4602

THOMPSON, MYRON H. federal judge; b. 1947; BA, Yale U., 1969, JD, 1972. Asst. atty. gen. State of Ala., 1972-74; sole practice Montgomery, Ala., 1974-79; ptnr. Thompson & Faulk, Montgomery, 1979-80; judge U.S. Dist. Ct. (mid. dist.) Ala., Montgomery, 1980-91, 98—, chief judge, 1991-98. Mem. ABA, Ala. Bar Assn., Nat. Bar Assn., Ala. Lawyers Assn. Office: US Dist Ct 203 US Courthouse PO Box 235 Montgomery AL 36101-0235

THOMPSON, MYRRAH MCCULLY TERZOLAS, music educator, director; b. Louisville, Miss., Jan. 13, 1955; d. William Wayne and Phoebe (Whitehead) McCully; divorced; 1 child, Stephanie Lauren Terzolas. B of Music Edn., Miss. State U., 1977; MusM, La. State U., 1979; postgrad., U. La., Monroe, 1983, U. La., 1987, postgrad., 2000. Counselor sch. svcs. U. La., Monroe, 1980—82; pvt. practice Monroe, 1982—; elem. tchr. music Monroe City Schs., 1986—92; sales staff 3M Corp.-Lanier, Monroe, 1990—92; instr. Yamaha music Paul Hewitt Music, Monroe, 1992—94; elem. tchr. music Ouachita Parish Schs., Monroe, 1993—97; dir. jr. high choir Ouachita Parish Jr. H.S., Monroe, 1997—. Adv. Gov.'s Blue Ribbon Commn. on Academe Excellence, Baton Rouge, 2004—, U. La., Monroe, 2003—04. Sponsor Hearts & Halos, Monroe, 2000—02. Named Miss La., Miss. La. Pageant, 1979, La. Mid. Sch. Tchr. of Yr., La. State Dept. Edn., 2004. Mem.: Music Educators Nat. Conf., Music Tchrs. Nat. Assn. (2d v.p. local chpt.), Am. Choral Dirs. Assn. (local-jr. high chair). Episcopalian. Avocations: travel, scrapbooks, ballroom dancing, dance. Home: 207 Warwick Dr Monroe LA 71203 Office: Ouachita Jr HS 5500 Blanks St Monroe LA 71203 Office Phone: 318-345-5100. Personal E-mail: mirrormc@aol.com.

THOMPSON, NANCY P. state legislator; b. Sioux Falls, S.D., Oct. 26, 1947; m. James Thompson, July 4, 1970; children: Kevin, Matthew, Cynthia, Joseph. BA, Creighton U., 1969, MA, 1982. Dist. staff mem. U.S. Rep. John Cavanaugh; dep. chief of staff Gov. Ben Nelson; former tchr.; mem. Nebr. Legislature from 14th dist., Lincoln, 1997—. Former exec. dir. Omaha Cmty. Partnership; mem. Sarpy County Bd. Commrs. Home: 1302 Western Hills Dr Papillion NE 68046-7036 Office: State Capitol Dist 14 PO Box 94604 Rm 1117 Lincoln NE 68509-4604 E-mail: nthompson@unicam.state.ne.us.

THOMPSON, NEAL PHILIP, food science and nutrition educator; b. Bklyn., July 18, 1936; s. Thomas I. and Ellenor (Backie) T.; m. Beverly Ethel Godshall, Oct. 4, 1958; children: Erick, Victor, Clifford, Karen, Stuart. BS, Wheaton Coll., 1957; MA, Miami U., 1962; PhD, Princeton U., 1965. Asst. prof. U. Fla., Gainesville, 1965-70, assoc. prof., 1970-76, prof., 1976—, asst. dean, 1980-86, assoc. dean, 1986-93. Capt. USNR, ret. Home: 27104 NW 203d Pl High Springs FL 32643 Office: U Fla Inst Food & Agrl Scis Food & Environ Toxicology Gainesville FL 32611-0720

THOMPSON, NEIL DANIEL, legal and genealogical researcher, retired lawyer; b. Calexico, Calif., Feb. 21, 1935; s. Francis Marion Thompson and Leah Harriet Howell. AB with honors, UCLA, 1957; PhD, Columbia U., 1963; LLB, Harvard U., 1963. Bar: N.Y. 1964, U.S. Dist. Ct. (so. dist.) N.Y. 1965, U.S. Customs Ct. 1967, U. S. Ct. Appeals (2d cir.) 1971, U.S. Supreme Ct. 1973. Assoc. Jas. Maxwell Fassett, N.Y.C., 1964-65, Doman & Ablondi, N.Y.C., 1965-69, Pollack & Kaminsky, N.Y.C., 1969-80; pvt. practice N.Y.C., 1980-86; rsch. cons. Salt Lake City, 1986—. Author: Family of Bartholomew Stovall, 1993; editor The Genealogist, 1980-96; contbr. articles to profl. jours. Trustee Bd. for Cert. of Genealogists, 1977-89, pres., 1983-86. Fellow Am. Soc. Genealogists (pres. 1992-95), Soc. Genealogists (London), Utah Geneal. Assn. (bd. dirs. 1988-89); mem. Phi Beta Kappa, Phi Mu Alpha. Democrat. Mem. Lds Ch. Avocations: music, stamp collecting/philately, book collecting. Home: 255 N 200 W Salt Lake City UT 84103-4545 Office Phone: 801-521-4732. Personal E-mail: gryphon801@aol.com.

THOMPSON, N(ORMAN) DAVID, insurance company executive; b. Rockville Centre, N.Y., July 30, 1934; s. Norman J. and Laurel H. (Johnson) T.; m. Joyce L. Angeletti, June 7, 1958; children: John L., Jennifer L., Sarah S. BA with distinction, Wesleyan U., 1956; LLB, Columbia U., 1959; postgrad., Harvard U., 1973. Bar: N.Y. Pvt. practice law, N.Y.C., 1961-62; corp. sec. Gen. Reins. Corp., N.Y.C., 1964-69, v.p. Greenwich, Conn., 1969, v.p., gen. counsel, sec., 1976-77; exec. v.p. N.Am. Reins. Corp., N.Y.C., 1977-78, pres., 1978-92; chmn., CEO Swiss Reins. Am. Corp. (formerly N.Am. Reins.), 1992-95, Swiss Re Am. Holding Corp. (formerly SwissRe Holding Co.), 1992-97; chmn. SwissRe Group Cos. (U.S.), 1992-95. Dir. Nat. Legal Ctr. for Pub. Interest, chmn., 1992-95; trustee Coll. Ins., 1992, 98. With U.S. Army, 1959-60. Mem. Reins Assn. Am. (chmn. 1982-83), Nat. Assn. Casualty and Surety Execs. (pres. 1986-87), Am. Arbitration Assn. (bd. dirs., chmn. fin. com. 1992-93), Am. Inst. Property and Casualty Underwriters (trustee, 1992-98), Univ. Club (N.Y.C.), Saugatuck Harbor Yacht Club (Westport, Conn.). Home: 47 Kettle Creek Rd Weston CT 06883-2208

THOMPSON, NORMAN WINSLOW, surgeon, educator; b. Boston, July 12, 1932; s. Herman Chandler and Evelyn Millicent (Palmer) T.; m. Marcia Ann Veldman, June 12, 1956; children: Robert, Karen, Susan, Jennifer. BA, Hope Coll., 1953; MD, U. Mich., 1957; MD (hon.), U. Linköping, Sweden, 1995. Diplomate Am. Bd. Surgery. From intern to prof. emeritus surgery U. Mich., Ann Arbor, Mich., 1957—2001, prof. emeritus surgery, 2001—. Contbr. articles to profl. jours. Trustee Hope Coll., Holland, Mich., 1973-88. Fellow Royal Australasian Coll. Surgeons (hon.), Royal Coll. Physicians and Surgeons of Glasgow; mem. ACS (gov. 1979-85), Ctrl. Surg. Assn., Western Surg. Assn. (1st v.p. 1992-93, pres. 1994-95), F.A. Coller Surg. Soc. (pres. 1986), Am. Surg. Assn., Am. Thyroid Assn., Soc. Surg. Alimentary Tract, Internat. Assn. Endocrine Surgeons (pres. 1989-91), Internat. Soc. Surgeons (v.p. 1995—), Am. Assn. Endocrine Surgeons (pres. 1980-81, 81-82), Royal Soc. Medicine, Brit. Assn. Endocrine Surgeons, Assn. French Endocrine Surgeons, Scandanvian Surg. Soc., Soc. Surg. Oncology, Turkish Assn. Endocrine Surgeons, Alpha Omega Alpha. Home: 465 Hillspur Rd Ann Arbor MI 48105-1048 Office: U Mich Med Ctr 2920 Taubman Bldg Ann Arbor MI 48109 Office Phone: 734-998-0167. Office Fax: 734-936-5830. Business E-Mail: normant@med.umich.edu.

THOMPSON, PAMELA, marketing executive; d. Glenn and Carol Thompson. AAS, Finger Lakes C.C., 1997; BS Magna Cum Laude, Ithaca Coll., 1999. Adminstrv. / devel. coord. Smith Opera Ho., Geneva, NY, 1999—2001; exec. dir. Geneva Bus. Improvement Dist., Geneva, 2002—. Grad. leadership Geneva Area C. of C., 2003, ex-officio bd. mem., 2004—. Recipient Ctrl. NY Women Who Make a Difference, Scotsman Cmty. Publ., 2002; grantee Ithaca Legacy Scholarship, Ithaca Coll., Dean's Scholarship, Emerson Scholarship. Mem.: Phi Theta Kappa. Avocations: soccer, swimming, travel, aerobics, photography, poetry.

THOMPSON, PAMELA A. nurse administrator; b. Silsbee, Tex., Apr. 7, 1949; d. John David and Peggy Gean (Gholson) Austin; m. Robert Laurence Thompson, May 26, 1979; children: Garrett Austin, Durete Abdella. BSN, U. Conn., 1971; MSN, U. Rochester, 1979. RN. Dir. maternal and child health Copley Meml. Hosp., Aurora, Ill., 1980-82; dir. emergency svcs. and pediatrics LaGrange (Ill.) Cmty. Hosp., 1982-86; v.p. Dartmouth Hitchcock Med. Ctr., Lebanon, N.H., 1986—. Pres. bd. Behavioral Health Network, Concord, N.H., 1997-99; chair Ctrl. and Eastern Europe Nursing Task Force, Washington, 1994-98. Sec., Andover (N.H.) After Sch. Program, 1994-96. Mem. ANA, Am. Coll. Healthcare Execs., Am. Orgn. Nurse Execs. (bd. dirs. 1997-98), N.H. Orgn. Nurse Execs. (pres. 1992-96), N.H. Hosp. Assn. (pres. bd. 1997-98), Ctr. for Nursing Leadership (mem. coun. 1998—). Democrat. Roman Catholic. Avocations: cooking, horseback riding, reading, sewing. Office: Dartmouth Hitchcock Med Ctr One Medical Center Dr Lebanon NH 03756 Home: 10524 Knollwood Dr Manassas VA 20111-2834

THOMPSON, PAMELA PADWICK, public relations executive; b. Columbus, Ohio, June 13, 1943; d. Frank John and Tiami Judith (Padwick) T.; stepfather, James William Bampton; m. Fairman Rogers Thompson, Jan. 10, 1942; children: Ryder McNeal, Darby McNeal. BA, U. Louisville, 1994; MA, U. Dayton, 1998. Ptnr. Crutcher, Kelly and Assocs., Louisville, 1979-83; owner Transl. Co., Louisville, 1981-83, Technigraphics, Louisville, 1984-87; v.p. dir. individual support Grtr. Louisville Fund for the Arts, Louisville, 1989-92; v.p. comms. John Templeton Found., Radnor, Pa., 1997—. Adj. prof. U. Louisville, 1997. Contbr. articles to profl. jours. including Small Group Behavior. Chair pub. rels. com. Keene Valley Libr., 2000-01; bd. dirs. Louisville Nature Ctr., 1996-97; mem. ad hoc com. State Ky. Biodiversity Coun., Louisville, 1996-97; city commr. City of Rolling Fields, Louisville, 1991-94; alliance bd. dirs. J.B. Speed Art Mus., Louisville, 1986-92. Mem. APA, Soc. for Consumer Psychology, Pub. Rels. Soc. Am., Jr. League Phila., Cosmo. Club Phila., Ausable Club. Episcopalian. Avocations: hiking, gardening, tennis, travel. Home: 4 Porter Ln Rose Valley PA 19086 Office: John Templeton Found Five Radnor Corp Ctr Ste 100 Radnor PA 19087 Fax: (610) 687-8961. E-mail: pthompson@templeton.org.

THOMPSON, PAUL C. labor union administrator; Pres. Local 298, United Transp. Union, 1968—70, chairperson, 1970—82; internat. v.p. United Transp. Union, 1983—99, gen. sec., treas., 1999—2001, asst. pres., 2001—04, internat. pres., 2004—. Labor rep. to Pres. Clinton's Sch./Work program com., 1993. Office: UTU 14600 Detroit Ave Cleveland OH 44107-4250 Office Phone: 216-228-9400. Business E-Mail: President@utu.org.

THOMPSON, PAUL GEORGE, lawyer; b. Des Moines, Nov. 17, 1963; BBA, U. Iowa, 1985; JD, U. Mich., 1989. Bar: Colo. 1989, D.C. 1990. Assoc. atty. Fried Frank Harris Shriver, Washington, 1989-90, Holme Roberts & Owen, Denver, 1990-95, ptnr. London, 1996—. Co-author: Securities Regulation in the Russian Federation, 1996; contbr. articles to profl. jours. Mem. ABA, Internat. Bar Assn., D.C. Bar, Colo. Bar Assn., Denver Bar Assn.

THOMPSON, PAUL HAROLD, university president; b. Ogden, Utah, Nov. 28, 1938; s. Harold Merwin and Elda (Skeen) T.; m. Carolyn Lee Nelson, Mar. 9, 1961; children: Loralyn, Kristyn, Shannyn, Robbyn, Daylyn, Nathan. BS, U. Utah, 1964; MBA, Harvard U., 1966, D Bus. Adminstrn., 1969. Rsch. assoc. Harvard U., Cambridge, Mass., 1966-69, asst. prof., 1969-73; assoc. prof. bus. Brigham Young U., Provo, Utah, 1973-78, prof., 1978-84, asst. dean, 1978-81, dean, 1984-89, v.p., 1989-90; pres. Weber State U., Ogden, Utah, 1990—. Cons. Goodyear, Hughes Aircraft, Portland GE, Esso Resources Ltd., GE. Co-author: Organization and People: Readings, Cases, and Exercises in Organizational Behavior, 1976, Novations: Strategies for Career Management, 1986; also articles. Named Outstanding Prof. of Yr., Brigham Young U., 1981; Baker scholar Harvard U., 1966. Mem. Am. Assn. State Colls. and Univs. (com. 1991—), Ogden C. of C. (exec. com. 1990—), Rotary (prograam com. Ogden 1991—, Harris fellow 1992—), Phi Beta Kappa. Office: Weber State U Presidents Office 3750 Harrison Blvd Ogden UT 84408-0001

THOMPSON, PAUL MICHAEL, lawyer; b. Dubuque, Iowa, Aug. 30, 1935; s. Frank W. and Genevieve (Cassutt) T.; m. Mary Jacqueline McManus, Jan. 30, 1960; children: Anne, Tricia, Paul, Tim, Jim. BA magna cum laude, Loras Coll., 1957; LL.B., Georgetown U., 1959. Bar: Iowa 1959, D.C. 1959, Va. 1966. Atty. appellate ct. br. NLRB, Washington, 1962-66; assoc. Hunton & Williams, Richmond, Va., 1966-71, ptnr., 1971—. Adj. prof. The T.C. Williams Sch. Law U. Richmond; adj. prof. law sch. Coll. William and Mary Sch. Law. Served with JAGC, USAF, 1960-62. Mem. ABA, Va. State Bar, Va. Bar Assn., Internat. Bar Assn., Commonwealth Club. Roman Catholic. Office: Hunton & Williams Riverfront Plaza E Tower 951 E Byrd St Richmond VA 23219 Personal E-mail: thompmerrypoint@aol.com. Business E-Mail: pthompson@hunon.com.

THOMPSON, PETER J. manufacturing executive; Pres. U.S. opers. Schweitzer-Mauduit Internat., Inc., Alpharetta, Ga., 1995—. Office: Schweitzer-Mauduit Internat Inc 100 N Point Ctr E Ste 600 Alpharetta GA 30022-8263

THOMPSON, PETER L. lawyer; s. David D. and Lynn P. Thompson; m. Amy A. Aldredge, Sept. 12, 1987; children: Elizabeth R., Bennett D., Miles M. BS, Bowdoin Coll., 1991; JD, U. Maine, 1994. Cert.: Maine 1994. Atty. Law Offices of Peter L. Thompson, Portland, Maine, 1994—. Dir. Consumer Health Law Program, Augusta, Maine, 1997—; bd. dirs. Brain Injury Assn. Maine, Augusta, 2001—. Mem.: Assn. Trial Lawyers Am., Maine Employment Lawyers Assn., Maine Bar Assn., Maine Trial Lawyers Assn. Office: Law Offices of Peter L Thompson 217 Commercial St Unit 200 Portland ME 04101 Office Phone: 207-874-0909. E-mail: peter@ptlawoffice.com.

THOMPSON, PETER LAYARD HAILEY, SR., landscape and golf course architect, architectural firm executive; b. Modesto, Calif., Apr. 26, 1939; BS in East Asian Studies, U. Oreg., 1962, B in Landscape Architecture, M in Urban Planning, U. Oreg., 1971; postgrad., U. Calif., Berkeley, 1975, Nat. U. Registered landscape arch., Calif., Oreg., Wash., Nev. With Oreg. Planning Commn., Lane County, 1965-70, commr. Eugene, 1981-83; sr. assoc. Ruff, Cameron, Lacoss, Eugene, 1971-75; prin. Peter L. H. Thompson & Assocs., Eugene, 1975-83, John H. Midby & Assocs., Las Vegas, Nev., 1983-86, Thompson-Wihlborg, Ltd., Corte Madera, Calif., 1982-89, Thompson Planning Group (now Thompson Golf Planning), Ltd., Novato, Calif., 1989—. With Oreg. Planning Commn., commr., 1981-83, Novato, Calif. Planning Commn., commr. 1989-93, pres. 1989-93; spkr. Oreg. Home Builders Conf., 1980, Pacific Coast Builders Conf., 1984, Tacoma Country Club Pro-Pres. Tournament, 1991, Madrona Links Men's Golf Club, 1991, Twin Lakes Country Club Pro-Pres. Tournament, 1992, Golf Expo, Palm Springs, Calif., 1993, 95, Golf Expo, Nashville, 1993, Golf Expo, Monterey, Calif., 1994, others. Contbr. articles to mags. Mem. citizen's adv. bd. City of Eugene, Oreg., City of Las Vegas. Mem. USGA, Am. Soc. Landscape Archs., Am. Assn. Planners, Nat. Golf Found., Urban Land Inst., Rotary Internat. Office: Thompson Golf Planning Ltd 1510 Grant Ave Ste 305 Novato CA 94945-3146 Office Phone: 415-878-2020.

THOMPSON, PETER M. retired food products executive; b. Australia; Student, Oxford U., Columbia U. Regional v.p. for Brazil Pepsi-Cola Internat., 1980—83; CEO Grand Met. PLC, 1984—94; pres. Snack Ventures Europe, Walkers Snack Foods Pepsi-Cola Internat., 1994—96, pres., COO, 1996—98, pres., CEO, 1998—2001, Pepsico Beverages Internat., Pepsico, Inc., Purchase, NY, 2001—04; ret., 2004. Office: Pepsico Beverages Internat 700 Anderson Hill Rd Purchase NY 10577

THOMPSON, RALPH GORDON, federal judge; b. Oklahoma City, Dec. 15, 1934; s. Lee Bennett and Elaine (Bizzell) T.; m. Barbara Irene Hencke, Sept. 5, 1964; children: Lisa, Elaine, Maria. BBA, U. Okla., 1956, JD, 1961. Bar: Okla. 1961. Spl. agt. Office of Spl. Investigations, USAF, 1957—60; ptnr. Thompson, Thompson, Harbour & Selph (and predecessors), Oklahoma City, 1961-75; judge U.S. Dist. Ct. for Western Dist. Okla., Oklahoma City, 1975—; chief judge U.S. Dist. Ct. (we. dist.) Okla., 1986-93. Mem. Okla. Ho. of Reps., 1966-70, asst. minority floor leader, 1969-70; spl. justice Supreme Ct. Okla., 1970-71; tchr. Harvard Law Sch. Trial Advocacy Workshop, 1981—; apptd. by chief justice of U.S. to U.S. Fgn. Intelligence Surveillance Ct., 1990-97; elected to jud. conf. of the U.S., 1997; apptd. to Edward J. Devitt Disting. Svc. Justice award selection com., 1997-99; apptd. by chief justice of U.S. to exec. com. of Jud. Conf. of the U.S., 1998-2000; coord. Long Range Planning for Fed. Judiciary, 1999-2000. Co-author: Bryce Harlow: Mr. Integrity, Bob Burke and Ralph G. Thompson, 2000 (nominee Pulitzer Prize, 2000). Rep. nominee for lt. gov., Okla., 1970; chmn. bd. ARC, Oklahoma City, 1970-72; chmn., pres. Okla. Young Lawyers Conf., 1965; mem. bd. visitors U. Okla., 1975-78. Lt. USAF, 1957-60, col. Res., ret. Decorated Legion of Merit; named Oklahoma City's Outstanding Young Man, Oklahoma City Jaycees, 1967, Outstanding Fed. Trial Judge, Okla. Trial Lawyers Assn., 1980; recipient Regents Alumni award U. Okla., 1990, Disting. Svc. award, 1993, Jour. Record Pub. Co. award for Disting. Svc., 2001, Humanitarian award Oklahoma City Pub. Schs. Found., 2003; inducted Okla. Hall of Fame, 1995, Fellow Am. Bar Found.; mem. ABA, Fed. Bar Assn., Okla. Bar Assn. (chmn. sect. internat. law and gen. practice 1974-75), Oklahoma County Bar Assn. (Jud. Svc. award 1988), Jud. Conf. U.S. (com. on ct. adminstrn. 1981-89, com. on fed.-state jurisdiction 1988-91), U.S. Dist. Judges Assn. 10th Cir. (pres. 1992-94), Rotary (hon.), Order of Coif, Am. Inns of Ct. (pres. XXIII 1995-96), Phi Beta Kappa (pres. chpt. 1985-86, Phi Beta Kappa of Yr. 1991), Beta Theta Pi, Phi Alpha Delta. Episcopalian. Office: US Dist Ct 200 NW 4th St Oklahoma City OK 73102-3027

THOMPSON, RALPH NEWELL, former chemical corporation executive; b. Boston, Mar. 4, 1918; s. Ralph and Lillian May (Davenport) T.; m. Virginia Kenniston, Jan. 31, 1942; children: Pamela, Nicholas, Diana. BS, MIT, 1940. Research engr. Middlesex Products Co., Cambridge, Mass., 1940-42; tech. dir. Falulah Paper Co., Fitchburg, Mass., 1945-48; staff engr. to v.p., div. gen. mgr. Calgon Corp., Pitts., 1948-70; v.p. mktg., corp. devel. Pa. Indsl. Chem. Corp., Clairton, 1970-74; gen. mgr. chem. div. Thiokol Corp., Trenton, N.J., 1974-76, group v.p.-chem. Newtown, Pa., 1976-82; marine artist, specializing in lighthouses and historic sailing vessels, 1982—. Dir. Mulford Co. Inc., Mass., 1956-82, Thiokol Can. Ltd., 1975-82, Thiokol Chems., Ltd., Eng., 1976-82, Toray Thiokol Co. Ltd., Japan, 1976-82, Nisso-Ventron K.K., Japan, 1977-82, S.W. Chem. Services Inc., Tex., 1978-82, S.W. Plastics Europe (S.A.), Belgium, 1978-82, Dynachem. Corp., Calif., 1979-82, Carstab Corp., Ohio, 1980-82 Patentee in field. Mem. Mt. Lebanon (Pa.) Civic League, 1950-74. Served with USNR, 1942-45. Recipient Goodreau Meml. Fund medal in chemistry, 1936 Fellow Am. Inst. Chemists; mem. TAPPI (contributor monograph series 1950-65), N.Y. Acad. Scis., Soc. Chem. Industry, Nat. Maritime Soc., Am. Soc. Marine Artists, Mil. Order World Wars, Pa. Soc., Soc. Descs. Colonial Clergy. Republican. Presbyterian. E-mail: corbet1006@aol.com.

THOMPSON, RAYMOND HARRIS, retired anthropologist, educator; b. Portland, Me., May 10, 1924; s. Raymond and Eloise (MacIntyre) T.; m. Molly Kendall, Sept. 9, 1948; children: Margaret Kelsey Luchetta, Mary Frances. BS, Tufts U., 1947; A.M., Harvard U., 1950, PhD, 1955. Fellow div. hist. research Carnegie Instn., Washington, 1950-52; asst. prof. anthropology, curator Mus. Anthropology, U. Ky., 1952-56; faculty U. Ariz., 1956-97, prof. anthropology, 1964—, Riecker Disting. prof., 1980-97, head dept., 1964-80; emeritus, 1997; dir. Ariz. State Mus., 1964-97; emeritus, 1997. Mem. adv. panel program in anthropology NSF, 1963-64, mem. mus. collections program, 1983-85; mem. NSF grad. fellowship panel Nat. Acad. Scis.-NRC, 1964-66; mem. research in nursing in patient care rev. com. USPHS, 1967-69; com. on social sci. commn. edn. in agr. and natural resources Nat. Acad. Scis., 1968-69; mem. anthropology com. examiners Grad. Record Exam., 1967-70, chmn., 1969-70; mem. com. recovery archaeol. remains, 1972-77, chmn., 1973-77; collaborator Nat. Park Service, 1972-76; mem. Ariz. Hist. Adv.

Commn., 1966-97, chmn., 1971-74, chmn. hist. sites rev. com., 1971-83; chmn. Ariz. Humanities Council, 1973-77, mem., 1979-85; adv. bd. Ariz. Hist. Recors, 1976-84; mem. research review panel for archaeology NEH, 1976-77, mem. rev. panel for museums, 1978, Ariz. Archaeology Adv. Commn., 1985-97; cons. task force on archaeology Adv. Council on Historic Preservation, 1978. Author: Modern Yucatecan Maya Pottery Making, 1958; editor: Migrations in New World Culture History, 1958, When is a Kiva, 1990; mem. editl. bd. Science, 1972-77. Trustee Mus. No. Ariz., 1969-84, 86-90; bd. dirs. Tucson Art Mus., 1974-77; cons. Nat. Mus. Act Coun., 1984-86. Served with USNR, 1944-45, PTO. Recipient Pub. Svc. award, Dept. Interior, 1990. Fellow AAAS (chmn. sect. H 1977-78), Tree-Ring Soc., Am. Anthrop. Assn. (Disting. Svc. award 1980); mem. Soc. Am. Archaeology (editor 1958-62, exec. com. 1963-64, pres. 1976-77, disting. svc. award 1998), Am. Soc. Conservation Archaeology (Conservation award 1980), Seminario de Cultura Maya, Am. Assn. Museums (accreditation vis. com. 1972, 82-90, cons. mus. assessment program 1983-89, repatriation task force 1987, steering com. mus. data collection program 1988-93), Internat. Coun. Museums (assoc.), Coun. Mus. Anthropology (dir. 1978-79, pres. 1980-83), Assn. Sci. Mus. Dirs. (sec.-treas. 1978-80), Ariz. Acad. Sci., Ariz. Archaeol. and Hist. Soc. (Byron Cummings award 1993), Mus. Assn. Ariz. (pres. 1983, 84), Phi Beta Kappa, Sigma Xi. Office: Univ Ariz Ariz State Museum Tucson AZ 85721-0026

THOMPSON, RICHARD, writer; b. Balt., Md., Sept. 26, 1946; s. John and Mary Thompson; m. Jeanne Dunn, July 21, 1969; children: Christopher, Kimberly. BS, U. of Balt., 1972—79. Systems specialist Social Security Adminstrn., Balt., 1966—2000. Author: The Tiger Cruise, North Star Bay. Petty officer 3rd class USN, 1967—68, Atlantic Fleet. Office: Kje Publishing PO Box 6672 Ellicott City MD 21042 Office Phone: 410-960-2208. Business E-Mail: publisher@kjepublishing.com.

THOMPSON, RICHARD DICKSON, lawyer; b. Lexington, Ky., Aug. 14, 1955; s. Lawrence Sidney and Algernon Smith (Dickson) T.; m. Bobbi Dale Magidoff, Aug. 3, 1980; children: Anne Katherine, Harrison Asher, Tracey Ruth. AB, Harvard U., 1977; JD, Stanford U., 1980. Bar: Calif. 1980, U.S. Dist. Ct. (so. dist.) Calif. 1980. Assoc. Rosenfeld Meyer & Susman, Beverly Hills, Calif., 1980-83, Silverberg Rosen Leon & Behr, L.A., 1983-86, assoc. ptnr., 1986-89; ptnr. Silverberg Katz Thompson & Braun, L.A., 1989-95, Bloom, Hergott, Dremer, & Cook, Beverly Hills, Calif., 1995—2000; sr. v.p., corp. devel. then COO The Brodia Group, San Francisco, 2000—02; of counsel Bloom, Hergott & Dremer, Beverly Hills, Calif., 2002—. Former bd. trustees L.A. Copyright Soc. (former pres.). Mem. Order of the Coif, Phi beta Kappa. Office: Bloom Hergott & Dremer 150 S Rodeo Dr Beverly Hills CA 90212

THOMPSON, RICHARD FREDERICK, psychologist, neuroscientist, educator; b. Portland, Oreg., 1930; s. Frederick Albert and Margaret St. Clair (Marr) T.; m. Judith K. Pedersen, May 22, 1960; children: Kathryn M., Elizabeth K., Virginia St. C. BA, Reed Coll., 1952; MS, U. Wis., 1953, PhD, 1956. Asst. prof. med. psychology Med. Sch. U. Oreg., Portland, 1959-63, assoc. prof., 1963-65, prof., 1965-67; prof. psychobiology U. Calif., Irvine, 1967-73, 75-80; prof. psychology Harvard U., Cambridge, Mass., 1973-74, Lashley chair prof., 1973; prof. psychology, Bing prof. human biology Stanford U., Palo Alto, Calif., 1980-87; Keck prof. psychology and biol. scis. U. So. Calif., L.A., 1987—, dir. neuroscience program, 1989—. Author: Foundations of Physiological Psychology, 1967, (with others) Psychology, 1971, Introduction to Physiological Psychology, 1975; Psychology editor (with others), W.H. Freeman & Co. publs., chief editor, Behavioral Neurosci., 1983—; editor: Jour. Comparative and Physiol. Psychology, 1981-83; regional editor: (with others) Physiology and Behavior; contbr. (with others) articles to profl. jours. Fellow AAAS, APA (Disting. Sci. Contbn. award 1974, governing coun. 1974—), Soc. Neurosci. (councilor 1972-76); mem. NAS, Am. Acad. Arts and Scis., Internat. Brain Rsch. Orgn., Am. Philos. Soc., Psychonomic Soc. (gov. 1972-77, chmn. 1976), Am. Psychol. Soc. (pres. 1994-96), Western Psychol. Assn. (pres. 1994-95), Soc. Exptl. Psychology (Warren medal). Office: Univ of So Calif Neuroscis Program HNB 122 Univ Park Los Angeles CA 90007 Office Phone: 213-740-7350. Business E-Mail: thompson@usc.edu.

THOMPSON, RICHARD L. manufacturing executive; B in Engring., Stanford U. With Caterpillar Inc., 1983—, v.p. Customer Services, Solar Turbines Inc., pres. Solar Turbines Inc., v.p. engring. divsn., 1990-95, group pres., 1995—. Office: Caterpillar Inc 100 NE Adams St Peoria IL 61629-0002

THOMPSON, RICHARD LEON, pharmaceutical company executive, lawyer; b. Rochester, N.Y., Dec. 5, 1944; s. Leslie L. and Marion (Cosad) T.; m. Catherine Jean Terry, July 6, 1974; children: Kristin Anne, Catherine Elizabeth. AB cum laude, SUNY, Albany, 1966; MA, Syracuse U., 1967; JD, Cath. U., 1975. Staff dir., counsel U.S. Ho. of Reps., Washington, 1973-78; dir. Abbott Labs., Washington, 1978-83; v.p. Squibb Corp., Washington, 1983-89, Bristol-Myers Squibb Corp., Washington, 1989—2001, sr. v.p. policy and govt. affairs, 2001—. Chmn. legis. adv. com. Proprietary Assn., Washington, 1984; bd. dirs. Bus. Govt. Rels. Coun. Mem. com. on changing enrollments Fairfax (Va.) County Pub. Sch., 1983-84, supts. adv. com., 1984-85, mem., 1988-98; mem. Fed. City Coun., 1992; chmn. legis. com. P.R.-U.S.A. Found., 1985-95; co-chair Edn. in 2010; bd. dirs. D.C. Hospice, Bryce Harlow Found., 1990-95; bd. dirs., treas. Ford Theater, 2000--; chmn. governance com. Meridian Internat. Ctr., 2000-02 1st lt. U.S. Army, 1968-69, Vietnam. Named one of Outstanding Young Men of Am., Jaycees, 1976. Mem. ABA, D.C. Bar Assn., Pharm. Mfrs. Assn. (chmn. Washington reps. com.1988), Congl. Country Club, City Club. Office: Bristol-Myers Squibb Corp 655 15th St NW Ste 300 Washington DC 20005-5717

THOMPSON, RICHARD LLOYD, retired pastor; b. Lansing, Mich., May 8, 1939; s. Lloyd Walter and Gladys V. (Gates) T.; m. Dianne Lee Tuttle, Nov. 14, 1958; children: Matthew, Beth Anne, Douglas. BA, Azusa Pacific U., 1969; MDiv, Concordia Theol. Sem., 1973; DD, Concordia U., Mequon, Wis., 1997. Aerospace industry test engr. Hycon Mfg. Co., Monrovia, Calif., 1961-69; pastor Trinity Luth. Ch., Cedar Rapids, Iowa, 1973-84, Billings, Mont., 1984-94, Good Shepherd Luth. Ch., Watertown, Wis., 1994—2001; ret., 2001. Chmn. mission com. Iowa E. dist. Luth. Ch. Mo. Synod, 1979-81, 2nd v.p. Iowa dist. E., Cedar Rapids, 1981-84, bd. mgr. Concordia plans, St. Louis, 1983-86, bd. dirs., St. Louis, 1986-98, chmn. bd. dirs., 1992-98, mem. commn. on theology and ch. rels., 2001; served on various task forces and coms. dealing with structure and vision setting for chs. at local, dist. and nat. level, 1975—. Mem. Nat. Exch. Club, Cedar Rapids, 1982-84, Billings, 1986; pro tem com. structure Commn. Doctrial Rev., 2001—. With USN, 1957-61. Mem. Kiwanis. Lutheran. Avocations: attending auctions, yard work, travel, exercise activity. E-mail: diarich39@msn.com., rltso@hotmai.com.

THOMPSON, RICHARD S. lawyer; b. Vidalia, Ga. m. Jennifer Darby; children: Loree Ann, Darby. Grad. cum laude, Mercer U., 1979, grad., 1982. Asst. dist. atty. Douglas County, Ga.; asst. atty. gen. State of Ga., 1986—88; pvt. practice Statesboro and Vidalia, 1989—95; ptnr. McNatt, Greene & Thompson, Vidalia, Ga., 1995—2001; U.S. atty. So. Dist. Ga., 2001—. Office: So Dist Ga PO Box 8999 Savannah GA 31412

THOMPSON, RICHARD THOMAS, academic administrator; b. Buffalo, Oct. 11, 1939; m. Nancy A. Streeter, July 29, 1959; children: Elizabeth Thompson Grapentine, Richard Thomas Jr., David Bryant. BA, Ea. Mich. U., 1961, MA, 1963; LLD (hon.), Walsh Coll., 2000. Cert. tchr. Mich. Tchr. Warren Consol. Sch., Mich., 1961—66; dean, pres. Highland Lake campus Oakland C.C., Union Lake, 1966—75, pres. Orchard Ridge campus Farmington, 1975—84, v.p. Bloomfield, 1984—88, vice chancellor, 1988—91, chancellor, 1996—, pres. Auburn Hills campus. Arbitrator Better Bus. Bur., Detroit, 1987—; bd. dirs., past chair Providence Hosp., Southfield; cons. examiner North Ctrl. Assn. Commn. Higher Learning, 1988—. Contbr. articles to profl. jours. Pres. Oakway Symphony Orch., Livonia, Mich., 1981—85; chair Oakland Literacy Coun., Pontiac, 1988—. Recipient Leadership award, Oakland County C. of C., 1987, Tricounty Disting. Svc. award, Detroit Coll. Bus., 1996, Shirley B. Gordon award Distinction, Phi Theta Kappa Internat., 2001. Mem.: Phi Delta Kappa. Home: 625 E Commerce St Milford MI 48381-1723 Office: Oakland Community Coll 2480 Opdyke Rd Bloomfield Hills MI 48304-2223

THOMPSON, ROBERT ALLAN, aerospace engineer; b. Cleve., June 10, 1937; s. Roy Henry and Viola Alverta (Nehls) T.; m. Louise Alberta Saari, Nov. 27, 1970. BSEE, Case Western Reserve U., 1958; postgrad. studies, Cleve. State U., 1959, John Marshall Law Sch., 1970; PhD, Union Inst., 1979. Registered profl. engr. Ohio, Wis., Conn., R.I. Tchr. Cleve. Bd. Edn., 1958-65; rsch. engr. Sohio Satellite Tracking Sta., Standard Oil Rsch. Lab., Cleve., 1958-63, acting dir., 1964-65; dir. Warrensville Hghts. (Ohio) Planetarium and Space Sci Program, 1964-65; tchr. spl. programs faculty Case Inst. Tech., Cleve., 1965; dir. planning phase sci. divsn. Cleve. Supplementary Edn. Ctr., 1965-66; dir. James A Lovell Regional Space Ctr., Milw., 1967-73; engring. and edn. cons. Chgo., 1973-78, Mystic, Conn., 1978—; pres., chmn. bd. Spatialworld Corp., 1982—. Chmn. secondary math. curriculum com. Cleve. Pub. Schs., 1963-64; mem. Wis. Aerospace Edn. Com., 1968-71; lectr. U. Wis., Milw., 1968-71; sec. Friends of Space Ctr., 1968-75. Author: The New Egoshell: An Individualized Space Age Realty; co-author (with L. Thompson) Egoshell-Planetary Individualism Balanced within Planetary Interdependence, 1987; contbr. articles to profl. jours. Kiwanian faculty adv. Collinwood Key Club, 1959—64. Recipient Leadership award, NE Cleve. Kiwanis, 1961; Goodwin Watson fellow, Union Inst., 1978—79. Fellow: Brit. Interplanetary Assn.; mem.: AIAA (chmn. Wis. sect. 1969—70, sr. mem. Conn. sect., coun. 1984—85, disting. lectr. 1987—89), AAAS, IEEE (sr. life) (chmn. membership com. Cleve. sect. 1965—66, exec. com.), Cleve. Astron. Soc. (exec. com. 1966—67), Cleve. Engring. Soc., Inst. Planetary Egology (pres. 1988—), Union Inst. Alumni Assn., Case Alumni Assn. Home: PO Box 624 Mystic CT 06355-0624 Office: PO Box 2001 Mystic CT 06355-0624 Office Phone: 860-572-0145. Personal E-mail: egoshell@aol.com.

THOMPSON, ROBERT CHARLES, lawyer; b. Council, Idaho, Apr. 20, 1942; s. Ernest Lavelle and Evangeline Montgomery (Carlson) T.; m. Marilyn Anne Wilcox, Jan. 17, 1960 (dec. Mar. 1962); m. Patricia Joan Price, June 1, 1963 (div. 1969); m. Jan Nesbitt, June 29, 1973 (dec. May 1998); m. Shari Lewis, Feb. 7, 1999; children: Tanya, Carrie, Christopher, Eric. AB, Harvard U., 1963, LLB, 1967. Bar: Mass. 1967, Calif. 1983, U.S. Dist. Ct. (ea. dist.) Mass. 1975, U.S. Ct. Appeals (1st cir.) 1976, U.S. Ct. Appeals (9th cir.) 1984, U.S. Dist. Ct. (no. dist.) Calif. 1983, U.S. Dist. Ct. (ea. dist.) Calif., 1996. Assoc. Choate, Hall & Stewart, Boston, 1967-73; asst. regional counsel EPA, Boston, 1973-75, regional counsel, 1975-82, assoc. gen. counsel, 1979-82, regional counsel San Francisco, 1982-84; ptnr. Graham & James, San Francisco, 1984-91, LeBoeuf, Lamb, Greene & MacRae LLP, San Francisco, 1992—99, of counsel, 2000—. Contbr. articles to profl. jours. Bd. dirs. Peninsula Indsl. and Bus. Assn., Palo Alto, Calif., 1986-98, chmn. Cambridge (Mass.) Conservation Commn., 1972-74; co-chmn. The Clift Confs. on Environ. Law, 1983-98; assoc. mem. Bay Conservation and Devel. Commn., 1998-2000. John Russell Shaw traveling fellow Harvard Coll., 1963-64; recipient Regional Administrs. Bronze medal EPA, 1976, 84. Mem. ABA (natural resources sect., com. on native Am. natural resources law, spl. com. on mktg.), Human Rights Watch, Phi Beta Kappa. Democrat. Episcopalian. Avocations: personal computers, yoga, antiques, wines, cooking, gardening. Office: LeBoeuf Lamb Greene & MacRae One Embarcadero Ctr San Francisco CA 94111

THOMPSON, ROBERT DOUGLAS, computer science educator, banker, consultant; b. Van Wert, Ohio, Apr. 2, 1944; s. Ernest Clinton and Gertrude Marcele (McBride) T.; m. Gail Joyce Knudson; children: Linda Marie Temple, Cheryl Elizabeth Christensen, Mark Robert. BS summa cum laude, Huntington Coll., 1966; MA, Mich. State U., East Lansing, 1967; student, Wright State U., 1974-90, Bowling Green State U., 1984, U. Dayton, 1985. Cert. tchr., Ohio. Office sec. United Brethren in Christ Denomination Ch., Huntington, Ind., 1963—66; grad. rsch. asst. Mich. State U., East Lansing, 1966—67; instr. Wright State U. Lake Campus, Celina, Ohio, 1976, 1993—97, Tri Star Career Compact, Celina, 1984—96; ptnr. Thompson Painting and Carpentry, Rockford, Ohio, 1969—95; tchr., dept. head, tech. coord. St. Henry Consol. Local Schs., Ohio, 1967—97; asst. v.p., br. mgr. Peoples Bank Co., Rockford, 1997—. Author, photographer numerous newspaper articles, 1974—, Business Professionals of America Ohio Association Handbook, 1989. Bd. dirs., pres., v.p. Oscar Figert Guidance Clinic, 1972-75; pres. Mercer County Mental Health Clinic, 1975; fin. chmn. Coldwater United Meth. Ch., 1982-90, 2000—, chmn. adminstrv. bd., 1994-99, lay leader, 1998—; solicitor Coldwater Combined Charities, 1982, 85; PRIDE evaluation svc. rep. State Dept. Edn., 1973, 78; troop treas. Coldwater area Boy Scouts Am., 1989-92; mem. office tech. adv. bd. Wright State U.-Lake Campus, Celina, Ohio, 1991—; gen. chairperson Rockford Combined Charities, 1997-2001; exec. officer Rockford Citizen Crime Awareness, 1998—; trustee Shanes Park, 1999—, Rockford Carnegie Libr., 1999—, v.p. 2001, pres. 2002; pres. Leota Braun Charitable Found., Inc., 2002--. Named super advisor Ohio Office Edn. Assn., 1983, 84, 85; recipient proclamation of excellence, Ohio State Dept. Edn. Mem. NEA, Am. Vocat. Assn., Bus. Profl. Am. (advisor 1973-97, star advisor and honor advisor award), Ohio Bus. Tchrs. Assn. (state exec. bd. 1976-77, 93-98, state conv. chmn. 1995, We. Ohio Bus. Tchr. of Yr. award 1983, 91, 95, Editor of Publs. 1996-98), Ohio Edn. Assn., St. Henry Edn. Assn. (local pres. 1970-72), Wabash Valley Dartball Assn. (sec. 1978-79, 87-88), Rockford C. of C. (treas. 1998—), Lions (Rockford chpt. v.p. 2001-04), Delta Pi Epsilon. Republican. Avocations: travel, antique autos, choir singing, home restoration. Home: 405 S Main St PO Box 242 Rockford OH 45882-0242 Office: Peoples Bank Co PO Box 475 101 N Main St Rockford OH 45882-0475 E-mail: rthompson@pbcbank.com.

THOMPSON, ROBERT FRANK, JR., career officer; b. Durham, N.C., Sept. 25, 1959; s. Robert Frank Sr. and Betty Ross (Connelly) T.; m. Vickie Marie Fjone, Nov. 17, 1979; children: Robert Frank III, Kimberly Anne. BA in English and History, Met. State Coll. Denver, 1993. Commd. 2d lt. U.S. Army Nat. Guard, 1989, advanced through grades to maj., 1998; stationed at Panama and Fort Polk, La., 1983-87; rural rt. carrier U.S. Postal Svc., Brighton, Colo., 1988-93; adminstrv. officer Colo. Army Nat. Guard, Denver, 1993-98, state family program dir., 1999-2000. Defense movement coord, 1998; master fitness trainer Colo. Army Nat. Guard, 1987, advisor work climate improvement program, 1995, facilitator increasing human effectiveness, 1996. Editor The Adv., 1990-91; founder Bob Thompson Freelance Writing and Editing Svcs., 2000; founder, gen. editor The Christian Fine Arts Review, 2000; contbr. poetry to publs. including The bible Advocate mag., The Sound of Poetry CD Set, 2001. Deacon Crossroads Bapt. Ch., Northglenn, Colo., 1997-99. Decorated Army Commendation medal (6); recipient Exceptional Acad. Achievement award ROTC, 1989, Metro State Coll. V.P.'s Honor Roll (3). Mem.: N.G. Assn. U.S., U.S. F.A. Assn. (Hon. Order St. Barbaras 1993), Poetry Soc. Colo., Pi Gamma Mu, Golden Key, Phi Alpha Theta. Republican. Avocations: marathons, freelance writing, travel, reading, sports. Home: 11033 Forest Way Thornton CO 80233 E-mail: bvthom@comcast.net.

THOMPSON, ROBERT KNOX, surgeon; b. Memphis, Jan. 4, 1957; MD, U. Tenn. Ctr. Health Scis., 1983. Diplomate Am. Bd. Surgery, Am. Bd. Gen. Vascular Surgery. Intern U. Tex., San Antonio, 1983-84, resident in gen. surgery, 1984-88; fellow in vascular surgery Baylor U. Med. Ctr., Dallas, 1988-89; pvt. practice San Antonio. Mem. staff Bapt. Meml. Hosp. Sys., San Antonio, Meth. Hosp., San Antonio; clin. assoc. prof. surgery U. Tex., San Antonio. Fellow ACS; mem. Soc. Vascular Surgery, Soc. Assocs. Vascular Surgery, San Antonio Vascular Surg. Soc., Bexar County Med. Soc., Tex. Med. Assn., Tex. Surg. Soc. Office: Peripheral Vascular Assocs 8715 Village Dr Ste 518 San Antonio TX 78217-5501

THOMPSON, ROBERT L., JR., pharmaceutical executive, lawyer; b. St. Paul, Aug. 9, 1944; s. Robert L. and Dorothy R. (Bergstrom) T.; m. Carolyn H. Foss, Aug. 4, 1973; children: Sarah, Kathryn, Jill. BA, Macalester Coll., St. Paul, 1967; JD, U. Oreg., 1973; LLM, NYU, 1988. Bar: Minn. 1973, U.S. Dist. Ct. Minn. 1978, N.Y. 1984. Corp. counsel Northrup King Co., Mpls., 1974-84; assoc. gen. counsel Sandoz Corp., N.Y.C., 1984-88, v.p., gen. counsel, sec., 1989-96; exec. v.p., gen. counsel Novartis Corp., N.Y.C., 1997-2001; vice chmn., pres., mng. dir. Novartis India, Ltd., Bombay, 2001—02; v.p., gen. counsel Novartis Insts. for BioMed. Rsch., Inc., 2002—. Mem. adv. bd. FM Global Ins. Co., N.Y.C., 1990-2001; mem. bd. visitors U. Oreg. Law Sch., 1995-2001. 1st lt. U.S. Army, 1968-70. Mem. ABA, Assn. Bar City N.Y. Republican. Presbyterian. Office: Novartis Insts for BioMed Rsch Inc 400 Technology Sq Cambridge MA 02139

THOMPSON, ROBERT LEE, agricultural economist, educator; b. Canton, N.Y., Apr. 25, 1945; s. Robert M. and Esther Louise (Weatherup) T.; m. Karen Hansen, Aug. 9, 1968; children— Kristina Marie, Eric Robert. BS, Cornell U., Ithaca, N.Y., 1967; MS, Purdue U., West Lafayette, Ind., 1969, PhD, 1974; LLD, Dalhousie U., 1999; DSc honoris causa, Pa. State U., 1999. Vol. agriculturalist Internat. Vol. Service, Pakse and Vientiane, Laos, 1968-70; vis. prof. Fed. Univ. Vicosa, Brazil, 1972-73; prof. Purdue U., West Lafayette, Ind., 1974-93, dean of agr., 1987-93; rsch. scholar Internat. Inst. for Applied Systems Analysis, Laxenburg, Austria, 1983; sr. staff economist Coun. Econ. Advisers, Washington, 1983-85; asst. sec. econs. U.S. Dept. Agr., Washington, 1985-87; pres., CEO Winrock Internat. Inst. Agrl. Devel., 1993-98; sr. advisor World Bank, Washington, 1998-99, dir. rural devel., 1999—2002; sr. advisor Ctr. for Strategic and Internat. Studies, 1998—, Nat. Ctr. for Food and Agr. Policy, Washington, 2003—; Gardner prof. agr. policy U. Ill., Urbana, 2004—. Vis. prof. Econ. Rsch. Svc., USDA, 1979-80; chmn. adv. coun. Nat. Ctr. for Food and Agrl. Policy, Washington, 1987-92; mem. Ind. Commn. on Agr. and Rural Devel., 1989-93, Nat. Commn. on Agrl. Trade and Export Policy, 1985-86, Nat. Commn. Internat. Trade, Devel., and Cooperation, 1996-97; mem. bd. agr. NRC, 1987-92; mem. Internat. Policy Coun. on Agr. and Trade, 1987—, chmn., 2000—; mem. USDA Joint Coun. on Food and Agrl. Scis., 1994-96; cons. USAID, OECD, Agr. Can., Ford Found., Brazilian Agr. Ministry, FAO, World Bank, Internat. Food Policy Rsch. Inst., Internat. Maize and Wheat Improvement Ctr., U.S. Feed Grains Coun., Nat. Planning Assn., USIA, Centre for Internat. Econs., Canberra, Club d'Experts en Economie Agricole Internat., Paris, Danish Coun. Rsch. Policy, FAO, Rome; bd. dirs. Cordell Hull Inst., Washington. Contbr. numerous articles to profl. publs. Author monographs, book chpts. Bd. dirs. Ind. 4-H Found., Ind. Inst. Agr. Food and Nutrition, 1987-93, Inst. for Sci. in Soc., 1991-93, USDA Grad. Sch., Washington, 1985-87; mem. nat. adv. coun. Minorities in Agr., Natural Resources and Related Sci.; bd. dirs. Farm Found., 1987-92, chmn. 1991-92. Recipient Agrl. Rsch. award Purdue U., 1983, Outstanding Alumni award Cornell U., 1988, Superior Svc. award USDA, 1989, Justin Smith Morrill award, 1995, Nat. 4-H Alumni award, 1992, Chgo. Farmers Agriculturalist of Yr. award, 1992, Bob Pim Agrl. Vision award Nat. Forum Agr., 1997; named Humanitarian of Yr., Am. Coll. Nutrition, 1999. Fellow AAAS, Am. Agrl. Econs. Assn. (editorial coun. 1983-85, quality com. award 1979, 91, 93); mem. Internat. Agribus Mgmt. Assn. (bd. dirs.), Am. Econ. Assn., Internat. Assn. Agrl. Economists (pres. 1993-96), Coun. on Fgn. Rels., Bretton Woods Com., Royal Swedish Acad. Agr. and Forestry (fgn.), Ukrainian Acad. Agrl. Scis., Cosmos Club (Washington), Sigma Xi, Alpha Gamma Rho, Alpha Zeta (Centennial Honor Role award 1997), Gamma Sigma Delta. Republican. Avocation: foreign language study. Office: 326 Mumford Hall 1301 W Gregory Dr Urbana IL 61801-3608 Office Phone: 217-333-1313. E-mail: rlt@uiuc.edu.

THOMPSON, ROBY CALVIN, JR., orthopedic surgeon, educator; b. Winchester, Ky., May 1, 1934; s. Roby Calvin and Mary Davis (Guerrant) T.; m. Jane Elizabeth Searcy, May 2, 1959; children: Searcy Lee, Roby Calvin, III, Mary Alexandria. BA, Va. Mil. Inst., 1955; MD, U. Va., 1959. Diplomate Am. Bd. Orthopaedic Surgery (mem. bd. 1983). Intern Columbia Presbyn. Med. Center, N.Y.C., 1959-60, asst. resident, then resident in orthopedic surgery, 1963-67; instr. orthopaedic surgery Coll. Phys. and Surg. Columbia U., 1967-68; mem. faculty Med. Sch. U. Va., 1968-74, prof. orthopaedic surgery, vice chmn. dept. Med. Sch., 1973—94; prof., chmn. dept. Med. Sch. U. Minn., 1974—94; chief med. officer U. Minn. Health Sys., 1995-96, v.p. clin. and acad. affairs, 1996—2001; assoc. dean clin. affairs U. Minn. Sch. Medicine, 1996—. Mem. merit rev. bd. VA, 1977-80; mem. study sect. on applied physiology and orthopedics NIH, 1980-83; adv. council mem. NIH, Nat. Inst. Arthritis, Musculoskeletal Disease and Skin, 1987-91; chmn. bd. dirs. U. Minn. Physicians, 2001—, CEO, 2001—. Trustee Jour. Bone and Joint Surgery, 1988-94, chmn. bd. trustees, 1991-94; contbr. articles to med. jours. Capt. M.C. USAR, 1960-61. Grantee John Hartford Found., NIH Mem. ACS, Orthopaedic Rsch. and Edn. Found. (bd. trustees 1990-96), Am. Acad. Orthopaedic Surgeons (bd. dirs. 1975-76, 83-90, pres. 1986), Orthopaedic Rsch. Soc. (pres. 1978), Am. Orthopaedic Assn., Musculoskeletal Tumor Soc. (pres. 1988-89), U. Va. Med. Alumni Assn. (bd. dirs. 1979-84), Woodhill Club (Wayzata). Republican. Presbyterian. Office: U Minn MMC 293 420 Delaware St SE Minneapolis MN 55455-0374

THOMPSON, RONALD EDWARD, lawyer; b. Bremerton, Wash., May 24, 1931; s. Melville Herbert and Clara Mildred (Griggs) T.; m. Marilyn Christine Woods, Dec. 15, 1956; children: Donald Jeffery, Karen, Susan, Nancy, Sally, Claire BA, U. Wash., 1953, JD, 1958. Bar: Wash. 1959. Asst. city atty. City of Tacoma, 1960—61; pres. firm Thompson, Krilich, LaPorte, West & Lockner, P.S., Tacoma, 1961—99. Judge pro tem Mcpl. Ct., City of Tacoma, Pierce County Dist., 1972—, Pierce County Superior Ct., 1972—. Chmn. housing and social welfare com. City of Tacoma, 1965-69; mem. Tacoma Bd. Adjustment, 1967-71, chmn., 1968; mem. Tacoma Com. Future Devel., 1961-64, Tacoma Planning Commn., 1971-72; bd. dirs., pres. Mcpl. League Tacoma; bd. dirs. Pres. Tacoma Rescue Mission, Tacoma Pierce County Cancer Soc., Tacoma-Pierce County Heart Assn., Tacoma Grand Cinema, Tacoma-Pierce County Coun. for Arts, Econ. Devel. Coun. Puget Sound, Tacoma Youth Symphony, Kleiner Group Home, Tacoma C.C. Found., Pierce County Econ. Devel. Corp., Wash. Transp. Policy Inst.; Coalition to Keep Wash. Moving, precinct committeeman Rep. party, 1969-73. With AUS, 1953-55; col. Res. Recipient Internat. Cmty. Svc. award Optimist Club, 1970, Patriotism award Am. Fedn. Police, 1974, citation for cmty. svc. HUD, 1974, Disting. Citizen award Mcpl. League Tacoma-Pierce County, 1985; named Lawyer of the Yr. Pierce County Legal Secs. Assn., 1992. Mem. ATLA, Am. Arbitration Assn. (panel of arbitrators), ABA, Wash. State Bar Assn. (Local Hero award 2002), Tacoma-Pierce County Bar Assn. (sec. 1964, pres. 1979, mem. cts. and judiciary com. 1981-82), Wash. State Trial Lawyers Assn., Tacoma-Pierce County C. of C. (bd. dirs., exec. com., v.p., chmn.), Downtown Tacoma Assn. (com. chmn., bd. dirs. exec. com., chmn.), Variety Club (Seattle), Lawn Tennis Club, Tacoma Club, Optimist (Tacoma, internat. pres. 1973-74), Phi Delta Phi, Sigma Nu. Roman Catholic. Home: 3101 E Bay Dr NW Gig Harbor WA 98335-7610 Office: Atty Law PO Box 1189 7525 Pioneer Way Ste 101 Gig Harbor WA 98335-1165 Office Phone: 253-853-7449. E-mail: retpllc@att.net.

THOMPSON, RONALD H. chemical engineer, educator; b. Memphis, Feb. 21, 1935; s. Roy H. and Marie T.; m. Peggy Jo Hillier; children: Bart, Russell, Robin, Charles. BS, La. Technol. U., 1961, MS, 1968; PhD, U. Ark., 1973. Chief chemist Western Electric Co., Shreveport, La., 1968-71; from asst. prof. to prof. chem. engring., dir. Nuclear Ctr., La. Technol. U., Ruston, 1973—. Exec. v.p. Enviromed. Labs., Ruston; cons. in field; pres. TBRAC Cons., Ruston. Grantee U.S. Dept. Energy, 1994, 95. Mem. AAAS, Am. Chem. Soc., Am. Nuclear Soc., Health Physics Soc. Democrat. Baptist. Home: PO Box 653 Ruston LA 71273-0653 Office: La Technol U W Arizona St Ruston LA 71273

THOMPSON, RONALD MACKINNON, former family physician, artist, writer; b. N.Y.C., Oct. 19, 1916; s. George Harold and Pearl Anita (Hatfield) T.; m. Ethel Joyce Chastant, June 30, 1950; children: Phyllis Anita, Walter MacKinnon, Charles Chastant, Richard Douglas. BS, U. Chgo., 1947, MS, 1948, MD, 1949. Diplomate Am. Bd. Family Practice. Intern U. Mich., Ann Arbor, 1950-51; resident in psychiatry U. Tex., Galveston, 1951-52; pvt. practice, family and internal medicine South Dixie Med. Ctr., West Palm Beach, Fla., 1952-85; ret., 1985. Instr. Anatomy, U. Chgo., 1946-47, Pharmacology, 1948-49. Contbr. more than 300 poems and short stories to lit. mags., also articles to med. jours.; 7 one-man shows (over 30 awards for painting in regional and nat. shows); represented in permanent collections at 6 mus. Former mem. bd. dirs. Norton Mus. of Art, West Palm Beach. With Fla. N.G., 1936-40; cadet USAAF, Force, 1943-44. Over thirty awards for painting in juried regional and nat. shows. Fellow Am. Acad. Family Physicians; mem.

AMA, Fla. Med. Assn., Fla. Acad. of Family Physicians, Palm Beach County Med. Soc., Nat. Watercolor Soc., Ariz. Watercolor Soc. Republican. Episcopalian. Avocations: country writing, square and round dancing. Home: 308 Leisure World Mesa AZ 85206-3142

THOMPSON, RONELLE KAY HILDEBRANDT, library director; b. Brookings, S.D., Apr. 21, 1954; d. Earl E. and Maxine R. (Taplin) Hildebrandt; m. Harry Floyd Thompson II, Dec. 24, 1976; children: Clarissa, Harry III. BA in Humanities magna cum laude, Houghton Coll., 1976; MLS, Syracuse U., 1976; postgrad., U. Rochester, 1980, 81; cert., Miami U., 1990. Libr. asst. Norwalk (Conn.) Pub. Libr., 1977; elem. libr. Moriah Ctrl. Schs., Port Henry, NY, 1977—78; divsn. coord. pediat. gastroenterology and nutrition U. Rochester (N.Y.) Med. Ctr., 1978—81, cons., pediat. housestaff libr. com., 1980—81; dir. Medford Libr. U. S.C., Lancaster, 1981—83; dir. Mikkelsen Libr., Libr. Assocs., Ctr. for Western Studies, mem. libr. com. Augustana Coll., Sioux Falls, SD, 1983—, adminstrv. pers. coun., 1989—94, 1997—. Presenter in field. Contbr. articles to profl. jours. Mem. S.D. Symphony; advisor pers. dept. City of Sioux Falls. Recipient leader award YWCA, 1991; Gaylord Co. scholar Syracuse U., 1976, named S.D. Libr. of Yr., 1998. Mem. ALA, AAUW, Assn. Coll. and Rsch. Librs. (nat. adv. coun. coll. librs. sect. 1987—), Mountain Plains Libr. Assn. (chair acad. sect., nominating com. 1988, pres. 1993-94), S.D. Libr. Assn. (chair interlibr. coop. task force 1986-87, pres. 1987-88, chair recommended minimum salary task force 1988, chair local arrangements com. 1989-90, 2002—), S.D. Libr. Network (adv. coun. 1986—, exec. com. 1992-96, 1998-2000, chair adv. coun. 1994-96, 98-2000). Office: Augustana Coll Mikkelsen Libr 29th & Smt Sioux Falls SD 57197-0001 Office Phone: 605 274-4921. E-mail: ronelle thompson@augie.edu.

THOMPSON, SADA CAROLYN, actress; b. Des Moines, Sept. 27, 1927; d. Hugh Woodruff and Corlyss Elizabeth (Gibson) T.; m. Donald E. Stewart, 1949; 1 dau., Liza. BFA, Carnegie Inst. Tech., 1949; DFA, Carnegie Mellon, late 1970's. Speech tchr. 92d St YMHA, N.Y.C. Stage debut in The Time of Your Life at Carnegie Inst. Tech. Drama Sch., 1945; co-founder Univ. Playhouse, Mashpee, Mass., 1947, appeared at Pitts. Playhouse, The Playhouse, Erie, Pa., summer stock prodns. at Henrietta Hayloft Theatre, Rochester, N.Y., Cambridge, Mass.; New York debut in Under Milk Wood, at YMHA, 1953; appeared in Off Broadway revival at Circle in the Sq. Theatre, 1961, and Nat. Edn. Television presentation, 1966; appeared in plays The Clandestine Marriage, Provincetown Playhouse, N.Y.C., 1954, The White Devil and, The Carefree Tree at, Phoenix Theatre, N.Y.C., 1955, The Misanthrope, Off Broadways Theatre East, 1956, The River Line, Carnegie Hall Playhouse, 1957; joined Am. Shakespeare Festival, Stratford, Conn., 1957 appearing in Othello, Much Ado About Nothing, 1957-58, The Merry Wives of Windsor, Alls Well That Ends Well, 1959, Twelfth Night, The Tempest and, Antony and Cleopatra, 1960; appeared in Off Broadway prodn. of Chekhov's Ivanov, 1958, Broadway prodn. of Juno and the Paycock, 1959, Tartuffe at Lincoln Center Repertory Theatre, 1965, Johnny No-Trump, 1967, The American Dream, 1968, The Effect of Gamma Rays on Man-in-the-Moon Marigolds, 1970, Twigs, 1971, Mourning Becomes Electra, 1971, At Sun.Mon early 1980's, Any Given Day 1995; motion pictures include You Are Not Alone, 1961, Desperate Characters, 1971, The Pursuit of Happiness, 1971; starred in TV series: Sandburg's Lincoln, 1974-76, Family, 1976-79 (Emmy award for outstanding actress in a dramatic series); TV spl. The Entertainer, 1976; appeared in TV mini-series Marco Polo, 1982, Princess Daisy, 1983, Queen, 1993, (TV movies) Adventures of Huckleberry Finn, 1985, My Love, 1986, Fatal Confession: A Father Dowling Mystery, 1987, Home Fires Burning, 1987, Fear Stalk, 1989, The Skin of Our Teeth, 1980's, Painting Churches, 1980's, Andre's Mother, 1990, Indictment: The McMartin Trial, 1995. Recipient Tony award 1972, New York Drama Critics award for best actress of year Variety 1971-72, 2 Obie awards, Atlanta Drama Critics Mask award as best actress for performance in The Vinegar Tree 1978; Any Mother's Son, 1997; The Patron Saint of Liars, 1998, tv.; Pollock, 1999, film. Office: Richard Bauman & Assocs 5757 Wilshire Blvd Ste 473 Los Angeles CA 90036-3635 Address: PO Box 490 Southbury CT 06488-0490

THOMPSON, SALLY ANN, editor; b. Hillsboro, N.D., Apr. 10, 1943; d. C. Hillman and Blanche E. (Bjerkan) Swenson; m. Arthur G. Thompson, July 1, 1965 (dec. Mar. 1990); 1 child, Laurie Kate Beth. Student, Concordia Coll., Moorhead, Minn., 1961-65. Reporter Valley Jour., Halstad, Minn., 1979-84; contbg. editor Prairie West Publs., Wahpeton, ND, 1982-84; editor Hillsboro Banner, Hillsboro, ND, 1984-95, Sun Newspapers, Minnetonka, Minn., 1995—. Lectr. Career Day Mayville State U., ND, 1985—92. Bd. dirs. Trail County Hist. Soc., 1979—95, Hillsboro Forestry Bd., 1990—93; mem. commns. com. Eastern N.D. Synod ELCA, 1990—93. Recipient numerous journalism awards. Lutheran. Avocations: photography, collages, reading, history. Home: 1805 Highway 101 Apt 203 Plymouth MN 55447-2715 Office: Sun Newspapers 10917 Valley View Rd Eden Prairie MN 55344 Office Phone: 952-392-7668. Personal E-mail: sally_thompson@hotmail.com.

THOMPSON, SALLY ENGSTROM, state official; b. Spokane, Wash., Feb. 17, 1940; d. Logan C. and Ava Leigh (Phillips) Engstrom; m. Donald Edward Colcun, 1981; children: Lauri Thompson, Tom Thompson, Tami Thompson, Sheri Colcun Trumpfheller. BS magna cum laude, U. Colo., 1975. CPA, Colo. 1976, Kans. 1986. Audit mgr. and mgmt. cons. Touche Ross & Co., Denver, 1975-82; v.p., mgr. planning and fin. analysis United Bank, Denver, 1982-85; pres., chief oper. officer Shawnee Fed. Svgs., Topeka, 1985-90; treas. State of Kans., 1991-98; CFO, acting asst. sec. for adminstrn. USDA, Washington, 1998—. Past editorial advisor New Accountant mag. Bd. dirs. Everywoman's Resource Ctr., Topeka, 1988-92, Community Svc. Found. Kans., Kids Voting Kans. (hon.); v.p., bd. dirs. Downtown Topeka Inc., YWCA, Topeka, 1986-93, Woman of Achievement award, 1984; mem. fin. com. Girl Scouts U.S., Kaw Valley, various coms., United Way of Greater Topeka; chmn. art auction com. KTWU-TV, summer concert, Topeka Civic Theatre. Recipient Disting. Community Leadership award Topeka Pub. Schs., 1989, Disting. Leadership award Nat. Assn. Community Leadership, 1991, 1991 Class Leadership Kans. Mem. AICPAs, Am. Soc. Women Accts., Kans. Soc. CPAs, Kansas C. of C. and Industry, Greater Topeka C. of C. (bd. dirs. 1989-92), Emporia State U. Bus. Sch. Adv. Bd., Nat. Assn. State Auditors, Controllers and Treas., Nat. Assn. State Treas. (v.p., Midwest regional chair), Women Execs. in Govt., Beta Alpha Psi. Democrat. Office: USDA 1400 Independence Ave SW Washington DC 20250-0002

THOMPSON, SAMUEL DONALD, assemblyman; b. Mobile, Ala., July 31, 1935; m. Jacqueline Thompson; children: Shaun, Vanessa, Richard. BS in Chemistry and Math, U. of Ark., 1960; PhD in Phys. Chemistry, La. State U., 1965. Del. Rep. Nat. Con., 1988, 1992, 1996, 2000, alt. del., 2004; dir. planning, analysis, and govt. rels. N.J. Turnpike Authority, 1994—97; assemblyman N.J. Gen. Assembly, 1998—; chmn. Old Bridge Rep. County Com., 2001. Rsch. scientist E.I. duPont de Nemours, 1965—68, J.P. Stevens and Co., 1968—71; dir. clin. lab improvement svc. N.J. State Dept. of Health, 1972—94; chmn. Middlesex County Rep. Com., 1986—94; mem. Old Bridge Twp. Environ. Commn., 1983, Old Bridge Twp. Planning Bd., 1983, U.S. Armed Forces Epidemiological Bd., 1983—90; co-chair Govs. Edn. Task Force, 1994. Mem. Task Force on Adolescent Violence, 1983, Commn. on Elder Care, 1999—2001. Republican. Baptist. Office: 725 Hwy 34 Matawan NJ 07747 Office Phone: 732-583-5558. Business E-Mail: AsmThompson@njleg.org.

THOMPSON, SAMUEL G. artist; b. Phila., Oct. 9, 1930; s. Samuel George and Helen Etta Thompson. Diploma, U. of Arts, Phila., 1953, Phila. Bibl. U., 1957. Instr. Saturday Sch. Phila. Mus. Sch. Art, 1952—59; instr. art appreciation Phila. Bibl. U., Langhorne, 1958—59; decorator John Wanamaker Store, Wynnewood, Pa., 1957—59; instr. watercolor S. Thompson Fine Art, Cambridge, Mass., 1987—89, Cambridge Pub. Libr., 2001, Boston Pub. Libr., 2002; host Watercolor Workshop CCTV Television, Cambridge, 1998. Spkr. painting Saturday Discussion Group, Oaxaca, Mexico, 1996—2001. Children Gospel Hour TV show, 1959, mag. illustrations, exhibitions include Rotenberg Gallery, Boston, 1997—98. Recipient 4-yr. scholarship, Dobbins Tech., 1950—53, 1st prize landscape painting, Fuller Art Mus. Mem. Show, 1989, Frances Roddy prize, Concord Art Assn., 2001. Mem.: Cambridge Artist Open Studios, Cambridge Art Assn. Home: 415 Putnam Ave Cambridge MA 02139 E-mail: samgthom@hotmail.com.

THOMPSON, SANDRA LEE, library administrator; b. Dover, Ohio, Jan. 23, 1968; d. Robert Leonard and Gwendolyn Ruth Stewart; m. Alan McKinney Thompson, Sept. 9, 1990; children: LeeAnna, Alisha, James. BS in Edn., Ohio U., 1989; M of Libr. Info. Sci., U. S.C., 2001. Tchr. Harrison Hills City Sch. Dist., Hopedale, Ohio, 1989-90; asst. dir. Puskarich Pub. Libr., Cadiz, Ohio, 1990-97, dir., 1998—. Mem. Ohio Libr. Coun., Columbus, 1994—; bd. dirs. Southeastern Ohio Libr. Orgn., Caldwell, 1997—, Ohio Pub. Libr. Info. Network. Mem.: Cadiz Rotary Assocs. (trustee), Am. Libr. Assn. Office: Puskarich Pub Libr 200 E Market St Cadiz OH 43907-1200 E-mail: sthompson@oplin.org.

THOMPSON, SCOTT L. automotive executive; BBA, Stephen F. Austin State U. CPA. Exec. v.p., oper. and fin. KSA Ind., Inc., 1991—96; sr. v.p., CFO, treas. Group1 Automotive, Houston, 1996—2002, exec. v.p., CFO, treas., 2002—. Office: Group 1 Automotive Inc 950 Echo Ln Ste 100 Houston TX 77024

THOMPSON, STANLEY B. church administrator; Pres., CEO, dir. The Free Meth. Found., Spring Arbor, Mich.; chmn., CEO, dir. King Trust Co., N.A.; CEO, chmn., dir. King Trust Charitable Gift Fund. Office: Free Methodist Foundation PO Box 580 Spring Arbor MI 49283-0580 Home: 227 Wickenham Dr Spring Arbor MI 49283 E-mail: sbthompson@kingtrust.org.

THOMPSON, STEPHEN ARTHUR, sales consultant; b. Englewood, N.J., Jan. 24, 1934; s. Stephen Gerard and Doris Lillian (Evans) T.; m. Joan Frances O'Connor, May 12, 1955 (div. 1978); children: Stephen Andrew, Craig Allen, David John; m. Sandra Rene Fingernut, May 27, 1979. BS, Ohio State U., 1961. Physicist Rocketdyne div. North Am. Aviation, Canoga Park, Calif., 1961-62, Marquardt Corp., Van Nuys, Calif., 1962-63; mem. tech. staff Hughes Rsch. Labs., Malibu, Calif., 1963-69; editor Electronic Engr. mag. Chilton Co., L.A., 1969-72, in advt. sales Instruments and Controls Sys., mag., 1972-77; regional advt. sales Design News mag. Cahners Pub. Co., L.A., 1977-84, sales mgr. Design News mag. Newton, Mass., 1984-87, pub. Design News mag., 1987-95, group. pub. mfg. group, 1989-93, sr. v.p. integrated mktg., 1993-94, gen. mgr. Boston divsn., 1995-96, gen. mgr. mfg. mktg. divsn., 1995-97, sr. v.p. tng., 1996-97; gen. mgr. OEM/processing group Advanstar Comms., Cleve., 1997-99; sales training cons. Bentleyville, Ohio, 1999-2000. Founder Design News Engring. Edn. Found., Newton, 1991-97; pub. Design News Mag., 1994-95; group pub. Mfg. Group. Author: Basketball for Boys, 1970; contbr. articles to Jour. Spacecraft/Rockets, 1966. Club leader YMCA, Canoga Park, 1963-78; active PTA, Canoga Park, 1961-80; bd. dirs. Chatsworth (Calif.) High Booster Club, 1972-80. 1st lt., jet fighter pilot USAF, 1952-58. Mem. Bus. Profl. Advt. Assn. (Golden Spike award 1980, 81, 82, 83), L.A. Mag. Reps. Assn. (life), Nat. Fluid Power Assn., BPA Internat. (bd. dirs.). Achievements include patents for ion source, system and method for ion implantation of semiconductors. Office: 7500 Old Oak Blvd Cleveland OH 44130-3343

THOMPSON, STEVE ALLAN, writer; b. Mpls., Sept. 10, 1951; s. John Thomas and Charlotte Joan (Ellis) T.; m. Michele Rae Jones, July 16, 1983; 1 child, Kent Lloyd. Student, U. Minn., 1969-73. Dept. supr. Hennepin County Libr., Edina, Minn., 1973-87; writer, 1987—. Cons. Okefenokee Glee & Perloo Inc., L.A., 1988—, Waycross/Ware County (Ga.) C. of C., 1990—, Phipps Ctr. for Arts, Hudson, Wis., 1996. Author: Walt Kelly Collector's Guide, 2d edit., 2004; co-author: Pogo Files for Pogophiles, 1992; editor The Fort Mudge Most 1988—; editl. bd. of Internatl. Jour. of Comic Art; contbr. articles to profl. jours. Mem. Internat. Soc. for Humor Studies, Bibliographical Soc. Am., Walt Kelly Soc. (pres. 1987—), Lewis Carroll Soc., Baker Street Irregulars, Grand Comics Database Project, Comics Scholars Consortium. Achievements include international recognized on life and career of Walt Kelly. Home: 6908 Wentworth Ave Richfield MN 55423-2363 E-mail: thompson_s@epi.umn.edu., thomp034@tc.umn.edu.

THOMPSON, STEVEN, zoological park administrator; PhD in Conservation Biology, U. Calif., Irvine. Rschr. Nat. Zool. Pk., Smithsonian Instn., 1983—90; v.p., Emily and John Alexander chair for conservation and sci. Lincoln Park Zoo, Chgo., 1990—. Office: Lincoln Park Zoo 2001 N Clark St Chicago IL 60614

THOMPSON, SYDNOR, JR., (CHARLES WILLIAM SYDNOR THOMPSON JR.), lawyer, mediator, arbitrator; b. Balt., Feb. 18, 1924; s. Charles William Sydnor Thompson and Helen Josephine Layne; m. Harriette Line, June 2, 1947; children: Darcy T. Kluttz, Charles William Sydnor III, Harriet T. Moore, Brenneman L., Mary Katherine Line T. Kelly. AB, Syracuse U., 1947; LLB, Harvard U., 1950; student, St. Andrews U., Scotland, 1945, Manchester U., Eng., 1950, London Sch. Econs., 1951. Cert.: N.C. Dispute Resolution Commn. (mediator), EEOC, Am. Arbitration Assn. (arbitrator), Nat. Assn. Securities Dealers. Assoc. Davis Polk & Wardwell, N.Y.C., 1951—54; ptnr. Parker Poe Thompson Bernstein Gage & Preston, Charlotte, NC, 1954—94; judge N.C. Ct. Appeals, Raleigh, NC, 1994; of counsel Parker, Poe, Adams & Bernstein, LLP, Charlotte, 1995—; prin. Mediation, Inc., Winston-Salem, NC, 1995—. Author: The Sydnor Family Saga, 2000, A Collection of Ad Hominem Verse, 2002; contbr. articles to law revs. Pres. Charlotte Symphony Orch., 1958—61, Charlotte Opera Assn., 1971—75; vice chair N.C. Arts Coun., Raleigh, 1981—84; pres. Mecklenburg Ministries, 1987—89, Wing Haven Found., 2001—02; chmn. Mecklenburg County Dem. Party, 1977—81. Served with U.S. Army, 1943—46, ETO. Decorated Bronze star; Fulbright scholar, 1950, 1951. Master: William H. Bobbitt Inn of Ct.; mem.: ABA (chmn. circuits subcom. 1977—95), Mecklenburg Bar Assn. (pres. 1990), N.C. Bar Assn. (chmn. appellate rules study com. 1989—91, chmn. local bar svcs. com. 1991—93), Old Catawba Soc., Horace Williams Philosophy Club, English Speaking Union, Sporadic Book Club, Charlotte Country Club, Tower Club. Avocations: genealogy, writing, tennis, acting. Office: Parker Poe Adams & Bernstein LLP Ste 3000 401 S Tryon St Charlotte NC 28202 Office Phone: 704-372-9000.

THOMPSON, TERENCE WILLIAM, lawyer; b. Moberly, Mo., July 3, 1952; s. Donald Gene and Carolyn (Stringer) T.; m. Caryn Elizabeth Hildebrand, Aug. 30, 1975; children: Cory Elizabeth, Christopher William, Tyler Madison. BA in Govt. with honors and high distinction, U. Ariz., 1974; JD, Harvard U., 1977. Bar: Ariz. 1977, U.S. Dist. Ct. Ariz. 1977, U.S. Tax Ct. 1979. Assoc. Brown & Bain P.A., Phoenix, 1977-83, ptnr., 1983-92, Gallagher and Kennedy, P.A., Phoenix, 1992—. Legis. aide Rep. Richard Burgess, Ariz. Ho. of Reps., 1974; mem. bus. adv. bd. Citibank Ariz. (formerly Great Western Bank & Trust, Phoenix), 1985-86. Mem. staff Harvard Law Record, 1974-75; rsch. editor Harvard Internat. Law Jour.,1976; lead author, editor-in-chief: Arizona Corporate Practice, 1996—; contbr. articles to profl. jours. Mem. Phoenix Mayor's Youth Adv. Bd. 1968-70, Phoenix Internat.; active 20-30 Club, 1978-81, sec. 1978-80, Valley Leadership, Phoenix, 1983-84, citizens task force future financing needs City of Phoenix, 1985-86; exec. coun. Boys and Girls Clubs of Met. Phoenix, 1990-2000, sr. coun. 2000—; bd. dirs. Phoenix Bach Choir, 1992-94; deacon Shepherd of Hills Congl. Ch., Phoenix, 1984-85; pres. Maricopa County Young Dems., 1982-83, Ariz. Young Dems., 1983-84, sec. 1981-82, v.p. 1982-83; exec. dir. Young Dems. Am., 1985, exec. com. 1983-85; others. Fellow Ariz. Bar Found.; mem. State Bar Ariz. (vice chmn. internt. law sect. 1978, sec. securities law sect. 1990-91, vice chmn. sect. 1991-92, chmn.-elect 1992-93, chmn. 1993-94, exec. coun. 1988-96, sec. bus. law sect. 1992-93, vice chmn. 1993-94, chmn. 1994-95, exec. coun. 1996-98), Nat. Assn. Bond Lawyers, Nat. Health Lawyers, Greater Phoenix Black C. of C. (bd. dirs. 1999-2001), Blue Key, Phi Beta Kappa, Phi Kappa Phi, Phi Eta Sigma. Home: 202 W Lawrence Rd Phoenix AZ 85013-1226 Office: Gallagher & Kennedy PA 2575 E Camelback Rd Phoenix AZ 85016-9225 Office Phone: 602-530-8515. Business E-Mail: twt@gknet.com.

THOMPSON, TERRIE LEE, graphic designer; b. Myrtle Creek, Oreg., Apr. 22, 1960; d. Claud Willie and Blanche Bernice Thompson. Student, Umpqua C.C., 1983-84; BFA, Pacific N.W. Coll. Art, 1988. Freelance graphic designer Terrie Thompson Design, Portland, 1987-90; graphic designer Promotion Products Inc., Portland, 1989-90, L. Grafix Inc., Portland, 1990-91, Warn Industries, Milwaukie, Oreg., 1991-92; pres. Thompson Typographics Inc., Portland, 1990—; typography contractor Nike Inc., Beaverton, Oreg., 1992—. Typography trainer for various design firms and agys., Portland, 1992-98, pres. Seeing Spots, Inc., 1998—. Work published in various design publs., including The Best in Catalogue Design, Comm. Arts Design Ann., How Mag. Computer Art and Design Ann.; creator cartoon character "Spot", 1989. Vol. graphic designer Washington Park Zoo, Portland, 1990; vol. art dir. Portland Mac Users Group, Portland, 1995; vol. beach clean-up crew Stop Oreg. Litter and Vandalism, 1990—. Recipient Bronze award Optima Design Awards, 1995, Digital Art and Design Ann. award Print Mag., 1997, Regional Design Ann. award Print Mag., 1997, Applied Arts Annual, 1997, 98, Good Neighbor award Forest Park Neighborhood Assn., 1999. Avocations: hiking, travel, camping, photography, music. Home and Office: Thompson Typographics Inc PO Box 83327 Portland OR 97283-0327

THOMPSON, THELMA BARNABY, English educator, university dean; b. Jamaica, West Indies, July 22, 1940; d. Claude Noel and Elaine Jordan (Robertson) Barnaby; m. Winston Lloyd Thompson, June 15, 1976; 1 child, Lisa Valdeen. BA, Howard U., Washington, D.C., 1970; MA, Howard U., 1972, PhD, 1978; diploma, Bethlehem Tchrs. Coll., Malvern, Jamaica, West Indies, 1960. Lectr. CUNY, 1972 74; asst. prof. Bowie (Md.) State Coll., 1974 76; assoc. prof., asst. chmn. English dept. U. D.C., Washington, 1976-88, dean Sch. Arts and Letters, 1988-90, Norfolk State U., 1990—. Asst. dean U. D.C., Washington. Author: The Seventeenth Century English Hymn; also articles. Recipient Bethlehem Coll. Medal of Distinction, scholarship and grad. fellowship. Mem. MLA, Coll. Lang. Assn. (pres., chmn. com. high sch./coll. rels.), South Atlantic MLA, Middle Atlantic Writers, Phi Beta Kappa, Phi Delta Kappa (award for disting. svc. and commitment to excellence in edn. 1991). Office: Norfolk State U Sch Arts and Letters Bos 4600 2401 Corprew Ave Norfolk VA 23504

THOMPSON, THEODIS, retired healthcare executive, health management consultant; b. Palestine, Ark., Aug. 10, 1944; s. Percy and Grozellia Monroves (Weaver) T.; m. Patricia Holley, Sept. 16, 1964; children: Gwendolyn Ware, Theodis E., Omari P. BS, Tuskegee Inst., 1968; MPA, U. Mich., 1969, PhD, 1972. Asst. chemist John T. Stanley Co., N.Y.C., 1964-66; news announcer, disc jockey KATZ Radio Sta., St. Louis, 1966-67; sr. rsch. assoc. U. Mich., Ann Arbor, 1969-71; asst. prof., chmn. Howard U., Washington, 1973-78; assoc. prof., dir. health planning U. So. Calif., L.A., 1978-79; dir. planning and evaluation Memphis Health Ctr., 1979-87, chief oper. officer, 1987-88; CEO Bklyn. Plz. Med. Ctr., 1988-99. Cons. Charles Mathis Assocs., Yonkers, N.Y., 1991—, USPHS, Bethesda, Md., 1993—; mem. adv. bd. N.Y. Urban League, Bklyn., 1991-93; lectr. St. Joseph's Coll., Bklyn., 1998—. Author, editor: Health Policy and Planning, 1975; contbr. articles to profl. jours. Bd. dirs. CHCANYS, Inc., N.Y.C., 1994, vice chair Cmty. Assocs. Devel. Corp., Inc., Bklyn., 1989. Recipient Disting. Svc. award N.Y. State Assn. Black and Puerto Ricans, Inc., 1992; named Disting. Man of Yr., 18th Senatorial Dist., 1996. Mem. APHA. Office Phone: 901-292-9684.

THOMPSON, THEODORE ROBERT, pediatric educator; b. Dayton, Ohio, July 18, 1943; s. Theodore Roosevelt and Helen (Casey) J.; m. Lynette Joanne Shenk; 1 child, S. Beth. BS, Wittenberg U., 1965; MD, U. Pa., 1969. Diplomate Am. Bd. Pediatrics (Neonatal, Perinatal Medicine). Resident in pediat. U. Minn. Hosp., Mpls., 1969-72, chief resident in pediat., 1971-72, fellow neonatal, perinatal, 1974-75, asst. prof., 1975-80, dir. divsn. neonatology and newborn intensive care unit, 1977-80, assoc. prof., 1980-85, prof., 1985—, co-dir. Med. Outreach, 1988-91, med. dir. med. outreach, 1991-00, assoc. chief pediat. svcs., 1988—2003, assoc. head pediat. edn. and cmty. programs, 2003—; med. dir. outreach, sec. bd. dirs. and exec. com. U. Minn. Physicians, 1992—, dir. clin. edn. med. students, 1999—. Mem. exec. com., sec.-treas. Fairview U. Med. Ctr., 2002—. Editor: Newborn Intensive Care: A Practical Manual, 1983. Bd. dirs. Life Link III, St. Paul, 1987—; cons. Maternal and Child Health, Minn. Bd. Health, 1975-94; bd. dirs. Minn. Med. Found., 1995-99. With USPHS. 1972-74. Recipient Avocacy award, U. Minn. Med. Sch. Fellow: Am. Acad. Pediats.; mem.: Gt. Plains Orgn. for Perinatal Health Care (Sioux Falls, SD Kunshe award 1989). Lutheran. Office: MMC 39 420 Delaware St SE Minneapolis MN 55455-0374 Office Phone: 612-626-2841. Business E-Mail: thomp005@umn.edu.

THOMPSON, THOMAS MARTIN, lawyer; b. Albion, Pa., Jan. 7, 1943; s. Donald C. and Mabel Louise (Martin) T.; m. Judith E. Daucher; children: Reid, Chad, Matthew, Molly. AB, Grove City Coll., 1965; JD cum laude, Harvard U., 1968. Bar: Pa. 1968. Ptnr. Buchanan Ingersoll, Pitts., 1968—, chair corp. fin. group. Adj. prof. law U. Pitts.; past chairperson, dir. Pa. Lawyer Trust Acct. Bd. Past pres. Neighborhood Legal Svcs. Assn.; bd. dirs., mem. exec. com. Pitts. Pub. Theater. Mem. ABA, Pa. Bar Assn. (chair-elect bus. law sect., Pro Bono award 1989), Allegheny County Bar Assn. (past chmn. pub. svc. com., past chmn. bus. law coun., past chair PBA legal opinion steering com.), Assn. for Corp. Growth (past pres. Pitts. chpt.). Democrat. Home: 1142 Dartmouth Rd Pittsburgh PA 15205-1705 Office: Buchanan Ingersoll One Oxford Ctr 301 Grant St Fl 20 Pittsburgh PA 15219-1410 Office Phone: 412-562-8855. E-mail: thompsontm@bipc.com.

THOMPSON, TINA MARIE, professional basketball player; b. LA, Feb. 10, 1975; B in sociology, U. So. Calif., 1997. Basketball player U. So. Calif., 1993—97; profl. basketball player Houston Comets, WNBA, 1997—. Named All-Star Game MVP, WNBA, 2000; named to First Team All-WNBA, 1997, 1998, WNBA All-Star Team, 1999, 2000, 2001, 2002, 2004. Achievements include No. 1 draft pick in 1997, the first WNBA draftee in the history of the league; mem. Houston Comets WNBA Championship Teams, 1997, 98, 99, 2000; mem. US Women's Basketball Team, Athens Olympics, 2004. Office: Houston Comets 2 E Greenway Plz Ste 400 Houston TX 77046-0202*

THOMPSON, TOMMY GEORGE, secretary of health and human services; b. Elroy, Wis., Nov. 19, 1941; s. Allan and Julia (Dutton) T.; m. Sue Ann Mashak, 1969; children: Kelli Sue, Tommi, Jason. BS in Polit. Sci. and History, U. Wis., 1963, JD, 1966. Polit. intern U.S. Rep. Thomson, 1963; legis. messenger Wis. State Senate, 1964-66; sole practice Elroy and Mauston, Wis., 1966-87; mem. Dist. 87 Wis. State Assembly, 1966-87, asst. minority leader, 1972-81, floor leader, 1981-87; self-employed real estate broker Mauston, 1970—; gov. State of Wis., 1987-2001; sec. U.S. Dept. Health & Human Svcs., Washington, 2001—. Alt. del. Rep. Nat. Conv., 1976; chmn. Intergovtl. Policy Adv. Commn. to U.S. Trade Rep.; chmn. Natl. Govs. Assn., 1995-96, mem. nat. govs. assn. exec. com.; chmn. bd. dirs., Amtrak, 1998-99. Served with USAR. Recipient med. award for Legis. Wis. Acad. Gen. Practice, Thomas Jefferson Freedom award Am. Legis. Exchange Coun., 1991, Most Valuable Pub. Official award City and State Mag., 1991, Governance award Free Congress Found., 1992, Governing Mag. Public Ofcl. of the Year, 1997, recipient Horatio Alger Awd., 1998, USA Mex. C of C, Good Neighbor Awd., 1999. Mem. ABA, Wis. Bar Assn., Rep. Govs. Assn., Phi Delta Phi. Republican. Roman Catholic. Office: Dept HHS Office of the Secy 200 Independence Ave SW Washington DC 20201-0004

THOMPSON, TRAVIS OGDEN, retired county official; b. Woodbury, N.J., May 2, 1935; s. Raymond Clark and Helen Pettit Thompson; m. Alice Isabel Woud, Sept. 6, 1958; children: Tarn Brian, Lynne Thompson Walsh. BS, U. Va., 1957; MBA, U. Wash., 1964. Bus. trainee GE, Bridgeport, Conn., 1957—59; fin. analyst Raytheon Co., Santa Barbara, Calif., 1961—62; mgr. The Boeing Co., Seattle, 1962—90; dir. fin. County of Maui, Wailuku, Hawaii, 1991—99; ret. Dir. Housing and Cmty. Devel. Corp. Hawaii, Honolulu, 2003—. Chair Big Bros. Big Sisters, Maui, Hawaii, 2002—04, Maui United Way, 1995—97; nat. committeeman Rep. Nat. Com., Hawaii, 2000—04; chair transition team Gov. Linda Lable, Hawaii, 2002—03; fin. chair Hawaii Bush-Cheney 04, Inc., Hawaii, 2003—04. 1st lt. USAF, 1959—61. Avocations: golf, walking, music, mandolin, reading. Home: 89 Pokolo Way Wailea HI 96753

THOMPSON, VERN, political organization executive; b. Maddock, N.D., Aug. 23, 1956; m. Cindy; one child, Will. Former city councilman; former twp. supr.; rep. N.D. State, 1989-91, state senator, 1997—2000. Exec. dir. ND Dem. Party, 2001—. Recipient N.D. Weekly N.D. POl. Figure of the Yr., 1995, Minnewaukan Citizen of the Yr., 1996. Democrat. Home: 1910 N Grandview Ln Bismarck ND 58503-0843

THOMPSON, VETTA LYNN SANDERS, psychologist, educator; b. Birmingham, Ala., Sept. 7, 1959; d. Grover and Vera Lee (King) S.; m. Cavelli Andre Thompson, May 27, 1990; children: Olajuwon, Malik Rashad, Kimberlyn, Assata Iyana. BA, Harvard U., 1981; MA, Duke U., 1984, PhD, 1988. Cert. psychologist and health svc. provider, State of Mo. Com. Psychologists. Psychology intern Malcolm Bliss Mental Health Ctr., St. Louis, 1985-86; psychotherapist, testing coord. Washington U. Child Guidance Clinic, St. Louis, 1986-87; psychologist, treatment team coord. Hawthorn Children's Psychiatric Hosp., St. Louis, 1987-89; asst. prof. U. Mo., St. Louis, 1989-95, assoc. prof., coord. black studies, 1995—. Tchg. asst. Duke U., Durham, N.C., 1982-84, rsch. asst., 1984-85; chair monitoring com. crisis access sys. Ea. Regional Adv. Coun. Dept. Mental Health, St. Louis, 1995-97; chair African Am. Task Force on Mental Health, Jefferson City, Mo., 1995-97; chair budget and planning com. Ea. Regional Adv. Coun., Dept. Mental Health, St. Louis, 1996-97, pres. Ea. Regional Adv. Coun., 1997-99; mem. children's mental health planning group St. Louis Mental Health Bd., 1996-97. Mem. editl. adv. bd. A Turbulent Voyage: Readings in African American Studies, 1995-96; mem. bd. editl. advisors Gt. Plains Rsch.; contbr. articles to profl. jours. Mem. adv. com. on violence prevention and investment in youth Mo. House, Jefferson City, 1995; mem. managed care steering com. Dept. Mental Health, Jefferson City, 1995—96, mem. strategic planning adv. coun., 1997; mem. Mo. Bd. for Respiratory Care, 1997; mem. state com. for psychologists Mo., 1997—; chair, 2000—02; sec., chair discipline com., 1999—2000; bd. dirs. St. Louis Mental Health Assn., sec., 2000—02, chair planning com., 2002, 2d v.p., 2002, pres., 2003. Kellogg Found.-Mo. Youth Initiative fellow, 1991-93; Ctr. for Great Plains Studies fellow U. Nebr., 1995—; recipient Disting. Svc. award Mental Health Assn. St. Louis, 1998, 99. Mem. APA (divsns. 1, 45), Assn. Black Psychologists, Am. Orthopsychiat. Assn. Methodist. Avocations: aerobics, walking, jazz. Office: U Mo 8001 Natural Bridge Rd Saint Louis MO 63121-4401

THOMPSON, WADE FRANCIS BRUCE, manufacturing executive; b. Wellington, New Zealand, July 23, 1940; came to U.S., 1961, naturalized, 1990. m. Angela Ellen Barry, Jan. 20, 1967; children: Amanda and Charles (twins). B in Commerce, Cert. Acctg., Victoria U., Wellington, 1961; MSc, NYU, 1963. Dir. diversification Sperry & Hutchinson, N.Y.C., 1967-72; v.p. Textsar Corp., N.Y.C., 1972-77; chmn. Hi-Lo Trailer Co., Butler, Ohio, 1977—2003; chmn., pres., chief exec. officer Thor Industries Inc., Jackson Center, Ohio, 1980—. Trustee Mystic Seaport Mus., Conn., 1984—; trustee Wade F.B. Thompson Charitable Found. Inc., 1985—, Mcpl. Art Soc., N.Y.C., 1993—, Seventh Regiment Armory Conservancy, N.Y.C., 1997—; founder The Drive Against Prostate Cancer. Mem. Union Club, N.Y. Yacht Club (N.Y.C.). Avocations: tennis, collecting contemporary art. Office: Thor Industries Inc PO Box 629 Jackson Center OH 45334-0629

THOMPSON, WADE S. artist, art and design educator; b. Moorhead, Minn., July 30, 1946; s. Roy S. and Nora A. (Hanson) T.; m. Maureen Larkey, June 14, 1975; children: Mora Eileen, Sarah Maria. BA in Art with distinction, Macalaster Coll., 1968; MA, MFA, Bowling Green U., 1972; postgrad., Pratt Inst., 1985. Graphic designer Assoc. Design, St. Paul, 1969-70; asst. prof. art Temple U., Phila., 1972-79; prof. art and design S.W. Mo. State U., Springfield, Mo., 1979—, asst. head dept. art and design, 1999—2001; acting head S.W. Mo. State Univ., Springfield, 2002—03. Lectr. U. Art and Design Helsinki, 1994; vis. prof. U. Minn., St. Paul, 1995; organizing chair 1998 Williamsburg Conf., 1996—; organizing chair Color and Design: 21st Century Tech. and Creativity Conf., 1998; organizing chair, moderator Artist and Digital Media Symposium, AIC Color, Rochester, NY, 2001; spkr., presenter in field. Contbr. articles to profl. jour.; one or two person shows include Alnico Gallery, NYC, 1977, Nat. Art Ctr., NYC, 1980, Jan Weiner Gallery, Kansas City, Mo., 1986, Peter Drew Galleries, Boca Raton, Fla., 1988, Mary Bell Galleries, Chgo., 1989, Still-Zinsel Contemporary Art, New Orleans, 1990, Aaron Gallery, Washington, 1990, Alexandre Hogue Gallery U. Tulsa, Okla., 1991, The Parthenon Mus., Nashville, 1995, Jack Meier Gallery, Houston, 1997, numerous others; group exhibn. include Provincetown (Mass.) Art Assn., 1976, Portsmouth (Va.) Art Ctr., 1976, The Smithsonian Traveling Exhibn., 1977-79, J.B. Speed Mus., Louisville, Ky., 1981, 84, The Nelson Gallery Atkins Mus., Kansas City, Mo., 1982, George Walter Vincent Smith Art Mus./Mus. Fine Arts, Springfield, Mass., 1984, 86, West Surrey Coll. Art and Design, Farnham, Surrey, Eng., 1984, Lamar Dodd Art Ctr., LaGrange, Ga., 1985, Arlington (Tex.) Mus. Art, 1989, Still-Zinsel Contemporary Fine Art, New Orleans, 1992, The Watkins Gallery Am. U., Washington, 1993, Elliot Smith Gallery, St. Louis, 1996, Keyes Gallery, Springfield, Mo., 1998, Malton Gallery, Cin., 2001, numerous others; featured in Am. Artist mag., catalog Color Archive Collections U. Art and Design Helsinki, The Oak Ridger, New Orleans Art Rev., New Art Examiner, The Kans. City Star, numerous others. Disting. scholar S.W. Mo. State U., 1992; recipient award for acrylic Chautauqua Nat. Exhbn., 1984, Color Archive Collection award U. Art and Design, Helsinki, Finland, 1997; grantee visual arts program Mo. Arts Coun., 1998. Mem. Inter-Soc. Color Coun. (nat. bd. dir. 1995-98, vice chair art, design, psychology interest group 1992-94, chair art, design, psychology interest group 1994-96). Home: 1910 E Cardinal St Springfield MO 65804-4329 Office: SW Mo State U Dept Art and Design 901 S National Ave Springfield MO 65804-0088

THOMPSON, WAITE, investment company executive, researcher; b. St. Louis, Nov. 5, 1940; s. Frank Charles Jr. and Jane (Waite) T. BA, Principia Coll., 1962. Polit. cons. Rep. Party of Calif., L.A., 1964-67, 72-74; traveling v.p. Club Universe, L.A., 1967-68, 69-72; comml. real estate investor Coldwell Banker, L.A., 1974-79; pres. Waite Thompson Inc., Santa Fe, 1979—. Author: The Santa Fe Guide, 1981—. Bd. trustees Hist. Santa Fe Found., 1989-94, Old Santa Fe Assn., 1994-96; mem. City of Santa Fe Hist. Design Review Bd., 1996-99; mem. coun. benefactors Santa Fe Cmty. Found., 1994—; mem. adv. bd. Rep. Nat. Com., Washington, 1964-67, 72-74. Mem. Santa Fe Opera Found., Mus. N.Mex. Found., Nat. Soc. Sons/Daughters of the Pilgrims, Nat. Soc. Sons of Am. Revolution. Republican. Mem. Christian Sci. Ch. Avocations: walking, swimming, reading, tennis, family history. Home and Office: 503 Johnson Ln Santa Fe NM 87505-2865

THOMPSON, WALLACE REEVES, III, physical education educator; b. Atlanta, Oct. 17, 1950; s. Wallace Reeves II and Annie Mae (Neal) T.; m. Sherrilyn Winkfield, Aug. 19, 1976 (div. 1985); 1 child, Sherrilyn M. m. Sandra Hicks, Feb. 28, 1994; 3 children: Garry C., Keneisha R., Ira. BA, Morehouse Coll., 1973. Cert. phys. edn. tchr., Ga. Phys. edn. tchr. Atlanta Pub. Schs., 1974—. Coach Saturday Sch. for the Arts, Atlanta, 1979-81. Vol. Nat. Black Arts Festival, Atlanta, 1990—, Ga. State Games, Atlanta, 1992—; coach Butler St. YMCA, Atlanta, 1982-85, AAU-Jr. Olympics, Atlanta, 1977-82, Centennial Olympics, Sports Video Viewing Room, Atlanta, 1996. Mem. AAHPERD. Baptist. Home: 119 Anderson Ave NW Atlanta GA 30314-1852 Office: Anderson Park Elem Sch 2050 Tiger Flowers Dr NW Atlanta GA 30314-1326

THOMPSON, WALTER DAVID, JR., systems analyst; b. Leakesville, N.C., Sept. 8, 1952; s. Walter David Sr. and Rachel Henderlite (Jones) T. Student, St. Andrews Coll., 1970-75. Beverage distributor N.Y. Seltzer, N.Y.C., 1975-76; restaurant mgr. Fountainhead Cafe, N.Y.C., 1976-77; newspaper delivery Greensboro (N.C.) Daily News, 1978-80; computer programmer Gary Brown Assocs., Greensboro, 1980-82; pvt. cons. Thompson Software Systems, Greensboro, 1982-86; asst. treas. corp. trust Bankers Trust, N.Y.C., 1987-88; computer analyst bond funds Merrill Lynch, N.Y.C., 1988; team leader, cons. corp. fin. Citibank, N.Y.C., 1988-89; v.p., sr. systems analyst Kidder, Peabody & Co., Inc., Manakin-Sabot, Va., 1989-94; dir. MIS James River Capital Corp., Manakin-Sabot, Va., 1995—. Rsch. grantee NSF, 1971. Mem. Am. Mensa Ltd. (membership coord. 1990-91). Home: 2236 Rockwater Ter Richmond VA 23233-3622 Office: James River Capital Corp 58 Broad Street Rd Manakin Sabot VA 23103-2213

THOMPSON, WARREN M. food franchise executive; BS, Hampden-Sydney Coll.; MBA, U. Va. V.p. Host Internat. divsn. Marriott Corp.; pres., CEO Thompson Hospitality, Reston, Va. Office: Thompson Hospitality Corp 45240 Business Ct Ste 200 Sterling VA 20166-6703

THOMPSON, WAYNE WRAY, historian; b. Wichita, Jan. 30, 1945; s. Clarence William and Elaine Maxine (Wray) T.; m. Lillian Evelyn Hurlburt, June 28, 1969 (div. 1999); m. Geraldine Kelleher Richter, Dec. 30 2000. BA, Union Coll., Schenectady, 1967; student, U. St. Andrews, Scotland, 1965-66; PhD, U. Calif., San Diego, 1975. Historian USAF, 1975—2004, Checkmate Air Campaign Planning Group, 1990—2004; sr. hist. advisor Gulf War Air Power Survey, 1991-93. Contbr. Congress Investigates (Arthur M. Schlesinger Jr. and Roger Bruns, editors), 1975; editor Air Leadership, 1986; contbr. War in the Pacific (Bernard Nalty, editor), 1991; contbr.: Winged Shield, Winged Sword, 1997; author: To Hanoi and Back, 2000. Served with AUS, 1971-72. Mem. Am. Hist. Assn., Orgn. Am. Historians, Air Force Hist. Found., Air Force Assn., Soc. Historians Am. Fgn. Rels., Soc. Mil. History, US Commn. Mil. History, Inter-Univ. Seminar Armed Forces, Assn. Asian Studies, Asia Soc., World History Assn., Phi Beta Kappa. Home: 2720 N Quincy St Arlington VA 22207

THOMPSON, WENOKA SHENAILE, television producer, writer; b. Laurel, Miss., July 23; d. Earnest Lee and Bettie Louise Thompson. Student, U. Md., 1995—. Talk show host, prodr. Sta. WXXV Fox 25, Gulfport, Miss., 1991—93; master control operator Sta. WBDC, Washington, 1993—98; asst. prodr. Am.'s Voice, Washington, 1999; prodr. Sta. WTOP News, CBS, Washington, 2000—. Pres. Sarah Elizabeth Co., Hyattsville, Md., 1998—; asst. prodr. Sta. NPR-WAMU, Washington, 1999. Author: John John's Adventure Book Series, 2002, (poem) Love Clearly Defined, 1987. Mem.: Sailing Club Washington. Achievements include tradmark for 1960's tee-The End of an Era. Avocations: golf, chess, sailing, tennis, photography.

THOMPSON, WILLARD SCOTT (W. SCOTT THOMPSON), social sciences educator; b. Providence, Jan. 1, 1942; s. Francis Willard and Loretta Belle Thompson; m. Phyllis Arina Nitze, Dec. 28, 1968 (div. May 1982); children: Phyllis Elizabeth Pratt, Nicholas Edwin Scott, Heidi Alexandra Nitze. BA with honors, Stanford U., 1963; PhD, Oxford (Eng.) U., 1967. Assoc. profl. internat. politics Fletcher Sch. Law and Diplomacy, Medford, Mass., 1967—93; asst. to sec. of def. Dept. Def., Washington, 1975—76; assoc. dir. U.S. Info. Agy. U.S. Govt., Washington, 1981—84; rsch. adj. prof. internat. politics Fletcher Sch. Law and Diplomacy, Medford, Mass., 2001—. Vis. prof. Asian Inst. Mgmt., Manila, 2001—; chair Universal Trading and Investment Co., Boston, 1993—, Internat. Ctr. for Instnl. Develop., Berkeley, Calif., 2000. Author: Ghana's Foreign Policy, 1969; co-author (with Nicholas Thompson): The Baobab and The Mango Tree, 2000, The Philippines in Crisis, 1992; contbr. articles to profl. jours. Co-chair Ams. for Effective Pres., Boston, 1980, Mass. Tomorrow, Boston, 1972—78; pres. Inst. Internat. Rels., Stanford U., 1962—63. Rhodes scholar, 1980, Fulbright fellow, Manila, 1989, Danforth fellows, 1965—67, Whtie House fellow, 1975—76. Mem.: Coun. on Fgn. Affairs, Internat. Inst. for Strategic Studies. Avocations: gardening, film, marathons, writing fiction. Home: 14398 Storybook Ln Amissville VA 20106 Office: Policy Ctr Asian Inst Mgmt Paseo de Roxas Makati Philippines Address: Villa Kusuma Seri Sukuwati, Bali Indonesia E-mail: thompsonwscott@yahoo.com.

THOMPSON, WILLIAM, director; s. William Edward and Carmella Thompson; m. Kathryn Gillen Thompson, Dec. 31, 1993; children: Charlotte, William. BA, Rutgers U., 1986, MA, 2003. Dir. bands Franklin Twp., Somerset, NJ, 1986—94, Branchburg (NJ) Twp., 1994—2000, Somerville (NJ) HS, 2000—. Owner Somerville Sch. Music, 1986—; music adjudicator Drum Corps Internat., 1994—. Trustee Branchburg Edn. Found., 1997—2000, Somerville Ednl. Found., 2000—. Recipient Tchr. award, NJ Gov., 1988, 1998. Methodist. Avocations: poker, fishing. Home: 855 N Branch Rd Bridgewater NJ 08807 Office: Somerville HS 222 Davenport St Somerville NJ 08876 Office Phone: 908-218-4151. Office Fax: 425-699-4490. Personal E-mail: jrthom@optonline.net.

THOMPSON, WILLIAM, JR., engineering educator; b. Hyannis, Mass., Dec. 4, 1936; s. William and Dinella Helen (Szeliga) T.; m. Martha Marion Cate, July 4, 1959; children: Melanie A., Sharon E., Jennifer L., Keith W. SB, MIT, 1958; MS, Northeastern U., 1963; PhD, Pa. State U., 1971. Staff engr. Raytheon Co., Wayland, Mass., 1958-60; sr. engr. Cambridge (Mass.) Acoustical Assocs., 1960-66; rsch. asst. Applied Rsch. Lab., State College, Pa., 1966-72; asst. prof. engring. sci. Pa. State U., University Park, 1972-78, assoc. prof., 1978-85, prof., 1985-2001, prof. emeritus, 2001—. Head transducer group Applied Rsch. Lab., State College, 1971-80; sabbatic leave Naval Rsch. Lab., Orlando, Fla., 1988-89; chairperson IBM Master Tchrs. Team, 1997-98. Contbr. articles to profl. jours.; patentee in field. Bd. dirs., treas., past pres. Nittany Mountain chpt. Am. Diabetes Assn., State College, 1979-92; bd. dirs., asst. treas., treas. Mid-Pa. affiliate, Bethlehem, 1980-90; bd. dirs. Sight-Loss Support Group of Ctrl. Pa., 1999, treas. 2000-. Recipient Disting. Svc. citation Mid-Pa. Affiliate Am. Diabetes Assn., 1981, and Affiliate Svc. award, 1988, J.R. Cardenuto award, Sight-loss Support Group of Ctrl. Pa., 1998. Fellow Acoustical Soc. Am. (patent reviewer of soc. jour. 1990-); mem. Soc. Engring. Sci., Lions (pres. State College 1981-82, 89-90, sec.-treas. 1984-88, 90-92, treas. 1992-, dist. diabetes chmn. 1983-88, 94-, chmn. Ctr. Lions Foresight Commn. 1992-2004, Melvin Jones fellow 1991, internat. leadership award 1998, dist. chmn. Habitat for Humanity, 2001-), Cen. Pa. Ballroom Dancers Assn. (pres.-elect 1997-98, pres. 1998-99). Republican. Avocations: sports, reading, photography, ballroom dancing. Home: 1245-62 Westerly Pky State College PA 16801 Office: Pa State U Dept of Engring Sci and Mechanics 212 Earth and Engring Scis University Park PA 16802-6812 E-mail: W1TESM@engr.psu.edu.

THOMPSON, WILLIAM DAVID, minister, homiletics educator; b. Chgo., Jan. 11, 1929; s. Robert Ayre and Mary Elizabeth (McDowell) T.; m. Linda Brady Stevenson, Nov. 2, 1968; children— Tammy, Kirk, Lisa, Rebecca, Gwyneth. AB, Wheaton Coll., Ill., 1950; BD, No. Bapt. Sem., 1954; MA, Northwestern U., 1955, PhD, 1960. Ordained to ministry Am. Baptist Ch., 1954. Instr. speech Wheaton Coll., 1952-55; pastor Raymond Baptist Ch., Chgo., 1956-58; assoc. prof. homiletics No. Bapt. Sem., Chgo., 1958-62; mem. faculty Eastern Bapt. Sem., Phila., 1962-87, prof. preaching, 1969-87; minister 1st Bapt. Ch., Phila., 1983-90. Pres. Thompson Comm., 1988-98, principal The Spirited Workplace, 1998—. Author: A Listener's Guide to Preaching, l966, Recent Homiletical Thought, 1967, Dialogue Preaching, l969, Preaching Biblically, l98l, Listening on Sunday for Sharing on Monday, 1983, Philadelphia's First Baptists, 1989, Public Speaking for Pleasure and Profit, 1997; editor Abingdon Preachers Libr., 12 vols., Essence of Public Speaking series, 10 vols. Mem. Phila. Hist. Commn., 1984-92, Ctr. for Baptismal Living Bd., 1999-, Singing City Bd., 2003-. Vis. fellow Cambridge U., 1968-69. Mem. Nat. Speakers Assn., Mid-Atlantic Speakers Assn. (pres. 1995), Acad. Homiletics (pres. l973), Religious Speech Comm. Assn. (v.p. 1983, pres. 1984), Union League Club. Democrat. Home: 765 Ormond Ave Drexel Hill PA 19026-2417 Personal E-mail: Thompcom@aol.com.

THOMPSON, WILLIAM IRWIN, educational consultant, writer; b. Chgo., July 16, 1938; s. Chester Andrew and Lillian Margaret (Fahey) Thompson; m. Gail Joan Gordon, Feb. 3, 1960 (div. Jan. 1979); children: Evan Timothy, Hilary Joan, Andrew Rhys; m. Beatrice Madeleine Rudin, Mar. 1, 1979. BA in Philosophy with honors, Pomona Coll., 1962; MA (Woodrow Wilson fellow), Cornell U., 1964, PhD (Woodrow Wilson dissertation fellow), 1966. From instr. to asst. prof. humanities MIT, Cambridge, 1965—67, assoc. prof., 1968, Old Dominion fellow, 1967; assoc. prof. York U., Toronto, Canada, 1968-72, prof., 1973; founding dir. Lindisfarne Assocs., 1972—97; curriculum designer, faculty cons. Ross Sch., East Hampton, NY, 1995—. Vis. prof. religion Syracuse (N.Y.) U., 1973; vis. scholar in polit. sci. U. Hawaii, 1981, vis. prof., 85; vis. prof. Celtic studies U. Toronto, 1984. Author: (book) Imagination of an Insurrection: Dublin, Easter 1916, 1967, At the Edge of History, 1971, Passages about Earth, 1974, Evil and World Order, 1976, Darkness and Scattered Light, 1978, The Time Falling Bodies Take to Light, 1981, From Nation to Emanation, 1981, Blue Jade from the Morning Star, 1983, Islands Out of Time, 1985, Pacific Shift, 1986, GAIA: A Way of Knowing, 1987, Imaginary Landscape, 1989, Selected Poems, 1959—89, GAIA TWO: Emergence, the New Science of Becoming, 1991, Reimagination of the World, 1991, The American Replacement of Nature, 1991, Coming into Being, 1996, Worlds Interpenetrating and Apart, 1997, Transforming History, 2001, Self and Society, 2004. Hon. colleague, Lindisfame scholar Cathedral St. John the Divine, N.Y.C., 1972—97. Recipient Obstfelder prize, Oslo Internat. Poetry Festival, 1986; grantee, Laurance S Rockefeller, 1992—98; Rockefeller scholar, Calif. Inst. Integral Studies, 1992—95. Address: PO Box 381561 Cambridge MA 02238

THOMPSON, WILLIAM MOREAU, radiologist, educator; b. Phila., Oct. 20, 1943; s. Charles Moreau and Aileen (Haddon) T.; m. Judy Ann Seel, July 27, 1968; children: Christopher Moreau, Thayer Haddon. BA, Colgate U., 1965; MD, U. Pa., 1969. Diplomate Am. Bd. Radiology. Intern Case Western Res. U., Cleve., 1969-70; resident in radiology Duke U., Durham, NC, 1972-75; asst. prof. Duke U. Med. Ctr., 1975—77, assoc. prof., 1977-82, prof. radiology, 1982-86, 2001—; prof., chmn. dept. radiology, Vilhelmina and Eugene Gedgared chair in Radiology U. Minn. Hosp. and Clinic, Mpls., 1986-2000, prof. radiology, dir. imaging rsch., 2000-01. Contbr. chpts. to books and articles to profl. jours. Served with USPHS, 1970-72. Recipient James Picker Found. Scholar in Acad. Medicine award, 1975-79, Disting. Scientist award, Armed Forces Inst. Pathology, Washington, 2001-02; R & D grantee VA, 1977-86. Fellow Am. Coll. Radiology; mem. AMA, Radiology Soc. N.Am. (program chmn. 1994-97), Minn. Med. Soc., Am. Roentgen Ray Soc., Assn. Univ. Radiologists (pres. 1989-90, Gold medal 2001), Soc. Gastrointestinal Radiology (pres. 1994-95, Cannon medal 2001), Assn. Program Dirs. (pres. 1995, Achievement award 2001), Soc. Chairs of Acad. Radiology Depts. (pres. 1997-98), Sigma Xi. Republican. Presbyterian. Home: 225 Galway Dr Chapel Hill NC 27517-6558 Office: PO Box 3808 Durham NC 27702-3808 Office Phone: 919-684-7448.

THOMPSON, WILLIAM REID, public utility executive, lawyer; b. Durham, N.C., Aug. 13, 1924; s. William Reid and Myrtle (Siler) T.; m. Mary Louise Milliken, Aug. 16, 1952; children: Mary Elizabeth, William Reid III, John Milliken, Susan Siler. BS, U. N.C., 1945; LLB, Harvard U., 1949. Bar: N.C. 1949. Ptnr. Barber and Thompson, Pittsboro, N.C., 1949-58; judge Superior Cts. N.C., 1958-60; assoc. gen. counsel Carolina Power & Light Co., 1960-63, v.p., gen. counsel, 1963-67, exec. v.p., 1967-71; chmn. bd., chief exec. officer Potomac Electric Power Co., Washington, 1971-89, chmn. bd., 1989-92. Adv. dir. Potomac Elec. Power Co. Bd. dirs. Nat. Orgn. on Disability; mem., former chmn. Fed. City Coun., N.C. Gen. Assembly from Chatham County, 1955-57. Served to lt. (j.g.) USNR, 1943-45, PTO. Mem. ABA, Edison Electric Inst. (bd. dirs., past chmn.), Southeastern Electric Exchange (past pres.), Assn. Edison Illuminating Cos. (past pres.), Bus. Coun., Met. Club, Burning Tree Club, Chevy Chase Club, Rotary, Phi Beta Kappa, Delta Kappa Epsilon. Republican. Methodist. Office: Potomac Electric Power Co 701 Ninth St NW Washington DC 20068-0002

THOMPSON, W(ILMER) LEIGH, pharmaceutical company executive, physician, pharmacologist; b. Shreveport, La., June 25, 1938; s. Wilmer Leigh and Mary Bissell (McIver) T.; m. Maurice Eugenie Horne, Mar. 29, 1957; 1 child, Mary Linton Bounetheau. BS, Coll. Charleston, 1958; MS in Pharmacology, Med U. S.C., 1960, PhD, 1963, ScD (hon.), 1994; MD, Johns Hopkins U., 1965. Diplomate Am. Bd. Internal Medicine. Intern Johns Hopkins Hosp., 1965-66, resident, 1966-67, 69-70; staff assoc. NIH, Bethesda, Md., 1967-69; asst. prof. medicine and pharmacology Johns Hopkins U., Balt., 1970-74, dir. critical care medicine and emergency medicine, 1974-82; prof. medicine, assoc. prof. pharmacology Case Western Res. U., Cleve., 1974-82, head critical care and clin. pharmacology, 1974-82; prof. medicine Ind. U., 1985-95; dir. Lilly Rsch. Labs., Eli Lilly & Co., Indpls., 1982, exec. dir., 1982-86, v.p., 1986-88, group v.p., 1988-91, exec. v.p., 1992-93, chief sci. officer, 1993-94; chmn., CEO Profound Quality Resources Com., Charleston, 1995—. Chair Inspire; bd. dirs. BAS, Diabetogen, Guilford Pharms., Depo Med, La Jolla Pharms., Sontra, Medarex. Author: Murder at Spoleto, 2003; editor: Textbook of Critical Care Medicine, 1984, 89, State of the Art: Critical Care, 1980-83. Served to surgeon USPHS, 1967-69. Recipient Faculty Devel. award Pharm. Mfrs. Assn. Found., Spl. citation FDA Commr., 2003; named Disting. Alumnus, Med. U. S.C., 1999, Disting. Med. Alumnus, Johns Hopkins U., 2003, Honor Alumnus award Coll. Charleston, 2004; Burroughs Wellcome Fund scholar, 1975-80. Fellow ACP, Am. Coll. Critical Care Medicine; mem. Soc. Critical Care Medicine (pres. 1981-82, hon. life mem. 1987), Ctrl. Soc. Clin. Rsch., Am. Soc. Pharmacology and Exptl. Therapeutics, John Hopkins Soc. Scholars (inducted). Episcopalian and Huguenot. Office: Profound Quality Resources Consulting 54 King St Charleston SC 29401-2731 Office Phone: 843-577-8936. Business E-Mail: electricpotato@jhu.edu.

THOMPSON, WINFRED LEE, university president, lawyer; b. Little Rock, July 28, 1945; s. Vester Lee and Willow Mae (Mills) T.; m. Carmen Angeles Tiongson; children: Emily, Michael. BA, U. Ark., 1967; MA, U. Chgo., 1970, PhD, 1987; JD, George Washington U., 1976, LLM, 1978. Congl. aide U.S. Ho. of Reps., Washington, 1973-77; exec. asst. to asst. sec. labor U.S. Dept. Labor, Washington, 1977-78; atty. Hatfield and Thompson, Searcy, Ark., 1978-81; dir. devel. Ark. State U., Jonesboro, 1981-82, v.p. for planning and devel., 1982-84; v.p. for fin. and adminstrn. U. Ark. System, Fayetteville, 1984-85; vice chancellor for fin. and adminstrn. U. Ark, Fayetteville, 1985-87; pres. U. Cen. Ark., Conway, 1988—2001; chancellor Am. U. of Sharjah, United Arab Emirates, 2002—. Bd. dirs. Ark. Sci. and Tech. Authority, Little Rock, 1984-89. Bd. dirs. Ark. Symphony Orch., 1991-94; mem. U.S. Peace Corps, The Philippines, 1967-69. 2d lt. USAR. Woodrow Wilson fellow U. Chgo., 1969-70. Mem. Phi Beta Kappa. Home: 140 Donaghey Ave Conway AR 72034-6252 Office: U Ctrl Ark Office of the President 201 Donaghey Ave Conway AR 72035-5001

THOMPSON, ZACHARY, city health department administrator; AS, El Centro Coll.; BS in Social Work, U. Tex., Arlington; MS, Amberton U., Garland, Tex. With W. Dallas Cmty. Ctr.; dep. dir. Dallas Co. Dept. Health and Human Svcs., Dallas, 1997—2004, dir., 2004—. Office: Dallas Co Dept Health and Human Svcs 2377 N Stemmons Fwy Dallas TX 75207-2710*

THOMPSON-CHRISTIE, HEATHER MARIE, adult education educator; b. Saginaw, Mich., Jan. 31, 1980; d. Thomas George and Linda Marie Thompson; m. Scott Robert Christie, Sept. 27, 2003; stepchildren: Adam Scott Christie, Caleb Michael Christie children: Jasmine Marie Thompson, Jenna Catherine Thompson. MA of Psychology, U. of Mich., Flint, 2000—02, MA in Edn., 2002—03. Lic. CAC Mich., 2001. Instr. ARC, Saginaw, Mich., 1999—; adult edn. Mich. Works, Port Huron, Mich., 2003—03; rschr. U. of Mich., Flint, 2000—03; mgr. of edn. Sylvan Edn. Solutions, Phila., 2003—. Author: (research) Everybody says I love you, Chivalry and sexism, Reaction in Witnesses of Fatal Construction Accidents. Recipient Saginaw County Hero Award, ARC, 2002; grantee Beatrice and William Caldwell Rsch. Fund, U. Of Mich., 2003. Mem.: ARC (life; chair of logistics 2001—02). R-Consevative. Bapt. Avocations: horse back riding, music playing, researching. Home: 8565 Dorwood Rd Birch Run MI 48415 Personal E-mail: collegegirluofm@yahoo.com. Business E-Mail: hethomps@umflint.edu.

THOMPSON CORNWALL, LONIETA AURORA, music educator, consultant; b. Newark, June 13, 1944; d. Wilmore and Hattie Stewart Thompson; children: Arminta Morant Cornwall, Ronald Pearson Cornwall. MusB, MusM, Manhattan Sch. Music, N.Y.C., 1962—66; M of Sacred Music, Union Theol. Sem., Sch. of Sacred Music, N.Y.C., 1970—73; EdD in Coll. Tchg. of Music, Teachers Coll., Columbia U., N.Y.C., 2001—04. Music tchr. Bd. Edn., N.Y.C., 1966—70; instr. music Shaw U., Raleigh, NC, 1984—. Organist Abyssinian Bapt. Ch., N.Y.C., 1965—68; dir. music Holy Trinity Luth. Ch., Hollis/Queens, NY, 1970—75; min. music First Bapt. Ch., Raleigh, NC,

1981—95; organist Christian Faith Bapt. Ch., Raleigh, 1999—2001; dir. music First Ref. Ch. of Cary, Cary, NC, 2001—. Composer: (musical score) Canticles for the Soul; co-author (with Marilyn Thompson): (paper) Embracing the Obvious: Direct Utilization of African Am. Musical Forms in Selected Art Songs by African Am. Composers. (Presentation for Nat. Assn. of African Am. Studies). Participant US EPA, Raleigh, NC, 2002, NC State Workers/ Dr. Martin Luther King Holiday Observance, Raleigh, NC, 2000—04; missionary to Zambia, South Africa Operation Reachback, Redlands, Calif., 2000; chair Gethsemane Seventh-day Adventist Ch. Sch., Raleigh, NC, 1995—2000; musical cons. Dr. Martin Luther King Celebration Com., Raleigh, 1995—2004. Recipient H.B. Caple Humanitarian award, The Shaw Players/Shaw U., 1997—98, The Crystal award, Women's Ministries/South Atlantic Conf. of Seventh-day Adventists, 1999, Lamplighter -Music Outreach award, Radio One-Hunter Industries, 2002. Mem.: Raleigh Chamber Music Guild (bd. directors 1994—95), N.C. Bach Festival (bd. directors 1990—94), Am. Guild of Organists, Alpha Chi. Seventh-Day Adventist. Avocations: writing (liturgies), walking, travel. Home: 2304 Foxtrot Rd Raleigh NC 27610 Office: Shaw Univ 118 East South St Raleigh NC 27601 Office Phone: 919-546-8412. Personal E-mail: lonieta@aol.com. E-mail: lcornwal@shawu.edu.

THOMPSON-DRAPER, CHERYL L. electronics executive, real estate executive; b. Houston, Dec. 11, 1950; d. J. R. and Mary Claude Thompson; m. John T. Draper, Aug. 17, 1991; children: Mary-Catherine, John M., Tom. Student, Houston C.C., Massey Bus. Coll. Various positions Warren Electric Group hdqrs., 1970-85; mgr. Warren Electric Co., 1985-89, v.p., bd. dirs., sec., 1990-92; chmn. bd., CEO, owner Warner Electric Co., 1992—, Warren Electric Del Caribe, 1992—, Warren Electric of La, 1992—, Warren Dominican Republic, 1992—, Warren Electric of Tex., 1992—; mgr., CEO, owner Warren Electric Telecomms.-Utility Co., 1995—; chmn., pres., CEO, owner Warren Electric Group Ltd.; chmn. bd., CEO, pres., owner Thompson Real Estate Ltd., 1995—. Cons. in field. Contbr. articles to profl. jours. Bd. dirs., v.p. San Jacinto coun. Girl Scouts U.S., chmn. fundraiser Urban Campout 1995-96, Houston Sports Found.; vice chmn. Theatre Under the Stars, 1997-2001, chmn. bd., 2001—; bd. dirs. Houston Livestock Show and Rodeo, 1994—; mem. spkrs. and internat. com. All Those Texans, pres., 1997; bd. dirs., mem. exec. com. Greater Houston Partnership, 1996—; mem. Tex Fedn. of Rep., Montgomery County Fair Adv. Bd., 1996—; bd. dirs. Nat. Edn. Found.; mem. med. adv. coun. and vet. med. adv. coun. Tex. A&M U., mem. tech. adv. coun. Coll. Engring.; chmn. indsl. distbn. adv. coun. U. Houston Coll. Engring.; mem. Am. Leadership Forum-Houston, 2000. Recipient Texan of Yr. award All Those Texans, 1994, Mktg. Excellence award-Indsl. Sales, Affiliated Distbrs., 1994, Woman on the Move award City of Houston, 1995, Outstanding Family Owned Bus. award State of Tex., 1995, 1st Largest Woman-Owned Bus. award Houston Bus. Jour., 1998, 99, 2000, 01, Warner Cable's Hometown Hero award, 1996, 3rd Largest Woman-Owned Bus. award State of Tex, Woman Enterprise Mag., 1996, 1997, Disting. Svc. award Houson Elec. League, 1996, Leadership Tex 1997 Class, Cora Bacon Foster award, 1997, 1998, Cmty. Svc. award Houston Bus. Jour., 1997, Indsl. Distbn. award of Distinction, Texas A&M U., 1997, Honeywell's Supplier of Yr. award, 1998. Fellow Paul Harris Rotary Club of Houston (bd. dirs.); mem. Nat. Assn. Elec. Distbrs. (bd. dirs., v.p. 1999-00); mem. NAFE, U.S. C. of C. (internat. com.), Am. Alliance of Family Bus., Nat. Assn. Corp. Dirs., Tex. Exec. Women, Exec. Women Internat., DAR, Petroleum Club of Houston, Pasadena C. of C., Women's C. of C. of Tex., Women's Contractor Assn. Republican. Methodist. Office: Warren Electric Group PO Box 67 Houston TX 77001-0067 Fax: 713-236-2188. E-mail: cheryltd@warrenelectric.com.

THOMS, DAVID MOORE, lawyer; b. N.Y.C., Apr. 28, 1948; s. Theodore Clark and Elizabeth Augusta (Moore) T.; m. Susan Rebecca Stuckey, Dec. 16, 1972. BA, Kalamazoo Coll., 1970; M in Urban Planning, Wayne State U., 1975, LLM in Taxation, 1988; JD, U. Detroit, 1979. Bar: Mich. 1980, N.Y. 1995. Planner City of Detroit, 1971-75; atty. Rockwell and Kotz, P.C., Detroit, 1980-87; pvt. practice David M. Thoms & Assocs., P.C., Detroit, 1987—2002, Miller Canfield Paddock and Stone, P.L.C., 2002—. Adj. assoc. prof. Madonna U., 1993—; presenter NYU Tax Inst. Editor Case and Comment U. of Detroit Law Rev., 1978-79. Mem. program com. Fin. and Estate Planning Coun. Detroit, 1980—; mem. adv. bd., chmn. nominating com., mem. exec. com. Met. Detroit Salvation Army, 1980—, sec.-treas., vice chmn., 1994-95, chmn., 1995-96; bd. dirs. bylaws and property com., mem. nominating com., devel. com., exec. com. Mich. chpt. ARC; bd. dirs. L'Alliance Française de Grosse Pointe, 1980-, pres., 1985-88, 94-95; bd. dirs. French Festival of Detroit, Inc., 1986-89, 91-94, pres.; bd. dirs. Fedn. of Alliances Françaises, 1989-95, 97-2002, also past treas., v.p., chmn. fin. com., pres., 2000-01, bd. dirs. Vis. Nurse Assn., 2003—, sec., 2004—; bd. dirs. Detroit Symphony Orch. Hall, Inc., 1996-97; trustee Kalamazoo Coll., 1993-97, mem. exec. com., 1995-97; dir. vis. com. European art DIA, 1995-97. Decorated Officier dans l'Ordre des Palmes Academiques, Knight Order of Salvador; recipient Prix Charbonnier; Burton scholar U. Detroit, 1979. Mem. ABA (chmn. subcom. on probate and estate planning, mem. charitable trust com.), Fed. Bar Assn., Oakland County Bar Assn., Detroit Bar Assn., State Bar Mich., N.Y. Bar Assn., Bar Assn. of City of N.Y., Am. Planning Assn. (Mich. chpt.), The Grosse Pointe Club. Mem. United Church of Christ. Avocations: tennis, architectural history, music, travel, art history. Office: 400 Renaissance Ctr Ste 950 Detroit MI 48243-1678 Office Phone: 248-267-3242. Business E-Mail: thoms@millercanfield.com.

THOMS, JOSEPHINE BOWERS, artist; b. Lansing, Mich., Sept. 14, 1922; d. Raymon Lyon and Adele (Hammond) Bowers; m. Bert Thoms, June 4, 1945 (dec.); 1 child, Adele Lucile Thoms; m. Peter Blackford Lauck, May 10, 1983. BA, Hillsdale Coll., 1944; MA, Md. Inst. Coll. Art, 1977. Instr. modern dance Hillsdale (Mich.) Coll., 1943-44; artist-in-residence St. John's Coll., Annapolis, Md., 1953-55, 68-70; instr. art Washington and Jefferson Coll., Washington, Pa., 1956, Bethany (W.Va.) Coll., 1963-65; illustrator Md. Dept. Natural Resources, Annapolis, 1977-95. Joint owner Onset Bay Gallery and Studio, Onset, Mass., portrait artist, colorist; instr. Washington Art Assn., 1958-69; art dir. Md. Fedn. Art, Annapolis, 1970-72, pres., 1972-74. Illustrator: Federal Prose, 1947; executed murals: History of Electricity, Hillsdale, 1942, The Harbor at Annapolis, Crownsville, Md., 1989. Mem. Caritas Soc. at St. John's Coll., 1969—, Md. Peace Action, Annapolis, 1983—. Recipient 1st prize for Exhbn. of Nature-Related Art, Adkins Arboretum, Tuckahoe State Pk., Denton, Md., 1995. Mem. Md. Soc. Portrait Painters (cert., exhibits chairperson 1995—), Annapolis Watercolor Club (1st prize 1993). Democrat. Episcopalian. Avocations: swimming, aerobics, piano, needlepoint design. Home: 61 Southgate Ave Annapolis MD 21401-2829

THOMSEN, PEGGY JEAN, mayor, educator; b. St. Louis, Feb. 28, 1940; d. Harold Herman and Crystal Mary (Margolf) Levora; m. John Henry Thomsen, Dec. 1, 1961; children: Dianna, James, Robert. BA, Calif. State U., Fresno, 1961, MA with honors, 1968; PhD, U. Calif., Berkeley, 1997. Gen. secondary credential, Calif. Instr. Ctrl. Tex. Coll., 1980-83, City Colls. Chgo., 1983-86, Heald Colls., San Francisco, 1987; mayor, coun. mem. City of Albany, 1997—. Mem. East Bay Econ. Alliance, 1997—, Nat. Mayors Conf., 1998-99, Alameda County Mayor's Conf., 1998-99; bd. alt. Waste Mgmt. Authority, 1999—; bd. dirs. Alameda County Congestion Mgmt. Agy., 1997—. Editor City of Albany (Calif.) Newsletter, 1987. Mem. sch. bd. Albany Unified Sch. Dist., 1978-97, pres. sch. bd., 1980-81, 85-86; pres. PTA, Albany, 1976-78, 69-71; leader Girl Scouts U.S.A., Albany, 1970-82; mem. fund-raising team YMCA, Albany, 1981-88; bd. dirs., sec. Bay Area chpt. March of Dimes, San Francisco, 1979-88, chmn., 1985-86, chmn. Alameda County chpt., 1985-88; mem. adminstrv. code Rev. com. Calif. Dept. Edn., 1981-83, chmn. sch. improvement program selection panel, 1981, mem. fin. com., 1982, state budget com., 1982; Acorn Br. Assoc. Children's Hosp., Oakland. Recipient Svc. award Jaycees, Albany, 1970, Svc. awards Calif. PTA, 1971, 78, Vol. of Yr. award March of Dimes, Alameda County, 1984; named Sta. KABL Citizen of Day, 1984. Mem. NEA, LWV, Nat. Sch. Bds. Assn., Calif. Sch. Bds. Assn., Calif. Elected Women's Edn. Asn., League Calif. Cities (pres.-bd. mem. East Bay divsn. 1997—), Calif. Elected Women's Assn. for Edn. and Rsch., Congestion Mgmt. Agy. (bd. mem. 1997—), Pi Gamma Mu. Democrat. Avocations: needlecrafts, editing, reading. Home: 757 Pierce St Albany CA 94706-1033 Office: City of Albany 1000 San Pablo Ave Albany CA 94706-2226

THOMSEN, SAMUEL BORRON, non-profit executive, consultant; b. St. Paul, July 10, 1931; s. Samuel W. and Margaret (View) T.; m. Judith Diane Wolf, June 17, 1961; children: Kathryn G., Samuel P.E., Robert J. BA in Polit. Sci., UCLA, 1957; postgrad., Cornell U., 1966-67. With U.S. Dept. State, Washington, 1960-90, U.S. Consul, Hue, Vietnam, 1964-66; polit. advisor U.S. Marines, Vietnam, 1965-66; dir. Office for Internat. Sci. Coop. Dept. State, Washington, 1980-83; dep. pres.'s rep. Office for Micronesian Status Negotiations, Washington, 1983-87; amb. U.S. Embassy, Majuro, Marshall Islands, 1987-90; pres. The Micronesia Inst., Washington, 1990—96. Mem. commissioning bd. U.S. Info. Agy., Washington, 1980-86; chmn. Washington tradecraft program Fgn. Svc. Inst., Dept. State, 1995-96, dir. Micronesian diplomatic tng. program, 1996-99; cons. The Mustard Seed Found., 2000—. Mem. editl. bd. Fgn. Svc. Jour., 1961-62. Mem. Rotary, Vientiane, Laos, 1968-70, Gaborone, Botswana, 1974-76; trustee Am. Anglican Coun., 2002—. With U.S. Army, 1951-54. Fellow Assn. Diplomatic Studies and Tng.; mem. Washington Inst. Fgn. Affairs, Diplomatic and Consular Officers Ret. (v.p.), Asia Soc., World Affairs Coun. Washington, Am. Fgn. Svc. Assn., Am. Legion. Republican. Episcopalian. Avocations: tennis, gardening, computing. Home: 6502 Kerns Ct Falls Church VA 22044-1402 E-mail: sthomsen@erols.com.

THOMSEN, THOMAS RICHARD, retired communications company executive; b. Avoca, Iowa, July 29, 1935; s. Howard August and Edna Mary (Walker) T.; m. Raylene Alice Tomes, Sept. 1, 1956; children: Jeffrey, Cathy. BSME, U. Nebr., 1958; MS, MIT, 1973. Engr. Western Electric Co., Omaha, 1957-64, mgr. Columbus, Ohio, 1964-72, v.p. Bell Sales West Morristown, N.J., 1979-80; asst. v.p. ops. staff AT&T, Basking Ridge, N.J., 1980-81; exec. v.p. Western Electric Corp., N.Y.C., 1981-82; pres. AT&T Tech. Systems, Berkeley Heights, N.J., 1982-90; chmn. bd. dirs. Lithium Tech. Corp., Pa., 1995-99; retired, 1999—. Bd. dirs. EFJ Inc., Peco II; exec. com. U. Nebr. Tech. Park. Mem. Telephone Pioneers Am. (former pres.), Pi Tau Sigma, Sigma Tau. Republican. Presbyterian. Avocations: golf, tennis. Home: 26 Bellinghamshire Pl New Hope PA 18938-5657

THOMSON, ALEXANDER BENNETT, JR., financial planner, tax and management consultant; b. Wyandotte, Mich., Sept. 1, 1954; s. Alexander Bennett and Norma Lee (Fields) T.; 1 child, Luis Joaquin Elizondo-Thomson; m. Carol Michaelsen, Oct. 10, 2002; student Eastern Mich. U., 1972-74, Kalamazoo Coll. 1975-77; MA, Antioch Sch. Law, 1983. Cert. fin. planner; chartered life underwriter, fin. cons.; investment adviser, health underwriter, enrolled agt. Pres. Thomson Mgmt. Group, Inc., Washington, 1977—; budget dir. The White House Conf. on Small Bus., 1979; asst. treas. Kennedy for Pres. Com. 1980, nat. scheduler, Geraldine A. Ferraro, 1984. Mem. Inst. Cert. Fin. Planners, Internat. Assn. Fin. Planners, Nat. Assn. Tax Profls. Democrat. E-mail: al@thomsonmanagement.com.

THOMSON, BASIL HENRY, JR., lawyer, university general counsel; b. Amarillo, Tex., Jan. 17, 1945; m. Margaret Shepard, May 4, 1985; children: Christopher, Matthew, Robert. BBA, Baylor U., 1968, JD, 1973. Bar: Tex. 1974, U.S. Ct. Mil. Appeals 1974, U.S. Supreme Ct. 1977, U.S. Dist. Ct. (we. dist.) Tex. 1988, U.S. Ct. Appeals (fed. cir.) 1990. Oil title analyst Hunt Oil Co., Dallas, 1971-73; atty., advisor Regulations and Adminstrv. Law divsn. Office of Chief Counsel USCG, Washington, 1973-77; dir. estate planning devel. dept. Baylor U., Waco, Tex., 1977-80, gen. counsel, 1980—2002; ret., 2002; assoc. gen. counsel So. Meth. U., Dallas, 2002—. Adj. prof. law Baylor U.; lobbyist legis. Ind. Higher Edn., 71st Session of Tex. Legislature; mem. legis. com. Gov.'s Task Force on Drug Abuse; dir. govtl. rels. Baylor U.; spkr. at meetings of coll. and univ. adminstrs.; assisted in drafting legis. for Texan's War on Drugs Tex. Legislature; mem. legal adv. com. United Educators Ins. Risk Retention Group, 1994-96. Active Longhorn Coun. Boy Scouts of Am.; mem. planning and zoning commn. City of Woodway, 2004—, mem. bd. adjustment, 1998—2004; bd. dirs. Heart of Tex. Coun. on Alcohol and Drug Abuse, 1987—91. Recipient Pres.'s award Ind. Colls. and Univs. of Tex., 1994, Dist. award of merit Boy Scouts Am. Fellow Coll. State Bar Tex.; mem. ABA, FBA, Nat. Assn. Coll. and Univ. Attys. (fin., nominations and elections coms. 1994-95, bd. dirs. 1988-91, 2000—, pres. 2004—), Nat. Assn. Ind. Colls. and Univs. (pres. 2004—), Tex. Bar Assn., Waco Bar Assn., McLennan County Bar Assn., Owners Assn. of Sugar Creek, Inc. (bd. dirs. 1991-95). Baptist. Avocations: backpacking, running, environmental concerns, acting. Home: 100 Sugar Creek Pl Waco TX 76712-3410 Office: So Meth U PO Box 750132 Dallas TX 75275-0137 Office Phone: 214-768-3233. Business E-Mail: bthomson@smu.edu.

THOMSON, CAROLINE HELEN, artist; b. Takapuna, New Zealand, Jan. 12, 1945; d. William Harvey Thomson and Phyllis Alwyn Morgan. Artist Provincetown Art Assn. and Mus. One-woman shows include Eye of Horus Gallery, Provincetown, 1993-94, Bangs St. Gallery, Provincetown, Mass., 1995-99; exhibited in group shows at Bangs St. Gallery, Provincetown, 1995-99, David Armstrong, Susanna Coffey, Jack Pierson, Caroline Thomson, 2000, two person exhbn., Susanna Coffey, Caroline Thomson, 1996-99, Provincetown Art Assn. and Mus., 1999, selections from the permanent collection, juried exhbn., Provincetown Art Assn. and Mus., 1989-97, Invitational exhbns., PAAM, 1989-98. Exhbn. include Charles Hawthorne, Varujan Boghosian, Lily Harmon, Provincetown Art Assn. and Mus. Documentary film based on the life of Caroline Thomson, London, 1967, directed by Sheldon Rochlin and Diane Rochlin. Avocations: singer-song writer, wildlife rehabilitation. Home Fax: 508-349-7922. Personal E-mail: dmschachter2000@yahoo.com.

THOMSON, DAVID, dancer, vocalist; b. N.Y.C. BA, SUNY Purchase. Mem. Trisha Brown Co., N.Y.C., 1987—93; vis. lectr. Sarah Lawrence Coll., 1994—95; founder, mem. Hot Mouth, Bklyn., 1995—. Cons., database programmer Random House, N.Y.C., 2000—. Recipient Bessie Ward award, 2002. Office: 70 Nevins St #3 Brooklyn NY 11217

THOMSON, DONALD ARTHUR, education educator; b. Detroit, Apr. 9, 1932; s. Arthur and Theresa Rita (Stasin) T.; m. M. Jenean Gruner, Apr. 6, 1957; children: Erin, Kurt, Lisa, Madelon. BS, U. Mich., 1955, MS, 1957; PhD, U. Hawaii, 1963. Asst. prof., curator of fishes & dir. mar. sci. to prof. U. Ariz., Tucson, 1963-98, prof. emeritus, 1998—. Author: Reef Fishes of the Sea of Cortez, 2000, Fishwater's Guide to the Gulf of Calif., 1976, Tide Calendar for the Northern Gulf of Calif., 1967-2003; contbr. articles to profl. jour. Democrat. Avocations: photography, fly fishing, aquaria, dogs. Office: Dept Ecol/Evol Biol Univ Ariz Tucson AZ 85721-0001

THOMSON, GARY R. political organization administrator, accountant; BS in acctg., Bob Jones U. CPA, ptnr. Goodman & Co., Chester, Va.; chmn. Rep. Party Va., 2002—03. Republican. Office: Goodman & Co 131 Temple Lake Dr, Ste 1 Colonial Heights VA 23834

THOMSON, GEORGE RONALD, lawyer, educator; b. Wadsworth, Ohio, Aug. 25, 1959; s. John Alan and Elizabeth (Galbraith) T. BA summa cum laude, Miami U., Oxford, Ohio, 1982, MA summa cum laude, 1983; JD with honors, Ohio State U., 1986. Bar: Ill. 1986, U.S. Dist. Ct. (no. dist.) Ill. 1986. Teaching fellow Miami U., 1982-83; dir. speech activities Ohio State U., Columbus, 1983-86; assoc. Peterson, Ross, Schloerb & Seidel, Chgo., 1986-87, Lord, Bissell & Brook, Chgo., 1987-94; asst. corp. counsel employment litig. divsn. City of Chgo., 1994—. Adj. prof. dept. comm. De Paul U., Chgo., 1988-90; presenter in field. Contbr. articles to profl. jours. Fundraiser Chgo. Hist. Soc., Steppenwolf Theater Co., AIDS Legal Counsel Chgo., Smithsonian Instn., Washington, 1988-90, U.S. Tennis Assn., 1990—; bd. dirs. Metro Sports Assn., 1992-94, Gerber-Hart Libr. and Archives, 1993-95, Gay and Lesbian Tennis Alliance Am., 1993-95, Team Chgo., 1994-96, Second City Tennis, 1999-2000, 02—; mem. coord. coun. Nat. Gay and Lesbian History Month; mem. Lawyer's Com. for Ill Human Rights; dir. Chgo. Internat. Charity Tennis Classic, 1993, 94, 95, 98. Recipient Spl. Commendation Ohio Ho. of Reps., 1984, 85, Nat. Forensics Assn. award, 1982. Mem. ABA, Chgo. Bar Assn., Lesbian and Gay Bar Assn., Speech Comm. Assn. Am., Mortar Bd., Phi Beta Kappa, Phi Kappa Phi, Omicron Delta Kappa, Delta Sigma Rho-Tau Kappa Alpha, Phi Alpha Delta. Presbyterian. Avocations: tennis, flute, antiques, folk arts and crafts, reading, travel. Home: 2835 N Pine Grove Ave Unit 2S Chicago IL 60657-6109 Office: City of Chgo Dept of Law 30 N La Salle St Ste 1020 Chicago IL 60602-2503

THOMSON, GERALD EDMUND, physician, educator; b. N.Y.C., 1932; s. Lloyd and Sybil (Gilbourne) T.; m. Carolyn Webber; children: Gregory, Karen. MD, Howard U., 1959; DSc (hon.), Morehouse Med. Coll., 1997. Diplomate Am. Bd. Internal Medicine (bd. govs. 1985-92, exec. com. 1988-91, chmn.-elect 1990-91, chmn. 1991-92). Resident in medicine SUNY-Kings County Hosp. Center, 1959-62, chief resident, 1962-63, N.Y. Heart Assn. fellow in nephrology, 1964-65, asst. vis. physician, 1963-70, clin. dir. dialysis unit, 1965-67; practice medicine specializing in internal medicine N.Y.C., 1963-64; attending physician SUNY Med. Bklyn. Hosp., 1966-70; instr. in medicine SUNY, Bklyn., 1963-68, clin. asst. prof. medicine, 1968-70; asso. chief med. services Coney Island Hosp., Bklyn., 1967-70; attending physician Presbyn. Hosp., 1970—; dir. nephrology Harlem Hosp. Center, N.Y.C., 1970-71, dir. med. services, 1971-85, pres. med. bd., 1976-78; assoc. prof. medicine Columbia Coll. Physicians and Surgeons, 1970-72, prof., 1972—, Samuel Lambert prof. medicine, 1980—, Robert Sonneborn prof. medicine, 1997—; exec. v.p. for profl. affairs, chief of staff Columbia-Presbyn. Med. Ctr., 1985-90; sr. assoc. dean Coll. Physicians and Surgeons, Columbia U., N.Y.C., 1990—. Mem. Health Rsch. Coun. City N.Y., 1972-75, mem. med. adv. bd. N.Y. Kidney Found., 1971-82; mem. Health Rsch. Coun., State N.Y., 1975-81, mem. hypertension info. and edn. adv. com. NIH, 1973-74, N.Y. State Adv. Com. on Hypertension, 1977-80; com. on non-pharm. treatment of hypertension Inst. of Medicine, Nat. Acad. Scis., 1980; mem. med. adv. bd. Nat. Assn. Patients on Hemodialysis and Transplantation, 1973-83; mem. adv. bd. Sch. Biomed. Edn., CUNY, 1979-83, Med. News Network, 1993-95; mem. com. on mild hypertension Nat. Heart and Lung Inst., 1976, mem. clin. trials rev. com., 1980-85, mem. rev. panel, 1979; bd. dirs. N.Y. Heart Assn., 1973-81, chmn. com. high blood pressure, 1976-81; bd. dirs. Primary Care Devel. Corp.; chmn. com. hypertension N.Y. Met. Regional Med. Program, 1974-76; mem. adv. com. Heart and Hypertension Inst. of N.Y. State, 1984; mem. N.Y. Gov.'s Health Adv. Coun., 1981-84, pub. Health Coun., N.Y., 1983-95, Joint Nat. Com. High Blood Pressure NIH, 1983-84, 87-88, mem. rev. panel hypertension detection and monitoring bd. study cardiovasc. risk factors in young Nat. Heart, Lung and Blood Inst., 1984-90; mem. panel on receiving and withholding med. treatment ACLU, 1984-88; mem. Grad. Med. Edn. Commn., State of N.Y., 1984-86, mem. Commn. on End-State Renal Disease, 1985, 89-90; pres. Washington Heights-Inwood Ambulatory Care Network Corp., 1986-91; bd. dirs. Primary Care Devel. Corp., 1993—. Mem. adv. bd. Jour. Urban Health, 1974-80, Med. News Network, 1993-94. Chmn. ad hoc com. on access to nursing homes Pub. Health Coun. State of N.Y., 1982-96; pres. Washington Heights-Inwood Ambulatory Care Network Corp., 1986-91; mem. Mayor's Commn. Health and Hosps. Corp.; dir. Harlem Ctr. for Health Promotion and Disease Prevention, 1993-95. Recipient Nat. Med. award Nat. Kidney Found., N.Y., 1984, Outstanding Alumnus award Howard U., 1987, Disting. Alumnus award, 1998, Dean's Outstanding Tchg. award Coll. Physicians and Surgeons Columbia U., 1986. Fellow ACP (Gov.'s coun. downstate region 1982-89, chmn. com. health pub. policy N.Y. chpt. 1982-89, health care professions com. 1987-90, bd. regents 1990-97, chmn. nat. health and pub. policy com. 1993-94, pres.-elect 1994-95, pres. 1995-96), N.Y. Acad. Medicine (mem. com. medicine in soc. 1974-76, chmn. com. medicine in soc. 1997-98); mem. AAAS, N.Y. Soc. Nephrology (pres. 1973-74), Am. Fedn. Clin. Rsch., Federated Coun. for Internal Medicine (chmn. 1991-92, 95-96), Soc. Urban Physicians (pres. 1972-73), Am. Soc. Artificial Internal Organs, Assn. Program Dirs. in Internal Medicine, Pub. Health Assn. N.Y.C. (dir. 1983-86), Physicians for Social Responsibility of N.Y. (dir. 1983), Assn. Acad. Minority Physicians (pres. 1988-90), Inst. of Medicine, Nat. Acad. Scis. Home: Premium Pt New Rochelle NY 10801-5327 Office: Coll Physicians & Surgeons Columbia U New York NY 10032

THOMSON, HELEN LOUISE, artist; b. Lewiston, Ill., Nov. 28, 1928; d. Clyde Arthur Pomeroy and Myrtle Lynch Cluney; m. William Edward Thomson, 1950; children: Persephone Ann, Lucinda Renee, Cynthia Louise. Student, Western Ill. U., 1972, 78, 85, U. Ill., 1972; diploma, North Light Art Sch. Artist, Table Grove, Ill., 1970—. Adj. prof. Western Ill. U., Macomb, 1985-94; mem. spkrs. roster Spoon River Coll., Canton, Ill., 1986-94; exec. dir. Two Rivers Arts Coun., Macomb, 1985-94. Exhibited in numerous one woman and group exhbns.; contbr. art to calendars United Fed. Savs. & Loan, 1980, 86. Pres. Spoon River Coll. Found., Canton, Ill., 1979-85, Fulton County Arts Coun., Canton, 1973-83; bd. dirs. Regional Arts Adv. Coun., Western Ill. U., 1978-85; mem. adv. panel Ill. Arts Coun., Chgo., 1980-83; officer PTA, Table Grove, 1957-85. Recipient Ruth Watts Svc. award Performing Arts Soc., Western Ill. U., 1994, award Two Rivers Arts Coun., 1994; selected for feature stories on pub. TV sta. WMEC, 1997, Canton Daily Ledger, Macomb Jour., Peoria (Ill.) Jour. Mem. PEO Sisterhood (pres., sec., chpalain, v.p.), Ill. Art League (exhbn. awards), Ill. Watercolor Soc., Galesburg Civic Art Ctr. (exhbn. awards), Chgo. Art inst. Avocations: antiques, antique dolls, family history, travel. Home: 404 S Broadway St Table Grove IL 61482-0163

THOMSON, JAMES ALAN, think-tank executive; b. Boston, Jan. 21, 1945; s. James Alan and Mary Elizabeth (Pluff) T.; m. Darlene Thomson; children: Kristen Ann, David Alan. BS, U. N.H., 1967; MS, Purdue U., 1970, PhD, 1972, DSc (hon.), 1992; LLD (hon.), Pepperdine U., 1996. Research fellow U. Wis., Madison, 1972-74; systems analyst Office Sec. Def., U.S. Dept. Def., Washington, 1974-77; staff mem. Nat. Security Council, White House, Washington, 1977-81; v.p. RAND, Santa Monica, Calif., 1981-89, pres., chief exec. officer, 1989—. Bd. dirs. L.A. World Affairs Coun., AK Steel Holding Corp., Encysive Pharms. Contbr. articles to profl. jours. and chpts. to books. Mem. Internat. Inst. for Strategic Studies (coun. 1985-99), Coun. Fgn. Rels. Office: RAND 1700 Main St Santa Monica CA 90401-3297

THOMSON, JESSICA LEE, biostatistician, educator, consultant, researcher; d. Lawrence Richard Heim and Margaret Ann Stegmann; m. Douglas Perkins Thomson, Aug. 27, 1994. BSc in Biology, U. Wis., Stevens Point, 1988; MS in Math., U. La., 1999, PhD in Stats., 2002. Chemist Hauser Chem. Co., Boulder, Colo., 1988—89; pharmacy technician St. Anthony's Hosp., Denver, 1989—90; quality control staff Senecca Foods, Janesville, Wis., 1990; rsch. assoc. Hazleton, Inc., Madison, Wis., 1991—96; rsch. asst. U. La., Lafayette, 1996, grad. asst., 1997—2002; asst. prof. Health Scis. Ctr. La. State U., New Orleans, 2002—. Contbr. articles to prof. jours. Mem.: Am. Statis. Assn., Am. Math. Soc. Avocations: boating, fishing, horseback riding, swimming, jogging. Home: 142 Bertinot Rd Opelousas LA 70570-1000 Office: LSU Health Scis Ctr Sch Pub Health 1600 Canal Street Ste 1100 New Orleans LA 70112

THOMSON, JOHN U. veterinarian, dean; BS in Animal Sci., Iowa State U., 1965, DVM, 1967; MS in Sci., N.W. Mo. State U., 1987. Pvt. practice, Clearfield, Iowa, 1967-87; ext. veterinarian SD State U., Brookings, 1987-90, acting head vet. sci. dept., 1990-93, head, 1993—, acting dir. S.D. Animal Disease Rsch. and Diagnostic Lab., 1990-93, dir., 1993—; dean Miss. State U. Coll. Vet. Med., Missisippi State, Miss. Pvt. vet. medicine cons., 1987-90. Contbr. articles to sci. jours. Grantee USDA, S.D. Agrl. Expt. Sta. Office: Miss State U Coll Vet Medicine Office of the Dean Box 9825 Mississippi State MS 39762-9825 Office Phone: 662-325-1131. Office Fax: 662-325-1498.*

THOMSON, KEITH STEWART, biologist, author; b. Heanor, Eng., July 29, 1938; s. Ronald William and Marian Adelaide (Coster) T.; m. Linda Gailbreath Price, Sept. 27, 1963; children: Jessica Adelaide, Elizabeth Rose. B.Sc. with honors, U. Birmingham, Eng., 1960; A.M., Harvard U., 1961, PhD (NATO fellow), 1963. NATO postdoctoral fellow Univ. Coll., London U., 1963-65; asst. prof. to prof. biology Yale U., 1965-87, dean Grad. Sch., 1979-87; dir. Peabody Mus. Natural History, 1976-79; pres. Acad. Natural Scis., Phila., 1987-95; disting. scientist-in-residence New Sch Social Rsch., N.Y.C., 1996-98; prof., dir. Mus. Natural History Oxford U., 1998—2003; sr. rsch. fellow Am. Philos. Soc., Phila., 2003—. Dir. Sears Found. Marine Rsch. and

Oceanographic History; hon. rsch. fellow Australian Nat. U., 1967; trustee, mem. corp. Woods Hole Oceanographic Inst.; bd. dirs. Wistar Inst., Ctrl. Phila. Devel. Corp., Wetlands Inst., Phila. Cultural Alliance, Charles Darwin Trust; rschr. in vertebrate evolution. Mem. editl. bd. Paleobiology, Jour. Morphology, 1988, Aspects of Lower Vertebrate Evolution, 1968, Origin of Terrestrial Vertebrates, 1968, Saltwater Fishes of Conn., 1971, 88, Priorities and Needs in Systematic Biology, 1981, Morphogenesis and Evolution, 1988, Living Fossil, 1991, The Common But Less Frequent Loon and Other Essays, 1993, HMS Beagle, 1995, 2003, Treasures on Earth, 2002. Fellow Linnean Soc. London, Zool. Soc. London; mem. Soc. Vertebrate Palaeontology, Sigma Xi.

THOMSON, KENNETH R. (LORD THOMSON OF FLEET), publishing executive; b. Toronto, Sept. 1, 1923; s. Lord Thomson of Fleet; m. Nora Marilyn Lavis, June 1956; children: David Kenneth Roy, Peter John, Taylor Lynne. Student, Upper Can. Coll., Toronto; BA, MA, U. Cambridge, Eng., 1947. With editl. dept. Timmins Daily Press, 1947; with advt. dept. Cambridge (Galt) Reporter, 1948-50, gen. mgr., 1950-53. Chmn., bd. dirs. The Woodbridge Co. Ltd.; pres., bd. dirs. Thomson Works of Art Ltd.; dir. The Thomson Corp. With RCAF, World War II. Mem. Granite Club, Hunt Club, Toronto Club, York Club. Avocations: collecting paintings and works of art, walking. Home: 8 Castle Frank Rd Toronto ON Canada M4W 2Z4 Office: Thomson Corp 65 Queen St W Toronto ON Canada M5H 2M8

THOMSON, PAUL RICE, JR., lawyer; b. Syracuse, NY, Dec. 28, 1941; s. Paul Rice and Marcella Elizabeth (Shea) T.; m. Elizabeth Ann Cutliff, Aug. 21, 1965; children: Paul R. III, Pamela Judeth. BA in History, Va. Mil. Inst., 1963; JD, Washington and Lee U., 1966. Bar: Va. 1966, U.S. Dist. Ct. (we. dist.) Va. 1966, U.S. Ct. Mil. Appeals 1967, U.S. Ct. Appeals (4th cir.) 1972. Assoc. Clement, Wheatley, Winston & Ingram, Danville, Va., 1969-71; asst. U.S. atty. Western Dist. Va., Roanoke, 1971-75, U.S. atty., 1975-79; gen. counsel natural resources The Pittston Co., Lebanon, Va., 1980—87; dep. asst. adminstr. EPA, Washington, 1987—90; ptnr. Woods Rogers PLC, Roanoke, Va., 1990—. Pres. Roanoke Valley Law Enforcement Coun., 1975-76; mem. Fed.-State Law Enforcement Coun., 1975-79; trustee Ea. Mineral Law Found., Pitts., 1980-82; adj. prof. Washington & Lee U., 1981-99. V.p. Danville Jr. C. of C., 1971. Capt. JAGC, USMC, 1966-69. Recipient Spl. Achievement award Dept. Justice, 1974 Mem. ABA, Va. Bar Assn., Fed. Bar Assn. (pres. local chpt. 1979), NRA, Trout Unltd. Roman Catholic. Avocations: fly fishing, bird hunting, raising labrador retreivers. Office: Woods Rogers PLC 10 S Jefferson St Roanoke VA 24011 Office Phone: 540-983-7742. Business E-Mail: thomson@woodsrogers.com.

THOMSON, RICHARD MURRAY, retired bank executive; b. Winnipeg, Man., Can., Aug. 14, 1933; s. H.W. and Mary Thomson. BASC in Engring., U. Toronto, 1955; MBA, Harvard U., 1957; fellow course in banking, Queen's U., 1958. With Toronto Dominion Bank, Canada, 1957—2004, asst. to pres. head office, 1963-68, chief gen. mgr., 1968-71, v.p., chief gen. mgr., dir., 1971-72, pres., 1972-77, pres., CEO, 1977-78, chmn., 1978-98, CEO, 1978-97, bd. dirs. Bd. dirs. S.C. Johnson & Son Inc., Prudential Fin., Inc., The Thomson Corp., Stuart Energy Systems Corp., Trizec Properties, Inc.; chmn. bd. dirs. Nexen Inc. Office: The Toronto Dominion Bank 66 Wellingto St W 10th Fl TD Bank Tow POB 1 Toronto Dominion Ctr Toronto ON Canada M5K 1A2

THOMSON, THYRA GODFREY, former state official; b. Florence, Colo., July 30, 1916; d. John and Rosalie (Altman) Godfrey; m. Keith Thomson, Aug. 6, 1939 (dec. Dec. 1960); children— William John, Bruce Godfrey, Keith Coffey. BA cum laude, U. Wyo., 1939. With dept. agronomy and agrl. econs. U. Wyo., 1938-39; writer weekly column Watching Washington pub. in 14 papers, Wyo., 1955-60; planning chmn. Nat. Fedn. Republican Women, Washington, 1961; sec. state Wyo. Cheyenne, 1962-86. Mem. Marshall Scholarships Com. for Pacific region, 1964-68; del. 72d Wilton Park Conf., Eng., 1965; mem. youth commn. UNESCO, 1970-71, Allied Health Professions Council HEW, 1971-72; del. U.S.-Republic of China Trade Conf., Taipei, Taiwan, 1983; mem. lt. gov.'s trade and fact-finding mission to Saudi Arabia, Jordan, and Egypt, 1985 Bd. dirs. Buffalo Bill Mus., Cody, Wyo., 1987—; adv. bd. Coll. Arts and Scis., U. Wyo., 1989, Cheyenne Symphony Orch. Found., 1990—. Recipient Disting. Alumni award U. Wyo., 1969, Disting. U. Wyo. Arts and Scis. Alumna award, 1987, citation Omicron Delta Epsilon, 1965, citation Beta Gamma Sigma, 1968, citation Delta Kappa Gamma, 1973, citation Wyo. Commn. Women, 1986; named Internat. Woman of Distinction, Alpha Delta Kappa, Keith and Thyra Honors Convocation in her honor Coll. of Arts and Scis. U. Wyo., 1997. Mem. N.Am. Securities Adminstrs. (pres. 1973-74), Nat. Assn. Secs. of State, Council State Govts. (chmn. natural resources com. Western states 1966-68), Nat. Conf. Lt. Govs. (exec. com. 1976-79) Republican. Home: 3102 Sunrise Rd Cheyenne WY 82001-6136

THOMSON, TODD STUART, corporate finance executive; b. Stanford, Calif., Jan. 30, 1961; s. Scott Dayton and Margaret Elaine (Guice) T.; m. Melissa Kay McKeithen, May 22, 1988. BA in Econs., Davidson Coll., 1983; MBA with distinction, U. Pa., 1987. With Barents Group LLC; cons., sr. cons. Booz Allen & Hamilton, Bethesda, Md., 1983-85; cons., mgr. Bain & Co., Boston, 1986-91; now exec. v.p., CFO Citigroup Inc. Office: EVP Fin CFO Citigroup Inc 399 Park Ave New York NY 10022

THONET, JOHN A. environmental planning and engineering consultant; b. Baldwin, N.Y., Aug. 4, 1950; s. John Chester and Grace W. (Keeling) T.; m. Kathi Lynn Blatt, May 1973; children: Hannah, Rebecca. BS in Forest Engring. cum laude, SUNY, Syracuse, 1972, MS, 1975. Registered profl. engr., Mass., N.J., Pa., Mich., W.Va., profl. planner, N.J. Environ. engr. Power Authority of State of N.Y., N.Y.C., 1973-74; project mgr., civil engr. Tippetts Abbett McCarthy Stratton Engrs. & Architects, N.Y.C., 1974-79; assoc. Dresdner Assocs. Environ. Land Use Planning Cons., Summit, N.J., 1979-80; pres. Thonet Assocs., Inc. Environ. Planning & Design Cons., South Orange, N.J., 1980—. Contbr. articles to profl. jours. Chmn. S. Orange Environ. Com., adv. coun. Environ. Resources and Forest Engring. Dept., SUNY; trustee N.J. Environ. lobby; mem. adv bd. Engring. and Computer Sci., Syracuse U. Mem. ASCE, Soc. Am. Foresters, N.J. Soc. Profl. Engrs., Nat. Assn. Environ. Profls. Avocations: guitar, tennis. Office: Thonet Assocs Environ Planning & Design Cons 14 S Orange Ave South Orange NJ 07079-1754 E-mail: jthonet@thonetassociates.com.

THONG, TRAN, biomedical company executive; b. Saigon, Vietnam, Dec. 8, 1951; came to U.S., 1969, naturalized, 1980. s. Vy and Vinh-Thi (Nguyen) T.; m. Thuy Thi-Bich Nguyen, Jan.12, 1978. BSEE, Ill. Inst. Tech., 1972; MS in Engring., Princeton U., 1974, PhD, 1975. Rsch. scientist Western Geophys., Houston, 1975-76; computer devel. engr. GE Co., Syracuse, N.Y., 1976-79; dir. electronic system lab. Tektronix, Inc., Beaverton, Oreg., 1980-90; v.p. engring., and digital signal processing gen. mgr. Tektronix Fed. Systems Inc., Beaverton, Oreg., 1990-93; v.p. systems design and devel. Micro Systems Engring., Inc., Lake Oswego, Oreg., 1993—; prin. N.W. Signal Processing, Inc. Adj. asst. prof. Syracuse U., 1979-81, Oreg. State U., Corvallis, 1980-83, U. Portland, Oreg., 1981-83; adj. prof. Oreg. Grad. Ctr., Beaverton, 1984—; mem. adv. bd. Biomed. Engring. Inst., U. Erlangen, Germany, 1996—. Author numerous sci papers and U. S. patents. Bd. dirs. S.E. Asia Scholarship Fund, 1994—. Fellow IEEE (com. chmn. 1982-88, assoc. editor Trans. 1979-81, gen. chmn, 1989, exec. v.p. circuits and sys. 1989); mem. Vietnamese Assn. for Computing Engring. Tech. and Sci. (founding mem., chmn. 1994-95, past pres, 1995-96, pres. 1998-99), Sigma Xi, Eta Kappa Nu, Tau Beta Pi. Republican. Office: Micro Sys Engring 6024 Jean Rd Lake Oswego OR 97035-5308

THONGBOONKERD, VISITH, nephrologist, researcher; b. Phichit, Thailand, Nov. 13, 1971; MD with first class honors(hon.), Chiang Mai (Thailand) U., 1994. Diplomate Thai Board of Nephrology Nephrology Soc. of Thailand. Clin. nephrology fellow Chiang Mai U., 1998—2000; Internat. Soc. of Nephrology fellow U. Louisville, 2000—. Recipient Best Fellow's Poster award, Internat. Soc. Nephrology, 2001. Office: U Louisville Proteomics Lab 570 South Preston St Ste 102 Louisville KY 40202

THONGSAK, VAJEEPRASEE THOMAS, business planning executive; b. Udonthani, Thailand, Feb. 10, 1935; came to U.S., 1970; s. Chanmar and Pee Vajeeprasee; m. Somchit; 1 child, Rosarine. BS in Sociology, BA in Philosophy, Mahamakut U., Bangkok, 1968; MA in Edn., Kean Coll. N.J., 1976; MA in Philosophy, NYU, 1989; PhD in Mgmt., AMA Mgmt. Inst., 1987. Cert. cash mgr. Tchr. Machimavas Sch., Udonthani, 1958-65; spl. instr. Chana Songkram Sch., Bangkok, 1965-68; tchrs. staff Thai Sripratoom U., Bangkok, 1968-70; salesman Met. Life of N.Y., 1974-76; rep. Mut. Life of N.Y., 1976-78; agt. Equitable Life Ins., N.Y.C., 1983-84; insp. IBI Security Svc. Inc., L.I., 1979-85; security police insp. Brandeis U., Waltham, Mass., 1985-86; U.S. chief legal investigator, pvt. investigator U.S. Legal Investigation, Inc., U.S. Bur.'s Security Agy., Boston, N.Y.C., Fresno, Calif., 1987—; chmn. Worldwide Bank Assocs. Investment, 2000—. Advisor Thai N.E. Assn., N.Y.C., 1980—, Rep. Nat. Com., Washingotn, 1980—; state advisor U.S. Congl. Adv., Washington, 1980; assoc. mem. Nat. Security Ctr., Citizen's Adv. Coun., Washington, 1989; pres., chief security agt. U.S. Bur. Security Agy., 1991; mem. Pres. Pvt. Sector Survey on Cost Control, Washington, 1989—; adv. bd. Am. Security Coun., Washington, 1983-88. Mem. G.O.P. Republican Conservative Party (recommendation pres. Gerald R. Ford 1977), 1977—. Nat. Republican Congl. Com. Victory Fund, Washington, 1982—, Republican Presdl. Task Force and Comsn. (recommendation chmn. Nat. Republican Senatorial Com. 1982, 93), 1982—, Am. Security Coun. Found., 1978—. Defense Dept., Defense Inst., 1982—, Nat. Rep. Senatorial Com., Washington, Chiefs of Police Nat. Drug Task Force, 1982—, Nat. Law Enforcement Officers Meml. Fund, Washington, 1982—, Natl. Wildlife Fedn., 1982—; apptd. state adviser U.S. Congl. Adv. Bd., 1979, 93; priest asst. U.S.A. Buddhayaram Temple, Bronx, 1970—; pres. S.E. Asia Found., 1970; mem. Citizens Against Govt. Waste, Washington; mem. U.S. Def. Com., Washington, 1982-86; sec. Wat Buddhamonthol United Buddhist Meditation Ctr., 1992—. Recipient Presdl. Seal, Rep. Orgn., 1983, 84, Rep. Presdl. Legion of Merit highest level of Govts. for Lifetime, 1993. Mem.: Nat. Constitution Ctr. (Pa. signer), Navy League U.S., Internat. Assn. Chiefs of Police, Rep. Presdl. Legion of Merit, Sen.'s Club, Pres.'s Club.

'T HOOFT, GERARDUS, physicist, researcher; b. Den Helder, The Netherlands, July 5, 1946; s. Hendrik 't Hooft and Margaretha Agnes (van Kampen) t' Hooft; m. Albertha Anje Schik, July 1, 1972; children: Saskia Anne, Ellen Marga. Ed., Utrecht U., The Netherlands; doctoraalexamen Theoretical Physics, Rijksuniversiteit Utrecht, The Netherlands, 1969, PhD, 1972; DSc (hon.), U. Chgo., 1981, U. Louvain, 1996, U. Bologna, 1998, Eurasian U., Astana, Kazakjstan, 2000, U. Western Cape, South Africa, 2001. Fellow European Ctr. Nuc. Rsch., Geneva, 1972—74; lectr., asst. prof. physics U. Utrecht, The Netherlands, 1974—77, prof., 1977—. Loeb lectr. Harvard U., Cambridge, Mass., 1976; Fairchild disting. scholar Calif. Inst. Tech., Pasadena, 1981; assoc. etranger Acad. des Scis., Paris, 1995. Assoc. editor Nuc. Physics B; contbr. articles to profl. jours. Decorated officer Legion of Honor France, comdr. Order Ned. Leeuw; recipient Dannie Heineman prize, Am. Phys. Soc., 1979, Am. Inst. Physics, N.Y.C., 1979, Wolf prize, Wolf Found., Jerusalem, 1981, Piou XI medal, Pontifica Accademia delle Sci. John Paul II, Vatican City, 1983, Spinoza premium, NWO, 1995, Franklin medal, Phila., 1995, Gian Carlo Wick commn. medal, Lausanne, 1997, HEP prize, European Phys. Soc., 1999, Nobel prize in physics, 1999. Mem.: Koninlijke Nederlandse Academie voor Wetenschappen (Lorentz medal 1986), Am. Acad. Arts and Scis. (hon.), U.S. Nat. Acad. Scis. (assoc.). Office: Spinoza Inst Leuvenlaan 4 PO Box 80 195 NL3508TD Utrecht Netherlands E-mail: g.thooft@phys.uu.nl.

THORBECKE, ERIK, economics professor; b. Berlin, Feb. 17, 1929; s. William and Madelaine (Salisbury) T.; m. Charla J. Westerberg, Oct. 17. 1954; children: Erik Charles, Willem, Jon. Student, Netherlands Sch. Econs., Rotterdam, 1948-51; PhD, U. Calif., 1957; hon. doctorate, U. Ghent, 1981. Asst. prof. econs. Iowa State U., 1957-60, assoc. prof., 1960-63, prof., 1963-73, Cornell U., 1974—, chmn. dept. econs., 1975-78, H.E. Babcock prof. econs. and food econs., 1978—. Econ. adviser Nat. Planning Inst., Lima, Peru, 1963-64; asso. asst. adminstr. for program policy AID, Washington, 1966-68, mem. research advisory com., 1976-81; sr. economist world employment program Internat. Labor Office, Geneva, 1972-73; vis. prof. Erasmus U., Rotterdam, 1980-81; mem. com. on internat. nutritional programs NRC-NAS, 1979-81; dir. program on comparative econ. devel., Cornell U., 1988—; sr. rsch. fellow USAID Inst. Policy Reform, 1990—. Author: The Tendency Towards Regionalization in International Trade, 1960, (with Irma Adelman) Theory and Design of Economic Development, 1966, (with K. Fox, J. Sengupta) Theory of Quantitative Economic Policy, 1968, Role of Agriculture in Economic Development, 1968, (with G. Pyatt) Planning Techniques for a Better Future, 1976; (with J. Defourny) Structural Path Analysis and Multiplier Decomposition within a Social Matrix, 1984, (with J. Foster, J. Greer) A Class of Decomposable Poverty Measures, 1984, (with J. Lecaillon, C. Morrisson) Economic Policies and Agricultural Performance of Low Income Countries, 1987, Planning Techniques for Social Justice In: The Balance between Industry and Agriculture in Economic Development, vol. 4, 1989, (with I. Adelman) The Role of Institutions in Economic Development, Special Issue of World Development, 1989, (with others) Adjustment and Equity in Indonesia, 1992, (with D. Berrian) Budgetary Rules to Minimize Societal Poverty in a General Equilibrium Context, 1992, (with T. van der Pluijm) Rural Indonesia: Socio-economic Development in a Changing Environment, 1993, (with A. de Janvry and E. Sadoulet) Impact of State and Civil Institutions on the Operation of Rural Market and Non-Market Configurations In: State, Market and civil Organizations: New Theories, New Practices, and Their Implications for Rural Development, 1995, (with A. Parikh) Impact of Rural Industrialization on Village Life and Economy: A Social Accounting Matrix, 1996, (with H-S Jung) A Multiplier Decomposition Method to Analyze Poverty Alleviation, 1996, (with others) Methods of Interregional and Regional Analysis, 1998, (with H. Wan) Taiwan's Development Experience: Lessons on Roles of Government and Market, 1999, (with C. Charumilind) Economic Inequality and its Socio-economic Impact, 2002; contbr. articles to profl. jours. Mem. Am. Econ. Assn., Am. Assn. Agrl. Econs. (Nat. award for best pub. research 1970) Office: Cornell U Dept Econs Ithaca NY 14853

THORBECKE, WILLEM HENRY, international company executive, consultant; b. Paris, July 4, 1924; s. Willem Johan Rudolf and Madelaine (Salisbury) T.; m. Sonya Stokowski, June 8, 1946; children; Noel Evangeline, Johan Rudolf, Willem Leif, Christine Louise. BS in Engring., BSBA, MIT, 1948. Exec. Royal Dutch Shell, N.Y.C., London, Tokyo, 1948-60, Mobil Corp., N.Y.C., 1960-69; cons. various cos., N.Y.C., Chgo., Houston, others, 1969-75; pres. Dravo Internat., Pitts., 1975-82, W.H. Thorbecke Assocs., Sewickley, Pa., 1982—. Chmn., chief exec. officer Energy Support Svcs. Inc., Coraopolis, Pa., 1982-87, dir., 1987-90; founder, chmn., CEO Thorbecke Enterprises, Inc., Sewickley, 1996—. Dir. World Affairs Coun., Pitts., 1978—; chmn. MIT Enterprise Forum, Pitts., 1987-89, 93-94. Flight lt. RAF. Named Tri-State Area Entrepreneur of Yr. Venture Mag., Ernst & Young, 1987. Mem. Am. Mgmt. Assn. (internat. coun. 1977-83), Nat. Assn. Corp. Dirs., Duquesne Club (Pitts.), Haagse Club (The Netherlands). Republican. Episcopalian. Home: Deer Haven Farm Stonedale Rd Sewickley PA 15143 E-mail: whthorbecke@aol.com.

THORBURN, JAMES ALEXANDER, retired humanities educator; b. Martins Ferry, Ohio, Aug. 24, 1923; s. Charles David and Mary Edna (Ruble) Thorburn; m. Lois McElroy, July 3, 1954; children: Alexander Maurice, Melissa Rachel; m. June Yingling O'Leary, Apr. 18, 1981. BA, Ohio State U., 1949, MA, 1951; postgrad., U. Mo., 1954—55; PhD, La. State U., 1977. Head English dept. high sch., Sheridan, Mich., 1951—52; instr. English U. Mo., Columbia, 1952—55, Monmouth (Ill.) Coll., 1955—56, U. Tex., El Paso, 1956—60, U. Mo., St. Louis, 1960—61, La. State U., Baton Rouge, 1961—70; prof. Southeastern La. U., Hammond, 1970—89, prof. emeritus English and linguistics; ret. Testing and cert. examiner English Lang. Inst., U. Mich., 1969—; participant Southeastern Conf. on Linguistics; mem. Conf. Christianity and Lit. Contbg. author Exercises in English, 1955, also poetry, short stories, book rev. editor Experiment, 1958—87; editor: Innisfree, 1984—89. With F.A. AUS, 1943—46. Mem.: MLA, La. Ret. Tchrs. Assn., La. Assn. for Coll. Composition, Am. Dialect Soc., Linguistic Soc. Am., Avalon World Arts Acad., Linguistic Assn. S.W., Sociedad Nacional Hispânica, Internat. Poetry Soc., Phi Kappa Phi (named emeritus life), Phi Mu Alpha Sinfonia, Sigma Delta Pi. Republican. Presbyterian. Home: 602 Susan Dr Hammond LA 70403-3444 Office: Southeastern La U # 739 Hammond LA 70402-0001 *I have always felt that no experience is wasted, if it is not selfish or vicious. Every such experience adds something, I believe, to that inner fund on which one draws, consciously or unconsciously, throughout one's life.*

THORBURN, LISA A. acoustical consulting company executive; BS in Scientific & Tech. Comm., Mich. Tech. U. With Sisters of St. Dominic, Anshen & Allen, IWERKS Entertainment, Don Dommer Assocs., STUDIOS Architecture, Harveys Resort Hotel/Casino, South Lake Tahoe, Helsing Group, Brava, Inc.; prin. designer Thorburn Assocs., Castro Valley, Calif. Contbr. tech. articles to profl. jours. Mem. AIA, NAFE, Soc. Tech. Comm., Soc. Mktg. Profl. Svcs., Constrn. Specifications Inst. Office: 2867 Grove Way Castro Valley CA 94546-6709

THORDARSON, WILLIAM, retired hydrogeologist; b. N.Y.C., Mar. 14, 1929; s. William and Lillian (Hirsch) T. BA, Columbia U., 1950; postgrad., U. Kans., Lawrence, 1953-55; MA, U. Colo., 1987. Hydrogeologist U.S. Geol. Survey, Denver, 1955-94. Author: Perched Groundwater, Nevada, 1965, Hydrogeology of Test Wells, 1975, Hydrogeology of South-Central Great Basin, 1983, Hydrogeologic Monitoring, Nevada, 1985, Hydrogeology of Anhydrite, 1989. Served with U.S. Army, 1950-52. Mem. Nat. Geog. Soc., Colo. Ground Water Assn., Colo. Sci. Soc., Geol. Soc. Wash. Home: 1453 Belcourt Lane Mount Pleasant SC 29466-8103

THORN, BRIAN EARL, Internet company executive; b. Tucson, Oct. 30, 1955; s. Charles Walter and Jacquelyn Grace (Sloat) T.; m. Mary L. Ayala, Nov. 23, 1979 (div. 1981); m. Brenda Anne Benson, Dec. 28, 1983; 1 child, Justin. Student, U. Ariz. Loss prevention mgr. HRT Industries, Tucson, 1977-82; sales mgr. Circuit City, 1982-86, ops. mgr., 1986-87, divsn. mgr., 1987-90; store mgr. Barnes & Noble, Houston, 1992-97; ops. mgr. Best Buy, The Woodlands, Tex., 1997-99; nat. sales mgr. Aerial/Voicestream Comm., Houston, 1999-2000; mgr. tech. InfoHighway Comms., Houston, 2000—. Bd. dirs. Infohighway Comms., Inc.; mem. advt./mktg. com. Woodlands Corp. Mem. planning com. Edn. for Tomorrow Alliance; mem. planning com., 4th of July planning com. Home for the Holidays Planning Com. Mem. Tex. Tech. Forum (treas.), Woodlands C. of C. (bd. dirs., mem. exec. nominating com., mem. affinity com., mem. visioning com.), Woodlands Libr. Guild (bd. dirs.), Montgomery County Sheriff Citizens Acad. Alumni Assn. Avocations: golf, reading, old cars, flying, computers.

THORN, ROD, professional basketball executive; b. 1941; m. Peggy Thorn; children: Jonathan, Amanda, Jessica. Student, W.Va. U. Player Balt. Bullets, NBA, 1963-64, Detroit Pistons and St. Louis Hawks, NBA, 1964-66, Seattle Supersonics, NBA, 1966-70, asst. coach, 1971-73, N.Y. Nets, Am. Basketball Assn., 1973-75; coach St. Louis Spirits, Am. Basketball Assn., 1975-76; asst. coach N.Y. Nets, 1976-78; gen. mgr. Chgo. Bulls, NBA, 1978-85; v.p. ops. NBA, N.Y.C., 1985-2000; pres. New Jersey Nets, East Rutherford, N.J., 2000—. Office: Nat Basketball Assn Olympic Tower 645 5th Ave Fl 10 New York NY 10022-5986 Address: NJ Nets Nets Champion Ctr 390 Murray Hill Pkwy East Rutherford NJ 07073-2109

THORN, ROSEMARY KOST, former librarian; b. N.Y.C., Dec. 15, 1954; d. Stephen John and Henrietta (Rosso) K.; m. Michael Thorn; children: Russell, Stephen. BA in Anthropology, Rutgers U., 1977; MLS, U. N.C., 1980. Head libr. U.S. EPA, Research Triangle Park, N.C., 1980-96; EPA. Avocations: running, gardening, travel, tae kwon do (2d degree black belt). Office Phone: 919-967-0339. E-mail: rosemarythorn@mindspring.com.

THORN, STUART WALLACE, marketing and financial executive; b. Glen Cove, N.Y., Mar. 20, 1956; s. Benjamin Chessman and Nancy Elizabeth (Libby) T.; m. Jean Marie Gillis, Oct. 7, 1979 (div.); children: Alexander Chessman, Jason Keane, Tyler Steven; m. Sharon Elizabeth Foreman, June, 2003. BS in Econs. magna cum laude, U. Pa., 1978, MBA in Fin., 1979. Market rsch. intern People's Savs. Bank, Bridgeport, Conn., 1987-88; fin. analyst, corp. control S.C. Johnson & Son, Inc., Racine, Wis., 1979-80, cost mgmt. analyst, prodn. support, 1980-81; project supr. Johnson Worldwide Assocs., S.C. Johnson & Son, Racine, 1982-83; fin. mgr. Porelon, Inc., Cookeville, Tenn., 1983-86; corp. acquistions dir. S.C. Johnson & Son, Inc., Racine, 1986-87, regional controller Africa and Nr. East Frimley, Eng., 1987-90, internat. mktg. assoc. Racine, 1990-91, dir. fin. N.Am. consumer products, 1991-94; v.p. internat. fin. Campbell Soup Co., 1994—; CFO Beaulieu of Am., 1995—2001; pres., CEO Southwire Co., Carrollton, Ga., 2001—. Solicitor United Way, Racine; bd. dirs. Explorers, Boy Scouts Am., 1986-87; bd. dirs. Racine County Opportunity Ctr., 1991—. Named Nat. Champion Nat. Collegiate Racing Assoc. Avocations: tennis, windsurfing, golf. Office: Southwire Co 1 Southwire Dr Carrollton GA 30119

THORN, SUSAN HOWE, interior designer; b. Washington, Apr. 22, 1941; d. James Bennett Cowdin and Lois (Fiesinger) Howe; m. William D. Thorn, June 22, 1963; children: Melissa Ann, William David. Lighting design, Parsons Sch. Design, 1975-77; BA, Syracuse U., 1962; AB, N.Y. Sch. Interior Design, 1995. Owner, designer Susan Thorn Interiors, Inc., Cross River, N.Y., 1965—. Designer total bldg. Cooper Labs, Bedford Hills, N.Y., 1973, total redesign Nycrest Corp., Cold Spring, N.Y., 1973-75, showrooms, model rooms stylist and coordinator France Voiles Co. Inc., N.Y.C., 1976, total design new corp. hdqrs. in Gen. Dynamics Bldg. (with Marjorie Borradaile Helsel), Robert E. Eastman Co., N.Y.C., 1967, Cummin & Friedland Capital Corp., 1982; designer offices, stores, employee areas comml., public, residential clients, including Waccabuc (N.Y.) Country Club, 1969, S. Salem (N.Y.) Library, St. Vincent's Hosp., N.Y.C., 1996; instr. adult edn. dept. John Jay High Sch.; spkr. civic orgns. Mem. Am. Soc. Interior Designers (profl.), Internat. Assn. Lighting Designers (assoc.), Decorators Club, Club of N.Y., Waccabuc Country Club. Episcopalian. Home: 88 N Salem Rd Cross River NY 10518 Office Phone: 914-763-5265. E-mail: thorninteriors@earthlink.net.

THORN, TERENCE HASTINGS, international energy industry executive; b. Takoma, Md., July 6, 1946; s. John Hastings and Norine R. (Freytag) T.; m. Judith Carol Bailey, Aug. 15, 1970; children: Kristin Lynn, Matthew Hastings. BA, U. Md., 1969, MA, 1973. Dir. congl. rels. Am. Gas Assn., Arlington, Va., 1975-79; dir. govt. rels. J. Walter Thompson Co., Washington, 1979-81; v.p. govt. rels. Houston Natural Gas Co., Washington, 1981-85; exec. v.p., chmn. bd. Mojave Pipeline Co., Houston, 1986-89; pres., CEO Transwestern Pipeline Co., Houston, 1993—; sr. v.p., exec. mgmt. com. bd. Enron Corp., Houston, 1993-98, exec. v.p. internat. govt. rels. and environ. affairs, 1998—2001, mng. dir. Middle East, 2001; cons. Houston Tex. Energy, Environment, Tech.; pres. JKM Cons., 2001—. Bd. dirs. Houston Pops, 1989-90, Pin Oak Charities, Houston, 1991-93, Greater Houston chpt. YMCA, 1994; city alderman, 1992-93; mem. Hermann Soc., 1993—. Energy Industry Sector Adv. Com. U.S. Dept. Commerce; prin. liason Pres.'s Coun. Sustainable Devel.; chmn. internat. com. Bus. Coun. of Sustainable Devel.; mem. adv. com. Commn. for Environ. Cooperation; trustee Tomas Rivera Policy Inst.; chmn. Internat. Gas Ctr. Mem. Pacific Coast Gas Assn. (chmn. 1994-95), Internat. Gas Union (chmn. com. 9), U.S. C. of C. (mem. internat. policy com.), Coun. of the Ams. (adv. com.), Wildlife Conservation Soc. (trustee), Nature Conservancy (trustee). Avocation: tennis. Home: 5800 Woodway Dr Apt 337 Houston TX 77057-1511

THORNBERRY, MAC, congressman; b. Clarendon, Tex., July 15, 1958; m. Sally Thornberry; 2 children. BA in History summa cum laude, Tex. Tech U., 1980; JD, U. Tex., 1983. Legis. coun. rep. Tom Loeffler, 1983-85; chief of staff Rep. Larry Combest, 1985-88; dep. asst. sec. legis. affairs U.S. State Dept., 1988-89; def. atty. Peterson, Farris, Doores & Jones, Amarillo, Tex., 1989-94; mem. U.S. Congress from 13th Tex. dist., 1995—; mem. armed svcs. com., budget com., oil and gas caucus, homeland sec. com., former mem. resources com. Family rancher. Mem. Tex. and Southwestern Cattle Raisers Assn. Republican. Office: US House Reps 2457 Rayburn HOB Washington DC 20515-4313

THORNBRO, WILLIAM GRADEN, writer; b. Muncie, Ind., July 8, 1952; s. William Wesley Thornbro and Bonnie Ather Marcum; m. Janice Kay Waters, Aug. 7, 1976; children: Christopher Wesley, Nicholas Dale. BS, Ball State U., 1978. Author: (book) An Uncertain Justice, A Question of Conspiracy. Mem.: Planetary Soc. Democrat. Avocations: reading /research, gardening. Home: 212 S Pasture Ln Muncie IN 47304-4120 Personal E-mail: wmthornbro@sbcglobal.net.

THORNBURG, FREDERICK FLETCHER, diversified business executive, lawyer; b. South Bend, Ind., Feb. 10, 1940; s. James F. and Margaret R. (Major) T.; children: James Brian, Charles Kevin, Christian Sean, Christopher Herndon; m. Patricia J. Malloy, Dec. 4, 1981. AB, DePauw U., 1963; postgrad., U. Notre Dame, 1965; JD magna cum laude, Ind. U., 1968. Bar: Ind. 1968, U.S. Tax Ct. 1970, U.S. Ct. Appeals (7th cir.) 1970, U.S. Supreme Ct. 1971. Tchr., coach U.S. Peace Corps, Colombia, 1963-65; law clk. to chief judge U.S. Ct. Appeals (7th cir.), 1968-69; assoc. Thornburg, McGill, Deahl, Harman, Carey & Murray, South Bend, 1969-75, ptnr., 1975-80; v.p. systems and svcs. group The Wackenhut Corp., Coral Gables, Fla., 1981-82, sr. v.p. adminstrn., 1982-86, exec. v.p., 1986-88, also bd. dirs.; pres. Wackenhut Internat. Corp. and Wackenhut Svcs., Inc.; v.p., legal counsel St. Thomas U., 1988-90, adj. prof. law, 1989-90; pres., CEO PropServ, Inc., 1991-94; pres. EPS Ltd., 1995—; CEO Practice Resources Corp., 1996-97; CEO, of counsel Stephens, Lynn, Klien & McNicholas, P.A., 1998-2000. Cons. MSC, Am. Tel. Corp.; legal and mgmt. cons., mem. bd. advisors Publix Supermarkets, Inc., 1994—95, St. Thomas U., 1990—95; bd. dirs., v.p. Doral Park Country Club; bd. dirs., mem. exec. com. RFBD, Inc.; bd. dirs. Genz, LLC, Carlos Albizu U. Found., 2002—; trustee U. Cmty. Hosp. Found., 1991—94; adj. prof. bus. St. Mary's Coll., 1975—78; vis. prof. CTA, 1985—95; vice chmn., pvt. sec. adv. coun. Fla. Sec. of State, 1985—90; chair ethics com. Miami Dade County Pub. Schs., 2002—; legal and mgmt. cons., mem. bd. adv. WLRN-PBS Radio and Television, 2003—; adj. prof. bus. St. Thomas U. Law Sch., 1999—2000, Carlos Albizu U., 2004, chair Bus. Sch. Adv. Bd., 2003—. Assoc. editor in chief Ind. Law Jour., 1967-68; contbr. articles to legal and bus. jours. Mem. Civic Ctr. Found., 1976—80; pres. Jaycees, 1974; bd. advisors PSC-TV, WLRN; bd. dirs. RFD&D, Inc.; former bd. dirs. Michiana YMCA, Channel 34, Symphony Orch. Assn., 1974—80, Boy Scouts of U.S.A.; bd. dirs., mem. exec. com. Doral and West Airport C. of C. Fulbright selectee, Halleck scholar. Mem. ABA, Ind. Bar Assn., Greater Miami C. of C. (former corp. rep. trustee), Elks Club, Doral Park Golf and Country Club (bd. dirs.), Order of Coif, Phi Delta Phi, Alpha Delta Sigma. Office: 10005 NW 52nd Ter Miami FL 33178-2608 Fax: (305) 591-6560. Office Phone: 305-513-0146. E-mail: MrFPT@aol.com.

THORNBURG, LACY HERMAN, federal judge; b. Charlotte, N.C., Dec. 20, 1929; s. Jesse Lafayette and Sarah Ann (Ziegler) T.; m. Dorothy Todd, Sept. 6, 1953; children— Sara Thornburg Evans, Lacy Eugene, Jesse Todd, Alan Ziegler. AA, Mars Hill Coll., 1950; BA, U. N.C., 1951, JD, 1954. Bar: U.S. Dist. Ct. (we. dist.) N.C. Practiced law, Webster, N.C., 1954-67; superior ct. judge State of N.C., 1967-83, atty. gen, 1985-92; emergency judge N.C. Superior Ct., Webster, 1993-94; mem. Nat. Indian Gaming Commn., 1994-95; judge U.S. Dist. Ct. for N.C., Asheville, 1995—. Mem. staff Congressman Taylor, Sylva, N.C., 1960, Congressman David Hall, Sylva, 1959-60; mem. N.C. Ho. of Reps., 1961-65; mem. N.C. Cts. Commn., N.C. Criminal Code Commn., Capital Planning Commn., Raleigh. Chmn. Jackson County Bd. of Health, Sylva, 1965-84; commr. Tryon Palace, New Bern, N.C. Served with U.S. Army, 1947-48. Mem. Lions, Masons, Shriners. Democrat. Avocations: fly fishing, skeet shooting. Office: US Dist Ct 200 US Courthouse 100 Otis St Asheville NC 28801-2611

THORNBURG, LEE ELLIS, film executive, director; b. Houston, Feb. 16, 1942; s. Richard Ellis and Lucyle (Comstock) T.; m. Jane Kaiser (div. 1981); children: Janette Mattas, Deanne Waddell; m. Patricia Ann Kirkham, June 16, 1987. Tech. svc. engr. Dresser Industries, Houston, 1970-76; pres. Lone Star Pictures Internat., Inc., Dallas, 1976—. Bd. dirs. TCI Wholesale. Dir. films including Hollywood High Part II, 1981, 6-Pack, 1991, Southwest, 1996, Memo, 1996; prodr. films including Kings of the Hill, 1976, Mr. Mean, 1978. Mem. Am. Film Market Assn. Republican. Methodist. Office: Lone Star Pictures 700 E Route 66 #77 Glendora CA 91740-3510 Office Phone: 214-522-2389. E-mail: lonestarpictures@aol.com.

THORNBURG, RON, newspaper editor; BA in Polit. Sci., Purdue U., 1971. Reporter Jour. and Courier, Lafayette, Ind., 1972-73; mng. editor The Evening Times, Melbourne, Fla., 1973-75; met. editor, asst. news editor, copy editor, bur. chief Today, Melbourne, 1975-78, mng. editor, 1978-80; exec. editor News Press, Fort Myers, Fla., 1980-86; news exec. Comty. Newspapers, Gannet Cot., Inc., Rosslyn, Va., 1986-88; editor Burlington (Vt.) Free Press, 1988-94; mng. editor Standard Examiner, Ogden, Utah, 1994—. Office: Standard Examiner 332 S Ward Ave PO Box 12790 Ogden UT 84412-2790 E-mail: rthornburg@standard.net.

THORNBURGH, DANIEL ESTON, retired university administrator, journalism educator; b. Terre Haute, Ind., Sept. 17, 1930; s. Lester D. and Dorothy (Green) T.; m. Adrianne Ames, Aug. 11, 1956; children: Debra Kay Thornburgh Considine, Stewart Beckett, Malcolm Noble. BS, Ind. State U., 1952; MA, U. Iowa, 1957; EdD, Ind. U., 1980. Reporter Terre Haute Star, 1952; publicity dir. Simpson Coll., Indianola, Iowa, 1955-57; info. dir. Marshall U., Huntington, W.Va., 1957-59, Ea. Ill. U., Charleston, 1959-65, chmn., prof. journalism, 1965-84, dir. univ. rels., 1992; ret. Vis. prof. U. Hawaii, 1982—83, U. Fla., 1993—94, Millikin U., 1996; mem. Gov.'s Coun. Health and Phys. Fitness, 1987—2003; pub. Casey Banner Times, Ill., 1967—69. Editor: (with others) Interpretative Reporting Workbook, 1982. Mem. Charleston City Coun., 1973-77; active Ill. Recreation Coun., Springfield, 1979-85; pres. Coles Hist. Soc., Charleston, 1972-74, 1992, trustee, 2004—; pres., trustee Five Mile House Found., 1998—; trustee Lincoln and Sargent Farm Found., 1999-2004; chmn. higher edn. and campus min. com. Meth. Ch., 2000-02. With U.S. Army, 1952—54. Named Outstanding Advisor, Coun. Coll. Publs. Advisors, 1971. Mem. Charleston C. of C. (Area Man of Yr. award 1971), Assn. Edn. Journalism and Mass Comm., Pub. Rels. Soc. Am., Soc. Profl. Journalists, Coun. Advancement and Support Edn. (Ea. Ill. U. PRSSA chpt.), Assn. Preservation Hist. Coles County (Merit award 2003), Masons (Cmty. Builder award 1997), Elks, Rotary (pres. Charleston 1976-77, dist. gov. 6490 2000-01, dist. hall officer 2004). Methodist. Avocations: tennis, writing. Home: 1405 Buchanan Ave Charleston IL 61920-2924

THORNBURGH, DICK (RICHARD L. THORNBURGH), lawyer, former United Nations official, former United States attorney general, former governor; b. Pitts., July 16, 1932; s. Charles Garland and Alice (Sanborn) T.; m. Virginia Walton Judson, Oct. 12, 1963; children: John, David, Peter, William. B in Engring., Yale, 1954; LLB, U. Pitts., 1957; hon. degrees, from 31 colls. and univs. Bar: Pa. 1958, U.S. Supreme Ct. 1965, D.C. 1998. Atty. Kirkpatrick & Lockhart, Pitts., 1959-69, 77-79, 87-88, 91-92, 94—; U.S. atty. for Western Pa. Pitts., 1969-75; U.S. asst. atty. gen. Dept. Justice, Washington, 1975-77; gov. State of Pa., Harrisburg, 1979-87; dir. Inst. Politics John F. Kennedy Sch. Govt., Harvard U., 1987-88; U.S. atty. gen. Washington, 1988-91; under-sec.-gen. for adminstrn. and mgmt. UN, N.Y.C., 1992-93. Del. Pa. Constl. Conv., 1967-68; vice chair World Com. on Disability; bd. dirs. Elan Corp. plc, Nat. Mus. Indsl. History, Gettysburg Nat. Battlefield Mus. Found. Mem. Coun. Fgn. Rels., Am. Law Inst.; trustee Urban Inst., U. Pitts. Fellow Am. Bar Found.; mem. Am. Judicature Soc. Republican. Office: Kirkpatrick & Lockhart LLP 1800 Massachusetts Ave NW, 2nd Flr Washington DC 20036-1800 Office Phone: 202-778-9080.

THORNBURGH, RICHARD EDWARD, bank executive; b. Cin., July 9, 1952; s. Robert Wesley and Frances (Cowing) Thornburgh; m. Cornelia Parsons, Aug. 6, 1983; children: Ainsley Frances, Katrina Parsons. BBA cum laude, U. Cin., 1974; MBA, Harvard U., Boston, 1976. Assoc. The First Boston Corp., N.Y.C., 1976-81, v.p., 1982-86, mng. dir. L.A., 1987—88; mng. dir., various roles including head global fin. institutions group Credit Suisse First Boston (formerly The First Boston Corp.), 1989—95; exec. bd, CFO Credit Suisse First Boston, 1995—96; CFO Credit Suisse Group, 1997—99; vice chmn. exec. bd Credit Suisse First Boston, 1999—2002, CFO, 2000—02; chief risk officer Credit Suisse Group, 2003—, mem. com. exec. bd., 2004—. Mem., oper. com. Credit Suisse First Boston, 2002—. Bd. dirs. L.A. Chamber Orch., 1989-91, First Congregational Ch. of Darien (Conn.), 1990-91. Mem. Harvard Club of N.Y.C., Racquet and Tennis Club, The Calif. Club, The Links. Avocations: sailing, golf, racquet sports, skiing. Office: Credit Suisse Group 11 Madison Ave New York NY 10010-3629*

THORNBURGH, RON E. secretary of state; b. Burlingame, Kans., Dec. 31, 1962; m. Annette Thornburgh. Student, Washburn U., 1985. Dep. asst. sec. of state, then asst. sec. of state State of Kans., Topeka, 1985-87; asst. sec. of state Sec. of State's Office, Topeka, 1991-95, sec. of state, 1995—. Vice chairperson blue ribbon panel on ethical conduct State of Kans., 1989. Mem. Kids Voting Kans. Exec. Com.; mem. adv. com. United Way. Toll fellow Henry Toll Fellowship Program, 1995. Mem. Washburn U. Alumni Bd., 20/30 Club Internat. Methodist. Office: Sec of State Statehouse 120 SW 10th Ave Fl 2D Topeka KS 66612-1504

THORNBURY, JOHN ROUSSEAU, radiologist, physician; b. Cleve., Mar. 16, 1929; s. Purla Lee and Gertrude (Glidden) T.; m. Julia Lee McGregor, Mar. 20, 1955; children: Lee Allison, John McGregor. AB cum laude, Miami U., Oxford, Ohio, 1950; MD, Ohio State U., 1955. Diplomate: Am. Bd. Radiology. Intern Hurley Hosp., Flint, Mich., 1955-56; resident U. Iowa Hosps., Iowa City, 1958-61; instr., asst. prof. radiology U. Colo. Med. Center, Denver, 1962-63; practice medicine specializing in radiology Denver, 1962-63, Iowa City, 1963-66, Seattle, 1966-68, Ann Arbor, Mich., 1968-79, Albuquerque, 1979-84, Rochester, N.Y., 1984-89, Madison, Wis., 1989-94. Mem. staff U. Wis. Hosp., Madison; prof. radiology, chief sect. body imaging, U. Wis. Med. Sch., 1989-94, prof. emeritus, 1994—; asst. prof. radiology U. Iowa Hosps., 1963-66, U. Wash. Hosp., Seattle, 1966-68; assoc. prof. radiology U. Mich. Med. Ctr., 1968-71, prof., 1971-79, chief uroradiology sect., 1971-79; prof. radiology, chief divsn. diagnostic radiology Sch. Medicine, U. N.Mex., 1979-84; prof. radiology U. Rochester Sch. Medicine, 1984-89, acting chmn., 1985-87; chmn. sci. com. on efficacy studies Nat. Coun. on Radiation Protection, 1980-95; rapporteur/mem. sci. group on indications/limitations of x-ray diagnostic procedures WHO, 1983; cons. com. on efficacy of magnetic resonance nat. health tech. adv. panel Australian Inst. Health, 1986; invited U.S. cons. MRI program, Nijmegen, The Netherlands, 1992; mem. planning group Low Back Pain Collaboratives and Nat. Congress, Inst. for Health Care Improvement, 1997-98; mem. methodologic rsch. issues working group NIH and Pub. Health Svc.-Office of Women's Health, 1998; cons., spkr. Royal Australasian Coll. Radiologists, Melbourne, Australia, 1997; cons. tech. assessment and outcomes rsch., 1994—; cons. in tech. assessment and outcomes rsch. to dept. neuroradiology Loma LInda Med. Ctr., 2002—; cons. to Am. Soc. Neuroradiology, 1995-2000; lectr. in field. Co-author/cons. Clin. Efficacy Assessment Project, Am. Coll. Physicians, 1986-89; assoc. editor: Yearbook of Radiology, 1971-82; mem. editl. bd.: Contemporary Diagnostic Radiology, 1977-84, Urologic Radiology, 1977-84 Bd. dirs. Sally Jobe Found., Denver, 1996—. Capt., M.C. USAF, 1956-58. Recipient Dist. Svc. award Am. Bd. Radiology, 2000, Alumni Achievement award Ohio State U. Coll. Medicine, 2000, Gold medal Assn. Univ. Radiologists, 2002; grantee Agy. Health Care Policy and Rsch., 1986-91, U. Rochester, 1986-89, U. Wis., Madison, 1989-91. Fellow Am. Coll. Radiology (mem. emeritus); mem. Am. Coll. Radiology Imaging Network (outcomes and quality of life subcom., urology com., NIH, 1999-2002), Soc. Uroradiology (pres. 1976-77, dir. 1977-79), Assn. Univ. Radiologists (pres. 1980-81), Radiol. Soc. N.Am., Am. Roentgen Ray Soc. (Caldwell medal 1993), Soc. for Health Svcs. Rsch. in Radiology (adv. com. to bd. dirs. 1998—), Colo. Radiol. Soc., Phi Beta Kappa, Delta Tau Delta, Omicron Delta Kappa, Phi Chi. Republican. Lutheran. Home: 185 Morgan Pl Castle Rock CO 80108 *"Mooring Post" relationships and sharing have been essential to success and achievements in my multidisciplinary research. "Mooring Post" persons range from expert mentors and stellar colleagues, to the bedrock of a loving and supportive family. Further, to me, Rule One in medicine has always been, "The patient comes first.".*

THORNDIKE, EDWARD HARMON, physicist; b. Pasadena, Calif., Aug. 2, 1934; s. Edward Moulton and Louise (Harmon) T.; m. Elizabeth H. Wenger, Sept. 8, 1955; children: Susan Lee, Patricia Lynn, Edward Harmon Jr. AB, Wesleyan U., Middletown, Conn., 1956; MS, Stanford U., 1957; PhD, Harvard U., 1960. Research fellow Harvard U., Cambridge, Mass., 1960-61; mem. faculty U. Rochester, N.Y., 1961—, asso. prof. physics, 1965-72, prof., 1972—. Vis. prof. U. Geneva, 1969-70; vis. scientist CERN, Geneva, 1969-70; mem. adv. coun. Ctr. Environ. Info., Rochester, 1974-93; mem. adv. com. Stanford Linear Accelerator Ctr. Exptl. Program, 1987-89; mem. vis. com. for Fermilab, Univs. Rsch. Assn., 1993-95. Author: Energy and Environment, a Primer for Scientists and Engineers, 1976; contbr. articles to profl. jours. Recipient W.K.H. Panofsky prize, 1999; NSF fellow, 1970, Guggenheim fellow, 1987-88. Fellow Am. Phys. Soc. Office: U Rochester Dept Physics/Astronomy Rochester NY 14627

THORNE, ANN LARAYNE, secondary school educator; b. Salt Lake City, Mar. 13, 1945; d. Ellvert Hiram and Mildred Anna (Harter) Himes; m. Conrad H. Thorne, Dec. 15, 1966 (div. 1986); children: Nathan, Jon Paul, Jason, Janna. BA, Utah State U., 1967; MA, U. Phoenix, 1997. Cert. K-12 secondary tchr. Ariz. Tchr. York Cmty. HS, Elmhurst, Ill., 1967—68, Shadow Mountain HS, Phoenix, 1984—, adviser newspaper journalism, 1994—2002, adviser lit. mag., 1996—99. Author: (novels) Somewhere in My Heart, 1996, Next Time My Love: Echoes of the Heart, 1997. Mem.: Ariz. Interscholastic Press Assn. (bd. dirs. 2001—, rec. sec. 2002—), Journalism Edn. Assn. Mem. Lds Ch. Avocations: writing, poetry, reading. Home: 3016 E Yucca St Phoenix AZ 85028 Office: Shadow Mountain HS 2902 E Shea Blvd Phoenix AZ 85028

THORNE, CARL F. gas industry executive; b. 1940; BS in Petroleum Engring., U. Tex.; JD, Baylor U. Bar: Tex. 1967. Dir. Sedco Inc., Dallas, 1986—, pres., CEO, 1987—, chmn. bd. dirs., 1987—; dir. Crescent Op., Inc., chmn. compensation com.; CEO, dir. Blocker Energy Corp., 1987—; ptnr. BEC Ventures; former pres. Sedco-Forex; pres., CEO ENSCO Internat. Inc., Dallas, 1987—, chmn. bd., 1987—. Mem. Nat. Ocean Industries Assn. (dir.). Office: ENSCO 500 N Akard St Ste 4300 Dallas TX 75201-3331

THORNE, FRANCIS, composer; b. Bay Shore, N.Y., June 23, 1922; s. Francis Burritt and Hildegarde (Kobbé) T.; m. Ann Cobb, Dec. 9, 1942; children: Ann Boughton (Mrs. William F. Niles), Wendy Oakleigh (Mrs. William H. Forsyth, Jr.), Candace Kobbé (Mrs. Anthony M. Canton). BA in Music Theory, Yale U., 1942. Founder, pres. Thorne Music Fund, Inc., 1965-75; pub. Edward B. Marks Music Corp., 1963—, Gen. Music Pub. Co., 1971—, G. Schirmer/AMP, 1985—, Theodore Presser Co., 1989—. Exec. dir. Lenox Arts Center, 1972-76, Am. Composers Alliance, 1975-85; co-founder, pres. Am. Composers Orch., 1976—. Composer: Elegy for Orch., 1964, Burlesque Overture, 1966, Lyric Variations for Orch., 1967, Symphony No. 1, 1963, No. II, 1966, No. III, 1970, No. IV, 1977, Fortuna, 1961-62, Liebesrock, 1969, Sonar Plexus, 1969, Six Set-Pieces, 1969, Contra Band Music, 1970, Antiphonies, 1970, Simultaneities, 1971, Quartessence, 1971, Fanfare, Fugue and Funk, 1972, Lyric Variations II, 1972, Piano Sonata, 1972, Lyric Variations III, 1973, Cantata Sauce, 1973, Evensongs, 1973, Cello Concerto, 1974, Piano Concerto, 1974, Violin Concerto, 1975, String Quartet 1, 1960, 2, 1967, 3, 1976, 4, 1983, Spoon River Overture, 1976, Grand Duo, 1976, Five Set Pieces, 1976, Love's Variations, 1976, Pop Partita, 1978, The Eternal Light for Soprano and Orchestra, 1979, Divertimento for Flute, Strings and Percussion, 1979, Lyric Variations IV for Solo Violin, 1980, Divertimento 2 for Bassoon and Stringed Instruments, 1980, Eine Kleine Meyermusik, 1980, Gems From Spoon River, 1980, Lyric Variations No. 6 for solo clarinet, 1981, Divertimento No. 3, 1982, Praise and Thanksgiving, 1983, Lyric Variations No. 5 for Orch., 1980-81, Symphony No. 5, 1984, Concerto Concertante, 1985, Rhapsodic Variations, No. 2, 1985, Humoresque for Orch., 1985, Rhapsodic Variations No. 3 for Oboe and Strings, 1986, The Affirming Flame for Soprano and Chamber Ensemble, 1987; seven simple syncopations for Piano solo, 1987, Rhapsodic Variations No. 4 For Viol Solo, 1987, Rhapsodic Variations No. 5 for Violins and Piano, 1988, Money Matters for Tenor and Chamber Ensemble, 1988, Piano Concerto No. 3, 1989, Remembering Dizzy for Brass Quintet, 1990, Pop Partita No. 2 for woodwinds and strings, 1991, Mario and The Magician, opera after Thomas Mann, in Prologue and 1 Act, 1991, Symphony No. 6 for Strings, 1992, Symphony No. 7 Along the Hudson for chorus and orch., 1994, Cello Concerto No. 2, 1995, Echo for Soprano and Mixed Chorus, 1996, Clarinet Concerto, 1997, Rhapsodic Variations No. 7 for Solo Piano, 1998, Lyric Variations No. 8, 1999, Flash Dances for Orchestra, 1999, Oboe Concerto, 1999-2000, SONG To Mark Stand's Poem, 2000, Concerto for Orchestra, 2000-2001, The Four Seasons, for mezzo and string trio, 2002; recs. on Composers' Recs., Inc., Serenus, Owl, Louisville Opus One and New World; founder, pres. Am. Composers Orch., 1976. Trustee Am. Symphony Orchestra League, Manhattan Sch. Music, Am. Music Center, MacDowell Colony, Walter W. Naumburg Found., Contemporary Music Soc., Theater Devel. Fund, Group for Contemporary Music., Am. Brass Quintet. Served to lt. USNR, 1942-45. Nat. Endowment Arts grantee, 1966, 73; fellow, 1976, 79; Nat. Inst. Arts and Letters grantee, 1968; N.Y. State Arts Council ballet commn., 1973 Mem. AAAL, BMI, Contemporary Music Soc. (bd. dirs.), Am. Composers Alliance, League Composers. Clubs: Century Assn. (N.Y.C.). Home: 116 E 66th St New York NY 10021-6504 E-mail: aco@americancomposers.org. *Having spent ten years as a businessman, I have been privileged to serve my composer colleagues as an administrator for musical organizations. The practical experience has also served me well as a creative artist in having instilled the virtues of discipline. Serving music as composer and administrator gives the highest sense of satisfaction, from participating in this life-giving world in a total comprehensive way.*

THORNE, JOHN REINECKE, business educator, venture capitalist; b. Pitts., Mar. 25, 1926; s. John Mueller and Louise (Reinecke) T.; m. Barbara Siebert, Aug. 31, 1951 (dec. Feb. 1995); children: John S., Barbara L., Richard W.; m. Helen L. Totzke, Dec. 29, 1999. BS, Brown U., 1947; MSEE, U. Pitts., 1949; MS in Indsl. Adminstrn., Carnegie Mellon U., 1952. Devel. engr. Westinghouse Elec. Corp., Pitts., 1947-50; mgr. fin. analysis Hughes Aircraft Co., L.A., 1952-54; dir. computer systems lab. Litton Industries, L.A., 1954-61; founder, chmn., pres. The Scionics Corp., L.A., 1961—69; cons., L.A., 1969-72; prof. bus. Carnegie-Mellon U., Pitts., 1972—2003, Morganthaler prof. entrepreneurship, 1987—2003, Morganthaler emeritus prof. entrepreneurship, 2003—, dir., Donald H. Jones Ctr. for Entrepreneurship, 1990—2000; founder, chmn. Enterprise Corp. Pitts., 1983-98; gen. ptnr. Pitts. Seed Fund, 1985—2000. Contbr. numerous articles on entrepreneurship to profl. jours. Named Fin. Svcs. Adv. of Yr. by SBA, 1988 Mem.: Rolling Rock Club, Duquesne Club. Unitarian Universalist. Home: 137 Furnace Run Laughlintown PA 15655-0369 Office: Dept of Bus Carnegie-Mellon U Pittsburgh PA 15213 Office Phone: 412-268-2263. Business E-Mail: thorne@andrew.cmu.edu.

THORNE, JOHN WATSON, III, advertising and marketing executive; b. Washington, Jan. 16, 1934; s. John Watson, Jr. and Mary Washington (Tucker) T.; m. Joan Kramer Vail, Mar. 2, 1957; children: Vail Tucker, Tracy Tucker, John Watson, IV. BA in Polit. Sci., George Washington U., 1955; MA in Sociology, New Sch. U., 1974. Asst. account exec. Young & Rubicam, Inc., N.Y.C., 1957-59; advt. mgr. GE, Decatur, Ill., 1959-63; dir. advt. promotion Brand Names Found., N.Y.C., 1963-66; account exec. Tatham-Laird & Kudner (advt.), N.Y.C., 1966-67; v.p., mgmt. supr. Wells, Rich, Greene, Inc., N.Y.C., 1973-76; v.p., account supr. Batten, Barton, Durstine & Osborn, Inc., N.Y.C., 1967-73, sr. v.p., mgmt. supr., 1976-81, exec. v.p., 1981-87, also dir., mem. oper. com.; chmn. Thorne & Assocs., Newtown, Pa., 1987—; pres. Telerx Mktg., Spring House, Pa., 1991-95; chmn. Alliance Mktg. Svcs. Group, Inc., Jamison, Pa., 1995—2004, Alliance Healthcare Info., Inc., Ivyland, Pa., 2004—. Mem. bus. program com. Proprietary Assn., Washington; adj. prof. advt. Syracuse (N.Y.) U. Pres. Hastings-on-Hudson (N.Y.) Bd. Edn.; bd. dirs. Young Concert Artists, N.Y.C.; mem. comm. coms. Nat. Urban League, Carnegie Hall. Served as 1st lt. USMCR, 1955-57. Mem. Buckingham Racquet Club, Lotos Club (N.Y.C.). Republican. Roman Catholic. Home: 100 Stoney Brook Rd Newtown PA 18940-2506 Office: Alliance Healthcare Info Inc One Ivybrook Blvd Ste 100 Ivyland PA 18974

THORNE, KIP STEPHEN, physicist, researcher; b. Logan, Utah, June 1, 1940; s. David Wynne and Alison (Comish) T.; m. Linda Jeanne Peterson, Sept. 12, 1960 (div. 1977); children: Kares Anne, Bret Carter; m. Carolee Joyce Winstein, July 7, 1984. BS in Physics, Calif. Inst. Tech., 1962; A.M. in Physics (Woodrow Wilson fellow, Danforth Found. fellow), Princeton U., 1963, PhD in Physics (Danforth Found. fellow, NSF fellow), 1965, postgrad. (NSF postdoctoral fellow), 1965-66; D.Sc. (hon.), Ill. Coll., 1979; Dr.h.c., Moscow U., 1981; D.Sc. (hon.), Utah State U., 2000, U. Glasgow, 2001; D.H.L. (hon.), Claremont Grad. U., 2002. Research fellow Calif. Inst. Tech., 1966-67, assoc. prof. theoretical physics, 1967-70, prof., 1970—, William R. Kenan, Jr. prof., 1981-91, Feynman prof. theoretical physics, 1991—. Fulbright lectr., France, 1966; vis. assoc. prof. U. Chgo., 1968; vis. prof. Moscow U., 1969, 75, 78, 82, 83, 86, 88, 90, 98; vis. sr. rsch. assoc. Cornell U., 1977, A.D. White prof.-at-large, 1968-92; adj. prof. U. Utah, 1971-98; mem. Internat. Com. on Gen. Relativity and Gravitation, 1971-80, 92-01, Com. on U.S.-USSR Coop. in Physics, 1978-79, Space Sci. Bd., NASA, 1980-83; co-founder, chair steering com. LIGO, 1984-87. Co-author: Gravitation Theory and Gravitational Collapse, 1965, Gravitation, 1973, Black Holes: The Membrane Paradigm, 1986, Black Holes and Time Warps: Einstein's Outrageous Legacy, 1994. Alfred P. Sloan Found. Rsch. fellow, 1966-68; John Simon Guggenheim fellow, 1967; recipient Sci. Writing award in physics and astronomy Am. Inst. Physics, 1969, 94, P.A.M. Dirac Meml. lectureship Cambridge U., 1995, Karl Schwarzschild medal Astron. Soc. Germany, 1996, J. Robert Oppenheimer Meml. lectureship U. Calif., 1999, Charles Darwin Meml. Lectureship Royal Astron. Soc., 2000, Arthur Holly Compton Meml. lectureship Washington U., 2001, Herzberg Meml. Lectureship Can. Assn. Physicists, 2001; Robinson Prize in Cosmology, U. Newcastle, 2002. Fellow Am. Phys. Soc. (Julius Edgar Lilienfeld prize 1996, chair topical group in gravity 1997-98); mem. Am. Philosophical Soc., Nat. Acad. Scis., Am. Acad. Arts and Scis., Am. Astron. Soc., Internat. Astron. Union, AAAS, Russian Acad. Scis., Sigma Xi, Tau Beta Pi. Office: California Inst Tech 130-33 Theoretical Astrophysics 1200 E California Blvd Pasadena CA 91125

THORNE, KRISTAN, newscaster; BJ, La. Tech. Broadcaster, La.; talk-radio show host; reporter ABC Affiliate, Alexandria, La., show anchor; DJ, news anchor KZMS; news dir. KXKZ-Radio, Ruston, La.; reporter WSAV-TV3, Savannah, Ga. Mem. state Bd. AP. Recipient 15 awards, AP. Avocations: scuba diving, skydiving, working out, pet Border Collie. Office: WSAV-TV3 1430 E Victory Dr Savannah GA 31404

THORNE, RICHARD MANSERGH, physicist; b. Birmingham, Eng., July 25, 1942; s. Robert George and Dorothy Lena (Goodchild) T.; children: Peter Baring, Michael Thomas, Thomas Mansergh. BSc, Birmingham U., 1963; PhD, MIT, 1968. Grad. asst. M.I.T., 1963-68; asst. prof. dept. atmospheric scis. UCLA, 1968-71, asso. prof., 1971-75, prof., 1975—, chmn. dept., 1976-79. Vis. fellow St. Edmund's Coll., Cambridge (Eng.) U., 1986-87, 92; cons. NATO Adv. Group for Aerospace R&D, 1973, Jet Propulsion Lab., Aerospace Corp. Contbr. articles to profl. jours. Recipient numerous grants NSF, NASA, NATO, Jet Propulsion Lab.; Fulbright scholar, 1963-70; fellow Royal Norwegian Coun. for Sci. and Indsl. Rsch., 1973, sr. vis. fellow U. Sussex, 1979-80, rsch. fellow Royal Soc. London, 1986-87. Fellow Am. Geophys. Union; mem. Internat. Union Radio Scis. Home: 10390 Caribou Ln Los Angeles CA 90077-2809 Office: UCLA Dept Atmospheric and Oceanic Scis Los Angeles CA 90095-0001 E-mail: rmt@atmos.ucla.edu.

THORNE, WILLIAM ALBERT, retired lawyer; b. Chgo., Feb. 20, 1924; s. William A. and Irma J. Thorne; m. Elizabeth Lee Douglas, June 19, 1948; children: Deborah, Elizabeth Ann, Margaret, Douglas. JD, Valparaiso U., 1949. Bar: Ind. 1949, U.S. Dist. Ct. (no. and so. dists.) Ind. 1949, U.S. Supreme Ct. 1960. Pvt. practice, Elkhart, Ind., 1949-63; ptnr. Thorne Grodnik, LLP, Elkhart, 1963-95; of counsel Thorne.Grodnik, LLP and predecessor, 1995—2002, ret., 2002. Bd. vis. Valparaiso U. Law Sch., 1990-96; chmn. City of Elkhart Parks and Recreation Bd., 1971-75; chmn. Elkhart Bd. Water Works, 1975-83, No. Ind. Conf. United Meth. Ch., Bd. Higher Edn. and Campus Ministry, 1994-2000; bd. trustees Meth. Theol. Sch. Ohio, 1993-2003. Cpl. U.S. Army, 1943-46. Fellow Ind. State Bar Assn. (chmn. bankruptcy sect. 1985-86, bd. govs. 1987-88). Democrat. United Methodist. Avocations: golf, reading. Personal E-mail: thollaw@msn.com.

THORNELL, JACK RANDOLPH, photographer; b. Vicksburg, Miss., Aug. 29, 1939; s. Benjamin O. and Myrtice (Jones) T.; divorced; children— Candice, Jay Randolph. Ed. pub. schs. Photographer Jackson (Miss.) Daily News, 1960-64; with A.P., 1964—. assigned, 1965, 1965, Democratic Nat. Conv., 1968. Served with AUS, 1958-60. Recipient Pulitzer prize for news photography of shooting of James Meredith, 1967; Headliners Photography award, 1967 Home: 6815 Madewood Dr Metairie LA 70003-4529 Office: 3800 Howard Ave New Orleans LA 70125-1429

THORNER, MICHAEL OLIVER, medical educator; b. Beaconsfield, Eng., Jan. 14, 1945; came to U.S., 1977; s. Hans and Ilse T.; m. Prudence Maria Ross, July 7, 1966; children— Benjamin Bruno, Anna Rosa MB, BChir, U. London, 1970. Intern, resident Middlesex Hosp., St. Bartholomew's Hosp., London; lectr. chem. pathology St. Bartholomews Hosp., London, 1974, research fellow, 1974-75, lectr. medicine, 1975-77; assoc. prof. medicine U. Va., Charlottesville, 1977-82, prof. medicine, 1982-90, head div. endocrinology and metabolism, 1986-98, dir. Clin. Research Ctr., 1984-97, assoc. dir. CRC, 1981-84, Kenneth R. Crispell prof. in internal medicine, 1990-98, Henry B. Mulholland prof. internal medicine, 1998—. Chmn. dept. internal medicine U. Va., 1997—. Contbr. articles to profl. jours. Recipient Albion O. Bernstein award, 1984, Virginia Scientist of Yr. award, 1985, Gen. Clin. Rsch. Ctrs. program award, 1995, The Pituitary Soc. Annual award for contbns. to understanding pituitary disease, 1995, Theodore E. Woodward Award 1996. Fellow Royal Coll. Physicians, ACP (John Phillips Meml. award 1999); mem. AAAS, Soc. Endocrinology, Endocrine Soc. (Edwin B. Astwood award 1992), Assn. Am. Physicians, Am. Soc. Clin. Investigations. Home: Mount Ammonett 3140 Plank Rd North Garden VA 22959-2312 Office: U Va Health Sys Dept Internal Medicine PO Box 800466 Charlottesville VA 22908-0466 Fax: 804-979-4967. E-mail: mot@virginia.edu.

THORNHILL, ARTHUR H., JR., retired book publisher; b. Boston, Jan. 1, 1924; s. Arthur Horace and Mary Josephine (Peterson) T.; m. Dorothy M. Matheis, Oct. 28, 1944; children: Sandra Susanne Thornhill Brushart, Arthur Horace. AB magna cum laude, Princeton U., 1948. With Little, Brown & Co., Inc., Boston, 1948-88, v.p., 1955-58, gen. mgr., 1960-87, chief exec. officer, pres., 1962-87, chmn. bd., 1970-87; chmn., pres., dir. Little, Brown & Co. (Can.), Ltd., 1955-84; v.p. Time, Inc., 1968-87; vice chmn. Time-Life Books, Inc., 1976-86. Mem. adv. council history dept. Princeton U., 1964-85; trustee, treas. Princeton U. Press, 1972-85; chmn. N.Y. Graphic Soc., 1974-79. Trustee Bennington Coll., 1969-76; fellow emeritus Ctr. for Creative Photography U. Ariz.; bd. dirs. Am. Book Pubs. Council, 1964-67. Served to 1st lt. USAAF, World War II. Decorated Air medal; recipient Princeton U. Press medal, 1985, Disting. Alumni award Dwight-Englewood Sch., 1998. Mem. Assn. Am. Pubs. (bd. dirs. 1978-81), Edgartown Yacht Club, Edgartown Reading Room (pres. 1990-92), Union Club (N.Y.C.), Princeton Club (N.Y.C.), Century Club (N.Y.C.), Publs. Lunch Club (N.Y.C.), Union Club (Boston), St. Botolph (Boston). Home: Apt 5303 250 Pantops Mountain Rd Charlottesville VA 22911-8703

THORNHILL, JOSHUA TAYLOR, IV, psychiatrist, academic administrator; b. Lynchburg, Va., Oct. 25, 1963; s. Joshua Taylor Thornhill, III and Jean Long Thornhill. BA, U. Va., 1985; MD, Ea. Va. Med. Sch., Norfolk, 1989. Diplomate Am. Bd. Psychiatry and Neurology. Dir., med. student edn. in psychiatry U. S.C. Sch. of Medicine, Columbia, SC, 1998—, asst. dean for clin. curriculum, 2000—. Oral bd. examiner Am. Bd. of Psychiatry and Neurology, Deerfield, Ill., 1999—. Contbr. articles to profl. jours. Recipient Humanism in Medicine award, Gold Found., 2002. Fellow: Am. Psychiat. Assn. (disting. fellow); mem.: S.C. Psychiat. Assn. (pres. 2001—02), Alpha Omega Alpha. Independent. Methodist. Office: U SC Sch Medicine 3555 Harden St Ext Ste 104-A Columbia SC 29203 Office Phone: 803-733-3367. Business E-Mail: jtt35@gw.med.sc.edu. E-mail: jthornh@medpark.sc.edu.

THORNLEY, EVAN, internet company executive; degree in Commerce, JD, U. Melbourne. Cons. McKinsey & Co.; co-founder LookSmart, San Francisco, 1995—. Office: LookSmart Ltd Headquarters 625 Second St San Francisco CA 94107

THORNLOW, CAROLYN, law firm administrator, consultant; b. Kew Gardens, N.Y., May 25, 1954; 1 child, Johanna Louise Ramm. BBA magna cum laude, Baruch Coll., 1982. Gen. mgr. Richard A. Ramm Assocs., Levittown, N.Y., 1972-78; adminstr. Tunstead Schechter & Torre, N.Y.C., 1978-82, Cowan Liebowitz & Latman, P.C., N.Y.C., 1982-84, Rosenberg & Estis, P.C., N.Y.C., 1984-85; contr. Finkelstein, Borah, Schwartz, Altschuler & Goldstein, P.C., N.Y.C., 1986-92; pres. Concinnity Svcs., Hastings, N.Y., 1984—. Instr. introduction to law office mgmt. seminars Assn. Legal Adminstrs., N.Y.C., 1984. Editor: The ABA Guide to Professional Managers in the Law Office, 1996; contbr. numerous articles to profl. jours. Mem. ABA (bd. dirs. law practice mgmt. div. 2000-01), N.Y. Assn. Legal Adminstrs. (v.p. 1982-83), Internat. Assn. Legal Adminstrs. (asst. regional v.p. 1983-84, regional v.p. 1984-85), Nat. Soc. Tax Profls. (cert. tax profl.), Am. Mgmt. Assn., Inst. Cert. Profl. Mgrs. (cert.), ABA, Inst. Cert. Mgmt. Accts., Mensa, Beta Gamma Sigma, Sigma Iota Epsilon. Home and Office: Concinnity Svcs 109 Washington Ave Hastings On Hudson NY 10706 Office Phone: 914-478-9000. Business E-Mail: cthornlow@concinnityservices.com., lawbucks@aol.com., crtinny@aol.com.

THORNSBERRY, WILLIS LEE, JR., chemist; b. Sturgis, Ky., Aug. 10, 1940; s. Willis Lee and Jane (Hall) T.; m. Mary Elizabeth Gaswint, June 19, 1965; children: Brian, Michele. BS, Murray State U., 1963; MS, U. Ark., 1967; PhD, Tulane U., 1974. Rsch. chemist Freeport-McMoran Inc., Belle Chasse, La., 1967-74, sr. rsch. chemist, 1974-92; pres. Tech. Devel. Svcs. Inc., Sturgis, Ky., 1995—. Contbr. articles to profl. jours. Coach, leader for youth groups Jefferson Parish Playgrounds, Gretna, La., 1970-84, Boy Scouts Am., Gretna, 1975-82. 1st lt. U.S. Army, 1963-65. Mem. Am. Chem. Soc. (sect. chmn. 1982), Sigma Xi. Democrat. Achievements include numerous patents for process for uranium recovery from phosphoric acid, recovery of silica from hydrofluorosilicic acid, stabilization of gypsum for construction purposes, preparation and use of fertilizer additives. Office: 1024 N Main St Sturgis KY 42459-1245 Office Phone: 270-333-2243. Personal E-mail: mwthorns@bellsouth.net.

THORNSBURY, MICHAEL, judge; b. Williamson, W.Va., July 6, 1956; s. John and Maggie Z. (Thocker) T.; m. Dreama K. Keith, June 25, 1977; children: Melissa, Matthew, Elizabeth Ann. BA, Pikeville (Ky.) Coll., 1977; JD summa cum laude, U. Ky., 1980. Bar: Ky. 1980, W.Va. 1980, U.S. Dist. Ct. (so. dist.) W.Va. 1980, U.S. Dist. Ct. (ea. dist.) Ky. 1980, U.S. Appeals 1988. Chief legal aid dept. Fed. Correctional Instn., Lexington, Ky., 1978-80; pvt. practice Williamson, 1980-96; city atty. Town of Gilbert, W.Va., 1985-90; cir. judge Mingo 30th Jud. Cir., Williamson, 1997-98. Re-elected to eight-yr. term, 2000; asst. pros. atty. County of Mingo, Williamson, 1981-85; special justice W.Va. Supreme Ct. Appeals; bd. trustees Pikeville Coll, 2000—. Mem. Mingo County Dep. Sheriff's Civil Svc. Commn., 1983-85. Recipient Amb. award Belfry H.S., 2000, Delbarton 2000 Cmty. Svc. award; Presdl. scholar Pikeville Coll., 1974. Mem. Assn. Trial Lawyer Am., Ky. Bar Assn., W.Va. Bar Assn., W.Va. Trial Lawyers Assn., W.Va. Jud. Assn., Ky. Trial Lawyers Assn., Mingo County Trial Lawyers Assn. (pres. Williamson chpt. 1986-88), Pike Coll. Alumni Assn. (bd. dirs.), Moose, Tug Valley Shriners (pres. 1999-2000), Kiwanis (bd. dirs. 1997—, pres. 2000-01), O'Brien Lodge 101, Scottish Rite, Temple Aide Beni Kedem Temple. Democrat. Methodist. Home: 1717 W 4th Ave Williamson WV 25661-3014 Office: Mingo Cir Judge PO Box 1198 75 E 2d Ave Williamson WV 25661

THORNTON, ANDREW JOHN, minister; b. Ukiah, Calif., Oct. 20, 1977; s. Gary Evan and Sandra Sue Thornton; m. Sarah Rebecca Ensor. BS in Christian Ministries, Southwestern Bapt. U., Bolivar, Mo., 1996—2000; MA in Bibl. Theology, MA in Christian Counseling, Luther Rice Theol. Sem., Atlanta, 2000—02. Summer missionary Mo. Bapt. Conv., Jefferson City, Mo., 1994—96; asst. min. students Golden Ave. Bapt. Ch., Springfield, Mo., 1996—98, assoc. pastor, 1999—2003; min. students First Bapt. Ch. of Ozark, Ozark, Mo., 2003—. Conservative. Baptist. Avocations: basketball officiating, reading, public speaking. Home: 104 E Lark Ozark MO 65721 Office: First Baptist Ch of Ozark 1400 W Jackson Ozark MO 65721 E-mail: athornton@fbcozark.org.

THORNTON, ANTHONY L, aerospace engineer; b. Fairfield, Calif., Mar. 19, 1956; s. Alfred Edward and Shirley Jean (Holbert) T. BS Aerospace Engring. Scis., U. Colo., 1978; MS Engring., Stanford U., 1980; PhD Aeronautics and Astronautics, Purdue U., 1992. Sr. mem. tech. staff Sandia Nat. Labs., Albuquerque, 1980-93, mgr., Univ. Outreach, 1993-94, dir., Diversity Leadership and Edn. Outreach, 1994-97; sr. rsch. and devel. engr. Lockheed Martin Skunk Works, Palmdale, CA, 1997—. Contbr. articles to profl. technical publs. Steering com. mem. NSF funded Utah, Colo., Ariz., N. Mex. Rural Systemic Initiative, 1994-97; charter mem. and adv. Norwest Bank Leadership Coun., 1995-96. Lt. USN-Reserve, Albuquerque, NM, 1983-86. Recipient Boeing Aircraft scholarship, 1974, 75, 76, Sandia award for excellence Sandia Nat. Labs., 1992, Disting. Engring. Achievement award Engring. Indsl. Coun., Inc., 2000; named Black Engr. of Yr. in Profl. Achievement U.S. Black Engr. & Info. Tech. mag., 2001; grantee SACHS Found., 1974-78, 1984-88; fellow Com. on Institutional Coop., Purdue U., 1984-89. Sr. mem. Am. Inst. Aeronautics and Astronautics. Independent. Baptist. Avocations: chess, track and field, investments. Office: PO Box 748 Fort Worth TX 76101 Fax: (661) 572-7157. E-mail: Anthony.Thornton@lmco.com., lcesaint@aol.com.

THORNTON, ARLAND, sociologist, educator; b. Boise, Idaho, July 18, 1944; s. Lavar and Alzina Thornton; m. Shirley Dray; children: Richard, Blake, Rebecca, Amy. PhD, U. Mich., 1975. Sr. rsch. scientist Survey Rsch. Ctr., U. Mich., Ann Arbor, 1975—; prof. sociology U. Mich., Ann Arbor, 1977—; sr. rsch. scientist Population Studies Ctr., U. Mich., Ann Arbor, 1983—. Mem. population rsch. subcommittee Nat. Inst. Child Health and Human Develop., Bethesda, 1996—2000; mem. Family and Child Well-Being Rsch. Network, Nat. Inst. Child Health and Hum Devel., Bethesda, 1993—99. Author: (book) Social Change and the Family in Taiwan, 1994 (Otis Dudley Duncan Book award and Goode Disting. Book award, 1995); editor: Ties That Bind, 2000, The Well Being of Children and Families: Research and Data Needs, 2001; contbr. articles to profl. jours. and chpts. to books. Lt. (j.g.) U.S. C.G., 1968—71. Recipient MERIT award, National Inst. Child Health and Human Devel., 2001. Mem.: Nat. Coun. on Family Rels., Am. Sociol. Assn. (various offices in population, family, and children sects., Disting. Career award family sect. 2000), Population Assn. Am. (pres. 2001). Avocations: bicycling, hiking, travel, sports. Office: U Mich Inst for Social Rsch Ann Arbor MI 48106

THORNTON, BILLY BOB, actor, film producer; b. Hot Springs, Ark., Aug. 4, 1955; m. Angelina Jolie, 2000 (div. 2003). Actor: (films) U-Turn, 1997, A Thousand Miles, 1997, The Apostle, 1997, Pushing Tin, 1999, A Gun, A Car, A Blonde, 1997, Primary Colors, 1998, Homegrown, 1998, Armageddon, 1998, A Simple Plan, 1998, Monster's Ball, 2001, Bandits, 2001, Waking up in Reno, 2002, Intolerable Cruelty, 2003, Love Actually, 2003, Levity, 2003, Bad Santa, 2003, The Alamo, 2004; writer (screenplays) For the Boys, 1991, Indecent Proposal, 1993, Tombstone, 1993, Trouble Bound, 1993, Floundering, 1994, On Deadly Ground, 1994, Some Folks Call It a Slingblade, 1994, Don't Look Back, 1996, A Family Thing, 1996, The Gift, 2000, guest appearance (TV episode) Ellen, 1997, (series) Hearts A Fire, 1992, dir., actor, writer Sling Blade, 1996 (Acad. award Best Adapted Screenplay), screenwriter, dir. Daddy and Them, 2001, dir., prodr. All the Pretty Horses, 2000. Office: Rogers & Cowan 1888 Century Park East Ste 500 Los Angeles CA 90067

THORNTON, CHARLES VICTOR, metals executive; b. Salt Lake City, Feb. 8, 1915; s. Charles Victor and Winnie May (Fitts) T.; m. Margaret Louise Wiggins, Apr. 17, 1937; children: Charles Victor III, Carolyn Louise (Mrs. John J. Moorhouse), David Frank. BS in Civil Engring., U. Utah, 1935; HHD, Ind. Inst. Tech., 1972. Registered profl. engr., Ohio, Tex. Engr. Truscon Steel Co., Youngstown, Ohio, 1935-37, dist. engr. Washington, 1937-40; chief engr. So. Iron Works, Inc., Alexandria, Va., 1940-45; pres. Thornton Industries, Inc., Ft. Worth, 1945-75, chmn. bd., 1975-88. Bd. dirs. Bank Commerce and Comml. Fin. Corp.; chmn. bd. dirs. Southview Corp. Author: American Association of Private Railroad Car Owners Roster of Private R.R. Cars, 1991, Autobiography, 1993, Charlie, 1994, Winnie, 1994. Chmn. bd. Southview Corp., 1980—, chmn. emeritus Shriners Hosps. for Children; mem. nat. adv. coun. U. Utah, 1985-96; chmn. investment com. Longhorn coun. Boy Scouts Am., 1985-88; v.p. campaign chmn. Ft. Worth Arts United, 1989; v.p. Tarrant County Arts Coun., 1989; pres. Tarrant County Water Bd., 1984-88; mem. policy com. Dallas-Ft. Worth Railtran, 1991-98; pres. Ft. Worth chpt. Internat. Good Neighbor Coun., 1991-92; bd. dirs. Ft. Worth Opera, 1997—; mem. World Affairs Coun. Ft. Worth, 1996, bd. dirs., 1997—, treas., 1998. Recipient Salesman of Yr. award Ft. Worth Sales and Mktg. Execs., 1984, Good Neighbor of Yr. award Internat. Good Neighbor Coun., 1984, Merit of Honor award U. Utah, 1986; holder airplane speed record Dallas to Wichita, Kans., 1969. Mem. ASCE (life) (Tex. sect. Svc. to People award 1995), Tex. Assn. Bus. (life), Ft. Worth C. of C. (pres. 1960), Am. Assn. Pvt. R.R. Car Owners (pres. 1982-83), Petroleum Club, Fort Worth Club, City Club, Exch. Club of Fort Worth (past pres.), La Cima Club, Oxford Club, Grand Coun. (Fort Worth chpt. Confrerie Saint Etienne), Masons (33 degree s.r.), Shriners (past imperial potentate), Kiwanis (past pres.), Elks, Petroleum Club, Tau Beta Pi. Office: PO Box 136397 Fort Worth TX 76136-0397 Home Fax: 817-237-0100.

THORNTON, CHARLES VICTOR, lawyer; b. Takoma Park, Md., July 18, 1942; s. Charles Victor and Margaret Louise (Wiggins) T.; m. Suzanne Thorne, May 16, 1970; children: Christopher, Matthew, Joshua, Jeremy. AB, Cornell U., 1964; JD, U. Mich., 1967. Bar: Calif. 1969, U.S. Dist. Ct. (ctrl. dist.) Calif. 1969. Instr. U. Pa. Law Sch., Phila., 1967-68; assoc. Paul, Hastings, Janofsky & Walker, L.A., 1968-74, ptnr., 1975—, mng. ptnr. L.A. office, 1992-96, mng. ptnr. San Francisco office, 1997-2000. Contbr. articles to publs. Pres. Info. and Referral Fedn. L.A. County, 1988-95; mem. exec. com. L.A. County United Way, 1988-92. Named Bd. Vol. of Yr. United Way, 1986. Mem. Calif. Club, L.A. Country Club, San Francisco YMCA (bd. dirs. 1998—, vice-chair 2003-). Avocations: running, golf. Office: Paul Hastings Janofsky & Walker 24th Flr 55 Second San Francisco CA 94105 Office Phone: 415-856-7001. E-mail: charlesthornton@paulhastings.com.

THORNTON, CLARENCE GOULD, electronics engineering executive; b. Detroit, Aug. 3, 1925; s. Lorenzo C. and Violet (Gould) T.; m. Gloria Fuchs, June 18, 1949; children: Susan Carol, Richard Scott. *Daughter Susan Carol, BA 1973, MS 1975 Penn State, PhD Molecular Biology 1983 U. Penn. Susan is employed by MDS Pharmaceutical Inc. 1992-2004, became President of Global Clinical Research and Central Laboratories employing 1300 Professionals in 20 countries on six continents. Her management resulted in top three international ranking and 25%+ per annum sales growth. Son Richard Scott, BS 1976 U. Vt., MD OBGYN 1979 U. Penn. Past Chairman OBGYN Holy Redeemer Hospital, Huntingdon Valley, Pa. Maintains Comprehensive Gynecology practice on active Medical Staff. Assistant Professor, Temple University Medical School. Served on Gloria Dei Church Council. Developed Adult Education/Christian Life program, and ministry for inner-city At-Risk Youths.* BS, U. Mich., 1949, MS, 1950, PhD, 1952. Project engr. Sylvania Electric Co., Woburn, Mass., 1951-52; sect. head to dir. Semiconductor div. Philco Corp., Lansdale, Pa., 1952-60; dir. R&D Philco Corp., Blue Bell, Pa., 1960-72; dir. Electronics Technology and Devices Lab., U.S. Army, Fort Monmouth, N.J., 1972-92; directorate exec. Army Rsch. Lab., 1992-95. Mem. Commn. on Engring. and Tech. Sys. Bd. on Army Sci. and Tech., Nat. Rsch. Coun., 1995—; sci., tech., bus. cons. 1995—; vol. lab. dir. emeritus, 2003-. *Over 50 years of progressive electronics R&D activity. Clarence Thornton's early contributions included invention and development of solid-state electronic devices, new types of transistors and integrated circuits, forerunners to today's electronic systems. Subsequently he directed the Army Electronics Technology and Devices Laboratory and co-directed Tri-Service/US Industry R&D in microelectronics, microwave devices, signal processing/computer chips, and power sources totaling over $1 billion. These enabling technologies are critical to ongoing development of components for secure communications, high-resolution radar, smart missiles, electronic warfare, and information systems for the modern Military. He remains professionally active as National Research Council Reviewer and Army Laboratory Consultant.* Contbr. articles to profl. jours.; patentee in field of electronics. Mem. Colts Neck Bd. Health, 1974-79. Served with USN, 1944-46. Recipient Local Svc. award Boy Scouts Am., 1963, Sci. Conf. award Dept. Army, 1976, Rsch. and Devel. Achievement award, 1976, Lab. of Yr. award, 1980, 83, 88, Lab. Excellence award, 1981, 85, 86, Sr. Exec. award, 1980-93, Gold medal Armed Forces Comms. and Electronics Assn., 1983, Handicapped Adv. Coun. award of achievement, 1985, Exceptional Civilian Svc. medal Dept. Army, 1985, Presdl. Rank award of Meritorious Svc., 1986, Presdl. Rank award of Disting. Sr. Exec., 1987, Crozier award, 1990, Superior Civilian Svc. medal, 1995, Exceptional Civilian Svc. medal, 1995. Fellow IEEE (Centennial medal 1994, Third Millennium medal 2000, Engring. Leadership Recognition award 1994, Joint Logistics Comdrs. award 1994); mem. AAAS, Nat. Def. Indsl. Assn., Assn. U.S. Army, Armed Forces Electronics Assn., Sr. Execs. Assn. (Exec. Achievement award 1994), Am. Defense Preparedness Assn., Alpha Chi Sigma, Phi Kappa Phi, Phi Lambda Upsilon. Mem. Reformed Ch. Home: 28 Glenwood Rd Colts Neck NJ 07722-1015 Office: AMSRL-EP Fort Monmouth NJ 07703

THORNTON, D. WHITNEY, II, lawyer; b. Miami, Fla., Oct. 17, 1946; s. Dade Whitney and Hilda (Bryan) T.; m. Jane Collis, Nov. 27, 1971; children: Bryan Whitney, Elizabeth Jane, Virginia Anne. BA, Washington and Lee U., 1968, JD cum laude, 1970. Bar: Va. 1970, D.C. 1976, U.S. Ct. Appeals (4th cir.) 1978, U.S. Supreme Ct. 1980, Calif. 1987, U.S. Ct. Appeals (9th cir.) 1987. Atty. Naval Air Sys. Command, Dept. Navy, Washington, 1970-73; asst. counsel to comptr. Dept. Navy, 1973-74, asst. to gen. counsel, 1974-76; assoc. Sullivan & Beauregard, Washington, 1976-77, ptnr., 1977-81, Bowman, Conner, Touhey & Thornton, Washington, 1981-83; pres. Continental Maritime Industries, Inc., San Francisco, 1983-87; ptnr. Dempsey, Bastianelli, Brown & Touhey, San Francisco, 1987-91, Seyfarth Shaw, San Francisco, 1992—2003; assoc. gen. counsel Lockheed Martin Space Systems Co., Sunnyvale, Calif., 2003—. Contbr. articles to profl. jours. Mem. ABA (pub. contract law sect., chmn. suspension and debarment com. 1977), FBA (vice chmn. govt. contracts coun., Disting. Svc. award 1981), Washington Golf and Country Club (Arlington, Va.). Republican. Methodist. Office: Lockheed Martin Space Systems Co ORGAN 26-01 Bldg 157 1111 Lockheed Martin Way Sunnyvale CA 94089-3504 E-mail: whit.thornton@lmco.com.

THORNTON, EDMUND B. philanthropist; b. Chgo., Mar. 9, 1930; s. George A. and Suzanne W. Thornton; children from previous marriage: Thomas, Jonathan, Susan, Amanda; m. Susan Feldhaus; 1 child, Taylor. BA, Yale U., 1954. With No. Trust Co., Chgo., 1957-59; asst. sec., asst. treas. Ottawa (Ill.) Silica Co., 1959-61, v.p. corp. devel., 1961-62, pres., CEO, 1962-75, chmn. bd., CEO, 1975-83, chmn. bd., 1983-86; dir., v.p. Ottawa Nat. Bank. Author various articles on historic preservation, history and military subjects. Del. Rep. Nat. Conv., 1964-88, precinct committeeman, 1978-92; chmn. LaSalle County Rep. Ctrl. Com., 1980-92, Ill. and Mich. Canal Nat. Heritage Commn., 1985-2004; pres. Ottawa Silica Co. Found., Edmund B. Thornton Found., Ottawa, 1986— 1st lt. USMC, 1954—56. Recipient Conservation Svc. award U.S. Dept. Interior, 1973. Mem. Nat. Assn. Mfrs., U.S. C. of C., Nat. Indsl. Sand Assn. (dir. 1968-73), Ill. Mfrs.' Assn. (dir. 1969-75, chmn. 1975), Ill. State C. of C. (dir. 1972-78), Explorers Club, Univ. Club (Chgo.), Elks. Republican. Congregationalist. Home: PO Box 1 Ottawa IL 61350-0001 Office: PO Box 949 Ottawa IL 61350-0949

THORNTON, FELICIA, food service executive, corporate financial executive; BSc Econs., Santa Clara U.; MBA Corp. Fin., Mktg., U. So. Calif. V.p., corp. planning and acctg. Ralphs Grocery Co., v.p., admin., 1998, group v.p., fin. and adminstrn., 1999—2001; group v.p. retail ops. Kroger Co., 2000—01; exec. v.p., CFO Albertson's, Inc., 2001—. Various exec. positions in fin. and adminstrn., retail ops. and corp. planning. Office: Albertson's Inc 250 Park Ctr Blvd Boise ID 83726

THORNTON, GEORGE WHITELEY, investment company executive; b. York, Pa., Aug. 11, 1936; s. Henry Moser and Virginia (Whiteley) T.; m. Dianne Fay George, Sept. 9, 1961; children: Sandra Whiteley, William Foster. BA, U. Va., 1958. Asst. to pres. mfg. Dentsply Internat., York, Pa., 1963-69, v.p. mfg., 1969-79, sr. v.p., 1979-85; pres., bd. dirs. Thornton Group Ltd., 1985—; chmn., chief exec. officer Thornton-White Inc., Charleston, S.C., 1986-92. Bd. dirs. Dentsply Internat., York, Commonwealth Nat. Bank (York region). Bd. dirs. United Way, York County, 1974-76; exec. com. Nat. Alliance Businessman, York, 1972-73, chmn., York metro, 1974-75; bd. dirs. Pennsylvanians for Right to Work, 1979-81; bd. trustees Right to Work Def. and Edn. Found., 1979-81. Recipient Dirksen Meml. award Pennsylvanians for Right to Work, 1979, Employer of Yr. award. Mem.: The Club at Pelican Bay (Fla.), Country Club of York (Pa.), Delta Phi. Republican. Presbyterian. Home: 1040 Box Hill Ln York PA 17403-4436

THORNTON, H MONTE, textiles executive; Pres. Hollytex Inc., 1984—90, Mohawk Industries (previously Karastan Bigelow), 1990—2000; pre. fashion and performance divsn. Mohawk Industries, 2000—01, pres., carpet group, 2001—. Office: Mohawk Industries P O Box 12069 Calhoun GA 30703-7002

THORNTON, J. DUKE, lawyer; b. Murray, Ky., July 11, 1944; s. Arthur Lee and Ruth Maxine (Billings) T.; m. Carol Caceres, Dec. 26, 1966 (dec.); children: Jennifer, Carey. BBA, U. N.Mex., Albuquerque, 1966, JD, 1969. Bar: N.Mex. 1969, U.S. Ct. Appeals (10th cir.) 1969, N.Y. 1985, U.S. Supreme Ct. 1992. With Butt, Thornton & Baehr, P.C., Albuquerque, 1971—, now chmn. bd. Legal counsel N.Mex. Jaycees, 1972; clk. N.Mex. Supreme Ct., Santa Fe, 1969; mem. com. N.Mex. Uniform Jury Instructions, 1987-88. Author: Trial Handbook for New Mexico Lawyers, 1992. Bd. dirs. N.Mex. Bd. of Dentistry, Santa Fe, 1987-88; commr. N.Mex. Racing Commn., Albuquerque, 1988-95. Mem. ABA, Assn. Coll. and Univ. Counsel, Internat. Assn. Ins. Counsel, Am. Bd. Trial Advs., Albuquerque Bar Assn. (bd. dirs. 1978-79), Nat. Collegiate Athletic Assn. (agt.). Avocation: pilot. Office: Butt Thornton & Baehr PC PO Box 3170 Albuquerque NM 87190-3170

THORNTON, J. PAT, lawyer; b. Omaha, Nov. 23, 1931; s. James Earl and Edna (Bridges) T.; m. Mary Lou Emery, Oct. 18, 1969; children: Earl Timothy, Bryan Patrick. BS in Fin., Creighton U., 1954, JD, 1959. Bar: Nebr. 1959. Law clk. Ct. Appeals, Omaha, 1961-63; assoc. Haney, Walsh & Wall, Omaha, 1963-64; pvt. practice Omaha, 1964—. Lt. U.S. Infantry, 1954-56. Mem. Nebr. Bar Assn., Nebr. Trial Lawyers Assn., Jay Busters. Republican. Roman Catholic. Avocations: coaching basketball, golf, hiking, travel. E-mail: jamesp5@aol.com.

THORNTON, J. RONALD, technology consultant; b. Fayetteville, Tenn., Aug. 19, 1939; s. James Alanda and Thelma White (McGee) T.; m. Mary Beth Packard, June 14, 1964 (div. Apr. 1975); 1 child, Nancy Carole; m. Martha Klemann, Jan. 23, 1976 (div. Apr. 1982); 1 child, Trey; m. Bernice McKinney, Feb. 14, 1986; 1 child, Paul Leon. BS in Physics and Math., Berry Coll., 1961; MA in Physics, Wake Forest Coll., 1964; postgrad., U. Ala., 1965-66, Rollins Coll., 1970. Rsch. physicist Brown Engring. Co., Huntsville, Ala., 1963-66; sr. staff engr. Martin Marietta Corp., Orlando, Fla., 1966-75; dep. dir. NASA, Washington, 1976-77; exec. asst. Congressman Louis Frey, Jr., Orlando, 1978; pres. Tens Tec, Inc., Orlando, 1978-79; dir. So. Tech. Applications Ctr. U. Fla., Gainesville, Fla., 1979—2002. Bd. dirs., treas. North Fla. Tech. Innovation Ctr., 1994—; mem. light wave tech. com. Fla. High Tech. and Indsl. Coun., Tallahassee, 1986—93, NASA Tech. Transfer Exec. Com., Washington, 1987—, Javits Fellowship Bd., Washington, 1986—91, Gov.'s New Porduct Award Com., Tallahassee, 1988—94, Fla. K-12 Math., Sci. and Computer Sci. Edn. Quality Improvement Adv. Coun., 1989—94, Fla. Sci. Edn. Improvement Adv.Com., 1991—92; bd. dirs. North Fla. Enterprise Corp., 2001—. Pres. Orange County Young Rep. Club, Orlando, 1970-71; treas. Fla. Fedn. Young Reps., Orlando, 1971-72; chmn. Fla. Fedn. Young Reps., Orlando, 1972-74; pres. Gainesville Area Innovation Network, 1988-89. Named Engr. Exhibiting Tech. Excellence and Accomplishment cen. Fla. chpt. Fla. Engring. Soc., 1975, Achievement award NASA, 1977. Mem. IEEE, Soc. Mfg. Engrs., Tech.

Transfer Soc. (pres. 1999, bd. dirs. 1996—2001, Thomas Jefferson award 1999), Nat. Assn. Mgmt. and Tech. Assistance Ctrs. (bd. dirs. 1988, pres. 1992). Republican. Avocations: music, travel, reading, golf. Home and Office: 17829 NW 20th Ave Newberry FL 32669-2143 Office Phone: 352-472-6026. Personal E mail: ronthornton@cox.net.

THORNTON, JERRY SUE, community college president; BA, MA, Murray (Ky.) State U.; PhD, U. Tex.; DHL, Coll. St. Catherine, St. Paul. Tchr. jr. high sch., Earlington, Ky., Murray H.S., Triton Coll., RiverGrove, Ill., dean arts ans scis.; pres. Lakewood C.C., White Bear Lake, Minn., 1985-92, Cuyahoga C.C., Cleve., 1992—. Bd. dirs. Nat. City Bank, Applied Indsl. Techs. Author books, book chpts. and articles. Bd. dirs. Greater Cleve. Growth Assn., Greater Cleve. Roundtable, Urban League of Greater Cleve., United Way Svcs., Rock and Roll Hall of Fame and Mus., Cleve. Found. Mem. Alpha Kappa Alpha. Office: Cuyahoga CC Office of Pres 700 Carnegie Ave Cleveland OH 44115-2833

THORNTON, JOE, professional hockey player; b. London, Can., July 2, 1979; Player Boston Bruins, 1997—. Mem. Team Can., World Cup of Hockey, 2004. Named to Second All-Star Team, NHL, 2003, All-Star Game, 2002, 2003, 2004. Achievements include mem. World Cup Champion Team Can., 2004. Office: 1 Fleetcenter Ste 250 Boston MA 02114*

THORNTON, JOHN WILLIAM, SR., lawyer; b. Toledo, July 3, 1928; s. Cletus Bernard and Mary Victoria (Carey) T.; m. Mary Feeley, Mar. 10, 1951; children: John W. Jr., Jane Thornton Mastrucci, Deborah Thornton Hasty, Michael; m. Gabriela Marin, 1994. AB magna cum laude, U. Notre Dame, 1950, LLB summa cum laude, 1956, JD, 1969; postgrad., U. Miami, Coral Gables, Fla. Bar: Fla. 1956, U.S. Dist. Ct. (no., mid. and so. dists.) Fla. 1956, U.S. Ct. Appeals (5th cir.) 1956, U.S. Ct. Appeals (11th cir.) 1982; cert. civil mediator Fla. Supreme Ct., arbitrator Fla. Supreme Ct.; cert. arbitrator AIDA-ARIAS U.S. and Reins. Assn. of Am. Assoc. area def. firm, Miami, Fla.; ptnr. Dixon, DeJarnette, et al, 1956-67, Stephens, Demos, Magill & Thornton, Miami, 1968-76; pvt. practice Thornton & Mastrucci, P.A. and predecessor firm, Miami, 1976—. Chairperson legis. com. Fla. Med. Malpractice Claims Coun., Inc., 1984—, legis. and adminstrv. code rep. on hosp. risk mgrs. qualifications, rules and liability and nursing home rules and liability, 1986—; lectr. Fla. tort ins. law hosp. and physician series on risk mgmt. Am. Inst. Med. Law, U. Miami Sch. Trial Techniques; lectr. South Fla. Hosp. Risk Mgmt. Soc.; legis. atty. Fla. Sch. Bd. Assn.; presenter legal, healthcare and ins. industry confs.; civil, state and fe. trial lawyer, 1956—; mem. ins. adv. bd., City of Coral Galbes, Fla., 2000—; lectr. in field. Contbr. articles to profl. publs. Mem. Dade County Sch. Bd., 1967—. Lt. USN, 1950-53, Korea. Mem. ABA (vice chmn. torts and ins. practice sect., chair sr. issues law com., torts and ins. practice sect., 1999—, active sr. lawyers divsn. 2001—), ATLA, Internat. Assn. Def. Counsel (chmn. med. malpractice com. 1975-76, chmn. profl. errors and omissions com. 1987—, chair excess, surplus lines and reins. law com. 1988), Def. Rsch. Inst. (chmn. practice and procedure com. 1976-77), Fedn. Def. and Corp. Counsel (chmn. auto and casualty ins. sect. 1987—, chmn. legis. com. 1984-88, vice chmn. ethics com. 1990-94, mem. task force on nursing home liability 1998—), Fla. Def. Lawyers Assn. (bd. dirs. 1976), Internat. Assn. Ins. counsel (chmn. med. malpractice 1972-74, com. 1975—, def. counsel com. 1976-91, reins. excess and surplus lines com. 1980-99, spkr. and presenter 1966-2003), Dade County Def. Bar Assn., Fed. Ins. Corp. Counsel (casualty ins. law com. 1972—, med. malpractice com. 1974—, excess surplus and reins. com. 1976—, publs. com. 1976-87), Maritime Law Assn. U.S., Fla. Def. Lawyers Assn. (bd. dirs., chmn. legis. com. 1974-77), Internat. Law Soc., Broward County Bar Assn., Am. Judicature Soc., Am. Health Care Assn., Congress Romanian Ams., Coral Gables Club, Ocean Reef Club, Riviera Country Club, Sapphire Valley Country Club. Roman Catholic. Office: 4080 Kiaora Ave Miami FL 33133-6348 Fax: 305-668-0400. E-mail: J.ThorMas@aol.com.

THORNTON, JOSEPH SCOTT, research institute executive, materials scientist; b. Sewickley, Pa., Feb. 6, 1936; s. Joseph Scott and Evelyn (Miller) T.; divorced; children: Joseph Scott III, Chris P. BSME, U. Tex., 1957, PhD, 1969; MSMetE, Carnegie Mellon U., 1962. Engr. Walworth Valve Co., Boston, 1958; metall. engr. Westinghouse Astronuclear Lab., Large, Pa., 1962-64; instr., teaching assoc. U. Tex., Austin, 1964-67; group leader Tracor Inc., Austin, 1967-69, dept. dir., 1973-75; dept. mgr. Horizons Rsch., Inc., Cleve., 1969-73; chmn., chief exec. officer Tex. Rsch. Internat., Inc. (formerly Tex. Rsch. Inst., Inc.), Austin, 1975—. Contbr. numerous tech. papers to profl. publs.; editor: WANL Materials Manual, 2 vols., 1964; patentee in field. Recipient IGS award, 2002; fellow Alcoa, Austin, 1964, RC Baker Found., 1967. Mem.: ASTM, Internat. Geosynthetics Soc. (award 2002), Adhesion Soc., Am. Soc. Metals Internat. (exec. com. 1965—66). Office: Tex Rsch Internat Inc 9063 Bee Caves Rd Austin TX 78733-6201 Office Phone: 512-263-2101. E-mail: jst@tri-intl.com.

THORNTON, KATHRYN C. physicist, astronaut; b. Montgomery, Ala., Aug. 17, 1952; d. William C. and Elsie Cordell; m. Stephen T. Thornton; children: Carol Elizabeth, Laura Lee, Susan Annette; stepchildren: Kenneth, Michael. BS in Physics, Auburn U., 1974; MS in Physics, U. Va., 1977, PhD, 1979. Physicist U.S. Army Fgn. Sci. & Tech. Ctr., Charlottesville, Va., 1980-84; with NASA, 1984—, astronaut Lyndon B. Johnson Space Ctr., 1985—, mission specialist Space Shuttle Discovery flight STS-33, 1989-96; prof. University of Virginia Sch of Engineering, VA, 1996—. Aboard maiden flight Space Shuttle Endeavor. 1992. Nato post-doctoral fellow Max Planck Inst. Nuclear Physics, 1979-80. Mem. AAAS, Am. Phys. Soc., Sigma Xi, Phi Kappa Phi. Office: U Va Charlottesville VA 22903

THORNTON, LARRY LEE, psychotherapist, author, educator, minister; b. Lake, Miss., Nov. 9, 1937; s. Harvey L. and Onzell (Goodson) T.; children: Matt Alan, Leigh Ann, Pamela; m. Helen Louise Thornton. BA, Miss. Coll., 1959; MDiv, New Orleans Bapt. Theol. Sem., 1963, MA, 1964; MS, U. So. Miss., 1966, PhD, 1969; postgrad., Harvard U., 1985. Dir. admissions Miss. Coll., Clinton, 1961; sr. prof. psychology Delta State U., Cleveland, Miss., 1968-99, prof. psychology emeritus, 1999—; founder, dir. Lic. Profl. Counseling, Assocs., Cleveland, 1988-98; pvt. practice Jackson, Miss., 1999—; founder Fellowship of Total Balance, Inst. of Vital Blance. Adj. prof. psychology Miss. Coll., Clinton, 1999—, New Orleans Bapt. Theol. Sem., 2000—; chmn. Miss. Bd. Lic. Profl. Counselors, 1992-93. Author: Insights into Human Development, 2002. Charter mem. Internat. Devel. Coun., Bapt. Theol. Sem., Rüschlikon, Zurich, Switzerland, 1992. Recipient Panhellenic Outstanding Faculty award, 1996, S.E. Kossman Outstanding Tchr. award, 1991. Mem. APA, ACA. Avocations: golf, tennis, walking. Home and Office: PO Box 13475 Jackson MS 39236

THORNTON, MICHAEL B. federal judge; Judge U.S. Tax Ct., Washington, 1998—. Office: US Tax Ct 400 2D St NW Washington DC 20217-0001

THORNTON, RAY, state supreme court justice, former congressman; b. Conway, AR, July 16, 1928; s. R.H. and Wilma (Stephens) Thornton; m. Betty Jo Mann, Jan. 27, 1956; children: Nancy, Mary Jo, Stephanie. BA, Yale U., 1950; JD, U. Ark., 1956. Bar: Ark. 1956, U.S. Supreme Ct. 1956. Pvt. practice in, Sheridan and Little Rock, 1956—70; atty. gen., 1971—73; mem. 93d-95th Congresses from 4th Ark. dist.; exec. dir. Quachita Bapt. U./Henderson State U. Joint Ednl. Consortium, Arkadelphia, Ark., 1979—80; pres. Ark. State U., Jonesboro and Beebe, 1984—89, U. Ark. Sys., Fayetteville, Little Rock, Pine Bluff, Monticello, 1984—89; mem. 102nd-104th Congresses from 2d Ark. dist., 1991—96; assoc. justice Ark. Supreme Ct., 1997—. Chmn. Ark. Bd. Law Examiners, 1967—70; del. 7th Ark. Constl. Conv., 1969—70. Chmn. pres.'s devel. coun. Harding Coll., Searcy, Ark., 1971—73. Served with USN, 1951—54, Korea. Mem.: AAAS (chmn. com. on sci., engring. and pub. policy 1980). Office: 625 Marshall St, 120 Justice Building Little Rock AR 72201

THORNTON, SPENCER P. ophthalmologist, educator; b. West Palm Beach, Fla., Sept. 16, 1929; s. Ray Spencer and Mae (Phillips) T.; m. Annie Glenn Cooper, Oct. 6, 1956; children: Steven Pitts, David Spencer, Ray Cooper, Beth Ellen. BS, Wake Forest Coll., 1951, MD, 1954. Diplomate: Am. Bd. Ophthalmology. Intern Ga. Bapt. Hosp., Atlanta, 1954-55; resident gen. surgery U. Ala. Med. Center, 1955-56; resident ophthalmology Vanderbilt U. Sch. Medicine, 1960-63; practice medicine specializing in ophthalmic surgery Nashville, 1960—; med. dir. Thornton Eye Ctr., 1995-99; clin. prof. ophthalmology U. Tenn., Memphis, 2002. Disting. vis. prof. dept. ophthalmology U. Tenn., Memphis 2001, Ridley medal lectr., 2001; mem. staff Bapt. Hosp., chief ophthalmology svc., 1982-87; guest prof., vis. lectr. U. Toronto, 1990-92, U. Paris, 1989, Rothchilds Inst., Paris, 1992, 94, U. Pretoria, 1991, 93, others; instr. Moscow Inst. Eye Microsurgery, 1981; instr. ophthalmic surgery Am. Acad. Ophthalmology Ann. Courses; lectr. lens implant symposiums Eng., Spain, Australia, Switzerland, Can., Sweden, Greece, Germany, France, Republic of South Africa, Japan; Berzelius lectr. U. Lund, Sweden, 1992; P.J. Hay Gold medal lectr. North of Eng. Ophthal. Soc., Scarborough, 1992; pres. Biosyntrx Inc., 2002—. King Features syndicated newspaper columnist, 1959-60, feature writer, NBC radio and TV, 1958-60; author, co-author textbooks on cataract and refractive surgery; mem. editl. bd. Jour. Refractive and Corneal Surgery, Jour. Cataract and Refractive Surgery, Video Jour. Ophthalmology, Ocular Surgery News (Ophthalmologist of Yr. 1996), Ophthalmic Practice (Can.), Eye Care Tech. Mag. (Lifetime Achievement award 1996); contbr. articles to profl. jours., inventor instruments and devices for refractive and lens implant surgery. Named one of 100 Best Ophthalmologists in Am., Ophthalmology Times mag., 1996; recipient Honor award Can. Implant Assn., 1993, Outstanding Achievement award Bowman Gray Sch. Medicine, 1995, Ridley medal U. Tenn., Memphis, Tenn., 2001. Fellow: ACS (life), Am. Coll. Nutritional Medicine (pres. 2000—), Am. Acad. Ophthalmology (honor award 1995); mem.: Am. Soc. Cataract and Refractive Surgery (pres. 1997—99), Can. Implant Soc. (life), South African Intraocular Implant Soc. (life), Am. Med. Soc. Vienna (life), Delta Kappa Alpha, Phi Rho Sigma. Baptist. Home and Office: 5070 Villa Crest Dr Nashville TN 37220-1425 Office Phone: 888-303-2111. Business E-Mail: sthornton@biosyntrx.com.

THORNTON, THOMAS NOEL, publishing executive; b. Marceline, Mo., Apr. 23, 1950; s. Bernard F. and Helen F. (Kelley) T.; m. Cynthia L. Murray, Nov. 26, 1971; children: T. Zachary, Timothy. B.J., U. Mo., 1972. Asst. to editor Universal Press Syndicate, Kansas City, Mo., 1972, v.p., 1974, dir. mktg., 1976; v.p., dir. mktg. Universal Press Syndicate and Andrews McMeel Pub., Kansas City, 1976-87; pres., COO Andrews McMeel Pub., 1987—2002, pres., CEO, 2003—. Bd. dirs. Andrews McMeel Universal. Office: Universal Press Syndicate 4520 Main St Ste 700 Kansas City MO 64111-7701 Business E-Mail: tthornton@amuniversal.com.

THORNTON, YVONNE SHIRLEY, physician, author, musician; b. N.Y.C., Nov. 21, 1947; d. Donald E. and Itasker F. (Edmonds) T.; m. Shearwood McClelland, June 8, 1974; children: Shearwood III, Kimberly Itaska. BS in Biology, Monmouth Coll., 1969; MD, Columbia U., 1973, MPH, 1996; DSc (hon.), Tuskegee U., 2003. Diplomate Am. Bd. Ob-gyn. Resident in ob-gyn Roosevelt Hosp., N.Y.C., 1973-77; fellow maternal-fetal medicine Columbia-Presbyn. Med. Center, N.Y.C., 1977-79; commd. lt. comdr. M.C. USN, 1979; asst. prof. ob-gyn Uniformed Svcs. U. Health Scis., 1979-82; assoc. prof. Cornell U. Med. Coll., N.Y.C., 1989-92; dir. clin. svcs. dept. ob-gyn N.Y. Hosp.-Cornell Med. Center, 1982-88; assoc. attending N.Y. Lying-In Hosp., 1982-89, assoc. clin. prof. ob-gyn. Columbia P&S, 1995-98, assoc. clin. prof., 2001—02; clin. prof. ob-gyn. U. Medicine and Dentistry N.J., 1998-2000; prof. clin. ob-gyn. Med. Coll. Cornell U., 2003—. Dir. Chorionic Villus Sampling Program, 1984-92; dir. perinatal diagnostic testing ctr. Morristown Meml. Hosp., 1992-2000, divsn. maternal-fetal medicine St. Luke's Roosevelt Hosp. Ctr., 2000-02; vice chair ob-gyn, dir. maternal-fetal medicine, Jamaica Hosp. Med. Ctr., 2002—; staff Nat. Naval Med. Ctr., Bethesda, Md.; saxophonist Thornton Sisters ensemble, 1955-76; vis. assoc. physician The Rockefeller U. Hosp., 1986-96; prof. clinical OB/GYN Cornell U. Med. Coll., 2003—; examiner Am. Bd. Ob-Gyn, 1997—; vice chmn. Dept. Ob-Gyn. Jamaica Hosp. Med. Ctr. Author: The Ditchdigger's Daughters, 1995, (named best books for young adults ALA, Excellence in Lit. award, N.J. Edn. Assn., nominated for Pulitzer Prize 1995) Primary Care for the Obstetrician and Gynecologist, 1997, Woman to Woman, 1997. Recipient Excellence in Literature award, N.J. Edn. Assn., 1996, winner Daniel Webster Oratorical Competition, Internat. Platform Assn., 1996; nominated Pulitzer Prize, 1995. Fellow: ACOG, ACS; mem.: AMA, Am. Fedn. Musicians, Soc. Maternal-Fetal Medicine, Assn. Women Surgeons, N.Y. Acad. Medicine. Democrat. Baptist. Office: 8900 Van Wyck Expressway New York NY 11418 Business E-Mail: ythornto@jhmc.org.

THORON, GRAY, lawyer, educator; b. Danvers, Mass., July 14, 1916; s. Ward and Louisa Chapin (Hooper) T.; m. Pattie Porter Holmes, Dec. 30, 1971 (dec. 2000); children from previous marriage: Claire, Louisa, Grenville C., Molly D., Thomas G. AB, Harvard U., 1938, LLB, 1941. Bar: N.Y. 1942. Assoc. Sullivan & Cromwell, N.Y.C., 1941-42, 45-48; assoc. prof. law U. Tex., 1948-50, prof. law, 1950-56; dean Law Sch. Cornell U., Ithaca, N.Y., 1956-63, prof. law, 1956-87, prof. emeritus, 1987—. Vis. prof. law U. Mich., 1951, U. Tex., 1970; faculty Salzburg Seminar in Am. Studies, 1959; asst. to solicitor gen. Dept. Justice, Washington, 1954-56; mem. NY State Laporte Legis. Ethics Com., 1964; spl. asst. atty. gen. NY State, 1965. Del. Rep. Nat. Conv., 1952; trustee Concord Acad., 1958-61. Served with inf. AUS, 1942-45. Decorated silver star, bronze star, purple heart with oak leaf cluster. Fellow Am. Bar Found. (life); mem. ABA, Am. Law Inst. (life), N.Y. State Bar Assn. (chmn. spl. com. to rev. code of profl. responsibility 1974-77, com. profl. ethics 1965-87, vice chmn. 1973-83, emeritus 1987—), Am. Arbitration Assn. (arbitrator 1965-90), Assn. Bar City NY, Lawyers Com. Civil Rights Under Law (trustee 1965-97), Phi Alpha Delta, Phi Kappa Phi, Century Assn., Harvard Club (NYC). Address: Savage Farm Dr Ithaca NY 14853

THORP, BENJAMIN A., III, retired paper company executive; b. Albany, N.Y., May 31, 1938; s. Benjamin A. Jr. and Anna C. (Head) T.; m. Barbara Sue Tellock, Aug. 1, 1964 (div. Mar. 1986); 1 child, Benjamin A. IV; m. Laurie Diane Murdock, Oct. 25, 1987. Student in elec. engring., Rensselaer Poly Inst., 1956-61, postgrad. in mgmt., 1967-68; BS in Physics, U. Md., 1964; postgrad. in engring., U. Bridgeport, 1966; postgrad. in mktg., U. Tenn., 1970. Product devel. mgr. Huyck Formex div. Huyck, Greenville, Tenn., 1969-71, mktg. mgr., 1971-73, v.p., gen. mgr., 1973-75, Huytech Systems div., Wake Forest, N.C., 1975-78; v.p., dir. research Huyck Corp., Rensselaer, N.Y., 1978-80; pres. Benjamin A. Thorp Inc., Albany, 1980-82, POYRY-BEK Inc., Raleigh, N.C., 1982-84; v.p. engring. BE&K Inc., Birmingham, Ala., 1984-85, James River Corp., Richmond, Va., 1984-95; v.p. mfg. tech. Chesapeake Corp., Richmond, Va., 1996-97; dir. pulp and paper engring. Ga. Pacific, Atlanta, 1998—2004, ret., 2004. Mem. exec. com. Pulp and Paper Found. Bd., Ga. Inst. Tech., 1991-95, pres., 1993-95; mem. indsl. adv. bd. Forest Web.com, 2000—, MTCI, Balt., Md., 2001—, Peregrine Energy, Greenville, S.C., 2002—; chmn. bd. Besicaf-Empire Devel. Co. Tech. editor Paper Machine Operations, Vol. 7, 3d edit., 1991; contbr. more than 100 articles to profl. jours.; patentee in field. Bd. dirs. Richmond Math. and Sci. Ctr., 1987-93, Sic. Mus. of Va. Found., 1989-98; chmn. papermaking project adv. com. Inst. Paper Sci. and Tech., 1990-94. Fellow TAPPI (chmn. papermakers com. 1984-86, vice chmn. paper and bd. divsn. 1988-90, chmn. 1990-92, bd. dir., Leadership award 1994); mem. Paper Industry Mgmt. Assn. (pres. 1996-97, chmn. bd. trustees 1999—2003, Glen T. Rinnegar award 1999), PIMA-CPBIS Mgmt. Excellence award, 2003, Exptl. Aircraft Assn., Meadowbrook Estates Civic Assn. (bd. dir. 1996-98). Presbyterian.

THORP, EDWARD OAKLEY, investment management company executive; b. Chgo., Aug. 14, 1932; s. Oakley Glenn and Josephine (Gebert) T.; m. Vivian Sinetar, Jan. 28, 1956; children: Raun, Karen, Jeffrey. BA in Physics, UCLA, 1953, MA, 1955, PhD in Math., 1958. C.L.E. Moore instr. MIT, Cambridge, Mass., 1959—61; asst. prof. N.Mex. State U., 1961—63, assoc. prof. math., 1963—65, U. Calif., Irvine, 1965—67, prof. math., 1967—77, prof. fin., 1977—82, regents lectr., 1992—93; gen. ptnr. Edward O. Thorp & Assocs., LP, Newport Beach, 1989—. Vis. prof. UCLA, 1991; chmn. Oakley Sutton Mgmt. Corp., Newport Beach, Calif., 1972-91; mng. gen. ptnr. Princeton/Newport Ptnrs., Newport Beach, 1969-91, OSM Ptnrs., MIDAS Advisors, Newport Beach, 1986-89; gen. ptnr. Ridgeline Ptnrs., Newport Beach, 1994-2002; portfolio mgr., cons. Glenwood Investment Corp., Chgo., 1992-94; prin., cons. Grosvenor Capital Mgmt., Chgo., 1992-93; pres. Noesis Corp., 1994-2002. Author: Beat the Dealer: A Winning Strategy for the Game of Twenty-One, 1962, rev. edit., 1966, Elementary Probability, 1966, The Mathematics of Gambling, 1984; co-author: Beat The Market, 1967, The Gambling Times Guide to Blackjack, 1984; columnist Gambling Times, 1979-84, Wilmott 2002—. Grantee NSF, 1954-55, 62-64, Air Force Office Sci. Rsch., 1964-73. Fellow NSF, Inst. Math. Stats.; mem. Phi Beta Kappa, Sigma Xi. Avocations: astronomy, distance running. Office: Edward O Thorp & Assocs LP 610 Newport Center Dr Ste 1240 Newport Beach CA 92660-6436

THORPE, DOUGLAS L. lawyer; b. Wahoo, Nebr., Jan. 25, 1937; BSCE, U. Nebr., 1959; JD cum laude, So. Meth. U., 1968. Bar: Calif. 1969. Mem. Perkins Coie, L.A., 1988—2002; pvt. law practice L.A., 2003—. Bd. dirs. Pub. Counsel, 1980-83. Mem. ABA (antitrust law sect., corp., banking and bus. law sect., litigation sect., econs. of law practice sect.); State Bar Calif., L.A. County Bar Assn. (del. to State Bar Conf. of Dels. 1981, 1983-84, exec. com. antitrust law sect. 1981-83), Century City Bar Assn. (bd. govs. 1982-85), Order of the Coif, Barristers, Phi Delta Phi, Sigma Tau, Tau Beta Pi, Chi Epsilon. Office: 11845 W Olympic Blvd Ste 1000 Los Angeles CA 90064

THORPE, JAMES, humanities researcher; b. Aiken, S.C., Aug. 17, 1915; s. J. Ernest and Ruby (Holloway) T.; m. Elizabeth McLean Daniells, July 19, 1941; children: John D., Sally Jans-Thorpe. AB, The Citadel, 1936, LL.D., 1971; MA, U. N.C., 1937; PhD, Harvard U., 1941; Litt.D., Occidental Coll., 1968; L.H.D., Claremont Grad. Sch., 1968; H.H.D., U. Toledo, 1977. Instr. to prof. English Princeton, 1946-66; dir. Huntington Libr., Art Gallery and Bot. Gardens, San Marino, Calif., 1966-83; sr. research assoc. Huntington Libr., San Marino, Calif., 1966-99. Author: Bibliography of the Writings of George Lyman Kittredge, 1948, Milton Criticism, 1950, Rochester's Poems on Several Occasions, 1950, Poems of Sir George Etherege, 1963, Aims and Methods of Scholarship, 1963, 70, Literary Scholarship, 1964, Relations of Literary Study, 1967, Bunyan's Grace Abounding and Pilgrim's Progress, 1969, Principles of Textual Criticism, 1972, 2d edit., 1979, Use of Manuscripts in Literary Research, 1974, 2d edit., 1979, Gifts of Genius, 1980, A Word to the Wise, 1982, John Milton: The Inner Life, 1983, The Sense of Style: Reading English Prose, 1987, Henry Edwards Huntington: A Biography, 1994, H.E. Huntington: A Short Biography, 1996, A Pleasure of Proverbs, 1996, Proverbs for Friends, 1997, Proverbs for Thinkers, 1998, The Gutenberg Bible, 1999, Poems Written at the Huntington Library, 2000, Proverbs for Our Time, 2003, Proverbs for the Future, 2004. Served to col. USAAF, 1941-46. Decorated Bronze Star medal.; Guggenheim fellow, 1949-50, 65-66. Fellow Am. Acad. Arts and Scis., Am. Philos. Soc.; mem. MLA, Am. Antiquarian Soc., Soc. for Textual Scholarship. Democrat. Episcopalian. Home: 20 Loeffler Rd Apt T320 Bloomfield CT 06002-2277

THORPE, JANET CLAIRE, judge; b. Bklyn., Dec. 8, 1953; d. Burton Walter and Phyllis Claire (Read) T.; m. David Frank Palmer, Aug. 26, 1978 (div. Aug. 1988); children: Katherine Elaine, Jennifer Claire; m. James Francis Box, June 29, 1991; children; Melissa Richelle, Maergrethe Cashel. Student, Boston U., 1972-74; BA in Polit. Sci. & History with honors, Union Coll., 1975; postgrad., Western New Eng. Sch. Law, 1975-76; JD, Emory U., 1978. Bar: Ga. 1978, U.S. Ct. Appeals (5th and 11th cirs.) 1978, 80, Fla. 1987, U.S. Dist. Ct. (mid. dist.) Fla. 1987. Law clk. to judge U.S. Dist. Ct., Atlanta, 1978; regional atty. Comptroller of Curency, Atlanta, 1978-80; assoc. corp. counsel Trust Co. Ga., Atlanta, 1980-86; dir. Trusco Properties, Inc., Atlanta, 1981-86; gen. counsel, corp. sec. SunTrust Banks Fla., Inc., Orlando, 1986-2000; gen. counsel SunTrust Bank N.A., Orlando, 1986-2000; group v.p. SunTrust Banks, Inc., 1995-2000; cir. ct. judge State of Fla. (9th cir.), Orlando, Fla., 2000—. Mem. Coun. Battered Women, Atlanta, 1983-86, bd. dirs., 1986; bd. visitors Cornell Mus. Fine Art, Rollins Coll., 1990-96; mem. bd. zoning variances City of Orlando, 1996-99; bd. dirs. Orange County Cmty. Alliance, 2000-03. Mem. Ga. Bar Assn., Fla. Bar Assn., Assn. Bank Holdings Cos (lawyers com. 1983-90), Am. Corp. Counsel Assn. (bd. dirs. ctrl. Fla. chpt. 1991-99), Am. Diabetes Assn. (bd. dirs. Fla. chpt. 1989-97), Leadership Orlando. Episcopalian. Avocations: gardening, child rearing, house renovation, photography. Office: Orange County Courthouse 425 N Orange Ave Orlando FL 32801

THORPE, SAMUEL STANLEY, JR., artist; b. Stoneham, Mass., July 15, 1933; m. Louise Harwood Gove; children: Michael, Scott, Craig, Heidi. Student, Sch. Mus. Fine Art, Boston. Represented in permanent collections at MBNA Am. Banks Corp. Collections, Aubuchon Hardware Corp., Nashua Fed. Savs. Bank, No. Middlesex Savings Bank, Indianhead Bank, Gardner Savs. Bank, Pepperell Bus. Assn., USA Distbg., Atty. Watnik & Watnik, PC, North Middlesex Savings Bank, Attys. Mitchell & Chenelle P.C., US Embassy, Vienna, numerous pvt. collections including Ambassador and Mrs. Wylie T. Buchanan and Pres. and Mrs. George H.W. Bush; illustrator Cameo Greetings, Maine, Doehler Card Corp., NH, Marion Heath Greetings, Mass., Airmar Corp., NH. Mem. So. Vt. Art Assn., Chaffee Art Ctr. (Rutland, Vt.), Artists Guild of the Kennebunks, Leominster Art Assn., New Haven Paint and Palette Club, Salmagundi Club (NYC), Copley Soc. (Boston). Home and Studio: 30 Elm Cir Townsend MA 01469-1236

THORSEN, JAMES HUGH, retired aviation director, retired airport manager; b. Evanston, Ill., Feb. 5, 1943; s. Chester A. and Mary Jane (Currie) T.; m. Nancy Dain, May 30, 1980. BA, Ripon Coll., 1965. FAA cert. comml. pilot, flight instr. airplanes and instruments. Bd. dirs. Internat. Northwest Aviation Coun. Pres. Thorsen Aviation Cons. Recipient Region Safety award FAA N.W. Mountain. Mem. Am. Assn. Airport Execs. (past pres. N.W. chpt., Disting. Svc. award 1999), Mensa, Idaho Falls W. Rotary Club (pres. 2002), Quiet Birdmen, Sigma Alpha Epsilon. Home: 334 Westmorland Dr Idaho Falls ID 83402-4607

THORSEN, MARIE KRISTIN, radiologist, educator; b. Milw., Aug. 1, 1947; d. Charles Christian and Margaret Josephine (Little) T.; M. James Lawrence Troy, Jan. 7, 1978; children: Katherine Marie, Megan Elizabeth. BA, U. Wis., 1969; MBA, George Washington U., 1971; MD, Columbia Coll. Physicians and Surgeons, 1977. Diplomate Am. Bd. Radiology. Intern. Columbia-Presbyn. med. Ctr., N.Y.C., 1977-78, resident dept. radiology, 1978-81; asst. prof. radiology Med. Coll. Wis., 1982-84, assoc. prof., 1984-89, prof., 1989-94; dir. computed tomography Waukesha Meml. Hosp., 1994—. Contbr. articles to profl. jours. Fellow computed body tomography Med. Coll. Wisc., Milw, 1981-82; Am. Coll. Radiology, Radiol. Soc. N. Am., Wis. Radiologic Assn. (sec., treas. 2001—). E-mail: mkthoren@aol.com.

THORSEN, NANCY DAIN, real estate broker; b. Edwardsville, Ill., 1944; d. Clifford Earl and Suzanne Eleanor (Kribs) Dain; m. David Massie, 1968 (div. 1975); 1 child, Suzanne Dain Massie; m. James Hugh Thorsen, May 30, 1980. BSc in Mktg., So. Ill. U., 1968, MSc in Bus. Edn., 1975; grad., Realtor Inst., Idaho, 1983. Cert. residential and investment specialist, fin. instr., luxury home mktg. specialist; designated real estate instr. State of Idaho; accredited buyer rep. Personnel officer J.H. Little & Co. Ltd., London, 1969-72; instr. in bus. edn. Spl. Sch. Dist. St. Louis, 1974-77; mgr. mktg./ops. Isis Foods, Inc., St. Louis, 1978-80; asst. mgr. store Stix, Baer & Fuller, St. Louis, 1980; assoc. broker Century 21 Sayer Realty, Inc., Idaho Falls, Idaho, 1981-88, RE/MAX Homestead Realty, 1989—. Spkr. in field; real estate fin. instr. State of Idaho Real Estate Commn., 1994; founder Nancy Thorsen Seminars, 1995. Bd. dirs. Idaho Vol., Boise, 1981-84, Idaho Falls Symphony, 1982; pres. Friends of Idaho Falls Libr., 1981-83; chmn. Idaho Falls Mayor's Com. for Vol. Coordination, 1981-84; power leader Power Program, 1995; mem. Mtn. River Valley Red Cross, chair capital campaign, cmty. gifts chair ARC. Recipient Idaho Gov.'s award, 1982, cert. appreciation City of Idaho Falls/Mayor Campbell, 1982, 87, Civilian Disting. Pres. award, 1990, Bus. Women of the Yr. award C. of C., 1998; named to Two Million Dollar Club, 1987, 88, Four Million Dollar Club, 1989, 90, Top Investment Sales Person for Eastern Idaho, 1985, Realtor of Yr. Idaho Falls Bd. Realtors, 1990, Outstanding Realtors Active in Politics, Women of Yr. Am. Biog. Inst., 1991, Profiles of Top Prodrs. award Real Estate Edn. Assn., Above the Crowd award 1997; named Western Region Power Leader, Darryl Davis Seminars. Mem. Nat. Spkrs. Assn., Idaho Falls Bd. Realtors (chmn. Orientation 1982-83, chmn. edn. 1983, chmn. legis. com. 1989, 95—, chmn. program com. 1990, 91), Idaho Assn. Realtors (pres. Million Dollar Club 1988-2001, edn. com. 1990-93, Mem. of Yr. 1991), Women's Coun. Realtors, Am. Bus. Women's Assn., So. Ill. U. Alumni Assn.,

Idaho Falls C. of C. (Bus. Woman of the Yr.-Professions, 1997), newcomers Club, Civitan (pres. Idaho Falls chpt. 1988-89, Civitan of Yr. 1986, 97, Outstanding Pres. award 1990, Hall of Fame 1998), Real Estate Educators Assn. Office: RE/MAX Homestead Inc 1301 E 17th St Ste 1 Idaho Falls ID 83404-6273 E-mail: thorsen@srv.net.

THORSNESS, JULIA MARIE, hospice administrator; b. Yakima, Wash., Apr. 8, 1958; d. Edward Gerhard William Rosin and Margaret Julia Franke; m. James Ray Thorsness; children: Rebecca, Timothy. BA in Social Work, Pacific Luth. U., 1980. Pub. rels. coord. Our Lady of Compassion Care Ctr., Anchorage, 1985-88; cmty. rels. mgr. Covenant Ho. Alaska, Anchorage, 1989-95; devel. dir. Camp Fire Boys and Girls, Anchorage, 1995-99; exec. dir. Hospice of Anchorage, 1999—. Editor, contbr. Hospice of Anchorage Newsletter, 2000— (awards). Mem. Pub. Rels Soc. Am. (bd. mem. Alaska chpt. 1996-98), Assn. Fundraising Profls. (past pres. Anchorage chpt.), Nat. Soc. Fund Raising Execs. (pres. Alaska chpt. 2000, Philanthropy Day chair 1997), Anchorage Lions Club (pres. 1998-99), Foraker Group (ops. bd. mem.). Lutheran. Home: 1161 W 77th Ave Anchorage AK 99518 Office: Hospice of Anchorage 500 W Int Airport Rd # C Anchorage AK 99518 E-mail: hospice@ak.net.

THORSON, LEE A. lawyer; b. Seattle, Nov. 10, 1949; s. Theodore Arthur and Irene Mary (Dakers) T.; m. Elizabeth Clayton Hay, June 7, 1975; children: Kirk Hunter, Alex Peter. BA, U. Wash., 1971; JD, U. Pacific, Sacramento, 1975; LLM Taxation, Boston U., 1976. Atty. Dahlgren & Dauenhauer P.S., Seattle, 1976-79, Lane Powell Spears Lubersky, Seattle, 1980-93; shareholder Birmingham Thorson & Barnett, P.C., 1993—; affiliate prof. U. Wash. Grad. Program in Taxation, 1995—. Mem. ABA (health law forum), Employee Benefits and Health Law coms., Wash. State Bar Assn. Avocations: bicycling, skiing. Office: Birmingham Thorson Barnett 601 Union St Ste 3315 Seattle WA 98101-4018 E-mail: lthorson@btbpc.com.

THORSON, STEVEN GREG, lawyer; b. Van Nuys, Calif., Feb. 7, 1948; s. Robert G. and Ruth C. T.; m. Patricia Lynn LaPointe, Aug. 3, 1974; 1 child, Kai Johannes. BA, St. Olaf Coll., 1977; JD, Hamline U., 1980. Bar: Minn. 1980, U.S. Dist. Ct. Minn. 1980, U.S. Tax Ct. 1980, U.S. Ct. Appeals (8th cir.) 1980. Pres. Thorson & Berg, Maple Grove, Minn., 1990—99; shareholder Barna, Guzy & Steffen, Ltd. Attys. at Law, Mpls., 1999—. Lectr. continuing legal edn., 1986—; apptd. to Minn. State Bar Assn. Commn. on Unauthorized Practice of Law, 1990-92; atty. for Columbus Twp. (Anoka County), 1981-96; mem. residential real estate com. Minn. State Bar Assn., 1992—. Mem. ch. coun. Peace Luth. Ch. Named a Super Lawyer, Minn. Law and Politics Mag., 2000—04; named one of Minn. Super Lawyers, Mpls./St. Paul mag., 1998, 2000—04. Mem. ABA, Minn. State Bar Assn. (real property coun., chair publs. com. 2001—), Hennepin County Bar Assn. (chmn. purchase agreement com. 1986-88), Anoka County Bar Assn. (pres. real estate sect. 1988). Avocation: alpine and nordic skiing. Home: 12071 Norway St NW Minneapolis MN 55448-2243 Office: 400 Northtown Fin Plz 200 Coon Rapids Blvd NW Ste 400 Minneapolis MN 55433-5894 Office Phone: 763-783-5124. E-mail: sthorson@bgslaw.com.

THORSTED, V. DARLEENE, neonatal and community health nurse; b. Albuquerque, Dec. 4, 1944; d. Charles F. and Violet J. (Keefe) Perry; m. Lawrence H. Thorsted, Nov. 1, 1974; children: Melanie, Dennis, Deidra. ADN, Coll. So. Idaho, 1973; BSN, Boise State U., 1987. RN, Idaho. Staff nurse Magic Valley Regional Med. Ctr., Twin Falls, Idaho, 1973; coord. med. care Intracorp, Missoula, Mont., 1987; case mgr. home care, primary nurse St. Luke's Regional Med. Ctr., Boise, Idaho, 1977-90, staff nurse neonatal ICU, 1977-90; exec. dir. Idaho Bd. Medicine, 1994—2000; RN Medicare coord. Boise Samaritan Village, 2000—. Mem. Idaho Nurses Assn., Sigma Theta Tau. Home: 1881 Hendricks Ct Meridian ID 83642-1337 Office Phone: 208-343-7726.

THORSTEINSSON, GUDNI, physiatrist; b. Vestmannaeyjar, Iceland, Aug. 5, 1941; came to U.S., 1971; s. Thorsteinn and Asdis Gudbjörg Einarsson; m. Elin Klein, Apr. 10, 1965; children: Arnar Karl, Asdis Thora. BS, Reykjavik (Iceland) Coll., 1961; candidatus med. et chirurg., U. Iceland, Reykjavik, 1968; MS, U. Minn., 1976. Diplomate Am. Bd. Phys. Medicine and Rehab. Dist physician Icelandic Govt., Djupivogur, 1970-71; resident dept. phys. medicine and rehab. Mayo Found., Rochester, Minn., 1972-75, mem. consulting staff, 1975-80; chair dept. Nat. Hosp., Reykjavik, 1980-81; dir. rehab. Mayo Clinic/St. Mary's Hosp., Rochester, 1981-85; dir. out-patient rehab. Mayo Clinic, Rochester, 1985-88, chair dept., 1987-91, chair dept. phys. medicine and rehab. Jacksonville, Fla., 1991-99. Physiatrist cons. Mayo Clinic, Rochester, 81-91, Jacksonville, 1991—. Author: (with others) Efficacy of Transcoutaneous Electrical Stimulation, 1977, Placebo Effect of Transcountaneous Electrical Stimulation, 1978, Electrical Stimulation for Anagesia, 1983, Management of Post Polio Syndrome, 1997. Mem. Am. Acad. Phys. Medicine and Rehab. Office: Mayo Clinic Jacksonville 4500 San Pablo Rd S Jacksonville FL 32224-1865

THORSTENBERG, LAURENCE (JOHN L. THORSTENBERG), oboe and English horn player; b. Salt Lake City, Dec. 6, 1925; s. Laurence Nathaniel and Alys Josephine (Blomquist) T. MusB, Curtis Inst. Music, Phila., 1951. Instrumental tchr., 1975-96, New Eng. Conservatory, Boston U., 1980-96; mem. Symphony Orch. Balt., 1951-52, Dallas Symphony Orch., 1952-54, Chgo. Symphony Orch., 1954-63, Boston Symphony Orch., 1964-93. Appeared summers, Marlboro (Vt.) Music Festival, 1952-54. With U.S. Army, 1944-46, ETO. Mem. Internat. Conf. Symphony and Opera Musicians (emeritus).

THORSTENSON, TERRY N. construction equipment company executive; b. Rugby, N.D., Apr. 1, 1938; s. Marvin Byron and Inez (Blessum) T.; m. Carol Trigg, Nov. 26, 1960; 1 child, Craig. BSME, U. N.D., 1959. Tng., sales, field rep. Caterpillar, Inc., Peoria, Ill., 1959-64, dist. rep., gen. supr., 1965-69, asst. sales mgr., 1969-74, mng. dir. sales, 1974-85, mgr. mktg. and engring devel., 1985-97; mgr. corp. pub. affairs and human resources Caterpillar, Peoria, Ill., 1997-99, dir. corp. pub. affairs, 1999—. Elder Westminster Presbyn. Ch., Peoria, 1979-81. Served to 2d lt., U.S. Army ROTC. Mem. Machinery and Allied Products Inst. (mem. mktg. council). Clubs: Peoria Country. Avocations: golf, tennis. Office: Caterpillar Inc 100 NE Adams St Peoria IL 61629-0002

THORTON, ANGELICA, newscaster; b. Mass. BA in Broadcast Journalism, Emerson Coll. Anchor, reporter KECI-TV, Missoula, Mont.; gen. assignment reporter NBC 17, Raleigh, NC, 1999—. Recipient award, Soc. Profl. Journalists, 1999. Avocations: skiing, hiking, soccer. Office: NBC 17 Studios 1205 Front St Raleigh NC 27609

THORUD, DAVID B. academic administrator; BS in Forestry, U. Minn., 1958, MS in Forest Hydrology, 1960, PhD in Forest Hydrology, 1964. Asst. prof. U. Minn., 1961—66; assoc. prof., prof. U. Ariz., 1966—72, head dept. watershed mgmt. Coll. Agr., 1972—74, dir. Sch. Renewable Natural Resources, 1974—77; asst. dir. Southeastern Forest Experiment Sta. USDA Forest Svc., 1977—78, prin. rsch. hydrologist Forest Environment Rsch., 1978—79, dir. Forest Expt. Sta., 1979—81; dir. govt. rels. U. Wash., Seattle, 1984—85, dean Coll. Forest Resources, 1981—94, acting provost, 1994—. Chair West Ctrl. Region Assn. State Coll. and Univ. Forestry Rsch. Orgns., 1972—74; chair U.S. Man and the Biosphere Project on Grazing Lands, 1976—78; pres. Internat. Soc. Tropical Foresters, 1982—83, Nat. Assn. Profl. Forestry Schs. and Colls., 1985—87; mem. U.S. Joint Coun. on Food and Agrl. Scis., 1987—89; mem. com. on forestry rsch. NRC, NAS, 1989—90, chair, 1990—91; trustee Ctr. for Internat. Forestry Rsch., 1994—97; chair bd. trustees Internat. Ctr. for Rsch. in Agro-forestry, 1994—97; bd. dirs. Evergreen Partnership, Port of Tacoma, Mountain to Sound Greenway. Contbr. articles to profl. jours. Fellow: Soc. Am. Foresters. Office: U Wash Office of the Provost 301 Gerberding Hall Box 351237 Seattle WA 98195-1237*

THOTTUPURAM, KURIAN CHERIAN, priest, college director, educator; b. Cherianad, Kerala, India; came to U.S., 1971; s. Cherian Koruth and Eliamma (Kandanavila) T.; m. Susan Grace Kompady, Dec. 29, 1969; children: Cherian, Kurian Jr., Theodore-George. BA, St. Joseph's Coll., India, 1964; grad. diploma in theology, Sem. of Lateran U., 1966; MA, Karnatak U., 1970, Mundelein Coll., Chgo., 1973; MEd, Loyola U., Chgo., 1979, PhD, 1981; DD, Notre Dame de Lafayette U., 1993. Ordained subdeacon, 1967, deacon, 1970, priest, 1970, chorbishop, 1986. Tchr. Mt. Tabor Monastery Coll., Pathanapuram, India, 1966-70; founder Malankarese Orthodox Syrian Ch., Chgo., 1971—; pastor St. John's Syrian Orthodox Ch., 1971-72; founder, pastor St. Thomas Orthodox Ch., 1972-80, St. Mary's Orthodox Ch., Oaklawn, Ill., 1982—; counseling psychologist Incentives Inst., Des Plaines, Ill., 1974-76; dir. social svc. Millardogden Ctr., Chgo., 1976-77; ednl. adminstr. ednl. program Chgo. Housing Authority, 1977-81; ecumenical officer Malankarese Orthodox Diocese, Chgo., 1981-85; dir. program planning and devel. Malcolm X Coll., Chgo. City Coll. System, 1985-91; english faculty Truman Coll., 1991-92; exec. dir. International Edn. Cons. and Evaluators of Ill., 1992; dir. curriculum/instrn. S.E.A. Ctr., 1993-94; mem. philosophy faculty Daley Coll., 1993-95, Triton Coll., 1995—. Pioneer Malankarese Orthodox Chs., 1971-81; adj. prof. philosophy Coll. of Lake County, 1995-96; pres. Am. Acad. Comparative-Internat. Edn., Chgo., 1993—; mem. Sch. Bd. Coun., 1991-93; presenter World Peace Conf., Istanbul, Turkey, 2004, spkr. World Peace Conf., 2004. Author: Dhyanamitram, 1966, Kalari, 1967, Perumpepadam, 1968, Foundations of Kerala Education, 1981, Bible Reading Guide of the Malankara Orthodox Church, Education and Social Change, 1987, The Mystery of Man, 1971, Personality of a Child: A Constant Process of Dualistic Eruption into Monism, 1972, Incarnation: A Theologico-mystical Study, 1981, Holy Spirit: The Life Giver, 1981, An Orthodox Introduction to Sacraments, 1983, The Book of Common Prayer of the Syrian Orthodox Ch., 1985, Book of Ordinations of the Syrian Orthodox Ch., 1987, Marriage After the Holy Priesthood, 1985, Contraception and Orthodox Theology, 1990, The Orthodox Christian Priesthood: An Anthology of Patristic Writings, 1995, Pre-British European Educational Activities in India, 1989; chief editor: Voice of Orthodoxy, 1986. Chmn. social action Diocese of Niraram, India, 1967-71; mem. Zonal coun. Diocese of Am., 1975-78, Diocesan Coun.; bd. regents Lafayette U., Aurora, Colo., 1989-95; exec. mem. Alleppey DT Kerala Congress, India, 1967-71; pres. Ecumenical Coun. Kerala Chs. Chgo., 1983-97; founder Voice of Orthodox Found., Chgo., 1995. Recipient Taylor award for High Achievement, Greek Orthodox Archdiocese, Schmitt Found. award, 1977, Pub. Svc. award Citizens Cultural Found., 1985. Mem. Am. Ednl. Studies Assn., Midwest History of Edn. Soc., Am. Assn. Biofeedback Clinicians, Internat. Assn. of Mission Studies, Germany. Mem. Eastern Orthodox Ch. Avocations: music, philanthropic work.

THOULESS, DAVID JAMES, retired physicist, educator; b. Bearsden, Scotland, Sept. 21, 1934; arrived in U.S., 1979, naturalized, 1994; s. Robert Henry and Priscilla (Gorton) T.; m. Margaret Elizabeth Scrase, July 26, 1958; children: Michael, Christopher, Helen. BA, U. Cambridge, Eng., 1955, ScD, 1986; PhD, Cornell U., 1958. Physicist Lawrence Berkeley Lab., Calif., 1958-59; rsch. fellow U. Birmingham, England, 1959—61, prof. math. physics, 1965—78; lectr., fellow Churchill Coll. U. Cambridge, England, 1961—65; prof. physics Queen's U., Kingston, Ont., Can., 1978; prof. applied sci. Yale U., New Haven, 1979-80; prof. physics U. Wash., Seattle, 1980—2003; ret. Author: Quantum Mechanics of Many Body Systems, 2d edit., 1972, Topological Quantum Numbers in Nonrelativistic Physics, 1998. Recipient Maxwell medal Inst. Physics, 1973, Holweck prize Soc. Francaise de Physique-Inst. Physics, 1980, Fritz London award for Low temperature physics, Fritz London Meml. Fund, 1984, Wolf prize in physics, 1990, Paul Dirac medal Inst. Physics, 1993, Lars Onsager prize Am. Phys. Soc., 2000; Edwin Uehling disting. scholar U. Wash., 1988-98. Fellow: Royal Soc.; mem.: NAS. Office: U Wash PO Box 351560 Seattle WA 98195-1560 Business E-Mail: Thouless@phys.washington.edu.

THOW, GEORGE BRUCE, surgeon; b. Toronto, Mar. 24, 1930; came to U.S., 1965; s. George and Helen Bruce (Smith) T.; m. Marion Bernice Perry, Sept. 7, 1956; children— Deborah, George, Helen, Catherine MD, U. Toronto, 1954. Diplomate Am. Bd. Gen. Surgery, Am. Bd. Colon and Rectal Surgery (pres. 1983-84, adv. coun. 1989—, sr. examiner 1989—). Intern Toronto East Gen. Hosp., 1954-55; gen. practice medicine Toronto, 1955-56; instr. anatomy U. Toronto; resident in gen. and colon and rectal surgery Mayo Postgrad. Sch. Medicine, Rochester, Minn., 1957-63; gen., colon and rectal surgeon Lockwood Clinic, Toronto, 1963-65; founder and dir. colon and rectal residency program U. Ill. Med. Sch. and Carle Found. Hosp., Urbana, 1974-85; dir. dept. colon and rectal surgery Carle Clinic Assocs., Urbana, Ill., 1974-85; clin. assoc. Sch. Basic Med. Scis., U. Ill., Urbana, 1973-77; clin. asst. prof. Coll. Medicine, U. Ill., Urbana-Champaign, 1975-78, clin. assoc. prof., 1978-85; prof. clin. nutrition, dept. food sci. U. Ill., Urbana, 1981-85; practice medicine specializing in colon and rectal surgery Chattanooga, 1985—. Vice chmn. Residency Rev. Bd. in Colon and Rectal Surgery, 1980-82; active Am. Bd. Med. Specialties, 1979-84; mem. interspecialty bd. AMA, Chgo., 1974-80 Assoc. editor Diseases of the Colon and Rectum Jour., 1978—; contbr. chpt. to book, numerous articles to profl. publs.; inventor Thow tube, Colovage operative irrigation tube. Cmty. coord. Urbana conv. Inter-Varsity Christian Fellowship, Ill., 1967-84. Recipient Med. Edn. award Carle Found., 1982 Fellow Royal Coll Surgeons (Can.) (cert. 1963), ACS (credentials com. 1980-82); mem. Priestley Surg. Soc., Mid-West Colon and Rectal Surg. Soc. (pres. 1985-86), Can. Assn. Gen. Surgeons, Am. Bd. of Colon and Rectal Surgery (chmn. exam. com.1980-83, pres. 1983-84, adv. coun. 1989), Soc. Surgery Alimentary Tract, Am. Cancer Soc. (pres. Champaign County unit 1975-77, Ill. Top Ten award 1973-74), United Ostomy Assn. (founding mem. Champaign-Urbana chpt.) Presbyterian. Address: PO Box 1350 Bend OR 97709-1350

THOW, JOHN H. music educator, composer; b. L.A., Oct. 6, 1949; s. George H. and Marie (Dykes) T.; m. Margaret Wait, June 24, 1971; children: Diana Corinna, Caroline Miranda. BMus in Composition magna cum laude, U. So. Calif., 1971; MA in Music Composition, Harvard U., 1973, PhD in Music Composition, 1977; diploma d'onore (Composition), Accademia Musicale Chigiana, Siena, Italy, 1974. Asst. prof. music theory and composition Boston U. Sch. for the Arts, 1978-80; asst. prof. in music composition U. Calif. Dept. Music, Berkeley, 1981-86, assoc. prof., 1986-90, prof., 1990—. Composer: Madrone (Bklyn. Philharm. commn. 1987), Image Double & Envoi, All Hallows, 1982 (NEA rec. grant 1983, Boston Musica Viva/New Eng. Found. for the Arts Commn. 1981), Breath of the Sun, 1993, Seven Charms for a New Day, Canto del Quetzal, Chinese Poems, Divergences, Trombone Concerto, Songs for the Earth, 1994 (Am. Acad. award 1994), Into the Twilight, 1988 (San Francisco Symphony commn. 1988), Trigon, 1974 (Debut Orchesta award 1976), Live Oak (Musical Elements N.Y. commn. 1983), Trilce, 1992, To Invoke the Clouds (award Nat. Flute Assn. 1997), Cantico, 1998; recs. include Neuma, Music and Arts, Cantilena. Guggenheim fellowship Guggenheim Fdn., 1986, Djerassi Fdn. fellowships, 1986, 87, Regents Jr. Faculty fellowship U. Calif., 1983, Goddard Lieberson fellowship Am. Acad. and Inst. of Arts and Letters, 1983, Dorland Mountain Colony fellow, 1981, Yaddo fellowships, 1976, 1980, John Knowles Paine Travelling fellowship (Harvard), 1976-77, Fulbright Grad. fellowship to Italy, 1973-74; Margaret Jory Fairbanks Copying Assistance grants (The Am. Music Ctr.), 1978, 92, Meet the Composer grants, 1980, 82, 86, 87, 92, 95; Acad. award in Music Composition AAAL, 1994, Newly Published Music award Nat. Flute Assn., 1997. Fellow Am. Academy in Rome (Rome Prize fellowship 1977); mem. BMI, Am. Music Ctr., Am. Composers Forum. Home: 1045 Ordway St Albany CA 94706-2522 Office: Univ of Calif-Berkeley Dept Music 208 Morrison Hl Berkeley CA 94720-0001

THOYER, JUDITH REINHARDT, lawyer; b. Mt. Vernon, N.Y., July 29, 1940; d. Edgar Allen and Florence (Mayer) Reinhardt; m. Michael E. Thoyer, June 30, 1963; children: Erinn Thoyer Rhodes, Michael John. AB with honors, U. Mich., 1961; LLB summa cum laude, Columbia U., 1965. Bar: N.Y. 1966, D.C. 1984. Law libr. U. Ghana, Accra, Africa, 1963-64; assoc. Paul, Weiss, Rifkind, Wharton & Garrison, N.Y.C., 1966-75, ptnr., 1975—. Mem. TriBar Opinion Com., 1995—. Bd. visitors Law Sch. Columbia U., N.Y.C., 1991—; bd. dirs. Women's Action Alliance, N.Y.C., 1975-89, pro bono counsel, 1975-97; mem. Women's Coun. Dem. Senatorial, campaign com., 1993-97; organizing com. Alumnae Columbia Law Sch., 1996—. Recipient medal for excellence, Columbia Law Sch., 2003. Mem. N.Y. County Lawyers Assn. (mem. securities and exchs. com. 1976-98), Assn. of Bar of City of N.Y. (mem. securities regulation com. 1976-79, mem. recruitment of lawyers com. 1980-82, mem. com. on mergers, acquisitions and corp. control contests 1996—). Home: 1115 5th Ave Apt 3B New York NY 10128-0100 Office: Paul Weiss Rifkind Et Al 1285 Ave of Americas New York NY 10019-6028

THRALL, ARTHUR ALVIN, artist, educator; b. Milw., Mar. 18, 1926; s. Irving and Helen (Fabich) T.; m. Winifred Rogers, 1960; children: Grant, Wade, Sara, Jay. BS, Milw. State Tchrs. Coll., 1950; MS, U. Wis., Milw., 1954; postgrad. (fellow), U. Ill., 1954-55. Tchr. art Lincoln Jr. High Sch., Kenosha, Wis., 1951-54; asst. prof. SUNY, Geneseo, 1955-56; assoc. prof. Milw.-Downer Coll., 1956-64; prof., Farrar-Marrs prof. fine arts Lawrence U., Appleton, Wis., 1964-90, prof. emeritus, 1990—. One-man shows include Smithsonian Instn., 1960, U. Dubuque, Iowa, 1993, Mt. Mary Coll., Milw., 1994, St. Norbert Coll, De Pere, Wis., 1995, Cardinal Stritch U., Milw., 1998, also others; group shows include Corcoran bienials, Washington, 1951, 53, 55, 57, 62, Bklyn. Mus. annuals, Mus. Modern Art, N.Y.C., NAD, N.Y.C, Audubon Artists, N.Y.C., 1985, S.A.G.A., N.Y.C., 1985, Charles Allis Art Mus., Milw., 1996, Miller Art Ctr., Sturgeon Bay, Wis., 1997, Elvehem Mus. Art, Madison, Wis., 1998, 99, Fairfield Gallery, Sturgeon Bay, Wis., 2001; represented in permanent collections Tate Gallery, Victoria and Alberta Mus., Brit. Mus., all London, Phila. Mus., Seattle Mus., Art Inst. Chgo., Bklyn. Mus., others. Served with U.S. Army, 1944-46, ETO. Recipient Bklyn. Mus. print awards 1952, 64; Pa. Acad. Arts award 1960; NAD awards 1956, 68); Louis Comfort Tiffany fellow, 1963 Mem. AAUP, Boston Printmakers (awards 1963, 65), Soc. Am. Graphic Artists (awards 1951, 52, 60, 78, 2000), Audubon Artists Inc. (award 1977). Home: 4225 N Woodburn St Milwaukee WI 53211-1504

THRALL, EILEEN FOWLER, real estate broker, government staff official; b. Washington, July 20, 1943; d. Edward Earl and Violet Wells (Ashford) Fowler; m. William Anthony Thrall, Feb. 2, 1963; children: James Edward, Jennifer Dianne, John Joseph. AS in Bus. Adminstrn., Am. U., 1964; BSBA, George Mason U., 1985. Cert. real estate broker. Girl Friday property mgmt. rental cashier The Carey Winston, Co., Washington, 1964-65; adminstrv. asst., asst. rental mgr. Reston, Va., Inc., 1965-67; cmty. columnist Potomac News, Woodbridge, Va., 1981-85; realtor, salesperson Old Mill Properties ERA Tatum, Inc., Prince William, Va., 1985-92; realtor, assoc. broker ERA Tatum, Inc., Better Homes Realty, Prince William, 1992—; asst. to chmn. bd., county supr. Prince William County Govt., Prince William, 1992-99. Bd. dirs. Prince William County Pub. Schs., 1991-92; mem. magisterial dist. chair Prince William County Dem. Com., 1975-2001; mem. steering com. No. Va. C.C. Tech. Consortium, Woodbridge, Va., 1991-98; mem. various offices Dumfries Meth. Ch., 1977—; mem. Bd. Zoning Appeals, 2002-, Prince William. Mem. Nat. Assn. Realtors, Va. Assn. Realtors, Prince William Assn. Realtors. Democrat. Methodist. Avocations: reading, bicycling, boating, camping, cooking. Home: 18312 Possum Point Rd Dumfries VA 22026-2817 Office: Better Homes Realty Inc 16150 Country Club Dr Dumfries VA 22026-1633

THRALL, GORDON FISH, publishing executive; b. Jamestown, N.Y., July 28, 1923; s. Clyde Lowell and Beulah Mae (Fish) T.; m. Betty Jane Roberts, Sept. 24, 1964; 1 dau., Jenifer Jane. A.B. in History and Polit. Sci., Alfred U., 1949; J.D., Baylor U., 1953. Bar: Tex. 1953, U.S. Supreme Ct. 1957, D.C. 1958, U.S. Ct. Appeals (D.C. cir.) 1958, U.S. Ct. Mil. Appeals 1958, U.S. Dist. Ct. (ea. dist.) Tex. 1976, U.S. Ct. Appeals (5th cir.) 1986. Law clk. U.S. Dist. Ct. (ea. dist.) Tex., 1953-54; asst. prosecutor Dallas County Dist. Atty., 1954-55; assoc. firm Phinney & Hallman, Dallas, 1955-56; asst. Tex. Atty. Gen., 1957; adviser, examiner ICC, Washington, 1957-59; asst. gen. counsel Tex. State Bar, Austin, 1959-61; county atty. Reagan County, Big Lake, Tex., 1961-72; ptnr. Norman, Thrall, Angle, Guy & Day, L.L.P., Jacksonville, Tex., 1972—2002; v.p. Heflin & Thrall Lang. Publs., Inc., 2002-- . Mem. exec. com. Tex. Baptist Gen. Conv., 1965-70, adminstrv. bd., 1991-95; deacon So. Bapt. Ch.; chmn. Permian Basin dist. Concho Valley council Boy Scouts Am., Big Lake, 1965-66; chmn. Jacksonville United Fund Drive, 1987, pres., 1989; pres. Cherokee County Health Facilities Devel. Corp., 1982—; v.p., bd. dirs. Travis Towers Retirement Facility, Jacksonville, 1980-2003; co-trustee Summers A. Norman Found., 1988-2002; mem. Nan Travis Meml. Hosp. Found. Bd., 1994—; pres. bd. visitors Jacksonville Coll., 1998—2003. Mem. Tex. State Bar, Tex. Bar Found. (vice chmn. UPL com. 1964), Big Lake C. of C. (pres. 1963, 67), Jacksonville C. of C. (pres. 1979), Cherokee Country Club, (dir. 1981-83), Kiwanis (pres. 1978, lt. gov. div. 34 1982), Big Lake Lions (pres. 1969), Masons (32 degree). Republican. Home: 702 Fort Worth St Jacksonville TX 75766-2610 Office: Heflin and Thrall Lang Publs Inc PO Box 1724 Jacksonville TX 75766 Business E-Mail: jheflin@language-publications.com.

THRALL, RICHARD CAMERON, JR., broadcasting executive; b. Delaware, Ohio, Nov. 13, 1929; s. Richard Cameron and Pauline (Taylor) T.; m. Nancy Burrows, June 7, 1952 (div. Jan. 1962); children: Vallerie E. Alm, Cynthia L. Graser; m. Shirley Annette Sturgeon, Oct. 6, 1962; children: Laurie Jo Woodward, James W. Hochberg. BA, Miami U., Oxford, Ohio, 1951. Producer, dir. Sta. WBNS-TV, Columbus, Ohio, 1951-57, Sta. KDKA-TV, Pitts., 1957-59, pub. affairs dir., 1959-63, asst. program dir., 1963-67; program mgr. Sta. WLWC, Columbus, 1967-68; mgr. corp. TV Avco Broadcasting, Cin., 1968-70, mgr. TV programming, 1970-76; v.p. programming Multimedia Broadcasting., Cin., 1976-82; sr. v.p. Multimedia Entertainment, Cin., 1982-84; sr. v.p., gen. mgr. Multimedia Entertainment of Tenn., Nashville, 1984-88; sr. v.p. ops. and adminstrn. Multimedia Entertainment, N.Y.C., 1988-94, sr. v.p. programming, 1994-96; ret., 1996. Freelance prodr., writer, program cons., 1996—. Writer numerous TV scripts and songs. Served with USN, 1947-48. Recipient Outstanding Country Special award Music City News, Nashville, 1983-87; named to Hon. Order Ky. Cols. Mem. Country Music Assn., NATAS (pres. Columbus/Dayton/Cin. chpt. 1980-83, bd. govs. 1985-87, chmn. nat. awards com. 1989-2002, winner regional Emmys and Emmy cert.). Congregationalist. Avocations: fishing, boating, skiing, travel.

THRASH, PATRICIA ANN, educational association administrator; b. Grenada, Miss., May 4, 1929; d. Lewis Edgar and Weaver (Betts) T. BS, Delta State Coll., 1950; MA, Northwestern U., 1953, PhD, 1959; cert. Inst. Edn. Mgmt., Harvard U., 1983; EdD (hon.), Vincennes U., 1997; DHL, Drake U., 1997, Adrian Coll., 1998. Tchr. high sch. English, Clarksdale, Miss., 1950-52; head resident Northwestern U., 1953-55, asst. to dean women, 1955-58, asst. dean women, 1958-60, lectr. edn., 1959-65, dean women, 1960-69, assoc. prof. edn., 1965-72, assoc. dean students, 1969-71; asst. exec. sec. Commn. on Instns. Higher Edn., North Central Assn. Colls. and Schs., 1972-73, assoc. exec. dir., 1973-76, assoc. dir., 1976-87, exec. dir., 1988-96; exec. dir. emeritus, 1997—. Mem. adv. panel Am. Coun. on Edn., MIVER program evaluation mil. base program, 1991-94; mem. nat. adv. panel Nat. Ctr. Postsecondary Tchg., Learning & Assessment, 1991-95. Author (with others): Handbook of College and University Administration, 1970; editor Jour. Northwestern U. Inst. for Learning in Retirement, 2000-02; contbr. articles to ednl. jours. Bd. dirs. Delta State U. Found., 2000-2002. Mem. Nat. Assn. Women Deans and Counselors (v.p. 1967-69, pres. 1972-73), Ill. Assn. Women Deans and Counselors (sec. 1961-63, pres. 1964-66), Am. Coll. Pers. Assn. (editl. bd. jour. 1971-74), Coun. Student Pers. Assns. in Higher Edn. (program nominations com. 1974-75, adv. panel Am. Coll. Testing Coll. Outcome Measures project 1977-78, staff Coun. on Postsecondary Accreditation project for evaluation nontraditional edn. 1977-78, mem. editl. bd. Jour. Higher Edn. 1975-80, guest editor Mar.-Apr. 1979, co-editor NCA Quar. 1988-96, vice-chair regional accrediting dirs. group 1993, exec. com. Nat. Policy Bd. for Higher Edn. Inst. 1993-95), Mortar Bd. (hon.), Phi Delta Theta, Pi Lambda Theta, Alpha Psi Omega, Alpha Lambda Delta. Methodist. Home: 2337 Hartrey Ave Evanston IL 60201-2552

THRASHER, DIANNE ELIZABETH, mathematics educator, computer consultant; b. Brockton, Mass., July 11, 1945; m. George Thomas Thrasher, Jan. 28, 1967; children: Kimberly Elizabeth, Noelle Elizabeth. BA in Math., Bridgewater State Coll., 1967, post grad in computer sci., 1987. Cert.

secondary math., history tchr. Tchr. math. Plymouth/Carver Regional Schs., Plymouth, Mass., 1976-78, Alden Sch., Duxbury, Mass., 1980-82, Marshfield (Mass.) H.S., 1982-84; computer cons. TC2I-Thrasher Computer Cons. and Instrn., Duxbury, Mass., 1988—; dir., owner Internat. Ednl. Franchise, 1991-95; owner Duxbury Math. Ctr. K-Adult, 1995—. Owner New Eng. Regional Kumon Ednl. Franchise, 1991-95, 2000—; Mass. State approved profl. point devel. provider for tchr. cert., 1996. Active U.S. Figure Skating Assn., Colorado Springs, 1978-85; 2d reader First Ch. Christ Scientist, Plymouth, 1971-73; bd. govs. Skating Club of Hingham, Mass., 1978-85, pres., 1983-85, dir. Learn to Skate program, 1983-85; mem. First Ch. Christ Scientist, Boston, 1964—; with New Eng. Regional Kumon Franchise Owners, 1991-95; charter mem. Nat. Adv. Coun. of the U.S. Navy Meml. Found., 1992, Mary Baker Eddy Libr. for the Betterment of Humanity, Boston, 2002. Recipient Presdl. Nomination for Excellence in Tng. Math., NSF, 1992, Ed Taylor Meml. Vol. Svc. award Skating Club Hingham, 1995, Amateur Photo award Internat. Libr. Photography, 1999. Mem. NAFE, AAUW, Math. Assn. Am., Am. Math. Soc., Am. Nat. Coun. Tchrs. Math, Duxbury Bus. Assn., Bostonian Soc., Nat. Hist. Trust and Preservation Soc., Smithsonian, Internat. Soc. Photographers (Amateur Photo award 1999). Avocations: antiques, bicycling, skating, sailing. Home: 140 Toby Garden St Duxbury MA 02332-4945 E-mail: sumizumi@aol.com.

THRASHER, FAY C. clinical psychologist; b. Wynne, Ark., Dec. 17, 1935; d. Andrew J. and Joy M. (Charles) Thrasher; children: Jeffrey K. Mitchell, Sidney J. Guidroz Jr. MEd, McNeese State U., 1963; MA, La. State U., 1967, PhD, 1970. Lic. psychologist. Chief psychologist Cmty. Mental Health, Lake Charles, La., 1970-73; clin. psychologist VA Hosp., Salisbury, N.C., 1973-76; chief psychologist VA Opt Clinic, San Antonio, 1976-77, Alvin C. York VA Med. Ctr., Murfreesboro, Tenn., 1977-87; clin. psychologist VA Med. Ctr., Alexandria, Va., 1990-95, chief psychologist, 1995—. Bd. dirs. Oasis Ministry, Pineville, La.; cons. to freedom cons., 1996—; bd. dirs. New Beginning Acad., Alexandria, treas., 1997—; cons. Bunkie Adolexcent Ctr., Bunkie Gen. Hosp., 1993—97. Chmn. Combined Fed. Campaign, Murfreesboro, 1985—86. Mem.: APA, Am. Coll. Forensic Examiners, Nat. Register. Avocations: duplicate bridge, antique collector, renovation of old homes, art, music. Home: 303 Rain Tree Pl Pineville LA 71360-5472 Office: Freedom Counseling Ctr 2809 Donahue Ferry Rd Pineville LA 71360-4513 Office Phone: 318-473-0010 x 2626.

THRASHER, JACK DWAYNE, toxicologist, researcher, consultant; b. Nashville, Kans., Aug. 13, 1936; s. Harold A. and Margaret E. (Bolin) T.; m. Diane L. Walton, June 29, 1963; children: Traci L., Kristen I. BS, Longbeach State U., 1959; PhD, UCLA, 1964. Asst. prof. U. of Colo. Sch. of Medicine, Denver, 1964-66, UCLA Sch. of Medicine, L.A., 1966-72; application specialist Millipore Corp., Bedford, Mass., 1973-75; cons. Thrasher and Assocs., L.A., 1975-92, Alto, N.Mex., 1992-96; mem. faculty E. N. Mex. U., Ruidoso, 1992-97; mentor Columbia Pacific U., San Rafael, Calif., 1992-96. Bd. dirs., chmn. Internat. Inst. Rsch. for Chem. Hypersensitivity, Alto, N. Mex., 1991-94; advisor Chem. Impact Project Mill Valley, Calif., 1993—. Author: (books) Cellular and Molecular Renewal in the Mammalian Body, 1971, The Poisoning of our Homes and Work Places, 1990; editor-in-chief Informed Consent, 1993-94. Grantee: USPHS, NIH, 1966-69. Avocations: golf, fishing, wood working. Home and Office: Sam 1 Trust PO Box 874 110 Raven Court Alto NM 88312 Office Phone: 505-336-8317. Personal E-mail: sam1trust@zianet.com.

THRASHER, JACQUELINE F. elementary school educator; b. Detroit, Sept. 23, 1957; d. Homer E. Premil and Frances H. Litchford; m. John A. Thrasher, Jan. 5, 1980; children: Jason, Jessica. BMus in Instrumental Music Edn., Ariz. State U., 1979. Instrumental music tchr. Alhambra H.S., Phoenix, 1980, Washington Elem. Sch. Dist., Phoenix, 1980—. Flutist Ariz. Winds Concert Band, Glendale, Ariz., 1980—. Candidate Ariz. legis. dist. 10 State Ho. of Reps., Phoenix, 2002, 2004; precinct committeeperson Ariz. Dem. Party D-10, Phoenix, 2002—04. Mem.: Washington Dist. Edn. Assn. (bargaining chair 1998—), Music Educators Nat. Conf. Democrat. Lutheran. Avocation: reading. Home: 4537 W Park Pl Glendale AZ 85306

THRASHER, JOHN, lawyer, former state legislator; b. Columbia, S.C., Dec. 18, 1943; BS, Fla. State U., 1965, JD with honors, 1972. Bar: Fla. Mem. Fla. Ho. of Reps., 1992—2001; co-chmn. rules, resolutions and ethics com., 1996-97; mem. utilities and comms., edn. appropriations coms., 1996-97; mem. civil justice and claims, ednl. facilities coms., 1996-97; attorney Smith, Hulsey & Busey, 2001—. Chmn. Clay County Del., 1993; mem. com. Rep. Caucus Policy, 1992, 93; v.p. Govtl. Affairs Clay County C. of C., 1989, 91, 92; mem. sch. bd. Clay County, 1986-90, chmn. 1989-90, vice chmn., 1988; mem. adv. bd. Children's Haven, Quigley House, 1993-94; bd. dirs. Clay Police Athletic League, Clay YMCA. Capt. U.S. Army, 1966-70, Germany, Vietnam. Decorated Bronze Star with oak leaf cluster; recipient Raymond B. Stewart Gavel of Authority award, Fla. Assn. Sch. Adminstrs., 1994; named 1st term Legislator of Yr., Fla. Sch. Bd. Assn., 1993, Ho. of Reps. Legislator of Yr., 1994. Republican. Presbyterian. Avocations: golf, basketball. Office: Smith, Hulsey & Busey 225 Water St, Ste 1800 Jacksonville FL 32202

THRASHER, ROSE MARIE, critical care nurse, community health nurse; b. Urbana, Ohio, Jan. 19, 1948; d. Jesse and Anna Frances (Clark) T. Student, Mercy Med. Ctr. Sch. Med. Tech., Springfield, Ohio, 1966—67, Wittenberg U., 1969—70; BSN, Ohio State U., 1974, BA in Anthropology, 1994, BA in Art History, 1997, BA in Geography, 2002. RN, Ohio; bd. cert. cmty. health nurse ANA; cert. provider BCLS and ACLS, Am. Heart Assn., CCRN, AACN; cert. asthma mgmt. edn. Am. Lung Assn. Ohio. Pub. health nurse Columbus (Ohio) Health Dept., 1977-78; critical care nurse VA Med. Ctr., San Francisco, 1981, Staff Builders Health Care Svc., Oakland, Calif., 1975-76, 81-85; supr., case mgr., home health nurse, passport program and intermittent care program Interim Health Care (formerly Med. Pers. Pool), Columbus, 1976-77, 85—, chart reviewer, 1996-98; IRP nurse Ohio State U. Hosps. East, Columbus, 1999—2003; ind. home health nurse, provider med. svcs. State of Ohio Dept. Human Svcs., 1999—. Chart reviewer Interim Health Care Support Svcs., Columbus, 1997. Acad. scholar Wittenberg U., Ohio State U. Mem. AACN, ANA (coun. cmty. health nursing), AAUW, AAAS, Internat. Union Anthrop. and Ethnol. Scis., NY Acad. Scis., Ohio Nurses Assn., Intravenous Nurses Soc., Ohio State U. Alumni Assn., Am. Anthrop. Assn., Midwest Art History Soc., Coll. Art Assn., Nat. Mus. Women in Arts, Nat. Women's Hall of Fame, Ohio Acad. Sci., Ohio State U. Coll. of Nursing Alumni Soc. Personal E-mail: thrasher.2@osu.edu.

THRASHER, WARREN ATTICUS, JR., telecommunications executive; b. Ft. Benning, Ga., Dec. 3, 1946; s. Warren Atticus and Caroline Amanda Thrasher; m. Emily Harrison Short, June 15, 1969; children: Warren Dean, Emily Amanda. BA in Econs., U. Ga., 1969; MBA in Mgmt., Ga. State U., 1979. Gen. mgr., network staff BellSouth, Atlanta, 1985—87, ops. mgr. North Ga. divsn., 1987—90, dir. network strategic planning, 1990—92, dir. network tng., 1992—93; dir. tng. and edn. Bellcore, Lisle, Ill., 1994—95; sr. dir., bus. devel. Advance Tech. Corp., Naperville, Ill., 1995—96; v.p. local infrastructure and access mgmt. AT&T, Oakton, Va., 1996—98; pres. Thrasher Techs., Inc., Vienna, Va., 1998—2000; gen. mgr. Qwest, Ballston, Va., 2000—02; mgr. Midatlantic region divsn. AT&T, Washington, 2002—. Capt. U.S. Army, 1969-73. Decorated Bronze Star U.S. Army. Mem. IEEE (assoc.), Rotary (Paul Harris fellow). Republican. Episcopalian. Avocations: sailing, skiing, model trains, reading. Home: 1850 Brenthill Way Vienna VA 22182-2587

THREATTE, GREGORY ALLEN, pathology educator, academic director; b. Smithdale, Pa., Aug. 28, 1947; s. James Hilton T. and Thelma Elizabeth (Wilson) Youngblood; m. Stephanie Ruth Mills, May 13, 1948; children: Leah Ruth, Renee Ruth, Lonnie Taylor. BA, Colgate U., 1969; MD, SUNY, Upstate, 1973. Diplomate Am. Bd. Pathology. Intern U. Hosp., Syracuse, N.Y., 1973-74; resident in anatomic pathology W. Penn Hosp., Pitts., 1974-76; resident in clin. pathology U. Calif., San Francisco, 1976-78; fellow Lawrence Berkeley Lab, Berkeley, Calif., 1978-81; asst. prof. Georgetown U., Washington, 1981-86; assoc. prof. pathology SUNY Upstate Med. U., Syracuse, 1986-98, prof. pathology, 1998—, chmn., 2001—. Contbr. chpt. to book. Trustee Univ. United Meth. Ch., Syracuse, N.Y., 1990-98, Syracuse Urban League, 1990-95, Colgate U., 1993-2002. Recipient Pres. award Affirmative Action, 1992, Excellence in Tchg. award, 1998. Mem. Am. Assn. Clin. Chemistry, Coll. Am. Pathologists, Assn. Academic Minority Profs., Assn. Pathology Chairs. Methodist. Avocations: skiing, golf. Office: SUNY Upstate Med U 750 E Adams St Syracuse NY 13210-2306 E-mail: threatte@upstate.edu.

THREET, JACK CURTIS, oil company executive; b. Dundas, Ill., Aug. 16, 1928; s. Ivy Clemon and Daryl (Curtis) T.; m. Catherine Irene Hall, Mar. 24, 1951; children— Linda Sue, Judith Ann. BA in Geology, U. Ill., 1951. Geologist, dist. geologist, div. exploration mgr., area exploration mgr. Shell Oil Co., various locations including Oklahoma City, Amarillo, Tex., Denver, Pitts., Lafayette, La., Billings, Mont., N.Y.C., L.A., 1951-69; gen. mgr. exploration and prodn. Shell Australia Ltd., Melbourne, 1969-71; v.p. exploration and prodn. Shell Can., Calgary, 1972-74, Shell Oil Co., New Orleans, 1974-75, v.p. internat. exploration and prodn. Houston, 1975-78, corp. v.p. exploration, 1978-87, ret., 1987; v.p., dir., co-founder Energy Exploration Mgmt. Co., Houston, 1989-92; pres., owner Threet Energy, Inc., Houston, 1989—, Threet, Inc., Houston, 1995—. Served with U.S. Army, 1953-55. Mem. Am. Assn. Petroleum Geologists, Lakeside Country Club (Houston), Rotary. Republican. Methodist.

THRELKEL, ROBERT HAYS, pediatrician; b. Beaver Dam, Ky., June 20, 1940; s. Frank Hays and Kathryn Taylor (Bentley) T.; m. Mireille Clivas Smith, May 24, 1995. BA magna cum laude, Vanderbilt U., 1962; MD, Duke U., 1966. Diplomate Am. Bd. Pediatrics. Physician/officer U.S. Army, 1964-71; intern in pediatrics Vanderbilt U. Hosp., Nashville, 1966-67, chief resident in pediatrics, 1968-69; ptnr. Carithers, Threlkel et al., Jacksonville, Fla., 1971—; trustee Wolfson Childrens Hosp., 1997—. Chief of staff Wolfson's Children's Hosp., Jacksonville, 1991-92. Maj. U.S. Army, 1969-71. Mem. Am. Bd. Pediatrics (ofcl. examiner 1987-93), Am. Acad. Pediatrics (alt. dist. chmn. 1989-94, Fla. chpt. chmn. 1981-85), Duval County Med. Soc. (pres. 1984), Phi Beta Kappa, Alpha Omega Alpha. Office: Drs Carithers Threlkel PA 2121 Park St Jacksonville FL 32204-3811 Office Phone: 904-387-6200.

THRELKELD, RICHARD DAVIS, broadcast journalist; b. Cedar Rapids, Iowa, Nov. 30, 1937; s. Robert M. and Lou Jane (Davis) T.; m. Sharon A. Adams, June 11, 1960 (div. 1983); children: Susan Anne, Julia Lynn; m. Betsy Aaron, May 15, 1983. BA, Ripon Coll., 1959; MS in Journalism, Northwestern U., 1961; LHD (hon.), Ripon Coll., 1989. Editor Sta. WHAS-TV, Louisville, 1961; reporter Sta. WMT-TV, Cedar Rapids, Iowa, 1961-66; corr. CBS News, N.Y.C. and San Francisco, 1966-82, nat. corr., 1989-96; chief corr. ABC News N.Y., N.Y.C., 1982-89; Moscow corr. CBS News, 1996-98, ret., 1998. Author: Dispatches From the Former Evil Empire, 2001; corr.: TV news documentary Defense of America, 1981 (Emmy award); TV news report Rhodesia Remembered, 1980 (Overseas Press Club award), TV news report Vietnam Remembered, 1985 (Emmy award), TV news series Status Reports, 1984 (Dupont award), TV new report Lebanon-Grenada 1983 (Overseas Press Club award). CBS News fellow, 1964 Mem.: Soc. Profl. Journalists.

THRO, WILLIAM EUGENE, lawyer; b. Elizabethtown, Ky., Nov. 8, 1963; s. Ernest Guernsey and Joan (Young) T.; children: Sandra Lucinda Grace Edwards-Thro, William Thomas Daniel Edwards-Thro, Noah Christopher James Edwards-Thro.; m. Julie Urback, Sept. 04, 2004. BA, Hanover Coll., 1986; MA, U. Melbourne, Australia, 1988; JD, U. Va., 1990. Bar: Ky. 1990, Colo. 1991, Va. 1998, U.S. Dist. Ct. (we. dist.) Ky. 1990, U.S. Dist. Ct. Colo. 1991, U.S. Ct. Appeals (6th and 10th cirs.) 1991, U.S. Ct. Appeals (3d cir.) 1993, U.S. Supreme Ct. 1993, U.S. Ct. Appeals (4th cir.) 1997, U.S. Dist. Ct. (ea. dist.) Va. 1998, U.S. Dist. Ct. (we. dist.) Va. 1998, U.S. Ct. Appeals (D.C. cir.) 1999, U.S. Bankruptcy Ct. (ea. and we. dists.) Va. 1999, U.S. Dist. Ct. (ea. dist.) Ky. 2003, U.S. Dist. Ct. (no. dist.) Ill. 2003. Jud. clk. Judge Ronald E. Meredith, U.S. Dist. Ct. (we. dist.) Ky., Louisville, 1990-91; asst. atty. gen. State of Colo., Denver, 1991-97, Commonwealth of Va., Richmond, 1997-99; gen. counsel Christopher Newport U., Newport News, Va., 2000—04; dep. state solicitor gen. Commonwealth Va., 2002—04, state solicitor gen., 2004—. Mem. authors' com. West's Edn. Law Reporter, St. Paul, 1992—. Author: Why You Cannot Sue State U: A Guide to Sovereign Immunity, 2001; co-author: Race Conscious Admissions and Financial Aid After the University of Michigan Decisions, 2004; co-editor: The NACUA Handbook for Lawyers New to Higher Education, 2003; mem. editl. bd. Jour. Coll. and Univ. Law, 2000—; contbr. articles to scholarly jours. Gen. counsel adv. bd. NCAA, 2001—04. Recipient Best Brief award, Nat. Assn. of Atty. Gen., 2004, Hardin County Sch. Disting. Alumni award, 2004; scholar U.S. Senate Youth scholar, Hearst Found., 1982, Harry S Truman scholar, Truman Scholarship Found., 1984, Rotary Internat. Ambassadorial scholar, Melbourne, 1987. Mem. Va. Bar Assn., Ky. Bar Assn., Nat. Assn. Coll. and Univ. Attys., Federalist Soc., Nat. Eagle Scout Assn., Inst. for Justice, Human Human Action Network. Republican. Presbyterian. Office: Atty Gen 900 E Main St Richmond VA 23219 also: 100 Bucktail Run Yorktown VA 23692 Office Phone: 804-786-2436. Personal E-mail: wthro@alumni.virgina.edu.

THRODAHL, MARK CRANDALL, medical technology company executive; b. Charleston, W.Va., Mar. 31, 1951; s. Monte Cordon and Josephine (Crandall) T.; m. Sudie Kenton, Oct. 21, 1978; children: Mary Elizabeth, Anne Katherine, Andrew Kenton. AB, Princeton U., 1973; MBA, Harvard U., Boston, 1975. Various positions Mallinckrodt, Inc., St. Louis, 1975-88; dir. corp. planning Becton Dickinson & Co., Franklin Lakes, NJ, 1988-91, pres. Nippon Becton Dickinson Tokyo, 1991-94, sector pres. Franklin Lakes, 1994-95, sr. v.p., 1995-2001; CEO Bespak Plc, London, 2001—. Mem. Old Warson Country Club, Ivy Club. Republican. Episcopalian. Home: 38 Carteret Rd Allendale NJ 07401-1850 Office: Bespak Plc Blackhill Dr Wolverton Mill So Milton Keynes MK12 5TS England Business E-Mail: mark.throdahl@bespak.co.uk.

THRONER, GUY CHARLES, JR., engineering executive, scientist, engineer, inventor, consultant; b. Mpls., Sept. 14, 1919; s. Guy Charles and Marie (Zechar) T.; m. Jean Holt, Dec. 5, 1943; children— Richard, Carol Anne, Steven BA, Oberlin Coll., 1943; postgrad., UCLA, 1960, 61. Registered profl. engr., Calif. Br. head Naval Weapon Ctr., China Lake, Calif., 1946-53; mgr. ordnance div., mgr. weapon systems div. Aerojet Gen. Corp., Azusa, Calif., 1953-64; v.p., div. mgr. FMC Corp., San Jose, Calif., 1964-74; research dir. Vacu Blast Corp., Belmont, Calif., 1976-78; v.p., devel. mfg. Dahlman, Inc., Braham, Minn., 1978-79; mgr. ordnance systems & tech. Battelle Meml. Inst., Columbus, Ohio, 1979-85; pres. Guy C. Throner & Assocs., tech. and mgmt. cons., 1985—. Dir. Omron Corp. Am., Chgo., 1976-77 Inventor, patentee indls., med. and mil. systems design Served as officer USNR, World War II Recipient Am. Order St. Barbara medal U.S. Army Arty, 1983, IR-100 award Indsl. Research Mag., Chgo., 1971, Congl. Commendation, 1985, Commendation, State of Ohio Ho. of Reps., 1995, also various commendations Mem. AIAA, Am. Def. Preparedness Assn. (Bronze medal 1974, Simon Silver medal 1985), Lake Wildwood Country Club, Sigma Xi. Republican. Avocations: astronomy, photography, golf. Home and Office: 17992 Jayhawk Dr Penn Valley CA 95946-9205 E-mail: guyt@nccn.net.

THROWER, RANDOLPH WILLIAM, lawyer; b. Tampa, Fla., Sept. 5, 1913; s. Benjamin Key and Ora (Hammond) T.; m. Margaret Munroe, Feb. 2, 1939; children: Margaret MacCary, Patricia Barmeyer, Laura (Mrs. David T. Harris, Jr.), Randolph William, Mary (Mrs. George B. Wickham). Grad., Ga. Mil. Acad., 1930; BPh, Emory U., 1934, JD, 1936. Bar: Ga. bar 1935, D.C. bar 1953. Partner Sutherland, Asbill & Brennan, Atlanta, Washington, 1947-69, 71—. Commr. internal revenue, 1969-71; Lectr. bar, legal meetings; spl. agt. FBI, 1942-43; mem. Arthur Andersen & Co. Bd. of Rev., 1974-80, Nat. Council on Organized Crime, mem. exec. com., 1970-71 Past pres. Ga., Met. Atlanta mental health assns.; chmn. City of Atlanta Bd. Ethics 1981-93; past trustee Emory U., Clark Coll.; past chmn., trustee Wesleyan Coll.; bd. govs. Woodward Acad.; past chmn. bd. visitors Emory U. Served as capt. USMCR, 1944-45. Mem. Atlanta Legal Aid Soc. (past pres.), Emory U. Alumni Assn. (past pres.), ABA (chmn. spl. com. on survey local needs 1971-78, past chmn. sect. taxation, mem. ho. of dels. 1964-66, 74-89), Ga. Bar Assn., Atlanta Bar Assn. (past pres.), Am. Bar Found. (dir. 1980-88, pres. 1986-88, medal 1993), Am. Law Inst., Atlanta Lawyers Club (past pres.), U.S. Claims Ct. Bar Assn. (pres. 1987-88), Phi Delta Phi. Clubs: Commerce (Atlanta), Capital City (Atlanta), Piedmont Driving (Atlanta). Republican. Methodist. Home: 2240 Woodward Way NW Atlanta GA 30305-4043 Office: Sutherland Asbill & Brennan Ste 2300 999 Peachtree St NE Atlanta GA 30309 E-mail: rwthrower@sablaw.com.

THUEME, WILLIAM HAROLD, secondary school educator, travel coordinator; b. St. Clair, Mich., Sept. 4, 1945; s. Harold Arthur and Delphine Betty (Buhl) Thueme; m. Katheen Koning, May 8, 1971; children: Benjamin William, Rebecca Kathleen, Jeffery William, Sarah Kathleen; m. Nora Thueme (div. Sept. 1993). Student, Port Huron Jr. Coll., 1963-64; BA, Mich. State U., 1967, MA, 1969; PhD in Counseling, Progressive Universal Life Ch., 1993, PhD in Motivation, PhD in Paranormal Psychology, Progressive Universal Life Ch., 1997, PhD in Psychometrics, 1999; postgrad., Oakland U., 1971, San Francisco State U., 1975, U. Hawaii, 1975; student, Spring Arbor Coll., 1968; PhD in Reading Edn., U. Mich., 1977; PhD (hon.), Aspen U., 2003. Cert. tchr., Mich. Ordained min. Universal Life Ch. Tchr. pub. schs., Charlotte, Mich., 1967-69, Ann Arbor, Mich., 1969—. Fgn. travel coord.-Ambs. Abroad Program, Amsterdam, The Netherlands, 1968—; regional driver coord. for Southeastern Mich. Avis Rent-a-Car, 1983—. Active UN Children's Found., Mich. Sheriffs Ednl. Found., Woods Rd. Assn., Normal Pk. Neighborhood Assn., US Legal Found., Found. for Nicaraguan Democracy, Habitat for Humanity Internat. (charter), Carter Ctr., Nat. Coun. Better Edn., participant Skyhook II Project; elections coord. Eaton County (Mich.) Rep. Party, 1968, nat. com., 1968—, nat. senatorial com.; troop com. Coun. Boy Scouts Am., Ypsilanti, merit badge counselor, 1988-89, cub scout summer camp instr.; Internat., Incorp. (life mem.). Shore Nat. Network of Poet's Soc. Wolverne Coun., 1987; coach of the angels Ypsilanti Am. Little League, 1988; parent adv. bd. The Childrens Devel. Lab. Ea. Mich. U., 1988-89; active Mich. United Conservation Clubs, Big Bros. Am., Charlotte, Mich., Human Rights Watch, Nat. Security Caucus US, 1988—, Heritage Found., 1988—, ofcl. sponsor Mandate for Leadership III, Policy Strategies for 1990's Project, Project Save Our Schs., 1988—, Citizens United for Better Edn., World Awareness, Inc., Group 61 Amnesty Internat., Legal Affairs Coun., Coun. for Inter-Am. Security, Nicaraguan Resistance Edn. Found., Nat. Right to Work Legal Def. Found., Citizens Against Govt. Waste, Citizens Commn. for Ethics in Govt., Citizens for Decency Through Law, Inc., Nat. Consumers League, Participating Parents for Progress in Ypsilanti Pub. Schs.; parents adv. bd. Chapelle Elem. Sch., Ypsilanti, 1989-90, West Mid. Sch., Ypsilanti, 1991-92, Ypsilanti Pub. Schs., 1990—, Ypsilanti HS; charter sponsor Victory over Communism Project; nominated charter mem. Presdl. Task Force; participant Imperial Congress: Crisis in the Separation of Powers Project, line-item veto project Heritage Found., 1989, campaign to revise medicare catastrophic coverage law project Nat. Assn. Uniformed Svcs., 1989, repeal of catastrophic coverage act program Conservative Caucus Inc., 1989, Srs. Coal. Against the Tax, 1989; nat. adv. coun. Citizens Com. for Right to Bear Arms; jr. and sr. choir, Sunday sch. tchr. St. Paul's Luth. Ch., 1959-64 (Perfect Attendance award 8 yrs.), Marine city, Mich., 1960-63; youth Sunday sch. tchr., dir. youth min. coun. Lawrence Ave. Meth. Ch., Charlotte, Mich., 1967-69, life ELCA Evang. Luth. Ch. in Am., Treas. St. Paul's Luther League, 1960; assoc. mem. for Gentlemen of All Ages Second Amendment Sisters, 2003, Internat. Amb. Goodwill World Peace and Diplomacy Forum, founding cabinet, life mem., 2003, amb., 2004; senator seat for lifetime term World Nations Congress Recipient Spl. Recognition award Richard Nixon, 1968-79, Gerald Ford, 1974-76, Ronald Reagan, 1971-88, George Bush, 1988-92, Spl. Recognition award Reagan Presdl. Campaign, 1981, Bush Presdl. Campaign, 1988, Citizen of Yr. award Citizens Com. for Right to Bear Arms, 1988, cert. recognition US Justice Found., 1991, Hale Found., Am. Security Coun. 30th Anniversary Spl. Recognition cert., cert. appreciation 2d Amendment Found., 1988, Appreciation of Devoted and Valuable Svc. award Chapelle Elem. Sch., 1988-89, Merit Badge, Wolverine Coun.; Internat. Peace prize, United Cultural Conv., 2002, Outstanding contributions to Literacy, Edn., Humanitarians and Peace, 2002; letters from First Lady Nancy Reagan, First Lady Barbara Bush, Mich. Gov. John Engler, Nelson Mandella, Tchg. Excellence award, Cmty. Svc. award, Global Rels. award, 2002, others. Mem. NEA, NRA (life, endowment), Lincoln Inst. for Rsch. Edn., United Conservatives of Am. (participant citizens against the catastrophic health act tax 1989), Mich. Edn. Assn., Internat. Reading Assn., Mich. Sheriffs Assn. (assoc.), Police Marksmanship Assn., Washtenaw Reading Coun., Southeastern Mich. Reading Assn., Mich. Reading Assn., Mich. ASCD, Ann Arbor Edn. Assn., Am. Security Coun., Am. Def. Inst., Found. for Christian Living, Am. Family Assn., Nat. Geog. Soc., Am. Film Inst., Internat. Freelance Photographers Orgn. (life), Taxpayers Edn. Lobby, Gun Owners Am., Nat. Assn. Federally Lic. Firearms Dealers, Nat. Consumers League, Conservative Caucus, Inc., Ams. for Freedom, Tri-County Sportsman League, Mich. United Conservation Clubs, Mich. State U. Alumni Assn. (Blue Water chpt.), Mich. State U. Coll. Comm. Arts Alumni Assn., Mich. State U. Coll. Social Sci. Alumni Assn., Inventors Assistance League (life), Shore Nat. Network Poets Soc. (life), Ft. Gratiot, Lions Club (v.p. 1998—), Lions Club Internat., Washtenaw Sportsmen's Club (Ypsilanti), Internat. Optimist Club (v.p. Ann Arbor chpt., bd. dirs. 1975-78), Port Huron Noon Optimist Club, Judo Black Belt Fedn. Am., Sigma Alpha Eta. Lutheran. Office Phone: 800-381-5111.

THUESEN, GERALD JORGEN, industrial engineer, educator; b. Oklahoma City, July 20, 1938; s. Holger G. and Helen S. T.; m. Harriett M. Thuesen; children: Karen T. Hannah, Dyan T. Jacobus. BS, Stanford U., 1960, MS, 1961, PhD, 1968. Engr. Pacific Tel. Co., San Francisco, 1961-62, Atlantic Richfield Co., Dallas, 1962-63; asst. prof. indsl. engring. U. Tex., Arlington, 1963, 67-68; assoc. prof. indsl. and sys. engring. Ga. Inst. Tech., Atlanta, 1968-76, prof., 1976-96, prof. emeritus, 1996—. Author: Engineering Economy, 4th edit., 1971, 5th edit., 1977, 6th edit., 1984, 7th edit., 1989, 8th edit., 1993, 9th edit., 2001, Economic Decision Analysis, 1974, 2nd edit., 1980, 3rd edit., 1998; assoc. editor: The Engring. Economist, 1974-80, editor, 1981-91. NASA/Am. Soc. Engring. Edn. summer faculty fellow, 1970 Fellow Inst. Indsl. Engrs. (dept. editor Trans. 1976-80, v.p. publs. 1979-80, divsn. dir. 1978-80, Wellington award 1989, Publs. award 1990, bd. trustees 1979-81), Am. Soc. Engring. Edn. (bd. dirs. 1977-79, Eugene L. Grant award 1977, 91); mem. Sigma Xi. Office: Ga Inst Tech Sch Indsl & System Engring Atlanta GA 30332-0205

THUESON, DAVID OREL, pharmaceutical executive, researcher, writer, educator; b. Twin Falls, Idaho, May 9, 1947; s. Orel Grover and Shirley Jean (Archer) T.; m. Sherrie Linn Lowe, June 14, 1969; children: Sean, Kirsten, Eric, Ryan, Todd. BS, Brigham Young U., 1971; PhD, U. Utah, 1976. Postdoctoral fellow U. Tex. Med. Br., Galveston, 1976-77, asst. prof., 1977-82; sr. rsch. assoc. Parke-Davis Pharms., Ann Arbor, Mich., 1982-88; dir. pharmacology Immunetech Pharms., San Diego, 1988-90; dir. immunopharmacology Tanabe Rsch. Labs., San Diego, 1990-92; v.p. discovery Cosmederm Techs., San Diego, 1992-97. Contbr. articles to profl. jours.; patentee in field. Scout leader Boy Scouts Am., Mich., Tex. and Calif., 1979—. NIH grantee, 1978-81. Mem. Am. Acad. Allergy and Clin. Immunology, Am. Assn. Immunologists, Am. Thoracic Soc. Republican. Mem. Lds Ch. Avocations: water-skiing, tennis, scuba diving. Home: 1356 Winchester Ave Mckinleyville CA 95519-8801 Office: 2330 Central Ave Ste 3 Mckinleyville CA 95519-3696 Office Phone: 707-840-0623. Business E-Mail: thueson@reninet.com.

THULEAN, DONALD MYRON, symphony conductor; b. Wenatchee, Wash., June 24, 1929; s. Elmer Edward and Mary (Myron) T.; m. Meryl Mary Parnell, Mar. 17, 1951; children— Dorcas Marie, Mark Myron, William Norton. BA, U. Wash., 1950, MA in Music, 1952; Mus.D. (hon.), Whitworth Coll., 1967. Faculty Pacific U., 1955-62; dean Pacific U. (Sch. Music), 1957-62. Assoc. conductor Portland (Ore.) Symphony, 1961-62, conductor, music dir. Spokane Symphony, 1962-84; v.p. profl. and artistic svcs. Am. Symphony Orch. League, 1983-99, condr. emeritus, 1998—; asst. conductor Seattle Symphony, 1966-69, chorus master, Aspen Music Festival, 1957-61; artistic cons. Title III project in performing arts, Wash., 1966-68, music dir. Tamarack Music Festival, 1971. Bd. dirs. Seattle Symphony, 2000—, Seattle Youth Symphonies, 2002--; mem. vis. com. U. Wash. Sch. Music, 2000--. Served with AUS, 1953-55. Unitarian (trustee).

THULIN, ADELAIDE ANN, design company executive, interior designer; b. Chgo., Nov. 15, 1925; d. Martin Evold and Kathleen Marie (Glennon) Peterson; m. Frederick Adolph Thulin, Jr., Aug. 18, 1945; children: Frederick, Kristin, Mary, Margaret, Francis, Peter, Andrea, Charles, Joseph, Kathleen, James, Suzanne, Patricia. Student, Northwestern U., 1943—47; AA in Interior Design, Harper Coll., 1977. Registered interior designer. Asst. prodn. mgr. Cruttenden & Eger, Chgo., 1946; editor Mt. Prospect (Ill.) Independent, 1960; real estate salesperson Homefinders, Northwest Chgo. and suburbs, 1965, 69-70; asst. v.p. advt. Littelfuse, Des Plaines, Ill., 1966-67; owner, pres. Applied Design Assocs., Mt. Prospect, 1977—; ptnr., sec. Applied Design Internat. Ltd., Mt. Prospect, 1992—. Career day spkr. local high schs., 1982—; bd. dirs. Works subs. Pvt. Industry Coun. Author, editor monthly newsletter Women's Archtl. Legue, 1983-85, The Binnacle, CYC, 1979-81. Organizer, Mothers March of Dimes, Mt. Prospect, 1953-54, Vols. for Stevenson, 1952, 56, Citizens for Douglas, 1954, Citizens for Kennedy, 1960; mem. Fair Rev. Coun., Chgo., 1983-84; mem. 13th Congl. Dist. Dem. Women's Club, publicity chmn., 1957-58; mem. Chgo. Symphony Orch. Chorus, 1972; del. Ill. Statehouse Conf. on Small Bus., 1984, 85; bd. dirs. Arts Coun. Mt. Prospect, 1986-93l organizer Mt. Prospect chpt. Internat. Sister Cities Program; chmn. Mt. Prospect Sign Rev. Bd.; mem. renovation com. Mt. Prospect Hist. Soc., 1988—; pres. cmty. edn. coun. H.S. Dist. 214, 1994-96; bd. dirs. Cmty. Edn. Foun.; reader for print-handicpped CRIS RAdio, 1982-92. Mem. AIA (profl. affiliate Chgo. chpt.), Am. Women Internat. Understanding, Nat. Small Bus. United (bd. dirs., v.p. state govt. affairs 1994), Ill. Coalition for N.Am. Free Trade Agreement, Women's Archt. League (publicity chmn. 1964-65), Mt. Prospect C. of C., Chgo. Women in Arch., Soc. Design Adminstrn., Internat. Soc. Poets (disting.), Gamma Alpha Chi. Roman Catholic. Avocations: choral singing, poetry writing. Home: 4 S Owen St Mount Prospect IL 60056-3309 Office: Applied Design Assocs Ltd 800 E Northwest Hwy Mount Prospect IL 60056-3457 E-mail: appldzn@aol.com.

THULIN, INGE G. manufacturing executive; b. Sweden; Mng. dir., Russian markets 3M Co., v.p., skin health divsn., v.p., Europe and Middle East, 2002—03, exec. v.p., internat. opers., 2003—. Office: 3M Co 3M Ctr Saint Paul MN 55144

THULL, TOM, state representative; m. Shelley Thull. Pres. Ctrl. Nat. Bank, Newton, Kans.; mem. Kans. Ho. of Reps., 2003—. Democrat. Office: State Capitol Rm 302-S 300 SW 10th Ave Topeka KS 66612 Home: 300 Campus Ct North Newton KS 67117

THUMMEL, ROSA, artist; b. Des Moines, Apr. 17, 1916; d. Sposeto Frank and Victoria Jaquinta; m. John W. Thummel-Senneich (dec. Mar. 1988); children: Randolph, Carl, Gabriella Student, Drake U., U. Iowa. One woman shows include Swiss Ctr. Gallery, N.Y.C., 1975, Nat. Art Ctr., N.Y.C., 1979, Tosta Gallery, Coconut Grove, Fla., 1980-83, Corridor Gallery, Summit, N.J., 1981; exhibited in group shows at Montclair (N.J.) Pub. Libr., 1976, Summit Art Ctr., 1978, 80, 82 (Beth Born Portrait award 1978, Best in Show 1980, First prize 1982), Painters & Scultpers Soc., N.Y.C., 1976-79, N.J., 1980-83, Bergen County (N.J.) Artist Guild, 1980, Sheila Nussbaum Gallery, Millburn, N.J., Lever House, N.Y.C., 1984, others; represented in pvt. collections. Home: 72 Holton Ln Essex Fells NJ 07021-1709

THUNE, JOHN, former congressman; b. Murdo, S.D., Jan. 7, 1961; m. Kimberley Thune; children: Brittany, Larissa. BBA, MBA, U. S.D. Legis. asst. Senator James Abdnor, 1985-87; dep. staff dir. to the ranking rep. Senate Small Bus. Com., 1987-89; exec. dir. South Dakota Rep. Party, 1989-91; state railroad dir. Gov. George Mickelson, 1991-93; exec. dir. S.D. Mcpl. League, 1993-96; mem. U.S. Congress from S.D., 1997—2002. Mem. agr. com., transp. and infrastructure com., small bus. com. Republican. Avocations: basketball, pheasant hunting.

THURBER, JAMES A. political scientist, educator; PhD in Polit. Sci., Ind. U., 1974. Dir., founder Ctr. Congl. and Presdl. Studies, Washington, 1979—; dir., rsch. scientist Battelle Human Affairs Rsch. Centers (HARC), 1980—84; prin. investigator Study Improve Campaign Conduct Congl. and Presdl. Elections, 1997—2000, Study Improve Campaign Conduct in Congl. and Presdl. Elections, 2000—4. Expert witness U.S. Ho. Reps., Select Com. Homeland Security, Washington, 2003—03, U.S. Dept. Justice, U.S. Supreme Ct. case on BCRA, 2002—03; advisor US Congress, Joint Com. Orgn. Congress, 1994—95; expert witness US Ho. Rep., Com. Rules, 1994—95; U.S. rep. IAEA Tech. Com. Mgmt. and Orgn. Nuc. Power Plants, 1991—95. Author: A Tribute to the House Appropriations Committee, 1865 - 1995, 130 Years of History; co-author: Setting Course: A Congressional Management Guide, 7th edition; editor: Rivals for Power: Presidential-Congressional Relations, The Battle for Congress; co-editor: Campaigns and Elections American Style, 2nd Edition, Congress and the Internet, Campaign Warriors: Political Consultants in Elections, Crowded Airwaves: Campaign Advertising in Elections. Recipient Outstanding Rsch. and Publ. award, Sch. Pub. Affairs, Am. U., 1992, 1992; fellow, Am. Polit. Sci. Assn., 1968—69; grantee, US Dept. Energy, 1993—95, The Pew Charitable Trusts, 1997—2000; NSF fellow, Ind. U., 1968—69. Master: Assn. Ctrs. Study Congress (steering com. mem. and founder 2003); mem.: Ctrs. Congress Ind. U. (bd. dirs. 1999), U. Md., Campaign Assessment & Candidate Outreach Project (bd. dirs. 1999—2003), Am. Assn. Polit. Cons. (mem. com. ethics, founding mem., com. on profl. edu 2002—), Pi Sigma Alpha (nat. bd., chair 1992—98). Office: American University 4400 Massachusetts Ave NW Ward 109 Washington DC 20016-8130

THURBER, JOHN ALEXANDER, lawyer; b. Detroit, Nov. 9, 1939; s. John Levington and Mary Anne (D'Agostino) T.; m. Barbara Irene Brown, June 30, 1962; children: John Levington II, Sarah Jeanne. AB in History, U. Mich., 1962, JD, 1965. Bar: Ohio 1965, Mich. 1968. Assoc. Hahn, Loeser and Parks, Cleve., 1965-67, Miller, Canfield, Paddock and Stone, Birmingham, Mich., 1967-73; sr. mem. Miller, Canfield, Paddock and Stone, P.L.C., Troy, Mich., 1974—. Treas. Birmingham Community House, 1971-73; pres. Birmingham Village Players, 1983-84; bd. dirs. Oakland Parks Found., Pontiac, Mich., 1984—, pres., 1989-92; mem. capital com. Lighthouse Found.; trustee Oakland Land Conservancy. Avocations: reading, theater, walking, sports. Office: Miller Canfield Paddock & Stone PLC 840 W Long Lake Rd Ste 200 Troy MI 48098-6358 E-mail: thurberj@millercanfield.com.

THURBER, PETER PALMS, lawyer; b. Detroit, Mar. 23, 1928; s. Cleveland and Marie Louise (Palms) T.; m. Ellen Bodley Stites, Apr. 16, 1955; children: Edith Bodley, Jane Chenoweth, Thomas, Sarah Bartlett BA, Williams Coll., 1950; JD, Harvard U., 1953. Bar: Mich., 1954. With Miller, Canfield, Paddock and Stone, Detroit, 1953-93, of counsel, 1994—. Trustee McGregor Fund, Detroit, 1979-2003. Bd. dirs. Detroit Symphony Orch., Inc., 1974-93; trustee Community Found. for Southeastern Mich., 1990-2000, Cun. Mich. Founds., 1991-2000. With U.S. Army, 1953-55. Fellow Am. Bar Found.; mem. ABA, Mich. Bar Assn. Clubs: Country of Detroit (Grosse Pointe Farms, Mich.). Roman Catholic. Avocations: reading; traveling; athletics. Home: 28 Provencal Rd Grosse Pointe Farms MI 48236-3038 Office: Miller Canfield Paddock & Stone 150 W Jefferson Ave Ste 2500 Detroit MI 48226-4416

THURBER, ROBERT EUGENE, physiologist, researcher; b. Bayshore, N.Y., Oct. 11, 1932; s. Hallett Elliot and Mary Jean (Winkler) T.; m. Barbara Meyer, June 24, 1953 (div. 1982); children: Robert, Joseph, Karl, Michael; m. Linda Boyd, Mar. 4, 1984; stepchildren: Janet, Barbara, Karen, Robert. BS, Holy Cross Coll., Worcester, Mass., 1954; MS, Adelphi U., 1961; PhD, U. Kans., 1964. Rsch. assoc. Brookhaven Nat. Lab., Upton, N.Y., 1956-61; rsch. asst. Iowa State U., Ames, 1961-62; asst. prof. Med. Coll. Va., Richmond, 1964-69; assoc. prof. Jefferson Med. Coll., Phila., 1969-70; prof., chmn. physiology Sch. Medicine East Carolina, Greenville, N.C., 1970-94, prof., 1994—. Contbr. articles to profl. jours. Sgt. U.S. Army, 1954-56, Korea. Predoctoral fellow USPHS, 1962, postdoctoral fellow NEH, 1977. Mem. Am. Physiol. Soc., Assn. Chairmen Depts. Physiology (councilor 1989-91), Am. Heart Assn. (pres. N.C. affiliate 1979), Greenville Country Club, River Bend Country Club. Avocations: music, sailing. Home: 108 Hyde Ct New Bern NC 28562-3724 Office: E Carolina U Sch Medicine Dept Physiology Greenville NC 27858 E-mail: thurberr@mail.ecu.edu.

THURBER, TIMOTHY NELS, historian, educator; b. Kenosha, Wis., Aug. 28, 1967; s. Winton Elmore and Mary Alice Thurber; m. Gretchen Marie White, July 20, 1996. BA, Gustavus Adolphus Coll., 1989; MA, U. N.C., 1991, PhD, 1996. Asst. prof. History SUNY at Oswego, 1997—2001, assoc. prof. History, 2002—04; history prof. Va. Commonwealth Univ., Richmond, 2004—. Author: The Politics of Equality, 1998. Grantee, Lyndon B. Johnson Found., 1999, Harry Truman Found., 1998, Everett Dirksen Ctr., 1998. Mem.: Orgn. Am. Historians, Am. Hist. Assn. Home: 3712 Milbranch Pl Richmond VA 23233 Office: Dept History Stagg Ho 912 W Franklin St Richmond VA 23284

THURM, KEVIN L. bank executive; b. Brooklyn, Apr. 5, 1961; BA Tufts, 1983, MA Oxford, 1986, JD Harvard Law Sch., 1989. Assoc. Cahill, Gordon & Reindel, 1989—91; deputy sec. Dept. Health & Human Svcs, Washington, 1996—2000; first dir. strategic planning, consumer div. Citigroup, Inc., 2001—.

THURMAN, ANDREW EDWARD, lawyer; b. Raleigh, N.C., May 11, 1954; s. William Gentry and Peggy Lou (Brown) T.; m. Patricia Thurman, May 19, 1979 (dec. 1989); children: Gentry Brown, Harrison Beauchamp, Andrew Guilford; m. Tracy Fletcher, Nov. 16, 1991; 1 child, Spencer Lee. BA, Columbia U., 1976; JD, Coll. William and Mary, 1979; MPH, U. Okla., 1984. Bar: Va. 1979, Okla. 1980, U.S. Ct. Appeals (10th cir.) 1981, U.S. Supreme Ct. 1985, Pa. 1988. Staff atty. Dept. of Human Services, Oklahoma City, 1979-80; counsel State of Okla. Teaching Hosps., Oklahoma City, 1980-84; mem. Miller, Dollarhide, Dawson & Shaw, Oklahoma City, 1984-87; ptnr. Berkman, Ruslander, Pohl, Lieber & Engel, Pitts., 1988-89; of counsel Buchanan Ingersoll, Pitts., 1989; sr. v.p. and gen. counsel Forbes Health System, Pitts., 1989-96; sr. counsel Allegheny Health Edn. & Rsch. Found., Pitts., 1997-98; dep. gen. counsel Allegheny U. Hosps. West, 1998-99; asst. gen. counsel Western Pa. Allegheny Health Sys., 1999—2002; assoc. prof. Carnegie-Mellon U., 2000—; pvt. practice, 2002—; assoc. prof. U. Pitts., 2003—. Pres. Council of Neighborhood Assns., Oklahoma City, 1984, Lincoln Terr. Neighborhood Assn., Oklahoma City, 1984; trustee Rader Trust, Oklahoma City, 1980—; treas. Bd. dirs. State Okla. Tchg. Hosps. Found., Oklahoma City, 1984-87, Newman Meml. Hosp., 1983-87, Willowview Hosp., Spencer, Okla., 1985-87, Allegheny U. Med. Ctrs., 1997—, AUMC/Cannonsburg Ambulance Svc., 1997—, Allegheny U. Hosps. West, 1998—, Diversified Health Group, 1998-99, Allegheny Med. Practices Network, 1999—, Allegheny Speciality Practice Network, 1999—; chair HCWP Ethics Task Force, 1993-2000. Fellow Am. Health Lawyers Assn.; mem. St. Anthony Hall Club of N.Y.C. (pres. 1976), Rivers Club. Democrat. Presbyterian. Avocation: reading detective novels. Home: 106 Richmond Dr Pittsburgh PA 15215-1039 Office: 1151 Freeport Rd # 391 Pittsburgh PA 15238 E-mail: andy@thrumanhealthlaw.com., andy@thurmans.net.

THURMAN, CYNTHIA DENISE, human services administrator; b. Ft. Myers, Fla., Mar. 14, 1970; children: Asia Naikee Garcia, Jai'ya Ja'V-ae Armani. Grad. high sch. Residential care coord. Sandy Pk. Redevelopment Ctr., North Fort Myers, Fla., 2001—; human services worker Gulf Coast Ctr., Ft. Myers, 2003—. Author: (poems) Soon. Recipient Shakespare Trophy of Excellence, Famous Poets Soc., 2004. Home: 4926 Gary Dr Fort Myers FL 33905 Office: Gulf Coast Center 5820 Buckingham Rd Fort Myers FL 33905 Office Phone: 239-694-2151 226. Personal E-mail: cind33905@aol.com.

THURMAN, KAREN L. former congresswoman, lobbyist; b. Rapid City, S.D., Jan. 12, 1951; d. Lee Searle and Donna (Altfillisch) Loveland; m. John Patrick Thurman, 1973; children: McLin Searl and Liberty Lee. BA, U. Fla., 1973. Mem. Dunnellon City Coun. (Fla.), 1975—83; mayor of Dunnellon Dunnellon, 1979-81; mem. Monroe Regional Med. Ctr. Governancy Com., Comprehensive Plan Tech. Adv. Com., Fla. State Senate, 1983—93, U.S. Congress from 5th Fla. dist., 1993—2002, ways and means com ., 1996—2002, House agrl. comm., com. on gov. reform and oversight; lobbyist eAppeals, Miami, 2004—, Freedom Healthcare, Hollywood, 2004—. Del. Fla. Dem. Conv., Dem. Nat. Conv., 1980; mem. Regional Energy Action com. Recipient Svc. Above Self award Dunnellon C. of C., 1980, Regional Coun. Appreciation for Svc. award. Mem. Dunnellon C. of C. (dir.), Fla. Horseman's Children's Soc. (charter). Democrat. Episcopalian.

THURMAN, ROBERT, philosophy, religious studies educator; m. Nena von Schlebrugge. Co-founder Am. Inst. Buddhism, 1973—; founder Tibet House, N.Y., 1987—; scholar, activist, chair religion dept. Columbia U., N.Y.C., 1988—, prof. religion dept. Named One of the Most Influential Americans, Time Mag. Buddhist. Office: Columbia U 1140 Amsterdam Ave New York NY 10027-7003

THURMAN, UMA KARUNA, actress; b. Boston, Apr. 29, 1970; d. Robert and Nena (von Schlebrugge) T.; m. Gary Oldman, 1990 (div. 1992); m. Ethan Hawke, 1998; 2 children. Appeared in films Kaze no tani no Naushika, 1984, Kiss Daddy Good Night, 1987, Johnny Be Good, 1988, Dangerous Liaisons, 1988, The Adventures of Baron Munchausen, 1989, Where the Heart Is, 1990, Henry and June, 1990, Cheerleader Camp II, 1990, Final Analysis, 1992, Jennifer Eight, 1992, Mad Dog and Glory, 1993, Even Cowgirls Get the Blues, 1993, Pulp Fiction, 1994 (Acad. award nom. Best Supporting Actress), A Month By the Lake, 1995, The Truth About Cats and Dogs, 1996, Beautiful Girls, 1996, Les Miserables, 1997, The Avengers, 1997, Batman & Robin, 1997, Gattaca, 1997, Vatel, 1999, Sweet and Lowdown, 1999, Tape, 2001, Chelsea Walls, 2001, Kill Bill: Volume 1, 2003, Paycheck, 2003, Kill Bill: Volume 2, 2004; TV movies include Robin Hood, 1991, Duke of Groove, 1996, The Golden Bowl, 2000, Hysterical Blindness, 2002 (also exec. prodr.). Office: Creative Artists Agy care Brian Lourd 9830 Wilshire Blvd Beverly Hills CA 90212-1804*

THURMAN, VIRGIL LEON, voice educator; b. Knoxville, Tenn., Nov. 4, 1940; s. Virgil Lee and Marie Campbell T. BA, David Lipscomb Coll., Nashville, 1962; MS, U. Ill., Urban-Champagne, Ill., 1965, EdD, 1977. K-12 vocal music educator Harlan (Ky.) County Schs., 1962-64; 4-12 vocal music educator North Royalton (Ohio) City Schs., 1965-68; grad. teaching asst. U. Ill., Urbana-Champaign, Ill., 1968-70; chorister Norman Luboff Choir, N.Y.C., 1970-71; announcer WILL-AM & FM Pub. Radio, Urbana-Champaign, Ill., 1971-73, 76-78; asst. prof. voice, choral music, music edn. Yankton (S.D.) Coll., 1973-76; instr. voice and choral music MacPhail Ctr. for the Arts, Mpls., 1977-86; artist-in-residence Mpls. Pub. Schs., 1977-78; vocal advisor Minn. Boychoir, 1981-86; sole proprietor, ptnr., specialist voice educator The Voice Ctr., Mpls., 1986-95; specialist voice educator Fairview Voice Ctr. Fairview-Univ. Med. Ctr., Mpls., 1995—. Bd. dirs., pres. Minn. chpt. Nat. Assn. Tchrs. of Singing, 1980-81, 84-86; assoc. dir. Interdisciplinary Voice Colloquium, U. Minn., Mpls., 1981-84' voice dept. asst. coord. MacPhail Ctr. for the Arts U. Minn., 1982-86; founder, bd. dirs., prin. faculty The VoiceCare Network, 1982—; mem. adv. bd. Ctr. Advanced Studies Music Edn., U. Surrey Roehampton, London; guest presenter, Am. Choral Dirs. Assn., Music Educators Nat. Conf., Internat. Soc. for Music Edn., The Choristers Guild, Voice Found. Am., N.Y.C., Alberta Music Conf., Assn. for Prenatal and Perinatal Psychology and Health, Am. Orff-Schulwerk Assn., Assn. Can. Choral Condrs., Orgn. Am. Kodaly Educators, Suzuki Assn. of the Ams., Internat. Soc. for Prenatal and Perinatal Psychology and Medicine, Austria, 1986, voice symposium Brit. Voice Assn., 1989, European Coun. Internat. Schs., 1992, Festival 500: Sharing the Voices, St. Johns, Nfld., Can., 1997, 2003, Internat. Symposium: The Phenomenon of Singing, Meml. U. of Nfld., Can., 1997, 2003, interdisciplinary voice seminar Utah State U., 1999, Internat. Conf. Music Perception and Cognition, 2000, Minn. Music Tchrs. Assn., 2002, Choral Fest 2004, Nat. Choral Assn., Early Childhood Music & Movement Assoc., 2002; vis. instr. U. Ill., Roosevelt U., Chgo., Queensland State Schs., Australia, 1988, Middle Tenn. State U., U. St. Thomas, St. Paul, 1998, 2000, 02, 04, U. Hartford, 1991, 93, 94, U. Iowa, 1987, U. Nebr., 2001, U. Alta., 1998, U. Queensland and Queensland Conservatorium, 1988, Westminster Choir Coll., Princeton, N.J., N.D. State U., U. Nebr., 2001, Mt. Alison U., New Brunswick, Canada, 2003, Meml. U. Newfoundland, St. John's, 2003; edn. cons. Nat. Ctr. for Voice and Speech, 2003-. Author, co-editor: Bodymind and Voice: Foundations of Voice Education, 1997, 2000; contbr. articles to profl. jours.; mem. editl. bd. Internat. Jour. Rsch. in Choral Singing; guest conductor: Male Australian Nat. Honours Choir, 2004. Music dir., conductor Betty Marin Hobby Singers, Mpls., 1977-80, Skyway Singers, Mpls., 1983-87, Choral Soc. Tri-Cities, Cumberland, Benham, Lynch, Ky., 1962-64; dir., actor Royalton Players Cmty. Theatre, North Royalton, Ohio, 1965-68; chorister Cleve. Orchestra Chorus, 1965-67, Cleve. Orchestra Chamber Chorus, 1967. Mem. ASCD, AAAS, Actors Equity Assn., Am. Choral Dirs. Assn., Am. Choral Dirs. Assn. of Minn., Am. Guild of Musical Artists, Am. Fedn. TV and Radio Artists, Assn. Canadian Choral Condrs., Assn. for Prenatal and Perinatal Psychology and Health, European Soc. for Cognitive Scis. of Music, Internat. Music Soc. for Prenatal Devel., Internat. Soc. for Music Edn., Nat. Assn. of Tchrs. of Singing, May Day Group, Music Educators Nat. Conf., Music Tchrs. Nat. Assn., N.Y. Acad. Scis., The Schubert Club, Thursday Musical, Voice and Speech Trainers Assn., The VoiceCare Network. Avocations: walking, jogging. Office: Fairview Voice Ctr 2450 Riverside Ave Minneapolis MN 55454-1450 E-mail: lthurma1@fairview.org.

THURMON, THEODORE FRANCIS, medical educator; b. Baton Rouge, Oct. 20, 1937; s. Theodore Francis and Gertrude Wilhemena (Arnette) T.; m. Virginia Ruth Strange, Sept. 1, 1961 (div. Oct. 1975); children: Penelope, Suzanna; m. Susonne Annette Ursin, Aug. 8, 1981 (div. Aug. 1992); children: Sarah Eileen, Amanda Aislinn; m. Suzanne Greenwood, Sept. 2, 1992. BS, La. State U., Baton Rouge, 1960; MD, La. State U., New Orleans, 1962. Diplomate Am. Bd. Pediatrics, Am. Bd. Med. Genetics. Commd. ensign USNR, 1957; transferred to USN, 1957, advanced through grades to lt. comdr., 1967; intern naval hosp. Pensacola, Fla., 1962-63; resident in pediatrics naval hosp. Phila., 1963-65; trainee in cytogenetics St. Christopher's Hosp., 1964-65; asst. cardiology naval hosp. St. Albans, N.Y., 1965-67; resigned USN, 1968; fellow in med. genetics Johns Hopkins Hosp., Balt., 1968-69; asst. prof. La. State U. Med. Ctr., New Orleans, 1969-72, assoc. prof., 1972-78, prof., 1978-86, Shreveport, 1986—. Author: Rare Genetic Diseases, 1974, Medical Genetics Primer, 1995, A Comprehensive Primer on Medical Genetics, 1999; contbr. articles to med. jours. Active birth defects ctr. Nat. Found./March of Dimes, New Orleans, 1969-81, La. Bd. Regents, New Orleans, 1982, La. Dept. Health, New Orleans, 1984—, La. Cancer & Lung Trust Fund, New Orleans, 1985-86. Fellow Am. Coll. Med. Genetics, Am. Acad. Pediat.; mem. AAAS, Am. Soc. Human Genetics, Assn. Profs. Human or Med. Genetics, La. Med. Soc. Home: 1732 Willow Point Dr Shreveport LA 71119-4108 Office: La State U Med Sch Pediat-Genetics 1501 Kings Hwy Shreveport LA 71103-4228 Office Phone: 318-675-6083. Business E-Mail: tthurm@lsuhsc.edu.

THURMOND, GEORGE MURAT, judge; b. Del Rio, Tex., Oct. 22, 1930; s. Roger H. and Day (Hamilton) T.; m. Elsiejean Davis, June 27, 1959; children: Carolyn Day, Georganna, Sarah Gail. BA, U. of the South, 1952; JD, U. Tex., 1955. Bar: Tex. 1955. Ptnr. Montague & Thurmond, Del Rio, 1955-69; judge Tex. Dist. Ct. (63rd dist.), Del Rio, 1970-2000, sr. judge, 2000—. Presiding judge 6th Adminstrv. Region, Del Rio, 1983-87; chmn. jud. sect. State Bar Tex., 1988-89. Editor: U. Tex. Law Review, 1955. Rep. Tex. Ho. of Reps., 1955-58. Mem. ABA, Tex. Bar Assn. Democrat. Episcopalian. Avocations: jogging, traditional jazz, model railroading. E-mail: gmthur@delrio.com.

THURMOND, J. STROM, JR., lawyer; b. S.C., Oct. 18, 1972; BA in English, U. S.C., 1995, grad. in Law, 1998. Bar: S.C. Ptnr. Strom, Young & Thurmond, LLP, Columbia, SC, 1998—99; asst. solicitor S.C. 2d Jud. Cir., 1999—2001; U.S. atty. Dist. S.C., 2001—. Chmn. dist. law enforcement coordinating com. Dist. S.C., mem. atty. gen.'s adv. coun. violent crime subcom. Office: First Union Bldg 1441 Main St Ste 500 Columbia SC 29201

THURMOND, JOHN PETER, II, bank executive, rancher, archaeologist; b. Elk City, Okla., Apr. 22, 1955; s. Arthur Leslie and Dorothea Jean (Lee) Thurmond; m. Susan Ide Smith, June 7, 1979; children: Katherine Anne, Allison Lee, Patrick Andrew. BA, U. Tex., 1976, MA, 1979. Pres., chmn. First Nat. Bank Leedey, Okla., 1984-92, Leedey Bancorporation, Inc., 1984-92, Thurmond Ranch, Inc., Cheyenne, Okla., 1982—. Pres., chmn. Dempsey Divide Rsch. Found., Inc., 2001—; vis. rsch. assoc. Sam Noble Okla. Mus. Natural History, U. Okla., 2001—; vice chmn. 1st Nat. Bank & Trust Co., Elk City, 1992—. Author: Archeology of the Cypress Basin, NE Texas, 1981, Late Paleoindian Utilization of the Dempsey Divide, 1990. EMT, sec. Leedey Ambulance Svc., Inc., 1981—88. Recipient Hist. Preservation award, Okla. Hist. Soc., 1991, 1997, Goodyear Conservationist award, 2000. Mem.: Okla. Hist. Soc. (dir. we. chpt. 2004—), Okla. Cattlemen's Assn., Geol. Soc. Am., Am. Quaternary Assn., Plains Anthrop. Soc., Tex. Archeol. Soc., Okla. Anthrop. Soc. (sec., treas. 1988—, Disting. Svc. award 1999), Cum Laude Soc., Phi Beta Kappa, Phi Kappa Phi.

THURNER, ARTHUR W. historian, educator; b. Mich., Oct. 16, 1924; s. Joseph and Frances Pauline Thurner; m. Virginia Katherine Peterson, Sept. 27, 1958 (dec. Aug. 15, 1993). BA, U. Chgo., MA, 1954, PhD, 1965. Cert. tchr. Ill. Head dept. N.Am. Life Ins., Chgo., 1955—62; tchr. Chgo. Pub. Schs., 1962—65; prof. history DePaul U., 1965—89, prof. emeritus, 1989—. Author: Calumet Copper and People, 1975 (Mich. Hist. Soc. award, 75), Rebels on the Range, 1984, Strangers and Sojourners, 1994. Precinct judge Bd. Elections, Chgo., 1980—94. Grantee, Am. Philos. Soc., 1981—84, Wayne State U., 1991; Woodrow Wilson fellow, U. Chgo., 1964—65. Democrat. Roman Catholic. Avocations: reading, writing poetry and fiction, walking, swimming. Home: 1642 E 56th St Apt 920 Chicago IL 60637

THURNER, HENRY, retired writer; b. Ulm, Germany, Mar. 3, 1924; s. Charles and Charlotte Thurner; m. Trudy Cecilia Eder, Aug. 16, 1945; children: Claudia, Ritchie. BA cum laude, Syracuse U., Syracuse, NY, 1947—53. Counter intelligence agt. US War Dept., 1945—47; tech. writer / editor GE, Syracuse, NY, 1950—69. Author: (novels) The Man Who Knew God, GECKO, Rufus in Heaven, others. Sgt. US Army, 1946—50, France / Germany. Decorated Cert. of Appreciation Electronic Systems Divsn., Air Force Systems Command. Avocations: painting, wood carving, poetry.

THURSBY, JERRY GILBERT, economics educator, consultant; b. Camp Le Jeune, N.C., Aug. 6, 1947; s. Gilbert Earl and Mary Kathleen (Bailey) T.; m. Marie Sloan Currie, Mar. 11, 1972; children: James, Mary. AB, U. N.C., 1969, PhD, 1975. Asst. prof. Syracuse (N.Y.) U., 1975-78; from asst. to assoc. prof. Ohio State U., Columbus, 1978-88; prof. Purdue U., West Lafayette, Ind., 1988-01; prof. econs., chmn. dept. Emory U., Atlanta, 2001—. Contbr. articles to profl. jours. With U.S. Army, 1969-71. Home: 910 Springdale Rd NE Atlanta GA 30306-4620 Office: Emory U Dept Econs Rich Meml Bldg Atlanta GA 30322 E-mail: jthursb@emory.edu.

THURSFIELD, DAVID W. automotive executive; Plant mgr. Ford Motor Co., 1979—84, gen. mfg. mgr. and gen. ops. mgr. various locations in Europe, 1984—92, dir. body and assembly ops. Ford of Europe, mgr. vehicle ops. Ford automotive ops., 1996—98, v.p. vehicle ops. Ford automotive ops., 1998—2001, group v.p. internat. ops. and global purchasing, 2001, chmn., CEO, and pres. Ford of Europe, 2001—02, exec. v.p and pres. internat. ops. and global purchasing, 2002—. Office: Ford Motor Co One American Rd Dearborn MI 48126-1899

THURSFIELD, FRED FALCONER, II, foundation administrator; b. Rochester, NY, Mar. 13, 1950; s. Richard Emmons and Alice (Hedges) T.; m. Kathi Suzanne Heathcote, Jan. 22, 1972 (div. Dec. 1996); children: Amy Christine Humphreys, Jennifer Anne Thursfield; m. Sara Garland Barr, Sept. 2, 1997; 1 stepchild, Shelby Blair Oktar. BA, U. Md., 1972. Cert. fund raising exec. Sales rep. Life of Va. Ins. Co., 1972-78; dir. alumni fund Johns Hopkins Med. Instns., Balt., 1978-82; major gift officer, dir. acad. programs Duke U., Durham, NC, 1982-92, asst. dir. devel. Sch. Environ, 1992-94; dir. ann. and capital programs Geisinger Found., Danville, Pa., 1994-95; assoc. dir. devel. Washington Hosp. Found., 1995-97; exec. dir. Peninsula Regional Found.,

Salisbury, Md., 1997—2001, Health First Found., Melbourne, Fla., 2001—04, Upper Chesapeake Health Found., Inc., 2004—. Mem. coun. Wildlife Preservation Trust, Internat., 1994-99. Mem.: Assn. Healthcare Philanthropy (regional sec. treas. 1998—99, chair elect 1999—2000, chair 2000—01, mem. Brevard County Zoo bd. 2002—04), U. Md. Alumni Assn. and Terrapin Club, Rotary. Republican. Methodist. Avocations: golf, reading, philately, art. Home: 520 Upper Chesapeake Dr Bel Air MD 21014 Office Phone: 443-643-3460. E-mail: ffalconert@aol.com.

THURSTON, BONNIE BOWMAN, religious educator, minister, poet; b. Bluefield, W.Va., Oct. 5, 1952; d. Ernest Venoy and Eleanor Sabina (King) Thurston; m. Burton Bradford Thurston, May 29, 1980 (dec. Nov. 1990). BA summa cum laude, Bethany Coll., 1974; MA, U. Va., 1975, PhD, 1979; postgrad., Harvard Div. Sch., 1983, Eberhard Karls U., Germany, 1983—84, Ecole Biblique, Jerusalem, 1993. Ordianed to ministry Disciples of Christ Ch., 1984. Instr., asst. dean U. Va., Charlottesville, 1979—80; adj. prof. Wheeling Coll. (now Wheeling Jesuit U.), W.Va., 1980—81, assoc. prof., chair dept. theology, 1985—95; asst. prof. Bethany Coll., W.Va., 1981—83; assoc. prof. N.T. Pitts. Theol. Sem., 1995—99, William F. Orr prof., chair, 1999—2002. Vis. scholar Harvard U. Div. Sch., Cambridge, Mass., 1983; tutor Inst. Study of Christian Origins, Tubingen, Germany, 1983—85; lectr. Sch. Religion Coun. of Chs., Wheeling, W.Va., 1980—81, Wheeling, 1985—90. Author: (books) The Widows, 1989, Wait Here and Watch, 1989, Spiritual Life in the Early Church, 1993, Women in the NT, 1998, To Everything a Season, 1999, Preaching Mark, 2002, (books of poetry) The Heart's Land, 2001, Hints and Glimpses, 2004; assoc. editor Cath. Biblical Quarterly; contbr. articles to profl. jours., poetry to jours. Mem.: Disciples Hist. Soc., Soc. for Buddhist-Christian Studies, Internat. Thomas Merton Soc. (bd. dirs.), Soc. Bibl. Lit., Cath. Bibl. Assn. Avocations: gardening, music, cooking. Office: PO Box 2258 Wheeling WV 26003

THURSTON, DONALD ALLEN, broadcast executive; b. Gloucester, Mass., Apr. 2, 1930; s. Joseph Allen and Helen Ruth (Leach) T.; m. Oralie Alice Lane, Sept. 9, 1951; children: Corydon Leach, Carolie Lane. Grad., Mass. Radio and Telegraph, 1949; HHD (hon.), North Adams (Mass.) State Coll., 1977; LHD (hon.), Emerson Coll., 1995. Announcer, engr. Sta. WTWN, St. Johnsbury, Vt., 1949-52; v.p., gen. mgr. Sta. WIKE, Newport, Vt., 1952-60; v.p., treas., gen. mgr. Sta. WMNB, North Adams, 1960-66; pres., treas. Berkshire Broadcasting Co., Inc., North Adams, 1966—2003. Bd. dirs. Broadcast Capital Fund, Inc., 1980-96, chmn. bd., 1981-89; bd. dirs. Broadcast Music, Inc., N.Y.C., 1990—, chmn. bd., 1994-97. Pres. No. Berkshire Indsl. Devel. Corp., 1965-67; commr. Mass. Cmty. Antenna TV Commn., 1972-74; trustee Mass. Coll. Liberal Arts, 1991-2000, vice chmn. bd. trustees, 1993-96, chmn., 1996-2001. Recipient Laymen's award Vt. Tchrs. Assn., 1958; Laymen's award Mass. Tchrs. Assn., 1962; Abe Lincoln Merit award So. Baptist Radio and TV Commn., 1975; named Man of Yr. Vt. Assn. Broadcasters, 1978 Mem. North Adams C. of C. (Hayden award 1967, pres. 1964-67), Nat. Assn. Broadcasters (dir. 1965-69, 73-77, chmn. radio 1976-77, chmn. bd., chmn. exec. com. 1977-79, Disting. Svc. award 1980), Mass. Broadcasters Assn. (pres. 1964, Disting. Svc. award 1964, 71, 78), Taconic Golf Club (Williamston, Mass.; bd. dirs. 1975-89). Republican. Methodist. Office: 466 Curran Hwy North Adams MA 01247-3919 *My goals have been to better my community, profession and life in general because I was a positive participant, and to provide independence, a sense of responsibility and a love of humanity for my family.*

THURSTON, GEORGE BUTTE, mechanical and biomedical engineering educator; b. Austin, Tex., Oct. 8, 1924; s. Rudolph D. and Olivia Ruth (Lester) T.; m. Carol A. McWharter, Apr. 5, 1947; children— John Douglas, Mary Elizabeth. BS, U. Tex., Austin, 1944, MA, 1948, PhD, 1952. Registered profl. engr., Tex. Supr. hydroacoustics sect. Def. Rsch. Lab., U. Tex., Austin, 1949-52; asst. prof. physics U. Wyo., Laramie, 1952-53, U. Ark., Fayetteville, 1953-54; physicist Naval Ordnance Test Sta., Inyokern, Calif., 1954-55; assoc. prof. Okla. State U., Stillwater, 1954-59; rsch. physicist U. Mich., Ann Arbor, 1958-59; prof. Okla. State U., 1959-68; vis. scientist Centre de Recherche sur les Macromolecules, Strasbourg, France, 1963-64; prof. mech. engring. and biomed. engring. U. Tex., Austin, 1968—; pres. Vilastic Scientific, Inc. Vis. prof. Helmholtz Inst. fur Biomedizinische Technik, Aachen, West Germany, 1975-76; cons. for govt., industry. Contbr. articles to profl. jours. Recipient Brown U. Calculus prize, 1942; Alexander von Humboldt Found. Sr. U.S. Scientist award, 1975; NSF faculty fellow, 1963-64; numerous grants. Fellow Am. Phys. Soc., Acoustical Soc. Am.; mem. ASME, Soc. Rheology, Internat. Soc. Biorheology, Brit. Soc. Rheology, Sigma Xi, Sigma Pi Sigma. Home: 1000 Madrone Rd Austin TX 78746-4320 Office: U Tex Dept Mech Engring Austin TX 78712

THURSTON, GEORGE R. lumber company executive; b. 1942; BS, Northwestern U., 1965, MBA, 1966. With Cummins Engine Co., 1966-78; exec. v.p. fin. and treas. North Pacific Lumber Co., Portland, 1987—. Office: PO Box 3915 Portland OR 97208-3915

THURSTON, KATHLEEN, academic administrator; Project mgr. Ideal Constrn., Inc., Honolulu, v.p. ops., pres., Thurston-Pacific, Inc., Honolulu, 1997—; commr. Dept. Hawaiian Home Lands; mem. bd. regents U. Hawaii, Honolulu, 2001—. Bd. dirs. Bishop Mus., Office of Hawaiian Affairs Native Hawaiian Revolving Loan Fund. Mem.: Gen. Contrs. Assn. of Hawaii (past pres.). Office: University of Hawaii 2444 Dole St Honolulu HI 96822

THURSTON, SALLY A. lawyer; b. Glens Falls, N.Y., 1961; BS, Cornell U., 1983; JD, Harvard U., 1986. Bar: N.Y. 1987. Ptnr. Skadden, Arps, Slate, Meagher & Flom, N.Y.C.; v.p., tax counsel NBC, Inc., N.Y.C., 1997—. Office: Skadden Arps Slate Meagher & Flom 4 Times Sq Fl 24 New York NY 10036-6595

THURSTON, STEPHEN JOHN, pastor; b. Chgo., July 20, 1952; s. John Lee and Ruth (Hall) T.; m. Joyce DeVonne Hand, June 18, 1977; children: Stephen John II, Nicole D'Vaugh, Teniece Rael, Christian Avery Elijah. BA in Religion, Bishop Coll., 1975; Hon. degree, Chgo. Baptist Inst., 1986. Co-pastor New Covenant Missionary Bapt. Ch., Chgo., 1975-79, pastor, 1979—. Third v.p. Nat. Bapt. Conv. Am., mem. exec. com. Christian Edn. Congress; pres. Ill. Nat. Bapt. State Conv.; mem. Christian Fellowship Dist. Assn.; lectr. various orgns.; instr. New Covenant Bapt. Ch., Fellowship Bapt. Ch. Co-chmn. religious affairs div. People United to Save Humanity (PUSH); bd. dirs. nat. alumni assn. Bishop Coll.; active NAACP; trustee, fin. chmn. Chgo. Bapt. Inst. Mem. Broadcast Ministers Alliance, Bapt. Ministers Conf. Chgo. (Ministerial Pioneer award). Clubs: Bishop Coll. (Chgo.). Office: New Cov Miss Baptist Church 740 E 77th St Chicago IL 60619-2553

THURSTON, WILLIAM PAUL, mathematician; b. Washington, Oct. 30, 1946; s. Paul Ambrose and Margaret (Martt) Thurston; m. Karen T. Barris, Dec. 10, 1993; children: Hannah, Nathaniel, Dylan, Emily. BS, New Coll., Sarasota, Fla., 1967; PhD, U. Calif., Berkeley, 1972. Mem. Inst. Advanced Study, Princeton, NJ, 1972—73; asst. prof. Sloan fellow MIT, Cambridge, 1973—74; prof. math. Princeton (N.J.) U., 1974—91, U. Calif., Berkeley, 1991—96, dir. Math. Sci. Rsch. Inst., 1992—96, prof. math Davis, 1996—. Recipient Waterman award, NSF, Fields medal, IMU, 1982. Fellow: Am. Acad. Sci., Nat. Acad. Scis.; mem.: Am. Math. Soc. Democrat. Office: Dept Mathematics UC Davis 1 Shields Ave Davis CA 95616-8633 E-mail: wpt@math.ucdavis.edu.

THURSWELL, GERALD ELLIOTT, lawyer; b. Detroit, Feb. 4, 1944; s. Harry and Lilyan (Zeitlin) T.; m. Lynn Satovsky, Sept. 17, 1967 (div. Aug. 1978); children: Jennifer, Lawrence; m. Judith Linda Bendix, Sept. 2, 1978 (div. May 1999); children: Jeremy, Lindsey. LLB with distinction, Wayne State U., 1967. Bar: Mich. 1968, N.Y. 1984, D.C. 1985, Colo. 1990, Ill. 1992, U.S. Dist. Ct. (ea. dist.) Mich. 1968, U.S. Ct. Appeals (6th cir.) 1968, U.S. Supreme Ct. 1994, U.S. Dist. Ct. (we. dist.) Mich. 2004. Student asst. to U.S. Atty. Eas. Dist. Mich., Detroit, 1966; assoc. Zwerdling, Miller, Klimist & Maurer, Detroit, 1967-68; st. prnt. The Thurswell Law Firm, Southfield, Mich. Arbitrator Am. Arbitration Assn., Detroit, 1969—; mediator Wayne County Cir. Ct., Mich., 1983—, Oakland County Cir. Ct. Mich., 1984—, also facilitator, 1991; twp. atty. Royal Oak Twp., Mich., 1982—; lectr. Oakland County Bar Assn. People's Law Sch., 1988. Pres. Powder Horn Estates Subdivsn. Assn., West Bloomfield, Mich., 1975, United Fund, West Bloomfield, 1976. Arthur F. Lederly scholar Wayne State U. Law Sch., 1965; Wayne State U. Law Sch. grad. profl. scholar, 1965, 66. Mem. ATLA (treas. Detroit met. chpt. 1986-87, v.p. 1989-90, pres. 1991-93), Mich. Bar Assn. (investigator/arbitrator grievance bd., atty. discipline bd., chmn. hearing panel), Mich. Trial Lawyers Assn. (legis. com. on govtl. immunity 1984, exec. bd., 2004), Detroit Bar Assn. (lawyer referral com., panel pub. adv. com. jud. candidates), Oakland County Bar Assn. Office: The Thurswell Law Firm 1000 Town Ctr Ste 500 Southfield MI 48075-1221 Office Phone: 248-354-2222.

THYDEN, JAMES ESKEL, diplomat, educator, lecturer; b. L.A., Apr. 10, 1939; s. Eskel A. and Mildred Aileene (Rock) T.; m. Patricia Irene Kelsey, Dec. 15, 1959; children: Teresa Lynn, Janice Kay, James Blaine. BA in Biology, Pepperdine U., 1961; MA in Scandinavian Area Studies, U. Wash., 1992. Cert. secondary tchr., Calif., Wash. Tchr. Gompers Jr. High Sch., L.A., 1962-64; fgn. svc. officer U.S. Dept. State, Washington, 1964-90; rschr. U. Wash., Seattle, 1992-93; exec. dir. Seattle chpt. UN Assn., 1993-96. Travel lectr. Cunard Lines' Royal Viking Sun, 1995, and Royal Caribbean's Splendour of the Seas, 1997. Editor govt. report, ann. human rights reports, 1983-86; author, editor in-house govt. reports, documents. Dir. Office of Human Rights, 1983-86; counselor Embassy for Polit. Affairs, Am. Embassy, Oslo, Norway, 1986-90. Named Outstanding Young Man Am., 1969, Alumnus of Yr., Pepperdine U., 1984. Mem.: Edmonds Libr. Bd., Soc. Advancement of Scandinavian Studies, World Affairs Coun. Seattle, Am. Fgn. Svc. Assn. Avocations: travel, reading, gardening. Home: 5631 153rd Pl SW Edmonds WA 98026-4239

THYEN, JAMES C. furniture company executive; b. Jasper, Ind., 1943; BS, Xavier U., 1965; MBA, Ind. U., 1967. With Kimball Internat. Inc., Jasper, 1967—, sr. exec. v.p., treas., 1982—, also bd. dirs. Home: 1440 W Schuetter Rd Jasper IN 47546-9545 Office: Kimball Internat Inc 1038 E 15th St Jasper IN 47546-2225

THYRET, RUSS, recording industry executive; Sales person L.A. WEA Br.; singles sales mgr. Warner Bros. Records Inc., 1971—73, sales mgr., 1973—75, v.p. sales dept., 1975—76, v.p. promotion, 1976—81, sr. v.p. mktg. dept., 1981—83, sr. v.p. mktg. and promotion, 1983, vice chmn., chmn., CEO, 1995—. Office: Warner Bros Records 3300 Warner Blvd Burbank CA 91505-4694

THYZEL, TIM, curator, artist, educator; b. Hamburg, Germany, Jan. 14, 1966; s. Werner and Freia Thyzel; m. Alexandra N Mitchell, Aug. 23, 2000. BFA, San Franciso Art Inst., 1988—91; MFA, Hochschule fur Bildende Kunste, 1991—95. Art tchr. Studio in a Sch., NYC, 2000—; sculpture instr. Sch. Visual Arts, NYC, 2004—. Bd. of directors Artist Ho., Wendenstrasse 45, Hamburg, Germany, 1994—96; ind. curator, NYC. One-man shows include Beton Museum, Cynthia Broan Gallery, NY, exhibited in group shows at Bill Maynes Gallery, Islip Art Mus., Ctr. for Curatorial Studies, Bard Coll., NY, Contemporary Mus., Balt., Dorsky Gallery, NY, Bronx Mus., Ethan Cohen Fine Arts, Design Ctr. of Austin. Recipient Installation Art award, Angel Orensanz Found., 1998; scholar Merit Scholarship, Sobel scholarship, San Francisco Art Inst., 1988; Arbeitsstependium (Artist Grant), City of Hamburg, 1996.

TIA, MANG, civil engineering educator; b. Phnom-Penh, Cambodia, Aug. 31, 1953; came to U.S., 1972; s. Chhay and You (Khou) T.; m. Liang Tsi Maria Mao, May 25, 1980; children: Samuel Q., Luke L., Timothy J. BSCE, BSME, MIT, 1976; MSCE, Purdue U., 1978, PhD in Civil Engring., 1982. Registered profl. engr., Fla. Vis. asst. prof. La. Tech. U., Ruston, La., 1982; vis. rsch. assoc. prof. Nat. Ctrl. U., Taiwan, 1989-90; asst. prof. U. Fla., Gainesville, 1982-87, assoc. prof., 1987-92, prof. civil engring., 1992—. Cons. in field. Contbr. articles to Jour. Asphalt Paving Technologists, ACI Material Jours., ASCE Transp. Jour., Transp. Rsch. Record. Deacon Gainesville Chinese Christian Ch., 1990—. Mem. ASCE, ASTM, Am. Concrete Inst., Am. Soc. Engring. Edn., Assn. Asphalt Paving Technologists, Transp. Rsch. Bd. Achievements include patent for Field Permeability Test Apparatus for Concrete. Home: 8214 NW 63rd Pl Gainesville FL 32653-6806 Office Phone: 352-392-9537 ext 1463. E-mail: tia@ce.ufl.edu.

TIAHRT, W. TODD, congressman, former state senator; b. Vermillion, S.D., June 15, 1951; s. Wilbur E. and Sara Ella Marcine (Steele) T.; m. Vicki Lyn Holland, Aug. 14, 1976; children: Jessica, John, Luke. Student, S.D. Sch. Mines & Tech., Rapid City, 1969-72; BA, Evangel Coll., 1975; MBA, S.W. Mo. State U., 1989. Property estimator Crawford & Co., Springfield, Mo., 1975-78; project engr. Zenith Electronics, Springfield, 1978-81; cost engr. Boeing, Wichita, Kans., 1981-94, proposal mgr., 1991-94; state senator State of Kans., Topeka, 1993—95; mem. U.S. Congress from 4th Kans. dist., Washington, 1995—; mem. appropriations com., 1997—. Chmn. 4th dist. Rep. party, 1990-92; exec. com. Kans. Rep. party, 1990-92, nat. security com., sci. com. Mem. Pachyderm (bd. dirs. 1991-92), Delta Sigma Phi. Republican. Home: 1329 Amity St Goddard KS 67052-9133 Office: 2441 Rayburn HOB Washington DC 20515-1604

TIAN, HONGQI, application developer, researcher; arrived in U.S., 2001; s. Tao Tian and Fengkun Li; m. Yan Li; children: Annie Miao, Tony Run. BS, Huazhong U. Sci. Tech., Wuhan, 1982, Master, 1984, PhD, 1989. Rschr. Chiba (Japan) U., 1991—94; sr. rsch. engr. Seiko Instruments Inc., Chiba, 1994—96; sr. software engr. Digital Dispatch Sys., Richmond, Canada, 1997—2000, Digital Control Inc., Renton, Wash., 2001—. Author: (book) Sliding Mode Control, 1994. Mem.: NY Acad. Sci. Achievements include patents for sliding mode control of magnetic bearing sys. Home: 14245 60th St SE Bellevue WA 98006

TIAN, QI, computer science educator; s. Huokang Tian and Keli Deng; m. Yanwei Wu, July 12, 1999. B in engring., Tsinghua U., China, 1992; MS, Drexel U., 1997; PhD, U. Ill., 2002. Chief software engr., co-founder Beijing Dongfang Ivy Multimedia Tech. Ltd., 1993—94; rsch. and tchg. asst. U. Ill., Urbana, 1997—2002, Drexel U., Philadelphia, Pa.; summer intern rschr. Mitsubishi Electric Rsch. Lab., Cambridge, Mass., 2000, 2001, vis. rschr., 2001; asst. prof. U. Tex., San Antonio, 2002—; adj. asst. prof. to asst profl. U. Tex. Health Sci. Ctr., San Antonio, 2002—; vis. prof. NEC Lab. Am., Inc., Cupertino, Calif., 2003. Mem.: IEEE (sr.). Achievements include patents pending for content-based visualization and user-modeling for interactive browsing and retrieval in multimedia databases; research in published 8 journal papers and over 30 conference papers in referred journals and international conferences. Office: U Tex 6900 N Loop 1604 W San Antonio TX 78249 E-mail: qitian@cs.utsa.edu.

TIAN, YONGLAI, electrical engineer; b. Shanghai, July 7, 1944; arrived in U.S., 1980; s. Liang Keng Tian and Yue Xiu Cao; married, May 1, 1972; children: Mark, Jerry. BS, Tsinghua U., Beijing, 1967; MS, Lehigh U., 1982, PhD, 1986. Rsch. assoc. Northwestern U., Evanston, Ill., 1986—88; assoc. prof. Shanghai Inst. Ceramics, 1988—90; rsch. engr. U. Wis., Madison, 1990—92; rsch. assoc. prof. George Mason U., Fairfax, Va., 1992—97; sr. R & D engr. Fusion Lighting, Inc., Rockville, Md., 1997—2002; sr. scientist FM Techs., Inc., Chantilly, Va., 2002—. Affiliate assoc. prof. George Mason U., Fairfax, 1998—2000. Honored fellow, Lehigh U., 1982—85. Mem.: IEEE, Am. Cermic Soc. Achievements include patents in field. Home: 3819 charles Stewart Dr Fairfax VA 22033 Office: FM Techs Inc 4431-H Brookfield Corp Dr Chantilly VA 20151 Office Phone: 703-818-9400 ext 106. Office Fax: 703-818-7090. Business E-Mail: ytian@cox.net.

TIANO, ANTHONY STEVEN, television producer, book publishing executive; b. Santa Fe, Mar. 27, 1941; s. Joseph A. and Marian (Adlesperger) T.; m. Kathleen O'Brien, Dec. 29, 1972; children: Mark A., A. Steven. BA, U. N.Mex., 1969, MA, 1971; LittD (hon.), Calif. Sch. Profl. Psychology, 1985. Dir. programming Sta. KNME-TV U. N.Mex., Albuquerque, 1968-72; sta. mgr. Sta. WHA-TV U. Wis., Madison, 1972-76; exec. dir. Sta. KETC-TV, St. Louis, 1976-78; pres., CEO KQED, Inc., San Francisco, 1978-93; chmn., CEO Santa Fe Ventures, Inc., San Francisco, 1993—. Vice-chair bd. dirs. Calif. Sch. Profl. Psychology, San Francisco, 1985-90. Mem. Nat. Assn. Pub. TV Stas. (vice chair bd. dirs. 1986). Office: Santa Fe Ventures 999 16th St 9 San Francisco CA 94107-2468

TIANO, LINDA V. lawyer; b. 1952; BA summa cum laude, U. Cin.; JD cum laude, Boston U. Assoc. Epstein Becker and Green, P.C., 1981—90, ptnr., stockholder, 1990—92; v.p. for legal and govt. affairs, gen counsel MVP Health Plan, 1992—95; sr. v.p., gen. counsel Empire BlueCross BlueShield, 1995—2002, WellChoice, Inc., N.Y.C., 2002—. Office: WellChoice Inc 11 W 42nd St New York NY 10036*

TIBBLE, DOUGLAS CLAIR, lawyer; b. Joliet, Ill., May 26, 1952; BA, DePaul U., 1974; JD, Syracuse U., 1977, MPA, 1978. Bar: Ill., US Dist. Ct. (no. dist.) Ill., US Ct. Appeals (7th cir.), US Supreme Ct. Ptnr. McBride, Baker & Coles, Oakbrook Terrace, Ill., 1996—2003, Brooks, Adams and Tarulis, Naperville, Ill., 2003—. Mem. ABA, DuPage County Bar Assn., Illinois State Bar Assn. Office: Brooks Adams and Tarulis 101 N Washington St Naperville IL 60540-4511

TIBBS, MARTHA JANE PULLEN, civic worker, retired social worker; b. Memphis, Feb. 12, 1932; d. John Thomas Jr. and Martha Frances (Gragg) Pullen; m. Eugene Edward Tibbs; children: Martha Katherine, Eugene Edward Jr. BSBA, U. Tenn., 1953; MA Edn., U. Memphis, 1958. Cert. tchr., social worker, Tenn. Tchr. Lausanne Sch., Memphis, 1954 55, Millington H.S., Memphis, 1955-56, Presbyn. Day Sch., Memphis, 1956-57, St. Mary's Episcopal Sch., Memphis, 1958-60; social worker Tenn. Dept. Pub. Welfare, Memphis, 1962-63. Author geneal. works. Mem. Memphis Vol. Svc. Bd., 1963-64; mem. Shelby County Hist. Comm., 1983-97, commr., 1983—; block worker Cancer, Kidney and Heart Fund, Memphis, 1984—; sec., treas. Eastland Presbyterian Ch. Mem.: DAR (past chpt. regent, sec.-treas. regents coun.), AAUW, NEA, Tenn. Geneal. Soc., Tenn. Tchrs. Assn., Tenn. Soc. Pres. Founders and Patriots of Am., Soc. Descendants of Knights Most Noble Order of Garter, Colonial Order of Crown, Tenn. State DAR (transp. chmn. 2001—), Cleve. Jr. Aux., Cleve. Med. Aux. (sec./treas.), West Tenn. Hist. Soc., Chicasaw Dist. DAR Sch. (Tenn. state vice chmn. DAR schs., parliamentarian Zachariah Davies chpt., chmn. Zachariah Davies chpt.), Nat. Registrar Daus. of Founders and Patriots Am. (v.p. Tenn. chpt., past Tenn. state registrar), Tenn. State Registrar Founders and Patriots (pres. 2003—), Nat. Soc. Colonial Dames XVII Century (1st v.p., pres. 2003—, 2d v.p. past treas. Chucaqua chpt.), Nat. Soc. So. Dames Am. (historian 2001—02, sec. 2002—, past pres. Memphis chpt., past state pres.), Colonial Dames Am., Tenn. State Dames of Ct. of Honor (pres. 2003—, historian, 1st v.p., nat. def. chmn.), Sovereign Colonial Soc. Ams. Royal Descent, Memphis Scottish Soc., Am. Clan Donald Soc., Am. Clan Gregor Soc., Family of Bruce Soc., Planetgenet Soc., Nat. Soc. Magna Charta Dames and Barons (past state sec. 2000—02, past Magna Carta sec. West Tenn. chpt. 2001—02, treas. West Tenn. chpt. 2002—), Cleve. Garden Club (past pres.), U. Club Memphis, Early Settlers Shelby County (registrar 1988, bd. dirs. 1992—, sec. 1998—, pres. 2002—), Nineteenth Century Club (newsletter editor 1985—88, sec. 1993—95, corr. sec. 1999—), Racquet Club, Cleve. Women's Club, Alpha Omega Pi. Republican. Presbyterian. Avocations: art, genealogy, computers, dance, tennis. Home: 2008 Massey Rd Memphis TN 38119-6404

TIBBS, SUE, state representative; b. Tulsa, Okla., Oct. 6, 1934; d. Clyde and Frances (VanSlyke) Sloan; m. Milton Homer Tibbs; children: Debra West, Kelli Dodd. Student, Tulsa Jr. Coll. Mem. Okla. Ho. of Reps., 2001—. Named Woman of Yr. Republican. Office: State Capitol 2300 N Lincoln Blvd Rm 323 Oklahoma City OK 73105

TIBERI, PATRICK J. congressman, former state legislator; b. Columbus, OH, Oct. 21, 1962; m. Denice Tiberi. BA, Ohio State Univ. Asst. dist. mgr. Congressman John Kasich; rep. from dist. 26 Ohio Ho. Reps., 1993—2001, majority fl. leader, mem. ins. and vets. affairs coms.; mem. U.S. Congress from 12th Ohio dist., 2001—, Armed Svcs. Com., Small Bus. Com. Pres. Windsor Terrace Learning Ctr. Mem. adv. bd. Columbus chpt. ARC, Columbus Italian Cultural Ctr., Com. Edn. & Workforce, Fin. Svcs.; past pres. Forest Park Civic Assn.; former rep. Northland Community Coun.; pres., co-founder Windsor Terrace Learning Ctr. Recipient Pres.'s award Northland Cmty. Coun., Vet. Admin Commendation award, Svc. award Am. Red Cross, Watchdog of Treas. award United Conservatives of Ohio. Mem. Sons of Italy. Republican. Home: 5208 Honeytree Loop W Columbus OH 43229-4631 Office: 113 Cannon Ho Office Bldg Washington DC 20515-3512 also: Dist Office 2700 E Dublin Granville Rd Ste 525 Columbus OH 43231

TIBLIER, FERNAND JOSEPH, JR., municipal engineering administrator; b. New Orleans, Mar. 11, 1960; s. Fernand Joseph and Dorothy May (Bosworth) T.; m. Janine Therese Cousineau, Sept. 1, 1990; children: Amanda, Christine. BA in Chemistry, Biology, Drury Coll., 1982; MS in Environ. Engring., U. Cen. Fla., 1986. Registered profl. engr., Fla. Rsch. asst. U. Cen. Fla., Orlando, 1983-86; asst. city engr., then acting city engr. City of Longwood, Fla., 1986-92, city engr., 1992-94, dir. pub. works, city engr., 1994-96; city engr., dir. pub. works City of Deltona, Fla., 1996-2000; engring. project mgr. McKim & Creed, P.A., 2000—. Mem. road impact fee com. Seminole County Citizen Adviser, Sanford, Fla., 1988-89; mem. water resources task force Seminole County Tech. Adviser, Sanford, 1992; advisor Pub. Works Acad. Oak Ridge High Sch., Orlando, 1996—; mem. Dean of Engring. adv. coun. U. Cen. Fla.; mem. tech. adv. com. Volusian Water Alliance. Lector, youth minister Nativity Ch., Lake Mary, Fla., 1987—; team capt. City of Longwood March of Dimes, 1992; mem. City of Longwood Planning Agy., 1997-98. Mem. ASCE, NSPE, Am. Pub. Works Assn., Am. Water Works Assn., Fla. Engring. Soc. (sec. Daytona Beach chpt. 2002, chmn. com. State Math Counts), Volusia Assn. Mcpl. Engrs. Republican. Roman Catholic. Avocations: home improvement, photography, travel, cooking, reading. Home: 407 Parson Brown Way Longwood FL 32750-4020 Office: McKim & Creed 1901 Mason Ave Ste 102 Daytona Beach FL 32117-5105

TIBSHRAENY, JAY, former mayor; b. Chandler, Ariz. m. Karen Tibshraeny; 1 child, Lauren. BS in Acctg., Ariz. State U. Owner property mgmt. firm, Chandler; citrus grower Chandler; mem. Chandler City Coun., 1986—; vice mayor City of Chandler, 1990—94, mayor, 1994—2002. Chmn. Regional Pub. Transp. Authority, City of Chandler; mem. Maricopa Assn. Govts. Regional Coun., Greater Phoenix Econ. Coun., Ariz. Mcpl. Water Users Assn., Ariz. League of Cities and Towns Resolutions Com., Williams Air Force Redevel. Partnership, Nat. League of Cities Transp. and Comm. Com. Mem. Chandler Friends of the Libr.; adv. bd. Chandler-Gilbert Assn. for Retarded Citizens, Child Crisis Ctr., Chandler; mem. City Coun. Pub. Safety com., Chandler Pub. Safety Retirement Sys. Bd., Chandler Vol. Firemen Pension bd. Mem. Chandler Hist. Soc., Chandler C. of C. (bd. dirs.).

TICE, BRADLEY SCOTT, humanities educator; b. Palo Alto, Calif., Oct. 6, 1959; s. Lilburn Trent and Paula Nanette (Osborne) T. AA, De Anza Coll., Cupertino, Calif., 1983; BA in History, San Jose State U., 1987; AA, De Anza Coll., Cupertino, Calif., 1995; PhD in Chemistry, Fairfax U., Baton Rouge, 1996; Diploma in Ayurvedic Medicine, The Ayurvedic Inst.; Diploma in Stress therapy, Internat. Yoga Sch.; LittD in Tchg., St. Clements Univ., The Carribean, 1998; DD (hon.), 1999; Doctor Philosophy in Comparative Religion, Am. Coll. Metaphysical Theology, Minn., 2001; PhD in Elec. Engring., Cambridge State U., 2001; PhD in Metaphysics, Am. Coll. of Metaphysical Theology, 2002; PhD in Religious Edn., Am. Coll. Metaphys. Theology, 2002; PhD in Elec. Engring., Northwestern Internat. U., Denmark, 2003, JD, PhD in Math., PhD in Telecomm., PhD in Physics, Northwestern Internat. U., Denmark, 2003; M in Law, Northwestern Internat. U., 2003. Cert. Cmty. Emergency Response Tng., Cupertino, Calif.; ordained to ministry Protestant Ch. Mem. staff Stanford Linear Accelerator Ctr., 1981-87, intern archives dept., 1991; prof. Pacific Lang. Inst., Cupertino, Calif., 1992—; dir. rsch. Advanced Human Design, Cupertino, 1992—; CEO Tice Pharms., San Jose; intern Ames Rsch. Ctr. NASA, Moffett Field, Calif., 1997-98, mission specialist astronaut candidate, 2001; substitute instr. Palo Alto (Calif.) Unified

Sch. Dist., 2001; assoc. Ames-NASA Rsch. Ctr., Moffett Field, Calif., 2003. Substitute libr. Robert Crown Law Libr. Stanford U., 1989; substitute instr. San Jose Unified Sch. Dist., 2002; adj. prof. Sch. Arts and Scis. Nat. U., San Jose, 2000—01; adj. prof. Nat. Hispanic U., San Jose, 2000—03, mem. faculty senate; grand awards judge engring. Intel Internat. Sci. and Engring. Fair, Louisville, 2002; mem. staff San Jose Giants Baseball Club, 2002. Editor: Jour. Pacific Lang. Inst., 1995—96; mem. editl. bd. The Story of Life.; contbr. articles to profl. jours. Vol. De Young Mus., San Francisco, 1990, Mus. Modern Art, San Francisco, 1990, Calif. Acad. Scis., San Francisco, 1990, Nat. Steinbeck Ctr., Salinas, Calif.; vol. guide Monterey Bay Aquarium, 1990; elected mem. Cupertino Pub. Safety Commn., 2000—02; mem. Santa Clara County Sheriff's Citizens Acad., San Jose, 2002; block leader tng. program Cupertino, 2002; mem. spl. events patrol dept. pub. safety Stanford U., Calif., 2001; candidate for bd. trustees Foothill-De Anza CC Dist., Los Altos Hills, Calif., 2002; neighborhood accountability bd. vol. Count of Santa Clara Probation Dept. Restorative Justice Program, Juvenile Probation Dept., San Jose, 2001; grand awards judge in chemistry Intel Internat. Sci. and Engring. Fair, San Jose, 2001; investor in preservation Computer History Mus., Moffett Field, Calif., 2001. Recipient Pres.'s award Nat. Author's Registry, 1996, editor's choice award (3), The Nat. Libr. of Poetry, 1995, (2), 1996, Cert. Merit for essay, Pharmacia Biotech and Sci. prize for young scientists, 1997, Commemorative Medal Honor, Hallmark, 2000, Jr. Engr. award A.G. Spalding and Bros., 1965; elected Order of Internat. Ambs., 1999, Internat. Man of the Year (medal of hon.), 1996, 97, Man of the Year (commemorative medal award), 1997, Internat. Order Merit, 2000, Commemmorative medal of honor Hallmark, 2000, Noble Prize Outstanding Achievement and Contbns. to Humanity, United Cultural Conv., Raleigh, N.C., 2001. Fellow Am. Coll. Metaphys. Theology; em. ACS, IEEE, AIAA, COSPAR (mem. com. space rsch.), Am. Physical Soc., N.Y. Acad. Scis., Assn. Computing Machinery, Am. Soc. Microbiology, Internat. Assn. Tchrs. English as a Fgn. Lang., Internat. Soc. Poets, Mars Soc. (found. mem.), Calif. Assn. for Health, Phys. Edn., Recreation and Dance (v.p. elect for recreation 1999), Internat. Pankration Assn. (founder). Avocations: weight training, fencing, bicycling, swimming, scuba diving. Office: Pacific Language Inst PO Box 2214 Cupertino CA 95015-2214

TICE, CAROL HOFF, intergenerational specialist, consultant; b. Ashville, N.C., Oct. 6, 1931; d. Amos H. and Fern (Irvin) Hoff; m. (div.); children: Karin E., Jonathan H. BS, Manchester Coll., North Manchester, Ind., 1954; MEd, Cornell U., 1955. Cert. tchr., Mich., N.Y., N.J. Tchr. Princeton (N.J.) Schs., 1955-60; tchr. Ann Arbor (Mich.) Schs., 1964—; dir. intergenerational programs Inst. for Study Children and Families Eastern Mich. U., Ypsilanti, 1985-96. Founder, pres. Lifespan Resources, Inc., Ann Arbor, 1979—; presdl. appointee to U.S. Nat. Commn. Internat. Yr. of the Child, Washington, 1979-81; del. to White House Conf. on Aging, Washington, 1995. Innovator; program, Tch. Learning Intergenerational Communities, 1971; author: Guide Books and articles, Community of Caring, 1980; co-producer, Film, What We Have, 1976 (award, Milan, Italy Film Festival 1982). Trustee Blue Lake Fine Arts Camp, Twin Lake, Mich., 1975—; dir. Visual Arts Colony, 1990—. Recipient Program Innovation award, Mich. Dept. Edn., 1974—80, C.S. Mott Found. award, 1982, Nat. Found. Improvement in Edn. award, Washington, 1986, Disting. Alumni award, Manchester Coll., 1979, A+ Break the Mold award, U.S. Sec. of Edn., 1992, Ann Arbor Sch. Supts. Golden Apple award, 1999, Disting. Svc. award, Mich. Art Edn. Assn., 2001; fellow Ford Found. fellow, Ithaca, N.Y., 1955. Mem. AAUW (agt. 1979, Agent of Change award), Generations United (hon. com. for Margaret Mead Centennial 2001, 1998—, Pioneer award 1989), Mich. Edn. Assn. (hon. mention Program Innovation 2000), Optimist Club (Humanitarian award). Democrat. Presbyterian. Office: Scarlett MS 3300 Lorraine St Ann Arbor MI 48108-1970

TICE, DOUGLAS OSCAR, JR., federal bankruptcy judge; b. Lexington, N.C., May 2, 1933; s. Douglas Oscar Sr. and Lila Clayton (Wright) T.; m. Janet N. Capps, Feb. 28, 1959 (div. Sept. 1976); children: Douglas Oscar III, Janet E.; m. Martha Murdoch Edwards, June 8, 1996. BS, U. N.C., 1955, JD, 1957. Bar: N.C. 1957, U.S. Ct. Appeals (4th cir.) 1964, Va. 1970, U.S. Dist. ct. (ea. dist.) Va. 1976, U.S. Bankruptcy Ct. (ea. dist.) Va. 1976. Exec. sec. N.C. Jud. Coun., Raleigh, 1958-59; assoc. Baucom & Adams, Raleigh, 1959-61; trial atty. Office Dist. Coun., IRS, Richmond, Va., 1961-70; corp. atty. Carlton Industries, Inc., Richmond, 1970-75; ptnr. Hubard, Tice, Marchant & Samuels, P.C., Richmond, 1975-87; judge U.S. Bankruptcy Ct. (ea. dist.), Richmond, Norfolk, Alexandria, Va., 1987-99, chief judge, 1999—. Mem. State-Fed. Jud. Coun. Va. Co-author: Monument & Boulevard, Richmond's Grand Avenues, 1996; contbr. articles to profl. jours. Vice pres. Richmond Pub. Forum, 1976-80, com. chmn. Richmond Forum, Inc., 1986-2001; past pres. Richmond Civil War Roundtable, mem., 1965—; bd. dirs. Epilepsy Assn. Va., Inc., 1976-87. Capt. USAR, 1957-66. Fellow Am. Coll. Bankruptcy; mem. ABA, Va. Bar Assn., City of Richmond Bar Assn., Am. Bankruptcy Inst., Nat. Conf. Bankruptcy Judges, So. Hist. Assn., Va. Hist. Soc., Old Dominion Sertoma (pres. Richmond chpt. 1967), Comml. Law League Am., Supreme Ct. Hist. Soc., State-Fed. Jud. Coun. Va., Am. Inn of Ct. Home: 5 Foxmere Dr Richmond VA 23238 Office: US Bankruptcy Ct 1100 E Main St Ste 339 Richmond VA 23219-3538 Office Phone: 804-916-2460. Personal E-mail: thetices2@comcast.net. E-mail: douglas_tice@vaeb.uscourts.gov.

TICE, GEORGE A(NDREW), photographer; b. Newark, Oct. 13, 1938; s. William S. and Margaret T. (Robertson) T.; m. Joanna Blaylock, 1958; m. Marie Tremmel, 1960; children: Christopher, Loretta, Lisa, Lynn, Jennifer. DHL(hon.), William Paterson U., 2003. Instr. photography New Sch. Social Research, 1970-98. Photographer (one-man shows) Met. Mus. Art, 1972, (group shows) Whitney Mus. Am. Art, 1974, (one-man shows) internat. Ctr. Photography, 2002, (group shows) Mus. Modern Art, 1979, (permanent collections), Met. Mus. Art, Art Inst. Chgo., Bibliotheque Nationale, Nihon U., Tokyo, books include Fields of Peace, 1970, Fields of Peace, reissued, 1998, Goodbye River, Goodbye, 1971, Paterson, 1972, Seacoast Maine, 1973, George A. Tice Photographs, 1953-73, 1975, Urban Landscapes, 1975, Artie Van Blarcum, 1977, Urban Romantic, 1982, Lincoln, 1984, Hometowns, 1988, Stone Walls, Grey Skies, 1991, George Tice: Selected Photographs, 1953-1999, 2001, George Tice: Urban Landscapes, 2002. Served with USN, 1956-59. Recipient Grand prix for best photography book of Year Arles, France, 1973; Guggenheim Found. fellow, 1973-74, Nat. Endowment for Arts fellow, 1973—; Bradford fellow, Eng., 1990-91, N.J. State Coun. on the Arts fellow, 1998. Address: 581 Kings Hwy East Atlantic Highlands NJ 07716-2825

TICE, PAMELA PARADIS, scientific editor, writer; b. Hutchinson, Minn., Sept. 1, 1955; d. Paul Edward, Sr. and Mary LaVerne (Hebert) Paradis; m. Jeffrey Johns Powell, June 17, 1977 (div. July 1982); m. Christopher Allen Tice, Aug. 25, 1997. BA, Coll. of St. Scholastica, 1977. Statis./sec. U. Tex. M.D. Anderson Cancer Ctr., Houston, 1978-87; data coord. Baylor Coll. Medicine, Houston, 1987-88, editl. asst., 1988-90, sr. editor, 1992-2000, rsch. assoc., 2000—; dept. editor U. Tex. Med. Sch., Houston, 1990-91; editor, Houston medicine HCA Ctr. for Health Excell., Houston, 1991-92; exec. asst. U. Tex. Sch. Nursing, Houston, 1991-92. Mem. scope and mandate task force, Coun. of Sci. Editors, Chgo., 1996. Editor-in-chief: Am. Med. Writers Assn. Jour., 1992-95 (Apex awards 1995, 96, 97, Matrix award 1996, 2000, 2001, others). Recipient Presdl. Alumni award, Coll. of St. Scholastica, 2003. Mem. AAAS, Am. Med. Writers Assn. (chpt. sec. 1989-90, chpt. treas. 1990-92, chpt. pres.-elect 1992-93, chpt. pres. 1993-94, chpt. past pres. 1994-95, chpt. dir.-at-large 2001-2003, chair McGovern Award com. 2003—, Chpt. Svc. award 1994, Assn. Pres. award 1993, Assn. Leadership award 1995), Coun. of Sci. Editors, Bd. of Editors in the Life Scis. (diplomate 2002), Assn. for Women in Comm. Office: Baylor Coll Medicine Dept Family & Cmty Medicine 3701 Kirby Dr Ste 600 Houston TX 77098-3926 Office Phone: 713-798-3652. Business E-Mail: pptice@bcm.tmc.edu.

TICE, RAPHAEL DEAN, army officer; b. Topeka, Kans., Dec. 4, 1927; s. Arthur Taylor and Mamie (McDonald) T.; m. Eunice Miriam Suddarth, Dec. 23, 1946; children: Karen Ann Tice Claterbos, William Dean. BS in Mil. Sci., U. Md., 1963; MSBA, George Washington U., 1970. Served as enlisted man U.S. Army, 1946-47; commd. 2d lt., 1947; advanced through grades to lt. gen., 1981; platoon leader and co. comdr. 1st Inf. div., W.Ger., 1949-52; co. comdr., regimental adj. 8th Inf. divsn., 1955-56; tng. advisor Vietnam, 1956-57; mem. staff Office of Dep. Chief of Staff for Pers., Dept. Army, 1960-63; chief pers. mgmt. divsn. Office of Under Sec. of Army, 1963-64; plans Officer So. Command, Panama, 1965-67; dep. comdr. 3rd Brig., 4th Inf. Divsn., 1967; comdr. 2nd Bn., 12th Inf. of 25th Inf. divsn., Vietnam, 1968; exec. for pers. procurement Office of Sec. Def. for Manpower and Res. Affairs, 1968-69; comdr. 1st Brig., 1st Inf. divsn., 1970, chief of staff, 1971; dep. dir. mil. pers. mgmt. Dept. Army, 1972-73; comdg. gen. Berlin Brigade, 1974-76; dep. chief of staff personnel U.S. Army Europe, 1976-77; comdg. gen. 3rd. Inf. divsn., 1977-79; dep. asst. sec. def. for mil. pers. and force mgmt. Dept. Def., 1979-85; exec. dir. Nat. Recreation and Pk. Assn., 1986—. Spl. adviser Pres.'s Coun. on Phys. Fitness and Sports; bd. dirs. Sports Pub. LLC, Class 6 Kayak, Inc. Decorated Silver Star, Legion of Merit with 2 oak leaf clusters, Air medal with V and 7 oak leaf clusters, Bronze Star with V, Vietnam Cross of Gallantry with Palm, Purple Heart., Def. Disting. Service medal, Army Disting. Service medal Mem. Assn. U.S. Army, Am. Chess Found. (hon. pres.) Home: 18077 Clendenning Cir Round Hill VA 20141-2580 Personal E-mail: rdt509@aol.com.

TICHENOR, CHARLES BECKHAM, II, food and beverage executive; b. Indpls. s. Norman and Esther (Bremmer) B.; m. Dr. Helen S. Tichenor. BS, Duke U.; postgrad., Harvard U.; PhD, Berne U., 1996. V.p. Sealtest-Kraft; pres., chmn. Champale Sparkling Beverage Corp., Trenton, N.J. Bd. dirs. Doughtie's Foods, Inc., Balt., Motor Coils Mfg., Pitts., Angostura, Trinidad, U.S. Fed. Res. Bank of Charlotte, Yoo Hoo Chocolate Beverage Co., Carlstadt, N.J., N.Y. Packaging Corp., Jersey City, South Tex. Oil Drilling, San Antonio, Dinamic Embellages, Rombach, France, Essex Bank, Va., Weisz Graphics, Columbia, S.C.; disting. corp. chief exec., prof. bus. Gardner-Webb U. Trustee Rider U., Lawrenceville, N.J. Lt. (j.g.) USNR, China-Okinawa, WWII. Mem. Davis Cup Tennis Team, 1942-43; recipient 2 Gold and 1 Silver medal U.S. tennis and racquet sports; Nat. Master in U.S. contract bridge. Mem. Am. Mgmt. Assn., Nat. Assn. Corp. Dirs., Merion Cricket Club (Phila.), Cleveland Country Club (Shelby, N.C.), Cosmos Club (Washington), Rotary Internat. Home: 137 Westfield Rd Shelby NC 28150-4856

TICHENOR, CHARLES BECKHAM, III, operations research analyst; b. Balt., Mar. 10, 1950; s. Charles Beckham II and Suzanne Nelson (Stevens) T.; m. Alison P. Walton, May 29, 1971; 1 child, Charles Beckham IV. BSBA, Ohio State U., 1972; MBA, Va. Tech., 1990; PhD in Bus., Berne U., 1999. Asst. prodn. supr. Champale Products, Norfolk, Va., 1977-80; ops. rsch. analyst IRS, Washington, 1989-93, tech. adv. info. sys. performance mgmt. office, 1999—2000; ops. rsch. analyst Dept. Def., Alexandria, Va., 2000—. Adj. prof. Strayer U., Balt. Lt. col. USAR, ret. Mem. Mensa. Roman Catholic. Avocations: tae kwon do (2d degree black belt), astronomy. Home: 6207 Cardinal Brook Ct Springfield VA 22152-1516 Office: Def Security Coop Agy Jefferson Davis Hwy Ste 203 Alexandria VA 22301 Business E-Mail: charley.tichenor@dsca.mil.

TICHMAN, NADYA ERICA, violinist; b. Freeport, N.Y., June 12, 1958; d. Herbert L. and Ruth Tichman. BMus, Curtis Inst. Music, 1980. Violinist, Aspen Music Festival 1975, 76, Opera Co. Phila. 1978, 79, Concerto Soloists of Phila. 1979-80, Santa Fe Opera Orch. 1979-81, San Francisco Symphony 1980—, assoc. concertmaster, 1990—, Grand Teton Music Festival 1982—, Chamber Music West, 1986, Midsummer Mozart Festival, New Albion Records; numerous solo and chamber music recitals; co-dir. Chamber Music Sundaes, San Francisco, Olympic Music Festival, Music in the Vineyards, Sir Georg Solti's World Orch.

TICKLE, PHYLLIS ALEXANDER, writer, publisher; b. Johnson City, Tenn., Mar. 12, 1934; d. Philip Wade and Mary Katherine (Porter) Alexander; m. Samuel Milton Tickle, June 17, 1955; children: Nora Katherine, Mary Gammon, Laura Lee, John Crockett II, Samuel Milton Jr., Philip Wade, Rebecca Rutledge. BA, East Tenn. State U., 1955; MA, Furman U., 1961. Tchr. Latin, English Memphis City Sch., 1955-57; fellow Furman U., Greenville, S.C., 1959-61; lectr. English Rhodes Coll., Memphis, 1961-64; dean humanities Memphis Coll. Art, 1964-71; mng. editor St. Luke's Press, Memphis, 1975-82; sr. editor St. Luke's Press, Iris Press, Memphis, 1982-85, Peachtree Pubs., Atlanta, 1988-90; dir. trade pub. group The Wimmer Cos., Memphis, 1990-92; religion editor Publishers Weekly, 1992-96; contbg. editor Pubs. Weekly, editor-at-large PW's Religion Bookline, 1996—2004. Poet-in-residence Brooks Meml. Gallery, 1981-89; poetry coord. Cumberland Valley Writer's Conf., 1977-83; mem. adv. bd. Iris Press, PBS Religion and Ethics Newsweekly, Forward Movement Publ., Mary Baker Eddy Libr., Garrett-McDill Ctr., Christy Awards, Dykes Found. Author: Syntactical Patterns in Indo-European Speech, 1968, The Story of Two Johns, It's No Fun to be Sick, 1976, On Beyond Koch, 1981, On Beyond Ais, 1982, The City Essays, 1982, What the Heart Already Knows, Stories for Advent, Christmas and Epiphany, 1985, Final Sanity: Stories of Lent, Easter and the Great Fifty Days, 1987, And Ordinary Time: Stories of the Days Between Ascensiontide and Advent, 1988, The Tickle Papers: Parables and Pandemonium, 1989, (dramas) Figs and Fury, 1976, Tobias and the Angels, 1983, Children of Her Name, 1987, (monograph) Of Snakes and Their Skins, 1980, (narrative poem) American Genesis, 1976, 3d edit., 1984, (poetry) Selections, 1984; contbg. author: Upper Room devotional, Disciplines, 1989, 365 Meditations for Women, 1990, 365 More Meditations for Women, 1992; gen. editor, contbr.: Confessing Conscience: Church Women on Abortion, 1990, Re-Discovering the Sacred: Spirituality for America, 1995, My Father's Prayer: A Remembrance, 1995; gen. editor: Home Works: An Anthology of Tennessee Writers, 1996; contbr. The Reader's Companion to "Crossing the Threshold of Hope," 1996, God-talk in America, 1997, The Divine Hours-Prayers for Summertime (Doubleday-Top Ten Books of Yr. 2000), 2000, The Divine Hours-Prayers for Autumn and Wintertime, 2000, The Shaping of a Life-A Spiritual Landscape, 2001, The Divine Hours-Prayers for Springtime, 2001; Greed-Matriarch of a Deadly Clan, 2004, The Graces We Remember, 2004, Eastertide- Prayers for Lent and Easter from The Divine Hours, 2004, Wisdom In the Waiting, 2004, Christmastide-Prayers for Advent Through Epephany from The Divine Hours, 2003, What The Land Already Knows, 2003, A Stitch and A Prayer, 2003, The Shaping of A Life-A Spiritual Landscape, 2001-2002, The Sharing of a Life-A Religious Landscape, 2005; poetry has appeared in Cumberland Poetry Rev., Front St. Trolley, Images, Kudzu, Mid-South Writer, Nexus, Old Hickory Rev., Painted Bride, Poets on, X-A Jour. of the Arts, Velvet Wings, others; also anthologized; columnist Dixie Flyer; writer mags. including Feminist Digest, Newsletter for Ctr. of So. Folklore, Ctr. City, The Tenn. Churchman, The Episcopalian, Alive Now!, John Milton mag., others. Chair lit. panel Tenn. Arts Commn., Nashville, 1990-92, mem. panel, 1978-82, past chair artists in edn., 1986-89; mem. exec. bd. Tenn. Humanities Coun., Nashville, 1986-90; vestrywoman St. Anne's Ch., Millington, 1988-92, 93-95; lay eucharistic min. Episcopal Ch., 1996—. Recipient Ind. Artist fellowship in lit. Tenn. Arts Commn., Nashville, 1985, Polly Bond award of excellence Episc. Comm., N.Y.C., 1988, Books of Excellence award Body, Mind and Spirit mag., 1996, Book of Yr. 1995 Catholic Press Assn., Mays award for lifetime contbn. to publ., 1996. Mem. Pub. Assn. of the South (bd. dir. 1986—, pres., chair 1985-86), Southeastern Booksellers Assn. (bd. dir. 1986-91), Tenn. Lit. Arts Assn. (pres. 1984-86). Office Phone: 901-357-5441. E-mail: tickrel@aol.com., thefarminLucy@aol.com.

TICKNOR, CAROLYN M. computer company executive; BA in Psychology, U. Redlands, Calif.; MA in Indsl. Psychology, San Francisco State U.; MBA, Stanford U. From programming, ops. mgr. to pres., CEO Hewlett-Packard Co., Palo Alto, Calif., 1977-94, pres., CEO laser jet imaging sys., 1994—. Office: Hewlett Packard Co 300 Hanover St Palo Alto CA 94304*

TIDBALL, CHARLES STANLEY, computer scientist, educator; b. Geneva, Apr. 15, 1928; (parents Am. citizens); s. Charles Taylor and Adele (Desmaison) T.; m. Mary Elizabeth Peters, Oct. 25, 1952. BA, Wesleyan U., 1950; MS (Univ. scholar), U. Rochester, 1952; PhD, U. Wis., Madison, 1955; MD (Shattuck fellow, Van Noyes scholar), U. Chgo., 1958; LHD (hon.), Wilson Coll., 1994; DSc (hon.), Hood Coll., 1999. Rotating intern Madison (Wis.) Gen. Hosp., 1958-59; physician I Mendota State Hosp., Madison, 1959; asst. research prof. physiology dept. George Washington U. Med. Center, Washington, 1959-63, USPHS spl. fellow, 1960-61, asso. prof., acting chmn. dept., 1963-64, prof., 1964-65, chmn. dept., 1964-71, Henry D. Fry prof., 1965-84, research prof. med., 1972-80; dir. Office Computer Assisted Edn. George Washington U. Med. Ctr., 1973-75, dir. Office Computer Assisted Edn. and Svcs., 1975-78; Lucie Stern disting. vis. prof. natural scis. Mills Coll., 1980; prof. edn. George Washington U., 1982-84, dir. ednl. computing tech. program Sch. Edn., 1982-84, prof. computer medicine Med. Ctr., 1984-92, prof. emeritus computer medicine, 1992, prof. neurol. surgery, 1990-92, prof. emeritus neurol. surgery, 1992; civil surgeon Immigration and Naturalization Svc., Dept. Justice, Washington, 1986-89; disting. rsch. scholar, co-dir. Tidball Ctr. for Study Ednl. Environments Hood Coll., Frederick, Md., 1994—. Trustee in residence Skidmore Coll., 1995. Author: (with others) Consolidated Index to For Thy Great Glory, 1993, (with others) Taking Women Seriously, 1999; editor: (with M. C. Shelesnyak) Frontiers in the Teaching of Physiology: Computer Literacy and Simulation, 1981; mem. editorial bd.: Jour. Applied Physiology, 1966-69, Jour. Computer-Based Instrn., 1974-89, Am. Jour. Physiology; assoc. editor physiology tchr. sect.; The Physiologist, 1979-85; contbr. articles to profl. jours. Trustee Cathedral Choral Soc., 1976-79, Wilson Coll., 1983-92, Everitt-Pomeroy, 1993-96, Population Reference Bur., 1987-94, 1996-2002, chmn. bd. trustees, 1992-94, sec., 1994-97; lay reader St. Albans Parish, 1965-67, Washington Nat. Cathedral, 1967-94, lay eucharist minister, 1994—, clergy asst., 1968—, homilist, 1977—, info. sys. specialist, 1986-93, vol. mgr. info. sys. program, 1993—; mem. commn. Episcopal Diocese Washington, 1976-78; mem. com. mgmt. YMCA Camp Letts, 1968-96, chmn., 1972-75, dir., chmn. Endowment Fund, 1977-96; bd. dirs. Met. YMCA, Washington, 1972-84, trustees coun., 1984-91, fin. com., 1972-93, v.p. internat. program, 1974-75, asst. treas., 1975-77, v.p., treas., 1977-79, vice chmn., 1979-80, chmn., 1980-82, pres. of found., 1991-93; bd. dirs., treas. Woodley Ensemble, 1993-2003; bd. dirs. Mid-Atlantic Region YMCA, 1974-83; bd. dirs., vice-chmn. Cathedral West Condo., 1983-84, chmn., 1984-87, 91-93, fin. com., 1979-94; bd. dirs. Buckingham's Choice Residents' Assn., 2000-02, chmn. resident svcs. com. Recipient award Washington Acad. Scis., 1967, Leader of Yr. award Met. YMCA, Washington, 1974, Red Triangle award, 1976, Service award, 1979; Dakota Indian name Am. Youth Found., 1976; Research Career Devel. award USPHS, 1961-63 Mem. Am. Physiol. Soc. (emeritus). Home: 3200 Baker Cir #I-235 Adamstown MD 21710 E-mail: ctidball@gwu.edu.

TIDBALL, M. ELIZABETH PETERS, physiologist, educator; b. Anderson, Ind., Oct. 15, 1929; d. John Winton and Beatrice (Ryan) Peters; m. Charles S. Tidball, Oct. 25, 1952. BA, Mt. Holyoke Coll., 1951, LHD, 1976; MS, U. Wis., 1955, PhD, 1959; MTS summa cum laude, Wesley Theol. Sem., 1990; DSc (hon.), Wilson Coll., 1973, Trinity Coll., 1974, Cedar Crest Coll., 1977, U. of South, 1978, Goucher Coll., 1979, St. Mary-of-The-Woods Coll., 1986; LittD (hon.), Regis Coll., 1980, Coll. St. Catherine, 1980, Alverno Coll., 1989; HHD (hon.), St. Mary's Coll., 1977, Hood Coll., 1982; LLD (hon.), St. Joseph Coll., 1983; LHD (hon.), Skidmore Coll., 1984, Marymount Coll., 1985, Converse Coll., 1985, Mt. Vernon Coll., 1986. Tchg. asst. physiology dept. U. Wis., 1952-55, 58-59; rsch. asst. anatomy dept. U. Chgo., 1955-56, rsch. asst. physiology dept., 1956-58; USPHS postdoctoral fellow NIH, Bethesda, Md., 1959-61; staff pharmacologist Hazleton Labs., Falls Church, Va., 1961, cons., 1962; assoc. in physiology George Washington U. Med. Ctr., 1960-62, asst. rsch. prof. dept. pharmacology, 1962-64, assoc. rsch. prof. dept. physiology, 1964-70, rsch. prof., 1970-71, prof., 1971-94, prof. emeritus, 1994—; asst. dir. M of Theol. Studies program Wesley Theol Sem., 1993-94; disting. rsch. scholar Hood Coll., Frederick, Md., 1994—, co-dir. Tidball Ctr. for Study of Ednl. Environments, 1994—. Lucie Stern Disting. vis. prof. natural scis. Mills Coll., 1980; scholar in residence Coll. Preachers, 1984, Salem Coll., 1985, Wesley Theol. Sem., 1992; Disting. scholar in residence So. Meth. U., 1985; vis. trustee prof. Skidmore Coll., 1995; cons. FDA, 1966-67, assoc. sci. coord. sci. assocs. tng. programs, 1966-67; com. on NIH tng. programs and fellowships NAS, 1972-75; faculty summer confs. Am. Youth Found., 1967-78; founder, dir. Summer Seminars for Women Am. Youth Found., 1987-95; cons. for instl. rsch. Wellesley Coll., 1974-75; exec. sec. com. on edn. and employment women in sci. and engring. Commn. on Human Resources, NRC/NAS, 1974-75, vice-chmn., 1977-82; cons., staff officer NRC/NAS, 1974-75; cons. Woodrow Wilson Nat. Fellowship Found., 1975-99, NSF, 1974-91; bd. mentor Assn. Governing Bds. of Univs. and Colls., 1991—, Gale Fund for the Study of Trusteeship Adv. Comm., 1992-98; cons. Women's Coll. Coalition Rsch. Adv. Com., 1992—; Single Gender Schooling Working Group, U.S. Dept. Edn., 1992-94, women's colls. roundtable, 1998; rep. to D.C. Commn. on Status of Women, 1972-75; nat. panelist Am. Coun. on Edn., 1983-90; panel mem. Congl. Office of Tech. Assessment, 1986-87; fellows selection com., fellows mentor Coll. Preachers, 1992—. Lead author: Taking Women Seriously, 1999; columnist Trusteeship, 1993-95; mem. editl. bd. Jour. Higher Edn., 1979-84, cons. editor, 1984—; mem. editl. bd. Religion and Intellectual Life, 1983—; contbr. articles to profl. jours. Trustee Mt. Holyoke Coll., 1968-73, vice chmn., 1972-73, trustee fellow, 1988—; trustee Hood Coll., 1972-84, 86-92, exec. com., 1974-84, 89-92, trustee emerita, 1997—; overseer Sweet Briar Coll., 1978-85, dir. emerita, 2003—; trustee Cathedral Choral Soc., 1976-90, pres. bd. trustees, 1982-84, hon. trustee, 1991—; trustee Skidmore Coll., 1988—, mem. exec. com., 1993—, trustee Bishop Claggett Ctr., 2003—; mem. governing bd. Coll. of Preachers, 1979-85, chmn., 1983-85; mem. governing bd. Protestant Episcopal Cathedral Found., 1983-85, mem. exec. com., 1983-85; bd. vis. Salem Coll., 1986-93; ctr. assoc. Nat. Resource Ctr., Girls Club Am., 1983-90; mem. governing bd. Buckinham's Choice Residents' Assn., 1999-2002. Named Outstanding Grad., The Penn Hall Sch., 1988; recipient Alumnae medal Honor, Mt. Holyoke Coll., 1971, Outstanding Svc. award, Am. Youth Found., 1975, Valuable Contbns. Gen. Alumni Assn. award, George Washington U., 1982, 1987, Pres.'s medal, 1999, Chestnut Hill medal Outstanding Achievement, Chestnut Hill Coll., Phila., 1987, Lifetime Svc. and Schoalrship award, Bd. Women's Coll. Coalition and Nation's Women's Coll. Presidents, 1998, Order of Merit, Cathedral Choral Soc., 2000, Shattuk fellowship, 1955—56, Mary E. Woolley fellowship, Mt. Holyoke Coll., 1958—59, postdoctoral fellowship, USPHS, 1959—61. Mem. AAAS, Am. Physiol. Soc. (chmn. task force on women in physiology 1973-80, com. on coms. 1977-80, mem. emeritus 1994—), Am. Assn. Higher Edn., Mt. Holyoke Alumnae Assn. (dir. 1966-70, 76-77), Histamine Club, Sigma Delta Epsilon, Sigma Xi. Episcopalian. Home: 4100 Cathedral Ave NW Washington DC 20016-3584 also: 3200 Baker Cir # I-235 Adamstown MD 21710

TIDWELL, GEOFFREY MORGAN, medical company executive; b. San Diego, Aug. 16, 1958; s. Morgan Alfred and Dorothy (Doolittle) T. BA in Psychology, U.S. Internat. U., 1991; MBA in Health Care Adminstrn., Nat. U., 1996. Rsch. asst. San Marcos (Calif.) Clinic, 1988-91; area svc. mgr. Nat. Med. Sys., Frederick, Md., 1993-94, Life Med. Svcs., San Diego, 1994-95; intern San Diego County Med. Soc., 1995-96; adminstrn. resident dept. interventional radiology U. Calif., San Diego, 1995-96; v.p., dir. clin. svcs. M&G Med. Svc., San Diego, 1995—. Vis. scholar U. Calif. Sch. Medicine, San Diego, 1996, 97, 98; radio personality Sta. KOWF, Escondido, Calif., 1989-90, Sta. KKYY, San Diego, 1990-91, Sta. KRMX, San Diego, 1990-91, Sta. KGB, San Diego, 1991-97; clin. svcs., v.p. sales and mktg. M&G Med. Svc., San Diego, 1995—; dir. client svcs. Calif. Anti-Aging Inst., Encinitas, Calif., 1999—. Co-author chpts. Podiatry Today, vol. 10 # 7, 1997. Vol. telethon Muscular Dystrophy Assn., San Diego, 1991, Easter Seals, San Diego, 1991. Mem. Am. Coll. Healthcare Execs. (assoc.), Med. Group Mgmt. Assn. (assoc.), Emergency Med. Assembly (assoc.), Healthcare Coalition San Diego County (assoc.), Psi Chi. Republican. Methodist. Avocations: fitness training, horseback riding, target shooting, reading, guitar. Office: M&G Med Svcs 4198 Convoy St San Diego CA 92111-3702 E-mail: kwoboy8@juno.com.

TIEDE, TOM ROBERT, journalist; b. Huron, SD, Feb. 24, 1937; s. Leslie Albert and Rose (Allen) T.; children: Kristina Anne, Thomas Patrick. BA in Journalism, Wash. State U., 1959. Mem. staff Kalispell (Mont.) Daily Interlake, 1960-61, Daytona Beach (Fla.) News Jour., 1961-63; war corr. Newspaper Enterprise Assn., N.Y.C., 1964—. Lectr. in field. Author: Your Men at War, 1965, Coward, 1968, Calley: Soldier or Killer?, 1971, Welcome to Washington, Mr. Witherspoon, 1979, The Great Whale Rescue, 1986, American Tapestry: Eye Witness Accounts of the 1900's, 1988, The Man Who Discovered Pluto, 1990, Fosser, 1994, Self Help Nation, 2001; permanent collections Boston U. Libr. Served as lt., inf. AUS, 1960. Recipient Ernie Pyle

Meml. award, 1965; Freedoms Found. award, 1966; George Washington medal, 1972 Mem. Internat. Platform Assn., Sigma Delta Chi, Lambda Chi Alpha. Clubs: Overseas Press, National Press, Nat. Headliners (award 1966 Atlantic City). Roman Catholic. Office: NEA 1090 Vermont Ave NW Washington DC 20005-4905 also: The Pinery 10599 Norwood Wingina VA 24599 Personal E-mail: ttiede@mindspring.com.

TIEDEMAN, DAVID VALENTINE, education educator; b. Americus, Ga., Aug. 12, 1919; s. Walter Dohlen and Edna M(arie) (Komfort) T.; m. Marjorie I(da) Denman, Sept. 26, 1942 (div. Jan. 2, 1973); children— David Michael, Jeffrey Denman; m. Anna Louise Miller, Jan. 6, 1973. AB, Union Coll., Schenectady, 1941; AM, U. Rochester, 1943; EdM, Harvard, 1948, EdD, 1949. Staff mem. NRC com. selection and tng. aircraft pilots U. Rochester, 1941-43; staff mem. test constrn. dept. Coll. Entrance Exam. Bd., 1943-44; assoc. head statistics div. Manhattan Project, 1944-46; Milton teaching fellow, instr. edn. Harvard Grad. Sch. Edn., 1946-48, Sheldon travelling fellow, 1948-49, instr. edn., 1949-51, asst. prof. edn., 1951-52, from lectr. edn. to prof., 1952-71, assoc. dir., research assoc. Center for Research in Careers, 1963-66, also chmn. exec. com., info. system for vocat. decisions, 1966-69; prin. research scientist Palo Alto office Am. Insts. for Research, 1971-73; prof. edn. No. Ill. U., DeKalb, 1973-80; dir. ERIC Clearinghouse in Career Edn., 1973-76; coordinator Office Vocat., Tech., and Career Edn., 1978-80; prof. career and higher edn. U. So. Calif., Los Angeles, 1981-84, prof. emeritus, 1984—; exec. dir. Nat. Inst. Advancement of Career Edn., 1981-84; pres. Internat. Coll., 1985-86; v.p. Lifecareer Found., 1985—; provost William Lyon U., 1988-91; faculty Walden U., 1992—. Mem. Adv. Council on Guidance Dept. Edn. Commonwealth Mass., 1957-63; chmn. commn. on tests Coll. Entrance Exam. Bd., 1967 70; mem. advisory screening com. in edn. Council Internat. Exchange of Scholars, 1975-79, chmn., 1978-79 Co-author 8 books.; editorial assoc.: Jour. Counseling Psychology, 1957-63, Personnel and Guidance Jour., 1960-63, Character Potential: A Record of Research, 1977-82, Jour. Career Edn., 1979-85; contbr. articles to profl. jours., chpts. to books. Bd. dirs. Mass. Com. Children and Youth, 1961 63. Fellow Ctr. for Advanced Study in Behavioral Scis.; spl. fellow NIMH, 1963-64 Fellow Am. Psychol. Soc., APA (prs. divsn. counseling psychology 1965-66); mem. ACA, Nat. Career Devel. Assn. (pres. 1965-66, Eminent Career award 1979), Nat. Coun. Measurement in Edn. (pres. 1962-63), Phi Beta Kappa, Sigma Xi, Phi Delta Kappa, Phi Kappa Phi. E-mail: anna@life-is-career.com.

TIEDGE-LAFRANIER, JEANNE MARIE, editor; b. N.Y.C., July 24, 1960; d. Richard Frederick and Joan Jean (Gerardo) Tiedge; m. John Daniel Lewis Lafranier, Oct. 8, 1989; children: Katelyn Ellen, John Richard. BA, Drew U., 1982. Asst. Denise Marcil Lit. Agy., N.Y.C., 1982-84; sr. editor New Am. Libr., N.Y.C., 1984-87, Warner Books, N.Y.C., 1987-95; editor corp. comm. Disticor, Ajax, Ont., Can., 1995—. Avocations: marathoner, equestrian.

TIEDJE, JAMES MICHAEL, microbiologist, educator, ecologist; b. Newton, Iowa, Feb. 9, 1942; married, 1965; 3 children. BS, Iowa State U., 1964; MS, Cornell U., 1966, PhD in Soil Microbiology, 1968. From asst. prof. to prof. Mich. State U., 1968 78, disting. prof., 1991—; dir. sci. and tech. ctr. microbial ecology NSF, 1988—. Vis. assoc. prof. U. Ga., 1974-75; cons. NSF, 1974-77; vis. prof. U. Calif. Berkeley, 1981-82; mem. biotech. sci. adv. com. EPA, 1986-89, chair sci. adv. coun. GPA, 1988-90. Editor: Applied Microbiology, 1974—, editor-in-chief, 1980-86. Recipient Carlos J. Finley prize, UNESCO, 1993. Mem. AAAS, Am. Soc. Agronomy (Soil Sci. award 1990), Internat. Inst. Biotech., Am. Soc. Microbiology (award in applied and environ. microbiology 1992), Soil Sci. Soc. Am., Ecol. Soc. Am., Internat. Soc. Soil Sci. (chair soil biology divsn.). Achievements include research in dentrification, microbial metabolism of organic pollutants, and molecular microbiol. ecology. Office: Michigan State U Microbial Ecology Ctr 540 Plant & Soil Scis Bldg East Lansing MI 48824-1325

TIEFEL, VIRGINIA MAY, librarian; b. Detroit, May 20, 1926; d. Karl and June Garland (Young) Brenkert; m. Paul Martin Tiefel, Jan. 25, 1947; children: Paul Martin Jr., Mark Gregory. BA in Elem. Edn., Wayne State U., 1962; MA in Library Sci., U. Mich., 1968. Librarian Birmingham Schs., Mich., 1967-68; librarian S. Euclid-Lyndhurst Schs., Cleve., 1968-69; acquisitions-reference librarian Hiram Coll., Ohio, 1969-77; head undergrad. libraries Ohio State U., Columbus, 1977-84, dir. library user edn., 1978-95, faculty outreach coord., 1995-98. Contbr. articles to profl. jours. Recipient Disting. Alumnus award U. Mich. Sch. Info. and Libr. Studies, 1993. Mem. ALA (v.p. Ohio sect. 1973-74, pres. 1974-75, Miriam Dudley Bibliographic Instrn. Librarian of Yr. 1986), Acad. Library Assn. Ohio (Outstanding Ohio Acad. Librarian 1984), Assn. Coll. and Research Libraries (chmn. bibliographic instrn. sect. com. on research 1983-84, chmn. com. on performance measures 1984-90). Lutheran. Home: 4711 Oak Bluff Ct Eau Claire WI 54701 E-mail: vtiefel@aol.com.

TIEFEL, WILLIAM REGINALD, hotel company executive; b. Rochester, N.Y., Mar. 30, 1934; s. William Reginald and Mary Hazel (Cross) T.; m. Vada Morell, Dec. 30, 1985 (dec. Apr. 1999); m. Norma Gewirz Kline, Nov. 25, 2000. Student, Williams Coll., 1952-54; BA with honors, Mich. State U., 1956; postgrad., Harvard Bus. Sch.; DBA in Hospitality Mgmt. (hon.), Johnson and Wales U. Gen. mgr. Marriott Hotels, Arlington, Va., 1964-65, Saddle Brook, N.J., 1966-69, Newton, Mass., 1969-71, regional v.p. Washington, 1971-80; corp. v.p. Marriott Corp., Washington, 1976-89; exec. v.p. Marriott Hotels and Resorts, Washington, 1980-88; pres. Marriott Hotels, Resorts and Suites, 1988-92; exec. v.p., mem. exec. and growth coms. Marriott Corp., 1988—2002; pres. Marriott Lodging Group, 1992-98; vice chmn. Marriott Internat., 1998—2002; chmn. Ritz-Carlton Hotel Co, 1998—2002, chmn. emeritus, 2002—; dir. Bulgari Hotels and Resorts, 2001—. Bd. dirs. Carmax, NY, N.Y. Stock Exch. Mem. bd. visitors Valley Forge Mil. Acad. and Jr. Coll., 1976-79, chmn., 1979, trustee, 1982-88, 89-92; chmn. Campaign for Valley Forge, 1985-88, chmn. com. on trustees, 1989-91, hon. life trustee; trustee Johnson and Wales U., 2002—; mem. adv. coun. Wilmer Eye Inst., Johns Hopkins U.; mem. bus. adv. com. Norton Mus. Art. Mem. Am. Hotel and Lodging Assn. (dir. Ednl. Inst., Arthur Landstreet award 1997), Soc. of the Four Arts, Cosmos Club (Washington). Republican. Roman Catholic. Home: 236 Via Las Brisas Palm Beach FL 33480-1643 E-mail: william.tiefel@marriott.com.

TIEFENBRUN, JONATHAN, surgeon; b. New York City, Feb. 5, 1943; s. Joseph and Helen (Henkin) Tiefenbrun; m. Susan Kissil, June 19, 1966; children: Michele, Jeremy, Gregory. MD, State Univ. N.Y., Bklyn., 1966. Diplomate Am. Bd. Surgery. Med. intern Kings County Hosp., Bklyn., 1966—67; resident in surgery Mt. Sinai Hosp., N.Y.C., 1967—73, chief resident in surgery, 1972—73, attending surgeon, 1973, Beth Israel Hosp., N.Y.C., 1981; sr. attending surgeon St. Luke's Roosevelt Hosp., N.Y.C., 1981; dir. clin. rsch. Lifescore Global Network, San Diego, 2001—03; dir. Balboa Nephrology Ultrasound Lab., San Diego, 2003—. Asst. prof. Mt. Sinai Sch. Medicine, N.Y.C., 1973; clin. prof. surgery U. Calif., San Diego, 2003. Contbr. articles to profl. journals. Fellow NIH, 1968—70. Fellow: ACS (instr. clin. ultrasound, dialysis access surgery); mem.: N.Y. Cardiovasc. Soc. Achievements include patents in field; inventor of catheters; endovascular grafts; ultrasonic and laser devices; gen. and vascular medicine and surgery diagnostice ultrasound. Avocation: classical guitar.

TIEFENBRUNN, ALAN JAMES, medical educator; b. St. Louis, Aug. 26, 1948; s. Kenneth Sylvester and Margaret Ann (Smith) T.; m. Sharon Kay Frost, June 3, 1972; children: Theresa, Curtis. AB cum laude, Washington U., St. Louis, 1970, MD, 1974. Intern, resident U. Calif., San Diego, 1974-77; fellow in cardiology Washington U., St. Louis, 1977-79, asst. prof. medicine, 1980-86, assoc. prof. medicine, 1986—, asst. prof. radiology, 1980—; assoc. physician Barnes Hosp., St. Louis, 1980—. Mem. adv. bd. Nat. Registry Myocardial Infarction, 1991—; mem. sci. steering com. Advancent Nat. CHF Registry, 2002--; cons. in field. Contbr. articles to profl. jours. Fellow Am. Coll. Cardiology, Am. Heart Assn. (coun. clin.cardiology), Alpha Omega Alpha. Avocations: skiing, scuba diving, shotgun sports. Home: 6255 Wydown Blvd Saint Louis MO 63105-2306 Office: Washington U Box 8086 660 S Euclid Ave Saint Louis MO 63110-1093 E-mail: atiefenb@im.wustl.edu.

TIEFENTHAL, MARGUERITE AURAND, school social worker; b. Battle Creek, Mich., July 23, 1919; d. Charles Henry and Elisabeth Dirk (Hoekstra) Aurand; m. Harlan E. Tiefenthal, Nov. 26, 1942; children: Susan Ann, Daniel E., Elisabeth Amber, Carol Aurand. BS, Western Mich. U., 1941; MSW, U. Mich., 1950; postgrad., Coll. of DuPage, Ill., 1988-90. Tchr. No. High Sch., Flint, Mich., 1941-44, Cen. High Sch., Kalamazoo, 1944-45; acct. Upjohn Co., Kalamazoo, 1945-48; social worker Family Svc. Agy., Lansing, Mich., 1948-50, Pitts., 1950-55; sch. social worker Gower Sch. Dist., Hinsdale, Ill., 1962-70, Hinsdale (Ill.) Dist. 181, 1970-89, cons., 1989—; sch. social worker Villa Park (Ill.) Sch. Dist. 45, 1989; addictions counselor Mercy Hosp., 1990-92; asst. prof. sch. social work, liaison to pub. schs. Loyola U., Chgo., 1990-98, ret., 1998. Field instr. social work interns U. Ill., 1979-88; impartial due process hearing officer; mem. adv. com. sch. social work Ill. State Bd. Edn. approved programs U. Ill. and George Williams Coll.; speaker Nat. Conf. Sch. Social Work, Denver, U. Tex. Joint Conf. Sch. Social Work in Ill.; founder Marguerite Tiefenthal Symposium for Ill. Sch. Social Work Interns. Co-editor The School Social Worker and the Handicapped Child: Making P.L. 94-142 Work; sect. editor: Sch. Social Work Quarterly, 1979. Sec. All Village Caucus Village of Western Springs, Ill., mem. village disaster com.; deacon Presbyn. Ch. Western Springs, Sunday sch. tchr., mem. choir; instr. Parent Effectiveness, Teacher Effectiveness, STEP; trainer Widowed Persons Service Tng. Program for Vol. Aides AARP. Recipient Ill. Sch. Social Worker of Yr., 1982. Mem. Nat. Assn. Social Workers (chmn. exec. council on social work in schs.), Ill. Assn. Sch. Social Workers (past pres., past conf. chmn., conf. program chmn.), Ladies Libr. Assn., Sch. Social Workers Supervisors Group (del. to Ill. Commn. on Children), Programs. for Licensure of Social Work Practice in Ill., Ladies Libr. Assn. (Kalamazoo), LWV, DKG, PEO. Avocation: sewing. Home: 4544 Grand Ave Western Springs IL 60558-1545 also: 3151 West B Ave Plainwell MI 49080

TIEFENWERTH, WILLIAM PHILIP, university program director; b. Bklyn., June 25, 1951; s. William Frederick and Catherine Florence (Klotz) T.; m. Karen Taylor, Aug. 15, 1977; 1 child, Casey Elizabeth. BS in Philosophy and Religion, Towson, U., 1973. Tchr., dept. dir. St. Mark Sch., Catonsville, Md., 1975-79; asst. to chaplain Johns Hopkins U., Balt., 1979-92, dir. vol. svcs., 1992-96, dir. cmty. rels., 1996—. Acad. advisor Johns Hopkins U., 1997, co-chairperson Mid-Atlantic region Am. Reads Regional Conf., 1997. Co-designer area mural (Balt.'s Best Mural award City Paper 1997). Founder cmty. ctr. Safe & Smart, 1994; bd. dirs. Homewood Literacy Adv., Balt., 1997, Charles Village Ben. Dist., Balt., 1996—; advisor Learn and Serve, Met. Balt., 1997, St. Paul St. Libr. Project, Balt., 1997; recruitment advisor Balt. Mentoring Partnership, 1997. Recipient award for Best Usage of Urban Property for Cmty. Use, 1994, 941st Point of Light award U.S. Pres. George Bush, Washington, 1992, Learning Loft award Abell Found., Balt., 1994. Mem. Md. Coun. Dirs. of Vol. Svcs., Student Affairs Adminstrs. Higher Edn. Democrat. Roman Catholic. Avocations: jazz, gardening, contemporary literature. Home: 2204 Grey Fox Ct Bel Air MD 21015-8905 Office: Johns Hopkins Univ 3400 N Charles St Baltimore MD 21218-2680

TIEGS, CHERYL, model, designer; b. Calif. Profl. model, appearing in nat. mags., including, Time, Life, Bazaar, Sports Illustrated, Glamour; appeared weekly on ABC's Good Morning America; also appearing in TV commls., Cheryl Tiegs line of sportswear, QVC, Cheryl Tiegs nationally-distributed line of women's eyeglass frames, Fashion Watches, Shoes and Hosiery, salon collection of wigs for Revlon; author: The Way to Natural Beauty, 1980; Sports Illustrated video Aerobic Interval Training with Cheryl Tiegs. Address: care Barbara Shapiro 15 E Putnam Ave Ste 3260 Greenwich CT 06830-5424

TIEKEN, ROBERT W. tire manufacturing company executive; b. Decatur, Ill., May 6, 1939; married; 2 children. BS, Ill. Wesleyan U. With GE Co., mem. corp. audit staff; mgr. fin. ops. GE Nuclear Energy, GE Transp. Sys.; with GE Aerospace, v.p. fin. and info. tech.; corp. v.p. GE Co., 1988; corp. v.p. fin. Martin Marietta, Bethesda, Md.; v.p. fin. Utah Internat., Inc.; exec. v.p., CFO Goodyear Tire and Rubber Co., Akron, Ohio, 1994—. Office: Goodyear Tire and Rubber Co 1144 E Market St Akron OH 44316-0002

TIELKE, JAMES CLEMENS, retail and manufacturing management consultant; b. St. Helena, Nebr., May 15, 1931; s. Joseph Hubert and Catherine Josephine (Schmidt) T.; m. Betty Merle Adams, Apr. 18, 1953; children: P.J., Michael J., Dawn M. BS in Bus. Adminstrn., U. S.D., 1959, MA in Speech and Econ., 1960. Partner, Tielke Motors, Yankton, S.D., 1952-54; owner Ft. Collins Motors, Colo., 1954-56; grad. tchg. asst. U. S.D., 1959-60; corp. buyer and mgr. auto, lawn/garden, paint, electronics Montgomery Ward, Chgo., 1960-77, v.p. mdse. adminstrn., 1978-81; pres. Midwest div. Structured Approaches, Inc., 1981-82; v.p. nat. accounts Dupli-Color Products, Elk Grove Village, Ill., 1983-85; pres. Black Leaf Products Co., 1985-89; v.p. Hysan Corp., Des Plaines, Ill., 1985-89; v.p. ice melter sales Koos, Inc., IMC Vigoro, Kenosha, Wis., 1989-97; pres. J.C. Tielke Assocs., Inc., 1997—. Mem. Nat. Ind. Conf. Bd. Pers. Mgmt. Conf., 1966, Am. Mgmt. Assn. Sr. Mgmt. Conf., 1977. Chmn. Chgo. Minority Bus. Opportunities Fair Devel. Commn.; bd. dirs. Chgo. Youth Ctrs., 1979-82. Recipient Honors award U. S.D. Sch. Bus., 1977 Mem. Internat. San. Supply Assn. Office Phone: 847-362-1225.

TIEMEYER, CHRISTIAN, conductor; m. Pattie Farris; children: Jeanie, Hank, Elisa. Grad., Peabody Conservatory; D of Musical Arts, Cath. U. of Am. Assoc. condr. Dallas Symphony, 1978-83; interim artistic dir., prin. guest condr. Omaha Symphony; music dir. Cedar Rapids Symphony, 1982—; founder Symphony Sch. of Music, 1986. Chmn. string and conducting faculties U. Utah; faculty Brigham Young U.; founding condr. Snowbird Summer Arts Inst.; founder Bear Lake Music Festival, 1992; guest condr. Preucil Orch. Prin. cellist Utah Symphony. Avocations: fly fishing, boating, outdoor activities. Office: Cedar Rapids Symphony Orch 205 2nd Ave SE Cedar Rapids IA 52401-1213

TIEMSTRA, JOHN PETER, economics professor; b. Chgo., July 15, 1950; s. Peter John and Margaret (Lamont) T.; m. Suzanne Spicer, Dec. 28, 1985; 1 stepchild: Remi Spicer Rakipi. AB, Oberlin Coll., 1971; PhD, MIT, 1975. Asst. prof. econs. Calvin Coll., Grand Rapids, Mich., 1975-81, assoc. prof., 1981-85, prof., 1985—. Vis. prof. Potchefstroom U., South Africa, 1992. Author: Economics: A Developmental Approach, 1999; editor, co-author: Reforming Economics, 1990; contbr. articles to profl. jours. Dean Grand Rapids Am. Guild of Organists, 1990-91; pres. West Mich. Irish Heritage Soc., Grand Rapids, 1988-91, Forest Hills Condo Assn., Cascade, Mich., 1988—; organist St. Paul's Epicopal Ch., Grand Rapids, 1990—, Working Group on Ethics and the Earth, Reformed Ch. in Am., 2002-04. Mem. Assn. for Social Econs., Assn. of Christian Economists, Am. Econ. Assn. Christian Reformed. Avocation: folk and church music. Office: Calvin Coll 1740 Knollcrest Cir SE Grand Rapids MI 49546-4301

TIENDA, MARTA, demographer, educator; b. Tex. PhD in Sociology, U. Tex., 1977. From asst. prof. to prof. rural sociology U. Wis., Madison, 1976—87; vis. prof. Stanford U., 1987; Ralph Lewis prof. sociology U. Chgo., 1994—97, chmn. dept. sociology, 1994—96; prof. sociology and pub. affairs Princeton U., NJ, 1997—, dir. office population rsch., 1998—2002, Maruice P. During '22 prof. demographic studies, 1999—. Rsch. assoc. office population rsch. Princeton U., 1997—; bd. dirs. Fed. Res. Bank N.Y. Co-author: Hispanics in the U.S. Economy, 1985, Hispanic Population of the United States, 1987, Divided Opportunities, 1988, The Color of Opportunity, 2001, Youth in Cities, 2002; contbr. articles to profl. jours. Trustee Corp. of Brown U., Jacobs Found. of Switzerland; bd. dirs. Princeton Med. Ctr. Guggenheim fellow. Fellow: AAAS, Am. Acad. Political Social Sci., Ctr. Advanced Study Behavioral Scis.; mem.: Internat. Union for Sci. Study of Population, Population Assn. Am. (past pres.), Am. Econ. Assn., Am. Sociol. Assn. Office: Office Population Rsch Princeton U 247 Wallace Hall Princeton NJ 08544-2091

TIENE, DREW, communications educator, consultant; b. Jersey City, June 21, 1948; s. Charles Drew Tiene and Dorothy Pepoon; m. Pamela Jean Luft, July 12, 1997. BA, U. Mich., Ann Arbor, 1970, MA, 1971; PhD, U. Tex., 1983. Cert. k-8 tchr. NY, Mich. Tchr. Village Cmty. Sch., NYC, 1972—79; instr. U. Tex., Austin, 1979—83; prof. Kent (Ohio) State U., 1983—. Cons. World Bank, Washington, 1985—87; mem. Assn. Ednl. Comm. and Tech., 1985—95; juror ednl. TV contest Japanese Broadcasting Co., Tokyo, 1991; cons. U.S. Agy. for Internat. Devel., Beijing and Bangkok, 1994—97; edit. bd. Ednl. Tech. Jour., Englewood Cliffs, NJ, 1997—; cons. Asian Devel. Bank, Manila, 2001. Author: (book) Exploring Current Issues in Ednl. Tech., 2001; prodr.: (documentaries) The Story of the Kent State Shootings, 1995; dir.: The Cuyahoga: Portrait of a River, 1995 (Environ. Video award, 1993). Grantee rsch., Japanese Broadcasting Found., 1994. Mem.: Soc. Info. Tech. in Edn. Home: 1873 Pine Ave Kent OH 44240 Office: Kent State Univ White Hall 405 Kent OH 44242 Business E-Mail: dtiene@kent.edu.

TIENKEN, ARTHUR T. retired foreign service officer; b. Yonkers, N.Y., Aug. 5, 1922; BA, Princeton U., 1947, MA, 1949. With U.S. Fgn. Svc., 1949-87, dep. chief mission, 1973-75, Addis Ababa, Ethiopia, 1975-77; Ambassador to Gabonese Republic and Democratic Republic of Sao Tome and Principe, Libreville, Gabon, 1978-81; dir. Fgn. Svc. Assignments and Career devel. Dept. State, 1981-85, sr. insp., 1985-87, ret., 1987. Diplomat-in-residence Marquette U., 1972-73 Served with U.S. Army, 1943-46. Mem. Diplomatic and Consular Officers Ret. (bd. govs. 1999—).

TIEP, PHAM HUU, mathematician, educator; DSc, Moscow State U., Russia. Assoc. prof. U. Fla., Gainesville, 2001—. Contbr. articles various profl. jours. Recipient 2nd prize, Internat. Math. Olympiad, 1979, Faculty Tchg. award, Coll. of Liberal Arts and Sciences, 2001—02; Rsch. fellowship, Alexander von Humboldt Found., 1993 - 1995. Mem.: Am. Math. Soc. Office: U Fla Dept Math 358 Little Hall PO Box 118105 Gainesville FL 32611-8105 Office Phone: 352-392-0281. E-mail: tiep@math.ufl.edu.

TIERNEY, BILL, university athletic coach; Head coach Princeton Tigers, 1988—. NCAA Divsn. 1A Champions, 1992, 94, 96, 97, 98; named Morris Touchstone Divsn. 1A Coach of the Yr.; elected to L.I. Lacrosse Hall of Fame, 1995. Office: Princeton U Dillon Gym Princeton NJ 08544-0001

TIERNEY, GORDON PAUL, real estate broker, genealogist; b. Ft. Wayne, Ind., Oct. 17, 1922; s. James Leonard and Ethele Lydia (Brown) T.; m. Carma Lillian Devine, Oct. 17, 1946; 1 child, Paul N. Student, Ind. U., 1940-41, Cath. U. Am., 1941-42; coll. tng. detachment, Clemson U., 1943. Br. mgr. Bartlett-Collins Co., Chgo., 1956-84; prin., broker Kaiser-Tierney Real Estate, Inc., Palatine, Ill., 1984-89; pres. Tierney Real Estate, Newburgh, Ind. Author: Burgess/Bryan Connection, 1978; assoc. editor Colonial Genealogist Jour., 1976-85. With U.S. Army, 1943—45, China. Decorated Legion of Honor; named Ky. Col. Fellow Am. Coll. Genealogists (pres. 1977-2000); mem. SAR (life mem., v.p. gen. 1984-85, genealogist gen. 1981-83, Silver and Bronze medals 1978-80, Patriot medal 1976, Meritorious Svc. award 1983, Minutemen award 1984), Huguenot Soc. Ill. (state pres. 1978-80), Huguenot Soc. S.C., Nat. Huguenot Soc., Huguenot Soc. Ind. (pres. 1993-95), Nat. Geneal. Soc., Ind. Hist. Soc., Soc. Ind. Pioneers, First Families Ohio, Ohio Geneal. Soc., Va. Geneal. Soc., Md. Geneal. Soc., Augustan Soc., Gen. Soc. War 1812 (state pres. 1985), Sons. and Daus. Pilgrims, Descs. Old Plymouth Colony, Mil. Order Stars and Bars, Soc. Descs. Colonial Clergy, Sons of Union Vets., Sons of Confederate Vets., Pioneer Wis. Families, Welcome Soc. Pa., Pa. Geneal. Soc., Nat. Soc. Archivists, Soc. Colonial Wars in Ill. (life mem.), Soc. Colonial Wars in Ind. (gov. 1992-94), Soc. Colonial Wars in Commonwealth Ky. (life mem.), Sons of Am. Colonists (nat. v.p. 1971-74), Mil. and Hospitalier Order St. Lazarus of Jerusalem, Clan Johnston/e in Am., Order Descs. Ancient Planters, Hump Pilots Assn., Nat. Bd. Realtors, Ill. Bd. Realtors, Sword Bunker Hill, Tri-State Geneal. Soc., Jamestowne Soc., Baronial Order Magna Charta, Royal Order Scotland, Masons, Shriners, Rolling Hill Country Club, Legion of Honor (comdr. 2001-02). Republican. Presbyterian. Home and Office: 8766 Hanover Dr Newburgh IN 47630-9327

TIERNEY, JOHN F. congressman, lawyer; b. Salem, Mass., Sept. 18, 1951; m. Patrice Tierney. BA, Salem State Coll., 1973; JD, Suffolk U., 1976. Ptnr. Tierney, Kalis, and Lucas, North Shore, Mass.; mem. U.S. Congress from 6th Mass. dist., 1997—; mem. com. edn. and workforce, com. gov. reform. Pres. Salem C. of C. Democrat. Office: US House Reps 120 Cannon House Office Bldg Washington DC 20515-0001

TIERNEY, KEVIN JOSEPH, lawyer, arbitrator, mediator, director; b. Lowell, Mass., Dec. 13, 1951; s. Joseph Francis and Esther Rowena T. BS cum laude, Bowdoin Coll., 1973; JD, U. Maine, 1976. Bar: Maine 1976. Atty. Union Mutual Life Ins. Co., Portland, Maine, 1976-80, asst. counsel, 1980, 2d v.p., counsel, 1980-84, 2d v.p., counsel, corp. sec., 1984-86, UNUM Corp., Portland, 1986-89, v.p., corp. counsel, sec., 1989-91, gen. counsel, sr. v.p., sec., 1991-99; atty. in pvt. practice Falmouth, Maine, 1999—. Bd. dirs. Vesta Ins. Group, MLIG Variable Ins. Trust. Bd. dirs. Pine Tree Alcoholism Treatment Ctr., Maine, 1977-84, So. Regional Alcoholism and Drug Abuse Coun., Maine, 1982-85; mem. radiation therapy tech. adv. com. So. Me. Vocat. Tech. Inst., 1985; trustee Portland Symphony Orch., 1990-99; trustee, treas. Falmouth Med. Libr. Mem. ARIAS-U.S., Assn. Life Ins. Counsel, Maine State Bar Assn., Cumberland County (Maine) Bar Assn., ABA.

TIERNEY, MAURA, actress; b. Boston, Feb. 3, 1965; m. Billy Morrissette, 1994. Student, NYU, Cir. in the Sq. Theatre Sch. Actor: (TV series) 704 Hauser St., —, News Radio, 1995—2000, ER, 2000—; (TV films) Flying Blind, 1990—, Out of Darkness, —, Student Exchange, —, Crossing the Mob, —, (guest appearance): (TV series) Growing Pains; (TV films) Family Ties; (TV series) Law & Order, The Van Dyke Show.; (films) Dead Women in Lingerie, 1991, The Linguini Incident, 1991, White Sands, 1992, Fly By Night, 1993, The Temp, 1993, Primal Fear, 1996, Primary Colors, 1997, Liar, Liar, 1997, Primary Colors, 1998, Forces of Nature, 1999, Instinct, 1999, Welcome to Mooseport, 2004. Office: c/o CAA 9830 Wilshire Blvd Beverly Hills CA 90212

TIERNEY, MICHAEL EDWARD, lawyer; b. N.Y., July 16, 1948; s. Michael Francis and Margaret Mary (Creamer) T.; m. Alicia Mary Boldt, June 6, 1981; children: Colin, Madeleine. BA, St. Louis U., 1970, MBA, JD, St. Louis U., 1978. Bar: Mo. Assoc., law clk. Wayne L. Millsap, PC, St. Louis, 1977-80; staff atty. Interco. Inc., St. Louis, 1980-83; textile divsn. counsel Chromalloy Am. Corp., St. Louis, 1984-87; v.p., sec. P.N. Hirsch & Co., St. Louis, 1983-84; sr. counsel, asst. sec. Jefferson Smurfit Corp., St. Louis, 1987-92, v.p., gen. counsel, sec., 1993-99, Kinexus Corp., St. Louis, 1999—2002. Adv. bd. St. Louis Area Food Bank, 1980—. U.S. Army Security Agy., 1970-73. Mem. Racquet Club St. Louis, Old Warson Country Club. Republican. Roman Catholic. Avocations: sailing, squash. Home: 10 Twin Springs Ln Saint Louis MO 63124-1139 Address: 18500 Edison Ave Chesterfield MO 63005-3629

TIERNEY, MICHAEL JOHN, mathematics and computer science educator; b. St. Louis, Feb. 19, 1947; s. John Thomas and Alice Marie (Krieger) T.; m. Edith L. Echelmeyer, Nov. 21, 1975 (div. Sept. 1984); 1 child, John E.; m. Virginia Lee Christian, Apr. 6, 1985. BS, St. Louis U., 1969, MS, 1971, PhD, 1974; MS, U. Va., 1995. Prof. math. and actuarial sci. Maryville Coll., St. Louis, 1974-83; prof. math. and computer sci. Va. Mil. Inst., Lexington, 1983—; dept. chair, 1995—. Mem. AAUP, AAAS, Am. Math. Soc., Math. Assn. Am., Soc. Indsl. and AppliedMath., Assn. Computing Machinery, Sigma Xi. Presbyterian. Avocations: tennis, landscaping. Home: 819 Gwynne Ave Waynesboro VA 22980-3342 Office: Va Mil Inst Lexington VA 24450

TIERNEY, PATRICK JOHN, information services executive; b. Denver, Oct. 9, 1945; s. Thomas Michael and Betty Ruth (Fairall) T.; m. Lois Bruce, Jan. 1, 1980; children: Christopher, Blake. BS, U. Colo., 1967, MBA, 1970. Pres. Gould E.P.C. Div., San Diego, 1980-84, Caterpillar Capital, San Diego, 1984-85; v.p., gen. mgr. TRW Info. Svcs., Orange, Calif., 1985-91; CEO Knight-Ridder Info., Mountain View, Calif., 1991-96; group CEO, The Thomson Corp., Stamford, Conn., 1996—. Mem. Info. Industry Assn. (chmn.). Republican. Office: The Thomson Corp 290 Harbor Dr Stamford CT 06902 E-mail: pat.tierney@tfn.com.

TIERNEY, THOMAS J. social entrepreneur; b. San Francisco, Mar. 5, 1954; s. Ralph Thomas and Eleanor Faye (Walker) T.; m. Joy Karen McGee, Sept. 23, 1984; children: Colin McGee, Braden Thomas. BA in Econs. with distinction, U. Calif., Davis, 1976; MBA with distinction, Harvard, 1980. Field engr. Bechtel Internat., Azrew, Algeria, 1976-78; cons. Bain & Co., San Francisco, 1980-82, mgr., 1982-83, v.p., 1983-87, mng. ptnr., 1987-92; pres. Bain & Co. Worldwide, San Francisco, 1992-2000, CEO, 1993-2000; founder & chmn. Bridgespan Group, 2000—; bd. dirs. eBay, Inc. Co-author: Aligning the Stars, 2002. Trustee Woods Hole Oceanographic Inst., The Hoover Inst., Harvard Bus. Sch. Social Enterprise; former bd. dirs. Nature Conservancy, Cath. Charities, WGBH, U. Calif.-Davis Alumni Assn., Bay Area United Way, United Way Mass. Bay, Stanford Bus. Sch.; bd. dirs. Inst. for Higher Edn., Nat. Acads. Recipient Winslow Meml. award U. Calif. Davis, 1976. Roman Catholic. Avocations: fishing, politics, non-profit sector. Home: 45 Old Farm Rd Wellesley MA 02481-1423 Office Phone: 617-572-3015.

TIERNO, PHILIP MARIO, JR., microbiologist, educator, researcher; b. Bklyn., June 5, 1943; s. Philip M. and Phyllis (Tringone) T.; m. Josephine Martinez, Apr. 2, 1967; children: Alexandra Lorraine, Meredith Anne. BS, LI U., 1965; MS, NYU, 1974, PhD, 1977. Microbiologist Luth. Med. Ctr., Bklyn., 1965-66; chief rsch. microbiologist hemodialysis unit VA Hosp., Bronx, NY, 1966-70; dir. microbiology divsn. NYU Med. Ctr. Goldwater Meml. Hosp., F.D. Roosevelt Island, 1970-81; assoc. and cons. microbiologist Maimonides Med. Ctr., Bklyn., 1970-79; dir. microbiology dept. Tisch-Univ. Hosp., NYU Med. Ctr., 1981—. Adj. asst. prof. CUNY, 1974—76, Bloomfield (NJ) Coll., 1975—82; assoc. prof. microbiology and pathology NYU Med. Sch., 1981—; cons. Office Atty. Gen. NY State, NIH, Coll. of Am. Pathologists, Dept. Health City of NY, 1981—; mem. Mayoral Task Force on Bioterrorism, NYC. Author: The Secret Life of Germs: Observations and Lessons from a Microbe Hunter, 2001, Protect Yourself Against Bioterrorism, 2002, Nuclear, Chemical and Biological Terrorism: Emergency Response and Public Protection, 2003, The Secret Life of Germs: What They Are, Why We Need Them, and How We Can Protect Ourselves Against Them, 2004; contbr. articles to profl. jours., chapters to books. Pres. Flushing Taxpayers Assn., 1973-77; bd. dirs. Comprehensive Health Planning Agy. City of NY, 1974-75, Norwood Bd. Adjustment, NJ, 1978-83, 86-98, Norwood Bd. Edn., 1983-86; chmn. Norwood Environ. Commn., 1986-98; co-founder, bd. dirs. Found. Sci. Rsch. in Pub. Interest, S.I., NY, 1985—. Mem. AAAS, NY Acad. Scis., Am. Acad. Microbiology, APHA, Am. Soc. Microbiology, Optimists (v.p. Norwood 1978-95), Knights of Malta (Knighthood). Home: 102 Harbor Cove Piermont NY 10968 Office: Tisch Hosp-Microbiology Dept NYU Med Ctr 560 1st Ave New York NY 10016-6402 Office Phone: 212-263-5905.

TIESZEN, RALPH LELAND, SR., hospital administrator, educator; b. Marion, SD, Sept. 21, 1928; s. Bernard D. and Hulda J. (Thomas) T.; m. Florence Morrill Johnson, July 25, 1952; children: Ralph Leland Jr., Stuart Carl, Stephan Lee. Student, Freeman Jr. Coll., 1946-48; BS, Wheaton Coll., 1950; postgrad., U. S.D., 1950-52; MD, Loma Linda U., 1954. Diplomate Am. Bd. Internal Medicine, Am. Bd. Geriatric Medicine. Intern LA County Hosp., 1954-55, resident TB and Chest, 1955-56; commd. 2d lt. med. corps. USAF, 1956, advanced through grades to maj., 1964, chief medicine hosp., 1962-64, ret., 1979; resident in internal medicine Mayo Found., Rochester, Minn., 1957-60; mem. active staff dept. internal medicine Carraway Meth. Med. Ctr., Birmingham, 1964—, dir. resident program, 1968-72, trustee, 1972-77, pres. staff, 1973-75, exec. com., fin. com., 1974-77, dir. geriatrics, 1989—; pvt. practice Carraway Internal Medicine Assoc., Birmingham, Ala.; asst. clin. prof. medicine Med. Coll. Ala., 1965-69, asst. clin. prof. dept. endocrinology, 1969-70, clin. assoc. prof. medicine, 1970-81, clin. prof. medicine, 1981—; clin. prof. gerontology and geriatric medicine U. Ala., Birmingham, 1999—; med. dir. Cmty. Hosp., 1989—. Mem. faculty joint commn. accreditation hosps., 1974-78; exec. com. Birmingham Regional Health Systems Agy.; investigator numerous clin. trials. Contbr. articles to profl. jours. Chmn. Birmingham String Quartet, 1970-74; v.p. ticket sales Ala. Symphony Assn., 1979, exec. com.; sec. men's com. Ala. Symphony, 1986-88, pres. 1990-91. Gen. Med. Officer USAR, 197984, comdr. U.S. Army Hosp., Birmingham, 1984-88, col., chief profl. svcs. 5th med. group, Birmingham, 1988-92, ret., 1992. Fellow ACP; mem. AMA, Am. Thoracic Soc. (sr.), Med. Assn. State Ala., Jefferson County Med. Soc. (past bd. censors, del. to state med. assn.), Birmingham Acad. Medicine (pres. 1987-88), Birmingham Internists Soc. (pres. 1972-73). Democrat. Avocations: opera, symphony, philosophy, medical ethics, astronomy. Office: Carraway Internal Medicine Assocs 1600 Carroway Blvd Ste 302 Birmingham AL 35234

TIET, QUYEN Q. clinical psychologist, researcher; b. Saigon, Vietnam, Dec. 11, 1964; BA, U. Calif., Berkeley, 1991; MA, U. Colo., Boulder, 1993; predoctoral fellow, Yale U., 1995—96; PhD, U. Colo., Boulder, 1996. Cert. clin. psychologist N.Y., 1998, Calif., 2001. Postdoctoral fellow Columbia U., N.Y.C., 1996—99, asst. prof. clin. psychology in psychiatry, 1999—2001; rsch. health sci. specialist, Dept. Vet. Affairs Palo Alto Health Care Sys. Stanford U. Sch. Medicine, Menlo Park, Calif., 2000—, consulting asst. prof. dept. psychiatry and behavioral scis., 2004—. Contbr. articles to profl. jours. Bd. dirs. Asian Am. Cmty. Involvement, San Jose, Calif., 2001. Recipient Young Investigator award, Nat. Alliance Rsch. of Depression and Schizophrenia, 1999. Mem.: APA. Office: Stanford U Sch Medicine Dept Vet Affairs Palo Alto Health Care Sys 795 Willow Rd # 152 Menlo Park CA 94025 Office Phone: 650-493-5000 27852. E-mail: quyen.tiet@med.va.gov.

TIETENBERG, THOMAS, economist, department chairman; b. Oct. 21, 1942; s. Harry Hall and Florence Elaine (Moxley) Tietenberg; m. Gretchen Ethel Sprague, Oct. 28, 1967; children: Heidi Leigh, Eric Justin. BS with distinction, U.S. Air Force Acad., 1964; MA in Econs., U. of East, Manila, 1965; MS in Econs., U. Wis., 1970, PhD in Econs., 1971. Asst. prof. econs. Williams Coll., Williamstown, Mass., 1971—77; assoc. prof. econs. Colby Coll., Waterville, Maine, 1977—84, prof. econs., 1984—, chmn., dept. econs., 1985—88, 1993—95, chmn., environ. studies program, 2000—, C.A. Johnson disting. tchg. prof., 1990—93, Mitchell Family prof. econs., 1993—. Mem. sci. adv. bd. environ. econs. com. U.S. EPA, 1993—96; editl. bd. Land Econs. Mgmt., 1981—, Jour. Environ. Econs. and Mgmt., 1992—98, Resource and Energy Econs., 1993—. Author: Emissions Trading: An Exercise in Reforming Pollution Policy, 1985, Environmental Economics and Policy, 2000, 4th edit., 2004, Environmental and Natural Resource Economics, 6th edit., 2003. Lay leader Pleasant St. United Meth. Ch., Waterville, 1984—88. Served from 2d lt. to capt. USAF, 1964—68. Fellow Gilbert T. White Resources for Future, Inc., 1984, econ. policy, Brookings Inst., 1974; scholar Fulbright, Inst. Internat. Edn., 1964. Mem.: Assn. Environ. and Resource Economists (pres. 1987—88). Avocations: golf, choral singing. Home: 2616 W River Rd Sidney ME 04330-2732

TIETKE, WILHELM, gastroenterologist, educator; b. Niengraben, Germany, Oct. 15, 1938; came to U.S., 1969, naturalized, 1979; s. Wilhelm and Frieda (Schmeding) T.; m. Imme Schmidt, Oct. 15, 1965; children: Cornelia, Isabel. MD, U. Goettingen, Germany, 1968. Diplomate Am. Bd. Internal Medicine, Am. Bd. Gastroenterology. Intern Edward W. Sparrow Hosp., Lansing, Mich., 1970; resident in internal medicine Henry Ford Hosp., Detroit, 1971-73, fellow in gastroenterology, 1973-75; practice medicine specializing in gastroenterology Huntsville, Ala., 1975—. Mem. vol. faculty, cons. U. Ala., Huntsville, 1976; clin. assoc. prof. internal medicine, 1979—; v.p. Huntsville Gastroenterology Assocs., P.C., 1979—. Fellow Coll. Gastroenterology; mem. AMA, ACP, Ala. Med. Soc., Am. Soc. Gastrointestinal Endoscopy, Rotary. Lutheran. Home: 2707 Westminister Way SE Huntsville AL 35801-2241 Office: 119 Longwood Dr Huntsville AL 35801 also: PO Box 2169 Huntsville AL 35804-2169

TIETZ, DIETMAR JUERGEN, website engineer, scientist; b. Berlin, Jan. 19, 1951; s. Alfred Georg Paul and Gertrud Klara (Schulz) T. m. Angelina (Osorio Ugalde). PhD, Hamburg U., 1982. Lectr. U. Hamburg, 1977-82; sr. scientist macromolecular analysis NIH, Bethesda, Md., 1983-93; pres., CEO, chmn. mktg. Forty Plus Greater Washington, 1992-93; sci. project mgr. dept. biostats. Justus-Liebig U., Giessen, Germany, 1993-95; web engring. team lead, software arch. Aerotek Md., NASA EOSDIS govt. project Raytheon Systems, 1996-99; dir. product devel. Dynamic Diagrams subs. Cadmus Profl. Comm., 1999—. Editor: Nucleic Acid Electrophoresis Lab Manual, 1998; mem. editl. bd. Electrophoresis Jour., VCH Weinheim, Germany, 1994-96. Mem. Am. Chem. Soc., Assn. German Naturforscher and Aerzte. Lutheran. Avocations: nature, computers, photography, electronic keyboard. Office: Cadmus Profl Comm 940 Elkridge Landing Rd Linthicum Heights MD 21090 E-mail: djt@his.com.

TIETZ, NORBERT WOLFGANG, clinical chemistry educator, administrator; b. Stettin, Germany, Nov. 13, 1926; s. Joseph and Anna (Kozalla) T.; m. Gertrud Kraft, Oct. 17, 1959; children— Margaret, Kurt, Annette, Michael Student, Tuebingen, Germany, 1945-46; D.Sc., Tech. U., Stuttgart, Ger., 1950. Chmn. dept. chemistry Reid Meml. Hosp., Richmond, Ind., 1956-59; prof., dir. clin. chemistry Mt. Sinai Med. Ctr. and Chgo. Med. Sch., Chgo., 1959-76, U. Ky. Med. Ctr., Lexington, 1976-96; prof. pathology U. Calif., San Diego, 1996—. Research fellow and asst. U. Munich, W.Ger., 1951-54; research fellow dept. pathology U. Chgo. and St. Luke's Hosp., Chgo., 1955-56, Rockford Meml. Hosp., Ill., 1954-55; cons. Ill. Dept. Pub. Health, 1967-76, VA Hosp., Hines, Ill., 1974-76; prof. biochemistry and pathology Rush Med. Coll., Chgo., 1975-76; vol. cons. VA Hosp., Lexington, 1976-96; cons. Dept. VA Med. Ctr., San Diego, 1997—. Editor: Fundamentals of Clinical Chemistry, 1970, 76, 87, Clinical Guide to Laboratory Tests, 1983, 90, 95, Textbook of Clinical Chemistry, 1986, A Study Guide to Clinical Chemistry, 1987, Applied Laboratory Medicine, 1992; assoc. editor: Dictionary and Encyclopedia of Laboratory Medicine and Technology, 1983; contbr. numerous articles to profl. jours. Recipient A. Dubin award Nat. Acad. Clin. Biochemistry, 1995, Disting. Internat. Svc. award Internat. Fedn. Clin. Chemistry, 1996. Fellow Acad. Clin. Lab. Physicians and Scientists, Am. Inst. Chemists; mem. Am. Assn. Clin. Chemistry (clin. chemist award 1971, award for outstanding efforts in edn. and tng. 1976, Disting. Alumnus award 1977, Steuben Bowl award 1978, Bernard F. Gerulat award N.J. chpt. 1988, award for Outstanding Contbns. to Clin. Chemistry 1989, Donald D. Van Slyke award N.Y. Met. chpt. 1989), AAAS, Am. Chem. Soc., Am. Soc. Clin. Pathologists, Man. Soc. Clin. Chemists (ann. Lectureship award 1987), Sigma Xi. Roman Catholic. Home: 7472 Caminito Rialto La Jolla CA 92037-3957 Office: U Calif Dept Pathology 9500 Gilman Dr La Jolla CA 92093-0612 E-mail: ntietz@ucsd.edu.

TIFFANY, JOSEPH RAYMOND, II, lawyer; b. Dayton, Ohio, Feb. 5, 1949; s. Forrest Fraser and Margaret Watson (Clark) T.; m. Terri Robbins, Dec. 1, 1984. AB magna cum laude, Harvard U., 1971; MS in Internat. Relations, London Sch. Econs., 1972; JD, U. Calif., Berkeley, 1975. Bar: U.S. Dist. Ct. (no. dist.) 1975, U.S. Dist. Ct. (ea. dist.) 1977, U.S. Ct. Appeals (9th cir.) 1982. Assoc. Pillsbury, Madison & Sutro, San Francisco, 1975-82, ptnr., 1983-2001, Pillsbury Winthrop LLP, Palo Alto, Calif., 2001—. Mem. ABA (antitrust, litigation sects.), Calif. Bar Assn. (antitrust and unfair competition sect.), Harvard Club. Office: Pillsbury Winthrop LLP 2475 Hanover St Palo Alto CA 94304-1115 Business E-Mail: jtiffany@pillsburywinthrop.com.

TIFFANY, SANDRA L. state legislator; b. Spokane, Wash., June 30, 1949; m. Ross M. Tonkens; 1 child, Courtney. Student, U. Calif. Mem. Nev. Assembly, 1993—. Mem. Nev. Rep. State Ctrl. com., Clark County Rep. Ctrl. com.; mem. adv. bd. Boys and Girls Club of Henderson; bd. dirs. Desert Rsch. Inst. Mem. Nat. Assn. Women Bus. Owners, Nat. Conf. State Legislatures, Nat. Orgn. Women Legislators, Am. Legis. Exchange coun., Nat. Rep. Leadership Assn., Exec. Devel. Assn., Henderson C. of C. (mktg. and tourism com., issues com.), Nev. Rep. Women's Club, Green Valley Cmty. Assn., Variety Club. Home: 61 Tanglewood Dr Henderson NV 89012-2117

TIFFANY-CASTIGLIONI, EVELYN, biomedical science educator, researcher; b. El Paso, Tex. d. Robert Samuel and Frances James Tiffany; m. Aldo Joseph Castiglioni Jr., Dec. 28, 1977; children: Anna Tiffany, Peter Vincent. BS in Biology, U. Tex., El Paso, 1975; PhD, U. Tex. Med. Branch, Galveston, 1979. Postdoc. fellow U. Calif., L.A., 1980-82; asst. prof. Tex. A&M U., College Station, 1982-87, assoc. prof., 1987-94; vis. assoc. prof. U. Tex. Health Sci. Ctr., San Antonio, 1989-90; prof. Tex. A&M U., College Station, 1994—; asst. dean for undergrad. edn. Coll. of Vet., Medicine Tex. A&M U., College Station, 1996-98, assoc. dean for undergrad. edn., 1998—, head dept. vet. anatomy and pub. health, 1999—. Mem. exec. com. U. Tex. Med. Br. Grad. Sch. Biomedicine, Galveston, 1999—. Author: (poems) Perspectives in Biology and Medicine, 1990; editor: In Vitro Neurotoxicology: Principles and Challenges, 2004; assoc. editor Neurotoxicology, 2004—; mem. editl. bd. Internat. Jour. Neurosci. Rsch., 2000—; contbr. articles to profl. jours. Recipient Faculty Disting. Achievement Award for Rsch., Tex. A&M U. Assn. Former Students, 1998; grantee NIH, 1993-97, EPA, 1985-89. Mem. Soc. Toxicologists, Am. Soc. Neurochemistry, Soc. for Neuroscience, Phi Kappa Phi. Avocations: harp, accordion. Office: Dept Vet Anatomy and Pub Health Texas A&M University College Station TX 77843-0001 Fax: 979-847-8981. Business E-Mail: ecastiglioni@cvm.tamu.edu.

TIFFT, WILLIAM GRANT, astronomer, educator; b. Derby, Conn., Apr. 5, 1932; s. William Charles and Marguerite Howe (Hubbell) T.; m. Carol Ruth Nordquist, June 1, 1957 (div. July 1964); children: Jennifer, William John; m. Janet Ann Lindner Homewood, June 2, 1965; 1 child, Amy, stepchildren: Patricia, Susan, Hollis. AB, Harvard Coll., 1954; PhD, Calif. Inst. Tech., 1958. Nat. sci. postdoctoral Australian Nat. U., Canberra, 1958-60; rsch. assoc. Vanderbilt U., Nashville, 1960-61; astronomer Lowell Obs., Flagstaff, Ariz., 1961-64; assoc. prof. U. Ariz., Tucson, 1964-73, prof., 1973—2002, prof. emeritus, 2002—; prin. scientist Sci. Assn. Study of Time in Physics and Cosmology, 2000—. Joint author: Revised New General Catalog, 1973; joint editor: Modern Mathematical Models of Time and Their Applications to Physics and Cosmology, 1997; contbr. over 100 articles to profl. jours. NSF Predoctoral fellow, 1954-58, NSF Postdoctoral fellow, 1958-60; grantee NASA, NSF, ONR, Rsch. Corp. Fellow Am. Astron. Soc.; mem. Internat. Astron. Union, Sci. Assn. Study in Physics and Cosmology (prin. scientist 2000-). Achievements include discovery of redshift quantization and correlations relating to it, including variability; first to detect voids in mapping of large scale supercluster structure; investigations of three-dimensional time in cosmology and particle physics. Office: U Arizona Dept Astronomy Tucson AZ 85721-0001 E-mail: wtifft@as.arizona.edu.

TIFT, MARY LOUISE, artist; b. Seattle, Jan. 2, 1913; d. John Howard and Wilhelmina (Pressler) Dreher; m. William Raymond Tift, Dec. 4, 1948. BFA cum laude, U. Wash., 1933; postgrad., Art Ctr. Coll., L.A., 1945-48, U. Calif., San Francisco, 1962-63. Art dir. Vaughn Shedd Advt., L.A., 1948; asst. prof. design Calif. Coll. Arts & Crafts, Oakland, Calif., 1949-59; coord. design dept. San Francisco Art Inst., 1959-62. Subject of cover story, Am. Artist mag., 1980, studio article, 1987; one-woman shows, Gumps Gallery, San Francisco, 1977, 1986, 90, Diane Gilson Gallery, Seattle, 1978, Oreg. State U., 1981, Univ. House, Seattle, Frye Art Mus., Seattle, 2000; exhibited in group shows including Brit. Biennale, Yorkshire, Eng., 1970, Grenchen Triennale, Switzerland, 1970, Polish Biennale, Crakow, 1972, Nat. Gallery, Washington, 1973, Madrid Biennale, 1980, U.S.-U.K. Impressions, Eng., 1988; represented in permanent collections, Phila. Mus. Art, Bklyn. Mus., Seattle Art Mus., Library Congress, Achenbach Print Collection, San Francisco Palace Legion of Honor, San Diego Mus. Art, U.S. Art in Embassies. Served to lt. USNR, 1943-45. Mem. Print Club Phila., World Print Council, Calif. Soc. Printmakers, Phi Beta Kappa, Lambda Rho. Christian Scientist. Studio: 4400 Stone Way N Apt 521 Seattle WA 98103-7487

TIGANI, BRUCE WILLIAM, lawyer; b. Wilmington, Del., May 10, 1956; s. J. Vincent Jr. and Josephine C. (DeAngelis) T.; m. Janice Rowe, Sept. 25, 1982; children: Jessica Lynne, Bruce William Jr. Student, Georgetown U., 1974-75; BBS, U. Del., 1978; JD, Villanova U., 1981. Bar: Del. 1981, Pa. 1982, U.S. Dist. Ct. Del. 1982, U.S. Dist. Ct. (ea. dist.) Pa. 1982, U.S. Tax Ct. 1982. Assoc. Lord & Mulligan, Media, Pa., 1981-84, resident atty. Wilmington, 1984-87, ptnr., 1987-88; mng. ptnr. Werb, Tigani, Hood & Sullivan, Wilmington, 1988-99, Tigani & Hood LLP, Wilmington, 2000—. Del. to IRS, Mid. Altantic Regional liason. Mem. lay adv. bd. The Little Sisters of Poor; active Rep. Com. of State Del. Mem. ABA, Del. State Bar Assn. (chmn. tax sect. 1991-92, real estate sect., chair trusts and estates sect. 1997-98, lectr. bus. and tax seminars), Wilmington Tax Group (chmn. 1994-95), Del. State C. of C. (commerce tax com.), Estate Planning Coun. Del., Inc. (bd. dirs. 1993-95), Concord Country Club, Univ. and Whist Club Wilmington, Blue and Gold Club. Avocations: golf, softball. Office: Tigani & Hood LLP PO Box 1471 1801 Mellon Bank Ctr 919 Market St Wilmington DE 19899-1471 E-mail: btigani@TiganihoodLaw.com.

TIGAR, MICHAEL EDWARD, law educator; b. Glendale, Calif., Jan. 18, 1941; s. Charles Henry and Margaret Elizabeth (Lang) T.; m. Pamet Ayer Jones, Sept. 21, 1961 (div. Mar. 1973); children: Jon Steven, Katherine Ayer; m. Amanda G. Birrell, Feb. 16, 1980 (div. Aug. 1996); 1 child, Elizabeth Torrey; m. Jane E. Blanksteen, Aug. 22, 1996. BA in Polit. Sci., U. Calif., Berkeley, 1962, JD, 1966. Bar: D.C. 1967, U.S. Ct. Appeals (2d, 4th, 5th, 6th, 7th, 8th, 9th, 10th, 11th, fed. and D.C. cirs.), U.S. Tax Ct., U.S. Supreme Ct. 1972, N.Y. 1993. Assoc. Williams & Connolly, Washington, 1966-69; editor-in-chief Selective Svc. Law Reporter, Washington, 1967-69; acting prof. law UCLA, 1969-71; pvt. practice law Grasse, France, 1972-74; assoc. William & Connolly, Washington, 1974, ptnr., 1975-77, Tigar & Buffone, Washington, 1977-84; prof. law U. Tex., Austin, 1984-87, Joseph D. Jamail Centennial prof. law, 1987-98; of counsel Haddon, Morgan & Foreman, Denver, 1996-98; prof. law, and Edwin A. Mooers, Sr., Scholar Am. U. Washington Coll. Law, Washington, 1998—. Reporter 5th Cir. Pattern Jury Instrns., Austin, 1988-90. Author: Practice Manual Selective Service Law Reporter, 1968, Law and the Rise of Capitalism, 1977, (with Jane B. Tigar) Federal Appeals: Jurisdiction and Practice, 3d edit., 1999, Examining Witnesses, 1993, Persuasion: The Litigator's Art, 1999; contbr. articles to profl. jours. Mem. ABA (vice chair 1987-88, chair elect 1988-89, chair 1989-90 sect. litigation). Avocations: sailing, cooking. Office: Washington Coll Law 4801 Massachusetts Ave NW Washington DC 20016-8196

TIGER, IRA PAUL, retired lawyer; b. Bklyn., Jan. 31, 1936; s. Sidney and Rebecca (Frankel) T.; m. Rosalind Silverman, July 4, 1957 (dec. Nov. 1972); children: Ruth, Lori; m. Ann Mae Gersh, May 5, 1974; stepchildren: Jimmie, Randy, Richard Riesenberg. BS in Econs., U. Pa., 1956, JD magna cum laude, 1959. Bar: Pa. 1960, U.S. Dist. Ct. (ea. dist.) Pa. 1960, U.S. Ct. Appeals (3d cir.) 1960, U.S. Supreme Ct. 1971, U.S. Ct. Appeals (7th cir.) 1996. Law clk. 3d cir., 1959-60; assoc. Schnader, Harrison, Segal & Lewis, Phila., 1960-67, ptnr., 1968—2002, chmn. litigation dept., 1986-90, chmn. standing com. on profl. conduct, 1992—2003, sr. counsel, 2003—04. Judge pro tem Phila. Ct. Common Pleas, 1994—2003; mediator U.S. Dist. Ct. (ea. dist.) Pa., 1991—2003. Rsch. editor U. Pa. Law Rev., 1958-59. Pres. Temple Sinai Synagogue, 1989-91, Elkins Park House Coun., 1996-98; mem. Planning Adv. Bd. Upper Dublin Twp., 1982-87, mem. ednl. adv. com., 1976-78; legal counsel Phila. Jr. C. of C., 1963-64, bd. dirs., 1962-66, sec. Jewish campus activities bd., 1971-73. Mem. ABA, Am. Judicature Soc., Inst. Jud. Adminstrn., Phila. Bar Assn. (chmn. fed. cts. com. 1985), Lawyers Club Phila., Order of Coif (exec. com. Pa. chpt. 1981-83), Beta Alpha Psi, Beta Gamma Sigma. Democrat. Office: Schnader Harrison 1600 Market St Ste 3600 Philadelphia PA 19103-7286 E-mail: itiger@schnader.com.

TIGER, LIONEL, social scientist, anthropology consultant; b. Montreal, Que., Can., Feb. 5, 1937; s. Martin and Lillian (Schneider) T.; 1 child, Sebastian Benjamin. BA, McGill U., 1957, MA, 1959; PhD, U. London, 1963. Instr. anthropology U. Ghana, Accra, 1960; asst. prof. dept. anthropology and sociology U. B.C., Vancouver, Canada, 1963—68; assoc. prof. anthropology Rutgers U., New Brunswick, NJ, 1969—74, prof. anthropology, 1974—, Charles Darwin prof. anthropology, 1990—. Cons., rsch. dir. Harry F. Guggenheim Found., N.Y.C., 1972-84; chmn. bd. social scientists U.S. News and World Report, 1986-88; sci. adv. bd. Am. Wine Inst., San Francisco; sr. rsch. assoc. Nat. Inst. Pub. Policy; mem. bd. advisors George Polk Awards, 2004—. Author: Men in Groups, 1969, 3d edit., 2004, (with Robin Fox) The Imperial Animal, 1971, 3d edit., 1998, (with Joseph Shepher) Women in the Kibbutz, 1975, Optimism: The Biology of Hope, 1979, 2d edit., 1994, China's Food, 1985, The Manufacture of Evil: Ethics, Evolution and the Industrial System, 1987; editor: Female Hierarchies, 1978, (with Michael Robinson) Man and Beast Revisited, 1992, The Pursuit of Pleasure, 1992, 2d edit., 2000, The Decline of Males, 1999, The Apes of New York, 2003; mem. editl. bd. Social Sci. Info., Ethology and Sociobiology jour., Jour. of Social Distress and the Homeless. Cultural laureate N.Y.C. Landmarks Found., 1999. Recipient W.I. Susman award for excellence in tchg., 1985, McNaughton prize for creative writing; Guggenheim fellow, 1969, rsch. fellow ASDA Found., 1985, Can. Coun., fgn. area tng. fellow Ford Found., Can. Coun.-Killam fellow for interdisciplinary rsch., Rockefeller fellow Aspen Inst., 1979, H.F. Guggenheim Found. fellow, 1988-891 Inst. for Law and Behavioral Rsch. fellow. Mem. PEN (mem. exec. bd., treas. 1988-91, v.p. 1991-94), Am. Anthrop. Assn., Internat. Humanist Assn. (humanist laureate), Can. Humanists Assn. (hon.), Soc. for Study of Evolution, Century Assn. Home: 248 W 23rd St Fl 4 New York NY 10011-2304 also: PO Box 965 Millbrook NY 12545 Office: Rutgers U 131 George St New Brunswick NJ 08901-1414 Office Phone: 732-932-9866., 732-932-7577. Business E-Mail: ltiger@rcl.rutgers.edu.

TIGERMAN, STANLEY, architect, educator; b. Chgo., Sept. 20, 1930; s. Samuel Bernard and Emma Louise (Stern) T.; m. Margaret I. McCurry; children: Judson Joel, Tracy Leigh. Student, MIT, 1948-49; BArch, Yale U., 1960, MArch, 1961. Archtl. draftsman firm George Fred Keck, Chgo., 1949-50, Skidmore, Owings and Merrill, Chgo., 1957-59, Paul Rudolph, New Haven, 1959-61, Harry Weese, Chgo., 1961-62; partner firm Tigerman & Koglin, Chgo., 1962-64; prin. firm Stanley Tigerman & Assos., Chgo., 1964-82; ptnr. Tigerman Fugman McCurry, Chgo., 1982-88, Tigerman McCurry, 1988—. Prof. architecture U. Ill.-Chgo., 1967-71, 80-93, dir. Sch. Architecture, 1985-93; vis. lectr. Yale U., 1974, Cornell U., Ithaca, N.Y., 1963, Cooper Union, 1970, U. Calif. at Berkeley, 1968, Cardiff (Wales) Coll., 1965, Engring. U., Bangladesh, 1967; chmn. AIA com. on design, coordinator exhbn. and book Chicago Architects, 1977; Charlotte Shepherd Davenport prof. architecture Yale U., 1979; architect-in-residence Am. Acad. in Rome, 1980; vis. prof. architecture Harvard U., 1982; William Henry Bishop Chair. prof. architecture Yale U., 1984, Sarrinen prof., 1993; dir. post-professional grad. program U. Ill.-Chgo.; co-founder Archeworks, Design Lab., Chgo., 1993; mem. adv. com. Princeton U., 1997. Prin. works include The Ounce of Prevention Educare Ctr., Chgo., Fukuoka Apt. Complex, Japan, The Power House, Zion, Ill., The Chgo. Children's Adv. Ctr.; author: Versus, 1982, Architecture of Exile, 1988, Stanley Tigerman: Buildings and Projects, 1966-89, 1989; contbr. Design of the Housing Site, 1966, Chicago on Foot, 1969, Art Today, 1969, New Direction in American Architecture, 1969, Contemporary Jewelry, 1970, Urban Structures for the Future, 1972, Spaces for Living, 1973, Chicago 1930-70, 1974, Interior Spaces Designed by Architects, 1976, 100 Years of Architecture in Chicago, 1976, 100 Years of Architecture in Chicago, 1986, Mies Reconsidered, 1986, Chicago Architecture 1872-1922, 1988, articles; exhibitions include Venice Biennale, 1976, 1980, Calif. Condition, 1982;, author essay; exhibitions include Chicago Architecture, The New Zeitgeist: In Search of Closure, 1989, 1989; author: (catalog) Chicago Architecture, The New Zeitgeist: In Search of Closure, 1989. Pres. Yale Arts Assn., 1969-70; mem. advisory com. Yale Archtl. Sch., 1976—; bd. dirs. Bangladesh Found. Served with USN, 1950-54. Recipient Alpha Rho Chi medal, Yale, 1961, Archtl. Record award, 1970, Masonry award, 1974, Masonry gold medal, 1974, Alumni Art award, Yale U., 1985, Design award for Art Inst. Chgo. Schinkel Exhbn., Am. Soc. Interior Designers, 1995, Humanitarian award, Holocaust Meml. Found. Ill., 2001, Grand award of Excellence, NAHB, 2001, 2003; grantee Advanced Studies in Fine Art, Graham Fedn., 1965. Fellow AIA (chmn. com. design 1976-77, adv. com., Disting. Svc. award Chgo. chpt. 1983, Chgo. Honor awards 1977-79, Nat. Honor award 1982, 84, 87, 91, 98, Nat. Modern Income Housing award 1970, Nat. Homes for Better Living award 1974, 75, Ill. award 1976, Nat. award of Merit 1970, 74, 75, named to Hall of Fame 1990, Disting. Bldg. award for pvt. residence Chgo. chpt. 1991, Chgo. Interior Archtl. Award of Excellence 1981, 83, 87, 91, 92, Nat. Interior Archtl. Award of Excellence 1992-93, Chgo. Disting. Bldg. award 1971, 73, 75, 77, 79, 81, 82, 84, 85, 86, 91, 94, Italian Ceramic Tile Design award 1995, Fukuoka Urban Beautification award 1995, 6 citations of merit Chgo. chpt. 1994, Interior Design award for A.I.C. Schinkel Exhibit 1996, Chgo. Interior Architecture award 1997, Chgo. Chpt. Arch. award 1998, Nat. Interior Architecture award 1998, Louis Sullivan award 2000), Ill./Ind. Masonry Coun. (Silver Award for Excellence in

Masonry 2003); mem. Arts Club of Chgo., Yale Club of N.Y.C., Century Assn. Club, Phi Kappa Phi. Office: Tigerman & McCurry Ltd 444 N Wells St Ste 206 Chicago IL 60610-4522 Office Phone: 312-644-5880.

TIGGES, JOHN THOMAS, writer, musician, lecturer; b. Dubuque, Iowa, May 16, 1932; s. John George and Madonna Josephine (Heiberger) T.; m. Kathryn Elizabeth Johnson, Apr. 22, 1954; children: Juliana, John, Timothy, Teresa, Jay. Grad., Loras Coll., 1950-54, 57; student, U. Dubuque, 1960. Night club entertainer, 1950-52; clk. John Deere Tractor Works, Dubuque, 1957-61; agt. Penn Mut. Life Ins. co., Dubuque, 1961-97; bus. mgr., bd. dirs. Dubuque Symphony Orch., 1960-68, 71-74; v.p., sec. Olson Toy and Hobby, Inc., 1964-66; pres. JKT, Inc., 1978-82; rsch. specialist Electronic Media Svcs. (Scripp-Howard), 1983-85; violinist. Tchr. continuing edn. creative writing N.E. Iowa C.C., 1975—98; tchr. writing U. Wis. Outreach Program's Ednl. Teleconf. Network; summer writing workshop U. Iowa; tchr. Rhinelander Sch. of the Arts, 1997—98; mem. faculty S.W. Writers Workshop, 1998; co-founder Dubuque Symphony Orch., 1960; founder Julien Strings, 1972; founder, bus. mgr. Dubuque Pops Orch., 1957—58, Dubuque Sch. of Novel, 1978, N.E. Iowa Writers Workshop, 1981; co-host Big Broadcast Radio Program, WDBQ Radio, 1979—82; founder Sinipee Critique/Editl. Svcs., 1988, Dubuque (Iowa) Sch. of the Novel, 1980, Sinipee Writers Workshop, 1985. Author: (novels) The Legend of Jean Marie Cardinal, 1976, Garden of the Incubus, 1982, Unto the Altar, 1985, Kiss Not the Child, 1985, Evil Dreams, 1986, The Immortal, 1986, Hands of Lucifer, 1987, As Evil Does, 1987, Pack, 1987, Venom, 1988, Vessel, 1988, Slime, 1988, Book of the Dead, 1989, From Below, 1989, Comes the Wraith, 1990, Breed, 1990, Mountain Massacre, 1990, Blood on the Rails, 1990, One Man Jury, 1991, The Curse, 1993, Monster, 1995, (book of short stories) Nightales, 1990, (plays) No More No Less, 1982, We Who Are About to Die, 1983; contbg. author Murder for Father, 1994, The New Amazons, 1997; co-author: (radio plays) Valley of Deceit, 1978; author: Rockville Horror, 1979, The Timid, 1982, All Bets are Down, 1991, (TV drama) An Evening with George Wallace Jones, 1983, (biographies) George Wallace Jones, 1983, John Plumbe Jr., 1983; prodr.: (TV series) The Loneliest Job, 1989; co-author: (nonfiction) The Milwaukee Road Narrow Gauge: The Bellevue, Cascade & Western, Iowa's Slim Princess, 1985, They Came from Dubuque, 1983, Milwaukee Road Steam Power, 1994, (non-fiction) Remember When...?, 1997, (nonfiction) Dubuque in the 19th Century, 2000, Dubuque in the 20th Century, 2000, Dubuque-Then and Now, 2000, The Mississippi River: Father of the Waters, 2000, Nightfeeders, 2002; editl. asst.: Julien's Jour.; contbg. editor: Over 49 News and Views; co-author, editor: A Cup and a Half of Coffee, 1977;; interviewer, spl. reporter: Editl. Assocs., 1982—84; columnist Memory Lane, What's the Difference, Telegraph Herald, syndicated columnist Tough Trivia Tidbits, Remember When..?, The 20th Century in Review; contbr. more than 2975 articles to profl. jours. Founder Better Quality Writing Pubs., 1996. Recipient Nat. Quality award, 1966-70, Carnegie-Stout Libr. World of Lit. honors award, 1981; John Tigges Writing contest named in his honor, John T. and Kathryn E. Tigges endowment scholarship for Writing Majors named in their honor, Loras Coll., Dubuque. Fellow World Lit. Acad.; mem. Horror Writers Am., Western Writers Am., Iowa Authors, Internat. Platform Assn., Toy Train Collectors Club, Dubuque Rails Model Railroad (co-founder 1987). Roman Catholic. Home: 2240 Coates St Dubuque IA 52003-7108

TIGHE, MARY ANN, real estate company executive; m. David Hidalgo; 1 child from previous marriage, Aaron. BA in art history, Cath. U.; MA in art history, U. Md. Staff mem. Smithsonian Instn.; arts adv. to v.p. Walter Mondale; dep. chmn. Nat. Endowment Arts; v.p. Am. Broadcasting Co.; sales assoc. Edward S. Gordon Inc. (name changed to Insignia/ESG Inc. 1997), 1984; exec. mng. dir. Insignia/ESG Inc., NYC, 1993—99, vice chmn., 1999—2002; pres., CEO NY Tri-State Region CB Richard Ellis, NYC, 2002—. Dir. Imperial Parking Corp. Bd. dirs. NYC Ballet, Parrish Art Mus., The New 42nd St., Joan's Legacy: The Joan Scarangello Found. to Conquer Lung Cancer. Recipient Woman Yr., Comml. Real Estate Women NY, 2001. Mem.: Real Estate Bd. NY (exec. com. bd. govs. 2001—, Henry Hart Rice award 1997, 2002, Robert T. Lawrence award 1992, 1998). Office: CB Richard Ellis Group Inc 200 Park Ave New York NY 10166

TIGHE-MOORE, BARBARA JEANNE, electronics executive; b. Wadsworth, Ohio, Jan. 12, 1961; d. Norton Raymond and Laura Alida (Frank) Tighe; m. Derek William Moore, June 26, 1982. Student, Hocking Tech. Coll., 1981, Sinclair Coll., 1986; BBA Honors Coll. magna cum laude, Kent State U., 1988. Lic. amateur radio operator. Tech. writer computer dept. Sinclair Coll., Dayton, Ohio, 1983; project mgr. O'Neil & Assocs., Dayton, 1983-84; biomed., bio-acoustic real-time flight simulation tempest developer Systems Rsch. Labs., Dayton, 1984-86; computer specialist Kent State U. Press, 1987-88; mgmt. analyst Electronic Warfare Frontier Engring. Inc., 1988-89; supr. small computer tech. svcs. Frontier Engring., Inc., 1989-90, project engr., 1990-92; ptnr., bd. dirs. MKCC, Dayton, 1990—, SDCC, Dayton, 1992—; regional mgr. User Tech. Assocs., Dayton, 1993-96; pres., owner Lida Ray Techs., Dayton, 1978—. Mem. graphics steering com., mem. sanctioned UNIX software adv. team Aero. Sys. Divsn.; program chair IEEE Internat. Wireless LAN Conf.; mem. Engring. Application Support Environ. Security Working Group, pres., 2000; proceedings chmn. Nat. Aerospace & Electronics Conf., 1995, 96, 97, bd. dirs., pres., 2000; bd. dirs. MKCC, Dayton, 1993—, Cin. Digital Women, SDCC; pres, bd. dirs. NAECON, 2000; spkr. Govt. Land Mobile Commn. Conf., 1993, Internat. Engring. Mgmt. Cons., 1994, Wireless '93, Calgary, Alta., Nat. Aerospace & Electronics Conf., 1995, 96, 97. Author: Job Search Strategies for the 90's, 1993, Through the Glass Ceiling, 1997, Riding the 5:15, 2000, Convergence of Socio-Economic and Technology Factors, 2001; co-author: Women on a Wire, 1996, Women on a Wire, vol. 2, 2001; editor: Graphics Directions, 1990—91; pub.: Team Advisor, SDCC Cleaning Times, IEEE Update; contbr. poetry to mags. and anthologies, papers, articles to profl. jours. Counselor Kwam's Kinder Kamp; tchr. Bible Sch.; cook Meals on Wheels; organizer/cook funeral Svcs. Dinners. Recipient Vol. Citizen award Wadsworth C. of C, 1979, Ohio Essayist award, 1979, Virginia Perryman award, 1979, Disting. Leadership award, 1990, 91. Mem.: IEEE (former treas., sec. Dayton sect., bd. dirs. 1995—97, chmn. bd. dirs. Dayton sect. 1999, region 2 chpt. coord. 2000—), Equestrian Team (point rider 1977—87), Armed Forces Comms. and Electronics Assn. (judge sci. fair western dist. 1992—), Internat. Film Soc. (pres. 1986—88), Assn. Internat. Students Econs. & Commerce (pres. 1986—87), Def. Planning Analysis Soc. (exec. bd.), Assn. Computer Machinery, Data Processing Mgmt. Assn., Tech. and Soc. of IEEE, Engring. Mgmt. Soc. of IEEE, Computer Soc. of IEEE (sec. 1991—92, vice chmn. 1992—93, chmn. 1994—95), Mortar Bd., Fencing Club, Beta Gamma Sigma, Omicron Delta Kappa, Phi Theta Kappa. Avocations: travel, investing, equestrian show jumping, soccer. Home: 729 Kyle Dr Tipp City OH 45371-1435 Office Phone: 937-667-4972. Personal E-mail: lidaray@siscom.net. Business E-Mail: bjmoore@lidaray.com.

TIGHT, DEXTER CORWIN, lawyer; b. San Francisco, Sept. 14, 1924; s. Dexter Junkins and Marie (Corwin) T.; m. Elizabeth Callander, Apr. 20, 1951; children: Dexter C. Jr., Kathyrn Marie Loken, Steven M., David C. AB, Denison U., 1948; JD, Yale U., 1951. Bar: Calif. 1951. Assoc. Pillsbury, Madison & Sutro, San Francisco, 1953-60; gen. atty. W.P. Fuller & Co., San Francisco, 1960-61; gen. counsel Schlage Lock Co., San Francisco, 1961-77; dir. govt. affairs Crown Zellerbach Corp., San Francisco, 1977-78; sr. v.p., internat. and gen. counsel The Gap Inc., San Bruno, Calif., 1978-90; gen. coun. The Nature Co., 1990—95. Bd. dirs. Shaw-Clayton Plastics, San Rafael, Calif., Granite Rock Co., Watsonville, Calif., Boys and Girls Club of the Peninsula; mem. World Affairs Coun., Internat. Diplomcay Coun.; chmn. That Man May See, San Francisco, 1997, 98. Trustee Denison U., 1978-99, chmn. capital fund dr., 1988-94; Trustee, Global Council, URI 2003-, trustee Calvary Presbyn. Ch., 1968, 73, elder, 1969-90; elder Valley Presbyn. Ch., 1992—; vol. Internat. Exec. Svc. Corps., participant People to People Internat. 2002. 2nd USAR, 1943—45, 1st Lt. USAR, 1951—52. Mem. ABA, Calif. Bar Assn., San Francisco Bar Assn. (chmn. various coms.), Commonwealth Club Calif. (past bd. dirs., exec. com.), Menlo Country Club, Bohemian Club (San Francisco), Guardsman Club (1st v.p. 1961), Phi Beta Kappa. Republican. Presbyterian. Avocations: horseback riding, fishing, tennis, golf, photography. Home: 170 Wildwood Way Redwood City CA 94062-2352

TIGUE, VIRGINIA BETH (GINNY TIGUE), volunteer; b. Owosso, Mich., Sept. 10, 1945; d. Joseph Frederick and Florence Marion Sahlmark; m. Joseph James Tigue Jr., Aug. 12, 1967; children: James Christopher, Molly Elizabeth. BS, cert. in phys. therapy, U. Mich., 1967. Registered phys. therapist, Mich., Calif. Phys. therapist at hosps., rehab. ctrs. and pvt. practice. Co-owner Tigue Property Co.; former co-owner Tex. Toyota of Grapevine. Councilman Pl. 5 City of Colleyville, 1998—2004, mayor pro tem, 2000—04, bond steering com., 1991, master plan revision com., 1997-98, chmn. cmty. ctr. adv. com. 1998; mem. Art Coun. Ft. Worth and Tarrant County Bd., Ft. Worth, 1997—, Tarrant County College Found. Bd., 2001-; founding bd. dirs. Grapevine-Colleyville Ind. Sch. Dist. Edn. Found., 1998-2004; bd. dirs. Colleyville C. of C., 1991—, chmn., 1994; founding chmn. Harris Hosp., 1992, 93, mem. women's adv. bd., 1992—, bd., HEB Hosp. trustees, 1999—, bd. Meth. Health Harris Found. 2001-; bd. dirs. Arts Coun. N.E. Tarrant, 1991-98, chmn., 1995-96; bd. dirs. Origins Mus., 1998—, v.p. 2000-2001; bd. dirs. Vol. Ctr. of Tarrant County, 1998-2002, chmn. 2000; bd. dirs. Dallas Mus. Art League, 1999-2000, United Way of Met. Tarrant County, 2000—, bd. dirs., 2002—; bd. dirs. N.E Leadership Forum, 1999—04, chmn., 2004; sustaining mem. Dallas Jr. League, 1991—; founding bd. dirs. Tarrant County Coll. Found., 2001—; sr. advisor Nat. Charity League, 1994,; bd. dirs. N.E. Tarrant County divsn. Am. Heart Assn., 1993-94, co-chmn. gala 1997; fund raising chmn. Friends of Colleyville Libr., 1992—; home tour com. Colleyville Women's Club, 1990, 93, 96, fashion show chmn., 1996; mem. adv. bd. Women's Shelter, 1996-98; mem. Women Leader's Summit, Washington, 1995, 96, 98, 99; mem. Women's Policy Forum, 1999—, Women's Found. of Tarrant County, 2000—. Named Most Influential Bus. Woman, The Bus. Press, 1997, Vol. of Yr., City of Colleyville, 1997, Colleyville Citien of Yr., 2001; recipient Legacy of Women award The Women's Shelter, 1995, Herman J. Smith Leadership award Colleyville C. of C., 1994, Proclamation as Outstanding Citizen of Colleyville, 1995. Mem. Colleyville Area C. of C. (bd. dirs. 1990-98, pres.-elect 1993, pres. 1994, vice-chmn. membership devel. 1997, vice-chmn. cmty. devel. 1998, 2003, vice chmn. bus. devel. 2004, Citizen of Yr. 2001, exec. bd. 2003-), Tex. Congress Parents and Tchrs. (hon. life mem.), Republican. Methodist. Avocations: golf, travel, reading, the arts. Home: 4415 Meandering Way Colleyville TX 76034-4513

TIJMANN, WILLEM BERT, civil engineer, consultant; b. Semarang, Java, Indonesia, Oct. 19, 1929; came to the U.S., 1956; s. Johan Hendrik and Alida Catharina (Deylius) T.; m. Martha Vanderlaan, Oct. 21, 1958 (div. 1986); children: Sonya Maria, John (dec.); m. Mirna Aeschlimann, Aug. 18, 1991. BS, Poly. Coll., Amsterdam, The Netherlands, 1953, M in Civil Engring., 1955. Registered profl. engr., Europe. Sr. hydraulics engr. Olarte, Ospina Arias y Payan Ltda, Civil Engrs., Bogotá, Colombia, 1955-56; soils and materials engr. Fay Spofford, Boston, 1956-62; sr. project engr. Dames & Moore, San Francisco, 1962-76; v.p. Slope Indicator Co., Seattle, 1976-87; pres. E&T Instrumentation, Stoneham, Mass., 1987—, W.B.T. Cons., Edmonds, Wash., 1987—. Inventor: holds 4 patents in U.S. and Can. Mem. ASCE (hon.), ASTM (sr.), Internat. Soc. Soil Mechanics and Engring. Found., Assn. Engring. Geologists (affiliate). Avocations: certified professional diver, diving, sailing, tennis, hiking. Home: 101A Pond St Stoneham MA 02180-2804 Office: 10628 W Deanne DR Sun City AZ 85351-4451 E-mail: 70@yahoo.com.

TIKALSKY, PAUL J. civil engineering educator, structural engineer; s. Lee J. and Marilyn A. Tikalsky; m. Julie A. Tikalsky; children: Peter, Daniel. BS in Civil and Environ. Engring., U. of Wis., 1983; MS in Structural Engring., U. of Tex., 1986, PhD in Structural Materials Engring., 1989. Lic. profl. engr., Calif. Housefellow U. of Wis., Madison, 1981—84; landscaping/equipment operator Sts. and Pks. Dept. City of New Holstein, Wis., 1978—82; tchg. asst. U. of Wis., 1984; rsch. asst. U. of Tex., Austin, 1984—89; from asst. to assoc. prof. Santa Clara (Calif.) U., 1989—95; consulting engr. TEI and Assocs., Santa Clara, 1989—94; assoc. prof. Pa. State U., University Park, 1995—. Prin. engr. Tikalsky Engring. Svcs., State College, Pa., 1993—. Contbr. scientific papers to profl. jours. Vice-chair, bd. mem. Habitat for Humanity, San Jose, Calif., 1992—95; bd. dirs. Stand Together, State College, 1998—2000. Grantee, PennDOT, U.S. Dept. Edn., Pvt. Founds., 1989—2003. Fellow: Am. Concrete Inst. (chair coms.); mem.: ASTM, ASCE, Sierra Club (life), Chi Epsilon (pres.). Achievements include research in development of 100-year highway program. Office: Pa State U 212 Sackett Bldg University Park PA 16802

TIKOSH, MARK AXENTE, lawyer; b. Arad, Banat, Romania, Aug. 17, 1955; arrived in U.S., 1981; s. Axente and Elena Ticosh; m. Mary Victoria Rotarescu, Sept. 10, 1979. BBA in Acctg. summa cum laude, Calif. State U., Fullerton, 1989; JD, U. of the Pacific, 1992, LLM, 1993. Bar: Calif. 1993. Acct., auditor II Orange County Probation Dept., 1984-88; pvt. practice Sacramento, Calif., 1993-94, Long Beach, Calif., 1994—. Cons. U. Banat Acad. Found., Timisoara, Romania, 1997—. Editor: The Transnational Lawyer, 1991. Mem. Town Hall L.A., 2002—. Scholarship McGeorge Legal Edn. Endowment Found., 1989-90, Dana Found., 1992-93. Mem. Calif. State Bar Assn. (estate planning trust and probate law sect.), L.A. County Bar Assn., Cato Inst., Beta Gamma Sigma. Republican. Avocations: travel, history, philosophy.

TILDEN, BRADLEY D. air transportation executive; b. Houston, Tex., 1960; Degree, Pacific Luth. U., 1983, U. Wash., 1997. From mem. staff to exec. v.p., CFO Alaska Air Group, Inc., Seattle, 1991—2000, exec. v.p. fin., 2000—, CFO, 2000—. Office: Alaska Air Group Inc 19300 Pacific Hwy south Seattle WA 98188*

TILDEN, RALPH FULTON, retired music educator, organist; b. High Point, N.C., Feb. 10, 1930; s. Thomas Alphonso and Ruth Eugenia (Fulton) T. BMus, Cin. Conservatory Music, 1952, MMus, 1954. Tchr., Fla. Prof. organ Cin. Conservatory Music, 1954-60; tchr. music, theology Cathedral Sch., Orlando, 1960-65; prof. Edison C.C., Ft. Myers, Fla., 1966-95. Organist, choirmaster Calvary Ch., Cin., 1954-60, St. Luke's Cathedral, Orlando, 1960-65, St. Luke's Ch., Ft. Myers, 1965-95; organ recitalist, U.S.A., France, Eng. Composer (choral works) Come, Holy Spirit, Come, 1987, His Voice as the Sound, 1997, Assumpta Est Maria, 2000. Vol., activist ACLU, 1960—, Nat. Gay & Lesbian Task Force, 1960—, Mtn. AIDS Support Coun., Boone, N.C., 1999. Mem. Am. Guild Organists (dean), Assn. Anglican Musicians, Organ Hist. Soc., Liturgy & Music Commn., Diocese of Western N.C. Democrat. Episcopal. Avocations: antique collecting, gardening. Home: 960 Meadow Ave Banner Elk NC 28604-9401

TILDEN, WESLEY RODERICK, writer, retired computer programmer; b. Saint Joseph, Mo., Jan. 19, 1922; s. Harry William and Grace Alida (Kinnaman) T.; m. Lorraine Henrietta Frederick, June 20, 1948 (dec. Mar. 1999). Grad., Navy Supply Corps Sch., 1945; BS, UCLA, 1948; BA, Park Coll., Mo., 1990. Purchasing agent Vortox Co., Claremont, Calif., 1951-61; lang. lab. dir. Mount San Antonio Coll., Walnut, Calif., 1962-65; computer programmer, operator General Dynamics, Pomona, Calif., 1967-70; ret., 1970. Author: Scota, The Egyptian Princess, 1994, Merit-Sekhet: Foster Mother of Moses?, 1996; photographer, textbooks, mags., newspaper, catalogs. Historian Claremont Sister City Assn., 1963-66. Lt. USNR, 1942-46 PTO. Recipient with Lorraine Tilden People to People award Reader's Digest Found., 1963-65; named Hon. Citizen Guanajuato, Mexico, 1963. Mem. Soc. Mayflower Descendants, Scottish Clans, UCLA Alumni Assn., Park Coll. Alumni Assn., Univ. Club of Claremont, The Scituate (Mass.) Hist. Soc. Republican. Avocations: history, genealogy, photography, gardening. Home: 351 Oakdale Dr Claremont CA 91711-5039

TILEWICK, ROBERT, lawyer; b. N.Y.C., Jan. 16, 1956; s. David and Helen (Fogel) T.; m. Susan Dara Tilewick; children: Naomi Seana, Benjamin Solomon. BA, Columbia U., 1977; JD, Temple U., 1985. Bar: N.Y. 1986, Ct. 1993, U.S. Dist. Ct. (so. and ea. dists.) N.Y. 1988, U.S. Ct. Appeals (2d cir.) 1989, U.S. Dist. Ct. Conn. 1991. Systems analyst, cons. Personnelmetrics, Inc., N.Y.C., 1977-80, 81-82; assoc. Cravath, Swaine & Moore, N.Y.C., 1985-87, Paul, Weiss, Rifkind, Wharton & Garrison, N.Y.C., 1987-91, 96-97, Wiggin & Dana, New Haven, Conn., 1991-96, Kalow, Springut & Bressler, N.Y.C., 1997-99, Graham & James, N.Y.C., 1999—. Co-designer race timing system for N.Y.C. Marathon, 1977-82. NIH grantee Marine Biol. Lab., Woods Hole, Mass, 1980. Mem. ABA, N.Y.C. Bar Assn., Conn. Bar Assn., New Haven Bar Assn., Supreme Ct. Hist. Soc. Avocation: music. Office: 885 3rd Ave New York NY 10022-4834

TILGHMAN, CARL LEWIS, lawyer; b. Detroit, Aug. 3, 1944; s. Clifford Raymond and Alma (Gillikin) T.; m. Nancy Ann Huff, Aug. 21, 1965; children: Jason Andrew, Amanda Carol. Student, Beaufort H.S., 1962; BA, Wake Forest U., 1966, JD, 1969. Bar: N.C. 1969. Asst. U.S. atty. U.S. Dept. Justice, Raliegh, N.C., 1973-76; U.S. atty. U.S. Dist. Ct. (ea. dist.) N.C., Raleigh, 1976-77; sole practice Beaufort, N.C., 1977-97; apptd. spl. Superior Ct. judge, 1997—2002; tax adminstr. Carteret County, 2003—. Vice chmn. Carteret County Commn., Beaufort, 1984—, vice chm. 1984-88, re-elected 1988, chmn., 1988-92. Served to capt. JAGC, U.S. Army, 1969-73. Mem. N.C. Bar Assn., Carteret County Bar Assn. (pres. 1983-84) N.C. Assn. County Commn. (bd. dirs.), Coastal Regional Solid Waste Authority (bd. dirs., chmn., 1991-92), Neuse River Coun. of Gov. (pres. 1991-92). Republican. Baptist. Avocations: playing saxaphone, singing. Home: RR 1 Box 214 Beaufort NC 28516-9801 Office: Attorney At Law PO Box 748 Beaufort NC 28516-0748

TILGHMAN, RICHARD GRANVILLE, bank executive; b. Norfolk, Va., Sept. 18, 1940; s. Henry Granville and Frances (Fulghum) T.; m. Alice Creech, June 28, 1969; children: Elizabeth Arrington, Caroline Harrison BA, U. Va., 1963. Asst. cashier United Va. Bank-Seaboard Nat., Norfolk, Va., 1968-70, asst. v.p., 1970-72, United Va. Mortgage Corp., Norfolk, Va., 1972, v.p., 1972-73, pres., chief exec. officer, 1974-76, United Va. Leasing Corp., Richmond, Va., 1973-74; sr. v.p. bank related United Va. Bankshares, Inc., Richmond, 1976-78; pres., chief adminstrv. officer United Va. Bank, Richmond, 1978-80; exec. v.p. corp. banking United Va. Bankshares, Inc., Richmond, 1980-84, vice chmn., 1984-85; pres., chief exec. officer United Va. Bankshares, Inc., now Crestar Fin. Corp., Richmond, 1985-99; chmn. SunTrust Bank-Mid-Atlantic (formerly Crestar Fin. Corp.), Richmond, 1986-2000; dir. Sysco Systems, 2002—. Bd. dirs. Chesapeake Corp., Richmond, 1986—; chmn. Va. Pub. Bldg. Authority, Richmond, 1982-87; prin. Va. Bus. Coun., 1987-2000; mem. Fed. Adv. Coun., 1994-97, pres. 1996-97. Chmn. bd. dirs. Richmond Symphony, 1984-85; bd. dirs., mem. gen. adv. coun. Sheltering Arms Hosp., Richmond, 1981-89; bd. dirs. Va. Free, 1989-90, Richmond Symphony Found., 1989-91, Va. Found. Ind. Colls., 1988—, bd. trustees, Norfolk Acad., 2001—, bd. dirs., Richmond Cmty. Found., 2002—,Va. Literacy Found., 1986-89; bd. govs. St. Catherine's Sch., 1989-95; bd. dirs. Va. Mus. Found., 1986-92, trustee, 1994—; trustee Randolph Macon Coll., 1985-93, Richmond Renaissance, 1986-99, Colonial Williamsburg Found., 1994—, founding trustee VCU Sch. Engring. Found., 1995—; co-chmn. NCCJ. 1st lt. U.S. Army, 1963-66. Mem. Bankers Rountable (dir. 1996-99), Am. Bankers Assn., Va. Bankers Assn. (bd. dirs. 1991-98, pres. 1996-97). Clubs: Commonwealth, Country of Va. Episcopalian. Office: 1390 Enclave Pkwy Houston TX 77077

TILGHMAN, SHIRLEY MARIE, academic administrator, biology professor; b. Toronto, Can. 2 children. PhD in Biochemistry, Temple U., 1975. Prof. molecular biology Princeton (NJ) U., 1986—, Howard A. Prior prof. in life scis., 1986—2001, pres., 2001—. Investigator Howard Hughes Med. Inst., 1988-2001; trustee The Jackson Lab., 1994-. Mem.: NAS, Am. Acad. Arts and Scis., Royal Soc. London, Inst. of Medicine, Am. Philos. Soc. Office: Princeton U Office of Pres One Nassau Hall Princeton NJ 08544-0001

TILL, JAMES EDGAR, medical educator, researcher; b. Lloydminster, Sask., Can., Aug. 25, 1931; s. William and Gertrude Ruth (Isaac) T.; m. Marion Joyce Sinclair, June 6, 1959; children: David William, Karen Sinclair, Susan Elizabeth. BA, U. Sask., 1952, MA, 1954; PhD, Yale U., 1957; DSc (hon.), U. Toronto, Can., 2004. Mem. physics divsn. Ont. Cancer Inst., Toronto, 1957-67, with divsn. biol. rsch., 1967-89, divsn. head, 1969-82, with divsn. epidemiology and stats., 1989—; assoc. dean U. Toronto, 1981-84, univ. prof., 1984-97, univ. prof. emeritus, 1997—. Contbr. articles on biophysics, cell biology and cancer control research to sci. jours. Recipient Gairdner Found. Internat. award, 1969, Order of Can., 1994; named to Canadian Med. Hall Fame, 2004. Fellow Royal Soc. Can., Royal Soc. London. Home: 182 Briar Hill Ave Toronto ON Canada M4R 1H9 Office: 610 University Ave Toronto ON Canada M5G 2M9 Office Phone: 416-946-2948. Business E-Mail: till@oci.utoronto.ca. *Albert Einstein said: "The most beautiful thing we can experience is the mysterious. It is the source of all true art and science." He also believed that concern for humanity must always form the chief interest of all technical endeavors— "in order that the creations of our mind shall be a blessing and not a curse to mankind." Is there a more eloquent summary of standards for the scientist than this?.*

TILLACK, THOMAS WARNER, pathologist, educator; b. Jacksonville, Fla., Nov. 16, 1937; s. Warner S. and Charlotte G. T.; m. Lynne Anne Beam, Oct. 30, 1970; children— Jonathan Allan, Allison Anne. BA, U. Rochester, 1959; MD, Yale U., 1963. Diplomate Am. Bd. Pathology. Intern Barnes Hosp., St. Louis, 1963-64, resident, 1964-66; staff assoc. NIH, Bethesda, Md., 1966-69, sr. staff fellow, 1969-71; asst. prof. pathology Washington U., St. Louis, 1971-73, assoc. prof., 1973-76; Walter Reed prof., chmn. dept. pathology U. Va. Med. Center, Charlottesville, 1976-2001; prof. U. Va. Health Sys., Charlottesville, 2001—. Served with USPHS, 1966-69. Mem. Am. Soc. Investigative Pathology, U.S. and Can. Acad. Pathology, Am. Soc. Cell Biology, Assn. Pathology Chairs, Phi Beta Kappa. Achievements include research publs. in cell biology and pathology. Home: 491 Ednam Cir Charlottesville VA 22903-4607 Office: U Va Health Sys Dept Pathology PO Box 800214 Charlottesville VA 22908-0214

TILLER, OLIVE MARIE, retired church worker; b. St. Paul, Dec. 13, 1920; d. Otto William and Myrtle Alice (Brougham) Foerster; m. Carl William Tiller, June 21, 1940; children: Robert W., Jeanne L. Peterson; m. Edward J. Alo, Dec. 15, 2001. BS, U. Minn., 1940. Spl. edn. tchr., Prince Georges County, Md., 1955-63; spl. asst. for profl. svcs. Kendall Demonstration Elem. Sch., Gallaudet Coll., Washington, 1971-78; spl. asst. for program Ch. Women United, N.Y.C., 1979-80; exec. asst. to gen. sec. Nat. Coun. Chs. of Christ in U.S.A., N.Y.C., 1981-87; dep. gen. sec. for coop. Christianity Am. Bapt. Chs. of U.S.A., Valley Forge, Pa., 1987-88. Author (with Carl W. Tiller): At Calvary, 1994. Mem. Human Rels. Commn. Prince George's County, 1967—73; bd. dirs. Am. Leprosy Missions, Greenville, SC, 1981—95, Bapt. Peace Fellowship of N.Am., Charlotte, NC, 1984—95; mem. Nat. Interreligious Svc. Bd. for Conscientious Objectors, 1991—98, treas., 1994—98, sec., 1997—98; mem. nat. coun. Fellowship of Reconciliation, 1985—88, 1996—97; mem. Study Commn. on Human Rights Bapt. World Alliance, 1995—2000, mem. Study Commn. on Freedom and Justice, 2000—, mem. World Aid com., 2000—; v.p. Am. Bapt. Chs. U.S.A., Valley Forge, 1976—77. Named to Hall of Fame, Ctrl. HS, 1993; recipient Dahlberg Peace award, Am. Bapt. Chs., 1991, Valiant Woman award, Ch. Women United, 1978, Meeker award, Ottawa U., 1995, Luke Mowbray Ecumenical award, Am. Bapt. Chs., 1999, Girls Dormitory at Ulaya Secondary Sch. in Tanzania named for Olive Marie Tiller. Baptist. Home: 283 Norman Dr Cranberry Township PA 16066-4235 E-mail: olivet@zoominternet.net.

TILLER, THOMAS C. manufacturing executive; BA, MIT, 1983; MBA, Harvard U., 1991; M in Mech. Engring., U. Vt. Engr. GE, 1983; mgr. GE Appliances; v.p., gen. mgr. GE Silicones; pres., COO Polaris Industries Inc., Mpls., 1998—. Office: Polaris Industries Inc 2100 Highway 55 Hamel MN 55340-9770

TILLERSON, REX W. oil industry executive; b. Wichita Falls, Tex. BS in Civil Engring., U. Tex., Austin. Joined Exxon Co., U.S.A., 1975, various positions, prodn. dept., 1975—87, bus. devel. mgr., natural gas dept., 1987—89, gen. mgr., ctrl. prodn. divsn., 1989—92; prodn. adv. Exxon Corp., Dallas, 1992; coord., affiliate gas sales Exxon Co. Internat., Florham Park, NJ, 1992—95; pres. Exxon Yemen Inc., Esso Exploration and Prodn. Khorat Inc., 1995—98; v.p. Exxon Ventures Inc., 1998—99; pres. Exxon Neftegas Ltd., 1998—99; exec. v.p. ExxonMobil Devel. Co., 1999—2001; sr. v.p. Exxon

Mobil Corp., 2001—04, pres., 2004—. Mem. Engring. Found. Adv. Coun. for the U. Tex. at Austin. Mem.: U.S.-Russia Bus. Coun., Soc. Petroleum Engrs., Am. Petroleum Inst. Office: ExxonMobil Corp 5959 Las Colinas Blvd Irving TX 75039-2298*

TILLEY, CAROLYN BITTNER, technical information specialist; b. Washington, July 29, 1947; d. Klaud Kay and Margaret Louise (Hanson) Bittner; m. Frederick Edwin Dudley, June 18, 1985 BS, Am. U., 1975; M.L.S., U. Md., 1976. With NIH, 1965-71; statis. research asst. Health Manpower Edn., Bethesda, Md., 1971-72; tech. info. specialist Nat. Libr. Medicine, Bethesda, Md., 1972-81, head medlars (med. lit. analysis and retrieval system) mgmt. sect., 1981—. Mem. editorial bd.: Med. Reference Services Quar. Mem. Nat. Fed. Abstracting and Info. Svc. Editl. Com. Recipient Merit award NIH, 1984, Rogers award Nat. Libr. Medicine, 1991. Mem. Med. Libr. Assn. Presbyterian. Avocation: horseback riding. Office: Nat Libr Medicine 8600 Rockville Pike Bethesda MD 20894-0002

TILLEY, JACK L. military officer; b. Vancouver, Wash., Dec. 3, 1948; With U.S. Army, 1966—69, 1971—, advanced through grades to sgt. maj., 2000—. Decorated Legion of Merit with two oak leaf clusters, Bronze Star with v device, Meritorious Svc. medal with one oak leaf cluster. Office: 200 Army Pentagon Washington DC 20310-0200

TILLEY, NORWOOD CARLTON, JR., federal judge; b. Rock Hill, S.C., 1943; s. Norwood Carlton and Rebecca (Westbrook) T. BA, Wake Forest U., 1966, JD, 1969. Bar: N.C. 1969, U.S. Dist. Ct. (middle dist.) N.C. 1971. Law clk. to Hon. Eugene A Gordon, U.S. Dist. Judge Middle Dist. N.C., 1969-71; asst. U.S. atty. Mid. Dist. N.C., Greensboro, 1971-73, U.S. atty., 1974-77, U.S. dist. judge Durham, 1988—; ptnr. Osteen, Adams, Tilley & Walker, Greensboro, 1977-88. Instr. Wake Forest U. Sch. Law, 1980. Office: US Dist Ct PO Box 3443 Greensboro NC 27402-3443

TILLEY, SHERMAINE ANN, investment company executive; b. Shawnee, Okla., Feb. 22, 1952; d. Cecil Fern and Zona Emma (Evans) T. BA in Chemistry summa cum laude, Okla. City U., 1973; PhD in Biochemistry, The Johns Hopkins U., 1980; MBA in Investment Banking/Corp. Fin., U. Toronto, 2000. Rsch. assoc. Albert Einstein Coll. Medicine, Bronx, 1980-85; rsch. asst. prof. NYU Sch. Medicine, NYC, 1985-94, rsch. assoc. prof., 1994-2000; asst. mem. Pub. Health Rsch. Inst., NYC, 1985-93, assoc. mem., 1994-2000. Ad hoc reviewer SBIR grants NIH, 1989-98; sec., staff coun. adv. com. Pub. Health Rsch. Inst., NYC, 1990-95; pres's. appointee bd. dirs. Pub. Health Rsch. Inst., 1993-95, Drug Royalty Corp., Toronto, 2000—. Contbr. articles to profl. jours.; patentee in field. Recipient Letzeiser medal, Okla. City U., 1973; Nat. Arthritis Found. fellow, 1982-85; Life and Health Ins. Med. Rsch. Fund grantee, 1986-89; NIH grantee, 1988-99; Can. credit mgmt. found. fellow, 1998-99. Mem. AAAS, Am. Assn. Immunologists, Am. Soc. Microbiology, Licensing Exec. Soc., Toronto Biotechnology Initiative, Rotman Advancement Bd.(U. Toronto Bus. Sch.). Achievements include demonstration of synergistic neutralization of HIV-1 by human monoclonal antibodies against the V3 loop and CD4 binding site of gpl20; completion of 8 biotechnology/pharmaceutical royalty financing transactions totaling over $US 66M as part of Drug Royalty's management group. Office: Drug Royalty Corp Royal Bank Plz Ste 3120 South Tower Box 122 200 Bay St Toronto ON Canada M5J 2J3 Business E-Mail: st@drugroyalty.com.

TILLEY, TANA MARIE, pharmaceutical executive; b. Athens, Ga., Dec. 28, 1955; d. Harry Sanford Pierce and Shirley Joanne Webster; m. Scott David Tilley, Aug. 28, 1977; children: Christopher Scott, Lauren Brooke. AD in Nursing, U. S.C., 1980, BS in Nursing cum laude, 1990. Asst. mgr. Brook's Fashions, 1975-78; staff nurse labor and delivery Spartanburg Regional Hosp., 1980-84, head nurse labor and delivery, 1984-89, staff nurse emergency rm., 1989-90; profl. sales rep. L'Nard & Assocs., 1989-90, TAP Pharm., 1990-92, regional hosp. liaison, 1992-95, dist. mgr., hosp. acct. execs., 1995-96, dist. mgr., 1996, 1997-2000, regional sales mgr., 2000—. Methodist. Home: 605 Shade Lake Ct Alpharetta GA 30004 Office: TAP Pharmaceuticals 1050 Crown Point Ste 1445 Atlanta GA 30338 E-mail: tanatilley@tap.com.

TILLINGHAST, CHARLES CARPENTER, III, marketing company executive; b. NYC, Nov. 16, 1936; s. Charles Carpenter, Jr. and Lisette (Micoleau) T.; m. Cynthia Branch, Sept. 28, 1974; children by previous marriage: Avery D., Charles W., David C. BS in Mech. Engring., Lehigh U., 1958; MBA, Harvard U., 1963. Asst. to dir. devel. Lehigh U., Bethlehem, Pa., 1958-61; adminstrv. asst. Boise Cascade Corp., Portland, Oreg., 1963; asst. to v.p. Boise (Idaho) Cascade Corp., 1964-65, gen. mgr. office supply divsn., 1965-67, gen. mgr. paper distbn. divsn., 1966, v.p. bus. products, 1967-69, sr. v.p. housing group, 1969-71, sr. v.p., 1971-73; pres. CRM divsn. Ziff-Davis Pub. Co., Inc., Del Mar, Calif., 1971-75; pres., treas. Value Communications, Inc., La Jolla, Calif., 1975-76; pres. Oak Tree Publs., Inc., San Diego, 1976-81, Advanced Mktg. Svcs. Inc., San Diego, 1982-94, chmn., 1994—2004, pres., CEO, 2004—. Served to 2d lt. AUS, 1959. Home: 1762 Nautilus St La Jolla CA 92037-6413 Office: Advanced Mktg Svcs Inc 5880 Oberlin Dr Ste 400 San Diego CA 92121-4794

TILLINGHAST, DAVID ROLLHAUS, lawyer; b. N.Y.C., Feb. 25, 1930; s. Charles Carpenter and Josephine Dorothy (Rollhaus) T.; m. Phyllis Van Horn, Sept. 24, 1955 (div. Jan. 1984); m. Lisa Sewell, Feb. 25, 1984; children: Gregory Barrett Sewell, Lauren Alexa. AB cum laude, Brown U., 1951; LLB cum laude, Yale U., 1954. Bar: N.Y. 1955, Oreg. 1956, U.S. Supreme Ct. 1978. Assoc. Hughes, Hubbard & Reed, N.Y.C., 1954-55, 57-61, ptnr., 1961-62, 65-90; assoc. King, Miller, Anderson, Nash & Yerke, Portland, Oreg., 1955-57; spl. asst. for internat. tax affairs U.S. Dept. Treasury, Washington, 1962-65; ptnr. Chadbourne & Parke, N.Y.C., 1990-99, Baker & McKenzie, N.Y.C., 1999—. Adj. prof. Sch. Law, NYU, 1977-87; cons. UN Ctr. on Transnat. Corps., 1978-87; reporter Am. Law Inst. Project on Internat. Aspects of U.S. Income Taxation, 1982-91; cons. to reporters Am. Law Inst. Revision of Restatement of Fgn. Relations Law of U.S., 1982-83. Author: Tax Aspects of Internat. Transactions, 1978, 2d edit., 1984; co-author: Income Tax Treaty Arbitration, 2004; contbr. articles to profl. publs. Mem. transition team Sec. of Treasury W. Michael Blumenthal, 1977. Estab. David L. Tillinghast lectr. on internat. taxation NYU Sch. Law. Mem.: Coun. Fgn. Rels., Tax Forum, Internat. Bar Assn. (vice chmn. com. on taxation bus. law sect. 1984—86), Internat. Fiscal Assn. (v.p. U.S. br. 1983—2000, permanent sci. com. 1983—2000, vice chmn. 1993—95, chmn. 1995—2000), Assn. of Bar of City of N.Y. (chmn. com. on taxation 1981—83). Democrat. Avocations: golf, tennis. Office: Baker & McKenzie 805 3rd Ave New York NY 10022-7513 Office Phone: 212-891-3526. E-mail: david.r.tillinghast@bakernet.com.

TILLINGHAST, JOHN AVERY, utilities executive; b. N.Y.C., Apr. 30, 1927; s. Charles C. and Dorothy J. (Rollhaus) T.; m. Mabel Healy, Sept. 11, 1948; children: Katherine Brickley, Susan Trainor, Abigail Ryan. BSME, Columbia U., 1948, MS, 1949. Registered profl. engr., Ky., Ind., Mich., N.Y., Ohio, Va., W.Va., N.H. With Am. Elec. Power Service Corp., N.Y.C., 1949-79, exec. v.p. engring. and constrn., 1967-72, sr. exec. v.p., vice chmn. engring. and constrn., 1972-79; sr. v.p. tech. Wheelabrator-Frye Inc., Hampton, N.H., 1979-83, Signal Advanced Tech. Group, The Signal Cos., Hampton, N.H., 1983-85; sr. v.p. Allied-Signal Internat., Hampton, 1985-86, Sci. Applications Internat. Corp., San Diego, 1986-88; pres. TILTEC, Portsmouth, N.H, 1987-94; CEO, Great Bay Power Corp., Dover, N.H, 1994-97; CEO BayCorp Holdings, Ltd., Dover, 1997-98, chmn. bd. Portsmouth, 1998—. Patentee generating unit control system. Elder Reformed Ch., 1976-79. Served with USN, 1944-46. Fellow ASME; mem. IEEE, NAE, Sigma Xi, Tau Beta Pi. Office: Great Bay 51 Dow Hwy Ste 7 Eliot ME 03903-2037

TILLMAN, BARBARA ANN, education educator, consultant; b. Waterbury, Conn., Oct. 20, 1945; d. Jehue and Carrie Lee Tillman. BSBA, Loyola, Paris, 1978; MA in Behavior Sci., Calif. State U., Dominguez Hills, 1994. Program mgr. Barclay Career Schs., New Port Beach, Calif., 1984-90, dir. edn. L.A., Cypress, Calif., 1984-90; vocat. rehab. counselor Am. Interant. Health and Rehab., L.A., 1990-92, Cascade Rehab. Co., Inc., L.A., 1992-94, Career Transition Ctr., Long Beach, Calif., 1994-96; instr. Nat. U., Costa Mesa, Calif., 1996—; ednl. cons. Fred Jefferson Foster Agy., Compton, Calif., 1996—. Cons. County L.A. Mem. Nat. Rehab. Assn., Internat. Assn. Personnel Employment Security, So. Calif. Mediation Soc. Democrat. Roman Catholic. Avocations: story telling, cooking. Office: Nat U 3390 Harbor Blvd Costa Mesa CA 92626-1502 Fax: 714-773-4644.

TILLMAN, CHARLES HERBERT, JR., cardiologist; b. Springfield, Mo., Feb. 16, 1956; m. Bonnie S. Hoover; children: Lauren, Robert. AB, Drury Coll., Springfield, Mo., 1978; MD, U. Mo., Columbia, 1982. Bd. cert. Internat. Medicine and Cardiovasc. Disease. Resident in internal medicine So. Ill. U., Springfield, 1982—85; cardiology fellow U. Mo., Columbia, 1985—87; pvt. med. practice Mexico (Mo.) Cardiovasc. Assocs., 1987—; chief of staff Audrain Med. Ctr., Mexico, 1994—95, 2002—. Fellow: ACP, Am. Coll. Cardiology; mem.: AAAS, Rotary Internat. Avocations: photography, tennis, amateur astronomy. Office: Mexico Cardiovasc Assocs 201 E Monroe Mexico MO 65265

TILLMAN, HOYT CLEVELAND, historian, educator, writer; b. Crestview, Fla., July 8, 1944; s. William Fred and Reba Elizabeth Tillman; m. Cristina Lian-ching Mih, June 27, 1970; children: Hoyt Langston, Margaret Mih. BA, Belhaven Coll., 1966; AM, Harvard U., 1970; MA, U. Va., 1968; PhD, Harvard U., 1976. Sr. tutor Harvard U., Cambridge, Mass., 1975—76; asst. prof. Ariz. State U., Tempe, 1976—81, assoc. prof., 1981—88, prof. history, 1988—. Exec. editl. com. Jour. Sung-Yuan Studies, Berkeley, Calif., 1991—; external rev. com. Inst. for Advanced Study, Princeton, NJ, 1999—2000; exec. adv. com. China Scholarship, Beijing, 1999—; vis. prof. U. Wash., Seattle, 1996, Ludwig-Maximilliam U., Munich, 2000—01, Academia Sinica's Inst. Chinese Lit. and Philosophy, Taipei, Taiwan, China, 1993, vis. rsch. prof., 96, Nat. Ctrl. Library's Ctr. Chinese Studies, 1994. Author: Ch'en Liang on Public Interest and the Law, Confucian Discourse and Chu Hsi's Ascendancy, Utilitarian Confucianism: Ch'en Liang's Challenge to Chu Hsi, Zhu Xi de Siwei Shijie (Zhu Xi's World of Thought); editor: China Under Jurchen Rule: Essays on Chin Intellectual and Cultural History; translator: Business as a Vocation: The Autobiography of Wu Ho-Su; contbr. articles to profl. jours., chpts., to books. Grant reviewer NEH, Washington, Am. Coun. Learned Societies, N.Y.C. Recipient Humboldt-Forschungspreis, Alexander von Humboldt Found., 2000, CIES award, J. William Fulbright Found., 2003—04; fellow, NEH, 1980, 1988—89, Fulbright-Hays Faculty Rsch. Abroad Program, 1982—83, Am. Coun. Learned Societies, 1989—90, Princeton U., N.J., 1990; grantee, Am. Coun. Learned Societies, 2004, NAS, 1982—84, Japan Found., 1993—96, Chiang Ching-kuo Found. Internat. Scholarly Exch., 1994—95, 2001—03; scholar, Chinese Acad. Social Scis., 1982—83, Peking U., 1982—84. Mem.: Soc. for Asian and Comparative Philosophy, Am. Hist. Assn. (com. John K. Fairbank prize 1996—98), Assn. Asian Studies. D-Liberal. Congregational. Achievements include the demonstration of greater intellectual and cultural diversity in 11th and 12th centuries Chinese Confucian philosophy. Avocations: travel, walking, reading, conversing. Home: 937 East Verde Ln Tempe AZ 85284-1507 Office: Ariz State U Dept History Tempe AZ 85287-4302 Office Phone: 480-965-5778 or -3025. Personal E-mail: htillman@asu.edu. E-mail: htillman@asu.edu.

TILLMAN, JOSEPH NATHANIEL, engineering executive; b. Augusta, Ga., Aug. 1, 1926; s. Leroy and Canarie (Kelly) T.; m. Alice Lavonia Walton, Sept. 5, 1950 (dec. 1983); children: Alice Lavonia, Robert Bertram; m. Areerat Usahaviriyakit, Nov. 24, 1986. BA magna cum laude, Paine Coll., 1948; MS, Northrop U., 1975, MBA, 1976; DBA, Nova U., 1989. Dir. Rockwell Internat., Anaheim, Calif., 1958-84; pres. Tillman Enterprises, Corona, Calif., 1985—. Guest lectr. UCLA, 1980-85. Contbr. articles to profl. jours. Capt. USAF, 1948-57, Korea. Recipient Presdl. Citation Nat. Assn. for Equal Opportunity in Higher Edn., 1986. Mem. Acad. Mgmt. (chmn. 1985-86), Soc. Logistics Engrs. (pres. 1985-86), Paine Coll. Alumni Assn. (v.p. 1976—), NAACP (pres. 1984-88). Avocations: duplicate bridge, travel, swimming, skiing, hiking. Office: Tillman Enterprises 1550 S Rimpau Ave Spc 45 Corona CA 92881-3206 Office Phone: 951-371-8179. Personal E-mail: josetman@juno.com.

TILLMAN, JUNE TORRISON, musician; b. Mpls., June 11, 1917; d. Odvin Olai and Anne Johanne (Andersen) Torrison; m. Jean Paul Tillman, July 19, 1941; 1 child, Paula Jeanne Tillman Morrow. BA, Macalester Coll., 1940; postgrad., MacPhail Coll Music, 1952-55, U. Minn., 1944-45; student, Dr. Hoch's Konservatorium, Frankfurt am Main, 1956-57. Cert. piano tchr., Fla., Mo. Clk. auditing dept. The Dayton Co., Mpls., summer 1935; tchr., libr. Howard Lake H.S., Minn., 1941; prin. clk. Army Office Chief of Fin., Washington, 1942-43; gold acct. Gen. Refineries, Inc., Mpls., 1944-45; asst. acct. First Acceptance Corp., Mpls., 1946-47, 51; property acct. clk. Army Quartermaster Commissary, Camp Wolters, Tex., 1959-61; music tchr. various orgns., 1953—. Nat. com. chmn. Music Tchrs. Nat. Assn., Ind. Music Tchrs. Forum Studio Policies, 1975-77; state conv. chmn. Fla. State Music Tchrs., Ft. Lauderdale, 1978; auditions ctr. chmn. Nat. Guild Piano Tchrs., Ft. Lauderdale, 1975-87; sponsor, tchr. Mus. Arts Jr. Club of Fla. Fedn. Music Clubs, Wilton Manors, 1976-87, Springfield, Mo., 1988-91, sr. club mem., 1987, pres., 1990-92, state conv. accompanist, 1988-90, v.p. S.W. region of Mo., 1989-91; organist, choir dir. various mil. chapels and civilian chs., U.S., Germany and Japan, 1935-65. Composer numerous works, 1958-87; reviewer (books, records, choral arrangements) 1978-86; editor Fla. Fedn. Music Clubs Publs., 1975-77, 81-84; music editor 12 Choral Octavos, 1981; composer, panelist state convention Minn. Fedn. Music Clubs, Bloomington, 1984; Soprano, Alto, Tenor, Bass, Organ anthem performed by Moramus Chorale at Moravian Music Festival, Winston-Salem, N.C., 1978; prodr., dir., accompanied Menotti's The Old Maid and the Thief, 1965, Argento's The Boor, 1966. Chmn. 10-piano concerts Broward County Music Tchrs., Plantation, Fla., 1969, 71;life mem. Women's Div. Boys Clubs of Broward, Fla., Ft. Lauderdale Symphony Soc.; organist, choir dir. Coral Ridge Moravian Ch., Ft. Lauderdale, 1966-85. Mem. Music Tchrs. Nat. Assn., Nat. Fedn. of Music Clubs (life, dist. pres. 1983-85, young artists auditions com. 1993-97), Morning Musicale of Ft. Lauderdale, Inc. (hon., life, pres. 1970-72), Am. Guild Organists (treas. 1967), Phi Beta (founder, pres. Pi Alpha Rho chpt., life, honor bracelet, scrolls 1971, 76, 83, citations 1988), Order Ea. Star (Richfield, Minn. chpt.), Masons (Fla. Grand chpt. Cmty. Svc. award 1987), Springfield Piano Tchrs. Forum, Toastmasters (gov. S.W. Mo. area 1988-89). Avocations: reading (especially biographies), crossword puzzles, langs. Home and Office: 845 Nottingham Dr Princeton IL 61356-2858

TILLMAN, KAREN SUE, lawyer; b. Garland, Tex., June 21, 1962; d. Franklin Willard and Mary Ruth Wright; m. Massie Tillman, July 2, 1993. BA, Baylor U., 1984, JD, 1986. Bar: U.S. Dist. Ct. (no. dist.) Tex. Law clk. U.S. Bankruptcy Ct., Ft. Worth, 1987-89; assoc. Hill & Gilstrap, Arlington, Tex., 1989-90; litigation atty. Radio Shack Corp., Ft. Worth, 1990—. Mem.: Ft. Worth Club. Republican. Baptist. Avocation: piano. Office: Radio Shack Corp 100 Throckmorton St Ste 1700 Fort Worth TX 76102-2847 Office Phone: 817-415-3767. E-mail: karen.tillman@radioshack.com.

TILLMAN, LYNNE (MERRILL), writer; b. Bklyn. d. Nathan and Sophie (Merrill) Tillman; m. David C. Hofstra. BA, Hunter Coll., 1967. Co-head writing dept. MFA program Bard Coll., 1993—2003; vis. critic Yale U., 1996; vis. assoc. prof. Brown U., 1998, Columbia U., 1999; assoc. prof., writer in residence U. Albany, 2002—; lectr. in field; vis. critic Yale U., 2002. Author: Living with Contradictions, 1982, Madame Realism, 1984, Tagebuch Einer Masochistin, 1986, Haunted Houses, 1987, Absence Makes the Heart, 1990, Motion Sickness, 1991, The Madame Realism Complex, 1992, Warhol's Factory: The Velvet Years 1965-67, 1996, Cast in Doubt, 1992, The Broad Picture, 1997, No Lease on Life, 1998 (Finalist, Nat. Book Critics Award in Fiction, 1998), Love Sentence, 1999, This is Not It, 2002; editor: Fence mag., 2003—; co-editor: Beyond Recognition: Representation, Power, Culture-Writings of Craig Owens, 1992; contbr. articles to profl. jours.; author: Bookstore: The Life and Times of Jeannette Watson and Books & Co., 1999. Grantee, Jerome Found., 1988, NYSCA, 1988, NYFA, 1990; MacDowell fellow, 1991, 1995—97, 1999—2001, 2003. Mem.: PEN. Home: PO Box 360 New York NY 10009

TILLMAN, MARY NORMAN, urban affairs consultant; b. Atlanta, Jan. 31, 1926; d. Mary Nellie Shehee; m. James A. Tillman Jr., Apr. 11, 1952; children: James A., Gina G. BA, Morris Brown Coll., 1947; postgrad., U. Minn., 1964, Old Dominion U., 1975—. Asst. bus. mgr. Morris Brown Coll., Atlanta, 1947-53; race rels. and urban affairs cons. Tillman Assocs. Cons. Social Engrs., Atlanta and Syracuse, N.Y., 1963—, sr. ptnr., treas., from 1965, now pres. Bd. dirs. The Tillman Inst. of Human Rels., Inc.; clin. prof. United Theol. Sem., New Brighton, Minn.; adj. prof. Gordon-Conwell Theol. Sem., South Hamilton, Mass. Author: What is Your Racism Quotient?, 1964, A Common Sense Approach to Racism and Other Exclusivities, 1998, (with James A. Tillman, Jr.) Why America Needs Racism and Poverty, 1972, Black Intellectuals, White Liberals and Race Relations: An Analytic Overview, 1973; What is your Exclusivity Quotient, 1978, A Common Sense Approach to Racism and Other Exclusivities, 2001; contbr. articles to profl. jours. Adv. coun. to urban ministries dept. So. Bapt. Conv., Cmty. Rels. Commn., Atlanta; bd. dirs. Christian Coun. Met. Atlanta, Tillman Inst. Human Rels. Mem. Tidewater Assn. Pub. Adminstrs. (dir.), Am. Acad. Cons., Nat. Black Writers Consortium (v.p.), Joint Ctr. for Polit. Studies. Office: 1765 Glenview Dr SW Atlanta GA 30331-2307 Office Phone: 404-349-3668.

TILLMAN, MASSIE MONROE, mediator, arbitrator, art gallery owner, retired federal judge; b. Corpus Christi, Tex., Aug. 15, 1937; s. Clarence and Artie Lee (Stewart) T.; m. Karen Wright, July 2, 1993; children: Jeffrey Monroe, Holly. BBA, Baylor U., 1959, LLB, 1961. Bar: Tex. 1961, U.S. Dist. Ct. (no. dist.) Tex. 1961, U.S. Ct. Appeals (5th cir.) 1969, U.S. Supreme Ct. 1969; formerly bd. cert. Personal Injury Trial Law, Tex. Ptnr. Herrick & Tillman, Ft. Worth, 1961-66; pvt. practice, Ft. Worth, 1966-70, 79-87; ptnr. Brown, Herman et al, Ft. Worth, 1970-78, Street, Swift et al, Ft. Worth, 1978-79; U.S. bankruptcy judge Ft. Worth divsn. No. Dist. Tex., 1987-2001; mediator, arbitrator, 2001—. Author: Tillman's Trial Guide, 1970; comments editor, case notes editor; mem. editl. bd. Baylor Law Rev., 1960-61. Bd. dirs. Fort Worth Acad. Fine Arts, Tex. Boys Choir, 2003—. Fellow Am. Bd. Trial Advocates, Tex. Bar Found.; mem. Ft. Worth/Tarrant County Bar (bd. dirs. 1969-70, v.p. 1970-71), Trial Attys.'s of Am., Nat. Conf. of Bankruptcy Judges, Coll. State Bar Tex., Am. Arbitration Assn. Republican. Baptist. Avocation: quail hunting. Address: PO Box 20213 Fort Worth TX 76102 Office Phone: 817-683-1422. E-mail: tillmanmediator@yahoo.com.

TILLMAN, MERCIA V. musician; b. Chatham, Eng. Singer Sid Mills Band, London, 1932—39; club hostess, catering mgr. U.S. Mil. Officer Clubs, 1955—69; owner Mercia Tillman Wedding Cons. & Catering, Manassas, Va., 1972—73; dir. svcs. Innisbrook Resort, Tarpon Springs, Fla., 1975—76; columnist West Coast Publs., Largo, Fla., 1977—78; owner Mercia Tillman Prodns., 1996—. Author: (songs) Florida, My State of Dreams, 1996, Walk Around the Mall, 1996, Goodbye Little Princess, 1998, Hello, My Love, Hello, 2000; author and pub.: Little Gems, 2004. Named Ms. Fla. Sr. Am., 1996; recipient Vol. Woman of Yr., Soroptimist Internat., Fla., 1997, Blue Cross/Blue Shield Ageless Hero award, State of Fla., 1999, 2000, Inductee Sr. Hall of Fame, City of St. Petersburg, Fla., 2000, KFC Col.'s Way award, State of Fla., 2000. Mem.: WWII Meml. Soc. (charter), Ms. Sr. Am. Fla. Cameo Club.

TILLMAN, VICKIE A. diversified financial services company executive; BA in comm., MPA in fin., U. Pitts. With Standard & Poor's, 1977—, exec. mng. dir. pub. fin. ratings dept., exec. v.p. structured fin. ratings, 1994—99, exec. v.p., 1999—, mem. exec. com. Office: Standard & Poor's 55 Water St New York NY 10041

TILLOTSON, MARY, cable television host; BA in Journalism, U. Ala. Anchor WSB-Radio, Atlanta; news anchor WMAL-Radio, Washington; reporter, anchor WTTG-TV, Washington; congl. reporter Ind. TV News Assn., Washington; news anchor Mutual Radio Network, Washington; reporter CNN, 1981-85, White House corr., 1985-88, Capitol Hill corr., 1988-91; TV talk show host CNN & Co. Atlanta, 1991—. Nominee CableACE award for best talk show interviewer, 1996. Office: Cable News Network One CNN Ctr 1 Cnn Ctr NW Atlanta GA 30303-2762

TILLSON, JOHN BRADFORD (BRAD), JR., newspaper publisher; b. Paris, Tex., Dec. 21, 1944; s. John Bradford Sr. and Frances (Ragland) T.; m. Patricia Hunt, June 14, 1966 (div. June 1978); children: John, Karen; m. Cynthia Wornom, Oct. 10, 1981. BA, Denison U., Granville, Ohio, 1966. Reporter Charlotte (N.C.) News, 1969-71, Dayton (Ohio) Daily News, 1971-76, city editor, 1977-80, asst. mng. editor, 1980-82, mng. editor features, 1982-84; editor Dayton Daily News and Jour. Herald, 1984-88, pub., 1988—; pres., CEO Cox Ohio Pub., 1996—. Lectr. Am. Press Inst., Reston, Va., 1980-84. Chair Inventing Flight/2003 Com., 1998—; mem. Centennial of Flight Commn., 1998—; chair Miami Valley Econ. Devel. Coalition, 1999-2001; pres. Dayton Art Inst., 1990-96; chair Alliance for Edn., 1992-94. Mem. Ohio Newspaper Assn. (treas. 2000—), Newspaper Assn. Am. Episcopalian. Office: Cox Ohio Pub 45 S Ludlow St Dayton OH 45402-1810

TILLY, JENNIFER, actress; b. Harbor City, Calif., Sept. 16, 1958; m. Sam Simon, 1984 (div., 1991). Grad., Stephens Coll., 1979. TV series include: Shaping Up, 1984, Key West, 1993; TV movies include: Heads, 1994; films include: No Small Affair, 1984, Moving Violations, 1985, He's My Girl, 1987, Inside Out, 1987, Rented Lips, 1988, High Spirits, 1988, Johnny Be Good, 1988, Remote Control, 1988, The Fabulous Baker Boys, 1989, Let It Ride, 1989, Far From Home, 1989, Scorchers, 1991, Shadow of the Wolf, 1992, Made in America, 1993, At Home With the Webbers, 1993, Double Cross, 1994, Bullets Over Broadway, 1994 (Academy award nomination best supporting actress 1994), The Getaway, 1994, The Pompatus of Love, 1996, Liar, Liar, 1996, House Arrest, 1996, Edie & Pen, 1996, Bound, 1996, American Strays, 1996, Bride of chucky, 1998, Music From Another Room, 1998, The Muse, 1999, Goosed, 1999, Do Not Disturb, 1999, (voice) Bartok the Magnificent, 1999, (voice) Stuart Little, 1999, Play It to the Bone, 1999, Bruno, 2000, Cord, 2000, The Crew, 2000, The Cat's Meow, 2001, Monsters, Inc. (voice), 2001, Jericho Mansions, 2003, The Haunted Mansion, 2003, Home on the Range (voice), 2004. Home: Care Carrol Gettko 118 S Beverly Dr Beverly Hills CA 90212-3003*

TILNEY, ELIZABETH A. marketing executive; B, U. Va; MBA, Dartmouth U. With media planning Benton & Bowles Advt., N.Y.C., 1979-81; with acct. mgmt. Ogilvy & Mather Advt., N.Y.C. and Houston, 1983-87; formerly with Russell Reynolds Assocs.; sr. v.p. mktg. comm. and adminstrn. Enron, Houston, 1996-99; sr. v.p. mktg. comm. and human resources Energy Svcs. subsidiary Enron, Houston, 1999—. Office: Enron Corp 1400 Smith St Houston TX 77002-7327

TILNEY, NICHOLAS LECHMERE, surgery educator; b. N.Y.C., Oct. 19, 1935; s. Robert Wallace and Olive van Rensallaer (Gawtry) T.; m. Henriette Beatrice Loudon, Sept. 20, 1958 (div. 1975); children: Rebecca, Louise Moore, Victoria; m. Mary Johanna Graves, June 17, 1978; 1 child, Frances. AB, Harvard U., 1958; MD, Cornell U., 1962. Surg. resident Peter Bent Brigham Hosp., Boston, 1962-71; rsch. fellow U. Oxford, Eng., 1968-69, 71-72; surg. registrar U. Glasgow, Scotland, 1972-73; asst. prof. surgery Harvard Med. Sch., Boston, 1974-76, assoc. prof. surgery, 1977-82, prof. surgery, 1983—, Francis D. Moore prof., 1992—, dir. Surg. Rsch. Lab., 1975—. Dir. transplant svcs. Brigham & Womens Hosp., Boston, 1976-92, Transplant Rsch. Ctr., 1992—. Contbr. articles to profl. jours. Lt. comdr. USN, 1966-68. Fellow ACS, Royal Coll. Physicians and Surgeons (Glasgow); mem. Am. Soc. Transplant Surgeons (pres. 1995), Am. Surg. Assn., Phi Beta Kappa. Avocation: boating. Office: Brigham and Womens Hosp 75 Francis St Boston MA 02115-6106

TILSON, HUGH HANNA, epidemiologist; b. New Kensington, Pa., Jan. 6, 1940; s. Donald Heath and Ann Coe T.; m. Judith Scullin, June 10, 1961; children: Hugh, Richard S., Ann C., Alice H. BA, Reed Coll., 1963; MD, Washington U., 1964; MPH, Harvard U., 1969, DPH, 1972. Diplomate Am. Bd. Preventive Medicine (trustee 1986-95, vice chmn. pub. health and preventive medicine, 1988-95). Intern Yale-New Haven Med. Ctr., 1964-65;

resident in preventive medicine Harvard Sch. Pub. Health, 1968-72; rsch. mem. John F. Kennedy Inst. Politics, 1969-70; rsch. assoc. Health Svcs. Rsch. Ctr., U. N.C., Chapel Hill, 1970-81; asst. prof. preventive medicine and pub. health U. Oreg. Med. Sch., 1971-74, assoc. prof., 1974-76, clin. prof., 1976-78, asst. health officer Multnomah County, Oreg., 1971-75, health officer, dir. divsn. health svcs., 1975-76, health officer, dir. dept. human svcs., 1976-78; dir. divsn. health svcs. State of N.C., Raleigh, 1979-81; with Burroughs Wellcome Co., Research Triangle Park, NC, 1981—94; internat. v.p. epidemiology, surveillance and policy rsch. GlaxoWellcome, Research Triangle Park, 1994-96. Adj. prof. epidemiology and health policy U. N.C. Sch. Pub. Health, clin. prof. family medicine U. N.C. Med. Sch., 1981—, sr. advisor to dean, 1997—; adj. prof. pharmacy U. N.C. Sch. Pharmacy; clin. prof. medicine Duke U. Sch. Medicine, 2002—; cons. in field; examiner Am. Bd. Preventive Medicine, 1974-75; cons. Nat. Ctr. for Health Svcs. Rsch., HEW, 1975-89; mem. external adv. bd. Health Svcs. Rsch. Ctr., U. Wash. Sch. Pub. Health, 1977-80; mem. pub. health stds. work group USPHS, 1977-92; chmn. external adv. bd. Health Svcs. Rsch. Ctr., U. N.C., 1979-93, mem. adv. bd., 1993—; mem. med. adv. bd. Planned Parenthood of Portland, 1973-79, Planned Parenthood Greater Raleigh, 1986-95; bd. dirs. N.W. Oreg. Health Systems Agy., 1976-79; vice chmn. policy adv. bd. Joint Commn. on Accrediation of Hosps., 1980-81; mem. bd. health promotion and disease prevention Inst. Medicine, 1993-99, mem. study panels, 1990—. Mem. editl. bd. Am. Jour. Pub. Health, 1980-85, assoc. editor, 1985-99, sr. advisor, 2000-01; mem. editl. bd. Jour. Cmty. Health, 1977-86, Jour. Pub. Health Policy, 1979-87, Jour. Clin. Rsch. and Pharmacoepidemiology, 1986-89, Am. Jour. Preventive Medicine, 1987-2004. Bd. dirs. United Way Columbia-Willamette, Oreg., 1977-78, Portland Opera Assn., 1977-79, Raleigh Chamber Music Guild, 1981-96, Partnership for Prevention, 1993—, Coun. on Linkages, 1995—; mem. Research Triangle Internat. Visitors Ctr., 1981-98, bd. dirs., v.p., 1981-85. With M.C. U.S. Army, 1963-68. Fellow Am. Coll. Preventive Medicine (regent 1988-92, pres.-elect 1993-95, pres. 1995-97, chair devel. 1997—), Maine Ctr. Pub. Health (sr.); mem. NAS (lifetime nat. assoc.) Nat. Assn. County Health Officers (pres. 1977-79), N.C. Med. Soc., English Speaking Union, N.C. Pub. Health Assn., APHA, Wake County Med. Soc. (v.p. 1981-82), AMA (alt. del. 2002—), Assn. Tchrs. Preventive Medicine, Pharm. Mfrs. Assn. (med. sect. steering com. 1988—96, sec. 1989-92, vice chmn. 1992—94, chmn. 1994—96), Internat. Soc. Pharmacoepidemiology (hon; life; founding co-pres. 1990-91, chmn. bylaws com. 1993—), Internat. Soc. Pharmacoecons. Outcomes Rsch. (founding mem., chmn. policy bylaws 1996—), Ctrs. for Edn. and Rsch. in Therapeutics (chmn. nat. steering com. 1999—), Wake County Med. Soc., Harvard Sch. Pub. Health Alumni Assn. (Alumni Award of Merit 2004), Am. Acad. Pharm. Physicians (bd. dirs. 1994—, hon. life mem. 1994—, policy com. chair 1996—), Maine Pub. Health Assn. Democrat. Episcopalian. Home: 1612 Oberlin Rd # 5 Raleigh NC 27608 Office: U NC Sch Pub Health Chapel Hill NC 27599-7400 Office Phone: 919-966-9275. E-mail: hugh_tilsone@unc.edu.

TILSON THOMAS, MICHAEL, symphony conductor; b. L.A., 1944; s. Ted and Roberta Tilson Thomas. Studies with, Ingolf Dahl, U. So. Calif., others; student conducting, Berkshire Music Festival, Tanglewood, Mass.; student conducting (Koussevitsky prize 1968); LL.D., Hamilton Coll.; L.H.D. (hon.), D'Youville Coll., 1976. Asst. condr. Boston Symphony Orch., 1969, assoc. condr., 1970-72, prin. guest condr., 1972-74; also Berkshire Music Festival, summer 1970, 74; music dir., condr. Buffalo Philharmonic Orch., 1971-79; music dir., prin. condr. Great Woods Ctr. for Performing Arts, 1985-88; prin. condr. London Symphony Orch., 1988-95; artistic dir. New World Symphony, Fla., 1988—; prin. guest condr. London Symphony Orch., 1995—; music dir. San Francisco Symphony, 1995—. Composer: Grace-A Song for Leonard Bernstein, 1988; composer: (for Empire Brass Quintet) Street Song, 1988; composer: (for orch. and narator Audrey Hepburn and New World Symphony) From the Diary of Anne Frank, 1990. Named Musician of Yr., Musical Am., 1970; recipient Koussevitsky prize, 1968, Grammy award, Carmina Burana with Cleve. Orch., 1976, Gershwin Live with L.A. Philharm., 1983, Grammy album for Best Classical Album, 2004. Office: 888 7th Ave Fl 37 New York NY 10106-3799 Mailing: Van Walsum Mgmt 4 Addison Bridge Pl London W14 8XP England

TILSWORTH, TIMOTHY, retired environmental/civil engineering educator; b. Norfolk, Nebr., Apr. 6, 1939; s. Brooke and Mildred (Palmer) T.; m. Joanne Novak, Apr. 19, 1966 (div. Jan. 1984); children: Craig Scott, Patrick Joseph; m. Debbie J. May, July 20, 1984. BSCE, U. Nebr., Lincoln, 1966, MSCE, 1967; PhD, U. Kans, 1970. Registered profl. engr., Alaska; diplomate Inst. Hazardous Materials Mgmt. Instr. U. Nebr., Lincoln, 1967; prof. environ. quality and civil engring. U. Alaska, Fairbanks, 1970-94, dir. program environ. quality engring. and sci., 1972-76, 78-94, asst. to pres. for acad. affairs, 1976-78, head dept. civil engring, 1990-91, chmn. grad. coun., chmn. chancellor search com., 1990-91; rschr. Antarctic Rsch. UAF/NSF, 1990—92; prof. emeritus civil engring. and environ. quality engring. U. Alaska, 1994—; co-owner Raven Press Pub. Co., Fairbanks, 1990—; with NSF Antarctic Rsch. McMurdo, 1991—92. Pres. faculty senate U. Alaska, 1992-93; owner Alaska Arctic Environ. Svcs., Fairbanks, 1972-99, DJT's Shelties Delight, Fairbanks, 1985-99, T2 Antiques, 1994-99; project mgr. superconducting super collider proposal State of Alaska, Fairbanks, 1987-88. Chmn. exec. com. Cowper for Gov. Alaska, Fairbanks, 1986. Recipient commendation State of Alaska, 1988. Mem. Assn. for Environ. Engring. Profs., ASCE (Outstanding Service award 1975), Am. Water Works Assn. Water Pollution Control Fedn., Fairbanks Golf and Country Club (bd. dirs. 2000-01), Chi Epsilon. Roman Catholic. Home and Office: 1900 Raven Dr Fairbanks AK 99709-6661 E-mail: fttt@uaf.edu.

TILTON, DAVID LLOYD, savings and loan association executive; b. Santa Barbara, Calif., Sept. 21, 1926; s. Lloyd Irvine and Grace (Hart) T.; m. Mary Caroline Knudtson, June 6, 1953; children: Peter, Jennifer, Michael, Catharine. AB, Stanford U., 1949, MBA, 1951. With Santa Barbara Savs. & Loan Assn., 1951-90, pres., 1965-84; now pres. Fin. Corp., Santa Barbara. Trustee, chmn. Calif. Real Estate Investment Trust, 1988. Served with USNR, World War II. Mem. Calif. Savs. and Loan League (dir. 1980), Delta Chi. Home: 630 Oak Grove Dr Santa Barbara CA 93108-1402 Office: Fin Corp Santa Barbara 311 E Carillo St Santa Barbara CA 93101-2761 E-mail: dtilton@earthlink.net.

TILTON, GLENN F. air transportation executive; b. Washington, Apr. 9, 1948; BA in Internat. Rels., U. S.C., 1970. Sales trainee U.S. mktg. ops. Texaco Inc., Washington, 1970, various assignments, 1970—76, div. supr. mktg. East Brunswick, NJ, 1976—78, area mgr. resale N.Y. div. N.Y.C., 1978, asst. to gen. mgr. northeastern region, 1978—79, mktg. mgr. resale Phila. div., 1979—81, staff coord. corp. planning and econs. dept., 1981—83; asst. gen. mgr. sales Texaco Europe, 1983—84, gen. mgr. mktg., 1984—87; v.p. mktg. Texaco U.S.A., Houston, 1984—88; pres. Texaco Refining and Mktg. Inc., Houston, 1988—91; v.p. Texaco Inc., 1989; chmn. Texaco Ltd., 1991—92; pres. Texaco Eruope, 1992—94, Texaco USA, Houston, 1994—2002; sr. v.p. Texaco Inc., 1995—2002; CEO Texaco, White Plains, NY, 2001; chmn., pres., CEO UAL Corp. and United Airlines, 2002—; pres. Texaco Global Bus. Unit. Mem.: bd. dirs., Chevron Texaco (chmn., 2002). Office: UAL PO Box 66100 Chicago IL 60666*

TILTON, WEBSTER, JR., contractor; b. St. Louis, Sept. 11, 1922; s. Webster and Eleanor (Dozier) T.; student St. Marks Prep. Sch., 1936-40, Pawling Prep. Sch., 1940-42; master brewers degree, U.S. Brewers Acad., 1949; m. Grace Drew Wilson, Feb. 14, 1948 (div. Oct. 1959); 1 son, Webster III; m. 2d, Nancy McBlair Payne, Jan. 5, 1963. Asst. brewing technologist F&M Schaffer Brewing Co., Bklyn., 1948-52; factory sales rep. Cole Steel Equipment Co., N.Y.C., 1957-68; dist. sales mgr. Scantlin Electronics, Inc., Washington, 1968-70; sales rep. Comml. Washer & Dryer Sales Co., Washington, 1970-72; propr. Webster Tilton, Jr., contractor, Washington, 1972-86. Served from cadet to chief mate Mcht. Marine Res.-USNR, 1942-45. Episcopalian. Home: 309 Briar Hill Rd Cooperstown NY 13326-3905

TILY, STEPHEN BROMLEY, III, bank executive; b. Phila., July 7, 1937; s. Stephen Bromley Jr. and Edith Helen (Straub) T.; m. Janet Anita Walz, July 10, 1965; children: Deborah Powell, Stephen Bromley IV, James Charles II. BS in Econs., Washington and Jefferson Coll., 1960; postgrad., Temple U. Sch. Law, 1963. Trust officer Indsl. Valley Bank & Trust Co., Phila., 1968—71; v.p. Farmers Bank Del., Wilmington, 1971—77; exec. officer G&T, Inc., Ltd., Wilmington, 1977—80; pres., COO DCG&T Co., Wilmington, 1977—91, chmn., CEO, 1991—93, chmn. emeritus, 1993—. Chmn. The Declaration Group, Conshohocken, Pa., 1985-97; trustee Declaration Fund, 1988-99; tchr. Am. Inst. Banking, 1970-79. Capt. USAR, 1960 61. Mem. Fin. Analysts of Phila., Barnegat Light Yacht Club (commodore 1988-89, trustee 1989-92), Kimberton Fish and Game Assn., Waynesborough Country Club, John's Island Golf Club, Merion Golf Club, Ducks Unltd. Republican. Episcopalian.

TIMBERLAKE, CHARLES EDWARD, history educator; b. South Shore, Ky., Sept. 9, 1935; s. Howard Ellis and Mabel Viola (Collier) T.; m. Patricia Alice Perkins, Dec. 23, 1958; children: Mark Brewster, Daniel Edward, Eric Collier BA, Berea Coll., 1957; Calif. State Teaching Credential, Claremont Grad. Sch., 1958, MA, 1962; PhD, U. Wash., 1968. Tchr. Barstow H.S., Calif., 1959-60, Claremont City Sch., Calif., 1960-61; tchg., rsch. asst. U. Wash., Seattle, 1961-64; asst. prof. history U. Mo., Columbia, 1967-73, assoc. prof., 1973-81, prof., 1981—, Byler disting. prof., 1996, chmn. dept., 1996—2000, asst. dir. Honors Coll., 1988-90. Exch. prof. Moscow State U., 1985, U. Manchester, England, 1987—88; hon. prof. history Lanzou U., China, 1991; dir. edn. svcs. Leisure Voyages, 1992—2000; vis. prof. Joensuu (Finland) U., 1996, 98, 2000, 03. Author: The Fate of Russian Orthodox Monasteries and Convents Since 1917, 1995; editor: Essays on Russian Liberalism, 1972, Detente: A Documentary Record, 1978, Religious and Secular Forces in Late Tsarist Russia, 1992, Profiles of Finland series, 1991-94, (microfiche) The St. Petersburg Collection of Zemstvo Publs., 1992—; contbr. chpts. to books, articles to profl. jours. Mem. Citizens Alliance for Progress, Columbia, Mo., 1969—75, pres., 1969—70; founding mem. High Edn. Rescue Operation, Mo., 1983—91; mem. Columbians Against Throw-Aways, 1980—83. Recipient Disting. Alumnus award Berea Coll., 2002; Fgn. Area fellow, 1965-66, fellow Internat. Rsch. and Exchs. Bd., 1971, 95, 2001, Am. Coun. Learned Socs., 1978-79, Fulbright-Hays fellow, 1995; grantee NEH, 1972, 79, 87. Mem. Am. Assn. Advancement Slavic Studies (bd. dirs. 1980-82, 84-86, chmn. council regional affiliates 1981-82, 85-86, chmn. permanent membership com. 1981-84), Western Slavic Conf., Am. Hist. Assn. (exec. council Conf. on Slavic and East European History 1987-89), Central Slavic Conf. (sec.-treas. 1967-68, pres. 1968-69, 76-77, 83-84, 88-89, 2001-02, exec. bd. 1972—, custodian archive 1972—), Mo. Conf. History (pres. 1992, sec.-treas. 1996-2000), State Hist. Soc. Mo., Fulbright Assn. (pres. Mo. chpt. 1997 2000). Avocations: hiking, travel. Home: 9221 S Rt N Columbia MO 65203-9312 Office: U Mo Dept History Columbia MO 65211-0001 Office Phone: 573-442-4580. E-mail: timberlakec@missouri.edu.

TIMBERLAKE, JUSTIN, vocalist; b. Memphis, Jan. 31, 1981; s. Randy Timberlake and Lynn Harless. Vocalist 'N Sync, 1996—; solo vocalist, 2002—. Singer: (albums) NSYNC, 1998, Home for Christmas, 1998, No Strings Attached, 2000, Celebrity, 2001, (solo album) Justified, 2003 (Grammy awards: Best Male Pop Vocal Performance for song "Cry Me A River", 2003, Best Pop Vocal Album, 2003). Founder J. Timberlake Found. Office: Jive Records 137-139 W 25th St 9th Floor New York NY 10012*

TIMBERLAKE, WILLIAM DAVID, psychology educator; b. San Francisco, Nov. 19, 1942; s. William Burman Timberlake and Lynn Louzelle Spradling; m. Kathleen Marie Nagy, Dec. 20, 1969 (div.); m. Susan Holly Stocking, Apr. 20, 1980; children: Anne Elizabeth, William Ryder. BA cum laude, Pomona Coll., 1964; MA, U. Mich., 1967, PhD in Exptl. Psychology with honors, 1969. From tchg. asst. to hon. faculty assoc. dept. psychology U. Mich., Ann Arbor, 1965-69; from lectr. to assoc. prof. psychology Ind. U., Bloomington, 1969-82, prof., 1982—, co-dir. Ctr. for Integrative Study Animal Behavior, 1992—2002. Hon. rsch. assoc. Harvard U., Cambridge, Mass., 1977-78; vis. assoc. prof. U. Calif., San Diego, 1978; adj. faculty cognitive and neural sis. Ind. U., 1987, adj. prof. biology, 1992—; vis. prof. zoology sub-dept. animal behavior Kings Coll., U. Cambridge, Eng., 1994-95, core faculty cognitive sci., 1995—, core faculty neural sci., 2000—; vis. prof. behavioral neuroscience Oreg. Health Scis. U., 2000-01; vis. scholar Reed Coll., 2000-01. Editor spl. issue Learning and Motivation, 1984; assoc. editor Animal Learning and Behavior, 1992-94, 94-96, 97-2002; mem. editl. bd. Jour. Exptl. Psychology: Animal Behavior Processes, Behavioural Processes, Behavior and Philosophy, Jour. of Exptl. Analysis of Behavior; contbr. articles to profl. jours. Bd. adv. Theatre Cir., Bloomington, 1993-2000; active Bloomington Chamber Singers, 1995—; bd. fellows Poynter Ctr. for Study of Ethics and Am. Instns., Ind. U., 1993-2003. Recipient FACET award for tchg. excellence Ind. U., 1999, James M. Catell Found. Sabbatical award, 2000; grantee NSF, 1979—, NIH, 1984—; NSF predoctoral fellow, 1965-68. Fellow APA (divsn. 1, 3, 6 and 25, coun. divsn. 6 1996-98, 2001-03), Am. Psychol. Soc., AAAS; mem. Animal Behavior Soc., Psychonomic Soc., Soc. for Rsch. Biol. Rhythms, Soc. for Study of Ingestive Behavior, Ea. Psychol. Assn., Midwestern Psychol. Assn., Assn. for Behavior Analysis, Internat. Soc. for Behavioral Ecology, Behavioral Brain Scis. Assocs., Am. Soc. Mammalogists, Soc. Neurosci., Soc. Quantitative Analysis of Behavior, Pavlovian Soc., Phi Beta Kappa, Phi Kappa Phi, Sigma Xi. Avocations: music, writing, art. Office: Ind U Psychology Dept 1101 E 10th St Bloomington IN 47405-7007 Business E-Mail: timberla@indiana.edu.

TIMBERS, JUDITH ANN, academic administrator, writer; b. Elmhurst, Ill., Dec. 10, 1946; d. James G.W. and Betty Timbers; children: Brandy, Pica. BA, U. Ill., 1968; MEd, U. Hawaii, 1972, EdD, 1982; MA, Forest Inst. Profl. Psychology, 1992; PsyD, Am. Sch. Profl. Psychology, 1999. Cert. tchr., Hawaii. Instr. U. Hawaii, Honolulu, 1974-76, coord., 1976-86, asst. prof., 1984-87; pres., founder, dir. Competency Tutoring Ctr., Honolulu, 1974—, Varsity Internat. Sch., Honolulu, 1980—. Grant writer to federally and locally funded grants; presenter in field. Contbr. articles to profl. jours. Active Pacific and Asian Affairs Coun. U.S. HEW fellow, 1971-72; recipient Profl. Svc. award State of Hawaii, 1984. Mem. NEA, NAFSA, Nat. Assn. Secondary Sch. Prins., Hawaii Assn. Children with Lca Avocations: japanese culture, golf, travel, reading. Office: Varsity Internat Sch 45-681 Maiaponi Pl Kaneohe HI 96744-1779

TIMCENKO, LYDIA TEODORA, biochemist, chemist; b. Beograd, Yugoslavia, July 4, 1951; arrived in U.S., 1975; d. Teodor Pavle and Branislava (Spasojevic) Timcenko; m. Ghazi Youssef, June 16, 1980 (div. Oct. 1989); children: Ali Alexander Youssef, Kareem Misha Youssef; m. Peter Porzio, Mar. 11, 1996. BS in Chemistry, U. Belgrade, Yugoslavia, 1975; MS, Wayne State U., 1977, PhD, 1984. Grad. asst. Wayne State U., Detroit, 1976-78, 81-84, rsch. assoc., 1986—88, lectr. in chemistry, 1989; postdoctoral fellow Mich. Cancer Found., Detroit, 1985; postdoctoral fellow Sch. Medicine Wayne State U., 1986—88; lectr. in chemistry Lawrence Tech. U., Southfield, Mich., 1989, 90-91; biochemist Strohtech, Inc., Detroit, 1990—91; prof. chemistry Sussex County Coll., Newton, NJ, 1997—99; asst. prof. chemistry N.Y. Techol. Coll., City U. Bklyn., 1999—; sci. tchr. New Milford (NJ) H.S., 2002, Newton (N.J.) H.S., 2002—; adj. prof. Pace Univ., N.Y.C., 2004—. Prin. investigator, rsch. scientist ICN Galenika Inst., Clin. Ctr. Serbia, Belgrade, 1991—96; rsch. scientist, mktg. cons. Huet Biol., Birmingham, Mich., 1987—91; adj. prof. chemistry Kean Coll.; adj. prof. dept. chemistry and chem. biology Stevens Inst. Tech., Castle Point on Hudson, Hoboken, NJ; adj. assoc. prof. organic chemistry Pace U., N.Y.C., 2002—04; adj. prof. in organic and biochemistry CUNY, 2004. Contbr. articles to profl. jours. Mem.: Am. Chem. Soc., Am. Soc. Microbiology, Phi Lambda Upsilon. Achievements include research in in shigella toxin in shigella and E. coli; mitoch GPO in advenal cortex; liberation of labile sufur from ferredoxins; adhesion shigella to HCTH and HELA; localization of GST and GP in adrenal. Home: 306 State Route 94 Columbia NJ 07832-2771

TIMINSKY, DALE, academic administrator; Pres. Sierra Nev. Coll., Incline Village, Nev. Office: Sierra Nevada Coll 999 Tahoe Blvd Incline Village NV 89451

TIMKEN, W. ROBERT, JR., manufacturing executive; b. 1938; married BA, Stanford U., 1960; MBA, Harvard U., 1962. With Timken Co. (formerly The Timken Roller Bearing Co.), Canton, Ohio, 1962—, asst. v.p. sales, 1964-65, dir. corp. devel., 1965-68, v.p., 1968-73, vice-chmn. bd., chmn. fin. com., 1973-75, chmn. bd., chmn. fin. com., 1975—, chmn. exec. com., 1983—, also dir. Office: Timken Co 1835 Dueber Ave SW Canton OH 44706-2798

TIMLIN, JAMES CLIFFORD, bishop; b. Scranton, Pa., Aug. 5, 1927; s. James C. and Helen E. (Norton) T. AB, St. Mary's Sem., Balt., 1948; STB, Gregorian U., Rome, 1950. Ordained priest Roman Cath. Ch., 1951. Asst. pastor St. John the Evangelist Ch., Pittston, Pa., 1952—53, St. Peter's Cathedral, Scranton, Pa., 1953—66; asst. chancellor, sec. Diocese of Scranton, 1966—71, chancellor, 1971—77, aux. bishop, vicar gen., 1976—84, bishop, 1984—2003, bishop emeritus, 2003—; pastor Ch. of Nativity, Scranton, 1979—84. Roman Catholic. Address: 300 Wyoming Ave Scranton PA 18503-1285

TIMLIN, ROBERT J. judge; b. 1932; BA cum laude, Georgetown U., 1954, JD, 1959, LLM, 1964. Atty. Douglas, Obear and Campbell, 1960-61, Law Offices of A.L. Wheeler, 1961; with criminal divsn. U.S. Dept. Justice, 1961-64; atty. U.S. Atty. Office (ctrl. dist.) Calif., 1964-66, Hennigan, Ryneal and Butterwick, 1966-67; city atty. City of Corona, Calif., 1967-70; prin. Law Office of Robert J. Timlin, 1970-71, 75-76; ptnr. Hunt, Palladino and Timlin, 1971-74, Timlin and Coffin, 1974-75; judge Mcpl. Ct., Riverside, Calif., 1976-80, Calif. Superior Ct., Riverside, 1980-90; assoc. justice Calif. Ct. Appeals, 1990-94; judge U.S. Dist. Ct. (ctrl. dist.) Calif., L.A., 1994—. Part-time U.S. Magistrate judge Ctrl. Dist. Calif., 1970-74. Served U.S. Army, 1955-57. Mem. Calif. Judges Assn. Office: US Dist Ct Central District of Calif Eastern Divsn 3470 12th St Riverside CA 92501 Office Phone: 909-328-4441.

TIMM, ROGER K. lawyer; b. Bay City, Mich., May 21, 1947; BS, U. Mich., 1969; JD, Harvard U., 1972. Bar: Mich. 1972. Mem. Dykema Gossett, Detroit. Mem. ABA, State Bar Mich. Office: Dykema Gossett 400 Renaissance Ctr Detroit MI 48243-1668 E-mail: rtimm@dykema.com.

TIMM-BROCK, BARBARA, chief product officer; b. St. Paul, Minn., Oct. 18, 1960; married; two children. BS in Chem. Engring., MS in Mgmt. of Tech., U. Minn. Sr. dir. Grand Metropolitan PLC/Pillsbury Co., 1982-92, Pizza Hut Inc., 1992-96; v.p. The Olive Garden, 1996-98; chief product officer Bakery Cafe Group, AFC Enterprises, 1998—. Avocation: golf. Office: Bakery Cafe Group 5555 Glnrdg Ctr N Atlanta GA 30342

TIMMCKE, ALAN EDWARD, colon and rectal surgeon; b. Madison, Wis., July 7, 1949; s. Wesley Eugene Timmcke; m. Deborah Cameron Brosseau (div.); m. Teresa Ann Watkins, Dec. 31, 1977; children: Gretchen Kristine, Alan Edward Jr. BS, Dickinson Coll., 1971; MD with honors, Temple U., 1975. Diplomate Am. Bd. Surgery, Am. Bd. Colon and Rectal Surgery; lic. physician, Pa., Maine, Mo., La. Intern in surgery Nat. Naval Med. Ctr., Bethesda, Md., 1975-76, resident in gen. surgery, 1976-79; rsch. fellow in colon and rectal surgery Jewish Hosp./Washington U. Med. Ctr., St. Louis, 1985-86, clin. fellow in colon and rectal surgery, 1986-87; asst. in surgery Washington U. Sch. Medicine, St. Louis, 1985-87; staff colon and rectal surgeon Ochsner Clinic, New Orleans, 1987—. Staff surgeon Nat. Naval Med. Ctr., Bethesda, 1979, Naval Regional Med. Ctr., Newport, R.I., 1979-82, dept. colon and rectal surgery Lahey Clinic Med. Ctr., Burlington, Mass., 1984-85; staff surgeon Rumford (Maine) Community Hosp., 1982-84, med. staff v.p., 1983-84; instr. surgery Uniformed Svcs. U. of Health Scis., Bethesda, 1978-79; lectr. in field. Contbr. articles and abstracts to profl. jours. Lt. comdr. M.C., USN, 1975-82. Recipient Harry E. Bacon Found. award for best original paper, 1987; NIH Summer Rsch. fellow, 1972. Fellow ACS, Am. Soc. Colon and Rectal Surgeons; mem. New Orleans Surg. Soc., Surg. Assn. of La., Internat. Soc. Univ. Colon and Rectal Surgeons, Soc. of Am. Gastrointestinal Endoscopic Surgeons, Am. Soc. Gastrointestinal Endoscopy, Alpha Omega Alpha. Office: Ochsner Clinic Dept Colon/Rectal Surgery 1514 Jefferson Hwy New Orleans LA 70121-2483 E-mail: atimmcke@aol.com.

TIMMER, BARBARA, state agency administrator; b. Holland, Mich., Dec. 13, 1946; d. John Norman and Barbara Dee (Folensbee) T. BA, Hope Coll., Holland, Mich., 1969; JD, U. Mich., 1975. Bar: Mich. 1975, U.S. Supreme Ct. 1995. Assoc. McCrosky, Libner, VanLeuven, Muskegon, Mich., 1975-78; apptd. to Mich. Women Commn. by Gov., 1976-79; staff counsel subcom. commerce, consumer & monetary affairs Ho. Govt. Ops. Com., U.S. Ho. of Reps., 1979-82, 85-86; exec. v.p. NOW, 1982-84; legis. asst. to Rep. Geraldine Ferraro, 1984; atty. Office Gen. Counsel Fed. Home Loan Bank Bd., 1986-89; gen. counsel Com. on Banking, Fin. and Urban affairs U.S. Ho. of Reps., Washington, 1989-92; asst. gen. counsel, dir. govt. affairs ITT Corp., Washington, 1992-96; sr. v.p., dir. govt. rels. Home Savs. of Am., Irwindale, Calif., 1996-99; ptnr. Manatt, Phelps & Phillips, Washington, 1999—; gen. counsel MyPrimeTime, Inc., San Francisco, 2000-01; asst. sec. U.S. Senate, 2001—02, asst. sgt. at arms, 2003; chief info. officer Calif. Dept. Transp., Sacramento, 2003—. Mem. info. tech. coun. Women's Transp. Seminar, Calif., 2004—. Editor: Compliance With Lobbying Laws and Gift Rule Guide, 1996. Bd. dirs. Women's HIgh Tech Coalition. Named to Acad. of Women Achievers, YWCA, 1993; recipient Affordable Housing award, Nat. Assn. Real Estate Brokers, 1990, Disting. Alumni award, Hope Coll., 2003. Mem. ABA (bus. law sect., electronic fin. svcs. subcom.), FBA (chair exec. coun. banking law com.), Exchequer Club, Women in Housing and Fin. (bd. dirs. 1992-94, gen. counsel 1994-98, Calif. state CIO coun. 2004—), Supreme Ct. Bar Assn., Supreme Ct. Hist. Soc., Mich. Bar Assn., Bar of D.C. Episcopalian. Office: 2629 Main St PMB 115 Santa Monica CA 90405 E-mail: btimmerdc@earthlink.net.

TIMMER, CHARLES PETER, agricultural and development economist; b. Troy, Ohio, July 29, 1941; s. Thomas Gerhart and Rose Marie (Hoffman) T.; m. Carol Falb, Aug. 31, 1963; children: Anne Carol, Ashley Susan. AB in Econs. magna cum laude, Harvard U., 1963, PhD in Econs, 1969. Commodity analyst W.R. Grace and Co., N.Y.C., 1964-66; asst. prof. econs. Food Research Inst., Stanford U., 1968-74, assoc. prof., 1974-75; econ. adv. Indonesian Nat. Planning Agy., Harvard Adv. Group, Jakarta, 1970-71; H.E. Babcock prof. food econs. Cornell U., 1975-77; prof. econs. of food and agr. Sch. Public Health Harvard U., Cambridge, Mass., 1977-80, John D. Black prof. agr. and bus., 1980-86, prof. devel. studies at large Bus. Sch., 1986-88, Thomas D. Cabot prof. devel. studies, at large, 1988-98; dean Grad. Sch. Internat. Rels., prof. devel. studies U. Calif., San Diego, 1998-2000, prof. devel. studies, 2000—03; chief economist Devel. Alternatives, Inc., 2003—04; sr. fellow Ctr. Global Devel., 2004—. Hibbard lectr. U. Wis., 1993; cons. on food and agr. Author: (with others) Choice of Technology in Developing Countries, 1975, (with Perkins et al) Small Scale Rural Industry in the People's Republic of China, 1977, (with Falcon and Pearson) Food Policy Analysis, 1983, (with Nelson et al) Food Aid and Development, 1981, Getting Prices Right: Scope and Limits of Agricultural Price Policy, 1986; editor, contbg. author: Rice Policy in Indonesia, 1974, The Political Economy of Rice in Asia, 1976, The Corn Economy of Indonesia, 1987, Agriculture and the State: Growth, Employment, and Poverty in Developing Countries, 1991; guest editor, contbg. author to Food Policy, 1995, Agriculture and Pro-Poor Growth, 2003. Recipient Bintang Jasa Utama medal Govt. Indonesia, 1992; named San Diego Citizen-Diplomat of Yr., 2000; John Harvard scholar, 1960-63; Fulbright fellow, 1963-64; NSF fellow, 1966-68 Mem. Am. Econ. Assn., Am. Agrl. Econs. Assn., AAAS, Phi Beta Kappa. Mailing: PO Box 1402 Kenwood CA 95452 Office: Ctr Global Devel 1776 Mass Ave NW Ste 301 Washington DC 20036 E-mail: peter_timmer@dai.com.

TIMMER, MARGARET LOUISE (PEG TIMMER), art educator; b. Osmond, Nebr., July 4, 1942; d. John Henry and Julia Adeline (Schilling) Borgmann; m. Charles B. Timmer, May 23, 1964 (div. June 1990); children: Jill Marie, Mark Jon. AA, N.E. Community Coll., Norfolk, Nebr., 1987; BA in Edn., K-12 art endorsement, Wayne (Nebr.) State U., 1988; MEd, Bank Street Coll./Parsons Sch. Design, N.Y.C., 1992. Cert. tchr., Nebr. Bookkeeper Goeres Electric, Osmond, 1960-61; tel. operator Northwestern Bell, Norfolk, 1961-64; with want advt. dept. Washington Post, 1964-65; saleswoman Jeannes Fashion Fabrics, Norfolk, 1970-72, Tripps, Norfolk, 1986-87; office and fin. mgr. Tim's Plumbing & Heating Inc., Norfolk, 1972-86; tchr. art

Norfolk Cath. Schs., 1988—, mem. bd., 1985-88. Instr. art history N.E. Community Coll., 1992—; mem. youth art bd. Norfolk Art Ctr., 1988—. One-woman show Uptown Restaurant, Norfolk, 1993, Norfolk Art Ctr., 1996; exhibited in group shows Sioux City (Iowa) Art Ctr., 1988, Columbus (Nebr.) Art Ctr., 1993. Mem. choir St. Mary's Cath. Ch., Norfolk, 1991—; mem. Norfolk Community Choir, 1991; bd. dirs. Norfolk Community Concerts Assn., 1984-87; treas. Norfolk Cath. Booster Club, 1985-86; leader 4-H, Madison County, 1973-78; judge art show Laurel (Nebr.) Women's Club, 1988. Named outstanding profl. vol. Norfolk Art Ctr., 1996; recipient Crystal Apple award Norfolk (Nebr.) C. of C., 1999. Mem. N.E. Nebr. Art Assn., Nebr. Art Edn. Assn. (3d place award 1988). Avocations: watercolor and oil painting, gardening, reading, gourmet cooking, sewing. Home: Rte 2 Box 239 55380 Warnerville Dr Norfolk NE 68701-9758 Office: Norfolk Cath Schs 2300 Madison Ave Norfolk NE 68701-4456 E-mail: ptimmer57@yahoo.com.

TIMMERHAUS, KLAUS DIETER, chemical engineering educator; b. Mpls., Sept. 10, 1924; s. Paul P. and Elsa L. (Bever) T.; m. Jean L. Mevis, Aug. 3, 1952; 1 dau., Carol Jane. BS in Chem. Engring, U. Ill., 1948, MS, 1949, PhD, 1951. Registered profl. engr., Colo. Process design engr. Calif. Rsch. Corp., Richmond, 1952-53; extension lectr. U. Calif., Berkeley, 1952; mem. faculty U. Colo., Boulder, 1953-95, prof. chem. engring., 1963—86, assoc. dean engring., 1963—86, dir. engring. rsch. ctr. coll. engring., 1983—86, chmn. aerospace dept., 1983—89, chmn. chem. engring. dept., 1986-89, Patten Chair Disting. prof., 1986-89, presdl. tchg. scholar, 1989—. Chem. engr. cryogenics lab. Nat. Bur. Standards, Boulder, summers 1955,57,59,61; lectr. U. Calif. at L.A., 1961-62; sect. head engring. div. NSF, 1972-73; cons. in field. Bd. dirs. Colo. Engring. Expt. Sta., Inc., Engring. Measurements Co. Editor: Advances in Cryogenic Engineering, vols. 1-25, 1954-80; co-editor: Internat. Cryogenic Monograph Series, 1965-. Served with USNR, 1944-46. Recipient Disting. Svc. award Dept. Commerce, 1957, Samuel C. Collins award for outstanding contbns. to cyrogenic tech., 1967, Meritorious Svc. award Cryogenic Engring. Conf., 1987, Disting. Pub. Svc. award NSF, 1984; named CASE Colo. Prof. of Yr., 1993, Disting. Lectr., L-T Fan, 2001. Fellow AAAS (v.p. 1985, pres. 1986, Southwestern and Rocky Mountain divsn. Pres.'s award 1989), Internat. Inst. Refrigeration (v.p. 1979-87, pres. 1987-95, US nat. commn. 1983-, pres. 1983-86, W.T. Pentzer award 1989, hon. co-chair, IIR World Congress, 2003), AIChE (v.p. 1975, pres. 1976, Alpha Chi Sigma award for chem. engring. rsch., 1968, Founders award 1978, Eminent Chem. Engr. award 1983, W.K. Lewis award 1987, F.J. Van Antwerpen award 1991, Inst. Lecture award 1995), Am. Soc. for Engring. Edn. (bd. dirs. 1986-88, George Westinghouse award 1968, 3M Chem. Engring. divsn. award 1980, Engring. Rsch. Coun. award 1990, Delos Svc. award 1991); mem. NAE, Am. Astron. Soc., Austrian Acad. Sci., Cryogenic Engring. Conf. (chmn. 1956-67, bd. dirs. 1967-), Internat. Cryocooler Conf. (bd. dirs. 1980-), Soc. Automotive Engrs. (Ralph Teetor award 1991), Sigma Xi (v.p. 1986-87, pres. 1987-88, bd. dirs. 1981-89), Verein Deitscher Ingenieure, Cryogenic Soc. Am., Sigma Tau, Tau Beta Pi, Phi Lambda Upsilon. Home: 905 Brooklawn Dr Boulder CO 80303-2708 Business E-Mail: klaus.timmerhaus@colorado.edu.

TIMMERMAN, THOMAS J. military planner, operations analyst; s. James G. and Jean M. Timmerman; m. Joan P. Davidson, Oct. 28, 2001. BS in Physics, USAF Acad., Colo., 1989; MS in Ops. Analysis, Air Force Inst. of Tech., Wright-Patterson Air Force Base, Ohio, 1996. Analyst Air Force Studies & Analyses Agy., Pentagon, DC, 1996—2000; chief of wing plans 33d Fighter Wing, Eglin AFB, Fla., 2000—02; chief of air analysis U.S. Forces Korea, 2003—. Decorated Young Turk Mil. Ops. Rsch. Soc.; recipient Impact award for Excellence, 1998. Home: PSC 303 Box 27 Apo AP 96204-3027

TIMMERMAN, WILLIAM B. utilities executive, accountant; b. Columbia, S.C., Nov. 12, 1946; s. William Bledsoe and Helen (Speissegger) T.; m. Janet Russell, Sept. 15, 1971; children: William III, Catherine Lucille. BA in Pub. Acctg., Duke U., 1968; postgrad., Harvard U., 1990. CPA, N.C. Auditor Arthur Andersen & Co., Charlotte, N.C., 1968-78; sr. v.p. Carolina Energies, Inc., Columbia, 1978-82; v.p. S.C. Electric & Gas Co., Columbia, 1982-83, v.p., group exec., 1983-84; chief fin. officer, sr. v.p. SCANA Corp., Columbia, 1984—94, exec. v.p., CFO, contr., 1994—95, pres., 1995—, chmn., CEO, 1997—. Exec. adv. com. Edison Electric Inst.; acctg. and fin. exec. com. Southeastern Electric Exchange; bd. dir. SCANA Corp.; chmn. bd. Standard Fed. Savs. Bank, Columbia. Trustee United Way of Midlands, Columbia, 1985—; vice chmn. fin. ARC, Columbia, 1986—; adv. bd. Sch. Bus. U. S.C., 1985—. Served with USN, 1968-72. Office: SCANA Corp 1426 Main St Ste 100 Columbia SC 29201-2834

TIMMERMANN, ALLAN GILLING, economics professor; b. Skovlund, Denmark, Oct. 9, 1964; came to U.S., 1994; s. Viggo Nielsen and Gyda Bente (Gilling) T.; m. Solange Maria Ferreli Fortes, Feb. 1, 1992. MS, London Sch. Econs., 1988; PhD, U. Cambridge, England, 1992. Lectr. fin. econs. U. London, 1991-94; asst. prof. U. Calif., San Diego, 1994-98, assoc. prof., 1999—2001, prof., 2001—. Cons. Barclay's Global Investors, 1998, IMF, Fed. Res. Bd., European Ctrl. Bank; prof. fin. London Sch. Econs., 1998-99. Dept. editor Jour. of Forecasting, 2000—; assoc. editor Jour. Bus. and Econ. Stats., 2001—; columnist Internat. Broker, London, 1992; contbr. articles to profl. jours. Hellman Faculty fellow, U. Calif., San Diego, 1997; British Coun. scholar, London, 1987; recipient Tress prize U. London, 1993. Mem. Am. Fin. Assn., Ctr. Econ. Policy Rsch. (rsch. fellow), Econometric Soc. Avocations: long distance running, tennis. Office: U Calif 9500 Gilman Dr La Jolla CA 92093-5004 E-mail: atimmerm@ucsd.edu.

TIMMERMANN, SANDRA, educational gerontologist, communication specialist; b. Orange, N.J., Mar. 25, 1941; d. Bernhard and Matilda (Schaaf) T.; m. George W. Bonham (dec.). BA with honors, U. Colo., 1963; MA, Columbia U., 1967, EdD, 1979. Account exec. Rowland Co., N.Y.C., 1964-67; dir. pub. info. The N.Y. TV Network/SUNY, N.Y.C., 1967-72; assoc. Hoefer/Amidei Pub. Rels./Mktg., 1972-74; assoc. dean, dir. inst. Inst. Lifetime Learning, AARP, Washington, 1974—84, dir. geriatric edn., 1984-86; exec. dir. Peninsula Ctr. for the Blind, Palo Alto, Calif., 1986-88; dir. western states region Am. Found. for the Blind, San Francisco, 1988-90; dir. edn. Am. Soc. on Aging, San Francisco, 1990-94, SeniorNet, San Francisco, 1995-97. Dir. Mature Market Inst., Met. Life Ins. Co., Westport, Conn., 1997—; bd. dirs. Calif. Coun. of Gerontology and Geriatrics, 1988-90; mem. tng. com. Nat. Ctr. for Black Aged; mgr. older adults sect. HEW Lifelong Learning Project; cons. Brookdale Ctr. on Aging, Hunter Coll.; cons. to bus. and industry; mem. adv. com. nat. project on counseling older people Am. Pers. and Guidance Assn.; mem. nat. adv. com. vocat. edn. and older adults U.S. Dept. Edn.; bd. dirs. Am. Soc. on Aging, 2000—; chair LEARN, 2000-03. Fin. gerontology columnist Jour. Fin. Svc. Profls.; contbr. articles to profl. jours. and newspapers. Trustee, chmn. adv. com. on later yrs. Am. Found. for the Blind; commr., v.p. Commn. on Status of Women, San Mateo County, Calif.; pres. bd. dirs. Sr. Coastsiders; chmn. youth and edn. Cmty. United Meth. Ch., Half Moon Bay, Calif.; mem. Nat. Adv. Coun. on Injury Prevention in Aging, 1998-2002; mem. exec. com., bd. dirs. Bridgeport (Conn.) YMCA, 1997-2003. Recipient Gloria Cavanaugh Nat. award for excellence in edn. and tng., Am. Soc. on Aging, 2003. Mem. Southwestern Conn. Agy. of Aging (bd. dirs. 1998—), Am. Assn. Adult and Continuing Edn. (editor Edn. and Aging newsletter, chmn. commn. on aging, bd. dirs.), Bus. Forum on Aging (governing coun. 1999—, chmn. bus. forum on aging 2003--), Coalition Adult Edn. Orgns. (dir., pres, 1984-85), Capital Spkrs. Club, Pi Beta Phi, Pi Lambda Theta, Kappa Delta Pi, Phi Delta Kappa. Home: 555 Hill Farm Rd Fairfield CT 06430-2149

TIMMINS, TIMOTHY A. telecommunications industry executive; BSBA, Portland (Oreg.) State U.; MBA, U. So. Calif. CPA. Formerly with investment banking divsn., former sr. v.p. Kemper Securities, Inc., 1985—93; exec. v.p., CFO Metro One Telecomm., Inc., Beaverton, Oreg., 1993—95, pres., CEO, 1995—. Office: Metro One Telecomm Inc 11200 Murray Scholls Pl Beaverton OR 97007

TIMMONS, EVELYN DEERING, pharmacist; b. Durango, Colo., Sept. 29, 1926; d. Claude Elliot and Evelyn Allen (Gooch) Deering; m. Richard Palmer Timmons, Oct. 4, 1952 (div. 1968); children: Roderick Deering, Steven Palmer. BS in Chemistry and Pharmacy cum laude, U. Colo., 1948. Chief pharmacist Meml. Hosp., Phoenix, 1950—54; libr. med. lit. rsch. Hoffman-LaRoche, Inc., Nutley, NJ, 1956—57; staff pharmacist St. Joseph's Hosp., Phoenix, 1958—60; relief mgr. various ind. apothecaries, Phoenix, 1960—68; asst. then mgr., dir. compounding Profl. Pharmacies, Inc., Phoenix, 1968—72; mgr. Mt. View Pharmacy, 1972—76, owner/mgr., 1976—; pres. Ariz. Apothecaries, Ltd., 1976—. Mem. profl. adv. bd., bereavement counselor Hospice of Valley, 1983-96; mem. profl. adv. bd. Upjohn Health Care and Svcs., Phoenix, 1984-86; bd. dirs. Am. coun. on Pharm. Edn., Chgo., 1986-92, v.p., 1988, 89, treas., 1990-91; mem. expert adv. bd. compounding pharms. U.S. Pharmacoepial Conv., 1992—; preceptor U. Ariz., 1965—, Midwestern Coll. Pharmacy, Ariz. Campus, 1998—; chief cons. bioidentical hormone replacement therapy and safety; disease mgmt. specialist; lectr. on NHRT and BHRT. Mem. editl. adv. bd. Internat. Jour. Pharm. Compounding, 1997-2000; author poetry; contbr. articles to profl. jours. Mem. Scottsdale (Ariz.) Fedn. Rep. Women, 1963-68; various other offices Rep. Fedn.; mem. platform com. State of Ariz., Nat. Rep. Conv., 1964; asst. sec. Young Rep. Nat. Fedn., 1963-65; active county and state Rep. coms.; adv. bd. Internat. Jour. of Pharm. Compounding, 1996-2001; fin. chmn. Internat. Leadership Symposium: Women in Pharmacy, London, 1987; treas. Leadership Internat. Women Pharmacy, 1991-2001; mem. founders circle Gladys Taylor McGarey Med. Found., 1996—. Named Outstanding Young Rep. of Yr., Nat. Fedn. Young Reps., 1965, Preceptor of Yr., U. Ariz./Syntex, 1984; recipient Disting. Pub. Svc. award Maricopa County Med. Soc., 1962, Disting. Alumni award Wasatch Acad., 1982, Career Achievement award Kappa Epsilon, 1983, Leadership and Achievement award Upjohn Labs., 1985-86, Outstanding Achievement in Profession award Merck, Sharp & Dohme, 1986, award of Merit Kappa Epsilon, 1988, Disting. Coloradoan award U. Colo., 1989, Vanguard award Kappa Epsilon, 1991, Unicorn award Kappa Epsilon, 1993, Compounding Pharmacist of the Yr. award Profl. Compounding Corp. of Am., 1994, 96, Healing Heart award Gladys Taylor McGarey Found., 1998, 50 Yr. Certificate U. Colo., 2000. Fellow Am. Coll. of Apothecaries (v.p. 1982-83, pres. elect 1983-84, pres. 1984-85, chmn. bd. dirs. 1985-86, adv. coun. 1986-92, Chmn. of Yr. 1980-81, Victor H. Morganroth award 1985, J. Leon Lascoff award 1990), Internat. Acad. of Compounding Pharmacists (bd. dirs. 1993-2000); mem. Ariz. Soc. of Hosp. Pharmacists, Am. Pharm. Assn. (Daniel B. Smith award 1990), Ariz. Pharmacy Assn. (Svc. to Pharmacy award 1976, Pharmacist of Yr. 1981, Bowl of Hygeia 1989, 1st Innovative Pharmacy award 1994, 50 Yr. Practice and Membership award 2001), Maricopa County Pharmacy Assn. (pres. 1977, Svc. to Pharmacy award 1977), Am. Soc. of Hosp. Pharmacists, Am. Aircraft Owners and Pilots Assn., Air Safety Found., Nat. Assn. of Registered Parliamentarians, Civinettes (pres. Scottsdale chpt. 1960-61), Kappa Epsilon (recipient Career Achievement award 1986, Vanguard award 1991, Unicorn award 1993). Avocations: flying, skiing, swimming, hiking, writing. Office: Mt View Pharmacy 10565 N Tatum Blvd Ste B-118 Scottsdale AZ 85253-1095 Business E-Mail: evelyn@mountainviewpharmacy.com.

TIMMONS, GERALD DEAN, pediatric neurologist; b. Rensselaer, Ind., June 1, 1931; s. Homer Timmons and Tamma Mildred (Spall) Rodgers; 1 child, Deanna Lynne; children from previous marriage: Jane Christina Timmons Mitchell, Ann Elizabeth, Mary Catherine. AB, Ind. U., 1953, MD, 1956. Diplomate Am. Bd. Psychiatry and Neurology. Intern Lima (Ohio) Meml. Hosp., 1956-57; resident Ind. U. Hosp., Indpls., 1957-59, 61-62; instr. neurology dept. Ind. U., Indpls., 1962-64; practice medicine specializing in psychiatry and neurology Indpls., 1962-64; practice medicine specializing in pediatric neurology Akron, Ohio, 1964—; chief pediatric neurology Children's Hosp. Med. Ctr., Akron, 1964—2000; chmn. neurology subcouncil Coll. Medicine Northeastern Ohio Univs., Rootstown, 1978-99. Sr. examiner Am. Bd. Neurology and Psychiatry. Contbr. articles to profl. and scholarly jours. Served to capt. USAF, 1959-61. Mem. Summit County Med. Soc., Ohio Med. Soc., AMA, Am. Acad. Pediatrics, Am. Acad. Neurology (practice com. 1980-86, sec. child neurology sect. 2000—), Child Neurology Soc. (chmn. honors and awards com. 1978-88), Am. Soc. Internal Medicine, Am. Electroencephalographic Soc. Republican. Methodist. Office: Akron Pediatric Neurology 300 Locust St Ste 460 Akron OH 44302-1804

TIMMONS, GORDON DAVID, economics professor, farmer; b. Elbert, Tex., May 21, 1919; s. Walter James and Ella Mae (McCarson) T.; m. Jean Betty Kulhanek, Feb. 11, 1947; children: Kathy, Linda, Scott, Jim, Tamara, Dallas, Timothy, Kelly, Susanna. Student, U. Tex., 1937-40, U. Mont., 1961-64; BS, Utah State U., 1955; MS, Mont. State U., 1958. Enlisted USAF, 1939, advanced through grades to col., ret., 1961; instr. Columbia Basin Coll., Pasco, Wash., 1966-86. Pres. Assn. Higher Edn., 1969-72. Decorated Legion of Merit, Croix de Guerre (France). Mem. Acad. Polit. Sci., N.W. Econ. Conf. Democrat. Avocation: horse breeding. Home and Office: Star Rte Box 39-A Olney TX 76374-0039 Office Phone: 940-862-5614. E-mail: Timmons@brazos.com.

TIMMONS, WILLIAM EVAN, corporate executive; b. Chattanooga, Dec. 27, 1930; s. Owen Walter and Doris (Eckenrod) T.; m. Mimi Bakshian, Sept. 28, 1966; children: Karen Leigh, Kimberly Anne, William Evan. Grad., Baylor Mil. Acad., Chattanooga, 1949; BS in Fgn. Svc., Georgetown U., 1959; postgrad., George Washington U., 1959-61. Aide to U.S. Senator Alexander Wiley, 1955-62; adminstrv. asst. to U.S. Rep. William Brock, 1963-69; dep. asst. to Pres. Richard M. Nixon, 1969-70, asst., 1970-74; asst. to Pres. Gerald R. Ford, 1974; pres. Timmons & Co. Inc., 1975-86, chmn. exec. com., 1986—. Mem. Fed. Property Rev. Bd., 1972-75, Pres.'s Trade Adv. Com., 1975-80; U.S. del. to Internat. Conf. on Viet Nam, Paris, 1973. Presdl. appointee U.S.-Japan Adv. Commn., 1983—85; nat. conv. dir. Reagan for Pres. Com., Detroit, 1980, Dallas, 1984, nat. polit. dir., 1980; exec. dir. Tenn. Rep. Com., 1962; mgr. Brock campaigns, 1962, 1964, 1966, 1968; dir. congl. rels. Nixon-Agnew campaign, 1968; coord. Nixon for Pres.; active Rep. Nat. Conv., Miami, Fla., 1968, 1972, dir. Pres. Ford com. Kansas City, 1976; mem. adv. com. Rep. Nat. Com. Conv., New Orleans, 1988, San Diego, 1996; mem. exec. com. Nat. Young Reps., 1965—67; dep. dir. for transition Office of Pres.-Elect, 1980—81; mem. faculty Nat. REp. campaign workshops, 1963—69; sr. adviser Bush for Pres. Com., New Orleans, 1988, Dole for Pres. Com., 1996; mem. adv. com. Bush for Pres., Rep. Nat. Conv., Phila., 2000; adviser Bush-Cheney Transition, 2000—01; bd. dirs. Radio Free Europe/Liberty, 1975—82, Georgetown U. Ctr. Strategic and Internat. Studies, 1982—85. With USAF, 1951—55. Named Outstanding Young Rep. of Year Nat. Rep. Com., 1965; recipient 1970 Ann. Achievement award Georgetown Alumni Club; citation for Disting. Service Baylor Mil. Acad. Alumni Assn., 1970 Mem. SCV, SAR, Soc. of the Cin., Columbia Country Club, George Towne Club, City Club, St. Alban's Tennis Club, Masons (33d degree). Home: 4426 Garfield St NW Washington DC 20007-1142 Office: Timmons & Co 1875 Eye St NW Ste 400 Washington DC 20006 Office Phone: 202-331-1760. E-mail: BTimmons@aol.com.

TIMMONS, WILLIAM MILTON, producer, freelance writer, retired cinema arts educator, publisher, film maker; b. Houston, Apr. 21, 1933; s. Carter Charles and Gertrude Monte (Lee) T.; m. Pamela Cadorette, Dec. 24, 1975 (div. 1977). BS, U. Houston, 1958; MA, UCLA, 1961; PhD, U. So. Calif., 1975. Child actor Houston Jr. Theater, 1945-46; staff announcer Sta. KMCO, Conroe, Tex., 1951-52; prodn. asst. Sta. KUHT-TV, Houston, 1953-54, 56-57; teaching fellow UCLA, 1960-61; ops. asst. CBS-TV, Hollywood, Calif., 1961-62; prof. speech and drama Sam Houston State U., Huntsville, Tex., 1963-67; chmn. dept. cinema Los Angeles Valley Coll., Van Nuys, Calif., 1970-91, ret., 1992. Prodr. Sta. KPFK, L.A., 1959-60, 83-95; pub. Acad. Assocs., L.A., 1976-2000; proofreader, cons. Focal Press Pub. Co., N.Y.C., 1983-92; mem. ind. investigations group Ctr. for Inquiry; lectr. Ctr. for Inquiry-West. Author: Orientation to Cinema, 1986, Everything About the Bible That you Never Had Time to Look Up, 2003, Regarding an Angel's Flight, 2004; contbr. articles to mags.; prodr., dir.: (radio programs) Campus Comments, 1963-67, numerous ednl. films, 1963—; prodr. ednl. series for cable TV, 1993—. With USNR, 1954-56. Named Hon. Tex. Ranger, State of Tex., Austin, 1946; U. Houston scholar, 1957. Mem. Mensa, U. So. Calif. Cinema-TV Alumni Assn., Red Masque Players, Humanist Assn. of L.A., Alpha Epsilon Rho, Delta Kappa Alpha. Democrat. Avocations: reading, writing, viewing movies. Office Phone: miltontimmons@adelphia.net.

TIMMS, EUGENE DALE, wholesale business owner, state senator; b. Burns, Oreg., May 15, 1932; s. Morgan Oscar and Dorothy Vera (Payne) T.; m. Edna May Evans, Aug. 24, 1953; children: Tobi Eugene, Trina Maria. BA, Willamette U., 1954; grad. studies, U. Wash. Mem. Oreg. Senate, Salem, 1982—; st. republican leader, 1992-94. Sen. State of Oreg., 1982, 84, 88, 92; pres. Harney City C. of C.; bd. trustees Assoc. Oreg. Industries; chmn. Parks & Recreation Dist. Bd.; mem. Harney City Hosp. Bd. Mem. SBA, Jaycees (state v.p.), Elk Lodge, Masonic Lodge, Al Kader Harney City Shrine Club. Presbyterian. Avocations: fishing, hunting, reading, going to the movies, sports. Home: 1049 N Court Ave Burns OR 97720-1016 Address: Oreg Senate S-219 State Capitol Salem OR 97310-0001

TIMMS, MICHELE, retired professional basketball player; b. Australia, June 28, 1965; Guard Australia's Women's Nat. Basketball League - Bulleen Boomers, 1984-85, Nunawading Spectres, 1985, Lotus Munchen, Germany, 1989-90, Perth Breakers, Australia, 1991-92, Basket Firenze, Italy, 1993-94, Sydney Flames, Australia, 1995, WTV Wuppertal, Germany, 1995-96, Phoenix Mercury, 1997—2001. Named WNBL Player of Yr., 1995, 96. Avocations: tennis, golf.

TIMONEY, PETER JOSEPH, veterinarian, virologist, educator, consultant; b. Dublin, June 5, 1941; came to U.S., 1983; s. John Francis and Evelyn Norah (Whittle) T.; m. Katherine Mary Murphy, Sept. 11, 1971; children: Peter, Caroline, Sarah, David. MVB, Nat. U., Dublin, 1964; MS, U. Ill., 1966; PhD, U. Dublin, 1974. Rsch. assoc. U. Ill., Urbana, 1964-66; rsch. officer Vet. Rsch. Lab., Abbotstown, Ireland, 1966-72; sr. rsch. officer equine diseases sect. Veterinary Rsch. Lab., Abbotstown, Ireland, 1972-79; assoc. prof. diagnostic lab., dept. microbiology Cornell U., Ithaca, N.Y., 1979-81; sci. dir. Irish Equine Ctr., Johnstown, Ireland, 1981-83; assoc. prof. virology vet. sci. dept. U. Ky., Lexington, 1983-87, prof. virology, assoc. chair for rsch., 1987-89, Frederick Van Lennep chair, 1988—, acting chair, 1989-90, chair, 1990-99, 2002—; bd. dirs. Gluck Equine Rsch. Ctr., 1990—. Cons. Daryl Labs., Inc., Santa Clara, Calif., 1981-86, Ft. Dodge (Iowa) Animal Health Lab., 1986-92, 94—. Fellow Royal Coll. Vet. Surgeons, World Equine Vet. Assn. (pres. 1995-99); mem. AAAS, Am. Assn. Equine Practitioners, Am. Soc. Microbiology, Am. Soc. Virology, U.S. Animal Health Assn. Avocations: reading, gardening. Office: Gluck Equine Rsch Ctr 108 Gluck Ctr Lexington KY 40506-0099 Office Phone: 859-257-4757 8-1085. Business E-Mail: ptimoney@uky.edu.

TIMOSHCHUK, VICTOR ARKADYEVICH, research scientist; b. Mary, Turkmenistan, Sept. 20, 1946; s. Arkady and Raisa Timoshchuk; m. Margarita Sergievsky, Feb. 16, 1990; m. Ludmila Gumenyuk, Aug. 10, 1979 (div. Feb. 13, 1990); children: Vladislav, Kirill, Sergey. MS in Organic Chemistry, St. Petersburg State U., Russia, 1964—69; PhD in Organic Chemistry, Rsch. Inst. Bio-organic Chemistry, Belarus Acad. Scis., Minsk, 1971—75. Sr. rschr. Rsch. Inst. Bio-organic Chemistry, Minsk, Belarus, 1976—81, Rsch. Inst. Peat, Minsk, Belarus, 1981—84; head, lab. Rsch. Inst. Microbiology and Epidemiology, Minsk, Belarus, 1984—88; sr. rschr. Rsch. Inst. Radiation Medicine, Minsk, Belarus, 1988—90; chief rschr. Belarus State U., Minsk, 1990—96; vis. rschr. Brigham Young U., Provo, Utah, vis. scientist, 1996—99; scientist TriLink Biotechnologies, Inc., San Diego, 1999—. Contbr. articles to profl. jours. Mem.: Internat. Soc. for Nucleosides, Nucleotides and Nucleic Acids. Achievements include discovery of a new type of isomery; patents for the syntheses of nucleosides of different types. Office: TriLink BioTechnologies Inc 9955 Mesa Rim Rd San Diego CA 92121 Office Phone: 858-546-0004. Personal E-mail: vatimoshchuk@yahoo.com. E-mail: vtimoshchuk@trilinkbiotech.com.

TIMOTHY, DAVID HARRY, retired biology educator; b. Pitts., June 9, 1928; s. David Edgar and Harriett P. (Stein) T.; m. Marian Claire Whiteley, Sept. 5, 1953; children: Marjory J., M. Elisabeth, David W. BS, Pa. State U., 1952, MS, 1955; PhD, U. Minn., 1956. Asst. geneticist Rockefeller Found., Bogota, Colombia, 1956-58, assoc. geneticist, 1958-61; assoc. prof. N.C. State U., Raleigh, 1961-66, prof., 1966-93, prof. emeritus, 1993—; ret. Cons. to fgn. and U.S. govts., also U.S. and internat. sci. orgns.; mem. USDA crop adv. com. on grasses, 1983-87, mem. policy adv. com., sci. and edn. grants program, 1982-84, chief scientist USDA Sci. and Edn. Competetive Rsch. Grants Office, 1985, 86; with Nat. Plant Genetic Resources Bd., 1984-91, vice chmn., 1991; bd. dirs., treas. Genetic Resources Comms. Sys., Inc., 1985-91, pres., 1991-93; mem. bd. on agr. NAS-NRC, work group on U.S. Nat. Plant Germplasm Sys., 1987-89. Co-author monographs; contbr. chpts. to books; contbr. articles to profl. jours. With AUS, 1946-48, PTO. Grantee NSF, 1965, 78, Rockefeller Found., 1968, 69, Pioneer Hi-Bred Internat., 1982, 83. Fellow AAAS (electorate nominating com., sect. O, Agr. 1988-90), Am. Soc. Agronomy, Crop Sci. Soc. Am. (editl. bd. 1982-84, assoc. editor Crop Sci. 1982-84, Frank N. Meyer medal for plant genetic resources 1994). Home: 13 Furches St Raleigh NC 27607-7048

TIMOUR, JOHN ARNOLD, retired librarian; b. Hartford, Conn., Jan. 20, 1926; s. John Alfred and Karin Elizabeth (Levin) Timour; m. Betty Jo Lord, Mar. 23, 1952; children: Jon, David, Alan. BA, Miami U., Oxford, Ohio, 1951; postgrad., Fla. State U., 1951-52; MA, George Washington U., 1960; M.L.S., U. Md., 1969. Tng. and Med. Lit. Analysis and Retrieval System liaison officer Nat. Library of Medicine, Bethesda, Md., 1966-69; dir. library services Conn. Regional Med. Program-Yale U., New Haven, 1969-73; dir. Mid-Eastern Med. Library Service Coll. Physicians of Phila., 1973-75; univ. librarian Thomas Jefferson U., Phila., 1975-87. Instr. USAR, Hamden, Conn., 1970—73; lectr. libr. sci. So. Conn. State Coll., New Haven, 1970—71; adj. prof. Drexel U., Phila., 1976—78. Contbr. articles to profl. jours. With USN, 1942—46, PTO, 2d lt. USAF, 1951—53, lt. col. USAR, 1953—73. Mem.: Spl. Librs. Assn. (pres. Phila. chpt. 1979—80), Acad. Health Info. Profls. (disting. mem.), Med. Libr. Assn. (bd. dirs. 1978—81, Eliot prize 1974), Am. Med. Writers Assn. (pres. Phila. chpt. 1986—87), Assn. Acad. Health Sci. Libr. Dirs., Conn. Assn. Health Sci. Librs. (hon.), Washington Yacht and Country Club, Sigma Xi (bull. editor Jefferson chpt. 1980—86, recognition cert. 1982), Beta Phi Mu. Episcopalian. Avocations: golf, chess, macintosh computers. Home: 6000 River Rd Apt 10 Washington NC 27889 E-mail: jtimour@coastalnet.com.

TIMPANE, PHILIP MICHAEL, education educator, policy analyst; b. Troy, N.Y., Nov. 27, 1934; s. Philip Thomas and Rita (Killeen) T.; m. Genevieve LaGrua, Nov. 30, 1957; children: Michael J., Joseph T., Paul J., David A. AB, Cath. U. Am., 1956, MA, 1964, LLD (hon.), 1991; MPA, Harvard U., 1970; LittD (hon.), Wagner Coll., 1986. Historian Joint Chiefs of Staff Dept. Def., 1961-65; spl. asst. civil rights Office of Sec. Def., 1965-68; edn. policy planner HEW, 1968-72; sr. fellow Brookings Instn., 1972-74; dir. edn. policy ctr. RAND Corp., 1974-77; dep. dir. Nat. Inst. Edn., Washington, 1977-80, dir., 1980-81; prof. edn. Columbia U. Tchrs. Coll., N.Y.C., 1981—, dean, 1981-84, pres., 1984-94; mem. Aspen Inst. Edn. Program, 1974-77, 87—; v.p. and sr. scholar Carnegie Found. for Advancement Tchg., Princeton, N.J., 1994-97; sr. adv. for edn. policy RAND, Washington, 1997—. Author: Corporate Interest in Public Education in the Cities, 1982; co-author: Youth Policy in Transition, 1976, Business Impact on Education and Child Development Reform, 1991, Rhetoric Versus Reality: What We Know and What We Need to Know about Vouchers and Charter Schools, 2001, Options for Restructuring the Safe and Drug-Free Schools and Communities Act, 2001; co-editor: Planned Variation in Education, 1975, Work Incentives and Income Guarantees, 1975, Ethical and Legal Issues in Social Experimentation, 1975, Higher Education and School Reform, 1998, Rediscovering the Democratic Purposes of Education, 2000; editor: Federal Interest in Financing Schooling, 1978. Mem. Arlington (Va.) Sch. Bd., 1972—76, chmn., 1973—74; bd. dirs. Children's TV Workshop, 1989—99, Jobs for the Future, 1995—2002, Inst. Ednl. Leadership, 1999—, So. Edn. Found., 1995—2003. Democrat. Roman Catholic. Office: Aspen Inst Edn Program 1 Dupont Cir Ste 700 Washington DC 20036 E-mail: mike.timpane@aspeninst.org.

TIMPANO, ANNE, museum director, art historian; b. Osaka, Japan, June 17, 1950; d. A.J. and Margaret (Smith) T. BA, Coll. William and Mary, 1972; MA, George Washington U., 1983. Program mgmt. asst. Nat. Mus. Am. Art, Washington, 1977-86; dir. The Columbus (Ga.) Mus., 1986-93, DAAP Galleries, U. Cin., 1993—. Grant reviewer Inst. Mus. Svcs., Washington,

1988—, Ga. Coun. for Arts, Atlanta, 1988-91. Mem. 1992 Quincentenary Commn., Columbus, 1987-92. Recipient David Lloyd Kreeger award George Washington U., 1980. Mem. Am. Assn. Mus. (surveyor mus. assessment program), Assn. of Coll. and Univ. Mus. and Galleries, Coll. Art Assn., Midwest Mus. Conf. Roman Catholic. Home: 85 Pleasant Ridge Ave Fort Mitchell KY 41017-2861 Office: U Cin PO Box 210016 Cincinnati OH 45221-0016 E-mail: anne.timpano@uc.edu.

TIMPE, RONALD ERNEST, insurance company executive; b. Atkinson, Kans., July 9, 1939; BS Math., Lewis & Clark Coll., 1961; grad. advanced mgmt. program, Harvard U., 1979. CLU. With Standard Ins. Co., Portland, Oreg., 1968—, asst. actuary, 1973—, asst. v.p., actuary, 1980—, v.p. group pensions, sr. v.p. group ins. and corp. fin. svcs., pres., CEO, 1993—, chmn., pres., CEO, also bd. dirs. Bd. dirs. Oreg. Bus. Coun., Oreg. Ind. Coll. Found., Oreg. Symphony. Fellow Soc. of Actuaries, mem. Portland Met. C. of C. (past chmn.). Office: StanCorp Fin Group Inc 1100 SW 6th Ave Portland OR 97204

TIMPERLAKE, EDWARD THOMAS, writer; b. Perth Amboy, N.J., Nov. 22, 1946; s. James Elwood Timperlake Jr. and Joan Dorothy (Conkling) Maurer; m. Barbette Runckel, Aug. 10, 1969 (div. 1993); children: Tara, Kimberly; m. Cathryn Porcelli Gekas, Apr. 8, 2000. BS, U.S. Naval Acad., 1969; MBA, Cornell U., 1977. Commd. 2d lt. USMC, 1969, advanced through grades to lt. col., 1985, ret., 1993; asst. venture mgr. Exxon Enterprise, N.Y.C., 1977-78; sect. mgr. T.A.S.C., Arlington, Va., 1978-81; dep. dir. Nat. Dir. Vietnam Vets. Leadership Program, Action Agy., Washington, 1981-83; dir. mobilization plans and requirements Office of Sec. Def., Washington, 1984; campaign staff George Bush for Pres., 1988; asst. sec. Dept. Vets. Affairs, Washington, 1989-93; pres. T-9 Group, 1993-95; profl. staff rules com. U.S. House of Reps., Washington, 1996—99; dir. tech. assessment internat. tech. security Office of the Sec. of Def., The Pentagon, Washington, 2003—. Author: Year of the Rat, 1998, Red Dragon Rising, 1999; contbr. articles to profl. jours. Mem.: Naval Acad. Alumni Assn., N.Y. Yacht Club, Army-Navy Club. Home: 1027 22d St Arlington VA 22202

TIMS, ROBERT AUSTIN, data processing official, pilot; b. Seattle, Dec. 21, 1942; s. Robert Mitchell Tims and Winifred Eileen (Dorgan) Bristol; m. Jane Moore, June 6, 1980. Student, Pacific Union Coll., 1960-61, Alpha Aviation Sch., 1976-77, BS in Computer Info. Sys. with honors, Ark. State U., 1998. Lic. comml. and instrument pilot; cert. flight instr. Engring. technician Tex. Instruments, Inc., Ridgecrest, Calif., 1966-67, various projects, Conn., N.Y. and N.J., 1967-70; homesteader Leslie, Ark., 1970-77; chief pilot/flight instr. Sharp Aviation Co., Jonesboro, Ark., 1977-79; chief pilot Pizza Inn of Ark., Jonesboro, 1979-83; data processing mgr., chief pilot Realty Assocs. Brokerage, Inc., Jonesboro, 1983-91, microanalyst, 1991-94. Pres., owner ABS Logic, Inc., computers and programming cons., Jonesboro, 1985—; programmer Jimco Lamp Mfg., Bono, Ark., 1998—99; programmer, analyst TEK Systems, Memphis, 2000—02; software engr. Northrop Grumman, Little Rock, 2003—04, Nextech, Memphis, 2003—04, Nucor Steel, Hickman, Ark., 2004—, JD Resources, Memphis, 2004—. Served with USN, 1962-66. Recipient Nat. Collegiate Bus. Merit award. Mem. CAP (squadron comdr. Jonesboro 1986-93), Am. Philatelic Soc., Planetary Soc., Nat. Space Soc., SETI Inst., Beta Gamma Sigma. Avocation: philately. Home and Office: 1616 Alonzo St Jonesboro AR 72401-4802 Office Phone: 870-219-8064.

TINAGLIA, MICHAEL LEE, lawyer; b. Chgo., Dec. 21, 1952; s. Michael Leo and Josephine (Esposito) T.; m. Lucia Yolando Guzzo, Oct. 14, 1978; children: Laura, Lisa, Elena. BA, Northwestern U., 1974; JD, DePaul U., 1977. Bar: Ill. 1977, U.S. Dist. Ct. (no. dist.) Ill. 1978, U.S. Dist. Ct. (ea. dist.) Wis. 1986. Assoc. Arnold & Kadjan, Chgo., 1977-79; ptnr. Leader & Tinaglia, Chgo., 1979-86; assoc. Laser, Schostok, Kolman & Frank, Chgo., 1987-92; prin. Law Office of Michael Lee Tinaglia Ltd., Chgo., 1992-93, 2000—; equity ptnr. DiMonte & Lizak, Park Ridge, Ill., 1994-99. V.p., corp. counsel Tiara Med. Sys., Inc., Oak Forest, Ill. Contbr. articles to profl. jours. Alderman City Coun., Park Ridge, 1997—, chmn. pub. safety com., 2003—, mem. fin. and budget com. Mem. Ill. Bar Assn., Chgo. Bar Assn. Roman Catholic. Avocations: skiing, guitar. Office: Law Offices of Michael Lee Tinaglia 161 N Clark St Ste 2550 Chicago IL 60601-3246

TINCHER, WAYNE COLEMAN, engineering educator; BA in Chemistry, David Lipscomb U., 1956; PhD in Physical Chemistry, Vanderbilt U., 1960. From rsch. chemist to rsch. group leader Monsanto Co., Research Triangle Park, N.C., 1960-71; from assoc. prof. to prof. Ga. Inst. Technology, Atlanta, 1971—. Recipient Olney medal Am. Assn. of Textile Chemists and Colorists, 1996. Office: Ga Inst Technology Sch Textile & Fiber Engring 801 Ferst Dr Atlanta GA 30332-0295 Office Phone: 404-894-2197. Business E-Mail: wayne.tincher@tfe.gatech.edu.

TINDALL, JON W. research scientist; b. Trenton, N.J., May 21, 1940; s. John William and Virginia K. (Snell) T.; m. Linda Mae Tindall, Apr. 21, 1983; children: William, Christine, Matthew. BA in Math., Claremont Men's Coll., Calif., 1972; MS in Indsl. Engring., UCLA, 1978; postgrad., U. So. Calif., 1975-77. Dept. mgr. Aerojet Gen., Azusa, Calif., 1965-69; staff engr. TRW, Redondo Beach, Calif., 1970-81; prin. investigator McDonald Douglas, Seal Beach, Calif., 1981-86; assoc. fellow Nichols Rsch., Newport Beach, Calif., 1986-93, fellow, sr. prin. investigator Colorado Springs, Colo., 1993—2000; chief engr. Millennium Engring., 2000—. Tech. project mgr. CSC/Nichols Rsch., Colorado Springs, 1997-2000; data fusion working group USAF, Colorado Springs, 1996-98, infared discrimination group, Newport Beach, Calif., 1990-94; radar systems analyst TRW, L.A., 1980-86. Designer: (realtime software) Engagement Coordination System, 1998; author tech. publs. in field. Recipient medal for acquisitions and technology Jacques Gansler, 1999. Mem. AIAA. Avocations: golf, bowling, computer games. Office: Millennium Engring 5450 Tech Center Dr Colorado Springs CO 80919 E-mail: tindallJ@nichols.com.

TINDALL, ROBERT EMMETT, lawyer, educator; b. NYC, Jan. 2, 1934; s. Robert E. and Alice (McGonigle) T.; children: Robert Emmett IV, Elizabeth. BS in Marine Engring., SUNY, 1955; postgrad., Georgetown U. Law Sch., 1960—61; LLB, U. Ariz., 1963; LLM, NYU, 1967; PhD, City U., London, 1975. Bar: Ariz. 1963. Mgmt. trainee GE, Schenectady, NY, Lynn, Mass., Glens Falls, NY, 1955-56, 58-60; law clk. Haight, Gardner, Poor and Havens, NYC, 1961; prin., mem. Robert Emmett Tindall & Assocs., Tucson, 1963—; assoc. prof. mgmt. U. Ariz., Tucson, 1969—. Vis. prof. Grad. Sch. of Law, Soochow U., China, 1972, Grad. Bus. Ctr., London, 1974, NYU, 1991—; dir. MBA program U. Ariz., Tucson, 1975-81, dir. entrepreneurship program, 1984-86; investment cons. Saudi Arabia, 1981—; lectr. USIA, Eng., India, Mid. East, 1974; lectr. bus. orgn. and regulatory laws Southwestern Legal Found., Acad. Am. and Internat. Law, 1976-80. Actor cmty. theatres, Schenectady, 1955-56, Harrisburg, Pa., 1957-58, Tucson, 1961-71; appeared in films Rage, 1971, Showdown at OK Corral, 1971, Lost Horizon, 1972; appeared in TV programs Gunsmoke, 1972, Petrocelli, 1974; author: Multinational Enterprises, 1975; contbr. articles on domestic and internat. bus. to profl. jours. Served to lt. USN, 1956-58. Fellow Ford Found., 1965-67; grantee Asia Found., 1972-73. Mem. Strategic Mgmt. Soc., State Bar Ariz., Acad. Internat. Bus., SAG, Honourable Soc. of Mid. Temple (London), Phi Delta Phi, Beta Gamma Sigma, Assn. Corp. Growth, Royal Overseas League (London). Home: PO Box 42196 Tucson AZ 85733-2196 Office: Coll Bus & Public Adminstrn U Ariz Dept Mgmt & Policy Tucson AZ 85721-0001

TINDALL, ROBERT J. architectural firm executive; Joined Callison Arch., Inc., Seattle, 1976—, COO, 1996—98, pres., 1998—. Acting exec. dir. Insight Alliance; spkr. in field. Mem. editl. adv. bd.: Retail Constrn. mag.; contbr. articles to profl. jours. Mem.: AIA (large firm roundtable), Urban Land Inst., Internat. Coun. on Shopping Ctrs. Office: Callison Arch Inc Ste 2400 1420 Fifth Ave Seattle WA 98101-2343*

TINDLE, CHARLES DWIGHT WOOD, broadcasting company executive; b. Bryn Mawr, Pa., Jan. 13, 1950; s. Charles Wood and Nancy (Sapp) T. Student, Kenyon Coll., 1968-71. Pres. Dwight Karma Broadcasting, Mesa, Ariz., 1971-76, Natural Broadcasting System, Mesa, 1976-79; producer, fellow Am. Film Inst. Ctr. for Advanced Film Studies, 1979-81; pres. Network 30, Scottsdale, Ariz., 1985—. Owner Sta. KDKB-AM-FM, Mesa, Sta. KSML-FM, Lake Tahoe, Calif., Sta. KNOT-AM-FM, Prescott, Ariz., Sta. KBWA, Williams, Ariz. Recipient Peabody award U. Ga., 1976. Republican. Seventh Day Adventist. Office: 644 N Country Club Dr Mesa AZ 85201-4948 Home: 7662 E Minnezona Ave Scottsdale AZ 85251-2102 Office Phone: 480-251-1597. E-mail: dwtindle@qwest.net.

TINERELLA, VINCENT P. librarian, protective services official; b. Evanston, Ill., May 3, 1957; s. Eileen R. and Bertil J. Anderson; m. Sheryle L. Pearson, June 14, 1962; children: Hilary I., Joseph P. MA in History, DePaul U., Chicago, Illinois, 1994; M of Libr. and Info. Sci., Dominican U., River Forest, Ill., 1998. Evaluation analyst Chgo. Police Dept., 1982—; reference libr. DePaul U., Chicago, 1999—. Author: (book reviews) Reference and User Services Quar., contbr. articles to profl. jours. Mem.: ALA, Reference and User Svcs. Assn., Ill. Libr. Assn., Beta Phi Mu, Phi Alpha Theta. Roman Catholic. Home: 5280 N Lawler Chicago IL 60630 Office: Chicago Police Dept 3510 S Michigan Ave Chicago IL 60653 Personal E-mail: vintin6360@msn.com.

TING, ALBERT CHIA, bioengineering researcher; b. Hong Kong, Sept. 7, 1950; came to U.S., 1957; s. William Su and Katherine Sung T.; m. Shirley Roung Wang, July 30, 1988. BA, UCLA, 1973; MS, Calif. State U., L.A., 1975, Calif. Inst. Tech., 1977; PhD, U. Calif., San Diego, 1983. Rsch. asst. Calif. Inst. Tech., Pasadena, 1975-77, U. Calif., San Diego, 1982-83; sr. staff engr. R&D Am. Med. Optics, Irvine, Calif., 1983-86; project engr., rsch. Allergan Med. Optics, Irvine, Calif., 1987-89, sr. project engr., rsch., 1989-92, sr. project engr., engring., 1993-94; bioengr. cons. Pharmacia Iovision, Inc., Irvine, Calif., 1995-97; sr. engr. D & E, 1997, sr. engr., project mgr., 1998-99; rsch. and devel. mgr., surg. Bausch & Lomb, Irvine, 1999—2001; R & D mgr. Visiogen, Inc., Irvine, 2001—02, sr. R & D mgr., 2002—. Inventor med. and optical devices, recipient patent awards 1988, 89, 91, 92, 93, 95, 2004; contbr. articles to sci. jours. Mem. AAAS, Biomed. Engring. Soc., Assn. for Rsch. in Vision and Ophthalmology, Biomed. Optics Soc. Office: Visiogen Inc 4 Jenner St # 180 Irvine CA 92618 Office Phone: 949-341-0700.

TING, ROBERT YEN-YING, physicist; b. Kwei-yang, China, Mar. 8, 1942; came to U.S. 1965; s. Chi-yung and Shou-feng (Yang) T.; m. Teresa Yen-chun Ting, June 3, 1967; children: Paul H., Peggy Y. BS, Nat. Taiwan U., 1964; MS, MIT, 1967; PhD, U. Calif., San Diego, 1971. Rsch. engr. U.S. Naval Rsch. Lab., Washington, 1971-77, supervisory engr., 1977-80, supervisory physicist Orlando, Fla., 1980-97; prof. dept. chemistry U. Ctrl. Fla., Orlando, 1997—. Prof. George Washington U., 1972-80. Contbr. over 100 articles in rheology, polymer and acoustics to profl. jours. Fellow Acoustical Soc. Am.; mem. Am. chem. Soc., Am. Ceramics Soc., Am. Inst. Chem. Engrs. Office: U Ctrl Fla Dept Chem Orlando FL 32816-2366 E-mail: rting@pegasus.cc.ucf.edu.

TING, SAMUEL CHAO CHUNG, physicist, researcher; b. Ann Arbor, Mich., Jan. 27, 1936; s. Kuan H. and Jeanne (Wong) Ting; m. Susan Carol Marks, Apr. 28, 1985; children: Jeanne Min, Amy Min, Christopher M. BS in Engring., U. Mich., 1959, MS, 1960, PhD in Physics, 1962, ScD (hon.), 1978, Chinese U. Hong Kong, 1987, U. Bologna, Italy, 1988, Columbia U., 1990, U. Sci. and Tech., China, 1990, Moscow State U., 1991, U. Bucharest, Romania, 1993, Nat. Tsinghua U., Taiwan, 2002, Nat. Jiaotong U., 2003. Ford Found. fellow CERN (European Orgn. Nuc. Rsch.), Geneva, 1963; instr. physics Columbia U., 1964, asst. prof., 1965—67; group leader Deutsches Elektronen-Synchrotron, Hamburg, Germany, 1966; assoc. prof. physics MIT, Cambridge, 1967—68, prof., 1969—; Thomas Dudley Cabot Inst. prof. M.I.T., 1977—. Program cons. divsn. particles and fields Am. Phys. Soc., 1970; hon. prof. Beijing Normal Coll., 1987, Jiatong U., Shanghai, 1987, U. Bologna, Italy, 1988. Assoc. editor Nuc. Physics B, 1970, editl. bd. Nuc. Instruments and Methods, Mathematical Modeling; contbr. articles to profl. jours. Recipient Nobel prize in Physics, 1976, De Gasperi prize in Sci., Italian Republic, 1988, Ernest Orlando Lawrence award, U.S. Govt., 1976, Gold medal in Sci., City of Brescia, Italy, 1988, Golden Leopard award, Town of Taormina, 1988, Forum Engelberg prize, 1996, Pub. Svc. medal, NASA, 2001; fellow Am. Acad. Arts and Scis., 1975. Mem.: NAS, Hungarian Acad. Sci., Deutsche Acad. Naturforscher Leopoldina (fgn. mem.), Russian Acad. Sci., Acad. Sinica, Pakistani Acad. Sci. Office: MIT Dept Physics 51 Vassar St Cambridge MA 02139-4308

TING, YU-CHEN, science educator, researcher; b. Hsia-Yi Hsien, China, Oct. 3, 1920; arrived in U.S., 1948; s. Jin-yung Ting and Yi-ying Wang; m. Jovina Chen, June 25, 1959; children: Andrew, Claire. BS, Nat. Henan U., Kaifeng, China, 1945; MS in Agr., Cornell U., 1951; PhD, La. State U., 1954. Tchg. asst. Nat. Henan U., 1944—48; rsch. asst. La. State U., Baton Rouge, 1951—54; postdoctoral rschr. Harvard U., Cambridge, Mass., 1954—58, rsch. fellow, 1958—62; asst. prof. Boston Coll., Chestnut Hill, Mass., 1962—64, assoc. prof., 1964—66, prof., 1966—91, prof. emeritus, 1991—. Cons. Cetus, Madison, Wis., 1982—85, Sci. Press of China, N.Y.C., 1992—; advisor Gerson and Lehrman, N.Y.C., 2001—. Author: Chromosomes of Maize-Teosinte Hybrids, 1964; contbr. articles to profl. jours. Com. mem. Nat. Assn. Chinese-Ams., Boston, 1975—86. Fellow sr. fellow, NAS, 1978; grantee rsch. grantee, NSF, 1983, Pioneer Hi-Bred Internat., Ames, Iowa, 1979. Fellow: AAAS. Achievements include discovery of meiosis and chromosome number of sweet potato plant; proposal that abnormal chromosome 10 in maize was originated by A-B translocation; investigation of inversion polymorphism of teosintes and maize; study of chromosome fine structures, anther culture and cloning of maize. Avocations: swimming, volleyball. Home: 230 Bonad Rd Chestnut Hill MA 02467 Office: Dept Biology Boston Coll 144 Commonwealth Ave Chestnut Hill MA 02467 E-mail: tiny@bc.edu.

TINGELSTAD, JON BUNDE, retired pediatrician, educator; b. McVille, N.D., Jan. 15, 1935; s. Sophus B. and Mabelle (Bunde) T.; m. Marcia Ayers, Dec. 17, 1960; children: Paul, Catherine, David. BA, U. N.D., 1957, BS, 1958; MD, Harvard U., 1960. Diplomate Am. Bd. Pediatrics. Intern Children's Hosp. Med. Ctr., Boston, 1960-61, resident, 1961-62, U. Colo. Med. Ctr., Denver, 1962-63; fellow in pediatric cardiology Children's Hosp., Buffalo, 1965-67; asst. prof. pediatrics Med. Coll. Va., Richmond, 1967-71, assoc. prof., 1971-76; prof., vice chmn. pediatrics East Carolina U. Sch. Medicine, Greenville, N.C., 1976-77, prof., chmn. pediatrics, 1977-2000. Mem. Greenville City Bd. Edn., 1978-82, chmn., 1981-82. Served to capt. USAF, 1963-65. Fellow Am. Acad. Pediatrics, Am. Coll. Cardiology; mem. Am. Bd. Pediatrics, Phi Beta Kappa, Phi Eta Sigma. Home: 103 Providence Pl Chocowinity NC 27817-8940 Office: E Carolina U Sch Med Dept Pediatrics Greenville NC 27858-4354 E-mail: JonBTing1@msn.com.

TINGLE, AUBREY JAMES, pediatric immunologist, research administrator; b. St. Paul, Alta., Can., June 28, 1943; s. Cyril Nisbet Tingle and Margaret Lucy (Fraser) Tarbuck; m. Valerie Jean Anderson, Nov. 2, 1968; children: Heather Lynn, Brian James. MD, U. Alta., Edmonton, 1967; PhD, McGill U., Montreal, Que., Can., 1974. Asst. prof. dept. pediatrics U. B.C., Vancouver, Can., 1974-79, head div. immunology dept. pediatrics, 1974-86, assoc. prof., 1979-86, prof., 1986—, prof. dept. pathology, 1986—; dir. rsch. B.C. Rsch. Inst. for Children's and Women's Health, Vancouver, 1992-2001; asst. dean rsch. Faculty of Medicine, U. B.C., Vancouver, 1992-2001; v.p. rsch. & edn. Children's & Women's Health Ctr B.C., Vancouver, 1997-2001; pres., CEO Michael Smith Found. for Health Rsch., Vancouver, 2001—. Fellow Royal Coll. Physicians and Surgeons Can., Soc. Pediatric Research, Am. Acad. Pediatrics; mem. Western Soc. Pediatric Research. Office: Michael Smith Found 1285 W Broadway Vancouver BC Canada V6H 3X8 E-mail: atingle@msfhr.org.

TINGLE, JAMES O'MALLEY, retired lawyer; b. N.Y.C., June 12, 1928; s. Thomas Jefferson and Mercedes (O'Malley) T. BS, U. Mont., 1950, BA, LL.B., U. Mont., 1952; LL.M., U. Mich., 1953, S.JD, 1958. Bar: Calif. 1959, Mont. 1952, N.Y. 1961. Asst. prof. law U. Mont., Missoula, 1955-56; atty. Shell Oil Co., N.Y.C., 1957-62; assoc. Pillsbury, Madison & Sutro, San Francisco, 1962-68, ptnr., 1969-2000. Author: The Stockholder's Remedy of Corporate Dissolution, 1959; editor: State Antitrust Laws, 1974. Served to 1st lt. USAF, 1953-55. William W. Cook fellow U. Mich. Mem. Mont. Bar Assn., Calif. Bar Assn., ABA Democrat.

TINGLEY, FLOYD WARREN, retired internist; b. Charlotte, N.C., Nov. 22, 1933; s. Floyd Warren Sr. and Janie (Suggs) T.; m. Sandra Carpenter, Aug. 20, 1955 (div. Dec. 1984); children: Sheryl Tingley Hagen, David Alan; m. Johnette Hill, Apr. 5, 1985. BA in English, Emory U., 1955, MD, 1959. Diplomate Am. Bd. Internal Medicine (bd. govs. 1986-92). Intern USAF Hosp., Lackland AFB, Tex., 1959-60; resident in internal medicine Parkland Meml. Hosp., Dallas, 1963-65, fellow in cardiology, 1965-66; pvt. practice specializing in internal medicine Arlington, Tex., 1966-88; med. dir. southwestern region Met. Life Ins. Co., Irving, Tex., 1988-90; regional practice leader William M. Mercer Inc., 1990-91; v.p., sr. med. dir. Provident Life and Accident Co., Chattanooga, 1991-92; v.p., nat. med. dir. Travelers Ins. Cos., Hartford, Conn., 1992-94; sr. v.p., chief med. officer Kemper Nat. Svcs., Plantation, Fla., 1995-2000, ret., 2000. Apptd. Tex. Commn. on Health Care Reimbursement Alternatives, 1987; bd. dirs. Riverside Nat. Bank, Grand Prairie, Tex. Contbr. articles to profl. jours. Pres. Arlington YMCA, 1971; chmn. budget com. Family Services, Ft. Worth, 1973; participant Health Policy Agenda for Am. People, Chgo., 1984-87; trustee Tex. Med. Liability Trust, Austin, 1987-88. Capt. USAF, 1958-63. Fellow ACP (pres. Tex. chpt. 1981); mem. AMA (chmn. sect. coun. internal medicine, 1979-88), Am. Soc. Internal Medicine (pres. 1986-87), Tex. Med. Assn. (treas. 1978-85, alt. del. to AMA 1985-91, commendation 1985), Tarrant County Med. Soc. (pres. Arlington br. 1974, del. to Tex. Med. Assn., Community Svc. award 1983). Presbyterian. Avocations: photography, sailing, gardening, computer hobbies. Home: 2709 Park Place Ct Arlington TX 76016-5891

TINGUS, STEVEN JAMES, physiologist researcher, educator, policymaker; b. Sacramento, Calif., Aug. 19, 1963; s. James George and Joanne Fotene (Kamilos) Tingus. BS in Biol. Sci., U. Calif., Davis, 1985, MS in Physiology, 1990, C.Phil. in Physiology, 1994. Dir. US dept. edn. Nat. Inst. on Disability and Rehab. Rsch., Washington, 2001—. Mem.: AAAS, Am. Assn. Polit. Cons. Republican. Greek Orthodox. Home: Apt 1101 2250 Clarendon Blvd Arlington VA 22201-3341 Office: Dir Nat Inst on Disability and Rehab US Dept Edn 400 Maryland Ave SW Washington DC 20202 Office Phone: 202-245-7549. Personal E-mail: stingus@earthlink.net.

TINKER, JOHN HEATH, anesthesiologist, educator; b. Cin., May 18, 1941; s. Leonard Henry and Georgia (Reeves) T.; m. Martha Iuen (div. Jan., 1989); children: Deborah H. Lynne, Karen Sue, Juliette Kay; m. Bonnie Howard, Mar. 18, 1989. BS magna cum laude, U. Cin., 1964, MS summa cum laude, 1968. Diplomate Am. Bd. Anesthesiology (sr. examiner 1976—). Surg. intern, resident Harvard Med. Sch., Peter Bent Brigham Hosp., Boston, 1969-70, resident in anesthesiology, 1970-72; cons. anesthesiology Mayo Clinic, Rochester, Minn., 1974-83, chief cardiovascular anesthesiology, 1978-83; prof. anesthesiology U. Iowa Coll. Medicine, Iowa City, 1983-97, chmn. dept., 1983-97; prof., chmn. anesthesiology U. Nebr., Med. Ctr., Omaha, 1997—. Mem. pharm. scis. rev. com., NIH, Bethesda, Md., 1986—; dir. Matrix Med. Inc., Orchard Park, N.Y., 1988—; frequent guest lectr. Author: Controversies in Cardiopulmonary Bypass, 1989 (monograph award Soc. Cardiovascular Anesthsiologists); editor: Anesthesia and Analgesia, Jour. Internat. Anesthesiology Rsch. Soc., 1983—; contbr. over 185 articles to profl. jours. Maj. U.S. Army, 1972-74. NIH grantee, 1977-87. Fellow Royal Coll. Surgeons Australia; mem. Am. Soc. Anesthesiologists (active numerous coms. 1972—), Soc. Cardiovascular Anesthesiologists, Assn. Univ. Anesthetists. Avocations: fishing, golf, modeling ships and airplanes. Office: U Nebr 984455 Nebr Med Ctr Omaha NE 68198-0001

TINKER, MARK CHRISTIAN, producer, director; b. Stamford, Conn., Jan. 16, 1951; s. Grant Almerin Tinker and Ruth Prince (Byerly) Fricke; m. Kristin Harmon, Apr. 16, 1988 (div. 2000); 1 child, James. BS, Syracuse U., 1973. Prodr.(dir., writer): (TV series) The White Shadow, 1978—81, St. Elsewhere, 1982—88 (Emmy, Peabody award, Peoples Choice award); dir.: (TV films) Babe Ruth, 1991, Bonanza: Under Attack, 1995; dir., prodr. (TV series) Civil Wars, 1991—93; dir.: (TV series, episode) ER (Going Home), 1994; (TV series) The Bob Newhart Show, 1972, Making the Grade, 1982, L.A. Law, 1986, Capital News, 1990, NYPD Blue, 1993—, Chicago Hope, 1994. Mem.: Nat. Acad. TV Arts and Scis.

TINKHAM, MICHAEL, physicist, researcher; b. Green Lake County, Wis., Feb. 23, 1928; s. Clayton Harold and LaVerna (Krause) T.; m. Mary Stephanie Merin, June 24, 1961; children: Jeffrey Michael, Christopher Gillespie. AB, Ripon (Wis.) Coll., 1951, Sc.D. (hon.), 1976; MS, MIT, 1951; PhD, 1954; MA (hon.), Harvard, 1966; DSc (hon), ETH Zurich, 1997. NSF postdoctoral fellow at Clarendon Lab., Oxford (Eng.) U., 1954-55; successively research physicist, lectr., asst. prof., asso. prof., prof. physics U. Calif. at Berkeley, 1955-66; Gordon McKay prof. applied physics Harvard U., 1966—, prof. physics, 1966-80, Rumford prof. physics, 1980—, chmn. physics dept., 1975-78. Cons. to industry, 1958—; participant internat. seminars and confs.; mem. commn. on very low temperatures Internat. Union Pure and applied Physics, 1972-78; vis. Miller rsch. prof. U. Calif.-Berkeley, 1987; vis. prof. Technical Univ., Delft, The Netherlands, 1993. Author: Group Theory and Quantum Mechanics, 1964, Superconductivity, 1965, Introduction to Superconductivity, 1975, 2d edit., 1996; contbr. articles to profl. jours. Served USNR, 1945-46. Recipient award Alexander von Humboldt Found. U. Karlsruhe, W. Ger., 1978-79; NSF sr. postdoctoral fellow Cavendish lab.; vis. fellow Clare Hall Cambridge (Eng.) U., 1971-72; Guggenheim fellow, 1963-64 Fellow Am. Phys. Soc. (chmn. div. solid state physics 1966-67, Buckley prize 1974, Richtmyer lectr. 1977), AAAS; mem. Am. Acad. Arts and Scis., Nat. Acad. Scis. Home: 98 Rutledge Rd Belmont MA 02478-2633 Office: Harvard Univ Physics Dept Lyman Lab of Physics 326 Cambridge MA 02138 E-mail: tinkham@RSJ.harvard.edu.

TINKLEPAUGH, WILLIAM C. food products executive; With fgn. agrl. svc. USDA; pres., CEO Master Dairies, Inc., 1995—2000; sr. v.p. govt. industry rels. Suiza Foods, 2000—01, Dean Foods, Dallas, 2002—. Mem.: Internat. Dairy Foods Assn. (v.p., dir.). Office: Dean Foods Co 2515 McKinney Ave Ste 1200 Dallas TX 75201-1945

TINNER, FRANZISKA PAULA, social worker, artist, apparel designer, educator, entrepreneur; b. Zurich, Switzerland, Sept. 18, 1944; arrived in U.S., 1968; d. Siegfried Albin and Gertrude Emilie (Sigg) Maier; m. Rolf Christian Tinner, Dec. 19, 1976; 1 child, Eric Francis. Student, U. Del., 1973-74, Va. Commonwealth U., 1974; BFA, U. Tenn., 1984; BA of Arts, U. Ark., Little Rock, 1991, postgrad. Lic. real estate broker. Dominican nun, Ilanz, Switzerland, 1961-67; waitress London, 1967-68; governess Bryn Mawr, Pa., 1969; saleswoman, 1970-90; model, 1983; artist, designer Made For You, Kerrville, Tex. and Milw., 1984-90; realtor Century 21, Milw., 1987-91; owner, entrepreneur Exquisite Treasures by Swiss Miss, 1998—. Intern Birch Community Ctr., 1992-93. Designer softsculptor doll Texas Cactus Blossom, 1984; author: (poems) The Gang (recorded by Nat. Libr. of Poetry), 1996, Cry Out for Help, 1998 (pres. choice award 1999), Springtime, 2000 (contest finalist). Ombudsman Action 10 Consumerline, Knoxville, Tenn., 1983—84; foster mother Powhatan, Va., 1976—81; vol. ARC, Knoxville, 1979; Va. Home for Permanently Disabled, 1975; vol., counselor Youth ofr Understanding-Fgn. Exch., Powhatan, 1975—77; tchr. pager/archiving host, mentor, area expert on Am. On Line, 1992—98; vol. Interactive Ednl. Svc., Ark., 1999—; vol. infant intensive care Ark. Children's Hosp., 1999—; vol. Online Internet Emotional/Psych Support BB (WWW), 1999—. Recipient Art Display award U. Knoxville, 1983, Prof. Choice of Yr. award, 1983, Outstanding Achievemnt award TV Channel 10, Knoxville, 1984, 1st place award for paintings and crafts State Fair Va., Tenn., 1st place award Nat. Dollmakers, 1985, finalist Best of Coll. Photography, 1991, Achievement award Coll. Scholar af Am., 1991, Achievement cert. in technique of anger therapy, 1993, Achievement cert. in crisis response team tng., 1994, Achievement cert. vol. work tchg. AOL. Mem. NASW, NAFE, Milw. Bd. Realtors,

Homemakers Club (pres. 1979-80), Newcomers Club, Bowlers Club (v.p.), Internat. Platform Assn. Avocations: art, cooking, teaching, writing, helping disabled and mentally ill. E-mail: elfqueenz@aol.com.

TINNEY, DIANE LINDA, publishing executive; b. Phila., Feb. 6, 1960; d. James Joseph and Roberta Molly Tinney; m. James Dixon Keene, Oct. 11, 1987; 1 child, David Zachary Keene. BS in Bus., Drexel U., 1983. Tax analyst Goldenberg, Rosenthal, LLP, Phila., 1979—83, IMS Internat., Blue Bell, Pa., 1983—84; sr. mgr. KPMG Peat Marwick, LLP, N.Y.C., 1984—90; owner, cons. Software Profl., Warwick, NY, 1990—2002; exec. dir. Assn. Computers and Taxation, Warwick, 1990—2002; pres. Moo Press, Inc., Warwick, 2002—. Bd. dirs., v.p. Warwick Valley PC Users Group, Warwick, 1995—2000; bd. dirs., treas., v.p. Temple Beth Shalom, Florida, NY, 1995—2004. Recipient scholarship program in her honor, Assn. for Computers and Taxation. Mem.: Pub. Mktg. Assn., Assn. of Am. Pub., Warwick Valley C. of C. Avocations: reading, skiing, boating, hiking, gardening. Office: Moo Press INc 6 High St 2d Fl Warwick NY 10990 Office Phone: 845-987-7750. Office Fax: 845-987-7845. Business E-Mail: dtinney@moopress.com.

TINNEY, HARLE HOPE HANSON, museum administrator, owner; b. Providence, Apr. 15, 1941; d. Frederick Charles and Grace Alma (Williamson) Hanson; m. Donald Harold Tinney, Dec. 2, 1960. Student, Albion Coll., 1959—60, Brown U., 1960. Tour guide Belcourt Castle, Newport, RI, 1959-60, mus. ptnr., owner, 1972—; stained glass crafter St. Luke Studio, Providence, 1961-89; exec. dir. Royal Arts Found. at Belcourt Castle, Newport, 2000—. Sec. founder Royal Arts Found., Newport, 1969—, events planner, 1984—, treas., 1996—; donor svcs. Mosaic Club, Newport, 1984-2000, Shake-A-Leg, Newport, 1980-1989, Newport Music Festival, 1964—; ch. organist St. Declan Chapel, 1998-2001. Mem. Sovereign Order Knights Hospitaller St. John Jerusalem (asst. editor newsletter 1998—), Royal Arts Found. (exec. dir. 2002-). Avocations: music, cello, church organ, antique restoration. Home: Belcourt Castle 657 Bellevue Ave Newport RI 02840-4280 Office Phone: 401-846-0669.

TINNIN, ROBERT PRIEST, JR., lawyer; b. Albuquerque, N.Mex., Aug. 15, 1939; s. Robert Priest and Frances Lee (Ferree) Tinnin; m. Carol Culbertson, Aug. 20, 1962 (div. 1975); 1 child, Joshua Robert; m. Marianne Hill Tinnin, July 23, 1976. BA, U. N.Mex., 1961; JD, Ind. U., 1964. Bar: N. Mex. 1964, US Dist. Ct./N.Mex. 1964, US Ct. Appeals (11th cir.) 1978, US Ct. Appeals (10th cir.) 1964, US Supreme Ct. Law clk., pres. justice US Ct. Appeals (10th cir.), Denver, 1964—65; ptnr. Poole, Tinnin & Martin PC, Albuquerque, 1965—, dir. Mem.: Albuquerque Bar Assn. (bd. dir. 1977—79), N. Mex. Bar Found. (pres. 1986—, bd. dir. 1984—), State Bd. of N. Mex. (bd. bar commissions 1980—85), ABA, Bernalillo County Labor Develop. Bd. (mem. 1980), Albuquerque Country (bd. dir. 1981—84). Democrat. Office: Poole Tinnin & Martin PO Box 1769 Albuquerque NM 87103-1769

TINNING, HERBERT PETER, association executive; b. Hoboken, N.J., Apr. 17, 1928; s. Peter Christian and Emmy Asta (Andersen) T.; divorced; children: Christian, Kirsten; m. Adeline Augusta Falk, Aug. 13, 1990. Degree in mech. engring., Stevens Inst. Tech., 1952. Engr. Good Housekeeping Inst., N.Y.C., 1954-56; dir. membership and sects. Am. Soc. Refrigerating Engrs., N.Y.C., 1956-58; application and sales engr. Dunham Bush Inc., N.Y.C., 1958-61; dir. tech. svcs. ASHRAE, N.Y.C., 1961-69; asst. tech. dir. Assn. Home Appliance Mfrs., Chgo., 1969-71; regional coord., dir. socioecon. program Nat. Assn. Accts., N.Y.C., 1972-77; adminstrv. exec. Compressed Gas Assn., N.Y.C., 1977-79; group dir., tech. affairs ASME, N.Y.C., 1980-93; exec. dir. Devils Foot Soc., Millburn, N.J., 1982—. Chmn. heating, refrigeration and air conditioning stds. bd. Am. Nat. Stds. Inst., N.Y.C., 1968-69; presenter in field. Contbr. articles to various publs. Mem. current affairs com. Berkeley Square Civic Assn., Arlington Heights, Ill., 1969-72; mem. pub. rels. and bylaws coms. Citizens Adv. Com., Arlington Heights, 1969-71; mem. mayor's action com. on drugs Village of Arlington Heights, 1970-71; mem. devel. com. Twp. of Weehawken, N.J., 1978-81; chmn. Brotherhood of St. Andrew, Arlington Heights, 1970-72; trustee Seabury-Western Theol. Sem., Evanston, Ill., 1972-75; deacon Episcopal Ch., 1974; fund capt. Stevens Inst. Tech., Hoboken, 1982-87. Recipient award of excellence U.S. Dept. Commerce, 1977. Mem. Am. Soc. Assn. Execs. (life, cert.), N.Y. Soc. Assn. Execs. (life, chmn. awards com., mem. human resources com.), Palisades Nature Assn. (life), Baker Street Irregulars (Horace Harker award 1973), Sherlock Holmes Soc. London, Priory Scholars (hon.), Millburn Old Guard (citation 1995). Avocations: sherlockian studies, gardening, natural history, reading. Home and Office: 93 Sagamore Rd Millburn NJ 07041-2154

TINSLEY, ADRIAN, college president; b. N.Y.C., July 6, 1937; d. Theodore A. and Mary Ethel (White) Tinsley. AB, Bryn Mawr Coll., 1958; MA, U. Wash., 1962; PhD, Cornell U., 1969. Asst. prof. English U. Md., College Park, 1968-72; dean William James Coll., Grand Valley State, Allendale, Mich., 1972-80; assoc. vice chancellor acad. affairs Minn. State U., St. Paul, 1982-85; exec. v.p., provost Glassboro (N.J.) State Coll., 1985-89; pres. Bridgewater (Mass.) State Coll., 1989—2002, pres. emerita, 2002—. Coord. women higher edn. adminstrn. Bryn Mawr & Hers Summer Inst., Bryn Mawr, Pa., 1977—. Editor: Women in Higher Education Administration, 1984. Office: Boyden Hall Bridgewater State Coll Bridgewater MA 02325-0001 Office Phone: 508-697-9656. Business E-Mail: atinsley@bridgew.edu.

TINSLEY, BOYD CALVIN, musician; b. Charlottesville, Va., May 16, 1964; s. George Franklin and Helen Carter Tinsley. Degree in History, U. Va.; studied violin with Isadore Saslav. Mem. Boyd Tinsley Band formerly Down Boy Down, 1987—92; mem. (violinist) Dave Matthews Band, 1992—. Musician (violinist with Dave Matthews Band): (albums) Remember Two Things, 1993, Crash, 1996, Live at Red Rocks 8.15.95, 1996, Before These Crowded Streets, 1998, Don't Drink the Water, 1998, Everyday, 2001, Busted Stuff, 2002, Central Park Concert, 2003, Gorge, 2004; musician: (violinist solo) True Reflections, 2003; musician: (violinst) Autopilot, The Samples, 1994, Kickin' & Screamin', Allgood, 1994, Best of Columbia Records Radio Hour, Vol. 2, Various Artists, 1996, Live on Letterman: Music from the Late Show, Various Artists, 1997, Scream 2 Original Soundtrack, 1997, Musical Chairs, Hootie & The Blowfish, 1998, Turnpike Diaries, The Getaway People, 2000, Return to Earth, The Samples, 2001, Wire, Third Day, 2004. Recipient (with Dave Matthews Band) Grammy award for Best Rock Performance by a Duo or Group with Vocal for So Much to Say, 1996, Chmns. award, NAACP Image Awards, 2004. Office: RCA Records 1540 Broadway New York NY 10036*

TINSLEY, JACKSON BENNETT, newspaper editor; b. Ewing, Tex., Dec. 14, 1934; s. Henry Bine and Sallie Alberta (Jackson) T.; m. Claudia Anne Miller, Oct. 3, 1965; children: Ben, Anna. BS, Sam Houston State U., 1958. Editor Diboll News-Bull., 1953-54, Corrigan Times, 1954; reporter Lufkin News, 1952, 56; news editor Port Lavaca Wave, 1955; mem. staff Ft. Worth Star-Telegram, 1959—60, 1962—2000, Sunday editor, 1967-71, asst. mng. editor, 1971-74, asst. to editor, 1974-75, exec. editor, 1975-82, v.p., exec. editor, 1982-86, v.p., editor, 1986-90, sr. v.p., editor, chmn., 1990—; info. asst. S.W. Bell Telephone Co., 1960-62. Part time instr., editor Tex. Christian U., 1971-72 Com. chmn. United Way Tarrant County, 1970-87, gen. chmn. Tex. Gridiron Show, 1981, 93-95; bd. dirs. Safety Coun. Ft. Worth, 1975-80; pres., bd. dirs. Parenting Guidance Ctr., 1989-90. 2d lt. U.S. Army, 1959. Recipient Nat. Writing award Edn. Writers Assn., 1965, citation Tex. Conf. AAUP, 1965; named Disting. Alumnus, Sam Houston State U., 1984; named to C.E. Shuford Journalism Hall of Honor, U. North Tex., 1987, his bust in U. Tex. Wall of Honor; established Jack B. Tinsley/Fort Worth Star Telegram endowed journalism scholarship. Mem. Soc. Profl. Journalists (pres. Ft. Worth chpt. 1991-92, chmn. journalism adv. com. U. North Tex. and Sam Houston State U. 1988-93), Am. Soc. Newspapers Editors, AP Mng. Editors Assn., Tex. AP Mng. Editors Assn. (pres. 1979-80), Press Club Ft. Worth (pres. 1970-71), Colonial Country Club, Ft. Worth Club, Rotary (v.p. Ft. Worth 1981, pres. 1983-84). Home: 3550 Wind River Ct Fort Worth TX 76116-9329 Office: Ft Worth Star-Telegram 400 W 7th St Fort Worth TX 76102-4793 E-mail: tinsley@star-telegram.com.

TINSLEY, NIKKI LEE, federal agency administrator; b. Apr. 23, 1948; BS in Bus. Admistrn., Ohio State U./Va. Commonwealth U., 1970; MS in Bus. Admistrn., U. Colo./U. No. Colo., 1981. Ednl. program asst. Office of Edn., Wash., 1971; bookstore mgr. U.S. Govt. Printing Office, Denver, 1971-76; auditor U.S. GAO, Denver, 1976-82; supervisory auditor Dept. of Interior, Minerals Mgmt. Svc., Lakewood, Colo., 1982-90; divsnl. insp. gen. EPA, Kansas City, Kans., 1990—95, dep. insp. gen. Washington, 1995-96, acting insp. gen., 1997-98, insp. gen., 1998—. Chair human resources com. Pres.'s Coun. on Integrity and Efficiency, 2002—04; mem. Adv. Coun. on Gobt. Auditing Stds., Comptroller Gen.'s Domestic Working Group. Recipient Bronze medal for commendable svc. EPA, 1995. Mem.: Colo. Soc. CPAs, Inst. Internal Auditors, Assn. Govt. Accts. (Disting. Fed. Leadership award 2004). Office: EPA MC 2410 1200 Pennsylvania Ave NW Washington DC 20460-0001

TINSMAN, MARGARET NEIR, state legislator; b. Moline, Ill., July 14, 1936; d. Francis Earl and Elizabeth (Lourie) Neir; m. Robert Hovey Tinsman Jr., Feb. 21, 1959; children: Robert Hovey III, Heidi Elizabeth, Bruce MacAlister. BA in Sociology, U. Colo., 1958; MSW, U. Iowa, 1974. Health care coord. Community Health Care, Inc., Davenport, Iowa, 1975-77; assoc. dir. Scott County Info., Referal, and Assistance Svc., Davenport, Iowa, 1977-79; county supr. Scott County Bd. Suprs., Davenport, Iowa, 1978-89; mem. Iowa Senate from 21st dist., Des Moines, 1989—, asst. minority leader, 1992—96, chmn. health and human svcs. appropriations subcom. Chair Iowa Adv. Commn. on Inter-govt. Rels., 1982—84; U.S. country rep. to the German-Am. Symposium German Marshall Plan, 1983; commr. Iowa Dept. Elder Affairs, Des Moines, 1983—89. Chair planning com. Quad City United Way, Davenport; bd. dirs. Bi-State Met. Planning Commn., Davenport, 1981-89, Quad City Devel. Group, Davenport, 1988-90, Am. Lung Assn. Ill., Iowa, Goodwill Industries S.E. Iowa; mem. structure commn. Nat. Episcopal Ch. Named Iowa Social Worker of Yr., NASW, 1978. Mem. Am. Lung Assn. of Ill.-Iowa (bd. dirs. 1989—), Davenport C. of C. (local/state govt. com. 1989—), Nat. Assn. Legislators, Nat. Assn. of Counties (bd. dirs. 1984-89, pres. Women Ofcl. 1984-89), Iowa State Assn. of Counties (bd. dirs. 1983-89, chair), Jr. League (sustaining mem. 1989), Vol. Action Ctr. (pres. 1989), Phi Beta Kappa. Republican. Avocations: tennis, golf, sailing, water and snow skiing. Home: 2865 Hickory Hill Ln Bettendorf IA 52722 Office: 3541 E Kimberly Rd Davenport IA 52807-2552 Office Phone: 563-359-3624.

TINSTMAN, DALE CLINTON, food products company consultant; b. Chester, Nebr., May 19, 1919; s. Clinton Lewis and Elizabeth Golashin (Gretzinger) T.; m. Jean Sundell, Oct. 1, 1942; children: Thomas C., Nancy Tinstman Remington, Jane C. Tinstman Kramer. BS, U. Nebr., 1941, JD, 1947. Bar: Nebr. 1947. Asst. sec., asst. mgr. investment dept. First Trust Co., Lincoln, Nebr., 1947-48; v.p., asst. treas. Securities Acceptance Corp., Omaha; fin. v.p., treas. Ctrl. Nat. Ins. Group, Omaha, 1958-60; pres., treas. Tinstman & Co., Inc., Lincoln, 1960-61; exec. v.p. First Med Am., Inc., Lincoln, 1961-68, pres., 1968-74, fin. cons., 1974—; pres., dir. Iowa Beef Processors, Inc., 1976-77, vice chmn., 1977-82, co-chmn., 1982-83, dir., cons., 1983—; chmn., dir. Eaton Tinstman Druliner, Inc., 1983—2000. Bd. dirs. IBP, Inc.; past chmn. Nebr. Investment Coun. Trustee, chmn. U. Nebr. Found.; trustee Lincoln Found., Nebr. Coun. Econ. Edn. Served with USAAF World War II, Korea; to col. Nebr. Air N.G. Mem. Nebr. Bar Assn., Nebr. Diplomats, Newcomen Soc. N.Am., Am. Legion, Nebr. State C. of C., Firethorn Country Club, Alpha Sigma Phi, Phi Delta Phi. Republican. Presbyterian (elder). Home and Office: 3500 Faulkner Dr B206 Lincoln NE 68516-6638

TINSTMAN, ROBERT ALLEN, former construction company executive; BS, Mining Engring., Univ. Wisconsin, Platteville, 1968. Underground engr. Reynolds Mining Corp., Bauxite, Ark., 1966-68, stripping engr., 1968-71, asst. mine superintendant, 1971-73; sr. mine engr. Texasgulf, Aurora, N.C., 1973-74, Morrison Knudsen Corp., Boise, Idaho, 1974-75, asst. mgr., mining engr., 1975-77, dir. mining engring., 1977-79, v.p., gen. mgr. mining engring., 1979-85; exec. v.p. Morrison Knudsen Engineers, Inc., Boise, Idaho, 1985-88, pres., 1988-89; pres. mining group Morrison Knudsen Co., Inc., Boise, Idaho, 1989-95; pres. CEO Morrison Knudsen Corp., Boise, Idaho, 1995-99; pres. Tinstman and Assoc., 1999—. Exec. comm. mem. Morrison Knudsen bd. dirs.; mng. dir. MK Peru; dir., Centennial Engring. Inc.; dir. Natl. Projects Inc.; bd. dirs. Home Fed., Ida Corp., Home Fed.; chmn. bd. Contractorhub.com. Bd. dirs. St. Lukes. Mem. Natl. Soc. of Professional Engrs., Soc. of Mining Engrs.

TINTLE, CARMEL JOSEPH, public relations executive; b. Paterson, N.J., Sept. 25, 1924; s. Herbert J. and Agnes (Merna) T.; m. Alice M. Hayes, Sept. 1, 1948; children: Joseph, Alice Maureen. BS, Fordham U., 1951; postgrad., NYU. Editl. asst. Newsweek mag., N.Y.C., 1946-50; news editor Beverage Retailer Weekly, N.Y.C., 1950-52; city editor Paterson Sunday Eagle, 1950-52; staff writer Carl Byoir & Assocs., Inc., N.Y.C., 1952-59, asst. account exec., 1959-64, assoc. account exec., 1964; account supr. Grey Pub. Rels., Inc., N.Y.C., 1964; v.p. Schenley Affiliated Brands Corp., subs. Schenley Industries, N.Y.C., 1964-72, sr. v.p., 1972-74; v.p. corp. affairs Am. Distilling Co., 1974—80; v.p. Banfi Vintners, Old Brookville, NY, 1980—90; CEO Vinum Comm., Inc., Old Brookville, 1980-90; cons. corp. comm. Banfi Vinters, Old Brookville, 1990—2002. Publicity dir., Jumby Bay Island, a Banfi resort property, Antigua, 1985-95. Vol. publicist Assumption Coll. Sis., Mendham, N.J., 2001—. Ensign U.S. Maritime Svc., 1943-46. Mem. N.Y. Press Club, SAR, KC, St. Patrick Guard of Honor N.J., U.S. Mcht. Marine Vets., Irish-Am. Cultural Inst., Fordham Univ.'s Golden Rams. Home: 14 Potter Ct Montclair NJ 07043-1514

TINTURIN, PETER, composer; b. Ekaterinoslav, Russia, June 1, 1910; arrived in U.S., 1929, naturalized; s. Leonid and Elizabeth Tinturin; m. Wela Davies (dec.); children: Leonid, Glenn. Student, Vienna Conservatory Music, 1924—29; BA, U. Vienna, 1929; MusB summa cum laude, Chapman U., 1953. Pvt. U.S. Army, 1943—44. Mem.: ASCAP (award for outstanding compositions 1934, 1937, 1941). Home: 464 26th St Santa Monica CA 90402-3106

TIO, ADRIAN RICARDO, artist, art educator; b. Ft. Wayne, Ind., Jan. 13, 1951; BA, Temple U., Phila., 1974; student, Tyler Sch. Art, Rome, 1975-76; MFA, U. Cin., 1979. Founds. coord. Sch. Art Bowling Green (Ohio) State U., 1979-87, drawing head, 1989-94, assoc. dir., 1991-94, assoc. dean arts and scis., 1994-96; chair dept. art Ind. State U., Terre Haute, 1996-2000; dir. sch. art No. Ill. U., Dekalb, 2000—. Cons. for migrant edn. Pa. Dept. Edn., Harrisburg, 1986-87; grant reviewer pub. artworks Ohio Arts Coun., Columbus, 1995-2000, artists/orgn. grants Arts Commn. Greater Toledo, Ohio, 1995-96. Represented in permanent collections Afro-Am. Mus. and Cultural Ctr., Chgo., Andy Warhol Found. Visual Arts, N.Y.C., Elvehejm Mus., U. Wis., Madison, Nat. Endowment for Arts, Washington, Ohio Arts Coun., Columbus, Rockefeller Found., N.Y.C., Toledo Mus. Art, White House, Washington, U. Cin., Villa Taverna Found., Washington, others, also pvt. collections. Bd. mem. Arts Illiana, Terre Haute, 1997-2000, Arts Commn. Greater Toledo, 1995-96. Recipient award new Partnerships for Artists, Arts Midwest/Nat. Endowment Arts, Mpls., 1990, new forms regional grant Nat. Endowment Arts, Chgo., 1992, individual artists fellowship Ohio Arts Coun., Columbus, 1994, Arts Endowment award Ind. State U., Terre Haute, 1997, Individual Artists grant Ind. Arts. Commn., 2000. Mem. Coll. Art Assn., Nat. Coun. Arts Adminstrs., Founds. in Art, Edn. and Theory (pres. 1984-86, editor 1982-86), Chgo. Artists Coalition, Chgo. Hand Bookbinders, Coll. Art Assn., Mid-Am. Print Coun., Mid-Am. Coll. Art Assn. Office: No Ill U Sch Art AB 216 Dekalb IL 60115-2854 Office Phone: 815-753-7850. Business E-Mail: artio@niu.edu.

TIPLER, FRANK JENNINGS, III, physicist; b. Andalusia, Ala., Feb. 1, 1947; s. Frank Jennings Jr. and Anne (Kearley) T.; m. Jolanta Rokicka; children: Allison Anne, Caroline Nicole. S.B., MIT, 1969; PhD, U. Md., 1976. Rsch. mathematician U. Calif., Berkeley, 1976-79; sr. rsch. fellow Oxford (Eng.) U., 1979; rsch. assoc. U. Tex., Austin, 1979-81; assoc. prof. physics and math. Tulane U., New Orleans, 1981-87, prof., 1987—. Vis. sr. scientist Max-Planck Inst. Astrophysics, Munich, 1987; vis. fellow U. Sussex, Brighton, Eng., 1987; vis. prof. Inst. Astrophysics, Liege, Belgium, 1988, U. Bern, Switzerland, 1988, U. Vienna, Austria, 1992. Author: l'Homme et le Cosmos, 1984, The Anthropic Cosmological Principle, 1986, The Physics of Immortality, 1994; editor: Essays in General Relativity, 1980; contbr. articles to profl. jour. Rsch. grantee NSF, 1984, 86. Libertarian. Business E-Mail: tipler@tulane.edu.

TIPPENS, DARRYL LEE, literature educator, writer; b. Elk City, Okla., May 30, 1947; s. Thomas E. and Patsy J. (Morgan) T.; m. Anne H. Bentley, Sept. 15, 1967; children: Timothy K., Jeffrey M. BA, Okla. Christian U., 1968; MA, La. State U., 1971, PhD, 1973. Asst. prof. Okla. Christian U., Okla. City, 1974-77, assoc. prof., 1978-83, prof., 1983-87, Abilene (Tex.) Christian U., 1987-2000; provost Pepperdine U., Malibu, Calif., 2001—. Vis. prof. Baylor U., Waco, Tex., 1982, Pepperdine U., Malibu, Calif., 1996. Editor: (book) Shadow and Light: Literature and the Life of Faith, 1997; assoc. editor Explorations in Renaissance Culture, 1995—; contbr. articles to literary jours. Faculty sponsor Amnesty Internat., Abilene (Tex.) Christian U., 1989—, Young Dems., 1996—. Named Grad. Prof. of Yr. Abilene Christian U., 1994, James W. Culp Disting. Prof., 1996-2000, Alumnus of Yr., Okla. Christian U., 1997. Mem. Conf. on Christianity and Lit. (treas. 1994—, bd. dirs.), Milton Soc. Am. (life), S. Ctrl. Renaissance Conf. (pres.). Democrat. Mem. Ch. of Christ. Office: Pepperdine U Provost's Office 24255 Pacific Coast Hwy Malibu CA 90263 E-mail: dltippens@aol.com.

TIPPING, WILLIAM MALCOLM, social services administrator; b. Oak Park, Ill., Mar. 31, 1931; s. William McKinley and Evelyn Amelia (Freier) T.; m. Lois A. Grife, Sept. 18, 1954 (dec. May 1986); children: William, Barbara, Robert; m. Babette J. Cumming, Oct. 10, 1987; children: Christopher Cumming, Courtney Barone. BA, Carleton Coll., Northfield, Minn., 1954. Sales rep. Gen. Mills, Inc., Mpls., 1954-56; account exec. Campbell Mithun, Inc., Mpls., 1956-63, v.p. mgmt., supr. Mpls. and Chgo., 1965-76; account supr., v.p. Lennen & Newell, Inc., N.Y.C., 1963-65; ptnr., mgr. Heidrick & Struggles, Inc., Chgo., 1976-88; exec. v.p., chief exec. officer Am. Cancer Soc., Atlanta, 1988-91; pres. Tipping and McRae, Inc., Atlanta, 1991-93; mng. dir. Ward Howell Internat., Inc., Atlanta, 1993-97. Trustee Carleton Coll., 1986-90; bd. dirs. Nat. Health Coun., N.Y.C., Ga. Conservancy, Families First; mem. fin. com. UICC, Geneva, 1990-91. Recipient Disting. Svc. award Carleton Coll., 1984. Mem. Capital City Club (Atlanta), Quechee (Vt.) Club, Comerce Club (Atlanta). Republican. Episcopalian.

TIPSON, BAIRD See TIPSON, LYNN

TIPSON, LYNN BAIRD (BAIRD TIPSON), academic administrator, religion educator; b. Plainfield, N.J., Oct. 22, 1943; s. Lynn Baird Sr. and Yvonne (Gaston) T.; m. Sarah Oden, May 16, 1970; children: David, Elizabeth. AB, Princeton U., 1965; M in philosophy, Yale U., 1969, PhD in religious studies, 1972. Asst. prof. religious studies U. Va., Charlottesville, 1970-76; asst. prof. religion Cen. Mich. U., Mt. Pleasant, 1976-77, assoc. prof., acting chair, 1977-78, assoc. prof., acting asst. dean Sch. Arts and Scis., 1978-81, assoc. dean Coll. Arts and Scis., 1981-87; provost, prof. religion Gettysburg (Pa.) Coll., 1987—95, acting pres., fall 1988; pres. Wittenberg U., Springfield, Ohio, 1995—2004, Washington Coll., Chestertown, Md., 2004—. Pres. North Coast Athletic Conf. Contbr. articles to profl. jours., dictionaries, and encys. Pres., bd. dirs. Springfield Symphony Orch. Fulbright-Hays fellow, 1965-66, Woodrow Wilson fellow, 1966-67, Rockefeller Dissertation fellow, 1969-70, NEH summer seminar grantee, 1977. Mem. Am. Soc. Ch. History (presented paper at nat. conf. 1984), Hist. Soc. of Protestant Episcopal Ch., Inst. Early Am. History and Culture, Phi Beta Kappa. Lutheran. Office: Washington Coll 300 Washington Ave Chestertown MD 21620*

TIPSORD, MICHAEL L. insurance company executive; B in Acctg., Ill. Wesleyan U.; JD, U. Ill. CPA; CLU, CPCU. Former lawyer; with State Farm Ins. Cos., 1988—, v.p., asst. treas., 1998—2001, v.p., treas., 2001—02, sr. v.p., CFO, 2002—. Office: State Farm Ins Cos 1 State Farm Plz Bloomington IL 61710-0001

TIPTON, CLYDE RAYMOND, JR., communications and resources development consultant; b. Cin., Nov. 13, 1921; s. Clyde Raymond and Ida Marie (Molitor) Tipton; m. Marian Gertrude Beushausen, Aug. 16, 1942 (dec. Aug. 2, 2000); children: Marian Page Ashley, Robert Bruce. BS, U. Ky., 1946, MS, 1947. Rsch. engr. Battelle Meml. Inst., Columbus, Ohio, 1947-49, sr. tech. adviser, 1951-62, coord. corp. comm., 1969-73, v.p. comm., 1973-75, asst. to pres., 1978-79, v.p., corp. dir. comm. and pub. affairs, 1979-86; staff mem. Los Alamos Sci. Lab., 1949-51; dir. research Basic, Inc., Bettsville, Ohio, 1962-64; asst. dir. Battelle Pacific N.W. Labs., Richland, Wash., 1964-69; pres., trustee Battelle Commons Co. for Cmty. Urban Redevel., Columbus, 1975-78; cons. bus. comm. and devel. Columbus, 1986—. Secretariat US del. 2d Internat. Conf. Peaceful Use Atomic Energy, Geneva, 1958; cons. U.S. AEC in Atoms for Peace Program, Tokyo, 1958, New Delhi, 1959—60, Rio de Janeiro, 1960. Author: (book) How to Change the World, 1982; editor: Jour. Soc. Nondestructive Testing, 1953—57, The Reactor Handbook, Reactor Materials, vol. 3, 1955, vol. 1, 1960, Learning to Live on a Small Planet, 1974. Past pres. Pilot Dogs, United Way Franklin County, Greater Columbus Arts Coun.; bd. dirs., treas. Pilot Guide Dog Found.; pres. emeritus Arhcs. Soc. Ohio Found.; trustee Episc. Retirement Homes, Inc. With USAAF, 1943. Named to U. Ky. Engring. Hall of Distinction, 1997; Haggin fellow, U. Ky., 1947, Sr. fellow, Otterbein Coll., 1978. Fellow: NSPE (past pres., Outstanding Svc. award 1992); mem.: Ohio Soc. Profl. Engr. (past pres., award of distinction, Uncommon Man award, Outstanding Svc. award 1993, 1998), Am. Soc. Metals, Torch Club Columbus, Lions, Sigma Xi, Alpha Chi Sigma. Episcopalian. Achievements include patents in field. Home and Office: 2218 Aschinger Blvd Columbus OH 43212-4620 Office Phone: 614-424-6077.

TIPTON, E. LINWOOD, trade association executive; b. Adrian, Mo., Nov. 19, 1934; s. Harlow Acklin and Mary Catherine (Lacy) T.; m. Marjorie A. Wolford, Dec. 17, 1955 (div. June 1983); children: Kelly A., Mark A.; m. Constance E. Eaton Broadstone, Oct. 8, 1983. BS in Agriculture, U. Mo., 1955, MS in Agriculture and Econs., 1956. Economist USDA Fgn. Agrl. Svc., Washington, 1956-57, Eastern Milk Prodrs., Syracuse, N.Y., 1960-62; exec. dir. Coop. Dairy Econ. Svc., Boston, 1962-65; v.p., exec. v.p., pres., chief exec. officer Internat. Dairy Foods Assn., Washington, 1965—. Founder Nat. Economist Club, Washington, treas., chmn. bd., 1967-73; founder Nat. Economist Ednl. Found., Washington, treas., chmn. bd., 1969-74; chmn. bd. Petlin, Inc., Washington; expert witness congl. coms., regulatory agencies; founder Internat. Sweetener Colloquium; apptd. to Nat. Commn. Agrl. Trade and Export Policy, 1984; advisor Sec. Agriculture, U.S. Trade Rep.; co-founder, chmn. bd. restaurant/motel chain, 1967—; chmn. The Food Group, The Ice Cream and Milk Polit. Action Com., Food Processors Steering Com. on Wage and Price Stability; elected to governance bd. dirs. Winn-Boll-Dann, Moscow, 2002. 1st lt. Army Fin. Corp., 1957-60. Recipient Citation of Merit U. Mo. Alumni Assn., 1988. Avocations: tennis, golf. Office: Internat Dairy Foods Assn 1250 H St NW Ste 900 Washington DC 20005-3952

TIPTON, GARY LEE, retired services company executive; b. Salem, Oreg., July 3, 1941; s. James Rains and Dorothy Velma (Dierks) Tipton. BS, Oreg. Coll. Edn., 1964. Credit rep. Std. Oil Co., Portland, Oreg., 1964—67; credit mgr. Uniroyal Inc., Dallas, 1967—68; ptnr., mgr. bus. Tipton Barbers, Portland, 1968—94; ret., 1994. Mem. U.S. Congl. adv. bd. Am. Security Coun., 1984—93; mem. steering com. Coun. on Fgn. Rels. Portland Com., 1983—84, chmn., 1984—86, mem. exec. com., 1988—90, bd. dirs., 1990—91; mem. Rep. Nat. Com., 1980—, Sen. Howard Baker's Presdl. Steering Com., 1980. Recipient World Culture prize, Accademia Italia, 1984, Presdl. Achievement award, 1982, Disting. Contbn. cert., Sunset H.S. Dad's Club, 1972, 1973, Cert. of Perfection award, Tualatin Valley Fire and Rescue Dist., 1994, Cert. of Recognition, Rep. Nat. Com., 2002, 2003, Cert. Appreciation, 2004. Fellow: Internat. Biog. Assn. (life; dep. dir. gen. 1987—, Key award, U.K. 1983); mem.: Sunset Mchts. Assn. (co-founder, treas. 1974—79, pres. 1982—83), World Affairs Coun. of Oreg., UN Assn. (steering com. UN day 1985), Internat. Platform Assn., Smithsonian Assocs., Portland Downtown Lions Club, City Club of Portland.

TIPTON, KENNETH WARREN, agricultural administrator, researcher; b. Belleville, Ill., Nov. 14, 1932; s. Roscoe Roy and Martha Pearl (Davis) T.; m. Barbara Adds, Mar. 2, 1957; children: Kenneth Warren Jr., Nancy Tipton O'Neal. BS, La. State U., 1955, MS, 1959; PhD, Miss. State U., 1969. Asst. prof. Agrl. Ctr., La. State U., Baton Rouge, 1959-70, assoc. prof., 1970-75, prof., 1975—, supt. Red River Rsch. Sta., La. Agrl. Expt. Sta. Bossier City, 1975-79, assoc. dir. La. Agrl. Expt. Sta. Baton Rouge, 1979-89, dir. La. Agrl. Expt. Sta., vice chancellor, 1989-96, vice chancellor, dir. emeritus, 1996—. Mem. com. nine USDA/Coop. State Rsch. Svc., 1986-88; Expt. State Com. Orgn. Policy, 1988-91. Contbr. articles to Agronomy Jour., Jour. Econ. Entomology, Grain Sorghum Conf. Coach baseball program Am. Legion, 1969-74; scoutmaster Boy Scouts Am., Baton Rouge, 1970-75. Capt. USAF, 1955-58. Mem. Am. Soc. Agronomy, Crop Sci. Soc. Am., Coun. Agrl. Sci. Tech. Achievements include research on inheritance of fiber traits in cotton, resistance of grain sorghum hybrids to bird damage, tannin content of grain sorghum and effects of phosphorus on growth of sorghum. Home: 732 Baird Dr Baton Rouge LA 70808-5916 Personal E-mail: barkentip@aol.com.

TIPTON, MARGARET ANN, religious organization administrator, writer; b. Covington, Tenn., Sept. 25, 1937; d. Hurtell Tipton and Jennie Anna Williams; 1 child, Cheryl Ann Brown-Dunbar. BA, Trinity Coll., Deerfield, Ill., 1985; postgrad., Moody Grad. Sch., Chgo., 1996. Underwriter Motors Ins. Corp., Chgo., 1963—70; youth coord. Monument of Faith Ch., Chgo., 1964—70, pres. personal evang. ministry, 1964—; pres., founder Effectual Door Bible Coll., Chgo., 1982—; editor, writer Beautiful for Him mag., Chgo., 1986—92; Christian edn. dir. Hope Tabernacle Ch., Chgo., 1988—91; pres., founder Jennie Williams Davis Found., Chgo., 2001—. Author: Personal Evangelism, 1 5, 1989, Mission, 2004, Most Misinterpreted Biblical Truths, 2004; host (cable TV program) The Margaret Tipton Show, Effectual Door Bible Coll. Radio Program, host (radio program) The EDBC Radio Teacher's Forum, 1985. Sec. Beat 322 Chgo. Alternative Policing Strategy Chgo. Police Dept., 1999—; pres. Bapt. Midwest Youth Conf., 1961—64; class leader Moody Bible Inst. Sch. Recipient Outstanding Svc. award, Midwest Youth Conf., 1982, Outstanding Cmty. Svc. award, Chgo. Police Dept., 2001. Mem.: NAACP, Nat. Black Evangel. Assn., Evangel. Tng. Assn., Nat. Urban League. Office: Effectual Door Bible Coll PO Box 20350 Chicago IL 60620 Office Phone: 773-487-7454.

TIPTON, SHEILA KAY, lawyer; b. Martins Ferry, Ohio, Aug. 4, 1951; d. Donald Duane and Elizabeth Julia T.; m. Orrin Frink, Nov. 2, 1973 (div.); m. William Llewellyn Dawe III, Dec. 6, 1985; children: Nicholas Albert, Alexander McNeill; stepchildren: William Llewellyn IV, Christopher Michael. BS, Ohio U., 1973; JD, Drake U., 1980. Bar: Iowa 1980, U.S. Dist. Ct. (no. and so. dists.) Iowa 1980, U.S. Ct. Appeals (8th cir.) 1980. Assoc. Bradshaw, Fowler, Proctor & Fairgrave, P.C., Des Moines, Iowa, 1980-85; ptnr., shareholder Bradshaw, Fowler, Proctor & Fairgrave, Des Moines, Iowa, 1985-99; ptnr. Dorsey & Whitney LLP, 1999—. Presenter in field. Contbr. articles to profl. jours. Pres. Polk County Legal Aid Soc., 1991-92; bd. dirs. Youth Home Mid-Am., 1990-97, sec., 1994-96, v.p., 1996-97; bd. dirs. des Moines Metro Opera Found., 1993-98, pres., 1997-98; bd. dirs. Des Moines Metro Opera, 1991—, v.p. devel., 1994-95, pres.-elect, 1995-96, pres., 1996-97, v.p. long range planning com., 1998-99; bd. counselors Drake U. Law Sch., 1996-98, 2003—. Recipient State of Iowa Govs. Vol. award, 1996. Mem. Iowa State Bar Assn. (adminstrv. law sect. coun. 1989-91, mem. bus. law sect. coun. 1993-97, co-chmn. quality life task force 1993-96, chair internat. trade com. 1992-94), Rotary (chmn. scholar com. 1994-95, bd. dirs. 1996-2003, sgt.-at-arms, 1997-98, sec.-treas. 1998-99, v.p. 1999-2000, pres.-elect 2000-01, pres. 2001-02). Avocations: opera, cooking, reading, golf, travel. Home: 13074 Lincoln Ave Des Moines IA 50325-7413 Office: Dorsey & Whitney LLP 801 Grand Ave Ste 3900 Des Moines IA 50309-2790 E-mail: tipton.sheila@dorsey.com., sheilatipton@mchsi.com.

TIRANA, BARDYL RIFAT, lawyer; b. Geneva, Dec. 16, 1937; s. Rifat and Rosamond English (Walling) T.; m. Anne Prather, June 22, 1985; children by previous marriage: Kyra, Amina. AB, Princeton U., 1959; LL.B., Columbia U., 1962. Bar: D.C. 1962, Md. 1986, N.Y. 1986, Va. 1986, Pa. 1992. Trial atty. Dept. Justice, 1962-64; assoc. Amram, Hahn & Sundlun, Washington, 1965-68, ptnr., 1969-72; dir., sec. Exec. Jet Aviation, Inc., Columbus, Ohio, 1970-77, Technics, Inc., Alexandria, Va., 1971-77; ptnr. Sundlun, Tirana & Scher, Washington, 1972-77; dir. def. civil preparedness agy. Dept. Def., Washington, 1977-79, mem. armed forces policy coun., 1977-79; chmn. bd. Technics, Inc., San Jose, Calif., 1979-85; of counsel Silverstein and Mullens, Washington, 1982-84, ptnr., 1984-90; pvt. practice law Washington, 1991—. Mem.-at-large D.C. Bd. Edn., 1970-74; trustee Jimmy Carter Inaugural Trust, Washington, 1977-87; co-chmn. 1977 Presdl. Inaugural Com., 1976-77; mem. exec. adv. coun. Calif. Commn. Indsl. Innovation, 1981-82; pres. China/USA Edn. Fund, Inc., Washington, 1981-2002; trustee The Waltz Group of Washington, 2000—; dir. Rocky Mountain Inst., Snowmass Colo., 1982-95. Recipient medal for disting. pub. svc. Dept. Def., 1979, Fuess award Phillips Acad., 1991, Svc. Commendation award YWCA of Nat. Capital Area, 1991. Mem. N.Y.C. Racquet and Tennis Club, D.C. Met. Club, The Century Assn. (N.Y.C.). Home: 3550 Tilden St NW Washington DC 20008-3121 E-mail: btirana@aol.com.

TIRAVANIJA, RIRKRIT, sculptor; b. Buenos Aires, 1961; Student, Ont. Coll. Art, Toronto, Can., 1981, Banff Ctr. Sch. Fine Arts, Can., 1984, Whitney Ind. Studies Program, N.Y.C., 1986, Sch. Art Inst. Chgo., 1985. Adj. asst. prof. Columbia U. Sch. Arts, N.Y.C. One-man shows include Paula Allen Gallery, N.Y.C., 1990, Randy Alexander Gallery, N.Y.C., 1991, 303 Gallery, N.Y.C., 1992, 95, Randolph St. Gallery, Chgo., 1993, Jack Hanley Gallery, San Francisco, 1994, Schipper & Krome, Koln, Germany, 1994, Kunsthalle St. Gallen, Switzerland, 1996, Kolnischer Kunstverien, Cologne, Germany, 1996, Mus. Modern Art, N.Y.C., 1997, Mus. for Gegenwartskunst, Zurich, 1998, Phila. Mus. Art, 1998, L.A. County Mus. Art, 1999, Gavin Brown's Enterprise, N.Y.C., 1999, Wexner Ctr. for the Arts, Columbus, Ohio, 1999, la Caixa, Barcelona, 1999, Galleria Emi Fontana, Milan, 2000, Galaria Salvador Diaz, Madrid, 2000; group shows at The New Mus. Contemporary Art, N.Y.C., 1991, Jack Tilton Gallery, N.Y.C., 1991, Ctr. Contemporary Arts, Ujazdowski Castle, Warsaw, Poland, 1991, 303 Gallery, N.Y.C., 1992, Goethe House, N.Y.C., 1992, Holly Solomon Gallery, N.Y.C., 1993, Aldrich Mus. Contemporary Art, Conn., 1993, Inst. Contemporary Arts, London, 1993, Musee d'Art Moderne de la Ville de Paris, 1994, Galerie Jennifer Flay, Paris, 1994, Whitney Mus. Am. Art, 1995, The Carnegie Mus. Art, Pitts., 1995, Walker Art Ctr., Mpls., 1995, CAPC Bordeaux, France, 1997, Wexner Ctr., Columbus, Ohio, 1999, The Ikon Gallery, Birmingham, Eng., 2003 04; film exhbns. include The New Film Maker, The Collective for Living Cinema, N.Y.C., 1985, Video Event, Tom Cugliani Gallery, N.Y.C., 1991; sculpture projects Munster, Germany, 1997, Venice Biennial, Italy, 1999. Fax: 212-941-9828.*

TIRONE, BARBARA JEAN, health insurance administrator; b. Celina, Ohio, Nov. 19, 1943; d. Vincent James and Theresa Barbara (Goettermoeller) G. BA, Miami U., 1965; MBA, U. Chgo., 1977. Asst. dir. for internat. trade State of Ill., Chgo., Brussels, Hongkong and Sao Paulo, Brazil, 1973-76; dir. office of mgmt. and planning Office Human Devel. Svcs., Chgo., 1976-79; dep. regional adminstr. Health Care Financing Adminstrn., Chgo., 1979-82, regional adminstr., 1982-87, dir. bur. of prog. ops. Balt., 1987-92; dir. health stds. and quality bur. Health Care Fin. Adminstrn., Balt., 1992-96; pres., CEO AdminaStar, Inc., Indpls., 1996-2001. Recipient Presdl. Disting. Rank award 1988, 94, Presdl. Meritorious Rank award 1987, 92; named Fed. Exec. of Yr., 1987. Home: 11212 Appaloosa Dr Reisterstown MD 21136 Office Phone: 410-833-5570. Personal E-mail: bgagel@comcast.net.

TIRRELL, JOHN ALBERT, organization executive, consultant; b. Boston, Feb. 11, 1934; s. George Howard and Helen Sarah (Hitchings) T.; m. Helga Ruth Eisenhauer, Jan. 29, 1966; children: Steffanie Ruth, Sabina Lisette, Monica Susanne. BA in Psychology, The King's Coll., Briarcliff Manor, N.Y., 1961; MEd, U. Ariz., 1975. Various positions for several orgns., 1962-68; analyst instrnl.-ednl. systems GE, Daytona Beach, Fla., 1969-72; dir. curriculum and program devel. Brookdale C.C., Lincroft, N.J., 1972; dir. learning and faculty resources Pima C.C., Tucson, 1972-76; dir. human resources planning and devel. Miami divsn. Cyprus Copper Co., Claypool, Ariz., 1976-79; exec. dir. Calvary Missionary Fellowship, Tucson, 1983-85; interim pastor Sagauro Evang. Ch., Tucson, 1985-86; pastor Midvale Evangelical Ch., Tucson, 1986-87; founder, pres. The Jethro Consultancy, Birmingham, Mich., 1979—; v.p. mgmt. svc. AA Gage, Ferndale, Mich., 1987-88; pastor Desert Hills Bapt. Ch., Tucson, 1993-95. Mem. adv. bd. UIM Internat., Flagstaff, Ariz., 1983-92, mem. fin. com., 1983-94, sec. support svcs. field bd., 1993-01, sec. bus. and devel. field bd., 2002--, sec. pers. com., 1997—, sec., 1998—, also bd. dirs., 1993—; assoc. faculty mem. Gila Pueblo Campus Ea. Ariz. Coll., Globe, 1978; adj. prof. Montclair State Coll., Upper Montclair, N.J., 1972; chmn. mgmt. and pers. com. Wildwood Ranch, Inc., Howell, Mich., 1989-92; interim pres., v.p. programs, v.p. devel. Detroit Rescue Mission Ministries, 1990-92; v.p. corp. planning, tng., productivity George Instrument Co., Royal Oak; mem. mgmt., comm., sociology So. Ariz. and Phoenix campuses U. Phoenix, 1997—, area chair for social scis., 2001—; adj. faculty mem. psychology Pima County C.C., 1999—. Contbr. articles to profl. jours. Mem. Ariz. Coun. for Econ. Conversion, 1992-94; mem. facilities task force Grace Evang. Free Ch., Birmingham, 1989-90, chmn. bylaws revision com., 1989-90, chmn. property devel. com., 1990-92; interim pastor Desert Hills Bapt. Ch., Tucson, 1992-93; elder 1st Evang. Free Ch., Tucson, 1979-81, 86-87, 97, supt. Sunday sch., 1981-84, supt. adult Sunday sch., 1992-93, chmn. gen. bd., elder bd., 1979-82, short-term missions coord., missions bd., 1992-93; bd. dirs. S.W. Border dist. Evang. Free Ch. Am., 1996-00, mem. comm. com., 1996-01, chmn. comm. com., 1998-99; bd. dirs. Clearing House of Operational Resources for Christian Orgns., Royal Oak, Mich., 1991; bd. dirs. Shadow Roc Homeowners Assn., 1996-98, treas., 1997; v.p. parent-tchr. fellowship Palo Verde Christian Sch., Tucson, 1980-81. Staff sgt. USAF, 1952-56. Mem. ASTD (treas., Old Pueblo chpt. 1982, bd. dirs.-at-large 1983, Human Resources Devel. award Valley of the Sun chpt. 1977), Birmingham-Bloomfield C. of C. (mem. profl. devel. edn. com. 1987-91, mem. pub. rels. mktg. com. 1989), King's Coll. Alumni Assn. (class gov. 1988-95, 2000--). Republican. Avocations: photography, Bible teaching. Home and Office: 1205 E Deer Canyon Rd Tucson AZ 85718-1069 E-mail: jack.tirrell@comcast.net.

TIRRO, FRANK PASCALE, music educator, author, composer; b. Omaha, Sept. 20, 1935; s. Frank and Mary Carmela (Spensieri) T.; m. Charlene Rae Whitney, Aug. 16, 1961; children: John Andrew, Cynthia Anne. B.M.E., U. Nebr., 1960; M.M., Northwestern U., 1961; PhD, U. Chgo., 1974. Chmn. lab. sch. U. Chgo., Ill., 1961—70; fellow of Villa I Tatti Harvard U., Florence, Italy, 1971—72; lectr. U. Kans., Lawrence, Kans., 1972—73; asst. prof. music Duke U., Durham, NC, 1973—74; dir. Southeastern Inst. Medieval and Renaissance Studies, Durham, NC, 1978—80; chmn., assoc. prof. music Duke U., Durham, NC, 1973—80; prof. Yale U., New Haven, 1980—, dean, 1980—89. Reader, cons. several univ. presses; jurist Parisot Internat. Cello Competition, Sao Paolo, Brazil, 1981. Author: Historia del Jazz Clásico, 2001, Historia del Jazz Moderno, 2001, Jazz: A History, 1977, rev. edit., 1993, Renaissance Choirbooks in the Archive of San Petronio in Bologna, 1986, Living With Jazz, 1996, (with others) The Humanities: Cultural Roots and Continuities, 1980, 7th edit., 2004; editor: Medieval and Renaissance Studies No. 9, 1982; mem. editl. bd. Wittenberg Rev.; composer American Jazz Mass, 1960; assoc. editor Am. Nat. Biography, 1994—. Bd. dirs. New Haven Symphony, 1980-89, Neighborhood Music Sch., New Haven, 1982-89, Chamber Orch. New Eng., 1980 82, Ctr. for Black Music Rsch., 1985-91. Recipient Standard Composer award Am. Soc. Composers, Authors and Pubs., 1966, 99, 2000, 01, Gustavus Fine Arts medal, 1988, Duke Ellington Fellow medal, 1989; travel grantee Am. Coun. Learned Socs., 1967; rsch. grantee Duke U., 1978; named to Omaha Ctrl. H.S. Hall of Fame, 2002. Mem. Am. Musicol. Soc. (council 1978-80), Coll. Music Soc. (council 1980-82, mem. exec. bd. 1984-86), Nat. Assn. Schs. of Music, Internat. Soc. Jazz Research, Renaissance Soc. Am., Mory's Club, Yale Club (NYC). Republican. Lutheran. Office: Yale U Sch Music PO Box 208246 New Haven CT 06520-8246 Office Phone: 203-432-5989. E-mail: frank.tirro@yale.edu.

TIRYAKIAN, EDWARD ASHOD, sociology educator; b. Bronxville, N.Y., Aug. 6, 1929; s. Ashod Haroutioun and Keghinee (Agathon) T.; m. Josefina Cintron, Sept. 5, 1953; children: Edmund Carlos, Edwyn Ashod. BA summa cum laude, Princeton U., 1952; MA, Harvard U., 1954, PhD, 1956; PhD (hon.), U. Rene Descartes, Paris, 1987. Instr. Princeton U., 1956—57, asst. prof., 1957—62; lectr. Harvard U., 1962—65; assoc. prof. Duke U., Durham, NC, 1965—67, prof., 1967—, chmn. dept. sociology and anthropology, 1969—72, dir. internat. studies, 1988—91. Vis. lectr. U. Philippines, 1954-55, Bryn Mawr Coll., 1957-59; vis. scientist program Am. Sociol. Assn., 1967-70; vis. prof. Laval U., Quebec City, Que., Can., 1978, Inst. Polit. Studies, Paris, 1992, Free U., Berlin, 1996; summer seminar dir. NEH, 1978, 80, 93, 89, 91, 96; lectr. Kyoto Am. Studies Summer Seminar, 1985, project leader Fulbright New Cent. Scholars Program, 2002-03. Author: Sociologism and Existentialism, 1962; Editor: Sociological Theory, Values and Sociocultural Change: Essays in Honor of P.A. Sorokin, 1963, The Phenomenon of Sociology, 1971, On the Margin of the Visible: Sociology, the Esoteric, and the Occult, 1974, The Global Crisis: Sociological Analyses and Responses, 1984; co-editor: Theoretical Sociology: Perspectives and Developments, 1970; New Nationalisms of the Developed West, 1985; Rethinking Civilizational Analysis, 2004. Fellow Ctr. for Advanced Study in Behavioral Scis., 1997-98; recipient Fulbright rsch. award, 1955; Ford faculty rsch. fellow, 1971-72, fellow Ctr. for Advanced Study in Behavioral Scis., 1997-98, Disting. New Century scholar Fulbright Scholar Program, 2002-03. Mem. Am. Sociol. Assn., African Studies Assn., Am. Soc. for Study Religion (co uncil 1975-78, pres. 1981-84), Assn. Internationale des Sociologues de Langue Française (v.p. 1985-88, pres. 1988-92), Soc. for Phenomenology and Existential Philosophy, Phi Beta Kappa. Clubs: Princeton, Century Assn. (N.Y.C.). Home: 16 Pascal Way Durham NC 27705-4924 Office Phone: 919-660-5632. *As a sociological researcher, I have sought to bring to light connections between seemingly unrelated social phenomena, realizing that only at the end of history will all connections become known. As a teacher, I have sought to encourage in students-undergraduates, graduates, and postgraduates-an unceasing gusto for intellectual curiosity in exploring the social world, as I have been stimulated by my undergraduate and graduate teachers.*

TISCH, ANDREW HERBERT, corporate executive; b. Asbury Park, N.J., Aug. 14, 1949; s. Laurence Alan and Wilma Zelda (Stein) T.; 2 children. BS, Cornell U., 1971; MBA, Harvard U., 1977. Brand mgr. Lorillard Co., N.Y.C., 1971-75; mgr. operational analysis Loews Corp., N.Y.C., 1977-79, v.p., 1985—; pres. Bulova Corp., Woodside, N.Y., 1985-89; chmn., chief exec. officer Lorillard Tobacco Co., N.Y.C., 1989—, also bd. dirs., Bulova Corp., Woodside, N.Y. Mem mgmt. com. Loews Corp., Bulova Systems and Instruments Corp. Contbr. articles to profl. jours. Mem. fgn. affairs com. Am. Jewish Com., N.Y.C., 1983—; bd. dirs. Outward Bound, Inc., Greenwich, Conn., 1983-88; trustee Central Synagogue, N.Y.C., 1984—; gen. chmn. United Jewish Appeal Fedn. of Jewish Philanthropies N.Y., vice chmn. United Jewish Appeal, chmn. Prime Minister's Coun., 1987—; bd. dirs. N.Y. Shakespeare Festival, 1987—; chmn. Children's Hearing Inst., 1988; bd. mem. N.Y.C. Sports Commn. Mem. 24 Karat Club N.Y., Century Country Club, Harmonie Club, Plumb Club, Achilles Track Club (bd. dirs.). Avocations: tennis, running. Office: Lorillard Tobacco Co 1 Park Ave New York NY 10016-5802

TISCH, JAMES SOLOMON, diversified holding company executive; b. Atlantic City, Jan. 2, 1953; s. Laurence A. and Wilma (Stein) T.; m. Merryl Hiat; children: Jessica, Benjamin, Samuel. BA, Cornell U., 1975; MBA, Wharton Grad. Sch., U. Pa., 1976. With Loews Corp., N.Y.C., 1977—, exec. v.p., 1987-94, pres., COO, 1994-99, pres., CEO, 1999—, also mem. mgmt. com. Chmn., CEO Diamond Offshore Drilling, Inc.; bd. dirs. CNA Fin., Vail Resorts, Inc., Loews Corp. Bd. dirs. Fedn. Employment and Guidance Svc., N.Y.C., 1985—; trustee Mt. Sinai Med. Ctr./NYU Med. Ctr., N.Y.C., 1988—; pres.-elect UJA Fedn. N.Y. Office: Loews Corp 667 Madison Ave Fl 7 New York NY 10021-8087

TISCH, JONATHAN MARK, hotel company executive; b. Atlantic City, Dec. 7, 1953; s. Preston Robert and Joan (Hyman) T. BA, Tufts U., 1976. Cinematographer, producer WBZ-TV, Boston, 1976-79; sales mgr. Loews Hotels, N.Y.C., 1980-81, dir. devel., 1981-82, v.p., 1982-85, exec. v.p., 1985-86, pres., 1986-89, CEO, 1986—, pres., 1999—. Mem. mgmt. com. Loews Corp.; bd. dirs. N.Y. Giants, 1991—. Trustee Robert Steel Found., N.Y.C., Gunnery Sch., Washington, Conn., 1983—, Tufts U., Medford, Mass., 1986—, Vice Pres.'s Residence Found., 1994; chmn. N.Y.C. host com. for Grammys, 1988, 92, 94; bd. dirs. Pediatric AIDS found.; vice chair econ. devel. com. N.Y.C. Partnership, 1994 . Mem. Am. Hotel and Motel Assn. (officer 1994-97), Travel Bus. Roundtable (chmn. 1995—, conf. chmn. 1995—), Friars Club. Avocations: golf, tennis, skiing. Office: Loews Hotels 51st St Levingston Ave New York NY 10021-8029

TISCH, PRESTON ROBERT, finance and sports executive; b. Bklyn., Apr. 29, 1926; s. Abraham Solomon and Sayde (Brenner) T.; m. Joan Hyman, Mar. 14, 1948; children: Steven E., Laurie M., Jonathan M. Student, Bucknell U., 1943—44; BA, U. Mich., 1948. Chmn., dir. Loews Corp., N.Y.C., 1960—; postmaster gen. U.S. Postal Svc., Washington, 1986—88; chmn., co-CEO, half owner N.Y. Football Giants, 1991—. Bd. dirs. CNA Fin. Corp., Bulova Watch Co., Loews Corp. Chmn. emeritus N.Y. Conf. and Visitors Bur., Nat. Dem. Conv., 1976, 80; chmn. Citymeals on Wheels, 1993-2002, chmn. emeritus, 2003--; trustee NYU; mem. Quadrennial Commn. on Exec., Legis. and Jud. Salaries, 1988; mem. Gov.'s Bus. Adv. Coun. for N.Y. State; founder, chmn. Take the Field (rebuilding N.Y.C. sch. athletic facilities). With AUS, 1943-44. Mem. Century Country Club, Sigma Alpha Mu. Office: Loews Corp 667 Madison Ave Fl 7 New York NY 10021-8087 also: NY Giants Giants Stadium East Rutherford NJ 07073

TISCH, STEVEN ELLIOT, television and movie producer; b. Lakewood, N.J., Feb. 14, 1949; s. Preston Robert and Joan (Hyman) T.; m. Patricia Keast, Sept. 27, 1981 (div. July 1991); m. Jamie Alexander, 1996; 5 children BA, Tufts U., 1971. Pres. Tisch-Avnet Prodns., L.A., 1981-88, Steve Tisch Co., L.A., 1988—. Exec. prodr. (films) Deal of the Century, 1983, The Long Kiss Goodnight, 1996, American History X, 1997, Wild America, 1997, Lock, Stock and Two Smoking Barrels, 1998, Wayward Son, 1999, Snatch, 2000, Looking for an Echo, 2000, Alex and Emma, 2003; prodr. Outlaw Blues, 1977, Coast to Coast, 1980, Risky Business, 1983, Soul Man, 1986, Big Business, 1988, Hot To Trot, 1988, Heart of Dixie, 1989, Heart Condition, 1990, Bad Influence, 1990 Forrest Gump, 1994, Corrina, Corrina, 1994, Dear God, 1996, Wild America, 1997, The Postman, 1997, Nico the Unicorn, 1997; TV prodr. Homeward Bound, 1980, Prime Suspect, 1982, Dirty Dancing, 1988, Lies of the Heart, 1991; co-prodr. Evil in Clear River, 1988, Mission Extreme, 2000; assoc. prodr. The Missing Are Deadly, 1975; exec. prodr. No Other Love, 1979, Something So Right, 1982, Calendar Girl Murders, 1984, The Burning Bed, 1984, Triplecross, 1985, In Love and War, 1987, Out on the Edge, 1989, Judgement, 1990, Afterburn, 1992, Keep the Change, 1992, The People Next Door, 1996; actor; Cry Uncle!, 1971, Dear God, 1996 Chmn. AIDS Project L.A., 1992-94. Office: care Steve Tisch Co 10202 W Washington Blvd Culver City CA 90232-2715

TISCHLER, ARTHUR STEVEN, pathologist, researcher; b. NYC, July 10, 1946; s. Louis Norman and Bertie (Brumberger) Tischler; m. Judith Samuels Tischler, May 1993; stepchildren: Sara Melrowitz, Eliana Melrowitz, Benyamin Melrowitz; m. Joanne Louise Greenfield Hager. BS, Pa. State U., 1967; MD, Thomas Jefferson U., 1971. Diplomate Am. Bd. Pathology. Prof. pathology Tufts U. Sch. Medicine, Boston; sr. pathologist Tufts New Eng. Med. Ctr., Boston. Editor: Endocrine Pathology, 2002—; contbr. articles to profl. jours. Pres. Endocrine Pathology Soc., 2000—01. Maj. U.S. Army, 1976—78. Rsch. grantee, Nat Cancer Inst., Nat. Inst. Neurol. Disorders & Stroke. Avocation: photography. Office: Tufts Univ New Eng Med Ctr Dept Pathology 750 Washington St Boston MA 02111-1526

TISCHLER, GARY LOWELL, psychiatrist, educator; b. N.Y.C., Oct. 30, 1935; s. Louis and Dorothy (Green) T.; m. Judith Post, Aug. 18, 1957; children: Laurie Dee, Marc David, Rachel Mara. AB, Hamilton Coll., 1957; MD, U. Pa., 1961; MS, Yale U., 1975. Intern Kings County Hosp., Bklyn., 1961-62; resident in psychiatry Yale U. Sch. Medicine, New Haven, 1962-65, asst. prof., 1967-70, assoc. prof., 1970-75, prof. psychiatry, 1975-90, chmn. dept. psychiatry, 1986-87; prof., chmn. dept. psychiatry and biobehavioral scis., dir. Neuropsychiatric Inst. UCLA Sch. Medicine, 1990-95; dir. Yale Psychiat. Inst., New Haven, 1978-87; chief psychiatry Yale-New Haven Hosp., 1986-87; clin. dir. Hill-West Haven divsn. Conn. Mental Health Ctr., New Haven, 1968-70, dir., 1970-77; prof. psychiatry UCLA, 1990-95, prof. emeritus, 1996—; prof., exec. vice chair dept. psychiatry, dir. Cornell U. Med. Coll., 1994—2002; dir. Westchester divsn., dir. mental health programs N.Y. Hosp., 1994-99, dir. Payne Whitney Clinic, 1996-97. Study dir. Pres.'s Commn. on Mental Health, Washington, 1977-79; cons. Arthur D. Little Inc., Boston, 1973-75, IBM Corp., Armonk, N.Y., 1986-87; mem. profl. adv. com. Am. Med. Internat., L.A., 1984-86; mem. bd. mental health and behavioral medicine Inst. Medicine, Washington, 1986—, com. on clin. evaluation, 1990-94. Author: Quality Assurance Thru Utilization and Peer Review, 1982; editor: Patient Care Evaluation in Mental Health, 1985, Diagnosis and Classification in Psychiatry, 1987; contbr. articles to profl. jours. Mem. Gov.'s transition staff on mental health, Conn., 1975; vice chmn. Bd. Mental Health State of Conn., 1986. Served to capt. U.S. Army, 1965-67, Vietnam. Fellow Am. Psychiat. Assn., Am. Coll. Mental Health Adminstrn., Am. Assn. for Social Psychiatry, Am. Coll. Psychiatry. Home: 36 Rock Hill Rd Bedford NY 10506-1522 E-mail: glt35@netscape.net.

TISCHLER, JUDITH BLANCHE, retired music publishing executive, educator; b. N.Y.C., May 14, 1933; d. Max and Anna (Drescher) Zucker; m. Alfred Tischler, Dec. 14, 1958; children: Marva, Mira, Gary. MA, CCNY, 1975; PhD, Jewish Theol. Sem., 1989. Editor, dir. Transcontinental Music Publs., N.Y.C., 1981—2000. Prof. music Jewish Theol. Sem., H.L. Miller Cantorial Sch. French hornist various concerts worldwide, 1952-71. Office: HL Miller Cantonal Sch Jewish Theol Sem of Am 3080 Broadway New York NY 10027 E-mail: tisch33@netvision.net.il., judithtischler@hotmail.com.

TISCHMAN, MICHAEL BERNARD, lawyer; b. Elizabeth, N.J., Oct. 8, 1937; s. Nathan and Ann (Goldberg) T.; m. Elinor Cohen, Aug. 16, 1959; children: David F., Susan F. BA, U. Pa., 1959; LLB, Harvard U., 1963; LLM in Taxation, NYU, 1968. Bar: N.J. 1964, Fla. 1979, N.Y. 1984. Law sec. Judge Walter J. Freund N.J. Appellate Div., 1963-64; assoc. Schiff, Cummis & Kent, Newark, 1964-67; ptnr. Cummis, Kent, Radin & Tischman, Newark, 1968-70, Sills, Beck, Cummis, Radin & Tischman, Newark, 1971-87, Sills, Cummis, Radin, Tischman, Epstein & Gross, Newark, 1988—2003, sr. counsel, 2004—. Panel chmn. fee arbitration com. N.J. Supreme Ct. Dist. Essex County, 1987-91; mem. health law and policy program adv. bd. Seton Hall Law Sch., 1997—. Mem. Mayor's Performing Arts Ctr. Task Force, Newark, 1988-96. Mem. N.J. Bar Assn. (com. on ltd. partnership act revisions 1983-88), Phi Beta Kappa. Home: 8 Wedgewood Way Scotch Plains NJ 07076-2727 Office: Sills Cummis Radin Tischman Epstein & Gross One Riverfront Pla Newark NJ 07102 E-mail: mtischman@sillscummis.com.

TISCORNIA, ANA MARIA, artist, educator, writer; b. Montevideo, Uruguay, Nov. 24, 1951; arrived in U.S., 1991; d. Carlos Tiscornia and Hilda Gascue. BArch, Inst. Vazquez-Acevedo, Montevideo, 1971. Prof. visual art Sch. Printmaking, Montevideo, 1984—87; prof. graphic expression Sch. Arch. U. de la Republica, Montevideo, 1985—89; prof. art U. de los Andes, Bogota, Colombia, 1992; adj. prof. SUNY, New Paltz, 1996—98, Jersey City U., 2000—02, SUNY, Old Westbury, 2000—03, asst. prof., 2003—. Dir. Club de Grabado de Montevideo, 1985—87; art editor Point of Contact, Syracuse, NY, 2002—. Contbr. articles to profl. jours. Recipient 1st prize, Fellowship Paul Cezanne, France/Uruguay, 1986, Hon. prize, II Havana (Cuba) Biennial, 1986; grantee, Pollock-Krasner Found., N.Y.C., 2000; fellowship, N.Y. Found. for the Arts, 2004. Home: 720 Greenwich St Apt 10G New York NY 10014 Office: SUNY Old Westbury Campus Ctr F-101 Old Westbury NY 11568 Office Phone: 516-876-3056. Business E-Mail: anatiscornia@earthlink.net.

TISDALE, DOUGLAS MICHAEL, lawyer; b. Detroit, May 3, 1949; s. Charles Walker and Violet Lucille (Battani) Tisdale; m. Patricia Claire Brennan, Dec. 29, 1972; children: Douglas Michael Jr., Sara Elizabeth, Margaret Patricia, Victoria Claire. BA in Psychology with honors, U. Mich., 1971, JD, 1975. Bar: Colo. 1975, U.S. Dist. Ct. Colo. 1975, U.S. Ct. Appeals

(10th cir.) 1976, U.S. Supreme Ct. 1979. Law clk. to chief judge U.S. Dist. Ct. Colo., Denver, 1975-76; ptnr. Brownstein Hyatt & Farber, P.C., 1976—92; shareholder Popham, Haik, Schnobrich & Kaufman, Ltd., 1992-97, dir., 1995-97; ptnr. Baker & Hostetler LLP, Denver, 1997—2002; owner Tisdale & Assocs., Denver, 2002—. Chmn. bd. dirs. Eagle Health Care Ctr., Inc.; treas. Vail Valley Med. Ctr. City councilman Cherry Hill Village, 2000—. Home: 4662 S Elizabeth Ct Cherry Hills Village CO 80113-7106 Office: Tisdale and Assocs LLC Colo State Bank Bldg Ste 2600 1600 Broadway Denver CO 80202-4989 Office Phone: 303-832-1800.

TISDALE, SHELBY JO-ANNE, museum director, consultant; b. London, Ontario, Canada, Oct. 25, 1950; d. Edith Ilene St. Clair and George Elgin Tisdale. BA, U. of Colo., 1977—80; MA, U. of Wash., 1982—85; PhD, U. of Ariz., 1989—97. Asst. collections mgr. Sch. of Am. Rsch., Santa Fe, 1984—85; asst. curator Palm Springs Desert Mus., 1985—87; chief curator Millicent Rogers Mus., Taos, 1987—89; tchg. assoc. U. of Ariz., 1990—95; adj. faculty Pima C.C., Tucson, 1992—97; curator, native am. art Philbrook Mus. of Art, Tulsa, 1999—2002; exec. dir. Millicent Rogers Mus., Taos, 2002—. Mus. planning cons. Ilwaco Heritage Found., Wash., 1983, Cocopah Indian Tribe, Somerton, 1993—97; cons. URS/Dames & Moore, Phoenix, 1997—2001. Contbr. articles to pubs. Fellow: Soc. for Applied Anthropology; mem.: Coun. for Mus. Anthropology (sec. 1988—90), Am. Anthrop. Assn. (assoc.), Am. Assn. of Mus., Rotary Internat. Avocations: travel, reading, hiking. Home: PO Box 2468 Taos NM 87571-2468 Office: Millicent Rogers Museum PO Box A/1504 Millicent Rogers Rd Taos NM 87571 Office Phone: 505-758-2462. E-mail: stisdale@newmex.com.

TISE, LARRY EDWARD, association executive, historian; b. Winston-Salem, NC, Dec. 6, 1942; s. Russell Edward and Lena Irene (Norman) T.; children: Larry Edward, Nicholas Allen, William Zane. AB, Duke U., 1965, M.Div., 1968; PhD (Ford Found. fellow, 1970, Research Triangle fellow, 1971), U. N.C., 1974. Part-time editor John Fries Blair, Pub., Winston-Salem, 1969-72; teaching fellow history dept. U. N.C., Chapel Hill, 1971, instr., 1972-73; dir. hist. publs. N.C. Bicentennial Com., 1973-74; asst. dir. N.C. Div. Archives and History, Raleigh, 1974-75, dir., 1975-81, N.C. State Hist. Preservation officer, 1975-81; exec. dir. Pa. Hist. and Mus. Commn., 1981-87; Pa. State Hist. Preservation officer, 1981-87; dir. Am. Assn. for State and Local History, Nashville, 1987-89; exec. dir. Benjamin Franklin Nat. Meml., Phila., 1989-97; pres., CEO Internat. Congress of Disting. Awards, 1997—. Adj. prof. grad. sch. fine arts U. Pa., 1984-87; vis. prof. Vanderbilt U., 1988-89, Temple U., 1989-91; Willbur Orville Wright vis. disting. prof. E. Carolina U., 2000-; mem. Nat. Hist. Publs. and Records Commn., 1982-88 Author, co-author writings in fields of archives, hist. preservation, hist. sites and museums, history, society, religion; author: The Southern Experience in the American Revolution, 1978, The Monitor: Its Meaning and Future, 1978, Writing North Carolina History, 1979, A House Not Made with Hands, 1966, The Yadkin Melting Pot: Methodism and the Moravians in the Yadkin Valley, 1750-1850, 1968, Proslavery: The Defense of Slavery in America, 1987, A Book About Children, 1992, The American Counterrevolution, 1998, Keep on Running, 1998, Benjamin Franklin and Women, 2000, The Soaring Place: The Untold Story of Kitty Hawk (2003); gen. editor: writings in fields of archives, hist. preservation, hist. sites and museums, history, society, religion including Winston-Salem in History, 13 vols, 1976; edit. bd. The Public Historian, 1980-86; editor N.C. Hist. Rev., 1974-81, Pa. Heritage, 1981-87, History News, 1987-89, Franklin Gazette, 1989-97; contbr. articles to books, newsletters, publs. Recipient William R. Davie History award, 1979, Herbert L. Feis award, Am. Hist. Assn., 1989, Benjamin Franklin Nat. Meml. awards 1990, Best New Book in History, Ind. Book Pubs., 1999; Nat. Endowment for the Humanities fellow, 1992-93; faculty fellow NASA-Langley Rsch. Ctr., 2000-03. Mem. Am. Hist. Assn. (various coms.), Orgn. Am. Historians (chmn. coms.), So. Hist. Assn., Am. Assn. State and Local History (mem. coun. and coms.), Nat. Assn. State Archives and Records Adminstrs. (pres. 1980-81), Nat. Conf. State Hist. Preservation Officers (bd. dirs. 1976-79, pres. 1979-81), Nat. Coun. on Pub. History (bd. dirs., exec. com. 1979-83, pres. 1983-85), N.C. Hist. Commn. (sec. 1975-81), N.C. Lit. and Hist. Assn. (sec., treas. 1977-81), Pa. Fedn. Hist. Socs. (sec. 1981-87), Friends of Franklin, Inc. (exec. sec. 1989-97). Methodist. E-mail: ltise@attglobal.net.

TISHER, C. CRAIG, nephrologist, educator, dean; MD, Wash. U., St. Louis, 1961. Resident Barnes Hosp., St. Louis, U. Wash. affiliated Hosps., Seattle; fellow in nephrology U. Wash., Seattle; positions at Walter Reed Hosp. and Walter Reed Army Inst. Rsch., Washington; joined faculty Duke U. Sch. Medicine, 1969; prof. medicine and pathology U. Fla. Coll. Medicine, Gainesville, Fla., 1980—, chief divsn. nephrology, hypertension and transplantation, 1980—87, named Ctrl. Fla. Kidney Ctr. Eminent Scholar Chair in Nephrology, 1989, prof. anatomy and cell biology, sr. assoc. dean, 1998—2002, Folke H. Peterson Disting. Professorship, 1999—, dean, 2002—; dir. Ctr. Clin. Trials Rsch U. Fla. Founding asst. editor Kidney Internat. jour.; chmn. med. adv. board Bioavailability Systems Inc., Cocoa Beach, Fla. Recipient Faculty Rsch. Prize in Clin. Scis., U. Fla., 1985. Mem.: Internat. Soc. Nephrology, Am. Soc. Nephrology (pres. 1990—91, jour. editor 1996—2001, John P. Peters Award 2001). Office: U Fla Divsn Nephrology Box J224 JHMHC Gainesville FL 32610 also: U Fla PO Box 100215 Gainesville FL 32610-0215*

TISHLER, WILLIAM HENRY, landscape architect, educator; b. Baileys Harbor, Wis., June 22, 1936; s. William John and Mary Viola (Sarter) T.; m. Betsy Lehner, Sept. 23, 1961; children: William Phillip, Robin Elizabeth. BS in Landscape Architecture, U. Wis., 1960; M in Landscape Architecture, Harvard U., 1964. Urban planner City of Milw., 1961-62; mem. faculty dept. landscape architecture U. Wis., Madison, 1964—; assoc. Hugh A Dega & Assocs. (Landscape Archs.), 1964-66; prin. Land Plans Inc. (Land and Hist. Preservation Planning Cons.), Madison, 1966—. Advisor emeritus Nat. Trust for Hist. Preservation; bd. dirs. The Hubbard Ednl. Trust. Author: American Landscape Architecture: Designers and Places, 1989, Midwestern Landscape Architecture, 2000, Wisconsin's Emerald Treasure: A History of Peninsula State Park, 2005; contbr. articles to profl. jours. With C.E., U.S. Army, 1960. Recipient Design Arts Program award NEA, 1981, Hawthorn award Friends of The Clearing, 1997, Outstanding Educator award Coun. Educators in Landscape Architecture, 1998; Attingham (Eng.) Program fellow Soc. Archtl. Historians, 1980; Dumbarton Oaks sr. fellow, 1990. Fellow Am. Soc. Landscape Archs. (Horace Cleve. vis. prof. U. Minn. 1993, nat. merit award 1971, 97, 99, honor award 1980, 89, Wis. chpt. Lifetime Achievement award 2000); mem. Assn. Preservation Tech., Wis. Acad. Arts, Letters and Scis., Pioneer Am. Soc. (Henry Douglas award), Hist. Madison (hon.), Vernacular Architecture Forum (past pres.), Madison Trust for Hist. Preservation, Alliance for Hist. Landscape Preservation (founder), The Clearing Landscape Inst. (founder, dir.), Phi Kappa Phi, Sigma Lambda Alpha, Gamma Sigma Delta, Sigma Nu. Lutheran. Home: 3925 Regent St Madison WI 53705-5222 Office: U Wis Dept Landscape Architecture Madison WI 53706 E-mail: wtishler@facstaff.wisch.edu.

TISHMAN, DANEL R, entrepreneur; b. July 1955; m. Sheryl C Tishman. BS, Evergreen State Coll.; MS, Lesley Coll. Grad. Sch. Chmn. and CEO Tishman Constrn., Interiors and Technologies Corp.; EVP Tishman Realty Corp. Recipient Zeckendorf award, CW Post Campus, Long Is. U., 2003. Office: TIshman Realty & Constrn 666 Fifth Ave New York NY 10103

TISHMAN, JOHN L. realty and construction company executive; b. N.Y.C., Jan. 24, 1926; s. Louis and Rose F. (Foreman) T.; m. Suzanne Weisberg; children: Daniel R., Katherine T. BS, U. Michigan. Chmn. bd. dirs., pres. Tishman Realty & Constrn. Co., Inc., N.Y.C., 1976—. Home: Mianus Riv Rd Bedford NY 10506 Office: Tishman Realty Const Corp NY 666 5th Ave Fl 36 New York NY 10103-0256

TISINGER, BILLY JOE, lawyer, educator; b. Woodstock, Va., Oct. 22, 1940; s. Laurence C. and Margarite L. Tisinger; m. Mate Fadely, June 17, 1962; children— Travis Joseph, Trent Coiner. B.A. in Sociology, Roanoke Coll., 1962; LL.B. magna cum laude, Washington and Lee U., 1969. Bar: Va. 1969, U.S. Dist. Ct. (we. dist.) Va. 1969. Tchr. sci., pub. schs., Greene County, Va., 1962-63; bldg. mgmt. specialist GSA, Washington, 1963-64, adminstrv. officer, 1964-66; ptnr. Harrison & Johnston, Winchester, Va., 1969—; instr. real estate Lord Fairfax Community Coll., 1975—; U.S. magistrate, 1973-83. Mem. Winchester-Frederick County Bar Assn. (pres. 1980, 81), Va. State Bar Assn., ABA, Order of Coif, Delta Theta Phi. Democrat. Mem. United Ch. of Christ. Office: PO Box 809 Winchester VA 22604-0809

TISINGER, CATHERINE ANNE, history and economics educator; b. Winchester, Va., Apr. 6, 1936; d. Richard Martin and Irma Regina (Ohl) T. BA, Coll. Wooster, 1958; MA, U. Pa., 1962, PhD, 1970; LLD (hon.), Coll. of Elms, 1985. Provost Callison Coll., U. of Pacific, Stockton, Calif., 1971-72; v.p. Met. State U., St. Paul, 1972-75, interim pres., 1976-77; dir. Ctr. for Econ. Edn., R.I. Coll., Providence, 1979-80; v.p. acad. affairs Ctrl. Mo. State U., Warrensburg, 1980-84; pres. North Adams State Coll., Mass., 1984-91; dean arts and scis. Shenandoah U., Winchester, Va., 1999—2001, prof. history and econs., 2001—, Disting. prof., 2001—. Cons. North Cen. Assn. Colls. and Schs., 1980-84, New Eng. Assn. Schs. and Colls., 1978-79, 85—, Minn. Acad. Family Physicians, 1973-77; mem. adv. bd. First Agrl. Bank, North Adams, 1985-91; pres. No. Berkshire Cooperating Colls., 1986-91; v.p. Coll. Consortium for Internat. Studies, 1989-90; cons. Inst. for Experiential Learning, 2002—. V.p. Med. Simulation Found., 1986-88; bd. dirs. Williamstown Concerts, 1988-91, Shawnee coun. Girl Scouts U.S.A., 1992-93, Parents' Choice, 1997-98, Parents Guide to Children's Media, Inc., 1998-2004. Mem. No. Berkshire C. of C. (bd. dirs. 1984-89, v.p. 1986-89). Avocations: fiber and textile arts, photography. Office: Shenandoah U 1460 University Dr Winchester VA 22601-5195 E-mail: ctisinge@su.edu.

TISINGER, DAVID HARVEY, lawyer; b. Carrollton, Ga., May 8, 1937; s. Robert D. and Naomi E. Tisinger; m. sharon Inman, Feb. 3, 1975; children: John David, Joel Wesley. BS, Ga. Inst. Tech., 1958; LLB, U. Ga., 1963. Bar: Ga. 1962. Ptnr. Tisinger Vance & Greer, Carrollton, 1963—. Instr. law U. Ga., Athens, 1964; chmn. bd. Carrollton State Bank, 1974-78. Mem. bd. regents U. Sys. of Ga., Atlanta, 1972-79. Lt. USNR, 1958-60. Fellow Am. Coll. Trial Lawyers; mem. ATLA, Def. Rsch. Inst. Avocations: farming, sailing. Office: Tisinger Tisinger Vance & Greer 100 Wagon Yard Plz Carrollton GA 30117-3490

TISMANEANU, VLADIMIR, political science educator, researcher; b. Brasov, Romania, July 4, 1951; s. Leonte and Hermina Tismaneanu; m. Mary Frances Sladek, Nov. 22, 1991; 1 child, Adam Volo. BA, MA, U. Bucharest, Romania, PhD, 1980; Doctor honoris causa, U. of the West, Timisoara, Romania, 2002, Nat. Sch. Polit. Studies, Bucharest, 2003. Rsch. assoc. Fgn. Policy Rsch. Inst., Phila., 1983-90; lectr. U. Pa., Phila., 1985-90; sr. asst. prof. U. Md., Coll. Pk., 1990-92, assoc. prof., 1992-97, prof., 1997—. Mem. E. Europe com. Am. Coun. Learned Socs., N.Y.C., 1997—. Author: Crisis of a Marxist Ideology in Eastern Europe, 1988, Reinventing Politics, 1992, Fantasies of Salvation, 1998, Slowly, Towards Europe, 2000, Letters from Washington, 2002; editor: Revolutions of 1989, 1999, Between Past and Future, 2000, Stalinism for All Seasons, 2003; mem. Jour. Democracy, 1996—, jour. editor East European Politics and Societies, 1998—; chair: editl. com. East European Politics and Societies, 2003—. Bd. dirs. Internat. Forum Dem. Studies, Washington, Civic Edn. Project. Recipient Vis. Disting. Lectr. award U.S. Dept. State, 1994; Book award Romanian-Am. Acad. Arts and Scis., 1998, award Romanian Cultural Found., 2000; Reagan Fascell Democracy fellow Nat. Endowment for Democracy, 2003-2004. Mem. Am. Assn. Advancement Slavic Studies, Am. Polit. Sci. Assn. Office: U Md Dept Govt & Politics Tydings Hall College Park MD 20742 Fax: 202-686-5131. E-mail: vtisman@gvpt.umd.edu.

TISSUE, MIKE, medical educator, respiratory therapist; b. Garfield, Wash., Aug. 24, 1941; s. Altha Lester and Fern Adeline (Willard) T.; m. Marjorie Lena Atkinson, Feb. 24, 1961 (div. June 1991); children: Sue Tipton, Pam Kromholtz, Paul, Donna Leach; m. Mary Emma Napier, Aug. 24, 1998. AAS (4 degrees) with honors, Spokane (Wash.) C.C., 1985; BS in Respiratory Therapy cum laude, Loma Linda (Calif.) U., 1987; MS in Respiratory Care, Ga. State U., 1999. Registered cardiovasc. invasive specialist, cardiac sonographer; registered respiratory therapist-neonatal pediat. specialist; registered pulmonary function technologist, respiratory care practitioner; diplomate sr. disability analyst. Respiratory intern, NICU therapist Loma Linda (Calif.) U. Med. Ctr., 1985-87; educator, therapist Riyadh (Saudi Arabia) Armed Forces Hosp., 1987-91; head dept. respiratory care Security Forces Hosp., Riyadh, 1991-93; asst. prof., dir. clin. edn. respiratory therapy program Morehead (Ky.) State U., 1993-94; program dir. assoc. degree respiratory therapy Chattahoochee Tech. Coll., Marietta, Ga., 1994—98; clin. instr. Ga. State U., Atlanta, 1999-2001; dir. respiratory therapy program Nat. Inst. Tech., Atlanta, 2001—. Pres., founder Riyadh Cardiorespiratory Soc., 1988-93; rschr. Loma Linda U., 1987, Riyadh Armed Forces Hosp., 1988; instr. and affil.various heart assns. at various times cons. ARC, Tacoma, 1984, instr. standard and advanced first aid and CPR, Inland Empire chpt., Spokane, 1975-94; instr. first aid San Bernardino/Redlands Svc. Ctr., Loma Linda, 1985-87, Am. Cmty. Svcs. U.S. Embassy, Riyadh, 1987-93, U.S. Mil. Operation Desert Storm, Riyadh, 1991-93; instr. Freedom From Smoking Clinic Program Am. Lung Assn., Calif., 1985-87, Saudi Arabia, 1987-93, Smyrna, Ga., 1994-96; mem. several coms. Chattahoochee Tech. Coll., 1994-98. Contbr. articles to profl. jours. Bd. dirs. Am. Heart Assn., Spokane, 1976-83, chair fin. com., 1981-83; chair programming and spkrs. bur. Am. Lung Assn., Smyrna, Ga., 1994-98, chmn. bd. dirs., 1995-96; sec. Cobb County Cmty. Coun., Marietta, 1995-96, spkr., 1995, v.p., 1996, pres. 1997; vol. Ga. Internat. Cultural Exch., 1995; registry exam. sr. proctor Cardiovasc. Credentialing Internat./Nat. Bd. Cardiovasc. Technologists, Riyadh, 1987-90; commr. Boy Scouts Am., Spokane, 1973-82. Named Citizen of Day KGA Radio, Spokane, 1983. Mem. AAUP (legis. com. Atlanta 1995-96), Am. Assn. Respiratory Care (therapist-driven protocol rev. com. 1994, ad hoc com. on patient-driven protocol rev. com. 1996, ad hoc com. for sects. rev. 1995-96, job analysis, neonatal pedit. specialist 2002), Applied Measurement Profls., Alliance of Cardiovasc. Profls., Ga. Soc. Respiratory Care (chmn. cardiopulmonary com. 1994-95, edn. com., smoking and health com.), Phi Delta Kappa (pub. rels. com. 1995-96). Avocations: photography, travel. Home: 1881 Arnold Dr SW Austell GA 30106-2907 Office: Nat Inst Tech Respiratory Therapy Program 1706 Northeast Pkwy Atlanta GA 30329 Personal E-mail: miketissue@juno.com.

TITCOMB, CALDWELL, music and theatre historian; b. Augusta, Maine, Aug. 16, 1926; s. Samuel and Lura Elizabeth (Smith) T. AB summa cum laude, Harvard U., 1947, MA, 1949, PhD, 1952. Univ. organist Brandeis U., Waltham, Mass., 1953-70, dir. undergrad. studies music, 1956-84, curator creative arts, libr., 1961-64, co-chmn. music dept., 1977-84, from instr. to prof. music, 1953-88, prof. emeritus, 1988—. Drama critic Harvard Crimson, 1953-82, Bay State Banner, 1975—, This Month on Stage, 1996-99, Totaltheater.com, 2000—; trustee Charles Playhouse, Boston, 1966-71 Editor: The Art of Fine Words, 1965, The Furies (Lucien Price), 1988; co-editor: Varieties of Black Experience at Harvard, 1986, Blacks at Harvard: A Documentary History of African-American Experience at Harvard and Radcliffe, 1993; contbr. articles to profl. jours., ency.; composer stage and film music scores. Bd. dirs. Cambridge (Mass.) Civic Symphony Orch., 1959-70; exec. bd. Mus. Fine Arts Friends Music, Boston, 1959-65; panelist Mass. Commn. Arts and Humanities, 1981-83; mem. selection com. Theater Hall of Fame, 1980—; juror Elliot Norton awards, 1985—; pres. Boston Theater Critics Assn., 1994—. With U.S. Army, 1944-46, PTO; with Mil. Intelligence Res., 1946-50. Mem. AAUP, Coll. Music Soc., Am. Theatre Critics Assn. (charter), New Eng. Theatre Conf. (adv. coun. 1961-81, coll. fellows 1981—), Am. Guild Organists, Am. Musicol. Soc. (coun. 1965-67), Soc. for Ethnomusicology, Eugene O'Neill Soc., Hist. Brass Soc., Signet Soc., Soc. for Am. Music, Phi Beta Kappa (sec. Mu chpt. Mass. 1984—). Avocations: philology, afro-american history and culture. E-mail: caldwell67@aol.com.

TITLE, GAIL MIGDAL, lawyer; b. Waldenberg, Germany, May 31, 1946; AB, Wellesley Coll., 1967; JD, U. Calif., Berkeley, 1970. Bar: Calif. 1971. Mng. ptnr. Katten Muchin Zavis (formerly Katten Muchin & Zavis), Beverly Hills. Adj. prof. law Loyola U., 1976-96; trustee Ctr. for Law in the Pub. Interest. Mem. ABA (litigation sect., forum com. entertainment), Assn. Bus. Trial Lawyers, State Bar Calif. (standing com. pub. interest law 1976—), L.A. County Bar Assn. (del. conf. dels. 1974-76, 88-89), Beverly Hills Bar Assn., L.A. Copyright Soc. (trustee), Office: Katten Muchin Zavis 1999 Ave Of Stars Ste 1400 Los Angeles CA 90067-6115

TITLE, PETER STEPHEN, lawyer; b. New Orleans, Nov. 24, 1950; s. Harold Benjamin and Beulah (Sterbcow) Title; m. Sheryl Gerber, June 14, 1981. BA, Columbia U., 1972; JD, Tulane U., 1975. Bar: La. 1975, U.S. Dist. Ct. (ea., we., mid. dists.) La., U.S. Ct. Appeals (5th cir.). Assoc. Session, Fishman & Nathan LLP, New Orleans, 1975—81, ptnr., 1982—. Instr. on property Tulane U., 1978; asst. examiner Com. on Admissions to Bar, 1980—88, examiner, 1988—; lectr. on real estate. Author: Louisiana Real Estate Transactions, 1991, 2000. Mem.: ABA, Am. Judicature Soc., Am. Coll. Mortgage Attys., New Orleans Bar Assn. (chmn. title examinations com. 1992—93), La. Bar Assn. (chmn. sect. on trust estates, probate and immovable property law 1983—84), B'nai B'rith, Order of Coif, Phi Delta Phi. Jewish. Home: 515 Hillary St New Orleans LA 70118-3833 Office: Sessions Fishman & Nathan 201 Saint Charles Ave Fl 35 New Orleans LA 70170-1000 Office Phone: 504-582-1500.

TITLEY, LARRY J. lawyer; b. Tecumseh, Mich., Dec. 9, 1943; s. Leroy H. and Julia B. (Ruesink) T.; m. Julia Margaret Neukom, May 23, 1970; children: Sarah Catherine, John Neukom. BA, U. Mich., 1965, JD, 1972. Bar: Va. 1973, Mich. 1973. Assoc. Hunton & Williams, Richmond, Va., 1972-73, Varnum, Riddering, Schmidt & Howlett, Grand Rapids, Mich., 1973—. Trustee Friends Pub. Mus., 1985—94; bd. dirs. Pub. Mus. Found., 1988—97, pres., 1992—95; bd. dirs. Camp Optimist YMCA, 1993—98, Peninsular Club, 1994—2003, pres., 1997. Mem. ABA, Mich. Bar Assn., Grand Rapids Bar Assn. Home: 520 Roundtree Dr NE Ada MI 49301-9707 Office: Varnum Riddering Schmidt & Howlett Bridgewater Pl PO Box 352 Grand Rapids MI 49501-0352 E-mail: ljtitley@vrsh.com.

TITLEY, ROBERT L. lawyer; b. Tecumseh, Mich., Dec. 15, 1947; AB, U. Mich., 1970; JD, Duke U., 1973. Bar: Wis. 1973, Mich. 1974. Ptnr. Quarles & Brady, Milw. Mem. editorial bd. Duke Law Jour., 1972-73. Mem. State Bar Mich., State Bar Wis., Order of Coif. Office: Quarles & Brady LLP 411 E Wisconsin Ave Milwaukee WI 53202-4497

TITO, JAMES P. software company executive; Founder, pres. The Belmont Group, mfrs. memory components and circuit bds.; pers. Interactive Mktg. Techs., online svcs. and mktg. co., from 1988; co-founder, chmn., CEO eShare Techs. software co., Norcross, Ga. Spkr., lectr. on devel. of interacitve na cmty. software tech.; appearanced include CNN, CNBC, numerous TV news programs and stas., N.Y. State Legislature; bd. dirs. LISTNet, L.I. Software Tech. Network. Mem. L.I. Econ. Devel. Adv. Bd., N.Y. Christian Fellowship; mem. adv. bd. L.I. U. Named One of Silicon Alley's Top 100 N.Y. Internet Industry Execs., 2 times. Office: ESHARE Technologies 5051 Peachtree Corners Cir Norcross GA 30092

TITONE, VITO JOSEPH, former state court justice; b. Bklyn., July 5, 1929; s. Vito and Elena (Ruisi) T.; m. Margaret Anne Viola, Dec. 30, 1956; children: Stephen, Matthew, Elena Titone Hill, Elizabeth. BA, NYU, 1951; JD, St. John's U., 1956, LL.D., 1984. Bar: N.Y. 1957, U.S. Dist. Ct. (ea. and so. dists.) N.Y., 1962, U.S. Supreme Ct. 1964, U.S. Ct. Appeals N.Y. 1985. Ptnr. Maltese & Titone, N.Y.C., 1957-65, Maltese, Titone & Anastasi, N.Y.C., 1965-68; assoc. counsel to pres. pro tem N.Y. State Senate, 1965; justice N.Y. State Supreme Ct, N.Y.C., 1969-75; assoc. justice appellate div. 2d dept., 1975-85; judge N.Y. State Ct. Appeals, Albany, 1985—98; of counsel Mintz & Gold LLP, N.Y.C., 1998—. Adj. prof. Coll. S.I., CUNY, 1969-72, St. John's U., Jamaica, N.Y., 1969-85. Bd. editors N.Y. Law Jour., 1999; contbr. articles to law jour. Bd. govs. Daytop Village Inc., N.Y.C.; bd. dirs. Boy Scouts Am.; bd. trustees The Am. Parkinson Disease Assn. With U.S. Army, 1951-53, to col. N.Y. State Guard. Named Citizen of Yr. Daytop Village, N.Y.C., 1969, Disting. Citizen Wagner Coll., S.I., 1983, Outstanding Contbr. Camelot Substance Abuse Network, 1983; recipient citation of merit S.I. Salvation Army Adv. Bd., 1983, Rapollo award Columbian Lawyers Assn., 1983, Disting. Judiciary award Cath. Lawyers Guild Diocese of Bklyn., 1991, Disting. Svc. award N.Y. State Lawyers Assn., Justice William Brennan award N.Y. Assn. Criminal Def. Lawyers, 1993, Life Achievement award N.Y. Conf. Italian Am. State Legislators, 1994, Ellis Island Medal of Honor, 1997, gold medal Bklyn. Bar Assn., 1997. Mem. ABA, N.Y. State Bar Assn., Richmond County Bar Assn., Supreme Ct. Justice Assn., VFW, Am. Legion (past comdr.), Charles C. Pinckney Tribute Def. Assn. of N.Y., Justinian Soc., K.C. Roman Catholic. Office: Mintz and Gold LLP 444 Park Ave S New York NY 10016-7321

TITRUD, OLIVER GEORGE, retired medical educator; b. Clarissa, Minn., May 11, 1926; s. Geroge Marius Titrud and Gunda Gjerstad; m. Dorothy Selma Lindborg, Oct. 9, 1949; children: Kermit Oliver, Cheryll Lu, Douglas Glenn, Bethine Joy, Debrah Lynn, Timothy Craig, Howard George, Rebecca Ann. BS, Bemidji (Minn.) State U., 1948; MS, U. Denver, 1951; MEdn, Macalester Coll., 1958; D of Chiropractic, L.A. Coll. Chiropractic, 1963; cert. advanced studies, No. Ill. U., 1972. Assoc. prof. Northwestern Coll., Roseville, Minn., 1952-57, Pasadena (Calif.) Coll., 1957-60; prof. biology Azusa (Calif.) Pacific U., 1960-63, Warner Pacific Coll., Portland, Oreg., 1963-69; prof. anatomy Nat. Coll. Chiropractic, Lombard, Ill., 1969-72; mem. faculty Can. Meml. Chiropractic Coll., Toronto, Ont., 1972-73; acad. dean, prof. anatomy Western States Chiropractic Coll., Portland, 1973-79; mem. faculty Palmer Coll. Chiropractic, San Jose, Calif., 1979-89; prof. Naturopathic Coll., Portland, 1989-93. Chmn. test com. Nat. Bd. Chriopractic Examiners, Denver, 1975-78. Author: Titrud's Method of Human Dissection, 1977. With USN, 1944-46. Grantee Western Mich. U., 1960. Avocations: studying languages, public speaking. Home: PO Box 351 Clarissa MN 56440-0351

TITTMANN, BERNHARD RAINER, engineering science and mechanics educator; b. Moshi, Tanganjika, East Africa, Sept. 15, 1935; came to U.S., 1950, naturalized, 1956; s. Gustav and Hermine Marie (Polland) T.; m. Katharine Shower, Dec. 17, 1966; children: Christine M., Heidi E., Raymond J., Monica M., Brian P.F. BS, George Washington U., 1957; MS, UCLA, 1961, PhD, 1965. Mem. staff Hughes Aircraft Co., Culver City, Calif., 1957-65; asst. prof. UCLA, 1965-66; mem. staff Rockwell Internat., Thousand Oaks, Calif., 1966-79, dept. mgr., 1979-89; Schell prof. engring. Pa. State U., University Park, 1989—. Co-author 6 books; contbr. over 300 articles to profl. jours.; patentee in field. George Washington fellow George Washington U., 1953, Howard Hughes fellow Hughes Aircraft Co., 1957, Fulbright fellow, 1998. Fellow IEEE (adminstrv. com. for ultrasonics, ferroelectrics, frequency control, major awards chmn. 1999—, disting. lectr. 1998-99), Acoustical Soc. Am., KC (4th degree); mem. Phi Beta Kappa. Home: 2466 Sassafras Ct State College PA 16803-3366 Office: Pa State U 212 Earth Engring Sci Bldg University Park PA 16802-6804

TITUS, ALICE CESTANDINA (DINA TITUS), state legislator; b. Thomasville, Ga., May 23, 1950; m. Thomas Clayton Wright. AB, Coll. William and Mary, 1970; MA, U. Ga., 1973; PhD, Fla. State U., 1976. Prof. polit. sci. U. Nev., Las Vegas, 1977—; mem. from dist. 7 Nev. Senate, 1989—, minority fl. leader, 1993—, mem. Legislative commn., 1991—. Chmn. Nev. Humanities Com., 1984-86; mem. Eldorado Basin adv. group to Colo. River Commn.; active Gov. Commn. Bicentennial of U.S. Constn.; former mem. Gov. Commn. on Aging. Author: Bombs in the Backyard: Atomic Testing and American Politics, 1986, Battle Born: Federal-State Relations in Nevada during the 20th Century, 1989. Mem. Western Polit. Sci. Assn., Clark County Women's Dem. Club, Amer. Pen Women, Aquavision, PEO. Greek Orthodox. Home: 1637 Travois Cir Las Vegas NV 89119-6283 Office: Nev Senate 401 S Carson St Rm 114F Carson City NV 89701-4747

TITUS, BRUCE EARL, lawyer; b. N.Y.C., June 5, 1942; BA, Coll. William and Mary, 1964, JD, 1971. Bar: Va. 1971, D.C. 1972, Md. 1984. Asst. dir. torts br., civil divsn. U.S. Dept. Justice, 1971-82; mem. Jones, Waldo, Holbrook and McDonough, Washington; ptnr. Venable, Baetjer and Howard, LLP, McLean, Va., 1986-976; prin. Rees, Broome & Diaz P.C., Vienna, Va., 1997—. Exec.

editor William & Mary Law Review, 1970-71. Mem. ABA, Va. State Bar, D.C. Bar, Fairfax Bar Assn. (pres. 1999-2000), Md. State Bar, Phi Delta Phi, Omicron Delta Kappa. Office: Rees Broome & Diaz PC 9th Fl 8133 Leesburg Pike Vienna VA 22182-2706

TITUS, JON ALAN, lawyer; b. Milw., Oct. 6, 1955; s. Mary Elna Irwin; m. Laura Jean Newman, Sept. 5, 1982; children: Katherine, Derek. BA, U. Ariz., 1977; JD, Ariz. State U., 1980. Bar: Ariz. 1980, U.S. Dist. Ct. Ariz. 1980; cert. real estate specialist. Pres. Titus, Brueckner & Berry, P.C., Scottsdale, Ariz., 1980—. Mem. Ariz. Kidney Found., 1984—, pres., 1991-92. Recipient Alumni Achievement award Ariz. State U., 1996. Mem. Ariz. Bar Assn. (chmn. securities regulation sect. 1986-87), Maricopa County Bar Assn., Scottsdale Bar Assn. (dir. 1993-95). Office: Titus Brueckner & Berry PC 7373 N Scottsdale Rd Ste B-252 Scottsdale AZ 85253-3513

TITUS, MICHELE R. state legislator; m. Eric DeBarry; 2 children. Grad., Albany Law Sch., 1998. Edn. lawyer, Brklyn.-Queens, NY, 1998—; state rep. State of N.Y., 2002—. Former exec. dir. N.Y. State Black and Puerto Rican Legis. Caucus. Democrat. Office: 19-31 Mott Ave Rm 301 Far Rockaway NY 11691

TITUS, ROGER WARREN, judge; b. Washington, Dec. 16, 1941; s. George R. and Margaret Titus; m. Catherine Mary Gaughen, Aug. 16, 1961; children: Paula Titus Laboy, Richard Roger, Mark William. BA, Johns Hopkins U., 1963; JD, Georgetown U., 1966. Bar: Md. 1966, D.C. 1966, U.S. Dist. Ct. Md. 1966, D.C. Dist. 1966, U.S. Ct. Appeals (4th cir.) 1966, U.S. Supreme Ct. 1970. Ptnr. Titus & Glasgow, Rockville, Md., 1966-88, Venable, Baetjer & Howard, Rockville, 1998—2003; judge U.S. Dist. Ct. for the Dist. of Md., Greenbelt, Md., 2003—. Asst. city atty. City of Rockville, 1966-69, city atty., 1970-82; spl. asst. Md. State Bd. of Law Examiners, 1969-72; adj. prof. law Georgetown U., Washington, 1972-78; mem. inquiry com. Atty. Grievance Commn., Annapolis, Md., 1975-80; mem. Trial Cts. Judicial Nominating Commn. Montgomery County, 1979-91; mem. standing com. on rules of practice and procedure Ct. of Appeals of Md., 1989—; mem. Appellate Jud. Nominating Commn., 1991-99. Trustee Suburban Hosp., Inc., Bethesda, Md., 1986-2000, chmn. bd., 1997-2000. Fellow: Am. Acad. Appellate Lawyers, Md. Bar Found. (bd. dirs. 1987—93, v.p. 1990—91, pres. 1991—93), Am. Bar Found., Am. Coll. Trial Lawyers; mem.: ABA (del. 1987—95), Montgomery County Bar Assn. (exec. com. 1983—84), Md. Mcpl. Attys. Assn. (pres. 1975), Am. Judicature Soc. (bd. dirs. 1995—2001), Md. Bar Assn. (sec. 1984—87, pres. 1988—89), Nat. Conf. Bar Pres. (mem. exec. coun. 1990—93), City Tavern Club. Office: US Dist Ct for Dist of Md 6500 Cherrywood Ln Greenbelt MD 20770

TITUS, TIMOTHY NEAL, aerospace scientist, military officer; b. Spirit Lake, Iowa, Sept. 6, 1962; s. DeWayne Orville and Alice Elizabeth Titus. PhD, U. Wyo., Laramie, Wyo., 1996. Space scientist U.S.G.S., Flagstaff, Ariz., 1999—; bn. comdr. 1-180th FA Bn., Ariz. Army N.G., Phoenix, Ariz., 2003—. R-Liberal. Free Methodist. Achievements include discovery of exposed water ice at the edge of the Martian southern polar cap. Avocations: travel, dance. Home: 2652 E Rt 66 Flagstaff AZ 86004 Office: US Geol Survey 2255 North Gemini Dr Flagstaff AZ 86001

TITUS, VICTOR ALLEN, lawyer; b. Nevada, Mo., Sept. 2, 1956; s. Charles Allen and Viola Mae (Cliffman) T.; m. Laraine Carol Cook, Oct. 13, 1974 (div. Feb. 1982); 1 child, Matthew; m. Deborah Diane Carpenter, Apr. 10, 1984; 1 child, Jacquelynn. BS, BA, Ctrl. Mo. State U., 1978; JD, U. Mo., 1981. Bar: N.Mex. 1981, U.S. Dist. Ct. N.Mex. 1981, Mo. 1982, U.S. Ct. Appeals (10th cir. 1983), U.S. Supreme Ct. 1986, Colo. 1989, Ariz. 1995. Lawyer Jay L. Faurot, P.C., Farmington, N.Mex., 1981-83; ptnr. Faurot & Titus, P.C., Farmington, N.Mex., 1983-85; lawyer, sole proprietor Victor A. Titus, P.C., Farmington, N.Mex., 1985—. Arbitrator in civil disputes Alternative Dispute Resolution-Arbitration; liquor lic. hearing officer City of Farmington, 1989-94. Contbr. articles to profl. jours. Adult Behind Youth, Boys & Girls Club, Farmington, 1987—; mem. hosp. adv. bd. San Juan Regional Med. Ctr., Farmington, 1988-93. Recipient San Juan County Disting. Svc. award N.Mex. Bar Assn., 1984; named one of Best Lawyers in Am., 1995-96, 97—. Mem. Assn. Trial Lawyers of Am., N.Mex. Trial Lawyers (bd. dirs. 1983—, pres. 1993-94), State Bar of N.Mex. (disciplinary bd. 1997—, specialization com. 1992-98, legal advt. com. 1990), San Juan County Bar Assn. (pres. 1984), Nat. Assn. Criminal Def. Lawyers (life), Colo. Trial Lawyers. Democrat. Avocation: sports. Home: 5760 Pinehurst Farmington NM 87402-5078 Office: Victor A Titus PC 2021 E 20th St Farmington NM 87401-2516 E-mail: vtitus@advantas.com.

TITUS-DILLON, PAULINE YVONNE, associate dean academic affairs, medical educator; b. Petersfield, Jamaica, Jan. 1, 1938; came to U.S., 1954; d. Ernest H. Titus and Vera I. (Tate) Harvey; m. Owen C. Dillon, Nov. 29, 1963. Student, Pratt Inst., 1954-57; BS in Chemistry summa cum laude, Howard U., 1960, MD, 1964. Diplomate Nat. Bd. Med. Examiners, Am. Bd. Internal Medicine. Intern Freedmen's Hosp. (name now Howard U. Hosp.), Washington, 1964-65, asst. resident, 1965-67, resident, chief resident, 1967-68, family practice physician, 1971, attending, 1971—; fellow in endocrinology and metabolism Georgetown U. Hosp., Washington, 1968-69; postdoctoral fellow NIH, Bethesda, Md., 1975-77; outpatient clinic physician Vets.' Adminstrn. Hosp., Columbia, S.C., 1969-71; from asst. prof. to assoc. prof. dept. medicine Howard U. Coll. Medicine, Washington, 1971-81, prof. internal medicine, 1981—, assoc. dean acad. affairs, 1980—2000; chief med. officer, residency prog. dir. Howard U. Med. Svc. D.C. Gen. Hosp., Washington, 1977-80, attending, 1977-80; sr. assoc. dean Howard U. Coll. Medicine, Washington, 2000—. Cons. Malawi, Africa project of Dept. Cmty. Health and Family Practice, 1989, Nat. Bd. Med. Examiners, 1995, Ednl. Commn. for Fgn. Med. Grads., 1997; Howard U. Coll. Medicine rep. Am. Assn. Med. Colls., 1980—, coord. activities, presenter, 1982-83, exec. devel. seminar for women, 1983, mem. Nat. Identification Prog. for Advancement of Women in Higher Edn., 1985, others; exec. chief proctor Nat. Bd. Med. Examiners, 1983—, liaison rep. for Howard U. Coll. Medicine, 1987—, mem. steering com. for liaison rep., 1989—, prin. investigator for Computer Based Exams. project, 1989—, mem. bd., 1997—; mem. numerous hosp., coll. coms., subcoms., reviews; lectr., presenter confs., workshops, symposiums. Contbr. articles to profl. jours. Recipient Joseph L. Johnson physiology award, 1961-62, Jacobi Soc. cert. of merit for proficiency in pediatrics, 1964, James E. Simpson Meml. prize Howard U., 1964, psychiatry prize, 1964, dept. surgery prize, 1964, Matilda Davis-Cunningham award, 1964, Am. Acad. Dental Medicine award, 1964, Daniel Hale Williams internship award, 1966, Daniel Hale Williams residency award, 1968, Nat. Rsch. Svc. award, 1975-77, inspirational leadership award Student Coun. Coll. of Medicine, 1979, superior performance as Chief Med. Officer award Howard U. Med. Svc., D.C. Gen. Hosp., 1980, student coun. award Howard U. Coll. Medicine, 1995, Pearl A. Watson award for excellence in delivery of health care Caribbean Am. Intercultural Orgn., 1996;; named Doctor of Year, D.C. Gen. Hosp., 1980; Alma Wells Givens scholar, 1962-63. Fellow ACP; mem. AMA, Nat. Med. Assn., Am. Med. Women's Assn. (liaison officer Howard U. Coll. Medicine, v.p. br. 1 Washington chpt. 1991-92, pres. 1992-93, Janet M. Glasgow Meml. award 1964), Nat. Bd. Med. Examiners, N.Y. Acad. Scis., D.C. Med. Soc., Phi Beta Kappa, Sigma Xi, Beta Kappa Chi, Alpha Omega Alpha (sec., treas. 1977-98, Gamma chpt. of Washington, councillor 1998—). Avocations: sewing, crochet, aerobics. Office: Howard Univ Coll Medicine 520 W St NW Washington DC 20059-0001 Fax: 202-806-7934.

TITZMAN, DONNA M. energy executive; BBA in Acctg., U. Tex. CPA. Acct. natural gas liquids Valero Energy Corp., San Antonio, 1986—89, various positions with fin. dept., 1989, v.p., treas., 1999—. Office: Valero Corp Hdqs 1 Valero Pl San Antonio TX 78212-3186

TIUMAN, ERICH LIM, textile company executive; b. Manila, Philippines, Nov. 20, 1935; s. Guat Ngo and Aytee Lim; m. Sofia Lu Tiuman, Dec. 25, 1960; children: Siegfried L., Luzono L. B Music Composition and Conducting, Centro Escolar U. Sch Music, Manila, 1968, M Music Composition, 1969. Prodn. mgr. Bee Lam Shirt Factory, Manila, 1954-63; pres. Peng Kong Grand Mason Band, Manila, 1954-63; dir., rsch. conductor China Youth Symphony Orchestra, Taipei, 1964-66; owner Tiuman Textile Distributors, Manila, 1968-75; pres., gen. mgr. Tiuman & Co., Manila, 1968-75; chmn., gen. mgr. Tiuman Ent. MLA, Manila, 1985-91; pre gen. mgr. Philtai Internat., Manila, 1985-88; owner Yecy Mfg., Manila, 1993—; with Izhu Inc., N.Y.C., 1995—. Composer orchestra lit., Symphony # 2, 1971, Tainoko Ballet Music, 1971. Recipient Philippine Swimming Championship/2nd pla., Philippines Athletic Assn., Manila, 1951, Chung Shan awards for Lit. and Arts, Csala Found., Taipei, 1971, Pres. Chiang Kai Sek Cultural award, MLA Literay Club, Manila, 1971. Mem. Asian Composers League/Philippines, Asian Pacific Ethnomusicology Soc. Avocations: swimming, rsch. in humanities, travel, composing, phy. tng. Home: Apt 40 B 1 Central Park W New York NY 10023 Office: 3-A Sta Agueda Ave Sto Niño Parañague Manila 1704 Philippines also: Izhu Inc 295 Greenwich St Apt 6P New York NY 10007-1052

TIZZIO, THOMAS RALPH, brokerage executive; b. Elmont, N.Y., Jan. 9, 1938; s. Anthony Thomas and Ann Marie (Pascale) T.; m. Mary Ann Gentile, Aug. 26, 1962; children: Anthony, Vincent, Thomas. BBA, Bklyn. Coll., 1962. Underwriter W.J. Roberts & Co., N.Y.C., 1957-65; sr. underwriter Atlantic Mut. Ins. Co., 1965-67; various positions AIG Am. Home Assurance Co., N.Y.C., 1967-74, sr. v.p. property underwriting, 1974-78; exec. v.p. AIG Transatlantic Reins. Co., N.Y.C., 1978-80, pres., bd. dirs., 1980-82; sr. v.p. reins. Am. Internat. Group, Inc., N.Y.C., 1982-85, pres. domestic brokerage divsn., 1985-91, pres. Brokerage divsn., 1986-91, pres., 1991-97, sr. vice chmn., 1997—. Mem. Am. Inst. for Property and Liability Underwriters (trustee), Ins. Inst. Am. (trustee). Office: Am Internat Group Inc 175 Water St New York NY 10038-4918

TJIAN, ROBERT TSE NAN, biochemistry educator, biology researcher, virology researcher; b. Hong Kong, Sept. 22, 1949; naturalized Brit. citizen. m. 1976. BA, U. Calif., Berkeley, 1971; PhD in Molecular Biology, Harvard U., 1976. Staff investigator molecular virology Cold Spring Harbor Lab., 1976-79, Robertson fellow, 1978; prof. biochemistry U. Calif., Berkeley, 1979—, prof. molecular and cell biology. Named Passano Found. laureate; recipient Lewis S. Rosentiel award for disting. work in basic med. rsch. Brandeis U., 1995. Mem. NAS (Molecular Biology award 1991). Achievements include research in oncogenic viruses and their interactions with the host cell; control of gene expression; simian virus 40; a small DNA containing oncogenic virus, tumor antigen, its structure and function. Office: U Calif Molecular and Cell Biology Dept 401 Barker Hall Berkeley CA 94720-0001*

TJOFLAT, GERALD BARD, federal judge; b. Pitts., Dec. 6, 1929; s. Gerald Benjamin and Sarita (Romero-Hermoso) Tjoflat; m. Sarah Marie Pfohl, July 27, 1957 (dec.); children: Gerald Bard, Marie Elizabeth; m. Marcia Penman Parker, Feb. 21, 1998. Student, U. Va., 1947—50, U. Cin., 1950—52; LLB, Duke U., 1957; DCL (hon.), Jacksonville U., 1978; LLD (hon.), William Mitchell Coll., 1993. Bar: Fla. 1957. Pvt. practice, Jacksonville, Fla., 1957—68; judge 4th Jud. Cir. Ct., Fla., 1968—70, U.S. Dist. Ct. Mid. Dist., Jacksonville, 1970—75, U.S. Ct. Appeals 5th Cir., Jacksonville, 1975—81, U.S. Ct. Appeals 11th Cir., Jacksonville, 1981—, chief judge, 1989—96. Mem. Adv. Corrections Coun. U.S., 1975—87, Jud. Conf. U.S., 1989—96, mem. com. adminstrn. probation sys., 1972—87, chmn., 1978—87; mem. Fed. Jud. Ct. Com. on Sentencing, Probation and Pretrial Svcs., 1988—90; U.S. del. 6th and 7th UN Congress for Prevention of Crime and Treatment of Offenders. Hon. life mem., bd. visitors Duke U. Law Sch., 2000; pres. North Fla. coun. Boy Scouts Am., 1976—85, 2000—01, chmn., 1985—90; trustee Jacksonville Marine Inst., 1976—90, Episc. H.S., Jacksonville, 1975—90; mem. vestry St. Johns Cathedral, Jacksonville, 1969—71, 1973—75, 1977—79, 1981—83, 1985—87, 1993, 1995—96, sr. warden, 1975, 1983, 1987, 1991, 1992. With U.S. Army, 1953—55. Recipient Merit award, Duke U., 1990, Fordham-Stein prize, 1996. Mem.: ABA, Am. Judicature Soc., Am. Law Inst., Fla. Bar Assn. Episcopalian. Office: 300 N Hogan St Ste 14-200 Jacksonville FL 32202-4257

TKACHUK, KEITH, professional hockey player; b. Melrose, Mass., Mar. 28, 1972; With Phoenix Coyotes formerly Winnipeg (Canada) Jets, 1992—2001, St. Louis Blues, 2001—. Mem. Team U.S.A., World Cup of Hockey, 1996, 2004, U.S. Olympic Hockey Team, Nagano, Japan, 1998, Salt Lake City, 2002. Named NHL Second Team All-Star, 1995, 1998; named to NHL All-Star Game, 1997—99, 2004. Achievements include mem. World Cup Champion Team U.S.A., 1996. Office: St Louis Blues Savvis Ctr Saint Louis MO 63103*

TKACZ, VIRLANA MARIA, theater director, writer, translator; b. Newark, June 23, 1952; BA, Bennington Coll., 1974; MFA, Columbia U., 1983. Assoc. prodr. Fox TV State of the Arts, N.Y.C., 1979—80; tchg. asst. Columbia U. Sch. of the Arts, N.Y.C., 1980—83; asst. dir., prodn. mgr. La MaMa Exptl. Theatre, N.Y.C., 1982—89; dir., dramaturg, asst. dir. N.Y.C., 1983—; assoc. dir., prodn. mgr. Ping Chong & Co., N.Y.C., 1989—96; resident dir. La MaMa Exptl. Theatre, N.Y.C., 1989—; artistic dir. and founder Yara Arts Group, N.Y.C., 1990—. Author: (book) Shanar: Dedicaiton Ritual of a Buryat Shaman in Siberia (Benjamin Franklin Award best book on religion, 2002); dir. and creator: (15 original theatre pieces) Swan, Howling, Obo: Our Shamanism, Song Tree, Circle, Flight of the White Bird, Virtual Souls, Wayward Wind, Waterfall/Refelctions, Yara's Forest Song, Blind Sight, Explosions, A Light From the East, The Warrior's Sister; translator: (poem) May (Transl. Prize from Agni Reveiw, 1992), (play) Forest Song (Nat. Theatre Transl. Fund Award, 1993), (poem) Ukrainian and Buryat Poetry (NY State Coun. on the Arts Lit.). Fellow Fulbright fellowship, Kiev, Ukraine, 2002; Internat. Creative Collaborations grant, Meet the Composer/Ford Found., 1997-1999. Mem.: Actors' Equity Assn., Am. Lit. Translators Assn. Office: Yara Arts Group 306 East 11th St #3B New York NY 10003 Office Phone: 212-475-6474. E-mail: yara@prodigy.net.

TKACZUK, NANCY ANNE, cardiovascular services administrator; b. Cambridge, Mass., Nov. 17, 1949; d. Ralph Aubrey and Eleanor Mae (Goding) Bedley; m. John Paul Tkaczuk, Apr. 9, 1977 (div. Apr. 1983); children: Timothy Aubrey, James Paul. AS in Social Svc., Endicott Coll., 1969; ADN, Clayton Coll., 1975. Coronary care nurse New England Meml. Hosp., Wakefield, Mass., 1975; cardiac cath lab nurse Saint Josephs Hosp., Atlanta, 1976-79; dir. cardiovascular svcs. Northside Hosp., Atlanta, 1979—. Founder Mitral Valve Prolapse Support, Atlanta, 1986—; BCLS instr., trainer Am. Heart Assn., 1976—, instr. ACLS, 1990—, pub. spkr., 1975—. Author: Mitral Valve Prolapse, The Heart With A Different Beat, 1986. Mem. Am. Coll. Cardiovascular Adminstrs., Atlanta Health Care Alliance, Am. Heart Assn., Ga. Hosp. Assn., Ga. Soc. Ambulatory Care. Methodist. Avocations: tennis, golf. Home: 715 Cranberry Trl Roswell GA 30076-2377 Office: Northside Hosp Cardiology Dept 1000 Johnson Ferry Rd NE Atlanta GA 30342-1611 E-mail: nancy.tkaczuk@northside.com.

TLOCZYNSKI, JOSEPH, psychology professor, researcher; b. Mt. Carmel, Pa., Oct. 10, 1958; s. Stephen Joseph Tloczynski and Mary Louise Hoffman Tloczynski; m. Andrea Shillingford, Nov. 14, 1987; children: Christian Joseph, Daniel Andrew, Eric Samuel. PhD in Psychology, Lehigh U., 1991. Prof. psychology dept. Bloomsburg (Pa.) U., 1990—. Contbr. articles to scholarly jours. Sch. bd. mem. St. Columba Sch., Bloomsburg, 2000—04. Mem.: APA (assoc.; mem. divsn. 36 Psychology of Religion). Roman Catholic. Achievements include research in Meditation, Contemplative Prayer, Intercessory Prayer, Spirituality, Personality, Health & Wellness. Avocations: family, health and fitness, music, landscaping and gardening. Office: Bloomsburg U Psychology Dept Bloomsburg PA 17815 Personal E-mail: jtloczyn@bloomu.edu. E-mail: jtloczyn@bloomu.edu.

TLSTY, THEA DOROTHY, research scientist, educator; b. Mobile, Ala., Jan. 28, 1952; d. Theodore H. and Josepine M. Tlsty. BS in zoology, U. South Fla., 1973; PhD in molecular biology, Washington U., 1980. Asst. prof. pathology U. NC, Chapel Hill, 1985-92, mem. Lineberger Comprehensive Cancer Ctr., 1985—95, assoc. prof. pathology, 1992—95, U. Calif., San Francisco, 1995—96, dir. molecular pathology, 1995—96, mem. Cancer Rsch. Inst., 1995—96, prof. pathology, 1996—, dir. Ctr. for Translational Rsch. in the Molecular Genetics of Cancer, 1996—, dir. program cell cycling and signaling, Comprehensive Cancer Ctr., 1996—. Predoctoral fellow cellular and molecular biology program, Wash. U., St. Louis, 1976-80, postdoctoral fellow dept. microbiology and immunology, 1980-81; postdoctoral fellow/sr. rsch. assoc. dept. biological sciences, Stanford U., 1981-85; vis. scientist U. Geneva, 1982; vis. scholar U. Zimbabwe, 1992; cons. Bristol-Meyers Co., 1987, Glaxo, 1990—94, Geron, 1993—95, Oncormed, 1995-97, Onyx, 1997-98, Day Casebeer, 1999-2000, Pennie and Edmonds, 2001-02; mem. editl. bd. Molecular Carcinogenesis, 1992-, Carcinogenesis, 1993-, Cancer Rsch., 1995-, Environ. Health Perspectives, 1996-, Am. Jour. Pathology, 1997-; mem. adv. coun., GM Cancer Rsch. Found. Contbr. numerous articles to sci. jours. Recipient Gold Key Honor Soc. Award; Starter Grant Award, Pharmaceutical Mfrs. Assn.; Avon Scholar, 2001-. Mem. AAAS, Am. Soc. Microbiology, Am. Assn. Cancer Rsch., Am. Soc. Biological Chemists and Molecular Biologists, Assn. for Women in Sci., Women in Cancer Rsch., Women in Cell Biology, Calif. Soc. Pathologists, Assn. Molecular Pathologists, Am. Soc. Investigative Pathology, Am. Soc. Cell Biology, Am. Soc. Biochemistry and Molecular Biology. Avocations: bicycling, sculpting, swimming. Office: U Calif Box 0506 San Francisco CA 94143-0506

TOAL, JAMES FRANCIS, academic administrator; b. N.Y.C., June 7, 1932; s. John Joseph and Catherine (Whyte) T. MA, St. John's U., 1966; PhD, Fordham U., 1976. Cert. elem. tchr., N.Y. cert. supt., adminstrn. and supervision, English 7-12. Athletic dir., tchr. English St. Francis Prep. High Sch., N.Y.C., 1957-60; tchr. Bishop Ford High Sch., N.Y.C., 1960-66, chmn. dept. English; prin. St. Francis Central Summer High Sch., N.Y.C., 1966-73, St. Francis Prep. High Sch., N.Y.C., 1966-73; exec. v.p., assoc. prof. dept. edn. adminstrn. and supervision Grad. Sch. St. Bonaventure U., N.Y., 1976-83; pres., prof. Quincy U., Ill., 1983-97; v.p. Siena Coll., Loudonville, N.Y., 1997—; also bd. trustees. Mem. Springfield Diocesan Bd. of Edn., Provincial Bd. of Edn., Franciscan Friars of Chgo. and St. Louis. Trustee Siena Coll., Loudonville, N.Y., 1977-83; bd. advisors Jamestown Community Coll., Olean, N.Y., 1979-83; bd. dirs. Am. Cancer Soc., Olean, 1981-83; mem. Mental Health Assn., 1981-83; mem. state legis. com. Commn. of Ind. Colls. and Univs., Albany, N.Y., 1980-83; mem. bd. trustees Padua Franciscan High Sch. Grantee Colgate U., 1967; grantee SUNY-Plattsburg, 1968, St. Bonaventure U., 1980 Mem. Am. Coun. on Edn., Associated Colls. of Ill., Ill. Bus. and Edn. Forum, Assn. of Governing Bds., West Ctrl. Ill. Ednl. Telecomm. Corp. (bd. dirs. exec. com., fin. com., pers. com.), Fedn. Ind. Ill. Colls. and Univs. (pub. rels. com.), Mid. States Accrediting Assn. (assoc., evaluation team for higher edn.), Nat. Assn. Secondary Sch. Prins., North Ctrl. Accrediting Assn. (evaluation team for higher edn., chair evaluation team 1986—), Soc. Coll. and U. Planning, Quincy C. of C. (transp. com. 1985-96, computer com. 1996—), Rotary, Univ. Club, KC, Phi Delta Kappa. Office: Siena Coll Office of VP Loudon Rd Loudonville NY 12211

TOAL, JEAN HOEFER, state supreme court chief justice; b. Columbia, S.C., Aug. 11, 1943; d. Herbert W. and Lilla (Farrell) Hoefer; m. William Thomas Toal; children: Jean Hoefer Eisen, Lilla Patrick. BA in Philosophy, Agnes Scott Coll., 1965; JD, U. S.C., 1968; LHD (hon.), Coll. Charleston, 1990; LLD (hon.), Columbia Coll., 1992, The Citadel, 1999, Francis Marion U., 1999, U. S.C., 2000. Bar: S.C. Assoc. Haynsworth, Perry, Bryant, Marion & Johnstone, 1968-70; ptnr. Belser, Baker, Barwick, Ravenel, Toal & Bender, Columbia, 1970-88; assoc. justice S.C. Supreme Ct., Columbia, 1988-00, chief justice, 2000—. Mem. S.C. Human Affairs Commn., 1972-74; mem. S.C. Ho. of Reps., 1975-88, chmn. house rules com., constitutional laws subcom. house judiciary com.; mem. parish coun. and lector St. Joseph's Cath. Ch.; chair S.C. Juvenile Justice Task Force, 1992-94; chair S.C. Rhodes Scholar Selection Com., 1994. Mng. editor S.C. Law Rev., 1967-68. Bd. visitors Clemson U., 1978; trustee Columbia Mus. Art; bd. trustees Agnes Scott Coll., 1996—. Named Legislator of Yr. Greenville News, Woman of Yr., U. S.C. Mortar Bd., 1989, Top 25 Doers, Dreamers & Drivers, Govt. Tech. Mag., 2003; recipient Disting. Svc. award S.C. Mcpl. Assn., U. Notre Dame award, 1991, Algernon Sydney Sullivan award U. S.C., 1991, Agnes Scott Coll. Outstanding Alumna award, 1991, John W. Williams award, Richland County Bar Assn., 1994, Jean Galloway Bissell award, S.C. Women Lawyers Assn., 1995, Margaret Brent Women Lawyers of Achievement award, 2004. Mem. ABA, S.C. Women Lawyers Assn., John Belton O'Neill Inn of Ct., Phi Beta Kappa, Mortar Bd., Order of the Coif. Office: Supreme Ct SC PO Box 11330 Columbia SC 29211-2456 E-mail: jtoal@sccourts.org.

TOALE, THOMAS EDWARD, school system administrator, priest; b. Independence, Iowa, Aug. 30, 1953; s. Francis Mark and Clara R. (DePaepe) T. BS in Biology, Loras Coll., 1975, MA in Ednl. Adminstrn., 1986; MA in Theology, St. Paul Sem., 1980; PhD in Ednl. Adminstrn., U. Iowa, 1988. Ordained priest Roman Cath. Ch., 1981; cert. tchr., prin., supt., Iowa. Tchr. St. Joseph Key West, Dubuque, Iowa, 1975-77, Marquette High Sch., Bellevue, Iowa, 1981-84, prin., 1984-86; assoc. supt. Archdiocese of Dubuque, 1986-87, supt. schs., 1987—. Assoc. pastor St. Joseph Ch., Bellevue, 1981-84; pastor Sts. Peter and Paul Ch., Springbrook, Iowa, 1984-86, St. Peter, Temple Hill, Cascade, Iowa, 1986—. Mem. Nat. Cath. Edn. Assn. (pres., chief adminstrs. Cath. edn.). Office: Archdiocese of Dubuque 1229 Mount Loretta Ave Dubuque IA 52003-7826

TOAN, BARRETT A. health products executive; s. Winthrop A. and Edith Byrne Toan; m. Polly O'Brien; children: Elliot, Frannie. BA in history, Kenyon Coll., 1969; MBA, U. Pa., 1974. With budget bur. State of Ill., Springfield; positions with State of Pa.; cons. PriceWaterhouse, Washington; commr. divsn. social svcs. State of Ark., 1979—81; dir. dept. social svcs. State of Mo., 1981—85; exec. dir., COO Sanus Health Plan of St. Louis, 1985—91; pres. Express Scripts Inc., Maryland Heights, Mo., 1990—2002, CEO, 1992—, chmn., 2000—. Bd. dirs. Pharm. Care Mgmt. Assn., Sigma-Aldrich Corp. Mem. bd. dirs., treas. Mentor St. Louis. Named Entrepreneur of Yr. Inc. Mag., 1994. Office: Express Scripts 13900 Riverport Dr Maryland Heights MO 63043-4827*

TOAY, THELMA M. columnist, poet; b. Anamosa, Iowa, Feb. 22, 1915; d. Frank Leroy and Edna May Stoughton; m. John S. Toay; 3 children. Student, St. Lukes Sch. Nursing, Davenport, IA, 1933, Highland Coll., 1966—67, Famous Writer's Course, Westport, CT; AA in Journalism, N.E. Iowa CC, Peosta, 1995—97. Contbr. various newspapers, Freeport, Ill., 1962—; contbr. Julien's Jour., Dubuque, Iowa, 1995—2003. Author: Bittersweet, 1979, Places for the Heart - Profiles of Life, 2001. Avocations: theater, music, reading, flower gardening.

TOBACH, ETHEL, retired curator; b. Miaskovka, USSR, Nov. 7, 1921; came to U.S., 1923; d. Ralph Wiener and Fanny (Schechterman) Wiener Idels; m. Charles Tobach, 1947 (dec. 1969). BA, Hunter Coll., 1949; MA, NYU, 1952, PhD, 1957; DSc (hon.), L.I. Univ., 1975. Lic. psychologist, N.Y. Rsch. fellow Am. Mus. Natural History, N.Y.C., 1958-61, assoc. curator, 1964-69, curator, 1969-90, emerita curator; rsch. fellow NYU, N.Y.C., 1961-64. Adj. prof. psychology and biology CUNY, N.Y.C., 1964—; disting. cons. faculty Saybrook Inst., San Francisco, 1998—. Co-editor: (series) T.C. Schneirla Conference Series, 1981, Genes & Gender Series, 1975; editor: International Jour. Comparative Psychology, 1987-93; assoc. editor: Peace and Conflict: Jour. of Peace Psychology, 1994—. Recipient Disting. Sci. Career, Assn. Women in Sci., 1974, NIHH Career Devel. award, 1964-74, Disting. Sci. Publ., Assn. for Women in Psychology, 1982, Kurt Lewin award Soc. for Psychol. Study of Social Issues, 1993, Gustavus Myers award for outstanding pub. on human rights in N.Am., 1996, Lifetime Peace Activity award Soc. for Study Peace, Conflict and Violence, 1999, Lifetime Achievement Psychology in Pub. Interest Gold Medal award Am. Psychol. Found., 2003. Fellow APA (pres. comparative psychology divsn. 1985, peace psycology divsn., 2003); mem. Internat. Soc. Comparative Psychology (sec. 1988-92, pres. (hon.)), Ea. Psychol. Assn. (pres. 1987, bd. dirs. 2001—, mem. exec. com. 2002—), N.Y. Acad. Scis. (v.p. behavioral scis. 1973-76), Psychologists for Social Responsibility), Soc. for Study of Peace, Conflict and Violence. Office: Am Mus Natural History Central Pkwy 79th St New York NY 10024-5192

TOBACK, PAUL A. recreational facility executive; Atty. Katten Muchin & Zavis, Chgo.; dir. adminstrn. City of Chgo.; exec. asst. to Chief Staff The White House, Washington; COO Globetrotters Engring. Corp.; from exec. v.p., COO to pres., CEO Bally Total Fitness Holding Corp., Chgo., 1997—2002, pres., 2002—, CEO, 2002—, bd. dirs. Office: Bally Total Fitness Holding Corp 8700 W Bryn Mawr Ave Chicago IL 60631*

TOBE, STEPHEN SOLOMON, zoology educator; b. Niagara-on-the-Lake, Ont., Can., Oct. 11, 1944; s. John Harold and Rose T. (Bolter) T.; m. Martha Reller. BSc, Queen's U., Kingston, Ont., 1967; MSc, York U., Toronto, Ont., 1969; PhD, McGill U., Montreal, Que., Can., 1972. Rsch. fellow U. Sussex, Eng., 1972-74; asst. prof. U. Toronto, 1974-78, assoc. prof., 1974-78, prof., 1982—, assoc. dean scis., faculty arts and sci., 1988-93, vice dean faculty arts and sci., 1995-96. Vis. prof. U. Calif., Berkeley, 1981, Nat. U. Singapore, 1987, 1993-94, U. Hawaii, 1988; mem. animal biology grant selection com. Natural Scis. and Engring. Rsch. Coun. Can., 1986-89, chair, 1988-89; lectr. Internat. Congress Entomology, Vancouver, B.C., Can., 1988; cons. in hydroponics. Editor Insect Biochemistry, 1987; mem. editl. bd. Jour. Insect Physiology, 1980—, Physiol. Entomology, 1985—, Life Scis. Advances, 1987—, Gen. and Comparative Endocrinology, 1995—; contbr. chpts. to books and articles to profl. jours. Recipient Pickford medal in comparative endocrinology, 1993; E.W.R. Steacie fellow Natural Scis. and Engring. Rsch. Coun. Can., 1982-84. Fellow Royal Soc. Can., Royal Entomol. Soc.; mem. AAAS, Entomol. Soc. Can. (C. Gordon Hewitt award 1982, gold medal 1990), Soc. Exptl. Biology. Avocations: amateur radio, gardening, hydroponics. Home: PO Box 695 Virgil ON Canada L0S 1T0 Office: U Toronto Dept Zoology 25 Harbord St Toronto ON Canada M5S 3G5 Office Phone: 416-978-3517. E-mail: stephen.tobe@utoronto.ca.

TOBEN, DOREEN A. corporate financial executive; b. Curacao; m. Ed Toben; 2 children. AB Polit. Sci., MBA Fin. and Mktg. . Dir. corp. planning AT&T, 1972; exec. dir. mktg. Bell Atlantic Enterprises Internat., Inc., 1989; various positions equipment engring., ops., and small bus. and consumer market mgmt. Bell Atlantic, Pa.; dir. fin. Bell Atlantic, 1983; divsn. mgr. strat. planning Bell Atlantic, 1984; asst. v.p.-comptroller Bell Atlantic, N.J., 1992; CFO Bell Atlantic, 1993; v.p. corp. fin. Bell Atlantic, vice pres., controller, 1995; mem. com. Bell Atlantic, v.p., CFO telecomm. network; sr. v.p., CFO telecomm. group Verizon, exec. v.p., CFO, 2002—. Office: Verizon 1095 Avenue of Americas New York NY 10036

TOBER, BARBARA D. (MRS. DONALD GIBBS TOBER), editor; b. Summit, N.J., Aug. 19, 1934; d. Rodney Fielding and Maude Starkey; m. Donald Gibbs Tober, Apr. 5, 1973. Student, Traphagen Sch. Fashion, 1954-56, Fashion Inst. Tech., 1956-58, N.Y. Sch. Interior Design, 1964. Copy editor Vogue Pattern Book, 1958-60; beauty editor Vogue mag., 1961; dir. women's services Bartell Media Corp., 1961-66; editor-in-chief Bride's mag., N.Y.C., 1966-94; chmn. Mus. Arts and Design; pres. Acronym, Inc., N.Y.C., 1995—, The Barbara Tober Found., 1995—. Sec.-treas., dir. Sugar Foods Corp.; adv. bd. Traphagen Sch.; coord. SBA awards; Am. Craft Coun., 1983—, benefit food com. chmn., 1984-87. Author: The ABC's of Beauty, 1963, China: A Cognizant Guide, 1980, The Wedding . . . The Marriage . . . And the Role of the Retailer, 1980, The Bride: A Celebration, 1984 Mem. Nat. Council on Family Relations, 1966; nat. council Lincoln Center Performing Arts, Met. Opera Guild; mem. NYU adv. bd. Women in Food Service, 1983; NYU Women's Health Symposium: Steering Com., 1983—. Recipient Alma award, 1968, Penney-Mo. award, 1972, Traphagen Alumni award, 1975, Diamond Jubilee award, 1983, Disting. Women award Northwood U., 1997. Mem. Fashion Group, Internat. Furnishings and Design Assn. (v.p., program chmn.), Am. Soc. Mag. Editors, Am. Soc. Interior Designers (press mem.), Intercorporate Group, Women in Communications (60 yrs. of success award N.Y. chpt. 1984), Nat. Assn. Underwater Instrs., Pan Pacific and S.E. Asia Women's Assn., Asia Soc., Japan Soc., China Inst., Internat. Side Saddle Orgn., Millbrook Hounds, Golden's Bridge Hounds, Wine and Food Soc., Chaines des Rotisseurs (chargée de press) (bd. dirs.), Dames d'Escoffier, Culinary Inst. Am. Home and Office: 620 Park Ave New York NY 10021-6591

TOBER, STEPHEN LLOYD, lawyer; b. Boston, May 27, 1949; s. Benjamin Arthur Tober and Lee (Hymoff) Fruman; m. Susan V. Schwartz, Dec. 22, 1973; children: Cary, Jamie. Grad., Syracuse U., 1971, JD, 1974. Bar: N.H. 1974, U.S. Dist. Ct. N.H. 1974, U.S. Supreme Ct. 1978, N.Y. 1981. Assoc. Flynn, McGuirk & Blanchard, Portsmouth, N.H., 1974-79; sole practice Portsmouth, 1979-81; ptnr. Aeschliman & Tober, Portsmouth, 1981-91; prin. Tober Law Offices, P.A., Portsmouth, 1992—. Lectr. Franklin Pierce Law Ctr., Concord, N.H., 1978-80. Contbr. articles to profl. jours. Mem. Portsmouth Charter Commn., 1976, Portsmouth Planning Bd., 1977-81; del. N.H. Constl. Conv., Concord, 1984; city councilman, Portsmouth, 1977-81. Fellow: Internat. Acad. Trial Lawyers, Am. Bar Found. (chair ea. region 2003—); mem.: ATLA (gov. 1980—86), ABA (state del., chair credentials and admissions com., mem. standing com. on fed. judiciary, chair tech. and comms. com.), N.H. Bd. Bar Examiners, N.H. Trial Lawyers Assn. (pres. 1977), N.H. Bar Assn. (pres. 1988—89, chair com. to redraft code of profl. responsibility, Disting. Svc. award 1986, 1994), New Eng. Bar Assn. (bd.dirs. 1988—91). Democrat. Jewish. Avocations: reading, tennis. Home: 55 T J Gamester Ave Portsmouth NH 03801-5871 Office: Tober Law Offices PA PO Box 1377 Portsmouth NH 03802-1377 Office Phone: 603-431-1003. Business E-Mail: stober@toberlaw.com.

TOBEY, PETER C. art dealer, conservator, consultant; b. Bklyn., May 2, 1962; s. Martin and Harriett Selma Tobey; m. Lorraine C. Williams, May 10, 1989. BFA, Sch. Visual Arts, N.Y.C., 1984. Art conservator Simon Parkes Art Conservation, N.Y.C., 1987—99; owner -pres. Tobey World Wide Corp, N.Y.C., 1997—; owner-dir. Tobey Fine Arts, N.Y.C., 1997—; owner-pres. Painting Restoration, N.Y.C., 1999—. Developer (digital TV-film and internet) True Image. Employer Coop. Internship Program, N.Y.C., 1997. Mem.: Am. Intitute Art Conservation (assoc.). Achievements include first internet arts program. Avocations: bicycling, martial arts. Office: Tobey World Wide Corp 580 Broadway New York NY 10012 E-mail: tobeyfinearts@juno.com.

TOBIAS, ANDREW PREVIN, columnist, lecturer; b. N.Y.C., Apr. 20, 1947; s. Seth D. and Audrey J. (Landau) T. BA, Harvard U., 1968, MBA, 1972. Pres. Harvard Agys. Inc., Cambridge, Mass., 1967-68; v.p. Nat. Student Mktg. Corp., N.Y.C., 1969-70; contbg. editor N.Y. Mag., 1972-77, Esquire mag., 1977-83; columnist Playboy mag., 1982-86; contbr. Time mag., 1989-94, Worth mag., 1995—. Co-host Beyond Wall Street, PBS series, 1997; daily internet columnist, 1996-. Author: The Funny Money Game, 1972, (under pen name John Reid) The Best Little Boy in the World, 1973, Fire and Ice, 1976, The Only Investment Guide You'll Ever Need, 1978, rev. edit., 1996, Getting by on $100,000 a Year and (Other Sad Tales), 1980, The Invisible Bankers, 1982, (software) Managing Your Money, 1984-94, Money Angles, 1984, The Only Other Investment Guide You'll Ever Need, 1987, Kids Say Don't Smoke, 1991, Auto Insurance Alert!, 1993, My Vast Fortune, 1997, the Best Little Boy in the World Grows Up, 1998. Treas. Dem. Nat. Com., 1999—; co-founder Alliance to Revitalize Calif.; bd. mem. Human Right's Campaign. Recipient Gerald Loeb award, 1984, Consumer Fedn. of Am. Media Svc. award, 1993, GLSEN Valedictorian award, 1997, Smith-Weld prize Harvard Mag., 1998.

TOBIAS, ANITA, publishing executive; V.p. U.S. syndication L.A. Times Syndicate, 1998—. Office: Los Angeles Times Syndicate Times Mirror Sq 145 S Spring St Fl 10 Los Angeles CA 90012-3601

TOBIAS, CHARLES HARRISON, JR., lawyer; b. Cin., Apr. 16, 1921; s. Charles Harrison and Charlotte (Westheimer) T.; m. Mary J. Kaufman, June 15, 1946; children— Jean M., Thomas Charles, Robert Charles. BA cum laude, Harvard U., 1943, LL.B., 1949. Bar: Ohio 1949. Assoc. firm Steer, Strauss and Adair, Cin., 1949-56; ptnr. firm Steer, Strauss, White and Tobias, Cin., 1956-90; mem. Kepley MacConnell & Eyrich, Cin., 1990-93; mediator U.S. Ct. Appeals (6th crct.), Cin., 1993—. Bd. dirs. Cin. City Charter Com., 1955-75; mem. Wyoming (Ohio) City Council, 1972-77, vice mayor, 1974-77; bd. govs., past chmn. Cin. Overseers, Hebrew Union Coll.-Jewish Inst. Religion; pres. Met. Area Religious Coalition of Cin., 1977-80, Jewish Fedn. Cin., 1972-74; mem. nat. bd. govs. Am. Jewish Com., 1981-87. With USN, 1943-46. Mem. Cin. Bar Assn., Losantiville Country Club. Office: US Ct Appeals Potter Stewart US Courthse 5th and Walnut St Cincinnati OH 45202 Home: 2115 Evergreen Ridge Dr Cincinnati OH 45215-5713 Office Phone: 513-564-7330.

TOBIAS, GEOFFREY, otolaryngologist, plastic surgeon; b. Paterson, NJ, Dec. 20, 1947; MD, Tufts U., 1973. Intern Tufts New England Med. Ctr., 1973—76; resident Mt. Sinai Hosp., NYC, 1976—78; attending surgeon and instr. Mt. Sinai Hosp. and Sch. Medicine, NYC; assoc. chief head and neck surgery Englewood Hosp., NJ. Mem. sci. adv. bd. Longevity mag. Named one of Top Doctors in NY, NY Mag., 2004. Mem.: Am. Acad. Otolaryngology - Head and Neck Surgery, Am. Acad. Facial Plastic Surgery. Office: 214 Engle St Englewood NJ 07631-2418 also: 815 Park Ave New York NY 10021-3276 Office Phone: 201-567-7966. Office Fax: 201-567-6770.

TOBIAS, LESTER LEE, psychological consultant; b. Bklyn., Oct. 11, 1946; s. Nathan and Charlotte T.; m. Andrea Furmanek, July 10, 1977; children: Lauren A., Julia E. AB, Grinnell Coll., 1967; AM, U. Ill., 1971, PhD, 1972. Diplomate Am. Bd. Profl. Psychology. Instr. dept. univ. extension U. Ill., Urbana, 1970-72, intern Psychol. and Counseling Ctr., 1970-71, clin. counselor, 1971-72; psychologist Jefferson County (Colo.) Mental Health Ctr., Denver, 1972-73, team leader, psychologist, 1973-74; psychol. cons. to Denver OEO Colo. Dept. Social Svcs., 1973-74; instr. Denver Community Coll., 1973-74; cons. psychologist Nordli, Wilson Assocs., Westborough, Mass., 1974-81; ptnr., cons. psychologist, 1981—. Pres. Psychol. Svcs. Internat., Inc., Westborough, 1983—. Author: Psychological Consulting to Management, 1990; contbr. articles to profl. and bus. publs. Bd. dirs. Worcester Big Bros., 1976, PMCS, 1983—. Meuhlstein Found. scholar, 1964-67; USPHS trainee, 1967-68. Fellow APA; mem. Nat. Psychol. Cons. to Mgmt. (Excellence award 1991), Mass. Psychol. Assn. Home: 6 John St Westborough MA 01581-2511 Office: Nordli Wilson Assocs Ste 212 18 Lyman St Westborough MA 01581-1474

TOBIAS, PAUL HENRY, lawyer; b. Cin., Jan. 5, 1930; s. Charles H. and Charlotte (Westheimer) T.; 1 child, Eliza L. AB magna cum laude, Harvard U., 1951, LLB, 1958. Bar: Mass. 1958, Ohio 1962. Assoc. Stoneman & Chandler, Boston, 1958-61, Goldman & Putnick, Cin., 1962-75; ptnr. Tobias, Kraus and Torchia, Cin., 1976—. Instr. U. Cin. Law Sch., 1975-77. Author: Litigating Wrongful Discharge Claims, 1987; co-author: Job Rights and Survivor Strategies, a Handbook for Terminated Employees, 1997; contbr. articles to profl. jours. Mem. Cin. Bd. of Park Commrs., 1973-81, Cin. Human Rels. Commn., 1980-84, Cin. Hist. Conservation Bd., 1990-91. With U.S. Army, 1952-54. Mem. ABA, Nat. Employment Lawyers Assn. (founder), Nat. Employee Rights Inst. (chmn.; editor-in-chief Employee Rights quar. 2000-02), Ohio State Bar Assn., Cin. Bar Assn. (past chmn. legal aid com.), Phi Beta Kappa. Home: 15 Hill And Hollow Ln Cincinnati OH 45208-3317 Office: Tobias Kraus Torchia 911 Mercantile Libr Bldg Cincinnati OH 45202 Office Phone: 513-241-8137. Business E-Mail: tkt@tktlaw.com.

TOBIAS, RANDALL LEE, ambassador, retired pharmaceutical executive; b. Lafayette, Ind., Mar. 20, 1942; m. Marilyn Jane Salyer, Sept. 2, 1966 (dec. May 1994); children: Paige Noelle, Todd Christopher; m. Marianne Williams, July 15, 1995; stepchildren: James Russell Ullyot, Kathryn Lee Ullyot. BS in Mktg., Ind. U., 1964; LLD (hon.), Galuedette U.; D of Engring. (hon.), Rose Hulman Inst. Tech., Sagamore of the Wabash, Ind.; LLD (hon.), Ind. U., 1997. Numerous positions Ind. Bell, 1964-77, Ill. Bell, 1977-81; v.p. residence mktg. sales and service AT&T, 1981-82, pres. Am. Bell Consumer Products, 1983, pres. Consumer Products, 1983-84, sr. v.p., 1984-85; chmn., CEO AT&T Comm., N.Y.C., 1985-91, AT&T Internat., Basking Ridge, N.J., 1991-93; vice chmn. bd. AT&T, N.Y.C., 1986-93; chmn., CEO Eli Lilly & Co., Indpls., 1993-98, chmn. emeritus, 1999; coord., U. S. Govt. Activities to Combat AIDS Globally U.S. Dept. State, Washington, 2003—. Bd. dirs. Kimberly-Clark, Knight-Ridder, Phillips Petroleum. Co-Author: Put The Moose On The Table, 2003 Chmn. bd. trustees Duke U.; trustee Colonial Williamsburg Found.; bd. govs. Indpls. Mus. Art; bd. dirs. Indpls. Symphony Orch., Ind. U. Found. (hon.), Econ. Club Indpls. Named one of Top 25 Mgrs. of Yr., Bus. Week, 1997, Family Champion, Working Mothers Mag., 1997. Mem. Bus. Coun., Indpls. Corp. Cmty. Coun., Coun. Fgn. Rels., Meridian Hills Country Club (Indpls.), Woodstock Club (Indpls.), Columbia Club (Indpls.), Athletic Club (Indpls.), Univ. Club (Indpls.), Amwell Valley Conservancy (N.J.), Theta Chi. Avocations: skiing, fly fishing, shooting. Office: US Dept State 2201 C St NW Washington DC 20520*

TOBIAS, ROBERT MAX, labor leader, lawyer; b. Detroit, Aug. 4, 1943; BA, U. Mich., 1965, MBA, 1968; JD, George Washington U., 1969. Lawyer Nat. Treasury Employees Union, Washington, 1968-70, gen. counsel, 1970-79, exec. v.p. and gen. counsel, 1979-83, pres., 1983-99; disting. adj. prof. pub. adminstrn., dir. Inst. for Study of Pub. Policy Implementation, Am. U., Washington, 1999—. Lectr. George Washington U. Law Sch., Washington, 1970-90; mem. IRS oversight bd., 2000—. Contbr. articles to law revs. Pres. Fed. Employee Edn. and Asst. Fund, Washington, 1986—. Fellow Nat. Acad. Pub. Adminstrn.; mem. ABA, Soc. for Labor Relations Profls. (1st Annual Union Leader award, 1987), Fed. Bar Assn. Democrat. Episcopalian. Office: Am U Sch Pub Affairs 4400 Massachusetts Ave Washington DC 20016-8070 E-mail: rtobias@american.edu.

TOBIAS, STEPHEN C. rail transportation executive; b. Bogota, Colombia, Dec. 11, 1944; BA in History, Citadel, 1967; postgrad., Harvard U., 1986. Jr. engr. Pocahontas divsn. Norfolk and Western Rlwy. Co., 1969-70, asst. roadmaster Scioto divsn., 1970, asst. trainmaster Pitts. divsn., 1970-71, gen. yardmaster Pitts. divsn., 1971-73, traimaster Bellevue terminal, 1973-74, asst. supt. Bellevue terminal, 1974-79, supt. Pitts. divsn., 1979-81, asst. gen. mgr. lake region, 1981, asst. gen. mgr. supt. eastern region, 1981-84; gen. mgr. eastern region Norfolk (Va.) So. Corp., 1984, gen. mgr. western lines, 1984-89, v.p. transp., 1989-92, v.p. strategic planning, 1992-93, sr. v.p. ops., 1993-94, exec. v.p. ops., 1994-98, vice chmn. and COO, 1998—. Trustee Norfolk Acad.; prin. Va. Bus. Coun.; bd. dirs. Plum Creek Timber Co., TTX Co., Inc. Dir. Va. law Enforcement Found.; mem. exec. adv. coun. Commonwealth Musical Stage. Capt. U.S. Army, 1967-69. Mem. Assn. Am. R.R.s. Office: Norfolk So Corp 3 Commercial Pl Norfolk VA 23510-2108

TOBIASSEN, BARBARA SUE, systems analyst consultant, educator, Peace Corps volunteer; b. Bklyn., Feb. 22, 1950; d. Vincent and Esther Alice (Hansen) M. BA in Math Edn., Rider Coll., 1972; postgrad., Montclair State U., 1973. Cert. secondary tchr., NJ. Math tchr. Westwood (NJ) H.S., 1973-80; programmer Prudential Ins. Co., Roseland, NJ, 1980-81; programmer, analyst Grand Union, Paramus, NJ, 1981-82; cons. Five Techs., Montvale, NJ, 1987-90; project mgr. Info. Sci., Inc., Montvale, 1982-84, cons., project mgr., 1987-90; pres. B. Maxwell Assoc., Inc., Westwood, 1990—; vol. Peace Corps; mem. Peace Corps., 2001—02; tchr. St. Paul's Luth., Accra, Ghana, 2002—. Guest spkr. Info. Sci., Best of Am., Computer Assocs. B.A.C.; educator, Ghana W. Africa, 2002-. Contbr. articles to profl. jours. Vol. Peace Corps, 2001—02. Mem.: APA (v.p. N.J. chpt. 1996), NAFE, Am. Payroll Assn., N.J. Info., Westwood Heritage Soc. Republican. Lutheran. Avocations: travel, reading, gardening, hiking. E-mail: btobiassen2003@yahoo.com.

TOBIN, AILEEN WEBB, educational administrator; b. Milford, Del., July 9, 1949; d. Wilson Webster Webb and Dorothy Marie (Benson) Rust; m. Thomas Joseph Tobin, Jr., July 31, 1971. BA cum laude, U. Del., 1971, MEd, 1975, PhD, 1981. Cert. tchr. secondary edn., cert. reading specialist, cert. reading cons., Del. Dir. Del. Tutoring Ctr., Wilmington, 1971-74; grad. teaching asst. U. Del., Newark, 1974-81, instr. Coll. Edn., 1978-82; ednl. specialist U.S. Army Ordnance Ctr. & Sch., Aberdeen Proving Ground, Md., 1982-85, chief internal eval. br., 1985-88, chief evaluation divsn., 1988, chief standardization and analysis div., 1988-90, dir. quality assurance, 1990-94, dir. tactical support equipment dept., 1994-98, dir. command planning office, 1998—. Cons. Dorchester County Sch. Dist., Dorchester County, Md., 1977-80; rsch. assoc., Ctr. for Ednl. Leadership, Newark, 1981-82; staff assoc., Rsch. for Better Schs., Inc., Phila., 1981-84. Author: (book chpt.) Approaches Informal Eval. of Reading, 1982, Dialogues in Literary Research, 1988, Cognitive & Social Perspectives for Literary Research & Instruction, 1989; contbr. articles to profl. jours. Recipient Silver award Fed. Exec. Bd., 1992, Comdr.'s award for Civil Svc. Dept. Army, 1994, 96, Order of Samuel Sharpe award Ordnance Corps Assn., 1994, Superior Civil Svc. award Dept. Army, 1995, 98. Mem. Internat. Reading Assn., Nat. Reading Conf., Am. Ednl. Rsch. Assn., Am. Evaluation Assn., Ordnance Corps Assn., Kappa Delta Pi. Methodist. Avocations: travel, reading, tennis, sailing. Home: 2515 Boston St # 205 Baltimore MD 21224 Office: US Army Ordnance Ctr & Sch ATSL CP Aberdeen Proving Ground MD 21005

TOBIN, BENTLEY, lawyer; b. Bklyn., Feb. 8, 1924; s. Nathan H. and Mildred E. (Aronoff) Tobin; m. Nancy Gurvitz, Sept. 13, 1947; children: Patricia E., Mitchell H.; m. Beverly Ann Mucciarone, Feb. 17, 1979. BS, CCNY, 1943; LLB, Harvard U., 1948. Bar: NY 1948, Mass. 1951, RI 1952. Atty. NYC Housing Authority, NYC, 1948—49; ptnr. Titiev, Greenman & Tobin, Boston, 1949—52; sr. ptnr. Tobin & Silverstein, Inc., Providence, 1952—84; ptnr. Hinckley, Allen, Tobin & Silverstein, 1984—87, Hinckley, Allen, Comen, 1987—92, Hinckley, Allen & Snyder, Providence, 1992—. Chmn. emeritus Landmark Med. Ctr. With USAR, 1943—46. Mem.: ABA, Woonsocket Bar Assn., RI Bar Assn. Office: Hinckley Allen Snyder 1500 Fleet Ctr Providence RI 02903-2319 Also: Landmark Med Ctr 115 Cass Ave Woonsocket RI 02895-4705 Office Phone: 401-274-2000. E-mail: tobinb@haslaw.com., bentley.tobin@cox.net.

TOBIN, CALVIN JAY, architect; b. Boston, Feb. 15, 1927; s. David and Bertha (Tanfield) T.; m. Joan Hope Fink, July 15, 1951; children— Michael Alan, Nancy Ann. B.Arch., U. Mich., 1949. Designer, draftsman Arlen & Lowenfish (architects), N.Y.C., 1949-51; with Samuel Arlen, N.Y.C., 1951-53, Skidmore, Owings & Merrill, N.Y.C., 1953; architect Loebl, Schlossman & Bennett (architects), Chgo., 1953-57, v.p., 1953-57, Loebl, Schlossman & Hackl, 1957—; retired, 1998. Chmn. Jewish United Fund Bldg. Trades Div., 1969; chmn. AIA and Chgo. Hosp. Council Com. of Hosp. Architecture, 1968-76 Archtl. works include Michael Reese Hosp. and Med. Ctr., 1954—, Prairie Shores Apt. Urban Redevel., 1957-62, Louis A. Weiss Meml. Hosp., Chgo., Chgo. State Hosp., Ctrl. Cmty. Hosp., Chgo., Gottlieb Meml. Hosp., Melrose Park, Ill., West Suburban Hosp., Oak Park, Ill., Thorek Hosp. and Med. Ctr., Chgo., Water Power Pl., Chgo., Christ Hosp., Oak Lawn, Greater Balt. Med. Ctr., Shriners Hosp. for Crippled Children, Chgo. Hinsdale (Ill.) Hosp., South Chgo. Cmty. Hosp., Chgo., Mt. Sinai Med. Ctr., Chgo., Alexian Bros. Med. Ctr., Elk Grove Village, Ill., Luth. Gen. Hosp., Park Ridge, Ill., Evanston (Ill.) Hosp., Resurrection Med. Ctr., Chgo., New Cook County Hosp., Chgo., also numerous apt., comml. and cmty. bldgs. Chmn. Highland Park (Ill.) Appearance Rev. Commn., 1972-73; mem. Highland Park Plan Commn., 1973-79; mem. Highland Park City Coun., 1974-89, mayor pro-tem, 1979-89; mem. Highland Park Environ. Control Commn., 1979-84, Highland Park Hist. Preservation Commn., 1982-89; bd. dirs. Highland Park Hist. Soc., Young Men's Jewish Coun., 1953-67, pres., 1967; bd. dirs. Jewish Community Ctrs. Chgo., 1973-78, bd. dirs., 1989-93; Ill. Coun. Against Handgun Violence, 1989-94; trustee Ravinia Festival Assn., 1990-98; bd. govs. Highland Park Cmty. House, 1994—; v.p Kohl Children's Mus. Wilmette, Ill., 1999—. With USNR, 1945-46. Recipient Boys Club Medallion award, Boys Club Am., 1968, Disting. Alumni award, Taubman Coll. Architecture and Urban Planning, U. Mich., 2004. Fellow AIA (2d v.p. Chgo. chpt.); mem. U. Mich. Alumni Soc. Coll. Architecture and Urban Planning (bd. govs. 1989-95), U. Mich. Alumni Assn. (bd. govs. 1990-95, v.p. 1993-95, pres. 1997-99, Disting. Alumni Svc. award 1996), Std. Club, Ravinia Green Country Club, Pi Lambda Phi. Jewish. Home: 814 Dean Ave Highland Park IL 60035-4749

TOBIN, CRAIG DANIEL, lawyer; b. Chgo., Aug. 17, 1954; s. Thomas Arthur and Lois (O'Connor) T. BA with honors, U. Ill., 1976; JD with high honors, Ill. Inst. Tech., 1980. Bar: Ill. 1980, U.S. Dist. Ct. (no. dist.) Ill. 1980, U.S. Dist. Ct. (no. dist.) Ind. 1986, U.S. Ct. Appeals (7th cir.) 1986, U.S. Supreme Ct. 1987. Trial atty. Cook County Pub. Defender, Chgo., 1980-82; trial atty. homicide task force Pub. Defender, Chgo., 1982-84; ptnr. Craig D. Tobin and Assocs., Chgo., 1984—. Lectr. Ill. Inst. for Continuing Legal Edn., Cook County Pub. Defender, Chgo., 1983, 92, Ill. Pub. Defender Assn., 1987; instr. Nat. Inst. Trial Advocacy. Recipient award for legal excellence Midwest Comm. Coun., 2002; named to Outstanding Young Men in Am., 1985. Mem. ABA, Chgo. Bar Assn., Nat. Assn. Criminal Def. Lawyers. Roman Catholic. Office: Craig D Tobin & Assocs 3 First National Plz Chicago IL 60602 Home: 6622 N Longmeadow Ave Lincolnwood IL 60712-3208

TOBIN, DENNIS MICHAEL, lawyer; b. Chgo., June 3, 1948; s. Thomas Arthur and Lois (O'Connor) T.; m. Sue Wynn Henslee, June 14, 1969 (div. 1977); m. Karen Thompson, Oct. 11, 1980; children: Kyle James, Daniel Patrick BA with honors, U. Ill., 1971; JD, Loyola U., Chgo., 1976. Bar: Ill. 1976, U.S. Dist. Ct (no. dist.) Ill. 1976, U.S. Ct. Appeals (7th cir.) 1985, U.S. Supreme Ct. 1985, Wis. 1989. Trial atty. Cook County Homicide Task Force, Chgo., 1976-84; prin. Dennis M. Tobin & Assocs., Chgo., 1984—. Gen. counsel Forest Health Systems and Found., Ill., Miss., Hawaii, 1986—, Manages Behavioral Care Inc., Psychiat. Ins. Co. Am. Dir. Forest Health Systems Found.; mem. Chgo. Coun. on Fgn. Rels. Mem. ABA (forum on health law), Nat. Assn. Criminal Def. Attys., Chgo. Bar Assn. (com. on health law), Am. Soc. Law and Medicine, Ill. Assn. Criminal Def. Attys. (v.p. 1984-87), Ill. Attys. for Criminal Justice, Wis. Bar Assn., Ill. Assn. Hosp. Attys., Nat. Health Lawyers Assn., U.S. Sporting Clays Assn., Nat. Sporting Clays Assn., Gateway Gun Club. Roman Catholic. Office: 335 Frost Dr Williams Bay WI 53191-9716

TOBIN, EUGENE MARC, foundation administrator, retired academic administrator; b. Newark, Mar. 23, 1947; s. Hyman and Clara (Pekersky) Tobin; m. Beverly Stethem, May 26, 1979; children: David Gehm, Leslie. BA in History, Rutgers U., 1968; MA in History Am. Civilization, Brandeis U., 1970, PhD in History of Am. Civilization, 1972; LLD (hon.), Hamilton Coll., 1994. Vis. instr. history Jersey City State Coll., 1972—75; vis. asst. prof. Kutztown State Coll., Pa., 1975—76; NEH postdoctoral fellow Vanderbilt U., Nashville, 1976—77; vis. asst. prof. Miami U., Oxford, Ohio, 1977—79, Indiana U., Bloomington, 1979—80; asst. prof. history Hamilton Coll., Clinton, NY, 1980—83, assoc. prof. history, 1983—88, prof. history, 1988—, dir. Am. studies program, 1983—88, chair dept. history, 1986—88, acting dean coll., 1988, dean faculty, 1989—93, pres., 1993—2003; sr. adv. Andrew W. Mellon Found., NYC, 2003—. Presenter in field. Co-author (with Michael H. Ebner): The Ape of Urban Reform: New Perspectives on the Progressive Era, 1977, Organize or Parish: America's Independent Progressives 1913-1933, 1986; co-author: (with Ann Fagan Ginger) The National Lawyers Guild: From Roosevelt Through Reagan, 1988; contbr. articles to profl. jours. With USAR, 1968—74. Recipient William Adee Whitehead award, N.J. Hist. Soc., 1976; fellow, NDEA, 1968—70; grantee rsch. grantee, Am. Philos. Soc., 1978—79, 1982—83. Mem.: Orgn. Am. Historians, Am. Hist. Assn. Office: Andrew W Mellon Found 140 E 62nd St New York NY 10023 Home: 151 E 80th St Apt 7B New York NY 10021-0444 E-mail: etobin@hamilton.edu.

TOBIN, GARY ALLAN, cultural and community organization educator; b. St. Louis, July 26, 1949; BA in History, Washington U., 1971; PhD in City and Regional Planning, U. Calif., Berkeley. Pres. Inst. for Jewish and Cmty. Rsch., San Francisco; dir. Abramson Program in Jewish Policy Rsch. U. Judaism, L.A.; former dir. Cohen Ctr. for Modern Jewish Studies Brandeis U., Waltham, Mass. Rsch. on antisemitism, racial and ethnic diversity, Jewish orgn. planning and philanthropy in Jewish Cmty. and Jewish Family Founds. Author: Jewish Perceptions of Antisemitism, Church and Synagogue Affiliation, Opening the Gates: How Proactive Conversion Can Revitalize the Jewish Community, Rabbis Talk About Intermarriage. Office: Inst Jewish & Cmty Rsch 3198 Fulton St San Francisco CA 94118

TOBIN, JAMES MICHAEL, lawyer; b. Santa Monica, Calif., Sept. 27, 1948; s. James Joseph and Glada Marie (Meisner) T.; m. Kathleen Marie Espy, Sept. 14, 1985. BA with honors, U. Calif., Riverside, 1970; JD, Georgetown U., 1974. Bar: Calif. 1974, Mich. 1987. From atty. to gen. atty. So. Pacific Co., San Francisco, 1975-82; v.p. regulatory affairs So. Pacific Comm. Co., Washington, 1982-83; v.p., gen. counsel Lexitel Corp., Washington, 1983-85;

v.p., gen. counsel, sec. ALC Comm. Corp., Birmingham, Mich., 1985-87, sr. v.p., gen. counsel, sec., 1987-88; of counsel Morrison & Foerster, San Francisco, 1988-90, ptnr., 1990—. Mem. ABA, Calif. Bar Assn., Fed. Comm. Bar Assn. Republican. Unitarian Universalist. Avocations: carpentry, travel. Home: 3134 Baker St San Francisco CA 94123-1805 Office: Morrison & Foerster 425 Market St Ste 3300 San Francisco CA 94105-2482 Office Phone: 415-268-7678. Business E-Mail: jtobin@mofo.com.

TOBIN, JAMES ROBERT, biomedical device manufacturing company executive; b. Lima, Ohio, Aug. 12, 1944; s. J. Robert and Doris L. (Hunt) T.; m. Janet Trafton, Dec. 30, 1971; children: James Robert III, Amanda Trafton. BA in Govt., Harvard U., 1966, MBA, 1968. Fin. analyst Baxter Internat., Inc., Deerfield, Ill., 1972-73, internat. contr., 1973-75, mng. dir. Japan, 1975-77, mng. dir. Spain, 1977-80; pres. IV Sys. Divsn. Baxter Internat. Inc., 1981-84; group v.p. Baxter Internat., Inc., 1984-88, exec. v.p., 1988-92, pres., COO, 1992-94, Biogen, 1994-97, pres., CEO, 1997-98, Boston Sci. Corp., 1999—, also bd. dirs. Bd. dirs. Creative Biomolecules, Pathogenesis, PE Corp. Bd. dirs. Beth Israel Deaconess Hosp. Lt. USN, 1968-72 Republican. Office: Boston Scientific 1 Boston Scientific Pl Natick MA 01760*

TOBIN, LOIS MOORE, retired home economist, educator; b. Johnstown, Pa., Oct. 8, 1928; d. William B and Ida L. (Diehl) Moore; m. Warner E. Tobin, June 7, 1953 (dec.); children: Brian W., Robert E. BS, Indiana State Tchrs. Coll., Pa., 1951; postgrad., U. Pitts., 1952, U. Colo., 1953; MEd, Pa. State U., 1967; postgrad., Indiana U. of Pa., 1977-85. Tchr. Allegheny Valley Joint Sch. Dist., Springdale, Pa., 1951-53, Kittanning (Pa.) Sch. Dist., 1953-55, Carlisle (Pa.) Joint Sch. Dist., 1964 66, State Coll. (Pa.) Sch. Dist., 1967-73; mem. faculty dept. food and nutrition Indiana U. of Pa., 1974, 76 77, mem. faculty home econs. edn., 1979-82, coord. Single Parent-Homemaker Svc. Ctr. Vocat. Pers. Prep., 1984-91. Mem. adv. com. Indiana Area Vocat.-Tech. Sch., 1981-94; presenter in field. Author: (booklet) Home Economics Education Bibliography on Special Needs, 1982, Teaching Special Needs Individuals in Home Economics, 1982; contbr. articles to profl. newsletters. Sec. Indiana County Human Svcs. Coun., 1990—91; vol. Bloodmobile, 1986—; tour guide Breezedale Restoration, 1986—; pres. Calvary Ch. Women's Club, 1975—76, Indiana County Newcomers Club, 1974, 1975; elder, session mem. Calvary Presbyn. Ch., 1996—2002. Grantee Dept. Edn. Bur. Vocat. Edn., 1980-82, 86-91, Human Svcs. Devel. Fund, 1989-91. Mem. Am. Vocat. Assn., Pa. Vocat. Assn., Nat. Trust for Hist. Preservation, Indiana County Hist. and Geneal. Soc., Indiana U. of Pa. Ret. Faculty Assn. (treas. 1998-2002), Indiana County Alumni Assn. (bd. dirs.), Pa. Home Econs. Assn. (treas. 1975-77), Pa. Vocat. Home Econs. Educators (sec. 1990-91). Avocations: swimming, travel, church choir. Home: 896 White Farm Rd Indiana PA 15701-1254

TOBIN, MARTIN JOHN, pulmonary and critical care physician; b. Kilkenny, Ireland, Apr. 23, 1951; came to U.S., 1980; s. Edmund and Johanna (Brennan) T.; m. Sareen Boland, Sept. 13, 1974; children: Damien, Kate, Kieran. MD, U. Coll., Dublin, Ireland, 1975. Diplomate Am. Bd. Internal Medicine, Am. Bd. Pulmonary Disease, Am. Bd. Critical Care Medicine. Resident in internal medicine U. Coll. and Trinity Coll., Dublin, Ireland, 1975-79; fellow Kings Coll. Med. Sch., London, 1978 80, Mt. Sinai Med. Ctr., Miami, 1980-82, U. Pitts., 1982-83; asst. prof. U. Tex. Med. Sch., Houston, 1983-88, assoc. prof., 1988-90; prof. medicine Loyola U. Chgo. Sch. Medicine, Maywood, Ill., 1990—, chief pulmonary and critical care, 1992, dir. fellowship tng. program, 1990—. Chief pulmonary and critical care Hines VA Hosp., Hines, Ill., 1990; 1996 lectr. in Pulmonary and Critcal Care Medicine, Harvard Med. Sch., Boston, D.H. Simmons lectr. UCLA Med. Sch., L.A., 1997; Balfour lectr. Mayo Clinic, Rochester, Minn.; Egan lectr. Am. Assn. Respiratory Care, Las Vegas, 1999; Wellcome lectr. Royal Soc. Medicine, London, 2000. Author: Principles and Practices of Mechanical Ventilation, 1994, Principles and Practice of Intensive Care Monitoring, 1998 and 5 other books; contbr. numerous articles to profl. internat. jours.; assoc. editor Am. Jour. Respirator Critical Care Medicine, 1992-99; N. Am. editor Intensive Care Medicine, Berlin, 1993-99; editor in chief Am. Jour. Respiratory & Critical Care Medicine, 1999—. Recipient Forrest M. Bird Achievement award, Am. Respiratory Care Found., Cin., 2000, Hon. Fellowship award of Faculty of Medicine, Univ. Coll. Dublin, Ireland, 2002. Mem. Am. Thoracic Soc. (bd. dirs. chair critical care assembly 1997-99). Avocations: reading, music. Office: Loyola U Chgo 2160 S 1st Ave Maywood IL 60153-3304

TOBIN, PATRICK JOHN, dermatologist; b. Bay City, Mich., Sept. 20, 1938; s. John Howard and Dorothy Ida (De Matio) T.; m. Suzanne Lane Bumstead, Apr. 11, 1959; children: Jennifer Lane, Suzannah Lane, Benjamin Lane. AS, Bay City Jr. Coll., 1958; MD, U. Mich., 1964. Diplomate Am. Bd. Dermatology. Intern Munson Med. Ctr., Traverse City, Mich., 1964-65, mem. active staff, 1970—; resident Univ. Hosp., Ann Arbor, Mich., 1965-68. Lt. comdr. USN, 1968-70. Fellow Am. Acad. Dermatology; mem. Mich. State Med. Soc., AMA, Am. Soc. for Dermatologic Surgery, Alpha Omega Alpha, Grand Traverse Yacht Club (commodore 1977), Grand Traverse Ski Club (pres. 1975). Avocations: skiing, bicycling, sailing, travel, reading. Home: 7777 Truesdale Ln Traverse City MI 49686-1667 Office: Northwestern Mich Dermatol 550 Munson Ave Ste 200 Traverse City MI 49686-3580 Office Phone: 231-935-8717.

TOBIN, PAUL EDWARD, JR., naval officer; b. Detroit, Oct. 24, 1940; s. Paul Edward and Mary Margaret (Atkinson) T.; m. Lynne Dawson Carter, June 12, 1963; children: Mary Elizabeth, Patricia Carter. BS in Naval Sci., U.S. Naval Acad., 1963; MS in Computer Sys., U.S. Naval Postgrad. Sch., 1969. Commd. ensign USN, 1963, advanced through grades to rear adm., 1988; commdg. officer USS Tattnall (DDG-19), 1979-81; chief engr. USS Forrestal (CV-59), 1981-83; commdg. officer USS Fox (CG-33), 1984-86, Surface Warfare Officers Sch., 1986-88; dir. USN Info. Sys. Mgmt., 1988-90; commdr. Surface Group Western Pacific, Subic Bay, The Philippines, 1990-92; asst. chief naval pers. USN, Washington, 1992-94, vice commdr. naval edn. and tng. Pensacola, Fla., 1994-96, oceanographer, 1996-98, ret., 1998; v.p. edn. Armed Forces Comms. and Electronics Assn., 1998—. Decorated D.S.M., Legion of Merit (4), Bronze Star. Mem. U.S. Naval Inst., Surface Navy Assn., Army Navy Country Club. Presbyterian. Avocations: classical music, running, computers, boating. Home: 114 Riverton Pl Edgewater MD 21037-1800 Office: 4400 Fair Lakes Ct Fairfax VA 22033-3801

TOBIN, RICHARD WILLIS, II, lawyer; b. Rantoul, Ill., Dec. 14, 1953; s. Richard Willis and Frances Irene (Kesler) T.; m. Deborah Lynne Grile, June 27, 1976; children: Richard Willis III, Michael L., Cathalain M. BS in History with honors, U.S. Air Force Acad., 1976; JD with honors, U. Fla., 1984; LLM with highest honors, George Washington U., 1993. Bar: Fla. 1984, U.S. Ct. Mil. Appeals 1985. Commd. 2d lt. USAF, 1976, advanced through grades to col., 1997, asst. staff Judge Adv., 1984—85, area def. counsel, 1985—86, dep. staff judge adv. Yokota Air Base, Japan, 1986—89, staff judge adv. Misawa Air Base, Japan, 1989, Altus AFB, Okla., 1989—92, regional counsel ctrl. region for environ. compliance Dallas, 1993—95, staff judge adv. Luke AFB, Ariz., 1995—97, chief environ. law and litig. divsn. Arlington, Va., 1997—2000, ret., 2000; dep. dir., acting dir., counselor to dir. Ariz. Dept. Environ. Quality, Phoenix, 2000—04, ret., 2004; of counsel Lewis and Roca, LLP, Phoenix, 2004—. Decorated Air Force Commendation medal (2), Air Force Meritorious Svc. medal (4), Legion of Merit. Mem. Order of the Coif. Republican. Presbyterian. Avocation: genealogy. Office Phone: 602-262-5774. E-mail: rtobin@lrlaw.com.

TOBIN, ROBERT EDWIN, regional director; b. Carlisle, Pa., Sept. 18, 1959; s. Dr. Warner E. and Lois Moore T.; m. Linda Drew, June 21, 1986; children: Emily May, Drew Warner. BA, Ind. Univ. of Pa., 1982; MBA, George Mason Univ., 1993. Rest. mgr. Pizza Hut, Myrtle Beach, S.C., 1982-85, area mgr. Fairfax, Va., 1985-91, divsn. tng. mgr. Washington, D.C., 1991-93, proj. mgr. Atlanta, 1993-94, dir. ops., 1994-97, Kansas City, 1997-98; reg. dir. ops. Denny's Restaurants, Pitts., 1998—2003; region dir. ops. Blockbuster, Fairfax, Va., 2003—. MBA mentor George Mason U., Fairfax, 1995-97. Dist. commr. Boy Scouts Am., Myrtle Beach, S.C., 1983-85; Sunday sch. tchr., mem. vestry and fin. com., Ch. of Ascension, Pitts., 1999—. Mem. Edgewood Club. Republican. Home: 6751 Jade Post Ln Centreville VA 20121 E-mail: RTobin02@sprynet.com.

TOBIN, ROBERT G. supermarket chain executive; b. 1938; With Stop & Shop Supermarket Co., 1960—, pres., COO, 1989-93, Stop & Shop Cos., Braintree, Mass., 1993-97, chmn. Quincy, Mass., 1995—, Ahold USA, Inc., Chantilly, Va. Office: Ahold USA Inc 14101 Newabrook Dr Chantilly VA 20151

TOBIN, TARY JEANNE, educational consultant, researcher; b. Des Moines, Sept. 18, 1940; d. Deam Hunter and Merle Bonne (Wildey) Ferris; m. David William Tobin, June 8, 1968; children: Robert, Jean, Mary Sue, Joseph, Anastasia, Teresa, Rebekah. BSc, U. Oreg., 1970, MEd, 1990, PhD, 1996. Cert. elem. tchr., tchr. of learning impaired, Oreg. Tchr. elem. sch. St. Mary's Cath. Sch., Eugene, Oreg., 1962-68; tchr. elem. and jr. high sch. St. Paul's Cath. Sch., Eugene, 1969-70, 72-74; mgr. adult foster care home Sr. and Disabled Svcs., Eugene, 1983-90; tchr. spl. edn. elem. sch. Springfield (Oreg.) Sch. Dist., 1991; rsch. assoc. U. Oreg., 1997—. Contbr. articles to profl. jours. Mem.: Am. Evaluation Assn., Coun. for Children with Behavioral Disorders, Coun. Exceptional Children. Avocation: digital photography. Home: 1055 W 18th Ave Eugene OR 97402 Office: Coll Edn 1235 U Oreg Eugene OR 97403-1235 Office Phone: 541-346-1423.

TOBIN, THOMAS F. lawyer; b. Chgo., Apr. 12, 1929; BSS, John Carroll U., 1951; JD, Loyola U., 1954. Bar: Ill. 1954. Ptnr. Connelly Robert and McGivney, Chgo. Office: Connelly Robert and McGivney 1 N Franklin St Ste 1200 Chicago IL 60606-3447

TOBIN, VINCENT MICHAEL, professional football coach, former sports team executive; b. Burlington Junction, Mo., Sept. 29, 1943; BE, U. Mo., 1965, M in Guidance and Counseling, 1966. Def. ends coach Missouri, 1967-70, def. coord., 1971-76, Brit. Columbia Lions CFL, 1977-82, Phila./Balt. Stars USFL, 1983-85, Chgo. Bears NFL, 1986-92, Indpls. Colts NFL, 1994-95; head coach Ariz. Cardinals, 1996—2000.

TOBIN, WILLIAM JOSEPH, newspaper editor; b. Joplin, Mo., July 28, 1927; s. John J. and Lucy T. (Shoppach) T.; m. Marjorie Stuhldreher, Apr. 26, 1952; children: Michael Gerard, David Joseph, James Patrick. BJ, Butler U., 1948. Staff writer AP, Indpls., 1947-52, news feature writer N.Y.C., 1952-54, regional membership exec. Louisville, 1954-56, corr. Juneau, Alaska, 1956-60, asst. chief bur. Balt., 1960-61, Helena, Mont., 1961-63, mng. editor Anchorage Times, 1963-73, assoc. editor, 1973-85, gen. mgr., 1974-85, v.p., editor-in-chief, 1985-89, editor editl. page, 1990, asst. pub., 1991; sr. editor Voice of the Times, 1991—. Mem. devel. com. Anchorage Winter Olympics, 1984-91, bd. dirs. Anchorage organizing com., 1985-91; bd. dirs. Alaska Coun. Econ. Edn., 1978-84, Boys Clubs Alaska, 1979-83, Anchorage Symphony Orch., 1986-87, Blue Cross Wash. and Alaska, 1987—, chmn., 1990-91; chmn. Premera Corp., 1994-99; mem. adv. bd. Providence Hosp., Anchorage, 1974-91, chmn., 1980-85. Sgt. U.S. Army, 1950-52. Mem. Alaska AP Mems. Assn. (pres. 1964), Anchorage C. of C. (bd. dirs. 1969-74, pres. 1972-73), Alaska World Affairs Coun. (pres. 1967-68), Alaska Press Club (pres. 1968-69), Commonwealth North Club (Anchorage). Home: 2130 Lord Baranof Dr Anchorage AK 99517-1257 Office: Anchorage Times PO Box 100040 Anchorage AK 99510-0040

TOBIS, JEROME SANFORD, physician; b. Syracuse, N.Y., July 23, 1915; s. David George and Anna (Feinberg) T.; m. Hazel Weisbard, Sept. 18, 1938; children: David, Heather, Jonathan. BS, CCNY, 1936; MD, Chgo. Med. Sch., 1943. Diplomate: Am. Bd. Phys. Medicine and Rehab. Intern Knickerbocker Hosp., 1943-44; resident Bronx VA Hosp., 1946-48; med. dir. state fever therapy unit USPHS, Brookhaven, Miss., 1944-46; practice medicine N.Y.C., 1948-70; prof. dir. dept. phys. medicine and rehab. N.Y. Med. Coll., Flower and Fifth Av. Hosps., 1948-61; prof. rehab. medicine Albert Einstein Coll. of Medicine, 1963-70; chief div. rehab. medicine Montefiore Hosp., 1961-70; dir. vis. physician Met., Bird S. Coler hosps., 1952-61; prof., chmn. dept. phys. medicine and rehab. Calif. Coll. Medicine, U. Calif. at Irvine, 1970-82, prof., dir. program in geriatric medicine and gerontology, 1980-86; mem. adv. com. Acad. Geriatric Resource program, 1984-86, 95—. Mem. expert med. com. Am. Rehab. Found., 1961-70; cons. Dept. Health, N.Y.C., Long Beach VA Hosp., 1970—, Fairview State Devel. Ctr., 1976—; mem. adv. coun. phys. medicine and rehab. for appeals com. Calif. Med. Assn., 1971-74, adv. com. U. Calif. Acad. Geriatric Resource Program, 1995—; NIH Internat. Fogarty fellow, hon. lectr., dept. geriatric medicine U. Birmingham, 1979-80; chair ethics com. U. Calif.-Irvine Med. Ctr., 1986—; mem. rev. panel musculoskeletal diseases NIH, 1996; rsch. prof. dept. phys. medicine & rehab. U. Calif., Irvine, 1986—, chair med. ethics com., 1986—; mem. Ctr. Health Policy Rsch. U. Calif., Davis, 1996—. Mem. editorial bd.: Heart and Lung, 1973-76, Geriatrics, 1975-80, Archives of Phys. Medicine and Rehab, 1958-73. Named Physician of the Year, 1957; recipient Distinguished Alumnus award Chgo. Med. Sch., 1972, Acad. award Nat. Inst. on Aging, 1981-86; named hon. faculty mem. Calif. Zeta chpt. Alpha Omega Alpha, 1981; Leavitt Meml. lectureship Baylor Coll. Medicine, 1983, Griffith Meml. lectureship Am. Geriatric Soc., 1984; Australian Coll. Rehabilitation Medicine, 1984; Jerome S. Tobis Ann. Conf. on Geriatric Medicine established in his name, U. Calif. at Irvine, 1986. Fellow ACP, Am. Coll. Cardiology, Am. Congress Rehab. Medicine (hon.); mem. AMA (mem. residency rev. com. Coun. Med. Edn. 1973), AAAS, Am. Acad. Cerebral Palsy, Am. Acad. Phys. Medicine and Rehab. (Disting. Clinician award 1993), Am. Congress Rehab. Medicine (pres. 1962), Calif. Coun. Gerontology and Geriatrics (bd. dirs. 1980-86, pres. 1985), N.Y. Acad. Medicine, N.Y. Acad. Sci., Orange County Med. Soc., Assn. U. Calif. Irvine (chair emeritae/i 1996-97). Home: 1115 Goldenrod Ave Corona Del Mar CA 92625-1508 Office Phone: 714-456-5626. Business E-Mail: jstobis@uci.edu.

TOBISMAN, STUART PAUL, lawyer; b. Detroit, June 5, 1942; s. Nathan and Beverly (Porvin) T.; m. Karen Sue Tobisman, Aug. 8, 1965; children: Cynthia Elaine, Neal Jay. BA, UCLA, 1966; JD, U. Calif., Berkeley, 1969. Bar: Calif. 1969. Assoc. O'Melveny & Myers, L.A., 1969-77, ptnr., 1977—. Contbr. articles to profl. jours. Trustee L.A. County Bar Assn., 1983-84. With USN, 1961-63. Fellow Am. Coll. Trust and Estate Counsel; mem. Phi Beta Kappa, Order of Coif. Office: O'Melveny & Myers LLP 1999 Avenue Of The Stars Los Angeles CA 90067-6035

TOBORG, ALFRED, history professor; b. Bklyn., Nov. 9, 1932; s. Willy Carl Heinrich Toborg and Gertrud Weck; m. Linda Onsruth, Aug. 17, 1963; children: Katherine Ann Toborg Franko, Louise Elaine Toborg Merrigan, William Lindell, Mary Elizabeth Toborg Boe. BA in History and German, Columbia U., 1954, PhD in History, 1965; MA in History, Xavier U., 1957. Lectr. in history Queens (N.Y.) Coll., 1959-60, Hunter Coll., N.Y.C., 1960; grad. asst. in history Columbia U., N.Y.C., 1959-60; prof. history Lyndon State Coll., Lyndonville, Vt., 1960-99, prof. history emeritus, 2000—. Lectr. in history L.I. U., Bklyn., summer 1961, U. Vt., Lyndonville br., summer 1963-65, 68. Contbr. articles, book revs. to profl. jours. Mem. Vt. Rep. State Com., 1999-; chmn. Lyndon Rep. Town Com., 1970-73; mem. Caledonia County Rep. Com., 1969-79, 81-83, 97-, vice chmn., 1971-73; chmn. Lyndon Town History Adv. Com., Lyndonville, 1993—; acad. assoc. Atlantic Coun. of U.S., Washington, 1987-99; deacon St. Elizabeth Ch., Lyndonville, 1990—; moderator Village of Lyndonville, 1999—. With U.S. Army, 1954—56, with U.S. Army, 1961—62. Humanities scholar Vt. Coun. on Humanities, 1985—, Fulbright scholar, 1958-59; Lyndon State Coll. grantee 1979-82, 85, 87, 92, 94-95, 98; Vt. State Colls. faculty fellow, 1989-90; recipient Appreciation award Lyndon State Coll. Alumni Assn., 1999, Vt. Pub. Svc. award Vt. Sec. of State, 1999. Mem.: KC (4th degree knight), Lyndon Hist. Soc. (pres. 1975—77, 2003—), Vt. Hist. Soc., Vt. Cursillo (treas. 1978—80), Am. Soc. 18th Century Studies, Am. Cath. Hist. Assn., Am. Hist. Assn., Am. Legion. Roman Catholic. Avocations: reading, writing, gardening, church activities, research. Home: 143 South St Lyndonville VT 05851-0272 E-mail: altoborg@upneat.com.

TOBY, JACKSON, sociologist, educator; b. N.Y.C., Sept. 10, 1925; m. Marcia Lifshitz, Aug. 1, 1952 (dec. Jan. 1997); children: Alan Steven, Gail Afriat. BA, Bklyn. Coll., 1946; MA in Econs, Harvard U., 1947, MA in Sociology, 1949, PhD in Sociology, 1950. Rsch. assoc. Lab. Social Relations, Harvard, 1950-51; mem. faculty Rutgers U., 1951—2002, prof. sociology, chmn. dept., 1961-68, prof. sociology emeritus, 2001, dir. Inst. for Criminological Rsch., 1969-94; vis. scholar Am. Enterprise Inst., 2004—. Cons. Youth Devel. Program, Ford Found., 1959-63 Author: (with H.C. Bredemeier) Social Problems in America, 1960, 2d edit., 1971; Contemporary Society, 1964, 2d edit., 1971; contbr. numerous articles to profl. jours., pub. policy jours., N.Y. Times, Wall St. Jour., L.A. Times, Chgo. Tribune, Washington Post, The Weekly Standard, Nat. Rev., Sociol. Rsch. Cons., Pres.'s Commn. Law Enforcement and Adminstrn. Justice, 1966; trustee NAMI-N.J., 1997-2000. Recipient numerous research grants Mem. Am. Sociol. Assn., Sociol. Rsch. Assn., Am. Soc. Criminology, Nat. Assn. Scholars. Achievements include spl. research adolescent delinquency in U.S., Sweden, Japan, other countries, on violence and dropouts in Am. public schools. Home: 17 Harrison Ave Highland Park NJ 08904-1813 Office: Rutgers U Dept Sociology Lucy Stone Hall Livingston Campus New Brunswick NJ 08903 E-mail: jtoby@rci.rutgers.edu.

TOBY, RONALD PAUL, historian; b. White Plains, N.Y., Dec. 6, 1942; s. Allen H. and Ruth (Hecht) T.; m. Yuko Kanai, Jan. 18, 1987. AB, Columbia U., 1965, MA, 1974, PhD, 1977. Preceptor Oriental studies Columbia U., N.Y.C., 1972-73; history lectr. U. Calif., Berkeley, 1977-78; from asst. prof. to prof. history and East Asian studies U. Ill., Urbana-Champaign, 1978—, head Dept. East Asian Langs. and Cultures, 1996—2000. Vis. prof. Inst. Rsch. in Humanities Kyoto U., Japan, 1995—96; prof. Tokyo (Japan) U., 2000—02. Author: State and Diplomacy in Early Modern Japan, 1984; co-author: Parades & Shows, 1994; co-editor: Great Historians, 2 vols., 1989, 91, Art and Culture in Circulation, 2002, Emergence of Economic Society in Japan, 1600-1859, 2004; mem. editl. bd. Internat. Jour. Japanese Diaspora, 1999 , Jour. Source Criticism, 2002—; contbr. articles to profl. jours. Exec. com. Internat. U. Ctr. for Japanese Lang. Studies, 1998—2002. Fulbright fellow, 1974-75, 84-85, Whiting Found. fellow, 1975-76, NEH fellow, 1988-89, Japan Found. fellow, 1989-90, Japan Soc. Promotion of Sci. fellow, 1993; Toyota Found. rsch. grantee, 1989-91. Mem. Assn. for Asian Studies (bd. dirs. 1988-89, N.E. Asia Coun. 1988-91). Office: U Ill Dept History 810 S Wright St Urbana IL 61801-3644 Office Phone: 217-333-6874. Business E-Mail: rptoby@uiuc.edu.

TOCCI, NEIL MICHAEL, marketing and corporate communications executive, educator; b. Boston, Feb. 15, 1949; s. Nildo Neil and Irene Marie (Rioux) T.; m. Marlene Perscheid, Apr. 22, 1972; 1 child, Margaux. BS, Boston Coll., 1971; MBA in Mktg., Fairleigh Dickinson U., 1976; MA, Seton Hall U., 1999. Pres. Carrera Graphic Assocs. Inc., Newark, 1976-94, Carrera Digital, Newark, 1994-97; digital color specialist AOE Ricoh, Fairfield, NJ, 1997-99; mgr., mktg. and corp. comm. Kyocera Mita Am. Inc., Fairfield, 1999—2002; sr. mktg. mgr. Fuji Hunt Photographic Chem., Inc., Allendale, NJ, 2003—. Adj. prof. psychology William Paterson U., Wayne, NJ, 2000—; panel, cons. mktg. strategy Essex County Coll., Newark, 1990; panelist, cons. comms. skills Seton Hall U., South Orange, NJ, 1992. Active Wyckoff YMCA, 1999—, coach recreation league, Wyckoff, 2002—. Mem.: ACA, NJ Psychol. Assn., High Mountain Golf Club. Roman Catholic.

TOCCO, ELAINE KAY, insurance policy specialist; b. Columbus, Ohio, May 20, 1957; d. Arthur Gene and Nancy Louise Lanker; m. Peter Joseph Tocco; children: Nicholas, Alexander; 1 child, Zachary. BA, Brescia U., 1981. Program cons. Disability Determination Svcs., Indpls., 1983—98; social ins. specialist Social Security Adminstrn., Balt., 1999—. Webelos leader Boy Scouts Am., Columbia, 1999—2001; coord. support group Multiple Sclerosis Soc., Indpls., 1985—86. Mem.: Nat. Assn. Disability Examiners, Mensa, Psy Chi, Alpha Chi. Roman Catholic. Avocations: reading, gardening. Home: 6048 Misty Arch Run Columbia MD 21044 Office: Social Security Adminstrn 6401 Security Blvd Baltimore MD 21207 Personal E-mail: elaine_tocco@hotmail.com. Business E-Mail: elaine.tocco@ssa.gov.

TOCCO, JAMES, pianist; b. Detroit, Sept. 21, 1943; s. Vincenzo and Rose (Tabbita) T.; 1 child, Rhoya. Prof. music Ind. U., Bloomington, 1977-91; eminent scholar, artist-in-residence U. Cin. Coll.-Conservatory Music, 1991—; prof. Musikhochschule, Lübeck, Ger., 1990—; artistic dir. Great Lakes Chamber Music Festival, 1994—; prof. Manhattan Sch. Music, 2002—. Debut with orch., Detroit, 1956, since performed with symphony orchs. including Chgo. Symphony, Los Angeles Philharmonic, Cin. Symphony, Detroit Symphony, Nat. Symphony, Balt. Symphony, Atlanta Symphony, Denver Symphony, Montreal Symphony, London Symphony, London Philharm., BBC Orch., Berlin Philharm., Moscow Radio-TV Orch., Amsterdam Philharmonic, Munich Philharmonic, Bavarian Radio Orch., Royal Concertebouw Orch., also recitals, U.S. and abroad, and performances, CBS and NBC networks; guest performer, White House; Recs. include the complete preludes of Chopin, collected piano works of Leonard Bernstein, complete piano works of Charles Tomlinson Griffes, 4 piano sonatas of Edward MacDowell, selected piano works of Aaron Copland, complete Bach-Liszt organ transcriptions, piano works of John Corigliano. concertos of Igor Stravinsky, Leonard Bernstein, and John Corigliano. Recipient Bronze medal Tchaikovsky Competition, Moscow 1970, Bronze medal Queen Elisabeth of Belgium Competition, Brussels 1972, 1st prize Piano Competition of Americas, Rio de Janeiro 1973, 1st prize Munich Internat. Competition 1973. Office: U Cin Coll Conservatory Musi Cincinnati OH 45221-0001

TOCCO, STEPHEN, former airport administrator; Exec. dir., CEO Boston Gen. Edward Lawrence Logan Internat. Airport, Mass. Pt. Authority, Boston; pres. ML Global Mintz Levin Cohen Ferris Glovsky & Popeo, PC, Boston; pres., CEO ML Strategies LLC, Boston. Office: Mintz Levin Cohen Ferris Glovsky & Popeo PC 1 Financial Ctr Fl 41 Boston MA 02111-2621

TOCHEFF, ROBERT DALE, music educator; b. Dayton, Ohio, May 18, 1952; s. George Edwin and Marie Tocheff; m. Diana Sue Tocheff, Mar. 22, 1957; children: Kimberly Brooke, Clayton Robert, Michael Samuel children: Kyle Wesley. AA, Mt. Vernon Nazarene U., 1972; BA in Music Edn., Olivet Nazarene U., 1974; MusM in Music Edn., Wright State U., 1978; PhD in Music Edn., Ohio State U., 1990. Cert. tchr. grades K-12 Ohio, 1974. Music specialist Kettering (Ohio) City Schools, 1974—81; min. music, worship leader First Ch. of the Nazarene, Dayton, 1977—81, Mt. Vernon, 1991—2003; music prof., dept. chmn. Mt. Vernon (Ohio) Nazarene U., 1981—; choir dir. Lakeholm Ch. of the Nazarene, Mt. Vernon, 2004—. Mem.: Ohio Music Educators Assn., Music Educators Nat. Conf., Am. Choral Dirs. Assn., Ohio Choral Dirs. Assn. (area rep. 1995—97). Home: 710 Wooster Rd Mount Vernon OH 43050 Office: Mount Vernon Nazarene Univ 800 Martinsburg Rd Mount Vernon OH 43050 Business E-Mail: btocheff@mvnu.edu.

TOCHTROP, LOIS, state legislator, nurse consultant; b. St. Louis, Jan. 31, 1942; d. Walter Louis Werner and Elizabeth Louise Brante; m. Paul Frederick Tochtrop, Oct. 14, 1961; children: Tony, Scott, Timothy. BSN and Health Care Adminstrn., Metro State Coll., 1988. RN; lic. nursing home adminstr. Staff nurse City Hosp., St. Louis, 1963-67; head nurse St. Louis U. Hosp., 1967-70; staff nurse Meml. Hosp., Jefferson City, Mo., 1970-75, nurse supr., 1975-79; office nurse, asst. DON Craig (Colo.) Med. Clinic, 1979-83; staff nurse Willowbrook Care, Denver, 1984-88, DON, 1988-90, Park Forest Care Ctr., Denver, 1990-98, nursing cons., 1998—. Pres. Colo. Nurses Assn. Dist. 23, 1992-96; legis. affairs specialist Abate of Co., 1993-96. Named Legislator of Yr., AARP, Denver, 1999, Colo. Sr. Lobby, Denver, 1999, Colo. Cancer Soc., Denver, 1999. Democrat. Roman Catholic. Avocations: reading, walking, word games, motorcycling.

TOCIO, MARY ANN, association executive; MS, Simmons Coll. Sch. Mgmt. Sr. v.p. ops. Health Stop Med. Mgmt., Inc., Boston; CEO Bright Horizons Family Solutions Family Ctrs., Cambridge, Mass. Office: Bright Horizons Family Solutions One Kendall Sw Bldg 200 Cambridge MA 02139

TODARO, ELISABETH M. lawyer; b. Easton, Pa., July 4, 1967; d. James Michael and Bernice Piparato Todaro. BA Econs., U. Va., 1989; JD, Harvard U., 1997. Bar: Mass. 1997, NY 2001. Analyst SNL Securities, Charlottesville, Va., 1989—91, ptnr., sr. analyst, 1991—94; summer assoc. Manatt, Phelps &

Phillips, Washington, 1995, Hogan & Hartson, 1996; assoc. Goodwin Procter LLP, Boston, 1997—. Mem.: ABA, Boston Bar Assn., Mass. Bar Assn. Office: Goodwin Procter LLP Exch Pl Boston MA 02109 Office Phone: 617-570-1000.

TODARO, GEORGE JOSEPH, pathologist, researcher; b. N.Y.C., July 1, 1937; s. George J. and Antoinette (Piccinni) Todaro; m. Jane Lehv, Aug. 12, 1962; children: Wendy C., Thomas M., Anthony A. BS, Swarthmore Coll., 1958; MD, NYU, 1963. Intern NYU Sch. Medicine, N.Y.C., 1963—64, fellow in pathology, 1964—65, asst. prof. pathology, 1965—67; staff assoc. Viral Carcinogenesis br. Nat. Cancer Inst., Bethesda, Md., 1967—70, head molecular biology sect., 1969—70; chief Viral Carcinogenesis br. Nat. Cancer Inst. (Lab. Viral Carcinogenesis), 1970—83; sci. dir., pres. Oncogen, Seattle, 1987—90; sr. v.p. exploratory biomed. rsch. Bristol-Myers Squibb Pharm. Rsch. Inst., 1990; pres., CEO Cytokine Networks, Inc., Seattle, 1998—; now prof. pathobiology U. Wash., Seattle. Adj. prof. pathology U. Wash., Seattle, 1983—, past chmn. dept. pathobiology; sr. v.p., sci. dir. Pathogenesis Corp., Seattle, 1992—95; mem. Fred Hutchinson Cancer Rsch. Ctr., Seattle, 1991—93. Editor: Cancer Rsch., 1973—86, Archives of Virology, 1976—, Jour. Biol. Chemistry, 1979; contbr. articles to profl. jours. Med. officer USPHS, 1967—69. Named Walter Hubert lectr., Brit. Cancer Soc., 1977; recipient Borden Undergrad. Rsch. award, 1963, Career Devel. award, USPHS, 1967, HEW Superior Svc. award, 1971, Gustav Stern award for virology, 1972, Parke-Davis award in exptl. pathology, 1975. Mem.: Am. Soc. Clin. Investigation, Am. Soc. hemists, Soc. Exptl. Biology and Medicine, Am. Assn. Cancer Rsch., Am. Soc. Microbiology, NAS. Home: 1940 15th Ave E Seattle WA 98112-2829 Office Phone: 206-336-5572. E-mail: gtodaro@targetedgrowth.com.

TODARO, MICHAEL PAUL, economics educator, consultant; b. May 14, 1942; s. George Joseph and Annette (Piccini) Todaro; m. Donna Renee Crickenberger, June 17, 1974; 1 child, Lenora Jean. BA, Haverford Coll., 1964; MPhil, Yale U., 1966, PhD, 1967. Vis. lectr. Makerere U. Uganda, 1964—65; vis. sr. lectr. U. Nairobi, Kenya, 1968—70, 1974—76; assoc. dir. Rockefeller Found., N.Y.C., 1968—76; vis. prof. U. Calif., Santa Barbara, 1976—77; dep. dir. Population Coun., N.Y.C., 1977, sr. assoc., cons., 1978—; prof. econs. NYU, N.Y.C., 1977—97. Cons. Fund for Peace (Inst. for Study of World Politics), N.Y.C., 1979—. Author: Internal Migration in Developing Countries, 1976, Economics for a Developing World, 1991, Economic Development in the Third World, 2000; co-author: Economic Theory, 1969; mem. editl. bd.: Population and Devel. Rev., 1976—. Fellow, Woodrow Wilson Found., 1966, NDEA, 1966; grantee, Compton Found., 1981—84. Mem.: Population Assn. Am., Internat. Union for Sci. Study of Population, Am. Econ. Assn., Coun. on Fgn. Rels., Phi Beta Kappa. Roman Catholic. Home: PO Box 432 York Harbor ME 03911 Office: Population Coun 1 Dag Hammarskjold Plz New York NY 10017

TODD, ANDREW CHRISTIAN, research scientist, consultant; b. Birmingham, Eng., Dec. 6, 1964; s. Robert Derrick and Rita T. BS, U. Birmingham (Eng.), 1986; phD, 1989. Chartered physicist. Vis. prof. U. Md., Balt., 1990-92; asst. prof. Mt. Sinai Sch. Medicine, N.Y.C., 1992-2000, assoc. prof., 2001—. Adj. asst. prof. Johns Hopkins U., Balt., 1995—. Contbr. numerous articles to profl. jours. Mem. Inst. Phyisics. Avocations: music, photography. Office: The Mt Sinai Med Ctr Box 1057 One Gustave L Levy Pl New York NY 10029-6574 Fax: (212) 423-9313. E-mail: andrew.todd@mssm.edu.

TODD, EDWARD WILLIAM, marketing professional; b. Tagbilaran, Bohol, The Philippines, Nov. 7, 1948; came to U.S., 1951; s. Edward Todd and Doris Julia Crozier-Todd; m. Janice Lynn Gustafson, July 2, 1983; children: Erin Kathleen, Kelsey Michelle. BA in Polit. Sci., Seattle Pacific U., 1970. Credit ctrl. supr. Sears, Seattle, Portland, Oreg., 1969-74; cost acct. Peerless Industries, Tualatin, Oreg., 1974-75; personal lines underwriter SAFECO Ins. Cos., Lake Oswego, Oreg., 1975-79, area underwriting mgr., 1979-96, cmty. involvement chmn., 1985—2002, sr. analyst, diversity mktg. coord., 1999—2002; N.W. region diversity mktg. specialist SAFECO Ins. Co., Redmond, Wash., 2002—. Mem. adv. bd. First Place, Seattle, 2003—. Wash. Latino Bus. Assn., 2003—; mem. session, elder, trustee Lake Grove Presbyn. Ch., 1989—92, mem. bd. deacons, 1986—89; bd. dirs. Lake Oswego C. of C., 1989—93, pres., 1992—93; co-founder Cmty. Cultural Diversity Week, 1997; bd. dirs., co-pres. Samaritan Counseling Ctr., 1997—98; co-chair legal budget com. Lake Oswego Sch. Dist., 1997—; bd. dirs. Lake Oswego Sch. Dist. Found., 1997—, pres., 1999—2000. Recipient Cmty. Leader of Year award, Lake Oswego C. of C., 2001. Democrat. Avocations: walking, reading, gardening, community service.

TODD, HAROLD WADE, retired association executive, retired air force officer; b. Chgo., Jan. 17, 1938; s. Harold Wade and Jeanne (Fayal) T.; m. Wendy Yvonne Kendrick, July 12, 1981; children by previous marriage: Hellen J. Wilson, Kenneth J., Stephen D., Joseph M., Michelle M. Adams, Mark A.; stepchildren: Jamie Y. White, James K. Mills, Timothy S. Emerson. BS, U.S. Air Force Acad., 1959; grad., Nat. War Coll., 1975. Commd. 2d lt. U.S. Air Force, 1959, advanced through grades to maj. gen., 1982; aide to comdr. (2d Air Force (SAC)), Barksdale AFB, La., 1970-71; exec. aide to comdr.-in-chief U.S. Air Forces Europe, Germany, 1971-74; spl. asst. chief of staff USAF, 1975-76; chief Concept Devel. Divsn., 1976-77; chief Readiness and NATO Staff Group, Hdqrs. USAF, 1977-78; exec. asst. to chmn. Joint Chiefs Staff, 1978-80; comdr. 25th region N. Am. Aerospace Def. Command McChord AFB, Wash., 1980-82; chief staff 4th Allied Tactical Air Force Heidelberg, 1982-85; commandant Air War Coll., 1985-89; vice comdr. Air U., 1985-89, ret., 1989; ind. cons. Colorado Springs, Colo., 1989-95; pres., CEO, Nat. Stroke Assn., Englewood, Colo., 1995-00. Founder, pres. Bossier City (La.) chpt. Nat. Assn. for Children with Learning Disabilities, 1970-71. Decorated Def. DSM, Air Force DSM (2), Legion of Merit (2), DFC, Air medal (8), Air Force Commendation medal. Mem. Air Force Assn., USAF Acad. Assn. Grads., Nat. War Coll. Alumni Assn. Home: 1250 Big Valley Dr Colorado Springs CO 80919-1015

TODD, HARRY WILLIAMS, aircraft propulsion system company executive; b. Oak Park, Ill., 1922; BSME, U. So. Calif., 1947, BSIE, 1948, MBA, 1950. With Rockwell Internat., Pitts., 1947-76, former v.p. ops.; pres., chmn., chief exec. officer, bd. dirs. The L.E. Myers Co., Pitts., 1976-80; with Rohr Industries, Inc., Chula Vista, Calif., 1980-90, chief operating officer, 1980-82, pres., chief exec. officer, chmn., 1982-90, retired, 1990; mng. ptnr. Carlise Enterprises, 1990-97; mng. dir. Carlisle Ent., Calif., 1990—. Bd. dirs. Rohr Industries, Pacific Scientific, Helmerich & Payne, Garrett Aviation Svcs. Trustee Scripps Clinic and Rsch. Found. With U.S. Army, 1944-46. Office: Carlisle Enterprises 7777 Fay Ave Ste 200 La Jolla CA 92037-4390

TODD, J. C. See COOPER, JANE

TODD, JAMES DALE, federal judge; b. Scotts Hill, Tenn., May 20, 1943; s. James P. and Jeanette Grace (Duck) T.; m. Jeanie M. Todd, June 26, 1965; 2 children. BS, Lambuth Coll., 1965; M Combined Scis., U. Miss., 1968; JD, Memphis State U., 1972. Bar: Tenn. 1972, U.S. Dist. Ct. (we. dist.) Tenn. 1972, U.S. Ct. Appeals (6th cir.) 1973, U.S. Supreme Ct. 1975. Tchr. sci., chmn. sci. dept. Lyman High Sch., Longwood, Fla., 1965-68, Memphis U. Sch., 1968-72; ptnr. Waldrop, Farmer, Todd & Breen, P.A., 1972-83; cir. judge div. II 26th Jud. Dist., Jackson, Tenn., 1983-85; judge U.S. Dist. Ct. (we. dist.) Tenn., Jackson, 1985-2001, chief judge, 2001—. Recipient Lifetime Achievement award Lambuth U., 2001; named Alumnus of Yr. Lambuth Coll. Alumni Assn., 1985. Fellow Tenn. Bar Found.; mem. Fed. Judges Assn. (bd. dirs. 1998-2002), Fed. Bar Assn., Jackson Madison County Bar Assn. (pres. 1978-79), Dist. Judges Assn. of 6th Cir. (pres. 2000-2001). Methodist. Office: US Dist Ct 111 S Highland Ave Jackson TN 38301-6107

TODD, JANET STAPLETON, law librarian; b. Selma, Ala., Apr. 2, 1950; d. Carl William and Louise Maxine (Starrett) Stapleton; m. Sammy Steven Todd, Nov. 27, 1971. B. U. N.Mex., 1972; MLS, La. State U., 1979; JD, U. Okla., 1982. Bar: Okla. 1983. Assoc. atty. Check Law Firm, Oklahoma City, 1983; instr. Oklahoma City U. Law Sch., 1983—84; law libr. Kornfeld Franklin & Phillips, 1983—85; jud. law clk. U.S. Dist. Ct., 1985—87, U.S. Bankruptcy Ct., 1987—89; Exxon Valdez law clk. U.S. Dist. Ct., Anchorage, 1989—92; law libr. Monroe County, Key West, Fla., 1993—95. Vol. Judge Advocate Office, Elmendorf AFB, Alaska, 1999. Vol. ARC, Elmendorf AFB, 1998—99; election ofcl. Oklahoma County Election Commn., Oklahoma City, 2002—; adminstrv. law judge Okla. Dept. Labor, 2004—. Mem.: Mid Del Investment Club. Avocations: genealogy, photography. Home: 6008 SE 57th St Oklahoma City OK 73135-5432

TODD, JAY MARLYN, retired editor; b. Granger, Utah, July 28, 1936; s. Kenneth Christian and Gertrude A. (Viehweg) T.; m. Janet Cutrer, Mar. 20, 1964; children: Deborah, Jay Randall, Deanna, Jason Cutrer, Sarah Janet. BS, U. Utah, 1961. Staff writer Deseret News, Salt Lake City, 1960-61; tchr. Ch. Edn. Sys., various cities in Utah, Idaho, 1961-65; asst. editor, asst. mng. editor Improvement Era, Salt Lake City, 1966-70; mng. editor New Era, Salt Lake City, 1971-72, Ensign, Salt Lake City, 1972-2001. Author: Curtain Time USA: Ambassador of Inspiration, 1965, Saga of the Book of Abraham, 1968, (booklets) The Creed Haymond Story, 1979, A Historical Walking Tour of Holladay, 1996; editor: A Treasury of Edward J. Wood, 1983.

TODD, JOE LEE, historian; b. Bartlesville, Okla., Sept. 28, 1946; s. Harold Albert and Mildred Viola Todd. Student, Okla. State U., 1964-66; BA in Anthropology, U. Okla., 1974; postgrad. in Anthropology, U. Tex., Austin, 1979-81. Curator of collections Okla. Hist. Soc., Oklahoma City, 1971-76; dir. 45th Infantry div. mus., Oklahoma City, 1976-78; curator Ft. Hood (Tex.) Mus., 1978-82; oral historian, archivist Okla. Hist. Soc., Oklahoma City, 1982—. Cons. Confederate Air Force, Midland, Tex., 1990—, Andersonville (Ga.) POW Ctr., 1991—. Author: Pipe-Tomahawks in the Oklahoma Historical Society, 1976, Native American Interveiws, oral histories, 1985, USS Oklahoma, Remembrance of a Great Lady, 1990. Bd. dirs. Sacred Heart (Okla.) Indian Mission, 1989-95. With U.S. Army, 1966-69, Okla. Nat. Guard, 1975-78, Tex. Nat. Guard, 1978-83, USAR, 1983-96. Decorated Air medal; recipient Humanitarian Svc. medal U.S. Army, 1992, Vietnam Svc. medal, 1969, Kuwaiti Liberation medal, 1991. Republican. Episcopalian. Office: Okla Hist Soc 2100 N Lincoln Blvd Oklahoma City OK 73105-4907 Home: RR 5 Box 415 Bartlesville OK 74003-9315

TODD, JOHN DICKERSON, JR., retired lawyer; b. Macon, Ga., June 30, 1912; s. J.D. and Hazel (McManus) T.; m. Mellicent McWhorter, Mar. 7, 1943; children— Rosalind (Mrs. Jack Harding Tedards, Jr.), John D. Student, Va. Mil. Inst., 1930-32; LLB, U. Ga., 1935. Bar: S.C. 1935. With firm Hingson & Todd, 1935-51; partner firm Leatherwood, Walker, Todd & Mann, Greenville, S.C., 1952-2000; sr. partner; judge Greenville City Ct., 1939; atty. County of Greenville, 1948-56; mem. bd. bar examiners State of S.C.; ret. Chmn. S.C. Judicial Study Commn., 1995. Served to maj. AUS, 1941-45. Mem. ABA, Am. Coll. Trial Lawyers, Am. Bar Found., 4th U.S. Cir. Jud. Conf., S.C. Bar Assn. (bd. govs., pres. 1978—), Greenville Jr. C. of C. (pres.), Greenville County Bar (past pres.), Greenville Kiwanis (past pres.), Greenville Country Club (past pres.), Summit Club, Poinsett Club, Phi Delta Phi, Sigma Nu. Baptist. Home: 200 Riverside Dr Greenville SC 29605-1133

TODD, JOHN J. computer company executive; BA, Longwood Coll.; MBA, Coll. William and Mary, 1960. CFO Boston Market, 1996-97, Allied Signal Aftermarket-Aerospace, Allied Signal Engines, Phoenix, Ariz.; sr. v.p., CFO Gateway, Inc., San Diego, 1998—. Held several exec. positions in fin., strategic planning, bus. devel. PepsiCo. Bd. dirs. Sharp HealtCare, Nat. Alzheimer's Assn., San Diego Internat. Sports Coun. Office: Gateway Inc San Diego CA 92121

TODD, JOHN JOSEPH, lawyer; b. St. Paul, Mar. 16, 1927; s. John Alfred and Martha Agnes (Jagoe) T.; m. Dolores Jean Shanahan, Sept. 9, 1950; children: Richard M., Jane E., John P. Student, St. Thomas Coll., 1944, 46-47; B.Sci. and Law, U. Minn., 1949, LL.B., 1950. Bar: Minn. 1951. Practice in, South St. Paul, Minn., 1951-72; partner Thuet and Todd, 1953-72; asso. justice Minn. Supreme Ct., St. Paul, 1972-85; sole practice West St. Paul, 1985-92; of counsel Brenner & Glassman Ltd., Mpls., 1992—99, Orme & Assoc., Eagan, Minn., 1999—. Served with USNR, 1945—46. Mem. state bar assns., VFW. Home: 6689 Argenta Trl W Inver Grove Heights MN 55077-2208 Office: Orme & Associates 4040 Nicols Rd Eagan MN 55121 Office Phone: 651-688-7646. Personal E-mail: jjbtodd@comcast.net. Business E-Mail: jtodd@ormelaw.com.

TODD, JUDITH F. lawyer; b. Chgo., Jan. 25, 1946; Student, Vassar Coll.; AB, U. Mich., 1968; JD cum laude, U. Miami, 1972. Bar: Fla. 1972, Ill. 1977, Ala. 1981. With Sirote & Permutt PC, Birmingham, Ala., now ptnr. Assoc. editor U. Miami Law Review, 1971-72. Fellow Am. Coll. Trust and Estate Counsel; mem. ABA, Fla. Bar, Ill. State Bar Assn. Office: Sirote & Permutt PC 2311 Highland Ave S Birmingham AL 35205-2972

TODD, KATHLEEN GAIL, physician; b. Portland, Oreg., Aug. 31, 1951; d. Horace Edward and Lois Marie (Messing) T.; m. Andrew Richard Embick, March 31, 1980; children: Elizabeth Todd Embick, Margaret Todd Embick. BA, Pomona Coll., 1972; MD, Washington U., St. Louis, 1976. Diplomate Am. Bd. Family Practice. Resident U. Wash. Affiliated Hosps., Seattle, 1976-79; pvt. practice Valdez (Alaska) Med. Clinic, 1980—; chief of staff Valdez Community Hosp., 1986—95. Mem. AMA, AAFP, Am. Acad. Family Practice, Alaska State Med. Assn. (counselor-at-large 1986-87). Democrat. Episcopalian. Avocations: skiing, kayaking, camping, music. Office: Valdez Med Clinic PO Box 1829 Valdez AK 99686-1829

TODD, KENNETH S., JR., parasitologist, educator; b. Three Forks, Mont., Aug. 25, 1936; s. Kenneth S. and Anna Louise (Seeman) T. BS, Mont. State U., 1962, MS, 1964; PhD, Utah State U., 1967. Asst. prof. U. Ill., Urbana, 1967-71, assoc. prof., 1971-76, prof. vet. parasitology, 1976-94, chmn. div. parasitology, 1983-90, asst. head vet. pathobiology, 1984-87, prof. vet. programs in agr., 1984-94, acting head vet. pathobiology, 1987-90, head, 1990-94; prof. emeritus, 1994. Affiliate scientist Ill. State Natural History Survey, 1987-94; adj. prof. microbiology Mont. State U., 1994—. Served with USAF, 1954-58. NSF grad. fellow, 1966-67 Mem. AVMA, Am. Assn. Vet. Parasitologists, Am. Micros. Soc., Am. Soc. Parasitologists, Am. Soc. Tropical Medicine and Hygiene, Helminthologic Soc. Washington, Midwest Conf. Parasitologists, Wildlife Disease Assn., Soc. Protozoologists, Mont. Acad. Scis., Rocky Mountain Conf. Parasitologists, World Assn. for Advancement of Vet. Parasitology. Office: Mont State U Dept Microbiology Bozeman MT 59715 E-mail: kstoddjr@hotmail.com.

TODD, LEE TROVER, JR., electrical engineer; b. Earlington, Ky., May 6, 1946; s. Lee T. Todd; m. Patricia Brantley; children: Troy, Kathryn. BSEE, U. Ky., 1968; MS, MIT, 1970, PhD, 1973. IBM postdoctoral fellow MIT, 1973-74; asst. prof. engring. U. Ky., Lexington, 1974-78, assoc. prof., 1978-87; chmn., chief exec. officer Databeam Corp., Lexington, 1983—; v.p. Hughes Display Products, Lexington. Chmn. Ky. Sci. & Tech. Coun., Lexington, 1987—; mem. Ky. Epscor Com., 1985—, Ky. Acad. Sci., 1988. Contbr. articles to profl. jours. Chmn., deacon Calvary Bapt. Ch., Lexington, 1989; bd. dirs. Ky. Econ. Devel. Corp., Frankfort, Georgetown Coll. (Ky.). Named Entrepreneur of Yr., INC mag., 1989; recipient Outstanding Alumnus award U. Ky. Coll. Engring., 1989, Small Bus. of Yr. award Lexington C. of C., U.S. Gt. Tchr. award, 1983; Hertz Found. fellow, 1968-73. Mem. Ky. Soc. Profl. Engrs. (Award of Achievement 1990), U. Ky. Alumni Assn., Leadership Ky., Louisville Adv. Tech. Coun. Baptist. Achievements include patents in field. Office: Presidents Office University of Kentucky 101 Gillis Building 0033 Lexington KY 40506

TODD, MURRAY, retail executive; B, Boise State U. With Super Thrift Drugstores, 1974—79; store mgr., dist. mgr. then v.p. ops. PayLess Drug Stores, 1979—89; v.p. of procurement Thrifty PayLess, 1994; group v.p. store svcs. and procurment Fred Meyer Stores, 1997—2000; sr. v.p., store ops. and procurement Rite Aid Corp., 2000—01. Office: Rite Aid Corp 30 Hunter Lane Camp Hill PA 17011

TODD, NORMA ROSS, retired government official; b. Butler, Pa., Oct. 3, 1920; d. William Bryson and Doris Mae (Ferguson) Ross; m. Alden Frank Miller, Jr., Apr. 16, 1940 (dec. Feb. 1975); 1 child, Alden Frank III; m. Jack R. Todd, Dec. 23, 1977 (dec. Sept. 1990). Student, Pa. State U., 1944-46, Yale U., 1954-57. Exec. mgr. Donora (Pa.) C. of C., 1950-57, pres., 1972; exec. mgr. Donora Cmty. Chest, 1950-57; office mgr. Donora Golden Jubilee, 1951; staff writer Donora Herald-American, 1957, city editor, 1957-70; assoc. editor Daily Herald, Donora, 1970-73; svc. rep. Pitts. Telesvc. Ctr., Social Security Adminstrn., HHS, 1977-83. Mem. Mayor's Adv. Coun., Donora, 1965-69, Citizens' Adv. Coun., Donora, 1965-69; mem. Donora Bd. Edn., 1954-60, pres., 1960; mem. Donora Borough Coun., 1970-72; bd. dirs. Mon Valley chpt. ARC, 1964-99, sec. bd., 1964-97, chmn. bd. dirs., 1997-99, mem. lifetime adv. bd., 2000; bd. dirs. Washington County Tourism Agy., 1970-90, sec., 1972-90; bd. dirs. Washington County History and Landmarks Found., 1971-80, 91-92, sec., 1975-80, 91-93, hon. life mem., 1996; bd. dirs. Mon Valley YMCA, 1960-66, Mon Valley coun. Camp Fire Girls, 1965-79, Mon Valley Drug and Alcoholism Coun., 1971-78; hon. life mem. Pa. Congress PTAs; bd. dirs. United Way Mon Valley, 1973-82, chmn. pub. rels., 1973-74. Recipient Fine Arts Festival of Pa. Poetry first prize award Fedn. Women's Clubs, 1987, 1st and 2d pl. awards for photography Washington County Fine Arts Festival, County Fedn. Women's Clubs, 1990, Disting. Svc. award Donora Rotary Club, 1997, Millenium Peace award, India, 2001, Two World Poets awards J. Mark Press, 2002, U.S. Rep. Senatorial Medal of Freedom, 2003, Congl. Order Merit, 2003; pub. in Best Poems of 1995 Nat. Libr. of Poetry, Best Poems of 1996, Best Poems of 1997, Outstanding Poets of 1998, Am. at the Millennium The Best Poets of the 20th Century, The Best Poems and Poets of 2001, The Best Poems and Poets of 2002, of 2003, and numerous anthologies in U.S., Italy, Great Britain and India. Mem. AAUW, Svc. Corps Retired Execs. (sec. 1998—), Pa. Soc. Newspaper Editors, Pitts. Press Club, Donora C. of C. (pres. 1971-72), DAR (regent Monongahela Valley chpt. 1974-77, treas. 1992-2001), Internat. Platform Assn. (finalist Acad. of Poets Competition, 2001), World Poetry Soc. Internat., Internat. Poets Acad., Famous Poet Soc., U.S. Poets, Metverse Muse, Washington County Poetry Soc. (pres. 1967-69), Donora Hist. Soc. (curator 1990—), Family of Bruce Soc. (descendants of King Robert the Bruce of Scotland 1987—), Mt. Vernon Ladies Assn., Washington County Fedn. Women's Clubs (rec. sec. 1964-66, pub. rels chmn. 1990-92), Order Ea. Star (worthy matron 1966-67, treas. 1986-94, 98—2003, bd. dirs. Western Pa. Eastern Star Home 1997-98, adv. bd. Masonic Eastern Star Home-West 1998-2000), White Shrine of Jerusalem (high priestess 1973-74, treas. 1995-2001), Order of Amaranth (royal matron 1966, dist. dep. 3 times, grand rep. W.Va. 1979-80), Donora Forecast (pres. 1957-59), Donora Unidon (pres. 1965-66, 56-57), Clan Ross Assn. U.S. Avocation: genealogy. Home: Overlook Ter Donora PA 15033 also: 1310 Mckean Ave Donora PA 15033-2200

TODD, ROBERT FRANKLIN, III, oncologist, educator; b. Granville, Ohio, Apr. 16, 1948; m. Susan Erhard, 1977; children: Currier Nathaniel, Andrew Joseph. AB, Duke U., 1970, PhD, 1975, MD, 1976. Diplomate Am. Bd. Internal Medicine. Intern Peter Bent Brigham Hosp., Boston, 1976-77, resident, 1977-78; fellow in oncology Sidney Farber Cancer Inst., Boston, 1978-80; clin. fellow in medicine Harvard Med. Sch., Boston, 1978-81; postdoctoral fellow divsn. tumor immunology Sidney Farber Cancer Inst., Boston, 1979-81; asst. prof. medicine Harvard Med. Sch., Boston, 1981-84; assoc. prof. internal medicine U. Mich., Ann Arbor, 1984-88, assoc. prof. cellular and molecular biology, 1985-88, assoc. dir. divsn. hematology-oncology internal medicine, 1987-91, prof. internal medicine, 1988—, assoc. chair for rsch. dept. internal medicine, 1989-91, assoc. chair dept. internal medicine, 1991-93, chief divsn. hematology-oncology dept. internal medicine, 1993—, assoc. v.p. rsch., 1999—, Frances and Victor Ginsberg prof. hematology/oncology, 1999—. Attending physician U. Mich. Hosps., 1984—. Contbr. numerous articles to profl. jours.; patentee in field. Mem.: Am. Soc. Clin. Investigation, S.W. Oncology Group, Ctrl. Soc. Clin. Rsch. (councilor 1997—, pres. 2001—02), Am. Fedn. Clin. Rsch. (councilor midwest chpt. 1986—89), Am. Soc. Hematology, Soc. Leukocyte Biology (councilor 1996—99), Am. Soc. Clin. Oncology, Am. Assn. Cancer Rsch., Am. Assn. Immunologists, ACP, Alpha Omega Alpha, Phi Beta Kappa. Office: U Mich Med Sch 1500 E Med Ctr Dr 7216 CCGC Ann Arbor MI 48109-0948

TODD, RONALD GARY, lawyer; b. Spokane, Wash., Dec. 12, 1946; s. Theodore H. and Dorothea I. (Swanson) T.; m. Natalie A., June 16, 1973; children: Russell E., Brian N., David E. AB, Cornell U., 1969; JD, Columbia U., 1972. Bar: N.Y. 1973, U.S. Dist. Ct. (so. and ea. dists.) N.Y. 1975, U.S. Ct. Appeals (2d cir.) 1975, U.S. Supreme Ct. 1976, D.C. 1993. Atty. Dewey Ballantine, N.Y.C., 1973-79, Simpson Thacher & Bartlett, N.Y.C., 1980-82; atty., ptnr. Golenbock & Barell, N.Y.C., 1982-89; ptnr. Reid & Priest (now Thelen Reid & Priest LLP), N.Y.C., 1989-2000; chief counsel J.P. Morgan Title Agy. LLC, 2000—; asst. gen. counsel JP Morgan Chase & Co., 2000—. Instr., guest lectr. NYU Sch. Continuing Edn., 1983-90; adv. bd. Commonwealth Land Title and TransAm. Title Ins. Co., N.Y.C., 1992-97. Contbr. articles to profl. jours. Pres., bd. dirs. Seven Bridges Field Club, 1982-85. Mem. ABA (real property sect. 1973—), N.Y. Bar Assn. (real property sect. 1973—), D.C. Bar Assn. (real property sect. 1992—). Avocations: instrumental music, tennis. Office: JP Morgan Title Agy 261 Madison Ave New York NY 10016-2303 Business E-Mail: ronald.todd@jpmchase.com.

TODD, SHIRLEY ANN, school system administrator; b. May 23, 1935; d. William Leonard and Margaret Judy (Simmons) Brown; m. Thomas Byron Todd, July 7, 1962 (dec. July 1977). BS in Edn., Madison Coll., 1956; MEd, U. Va., 1971. Cert. tchr. Va. Elem. sch. tchr. Fairfax County Sch. Bd., Fairfax, Va., 1956—66, mid. sch. tchr., 1966—71; guidance counselor James F. Cooper Mid. Sch., McLean, Va., 1971—88, dir. guidance, 1988—96; chmn. mktg. Lake Anne Joint Venture, Falls Church, Va., 1979—81, mng. ptnr., 1980—82. Del. Fairfax County Rep. Conv., 1985. Fellow: Fairfax Edn. Assn. (bd. dirs. 1968—70, profl. rights and responsibilities commn. 1970—72); mem.: ASCD, NEA, Va. Sch. Counselors Assn., Va. Counselors Assn., Va. Counselors Assn. (exec. com. 1987), No. Va. Counselors Assn. (exec. bd. 1982—83, hospitality and social chmn.), Va. Edn. Assn. (state com. on local assns. and urban affairs 1969—70), Vintage Ladies of No. Va. (newsletter editor 2002—03), Women's Golf Assn. (pres. 1997—98), Welcome Club of No. Va. (pres. 2003—04), Chantilly Nat. Golf and Country Club (v.p. social 1981—82). Baptist. Avocations: golf, tennis. Home: 6543 Bay Tree Ct Falls Church VA 22041-1001

TODD, THOMAS ABBOTT, architect, urban designer, city planner; b. North Stonington, Conn., May 5, 1928; s. James Arnold and Isabel Nisbet (Downs) T.; m. Carol Roberts, July 7, 1956; children: Christopher, Suzannah, Cassandra. BA, Haverford Coll., 1950; MCP, MArch with honors, U. Pa., 1959. Designer Geddes Brecher Qualls Cunningham, Phila., 1961; chief designer Eshbach Pullinger Stevens Bruder, Phila., 1962; ptnr. Grant & Todd, Phila., 1963, Wallace McHarg Roberts Todd, Phila., 1963-79, Wallace Roberts & Todd, Phila., 1979-91, Warner, Todd Gaffney, Jamestown, R.I., 1993-01. Prin. works include The master plan for Abuja, capitol city of, Nigeria; urban design concept, master plan and public architecture for Balt. Inner Harbor; master plan U.S. Capitol Grounds, Washington, D.C., McKeldin Sq., Balt., Norfolk waterfront master plan, (Va.), Atlantic City Conv. Ctr./Rail Terminal, Lower Manhattan Plan, N.Y.C., Downtown L.A. devel. Plan, plan for State facilities, Annapolis, Md., master plan Haverford Coll., 6th St Market Place, Richmond, Va., Tredegar Galleries Valentine Mus., Richmond, Waterside Festival Market, Town Point Pk. and Waters Edge Promenade, Norfolk, Va., Liberty State Pk., Jersey City, N.J., Wiggins Waterfront State Pk., Camden, N.J., Downtown Buffalo master plan, Quadrangle Life Care Community, Haverford, Pa., Liberty Pl. master plan and designers concept, Phila., long range devel. plan U. Pa., Performing Arts Ctr., Haverford Coll., Assembly Hall, Germantown Friends Sch., plan for downtown Westerly, R.I., Newport, R.I., Harborfront and South Thames Street Demonstration Plan, Newport, also numerous pvt. residences, landscape plans, instl. and pub. master plans and buildings; one-man painting exhbns. include Phila. Independence Seaport Mus., 2000, Newport (R.I.) Art Mus., 2001; contbr. articles to profl. jours. Bd. dirs. Germantown Friends Sch., Phila., 1972-74, Green St. Friends Sch., Phila., 1973-75, Phila. Maritime Mus., 1986-90, Philomel Ancient Instruments, Phila., 1986-91, Maxwell Mansion, Phila., 1983-86, Save the Bay, Naragansett

Bay, 1997, Grow Smart R.I., 1997; v.p. Haverford Coll. Arboretum, 1983; chmn. ann. giving Haverford Coll., 1987; mem. Jamestown (R.I.) Planning Bd.; advisor Ft. Adams Found., Newport. Theophilus Parsons Chandler fellow, 1959; recipient numerous design awards. Fellow AIA; mem. Am. Inst. Cert. Planners. Independent. Quaker. Home: 118 Highland Dr Jamestown RI 02835-2900

TODD, THOMAS ALEXANDER, secondary school educator; b. Lowell, Mass., June 14, 1945; s. Thomas Alexander Todd and Evangeline Slade Spence. BA in English, Bates Coll., 1967; MA in English, NYU, 1968. English instr. The Franklin Sch., NYC, 1969—74; English dept. chmn. The Rhodes Sch., NYC, 1974—87; English instr. The Lenox Sch., NYC, 1987—91, St. Hilda's and St. Hugh's Sch., NYC, 1991—93; English/drama instr. Bronx H.S. of Sci., NY, 1993—. Editor: (book) Water: Source, Sustainer, Destoryer of Life, 1971. Mem.: Drama League, The Dramatists Guild of Am., Inc. (assoc.). Avocations: theater, poetry, acting. Home: 72 Park Terrace West Apt E-87 New York NY 10034 Office: The Bronx HS of Sci 75 W 205th St Bronx NY 10468 Office Phone: 718-817-7700. E-mail: thoastodd2@yahoo.com.

TODD, VIRGIL HOLCOMB, clergyman, religion educator; b. Jordonia, Tenn., June 22, 1921; s. George Thurman and Nellie Mai (Dutton) T.; m. Irene Rolman, Sept. 21, 1941; 1 child, Donald Edwin. BA, Bethel Coll., 1945; BD, Cumberland Presbyn. Sem., 1947; MA, Scarritt Coll., 1948; PhD, Vanderbilt U., 1956. Ordained to ministry Presbyn. Ch., 1944. Minister Cumberland Presbyn. Chs., Tenn. and Ky., 1943-52; assoc. prof. Bethel Coll., McKenzie, Tenn., 1952-54; prof. of Old Testament Memphis Theol. Sem., 1954-2001, ret., 2001. Interim minister Presbyn. chs. in Tenn., Ky. and Miss., 1952 ; vice-moderator Gen. Assembly Cumberland Presbyn. Ch., 1984 85, moderator, 1985-86. Author: Prophet Without Portfolio (2d Isaiah), 1972, A New Look at an Old Prophet (Ezekiel), 1977, Biblical Eschatology, 1985. Active Shelby (County) United Neighbors, Memphis, 1973-74, United Way of Greater Memphis, 1974-82. Mem. Soc. Bibl. Lit., Memphis Ministers' Assn. Lodges: Civitan (chaplain, bd. dirs. local chpt.). Democrat. Presbyterian. Avocations: travel, golf. Home: 3095 E Glengarry Rd Memphis TN 38128-2911

TODD, WILLIAM K., JR., information technology executive; BS in Bus. Mgmt., NH Coll. Sr. v.p. distbn. mfg. Entex Info. Svcs., Rye Brook, NY, 1999; v.p., gen. mgr. configuration and assembly Tech Data Corp., Clearwater, Fla., 1999—2000, sr. v.p. logistics and integration svcs., 2000—. Office: Tech Data Corp 5350 Tech Data Dr Clearwater FL 33760-3122

TODD, WILLIAM MICHAEL, lawyer; b. Cleve., Dec. 13, 1952; s. William Charles and Jennie Ann (Diana) T. BA, U. Notre Dame, 1973; JD, Ohio State U., 1976. Bar: Ohio 1976, U.S. Dist. Ct. (so. dist.) Ohio 1977, U.S. Supreme Ct. 1987. Assoc. Porter, Wright, Morris & Arthur, Columbus, Ohio, 1976-82, ptnr., 1983-93; Squire, Sanders & Dempsey, Columbus, 1993—. Trustee Callvac Svcs., Columbus, Ohio, 1985—91, pres., 1988; trustee Opera Columbus, 2004—. Mem. ABA (governing com. forum on health law 1988-91), Ohio Bar Assn., Columbus Bar Assn., Am. Soc. Med. Assn. Counsel, Am. Bd. Trial Advocates, Ohio Soc. Healthcare Attys. (pres. 1999-2000), Am. Health Lawyers Assn., Columbus Athletic Club. Roman Catholic. Avocations: music, recreational sports. Office: Squire Sanders & Dempsey 41 S High St Columbus OH 43215-6101 Office Phone: 614-365-2712. Business E-Mail: wtodd@ssd.com.

TODD, ZANE GREY, retired utilities executive; b. Hanson, Ky., Feb. 3, 1924; s. Marshall Elvin and Kate (McCormick) T.; m. Marysnow Stone, Feb. 8, 1950 (dec. 1983); m. Frances Z. Anderson, Jan. 6, 1984. Student, Evansville Coll., 1947-49; BS summa cum laude, Purdue U., 1951, DEng (hon.), 1979; postgrad., U. Mich., 1965; DHL, U. Indpls., 1993. Fingerprint classifier FBI, 1942-43; electric system planning engr. Indpls. Power & Light Co., 1951-56, spl. assignments supr., 1956-60, head elec. system planning, 1960-65, head substation design div., 1965-68, head distbn. engring. dept., 1968-70, asst. to v.p., 1970-72, v.p., 1972-74, exec. v.p., 1974-75, pres., 1975-81, chmn., chief exec. officer, 1976-89, dir., chmn. exec. com., 1989-94, chief exec. officer, 1981-89; chmn., pres. IPALCO Enterprises, Inc., Indpls., 1983-89, dir., chmn. exec. com., 1989-94; chmn. bd., chief exec. officer Mid-Am. Capital Resources, Inc. subs. IPALCO Enterprises, Inc., Indpls., 1984-89, also bd. dirs., 1984-94. Gen. mgr. Mooresville (Ind.) Pub. Svc. Co., Inc., 1956-60; bd. dirs. Nat. City Bank Ind. (formerly Mchts. Nat. Corp.), 1975-94, Am. States Ins. Co., 1976-94; hon. dir. 500 Festival Assocs., Inc., pres. 1987. Originator probability analysis of power system reliability; contbr. articles to tech. jours. and mags. Past pres. adv. bd. St. Vincent Hosp.; past chmn., bd. trustees Ind. Cen. U. (now U. Indpls.); Nat. and Greater Indpls. adv. bds. Salvation Army, 1984-96; bd. govs. Associated Colls. of Ind., 1979-92. Sgt. AUS, 1943-47. Recipient William Booth award Salvation Army, 1994; named Disting. Engring. Alumnus Purdue U., 1976, Outstanding Elec. Engr. Purdue U., 1992, Knight of Malta, Order of St. John of Jerusalem, 1986. Fellow IEEE (past chmn. power sys. engring. com.); mem. ASME, NSPE, Power Engring. Soc., Ind. Fiscal Policy Inst. (bd. govs.), Ind. C. of C., Indpls. C. of C., Mooresville C. of C. (past pres.), PGA Nat. Country Club, Ulen Country Club, Indpls. Athletic Club (past bd. dirs.), Meridian Hills Country Club (past bd. dirs.), Skyline Club (bd. govs.), Newcomen Soc. (past chmn. Ind.), Rotary, Lions (past pres.), Eta Kappa Nu, Tau Beta Pi. Home: 7645 Randue Ct Indianapolis IN 46278-1565

TODD COPLEY, JUDITH A. materials and metallurgical engineering educator; b. Wakefield, West Yorkshire, Eng., Dec. 13, 1950; came to U.S., 1978; d. Marley and Joan Mary (Birkinshaw) Booth; m. David Michael Todd, June 17, 1972 (div. June 1981); m. Stephen Michael Copley, Aug. 3, 1984; 1 child, Amy Elizabeth. BA in Materials Sci., Cambridge (Eng.) U., 1972, MA, PhD in Metall./Materials Sci., 1977. Rsch. asst. Imperial Coll. Sci. and Tech., London, 1976-78; rsch. assoc. SUNY, Stonybrook, 1978; rsch. engr. U. Calif., Berkeley, 1979-81; asst. prof. materials sci. and mech. engring. U. So. Calif., L.A., 1982—90; assoc. prof. metall. and materials engring. Ill. Inst. Tech., Chgo., 1990-97, assoc. chair mech. materials and aerospace engring., 1995—2001, prof. materials and mech. engring., 1997—2002, assoc. dean rsch. Armour Coll. Engring. and Sci., 2001—02; P.B. Breneman dept. head chair chair dept. engring. sci. and mechanics Pa. State U., University Park, 2002—. Mem. task force Materials Property Coun., N.Y.C., 1979—89; prof. Iron and Steel Soc., 1996—2002; mem. editl. bds. Contbr. articles to profl. jours.; patentee in field. Recipient Brit. Univs. Student Travel award, 1972, Brit. Fedn. Univ. Women award, 1972, Faculty Rsch. award Oak Ridge (Tenn.) Nat. Lab., 1986, Vanadium award British Inst. Materials, 1990; Kathryn Kingswell Meml. scholar, 1972, Julia Beveridge Award, IIT, 1998, Cert. Appreciation Am. Soc. Mech. Engrs., 1995, 97, Forging Industry Ednl. Rsch. Found., 1993, Booz-Allen and Hamilton Award for Tchg. and Svc., Ill. Inst. Tech., 1996, Mary Ewart Traveling Scholarship, Cambridge Univ., 1972, Sci. Rsch. Coun. Fellowship and Overseas Travel Award, 1972. Fellow ASME Internat. (chmn. materials and fabrication com. 1993-97, pressure vessel and piping divsn. membership chair PVP divsn., 1997-2001, assoc. editor Jour. Pressure Vessel and Piping Tech. 1994-2001, mem. exec. com. and publs. chair PVP divsn. 2001—, pubs. chair, PVP divsn. 2001-2005, v.p. mfg. group 2002—, bd. on women and miniorites award 1997), Assn. Women in Sci., ASM Internat. (chmn. L.A. chpt. 1986-87, coun. mem. materials sci. divsn. 1984-89); mem. AIME (Rsch. award 1983), ASTM, Soc. Women Engrs. (sr.), Electron Microscopy Soc., Electrochemical Soc., Hist. Metallurgy Soc., Nat. Soc. Corrosion Engrs. (Seed grant award 1983), Microbeam Analysis Soc., Soc. Mfg. Engr., Am. Assn. Univ. Women, Instn. Materials, Chartered (Sr.) Engr. Status, Minerals, Metals, Materials Soc. of the Am. Inst. Mining, Metall. Petroleum Engrs., Am. Ceramics Soc., Ill. Microscopical Soc. Avocation: archaeometry. Office: Pennsylvania State Univ Dept Engring Sci and Mechanics 212 Earth-Engring Sci Bldg University Park PA 16802-6812 Office Phone: 814-863-0771. E-mail: jtodd@psu.edu.

TODHUNTER, JOHN ANTHONY, toxicologist, consultant; b. Cali, Valle, Colombia, Oct. 9, 1949; s. John Arthur and Teresa Maria (Torres) T.; divorced, 1986; children: Jennifer, Julia; m. D. Holli Wilson, Apr. 19, 1986; 1 child, Jacqueline Rose. BSc, UCLA, 1971; MSc, Calif. State U., 1973; PhD, U. Calif., Santa Barbara, 1976. Diplomate Am. Bd. Toxicology, Am. Bd. Forensic Examiners; regulatory affairs cert. Instr. Calif. State U., L.A., 1972-73; rsch. asst. U. Calif., Santa Barbara, 1973-76; fellow Roche Inst. Molecular Biology, Nutley, N.J., 1976-78; asst. prof. Cath. U. Am., Washington, 1978-81, chmn. Biochemistry Program, 1980-81; asst. adminstr. U.S. EPA, Washington, 1981-83, cons. Sci. Regulatory Svcs. Internat., Washington, 1983-91; pres. SRS Internat. Corp., 1991—, SRS Internat. Health Care Group, 1995—. Expert advisor European regional office WHO, Stockholm, 1984; mem. Hazardous Waste Siting Bd., Annapolis, Md., 1980-81. Contbr. articles to profl. jours. Bd. dirs. Reagan Alumni Assn., Washington, 1985—; vol. Am. Cancer Soc., Washington, 1988—; mem. Presdl. Transition Team, Washington, 1980. U. Calif. Bd. Regents fellow, 1975, B.R. Baker Meml. fellow dept. chemistry U. Calif., Santa Barbara, 1976. Fellow Am. Inst. Chemists (dir. at large 1989-92, vice chmn. bd. 1992); mem. Soc. of Toxicology, Am. Chem. Soc., Soc. for Risk Analysis, N.Y. Acad. Sci. Office: SRS Internat 1625 K St NW Ste 1000 Washington DC 20006-1619 E-mail: todhunter@srsinternational.com.

TODMAN, MICHAEL A. manufacturing executive; b. St. Thomas, U.S. V.I. BBA, Georgetown U. Formerly with Price Waterhouse and Co., Wang Labs., Inc.; dir. fin. United Kingdom Whirlpool, Inc., 1993—95, from gen. mgr. No. Europe to v.p. consumer svcs. Whirlpool Europe, 1993—95, contr. N.Am., 1995—96, v.p. product mgmt., 1996—97, v.p. Sears sales and mktg., 1997—99, sr. v.p. sales and mktg. N.Am., 1999—2001, exec. v.p. N.Am., mem. corp. exec. com., 2001, corp. exec. v.p., pres. Whirlpool Europe, 2001—. Office: Whirlpool Inc 2000 N M-63 Benton Harbor MI 49022

TODREAS, NEIL EMMANUEL, nuclear engineering educator; b. Peabody, Mass., Dec. 17, 1935; s. David and Anna (Gendleman) T.; m. Carol S. Schonberg, June 19, 1958; children: Timothy, Ian. BSM.E., MS, Cornell U., 1958; ScD in Nuc. Engring., MIT, 1966. Asst. prof. dept. nuc. engring. MIT, Cambridge, Mass., 1970-71, assoc. prof., 1971-75, prof., 1975—. Kepco prof. nuc. engring. and prof. mech. engring., 1992—, head dept. nuc. engring., 1981-89. Served to lt. (j.g.) USN, 1958-62. Named Disting. Tchr., Ruth and Joel Spira award MIT Sch. Engring., 1995. Fellow ASME, Am. Nuc. Soc. (Arthur Holly Compton award for outstanding educators in nuc. engring. 1995, Tech. Achievement award for outstanding contbns. to thermal hydraulics 1994); mem. Nat. Acad. Engring., Sigma Xi, Tau Beta Pi, Pi Tau Sigma. Office: MIT Bldg 24 Rm 205 77 Massachusetts Ave Cambridge MA 02139-4307

TODSEN, DANA ROGNAR, health care executive; b. St. Petersburg, Oct. 8, 1947; s. Birger Rognar and Elsie (Ewing) T.; m. Janis Hellman, June 13, 1970; children: Matthew Kristian, Jennifer Alana. BA, U. South Fla., 1970, MA, 1976. Assoc. dir. So. Health Found., Tampa, Fla., 1976-78; dir. U. Tampa, 1978-82; mng. dir. St. Anthony's Health Care Found., St. Petersburg, 1982-85; dir. devel. Moffitt Cancer Ctr., Tampa, 1985-91; CEO Meml. Health Trust, 1991-98; pres., CEO Bapt. Health Found., Birmingham, Ala., 1998—2001; exec. dir. CHOC Found. for Children, Orange, Calif., 0002—. Found. cons. Quorum Health Resources, Brentwood, Tenn., 1997—; pres. Todsen & Assocs., Laguna Niguel, Calif., 1997—; adj. instr. Hillsborogh C.C., 1978, U. South Fla., 1980; assoc. faculty the Kaiser Inst., Colo., 2001; keynote spkr. in field. Contbr. articles to profl. jours. Bd. trustees Cmty. Found. Greater Tampa; bd. dirs. Savannah Maritime Festival, 1991-98, Ga. Nonprofit Resource Ctr. Ala., 1998—, Ga. Med. Soc. Growing Health Partnership, 1996-98, Pres.'s Summit for Am.'s Future, The Alliance for Youth, 1997-98, Ptnrs. for Cmty. Health, 1996-98, Ronald McDonald House Charities of the Coastal Empire, 1992-98, St. Andrew's Prep. Sch., 1993-96, United Way of the Coastal Empire, 1993, Centennial Olympic Games Yachting Com., 1993-96, Children's Home Soc., 1983-91, Leadership, Tampa Bay, 1987—, bd. dirs., 1987-91, pres., 1990-91; mem. Leadership Tampa, 1981—; cons. Coffeeville (Kans.) Health Found., Monroe Health Found., Monroeville, Ala., Hubbard Regional Hosp., Webster, Mass., Gibson Meml. Hosp., Gibson City, Ill., Jordan Health Sys., Plymouth, Mass., Hickory (N.C.) Day Sch., Beaufort (S.C.) Acad., Spring of Tampa Bay, McLaughlin Rsch. Inst., Great Falls, Mont., Big Bros./Big Sisters Tampa, Met. Ministries, Tampa Cmty. Health Ctr., Suicide and Crisis Ctr., Exec. Svc. Corp. Tampa. Fellow AHA Health Forum, 2000. Mem. Am. Coll. Healthcare Execs., Nat. Soc. Fund Raising Execs. (cert., bd. dirs. 1992—, pres. 1992—), Assn. Am. Med. Coll., Nat. Ctr. for Nonprofit Bd., Acad. for Health Svc. Mktg., Am. Mktg. Assn., Assn. for Healthcare Philanthropy (cert.), Am. Coll. Healthcare Mktg., Sales & Mktg. Execs. Internat., Mil. Affairs Coun., Coun. for Advancement and Support Edn., Philanthropic Action Coun., Savannah Area C. of C. (mil. and civilian affairs coun.), Greater Tampa C. of C., Tampa Tiger Bay, Greystone Country Club, Summit Club, Savannah Yacht Club, Chatham Club, First City Club, Rotary Club Birmingham, Alpha Tau Omega. Democrat. Methodist. Home: 12 Hastings Laguna Niguel CA 92677 Office: CHOC Found for Children 455 S Main St Orange CA 92868 Office Phone: 714-532-8356. Personal E-mail: dtodsen@msn.com.

TODTENKOPF, MARK STEVEN, neuroscientist; b. Waltham, Mass., Dec. 27, 1970; s. Norbert Frank and Victoria Martha Todtenkopf; m. Robin Ellen Wurtzel, Sept. 12, 1970; 1 child, Alyse Hope. PhD, Northeastern U., Boston, 2001. Rsch. technician McLean Hosp., Belmont, Mass., 1992—97; rsch. fellow Harvard Med. Sch. / McLean Hosp., Belmont, Mass., 2001—. Contbr. articles to profl. jours. Grantee NRSA gramtee, NIH/NIDA, 2024—. Mem.: Soc. for Neurosci. Office: Harvard Med School / McLean Hospital 115 Mill St 001 MRC Belmont MA 02478 E-mail: mtodtenkopf@mclean.harvard.edu.

TOEDT, D(ELL) C(HARLES), III, lawyer; b. Maxwell AFB, Ala., Nov. 17, 1954; m. Maretta A. Comfort. BA with high honors, U. Tex., 1973, JD, 1981. Bar: Tex. 1982, U.S. Patent and Trademark Office 1983, U.S. Dist. Ct. (so. dist.) Tex. 1984, U.S. Ct. Appeals (fed. cir.) 1984, U.S. Supreme Ct. 1991, Calif. 1996. Atty. Schlanger, Cook, Cohn, Mills & Grossberg, Houston, 1982-83, Arnold, White & Durkee, Houston, 1983-99; v.p., gen. counsel BindView Corp., Houston, 1999—. Adj. prof. S. Tex. Coll. Law, 1988—90. Assoc. editor: Tex. Law Rev., 1981—82, author, editor: book Licensing Law Handbook: Computer Software Issues, 1987; editor: Law and Bus. Computer Software, 1989—92; contbr. articles to profl. jours. Served to lt. USN, 1974—79. Mem.: ABA (chmn. computer-related coms. 1985—96, elected mem. coun. sect. intellectual property law 1999—2000). Office: BindView Corp 5151 San Felipe 25th Fl Houston TX 77056- Office Phone: 713-561-4001. E-mail: dc.toedt@bindview.com.

TOEDTMAN, JAMES SMITH, newspaper editor, journalist; b. Dayton, Ohio, Dec. 1, 1941; s. James Christian and Ella Barnes (Smith) T.; m. Haydee N. Sicart, Aug. 23, 1969; children: Eric, Kristen. AB, Coll. Wooster, 1963; postgrad., U. Queensland, Brisbane, Australia, 1964; MSc in Journalism, Columbia U., 1967. Pub. dir. Coll. Wooster, Ohio, 1963, 65; reporter, city editor, Sunday news editor, Washington Bur. news editor Newsday, L.I., NY, 1967-79; exec. editor Boston Herald Am., 1979-82; editor Balt. News Am., 1982-86; mng. editor N.Y. Newsday, 1986-95, Washington bur. chief, 1995—2001, assoc. editor, 2001—. Adv. bd. comm. dept. Flagler Coll., 2003—. Recipient shared award Silurian Soc., Polk award, Pulitzer Prize, 1970, 92, 97, spl. citation Inter-Am. Press Assn., 1979, Best Editl. award Md.-Del.-D.C. Press Assn., 1984, 86; Rotary Found. fellow, 1964, Internat. fellow Columbia U., 1966-67. Mem. Coll. of Wooster Alumni Assn. (pres. 1980-81). Methodist. Home: 2604 Geneva Hill Ct Oakton VA 22124-1534 Office: Ste 850 1730 Pennsylvania Ave NW Washington DC 20006-4706 Office Phone: 202-626-8483. E-mail: toedtman@newsday.com.

TOELKES, DIXIE E. state legislator; m. Roger Toelkes. Educator; mem. from dist. 53 Kans. State Ho. of Reps., Topeka. Address: 3811 SE 33rd Ter Topeka KS 66605-3077 Office: Kans House of Reps State House Topeka KS 66612

TOENSING, VICTORIA, lawyer; b. Colon, Panama, Oct. 16, 1941; d. Philip William and Victoria (Brady) Long; m. Trent David Toensing, Oct. 29, 1962 (div. 1976); children: Todd Robert, Brady Cronon, Amy Victoriana; m. Joseph E. diGenova, June 27, 1981. BS in Edn., Ind. U., 1962; JD cum laude, U. Detroit, 1975. Bar: Mich. 1976, D.C. 1978. Tchr. English, Milw., 1965-66; law clk. to presiding justice U.S. Ct. Appeals, Detroit, 1975-76; asst. U.S. atty. U.S. Atty.'s Office, Detroit, 1976-81; chief counsel U.S. Senate Intelligence Com., Washington, 1981-84; dep. asst. atty. gen. criminal div. Dept. Justice, Washington, 1984-88; spl. counsel Hughes Hubbard & Reed, Washington, 1988-90; ptnr. Cooter and Gell, Washington, 1990-91; ptnr., co-chmn. nat. white collar group Manatt, Phelps and Phillips, Washington, 1991-95; founding ptnr. diGenova & Toensing, Wasington, 1996—. Mem. working group on corp. sanctions U.S. Sentencing Commn., 1988-89; co-chairperson Coalition for Women's Appts. Justice Judiciary Task Force, 1988-92; spl. counsel for Teamsters investigation, U.S. Ho. of Reps., Subcom. on Oversight and Investigations of com. on Edn. and the Workforce, 1997-98. Author: Bringing Sanity to the Insanity Defense, 1983, Mens Rea: Insanity by Another Name, 1984; contbg. author: Fighting Back: Winning The War Against Terrorism, Desk Book on White Collar Crime, 1991; contbr. articles to profl. jours. Founder, chmn. Women's Orgn. To Meet Existing Needs, Mich., 1975-79; chmn. Republican Women's Task Force, 1979-81; bd. dirs. Project on Equal Edn. Rights, Mich., 1980-81, Nat. Hist. Intelligence Mus., 1987-95, America's Talking Legal Analyst, 1995; MSNBC legal analyst, 1998-99. Recipient spl. commendation Office U.S. Atty. Gen., 1980, agy. seal medallion CIA, 1986, award of achievement Alpha Chi Omega, 1992; featured on cover N.Y. Time Mag. for anti-terrorism work, April 1991. Mem. ABA (mem. standing com. on law and nat. security, mem. coun. criminal justice sect., mem. adv. com. complex crimes and litigation, vice chmn. white collar crime com., chmn. subcom. on corp. criminal liability). E-mail: dt@digenovatoensing.com.

TOEPFER, SUSAN JILL, editor; b. Rochester, Minn., Mar. 9, 1948; d. John Bernard and Helen Esther (Chapple) T.; m. Lorenzo Gabriel Carcaterra, May 16, 1981; children: Katherine Marie, Nicholas Gabriel. BA, Bennington Coll., 1970. Mng. editor Photoplay Mag., N.Y.C., 1971-72; freelance writer N.Y.C., 1972-78; TV week editor N.Y. Daily News, N.Y.C., 1978-79, leisure editor, 1979-82, features editor, 1982-84, arts and entertainment editor, 1984-86, exec. mag. editor, 1986-87; sr. writer People Mag., N.Y.C., 1987-89, sr. editor, 1989-91, asst. mng. editor, 1991-94, exec. editor, 1994—2000, dep. mng. editor, 2000—02; editor-in-chief Rosie Mag., 2002; editor-at-large G+J USA, N.Y.C., 2003—04. Office: G+J USA 375 Lexington Ave New York NY 10017-5514

TOEPPE, WILLIAM JOSEPH, JR., retired aerospace engineer; b. Buffton, Ohio, Feb. 27, 1931; s. William Joseph Sr. and Ruth May (Hipple) T. BSEE, Rose-Hulman Inst. Tech., Terre Haute, Ind., 1953. Engr. Electronics divsn. Ralph M. Parsons Co., Pasadena, Calif., 1953-55; pvt. practice cons. Orange, Calif., 1961-62; engring. supr. Lockheed Electronics Co., City of Commerce, Calif., 1962-64; staff engr. Interstate Electronics Corp., Anaheim, Calif., 1957-61, engring. supr., 1964-89, ret., 1989. Author: Finding Your German Village, 1990, Gazetteers and Maps of France for Genealogical Research, 1990, German Geneal. Soc. Am. Library User's Guide, 1995, Sandusky County, Ohio, Births, Infant-Name Soundex Index, 1997, Osnabrück Farm Histories, 1999, GCSA Libr. Shelf List Catalog, 1999. Pres. Golden Cir. Home Owners' Assn., Orange, 1989-95. With U. S. Army, 1955-57. Mem. Ohio Geneal. Soc. (life), So. Calif. Geneal. Soc., German Geneal. Soc. Am. (bd. dirs. 1993-97). Avocations: genealogy, music. Home: PO Box 11526 Santa Ana CA 92711-1526

TOEVS, ALDEN LOUIS, management consultant, researcher; b. American Falls, Idaho, Jan. 25, 1949; s. Alden Louis and Wilma Christen (Coffee) T. BS, Lewis and Clark Coll., 1971; PhD, Tulane U., 1975. NSF fellow MIT Energy Lab., Boston, 1975-76; prof. econs. La. State U., Baton Rouge, 1976-77, U. Oreg., Eugene, 1978-83; dir. mortgage rsch. Morgan Stanley and Co., N.Y.C., 1983-90; exec. v.p. First Manhattan Cons. Group, N.Y.C., 1990—. Vis. scholar Fed. Home Loan Bank, San Francisco, 1983, Fed. Reserve Bank, 1982; dir. capital market research U. Oreg., Eugene, 1982-83; instnl. investor All-Am. Rsch. Team, 1990. Author: Innovations in Bond Portfolio Managements, 1983, Winning the Credit Cycle Game, 1998; contbr. articles to profl. jours. Trustee Orch. St. Lukes, 1990—, Creative Glass Ctr. Am., Contemporary Glass Ctr. Am., 2004—. Recipient Graham and Dodd scroll Fin. Analysts Fed., 1983.

TOFEL, RICHARD JEFFREY, communication executive; b. N.Y.C. s. Robert Leonard and Carol T.; m. Jeanne Helen Straus, Feb. 26, 1983; children: Rachel Straus, Colin Straus. AB, Harvard U., 1979; MPP, JFK Sch. Govt., 1983; JD, Harvard U., 1983. Bar: N.Y. 1984, U.S. Dist. Ct. (so. and ea. dists.) N.Y. 1984, U.S. Ct. Appeals (2d cir.) 1987, U.S. Dist. Ct. (no. dist.) N.Y. 1988, U.S. Supreme Ct. 1990. Assoc. Patterson, Belknap, Webb & Tyler, N.Y.C., 1983-86; exec. dir. Mayor's Commn. Human Svcs. Reorganization, N.Y.C., 1984-85; assoc. Gibson, Dunn & Crutcher, N.Y.C., 1986-89; counsel Dow Jones & Co., N.Y.C., 1989-91, asst. gen. counsel, 1991-92; asst. mng. editor Wall Street Jour., N.Y.C., 1992-95; dir. internat. devel. and adminstrn. Dow Jones & Co., N.Y.C., 1995-97, v.p. corp. comm., 1997-2000, v.p., asst. to publ. Wall Street Jour., 2000—02, v.p., asst. publ. Wall Street Jour., 2002—. Bd. dirs. Wildcat Svc. Corp., Roper Ctr. for Pub. Opinion Rsch. Author: A Legend in the Making: The New York Yankees in 1939, 2002, Vanishing Point: The Disappearance of Judge Crater, and the New York He Left Behind, 2004; contbr. articles to profl. jours. Bd. dirs. Yogi Berra Mus. and Learning Ctr. Democrat. Jewish. Home: 5205 Sycamore Ave Bronx NY 10471-2835 Office: Dow Jones & Co 200 Liberty St 11th Fl New York NY 10281-1003 Business E-Mail: dick.tofel@dowjones.com.

TOFF, NANCY ELLEN, book editor; b. Greenburgh, N.Y., Aug. 29, 1955; d. Ira N. and Ruth (Bluthenthal) T. AB, Harvard U., 1976. Editor, prodr. Music Minus One, N.Y.C., 1973-75; rschr. Time-Life Books, Alexandria, Va., 1976-80; editor, asst. prodr. Time-Life Music, Alexandria, Va., 1980-84; prodn. mgr. Vanguard Recording Soc., N.Y.C., 1984-86; editor Grove's Dictionaries of Music, N.Y.C., 1984-85; v.p., editor-in-chief Chelsea House Pubs., N.Y.C., 1986-89, v.p., dir. book devel., 1990; editl. dir. Julian Messner/Silver Burdett Press, Englewood Cliffs, N.J., 1990-91; editl. dir. children's and young adult books Oxford U. Press, N.Y.C., 1991-98, editl. dir. young adult reference, 1998—, v.p., 1999—. Editorial cons., Music Div. Lib. of Congress, 1983; hist. cons., Dept. of Musical Instruments, Met. Mus. of Art, N.Y.C., 1986. Author: The Development of the Modern Flute, 1979, The Flute Book, 1985, 2d edit., 1996, Georges Barrère and the Flute in America, 1994; cons. editor Flutist Quar., 1990-99; contbr. articles to profl. jours.; curator Georges Barrère and the Flute in America, N.Y. Pub. Libr., 1994. Bd. dirs., Radcliffe Coll. Alumnae Assn. 1979-80. Recipient Dena Epstein award Music Libr. Assn., 1997; Sinfonia Found. rsch. grantee, 1999. Mem. Nat. Flute Assn. (asst. sec. 1988-89, sec. 1989-90, bd. dirs. 1990-92), N.Y. Flute Club (bd. dirs. 1986—, sec. 1991-92, 98-2000, pres. 1992-95, 1st v.p. 1995-98). Home: 425 E 79th St Apt 6F New York NY 10021-1011 Office: Oxford U Press 198 Madison Ave New York NY 10016-4341 E-mail: toffn@oup-usa.org.

TOFFEL, ALVIN EUGENE, corporate executive, business and governmental consultant; b. Los Angeles, July 14, 1935; s. Harry and Estelle Charlotte Toffel; m. Neile McQueen; children: Stephanie, Elizabeth, Michelle; stepchildren: Terry (dec.), Chad. BA, UCLA, 1957. Dir. mgmt. systems and organizational planning Rockwell Internat., 1963-69; Exec. Office for the Pres. White House, Washington, 1969-70; nat. chmn., campaign dir. McCloskey for Pres., 1971-72; polit. cons., 1971—. Cons. personal bus. and govt. Norton Simon and Norton Simon, Inc., Los Angeles, 1972-80; pres. Norton Simon Found., Pasadena, Calif., 1977-80; cons. exec. asst. to pres. Twentieth Century Fox Film Corp., 1980; bd. dirs. Geometrics, Inc.; pres. So. Shellfish Inc., Atlantic Internat. Ins. Ltd., Toffel Thoroughbred Racing; lectr. mgmt. UCLA, Stanford U. Pres. Norton Simon Mus. Art, Pasadena; vice chmn. U.S. Pension Svcs., Inc. With SAC USAF, 1958-63. Recipient White House Interchange Exec. Outstanding Achievement, 1971; recipient Achievement Am. Advtg. Council, 1972 Mem. Ky. Cols., Presdl. Interchange Execs. Assn., Assn. Old Crows Achievements include developing standard U.S. govt. program performance measurement system, aerospace engring. techniques of program mgmt., aerospace manuals. Home and Office: 2323 Bowmont Dr Beverly Hills CA 90210-1808 *My legacy derives from my grandparents leaving the familiar to come to America. Here, anything can be accomplished if one honestly defines what he wants. It then becomes a matter of choosing among the many ways to accomplish anything. The character of the individual can be seen by the choices he makes.*

TOFFOLON, JOHN, JR., investment company executive; CAO, CO, CFO, exec. mng. dir. Nomura Securities Internat., N.Y.C., until 2000. Office: Nomura Securities Internat 2 World Financial Ctr Bldg B New York NY 10281-1077

TOFIAS, ALLAN, accountant; b. Boston, Apr. 13, 1930; s. George I. and Anna (Seidel) T.; m. Arlene Shube, Aug. 30, 1981; children: Bradley Neil, Laura Jean Silver. BA, Colgate U., 1951; MBA, Harvard U., 1956. CPA, Mass. Sr. acct. Peat, Marwick, Mitchell & Co., Boston, 1956—60; mng. ptnr. Tofias, Fleishman, Shapiro & Co., P.C., Boston, 1960-96; chmn. bd., 1996-97. Bd. dir. Rowe Cos., One Price Clothing Stores, Inc.; former trustee Gannett, Welch & Kotler Mut. Funds. Mem. Brookline (Mass.) Town Meeting, 1970-77, mem. fin. adv. bd., 1975-81; mem. New Eng. Bapt. Health Care Corp., 1985—, trustee, 1998-, chmn. fin. com., 1998-2002 (trustee 1998-); bd. dir. West Newton YMCA, 1986-89; mem. exec. com. Boston Aid to Blind, bd. dir., 1988-97, pres., 1993-94. Lt. USNR, 1951-54. Mem. AICPA (coun. 1995-99), Mass. Soc. CPA's (pres. 1995-96), Nat. CPA Group (exec. com. 1983-88, vice chmn. 1985-88), BKR Internat. (world bd. dirs. 1988-97, chmn. 1994-96), Wightman Tennis Club (treas. 1974-76), Newton Squash and Tennis Club (bd. dirs. 1966-99), Masons. Home: 59 Monadnock Rd Wellesley MA 02481-1334 Office: 2044 Beacon St Waban MA 02468-1445

TOFLE, RUTH BRENT, design educator, researcher; b. Washington, Mo., Sept. 11, 1951; d. Clarence Frank and Dorothy May (Horstick) Stumpe; m. Edward Everett Brent, May 14, 1972 (div. Mar. 1999); 2 children; m. Marvin Tofle, Nov. 17, 2001. BS cum laude, U. Mo., 1972; MA, U. Minn., 1974, PhD, 1978. Cert. of qualification Nat. Coun. Interior Design Qualification; registered comml. interior designer, Mo., 2000; accredited profl. Leadership in Environmental Design. Postdoctoral fellow in socio-clin. geriatrics NIMH, 1978-79; asst. prof. U. Mo., Columbia, 1981-86, assoc. prof. design, 1986-92, prof., 1992—, acting dept. chair, 1984-85, chair dept. archtl. studies, 1985—. Project dir. Adminstrn. on Aging Grant, 1979-81; v.p. Idea Works, Inc., Columbia, 1981-99; chair campus planning com. for facilities and grounds, U. Mo., Columbia, 1993—. Co-author: (computer software) Home-Safe-Home, 1989, Color in Health Care Environments; co-editor: Popular American Housing, 1995, Aging, Autonomy and Architecture: Advances in Assisted Living, 1999; dep. editor: Jour. Housing for Elderly; assoc. editor: Jour. Archtl. and Planning Rsch.; contbr. articles to profl. jours. Active Mayor's Task Force, Columbia Low-Income Housing, 1984-85; mem. Main St. adv. coun. dept. econ. devel. State of Mo., 1989-90; regional chairperson dists. 84 and 85 United Way, Columbia, 1989, 90, 98, 99, 2000, 2001; mem. adv. bd. Pub. Housing Authority, Columbia, 1984-85; chairperson North Cen. Region-54 Agrl. Expt. Sta. Rsch., 1989-91; mem. Columbia Regional Home Health and Hospice Adv. Bd., Columbia Regional Hosp., 1993-2000; mem. pub. bldg. devel. and fin. com. City of Columbia, 2000—; bd. trustees The Mo. 4-H Found., 1997—, co-chair mktg. and pub. rels. com.; chair campus planning com. for facilities and grounds U. Mo., 1993—. Grantee Adminstrn. on Aging, 1979-81, VA, 1981, Am. Home Econs. Assn., 1981-82, 2 Joel Polsky Found. Interior Design Rsch. grantee, 1986, 87; recipient Fulbright award Chinese History and Culture, 1988, exch. faculty award Prince of Sonkla U., Thailand, 1990, Chonnam U., Korea, 1992; Fulbright fellow to Morocco and Tunisia, 1993. Mem. Am. Home Econs. Assn. (chmn. art/design sect. 1984-87, New Achievers award 1987), Am. Assn. Housing Educators, Am. Soc. Interior Designers (allied mem., chmn. position papers com. 1988-90, Presdl. citation 1990), Interior Design Educators Coun., Nat. Coun. for Interior Design (cert.), Environ. Design Rsch. Assn., Illuminating Engring. Soc. (participant workshop for tchrs.), Gerontol. Assn., Mo. Fulbright Alumni Assn. (membership chmn. 1989-90, v.p. 1990-92, pres. 1992-94), Univ. Club Inc. (pres. 1991-92, bd. dirs., sec. 1993-95, U. Mo. faculty alumni award 1992), Gamma Sigma Delta (pres. 1993-94, Disting. Adminstrn. award 1997), Omicron Nu, Phi Upsilon Omicron. Home: 1805 Cliff Dr Columbia MO 65201 Office: U Mo Dept Archtl Studies 142C Stanley Hall Columbia MO 65211-7700 Business E-Mail: TofleR@missouri.edu.

TOFTNER, RICHARD ORVILLE, engineering executive; b. Warren, Minn., Mar. 5, 1935; s. Orville Gayhart and Cora Evelyn (Anderson) T.; m. Jeanne Bredine, June 26, 1960; children: Douglas, Scott, Kristine, Kimberly, Brian. BA, U. Minn., 1966; MBA, Xavier U., 1970. Registered environ. assessor, Calif. Sr. economist Federated Dept. Stores, Inc., Cin., 1967-68; dep. dir. EPA, Washington and Cin., 1968-73; mgmt. cons. environ. affairs, products and mktg., 1973-74; prin. PEDCo Environ., Cin., 1974-80; trustee PEDCo trusts, 1974-80; pres. ROTA Mgmt., Inc., Cin., 1980-82; gen. mgr. CECOS, 1982-85; cons., 1985—; v.p. Smith, Stevens & Young, 1985-88; real estate developer, 1980—. Pres., CEO Toxitrol Internat., Inc., 1988-89; dir. Environ. Svcs. Belcan Engring. Group, Inc., Cin., 1989-92; prin. exec. cons. Resource Mgmt. Internat., Inc., 1994—; adj. prof. environ. engring. U. Cin., 1975-86; lectr. Grad. fellowship rev. panel Office of Edn., 1978-79; advisor, cabinet-level task force Office of Gov. of P.R., 1973; pvt. investor, 1991—; bd. dirs. EnviroAudit Svcs., Inc., pres., CEO, 1992—; mem. legis. com. Ohio Chem. Coun., 1995—; v.p. environ. engring. CSA Architects & Engrs., 1996-2001; client svc. mgr. Weston Solutions, Inc. Environ. Cons., 2001—; subcom. Nat. Safety Coun., 1972; mem. exec. environ. briefing panels Andersen Consulting, 1991-92; nominee commr. PUCO, Ohio; chmn. Cin. City Waste Task Force, 1987-88; co-chair Hamilton County Resource Recovery Com., 1989—. Contbr. articles on mgmt. planning and environ. to periodicals, chpts. to books; inventor, developer Toxitrol Waste Minimization; inventor EnviroAudit. With AUS, 1954-57. Mem. U.S. Tennis Assn., Nat. Registry Environ. Profl. Rep., Engring. Soc. Cin., Assn. Corp. Environ. Execs., Cin. C. of C., Global Assn. Corp. Environ. Execs. (charter). Republican. Lutheran. Home: 9175 Yellowwood Dr Cincinnati OH 45251-1948 Office: 4100 Executive Park Dr Ste 16 Cincinnati OH 45241-4026

TOGASAKI, SHINOBU, computer scientist; b. San Francisco, Aug. 17, 1932; s. Kikumatsu and Sugi (Hida) T.; m. Toshiko Kawaguchi, Nov. 24, 1959; children: John Shinobu, Ann Mariko. BS in Math., Duke U., 1954; postgrad., Stanford U., 1954-56. Math. programmer IBM, 1956—69, sr. programmer, 1970-87; mgr. applications devel. Service Bur. Corp., Palo Alto, 1961-64, sr. analyst, 1964-68, systems architect devel. lab. San Jose, Calif., 1968-70; chief fin. officer Robin Hood Ranch, Inc., 1976-86; mgr. architecture & strategy Hewlett Packard Corp., Cupertino, Calif., 1987-89, mgr. strategic planning, 1989-93; chief architect MFA Hewlett Packard, 1993—2002; strategic cons., 2002—. Mem. Am. Mgmt. Assn., AAAS, Am. Statis. Assn., Assn. Computing Machinery, Inst. Mgmt. Sci., Sigma Pi Sigma. Home: 2367 Booksin Ave San Jose CA 95125-4705 E-mail: togasaki@alumni.duke.edu.

TOGERSON, JOHN DENNIS, retired computer software company executive; b. Newcastle, England, July 2, 1939; arrived in Can., 1949; s. John Marius and Margaret (McLaughlin) T.; m. Donna Elizabeth Jones, Oct. 3, 1964 (div. 1972); children: Denise, Brenda, Judson; m. Patricia Willis, May 5, 1984. BME, GM Inst., Flint, Mich., 1961; MBA, York U., Toronto, Ont., 1971. Sr. prodn. engr. GM of Can., Oshawa, Ont., 1961-69; with sales, investment banking Cochran Murray, Toronto, 1969-72; pres. Unitec, Inc., Denver, 1972-79, All Seasons Properties, Denver, 1979-81, Resort Computer Corp., Denver, 1981—; mng. dir. VCC London (subs. of Resort Computer Corp.), 1992; retired, 1996. Bd. dirs. VCC London (sub. of 1st Nat. Bank U.K.), London, 1989—, mng. dir., 1992; pres., bd. dirs. Resort Mgmt. Corp., Dillon, Colo., 1980-81; presenter Assn. of Resort Developers Nat. Conv., 1993, Internat. T.S. Found. Think Tank, 1993, and others; cons for computer sys., including Expert Witness assignment; internat. bus. devel. cons. Contbr. articles to profl. jours. Avocations: mountain biking, ice hockey, international business development consulting.

TOGNINO, JOHN NICHOLAS, financial services executive; b. N.Y.C., Sept. 20, 1938; s. Gennaro and Catherine (Barbieri) T.; m. Norma Lucille Borrelli, Nov. 7, 1959; children: Katherine Ann, John Nicholas Jr., Michael A. BA in Econs. summa cum laude, Fordham U., 1975. Instnl. sales trader A.G. Becker & Co., N.Y.C., 1970-72; trader Merill Lynch, N.Y.C., 1957-69, instnl. salesman, 1972-74, mgr. over-the-counter sales trading, 1974-83, dir. over-the-counter dept., 1983-87, dir. unlisted trading, 1987-88, mng. dir. non-dollar equities London, 1988-91, mng. dir. global equities, ret. N.Y.C., 1991-93; exec. v.p. Charles Schwab & Co., Inc., Jersey City, 1993-96; pres., CEO Security Traders Assn., N.Y.C., 1996-99, EVP NASDAQ, 1999—2001; chmn., CEO Pepper Fin. Group, 2001—. Bd. dirs. Nat. Assn. Security Dealers Automated Quotations Inc. Contbg. author: Market Maker Sponsorship: A Synergistic Package of Services, 1987. Mem. Ardlsey Bd. Edn., 1977—84, pres., 1979; v.p. Ardsley Sch. Dist. Bd., 1978, 1981; trustee, vice chmn. St. Barnabas Hosp., Bronx, 1996—; mem. health sci. adv. coun., Coll. of Phys. and Surgeons Columbia Presbyn. Med. Ctr., 1998—; pres. Ardsley Rep. Club, 1967—68; mem. exec. com. of laity Archdiocese of N.Y.C., 1988; trustee Fordham U., 2000—, chmn. bd. trustees, 2004; dir. Muscular Dystrophy Assn., 2000—; bd. dirs. Bus. Coun. for Internat. Understanding, 2000—01. Named Trader of Yr., Security Traders Monthly mag., 1984, Over-the-Counter Man of Yr., Equities mag., 1986; recipient lifetime achievement award Chgo. Stock Exch., 1997. Mem. Nat. Security Traders Assn. (various offices 1981-88, chmn. fin. com. Found. 1992—), Nat. Assn. Security Dealers (bus. conduct com. 1984-86), Security Traders Assn. N.Y. (various offices 1973-83, pres. 1980-81), St. Andrews Golf Club (Hastings, N.Y.), Grey Oaks Country Club (Naples, Fla.), Alpha Sigma Lambda, Alpha Sigma nu. Republican. Roman Catholic. Avocations: jogging, tennis, golf. Home: Two Stoneleigh Plz Apt 4H Bronxville NY 10708 Office: Pepper Fin Group 2 Hollyhock Ln Bedford NY 10506 Office Phone: 914-234-4580.

TOGNOLI, ERA M. performing company executive, artistic director; Gen. mgr., artistic dir., founder Metro Lyric Opera, Allenhurst, NJ, 1959—. Office: Metro Lyric Opera PO Box 35 Allenhurst NJ 07711-0035

TOHE, LAURA, English educator; d. Benson Tohe and Laura Florence; children: Jerame Tillman, Deswood Tillman. BA, U. N.Mex., 1975; MA, U. Nebr., 1985, PhD, 1993. Faculty assoc. women's studies Ariz. State U., Tempe, 1994—, asst. prof. English, 1994—2000, assoc. prof. English, 2000—. Cons. ACT, Iowa, 1996—; mem. adv. bd. Diné Tchr. Edn. Program, Tsaile, Ariz., 1996—; humanities spkr. Ariz. Humanities Coun., Phoenix, 1995—. Co-editor: (anthology) Sister Nations: Native American Women Writers on Community, 2002; author: (book of poetry and stories) No Parole Today, 1999 (Poetry of the Yr., 1999), (poetry) Making Friends with Water, 1986. Recipient Poetry prize, Blue Mesa Rev., 1999, Lila Wallace award, 1999. Avocations: hiking, photography. Office: Ariz State Univ Dept English PO Box 870302 Tempe AZ 85287-0302 E-mail: l.tohe@asu.edu.

TOHME, JACK FOUAD, endocrinologist; b. Lebanon, 1950; MD, Am. U., Beirut, 1974. Diplomate Am. Bd. Internal Medicine, Am. Bd. Endocrinology. Resident in internal medicine Am. U. Hosp., Beirut, 1974—76; fellow in endocrinology Columbia-Presbyn. Med. Ctr., N.Y.C., 1976—77, Barnes Hosp./Washington U., St. Louis, 1977—79; chief endocrinology The Valley Hosp., Ridgewood, NJ. Asst. clin. prof. medicine Columbia U. Coll. Physicians and Surgeons, N.Y.C., 1984—. Named one of Top Drs. 2003, Castle Connolly and N.J. Monthly Mag. Avocations: fishing, skiing. Office: Endocrine Assocs 265 Ackerman Ave # 101 Ridgewood NJ 07450-4299

TOKAR, BETTE LEWIS, economics professor; b. Mar. 26, 1935; d. Howard H. and Irma Rhodes (Pixton) Lewis; m. Jacob John Tokar, Oct. 1, 1955; children: Teresa, Bonnie, Michael, Robert. Student, Ursinus Coll., 1953—55; BA in Polit. Economy, Holy Family U., 1967; MA in Econs., Temple U., 1973, EdD, 1993. Lectr. Holy Family U., Phila., 1972—75, instr., 1975—78, asst. prof., 1978—82, dept. chair, 1977—85, assoc. prof., 1982—96, prof., 1986—. Lectr. La Salle Coll., Phila., 1977, Cmty. Coll. Phila., 1986—96; assessor CLEO, Phila., 1979—85. Bd. dirs. St. Andrews-in-the-Field; candidate for auditor Lower Southampton Township, Bucks County, Pa., 1967, 1969, dem. committeewoman, 1968; treas. Dem. Club Lower Township, Bucks County, 1968; bd. dirs. Chapel of Four Chaplins, 1994—2002, Pine Tree Farms Assoc., Feasterville, Pa., 1968. Mem.: MENSA, Fin. Mgmt. Assn., Internat. Trade & Fin. Assn., Am. Mgmt. Assn., Am. Econ. Assn., Am. Acctg. Assn., Nat. Bus. Edn. Assn., Assn. Social Edn., Acad. Internat. Bus., Pi Gamma Mu, Delta Pi Epsilon. Episcopalian. Office: Holy Family Univ Grant And Frankford Ave Philadelphia PA 19114-2094 Office Phone: 215-637-7700 3274.

TOKER, KAREN HARKAVY, physician; b. New Haven, Oct. 23, 1942; d. Victor M. and Nedra (Israel) Harkavy; m. Cyril Toker, Sept. 1, 1968; children: David Edward, Rachel Lee. BS in Chemistry, Coll. William and Mary, 1963; MD, Yale U., 1967. Diplomate Am. Bd. Pediat., 1974. Intern dept. pediat. Bronx Mcpl. Hosp. Ctr., Albert Einstein Coll. Medicine, N.Y., 1967-68, asst. resident dept. pediat., 1968-69, sr. resident dept. pediat., 1969, 70-71, attending pediatrician, 1971-72, 73-76; pediatrician Montgomery Health Dept., Silver Springs, Md., 1976-83; pediatric cons. Head Start Program Montgomery County Pub. Schs., Rockville, Md., 1976-83; pvt. practice gen. pediat. Rockville, 1983-89; pediatrician Nemours Children's Clinic, Jacksonville, Fla., 1991-95; med. dir. Pearl Plaza Pediatrics, Duval County Pub. Health Unit, 1995-97; instr. pediat. Albert Einstein Coll. Medicine, N.Y., 1971-74, asst. prof. pediat., 1974-76; clin. asst. prof. U. Fla., 1995—2003; med. dir. Ctr. for Women and Children, Duval County Health Dept., 1997—2003; pediatric cons. Urban Child Health, 2003—. Exec. bd. sec. Congregation Har Shalom, Potomac, 1989-91. Fellow Am. Acad. Pediat.; mem. Fla. Med. Assn., Duval County Med. Soc., Ambulatory Pediatric Assn. Democrat. Jewish. Avocations: piano, opera, ballet, swimming. Home and Office: 6030 Oakbrook Ct Ponte Vedra Beach FL 32082 Office Phone: 904-285-6851.

TOKERUD, ROBERT EUGENE, retired electrical engineer; b. Great Falls, Mont., Aug. 30, 1936; s. Fred Eugene Tokerud and Helen A. (Tadevich) Thomas; m. Marsha Kay Tokerud; children: Pamela, Torri, Marc, Camille, Corinne, David, Jeramie, Autumn, Melanie. BSEE, U. Calif., Berkeley, 1959; cert. Inst. Mgmt., Northwestern U., 1975. Sr. project engr. Sperry Utah Co., Salt Lake City, 1959—65; mgr. infosystems Lockheed Electronics Co., Houston, 1965—69; mgr. earth resources Lockheed Engring. and Sci. Co., Houston, 1969—74, asst. dir. sci. and applications, 1974—79, dir. bus. devel., 1980—87, life sci. program mgr. Washington, 1987—89; pres. Lockheed Martin Logistics Mgmt., Arlington, Tex., 1989—97; v.p. Lockheed Corp., 1993—97; exec. v.p. Lockheed Martin Aircraft and Logistic Ctrs., 1997; ret., 1997. Cons. Aerospace, 1997-2000; pres., CEO Operational Tech. Inc., 2000-02; exec. mgmt. cons. Human Dynamics, 2003-04. Author conf. procs., other profl. publs. Commr. Tex. Strategic Mil. Planning Commn., 1997—2002; bd. dir. El Lago (Tex.) Water and Waste Mgmt. Dist., 1974. Office Phone: 972-256-0061. E-mail: rtokerud@gte.net.

TOKOFSKY, JERRY HERBERT, film producer; b. N.Y.C., Apr. 14, 1936; s. Julius H. and Rose (Trager) T.; m. Myrna Weinstein, Feb. 21, 1968 (div.); children: David, Peter; m. Fiammetta Bettuzzi, 1970 (div.); 1 child, Tatianna; m. Karen Oliver, Oct. 4, 1981. BS in Journalism, NYU, 1956, LLD, 1959, M in Am. Lit., 1999. Talent agt. William Morris Agy., N.Y.C., 1953-59, v.p. L.A., 1959-64; exec. v.p. Columbia Pictures, L.A., 1964-69; v.p. Paramount Pictures, London, 1970; exec. v.p. MGM, London, 1971; pres. Jerry Tokofsky Prodns., L.A., 1972-82; exec. v.p. Zupnik Enterprises, L.A., 1982-92; pres. Jerry Tokofsky Entertainment, Encino, Calif., 1992—; CEO TKO Comm. Prof. Sch. TV and Film U. So. Calif. Sch. Bus. Prodr. films: Where's Poppa, 1971, Born to Win, 1972, Paternity, 1981, Dreamscape, 1985, Fear City, 1986, Wildfire, 1988, Glengarry Glen Ross, 1992, The Grass Harp, 1995, American Buffalo, 1995, Double Down, 1997, Life on Mars, 1998, John Steinbecks In Dubious Battle, 2004, Puccini, 2004, Daisy Winter, 2004, Gods House of Style, 2004, High Desert, 2004. With U.S. Army, 1959, res. 1959-63. Named Man of Yr. B'nai B'rith, 1981; recipient L.A. Resolution City of L.A., 1981. Mem. Variety Club Internat. Avocations: skiing, tennis, golf, chess. *Passion for family, life, work, with patience and intelligence and you have a chance to grab that winning ring.*

TOKUHATA, GEORGE K. retired medical educator, epidemiologist, consultant; b. Matsue, Japan, Aug. 25, 1924; arrived in U.S., 1951; s. Yujiro and Hama Tokuhata; m. Sumiko Matsui, June 10, 1949. BA, Keio U., Tokyo, 1950; MA, Miami U., Oxford, Ohio, 1952; PhD, U. Iowa, 1955; Dr.PH, Johns Hopkins U., 1962. Chief epidemiology chronic disease div. USPHS, Washington, 1961—64; assoc. prof. preventive medicine U. Tenn., Memphis, 1965—67; dir. rsch. Pa. Dept. Health, Harrisburg, 1968—89; prof. behavioral sci. Pa. State U. Coll. Medicine, Hershey, 1970—95; prof. epidemiology U. Pitts., Pitts., 1970—90; ret. Cons. product safety U.S. FDA, Washington, 1970—73; cons. maternal child health rsch. U.S. Children's Bur., 1974—77; cons. rsch. grant svcs. Nat. Cancer Inst., 1982—86. Contbr. chapters to books, articles over 100 articles to profl. jours. Grantee, USPHS, U.S. FDA. Fellow: APHA, Am. Coll. Epidemiology; mem.: Fgn. Policy Assn. (bd.dirs. 1995—2000), Torch Club Internat. (bd.dirs. 1999—2002). Achievements include first to find genetic role played in lung cancer; research in radiation, stress and health; first to new method of finding familial aggregation of chronic diseases. Avocations: classical music, landscape design, gardening. Home: 410 Rupley Rd Camp Hill PA 17011

TOKUTANI, MASAO, risk management educator; b. Tokyo, Nov. 1, 1940; s. Takeo and Matsu (Hagiwara) T. B, Chuo U., 1964, Dr., 1978; Mr., Waseda U., 1967. CPA, Tokyo. Asst. prof. Chiba U. Commerce, 1967-73; assoc. prof. Seikei U., Tokyo, 1974-78, full prof., 1979-2001, prof. emeritus, 2001—; prof. Grad. Sch. Internat. Acctg. Chuo U., 2002. Cons. in field. Author: Corporate Social Accounting, 1977, Risk Management, 1983. Mem. Japan Acctg. Assn., Secom Sci. and Tech. Found. (Risk Measurement and Bus. Behavior award 1983), Asian-Pacific Rsch. Ctr. Seikei U. Avocations: golf, fishing. Home: 63-25 Isshiki Hayama Miuragun, Kanagawa 240-0111 Japan Office: 1-19-403 Sakaecho-Kanagawku Yokohama 221-0052 Japan E-mail: mt@miraisitu.com.

TOLAN, ROBERT WARREN, pediatric infectious disease specialist; b. Bowling Green, Ohio, Nov. 20, 1960; s. Robert Warren Tolan and Margaret Delores (Petter) Cardwell. BA, Ind. U., 1982, MA, 1983; MD, Washington U., St. Louis, 1987. Diplomate Nat. Bd. Med. Examiners, Am. Bd. Pediatrics, sub-bd. of pediat. infectious diseases. Resident in pediat. Riley Hosp. for Children, Indpls., 1987-90; fellow in infectious diseases St. Louis Children's Hosp., 1990-94; pvt. practice pediatrics and pediatric infectious diseases, 1994—; clin. instr. pediat. Washington Univ. Sch. Med., 1994—98; clin. assoc. prof. pediat. Drexel U. Coll. Medicine, 2002—. Co-author: Fever of Unknown Origin in Children, 1991; contbr. articles to profl. jours. Pediatric Scientist Devel. Program fellow, 1990—94. Fellow: Am. Acad. Pediatrics; mem.: AMA, Pediatric Infectious Diseases Soc., Infectious Diseases Soc. Am., Am. Soc. Microbiology, Physicians for Social Responsibility, Soc. for Preservation and Encouragement of Barbershop Quartet Singing in Am. Democrat. Episcopalian. Achievements include patent for a cloned outer membrane protein from Haemophilus influenzae type b which is being developed as a vaccine candidate; reviews of surgical management of pediatric endocarditis and of toxic shock syndrome and influenza; description of systemic pseudomalignant form of cat-scratch disease in normal children, the cloning of an outer membrane protein from Haemophilus influenzae type b, the lack of epidemiologic utility of analysis of lipopolysaccharide from the same organism. Office: St Christopher's Hosp for Children Specialty Care at Capital Health Sys 416 Bellevue Ave Ste 103 Trenton NJ 08618-4502 Personal E-mail: pedIDBob@aol.com.

TOLAND, JOHN ROBERT, lawyer; b. Iola, Kans., Oct. 7, 1944; s. Stanley E. and June Elizabeth (Thompson) T.; m. Karen Alice Jeffries, Apr. 26, 1980; children: Carol Jane, Mark Charles, Scott Robert, Kent William. BA with highest distinction, U. Kans., 1966, JD, 1969. Bar: Kans. 1969, U.S. Dist. Ct. Kans. 1969, U.S. Ct. Appeals (10th cir.) 1969, U.S. Supreme Ct. 1976. Ptnr. Toland and Thompson, LLC, Iola, 1973—. City atty., Yates Center, Kans., 1976-82; spkr. in field. Editor-in-chief Kans. Law Rev., 1968-69; mem. bd. editors Kans. Bar Assn. Jour., 1988-92. Trustee Allen County Hosp., Iola, 1979-82; bd. dirs. Iola Pub. Library, 1980-88, pres., 1983-88; bd. dirs. United Fund of Iola Inc., 1975-79, treas., 1975-77; bd. dirs. Iola Area Symphony Orch., 1994-97; ruling elder 1st Presbyn. Ch., Iola, 1983-85, 97-98; mem. Allen County Hist. Soc., Kans. State Hist. Soc., The Friends of the Eisenhower Found., U. Kans. Alumni Assn.; mem. com. on ministry John Calvin Presbytery, Presbyn Ch. (USA), 1986-88; mem. Permanent Jud. Commn., 1998—; coach Boys Basketball Youth League. Capt. JAGC, U.S. Army, 1969-73, Vietnam. Decorated Bronze Star, Army Commendation medal with oak leaf cluster; John Ise scholar in Econ., 1965-66, Summerfield scholar, U. Kans., 1962-66, Nat. Merit scholar, 1962-66. Fellow Kans. Bar Found.; mem. ABA, Kans. Bar Assn., Kans. Sch. Attys. Assn. (bd. dirs. 1989-93, spkr. at sch. law seminars), Allen County Bar Assn. (pres. 1980-81), Am. Legion, Rotary (pres. Iola chpt. 1980-81, Paul Harris fellow 1986), Order of Coif, VFW, Phi Beta Kappa, Phi Delta Phi, Beta Theta Pi, Sigma Pi Sigma. Home: PO Box 312 Iola KS 66749-0312 Office: Toland and Thompson LLC 103 E Madison St Iola KS 66749-3330 Office Phone: 620-365-6901.

TOLANEY, MURLI, environmental engineering executive; b. Aug. 1, 1941; BS in Civil Engring., MS in Environ. Engring., U. Kans.; attended Advanced Mgmt. program, Harvard Bus. Sch. Jr. engr. Coun. Sci. and Indsl. Resources, New Delhi, 1963-66; project engr. L.A. County Sanitary Dist., 1966-70; with Montgomery Watson Assn., MWH Global Inc., Pasadena, Calif., 1970—, CEO, chmn. Program mgr., Wastewater Capital Improvement Program City of LA. Author of several technical papers. Bd. dir. San Gabriel Valley Coun., Calif., Boy Scouts Am., Methodist Hosp. Found., Arcadia, Calif., Water Environment Rsch. Found., U. Kans., Sch. Engring. Recipient Asian Am. Engr. Yr., Chinese Inst. Engrs./U.S.A., 2003. Office: Montgomery Watson Ams 300 N Lake Ave Ste 1200 Pasadena CA 91101-4184*

TOLBERT, BERT MILLS, biochemist, educator; b. Twin Falls, Idaho, Jan. 15, 1921; s. Ed. and Helen (Mills) T.; m. Anne Grace Zweifler, July 20, 1959; children— Elizabeth Dawn, Margaret Anne, Caroline Joan, Sarah Helen. Student, Idaho State U., 1938-40; BS, U. Calif. at Berkeley, 1942, PhD, 1945; postgrad., Fed. Inst. Tech., Zurich, Switzerland, 1952-53. Chemist Lawrence Radiation Lab., Berkeley, 1944-57; faculty U. Colo., Boulder, 1957-89, prof., 1961-89, prof. emeritus, 1989—, assoc. chmn. dept. chemistry and biochemistry, 1980-88. Bd. dirs. Hauser Chem. Rsch., Boulder, 1983-99; dirs. Hauser Inc., Boulder, 1983-99, vis. prof. IAEA, Buenos Aires, Argentina, 1961-62; Biophysicist U.S. AEC, Washington, 1967-68; cons. pvt. cos, govt. agys. Author: (with others) Isotopic Carbon, 1948; contbr. (with others) articles to profl. jours. Fellow AAAS; mem. Am. Chem. Soc., Am. Soc. Biochemistry and Molecular Biology, Radiation Rsch. Soc., Soc. for Exptl. Biology and Medicine. Achievements include rsch. on organic chemistry, including use of isotopes in chemistry and biochemistry, radiation chemistry, radiation effects in protein, intermediary metabolism, metabolism of ascorbic acid, nutritional biochemistry, instrumentation in radioactivity. Home: 444 Kalmia Ave Boulder CO 80304-1732

TOLBERT, BETH WILLDEN, real estate company executive, real estate broker; b. Delta, Utah, Apr. 7, 1935; d. Delbert B. and Mildred (Twitchell) Willden; m. Stanley Tolbert, May 12, 1955; children: Keven, Tracy, Troy. Student, Brigham Young U., 1953-54. Cert. residential specialist. Realtor Harding Realty, Am. Fork, Utah, 1976-82; associate broker Pine Valley Realty, Alpine, Utah, 1982-97; prin., owner Beth Tolbert Realty Group, St. George, Utah, 1997—; ptnr., prin. broker Tolbert & Nielsen Realty Group, LLC, St. George, Utah, 2003—. Apptd. Utah Real Estate Commn., Salt Lake City, 1993—, chair 1993-94; bd. trustees Utah Valley State Coll., Orem, 1991—, chair 1996-97; pres. Nat. Womens Coun. Realtors, 1994; bd. trustees Leadership Dixie, 2000-01. Recipient Realtor of Yr. award Utah Assoc. Realtors, 1984, Distinguished Svc. award 1994, 97, Realtor of Yr. award Utah County Bd. Realtors, 1984. Home: 656 Country Ln Santa Clara UT 84765-5471

TOLBERT, CLINTON JAME, army officer, machinist; b. Auburn, Ala., Dec. 22, 1953; s. Clinton and Rosia Love (Fillmore) T.; m. Gloria Jean Fitzpatrick, Sept. 23, 1974; children: Christopher, Mark, Marcella. BS, Tukegee U., 1983; MBA, Troy State U., 1987, MS, 1990; AS in Applied Sci., So. U., Opelika, Ala., 1996. EMT U.S. Army, Fort Benning, Ga., 1972-75; machine operator West Point Pepperll, Inc., Valley, Ala., 1975-82; 1st lt. Army Nat. Guard, Roanoke, Ala., 1982-86, capt., 1986-92, major Montgomery, Ala., 1992-96; machinist Falk Corp., Auburn, Ala, 1996—. Elder Methodist Ch., Auburn, Ala., 1996— Named All- Am. Scholar, U.S. Achievement Acad., Lexington, Ky., 1996; recipient Minority Leadership award, U.S. Achievement Acad., Lexington, 1996. Mem. Nat. Guard Assn. Democrat. Avocations: reading, golf. Home: 989 Fitzpatric Rd Auburn AL 36830

TOLBERT, GARY J. minister; b. Allentown, Pa., Sept. 5, 1952; s. James Warren and Louise Bitto Tolbert; m. Malia H. Tolbert, Dec. 22, 1974; 1 child, Matthew W. BA in Theology, So. Adventist U., 1977; MA in Ministry, Andrews U. Ordained to gospel ministry Fla. Conf. Seventh Day Adventist, 1982. Sr. pastor various Seventh-Day Adventist chs., Fla., 1978—91, Seventh-Day Adventist Ch., Yakima, Wash., 1991—2000, Fletcher, NC, 2000—. Mem. exec. com. Upper Columbia Conf., Spokane, Wash., 1991—98, Carolina Conf., Charlotte, NC, 2000—; lectr. in field. Recipient Bronze award, Apple Valley Toastmasters, 1999. Mem.: Blue Ridge Ministerial Assn. (pres. 2002—). Avocation: art. Office: Fletcher SDA Ch PO Box 409 Fletcher NC 28732 Office Phone: 828-684-0332. E-mail: pastorgary@bellsouth.net.

TOLBERT, MARGARET A. geochemistry educator; Prof. dept. chemistry U. Colo., Boulder. Recipient James B. Macelwane Young Investigator medal Am. Geophys. Union, 1993. Office: U Colo Dept Chemistry PO Box 215 Boulder CO 80309-0215

TOLCHIN, JOAN GUBIN, psychiatrist, educator; b. N.Y.C., Mar. 10, 1944; d. Harold and Bella (Newman) Gubin; m. Matthew Armin Tolchin, Sept. 1, 1966; 1 child, Benjamin. AB, Vassar Coll., 1964; MD, NYU, 1972. Diplomate Am. Bd. Gen. Psychiatry, Am. Bd. Child Psychiatry. Rsch. asst. Albert Einstein Coll. Medicine, N.Y.C., 1964-68; instr. psychiatry med. coll. Cornell U., N.Y.C., 1977-78, clin. instr., 1978-86, clin. asst. prof., 1986—2004, clin. assoc. prof., 2004—. Contbr. articles to profl. jours., chapters to books. Fellow: Am. Acad. Child and Adolescent Psychiatry; mem.: N.Y. Coun. Child and Adolescent Psychiatry (bd. dirs. 1992—96, pres. 1994—95, bd. advisors 2001—), Am. Acad. Psychoanalysis and Dynamic Psychiatry (sec. 1998—2001), Alpha Omega Alpha (mem. disaster psychiatry outreach). Office: 35 E 84th St New York NY 10028-0871

TOLCHIN, KAREN REBECCA, adult education educator; b. NYC, June 26, 1970; d. Martin and Susan Jane Tolchin; m. Todd Vance, July 29, 2000 (div. Jan. 2002). BA, Bryn Mawr Coll., 1992; MA, Brandeis U., 1998; PhD, Brandeis U., 2000. Asst. prof. humanities Nova Southeastern, Ft. Lauderdale, Fla., 2001—. Vis. prof. Nova Southeastern, Ft. Lauderdale, 2000—01. Mem.: MLA. Office: Nova Southeastern U 3301 Coll Ave Fort Lauderdale FL 33314 Home: Apt 5M 3901 S Ocean Dr Hollywood FL 33019

TOLCHIN, MARTIN, retired newspaper reporter, author; b. N.Y.C., Sept. 20, 1928; s. Charles T. and Evelyn (Weisman) Tolchin; m. Susan Jane Goldsmith, Dec. 23, 1965; children: Karen. Student, U. Utah, 1947-49; LL.B., N.Y. Law Sch., 1951. Reporter N.Y. Times, N.Y.C., 1954—94; publisher and editor-in-chief The Hill, Washington, 1994—2002. Author (with Susan Jane Tolchin): To The Victor, 1971; author: Clout-Woman Power and Politics, 1974, Dismantling America-The Rush to Deregulate, 1983, Buying Into America: How Foreign Money is Changing the Face of Our Nation, 1988, Selling Our Security-The Erosion of American's Assets, 1992, Glass Houses: Congressional Ethics and the Politics of Venom, 2001. Served with U.S. Army, 1951-53. Recipient Schaeffer Gold Typewriter award E.M. Schaeffer Co., 1967; recipient Page One award Newspaper Guild N.Y., 1967, 69, 73, Citizens Budget Commn. award, 1967, Sigma Delta Chi award, 1973, Everett M. Dirksen award for disting. reporting of Congress, 1983; named to Journalism Hall Fame, Soc. Profl. Journalists, 2004. Mem. Nat. Press Club (Washington), Univ. Club. Jewish. Home: 3525 Winfield Ln NW Washington DC 20007-2378 Personal E-mail: mtolchin@aol.com.

TOLCHIN, SUSAN JANE, public administration educator, writer; b. N.Y.C., Jan. 14, 1941; d. Jacob Nathan and Dorothy Ann (Markowitz) Goldsmith; m. Martin Tolchin, Dec. 23, 1965; 1 child, Karen Rebecca. BA, Bryn Mawr Coll., 1961; MA, U. Chgo., 1962; PhD, NYU, 1968. Lectr. in polit. sci. CCNY, N.Y.C., 1963-65, Bklyn. Coll., 1965-71; adj. asst. prof. polit. sci. Seton Hall U., South Orange, N.J., 1971-73; assoc. prof. polit. sci., dir. Inst. for Women and Politics, Mt. Vernon Coll., Washington, 1975-78; prof. pub. adminstrn. George Washington U., Washington, 1978-98; prof. pub. policy Sch. Pub. Policy George Mason U., Fairfax, Va., 1998—. Disting. lectr. Indsl. Coll. Armed Forces, 1994. Author: The Angry American: How Voter Rage is Changing the Nation, 1996, 2d edit., 1998; author: (with Martin Tolchin) To the Victor: Political Patronage from the Clubhouse to the White House, 1971, Clout--Womanpower and Politics, 1974, Dismantling America--The Rush to Deregulate, 1983, Buying Into America--How Foreign Money Is Changing the Face of Our Nation, 1988, Selling Our Securit--The Erosion of America's Assets, 1992, Glass Houses--Congressional Ethics and the Politics of Venom, 2001. Bd. dirs. Cystic Fibrosis Found., 1982—; county committeewoman Dem. Party, Montclair, N.J., 1969-73. Recipient Founder's Day award NYU, 1968, Trachtenberg award for rsch. George Washington U., 1998; named Tchr. of Yr., Mt. Vernon Coll., 1978; Dilthey fellow George Washington U., 1983, Aspen Inst. fellow, 1979. Fellow Nat. Acad. Pub. Adminstrn.; mem. Am. Polit. Sci. Assn. (pres. Women's Caucus for Polit. Sci. 1977-78), Am. Soc. Pub. Adminstrn. (chair sect. natural resources and environ. adminstrn. 1982-83, Marshall Dimock award 1997). Democrat. Office: Inst Pub Policy George Mason U Fairfax VA 22030 Office Phone: 703-993-4035. Business E-Mail: tolchin@gmu.edu.

TOLCHINSKY, PAUL DEAN, organization design psychologist; b. Cleve., Sept. 30, 1946; s. Sanford Melvin and Frances (Klein) T.; m. Laurie S. Schermer, Nov. 3, 1968 (div. Jan. 1982); m. Kathy L. Dworkin, June 19, 1988; children: Heidi E., Dana M. BA, Bowling Green State U., 1971; PhD, Purdue U., 1978. Asst. br. mgr., tng. instr. Detroit Bank and Trust, 1971-73; mgr. tng. and devel. nuclear divsn. Babcock and Wilcox Co., Barberton, Ohio, 1973-75; internal cons. food products divsn. Gen. Foods Corp., West Lafayette, Ind., 1975-77; grad. tchg. asst. Krannert Grad. Sch. Mgmt. Purdue U., West Lafayette, 1975-78; asst. prof. mgmt. Coll. Bus. Adminstrn. Fla. State U., Tallahassee, 1978-79, U. Akron, Ohio, 1979-81; pres. Performance Devel. Assocs., Cleve., 1975—; ptnr. Dannemiller Tyson Assocs., Cleve., 1994-99; mng. ptnr. Performance Devel. Assocs., 2000—. Contbr. articles to profl. publs. Bd. dirs. Temple Tiferth Israel, Cleve., 195. With U.S. Army, 1966-69, Vietnam. Mem. APA, Acad. Mgmt. Democrat. Jewish. Avocations: running, travel. Office: Performance Devel Assocs 50 Fox Glen Rd Moreland Hills OH 44022 Office Phone: 440-349-1990.

TOLDALAGI, MARIANNE, foundation administrator; Bd. dirs. Am. Womans Econ. Devel. Corp., N.Y.C. Sr. v.p./gen. mgr. Leisure Travel, Am. Express. Office: Am Womans Econ Devel Corp 71 Vanderbilt Ave Ste 320 New York NY 10169-0005

TOLEDANO, RALPH DE, columnist, author, poet; b. Internat. Zone of Tangier, Aug. 17, 1916; m. Nora Romaine, July 6, 1938 (div. 1964); children: James, Paul Christopher; m. Eunice Marshall, Apr. 19, 1979 (dec. Aug. 1999). BA, Columbia Coll., 1938; postgrad., Cornell U., 1943. Founder, co-editor Cross-Town, 1932-33; Founder, co-editor Jazz Info., 1938-39; assoc. editor The New Leader, 1941-43; editor The Standard, 1946; mng. editor Plain Talk, 1946-47; pub. dir. Dress Joint Bd., Internat. Ladies Garment Workers Union, 1947-48; asst. editor Newsweek, 1948, nat. reports editor, 1950-60, asst. chief Washington Bur., 1956-60; syndicated columnist King Features, 1960-71, Nat. News Research Syndicate, 1971-74, Copley News Service, 1974-89, Heritage Features Syndicate, 1989-91, Creators Syndicate, 1991-98, Nat. News Rsch. Syndicate, 1998—; editor House Republican Leadership report Am. Mil. Strength and Strategy, 1960; chief Washington Bur., Taft Broadcasting Co., 1960-61; dir. polit. intelligence Goldwater Presdl. Campaign, 1963-64; contbg. editor Nat. Rev., 1960—2001; pres. Nat. News-Rsch., 1960—, Anthem Books, 1960—; editor-in-chief Washington World, 1961-62. Vice-chmn. Am. Conserva-Union, 1965-66; mem. 20th Century Fund Task Force on Freedom Press, 1971-72. Author: Seeds of Treason, 1950, Spies, Dupes and Diplomats, 1952, Day of Reckoning, 1955, Nixon, 1956, Lament for a Generation, 1960, The Greatest Plot in History, 1963, The Winning Side, 1963, The Goldwater Story, 1964, RFK: The Man Who Would be President, 1967, America, I-Love-You, 1968, One Man Alone: Richard M. Nixon, 1969, Claude Kirk: Man and Myth, 1970, Little Cesar, 1971, J. Edgar Hoover: The Man in His Time, 1973, Hit and Run: The Ralph Nader Story, 1975, Let Our Cities Burn, 1975, Poems: You & I, 1978, Devil Take Him, 1979, The Apocrypha of Limbo (poems), 1994, Notes from the Underground: The Chambers-Toledano Letters, 1997, Prelude to Terror: The Secret War on America, 2003; editor: Frontiers of Jazz, 1947, Mark Twain on Practically Anything, 2001; co-editor: (with Melvin Laird) The Conservative Papers, 1962,; editor-in-chief. Political Success, 1968 69; mem. editl. bd. Yale Lit. Mag, 1981-86; contbg. editor Insight, Washington Times; contbr. articles to nat. mags. Bd. dirs. Americans for Constitutional Action, 1966-67, Constructive Action, 1990—2000 With OSS, AUS, 1943-46. Recipient Freedoms Found. award, 1950, 61, 74; Americanism award VFW, 1953; Disting. Journalism fellow Heritage Found. Mem. Internat. Mark Twain Soc., Bibl. Archeology Soc., Dutch Treat Club (N.Y.), Nat. Press Club, Naval and Mil. Club (London), Am. Legion (vice comdr. Pershing post), Sigma Delta Chi. Office: 500 23rd St NW Washington DC 20037-2828

TOLEDO, FRANCK MARC, geneticist, molecular biologist; b. Lille, France, Nov. 27, 1966; s. Robert Louis Raymond Toledo and Janine Benhamou; m. Floriane Bernard, June 5, 1999 (div. July 24, 2003). PhD, Univ. Pierre et Marie Curie, Paris, France, 1994. Tchg. asst. Univ. Pierre et Marie Curie, Paris, 1995—96; jr. scientist Pasteur Inst., Paris, 1996—99, sr. scientist, 2000—02; scientist Salk Inst., San Diego, 2000—. Fellow, Ligue Nationale contre le Cancer, 1994, Assn. pour la Recherche sur le Cancer, 1995, 2000. Achievements include discovery of Mechanisms of chromosome rearrangements in cancer cells; mammalian DNA replication origin. Office: Salk Inst GEL-W 10010 N Torrey Pines Rd La Jolla CA 92037 Business E-Mail: toledo@salk.edu.

TOLEDO, FREDERICO GRANCHI STEIDEL, physician, scientist; b. Rio de Janeiro, Jan. 21, 1972; s. Jose Augusto Toledo and Francisca Granchi. MD, U. Fed. Rio de Janeiro, 1996. Rsch. trainee U. Fed. Rio de Janeiro, 1990-93; spl. project assoc. Mayo Clinic, Rochester, Minn., 1994, rsch. fellow, 1996-98; resident in internal medicine U. Miami, 1999—2002; endocrinology fellow U. Pitts., 2002—04, clin. instr. of medicine, 2004—. Mem.: Am. Diabetes Assn., Am. Assn. Clin. Endocrinologists, Endocrine Soc. Avocation: computers. Office: 1605 Teal Trace Pittsburgh PA 15237

TOLEDO-PEREYRA, LUIS HORACIO, transplant surgeon, researcher, historian educator; b. Nogales, Ariz., Oct. 19, 1943; s. Jose Horacio and Elia (Pereyra) Toledo; m. Marjean May Gilbert, Mar. 21, 1974; children: Alexander Horacio, Suzanne Elizabeth. BS magna cum laude, Regis Coll., 1960; MD, Nat. U. Mex., 1967, MS in Internal Medicine, 1970; PhD in Surgery, U. Minn., 1984. Intern Hosp. Juarez, Nat. U. Mex., 1966; resident in internal medicine Instituto Nacional de la Nutricions, Nat. U. Mex., 1968, 70; resident in surgery U. Minn., 1970-76; resident in thoracic and cardiovascular surgery U. Chgo., 1976-77; dir. surg. rsch. Henry Ford Hosp., Detroit, 1977-79; co-dir. transplantation, 1977-79; chief transplantation, dir. surg. rsch. Mt. Carmel Mercy Hosp., Detroit, 1979-89; chief transplantation, dir. rsch. Borgess Med. Ctr., Kalamazoo, 1990-99, 90—; clin. prof. surgery Mich. State U., 1993-96, prof. surgery, 1996—. Adj. prof. Sch. Health Sci. Mercy Coll., Detroit, 1983-91, history Western Mich. U., 1990—, biol. sci., 1991-96; prof. surgery Nat. U. Mex., 1990-96. Guest editor various med. and transplant jours.; mem. editl. bd. Dialysis and Transplantation, 1979—, Rsch. in Surgery, 1991—, Cirugia Iberoamericana, 1992—, clin. adv. bd. Transpl. Proc., 1993—, Medico Interamericano, 1993—, Cirugia Espanola, 1994—; assoc. editor Transplantology, 1990—; contbr. over 800 publs. on organ preservation, transplantation, other surg. and med. related areas, and the history of medicine to profl. jours. Recipient Outstanding Achievement award U. Mex., 1961, 64, 67; Resident Rsch. award Assn. Acad. Surgery, 1974; Cecil Lehman Mayer Rsch. award Am. Coll. Chest Physicians, 1975, Surgery Rsch. Nat. award Mex. Assn. Gen. Surgery, 1993. Mem. AMA, Transplantation Soc., Assn. Acad. Surgery, Am. Soc. Transplant Surgery, Soc. Organ Sharing (pres., founder), Am. Assn. History Medicine, Am. Soc. Nephrology, Am. Assn. Immunologists, Am. Physiol. Soc., Soc. Exptl. Biology and Medicine, Am. Soc. Artificial Organs, Am. Diabetes Assn., European Soc. Study of Diabetes, No. Am. Soc. Dialysis Transplantation (pres., founder), Pan Am. Soc. Dialysis Transplantation (pres. elect, founder), Transplantation Soc. Mich. (pres., exec. bd.). Roman Catholic. Home: 3598 Whistling Ln Portage MI 49024-5545 Office: Borgess Med Ctr 1631 Gull Rd Ste 110 Kalamazoo MI 49048-1626

TOLER, PENNY, former professional basketball player, sports team executive; b. Mar. 24, 1966; B of Psychology, Long Beach State U., 1989. Guard, Montecchio, Italy, 1989—91, Pescara, Italy, 1991—94, Sporting Flash, Greece, 1994—96, Ramat HaSharon, Israel, 1996—97, Los Angeles Sparks, (WNBA), 1997—99; gen. mgr. L.A. Sparks, 1999—. Mem. U.S. Basketball Olympic Com., 1999—. Founder Points from Penny Program, 1998. Named All-Am. & Co-Player of Yr./Big West, 1988, 1989. Achievements include scored first ever basket in WNBA history. Avocations: ping pong/table tennis, tennis, craps. Office: LA Sparks Great Western Forum 555 N Nash St El Segundo CA 90245-2818

TOLES, THOMAS GREGORY, editorial cartoonist; b. Buffalo, Oct. 22, 1951; s. George Edward and Rose Elizabeth (Riehle) Toles; m. Gretchen Amanda Saarnijoki, May 26, 1973; children: Amanda Laurel, Seth August. BA in English, SUNY, Buffalo, 1973. Artist Buffalo Courier-Express, NY, 1973—80, cartoonist, 1980—82, Buffalo News, NY, 1982—2002, UPS, 1982—, US News & World Report, 1994—99, The New Republic, 2000—02, Washington Post, Wash., DC, 2002—. Author: My School Is Worse than Yours, 1997; cartoon collection, The Taxpayer's New Clothes, 1985, Mr. Gazoo: A Cartoon History of the Reagan Era, 1987, At Least Our Bombs Are Getting Smarter: A Cartoon Preview of the 1990's, 1991, My Elected Representatives Went to Washington, 1993, Duh, 1996, comic strip, Curious Avenue, 1992—94, Randolph Itch, 2a.m., 2000—02. Recipient John Fischetti Editorial Cartoon award, Columbia Coll., Chgo., 1984, Pulitzer Prize for edit. cartooning, 1990, Editl. Cartoonist of the Yr., 2002. Mem.: Am. Assn. Editorial Cartoonists. Home: 4625 46th St NW Washington DC 20016 Office: WA Post 1150 15th St NW Washington DC 20071

TOLF, ROBERT WALTER, writer; b. Chgo., Aug. 3, 1929; s. Carl Oscar and Margaret Emilia (Zeltner) T.; m. Nancy Ellen List, Aug. 9, 1952; 1 child, Carolyn Anne. BA cum laude, Harvard U., 1951; PhD, U. Rochester, 1957. Attache, 2d sec. U.S. Dept. State, various locations, 1957-70; editor Fla. Trend, St. Petersburg, 1973—; columnist, critic Sun-Sentinel, Ft. Lauderdale, Fla., 1975—; sr. sch. fellow Hoover Instn., 1976—77; exec. dir. Phileas Soc., Ft. Lauderdale, 1988—; producer, writer, narrator Columbus Documentaries, Ft. Lauderdale, 1989-92. Sr. rsch. fellow Hoover Inst., 1977. Author: The Russian Rockefellers, 1976, Addison Mizner, 1983, Chicago Sketch Book, 1988, Paris Sketch Book, 1990, Discover Florida, 1982, Country Inns of the Old South, 1978, 83, Country Inns of New York State, 1984, Country Inns of the Mid-Atlantic, 1986, Florida Weekends, 1990, 94, Florida's Best Beach Vacations, 1992, Florida Country Inns, 1993, 96, Destination Florida--Sanibel and Captiva, 1993, Destination Florida--South Beach Miami, 1993, 17 Florida Restaurant Guides, 1973-96, Trumpy, 1996, others; editor: Columbus Documents, 1992; author, prodr. narrator 15 videos in The Great Explorers Series. Lt. U.S. Army, 1954-57. Mem. Harvard Varsity Club, Fox Club, Harvard Club Broward County. Office: 3100 S Ocean Blvd Apt 422 Highland Beach FL 33487

TOLFORD, FRANK STEFAN, bookstore executive; b. Bremen, Germany, June 30, 1949; came to U.S., 1955; s. Charles Lawrence and Marta Sophia Tolford. AA, St. Johns River Jr. Coll., Palatka, Fla., 1973; BA, U. North Fla., Jacksonville, 1976. Warehouse mgr. Smith & Royals Elec. Svc. Co., Jacksonville, 1977-80; gen. mgr. Chamblin Bookmine, Jacksonville, 1981—. Donor Fla.-Ga. Blood Alliance, Jacksonville, 1982—. Mem. Fla. Antiquarian Booksellers Assn. (v.p. 1990-91, pres. 1991-94). Republican. Episcopalian. Avocations: stamps, chess, books. Office: Chamblin Bookmine 4551 Roosevelt Blvd Jacksonville FL 32210-3314

TOLIA, VASUNDHARA K. pediatric gastroenterologist, educator; b. Calcutta, India; came to U.S., 1975; d. Rasiklal and Saroj (Kothari) Doshi; m. Kirit Tolia, May 30, 1975; children: Vinay, Sanjay. MBBS, Calcutta U., 1968-75. Intern, resident Children's Hosp. Mich., Detroit, 1976-79, fellow, 1979-81, dir. pediat. endoscopy unit, 1984-90, dir. pediat. gastroenterology and nutrition, 1990—; instr. Wayne State U., Detroit, 1981-83, asst. prof., 1983-91, assoc. prof., 1991-97, prof., 1997—. Mem. editl. bd. Inflammatory Bowel Diseases, 1999— Am. Jour. Gastroenterology, 1999, Rev. of World Lit. in Pediatrics, 1999—; contbr. articles to profl. jours. Named Woman of Distinction, Mich. chpt. Crohn's and Colitis Found. Am., 1991 Fellow Am. Coll. Gastroenterology (chair ad-hoc com. pediat. gastroenterology 1998-2000), Am. Acad. Pediats.; mem. Am. Gastroenterology Assn., N.Am. Soc. Pediat. Gastroenterology and Nutrition, Soc. Pediat. Rsch. Office: Childrens Hosp Mich 3901 Beaubien St Detroit MI 48201-2119

TOLINS, ROGER ALAN, lawyer; b. Bklyn., Jan. 25, 1936; s. Albert and Claire (Rothstein) T.; m. Doris Levine, May 15, 1960; children: Fran, Jonathan. AB with distinction, Dartmouth Coll., 1956; LLB, NYU, 1959, LLM in Taxation, 1961. Bar: N.Y. 1959. Assoc. Brennan, London & Buttenwieser, N.Y.C., 1961 67; ptnr. Goldfeld, Charak, Tolins & Lowenfels, N.Y.C., 1967-74, Tolins & Lowenfels, N.Y.C., 1975—. Guest lectr. in securities law Seton Hall U. Sch. Law, 1989—. With U.S. Army, 1959-60. Mem. ABA (sect. on taxation), N.Y. State Bar Assn.

TOLIVER, LEE, mechanical engineer; b. Wildhorse, Okla., Oct. 3, 1921; s. Clinton Leslie and Mary (O'Neal) T.; m. Barbara Anne O'Reilly, Jan. 24, 1942 (dec. Jan. 1999); children: Margaret Anne, Michael Edward. BSME, U. Okla., 1942. Engr. Douglas Aircraft Co., Santa Monica, Calif., 1942, Oklahoma City, 1942-44, Los Alamos (N.Mex.) Sci. Lab., 1946; instr. mech. engring. Ohio State U., Columbus, 1946-47; engr. Sandia Nat. Labs., Albuquerque, 1947-82; instr. computer sci. and math. U. N.Mex., Valencia County, 1982-84; number theory researcher Belen, N.Mex., 1982—. Author: Relations Between Prime and Relatively Prime Integers, 1998. With Manhattan Project (Atomic Bomb) U.S. Army, 1944-46. Home: 206 Howell St Belen NM 87002-6225

TOLL, BARBARA ELIZABETH, art gallery director; b. Phila., June 8, 1945; d. Joseph M. and Evelyn Toll BA, Goucher Coll., 1967; MFA, Pratt Inst., 1969. Asst. dir. jr. coun. Mus. Modern Art, N.Y.C., 1969-70; dir. Hundred Acres Gallery, N.Y.C., 1971-76; curator David Rockefeller Collection, N.Y.C., 1975-81; pres., dir. Barbara Toll Fine Arts, N.Y.C., 1981-94, dir., 1994—. Bd. dirs. Corp. Yaddo; curator Focus: Donald Judd Furniture, Parrish Art Mus., Southampton, NY, 1996, Friendships in Arcadia: Writers and Artists at Yaddo in the 90s, 2000, Follies: Fantasy in the Landscape, Parrish Art Mus., 2001, Reconfiguring Space: Blueprints for Art in Gen., 2003. Trustee Ind. Curators Internat.; nat. bd. dirs. ArtTable, 2001—04. Avocation: gardening. Office: 138 Prince St New York NY 10012-3135

TOLL, JOHN SAMPSON, university president, physics educator; b. Denver, Oct. 25, 1923; s. Oliver Wolcott and Merle d'Aubigne (Sampson) T.; m. Deborah Ann Taintor, Oct. 24, 1970; children: Dacia Merle Sampson, Caroline Taintor. BS with honors, Yale U., 1944; AM, Princeton U., 1948, PhD, 1952; DSc (hon.), U. Md., 1973, U. Wroclaw, Poland, 1975; LLD (hon.), Adelphi U., 1978; PhD (hon.), Fudan U., Peoples Republic China, 1987; LHD (hon.), SUNY, Stony Brook, 1990; LLD (hon.), U. Md., Eastern Shore, 1993. Mng. editor, acting chmn. Yale Sci. mag., 1943-44; with Princeton U., 1946-49, proctor fellow, 1948-49; Friends of Elementary Particle Theory Research grantee for study in France, 1950; theoretical physicist Los Alamos Sci. Lab., 1950-51; staff mem., assoc. dir. Project Matterhorn, Forrestal Rsch. Ctr., Princeton U., 1951-53; prof., chmn. physics and astronomy U. Md., 1953-65; pres., prof. physics SUNY, Stony Brook, 1965-78, U. Md., 1978-88, chancellor, 1988-89, chancellor emeritus, prof. physics, 1989—; pres. Univs. Rsch. Assn., Washington, 1989-94, Washington Coll., Chestertown, Md., 1995—. 1st dir. chancellor's panel on univ. pruposes SUNY, 1970; physics cons. to editl. staff Nat. Sci. Tchrs. Assn., 1957—61; U.S. del., head scientist, secretariat Internat. Conf. High Energy Physics, 1960; mem.-at-large U.S. nat. com. Internat. Union Pure and Applied Physics, 1960—63; chmn. rsch. adv. com. on electrophysics NASA, 1961—65; mem. gov. Md. Sci. Resources Adv. Bd., 1963—65; mem., chmn. adv. panel for physics NSF, 1964—67; mem. N.Y. Gov.'s Adv. Com. Atomic Energy, 1966—70; mem. commn. plans and objectives higher edn. Am. Coun. Edn., 1966—69; mem. Hall of Records Commn., 1979—88; mem., chmn. adv. coun. Princeton Plasma Physics Lab., 1979—85; mem. adv. coun. pres.'s Assn. Governing Bds., 1980—88, So. Regional Edn. Bd., 1980—90; mem. exec. com. Washington/Balt. Regional Assn., 1980—89, Nat. Assn. State Univs. and Land Grant Colls., 1980—88, Ctr. Study of the Presidency, 1983—84; mem. univ. programs panel of energy rsch. bd. Dept. Energy, 1982—83; mem. adv. com. SBHE, 1983—89, Md. Gov.'s Chesapeake Bay Coun., 1985; mem. resource com. state trade policy coun. Gov.'s high tech roundtable Md. Dept. Econ. Devel., 1986—89; chmn. marine divsn. NASULGC, 1986; bd. trustees Aspen Inst. Humanities, 1987—89; mem. commn. higher edn. Middle States Assn. Colls. and Schs., 1987; chmn. adv. panel on tech. risks and opportunities for U.S. energy supply and demand U.S. Office Tech. Assessment, 1987—91, chmn. adv. panel on internat. collaboration in def. tech., 1989—91; mem. Sea Grant rev. panel U.S. Dept. Commerce, 1992—, chair, 1996—97; mem. com. financing higher edn. Nat. Assn. Ind. Colls. and Univs., 1996—98; bd. govs. Chesapeake Bay Maritime Mus., 1996—; dir. Md. Gov.'s Blue Ribbon Citizens Pfiesteria Action Commn., 1997; mem. governing coun. Wye Faculty Seminar, 1997—; dir. Eastern Shore Assn. Coll. Pres., 1998—; mem. bd. dirs. Md. Ctr. Agro-Ecology, Inc., 1999—; vis. prof. Nordic Inst. Theoretical Physics, Niels Bohr Inst., Denmark, U. Lund, Sweden, 1975—76; mem. math. scis. edn. bd. NAS; mem. Higher Edn. Heritage Action Com., 2002—. Contbr. articles to profl. jours. Mem. adv. coun. Del-Mar-Va coun. Boy Scouts Am., 1999—; mem. Higher Edn. Heritage Action Com., 2002—; bd. dirs. Hodson Scholarship Found., 1996, Mid-Shore Cmty. Found., 2002—. Recipient Benjamin Barge prize in math. Yale U., 1943, George Beckwith medal for Proficiency in Astronomy, 1944, Outstanding Citizen award City of Denver, 1958, Outstanding Tchr. award U. Md. Men's League, 1965, Copernicus award govt. of Poland, 1973, Stony Brook Found. award for disting. contbns. to edn., 1979, Disting. Svc. award State of Md., 1981, Silver medal Sci. U. Tokyo, 1994, Internat. Landmark award U. Md., 1994, first recipient Lifetime Achievement award Md. Assn. for Higher Edn., 2000, Chief Exec. Leadership award Coun. for Advancement and Support Edn., 2000; named Washingtonian of Yr., 1985, Citizen of Yr. Chestertown Optimist Club, 1997, John S. Toll Physics Bldg., Univ. Md., 2001; John Simon Guggenheim Meml. Found. fellow Inst. Theoretical Physics U. Copenhagen, U. Lund, Sweden, 1958-59. Fellow AAAS, Am. Phys. Soc., Washington Acad. Scis. (pres. 1995-96), N.Y. Acad. Scis.; mem. NSTA, Am. Coun. Edn. (bd. dirs. 1986-89, NAACP (life), Am. Assn. Physics Tchrs., Fedn. Am. Scientists (chmn. 1961-62), Philos. Soc. Washington, Assn. Higher Edn., Yale U. Sci. and Engring. Assn. (award for disting. contbns. 1996), Cosmos Club, Hamilton St. Club, Baltimore, Univ. Club (Washington and N.Y.), Phi Beta Kappa, Phi Kappa Phi (disting., Marylander of Yr. 2000 award), Sigma Xi (Sci. Achievement award 1965), Omicron Delta Kappa (hon.), Sigma Pi Sigma. Achievements include research on elementary particle theory, scattering. Office: U Md Dept Physics College Park MD 20742-4111 also: Washington Coll Pres's Office Chestertown MD 21620 E-mail: johntoll@physics.umd.edu., jtoll2@washcoll.edu. *Throughout my life I have tried mainly to do whatever seemed most important and useful.*

TOLL, PERRY MARK, lawyer, educator; b. Kansas City, Mo., Oct. 28, 1945; s. Mark Irving and Ruth (Parker) T.; m. Mary Anne Shottenkirk, Aug. 26, 1967; children: Andrea Lynne, Hillary Anne. BS in Polit. Sci. and Econs., U. Kans., 1967, JD, 1970. Bar: Mo. 1970 1970, U.S. Dist. Ct. (we. dist.) Mo. 1970, U.S. Tax. Ct. 1979, U.S. Supreme Ct. 1979. With Shughart, Thomson & Kilroy P.C., Kansas City, 1970—, pres., 1995—, chmn. bus. dept., 1999—. Asst. prof. deferred compensation U. Mo., Kansas City, 1979-83; bd. dirs., pres. Heart of Am. Tax Inst., Kansas City, 1975-87. Mem., chmn. Prairie Village (Kans.) Bd. Zoning Appeals, 1977-95. Mem. ABA, Mo. Bar Assn., Am. Health Lawyers Assn., Am. Agr. Law Assn., Mo. Merchants and Mfrs. Assn., Greater Kansas City Med. Mgrs. Assn., Lawyers Assn. Kansas City, East Kans. Estate Planning Coun. (bd. dirs., pres.), Phi Kappa Tau (bd. dirs. Beta Theta chpt.). Office: Shughart Thomson & Kilroy 12 Wyandotte Plz 120 W 12th St Ste 1500 Kansas City MO 64105-1929

TOLL, ROBERT IRWIN, lawyer, real estate developer; b. Elkins Park, Pa., Dec. 30, 1940; s. Albert A. and Sylvia (Steinberg) T.; m. Norma (div.); children: Laurie, Deborah; m. Jane Snyder; children: Rachel, Jacob; stepson, Joshua Goldfein. AB, Cornell U., 1963; LLB cum laude, U. Pa., 1966. Bar: Pa. 1967. Atty. Wolf, Block Schorr Solis-Cohen, Phila., 1966-67; chmn., chief exec. officer Toll Bros. Inc., Huntingdon Valley, Pa., 1967—. Mem. Mayor's Coun. on Housing in Phila.; mem. bd. overseers U. Pa. Law Sch.; mem. real estate coun. Cornell U. Real Estate Coun. Bd. dirs. Pa. Campaign for Choice, Phila., Beth Sholom Synagogue, Elkins Park, Southeastern chpt. ARC; sponsor Say Yes to Edn., Phila.; mem. bd. trustees Abington Meml. Hosp. Found. Named Profl. Builder of Yr., Builder Mag., 1988. Mem. Nat. Assn. Home Builders, Philmont Country Club (Huntingdon Valley), Equity Lodge 591. Avocations: racing j/35 sailboats, tennis, skiing. Office: Toll Brothers Inc 3103 Philmont Ave Huntingdon Valley PA 19006-4298

TOLL, SHELDON SAMUEL, lawyer; b. Phila., June 6, 1940; s. Herman and Rose (Ornstein) T.; m. Roberta Darlene Pollack, Aug. 11, 1968; children: Candice Moore, John Maitland, Kevin Scott. Bar: Pa. 1967, Mich. 1972, Ill. 1990, Tex. 1990, U.S. Dist. Ct. (ea. dist.) Pa. 1968, U.S. Ct. Appeals (3d cir.) 1970, U.S. Supreme Ct. 1971, Mich. 1972, U.S. Dist. Ct. (ea. dist.), U.S. Ct. Appeals (6th cir.) 1973, U.S. Ct. Appeals (5th cir.) 1978, U.S. Dist. Ct. (no. dist.) Calif. 1986, U.S. Ct. Appeals (9th cir.) 1987, U.S. Dist. Ct. (ea. dist.) Wis. 1989. Assoc. Montgomery, McCracken et al, Phila., 1967-72; sr. ptnr. Honigman Miller Schwartz and Cohn, Detroit, 1972—2003; prin. Sheldon S. Toll PLLC, Southfield, Mich., 2003—. Panelist Bankruptcy Litigation Inst., N.Y.C., 1984-94. Author: Toll's Pennsylvania Crime Code, 2003, Bankruptcy Litigation Manual, 1988. Bd. dirs. Southeastern Mich. chpt. ARC, Detroit. Mem. Fed. Bar Assn. (past pres. Detroit chpt.), ABA, Pa. Bar Assn., Phila. Bar Assn., Detroit Bar Assn., Franklin (Mich.) Hills Country Club, Phi Beta Kappa. Democrat. Jewish. Office: Sheldon S Toll PLLC 2000 Town Ctr Ste 2550 Southfield MI 48075 Business E-Mail: lawtoll@comcast.net.

TOLLE, GORDON J. political science educator; b. South Bend, Ind., Dec. 1, 1942; s. Wilmer H. and L. Jeannette Tolle; m. Mary Louise Crow, Aug. 6, 1977; children: Jay E., Steven. AB, Oberlin Coll., 1965; MA in Govt., U. Notre Dame, 1967; PhD in Polit. Sci., U. Colo. Instr. S.Dak. State U., Brookings, 1967—71, 1973—75, asst. prof., 1975—79, assoc. prof., 1979—84, prof. polit. sci., 1984—87, 1988—; prof. Ariz. State U., Tempe, 1987—88. Bd. dirs. Upper Midwest Honors Coun., 1977—81, 1982—85; coord. European Studies Program, Brookings, 1981—. Author: Human Nature Under Fire: The Political Philosophy of Hannah Arendt, 1982; contbr. articles, book revs. to profl. publs. Recipient Merit Tchg. award, Regents of SD, 1985. Mem.: L.Am. Studies Assn., Am. Polit. Sci. Assn. Avocations: biking, euphonium. Office: SDak State U Polit Sci Dept Scobey Hall Box 504 Brookings SD 57007

TOLLE, MELINDA EDITH, engineer, scientist; b. N.Y., Aug. 8, 1964; d. Robert Dale and Mildred Elva Tolle. BS in Physics, BS in Geophysics, U. Utah, 1986, MS in Mech. Engring., 1988. Cert. quality engr. Am. Soc. for Quality; cert. quality mgr. Am. Soc. for Quality. Engr. assoc. Thiokol, Brigham City, Utah, 1987-88, sr. engr. assoc., 1988-90, engr., 1990-92, sr. scientist, sr. engr., 1992-98, prin. scientist, prin. engr., 1998-2000; sr. prin. scientist, sr. prin. engr. Alcoa, Brigham City, Utah, 2000—. Adj. instr. Weber State U., Ogden, Utah, 1996—. Mem. AIAA (regional dep. dir. Meb 2000—, Utah sect. chair-elect 1998-99, chair 1999—), Am. Soc. for Quality (sect. chair 1997-98, mem. chair 1995-96, vice chair 1996-97, strategic mgmt. plan chair 2000—), Am. Nuc. Soc., Utah Engring. Coun. (bd. dirs. 1998—), Alpha Nu Sigma (pres. 1988). Office: Thiokol PO Box 707 Brigham City UT 84302-0707

TOLLE, SUSAN W. internist, educator, educational administrator; b. Nov. 21, 1951; BS, Lewis & Clark Coll., Portland, Oreg., 1973; MD, Oreg. Health Sci. U., 1977. Chief resident U. Calif., San Diego, 1977-81; gen. internal medicine faculty Oreg. Health Sci. U., Portland, 1981—, dir. Ctr. for Ethics in Health Care, 1989—. Fellow in Ethics U. Chgo., 1988—89. Contbr. articles to profl. jours. Mem. Task Force to Improve the Care of Terminally Ill Oregonians. Office: Ethics in Health Care Ctr Oreg Hlth Sci U 3181 SW Sam Jackson Park Rd UHN 86 Portland OR 97239-3098

TOLLEFSON, BEN C. state legislator, retired utility sales manager; b. Minot, N.D., June 14, 1927; s. Ben K. and Hannah G. (Espeseth) T.; m. Lila R. Adams, Apr. 11, 1949; children: Robb, LuAnn, David, Richard. Student, Minot State U., 1946-48. Advt. salesman Minot Daily News, 1956-57; utility salesman No. States Power Co., Minot, 1957-72, sales mgr., 1972-89; retired, 1989; advisor Ctrl. Venture Capital, Minot, 1990-95; mem. N.D. Ho. of Reps., Bismark, 1984-99, N.D. Senate from 38th dist., Bismark, 2001—. Pres. Minot Jaycees, 1957. Served with USN, 1945-47. Recipient Clara Barton Svc. award Am. Red Cross, 1969; named one of Outstanding Young Men Am., Minot Jaycees, 1958, State Ofcl. Yr., Nat. Assn. Home Builders, 1992. Mem. Kiwanis (Minot lt. gov. 1973, Outstanding Lt. Gov. 1973), Elks. Republican. Lutheran. Avocations: hunting, public speaking. Home: 500 Twenty Fourth St NW Minot ND 58701

TOLLEFSON, LEE, architect; BArch, U. Minn.; MArch, U. Pa. Adj. prof. U. Minn., Mpls., 1970—; ptnr. Rafferty, Rafferty, Tollefson Archs., St. Paul, 1983—. Fellow: AIA. Office: CALA Ralph Rapson Hall 89 Church St SE Minneapolis MN 55455

TOLLENAERE, LAWRENCE ROBERT, retired industrial products company executive; b. Berwyn, Ill., Nov. 19, 1922; s. Cyrille and Modesta (Van Damme) T.; m. Mary Elizabeth Hansen, Aug. 14, 1948; children: Elizabeth, Homer, Stephanie, Caswell, Mary Jennifer. BS in Engring., Iowa State U., 1944, MS in Engring., 1949; MBA, U. So. Calif., 1969; LLD (hon.), Claremont Grad. Sch., 1977. Specification engr. Aluminum Co. Am., Vernon, Calif., 1946-47; asst. prof. indsl. engring. Iowa State U., Ames, 1947-50; sales rep. Am. Pipe and Constrn. Co. (now AMERON), South Gate, Calif., 1950-53, spl. rep., 1952-54, 2nd v.p., mgr. Columbian divsn., 1955-57, divsn. v.p., mgr., 1957-63, v.p. concrete pipe ops., 1963-65, pres. corp. hdqrs., 1965-67; pres., CEO Ameron Inc., Monterey Park, Calif., 1967-89, CEO, pres. Pasadena, 1989-93, chmn. bd. dirs., 1989-94, ret., 1994. Trustee The Huntington Library, Art Gallery and Bot. Gardens; emeritus mem. bd. fellows Claremont U. Ctr.; bd. gov.'s Iowa State U. Found. Mem. Newcomen Soc. N.Am., Calif. C. of C. (bd. dirs. 1977-92), Calif. Club (past pres.), Jonathan Club, Bohemian Club, San Francisco Club, Commanderie de Bordeaux Club, L.A. Confrerie des Chevaliers du Tastevin Club, Twilight Club, Lincoln Club, Beavers Club (past pres., hon. dir.), Valley of Montecito Club, Alpha Tau Omega. Republican. Avocations: fishing, hunting, equestrian, stamp collecting/philately. Home: 1400 Milan Ave South Pasadena CA 91030-3930 Office: 2452 E Foothill Blvd Ste 230 Pasadena CA 91107

TOLLES, BRYANT FRANKLIN, JR., history and art history educator; b. Hartford, Conn., Mar. 14, 1939; s. Bryant Franklin and Grace Frances (Ludden) T.; m. Carolyn Coolidge Kimball, Sept. 15, 1962; children: Thayer Coolidge, Bryant Franklin III. BA, Yale U., 1961, MA in Tchg., 1962; PhD, Boston U., 1970. Instr. history King Sch., Stamford, Conn., 1962-63; tchr. history St. George's Sch., Newport, RI, 1963-65; instr., asst. dean Tufts U., Medford, Mass., 1965-71; asst. dir., libr., editor publs. N.H. Hist. Soc., Concord, 1972-74; exec. dir., libr. Essex Inst., Salem, Mass., 1974-84; dir. mus. studies program, prof. history and art history U. Del., Newark, 1984—, chmn. art conservation dept., 1997-2000. Mem. Com. for a New Eng. Bibliography, Inc. Author: New Hampshire Architecture, 1979, Architecture in Salem, 1983, The Grand Resort Hotels of the White Mountains: A Vanishing Architectural Legacy, 1998, Summer Cottages in the White Mountains: The Architecture of Leisure and Recreation, 1870-1930, 2000, Resort Hotels of the Adirondacks: The Architecture of a Summer Paradise, 1840-1940, 2003; editor: Leadership for the Future, 1991; contbr. articles and book revs. to profl. jours. Trustee Mt. Washington Obs., N.H., N.H. Hist. Soc. Ford. Found. fellow Yale U., 1962. Mem. Colonial Soc. Mass., Orgn. Am. Historians, Soc. Archtl. Historians, Soc. Indsl. Archaeology, Am. Assn. Mus., New Eng. Mus. Assn., Mid-Atlantic Mus. Assn., Am. Assn. for State and Local History, Wilmington Rowing Club, Appalachian Mountain Club. Home: 1002 Kent Rd Wilmington DE 19807-2820 Office: U Del Mus Studies Program 301 Old Coll Newark DE 19716 Business E-Mail: bftolles@udel.edu.

TOLLESTRUP, ALVIN VIRGIL, physicist; b. Los Angeles, Mar. 22, 1924; s. Albert Virgil and Maureen (Petersen) T.; m. Alice Hatch, Feb. 26, 1945 (div. Nov. 1970); children: Kristine, Kurt, Eric, Carl; m. Janine Cukay, Oct. 11, 1986. BS, U. Utah, 1944; PhD, Calif. Inst. Tech., 1950. Mem. faculty Calif. Inst. Tech., Pasadena, 1950-77, prof. physics, 1968-77; scientist Fermi Nat. Lab., Batavia, Ill., 1977-93; co-spokesman CDF Collaboration, 1977-93. Co-developer superconducting magnets for Tevatron, Fermi Lab. Served to lt. (j.g.) USN, 1944-46. NSF fellow; Disting. Alumni award Calif. Inst. Tech., 1993. Fellow AAAS, NAS, Am. Phys. Soc. (R.R. Wilson prize 1989, Nat. medal for tech. 1989). Democrat. Office: Fermi Nat Lab PO Box 500 Batavia IL 60510-0500

TOLLEY, AUBREY GRANVILLE, psychiatrist, health facility administrator; b. Lynchburg, Va., Nov. 15, 1924; married. Student, Duke U., 1942—43, U. Va., 1946—48, MD, 1952. Diplomate Am. Bd. Psychiatry and Neurology. Intern St. Elizabeths Hosp., Washington, 1952-53; asst. resident psychiatry U. Va. Hosp., Charlottesville, 1953-54; resident psychiatry VA Hosp., Roanoke, Va., 1955-56; instr. U. N.C. Sch. Medicine, 1956-61, asst. prof., 1961-66, clin. asst. prof. psychiatry, 1966-72, clin. assoc. prof., 1972-76, clin. prof., 1976—; dir. psychotherapy Dorothea Dix Hosp., Raleigh, NC, 1962-67, dir. hosp., 1973-88. Dir. resident tng. John Umstead Hosp., Butner, N.C., 1966-67; dir. profl. tng. and edn. N.C. Dept. Mental Health, Raleigh, 1967-72, asst. dir., 1972-73; prin. investigator USPHS grant, 1957-59; cons. VA Hosp., Fayetteville, N.C., 1957-78; sr. cons., supervising faculty, cmty. psychiatry sect. dept. psychiatry U. N.C. Sch. Medicine, 1971-88; exec. sec. Multiversity Group, 1968-73 Trustee Found. Hope, Raleigh, 1984—. Served with USNR, 1943-46. Fellow Am. Psychiat. Assn. (disting. life; assembly rep. N.C. Dist. br. 1969-82, 86-2000, mem. joint commn. on pub. affairs 1984-87, mem. constl. membership com. 1990-96, mem. commn. on subspecialization 1990-94, Warren Williams award 1987), Am. Coll. Psychiatrists (life); mem. AMA, N.C. Med. Soc., Durham-Orange County Med. Soc., N.C. Psychiat. Assn. (pres. 1984-85, Lifetime Disting. Svc. award 1999), N.C. Hosp. Assn. (life), George C. Ham Soc. (Disting. Alumni award 1992). Home and Office: 110 Laurel Hill Rd Chapel Hill NC 27514-4323

TOLLEY, EDWARD DONALD, lawyer; b. San Antonio, Jan. 31, 1950; s. Lyle Oren and Mary Theresa Tolley; m. Beth Dekle Tolley; 1 child, Edward Spencer. BBA, U. Ga., 1971, MBA, 1974, JD, 1975. Bar: Ga. 1975, U.S. Dist. Ct. (5th cir.) 1976, U.S. Supreme Ct. 1978, U.S. Ct. Appeals (11th cir.) 1981. Ptnr. Cook, Noell, Tolley Bates and Michael and predecessor firms, Athens, Ga., 1975—. Lectr. various colls., univs., civic and profl. groups. Mem. Family Counseling Assn. of Athens, Inc., mem. Gov.'s Commn. on Criminal Sanctions and Correctional Facilities, 1988-90; past bd. dirs. Am. Cancer Soc.; pres. Clarke County Bd. Edn., 1992-93. Recipient award for cmty. svc. Chief Justice Ga. Supreme Ct., 2000. Fellow Ga. Bar Found., Am. Bd. Criminal Lawyers (bd. dirs. 1987, pres. 1996); mem. Fed. Bar Assn. (sec. 1983, treas. 1985, pres. Macon chpt. 1997-98), Ste Bar Ga. (chmn. law office and econ. com., bd. govs. 1985—, formal adv. opinion bd.), Ga. Trial Lawyers (v.p.), Ga. Assn. Criminal Def. Lawyers (pres. 1985, Indigent Def. award 1983, 88), Athens Bar Assn. (past pres.), Am. Judicature Soc., Order of Barristers (Cmty. Svc. award Chief Justice Ga. Supreme Ct., 2000). Office: Cook Noell et al 304 E Washington St Athens GA 30601-2751

TOLLEY, JERRY RUSSELL, university administrator; b. Goldsboro, N.C., Nov. 6, 1942; s. Elva Russell Tolley and Clara (Smith) Tolley-Bunch; m. Joan Morrison, June 8, 1965; children: Jerry R. Jr., Justin Clay. BS, East Carolina U., 1965, MEd, 1966; EdD, U. N.C., Greensboro, 1982; exec. mgmt. courses, Duke U. Tchr., coach Fayetteville (N.C.) Sr. High Sch., 1966; asst. football coach, head track and tennis coach Elon Coll., N.C., 1967-77, head football coach, 1977-81, dir. athletic sholarship fund, 1982, dir. corp. and ann. resources, 1983, coordinator Pride II Capital Campaign, 1984, assoc. dir. devel., 1985, officer corp. and major gifts, maj. gifts officer, 1999, dir. ann. giving, 2003; asst. v.p. tng., nat. dir. tng. & pub. affairs Lab. Corp. of Am., Burlington, N.C., 1986—. Author: Intercollegiate History of Athletics and Elon College, 1982, American Football Coaches Guidebook to Championship Football Drills, 1985, 101 Winning Football Drills -From the Legends of the Game, 2003; co-author: 101 Winning Plays, 1977, Leadership Education: A Source Book, 1989; contbr. articles. Treas. Town of Elon Coll., 1984-87, mayor protem, 1988, mayor, 1990-98, mayor emeritus, 1998—, chmn. recreation commn.; convenor City County Govt. Assn., 1987-98, Alamance County, N.C., 1986—; mem. exec. bd. dirs. Cherokee Coun. Boy Scouts Am., 1986, Thomas E. Powell Jr. Biology Found., Alamance Found.; exec. bd. N.C. Health & Fitness Found.; visitors Elon Coll.; mem. exec. com. Alamance County Ptnrs. in Edn.; bd. govs. 2 Those Who Care; dir. Alamance Edn. Alliance; bd. dirs. Cmty. Found. Greensboro; chmn. Citizens for Schs.; mktg. advisory com. Village of Brookwood; bd. advisors Morris Plan Bank. Named one of Outstanding Young Men Am., 1980, Internat. Men of Achievement, 1990, Cmty. Leaders Am., 1990, Mayors Hall of Fame, 1995; recipient Dwight D. Eisenhower award Nat. Football Hall of Fame, 1980, 81, Nat. Collegiate Football Championship award Eastman Kodak, Meritorious Svc. award Tom Sawyer-Huck Finn Tennis Classic, 1986, Order of the Long Leaf Pine, 1997, Laurel Wreath award State of N.C., 2002; named Nat. Football Coach of Yr., Nat. Assn. Intercollegiate Athletics, 1980, Elon Coll. Sports Hall of Fame, East Carolina U. Athletic Hall of Fame, 1991. Mem.: All-Am. Football Found. (Lifetime Achievement award 2003), Coun. Advancement of Edn., Am. Football Coaches Assn. (life Lifetime award 2003), Omicron Delta Kappa, Phi Delta Kappa. Avocations: writing, racquet sports, jogging. Home: Box 463 1322 Westbrook Ave Elon NC 27244-9358 Office: Elon Univ 2600 Campus Box # 2600 Elon NC 27244-2010

TOLLINCHE, CHARLES R. physician; b. Bayamon, P.R., Aug. 16, 1942; s. Felix and Beba (Portell) T.; m. Maria Pilar Bartolomé; children: Maria, Charles, Luis, Evelyn, Felix. BA, Inter.-Am. U., San German, P.R., 1963; MD, U. Zaragoza, Spain, 1972. Diplomate Am. Bd. Surgery. Intern Mayaguez Med. Ctr., 1972-73, resident in gen. surgery, 1973-74, San Juan Mcpl. Hosp., 1974-77; chief surg. svcs. 4th Med. Group Seymour Johnson AFB, N.C., 1995—; mem. staff St. Mary's Hosp., Hoboken, NJ, 2002—. Served to col. USAF, 1979—2002. Fellow: ACS; mem.: Am. Soc. Gen. Surgeons, KC. E-mail: espana@optonline.net.

TOLLISON, JOSEPH W. family practice physician; Pres. Am. Bd. Family Practice, Lexington, Ky., 1997, dep. exec. dir., 1999—. Office: Am Bd Family Practice 2228 Young Dr Lexington KY 40505-4219

TOLLIVER, DOROTHY, librarian; b. N.Y.C., Apr. 10, 1937; d. Morris and Rose (Poliner) Lamm; m. Robert F. Tolliver, Sept. 3, 1956; children: Craig Lee, Marc Alan. BA, Ind. U., 1958; MSLS, U. Ill., Champaign-Urbana, 1973. Inter-libr., reference libr. L.A. County Libr., 1958-59; dir. libr. Temple City (Calif.) Pub. Libr., 1959-60; reference, young adult libr. Burbank (Calif.) Pub. Libr., 1960-62; PTA libr. Roselawn Elem. Sch., Danville, Ill., 1970-72; reference libr. Danville Area C.C., 1970—72, head libr., 1973—88; libr. dir. Kahului Pub. Libr., 1988—89; head libr. UH Maui C.C., Kahului, 1989—. Cons. Ill. Office Edn., 1980-88, Hawaii Dept. Edn., 1992—. Mem. Commn. Status of Women, 1992—98; sec. Maui County Com. Status of Women, 1991—96; dir. Jewish Arts and Edn. Coun. Maui, 1996—99; mem. Hawaii Book Acad., judge Ka Pala Pala Po'okela awards, 2002—; chair Maui County Women's Conf., 1993; vice chair Maui County Commn. Persons with Disabilities, 1996—2001; pres. S&M Katz Jewish Libr. of Maui, 1996—. Hawaii Ctr. for the Book, 2002—; bd. dirs. Congregation Gan Eden, 1990—, pres., 1991—95; bd. dirs. Congregation Israel, pres., 1983—87; bd. dirs. Maui Cmty. Theater, 1997—; actor, dir. Voices on the Wind Readers' Theater, 1992—. Recipient Little Red Schoolhouse award Danville Schs. Citizens Com., 1972, Hawaii State award for leadership in promoting postive soc. change, edu. and womens equity, 1997. Mem.: AAUW (pres. Maui chpt. 1993—97, state bd. dirs. 1993, Hawaii State award), ALA, Am. Coll. and Rsch. Librs., Maui County Libr. Assn. (pres. 1990—96), Hawaii Libr. Assn. (bd. dirs.), Phi Beta Mu (alpha chpt.). Jewish. Avocations: reading, theater, travel. Office: Maui Community Coll 310 W Kaahumanu Ave Kahului HI 96732-1617 Office Phone: 808-984-3583. E-mail: tolliver@hawaii.edu.

TOLLIVER, ELKIN, JR., judge; b. Phila., Jan. 29, 1950; s. Elkin and Vernetta Tolliver; m. Toni Diane Bennett, Oct. 3, 1998; 1 child, Nia B. BA in Polit. Sci., Dickinson Coll., 1970; JD, Villanova U., 1976; LLM in Trial Advocacy, Temple U., 1994. Bar: Pa. 1976, U.S. Dist. Ct. (ea. dist.) Pa. Atty. Broujos & Andrews, Carlisle, Pa., 1976—78, U.S. Dept. HEW, Office Gen. Counsel, Phila., 1978—82, U.S. Dept. Edn., Office Civil Rights, 1982—85; trial atty. Pub. Defender Assn. Phila., 1985—88, State Workers' Ins. Fund, 1988—90, Rubinate Jacobs & Saba, 1990—2000; dist. justice Pa. Judiciary, Delaware County, 2000—. Pre-law advisor and prof. Lincoln U., Oxford, Pa., 2000—04. Co-author: (legal digest) Digest & Index of Court Cases of the Pennsylvania State Civil Service Commission, 1975. Office: 821 Baltimore Pike East Lansdowne PA 19050 E-mail: elkin.tolliverjr@verizon.net.

TOLLIVER, GLENDA REEDER, social worker; b. Tyler, Tex., May 12, 1949; d. Nathaniel and Jessie Mae Reeder; m. Cletis Frank Tolliver, Feb. 23, 1985; 1 stepchild, Cletis K. Student in psychology, Tyler Jr. Coll., 1967—69, Tex. So. U., 1969—71, student in psychology, 1975—77. LCSW. Day care counselor Neighborhood Ctr., Inc., Houston, 1973—77; child protective svc. specialist Tex. Dept. Protective and Regulatory Svcs., Houston, 1977—99, supr., child protective svcs., 1999—. Adv. mem. 5th Ward Enrichment Program, Houston, 1992. Mem.: NAACP, Nat. Black Child Devel., Inc. (pub. rels. 1981—, Pres. award, Houston chpt. 1994), Nat. Coun. Negro Women (v.p. Houston chpt. 1982—83), Toastmasters (pin), Gamma Phi Delta (pres. 1985—91). Avocations: sign language, writing poetry and novellas, piano, reading, studying cultures.

TOLLIVER, LISA MARIE, management consultant; AB, Harvard U.; MBA, Columbia U., N.Y.C., 1990; postgrad., Columbia U. Registered arbitrator NASD, 2001, cert. def. contr. US Dept. of Def., homeland security safety. Mgmt. cons. legal dept. AT&T, NYC, 1982—83; mgmt. trainee - regulatory/revenue matters New Eng. Tel. and Telegraph, Boston, 1983—84; asst. staff mgr. regulatory/revenue matters New Eng. Tel. and Tel., Boston, 1984—85; mgr. mktg. and regulatory NYNEX Svc. Co., White Plains, NY, 1985—87; talk show host, prodr. Whitney Radio WVOX, New Rochelle, NY, 2000—; staff mgr. corp. planning NYNEX Svc. Co., White Plains, NY, 1987—88, staff dir. corp. planning, 1988—90; assoc. dir. mktg. and planning for large bus. mkts. NYNEX Telesector Resources Group, White Plains, 1990—92; dir. bus. planning Taco Bell Hdqs. PepsiCO, Irvine, Calif., 1992—93; mgmt. cons. Mitchell Madison Group, N.Y.C., NY, 1997—98; prin. 360 Meridian, LLC, Scarsdale, NY, 1995—. Vol. rschr. of post traumatic stress disorder in WTC bombing victims and hiv/aids patients Anxiety Disorders Clinic, Dept. of Psychiatry at NY Hosp.-Cornell Med. Ctr., NYC, 1993; adj. prof. CUNY Hunter Coll., NYC, 2002—; prof. Met. Coll. NY Sch. for Bus., NYC, 2003—; lectr. in field. Contbr. articles, poetry to profl. jours. Mentor Westchester Enterprise Devel. Program, White Plains, NY, 2000—; exec. advisor and instr. Jr. Achievement, Boston, 1983—85; founder Women's Lit. Guild and Self-Empowerment Group of So. Calif., Irvine and L.A., 1992—93; vol. Silicon Alley Cares, NYC, 2001—03; active Minority Bus. Relief Task Force, Bklyn., 2001—02; co-founder, study group host CoachVille, 2003—; ofcl. ptnr. vets. history project Libr. of Congress, 2003—; pub. rels. and media com. Grace Bapt. Ch., Mount Vernon, NY, 2000—01; vol. radio host, bus. counselor and instr. SCORE Chpt. 306, White Plains, 2000—03; entrepreneur African Am. Leadership Forum, White Plains, 2000—03; bus. mem. Nat. Health and Safety Coun., White Plains, 2000—; co-founder NYNEX Assn. Mgmt. Women, White Plains, 1983—85, Tng. Com. of NYNEX Minority Mgmt. Assn.; pub. rels. com. Westchester Assn. of Women Bus. Owners, White Plains, NY, 2001—03; adv. coun. mem. Nassau Educators Fed. Credit Union, Valley Stream, NY, 2001—04; bd. dirs. Boys and Girls Club, Mt. Vernon, 2004—; entrepreneur mem. Interracial Women's Leadership Round Table, White Plains; open book com. PEN Am. Ctr., N.Y.C.; grad. sch. rep. to Columbia APA, Washington, 1994—2003; entrepreneur com. Nat. Black MBA Assn. Westchester/Greater Conn., White Plains, 2001—02. Recipient Svc. award, Nat. Assn. of Minority Contrs. and Turner Constrn., 2001, SCORE Success Story, SCORE, 2001; scholar Coleman scholar, US Assn. of Small Bus. Enterprise, 2002—03, Minority Student and Gen. scholar, Columbia Tchrs. Coll., 1994, NYNEX Corp. scholar, 1988—90. Mem.: Orgn. of Women in Trade, Orgn. Devel. Network, N.Y.New Media Assn., Nat. Writers Union, Inst. for Supply Mgmt., Internat. Webmasters Assn. - HTML Writers Guild, Assn. of Black Psychologists, Womens Sports Found., Columbia Women Bus. Owners, U.S. Assn. of Small Bus. and Entrepreneurship, Silicon Alley Entrepreneurs Club, Acad. of Mgmt., Tel. Co. Pioneers (life), Nat. Brotherhood of Skiers, Black Ivy, Nat. Assn. of Black Scuba Divers, Aquatic Voyagers Scuba Club, Columbia Bus. Sch. Alumni Club, Assoc. African Am. Harvard Alumni. Avocations: downhill skiing, scuba diving, sailing, art, travel. Office: 360 Meridian LLC 648 Central Park Ave #405 Scarsdale NY 10583-2512

TOLMIE, KENNETH DONALD, artist, author; b. Halifax, N.S., Can., Sept. 18, 1941; s. Archibald and Mary Evelyn (Murray) T.; m. Ruth MacKenzie, Aug. 11, 1962; children: Sarah Katherine, Jane Marianna. B.F.A., Mt. Allison U., 1962. Owner Tolmie Film Prodns., Kendog Films, Tolmie Gallery, Toronto. Chmn. Visual Arts Ottawa, 1975-76; founding mem. Bridgetown and Area Hist. Soc., James House Mus. Author: (children's book) Tale of an Egg, 1974, (art book) A Rural Life: An Artist's Portrait, 1986; 3 TV documentary films produced on his work by CBC and by TV-Ont., producer, Tolmie films prodn. in assn. with CBC, 2002 (aired nat. on CBCTV, 2002); one-man shows include Dorothy Cameron Gallery, Toronto, 1963, Beckett Gallery, Hamilton, 1986, Kaspar Gallery, Toronto, 1988; Mt. Allison Univ. solo cross Can. touring exbn. Bridgetown Series, 1982-84; group shows include Banfer Gallery, N.Y.C., 1963, Nat. Gallery Can., Watercolors Prints and Drawing, 1964, 66, London Art Mus., Ont., 1966, Can. Soc. Graphic Art, 1973, Art Gallery N.S., 1980, 81, N.S. Art Bank, 1981; represented in permanent collections Nat. Gallery Can., Ottawa, Montreal Mus. Fine Arts, N.S. Art Bank, Art Gallery N.S., Confedn. Centre for Arts, Hirshhorn Collection, Washington, Owens Art Gallery, Mt. Allison U., Dofasco Ltd., Husky Oil Ltd., Procter & Gamble Ltd., Slater Steels Ltd., Crownx Ltd., Moving Products, Inc. Bd. dirs. Art Gallery N.S., 1979-81. Recipient prodn. grant Nova Scotia Film Devel. Corp., 1999. Mem. Visual Arts N.S., Visual Arts Ont., Visual Arts Ottawa (chmn. 1975-76), Bridgetown Hist. Soc. (hon. life) Address: 39 Kenneth Ave Toronto ON Canada M6R 2J2 E-mail: ken@kentolmie.com.

TOLO, VERNON THORPE, orthopedist, educator; b. Onawa, Iowa; MD, Johns Hopkins U., 1968. Diplomate Am. Bd. Orthopaedic Surgery. Intern Johns Hopkins Hosp., Balt., 1969—70, resident orthop. surgery, 1972—75; fellow pediat. orthop. Hosp. Sick Children, Toronto, Canada, 1975—76; asst. prof. Johns Hopkins U. Sch. Medicine, Balt., 1976—82, assoc. prof., 1982—87; prof. U. So. Calif., L.A., 1987—. Attending physician Johns Hopkins Hosp., Balt., 1976—87, Children's Hosp., L.A., 1987—. Mem.: Scoliosis Rsch. Soc., Pediat. Orthopedics Soc., Am. Acad. Pediatricians, Am. Orthop. Assn., Am. Acad. Orthop. Surgeons (1st v.p. 2001—02, pres. 2002—03). Office: Children's Hosp 4650 W Sunset Blvd Los Angeles CA 90027-6062

TOLON, MICHAEL ODED, music educator, director; b. Midway City - Tinker AFB, Okla., Jan. 30, 1958; s. Oded and Mattie Loren Tolon; m. Joni Beth - Hamilton Tolon, Apr. 9, 1983; children: Cathryn Marye, Elizabeth Ashley, Joel David Michael, Rachel Ruth. BA, Columbia Christian Coll.; MSc in Music Edn., Portland (Oreg.) State U., 1988. Cert. tchr. Tchr. Standards and Practices, Oreg., 1989. Dir. of bands Marshall H.S., 1989—93, Tigard (Oreg.) HS, 1993—98, Parkrose HS, Portland, Oreg., 1998—. Adj. instr. Cascade Coll., Portland, 1997—. Musician: (band) Jazz Express. Ch. leader Metro Ch. of Christ, Gresham, Oreg., 1992—2002. Grantee, Guitar Workshops Ltd., 2001. Mem.: Oreg. Music Educator Assn. (assoc.). Republican. Avocations: church work, camping, fishing. Home: 3505 Southwest Victoria Place Gresham OR 97080 Office: Parkrose High School 12003 NE Shaver Street Portland OR 97220 Office Phone: 503-408-2605. Personal E-mail: michael_tolon@parkrose.k12.or.us. E-mail: mitolon@yahoo.com.

TOLOR, ALEXANDER, psychologist, educator; b. Vienna, Oct. 21, 1928; s. Stanley and Josephine (Kellner) T.; m. Belle Simon, Sept. 2, 1951; children: Karen Beth, Lori Ann, Diana Susan. BA, NYU, 1949, MA, 1950, PhD, 1954. Diplomate Am. Bd. Profl. Psychologists. Grad. asst. NYU, 1950-52; intern Neurol. Inst., N.Y.C., 1952-53, clin. psychologist, 1953-55; sr. clin. psychologist Inst. of Living, Hartford, Conn., 1957-59; dir. psychol. services Fairfield Hills Hosp., Newtown, Conn., 1959-64; clinic dir. Kennedy Center, Bridgeport, Conn., 1964-65; dir. Inst. Human Devel., Fairfield U., 1965-77, assoc. prof. psychology, 1965-68, research prof. psychology, 1968-75, prof. psychology, 1975-89, dir. school psychology div., 1975-77, dir. sch. and applied psychology program, 1982-86, prof. emeritus, 1989—; practice psychology Danbury, Conn., 1960-96; clin. instr. psychology Yale U., 1963-67. Cons. West Haven VA Hosp., 1962-66, Bridgeport Bd. Edn., Silver Hill Found., 1972-75, Fairfield Hills Hosp., 1973-94, Hallbrooke Hosp., 1975-92. Author: (with H.C. Schulberg) An Evaluation of the Bender-Gestalt Test, 1963, (with G.G. Brannigan) Research and Clinical Applications of the Bender-Gestalt Test, 1980, (with M. Deignan) Adjustment Problems in Children, 1984; editor: Effective Interviewing, 1985; adv. editor Jour. Cons. and Clin. Psychology; cons. editor Personality: An Internat. Jour.; contbr. articles to profl. jours. Served to 1st lt. USAF, 1955-57. Fellow Am. Psychol. Assn., Soc. Personality Assessment, Conn. Psychol. Assn. (mem. council 1964, pres. 1984); mem. Eastern Psychol. Assn., Psi Chi, Delta Phi Alpha, Beta Lambda Sigma, Phi Delta Kappa Home: 6 Brittania Dr Danbury CT 06811-2606 E-mail: atbt51@aol.com.

TOLOSA, GUSTAVO ALBERTO, music educator; arrived in U.S., 1987; s. Luis Benito and Maria Raquel Tolosa; m. Diana Lynne Ellis, Dec. 17, 1988; children: Elena Raquel, Julia Elizabeth, Stefan Ellis. BA, Abilene Christian U., 1990; MusM, U. Redlands, 1993; MusD in Piaho, Eastman Sch. Music, 1997. Tchg. asst. Eastman Sch. Music, Rochester, NY, 1993—96; dir. piano studies Abilene Christian U., 1996—. Musician: (piano recital) Inter-Disciplinary Recital: Music and Art. Scholar, Eastman Sch. Music, 1993—96. Mem.: Music Tchrs. Nat. Assn. Church Of Christ. Achievements include development of an inter-disciplinary series of concerts; specialist in 20th century music and Argentine music. Avocations: travel, business. Office: Abilene Christian Univ ACU Box 28274 Abilene TX 79699-8274

TOLSTEDT, CARRIE L. bank executive; BS in Bus. Adminstrn., U. Nebr.; degree in Banking, U. Wash. From credit tng. program to corp. banking officer United Bank Denver, corp. banking officer; from v.p. corp. banking to sr. v.p. downtown Omaha (Nebr.) retail banking Norwest Bank Nebr., Omaha, 1986—95; sr. v.p. corp. retail FirstMerit Corp., Akron, Ohio, 1995—96, pres., CEO Citizens Nat. Bank and Peoples Nat. Bank, 1996—98, exec. v.p., 1996—98; with Norwest Corp., 1998; regional pres. Ctrl. Calif. Wells Fargo & Co., San Francisco, 1998—2001, exec. v.p. regional banking, 2001—. Bd. dirs. The Cmty. Coll. Found. Mem.: Consumer Bankers Assn. (bd. dirs.), U. Nebr. Alumni Assn. (bd. dirs.), Calif. C. of C. (bd. dirs.). Office: Wells Fargo & Co 420 Montgomery St San Francisco CA 94163

TOLU, TOLU, foundation administrator; b. Washington; BBA, BS in Bus. Mgmt. Radiation Therapy Tech., Howard U. Lic. real estate broker; former lic. ins. broker, gen. agent. Fin. planner, life ins. broker, agt. recruiter and trainer EWW Fin. Svcs., 1977-86; br. mgr. Medox Health Care Svcs., 1982-83; founder, exec. dir. Tolu Found., 1986—; pres., broker EWW Real Estate, Inc., 1990-96. Pub. spkr. in field, 2001—. Author: Why and How Women Are Exploited By Men Worldwide, 1999. Mem. Internat. Toastmistress. Avocations: body building, anthropology, world politics, travel, gender bias issues. Home: PO Box 48331 Washington DC 20002-0331 E-mail: tolu2@aol.com.

TOLUIE, KAMRAN, cardiologist, physiologist; b. Tehran, Iran, June 29, 1961; arrived in U.S., 1991; s. Kiumars Toluie and Shahin Noor Bakhsh; m. Fereshteh Salim Shahshahani, June 14, 1990; children: Sherwin, Ava. MD, Tabriz (Iran) U., 1986. Diplomate Am. Bd. Internal Medicine, Am. Bd. Cardiovascular Diseases, Am. Bd. Cardiac Electrophysiology. Resident in internal medicine SUNY, Bklyn., 1993-96; cardiology fellow Metrohealth Med. Ctr./Mt. Sinai Med. Ctr., Cleve., 1996-98; electrophysiology fellow Hosp. U. Pa., Phila., 1998-2000; dir. cardiac electrophysiology Kaiser Permanente Med. Ctr., L.A., 2000—. Translator: Introdction to ECG, 1990, Manual of Medical Procedures; contbr. chapters to books, articles to profl. jours. Fellow: ACP, Am. Coll. Cardiology. Achievements include performed first FDA-approved biventricular ICD in a non-clinical site in the U.S; performed first atrial fibrillation ablation under phased array intracardiac echocardiography guidance and 3-D electroanatomical mapping in Iowa; performed first biventricular pacer in Cedar Rapids, Iowa. Avocation: tennis. Home: 18100 Lake Encino Dr Encino CA 91316 Office: Kaiser Permanente LA Med Ctr 4867 Sunset Blvd 6th Fl Los Angeles CA 90027 Office Phone: 323-783-5850. E-mail: ktoluie@pol.net.

TOM, HOWARD S. company executive; b. NYC, June 23, 1952; s. Hall Bing and Yvonne Quan Tom; m. Elena Nieves, Jan. 22, 1994. AB, Columbia U., 1974, MBA, 1976, postgrad.; MSSM, U. So. Calif., 1982; MPM, Keller Grad. Sch. Mgmt., 2004. Cert. LAN. Cost adminstr. AIL div. Eaton Corp., Deer Park, N.Y., 1984-85; fin. cons. Equitable, Citibank, J. Gregory, N.Y.C., 1986-95; tech. cons. Green Star Enterprises, Inc., L.I., 1997; v.p. contracts RK Group, Inc., N.Y.C., 1998; v.p. tech. cons. Concepts in Staffing, N.Y.C., 1999; in bus. devel. franchisexchange.com, 2000-01; account exec. Konica Office Products, Inc., 2001, Salience Assocs. Inc., 2001. Lt. USN, 1976-82. Mem. Project Mgmt. Inst., Columbia Bus. Sch. Alumni Club, Guggenheim Mus., Met. Mus. Art. Republican. Roman Catholic. Avocations: opera, ballet, classical music, modern dance. Home: 229 E 12th St Apt 21 New York NY 10003-9120 Office Phone: 917-532-3892. Personal E-mail: hstom@msn.com.

TOM, JAMES ROBERT, accountant; b. Odessa, Tex., Apr. 21, 1939; s. George Ellison and Mattie Inez (Zimmerman) T.; m. Frances Kay Mackey, Sept. 16, 1961; children: Susan Kay, James Robert Jr., Emily Christian. Student, Tex. A&M U., 1957; BBA in Acctg., Tex. Tech. U., 1961; postgrad., Colo. State U., 1961—62. CPA Tex. Jr. acct. Peat, Marwick, Mitchell & Co., Midland, Tex., 1965; asst. trust officer 1st City Nat. Bank, Midland, 1966-67, v.p., trust officer, 1969-72; sr. acct. Main Hurdman, Midland, 1967-68; pres. Gibson Mfg. Co., Midland, 1972-73; exec. v.p., CEO Teraco, Inc., Midland, 1974-75, fin. cons., 1975-76, acct., 1976—. Bd. dirs. Am. Heart Assn., Midland, 1966, Arthritis Found., Midland, 1971-72, 75, Midland County Livestock Assn., Midland, 1966-72, ARC, Midland, 1970-80, Boys Club, Midland, 1971-72. 1st lt. U.S. Army, 1963-65. Mem. AICPAs, Tex. Soc. CPAs, Permian Basin CPAs. Republican. Roman Catholic. Avocations: fishing, hunting, reading. Home: 3104 Humble Ave Midland TX 79705-8207 Office: 1010 W Texas Ave Midland TX 79701-6170

TOM, LAUREN, actress, singer; b. Chgo., Aug. 4, 1959; d. Chan and Nancy (Dare) T.; m. Glenn Lau-Kee, Oct. 23, 1982. Student, Northwestern U., 1977; BA, NYU. Plays include A Chorus Line, 1978-79, The Music Lessons, 1980, Family Devotions, 1981, Doonesbury, 1983-84, Hurlyburly, 1985, (film) Nothing Lasts Forever, 1982, (TV shows) The Facts of Life, 1982, ABC Afterschool Special, 1984, CBS Afterschool Break, 1984. Supporter Asia Inst., Washington. Mem. Actors' Equity Assn., Screen Actors Guild, AFTRA.

TOM, LAWRENCE, technology executive; b. L.A., Jan. 21, 1950; BS, Harvey Mudd Coll., 1972; JD, Western State U., San Diego, 1978; spl. diploma, U. Calif., San Diego, 1991. Design engr. Rockwell Internat., L.A., 1972-73, Goodrich Corp. (formerly Rohr, Inc.), Chula Vista, Calif., 1973-76, sr. design engr., 1980, computer graphics engring. specialist, 1980-83, chief engring. svcs., 1989-91, chief engring. quality, 1991-93, project mgr., 1993-98, info. tech. specialist, 1998—2002. Sr. engr. Rohr Marine, Inc., Chula Vista, 1977-79; chief exec. officer Computer Aided Tech. Svcs., San Diego, 1983-87; software cons. Small Systems Software, San Diego, 1984-85; computer graphics engring. specialist TOM & ROMAN, San Diego, 1986-88; dir. Computervision Users Group, 1986-88, vice chmn. 1988-91, pres., 1991-93, exec. chmn., 1992-94; bd. dirs. Exec. Program for Scientists and Engrs.-Alumni Assn. U. Calif., San Diego, 1991—; CFO Global Peregrine Users Group, 2001-03; pres. Art to Art, San Diego, 1994-99; pres. SGL Computer Profls., San Diego, 1999—; cons. in field. George H. Mayr Found. scholar, 1971, Bates Found. Aero. Edn. scholar, 1970-72. Mem. Nat. Mgmt. Assn. (chpt. v.p.), Aircraft Owners and Pilots Assn., Infiniti Club. Office: 7770 Regents Rd Ste 113-190 San Diego CA 92122-1967 Office Phone: 619-985-9850. E-mail: larry.tom@sglpro.com.

TOMAIN, JOSEPH PATRICK, dean, law educator; b. Long Branch, N.J., Sept. 3, 1948; s. Joseph Pasquale and Bernice M. (Krzan) T.; m. Kathleen (Corcione), Aug. 1, 1971; children: Joseph Anthony, John Fiore. BA, U. Notre Dame, 1970; JD, George Washington U., 1974. Bar: NJ, Iowa. Assoc. Giordano and Halleran, Middletown, NJ, 1974-76; asst. to prof. law Drake U. Sch. Law, Des Moines, 1976-83; prof. law U. Cin., 1983—, acting dean, 1989-90, dean, 1990—, Nippert prof. law, 1990—. Vis. prof. law, U. Tex., Austin, 1986-87. Author: Energy Law in a Nutshell, 1981, Nuclear Power Transformation, 1987; co-author: Energy Decision Making, 1983, Energy Law and Policy, 1989, Energy and Natural Resources Law, 1992, Regulatory Law and Policy, 1993, 2d edit., 1998, 3rd edit., 2003, Energy, The Environment and the Global Economy, 2000. Trustee Ctr. for Chem. Addictions Treatment, Cin., Vol. Lawyers for Poor, Cin.; mem. steering com. BLAC/CBA Round Table, Cin.; chair Knowledge Works Found. Served in USAR, 1970-76. Mem. ABA, Am. Law Inst., Ohio State Bar Assn. (del.), Cin. Bar Assn. (trustee). Roman Catholic. Home: 3009 Springer Ave Cincinnati OH 45208-2440 Office: U Cin Coll Law Office Dean PO Box 210040 Cincinnati OH 45221-0040 Office Phone: 513-556-0121. E-mail: joseph.tomain@uc.edu.

TOMAINO, JOSEPH CARMINE, former retail executive, former postal inspector; b. Danbury, Conn., Dec. 12, 1948; s. Joseph and Lena Marie (LaCava) T.; m. Eileen M. Pulver (div. Feb. 1978); m. Ann C. Underriner, Sept. 20, 1986; children: Joseph Richard, Robert John. BS, Western Conn. State U., 1970; MBA, Roosevelt U., 1978, MS in Acctg., 1986. Cert. fraud specialist; cert. fraud examiner; diplomate Am. Bd. Law Enforcement, Am. Coll. Forensic Examiners; expert, lic. pvt. investigator, Ill. Post office clk. U.S. Postal Svc., Ridgefield, Conn., 1970-71, postal inspector Chgo., 1971-80, supervisory postal inspector, 1980-93; mgr. we. ops. loss prevention dept. Walgreen Co., Deerfield, Ill., 1993-96; sr. mgr. litigation svcs. Altschuler, Melvoin & Glasser CPAs, 1996-98; dir. litigation svcs. Altschuler, Melvoin & Glasser/Am. Express Co., Chgo., 1999-2000; ptnr. Altschuler, Melvoin & Glasser CPAs, Chgo., 2000—; mng. dir. Am. Express Tax & Bus. Svcs., Chgo., 2000—02; sr. mng. dir. Chgo. region Citigate G.I., Chgo., 2002—. Mem. Am. Soc. Indsl. Security, Fed. Law Enforcement Officers Assn., Nat. Assn. Chiefs Police, Ill. Chiefs Police, Spl. Agts. Assn., Ill. Police Assn., Nat. Soc. Pub. Accts., Assn. Cert. Fraud Examiners, Assn. Cert. Fraud Specialists, Am. Coll. Forensic Examiners, Ill. Soc. CPAs. Office: Citigate GI PO Box 966 Chicago IL 60690-0966

TOMAN, MARY ANN, federal official; b. Pasadena, Calif., Mar. 31, 1954; d. John James and Mary Ann Zajec T.; m. Milton Allen Miller, Sept. 10, 1988; 1 child, Mary Ann III. BA with honors, Stanford U., 1976; MBA, Harvard U., 1981. Mgmt. cons. Bain and Co., Boston, 1976-77; brand mgr. Procter & Gamble Co., Cin., 1977-79; summer assoc. E.F. Hutton, N.Y.C., 1980; head corp. planning The Burton Group, PLC, London, 1981-84; pres., founder Glenclair Ltd., London, 1984-86; pres. London Cons. Group, London, Beverly Hills, Calif., 1987-88; mem. U.S. Presdl. Transition Team, Bus. and Fin., 1988-89; dep. asst. sec. commerce, automotive affairs, consumer goods U.S. Dept. Commerce, Washington, 1989-93; commr., chmn. L.A. Indsl. Devel. Authority, 1993-95; dep. treas. State of Calif., Sacramento, 1995-99. Bd. dirs. U.S. Coun. of Devel. Fin. Agencies, 1994-97. Founder, chair Stanford U. Fundraising, London, 1983-88; chair Reps. Abroad Absentee Voter Registration, London, 1983-88; bd. dirs. Harvard Bus. Sch. Assn., London, 1984-87; vol. Bush-Quayle Campaign, 1988; trustee Bath Coll., Eng., 1988—; apptd. by Gov. Wilson to State of Calif. Econ. Devel. Adv. Coun., 1994-97, Jobs Tng. Coordinating Coun., 1998-2000; first vice chmn. Rep. Party L.A. County, 1996-99; chmn. Republican Party Los Angeles County, 1999—; mem. exec. bd. Coun. Calif. County Chairmen, 1999—; mem. U.S. Presdl. Transition Team, 2000-2001; Rep. candidate for Calif. State Treas., 2002. Named Calif. Mother of Yr., 1997. Mem. Stanford Club U.K. (pres. 1983-88), Harvard Club N.Y., Harvard Club Washington, Nat. Assn. of Urban Rep. County Chmn. Roman Catholic. Home: 604 N Elm Dr Beverly Hills CA 90210-3421 Office: PO Box 71483 Los Angeles CA 90071-0483 Office Phone: 310-274-4822.

TOMAR, RUSSELL HERMAN, pathologist, educator, researcher; b. Phila., Oct. 19, 1937; s. Julius and Ethel (Weinreb) T.; m. Karen J. Kent, Aug. 29, 1965; children: Elizabeth, David. BA in Journalism, George Washington U., 1959, MD, 1963. Diplomate Am. Bd. Pathology, Am. Bd. Allergy and Immunology, Am. Bd. Pathology, Immunopathology. Intern Barnes Hosp., Washington U. Sch. Medicine, 1963-64, resident in medicine, 1964-65; asst. prof. medicine SUNY, Syracuse, 1971-79, assoc. prof., 1979-88, assoc. prof. microbiology, 1980-84, prof., 1984-88, asst. prof. pathology, 1974-76, assoc. prof., 1976-83, prof., 1983-88, dir. immunopathology, 1974-88, attending physician immunodeficiency clinic, 1982-88, acting dir. microbiology, 1977-78, 82-83, interim dir. clin. pathology, 1986-87; prof. pathology and lab. medicine U. Wis. Ctr. for Health Scis., Madison, 1988—2003; dir. div. lab medicine U. Wis., Madison, 1988-95, dir. immunopathology and diagnostic immunology, 1995-98, prof. population health scis., 1999—2003, vis. prof. population health scis., 2003—; chair dept. pathology Stroger Hosp. Cook County, Chgo., 1999—; prof. pathology Rush U., 1999—. Past mem. numerous coms. SUNY, Syracuse, U. Wis., Madison; mem. exec. com., chair and med. cons. AIDS Task Force Cen. N.Y., 1983-88. Assoc. editor Jour. Clin. Lab. Analysis; contbr. articles, rev. to profl. jours. Mem. pub. health com. Onondaga County Med. Soc., 1987-88. Lt. comdr. USPHS, 1965-67. Allergy and Immunology Div. fellow U. Pa. Fellow Coll. Am. Pathologists (diagnostics immunology rsch. com. 1993-2003, stds. com. 1995-97, commn. on clin. pathology 1997-2003), Am. Soc. Clin. Pathology (com. on continuing edn. immunopathology 1985-91, pathology data presentation com. 1976-79), Am. Acad. Allergy (penicillin hypersensitivity com. 1973-77); mem. AAAS, Am. Assn. Immunologists, Am. Assn. Pathology, Acad. Clin. Lab. Physicians and Scientists (com. on rsch. 1979-81, chairperson immunology 1979), Clin. Immunology Soc. (clin. lab. immunology com., chair coun. 1991-96). Office: Stroger Cook County Dept Pathology 1901 W Harrison St Chicago IL 60612 Business E-Mail: russell.tomar@hektoen.org.

TOMAR, WILLIAM, lawyer; b. Camden, N.J., Oct. 10, 1916; s. Morris and Katie (Sadinsky) T.; m. Bette Brown, Nov. 28, 1942; children: Richard T., Dean Jonathon. LLB cum laude, Rutgers U., 1939. Bar: N.J. 1940, U.S. Ct. Appeals (3d cir.) 1953, U.S. Supreme Ct. 1953, Fla. 1975, D.C. 1978. Sr. ptnr. Tomar, O'Brien, Kaplan, Jacobi & Graziano, Haddonfield, N.J., 1958—. Mem. faculty Ctr. Trial and Appellate Advocacy, Hastings Coll. Law, U. Calif., 1971-86, Nat. Coll. Advocacy, Harvard U. Law Sch., 1973-75. Mem. UN Speakers Bur., UNICEF, 1960—; mem. adv. bd. Salvation Army, 1967-84, Inst. Med. Rsch., 1967—, N.J. Capital Punishment Study Commn., 1972-73, Touro Law Sch., 1981; mem. adv. bd. N.J. Student Assistance Bd., 1987-98, vice chmn., 1992-98; bd. dirs. South Jersey Assn. Performing Arts, Haddonfield Symphony Soc., 1985—; bd. dirs., pres. 1992-99; mem. exec. bd. So. N.J. Coun. Boy Scouts Am., 1985—, pres. 1992—, Disting. Citizen award, 2001; vice chmn., mem. bd. trustees Cooper Hosp., Univ. Med. Ctr. 1979-97, bd. mem. emeritus 1998; mem. planning com. World Peace Through Law Ctr., 1970—; trustee Cooper Med. Ctr., 1979—. Recipient Disting. Alumni award Rutgers U. Sch. Law, 1996, Neighbor of Yr. award N.J. chpt. ARC, 1999; honored at Juvenile Diabetes Found. South Jersey ann. gala, 2000. Fellow Am. Coll. Trial Lawyers; mem. ABA, Assn. Trial Lawyers Am. (assoc. editor jour. 1962-68, gov. 1963-64, nat. parliamentarian 1964-70, nat. exec. com. 1964-70, chmn. seminars 1965 lectr. student adv. program 1968—), World Jurist Assn. (founding mem. 1974—), N.J. Bar Assn. (fee arbitration com. 1972-74, 75-77), Trial Lawyers of N.J. (cert. by Supreme Ct. of N.J. as civil trial atty, Trial Bar award 1977), N.J. Workers Compensation Assn. (trustee 1958-83), N.Y. Trial Attys. Assn., Phila. Trial Lawyers Assn., Camden County Bar Found. (bd. trustees 1986—), Camden County Bar Assn., (com. on rels. of bench and bar 1964—, adult edn. com. 1975—). Office: 20 Brace Rd Cherry Hill NJ 08034-2634

TOMASELLI, FRED, artist; b. Santa Monica, Calif., 1956; m. Laura Miller; 1 child. BA in Painting and Drawing, Calif. State U., Fullerton, 1982. One-man shows include Contemporary Arts Ctr., Cin., 1997, White Cube, London, 2001, Alright-Knox Gallery Art, N.Y.C., 2003, James Cohan Gallery, 2003, exhibited in group shows at Whitney Mus. Am. Art, 1997, The Barbican Gallery, London, 2001, Malborough Gallery, N.Y.C., 2003; co-author (with Michael Rush, Amy Cappellazzo): Fred Tomaselli: Ten Year Survey, 2003; co-author: (with Franz Ackerman, Eija-Liisa Ahtila, Dan Graham, John Boc) Parkett #68: Eija-Liisa Ahtila, 2003; co-author: (with Peter Buchanan-Smith and Rick Mooty) The Wilco Book, 2004. Named Invited Exhibitor, Biennial Exhbn., Whitney Mus. Am. Art, N.Y.C., 2004; recipient Art Commn. award for excellence in design, City Hall, N.Y.C., 1993. Home: 424 Humboldt St Brooklyn NY 11211*

TOMASH, ERWIN, retired computer equipment company executive; b. St. Paul, Nov. 17, 1921; s. Noah and Milka (Ehrlich) T.; m. Adelle Ruben, July 31, 1943; children: Judith Sarada Tomash Diffenbaugh, Barbara Ann Tomash Bussa. BS, U. Minn., 1943; MS, U. Md., 1950. Instr. elec. engring. U. Minn., 1946; assoc. dir. computer devel. Univac div. Remington Rand Corp., St. Paul, 1947-51; dir. West Coast ops. Univac div. Sperry Rand Corp., L.A., 1953-55; pres. Telemeter Magnetics, Inc., L.A., 1956-60; v.p. Ampex Corp., L.A., 1961; founder, pres. Dataproducts Corp., L.A., 1962-71, chmn. bd., 1971-80, chmn. exec. com., 1980-89; chmn. bd., dir. Newport Corp., Irvine, Calif., 1982-94. Founder, trustee, dir. Charles Babbage Found., U. Minn.; dir. and nat. gov. Coro Found., L.A. Served to capt. Signal Corps AUS, 1943-46. Decorated Bronze Star; recipient Outstanding Grad. award U. Minn., 1983. Mem. IEEE (sr., computer entrepreneur award 1988), Am. Soc. for Technion, History of Sci. Soc., Soc. for History of Tech., Assn. Internationale du Bibliophile. Home: 3918 Mainsail Pl Los Angeles CA 95073 E-mail: etomash@ieee.org.

TOMASI, DONALD CHARLES, architect; b. Sacramento, Calif., Oct. 24, 1956; s. Thomas M. and Anita (Migliavacca) T.; m. Loretta Elaine Goveia, Feb. 1, 1986; children: Jeffrey, Genna, Michael. AB in Architecture with honors, U. Calif., Berkeley, 1979; MArch, U. Wash., 1982. Registered architect, Calif. Project mgr. Robert Wells and Assocs., Seattle, 1982-84, Milbrandt Architects, Seattle, 1984, T.M. Tomasi Architects, Santa Rosa, Calif., 1984-86; prin. Tomasi Architects, Santa Rosa, 1986-93, sr. prin.; prin. TLCD Architecture, Santa Rosa, 1993—. Grad. Leadership Santa Rosa, 1992; mem. design rev. com. Sonoma County, 1988-90; chmn. Santa Rosa Design Rev. Bd., 1990-97. Recipient Honor award Coalition for Adequate Sch. Housing, 1991, 93, 96, 99, 2000, 02, 04, Merit award, 1991. Mem. AIA (chpt. bd. dirs. 1990-91, 98, v.p. 1999, pres. 2000, Calif. Coun. bd. dirs. 2002-03, Merit award 1986). Avocations: skiing, wine, travel.

TOMASI, THOMAS B. cell biologist, administrator; b. May 24, 1927; s. Thomas B. and Ivis (Ratazzi) T.; m. Barbara Betzold, May 27, 1995; children: Barbara, Theodore, Anne. AB, Dartmouth Coll., Hanover, N.H., 1950; MD, U. Vt., Burlington, 1954; PhD, Rockefeller U., 1965. Intern, resident, chief resident Columbia Presbyn. Hosp., N.Y.C., 1954-58, instr. medicine, 1958-60; prof., chmn. div. exptl. medicine U. Vt., Burlington, 1960-65; prof. medicine, dir. immunology SUNY, Buffalo, 1965-73; prof., chmn. immunology dept. Mayo Med. Sch., Rochester, Minn., 1973-81; dir. Cancer Ctr., Disting. Univ. prof., chmn. dept. cell biology U. N. Mex., Albuquerque, 1981-86; pres., CEO Roswell Park Cancer Inst., Buffalo, 1986-96, chmn. dept. molecular medicine, 1986-97, prof. microbiology, 1997—, prof. immunology, 1997—. Author: The Immune System of Secretions, 1976; contbr. over 200 articles to profl. jours. Served with USN, 1945-46 Mem. Am. Soc. Cell Biology, Am. Assn. Immunologists, Am. Assn. Cancer Research, Am. Soc. Clin. Investigation, Am. Fedn. Clin. Research, Assn. Am. Physicians Roman Catholic. Avocations: skiing, tennis, hunting, fishing, gardening. Office: Roswell Park Cancer Inst Elm And Carlton St Buffalo NY 14263-0001

TOMASKO, EDWARD A. financial planner; b. Stafford Springs, Conn., Sept. 18, 1943; s. Edward A. Sr. and Gertrude Ann (Burr) T.; m. Helen F. Flanagan, Oct. 18, 1969; children: Felicia, Joy. BA, Quinnipac Coll., 1966; MBA, Am. U., 1968. CFP. Direct mktg. & sales Iroquois Brands, Stamford, Conn., 1979-81; owner Tomasko Bus. Cons., Bethel, Conn., 1981-82; v.p. mktg. & consulting Excell Mktg., New Canaan, Conn., 1982; market mgr. Stauffer Chem., Westport, Conn., 1982-85; direct mktg. & sales Folz Vending, L.I., N.Y., 1986; registered rep. Moseley Securities, New Haven, 1987-88, Fahnestock & Co. Inc., Danbury, Conn., 1988-90; prin. Titan Value Equities, Hamden, Conn., 1990—. V.p. bd. govs. Quinnipac Coll.; chmn. pension and ins. commn. Town of Bethel, Conn. Mem. FPA (pres. So. Conn. chpt. 1993-96, chmn. state conf. 1992-93, adv. coun. 1997—). Republican. Avocations: photography, choir singing. Home: 20 Spring Hill Ln Bethel CT 06801-2726 Office: Mut Svc Corp Fin Strategies Investment Advisors Svc LLP 2600 Dixwell Ave Ste 1 Hamden CT 06514-1833 E-mail: edward_a-tomasko@sbcglobal.net.

TOMASKY, SUSAN, corporate officer; b. Morgantown, W.Va., Mar. 29, 1953; m. Ron Ungvarsky; 1 child, Victoria. BA cum laude, Univ. Ky., 1974; JD (hons.), George Washington Univ., 1979. Staff mem. House Com. Interstate and Fgn. Commerce, Washington, 1974—76; with FERC's Office of Gen. Counsel., Washington, 1979—81; assoc. Van Ness, Feldman & Curtin, Washington, 1981—86; ptnr. Van Ness, Feldman & Curtis, Washington, 1986—93; gen. coun. Federal Energy Regulatory Commn., Washington, 1993—97; 1997ptnr. 1998Hogan & Harts, Washington, 1997-98; senior v.p., gen. coun. & Sec. Am. Electric Power Svc. Corp., Columbus, Ohio, 1998—2000, exec. v.p., gen. counsel, sec., 2000—01, exec. v.p., CFO, 2001—. Staff mem. George Washington U. Law Rev., 1979. Trustee Columbus Symphony Orch., Columbus Sch. for Girls; co-chair Keystone Energy Bd. Mem. Greater Columbus C. of C., Phi Beta Kappa.

TOMASSON, HELGI, dancer, choreographer, dance company executive; b. Reykjavik, Iceland, 1942; m. Marlene Rizzo; children: Kristinn, Erik. Student, Sigridur Arman, Erik Bidsted, Vera Volkova, Sch. Am. Ballet, Tivoli Pantomime Theatre, Copenhagen. With Joffrey Ballet, 1961-64; prin. dancer Harkness Ballet, 1964-70, N.Y.C. Ballet, 1970-85; artistic dir. San Francisco Ballet, 1985—, also dir. Dancer debut Tivoli Pantomime Theatre, 1958, A Season of Hell, 1967, Stages and Reflections, 1968, La Favorita, 1969, The Goldberg Variations, 1971, Symphony in Three Movements, 1972, Coppelia, 1974, Dybbuk Variations, 1974, Chansons Madecasses, 1975, Introduction and Allegro, 1975, Allegro, 1975, Union Jack, 1976, Vienna Waltzes, 1977, choreographer Theme and Variations, Polonaise, Op. 65, 1982, Ballet d'Isoline, 1983, Menuetto, N.Y.C. Ballet, 1984, Beads of Memory, 1985, Swan Lake, 1988, Handel-a Celebration, 1989, Sleeping Beauty, 1990, Romeo and Juliet, 1994. Decorated Knight Order of Falcon Iceland, Comdr. Order of Falcon; recipient Silver medal, Internat. Moscow Ballet Competition, 1969, Golden Plate award, Am. Acad. Achievement, 1992, Dance Mag. award, 1992. Office: c/o San Francisco Ballet 455 Franklin St San Francisco CA 94102-4438

TOMASULO, VIRGINIA MERRILLS, retired lawyer; b. Belleville, Ill., Feb. 10, 1919; d. Frederick Emerson and Mary Eckert (Turner) Merrills; m. Nicholas Angelo Tomasulo, Sept. 30, 1952 (dec. May 3, 1986); m. Harrison I. Anthes, Mar. 5, 1988. BA, Wellesley Coll., 1940; LLB (now JD), Washington U., St. Louis, 1943. Bar: Mo. 1942, U.S. Ct. Appeals (D.C. cir.) 1958, Mich. 1974, U.S. Dist. Ct. (ea. dist) Mo. 1943, U.S. Supreme Ct. 1954, U.S. Tax Ct. 1974, U.S. Ct. Appeals (6th cir.) 1976. Atty. Dept. of Agr., St. Louis and Washington, 1943-48; Office of Solicitor, Chief Counsel's Office IRS, Washington and Detroit, 1949-75; assoc. Baker & Hostetler, Washington, 1977-82, ptnr., 1982-89, of counsel, 1989, ret., 1989. Sec. S.W. Day Care Assn., Washington, 1971—73; state bd. mem., dir. region IV Fla. Life Care Residents Assn., 2002—04; mem. adv. bd. Brede-Wilkins Scholarship Found., 2002—. Mem.: FBA, ABA, Mo. Bar, Village on the Green Residents Assn. (mem. coun. 1998—2000, chair health care com. 1999—2001, mem. fin. com., chair fin. com. 2004—), Wellesley Club (Ctrl. Fla.). Episcopalian. Home: 570 Village Pl Apt 300 Longwood FL 32779-6037

TOMASZEWSKI, RICHARD PAUL, market representation executive; b. Flushing, NY, Jan. 8, 1958; s. Francis Richard and Agatha Jean (Corsaro) T.; m. Joann L. Turone, Aug. 2, 1980; children: Elizabeth Jean, Annamaria Concetta. BA in Econs. and polit. sci. cum laude, Union Coll., Schenectady, N.Y., 1980; MBA in Mktg., Fin., Syracuse U., 1982. Grad. asst. Syracuse (N.Y.) U., 1981; field ops. analyst Ford Motor Co., Charlotte, N.C., 1982-83, zone mgr., 1983-93, mkt. representation specialist Atlanta, 1993-98, nat. employee involvement rep. Atlanta region, 1994-98, mkt. representation mgr., 1998—. Mem. Ford Motor Co. Polit. Action Com., Atlanta, 1993, Cmty. Rels. Com., 1999-2002. Tidmarsh scholar Union Coll., Schenectady, 1977; co-recipient Total Market Representation award, 1997, 99-2003. Mem. Union Coll. Alumni Assn., Syracuse U. Alumni Assn., U.S. Tennis Assn., Atlanta Lawn Tennis Assn., Omicron Delta Epsilon, Alpha Mu Alpha. Republican. Roman Catholic. Avocations: tennis, swimming, chess, walking. Office: Ford Motor Co 1455 Lincoln Pkwy E Ste 530 Atlanta GA 30346-2288 E-mail: rtomasze@ford.com.

TOMAZI, GEORGE DONALD, retired electrical engineer; b. St. Louis, Dec. 27, 1935; s. George and Sophia (Bogovich) T.; m. Lois Marie Partenheimer, Feb. 1, 1958; children: Keith, Kent. BSEE, U. Mo., Rolla, 1958, Profl. EE (hon.), 1970; MBA, St. Louis U., 1965, MSEE, 1971. Registered profl. engr., Mo., Ill., Wash., Ohio, Calif. Project engr. Union Electric Co., 1958-66; dir. corp. planning Gen. Steel Industries, 1966-70; exec. v.p. St. Louis Research Council, 1970-74, Hercules Constrn. Co., St. Louis, 1974-75; dir. design and constrn. div. Mallinckrodt, Inc., St. Louis, 1975-93; ret., 1993. Author: P-Science: The Role of Science in Society, 1972, The Link of Science and Religion, 1973. Active Nat. Kidney Found.; bd. dirs. U. Mo. Devel. Council, St. Louis Artists Coalition, Citizens for Modern Transit; elder Luth. Ch.; v.p. Coun. Luth Chs., St. Louis; mem. adv. com. grad. sch. U. Mo., Columbia, mem. pres.'s role and scope comm.; dir. Coun. Luth. Chs. Greater St. Louis; mem. bldg. com. Humane Soc. Mo.; pres. coun. Luth. Ch. of the Living Christ. Served with U.S. Army, 1959-61. Recipient award Acad. Elec. Engrs., U. Mo., Rolla, Achievement award Humane Soc. of Mo., special award, 1998, Achievement award Engrs. Club St. Louis, 2002, Order of the Golden Shillaleagh, U. Mo., Rolla, 2004, Legacy Circ. award U. Mo., Columbia, 2004. Mem. NSPE (life), IEEE (life, chmn. state govt. activities com. 1990-93), Japan-Am. Soc., AAAS, AIChE, Profl. Engrs. in Industry, Mo. Soc. Profl. Engrs. (Profl. Engr. in Industry 1989, pres. St. Louis chpt.), Profl. Engrs. and Land Surveyors (chmn. Mo. bd. for architects 1989-95), Am. Def. Preparedness Assn., U. Mo. Alumni Assn. (bd. dirs. 1972-78), Engrs. Club (pres. 1985-86, Achievement award 2002), Mo. Athletic Club, Rotary, Sigma Pi. Address: #44 Jamestown Farm Dr Florissant MO 63034-1405 Office: 44 Jamestown Farm Dr Florissant MO 63034-1405 E-mail: G-L-Tomazi@worldnet.att.net.

TOMB, DIANE LENEGAN, federal agency administrator; Grad., Mt. St. Mary's, Md. Assoc. dir. Office Bus. Liaison U.S. Dept. Commerce, 1991—93, dir. pub. affairs for Internat. Trade Adminstrn.; dir. pub. affairs practice, mktg. dir. Washington regional office Burson-Marsteller, 1994—97; sr. v.p. for comm. Fannie Mae Found.; asst. sec. for pub. affairs Dept. HUD, Washington, 2002—. Office: Dept HUD Pub Affairs 451 7th St SW Washington DC 20410-9000

TOMBAUGH, DOROTHY ELVE, retired secondary school educator, author, lecturer; b. Newark, N.Y., Mar. 19, 1917; d. John E. and Edith Deming Elve; m. Roy Wilson Tombaugh, Aug. 10, 1940; children: Sandra Tombaugh Ehrman, Karen Tombaugh Dean. BS, Alfred U., 1938, DSc, 1983; MAT, Siena Heights U., 1965, DHL (hon.), 1982. Cert. med. technologist, Am. Soc. Clin. Pathologists. Med. technologist Rochester (N.Y.) Gen. Hosp., 1938-39, Sage Meml. Hosp., Ganado, Ariz., 1940, Cedars of Lebanon Hosp., L.A., 1941; spectographer, rsch. asst. Applied Rsch. Labs., Glendale, Calif., 1942-44; tchr. chemistry and biology Euclid (Ohio) H.S., 1963-79; lectr. NSF Grant, 1979-81, mainstreamed blind students in biology classes and labs, 1970-75. Judge for state and internat. sci. fairs N.E. Ohio, So. Ariz., 1965-98; lectr. NSF Chatauqua for Coll. Tchrs., 1977-80; lectr. in field. Author: Biology for the Blind, 1973; contbr. articles to profl. jours. Troop leader Girl Scouts, Eagle Rock, Calif., 1943-44, Bethel Park, Pa., 1954-55, Dayton, Ohio, 1957-59; deacon Presbyn. Ch., North Elmonte, Calif., 1947-50, Tucson, 1990-93, 1998-2002; fin. com. YWCA, Pitts., 1954-56. Named Outstanding Biology Tchr., Nat. Assn. Biology Tchrs., Ohio, 1975. Presbyterian. Avocation: greenhouse and gardening. Home: 2341 S Circle X Pl Tucson AZ 85713-6703

TOMBLIN, EARL RAY, state legislator; b. Logan County, W.Va., Mar. 15, 1952; s. Earl and Freda (Jarrell) T.; m. Joanne Jaeger, Sept. 8, 1979; 1 child, Brent Jaeger. BS, W.Va. U.; MBA, Marshall U.; postgrad., U. Charleston. Former sch. tchr.; businessman; mem. W.Va. Ho. Dels., 1974-80, W.Va. State Senate, 1980—, pres., 1995—; lt. gov. State of W.Va., Charleston, 2000—. Chmn. So. Legis. Conf. Former pres., bd. dirs. Appalachia Ednl. Lab., Inc.; mem. Logan County Devel. Authority. Mem. Kappa Alpha. Democrat. Presbyterian. Office: Capitol Bldg Rm 229M Charleston WV 25305 Address: PO Box 116 Chapmanville WV 25508-0116

TOMBLINSON, JAMES EDMOND, architect; b. Flint, Mich., Feb. 12, 1927; s. Carl and Edna Ethel (Spears) T.; m. Betsy Kinley, Sept. 26, 1959; children: Amy Lisa, John Timothy (dec.). B.Arch., U. Mich., 1951. Draftsman firms in, Detroit, 1951-53, Flint, 1953-54, 56-57, San Francisco, 1955-56; field engr. Atlas Constructors, Morocco, 1952-53; architect Tomblinson, Harburn, & Assocs., Inc. (and predecessors), Flint, 1958—, pres., 1969-95; chmn. bd. Tomblinson, Harburn & Assocs., Inc (and predecessors), 1995—2001; chmn. Mich. Bd. Registration Architects, 1975-77; sec. Mundy Twp. Planning Commn., 1974-85, Grand Blanc Planning Commn., City of Mich., 1985—; chmn., 1988—. Pres. Flint Beautification Commn., 1968-69; bd. dirs. Grand Blanc Beautification Commn., 1969-84; founding mem. bd. dirs. Flint YMCA, 1969-75, chmn. camp com., 1971-75; founding mem. bd. dirs. Flint Environ. Action Team, 1971-77, v.p., 1971-73; elder First Presbyn. Ch. Flint, 1983, trustee, 1986-99; exec. com. Tall Pine council Boy Scouts Am., 1975—; bd. dirs. New Paths, 1994-2004, pres., 1985-86, 94—; trustee Grand Blanc Cmty. Found., 1997-2004; mem. vestry St. Christopher's Ch., 2004—. Served with AUS, 1945-46. Recipient various civic service awards. Fellow AIA; mem. Mich. Soc. Architects, Flint Area C. of C. Clubs: Greater Flint Jaycees (dir. 1957-63, v.p. 1963), Flint City, U. Mich. (pres. Flint chpt. 1980—). Lodges: Rotary (pres. 1984-85). Home: 686 Applegate Ln Grand Blanc MI 48439-1669 Office: THA Architects Engrs 817 E Kearsley St Flint MI 48503-2076 E-mail: jtomblinson@tha-flint.com., jetomblinson@aol.com.

TOMBRELLO, THOMAS ANTHONY, JR., physics educator, consultant; b. Austin, Tex., Sept. 20, 1936; s. Thomas Anthony and Jeanette Lilian (Marcuse) T.; m. Esther Ann Hall, May 30, 1957 (div. Jan. 1976); children: Christopher Thomas, Susan Elaine, Karen Elizabeth; m. Stephanie Carhart Merton, Jan. 15, 1977; 1 stepchild, Kerstin Arusha. BA in Physics, Rice U., 1958, MA, 1960, PhD, 1961, Uppsala (Sweden) U., 1997. Rsch. fellow in physics Calif. Inst. Tech., Pasadena, 1961-62, 64-65, asst. prof. physics, 1965-67, assoc. prof., 1967-71, prof., 1971—, William R. Kenan Jr. prof., 1997—, tech. assessment officer, 1996—, chair divsn. physics, math. and astronomy, 1998—; asst. prof. Yale U., New Haven, 1963. Cons. in field; disting. vis. prof. U. Calif.-Davis, 1984; v.p., dir. rsch. Schlumberger-Doll Rsch., Ridgefield, Conn., 1987-89; mem. U.S. V.P.'s Space Policy Adv. Bd., 1992; mem. sci. adv. bd. Ctr. of Nanoscale Sci. and Tech., Rice U., 1995—; bd. dirs. Schlumberger Tech. Corp., Schlumberger Found., 1987-89. Assoc. editor Nuc. Physics, 1971-91, Applications Nuc. Physics, 1980-89, Radiation Effects, 1985-88, Nuc. Instruments and Methods B, 1993-96. Recipient Alexander von Humboldt award von Humboldt Stiftung, U. Frankfurt, Germany, 1984-85; named Disting. Alumnus, Rice U., 1998; NSF fellow Calif. Inst. Tech., 1961-62, A.P. Sloan fellow, 1971-73. Fellow Am. Phys. Soc.; mem. AAAS, Phi Beta Kappa, Sigma Xi, Delta Phi Alpha. Democrat. Avocations: reading, jogging. Office: Calif Inst Tech Dept Physics Mail Code 200 36 Pasadena CA 91125-0001 Office Phone: 626-395-4241. E-mail: tat@its.caltech.edu.

TOMBROS, PETER GEORGE, pharmaceutical company executive; b. Oak Hill, W.Va., June 12, 1942; s. George P. and Mary Jane (Boliski) T.; m. Ann Riblett Cullen, June 12, 1965. BS, Pa. State U., 1964, MS, 1966; MBA, U. Pa., 1968. Mktg. asst. Pfizer Labs. div. Pfizer Inc., N.Y.C., 1968; asst. product mgr. Pfizer Inc., N.Y.C., 1969, product mgr., 1970-71, group product mgr., 1972-74, v.p. mktg., 1975-80; sr. v.p., gen. mgr. Roerig div. Pfizer Inc., N.Y.C., 1980-86; exec. v.p. Pfizer Pharms. div. Pfizer Inc., N.Y.C., 1986-90, v.p. corp. strategic planning, 1990-94; also corp. officer Pfizer Inc., N.Y.C.; ret. pres., CEO Enzon, Inc., Piscataway, 1994—2001, also bd. dirs.; chmn., CEO VivoQuest Inc., 2001—, also bd. dirs.; dir. Cambrex Corp., East Rutherford. Alumni fellow Penn State, 1993; bd. dirs. Pfizer Pharm. Inc., 1986-1992, Alpharma Inc., Oslo, Norway, NPS Pharm., Inc., Salt Lake City, Paradigm Genetics, Rsch. Triangle Park, N.C. Bd. dirs. Am. Found. for Pharm. Edn., North Plainfield, N.J., 1980-2001, past chmn.; trustee Fisk U., Nashville, 1986-96, Dominican Coll., Orangeburg, N.Y., 1987—2002; trustee Bklyn. Borough Hall Restoration, 1987-92; mem. corp. devel. com. Cen. Park Conservancy, N.Y.C., 1986-94; bd. dirs. Vote America, 1990; bd. dirs. Cancer Care; chmn. bd. dirs. NJ Tech. Coun., 2001-2003. Mem. Pharm. Mfrs. Assn. (past chmn. mktg. steering com., 1986-1992), Links Club, Blind Brook Club, Masons. Avocations: marathon running, golf, tennis, skiing, bridge. Office: VivoQuest Inc 711 Executive Blvd Valley Cottage NY 10989

TOME, CAROL, corporate financial executive; b. Jackson, Wyoming; BS in Communications, U. of Wyoming; MBA in Finance, U. of Denver. Comml. lender Bank of Denver (now Wells Fargo); dir. banking Johns-Manville Corp.; v.p., treas. Riverwood Internat. Corp., Home Depot, 1995, sr. v.p. fin., CFO, 2001—. Bd. dirs. UPS, 2003—. Bd. dirs. Girls Inc.; trustee Ga. Substance Abuse Advisory Coun., Home Fund; advisory bd. Met. Atlanta Arts Fund. Office: Home Depot 2455 Paces Ferry Rd Atlanta GA 30339-4029

TOMÉ, WOLFGANG AXEL, physicist, researcher, educator; b. Ludwigsburg, Fed. Republic Germany, May 15, 1962; came to U.S., 1987, permanent resident, 1999; s. Kurt Wolfgang and Monika Else (Bub) T.; m. Marie-Jacqueline Lamoth, Aug. 24, 1990; children: Anne-Sophie, Marie-Hèlène. Vordiplom in Physik, Eberhard-Karls U., Tuebingen, Fed. Republic of Germany, 1986; MS in Physics, U. Denver, 1989; PhD in Physics, U Fla., 1995. Diplomate Am. Bd. Radiology, Am. Bd. Therapeutic Radiol. Physics. Grad. teaching asst. U. Denver, 1987-89, grad. rsch. asst., 1988, U. Fla., Gainesville, 1989-95, postdoctoral assoc. in med. physics, 1995-98, asst. prof. human oncology and med. physics, 1998—2003, assoc. prof. human oncology and med. physics, 2003—. Author: Path Integrals on Group Manifolds, 1998; contbr. articles to Founds. of Physics, Jour. Math. Physics, Acta Physics Polonica, Annales Inst. Henri Poincaré, Med. Physics, Physics in Medicine and Biology, Internat. Jour. Radiation Oncology, Biology and Physics, Radiotherapy and Oncology, Internat. Jour. of Cancer, Med. Dosimetry, Tech. in Cancer Rsch. and Treatment, others. Doctoral fellow Studienstiftung des deutschen Volkes, 1992; fellow Studienstiftung des deutschen Volkes, 1986. Mem. Am. Soc. for Therapeutic Radiology and Oncology, Am. Assn. Physicists in Medicine, Internat. Assn. Math. Physics, Am. Coll. Med. Physics, European Soc. for Therapeutic Radiology and Oncology, Sigma Xi Rsch. Soc., Alpha Nu Sigma, Pi Mu Epsilon, Phi Beta Delta. Office: U Wis Dept Human Oncology Madison WI 53792 E-mail: tome@humonc.wise.edu.

TOMEI, CAROLYN, state representative; m. Gary Michael. BS in Psychology, MSW, Portland State U. State rep., dist. 41 Oreg. House Rep., Salem, 2001—; mayor City of Milwaukie, Oreg.; child devel. specialist Portland Pub. Schs. Vice-chair Health and Human Svcs. Com.; mem. Water Com.; instr. Portland C.C. Democrat. Office: 900 Court St NE H-388 Salem OR 97301 Office Phone: 503-986-1441. E-mail: rep.carolyntomei@state.or.us.

TOMEI, MARISA, actress; b. Bklyn., Dec. 4, 1964; d. Gary and Patricia Tomei. TV appearances include (series) As the World Turns, 1983-88, A Different World, 1987, Only Love, 1998, My Own Country, 1998, Since You've Been Gone, 1998, (films) Parker Kane, 1990; film appearances include: The Flamingo Kid, 1984, Playing for Keeps, 1986, Oscar, 1991, Zandalee, 1991, My Cousin Vinny, 1992 (Acad. award best supporting actress 1993), Chaplin, 1992, Untamed Heart, 1993, Equinox, 1993, The Paper, 1994, Only You, 1994, The Perez Family, 1994, Four Rooms, 1995, Unhook the Stars, 1996, What Women Want, 2000, Dirk and Betty, 2000, Driven, 2000, King of the Jungle, 2000, In the Bedroom, 2001 (ShoWest award best supporting actress, 2002), Someone Like You, 2001, The Guru, 2002, The Wild Thornberrys Movie (voice), 2002, Anger Management, 2003, Loverboy, 2004; theatre appearances include Slavs! Thinking About the Longstanding Problems of Virtue and Happiness, 1994, Welcome to Sarajevo, 1997. Office: United Talent Agy 9560 Wilshire Blvd Ste 500 Beverly Hills CA 90212*

TOMEK, WILLIAM GOODRICH, agricultural economist; b. Table Rock, Nebr., Sept. 20, 1932; s. John and Ruth Genevieve (Goodrich) T. BS, U. Nebr., 1956, MA, 1957; PhD, U. Minn., 1961. Asst. prof. Cornell U., Ithaca, N.Y., 1961-66, NSF fellow, 1965, assoc. prof. agrl. econs., 1966-70, prof., 1970-99, grad. sch. prof., 2000—, chmn. dept. agrl. econs., 1988-93. Vis. econ. USDA, 1978-79; vis. fellow Stanford U., 1968-69, U. New Eng., Australia, 1988; mem. adv. panel Rev. Agrl. Econs., 1996-98. Author: Agricultural Product Prices, 2003; editor: Am. Jour. Agrl. Econs., 1975-77; co-editor: Chgo. Bd. Trade Rsch. Symposia, 1993-2001; mem. editl. bd. Jour. Futures Markets, 1992-95; contbr. articles to profl. jours. Served with U.S. Army, 1953-55. Recipient Earl Combs Jr. award Chgo. Bd. Trade Found. Mem. Am. Agrl. Econs. Assn. (pres. 1985-86), Am. Econ. Assn., Econometric Soc., Northeastern Agrl. Econs. Assn., Am. Agrl. Econs. Assn. (awards 1981, 89, 97, fellow), Gamma Sigma Delta (rsch. award 1994). Democrat. Methodist. Office: Cornell U Warren Hall Ithaca NY 14853-7801 Office Phone: 607-255-2189. E-mail: wgt1@cornell.edu.

TOMEY, ANN LOUISE MARRINER, nursing educator; b. Holdrege, Nebr., Jan. 25, 1943; d. Wilbur Dodge and Arlene Mae (Hanni) Clawson; m. Gerald Lynn Marriner, Feb. 10, 1964 (div. 1985); m. H. Keith Tomey, Feb. 14, 1987. BSN, U. Colo., Boulder, 1967; MSN, U. Colo., Denver, 1970; PhD, U. Colo., Boulder, 1975. RN, Ind. Instr. U. Tex., San Antonio, 1970-71; asst. prof. N.Y. State U., Plattsburgh, 1971-72; lectr. Humboldt State U., Arcata, Calif., 1973-74; pub. health nurse, supr. Humboldt County Health Dept., Eureka, Calif., 1974-75; assoc. prof. nursing U. Colo., Denver, 1975-80; prof. nursing Ind. U., Indpls., 1980-92, Ind. State U., Terre Haute, 1991—. Gen. duty nurse Boulder Meml. Hosp., 1964-67; pub. health nurse Tri-County Health Dept., Aurora, Colo., 1966-67, sch. nurse Boulder City and County Health Dept., 1968-70; ind. cons., 1975—; peer mentor, S. Am., 1999—. Editor: Current Perspectives in Nursing Management, 1979 (Book of Yr.), Dimensions of Nursing Administration, 1989 (Book of Yr.); author, editor: 40 books; contbr. chapters to books, over 65 articles to profl. jours. Mem. adv. com. Ind. U. Sch. Medicine, Terre Haute, 1992-98, Ivy Tech State Coll., Terre Haute, 1992-98; mem. rev. panel United Way, Terre Haute, 1994—; chair adv. com. Midwest Ctr. for Rural Health, Terre Haute, 1996-98. Disting. lectr. Sigma Theta Tau, 1988—. Fellow: Am. Acad. Nursing; mem.: Ind. Nurses Found. (treas. 1996—99, 2001—02), Ind. Nurses Assn. (2d v.p. 1985—89, 1st v.p. 1989, pres. 1989—91, PAC chair 2001—), Phi Kappa Phi (pub. rels. officer 2001—03, v.p. 2003—, pres. 2003—). Avocations: reading, writing, cooking, gardening, walking. Home: 3939 S Willowbrook Ct Terre Haute IN 47802-8842 Office: Ind State U 8th And Chestnut Terre Haute IN 47809-0001 Office Phone: 812-237-3480. E-mail: A-Tomey@indstate.edu.

TOMEY, DICK, university football coach; b. Bloomington, Ind., June 20, 1938; m. Nanci Kincaid, 1998; children: Rich, Angie, Alli, Leigh; stepchild, Sonny Arquette. BA, DePauw U., 1964. Grad. asst. Miami U., Oxford, Ohio, 1962-63; asst. coach, freshman coach No. Ill. U., DeKalb, 1964; asst. coach, backs coach Davidson Coll., 1965-66; asst. coach, coach defensive backs U. Kans., Manhattan, 1967-70; asst. coach UCLA, 1971-76; head coach U. Hawaii, 1977-86, U. Ariz., Tucson, 1987—. Named Pac-10 Coach of Yr., 19932; winner Fiesta Bowl, 1993. Mem. Am. Football Coaches Assn. (trustee 1996—, mem. I-A All-Am. team selection com., hon. membership com., Kodah Region 5 Coach of Yr. 1992). Avocations: golf, skiing. Office: Am Football Coaches Assn 5900 Old Mcgregor Rd Waco TX 76712-6166

TOMICH, LILLIAN, lawyer; b. L.A. d. Peter S. and Yovanka P. (Ivanovic) T. AA, Pasadena City Coll., 1954; BA in Polit. Sci., UCLA, 1956, cert. secondary tchg., 1957, MA, 1958; JD, U. So. Calif., 1961. Bar: Calif., U.S. Ct. Appeals (9th Cir.) 1978, 2002. Sole practice, 1961-66; house counsel Mfrs. Bank, L.A., 1966; assoc. Hurley, Shaw & Tomich, San Marino, Calif., 1968-76, Driscoll & Tomich, San Marino, 1976—. Dir. Continental Culture Specialists Inc., Glendale, Calif. Trustee St. Sava Serbian Orthodox Ch., San Gabriel, Calif. Recipient Episcopal Gramata award Serbian Orthodox Met. of Midwestern Am., 1993, Episcopal Gramata award Serbian Orthodox Bishop of Western Am., 1996, 2002; Charles Fletcher Scott fellow, 1957; U. So. Calif. Law Sch. scholar, 1958. Mem.: ABA, ATLA, Women Lawyers Assn., Los Angeles County Bar Assn., Calif. Bar Assn., Order Mast and Dagger, San Marino C. of C., UCLA Alumni Assn., Town Hall and World Affairs Coun., Pi Kappa Delta, Alpha Gamma Sigma, Iota Tau Tau. Office: 2460 Huntington Dr San Marino CA 91108-2643 Office Phone: 626-287-1248.

TOMICH, PAUL, medical association administrator, obstetrician, gynecologist; Pres. Cen. Assn. of Obstetricians and Gynecologists, Washington, 2001—02. Office: Cen Assn of Ob/Gyn 409 12 St SW Washington DC 20024

TOMICH-BOLOGNESI, VERA, secondary school educator; b. L.A. d. Peter S. and Yovanka (Ivanovich) T.; m. Gino Bolognesi, July 12, 1969. AA, John Muir Jr. Coll., Pasadena, Calif., 1951; BA in Polit. Sci., UCLA, 1953, MEd, 1955, EdD, 1960. Cert. secondary tchr., Calif.; cert. secondary sch. adminstrn., Calif.; cert. jr. coll. tchr., Calif. Tchg. asst. dept. edn. UCLA, 1956; tchr., dept. chmn. Culver City (Calif.) Unified Sch. Dist., 1956-91; rschr., writer U.S. Dept. Edn., Washington, 1961, del. to Yugoslavia, 1965; co-owner, exec. Metrocolor Engring., San Gabriel, Calif., 1973—. Cons., Continental Culture Specialists, Inc., Glendale, Calif., 1985-92; rsch. asst. Law Firm of Driscoll & Tomich, San Marino, Calif., 1989—. Author: Education in Yugoslavia and the New Reform, 1963, Higher Education and Teacher Training in Yugoslavia, 1967; screenplay editor 1996—. Bd. trustees St. Sava Serbian Orthodox Ch., San Gabriel, 1975—, mem., 1960—. Named an Outstanding Young Women of Am., 1966; recipient Episcopal Gramata, Serbian Orthodox Ch. of Western Am., 1996, 2002. Mem. NEA (life), Calif. Tchrs. Assn., UCLA Alumni Assn., Alpha Gamma Sigma, Pi Lambda Theta. Home: 100 E Roses Rd San Gabriel CA 91775-2343 Office: Metrocolor Engring 5110 Walnut Grove Ave San Gabriel CA 91776-2026

TOMITA, KAZUO (JOE), automotive executive; m. Sawako Tomita; 4 children. Degree in Tech., Tokyo U., 1969. Staff engr., R&D Ctr. Toyota, Higashifuji, Japan, 1969—72, 1975—87, staff engr. Factory Rep. Office Ann Arbor, Mich., 1972—75, mgr. Toyota City, Japan, 1987, group v.p. Tech. Ctr. Torrance, Calif., 1990—93, with Toyota City, 1993—96, gen. mgr. quality control Kamigo, Japan, 1997—99, project gen. mgr. Higashifuji, 2000—01; group v.p. tech. and regulatory affairs Toyota Motor N.Am., Washington, 2001—. Office: Ste 600 1850 M St NW Washington DC 20036

TOMIYASU, KIYO, consulting engineer; b. Las Vegas, Nev., Sept. 25, 1919; s. Yonema and Toyono (Kawamura) T.; m. Eiko Nakamizo, Aug. 31, 1947. BS, Calif. Inst. Tech., 1940; MS, Columbia U., 1941; M.E.S., Harvard U., 1947, PhD, 1948. Instr. Harvard U., 1948-49; head engring. sect. Sperry Gyroscope Co., Gt. Neck, N.Y., 1949-55; with GE, 1955-93; cons. engr. microwave techniques GE Valley Forge Space Ctr., Phila., 1969-93; with Martin Marietta Corp., Phila., 1993-95, Lockheed Martin Corp., Phila., 1995—. Author: The Laser Literature-An Annotated Guide, 1968; articles; patentee in field. Exec. bd. Friendship Hill Civic Assn., Paoli, Pa., 1972-73, pres., 1973. Recipient Steinmetz award Gen. Electric Co., 1977; Mgmt. and Data Systems fellow Martin Marietta Corp., 1993; established Tomiyasu Meml. ann. scholarship Calif. Inst. Tech., 1977. Fellow IEEE (life, hon. life mem. Microwave Theory and Techniques Soc. 1973, tech. activities bd., awards bd., publs. bd., bd. dirs. div. IV 1985-86, ednl. activities bd. 1987-88, Microwave Career award, 1981, Centennial medal 1984, Millennium medal 2000, established Kiyo Tomiyasu award 2000), Geosci. and Remote Sensing Soc. (hon. life; Geosci. and Remote Sensing Outstanding Svc. award 1986, Microwave Disting. Svc. award 1987); mem. Am. Phys. Soc. Home: 366 Hilltop Rd Paoli PA 19301-1211 Office: Lockheed Martin Corp PO Box 8048 Philadelphia PA 19101-8048

TOMJACK, T.J. wholesale distribution executive; b. Aug. 25, 1942; BBA, U. Notre Dame, 1964. With Peat Marwick Mitchell & Co., 1964-71, Potlatch Corp., 1971-85; exec. v.p. sales North Pacific Lumber Co., Portland, Oreg., 1971-85, exec. v.p., COO, 1987, pres., 1988—, chmn., CEO, 1989—. Office: 815 NE Davis St Portland OR 97232-2987

TOMJANOVICH, RUDOLPH, professional basketball coach; b. Hamtramck, Mich., Nov. 24, 1948; Grad., Univ. Michigan, 1970. Player Houston Rockets, 1970—81, scout, 1981-83, asst. coach, 1983-92, head coach, 1992—2003, personnel consultant, 2003—04; head coach Los Angeles Lakers, 2004—. Named NBA Coach of the Year, Sporting News, 1993, head coach, Western Conference All-Star Team, 1997. Achievements include coach NBA Championship Team, 1994, 1995; coach gold medal men's Basketball Team, Sydney Olympic Games, 2000. Office: c/o Los Angeles Lakers 555 N Nash st El Segundo CA 90245*

TOMKA, PETER, Slovakian diplomat, lawyer, judge, arbitrator; b. Banská, Bystrica, Slovakia, June 1, 1956; s. Ján and Kornélia (Plai) T.; m. Zuzana Halgasová, June 30, 1990. Grad., Charles U., Prague, Czechoslovakia, 1979; PhD in Internat. Law, Charles U., 1985. Lectr. Law Sch., Charles U., Prague, 1980-86, assoc. lectr. in internat. law, 1986-91; asst. legal advisor Fed. Ministry of Fgn. Affairs, Czechoslovakia, 1986-90, head pub. internat. law divsn., 1990-91; counsellor, legal advisor Permanent Mission to UN, N.Y.C., 1991-92, amb., dep. permanent rep. of Slovakia, 1993-97, charge d'affaires, 1994-97; legal advisor Ministry Fgn. Affairs, Bratislava, Slovakia, 1997-98, dir. gen. legal and consular affairs, 1998-99; permanent rep. of Slovakia to UN, N.Y.C., 1999—2003; judge Internat. Ct. Justice, The Hague, Netherlands, 2003—; arbitrator Iron Rhine Case, Belgium, Netherlands, 2003—. Former agt. of Slovakia Internat. Ct. Justice in Gabcikovo-Nagymaros Project Case, Hungary/Slovakia; mem. Permanent Ct. Arbitration, 1995; chmn. UN Legal Com., 1997; vice chair com. legal advisors Coun. of Europe, 1998—99, chmn. com. legal advisors, 2001—02; mem. UN Internat. Law Commn., 1999—2003, vice chmn., 2000. Office: Internat Ct Justice Peace Palace 2517 KJ The Hague Netherlands Office Phone: (31-70)3022323.

TOMKINS, CALVIN, writer; b. Orange, N.J., Dec. 17, 1925; s. Frederick and Laura (Graves) T.; m. Grace Lloyd Fanning, Sept. 11, 1948; children: Anne Graves, Susan Temple, Spencer; m. Judy Johnston, Nov. 11, 1961 (div. Feb. 1981); m. Susan Cheever, Oct. 1, 1981; 1 child, Sarah Liley Cheever; m. Dodie Kazanjian, May 28, 1988. BA, Princeton U., 1948. Assoc. editor Newsweek mag., N.Y.C., 1955-57, gen. editor, 1957-59; staff writer The New Yorker, N.Y.C., 1960—. Author: The Bride and The Bachelors, 1965, Merchants and Masterpieces, 1970, Living Well Is the Best Revenge, 1971, Off the Wall, 1980, Post- to Neo-, 1988, (with Dodie Kazanjian) Alex: The Life of Alexander Liberman, 1993, Duchamp: A Biography, 1997. Bd. dirs. Cunningham Dance Found., N.Y.C., 1963-90. With USN, 1944-46. Guggenheim fellow, 1978 Mem. Authors League Am. Inc., Pen Am. Ctr. Clubs: Century (N.Y.C.). Home: 145 E 74th St New York NY 10021-3225 Office: New Yorker Mag 4 Times Sq New York NY 10036-6561

TOMKINS, MARK E. manufacturing executive; b. Ill. BS, MBA, Ea. Ill. U. CPA Ill. V.p. fin. and bus. devel. electronic materials divsn. to v.p. fin. and bus. devel. polymers divsn. Allied Signal, 1996—98; sr. v.p., CFO Great Lakes Chem. Co., 1998—2001, Vulcan Materials Co., Birmingham, Ala., 2001—. Office: Vulcan Materials Co 1200 Urban Ctr Dr Birmingham AL 35242

TOMKOW, GWEN ADELLE, artist; b. Detroit, May 16, 1932; d. Galen A. and Edythe Christine (Barr) Roberts; m. Michael Tomkow, Nov. 14, 1953; children: Eric Michael, Thomas Edward, Nikola Christine, Kit Adair. A of Bus., Detroit Bus. Inst., 1952; student, Birmingham Bloomfield Art Assn., Assn., Mich., 1985-87, Visual Art Assn., Livonia, Mich., 1984-89. Tchr. watercolor Visual Art Assn., Livonia, 1989—; tchr. watercolor workshop

Village Fine Art Assn., Milford, Mich., 1996; tchr. workshop Ella Sharp Mus. Jackson Civic Art, Mich., 1996—2003; slide lectr. Livonia Artist Club, 1995, Palette and Brush Club, Southfield, Mich., 1995, Pontiac (Mich.) Oakland Artists, 1995, Ea. Mich. U. Watercolor Soc., 1994; tchr. watercolor workshop Ann Arbor Women Painters U. Mich. Art Sch., 1997; slide lectr. Western Ohio Water Color Soc., 1999; tchr. watercolor workshop Awakening Artist Inside Art Imporium, 2004. Artist-in-residence Farmington Art Commn., Farmington Hills, 1988; slide lectr. Springfield (Ohio) Art Mus; mem. Framington Hills Art Commn., 2002—; tchr. cultural arts Farmington Heritage Studios, 2003—; juror Livonia Fine Arts Exhibit, 2004. One-woman shows include Cary Gallery, 1997—2003; artist (exhibitions) Joppich's Bay St. of Northport, 1988—98; exhibitions include Joppich's Bay St. of Northport, 2000—03, Cary Gallery, 1995—, Art Corridor, 1998, Cary Gallery, 2003, Represented in permanent collections E. Carothers Dunnegan Gallery of Art Mus., Bolivar, Mo., Atrium Gallery, Northville, MI. Recipient Purchase awards U.S.A. Springfield (Mo.) Art Mus., 1990, 93, 94, Watercolor U.S.A., 1999, 1st prize Helen de Roy Competition, Oakland C.C., Farmington, Mich., 1988, 92, Grumbacher Gold medal Farmington Artists Club, 1992, 2001, Farmington Hills, Mich., 1995, 98. Mem. Nat. Watercolor Soc. (signature, Alex Nepote Meml. award 1998), Mich. Watercolor Soc. (Meml. award 1992), Farmington Art Assn. (pres. 1987-89), Detroit Soc. Women Painters Sculptors (sec. 1994-95, award 1999), Palette and Brush (v.p. 1982-83), Founders Soc. Detroit Inst. Arts, Nat. Mus. Women in the Arts, Birmingham Soc. Women Painters. Presbyterian. Avocations: tennis, golf, choir singer, theater.

TOMLIN, JAMES MILTON, lawyer; b. Springfield, Ill., July 16, 1942; s. Bernard A. and Iona M. T.; m. Carol L. Wandell, Dec. 23, 1966 (div. Mar. 1994); children: Brian, Brad, Mitch; m. Barbara Soldwedel, Aug. 24, 1998. BS, U. Ill., 1964, JD, 1967. Bar: Ill. 1968, U.S. Dist. Ct. (no. dist.) Ill. 1973. Judge adv. gen. corps. USN, 1968-71, USNR, 1971-91; atty. Westervest, Johnson, Nicol & Keller, Peoria, Ill., 1971-73; asst. corp. counsel City of Peoria, 1973-74; pvt. practice Peoria, 1974—. Mem. law adv. bd. Ctrl. Ill. C.C., Peoria, 1990-94. Bd. dirs. Neighborhood House Assn., Peoria, 1985—, former pres., Tower Pk., Peoria Heights, 1974-84; former pres. Forest Pk. Found., Peoria, bd. dirs. treas. David Boyd Meml. Found., 2001—. Recipient Cmty. Svc. award, Ill. State Bar Assn., 2001. Avocations: skiing, golf, bicycling. Office: 5823 N Forest Park Dr Peoria IL 61614-3559 Fax: 309-688-7581. E-mail: jtomlinlaw@aol.com.

TOMLIN, JEANNE BRANNON, real estate broker, small business owner; b. Carroll, Iowa; d. James Leonard and Mary Agnes (Cavenaugh) Brannon; widowed; children: David, Elizabeth; m. James W. Tomlin; stepchildren: Angela, Julie, Lori, Fran. A in Archtl. Tech., Ind. U. Purdue U., Indpls., 1970, student. Lic. real estate broker. Salesperson F.C. Tucker, Indpls.; mgr. Dan Nichols Builder, Greenwood, Ind.; asst. mgr. Carpenter Better Homes and Gardens, Carmel, Ind., sales broker, 1989-92, Tomlin Realtors, Greenwood, 1992-97, pres., CEO, 1997—. Mem. com. Nat. Handicapped Sports, Indpls., 1986-88; mem tech. task force Met. Indpls. Bd. Realtors, 1993-94, mem. comm. com., 1998—. Mem. Indpls. C. of C., Greenwood C. of C., Golden Key Nat. Honor Soc., Alpha Sigma Lambda. Avocations: scuba diving, skiing. Office: Tomlin Realtors 243 S Madison Ave Greenwood IN 46142-3123

TOMLINSON, ALEXANDER COOPER, investment banker, consultant; b. Haddonfield, N.J., May 13, 1922; s. Alexander Cooper and Mary (Buzby) T.; m. Elizabeth Anne Brierley, Jan. 10, 1953 (div.); children: William Brierley, Deborah T. Marple, Alexander Cooper III; m. Margaret L. Dickey, Nov. 15, 1986. BS, Haverford Coll., 1943; postgrad., London Sch. Econs. and Polit. Sci., 1947-48; MBA, Harvard U., 1950; LLD (hon.), Haverford Coll., 1995. With Morgan Stanley & Co., N.Y.C., 1950-76, ptnr., 1958-76, mng. dir., 1970-76; dir., pres. Morgan Stanley Can. Ltd. div., Montreal, Que., 1972-76; chmn. exec. com. First Boston, Inc., N.Y.C., 1976-82, dir., 1976-88; pres. Nat. Policy Assn., Washington, 1982-85; exec. dir. Ctr. for Privatization, Washington, 1985-88; pres. Hungarian-Am. Enterprise Fund, Washington, 1990-93; chmn. Fund for Arts and Culture in Ctrl. and Ea. Europe, 1994-97. Mem. U.S. adv. bd. Que. Hydro, 1984-95. Trustee Incorp. Village, Cove Neck, N.Y., 1958-72, 76-82, Cold Spring Harbor Lab., 1976-87, N.Y. Infirmary-Beekman Downtown Hosp., 1968-82, East Woods Sch., Oyster Bay, N.Y., 1962-70, Nature Conservancy, L.I., N.Y., 1970-82, Salisbury Sch., Conn., 1976-87, Carnegie Found. for Advancement Tchg., 1984-90; bd. mgrs. Haverford Coll., 1979-01; bd. dirs. Nat. Bldg. Mus., 1987-94, Nat. Policy Assn., 1982-90, Decatur House Coun., 1990-94; chmn. Am. Friends Can., Inc., 1982-91, Harvard Bus. Sch. Fund, 1981-83. Lt. USNR, 1943-46. Mem. Coun. on Fgn. Rels., Metropolitan Club (Washington), Links (N.Y.). Home: 3314 P St NW Washington DC 20007-2701

TOMLINSON, J. RICHARD, engineering services company executive; b. Newtown, Pa., Mar. 26, 1930; s. Robert K. and Margaret (Wright) T.; m. Barbara Elizabeth Brazill, Apr. 30, 1955; children: Karin Kathleen Tomlinson Pizzitola, Kimberly Ann Tomlinson Donahue. BA, Swarthmore Coll., 1952; postgrad., George Washington U., 1952-53, U. Mich., 1955-57, Drexel Inst. Tech., 1954-57, Am. U., 1965. Mgmt. analyst Dept. State, Washington, 1952-53; with Old Republic Life Ins. Co., Washington, 1953-54; supr. financial analysis Ford Motor Co., Detroit, 1954-61; cons. McKinsey & Co., Washington, 1961-65; v.p. finance, dir. passenger svcs. Reading Co., Phila., 1965-69; v.p. finance Rollins Internat., Inc., 1969-71; exec. v.p. Amtrak, Washington, 1972-74; ptnr. L.T. Klauder and Assocs., 1974-75, 79-83; exec. v.p. Penn Central Transp. Co., 1975-78; pres. LTK Engrng. Svcs., 1984-95; retired. Named Man of Month, Phila. C. of C., 1967 Mem. Union League, Aronimink Golf and Country Club, Phila. Aviation Country Club. Home: 451 Inveraray Rd Villanova PA 19085-1139

TOMLINSON, JAMES FRANCIS, retired news agency executive; b. Long Beach, Calif., Oct. 18, 1925; s. Lilburn Jesse and Margaret (Roemer) T.; m. Sally JoAnne Ryan, Aug. 12, 1967; children— Elizabeth Anne, Victoria Alexandra. BA, U. Va., 1950; student, Harvard U., Grad. Sch. Arts and Scis., 1950-51; grad., Advanced Mgmt. Program, Harvard U., 1977. With A.P., 1951-92, chief bur., 1957-63, bus. news editor N.Y.C., 1963-67, dep. treas., 1967-68, treas., 1968-87, v.p., 1972-92, sec., 1978-92, asst. to pres., 1987-92. Served with AUS, 1943-46, ETO. Mem. Phi Beta Kappa, Phi Eta Sigma. Clubs: N.Y. Athletic (N.Y.C.), Harvard (N.Y.C.). Home: 222 E 71st St New York NY 10021-5164

TOMLINSON, JAMES LAWRENCE, mechanical engineer; b. Detroit, Sept. 12, 1935; s. James Emmet and Ethel Pearl (Williams) T.; m. Marilyn Joyce Peterson, Aug. 24, 1957; children: James, Mary, Robert, Susan. BSME, Mich. Tech., 1957. Registered profl. engr., Mich. Design engr. Buick Motor div. GMC, Flint, Mich., 1960-61, project engr., 1961-66, sr. project engr., 1966-71; staff analysis engr. GM Corp., Warren, Mich., 1971-82, sr. staff analysis engr., 1983-88; pres. Eastport (Mich.) Engrng., 1989—. Mayor City of Grand Blanc, 1985-89, city councilman, 1969-84, police liaison/commr., 1971-82, planning adv. bd., 1978-80, planning commn., 1985-89; nat. coun. mem. Boy Scouts Am., 1979-90, 93—, regional bd. mem., 1995—, coun. commr., 1979-84, coun. v.p., 1984—, nat. camp sch. staff, 1986-88, regional camp inspector/accreditation team, 1988—, subcamp chief nat. jamboree, 2001, 05; vice chmn. Genesee County Sml. Cities and Villages Assn., 1986, chmn., 1987; bd. dirs. Three Lakes Assn., Inc., 1997-2003. Capt. USAF, 1958-60. Recipient Silver Beaver Tall Pine coun. Boy Scouts Am., 1980, Silver Antelope Ctrl. region, 1996. Mem. NSPE (treas. Flint chpt. 1968-72, Engr. of the Yr. Flint chpt. 1990), SAE (mem. com. 1992-94, 96-98), ASME (exec. bd. Saginaw Valley chpt. 1968-70), Friends of Torch Lake Twp., Inc. (pres. 1994—). Mem. Congl. Ch. Home: PO Box 25 Eastport MI 49627-0025 Office Phone: 231-599-2440.

TOMLINSON, JOHN, news agency executive; Sr. v.p. news Metro Network News, Houston, 1997—. Office: Westwood One Inc 2800 Post Oak Blvd Ste 4000 Houston TX 77056-6109

TOMLINSON, JOHN RANDOLPH, lawyer; b. Seattle, Jan. 11, 1931; s. Charles Lawrence and Irma (Schnauffer) T.; m. Susan Jo Weaver, June 15, 1953; children: John R. Jr., Lynn M., James L., Anne E. BBA, U. Wash., 1953, JD, 1955. Bar: Wash. 1955, U.S. Dist. Ct. (we. and ea. dists.) Wash. 1955, U.S. Ct. Appeals (9th cir.) 1957, U.S. Supreme Ct. 1975. Assoc. Jones, Grey & Bayley, Seattle, 1957-61, ptnr., 1962-78, Lane Powell Spears Lubersky, Seattle, 1979—. Lectr. on continuing legal edn. Editorial bd. U. Wash. Law Rev., 1953. Served to 1st lt. USAFR, 1953-77. Fellow Am. Coll. Trial Lawyers; mem. ABA (chmn. litigation sect. 1986-87, vice chmn. 1984-85, chmn. elect 1985-86), Wash. State Bar Assn., Seattle Bar Assn., Phi Gamma Delta. Lodges: Rotary. Republican. Avocations: golf, skiing, fishing, hunting. Home: 8435 NE 21st Pl Bellevue WA 98004-2405 Office: Lane Powell Spears Lubersky 1420 5th Ave Ste 4100 Seattle WA 98101-2338

TOMLINSON, WILLIAM HOLMES, management educator, retired army officer; b. Thornton, Ark., Apr. 12, 1922; s. Hugh Oscar and Lucy Gray (Holmes) T.; m. Dorothy Payne, June 10, 1947 (dec.); children: Jane Axtell, Lucy Gray, William Payne; m. Florence Mood Smith, May 1, 1969 (div.); m. Suzanne Scollard Gill, Mar. 16, 1977. *Since Farrar's Island, VA, the family has been dedicated to duty, honor and country. Ancestral grandparents, Judith Jefferson Farrar (VA), George Gray Sr. (NC), Humphrey Beckett Tomlinson (MD), William Hudson (VA), Samuel Davis (VA), John Timmons (SC) and others served in the Revolution. Great grandfather Jesse Russell (TN) fought under Jackson at New Orleans. Great grandfathers Noah Dortch Holmes (AR), Alexander Mason (AR), and Phillip George Henry (AR) fought for the Confederacy. Father Hugh Oscar Tomlinson (AR) served in the AEF (France) in WWI. Brother Hugh Pat Tomlinson left Byrd HS, Shreveport,LA, to join Navy on his 17th birthday February 2, 1942-April 18, 1997, and fought as amphibious sailor (LST 449) on beacheads from Guadalcanal to Iwo Jima and Okinawa. After LSU (1950), Regular Army Commission in Field Artillery, Korea, later airborne, Special Forces.* Student, Centenary Coll., 1938-39; BS, U.S. Mil. Acad., 1943; grad., Field Arty. Sch., 1951, Air Command Staff Coll., 1958; MBA, U. Ala., 1960; MS in Internat. Affairs, George Washington U., 1966; grad., U.S. Army War Coll., 1966, Indsl. Coll. Armed Forces, 1968; PhD in Bus. Adminstrn., Am. U., 1974; grad. Advanced Mgmt. Program, Harvard Bus. Sch., 1968, 69. Commd. 2d lt. U.S. Army, 1943, advanced through grades to col., field arty., 1966; combat svc. in Leyte and Cebu Philippines 246 Field Arty. Bn. Americal Divsn., 1945; aide de camp to comdg. gen. Robert Eichelberger 8th U.S. Army, Japan, 1945-48; exec. officer 34 FA Bn, ops. officer 9th Divsn. Arty. Germany and Ft. Carson, Colo., 1954-57; with ODCSPER, 1960—61, Office of Undersec. Army, The Pentagon, Washington, 1961-64; comdr. 2d Bn. 8th Arty. and 7th Divsn. Arty. UN Comd. South Korea, 1964-65; faculty Indsl. Coll. Armed Forces, Ft. McNair, Washington, 1966-72, U. North Fla., Jacksonville, 1972—2002, prof. mgmt., prof. emeritus, 2002—. Vis. prof. U. Glasgow, Scotland, 1987; vis. lectr. Moscow Linguistics U., Plekhanov Econ. Acad., Ulyanovsk U., Russia, 1993; mem. Nat. Def. Exec. Res., Fed. Emergency Mgmt. Agy., 1976—. Author: Assessment of the National Defense Executive Reserve, 1974; co-author: International Business, Theory and Practice, 1991, Business Policy and Strategy, 2000; contbr. articles to profl. jours. Mem. exec. bd. Jacksonville Campus Ministry, 1991—, pres., 2002-. Decorated Bronze Star, Legion of Merit, Philippine Liberation medal, Japanese Occupation, Asiatic Pacific with Invasion Arrow; recipient Freedom Found. award, 1967-71, Sr. Profl. in Human Resources, Tchg. Incentive award State Univ. Sys., 1994-95. Mem. SAR, Sons Confederate Vets., Soc. Human Resource Mgmt., Acad. Mgmt., Indsl. Rels. Rsch. Assn., Acad. Internat. Bus., European Internat. Bus. Assn., Internat. Trade and Fin. Assn., Exec. Svc. Corp. Bd., Co. Mil. Historians, Nat. Eagle Scout Assn., N.E. Fla. Employee Svcs. Mgmt. Assn. (charter pres. 1987-89), Stewart Soc. (Edinburgh, regional commr.), West Point Soc. North Fla. (pres. 1976-77), Mil. Order Stars and Bars (comdr. 1980-90), Army Navy Club, Fla. Yacht Club, Masons, Shriners, Rotary, Beta Gamma Sigma (pres. 1988-89), Kappa Alpha. Presbyterian (elder, trustee). Home: 1890 Shadowlawn St Jacksonville FL 32205-9430 Office: 1890 Shadowlawn St Jacksonville FL 32205-9430 Office Phone: 904-388-1148. E-mail: wtomlins@comcast.net.

TOMLINSON-KEASEY, CAROL ANN, university administrator; b. Washington, Oct. 15, 1942; d. Robert Bruce and Geraldine (Howe) Tomlinson; m. Charles Blake Keasey, June 13, 1964; children: Kai Linson, Amber Lynn. BS, Pa. State U., 1964; MS, Iowa State U., 1966; PhD, U. Calif., Berkeley, 1970. Lic. psychologist, Calif. Asst. prof. psychology Trenton (NJ) State Coll., 1969-70, Rutgers U., New Brunswick, NJ, 1970-72; prof. U. Nebr., Lincoln, 1972-77, U. Calif., Riverside, 1977-92, acting dean Coll. Humanities and Social Scis., 1986-88, chmn. dept. psychology, 1989-92, vice provost for acad. planning and pers. Davis, 1992-97, vice provost for acad. initiatives, 1997-99, chancellor, 1999—. Author: Child's Eye View, 1980, Child Development, 1985, numerous chpts. to books; contbr. articles to profl. jours. Recipient Disting. Tchr. award U. Calif., 1986. Mem. APA, Soc. Rsch. in Child Devel., Riverside Aquatics Assn. (pres.). Office: PO Box 2039 Merced CA 95344 Office Phone: 209-724-4417.

TOMLJANOVICH, ESTHER M. retired judge; b. Galt, Iowa, Nov. 1, 1931; d. Chester William and Thelma L. (Brooks) Moellering; m. William S. Tomljanovich, Dec. 26, 1957; 1 child, William Brooks Tomljanovich. AA, Itasca C.C., 1951; BSL, St. Paul Coll. Law, 1953, LLB, 1955. Bar: Minn. 1955, U.S. Dist. Ct. Minn. 1958. Asst. revisor of statutes State of Minn., St. Paul, 1957-66, revisor of statutes, 1974-77, dist. ct. judge Stillwater, 1977-90; assoc. justice Minn. Supreme Ct., St. Paul, 1990—98, ret., 1998. Adv. bd. women offenders Minn. Dept. Corrections, 1999—; leadership com. So. Minn. Legal Svcs. Corp., 1999—. Former mem. North St. Paul Bd. Edn., Maplewood Bd. Edn., Lake Elmo Planning Commn.; trustee William Mitchell Coll. Law, 1995—2004, Legal Rights Ctr., 1995—2004, pres., 1999; bd. dirs. Itasca C.C. Found., 1996—2004, Medica Health Ins. Co., 2001—, vice chair, 2003—. Recipient Centennial 2000 award William Mitchell Coll., Disting. Alumna award; named one of One Hundred Who Made a Difference William Mitchell Coll. Law Mem. Minn. State Bar Assn., Bus. and Profl. Women's Assn. St. Paul (former pres.), Minn. Women Lawyers (founding mem.). Office: 8533 Hidden Bay Trail Lake Elmo MN 55042

TOMME, CURTIS RABON, lawyer; b. Brady, Tex., Feb. 18, 1956; s. William Rabon Tomme and Hannah Mae Curtis; m. Elizabeth Ann Watson, Nov. 1, 1997. BS in Indsl. Distribution, Tex. A&M U., 1978; JD, Tex. Tech U., 1988. Bar: Tex. 1989. Asst. dist. atty. Taylor County, Abilene, Tex. Bd. dirs. Salvation Army, Abilene, sec., 1999-2000, vice chair 2001-03; bd. dirs. Habitat for Humanity, vice chmn. 1999—; staff mem. Rudy Issard for Congress Camp, Abilene, 1995-96. Mem. Abilene Bar Assn., Abilene C. of C., Abilene A&M Club (pres. 2000). Office: Taylor County Criminal Dist Atty 400 Oak St Ste 110 Abilene TX 79602-1527

TOMMEY, CHARLES ELDON, retired surgeon; b. Nashville, Ark., Jan. 13, 1922; s. William Robert and America Anna (Compton) T.; m. Clara Blair Newman, Aug. 28, 1948; children: Robert, Jean, Phillip, Dale, Scott. Student, Henderson State Tchrs. Coll., 1940-42; BSM, U. Ark. Sch. Medicine, 1944, MD, 1945. Diplomate Am. Bd. Surgery. Intern City Hosp., Columbus, Ga., 1945-46; surg. resident Bapt. Hosp., Little Rock, 1948-49, VA Hosp., Cleve., 1950-54; pvt. practice surgery El Dorado, Ark., 1954-95; ret., 1995. Asst. clin. instr. surgery U. Ark. Coll. Medicine. Capt. U.S. Army Med. Corps, 1943-45, 46-48. Fellow ACS. Baptist. Avocations: golf, photography. Home: 123 Glenridge Pky El Dorado AR 71730-3117

TOMNITZ, DONALD J. construction executive; Divsn. v.p. D.R. Horton, Inc., Arlington, Tex., 1983, v.p. western region, 1994, pres. home bldg. divsn., 1996, exec. v.p., CEO, 1998—, also bd. dirs. Office: DR Horton Inc 1901 Ascension Blvd Ste 100 Arlington TX 76006-6521

TOMOMATSU, HIDEO, chemist; b. Tokyo, June 8, 1929; arrived in U.S., 1959; s. Shinsai Nasu and Suma T.; m. Yuko Ito, Nov. 12, 1967; 1 child, Tadao. BSChemE., Waseda U., 1952; MS in Chemistry, U. of the Pacific, 1960; PhD in Chemistry, Ohio State U., 1964. Registered profl. engr., Tex., U.S. patent agt. Chem. Hodogaya Chem. Co., Tokyo, 1952-59, Texaco Chems. Co., Austin, Tex., 1964-72; Quaker fellow Quaker Oats Co., Barrington, Ill., 1972-96; cons. Functional Food Resources, Inc., Escondido, Calif., 1996—. Contbr. articles to profl. jours.; patentee in field. Mem. Am. Chem. Soc., Am. Assn. Cereal Chemists, Inst. Food Technologists. Home: 2555 Seascape Gln Escondido CA 92026-3862 Personal E-mail: hitomoyuko@earthlink.net.

TOMOVIC, MILETA MILOS, mechanical engineer, educator; b. Belgrade, Yugoslavia, Dec. 29, 1955; came to U.S., 1979; naturalized, 1995; s. Milos Nedeljko and Danica Dane (Lemaic) T.; m. Cynthia Lou Bell, Apr. 15, 1994; children: Adriane, Milos, Senja. BS, U. Belgrade, 1979; MS, MIT, 1981; PhD, U. Mich., 1991. Rsch. asst. MIT, Cambridge, Mass., 1979-81, 83-85; design engr. Foundry Belgrade, 1982-83, sys. engr. Energoprojekt, Belgrade, 1985-86; assoc. prof. Purdue U., West Lafayette, Ind., 1991—2003, W.C. Furnas prof., 2003—; v.p. Metalcasting Engring., Inc., 1996—; spl. asst. to dean, advanced man. Purdue U., 2004—. Cons. Tech. Assistance Program, 1993—; mem. adv. bd. Engineered Casting Solutions. Assoc. editor Foundry, 1995—, also conf. procs. in field; author textbook on materials and mfg. processes. Named Key prof., Foundry Edn. Found., 1991—, Ind. Rep. of Yr., 2002; recipient Rep. Gold medal, 2002, 2003, Dir.'s award, Am. Metal Casting Consortium, 2002, Outstanding Faculty, 1967, 2001; grantee, Purdue Rsch. Found., 1994—95. Mem.: ASME (chpt. bd. dirs. 1993—95), Am. Foundrymen Soc. (chpt. bd. dirs. 1995—), Am. Soc. Engring. Educators, Am. Soc. Metals (chpt. chmn. 1994—95). Christian Orthodox. Achievements include patents in areas of metalcasting refiner plates for pulp and paper industry, mill balls for cement and metal extraction industry; research on wear and impact resistant materials, new metalcasting technologies, welding processes. Home: 3344 Dubois St West Lafayette IN 47906-1199 Office: Purdue U MET Dept Knoy Hall West Lafayette IN 47907 Office Phone: 765-494-5866. E-mail: tomovicm@purdue.edu.

TOMPKINS, CHRISTOPHER ROBIN, director, educator; b. Mt. Kisco, N.Y., Apr. 2, 1967; s. John Roger Tompkins, Sr. and Marie Helen Tompkins; m. Katherine Ann Ide Tompkins, July 31, 1993; children: Hannah Elizabeth Ide, Phoebe Neel DeVoe. BA, Colby Coll., 1989; MSSc, Syracuse U., 2000. History tchr. Wellington Sch., Columbus, Ohio, 1989—90, Greens Farms Acad., Greens Farms, Conn., 1990—93; tchr., coll. counselor Acad. Cotopax, Quito, Ecuador, 1993—94; dir. admission South Kent Sch., Kent, Conn., 1994—96; dir. admission and fin. aid St. Andrews Sewanee Sch., Sewanee, Tenn., 1996—99; asst. headmaster Canterbury Episcopal Sch., DeSoto, Tex., 1999—2000; dir. admission and fin. aid Mercersburg Acad., Mercersburg, Pa., 2000—. Chair admission com. Colby Alumni Coun., Waterville, Maine, 1997—2001; bd. dirs. Chambersburg Montessori Sch., Chambersburg, Pa., Cloud Forest Sch. Found., Costa Rica. Author: (novels) Croton Dams and Aqueduct, 2000; contbg. author: Far and Wide: Diversity in Boarding School, 1998. Founding dir. Southeastern Assn. of Boarding Schs., 1997; vice chair bd. dirs. Cloud Forest Sch. Found., 2004—; active St. Johns Episcopal Ch., Hagerstown, Md., 2000—. Mem.: Fountain Head C.C., Yorktown Sportsman's Club. Avocations: model railroading, stamps, golf, cross country skiing, hiking. Home and Office: 300 E Seminary St Mercersburg PA 17236-1550 E-mail: ct3408@hotmail.com.

TOMPKINS, JOSEPH BUFORD, JR., lawyer; b. Roanoke, Va., Apr. 4, 1950; s. Joseph Buford and Rebecca Louise (Johnston) T.; children: Edward Graves, Claiborne Forbes. BA in Politics summa cum laude, Washington and Lee U., 1971; M Pub. Policy, JD, Harvard U., 1975. Bar: Va. 1975, U.S. Ct. Appeals (D.C. cir.), U.S. Ct. Appeals (5th cir.), 1977, U.S. Supreme Ct. 1977, U.S. Dist. Ct. D.C. 1982, U.S. Ct. Appeals (11th cir.) 1982, U.S. Ct. Appeals (3d cir.) 1983, U.S. Ct. Appeals (6th cir.) 1985, U.S. Ct. Appeals (7th cir.) 1991, U.S. Ct. Appeals (4th cir.) 1993, U.S. Ct. Internat. Trade 1996. Assoc. Sidley & Austin (now Sidley Austin Brown & Wood LLP), Washington, 1975-79, ptnr., 1982—; assoc. dir. Office Policy and Mgmt. Analysis criminal divsn. U.S. Dept. Justice, Washington, 1979-80, dep. chief fraud sect. criminal divsn., 1980-82. Contbr. articles to profl. jours. Mem. Va. Bd. Health Professions, Richmond, 1984-92, vice chmn., 1984-86, chmn., 1986-88, 90-91. Mem. ABA (white collar crime com. criminal justice sect. 1980—, chmn. task force on computer crime 1982-92), Va. Bar Assn., D.C. Bar Assn., Phi Beta Kappa. Home: 8146 Wellington Rd Alexandria VA 22308-1214 Office: Sidley Austin Brown & Wood LLP 1501 K St NW 8th Fl Washington DC 20005 Fax: 202-736-8711. E-mail: jtompkins@sidley.com.

TOMPKINS, RAYMOND EDGAR, lawyer; b. Oklahoma City, July 13, 1934; s. Charles Edgar and Eva Mae (Hodges) T.; m. Sue Anne Sharpe, June 10, 1963; children: Matthew Stephen, Christopher T., Katherine Anne. BS, Okla. State U., 1956; JD, U. Okla., 1963. Bar: Okla. 1963, U.S. Dist. Ct. (no. dist.) Okla. 1963, U.S. Dist. Ct. (we. dist.) Okla. 1964, U.S. Ct. Appeals (10th cir.) 1965, U.S. Supreme Ct. 1968, U.S. dist. Ct. (ea. dist.) Okla. 1969, U.S. Ct. Appeals (9th cir.) 1981, U.S. Ct. Appeals (4th cir.) 1986. Adminstrv. asst. U.S. Congress, 1966-68; ptnr. Linn & Helms, Oklahoma City, 1980-90, Daughery, Bradford, Haught & Tompkins, P.C., Oklahoma City, 1990-94; shareholder Conner & Winters, P.C., Oklahoma City, 1994—2003; sole practitioner Oklahoma City, 2003—. Past chmn. bd. trustees Okla. Ann. Methodist Conf., St. Luke's United Meth. Ch.; past chmn. adminstrv. bd.; mem. Okla. Bur. Investigation Commn., past chmn.; past gen. counsel Rep. State com., Interstate Oil Compact. Maj. USAR. Recipient award of Honor Oklahoma City Bi-Centennial Commn., 1976. Fellow Am. Coll. Civil Trial Mediators; master William S. Holliway Am. Inns of Ct. (emeritus, pres.), Robert J. Turner Am. Inn of Ct. (pres.); mem. ABA, Okla. County Bar Assn. (Pres.'s award 1988), Okla. Bar Assn. (chmn. bench and bar com. 1995-97, chmn. ADR sect., Law Day award), Nat. Arbitration Forum, Am. Arbitration Assn. (mediator/arbitrator), NASD (mediator, arbitrator), NYSE (mediator, arbitrator), Am. Judicature Soc., Assn. Atty.-Mediators (past pres. Okla. chpt., nat. dir. and sec., Nat. President's award 2000), Blue Key, Lions (pres. Oklahoma City chpt.). Home: 3148 Birch Bark Ln Oklahoma City OK 73120 Office: 1001 NW 63d St Ste 200 Oklahoma City OK 73116 Office Phone: 405-607-8303.

TOMPKINS, RONALD GARY, surgeon, educator, biomedical investigator; b. Many, La., Sept. 24, 1951; s. Horace and Ruby (McFerrin) T.; m. Denise Marie Clougherty, Mar. 7, 1985; children: Megan Elizabeth, Ryan Coleman, Caitlin Maureen. BS in Chemistry summa cum laude, Tulane U., 1972, MD, 1976; SM in Chem. Engring., ScD in Med. and Chem. Engring., MIT, 1983. Diplomate Am. Bd. Surgery (bd. dirs. 1994—), Am. Bd. Surg. Critical Care. Intern in surgery Mass. Gen. Hosp., Boston, 1976-77, asst. resident, then resident, 1977-79, 83-85, asst. in surgery, 1985-87, asst. surgeon, 1988-90, assoc. chief trauma and burn svcs., 1987-90, chief, 1990—, assoc. vis. surgeon, then vis. surgeon, 1991—; clin. fellow in surgery Harvard Med. Sch., Boston, 1977-79, 92-85, instr., then asst. prof. surgery, 1985-90, assoc. prof., 1990-96, John F. Burke prof. surgery, 1996—. Rsch. assoc. MIT, Cambridge, Mass., 1985-86; asst. in surgery Shriners Burns Inst., Boston, 1987-88, asst. surgeon, 1988-90, chief staff, 1990—; numerous presentations in field at regional, nat. and internat. orgns. Mem. editl. bd. Critical Care Medicine, 1991—, Jour. Tissue Engring., 1994—, Jour. Am. Soc. Artificial Internal Organs, 1994—; contbr. over 217 articles and revs. to med. jours., chpts. to books; patent for culturing liver cells. DuPont fellow MIT, 1979-80, E.R. Gilliland fellow, 1980-81, William Prince fellow, 1981-83; Edward D. Churchill rsch. fellow Mass. Gen. Hosp., 1981-82, fellow Am. Surg. Assn. Found., 1987-88; grantee Link Found., 1985—, NIH, 1987-91, Whitaker Found., 1988-91, Nat. Inst. Gen. Med. Scis., 1992—, Nat. Inst. Digestive Diseases and Kidney, 1987-94, Shriners Hosps., 1988—. Fellow ACS; mem. AMA, AAAS, AIChE, Assn. for Acad. Surgery, Am. Chem. Soc., Am. Burn Assn., Am. Fedn. for Clin. Rsch., Soc. Critical Care Medicine, Surg. Infection Soc., Am. Soc. for Artificial Internal Organs, Shock Soc., Am. Assn. for Surgery of Trauma, Am. Soc. for Laser Medicine and Surgery, Soc. for Cryobiology, Soc. Univ. Surgeons, Am. Assn. for Study Liver Diseases, Am. Trauma Soc., New Eng. Surg. Soc., Cell Transplant Soc., Phi Beta Kappa, Alpha Omega Alpha, numerous others. Office: GRB1302 Mass Gen Hosp 55 Fruit St Boston MA 02114-2622 Home: 2 Hawthorne Pl Apt 8N Boston MA 02114-2309

TOMPKINS, RONALD K. surgeon; b. Malta, Ohio, Oct. 14, 1934; s. Kenneth Steidley and Mildred Lillian (Loomis) T.; m. Suzanne Colbert, June 9, 1956; children: Gregory Alan, Teresa Susan, Geoffrey Stuart. BA, Ohio U., 1956; MD, Johns Hopkins U., 1960; MS, Ohio State U., 1968; DSc (hon.), U. Bordeaux, 1995. Diplomate Am. Bd. Surgery. Intern in surgery Ohio State U., 1960-61, resident in surgery, 1964-68, adminstrv. chief resident in surgery, 1968-69, NIH trainee in acad. surgery, instr. physiol. chemistry, 1966-69; asst. prof. surgery UCLA, 1969-73, assoc. prof., 1973-79, prof., 1979-2001, prof.

emeritus, 2001—, chmn. basic surg. tng. program, 1970-79, asst. dean student affairs, 1979-82, chief divsn. gen. surgery, 1982-88, chief gastrointestinal surgery, 1986-97, assoc. dean, 1988-91, dir. surg. edn., 1996—2004. Cons. VA Hosps. Editor-in-chief World Jour. Surgery, 1993-2004. With M.C. USAF, 1961-64. Recipient Disting Alumni award, Ohio U. Arts & Scis., 2001; fellow, Royal Soc. Medicine Eng., 1976—77; grantee, NIH, 1968—70, John A. Hartford Found., 1970—79. Fellow ACS (So. Calif. chpt. pres. 1987); mem. Am. Surg. Assn., Am. Gastroenterol. Assn., Am. Fedn. Clin. Rsch. Am. Inst. Nutrition, AMA, Assn. Acad. Surgery, Pacific Coast Surg. Assn. (recorder 1986-91, pres. 1995), Soc. Clin. Surgery, Soc. Surgery Alimentary Tract (sec. 1982-85, pres.-elect 1985, pres. 1986, chmn. bd. trustees 1987), Soc. Univ. Surgeons, Societe Internationale de Chirurgie (U.S. chpt. sec. 1990-94, pres. 1996-98), Internat. Biliary Assn. (pres. 1979-81), Bay Surg. Soc., LA Surg. Soc. (pres. 1981), Robert M. Zollinger/Ohio State U. Surg. Soc. (pres. 1988-90), Longmire Surg. Soc. (pres. 1997-99), Phi Beta Kappa, Sigma Xi, Alpha Omega Alpha, Delta Tau Delta. Republican. Achievements include research numerous publs. in gastrointestinal surgery and gastrointestinal metabolism and biochemistry. Office: U Calif Dept Surgery Los Angeles CA 90024

TOMPKINS, SUSIE, apparel company executive, creative director; children: Quincey, Summer. Design cons. Esprit de Corp, San Francisco. Office: Esprit de Corps Internat 3 Embarcadero Ctr Ste 2290 San Francisco CA 94111-4045 also: 1370 Broadway Fl 16 New York NY 10018-7302

TOMPSON, MARIAN LEONARD, professional society administrator; b. Chgo., Dec. 5, 1929; d. Charles Clark and Marie Christine (Bernardini) Leonard; m. Clement R. Tompson, May 7, 1949 (dec. 1981); children: Melanie Tompson Kandler, Deborah Tompson Frueh, Allison Tompson Fagerholm, Laurel Tompson Davies, Sheila Tompson Doucet, Brian, Philip. Student public and parochial schs., Chgo. and Franklin Park, Ill. Co-founder La Leche League (Internat.), Franklin Park, 1956, pres., 1956-80, dir., 1956—, pres. emeritus, 1990—; exec. dir. Alternative Birth Crisis Coalition, 1981-85; founder, exec. dir. AnotherLook, Inc., 2001—. Cons. WHO; bd. dirs. N.Am. Soc. Psychosomatic Ob-Gyn, Natural Birth and Natural Parenting, 1981-83; mem. adv. bd. Nat. Assn. Parents and Profls. for Safe Alternatives in Childbirth, Am. Acad. Husband-Coached Childbirth; mem. adv. bd. Fellowship of Christian Midwives; mem. profl. adv. bd. Home Oriented Maternity Experience; guest lectr. Harvard U. Med. Sch., UCLA Sch. Pub. Health, U. Antioquia Med. Sch., Medellín, Columbia, U. Ill. Sch. Medicine, Chgo., U. W.I., Jamaica, U. N.C., Nat. Coll. of Chiropractic, Am. Coll. Nurse Midwives, U. Parma, Italy, Inst. Psychology, Rome, Rockford (Ill.) Sch. Medicine, Northwestern U. Sch. Medicine, NGO Forum/4th World Conf. on Women, Beijing; mem. family com. Ill. Commn. on Status of Women, 1976-85; mem. perinatal adv. com. Ill. Dept. Pub. Health, 1980-83; mem. adv. bd. Internat. Nutrition Comm. Svc., 1980—; bd. cons. We Can, 1984—; exec. adv. bd. United Resources for Family Health and Support, 1985-86; mem. internat. adv. coun. World Alliance of Breast Feeding Action, 1996. Author: (with others) Safe Alternatives in Childbirth, 1976, 21st Century Obstetrics Now!, 1977, The Womanly Art of Breastfeeding, 6th edit., 1997, Five Standards for Safe Childbearing, 1981, But Doctor, About That Shot..., 1988, The Childbirth Activists Handbook, 1983; author prefaces and forwards in 11 books; columnist La Leche League News, 1958-80; columnist People's Doctor Newsletter, 1977-88, mem. adv. bd., cons., 1988-92; assoc. editor Child and Family Quar., 1967—; mem. med. adv. bd. East West Jour., 1980—; also articles. Mem. adv. bd. Shelters for Healthy Environments, 1998—2002, The Beginning Project, 2000. Recipient Gold medal of honor Centro de Rehabilitacao Nossa Senhora da Gloria, 1975, Night of 100 Stars III Achiever award Actors Fund Am., 1990, N.Y. Soc. Ethical Culture Ethical Humanist award, 1999, 100 Women Making a Difference Today's Chgo. Woman. Mem. Nat. Assn. Postpartum Care Svcs. (adv. bd.), Chgo. Cmty. Midwives (adv. bd.), World Alliance for Breast Feeding Action (mem. internat. adv. coun. 1997). Office: 1400 N Meacham Rd Schaumburg IL 60173-4808 Personal E-mail: m.tompson@comcast.net.

TOMS, JUSTINE WILLIS, educational organization executive; b. Evanston, Ill., Oct. 16, 1942; d. Robert Jacques and Ruth (Herzfeld) W.; m. Donald Carroll Welch, Nov. 1962 (div. 1969); 1 child, Robert Gregory Welch; m. Michael Anthony Toms, Dec. 16, 1972. BS, Auburn U., 1967. Elem. sch. tchr. Sylacauga (Ala.) Sch. System, 1966-69; exec. dir. New Dimensions Radio, Ukiah, Calif., 1973—. Seminar leader in field. Co-author: True Work: Doing What You Love and Loving What You Do, 1998; editor (quar. jour.) New Dimensions Jour., 1987—. Democrat. Buddhist. Avocations: horseback riding, drumming.

TOMS, KATHLEEN MOORE, nurse; b. San Francisco, Dec. 31, 1943; d. William Moore and Phyllis Josephine (Barry) Stewart; m. Benjamin Peskoff (dec. Aug. 2002); children from previous marriage: Kathleen Marie Toms Myers, Kelly Therese Toms Shaver. AA, City Coll., San Francisco, 1963; BPS in Nursing Edn., Elizabethtown (Pa.) Coll., 1973; MS in Edn., Temple U., 1977; MS in Nursing, Gwynedd Mercy Coll., 1988; grad., U.S. Army War Coll., 1999. RN, Calif. Med.-surg. nurse St. Joseph Hosp., Fairbanks, Alaska, 1963-65, emergency rm. nurse Lancaster, Pa., 1965-69, blood, plasma and components nurse, 1969-71; pres. F.E. Barry Co., Lancaster, 1971—; dir. insvc. edn. Lancaster Osteo. Hosp., 1971-75; coord. practical nursing program Vocat. Tech. Sch., Coatesville, Pa., 1976-77; dir. nursing Pocopson Home, West Chester, Pa., 1978-80, Riverside Hosp., Wilmington, Del., 1980-83; assoc. Coatesville VA Hosp., 1983-89, chief nurse, 1984-89; with VA Ctrl. Office; supr. psychiat. nursing Martinez (Calif.) VA Med. Ctr., 1989-94; assoc. chief nursing svc. edn. VA Ho. Calif. Sys. Clinics, Pleasant Hill, 1994—; nurse mgr. VA Ctr. Rehab. and Extended Care, Martinez, 1996—; patient health edn. coord. VA No. Calif. Health Care Sys., Martinez, 2000—. Trainee assoc. chief Nursing Home Care Unit, Washington; mem. Pa. Gov.'s Coun. on Alcoholism and Drug Abuse, 1974-76; mem. Del. Health Coun. Med.-Surg. Task Force, 1981-83; dir. Lancaster Cmty. Health Ctr., 1973-76; lectr. in field. Col. Nurse Corps, USAR. Decorated Army Commendation medals (6), Meritorious Svc. medals (2); recipient Cmty. Svc. award Citizens United for Better Pub. Rels., 1974; award Sertoma, Lancaster, 1974; Outstanding Citizen award Sta. WGAL-TV, 1975; U.S. Army Achievement award, 1983. Mem. Elizabethtown U. Alumni Assn., Temple U. Alumni Assn., Pa. Nurses Assn. (bd. dirs. 1972-76), Sigma Theta Tau, Beta Gamma. Achievements include invention of auto-infuser for blood or blood components. Home: 208 Sea Mist Dr Vallejo CA 94591-7748 E-mail: ktoms007@aol.com.

TOMS, MICHAEL ANTHONY, broadcast journalist, editor, writer, producer; b. Washington, June 7, 1940; s. Austin Herman Toms and Margaret Dorothy (Pitcher) Slavinsky; m. Justine Willis, Dec. 16, 1972; children: Michael Anthony, Robert Welch. Student, U. Miami, 1959-60, U. Va. Extension, 1961-63; postgrad., Calif. Inst. Integral Studies, San Francisco, 1973-75; DrTheology, Sem. St. Basil the Great, Sydney, Australia, 1981; DHL (hon.), U. Humanistic Studies, San Diego, 1983. Field govt. rep. VariTyper Corp., Washington, 1960-64, sales mgr. San Francisco, 1964-67, regional sales mgr. San Bernardino, 1967-68; pres. Creative Mktg. Assocs., San Francisco, 1968-73; chmn. bd. The Response Mktg. Group, San Francisco, 1971-73; CEO Michael A. Toms & Assocs., San Francisco, 1973-76; pres. New Dimensions Found., San Francisco, 1973—. Sr. acquisitions editor Harper Collins, San Francisco, 1989-95; exec. prodr., host nat. pub. radio interview series New Dimensions, 1980—, on-line radio series Spirit of the Times, 1999—; chmn. bd. emeritus Calif. Inst. Integral Studies, San Francisco, 1979-83; exec. dir. Audio Inds., Inc., San Francisco, 1981-83; adj. prof. Marylhurst Coll. Grad. Sch. of Bus., 1993—, Union Grad. Sch., 1994—; founder, CEO New Dimensions Broadcasting Network, 1994—; exec. editor New Dimensions Book Series, 1993—; mem. bd. dirs. KQED, Inc., San Francisco, 1980-83, Green Earth Found., 1989-95, KZYX-FM, Mendocino County, Calif., 1989-91; mem. bd. adv. The Great Round, 1989-95. Author: Worlds Beyond, 1978, The New Healers, 1980, An Open Life, 1988, At The Leading Edge, 1991, Wise Words, 1997, The Power of Meditation and Prayer, 1997, The Well of Creativity, 1997, The Soul of Business, 1997, Roots of Healing, 1997, Money, Money, Money, 1998, Buddhism in the West, 1998; co-author: True Work, 1998; exec. prodr.: Spirit of the Times, Deep Ecology for the 21st Century; editor The Inner Edge newsletter, 1997—. Mem. Task Force to Promote Self Esteem and Personal and Social Responsibility, Mendocino County, Calif., 1988-89; mem. internat. adv. bd. Radio for Peace Internat., 1988—; bd. dirs. Human Potential Audio Found., 1994-97; mem. adv. bd. New Road Map Found., 1991—. Mem. Internat. Assn. for Socially Responsible Radio (founding dir. 1991—). Avocations: travel, writing, reading, birdwatching. Home: PO Box 1029 Ukiah CA 95482-1029 Office: New Dimensions Found PO Box 569 Ukiah CA 95482-0569

TOMSON, JON SCOTT, business professional; b. Rochester, N.Y., Dec. 13, 1948; s. Peter and Genevieve Helen Tomson; m. Carol Neuman, June 24, 1973; children: Brett Neuman, Christopher William. B of Indsl. Engring., Kettering U., 1971; M of Urban Planning, CUNY, 1974. Asst. dir. N.J. Dept. Higher Edn., Trenton, 1974—77; dir. human resources N.J. Dept. Human Svcs., Trenton, 1977—81; dir. sales and mktg. Getinge Internat., Lakewood, NJ, 1981—90; prin. CUH2A, Inc., Princeton, NJ, 1990—. Trustee Forum Inst. for Pub. Policy, Princeton, 1999—, Friends of Old Yellow Meeting House, Allentown, N.J., 1980—. Mem.: Internat. Soc. Pharm. Engring. (officer 1995—, chmn. bd. 2002, Mem. of Yr. 1995), Soc. Coll. and Univ. Planning, Soc. Mktg. Profl. Svcs., Am. Inst. Cert. Planners. Avocations: soccer, skiing, scuba diving. Office: CUH2A Inc 211 Carnegie Ctr Princeton NJ 08540

TON, PAUL, investor, educator; b. Buffalo, N.Y., Apr. 30, 1926; s. Edward Cornelius Ton and Laura Delia Slotboom; m. Joan Karen Marshall, June 18, 1951; children: Scott, Elizabeth, Robert, John. BS, Union Coll., Schenectady, N.Y., 1949; MA, Stanford U., Palo Alto, Calif., 1951, U. Denver, 1953, PhD, 1969. Instr. electronics USAF, Denver, 1951—52; tchr. history Denver Pub. Schs., 1952—89; adj. prof. history Metro State Coll., Denver, 1990—2003. Dept. head, Driver Edn. Am. Auto Assn., Denver, 1957—64; dept. chair South H.S., Denver, 1972—77; history cons. Am. Frontier TV series, 1985—87; mng. dir. Westton Prodns., 1995—. Contbr. (book) The Mining Frontier, 1967, Henry M. Porter, Empire Builder, 1991. Cpl. U.S. Army, 1944—46, PTO. Mem.: Western Hist. Assn., Orgn. of Am. Historians, Am. Hist. Assn. Republican. Presbyterian. Avocation: photography. Home: 390 Lansing St Aurora CO 80010 Personal E-mail: forpton@comcast.net.

TONACK, DELORIS, elementary school educator; Elem. tchr. math. and sci. Goodrich Jr. High Sch., 1996—. Recipient Nebr. State Tchr. of Yr. award math./sci., 1992. Office: Sci Focus Program 1222 S 27th St Lincoln NE 68502-1832

TONAPI, SANDEEP SHRIKANT, engineer; s. Shrikant Vasant and Meera Tonapi; m. Leena Vaidya, Apr. 6, 1999; children: Soumitra, Siddhant. PhD, SUNY, 2001. Rsch. assoc. Rsch. Found., SUNY, Binghamton, NY, 1996—2001; rsch. engr. Gen. Electric Global Rsch., Niskayuna, NY, 2001—. Principal investigator (research) Nanoengineered thermal interfaces for next generation microelectroncis ($7.2MM from NIST, 2002); contbr. articles various profl. jours. Grantee $7.2MM, NIST - US Dept. of Commerce, 2002. Mem.: Am. Soc. Mech. Engineers (assoc.). Achievements include invention of 9 patent applications with US patent Office in the areas of nanostructured materials and thermal management of microelectronics; Chaired 5 sessions in the past 2 years at leading ASME conferences. Avocations: travel, history. Personal E-mail: tonapi@crd.ge.com. E-mail: tonapi@crd.ge.com.

TONDEUR, PHILIPPE MAURICE, mathematician, educator; b. Zurich, Switzerland, Dec. 7, 1932; came to U.S., 1964, naturalized, 1974; s. Jean and Simone (Lapaire) T.; m. Claire-Lise Ballansat, Dec. 20, 1965. PhD, U. Zurich, 1961. Rsch. fellow U. Paris, 1961-63; lectr. math. U. Zurich, 1963-64, U. Buenos Aires, 1964, Harvard U., Cambridge, Mass., 1964-65, U. Calif., Berkeley, 1965-66; asso. prof. Wesleyan U., Middletown, Conn., 1966-68; assoc. prof. U. Ill., Urbana, 1968-70, prof., 1970—2002, prof. emeritus, 2002—, chair dept. math., 1996-99. Vis. prof. Auckland U., 1968, Eidg. Techn. Hochschule U. Heidelberg, 1973, U. Zurich, 1987, U. Rome, 1984, Ecole Poly., Paris, 1987, U. Santiago de Compostela, Spain, 1987, Max Planck Inst., 1987, U. Leuven (Belgium), 1990, Keio U., Yokohama, Japan, 1993; assoc. mem. Ctr. Advanced Study U. Ill., 1977—78, 1991—92; dir. divsn. math. sci. NSF, 1999—2002. Contbr. articles to profl. jours. Recipient Divsn. Math. Scis. Govtl. Math. award; fellow Swiss Nat. Sci. Found., Harvard U., U. Ill. Mem.: Math. Assn. Am., Soc. Indsl. and Applied Math. (Frederick A. Howes pub. svc. award), Soc. Math. France, Schweiz Math. Gesellschaft, Am. Math. Soc. Office: U Ill Math Dept Urbana IL 61801 E-mail: tondeur@math.uiuc.edu.

TONEGAWA, SUSUMU, biology professor; b. Nagoya, Japan, Sept. 5, 1939; arrived in U.S., 1963; s. Tsutoma and Miyoko T. (Masuko) Tonegawa; m. Mayumi Yoshinari, Sept. 28, 1985; children: Hidde, Hanna, Satto. BS, Kyoto U., Japan, 1963; PhD, U. Calif., San Diego, 1968. Rsch. asst. U. Calif., San Diego, 1963—64, teaching asst., 1964—68; mem. Basel (Switzerland) Inst. Immunology, 1971—81; Whitehead prof. biology MIT, Cambridge, 1981—. Investigator Howard Hughes Med. Inst., 1988—; dir. MIT Ctr. for Learning and Memory, 1994—; professorship Amgen, Inc., 1994. Mem. editl. bd. Immunity. Decorated Order of Culture Emperor of Japan; co-recipient Albert Lasker Med. Rsch. award, 1987; named Person with Cultural Merit, Japanese Govt., 1983; recipient Cloetta prize, 1978, Avery Landsteiner prize, Gesselschaft fur Immunologie, 1981, Louisa Gross Horwitz prize, Columbia U., 1982, Gardiner Found. Internat. award, Toronto, Ont., Can., 1983, Robert Koch Found. prize, Bonn, Germany, 1986, Nobel prize in physiology or medicine, 1987. Mem.: NAS (fgn. assoc.), Scandinavian Soc. Immunology (hon.), Am. Assn. Immunologists (hon.). Office: MIT Rm E17-353 77 Massachusetts Ave Cambridge MA 02139-4307*

TONELLO-STUART, ENRICA MARIA, political economist; b. Monza, Italy; d. Alessandro P. and Maddalena M. (Marangoni) Tonello; m. Albert E. Smith; m. Charles L. Stuart. BA in Internat. Affairs, Econs., U. Colo., 1961; MA, Claremont Grad. Sch., 1966, PhD, 1971. Sales mgr. Met. Life Ins. Co., 1974-79; pres., CEO, ETS R&D, Inc., Palos Verdes Peninsula, Calif., 1977—. Dean internat. studies program Union U., L.A. and Tokyo; lectr. internat. affairs and mktg. UCLA Ext., Union U. Pub., editor Tomorrow Outline Jour., 1963—, The Monitor, 1988; pub. World Regionalism-An Ecological Analysis, 1971, A Proposal for the Reorganization of the United Nations, 1966, The Persuasion Technocracy, Its Forms, Techniques and Potentials, 1966, The Role of the Multinationals in the Emerging Globalism, 1978; developed the theory of social ecology and econsociometry. Organizer 1st family assistance program Langley FB Tactical Air Command, 1956-58. Recipient vol. svc. award VA, 1956-58, ARC svc. award, 1950-58. Mem. Corp. Planners Assn. (treas. 1974-79), Investigative Reporters and Editors, World Future Soc. (pres. 1974-75), Asian Bus. League, Soc. Environ. Journalists, Chinese Am. Assn. (life), Japan Am. Assn., L.A. World Trade Ctr., Palos Verdes C. of C. (legis. com.), L.A. Press Club (bd. dirs.), Zonta (chmn. internat. com. South Bay), Pi Sigma Alpha. Avocations: writing, collecting old books and maps, community service, travel.

TONER, DONALD THOMAS, music educator; m. Christina Elisabeth Otten, Aug. 8, 1997. MusB, U. of Mass., 1981; MusM, Yale U., 1991; diploma, Yale U., New Haven, CT, 1992; cert. in Performing, Eastman Sch. of Music, 1994; D in Musical Arts, Eastman Sch. of Music, N.Y., 1994. Instr. SUNY, Plattsburgh, NY, 1985—89, vis. prof. Fredonia, NY, 1993—94, instr. Plattsburgh, 1995—96; asst. prof. U. of Vt., Burlington, 1995—2003, assoc. prof., 2003—. Prin. percussionist Vt. Symphony Orch., 1983—; substitute percussionist Rochester (N.Y.) Philharm. Orch., 1992—95; condr. Vt. All-State Orch., 1993. Scholar, Yale Sch. of Music, 1992. Mem.: Coll. Band Dirs. Nat. Assn. (state pres. 1999—2002), Vt. Musicians Union (vice-president 1996—98), Percussive Arts Soc. (pres. Vt. Chpt. 1999—2002). Home: 47 Sandy Lane Burlington VT 05401 Office: University of Vermont So Prospect St Burlington VT 05401

TONER, MICHAEL E. commissioner; BA with distinction, U. Va, 1986; MA in polit. sci., Johns Hopkins U., 1989; JD cum laude, Cornell Law Sch., 1992. Bar: DC, Va., US Supreme Court, 4th US Circuit Court of Appeals, US Dist. Courts, DC and Eastern Dist. Va. Chief counsel Rep. Nat. Com., 2001; gen. counsel Bus-Cheney Transistion, 2000, Bush-Cheney 2000 Presidential Campaign, 2000; deputy counsel Rep. Nat. Com., 1997—99; counsel Dole-Kemp Presidential Campaign, 1996; assoc. atty. Wiley, Rein, & Fielding, Washington, 1992—96. Office: Fed Election Commn 999 E St NW Washington DC 20463

TONER, MICHAEL F. journalist; b. LeMars, Iowa, Mar. 17, 1944; s. Francis F. and Mary Ann (Delaney) Toner; m. Patricia L. Asleson, Aug. 28, 1966; children: Susan Michelle, Sharon Lynn. BA cum laude, U. Iowa, 1966; postgrad., U. Okla., Peru; MS cum laude, Northwestern U., 1967. Reporter UPI, Chgo., 1966—67; bur. chief Miami Herald, Key West, Fla., 1967—68, reporter, 1968—69, asst. city editor, 1970—72; sci./environ. writer Miami (Fla) Herald, 1973—84; sci. editor Atlanta Jour. and Constn., 1984—91, sci. writer, 1991—. Co-author: Florida by Paddle and Pack, 1979; contbr. articles to mags. Recipient Pulitzer Prize for explanatory journalism, 1993, Stanford U. Profl Journalism fellow, 1973. Avocations: photography, swimming, cooking, stamp collecting/philately. Office: Atlanta Journal and Constn 72 Marietta St NW Atlanta GA 30303-2804

TONEVA, ELENA T. education educator, researcher; d. Todor Lubenov Angelov and Jordanka S. Angelova; m. Thomas V. Tonev, Dec. 29, 1974; children: Daniela T., Vassi T. PhD, Sofia U., Bulgaria, 1979. Rsch. fellow Bulgarian Acad. of Scis., Sofia, 1979—83; asst. prof. Sofia U., Bulgaria, 1983—89; vis. instr. U. Toledo (Ohio), 1990—93; vis. asst. prof., assoc. prof. U. Mont., Missoula, 1993—2000; asst. prof. Ea. Wash. U., Cheney, 2000—. Cons. Bulgarian Pension Fund, Sofia. Author: Continued Fractions, 1989, Problems in Analysis, part 1, 1997, Problems in Analysis, part 2. Mem.: Am. Math. Soc., Math. Assn. of Am. Office: Eastern Washington Univ Kgs 216 526 5th St Cheney WA 99004 Office Phone: 509-359-4232. Office Fax: 509-359-4700. E-mail: etoneva@mail.ewu.edu.

TONEY, ANGELA M. medical administrator and educator; b. Southbridge, Mass., June 1, 1970; d. Alvin Darryl Toney; 1 child, Meghan. BS i Biology, BA in English, Harvard U., 1993, MPH, 1996. Med. asst., Boston, 1989-96; emergency med. technician EMT-I Boston EMS, 1991-95; rschr. Premier Rsch. Worldwide, Phila., 1997-98; med. instr. Star Tech. Inst., Upper Darby, Pa., 1997—, asst. dir., 1997-98, med. dir., 1998—, U. Pa., 1998—. Advisor Delaware County Intermediate Unit, 1997—; Disaster Health Svcs. vol. ARC, Phila., 1998—, vol. trainer, 1997—; med. exam. proctor NCCT, Overland Park, Kans., 1997—. Mem. Am. Assn. Med. Assts., Internat. Congress Med. Profls., Am. Soc. Clin. Lab. Sci., Tri-County Chpt. Med. Assts., Delaware County Computer Assn. (dir. pub. rels. 1998—), Delaware County C. of C., Alpha Beta Kappa Delta Pa. Democrat. Ropman Catholic. Avocations: black and white photography, travel, classical literature, foreign films. Office: Star Tech Inst 1570 Garrett Rd Upper Darby PA 19082-4500 also: U Pa 3400 Spruce St Philadelphia PA 19104-4206 E-mail: Angeland45@yahoo.com.

TONG, ALEX WAIMING, immunologist; b. Hong Kong, Apr. 8, 1952; came to U.S., 1970; s. Robert S. and Agnes M. (Cheng) Tong; m. Susan J. Radtke, May 23, 1980 (div. Mar. 1988); 1 child, Nicole L.; m. S. Quay Mercer, May 13, 1995 (div. Oct. 2003); children: Alexander C., Caitlyn Y., Madeleine H. BA in Biology, U. Oreg., 1973; PhD in Microbiology and Immunology, Oreg. Health Scis. U., 1980. Undergrad. teaching asst. biology dept. U. Oreg., Eugene, 1972-73; postdoctoral fellow Surg. Rsch. Lab. Portland VA Med. Ctr., 1980-82; rsch. assoc. in immunology Charles A. Sammons Cancer Ctr., Baylor U. Med. Ctr., Dallas, 1982-86; assoc. dir. immunology lab. Baylor U. Med. Ctr., 1986; asst. prof. Inst. Biomed. Studies, Baylor U., Waco, Tex., 1988-97, assoc. prof., 1997—2001, prof., 2002—; scientific dir. molecular & cell processing ctr., U.S. oncology rsch. Ctr., Dallas, 2002—04; dir. lab. rsch. Mary C. Crowley Med. Rsch. Ctr., 2004—. Prin. investigator Nat. Cancer Inst., Bethesda, Md., 1994—; adj. assoc. prof. immunology grad. studies program U. Tex. Southwestern Med. Ctr., Dallas, 1982—. Contbr. articles to profl. jours. Tatar rsch. fellow Med. Rsch. Found. Oreg., Portland, 1981-83. Mem.: Am. Soc. Gene Therapy, Am. Soc. Hematology, Am. Assn. Cancer Rsch., Am. Assn. Immunologists, Am. Amateur Karate Fedn. (dir. S.W. region), Internat. Traditional Karate Fedn. (cert. coach 1990—, cert. referee 1988—), Japan Karate Assn. Dallas (dir.). Democrat. Avocations: traditional karate, alpine skiing, scuba diving. Office: Baylor U Med Ctr Cancer Immunology Rsch Lab 3500 Gaston Ave Dallas TX 75246-2096

TONG, FREDA MADELINE, writer; b. Cooper, Maine, Mar. 19, 1942; d. Cecil Arthur and Edith May (Keen) Hatfield; m. Peter Chung-Ping Tong, Sept. 4, 1965; children: Peter Wendell, Joanna Tong Armour, Linda Tong Feldman. Grad., Glen Cove (Maine) Bible Sch., 1965; MA in Chinese Studies, Soochow U., Taipei, Taiwan, 1983. Missionary Christian Reformed World Missions, Taiwan, 1966—97. Author: (non-fiction) Sons for the Master, Chinese transl. Mem.: Writers' Critique Group. Republican. Christian Reformed. Avocations: travel, reading, needlecrafts, sewing. Home: 15459 El Molino St Fontana CA 92335

TONG, HING, mathematician, educator; b. Canton, China, Feb. 16, 1922; s. Shen-Beu and Fung-Kam (Cheng) T.; m. Mary Josephine Powderly, Aug. 19, 1956; children— Christopher Hing, Mary Elizabeth, William Joseph, Jane Frances, James John. AB, U. Pa., 1943; PhD, Columbia, 1947; MA (hon.), Wesleyan U., Middletown, Conn., 1961. NRC postdoctoral fellow Inst. Advanced Study, Princeton, 1947-48; lectr. Canton (China) U., 1949; Cutting travelling fellow Inst. Henri Poincare, Paris, France, 1950-51; asst. prof. Reed Coll., 1952-53; vis. asst. prof. Barnard Coll., 1953-54; mem. faculty Wesleyan U., 1954-67, prof. math., 1960-67, chmn. dept., 1962-64; prof. math. Fordham U., Bronx, N.Y., 1966-84, chmn. dept., 1967-74. Mem. U.S. subcom. World Orgn. Gen. Systems and Cybernetics. Contbr. profl. jours. Mem. Phi Beta Kappa, Sigma Xi. Home: 725 Cooper Ave Oradell NJ 07649-2334

TONG, KAITY, anchor; BA, Bryn Mawr Coll.; MA, Stanford U. Street reporter various West Coast radio/tv networks; anchor WABC Eyewitness News, WB-11 News at 10/WPIX-TV, N.Y.C. Recipient Exceptional Achievement award, Disting. Woman award, Star award, Edward R. Murrow award. Acitve United Cerebral Palsy, Children's Mus. of Manhattan, Juvenile Diabetes Found., Friends for Life, League for the Hard of Hearing. Office: WPIX-TV/Tribune Co 220 E 42d St New York NY 10017

TONG, ROSEMARIE, medical humanities and philosophy educator, consultant and researcher; b. Chgo., July 19, 1947; d. Joseph John and Lillian (Nedued) Behensky; m. Paul Ki-King Tong, Aug. 15, 1971 (dec. Apr. 1988); children: Paul Shih-Mien Tong, John Joseph Tong; m. Jeremiah Putnam, Aug. 1, 1992. BA, Marygrove Coll., 1970; MA, Cath. U., 1971; PhD, Temple U., 1978; LLD (hon.), Marygrove Coll., 1987; LHD (hon.), SUNY, Oneonta, 1993. Asst. and assoc. prof. philosophy Williams Coll., Williamstown, Mass., 1978-88; vis. disting. prof. humanities Davidson (N.C.) Coll., 1988-89, Thatcher Prof. in med. humanities and philosophy, 1989-99; prof. humanities and philosophy U. N.C., Charlotte, 1999—; dir. Ctr. for Profl. and Applied Ethics, Charlotte, 2002—. L. Stacy Davidson vis. chair in liberal arts U. Miss., Oxford, 1998; Louise M. Olmstead vis. prof. philosophy and women's studies, Lafayette Coll., Easton, Pa., 1993; disting. prof. health care ethics U. N.C., Charlotte, 1999—; manuscript reviewer Wadsworth Pub. Co., 1985-92; curriculum reviewer philosophy dept. Carlton and Bowdoin Colls., 1986; honors examiner Hobart and William Smith Colls., 1990; dissertation dir., adj. faculty The Union Inst., 1992-93; cons., judge, panelist, organizer and speaker in field; mem. numerous U. coms. Author: Women, Sex and the Law, 1984, Ethics in Policy Analysis, 1985, Feminist Thought: A Comprehensive Introduction, 1989, Feminist Philosophies: Problems, Theories, and Applications, 1991, Feminine and Feminist Ethics, 1993, Feminist Thought: A More Comprehensive Introduction, 1998, (with Larry Kaplan) Controlling Our Reproductive Destiny, 1994, Feminist Philosophy: Essential Readings in Theory, Reinterpretation and Application, 1994, Feminist Bioethics, 1997, Feminist Thought: A More Comprehensive Ethics, 1998, Globalizing Feminist Bioethics: Crosscultural Perspectives, 2000; contbr. numerous articles to profl. jours.; mem. various editl. bds. Project reviewer Annenberg/CPB Project, Washington, 1986; policy writer dvsn. health svcs. rsch. and policy U. Minn., 1988, Frank Graham Porter Early Childhood Ctr., U. N.C. Chapel Hill, 1988; mem. Charlotte task force Congl. Task Force Health Care, Congressman Alex

McMillan, 1991, standards and ethics com. Hospice N.C., 1991, resource and ethics coms. McMillan-Spratt Task Force Health Care Policy, 1992, pastoral care com. Carolinas Med. Ctr., 1990—, ethics com. Presbyn. Hosp., 1990—, N.E. Regional Hosp., 1991, Nat. Adv. Bd. Ethics in Reproduction, Washington, 1993; active Hastings Ctr. Project Undergrad. Values Edn., Briarcliff Manor, N.Y., 1993, N.C. Found. Humanities and Pub. Policy; mem. bioethics Resource Group, 1992—; mem. feminist approaches to bioethics network, 1996—; dir. med. humanities program Davidson Coll., 1988-98. Named Prof. of Yr., Carnegie Found. and Coun. Advancement and Support of Edn., 1986. Mem. Internat. Assn. for Feminist Approaches to Bioethics Network (coord. 1999—), Internat. Assn. Bioethics (chair 2003—), Am. Assn. for Bioethics and Humanities, Am. Cath. Philos. Assn., Am. Philos. Assn. (ad hoc com. computers, pub. and role of Am. Philos. Assn. 1984, adv. com. to program com. 1986-88, nomination com. 1989-91, nat. com. on status of women 1989-93, 2003—), Am. Legal Studies and Assn., Am. Soc. Pol. and Legal Philosophy, Am. Soc. Law and Medicine, Nat. Coun. Rsch. on Women, Nat. Women Studies Assn., Internat. Assn. Philosophy Law and Social Philosophy, Assn. Practical and Profl. Ethics, Society Christian Ethics, Soc. Women in Philosophy, Soc. Philosophy and Tech., Soc. Philosophy and Pub. Affairs, Soc. Study of Women Philosophers, Network Feminist Approaches to Bioethics, The Hastings Ctr., Triangle Bioethics Group, So. Soc. Philosophy and Psychology. Avocations: aerobics, boating, hiking. Office Phone: 704-687-2850.

TONG, SIU WING, computer programmer; b. Hong Kong, May 20, 1950; came to U.S., 1968; BA, U. Calif., Berkeley, 1972; PhD, Harvard U., 1979; MS, U. Lowell, 1984. Rsch. assoc. Brookhaven Nat. Lab., Upton, N.Y., 1979-83, software engr. Honeywell Info. Systems, Billerica, Mass., 1984-85, sr. programmer, analyst Hui Computer Cons., Berkeley, Calif., 1985-88; sr. v.p. devel., chief fin. officer Surgicenter Info. Systems, Inc., Orinda, Calif., 1989-94; sr. sys. specialist Info. Sys. Divsn. Contra Costa County Health Svcs., Martinez, Calif., 1995-97, info. tech. supr. Info. Sys. Divsn., 1997—. Vol. tchr. Boston Chinatown Saturday Adult Edn. Program of Tufts Med. Sch., 1977-79. Muscular Dystrophy Assn. fellow, 1980-82. Mem. AAAS, IEEE, Assn. Computing Machinery, N.Y. Acad. Scis. Home: 17 Beaconsfield Ct Orinda CA 94563-4203 Office: Contra Costa County Health Svcs 595 Center Ave Ste 210 Martinez CA 94553-4634 E-mail: swtong@hsd.co.contra-costa.ca.us.

TONGUE, PAUL GRAHAM, financial executive; b. Phila., Dec. 30, 1932; s. George Paul and Florence Amelia (Kogel) T.; m. Marjorie Joan Meyers, May 26, 1954; children: Suzanne Marjorie, Douglas Paul BS in Commerce, Drexel U., 1957; MBA, NYU, 1965. With Chase Manhattan Bank, N.Y.C., 1957-87; chmn. Plus Systems Inc., Denver, 1985; pres. Eppley-Tongue Assocs., Inc., Towson, Md., 1988—; exec. v.p. Veritas Venture Inc., Scotch Plains, N.J., 1990-91. Pres. Our Saviour Luth. Ch., Manhasset, N.Y., 1984; pres. 1st Night of Williamsburg, Inc.; bd. dirs. Ronald Reagan Club, Ford's colony Homeowners' Assn., Williamsburg Area Civic and Cultural Ctr., Inc., Sr. Exec. Resource Corps, Coll. William and Mary. Mem. Ford's Colony Country Club. Avocations: golf, classical music. E-mail: pgtongue@cox.net.

TONGUE, WILLIAM WALTER, economics and business consultant, educator; b. Worcester, Mass., May 24, 1915; s. Walter Ernest and Lena (Brown) T.; m. Beverly Harriet Cohan, Dec. 26, 1936; children— Barbara Tongue Duggan, Kathleen Tongue Alligood. AB, Dartmouth, 1937, M.C.S., 1938; PhD, U. Chgo., 1947. Jr. acct. Price, Waterhouse & Co. (C.P.A.'s), N.Y.C., 1938; instr. Coe Coll., Cedar Rapids, Iowa, 1941-42; spl. cons. OSS, 1942; fin. economist Fed. Res. Bank Chgo., 1942-44; economist Jewel Companies, Inc., Chgo., 1944-64; prof. econs. and finance U. Ill. Chgo., 1965-80. Prof. emeritus, 1980—; econ. cons. LaSalle Nat. Bank, Chgo., 1968-91; mem. com. CNA Fin. Separate Fund B., 1997-2003; dir. St. Joseph Light & Power Co., Mo., 1965-86; trustee Signode Employees' Savs. and Profit Sharing Trust Fund, 1980-89. Author articles; contbr.: to books including How We Can Halt Inflation and Still Keep Our Jobs, 1974. Bd. dirs., v.p. rsch. and stats. Chgo. Assn. Commerce and Industry, 1968-69; bd. dirs. Luther Village Owners Corp., v.p., 2002—. Mem. Nat. Assn. Bus. Economists (pres. 1962-63), Conf. Bus. Economists, Am. Statis. Assn. (pres. Chgo. chpt. 1951-52), Econ. Club Chgo., Investment Analysts Assn. Chgo., Inst. Chartered Fin. Analysts (chartered fin. analyst 1963), Midwest Fin. Assn. (pres. 1972-73). Home and Office: 1220 Village Dr Apt 427 Arlington Heights IL 60004-8123 Office Phone: 847-670-7836. Personal E-mail: williamtoungue@msn.com.

TONINI, LEON RICHARD, sales professional; b. Pittsfield, Mass., May 16, 1931; s. John Richard and Mabel Grayce (Rushbrook) T.; m. Helen Jo, Aug. 15, 1966; 1 son, John Richard II. BA in Mgmt., U. Md., 1951. Enlisted in U.S. Army, 1947, advanced through grades to master sgt., 1968; service in W.Ger., Korea and Vietnam; ret., 1974; dir. vets. employment and assistance Non-Commd. Officers Assn., San Antonio, 1974-75; supr. security Pinkerton's Inc., Dallas, 1975-78; gen. mgr. civic ctr. Travelodge Motor Hotel and Restaurant, San Francisco, 1978-85; sales rep. Vernon Co., 1985—. Chmn. San Francisco Vets. Employment Com., 1981. Served as sgt. maj. Calif. N.G., res. Decorated Bronze Star, Republic Vietnam Honor medal, 2d class. Mem. Non-Commd. Officers Assn. (dir. Calif. chpt.), Am. Legion, Assn. U.S. Army Res. Officers Assn., Amvets, Patrons of Husbandry, Masons. Baptist. Home and Office: 205 Collins St Apt 9 San Francisco CA 94118-3429 E-mail: toninIblackjack@cs.com. *Personal philosophy: You can be what you want to be, go beyond the rest.*

TONJES, MARIAN JEANNETTE BENTON, education educator; b. Rockville Center, NY, Feb. 16, 1929; d. Millard Warren and Felicia E. (Tyler) Benton; m. Charles F. Tonjes (div. 1965, dec.); children: Jeffrey Charles, Kenneth Warren. BA, U. N.Mex., 1951, cert., 1966, MA, 1969; EdD, U. Miami, 1975. Dir. recreation Stuyvesant Town Housing Project, N.Y.C., 1951-53; tchr. music., phys. edn. Sunset Mesa Day Sch., Albuquerque, 1953-54; tchr. remedial reading Zia Elem. Sch., Albuquerque, 1965-67; tchr. secondary devel. reading Rio Grande High Sch., Albuquerque, 1967-69; rsch. asst. reading Southwestern Coop. Ednl. Lab., Albuquerque, 1969-71; assoc. dir., vis. instr. Fla. Ctr. Tchr. Tng. Materials U. Miami, 1971-72; asst. prof. U.S. Internat. U., San Diego, 1972-75; prof. edn. Western Wash. U., Bellingham, 1975-94, prof. emerita, 1994—; dir. summer study at Oriel Coll. Oxford (Eng.) U., 1976—93. Adj. prof. U. N.Mex., Albuquerque, 1995—, reading supr. Manzanita Ctr., 1968; vis. prof. adult edn. Palomar (Calif.) Jr. Coll., 1974; vis. prof. U. Guam, Mangilao, 1989-90; invited guest Russian Reading Assn., Moscow, 1992; internat. travel adv. Vantage Deluxe Travel, 2002—; spkr. European Conf. reading, Tallinn, Estonia, 2003; cons. in field. Author: (with Miles V. Zintz) Teaching Reading/Thinking Study Skills in Content Classroom, 3rd edit., Secondary Reading, Writing and Learning, 1991, (with Roy Wolpow and Miles Zintz) Integrated Content Literacy, 1999. Trustee White Mountain Sch., 2000—; tour dir. In the Footsteps of Dickens, England, 2001; read by three com. Albuquerque Bus. and Edn. Compact. Tng. Tchr. Trainers grantee, 1975; NDEA fellow Okla. State U., 1969. Mem.: Am. Reading Forum, Internat. Reading Assn., PEO (past chpt. pres.), World Congress in Reading Buenos Aires, European Coun. Internat. Schs., European Conf. in Reading, UK Reading Assn., Internat. Reading Assn. (non-print media and reading com. 1980—83, workshop dir. S.W. regional confs. 1982, travel, interchange and study tours com. 1984—86, com. internat. devel. N.Am. 1991—96, symposium chair World Congress, Manila 2004, Outstanding Tchr. Educator award 1981), Am. Reading Forum (chmn. bd. dirs. 1983—85), Albuquerque Tennis Club, Internat. Soc. Rwy. Travelers, Delta Delta Delta. Presbyterian. Avocations: miniatures, tennis, bridge, art, travel. E-mail: mtonjes@unm.edu.

TONKERY, DAN, Internet company executive; b. Fairmont, W. Va., July 21, 1946; s. Thomas H. and Jean D Tonkery; m. Linda E. Persons, May 2, 1981; children: Andrew D., John C. Fiero, Steven C. Fiero. BA, David Lipscomb U., 1968; MLS, U. Ill., 1970. Pres. The Faxon Co., Westwood, Mass., 1996—2001; vp of bus. devel. EBSCO Info. Services, Birmingham, Ala., 2001—. Founder and prisident TDT Ventures, Morristown, NJ, 1995—96; pres. ceo Readmore Co., N.Y.C., 1986—95; founder, pres. Horizon Info. Svcs., LA, 1984—86; sr. v.p. The Faxon Co., Westwood, Mass., 1982—84; assoc. u. libr. U. Calif., LA, 1979—82; chief tech. svcs. divsn. Nat. Libr. Medicine, Bethesda, Md., 1970—79. Treas. Coun. on Libr. Info. Resources, Washington, 1996—2004. Fellow Pub. Health Svc. fellow, Pub. Health Svc, NIH, 1970. Avocation: golf. Home: 15 Old Mendham Rd Morristown NJ 07960 Office: EBSCO Info Svcs PO Box 1943 Birmingham AL 35201 Personal E-mail: tonkery@mindspring.com. E-mail: dtonkery@ebsco.com.

TONKIN, HUMPHREY RICHARD, academic administrator, educator; b. Truro, Cornwall, Eng., Dec. 2, 1939; came to U.S., 1962; s. George Leslie and Lorna Winifred (Sandry) T.; m. Sandra Julie Winberg, Mar. 9, 1968 (div. 1981); m. Jane Spencer Edwards, Oct. 1, 1983; 1 child, Sebastian George. BA, St. John's Coll., Cambridge, Eng., 1962, MA, 1966; AM, PhD, Harvard U., 1966; DLitt (hon.), U. Hartford, 1999. Asst. prof. English U. Pa., Phila., 1966-71, assoc. prof., 1971-80, prof., 1980-83, vice-provost undergrad. studies, 1971-75, coord. internat. programs, 1977-83, master Stouffer Coll. House, 1980-83; pres. State Univ. Coll., Potsdam, N.Y., 1983-88, U. Hartford, Conn., 1989-98, prof. humanities, pres. emeritus, 1998—; vis. fellow Whitney Humanities Ctr. Yale U., 1998-99. Vis. prof. English Columbia U., N.Y.C., 1980-81; exec. dir. Ctr. Rsch. and Documentation on World Lang. Problems, Rotterdam and Hartford, 1974—. Editor: Language Problems and Language Planning; author: (bibliography) Sir Walter Raleigh, 1971, Esperanto and International Language Problems, 4th edit., 1977, Spenser's Courteous Pastoral, 1972; author: (with Jane Edwards) The World in the Curriculum, 1981, The Faerie Queene, 1989; editor (with Allison Keef): Language in Religion, 1989, Esperanto, Interlinguistics and Planned Language, 1997; editor: (with Timothy Reagan) Language in the 21st Century, 2003; editor, translator Esperanto: Language, Literature and Community (Pierre Janton), 1993, Maskerado: Dancing Around Death in Nazi Hungary (Tivadar Soros), 2000; contbr. articles to profl. jours. Pres. Pa. Coun. Internat. Edn., 1980-81; bd. dirs. World Affairs Coun. Phila., 1979-83, Zamenhof Found., 1987-94, Hartford Symphony Orch., 1989-98, World Affairs Coun. Conn., 1989-2003, Greater Hartford Arts Coun., 1989-99, Can.-U.S. Found. Ednl. Exchange, 1997-2003, chmn. 1999-2000; bd. dirs. World Learning, 1998—; chmn. Coun. Internat. Exch. Scholars, 1988-94, Esperantic Studies Found., 1991—, Partnership for Svc.-Learning, 1991-96, v.p., 2001—; bd. dirs. Am. Forum, 1985—, chmn., 1998-2003. Recipient Lindback award for disting. teaching, 1970; Frank Knox fellow Harvard U., 1962-66; Guggenheim fellow, 1974. Fellow Acad. Esperanto; mem. Universal Esperanto Assn. (pres. 1974-80, 86-89, rep. to UN 1974-83, hon. com. 1995—), Spenser Soc. (pres. 1983-84, former dir.), Internat. Acad. Scis. San Marino, Conn. Acad. Arts and Scis., Cosmos Club. Home: 279 Ridgewood Rd West Hartford CT 06107-3542 Office: U Hartford Mortensen Libr 200 Bloomfield Ave West Hartford CT 06117-1599 Office Phone: 860-768-4448. Business E-Mail: tonkin@hartford.edu.

TONKIN, INA LYNN DYER, cardiovascular radiologist, educator; b. Louisville, Apr. 26, 1944; d. Robert S. and Nancy E. (Camp) Dyer; m. Allen K. Tonkin, June 29, 1968; children: Allison Elizabeth-Ann, Kieth Allen. BA, DePauw U., 1966; MD, U. Louisville, 1970. Diplomate Am. Bd. Radiology, 1974; Am. Bd. Vascular Interventional Radiology, 1994; Am. Bd. Pediatric Radiology, 1996. Pediatric intern U. Fla., Gainesville, 1970-71, resident in radiology, 1971-73, fellow in cardiovasc. radiology, 1974-75; asst. prof. U. Ariz. Health Sci. Ctr., Tucson, 1975-77, U. Ala.-Birmingham, 1977-79; assoc. prof. radiology U. Tenn., Memphis, 1979-84, prof., 1984, prof. pediat, 1985—. Exec. com. LeBonheur Children's Med. Ctr., Memphis, 1981-85, chief of med. staff, 1987; disting. scientist Armed Forces Inst. of Radiologic Pathology, Washington, 1992-93; prof. radiology & pediat. U. Tenn. Hlth. Sci. Ctr., Memphis. Editor: (book) Pediatric Cardiovascular Imaging, 1992; contbr. chpts. to books, rsch. articles to profl. jours. Recipient Disting. Alumnus award U. Louisville Med. Sch., 1999. Fellow Soc. Interventional Radiology, 1988, Am. Coll. Radiology, 1990; mem. Soc. Pediatric Radiology (treas.), Jour. Rev. Club of Memphis (sec. 1984, pres. 1985), Soc. Interventional Radiology, N.Am. Soc. Cardiac Imaging (pres.), Nat. and Internat. Lectr. (1976-2004). Methodist. Home: 3415 Chambers Chapel Rd Lakeland TN 38002-9573 Office: LeBonheur Children's Med Ctr 50 N Dunlap St Memphis TN 38103-4909 also: Univ Tenn Health Sci Ctr Prof Radiology and Pediat 50 N Dunlap St Memphis TN 38103-4909 E-mail: Drs.Tonkin@mindspring.com.

TONKIN, LEO SAMPSON, educational foundation administrator; b. Suffern, N.Y., Apr. 2, 1937; s. Leo S. and Ann (Petrone) T. AB, Johns Hopkins, 1959; postgrad., Sch. Advanced Internat. Studies, 1962-63; JD, Harvard, 1962; Dr. Pedagogy, SUNY, 1973. Legis. asst. to U.S. Congressman; then Sen. Charles McC. Mathias, Jr., of Md., 1962-63; assoc. counsel U.S. Ho. of Reps. Select Com. on Govt. Research, 1964; spl. cons. Ho. Spl. Subcom. on Edn., 1965-66; exec. dir. Commrs. Council on Higher Edn., Washington, 1965-66; pres. Leo S. Tonkin Assos., Inc., 1966—; founder, dir., chmn. bd. Washington Workshops Found., 1967—; pres. Travel Seminars, Ltd., 1999—. Mem. White House Conf. on Edn., 1965, White House Conf. on Youth, 1971; spl. asst. to chmn. U.S. Ho. of Reps. Select Com. on Crime, 1972; mem. bd. plebe sponsors U.S. Naval Acad., 1977—; v.p. London Fedn. Boys' Clubs, 1980—; mem. adv. panel Nat. Commn. for Protection of Human Subjects of Biomed. and Behavioral Research, HEW, 1976-77; bd. dirs. Star Scientific, Inc., 1998—; nat. adv. coun. Retinitis Pigmentosa Found., 1999—. Contbr. articles to mags. Bd. dirs. Washington Choral Arts Soc., 1971-73, Nat. Coordinating Council on Drug Edn., 1973, Nat. Student Ednl. Fund, 1974—; chmn. Wall Street Seminar Found., 1978—; chmn. bd. trustees St. Thomas Aquinas Coll., 1966-73, continuing trustee, 1973-78, trustee, chmn. emeritus, 1978—; chmn. bd. trustees City of Phila. Govt. Honors Program; trustee Southeastern U., 1966-73; asso. bd. trustees Immaculata Coll., 1966-73; mem. advisory bd. Pub. Affairs and Govt. Degree Program, Mt. Vernon Coll., 1971-74; bd. dirs. YMCA, Washington, 1969-71. Recipient Americanism award, Valley Forge Freedoms Found, 1973 Mem. Johns Hopkins Alumni Assn. of Washington (pres. 1969-72) Clubs: Georgetown (Washington), City Tavern (Washington), Nat. Press (Washington), Capitol Hill (Washington), Capitol Yacht (Washington); Harvard (N.Y.C.). Home: 4368 Sunset Ct Warrenton VA 20187-3584 Office: 3222 N St NW Washington DC 20007-2849 Office Phone: 202-965-3434.

TONKONOGY, JOSEPH MOSES, physician, neuropsychiatrist, researcher; b. Belaya Tserkov, Kiev, Ukraine, Oct. 22, 1925; came to U.S., 1979, naturalized, 1985; s. Moysey Iosifovich and Beyla (Gdalievna (Schvachkina) T.; married; children: Vitaly, Milla, Bella. MD, Military Med. Acad., Leningrad, USSR, 1947; PhD, All Union Acad. Med. Sci., Moscow, 1956; DSc, 1st Med. Inst., Leningrad, 1966. From asst. to prof. The Bechterev Inst., Leningrad, 1956-66, prof., chmn., 1966-78; assoc. Boston U. Sch. Medicine, 1980-81; physician VA Med. Ctr., Northampton, Mass., 1981-87; assoc. prof. U. Mass. Med. Ctr., Worcester, 1987-95, prof., 1995—. Dir. neuropsychiatry svc. Worcester State Hosp., Mass., 1989—. Author: Introduction to Clinical Neuropsychology, 1973, Vascular Aphasia, 1986, The Brief Neuropsychological Cognitive Examination, 1997; editor: Problems of Contemporary Psychoneurology, 1966, Psychological Experiment in Psychiatry and Neurology, 1969, Mathematical Methods in Psychiatry and Neurology, 1971, Current Problems of Clinical Psychology, 1975; cons. (book) Soviet Military Psychiatry, 1986; contbr. numerous articles to profl. jours. Capt. Med. Corps, Germany, 1947-48. Recipient The Bechterev Prize, All Union Acad. Med. Scis., Moscow, 1974. Fellow: The Royal Soc. Medicine (U.K.); mem.: Internet Psychogeriatric Soc., Soc. Neurosci., Internat. Neuropsychol. Soc., Am. Acad. Neurology, Am. Neuropsychiat. Assn. Jewish. Office: U Mass Med Ctr Dept Psychiatry 55 Lake Ave N Worcester MA 01655-0002

TONKS, ROBERT STANLEY, pharmacology and therapeutics educator, former university dean; b. Aberystwyth, Wales; emigrated to Can., 1973; s. Robert Patrick Dennis and Prudence Violet (Williams) T.; m. Diana Mary Cownie; children: Pamela Mary, Julia Rosalind, Robert Michael, Sara Katharine. Student, U. Coll. of South Wales, Welsh Coll. Pharmacy; B.Pharm., PhD, Welsh Nat. Sch. Medicine, Cardiff. Organon postdoctoral fellow Med. Sch., Cardiff, Nat. Health Service postdoctoral fellow; Nat. Health Service sr. fellow Cardiff and Nevill Hall Hosp., Abergavenny; lectr. pharmacology U. Wales, Cardiff, 1958-72; vis. fellow Claude Bernard Research Assn., Faculté de Medicine, Paris, 1959; sr. lectr. pharmacology and therapeutics Med. Sch. and U. Wales Hosp., Cardiff, 1972-73; dir., prof. Coll. Pharmacy, Dalhousie U., Halifax, N.S., Can., 1973-77, dean Faculty of Health Professions, 1977-88, prof. geriatric pharmaco-therapeutics, 1988—, acting head divsn. geriatric medicine, 1991-94. Cons. pharm. industry in U.K., Govt. of N.B., Can., Health and Welfare Dept. Can.; advisor health manpower Govt. of N.S.; coordinator N.E. Can./Am. Health Coun. co-chmn., 1974-91; emeritus chmn., mem. Health and Welfare Personnel Career Rev. Com., 1977-91; pharm. scis. grants com. Med. Rsch. Council Can., chmn.; mem. rev. com. health protection br. fed. govt. div. pharm. chemistry, Can.; chmn. advisory com. N.B. Minister of Health; mem. joint com. on devel. rsch. in nursing Med. Rsch. Coun.-Nat. Health Rsch. Devel. Program; mem. nat. adv. panel on risk/benefit mgmt. of drugs.; adv. com. on restructuring Health Canada's Personnel Career Awards; trustee Lakeridge Health Corp., Oshawa, Ont., 2001-02, Lakeridge Health Whitby Found., Ont., 2003-04. Contbr. articles on pharmacology and pathology to profl. jours. Fellow: Inst. Biology, Pharm. Soc. Gt. Britain; mem.: Welsh Cultural Soc. (past pres.), Med. Soc. N.S. (task force on pharmacare), N.S. Pharm. Soc. (coord. drug and med. supplies Ethiopia airlift, cert. of merit), N.B. Pharm. Soc. (hon.), Can. Soc. Hosp. Pharmacy (hon.), Can. Geriatrics Soc., Am. Soc. Clin. Pharm. and Therapeutics, Canadian Soc. Clin. Investigation, Brit. Pharmacol. Soc. Anglican. Mailing: 6 Tom Edwards Dr Whitby ON Canada L1R 2R4 Office: Dalhousie U Coburg Rd Halifax NS Canada Personal E-mail: bobtonks@dal.ca.

TONN, ELVERNE MERYL, pediatric dentist, dental benefits consultant, forensic odontologist; b. Stockton, Calif., Dec. 10, 1929; s. Emanuel M. and Lorna Darlene (Bryant) T.; m. Ann G. Richardson, Oct. 28, 1951; children: James Edward, Susan Elaine Tonn. AA, La Sierra U., Riverside, Calif., 1949; DDS, U. So. Calif., 1955; BS, Excelsior Coll., 1984; diploma, Citizens Police Acad., Manteca, 2003. Lic. dentist; diplomate Am. Bd. Forensic Dentistry, Am. Bd. Quality Assurance and Utilization Rev. Physicians; cert. dental benefits cons. Pediatric dentist, assoc. Walker Dental Group, Long Beach, Calif., 1957-59, Children's Dental Clinic, Sunnyvale, Calif., 1959-61; pediatric dentist in pvt. practice Mountain View, Calif., 1961-72; pediatric dentist, ptrn. Pediatric Dentistry Assocs., Los Altos, Calif., 1972-83; pediatric dentist, ptnr. Valley Oak Dental Group, Manteca, Calif., 1987—2003; from clin. instr. to assoc. prof. U. Pacific, San Francisco, 1964-84; assoc. prof. U. Calif., San Francisco, 1984-86. Pediat. dental cons. Delta Dental Plan, San Francisco, 1985—2002; chief dental staff El Camino Hosp., Mountain View, Calif., 1964—65, 1984—85; dental cons. Interplast program Stanford U. Sch. Medicine. Weekly columnist Manteca Bull., 1987-92; producer 2 teaching videos, 1986; contbr. articles to profl. jours. Capt. U.S. Army, 1955—57. Fellow Am. Coll. Dentists, Internat. Coll. Dentists, Am. Acad. Pediatric Dentistry, Royal Soc. Health (Eng.), Acad. of Dentistry for Handicapped, Pierre Fauchard Acad., Acad. Dental Materials, Am. Soc. Dentistry for Children (mastership award 2001); mem. ADA, Internat. Assn. Pediatric Dentistry, Internat. Assn. Dental Rsch., Am. Acad. Forensic Scis., Am. Soc. Forensic Odontology, Fedn. Dentaire Internationale, Am. Assn. Dental Cons., Calif. Dental Assn., Calif. Soc. Dentistry for Children (pres. 1968), Calif. Soc. Pediatric Dentistry, N.Y. Acad. Scis., Calif. Acad. Sci., Rotary Internat., Manteca Police Dept. (Badge 2003), Disaster Mortuary Org. Response Team, Am. Coll. Med. Quality, Manteca Cert. Emergency Response Team. Republican. Avocations: photography, travel, medieval history. Home and Office: Tonn Consulting Services 374 Laurelwood Cir Manteca CA 95336-7122 Office Phone: 209-815-4824. Personal E-mail: emtonn@comcast.net.

TONN, ROBERT JAMES, retired entomologist; b. Watertown, Wis., June 23, 1927; s. Harry James and Elise (Foogman) T.; m. Noemi C. Tonn; children: Sigrid M., Monica E. BS, Colo. State U., 1949, MS, 1950; MPH, Okla. Med. Sch., 1963; PhD, Okla. State U., 1959. Rsch. assoc La. State U., Costa Rica/New Orleans, 1961-63; dir. Taunton Field Sta., Taunton, Mass., 1963-65; chief PMO unit WHO, various locations, 1965-87. Adj. prof. of parasitology U. Tex.-El Paso, 1988—; cons. USAID/VBC, 1987—. Contbr. numerous articles to profl. jours. Mem. Am. Soc. Tropical Medicine, Soc. Vector Ecology (pres. 1984), Am. Mosquito Control Assn., U.S./ Mex. Border Health Assn., Royal Soc. Tropical Medicine and Hygiene, Masons. Congregationalist. Home: 4247 Winchester Rd Las Cruces NM 88011 Personal E-mail: tonnapollo@aol.com.

TONSETH, RALPH G. airport executive; Dir. aviation San Jose (Calif.) Airport, 1990—. Office: San Jose Airport 1732 N 1st St Ste 600 San Jose CA 95112-4544

TONTIRUTTANANON, CHANNARONG, electrical engineer, researcher; b. Muang, Surin, Thailand, 1971; B in Engring., Chulalongkorn U., Bangkok, 1992; MS, Auburn U., 1997, PhD, 1998. Instr. Assumption U., Bangkok, 1992—95; grad. rsch. asst. Auburn (Ala.) U., 1995—98; postdoctoral rsch. fellow U. Iowa, Iowa City, 1999; sr. mem. sci. staff Nortel Networks Inc., Richardson, Tex., 1999—. Contbr. articles to profl. jours. Mem.: IEEE, Am. Math. Soc., Phi Kappa Phi, Eta Kappa Nu. Achievements include patents for overload control system and method for a telecommunication system. Office Phone: 972-685-4924. E-mail: ctont@nortelnetworks.com.

TOOBIN, JEFFREY ROSS, writer, legal analyst; b. N.Y.C., May 21, 1960; s. Jerome and Marlene Sanders T.; m. Amy Bennett McIntosh, May 31, 1986; children: Ellen Frances, Adam Jerome. AB, Harvard U., 1982, JD, 1986. Bar: N.Y. 1987. Law clerk Hon. J. Edward Lumbard, N.Y.C., 1986-87; assoc. counsel Indep. Counsel Lawrence Walsh, Washington, 1987-89; asst. U.S. Atty. Ea. Dist. N.Y., Bklyn., 1990-93; legal analyst ABC News, N.Y.C., 1996—2002; staff writer The New Yorker, N.Y.C., 1993—; sr. legal analyst CNN, N.Y.C., 2002—. Author: Opening Arguments: A Young Lawyer's First Case-United States v. Oliver North, 1991, The Run of His Life: The People v. O.J. Simpson, 1996, A Vast Conspiracy: The Real Story of the Sex Scandal that Nearly Brought Down a President, 2000, Too Close To Call: The Thirty Six Day Battle To Decide the 2000 Election, 2001; contbr. articles to The New Yorker. Office: The New Yorker 4 Times Sq New York NY 10036-6592

TOOHEY, BRIAN FREDERICK, lawyer; b. Niagara Falls, N.Y., Dec. 14, 1944; s. Matthew and Marilyn (Hoag) T.; m. Mary Elizabeth Monihan; children: Maureen Elizabeth, Matthew Sheridan, Margaret Monihan, Mary Catherine, Elizabeth Warner. BS, Niagara U., 1966; JD, Cornell U., 1969. Bar: N.Y. 1969, N.Mex. 1978, Ohio 1980. Ptnr. Jones Day, Cleve., 1981—. Lt. JAG Corps, USNR, 1970-73. Mem. ABA, N.Y. State Bar Assn., State Bar N.Mex., Ohio State Bar Assn., Greater Cleve. Bar Assn. Roman Catholic. Home: 25 Pepper Creek Dr Cleveland OH 44124-5279 Office: Jones Day N Point 901 Lakeside Ave E Cleveland OH 44114-1190 E-mail: bftoohey@jonesday.com.

TOOHEY, EDWARD JOSEPH, financial services company executive, retired; b. Jersey City, Jan. 15, 1930; s. John Joseph and Estelle Anita (Hudson) T.; m. Ruth Phyllis Scheidecker, Mar. 13, 1948; 1 child, Phyllis Karen. BA, Yale U., 1953. From with to mgr. dir. Merrill Lynch, Pierce, Fenner & Smith, Inc., N.Y.C., 1956—94, mgr. dir. instl. nat. sales, 1994—2001, ret., 2001. Pres. Bunbury Co., N.Y.C. Trustee Windham Found., Grafton, Vt., 1978—; vice chmn. Peddie Sch., Highstown, N.J., 1981—, trustee, 1976—; bd. dirs. N.Y.C. Ballet, 1993-96, emeritus, 1996—. Maj. USMC, 1953-55. Mem. Canoe Brook Country Club (Summit, N.J.), Yale Club, Sky Club, Univ. Club (N.Y.C.), Georgetown Club (Washington). Home: 1 Gracie Ter New York NY 10028-7955 E-mail: etoohey@exchange.ml.com.

TOOHEY, JAMES KEVIN, lawyer; b. Evanston, Ill., July 16, 1944; s. John Joseph and Ruth Regina (Cassidy) T.; m. Julie Marie Crane, Nov. 1, 1969 (div. Aug. 1977); children: Julie Colleen, Jeannne Christine; m. Anne Margaret Boettingheimer, May 28, 1983; children: James Robert, Kevin John, Casey Anne. BBA, U. Notre Dame, 1966; JD, Northwestern U., 1969. BAr: Ill. 1969, U.S. Dist. Ct. (no. dist.) Ill. 1971, U.S. Dist. Ct. (ctrl. dist.) Ill. 1991, U.S. Ct. Appeals (7th cir.) 1973, U.S. Ct. Appeals (8th cir.) 1975, U.S. Supreme Ct. 1988. Assoc. Taylor, Miller, Magner, Sprowl & Hutchings, Chgo., 1970-71; asst. U.S. Atty. Office U.S. Atty., Chgo., 1971-74; assoc. Ross, Hardies, O'Keefe, Babcock & Parsons, Chgo., 1974-77; ptnr. Ross & Hardies, Chgo., 1978—2003, McGuire Woods, LLP, 2003—. Mem. St. Mary of the Wood Parish Coun., 1999-2002 Mem. Ill. State Bar Assn., Soc. Trial Lawyers, Assn. Advancement of Automotive Medicine, Ill. Assn. Def. Attys., Trial Lawyers

Club Chgo., Edgebrook Sauganash Athletic Assn. (bd. dirs., commr. 1993-96; softball, baseball, and basketball coach). Office: McGuirewoods LLP 77 W Wacker Dr Chicago IL 60601 E-mail: james.toohey@rosshardies.com.

TOOHEY, PHILIP S. lawyer; b. 1943; BA, Hamilton Coll., 1965; JD, Cornell U., 1968. Bar: N.Y. 1968. Law clk. Hon. Louis M. Greenblatt Appellate Divsn., 1968-69; assoc. Phillips, Lytle, Hitchcock, Blaine & Huber, 1969-74, ptnr., 1975-84; sr. bank counsel Marine Midland Banks, Inc., Buffalo, 1984-88, dep. gen. counsel, 1988-91, gen. counsel, sec., 1991-2000; sr. exec. v.p., gen. counsel, sec. HSBC Bank USA, 2000—. Mem. N.Y. State Bar Assn. (chmn. bus. law com. of banking, corp. & bus. law sect. 1985-88, sec. bus. law sect. 1988-89, vice chmn., treas. bus. law sect. 1989-90, 1st vice chmn. bus. law sect. 1990-91, chmn. bus. law sect. 1991-92). Office: HSBC Bank USA 1 Hsbc Ctr Buffalo NY 14203-2840

TOOKER, GEORGE, artist; b. Bklyn., Aug. 5, 1920; s. George Clair and Angela Montejo (Roura) T. BA, Harvard U., 1942; student, Art Students League, N.Y.C., 1943-44. Instr. Art Students League, N.Y., 1965-68. One man shows include Edwin Hewitt Gallery, 1951, 55, Robert Isaacson Gallery, 1960, 62, Durlacher Bros., 1964, 67, Hopkins Center at Dartmouth Coll., 1967, Fine Arts Mus., San Francisco, 1974, Mus. Contemporary Art, Chgo., 1974, Whitney Mus., N.Y.C., 1975, Indpls. Mus. Art, 1975, D.C. Moore Gallery, 1997, 98, 2000; exhibited in group shows at Whitney Mus., 1947-50, 53, 55-58, 61, 64, 65, 67, 75, Venice Biennale, 1956, Art Inst. Chgo., 1951, 52, 54, 59, Inst. Contemporary Arts, London, 1950, Va. Mus., 1954, 62, Pa. Acad., 1966, Marisa Del Re Gallery, 1985, 88, 92, Spoleto Festival, Gibbes Mus. Art, Charleston, S.C., 1987, Robert Hall Fleming Mus. U. Vt., 1987, Marsh Gallery, U. Richmond, Va., 1989, Addison Gallery of Am. Art, 1994; represented permanent collections at Smithsonian Nat. Mus. of Am. Art, Smithsonian Hirshhorn Mus., Whitney Mus., Dartmouth Coll., Met. Mus., Walker Art Center, Mus. Modern Art, S.C. Johnson & Sons, Inc., Art, U.S.A., Sara Roby Fund Collection Am. Art, Addison Gallery, Ariz. State Univ. Gallery, Bklyn. Mus. Columbus (Ohio) Mus. Recipient Vt. gov.'s award for excellence in arts, 1983; Grantee Nat. Inst. Arts and Letters, 1960 Mem. NAD., Acad. Arts and Letters Address: PO Box 385 Hartland VT 05048-0385 Office: care DC Moore Gallery 724 5th Ave New York NY 10019-4106

TOOKER, JOHN PHILLIP, internist, educator; b. Denver, Colo. m. Nancy Tooker; 2 children. MD, U. Colo. Med. Sch., 1970; MBA, Temple U. Diplomate Am. Bd. Internal Medicine, Am. Bd. Critical Care Medicine, Am. Bd. Pulmonary Disease. Intern Belevue Hosp. Ctr., N.Y.C., 1970—71, resident med., 1971—72, U. Colo., 1972—73; fellow Maine Med. Ctr., Portland, 1975—76; fellow internal medicine U. Wash., Seattle, 1976—77; asst. chief dept. internal medicine, program dir. Maine Med. Ctr., Portland; CEO, exec. v.p. ACP-Am. Soc. Internal Medicine, Phila., 2002—. Assoc. prof. medicine Vermont U.; attending physician Salr Hosp.; adj. prof. U. Pa. Fellow: Coll. Physicians Phila., Am. Coll. Chest Physicians; mem.: AMA, Phila. County Med. Soc., Pa. Med. Soc., Am. Thoracic Soc., Am. Coll. Physician Execs., Alpha Omega Alpha. Office: 22 Bramhall St Portland ME 04102-3134 Address: ACP-Am Soc Internal Medicine 190 N Independence Mall W Philadelphia PA 19106-1572

TOOKES, JAMES NELSON, real estate investment company executive; b. Tallahassee, Sept. 16, 1934; m. Hortense Latricia James, June 22, 1958; 1 child, Gerald Ray. BS, Fla. A&M U., 1955, MEd, 1956. Tchr. Griffin Elem. Sch., Tallahassee, 1957-58, Douglas Elem. Sch., Wabasso, Fla., 1958-59, Barrow Hill Sch., Tallahassee, 1959-60, prin., 1960-67; tchr. various sch. ctrs. Leon County Dist., Tallahassee, 1960-65; prin. Pineview Elem. Sch., Tallahassee, 1967-73. Pres. Geray Petroleum, Inc., Tallahassee, 1980—, J.N.T. Properties, Inc., Tallahassee, 1973-77; broker Tookes Realty, Tallahassee, 1973-85; adv. bd. Barnett Bank of Tallahassee, 1977-79; bd. dirs. Marine State Bank. Bd. dirs. Tallahassee Youth Ctr., 1952-54, Tallahassee Meml. Regional Med. Ctr., 1977-82; chmn. divsn. United Fund campaign, 1962; trustee Tallahassee C.C., 1974-82, chmn. bd., 1976-77. Recipient Sch. Adminstr. Svc. award Pineview Elem. Sch. Student Coun., 1967-73, commednation award Bert Roger's Sch. Real Estate, 1973, Contbns. to Cmty. award Phi Beta Lambda, 1974; named One of 5 Most Outstanding Black Businessmen in State of Fla., Fla. A&M U. Sch. Bus. and Industry, 1974. Mem. Phi Delta Kappa, Kappa Alpha Psi (Man of Yr. 1973). Home: 925 E Magnolia Dr Apt 5C Tallahassee FL 32301-6606 Office: JNT Properties Inc 525 John Knox Rd Ste C Tallahassee FL 32303 E-mail: tookesj@jntprop.com.

TOOKEY, ROBERT CLARENCE, actuary, consultant; b. Santa Monica, Calif., Mar. 21, 1925; s. Clarence Hall and Minerva Maconachie (Anderson) T.; m. Marcia Louise Hickman, Sept. 15, 1956; children: John Hall, Jennifer Louise, Thomas Anderson. BS, Calif. Inst. Tech., 1945; MS, U. Mich., 1947. With Prudential Ins. Co. Am., Newark, 1947-49; assoc. actuary in group Pacific Mut. Life Ins. Co., L.A., 1949-55; asst. v.p. in charge reins. sales and svc. for 17 western states Lincoln Nat. Life Ins. Co., Ft. Wayne, Ind., 1955-61; dir. actuarial svcs. Peat, Marwick, Mitchell & Co., Chgo., 1961-63; mng. prin. So. Calif. office Milliman & Robertson, cons. actuaries, Pasadena, 1963-76; pres. Robert Tookey Assocs., Inc., 1977—. Committeeman troop 501 Boy Scouts Am., 1969-72. Served to lt. (j.g.) USNR, 1943-45, 51-52. Fellow Soc. Actuaries, Conf. Consulting Actuaries; mem. Am. Acad. Actuaries, Pacific Ins. Conf., Rotary Club (Pasadena), Union League Club (Chgo.). Home and Office: PO Box 646 La Canada CA 91012-0646

TOOLAN, BRIAN PAUL, newspaper editor; b. Carbondale, Pa., June 29, 1950; s. Walter William and Elizabeth (Cleary) T.; m. Maureen Ellen Connolly, Sept. 7, 1974; children: Brendan, Seamus, Bridget, Colin, Molly. BA in English, St. Bonaventure U., Olean, N.Y., 1972. Reporter Scranton (Pa.) Tribune, 1972-79; copy editor Dayton (Ohio) Jour. Herald, 1979-81; layout editor Balt. News Am., 1981; copy editor Phila. Daily News, 1982-84, sports editor, 1984-89, asst. mng. editor, 1989-91, mng. editor, 1991-98; editor Hartford (Conn.) Courant, 1998—. Mem. AP Mng. Editors, Am. Soc. Newspaper Editors, Pa. Soc. Newspaper Editors (dir. 1989-92). Roman Catholic. Office: Hartford Courant 285 Broad St Hartford CT 06115-2510

TOOLE, BRUCE RYAN, retired lawyer; b. Missoula, Mont., June 21, 1924; s. John Howard and Marjorie Lee (Ross) T.; m. Loris Knoll, Sept. 29, 1951; children: Marjorie, Ryan, Allan. JD, U. Mont., 1949. Bar: Mont., U.S. Ct. Appeals (9th & Fed. cirs.), U.S. Supreme Ct., U.S. Claims Ct. Sole practice, Missoula, 1950; dep. county atty. Missoula County, 1951; ptnr. Crowley Law Firm, Billings, Mont., 1951-92, of counsel, 1992—; ret. Editor Mont. Lawyer, 1979-83. Mem. Mont. Com. for Humanities, Missoula; v.p. Billings Preservation Soc.; precinctman Yellowstone County Reps. With U.S. Army, 1944-45, ETO. Fellowship grantee NEH, Harvard U., 1980. Fellow Am. Coll. Trial Lawyers, Am. Bar Found.; mem. Am. Bd. Trial Advs., State Bar Mont. (pres. 1977-78), Yellowstone County Bar (pres. 1973, chmn. com. on mediation 1992), Internat. Assn. Def. Counsel. Avocations: politics, history, photography, metal work. Home: 3019 Glacier Dr Billings MT 59102-0711 Office: Crowley Law Firm 490 N 31st St Ste 500 Billings MT 59101-1288 E-mail: crowley@crowleylaw.com.

TOOLE, JAMES FRANCIS, medical educator; b. Atlanta, Mar. 22, 1925; s. Walter O'Brien and Helen (Whitehurst) T.; m. Patricia Anne Wooldridge, Oct. 25, 1952; children: William, Anne, James, Douglas Sean, Lauren, Robert, Dean Tyler, Kyle, Kaitlin, Grace. BA, Princeton U., 1947; MD, Cornell U., 1949; LLB, LaSalle Extension U., 1963; Dr. Honoris Causa, U. Targu Mures, Romania, 1998. Intern, then resident internal medicine and neurology U. Pa. Hosp., London, 1949—55, Nat. Hosp., London, 1955—56; mem. faculty U. Pa. Sch. Medicine, 1959—61; prof. neurology, chmn. dept. Bowman Gray Sch. Medicine Wake Forest U., 1962—83. Vis. prof. neurosci. U. Calif. San Diego, 1969—70; vis. scholar Oxford U., 1989; mem. Nat. Bd. Med. Examiners, 1970—76; mem. task force arteriosclerosis Nat. Heart Lung & Blood Inst., 1970—81; chmn. 6th and 7th Princeton confs. cerebrovascular diseases; cons. epidemiology WHO, Japan, 1972, 73, 93, USSR, 68, Switzerland, 74, Côte d'Ivoire, 77; mem. Lasker Awards com., 1976—77; chmn. neuropharmacologic drugs com. FDA, 1979; chair Commn. on Presdl. Disability, 1994—97; cons. NASA, 1966. Author: Cerebrovascular Diseases, 5th edit., 1999; editor: Current Concepts in Cerebrovascular Disease, 1969—73, Jour. Neurol. Sci., 1990—97; mem. editl. bd. Annals Internal Medicine, 1968—75, Stroke, 1972—74; mem. editl. bd. Jour. AMA, 1975—77; mem. editl. bd. Ann. Neurology, 1980—86, Jour. of Neurology, 1985—89. Pres. N.C. Heart Assn., 1976-77. Served with AUS, 1950-51; flight surgeon USNR, 1951-53. Decorated Bronze Star with V, Combat Med. badge. Master: ACP (licentiate); fellow: Royal Coll. Physicians, AAAS (life); mem.: AMA, Soc. for Neurosci., Hungarian Neurol. Soc., Polish Neurol. Soc., N.C. Stroke Assn. (pres. 1999—2001), Nat. Stroke Assn. (bd. dirs. 1993—, exec. com. 1994—, chmn. Commn. on U.S. Presdl. Disability 1994—), Internat. Stroke Soc. (exec. com. 1989—97, program chmn. 1992, pres. 2000—04), Irish Neurol. Assn. (hon.), Am. Clin. and Climatol Assn. (life), Assn. Brit. Neurologists (hon.), German Neurol. Soc. (hon.), Austrian Soc. Neurology (hon.), Russian Acad. Neurology (hon.), Am. Soc. Neuroimaging (pres. 1992—94), Am. Acad. Neurology, World Fedn. Neurology (sec.-treas. 1982—89, mgmt. com. 1990—98, pres. 1998—2001, chmn. Rsch. and Edn. Found. 1999—2004), Am. Neurol. Assn. (sec.-treas. 1978—82, pres. 1984—85, historian 1988—, archivist 2004), Am. Physiol. Soc., Am. Heart Assn. (chmn. com. ethics 1970—75). Home: 1836 Virginia Rd Winston Salem NC 27104-2316 Office Phone: 336-716-2338. Business E-Mail: jtoole@wfubmc.edu.

TOOLE, JOHN HARPER, lawyer; b. Johnson City, N.Y., Apr. 4, 1941; s. Edward Joseph and Anne (Junius) T.; m. Lamar Sparkman, May 30, 1969; children: John Carter, Lucy Bland. BS, U. Va., 1963; JD, Washington Coll. of Law, 1971. Bar: Va. 1971, D.C. 1972. From assoc. to ptnr. Lewis, Mitchell & Moore, Tysons Corner, Va., 1971-77; ptnr. Watt, Tieder, Killian, Toole & Hoffar, Tysons Corner, 1978-82; of counsel, ptnr. McGuire, Woods, Battle & Boothe, Tysons Corner, 1983-90, McLean, Va., 1990-99; ptnr. Cooley Godward LLP, Reston, Va., 2000—. 1st lt. U.S. Army, 1963—66. Mem. ABA, Va. State Bar, Va. Bar Assn., D.C. Bar Assn. Office: Cooley Godward LLP 11951 Freedom Dr Reston VA 20190-5601 Fax: 703 456-8100. E-mail: jtoole@cooley.com.

TOOLE, KENNETH R., JR., state senator; b. Missoula, Mont., June 18, 1955; m. Nancy Toole; 3 children. BA, U. Mont., 1981. Program dir. Rural Employment Opportunities; investigator Mont. Human Rights Commn.; personnel dir. Mont. Office Pub. Interest; co-dir. Mont. Human Rights Network, 1996-2000; Dem. senator dist. 27 Mont. State Senate, 2000—. Mem. Mont. Adv. Com. to U.S. Commn. on Civil Rights. Caucus chair N.W. Energy Coalition; bd. dirs. No. Plains Resource Coun., Plan Helena, Renewable N.W.; chair Local Ctrl. Com. Dems.; west chair rep. Mont. State Dem. Bd. Office: PO Box 1462 Helena MT 59624 E-mail: samt@mcn.net.

TOOMAJIAN, WILLIAM MARTIN, lawyer; b. Troy, N.Y., Sept. 26, 1943; s. Leo R. Tooomajian and Elizabeth (Gundrum) Toomajian; children: Andrew, Philip. AB, Hamilton Coll., 1965; JD, U. Mich., 1968; LLM, NYU, 1975. Bar: N.Y. 1968, Ohio 1978. Mem. firm Cadwalader, Wickersham & Taft, N.Y.C., 1971—77, Baker & Hostetler, Cleve., 1977—. Lt. U.S. Coast Guard, 1968—71. Mem.: ABA, Cleve. Tax Club, Cleve. Bar Assn., Ohio Bar Assn. Home: 3582 Lytle Rd Cleveland OH 44122-4908 Office: Baker & Hostetler 3200 National City Ctr 1900 E 9th St Ste 3200 Cleveland OH 44114-3475 Business E-Mail: wtoomajian@bakerlaw.com.

TOOMAN, STEPHANIE, performing arts educator; BFS, Julliard Sch.; MFA, Purchase Coll. Rehearsal dir. Neta Pulvermacher, Errol Grimes, The Purchase Dance Corps; dancer, rehearsal dir. Kazuko Hirabayashi, Tokyo; tchr. dance Alvin Ailey Am. Dance Ctr., the Netherlands Dance Theatre, 1st and 2d Cos., the Hague, Netherlands, The Rotterdam Dance Acad., The Inst. del Theatre, Barcelona; with Merian Soto/Pepatian, EarlMosley Diversity of Dance, Nathan Trice, Errol Grimes Dance Group; collaborator, dancer Reggie Wilson, 1989—.

TOOMBS, KENNETH ELDRIDGE, librarian; b. Colonial Heights, Va., Aug. 25, 1928; s. Garnett Eldridge and Susie W. (Bryant) T.; m. Ada Teresa Hornsby, Aug. 29, 1949; children— Susan Elizabeth Shealy, Cheri Lynn Morris, Teresa Ann Heilman. AA, Tenn. Wesleyan Coll., 1950; BS, Tenn. Poly. Inst., 1951; MA, U. Va., 1955; MLS, Rutgers U., 1956; student, La. State U., 1961-63. Reference asst. Alderman Library, U. Va., 1954-55; research asst. Grad. Sch. Library Sci., Rutgers U., 1955-56; mem. staff and faculty La. State U., 1956-63, asst. dir. charge pub. services, 1962-63; dir. libraries, prof. library sci. U. Southwestern La., 1963-67; dir. libraries U. S.C., Columbia, 1967—88; bd. dirs. Southeastern Library Network, 1967-88; disting. dir. of librs. emeritus U. S.C., Columbia, 1988—; vice chmn. Southeastern Library Network, 1973-74, 83-84, chmn., 1974-75, treas., 1984-85. Libr. cons. for bldgs. and adminstrn. for 60 colls. and univs. in past 30 yrs.; chmn. librarians sect. La. Coll. Conf., 1965-67; mem. Bd. La. Libr. Examiners, 1966-67; participant Libr. Mgmt. Inst., U. Wash., Seattle, 1969, Libr. Bldg. Problems Inst., UCLA, 1970; co-founder Southeastern Libr. Network with John Gribbin. Contbr. articles to profl. jours.; editor: Bull. La. Library Assn, 1959-62; mng. editor: SW La. Jour, 1963-67; adv. bd.: Linguistic Atlas Am. Treas. Wesley Found.; v.p. Am. Field Services Internat. Scholarships; bd. dirs. U. S.C. Ednl. Found., 1975-82; Danforth assoc., 1967—; AIA/ALA Bldg. Awards Jury, 1987. Served to 1st lt. AUS, 1946-47, 51-53. Mem. ALA (life), La. Library Assn. (parliamentarian 1962-63, 66-67), Southeastern Library Assn. (Life mem., exec. bd. 1981-85, Rothrock award 1978), Southwestern Library Assn., S.C. Library Assn. (Life mem., pres. 1976, exec. bd. 1981-85), Assn. Southeastern Research Libraries (chmn. 1973-75, adv. com. to OCLC 1979-84), AAUP (sec.), La. Hist. Assn., La. Tchrs. Assn., Soc. Tympanuchus Cupido Pinnatus, South Caroliniana Soc., Nat. Library Bldg. Consultants List (chmn. 1981-84), Tenn. Squire (Ky. col.), Assn. of S.C. Retirees (bd. dirs. 1995—), Omicron Delta Epsilon. Clubs: Mason (Shriner), Kiwanis, Torch Club. Methodist. Home: 16 Garden Springs Rd Columbia SC 29209-1716

TOOMEY, JEANNE ELIZABETH, animal activist; b. NYC, Aug. 22, 1921; d. Edward Aloysius and Anna Margaret (O'Grady) Toomey; m. Peter Terranova, Sept. 28, 1951 (dec. 1968); children: Peter Terranova (dec.), Sheila Terranova Beasley. Student, Hofstra U., 1938-40; student law sch., Fordham U., 1940-41; BA, Southampton Coll., 1976; postgrad., Monmouth Coll., 1978-79. Reporter, columnist Bklyn. Daily Eagle, 1943-52; with The Fitzgeralds, NBC Radio, N.Y.C., 1952-53; reporter, writer King Features Syndicate, N.Y.C., 1953-55; reporter, columnist N.Y. Jour.-Am., N.Y.C., 1955-61; newsman AP, N.Y.C., 1963-64; stringer, columnist News Tribune, Woodbridge, N.J., 1976-86; editor Calexico (Calif.) Chronicle, 1987-88; editor community sect. Asbury Park (N.J.) Press, 1988; pres., dir. Last Post Animal Sanctuary, Falls Village, Conn., 1989—. Author: Murder in the Hamptons, 1994, Assignment Homicide, 1998. Named Woman of the Yr. N.Y. Women's Press Club, 1960. Mem. Newswomen's Club of N.Y., Overseas Press Club, N.Y. Press Club, Silurians. Roman Catholic. Address: PO Box 259 Falls Village CT 06031-0259 Office: 95 Belden St Falls Village CT 06031 Office Phone: 860-824-0831. Office Fax: 860-824-5460.

TOOMEY, KATHLEEN ELIZABETH, state agency administrator; b. Aspinwall, Pa., Nov. 21, 1951; AB in biology cum laude, Smith Coll., 1973; MPH, MD, Harvard U., 1979. Diplomate Am. Bd. of Family Practice, Nat. Bd. of Med. Examiners. Resident dept. family medicine U. Wash., Seattle, 1979-82; clin. dir. Alaska Native Hosp., Kotzebue, 1982-85; Pew Health Policy fellow Inst. for Health Policy Studies, U. Calif. Sch. Medicine, San Francisco, 1985-87; Epidemic Intelligence Svc. officer Nat. Ctr. for Prevention Svcs., Ctrs. for Disease Control, Atlanta, 1987-89; legis. asst. on health issues to Senator John Chafee, U.S. Senate, Washington, 1991; asst. to dir. for external rels., 1989-90; state epidemiologist, dir. epidemiology and prevention br. Divsn. of Pub. Health, Ga. Dept. of Human Resources, 1993-97, dir., 1997—. Adj. assoc. prof. in epidemiology Rollins Sch. of Pub. Health, Emory U.; clin. assoc. prof. Morehouse U. Sch. Medicine, Emory U.; mem. Statewide Child Fatality Rev. Panel, 1998; mem. Bd. Health Promotion and Disease Prevention, Inst. of Medicine, 1998—; mem. Tech. Adv. Group on Devolution and Federalism, Nat. Health Policy Forum, George Washington U., 1998—. Mem. task force The Nat. Campaign to Prevent Teen Pregnancy, 1996-99. Fulbright scholar, 1973-74. Mem. Am. Acad. Family Physicians, Am. Pub. Health Assn. (governing coun. Ga. state chpt. rep. 1997-99), Am. Sexually Transmitted Diseases Assn., Assn. State and Territorial Health Ofcls. (exec. com. 1998—), Ga. Acad. Family Physicians, Ga. Pub. Health Assn., Med. Assn. Atlanta, Med. Assn. Ga. (pub. health and preventative health care com. 1997—). Office: Divsn of Pub Health 2 Peachtree St NW Ste 15-470 Atlanta GA 30303-3142 E-mail: ket1@dhr.state.ga.us.

TOOMEY, PATRICK J. congressman; b. Providence, R.I., Nov. 17, 1961; m. Kris.; children: Bridget, Patrick. BA cum laude, Harvard U., 1984. Investment banking Chem. Bank N.Y.; v.p., dir. U.S. subsidiary British merchant bank; co-founder internat. fin. svcs. consulting firm; founder Toomey Enterprises, Inc., Allentown, Pa.; mem. U.S. Congress from 15th Pa. dist., 1999—. Serves on Banking and Fin. Svcs., Budget and Small Bus. coms. Elected to Allentown Govt. Study Commn., 1994. Elected in 1998 to U.S. Ho. Reps. seat vacated by retiring Rep. Paul McHale. Served an internship with Sen. John Chafee (R-R.I.). Republican. Achievements include Toomey Enterprises, Inc., a family restaurant bus., operates 2 Rookies Restaurants located in Allentown and Lancaster, Pa. Office: 224 Cannon Hob Washington DC 20515-3815 also: 2020 Hamilton Street Allentown PA 18104

TOOMEY, RICHARD ANDREW, JR., lawyer; b. Portsmouth, NH, Oct. 21, 1944; s. Richard Andrew and Elizabeth Neal (Rylander) T.; m. Jeanne Zurmuhlen; 1 child, Samuel Van Pelt. BA, U. N.H., 1966; JD, NYU, 1969. Bar: N.Y. 1969, Mass. 1989. Atty. VISTA, Mpls., 1969-71; assoc. Carter, Ledyard & Milburn, N.Y.C., 1971-77; v.p., sr. assoc. counsel Chase Manhattan Bank, N.Y.C., 1977-89; gen. coun. Shawmut Bank NA, Boston, 1989-94; dep. gen. coun. Shawmut Nat. Corp., Boston, 1995; group sr. counsel Fleet Fin. Group, Boston, 1996-2000; gen. counsel Fleet Bank NA, Jersey City, 1996—2000; asst. gen. counsel Sovereign Bank, Boston, 2000—. Mem.: Boston Bar Assn. E-mail: rtoomey@sovereignbank.com.

TOOMEY, SISTER STEPHANA, liturgical space designer, nun; b. Wilmington, Del., Nov. 19, 1930; d. Hugh Jeremiah and Ellen (Vahey) Toomey. BS in Art Edn., Moore Coll. Art, Phila., 1952; MEd in Art, Temple U., 1960; cert., Internat. Ctr. Glass-Mosaics, Ravenna, Italy, 1975; postgrad., Paros (Greece) Sch. Fine Arts, 1975. Lic. lic. liturgical cons. and designer; joined Dominican Order, Roman Cath. Ch., 1956. Tchr. art pub. schs., Camden, N.J., 1952-54, Oak Grove, Del., 1954-56; founder, pres. Efharisto Studio Inc., worship space design studio, Balt., 1976—. Cons., mem. liturgical adv. com. Archdiocese of Balt., 1986—91. Contbr. articles and photogs. to various publs.; 5 nat. TV documentaries produced on her work; Represented in permanent collections Nat. Mus. Women in Arts. Mem. New Ventures. Named Top Winner for stained glass in chs., Bene Competition, San Jose, 2000—01; recipient hon. mention for stained glass in chs., 1991, 1993, 1998. Mem.: Dominican Order's Internat. Inst. Arts (founding mem. Dominican Inst. Arts 1997, Fra Angelico Lifetime Achievement award 1999), Balt. Writers Alliance, Form Reform, Faith and Form of AIA, Constrn. Specifications Inst., Art Architecture of AIA, Interfaith Forum Religion. Avocations: being with nature, classical music, assisting all religious traditions in design of worship space, liturgical appointments, stained glass. Office: Efharisto Studio Inc 5130 Franklintown Rd Baltimore MD 21207 Fax: 410-448-3259. Office Phone: 410-448-1711.

TOOMRE, ALAR, applied mathematician, theoretical astronomer; b. Rakvere, Estonia, Feb. 5, 1937; came to U.S., 1949, naturalized, 1955; s. Elmar and Linda (Aghen) T.; m. Joyce Stetson, June 15, 1958; children: Lars, Erik, Anya. BS in Aero. Engring., BS in Physics, MIT, 1957; PhD in Fluid Mechanics, U. Manchester, Eng., 1960. C.L.E. Moore instr. math. dept. MIT, Cambridge, 1960-62, asst. prof. applied math., 1963-65, assoc. prof., 1965-70, prof., 1970—; fellow Inst. for Advanced Study, Princeton, N.J., 1962-63. Contbr. articles to profl. jours. Guggenheim fellow, 1969-70, MacArthur fellow, 1984-89; Fairchild scholar, 1975, Marshall scholar, 1957-60 Fellow AAAS; mem. Am. Astron. Soc. (Dirk Brouwer award 1993), Internat. Astron. Union, Am. Acad. Arts and Scis., Nat. Acad. Scis. Office: MIT 77 Massachusetts Ave Rm 2-371 Cambridge MA 02139-4307 Office Phone: 617-253-4326. E-mail: toomre@math.mit.edu.

TOON, MALCOLM, former ambassador; b. Troy, N.Y., July 4, 1916; s. George and Margaret Harcomb (Broadfoot) T.; m. Elizabeth Jane Taylor, Aug. 28, 1943; children: Barbara, Alan, Nancy. AB, Tufts U., 1937, LL.D. (hon.), 1977; MA, Fletcher Sch. Law and Diplomacy, 1938; student, Middlebury Coll., 1950, Harvard U., 1950-51; LL.D. (hon.), Middlebury Coll., 1978, Drexel U., 1980, Am. Coll. Switzerland, 1985, Grove City Coll., 1990. Fgn. service officer, 1946-79; assigned successively, 1946-60; assigned Am. embassy, London, 1960-63, counselor political affairs Moscow, 1963-67; with Dept. of State, Washington, 1967-69; ambassador to Czechoslovakia, 1969-71; to Yugoslavia, 1971-75; to Israel, 1975-76; to USSR, 1976-79. Mem. U.S. del. Nuclear Test Conf., Geneva, 1958-59, Four Power Working Group, Washington, London, Paris, 1959, Fgn. Ministers Conf., Geneva, 1969, Ten Nation Disarmament Com., Geneva, 1960; mem. SALT II del., 1977-79, U.S.-Soviet Summit Conf., Vienna, 1979; Brennen prof. U. N.C., Asheville, 1981; Finch prof. Miami U., Oxford, Ohio, 1982; Allis-Chalmers chair Marquette U., Milw., 1982 Trustee emeritus Tufts U.; bd. overseers Fletcher Sch. Law and Diplomacy, 1992; former chmn. U.S. Delegation to Joint U.S. Russian Commn. on POW's, MIA's. Served from ensign to lt. comdr. USNR, 1942-46. Decorated Bronze Star with combat V; recipient Freedom Leadership award Hillsdale Coll., 1980, Valley Forge Freedom award, 1981, Disting. Honor award Dept. State, 1980, Wallace award, 1984, Gold medal Nat. Inst. of Social Scis., 1987, Degree of Prof., Acad. Natural Scis. of the Russian Fedn., 1996. Silver medal, 1996. Home: 375 Pee Dee Rd Southern Pines NC 28387-2118

TOOTE, GLORIA E. A. real estate developer, lawyer, columnist; b. N.Y.C. d. Frederick A. and Lillie M. (Tooks) Toote Student, Howard U., 1949-51; JD, NYU, 1954; LLM, Columbia U., 1956. Bar: N.Y. 1955, U.S. Dist. Ct. (so. and ea. dists.) N.Y. 1956, U.S. Supreme Ct. 1956. With firm Greenbaum, Wolff & Ernst, 1957; mem. editorial staff Time mag., 1957-58; asst. gen. counsel N.Y. State Workmen's Compensation Bd., 1958-64; pres. Toote Town Pub. Co. and Town Sound Studios, Inc., 1966-70; asst. dir. Action Agy., 1971-73; asst. sec. Dept. HUD, 1973-75; vice chmn. Pres.'s Adv. Council on Pvt. Sector Initiatives, 1983-85; housing developer, 1976—; pres. Trea Estates and Enterprises, Inc.; newspaper columnist. Chairperson The Policy Coun. Former bd. dirs. Citizens for the Republic, Nat. Black United Fund, Fed. Exec. Women in Govt., Am. Arbitration Assn., Consumer Alert; bd. overseers Hoover Inst., 1985-95; vice chair Nat. Polit. Congress of Black Women, 1984-92; former mem. Coun. Econ. Affairs, Rep. Nat. Com.; pres. N.Y.C. Black Rep. Coun.; exec. trustee Polit. Action Com. for Equality; mem. NYNEX Consumer Adv. Coun., 1995-98. Recipient citations Nat. Bus. League, Alpha Kappa Alpha, U.S. C. of C., Nat. Assn. Black Women Attys. Mem. N.Y. Fedn. Civil Svc. Orgns., Nat. Assn. Real Estate Brokers, Fed. Nat. Mortgage Assn. (bd. dirs. 1992-94), Nat. Citizens Participation Coun., Nat. Bar Assn., Delta Sigma Theta, others. Address: 282 W 137th St New York NY 10030-2407

TOOTHE, KAREN LEE, elementary and secondary school educator; b. Seattle, Dec. 13, 1957; d. Russell Minor and Donna Jean (Drolet) McGraw; m. Edward Frank Toothe, Aug. 6, 1983; 1 child, Kendall Erin. BA in Psychology with high honors, U. Fla., 1977, MEd in Emotional Handicaps and Learning Disabilities, 1979. Cert. behavior analysis Fla. Dept. Profl. Regulation, behavior analyst Nat. Behavior Analyst Bd. Alternative edn. self-contained tchr. grades 2 and 3 Gainesville Acad., Micanopy, Fla., 1979; emotional handicaps self-contained tchr. Ctr. Sch. Alternative Sch., Gainesville, Fla., 1979-80; learning disabilities resource tchr. grades 2 and 3 Galaxy Elem. Sch., Boynton Beach, Fla., 1980-81, learning disabilities self-contained tchr. grades 1-3, 1981, varying exceptionalities self-contained tchr. grades 3-5, 1981-83, chpt. one remedial reading tchr. grades 3 and 4, 1982-83; sec. and visual display unit operator Manpower, London, 1983-84; dir. sci./geography/social studies program Fairley House Sch., London, 1984-86, specific learning difficulties self-contained tchr. ages 8-12, dir. computing program, 1984-89; specific learning difficulties resource tchr. ages 8-16 Dyslexia Inst., Sutton Coldfield, Eng., 1990; behavior specialist, head Exceptional Student Edn. dept. Gateway High Sch., Kissimmee, Fla., 1990, behavior specialist, head ESE dept., 1991, resource compliance specialist, head ESE dept., 1991-93, tchr. summer youth tng. and enrichment program, 1993, Osceola High Sch.,

Kissimmee, 1992; resource compliance specialist, program specialist for mentally handicapped, physically impaired, occupational and phys. therapy programs St. Cloud (Fla.) Mid. Sch., 1993-96, local augmentative/assistive tech. specialist, 1995—; resource compliance specialist, program specialist physically impaired occupl./phys. therapy programs, local augmentative/assistive tech. specialist Hickory Tree Elem. Sch., 1996-97, program specialist assistive tech., occpl., and phys. therapy, physically impaired programs, 1997-99, program specialist assistive tech., 1999—. Sch. rep. CREATE, Alachua County, Fla., 1979-80, Palm Beach County South Area Tchr. Edn. Ctr. Coun., 1980-83, chmn., 1982-83; mem. writing team Title IV-C Ednl. Improvement Grant, Palm Beach County, Fla., 1981; mem. math. curriculum writing team Palm Beach County (Fla.) Schs., 1983; mem., co-dir. Fairley House Rsch. Com., 1984-90; co-founder, dir. Rsch. Database, London, 1984-89; co-chmn. computer and behavior/social aspects writing teams Dyslexia Inst. Math., Staines, Eng., 1990; lectr., course tutor Brit. Dyslexia Assn., Crewe, Eng., 1990; mem. Vocat.-Exceptional Com., 1991-93; mem. Osceola Reading Coun., 1991-98; mem. sch. adv. com. Gateway High Sch., 1991-93, St. Cloud Mid. Sch., 1993-96; mem. sch. adv. com. Hickory Tree Elem. Sch., 1999-2000, Ctr. for Ind. Living Assitance for Tech. Divsn.; presenter in field. Mem. bd. assistive tech. divsn. Ctr. for Ind. Living. Named Mid. Sch. Profl. of Yr. Osceola chpt. Coun. Exceptional Children, 1995, 96, Profl. Recognized Spl. Educator, 1997; winner Disney's Teacherific Spl. Judges award, 1997; recipient Outstanding Svcs. to Coun. for Exceptional Children award, 2002, 2003, Outstanding Related Svcs. Tchr. of Yr., 2003, Outstanding Support Svcs. award, 2003. Mem. CEC (named local chpt. Mid. Sch. Profl. of Yr. 1995, 96, exec. com. 1997—, C.A.N. rep. 1997-99, pres.-elect 1999-2000, pres. 2000 01, Outstanding Svcs. to CEC award 2002, 03, Outstanding Related Svcs. Tchr. of Yr. 2003, Outstanding Support Svcs award 2003), Fla. Soc. for Augmentative and Alt. Comm., Phi Beta Kappa. Avocations: travel, reading, physical fitness, scuba diving, arts and crafts. Home: 2175 James Dr Saint Cloud FL 34771-8830 Office: Osceola Dist Schs ESE Adminstrv Annex 805 Bill Beck Blvd Kissimmee FL 34744-4492 Office Phone: 407-348-2984. Business E-Mail: toothek@osceola.k12.fl.us.

TOPALIAN, NAOMI GETSOYAN, writer; b. Beirut, Jan. 26, 1928; came to the U.S., 1953; d. Avedis S. and Zarouhi T. (Yezegelian) G.; m. Paul G. Topalian, Sept. 18, 1954; children: Andrew P., Janet Z. Topalian Moffatt. Diploma, Am. U. Hosp. Sch. Nursing, Beirut, 1952; BS, Boston U., 1967. RN, Mass. Pediat. nurse Children Med. Ctr., Boston, 1954-55; inservice edn. supr. Winchester (Mass.) Hosp., 1967-70; tchr. nursing Northeastern Vocat. H.S., Wakefield, Mass., 1970-72; med. and surg. nurse various tchg. hosps., Boston, 1973-87. Author: Dust to Destiny, 1986, People, Places and Moultonborough, 1989, Legacy of Honor, 1995; contbr. Personality and Presidency: A Scientific Inquirey, 1998, Breaking the Rock of Tradition, 2000; contbr. articles to profl. jours. Supt. primary divsn., Sunday sch. tchr., mem. pulpit com., co-pres. couples club Armenian Meml. Ch., Watertown, Mass.; Armenian lang. tchr. First Armenian Ch. of Belmont; active Belmont Coun. Chs., chair religious edn. com.; pres. Armenian Women's Edn. Club. Mem. Armenian Internat. Womens Assn. Avocations: needle work, knitting, counseling the bereaved. Home: 46 Circle Rd Lexington MA 02420-2926

TOPEL, DAVID GLEN, agricultural studies educator; b. Lake Mills, Wis., Oct. 24, 1937; BS, U. Wis., 1960; MS, Kans. State U., 1962; PhD, Mich. State U., 1965; DSc (hon.), Szent Istvan U., Godallo, Hungary, 2002. Assoc. prof. animal sci. and food tech. Iowa State U., Ames, 1967-73, prof. animal sci. and food tech., 1973-79, dean Coll. Agr., 1988-2000, dir. agr. and home econs. experiment sta., 1988-2000; prof., head dept. Auburn U., Ala., 1979—88, M.E. Ensminger endowed chair animal sci., 2000—. Cons., presenter, lectr. in field; mem. Gov. of Iowa's Sci. Adv. Coun., 1990-2000, Gov. of Iowa's Livestock Revitalization Task Force, 1993-98; chair Gov.'s Environ. Agr. Com., 1994; mem. Iowa Corn Promotion Bd.; mem. faculty Royal Vet. and Agrl. U., Denmark, 1971-72; vis. prof. Nat. Taiwan U., 1972. Author: The Pork Industry - Problems and Progress, 1968. Secretariat World Food Prize, Iowa State U., Ames, 1991-96. Fulbright-Hays scholar Royal Vet. and Agrl. U., 1971-72; recipient award of merit Knights of Ak-Sar-Ben, 1973, Commr.'s award Agrl. Commr. Republic of China, 1977, disting. Achievement award Block and Bridle Club, 1979, Ala. Cattlemen's Assn.,1 984, Hon. State Farmer Degree, Ala., 1986, Harry L. Rudnick Educator's award Nat. Assn. Meat Purveyors, 1989, USDA Honor award, 1999, Hon. Prof. award Gyöngyös Coll., Hungary, 2000; named hon. prof. Ukrainian State Agrl. U., 1993. Fellow Am. Soc. Animal Sci. (Disting. Rsch. award in meat sci. 1979, Bouffault Internat. Agr. award 2002); mem. Am. Meat Sci. Assn., Inst. Food Tech., Iowa Crop Improvement Assn., Extension and Tchg. (pres. North Ctrl. Region 1992), Nat. Assn. State Univs. and Land-Grant Colls. (chair bd. agr. 1993, mem. commn. on food, environ. and renewable resources 1992-99), Ukrainian Acad. Agrl. Scis., Sigma Xi (Outstanding Achievement award Iowa chpt. 1993), Alpha Zeta, Gamma Sigma Delta (Internat. award). Presbyterian. Avocations: fishing, golf. Office: Iowa State U Coll Agriculture 2374 Kildee Hall Ames IA 50011-0001 Home: 4108 Laura Ct Ames IA 50010 Office Phone: 515-294-6304.

TOPELIUS, KATHLEEN ELLIS, lawyer; b. July 15, 1948; BA, U. Conn., 1970; postgrad., U. Md., 1971-74; JD, Cath. U. Am., 1978. Bar: D.C. 1978, U.S. Supreme Ct. 1988. Atty. office of gen. counsel Fed. Home Loan Bank Bd., 1978-80; ptnr. Morgan, Lewis & Bockius, Washington, 1985-93, Bryan Cave, Washington, 1993—. Recipient Alpha award Fed. Home Loan Bank Bds., 1979. Office: Bryan Cave 700 13th St NW Fl 7 Washington DC 20005-5921 Office Phone: 202-508-6140. Business E-Mail: ketopelius@bryancave.com.

TOPHAM, SALLY JANE, ballet educator; b. N.Y.C., June 2, 1933; d. William Holroyd Topham and Marian Phyllis (Thomas) Topham Halligan; m. Joseph Vincent Ferrara, Dec. 27, 1958 (div. 1977); children: Gregory Paul, Mark Edward. Student Ballet Theatre Sch., Royal Acad. Dance, London; trained in Europe. Freelance profl. dancer ballet, opera ballet, summer stock, 1956-59; founder, dir. Monmouth Sch. Ballet, N.J., 1963-83; dir. Shore Ballet Theatre Sch., 1986-95; freelance tchr., choreographer, 1996—. Tchr., dir. Mount Allison U. Summer Sch., New Brunswick, Canada, 1973—77; dir. Westfield Sch. Ballet, NJ, 1976—77; artistic dir. Shore Ballet Co., 1977—; prof. ballet Monmouth Coll., West Long Branch, NJ, 1981—83; founder Ctrl. Jersey Acad. Ballet, Red Bank, NJ, 1983—85; dir. Acad. of Shore Ballet, 1995—2000; cons. formulation dance curriculum for N.J. pub. schs. State Bd. Edn., 1997; tchr. Colts Neck Dance Acad., 2000—03, Middletown Dance Acad., 2003, Spring Lake Sch. Dance, 2003—. Choreographer (ballet) Coppelia, 1981, 90, 96, Shubert Songs, 1980, Homage to Bournonville, 1977, Nutcracker, 1985, Cinderella, 1988; staged many ballets and opera ballets. Bd. dirs. Monmouth Arts Found., Red Bank, 1972—, Shore Ballet Co., Red Bank, 1976—; founder, bd. dirs. Monmouth Civic Ballet, Red Bank, 1972-75. Mem.: English Speaking Union (bd. dirs., treas. 2004), Am. Acad. Ballet (assoc.), Royal Acad. Dance (assoc.; reg. tchr., advanced tchg. diploma 1979). Avocations: theater, music, books, travel. Office: Shore Ballet Co 8 Hunt St Rumson NJ 07760-1428

TOPIEL, MARTIN STANLEY, epidemiologist; b. 1953; 2 children. MD, NYU, 1979. Diplomate Am. Bd. Internal Medicine, Am. Bd. Infectious Disease. Intern George Washington U. Med. Ctr., Washington, 1979—80, resident in internal medicine, 1980—82, fellow in infectious disease, 1982—84; epidemiologist Virtua Meml. Hosp.-Burlington, Mt. Laurel, NJ. Named one of Top Drs. 2003, N.J. Monthly Mag. Office: Virtua Meml Hosp-Burlington 1001 Briggs Rd Ste 250 Mount Laurel NJ 08054-4111

TOPIK, STEVEN CURTIS, historian, educator; b. Montebello, Calif., Aug. 6, 1949; s. Kurt and Trudy Topik; m. Martha Jane Marcy, Feb. 3, 1979; children: Julia, Natalia. BA, U. Calif., San Diego, 1971; MA, U. Tex., 1973, PhD, 1978. Asst. prof. U. Fed. Fluminense, Rio de Janeiro, 1978-81, Colgate U., Hamilton, NY, 1981-84; prof. U. Calif., Irvine, 1984-96, chair history dept., 1996-2000. Vis. prof. Universidade Fed. Fluminense, Rio de Janeiro, 1984—, U. Ibero Americana, Mexico City, 1982, Ecoles des Hautes Etudes en Sci. Social, Paris, 1990, London Sch. Econs., 2002; cons. in field. Author: (book) The Political Economy of the Brazilian State, 1987, Trade and Gunboats, The United States and Brazil in the Age of Empire, 1996; author: (with Allen Wells) The Second Conquest of Latin America, 1998; author: (with Kenneth Pomeranz) The World Trade Created, 1999; editor (with Dorothy Solinger and David Smith): States and Sovereignty in the Global Economy, 1999; editor: (with William Clarence-Smith) The Global Coffee Economy in Africa, Asia and Latin America 1500-1989, 2003; contbr. revs. to profl. publs.; mem. editl. com. U. Calif. Press, Berkeley, 1987—89. Mem. Mayor's Adv. Bd. Sister Cities, Irvine, 1989—90; mem. adv. bd. Orange County (Calif.) Com. L.Am., 1989—90. Fellow, Rockerfeller Found., 1977, Fulbright-Hayes Found., 1978—79, 1984, Social Sci. Rsch. Coun. Mexico City, 1982—83, NEH, 1987, 1989—90, U. Calif., 1988—89. Mem.: Pacific Coast Coun. L.Am. Studies (bd. govs. 1987—90), Conf. L.Am. History (mem. com. hist. stastis., mem. com. projects and publs., chair Brazilian studies com. 1988—90), Am. Hist. Assn., L.Am. Studies Assn. Office Phone: 949-824-8053. E-mail: sctopik@uci.edu.

TOPINKA, JUDY BAAR, state official, political organization worker; b. Riverside, Ill., Jan. 16, 1944; d. William Daniel and Lillian Mary (Shuss) Baar; 1 child, Joseph Baar. BS, Northwestern U., 1966. Features editor, reporter, columnist Life Newspapers, Berwyn and LaGrange, Ill., 1966-77; with Forest Park (Ill.) Rev. and Westchester News, 1976-77; coord. spl. events dept. fedn. comm. AMA, 1978-80; rsch. analyst Senator Leonard Becker, 1978-79; mem. Ill. Ho. of Reps., 1981-84, Ill. Senate, 1985-94; treas. State of Ill., Springfield, 1995—; chmn. State Rep. Party, 2002—. Former mem. judiciary com., former chmn. senate health and welfare com.; former mem. fin. instn. com.; former co-chmn. Citizens Coun. on Econ. Devel.; former co-chmn. U.S. Commn. for Preservation of Am.'s Heritage Abroad, serves on legis. ref. bur.; former mem. minority bus. resource ctr. adv. com. U.S. Dept. Transp.; former mem. adv. bd. Nat. Inst. Justice. Founder, pres., bd. dirs. West Suburban Exec. Breakfast Club, from 1976; chmn. Ill. Ethnics for Reagan-Bush, 1984, Bush-Quayle 1988; spokesman Nat. Coun. State Legislatures Health Com.; former mem. nat. adv. coun. health professions edn. HHS; mem., GOP chairwoman Legis. Audit Commn. of Cook County; chmn. Riverside Twp. Regular Republican Orgn., 1994—. Recipient Outstanding Civilian Svc. medal, Molly Pitcher award, Abraham Lincoln award, Silver Eagle award U.S. Army and N.G. Office: Office of Ill State Treasurer 100 W Randolph St Ste 15-600 Chicago IL 60601-3232

TOPLITT, GLORIA H. voice educator, singer, actress; b. St. Louis, May 22, 1925; d. Wade Fitzgerald Hamilton and Neyneen Farrell Pires; m. James Parnell, 1942 (div. July 1949); 1 child, Dennis James Parnell; m. Abraham Toplitt, Aug. 19, 1968. Student, Guy Bates Post Acad. Dramatic Arts, L.A., 1941-43. Stage performer, N.Y.C., 1944-59; dir. entertainment Holland Am. Lines, 1959-61; voice tchr. North Hollywood (Calif.) Conservatory, 1965-67; pvt. voice tchr. North Hollywood, 1968-95; music specialist outreach program NASA Space Sci. and Tech., Inc., Springfield, Va., 1997—. Dir. Workshop Theatre Program, North Hollywood, 1968-78; coach for impaired voices, North Hollywood, 1968—. Author, composer: Parade of Planets, 1998, Space Challenge, 1999 actor: (plays, N.Y. stage prodns.) appeared as leading lady Oklahoma, Chocolate Soldier, Lend an Ear, Courtin' Time, Showboat, Take Me Along, Auld Lang Syne, Three Musketeers, Carousel, Oh! Captain, Brigadoon, Guys and Dolls, Hit the Deck, Finian's Rainbow, others. Mem. election bd. Office of Voter Registrar, North Hollywood, 1996-98. Avocations: poetry, travel, theater, elderhostel classes, reading. Home: 4405 Carpenter Ave North Hollywood CA 91607-4110

TOPP, ALPHONSO AXEL, JR., environmental scientist, consultant; b. Indpls., Oct. 15, 1920; s. Alphonso Axel and Emilia (Karlsson) T.; m. Mary Catherine Virtue, July 7, 1942; children: Karen, Susan, Linda, Sylvia, Peter, Astrid, Heidi, Eric, Megan, Katrina. BS in Chem. Engring., Purdue U., 1942; MS, UCLA, 1948. Commd. 2d lt. U.S. Army, 1942, advanced through grades to col., 1966, ret., 1970; environ. protection scientist radiation protection sect. State of N. Mex., Santa Fe, 1970-78, program mgr. licensing and registration sect., 1978-81, chief radiation protection bur., 1981-83, cons., 1984—. Decorated Legion of Merit, Bronze Star with 2 oak leaf clusters, U.S. Army. Mem. Rotary, Triangle, Sigma Xi. Republican. Methodist. Home and Office: 1200 Calle Cordoniz Los Osos CA 93402-4428 E-mail: alphons188@aol.com.

TOPPETA, WILLIAM JOHN, insurance company executive, lawyer; b. N.Y.C., Sept. 18, 1948; s. John Francis and Rita Ann (Carretta) T. BA, Fordham u., 1970; JD, NYU, 1973, ML, 1977. Bar: N.Y. 1974, U.S. Supreme Ct. 1977. Atty. Met. Life, N.Y.C., 1973-79, asst. v.p., 1979-81, asst. gen. counsel, 1981-82, assoc. gen. counsel, 1982-83, v.p., assoc. gen. counsel, 1983-92; pres., CEO MetLife Can. Ops., 1993-95, sr. v.p. corp. re-engring., 1995-97, exec. v.p., 1995-97; sr. exec. v.p. Met. Life, 1997-99, pres., chief admin. officer, 1999—, pres. internat., 2001—. Adj. prof. Pace U. Law Sch., White Plains, N.Y., 1984—, Bklyn. Law Sch., 1985—. Mem. ABA (vice-chairperson com. on trial techniques 1986—), N.Y. State Bar Assn., Assn. Bar of City of N.Y. Democrat. Roman Catholic. Office: Met Life 1 Madison Ave New York NY 10010-3603 E-mail: btoppeta@metlife.com.

TOPPING, AUDREY RONNING, photojournalist; b. Camrose, Alta., Can., May 21, 1928; arrived in U.S., 1967; d. Chester Alvin and Inga Marie (Horte) Ronning; m. Seymour Topping, Nov. 10, 1949; children: Susan, Karen, Lesley, Robin, Joanna. Student, Augustana Univ., Camrose, 1943-46, Nanking (China) U., 1947-48, Berlin Art Sch., 1956-58, U. B.C., 1949-50; D of Arts (hon.), Rider Coll., N.J., 1983. Freelance journalist N.Y. Times Mag., N.Y.C., 1966—2001; writer, photographer Nat. Geographic, Washington, 1971-79; columnist Earth Times, N.Y.C., 1996—; spl. corr. Houston Chronicle, 1997—2001; photjournalist-at-large Earthuman Mag., 2002—. Advisor U.S.-China Arts Exch., 1997—; commentator, writer Great Wall Across The Yangtze (PBS), Homecoming (Chinese TV), 2002; TV scriptwriter China Mission, 1975. Author: Dawn Wakes In the East, 1972, The Splendors of Tibet, 1981, Charlie's World, 2000; A Day in the Life of Can., 1986, two children's books, N.Y. Times, Nat. Geographic, Readers Digest, Time, Life, Geo, Sci. Digest, Earth Times, others, exhibitions include Royal Ont. Mus., Toronto, 1980, Hallmark Gallery, NYC, 1973, Overseas Press Cub, 1975, Westchester C.C., 1989, 2004, Libby Gallery, Purchase, NY, 2004, Bhutan UN Embassy, NY, 2004. Recipient Alumni award Augustana Univ. Coll., 1989, Medallion award Westchester C.C., 1989, Greenway Winship award Internat. Ctr. Journalists, 2000. Mem.: Coun. of Fgn. Relations, Soc. Woman Geographers, Asia Soc., Fgn. Policy Assn., Fox Meadow Tennis Club. Jr. Fortnightly. Avocations: sculpture, painting, tennis, skiing, exploring. Home and Office: 5 Heathcote Rd Scarsdale NY 10583-4413 E-mail: topaud@aol.com.

TOPPING, JENNIFER, Olympic athlete; b. May 30, 1980; Student, U. Wash., 1999; grad., Calif. State, Fullerton, 2003. Mem. U.S. Nat. Team, 2002—, U.S. Women's Softball Team, Athens Olympic Games, 2004. Named Big West Conference Player of the Yr., 2001, 2002, 2003, NFCA First Team All-Am., 2000, 2001, 2002, 2003. Achievements include mem. Gold medal U.S. Nat. Team, Pan Am. Games, 1999, 2003. Office: USA Softball Complex 4845 S Shields Blvd Oklahoma City OK 73129*

TOPPING, SEYMOUR, author, educator; b. N.Y.C., Dec. 11, 1921; s. Joseph and Anna (Seidman) Topolsky; m. Audrey Elaine Ronning, Nov. 10, 1949; children: Susan, Karen, Lesley, Rebecca, Joanna. BJ, U. Mo., 1943; LittD (hon.), Rider Coll., 1983. With I.N.S. (China civil war), 1946-47; with AP, 1948-59, corr., 1957-59; mem. staff N.Y. Times, 1959-93, chief corr. Moscow, 1960-63, chief corr. S.E. Asia, 1963-66, fgn. editor, 1966-69, asst. mng. editor, 1969-76, dep. mng. editor, 1976-77, mng. editor, 1977-86; dir. editl. devel. N.Y. Times Regional Newspapers, 1987-93; chmn. New Directions for News, 1990-91; pres. Am. Soc. Newspaper Editors, 1992—93; prof. Grad. Sch. Journalism Columbia U., N.Y.C., 1993—2002, adminstr. Pulitzer Prizes, 1993—2002, Sanpaolo prof. emeritus of internat. journalism, 2002—. Adviser Internat. Ctr. for Journalists, Found. Am. Comm.; juror Pulitzer Prize com.; lectr. in field. Author: Journey Between Two Chinas, 1972, The Peking Letter, A Novel of the Chinese Civil War, 1999, Fatal Crossroads, A Novel of Vietnam 1945, 2004. Spl. advisor to Sec.-Gen. UN to Earth Summit, Rio de Janeiro, 1992; mem. Nat. Com. U.S.-China Rels.; Served with inf. AUS, 1943-46, PTO. Recipient Greenway-Winship award for contbns. to internat. journalism, 2000, Disting. Svc. award, Mo. Sch. of Journalism, 1968, Disting Alumni award, 1993. Mem. Coun. Fgn. Rels., Asia Soc., Am. Soc. Newspaper Editors, Am. Bd. of Dirs. Internat. Press Inst., Century Assn. Home: 5 Heathcote Rd Scarsdale NY 10583-4413 Personal E-mail: st122@columbia.edu.

TORAK, ELIZABETH LICHTENSTEIN, artist; b. N.Y.C., Apr. 12, 1959; d. Immanuel and Nancy (Rabi) Lichtenstein; m. Thomas John Torak, Jan. 5, 1985. BA in Math., U. Chgo., 1981; postgrad., Art Students League N.Y., 1981-85. One-woman shows include Capricorn Galleries, Bethesda, Md., 1993, G.C. Lucas Gallery, 1999; two-person shows include Tilting at Windmills Gallery, Manchester, Vt., 1998, 2000, 01, 03, 04, G.C. Lucas Gallery, Indpls., 1995-98, So. Vt. Art Ctr., Manchester, 1995, Clapp & Tuttle Galley, Woodbury, Conn., 1992, N.J. Mus. Agr., New Brunswick, 1992; exhibited in group shows at Butler Inst. Am. Art, Youngstown, Ohio, 1992-95, 97-99, 2000-02, Conn. Valley Hist. Mus., Springfield, Mass., 1996, Wiregrass Mus. Art, Dothan, Ala., 1996, Arlington (Tex.) Mus. Art, 1991, San Diego Art Inst., 1989, First Ch. Gallery, Court Square, Springfield, 1997, 93, Salmagundi Club, N.Y.C., 1993-99, Francesca Anderson Fine Art, Lexington, Mass., 1994, 96-98, Nat. Arts Club, N.Y.C., 1993-96, Greenhouse Gallery of Fine Art, San Antonio, 1995-96, Copley Soc. Boston, 1994, Gallery 128, N.Y.C., 1994, Wyckoff (N.J.) Gallery, 1994; represented in permanent collections Pierre Hotel, Reliance Nat. Ins. Co., Miss. Chem. Corp.; commd. by Fatima Retreat House, Indpls., Our Lady of Grace Ch., Bronx. Mem. Am. Artists Profl. League, Acad. Artists Assn., Audubon Artists, Catherine lorellard Wolfe Art Club. Democrat. Avocations: reading, gardening, hiking, cello.

TORBET, LAURA, writer, artist, photographer, graphic designer; b. Paterson, N.J., Aug. 23, 1942; d. Earl Buchanan and Ruth Claire (Ehlers) Robbins; m. Bruce J. Torbet, Sept. 9, 1967 (div. 1971); m. Peter H. Morrison, June 19, 1983 (dec. Nov. 1988); m. Salam Habibi, Aug. 23, 1995 (div. 2000). BA, BFA, Ohio Wesleyan U., 1964. Mng. editor Suburban Life mag., East Orange, N.J., 1964-65; asst. pub. rels. dir. United Funds N.J., Newark, 1965-67; art dir. Alitalia Airlines, N.Y.C., 1967-69; propr. Laura Torbet Studio, N.Y.C., 1969-84. Author: Macrame You Can Wear, 1972, Clothing Liberation, 1973, Leathercraft You Can Wear, 1975, The T-Shirt Book, 1976, The Complete Book of Skateboarding, 1976, How To Do Everything with Markers, 1977; (with Doug McLaggan) Squash: How to Play, How to Win, 1977, The Complete Book of Mopeds, 1978; (with Luree Nicholson) How to Fight Fair With Your Kids...and Win!, 1980; editor: Helena Rubenstein's Book of the Sun, 1979, The Encyclopedia of Crafts, 1980; (with George Bach) A Time for Caring, 1983, The Inner Enemy, 1983; (with Hap Hatton) Helpful Hints for Hard Times, 1982, The Virgin Homeowners Handbook, 1984, Helpful Hints for Better Living, 1984; (with James Braly) Dr. Braly's Optimum Health Program, 1985; (with Bernard Gittelson) Intangible Evidence, 1987; (as writer for Harville Hendrix) Keeping the Love Your Find, 1992, The Couples Companion, 1994, The Personal Companion, 1996, (as writer for Peter Lambrou and George Pratt) Instant Emotional Healing, 1999, (as writer for Lisa Fittipaldi) A Brush with Darkness, 2004; editor, ghostwriter, co-author books. Pres., bd. dirs. The Living/Dying Project. Mem. Boss Ladies. Home and Office: 503 The Alameda San Anselmo CA 94960 Office Phone: 415-485-1615. Personal E-mail: lulutorbet@aol.com.

TORBICA, ZELJKO MARKO, construction executive, educator; arrived in U.S.A., 92; s. Marko and Nadezda Torbica; m. Maria Jovanov, Oct. 30, 1999; children: Talia, Nada, Dara, Djordje. PhD, U. Fla., 1997—97; diploma, U. of Belgrad, 1986. Cert. quality engr., Am. Soc. Quality; project mgmt. profl. Project Mgmt. Inst. Engr. Energoprojekt, Belgrade, Serbia and Montenegro, 1986—92; asst. prof. Minn. State U., Mankato, 1996—97; constrn. mgmt. educator Fla. Internat. U., Miami, Fla., 1997—.

TORCHETTI, JOHN, professional athletics coach; Asst. Greensboro Monarchs, 1992—93; head coach, dir. hocky ops. San Antonio (Tex.) Iguanas, 1994—95; asst. gen. mgr., asst. coach San Antonio (Tex.) Dragons, 1996; coach Komets, 1996—98; gen. mgr. Detroit (Mich.) Vipers, 1998—2002; head coach devel. affiliate Fla. Panthers, San Antonio, 2002—03, asst. coach Sunrise, Fla., 2003—04, head coach, 2004—. Asst. scouting dir. Tampa Bay (Fla.) Lightning, 2001—02. Named Coach of Yr., CHL, 1995. Office: One Panther Pkwy Fort Lauderdale FL 33323*

TORCHIN, MIMI, periodical editor; Founder, editor-in-chief Soap Opera Weekly, N.Y.C, 1989—. Office: Soap Opera Weekly 261 Madison Ave Fl 9 New York NY 10016-2303

TORESCO, DONALD, automotive executive; b. 1936; With Dom's Auto Sales, Inc., Plainfield, N.J., 1958-91; CEO mng. group for Autoland Toresco Enterprises, Springfield, N.J., 1984—. Office: Toresco Enterprises 170 Route 22 Springfield NJ 07081-3123

TORG, JOSEPH STEVEN, orthopaedic surgeon, educator; b. Phila., Oct. 25, 1934; m. Barbara Jane Groenendaal, May 23, 1959; children: Joseph Steven, Elisabeth, Jay Michael. AB, Haverford Coll., 1957; MD, Temple U., 1961. Diplomate: Am. Bd. Orthopaedic Surgeons. Intern San Francisco Gen. Hosp., 1961-62; resident in orthopaedic surgery Temple U. Hosp., Phila., 1964-68, Shriners Hosp. for Crippled Children, Phila., 1966-67; asst. surgeon Episcopal Hosp., Phila., 1968-70; surgeon Shriners Hosp. Crippled Children, 1970-78; mem. staff Temple U. Hosp., 1970-78, instr. orthopaedic surgery, 1968-70, asst. prof., 1970-75, assoc. prof., 1976-78; dir. Center for Sports Medicine and Sci., 1974-78; chief orthopaedic sect. St. Christopher's Hosp. for Children, Phila., 1971-74, mem. staff, 1974—; active staff St. Joseph's Hosp., Phila., 1977—; prof. U. Pa., 1978—, active staff hosp., 1978—; dir. Sports Medicine Center, 1978—; prof. orthopaedic surgery Temple U., 1995. Mem. active staff Children's Hosp., Phila., 1978; med. cons. Pres.'s Council on Phys. Fitness and Sports Mem. editorial bd. Sports Medicine, Yearbook of Sports Medicine, Contemporary Orthopaedics, Jour. Clin. Sport Medicine, Am. Jour. Knee Surgery, Orthopaedic Rev.; contbr. articles to profl. jours. Served with M.C. U.S. Army, 1962-64. Recipient Layman Honor award Pa. State Assn. Health, Phys. Edn. and Recreation, 1970, Grad. Honor award, 1975; Commendation of Merit Phila. Public High Sch. Football Coaches, 1974 Fellow Am. Acad. Orthopaedic Surgeons, Am. Coll. Sports Medicine (trustee 1975-78), Phila. Coll. Physicians; mem. AMA, Eastern Orthopaedic Soc., Am. Orthopaedic Soc., Sports Medicine, Phila. County Med. Soc., Phila. Orthopaedic Soc., Pa. State Med. Soc., Pa. State Orthopaedic Soc. Home: 401 Conestoga Rd Wayne PA 19087-4811 Office: Temple U Hospital 6th Floor 3401 N Broad St Philadelphia PA 19140 Office Phone: 215-707-1321. Personal E-mail: torgmd@aol.com.

TORGERSEN, PAUL ERNEST, academic administrator, educator; b. N.Y.C., Oct. 13, 1931; s. Einar and Frances (Hansen) T.; m. Dorothea Hildegarde Zuschlag, Sept. 11, 1954; children: Karen Elizabeth, Janis Elaine, James Einar. BS, Lehigh U., 1953, DEng, 1994; MS, Ohio State U., 1956, PhD, 1959. Grad. tchg. asst. Ohio State U., Columbus, 1957, instr., 1957-59; asst. to assoc. prof. Okla. State U., Stillwater, 1959-66; prof., dept. head, dean Coll. Engring. Va. Tech, Blacksburg, 1967-93, pres., 1993-2000, John W. Hancock chair of engring. Dir. Roanoke (Va.) Electric Steel, 1986-2001, Luna Innovations, 2000—, EDD, 1996—. Author 5 books. Mem. Gov. Mark Warner's Commn. on Bd. of Visitor Appts., Richmond, Va., 2002--; So.State Energy Bd., Richmond, 1986-90. 1st lt. USAF, 1953-55. Fellow Am. Soc. Engring. Edn. (Lamme medal 1994), Inst. Indsl. Engring (Frank and Lillian Gibreth award 2001); mem. Nat. Acad. Engring. (coun. 1999—). Avocation: tennis. Office: Va Tech 302A Whittemore Blacksburg VA 24061-0118

TORGERSON, KATHERINE P. diversified business media company executive; Now v.p. human resources and exec. adminstrn. Penton Media, Inc., Cleve., with. Office: Penton Media Inc Ste 316 1300 E 9th St Cleveland OH 44114-1503

TORGERSON, LARRY KEITH, lawyer; b. Albert Lea, Minn., Aug. 25, 1935; s. Fritz G. and Lu (Hillman) Torgerson. BA, Drake U., 1958, MA, 1960, LLB, 1963, JD, 1968; MA, Iowa U., 1962; cert., The Hague Acad. Internat. Law, The Netherlands, 1965, 69; LLM, U. Minn., 1969, Columbia U., 1971, U. Mo., 1976; PMD, Harvard U., 1973; EdM, 1974. Bar: Minn. 1964, U.S.

Dist. Ct. Minn. 1964, Wis. 1970, Iowa 1970, U.S. Dist. Ct. (no. dist.) Iowa 1971, U.S. Tax Ct. 1971, U.S. Supreme Ct. 1972, U.S. Dist. Ct. (ea. dist.) Wis. 1981, U.S. Ct. Appeals (8th cir.) 1981. Asst. corp. counsel 1st Bank Stock Corp. (88 Banks), Mpls., 1963-67, 1st Svc. Corp. (27 ins. agys., computer subs.), Mpls., 1965-67; v.p., trust officer Nat. City Bank, Mpls., 1967-69; sr. mem. Torgerson Law Firm, Northwood, Iowa, 1969-87; trustee, gen. counsel Torgerson Farms, Northwood, 1967—, Redbirch Farms, Kensett, Iowa, 1987—2002, Sunburst Farms, Grafton, Iowa, 1987—, Gold Dust Farms, Bolan, Iowa, 1988—, Torgerson Grain Storage, Bolan, 1988—, Indian Summer Farms, Bolan, 1991—, Sunset Farms, Bolan, 1992—, Sunrise Farms, Grafton, 1994—. CEO, gen. counsel Internat. Investments, Mpls., 1983-96, Transoceanic, Mpls., 1987-96, Torgerson Capital, Northwood, 1996—, Torgerson Investments, Northwood, 1984—, Torgerson Properties, Northwood, 1987—, Torgerson Ranches, Sundance, Wyo., 1998—, Hawaiian Investments Unltd., Maui, Hawaii, 1998—, Internat. Investments Unltd., San Pedro, Belize, 1999—. Recipient All-Am. Journalism award Thomas Arkle Clark Outstanding Achievement award, 1958, Dennis E. Brumfield Outstanding Achievement award, 1958, Johnny B. Guy Outstanding Leadership award, 1958; named to Outstanding Young Men of Am., U.S. Jaycees; Hagen scholar, Honor scholar. Mem. ABA, Am. Judicature Soc., Iowa Bar Assn., Minn. Bar Assn., Wis. Bar Assn., Hennepin County Bar Assn., Mensa, Drake Student-Faculty Coun., Drake Student Alumni Coun. (chmn.), Jaycees, Harvard Bus. Sch. Study (pres., exec. com., univ. editor in chief), Psi Chi, Circle K (pres. local chpt.), Phi Alpha Delta, Omicron Delta Kappa (pres. local chpt.), Pi Kappa Delta (pres. local chpt.), Alpha Tau Omega (pres. local chpt., Silver Bullet Outstanding Leadership award, 1965, 66), Pi Delta Epsilon (founder, chpt. pres.), Alpha Kappa Delta, Alpha Scholastic Hon. (U. editor-in-chief), Harvard Bus. Sch. Exec. Com. (U. editor-in-chief). Lutheran.

TORGERSON, LINDA BELLE, music educator; b. Sioux City, Iowa, Dec. 16, 1951; d. Fredric William and Clara Jeanette Wilson; m. Peter Kinsey Torgerson; children: Christopher, Patricia. Diploma, Ctrl. H.S., 1971; MusB Edn., Morningside Coll., 1976; MEd, City U., 1999. Cert. Iowa tchr., tchr. Mont., Washington. Choral dir. First United Meth. Ch., Sioux City, Iowa, 1974—76, First Presbyn. Ch., Kalispell, Mont., 1976—80; pvt. music instr. Self-employed, Kalispell, Mont., 1976—80; music tchr. St. Matthews Sch., Kalispell, Mont., 1976—77; music dir., coord. Flathead County Rural Schools, Kalispell, Mont., 1979—85; music dir. Clarkston Sch. Dist., Clarkston, Wash., 1985—. Treas. Clarkston Edn. Assn., Clarkston, Wash., 1988—90, v.p., 1990—92, Clarkston, 2001—03, pres., 1991—92; sec. Wash. uniserv polit. action com. Wash. Edn. Assn., Olympia, Wash., 1992—93; bldg. rep. Clarkston Edn. Assn., Clarkston, Wash., 1993—94; jazz band dir. Lincoln Mid. Sch., Clarkston, Wash., 1996—; bldg. rep. Clarkston Edn. Assn., Clarkston, Wash., 2000—01, v.p., 2001—03; co-director for asotin county teens against smoking Asotin County Devel. Services, Clarkston, Wash., 2001—02. Singer (composer): (commercial) Flathead County Milk Music Ad for the Radio, 1978; contbr. articles to profl. jours. Mem. U-Pac bd. for SE Wash. Edn. Assn., Kennewick, Wash., 1992—93. Grantee Dist., Clarkston Sch. Dist., 1994, 1995. Mem.: NEA, Clarkston Edn. Assn. (v.p. 2001), Clarkston Edn. Assn. (bldg. rep. 1992—94), Clarkston Edn. Assn. (pres./past pres. 1991—92), Clarkston Edn. Assn. (v.p. 1989—91), Clarkston Edn. Assn. (treas. 1987—89), SE Wash. Music Educators Assn. (pres. 2002—), Wash. Music Educators Assn., Music Educators Nat. Conf. Home: 1505 8th St Clarkston WA 99403 Office: Lincoln Mid Sch 1945 4th Ave Clarkston WA 99403 Personal E-mail: torgersonl@csdk12.org.

TORGOW, EUGENE N. electrical engineer; b. Bronx, N.Y., Nov. 26, 1925; s. Frank and Blanche Anita (Revzin) T.; m. Cynthia Silver, Mar. 19, 1950; children: Joan, Martha, Ellen. BSEE, Cooper Union, 1946; MSEE, Poly. Inst. Bklyn., 1949; Engr. in E.E., Poly. Inst. N.Y., 1980; postgrad., UCLA, 1983. Rsch. assoc., sect. leader Microwave Rsch. Inst., Poly. Inst. Bklyn., 1947-51, 53-60, instr., 1954-59; mgr. microwave lab. A.B. Dumont Labs, East Paterson, N.J., 1951-53; chief engr., mgr. microwave products Dorne & Margolin, Inc., Westbury, L.I., N.Y., 1960-64; chief engr., dir. rsch., dir. mktg. Rantec divsn. Emerson Electric, Calabasas, Calif., 1964-68; with Missle Sys. Group, Hughes Aircraft Co., Canoga Park, Calif., 1968-85, assoc. labs. mgr., 1981-85. Cons. various electronics firms, N.Y.C., 1956-59; cons., 1986—; cons. Exec. Svc. Corps of So. Calif., 1996—; pres. Cons. Adv. Coun., 1999-2000; lectr. Calif. State U., Northridge, 1986-91. Contbr. articles to profl. jours.; patentee in field. Mem. Fair Housing Coun. San Fernando Valley, L.A., 1967—, L.A. Co. Mus. Assn., 1976—2001. Served with USAAC, 1946—47. Recipient Engr. '85 Merit award San Fernando Valley Engrs. Coun., 1985. Fellow IEEE, Inst. for Advancement Engring.; mem. WINCON (bd. dirs. 1984-89, chmn. bd. dirs. 1988-89), Microwave Theory and Techniques Soc. of IEEE (pres. 1966, mem. adminstrn. com. 1962-72, Svc. award 1978), Accreditation Bd. Engring. and Tech. (mem. engring. accreditation com. 1994-99), Amiotropic Lateral Sclerosis Assn. (trustee greater L.A. chpt. 1999-2004, adv. trustee 2004-), Hughes Mgmt. Club (edn. chmn. 1979-80), Sigma Xi. Democrat. Office: 9531 Donna Ave Northridge CA 91324-1816

TORGUSON, MARLIN F. entertainment company executive; b. 1945; Owner, prin. Torgy's Inc., Glenwood, Minn., 1965—; with G M T Mgmt. Co., 1984-91; prin., v.p. Jackpot Junction Casino, Morton, Minn.; founder Mardi Gras Casino Corp., 1990—, Atlantic-Pacific Corp., 1990—, Bay St. Louis Casino Corp., 1992—, Biloxi Casino Corp., 1992—; pres., CEO Casino Magic Corp., 1992-94, CFO, treas., 1992-93, chmn., 1994—. Bd. dirs. Hollywood Pk. Inc. Office: Casino Magic Corp PO Box 8003 Bay Saint Louis MS 39521-8003

TORISKY, EUGENE VINCENT, JR., philosopher, educator; b. Pitts., Dec. 20, 1963; s. Eugene and Althea Torisky; m. Theresa Mazzaferri, Mar. 22, 1965; 1 child, Justin Bartholomew. BA magna cum laude, Bowling Green (Ohio) State U., 1986, M.A. in Applied Philosophy, 1993, PhD in Applied Philosophy, 2001. Vis. asst. prof. philosophy Stetson U., DeLand, Fla., 1998—2000, Ithaca (N.Y.) Coll., 2001—02; asst. prof. philosophy St. Vincent Coll., Latrobe, Pa., 2002—. Contbr. articles to profl. jours. Mem.: Am. Philos. Assn., Amnesty Internat. Office: Saint Vincent Coll 300 Fraser Purchase Rd Latrobe PA 15650-2690 Business E-Mail: eugene.torisky@email.stvincent.edu.

TORIUMI, DEAN MICHAEL, facial, plastic and reconstructive surgery, educator; b. Chgo., Ill., 1958; Degree in biology, Knox Coll., 1980; grad., Norwestern U. Med. Ctr.; MD, Rush Med. Coll., 1981. Cert. otolaryngology 1988. Resident, gen. surgery U. Ill., Chgo., 1983—85; resident, otolaryngology Northwestern U. Med. Sch., Chgo., 1985—87; fellowship, facial plastic and reconstruction surgery Tulane Med. Sch., New Orleans, 1988, Va. Mason Med. Ctr., Seattle, 1989; assoc. prof. U. Ill., Dept. Otolaryngology, Chgo. Co-author: Open Structure Rhinoplasty; contbr. articles various profl. papers, chapters to books. Mem.: Am. Acad. Facial Plastic and Reconstructive Surgery (pres.). Office: U Ill Chgo Coll Medicine Dept Otolaryngology 1855 W Taylor St Rm 242 Chicago IL 60612-7242 Address: 60 E Del Pl Chicago IL 60611-1495 also: 900 N Mich Ave Chicago IL 60611-1542

TORKELSON, JODIE RAE, charitable organization executive; b. Cudahy, Wis., May 13, 1958; d. Wallace Keith and Delores Helen (Hagen) T. BA in Polit. Sci., Moorhead State U., 1980. Staff asst. Congressman Richard Nolan, Washington, 1980-81; office mgr. Congressman Leon E. Panetta, Washington, 1981-86, adminstrv. asst., 1988-89; acting exec. dir. Life Underwriters for Lutheran Charities, Mpls., 1986-88; dir. adminstrn. com. on budget U.S. Ho. of Reps., Washington, 1989-93, assoc. dir. for adminstrn. Office of Mgmt. and Budget, 1993-94; asst. to pres. for mgmt. and adminstrn. The White House, Washington, 1994-97; chief of staff, sr. advisor to dir. Voice of Am., Washington, 1997-99; v.p. ops. Children's Def. Fund, Washington, 2000. Lutheran. Office: Children's Def Fund 25 E St NW Washington DC 20001-1591

TORKILDSEN, PETER G. state agency administrator; b. Milw., Jan. 28, 1958; s. Robert Allan and Mary Ellen (Hill) T.; m. Gail Bloomgarden, Jan. 1996. BA, U. Mass., 1980; MPA, Harvard U., 1990. Mem. Mass. House of reps., 1985-91, 103rd and 104th Congress from 6th Mass. dist., 1993-97; pres. Thunder Hill Inc., Peabody, Mass., 1997—; commr. Mass. Labor Rels. Commn., Boston, 2001—. Mem. Danvers Town Meeting, 1983-85, Mass. Rep. State Com., Boston, 1984-93. Mem. Am. Legis. Exchange Council, Mass. Legislator's Assn., Nat. Rep. Legislator Assn. Lodges: Sons of Norway. Republican. Roman Catholic. Home: Box 395 Danvers MA 01923-395 Office: 399 Washington St 4th Fl Boston MA 02108

TORKILDSON, RAYMOND MAYNARD, lawyer; b. Lake City, S.D., Nov. 19, 1917; s. Gustav Adolph and Agnes (Opitz) T.; m. Sharman Elizbeth Vaughn, Sept. 8, 1956; children: Stephen, Thomas. S.B., U. S.D., 1946; JD, Harvard U., 1948. Bar: Calif. 1949, Hawaii 1950. Assoc. James P. Blaisdell, Honolulu, 1949-52; ptnr. Moore, Torkildson & Rice and successors, Honolulu, 1955-64; exec. v.p. Hawaii Employers Council, Honolulu, 1964-67; ptnr. Torkildson, Katz, Fonseca, Jaffe, Moore & Hetherington and predecessors, Honolulu, 1967-72; sr. ptnr., 1972-92; of counsel, 1993—. Mem. mgmt. com. Armed Forces YMCA, Honolulu, 1971; treas. Hawaii Republican Com. 1977-83. Served with U.S. Army, 1941-46; lt. col. Res. ret. Mem. ABA, Hawaii Bar Assn. Clubs: Oahu Country, Pacific (Honolulu). Roman Catholic.

TORME, MARGARET ANNE, public relations executive, communications consultant; b. Indpls., Apr. 5, 1943; d. Ira G. and Margaret Joy (Wright) Barker; children: Karen Anne, Leah Vanessa. Student, Coll. San Mateo, 1961—65. Pub. rels. mgr. Hoefer, Dieterich & Brown (now Chiat-Day), San Francisco, 1964-73; v.p., co-founder, creative dir. Lowry & Ptnrs., San Francisco, 1975-83; pres., founder Torme and Lauricella Comm., San Francisco, 1983—. Cons. in comm. Mem. Coun. Pub. Rels. Firms, San Francisco C. of C. (Outstanding Achievement award for Women Entrepreneurs 1987), Jr. League (adv. bd.), Pub. Rels. Orgn. Internat. (v.p., dir.). Office: 847 Sansome St San Francisco CA 94111-2908 E-mail: margaret@torme.com.

TORN, RIP (ELMORE RUAL TORN JR.), actor, director; b. Temple, Tex., Feb. 6, 1931; s. Elmore and Thelma (Spacek) T.; m. Ann Wedgeworth, Jan. 15, 1955 (div.); 1 dau., Danae; m. Geraldine Page; children: Angelica, Anthony, Jonathan. Student, Tex. A & M Coll., 1948-50; BSF.A., U. Tex. Performances include: (stage) Cat on a Hot Tin Roof, 1955, Orpheus Descending, 1958, Chaparral, 1958 (Theatre World award 1959), Sweet Bird of Youth, 1959, on tour, 1960, Daughter of Silence, 1961, Macbeth, 1962, Desire Under the Elms, 1963, Strange Interlude, 1963, Blues for Mr. Charlie, 1964, The Kitchen, 1966, The Country Girl, 1966, The Deer Park, 1967 (Obie award), The Cuban Thing, 1968, The Honest-to-God Schnozzola, 1969, Dream of a Blacklisted Actor, 1969, The Dance of Death, 1970-71, The Marriage Proposal, 1971, Marriage and Money, 1971, Barbary Shore, The Little Foxes, 1974, The Father, 1975, The Glass Menagerie, 1975, Fever for Life, 1975, Creditors, 1977, Night Shift, 1977, Seduced, 1979, Anna Christie, 1992; (motion pictures) Baby Doll, 1956, A Face in the Crowd, 1957, Time Limit, 1957, Pork Chop Hill, 1959, King of Kings, 1961, Hero's Island, 1962, Sweet Bird of Youth, 1962, Critic's Choice, 1963, The Cincinnati Kid, 1965, One Spy Too Many, 1966, Beach Red, 1967, You're a Big Boy Now, 1967, Beyond the Law, 1968, Sol Madrid, 1968, Coming Apart, 1969, Tropic of Cancer, 1970, Slaughter, 1972, Payday, 1973, Crazy Joe, 1974, Birch Interval, 1976, Maidstone, The Man Who Fell to Earth, 1976, Nasty Habits, 1977, Coma, 1978, The Seduction of Joe Tynan, 1979, First Family, 1980, Heartland, 1980, One Trick Pony, 1980; Jinxed, 1982, Airplane II: The Sequel, 1982, The Beastmaster, 1982, A Stranger is Watching, 1982, Cross Creek, 1983, City Heat, 1984, Misunderstood, 1984, Night Shadows, 1984, Song Writer, 1984, Flashpoint, 1984, Summer Rental, 1985, Beer, 1985, Extreme Prejudice, 1987, Defending Your Life, 1991, Beautiful Dreamers, 1992, Hard Promises, 1992, Robocop 3, 1993, Where the Rivers Flow North, 1994, How to Make an American Quilt, 1995, Down Periscope, 1996, Trial and Error, 1997, Men in Black, 1997, Hercules, 1997, The Mouse, 1997, Senseless, 1998, Wonder Boys, 1999, Man of the People, 1999, Welcome to Mooseport, 2004, Dodgeball: A True Underdog Story, 2004; (TV films and miniseries) Two Plays, 1971, The President's Plane Is Missing, 1973, The FBI Versus the Ku Klux Klan, 1975, Song of Myself, 1976, Betrayal, 1976, The Gift of Love, 1978, Blind Ambition, 1979, A Shining Season, 1979, Sophia Loren: Her Own Story, 1980, Rape and Marriage: The Rideout Case, 1980, The Blue and the Gray, 1982, When She Says No, 1984, Dream West, 1986, April Morning, 1988, Sweet Bird of Youth, 1989, By Dawn's Early Light, 1990, Another Pair of Aces: Three of a Kind, 1991, My Son Johnny, 1991, Death Hits the Jackpot, 1991, T-Bone and Weasel, 1992, Dead Ahead: The Exxon Valdez Disaster, 1992, A Mother's Right: The Elizabeth Morgan Story, 1993, The Almost Perfect Bank Robbery, 1996, Balloon Farm, 1997, Seasons of Love, 1998, Passing Glory, 1999; (TV series) The Larry Sanders Show, HBO, 1992— (Emmy nominee for best supporting actor 1993, 94, Cable Ace award for best supporting actor 1994), Ghost Stories, 1997 (narrator); dir. plays: The Beard, 1968 (Obie award), Look Away, 1973. Mem. AFTRA, SAG, Actors Equity Assn., Actors' Studio (bd. dirs., prodn. bd., 1st chmn. founding com.), Dirs. Guild Am. Office: Gersh Agency 130 W 42nd St Ste 1804 New York NY 10036-7901

TORNABENE, RUSSELL C. communications executive; b. Gary, Ind., Sept. 18, 1923; s. Samuel Tornabene and Marion LaVorci Roush; m. Audrey F. Shankey, June 21, 1952; children: Joseph, Leigh, David, Lynn. AA, Gary Jr. Coll., 1941, 46-47; BA, Ind. U., 1949, MA, 1950. Radio, TV newswriter WRC-AM-TV, Washington, 1951-55; network supr. NBC Network News, Washington, 1955-61, network gen. mgr. NYC, 1961-75; v.p. NBC News, NYC, 1975-81; exec. officer Soc. Profl. Journalists, Chgo., 1981-87; Midwest dir. Exec. TV Workshop, Chgo., 1987-96; pres. Russell Communications Cons., 1996—. Bd. dirs. LifeLine Pilots. Contbr. articles on news to mags. and newspapers. Mem. N.Y. Catholic Archdiocese Sch. Bd., N.Y.C., 1972 Recipient Disting. Service award, Sigma Delta Chi, 1949; Ernie Pyle scholar, 1949 Mem. Acad. TV Arts and Scis., Radio TV News Dirs. Assn., Overseas Press Club (former v.p.). Avocation: photography. Office: 626 Sheridan Sq Apt 2 Evanston IL 60202

TORNBLOM, CLAUDIA L. civilian military employee; BSc, Iowa State U.; MPA, U. Minn.; graduate, Nat. Defense U., 1992. From fiscal programs mgmt. officer to dep. asst. sec. U.S. Army Civil Works Program, Washington, dep. asst. sec. mgmt. & budget. Office: Office of Secretary of Army for Civil Works Army Pentagon Washington DC 20310-1500

TORNESE, JUDITH M. financial institution executive; b. Pitts., Aug. 26, 1942; d. Ilario and Rose Mary Tornese; m. Jerry E. Winters. Student, U. Pitts., Golden Gate U. CPCU. Various positions Transam Corp., San Francisco, 1971-81; dir. risk mgmt. TransAm. Corp., San Francisco, 1981-87; dir. X.L. Ins. Co., 1987-92; v.p. risk mgmt. TransAm. Corp., San Francisco, 1987—; dir., chair devel. com. St. Vincent de Paul Soc., 1994—. Dir. San Francisco Suicide Prevention, 1984-90; mem. Earthquake Ins. and Recovery Fin. Com. of Seismic Safety Commn., 1988-91. Named Risk Mgr. of Yr. Bus. Ins. Mag., 1992. Mem. Risk and Ins. Mgmt. Soc. (soc. dir. 1981—, chair nominating com. 1987-92, strategic planning com., 1996—), Mfr.'s Alliance Productivity and Innovation (risk mgmt. coun. 1981-85). Office: Transam Corp 600 Montgomery St San Francisco CA 94111-2702

TORNEY, ANNE, architectural firm executive; MA arch., Univ. of Calif., Berkeley, Calif.; BA arch., Princeton Univ. Lic. David Baker & Assoc., San Francisco, Calif. Ptnr. Solomon ETC, San Francisco, 1994—99, prin., 2000—02, project arch./mgr., 2002—. Achievements include design of projects included: Vermont Village Plaza, the mixed-use complex in So. Ctrl. LA, the 50-unit Alcantara Court in San Francisco, 101 San Fernando and 324 apt. currently under construction in San Jose. Office: Solomon ETC 1328 Mission St 4th Fl San Francisco CA 94103

TORNOW, L. WILLIAM, musician; b. Devils Lake, ND, Feb. 1, 1949; s. E. Edward and Ellen Naomi Tornow. BMus in Pub. Sch. Music, Concordia Coll., Moorhead, Minn., 1971; MA in Music, Trinity U., San Antonio, 1978; DMA in Piano Performance, U. Minn., Mpls., 1983. Artist in residence Cmty. Music Ctr., Fargo, ND, 1978—79; organist Our Saviour's Evang. Luth. Ch., Cannon Falls, Minn., 1984—85, St. George's Episc. Meml. Ch., Bismarck, ND, 1985—86. Composer: Elegy, 1971, Symphony No. 1 for Chamber Orch., 1989, Overture to Spring on Themes of Beethoven for orchestra, 1998, Symphony No 2 for Piano and Orch., 2002. Spl. 4 (E-4) U.S. Army, 1971—74, Germany and Tex. Fellow: Nat. Music Tchrs. Assn.; mem.: Am. Guild of Organists. Avocations: fishing, golf. Home and Studio: 1107 W Capitol Ave Apt 62 Bismarck ND 58501

TORNQVIST, ERIK GUSTAV MARKUS, chemical engineer, research scientist, consultant; b. Lund, Sweden, Jan. 13, 1924; came to U.S., 1951; s. Gustav Ivar and Anne Marie (Lassen) T.; m. Linnéa Dagmar Lindborg, June 28, 1969; children: Gunvor, Karin, Carl-Erik. MSChemE, Royal Inst. Tech., Stockholm, 1948; MS in Biochemistry, U. Wis., 1953, PhD in Biochemistry/Organic Chemistry, 1955. Registered engr., Sweden. 1st rsch. asst. divsn. food chemistry Royal Inst. Tech., 1949—51; rsch. asst. dept. biochemistry U. Wis., Madison, 1951—55; rsch. chemist chem. divsn. Esso Rsch. and Engring. Co., Linden, NJ, 1955—58, rsch. assoc., 1958—66, sr. rsch. assoc., 1966—72, Exxon Chem. Co., Tech., Linden, NJ, 1972—86; internat. cons. Watchung, NJ, 1986—90, 2003—; pres. PolymErik, Inc., Watchung, 1990—2003. Vis. prof. Royal Inst. Tech., 1987; invited prin. speaker Scandinavian Day, Chautauqua (N.Y.) Instn., 1983, 87; invited speaker, chmn. numerous nat. and internat. meetings. Co-editor: Polymer Chemistry of Synthetic Elastomers, 2 vols., 1968, 69; patentee in field; contbr. articles to profl. jours., chpts. to books. Treas. United Swedish Socs., N.Y.C., 1972-86, Swedish Sch. Assn. N.J., 1988-91; bd. govs. Am. Swedish Hist. Mus., Phila., 1974-89; trustee New Sweden Co., Bridgeton, N.J., 1986-89, Kalmar Nyckel Found., Wilmington, Del., 1987-96, hon. trustee, 1996; bd. dirs. Watchung Hills Soccer Assn., Watchung/Warren, N.J., 1989-95. Recipient award 1st Nat. Inventors Day, 1973, gold Bicentennial medal King of Sweden, 1980, John Hanson award for excellence in pub. svc. Am.-Swedish Cultural Found., Mpls., 1981, citation Swedish Coun. of Am., 1983, cert. of appreciation Swedish New Sweden '88 Com., 1989; grad. fellow Roos' Found., Stockholm, 1949, 51, Govt. of Sweden, 1948, State Coun. for Technol. Rsch., Stockholm, 1949, Adelsköld fellow Royal Acad. Sci., 1951, 53, Univ. fellow Sweden-Am. Found., Stockholm, 1951. Fellow: Swedish Colonial Soc. (hon. gov. Ad Vitam 1982, gov. 1977—82, 1986—89); mem.: John Ericsson Soc., Internat. Union Pure and Applied Chemistry (affiliate), Swedish Assn. Grad. Engrs., Am. Soc. Swedish Engrs. (life; sec. 1965—68, pres. 1968—72, John Ericsson Gold medal 1984), Swedish Soc. Chem. Engrs., Am. Chem. Soc., NY Acad. Scis., Schlaraffia, Wis. Alumni Assn. (life), Svensk I Varlden (life), Am.-Scandinavian Soc., KTH Alumni, Swedish-Am. C. of C., Swedish Ski Club (pres. 1972—74), Vasa Order Am. (co-cultural leader NJ Dist. 6, 1997, chmn. Lodge Skandia 2000—), Sigma Xi, Phi Lambda Upsilon. Lutheran. Achievements include invention and development of numerous catalysts for polymerization of olefins and dienes, especially the catalyst for making most of the isotactic polypropylene over a period of more than 20 years (from about 1958) and still in large-scale use, having resulted in production of billions of dollars worth of polymer, also, elucidation of many aspects of the mode of action of these and other catalysts and the preparation of numerous novel polymers. Home and Office: 38 Mareu Dr Watchung NJ 07069-5025 E-mail: erikgmt@yahoo.com.

TORNSTROM, ROBERT ERNEST, lawyer, oil company executive; b. St. Paul, Jan. 17, 1946; s. Clifford H. and Janet (Halle) T.; m. Betty Jane Hermann, Aug. 5, 1978; children: Carter, Gunnar, Katherine. BA, U. Colo., 1968, JD, 1974; diploma grad. sch. mgmt. exec. program, UCLA, 1990. Bar: Colo. 1974, U.S. Dist. Ct. Colo. 1974, Calif. 1975, U.S. Dist. Ct. (cen. dist.) Calif. 1975. Atty. Union Oil Co. of Calif., L.A., 1974-76, counsel internat. div., 1977-78, regional counsel, 1976-77; sr. atty. Occidental Internat. Exploration and Prodn. Co., Bakersfield, Calif., 1978-81, mng. counsel, 1981-85, v.p., assoc. gen. counsel, 1985-88, v.p., regional ops. mgr., 1988-91; pres. Occidental Argentina, Buenos Aires, 1991-93, Occidental of Russia, Moscow, 1993-94; dir. comml. negotiations Occidental Internat., 1994-96; chmn. of bd. Sullivan Petroleum Co., 1997—. Bd. dir. and chmn. bd. Parmaneft Joint Venture, Vanyogannef JV, Moscow; bd. dir. Calif. Land and Cattle Co., King City, 602 Operating Corp.; legal cons. Island Creek Coal Co., Lexington, Ky. Exec. bd. Cmty. Ho., Bakersfield; pres. Snowbird Assn., Mammoth Lakes. Capt. U.S. Army, 1968—71, Vietnam. Decorated Bronze Star. Mem. Am. Soc. Internat. Law, Am. Corp. Counsel Assn., Soc. Mayflower Descendants, Moscow Country Club, Stockdale Country Club. Republican. Episcopalian. Avocations: skiing, tennis, golf, riding, collecting classic automobiles. Home: 310 Mount Lowe Dr Bakersfield CA 93309-2468 Office: 1508 18th St Ste 222 Bakersfield CA 93301 Office Phone: 661-327-5008.

TOROK, MARGARET LOUISE, insurance company executive; b. Detroit, June 22, 1922; d. Perl Edward Ensor and Mary (Seggie) Armstrong; m. Leslie A. Torok, Aug. 14, 1952; 1 child, Margaret Mary Ryan. Lic. Ins. Agy. From ins. agt. to corp. officer Grendel-Wittbold Ins., Southgate, Mich., 1961-72, pres. of corp., 1972—2001. Bd. dirs. Ind. Ins. Agts. of Mich., Lansing, 1984-92, Ind. Ins. Agts. of Wayne County, Dearborn, 1967—, pres. 1978. Bd. dirs. So. Wayne County C. of C., Taylor, 1975—, CEO, chmn. bd. dirs., 1997-98; bd. dirs. City of Southgate Tax. Increment Fin. Authority Dist. and Econ. Devel. Commn., 1987—, YMCA, mem. endowment coun., Wyandotte, 1978—, chmn. Leadership, 1980-88; bd. dirs. Downriver Cmty. Alliance, 1990-94; lay chmn. Cath. Svc. Appeal for Archdiocese of Detroit, 1989; co-chair fundraiser Sacred Heart Ch.; mem. bd. MESC Employers Com., 1991-95; com. mem., bd. dirs. New Workforce Devel. Com., gov. appt., charter mem.; hon. chmn. Art Ambience, 2002; chmn. bd. MESC com., 1991-95; mem. U.S. Power Squadron, 1988—. Recipient Capital award Ind. Ins. Agts. of Mich., 1988, Lifetime Achievement award, Amb. award, 1994, Woman of Yr. AAUW, 1994, Salute to Excellence award Downriver Coun. of Arts, 1993-94, Chmn. of Yr. award MESC Job. Svc. Employers Com., 1991, Robert Stewart award Wyandotte Svc. Club Coun., 1994, Partnership award The Info. Ctr., 1996, 2001, W.O. Hildebrand award Mich. Assn. Ins. Agts., 1997; named to Ins. Hall of Fame, Olivet Coll., 1998. Mem.: Mich. Assn. Ins. Agts., Soroptimist Club of Wyandotte Southgate Taylor (pres. 1984—86, Advancing Status Women award 1988, Soroptimist of Yr. award 1993—94), Wyandotte Yacht Club. Roman Catholic. Office: Grendel Wittbold Agy Inc 12850 Eureka Rd Southgate MI 48195-1344 Office Phone: 734-284-4740.

TOROP, PAUL, psychiatrist; b. N.Y.C., Oct. 18, 1940; s. Ralph and Betty Torop; m. Karen Torop, Dec. 19, 1965; children: Jonathan, Daniel. BA, Yale U., 1962; MD, Harvard U., Boston, 1966. Diplomate Am. Bd. Psychiatry and Neurology. Intern Mt. Zion Hosp., San Francisco, 1966-67; resident McLean Hosp., Belmont, Mass., 1967-70; instr. psychiatry Harvard Med. Sch., 1970; psychiatrist Underclift Mental Health Ctr., Meriden, Conn., 1972-73; asst. clin. prof. psychiatry Yale U., New Haven, 1973—; pvt. practice psychiatry Middletown, Conn., 1973—. Sr. attending psychiatrist Middlesex Hosp., Middletown, Conn., 1973—; psychiatrist Wesleyan U. Student Mental Health Svc., Middletown, Conn., 2000—. Contbr. articles to profl. jours., chpts. to books. Pres., bd. dirs. Gilead Cmty. Svcs., Middletown, 1991-94. Maj. USAF, 1970-72. Fellow Am. Psychiat. Assn.; mem. AMA, Conn. Psychiat. Assn. (New Haven/Middlesex br. pres. 1987-88). Office: 267 William St Middletown CT 06457

TORQUATO, SALVATORE, materials science and chemistry educator; b. Falerna, Calabria, Italy, Feb. 10, 1954; came to U.S., 1955; s. Vincent and Palma (Vaccaro) T.; m. Kim Tracey Hoberock, Nov. 8, 1975; children: Michelle, Lisa. BSME, Syracuse U., 1975; MSME, SUNY, Stony Brook, 1977, PhD in Mech. Engring., 1980. Rsch. engr. Grumman Aerospace Corp., Bethpage, N.Y., 1975-78; rsch. asst. dept. mech. engring. SUNY, Stony Brook, 1978-80; asst. prof. dept. mech. engring. GM Inst., Flint, Mich., 1981-82; from asst. to assoc. prof. depts. mech., aerospace & chem. engring. N.C. State U., Raleigh, 1982-90, prof. depts. mech., aerospace & chem. engring., 1991-92; prof. Civil Engring. Princeton (N.J.) U., 1992-99, prof. chemistry, 2000—. Vis. prof. Courant Inst. Math. Scis., N.Y.C., 1990-91; cons. Eastman Kodak, Rochester, N.Y., 1989—; mem. Inst. Advanced Study, 1998-99. Contbr. articles to profl. jours. Grumman Masters fellow, 1975-77; fellow Guggenheim, 1998; grantee NSF, 1982—, U.S. Dept. Energy, 1986—; recipient Engring. Rsch. Achievement award Alcoa Co., 1987, Disting. Engring. Rsch. award, 1989, Gustus L. Larson Meml. award, 1994. Fellow ASME; mem. Am. Inst. Chem. Engrs., Am. Phys. Soc., Soc. Engring. Sci., Soc. for Indsl. and Applied Math. Avocations: racquetball, reading, music. Office: Princeton U Princeton Materials Inst Dept Chemistry Princeton NJ 08544-0001

TORRAS, JOSEPH HILL, pulp and paper company executive; b. Americus, Ga., Nov. 14, 1924; s. Fernando Joseph and Nell Wilson (Hill) T.; m. Mary Ravenel Robertson, Sept. 20, 1952; children: Mary Martin, Fernanda Maria, Joseph Hill. S.B., Yale U., 1948; MBA, Harvard U., 1950; D in Bus. Adminstrn., Piedmont Coll., 1997. Asst. to fin. v.p. Seatrian Lines, Inc., 1950-51; with St. Regis Paper Co., 1951-60, sales mgr. printing papers div., 1956-60; exec. v.p. Brown Co., Boston, 1960-64; pres., chmn. bd. Premoid Corp., West Springfield, Mass., 1964-87; pres. Precon, Inc., Ludlow, 1967-87, Astro Tissue Co., Battleboro, Vt., 1968-72; chmn. bd. Whitman Products, Ltd., West Warwick, R.I., 1976-89; pres., CEO, Preco Corp., Amherst, Mass., 1976—; chmn., CEO Lincoln Pulp & Paper Co., Lincoln, Maine, 1968—, Eastern Fine Paper, Inc., Brewer, Maine, 1989—, Eastern Pulp & Paper Corp., 1995—. CEO, Shelburne Corp., 1999—; bd. dirs. Bay Banks, Inc., Boston; adv. dir. Liberty Mut. Ins. Mem. Mass. Gov.'s Bus. Adv. Coun., 1985-89, devel. bd. Yale U., 1989—; bd. govs. Mass. Gen. Hosp.; bd. dirs. Mass. Taxpayers Assn., 1976-86; trustee Hist. Deerfield, 1990—, Piedmont Coll., Ga., 1991-99. Lt. (j.g.), aviator USNR, 1943-46. Mem. Tissue Paper Mfrs. Assn. (dir. 1963-64), Am. Pulp and Paper Mill Supts. Assn., Salesman's Assn. Paper Industry, NAM (dir. 1981-85), Colony Club. Home: 264 Bardwells Ferry Rd Shelburne Falls MA 01370-9744

TORRAS, MARIANO, economist, educator; b. N.Y., N.Y., Aug. 26, 1965; s. César Augusto and Sile Elizabeth Torras; m. Athena Demetra Spelios, June 26, 1993; children: Teseo Lukas, Lisandro Dionisio. BS in Fin., NYU, 1988; MA in Internat. Polit. Economy Devel., Fordham U., 1993; MA in Econs., U. Mass., 1995, PhD in Econs., 2000. Defined contbn. tech. Corroon & Black, Stamford, Conn., 1989—90; benefits analyst Williams, Thecher & Rand, N.Y., 1990—91; rsch. asst. Fordham U., Bronx, NY, 1992—93; tchg. asst. econs. U. Mass., Amherst, Mass., 1994—96, lectr. econs., 1997; adj. prof. econs. NYU, N.Y., 1998; asst. prof. econs. Adelphi U., Garden City, NY, 1999—. Cons. Rendazzo & Giffords, Inc., Great Neck, NY, 2001—. Author: Welfare, Inequality, and Resource Depletion, 2003; contbr. articles to profl. jours. Parent rep. Sch. Leadership Team Pub. Sch. 39, Bklyn., 2003—. Grantee Fgn. Lang. Area Studies grant, U. Mass., 2001; scholar, Nat. Hispanic Scholarship Fund, 1991—94. Avocations: chess, cooking, music. Home: Adelphi Univ 1 South Ave Brooklyn NY 11215

TORRE, JOSEPH PAUL (JOE TORRE), professional baseball team manager; b. Bklyn., July 18, 1940; m. Alice Torre; children: Michael, Lauren, Tina, Andrea Rae. Profl. baseball player Milw. Braves, 1960-69, St. Louis Cardinals, 1969-74, N.Y. Mets, 1974-77, player-mgr., 1977-82; mgr. Atlanta Braves, 1982-84; TV broadcaster Calif. Angels, 1984-90; mgr. St. Louis Cardinals, 1990-94, N.Y. Yankees, 1995—. Author: (novels) Chasing the Dream: My Lifelong Journey to the World Series, 1997, Joe Torre's Ground Rules for Winners: 12 Keys to Managing Team Players, Tough Bosses, Setbacks, and Success, 1999. Named Nat. League's Most Valuable Player, 1971, Player of Yr., Sporting News, 1971, Mgr. of Yr., 1982, 1996, 1998; named to All-Star Team, 1963-67, 70-73, coach 1997, 1999-2002, 2004; recipient Gold Glove award, 1965; hit for cycle, 1973; winner World Series N.Y. Yankees, 1996, 1998, 1999, 2000. Office: New York Yankees Yankee Stadium E 161 St & River Ave Bronx NY 10451*

TORRE-AMIONE, GUILLERMO, cardiologist, researcher; s. Guillermo Torre and Gloria Amione de Torre; m. Maria Eugenia Martinez, Jan. 31, 1986; children: Guillermo Torre, Federico Torre. MD, PhD, Monterrey Tecnologico, 1985. Diplomate Am. Bd. Internal Medicine. Asst. prof. medicine Baylor Coll. Medicine, Houston, 1996—; med. dir. heart transplant program The Meth. Hosp., Houston, 1996—. Office: Baylor Coll Medicine Ste 1901 6550 Fannin Houston TX 77030

TORRENCE, GWEN, Olympic athlete; b. Atlanta, June 12, 1965; m. Manley Waller Jr.; 1 child, Manley Waller III. BA, U. Ga., 1987. Runner Olympic Games, Atlanta, 1996. Named 2d pl., NCAA 100, 1985, 7th pl., USA/Mobil 100, 1985, 5th pl., USA/Mobil 200, 1985, champion, NCAA 100, 1987, NCAA 200, 1987, winner, Pan Am. Games 200, 1987, USA/Mobil 200, 1991, winner 100 meters, 200 meters, USA/Mobil Track & Field Championships, 1995, 5th pl., U.S. World Championships 200, winner, Sprints WOrld Univ. Games; recipient 3d pl. in both 100 and 200 trials, Olympic Games, 1988, 2d pl. USA/Mobil 100, 1991, Gold medal 200 Meter, Barcelona Spain, 1992, Gold medal 100 Meters, World Track & Field Championships, Gutenborg, Sweden, 1995, winner 100 Meters, World Athletic Championships, 1995, Gold medal 100 meters, 200 meters, Goodwill Games, 1995, Gold medal 4 X 400 meter relay, Atlanta Olympic Games, 1996, Bronze medal 100 meters, 1996. Achievements include ranked 5th in the world at 200 meters Track & Field News, 1987; ranked number 3 sprinter in the world, 1991; ranked 3d place in the workd in the 100, 1993; ranked 2d place in the work in the 200, 1993; ranked 4th place in the work in the 400, 1993. Address: US Track & Field 1 RCA Dome Ste 140 Indianapolis IN 46225-1023

TORRENCE-THOMPSON, JUANITA LEE, public relations executive; b. Brockton, Mass., Nov. 08; d. James Lee Torrence and Zylpha Odyselle Mapp-Robinson; m. Hugh Warren Thompson, Dec. 19, 1965; 1 child, Derek Rush. BS in Bus. & Comm., Empire State Coll., Old Westbury, N.Y., 1983; MA in Comm., Fordham U., 1989. Newsletter editor UN Internat. Sch., 1976-77; pub. rels., editl. asst. Nat. Assn. Theatre Owners, 1979-80; asst. acct. exec. Richard Weiner, Inc., 1984; newsletter editor SUNY Empire State Coll., 1985-87; editor Dorf & Stanton Comm., Inc., 1987-88; pub. rels. exec. pvt. practice, 1988—. Adj. prof. pub. rels. Coll. New Rochelle, N.Y., 1997. Author: Spanning The Years, Wings Span to Eternity, Celebrating a Tapestry of Life, Spanning the Years Wing Span to Eternity; contbr. articles, poems, short stories, essays to mags., newspapers and newsletters. Bd. dirs. So. Queens Park Assn., Jamaica, N.Y., 1988-91; mem. parent faculty soc. UN Internat. Sch., N.Y.C., 1976-80; pub. rels. cons. UN Coll. Fund, N.Y.C., 1994. Recipient Feature Article award Writers Digest, 1985, Meritorious Svc. award United Negro Coll. Fund, 1994, Editors Choice award Nashville Newsletter, 1994, Robins Nest Mag., 1996, First prize N.Y. Pub. Libr. Contest, 1996, Outstanding Achievement award SUNY, Empire State Coll., Old Westbury, honoree SUNY, Margaret A. Walker Short Story Competition award 1999, 2000. Mem. AAUW, Nat. Assn. Black Journalists, Poetry Soc. Am., Acad. Am. Poets, Native Am. Journalists Assn., Black Ams. in Pub., Poets and Writers, Fresh Meadows Poets. Avocations: travel, theater, films, opera, concerts. Office: PO Box 751205 Forest Hills NY 11375-8805 E-mail: poetrytown@earthlink.net.

TORRENZANO, RICHARD, public affairs executive; BS, N.Y. Inst. Tech., 1972, LittD (hon.), 1990; postgrad., Stanford Univ., 1986. With NY Stock Exch., 1982—91, sr. v.p., mgmt. and exec. com., chief spokesman; sr. v.p., dir. corp. affairs, mgmt. com. SmithKline Beecham, London, 1990—94; chmn., CEO The Torrenzano Group, N.Y.C., 1995—. Coord. Pres. Reagan's Bd. Advisors on Pvt. Sector Initiatives, Washington, 1986—89; pvt. sector adv. com. USIA, Washington, 1983—92; coord. program USSR-USA Conf. on Stock Markets, Moscow, 1990, PRC-USA Conf. on Stock Markets, Beijing, 1986; lectr. in field. Contbr. articles to profl. journals. Trustee, mem. exec. com. N.Y. Inst. Tech., 1985—; trustee John Cabot Univ., Rome, 1998. Decorated knight of Malta, knight comdr. Order of Holy Sepulchre, knight ofcl. Order of Saints Maurice and Lazarus' House of Savoy, knight comdr. Constantinian Order of St. George, knight comdr. Royal Order of Francis I, knight Order of Merit Republic of Italy; recipient Silver Anvil Award, Pub. Rels. Soc. Am., Ellis Island Medal of Honor, 1997. Mem.: Royal Soc. Medicine (London), N.Y. Press Club, Nat. Press Club, Washington. Office: The Torrenzano Group 551 Fifth Ave Ste 1400 New York NY 10176-1400 Office Fax: 212-681-6961. Business E-Mail: richard@torrenzano.com.

TORRES, ARELIS, elementary school educator; arrived in U.S., 1988; d. José Luis Torres and Elizabeth Gómez. B in Psychology, U. P.R., 1988; EdM, Adelphi U., 1991. Tchr. Pub. Sch. 143, Queens, NY, 1988—99, Pub. Sch. 16, Corona, NY, 1999—. Activist, educator SHARE, N.Y.C., 1996—, translator, 1998—; mem. SHARE-Latina SHARE, N.Y.C., 1998—; vol. Learning Leaders, N.Y.C., 2000—01. Named Most Valuable Vol., SHARE, 2000; recipient Citizenship award, N.Y.C. Coun., 2000. Mem.: United Fedn. Tchrs. Avocations: poetry, painting, music, bicycling.

TORRES, ART, former state legislator; b. L.A. children: Joaquin, Danielle. AA, East L.A. C.C.; BA, U. Calif., Santa Cruz; JD, U. Calif. John F. Kennedy teaching fellow Harvard U.; with State Assembly, 1973—81; former senator state legislator State of Calif., L.A., 1982—93; chmn. Calif. Dem. Party, 1996—. Chmn. Senate Com. Ins., Claims and Corps., Assembly Health Com., Senate Toxics and Pub. Safety Mgmt. Com., Select Com. Pacific Rim, Senate Spl. Rask Force on New L.A.; founder Calif. EPA; sr. mem. Senate Edn. Com.; author 1992 Immigrant Workforce Preparation Act; mem. Nat. Conf. State Legislatures Coalition on Immigration, Senate Appropriations Com., Senate Energy and Pub. Utilities Com., Senate Govtl. Orgn. Com., Senate Judiciary Com., Senate Natural Resources Com., Senate Transp. Com., chmn. California Dem. Party. Mem. Coun. Fgn. Rels., N.Y., Nat. Commn. Internat. Migration and Econ. Devel.; participant IVth Nobel Prizewinners Meeting Nova Spes Internat. Found., Vatican, Rome, 1989—. Recipient Legislator of Yr. award Calif. Orgn. Policy and Sheriffs, 1990, Outstanding Legislator of Yr. award Calif. Sch. Bd. Assn., 1990, Outstanding Alumnus award U. Calif. Santa Cruz, Dreamer award Boys and Girls Club Am., 1990, Achievement award Latin Am. Law Enforcement Assn., 1992. Democrat. Office: 911 20th St Sacramento CA 95814-3115 Address: 1401 21st St Ste 100 Sacramento CA 95814

TORRES, ARTHURO G. toy company executive; Chmn., CEO Play by Play Toys & Novelties, Inc., San Antonio, 1992—. Office: Play By Play Toys & Novelties Inc 1153 E Commerce St San Antonio TX 78205-3305

TORRES, DALYS E. music educator, consultant; b. Panama, Republic of Panama, Nov. 20, 1948; arrived in U.S., 1970; d. Victor Manuel Torres and Felicidad Bethancourth. Attended, Johnny Colon Sch. Music, 1985—87; studied with Edwina Tyler, 1985—87; BS in Bus. Adminstrn., Boricua Coll., 1986; postgrad. in Bilingual Edn./TESOL (Tchg. English to Students of Other Languages), L.I. U., 1992—94. Eligibility specialist I HRA/Food Stamp Dept. F-14, N.Y.C., 1985—86; eligibility specialist spl. projects HRA/Food Stamp Dept. F-12, N.Y.C., 1986—87; group supr. HRA/Food Stamp Dept. F-16, N.Y.C., 1988—89; classroom bilingual tchr. Bd. Edn. Pub. Sch. 28A Dist. 6, N.Y.C., 1989—92, Bd. Edn. Pub. Sch. 152 Dist. 6, N.Y.C., 1992—95; percussion and creative movement specialist Bd. Edn. Pub. Sch. 27 Dist. 7, Bronx, NY, 1995—98, Bd. Edn. Pub. Sch. 145 Dist. 3, N.Y.C., 2000—; percussion and creative movement instr., cons. and performer, 1992—. Dir. multicultural music activities Pub. Sch. 28A Dist. 6 N.Y.C., 1989—92; percussion specialist N.Y. Pub. Librs., N.Y.C./Bronx, 1993—2000; percussion and creative movement specialist Mich. Internat. Women Music Festival, Grand Rapids, 1998; percussion specialist for HIV Montekiori Hosp./Staten Island Task Force, N.Y.C./Staten Island, 1999; percussion instr. Vision at Selis Manor, N.Y.C., 2002—; marching percussionist Pan-Am. Marching Band, Bklyn., 1999. Recipient Cultural Music Contbn. award, UFT/Afro Am. Heritage Com., N.Y.C., 1996, Art Edn. awards, Bravo's 2000 Nat. Awards, N.Y.C., 2000. Roman Catholic. Achievements include design of Percussion and Creative Movement Program for Pub. Sch. at P.S. 27 (Dist. 7); Percussion Program for N.Y. Pub. Libr., 1993-2000; Percussion and Creative Movement for Women, Women with HIV, and Women with Other Diseases, 1999-; Percussion Program for the Blind: Percussion with a Passion at Vision Selis Manor, N.Y.C., 2002-. Avocations: reading, films, rollerskating. Home and Office: 646 9th Ave #5FN New York NY 10036 Office Phone: 212-757-3384.

TORRES, DANIEL, literature educator; b. Caguas, P.R., Mar. 9, 1961; arrived in U.S., 1984; s. Vicente Torres and Antonia Rodriguez. BA in Comparative Lit., U. P.R., Rio Piedras, 1984; MA in L.Am. Poetry, SUNY, Stony Brook, 1986; PhD in L.Am. Baroque, U. Cin., 1990. Tchg. asst. SUNY, Stony Brook, 1984—86, U. Cin., 1986—88; instr. Ohio State U., Columbus, 1988—90; prof. Ohio U., Athens, 1990—. Author Moriras si da una primavera novels; contbg. editor: Cin. Roman Langs. Rev., 1990—, Chasqui: L.Am. Rev., 2000—, author poetry and criticism. Activitst, bd. mem. United Campus Ministry, Athens, Ohio, 1993—2003. Named Book of Yr., Pen Club, P.R., 1990. Mem.: MLA, Internat. Inst. Iberoamerican Lit., L.Am. Studies Assn. Avocations: reading, dance, travel, music, driving. Office: Ohio U Modern Langs 283 Gordy Hall Athens OH 45701 Office Phone: 740-592-1084. Business E-Mail: torres@ohio.edu.

TORRES, DARA, Olympic athlete; b. Beverly Hills, Calif., Apr. 15, 1967; Degree in broadcasting, U. Fla. Intern CNN and NBC Sports; commentator TV sports NBC, ESPN, TNT, Fox News, Fox Sports; ret. swimmer TV reporter: Good Morning America, Inside Edition; host Oxygen Sports. Spokesperson Tae Bo workout tapes. Host sci. and tech. show Discovery Channel. Recipient Gold medal (2) 4 x 100-meter freestyle, 4 x 100-meter medley (team), Bronze medal (3) 50 and 100-meter freestyle, 100-meter fly Sydney Olympics, 2000, Gold medal 100-meter freestyle, 4 x 100-meter freestyle, 4 x 100-meter relay (team) Pan Pacific Championships, 1987, Gold medal 4 x 100-meter freestyle relay (team) L.A. Games, 1984, Bronze medal 4 x 100-meter freestyle relay (team), Silver medal 4 x 100-meter medley (team), 1988, Gold medal 4 x 100-meter free relay (team) Barcelona Olympics, 1992; 12-time nat. champion; former world-record holder 50-meter freestyle, Am.-record holder 50-meter freestyle and 100-meter fly, 1991 Summer Nationals Kiphuth award, 1991, Summer Nationals Comeback award Achievements include first american to swim in four Olympics, five time US Open champion, seven time National A team member, two time All Star team. Office: USA Swimming 1 Olympic Plz Colorado Springs CO 80909-5746

TORRES, ERNEST C. federal judge; b. 1941; AB, Dartmouth Coll., 1963; JD, Duke U., 1968. Assoc. Hinckley, Allen, Salisbury & Parsons, 1968-74; ptnr. Saunders & Torres, 1974-80; assoc. justice R.I. Superior Ct., 1980-85; asst. v.p. Aetna Life and Casualty, 1985-86; ptnr. Tillinghast, Collins & Graham, 1986-87; chief judge U.S. Dist. Ct. R.I., Providence, 1988—. Pres. East Greenwich (R.I.) Town Coun., 1972-74; state rep. R.I. Ho. of Reps., 1975-80, dep. minority leader, 1977-80. Recipient Disting. Svc. award Jaycees, 1974; named Man of Yr., Prince Henry Soc. R.I., 1988, Prince Henry Soc. Mass., 1995; Alfred P. Sloan scholar Dartmouth Coll. Mem. ABA, ATLA, FBA, R.I. Bar Assn., Jaycees (Dist. Svc. award 1974), Prince Henry Soc. of R.I., Prince Henry Soc. of Mass. Office: US Dist Ct One Exchange Terrace Providence RI 02903

TORRES, ESTEBAN EDWARD, former congressman, business executive; b. Miami, Ariz., Jan. 27, 1930; s. Esteban Torres and Rena Baron (Gomez) T.; m. Arcy Sanchez, Jan. 22, 1955; children: Carmen D'Arcy, Rena Denise, Camille Bianca, Selina Andre, Esteban Adrian. Student, East Los Angeles Coll., 1960, Calif. State U., Los Angeles, 1963, U. Md., 1965, Am. U., 1966; PhD (hon.), Nat. U., 1987; DHL (hon.), Whittier Coll., 2001. Chief steward United Auto Workers, local 230, 1954-63, dir. polit. com., 1963; organizer, internat. rep. United Auto Workers, local 230, Washington, 1964; asst. dir. Internat. Affairs Dept., 1975-77; dir. Inter-Am. Bureau for Latin Am., Caribbean, 1965-67; exec. dir. E. Los Angeles Community Union (TELACU), 1967-74; U.S. ambassador to UNESCO, Paris, 1977-79; chmn. Geneva Grp., 1977-78; chmn. U.S. del. Gen. Conf., 1978; spl. asst. to pres. U.S., dir. White House Office Hispanic Affairs, 1979-81; mem. 98th-103rd Congresses from 34th Dist. Calif., 1983-98; mem. appropriations com., subcom. fgn. ops., subcom. transp. Campaign coordinator Jerry Brown for Gov., 1974; Hispanic coordinator Los Angeles County campaign Jimmy Carter for Pres., 1976; mem. Sec. of State Adv. Group, 1979-81; v.p. Nat. Congress Community Econ. Devel., 1973-74; pres. Congress Mex.-Am. Unity, 1970-71, Los Angeles Plaza de la Raza Cultural Center, 1974; dir. Nat. Com. on Citizens Broadcasting, 1977; cons. U.S. Congress office of tech. assessment, 1976-77; del to U.S. Congress European Parliament meetings, 1984; ofcl. congl. observer Geneva Arms Control Talks; chmn. Congl. Hispanic Caucus, 1987; speaker Wrights Del. to USSR, 1987; Dem. dep. Whip, 1990; chmn. Nat. Latino Media Coun. Contbr. numerous articles to profl. jours. Co-chmn. Nat. Hispanic Dems., 1988—; chmn. Japan-Hispanic Inst. Inc.; bd. visitors Sch. Architecture UCLA, 1971-73; bd. dirs. Los Angeles County Econ. Devel. Com., 1972-75, Internat. Devel. Conf., 1976-78; chmn. Congrl. Hispanic Caucus, 1985-86; pres. Plaza de la Raza Cultural Ctr., 1972-73; trustee Am. Coll. Paris, 1977-79; mem. Calif. Transp. Commn., Sacramento. Served in AUS, 1949-53, ETO. Recipient Congrl. award Nat. Leadership award 1997. Mem. Americans for Dem. Action (exec. bd. 1975-77), VFW Post 6315, Pico Rivera, Calif., Am. Legion, Smithsonian Inst. (regent 1997—), S.W. Voter Inst., Calif. Transp. Commn. Democrat. Address: 908 E Lucille Ave West Covina CA 91790-5221

TORRES, JACQUELINE, television director, actress; d. Wenceslao Torres and Violeta M. Rolon; m. Mario Ramirez, Jan. 28, 1996. B in Radio, TV, and Film, U. of Md., College Park, 1986; M in Comm., U. of P.R., Rio Piedras, 1993. Prodr., dir., writer Telemundo, San Juan, PR, 1990—95; prodr., writer, dir. Telemundo Network, L.A., 1995—96; dir., prodr., writer Laguna Films, Van Nuys, Calif., 1996—2002; actress various prodns., L.A., 1997—; pres. Jakmar Entertainment, North Hollywood, Calif., 2002—. Actor, dir.: (films) The Price of the American Dream; prodr., reporter: (TV series) La Hora Lunatica; prodr., writer: (TV spls.) Pequenos.Grandes Lecciones I, II & III; (TV series) Marcano.El Show (Paoli award, 1991); actor, dir. Crossing Frontiers, writer, prodr. (films) Atrapamos A Bin Laden; actor: (TV series) ER, The District; (films) Miss Castaway, La Paloma y El Gavilan, Clave Secreta, El Guero Estrada, Cuatro Meses de Libertad, La Verdadera Historia De Sergio; prodr.: (film) Carga Blanca; dir.: (films) East LA King. Mem.: SAG (life). Office: Jakmar Entertainment PO Box 8776 Universal City CA 91618 Home: PO Box 2771 Toluca Lake CA 91610 E-mail: jackie@jackietorres.com.

TORRES, JACQUES, food service executive; Master Pastry Chef, Culinary Sch., Cannes, France, 1983. Chef Hotel Negresco; opened Ritz-Carlton Rancho Mirage; exec. pastry chef Le Cirque 2000, N.Y.C. Dean pastry studies French Culinary Inst. N.Y.; cons. Cointreau and Valrhona chocolate; participant Pierre Franey's Birthday Celebrations, Merci Julia for Julia Child; spent culinary weeks, Tokyo, Sydney, Australia, Melbourne, Australia, Spain. Appeared (TV series) Julia Child's Master Chef. Active God's Love We Deliver, ARC, Meals on Wheels. Named Pastry Chef of Yr., James Beard Found., Am. Pastry Chef of Yr., Chef's of Am.; named one of 10 Best Pastry Chefs, Chocolatier Mag.; recipient award, French Championship of Desserts, 1986, Gold medal, Japanese Pastry Chef Assn. Office: Le Cirque 2000 455 Madison Ave New York NY 10022

TORRES, JUDITH, lab administrator; b. NYC; d. Benigno Rodriguez and Luz Maria Ruiz; m. William Torres Rodriguez, Dec. 29, 1991; 1 chld, William Elijah. BS in Indsl. Chemistry, U. P.R., 1985; postgrad. student, McCrone Rsch. Inst., Chgo., 1987-92. Analytic chemist Bristol Meyers Squibb, Humacao, P.R., 1984-88, supr. quality control, 1988-91; pharm. chemist Eli Lilly and Co., Indpls., 1991-95, head dept. quality control labs., 1998—. Office: Eli Lilly and Co Lilly Corp Ctr Drop Code 5532 Indianapolis IN 46256 Fax: (317)276-5727. E-mail: torres_judith@lilly.com.

TORRES, RALPH CHON, minister; b. San José, Calif., Oct. 18, 1948; s. Chon Poncé and Dora (Grijalva) T.; m. Pamela Ellen Hansen, Mar. 6, 1971; children: Chon, Brita, Samuel, Sarah. BTh, L.I.F.E. Bible Coll., L.A., 1970. Ordained to ministry Internat. Ch. of the Foursquare Gospel, 1981. Missionary asst. Internat. Ch. of Foursquare Gospel, Mexicali, Mex., 1970, youth pastor Redondo Beach, Calif., 1971-72, Pueblo, Colo., 1972-74; sr. pastor Internat. Ch. of Foursquare Gospel., Pasadena, Calif., 1984—; youth pastor Ch. on the Way, Van Nuys, Calif., 1975-84. Asst., dir. children's camps, Jr. and Sr. High camps for So. Calif. Dist. Foursquare Chs., 1978—; tchr. L.I.F.E. Bible Coll., L.A., 1979-86; bd. dirs. Holy Ghost Repair Svc., Hollywood, Calif., Centrum of Hollywood, Christians in Govt., L.A., Camp Cedar Crest, Running Springs, Calif.; bd. dirs., speaker Mainstream Inc., Tacoma, 1978-83. Composer: Kids of the Kingdom, 1976. Mem. Prop. 98 Sch. Report Card Com., Pasadena, 1989-90; adv. com. Marshall Fundamental Sch., Pasadena, 1989-90, Pasadena Unified Sch. Dist., 1990—. Recipient commendation for svc. Mayor of Pasadena, 1990. Office: Pasadena Foursquare Ch 174 Harkness Ave Pasadena CA 91106-2007

TORRES, RUDY ARNOLD, artist; b. LA, Dec. 21, 1957; s. Benjamin Tiburcio and Josephine Irene Torres. Student, East Los Angeles Coll., 1981—83, Pacific Inst. Comml. Art, 1984—85, Otis Parsons Sch. Design, 1985—86. Artist, co-owner Echo Park Gallery, L.A., 1989—91. One-man shows include Minus Zero Gallery, Torrance, Calif., 1990, Mary Norton Clapp Libr., Occidental Coll., L.A., 2000, exhibitions include Alpha Contemporary Exhibits, 1983—86, Mac Houston Art Gallery, Pasadena, Calif., 1986, Brand Libr. Art Gallery, Glendale, Calif., 1987, Design Ctr. L.A., 1987, L.A. Photography Ctr., 1987, 1989, L.A. Mcpl. Gallery, 1989, L.A. Art Assn., 1989, Echo Park Gallery, L.A., 1990—91, Boathouse Gallery, 1992, Weingart Gallery, 1992, Arthur Coons Gallery, 1992, Galeria Las Americas, 1992—94, 1996, Art & Barbee Art Gallery, Hollywood, Calif., 1993, Hilles Libr. at Harvard U., 1995, Palette Des Artists, Pasadena, 1996, Galeria Otravez, East Los Angeles, Calif., 1996, 2001, Olvera St. Gallery, L.A., 1996, Long Beach (Calif.) Gallery, 1998, Calif. State U. Fullerton grand Ctrl. Art Ctr., Santa Ana, 2001, Guggenheim Gallery, Chapman U., Orange, Calif., 2001, Huntington Beach (Calif.) Gallery, 2002, City of Brea (Calif.) Gallery, 2002, Showcase North Gallery, Santa Ana, 2001—02. Recipient cert. of appreciation for mural in Herman Dist., 14th Dist. City of L.A., 1986. Avocations: body building, swimming, jogging, camping, fishing. Home: 700 W La Veta Ave # R5 Orange CA 92868

TORRES, SHELBY CREDLE, English educator; d. Leroy Credle. AA in Liberal Arts, NYC Tech. Inst., 1971; BA in English, Herbert H. Lehman Coll., 1972; MEd, Rutgers U., 1982. Cert. tchr. NY, profl. tchg. stds. cert. NY. Tchr. English Rahway (NJ) Bd. Edn., 1974—2001; comms. instr. Upward Bound Rutgers U., New Brunswick, NJ, 1978—92; tchr. English N.Y.C. Bd. Edn., 2000. Asst. chairperson Middlestates Assn. Schs. and Colls., 1999, mem. vis. com., 1994—2000. Organizer toy and clothing dr. Rahway HS, 1991; mem. vestry St. Luke's Episc. Ch., Metuchen, NJ. Recipient cert. of appreciation, Elijah's Promise Helping the Homeless. Democrat. Avocations: collecting diverse music, dance, tennis, reading, decorating.

TORRESE, DANTE MICHAEL, prosthodontist, educator; b. Yonkers, N.Y., Feb. 12, 1949; s. Dante Angelo and Matilda (Dal Lago) T.; m. Camille Patricia DiPaola, Aug. 7, 1982. BS in Biology, Manhattan Coll., 1971; DDS, Columbia U., 1975; prosthodontic cert., NYU, 1983. Resident in dentistry Presbyn. Hosp., N.Y.C., 1975-76; clin. instr. dentistry Columbia U., N.Y.C., 1976-78, asst. clin. prof. dentistry, 1978—; pvt. practice dentistry Yonkers, N.Y., 1976—. Attending dentist Presbyn. Hosp., N.Y.C., 1976-86; lectr. in field. Recipient Am. Acad. Oral Pathology Grad. award 1975, Densply Corp. award for removable prosthodontics, 1975, Psi Omega Scholastic Achievement award, 1975. Fellow Am. Coll. of Dentists, Royal Soc. Health; mem. NRA (life), Yonkers Dental Soc., 9th Dist. State Dental Soc., Invested Baker St. Irregular, Sherlock Holmes Wireless Soc., Single Action Shooting Soc. (life), Yonkers Amateur Radio Club, Westchester Astronomy Club, Exch. Club (sec. 1979—), Three Garridebs of Westchester, Priory Scholars of N.Y.C. Club, Montague Street Lodgers of Bklyn. Club, Omicron Kappa Upsilon. Office: 984 N Broadway Ste 503 Yonkers NY 10701-1308

TORRES-GIL, FERNANDO M. federal official, academic administrator; b. Salinas, Calif., June 24, 1948; BA in Polit. Sci., San Jose State U., 1970; MSW, Brandeis U., 1972, PhD, 1976. Spl. asst. to sec. Dept. Health, Edn. and Welfare, Washington, 1978-79, Dept. Health and Human Svcs., Washington, 1979-80, asst. sec. for aging, 1993—; prof. gerontology and pub. adminstrn. U. So. Calif., 1981-91, assoc. dir. Nat. Resource Ctr. on Minority Aging Populations, 1988-92, prof. social welfare, 1991-93; assoc. dean Sch. Pub. Policy and Soc. Rsch. UCLA. Staff dir. Select Com. on Aging, U.S. Ho. of Reps., Washington, 1985-87. Contbr. articles to profl. jours. White House fellow, 1978-79. Mem. Am. Soc. Aging (pres. 1989-92). Office: UCLA Sch Pub Plicy & Social Rsch Box 951656 3250 Public Policy Blvd Los Angeles CA 90095-1656

TORRES-PADILLA, JOSE LUIS, English educator; b. Cayey, P.R., Dec. 23, 1954; PhD. English, U. of Southern Calif., 1994; M.A. English, U. of Southern. Calif., 1989; M.F.A Creative Writing, Columbia U., 1981; B.A. Hispanic Studies & Psychology, Vassar Coll., 1976. Editor Latin N.Y. Mag., 1977—78; assoc. prof. English UPR- Cayey, Cayey, PR, 1981—2000, SUNY,

Plattsburgh, NY, 2000—. Writer (short stories, poems and journals). Recipient Hon. Mention, Ford Found. Dissertation Fellowships for Minorities, 1992; grantee Recovering Hispanic and Lit. Heritage: Scholars for the Dream award, Conf. on Coll. Composition and Comm. Mem.: Soc. for the Study of Multi Ethnic Lit. of the U.S., Modern Lang. Assoc. Avocations: music, sports. Mailing: 8 Olivetti Pl Plattsburgh NY 12901

TORREY, BARBARA BOYLE, research council administrator; b. Pensacola, Fla., Nov. 27, 1941; d. Peter F. and Elsie (Hansen) Boyle; m. E. Fuller Torrey, Mar. 23, 1968; children: Michael, Martha. BA, Stanford U., 1963, MS, 1970. Vol. Peace Corps, Tanzania, 1963-65; fiscal economist Office Mgmt. and Budget, Washington, 1970-80; dept. asst. sec. HHS, Washington, 1980-81; dir. Ctr. for Internat. Rsch. Census Bur., Washington, 1984-92; pres. Population Reference Bur., Washington, 1992-93; exec. dir. Commn. on Behavioral and Social Scis. and Edn. NRC, NAS, Washington, 1993—. Bd. dirs. Luxembourg Income Study. Co-editor: The Vulnerable, 1987, Population and Land Use, 1992; contbr. articles to profl. jours. Fellow AAAS; mem. Population Assn. Am. (bd. dirs. 1993—). Office: Population Ref Bur 1875 Connecticut Ave NW Ste 520 Washington DC 20009-5728

TORREY, CLAUDIA OLIVIA, lawyer; b. Nashville, June 10, 1958; d. Claude Adolphus and Rubye Mayette (Prigmore) T. BA in Econ., Syracuse U., 1980; JD, N.Y. Law Sch., 1985. Bar: NY 1988. Legal intern Costello, Cooney & Fearon, Syracuse, NY, 1979; legal clk. First Am. Corp., Nashville, 1981; legal asst. James I. Meyerson, N.Y.C., 1982-85; jud. law clk. N.Y. State Supreme Ct., N.Y.C., 1985; interim project supr., legal asst. CUNY Ctrl. Office, 1985-86; legal analyst Rosenman & Colin Law Firm, N.Y.C., 1986-87; asst. counsel N.Y. State Legis., Albany, 1988-90; atty., cons. pvt. practice, Nashville, Cookeville, Tenn., 1991—. Bd. dirs. Children's Corner Day Care Ctr., Albany, 1989-90. Author column Health Law Jour. of N.Y. State Bar Assn., 1996—; co-author Legal Manual for New York Physicians, 2003. Ch. rep. FOCUS exec. coun. Westminster Presbyn. Ch., Albany, 1990; mem. PDS/USN Alumni Bd., Nashville, 2001—; interim chair Synod of Living Waters COR Com., Presbyn. Ch. (U.S.A.), 2002. Mem. ABA (young lawyers divsn. liaison to ABA forum on health law 1994-96), Internat. Platform Assn., N.Y. State Bar Assn. (chmn., membership sub-com. on non-resident mems. 2004—, chmn. health law sect. study group on health info., privacy and confidentiality 1998-99, mem.-at-large health law section exec. com., 2002-04), Alpha Kappa Alpha (treas., pres., corr. sec. Iota Upsilon Chpt. Syracuse U.) Avocations: singing, reading, harp, travel, art. Home and Office: PO Box 150234 Nashville TN 37215-0234 Office Phone: 931-528-4280. E-mail: jewel3@prodigy.net.

TORREY, DAVID LEONARD, investment banker; b. Ottawa, Ont., Can., Oct. 6, 1931; s. Arthur Starratt and Josephine Edith (Leonard) T.; divorced; children: Heather Torrey Murphy, John Winthrop, Diana Bruce, Arthur Bruce, David Molson. BA in Econs., St. Lawrence U., 1953; diploma, Ivey Sch. Bus., U. Western Ont., 1954. With Pitfield Mackay Ross Ltd., Toronto, Ont., Can., 1954-84, v.p., 1963-73, sr. v.p., 1973-80, vice chmn., 1980-82, pres., 1982-84, also bd. dirs.; vice chmn. Dominion Securities, Inc., 1984-88, RBC Dominion Securities, Inc., 1988-91. Chmn. Montreal Stock Exch., 1971-73, Phillips Cables Ltd., 1991-96; bd. dirs. Wajax Ltd., 1963-2002, Can. Stebbins Engring. and Mfg. Co. Ltd.; mem. coun. Montreal Bd. Trade, 1971-72. Chmn. Montreal Downtown YMCA, 1972-74; trustee St. Lawrence U., 1980-92; bd. dirs. Montreal Gen. Hosp. Found. Mem. Investment Bankers Assn. (gov. 1971-72), Securities Industries Assn. (bd. govs. 1972-73), Multiple Sclerosis Can. (past pres., bd. dirs.), Royal Montreal Golf Club, Mt. Royal (Montreal) Club, Toronto Club, Saifish Club Fla. (Palm Beach), Beta Theta Pi. Home: 389 Carlyle Ave Montreal QC Canada H3R 1T3 Office: PO Box 6001 1 Pl Ville Marie 2E Montreal QC Canada H3C 3A9 Office Phone: 514-399-9932.

TORREY, JAMES D. mayor, communications executive, consultant; b. Drayton, N.D., July 16, 1940; s. Howard J. Torrey and Gertrude (Carpenter) Steenson; m. Katherine Joann Kowal, Sept. 2, 1958; children: Tamara, Timonthy (dec.), Teresa, Todd. Student, U. Oreg., 1959-61. Mgr. Waldport (Oreg.) Food Market, 1959-67; dist. mgr. Obie Outdoor Advt., Aberdeen, Wash., 1967-68; dir. sales Obie Media Corp., Eugene, Oreg., 1968-71, exec. v.p., 1971-78, pres., CEO, 1980-88, Total Comm., Inc., Eugene, Oreg., 1989-91; N.W. area market mgr. 3M Nat. Advt., Eugene, Oreg., 1978-80; dir. mktg. State Accident Ins. Fund, Salem, Oreg., 1988-89. Mem. exec. com. affiliate bd. Mut. Broadcasting, 1981-87. Pres. Waldport City Coun., 1962-67; coach Eugene Kidsports, 1968-92, Am. Softball Assn. Girls Softball Team, 1988; mem. adv. com. 4 J Sch. Dist., 1988-90; bd. dirs. Lane County United Way, 1983-86, dir., 1992, Lane County Goodwill Industries, 1989-90; mem. Eugene City Budget Com., 1992-94, Eugene City Coun., 1994-97; mayor City of Eugene, Oreg., 1997—. Named JCI senator, Oreg. State Jaycees, 1966, Citizen of Yr., City of Waldport, 1967, Outstanding Vol., City of Eugene, 1991, First Citizen, Eugene, Oreg., 2001—. Mem. Oreg. Outdoor Advt. Assn. (pres. 1971-80), Oreg. Assn. Broadcasters (dir. 1984-87), Eugene C. of C. (bd. dirs., pres. 1991-92), Eugene Rotary (dir., pres. 1984, Paul Harris fellow 1985). Republican. Roman Catholic. Avocation: youth coaching. Office: Mayor's Office 777 Pearl St Ste 105 Eugene OR 97401-2720

TORREY, RICHARD FRANK, utility executive; b. Saratoga Springs, N.Y., Dec. 31, 1926; s. Reginald Frank and Marian (Currey) T.; m. Betty Louise Stetson, July 2, 1949; children: Patricia Ann Torrey, Carol Louise Torrey Kress, Barbara Jean Torrey Friedman. BA cum laude, Syracuse U., 1951. News reporter, Syracuse (N.Y.) Post Standard, 1947-51; pub. rels. account exec. Syracuse, 1951-53; home sec. 35th Congl. Dist., Syracuse, 1952-53; exec. sec. to mayor Syracuse, 1954-58; dir. area devel. Niagara Mohawk Power Corp., Syracuse, 1958-66, comml. v.p. Buffalo, 1966-68, adminstrv. v.p., 1968-72, v.p., gen. mgr., 1972-76, sr. v.p., 1976-88, ret., 1988; pres. Can. Niagara Power Co. Ltd., Niagara Falls, Ont., Can., 1968-88, dir., 1968-89. Pres., dir. Caragh Investments Ltd., 1981-85; pres. Opinac Investments Ltd., Toronto, 1982-88, bd. dirs., 1982-89; pres. Opinac Energy Ltd., Calgary, Alta., 1983-88, bd. dirs., 1983-89. Pres. Syracuse USO, 1959-61, mem. nat. coun., 1959-62, 68-74; co-chmn. Ctrl. N.Y. Interim Coun. Regional Planning, 1965-66; gen. chmn. Dunbar-Huntington Bldg. Fund, Syracuse, 1963; state campaign chmn. N.Y. Job Devel. Authority, 1961; gen. chmn. United Way of Buffalo and Erie County, 1971; mem. Syracuse U. Corp. Adv. Coun., 1972-76; trustee Elmcrest Children's Ctr., 1962-63, Camp Good Will, Syracuse, 1964-66, Syracuse Area Coun. Chs., 1959-64; bd. dirs. United Way Buffalo and Erie County, 1967-76, Greater Buffalo Devel. Found., Kenmore Mercy Hosp., 1970-76, Crouse Irving Meml. Hosp. Found., 1978-87, Nat. Kidney Found., 1987-89, Bon Secours-Venice (Fla.) Hosp. Found., 1992-98, vice chmn. 1995-96, chmn. 1996-98; bd. dirs. Plantation Cmty. Found., Venice, 1989, pres., 1990-93, pres. emeritus, 1993—; mem. bd. adv. Sisters of St. Joseph, 1967-76; elder Trinity Presbyn. Ch., Venice, 1992-94; assoc. mem. Dewitt Cmty. Ch. Served with Air Corps U.S. Army, 1944-47. Recipient Syracuse Young Man of Yr. award, 1962; Outstanding Citizen award Buffalo Evening News, 1973. Mem. Empire State (v.p., bd. dirs. 1963-80), Buffalo Area (v.p. 1968-72, bd. dirs. 1968-76, pres. 1972-73, chmn. bd. 1973-74, Man of Yr. 1974) C. of C., Associated Industries of N.Y. (bd. dirs. 1978-80), Bus. Coun. N.Y. (bd. dirs. 1980-82), Mfrs. Assn. Cen. N.Y. (bd. dirs. 1977-88), Augusta Villa Assn. (bd. dirs. 1989-92), Buffalo Club (past 2d v.p., dir.), Syracuse Century Club (gov. 1980-83), Onondaga Golf Club, Plantation Golf and Country Club, Automobile Club Western N.Y.(bd. dirs. 1971-73, pres. 1973), N.Y.S. Automobile Assn. (dir. 1975-76), Venice Yacht Club. Home and Office: 7333 Scotland Way #2303 Sarasota FL 34238

TORREY, WILLIAM ARTHUR, professional hockey team executive; b. Montreal, Que., Can., June 23, 1934; BS, St. Lawrence U., 1957. From dir. pub. rels. to bus. mgr. Pitts. Hornets Am. Hockey League team, 1960-68; exec. v.p. Calif. Golden Seals, 1967-72; gen. mgr. N.Y. Islanders, 1972-93, pres., 1980-89, chmn. bd., 1989-92, cons., 1993; pres. Fla. Panthers, Sunrise, 1993—. N.Y. Islanders NHL Stanley Cup Champions, 1980-83. Office: Florida Panthers Hockey Club Office Depot Ctr 1 Panther Pkwy Sunrise FL 33323-5315

TORRIANI-GORINI, ANNAMARIA, microbiologist, educator; b. Milan, Dec. 19, 1918; came to U.S., 1955, naturalized, 1962; d. Carlo and Ada (Forti) Torriani; m. Luigi Gorini (dec. Aug. 1976); 1 child, Daniel. PhD, U. Milan, Italy, 1942. Research assoc. Istituto Ronzoni Chimica-Biochimica, Milan, 1942-48; charge de recherche Institut Pasteur, Paris, 1948-56; research assoc. NYU, 1956-58, Harvard U., Cambridge, Mass., 1958-60, MIT, Cambridge, 1960-71, assoc. prof. microbiology, 1971-76, prof., 1976—; prof. emerita, 1989. Recipient NIH Career award, 1962-72; Fulbright fellow, 1956-58. Mem. Am. Soc. Microbiology, Soc. Française de Microbiologie (hon.). Home: 115 Longwood Ave Brookline MA 02446-6625 Office: MIT Dept of Biology 68-371 Cambridge MA 02139 E-mail: Pho@mit.edu.

TORRICELLI, ROBERT G. former senator; b. Franklin Lakes, N.J., Aug. 26, 1951; BA, Rutgers U., 1974, JD, 1977; MPA, Harvard U., 1980. Bar: N.J. 1978. Dep. legis. counsel Office Gov. N.J., 1975-77; counsel to V.P. Mondale, Washington, 1978-81; pvt. practice Washington, 1981-82; mem. 98th-104th Congresses from 9th Dist. N.J., Washington, 1983-96, sci., space and tech. com., fgn. affairs com., select com. on intelligence, chmn. Western Hemisphere subcom., 1992-94; U.S. senator from N.J., 1996—2002. Mem. rules, govt. affairs, judiciary and fgn. rels. coms. Bd. govs. Rutgers U., 1977-83. Mem. ABA, N.J. Bar Assn. Democrat. Address: PO Box 229 Rosemont NJ 08556-0229

TORRIERI, DON JOSEPH, electronics engineer, mathematician, researcher; b. Balt., Nov. 19, 1942; s. Peter and Mary Torrieri; m. Nancy Karen Weir, Jan. 27, 1971; children: Karen Marisa, Peter. BS, MIT, 1964; MS, Poly. U., Farmingdale, N.Y., 1966, U. Md., 1969, PhD, 1971. Electronics engr. Naval Rsch. Lab., Washington, 1971-77; mathematician Dept. of the Army, Adelphi, Md., 1977—. Faculty George Washington U., Washington, 1988-92, Johns Hopkins U., Balt., 1993—. Author: Principles of Military Communication Systems, 1981, Principles of Secure Communication Systems,1985, 2d edit., 1992, Principles of Spread-Spectrum Communication Systems, 2004; contbr. chpt. to book Principles of Spread-Spectrum Communication Systems, 2004, articles to profl. jours. Coach many soccer, basketball, baseball & softball youth teams, 1990-2000. Mem. IEEE (sr., Best Paper award Mil. Comms. Conf. 1991), Sigma Xi. Achievements include authorship of a textbook that is the standard in the field. Home: 2204 Hidden Valley Ln Silver Spring MD 20904-5240 Office: Army Rsch Lab 2800 Powder Mill Rd Adelphi MD 20783-1138 E-mail: dtorr@arl.army.mil.

TORRUELLA, JUAN R. federal judge; b. San Juan, P.R., June 7, 1933; BS in Bus. and Fin., U. Pa., 1954; LLB, Boston U., 1957; LLM, U. Va., 1984; MPA, U. P.R., 1984; MSt, Oxford U., 2003; LLD (hon.), St. John's U., 1995, Roger Williams U., 1995. Judge U.S. Dist. Ct. P.R., San Juan, 1974—82, chief judge, 1982—84; judge U.S. Ct. Appeals (1st cir.), San Juan, 1984—, chief judge, 1994—2001. Former mem. jud. conf. com. Adminstrn. Fed. Magistrate Sys.; former mem. jud. conf. exec. com. Adminstrn. Fed. Magistrate Sys.; former mem. jud. conf. com. Internat. Jud. Reform. Mem.: FBA, ABA, P.R. Bar Assn., D.C. Bar Assn., Assn. Labor Rels. Practitioners P.R. and V.I. Office: John J Moakley US Courthouse 1 Courthouse Ste 2500 Boston MA 02210

TORTI, FRANK MICHAEL, physician, healthcare administrator; BA, MA, Johns Hopkins U., 1969; MPH, Harvard U., 1973, MD, 1974. Diplomate in internal medicine and med. oncology Am. Bd. Internal Medicine. Asst. prof. medicine Stanford (Calif.) U., 1979-84, clin. assoc. prof. medicine, 1984-86, assoc. prof. medicine, 1986-93; prof. medicine Wake Forest U. Sch. Medicine, Winston-Salem, N.C., 1993—, dir. Comprehensive Cancer Ctr., 1993—, chmn. dept. cancer biology, 1993—. Chair N.C. Gov.'s Commn. on Cancer Coordination and Control, 1993—; v.p., founding mem. Nat. Bladder and Prostate Cancer Found., 1990—; mem. study sect. Am. Inst. for Cancer Rsch., Bethesda, Md., 1989—. Mem. Am. Assn. for Cancer Rsch., Am. Soc. Clin. Oncology, Am. Soc. Cell Biology, Internat. Soc. Interferon Rsch., Am. Fedn. for Clin. Rsch., Soc. for Biol. Therapy. Office: Wake Forest U Sch Medicine Medical Center Blvd Winston Salem NC 27157-1082 E-mail: ftorti@wfubmc.edu.

TORTO, CHRISTOPHER, communications executive; BS in Fin., U. Maine; MBA, Harvard U. Gen. mgr. GTECH do Brasil (subs. GTECH Corp.), 1992-96; pres., CEO Horizon Cablevision do Brasil, 1996-98; CEO Voyager-.net, 1998—, pres., vice chmn. of bd., 1999—. Office: Voyager net Inc 4660 S Hegadom Rd Ste 320 East Lansing MI 48823

TORTOLANI, ANTHONY JOHN, surgeon, educator; b. Eastchester, N.Y., Oct. 15, 1943; s. Salvatore Paul and Yolanda (Vecciarelli) Tortolani; m. Beth Callahan, Dec. 15, 1967 (dec. Oct. 1993); children: Julia Sue, Paul Justin; m. Katherine Gormley, Sept. 25, 1999. BS, Fordham U., 1965; MD, George Washington Sch. Medicine, 1969. Diplomate Am. Bd. Surgery, Am. Bd. Thoracic Surgery. Chief divsn. cardiovascular & thoracic surgery North Shore U. Hosp., Manhasset, N.Y., 1978-90, chmn. dept. surgery, 1988-96, chmn. med. bd., 1994-96, chmn. dept. surgery Glen Cove, N.Y., 1990-96; John D. Mountain chair surgery North Shore U. Hosp.- Cornell U. Med. Coll., Manhasset, 1989-96, program dir. surg. residency program, 1992-96; prof. surgery Cornell U. Med. Coll., N.Y.C., 1993-97, prof. cardiothoracic surgery, 1997-99; mem. staff N.Y. Hosp., N.Y.C., 1997-99; dir., prof. cardiothoracic surgery Jack D. Weiler Hosp./Montefiore Med. Ctr. Albert Einstein Coll. of Medicine, N.Y.C., 1999-2001; prof. clin. cardiothoracic surgery Weill Med. Coll. Cornell U., 2001—. Vice chmn. N.Y. Presbyn. Cornell Cardiothoracic Surgery Network. Active Columbus Citizens Found., N.Y.C. Maj. USAF, 1974-76. Roman Catholic. Avocation: breeding arabian horses. Office: NY Presbyn Hosp 525 E 68th St Rm M-404 New York NY 10021

TORTORA, LESLIE C. finance company executive; With Goldman Sachs & Co., N.Y.C., 1984—, ptnr., 1992—, mng. dir., 1996—, mem. mgmt. com., 1999—. Office: Goldman Sachs & Co 85 Broad St New York NY 10004-2456

TORTORELLA, JOHN, professional athletics coach; b. Boston, Mass., June 24, 1958; Coach Va. Lancers Atlantic Coast Hockey League, 1986—88; asst. coach Buffalo Sabres, 1989—95; coach Rochester Am. Am. Hockey League, 1995—97; asst. coach Phoenix Coyotes, 1997—99, N.Y. Rangers, 1999—2001; coach Tampa Bay Lightning, 2001—. Named Coach of Yr., Atlantic Coast Hockey League, 1986—87. Achievements include coached Stanley Cup Championship Team, Tampa Bay Lightning, 2004. Office: Tampa Bay Lightning Hockey Club Ice Palace Arena 401 Channelside Dr Tampa FL 33602

TORTORELLO, NICHOLAS JOHN, public opinion and market research company executive; b. Maspeth, NY, Dec. 1, 1948; s. John Anthony and Verla Jean (Odel) T.; m. Joan Elizabeth King, Jan. 13, 1973; children: Kerry Ann, Jennifer Joan. BA in Polit. Sci. with highest honors, Williams Coll., l97l; M Religious Studies, St. Joseph's Sem., Yonkers, N.Y., l988. V.p. Louis Harris & Assocs., N.Y.C., 1971-73, sr. v.p., 1973-79; exec. v.p. DMT Inc., N.Y.C., 1979-83; pres. Tortorello Corp., Pearl River, N.Y., 1983-85; pres. Tortorello group Market Facts Inc.-N.Y., N.Y.C., 1985-86; v.p. Total Rsch. Corp., Princeton, N.J., 1986-88; chmn. Rsch. and Forecasts Inc., N.Y.C., 1989-93; sr. v.p. Roper Starch Worldwide Inc., N.Y.C., 1993-98; pres. Guideline Consulting, N.Y.C., 1998—2002; v.p., gen. mgr. Lieberman Rsch. Worldwide Inc., 2003—. Editor, author Tortorello Trendline, 1983-85, Rsch. and Forecasts Trendline, 1989-91. Trustee Riverdale (N.Y.) Country Sch., 1982-90, v.p., 1986-89; trustee Marymount Manhattan Coll., N.Y.C., 1986-88; lectr., tchr. religion St. Anthony's Ch., Nanuet, N.Y., 1984-86; mem. CARA Bd. Georgetown U., Washington, 1992-98, rsch. adv. coun., 2000—; mem. Hosp. Chaplaincy Bd., 1991-97; v.p. Class of '71, Williams Coll., 2001. Recipient Am. Legion award for leadership, scholarship, honor and svc., 1967, Disting. Alumnus of Yr. award Riverdale Country Sch., 1984. Mem. Am. Dirs. Inst. (trustee 1984-87), Coun. Am. Survey Rsch. Orgn. (chmn. bd. dirs. 2001, chmn. publs. com. 1991-94, chmn. pub. rels. com. 1995-97, chmn. mktg. and comms. com. 1997-99, bd. dirs., chmn. 1999 ann. conf., chmn. bd. dirs. 1999, chmn. bd. trustees 2001, chmn. nominating com. 2002), Am. Assn. Pub. Opinion Rsch.(Counselor-AT Large, 2004—), Williams Club. Democrat. Avocations: collecting Lionel trains, collecting stereo equipment, softball, golf, collecting american coins. Office: Liebermen Rsch Worldwide Office Meadows Complex 201 Rt 17 N Ste 405 Rutherford NJ 07070 Office Phone: 914-907-7926. Business E-Mail: ntortorello@lrwonline.com.

TORTORICE, DONALD A. law educator; s. Frank C. and Leila Bridges Tortorice; m. Nancy Mutschler; children: Jonathan, Jeffrey, Christopher. BA, U. Tex., Austin, 1964; JD, U. Calif., Berkeley, 1972. Cert.: U.S. Supreme Ct., Supreme Ct. of Pa. Officer U.S. Navy, 1964—69; atty. Duane Morris & Heckescher, Phila., 1969—98; law prof. Coll. of William and Mary, Williamsburg, Va., 1998—. Dir. Cardinal Industries, Lancaster, Pa., 1986—96, Eastern Alliance Corp., Cayman Islands, 1989—98, Westmoreland Coal Co., Colorado Springs, Colo., 2002—. Author: (book) The Modern Rules of Order, 1997, (textbook) Bioethics and the Law, 1999; editor: (book) Pennsylvania Corporate Practices, 1995. Pres. Pa. Def. Inst., Harrisburg, Pa. Bar Corp. Section, Harrisburg. Fellow: Am. Bar Found.; mem.: Williamsburg Club, Queens Lake Club (pres. 2001). Office: Coll of William and Mary Law Sch S Henry St Williamsburg VA 23187

TORUÑO, RHINA M. Literature educator, researcher, writer; b. San Salvador, El Salvador; came to U.S., 1981; d. Juan Felipe and Juana (Contreras) Toruño; m. Henriquez Trujillo, Nov. 4, 1967 (div.); children: Mario Felipe, José Rodrigo; m. Hector-Neri Castañeda (dec.). Grad., Santa Ines Coll., Nueva San Salvador, El Salvador, 1961; BA in Philosophy, Nat. U .El Salvador, 1971; MA in Philosophy, Cath. U. Louvain, Belgium, 1973, PhD in French Contemporary Philosophy, 1978; MA in Hispanic and Latin Am. Lit., Nat. U. Paris/Sorbonne, 1976; PhD in Latin Am. Lit., Ind. U., Bloomington, 1994. Tchr. asst. Nat. U. El Salvador, San Salvador, 1968-71, prof. philosophy, 1976-81; vis. scholar Sch. Edn. Stanford U., Palo Alto, Calif., 1981-82; vis. asst. prof. Fla. State U., 94-95; asst. prof. U. Tex. of the Permian Basin, Odessa, 1995-97, assoc. prof., 1997-00, prof., 01—, Kathlyn Cosper Dunagan prof. humanities, Spanish area coord., 1997—. Cons. for edn. com. Mexican-Am. Network of Odessa, 1997—. Author: Time, Destiny and Oppression on the Work of Elena Garro, 1996, 2d edit., 1998; assoc. editor Chiricu, Ind. U., Bloomington, 1985-90, Third Woman, Berkeley U., 1986-87; author more than 50 articles on literary criticism in English, French, Spanish. Recipient Ednl. Rshc. award, Pan Am. Round Table, Odessa, Tex., 1996, Internat. Prize Emmanuel Mounier, French Assn. of Friends of Emmanuel Mounier, Paris, 1974, Damas de Oro, Odessa, Tex., 2000; grantee U Tex., Odessa, 2000, 02, 03; fellow Internat. Fedn. Univ. Women, Geneva, 1981-82. Mem. Soc. des Amis d'Emmanuel Mounier, Fedn. Internat. des Femmes Deplomees de Univs. Internat., Salvadoran Acad. Scis. (1st female mem.), Salvadoran Acad. Lang. (Royal Acad. of Spain br.), Pan Am. Round Table, Spanish Book Club (pres. 1996—), Hispanic C. of C. Democrat. Roman Catholic. Avocations: reading short stories for children, aerobics, gardening, travel. Home: 4305 Buck Pl Odessa TX 79762-4650 Office: U Tex Permian Basin 4901 E University Blvd Odessa TX 79762-0001 E-mail: toruno_r@utpb.ed.

TORVALDS, LINUS (BENEDICT), application developer; b. Helsinki, Finland, Dec. 28, 1969; married; children: Patricia Miranda, Daniela. Student, Helsinki U. Developer Transmeta Corp., Santa Clara, Calif., 1997—2003; fellow Open Source Develop. Labs (OSDL), Beaverton, Oreg., 2003—. Recipient Nokia Found. Award, 1997, Lifetime Achievement Award, Uniforum, 1997. Achievements include invention of Linux operating system. Office: OSDL 12725 SW Millikan Way, Ste 400 Beaverton OR 97005*

TORYKIAN, JOAN MARIE, archivist; b. N.Y.C., Sept. 13, 1936; BA in Polit. Sci., U. Calif. Berkeley, 1958; cert. de français usuel, U. Paris, 1961; postgrad., U. Oslo, 1963—67; MA in Pub. Adminstrn., U. Calif. Berkeley, 1970; postgrad., U. Calif. Davis, 1970—73; cert., We. Archives Inst., 1992. Secretariat 1st Peacekeeping Conf. Nobel Inst., Oslo, 1964; libr. Norwegian Inst. Internat. Affairs, Oslo, 1963; exec. dir. Svc. Civil Internat., Oslo, 1965; rschr. Internat. Population and Urban Rsch. Inst. U. Calif. Berkeley, 1967—68, rschr. Sch. Law, 1976; career cons. Berkeley, 1977—95. Conf. coord., writing group chair Sociologists for Women in Soc., San Francisco, 1980—86; adv. to bd. dirs. Easy Bay Women in Sci., San Francisco, 1993—; founder, adv. Armenian Women's Archives, 1988—. Author: Dialogues with the Gods: Poems for John, 1980, The Wounding Animus: Its Socio-Archetypal Influences on Intellectual Integrity, 2000; co-author (booklet): The A B Cs of Rent Control for Tenants. Friend Bancroft Libr. U. Calif. Berkeley, 2001—. Mem.: Women's Classical Caucus, Soc. Calif. Archivists. Home and Office: North Berkeley Sta PO Box 9267 Berkeley CA 94709-0267

TOSCANO, JAMES VINCENT, medical institute administration; b. Passaic, N.J., Aug. 8, 1937; s. William V. and Mary A. (DeNigris) T.; m. Sharon Lee Bowers; children: Shawn Truelson, Lauren Bjorklund, David Brendan, Dania Toscano Miwa. AB summa cum laude, Rutgers Coll., 1959; MA, Yale U., 1960. Lectr. Wharton Sch., U. Pa., 1961-64; chief opinion analyst Pa. Opinion Poll, 1962-64; mng. dir. World Press Inst., St. Paul, 1964-68, exec. dir., 1968-72; dir. devel. Macalester Coll., St. Paul, 1972-74; v.p. resource devel. and pub. affairs Mpls. Soc. Fine Arts, 1974-79; pres. Minn. Mus. Art, 1979-81; exec. v.p. Park Nicollet Inst., 1981—; corp. sec. Park Nicollet Clinic, 1983-86; sr. v.p. Am. Med. Ctrs., Inc., 1985-87. Adj. prof. sch. of mgmt. U. St. Thomas, 1989-2001; co-chair prin. practices nonprofit excellence com. MCN, 1994-98; lectr. Grad. Sch. Pub. Adminstrn. and Non-profit Mgmt., Hamline U., 2003—. Author: The Chief Elected Official in the Penjerdel Region, 1964; co-author, co-editor: The Integration of Political Communities, 1964. Bd. dirs., exec. com., sec., World Press Ins., 1972—; bd. dirs., chmn. Southside Newspaper Mpls., 1975-79; chmn. com. to improve student behavior St. Paul Pub. Schs., 1977-79; bd. dirs. Planned Parenthood St. Paul, 1965-72, Mpls. Action Agy., 1976-79; emeritus dir. Help Enable Alcoholics Receive Treatment; mem. St. Paul Heritage Preservation Commn., 1979-82, vice chmn., 1981; mem. Citizens Adv. Com. on Cable Comm.; bd. dirs. Citizens League, 1980, African-Am. Culture Ctr., 1979-82, Am. Composers Forum, 1981-85, St. Paul Chamber Orch., 1976-80, 83-89, United Theol. Sem., 1985-88; dir. emeritus Minn. Citizens for the Arts; bd. dirs., mem. exec. com., chmn. Med. Alley Assn., 1986-96; mem. task force on tech. assessment Med. Alley, 1992-93; mem. health affairs adv. com. Acad. Health Ctr. U. Minn., 1988-95; bd. dirs. Mother Cabrini House, 1985-92, Minn. Civil Justice Coalition, 1987-91, also chmn.; chmn. Gov.'s Task Force on Health Care Promotion, 1985-86, mem. Gov.'s Com. Promotion Health Care Resources, 1986-87; chmn. bd. Minn. Fin. Counseling Svcs., Inc., 1990-93; mem. task force cost effectiveness Med. Alley, 1994-95; bd. dirs. Meml. Blood Bank, 1995-2001, mem. exec. com., 1996-2001; bd. dirs. Bakken Mus., 1997-2003, Stevens Sq. Cmty. Orgn., 1997-99; bd. dirs. Rainbow Rsch., Inc., 2002-, chmn. bd., 2004-; bd. dirs. Friends of the St. Paul Libr., 2004-. Woodrow Wilson Nat. fellow, 1960. Mem. Minn. Newspaper Found. (bd. dirs. 1987-92), Minn. Coun. Nonprofits (bd. dirs. 1989-95, 97-2003, bd. mem. Vocal Essence 1993-96, alt. Minn. Healthcare Commn., 1993-95, mem. Minn. Healthcare Commn., 1995-97, chair task force on med. edn. and rsch. costs 1994-96; mem. com. on med. rsch. and edn. costs, 1996-2003, chair 1996-99; liaison health tech. adv. com. 1993-97; pres. 2000-03, bd. dirs. Summit Ave Residential Preservation Assn., 2000—), Skylight Club, Informal Club. Address: 1982 Summit Ave Saint Paul MN 55105-1460 Office: Pk Nicollet Inst 3800 Park Nicollet Blvd Minneapolis MN 55416-2527 Office Phone: 952-993-3142. Personal E-mail: jvt2@comcast.net. Business E-Mail: Toscaj@parknicollet.com.

TOSCANO, SAMUEL, JR., wholesale distribution executive; b. 1948; With Manhattan Drug Co. and Hillside (N.J.) Drug Co., 1967-72, Neuman Distributors, Inc., Ridgefield, NJ, 1972—2000, mgr. sales, dir. sales, v.p. sales, CEO, chmn. Moonachi, NJ, 1979—2000.

TOSHEFF, JULIJ GOSPODINOFF, psychiatrist; b. Svishtov, Bulgaria, July 3, 1925; came to U.S., 1968; s. Gospodin P. and Mara A. (Karaivanova) T.; m. Finnie I. Kancheva, Feb. 10, 1927; 1 child, Deana. MD, Higher Med. Inst., Sofia, Bulgaria, 1952. Resident Higher Inst. Specialization of Physicians, Sofia, Bulgaria, 1953-56, 59-62, staff physician, 1957-59, staff psychiatrist clinic psychiatry, 1962-67; staff internist Gen. City Hosp., Tetovo, Yugoslavia, 1967; rsch. assoc. dept. psychiatry Johns Hopkins U. Sch. Medicine, Balt., 1968-69, instr. behavioral biology, dept. psychiatry, 1969-72; intern South Baltimore Gen. Hosp., 1972-73; resident L.I. Jewish Med. Ctr., Hillside Hosp.,

Glen Oaks, N.Y., 1973-76, staff psychiatrist, 1976—. Contbr. articles to profl. jours. Lt. Bulgarian Army. Mem. APA. Avocations: classical music, opera, reading. Office: 45 N Station Plz Great Neck NY 11021-5011

TOSI, GLORIA C. labor union administrator; Adminstrv. asst. Fed. Maritime Commn., 1969; dir. govtl. affairs Internat. Longshoremen's Assn.; from dir. corp. affairs to pres. Am. Maritime Congress, Washington, 1981—2000, pres., 2000—. Office: American Maritime Congress 1300 I St NW Ste 250 West Washington DC 20005

TOSKES, PHILLIP PAUL, gastroenterologist, educator, clinical researcher; b. Balt., Md., Jan. 4, 1940; s. John F. and Mary R. (Vonelli) T.; m. Patricia A. Sponsel, June 3, 1961; children: Tammy Lynn Price, Tracey Lynn, Steven D. BA, Johns Hopkins U., 1961; MD, U. Md., 1965. Diplomate Am. Bd. Internal Medicine (bd. dirs.), Am. Bd. Gastroenterology. Intern, resident U. Md. Hosp., Balt., 1965-68; fellow in gastroenterology Hosp. U. Pa., Phila., 1968-70; asst. prof. medicine U. Fla., Gainesville, 1973-75, assoc. prof. medicine, 1975-78, prof. medicine, 1978—, dir. divsn. gastro, hepatology, 1978-97, prof., chmn. dept. medicine, 1997—2002. Chief gastro sect. Gainesville VA Med. Ctr., 1973-92; chmn. Nat. Digestive Disease Adv. Bd., Washington, 1992-94. Author chpts. to books. Maj. U.S. Army, 1970-73. Recipient Disting. Achievement award Can. Gastroenterol. Assn., 1982. Fellow ACP (Meade Johnson scholar 1966-68); mem. Am. Soc. Clin. Investigation, Am. Fedn. Clin. Rsch., Am. Gastroenterol. Assn. (pres. 1997-98). Avocations: travel, swimming, boating. Home: 202 NW 114th Way Gainesville FL 32607-1122 Office: U Fla Box 100214 1600 SW Archer Rd Gainesville FL 32610-3001 Office Phone: 352-392-2877. Business E-Mail: toskepp@medicine.ufl.edu.

TOSSI, ALICE LOUISE, special education educator; b. St. Augustine, Fla., Feb. 25, 1941; d. Hubert Parker and Marie Francis (Mecca) Hahn; m. Donald Joseph Tossi, Feb. 19, 1966; children: Kevin, Craig, Raymond. BA, Rollins Coll., 1978. Cert. elem. tchr., Fla. Sec. Diocese of St. Augustine, Fla., 1958-59, Fla. East Coast Ry., St. Augustine, 1959-60; legal sec. Mahon & Stratford, Jacksonville, Fla., 1960-61; sec. comptroller's dept. Esso Standard Oil S. A., Ltd., Coral Gables, Fla., 1962-63; sec. Kelly Temporary, Maitland, Fla., 1976-78; tchr. All Souls Elem., Sanford, Fla., 1979-81, Harbor Elem., Maitland, 1981-82; sec., tech. asst. physically impaired Seminole County Sch. Bd., Sanford, 1983—; chorus pars profl. Sweet Adelines show Lakeview Mid. Sch., 1957—2003; asst. Highlands Elem. Sch., Winter Springs, Fla. Bd. dirs. Seminole County Dem. Assn., 1983. Mem. Coun. of Exceptional Edn. (sec. 1986-90, Placque 1987), Seminole County Sch. Bd. Assn. (sec. polit. action com.). Roman Catholic. Home: 114 W Woodland Dr Sanford FL 32773-5706

TOSTE, ANTHONY PAIM, chemistry educator, researcher; b. Mountain View, Calif., June 26, 1948; BS in Chemistry with honors, Santa Clara (Calif.) U., 1970; PhD in Biochemistry and Chemistry, U. Calif., Berkeley, 1976. Rsch. fellow Cardiovasc. Rsch. Inst., San Francisco, 1977-79; rsch. scientist Battelle Meml. Inst. Pacific N.W. Nat. Lab., Richland, Wash., 1980-88; asst. prof. S.W. Mo. State U., Springfield, 1988-94, assoc. prof., 1994-99, full prof., 1999—. Cons. Mitsubishi Metal Corp., Tokyo, 1984-87, Dow Chem., Tex., 1994-96; presenter in field. Contbr. articles to jours. in field, cmty. svc. presentations. Bd. dirs. Mid Columbia Arts Coun., Richland, 1987-88, Bot. Soc. S.W. Mo., Springfield, 1997-2002; pres. bd. dirs. Springfield Sister Cities Assn., 1993-96; co-founder, leader Internat. Friendship Dels. to Japan, 1996, 99, 2001, 03. Rsch., equipment grantee NSF, 1990; recipient Diverse Cmty. award Sister Cities Internat., Boston, 1996. Mem. Am. Chem. Soc. (treas. Ozark sect. 1989-91, chmn.-elect 2000, chmn. 2000-01), Am. Nuc. Soc. (Best Poster award 1987), Assn. Ofcl. Analytical Chemists (program chair 1986, 90), Mo. Acad. Sci. (program chair 1997, 2002). Avocations: picture framing, collecting fine art, woodworking, reading, cinema. Home: 2113 E Woodhaven Pl Springfield MO 65804-6767 Office: SW Mo State U Dept Chemistry 901 S National Ave Springfield MO 65804-0088 Office Phone: 417-836-5150. Business E-Mail: anthonytoste@smsu.edu.

TOSTESON, DANIEL CHARLES, physiologist, medical school dean emeritus; b. Milw., Feb. 5, 1925; s. Alexis H. and Dilys (Bodycombe) T.; m. Penelope Kinsley, Dec. 17, 1949 (div. 1969); children: Carrie Marias, Heather Tosteson, Tor, Zoe Losada; m. Magdalena Tieffenberg, July 8, 1969; children: Joshua, Ingrid. Student, Harvard U., 1942-44, MD, 1949; DSc (hon.), U. Copenhagen, 1979; Dr. hon. causa, U. Liege, 1983; DSc (hon.), Med. Coll. Wis., 1984, NYU, 1992; DHL (hon.), Johns Hopkins U., 1993; Dr. honoris causa, Cath. U. Louvain, 1996, Duke U., 1996, Emory U., 1996; DMed (hon.), Ludwig Maximilians U., 2002. Fellow physiology Harvard Med. Sch., 1947-48; intern, then asst. resident medicine Presbyn. Hosp., N.Y.C., 1949-51; research fellow medicine Brookhaven Nat. Lab., 1951-53; lab. kidney and electrolyte metabolism Nat. Heart Inst., 1953-55, 57, research fellow biol. isotope research lab., 1955-56; research fellow Physiol. Lab., Cambridge, Eng., 1956-57; assoc. prof. physiology Washington U. Sch. Medicine, St. Louis, 1958-61; prof., chmn. dept. physiology and pharmacology Duke U. Sch. Medicine, 1961-75, James B. Duke Distinguished prof., 1971-75; dean div. biol. scis., dean Pritzker Sch. Medicine U. Chgo., Lowell T. Coggleshall prof. med. scis., v.p. for Med. Center, 1975-77; dean, Caroline Shields Walker prof. cell biology Harvard Med. Sch., Boston, 1977-97, dean emeritus, Caroline Shields Walker prof., 1997—, pres. Med. Ctr., 1977-97. Mem. molecular biology panel NSF, 1959-62; cons. sci. rev. com. NIH, 1964-67, nat. adv. gen. med. scis. coun., 1982-86; mem. U.S. Office Tech. Assessment, 1976; ethics adv. bd. HEW, 1977-80; nat. adv. gen. med. scis. coun. NIH, 1982—; mem. governing bd. NRC, 1977; mem. sci. com. Found. pour l'Etude du Systeme Nerveux Central et Peripherique, 1982—; nat. adv. com. biomed. scis. PEW Scholars Program, 1984-87. Recipient Harvard medal, 2002. Mem. Inst. Medicine NAS (coun. 1975-78, adv. bd. PEW scholars program 1984-85), AAAS, Acad. Arts and Scis. (pres. 1997-00), Am. Physiol. Soc. (council 1967-75, pres. 1973-74), Soc. Gen. Physiologists (pres. 1968-69), Biophys. Soc. (council 1970 73), Assn. Am. Med. Colls. (chmn. coun. acad. socs. 1969-70, chmn. assembly 1973-74, chmn. physician supply task force 1988-90, Abraham Flexner award 1991), Assn. Am. Physicians, Am. Acad. Arts and Scis. (pres. 1997-2000), Red Cell Club, Soc. Health and Human Values, Danish Royal Soc. (fellow), Alpha Omega Alpha. Achievements include spl. research cellular transport processes, red cell membranes. Office: Harvard Med Sch Goldenson Bldg B-243 220 Longwood Ave Boston MA 02115-5701

TOSTI, DONALD THOMAS, psychologist, consultant; b. Kansas City, Mo., Dec. 6, 1935; s. Joseph T. Tosti and Elizabeth M. (Parsons) Tosti Addison; m. Carol J. Curless, Jan. 31, 1957 (dec. 1980); children: Rene, Alicia, Roxanna, Brett, Tabitha, Todd Marcus; m. Annette Brewer, Dec. 29, 1989. BSEE, U. N.Mex., 1957, MS in Psychology, 1962, PhD in Psychology, 1967. Chief editor Tchg. Machines, Inc., Albuquerque, 1960-64; divsn. mgr. Westinghouse Learning Corp., Albuquerque, 1964-70; founder, sr. v.p. Ind. Learning Sys., San Raphael, Calif., 1970-74, pres., 1974-76; chmn. bd. Omega Performance, San Francisco, 1976-77; pres. Operants, Inc., San Rafael, 1978-81; v.p. Forum Corp., San Rafael, 1981-83; mng. ptnr. Vanguard Cons. Group, San Francisco, 1983—. Author: Basic Electricity, Advanced Algebra, Fundamentals of Calculus, TMI Programmed Mathematics Series, 1960-63, Behavior Technology, 1970, A Guide to Child Development, Tactics of Communication, 1973; co-author: Learning Is Getting Easier, 1973, Indtroductory Psychology, 1981, Usibility Factors in Hardware and Software Design, 1982, Comparative Usibility, 1983, Performance Based Management, Positive Leadership, 1986, Strategic Alliances, 1990, The Professional Manager, 1995, Power and Governance, 1996, Global Fluency, 1999, Organizational Alignment, 2000, Internal Branding, 2000, Principles of Performance Consulting, 2001. Mem. AAAS, APA, Internat. Soc. for Performance Improvement (v.p. rsch. 1983-85, treas. 1997-99, pres., 2003-, Outstanding Mem. award 1984, Life Membership award 1984, Outstanding product award 1974), Sigma Xi. Home: 41 Marinita Ave San Rafael CA 94901-3443

TOT, ZVONIMIR, musician, composer, music educator; b. Novi Sad, Serbia-Monteneg, May 26, 1967; s. Milica Čudanov and Ivan Tot. MusB, Franz Liszt Acad. Musical Arts, Budapest, Hungary, 1995, Amsterdam Conservatory, The Netherlands, 1999; MusM, No. Ill. U., 2002. Music theory, aural skills, and guitar instr. Coll. DuPage, Glen Ellyn, Ill., 2001—; vis. prof., music theory and aural skills U. Ill., Chgo., 2002—03, 2004—. Guitar instr. McHenry County Coll., Ill.; resident composer-conductor George Soros Found. Jazz Seminars, Serbia and Montenegro, 1995—97. Musician: (compact disk) Travels and Dreams; composer: (concert music classical compositions) Missa Brevis, Ave Maria, Wat Buigt gij u neder, o mijn ziel (psalm 42), numerous jazz compositions. Fellow, No. Ill. U., 2001—02. Mem.: Internat. Assn. Jazz Edn., Am. Composers Forum, ASCAP, Jazz Inst. Chgo., Pi Kappa Lambda. Home: 22S Fernwood Dr Bolingbrook IL 60440 Personal E-mail: zt@zt-music.com.

TOTAKURA, SATYANARAYANA RAJU, secondary school educator; b. Andhra Pradesh, India, Apr. 10, 1937; s. Narasimha Raju and Suramma Totakura; m. Sarada Totakura, June 22, 1961; children: Usharani, Srinivasa Raju, Raghurama Raju. BSc, W.G.B. Coll., 1959; BEd, M.R. Coll., 1961; MSc, Banaras Hindu U., 1969; MEd, Andhra U., 1985; PhD, World U., 1987. Vis. prof. of math. Telugu Assn. of North Am., New York, 1993—98; math tchr. Bd. of Edn., Flushing, NY, 1996—; lectr. in math. DNR Coll., 1970—93. Pres. Inst. of Vedic Math., Detroit, 1993—96, Inst. of Vedic Math. Edn. Found., New York, 1997—. Author: (book) Vedic Mathematics, 1995, Fingers Calculator, 1995, Recreational Mathematics, 1995, Vedaganitam, 1980, Mathematical Shortcuts, 1988, Wonders with Numbers, 1989. Recipient Kannadakoota award, Kannadakoota N.Y., 1996, TLC award, Telugu Lit. and Culture Assn., 1996, TTD grant, Tirumal Tirupati Devastanam, 1987. Mem.: Indian Sci. Congress. Achievements include invented and re-invented novel techniques that a student of mathematics can follow without any difficulty to not only learn but also master mathematics; disseminated his techniques of learning mathematics through TV programs, radio lectures, lectures, seminars and workshops throughout India and U.S.A. Home: 43-32 Kissena Blvd 10-L Flushing NY 11355 E-mail: srajutotakura@hotmail.com.

TOTENBERG, NINA, journalist; b. N.Y.C., Jan. 14, 1944; d. Roman and Melanie (Shroder) T.; m. Floyd Haskell, Feb. 3, 1979 (dec.); m. H. David Reines, 2000. Student, Boston U.; LLD (hon.), Haverford Coll., Chatham Coll., Gonzaga U., Northeastern U., St. Mary's, SUNY; LHD, Lebanon Valley Coll., Westfield State Coll., Pa. State U., Pine Manor Coll., De Paul U., Simmons Coll. Reporter Boston Record Am., 1965, Peabody Times, 1967, Nat. Observer, 1968-71, Newtimes, 1973, Nat. Pub. Radio, Washington, 1974—, Inside Washington, 1992—; reporter Nightline ABC, 1993-98. Contbr. articles to N.Y. Times Mag., Harvard Law Rev., Christian Sci. Monitor, N.Y. Mag., Parade. Recipient Sidney Hillman award, 1983, Alfred I. Dupont award Columbia U., 1988, 91, George Foster Peabody award, 1991, George Polk award, 1991, Joan Barone award, 1991, Silver Gavel award ABA, 1968-98, Woman of Courage award Women in Film, 1991, Athena award, 1994, Presdl. Commendation, Radcliffe Coll., 1998; named outstanding broadcast journalist of yr. Nat. Press Found., 1999. Mem. Sigma Delta Chi (award 1991). Office: NPR 635 Massachusetts Ave NW Washington DC 20001-3740

TOTENBERG, ROMAN, violinist, music educator; b. Lodz, Poland, Jan. 1, 1911; came to U.S., 1935; s. Adam and Stanislava (Vinaver) T.; m. Melanie Shroder, July 30, 1941; children: Nina, Jill, Amy. Grad., Chopin Sch. Music, Warsaw, Poland, 1928, Hochschule für Music, Berlin, 1931, Paris Inst. Instrumental Music, 1933; PhD (hon.), Symmons Coll., 2002. Head violin dept. Peabody Conservatory, Balt., 1943-44, Mannes Coll. Music, N.Y.C., 1951-57; chmn. string dept. Boston U., 1962-78, prof., 1978—, co-chmn. string dept. Prin. soloist, dir. chamber music Interstate Broadcasting Co., N.Y.C., 1937-42; prin. soloist, head string dept. Music Acad. West, Santa Barbara, Calif., summers 1948-51; with Music Assocs., Aspen, Colo., summers 1951-62; dir. Totenberg Instrumental Ensemble, 1953-60; George Miller vis. prof. U. Ill., 1960-61; head string dept. Boston U. Tanglewood Inst., summers 1966-74; performer, tchr. Kneisel Hall Festival, Blue Hill, Maine, 1975—, acting dir., 1984-87; dir. Longy Sch. Music, Cambridge, Mass., 1978-85; judge Paganini, Wieniawski, Carnegie Hall competitions, Kreisler and Japan Internat. Competition. Performer worldwide concerts and tours; rec. artist with Vanguard, DGG, Mus. Heritage Soc. records, Titanic compact disk, Omega Records, VGR Records, Eisenkolis Records. Chmn. Music Project, Newton Tricentenary, 1988. Recipient Mendelssohn prize, 1932, Wieniawski Soc. medal, 1970, Eugene Ysaye Soc. medal, 1975, Polish Nat. medal of Cultural Achievement, 1988. Mem. Am. String Tchrs. Assn. (named Artist-Tchr. of yr. 1983), AAUP, Music Tchrs. Nat. Assn., Phi Kappa Lambda. Avocations: photography, tennis. Office: Boston U 855 Commonwealth Ave Boston MA 02215-1303 *Devotion to human values expressed through music as well as through daily activities in public life.*

TOTH, ROBERT CHARLES, retired polling consultant, journalist, writer; b. Blakely, Pa., Dec. 24, 1928; s. John and Tillie (Szuch) T.; m. Paula Goldberg, Apr. 12, 1954; children: Jessica, Jennifer, John. BS in Chem. Engring., Washington U., St. Louis, 1952; MS in Journalism, Columbia U., 1955; postgrad., Harvard U., 1960-61. Started as engr. in Army Ordnance Dept., 1952—54; reporter Providence Jour., 1955—57; sci. reporter N.Y. Herald Tribune, 1957—62, N.Y. Times, 1962—63; mem. staff Los Angeles Times, 1963—93, bur. chief London, 1965—70, diplomatic corr., 1970—71, White House corr., 1972—74, bur. chief Moscow, 1974—77, nat. security corr. Washington bur., 1977—93; ret. Cons. opinion poll in U.S. and abroad by Times Mirror Ctr. (now Pew Rsch. Ctr.) for People and Press, 1990, sr. assoc., 1993-98. Co-author: The Dimishing Divide, Religion's Changing Role in American Politics, 2000. Served with USMC, 1946-48. Recipient Overseas Press Club award, 1977, Sigma Delta Chi award, 1977, George Polk award in Journalism for fgn. reporting L.I. U., 1978, Columbia U. Alumni award, 1978, Wienthal award Fgn. Service Inst., Georgetown U., 1986, Edwin N. Hood award Nat. Press Club, 1986; Pulitzer Travelling scholar, 1955; Nieman fellow Harvard U., 1960-61 Mem. Coun. on Fgn. Rels. Home: 21 Primrose St Chevy Chase MD 20815-4228 E-mail: tothrc@aol.com.

TOTLIS, GUST JOHN, retired title insurance company executive; b. Highwood, Ill., May 15, 1939; s. John Chris and Agape (Galelis) T.; m. Joyce Elaine Edholm, June 5, 1960; children: Kenneth Chris, Charles Gust. BA, Lake Forest Coll., 1962; MBA, U. Chgo., 1964. Fin. planning mgr. Gen. Foods Corp., Battle Creek, Mich., 1964-68; fin. analyst Irving Trust Co., N.Y.C., 1968-69, asst. sec., 1969-71, asst. v.p., 1971-72, v.p., 1972-75; corp. contr. Irving Bank Corp., N.Y.C., 1975-82; exec. v.p., CFO Fidelity Union Bancorp, Newark, 1982-85, Star Banc Corp (formerly First Nat. Cin. Corp.), Cin., 1985-93; sr. v.p., CFO Chgo. Title and Trust Co., 1993-99. Bd. dirs. Ticor Title Ins. Co., Security Union Title Ins. Co., Chgo. Tech. Corp., Credit Data Reporting Svcs., Inc., Market Intelligence, Inc., Nat. Flood Info. Svcs., Inc.; chmn. gov. bd. Ill. Coun. Econ. Edn., 1997-99. Adv. bd. dirs., treas. Salvation Army, Cin., 1987-93; bd. dirs., pres. Cin. Chamber Orch., 1988-93; pres. May Festival Assn., 1988-93; v.p. Spl. Olympics, 1990-93; vice chmn. United Way, 1991-94; bd. trustees Cin. Inst. Fine Arts, 1991-93. Mem. Fin. Execs. Inst., Univ. club, Kenwood Country Club, Univ. Club Chgo. Presbyterian. Home: 111 E Bellevue Pl Chicago IL 60611-1115

TOTMAN, CONRAD DAVIS, history professor; b. Conway, Mass., Jan. 5, 1934; s. Raymond Smith and Mildred Edna (Kingsbury) T.; m. Michiko Ikegami, Jan. 21, 1958; children: Kathleen Junko, Christopher Ken. BA, U. Mass., 1958; MA, Harvard U., 1960, PhD, 1964. Asst. prof. U. Calif., Santa Barbara, 1964-66; asst. prof. Northwestern U., Evanston, Ill., 1966-68, assoc. prof., 1968-72, prof. Japanese history, 1972-84, chmn. dept. history, 1977-80; prof. Japanese history Yale U., New Haven, 1984-97, prof. emeritus, 1997—, acting chmn. Dept. History, 1989-90; prof. Kyoto Ctr. for Japanese Studies, 1992-93. Vis. prof. Stanford U., 1997, Yale U., 1999. Author: Politics in the Tokugawa Bakufu 1600-1843, 1967, paperback edit., 1988, The Collapse of the Tokugawa Bakufu 1862-1868, 1979 (John K. Fairbank prize Am. Hist. Assn. 1981), Japan Before Perry: A Short History, 1981, Tokugawa Ieyasu: Shogun, 1983, The Origins of Japan's Modern Forests, 1985, The Green Archipelago: Forestry in Preindustrial Japan, 1989, paperback edit., 1998 (Japanese translation 1998), Early Modern Japan, 1993, paperback edit., 1995, The Lumber Industry in Early Modern Japan, 1995, A History of Japan, 2000, Pre-Industrial Korea and Japan in Environmental Perspective, 2004. Served with U.S. Army, 1953-56. Recipient Carstensen prize for essay Agrl. History Soc., 1982; Woodrow Wilson nat. fellow, 1958-59; Social Sci. Research Council-Am. Council Learned Socs. fellow, 1968-69; NEH sr. fellow, 1972-73; Fulbright-Hays research grantee, 1968-69; Japan Found. grantee, 1981-82 Mem. Assn. Asian Studies (N.E. Asia coun. 1977-80, chmn. 1978-80, exec. com. 1978-80, pres. New Eng. Conf. 1985-86, coun. of confs. 1992-95), Forest History Soc. Office: Yale U Dept History New Haven CT 06520

TOTTEN, GEORGE OAKLEY, III, political science educator; b. Washington, July 21, 1922; s. George Oakley Totten Jr. and Vicken (von Post) Börjesson Totten Barrois; m. Astrid Maria Anderson, June 26, 1948 (dec. Apr. 26, 1975); children: Vicken Yuriko, Linnea Catherine; m. Lilia Huiying Li, July 1, 1976; 1 child, Blanche Maluk Lemes. Cert., U. Mich., 1943; AB, Columbia U., 1946, AM, 1949; MA, Yale U., 1950, PhD, 1954; docentur i japanologi, U. Stockholm, 1977. Lectr. Columbia U., N.Y.C., 1954-55; rsch. assoc. Fletcher Sch. Law and Diplomacy Harvard U. and Tufts U., Mass., 1956—58; asst. prof. MIT, Cambridge, 1958-59, Boston U., 1959-61; assoc. prof. U. R.I., Kingston, 1961-64, Mich. State U., 1964—65; assoc. prof. polit. sci. U. So. Calif., L.A., 1965-68, prof., 1968-92, chmn. dept., 1980-86, prof. emeritus, 1992—96, disting. prof. emeritus, 1996—. Dir., founder Calif. Pvt. Univs. and Colls. Yr.-in-Japan program Weseda U., 1967-73; 1st dir. East Asian Studies Ctr., 1974-77; 1st dir. USC-UCLA Joint East Asian Studies Ctr., 1976-77; sr. affiliated scholar Ctr. for Multiethnic and Transnat. Studies, 1993-98; chair USC Korea Project, 1998—; vis. prof. U. Stockholm, 1977-79, 1st dir. Ctr. Pacific Asia Studies, 1986-89, sr. counselor bd. dirs., 1989—; hon. pres. Huaxiu Pvt. Sch., Anyang City, Henan Province, China, 1999—; vis. prof. Ctr. for Japanese Studies, U. Hawaii, Manoa, 1992-93. Author: Social Democratic Movement in Prewar Japan, 1966, Chinese edit., 1987, Korean edit., 1997; co-author: Socialist Parties in Postwar Japan, 1966, Japan and the New Ocean Regime, 1984, Japan in the World, the World in Japan, Fifty Years of Japanese Studies at Michigan, 2001; editor: Democracy in Prewar Japan: Groundwork or Facade?, 1965, Helen Snow's Song of Ariran, 1973, Korean edit., 1991, Chinese edit., 1993, Kim Dae-jung's A New Beginning, 1996, Lee Hee-ho's (Mrs. Kim Dae-jung's) Praying for Tomorrow: Letters to My Husband in Prison, 1999; author, co-editor: Developing Nations: Quest for a Model, 1970, Japanese edit., 1975, The Whaling Issue in U.S.-Japan Relations, 1978, China's Economic Reform: Administering the Introduction of the Market Mechanism, 1992, Community in Crisis: The Korean American Community After the Los Angeles Civil Unrest of April 1992, 1994, Korean edit., 2003; co-translator: Ch'ien Mu's Traditional Government in Imperial China, 1982, 1st paperback edit., 2000; contbr. Sources of the Japanese Tradition, 1958, Aspects of Social Change inModern Japan, 1967, Japan in Crisis: Essays on Taishō Democracy, 1974, The Politics of Divided Nations, 1991, Chinese edit., 1995, Japanese edit., 1997; editl. bd. Acta Koreana, 1997—2003. Mem. U.S.-China People's Friendship Assn., Washington, 1974—, World Feds., 1962—2004, Citizens for Global Solutions, 2004—; mem. Com. on U.S.-China Rels., N.Y.C., 1975—; chmn. L.A.-Pusan Sister City Assn., L.A., 1976-77; founding mem. L.A.-Guangzhou Sister City Assn., 1981, bd. dirs., 1990—; mem. nat. adv. com. Japan Am. Student Conf., 1984—, Assn. Korean Polit. Studies in N.Am., 1992—, v.p. 1996-98; v.p. China Semina, 1985—; bd. dirs. Assn. for the Study of Korean Culture and Identity, Korea, 1999-2000; mem. coun. China Soc. for People's Friendship Studies, Beijing, 1991—; adv. Chinese American Alliance China's Peaceful Reunification, 2002—. 1st lt. AUS, 1942-46, PTO. Recipient Plaque for program on Korean studies Consulate Gen. of Republic of Korea, 1975, Disting. Emeritus award U. So. Calif., 1996; Social Sci. Rsch. Coun. fellow, 1952-53; Ford Found. grantee, 1955-58, NSF grantee, 1979-81, Korea Found. grantee, 1993, Rebuild L.A. grantee, 1993, Philippine Liberation medal, 1994. Mem.: U. So. Calif. Faculty Ctr., European Assn. Japanese Studies, Japan-Am. Soc. Calif. (bd. dirs. 1990—94), Japanese Polit. Sci. Assn., Internat. Studies Assn., Internat. Polit. Sci. Assn., Asia Soc., Am. Polit. Sci. Assn., Assn. Asian Studies, Swedish Club of L.A., Phi Beta Delta (founding mem. Beta Kappa chpt. 1993—). Episcopalian. Home: 5129 Village Green Los Angeles CA 90016-5205 Office: USC Korea Project Dept Polit Sci VKC 327 Los Angeles CA 90089-0044 Business E-Mail: totten@usc.edu.

TOTTEN, LISA ANN, science educator; b. Kettering, Ohio, June 5, 1969; d. Walter William and Margaret Louise Rodenburg; m. Jeffrey Andrew Totten, Oct. 3, 1992; children: Benjamin Andrew, William Jonathan. PhD, John Hopkins U., 1998. Prof. Rutgers U., New Brunswick, NJ, 2001—. Nat. Merit scholar, Nat. Merit Scholarship Corp., 1987-1991, Grad. Student fellowship, NSF, 1994-1997, Post-Doctoral fellowship in Environ. Chemistry, Camille and Henry Dreyfus Found., 1998-2000. Mem.: Assn. of Environ. Engring. and Sci. Prof., Soc. of Environ. Toxicology and Chemistry, Am. Chem. Soc. (Grad. Student Award 1998). Office: Rutgers U 14 Coll Farm Rd New Brunswick NJ 08901

TOTTON, GAYLE, professional sports team executive; CEO Sacramento (Calif.) Sirens. Office: Sacramento Sirens PO Box 15920 Sacramento CA 95813-9998

TOUBY, KATHLEEN ANITA, lawyer; b. Miami Beach, Feb. 20, 1943; d. Harry and Kathleen Rebecca (Hamper) T.; m. Joseph Thomas Woodward; children: Mark Andrew, Judson David Touby. BS in Nursing, U. Fla., 1965, MRC in Rehab. Counseling, 1967; JD with honors, Nova U., 1977. Bar: Fla. 1978, D.C. 1978. Counselor Jewish Vocat. Svc., Chgo., 1967-68; rehab. counselor Fla. Dept. Vocat. Rehab., Miami, 1968-70; spl. asst., asst. U.S. atty. U.S. Dept. Justice, Miami, 1978-80; assoc. Pyszka & Kessler, P.A., Miami, 1980-83; ptnr. Touby & Smith, P.A., Miami, 1983-89, Touby, Smith, DeMahy & Drake, P.A., Miami, 1989-94, Touby & Woodward, P.A., Miami, 1994—. Chmn. adv. exec. bd. Paralegal Edn. program Barry U., 1986-87; lectr. Food and Drug Law Inst., 1987-89, 91; lectr. environ. law Exec. Enterprises, 1987-88; lectr. trial techniques, Hispanic Nat. Bar Assn., St. Thomas Law Sch.; adj. prof. product liability Can. Govt., U.S. Trade and Mktg. Dept., 1989-95. Co-author: The Environmental Litigation Deskbook, 1989; contbr. chpts. to books, articles to profl. jours. Mem. ABA, Am. Inns of Ct. (pres. 1998-99, pres.-elect St. Thomas Law Sch. chpt. 1997-98, pres. 1998-99), Dade County Bar Assn. (legal aid, pub. svcs. com. 1988), Fed. Bar Assn. (bd. dirs. 1989—, v.p. 1991-92, pres.-elect So. Fla. chpt. 1992-93, pres. 1993-94), Cuban-Am. Bar Assn., Phi Delta Phi (province pres. 1982-85, bd. dirs. 1985-87). Roman Catholic. Home: 4150 Bay Point Rd Miami FL 33137-3352 Office: Touby & Woodward PA 250 Bird Rd Ste 308 Miami FL 33146-1424 Office Phone: 305-442-2318.

TOUCHY, DEBORAH K.P. lawyer, accountant; b. Pasadena, Tex., Dec. 9, 1957; d. Donald Carl and Bobbie Jo (Jackson) Putzka; m. Harry Roy Touchy, Jr., Feb. 23, 1980. BBA, Baylor U., 1979; JD, U. Houston, 1988. Bar: Tex. 1989; CPA, Tex.; cert. in estate planning and probate law Tex. Bd. Legal Specialization. Sr. mgr. tax KMPG Peat Marwick, Houston, 1980-86; assoc. Fizer Beck Webster & Bentley, Houston, 1989-90; pvt. practice law Houston, 1990—; chmn. spl. events Jr. League Houston, 1997-98. Editor Houston Law Rev., 1988-89. Chmn. ticket sales incentives Chi Omega, Houston, 1985; active ticket sales Mus. Fine Arts, Houston, 1984; facilities chmn. Woodland Trails West Civic Orgn., Houston, 1982-83; pres. Women Attys. in Tax & Probate, 1994-95, pres., 2004; bd. dirs. Episcopal Ch. Women at St. John the Divine; active St. John's Sch., 1999-, Lower Sch. Scrapbook Chmn. 2001-02; mem. steering com. Girl Scouts of San Jacinto County Capital Campaign, 2003-. Recipient Outstanding Alumni award, Beta Alpha Psi, 1997. Mem. ABA (estate-probate sect. 1989—, vice chmn. commn. property com. 1994—), AICPA (taxation sect., estate and gift tax com. 1992-95, 98-2000), Tex. Soc. CPAs (bd. dirs. 1995—, chmn. tax inst. com. 1996-97, estate planning com. 1990-94, 96—), Houston Chpt. CPAs (chmn. taxpayer edn. 1985-86, chmn. membership com. 1992-93, v.p. 1993-94, 96-97, chmn. tax forums 1994-95, long range planning com. 1995-96, chmn. leadership devel. 1997-98, treas. 1998-99, chmn. ann. charity event 1999-2000, bd. dirs. 1999-2000, 2002-03, pres. 2001-02), Houston Bar Assn. (estate-probate sect. 1989—), State Bar Tex. (estate-probate sect. 1989—, mem. elder law com. 1991-97), Houston Estate and Fin. Forum, Baylor U. Women's Assn. (treas. 1993-94, chmn. fin. com. 1994-95, parliamentarian 1995-96, sec. 1996-97, pres. 1997-98, chmn. audit com. 1999-2000), Chief Justice-Advocates, Tex.

Bd. Legal Specializations (cert. estate planning, probate law 1994), Order of Coif, Omicron Delta Kappa, Phi Delta Phi, Beta Alpha Psi (Outstanding Alumni 1997). Office: PO Box 130122 Houston TX 77219-0122 E-mail: dtouchy@swbell.net.

TOUFEILI, IMAD, science educator; s. Ali Toufeili and Waheeba Salim; m. Diana Hijazi Toufeili, Sept. 1, 1989; children: Grace, Abbas, Basil. BS in Chemistry, Lebanese U., 1978; MS in Food Sci., U. Reading, 1981, PhD in Food Sci., 1985. Asst. prof. Am. U. Beirut, 1987—93, assoc. prof., 1993—2002, prof., 2002—. Cons. WHO, Geneva; tech. advisor FAO, Rome, 1996—98. Contbr. articles to profl. jours. Recipient Fulbright award, U.S. Govt., Washington, 1998; fellow, Inst. Food Sci. Tech., London, 1997. Mem.: N.Y. Acad. Scis., Inst. Food Technologists, Am. Assn. Cereal Chemists. Avocations: reading, swimming. Office: Am U Beirut Riad El-Solh Beirut 11072020 Lebanon

TOUGIAS, MARK A. artist; b. Springfield, Mass., Nov. 1, 1957; s. Arthur E. and Geraldine M. (Loncrini) T. BA in Edn., U. Mass., 1979. One-person shows include Cambridge Gallery, Worcester, Mass., 1988, Clarke Gallery, Stowe, Vt., 1991, 99, Ivory Treasures Gallery, Montreal, 1993, So. Vt. Art Ctr., Manchester, Vt., 1995, 98, 2002, Blue Heron Gallery, South Burlington, Vt., 2000, Gallery of Graphic Arts, N.Y.C., 2000, 03, Framework Gallery, Saratoga Springs, N.Y., 2001, Green Mountain art gallery, Stowe, Vt., 2002; exhibited in small group shows Hardcastles Gallery, Wilmington, Del., 1993, Gallery of Graphic Arts, N.Y.C., 1999, Mary Bryan Gallery, Jeffersonville, Vt., 1994—, Noroton Gallery, Darien, Conn., 2000; large group exhbns. include Springfield (Mass.) Mus. Fine Arts, 1985-88, Whistler House Mus., Lowell, Mass., 1988, Cape Cod Art Assn., Barnstable, Mass., 1989, Salmagundi Club, N.Y.C., 1993, Stratton (Vt.) Arts Festival, 1995-98, North Shore Arts Assn., Gloucester, Mass., 1998—; co-author: Autumn Rambles of New England, 1998. Mem. Am. Soc. Marine Artists, No. Vt. Artist Assn. (Harold Knight award 1996, Best in Oils 1996, 2000), North Shore Arts Assn. (Guild of Boston Artists-Roger Curtis award for excellence 1998), Helen Day Art Ctr. (artist mem., Artists' Choice award 1999), So. Vt. Art Ctr. Avocations: travel, cultural studies, music. Home: PO Box 422 Cambridge NY 12816-0422

TOUHILL, BLANCHE MARIE, retired university chancellor, history-education educator; b. St. Louis, Mo., July 1, 1931; d. Robert and Margaret (Walsh) Van Dillen; m. Joseph M. Touhill, Aug. 29, 1959. BA in History, St. Louis U., 1953, MA in Geography, 1954, PhD in History, 1962. Prof. history and edn. U. Mo., St. Louis, 1965-73, assoc. dean faculties, 1974-76, assoc. vice chancellor for acad. affairs, 1976-87, vice chancellor, 1987-90, chancellor, 1991—2002, chancellor emeritus, 2002—. Bd. dirs. Peabody Energy, Inc. Author: William Smith O'Brien and His Irish Revolutionary Companions in Penal Exile, 1981, The Emerging University UM-St. Louis, 1963-83, 1985; editor: Readings in American History, 1970, Varieties of Ireland, 1976. Named Outstanding Educator St. Louis chpt. Urban League, 1976; recipient Leadership award St. Louis YWCA, 1986. Mem. Nat. Assn. State Univs. and Land Grant Colls. (exec. com. 1988—), Am. Com. on Irish Studies (pres. 1991—), Phi Kappa Phi, Alpha Sigma Lambda. E-mail: j_touhill@hotmail.com.

TOUHILL, C. JOSEPH, environmental engineer; b. Newark, Aug. 27, 1938; s. Charles J. and Caroline A. T.; m. Helen Elizabeth O'Malley, June 11, 1960; children: Gregory Joseph, Stephen Mark, Christopher Alan, Kathleen Elizabeth. BCE, Rensselaer Poly. Inst., 1960, PhD in Environ. Engring., 1964; SM, MIT, 1961. Diplomate Am. Acad. Environ. Engrs. Mgr. water and land resources dept. Battelle Meml. Inst., Richland, Wash., 1964-71; pres. Baker/TSA Inc., Pitts., 1977-90; group sr. v.p. ICF Kaiser Engrs. Inc., Pitts., 1990-94; exec. v.p. EG&G Environ. Inc., Pitts., 1994-97; pres. Touhill Tech. Mgmt. Corp., Jamison, Pa., 1997-99, 2003—; nat. discipline lead for process and environ. engring. Tetra Tech FW, Inc. (formerly Foster Wheeler Environ. Corp.), Langhorne, Pa., 1999—2003. Co-author: Hazardous Materials Spills Handbook, 1982, Hazardous Waste Management Engineering, 1987; editor: Resource Management in the Great Lakes Basin, 1971; mem. editorial bd. Environ. Progress Jour., 1979-93. Bd. dirs. Suburban Gen. Hosp., Pitts., 1986-96; vice chmn. Franklin Park (Pa.) Authority, 1977-96, chmn. adv. com., dept. Environ. and energy Engring., Rensselaer Polytech Inst., 1996-98, mem. adv. bd. dept. civil and environ. engring., 2000-. Recipient fellow award Rensselaer Alumni Assn., 1994. Fellow ASCE (life), AIChE (chmn. environ. engring. div. 1977, Inst. fellow 2000), Am. Chem. Soc. (editl. adv. bd. 1975-77), Am. Water Works Assn. (life), Water Environment Fedn. (life). Office: 2269 Sunrise Way Jamison PA 18929 Office Phone: 215-491-5617. E-mail: jtouhill@alum.mit.edu.

TOULANTIS, MARIE, retail executive; V.p. The Chase Manhattan Bank, New York, NY, 1987-96, sr. v.p., 1996-97; exec. v.p. fin. Barnes & Noble Inc., N.Y.C., 1997-99, CFO barnesandnoble.com Inc., 1999—. Office: Barnesandnoble dot com Inc 76 9th Ave Fl 11 New York NY 10011-5201

TOULMIN, PRIESTLEY, retired geologist; b. Birmingham, Ala., June 5, 1930; s. Priestley and Catharine Augusta (Carey) T.; m. Martha Jane Slason, Aug. 30, 1952; children: Catharine Bosier (Mrs. Robert G. Gibson), Priestley Chewning. AB, Harvard U., 1951, PhD, 1959; MS, U. Colo., 1953. With U.S. Geol. Survey, Washington, 1953-56, 57-89, staff geologist for exptl. geology, 1966, chief br. exptl. geochemistry, 1966-71, geologist geologic div., 1971-89, 1974-89, ret., 1989; also leader inorganic chemistry team NASA (Viking Project). Adj. prof. Columbia U., 1966; research asso. in geochemistry Calif. Inst. Tech., 1976-77; vis. lectr. Am. Geol. Inst.; dir. petrogenesis and mineral resources program NSF, 1985; bd. dirs., treas. 28th Internat. Geol. Congress, 1985-86 Mng. sci. editor Geochemistry Internat., 1965-68; assoc. editor Am. Mineralogist, 1974-76; contbr. articles to profl. jours. Mem. advisory com. spl. edn., Alexandria, Va., 1977-80. Recipient Exceptional Service medal NASA, 1977; Meritorious Service award U.S. Dept. Interior, 1978 Fellow Geol. Soc. Am., Mineral Soc. Am. (bd. assoc. editors 1974-76), Soc. Econ. Geologists; mem. AAAS, Geol. Soc. Washington (2d v.p. 1977, councillor 1973-74, 90-91, 1st v.p. 1981, pres. 1982), Am. Geophys. Union, Soc. Mayflower Descs., S.R., SAR, Soc. Colonial Wars (D.C.), Aztec Club of 1847, St. Andrews Soc. (Washington), Cosmos Club (pres. 1993-94, found. trustee 1994—, chmn. 1996-2001), Sigma Xi, Sigma Gamma Epsilon. Home: 418 Summers Dr Alexandria VA 22301-2449 Office: PO Box 183 Alexandria VA 22313-0183

TOULMIN, STEPHEN EDELSTON, humanities educator; b. London, Mar. 25, 1922; BA in Math. and Physics, King's Coll., Cambridge, Eng., 1942; PhD, King's Coll., 1948; D Tech. (hon.), Royal Inst. Tech., Stockholm, 1991. Lectr. in philosophy of sci. Oxford U., Eng., 1949-55; prof., chmn. dept. of philosophy U. Leeds, Yorkshire, Eng., 1955-59; dir. unit for history of ideas Nuffield Found., London, 1960-65; prof. history of ideas and philosophy Brandeis U., Waltham, Mass., 1965-69; prof. philosophy Mich. State U., East Lansing, 1969-72; prof. humanities U. Calif., Santa Cruz, 1972-73; prof. com. social thought U. Chgo., 1973-86; Avalon prof. humanities Northwestern U., Evanston, Ill., 1986-92, Avalon prof. emeritus, 1992—; prof. U. So. Calif., L.A., 1993-2001, 2001—. Vis. prof. U. Melbourne, Australia, 1954-55, Stanford U., 1959, Columbia U., N.Y.C., 1960, Hebrew U., Jerusalem, 1964, U. South Fla., 1972, Dartmouth Coll., 1979, SUNY, Plattsburgh, 1980, Colo. Coll., 1980, 82, MacMaster U., 1983, Harvard Project Physics Grad. Sch. Edn., Harvard U., 1965; counselor Smithsonian Inst., Washington, 1967-77; cons., staff mem. Nat. Commn. Protection Human Subjects Biomed. Behavioral Rsch., 1975-78; sr. vis. scholar, fellow Inst. Soc. Ethics and Life Scis., Hastings-on-Hudson, N.Y., 1981-2001; regent's lectr. U. Calif. Med. Sch., Davis, 1985; Mary Flexner lectr. Bryn Mawr Coll., 1977; Reyerson lectr. U. Chgo., 1979, John Nuveen lectr., 1980; Tate-Wilson lectr. So. Meth. U., 1980; Or Emet lectr. Osgoode Hall Law Sch., 1981; McDermott lectr. U. Dallas, 1985; lectr. Sigma Xi, 1965-66, Phi Beta Kappa, 1978-79, Phi Beta Kappa-AAAS, 1984, Thomas Jefferson lectr. NEH, Washington, 1997; Tanner lectr. Clare Hall, Cambridge U., 1998; guest prof. social and human scis. Wolfgang Goethe Universitat, Frankfurt, Germany, 1987; vis. fellow Internationales Forschungszentrum Kulturwissenschaften (IFK), Vienna, 1995. Author: The Place of Reason in Ethics, 1949, The Philosophy of Science: an Introduction, 1953, The Uses of Argument, 1958, Foresight and Understanding, 1961, Human Understanding, vol. 1, 1972, Knowing and Acting, 1976, The Return to Cosmology, 1982, Cosmopolis, 1989; (with J. Goodfield) The Fabric of the Heavens, 1961, The Architecture of Matter, 1963, The Discovery of Time, 1965; (with A. Janik) Wittgenstein's Vienna, 1973; (with R. Rieke and A. Janik) An Introduction to Reasoning, 1978; (with A. Jonsen) The Abuse of Casuistry, 1987; (with B. Gustavsen) Beyond Theory, 1996, Return to Reason, 2001; contbr. numerous sci. articles to profl. jours. Recipient Honor Cross 1st class (Austria), 1991; Getty Ctr. for History of Art and Humanities scholar, 1985-86, First Book of the Year prize Am. Soc. Social Philosophy, 1992; Ctr. for Psychosocial Studies fellow, 1974-76. Fellow Am. Acad. Arts and Scis.

TOUMEY, DONALD JOSEPH, lawyer; BA, Williams Coll., 1978; JD, Yale U., 1981. Bar: N.Y. 1982, D.C. 1985, U.S. Supreme Ct. 1986. Law clk. to judge U.S. Ct Appeals (2d cir.), N.Y.C., 1981-82; spl. asst. to gen. counsel U.S. Dept. Treasury, Washington, 1982-85; assoc. Sullivan & Cromwell, N.Y.C., 1985-90; ptnr., 1990—. Republican. Office: Sullivan & Cromwell LLP 125 Broad St New York NY 10004-2489 Office Phone: 212-558-4077.

TOUPIN, HAROLD OVID, retired chemical company executive; b. Hibbing, Minn., Jan. 21, 1927; s. Ovid Pascal and Ellen (Holt) T.; m. Edna F. Sallila, Feb. 8, 1948 (div. Feb. 1973); m. Colleen Beverly Lange, Apr. 18, 1981; children: James, Ronald. BS, U. Minn., 1954, MA, 1955, postgrad, 1968; PhD (hon.), Internat. Acad. Color, Las Vegas, Nev., 1982, U. Mont., 1990. Mgr. Firestone Tire Co., East Los Angeles, Calif., 1948-51; dir. vocat. edn. Hopkins (Minn.) Pub. Schs., 1955-75; with research and devel. Power-o-Peat Co., Gilbert, Minn., 1956-67; chief exec. officer, cons. Color Specialties Inc., Mpls., 1976-98; ret., 1999. Pres., founder travel, meeting planners svc. co., 1990; founder internat. office for color specialties, 1994; bd. dirs. Vu-tek Inc., St. Paul, Airport Auto Sales, St. Paul Color Specialties of Nev., Las Vegas, Instant Air Inc., Mpls., Freedom Fin.; cons. Runs Hot Cons. Svc., 1966-75; ptnr. Vermes Jewelry, Mpls., 1956-80. Contbr. articles to profl. jours. Bd. dirs. Hopkins Jaycees, 1958-60. Served with USAAF, 1944-47. Mem. Am. Assn. Mfrs., Internat. Assn. Color, Nat. Ret. Tchrs. Assn., Am. Assn. Self Employeed, Met. Area Dist. Edn. Instrs. Assn. (pres.), Mpls. C. of C. (Super Bowl com. 1992), Am. Legion, VFW. Lodges: Lions (sec. Hopkins club 1956-76). Democrat. Roman Catholic. Avocations: travel, golf, writing.

TOUPS, BYRON JOSEPH, musician, educator; b. Thibodaux, La., Jan. 24, 1969; s. Alphonse Toups, Jr. and Marlene Mary Toups; children: Madeline Elizabeth, Tristan Joseph. MusB, Univ. Southwestern LA., 1987—93. Cert. tchr. LA. Bd. Ed., 1997. Dir. bands Destrehan H.S., La., 1999—. Mem.: LMEA (assoc.). Avocations: travel, cooking, sports, music. Home: 102 Edna Dr Des Allemands LA 70030 Office: Destrehan High School 1 Wildcat Ln Destrehan LA 70047 Personal E-mail: byrontoups@msn.com.

TOURINO, RALPH GENE, aerospace transportation executive; b. L.A., Mar. 11, 1941; s. John Tourino and Zalia Rose (Perez) Chacon; m. Sherry Lane Tisdail, Sept. 5, 1964; children: Christina Marie, Rebecca Kathleen. BS, UCLA, 1964; MPA, Auburn U., 1973; MBA, U. So. Calif., 1975; postgrad. sr. officials in nat. security, Harvard U., 1988. Commd. 2d lt. USAF, 1964, advanced through grades to maj. gen., 1992; student Undergrad. Navigator Tng., James Connally AFB, Tex., 1964-65; C-97 navigator AF Western Test Range, Vanderberg AFB, Calif., 1965-66; navigator HQ 7th AF Flight Ops., Tan Son Nhut AB, Vietnam, 1966-67; mem. KC135 Crew, March AFB, Calif., 1967-70; sect. comdr. Squadron Officer Sch., Maxwell AFB, Ala., 1970-73; program control Space Div., L.A. AF Sta., 1975-78; dir. program control NAVSTAR Global Positioning System, L.A. AF Sta., 1978-80; dir. contracts Space Def. Systems Program Office, L.A. AF Sta., 1980-82; systems program dir. Inertial Upper Stage Program, L.A. AF Sta., 1982-85; asst. dep. cmdr. for Small ICBM Ballistic Missile Office, Norton AFB, Calif., 1985-87; asst. dep. chief of Staff Systems AF Systems Command, Andrews AFB, Md., 1987-88, insp. gen., 1988-89; comdr. Ballistic Missile Orgn., Norton AFB, 1989-91; program dir. B-2 System Program Office, Wright-Patterson AFB, Ohio, 1991—94; retired as maj. gen. USAF, 1994; v.p., space support systems Lockheed Martin, Santa Maria, Calif. Decorated Legion of Merit, Def. Meritorious Svc. medal, Meritorious Svc. medal, Air medal, Air Force Commendation medal. Mem. Air Force Assn., AIAA. Republican. Avocation: exercising. Office: Lockheed Martin 6801 Rockledge Dr Bethesda MD 20817*

TOURKOW, JOSHUA ISAAC, lawyer; b. Fort Wayne, Ind., Mar. 5, 1947; s. Frederick Rhinehold and Leah Sarah (Schwartz) T.; m. Donna Susan Dubin, Aug. 30, 1970; children— Illana Joy, Lisa Michelle, Benjamin Ahron. Student Bar Ilan U., Israel, 1968; B.S. in Indsl. Mgmt., Purdue U., 1970; J.D., Ind. U.-Indpls., 1973. Bar: Ind. 1973, U.S. Dist. Cts. (no. and so. dists.) Ind. 1973, U.S. Ct. Appeals (7th cir.) 1973. Asst. dep. prosecutor Marion County, Indpls., 1972-73; ptnr. Tourkow, Crell, Rosenblatt & Johnston, Ft. Wayne, 1973— . Bd. dirs. Housing & Neighborhood Devel. Services, Inc., Ft. Wayne, 1980-84, Ft. Wayne Redevel. Com., 1983; atty. Ft. Wayne Housing Authority, 1983—87; advisor, atty. Parents Without Partners, Ft. Wayne, 1981-85, Fathers United for Equal Rights, Ft. Wayne, 1980— . Mem. ABA, Ind. Bar Assn. (chair of family law, 1992-994), Allen County Bar Assn (chair family law sect. 2000-02). Home: 7022 Winchester Rd Fort Wayne IN 46819-1530 Office: Tourkow Crell Rosenblatt & Johnston 814 Anthony Wayne Building Fort Wayne IN 46802

TOURLENTES, THOMAS THEODORE, psychiatrist; b. Chgo., Dec. 7, 1922; s. Theodore A. and Mary (Xenostathy) T.; m. Mona Belle Land, Sept. 9, 1956; children: Theodore W., Stephen C., Elizabeth A. BS, U. Chgo., 1945, MD, 1947. Diplomate Am. Bd. Psychiatry and Neurology (sr. examiner 1964-88, 90). Intern Cook County Hosp., Chgo., 1947-48; resident psychiatry Downey (Ill.) VA Hosp., 1948-51; practice medicine specializing in psychiatry Chgo., 1952, Camp Atterbury, Ind., 1953, Ft. Carson, Colo., 1954, Galesburg, Ill., 1955-71; staff psychiatrist Chgo. VA Clinic, 1952; clin. instr. psychiatry Med. Sch., Northwestern U., 1952; dir. mental hygiene consultation service Camp Atterbury, 1953-54, Ft. Carson, 1953-54; asst. supt. Galesburg State Research Hosp., 1954-58, supt., 1958-71; dir. Comprehensive Community Mental Health Ctr. Rock Island and Mercer Counties; dir. psychiat. services Franciscan Hosp., 1971-85; chief mental health services VA Outpatient Clinic, Peoria, Ill., 1985-88; clin. prof. psychiatry U. Ill., Chgo. and Peoria, 1955—; preceptor in hosp. adminstrn. State U. Iowa, Iowa City, 1958-64. Councilor, del. Ill. Psychiat. Soc.; chmn. liaison com. Am. Hosp. and Psychiat. Assns., 1978-79, chmn. Quality Care Bd., Ill. Dept. Mental Health, 1995-97. Contbr. articles profl. jours. Mem. Gov. Ill. Com. Employment Handicapped, 1962-64; zone dir. Ill. Dept. Mental Health, Peoria, 1964-71; mem. Spl. Survey Joint Commn. Accreditation Hosps.; chmn. Commn. Cert. Psychiat. Adminstrs., 1979-81; pres. Knox-Galesburg Symphony Soc., 1966-68; bd. dirs. Galesburg Civic Music Assn., pres., 1968-70; chair Knox county United Way Campaign, 1989; pres. Civic Art Ctr., 1990-92. Capt. M.C. AUS, 1952-54. Fellow AAAS, AMA, Am. Psychiat. Assn. (chair hosp. and cmty. psychiatry award bd. 1989-90, dist. life fellow, 2002), Am. Coll. Psychiatrists, Am. Coll. Mental Health Adminstrs.; mem. Ill. Med. Soc. (chmn. aging com. 1968-71, coun. on mental health and addictions 1987-89), chair mental health substance abuse com. 1987-89), Ill. Psychiat. Soc. (pres. 1969-70), Am. Pub. Health Assn., Soc. Biol. Psychiatry, Ill. Hosp. Assn. (trustee 1968-70), Am. Coll. Hosp. Adminstrs., Assn. for Rsch. Nervous and Mental, Am. Assn. Psychiat. Adminstrs. (pres. 1980), Ctrl. Neuorpsychiat. Assn. (pres. 1988-89). Home and Office: 138 Valley View Rd Galesburg IL 61401-8524 Office Phone: 309-344-1177. E-mail: tourlentes@gallatinriver.net. *Feeling useful and needed is the greatest recognition and reward.*

TOURLITSAS, JOHN CONSTANTINE, radiologist; b. Cavala, Greece, Oct. 4, 1926; came to U.S., 1956; s. Constantine Nacos and Marica Constantine (Athanasiou) T. MD, U. Athens, Greece, 1955. Diplomate Am. Bd. Radiology. Intern Sioux Valley Hosp., Sioux Falls, S.D., 1956-57; resident Midway Hosp., Mpls.-St. Paul, 1957-59, New Eng. Deaconess Hosp./Harvard U., Boston, 1959-60, Mass. Meml. Hosps./Boston U., 1960-61, Toronto (Ont., Can.) Western Hosp.-U. Toronto, 1961-62; rsch. fellow in radiology Postgrad. Rsch. Inst. Hosp for Sick Children, U. Toronto, 1962; resident Sunnybrook VA Hosp.-U. Toronto, 1963, Royal Victoria Hosp., McGill U., Montreal, 1963-65; attending radiologist, vis. radiologist Maimonides Med. Ctr., Coney Island Hosp., Bklyn., 1966-68; attending, cons. radiologist Bronx (N.Y.)-Lebanon Hosp. Ctr.-Albert Einstein Coll. Med., 1968-95; ret., 1995. Instr. radiology Albert Einstein Coll. Medicine, 1972-77. Joslin Clinic fellow, Boston, 1959-60. Fellow Am. Coll. Chest Physicians; mem. AMA, Am. Coll. Radiology, Am. Roentgen Ray Soc., Radiol. Soc. N.Am., N.Y. State Med. Soc. Avocations: reading, walking, travel. Home: 372 Fifth Ave Apt 8C New York NY 10018-8109

TOURTELLOTTE, CHARLES DEE, internist, rheumatologist, educator; b. Kalamazoo, Aug. 28, 1931; s. Dee and Helen May (Lotz) T.; m. Barbara Richwine, June 25, 1955; children: Daniel DeWitt, Elizabeth Anne, William Charles, Scott David. AB, Johns Hopkins U., 1953; MS in Biochemistry, MD, Temple U., 1957. Diplomate Am. Bd. Internal Medicine. Intern, resident in medicine U. Mich. Hosp., Ann Arbor, 1957-60; fellow in rheumatology Temple U. Hosp., Phila., 1960-61; fellow in biochemistry Rockefeller U., N.Y.C., 1961-63; faculty Sch. Medicine, Temple U., 1963—, prof. medicine, 1972-97, prof. emeritus, 1997—; chief rheumatology Temple U. Hosp., 1994-97, pres. med. staff, bd. govs., 1984-86. Dir. Greater Delaware Valley Arthritis Control Program, 1974-77; pres. Eastern Pa. chpt. Arthritis Found., 1972-74; mem. active/cons. staff 10 area and regional hosps. Contbr. chpts. to textbooks, articles to profl. jours.; mem. editl. bd.: Arthritis and Rheumatism, 1969-77, 19th-24th Rheumatism Revs, 1969-81. Mem. Haddonfield (N.J.) Bd. Edn., 1968-74, pres., 1974; mem. Borough of Haddonfield Environ. Comm., 1975-87, chmn., 1977-85; mem. Haddonfield Civic Assn., 1963—; South N.J. chmn. Johns Hopkins U. Alumni Schs. Com., 1975-90; trustee Bobby Fulton Meml. Fund, 1979—, 1st Presbyn. Ch. of Haddonfield, 1998-2000. With AUS, 1953-61. Helen Hay Whitney Found. fellow, 1962-63; Arthritis Found. fellow, 1963-66 Fellow ACP, Phila. Coll. Physicians, Am. Coll. Rheumatology (founding fellow); mem. Pa. Med. Soc., Phila. County Med. Soc., Babcock Surg. Soc., Phila. Rheumatism Soc. (pres. 1968-69), Pa. Rheumatology Soc. (founding pres. 1985-86), N.J. Soc. of Pa., Nat. Huguenot Soc. (surgeon gen. 2002—), Huguenot Soc. Pa., Temple U. Med. Alumni Assn. (pres. 1997-99), Tavistock County Club (N.J.), Little Egg Harbor Yacht Club, Med. Club of Phila. (bd. dirs., pres. 1998-99), Sixty-five Club of Haddonfield (dir. 2003-), Interfaith Caregivers (trustee 2004-), Sigma Xi, Alpha Omega Alpha, Delta Upsilon, Phi Chi. Presbyterian. Home: 6 Lane Of Acres Haddonfield NJ 08033-3505 Office: Temple Univ Hosp Dept Rheumatology Philadelphia PA 19140-5192 Office Phone: 215-221-2000. Personal E-mail: cd_tourte@prodigy.net.

TOURTELLOTTE, MILLS CHARLTON, mechanical and electrical engineer; b. Great Falls, Mont., Dec. 16, 1922; s. Nathaniel Mills and Frances Victoria (Charlton) T.; m. Dorothy Elsie Gray, Sept. 16, 1947 (dec. 1994); children: Jane Tourtellotte Collins, Kathryn Tourtellotte Bauman, Thomas; m. Linda M. Merritt, July 1, 1995. BS, Ill. Inst. Tech., 1947, MS, 1952. Registered profl. engr., Ill., Mich., Tex. Engr. Automatic Electric Co., Chgo., 1947-49, Inland Steel Co., East chicago, Ind., 1952-56; sr. project engr. Gulf States Tube divsn. Vision Metals, Rosenberg, Tex., 1956—2001; fallout shelter analyst Fed. Emergency mgmt., Washington, 1970—; dealer Amsoil, 1977—; pres. Fabricators, Inc., Rosenberg, Tex. Substitute tchr. Lamar Consol. Ind. Sch. Dist., Rosenberg, 2001—03. Contbr. articles to profl. jours.; patentee mech. and elec. devices. Election judge Ft. Bend County Republican party, 1965; chmn. 4H Adult Leaders Assn., 1968. With USN, 1944-46, WWII. Named Friend of 4H, Ft. Bend County Extension Svc., 1968. Mem. NSPE, ASME (life), Tex. Soc. Profl. Engrs. (edn. chmn. 1969), Fluid Power Soc., Am. Soc. for Engring. Edn. (industry chmn. 1969), Assn. Iron and Steel Engrs. (life), Mich. Soc. Profl. Engrs., Ill. Soc. Profl. Engrs., VFW (life, quartermaster 1984), Am. Legion, Houston Inventors Assn., Handyman Club Am. Office: Fabricators Inc PO Box 242 Rosenberg TX 77471 Office Phone: 281-232-3407.

TOURTELLOTTE, WALLACE WILLIAM, neurologist, educator; b. Great Falls, Mont., Sept. 13, 1924; s. Nathaniel Mills and Frances Victoria (Charlton) T.; m. Jean Esther Toncray, Feb. 14, 1953; children: Wallace William, George Mills, James Millard, Warren Gerard. PhB, BS, U. Chgo., 1945, PhD, 1948, MD, 1951. Intern Strong Meml. Hosp. U. Rochester Sch. Medicine and Dentistry, NY, 1951-52; resident in neurology U. Mich. Med. Ctr., Ann Arbor, 1954-57, asst. prof. neurology, 1957-59, assoc. prof., 1959-66, prof., 1966-71; prof. dept. neurology UCLA, L.A., 1971—, vice chmn. dept. neurology, 1971-98, emeritus vice chmn. dept. neurology, 1998; chief neurology svcs. VA Wadsworth, West Los Angeles, 1971-99, emeritus, 1999—, emeritus dir. tng. program, 1999—, staff neurologist, neuroscientist, 1999—. Vis. assoc. prof. Washington U., St. Louis, 1963-64; hon. mem. med. adv. bd. Nat. Multiple Sclerosis Soc., 1968—, 1994—, So. Calif. Multiple Sclerosis Socs., 1972—; dir. Multiple Sclerosis Rsch. and Treatment Ctr., Human Brain and Spinal Fluid Resource Ctr., 1971—. Co-editor (with Cedric Raines, Henry McFarland): Multiple Sclerosis, Clinical and Pathogenetic Basis, 1997; mem. editorial bd. Jour. Neurol. Sci., Revue Neurologica, Italian Jour. Neurol. Sci., Multiple Sclerosis Jour.; dedicated The Wallace W. Tourtellotte Clin. and Neurosci. Libr., 1999. Lt. (j.g.) M.C., USNR, 1952-54. Recipient Disting. Alumni Service award U. Chgo., 1982. Fellow Am. Acad. Neurology (S. Weir Mitchell Neurology Reseach award 1959); mem. Am. Neurol. Assn. (counselor 1982—, v.p. 1992), World Fedn. Neurology (founding mem.), Am. Assn. Neuropathologists, Internat. Soc. Neurochemsitry (founding mem.), Am. Soc. Pharmacology and Exptl. Therapeutics, Am. Soc. Neurochemistry (founding mem.), Soc. Neurosci., Confrerie de la Chaine des Rotisseur, Argentier du Baillage de Los Angeles (vice chanceller, comdr.), Ordre Mondial des Gourmets Degustateurs Etats-Unis Chevalier, Pasadena Wine and Food Soc., Physician Wine & Food Soc., Sigma Xi. Republican. Presbyterian. Achievements include the 13th most quoted neurologist in world, 1999. Home: 1140 Tellem Dr Pacific Palisades CA 90272-2244 Fax: 310-454-7650. E-mail: wtourtel@ucla.edu.

TOURTET, CHRISTIANE ANDRÉE, writer, human rights activist, photojournalist, reporter; b. Grenoble, France, June 18, 1945; came to U.S., 1965; d. André and Maria Tourtet. Cert. completion humanistic psychology, Fla. Jr. Coll., Jacksonville, 1969, AS with high honors, 1973, AA with high honors, 1974; BA with honors, Jacksonville U., 1975. Hostess interpreter-translator Credit Lyonnais, Grenoble, 1963-65; instr. French Albany (N.Y.) Acad. for Girls, 1965-66; instr. French, asst. lang. lab. Coll. of St. Rose, Albany, 1966-67; instr. French Bartram Sch., Jacksonville, 1970; instr. French and modeling Fla. Jr. Coll., Jacksonville, 1971-74; producer-dir., radio personality ednl. French program Sta. WFAM FM radio, Jacksonville, 1977-79; interpreter, translator French Lang. Bank, Jacksonville, 1980-83. Tutor pvt. and small group classes in French; model for publicity ads, brochures in major mags., newspapers; lectr. in field. Author: Fruits of Life (Silver medal Arts Scis. Letter, Paris, 1977); editor, contbr. New Leaf News, Fla. Flambeau, Back to School Mag.; editor, pub., contbr. Environ. Med. and Disability Corner, Tallahassee Area Ch. News, FSView, AARP Newsletter, Tallahassee Alliance with Disabilities Newsletter; recs. Flamingo Studios, Tallahassee, Fla., 1986-87 (Internat. Woman of Yr., 1991-92, 1996-97, Internat. Woman of Millenium 2000, International Personality of the Year, 2001; exhibited in group shows at North Fla. Fair, Tallahassee, 2002 (1st, 2d, and 3d pl. in photography, 2d pl. 2003); paintings exhibited in France, Monte Carlo and U.S.; photography exhibited in galleries, pub. in mags. including Today's Photographer; guest appearance Phyllis Fouraker Show, Jacksonville, Fla.; actress in over 28 TV commls. Pres. Le Cercle Francais, Albany, 1965. Named Woman of Yr., Romanian Prince Paltin Sturdza, Princess Cornelia Sturdza and Prince Michael Sturdza, 1995; named to Millenium Hall of Fame, Permanent Honor Roll, Internat. Freelance Photographers Orgn., 2004; recipient 1st prize Solfège Artistic Competition, 1957, 1st prize, Accordion Acad. Grenoble, 1958, Bronze medal accordion solo, Cup of France, City of Lyon, 1958, Gold medal Cup of France, 1959, Cup of Europe, 1959, 2d prize in singing, City of Grenoble, 1961, medal of City of Grenoble, 1977, medal of Dauphine County, 1977, medal of Chevalier of Order of Merit, Paris, 1976, medal of Chevalier of French Courtesy, 1977, medal of Nat. Merit, 1976, Silver medal honor, Twentieth Century Achievement award, 1993, U.S. flag flown over Capitol in her honor, Washington, 1999—2001, Internat. Woman of Yr., Romanian Prince Paltin Sturdza, Princess Cornelia Sturdza and Prince Michael Sturdza, 1996—97, Lifetime Distinction of Honor for Photographic Achievement, Am. Image Press, 2004, Meritorious Achievement award. Mem. NAFE, APHA, Am. Acad. Environ. Medicine (assoc.), Environ. Illness Assn. Tallahassee (founder, pres. 1989—), Chem. Injury Info. Network (judge arts and talent

contest 1999), Nat. Ctr. Environ. Strategies, Share, Care, Prayers, H.E.A.L., Am. Med. Writers Assn., Internat. Platform Assn., Nat. Assn. Sci. Writers, Freelance Media Svcs., India Assn. Tallahassee (publicity officer, fashion show judge), Internat. Freelance Photographers Orgn., World Nat. Congress (senator 2003—), Am. Image Press, Phi Theta Kappa. Address: PO Box 20517 Tallahassee FL 32316-0517

TOUSSAINT, ALLEN RICHARD, recording studio executive, composer, pianist; b. New Orleans, Jan. 14, 1938; s. Clarence Matthew and Naomi (Neville) Toussaint; children: Naomi, Clarence, Alison. Student pub. and pvt. schs., New Orleans. Pres. Sea-Saint Rec. Studios, Inc., New Orleans; founder NYNO Music, 1998. Lectr. in field. Pianist for: Shirley & Lee, 1957, U.S. Army Soldiers Choir, 1963—65, recorded albums: Tousan-Wild Sounds of New Orleans, 1958, Life, Love & Faith, 1972, Southern Nights, 1975, Motion, 1978, Connected, 1996, founder, v.p. recorded albums: Sansu Enterprises, Inc., 1965—; composer: (songs) Southern Nights (Country Music Assn. Song of Yr., Broadcast Music, Inc. citation of achievement), The Greatest Love, The Optimism Blues, Viva La Money, Whipped Cream, With You In Mind, Working In A Coal Mine, Yes We Can, Can, All These Things (Broadcast Music, Inc. citation of achievement); performer, dir., choreography: (Broadway plays) The High Rollers Social and Pleasure Club, 1992; performer: New Orleans Jazz Festival, annually. With U.S. Army, 1963—65. Named to, Rock and Roll Hall of Fame, 1998. Mem.: Contemporary Arts Ctr., Am. Fedn. Musicians, Broadcast Music, Inc. Office: NYNO Music Inc 135 W 50th St Fl 8 New York NY 10020-1201

TOUSSIENG, YOLANDA, make-up artist; Television work includes: (movies) Fallen Angel, 1981, 1981, Blue de Ville, 1986, (series) Pee-wee's Playhouse, 1986, (mini-series) North and South, Book II, 1986, films include Blue City, 1986, No Man's Land, 1987, Beetlejuice, 1988, Gross Anatomy, 1989, Three Fugitives, 1989, Farewell to the King, 1989, Edward Scissorhands, 1990, Flatliners, 1990, Everybody Wins, 1990, Hoffa, 1992, Batman Returns, 1992, Mrs. Doubtfire, 1993, Rising Sun, 1993, Ed Wood, 1994 (Acad. award for Best Make-up, 1994), Being Human, 1994, Junior, 1994. Office: IATSE Local 706 11519 Chandler Blvd North Hollywood CA 91601-2618

TOUSTER, SAUL, law educator; b. Bklyn., Oct. 12, 1925; s. Ben and Bertha (Landau) T.; m. Helen Davidson, Nov. 23, 1954 (div. 1967); children: Natasha Ann, Jonathan Bach; m. Irene Tayler, Jan. 14, 1978. AB magna cum laude, Harvard U., 1944, JD, 1948. Bar: N.Y. 1949. Practiced in, N.Y.C., 1949-55; prof. law SUNY-Buffalo, 1955-69, asst. to pres., 1966-68, mem. adj. faculty in medicine, edn., psychology, 1964-69; prof. law and social scis. State Coll. at Old Westbury, 1969-71; prof., provost, acad. v.p. CCNY, 1971-73; acting pres. Richmond Coll. City U. N.Y., 1973-74; prof. law CUNY Grad. Sch. also John Jay Coll. of Criminal Justice, 1974-80; prof., dir. legal studies, humanities, professions programs Brandeis U., Waltham, Mass., 1980-93, prof. emeritus, 1993. Legis. cons. N.Y. State Law Rev. Commn., 1956-61; vis. prof. U. Brussels, summer, 1968, Boston Coll. Law Sch., 1994. Author: Still Lives and Other Lives, 1966, Surrealism and the Art of Samuel Book, in Between Worlds, 2002; editor, author introduction: A Survivors' Haggadah, 1998, Beyond Words: A Holocaust History in Sixteen Woodcuts done in 1945 by Miklos Adler, A Hungarian Survivor, 2001; contbr. articles to legal periodicals. Served to lt. (j.g.) USNR, 1944-46. NEH fellow, 1978; Am. Bar Found. Legal History fellow, 1977-78 Mem. Internat. Inst. Boston (bd. advisors), Phi Beta Kappa. Home: 180 Beacon St Boston MA 02116-1408 E-mail: stouster@mac.com.

TOUTANT, SYLVAIN, retail executive; Pres., CEO Réno-Dépôt/Bldg. Box Inc, Montreal, Canada. Office: Réno Dépôt 1011 Rue du Marche-Central Montreal QC Canada H4N 3J6

TOUTONGHI, MICHAEL, information technology executive; Steel worker; jewelry designer; co-founder Sunny Hill Software, CAD Innovations; dir. software devel. SOTA Tech.; dir. R&D Gibson Rsch. Corp.; from mem. staff to corp. v.p. Microsoft, Redmond, Wash., 1992, corp. v.p. Office: One Microsoft Way Redmond WA 98052-6399

TOVAR, NICHOLAS MARIO, mechanical engineer; b. Ogden, Utah, Jan. 18, 1960; s. Gerdo and Alice (Martinez) T.; m. Suzanne Oxborrow, Sept. 17, 1982; children: Ashley, Nicholas Brock, Clinton Gregory, Lance Edward, Marshall Prescott, Jarrett Stanley, Hathaniel William. BSME in Logistics Engring., Weber State U., 1986; BSME in Mech. Engring. and Mfg., Nat. U., 1990. Logistics contr. Utah-Idaho Supply Co., Salt Lake City, 1985-86; sr. manufacturing engr. Aerojet Propulsion div. GenCorp., Sacramento, 1986-93; sr. quality engr. BP Chems. Adv. Materials Divsn., Stockton, 1993-94; dir. quality engring. Indsl. Testing Internat., Lincoln, 1994-95; quality assurance mgr. Siemens Transp. Systems, Sacramento, 1996-98; v.p. quality assurance Precision Components Group - RPMI, 1998—. Republican. Mem. Lds Ch. Avocations: athletics, wargames, history, music. Home: 11428 Sabalo Way Gold River CA 95670-6207 Office: Precision Comppnent Group - RPMI 4180 Duluth Ave Rocklin CA 95765-1400 E-mail: nmtovar@rocklinprecision.com.

TOVEY, JOSEPH, investment banker; b. Tel Aviv, Nov. 5, 1938; came to U.S., 1940, naturalized, 1947; s. Samuel and Rachel (Weiman) T.; m. Anita Beverly Losice, Feb. 20, 1961; children: David, Debra, Nissan Chaim, Seth Reuven, Shaina Nava. BS summa cum laude, Bklyn. Coll., 1959; MBA, NYU, 1961, PhD, 1969. CPA. Staff acct. Machtiger Green & Co., N.Y.C., 1959—60, Loeb & Troper, N.Y.C., 1960—61; tax rschr. Lybrand, Ross Bros. & Montgomery, 1961—63; planning assoc. Mobil Oil Corp., N.Y.C., 1963—67; asst. v.p. A.G. Becker & Co., N.Y.C., 1967—70; assoc. Roth, Gerard & Co., N.Y.C., 1970—73; v.p. Faulkner, Dawkins & Sullivan, Inc., N.Y.C., 1973—76, Shields Model Roland, Inc., N.Y.C., 1976—77; ptnr. Tovey & Co., N.Y.C., 1977—. Pres. Joint Trading Ltd., 1977-83, Tovey & Co., Inc., 1978-96, Midwood Petroleum Corp., 1980-91, Joint Trading (Del.) Ltd., 1984-96; chmn. Midwood Asset Mgmt. Co., Inc., 1985-96; CEO Terra Link Comm. Corp., 1997-2001; mem. exec. bd. Agudath Israel Am., 1963-67; CEO Hearthside Comm. Ltd. LLC, 1998-2001; adj. assoc. prof. fin. Sy Syms Sch. Bus., 2002—. Author: (with H.C. Smith) Federal Tax Treatment of Bad Debts and Worthless Securities, 1964; assoc. editor Tax Letter, 1961-66; contbr. articles to profl. jours. Mem. Am. Newcomen Soc., NYU Alumni Assn., Bklyn. Coll. Alumni in Fin. Home: 1170 E 19th St Brooklyn NY 11230-4902 Office: PO Box 1524 40 Wall St New York NY 10268-1524

TOVI, MURRAY, futurist, research scientist; b. N.Y.C., Mar. 18, 1937; s. Louis Tovi and Jean Cohen; m. Joan H. Granoff, Oct. 30, 1965; 1 child, Rosanna. BBA, CCNY, 1961. Exec v.p. Tovi and Perkins, Inc., N.Y.C., 1969—73; pres. Murray Tovi Designs, Inc., N.Y.C., 1975—78, Concepts in Art and Sci. Inc., Colorado Springs, 1982—89, Transflectors, Inc., Colorado Springs, 1988—90, Theoretical Optics Inc., Colorado Springs, 1988—90, Tovi Scis., Ocala, Fla., 1991—. Cons. Am. Soc. Interior Designers, N.Y.C., 1985—86. Author: Introduction to Neo-Classical Physics, 2001, The Relative Speed of Light Theory, 2003. Achievements include invention of first discreet surveillance system. Office: Tovi Scis PO Box 116 Sparr FL 32192 Office Phone: 352-671-6600. Business E-Mail: ToviSciences@aol.com.

TOWBIN, A(BRAHAM) ROBERT, investment banker; b. NYC, May 26, 1935; s. Harold Clay and Minna (Berlin) T.; children: Minna Joyce Pinger, Abraham Robert Jr., Zachary Harold. BA, Dartmouth Coll., 1957. With Asiel & Co., N.Y.C., 1958-59; with L.F. Rothschild, Unterberg, Towbin Holdings, Inc. (merged with C.E. Unterberg, Towbin Co. 1977), N.Y.C., 1959-86, vice chmn., 1961-86; mng. dir. Lehman Bros., NY, 1987—94; pres. Russian Am. Enterprise Fund., Moscow and N.Y.C., 1994-95; vice chmn. U.S. Russia Investment Fund, Moscow and N.Y.C., 1995; mng. dir. C.E. Unterberg, Towbin, N.Y.C., 1995—99, co-chmn., 1999—2002; mng. dir. Stephens, Inc. and Stephens Fin. Group, N.Y.C., 2002—. Bd. dirs. Gerber Sci. Inc., Globalcomm Sys. Inc., K&F Industries, Northfork Bancorp. Hon. mem. N.Y. State Coun. Arts., bd. dirs.; trustee N.Y. State Hist. Assn., South St. Seaport. Mem.: Securities Industry Assn., Nat. Golf Links Am., Century Assn., Chelsea Art Club (London), Antigua Yacht Club, N.Y. Yacht Club (trustee 2004—), Stock Exch. Luncheon Club, Bond Club N.Y. Office: Stephens Inc 65 E 55th St New York NY 10022 Office Phone: 212-891-1720. Business E-Mail: rtowbin@stephens.com.

TOWE, THOMAS EDWARD, lawyer; b. Cherokee, Iowa, June 25, 1937; s. Edward and Florence (Tow) T.; m. Ruth James, Aug. 21, 1960; children: James Thomas, Kristofer Edward. Student, U. Paris, 1956; BA, Earlham Coll., 1959; LLB, U. Mont., 1962; LLM, Georgetown U., 1965. Ptnr. Towe, Ball, Enright, Mackey & Sommerfeld, Billings, Mont., 1967—; legislator Mont. House of Rep., Billings, 1971-75, Mont. State Senate, Billings, 1975-87, 91-94. Served on various coms. Mont. Senate, 1975-87, 91-94. Contbr. articles to law revs. Mem. Alternatives, Inc., Halfway House, Billing, 1977-99, pres., 1985-86; mem. adv. com. Mont. Crime Control Bd., 1973-78, Youth Justice Coun., 1981-83; mem. State Dem. Exec. Com., 1969-73; Dem. candidate for Congress, 1976; bd. dirs. Mont. Consumer Affairs Coun., Regl. Cmty. Svcs. for the Devel. Disabled, 1975-77, Rimrock Guidance Found., 1975-80, Vols. of Am., Billings, 1984-89, Youth Dynamics Inc., 1989-96, Zoo Mont., 1985-2001, Inst. for Peace Studies, 1993—, Mont. State Parks Assn., 1993—. Capt. U.S. Army, 1962-65. Named as one of 100 Most Influential Montanans in 20th Century, Missoulian newspaper. Mem. Mont. Bar Assn., Yellowstone County Bar Assn., Billings C. of C. Mem. Soc. Of Friends. Avocation: outdoor recreation. Home: 2739 S Gregory Dr Billings MT 59102-0509 Office: Towe Ball Enright Et Al 2525 6th Ave N Billings MT 59101-1358 Office Phone: 406-248-7337. E-mail: t.towe@bresnan.net.

TOWERS, JOHN R. manufacturing executive, lawyer; b. N.Y.C., 1941; AB in Econs., Princeton U., 1963; LLB, U. Va., Richmond, 1966. V.p. client adminstrn. State Street Bank, Boston, 1969-81; v.p. product devel. Fidelity Investments, Boston, 1981-89; sr. v.p. mutual funds U.S. Trust Co. of N.Y., 1989-90; sr. v.p. securities Bank of Boston, 1990-94; sr. v.p. State St. Bank & Trust, Boston, 1994-97; exec. v.p., gen. counsel State St. Boston Corp., Boston, 1997-2000, vice chmn., chief adminstrv. officer, 2000—. Mem. ABA, Boston Bar Assn., N.Y. State Bar Assn., Mass. Bar Assn., Am. Soc. Corp. Secs. Office: State Street Corp 225 Franklin St Boston MA 02110-2804

TOWERS, KENNETH DALE, journalism educator; b. Chgo., July 4, 1935; s. Albert M. and Irene D. Towers; m. Rita Kennedy, Feb. 28, 1959 (dec. Nov. 1993); m. Susan J. Culliton, May 13, 2000. B of Philosophy, Northwestern U., 1960. Editor, mng. editor, city editor, reporter Chgo. Sun-Times, 1955-90; exec. dir. Ill. Ins. Info. Svc., Chgo., 1990-92; journalism prof. Northwestern U., Evanston, Ill., 1994—. Staff sgt. U.S. Army, 1957-63. Mem. Soc. Profl. Journalists (regional dir. 1980), Chgo. Coun. Fgn. Rels., Internat. Press Club, Chgo. Press Club (pres. 1976), Chgo. Headline Club (pres. 1972). Roman Catholic. Avocations: reading, writing, spectator sports. Home: 444 W Oakdale Chicago IL 60657 E-mail: k.towers@attbi.com.

TOWERY, CURTIS KENT, lawyer; b. Hugoton, Kans., Jan. 29, 1954; s. Clyde D. and Jo June (Curtis) Towery. BA, Trinity U., 1976; JD, U. Okla., 1979; LLM in Taxation, Boston U., 1989. Mem. Curtis & Blanton, Pauls Valley, Okla., 1980-81; lawyer land and legal dept. Trigg Drilling Co., Oklahoma City, 1981-82; adminstrv. law judge Okla. Corp. Commn., Oklahoma City, 1982-85; counsel Curtis & Blanton, Pauls Valley, Okla., 1985-88; adminstrv. law judge Okla. Dept. Mines, Oklahoma City, 1985-88, assoc. gen. counsel, 1989-92; contracts and purchasing adminstr., atty. Okla. Turnpike Authority, Oklahoma City, 1992-93; asst. gen. counsel Okla. Corp. Commn., 1993-97; spl. judge City of Oklahoma City, 1997—2000; adminstrv. law judge Okla. Dept. of Labor, 1998, 2002—04; v.p., trust officer Bank One Trust, Oklahoma City, 1998-2000; mgr. Cherokee Capital Holdings, 2000—. Sr. adminstrv. law judge Okla. Corp. Commn., 2003—04; dept. special trustee Office of Special Trustee, dept. interior, 2004. Assoc. bd. Okla. Mus. Art, 1985—88, Okla. Symphony Orch., 1987—92, Ballet Okla., 1987—92, sec., 1990—91, v.p., 1988—89. Mem.: ABA, Okla. Bar Assn., Tex. Bar Assn., Faculty Ho., Elks, Rotary, Sigma Nu, Phi Alpha Delta. Democrat. Presbyterian. Avocations: flying, golf, travel, investment analysis. Home: 11300 N Pennsylvania Ave Oklahoma City OK 73120 also: 4160 E 47th St Tulsa OK 74135 Office: PO Box 440 Pawnee OK 74058

TOWERY, JAMES E. lawyer; b. Los Alamos, N.Mex., July 12, 1948; s. Lawson E. and Irma (Von Apeldorn) T.; m. Kathryn K. Meier, July 20, 1991; 1 child, Mark J. BA, Princeton U., 1973; JD, Emory U., 1976. Assoc. Morgan Beauzay Hammer, San Jose, Calif., 1977-79; ptnr. Morgan & Towery, San Jose, Calif., 1979-89; assoc. Hoge Fenton Jones & Appel, San Jose, Calif., 1989-90, ptnr., 1990—. Chmn. bd. trustees Alexian Bros. Hosp., San Jose, Calif., 1995-98. Mem. ABA (ho. of dels. 1989-98, standing com. client protection 1996—, chair 1998-00), State Bar Calif. (v.p. and chair discipline com. 1994-95, pres. 1995-96, bd. govs. 1992-96, pres. 1995-96, presiding arbitrator, fee arbitration program 1990-92), Santa Clara County Bar Assn. (counsel 1984-85, treas. 1987, pres. 1989). Office: Hoge Fenton Jones 60 S Market St San Jose CA 95113-2351

TOWEY, AUGUSTINE DENIS, theater educator, theater director; b. Hempstead, N.Y., June 30, 1937; s. Patrick Joseph and Ann Marie Towey. BA, St. Johns U., 1958; MA, St. John's U., 1960; diploma, U. Birmingham, 1960; PhD, NYU, 1973. Instr. St. John's U., Jamaica, NY, 1960—61; prof. theatre studies Niagara U., Niagara Falls, NY, 1964—. Assoc. artistic dir. Artpark, Lewiston, NY, 1975—2004; dir. Irish Classical Theatre, Buffalo, 1993—99. Author: (book) Waiting for Snow in Lewiston, 1990, The Things of Man, 1991, Silences, 1996, Later Enchantments, 2000, (tv drama) The Guardian. Recipient Citizen of the Yr. award, Buffalo Evening News, 1991, Career Achievement award, Artvoice, 1997, Arts award, Nat. Conf. Cmty. Justice, 2004. Mem.: Dramatists' Guild, Soc. of Stage Dirs./Choreographers. Roman Catholic. Office: Niagara Univ 555 Lewiston Rd Niagara Falls NY 14109 Office Phone: 716 286 8481. Business E-Mail: atowey@niagara.edu.

TOWEY, CARROLL FRANCIS, senior education specialist; b. Boston, Jan. 30, 1932; s. Thomas Patrick and Marietta V. (Alcock) T.; m. Marie Elizabeth Linehan, Aug 24, 1957 (dec. Apr., 1992); children Mary Ellen Roth, Michael Carroll, Kevin James; m. Miriam A. Quinlan, Sept. 4, 1993. BS in Edn., Salem State Coll., 1953; MEd, Boston U., 1957, cert. advanced grad. study (adult edn.), 1967; EdD, U. Mass., 1973. Sr. supr. Mass. Dept. Edn., Boston, 1965-67; sr. program advisor U.S. Dept. Edn., Washington, 1967—. Mem. Met. Wash. Assn. for Adult and Continuing Edn., Washington, 1981-85, pres. 1983-84; author: reports to U.S. Dept. Edn. on model programs, evaluation of adult education, and compliance by states to federal regulations; bd. dirs. Northern Va. Chpt. Retired Officers Assn., 1997. Mem. Mass. Soc. Washington, D.C., 1982—, v.p. 1993-95, pres. 1995-96, treas., 1996-97. With U.S. Army, 1955-57, Korea. Recipient Appreciation certs. Nat. Defense U., 1990, Nev. Dept. Edn., 1991, Pima County, Ariz., 1992. Mem. Fed. Vocat. Edn. Assn. (pres. 1993-94), Am. Assn. Adult and Continuing Edn. (founding mem., pres. Met. Washington 1983-84, Appreciation cert. 1988), Ret. Officers Assn. (bd. dirs. Nova Troa 1997, 2d v.p. 1998-99, 1st v.p. 2000), Phi Delta Kappa Boston U. Democrat. Roman Catholic. Avocations: gardening, reading, financial management, sports. Home: 1016 S Wayne St Apt 309 Arlington VA 22204-4435 Office: US Dept Edn 400 Maryland Ave SW # Wdc Washington DC 20202-0001

TOWLE, ALEXIS CHARLES (LEX TOWLE), education advocate; b. Newburyport, Mass., Mar. 23, 1946; s. Sidney Norwood and Nancy Lois (Roberts) Towle; m. Maryellen Foote, Oct. 19, 1991; children: Ian, Devon. BA, Oundle Coll., Northants, Eng., 1964, Yale U., 1968. V.p., trust officer Nat. Shawmut Bank, Boston, 1973-78; v.p., fin. cons. Merrill Lynch & Co., Boston, 1979-82, Kidder, Peabody & Co., Boston, 1983-88; v.p., investment banker Boston Bay Capital, Inc., Boston, 1988-93; dir. devel., campaign Boston Renaissance Charter Sch., 1994-95; pres. Appletree Inst. Edn. Innovation, Washington, D.C., 1995—. Treas., trustee Stoneridge Montessori Sch., Beverly Mass., 1994-2003; co-founder, trustee Cesar Chavez Charter Sch., Washington, 1998-99, Washington Math Sci. Charter Sch., 1998-2001, Paul Jr. High Charter Sch., Washington, 1999-2001, Apple Early Literacy Presch., Washington, 2001. Author (with others) amendments to D.C. School Reform Act of 1995. Lt USMC, 1968—71, Vietnam. Mem.: Nat. Soc. Fundraising Execs. (edn. com.). Republican. Episcopalian. Avocations: skiing, ice hockey, gardening. Home: 21 Fellows Rd Ipswich MA 01938-2710 Office: Apple Tree Inst Edn Innovation 907 Sixth St SW Ste 615 Washington DC 20024 Fax: 202 488 3991. Personal E-mail: lextowle@aol.com.

TOWLE, LELAND HILL, retired government official; b. Boston, Mar. 29, 1931; s. Leland and Bertha Mary (Hill) T.; m. Carol Peterson, June 5, 1953; children— Peter Kimball, Gretchen Towle Maynard, Michele. BS, U. N.H., 1952; MS, M.I.T., 1953; Cert. in Bus. and Mgmt, U. Calif., Berkeley, 1962. Nuclear chemist Stanford Research Inst., Menlo Park, Calif., 1956-59, community systems economist, economist, nuclear economist, 1959-68, mgr. health scis. research, 1968-74; asst. dir. Nat. Center for Alcohol Edn., Arlington, Va., 1974-75. Cons. Medicine in the Pub. Interest, Washington, 1975, Internat. Ctr. for Alcohol Policies, 1995-98—; vis. scientist Nat. Inst. on Alcohol Abuse and Alcoholism, Rckville, Md., 1975-76, dep. dir. office of program devel. and analysis, 1976-77, assoc. dir. office of program devel. and analysis, 1977-81, dir. internat. and intergovtl. affairs, 1981-95; dir. LHT Assocs., Inc., 1995-98. Contbr. articles to profl. jours. Bd. dirs. Med. Resources Found., Palo Alto, Calif., 1972-73. Served with USAF, 1952-56. Mem. Am. Pub. Health Assn., Sci. Research Soc. Am., Am. Nuclear Soc., Am. Chem. Soc., Sigma Xi, Phi Kappa Phi. Home: PO Box 516 Burgess VA 22432

TOWLE, LEX See TOWLE, ALEXIS

TOWLEN, TRACEY, physical therapist; BS magna cum laude, Quinnipiac Coll., 1999; M in Phys. Therapy, Quinnipiac U., 2001. Student phys. therapist Nova Care Sports Rehab., 1998, JFK-Johnson Rehab. Inst., Edison, NJ, 1999, San Diego Children's Hosp., 2000; phys. therapist Monmouth Med. Ctr., 2001—04, Robert Freidman Phys. Therapy, Englishtown, NJ, 2002, The Rehab. Hosp., Tinton Falls, NJ, 2004—; owner, founder Hope For Life, 2004—. Mem.: Spl. Athletics (buddy 1998—99), Quinnipiac Phys. Therapy Club, Am. Phys. Therapy Assn. (sec. mem. Orthop. and Women's Health), Nat. Lymphedema Network, Quinnipiac Dance Co. (costume coord. 1998, pres. 1999). Business E-Mail: Tracey@Hopeforlifeclinic.com.

TOWLER, EVELYN WHEELER, elementary school educator; b. Northport, Mich., June 29, 1924; d. Lennis H. and Caroline Greiner Wheeler; m. Charles F. Towler (dec.); children: Jacquetta Sue, Charles F. Towler Jr. BA in History, BA in English Bible, Bob Jones U., Greenville, S.C., 1949; postgrad., U. Fla., 1950—54, Fla. So. Coll., Lakeland, 1966—67, U. S. Fla., 1968, Rollins Coll., Winter Park, Fla., 1970, Fla. Technol. U., 1970—75. Cert. elem. tchr., media specialist Fla. Kindergarten tchr., LaBelle, Fla., 1943—44; primary grades tchr. Spring Lake (Fla.) Elem. Sch., 1950—52; youth dir. Presbyn. Ch., Lakeland, Fla., 1952—54; tchg. prin., co-founder Lakeland Christian Sch., 1954—63; asst. to dean of edn. Fla. So. Coll., Lakeland, 1964—67; tchr., lang. arts coord., media specialist Longwood Elem. Sch., Fla., 1967—85; media specialist, libr. Keswick Christian Sch., St. Petersburg, Fla., 1985—91. Writer Lifepacs Alpha-Omega Pubs., Tempe, Ariz., 1977. Author: (novels) Under Sheltering Wings, 2001, The Road to Home, 2003, Teach Your Child to Write Creatively, 1985, Chronicles of a Hometown Church, 1993, Visitors Guide to Delightful Dunedin, 1993. Vol. Dunedin Hist. Mus.; mem. Dunedin Hist. Soc., Dunedin Friends of the Libr.; camp counselor Children's Bible Mission; bd. dirs. Dunedine Hist. Soc. Named one of Leaders of Am. Elem. Edn., 1971, Outstanding Elem. Tchrs. of Am., 1973; recipient History-Maker award, Dunedin Hist. Soc., 2000. Republican. Methodist. Avocation: genealogy.

TOWLES, DONALD BLACKBURN, retired publishing executive; b. Lawrenceburg, Ky., Sept. 10, 1927; s. Joseph Sterling and Marjorie (Blackburn) Towles; m. Geraldine Gooch, Dec. 20, 1947 (dec. Nov. 1980); children: Sally Blackburn Towles Clark, Rebecca Neale Towles Brown; m. Julia Mason, Dec. 3, 1981. AB in Journalism, U. Ky., 1948. Asst. dir. publicity, editor In Ky. Mag. Commonwealth of Ky., Frankfort, 1948—55; pub. svc. mgr. Courier-Jour. and Louisville Times Co., Louisville, 1956—66, dir. pub. svc. and promotion, 1966—71, v.p., 1974—92, v.p., dir. circulation, 1971—76, v.p., dir. pub. affairs, 1976—92; ret., 1993. Author: (book) The Press of Kentucky 1787-1994; editor: Newspaper Promotion Handbook, 1983. Chmn. Louisville area chpt. ARC, 1987—89; mem. adv. bd. Salvation Army, 1982—97; elder emeritus Discple of Christ; chmn. program adv. com. Louisville Devel. Program, 1971—80; bd. dirs. Louisville Med. Ctr., 1982—97; pres. Heritage Corp. Louisville, 1982—85; chmn. Thos. D. Clark Found., 2000—04; adv. bd. Christian Ch. Homes Ky., 1992—96; chmn. Sr. Citizens East, 1996—97. With U.S. Army, 1952—54, Korea. Named Outstanding Chpt. Vol., Louisville area ARC, 1993, Outstanding State Vol., 1994; named to Ky. Journalism Hall of Fame, 1992; recipient Cmty. Svc. award, Louisville Devel. Com., 1980. Mem.: Soc. Profl. Journalists (pres.Louisville chpt. 1991—92), Ky. Press Assn. (pres. 1982, Pres.'s Cup Leadership 1982, Disting. Svc. award 1987), Internat. Newspaper Promotion Area (pres. 1980—82, Silver Shovel 1983), Journalism Alumni Assn. U. Ky. (pres. 1979—94, Outstanding Alumnus award 1976, All-Am. Alumni award 1994). Democrat. Home: 3536 Norbourne Blvd Louisville KY 40207-3753

TOWLES, STOKLEY PORTER, commercial and investment banking executive; b. St. Louis, Dec. 12, 1935; s. Harold Robert Towles and Margaret (Salmon) Derrick; m. Eleanor Hollingsworth, June 19, 1960 (div. 1983); children: Stokley Porter, Amor Hollingsworth, Holly Kimbrough; m. Jeanne Glass, Dec. 28, 1983. AB, Princeton U., 1957; MBA, Harvard U., 1960. With Brown Bros. Harriman & Co., Boston, 1960—, asst. mgr., 1964-67, dep. mgr., 1967-69, mgr., 1969-78, ptnr., 1978—. Bd. dirs. Groveland Mutual Ins. Co., Auto-HomePage Ins. Agy., Dorchester Mut. Ins., Dedham, Brown Bros. Harriman S.A., Luxembourg, Brown Bros. Harriman Trustee Svcs. (Ireland) Ltd., Dublin, Norfolk & Dedham Mut. Fire Ins. Co., Assn. of Global Custodians; corporator Dedham Instn. for Savs.; mem. Dean's Com. Internat. Devel. John F. Kennedy Sch. Govt. Harvard U. Overseer Boys and Girls Clubs, Boston, 1965, Vincent Meml. Hosp., Boston, 1978, Noble and Greenough Sch., Dedham, 1985; treas., trustee St. Philip's Ch.; trustee Sears Found., Com. for Econ. Devel., Mus. Fine Arts, Boston; bd. visitors Mary Inst. and St. Louis Country Day Sch. Mem. Somerset Club, The Country Club (gov. 1967-73), Kittansett Club, Birnam Wood Golf Club, Phi Beta Kappa. Avocations: tennis, golf, jogging, reading. Office: Brown Bros Harriman & Co 40 Water St Boston MA 02109-3661

TOWNE, EDGAR ARTHUR, theologian, educator; b. Albany, NY, Feb. 27, 1928; s. Arthur Bethuel and Margaret (Shug) T.; m. Sara Jean Wright, June 14, 1952 (div. 1961); children: Mary Michal, Jonathan Wright, Nathan Arthur; m. Marian Kleinsasser, Dec. 18, 1961; 1 child, Stephen Edgar. BA, Coll. Wooster, 1949; BD, Pitts. Theol. Sem., 1952; MA, U. Chgo., 1962, PhD, 1967. Ordained to ministry Presbyn. Ch. (USA), 1952. Assoc. prof. systematic theology Winebrenner Theol. Sem., Findlay, Ohio, 1962-67; prof. philosophy and religion Findlay Coll., 1967-70; min. Hyde Park Union Ch., Chgo., 1971-75; prof. theology Christian Theol. Sem., Indpls., 1975-93, prof. theology emeritus, 1993—. Vis. prof. theology Christian Theol. Sem., Indpls., 1970-71; vis. scholar Grad. Theol. Union, Berkeley, Calif., 1981-82, Pitts. Theol. Sem., 1988-89; co-moderator com. on pub. ministry Synod of Lincoln Trails, Ind., Ill., 1986-88. Author: Two Types of New Theism: Knowledge of God in the Thought of Paul Tillich and Charles Hartshorne, 1997. Mem. ethics com. Meth. Hosp. Ind., Indpls., 1985-90 Mem. Am. Theol. Soc. (pres. Midwest divsn. 1986-87, 2003-04), Am. Acad. Religion, Ctr. Process Studies, Soc. Christian Ethics, Highlands Inst. for Am. Religious and Philos. Thought. Independent. Home: 5129 N Illinois St Indianapolis IN 46208-2613

TOWNE, JONATHAN BAKER, vascular surgeon; b. Youngstown, Ohio, Jan. 10, 1942; m. Sandra Green Towne, Aug. 24, 1963; children: Timothy, Heidi, Crista. BS, U. Pitts., 1963; MD, U. Rochester, N.Y., 1967. Intern in surgery U. Mich., Ann Arbor, 1967-68, resident I, 1968-69; resident II, III, IV U. Nebr., Omaha, 1969-72; chief gen. surgery USAF Hosp., Vandenberg AFB, Calif., 1972-74; asst. prof. surgery Med. Coll. Wis., Milw., 1975-79, assoc. prof., 1979-84, prof., 1984—, chair vascular surgery, 1984—. Editor: (book) Complications Vascular Surgery, 1980, Complications Vascular Surgery, II,

1985, Complications Vascular Surgery, III, 1991. Mem.: Wis. Surg. Soc. (pres. 1991—92), Assn. Program Dirs. Vascular Surgery (pres. 1997—98), Ctrl. Surg. Assn. (recorder 1992—97, pres.-elect 2001), Soc. Vascular Surgery (sec. 1994—98, pres.-elect 1999, pres. 2000). Avocation: photography. Office: Med Coll Wis 9200 W Wisconsin Ave Milwaukee WI 53226-3522 Office Phone: 414-456-6970. E-mail: jtowne@mcw.edu.

TOWNE, RUTH H. state legislator; b. Manchester, Conn., June 17, 1928; m. Roderick E. Towne (dec.); 2 children. BS, U. Conn., 1949. Dairy farmer, Berlin, Vt.; rep. Dist. 5 State of Vt., 1977—. Breeder Morgan horses; mem. U-32 H.S. Bd. Dirs., chairwoman; treas. Washington Ctrl. Supervisory Union; consumer mem. Bd. Vet. Registration and Exam.; mem. Vt. Ext. Svc., 1949-52; rep. dist. 4-2 Barre City Berlin. Named Woman of Yr. Vt. Farm. Bur., 1989. Mem. DAR Marquis de Lafayette chpt., Vt. Farm Bur., Washington County 4-H Club (agt.), Berlin Hist. Soc. (v.p. 1985-2000). Home: Box 4285 523 Three Mile Bridge Rd Berlin VT 05602-9288 Office: Vt House of Reps Office Of House Mems Montpelier VT 05602

TOWNES, BOBBY JOE, travel agency executive; b. Pickens, S.C., Aug. 29, 1932; s. James Harold and Coda Lenora (Nations) T.; m. Addie Elise Ray, May 2, 1956; children: John William, Robert Scott. Assoc. BA, Mars Hill (N.C.) Jr. Coll., 1952; BA, Furman U., Greenville, S.C., 1955; diploma, Grad. Sch. Banking, Rutgers U., 1969. V.p. Peoples Nat. Bank, Greenville, 1954-73; exec. v.p. Community Bank, Greenville, 1973-76; pres. Piedmont Travel, Inc., Greenville, 1976-93, chmn., 1993—; mng. ptnr. Long Beach Properties, 1992—, Pawleys Promise, Pawleys Island, S.C., 1998—. Chmn. Greenville World of Travel, 1976-80; pres. Piedco Assocs., Greenville, 1973—; mng. ptnr. Cutter Joint Ventures, Hilton Head, S.C., 1972—; pres. Piedco II, 1992—; chmn. Boutique Ltd., 1971-75; mng. ptnr. Townes Properties, Greenville, 2002, Townes Family Partnership, 2002; instr. Am. Inst. Banking, 1964-70, Charter Life Underwriters, Greenville, 1968; mem. adv. com. KLM Dutch Airlines, Atlanta, 1982, System One Automation, Miami, Fla., 1980, Eastern Airlines, Miami, 1983-87; mem. adv. bd. Mars Plus Data Systems, Miami, 1976-79; bd. dir., Townes Family Charitable Trust Author: Independent Bank Survival, 1968, Townes and Allied Families, 1995. Chmn. United Way, Greenville, 1973; v.p. ARC, Greenville, 1970, Cancer Soc., Greenville, 1966; v.p. Furman U. Alumni Bd., Greenville, 1968-70, Furman U. Paladin Bd., Greenville, 1972-74; mem. Furman U. Com. for Self Study, Greenville, 1976; com. Gov.'s Econ. Coun., Columbia, SC, 1972; v.p., mem. founders com. Cmty. Concerts, Greenville, 1976; pres. YMCA Youth Guides, Greenville, 1970; v.p., organizer Centurian Club, 1978; mem. nat. alumni bd. Mars Hill Coll., 1998; Presidents Bd. of Advisors, Mars Hill Coll., 2003; mng. ptnr. Townes Family Charity Trust, 2001; bd., Greenville Little Theatre, 2003. Recipient Sertoma Internat. Disting. Club Pres. award, 1967, Outstanding Young Mem. of Am. award, 1968, Finalist Ernst & Young Entrepreueur of Yr., 2000. Mem. Am. Inst. Banking (pres. 1964, bd. dirs. 1966), Young Bankers S.C. (bd. dirs. 1965), S.C. Bankers Assn. (bd. dirs. 1969), Greenville Wine Soc. (pres., organzer 1968, 72), S.C. Hist. Soc., Greenville County Hist. Soc., Poinsett Club, Commerce Club, Colonial Club (v.p. 1989, pres. 1991), Sertoma (v.p. 1982, pres. 1968, Gold Honor club 1967), Exec. Sertoma Club (v.p. 1982). Republican. Episcopalian. Avocation: genealogy. Home: 14 Selwyn Dr Greenville SC 29615-1727 E-mail: btownes@bellsouth.net.

TOWNES, CHARLES HARD, physics educator; b. Greenville, S.C., July 28, 1915; s. Henry Keith and Ellen Sumter (Hard) Townes; m. Frances H. Brown, May 4, 1941; children: Linda Lewis, Ellen Screven, Carla Keith, Holly Robinson. BA, BS, Furman U., 1935; MA, Duke U., 1937; PhD, Calif. Inst. Tech., 1939. Mem. tech. staff Bell Telephone Lab., 1939—47; assoc. prof. physics Columbia U., 1948—50, prof. physics, 1950—61; exec. dir. Columbia Radiation Lab., 1950—52, chmn. physics dept., 1952—55; provost and prof. physics MIT, 1961—66, Inst. prof., 1966—67; v.p., dir. rsch. Inst. Def. Analyses, Washington, 1959—61; prof. physics U. Calif., Berkeley, 1967—86, 1994, prof. physics emeritus, 1986—94, prof. grad. sch., 1994—. Guggenheim fellow, 1955—56; Fulbright lectr. U. Paris, 1955—56, U. Tokyo, 1956; dir. Enrico Fermi Internat. Sch. Physics, 1963; Richtmeyer lectr. Am. Phys. Soc., 1959; Scott lectr. U. Cambridge, 1963; Centennial lectr. U. Toronto, 1967; Lincoln lectr., 1972—73; Halley lectr., 1976; Krishnan lectr., 92; Nishina lectr., 92; Weinberg lectr. Oak Ridge (Tenn.) Nat. Lab., 1997; Rajiv Gandhi lectr., 97; Henry Norris Russell lectr. Am. Astron. Soc., 1998; dir. Gen. Motors Corp., 1973—86; dir. Perkin-Elmer Corp., 1966—69; mem. Pres.'s Sci. Adv. Com., 1966—69, vice chmn., 1967—69; chmn. sci. and tech. adv. com. for manned space flight NASA, 1964—70; mem. Pres.'s Com. on Sci. and Tech., 1976; rschr. on nuc. and molecular structure, quantum electronics, interstellar molecules, radio and infrared astrophysics. Author (with A.J. Schawlow): Microwave Spectroscopy; author: Making Waves, 1996, How the Laser Happened. Adventures of a Scientist, 1999; author, co-editor Quantum Electronics, 1960, Quantum Electronics and Coherent Light, 1964, editl. bd. Rev. Sci. Instruments, 1950—52, Phys. Rev., 1951—53, Jour. Molecular Spectroscopy, 1957—60, Procs. NAS, 1978—84, Can. Jour. Physics, 1995—, contbr. articles to sci. publs., patentee masers and lasers. Mem. corp. Woods Hole Oceanographic Instn.; bd. mem. Calif. Inst. Tech., Carnegie Instn. Washington, Ctr. for Theology and Natural Scis., Mount Wilson Inst. Decorated officier Légion d'Honneur (France); named to Nat. Inventors Hall of Fame, 1976, Engring. and Sci. Hall of Fame, 1983; recipient numerous hon. degrees and awards including Nobel prize for Physics, 1964, Stuart Ballantine medal, Franklin Inst., 1962, Thomas Young medal and prize, Inst. Physics and Phys. Soc., Eng., 1963, Disting. Pub. Svc. medal, NASA, 1969, Wilhelm Exner award, Austria, 1970, Niels Bohr Internat. Gold medal, 1979, Nat. medal of Sci., 1982, Berkeley citation, U. Calif., 1986, Common Wealth award, 1993, ADION medal, Obs. Nice, 1995, Mendel award, Villanova U., Frank Annunzio award, Christopher Columbus Fellowship Found., 1999, Rabindranath Tagore Birth Centenary plaque, Asiatic Soc., 1999, Karl Schwarzschild medal, Astronomische Gesellschaft, 2002, Drake award, SETI Inst., 2003. Fellow: IEEE (life medal of honor 1967), Calif. Acad. Scis., Indian Nat. Sci. Acad., Optical Soc. Am. (Mees medal 1968), Am. Phys. Soc. (pres. 1967, Plyler prize 1977, Frederick Ives medal 1996); mem.: NAE (founders award 2000), NAS (coun. 1968—72, 1978—81, chmn. space sci. bd. 1970—73, Comstock award 1959, Carty medal 1962), N.Y. Acad. Scis., Max-Planck Inst. Physics and Astrophysics (fgn. mem.), Pontifical Acad. Scis., Russian Acad. Scis. (Lomonosov medal 2000, fgn. mem.), Royal Soc. (fgn. mem.), Am. Acad. Arts and Scis., Am. Astron. Soc., Am. Philos. Soc. Office: U Calif Dept Physics 366 Leconte # 7200 Berkeley CA 94720-0001 Office Phone: 510-642-1128. Business E-mail: cht@ssl.berkeley.edu.

TOWNES, PHILIP LEONARD, pediatrician, educator; b. Salem, Mass., Feb. 18, 1927; s. Saul and Lillian (Kravetsky) T.; m. Marjorie Joan Greenstone, Aug. 27, 1956; children: Elizabeth Ann, Susan Jane, David Andrew. AB, Harvard, 1948; PhD, U. Rochester, 1952, MD, 1959. Diplomate: Am. Bd. Pediatrics, Am. Bd. Med. Genetics. Intern Strong Meml. Hosp., Rochester, 1959-60, asst. resident, 1963, chief resident pediatrics, 1965; mem. faculty U. Rochester Sch. Medicine, 1952-79, prof. pediatrics, 1969-79; prof. anatomy (genetics), chmn. div. genetics, dir. Genetic Clinic, 1966-79; prof. pediatrics U. Mass. Sch. Medicine, 1979-95, dir. Genetic Clinic, 1979-95, dir. Cytogenetics Lab., 1981-95, prof. pediatrics/ob-gyn. emeritus, 1995—; pediatrician Strong Meml. Hosp. Cons. attending Newark State Hosp., Genesee Hosp.; hon. research asst. Univ. Coll., London, Eng., 1965-66; mem. adv. com. for genetics services Mass. Dept. Pub. Health, 1979-84, chmn. com., 1982-83; mem. steering com. New Eng. Regional Genetics Group, 1981-82. Contbr. articles to med. jours. Mem. com. qualifications cytogenetics N.Y. State Dept. Health, 1968-74; bd. dirs. Monroe County chpt. Nat. Found., 1965-79, chmn. med. adv. com., 1967-79, hon. bd. dirs., 1979—, also cons.; trustee Seven Hills Found., 1996—. USPHS predoctoral fellow, 1951-52; sr. research fellow, 1960-61; research career devel. award, 1961-66 Mem. Am. Acad. Pediatrics, Am. Assn. Anatomists, Soc. Pediatric Research, Am. Soc. Human Genetics, Am. Pediatric Soc., Teratology Soc., Sigma Xi, Alpha Omega Alpha. Home: 14 Spring Valley Rd Worcester MA 01609-1151

TOWNLEY, JOHN JOE, music educator, writer, musician; b. Tampa, Fla., Apr. 22, 1951; s. John Joseph Townley and Lucille Marie Campanella; m. Shirley He, Oct. 22, 1999. MA in Humanities, Calif. State U., 1988. Webmaster www.JoeTownley.com, L.A., 2000—. Author: (novels) The Apocalypse Project, 2000, On Ghost Trails, 2002; musician (concert pianist): Joe Townley Plays Chopin & Rachmaninoff. Mem.: Music Tchrs. Assn. Calif. Avocations: filmmaking, stage production, videotaping, popular song composing, mentoring aspiring concert pianists. Home: PO Box 50955 Los Angeles CA 90050 Personal E-mail: johnjoetownley1@aol.com.

TOWNS, DEBI, state legislator; b. Feb. 12, 1956; MSE, U. Wis., Whitewater, 1999. Dairy farm owner; former fin. cons. and sch. adminstr.; mem. Wis. State Assembly, Madison, 2002—, vice chair com. on edn., mem. agr. com., mem. coll. and univ. com., mem. edn. reform com., mem. fin. instns. com. Republican. Office: State Capitol Bldg Rm 302 N PO Box 8953 Madison WI 53708 Address: 7930 N Eagle Rd Janesville WI 53545

TOWNS, EDOLPHUS, congressman; b. Chadbourn, N.C., July 21, 1934; m. Gwendolyn Forbes, 1960; children: Darryl, Deidra. BS, N.C. A & T State U., Greensboro, 1956; MSW., Adelphi U., Garden City, N.Y., 1973; PhD (hon.), N.C. A&T, Shaw U. Tchr. Medgar Evers Coll., Bklyn., N.Y.C. Pub. Schs.; dep. hosp. adminstr., 1965-71; dep. pres. Borough of Bklyn., 1976-82; mem. U.S. Congress from 11th N.Y. dist. Washington, 1983—91; mem. U.S. Congress from 10th N.Y. dist., 1992—; mem. energy and commerce com., govt. reform com. Mem. adv. council Boy Scouts Am.; active Salvation Army. Served with U.S. Army, 1956-58. Named to Acad. of Distinction Adelphi U. Mem. Kiwanis, Phi Beta Sigma. Democrat. Office: US Ho of Reps 2232 Rayburn Ho Office Bldg Washington DC 20515-0001

TOWNSEND, ALAIR ANE, publisher, municipal official; b. Rochester, N.Y., Feb. 15, 1942; d. Harold Eugene and Dorothy (Sharpe) T.; m. Robert Harris, Dec. 31, 1970 (div. 1994). BS, Elmira Coll., 1962; MS, U. Wis., 1964; postgrad., Columbia U., 1970-71. Assoc. dir. budget priorities Com. on Budget, U.S. Ho. of Reps., Washington, 1975-79, dep. asst. sec. for budget HEW, 1979-80, asst. sec. for mgmt. and budget, 1980-81; dir. N.Y.C. Office Mgmt. and Budget, 1981-85; dep. mayor for fin. and econ. devel. City of N.Y., 1985-89; pub. Crain's N.Y. Bus., N.Y.C., 1989—. Bd. overseers Tchrs. Ins. and Annuity Assn.-Coll. Retirement Equities Fund; former mem. adv. bd. Ford Motor Credit Corp.; former bd. dirs. Armor Holdings Inc. Former vice-chmn., trustee Elmira Coll.; former mem. Coun. Fgn. Rels.; former bd. govs. Am. Stock Exch.; chmn. Am. Woman's Econ. Devel. Corp.; former chmn. N.Y.C. Sports Commn.; former chmn. Consol. Corp. Fund of Lincoln Ctr.; bd. dirs. Lincoln Ctr.; vice-chmn. Buffalo Fiscal Stability Auth. Mem. Women's Forum, Partnership for NYC (bd. dirs.), N.Y. State Bus. Coun. (bd. dirs.), Econ. Club N.Y. (bd. dirs.). Office: Crain's NY Bus 711 3d Ave New York NY 10017

TOWNSEND, ANN VAN DEVANTER, foundation administrator, art historian; b. Washington, June 20, 1936; d. John Ward and Ellen Keys (Ramsey) Cutler; m. Willis Van Devanter, Dec. 27, 1958 (div. May 1974); 1 child, Susan Earling Van Devanter (Mrs. John Philip Newell); m. Lewis Raynham Townsend, Dec. 10, 1983. BA, Brown U., 1958; MA, George Washington U., 1975. Grantsmanship cert. Guest curator Balt. Mus. Art, 1971-77; dir. cultural affairs Chevy Chase (Md.) Savs. & Loan, Inc., 1978-81; dir. spl. partnership projects NEA, Washington, 1982-83; founding pres. The Trust for Mus. Exhbns., Washington, 1984—. Organizer over 60 nat. and internat. mus. exhbns. for more than 240 mus. Co-author: Self-Portraits of American Artists, 1670-1973, 1974; author: Anywhere So Long As There Be Freedom, 1975, Two Hundred Years of American Painting, 1976; contbr. articles to mags. U.S. commr. Cagnes-Sur-Mer Internat. Afts Festival, France, 1977, 78; mem. women's com. Washington Opera, 1993—; bd. dirs. Friends of Corcoran Gallery of Art, Washington, 1975-76, Strathmore Hall Arts Ctr., Rockville, Md., 1978-80, Am. Swedish Hist. Mus., Phila., 1987-89, U.S. World Fedn. Friends of Mus., 1995—. Acad. grad. fellow Johns Hopkins Sch. Advanced Internat. Studies, 1958. Mem. Nat. Soc. Arts and Letters, Soc. Women Goegraphers, Am. Assn. Mus., Internat. Coun. Mus., Am. Assn. Royal Acad. Trust, Am. Friends of the Hermitage Mus., Am. Friends of French Heritage, Cir. of the Nat. Gallery of Art, Sulgrave Club, Cosmos Club. Episcopalian. Avocations: backgammon, gourmet cooking, ballroom dancing, bridge. Office: The Trust for Mus Exhbns 1424 16th St NW Ste 600 Washington DC 20036-2239 Office Phone: 202-745-2566. E-mail: atownsend@tme.org.

TOWNSEND, BRENDA S. educational association administrator; Dir. profl. devel. Internat. Reading Assn., Newark, Del., 1992—, dir. con. and affiliate svcs. Mem. adv. bd. The Gooding Inst. Rsch. in Family Literacy. Office: Internat Reading Assn 800 Barksdale Rd PO Box 8139 Newark DE 19714-8139

TOWNSEND, BRIAN DOUGLAS, paralegal; b. Tokyo, Sept. 22, 1961; s. Thomas and Juanita Evora (Sanford) T.; m. Gloria Ann Wigfall, Aug. 23, 1986; children: Brian D. Jr., Brianna A. BA in Criminology, U. Md., 1983. Legal aide Kirkland & Ellis, Washington, 1984-85; legal asst. to mng. clk. Cadwalader, Wickersham & Taft, Washington, 1985-87; paralegal specialist, Office of Chief Counsel U.S. Dept. Transp. Maritime Adminstrn., Washington, 1987-90, U.S. Dept. Treasury, IRS, Washington, 1990-92; litigation support specialist U.S. Dept. Justice, Tax Divsn., Washington, 1992-93; paralegal specialist Resolution Trust Corp., Washington, 1993-95, FDIC, Washington, 1996-98, U.S. Dept. Treasury, OIG, Washington, 1998-99; program specialist FOIA/PA U.S. Dept. Treasury, OFAC, Washington, 1999-2000; mgmt. analyst USDA, Washington, 2000—02; program analyst IRS/OPA, U.S. Dept. Treasury, Washington, 2002—. Avocations: bowling, fishing, swimming, chess, football. Office: US Dept Treasury IRS/OPA 1111 Constitution Ave NW Washington DC 20224-0002 E-mail: briandouglastownsend@yahoo.com., brian.d.townsend@irs.gov.

TOWNSEND, C. EDWARD, publishing executive; b. Belle Plaine, Minn., Dec. 17, 1930; s. Daniel Charles and Pearl Townsend; m. Susan M. Strumwell; children: Dana, Daniel, Amy, Jeff, Caroline. BA, U. Minn., 1952. Publ. Belle Plaine Herald. Pres. Belle Plaine Devel. Corp., 1978—86; publ. Henderson (Minn.) Ind. Pres. Belle Plaine C. of C., 1993—94; planning and zoning bd. Belle Plaine City, 1970—80, city coun., 1981—90. Named Townsend Park in his honor, City of Belle Plaine, 2001. Home: PO Box 7 Belle Plaine MN 56011

TOWNSEND, CHARLES H. publishing executive; m. Joanna E. Townsend. Pres., pub. Family Cir. Mag., 1986—90; pres., CEO N.Y. Times Co. Women's Mag. Group, 1990—94; pub., Glamour Mag. Conde Nast Publs. Inc., N.Y.C., 1994—95, exec. v.p., 1995—2000, COO, 2000—04, pub., CEO, 2004—; COO Advance Mag. Group, N.Y.C., 2001—. Office: Conde Nast Publications Inc 4 Times Sq New York NY 10036-6561*

TOWNSEND, CHRISTOPHER GORDON, lawyer; b. New Bedford, Mass., June 9, 1947; s. Christopher Gordon and Rita Mary (Fitzgerald) T.; m. Christine P. Davis, June 17, 1972; children: Christopher IV, Jessica C. BA, Providence Coll., 1969; JD, Georgetown U., 1975. Bar: D.C. 1975. Jud. clk. Supreme Ct. Del., Wilmington, 1975-76; atty. U.S. Dept. Justice, Washington, 1976-77, U.S. SEC, Washington, 1977-82; asst. gen. counsel Marriott Corp., Bethesda, Md., 1982-93; dep. gen. counsel Host Marriott Corp., Bethesda, 1993-96, gen. counsel, 1996-01; ptnr. Patton, Boggs LLP, 2001—. Editor: Am. Criminal Law Rev., 1974-75. Lt. USN, 1969-72. Mem. ABA. Office: Patton Boggs LLP 8484 Westpark Dr Mc Lean VA 22102

TOWNSEND, COURTNEY M. surgeon; b. Lubbock, Tex., 1943; MD, U. Tex., Galveston, 1969. Specialty bd. 1 Surgery 1975. Intern U. Tex. Med. Br., 1969—70, resident surgery, 1970—74; fellow surgical oncology U. Calif., L.A., 1974—76; prof. U. Tex. Med. Br. James IV Surg. Traveller U. Tex. Med. Br., 1986; pres. Am. Pancreatic Assn., 1992—95; mem. Tex. Cancer Coun., 1992—2004; bd. dirs. James IV Assn. Surgeons, Inc., 1999—2002; residency rev. com. surgery AMA, 1999—2003; sec. So. Surg. Assn., 1999—2004; dir. Am. Bd. Surgery, 2000—. Editor-in-chief: Sabiston Textbook of Surgery: The Biological Basis of Modern Surgical Practice, 16th edit. Recipient Rsch. Career Devel. award, NIH, 1982, Asbel Smith Disting. Alumnus, 1986. Fellow: ACS (exec. com. 1999—2003). Office: 301 University Blvd Galveston TX 77555-0527

TOWNSEND, EARL C., JR., lawyer, writer; b. Indpls., Nov. 9, 1914; s. Earl Cunningham and Besse (Kuhn) T.; m. Emily Macnab, Apr. 3, 1947 (dec. Mar. 1988); children: Starr, Vicki M., Julia E. (Mrs. Edward Goodrich Dunn Jr.), Earl Cunningham III, Clyde G. Student, De Pauw U., 1932-34; AB, U. Mich., 1936, JD, 1939. Bar: Ind. 1939, Mich. 1973, U.S. Supreme Ct. 1973, U.S. Ct. Appeals (4th, 5th, 6th, 7th cirs.), U.S. Dist. Ct. (no. and so. dists.) Ind., U.S. Dist. Ct. (ea. dist.) Va., U.S. Dist. Ct. (ea. dist.) Mich. Sr. ptnr. Townsend & Townsend, Indpls., 1941-64, Townsend, Hovde & Townsend, Indpls., 1964-84, Townsend & Townsend, Indpls., 1984—. Dep. prosecutor, Marion County, Ind., 1942-44; radio-TV announcer WIRE, WFBM, WFBM-TV, Indpls., 1940-53, 1st TV announcer Indpls. 500 mile race, 1949, 50; Big Ten basketball referee, 1940-47; lectr. trial tactics U. Notre Dame, Ind. U., U. Mich., 1968-79; chmn. faculty seminar on personal injury trials Ind. U. Sch. Law, U. Notre Dame Sch. Law, Valparaiso Sch. Law, 1981; mem. Com. to Revise Ind. Supreme Ct. Pattern Jury Instrns., 1975-83; lectr. Trial Lawyers 30 Yrs. Inst., 1986; counsel atty gen., 1988-92. Author: Birdstones of the North American Indian, 1959; editor: Am. Assn. Trial Lawyers Am. Jour., 1964-88; contbr. articles to legal and archeol. jours.; composer (waltz) Moon of Halloween. Trustee Cathedral High Sch., Indpls., Eiteljorg Mus. Am. Indian and Western Art, Cale J. Holder Scholarship Found. Ind. U. Law Sch.; life trustee, bd. dirs., mem. fin. and bldg. coms. Indpls. Mus. Art; life trustee Ind. State Mus.; founder, dir. Meridian St. Found.; mem. dean's coun. Ind. U.; founder, life fellow Roscoe Pound/Am. Trial Lawyers Found., Harvard U.; fellow Meth. Hosp. Found. Recipient Ind. Univ. Writers Conf. award, 1960, Hanson H. Anderson medal of honor Arsenal Tech. Schs., Indpls., 1971; named to Coun. Sagamores of Wabash, 1969; Rector scholar, 1934, Ind. Basketball Hall of Fame; hon. chief Black River-Swan Creek Saginaw-Chippewa Indian tribe. Fellow: Ind. Bar Found. (life trustee, disting. fellow award), Internat. Soc. Barristers, Internat. Acad. Trial Lawyers; mem.: ATLA (v.p.), ABA (com. on trial techniques 1964—76, aviation and space 1977—), ASCAP, Mich. Trial Lawyers Assn., Bar Assn. 7th Fed. Cir. (bd. govs. 1966—68), 34th Jud. Cir. Bar Assn., Roscommon County Bar Assn., State Bar of Mich. (Champion of Justice award 1989), Am. Judicature Soc., Am. Arbitration Assn. (nat. arbitrators panel), Am. Bd. Trial Advocates (diplomate, pres. Ind. chpt. 1980—86), Ind. Trial Lawyers Assn. (pres. 1965, pres. Coll. Fellows 1984—90), Indpls. Bar Found. (disting. charter 1986), Ind. State Bar Assn. (Golden Career award 1989), Genuine Indian Relic Soc. (founder, pres., chmn. frauds com.), Trowel and Brush Soc. (hon.), Marion County/Indpls. Hist. Soc. (bd. dirs.), Ind. Hist. Soc., Soc. Mayflower Descendants (gov. 1947—49), Columbia Club, U. Mich. Pres. Club, Key Biscayne Yacht Club, The Players Club, U. Mich. Victors Club (founder, charter mem.), Shriners, Masons (33 degree), Scottish Rite, Phi Kappa Phi, Delta Kappa Epsilon. Republican. Methodist. Avocations: art, Indian relics. Home: 5008 N Meridian St Indianapolis IN 46208-2624

TOWNSEND, ELIZABETH, state legislator; Mem. from dist. 31 Maine State Ho. of Reps., 1993-95, mem. from dist. 36, 1995—. Address: 44 Country Ln Portland ME 04103-6206 Office: Maine Ho of Reps State Capitol Augusta ME 04333-0001

TOWNSEND, FRANCES (FRAN TOWNSEND), healthcare educator, writer; b. Fort Worth, May 25, 1926; d. Robert Emory Hicks and Ida Belle Hagendoorn; m. William Brice Townsend III; children: William Brice IV children: Mary Townsend Seeley. BA, BS, Tex. Women's U., 1946. Cert. clin. nutritionist Clin. Nutrition Certification Bd., dietitian/nutritionist NY, Accictionolotist Am. Coll. of Addictionology and Compulsive Disorders. Cons., counselor, wholistic health educator Well Body / Well Mind, LLC, Springfield, Mo., 1996—; assoc. editor Tree of Light Pub., St. George, Utah, 2000—. Founding pres. Ritecare Internat., Inc., Springfield, 1976—2003. Author: (column) Today's Healthy Woman, Wellness Way. Avocations: gardening, jewelry making, birdwatching, writing. Office Phone: 417-883-5661. Personal E-mail: ftownsend3@mchsi.com.

TOWNSEND, FRANCES FRAGOS, federal agency administrator; m. John Townsend; 2 children. BA, BS, Am. U., 1982; JD, San Diego U., 1984. Asst. dist. atty., Bklyn., 1985—88; chief to staff to asst. atty. gen. criminal divsn. Dept. Justice, 1993—95, acting dep. asst. atty. gen., 1997—98, counsel Office of Intelligence Policy and Re., 1998—2001; asst. commandant for intelligence U.S.C.G., Dept. Homeland Security, 2001—03; dep. asst. to Pres. Bush, dep. nat. security advisor for combating terrorism Nat. Security Coun., 2003—. Office: Eisenhower Exec Office Bldg Rm 313 17th St & Pennsylvania Ave NW Washington DC 20504

TOWNSEND, GREGORY WILLIAMS, music educator; b. Saint Louis, Mo., June 3, 1970; s. Frederick Dalton and Joyce Williams Townsend. MusB, So. Ill. U., 1988—93, MA in Music Edn., 1998—. Cert. tchr. Ill. State Bd. Edn., 1996, Mo. State Bd. Edn., 1993. Music dept. chairperson Althoff Cath. H.S., Belleville, Ill., 1995—2000; instrumental music instr. Salem Cmty. H.S., Ill., 2000—02; band dir. Carbondale Cmty. H.S., Ill., 2002—. Composer: (wind band music) The Course, Walking Away. Mem. Salem Theatre Found., Salem, Ill., 2001—01. Recipient Grand Champion Instrumental Ensemble (as Dir.), Music Showcase Festivals, 1999; grantee Music Performance Scholarship, So. Ill. U. at Edwardsville, 1988-1993. Mem.: NEA, Ill. Educator's Assn., Music Educator's Nat. Conf., Ill. Music Educator's Assn. (band divsn. co-chairperson/chairperson 2001—03). Avocations: scuba diving - advanced certification, computers, tennis, volleyball. Office: Carbondale Community High School 1301 E Walnut St Carbondale IL 62902 Personal E-mail: gregtownsend@mac.com.

TOWNSEND, IRENE FOGLEMAN, accountant, tax specialist; b. Birmingham, Ala., May 29, 1932; d. James Woods and Virginia (Martin) Fogleman; m. Kenneth Ross Townsend, Mar. 18, 1951; children: Marietta Irene, Martha Shapard, Kenneth Ross Jr., Elizabeth Buchanan. BSBA, East Carolina U., 1980. CPA, N.C., Va. Acct. Norwood P. Whitehurst & Assocs., Greenville, N.C., 1981-86; asst. v.p. Tenet Healthcare Corp., Vienna, Va., 1995—; v.p. NME Psychiatric Hosps., Inc., Vienna, Va., 2001—. Fellow AICPA, N.C. Assn. CPAs, D.C. Inst. CPAs, Va. Soc. CPAs; mem. DAR, N.C. Soc. Daus. of Colonial Wars, Colonial Dames 17th Century. Democrat. Episcopalian (lay reader, chalice bearer). Avocations: bicycling, genealogy. Home: 2521 Paxton St Woodbridge VA 22192-3414 Office: Tenet Healthcare Corp 501 Church St NE Ste 301 Vienna VA 22180-4734 E-mail: irene_townsend@hotmail.com.

TOWNSEND, JAMES DOUGLAS, accountant; b. Kokomo, Ind., May 20, 1959; s. Lemon Dale and Diamond Sue (Turner) T.; m. Ariane Antonia Atkins, May 7, 1983 (div. July 1992); 1 child, Bradley Alan; m. Mildred Ann Kurtz, Oct. 18, 1992; children: Heather Marie, Tyler Neil. Student, Ind. U., 1977, Ind. State U., 1977-78; BS in Acctg. summa cum laude, Ball State U., 1980. CPA, Ind., Colo.; cert. mgmt. acct. Acctg. intern Chevrolet Motor Div. Gen. Motors Corp., Muncie, Ind., 1979; from staff acct. to sr. mgr. Price Waterhouse, Indpls., 1980—89; from contr. to v.p. fin. Raffensperger, Hughes & Co., Inc., Indpls., 1989—95; sr. v.p., chief adminstrv. officer Nat City Investments, Inc., Indpls., 1995-99; pres. Fin. Mgmt., Inc., Indpls., 1994—; sr. v.p. Madison Ave. Capital Group LLC, 1999-2000; CFO Colo.'s Ocean Journey, 2000-01, exec. v.p., COO, 2001, pres., CEO, 2001—; v.p., contr. Curian Capital LLC, 2004—, Jackson Nat. Life Distbr., Inc., 2004—. Coord. Seek Program Ind. U., Indpls., 1985-86; cons. project bus. Jr. Achievement, Indpls., 1986; treas., asst. sec. Sagamore Funds Trust, 1991-94; treas. Raffensberger Hughes Capitol Corp., 1991-94, RHGP, Inc., 1993-95. Baseball coach Pike Twp. (Ind.) Youth League, 1986-87; cubmaster Pike Twp. Coun. Boy Scouts Am., 1987-88; mem. Pike Twp. Sch. Bd., 1988-92, v.p., 1989-90, pres., 1990-92; bd. dirs. Project I-Star, 1992-94, Crooked Creek Villages Homeowners Assn., 1998-99; fin. com. Highlands Ranch Cmty. Assn., 2000—02. Fellow Life Mgmt. Inst.; mem. AICPA, Inst. Mgmt. Accts., Ind. CPA Soc. (vice chmn. edn. com. 1988-89, chmn. 1989-90, chmn. govt. rels. com. 1999), Colo. Soc. CPAs, Indpls. C. of C. (SKLA exec. coun. 1992-94), Swallow Hill Music Assn. Republican. Avocations: boating, golf, guitar, chess, scuba diving. Mailing: PO Box 3415 Dillon CO 80435-3415 Home: 0052 Hunki Doil Ct Dillon CO 80435

TOWNSEND, JAMES WILLIS, computer scientist; b. Evansville, Ind., Sept. 9, 1936; s. James Franklin and Elma Elizabeth (Galloway) T.; m. Leona Jean York, Apr. 20, 1958; 1 child, Eric Wayne. BS in Arts and Scis., Ball State U., 1962; PhD, Iowa State U., 1970. Rsch. technologist Neuromuscular div. Mead Johnson, Evansville, 1957-60; chief instr. Zoology dept. Iowa State U., Ames, 1965-67; asst. prof. Ind. State U., Evansville, 1967-72; cons. electron microscopy Mead Johnson Rsch. Ctr., Evansville, 1971-73; mgr. neurosci. Neurosci. Lab., Kans. State U., Manhattan, 1974-76; head electron microscopy Nat. Ctr. for Toxicology Rsch., Jefferson, Ark., 1976-82; dir. electron microscopy U. Ark. Med. Sci., Little Rock, 1982-87; dir. computer ops. pathology dept. Univ. Hosp., Little Rock, 1987-99, sr. analyst clin. info. sys., 1999-2000; sr. cons. Soft Computer Consultants, Palm Harbor, Fla., 2000—03; mktg. mgr. Profl. Benefits Group, 2003—. Workshop presenter Am. Soc. Clin. Pathology, 1980-81, Nat. Soc. Histotechnologists, 1984-88. With USAF, 1957. Contbr. articles to profl. jours.; reviewer Scanning Electron Microscopy, 1977-78. Nat. Def. fellowship NDEA, Iowa State U., 1962-65; recipient Chgo. Tribune award Chicago Tribune, 1955. Mem. Sigma Xi, Sigma Zeta. Baptist. Avocations: genealogy, american civil war, scuba. Home and Office: 116 Trelon Way Little Rock AR 72223 Office Phone: 501-868-3008.

TOWNSEND, JANE KALTENBACH, biologist, educator; b. Chgo., Dec. 21, 1922; BS, Beloit Coll., 1944; MA, U. Wis., 1946; PhD, U. Iowa, 1950. Asst. in zoology U. Wis., 1944-47, asst., project assoc. in pathology, 1950—53; asst., instr. U. Iowa, 1948-50; rsch. fellow Wenner-Grens Inst. Am. Cancer Soc., Stockholm, 1953—56; asst. prof. zoology Northwestern U., 1956-58; asst. prof. to assoc. prof. zoology Mt. Holyoke Coll., South Hadley, Mass., 1958-70, prof., 1970-93, chmn. biol. scis., 1980-86, prof. emeritus, 1993—. Fellow AAAS (sec. sect. biol. sci. 1974-78); mem. Am. Assn. Anatomists, Am. Inst. Biol. Scis., Soc. Integrated Comparative Biology, Soc. Exptl. Biology and Medicine, Soc. Devel. Biology, Corp. of Marine Biol. Lab., Sigma Xi, Phi Beta Kappa. Office: Mount Holyoke Coll Dept Bio Scis South Hadley MA 01075 Office Phone: 413-538-2124. Business E-Mail: jtownsen@mtholyoke.edu.

TOWNSEND, JOHN MICHAEL, lawyer; b. West Point, N.Y., Mar. 21, 1947; s. John D. and Vera (Nachman) T.; m. Frances M. Fragos, Oct. 8, 1994; children, James E., Patrick M. BA, Yale U., 1968, JD, 1971. Bar: N.Y. 1972, U.S. Dist. Ct. (so. and ea. dists.) N.Y. 1975, U.S. Ct. Appeals (2nd cir.) 1975, U.S. Supreme Ct. 1975, U.S. Ct. Appeals (8th cir.) 1982, U.S. Ct. Appeals (7th and 10th cirs.) 1986, D.C. 1990, U.S. Dist. Ct. D.C. 1990, U.S. Ct. Appeals (D.C. cir.) 1990, U.S. Ct. Appeals (4th cir.) 1991, U.S. Ct. Appeals (fed. cir.) 2000, U.S. Ct. Appeals (11th cir.) 2001, U.S. Ct. Fed. Claims, 2000, U.S. Ct. Appeals (1st cir.) 2003. Assoc. Hughes Hubbard & Reed, LLP, N.Y.C., 1971-73, 75-80, ptnr., 1980—; assoc. Hughes Hubbard & Reed, Paris, 1973-74. Bd. dirs., chair exec. com., law com. Am. Arbitration Assn.; trustee U.S. Coun. Internat. Bus. 1st lt. USAR, 1971-75. Mem. ABA, Am. Law Inst., Internat. Bar Assn. (chair mediation com.), Assn. Bar City N.Y., Union Internat. des Avocats, Coll. Comml. Arbitrators, Univ. Club, Yale Club (N.Y.C.). Democrat. Episcopalian. Office: Hughes Hubbard & Reed LLP 1775 I St NW Washington DC 20006 2401 Fax: (202) 721-4646. Office Phone: 202-721-4600. E-mail: townsend@hugheshubbard.com.

TOWNSEND, JOHN WILLIAM, JR., physicist, retired federal aerospace agency executive; b. Washington, Mar. 19, 1924; s. John William and Elenore (Eby) T.; m. Mary Irene Lewis, Feb. 7, 1948; children: Bruce Alan, Nancy Dewitt, John William III, Megan Lewis; m. JoAnn C. Clayton, Sept. 17, 1996. BA, Williams Coll., 1947, MA, 1949, ScD, 1961. With Naval Research Lab., 1949-55, br. head, 1955-58; with NASA, 1958-68, dep. dir. Goddard Space Flight Ctr., 1965-68; dep. adminstrn. Environ. Scis. Svcs. Adminstrn., 1968-70; asso. adminstr. NOAA, 1970-77; pres. Fairchild Space and Electronics Co., 1977-82; v.p. Fairchild Industries, 1979-85; pres. Fairchild Space Co., 1983-85; sr. v.p. Fairchild Industries, 1985-87; chmn. bd. Am. Satellite Co., 1985, sr. v.p., exec. aerospace group, 1987, exec. v.p., 1987; dir. NASA Goddard Space Flight Ctr., 1987-90; ret., 1990. Mem. U.S. Rocket, Satellite Rsch. Panel, 1950-60; chmn. space applications bd. NRC, 1985-87; bd. dirs., trustee Telos Corp., 1990-92; mem. adv. bd. Loral Corp., 1990-92; mem. coms. NRC, 1990—; bd. dirs CTA, Inc., 1990-98. Author numerous papers, reports in field. Pres. town council, Forest Heights, Md., 1951-55. Served with USAAF, 1943-46. Recipient Profl. Achievement award Engrs. and Architects Day, 1957; Meritorious Civilian Service award Navy Dept., 1957; Outstanding Leadership medal NASA, 1962; Distinguished Service medal, 1971, 90; recipient Arthur S. Fleming award Fed. Govt., 1963, Edward A. Flinn III award, 1999. Fellow AIAA, AAAS, Am. Meteorol. Soc.; mem. NAE (com. 1990-93), Am. Phys. Soc., Am . Geophys. Union. (fin. com. 1991-98, Edward A. Flinn III award, 1999), Internat. Astronautical Fedn. (mem., tru stee internat., acad. astronautics), Sigma Xi. Home: 6532 79th St Cabin John MD 20818-1201

TOWNSEND, JUNE H. foreign language educator; b. Dunbar, W. Va. d. Lawrence Hobart and Naomi Jane Hickman; m. Horace Raymond Townsend; children:Horace Raymond III, Timi Jane, Thomas Lawrence, Christopher Randolph. MEd, Xavier U., Cin., 1973; MA, Ohio State U., 1988, PhD, 1993. Tchr. pub. schs. of Ohio, 1960-84; tchg. assoc. Ohio State U., Columbus, 1986-89; prof. of Spanish Wilmington (Ohio) Coll., 1989—. Spkr. Congress Internat., Madrid, 1995, U. Louisville, 1994, 1993, U. Cin., 1993, Duquesne U., Pitts., 1993, AATSP Ann. Mtg., Cancun, Mexico, 1992, E. Carolina U., Greenville, N.C., 1991. Contbg. author: Ency., 1999; author: The Influence of William Faulkner in the Spanish Post Civil War Novel, 2000. Mem. Am. Assn. of Tchrs. of Spanish and Portuguese, Assn. Internat. Hispanica de las Humanidades (sec. 1995), MLA, Soc. Nat. Honararia Hispanica, Ohio Humanities Coun. Directory of Scholars, Sigma Delta Pi. Mem. Soc. Of Friends. Avocations: travel, reading, music. Office: Wilmington Coll 25 Ludovic St Wilmington OH 45177 E-mail: june_townsend@wilmington.edu.

TOWNSEND, KATHLEEN KENNEDY, former lieutenant governor; b. Greenwich, Connecticut, July 4, 1951; d. Robert F. and Ethel S. Kennedy; m. David Townsend; children: Meaghan, Maeve, Kate, and Kerry. BA cum laude, Harvard Univ., 1974; JD, U. N.Mex., 1978. Instr. Dundalk Cmty. Coll., 1985-86, Essex Cmty. Coll., 1986-87, U. Pa., 1987-88; exec. dir. Md. Student Svc. Alliance, State dept. of Edn., 1987—93; dep. asst. atty. gen. U.S. Dept. Justice, Washington, 1993-94; lt. gov. State of Md., 1995—2003; pres. Operation Respect, 2003; adj. prof. Georgetown's Sch. of Pub. Policy, 2003. Chair so. region Nat. Conf. Lt. Gov., chair oversight com. Johns Hopkins U., Peabody Inst., 1995-96; nat. adv. bd. Export-Import Bank U.S.; bd. adv. Johns Hopkins U. Sch. Advanced Internat. Studies, Inst. Human Virology U. Md; chair, State House Trust, 1995-2003, Adv. Bd., After-School Opportunity Programs, 1999-, co-chair, Safe Schools Interagency Steering Com., 1999-2003; Delegate, Dem. Party Nat. Conv., 1988, 1996, 2000; chair, Dem. Caucus of Lt. Gov. Editor U. N.Mex. Law Rev.; contbg. articles to profl. jour. and newspapers. Founder Robert F. Kennedy Human Rights Award; chair Cabinet Coun. Criminal and Juvenile Justice, 1995-2003; chair Cabinet Coun. for Bus. and Econ. Devel.; chair Md. del. Pres. Summit Am. Future, 1997; chair State Sys. Reform Task Force for Children and Youth Reform, 1996, Task Force to study increasing availability of substance abuse programs, 1998-2001, Gov.of the Yr. 2000 Pub. Info.; chair adv. bd. after sch. opportunity programs; co-chair Md. Family Violence Coun.; bd. dir. John F. Kennedy Libr. Found., Nat. Inst. Women's Policy Rsch.; chair external adv. bd. Kennedy Krieger Inst. Early Infant Transition Ctr.; sr. advisor, Appropriations Com., House of Delegates, 1984-85; asst. Atty. Gen., Md., 1985-86; bd. ptnr. Radcliffe Coll. Recipient 4 hon. degrees; Visionary Leadership Award, Healthy Families Am., 2000, Clinton Ctr. Award for Leadership, Dem. Leadership Coun., 2002. Mem., Econ. Devel. Commn., Baltimore County, 1987, Gov. Exec. Coun., Gov. Commn. on Svc. and Volunteerism, 1998-. Democrat. Office: Operation Respect 5th Fl 2 Penn Plaza New York NY 10121*

TOWNSEND, KENNETH ROSS, retired priest; b. Holly Grove, Ala., Oct. 31, 1927; s. James Ernest and Mary H. (Jordan) T.; m. Irene Fogleman, Mar. 18, 1951; children: Marietta, Martha, Kenneth Ross, Elizabeth. AB, Birmingham South Coll., 1956; postgrad., Union Theol. Sem., 1960-63; MDiv, Va. Theol. Sem., 1964. Ordained priest Episcopal Ch., 1965. Pastor meth. chs. N.C. and Va. Confs., 1954-63; priest Bath Priest Parish, Dinwiddie, Va., 1964-69, St. Paul's Ch., Vanceboro, N.C., 1969-89; ret., 1989. Lectr. philosophy Richard Bland Coll. of Coll. William and Mary, Williamsburg, Va., 1966-68; del. to synod Province IV, 1973; mem. liturgical com. Episcopal Diocese of East Carolina, Wilmington, N.C., 1971-82, mem. prison commn., 1984; resident priest Olivet Ch., Franconia, Va., 1995—. Writer, painter With USNR, 1945-46. Mem.: VFW, Delta Sigma Phi. Home: 2521 Paxton St Lake Ridge Woodbridge VA 22192 Personal E-mail: ktownsend22@hotmail.com. *The world has too much to lose by literary and academic silence: we live in an unavoidable relationship to the Cosmos.*

TOWNSEND, MARJORIE RHODES, aerospace engineer, engineering executive; b. Washington, Mar. 12, 1930; d. Lewis Boling and Marjorie Olive (Trees) Rhodes; m. Charles Eby Townsend, June 7, 1948; children: Charles Eby Jr., Lewis Rhodes, John Cunningham, Richard Leo. BEE, George Washington U., 1951. Electronic scientist Naval Rsch. Lab., Washington, 1951-59; rsch. engr. to sect. head Goddard Space Flight Ctr.-NASA, Greenbelt, Md., 1959-65, tech. asst. to chief systems divsn., 1965-66, project mgr. small astronomy satellites, 1966-75, project mgr. applications explorer missions, 1975-76, mgr. preliminary systems design group, 1976-80; aerospace and electronics cons. Washington, 1980-83; v.p. systems devel. Space Am., 1983-84; aerospace cons. Washington, 1984-90; dir. space systems engring. BDM Internat., Inc., Washington, 1990-91; dir. space applications BDM ESC, Washington, 1991-92; sr. prin. staff mem. BDM Fed., Inc., Washington, 1992-93. Aerospace cons., Washington, 1993—. Patentee digital telemetry system. Decorated Knight Italian Republic Order, 1972; recipient Fed. Women's award, 1973, EUR award for Culture, 1974, Engr. Alumni Achievement award George Washington U., 1975, Gen. Alumni Achievement award George Washington U., 1976, Exceptional Svc. medal NASA, 1971, Outstanding Leadership medal NASA, 1980, Eye-of-the-Needle award NASA, 1991. Fellow IEEE (chmn. Washington sect. 1974-75), AIAA (chmn. nat. capitol sect. 1985), AAAS (coun. del. 1985-88), Washington Acad. Sci. (pres. 1980-81); mem. Internat. Acad. Astronautics, Am. Geophys. Union, Soc. Women Engrs., Wing of Aerospace Med. Assn., Inc. (hon.), DAR, Daus. Colonial Wars, Mensa, Sigma Kappa, Sigma Delta Epsilon (hon.). Republican. Episcopalian. Home and Office: 3529 Tilden St NW Washington DC 20008-3122 E-mail: mrtownsend@aol.com.

TOWNSEND, MILES AVERILL, aerospace and mechanical engineering educator; b. Buffalo, N.Y., Apr. 16, 1935; s. Francis Devere and Sylvia (Wolpa) T.; children: Kathleen Townsend Hastings, Melissa, Stephen, Joel, Philip. BA, Stanford U., 1955; BS MechE, U. Mich., 1958; advanced cert., U. Ill., 1963, MS in Theoretical and Applied Mechanics, 1967; PhD, U. Wis., 1971. Registered profl. engr., Ill., Wis., Tenn., Ont. Project engr. Sundstrand, Rockford, Ill., 1959-63, Twin Disc Inc., Rockford, 1963-65, 67-68; sr. engr. Westinghouse Electric Corp., Sunnyvale, Calif., 1965-67; instr., fellow U. Wis., Madison, 1968-71; assoc. prof. U. Toronto, Ont., Can., 1971-74; prof. mech. engring. Vanderbilt U., Nashville, 1974-81; Wilson prof. mech. and aerospace engring. U. Va., Charlottesville, 1981—, chmn. dept., 1981-91. Ptnr., v.p. Endev Ltd., Can. and U.S., 1972—; cons. in field. Contbr. numerous articles on dynamics, design dynamical systems, controls and optimization to profl. jours.; 7 patents in field. Recipient numerous research grants and contracts. Fellow ASME, AAAS; mem. N.Y. Acad. Scis., Sigma Xi, Phi Kappa Phi, Pi Tau Sigma. Avocations: running, reading, music. Home: 212 Alderman Rd Charlottesville VA 22903-1704 Office: U Va Dept Mech and Aerospace Engring Thornton Hall Charlottesville VA 22903-2442 Business E-Mail: mat@virginia.edu.

TOWNSEND, P(RESTON) COLEMAN, agricultural business executive; b. Salisbury, Md., Dec. 27, 1945; s. Preston Coleman and Rachel (Morris) T.; m. Susan Marshall, Dec. 8, 1981. BS, U. Del., 1969. Chmn., CEO Townsends, Inc., Millsboro, Del., 1969-99, chmn., 1999—. Bd. visitors Del. State U. Mem. Nat. Broiler Council (bd. dirs.). Republican. Office: Townsends Inc 919 N Market St Ste 420 Wilmington DE 19801-3014

TOWNSEND, ROBERT, film director; b. Chgo., Feb. 6, 1957; s. Robert and Shirley (Jenkins) T. Film dir. Creative Artists Agy., Beverly Hills, Calif., 1979—. Actor: (stage) Take It From the Top, 1979, Bones, 1980, (films) Cooley High, 1974, Willie and Phil, 1980, Streets of Fire, 1983, A Soldier's Story, 1983, American Flyers, 1984, Odd Jobs, 1984, Ratboy, 1985, The Mighty Quinn, 1989, That's Adequate, 1990, Joseph's Gift, 1998, The Tax Man, 1999, (TV movies) Women At West Point, 1979, Senior Trip!, 1981, In Love With an Older Woman, 1982, Bliss, 1995, Mercenary II: Thick and Thin, 1997, Love Songs, 1999, Jackie's Back!, 1999, Up Up and Away, 2000; actor, prod., dir., co-writer: (films) Hollywood Shuffle, 1987, The Five Heartbeats, 1990, The Meteor Man, 1993; dir.: (films) Eddie Murphy Raw, 1987, B.A.P.S., 1997, Fraternity Boys, 1999 (TV films) Love Songs, 1999, Jackie's Back!, 1999, The 20th Century: From Behind Closed Doors, 1999, Up Up and Away, 2000, Little Richard, 2000, Holiday Heart, 2000; stand-up comedian: (TV spls.) Robert Townsend and His Partners in Crime, Take No Prisoners, Robert Townsend and His Partners in Crime II; TV series: Townsend Television, 1992, The Parent 'Hood, 1995. Office: Tinsel Townsend 8033 W Sunset Blvd Ste 890 Los Angeles CA 90046-2401 also: Creative Artists Agy 9830 Wilshire Blvd Beverly Hills CA 90212-1804

TOWNSEND, SANDRA L. state representative; b. Buffalo, Okla., Dec. 25, 1936; 3 children. County clk., chief dep. San Juan County, Aztec, N.Mex., 1967—91; ret., 1991; state rep. dist. 3 N.Mex. State Legis., Santa Fe, 1995—. Mem. Agr. and Water Resources com. N.Mex. State Legis., Santa Fe, mem. Appropriations and Fin. com. Republican. Methodist. Home: PO Box 1292 Aztec NM 87410 Office: New Mexico State Capitol Rm 201B Santa Fe NM 87504

TOWNSEND, SUSAN ELAINE, religious organization officer; b. Phila., Sept. 5, 1946; d. William Harrison and Eleanor Irene (Fox) Rogers; m. John Holt Townsend, May 1, 1976. BS in Secondary Edn., West Chester State U., 1968; MBA, Nat. U., 1978; PhD in Human Behavior, La Jolla U., 1984. Biology tchr. Methacton Sch. Dist., Fairview Village, Pa., 1968-70; bus. mgr., analyst profl. La Jolla Research Corp., San Diego, 1977-79; pastoral asst. Christ Ctr. Bible Therapy, San Diego, 1980-82, also bd. dirs.; v.p., pub. relations World Outreach Ctr. of Faith, San Diego, 1981-82, also bd. dirs.; owner, pres., cons. Townsend Research Inst., San Diego, 1983-89; propr. Pop "N" Stuff Vending, 2004—. Teaching assoc. La Jolla U. Continuing Edn., 1985-86, adminstr., assoc. registrar, adj. faculty, 1990. Author: Hostage Survival-Resisting the Dynamics of Captivity, 1983; contbr. articles to profl. jours. Instr. USN Advanced Survival Evasion Resistance Escape Sch., 1986-89; security officer Shield Security, San Diego, 1991-92; COO Matthew 25:34-40 Ministries, San Diego, 2000—; bd. dirs. Christ Fellowship Ch. of San Diego, 1987-96, music dir., 1992-2000; religious vol. Met. Correctional Ctr., San Diego, 1983-89; vol. San Diego County Jail Ministries, 1978-2000, scheduling coord., 1993-99, sec., 1998-2000. Comdr. USN, 1970-76, USNR, 1976-93. Mem. Naval Res. Assn. (life), Res. Officers Assn.(outstanding Jr. Officer of Yr. Calif. chpt. 1982), Navy League U.S. (life), West Chester U. Alumni Assn., Nat. U. Alumni Assn. (life), La Jolla U. Alumni Assn., Gen. Fedn. Women's Club (pres. Peninsula Women's Club 1983-85, 94-96, pres. Parlimentary Law Club 1984-86, 96-98, rec. sec. Past Pres.' Assn. 1994-96, pres. 2000-02), Calif. Fedn. Women's Clubs (v.p.-at-large San Diego dist. 25 1982-84, rec. sec. 1994-96, 1st v.p./dean of chmn. 1996-98, pres. 1998-2000). Office Phone: 619-223-1504. E-mail: pop-n-stuff@cox.net.

TOWNSEND, TERRY, publishing executive; b. Camden, N.J., Dec. 14, 1920; d. Anthony and Rose DeMarco; m. Paul Brorstrom Townsend, Dec. 8, 1961; 1 child, Kim. BA, Duke U., 1942; LHD (hon.), Dowling Coll., 1991. Pub. rels. dir. North Shore U. Hosp., Manhasset, N.Y., 1956-68; pres. Theatre Soc., L.I., 1967-70, Townsend Comm. Bur., L.I., 1970-98; ptnr. L.I. Communicating Svc., Bellport, 1977—; sales rep. Zere Comml. Real Estate Svcs., 2003—. Pub. L.I. Bus. News, 1979-98, pub. emeritus, 1998—; v.p. ParrMeadows Racetrack, Yaphank, N.Y., 1977; mem. Bellport Archtl. Rev. Bd., 1997—. Columnist, writer L.I./Bus., Ronkonkoma, 1970-75. Assoc. trustee North Shore U. Hosp., 1968—; bd. govs. Adelphi U. Friends Fin. Edn., 1978-85; chmn. ann. archtl. awards competition N.Y. Inst. Tech., 1970-83; trustee Dowling Coll., 1984-2000; trustee L.I. Fine Arts Mus., 1984-85; pub. broadcasting PBS Sta. WLIW TV, Garden City, L.I., N.Y., 1990-93; bd. dirs. Family Svc. Assn. Nassau County, 1982-92; dinner chmn. L.I. 400 Ball, 1987; trustee L.I. Mus. Art, 1994-2003; pres. Bellport Women's Golf Club, 2004. Recipient Media award 110 Ctr. Bus. and Profl. Women, 1977, Enterprise award Friends of Fin. Edn., 1981, L.I. Loves Bus. Showcase Salute, 1982, Cmty. Svc. award N.Y. Diabetes Assn., 1983, Disting. Long Islander in Comm. award L.I. United Epilepsy Assn., 1984, Spl. award Dowling Coll. Spring Tribute, 1989, Disting. Svc. award Episcopal Health Svcs., 1989, Disting. Citizen award Dowling Coll., 1991, Gilbert Tilles award Nat. Assn. Fundraising Execs., 1994, Hadassah Cmty. Svc. award, 1996, Golden rule award Little Village Sch., 1997, Lifetime Achievement award L.I. Assn., 1998, Promote L.I. Achievement award, 1998, Lifetime Achievement award Advancement for Commerce & Industry, 1999; named 1st Lady of L.I., L.I. Pub. Rels. Assn., 1973, L.I. Woman of Yr. L.I. Assn. Action Com., 1989; Paul and Terry Townsend Sch. of Bus., Dowling Coll., designated in her honor, 2004. Mem.: Bellport Women's Golf Club (pres. 2003—04). Office: LI Communicating Svcs PO Box 915 Bellport NY 11713-0915 E-mail: terytowns@aol.com.

TOWNSEND, WILLIAM JACKSON, lawyer; b. June 4, 1932; s. Robert Glenn and Lois Juanita (Jackson) T. BS, Wake Forest U., 1954; student, U. Ky., 1957, U. Louisville, 1958; JD, U. N.C., 1960. Lawyer; b. Grayson, Ky., June 4, 1932; s. Robert Glenn and Lois Juanita (Jackson) T. BS, Wake Forest U., 1954; Student U. Ky., 1957, U. Louisville, 1958, U. N.C., 1960. Bar: N.C. 1965. Claims adjuster State Farm Ins. Co., 1963; sole practice, Fayetteville, N.C., 1965—; pub. adminstr. Robeson County, N.C., 1966; dir., treas. Colonial Foods, Inc., St. Paul, N.C., 1959—; tax atty. City of Lumberton, 1966-67 . Served as 1st lt. U.S. Army, 1954-56. Mem. N.C. Bar Assn., N.C. State Bar, Cumberland County Bar Assn., N.C. Bar Assn., Scabbard and Blade (pres.), Delta Theta Phi. Presbyterian. Club: Kiwanis (treas. Fayetteville 1973-82). Office: PO Box 584 Fayetteville NC 28302 Office Phone: 910-483-4462.

TOWSLEE, JANET L. special education educator; b. Louisville, Apr. 4, 1942; d. James and Juanita (Flowers) T.; m. Donald Collier, Aug. 28, 1964; children: Richard Louis, Rebecca Elizabeth. BS in Russian Studies, Fla. State U., 1963; MA in Spl. Edn., U. Louisville, 1967; EdD in Spl. Edn., Ind. U., 1974. Cert. tchr. spl. edn. Tchr. Jefferson County Schs., Louisville, 1963-69; teaching asst. Ind. U., Bloomington, 1969-72; with dept. spl. edn. Ga. State U., Atlanta, 1972—, assoc. dean, dir. ednl. field svcs. dean's office, 1978-91; faculty dept. spl. edn. Clayton State Coll., 1992—. Instr. edn. U. Louisville, 1966-67, 69; tchr. basic adult edn. Jefferson County Bd. Edn., 1963-69. Author: Future Educator of America Handbook, 1989, 91, 93; editorial cons. Profl. Educator, 1986—; contbr. articles, book revs. to profl. jours. Bd. dirs. Tommy Nobis Ctr., 1987—, also twice pres. Recipient Outstanding Svc. award Tommy Nobis Ctr., 1987; named Disting. Adminstr. of Yr. Mortar Bd. Ga. State U., 1983. Mem. Assn. Tchr. Educators (one of 70 Leaders Tchr. Edn. 1990, pres. 1987-88, Pres. award for Svc. 1983, 86, Honor Roll 1984), Comparative and Internat. Edn. Soc., Nat. Coun. States Insvc. Edn., U.S.-China Tchr. Edn. Consortium, Assn. Spl. Edn. Tech., Coun. Exceptional Children Internat. (divs. mental retardation, tchr. edn., career devel. internat. edn. and svcs.), Am. Assn. Colls. Tchr. Edn. (NCATE exec. bd.), S.E. Regional Assn. Tchr. Educators, Ga. Assn. Tchr. Educators, Ga. Staff Devel. Coun., Ga. Coun. Exceptional Children, Met. Atlanta Tchr. Edn. Group. Home: 1194 W Nancy Creek Dr NE Atlanta GA 30319-1644

TOWSNER, CYNTHIA MERLE, vocational school educator; b. Washington, Apr. 23, 1939; d. Philip and Edith Towsner; married, 1963; children: Scott David Garrison, Katrina L. Goldbrand. BS, U. Md., 1961, postgrad., 1964-65, Am. U., 1987. Adv. cert. contracting officer's tech. rep. U.S. Dept. Edn. Tchr. Montgomery County Pub. Schs., Rockville, Md., 1961-66, 72-80; spl. asst. to commr. rehab. svcs. adminstrn. U.S. Dept. Edn., Washington, 1981-85, spl. asst. to the dir. Office Intergovtl. & Interagy. Affairs, 1985-87, acting dir. intergovtl. affairs office, 1987, ednl. program specialist Office Bilingual Edn. & Minority Languages Affairs, 1987-93, edn. program specialist Bilingual Vocat. Tng., 1993-96, nat. coord. family literacy and literacy vols. for adults, 1996—2002, coord lit. vols., 1996—. Pres. Office Vocat. Adult Edn., U.S. Dept. Edn., Educare Programs, Inc., Chevy Chase, Md., 1988—; cons. R.J. Comer Comm., Inc., Jacksonville, Fla., 1995-97; v.p. Dalmahoy Group Internat., Chevy Chase, 1997-99. Photographer Project Education Reform: Time for Results, vol. 1, 1987. Vol. Holy Cross Hosp., Silver Spring, Md., 1969-74; asst. to pres. for edn. issues, chair nominating com., chair cmty. directory Rock Creek Hills Civic Assn., Kensington, 1968-85; v.p. D.C., Md. and Va. region, chair youth rally, chair radiothon publicity St. Jude's Children's Rsch. Hosp., Aiding Leukemia Stricken Am. Children, Memphis, 1969-81; chair internat. festival Larchmont Elem. Sch. PTA, Montgomery County, MD, 1976-78; bd. dirs., mem., chair Citizens for Edn., Montgomery County, Md., 1977-82; active Renaissance Women, Washington, 1983-87; chair corp. and bus. contbns. Hosp. Relief Fund for the Caribbean, Chevy Chase, 1989-91, annual ball com., 1989-94; vol. tutor Laubach Literacy Action and Literacy Vols. Am., Chevy Chase, 1989-93. Recipient Meritorious Svc. medal Am. Automobile Assn., Washington, Honors award Rock Creek Hills Civic Assn., Kensington, Md., 1979, Pres.'s award Combined Fed. Campaign, Washington, 1987, Hammer award V.P. of the U.S., Washington, 1996, 1st place ribbon in photography Montgomery County Agrl. Fair, Gaithersburg, Md., 1998, 1st, 2nd and 3rd place ribbons in photography Montgomery County Agrl. Fair, Gaithersburg, 1999, 1st and 2nd place ribbons in photography Md. State Fair, Timonium, 1999, 1st pl. award Md. State Fair, 2000. Mem. AAUW, Internat. Freelance Photographers Orgn. (named Master Photographer 2002, life), Assn. for Career and Tech. Edn., Soc. Govt. Meeting Profls., Nat. Trust for Scotland, Nat. Mus. Women in the Arts (founding mem.). Avocations: photography, reading, travel. Home: 4620 N Park Ave Apt 1404E Chevy Chase MD 20815-4563 E-mail: cindymt@comcast.net.

TOY, CHARLES DAVID, lawyer; b. NYC, June 29, 1955; s. Frank H.F. and Louise S.K. (Louie) Toy; m. Sandra Lynn Youla, Mar. 10, 1984; 1 child, Alana May Youla. BA cum laude, Harvard U., 1977, JD, 1980. Bar: NY 1981, DC 2001. Assoc. Milbank, Tweed, Hadley & McCloy, NYC, 1980-84, Kaye, Scholer, Fierman, Hays & Handler, Hong Kong, 1984—88, ptnr., 1989—91, NYC, 1991—93; v.p., gen. counsel Overseas Pvt. Investment Corp., Washington, 1993-2001, v.p. fin., 1995-96, v.p. investment funds, 1998-99; ptnr. Wilmer, Cutler & Pickering, Washington, 2001—02; mem. bd. advisors GMI Capital Corp., Chevy Chase, Md., 2002—04, exec. v.p., 2004—. Spkr. in field; profile subject Internat. Fin. Law Rev., 1996, Ave. Asia, 1996, 97, ABA 1997, 98, 99, 2002, Am. Conf. Inst., 1996, 98, Am. Soc. Internat. Law, 1996, 97, Assn. Bar City NY, 2000, World Econ. Devel. Conf., 1996, Corp. Legal Times Roundtable, 1996, Com. of 100, 1996, Asian Am. Bar Assn., 1996, Asian Bus. Assn., 1996, Asian Pacific Am. Bar Assn., 1996, Forbes, 1997, Adam Smith Inst., 1998, Jerome Levy Econs. Inst. Bard Coll., 1998, Asian Pacific Am. Inst. Congl. Studies, 1998, Embassy South Africa, 1998, Harvard Inst. Internat. Devel., 1998, 99, Insight Info., 1998, 99, Nat. Asian Pacific Am. Bar Assn., 1998. U. Fla. Levin Coll. Law, 1999, CNA/Schinnerer Conf., 1999, Case We. Res. U. Sch. Law, 1999, Practising Law Inst., 1999, 2000, U. Iowa Tippie Sch. Mgmt., 2000, Met. Corp. Counsel Interview, 2000, Internat. Project Fin. Assn., 2000, Am. Corp. Counsel Assn., 2000, US Inst. Peace, 2001; interview Legal Times, 2001, Bloomberg, 2002. Contbg. editor Taxes and Investment in Asia and the Pacific, 1985, Tax News Service, 1986—, Bulletin for International Fiscal Documentation, 1986—; bd. editors Strategic Alliance Alert, 1994-95. Bd. trustees Lower East Side Tenement Mus., 1994-98. Mem. ABA, NY State Bar Assn., Assn. Bar City of NY, Nat. Asian Pacific Am. Bar Assn., Asian Pacific Am. Bar Assn., Harvard Law Sch. Assn., Am. Club (Hong Kong), Ladies Recreation Club (Hong Kong), Phi Beta Kappa Democrat. Roman Catholic. Office: GMI Capital Corp 4701 Willard Ave Ste 413 Chevy Chase MD 20815-4610 E-mail: toy@gmicc.com.

TOY, STEPHEN J. corporate financial executive; b. Nov. 1972; BS in Bus. Adminstrn., SUNY, 1994. Corp. auditor Kansai Sawayawa; corp. fin. O'Brien Ptnrs., Inc.; mng. dir. WL Ross & Co. LLC, N.Y. Office: WL Ross & Co LLC Manhattan Tower 19th Fl 101 East 52d St New York NY 10022

TOYODA, SHOICHIRO, automobile company executive; b. Nagoya, Japan, Feb. 27, 1925; s. Kiichiro and Hatako Toyoda; m. Hiroko Mitsui, Nov. 30, 1952; children: Atuko, Akio. B in Engring., Nagoya U., 1947, D in Engring., 1955. Dir. Toyota (Japan) Motor Co., Ltd., 1952-61, mng. dir., 1961-67, sr. mng. dir., 1967-72, exec. v.p., 1972-81; pres. Toyota Motor Sales Co., Ltd., 1981-82, Toyota Motor Corp., 1982-92, chmn., 1992-99, hon. chmn., 1999—. Bd. dirs. Denso Co., Ltd., Nagoya Broadcasting Network; chmn. bd. dirs. Inst. Internat. Econ. Studies. Chmn. Keidanren, Tokyo, 1994-98; hon. chmn. KDDI, 2000; consul gen. Honorario de Costa Rica, Nagoya, 1984—. Recipient Medal with Dark-Blue Ribbon, Govt. of Japan, 1972, The Deming Prize, 1980, Medal with Blue Ribbon, Govt. of Japan, 1984, FISITA medal, France, Medal of Isabel la Cath., King of Spain, 2000; decorated knight comdr. Most Noble Order of the Crown (Thailand), gran cruz Order Nacional al Merit, Colombia, knight comdr. Brit. Empire, grand cordon Order of the Sacred Treasure (Japan), Order Francisco de Miranda First Class (Venezuela), Ordem Nat. do Cruzeiro do Sul (Brazil), Order of Merit (Turkey), comdr. Legion of Honor (France), Grande Ufficiale, Govt. of Italy, hon. companion Gen. divsn. Order of Australia, grand decoration of honor in gold with star, Austria. Office: Toyota Motor Corp 1 Toyota-cho Toyota 471-8571 Japan

TOZER, ELIZABETH FARRAN, interior and floral designer; b. Cleve., Jan. 25, 1942; d. Charles and Irma (Gaensslen) Farran; m. W. James Tozer Jr., July 30, 1965; children: Farran Tozer Brown and Katherine Tozer Roddy. BFA, Ohio Wesleyan U., 1964. Residential and comml. interior and floral designer Elizabeth Farran Tozer Design, N.Y.C., 1982—. Interior design cons. N.Y. Found. for Sr. Citizens, N.Y.C., 1982—; pres. The Flower Svc. Store, N.Y.C., 1972-92; spokesperson Am. Florists Mktg. Coun., 1987; appeared in numerous radio, TV, and newspaper interviews in eleven maj. U.S. cities. Author: The Art of Flower Arranging, 1981; contbr. articles to profl. publs. Chmn. N.Y. Flower Show, 1996; mem. exec. com., mem. nominating com. Mus. of the City of N.Y., 1994—; vice chmn., chmn. nominating com., bd. dirs. N.Y. Found. for Sr. Citizens, 1980-; mem. nominating com. Sch. Am. Ballet, Lincoln Ctr., 1977—; chmn. more than 30 maj. fundraising events in N.Y.C. and Dutchess County, N.Y., 1977—; mem. adv. bd. Nat. Acad. Design, 1999-; chmn. Inst. Ecosys. AldoLeopold Soc., 2001-. Recipient award Mcpl. Arts Soc., 1997, award YWCA Acad. Women Achievers, 1995, Pillars of Industry award, Best Srs. Mid-Rise Bldg. award Nat. Assn. Home Builders, 1995, Spl. Merit award Associated Builders and Owners of Greater N.Y., 1993. Mem. N.Y. Hort. Soc. (nominating com.). Avocation: raising miniature horses. Office: EFT Design Ltd 1112 Park Ave # 6A New York NY 10128-1235

TOZER, W. JAMES, JR., investment company executive; b. Salt Lake City, Feb. 9, 1941; s. W. James and Virginia (Somerville) T.; m. Elizabeth Farran, July 30, 1965; children: Farran Virginia, Katharine Coppins. BA cum laude, Trinity Coll., 1963; MBA, Harvard U., 1965. Investment officer First Nat. City Overseas Investment Corp., N.Y.C., 1965-70; v.p. corp. devel. Citicorp, N.Y.C., 1970-71; sr. v.p. and head Citicorp Subs. Group, 1971-74; sr. v.p., gen. mgr., head Merchant Banking Group, 1974-75, sr. v.p., gen. mgr. N.Y. banking div., 1975-77; sr. exec. v.p., dir. and head investment banking div. Shearson Hayden Stone, Inc., N.Y.C., 1978-79; sr. exec. v.p. Marine Midland Bank and Marine Midland Banks, Inc., 1979-80, sr. exec. v.p. ops., fin. and strategic staff units, 1980-85, mem. office of chmn., sector exec. corp., instl. and internat. banking, 1985-87; chmn. Mountain West Banking Corp., Denver, 1988-89; pres., chief operating officer Prudential-Bache Securities, Inc., N.Y.C., 1989-90; pres., CEO Lincolnshire Mgmt., Inc., N.Y.C., 1993-94; mng. dir. Vectra Mgmt. Group, 1990—. Bd. dirs. Lending Tree, Inc., 1998—2003. Chmn. bd. Fellows Trinity Coll., 1972-78; trustee, treas. Community Service Soc., 1976-87; trustee, treas. The Sch. for Field Studies, 1995—; trustee Citizens Budget Commn., 1986—; adv. council Atlanta U. Sch. Bus. Adminstrn., 1985-89; bd. Episcopal Charities. Mem. N.Y. State Bankers Assn. (legis. policy com. 1981-87), Assn. Res. City Bankers (govt. rels. com. 1984-87), Am. Bankers Assn. (govt. rels. coun. 1985-87), Economic Club, University Club, Bond of N.Y. Club, Millbrook Club, Mashomack Club, River Club (N.Y.C.), Alta Club, (S.L.C). Home: 550 Park Ave New York NY 10021-7369 Office: 424 W 33St Ste 540 New York NY 10001-2614 Office Phone: 212-631-0202., 212-631-0202.

TOZER, WILLIAM EVANS, entomologist, educator; b. Binghamton, NY, July 7, 1947; s. William Evans and Gertrude Genevieve (Lewis) T. BS in Natural Sci., Niagara U., 1969; MS in Biology, Ball State U., 1979; PhD in Entomology, U. Calif., Berkeley, 1986. Cert. C.C. biology and zoology tchr. Calif. Jr. H.S. sci. and English tchr. St. Patricks Sch., Corning, NY, 1969-71; tchg. asst. biology Ball State U., Muncie, Ind., 1974-76; pvt. practice biol. environ. cons. Berkeley, Calif., 1976-79, 86-88; rsch. asst. U. Calf., Berkeley, 1979-86; dept. head edn. and tng. USN Disease Vector Ecology and Control Ctr., Poulsbo, Wash., 1988—. Mem., acting chmn. San Francisco Bay Area Mosquito Control Coun., Alameda, 1988-96; chmn. com., mem. Armed Forces Pest Mgmt. Bd., Washington, 1994—; bd. dirs. Cert. and Tng. Assessment Group, EPA/USDA, 2001-. Editor (field handbook) Navy Environmental Health Center, 1994; contbr. articles to profl. jours. With U.S. Army, 1971-73. Mem. Am. Entomol. Soc., Sigma Xi. Achievements include first to publish evidence for underwater behavioral thermoregulation in adult insects. Home: 1407 NW Santa Fe Ln Apt 304 Silverdale WA 98383-7915 Office: USN Disease Vector Ecol Control Ctr 2850 Thresher Ave Silverdale WA 98315- Office Phone: 360-315-4450. Business E-Mail: william.tozer@ndvecc.navy.mil.

TRABER, PETER GEORGE, academic administrator, educator; b. Johnstown, NY, 1955; m. K. Bobbi Traber; 2 children. Grad., U. Mich., 1977; MD, Wayne State U. Med. Sch., 1981; completed Mgmt. Devel Program for Physician Exec., Wharton Sch. U. Pa. Resident in internal medicine Northwestern U. Med. Sch., Chgo., fellow in gastroenterology, U. Mich. Sch. Medicine, faculty mem., 1987—92; chief gastroenterology U. Pa. Sch. Medicine, 1992—97, T. Grier Miller prof. medicine, 1993—97, Frank Wistar Thomas prof. and chair dept. medicine, 1997—2000, interim dean, 2000; interim CEO U. Pa. Health Sys., Phila., 2000; sr. v.p. clinical devel. and med. affairs and chief med. officer GlaxoSmithKline, 2000—03; pres., CEO, prof. medicine Baylor Coll. Medicine, 2003—. Bd. dir. Tanox Inc., 2004—. Recipient Disting. Alumni award, Wayne State U. Sch. Medicine. Mem.: Assn. Am. Physicians, Am. Soc. Clinical Rsch., Am. Gastroenterologic Assn. Office: Baylor Coll Medicine One Baylor Plz Houston TX 77030

TRABITZ, EUGENE LEONARD, aerospace company executive; b. Cleve., Aug. 13, 1937; s. Emanuel and Anna (Berman) T.; m. Caryl Lee Rine, Dec. 22, 1963 (div. Aug. 1981); children: Claire Marie, Honey Caryl; m. Kathryn Lynn Bates, Sept. 24, 1983; 1 stepchild, Paul Francis Rager. BA, Ohio State U., 1965. Enlisted USAF, 1954, advanced through grades to maj.; served as crew comdr. 91st Strategic Missile Divsn., Minot, SD, 1968-70; intelligence officer Fgn. Tech. Divsn., Dayton, Ohio, 1970-73; dir. external affairs Aero. Systems Divsn., Dayton, 1973-75; program mgr. Air Force Armament Divsn., Valparaiso, Fla., 1975-80; dir. ship ops. Air Force Ea. Test Range, Satellite Beach, Fla., 1980-83; dep. program mgr. Air Force Satellite Text Ctr., Sunnyvale, Calif., 1983-84; ret., 1984; sr. staff engr. Ultrasystems Inc., 1984-86; pres. TAWD Systems Inc., Palo Alto, Calif., 1986-92, Am. Telenetics Co., San Mateo, Calif., 1992—; pres., CEO Enterprise Def. Inst., Inc., San Mateo, 2002—. Cons. Space Applications Corp., Sunnyvale, 1986-87, Litton Computer Svcs., Mountain View, Calif., 1987-91, Battelle Meml. Inst. Columbus, 1993—. V.p. Bd. County Mental Health Clinic, Ft. Walton Beach, Fla., 1973-75. Decorated Bronze Star. Mem. DAV (life), ASIS Internat., Nat. Def. Indsl. Assn., Armed Forces Comm. and Electronics Assn., Am. Soc. for Indsl. Security Internat., U.S. Space Found. (charter), Air Force Assn. (life), Nat. Sojourners, Masons (32d degree). Avocations: golf, tennis, racketball, sailing, bridge. Home: 425 Anchor Rd Apt 317 San Mateo CA 94404-1058 Office Phone: 650-345-5694. E-mail: gene@amtelenet.com.

TRABULSI, JUDY, advertising and marketing executive; b. Houston; d. Richard Joseph and Genevieve (Jamail) T. BS in Comm., U. Tex., 1971. Exec. v.p., exec. media dir. Gurasich, Spence, Darilek & McClure, Austin, Tex., 1971—. Mem. nat. adv. coun. SBA, Washington, 1994-96; adv. coun. U. Tex. Comm. Sch., Austin, 1996—; adv. mem. 21st Century Dems., 1996. Office: Gurasich Spence Darilek & McClure 828 W 6th St Austin TX 78703-5420

TRACEY, MATTHEW SEAN, music educator, musician; b. Teaneck, NJ, Feb. 4, 1965; s. Patrick Edward and Kathleen Teresa Tracey; m. Dawn C. Cusimano, Nov. 3, 1990. MusM, Montclair State U., NJ, 1987—89; MusB, William Paterson U., Wayne, NJ, 1983—87. Cert. K-12 tchr. of music NJ, 1987. Musician Ray Sepulveda Orch., New York, 1993—, Tito Nieves Orch., New York; musical dir. Frankie Negron Orch., New York, 1994—96; k-12 music dept. chairperson Ridgefield Pub. Schools, NJ, 1990—; dir. of bands Ridgefield Meml. HS, 1987—. Hon. lifetime mem. Nat. PTA, NJ; mem. Music Educators Nat. Conf., NJ, 1983—, Internat. Assn. of Jazz Educators, NJ, NEA, NJ. Edn. Assn., Music Educators of Bergen County, NJ. Musician: (studio/ recording musician) commercial jingles, Pop, Jazz, Latin recordings; profesional marching drill designer, Drill Designer; composer: (composer/arranger) various works. Recipient World Champion Bushwacker Drum & Bugle Corps, Drum Corps Associates, 1986, 198, 1989, 1990, World Champion-Garfield Cadets, Drum Corps Internat., 1984. Mem.: Nat. PTA (hon. Hon. Lifetime Mem. 2004). Achievements include NJ Governors's Tchr. of the Year. Avocations: family, music, travel, gastronomy. Office: Ridgefield Memorial High School 555 Walnut street Ridgefield NJ 08657 E-mail: contactus@ridgefieldband.com.

TRACEY, PATRICIA A. career officer; b. Bronx, N.Y. m. Richard Metzer. Grad., Women Officers Sch., 1970; BA in Math., Coll. New Rochelle; MS in Ops. Rsch., Naval Postgrad. Sch. Ensign USN, 1970; advanced through grades vice admiral; cmd. ctr. officer naval space surveillance sys.; staff tour of comdr. in chief Pacific fleet; bur. naval personnel placement officer; extended planning analyst sys. analysis divsn. chief naval ops. staff, 1980-82, exec. officer recruiting dist., 1982-84, manpower and personnel analyst program appraisal divsn., 1984-86; comdr. Naval Tech. Tng. Ctr. Treasure Is., 1986-88; head enlisted plans, cmty. mgmt. br. Chief Naval Personnel, 1988-90; comdr. Naval Sta. Long Beach (Calif.), 1990; fellow chief naval ops.'s strategic studies group Naval War Coll.; dir. manpower and personnel J-1 joint staff, 1993-95; comdr. Naval Tng. Ctr., 1995-96; chief naval edn. and tng., dir. naval tng. chief naval ops. Pensacola, Fla., 1996-98; dep. asst. sec. of def., 1998—. Decorated 3 Legions of Merit, Def. Disting. Svc. medal, Navy Disting. Svc. medal, 3 Meritorious Svc. medals. Office: Dep Asst Sec of Def Mil Personnel Policy 4000 Defense Pentagon 3E767 Washington DC 20301-4000

TRACHSEL, WILLIAM HENRY, corporate lawyer; b. El Paso, Tex., Apr. 20, 1943; BS in Aerospace Engring., U. Fla., 1965; JD, U. Conn., 1971. Bar: Conn. 1971. V.p., counsel Hamilton Standard, Hartford, Conn., 1978; v.p., counsel automotive div. United Tech. Corp., Hartford, Conn., 1979—83, deputy general counsel, 1983—86, v.p., dep. gen. counsel, 1986—93, v.p., sec. and dep. gen. counsel, 1993-98, sr. v.p., gen. counsel, sec., 1998—2004, sr. v.p., gen. counsel, 2004—. Mem.: U. Conn. Found. (bd. dir.), U. Conn. Capital Campaign Steering Comm., Am. Bar Assoc., Conn. Bar Assoc., Conn. Bar Found. (bd. dir.), Hartford Hosp. (bd. dir.), MetroHartford Alliance. Office: United Tech Corp Bldg Hartford CT 06101 Business E-Mail: william.trachsel@utc.com.

TRACHTENBERG, MATTHEW J. bank executive; b. NYC, June 20, 1958; s. Mark Trachtenberg and Joanne Horne. BA magna cum laude, NYU, 1974; JD, Bklyn. Law Sch., 1977; MBA in Fin., Fordham U., 1982. Bar: NY 1979. Mgmt. trainee Mfrs. Hanover Trust Co., NYC, 1977-78, credit analyst, 1978-79, corp. banking rep., 1979-80, asst. sec., 1980-82, asst. v.p., 1982, v.p., 1982-86, v.p., corp. sec., 1987-92; dir. Mfrs. Hanover Found., NYC, 1987-92; v.p., sec. regional bd. Chem. Bank, NYC, 1992-96, v.p., dep. corp. sec., 1992-96, sec. regional bd., 1992-96, v.p., 1992-96, Chem. Banking Corp., NYC, 1992-96; v.p. asst. corp. sec. Chase Manhattan Bank, NYC, 1996—98; sec. Chase Manhattan Regional Bd., NYC, 1996—98; v.p., sr. pvt. banker PNC Bank, NYC, 1999—2000, Fleet Bank, NYC, 2000—02; mng. dir. First Republic Bank, NYC, 2002—04; sr. v.p. US Trust Co., 2004—. Bd. dirs., pres. Nat. Orch. Assn.; bd. dirs., past pres. USO Met. NY; mem. adv. edn. com. Lighthouse for the Blind; bd. dirs., treas. NY Eye and Ear Infirmary; bd. dirs. Continuum Health Ptnrs. NY State Regents scholar. Mem.: Am. Soc. Corp. Secs., NY State Bar Assn., Phi Beta Kappa, Pi Sigma Alpha. Avocations: music, fishing, painting, writing. Office: First Republic Bank 1230 Ave of the Americas New York NY 10020

TRACHTENBERG, STEPHEN JOEL, university president; b. Bklyn., Dec. 14, 1937; s. Oscar M. and Shoshana G. (Weinstock) Trachtenberg; m. Francine Zorn, June 24, 1971; children: Adam Maccabee, Ben-Lev. BA, Columbia U., 1959; JD, Yale U., 1962; M in Pub. Adminstrn., Harvard U., 1966; LHD (hon.), Trinity Coll., 1986; HHD (hon.), U. Hartford, 1989; LLD (hon.), Hanyang U., Seoul, 1990; DPA (hon.), Kyonggi U., Seoul, 1994; LLD (hon.), Richmond Coll., London, 1995; MD (hon.), Odessa State Med. U., Ukraine, 1996; LLD (hon.), Mount Vernon Coll., 1997; LHD (hon.), Boston U., 1999, Gratz Coll., 1999; LLD (hon.), So. Conn. State U., 2001, U. New Haven, 2002. Bar: N.Y. 1964, U.S. Supreme Ct. 1967. Atty. AEC, 1962—65; legis. asst. to Congressman John Brademas of Ind., Washington, 1965; tutor law Harvard Coll.; tchg. fellow edn. and pub. policy J.F. Kennedy Grad. Sch. Govt., Harvard U., 1965—66; spl. asst. to U.S. edn. commr. Office of Edn., HEW, Washington, 1966—68; assoc. prof. polit. sci. Boston U., 1969—77, assoc. dean, 1969—70, dean, 1970—74, assoc. v.p., co-counsel, 1974—76, v.p. acad. svcs., 1976—77; pres., prof. pub. adminstrn. U. Hartford, Conn., 1977—88, George Washington U., Washington, 1988—. Mem. joint editl. bd. The Presidency and ACE/Praeger Series on Higher Edn.; mem. Fed. City Coun.; bd. dirs. Consortium of Univs. Washington Met. Area, Riggs Bank, Greater Washington Bd. Trade, Nat. Edn. Telecom. Orgn., Washington Rsch. Libr. Consortium, DC Com. to Promote Washington; exec. adv. coun. SCT Edn. Sys. Contbr. articles to profl. jours. Trustee Al-Akhawayn U., Morocco, Com. for Econ. Devel.; active 2001 U.S. Savs. Bonds Vol. Com.; chmn. Md./D.C. Selection Com., 1998—2004, Rhodes Scholarships; mem. Washington Regional Panel for Selection of 2004-05 Class of White House Fellows; active D.C. Mayor's Bus. Adv. Coun.; exec. panel Chief Naval Ops.; bd. overseers List Coll. Jewish Theol. Sem. Am.; chair, bd. dirs. D.C. C. of C.; chair, pres. council Atlantic 10 Conf.; bd. dirs. Chiang Chen Indsl. Charity Found. Ltd., Hong Kong. Decorated grand officier du Wissam Al Alaoui King Mohammed VI of Morocco; named Outstanding Young Person, Boston Jr. C. of C., 1970, Alumnus of Yr., James Madison H.S., Bklyn., 1982, Washingtonian of Yr., Washingtonian Mag., 2000, Jan. 22, 1998 Stephen Joel Trachtenberg Day, D.C. City Council, Feb. 2, 1999 Stephen Joel Trachtenberg Day, Mayor of San Francisco; named one of 100 Young Leaders, Acad. Am. Council Learning, 1978, Fifty Outstanding Alumni Problem Solvers, Harvard's John F. Kennedy Sch. Govt., 1987, "The 2002 Forty Forward" Ann. List 40 Most Influential People in Town, Washington Bus. Forward mag., 2002; recipient Myrtle Wreath award, Hadassah, 1982, Scopus award, Am. Friends of Hebrew U., 1984, Human Rels. award, NCCJ, 1987, NAACP award, 1988, Conn. Bar Assn. citation, 1988, Univ. medal of highest honor, Kyung Hee U., Korea, 1990, Martin Luther King, Jr. Internat. Salute award, 1992, Hannah G. Solomon award, Nat. Coun. Jewish Women, 1992, Father of Yr. award, Washington Urban League, 1993, Univ. Pres. medal, Kyonggi U., Korea, 1993, Merit award, Am. Czech and Slovak Assn., 1993, John Jay award, Columbia U., 1995, Spirit of Democracy award, Am. Jewish Congress, 1995, Newcomen Soc. award, 1995, Disting. Achievement medal, Greenberg Ctr. for Judaic Studies U. Hartford, 1995, Humanitarian award, B'nai B'rith, 1996, Disting. Pub. Svc. award, U.S. Dept. of State Sec.'s Open Forum, 1997, Tree of Life award, Jewish Nat. Fund, 1999, High Twelve Internat. Founders award, 2000, Key of Life award, Egypt's Internat. Econ. Forum, 2001, medal of merit, U.S. Dept. Treasury, 2001, Father Yr. award, Am. Diabetes Assn., 2002, Humanitarian award, The Albert B. Sabin Vaccine Inst., 2003, Madison Freedom award, 2004; Winston Churchill fellow, Eng., 1969, Hon. Wolcott fellow, 1999, Morse Coll. Yale U. assoc. fellow. Fellow: Am. Acad. Arts and Scis.; mem.: Bus.-Higher Edn. Forum, Ind. Retail Cattleman's Assn. (adv. coun.), Sr. Soc. Sachems, Coun. Fgn. Rels., Newcomen Soc. U.S. (life; former trustee), Am. Coun. Learned Soc. (assoc.), Internat. Assn. Univ. Pres. (N.Am. coun.), N.Y. Acad. Scis., Am. Assn. Univ. Adminstrs. (pres. 1998—2000, Disting. Svc. award 1996), Am. Coun. for the UN U. (vice chair), Hannibal Club, Nat. Press Club, Cosmos Club, Harvard Club, Tumble Brook Country Club, Univ. Club, George Washington U. Club, Masons (33d degree, Grand Cross award), Phi Beta Kappa. Office: George Washington U Office of Pres 2121 Eye St N W Rm 802 Washington DC 20052-0001

TRACT, MARC MITCHELL, lawyer; b. NYC, Sept. 20, 1959; s. Harold Michael and Natalie Ann (Meyerowitz) T.; m. Sharon Beth Widrow; children: Melissa Hope, Harrison Michael, Sarah Michelle. BA in Biology, Ithaca Coll., 1981; JD, Pepperdine U., 1984. Bar: NY 1985, NJ 1985, DC 1986. Assoc. Kroll & Tract, NYC, 1985—90, ptnr., 1990—94, Rosenman & Colin LLP, NYC, 1994—2002, Katten Muchin Zavis Rosenman, NYC, 2002—. Bd. dirs. Rampart Ins. Co., Navigators Group Inc., NYC, MAPFRE Reins. Corp., Florham Park, NJ, AXA Art Ins. Corp., NYC. Bd. dirs. Italian Acad. Found. Decorated Order of Merit of Savoy. Mem. ABA, Assn. Bar City of NY, NY State Bar Assn., NJ State Bar Assn., NY County Lawyers Assn., Am. Coun. Germany, Old Westbury Golf and Country Club, Met. Club, Econ. Club NY. Republican. Office: KMZ Rosenman 575 Madison Ave Fl 11 New York NY 10022-2511

TRACY, ALAN THOMAS, trade association administrator; b. Janesville, Wis., May 3, 1947; s. Robert Elmer and Frances Dina (Daane) T.; m. Kris Cunningham; children: Chad, Paul, Sarah. BS in Agrl. Econs., Cornell U., Ithaca, N.Y., 1969; MBA, U. Wis., 1970. With Tracy & Son Farms, Inc., Janesville, Wis., 1970-81, v.p., 1973-76, pres., 1976-81; gen sales mgr., assoc. adminstr. Dept. Agr., Washington, 1981-82, dep. undersec. for internat. affairs and commodity programs, 1982-85, dep. asst. sec. dor mktg. and inspection services, 1985-86; spl. asst. to pres. for agrl. trade and food assistance The White House, 1986-89; sec. Wis. Dept. Agr., Trade and Consumer Protection, Madison, 1990-97; pres. U.S. Wheat Assocs., Washington, 1997—. Dir. Heritage Bank, Beloit, Janesville, 1978-81; pres. Mid. Am. Intrnat. Agrl. Trading Coun., 1994, Nat. Assn. State Depts. Agr., 1995-96. Trustee Beloit Coll., Wis., 1980-83; chmn. Republican party Rock County, 1972-74. Named Outstanding Young Farmer Wis. Wis. Jaycees, 1980; Nat. Merit scholar, 1965 Mem. Janesville C. of C. (chmn. agribus. com. 1978-79) Lodges: Rotary-Janesville (dir. 1980-81). Methodist. Office: US Wheat Assocs 1620 I St NW Ste 801 Washington DC 20006-4005

TRACY, HAROLD DEWAYNE, retired secondary school educator; b. Midwest, Wyo., Nov. 10, 1928; s. Lester Otto and Edith Grace (Fraley) Tracy; m. June A. Burch, Sept. 9, 1950 (div.); children: Kim D., Todd R., Lisa A.; m. Barbara Ann Schurman; children: Matthew D., Elizabeth L. AA in Edn., North Idaho Jr. Coll., 1952; BA in Edn., Whitworth Coll., 1954; postgrad., San Francisco State U., 1959. Tchr. Coeur D'Alene (Idaho) Sch., 1952-54, Oswego (Oreg.) Sch. Dist., 1954-60, D.O.D., Subic Bay, The Phillipines, 1960-64, Forest Grove (Oreg.) Dilley, 1964-66; ins. rep. Northwestern Marsh, Portland, 1966-71; pres. Red Barn Rest Corp., Redmond, Oreg., 1971-79; owner, mgr. Thrifty Ads, Bend, Oreg., 1979-87. Sgt. USAF, 1946-49. Democrat. Presbyterian. Avocations: flying, hunting, fishing, reading, travel. Home: 2720 Roberts Rd Medford OR 97504

TRACY, JAMES DONALD, historian, educator; b. St. Louis, Feb. 14, 1938; s. Leo W. and Marguerite M. (Meehan) T.; m. Nancy Ann McBride, Sept. 6, 1968 (div. 1993); children: Patrick, Samuel, Mary Ann; m. Suzanne K. Swan, May 2, 1997. BA, St. Louis U., 1959; MA, Johns Hopkins U., 1960, Notre Dame U., 1961; PhD, Princeton U., 1967. Instr. U. Mich., 1964-66; instr. to prof. history U. Minn., Mpls., 1966—, dept. chmn., 1988-91, Union Pacific prof. early modern history, 2001—04. Vis. prof. U. Leiden, Netherlands, 1987, U. Paris IV, 2001, U. Amsterdam, 2004. Author: Erasmus: The Growth of a Mind, 1972, The Politics of Erasmus: A Pacifist Intellectual and His Political Milieu, 1979, True Ocean Found.: Paludanus's Letters on Dutch Voyages to the Kara Sea, 1980, A Financial Revolution in the Habsburg Netherlands: Renten and Renteniers in the County of Holland, 1515-1565, 1985, Holland Under Habsburg Rule: The Formation of a Body Politic, 1506-1566, 1990, Erasmus of the Low Countries, 1996, Europe's Reformations, 1450-1650, 1999, Emperor Charles V, Impresario of War, 2002; editor: Luther and the Modern State in Germany, 1986, The Rise of Merchant Empires: Long Distance Trade in the Early Modern Era, 1350-1750, 1990, The Political Economy of Merchant Empires: Long Distance Trade and State Power in the Early Modern World, 1991; editor: (with T.A. Brady and H.A. Oberman) Handbook of European History in the Late Middle Ages, Renaissance and Reformation, Vol. 1, 1994, Vol. 2, 1995; editor: City Walls: The Urban Enceinte in Global Perspective, 2000; editor: (with T.A. Brady, K.G. Brady and S. Karant-Nunn) The Work of Heiko A. Oberman, 2003; mem. editl. bd. Sixteenth Century Jour., 1979—2000; co-editor: Jour. Early Modern History, 1997—2000; editor, 2000—. Guggenheim fellow, 1972-73; NEH summer grantee, 1977, 85; Fulbright rsch. grantee, Belgium, 1979, Netherlands, 1980; resident fellow Netherlands Inst. for Advanced Studies, 1993-94. Mem. Am. Cath. Hist. Soc. (pres. 1999-00), Soc. Reformation Rsch. (pres. 1995-97), 16th Century Studies Conf. (pres. 1985-86). Republican. Roman Catholic. Home: 757 Osceola Ave # 2 Saint Paul MN 55105-3327 Office: U Minn History 614 Social Sci Bldg Minneapolis MN 55455 Office Phone: 612-624-0808. Business E-Mail: tracy001@umn.edu.

TRACY, JAMES JARED, JR., accountant, financial executive, law firm administrator; b. Cleve., Jan. 17, 1929; s. James Jared and Florence (Comey) T.; m. Elizabeth Jane Bourne, June 30, 1953 (div. 1988); children: Jane Tracy Ahrens, Elizabeth Tracy Jenkins, James Jared IV, Margaret Tracy Rosen; m. Judith Anne Cooper, Feb. 18, 1989. AB, Harvard U., 1950, MBA, 1953. CPA, Ohio. Acct., sr. mgr. Price Waterhouse & Co., Cleve., 1953-65; treas., CFO Clevite Corp., Cleve., 1965-69; from asst. treas. to treas. Republic Steel Corp., Cleve., 1969—75; v.p., treas. Johns-Manville Corp., Denver, 1976-81; v.p., treas., CFO Internat. Techs. Corp., LA, 1981—82; exec. dir. Hufstedler, Miller, Carlson & Beardsley, LA, 1983—84, Shank, Irwin & Conant, Dallas, 1984-85, Pachter, Gold & Schaffer, LA, 1985—86; v.p., sr. cons. Right Assocs., LA, 1987—91; dir. adminstrn. Larson & Burnham, Oakland, Calif., 1991-95; adminstrv. dir. Law Offices of Thomas E. Miller, Newport Beach, Calif., 1996-97; human resources adminstr. Baker & McKenzie, San Francisco, 1997-98; dir. adminstrn. Wartnick, Chaber, Harowitz & Tigerman, San Francisco, 1998-2000, Kasdan, Simonds, & Epstein, Irvine, Calif., 2000—03; instr. bus. planning Santa Anna Coll., 2004—. Trustee, v.p. Miss Hall's Sch., Pittsfield, Mass., 1970-78; adv. bd. Arkwright-Boston Ins. Co., 1976-81. Trustee, v.p. Cleve. Soc. for Blind, 1965-76; trustee Western Res. Hist. Soc., Cleve., 1972-76; treas. St. Peters by the Sea Presbyn. Ch., Palos Verdes, Calif., 1981-91, Literacy Coun. Newport Beach (Calif.) Pub. Libr., 2002—; pres. Harvard Club, Cleve., 1958-59, Harvard Bus. Sch. Club, Cleve., 1959-60, Rocky Mountain Harvard Club, Denver, 1978-79; bd. dirs. Met. YMCA, Cleve., 1972-76, Fedn. for Cmty. Planning, Cleve., 1971-76, v.p. Recipient Alumni award Harvard U., Denver, 1981. Mem. AICPA, Ohio Soc. CPAs, Assn. Legal Adminstrs., Rotary (pres. Piedmont Montclair chpt. 1995-96), Harvard Radcliffe Club So. Calif., Harvard Bus. Sch. Assn. Orange County (treas. 2004—). Avocations: sailing, golf, gardening. Home: 2204 Fortuna Newport Beach CA 92660 E-mail: jimjudytracy@adelphia.net.

TRACY, JIM, professional sports team executive; m. Debra Tracy; children: Brian, Chad, Mark. Attended, Marietta Coll. Bench coach, coord. all on-field activities L.A. Dodgers; mgr. Midwest League Single-A Peoria, Cubs' affiliate, 1987; minor league mgr. Chgo. Cubs, Cin. Reds, Expos, 1987—91, 1993—94; with Reds, 1989—91, minor league field coord., 1992; mgr. Triple-A Ottawa, Montreal's affiliate, 1994; bench coach Felipe Alou, Montreal Expo mgr., 1993—; interim mgr. L.A. Dodgers, 2000, mgr., 2000—. Named The Sporting News' Mgr. of Yr., 1993, Ea. League's Mgr. of Yr., 1993, NCAA Divsn. III All-Am. selection, Marietta Coll., Ohio. Mem.: Marietta Coll. Sports Hall of Fame. Office: LA Dodgers 1000 Elysian Park Ave Los Angeles CA 90012

TRACY, JOHN PATRICK, state legislator; b. Springfield, Vt., Apr. 12, 1952; m. Lynn Richardson Pitcher; five children. BA, U. Vt., 1984. Rep. State Vt., 1995—. Restaurant mgr. Vice chair Burlington & Chittenden County Dem. Coms.; mem. Ward 5 Dem. Com.; active Burlington Waterfront Bd. Mem. VFW. Address: 92 Park St Burlington VT 05401-4327

TRACY, LAREE ANN, statistician, medical researcher; b. Rock Springs, Wyo., Sept. 15, 1974; d. Robert Donald Harrision and Janice LouAnn Tracy. BS in Math., Creighton U., 1996; MA in Math. Statis., U. Md., 2002. Telemetry tech. Meth. Hosp., Omaha, 1995—96; clin. rsch. coord. Creighton U. Endocrinology Ctr., 1995—97; project leader Baxter Pharmaceuticals, Liberty Corner, NJ, 1997—98; med. logistician U.S. Army, Seoul, 1999—2000; rschr. Walter Reed Army Inst. Rsch., Washington, 2000—02, statistician, 2001—02; project mgr. FDA, Rockville, Md., 2002—03, math. statistician, 2003—. Sci. reviewer Walter Reed Army Inst. Rsch., 2000—02, statis. reviewer, 2001—02, grant writer, 2001—01. Treas. Home Owners Assn., Laurel, Md., 2001—02. With US Army and US Pub. Health Svc., 1998. Decorated Commendation medal US Army, Achievement medal (2), Meritorious Svc. medal; recipient Disting. Mil. Grad., US Army ROTC, 1996; scholar Dean's Leadership Scholarship, Creighton U., 1992, ROTC Scholarship, US Army, 1992, US Air Force, 1992. Mem.: Am. Soc. Tropical Medicine and Hygiene, Am. Math. Assn., Am. Statis. Assn., Saki do Kwan Tae kwon Do Assn. Avocations: running, martial arts, travel, painting, bicycling. Home: 3211 Foster Ave Baltimore MD 21224 Office: US FDA CDER 9201 Corp Blvd Rockville MD 20850 Office Phone: 301-827-2212. Personal E-mail: tracyl@cder.fda.gov. Business E-Mail: tracyl@cder.fda.gov.

TRACY, MICHAEL CAMERON, choreographer, performer, educator; b. Florence, Italy, Feb. 1, 1952; s. Stanley B. and Elizabeth Lee (McIntosh) T. BA Magna cum laude, Dartmouth Coll., 1973. Adj. faculty Yale U., New Haven, Conn., 1992. Artistic dir. Pilobolus Dance Theatre, Washington, Conn., 1974—; choreographer Die Zauberflöte, European prodn. with John Eliot Gardiner's Monteverdi Choir and English Baroque Soloists, 1995; co-choreographer: Ciona, 1974, Monkshood's Farewell, 1975, Untitled, 1976, Day Two, 1980, Pyramid of the Moon, 1996, Aeros, 1996, Elysian Fields, 1997, Apoplexy, 1998, The Hand That Mocked, The Heart That Fed, 1998, A Selection, 1999, Sweet Dreams, 2000, Symbiosis, 2001, The Brass Ring (commissioned by Olympic Arts Festiveal), 2002, My Brother's Keeper, 2003; choreographer Curiouser and Curiouser Nat. Theatre of Deaf, 1996. Recipient Berlin Critics award, 1975, New Eng. Theatre Conf. prize, 1977, Brandeis award, 1978, Excellence in Arts award Conn. Commn. on the Arts, 1981, Emmy award 1997, Scripps award, 2000; sr. fellow Dartmouth Coll., 1973. Mem. Dartmouth Players. Office: PO Box 388 Washington Depot CT 06794-0388 E-mail: mtracy@pilobolus.com.

TRACY, PATRICK F. food products executive; CEO Dot Foods, Mt. Sterling, Ill. Office: Dot Foods Route 99 S Mount Sterling IL 62353

TRACY, PAUL ANTHONY, race car driver; b. Scarborough, Ont., Can., Dec. 17, 1968; m. Lisa Hunter, 1998; children from previous marriage: Alysha, Conrad. Cart/Indy car driver Coyne Penske, 1991, Penske, 1992—94, 1996—97, Newman/Haas, 1995, Team KOOL Green, Indpls., 1998—. Achievements include winner 1999 Milw. Mile (Miller Lite 225), numerous others. Office: Team Kool Green 7615 Zionsville Rd Indianapolis IN 46268-2174

TRACY, RICHARD E. medical educator; b. Klamath Falls, Oreg., Apr. 30, 1934; BA, U. Chgo., 1955, MD, PhD, 1961. Diplomate Am. Bd. Anatomic Pathology, Am. Bd. Forensic Pathology. Prof. Sch. Medicine La. State U., New Orleans, 1967. Office: Sch of Medicine La State U Health Sci Ctr New Orleans LA 70112 Office Phone: 504-568-6072. E-mail: rtracy@lsuhsc.edu.

TRACY, SAUNDRA J. academic administrator; m. Doug Tracy; children: Steve, Elaine. BA in Spanish, Carroll Coll., Waukesha, Wis., 1968; M Ed in Fgn. Lang. Instrn., U. Pitts., 1971; PhD in Edn. Adminstrn., Purdue U., West Lafayette, Ind., 1981. Dir. Greater Cleve. Adminstr. Assessment Ctr., 1968—88; asst. to assoc. prof. edn. Cleve. State U., 1981—88; exec. dir. sch. study coun. Lehigh U., 1989—91, dir. ednl. programs Lee Iacocca Inst., 1990—92, assoc. prof. to prof. edn., 1988—94; dean of coll. of edn. Butler U., 1994—98; v.p. acad. affairs Mt. Union Coll., 1998—2001; pres. Alma Coll., 2001—. Fellow, Am. Coun. of Edn., 1992—93. Office: Alma Coll 614 West Superior St Alma MI 48801-1599 Office Phone: 989-463-7146.

TRACY, SUSANNE MARY, nursing educator; b. Rochester, N.Y., June 9, 1945; d. Edward and Ann (Bihun) Koszalka; m. Daniel A. Tracy, III, June 17, 1967; children: Lisa, Michael, Scott, Erin. BSN, Niagara Univ., 1967; MN, U. S.C., 1975; MA, Rivier Coll., 1992; PhD, U. R.I., 2003. Registered nurse, N.H., Mass. Navy nurse U.S. Navy, Niagara Falls/Pensacola, N.Y./Fla., 1966-68; instr. of nursing Columbus State Univ., Columbus, Ga., 1975-77; asst. prof. nursing Jefferson Cmty. Coll., Watertown, N.Y., 1977-81; asst. head nurse of rehab. Penrose Hosp., Colorado Springs, Colo., 1981-82; edn. cons. Penrose & St. Mary Corwin Hosp., Colorado Springs, Pueblo, Colo., 1982-85; asst. prof. nursing Rivier Coll., Nashua, N.H., 1985-91, assoc. prof. nursing, 1991—. Contbr. articles to profl. jours. Decorated Nat. Svc. medal U.S. Navy, 1967; named Outstanding Young Women of Am. Nat. Awards Program, 1977. Mem.: ANA, Nat. League Nursing, Am. Assn. Higher Edn., New Eng. Edn. Assessment Network (bd. dirs. 1995—), Ea. Nursing Rsch. Soc., Sigma Theta Tau. Avocations: research, travel. E-mail: olsldr@aol.com.

TRACY, THOMAS FRANCIS, JR., pediatric surgeon, resarcher, educator; b. Albany, N.J., June 26, 1952; s. Thomas Francis Tracy and Tracy (Portley) Mary; m. Elizabeth Alexander; children: Aaron Patrick, Anthony Michael, Adam Alexander. BA, Colgate U., N.Y., 1974; MS, Albany Med Coll., 1975; MD, Sackler Sch. of Medicine, Tel Aviv U., Israel, 1981; MA (hon.), Brown Med. Sch., R.I., 1998. Cert. General Surgery Am. Bd. of Surgery, 1987, Pedat. Surgery Am. Bd. of Surgery, 1992, General Surgey Recertification Am. Bd. of Surgery, 1996, Recertification Pediat. Surgery Am. Bd. of Surgery, 2002. Attending surgeon Cardinal Glennon Children's Hosp., St. Louis, 1988—97, St. Louis U. Health Scis .Ctr., St. Louis, 1988—97; pediatric surgeon-in-chief R.I. Hosp., Providence, 1997—; surg. dir. Hasbro Children's Hosp., Providence, 1997—; chief pediatric surgery Women & Infants Hosp., Providence, 1997—; dept. of surgery The Miriam Hosp., Providence, 2001—. Exam. cons. gen. surgery Am. Bd. of Surgery, 1997—, examiner, 1998—; ethics and advocacy com. Am. Pediatric Surg. Assn., 2000—; exec. bd., ri chpt. Am. Acad. of Pediat., 1998—; curriculum coun. Assn. of Pediatric Surgery Tng. Program Directors, 1998—; exec. bd. dirs. found. Soc. of U. Surgeons, 1999—; apsa rep. Adv. Bd. to create a model pediatric component for state disaster plans, 2002—. Section editor (book) The practice of general surgery, 1st edit.; editor: (numerous chpts. and med. texts) Pediatric Surgery And Liver Rsch.; author: (0ver 90 peer reviewed papers) Clin. and Basic Sci. Surg. co-investigator Children's Oncology Group, 2000—02; strategic planning com. Ronald McDonald Ho., Providence, 1997—2002; corporator Morton Health Found., Taunton, Mass., 2000—02; splty. practice adv. bd. Blue Cross/Blue Shield of R.I., Providence, 2002. Grantee, FDA, 1997—2002, NIH, 2001—. Fellow: Am. Acad. of Pediat. (mem. surgical sect.), ACS; mem.: Am. Assn. for the Study of Liver Diseases, Boston Surg. Soc., Surg. Biology Club III, New Eng. Surg. Soc., Soc. of U. Surgeons, Am. Pedaitric Surg. Assn. (chmn. publs. com. 2000—02), Humera Surg. Soc., Assn. for Academic Surgery, Gastroenterology Rsch. Group, Am. Soc. for Cell Biology. Office: RI Hosp 593 Eddy St Hasbro 147 Providence RI 02903 E-mail: thomas_tracy@brown.edu.

TRACY, THOMAS MILES, international health organization official; b. Great Barrington, Mass., July 8, 1936; s. Thomas Paul and Marion (Miles) T.; m. June Betts, June 17, 1967; children: Miles Christopher, Keir Thomas John. BA, Colgate U., 1958; MA, Stanford U., 1959; MBA, Columbia U., 1973. Fgn. service officer Dept. State, Washington, 1960-84; counselor Am. Embassy, Moscow, 1975-78, Bonn, Germany, 1978-79; asst. sec. Dept. State, Washington, 1979-83; chief administrn. Pan Am./WHO, Washington, 1983-98; mgmt. cons. Dept. State, 2003—. V.p. Pan-Am. Health and Edn. Found., treas. Trustee, vice chmn. Chelsea Sch., 1988—. With U.S. Army, 1959-60. Recipient Superior Honor award Dept. State, 1978 Mem. Am. Fgn. Svc. Assn. (dir. 1970-72), Am. Fgn. Svc. Protective Assn. (dir. 1988—, v.p. 1997—), Am. Fgn. Svc. Protective Found. (sec., treas.). Home: 5902 Devonshire Dr Bethesda MD 20816-3416

TRACY, TRACY FAIRCLOTH, special education educator; b. Washington, Aug. 22, 1961; d. James Claybert and Esther (Harrell) Faircloth; m. Charles Randall Tracy, Aug. 16, 1986; children: James Wren, Corissa Estelle. BS in Spl. Edn.-Mental Retardation, Old Dominion U., 1983. Tchr. Newport News (Va.) Pub. Schs., 1983—, cmty.-based instrn. specialist, 1992—2000, cmty.-based program adminstr., 2001—. Leader Camp Fire, Inc., Newport News, 1983—92; vol. Newport News Spl. Olympics, 1984—, treas., 1987—; active Va. PTA, Nat. PTA. Named to Outstanding Young Women Am., 1988; recipient Outstanding Svc. award, Newport News Spl. Olympics, 1986, 1988, 1990, Citizenship award, Denbigh Kiwanis, 1988, Appreciation award, Hampton-Newport News Cmty. Svcs. Bd., 1989, included in Am. Registry of Outstanding Profl. Mem.: Student Coun. Exceptional Children (pres. 1982—83), Coun. Exceptional Children, Assn. Retarded Citizens, Alpha Chi, Kappa Delta Pi (Nu Eta chpt.). Democrat. Methodist. Avocations: arts and crafts, swimming, walking. Home: 4708 Harlequin Way Chesapeake VA 23321-1247 Office: Enterprise Acad 813 Diligence Dr Ste 110 Newport News VA 23606-4237 E-mail: ctracywin@cox.net.

TRADER, JOSEPH EDGAR, orthopedic surgeon; b. Milw., Nov. 2, 1946; s. Edgar Joseph and Dorothy Elizabeth (Senzig) T.; m. Janet Louise Burzycki, Sept. 23, 1972 (div. Nov. 1987); children: James, Jonathan, Ann Elizabeth; m. Rhonda Sue Schultz, May 26, 1990. Student, Marquette U., 1964-67; MD, Med. Coll. Wis., 1971. Diplomate Am. Bd. Orthopaedic Surgery. Emergency rm. physician columbia, St. Joseph's Hosps., Milw., 1972-76; orthopaedic surgeon Orthopaedic Assn., Manitowoc, Wis., 1978—. Mem. exec. com. Holy Family Meml. Med. Ctr., Manitowoc, 1985-96, chief-of-staff, 1994-96, ethics com., 1995—, chair instnl. rev. com. Former pres., bd. dirs. Holy Innocents Mens Choir; county del. State Med. Soc. Charitable Sci. and Edn. Found. Fellow ACS, Am. Acad. Orthopaedic Surgeons; mem. AMA, Wis. State Med. Soc., Wis. Orthopaedic Soc., Midwest Orthopaedic Soc., Milw. Orthopaedic Soc., Am. Coll. Sports Medicine, Crown and Anchor, Manitowoc Yacht Club,Phi Delta Epsilon, Psi Chi . Roman Catholic. Avocations: singing, piano, scuba diving, tennis, skiing, sailing. Home: 1021 Memorial Dr Manitowoc WI 54220-2242 Office: Orthopaedic Assocs 501 N 10th St Manitowoc WI 54220-4039 Office Phone: 920-682-6376.

TRAFFORD, ABIGAIL, columnist, editor, writer; b. N.Y.C., July 14, 1940; d. William Bradford and Abigail (Sard) T.; children: Abigail Brett Miller, Victoria Brett. BA cum laude, Bryn Mawr Coll., 1962. Researcher Nat. Geog. Soc., Washington, 1964-67; tchr. Hermansberg Mission, Northern Ter., Australia, 1967-68; spl. corr. Time mag., The Washington Post, Houston, 1969-74; writer, asst. mng. editor U.S. News & World Report, Washington, 1975-86; health editor The Washington Post, 1986-00, columnist, 2000—. Author: Crazy Time: Surviving Divorce and Building a New Life, 1982, revised edit., 1992, My Time: Making the Most of the Rest of Your Life, 2004. Journalism fellow Harvard Sch. Pub. Health, 1980. Mem. Washington Press Club Found. (bd. mem. 1989—, pres. 1993-95). Home: 2600 Upton St NW Washington DC 20008-3826 Office: The Washington Post 1150 15th St NW Washington DC 20071-0002 Office Phone: 202-334-7678.

TRAFTON, STEPHEN J. bank executive; b. Mt. Vernon, Wash., Sept. 17, 1946; m. Diane Trafton; children: John, Roland. BS in Zoology, Wash. State U., 1968. V.p., mgr. dept. money market Seattle-First Nat. Bank, 1968-79; v.p., mgr. bank consulting group Donaldson Lufkin Jennrette, N.Y.C., 1980; exec. v.p., treas. Gibraltar Savings Bank, L.A., 1980-84; banking cons., 1984-86; v.p., treas. Hibernia Bank, San Francisco, 1986-88; sr. v.p., treas. Goldome Bank, Buffalo, N.Y., 1988-90; sr. exec. v.p., CFO Glenfed Inc., 1990-91, vice chmn., CFO, 1991—, pres., 1992—; sr. exec. v.p., CFO Glendale Fed. Bank, 1990-91, vice chmn., CFO, 1991, pres., COO, 1991-92, chmn. bd., pres., CEO, 1992-99, COO, also bd. dirs.; exec. v.p. Golden State Bancorp, 1999—. Mem. Phi Eta Sigma. Office: Golden State Bancorp Inc 135 Main St San Francisco CA 94105

TRAGEN, IRVING GLENNE, consultant; b. May 18, 1922; m. Eleanor May Dodson, Aug. 7, 1947. AB, U. Calif., Berkeley, 1943; LLM, U. Chile, Santiago, 1946; JD, U. Calif., 1945. Personnel officer Mex.-U.S. Commn. Eradicate Foot & Mouth Disease, Mex., 1948-49, WHO/Pan Am. Sanitary Bur., Washington, 1950-53; with U.S. Dept. State & AID, El Salvador, Chile, Peru, Venezuela, Washington, Calif., 1953-63; dir. L.Am. bur. instl. devel. AID, Washington, 1963-65; dir. AID Mission, La Paz, Bolivia, 1965-68; country dir. Argentina, Paraguay, Uruguay U.S. Dept. State, Washington, 1969-71; v.p. Inter-Am. Found., Rosslyn, Va., 1971-73; chief Ctrl. Am. Regional Office U.S. Dept. State & AID, Guatemala, 1973-75, dir. USAID & econ. counselor U.S. Embassy, 1975—77; deputy U.S. rep. U.S. Mission fo OAS, U.S. Dept. State, Washington, 1977-80; exec. dir. Inter-Am. ECOSOC, Washington, 1980-84; exec. sec. Inter-Am. Drug Abuse Control Commn., Washington, 1984-94; prin. advisor Regional C.Am. Legal Devel., San Jose, Costa Rica, 1995-97; cons. L.Am./European Orgns. on Drug Trafficking, Hanford, Calif., 1999—2002. Mem. adv. bd. U. Pacific, Stockton, Calif., 2000-2003. Mem. editl. bd. (Spanish edit.) Money Laundering Alert Internat., 2000-01. Trustee emeritus Museo de las Americas, Denver, 2000. Home and Office: 3890 Nobel Dr Ste 1303 San Diego CA 92122

TRAGER, D. DAVID, retired pharmacist, general consultant; b. Napa, California, Oct. 4, 1931; s. Louis D. (dec.) and Frances Amanda (Brose) T. (dec.); m. Ruth (Pacovsky), June 15, 1952 (div. Sept. 1978); children: Louis, Solomon; m. Sarah Ann (Brancato), Dec. 28, 1983 (dec. May 2000); children: Daryl, Randy, Missi Hasnas; m. Phyllis Baldwin (Douglas), Oct. 7, 2001; 1 stepchild, Robert Gordon Douglas. BS in Pharm., U. Calif., San Francisco, 1953; post grad. in Clin. pharmacy, U. So. Calif., 1976, post grad. in Drug action, 1978. Registered pharmacist Calif. Pharmacist multiple locations, Calif., 1953-59; pharmacist, pharmacy mgr. Longs Drugs, West Covina, Calif., 1959-60; pharmacist Bay Pharmacy, Pacific Palisades, Calif., 1960-65; pharmacist, v.p. Palisades Drug Co., Pacific Palisades, Calif., 1965-67; pharmacist Bi Rite, Westwood and Santa Monica, Calif., 1967-68; pharmacist, owner Trager, Pacific Palisades, Calif., 1968-72; pharmacist Kaiser Found. Hosp. Pharmacy, Panorama City, Calif., 1973-90, Woodland Hills, Calif., 1990-98; ret. Simi Valley, Calif., 1998. Script cons., patient cons., Calif., 1963—69; propr. P-I-E Software, Calif., 1995—; mentor first yr. pharmacy students U. Pacific, Calif., 1998—2001, tech. lit. cons., Calif., 2001—; per diem overnight pharmacist Kaiser Permanent Pharmacy, Woodland Hills, Calif., 2001—. Mem.: Am. Inst. History of Pharmacy, Calif. Employee Pharmacist Assn., Am. Pharm. Assn., Ancient and Accepted Scottish Rite, Scottish Rite Rsch. Soc. (life), Royal Arch Mason, Masons (life), Shriners, Kappa Psi. Republican. Jewish. Avocations: computers, reading, masonic rsch. Home: 1531 Yosemite Ave Simi Valley CA 93063-4548 Fax: 805-582-1844.

TRAGER, DAVID G. federal judge; b. Mt. Vernon, N.Y., Dec. 23, 1937; s. Sol and Clara (Friedman) T.; m. Roberta E. Weisbrod, May 2, 1972; children: Mara Emet, Josiah Samuel, Naomi Gabrielle. BA, Columbia Coll., 1959; LL.B., Harvard U., 1962. Bar: N.Y. Assoc. Berman & Frost, 1963-65, Butler, Jablow & Geller, 1965-67; asst. corp. counsel Appeals Div. City of N.Y., 1967; law clk. Judge Kenneth B. Keating, N.Y. State Ct. Appeals, 1968-69; asst. U.S. atty. chief, appeals div., 1970-72; U.S. atty. Ea. Dist. N.Y., Bklyn., 1974-78; prof. Bklyn. Law Sch., 1972-94, dean, 1983-94; judge U.S. Dist. Ct. (ea. dist.) N.Y., Bklyn., 1994—; mem. adv. com. on criminal rules Jud. Conf. U.S., 2000—. Chmn. Mayor's Com. on Judiciary, 1982-89, N.Y. State Temp. Commn. on Investigation, 1983-90. Mem. N.Y.C. Charter Rev. Commn., 1986-89. With USAR, 1962-65, USNR, 1965-69. Mem.: Am. Law Inst., Fed. Bar Coun. (pres. 1986—88). Office: US Courthouse 225 Cadman Plz E Brooklyn NY 11201-1818

TRAGER, GARY ALAN, endocrinologist, diabetologist; b. N.Y.C., July 30, 1950; s. Jacob Morris and Elena (Tanzer) T.; m. Marie-Christine Nicole Lachal, Dec. 26, 1976; children: Ashley Audrey, Brendon Alden. BA in Biology and Anthropology, SUNY, Binghamton, 1972; MD, U. Cen. del Este, Dominican Republic, 1980. Subintern-rotating Jamaica (N.Y.) Hosp., 1979-80; intern and resident medicine Bklyn.-Cumberland Med. Ctr., 1980-83; fellow endocrinology SUNY, Stony Brook, 1983-85, clin. asst. instr., 1983-85; asst. attending Huntington (N.Y.) Hosp., 1985-90, assoc. attending, 1990-97, sr. attending, 1997—. Adv. bd. Sankyo-Park Davis, Merck & Co., Bayer Pharms., Hoechst Marion Roussel, Boehringer Mannheim, Eli Lilly & Co., Park Davis, Pratt Pharms., Upjohn, Johnson and Johnson, Pfizer, Inc. and Roerig Divsn.; nat. adv. bd., nat. speaker bureaus Parke Davis, Novodisc, Sherring-Plough, spkr. Forest Pharms., Ciba Geisy, Knoll; mem. nutrition com. Huntington Hosp., 1987—, dir. diabetes club, 1985—; mem. Nassau-Suffolk Hosp. Coun. on Diabetes, with Nat. Diabetes Ednl. Initiative, lab com. H.H., 1997—, pharm. and therapy com., 1998— Mem. profl. edn. com. Am. Diabetes Assn., Long Island, Melville, N.Y., 1985—; mem. Am. Diabetic Assn. Fund, Long Island, N.Y., 1989—; ad hoc mem. Eaton's Neck Emergency Squad, Long Island, 1985-89; I.P.R.O. Nassau-Suffolk Counties, 1998—. Mem. AMA, Am. Fertility Soc., Am. Diabetes Assn., Am. Soc. Internal Medicine, Am. Soc. Andrology, Am. Assn. Clin. Endocrinologists, Peripheral Neuropathy Inst., Am. Soc. Hypertension, Adrenal Soc. Office: 158 E Main St Huntington NY 11743-2988

TRAGER, WILLIAM, biology professor; b. Newark, Mar. 20, 1910; s. Leon and Anna Emilfork T.; m. Ida Sosnow, June 16, 1935; children: Leslie, Carolyn, Lillian. BS, Rutgers U., 1930, Sc.D. (hon.), 1965; MA, Harvard U., 1931, PhD, 1933; Sc.D. (hon.), Rockefeller U., 1987. Fellow Rockefeller Inst., Princeton, NJ, 1934—35; mem. faculty Rockefeller U., N.Y.C., 1935—, assoc. prof., 1950—64, prof. biology, 1964—81, prof. emeritus, 1981—. Guest investigator West African Inst. Trypanosomiasis Research, 1958—59, Nigerian Inst. Trypanosomiasis Research, 1973—74; vis. prof. Fla. State U., 1962, U. P.R. Med. Sch., 1963, U. Mex. Med. Sch., 1965; mem. study sect. parasitology and tropical medicine Nat. Inst. Allergy and Infectious Diseases, 1954—58, 1967—70, mem. tng. grant com., 1961—64, mem. microbiology and infectious diseases adv. com., 1978—79; mem. malaria commn. Armed Forces Epidemiol. Bd., 1965—73; mem. study group parasitic diseases Walter Reed Army Inst. Research, 1977—79; chmn. sci. adv. council Liberian Inst. Tropical Medicine, 1965—66; rapporteur 6th, 7th Congresses Tropical Medicine; pres. Am. Found. for Tropical Medicine, 1966—69; mem. steering com. Malaria Immunology Group, WHO, 1977—80; cons. WHO, Bangkok, 1978, Panama, 79, Shanghai, 79; hon. pres. Asia and Pacific Conf. on Malaria, 1985. Author: Symbiosis, 1970, Living Together: The Biology of Animal Parasitism, 1986; editor: Jour. Protozoology, 1954—65; contbr. articles to profl. jours. Capt. AUS U.S. Army, 1943—45. Recipient Darling medal, WHO, 1980, Leuckart medal Deutsche Gesellschaft fur Parasitologie, 1982, First Rameshwardas Birla Internat. award in Medicine, 1982, Manson medal, Royal Soc. Tropical Medicine and Hygiene, 1986, Prince Mahidol award in Med. Sci., 1994; fellow, NRC, 1933—34, Guggenheim Found., 1973—74, Avivah Zuckerman fellow, Kuvin Ctr. Infections and Tropical Diseases, Hebrew U., 1982. Fellow: AAAS, N.Y. Acad. Scis.; mem.: NAS, Am. Soc. Tropical Medicine and Hygiene (pres. 1978—79, Le Prince medal 1991), Soc. Protozoologists (pres. 1960—61), Am. Soc. Parasitologists (council 1956—57, v.p. 1973, pres. 1974). Office: Rockefeller U York Ave At 66th St New York NY 10021 Office Phone: 212-327-8630. E-mail: trager@mail.rockefeller.edu.

TRAGOS, GEORGE EURIPEDES, lawyer; b. Chgo., July 15, 1949; s. Euripedes G. and Eugene G. (Gatziolis) T.; m. Donna Marie Thalassites, Nov. 18, 1978; children: Louise, Gina, Peter. BA, Fla. State U., 1971, JD, 1974. Bar: Fla., U.S. Dist. Ct. (mid., so. dists.) Fla., U.S. Dist. Ct. (we. dist.) Tenn., U.S. Ct. Appeals (5th, 11th cirs.). Legis. aide Fla. Ho. of Reps., 1972-73; tax analyst tax and fin. com., 1973-74; chief, felony asst. states atty. State of Fla., Clearwater, 1974-78; partner firm Case, Kimpton, Tragos & Burke, P.A., Clearwater Beach, 1978-83; chief criminal div. U.S. Atty.'s Office for Middle Dist. Fla., Tampa, 1983-85; lead trial asst. Pres. Organized Crime Drug Enforcement Task Force, Tampa, 1985; sole practice Clearwater, 1985—. Contbr. articles to profl. jours. and frequent lectr. Mem. Clearwater Bar (pres. 1994), Fla. Bar Assn. (chmn. fed. practice com. 1986, chmn. criminal law sect. 2000, chmn. bar evidence com. 1990), Fla. Assn. Criminal Def. Lawyers (pres. 1991), Fla. State U. Alumni Assn. Law Sch. (bd. dirs.), Tampa Bay Fed. Bar Assn. (v.p. 1989), Clearwater Beach Jaycees (pres. 1979), Fla. U. Gold Key Club (pres. 1972), Ahepa. Mem. Greek Orthodox Ch. Avocations: boating, tennis. Office: 600 Cleveland St Ste 700 Clearwater FL 33755-4158 E-mail: greek.law@verizon.net.

TRAHAN, GRACE, newscaster; m. Joe Rodecap; 1 child. BA in Mass Comms., Okla. City U., 1987. Anchor KFDM-TV, Beaumont, Tex.; reporter Sta. WRTV-TV, Indpls., 1994, anchor, 1994—. Recipient Tex. Sch. Bell award. Office: WRTV TV 1330 N Meridian St Indianapolis IN 46202*

TRAIER, JOHN, state agency administrator; Banking dep. commr. N.J. Banking and Ins. Dept., Trenton, 1999; dep. treas. N.J. Transit, Newark, 1999—. Office: NJ Transit 1 Penn Plaza E Newark NJ 07105

TRAIL, MARGARET ANN, retired employee benefits company executive, beef cattle producer, sterling silver merchant; b. Bryan, Tex., July 17, 1941; d. Louis Milton and Margaret (Stromberg) Thompson; m. Robert A. Rosemier, Aug. 25, 1962 (div. Feb. 1973); 1 child: Gretchen Elisabeth; m. Newt Shands Trail, Dec. 4, 1989. BSN, U. Iowa, 1963; MS, No. Ill. U., 1971. Instr. Cooley Dickinson Hosp., Northampton, Mass., 1964-65; dir. nursing De Kalb (Ill.) Pub. Hosp., Kishwaukee Cmty. Hosp., 1972—76, Terre Haute (Ind.) Regional Hosp., 1976—78; from mgr. clin. systems to dir. spl. projects Hosp. Corp. Am., Nashville, 1978-86; from dir. med. mgmt. to v.p. Equicor, Nashville, 1986-90; divsn. v.p. The Travelers Ins. Co., Hartford, Conn., 1990-93; asst. v.p. health svcs. quality mgmt. Aetna, Hartford, 1993—2003, ret., 2003. Mem. LWV (pres. DeKalb chpt. 1970-72). Avocation: gardening. E-mail: matrail@earthlink.net.

TRAILL, DAVID ANGUS, classics educator; b. Helensburgh, Scotland, Jan. 28, 1942; came to U.S., 1965; s. Angus Nicolson and Elizabeth Blyth (Wilson) Trail. MA, U. St. Andrews, Scotland, 1964; PhD, U. Calif., Berkeley, 1971. Lectr. classics McGill U., Montreal, Que., Can., 1964-65; tchg. asst. U. Calif., Berkeley, 1965-68, asst. prof. Davis, 1970-78, assoc. prof., 1978-85, prof., 1985—. Cons. prodn. documentaries on Schliemann and Troy, Brit. Broadcasting Corp., London, 1980-81, 84, Nat. Geographic, 1999. Author: Walahfrid Strabo's Visio Wettini: Text, Translation and Commentary, 1974; co-editor: Myth, Scandal, and History: The Heinrich Schliemann Controversy, 1986, Excavating Schliemann, 1993, Schliemann of Troy: Treasure and Deceit, 1995; contbr. articles to profl. jours. Mem. Am. Philol. Assn., Archaeol. Inst. Am., Medieval Acad. Am. Home: 1351 Monarch Ln Davis CA 95616-1636 Office: Classics Dept U Calif Davis CA 95616 Office Phone: 530-752-6441. E-mail: datraill@ucdavis.edu.

TRAIN, HARRY DEPUE, II, retired naval officer; b. Washington, Nov. 5, 1927; s. Harold Cecil and May (Philipps) T.; m. Catharine Peck Kinnear, July 8, 1950; children: Louise Lucas, Catharine Philipps, Elizabeth Langdon, Cecilia Spencer. BS, U.S. Naval Acad., 1949. Commd. ensign U.S. Navy, 1949, advanced through grades to adm., 1978; comdr. Cruiser-Destroyer Flotilla 8, 1971-72; dir. internat. security affairs East Asia and Pacific Region Office Asst. Sec. Def., 1972-73; dir. Systems Analysis Div., Office Chief Naval Ops., 1973-74; dir. joint staff Orgn. Joint Chiefs of Staff, 1974-76; comdr. U.S. 6th Fleet, 1976-78; comdr.-in-chief U.S. Atlantic Fleet and supreme allied comdr. Atlantic, 1978-82, U.S. Atlantic Commd.; ret. U.S. Atlantic Fleet and supreme allied comdr. Atlantic, 1982. Mgr. Hampton Rds. Ops. Sci. Applications Internat. Corp. Mem. Hart-Rudman Commn. Decorated D.S.M. with 3 gold stars, Def. Disting. Svc. medal, Legion of Merit with 3 gold stars, Meritorious Svc. medal, Joint Svcs. Commendation medal, Navy Commendation medal; comdr. Order Republic of Tunisia; Order Naval Merit Brazil; Pedro Campbell medal Uruguay; Order of Pres. of Republic Chile; decorated Portuguese Mil. Order Christ; Netherlands Order Orange-Nassau; German Order Merit; French Legion of Honor; Colombian Naval Order Admiral Padilla; Mex. Order Spl. Merit; sr. fellow Joint and Combined Warfighting Sch., Joint Forces Staff Coll. Mem. U.S. Naval Inst., Coun. on Fgn. Rels., Columbia Country Club, Town Point Club(chmn. bd. govs.). Home: 401 College Pl Apt 10 Norfolk VA 23510-1130

TRAIN, JOHN, investment counselor, writer, government official; b. N.Y.C., May 25, 1928; s. Arthur Cheney and Helen (Coster) T.; m. Maria Teresa Cini di Pianzano, 1961 (div. 1976); children: Helen, Nina, Lisa; m. Frances Cheston, July 23, 1977. BA magna cum laude, Harvard U., 1950, MA, 1951. Founder, mng. editor Paris Rev., 1952-54; staff Asst. Sec. Army, Washington, 1954-56; assoc. de Vegh & Co., 1956-58; chmn. Train, Babcock Advisors (and predecessor firms), N.Y.C., 1958-94, chmn. emeritus, 1995—; co-chmn., then hon. dir. ICAP, S.A., Athens, 1964—; chmn. Montrose Fin. Group, N.Y.C., 1992—; pres. Chateau Malescasse, Lamarque-Margaux, Bordeaux, France, 1970-81; columnist Forbes mag., 1977-83, Harvard mag., 1983-95, Wall St. Jour., 1984—, Worth Mag., Boston, 1991-93, Town and Country mag., 1994-95, Fin. Times, London, 1994—2002, Strategic Rev., 1998—2002. Bd. dirs. African Devel. Found., Washington, 1988-94; bd. dirs. Bulgarian-Am. Enterprise Fund, Washington, Genesis Funds, London, Internat. Rescue Com., N.Y.C.; chmn. Northcote Parkison Fund, 1988—; bd. govs. East-West Ctr., Hawaii, 1993-96. Author: Dance of the Money Bees, 1973, Remarkable Names, 1977, Even More Remarkable Names, 1979, Remarkable Occurrences, 1978, Remarkable Words, 1980, The Money Masters, 1980, Remarkable Relatives, 1971, Preserving Capital and Making it Grow, 1983, Famous Financial Fiascos, 1984, John Train's Most Remarkable Names, 1985, The Midas Touch, 1987, The New Money Masters, 1989, Valsalva's Maneuver, 1989, John Train's Most Remarkable Occurences, 1990, Wit, 1991, Love, 1993, The Craft of Investing, 1994, Crazy Quilt, 1996, Oriental Rug Symbols, 1997, Investing and Managing Trusts under the New Prudent Investor Rule, 1999, Money Mastery of Our Time, 2001; contbr. articles to profl. publs. Chmn. Italian Emergency Relief Com., 1976-77; pres. Afghanistan Relief Com., 1986-95; trustee Harvard Lampoon, Cambridge, Mass., 1974-90, World Monuments Fund, 1988-92; chmn. Free Elections Project, 1990, Brit. Mus. Nat. Hist. Internat. Trust, 1990—, Northcote Parkinson Fund, 1990—; trustee univ. coun. Am. U. Bulgaria, 1996—. With U.S. Army, 1954-56. Decorated commendatore Ordine del Merito della Repubblica, commendatore Ordine Della Solidarieta, medal Provincia di Udine (Italy); recipient Disting. Grotonian award, 1996, Queen's Birthday honors Order of St. John, 1997. Mem.: Fgn. Policy Assn. (trustee), Internat. Inst. Strategic Studies (London), Order Colonial Lords of Manors, Coun. on Fgn. Rels., Union Club, Racquet & Tennis Club, Met. Club (Washington), Century Club. Office: 667 Madison Ave New York NY 10021-8029

TRAIN, RUSSELL ERROL, environmentalist; b. Jamestown, R.I., June 4, 1920; s. Charles R. and Errol C. (Brown) T.; m. Aileen Bowdoin, May 27, 1954; children: Nancy, Emily, Bowdoin, Errol. AB, Princeton U., 1941, LL.D. (hon.), 1970; JD, Columbia U., 1948, LL.D. (hon.), 1970, Bates Coll., 1970, Drexel U., 1970; D.E. (hon.), Worcester Poly. Inst., 1970, U. Md., 1975; Sc.D. (hon.), St. Mary's Coll., 1970, Clarkson Coll. Tech., 1973, Salem Coll., 1975, Southwestern U., 1976, Mich. State U., 1976; D.C.L. (hon.), U. of South, 1973; D public svc., Washington Coll., 1996. Bar: D.C. bar 1949. Atty. staff joint com. on internal revenue taxation U.S. Congress, 1949-53; chief counsel Ways and Means Com., U.S. Ho. of Reps., 1953-54, minority adviser, 1955-56; asst. to sec., head legal adv. staff Treasury Dept., 1956-57; judge U.S. Tax Ct., 1957-65; pres. Conservation Found., 1965-69; also trustee; undersec. Dept. Interior, 1969-70; chmn. Council on Environ. Quality, 1970-73; adminstr. EPA, Washington, 1973-77; sr. assoc. Conservation Found., 1977; pres., chief exec. officer World Wildlife Fund, Washington, 1978-85, chmn. bd., 1985-94, chmn. emeritus, 1994—; chmn. bd. Conservation Found., 1985-90; chmn. Nat. Commn. on the Environment, 1991-93; chmn. Nat. Coun. World Wildlife Fund, Washington, chmn. emeritus. Mem. Washington Nat. Monument Assn., Nat. Water Commn., 1968—69; head U.S. del. UN Conf. Human Environment, 1972; rep. Internat. Whaling Commn., 1972, other internat. confs.; mem. Pres.'s adv. com. on trade and trade negotiations, 1991—93. Author: The Bowdoin Family, 2000, The Train Family, 2000, A Memoir, 2000, Politics, Pollution, and Pandas, 2003. Trustee emeritus African Wildlife Found.; adv. trustee Rockefeller Bros. Fund. Decorated Order of the Golden Ark (The Netherlands); recipient Albert Schweitzer medal, Animal Welfare Inst., 1972, Aldo Leopold medal, Wildlife Soc., 1975, Conservationist of Yr. award, Nat. Wildlife Fedn., 1974, 1986, John and Alice Tyler Ecology award, 1978, Freese award, ASCE, 1978, Pub. Welfare award, Nat. Acad. Scis., 1981, Elizabeth Haub prize in internat. environ. law, 1981, Frances K. Hutchinson medal, Garden Club of Am., 1984, Lindbergh award, 1985, Environ. Law Inst. award, 1986, Presdl. Medal of Freedom, 1991, Heinz Chmns. medal, 2001. Fellow: AAAS; mem.: Am. Acad. Arts and Scis., Atlantic Coun., Coun. Fgn. Rels. Office: World Wildlife Fund 1250 24th St NW Fl 6 Washington DC 20037-1193

TRAINA, ALBERT SALVATORE, publishing executive; b. Bklyn., Apr. 30, 1927; s. Salvatore and Guilia (LeBarbara) T.; m. Vail Devereux, June 27, 1957; children— Caroline Vail, Robert Brooks. BS (N.Y. State War Service scholar), Seton Hall U., 1950; postgrad., Columbia U., 1950-51; MBA, NYU, 1954. Circulation promotion advt. space salesman Fairchild Publs., N.Y.C., 1951-53; Eastern advt. mgr. Modern Bride mag. Ziff-Davis, N.Y.C., 1953-58; advt. mgr. Bride and Home mag. Hearst Mags., N.Y.C., 1958-60, pub. Bride and Home mag., 1960-64; pub. Sports Afield mag., 1964-65, Town and Country mag., 1965-67, Harpers Bazaar mag., 1967-70; pres., chief exec. officer Bartell Media Corp., 1970-74; pres. Ziff-Davis Mag. Network, 1974-76, group v.p., 1976-78; sr. v.p. Ziff-Davis Pub. Co., 1978-81; pres. Ziff-Davis Consumer Mag., 1981-85; exec. v.p. mags. CBS, N.Y.C., 1985; pres. Traina Assocs., N.Y.C., 1985—. Mem. Scarsdale Bi-Partisan Com., 1975-78; bd. dirs. Crane Berkeley Assn., 1978-88, pres., 1983-84; mem. nat. bd. dirs., chmn. comms. com., treas. Goodwill Industries of Am., 1979-92, chmn. bd., 1988-92; chmn. bd. trustees Chebeague Island Libr., 1997-2001; pres. bd. dirs. Chebeague Recreation Ctr., 1998-2003. With USNR, 1945-46. Mem. NYU Grad. Sch. Bus. Adminstrn. Alumni Assn., NYU Alumni Fedn. (comms. com. 1970-73), Union League Club (N.Y.C.). Home: 11 Springettes Rd Chebeague Island ME 04017-9723

TRAINES, ROSE WUNDERBAUM, sculptor, educator; b. Monroeville, Ind., Sept. 13, 1928; d. Louis and Leah (Fogel) Wunderbaum; m. Robert Jacob Traines, June 25, 1949; children: Claudia Denise Traines Lang, Monica Rae Traines Martin. Student, Ind. State Tchr.'s Coll., 1946—48, Mich. State U., 1948—49; BS, Ctrl. Mich. U., 1951. Lectr. in field. One person shows include Ctrl. Mich. U., Mt. Pleasant, 1964, Alma Artmobile, Mich., 1972, Ctrl. Mich. Homecoming, Mount Pleasant, Mich., 1982, Internat. Inst. Scrap Iron and Steel, Inc., Washington, 1983, Fontainebleau Hotel, Miami Beach, Fla., 1983, Elliott Mus. Art Gallery, Stuart, Fla., 1988, 98, Walt Kuhn Gallery, Cape Neddick, Maine, 1988, Coll. Club of Boston, 1990, Brass Latch Gallery, Montpelier, Ind., 1991, 96, 98, Vero Beach Ctr. for the Arts, Fla., 1992, Maritime and Yachting Mus., Stuart, Fla., 1997, Mid-Mich. Regional Med. Ctr., Healing Arts Gallery, Midland, 1997, Northwood Gallery, Midland, Mich., Commerca Bank Art Series, Palm Beach Gardens, 2002, Gallery Five, Tequesta, Fla., 2002, Michigan U. Park Libr. Gallery, 2002, Art Reach of Mid. Mich., Mt. Pleasant, 2002, Arthur Glick Jewish Cmty. Ctr., Indpls., Ind., 2004; two-person shows include Gallery One, North Palm Beach, 1973, Midland Ctr. for the Arts, Mich., 1976, Springfield Art Mart, Ohio, 1977, Hillel Student Ctr. Gallery-U. Cin., 1993, others; exhibited in group shows including Saginaw Mus. Art, Mich., 1965, Grand Rapids Mus., Mich., 1966, Kalamazoo Mus., Mich., 1967, Kellogg/Kresge Art Ctr., Mich. State U., East Lansing, 1967, Art Reach Mid-Mich., Mount Pleasant Mich., 1987, Salmagundi Club, N.Y.C., 1988, 91-92, 96, Copley Soc., Boston, 1990, 95, Allied Artists of Am., Inc., N.Y.C., 1995-96, Self Family Arts Ctr., Hilton Head Island, S.C., 1996-97, Palm Beach Gardens Fla. City Hall, 2003, Palm Beach Gardens Cmty. Ctr., 2003, others; represented in permanent collections at Dow-Corning Corp. Collection, Midland Ctr. for the Arts, Elliott Mus., Stuart, Fla., Walt Kuhn Gallery, Maine, Norman Cousins, Tom Keating, Marge Fishbain, Kitti Pyne, Donny Hersee, Phyllis Troth, Alden Dows, Carl Gerstackers, Coll. Club Boston, Pullen Elem. Sch., Isabella Bank and Trust Co., Ctrl. Mich. U., Blake Libr, Stuart, Fla., La Belle Mgmt. Corp., Morey Bandit Industries, Mich., Ctrl. Mich. Cmty. Hosp., Northwood U., The Vets. Meml. Libr., Mt. Pleasant, Mich., Pub. Libr., Clare, Mich., Brass Latch Gallery, Northville (Mich.) Pub. Libr, others, also pvt. collections. Tchr. Jewish Sunday Sch., Mt. Pleasant, 1955-70; officer Child and Youth Study Clubs, Mt. Pleasant, 1963-73; mem. City Recreation Commn., Mt. Pleasant, 1963-73, Area Health Planning Coun., Mt. Pleasant, 1974-80; pres., vol. Hosp. Aux. Med. Care, Red Cross Blood Bank, United Fund Cancer Dr., Mt. Pleasant, 1960-80; storyteller pub. libr., Mt. Pleasant, 1957-79. Recipient Northwood U. Artist award, Midland Ctr. for Arts, Mich., 2002. Mem.: Brass Latch Gallery, Art Reach of Mid-Mich., Hilton Head Art League S.C. (Lifetime of Creative Excellence award 1998), Copley Soc. Boston (signature mem.), Allied Artists of Am. (Mems. award of merit 1996, Raymond H. Brumer Meml. award 1999), Nat. Mus. of Women in Arts (charter), Salmagundi Club (Philip Isenberg award 1993, Pamela Singleton award 1997, Elliot Liskin Meml. award 1998, Anonymous award 1998, Peters Sculpture Materials award 2001, Alphaeus P. Cole Meml. award 2001, Mems. Meml. award 2003). Jewish. Avocations: lecturing, community work, tennis, presenting humorous programs, drums. Home: 1151 Nettles Blvd Jensen Beach FL 34957-3388 Office Phone: 989-773-3873.

TRAINOR, BERNARD EDMUND, retired military officer; b. N.Y.C., Sept. 2, 1928; s. Joseph Patrick and Ann Veronica (Whelan) T.; m. Margaret Ann Hamilton, June 13, 1959; children: Kathleen Marie, Theresa Ann, Eileen Cecile, Claire Hamilton. BS, Coll. of Holy Cross, 1951; MA, U. Colo., 1963, postgrad., 1970-73; ed., Air War Coll., Montgomery, Ala., 1969-70. Commd. 2nd lt. USMC, 1951, advanced through grades to lt. gen., 1983, inf. comdr., 1952, assigned to USS Columbus, 1953-55, mem. staff Marine Corps Hdqrs., 1955-58, with exch. office Royal Marine Commandos, 1958-59, inf. comdr. 1st Marine divsn., 1959-61; asst. prof. naval sci. U. Colo., Boulder, 1961-64; assigned to Marine Corps Command and Staff Coll., 1964-65; adv. Republic of Vietnam, 1965-66; instr. Marine Corps Command and Staff Coll., 1966-69; bn. comdr. Vietnam, 1970-71; staff officer Hdqrs. Marine Corps, Washington, 1970-71; dir. First Marine Corps Dist., N.Y.C., 1974-76; asst. depot comdr. Marine Corps Recruit Depot, Parris Island, S.C., 1976-78; dir. Edn. Ctr., Quantico, Va., 1978-81; dep. chief of staff for plans, policies and ops. Hdqrs. Marine Corps, 1981-85; ret., 1985; mil. corr. N.Y. Times, 1986-90; dir. nat. security program Kennedy Sch. Govt. Harvard U., Cambridge, Mass., 1990-96, assoc. Ctr. Sci. and Internat. Affairs, 1996—; sr. fellow nat. security Coun. on Fgn. Rels., 1999—. Retired USMC, 1985. Author: History of the U.S. Marine Corps, 1968, The Generals' War, 1995; contbg. author: American Defense Annual, 1990, 2d edit., 1996, Defense Beat, 1991, After the Storm, 1992, The Almanac of Seapower, 1993, Newsmen and National Defense, 1991, Perspectives on Warfighting, 1992; mem. editl. adv. bd. Naval War Coll. Rev.; contbr. articles to profl. jours. Mil. analyst NBC News. Decorated D.S.M., Legion of Merit with Combat V and two stars, Bronze Star with Combat V, Navy Commendation medal with Combat V and two gold stars, others; recipient Anderson Meml. award Air War Coll., 1970. Mem. Naval Inst., Marine Corps Assn., Coun. Fgn. Rels., World Affairs Coun. (bd. dirs.), Army-Navy Club, Wardroom Club Boston. Roman Catholic. Home: 80 Potter Pond Lexington MA 02421-8247 E-mail: mc151rvn@aol.com.

TRAINOR, JOHN FELIX, retired economics educator; b. Mpls., Dec. 1, 1921; s. James Patrick and Myra Catherine (Pauly) T.; m. Margaret Dolores Pudenz, July 3, 1965 (dec. 1977); children: John Anthony, Patrick James. BA cum laude, Coll. St. Thomas, 1943; MA, U. Minn., 1950; PhD, Wash. State U., 1970. Instr. De LaSalle H.S., Mpls., 1946-47, Coll. St. Thomas, 1949-50; v.p. Trainor Candy Co., Mpls., 1949-56; instr., asst. prof. econs. Rockhurst Coll., Kansas City, Mo., 1956-62; instr. Wash. State U., Pullman, 1966-67; asst. prof. Minn. State U., Moorhead, 1967—70, assoc. prof. econs., 1971-87, prof. econ., 1988-89, chmn. dept. econs., 1981-89; prof. emeritus, 1989—. Pres. Minn. Econs. Assn., 1976—77. Author: (with Frank J. Kottke) The Nursing Home Industry in the State of Washington, 1968. Ensign to Lt. (j.g.) USNR, 1943-46, ETO. Mem. Assn. Social Econs., Omicron Delta Epsilon. Roman Catholic. Avocations: hiking, reading, solving and constructing crossword puzzles. Home: 1333 4th Ave S Moorhead MN 56560-2971

TRAINOR, LILLIAN (MIDGE TRAINOR), elections official, campaign consultant; b. Oct. 30, 1936; d. Loenell Lesley and Lillie Ara (Kenyon) Barber; m. Arthur James Trainor, Mar. 9, 1959; children: Michael, Arthur, Lynn Marie. Student pub. schs., Pleasantville, N.J. Chair Burlington County Bd. Elections, Mount Holly, N.J., 1978-81, commr. of registration, 1981-83, chair, 1983-90; dir. N.J. Divsn. Elections, 1990-94. Vice chair, mem. exec. bd. Burlington County Dem. Com., 1977-90, 94-2002; chair Southampton Twp. Dem. County Com., 1976-79, 94-2002; bd. dirs. County Canvassers, Burlington County, 1978-90; v.p. Southeastern Dem. Coalition, 1977-87; mgr. Florio for Gov. Campaign, N.J., 1981, Carter for Pres. Campaign, Burlington County area, 1980; del. Dem. Nat. Conv., 1984, 88; coord. Women for Florio Gubanatorial campaign, 1989. With WAC, 1955-57. Mem. Nat. Assn. State Election Dirs., N.J. State Assn. Election Ofcls., VFW Aux., Big Six Club (pres. 1973-79). Avocations: accordion, piano, painting, birdwatching. Home: 20 Pleasant St Vincentown NJ 08088

TRAISMAN, HOWARD SEVIN, pediatrician; b. Chgo., Mar. 18, 1923; s. Alfred Stanley and Sara (Sevin) T.; m. Regina Gallagher, Feb. 29, 1956; children: Barry D. Lifschultz, Edward S., Kenneth N. BS in Chemistry, Northwestern U., 1943, MB, 1946, MD, 1947. Intern Cook County Hosp., Chgo., 1946-47; resident in pediat. Children's Meml. Hosp., Chgo., 1949-51, attending physician divsn. endocrinology, 1951—; mem. faculty Med. Sch. Northwestern U., Evanston, Ill., 1951—, prof. pediat., 1973—, pres., 1999—. Author articles in field, chpts. in books. Capt. M.C. AUS, 1943-46, 47-49. Recipient Northwestern U. Alumni Merit award, 1995. Mem. Am. Diabetes Assn. (Disting. Svc. award 1976), Am. Pediatric Soc., Am. Acad. Pediat., Endocrine Soc., Lawson Wilkins Pediatric Endocrine Soc., AMA, Midwest Soc. Pediatric Rsch., Ill. Med. Soc., Chgo. Pediatric Soc., Chgo. Med. Soc., Inst. Medicine Chgo. Democrat. Jewish. Office: 1325 Howard St Evanston IL 60202-3766

TRAKATELLIS, DEMETRIOS See DEMETRIOS

TRALDI, LORENZO, mathematician, educator; b. Rome, May 22, 1955; arrived in U.S., 1955; s. Giuseppe Alberto Traldi, Ila Dawson Little, Charles Little (Stepfather); m. Sharon Richter; children: Arthur, Matthew, Oliver, Rebecca. BA, CUNY, Flushing, NY, 1976; PhD, Yale U., 1980. Asst. prof. Lafayette Coll., Easton, Pa., 1980—86, assoc. prof., 1986—94, prof., 1994—2001, Marshall R. Metzgar prof. math., 2001—. Contbr. articles and revs. to profl. jours. Grantee, Lafayette Coll., 1983, 1987, 1991, 1996, 1997, 2000, 2001, USAF Office Sci. Rsch., 1991—92, rsch. experience for undergrads. grants, NSF, 1994, 2001, 2003. Mem.: IEEE, Inst. for Combinatorics and its Applications, Am. Math. Soc. Independent. Home: 725 Coleman St Easton PA 18042 Office: Dept Math Lafayette Coll Easton PA 18042 Office Phone: 610-330-5276. Personal E-mail: traldil@lafayette.edu. Business E-Mail: traldil@lafayette.edu.

TRAMMELL, ALAN STUART, professional baseball manager; b. Garden Grove, Calif., Feb. 21, 1958; m. Barbara Leverett, Feb. 21, 1978; children: Lance, Kyle, Jade Lynn. Shortstop Detroit Tigers, 1977—96, asst. to baseball ops., 1996—98; first base coach San Diego Padres, 2000—02; mgr. Detroit Tigers, 2002—. Named Most Valuable Player, So. League, 1977; winner Gold Glove award, 1980, 81, 83, 84, Silver Slugger award, 1987, 88, 90; mem. Am. League All-Star Team, 1980, 84, 87, 88, 90, World Series Championship Team, 1984; named Most Valuable Player 1984 World Series. Office: Detroit Tigers Comerica Park 2100 Woodward Ave Detroit MI 48216

TRAMMELL, HERBERT EUGENE, physicist, laboratory executive; b. Laurel, Miss., Apr. 19, 1927; s. Homer Lee and Evie Louisa (Breazeale) T.; m. Jane Walker, Dec. 28, 1948; children— Carmen, Bert, Lisa, Brian. BA in Physics, U. Miss., 1947, MA, 1948. With Nuclear div. Union Carbide, Oak Ridge, 1949-89, mgr. barrier devel. programs, 1967-69, dir. gaseous diffusion devel. div., 1969-77; dir. engring. tech. div. Oak Ridge Nat. Lab., 1977-89, ret., 1989; with Martin Marietta Energy Systems, 1983-89. Bd. dirs. Emory Valley Sch. for Retarded Children, 1962-68, v.p., 1966-68; mem. Tenn. Med. Malpractice Rev. Bd., 1974-80; active PTA. Served with U.S. Navy, 1944-45. Mem.: Rotary (pres. 1980-81). Methodist. Home: 901 Johnson St Key West FL 33040-4745 E-mail: htrammell@aol.com.

TRAMMELL, JOSEPH EMANUEL, small business owner, media consultant; arrived in U.S., 1950; s. Webster Benjamin and Elizabeth Trammell; children: Aaron, Sarah. Grad., Upper Freehold Twp. H.S., Allentown, NJ, 1967. Engring. aide Frequency Engring. Labs., Farmingdale, NJ, 1969—71, Reeves Teletape Sound Shop, N.Y.C., 1977—79; maitre d Inkwell Coffeehouse, West Long Branch, NJ, 1971—73; motion picture craftsman NABET Local 15, N.Y.C., 1973—85, IATSE Local 52, N.Y.C., 1985—; pres., owner Navesync Inc., N.Y.C., 1979—. Elec., mech. optical, visual cons. to TV programs and films. Vol. Boy Scouts Am., Atlanta Highlands, NJ, 1986—88. Recipient Outstanding Achievement in Motion Picture Industry award, U.S. Dept. Commerce, 1995. Mem.: IATSE (mem. exec. bd. local unit 1990—98). Achievements include patent in field. Avocations: computers, cooking, gardening. Office: Navesync Inc 306 W 38t St 5th Fl New York NY 10018

TRAMMELL, KENNETH R. automotive executive; married; 2 children. BBA in acctg., U. Houston. Cert. CPA Tex. Sr. mgr. Arthur Andersen LLP; asst. contr. Tenneco Automotive, 1996—97, corp. contr., 1997—99, v.p., contr., 1999—2003, sr. v.p., CFO, 2003—. Office: Tenneco Automotive 500 N Field Dr Lake Forest IL 60045

TRAMONTINE, JOHN ORLANDO, retired lawyer; b. Iron Mountain, Mich., Sept. 21, 1932; s. Orlando F. and Susan M. (Hollar) Tramontine; m. Nancy A. McCabe, July 14, 1956; 1 child, Margaret A. BSChemE, U. Notre Dame, 1955; postgrad., Georgetown U., 1956—58; LLB, NYU, 1960. Bar: N.Y. 1960, U.S. Dist. Ct. (no. dist.) Ill. 1963, U.S. Dist. Ct. (so. and ea. dists.) N.Y. 1965, U.S. Ct. Appeals (2d and 5th cirs.) 1967, U.S. Supreme Ct. 1970, U.S. Ct. Appeals (8th cir.) 1970, (3d cir.) 1973, (7th cir.) 1976, (fed. cir.) 1979, U.S. Dist. Ct. (we. dist.) N.Y. 1981. Examiner U.S. Patent Office, 1956-58; patent agt. Arthur, Dry & Dole, N.Y.C., 1958-60; assoc. Arthur, Dry, Kalish, Taylor & Wood, N.Y.C., 1960-62, Wolfe, Hubbard, Voit & Osann, Chgo., 1962-63, Fish & Neave, N.Y.C., 1963-70, ptnr., 1970-2000; ret., 2000. 2nd lt. USMCR, 1955. Fellow Am. Coll. Trial Lawyers, Am. Bar Found.; mem. ABA, Assn. of Bar of City of N.Y. (chmn. patent com. 1974-77), Fed. Cir. Bar Assn., N.Y. Intellectual Property Law Assn. (pres. 1985-86), St. Andrews Golf Club (sec. 1981-83). Office: Fish & Neave 1251 Avenue of the Americas New York NY 10020-1105

TRAMONTO, RICK, chef; b. Rochester, NY; m. Gale Gand. Grill/saute cook The Scotch & Sirloin; chef Strathallen; garde-mgr. chef Tavern on the Green; chef Gotham Bar & Grill, Aurora, Avanzare, Chgo., The Pump Room, Chgo., Scoozi!, Chgo., Charlie Trotter's, Chgo., Stapleford Park Hotel, London; owner, chef Tru, Chgo., 1999—, Brasserie T., Chgo. Appeared on Oprah TV program. Named one of Am.'s rising Star Chefs, Robert Mondavi, 1995; named to Ten Best New Chefs, Food & Wine, 1994. Office: 676 N St Clair St Chicago IL 60611

TRAMUTOLA, JOSEPH LOUIS, lawyer, educator; b. Union City, NJ, Mar. 6, 1931; s. Joseph Emil and Elda (Brioli) T.; m. Mary Ann Banull, Sept. 4, 1965; children Karen, Kim, Karla. BA, St. Peter's Coll., Jersey City, 1953; JD, Fordham U., 1959. Bar: N.J. 1961. Atty. Toolan, Haney, Romand, Perth Amboy, N.J.; prof. law Fairleigh Dickinson U., Madison, N.J., 1965—, creator, dir. ednl. program for older persons, 1972-2001, ret., 2001. Pre-legal advisor Silberman Coll. bus., Fairleigh Dickinson U.; cons. Am. Coun. on Edn., Washington, Am. Edn. Assn., Washington, Thomas Edison Coll., Trenton, N.J., Chartered Pub. Underwriters, East Orange, N.J., USDA; adj. faculty U. Mich., dir. Fairleigh Dickinson U. Patent Inst. dir. ednl. seminars on student law; seminar dir. student law, Calif., Ill., Mass., N.Y., Ga. Author: Guide Book for Student Rights, Legal Perspective for Student Personal Administration, Legal Overview of the New Student; dir. CPA Law Rev. With U.S. Army, 1955-57. Named Outstanding Educator Outstanding Educators Inc., 1973, 1974, Commendation for Civic Contb. N.J. Legis., 1993. Roman Catholic. Avocations: bonsai, clock making, gardening, zymology, music. Home: 12 Browning Ct Mendham NJ 07945-3301 Fax: 973-543-6621. Personal E-mail: jltramutola@aol.com.

TRAN, CAN NGOC, educator, researcher; b. Saigon, Vietnam, Jan. 24, 1924; arrived in U.S., 1985; s. Dan Van Tran and Day Thi Le; m. Loc Thi Nguyen, Mar. 21, 1951; children: Raymond, Hung, Oanh, Thu, Bao, Son. Author: Unforgettable Stories, 1991, Mot Chuyen Tinh Tho Mong, 1999, Nhung Ky Niem Khong Quen, 2001; rschr.: Four Very Dangerous Diseases of the Contemporary Which Could Be Mortal, 2002; author: A Love Story Between City and Mountain, 2003. Gen. sec. Popular Revolutionary Com., Giadinh Province, Vietnam, 1945—48. Home: 1095 Ricco Dr Sparks NV 89434

TRAN, HENRY BANG Q. social work case manager; b. Binh Dinh, Vietnam, Dec. 28, 1952; came to U.S., 1975; s. Mau Dinh and Ho Thi Tran; m. Thuhong T. Ngo; children: John, Michael, Robert, Richard, Jennifer. BA, Northeastern Ill. U., 1977, MA, 1978. Cert. social worker, real estate broker. Social worker Tex. Dept. Human Svcs., Houston, 1980-96; founder, pres. Texo Properties, Inc., Houston, 1984-85; pres. N.E.W.S. Properties, Houston, 1985—; case mgr. Tex. Workforce Commn., 1996—. Instr. math. City Colls. Chgo., 1977, Vietnamese lang. U. Houston, 1985, pres. H Trans Corp. V.p. Buddhist Assn. for Services of Humanity in Am., Houston, 1985—; pres. Quang Trung Mut. Assistance Assn., Houston, 1984—. Fellow U. Miami, 1979. Mem. Nat. Assn. Realtors, Tex. Pub. Employee Assn., Dalat U. Alumni Assn., Asia Soc., Houston Vietnam Lions Club (pres. 1991). Avocations: tennis, soccer, jogging.

TRAN, JACK NHUAN NGOC, gas and oil reservoir engineer; b. Quang Binh, Vietnam, Sept. 21, 1933; came to U.S., 1975; s. Dieu Ngoc and Ly Thi (Nguyen) T.; m. Christine Quang Huynh; children: Quoc Dung, Ann Nga Huyen, Ephram Anh Dung, John Hung Dung. BS, U. San Francisco, 1977, MBA, 1978. With Republic of Vietnam Mil., 1952-67; cadet Rep. Vietnam Mil. Acad., Dalat, 1952-53; 1st lt., co. comdr. 1st Republic of Vietnam Bn., South Vietnam, 1953-54; editor-in-chief Republic of Vietnam Revs., Saigon, 1955-57; commandant Republic of Vietnam Aerial Photo Ctr., Saigon, 1958-61, Republic of Vietnam Mil. Intelligence Sch., Caymai and Saigon, 1962-67; mem. Republic of Vietnam Senate, 1967-73; v.p. The Meteco Corp., Saigon, Vietnam, 1971-72; pres., chmn. bd. Meteco-Vinaseco Co., Saigon, 1972-75; air photo analyst Std. Oil Co., San Francisco, 1975-79; gas and oil engr. Chevron Oil Co., San Francisco, 1980—; col. U.S. Intelligence, Calif., 1980-90. Author: Flower in the Battle Field, 1956, Geological Survey of the Kndu, CA, 1982, Beluga River Oil Development, 1984, The Military Life, 1992; editor-in-chief Chien-Si Quoc-Gia Mag. Recipient Hon. Key of the City, City of Omaha, Nebr., 1989, Hon. Citizen City of Fayetteville, N.C., 1969; Resolution of Recognition, Senate of State of Hawaii, 1969, Senate of State of Tex., 1969. Mem. The U. of San Francisco Alumni Assn., Rotary Internat. Roman Catholic. Avocations: swimming, music, reading, travel. Home: 1418 Lundy Ave San Jose CA 95131-3310

TRAN, KHANH T. insurance company executive; CFO, Pacific Life Ins. Co., Newport Beach, Calif. Office: Pacific Life Ins Co PO Box 9000 Newport Beach CA 92658-9030

TRAN, LAN P. writer, performer; b. Austin, Tex., June 2, 1973; d. Huy B. and Bay T. Tran. BA, UCLA, 1996; MA, NYU, 1999. Author: Lone Stars in Falling Backwards: Stories of Fathers & Daughters, 2004, How To Unravel Your Family, 2003, Lemongracias, 2002; performer: The American Living Room Festival, 2002, National Literary Caravan, 2002, ONE Festival, 2003, The Quarterly Report, 2004, many others. Finalist Heideman award, 2003; recipient York Prize, 2002;, Hedgebrook Found., 2002, Ragdale Found., 2002, Vt. Studio Ctr., 2002, Va. Ctr. for the Creative Arts, 2001.

TRAN, LONG TRIEU, industrial engineer; b. Saigon, Vietnam, Oct. 10, 1956; arrived in US, 1973; s. Nguyen Dinh and Thiet Thi (Nguyen) T.; m. Khanh Thi-Hong Phan, Aug. 3, 1988. BS in Mech. Engring. with honors, U. Kans., 1976; MS in Mech. Engring., MIT, 1980; MBA in Bus. Adminstrn. with honors, U. Louisville, 1993. Cert. quality engr., mfg. engr., project mgmt. profl. Tchg. asst. U. Kans., 1975-76, U. Calif., Berkeley, 1977; rsch. asst. Lawrence Berkeley Labs., 1977, MIT, 1977-80; libr. staff Harvard U. Med. Sch. Libr., 1977-78; mem. staff New England Deaconess Hosp., Boston, 1978-80; prodn. programming engr. GE, Cleve., 1980-81, advanced mfg. engr. Louisville, 1981-82, quality sys. engr., 1982-84, quality control engr., 1984-

86, sr. quality info. equipment engr., 1986-89, sr. quality indsl. engr., 1990-94, sr. supplier tech. assistance engr., 1995-96, sr. advanced supplier quality engr., 1996-98, program mgr. purchased material quality, 1999, combo blackbelt leader supplier quality, 1999-2000, Six Sigma program mgr., 2000—02, sr. purchased material quality engr., 2003—. Exec. advisor Jr. Achievement Inc., Louisville, 1983-84; monitor/reader Rec. for the Blind, 1994—; fundraiser The Dream Factory Inc., 1994—. Vol. NCCJ, 1994—, Clothe-A-Child, 1993—, Dare-To-Care, 1994—, Ronald McDonald House, 1994—. Mem. AAAS, ASME, Am. Soc. Quality Control, Computer and Automated Sys. Assn. (charter), Am. Prodn. and Inventory Control Soc., Robot Inst. Am., Robotics Internat. (charter), Soc. Mfg. Engrs. (sr.), Instrument Soc. Am. (sr.), Am. Mgmt. Assn., N.Y. Acad. Scis., Internat. Platform Assn., Indsl. Computing Soc. (founding), Project Mgmt. Inst., Nat. Pks. Conservation Assn., U.S. Libr. Congress Assocs. (founding), Assn. Compassion (bd. dirs. 2003—), (life) Handyman Club of Am., (life) PGA Tour Partners Club, Sigma Xi, Pi Tau Sigma, Tau Beta Pi, Phi Kappa Phi, Beta Gamma Sigma. Republican. Achievements include research on grinding processes and material surface analysis, also manufacturing project management. Home: 3642 Windward Way Louisville KY 40220-1818 Office: Gen Electric Co Appliance Park AP2-117 Louisville KY 40225-0001 Office Phone: 502-452-7082.

TRAN, NANG TRI, engineering executive, electrical engineer; b. Binh Dinh, Vietnam, Jan. 2, 1948; came to the U.S., 1979, naturalized, 1986; s. Cam Tran and Cuu Thi Nguyen; m. Thu-Huong Thi Tong, Oct. 14, 1982; children: Helen, Florence, Irene, Kenneth. BSEE, Kyushu Inst. Tech., Kitakyushu, Japan, 1973, MSEE, 1975; PhD in Materials Sci./Solid State Device, U. Osaka Prefecture, Sakai, Japan, 1979. Rsch. assoc. U. Calif. Irvine, 1979; engr., rsch. scientist Sharp Electronics, Irvine, 1979-80; sr. rsch. scientist Arco Solar Industries, Chatsworth, Calif., 1980-84; sr. rsch. specialist, group leader 3M Co., St. Paul, 1985-96; staff scientist Imation Corp., Oakdale, Minn., 1996—; exec. Khanti Inc. Adj. prof. Inst. Tech., U. Minn., Mpls.; cons., lectr. Japan industry mgmt.; reviewer NSF. Author: (poetry) My Journey; contbr. articles to profl. jours. Mem. tech. com. various internat. confs. Recipient R&D awards, Photonic Cir. Excellence award; fellow, Govt. South Vietnam, Japan, USAID, Rotary Internat., 1968—79. Mem. IEEE (sr.), Japan Soc. Applied Physics, N.Y. Acad. Scis. Achievements include invention of direct digital x-rays; transparent conducting zinc oxide doped with group III elements; thin film transistors on flexible substrate; structured phosphors in se-based thin film solar cells; patents in field; research in amorphous silicon solar cells; image sensors; solid state memory; photoconductors; CD; high density data storage media; diamond like carbon evaporated lubricant; transparent conducting oxide films. Office: Imation Corp Materials Media Tech 1 Imation Pl Discovery 1D-20 Oakdale MN 55128-3414 Office Phone: 651-704-4448. Business E-Mail: nttran@imation.com.

TRAN, NICHOLAS Q. computer scientist, educator; b. Saigon, Vietnam; PhD, U. Calif., Santa Barbara, 1992. Tech. staff mem. IBM, Raleigh, NC, 1993—94; lectr. U. Pa., Phila., 1993—97; asst. prof. Wichita State U., Kans., 1997—2000; assoc. prof. Santa Clara U., Calif., 2000—. Grantee A Theory of Hiding Functions and Its Applications in Digital Watermarking, AFSOR EPSCoR, 2000-2004, 'A Complexity-Theoretic Found. for Digital Image Watermarking Sys., NSF, 2003-2006, Modeling and Benchmarking Digital Watermarking, NSF EPSCoR, 1999-2000. Mem.: European Assn. for Theoretical Computer Sci., Assn. for Computing Machinery. Office: Santa Clara Univ 500 El Camino Real Santa Clara CA 95053-0290 Business E-Mail: ntran@scu.edu.

TRAN, QUI-PHIET, English educator; b. Dalat, Vietnam, Jan. 6, 1937; came to U.S., 1972; s. But Qui and Anh Nguyen Thi Tran; m. Ngan Vo Thi, Aug. 30, 1963; children: Hung, Thuy, Long, Kien. BA, U. Hue, Vietnam, 1960; MA, U. Tex., 1974, PhD, 1977. English tchr. Votanh H.S., Nhatrang, Vietnam, 1960-64, Petrus Ky H.S., Saigon, Vietnam, 1964-65; instr. English U. Hue, 1965-72, U. Tex., Austin, 1977-78; resource specialist Arlington (Va.) Pub. Schs., 1980-81; asst. prof., then assoc. prof. Schreiner U., Kerrville, Tex., 1982-90, prof. English, 1990—2002, prof. emeritus, 2002—. Document analyst Congl. Info. Svc., Washington, 1979-80; refugee resettlement cons. Ctr. for Applied Linguistics, Washington, 1980-81, Action, U.S. Govt., Washington, 1982; Fulbright lectr. Nat. U. Vietnam, Ho Chi Minh City, 1999-2000. Author: William Faulkner, 1980; contbr. articles to profl. publs. Advisor Vietnamese Parents Assn., Arlington, 1980-81. Grantee Mellon Found., 1983, NEH, 1983, 89, Am. Coun. Learned Socs., 1984-85. Mem. MLA, Fulbright Assn. Avocation: gardening. Home: 15842 Clayton Bend Dr Houston TX 77082-4077 E-mail: qui-phiet.tran@comcast.net.

TRAN, TUAN DIEP, pediatrician, educator; b. Saigon, Vietnam, May 18, 1967; s. Phuong Huan Tran and Anh Tu Diep; m. MyLien Thi Tu; children: KhanhHoa Lien, Khang Vi. MD, U. Medicine and Pharmacy, HoChiMinh City, Vietnam, 1989; PhD, U. Tokyo, Japan, 2003. Asst. lectr. dept. pediat. U. of Medicine and Pharmacy, HoChiMinh City, 1989—93, lectr., 1993—. Postdoctoral fellow Nat. Inst. Physiol. Sci., Japan, 2003; exch. scholar U. Mich., 2004—. Contbr. articles to profl. jours., chapters to books. Recipient Silver medal All Univs. Basketball Championship, Ministry of Edn., Vietnam, 1986, 3rd prize Med. Young Investigator awards, Ministry of Health and Ministry of Youth, Vietnam, 1990; fellow Asian Youth Fellowships, Ministry of Fgn. Affairs, Japan, 1997, Monbusho Fellowships, Ministry of Edn., Sci., Sport, and Culture, Japan, 1998, John J. Bonica Trainee Fellowship, Internat. Assn. Study of Pain, 2002, Japan Soc. Promotion Sci., 2003, NIH/WHO, 2004; Outstanding fellow, Inst. Brain Rsch. Orgn., 2003. Mem.: Internat. Assn. Study of Pain, Soc. for Neurosci. Achievements include development of new method to directively and selectively activate C-fibers (relate to second pain). Home: 2209 Stone Rd Ann Arbor MI 48105 Address: 456A Nguyen Chi Thanh St P4Q11 Hochiminh City Vietnam Business E-Mail: dieptuan@umich.edu.

TRANI, EUGENE PAUL, university president, educator; b. Bklyn., Nov. 2, 1939; s. Frank Joseph and Rose Gertrude (Kelly) T.; m. Lois Elizabeth Quigley, June 2, 1962; children: Anne Chapman, Frank. BA in History with honors, U. Notre Dame, 1961; MA, Ind. U., 1963, PhD, 1966. Instr. history Ohio State U., Columbus, 1965-67; asst. prof. So. Ill. U., Carbondale, 1967-71, assoc. prof., 1971-75, prof., 1975-76; asst. v.p. acad. affairs, prof. U. Nebr., 1976-80; prof., vice chancellor acad. affairs U. Mo. Kansas City, 1980-86; prof., v.p. acad. affairs U. Wis. System, 1986-90; pres. Va. Commonwealth U., 1990—; pres. bd. dirs. Va. Biotech Rsch. Park, 1992-97, chmn., 1997—; pres., chmn. VCU Health Sys., 2000—. Vis. asst. prof. U. Wis., Milw., 1969; bd. dirs. Met. Richmond SunTrust Mid-Atlantic Bank, Universal Corp., LandAm. Fin. Group, Inc.; mem. commn. Internat. Edn. Am. Coun. Ed., 1991—; bd. gov. Ctr. Russian Am. Bus., Washington, 1993-98; adv. coun. on Grad. Studies and Rsch., U. Notre Dame, 1994—, NASULGC, 1980—, chair commn. on internat. affairs, 1993-94; vis. prof. Univ. Coll., Dublin, 2002; bd. advisors Inst. for U.S. Studies, U. London, 1993-99; cons. in field. Author, editor: Concerns of a Conservative Democrat, 1968, The Treaty of Portsmouth: An Adventure in American Diplomacy, 1969; (with Donald E. Davis) The First Cold War, 2002; (with David Wilson) The Secretaries of the Department of the Interior, 1849-69, 1975;) The Presidency of Warren G. Harding, 3d edit., 1989; contbr. articles to profl. jours., newspapers; book reviewer. Permanent mem. Coun. Fgn. Rels., N.Y.C., 1979—; bd. dirs. Richmond Ballet, 1991-96, NCCJ, Richmond, 1991-94, Va. Spl. Olympics, 1991-96, YMCA of Greater Richmond, 1992—, Richmond Renaissance, 1992-96, 2001—, chmn., 2001—; bd. dirs. Met. Bus. Found., 1992-98, Va. Tech. Fund Found., 1993--, Met. Bus. League, 1994--; mem. U.S. Savs. Bond Vol. Com., chmn. higher edn. area, 1992-93; adv. bd. Greater Richmond chpt. ARC, 1992—; mem. Gov.'s Commn. Info. Tech. in Va., 1998-2000; bd. dirs. Collegiate Sch., 1998—; adv. bd. Black History Archives Project, 1992-96; bd. dirs. Va. Ctr. for Innovative Tech., 1990-96, Capital Area Assembly, 1990-93, Richmond Symphony, 1991-94, Richmond Symphony Coun., 1995—; mem. coun. advisors Christian Children's Fund, 1992-95; mem. Ctrl. Richmond Assn., 1992-96; bd. trustees Va. Hist. Soc., 1994-96, Theatre Va., 1994-97, Richmond Children's Mus., 1994—, World Affairs Coun. of Greater Richmond, 1999-2003; bd. dirs. Sci. Mus. of Va. Found., 1994—; mem. Gov.'s Biotech. Initiative Adv. Bd., 2002—; bd. dirs. Qatar Found. for Edn. Sci. Comm. Devel., Va. Tech. Fund Found., 1993—. Fellow Russian and East European Inst., 1964-65, Nat. Hist. Publs. Commn., 1969-70, Woodrow Wilson Internat. Ctr. Scholars, 1972-73, So. Ill. U. Sabbatical Leave, 1975-76, Coun. Internat. Exchange Scholars, 1981, U. Mo. Faculty, 1981; grantee U.S. Dept. Interior Rsch., 1965-66, So. Ill. U. Office Rsch. and Projects, 1967-74, Am. Philos. Soc., 1968, 72, So. Ill U. Summer Rsch. 1970, 72, 75, Lilly Endowment, 1975-76, Sloan Commn. Govt. and Higher Edn., 1978, USIA Am. Participants Program, 1984-86, 88, 90; Inst. for U.S. Studies fellow U. London, 1995, fellow commoner St. John's Coll., Cambridge, 1998; recipient Younger Humanist award NEH, 1972-73, Leadership and Achievement award Ctrl. Richmond Assn., 1992, Biotech. Leadership award Va. Biotech. Assn., 1999; recipient Disting. Leadership award, Nat. Assn. Cmty. Leaders, 1994, Richmond Humanitarian award, NCCJ, 1995, Flame Bearer of Edn. award Coll. Fund/UNCF, 1998, Richmond Joint Engrs. Coun. Cmty. Svc. award, 2002; named Style Mag. Richmonder of Yr., 1998, Hope award, Nat. MS Soc., 2003, others. Mem. Internat. Inst. Strategic Studies, Am. Assn. Advancement Slavic Studies, Orgn. Am. Historians, Soc. Historians Am. Fgn. Rels., Greater Richmond C. of C. (bd. dirs. 1991-96, chmn. 1997-98), Phi Kappa Phi. Roman Catholic. Avocations: reading, travel, basketball, golf. Office: Va Commonwealth U Box 842512 910 W Franklin St Richmond VA 23284-2512 E-mail: etrani@vcu.edu.

TRANI, JOHN M. former consumer products company executive; b. N.Y.C., 1946; B in Aerospace Engring., Bklyn. Poly. Inst., 1960, M in Indsl. Mgmt., Ops. Rsch. With GE, 1978—97; pres., CEO GE Med. Svcs. divsn. GE Co., 1986—97; chmn., CEO Stanley Works, New Britain, Conn., 1997—2003.

TRANK, DOUGLAS MONTY, rhetoric and speech communications educator; b. Lincoln, Nebr., Sept. 8, 1944; s. Walter John and Hazel Elaine (Stegeman) T.; children: Heather Nicole, Jessica Celeste; m. Christine Marie Quinn, 1992. BA in English, U. Nebr., Kearney, 1967, MS in Comm., 1970; PhD in Comm., U. Utah, 1973. Tchr. Ogallala (Nebr.) High Sch., 1967-70; teaching fellow in communications U. Utah, Salt Lake City, 1970-72; prof. communications Old Dominion U., Norfolk, Va., 1972-74; prof. rhetoric and edn. U. Iowa, Iowa City, 1974—, chmn. rhetoric dept., 1984-89, 2001—. Chmn. bd. control athletics, faculty senate, mem. ednl. policy com., faculty adv. com., faculty assembly, exec. com. U. Iowa. Author 3 books; editor Communication Edn., 1993-96; assoc. editor Communication Studies; contbr. numerous articles to profl. jours. Recipient Admiral award Ace Adventures, Inc., Iowa, 1987, Hemingway prize, 1992. Mem. Speech Communication Assn., Iowa Communication Assn. (pres. 1980-82, editor 1977-81, mem. jour. editorial bd.), Cen. States Communication Assn. (pres. 1990-91), Fedn. Iowa Speech Orgns. (pres. 1977-79), Iowa City Optimist Club (dir. 1982-89, pres. 1987-88). Democrat. Avocations: ice sailing, hunting, fishing, canoeing. Office: U Iowa Dept Rhetoric Iowa City IA 52242 E-mail: douglas-trank@uiowa.edu.

TRANQUADA, ROBERT ERNEST, internist, educator; b. L.A., Aug. 27, 1930; s. Ernest Alvro and Katharine (Jacobus) Tranquada; m. Janet Martin, Aug. 31, 1951; children: John Martin, Katherine Anne, James Robert. BA, Pomona Coll., 1951; MD, Stanford U., 1955; D.Sc. (hon.), Worcester Poly. Inst., 1985. Diplomate Am. Bd. Internal Medicine. Intern in medicine UCLA Med. Center, 1955—56, resident in medicine, 1956—57; resident Los Angeles VA Hosp., 1957—58; fellow in diabetes and metabolic diseases UCLA, 1958—59; fellow in diabetes U. So. Calif., 1959—60, asst. prof. medicine, 1960—63, assoc. prof., 1964—68, chmn. dept. community medicine, 1967—70; med. dir. Los Angeles County/U. So. Calif. Med. Center, 1969—74; assoc. dean U. So. Calif. Sch. Medicine, 1969—76; regional dir. Central Region, Los Angeles County Dept. Health Services, 1974—76; assoc. dean UCLA Sch. Medicine, 1976—79; chancellor and dean U. Mass. Med. Sch., 1979—86; dean U. So. Calif. Sch. Medicine, 1986—91; prof. medicine U. So. Calif., L.A., 1986—92, Norman Topping/Nat. Med. Enterprises prof. med./pub. policy, 1992—97; prof. emeritus, 1997—. Mem, chair L.A. County Task Force on Health Care Access, 1992—94. Corporator Worcester Art Mus., 1980—86; mem. Ind. Commn. on L.A. Police Dept., 1991—92; mem. governing bd. L.A. County Local Initiative Health Authority, 1994—, chmn., 2001—; emeritus Keck Grad. Inst. Applied Life Scis., 2000—; bd trustees Pomona Coll., 1969—, vice chmn., 1971—79, chmn., 1991—2000, hon., 2000—; bd. fellow Claremont U. Ct., 1971—79, 1991—2000; chmn. bd. overseers Claremont U. Consortium, 2000—; bd. trustees Keck Grad. Inst. Applied Life Scis., 1997—, vice-chmn., 1997—2000; bd. dirs. Nat. Med. Fellowships, Inc., 1973—, chmn., 1980—85; bd. trustees Charles Drew U. Med. and Sci., 1968—79, 1986—95, Orthopaedic Hosp., 1986—91, Barlow Hosp., 1987—89; bd. dirs. Worcester Acad., 1984—86, U. So. Calif. Univ. Hosp., 1988—91, Alliance for Childrens Rights, 1991—95, Cmty. Health Coun., Inc., 1993—, Good Hope Med. Found, 1994—, Ralph M. Parsons Found., 2000—. Fellow Milbank Found., 1967—72. Fellow: AAAS, Am. Antiquarian Soc.; mem.: Inst. Medicine of Nat. Acad. Scis., Calif. Med. Assn., L.A. Acad. Medicine, L.A. County Med. Assn., AMA, Alpha Omega Alpha, Sigma Xi, Phi Beta Kappa.

TRANSOU, LYNDA LOU, advertising art administrator; b. Atlanta, Dec. 11, 1949; d. Lewis Cole Transou and Ann Lynette (Taylor) Putnam; m. Lue Gregg Loso, Oct. 25, 1991. BFA cum laude, U. Tex., 1971. Art dir. The Pitluk Group, San Antonio, 1971, Campbell, McQuien & Lawson, Dallas, 1973-74, Bozell & Jacobs, Dallas, 1974-75; art dir., ptnr. The Assocs., Dallas, 1975-77; art dir. Belo Broadcasting, Dallas, 1977-80; creative dir., v.p. Allday & Assocs., Dallas, 1980-85; owner Lynda Transou Advt. & Design, 1986—. Recipient Merit award, N.Y. Art Dirs. Show, 1980, Gold award, Dallas Ad League, 1980, Silver award, 1980, 1981, 1982, 2 Merit awards, Houston Art Dirs. Club, 1978, Dallas Ad League, 1986, Merit award, Broadcast Designers Assn., 1980, Merit awards, Dallas Ad League, 1978, 1987, Silver award, Houston Art Dirs. Show, 1982, Gold award, Tex. Pub. Rels. Assn., 1985, N.Y. One Show, 1982, Creativity awrd, Art Direction mag., 1986, Print award, Regional Design Annual, 1988, 2 Gold Adrian awards, 1997, Katy award, Dallas Press Club, 2001. Mem. Am. Inst. Graphic Arts, Dallas Soc. Visual Comm. (Bronze award 1980, Merit award 1978-86), Delta Gamma (historian 1969-70).

TRANSUE, DAVID LOWELL, illustrator, writer; s. Lowell Wayne and Ruth Jeannette Transue; m. Julie Parker, Nov. 17, 1978 (div. Jan. 1, 1982); 1 child, Justin David. Degree in Illustration, Famous Artist Schs., Westport, Conn., 1972; student in Graphic Design, Elmira (N.Y.) Coll., 1972—75. Art dir. Poesie India, Orissa, India, 1984—. Contbg. editor: Doll World, Ithaca House Books; contbr. poetry to mags. including Prophetic Voices, An Internat. Lit. Jour., 1983-90, illustrations to mags., short stories to mags. including Abiko Annual, cover paintings for ESA Pub., 1991, Modern Pub., 1984, Tapestry, 2002, Angel Records, 1984, others. Recipient Pres.'s award, Nat. Authors Registry, 2002. Republican. Nazarene Ch. Avocations: jazz, music, reading, poetry, physics. Home and Office: 124 Kingston Rd Greenwood SC 29649 Office Phone: 864-229-9800.

TRANYHAM, DAVID FRANCIS, United States Government administrator; b. Baton Rouge, La. m.; 3 children. BA in Polit. Sci., La. State U., 1973; postgrad. studies, Vanderbilt U., 1973-77. Rsch. analyst U.S. Dept. Transp., Washington; mem. staff aviation subcom. U.S. Ho. of Reps., Washington, 1979-97; asst. adminstr. policy, planning, internat. aviation FAA, Washington, 1998—. Exec. dir. Nat. Civil Aviation Rev. Commn., 1997-98. Office: Nat Hdqtrs Fed Aviation Adminstrn 800 Independence Ave SW Washington DC 20591-0001

TRAPOLIN, FRANK WINTER, retired insurance executive; b. New Orleans, Jan. 29, 1913; s. John Baptiste and Florence Bertha (Winter) T.; m. Thelma Mae Mouledoux, Oct. 27, 1937; children: Timothy, Patricia Couret, Jane Oaksmith, Anne Britt. BS in Econs., Loyola U., New Orleans. cert. ofcl. U.S.A. Track and Field. Agt. Godchaux & Mayer, New Orleans, 1935-42m 46-51; pres. Trapolin-Couret Ins. Agy., Inc., New Orleans, 1953-92; v.p. Gillis, Ellis & Baker, Inc., New Orleans, 1993-94; ret., 1994. Mem. faculty Loyola U., 1938-40; TV lectr., instr. seamanship USCG Aux., New Orleans. Former pres. Cath. Human Rels. Commn. Greater New Orleans, Associated Cath. Charities, Maryland Drive Homeowners Assn., Loyola U. Alumni Assn; former chmn. adv. bd. Ursuline Nuns New Orleans, New Orleans Juvenile Cts.; past scoutmaster Boy Scouts Am., former chmn. troop com.; former v.p. Cmty. Rels. Coun. Greater New Orleans, New Orleans Jr. C. of C.; former v.p. La. Interch. Conf., now treas. emeritus; former trustee United Fund Greater New Orleans Area; dir. emeritus Cath. Book Store Found.; tng. officer 8th USCG Aux.; former mem. adv. bd. Coll. Bus. Adminstrn., Loyola U., Mother-house Sisters of Holy Family, Immaculate Conception Cath. Ch.; group capt. Manresa Retreats, 1947-97; former bd. dirs. St. John Berchman Orphanage, New Orleans Interfaith Conffn.; St. Elizabeth's Home for Girls, Manresa Retreat House; mem. adv. bd. New Orleans Track Club; founder Serra Run for Vocations; bd. dirs. Aubudon Blvd. Assn.; participant U.S. Sr. Olympics, 1997; lector Cath. Ch., 1964-87, eucharist min., 1986-2001. With USN, 1942-46, 51-53; capt. USNR ret. Decorated Order of St. Louis; recipient merit cert. City of New Orleans, 1972; winner 80 and over category La. Sr. Olympics 5000 meter walk, 1995, 96. Mem. La. Assn. Ins. Agts., Nat. Assn. Ins. Agts., New Orleans Ins. Exch., Navy League, Mil. Order World Wars, Greater New Orleans Execs. Assn. (hon. life, pres. 1985, Exec. of Yr. award 1985), New Orleans Photog. Soc., New Orleans Runners Assn., World Trade Ctr. New Orleans (hon.), Serra Club (pres. New Orleans 1973-74), Sertoma Club (pres. New Orleans 1955-56), Internat. House, New Orleans Track Club, New Orleans Yacht Club, Pass Christian Yacht Club, KC (4th degree), Blue Key. Democrat. Achievements include patents for gunnery, training and machinery devices with US Navy. Home: 119 Audubon Blvd New Orleans LA 70118-5538

TRAPP, BRUCE D. neurologist; PhD, Loyola U. Neurology faculty Johns Hopkins U. Sch. Medicine; prof. chemistry Cleve. State U.; prof. neurosci. Case Western Res. U., Cleve.; prof. cell biology, neurobiology and anatomy Ohio State U., Columbus; fellow Nat. Inst. Neurol. Disorders and Stroke NIH, Bethesda, Md.; chmn. dept. neuroscis. Lerner Rsch. Inst., Cleve. Clinic Found., 1994—. Contbr. chapters to books, articles to profl. jours. Recipient Jordi Folch Pi award, Am. Soc. Neurochemistry, 1985, John Dystel prize for multiple sclerosis rsch., Am. Acad. Neurology, 2003; Harry Weaver Neurosci. scholar, Nat. MS Soc., 1986. Office: Cleve Clinic Found Dept Neuroscis 9500 Euclid Ave Cleveland OH 44195

TRAPP, JAMES MCCREERY, lawyer; b. Macomb, Ill., Aug. 11, 1934; BA, Knox Coll., 1956; JD, U. Mich., 1961. Bar: Ill. 1961. Ptnr. McDermott, Will & Emery, Chgo., 1961-98, sr. counsel, 1998—. Chmn. Ill. Inst. Continuing Legal Edn., 1978-79, bd. dirs., 1980-86, pres., 1984-85. Fellow Am. Coll. Trust and Estate Coun. (Ill. chmn. 1980-83, nat. regent 1983—, treas. 1989-90, sec. 1990-91, v.p. 1991-92, pres.-elect 1992-93, pres. 1993-94, exec. com. 1986-94), Am. Bar Found., Ill. Bar Found.; mem. ABA, Ill. State Bar Assn., Chgo. Bar Assn. (chair trust law com. 1972-73, com. on coms. 1972-74), Internat. Acad. Estate and Trust Law, Am. Law Inst. (pres.), Chgo. Estate Planning Coun. Office: McDermott Will & Emery 227 W Monroe St Chicago IL 60606-5096

TRAPP, MARY JANE, lawyer; b. Columbus, Ohio, July 6, 1956; AB cum laude, Mount Holyoke Coll., 1978; JD, Case Western Reserve U., 1981. Bar: Ohio 1981, U.S. Supreme Ct. 1987. Ptnr. Apicella and Trapp, Cleve. Commr. Supreme Ct. Ohio Bd. Commrs. on Unauthorized Practice of Law, 1986—89; mem. Supreme Ct. Rules adv. com., 1997—2002. Fellow: Ohio State Bar Found., Am. Bar Found.; mem.: Cleve. Bar Assn. (trustee 1995—98), Cuyahoga County Bar Assn. (trustee 1986—93, 1999—), Ohio Acad. Trial Lawyers, Ohio State Bar Assn. (pres. 2001—02), ABA. Office: Apicella and Trapp 1200 Penton Media Bldg 1300 E 9th St Cleveland OH 44114-1503

TRAPP, PETER JARL RUDOLF, portfolio manager, farmer; b. Darlington, Eng., Oct. 5, 1945; arrived in U.S., 1971; s. Jarl Rudolph and Olive Lindsay (Fairley) Trapp; m. Regina Antoinette Thomas, Sept. 6, 1969 (div. Dec. 1986); children: Sophia Antoinette, Alexander Rudolf, Olivia Henrietta Elizabeth. Mi-Lic, Fribourg U., Switzerland, 1971; MBA, Columbia U., 1973. V.p. First Boston Corp., N.Y.C., 1973-78, Goldman Sachs & Co., N.Y.C., 1978-81; mgr. dir. Dean Witter Reynolds Inc., N.Y.C., 1982-84; mgr. dir., exec. officer Marine Midland Bank N.A., N.Y.C., 1985-89; sr. v.p. Gerard Klauer Mattison & Co., N.Y.C., 1990-94; mgr. dir. Needham & Co., N.Y.C., 1994—2003; exec. v.p., portfolio mgr. Needham Investment Mgmt., N.Y.C., 1998—2003; founding ptnr. Bifrost Ptnrs. LLC, N.Y.C., 2003—. Bd. dirs. Carmel Bach Festival. Cadet sgt. Swedish Army, 1968—69. Mem.: Coral Beach Club (Bermuda), Annabel's (London), Leash and Doubles Club (N.Y.). Avocations: skiing, fishing, shooting, farming. Home: Bean Creek Farm 341 Tripp McGhee Rd Box 948 Pine Plains NY 12567-0948 Office: Bifrost Ptnrs LLC Ste 801 250 Park Ave 2d Fl New York NY 10177 Office Phone: 212-297-5656. Business E-Mail: pt@bifrostcapital.com.

TRASK, THOMAS EDWARD, religious organization administrator; b. Brainard, Minn., Mar. 23, 1936; m. Shirley Burkhart; children: Kimberly, Bradley, Todd, Tom. BA, North Ctrl. Bible Coll., 1956, DDiv (hon.), 1994. Ordained min. Assemblies of God, 1958. Pastor First Assembly of God, Hibbing, Minn., 1956-60, pastor Vicksburg, Mich., 1960-64; Mich. dist. youth and Sunday sch. dir. Assembly of God, 1964-68; pastor First Assembly of God, Saginaw, Mich., 1968-73, Brightmoor Tabernacle, Southfield, Mich., 1976-88; supt. Mich. Dist. Coun., Dearborn, 1973-76; gen. treas. The Gen. Coun. Assemblies of God, Springfield, Mo., 1988-93, gen. supt., 1993—. Co-author: Back to the Altar: A Call to Spiritual Awakening, 1994, Back to the Word, A Call to Biblical Authority, 1996, The Battle: Defeating the Enemies of Your Soul, 1997, The Blessing: Experiencing the Power of the Holy Spirit Today, 1998, The Choice: Embracing God's Vision in the New Millennium, 1999, The Fruit of the Spirit, 2000, Ministry for a Lifetime, 2001. Mem. Assemblies Of God Ch. Office: Assemblies of God 1445 N Boonville Ave Springfield MO 65802-1894

TRAUB, J(OSEPH) F(REDERICK), computer scientist, educator; b. June 24, 1932; m. Pamela Ann McCorduck, Dec. 6, 1969; children: Claudia Renee, Hillary Anne. BS, CCNY, 1954; PhD, Columbia U., 1959; DSc (hon.), U. Cen. Fla., 2001. Tech. staff Bell Labs., Murray Hill, N.J., 1959-70; prof. computer sci. and math., head dept. computer sci. Carnegie-Mellon U., Pitts., 1971-79; Edwin Howard Armstrong prof. computer sci., chmn. dept., prof. math. Columbia U., 1979-86; prof. computer sci. Princeton (N.J.) U., 1986-87; pres. John Von Neumann Nat. Supercomputer Ctr., Consortium for Sci. Computing, Princeton, 1986-87; Edwin Howard Armstrong prof., chmn. dept. computer sci., prof. math. Columbia U., N.Y.C., 1987-89, Edwin Howard Armstrong prof. computer sci., math., 1989—; external prof. Santa Fe Inst., 1995-98, 2004—; fellow Biosgroup, 1998—2003. Dir. N.Y. State Ctr. Computers and Info. Systems, 1982-88; disting. lectr. MIT, 1977; vis. Mackay prof. U. Calif., Berkeley, 1978-79; cons. Hewlett-Packard, 1982, IBM, 1984, Schlumberger, 1986, Signet Bank, 1994, Lucent Techs., 1996, Bios Group, 1998—; mem. pres.'s adv. com. computer sci. Stanford U., 1972-75, chmn., 1975-76; adv. com. Fed. Jud. Center; mem. sci. council I.R.I.A., Paris, 1976-80; central steering com., computing sci. and engring. research study NSF, also liaison to panel on theoretical computer sci. and panel on numerical comp., 1974-80; mem. adv. com. Carnegie-Mellon Inst. Research, 1978-79; mem. applied math. div. rev. com. Argonne Nat. Lab., 1973-75; mem. adv. com. math. and computer sci. NSF, 1978-80; chmn. computer sci. and tech. bd. NRC, 1986-90; chmn. computer sci. and telecommunications bd. NRC, 1990-92; trustee Columbia U. Press, 1983-85; founding chair Spl. Interest Group on Numerical Math., 1965-71. Author: Iterative Methods for the Solution of Equations, 1964, Russian edit., 1985; (with H. Wozniakowski) A General Theory of Optimal Algorithms, 1980, Russian edit., 1983, Chelsea, 1998; (with G. Wasilkowski and H. Wozniakowski) Information, Uncertainty, Complexity, 1983, Information-Based Complexity, 1988; (with A.G. Werschulz) Complexity and Information, 1998; editor: Complexity of Sequential and Parallel Numerical Algorithms, 1973, Analytic Computational Complexity, 1976, Algorithms and Complexity: New Directions and Recent Results, 1976, Jour. Assn. Computing Machinery, 1970-76, Transactions on Math. Software, 1974-76, Jour. Computer and Sys. Scis., 1973-86, Internat. Jour. on Computers and Math. with Applications, 1974—, Cohabiting With Computers, 1985; (with P. Hut and D. Ruelle) Fundamental Sources of Unpredictability, 1997; founding editor Jour. Complexity, 1985—, Ann. Rev. Computer Sci., 1986-92; assoc. editor Complexity, 1995—. Sherman Fairchild Disting. scholar Calif. Inst. Tech., 1991, 92; recipient Award for Disting. Svc. to Computing Rsch. Computer Rsch. Assn., 1992, Lezione Lincee Acad. Nazionale dei Lincei,

1993, Sr. Scientist award Alexander Von Humboldt Found., 1992-98, City of N.Y. Mayor's award for excellence in sci. and tech., 1999. Fellow AAAS (coun. 1971-74), ACM (chmn. award com. 1974-76), N.Y. Acad. Scis.; mem. IEEE (Emanuel R. Piore Gold medal 1991), NAE (membership com. for computer sci., elec. engring. and control 1986-87, membership com. for computer sci. and engring. 1987-91, presdl. search com. 1993-94), Conf. Bd. Math. Scis. (coun. 1971-74), Soc. Indsl. and Applied Math., Am. Math. Soc. Office: Columbia University Dept Computer Sci 1214 Amsterdam Ave #MC0401 New York NY 10027-7003 Business E-Mail: traub@cs.columbia.edu.

TRAUB, RICHARD KENNETH, lawyer; b. Lakewood, NJ, Aug. 4, 1950; s. Harold W. and Muriel N. (Zurlin) T.; m. Barbara Lynn Wright, July 9, 1972; children: Russell S., Melissa L. BBA, U. Miami, Coral Gables, Fla., 1972, JD cum laude, 1975. Bar: Fla. 1975, N.Y. 1976, N.J. 1976, U.S. Dist. Ct. N.J. 1976, U.S. Supreme Ct. 1979, U.S. Dist. Ct. (ea. & so. dists.) N.Y. 1981. Ptnr. Wilson, Elser, Moskowitz, Edelman & Dicker, N.Y.C., 1975-95, Traub Eglin Lieberman Straus, Hawthorne, N.Y., 1996—. Ptnr. Time for Patty Stables, N.J., 1992—; officer, dir. X-Ray Duplications, Inc., N.J.; ptnr., founder Fractured Greetings, N.J.; mem., lectr. Fedn. Ins. and Corp. Counsel, 1993—,chair tech. com., mem. admissions com., industry cooperation ins. coverage alt. dispute resolution coms. and tech. sect.; lectr. Inst. for Internat. Rsch., Washington, 1988, Engring. News Record Constrn. Claims Conf., 1991. Author: Legal and Professional Aspects of Construction Management, 1990, The Year 2000 and Potential Liabilities and Otherwise, 1999, Litigating Year 2000 Cases, Chapter 8, Insurance Coverage, 1999, Practical Environmental Forensics--Process and Case Histories, 2000; contbr. chpt.: Data Security and Privacy Law-Combatting Cyberthreats, The West Group, 2002; contbr. articles to profl. jours. Mem. ABA (forum com. on constrn. industry 1989, tort and ins. practice sect. 1985—), NY State Bar Assn., NJ Bar Assn., Fla. Bar Assn., Fedn. Def. and Corp. Counsel (spkr. The Millennium Bug ins. coverage sect., vice chair tech. and e-commerce sect., chair tech. com.), Def. Rsch. Inst., Assn. Def. Trial Atty. Office: Traub Eglin Lieberman Straus Mid-Westchester Exec Park Three Skyline Dr Hawthorne NY 10532 also: 100 Metroplex Dr Ste 203 Edison NJ 08817- Office Phone: 732-985-1000. E-mail: rtraub@tels.com.

TRAUDT, MARY B. elementary school educator; b. Chgo., Jan. 1, 1930; d. Lloyd Andrews Haldeman and Adele Eleanor (MacKinnon) Haldeman-Oliver; m. Eugene Peter Traudt, Dec. 6, 1952 (dec.); 1 child, Victoria Jean. BS, Cen. Mich. U., 1951; MA, Roosevelt U., 1978; postgrad., U. Ill., 1982. Asst. editor Commerce Clearing House, Chgo., 1951-53; tchr. Cleve. Elem. Sch., 1954-56, Chgo. Sch. System, 1956-57, Community Consolidated # 54, Hoffman Estates, Ill., 1957-64, Avoca Elem. Sch., Wilmette, Ill., 1964—; ret., 1995. Recipient Computer award Apple Computer Co. Mem. NEA (life), Ill. Assn. of Ret. Tchrs. (life), North Shore Assn. of Ret. Tchrs. (life), Avoca Edn. Assn. (v.p. 1986-91), Alpha Psi Omega. Presbyterian. Avocations: reading, sewing, music, travel, gardening. Home: 512 N McClurg Ct #2201 Chicago IL 60611-4117

TRAUGER, ALETA ARTHUR, judge; BA in English magna cum laude, Cornell Coll., Iowa, 1968; MAT, Vanderbilt U., 1972, JD, 1976. Tchr., Tenn., Eng., 1970-73; assoc., law clk. Barrett, Brandt & Barrett, P.C., Nashville, 1974-77; asst. U.S. atty., first asst., chief of criminal divsn. Mid. Dist. Tenn., 1977-82, No. Dist. Ill., 1979-80; assoc. Hollins, Wagster & Yarbrough, P.C., Nashville, 1983-84; legal counsel Coll. of Charleston, S.C., 1984-85; counsel, ptnr. Wyatt, Tarrant, Combs, Gilbert & Milom, Nashville, 1985-91; judge Tenn. Ct. of the Judiciary, 1987-93; chief of staff Mayor's Office, Nashville, 1991-92; bankruptcy judge U.S. Bankruptcy Ct. (mid. dist.) Tenn., Nashville, 1993-98; dist. judge U.S. Dist. Ct. (mid. dist.) Tenn., Nashville, 1998—. Mem. hearing panel bd. profl. responsibility Tenn. Supreme Ct., 1983-84, mem. adv. com. on rules of civil and appellate procedure, 1989-96; lectr. Vanderbilt U. Sch. Law, 1986-88, mem. Law Sch. alumni bd., 1989-92; master of bench Harry Phillips Am. Inn of Ct., 1990-94; mem. Internat. Women's Forum, 1993—, v.p. Tenn. chpt., 1996-97; mem. Nat. Conf. Bankruptcy Judges, 1994-98, chmn. ethics com., 1994-98; trustee Cornell Coll., 1998—. Bd. dirs. Nashville Inst. for Arts, 1992-99, Miriam's Promise (adoption agy.), 1995-98, Renewal House, 1996-98. Fellow: Nashville Bar Found., Tenn. Bar Found. (life), Am. Bar Found. (life); mem.: FBA (v.p. 1983—84, 1985—86), ABA, Fed. Judges Assn., Nat. Assn. Women Judges (liaison to ABA commn. on the status of women in the profession 2000—01), Tenn. Lawyers Assn. for Women (v.p. 1988—89, pres. 1989—90, bd. dirs. 1990—91), Lawyers Assn. for Women (pres. 1982—83, bd. dirs. 1983—84, 1986—88), Nashville Bar Assn. (bd. dirs. 1984, 1989—91). Office: 825 US Courthouse 801 Broadway Nashville TN 37203-3816 Office Phone: 615-736-7143.

TRAUGER, DONALD BYRON, nuclear engineering laboratory administrator; b. Exeter, Nebr., June 29, 1920; s. Charles C. and Ethel L. (Downey) T.; m. Elaine Causey, Sept. 2, 1945; children: Byron Roscoe, Thomas Charles. AB, Nebr. Wesleyan U., 1942, D.Sc. (hon.), 1974; postgrad., Columbia U., 1942-46, U. Tenn., 1946-49; D.Sc. (hon.), Tenn. Wesleyan Coll., 1977. Supr. test equipment devel. Manhattan Dist. Project, 1942-46; supr. Devel. Lab., Oak Ridge Gaseous Diffusion Plant, 1946-54; with Oak Ridge Nat. Lab., 1954-93, assoc. dir. nuclear and engring. technologies, 1970-84, sr. staff asst. to dir., 1984-93; cons. in energy tech., 1993—. Bd. dirs. Gene Rsch. Access Corp. Editorial advisor Anns. Nuclear Engring, 1973—; design features editor sect. IV Nuclear Safety Jour., 1989-98. Mem. Oak Ridge Bd. Edn., 1961-67; pres. Oak Ridge PTA Coun., 1969-70, Oak Ridge Parents Adv. Coun., 1958-59; chmn. exec. com., trustee Tenn. Wesleyan Coll., 1976-81, chmn. bd. govs., 1986-90, chmn. bd. trustees, 1990-93. Recipient Alumni Achievement award Nebr. Wesleyan U., 1962 Fellow Am. Nuclear Soc. (chmn. planning com. 1981-83); mem. AAAS, Am. Phys. Soc., Rotary, Sigma Xi (pres. Oak Ridge chpt. 1987-88), Sigma Pi Sigma. Methodist. Office Phone: 865-483-1006. Personal E-mail: dbtrauder@aol.com.

TRAUGOTT, ELIZABETH CLOSS, linguist, educator, researcher; b. Bristol, Eng., Apr. 9, 1939; d. August and Hannah M. M. (Priebsch) Closs; m. John L. Traugott, Sept. 26, 1967; 1 child, Isabel. BA in English, Oxford U., Eng., 1960; PhD in English lang., U. Calif., Berkeley, 1964. Asst. prof. English U. Calif., Berkeley, 1964-70; lectr. U. East Africa, Tanzania, 1965-66, U. York, Eng., 1966-67; lectr., then assoc. prof. linguistics and English Stanford (Calif.) U., 1970-77, prof., 1977—2003, chmn. linguistics dept., 1980-85, vice provost, dean grad. studies, 1985-91, mem. grad. record examinations bd., 1989-93, mem. test of English as a fgn. lang. bd., 1990—92, chmn. test of English as a fgn. lang. bd., 1991—92. Mem. higher edn. funding coun. Eng. Assessment Panel, 1996, 2001. Author: (book) A History of English Syntax, 1972; author: (with Mary Pratt) Linguistics for Students of Literature, 1980; author: (with Paul Hopper) Grammaticalization, 1993, rev. edit., 2003; author: (with Richard Dasher) Regularity in Semantic Change, 2002; editor (with ter Meulen, Rielly, Ferguson): On Conditionals, 1986; editor: (with Heine) Approaches to Grammaticalization, 2 vols., 1991; series co-editor: Topics in English Linguistics; contbr. articles to profl. jours. Am. Coun. Learned Socs. fellow, 1975—76, Guggenheim fellow, 1983—84, Ctr. Advanced Study Behavioral Scis. fellow, 1983—84. Fellow: AAAS; mem.: AAUW, AAUP, MLA, Internat. Pragmatics Assn. (bd. dirs. 2000—), Internat. Soc. Hist. Linguistic (pres. 1979—81), Linguistic Soc. Am. (pres. 1987, sec.-treas. 1994—98). Office: Stanford Univ Dept Linguistics Bldg 460 Stanford CA 94305-2150 Business E-Mail: traugott@stanford.edu.

TRAUPMAN-CARR, CAROL ANN, dean, musicologist; b. Allentown, Pa., May 7, 1964; d. John Henry and Carol Jean Traupman; m. David Francis Carr, May 20, 1995; children: Andrew John Carr, Allison Rose Carr. MusB with honors, BA summa cum laude, Moravian Coll., 1986; MA, Cornell U., 1989, PhD, 1995. Tchr. vocal music Ithaca City Schs., NY, 1990—92; dir. Moravian Coll. Music Inst., Bethlehem, Pa., 1993—94; asst. prof. music Moravian Coll., 1994—2001, chair music dept., 2000—01, assoc. dean acad. affairs, 2001—, assoc. prof. music, 2001—; choral dir. St. Ann's R.C. Ch., Emmaus, 1992—. Arranger-in-residence Mainst. Brass Quintet, Bethlehem, 2002—; adj. faculty mem. Moravian Coll., 1992—93. Editor: (collection of essays) Pleasing for Our Use: David Tannenberg and the Organs of the Moravians, (exhibition catalogue) The Square Piano in Rural Pennsylvania, 1760-1830; arranger (brass quintet arrangement) O Come, O Come, Emanuel, Tri-angels, The Boar's Head Carol, Here We Come A-wassailing, Alleluia, the Strife is O'er, Shenandoah, (choral arrangement) O Sanctissima, Were You There?. Fellow, Cornell U., 1989—90; grantee, Pa. Humanities Coun., 1997—98; From Archives to Alive grantee, Pharo Found., 1998. Mem.: Am. Coun. Edn. (assoc.), Am. Musicological Soc. (assoc.). Roman Catholic. Office: Moravian College 1200 Main Street Bethlehem PA 18018 E-mail: caroltcarr@moravian.edu.

TRAUT, CHRISTOPHER D. educational materials distribution executive; Pres., elem. and HS group Follett Corp., River Grove, Ill., 1997—2000, CEO, 2000. Office: Follett Corp 2233 West St River Grove IL 60171-1895

TRAUTH, DAVID E. dairy company executive; b. Covington, Ky., Oct. 8, 1946; s. Louis J. Jr. and Mary B. Trauth. BBA, U. Cin., 1970. V.p. Louis Trauth Dairy Inc., Newport, Ky., 1972-80, pres., CEO, 1981-2000, Louis Trauth Dairy/Suiza Foods, Newport, 2000—. Bd. dirs. Holly Hill Children's House, Alexandria, Ky., 1996-2002. Mem. Cin. Dairy Tech. Soc. (pres. 1982-83), No. Ky. C. of C. (bd. dirs. 1990-96, Entrepreneur of Yr. 1986), Quail Unltd., Ducks Unltd., Ruffed Grouse Soc., Wild Turkey Fedn., Ohio Valley Beagle Club (sec. 1974—). Office: Louis Trauth Dairy Dean Foods PO Box 1770 Newport KY 41071

TRAUTH, JEANETTE M. healthcare educator; b. Cincinnati, Ohio, Apr. 23, 1953; d. Albert E. and Martha B. Trauth; m. Stephen J. Jurman, July 21, 1984; children: Beryl Lee Trauth-Jurman, Danielle Miriam Trauth-Jurman. PhD, U. Pitts., 1981—88. Assoc. prof. U. Pitts., 1988—. Office: U Pitts 130 De Soto St Pittsburgh PA 15261

TRAUTH, JOSEPH LOUIS, JR., lawyer; b. Cin., Apr. 22, 1945; s. Joseph L. and Margaret (Walter) Trauth; m. Barbara Widmeyer, July 4, 1970; children: Jennifer, Joseph III, Jonathan, Braden, Maria. BS in Econs., Xavier U., 1967; JD, U. Cin., 1973. Bar: Ohio 1973, U.S. Dist. Ct. (so. dist.) Ohio 1973, U.S. Ct. Appeals (6th cir.) 1973, U.S. Supreme Ct. 1988, Ky. 2000. Ptnr. Keating, Muething & Klekamp, PLL, Cin., 1973-80, Keating, Muething & Klekamp, Cin., 1980—. Spkr. real estate law, 1974—. Contbr. articles to profl. jours. Mem. Parish Coun., Cin., 1990. Mem.: Cin. Bar Assn. (mem. grievance com., mem. real estate com., mem. negligence com.). Roman Catholic. Avocations: running, tennis, reading. Office: Keating Muething & Klekamp 1400 Provident Tower 1 E 4th St Ste 1400 Cincinnati OH 45202-3717 Office Phone: 513-579-6515. E-mail: jtrauth@kmklaw.com.

TRAUTHWEIN, CHRISTINA, editor-in-chief; Asst. editor Archtl. Lighting Mag., 1989, editor-in-chief. Mem.: IESNA (mem. N.Y. Designer's Lighting Forum), IALD (mem. press affiliate, co-chair awards com.). Office: 770 Broadway New York NY 10003

TRAUTMAN, DONALD W. bishop; b. Buffalo, June 24, 1936; Ed., Our Lady of Angels Sem., Niagara Falls, N.Y., Theology Faculty, Innsbruck, Austria, Pontifical Biblical Inst., Rome, Cath. U., St. Thomas Aquinas U., Rome. Ordained priest Roman Cath. Ch., 1962, consecrated bishop Roman Cath. Ch., 1985. Titular bishop of Sassura and aux. bishop Diocese of Buffalo, 1985; bishop, Erie, Pa., 1990—. Past mem. Prolife com. doctrine and migration Nat. Conf. Home: 205 W 9th St Erie PA 16501-1304 Address: 429 E Granview Blvd Erie PA 16514-0397

TRAUTMAN, HERMAN LOUIS, lawyer, educator; b. Columbus, Ind., Sept. 26, 1911; s. Theodore H. and Emma (Guckenberger) T.; m. Marian Lucille Green, Sept. 1, 1940; children: Stephen M., Pamela C.; LLB with distinction Ind. U., 1937, BA, 1946, JD with distinction, 1946; postgrad., NYU, 1953, Ford Found. faculty fellow, Harvard U., 1954-55. Bar: Ind. 1937, U.S. Tax Ct., U.S. Ct. Appeals (6th cir.) Tenn. Sole practice, Evansville, Ind., 1937-43; pres. Crescent Coal Co., Evansville, 1941-43; prof. law U. Ala. Tuscaloosa, 1946-49; prof. law Vanderbilt U., 1949—, prof. law emeritus, 1977; NYU vis. prof., 1955, U. Mich., Ann Arbor, 1963-64; ptnr. Trautman & Trautman, Nashville, 1976-85; sole practice, Nashville, 1986—. Served to lt. comdr. USN, 1943-46. Mem. ABA, Am. Law Inst., Tenn. Bar Assn., Nashville Bar Assn., Nat. Conf. Jud. Adminstrs., Estate Planning Coun., Order of Coif, Phi Gamma Delta, Belle Meade Club, Univ. Club, Kiwanis. Methodist. Address: PO Box 150862 Nashville TN 37215-0862

TRAUTMAN, WILLIAM ELLSWORTH, lawyer; b. San Francisco, Nov. 27, 1940; s. Gerald H. and Doris Joy (Tucker) T.; m. Dorothy (Williamson), June 17, 1962; children: Darcey, Torey. BA, U. Calif., Berkeley, 1962, LLB, 1965. Bar: Calif., 1965; U.S. Supreme Ct.; Calif. Dist. Ct.; U.S. Ct. Appeals (9th and Fed. Cir.). Assoc. Chickering and Gregory, San Francisco, 1965-71, ptnr., 1972-81, Brobeck, Phleger, and Harrison, San Francisco, 1981—2003, litig. dept. chair, 1984-91, San Francisco mng. ptnr., 1992-96; ptnr. Morgan, Lewis, and Bockius, San Francisco, 2003—. Pres. Oakland, Calif. Mus. Assn., 1981-83; mem. profl. ethics com. State Bar Calif., 1974-77. Fellow: Am. Coll. Trial Lawyers; mem.: Barrister's Club of San Francisco (v.p. 1973), Calif. Barristers (bd. dirs., v.p.), Bar Assn. San Francisco (bd. dirs. 1972—73), Legal Aid Soc. (bd. dirs. 1982—93, pres. 1985—88), U. Calif.-Berkeley Found. (trustee 1998—2000), Boalt Hall Alumni Assn. (bd. dirs. 1993—99, pres. 1997—98). Office: Morgan Lewis & Bockius 1 Market St San Francisco CA 94105-1420 E-mail: wtrautman@morganlewis.com.

TRAUTMANN, THOMAS ROGER, history and anthropology educator; b. Madison, Wis., May 27, 1940; s. Milton and Esther Florence (Trachte) T.; m. Marcella Hauolilani Choy, Sept. 25, 1962; children: Theodore William, Robert Arthur. BA, Beloit Coll., 1962; PhD, U. London, 1968. Lectr. in history Sch. Oriental and African Studies, U. London, 1965-68; asst. prof. history U. Mich., Ann Arbor, 1968-71, assoc. prof., 1971-77, prof., 1977—, Richard Hudson rsch. prof., 1979, prof. history and anthropology, 1984—, chmn. dept. history, 1987-90, Steelcase rsch. prof., 1993-94, dir. Inst. Humanities, Mary Fair Croushore prof. humanities, 1997—2002, Marshall D. Sahlins coll. prof. history and anthropology, 1997—. Author: Kautilya and the Arthasastra, 1971, Dravidian Kinship, 1981, Lewis Henry Morgan and the Invention of Kinship, 1987; author: (with K.S. Kabelac) The Library of Lewis Henry Morgan, 1994; author: (edit. with Diane Owen Hughes) Time: Histories and Ethnologies, 1995, Aryans and British India, 1997; author: (edit. with Maurice Godelier and Franklin Tjon Sie Fat) Transformations of Kinship, 1999; editor: Comparative Studies in Society and History, 1997—; contbr. articles on India, kinship and history of anthropology. Sr. Humanist fellow NEH, 1984. Mem. Am. Anthrop. Assn., Assn. Asian Studies, Am. Inst. Indian Studies (mem. exec. com. trustee, sr. rsch. fellow in India 1985, 97), Phi Beta Kappa. Office: U Mich Dept History Ann Arbor MI 48109-1003

TRAUTNER, JOHN JAMES, real estate executive; b. Simpson, Minn., Dec. 4, 1935; s. John Sylvester and Oridena Francis (Baker) T.; m. Donna L. Jones, June 1960 (div. Dec. 1969); children: Theresa, Carrie, John; m. Carol Lee Rowberry, July 12, 1974 (div. May 1981); 1 child, Lindsey D.; m. Kathy N. Bucy, July 19, 1992; 1 stepchild, Victor. BA, Anchorage C.C., 1968; BBA, U. Alaska, 1970, MBA, 1998. Masters lic. U.S. Coast Guard, lic. comml. pilot. Adminstr., pub. affairs RCA Svc. Co., Anchorage, 1965-70; dir. adminstrn. & pub. rels. Alaska Resort, Inc., Girdwood, 1970-71; mgmt. cons. State of Alaska, 1972-73; exec. dir. City of Lost River (Alaska), 1973-74; v.p., gen. mgr. C. Bruce Ficke Investments, Girdwood, 1974-76; pres., gen. mgr. Gateway, Inc., Girdwood, 1976-85; CEO Alyeska Mgmt. Svcs., Inc., Girdwood, 1985—. Mem. MD49 Coun. Govs., Fairbanks, Alaska, 1996-97, chmn., 1999-2000; marriage commr. 3d Jud. Dist., Anchorage, 1973-93. Patentee in field. Chmn., mem. Girdwood Bd. Suprs., 1992-95; fire chief Girdwood Fire Dept., 1972-75; chmn. Girdwood Cmty. Coun., 1976-78, Jr.-Inter-Fraternity Coun., Seattle, 1957-58. Sgt. U.S. Army, 1953-64. Melvin Jones fellow, chgo., 1993-94. Mem. N.Am. Nature Photographers Assn., Am. Legion, Lions, Disabled VFW, Alaska Airmens Assn., San Francisco Tennis Club. Republican. Roman Catholic. Avocations: photography, music, art, humanitarianism, flying. Office: Alaska Mgmt Svcs Inc PO Box 909 Girdwood AK 99587-0909 E-mail: outsidermining@msn.com.

TRAUTWEIN, GEORGE WILLIAM, conductor, educator; b. Chgo., Aug. 5, 1927; s. William Jacob and Hilda (Martin) T.; m. Barbara Wilson, Jan. 20, 1955; children: Paul Martin, Matthew Richard. MusB, Oberlin Conservatory, Ohio, 1951; MusM, Cleve. Inst. Music, 1955; MusD, Ind. U., 1961. Mem. faculty U. Minn., U. Tex., Austin, Armstrong (Ga.) State Coll.; arts cons. Nat. Endowment Arts; dir. internat. study program for Wake Forest U. at Tokai U., Japan, 1995. Violinist Indpls. Symphony Orch., 1947-48, Balt. Symphony Orch., 1951-52, Nat. Symphony Orch., Washington, 1952-53, Cleve. Orch., 1953-57, Chautauqua Symphony Orch., N.Y., 1953-59, Camerata Acad., Salzburg, 1957-58, Mozarteum Orch., Salzburg, 1958 (Fulbright grantee 1958), assoc. condr. Dallas Symphony Orch., 1962-66, Mpls. Symphony, 1966-73; music dir. S.D. Symphony, 1971-75, Internat. Congress Strings, Ohio, 1973-75; music dir., condr. Savannah (Ga.) Symphony Orch., 1974-77; music adv., prin. guest condr. Evansville (Ind.) Philharm., 1979-80; music dir., condr. RIAS Edn. Network, Berlin, 1979, Tucson Symphony Orch., 1977-81; artistic dir., condr. Piedmont Chamber Orch.; prin. condr. Internat. Music program; dir. orchestral programs, N.C. Sch. of Arts, 1981-83; dir. instrumental ensembles, Wake Forest U., 1983-96, dir. Artists series, 1985-98; guest appearances with orchs., U.S., Germany, Sweden, France, Rumania, Jugoslavia, Portugal, Hong Kong, India, P.R., Mex. Adv. bd. Avery Fisher Found., N.Y.C. Served with USN, 1948-49. Recipient Orpheus award Phi Mu Alpha, 1971, ASCAP award, 1979, 82, World Peace award Ministry of World Harmony, 1983; Fulbright grantee Mozarteum, Salzburg, 1958; Sr. Fulbright lectr., India, 1989-90. Mem. Am. Fedn. Musicians, Chamber Music Soc. Am., Sir Thomas Beecham Soc., Erich Wolfgang Korngold Soc., Condrs. Guild Am. Avocations: chamber music, art reproduction, W.B. Yeats, James Joyce. Office: Wake Forest U PO Box 7411 Winston Salem NC 27109-7411

TRAVAGLINI, JOSEPH, educational consultant; b. Phila., Sept. 17, 1932; m. Marilyn Irene Gordon, Dec. 26, 1956; children: Mark D., David H. BSBA, Drexel U., 1955; M of Govtl. Adminstrn., U. Pa., 1960; PhD, U. Md., 1974. Dir. personnel svcs. Antioch Coll., Yellow Springs, Ohio, 1960-65; mgr. adminstrv. svcs. U. Chgo., 1965-66; asst. bur. chief Pa. State Dept. Edn., Harrisburg, 1966-67; asst. to pres. Essex C.C., Baltimore County, Md., 1967-75; program mgr. individualized degree programs Ctrl. Mich. U., Mt. Pleasant, 1975-88; dean grad. and external programs Coll. Santa Fe, 1988-89; assoc. dean, dir. The Union Inst., San Diego Ctr., Cin., 1989-92; ednl. cons. San Diego, 1993—. Co-chair accreditation study Essex C.C., 1969-70; team leader program learning seminar U. Mich., Ann Arbor, 1982; reviewer Calif. Postsecondary Edn. Commn., Sacramento, 1990-91; cons. to pres. La Jolla U., San Diego, 1993. Author: (chpt.) Personalized Instruction in Education Today, 1970; co-author: (chpt.) The University and the Inner City, 1980. Pres. Joppatowne (Md.) Civic Assoc., 1969-74; county coun. candidate Harford County, Bel Air, Md., 1974; alumni amb. Drexel U., Phila., 1997—; vol. auditor Balboa Pk. Japanese Friendship Garden, San Diego, 1995—. With U.S. Army, 1955-57. Recipient Samuel S. Fels scholarship U. Pa., 1958-60, fellowship U. Colo., 1968. Mem. Wharton Alumni Club So. Calif., Sierra Club, World Wildlife Fund, Nature Conservancy, Phi Delta Kappa (emeritus). Democrat. Avocations: environment, international travel, jogging, music, politics. Home: 3375 Date St San Diego CA 92102-1635

TRAVAGLINI, ROBERT E. state legislator; m. Kelly Holtz; 1 child, Taylor Rae. BS, Boston State Coll., 1974; postgrad., Boston U. Exec. asst. Mass. Atty. Gen., 1975-81; adminstrv. asst. Mayor's Office, Boston, 1981-83; councilor Boston City Dist. 1, chmn. transp. and commerce, 1983-92, chmn. edn., 1983, chmn. pub. works and urban resources, 1984, chmn. transp., 1986-87, chmn. environ. and pub. works, 1988-89, chmn. plannind and devel. com., 1992; mem. Mass. Senate, Boston, 1992—, pres., 2003—; chmn. join com. on local affairs; vice chmn. joint com. on govt. regulations; mem. transp., housing and urban devel. coms. Home: 51 Saint Andrews Rd Boston MA 02128-1223 Office: Room 511B State House Boston MA 02133

TRAVELSTEAD, CHESTER COLEMAN, former educational administrator; b. Franklin, Ky., Sept. 25, 1911; s. Conley and Nelle (Gooch) T.; m. Marita Hawley, Aug. 1, 1936; children: Coleman, Jimmie. AB, Western Ky. State Coll., Bowling Green, 1933; M of Music, Northwestern U., 1947; PhD, U. Ky., 1950; HHD, Morehead (Ky.) State U., 1975; PhD, John F. Kennedy U., Buenos Aires, 1975; LHD, U. N.Mex., 1980. Tchr., prin. rural and consol. schs., Mecklenberg County, Va., 1931-32, 33-35; tchr. gen. sci., math., music Picadome H.S., Lexington, Ky., 1935-37; dir. music Henry Clay H.S., Lexington, 1937-42; personnel supr. Lexington Signal Dept., Dept. War, 1942-43; supr. music Lexington pub. schs., 1945-47; rep. Investors Diversified Services, Inc., 1947-48; coordinator in-service tchr. edn. Ky. Dept. Edn., 1950-51; asst. prof. edn., asst. dean Coll. Edn., U. Ga., Athens, 1951-53; dean Sch. Edn., U. S.C., Columbia, 1953-56; dean Coll. Edn. U. N.Mex., Albuquerque, 1956-68, v.p. acad. affairs, 1968-76, provost, 1976-77. Mem. Nat. Council Accreditation Tchr. Edn., 1960-66, chmn., 1963-65 Author books; contbr. articles in field to profl. jours. Pres. bd. dirs. N.Mex. Symphony Orch., 1977-78, 84-85; mem. N.Mex. Jud. Stds. Commn., 1995-96. With USNR, 1943-45; PTO. Mem. AAUP, NEA, Nat. Assn. Scholars, Soc. Advancement Edn., Phi Kappa Phi, Phi Delta Kappa., Kappa Delta Pi. Home: Montebello # 128 10500 Academy Rd NE Albuquerque NM 87111-7306 Office Phone: 505-275-6112.

TRAVER, ROBERT WILLIAM, SR., management consultant, writer, engineer; b. Waterbury, Conn., Oct. 13, 1930; s. Alfred Matthew, Sr. and Dorothy Viola (Thomson) Traver; m. Eleanor Jean Finnemore (div. Feb. 1963); children: Robert William Jr., Jeffrey Matthew, Elizabeth; m. Valarie Jane Mason. B in Mech. Engring., Clarkson U., 1955; MBA, U. Mass., 1963. Registered profl. engr., N.Y. Quality control engr. Gen. Electric Co., Pittsfield, Mass., 1955-62; mgr. reliability and quality assurance Tansitor Electronics, Inc., Bennington, Vt., 1962-65; sr. cons. Rath & Strong, Inc., Lexington, Mass., 1965-70; regional mgr. TAC, Inc., Albany, N.Y., 1970-72; dist. mgr. IDS, Inc., Albany, 1972-81; v.p. Reddy, Traver & Woods, Inc., Lexington, 1981-96; owner Traver Assocs., Averill Pk., N.Y., 1996—. Participant in ednl. exch., China, 1985, Australia, New Zealand, 86. Author: Manufacturing Solutions for Consistent Quality and Reliability; contbr. articles to profl. jours. Chmn. lake com. Crooked Lake Improvement Assn., Averill Park, NY, 1973—74; v.p. Sand Lake (N.Y.) Businessmen's Assn., 1974—76. With U.S. Army, 1950. Fellow: Am. Soc. Quality; mem.: Trout Unlimited. Republican. Congregationalist. Avocations: fishing, gardening. Home and Office: 184 Eastern Union Tpke Averill Park NY 12018-9563 Office Phone: 518-674-2130. Personal E-mail: rwtraver@aol.com.

TRAVERS, JAMES M. application developer; Grad., Pa. State U. Various managerial positions Tex. Instruments, Inc., 1978-94; pres., gen. mgr. Harbinger Corp., Atlanta, 1995-98, pres., chief oper. officer, 1998—. Office: Harbinger Corp 11720 Amberpark Dr Ste 100 Alpharetta GA 30004-2271

TRAVERS, PAUL, company executive; With Strand Hotels Ltd., Grand Met. Group; fin. dir. Europe Inter-Continental Hotels and Resorts, fin. dir. Forum Hotels, v.p. fin. Middle East and Africa, sr. v.p., group fin. contr., sr. v.p. property mgmt.; CFO REZsolutions, Inc., until 1999; pres. REZsolutions Hospitality Group. Office: Pegasus Solutions 14000 N Pima Rd 100 Scottsdale AZ 85260-3603

TRAVERS, W. LAWRENCE, healthcare executive; b. Syracuse, N.Y., Nov. 1, 1943; s. Walter Roy and Elizabeth Laurene (Hicks) T. BS, Coll. of Emporia, Kans., 1965; MSW, Syracuse U., 1972. Diplomate in clin. social work N.Y.; cert. addictions counselor. Cons. alcoholism treatment Hutchings Psychiat. Ctr. N.Y. State, Office of Mental Health, Syracuse, 1972-73, program dir. alcoholism rehab. unit, 1973-76, program dir. psychogeriatric day treatment/outpatient svcs., 19976-80, mental health outpatient svc., 1980-86, program dir. mentally ill chem. abuse sr. adv. panel, 1986-91; rehab. coord. Capital Dist. Psychiat. Ctr., Albany, N.Y., 1991-94; edn. and tng. cons., 1994-97; cons. to med. dir. managed care N.Y. State/Office of Mental Health, Albany, 1997-98, dir. co-occurring psychiat. and addictive disorders, 1998-2000, dir. health systems transition, 2000—; cons. N.Y.C. Office of Mental Hlth., 2000—; pvt. practice Albany, N.Y. Dir. Health Systems Teransition, Albany,NY, bd. dirs. Franklin Med. Lab. Sch., Westbury, N.Y., 1980. Dem. Party ofcl., 1974-76. Recipient Sci. Achievement award Chem. Rubber Co.,

1965. Fellow Am. Orthophychiat. Assn.; mem. NASW (clin. register), Acad. Cert. Social Workers (diplomate), Am. Coll. Addiction Treatment Adminstrs., Am. Bd. Examiners in Clin. Social Work, Nat. Assn. Drug Abuse and Alcoholism Commn. (master addiction counselor), Am. Coll. Health Care Execs. Presbyterian. Office: NY State Office Mental Health 44 Holland Ave Albany NY 12208-3411 Home: 1598 Yarrow Cir Bellport NY 11713-3041 E-mail: lawrencetravers@compuserve.com.

TRAVERSO, ANTHONY A. lawyer; b. Northampton, Mass., June 8, 1962; s. Edmund and Georgina J. (Nee Bolas) Traverso. BA cum laude, U. Mass., 1987; JD, Northeastern U. Sch. of Law, 1995. Bar: Mass. 1995, NY 1996; cert. french language La Sorboune, Paris IV, 86. Law clk. Hon. A.S. Chrein, Judge US Dist. Ct., Bklyn., 1995—96; assoc. Hawkins Delafield & Wood, N.Y.C., 1996—99, Bryan Cave LLP, N.Y.C., 1999—2001; regional counsel The Trust for Pub. Land, N.Y.C., 2001—. Environ. cons. Essex County Greenbelt Assn., Essex, Mass., 1990—92, The Trustees of Reservations, Beverly, Mass., 1990—92; exec. cons. The Inst. for Cmty. Economics, Springfield, Mass., 1991; lead attorney The Trust of Pub. Land, Preservation of Stafford, Horse Farm, and Voorhees, NJ, 2004. Vol. US Peace Corps, Kinshasa, Republic of the Congo, 1987—89; supporter 20/20 Vision, Wash., DC, 1999—. Mem.: Transp. Alternatives, Land Trust Alliance, Essex County Greenbelt Assn., Appalachian Mt. Club. Avocations: travel, art, bicycling, outdoors. Home: 110 Third Pl Brooklyn NY 11231 Office: The Trust for Public Land 666 Broadway 9th Fl New York NY 10012 Office Phone: 212-677-7171.

TRAVIS, ALBERT HARTMAN, retired ancient language educator; b. L.A., Dec. 22, 1913; s. Hartman Porter and Adelaide (Ball) Travis; m. Lucile A. Diehl, May 8, 1938; m. Barbara Brown Bettingen, Jan. 25, 1957. BA, U. So. Calif., 1936; MA, Harvard U., 1938, PhD, 1940. Instr. Greek and Latin Harvard and Radcliffe Coll., 1940—42; asst. prof. U. So. Calif., 1946—47; mem. faculty UCLA, 1947—76, prof. classics, 1959—76, prof. emeritus, 1976—, chmn. dept. classics, 1954—62, 1965—68, acting chmn., 1975—76. Author: Servianorum in Vergilii Carmina Commentariorum, Vol. III, 1965; editor: U. Calif. Studies in Classical Antiquity, vol. IV, 1971, U. Calif. Studies in Classical Antiquity, vol. V, 1972; contbr. articles to profl. jours. Lt. comdr. USNR, 1942—46. Decorated Bronze Star with combat V. Mem.: Presdl. Unit Citation, Renaissance Conf. So. Calif., Mediaeval Assn. Pacific, Mediaeval Acad. Am., Calif. Classical Assn., Philol. Assn. Pacific Coast, Archaeol. Inst. Am., Am. Philol. Assn., Kappa Alpha, Phi Kappa Phi, Phi Beta Kappa. Home: 1166 Mill Ln San Marino CA 91108

TRAVIS, ALICE DIMERY, journalist; b. Kingstree, S.C., Sept. 23, 1943; d. Virgil Cornelius Dimery and Mary Agnes (Fassitt) Dimery-Murphy; m. William Daniel Travis, Sept. 9, 1967 (div. July 1973); m. Antonio Maugeri, Oct. 30, 1980; 1 child, Alexander Virgil. AB in Sociology, Immaculata Coll., 1965; postgrad., U. Pa., 1965-66, Temple U., 1966-69. Staff technician, mgmt. trainee Bell Telephone Co. of Pa., Phila., 1965-68; dir. tng. comprehensive health svcs. Temple U., Phila., 1968-70; co-host Panorama Metromedia TV, Washington, 1970-73; co-host AM New York ABC TV/WABC, N.Y.C., 1973-75; rsch. cons. Paterson, Michael, Jones, London, 1975-76; host Gerber Carter Comm., N.Y.C., 1977-78; comm. cons. Alice Travis, Inc., N.Y.C., 1976-88; rsch. journalist Mahopac Falls, N.Y., 1988—. Comm. cons. J. Ray McDermott, Bell Labs., 1977—; tng. analyst Ciba Geigy, Hooker Chem., 1988. Author: Cognitive Evolution: The Biological Imprint of Applied Intelligence, 1995; moderator 26 programs, You series, U.S. Dept. HEW, 1972, 73; host, creator spl. programming People, 1973. Recipient Annie E. Gorman award in sociology Immaculata Coll., 1965, Comm. award Inst. Fgn. Svc., U.S. Dept. State, 1971, media awards Fed. Editors Assn., 1973, Am. Women in Radio and TV, 1973, AAUW, 1975; named Media Woman of the Yr., Nat. Assn. Media Women, 1978, numerous others; keys to cities of Savannah, Ga., West Orange, N.J. Roman Catholic. Avocations: fashion designing, real estate development. Office: PO Box 365 Mahopac Falls NY 10542-0365

TRAVIS, DEMPSEY JEROME, real estate company executive; b. Chgo., Feb. 25, 1920; s. Louis and Mittie (Strickland) T.; m. Moselynne Hardwick, Sept. 17, 1949. BA, Roosevelt U., 1949; grad., Sch. Mortgage Banking, Northwestern U., 1969; D.Econs., Olive Harvey Coll., 1974; D.BA (hon.), Daniel Hale Williams U., Chgo., 1976; PhD (hon.), Kennedy-King Coll., 1982; DHL (hon.), Governor State U., 2001. Cert. property mgr.; cert. real estate counselor. Pres. Travis Realty Co., Chgo., 1949—, Urban Rsch. Press, 1969—. Author: Don't Stop Me Now, 1970, An Autobiography of Black Chicago, 1981, An Autobiography of Black Jazz, 1983, An Autobiography of Black Politics, 1987, Real Estate is the Gold in Your Future, 1988, Harold: The People's Mayor, 1989, Racism: American Style a Corporate Gift, 1990, I Refuse to Learn to Fail, 1992, Views From the Back of the Bus During World War II and Beyond, 1995, The Duke Ellington Primer, 1996, The Louis Armstrong Odessey: From Jazz Alley to America's Jazz Ambassador, 1997, Racism: Revolves Like a Merry Go 'Round: 'Round 'n 'Round It Goes, 1998, They Heard a Thousand Thunders, 1999, The Life and Times of Redd Foxx, 1999, The Victory Monument: The Beacon of Chicago's Bronzeville, 1999, J. Edgar Hoover's FBI Wired the Nation, 2000, The FBI Files on the Tainted and the Damned, 2001, An American Story: In Red, White and Blue, 2002, Norman Granz The White Moses of Black Jazz, 2003, Jimmie Lumceford: The King of Jazzmocracy, 2004. Trustee Northwestern Meml. Hosp., Chgo., Chgo. Hist. Soc., Auditorium Theater, Chgo., Roosevelt U.; bd. dirs. Columbia Coll. With AUS, 1942-46. Recipient award Soc. Midland Authors, 1982, Chgo. Art Deco Soc., 1985, The Human Rights award The Gustavus Myers Ctr. for Study of Human Rights in N.Am., 1995, Humanitarian award Kennedy-King Coll., 1997, Art Deco award, 1983, Soc. Midland Authors award for nonfiction, 1981; named to Jr. Achievement Chgo. Bus. Hall of Fame, 1995; named embedded in sidewalk of Bronzeville Walk of Fame, Chgo; inductee Internat. Literary Hall of Fame, Chgo. State U., 2000. Mem. United Mortgage Bankers Assn. Am. (pres. 1961-74), Dearborn Real Estate Bd. (pres. 1957-59, 70-71), Nat. Assn. Real Estate Brokers (1st v.p. 1959-60), Inst. Real Estate Mgmt., Soc. Profl. Journalists, Soc. Midland Authors (pres. 1988-90), NAACP (pres. Chgo. 1959-60), Econs. Club, Forty Club Chgo., Assembly Club, Cliff Dwellers, The Caxtons Club. Office: Travis Realty Co 840 E 87th St Chicago IL 60619-6298 E-mail: travisDT88@aol.com.

TRAVIS, GRANT CARNER, lawyer; b. Cin., Sept. 24, 1969; BS in Polit. Sci., N.Y. Inst. Tech., Old Westbury, 1992; JD, Duquesne U., Pitts., 1995. Bar: Pa. 1995, U.S. Dist. Ct. (we. dist.) Pa. 1995, Erie County, Pa. Ct. of Pleas 1995. Law clk. Conner & Riley, Erie, Pa., 1993—95, atty., 1995—99; pvt. practice The Travis Law Firm, Edinboro and Erie, 1999—. Bd. dirs. Erie County YMCA, Edinboro, 2000—, pres. bd. dirs., 2001—. Mem.: ATLA, Pa. Trial Lawyers Assn. (bd. govs. 2001—), We. Pa. Trial Lawyers Assn. (bd. govs. 1998—), Nat. Assn. Criminal Def. Lawyers, Pa. Assn. Criminal Def. Lawyers, Erie County Bar Assn. (Spkrs. Bur. 1999—), Pa. Bar Assn. Office: The Travis Law Firm Travis Law Bldg 102 Lorna Ln Edinboro PA 16412

TRAVIS, JAY A., III, lawyer; b. McComb, Miss., June 8, 1940; s. J.A. and Katharine (Brennan) T., Jr.; m. Judith Thompson, Sept. 8, 1965; children: Kathy, John E., William. BBA, U. Miss., 1962, JD, 1965. Bar: Miss. 1965, U.S. Dist. Ct. (so. dist.) Miss. 1967, U.S. Ct. Appeals (5th cir.) 1970. Assoc. Thompson, Alexander & Crews, Jackson, Miss., 1967-69; ptnr. Butler, Snow, O'Mara, Stevens & Cannada, Jackson, 1969—. Chmn. Miss. Law Inst., 1974; pres. Estate Planning Coun. Miss., 1975-76. Mem. vestry, cathedral warden St. Andrew's Episc. Ch., 1983-87. Capt. JAGC, USAR, 1965-73. Fellow Am. Coll. of Trust & Estate Counsel (bd. of regents, 1994-2000, state chmn. 1987-92), Am. Bar Found.; mem. ABA (fellow young lawyers sect.), Miss. State Bar (pres. young lawyers sect. 1975-76), Miss. Bar Assn. (chmn. estates and trusts sect. 1987-88), Hinds County Bar Assn. (pres. 1988-89), Univ. Club, River Hills Club, Phi Delta Phi. Office: PO Box 22567 Jackson MS 39225-2567 E-mail: jay.travis@butlersnow.com.

TRAVIS, JEREMY, academic administrator; b. Worcester, Mass., July 31, 1948; BA in Am. studies cum laude, Yale Coll., 1970; MPA, NYU, 1977, JD cum laude, 1982. Exec. dir. victim/witness assistance project Vera Inst. Justice, 1975—77; exec. dir. NYC Criminal Justice Agy., 1977—79; cons. NYC Bd. of Correction, 1979—82; law clerk to Judge Ruth Bader Ginsburg US Court of Appeals, DC, 1982—83; spl. counsel to police commr. NYC Police Dept., 1984—86; spl. counsel to first dep. mayor and asst. dir. law enforcement services, Mayor's Office of Ops. City of NY, 1986, spl. advisor to mayor, 1986—89; chief counsel to subcommittee on criminal justice U.S. Ho. of Reps. Com. on the Judiciary, Washington, 1990; dep. commr. legal matters NYC Police Dept., 1990—94; dir. Nat. Inst. Justice, Dept. Justice, Washington, 1994—2000; sr. fellow Justice Policy Ctr., The Urban Inst., Washington, 2000—04; pres. John Jay Coll. of Criminal Justice CUNY, 2004—. Vis. lectr. Yale Coll., 1979; adj. prof. Wagner Grad. Sch. Pub. Svc., NYU, 1985-90; adj. assoc. prof., NY Law Sch., 1992-94; vis. prof., George Washington U., 2004; nat. adv. bd., program on State Crime Prevention Initiatives, Nat. Crime Prevention Coun., 2001-, Join Together program, Robert Wood Johnson Found., 2001-, Nat. H.I.R.E. Network, Legal Action Ctr., 2001-, Ctr. for Rsch. on Criminal and Mental Health, Rutgers U., 2002-; nat. adv. com. on Reclaiming Futures, Robert Wood Johnson Found., 2000-; adv. bd., Ctr. for Cmty. Safety, Winston-Salem State U., 2001-; Aspen Inst. Roundtable on Comprehensive Cmty. Initiatives, 1999-. Rockefeller Fellow, Yale Div. Sch., 1970-71; Marden and Marshall Fellow in Criminal Law, NYU Sch. Law, 1983-84; recipient Disting. Alumnus Award, NYU, 1986, Outstanding Pub. Svc. Award, NY County Lawyers Com., 1992, Edmund S. Randolph Award, US Atty. Gen., 2000, August Vollmer Award, Am. Soc. Criminology, 2002, Gerhard O.W. Mueller Award, Internat. Sect., Acad. Criminal Justice Sciences, 2003, Margaret Meade Award, Internat. Cmty. Corrections Assn., 2003. Mem.: NY State Bar. Office: CUNY John Jay Coll Criminal Justice 899 Tenth Ave New York NY 10019

TRAVIS, JOHN D. bank commission official; Former mem. La. Ho. Reps.; local pres. Hancock Bank La., St. Francisville; commr. La. Office Financial Inst. Mem. House Governmental Comm., House Ways and Means Comm., House Judicial, Agriculture, Budget and Joint Capital Outlay Comm. Mem. East Feliciana Parish Sch. Bd., 1973—84, Jackson Town Bd., 1969—76. Office: PO Box 94095 Baton Rouge LA 70804-9045

TRAVIS, LAWRENCE ALLAN, accountant; b. Bloomington, Ill., Sept. 17, 1942; s. Willard Burns and Florence May (Harvey) T.; m. Katy Quinones, Apr. 16, 1965 (div. Feb. 1978); children: Lawrence Allan Jr., Matthew B.; m. Kathleen Lucas, May 20, 1995. BS in Bus. Edn., Ill. State U., 1968; MA in Pub. Adminstrn., U. Ill., Springfield, 1976. CPA, Ill. Staff acct. Alexander Grant & Co., Chgo., 1969; internal auditor State Farm Ins., Bloomington, 1969-73; dep. dir. Ill. Dept. Ins., Springfield, 1973-74; audit mgr. Ill. Auditor Gen., Springfield, 1974-81; pres. Lawrence Travis & Co., P.C., CPAs, Virden, Normal, Springfield and Jacksonville, Ill., 1979—, also bd. dirs.; registered rep. Terra Securities, 1994—. Pres., bd. dirs. Travco, Inc., Virden; v.p., bd. dirs. Ka-Lar Enterprises, Inc., Springfield, Miller Comm., Inc. Mem. Ill. Common Cause, Springfield. Mem. AICPA, Assn. Govt. Accts., Ill. CPA Soc., Internat. Platform Assn., Nat. Space Soc., Smithsonian Assocs., World Future Soc., Internat. Traders. Democrat. Roman Catholic. Avocation: sports. Home: 2409 Idlewild Dr Springfield IL 62704-5403 Office: Lawrence Travis & Co PC 1700 S 1st St Springfield IL 62704-3902

TRAVIS, MARTIN BICE, political scientist, educator; b. Iron Mountain, Mich., Sept. 22, 1917; s. Martin Bice and Helen (Carrett) T.; m. Olivia Brewster Taylor, Nov. 29, 1942; children: Elizabeth Nichols (Mrs. Usama Mugharbil), Helen Willard. AB, Amherst Coll., 1939; student, Heidelberg (Germany) U., 1937; MA, Fletcher Sch. Law and Diplomacy, 1940; PhD, U. Chgo., 1948. Asst. prof. internat. relations Syracuse U., 1948-49; asst. prof. polit. sci. Duke U., 1949-52; asst. prof., then assoc. prof. polit. sci. Stanford U., 1953-61; prof. polit. sci. SUNY-Stony Brook, 1961-92; coordinator SUNY Program Am. U., Beirut, Lebanon, 1972-73; chmn. dept., 1961-68; dir. Inst. Am. Studies SUNY-Stony Brook, 1965-93. Vis. prof. Sch. Internat. Affairs, Columbia, 1956-57; vis. summer prof. U. Guadalajara, Mex., 1959, 62, U. Wash., 1961; Bd. dirs. State U N.Y. Inst. Am. Studies in France, 1966-77; cons. to industry. Author: (with E.E. Robinson) Powers of the President in Foreign Affairs, 1966; Co-editor, contbr.: (with Philip W. Buck) Control of Foreign Relations in Modern Nations, 1957; bd. editors: Western Polit. Quar, 1956-58; adv. bd.: Almanac of Current World Leaders, 1957—; editorial critic for book pubs. Mem. sch. bd., Cold Spring Harbor, N.Y., 1965-71, v.p. 1967-68, pres. 1968-69; trustee Village of Laurel Hollow, 1983-95, police com., 1983-85, mayor, 1985-95; established Martin B. Travis Scholarship fund for pre-law majors at SUNY, Stonybrook, 1995. Grantee Ford Found. 1960-61; recipient Hugh Cleland Meml. Outstanding Prof. award Alumni Assn. SUNY Stony Brook, 2000. Mem. Coun. Fgn. Rels., Phi Delta Theta, Phi Delta Kappa. Home: 533 Cold Spring Rd Syosset NY 11791-1206 Office: Dept Polit Science Suny Stony Brook NY 11794-0001

TRAVIS, RANDALL HOWARD, retired physiologist, retired endocrinologist; b. Curdsville, Ky., July 11, 1924; s. Charles Spaulding and Celestine Frances Travis; m. Priscilla Beryl Korabeck, June 24, 1949 (div.); m. Ilona Marie Engel, June 14, 1974; children: Randall Howard, Laura Jane. BS, U. Chgo.; MD, Western Res. U., 1948—52. Assoc. prof. Case Western Res. U., Physiology Dept., Cleve., 1968—85; asst. prof. dept. medicine Case Western Res. U., 1963—85; retired, 1985. Assoc. physician, medicine Cleve. Met. Gen. Hosp., 1974—85. Contbr. articles to biomed. jours. Panel mem., reparations bd. Dept. of Corrections, Waterbury, Vt., 2000—03; adv. RSVP, Morrisville, Vt., 1996—2003, Sr. Companions Program, Barre, Vt., 2000—03. Sgt. USMC, 1943—46. Grantee Established Investigator, Am. Heart Assn., 1956-1959, Rsch. grants, NIH, 1959-1974. Mem.: AAAS, Endocrine Soc., Ctrl. Soc. for Clin. Rsch. (assoc.), Vt. Med. Soc. (life). Liberal. Avocations: boating, skiing, bicycling, hiking. Home: PO Box 553 Waterbury VT 05676

TRAVIS, RANDY BRUCE, musician; b. Monroe, N.C., 1959; married. Musician Country City U.S.A., 1977-82, Nashville Palace, 1982-85; recording artist, 1986—. Rec. artist Warner Bros. Records, 1985-97, DreamWorks Records, 1997-2000, Inspirational Journey Warner Bros. and Atlantic Christian Music Divsn. (Dove award 2001); albums include debut Storms of Life, 1986 (Album of Yr., Acad. Country Music 1987, Album of Yr., Music City News 1987), Always & Forever, 1987 (Album of Yr., Country Music Assn. 1987), Old 8x10, 1988, No Holdin' Back, 1989, An Old Time Christmas, 1989, Heroes and Friends, 1990, High Lonesome, 1991, Greatest Hits, 1992, Wind in the Wire, 1993, This is Me, 1994, Full Circle, 1996, You And You Alone, 1998, Man Ain't Made of Stone, 1999; songs include On the Other Hand (Best Song, Acad. Country Music 1987, Best Single, Acad. Country Music 1987, Single of Yr., Music City News 1987), Diggin' Up Bones, No Place Like Home, Forever and Ever, Amen (Single of Yr., Song of Yr.,Country Music Assn. 1987, Best Country Record, AMOA Jukebox 1987), I Won't Need You Anymore, No Holding Back, 1989, Full Circle, 1996, You and You Alone, 1998 (Dove award 2001, Best Blue Grass album), Baptism (Best Country song); film appearances include: Frank and Jesse, 1994, Wind in the Wire, 1994, A Holiday to Remember, 1995, The Legend of O.B. Taggart, 1995, Edie & Pen, 1996, Boys Will Be Boys, 1996, Fire Down Below, 1997, Steel Chariots, 1997, The Rainmaker, 1997, White River Kid, 1998, Texas Rangers, 1999, John John In The Sky, 1999, Major Reno, 1999, Trial Of Old Drum, 2000, Fathers Of Our Country, 2000, (animated children's movie) Annabelle's Wish, 1997, The Shooter, 1997, T-N-T, 1998, Black Dog, 1998, Baby Geniuses, 1998, Casper's Christmas, 2000, (TV Movie) A Holiday To Remember, 1995 (TV mini series) Texas, 1994, Touched by an Angel, 1994, 95, 97, 2001, Matlock, 1992, 93; (TV movie) Dead Man's Revenge, 1994, At Risk, 1993; (TV spl.) Down Home, 1990, Happy Trails, 1990. Named Top Male Vocalist, Acad. Country Music, 1987, Male Vocalist of Yr., Music City News, 1987, Star of Tomorrow, Music City News, 1987, Male Vocalist of Yr., Country Music Assn., 1987, Entertainer of Yr. Music City News, 1988, Male Artist of Yr., 1988, Favorite Entertainer, Favorite Entertainer, Nashville Network Viewers Choice Awards, 1988; recipient Horizon award Country Music Assn., 1986, Grammy award, 1987, Am. Music award, best country album, 1988, Am. Music award, best country single, 1988, Country Music Assn. best male vocalist, 1988. Mem. Grand Ole Opry. E-mail: traviscorp@home.com.

TRAVIS, TONI-MICHELLE C. political analyst, educator; d. Mark E. and Ada Deans Chapman; m. Theodore W. Travis. BA, Bard Coll., Annandale-on-Hudson, N.Y., 1969; MA, U. Chgo., 1973, PhD, 1983. Asst. prof., govt. George Mason U., Fairfax, Va., 1984—90, asst. dean, Coll. Arts & Scis., 1993—95, host, prodr., Capital Region Roundtable, 1998—2002, assoc. prof., govt., 1990—2004; vis. prof. Simmons Coll., Boston, 1998—2000. Pres. Women's Caucus, Washington, 1994—95. Co-author: (book) The Meaning of Difference, 1996, 2000, 2003, editor: (book series) Race and Politics, 1995—2002. Bd. mem. Make Women Count, Richmond, Va., 1998—2000; mem. Higher Edn. Group, Washington, 1997—2003. John Bard Scholar, Bard Coll., 1968, Ford Found Fellowship, U. Chgo., 1969—73. Mem.: Nat. Capital Area Polit. Sci. Assn. (pres. 1994—95), Am. Polit. Sci. Assn. (coun. mem. 1994—96), Fairfax Com. of 100. Avocation: walking. Office: Dept Pub and Internat Affairs George Mason Univ MS 3F4 4400 University Dr Fairfax VA 22030 Business E-Mail: ttravis@gmu.edu.

TRAVIS, TRACEY THOMAS, retail executive; MBA in Fin. and Ops. Mgmt., Columbia U. With Pepsi, 1987—97; CFO Rexam Beverage Can Ams., 1997—99; v.p. fin., CFO Intimate Brands, Inc., 2001—02; sr. v.p. fin. Ltd. Brands, Inc., Columbus, Ohio, 2003—. Bd. dirs. Jo-Ann Stores, Inc. Office: Ltd Brands Three Ltd Pkwy Columbus OH 43230

TRAVIS, TRACY LEIGH, emergency physician; b. Lynchburg, Va., Aug. 27, 1957; d. Charles C. Jr. and Mildred (Lindsay) T.; m. David Stephens; children: Jennifer Koecke, Travis Stephens. BS in Biology, Lynchburg Coll., 1979; MD, Eastern Va. Med. Sch., 1982. Diplomat Am. Bd. Emergency Medicine. Resident Butterworth Hosp., Grand Rapids, Mich., 1987; emergency physician Mary Washington Hosp., Fredericksburg, Va., 1988-93, ExpressCare, Stafford, Va., 1992-96, Inova Emergency Care, Fairfax, Va., 1996—, Inova Fairfax Hosp., 1998—. Fellow Am. Coll. Emergency Physicians; mem. Phi Kappa Phi. Home: 10856 Meadow Pond Ln Oakton VA 22124-1446 Office: Emergency Physicians No Va Ltd 3300 Gallows Rd Falls Church VA 22042-3307

TRAVIS, VANCE KENNETH, petroleum business executive; b. Coriander, Sask., Can., Jan. 30, 1926; s. Roy Hazen and Etta Orilla (Anderson) T.; m. Louise Mary, Nov. 30, 1948 (div. 1979); children: Stuart, Shirley, Gordon, Donald, Marian; m. Mildred Elaine, June 29, 1979; stepchildren: Susan, Nancy, Gordon, Sandra, Karen. Chmn. bd. Turbo Resources Ltd., 1970-83, Challenger Internat., 1977-83, Bankeno Mines Ltd., 1977-83, Queenston Gold Mines Ltd., Toronto, Canada, 1977-84, Health Risk Mgmt. Inc., Mpls., 1984-86, Triad Internat. Inc., 1985—; dir. Health Resource Mgmt. Ltd., Edmonton, Canada, 1990-97. Bd. dirs. Vencap Equities Alta. Ltd., Edmonton, 1981-86, L.K. Resources Ltd., Calgary, 1973-84. Mem. Young. Pres.'s Orgn., Calgary, 1964-76, World Pres. Orgn. Recipient Presdl. pin Jr. Achievement, 1963, Best Pitcher award Petroleum Fastball League, 1955. Mem.: Calgary Petroleum Club. E-mail: kentravis@telus.net.

TRAVOLTA, JOHN, actor; b. Englewood, N.J., Feb. 18, 1954; s. Salvatore and Helen (Burke) T.; m. Kelly Preston; children: Jett, Ella Bleu. Appeared in TV series Welcome Back Kotter, 1975-77; TV movies: The Boy in the Plastic Bubble, 1976, Chains of Gold, 1980; films: Carrie, 1976, Saturday Night Fever, 1977 (Best Actor award Nat. Bd. Rev., 1977, Best Actor Acad. award nominee 1977, Best Actor 1st runner up Nat. Soc. Film Critics 1977, Best Actor 2nd runner up N.Y. Film Critics Circle 1977), Grease, 1978 (Golden Globe World Film Favorite 1978), Moment-By-Moment, 1978, Urban Cowboy, 1980, Blow Out, 1981, Staying Alive, 1983 (Male/Box Office Star of Yr., Nat. Assn. Theatre Owners Show East 1983), Two of a Kind, 1983, Perfect, 1985, The Dumb Waiter, 1987, The Experts, 1989, Look Who's Talking, 1989 (Male/Box Office Star of Yr., Nat. Assn. Theatre Owners ShowEast 1989), Look Who's Talking Too, 1990, The Tender, 1991, Shout, 1991, Look Who's Talking Now, 1993, Pulp Fiction, 1994 (Best Actor Acad. award nominee 1994, Best Actor award nominee Brit. Acad. Film and TV Arts 1994, Golden Globe Best Actor award nominee 1994, Best Actor award nominee SAG 1994, Best Actor award nominee Chgo. Film Critics 1994, Best Actor award nominee Comedy awards 1994, Best Actor award L.A. Film Critics 1994, Best Actor award Stockholm Film Festival 1993, Best Actor award London Film Critics Cir. 1994), Get Shorty, 1995, White Man's Burden, 1995, Broken Arrow, 1996, Phenomenon, 1996, Michael, 1996, Face Off, 1997, Mad City, 1997, She's So Lovely (also dir.), 1997, Primary Colors, 1998 (Golden Globe nominee), A Civil Action, 1998, General's Daughter, 1999, Battlefield Earth, (also prodr.) 2000, Lucky Numbers, 2000, Swordfish, 2001, Domestic Disturbance, 2001, Basic, 2003, The Punisher, 2004; author: Staying Fit, 1984, Propeller One Way Night Coach; rec. artist album, 1976, 77. Recipient Best Male Vocalist Billboard award, 1976, Best Male Vocalist award Record World and Music Retail mag., 1976, Best Actor Golden Apple award Cue mag., Juno award Can. Acad. Rec. Arts and Scis., 1978, Golden Apple award 1998, Lifetime Achievement award British Acad. Film and TV Assn., 1998, Chgo. Internat. Film Festival, 1998, Palm Springs Internat. Film Festival, 1999, Alan J. Pakula award U.S. Broadcast Film Critics Assn., 1999,; nominated Best New Male Star Women's Press Club, 1976; named Man of Yr., Hasty Pudding Club, Harvard U., 1981. Office: William Morris Agency 151 El Camino Dr Beverly Hills CA 90212

TRAXLER, EVA MARIA, marketing professional; b. Phorzheim, Germany, June 1, 1955; d. Wayne Delmar and Ruth Lydia (Mischak) Frasure; m. Richard John Traxler, Mar. 25, 1986. BS, U. Minn., 1980; MBA, U. St. Thomas, 1987. Ops. control planner Gen. Mills, Mpls., 1981; asst. prodn. planner Pillsbury, Mpls., 1982-87, planning specialist, 1987-88; new products planner Land O'Lakes, Mpls., 1988-89, mktg. asst., 1989-90; sr. product mgr., mgr. mdse. svcs. Newell/Rubbermaid, St. Paul, 1990-94; mktg. mgr. Jostens, Mpls., 1995-96; brand mgr. Metacom, 1996-98; mgr. sml. bus. mktg. Am. Express, 1998—, advice mgr., 2001—. Big sister Big Bros./Big Sisters, St. Paul, 1982-89, bd. mem., 1986-92, Courage Ctr., 1998—. Avocations: exercise, travel, old house renovation. E-mail: evatraxler@hotmail.com.

TRAXLER, WILLIAM BYRD, JR., federal judge; b. Greenville, S.C., May 1, 1948; s. William Byrd and Bettie (Wooten) Traxler; m. Patricia Alford, Aug. 21, 1972; children: William Byrd III, James McCall. BA, Davidson Coll., 1970; JD, U. S.C., 1973. Assoc. William Byrd Traxler, Greenville, 1973—75; asst. solicitor 13th Jud. Ct., Greenville, 1975—78, dep. solicitor, 1978—81, solicitor, 1981—85, resident cir. judge, 1985—92; U.S. Dist. judge Dist. of S.C., Greenville, 1992—98; judge U.S. Ct. of Appeals (4th cir.), Greenville, 1998—. Recipient Outstanding Svc. award, Solicitors Assn., S.C., 1987, Leadership award, Probation, Parole & Pardon Svcs., S.C., 1990. Office: PO Box 10127 Greenville SC 29603-0127

TRAYLOR, ANGELIKA, stained glass artist; b. Munich, Bavaria, Germany, Aug. 24, 1942; Came to U.S., 1959; d. Walther Artur Ferdinand and Berta Kreszentia (Boeck) Klau; m. Lindsay Montgomery Donaldson, June 10, 1959 (div. 1970); 1 child, Cameron Maria Greta; m. Samuel William Traylor III, June 12, 1970. Student, Pvt. Handelsschule Morawetz Jr. Coll., Munich, 1958. Freelance artist, 1980—. Works featured in profl. jours. including the Daylily Jour., 1987, Design Jour., South Korea, 1989, The Traveler's Guide to American Crafts, 1990, Florida Mag., 1991, Florida Today, 1993, Adventures in Art, vol. 3, 1993, Melbourne Times, 1994, The Orbiter, 1996, The Glass Collector's Digest, 1996, (TV appearances) Focus on History, 1993, Focus, 1998, Space Coast Press, 1999, Weekend Decorating Projects-Women's Day, 1999, Pen Women, 1999, Stained Glass for the First Time, 2000, Creative Stained Glass, 2004; represented in permanent collections White House Christmas Ornament Collection, 1993, 97, Holmes Regional Med. Ctr., Melbourne, Fla., other pvt. and corp. collections. Recipient Fragile Art award Glass Art mag., 1982, 1st Yr. Exhibitor award Stained Glass Assn. Am., 1984, 2d pl. Non-figurative Composition award Vitraux des USA, 1985, Best of Show Stained Glass Assn. Am., 1989, 3d pl., 1989, Merit award George Plimpton All-Star Space Coast Art Open, 1994; named Hist. Woman of Brevard, Brevard Cultural Alliance, 1991, one of 200 Best Am. Craftsmen Early Am. Life mag., 1994, 95, 97, 98, 2000. Home and Office: 100 Poinciana Dr Indian Harbor Beach FL 32937-4437 Office Phone: 321-773-7640.

TRAYLOR, CHET D. state supreme court justice; b. Columbia, La., Oct. 12, 1945; s. John Hardy and Bernice (Bogan) T.; children: Mary Therese, Leigh Ann, Anna Marie. BA in Govt., N.E. La. State U., 1969; JD, Loyola U., 1974.

Bar: La. Judge 5th Jud. Dist. Ct., Franklin, Richland and West Carroll Parishes, La., 1985-97; assoc. justice La. Supreme Ct., 1997—. Past legal advisor La. State Police; past investigator La. Dept. Justice; asst. dist. atty., Franklin Parish, 1975-76. Founding bd. mem. Winnsboro Econ. Devel. Found.; mem. Rocky Mountain Conservation Fund. With U.S. Army. Mem. ABA, La. Bar Assn., La. Dist. Judges Assn., NRA (life), Franklin Parish Mental Health Assn. (past bd. dirs.), Winnsboro Lions Club (past bd. dirs.), Greenwings (founder John Adams chpt.). Methodist. Office: Supreme Ct 301 Loyola Ave New Orleans LA 70112-1814

TRAYLOR, DONALD REGINALD, mathematics educator; b. Shreveport, La., Aug. 14, 1937; s. Guy Kirby and Eva (Hunt) T.; m. Jacqueline Rose Pearson, June 4, 1959; children: Chapman Parker, Kirby Russell, Pearson Hunt. BA, U. Tex., 1959; MS, Auburn U., 1960, PhD, 1962. Asst. prof. Auburn (Ala.) U., 1962-63, U. Houston, 1963-66, assoc. prof., 1966-71, pres., prof., 1972-77; fellow Am. Coun. on Edn., Washington, 1971-72; pres. Traylor Products & Svcs., San Antonio, 1977-90; prof. math. U. of the Incarnate Word, San Antonio, 1990—, interim v.p. acad. affairs, 1993-95, acting dean Sch. Math., Nursing and Sci., 1995-96, dean Sch. Grad. Studies and Rsch., 1996—, v.p. for extended acad. programs, 1999—. Mem. adv. coun. Auburn U., 1966-96, St. Mary's U., San Antonio, 1978-85. Author: Advanced Calculus, 1970, Creative Teaching: Heritage of R.L. moore, 1972; editor: Proceedings of Topology Conference, 1968; inventor tactile drawing and writing device. Grantee NASA, 1964, NSF, 1965-67, NIH, 1985-89, NSF and Eisenhower, 1992—. Office: U of the Incarnate Word 4301 Broadway St San Antonio TX 78209-6318 E-mail: traylor@universe.uiwtx.edu.

TRAYLOR, ORBA FOREST, economist, lawyer, educator; b. Providence, Ky., June 16, 1910; s. Eddie Ewing and Dillie (Stuart) T.; m. Josephine Zananiri, Nov. 17, 1945; children— Joseph Marion, Robert Forest, John Christopher. BA, Western Ky. U., 1930; MA, U. Ky., 1932, PhD, 1948; JD, Northwestern U., 1936. Bar: Ky. 1941. Head dept. econs. Ashland Coll., 1935-36; legal asst. trust dept. 1st Nat. Bank, Chgo., 1936-37; assoc. prof. econs., sociology Western Ky. U., 1938-40; rsch. asst. Bur. Bus. Rsch., U. Ky., 1939; rsch. dir. Ky. Legis. Coun., 1939-41; dir. rsch. and stats. Ky. Dept. Welfare, 1941; assoc. econ. analyst div. tax research U.S. Treasury Dept., 1942; acting chief acctg. UNRRA, Balkan Mission, 1944-45; asst. prof. econs. and bus. U. Denver, 1946-47, U. Mo., 1947-50; tax specialist, asst. econ. commr. ECA, Greece, 1950-53; coord. exec. devel. programs Ordnance Corps, Dept. Army, 1954; pub. fin. expert UN; lectr. fin. adminstrn. Inst. Pub. Adminstrn., Egypt, 1954-56; exec. asst. to lt. gov. Ky. Legis. Rsch. Commn., Frankfort, 1956-58; commr. fin. State of Ky., Frankfort, 1958-59; dir. finance Office High Commr., Ryukyu Islands, 1960-64, dir. econ. affairs, 1964-65; prof. econs. and pub. adminstrn. U. Ala., Huntsville, 1965-75, chmn. dept. bus. and pub. adminstrn., 1966-68, chmn. econs., 1968-70; vis. prof. pub. adminstrn. San Diego State U., 1975-76, U. Mo., 1976-77; fin. economist AID, U.S. State Dept., 1977-78; adj. prof. Ala. A&M U., 1978-81, NYU and Rider Coll., 1981-82, Columbia Coll., 1982—2001; cons. economist Am. Tech. Services, Inc., 1982-91. Cons. ops. research Johns Hopkins U., 1957-61; fiscal cons. various orgns.; vis. lectr. econs. various univs. and colls.; lectr. U. Md. Far East Div., 1960-65, Ala. A&M U., 1976-77, Fla. Inst. Tech., 1977; sr. adv. Bank of Ryukyus, 1960-65, Joint Fgn. Investment Bd., 1964-65; chmn. bd. Ryukyuan Devel. Loan Corp., 1960-65, Joint Petroleum Bd., 1960-65; counsellor Oak Ridge Asso. Univs., 1966-67 Mem. editorial bd.: Public Adminstrn. Rev, 1973-79; contbr. articles to profl. publs. Mem. Ala. Edn. Study Commn. Fin. Task Force, 1968-69; chmn. fin. com. Top of Ala. Health Planning Agy., 1974-75; mem. adv. com. Ala. Legislature, 1981-94. With AUS, 1942-46; lt. col. Res. (ret.). Mem. Am., So. econs. assns., Am. Soc. for Pub. Adminstrn. (council 1973-75), Am., Ky. bar assns., Nat. Tax Assn. (dir. 1971-74), local C. of C., Res. Officers Assn., Mil. Order World Wars, Beta Gamma Sigma, Delta Sigma Pi. Clubs: Rotary. Democrat. Baptist. Address: 216 Westmoreland Ave SE Huntsville AL 35801-2726

TRAYLOR, ROBERT ARTHUR, lawyer; b. Syracuse, N.Y., Jan. 15, 1949; s. Robert Arthur and Julia Elizabeth (McNulty) T.; m. Bonita Lynn Schmidt, Nov. 26, 1977. BS, LeMoyne Coll., 1970; JD cum laude, Syracuse U., 1975. Bar: N.Y., U.S. Dist. Ct. (no. dist.) N.Y., U.S. Tax Ct. Assoc. Love, Balducci & Scaccia, Syracuse, N.Y., 1976-77; estate tax atty. IRS, Syracuse, 1977-81; assoc. Scaccia Law Firm, Syracuse, 1981—. Contbr. articles to profl. jours. Of counsel St. Ann Sch., Syracuse, 1981—, mem. coordinating com. Vision 2000 1994—, mem. bd., 1998—. With U.S. Army, 1970-72. Mem. ABA, Onondaga County Bar Assn. (vol. lawyer program 1993—, Vol. Lawyer of Month 1994), World Wildlife Fedn. Republican. Roman Catholic. Avocations: motorsports, military history, catholic education. Home: 112 Knowland Dr Liverpool NY 13090-3130 Office: Scaccia Law Firm State Tower Bldg Ste 402 Syracuse NY 13202-1798

TRAYLOR, WILLIAM ROBERT, publisher; b. Texarkana, Ark., May 21, 1921; s. Clarence Edington and Seba Ann (Talley) T.; m. Elvirez Sigler, Oct. 9, 1945; children: Kenneth Warren, Gary Robert, Mark Daniel, Timothy Ryan. Student, U. Houston, 1945-46, U. Omaha, 1947-48. Div. mgr. Lily-Tulip Cup Corp., N.Y.C., 1948-61; asst. to pres. Johnson & Johnson, New Brunswick, N.J., 1961-63; mgr. western region Rexall Drug & Chem. subs. Dart Industries, L.A., 1963-67; pres. Prudential Pub. Co., Diamonds Springs, Calif., 1967—. Cons. to printing industry, 1976-98; syndicated writer (under pseudonym)s. Bill Friday's Bus. Bull., 1989—. Author: Instant Printing, 1976 (transl. into Japanese), Successful Management, 1979, Quick Printing Encyclopedia, 1982, 8th edit., 1998, How to Sell Your Product Through (Not to) Wholesalers, 1980; pubr. Professional Estimator and Management Software for Printing Industry, 1997, Small Press Printing Encyclopedia, 1994. With USCG, 1942-45. Named Man of Yr. Quick Printing Mag., 1987. Mem. Nat. Assn. Quick Printers (hon. lifetime), C. of C., Kiwanis, Toastmasters. Democrat. Avocations: skiing, boating. Address: 685 E College PKWY Apt 11 Carson City NV 89706-2902

TRAYNHAM, JAMES GIBSON, chemist, educator; b. Broxton, Ga., Aug. 5, 1925; s. James G. and Eddie Louise (Greer) T.; m. Margaret A. Egert, 1948; children: David F., Peter C.; m. Gresdna A. Doty, 1980. Student, South Ga. Coll., 1942-43; BS, U. N.C., 1946; PhD, Northwestern U., 1950. Instr. Northwestern U., 1949-50; asst. prof. Denison U., 1950-53; mem. faculty La. State U., Baton Rouge, 1953—, prof. chemistry, 1963-88, prof. emeritus, 1988—, chmn. dept. chemistry, 1968-73, vice chancellor for advanced studies and rsch., dean Grad. Sch., 1973-81. Postdoctoral research fellow Ohio State U., 1951-53; oral history cons. Chem. Heritage Found., 1997-2002. Author: Organic Nomenclature: A Programmed Introduction, 1966, 5th edit., 1997; editor: Essays on the History of Organic Chemistry, 1987; contbr. articles to profl. jours. Bd. dirs. Council Grad. Schs. in, U.S., 1981. Recipient Petroleum Research Fund-Am. Chem. Soc. Type D award Eidg. Technische Hochschule, Zurich, Switzerland, 1959-60; Charles E. Coates award Baton Rouge sects. Am. Chem. Soc. and Am. Inst. Chem. Engrs., 1965; NATO sr. fellow in sci. Universität des Saarlandes, Saarbrücken, Fed. Republic Germany, 1972 Mem. Am. Chem. Soc. (councilor, past chmn. Baton Rouge sect., chmn. divsn. history of chemistry 1988), La. Acad. Sci., Internat. Union Pure and Applied Chemistry (former titular mem. commn. on nomenclature of organic chemistry, sec. 1994-99), Phi Beta Kappa, Sigma Xi, Phi Lambda Upsilon, Phi Kappa Phi (past pres. La. State U. chpt.). Home: 122 Highland Trace Dr Baton Rouge LA 70810-5061 Office Fax: 225-769-7801. Personal E-mail: jimtraynham@msn.com.

TRAYNOR, DANIEL M. state representative; Postgrad in law, U.N.D., 1997. Lic.: N.D. (Law). Elected state chmn. N.D. Rep. party, 2001—; law clerk N.D. Supreme Court. District 15 chmn.; vol. Political Campaigns, 1988; dir. N.D. Rep. Party Election, 1992; mem., delegate rules com. Rep. Nat. Convention, Phila., 2000. Republican. Office: PO Box 1917 Bismarck ND 58502-1917

TRAYNOR, JOHN MICHAEL, lawyer; b. Oakland, Calif., Oct. 25, 1934; s. Roger J. and Madeleine (Lackmann) Traynor; m. Shirley Williams, Feb. 11, 1956; children: Kathleen Traynor Millard, Elizabeth Traynor Fowler, Thomas. BA, U. Calif., Berkeley, 1955; JD, Harvard U., 1960. Bar: Calif. 1961, U.S. Supreme Ct. 1966. Dep. atty. gen. State of Calif., San Francisco, 1961—63; spl. counsel Calif. Senate Com. on Local Govt., Sacramento, 1963; assoc. firm Cooley Godward, LLP, San Francisco, 1963—69, ptnr., 1969—. Adviser 3d Restatement of Unfair Competition, 1988—95, 3d Restatement of Torts, Products Liability, 1992—97, Apportionment, 1994—99, 2d Restatement of Conflict of Laws revs., 1988, 3d Restatement of Restitution and Unjust Enrichment, 1997—; lectr. Boalt Hall Sch. Law U. Calif., Berkeley, 1982—89, Berkeley, 1996—98; chmn. EarthJustice Legal Def. Fund (formerly Sierra Club Legal Def. Fund), 1991—92, trustee, 1974—96. Mem. bd. overseers Inst. for Civil Justice RAND, 1991—97; bd. dirs. Environ. Law Inst., 1991—97, 2000—; Sierra Legal Def. Fund. Canada, 1990—96. 1st lt. USMC, 1955—57. Recipient John P. Frank award, 2004. Fellow: AAAS, Am. Acad. Arts and Scis., Am. Bar Found. (life); mem.: Calif. Acad. Appellate Lawyers, Bar Assn. San Francisco (pres. 1973), Am. Law Inst. (coun. 1985—, pres. 2000—). Home: 3131 Eton Ave Berkeley CA 94705-2713 Office: Cooley Godward LLP 1 Maritime Plz Ste 2000 San Francisco CA 94111-3580 Office Phone: 415-693-2110. E-mail: mtraynor@cooley.com.

TREACY, GERALD BERNARD, JR., lawyer; b. Newark, July 29, 1951; s. Gerald B. Sr. and Mabel L. (Nesbitt) T.; m. Joyce M. Biazzo, Apr. 6, 1974. BA summa cum laude, Rider Coll., 1973; JD, UCLA, 1981. Bar: Calif. 1981, Wash. 1982, D.C. 1995. Tchr. English Arthur L. Johnson Regional High Sch., Clark, N.J., 1973-77; assoc. Gibson, Dunn & Crutcher, L.A., 1981-82; ptnr. Perkins Coie, Bellevue, Wash., 1982-94, McGuire Woods Battle & Boothe, McLean, Va. and Bellevue, Va., 1994-96, Egger, Betts, Austin, Treacy, Bellevue, Wash., 1996-98; mem. Treacy Law Group, Bellevue, 1998—; of counsel Montgomery Purdue Blankinship and Austin, Seattle, 2000—. Chmn. bd. dirs. estate planning adv. bd. U. Wash., Seattle, 1990-92; presenter TV Seminar, Where There's a Will, PBS affiliate. Author: Washington Guardianship Law, Administration and Litigation, 1988, supplemented, 1991, 3d edit. supplemented, 2002, Supporting Organizations, 1996, 2d edit., 2002. Endowment fund com. Unitd Way, Seattle, 1987—89; exec. com. Wash. Planned Giving Coun., 1993—94, 1996—98; bd. dirs., adv. bd. ARC, Seattle, 1985—89, Arthritis Gift, 1987—89, Seattle Symphony, 1992, Seattle U., 1996; bd. dirs. Kitsop Opera, 2003—04; founder, prodr. West Sound Lyric Theater, 2003—. Mem. Eastside King County Estate Planning Coun., Order of Coif. Avocations: photography, hiking, ethnic and classical music, poetry, host/writer gilbert & sullivan radio show. Office: PO Box 710 Keyport WA 98345 Office Phone: 360-697-4142. E-mail: gbtreacy@aol.com.

TREACY, JOHN C. insurance company executive; b. 1963; With Ernst & Young, 1984—89; with investment reporting dept. St. Paul Co., 1989—96, fin. reporting officer, 1996—99, v.p., contr. fire and marine, 1999—2001, corp. contr., 2001—. Bd. dirs. Cath. Charities. Mem.: Am. Ins. Assn. (mem. fin. mgmt. issues com.). Office: St Paul Cos Inc 385 Washington St Saint Paul MN 55102

TREACY, VINCENT EDWARD, lawyer; b. Mass., Jan. 30, 1942; AB, Boston Coll., 1964; JD with honors, George Washington U., 1971. Bar: Va. 1972, D.C. 1973, Md. 1999; U.S. Supreme Ct. 1976. Atty. Fed. Labor Rels. Coun., Washington, 1971-73; legis. atty. Am. law divsn. Congrl. Rsch. Svc., Libr. Congress, Washington, 1973-98; sole practitioner Washington, 1998—. Cons. Romanian Legal Analysis and Legis. Drafting Conf., Senate and Chamber Duputies Romania, Bucharest, 1996. Mem. law rev. staff George Washington Law Rev., 1970. Mem. George Washington Law Alumni Assn. (pres. Capitol Hill chpt. 1986-87), Order of Coif. Office Phone: 202-966-1497. E-mail: vtreacy@msn.com.

TREACY, WILLIAM JOSEPH, electrical and environmental engineer; b. NYC, Jan. 16, 1959; s. William Joseph and Angela Bridget (Keane) T.; 1 child, Denise Marie. BSEE, Manhattan Coll., 1981; M in Aero. Sci., Embry-Riddle U., 1987. Registered profl. engr., N.Y. Commd. 2d lt. USAF, 1981, advanced through grades to capt., project mgr., 1981—84, dept. chief Netherlands GLCM program office Ramstein, Germany, 1984—88, chief engr. Soesterberg, Netherlands, 1988—91, heavy repair supt. Plattsburgh, NY, 1991—92, CFO, 1992—94, chief environ. engr., 1994—95; bldg. sys. supr. Plattsburgh Airbase Redevel. Corp., 1995—2004, Plattsburgh Mcpl. Lighting Dept., 2004—. Computer technician, Plattsburgh, 1992—. Active Red Cross, Plattsburgh, 1992. Decorated Meritorious Svc. medal, Air Force Commendation medal with one oak leaf cluster, others; USAF ROTC Program Acad. scholar, 1978. Mem. IEEE, ASHRAE, Nat. Fire Protection Assn., Internat. Assn. Elec. Insps., Assn. for Facilities Engring., Aircraft Owners and Pilots Assn., Friends of Ft. Ticonderoga, Am. Legion. Republican. Roman Catholic. Avocations: flying, star trek memorabilia, cross country skiing. Home: 60 Leonard Ave Plattsburgh NY 12901-2565 Office: Plattsburgh Mcpl Lighting Dept 32 Green St Plattsburgh NY 12903 Office Phone: 518-563-2200.

TREADWAY, JAMES CURRAN ERIK CORBETT, lawyer, investment company executive, former government official; b. Anderson, S.C., May 21, 1943; s. James C. and Maxine (Hall) T.; m. Susan Pepper Davis, Sept. 6, 1969; children: Elizabeth Pepper Hall, Caroline Worrell Harper Corbett. AB summa cum laude, Rollins Coll., 1964; JD summa cum laude, Washington and Lee U., 1967. Bar: Ga. 1967, Mass. 1968, D.C. 1970. Assoc. Candler, Cox, McClain & Andrews, Atlanta, 1967-68, Gadsby & Hannah, Boston and Washington, 1968-72; ptnr. Dickstein, Shapiro & Morin, Washington, 1972-82; commr. SEC, Washington, 1982-85; ptnr. Baker & Botts, Washington, 1985-87; exec. v.p., chmn. merchant banking dept., exec. com. Paine Webber Group Inc., N.Y.C., 1987—. Chmn. Nat. Commn. on Fraudulent Fin. Reporting, 1985—87; chmn. bds. dirs. Washington & Lee U. Sch. Law, 1992—94; dir. U. So. Calif., Sch. of Acctg. and Fin. Disclosure, 1985—93; mem. planning com. Garret Securities Law Inst., Northwestern U., 1985—92; spl. expert adviser, witness various U.S. congl. coms.; lectr. and author in field. Editor-in-chief Wash. & Lee U. Law review, 1966-67. Recipient Wildman Medal Am. Acctg. Assn., 1989. Mem. Mass. Bar Assn., Ga. Bar Assn., D.C. Bar Assn., Chevy Chase (Md.) Club, Bedford (N.Y.) Golf and Tennis Club, City Tavern Club, Met. Club, Univ. Club (Washington), Verbank Hunting and Fishing Club (Uniondale N.Y.; dir. 1995—), Order of Coif, Phi Beta Kappa, Omicron Delta Kappa. Home: Laurel Ledge Farm RD 4 Croton Lake Rd Bedford Corners NY 10549-4227 Office: PaineWebber Group Inc 1285 Ave of Americas New York NY 10019-6028

TREADWAY, SANDRA GIOIA, library director; b. Jersey City, N.J., Jan. 15, 1950; d. Robert Peter and Essey Grace (Graham) Gioia; m. John David Treadway, Sept. 4, 1976 (div. 2003); 1 child, Robyn Grace. BA in History, Manhattanville Coll., 1971; MA in History, U. Va., 1972, PhD in History, 1978. Instr. history Va. Polytech Inst. & State U., Blacksburg, 1976-78; editor Va. State Libr., Richmond, 1978-91, dir. pubs., 1991-96; deputy dir. Libr. Va., Richmond, 1996—. Author: Women of Mark, 1995; co-author: The Common Wealth: Treasures from the Collections of the Library of Virginia, 1997; co-editor: Dictionary of Virginia Biography, vol. 1, 1999, vol. 2, 2001. Mdm. bd. St. Mary Sch., Richmond, 1988-96. Mem. Am. Hist. Assn., Orgn. Am. historians, So. Historical Assn., So. Assn. Women Historians (pres. 2002), Va. Hist. Soc., Va. Libr. Assn., Serra Internat. (bd. dirs. 1985—). Roman Catholic. Avocations: reading, travel. Home: 8201 Gaylord Rd Richmond VA 23229-4121 Office: Libr LVa 800 E Broad St Richmond VA 23219-1905

TREADWAY-DILLMON, LINDA LEE, athletic trainer, actress, stuntwoman; b. Woodbury, N.J., June 4, 1950; d. Leo Elmer and Ona Lee (Wyckoff) Treadway; m. Randall Kenneth Dillmon, June 19, 1982. BS in Health, Phys. Edn. & Recreation, West Chester State Coll., 1972, MS in Health and Phys. Edn., 1975; postgrad., Ctrl. Mich. U., 1978; Police Officer Stds. Tng. cert. complaint dispatcher, Goldenwest Coll., 1982. Cert. in safety edn. West Chester State Coll.; cert. EMT, Am. Acad. Orthopaedic Surgeons. Grad. asst., instr., asst. athletic trainer West Chester (Pa.) State Coll., 1972-76; asst. prof., program dir., asst. athletic trainer Ctrl. Mich. U., Mt. Pleasant, 1976-80; police dispatcher City of Westminster, Calif., 1980-89; oncology unit sec. Children's Hosp. Orange County, Orange, Calif., 1989-96; control clk. food and beverage Marriott Hotel, Anaheim, Calif., 1996—2003. Stuntwoman, actress United Stunt Artists, SAG, L.A., 1982—; dancer Disneyland, Anaheim, Calif., 1988—; contbr. articles to profl. jours. Athletic trainer U.S. Olympic Women's Track and Field Trials, Frederick, Md., 1972, AAU Jr. World Wrestling Championships, Mt. Pleasant, Mich., 1977, Mich. Spl. Olympics, Mt. Pleasant, 1977, 78, 79. Recipient bronze and gold Spirit of Disneyland Resort awards, 1997; named Outstanding Phys. Educator, Delta Psi Kappa, Ctrl. Mich. U., 1980, Outstanding Young Woman of Am., 1984; named to Disneyland Entertainment Hall of Fame, 1995. Mem. SAG, Nat. Athletic Trainers Assn. (cert., women and athletic tng. ad hoc com. 1974-75, placement com. 1974-79, program dirs. coun. 1976-80, ethics com. 1977-80, visitation team 1978-80, 25 Yr. award 1997), U.S. Field Hockey Assn. (player), Pacific S.W. Field Hockey Assn. (player, Nat. Champion 1980, 81, 82), L.A. Field Hockey Assn. (player), Swing Shift Dance Team (dancer). Presbyterian. Avocations: flying, piano, athletics, stitchery, travel. Home: 18073 Scanlan Ct Fountain Valley CA 92708-5865

TREADWELL, ALEXANDER F. former state official, political party chairman & leader; b. London, Mar. 25, 1946; m. Libby, 1970; children: Carrie, Zach. BA, U. N.C. Former chmn. Essex Cty. Rep. Committee; vice chmn. NY St. Rep. Party, 1989; sec. of state State of N.Y., 1995—2001; chmn. Rep. State Com., 2001—. Reporter & freelance journalist, Sports Illustrated, writer, Classic Magazine, NY Magazine. Author: The World of Marathons, Stewart, Tabori & Chang, 1987. NY Army Natl. Guard, 1968-74. Republican. Office: New York Republican State Committee 315 State Street Albany NY 12210

TREADWELL, HUGH WILSON, retired publishing executive; b. Waurika, Okla., Nov. 21, 1921; s. Hugh and Jessie Ellen (Cogdell) T.; m. Edith Albena Doolittle, June 20, 1959; children— Pamela, Hugh, Cynthia. BA, U. Okla., 1949, MA, 1952; diploma in French Studies (Rotary Found. fellow), Institut de Touraine, U. Poitiers, France, 1950. Asst. editor internat. lit. quar. Books Abroad, U. Okla., 1952-53; field rep. coll. dept. The Macmillan Co., 1953-60, Holt, Rinehart & Winston, Inc., Okla. and Tex., 1960-62, mgr. coll. programs in fgn. lang. dept., 1962-67; sr. editor coll. dept. Random House-Knopf, N.Y.C., 1967-72; dir. U. N.Mex. Press, Albuquerque, 1973-80, Tex. Western Press, U. Tex., El Paso, 1981-85; pvt. practice cons., 1985—; field rep. coll. dept. W.W. Norton & Co., Tex., N.Mex., Okla., 1988-93; instr. ESL El Paso C.C., 1994—. Instr. French U. Okla., 1952-53; Industry rep. Nat. Com. Support of Fgn. Langs., 1971, freelance translator (French-English), 1996—. Pres. El Paso Coun. for Internat. Visitors, 1987-88. With USAAF, 1943-46. Decorated Air medal. Mem. Phi Beta Kappa. Clubs: Alliance Francaise (El Paso). Democrat. Home: 6832 La Cadena Dr El Paso TX 79912-2810 *In my mind, the pursuit of happiness has always been bound up with the pursuit of knowledge— knowledge not in a purely abstract sense, but purposeful knowledge humanely applied. The professions of teaching and publishing, if practiced in the light of the highest ethical standards associated with each, make this pursuit possible and offer the greatest satisfaction to those who view life as I do. I consider myself fortunate to have served in both of these professions.*

TREADWELL, KENNETH, JR., obstetrician/gynecologist; b. Perth Amboy, N.J., Sept. 28, 1947; s. Kenneth and Vivian Leona (Broadsdale) T.; children: G. Ryan, Raven Suzanne. MD, U. Rochester, 1977. Diplomate Am. Col. Ob-gyn. Resident in obstetics/gynecology U.N.C. Meml. Hosp., Chapel Hill, 1977-81; mem. staff USPHS Commissioned Corps, Newark, N.J., 1981-84, Newark (N.J.) Beth Israel Hosp., 1981—, U. Med. & Dentistry N.J., Newark, 1981—; capt. Naval Reserve Med. Corps, 1984—; mem. staff Columbus Hosp., Newark, N.J., 1989—, Trinitas Hosp., Livingston, NJ, 1990—, St. Barnabas Med. Ctr., Livingston, N.J., 1990—, Raritan Bay Med. Ctr., Perth Amboy, N.J., 1994—. Clin. instr. U. Med. & Dentistry N.J., Newark, 1981—. Fellow Acad. Medicine N.J.; mem. AMA, Assn. Gynecological Laparoscopy, N.J. Obstetrics Soc., Nat. Med. Assn., Robert & Ross Obstetrics Soc. Office: 1387 Clinton Ave Irvington NJ 07111-1442

TREADWELL-RUBIN, PAMELA A. lawyer; b. Arlington, Tex., Dec. 15, 1960; BA in Polit. Sci., U. Ariz., 1982, JD, 1985. Bar: Ariz. 1985. Prosecutor, Tucson City, 1985—87; dep. atty. Pima County, 1987—93; atty. Goering, Roberts, Rubin, Brogna, Enos & Hernandez, P.C., Tucson. Mem. Ariz. Juvenile Justice Adv. Coun., 1993—96. Fellow: Ariz. Bar Found. (bd. dirs. 1991—94, chair victims' rights pro bono panel 1992—93); mem.: Pima County Bar Assn. (bd. dirs. 1989—90, pres. Young Lawyers divsn. 1989—90, bd. dirs. 1996—), Ariz. Women Lawyers Assn., State Bar Ariz. (pres. Young Lawyers divns. 1994—95, cert. specialist worker's compensation 1995—, bd. govs. 1996—, pres. 2003—04, Outstanding Young Lawyer 1997). Office: Goering Roberts Rubin Brogna Enos & Hernandez PC Ste 200 3320 N Campbell Ave Tucson AZ 85719 Office Phone: 520-577-9300.

TREANOR, CHARLES EDWARD, scientist; b. Buffalo, Oct. 22, 1924; s. William Michael and Margaret Mary (Powers) T.; m. Ruth Ziegelmaier, Jan. 28, 1950; children: Timothy, John, Peter, Michael, Melissa. BA, U. Minn., 1947; PhD, U. Buffalo, 1952-53. Instr. physics U. Buffalo, 1952-53; physicist Cornell Aero Lab., Buffalo, 1954-68, head aerodynamic rsch. dept., 1968-78; v.p. phys. sci. group Calspen Corp., Buffalo, 1978-83, v.p., chief scientist, 1983-90; pres. CTSA, Inc., 1990—2004; ret. Contbr. articles to profl. jours.; patentee in field. Served to lt. U.S. Army, 1943-46. Recipient C.C. Furnas award SUNY, Buffalo, 1989. Fellow Am. Phys. Soc. (div. chmn. 1977), AIAA (com. chmn. 1975-76, 87-89, Fluid and Plasma Dynamics award 1978); mem. NAE. Home: 535 Seabrook Drive Buffalo NY 14221-1919 Fax: (716) 633-6540. E-mail: ctreanor@aol.com.

TREANOR, MARK C. lawyer, diversified financial services company executive; b. Proctor, Vt., Dec. 2, 1946; BS, U.S. Naval Acad., 1968; JD with honors, U. Md., 1976. Bar: Md. 1976, U.S. Dist. Ct. Md. 1977, U.S. Ct. Appeals (4th cir.) 1979, U.S. Tax Ct. 1980, U.S. Supreme Ct. 1980, Vt. 1997. Ptnr. Miles & Stockbridge, 1982—85, Treanor, Pope & Hughes, 1987—98; sr. exec. v.p., gen. counsel, sec. Wachovia Corp., Charlotte, NC, 1998—. Mem. Md. Law Rev., 1975—76. Bd. visitors U. Md. Sch. Law; bd. advisors U. N.C. Sch. Law Banking Inst., NC. Capt. USMC, 1968—73. Mem.: ABA, Order of Coif, Md. State Bar Assn., Phi Alpha Delta. Office: Wachovia Corp 1 Wachovia Ctr 301 S College St Charlotte NC 28288-0630

TREASURE-TERRELL, SUZANNE MARIE, marketing and sales professional, writer, poet, lyricist; b. Chgo., Aug. 18, 1963; d. James Allen Olejarz and Christeen Joy Lindblom; adopted by James DuWayne and Mary Frances (Urban) T.; m. Kenneth Dwayne Terrell, Apr. 1, 2000. Student part time, Dallas Bapt. U., 1988-99. Toll assistance operator Southwestern Bell Tel./AT&T, Dallas, 1982-88; bus. office clk. Southwestern Bell Tel., Dallas, 1988-93, drafting clk., 1993-94, svc. rep., 1994-2000; ret., 2000; customer svc. rep. Blockbuster Video, Dallas, 1994-95; sales rep. Up in Smoke Tobacco Shop, Dallas, 1995-96; sec. bd. Irving Writers Connection, 1994. Telefundraiser Stephen Dunn & Assoc., Myerson Symphony Ctr., Dallas, 1992-93; mem. V.I.P. security staff Tex. Rangers Ballpk., Arlington, 1993-94; job steward Comm. Workers of Am., Dallas, 1982-2000, ret. mem., 2000—; cons., advisor participative mgmt. and employee interactive com., Dallas, 1991-93; owner Treasured Thoughts; co-owner The Revolving Door Inn. Contbr. poetry to Amherst Soc., Am. Poetry Ann. (Poetic Achievement award 1994); contbr. articles to newsletters, Alzheimer's Assn., Tex. Scottish Rite Hosp. for Children, Irving Writers Connection, SBC PM/EI Com.; lyricist for Fatal Fate. Fundraiser United Way, Dallas, 1992-93; cert. ct. appointed advocate Dallas CASA, 1992—; cert. tel. counselor Contact 214, Dallas, 1995-97; press ops. rep. World Cup USA 94, Dallas. Recipient award of merit World of Poetry, Sacramento, 1987, 91, Editor's Choice award The Nat. Libr. of Poetry, Ownings Mills, Md., 1998, Commendation Letter Pres. Bill Clinton for positive contbn. and dedication to volunteerism in local cmty., Dallas, 1993; named Famous Poet for 1998, 99, 2003, Famous Poets Soc., Hollywood, Calif., Talent, OR, 1998, 99, 2003; nominee Golden Rule award JC Penney, Dallas, 1993. Mem. Comm. Workers of Am. (job steward 1982-2000, CWA-COPE Platinum Quorum 1993-96, Outstanding Contbn. award 1994, CWA-COPE Triple Quorum 1996-97, Outstanding Contbn. award 1996, 99), Tel. Pioneers of Am. (life mem.), Irving Writers Connection (sec. bd. 1994), Allen Area Rep. Women's Club. Methodist. Avocations: writing poetry and short stories, arts and crafts, volunteering for children-oriented organizations, illness-related orgns. and nat. events. Home: 514 Bending Bough Dr Spring TX 77388-6102 also: PO Box 1171 Ozark MO 65721-1171

TREAT, JOHN ELTING, entrepreneur; b. Evanston, Ill., June 20, 1946; s. Carlin Alexander and Marjorie Ann (Mayland) T.; adopted s. Howard Elting Jr.; m. Barbara Laflin, May 27, 1984; children: Charles, Luli, Tyler, Tucker, Mayland. BA, Princeton U., 1967; MA, Johns Hopkins U., 1969. Legis. asst. U.S. Senate, 1966; assoc. ops. officer Office of Sec., U.S. Dept. State, 1971-73; research coordinator Presdl.-Congressional Commn. on Orgn. of Govt. for Conduct of Fgn. Policy, Washington, 1973-74; dir. research trade U.S. Fed. Energy Adminstrn., Washington, 1974-78; dep. asst. sec. U.S. Dept. Energy, Washington, 1979-80; staff mem. Nat. Security Council, 1980-81; sr. v.p. N.Y. Merc. Exchange, N.Y.C., 1981-82, pres., 1982-84; ptnr. Bear Stearns & Co., Los Angeles, 1984-85; exec. pub. Petroleum Intelligence Weekly, N.Y.C., 1985-87; pres. Regent Internat., Washington and The Hague, 1987-89; v.p., ptnr. Booz, Allen & Hamilton, Inc., San Francisco, 1989—2001; chmn. Sanctuary Devel. LLC, 2001—. Chmn. spl. gifts Am. Cancer Soc., 1983; chmn. bd. dirs. Mirror Repertory Co., 1987—90; trustee, mem. exec. com., chmn. corp. rels. com. No. Calif. World Affairs Coun.; mem. San Francisco Fgn. Rels. com.; bd. trustees Am. U. of Cairo; trustee Yosemite Nat. Insts., 2001—. With USNR, 1969—71. Decorated AF Commendation medal; Ford Found. European Area Travel grantee, 1972; Woodrow Wilson fellow, 1967; McConnell fellow, 1966 Mem. Coun. Fgn. Rels., Internat. Assn. for Energy Econs. Clubs: Colonial (Princeton, N.J.), St. Francis Yacht Club, Bankers (San Francisco). Democrat. Unitarian Universalist. Home: PO Box 544 Twin Meadows Ranch Placerville CO 81430 E-mail: treat_john@bah.com.

TREAT, SHARON ANGLIN, state legislator; b. Brattleboro, Vt., Jan. 30, 1956; d. Robert Sherman and Mary Lou (Strassburger) T. AB, Princeton U., 1978; JD cum laude, Georgetown U., 1982. Bar: Maine, N.J. Asst. dep. pub. adv. N.J. Dept. of the Pub. Adv., Trenton, 1982-85; assoc. atty. Ball, Livingston & Tykulsker, Newark, 1985-86; staff atty. Natural Resources Coun. Maine, Augusta, 1986-90; state rep. Maine State Legis., Augusta, 1991-96; mem. dist. 18 Maine Senate, Augusta, 1997—; pvt. practice Gardiner, Maine, 1991—. Leader Ctr. for Policy Alternatives, Washington, 1992—; house chair Human Resources Com., 1993-94, Judiciary Com., 1995-96; senate chair natural resources com., 1997—; mem. labor com. 1997—, mem. Adv. Commn. on radioactive Waste, 1997—. Bd. dirs. N.J. Environ. Lobby, Trenton, 1984-86, Maine People's Resource Ctr., Augusta, 1991—, N.E. Citizen Action Resource Ctr., Hartford, Conn., 1992—, Maine Assn. Conservation Commns., 1994—; co-founder, dir. Alliance, Portland, Maine, 1987; trustee Class of 1978 Found., White Plains, N.Y., 1988—; mem. adv. bd. Augusta Area Rape Crisis Ctr., 1992—; mem. adv. coun. Divsn. of Deafness, 1994—; mem. Natural Resources Coun. Maine, Maine Women's Lobby. Mem. Gardiner Libr. Assn., Rotary. Democrat. Office: PO Box 12 Gardiner ME 04345-0012 also: Maine State Senate 3 State House Sta Augusta ME 04333-0003

TREBEK, ALEX, television game show host; b. Sudbury, Ont., Can., July 22, 1940; came to U.S., 1973; s. George Edward and Lucille (Lagace) T.; m. Elaine Callei (div. 1981); m. Jean Currivan, Apr. 30, 1990; 2 children. BA and PhB, U. Ottawa, Ont., 1961. Staff announcer CBC, Toronto, Ont., 1961-73; game show host Wizard of Odds for NBC, Calif., 1973-74, Stars on Ice for Can. TV, 1974-77, High Rollers for NBC, Calif., 1974-79, $128,000 Question for Global TV, Can., 1976-77, Double Dare for CBS, Calif., 1977-78, Battle Stars for NBC, Calif., 1981-82; producer Jeopardy!, Calif., 1984-87, game show host, 1984—, Classic Concentration, Calif., 1987-90, To Tell the Truth, 1991. Owner Creston Vineyards. Film appearances include: Short Cuts, 1993, Spy Hard, 1996, Ellen's Energy Adventure, 1996, Mafia!, 1998, Random Hearts, 1999, The Male Swagger, 1999. Recipient Star on the Walk of Fame, 1999. Mem. Screen Actors Guild, AFTRA, Assn. Can. TV and Radio Artists. Roman Catholic. Avocations: golf, hockey, tennis. Office: Jeopardy! 1020 W Washington Blvd Culver City CA 90232*

TREBING, DAVID MARTIN, automotive executive; b. Lincoln, Nebr., June 2, 1961; s. Harry Martin and Joyce Alice (Christie) T. BA in Mktg., Mich. State U., 1984; MBA in Fin., Wake Forest U., 1986. Project mgr. mktg.-sales Gilbarco div. Exxon Corp., Greensboro, N.C., 1984-86; cash mgmt. analyst Chrysler Fin. Corp., Troy, Mich., 1986-87; sr. corp. fin. specialist Chrysler Corp., Auburn Hills, Mich., 1987-92, mgr. activity-based costing implementation Detroit, 1993-96, mgr. Asia-Pacific Sales Fin., 1996-98; v.p. fin. and adminstrn. Daimler Chrysler Taiwan Co. Ltd., 1998—2001; sr. corp. mgr. regional govt. affairs Daimler Chrysler Corp., Auburn Hills, Mich., 2001—. Mem. Internat. Armed Forces Coun., Detroit, 1987-92, St. George's Soc. N.Y., N.Y.C.; trustee Detroit Hist. Soc.; mem. exec. com., bd. dirs. Meadow Brook Theatre and Festival; Chgo. com. Coun. on Fgn. Rels.; mem. Nat. Com. U.S.-China Rels.; bd. dirs. devel. fund Mich. State U.; bd. dirs. Nat. Flag Found. Lt. (j.g.) USNR, 1987-90. Inst. fellow Inst. Pub. Utilities, 1983. Mem. Econ. Club Detroit, Detroit Com. on Fgn. Rels., Army and Navy Club, Detroit Athletic Club, Grosse Pointe Club, Church Club of N.Y., Vet. Corps Arty. State N.Y., SAR (pres. Detroit chpt. 1987-89), Soc. War 1812, Soc. Colonial Wars (sec. gen., dep. gov. gen. Mich. Soc.), English-Speaking Union, Am. C. of C. in Taipei (bd. suprs.), Pres. Club Mich. State U., Royal New Zealand Yacht Squadron, Chgo. Yacht Club. Avocations: skiing, tennis, travel, skeet/trap shooting, sailing. Office: Daimler Chrysler Corp CIMS 485-10-95 1000 Chrysler Dr Auburn Hills MI 48326-2766 E-mail: DMT@dcx.com.

TREBON, LAWRENCE ALAN, lawyer; b. Waterloo, Iowa, Mar. 28, 1949; s. Al C. and Ann (Ryan) T.; m. Lynn Kutsch, June 12, 1971; children: Scott, Luke. BA, Loras Coll., 1971; JD, Marquette U., 1974. Ptnr. Stepke & Trebon, Milw., 1974-76, Stepke, Kossow, Trebon & Stadtmueller, Milw., 1976-78, Stepke, Trebon & Schoenfeld, Milw., 1978-80, Trebon & Schoenfeld, Milw., 1980-85, Trebon & Polsky, Milw., 1985-94, Trebon & Mayhew, Milw., 1994—. Coach basketball and t-ball, Milw., 1981-90; chmn. fin. com. St. Monica Parish, Whitefish Bay, Wis., 1986-87, chmn. fin. resources com., 1990-94; pres. home and sch. com. St. Monica Sch., Whitefish Bay, 1987-88. Mem. Tripoli Country Club (bd. govs. 1991-94). Republican. Roman Catholic. Avocations: golf, tennis, downhill skiing. Office: Trebon & Mayhew 733 N Van Buren St Ste 770 Milwaukee WI 53202-4768 Office Phone: 414-224-1000.

TREBON, THOMAS, academic administrator; m. Scottie Trebon. B magna cum laude, Seattle U.; M, PhD, U. Denver. Tchr., adminstr. Seattle U.; acad. dean Coll. Arts and Scis. Rockhurst Coll., Kansas City; provost, v.p. acad. affairs Sacred Heart U., Trumbull, Conn.; with St. Norbert Coll., 1995 -2001; v.p. acad. affairs, dean Carroll coll., Helena, Mont.; pres. Carroll Coll., 2001—. Office: Carroll Coll 100 N East Ave Waukesha WI 53186

TRECEK, TIMOTHY SCOTT, lawyer; b. Racine, Wis., Sept. 26, 1968; s. Robert Thomas and Mona Marie Trecek; m. Karyn Marie Kwiatkowski, Aug. 27, 1994; children: Gabrielle Grace, Danielle Terese. BS in Polit. Sci., Marquette U., 1990, JD, 1993. Bar: Wis. 1993, U.S. Dist. Ct. (ea. dist.) Wis. 1993. Atty. Kasdorf, Lewis & Swietlik, Milw., 1993—95, Habush, Habush & Rottier, S.C., Milw., 1995—. Mem. ABA, Wis. Acad. of Trial Lawyers (com. Office Lawyer Regulation), Wis. State Bar Assn., Assn. of Trial Lawyers of Am. Roman Catholic. Avocations: golf, family. Office: Habush Habush & Rottier 777 E Wisconsin Ave 2300 Milwaukee WI 53202-5381 E-mail: ttrecek@habush.com.

TRECHSEL, GAIL, museum director; Curator, adminstr. Birmingham (Ala.) Mus. Art, 1976—96, dir., 1996—. Mem. Ala. State Arts Coun. Office: Birmingham Mus Art 2000 8th Ave North Birmingham AL 35203-2278*

TRECKELO, RICHARD M. lawyer; b. Elkhart, Ind., Oct. 22, 1926; s. Frank J. and Mary T.; m. Anne Kosick, June 25, 1955; children: Marla Treckelo Buck, Mary Treckelo Lucchesi. AB, U. Mich., 1951, JD, 1953. Bar: Ind. 1953, U.S. Dist. Ct. (no. and so. dists.) Ind. Pvt. practice, Elkhart, 1953-70; ptnr. Barnes and Thornburg, Elkhart, South Bend, others, 1971-91, of counsel, 1992—. Sec. Skyline Corp., Elkhart, 1959-94, bd. dirs., 1961-91. Bd. dirs. Elkhart Gen. Hosp. Found., Elkhart Park Found.; co-chmn. Elkhart Constl. Bicentennial Commn. Served with USAF, 1945-46. Mem. ABA, Elkhart City Bar Assn. (pres. 1975), Ind. Bar Assn., Elkhart County Bar Assn., Pres.'s Club (U. Mich.), Christiana Country Club, Michiana Club (chmn., U. Mich. Elbel Scholarship award), Rotary. Republican. Office: Barnes & Thornburg 121 W Franklin St Ste 200 Elkhart IN 46516-3200

TREDWAY, THOMAS, college president; b. North Tonawanda, N.Y., Sept. 4, 1935; s. Harold and Melanya (Scorby) T.; m. Catherine Craft, Jan. 12, 1991; children: Daniel John, Rebecca Elizabeth. BA, Augustana Coll., 1957; MA, U. Ill., 1958; BD, Garrett Theol. Sem., 1961; PhD, Northwestern U., 1964. Instr. history Augustana Coll., Rock Island, Ill., 1964-65, asst. prof., 1965-69, assoc. prof., 1969-71, prof., 1971—, v.p. acad affairs, 1970-75, pres., 1975—. Vis. prof. ch. history Waterloo Lutheran Sem., 1967-68 Mem. Phi Beta Kappa, Omicron Delta Kappa Lutheran. Office: Augustana Coll Office of President 639 38th St Rock Island IL 61201-2210

TREE, MICHAEL, violinist, violist, educator; b. Newark, Feb. 19, 1934; s. Samuel and Sada (Rothman) Applebaum; m. Johanna Kreck, Sept. 8, 1966; children: Konrad Efrem, Anna Louise. Diploma, Curtis Inst. Music, Phila., 1955; DFA (hon.), U. South Fla., 1975, SUNY, Binghamton, 1983. Faculty Harpur Coll., Binghamton, 1965-70, Curtis Inst. Music, 1970—, U. Md., College Park, 1981—, St. Louis Conservatory Music, 1982-88, Rutgers U., 1988—2000, Manhattan Sch. Music, 1993—, Juilliard Sch., NYC, 2002—. Co-artistic dir. Phila. Chamber Orch., 1985-88; Misha Elman chair Manhattan Sch. Music, 1991. Violin recital debut at Carnegie Hall, 1954; soloist with major orchs. and at maj. internat. festivals, 1958—; founding mem. Guarneri String Quartet, 1964—, rec. artist for Philips, RCA, Columbia, Nonesuch, Vanguard, Sony Classics, Arabesque records. Recipient Seal of Recognition City of N.Y., 1982. Avocations: hiking, tennis. Home: PO Box 193 Marlboro VT 05344-0193 Office: care Herbert Barrett Mgmt Inc 1776 Broadway Ste 1610 New York NY 10019-2002

TREECE, JAMES LYLE, lawyer; b. Colorado Springs, Colo., Feb. 6, 1925; s. Lee Oren and Ruth Ida (Smith) T.; m. Ruth Julie Treece, Aug. 7, 1949 (div. 1984); children: James (dec.), Karen Pelletier, Teryl Wait, Jamilyn Smyser, Carol Crowder. Student, Colo. State U., 1943, Colo. U., 1943, U.S. Naval Acad., 1944-46; BS, Mesa Coll., 1946; JD, U. Colo., 1950; postgrad., U. N.C., 1976-77. Bar: Colo. 1952, U.S. Dist. Ct. Colo. 1952, U.S. Ct. Appeals (10th cir.) 1952, U.S. Supreme Ct. 1967. Assoc. Yegge, Hall, Treece & Evans and predecessors, 1951—59, ptnr., 1959—69; U.S. atty. Colo., 1969—77; pres. Treece & Bahr and predecessor firms, Littleton, Colo., 1977—91; mcpl. judge, 1967—68; mem. faculty Nat. Trial Advocacy Inst., 1973—76, Law-Sci. Acad., 1964. Chmn. Colo. Dept. Pub. Welfare, 1963-68; chmn. Colo. Dept. Social Svcs., 1968-69; mem. Littleton Bd. Edn., 1977-81. Served with USNR, 1944-46. Recipient awards Colo. Assn. Sch. Bds., 1981, IRS, 1977, FBI, 1977, DEA, 1977, Fed. Exec. Bd., 1977. Mem. Fed. Bar Assn. (pres. Colo. 1975, award 1975), Colo. Bar Assn. (bd. govs.), Denver Bar Assn. (v.p., trustee). Republican. Episcopalian. Home: 12651 N Pebble Beach Dr Sun City AZ 85351-3327 Personal E-mail: jltreece@juno.com.

TREFFER, KEVIN DUANE, physician, educator; b. Kansas City, Mo., Aug. 31, 1961; s. Frederick Anton and Abbie Jane (Evans) T.; m. Connie R. Treffer, Apr. 4, 1992; 1 stepchild, Jerry Kilgore. BS, Bob Jones U., 1983; DO, Univ. Health Scis., Kansas City, 1987. Diplomate Am. Bd. Family Practice; cert. osteopathic manipulatice med. Am. Bd. Osteopathic Neuromusculoskeletal Med. Intern Univ. Hosp., Kansas City, 1987-88; faculty, gen. family practice Univ. Health Scis., Coll. Osteo. Medicine, Kansas City, 1988—, coord. osteo. manipulative medicine, 2002—, mem. faculty osto. principles and practice dept., 1992—; pvt. practice, gen. family practice Univ. Family Care Ctr., Kansas City, 1988—; pvt. practice, emergency medicine Lafayette Regional Hosp., Lexington, Mo., 1988-95, program co-dir. family medicine/osteo. manipulative medicine residency, 2002—; coord. osteop. manipulative medicine UHS-COM, 2002—. Med. dir. Clay County Pub. Health Dept., Liberty, Mo., 1995-97; cons. Nat. Bd. Osteo. Med. Examiners, 1994—. Mem. Am. Osteo. Assn., Mo. Assn. Osteo. Physicians, Am. Coll. Osteo. Family Practitioners (past chmn. awards and scholarship com. Mo. chpt., bd. govs. Mo. chpt. 1997-2000), Jackson County Osteo. Assn. (bd. gov. 1992—, pres. 1995-97, del. 1997—), Am. Acad. Osteopathy, Ednl. Coun. Osteo. Prin., Alpha Phi Omega. Home: 3110 Gateway Dr Independence MO 64057-3319 Office: UHS-Com 1750 Independence Ave Kansas City MO 64106-1453

TREFFERT, DAROLD ALLEN, psychiatrist, author, hospital director; b. Fond du Lac, Wis., Mar. 12, 1933; s. Walter O. and Emma (Leu) T.; m. Dorothy Marie Sorgatz, June 11, 1955; children: Jon, Joni, Jill, Jay. BS, U. Wis., 1955, MD, 1958. Diplomate Am. Bd. Psychiatry and Neurology. Resident in psychiatry U. Wis. Med. Sch., 1959-62, clin. prof. psychiatry, 1965—; chief children's unit Winnebago (Wis.) Mental Health Inst., 1962-64, supt., 1964-79, Ctrl. State Hosp., Waupun, Wis., 1977-78; dir. Dodge County Mental Health Ctr., Juneau, Wis., 1964-74; mem. staff St. Agnes Hosp., Fond du Lac, 1963—; exec. dir. Fond du Lac County Mental Health Ctr., 1979-92. Chmn. Controlled Substances Bd. Wis.; chmn. med. examining bd. State of Wis. Author: Extraordinary People: Understanding Savant Syndrome, 1989, re-issued, 2000, edits. in U.S., U.K., Italy, Japan, The Netherlands, Sweden; autism cons. (movie) Rainman, 1988. Fellow Am. Coll. Psychiatrists; mem. AMA, Wis. Med. Soc. (pres. 1979-80), Wis. Psychiat. Assn. (pres.), Am. Assn. Psychiat. Adminstrs. (pres.), Alpha Omega Alpha. Home: W 4065 Maplewood Ln Fond Du Lac WI 54935-9562 Office: 430 E Division St Fond Du Lac WI 54935-4560 Office Phone: 920-926-4297. Personal E-mail: savants@dotnet.com. Business E-Mail: dtreffert@pol.net. *People often spend too much time regretting what they are not and far too little time savoring that which they are.*

TREFNY, JOHN ULRIC, college president; b. Jan. 28, 1942; s. Ulric John and Mary Elizabeth (Leech) T.; m. Sharon Livingston, 1992; 1 child from previous marriage, Benjamin Robin. BS, Fordham U., 1963; PhD, Rutgers U., 1968. Rsch. assoc. Cornell U., Ithaca, N.Y., 1967-69; asst. prof. physics Wesleyan U., Middletown, Conn., 1969-77, Colo. Sch. Mines, Golden, 1977-79, assoc. prof., 1979-85, prof., 1985—, assoc. dean rsch., 1988—90, head physics dept., 1990—95, v.p. for acad. affairs, dean faculty, 1995—2000, pres., 2000—. Dir. Amorphous Materials Ctr. Colo. Sch. Mines, 1986-90; cons. Solar Energy Rsch. Inst., Golden, Energy Conversion Devices, Troy, Mich., others. Contbr. articles to profl. jours. Recipient Tchg. award AMOCO Found., 1984, Friend of Sci. Edn. award, 1990. Mem. Colo. Assn. Sci. Tchrs. (bd. dirs. 1986-88), Sigma Xi (N.W. region co-dir. 1994-2000), Sigma Pi Sigma. Avocations: golf, travel. Home: 1722 Illinois St Golden CO 80401-1836

TREFRY, ROBERT J. healthcare administrator; b. Springfield, Vt., Mar. 29, 1947; married. Bachelors' degree, Ga. Inst. Tech., 1970; Masters' degree, George Washington U., 1974. With Greater Southeast Community Hosp., Washington, 1973, adminstrv. asst., 1973-74, asst. adminstr., 1974-79; sr. v.p. North Kansas City (Mo.) Community Hosp., 1979-83; exec. v.p., chief exec. officer St. Agnes Hosp., White Plains, N.Y., 1983-88; exec. v.p., chief operating officer Carle Found. Hosp., Urbana, Ill., 1988-91; exec. v.p., chief oper. officer Bridgeport (Conn.) Hosp., 1991-94, pres., CEO, 1994—; exec. v.p. Yale New Haven Health Sys., 1996—. With U.S. mil. 1970-71. Office: Bridgeport Hosp 267 Grant St Bridgeport CT 06610-2870

TREFTS, JOAN LANDENBERGER, retired educator, administrator; b. Pitts., Jan. 31, 1930; d. William Henry III and Eleanore (Campbell) Landenberger; m. Albert Sharpe Trefts Sr., June 20, 1952 (dec.); children: Dorothy, Albert Jr., William, Deborah, Elizabeth. AB, Western Coll. for Women, 1952; M, John Carroll U., 1982, M, 1984. Lic. and cert. home economist, cert. prin., N.Y., Ohio, supr., biol. sci., econs., voact. edn., pre-kindergarten edn. Summer sch. prin. John Adams H.S., Collinwood and South High, Cleve., 1972-95. Cons. Cleve. Partnership Program. Trustee Chautauqua Literacy and Sci. Cir., Presbyn. Assn. Chautauqua, NY. Named Tchr. of Yr., Cleve., 1994. Mem.: DAR (state officer 2000—), Ohio Vocat. Assn. (bd. dirs.), Am. Vocat. Assn. (nat. com.), Am. Home Econs. Assn., Presbyn. Assn. (trustee), Dames of Ct. of Honor (pres. gen. 2001—), Colonial Daus. of 17th Century (nat. officer), Daus. Am. Colonists (state officer), Nat. Officers Colonial Clergy (nat. officer, chancellor), Colonial Dames Am. (pres. chpt. 18, nat. officer ct. honor), U.S. Daus. of 1912, Colonial Dames of XVII Century, New Eng. Soc. of Western Res. (pres.), Clearwater Country Club, Cleve. Skating Club, Union Clubs. Republican. Presbyterian. Avocations: curling, rug hooking, needlepoint. Home: 20101 Malvern Rd Shaker Heights OH 44122-2825

TREFZGER, RICHARD CHARLES, surgeon; b. Peoria, Ill., Jan. 27, 1948; s. John Dennis and Marilyn Leslie (Wilson) Trefzger; m. Nancy Ellen Guy, Dec. 19, 1971; children: Emily Jean, Michael Guy. BS, U. Ill., 1970, MD, 1973. Diplomate Am Bd Surgery. Intern in surgery Med. Coll. Wis., Milw., 1973-74, resident in surgery, 1974-75, Presbyn.-St. Luke's Hosp., Chgo., 1975-78; instr. surgery Rush Med. Coll., Chgo., 1977-78; med. dir. Westminster Village Retirement Ctr., Bloomington, Ill., 1980-84, St. Joseph's Trauma Ctr., Bloomington, 1986-96, BroMenn Regional Trauma Ctr., Normal, Ill., 1994-96; chief surgery Bromenn Regional Med. Ctr., Normal, Ill., 1987-88, 94-96, St. Joseph's Med. Ctr., Bloomington, 1989-91, pres. med. staff, 1991-92. Clin. instr. U. Ill. Coll. Medicine, 1980—; chmn. bd. dirs. BroMenn Physician Hosp. Orgn., 1995—96; sec. med. staff BroMenn Regional Med. Ctr., 1998, v.p., 99, bd. dirs., 1999—2002, pres. med. staff, 2000—02. Mem Ill State Univ Civic Chorale, Normal, 1991—98; bd dirs Community Cancer Ctr, Bloomington, 1996—, pres, 2000; vpres ofcl bd First Christian Ch, Bloomington, 1981, 1999—2002, elder, 1980—; rector Cursillo in Christianity, 2001; bd dirs Barton Stone Christian Home, Jacksonville, Ill., 1979—82. Fellow: ACS (councilor Ill. chpt. 1986—88, mem. Ill. chpt. com. trauma 1996—2003); mem.: AMA, Ill. Surg. Soc. (gov. 1990—94, v.p. elect 1997, v.p. 1998, pres. elect 1999, pres. 2000, trustee 2001—04), Danvers Cmty. Band-Saxophone, Scottish Rite, Rotary (dir. 1982—85, 1994—99, sec. 1995—96, v.p. 1996—97, pres. 1997—98, band-saxophone, Paul Harris fellow 1989), Masons, Alpha Omega Alpha. Avocations: running, skiing, music, travel. Home: 41 Pendleton Way Bloomington IL 61704-6243 Office: Surg Assocs 1404 Eastland Dr Bloomington IL 61701-3532 Office Phone: 309-663-4351. Personal E-mail: MENDR2@aol.com.

TREGENZA, NORMAN HUGHSON, investment banker; b. Morristown, N.J., Feb. 1, 1937; s. Norman J. and Marion Esther (Hughson) T.; m. Alyce Virginia Bruene, Aug. 27, 1966; children: Norman Arthur, Suzanne Carol. BA, St. Lawrence U., 1959; MBA, NYU, 1963. Sr. investment officer Tchrs. Ins. and Annuity Assn., N.Y.C., 1960-71; sr. v.p. Republic Funding Corp., N.Y.C., 1971-82; pres. Convent Capital Corp., 1982—. Bd. dirs. Amerityre Corp., Boulder City, Nev. Chmn. stewardship com. Presbyn. Ch., Morristown, 1978, ruling elder, 1979, pres. bd. trustees, 1982; trustee St. Lawrence U., Canton, N.Y., 1983-95, Gill/St. Bernards Sch. (hon.), 1982-96, The Morris Mus., Morristown, 1983—. Mem. St. Lawrence U. Alumni Assn. N.J. (pres. 1970-72), Nat. Coun. USS Constitution Mus. Clubs: Baltusrol Golf, Park Ave., Indian Mound Golf. Home and Office: West Shore Dr Silver Lake NH 03875

TREGO, CHARLES R., JR., food products company executive; m. Peg Trego, 1973; children: Seth, Sara, Courtney. BS in Acctg., MBA, U. Dayton; postgrad., Stanford U. Auditor Ernst & Ernst, 1971-75; v.p., contr. Ponedrosa, Inc., 1976-84; sr. v.p., CFO, Bojangles of Am., 1984-86; exec. v.p., CFO, Rich Products Corp., Buffalo, 1986—. Mem. coun. on accountancy Canisius Coll; active Am. Diabetes Assn., Children's Hosp. Found., Nativity of Our Lord Parish, Sisters of Mercy Hosp., Trocaire Coll., girls softball coach. Office: Rich Products Corp 1150 Niagara St Buffalo NY 14213

TREGURTHA, JAMES DAVID, retired career Navy officer, engineer; b. Orange, NJ; s. James D. Sr. and Dorothy Elizabeth (Clinton) T.; m. Gloria Dealey, Dec. 27, 1955; children: Diane Elizabeth Churchyard, Catherine Elizabeth Galusha. BS in Life Scis., BS in Naval Scis. and Engring., Cornell U., 1950; diploma, U.S. Naval Submarine Sch., 1953; MS in Bus. Mgmt. & Personnel Adminstrn., U.S. Naval Post Grad. Sch., 1971. Commd. ensign USN, 1950, advanced through grade to capt., 1971; lt. (j.g.) Destroyer Force, 1950-53; lt. USS Becuna, 1953—55, Guided Missle Unit, 1956-58, USS Grayback, 1958-60; lt. comdr. USS Razorback, 1960-61, USS Rasher, 1961-63; lt. Seventh Fleet Subrep., 1963—66; comdr., submarine rep. fleet ops. Pentagon, Washington, 1966-68; comdr. cheif of staff officer submarine squadron eight, 1968-69; comdr. Submarine Dvsn. Eighty One, 1969; capt., chief staff officer Submarine Flotilla Seven, 1971-72; capt., comdr. USS Durham, 1972-74; capt., commodore Amphibious Squadron, 1974-76; capt. head amphibious ship Pentagon, Washington, 1976—78, capt., dep. dir. ships acqisition, 1978-79; capt., chief staff Eastern Pacific Fleet Amphibious Forces, 1979-80; ret. USN, 1980. Dir. phys. plant svc. and biomedical engring. Anaheim (Calif.) Meml. Hosp., 1980-83, dir. plant engring. and biomedical engring. St. John's Hosp. & Health Ctr., Santa Monica, Calif., 1983-89; asst. chief engr., Long Beach State U., 1989-94. Decorated Legion of Merit. Mem. Retired Officers Assn. (pres. 1999-2003), Submarine Vets. WWII (assoc.), Naval Submarine League, Navy League.

TREGURTHA, PAUL RICHARD, marine transportation company executive; b. Orange, NJ, 1935; married. BSME, Cornell U., 1958; MBA, Harvard U., 1963. Contr., v.p. Brown & Sharpe Mfg. Co., 1969-71; v.p. fin. Moore McCormack Resources, Inc., Stamford, Conn., 1971-73, exec. v.p. fin., 1973-78, pres., COO, from 1978, pres., CEO, chmn., 1987-88; chmn., CEO, co-owner Mormac Marine Group, Inc., Stamford, 1988—. Vice chmn., co-owner The Interlake Steamship Co., 1988—; chmn., CEO Moran Transp. Co., 1994—; bd. dirs. FPL Group, Inc. Trustee emeritus Cornell U., Ithaca, NY; trustee Tchrs. Ins. and Annuity Assn. 1st lt. USAF, 1958—61. Named Baker Scholar, Harvard U., 1963. Office: Mormac Marine Group Inc One Landmark Sq Stamford CT 06901-2608 Office Phone: 203-977-8950.

TREIBLE, KIRK, retired academic administrator, foundation administrator; b. Newton, N.J., Mar. 29, 1941; s. William Bryan and Grace Almond T.; 1 cons, Todd. BS, W.Va. Wesleyan Coll.; MBA, W.Va. U.; LLD, LaGrange Coll. Bus. mgr. Parkersburg (W.Va.) C.C., 1969-71; devel. officer W.Va. Wesleyan Coll., 1972-75, acting treas., 1975-77; v.p. fin. Southwestern U., Georgetown, Tex., 1977-88; pres. Andrew Coll., Cuthbert, Ga., 1998—2002, now pres. emeritus; ednl. cons., 2002—; exec. dir. United Meth. Found. for Comm., 2003—. Bd. dirs. Citizen Bank, Geogetown, Tex., 1978-88; bd. dirs. Regions Bank, Cuthbert, Ga., 1989-99; cons. Nebr. Wesleyan U.; cons. So. Assn. Schs. and Colls. Chmn. adminstrv. bd. First United Meth. Ch., 1983-85, univ. senate; mem. W.I.H. and Lula E. Pitts Found., Peed scholarship Trust, United Meth. Ch. Served with USAF, 1966-69. Mem. Assn. Pvt. Colls. and Univs. Ga. (pres. dir.), Nat. Assn. Schs. and Colls. Methodist. Home: Apt 605 2000 Grand AVe Nashville TN 37212 E-mail: ktreible@aol.com.

TREICHEL, HELMUTH W.A. technology executive; b. Hessberg, Germany, Aug. 26, 1953; s. Otto Treichel, Elise Treichel; m. Ursula M. Fischer; 1 child, Nicola. BSChemE, Acad. Sci. and Tech., Isny, Germany, 1986. Process devel. engr. Siemens AG, Munich, 1986—92; lead engr. Siemens Components, Burlington, Vt., 1992—94; dept. mgr. multilevel metallization, pilot prodn. mgr. Fraunhofer Inst. for Solid State Tech., Munich, 1994—97; sr. engring. mgr. Lam Rsch. Corp., Fremont, Calif., 1997—2000; dir. tech. Novellus Sys., Inc., San Jose, 2000—02. Presenter in field. Contbr. articles to profl. jours. Mem.: Materials Rsch. Soc. Achievements include patents in field. Home: 859 Pheland Ct Milpitas CA 95035 Personal E-mail: treichel@yahoo.com. Business E-Mail: helmuth.treichel@novellus.com.

TREIGER, IRWIN LOUIS, lawyer; b. Seattle, Sept. 10, 1934; s. Sam S. and Rose (Steinberg) T.; m. Betty Lou Friedlander, Aug. 18, 1957; children: Louis H., Karen I., Kenneth B. BA, U. Wash., 1955, JD, 1957; LLM in Taxation, NYU, 1958. Bar: Wash. 1958, D.C. 1982, U.S. Dist. Ct. (we. dist.) Wash., U.S. Ct. Appeals (9th cir.), U.S. Supreme Ct. Assoc. Bogle & Gates, Seattle, 1958-63, ptnr., 1964-99, chmn., 1986-94; ptnr. Dorsey & Whitney LLP, Seattle, 1999—. Trustee Am. Tax Policy Inst., 2004—. Pres. Jewish Fedn. Greater Seattle, 1993-95; chmn. Mayor's Symphony Panel, 1986, Corp. Coun. for the Arts, 1987-88; pres. Seattle Symphony Found., 1986—; trustee, co-chmn. Cornish Coll. of the Arts, 1990-96, chair elect 2003—; trustee The Seattle Found., 1992—, vice chair, 1999-2003, chair, 2003—; trustee., sec. Samis Found., 1989—; chmn. King County Baseball Pk. Commn., 1995. Fellow Am. Coll. Tax Counsel; mem. ABA (chmn. taxation sect. 1988-89, sect. del. 1990-96, bd. govs. 2000-03), Wash. State Bar Assn. (chmn. taxation

sect. 1975, co-chmn. nat. conf. lawyers and accts. 1997-2000), Greater Seattle C. of C. (chmn. 1993-94), Seattle Rotary (trustee 1998-2000), Seattle Rotary Svc. Found. (v.p. 1995-96, pres. 1996-97). Jewish. Office: Dorsey & Whitney LLP Ste 3400 1420 5th Ave Seattle WA 98101-4010 Office Phone: 206-903-8705. E-mail: treiger.irwin@dorseylaw.com.

TREIMAN, DAVID MURRAY, neurology educator; b. St. Louis, Oct. 13, 1940; s. Alfred Abraham and Dorothea Bader (Collins) T.; m. Lucy Ellen Jones, Apr. 9, 1967; children: Stephen Brant, Michael Andrew, Matthew Laurence, Daniel Robert. BA in Zoology, U. Calif., Berkeley, 1962; MD, Stanford U., 1967. Diplomate Am. Bd. Psychiatry and Neurology. Intern Duke U. Med. Ctr., Durham, N.C., 1967-68; resident in internal medicine, postdoctoral fellow Duke U., Durham, 1967-70, resident in neurology svc., postdoctoral fellow, 1970-73; chief neurology USN Med. Ctr., Jacksonville, 1973-75, Yokosuka, Japan, 1975-78; from asst. to assoc. prof. neurology UCLA Sch. Med., 1978-90, prof. neurology, 1990—. Editor: Status Epilepticus, 1983, Neurobehavioral Problems in Epilepsy, 1991; contbr. articles to New England Jour. Medicine, Neurology, Epilepsy Rsch. Comdr. USN, 1973-78. Grantee VA, NIH. Fellow Am. Acad. Neurology; mem. Am. Epilepsy Soc., Am. Neurol. Assn., Neurosci. Soc. Achievements include research in clinical and electrical characteristics of generalized convulsive status epilepticus. Office: Clinical Academic Bldg Ste 6100 125 Paterson St New Brunswick NJ 08901 E-mail: treiman@umdnj.edu .

TREINAVICZ, KATHRYN MARY, application developer; b. Nov. 25, 1957; d. Ralph Clement and Frances Elizabeth (O'Leary) T. BS, Salem State Coll., Mass., 1980. Tchr. Brockton Pub. Schs., 1980-81; instr. Quincy CETA Inc., Mass., 1981-82; programmer Systems Architects Inc., Randolph, Mass., 1982; programmer analyst Dayton, Ohio, 1982-84; sr. programmer analyst System Devel. Corp., Dayton, 1984-86; project mgr. Unisys Inc., Dayton, 1986-87; software engr. Computer Scis. Corp. (formerly Systems & Applied Corp. 1988), 1987-89; project mgr. Computer Sci. Corp. (formerly Atlantic Rsch. Corp. 1994), Fairborn, Ohio, 1989-96; dept. mgr., 1996-98; sr. test analyst, 1998—. Mem. NAFE. Democrat. Roman Catholic. Avocations: steven king novels, needlepoint, knitting, crocheting.

TREISTER, GEORGE MARVIN, lawyer; b. Oxnard, Calif., Sept. 5, 1923; s. Isadore Harry and Augusta Lee (Bloom) T.; m. Jane Goldberg, Jan. 24, 1946; children: Laura, Neil, Adam, Dana. BS, UCLA, 1943; LL.B., Yale U., 1949. Bar: Calif. 1950. Law clk. to chief justice Calif. Supreme Ct., 1949-50; law clk. to Assoc. Justice Hugo L. Black U. S. Supreme Ct., 1950-51; asst. U.S. atty. So. Dist. Calif., 1951-53; dep. atty. gen. Calif., 1953; practiced in, 1953—; mem. Stutman, Treister and Glatt, 1953—; instr. U. So. Calif. Law Sch., 1954-98, Stanford U. Law Sch., 1977-81. Mem., former vice chmn. Nat. Bankruptcy Conf.; former mem. adv. com. on bankruptcy rules Jud. Conf. U.S. Contbr. articles to profl. jours. Served with USNR, 1943-46. Mem. Am. Law Inst. Home: 1201 Neil Creek Rd Ashland OR 97520-9778 Office: 1901 Ave of the Stars 12th fl Los Angeles CA 90067 Office Phone: 541-488-3100.

TREITEL, CORINNA, social studies educator; PhD, Harvard, Cambridge, MA, 1999; MA, Ind. U., Bloomington, IN, 1992; BA, Carleton Coll., Northfield, MN, 1988. Vis. asst. prof. of history Claremont-McKenna Coll., Claremont, Calif., 2000—01; asst. prof. of history Wellesley Coll., Wellesley, Mass., 2001—04; fellow Radcliffe Inst. for Advanced Study, 2004—05. Recipient Bernadotte Schmitt Award, Am. Hist. Assn., 1999; fellow Charlotte Newcombe Award, Woodrow Wilson Found., 1998-1999; scholar Nat. Merit Scholarship, Nat. Merit Found., 1984-1988. Mem.: AAAS, German Studies Assn., Am. Hist. Assn., Sigma Xi. Office: Radcliffe Inst for Advanced Study 34 Concord Ave Cambridge MA 02138

TREITEL, DAVID HENRY, financial consultant; b. Lynn, Mass., Apr. 22, 1954; s. Henry David and Lotte (Elkeses) T.; m. Madelynn Drimmer, Sept. 1982 (div. Oct. 1988); m. Amy Gail Granowitz, Apr. 18, 1990. BA in Econs. with honors, Middlebury Coll., 1976; MBA, Columbia U., 1978. Sr. assoc. Simat Helliesen & Eichner, Inc., N.Y.C., 1980-84, 1980-84, v.p., 1984-88, sr. v.p., 1988-90, exec. v.p., 1990-95; pres. Simat Helliesen & Eichner, Inc., N.Y.C., 1995—. CEO, chmn., 1996—. Bd. dirs. Midwest Express Airlines, Milw., Aircraft Fin. Trust, Wilmington, Del. Contbr. articles to profl. jours. Bd. dirs. Riverside Symphony, N.Y. Mem. The Wings Club (bd. dirs.). Republican. Avocations: golf, tennis, tournament bridge, travel. Office: Simat Helliesen & Eichner 90 Park Ave Fl 27 New York NY 10016-1308

TREJO, JOANN, medical researcher; b. Stockton, Calif., Jan. 23, 1964; BS, U. Calif., Davis, 1986; PhD, U. Calif., San Diego, 1992. Postdoctoral fellow Cardiovasc. Rsch. Inst., U. Calif., San Francisco, 1992—2000; asst. prof. pharmacology U. N.C., 2000—. Undergrad. rsch. asst. Lawrence Berkeley Lab. Divsn. Biology and Medicine, 1983—86; tchg. asst. dept. environ. toxicology U. Calif., Davis, 1986, dept. pharmacology, San Diego, 1988—91, dept. biology, 1989. Contbr. articles to profl. jours. Recipient Nat. Hispanic Scholarship Fund award, 1990—91, Minority Scientist Career Devel. award, Am. Heart Assn., 1995; fellow San Diego and Grad. Opportunity, 1986—88, Dissertation, Nat. Rsch. Coun. Ford Found., 1991—92, Pres.'s Postdoctoral, U. Calif., 1993—95; grantee Tng., NIH/NHLBI Cardiovasc. Rsch. Inst., 1992—93; scholar Katherine Larcara, 1982, Jack O'Keefe, 1982, Kiwanis Club Undergrad., 1982. Mem.: LWV, AAAS, Am. Soc. Cell Biology, Soc. Advancement of Chicanos and Native Americans in Sci. Home: 303 Lorraine St Carrboro NC 27510-1121 Office: UNC-Sch Medicine Dept Pharmacology 1106 Mary Ellen Jones Bldg Chapel Hill NC 27514

TREJOS, FRANKLIN ANTHONY, physician assistant; b. Spokane, Wash., July 6, 1955; s. Frank Trejos and Lloydene Louise (Small) Mielbrecht; children: Cerena, Cebrena, Alyssa. Student, Western Coll., 1978; diploma in physician asst., U. Utah, 1984. Advanced EMT Kootenai County Emergency Med. Rescue Svc., Coeur d'alene, Idaho, 1980—82; phys. asst. Franklin Park Minor Emergency Ctr., Spokane, 1984—85; phys. asst. family practice Cigna Health Plan, Mesa, Ariz., 1985—87; phys. asst. gen. surgery, orthopedic surgery, neurosurgery Mayo Clinic Scottsdale, Ariz., 1987—97; faculty physician asst. program, physician asst. Midwestern U., Glendale, Ariz., 1997—2000; physician asst. Sonoran Med. Ctrs., Phoenix, 2001—02; with Desert Pain Inst., Mesa. Adj. faculty Midwestern U. Coll. Osteo. Medicine, Glendale. Fellow: Am. Acad. Physician Assts. Avocations: water-skiing, mountain biking, astronomy, photography, marine life. Office: Desert Pain Institute 6309 E Baywood Mesa AZ 85206 Office Phone: 480-325-3801. Personal E-mail: f.trejos@cox.net.

TRELEASE, ALLEN WILLIAM, historian, educator; b. Boulder, Colo., Jan. 31, 1928; s. William, Jr. and Helen (Waldo) T.; children— William C. (dec. 1990), Mary E., John A. AB, U. Ill., 1950, MA, 1951; PhD, Harvard U., 1955. Mem. faculty Wells Coll., Aurora, N.Y., 1955-67, prof. history, 1965-67, chmn. dept. history and govt., 1963-67; prof. history U. N.C., Greensboro, 1967-94, head dept., 1984-92, prof. emeritus, 1994—. Author: Indian Affairs in Colonial New York: The Seventeenth Century, 1960, White Terror: The Ku Klux Klan Conspiracy and Southern Reconstruction, 1971, Reconstruction: The Great Experiment, 1971, The North Carolina Railroad, 1849-1871, and the Modernization of North Carolina, 1991, Changing Assignments: A Pictorial History of the U. of N.C. at Greensboro, 1991, Making North Carolina Literate: The University of North Carolina, from Normal School to Metropolitan University, 2003. Mem. Am., So. Hist. assns., Orgn. Am. Historians, Hist. Soc. N.C. (pres. 1986-87), AAUP, Phi Beta Kappa, Phi Kappa Phi, Phi Eta Sigma, Phi Kappa Psi.

TRELFA, RICHARD THOMAS, paper company executive; b. Alpena, Mich., July 5, 1918; s. Fred R. and Mable (Hagen) T.; m. Heidi Brigitte Ruckstuhl (dec. 1996); children: Thomas W., Barbara E. (dec.), Jeffrey C., Michael F.; m. Jennifer Thorlby Trelfa, Jan. 30, 1999. BS, U. Mich., 1940. With Hercules Powder Co., 1941-52, Watervliet Paper Co., Mich., 1952-58; exec. v.p., treas., dir. Perkins-Goodwin Co., Inc., N.Y.C., 1958-70, v.p., treas., CFO, 1970, sr. v.p., 1974-82; chmn. bd. Elcon, Inc., Houston, 1983-91; vice-chmn. bd. B.S. & W Whiteley Ltd., Eng., 1983-88, also bd. dirs. Treas., dir. Kennebec River Pulp & Paper Co., Madison, Maine, 1967-69, chmn. bd., treas., 1969-72, chmn. bd., mem. exec. com., 1972-73, dir., mem. exec. com., 1973-75; pres. Castle & Overton (Can.) Ltd., 1971-82; chmn. bd. EHV Weidmann Industries, Inc., St. Johnsbury, Vt., 1974-84, Franconia Paper Co. Inc., Lincoln, N.H., 1978-80; N.H. State rep. to Gen. Ctr., 1990-98; water commr. Lisbon, N.H., 1990-97, selectman, Lisbon, 1995-2002. Fellow Am. Soc. Quality Control, TAPPI (past divsn. chmn., dir.); mem. Paper Industry Mgmt. Assn. (past divsn. chmn.), Am. Inst. Chem. Engrs., Am. Chem. Soc., Soc. Rheology, Masons, Univ. Mich. Club. Republican. Home: 245 Northey Rd Lisbon NH 03585-7016 Personal E-mail: rttrelfa@aol.com.

TRELSTAD, ROBERT LAURENCE, pathology educator, cell biologist; b. Redding, Calif., June 16, 1940; s. Bertram Laurence and Dorothy (Axt) T.; m. Barbara Stanton Henken, Aug. 27, 1961; children: Derek, Graham, Brian, Jeremy. BA, Columbia U., 1961; MD, Harvard U., 1966. From asst. to assoc. prof. Harvard Med. Sch., Boston, 1972-81; chief pathology Shriners Burns Inst., Boston, 1975-81; staff pathologist Mass. Gen. Hosp., Boston, 1972-81; prof., chair pathology Robert Wood Johnson Med. Sch., Piscataway, New Brunswick, NJ, 1981-98; acting dir. Child Health Inst. of NJ, 1998—, Paz chair devel. biology, 1999—. Mem. study sect. NIH, Bethesda, Md., 1971-75, 86-90; mem. adv. coun. Nat. Inst. Child Health and Human Devel., 1993-97; chmn. health professions adv. com. Princeton U., 2002—. Co-founder, editor-in-chief: Keyboard Pub., Inc., 1990; past mem. editl. bd. various profl. jours. including Jour. Cell Biology, Am. Jour. Pathology, Devel. Biology, Devel. Dynamics. Lt. comdr. USPHS, 1967—69. Helen Hay Whitney Found. fellow, 1969-72; recipient Rsch. Faculty award Am. Cancer Soc., 1972-76, Disting. Tchr. in Basic Scis. award Alpha Omega Alpha and Assn. Am. Med. Colls., 1992. Mem. Am. Soc. Cell Biology (sec. 1982-88), Soc. Devel. Biology (pres. 1983). Home: 35 Westcott Rd Princeton NJ 08540-3038 Office: Robert Wood Johnson Med Sch Child Health Inst New Brunswick NJ 08901 Office Phone: 732-235-9525. E-mail: trelstad@umdnj.edu.

TREMAIN, ALAN, hotel executive; b. Kent, England, Aug. 18, 1935; arrived in U.S., 1966; s. Archibald and Elizabeth (Morris) T.; m. Ingrid K. Olbrich, Dec. 1997; 1 child, Warren. Grad., Westminster Hotel Sch., 1952, Canterbury Sch. Econs., 1962; LL.B., La Salle Sch., Chgo., 1971. Chef de Partie Grosvenor House, London, 1954-55; food and beverage mgr. Peninsula, Hong Kong, 1956-57; gen. mgr. Warners Hotel, also The Russley, Christchurch, New Zealand, 1958-64, Menzies, Sydney, Australia, 1964-65, Empress Hotel, Vancouver, Canada, 1966-69; pres. Planned Food Facilities (Internat.) Ltd., Toronto, Canada, 1970-72; resident mgr. Sheraton Boston, 1972; mng. dir. Copley Plaza Hotel, Boston, 1972—. Chmn. Hotels of Distinction, Inc., Boston; dir. The China Fund, Inc., 1992, chmn., 1999—. Author: A Guide to the Fine Art of Living, 1963, A Meal for To-Night, 1965. Decorated officer Order Brit. Empire; recipient Culinary Merit award from Cercle Epicurien Mondel, Paris, 1956. Fellow Hotel and Catering Inst. (U.K.); founding mem. Internat. Soc. Chefs de Cuisine (chmn. 1954), Masons, Montreal Badminton and Squash Club, The Beach Club, Palm Beach Club, Les Ambs. Club, London Club, Rolls Royce Owners Club. Address: 4100 N Ocean Dr #1001 Singer Island FL 33404 E-mail: atremain@aol.com.

TREMAINE, SCOTT DUNCAN, astrophysicist; b. Toronto, May 25, 1950; s. Vincent Joseph and Beatrice Delphine (Sharp) T. BSc, McMaster U., Hamilton, Ont., 1971; PhD, Princeton U., 1975. Postdoctoral fellow Calif. Inst. Tech., Pasadena, 1975-77; rsch. assoc. Inst. Astronomy, Cambridge, Eng., 1977-78; long-term mem. Inst. for Advanced Study, Princeton, N.J., 1978-81; assoc. prof. MIT, Cambridge, 1981-85; prof., dir. Can. Inst. for Theoretical Astrophysics U. Toronto, 1985-96; dir. program in cosmology and gravity Can. Inst. Advanced Rsch., Toronto, 1996—2002; prof. Princeton U., 1997—, chair dept. astrophys. scis., 1998—. Author: Galactic Dynamics, 1987; contbr. articles to profl. jours. E.W.R. Steacie fellow Natural Scis. and Engring. Rsch. Coun., 1988; recipient H.B. Warner prize Am. Astron. Soc., 1983, Steacie prize, 1989, C.S. Beals award Canadian Astron. Soc., 1990, Rutherford medal Royal Soc. Can., 1990, Heinemann prize for Astrophysics, 1997, Brouwer award, 1997. Fellow Royal Soc. London, Royal Soc. Can.; mem. Am. Acad. Arts and Scis. (fgn. hon.), Nat. Acad. Scis. Office: Princeton U Dept Astrophys Sci Peyton Hall Princeton NJ 08544-1001 E-mail: tremaine@astro.princeton.edu.

TREMAYNE, ERIC FLORY, lawyer; b. Washington, Nov. 29, 1945; s. Bertram William and Frances (Lewis) Tremayne; m. Barbara Ann Williams, Sept. 18, 1982. BA, Westminster Coll., 1967; JD, Washington U., St. Louis, 1973. Bar: Mo. 1973, U.S. Dist. Ct. (ea. and we. dists.) Mo. 1973, U.S. Tax Ct. 2003. Assoc. Tremayne, Lay, Carr, Bauer, Clayton, Mo., 1973—77, ptnr., 1978—; prosecuting atty. City of Wildwood, Mo., 1996—2000. Dir. Option Computer Corp., St. Louis. Bd. dirs. YMCA of Ozarks; campaign aide Citizens for Kit Bond, St. Louis, 1972. With U.S. Army, 1968—70. Mem.: Bar Assn. Met. St. Louis, St. Louis County Bar Assn. (pres. 1983—84, Outstanding Young Lawyer 1981), Sports Car Club Am. (instr. 1979—), Beta Theta Pi (v.p. 1978—90). Home: 433 Eatherton Valley Rd Wildwood MO 63005-4103 Office: Tremayne Lay & Coleman LLP 7777 Bonhomme Ave Ste 1600 Clayton MO 63105-1911 Office Phone: 314-863-4151. Business E-Mail: etremayne@tremayne.org.

TREMBLAY, ANDRE GABRIEL, lawyer; b. Saguenay, Que., Can., Nov. 10, 1937; s. Jean-Charles Tremblay and Julienne (Tremblay) Laberge; children: Jean-Francois, Frederic, Alexandre Reynold. BA, U. Laval-Que. Can., 1959, LL.L., 1962; LLM, U. Ottawa-Ont. Can., 1964, LL.D., 1966. Bar: Que 1963. Asst., law U. Ottawa, 1966—70; assoc. U. Montreal, 1970—75, prof. law, 1972—2003, pres. Can. Assn. Profs.; dir. Pub. Law Ctr., 1972—76, vice dean Law, 1982—86; v.p. Com. on Human Rights, Montreal, 1981—83; legal adv. to bar, govts., law firms, 1972—. Sr Const advisor to Que Govt, 1986—92; pres Prof's Union Univ Montreal, 1995—98; co-counsel Int Criminal Tribunal Rwanda, UN. Author: (book) Les competences legislatives, 1967 (1st Prize Govt Que, 1968), Precis de droit municipal, 1973, Precis de droit constitutionnel, 1982, Droit Constitutionnel-Principles, 1993, Droit Constitutionnel-Principles, 2d ed, 2000, La Revision Constitutionnelle, 1997, Droit Constitutionnel-Documents, 1999; contbr. chapters to books, articles to profl jours. Mem observer's mission Int Comn Jurists, Geneva, 1981—. Mem.: Asn Can Law Teachers. Office: Faculty Law U Montreal CP 6228 succ A Montreal QC Canada H3C 3J7 E-mail: agtremblay@videotron.ca.

TREMBLAY, ANDRÉ-MARIE, physicist; b. Montreal, Que., Can., Jan. 2, 1953; m. Marié à Guylaine Séguin; children: Noémie, Rachel. BSc, U. Montreal, 1974; PhD, MIT, 1978. With Energie Atomique du Can. Limitée, 1973-74, MIT, Boston, 1974-75, Inst. de Recherche de l'Hydro-Que., 1976, Cornell U., Ithaca, N.Y., 1978-80; prof. physics U. Sherbrooke, Que., 1980—, dir. Rsch. Ctr. Physics of Solids, 1991-99. Cons. Cornell U., 1981, Ohio State U., 1982, IBM, 1984; vis. scientist Cornell U., 1986-87, Yale U., 2003; vis. rsch. physicist Inst. for Theoretical Physics, Santa Barbara, Calif., 1989, 96, 2000; vis. scientist Brookhaven (N.Y.) Nat. Lab, 1984; assoc. prof. U. Provence, France, 1982, 83, 97, 99, 2000, 02; Can. Rsch. chair in condensed matter physics, 2000—. Contbr. over 110 articles to profl. publs. Recipient Herzberg medal Can. Assn. Physics, Steacie prize Natural Scis. and Engring. Rsch. Coun., 1987, CAP-CRM prize in Theoretical and Math. Physics, 2001, Urgel-Archaubault prize Assn. francophone pour le savoir, 2003; Killam fellow, 1992-94. Mem. Can. Inst. Advanced Rsch; fellow Royal Soc. of Canada. Office: Sherbrooke U Dept Physics Sherbrooke QC Canada J1K 2R1 E-mail: tremblay@physique.usherbrooke.ca.

TREMBLAY, FRANCOIS-LOUIS, Olympic athlete; b. Alma, Que., Can., Nov. 13, 1980; Profl. speed skater, Canada, 1998—. Recipient 1st pl. overall award, World Jr. Championships, 1998, 1st pl., World Team Championships, 2000, 2001, Gold medal 5000m men's short track speed skating relay, 2002 Olympic Games, 1st pl., World Cup Sofia relay, 2002. Office: Speed Skating Can 2781 Lancaster Rd Ste 402 Ottawa ON K1B 1A7 Canada

TREMBLAY, MARC ADÉLARD, anthropologist, educator; b. Les Eboulements, Que., Can., Apr. 24, 1922; s. Willie and Laurette (Tremblay) T.; m. Jacqueline Cyr, Dec. 27, 1949; children: Geneviève, Lorraine, Marc, Colette, Dominique, Suzanne. AB, U. Montreal, 1944, L.S.A., 1948; MA, Laval U., 1950; PhD, Cornell U., 1954; PhD (hon.), Ottawa U., 1982, Guelph U., 1983, U. N. B.C., 1994, Carleton U., 1995, U. Ste. Anne, 1997, McGill U., 1998. Research asso. Cornell U., 1953-56; mem. faculty Laval U., 1956-93, prof. anthropology, 1963-68, 81-93, prof. emeritus, 1994, vice dean social scis., 1968-71, dean Grad. Sch., 1971-79, also mem. univ. council.; pres. Quebec Coun. Social Rsch., 1987-91. Dir. Inuit and Circupolar Study Group Laval U., 1991—93; mem. Nunavik Commn., 1999—2001. Author 25 books and monographs in social scis., about 200 articles. Decorated officer Order of Can., gt. officer Order of Que.; recipient Que. Lit. prize, 1965, Innis-Gerin prize Royal Soc. Can., 1979, Molson prize Can. Coun., 1987, Prix Marcel Vincent ACFAS, 1988, Contbn. exceptionnelle Societé de sociologie et d'anthropolotie, 1990, Esdras Minville award Soc. St.-Jean Baptiste, 1991; named to Internat. Order of Merit, Internat. Biog. Inst., Cambridge, Eng., 1990. Mem. Royal Soc. Can. (pres. 1981-84), Acad. des Scis. Morales et Politiques (sec.), Rsch. Inst. Pub. Policy, Am. Anthrop. Assn. (past fellow), Am. Sociology Soc. (past fellow), Can. Soc. Applied Anthropology, Can. Sociology and Anthropology Assn. (founding pres.), Can. Ethnology Soc. (past pres.), Assn. Can. Univs. for Northern Studies (past pres.), Assn. Internat. Sociology, Societe des savants et sci. Can. (v.p., pres. nat. order Quebec 1998-2000). Home: 835 N Orléans St Sainte Foy QC Canada G1X 3J4 Office: Laval Univ Dept Anthropology Quebec City PQ Canada G1K 7P4 Fax: (418) 653-9865. Office Phone: 418-653-5411. E-mail: matremgt@globetrotter.net.

TREMBLAY, RICHARD ERNEST, psychology educator; b. Nov. 23, 1944; BA, U. Ottawa, Can., 1966; MPsed, U. Montreal, 1970; PhD, U. London, 1976. Asst. prof. U. Montreal, 1976-81, assoc. prof., 1981-86, prof., 1986—, Can. Rsch. chair in child devel., 2001—, dir. Ctr. of Excellence for Early Child Devel., 2001—; clinician St. Charles Psychiat. Hosp., Joliette, Can., 1966-69, Boscoville, Montreal, Can., 1967-70, Phillippe Pinel Psychiat. Inst., Montreal, 1970-73. Chmn. Sch. of Psycho-Edn., Faculty of Arts and Scis., U. Montreal, 1986-90; invited prof. ethology lab. U. Rennes I, 1993-94, dept. psychology U. Jyväskylä, Finland, 1991; invited scientist psychophysiology lab. U. Franche-Com., 1982-83; presenter in field. Author (with others): Face to Face with Giftedness, 1983, Ethologie et Development de l'enfant, 1985, Le Traitement des Adolescents Delinquants, 1985, Les Relations Entre Enfants, 1988, Human Development and Criminal Behavior: New Ways of Advancing Knowledge, 1991, Famille, Inadaption et Intervention, 1991, Les enfants agressifs: Perspective Development Interculturelle, 1991, Preventing Antisocial Behavior from Birth to Adolescence, 1992, Juvenile Crime, Juvenile Justice, 2001. Molson fellow Can. Inst. of Advanced Rsch. Fellow Royal Soc. of Can., Can. Psychol. Assn.; mem. AAAS, Internat. Soc. for the Study of Behavioral Devel. (exec. com. 1994—), Internat. Soc. for Rsch. on Agression (coun. mem. 1992-96), Am. Soc. of Criminology, Assn. Canadienne-Française pour l'Avancement des Scis., European Assn. for Psychology and Law, Internat. soc. for Human Ethology, N.Y. Acad. Scis., Soc. for Rsch. in Child Devel.

TREMBLAY, WILLIAM ANDREW, English language educator, writer; b. Southbridge, Mass., June 9, 1940; s. Arthur Achille and Irene (Fontaine) T.; m. Cynthia Ann Crooks, Sept. 28, 1962; children: William Crooks, Benjamin Philip, John Fontaine. BA, Clark U., 1962, MA, 1969; MFA in Poetry, U. Mass., 1972. English tchr. Southbridge (Mass.) High Sch., 1962-63, Sutton (Mass.) High Sch., 1963-65, Tantasqua Regional High Sch., Sturbridge, Mass., 1965-67; asst. prof. Leicester (Mass.) Jr. Coll., 1967-70; teaching asst. U. Mass., Amherst, 1970-72; instr. Springfield (Mass.) Coll., 1972-73; prof. English Colo. State U., Fort Collins, 1973—, dir. MFA program in creative writing. Fulbright-Hays lectureship, Lisbon, Portugal, 1979, NEH summer program, 1981; mem. program dirs. coun. Associated Writing Programs, 1984-86. Author: The June Rise: The Apocryphal Letters of Antoine Janis, 1994, (poetry) Shooting Script: Door of Fire, 2003, Rainstorm Over the Alphabet, 2001, Duhamel: Ideas of Order in Little Canada, 1986, Second Sun: New and Selected Poems, 1985, Home Front, 1978, The Anarchist Heart, 1977, Crying in the Cheap Seats, 1971; editor-in-chief: Colo. Rev., 1983-91. Nat. Endowment for the Humanities, 1981, Summer writing fellow Corp. of Yaddo, 1989, Creative Writing fellow Nat. Endowment for Arts, 1985; recipient Pushcart prize Pushcart Prize Anthology, 1987, Best Am. Poetry, 2003. Mem.: Puerto del Sol (bd. advisors, John F. Stern Dist. Prof. award 2002), Am. Acad. Poetry, Poudre Wilderness Vol. Home: 3412 Lancaster Dr Fort Collins CO 80525-2817 Office: Colo State U Dept English Fort Collins CO 80523-0001

TREMBLEY, MARK MICHEL, geographer, educator; b. Glendale, Calif., Apr. 21, 1941; s. Stanley Alexander and Elaine Blanche (Rendahl) T.; m. (div.); 1 child, Kirsten Perri. BA in Geography, Calif. State U., Northridge, 1964; MA in Geography, U. Calif., Berkeley, 1970, MLA in Landscape Arch., 1975. City planner City of Hayward, Calif., 1968-71; instr. earth sci. Fresno (Calif.) City Coll., 1971-73; pvt. practice environ. planner Berkeley, Calif., 1975-79; dir. grad. program in urban and regional planning Antioch U., 1978-81; project mgr. Edaw, Inc., San Francisco, 1981-85; sr. assoc. EIP Assoc., San Francisco, 1985-90; prof. urban geography San Diego Mesa Coll., 1990—. Developer AS degree program in geog. info. sys. San Diego Mesa Coll., 1999-2000; cons. in field. Vol. County Dem. Party, 1996-97. Beatrix Ferrand fellow U. Calif./Oreg. State U., 1973; Nat. Sci. Found. grant Nat. Sci., 1973, Chancellors grant for innovative edn. San Diego C.C. Dist., 1998. Mem. Assn. Am. Geographers, Nat. Coun. for Geographic Edn., Am. Soc. Landscape Architects. Democrat. Unitarian Universalist. Avocations: fly fishing, history, community theater. Home: 3424 Sixth Ave San Diego CA 92103 Office: San Diego Mesa Coll 7250 Mesa Coll Dr San Diego CA 92111 E-mail: mtremble@sdccd.net.

TREMBLY, DENNIS MICHAEL, musician; b. Long Beach, Calif., Apr. 16, 1947; s. Fred Lel and Jewel Fern (Bouldin) T. Student, Juilliard Sch. Music, 1965-68. Sr. lectr. U. So. Calif., L.A., 1981—. Bass player, 1959—, with Los Angeles Philharmonic Orch., 1970-73, co-prin. bass, 1973— . Recipient 2d pl. Internat. Solo Bass competition, Isle of Man, 1978 Mem. Internat. Soc. Bassists. Office: L A Philharm Orch 151 S Grand Ave Los Angeles CA 90012

TREML, VLADIMIR GUY, economist, educator; b. Kharkov, USSR, Mar. 27, 1929; came to U.S., 1950, naturalized, 1953; s. Guy Alexey and Lydia Vladimir (Timofeev) T.; m. Emma Miro, July 12, 1952; children— Irene Treml Cagney, Tatiana, Alexey. BA in Econs, Bklyn. Coll., 1955; MA in Econs, Columbia U., 1956; PhD in Econs, U. N.C., 1963. Dept. supr. Bache & Co., N.Y.C., 1953-58; research asso. Inst. for Social Scis., U. N.C., Chapel Hill, 1958-61; asso. prof. econs. Franklin and Marshall Coll., 1961-66; research asso. Inst. Study USSR, Munich, Germany, 1966-67; prof. econs. Duke U., 1967—; dir. Ctr. for Slavic Studies U.S. Dept. Edn. of Duke U., 1991—. Cons. in field; expert Dept. Commerce, The World Bank, other fed. agys., 1971—; vis. Ford research prof. U. Calif., Berkeley, 1984-85; vis. research prof. U. Hokkaido, Sapporo, Japan, 1985. Author: (with others) Structure of the Soviet Economy, 1972, Input-Output Analysis and the Soviet Economy, 1975, Western Sovietology in the Soviet Union, 1999; contbr. reports to publs. of Joint Econ. Com., U.S. Congress; contbr. articles to profl. publs.; editor: Soviet Economic Statistics, 1972; editor, contbg. author: Studies in Soviet Input-Output Analysis, 1977, Alcohol in the USSR, 1982; contbg. editor: Soviet Economy Jour. Trustee Nat. Council for Soviet and East European Research, Inc., Washington, 1978-84. Served with USMC, 1951-53. Ford Found. grantee, 1972-81, Dept. Def.-Advanced Rsch. Project Agy. grantee, 1975-76, Dept. State grantee, 1976-77, Dept. Def. grantee, 1985-90, Georgetown U. grantee, 1984-86, Olin Found. grantee, 1989, Internat. Rsch. and Exch. Bd. grantee, 1993-96, Nat. Coun. for Eurasian Rsch. grantee, 1996-98; Fulbright fellow Moscow U., 1992. Mem. So. Econ. Assn., Am. Econ. Assn., Assn. Comparative Econ. Studies (exec. com. 1972-74), Am. Assn. Advancement Slavic Studies, So. Conf. on Slavic Studies (pres. 1977-78), Phi Beta Kappa. Democrat. Eastern Orthodox. Home: 603 Longleaf Dr Chapel Hill NC 27517-3039

TRENBEATH, THOMAS L. state legislator, lawyer; b. Neche, N.D., July 23, 1948; m. Rose Trenbeath; children: Ian, Britta. BS, U. N.D., 1970, JD, 1978. Underwriting atty. Chgo. Title Ins. Co., Denver, 1981-84; v.p. Ticor Title Ins. Co., Denver, 1984—86; ptnr. Fleming, DuBois & Trenbeath, Attys., 1986-97; city adminstr., atty., 1997—; mem. N.D. Senate from 10th dist.,

2001—. Mem. ct. svcs. adminstrn. com. N.D. Supreme Ct., 1995—; dir. Red River Regional Coun., 1999—. Capt. USAR, 1971-78. Mem. N.D. Assn. Mcpl. Power Sys. (v.p. 1999—), N.D. Bar Assn., N.D. Humanities Coun. Republican. Lutheran. Office: PO Box 361 Cavalier ND 58220-0361 E-mail: rosentom@polarcomm.com., ttrenbea@state.nd.us.

TRENBERTH, KEVIN EDWARD, atmospheric scientist; b. Christchurch, New Zealand, Nov. 8, 1944; came to U.S., 1977; s. Edward Maurice and Ngaira Ivy (Eyre) T.; m. Gail Neville Thompson, Mar. 21, 1970; children: Annika Gail, Angela Dawn. BSc with honors, U. Canterbury, Christchurch, 1966; ScD, MIT, 1972. Meteorologist New Zealand Meteorol. Service, Wellington, 1966-76, supt. dynamic meteorology, 1976-77; assoc. prof. meteorology U. Ill., Urbana, 1977-82, prof., 1982-84; scientist Nat. Ctr. Atmospheric Research, Boulder, Colo., 1984-86, sr. scientist, 1986—, leader empirical studies group, 1987, head sect. climate analysis, 1987—; dep. dir. climate and global dynamics divsn. Nat. Ctr. Atmospheric Rsch., Boulder, Colo., 1991-95. Mem. joint sci. com. for world climate rsch. programme, com. climate changes and the ocean Tropical Oceans Global Atmosphere Program Sci. Steering Group, 1990-94; mem. Climate Variability and Predictability Sci. Steering Group, 1995—, co-chair, 1996-99; mem. joint sci. com. World Climate Rsch. Program, 1999—, officer 2002—. Editor: Climate System Modeling, 1992, Earth Interactions, 1996-98; contbr. Intergovernmental Panel on Climate Change, 1990, 92, lead author, 1995, 2001; contbr. articles to profl. jours. Recipient Disting. Achievement award Nat. Ctr. Atmospheric Rsch., 2003; grantee NSF, NOAA, NASA. Fellow Am. Meteorol. Soc. (editor sci. jour. 1981-86, com. chmn. 1985-87, Editor's award 1989, Jule G. Charney award 2000), AAAS (coun. del. sect. atmosphere and hydrosphere sci. 1993-97), Royal Soc. New Zealand (hon.); mem. NAS (earth scis. com. 1982-85, tropical oceans global atmosphere adv. panel 1984-87, polar rsch. bd. 1986-90, climate rsch. com. 1987-90, global oceans atmosphere land sys. panel 1994-98, panel on reconciling temperature observations, 1999-2000, com. on global change rsch. 1999-02), Meterol. Soc. New Zealand. Home: 5697 Pennsylvania Pl Boulder CO 80303 Office: Nat Ctr Atmospheric Rsch PO Box 3000 Boulder CO 80307-3000 Office Phone: 303-497-1318. Business E-Mail: trenbert@ucar.edu.

TRENCH, WILLIAM FREDERICK, mathematician, educator; b. Trenton, N.J., July 31, 1931; s. George Daniel and Anna Elizabeth (Taylor) Trench; m. Lucille Ann Marasco, Dec. 26, 1954 (div. Dec. 1978); children: Joseph William, Randolph Clifford, John Frederick, Gina Margaret; m. Beverly Joan Busenshut, Nov. 22, 1980. BA in Math., Lehigh U., 1953; AM, U. Pa., 1955, PhD, 1958. Applied mathematician Moore Sch. Elec. Engring., U. Pa., 1953-56; with GE Corp., Phila., 1956-57, Philco Corp., Phila., 1957-59, RCA, Moorestown, NJ, 1959—64; assoc. prof. math. Drexel U., Phila., 1964-67, prof., 1967-86; Andrew G. Cowles disting. prof. math. Trinity U., San Antonio, 1986-97, prof. emeritus, 1997—. Author: Multivariable Calculus with Linear Algebra and Series, 1972, Elementary Differential Equations, 2000, Elementary Differential Equations with Boundary Value, 2001, Advanced Calculus, 1978, Introduction to Real Analysis, 2003; author: (with Bernard Kolman) Elementary Multivariable Calculus, 1971; contbr. articles to profl. jours. Mem.: Internat. Linear Algebra Soc., Soc. Indsl. and Applied Math., Am. Math. Soc., Phi Beta Kappa, Pi Mu Epsilon, Eta Kappa Nu. Achievements include development of of Trench's Algorithm for inversion of finite Toeplitz matrices; of fast algorithms for computing eigenvalues of structured matrices; of asymptotic theory of solutions of nonlinear functional differential equations under mild integral smallness conditions; of Trench's canonical form for disconjugate differential operators. Home: 95 Pine Ln Woodland Park CO 80863-9535 E-mail: wtrench@trinity.edu.

TRENCHER, WILLIAM MANNES, lawyer; b. Bklyn., Mar. 9, 1947; s. B. Bernard and Lillian (F.) T.; m. Susan, June 20, 1970; children— Emily, Julie, Daniel. BA, Am. U., 1969, JD, 1972. Bar: Va. 1973, D.C., Md. Adminstr. Am. U. Law Inst., Washington, 1972-75, dir. Moot Ct. program; assoc. rsch. sci. Am. Inst. for Rsch., Washington, 1975-80; atty. Adminstrv. Office of U.S. Cts., Washington, 1980-88; trial atty. tax divsn. Dept. Justice, Washington, 1988-90; prin., founding ptnr. Steffan & Trencher, P.C., Fairfax, Va., 1990-92; counsel Bayh, Connaughton & Malone, P.C., Washington, 1992-95; gen. counsel Commerce Funding Corp., Vienna, Va., 1995-98; chief counsel U.S. Internat. Trade Commn. Fellow Am. U. Law Inst.; mem. Legal Aid Soc. Home: 9723 St Andrews Dr Fairfax VA 22030-1856 Office: USITC 500 E St NW Washington DC 20436-0003

TRENEFF, CRAIG PAUL, lawyer; b. Columbus, Ohio, July 16, 1952; s. Christ and Marlene Sue (Bach) T.; m. Loraine Marsh Treneff, July 12, 1986. BA, Ohio State U., 1974; JD, Capital U., 1981. Bar: Ohio 1981, U.S. Dist. Ct. (so. dist.) Ohio 1982. Legis. asst. Ohio House Rep., Columbus, 1974-81; law clk. Ohio Supreme Ct., Columbus, 1981-83; assoc. Morrow, Gordon & Byrd, Newark, 1983-84; counsel atty. Teaford, Rich & Dorsey, Columbus, 1984-85; ptnr. Schottenstein, Treneff & Williams, Columbus, 1985-97, Treneff & Williams, Columbus, 1997-2001; prin. Craig P. Treneff Law Office, 2001—. Del. coord. Gore for Pres., Ohio, 1988; mgr. Franklin County Treas. campaign, 1988; rsch. coord. Brown for Ohio Sec. campaign, 1982, 90, Franklin County Profls. campaign, 1980; treas. Ohioans with Sherrod Brown; pres. bd. trustees Directions for Youth; mem. Zoning Bd. Appeals, Westerville, Ohio, 1990-95, 96; chmn. Planning Commn., Westerville, Ohio, 1996—. Fellow Am. Acad. Matrimonial Lawyers; mem. ABA, Columbus Bar Assn., Ohio Bar Assn. (bd. cert. family rels. law specialist). Democrat. Lutheran. Home: 148 Executive Ct Westerville OH 43081-1474 Office: Craig P Treneff Law Offices 555 S Front St Ste 320 Columbus OH 43215-5668 E-mail: cptreneff@cs.com.

TRENNEPOHL, GARY LEE, university administrator, finance educator; b. Detroit, Dec. 6, 1946; s. Leo Donald and Wilma Mae (Tiesnvold) T.; m. Sandra K. Yeager, June 9, 1968; children: Paige E., Adrienne A. BS, U. Tulsa, 1968; MBA, Utah State U., 1971; PhD, Tex. Tech. U., 1976. Asst. prof. aero. studies Tex. Tech. U., Lub 1972-74; asst./assoc. prof. fin. Ariz. State U., Tempe, 1977—82; prof. U. Mo., Columbia, 1982-86, dir. Sch. Bus., 1984-86; prof., head dept. fin. Tex. A&M U., College Station, 1986-91, assoc. dean Coll. Bus., 1991-93, Peters prof. fin., 1992-95, exec. assoc. dean, 1994-95; dean Coll. Bus. Okla. State U., Stillwater, 1995-99; pres. Okla. State U.-Tulsa, 1999—. Mem. faculty Options Inst., Chgo. Bd. Options Exch., 1987—; bd. dirs. NCCJ, Blue Cross/Blue Shield. Author: An Introduction to Financial Management, 1984, Investment Management, 1993; assoc. editor Jour. Fin. Rsch., 1983-96; contr. chpts. Encyclopedia of Investments, Options: Essential Concepts; contbr. articles to profl. jours. Capt. USAF, 1968-72. Decorated Commendation medal with oak leaf cluster, Vietnam Svc. medal. Mem. Fin. Mgmt. Assn. (v.p. program 1993, pres. 1993-94), Met. Tulsa C. of C. (bd. dirs.). Lutheran. Office: Okla State U Tulsa 700 N Greenwood Ave Tulsa OK 74106-0702 Office Phone: 918-594-8001. Business E-Mail: garyt@osu-tulsa.okstate.edu.

TRENSE, SHARON, state legislator; b. Nov. 23, 1939; m. Charles Trense; 2 children. Student, Northwestern U. Owner Sharons of Dunwoody; mem. Ga. Ho. of Reps., 1992—. Mem. edn., human rels. and aging coms., mem. state inst. and property coms. Republican. Methodist. Office: Ga Ho of Reps State Capitol Atlanta GA 30334 Home: 2296 Littlebrooke Dr Atlanta GA 30338-3154

TRENT, CHARLES H., JR., social work educator; b. Abingdon, Va., Sept. 25, 1939; s. Charles Howard Sr. and Sue Sheffey (Coffee) T.; m. Gina Fiering, May 30, 1993. BA, Pace U., 1972; MSW, NYU, 1974; PhD, Fordham U., 1985. Admissions counselor Cooper Union, N.Y.C., 1969-74; supr. II social worker Rapid Intervention Project, N.Y.C., 1974-75; coord. SSI Advocacy Ctr., Hempstead, N.Y., 1975-77; dir. Project Life, N.Y.C., 1977-88; exec. dir. East Harlem Com. on Aging, Inc., N.Y.C., 1977—; asst. prof. Yeshiva U., N.Y.C., 1985-88, assoc. prof., 1985—. Adj. instr., assoc. prof. Fordham U., N.Y.C., 1983—; bd. dirs. Welfare Rsch. Inc., Albany, N.Y. With USAF. Fellow NIMH, 1972-74, Coun. on Social Work Edn. fellow NIMH, 1981-85; Brookdale Inst. scholar, 1981. Mem. NASW, Soc. for Study of Social Problems, Coun. on Social Work Edn., Soc. for Social Work Rsch., Assn. Cmty. Organizers and Social Adminstrs., Fifth Ave. Com. Avocations: writing, reading, computers, sports. Office: Yeshiva U 2495 Amsterdam Ave New York NY 10033-3312 Home: 118 Penn Est East Stroudsburg PA 18301-9029 E-mail: CO925S@aol.com.

TRENT, DARRELL M. academic and corporate executive; b. Neosho, Mo., Aug. 2, 1938; s. Clarence Melvin and Edna Ruth T.; m. Judith Mercy Turner; children: Darrell Michael, Derek Montgomery, Mercy Ruth. AB, Stanford U., 1961; postgrad., Internat. Law Sch., The Hague, Netherlands, summer 1961, Wharton Grad. Sch. Bus., U. Pa., summer 1962; MBA, Columbia U., 1964. Owner, mgr. Trent Enterprises, Kans. and Mo., 1963-66; pres., chief exec. officer N.Am. Carmen, Ltd., Del., 1965-68, Assoc. Stores, Inc., Okla., 1967-69, Plaza Supermarkets, Inc., Kans., 1966-69, Food Service, Inc., Kans., 1966-69, Supermarkets, Inc., Kans., 1966-69, Acton Devel. Co., Inc., Kans., 1966-81; research/writer Nixon for Pres., 1968; staff dir. for personnel Presdl. Transition, 1968-69; commr. Property Mgmt. and Disposal Service, GSA, 1969; dep. asst. to Pres. U.S., 1969-70; exec. dir. Property Rev. Bd., Exec. Office of Pres., 1969-73; dep. dir. Office Emergency Preparedness, 1970-72, acting dir., 1973; mem. Cost of Living Council, 1973, Oil Policy Com., 1973; chmn. Joint Bd. Fuel Supply and Fuel Transp., 1973, mem. NSC, 1973; chmn. Pres.'s Adv. Council CD, 1973; U.S. mem. NATO Sr. Civil Emergency Planning Com., 1973; sr. research fellow Hoover Inst., Stanford U., 1974-81, 89-94, sr. advisor, 1998—, assoc. dir., 1974-81, bd. overseers, 1985-89; dep. campaign mgr. Citizens for Reagan, 1976; dep. campaign mgr., cons. Reagan for Pres. Com., 1979-80, sr. policy advisor, 1980; dir. Office Policy Coordination, Presdl. Transition, 1980-81; U.S. alt. rep. Nato Com. Challenges of Modern Soc., 1982-83; dep. sec. U.S. Dept. Transp., 1981-82, acting sec., 1982-83; chmn. U.S. del. European Civil Aviation Com. with rank ambassador, 1983-88; chmn. Action Devel. Corp., Inc., 1988—; chmn., chief exec officer Rollins Environ. Svcs., Inc., 1983-88, TEC Systems, Inc., 1990-91, Clean Earth Tech., Inc., 1992-93. Chmn. Fed. Home Loan Bank Pitts., 1983-91; cons. ACDA, 1974-81, HUD, 1974, Dept. Commerce, 1974-76; bd. advisors Chronicle Info. Svcs., Inc., 1984-87. Author: The U.S. and Transnational Terrorism, 1980, Transportation: Policy, Goals, Accomplishments, 1984; co-author: Terrorism: Threat, Reality, Response, 1979; contbr. articles to profl. publs. Bd. regents Pepperdine U., 1985-92; bd. dirs. Found. Teach Econs., 1988-90; dep. chmn. Ronald Reagan Presdl. Found., 1985-88. Mem. Bohemian Club. Republican. Methodist. Office: 1610 S Broadway St Ste C Pittsburg KS 66762-5845

TRENT, DONALD STEPHEN, thermo fluids engineer; b. Cloverdale, Oreg., Mar. 29, 1935; s. James Charles and Emma (Bauer) T.; (div. Jan., 1986); children: Steve, Lynn Trent Wooldridge, Greg; m. Alta Mae Brown, Aug. 20, 1994. BSAE, Oregon State U., 1962, MSME, 1964, PhD in Mech. Engring., 1972. Chief scientist (emeritus) Battelle Meml. Inst., Richland, Wash., 1965-96; retired, 1996; cons., 1996—. Cons. in field, 1996—; courtesy prof. Oreg. State U., Corvallis, 1987—; rsch. affiliate MIT, Cambridge, Mass., 1990—; mem. tchg. staff Wash. State U., Richland, 1991—; vis. U. Md., College Park, 1995—. Sgt. U.S. Army, 1958-61. Recipient Fed. Lab. Consortium award, 1992. Mem. ASME, Phi Kappa Phi, Sigma Xi. Achievements include patent on a heat pipe; 2 copyrights on computational fluid dynamics software. Home: 1225 Country Ridge Dr Richland WA 99352-7763 Address: 1225 Country Ridge Dr Richland WA 99352-7763

TRENT, GRACE CHEN, communications executive; Sr. v.p. pub. rels., chief of staff MCI, Inc., Ashburn, Va., 2003—. Named Pub. Rels. Profl. of Yr., Pub. Rels. Soc. Am., 2004. Office: MCI Inc 22001 Loudoun County Pkwy Ashburn VA 20147*

TRENT, JOHN THOMAS, JR., lawyer; b. Hammond, Ind., Mar. 11, 1954; s. John Thomas and Sally (Ritter) T.; m. Laura Marie Nelson, Aug. 5, 1978; children: Lauren, Valerie, Alex. AB, Wabash Coll., 1976; JD, Vanderbilt U., 1979. Bar: Tenn. 1979, U.S. Dist. Ct. (mid. dist.) Tenn. Mng. dir. Boult, Cummings, Conners & Berry P.L.C., Nashville, 1979—. Spkr., panelist real estate and other groups. Chmn. adminstrv. bd. and other coms. and offices West End United Meth. Ch., Nashville, 1983—99; bd. dirs. Cumberland Sci. Mus., 1997—, Jr. Achievement Middle Tenn. Fellow Nashville Bar; mem. ABA, Nat. Assn. Indsl. and Office Parks (past bd. dirs. Nashville chpt.), Tenn. Bar Assn., Nashville Bar Assn., Nat. Assn. Bond Lawyers, Assn. Attys. and Execs. in Corp. Real Estate. Office: Boult Cummings Connors & Berry PLC 414 Union St Ste 1600 Nashville TN 37219-1744

TRENT, LUTHER E. airport executive, state agency executive; Dir. airports Oklahoma City Dept. Airports; exec. dir Will Rogers World Airport, Oklahoma City, 1993—. Office: Will Rogers World Airport 7100 Terminal Dr Unit 937 Oklahoma City OK 73159-0937

TRENT, ROBERT HAROLD, retired business educator; b. Norfolk, Va., Aug. 3, 1933; s. Floyd Murton and Myrtle Eugenia (White) T.; m. Joanne Bell, Aug. 17, 1951; 1 child, John Thomas BS, U. Richmond, 1963; PhD, U. N.C., 1968. Asst. prof. U. N.C., Chapel Hill, 1968-69; assoc. prof. commerce McIntire Sch. Commerce U. Va., Charlottesville, 1970-74, prof. commerce, 1975-84, Ralph A. Beeton prof. free enterprise, 1985-91; C. & P. Telephone Co. prof. commerce U. Va., Charlottesville, 1991-98, prof. commerce emeritus, 1998—. Co-author: Marketing Decision Making, 1976, 4th edit., 1988; editor: Developments in Management Information Systems, 1974 Mem. Beta Gamma Sigma, Omicron Delta Kappa.

TRENT, WENDELL CAMPBELL, business owner; b. Sneedville, Tenn., Nov. 1, 1940; s. William Campbell and Inez Hall (Dauherty) T.; m. Donne Lee Posey, May 31, 1964. BA, Berea Coll., 1963; MPH, UCLA, 1971; D in Pub. Adminstrn., Nova U., 1980. Asst. USPHS UCLA, 1969; pres. Lockwood MacDonald Hosp., Petoskey, Mich., 1971-75, Allegan Gen. Hosp., Mich., 1984-85, Bethany Meth. Hosp., Chgo., 1979-84, St. Ansgar Hosp., Moorhead, Minn., 1984-85, Meml. Hosp., Lawrenceville, Ill., 1985-89; midwest devel. dir. Brim Healthcare, 1989-90; prin. Larson & Trent Assocs., Jefferson City, Tenn., 1990—. Mem. Gov.'s Health Care Task Force; mem. Govs. Com. on Healthcare. Contbr. articles to profl. jours. Maj. USAF, 1963-69. Decorated Bronze Star. Fellow Am. Coll. Hosp. Adminstrs. (article of yr. com.); mem. Rotary, Kiwanis. Republican. Presbyterian. Avocations: photography, amateur radio. Home: 1290 Hickory Hills Rd Jefferson City TN 37760-5316

TRENTANELLI, JOHN ANTHONY, educational administrator; b. Cleve., Oct. 18, 1939; s. Frank Joseph and Marie Theresa Trentanelli; m. Barbara Kay Trentanelli, Apr. 30, 1977; 1 child, Angela Rose. BS in Edn., S.E. Mo. State U., 1969; postgrad., Cleve. State U., 1980-81; M. Edn. and Adminstrn., Prarie View A&M U., Tex., 1987. Substitute tchr. Parma (Ohio) Pub. Sch. Dist., 1977-78; social studies tchr., Am. Fedn. Tchrs. rep. Cleve. Pub. Schs., 1978-81; social studies tchr., dept. chmn. Houston Ind. Sch. Dist., 1981-87, asst. prin., 1987-99, Yonkers (N.Y.) Pub. Sch. Dist., 1999—. Editor Galveston Bay Power Squadron, Bay Breeze, 1999. Treas. Galveston Bay Power Squadron, Clear Lake, Tex., 1999. Mem. ASCD, Pi Kappa Alpha (pres. Dist. 15, 1972-73). Avocation: power and sail boating. Office: Lincoln H S 375 Kneeland Ave Yonkers NY 10704 Home: 25 Spring Pond Dr Ossining NY 10562-2036 E-mail: jtrentanelli@yonkerspublicschool.org.

TREPANI, JOSEPH B. information technology executive; BS in Acct., Florida State U. CPA. V.p fin. Action Staffing, Inc., 1989—90; contr. Tech Data Corp., Clearwater, Fla., 1990—91, dir. ops., 1991—95, v.p. worldwide contr., 1995—98, sr. v.p., corp. contr., 1998—. Office: Tech Data Corp 5350 Tech Data Dr Clearwater FL 33760-3122

TREPP, LEO, rabbi; b. Mainz, Germany, Mar. 4, 1913; s. Maier and Selma (Hirschberger) T.; m. Miriam de Haas, Apr. 26, 1938 (dec. Dec. 15, 1999); 1 child, Susan Trepp Lachtman. PhD, U. Wurzburg, Germany, 1935, U. Oldenburg, 1989; DD, Hebrew Union Coll., 1985; postgrad., Harvard U., 1944-45; PhD (hon.), U. Wurzburg, 1985. Ordained rabbi, 1936. Rabbi various temples, various locations, 1940-51; part-time rabbi Santa Rosa, Calif., 1951-61, Eureka, Calif., 1961-90; rabbi emeritus, 1990; Jewish chaplain Vets. Home of Calif., Yountville, Calif., 1954-98; prof. philosophy Napa Valley Coll., 1951-83, prof. emeritus, 1983—; prof. Judaic studies U. Mainz, 1983—. Guest lectr. Humboldt Univ., Berlin, 2003. Author: Eternal Faith, Eternal People - A Journey into Judaism, 1962, Judaism, Development and Life, 1966, 4th edit., 2000, A History of the Jewish Experience, 1974, 2d edit., 2001, The Complete Book of Jewish Observance, 1980, Judaism and the Religions of Humanity, 1985, What if Shylock were a Marrano, 1985, The Controversy between Samson Raphael Hirsch and Seligmann Baer Bamberger—Halakhical and Societal Implications, 1991, Yamim Nora'im: The Traditional Liturgy and "Gates of Repentance", 1991; author numerous books in other langs.; major works include Die Juden, 1982, 2d edit., 1998, Jüdische Ethik, 1988, Der jüdische Gottesdienst—Form und Entfaltung, 1991, enlarged edit., 2003, Die Amerikanischen Juden—Profil einer Gemeinschaft, 1991, Jüdisches Denken im 20 Jahrhundant, 1992; (with G. Mayer) Abriss der jüdischen Geschichte, 1992; Gerchichte der Deutschen Juden, 1996, Das Vermächtnis der deutschen Juden, 2000, Liturgical Chants of the Synagogue at Mainz, 2001, (CD) Niguney Magenza, 2001; contbr. articles to profl. jours. Mem. Napa Planning Commn., 1964-69. Recipient Great Seal, City of Oldenburg, 1971, George Washington Honor medal, Freedoms Found., 1979; hon. freeman City of Oldenburg, 1990, Hon. Senator, U. Mainz, 1996, Gutenberg Plaquette, City of Mainz, 1993, Cross of Merit 1st class Germany, 1997, Ring of Honor, City of Mainz, 2003, Price Land of Oldenburg, 2003, Symposium in his honor, Univ. of Mainz, 2003; new Jewish chapel named in his honor Vets. Home Calif., 1997; commendation Assembly Calif. Legis., 1998. Mem. Ctrl. Conf. Am. Rabbis, Rabbinical Assembly, Am. Philos. Assn., Am. Acad. Religion, No. Calif. Bd. Rabbis. Home: 820 Mission Ave Apt 9 San Rafael CA 94901-3251 E-mail: leotrepp@worldnet.att.net.

TREPPLER, IRENE ESTHER, retired state senator; b. St. Louis County, Mo., Oct. 13, 1926; d. Martin H. and Julia C. (Bender) Hagemann; student Meramec Community Coll., 1972; m. Walter J. Treppler, Aug. 18, 1950; children: John M., Steven A., Diane V. Anderson, Walter W. Payroll chief USAF Aero. Chart Plant, 1943-51; enumerator U.S. Census Bur., St. Louis, 1960, crew leader, 1970; mem. Mo. Ho. of Reps., Jefferson City, 1972-84; mem. Mo. Senate, Jefferson City, 1985-96; chmn. minority caucus, 1991-92. Active Gravois Twp. Rep. Club, Concord Twp. Rep. Club; alt. del. Rep. Nat. Conv., 1976, 84; mem. Mo. Adv. Coun. on Hist. Preservation, 1998—; gov. apptd. Mo. Adv. Coun. on Hist. Preservation, 1998—. Recipient Spirit of Enterprise award Mo. C. of C., 1992, appreciation award Mo. Med. Assn., Nat. Otto Nuttli Earthquake Hazard Mitigation award, 1993, Disting. Legislator award Cmty. Colls. Mo., 1995; named Concord Twp. Rep. of Yr., 1992. Mem. Nat. Order Women Legislators (rec. sec. 1981-82, pres. 1985), Nat. Fedn. Rep. Women. Mem. Evangelical Ch.

TRESCOTT, PAUL BARTON, economics professor; b. Bloomsburg, Pa., Nov. 22, 1925; s. Paul Henry and Stella Henrietta (Potts) T.; children by previous marriage: Jeffrey A., Jill V., Andrew B. (dec.); m. Kathleen Colcord, Aug. 15, 1982. BA, Swarthmore Coll., 1949; MA, Princeton U., 1951, PhD, 1954. Reporter Evening Bulletin, Phila., 1948; instr. in econ. Princeton (N.J.) U., 1952-54; asst. assoc. prof. Kenyon Coll., Gambier, Ohio, 1954-67; prof. in econs. Miami U., Oxford, Ohio, 1967-69; prof. in econs., history So. Meth. U., Dallas, 1969-76; prof. in econs. So. Ill. U., Carbondale, 1976—. Vis. prof. in econs. Thammassat U., Bangkok, 1965-67, People's U., Beijing, 1992; vis. prof. in fin. U. Ill., Champaign and Urbana, 1981; acad. adv. commn. to Thailand U.S. Dept. State, Washington, 1968-70. Authors: Money, Banking and Economic Welfare, 1960, 2d edit., 1965, Financing American Enterprise, 1963, rep., 1982, The Logic of the Price System, 1970, Thailand's Monetary Experience, 1971. Sgt. U.S. Army, 1944-46. Rsch. grantee Brookings Inst., Washington, 1961-62; Fulbright scholar U.S. Govt., Peking U., China, 1983-84, Tech. U., Czestochowa, Poland, 1996. Mem. Am. Econs. Assn., History Econs. Soc. Avocations: music, travel. Office: So Ill U Dept Econs Carbondale IL 62901 Office Phone: 618-536-7746.

TRESHIE, R. DAVID, former newspaper publishing executive; Publ. The Orange County Register, Santa Ana, Calif., ret., 1999. Office: The Orange County Register 625 N Grand Ave Santa Ana CA 92701-4347

TRESKOV, YAKOV MAKS, engineer; b. St. Petersburg, Russia, May 13, 1936; arrived in U.S., 1994; s. Maks Treskov and Erena Beylenson; m. Zinaida Treskov; children: Erena, Tatiana. Diploma in engring., Inst. Elec. Engring., Leningrad, Russia, 1965. Specialist radar equipment on submarines, Leningrad, 1965—92; P.S. technician Block Sci. Inc., NJ, 1994—2001. Home: 2329 Hudson Terr Apt B5 Fort Lee NJ 07024 Home Fax: 201-461-4703.

TRESSLAR, NOLA V. artist, retired marketing professional, retired foundation administrator; b. Tacoma, Mar. 10, 1942; d. Arthur and Viola Mafalda (Sirianni Di Carlo) De Caro; m. Lloyd E. Montgomery, Dec. 8, 1961 (div. 1971); children: Gina N. Montgomery, Melissa R. Montgomery; m. Walter B. Swain, Mar. 11, 1977 (div. 1994); m. Guy E. Tresslar, May 16, 1997. Student, U. Puget Sound, 1959-62. First woman cert. real estate appraiser Wash. Appraiser/assessor Pierce County Assessors Office, Tacoma, 1971-77; chief appraiser Otero Savs. & Loan, Colorado Springs, 1977-78; pvt. fee appraiser, co-owner N.W.S. & Assocs., Colorado Springs, 1978—. Pres., designer N.V.S. Enterprises, Colorado Springs, 1980—89; dir. mktg. U.S. West Edn. Found., Seattle, 1990—92; exec. dir. N.W. Baby Talk, 1993—95; designer numerous gift items. Fund devel., pub. rels. mgr. Child Abuse Prevention Resources, 1995—; mem. cultural enrichment adv. coun. MetroParks of Pierce County, 1997—. Recipient Women at Work award, Coun. Working Women, 1985, Pub. Svc. award, Colorado Springs Assn. Life Underwriters, 1985, Booster of the Yr. award, Salesman With a Purpose, 1986. Mem.: NOW, NAFE, Sumi Coll. and Mixed Media Painting, Cultural Enrichment Adv. Coun. Met. Parks, Soc. Real Estate Appraisers (candidate, treas. 1978, bd. dirs. 1982—84), Tacoma Jr. League (cmty. adv. bd.), Urban League, Chi Omega Alumnae. Democrat. Avocations: travel, sumi painting, crafts, photography, volunteering.

TRESTMAN, FRANK D. distribution company executive, director; b. Mpls., Sept. 3, 1934; s. Saul and Rose (Hyster) T.; m. Carol Lynn Wasserman, Apr. 3, 1960; children— Lisa Ellen, Jill Susan BBA with high distinction, U. Minn., 1955. Exec. v.p., treas. Napco Industries, Inc., Mpls., 1965-74, pres., dir., 1974-84; chmn, CEO Mass Merchandisers, Inc., Hopkins, Minn., 1984-86; pres. Trestman Enterprises, Golden Valley, Minn., 1987—. Bd. dirs. Best Buy Co., Mpls., Western Container Corp., Mpls., T.C.F. Industries, Metris Cos., Inc., Where to Live.com; chmn. Avalon Real Estate Group., Mpls., Camir Investment Co., Mpls. Mem. bd. govs. Mt. Sinai Hosp., Mpls., 1978-91, Abbott Northwestern Hosp., 1993-2002; chmn. bd. trustees Mpls. Fedn. Endowment Fund; bd. dirs. Harry Kay Found. With USN, 1957-58. Mem. Oak Ridge Country Club (Hopkins). Office: Trestman Enterprises 5500 Wayzata Blvd Ste 1045 Minneapolis MN 55416-1241

TRETHEWEY, NATASHA, poet, literature educator; b. Gulfport, Miss., 1966; BA in English, U. Ga.; MA in English and Creative Writing, Hollins U.; MFA in Poetry, U. Mass. Instr. Auburn U.; poet, assoc. prof. English Emory U., Atlanta, 2001—. Author: Domestic Work, 2000 (Cave Canem Poetry prize, 1999, Miss. Inst. of Arts and Letters Book prize, 2001, Lillian Smith award for peotry, 2001), Bellocq's Ophelia; contbr. poetry to publs. Recipient Disting. Young Alumna award, U. Mass., Julia Peterkin award, Converse Coll., Grolier Poetry prize, Grolier Bookstore, Cambridge, Mass., Margaret Walker award for poetry, Poets and Writers mag. and QBR: The Black Book Rev., Jessica Nobel-Maxwell Meml. award for poetry, Am. Poetry Rev.; fellow, John Simon Guggenheim Meml. Found., 2003, Nat. Endowment for the Arts, Ala. State Coun. on the Arts, Money for Women/Barbara Deming Meml. Fund; Bunting fellow, Radcliffe Inst. for Advanced Study, Radcliffe U., 2000—01. Office: Emory Univ Creative Writing Program 537 Kilgo Cir Atlanta GA 30322

TRETZ, CHRISTOPHE ROBERT, electrical engineer; b. Strasbourg, France, Mar. 22, 1968; arrived in U.S., 1991; s. Philippe and Liliane (Gué) T. Diplôme d'Ingénieur, Ecole Nationale Supérieure d'Electronique, d'Electrotechnique, d'Informatique, d'Hydraulique de Toulouse, Toulouse, France, 1991; MS, Columbia U., N.Y.C., 1992; MPh, Columbia U., 1995, PhD, 1997. Rsch. asst. Columbia U., N.Y.C., 1992-97; adv. engr. IBM Rsch., Yorktown Heights, N.Y., 1997-2000, rsch. staff mem., 2000; mem. tech. staff

design engr. Advanced Micro Devices, Sunnyvale, Calif., 2000—03; sr. cir. design engr. IBM Engring. and Tech. Svcs., San Jose, Calif., 2003—. Rsch. mentor Semiconductor Rsch. Corp., Durham, N.C., 1997—. Mem. IEEE (tech. com. internat. soi conf. 1998-2001, pub. rels. and publicity chair internat. soi conf. 2001-02, sr. com. internat. soi conf. 2001-02, short course chair internat. soi conf. 2002, treas., exec. com. internat. soi conf. 2003—, treas. internat. soi conf., 2003, local arrangement chair internat. sci. conf. 2004). Roman Catholic. Achievements include inventor reduction of hysteresis in soi cmos circuits, method and system to tune integrated circuit, method and system for selecting sizes of components for integrated circuits. Avocations: skiing, golf, wine-tasting, gourmet cooking. Home: 235 Briar Ridge Dr San Jose CA 95123-2667 Office: IBM E&TS San Jose Design Ctr 5600 Cottle Rd Mail Stop F010 San Jose CA 95193 E-mail: ctretz@us.ibm.com.

TREU, JESSE ISAIAH, venture capitalist; b. N.Y.C., Apr. 10, 1947; BS, Rensselaer Poly. Inst., 1968; MA, Princeton U., 1971, PhD, 1973. Physicist, liaison sci. components, materials group Gen. Electric Co., Schenectady, N.Y., 1973-77; tech. dir. Technicon Corp., Tarrytown, N.Y., 1977-82; v.p. Channing Weinberg-CW Ventures, N.Y.C., 1982-85; gen. ptnr. Domain Assocs., Princeton, N.J., 1986—. Office: Domain Assocs 1 Palmer Sq Princeton NJ 08542-3718

TREUMANN, WILLIAM BORGEN, university dean; b. Grafton, N.D., Feb. 26, 1916; s. William King and Dagny Helen (Borgen) T.; m. Mildred Elizabeth Jenkins, Aug. 14, 1948; children— Richard Roy, Robert Evan, Beverly Kay. BS, U. N.D., 1942; MA, U. Ill., 1944, PhD, 1947. Teaching asst. chemistry U. Ill., 1942-45, teaching asst. math., 1945-46, vis. prof., summers 1948-50; from asst. prof. to prof. chemistry N.D. State U., 1946-55; mem. faculty Minn. State U. Moorhead, 1960—, prof. chemistry, 1962—, asso. dean acad. affairs, 1968-70, dean faculty math. and sci., 1970—. Contbr. to profl. jours. Research Corp. Am. grantee, 1954; Minn. U. Bd. grantee, 1967 Fellow Am. Inst. Chemists; mem. Am. Chem. Soc., Am. Assn. U. Profs., Minn. Acad. Sci., Fedn. Am. Scientists, Phi Beta Kappa, Sigma Xi. Home: 1809 11th Ave S Fargo ND 58103 Office: Math Dept Moorhead State U Moorhead MN 56560

TREUSCH, PAUL ELLSWORTH, law educator, lawyer; b. Chgo. m. Phyllis Freedman, 1941; 1 child, Karen Treusch Lord. PhB, U. Chgo., 1932; JD cum laude, 1935. Bar: Ill. 1935, D.C. 1945, Mass. 1974, U.S. SUpreme Ct. 1939. Ovt. practice, Chgo., 1935-37; mem. law faculty La. State. U., Baton Rouge, 1937-38; atty. Office of Chief Counsel IRS, Washington, 1938-70; mem. excess profits tax coun., 1948-51; asst. chief counsel (litigation), 1951-70; adj. prof. law Howard U., Washington, 1965-70; prof., 1970-73, 76-79; prof. emeritus, 1979—. Professorial lectr. law George Washington U., 1966-73; prof. law Boston U., 1973 -76, prof. emeritus, 1976—; head Washington office Winston Strawn, Chgo., 1970-73; prof. Southwestern U. L.A., 1979—; lectr. Zhongshan U. Law Dept., 1991—, Hong Kong U. and City U. Law Schs., 1991—. Co-author: treatise: Tax Exempt Charitable Organizations, 1978, 83, sole author 3d edit., 1988; contbr. to numerous pubs. Bd. dirs., legal counsel Burgundy Farm Country Day Sch.; bd. dirs. Washington Inst. Mental Hygiene. Mem. Fed. Bar Assn. (nat. pres. 1969-70, nat. coun.), Fed. Bar Found (dir.), ABA (life; exempt orgn. and internat. law coms.), Am. Law Inst. (life). Clubs: Cosmos (Washington); Nat. Press (Washington); Los Angeles Athletic. Office: Southwestern U Sch Law 675 S Westmoreland Ave Los Angeles CA 90005-3992 Fax: 213-383-1688. Office Phone: 213-738-6756. E-mail: PTreusch@swlaw.edu.

TREUTING, EDNA GANNON, retired nursing administrator, retired nursing educator; b. New Orleans, Dec. 16, 1925; d. Alphonse Joseph and Clara Josephine (David) Gannon; m. August Raymond Treuting, Sept. 4, 1948 (dec.); children: Keith, Karen Treuting Stein, Madeline Treuting LeBlanc, Jaime Treuting Gonzales, Jay (dec.). Diploma, Charity Hosp. Sch. Nursing, New Orleans, 1946; BS in Nursing Edn., La. State U., 1953; MPH, Tulane U., 1972, DPH, 1978. RN, La.; cert. family nurse practitioner Tulane U. Head nurse premature nursery Charity Hosp., New Orleans, 1946-47, head nurse pediatrics, 1947-49; instr. pediatrics Charity Hosp. Sch. Nursing, New Orleans, 1949-52, 54, instr., LPN, 1953; pvt. duty Touro, Hotel Dieu, New Orleans, 1957-59; instr. maternal and child health La. State U. Sch. Nursing, New Orleans, 1960, 65, 69-71; from instr. to prof., sect. head Tulane Sch. Pub. Health and Tropical Medicine, New Orleans, 1972-83; dean, prof. Our Lady Holy Cross Coll. Nursing Div., New Orleans, 1983-84; chief nurse Dept. Health and Hosp., New Orleans, 1987-94. Region IV nurse practitioner Baylor U., Health Edn. and Welfare, 1974-76; citizen amb. to South Am. People to People, 1979; presentor U. Hawaii Pub. Health and Nursing, 1977; planner, advisor, reviewer continuing edn. U. Tenn., Memphis, 1990-95. Author, editor: Occupation Health Nursing, 1979; sect. head, prin. investigator Practitioner Programs Family and Pediatric, 1973-83; item writer Nurse Practitioners, Community Health and Occupational Nursing, 1974-80; mem. editl. bd. to sci. jours. and Nurse Practitioner Jour. Pres. Oti-Mrs. Internat., New Orleans, 1955-68; sponsor bd. dirs. Holy Cross H.S. Treuting Scholarship, New Orleans, 1966—; hurricane and disaster nurse ARC, New Orleans, 1966-77; v.p. Pandora Carnival Club, New Orleans, 1968-78; alternate state health dept. Commn. Nursing Supply and Demand by Legislation, 1991-94; planner, presentor La. State Rsch. Day, 1990-92. Named outstanding woman in the mainstream world's fair women of achievement, 1984. Mem. AARP (chpt. 3086 pres. 2000—. pres. 2001—), New Orleans Dist. Nurses Assn. (First J.B. Hickey Meml. Cmty. award 1985, Great 100 Nurse-First Yr. 1987), La. Pub. Health Assn. (Dr. C.B. White Merritorious Diligent Svc. 1990), La. Nurse Practitioners Assn.(Edna Treuting scholarship named in her honor), AARP (sr. mem., chpt. pres. 2001—), Tulane U. Alumni Assn. (past pres.), Tulane Med. Alumni Assn. (past pres.), New Image Club of Mandeville (chmn. 1986-2003), Mandeville Rep. Women, Young at Heart, Delta Omega (nat. and chpt. past pres.), Sigma Theta Tau. Republican. Roman Catholic. Avocations: travel, dance, swimming, photography, reading. Home: 1914 Marlin Dr Mandeville LA 70448-1069

TREVATHAN, EDWIN, neurologist, educator; b. Louisville, Nov. 3, 1956; s. Norman Edwin, Jr. and Joyce Brent (Sawyer) Trevathan; m. Linda Scott, Dec. 31, 1977; children: Scott, Daniel, Luke. BS in Biochemistry and Math., Lipscomb U., 1977; MD, MPH in Chronic Disease Epidemiology, Emory U., 1982. Diplomate Am. Bd. Psychiatry and Neurology, Am. Bd. Pediat., Am. Bd. Clin. Neurophysiology. Resident in pediats. Yale U. Sch. Medicine, New Haven, 1982-84; resident and fellow in neurology/child neurology Mass. Gen. Hosp., Harvard Med. Sch., Boston, 1984-87; fellow in neurophysiology and epilepsy Boston Children's Hosp., 1986-87; epidemic intelligence officer Ctrs. for Disease Control & Prevention, Atlanta, 1987-89; dir. Children's Epilepsy Ctr., chief neurology Scottish Rite Children's Med. Ctr., Atlanta, 1989-95; ptnr. Child Neurology Assocs., P.C., Atlanta, 1989-95; dir. Comprehensive Epilepsy Ctr. U. Ky. Coll. Medicine, Lexington, 1995-98; dir. Pediat. Epilepsy Ctr. Washington U. Sch. Medicine, St. Louis Children's Hosp., 1998—, prof. neurology & pediatrics, 2004—. Assoc. chief neurology svc. U. Ky. Coll. Medicine, Lexington, 1996—98. Contbr. articles to profl. jours. Bd. dirs., mem. Epilepsy Found. Am., Atlanta, 1991—95; bd. dirs. PREDISAN, Atlanta, 1994—; pres. profl. adv. bd. Epilepsy Found. Greater St. Louis, 1999—2003. With USPHS, 1987—89. Fellow: Royal Soc. Medicine (London); mem.: Am. Acad. Neurology, Alpha Omega Alpha. Office: Pediatric Epilepsy Ctr Washington U Dept Neurology PO Box 8111 660 S Euclid Ave Saint Louis MO 63110 Fax: (314) 454-4225. Business E-Mail: Trevathan@wustl.edu.

TREVENA, JOHN HARRY, lawyer; b. Dunedin, Fla., Dec. 28, 1961; s. Ernest Lewis and Lenora Geraldine (Adelson) T.; m. Susan Lee Corris, Nov. 23, 1988; 1 child, Samuel Alan. BA in criminal justice, Univ. S. Fla., 1982; Fla. Police standards, Pinellas Police Acad., 1982; JD, Stetson Univ., 1985. Bar: Fla., U.S. Dist. Ct. (mid. dist.) Fla. 1986; bd. cert. criminal trial lawyer, Fla. Pvt. practice, Largo, Fla. Editorial bd. Fla. Bar Jour., Fla. Bar News, 1990-93. Mem.: Tampa Bay Cath. Lawyers Guild, Inc., Am. Judicature Soc., Pinellas County Criminal Def. Lawyers Assn., Pinellas County Trial Lawyers Assn., Fla. Bar Assn., Clearwater and Am. Bar Assn., Nat. Assn. Criminal Def. Lawyers (life), Fla. Assn. Criminal Def. Lawyers (life). Roman Catholic. Democrat. Home: 423 Buttonwood Ln Largo FL 33770-4060 Office: 801 W Bay Dr Ste 509 Largo FL 33770-3220 E-mail: trevenalaw@aol.com.

TREVETT, THOMAS NEIL, lawyer; b. Rochester, N.Y., Mar. 14, 1942; S. Frank E. and Andrea (Kuhn) T.; m. Margaret H. Hepburn, July 29, 1967; children; Monica, Millicent, Thomas. BS, St. John Fisher Coll., 1964; JD, Albany Law Sch., 1967. Bar: N.Y. 1967, U.S. Dist. Ct. (we. dist.) N.Y. 1968. Assoc. Thomas J. Meagher, Rochester, 1967-68, Trevett, Lenweaver, Salzer, and predecessor Gough, Skipworth, Summers, Eves & Trevett, Rochester, 1968—; pres. Trevett, Lenweaver, Salzer, and predecessor Gough, Skipworth, 1985-89. N.Y. estate tax atty., 1974-92. State Dem. committeeman; bd. dirs. Genesee region March Dimes, Rochester Area Multiple Sclerosis Soc., chmn. bd., 1992-94; chmn. bd. trustees McQuaid Jesuit H.S., 1997-2003. Mem. ABA, N.Y. State Bar Assn., (ho. of dels. 1981, chmn. Ins. Negligence and Compensation Law sect. 1989-90, John E. Leach award, 1996), Monroe County Bar Assn. (trustee 1996—, pres. 1999—), Def. Rsch. Inst., Fedn. Def. and Corp. Counsel, Wayne County Bar. Assn. (pres. 1978-79). Roman Catholic. Office: 2 State St Ste 1000 Rochester NY 14614-1803 also: 2003 Ridge Rd Ontario NY 14519 Office Phone: 585-454-2181. E-mail: ttrevett@trevettetal.com.

TREVILLIAN, WALLACE DABNEY, retired economics professor, retired dean; b. Charlottesville, Va., May 1, 1918; s. Robert Carr and Mary Anna (Perry) Trevillian; m. Mary Lou McEachern, Nov. 28, 1963 (dec. Dec. 2001); children: Malcolm McEachern, Edward Dabney. BS, U. Va., 1940, MA, 1947, PhD, 1954; postgrad., U. Calif., 1950-51. Mem. faculty Clemson (S.C.) U., 1947—, from instr. to assoc. prof., 1947-55, prof., head dept. indsl. mgmt., 1955-63, founding dean bus. edn., 1963-80, prof., dean emeritus, 1983—. Mem. Regional Export Expansion Coun., 1965—77; sec. commn. edn. for bus. professions Nat. Assn. State Univs. and Land-Grant Colls., 1975—77; pres. Nat. Coun. Textile Edn., 1978—80. Master sgt. U.S. Army, 1941—45. Vis. scholar, U. Sussex, Eng., 1980—; Econ. in Action fellow, Cast Inst. Tech., 1958. Mem.: Thomas Jefferson Soc. Alumni U. Va., Poinsett Club (Greenville, S.C.), Piedmont Econs. Club, Newcomen Soc., St. Andrews Soc. Upper S.C. Episcopalian. Home: 305 Jones Ave Greenville SC 29605-2862

TREVINO, GUILLERMO PRIETO, brokerage house executive; Chmn., pres. Mexican Stock Exch., 2001—. Office: Mexican Stock Exch Paseo de la Reforma No 255 Col Cuauhtemoc 06500 Mexico City Mexico

TREVINO, JERRY ROSALEZ, retired secondary school principal; b. Bee County, Tex., July 9, 1943; s. Geronimo R. and Hilaria (Rosalez) T.; m. Juanita Escalante, Jan. 1, 1985; 1 child, John-Michael. BA, U. Houston, 1967, MEd, 1974; PhD, Kennedy-Western U., 1988; postgrad., U. Tex., Permian Basin, 1988-92. Cert. tchr., adminstr., supt., Tex. Tchr. N.E. Houston Sch. Dist., 1966-70, pub. rels. officer, 1970-72, asst. prin., 1972-76; tchr. Harris County Dept. Edn., Houston, 1968-72, Austin (Tex.) Ind. Sch. Dist., 1977-87; asst. prin. Tex. Youth Commn., Pyote, 1987-91, prin., 1991-96, ret., 1996. Chair edn. seminar, 24th Internat. Congress, Oxford (Eng.) U., 1997; reader, U.S. Dept. Edn., 1996-97; mentor Austin Ind. Sch. Dist., 1996-98; Title VII project dir. U.S. Dept. Edn., Pyote, 1988-96; instr. Austin C.C., 1980-84, chair, Prin. Coun. for Edn. of Lang. Minority Students, S.W. Ednl. Devel. Lab., Austin, 1994-96; rschr. and ednl. cons. Bentiva Edn. Solutions, 2002—. Editor newsletter The Flyer, 1970-72; contbr. articles to profl. pubs. Mem. Community Adv. Coun., Pyote, 1987-96; mem. Tex. Children's Mental Health Plan, Monahans, Tex., 1991-96; mem. planning com. Permian Basin Quality Work Force, Midland, Tex., 1992-96; mem. Supt.'s Coun., Pyote, 1987-96. Named Outstanding Adminstr. of Permian Basin (Golden Apple award) Permian Basin Private Industry Coun., 1994. Mem. ASCD, Nat. Assn. for Bilingual Edn., Order Internat. Ambs., Tex. Assn. Secondary Sch. Prins., Civil Air Patrol, Soc. of Leading Intellectuals of the World, Tex. Coun. Humanities, League United L.Am. Citizens. Presbyterian. Avocations: flying, travel, reading, landscaping. Address: PO Box 299 Paige TX 78659 E-mail: jerryrtrevino@hotmail.com.

TREVINO, LEE BUCK, professional golfer; b. Dallas, Dec. 1, 1939; s. Joe and Juanita (Barrett) T.; m. Claudia Bove; children: Richard Lee, Lesley Ann, Tony Lee, Troy Liana, Olivia Leigh, Daniel Lee. Ed. pub. schs. Head profl. Hardy's Driving Range, Dallas, 1961-65; asst. profl. Horizon Hills Country Club, El Paso, Tex., 1966-67; chmn. bd. Lee Trevino Enterprises, Inc., 1967—; joined PGA Tour, 1967, PGA Sr. Tour, 1989. Hon. chmn. Christmas Seal campaign, 1969-72, sports ambassador, 1971; mem. Pres.'s Conf. on Phys. Fitness and Sports; grand marshal Sun Carnival Parade, 1969-70, 71-72; mem. sports com. Nat. Multiple Sclerosis Soc. Served with USMCR, 1956-60. Mem. Spl. Svcs. Unit USMC. Recipient Hickok Belt award, 1971; named Golf Rookie of Yr., 1967, PGA Player of Yr., 1971, Tex. Pro Athlete of Yr., 1970, Gold Tee award, 1971, AP Pro Athlete of Yr., 1971, Player of Yr. Golf Mag., 1971, Sportsman of Yr. Sports Illustrated, 1971, PGA Sr. Tour Players of Yr., 1990, 92, 94, Internat. Sports Personality of Yr. Brit. Broadcasting Assn., 1971, Rookie and Player of Yr., Sr. PGA Tour, 1990; mem. Tex. Hall of Fame, Am. Gulf Hall of Fame, World Golf Hall of Fame. Achievements include Tournament winner Tex. Open, 1965, 66, N.Mex. Open, 1966, U.S. Open, 1968, 71, Amana Open, 1968, 69, Hawaiian Open, 1968, Tucson Open, 1969, 70, World Cup, 1969, 71, Nat. Airlines Open, 1970, Brit. Open, 1971, 72, Canadian Open 1971, 77, 79, Can. PGA, 1979, Danny Thomas-Memphis Classic, 1971, 72, 80, Tallahassee Open, 1971, Sahara Invitational, 1971, St. Louis Classic, 1972, Hartford Open, 1972, Jackie Gleason Classic, 1973, Doral-Eastern Open, 1973, Mexican Open, 1973, 75, Chrysler Classic, Australia, 1973, PGA Championship, 1974, 84, World Series Golf, 1974, Greater New Orleans Open, 1974, Fla. Citrus Open, 1975, Colonial Nat. Invitational, 1976, 78, Colgate Mixed Team Matches, 1979, Brit. Masters, 1985, U.S. Sr. Open, 1990; King Hassan Moroccan trophy II, 1977; Lancome trophy Benson & Hedges, 1978, 80; 1st golfer to have scored four sub-par rounds in U.S. Open Competition, 1968; leading Money winner, 1970, 2d pl. money winner 1971, 1972; Vardon trophy winner, 1970 1972, 74, 80; Can. PGA, 1983; PGA Seniors Championship, 1994; capt. Ryder Cup Matches, 1985; first golfer to have scored 4 sub-par rounds in PGA competition. Office: Assured Mgmt Co 1901 W 47th Pl Ste 200 Mission KS 66205-1834

TREVISAN, MAURIZIO, epidemiologist; b. Naples, Italy, Jan. 31, 1952; came to U.S., 1979; s. Ilario and Bianca (Bruni) T.; m. Lisa Monagle, Dec. 22, 1983; children: Simona, Alessia, Stefan. MD magna cum laude, U. Naples, Italy, 1977; MS, SUNY, Buffalo, 1989. Cert. in medicine and surgery, Italy, 1977, diabetes and metabolic disease, Italy, 1980. Resident dept. internal medicine Med. Sch. U. Naples, 1977-79; rsch. fellow dept. community health and preventive medicine Med. Sch. Northwestern U., 1979-82; cons. dept. medicine U. Naples, 1983-85; asst. prof. dept. social and preventive medicine SUNY, Buffalo, 1985-88, clinical asst. prof. dept. family medicine, 1988-89, assoc. prof. dept. social and preventive medicine, 1988-92, clinical assoc. prof. nutrition program, 1989-94, assoc. prof. dept. family medicine, 1989-94, interim chair dept social and preventive medicine, 1991-92, prof. dept. social and preventive medicine, 1993—, prof. dept. family medicine, 1994—, interim dean Sch. Health Related Professions, 2001—03, interim dean Sch. Pub. Health and Health Professions, 2003—; prin. investigator Women's Health Initiative WNY Vanguard Clin. Ctr., 1993—2003, co-investigator Women's Health Initiative, 2003—; chair dept. social and preventive medicine SUNY, 1992—2003. Vis. physician dept. physiology Harvard Med. Sch., 1982; adj. asst. prof. dept. cmty. health and preventive medicine Northwestern U. Med. Sch., 1987-96; adj. prof. nutrition program SUNY, Buffalo, 1994—, dir., health in housing, SUNY, Buffalo, 1996—; adj. prof. dept. cmty. health and preventive medicine Northwestern U. Med. Sch., 1996—. Fellow Am. Heart Assn. Coun. on Epidemiology. Recipient Rsch. Career Devel. award NIH, 1989-94. Fellow, Am. Coll. of Epidemiology; mem. Am. Epidemiol. Soc. Achievements include research in population-based epidemiological investigation of risk factors for essential hypertension and coronary heart disease. Office: SUNY Buffalo Sch Pub Health and Health Professions 435 Kimball Tower Buffalo NY 14214-3000 E-mail: trevisan@buffalo.edu.

TREVOR, ALEXANDER BRUEN, technology consultant; b. N.Y.C., Apr. 12, 1945; s. John B. Jr. and Evelyn (Bruen) T.; m. Ellen Ruth Armstrong, Sept. 21, 1974; children: Anne Wood, Alexander Jay Bruen. BS, Yale U., 1967; MS, U. Ariz., 1971. Rsch. asst. U. Ariz., Tucson, 1971; systems analyst CompuServe Inc., Columbus, Ohio, 1971-73, dir. systems, 1973-74, v.p., 1974-81, exec. v.p., chief tech. officer, 1981-96, also bd. dirs., 1985-96; pres. Nuvocom, Inc., Columbus, 1996—. Bd. dirs. Applied Innovation, Inc., Dublin, Ohio, CMHC Sys., Dublin. Author (software program) CB Simulator, 1980. Trustee Trudeau Inst., Saranac Lake, N.Y., Aviation Safety Inst., Worthington, Ohio. 1st lt. Signal Corps, U.S. Army, 1968-70, Vietnam. Decorated Bronze Star. Mem. IEEE, SAR (N.Y.), Union Club (N.Y.). Republican. Episcopalian. Office: Box 340876 Worthington OH 43234-0876

TREVOR, KIRK DAVID NIELL, orchestra conductor, cellist; b. London, Feb. 8, 1952; Student, Dartington Coll., 1968-69; grad. with distinction, Guildhall Sch. Music and Drama, 1974; student, N.C. Sch. Arts, 1975-77. Asst. condr. Guildhall Opera Sch., 1973-74; music dir. Youth Symphony of Carolinas, 1978-82; music dir., condr. Knoxville (Tenn.) Symphony Orch., 1985—; chief condr. Martinu Philharmonic Czech Rep., 1995—; assoc. condr. Charlotte (N.C.) Symphony Orch., 1978-82, Exxon Art Endowment and Dallas Symphony, 1982-85; former resident condr. Dallas Symphony; dir. music Indpls. Chamber Orch., 1988—; asst. prof. U. Tenn., 1985—. Guest condr. U.S., S.Am., USSR, Czech Republic, Poland, Romania, Switzerland; tchr. Condrs. Symphonic Workshop in Zlin, Czech Republic, 1991—, Artistic Dir. Recipient Libottom Meml. prize, 1972, Kappilis Condr. prize, 1974, Toussant prize, 1974; winner Am. Condrs. Program, 1990; Fulbright Exchange grantee U.K. and U.S. Dept. State, 1975, Am. Condrs. Program grantee, 1990. Mem. Condrs. Guild, Am. Symphony Orch. League. Office: Knoxville Symphony Orch 406 Union Ave, Ste 100 Knoxville TN 37902

TREXLER, EDGAR RAY, minister, editor; b. Salisbury, N.C., Sept. 17, 1937; s. Edgar Ray and Eula Belle (Farmer) T.; m. Emily Louise Kees, Aug. 21, 1960; children: David Ray, Mark Raymond, Karen Emily. AB, Lenoir-Rhyne Coll., 1959, LittD, 1978; MDiv, Luth. Theol. So. Sem., 1962; MA, Syracuse U., 1964; postgrad., Boston U., 1960, Luth. World Fedn. Study Project, Geneva, 1977, 81; LittD (hon.), Midland Coll., 1990; DD, Wittenberg U., 1994. Ordained to ministry United Luth. Ch. Am., 1962; pastor St. John's Luth. Ch., Lyons, N.Y., 1962-65; features editor Luth. Mag., Phila., 1965-72, assoc. editor, 1972-78, editor, 1978-87, Chgo., 1988-99. Sec. Commn. Ch. Papers, Luth. Ch. Am., 1971-72, mem. staff team comm., 1972-78; chmn. Interch. Features, 1971-76; chmn. postal affairs com. Assoc. Ch. Press, 1983-90, Work Group on New Ch. Periodical, 1985-86; Evangelical Luth. Ch. Am. Cabinet of Execs., 1988-99. Author: Ways to Wake Up Your Church, 1969, Creative Congregations, 1972, The New Face of Missions, 1973, Mission in a New World, 1977, LWF/6, 1978, Anatomy of a Merger, 1991, High Expectations: Understanding the ELCA's Early Years, 1988-2002, 2003; mem. editl. adv. bd. The New World, Roman Cath. Archdiocese of Chgo., 1994-96. Pres. Lyons Coun. Chs., 1964; trustee Lenoir Rhyne Coll., 1975-84, 97—. Luth. Theol. So. Sem., 2003—. Recipient Disting. Alumnus award Lenoir-Rhyne Coll., 1991, Disting. Svc. award Newberry Coll., 1992, Bachman award for disting. leadership Luth. Theol. So. Sem., 1993, Mauney Leadership Awd., Luth. Theol. So. Seminary (alumni awd.), 1999, award of merit for editls. Assoc. Ch. Press, 1991, 98, award of merit for articles in mission mags. Assoc. Ch. Press, 1974, hon. life mem., Assoc. Ch. Press, 1999. Mem. Nat. Luth. Editors Assn. (pres. 1975-77). Home: 2504 Carriage Falls Ct Hendersonville NC 28791-1816 E-mail: etrexler@bellsouth.net.

TREXLER, JOHN PETER, retired geology educator, researcher; b. Allentown, Pa., Nov. 8, 1926; s. Robert William and Hilda (Seip) T.; m. Virginia Hamilton, Jan. 29, 1950; children: Margaret T. Hessen, Virginia P. Trexler-Myren. BA, Lehigh U., 1950, MS, 1953; PhD, U. Mich., 1964. Indsl. geologist Lehigh Portland Cement Co., Allentown, Pa., 1950, 51; geologist U.S. Geol. Survey, 1953-62; mem. faculty, prof. Juniata Coll., Huntingdon, Pa., 1962-89, founder, developer geol. dept., chmn. geology dept., 1962-79, emeritus prof. geology, 1989—. Author, co-author numerous articles, reports, and maps. With USNR, 1945-46. Fellow NSF, 1970-71. Fellow Geol. Soc. A.; mem. Rotary (pres. 1972). Republican. Presbyterian. Avocations: horseback riding, sailing, reading, music. Home: RR 2 Box 294 Huntingdon PA 16652-9113

TREYNOR, JACK LAWRENCE, financial advisor, educator; b. Council Bluffs, Iowa, Feb. 21, 1930; s. Jack Vernon and Alice (Cavin) T.; m. Elizabeth Glassmeyer, Aug. 29, 1968; children: Elizabeth Childs, Wendy F.C., Thomas Pirrie V. BA, Haverford Coll., 1951; MBA with distinction, Harvard U., 1955; postgrad., MIT, 1962-63. Jr. faculty Harvard U. Sch. Bus., Cambridge, Mass., 1955-56; ops. research staff Arthur D. Little, Cambridge, 1956-66; mgr. computer applications Merrill Lynch, N.Y.C., 1966-69; editor Fin. Analysts Jour., N.Y.C., 1969-81; chief investment officer Treynor-Arbit Assocs., Chgo., 1981-85; assoc. vis. prof. dept. of fin. and bus. econs. U. So. Calif., Los Angeles, 1985-88; pres. Treynor Capital Mgmt., Palos Verdes Estates, Calif. Gen. ptnr., trustee, dir. certain mutual funds Eaton Vance, 1970-2003; mem. Investment Adv. Coun. City of NY, 1980-81. Author: (with Patrick Regan and William Priest) The Financial Reality of Pension Funding Under ERISA, 1976; mem. editl. bd. Fin. Analysts Jour., 1969-2002, mem. editl. adv. coun., 2003—; mem. editl. adv. bd. Jour. Investment Mgmt., 2003—; co-author and contbr. numerous articles in fin. jours. (Graham and Dodd Scroll award 1968, 82, twice in 1987, Graham and Dodd Plaque for best paper in Fin. Analysts Jour. 1981, Graham & Dodd Scroll award 1998, 99). Trustee Fin. Analysts Research Found., 1970-85; mem. vis. com. Grad. Sch. Bus. Adminstrn. U. Chgo., 1984-89. Served with U.S. Army, 1951-53. Recipient James R. Vertin award Fin. Analysts Rsch. Found., 1997, Lillywhite award Employee Benefit Rsch. Inst., 1997. Fellow Inst. for Quantitative Rsch. in Fin. (disting. bd. dirs. 1990—); mem. Fin. Analysts Fedn. (Nicholas Molodovsky award 1985), Investment Adv. Coun. City N.Y., Am. Fin. Assn. (dir. 1979-81), Haverford Varsity Club, Longwood Cricket Club (Chestnut Hill, Mass.), N.Y. Athletic Club, Manursing Island Club (Rye, N.Y.), Winter Club (Lake Forest, Ill.),), Palos Verdes Tennis Club, Palos Verdes Beach and Athletic Club. Episcopalian. Avocations: jazz piano, sports cars, antique trains. Office Phone: 310-378-3900.

TREYZ, JOSEPH HENRY, librarian; b. Binghamton, N.Y., Nov. 23, 1926; s. Joseph Henry and Edna Belle (Leonard) T. BA, Oberlin Coll., 1950; postgrad., Harvard U., 1951; M.L.S., Columbia U., 1952. Circulation asst. N.Y. Acad. Medicine Library, 1950-51; cataloger Columbia Libraries, N.Y.C., 1951-53, Stevens Inst. Tech., Hoboken, N.J., 1953-54; adminstrv. asst. Yale Library, 1955, asst. head catalogue dept., 1955-61; head new campuses program U. Calif., La Jolla, 1961-65; asst. dir. U. Mich. Library, Ann Arbor, 1965-71; dir. libraries U. Wis., Madison, 1971-83, asst. to chancellor, 1983-85; sec.-treas. L.D. Repos, Inc., 1985-87, pres., 1987—. Univ. rep. Consumer Reaction Project for Catalog Card Reprodn. Study, 1961; condr. survey tech. services Fordham U. Libraries, 1967-69, Brandeis U. Libraries, 1970-71; mem. Wis. Gov.'s Com. on Library Devel., 1973-81, Wis. com. Library Services and Constrn. Act, 1979-81; del. U.S. Mission to China on Libraries, 1979 Author: Books for College Libraries, 1967, also articles. Bd. dirs. Wis. Center for Theatre Research. Served with AUS, 1945-46. Mem. Universal Serials and Book Exchange (v.p. 1976, pres., chmn. bd. dirs. 1977), ALA (councilor 1970-74, 77-81, chmn. various coms. 1967-69, recipient Melvil Dewey medal 1970), Assn. Research Libraries (commn. orgn. materials, dir. 1975-78), Midlnet (v.p. 1978-79, pres. 1979-80), Assn. Coll. and Research Libraries (chmn. editorial bd. Choice 1968-70), Wis. Library Consortium (pres. 1975-76), Wis. Assn. Acad. Libraries (chmn. 1973-74), Council U. Wis. Librarians (chmn. 1975-76, 79-80, 81-83), Wis. Library Assn. (bd. dirs. 1973-74, mem. White House Conf. com. 1977-78), Madison Area Library Council (v.p. 1973-74), Mich. Library Assn. (chmn. tech. services sect. 1968-69), N.Y. Tech. Services Librarians (pres. 1959-60). Methodist. Home: 801 N Venetian Dr Miami FL 33139-1031

TREZZA, ALPHONSE FIORE, librarian, educator; b. Phila., Dec. 27, 1920; s. Vincent and Amalia (Ferrara) T.; m. Mildred Di Pietro, May 19, 1945; children: Carol Ann Trezza Johnston, Alphonse Fiore. BS, U. Pa., 1948, MS, 1950, postgrad.; LHD (hon.), Rosary Coll., 1997. Page Free Library, Phila., 1940-41, 45-48, library asst., 1948-49; cataloger, asst. reference librarian Villanova U., 1949-50, instr., 1956-60; head circulation dept. U. Pa. Library, 1950-56; lectr. Drexel Inst. Sch. Library Sci., 1956—60; editor Cath. Library world, 1956-60; exec. sec. Cath. Library Assn., 1956-60; assoc. exec. dir. ALA, exec. sec. library adminstrn. div., 1960-67, assoc. dir. adminstrv. services, 1960—69; dir. Ill. State Library, Springfield, 1969-74; lectr. Grad. Sch. Library and Info. Sci., Cath. U., 1975-82; exec. dir. Nat. Commn. on Libraries and Info. Scis., Washington, 1974-80; dir. intergovt. library Coop-

eration Project Fed. Library Com./Library of Congress, Washington, 1980-82; assoc. prof. Sch. Library and Info. Studies Fla. State U., Tallahassee, 1982-87, prof., 1987-93, emeritus prof., 1993— Mem. Ill. Library LSCA TITLE I-II Adv. Commn., 1963-69; mem. network devel. com. Library of Congress, 1977-82; bd. visitors Sch. Library and Info. Sci., U. Pitts., 1977-80; cons. Becker & Hayes, Inc., 1980-84, King Research, Inc., 1981-82; mem. planning com and steering com. Fla. Gov.'s Conf. on Library and Info. Svcs., 1988-91. Nat. chmn. Cath. Book Week, 1954—56; pres. Joliet Diocesan Bd. Edn., 1966—68; auditor Borough of Norwood, Pa., 1958—60; mem. patron's bd. Fla. State U. Sch. Theater, 2000—; bd. mem. Lafayette Oaks Home Assn., 2002—; Dem. committeeman Lombard, Ill., 1961—69; extraordinary min. of Eucharistic Blessed Sacramento Cath. Ch., 1984—, mem. parish coun., 2000—. 1st lt. USAF, 1942—45. Decorated Air medal; recipient Ofcl. commendation White House Conf. on Libr. and Info. Svc., 1979, citation State Libr. Agys., 1994, Silver award Commn. Libr. Info. Sci., 1996. Mem. ALA (coun. 1973-82, 88-92, mem. exec. bd. 1974-79, chmn. stats. coordinating com. 1970-74, mem. pub. com. 1975-78, 81-83, 87-89, chmn. adv. com. interface 1979-83, chmn. membership com. 1983-84, chmn. nominating com. 1988-89, mem. legis. com. 1989-91, adv. bd. ALA Yearbook 1976 91, Assn. Specialized and Coop. Library Agys. legis. com., 1987-89, ad hoc com. White House Conf. on Libr. and Info. Svcs. 1989-91, chmn. awards com. 1990-92, Exceptional Achievement award 1981, J.B. Lippincott award 1989), Cath. Library Assn. (life, adv. coun. 1960—), Ill. Library Assn. (chmn. legis.-library devel. com. 1964-69, mem. exec. bd., libr's. citation 1974), Fla. Library Assn. (bd. dirs. 1987-93, pres. 1991-92, intellectual freedom com., chmn. com. on Fla. Librs. publ., editor, publ. com., planning com., 1991, site com.), Continuing Libr. Edn. Network and Exchange (pres. 1982-83), Internat. Fedn. Library Assns. and Institutions (statistics standing com. 1976 85, planning com.), Coun. Nat. Library Assns. (chmn. 1959-61), Assn. Coll. and Research Librarians (pres. Phila. chpt. 1953-55), Drexel Inst. Library Sch. Alumni Assn. (pres. 1955-56, exec. bd. 1956-60, chmn. chief officers State Library Agys. 1973-74), Chgo. Library Club (pres. 1969), Assn. Library and Info. Sci. Edn. (govt. relation com. 1985-87), Drexel U. Alumni Assn. (Outstanding Alumnus award 1963), Kappa Phi Kappa (chpt. pres. 1948), Beta Phi Mu (hon.). Lodges: K.C. E-mail: atrezza@mailer.fsu.edu. *You can't do anything alone. You need support and you need opposition. Opposition provides you with challenge. Challenge brings out the best in you.*

TRIANTAFYLLOU, MICHAEL STEFANOS, ocean engineering educator; b. Athens, Greece, Oct. 27, 1951; came to U.S., 1974; s. Stefanos M. and Penelopi I. (Koutras) T.; m. Joan L. Kimball, Sept. 22, 1985; children: Stefanos R., Kimon K. MS in Ocean Engring., MSME, MIT, 1977, ScD, 1979. Rsch. assoc. MIT, Cambridge, Mass., 1978-79, asst. prof., 1979-83, assoc. prof., 1983-86, tenured assoc. prof., 1986-90, prof., dir. ocean engring. testing tank, 1990—. Vis. scientist Woods Hole (Mass.) Oceanographic Inst., 1990—; com. chair MIT/Woods Hole Joint Program in Oceanography. Featured cover Scientific American Science; contbr. articles to profl. jours. Rsch. grantee OFfice NAval Rsch., Office Naval Tech., NSF, Doherty Found. Dept. Commerce, 1979—. Mem. Internat. Soc. Offshore and Polar Engrs. (founding mem.), Soc. Naval Architects and Marine Engrs. (papers com., vice chmn. OC-2 com.), Am. Phys. Soc. Office: MIT 77 Massachusetts Ave Rm 5-323 Cambridge MA 02139-4307 Office Phone: 617-253-4335.

TRIANTAPHYLLOU, H. H. plant pathologist; b. Fuerth, Bavaria, Germany, Jan. 16, 1927; came to U.S., 1954; d. Friedrich and Ferdinandine (Schonleben) Hirschmann; m. Anastasios Christos Triantaphyllou, July 9, 1960; 1 child, Christos F. PhD, U. Erlangen, Erlangen, Germany, 1951. From tech. asst. to prof. N.C. State Univ., Raleigh, N.C., 1954-92; ret. Contbr. articles to profl. jours., chpts. to books in field. Recipient rsch. award Soc. Sigma Xi, 1962, Ruth Allen award Am. Phytopathol. Soc., 1993, Soc. Nematologists fellowship, 1981. Mem. Helminthological Soc. Wash., Soc. European Nematologists, Soc. of Nematologists, Soc. Sigma Xi. Avocations: sailing, music, piano. Office: N C State U Dept Plant Pathology PO Box 7616 Raleigh NC 27695-0001

TRIBBETT, CHARLES, executive recruiter; BA magna cum laude, Marquette U.; JD, U. Va. Former atty. Skadden, Arps, Slate, Meagher & Flom, N.Y.C.; mng. dir. Russell Reynolds Assocs., Chgo. Bd. trustees Northwestern J.L. Kellogg Bus. Sch.; bd. dirs. Chgo. Children's Mus., AON Pension and Investment Fund, Chgo. Union League. Office: Russell Reynolds Assoc 200 S Wacker Dr Ste 2900 Chicago IL 60606

TRIBBLE, RICHARD WALTER, brokerage executive; b. San Diego, Oct. 19, 1948; s. Walter Perrin and Catherine Janet (Miller) T.; m. Joan Catherine Sliter, June 26, 1980. BS, U. Ala., Tuscaloosa, 1968. Grad. Gulf Coast Sch. Drilling Practices, U. Southwestern La., 1976. Registered rep. ITT-Hamilton, Woodridge, Va., 1969-71; stockbroker Shearson, Loeb & Rhoades and Co., Washington, 1971-76; ind. oil and gas investment sales Falls Church, Va., 1976-77; pres. Monroe & Keusink, Inc., Falls Church, Va., 1977-87; instnl. investment officer FCA Asset Mgmt., Columbus, Ohio, 1983-85; fin. cons. Merrill Lynch Pierce Fenner & Smith, Inc., Phoenix, 1987—, cert. fin. mgr., 1989—, sr. fin. cons., 1992—, asst. v.p., 1993—2002, v.p., 2002—, wealth mgmt. advisor, 2003—. Mem. adv. bd. Samaritan Found., 1999—. With USMC, 1969-70. Mem. Ariz. Fiduciary Assn., Ctrl. Ariz. Estate Planning Coun., Ariz. Chpt. Investment Mgmt. Cons. Assn. (dir.). Republican. Methodist. Office: # 900 2555 E Camelback Rd Phoenix AZ 85016-4219 Office Phone: 602-954-5055. E-mail: richard_tribble@ml.com.

TRIBE, LAURENCE HENRY, lawyer, educator; b. Shanghai, Republic of China, Oct. 10, 1941; s. George Israel and Paulina (Diatlovitsky) T.; m. Carolyn Ricarda Kreye, June 20, 1964; children: Mark Alexander, Kerry Katrina. AB summa cum laude in Math., Harvard U., 1962, JD magna cum laude, 1966; LL.D. (hon.), Gonzaga U., 1980, Pacific U., 1987, Am. U., 1987, Ill. Inst. Tech., 1988, Colgate U., 1997; LH.D. (hon.) (hon.), Hebrew U., 1998. Bar: Calif. 1966, U.S. Supreme Ct. 1966. Law clk. Calif. Supreme Ct., 1966-67, U.S. Supreme Ct., 1967-68; exec. dir. tech. assessment panel Nat. Acad. Scis., 1968-69; asst. prof. law Harvard U., 1969-72, prof., 1972-82, Ralph S. Tyler, Jr. prof. constl. law, 1982—; chmn. Marshall Islands Jud. Service Commn., 1979-80. Chief appellate counsel Calif. Nuclear Litigation, 1978-83; spl. dep. atty. gen. Hawaii, 1983-84; cons. NSF, Nat. Endowment Humanities, White House, others; cons. Marshall Islands for drafting new constitution, 1978-79. Author: American Constitutional Law, 1978 (recipient awards), 2d edit., 1988, Constitutional Choices, 1985, God Save this Honorable Court, 1985, Abortion: The Clash of Absolutes, 1990, (with Mike Dorf) On Reading the Constitution, 1991; contbr. articles to profl. jours. Nat. scholar; recipient Triennial Coif award for the outstanding work of legal scholarship in U.S., 1978-80, Scribe award, 1980, Beale prize; 1966 Detur prize, 1969; nat. debate champion, 1961; NSF fellow, 1962-63. Fellow Am. Acad. Arts and Scis.; mem. ABA (Silver Gavel award 1991), ACLU, Phi Beta Kappa. Office: Harvard U Law Sch Hauser Hall 420 Cambridge MA 02138 E-mail: tribe@law.harvard.edu.*

TRIBLE, PAUL SEWARD, JR., former United States senator; b. Balt., Dec. 29, 1946; s. Paul Seward and Katherine (Schilpp) T.; m. Rosemary Dunaway; children: Mary Katherine, Paul Seward III. BA, Hampden-Sydney Coll., 1968; JD, Washington and Lee U., Lexington, Va., 1971. Bar: Va. 1971. Law clk. to U.S. dist. judge Albert V. Bryan, Jr., 1971-72; asst. U.S. atty. Office U.S. Atty. Eastern Dist. Va., 1972-74; commonwealth's atty. Essex County, Va., 1974-76; U.S. Congressman 1st Va. Dist., Washington, 1976-82; U.S. Senator from Va., 1982-89; of counsel Shuttleworth, Ruloff & Giordano, Va., 1989—95, Laxalt, Washington, Washington, 1989—91; pres. Jefferson Group, Washington, 1991-95, Christopher Newport U., Newport News, Va., 1996—. Mem.: Washington and Lee Law Rev. Republican. Episcopalian. Office: Christopher Newport Univ Office of President 1 University Pl Newport News VA 23606-2998

TRIBUS, MYRON, retired quality counselor, engineer, educator; b. San Francisco, Oct. 30, 1921; s. Edward and Marie D. (Kramer) T.; m. Sue Davis, Aug. 30, 1945; children— Louanne, Kamala. BS in Chemistry, U. Calif. at Berkeley, 1942; PhD in Engring, U. Calif. at Los Angeles, 1949; DSc (hon.) (hon.), Rockford (Ill.) Coll., 1965, Oakland (Mich.) U., 1971. Registered profl. engr., Mass.; cert. trainer Feuerstein's method, 1996. Instr. to prof. engring. U. Calif. at Los Angeles, 1946-61; dir. aircraft icing research U. Mich., 1951-54; dean engring. Thayer Sch. Engring., Dartmouth Coll., 1961-69; asst. sec. sci. and tech. Dept. Commerce, Washington, 1969-70; sr. v.p. tech. and engring. info. tech. group Xerox Corp., Rochester, N.Y., 1970-74; dir. Center for Advanced Engring. Study, Mass. Inst. Tech., Cambridge, 1974-86; cons. in quality mgmt., 1986—; dir. rsch., co-founder Exergy, Inc., Hayward, Calif., 1987-99. Cons. heat transfer Gen. Electric Co., 1950; cons. Fed. Office Saline Water; tech. adv. bd. Dept. Commerce; adviser to NATO, 1953; mem. Nat. Adv. Com. Oceans and Atmosphere, 1971-72. Author: Thermostatics and Thermodynamics, 1961, Rational Descriptions, Decisions and Designs, 1969; Contbr. articles to profl. jours. Bd. govs. Technion, Haifa, Israel, 1973-84. Served to capt. USAAF, 1942-46. Recipient Thurman H. Bane award Inst. Aero. Scis., 1945, Wright Bros. medal Soc. Automotive Engrs., 1945; Alfred Noble prize Engring. Socs., 1952, Robert Fletcher awrd Thayer Sch. Engring., Dartmouth Coll., 1994; named UCLA Alumnus of Yr., 1972. Mem. ASME, IEEE, NSPE. E-mail: mtribus@earthlink.net.

TRICARO, ROBERT COLLET, science educator, editor; b. N.Y.C., Jan. 30, 1931; s. Robert and Frances Tricaro. BS cum laude, Adelphi Coll., 1959, MA in Ednl. Philosophy, 1961; MS in Biology, Adelphi U., 1966. Asst. prof., then assoc. prof. Miami-Dade C.C., Miami, 1965—80; pres. Med. Data Control, Inc., San Francisco, 1980—95; adj. faculty mem. City Coll. San Francisco, 1981—; co-editor poetry mag. Mother Earth Internat., San Francisco, 2003—. Cons. in med. mgmt. Contbr. poetry to lit. jours. Pub. rels. specialist L'Alliance Française, Miami, 1974—78. With U.S. Army, 1954—56. Recipient Svc. award, L'Alliance Française, 1976; biology grantee, NSF, 1963—65. Mem.: Bay Area Poets' Coalition (mem. com. 2002—). Lutheran. Avocations: opera, symphony, exercise, poetry reading. Home: 601 Van Ness Ave Unit 22 San Francisco CA 94102 Office: Internat Poetry Soc 934 Brannan St 2d Fl San Francisco CA 94103

TRICASE, ELIZABETH, gymnast; b. Elmhurst, Ill., July 26, 1986; d. Pino and Sheila. Gymnast Ill. Gymnastics Inst./U.S. Natl. Team, 2001—; competed in U.S. Gymnastics Championships, Cleve., 2001, 2002, 2003, Spring Cup, Burlington, Canada, 2002, Pacific Alliance Championships, Vancouver, Canada, 2002, U.S. Classic, Pomona, Calif., 2001, Virginia Beach, Va., 2002, San Antonio, 2003, FL Gym Open, Luxembourg City, Luxembourg, 2004, Am. Classic, Ontario, Calif., 2004, Nat. Elite Podium Meet, NYC, 2004. Named U.S. Nat. Vault Champion, 2002; recipient 1st place vault, U.S. Gymnastics Championships, 2002, FL Gym Open, 2004. Avocations: soccer, basketball, running track. Office: 145 Plaza Dr Westmont IL 60559

TRICE, WILLIAM HENRY, paper company executive; b. Geneva, N.Y., Apr. 4, 1933; s. Clyde H. T.; m. Sandra Clayton, July 16, 1955; children: Russell, Amy. BS in Forestry, State U. N.Y., 1955; MS, Inst. Paper Chemistry, Appleton, Wis., 1960, PhD, 1963. With Union Camp Corp., 1963—, tech. dir. bleached div., 1972-74, v.p., corp. tech. dir. research and devel., 1974-79, sr. v.p. tech., 1979-85, exec. v.p., 1985-96. Chmn. bd. dirs. Bush Boake Allen, Inc. Trustee, pres. Western Mich. U.-Paper Tech. Found., Syracuse Pulp and Paper Found. With USAF, 1955-57. Fellow TAPPI (bd. dirs. 1978-81), Inst. Paper Sci. and Tech. (trustee, exec. commn. alumni assn.).

TRICKETT, PAULA J. assistant principal; b. Detroit, Oct. 2, 1961; d. Paul and Theresa Ann Estes; m. Edward H. Adair, May 15, 1982 (div. July 1994); 1 child, Allison Marie Adair; m. Dennis J. Trickett, Nov. 1, 1996. BS in Mathematics & Acctg., Cumberland Coll., Williamsburg, Ky., 1982, MS in Math Edn., 1995; Rank I in Ednl. Administrn., Union Coll., Barbourville, Ky., 1996. Cert. tchr. in mathematics Ky., 1991. Staff acct. Jerrico, Inc., Lexington, Ky., 1982—83, sr. staff acct., 1983—84, acctg. supr., 1984—85; sr. acct. Cumberland Coll., Williamsburg, Ky., 1985—91; ADD HS mathematics tchr. Whitley County H.S., Williamsburg, Ky., 1991—96, asst. prin., 1996—, curriculum coord., 2001—. Adv. dir. Town & Country Bank, Williamsburg, Ky., 2000—; mem. Ky. Leadership Acad., 2001—03; mem., Mathematics Adv. Coun. Cumberland Coll., Williamsburg, Ky., 1998—2000. Coach Little League T-Ball, Williamsburg, Ky., 1990—92; fin. com. mem. First Baptist Ch., Williamsburg, Ky., 1993—96, bldg. & grounds com. mem., 2001—. Mem.: Ky. Assn. Sch. Adminstrs., Ky. Assn. Secondary Sch. Prins., Delta Kappa Gamma. Avocations: cooking, reading, travel, fishing. Home: 329 Denham St Williamsburg KY 40769 Office: Whitley County HS 350 Blvd of Champions Williamsburg KY 40769 Office Phone: 606-549-7025.

TRICKEY, SAMUEL BALDWIN, physics educator, researcher, university administrator; b. Detroit, Nov. 28, 1940; s. Samuel Miller and Betty Irene (Baldwin) T.; m. Lydia Hernandez, Dec. 28, 1962 (div. June 1981); children: Matthew J., Phillip J.; m. Cynthia Karle, Aug. 13, 1983. BA in Physics, Rice U., 1962; MS, Tex. A&M U., 1966, PhD in Theoretical Physics, 1968. Rsch. scientist Mason & Hanger-Silas Mason Corp., 1962-64; asst. prof. physics U. Fla., Gainesville, 1968-73, assoc. prof., 1973-77, prof. physics and chemistry, 1979—, dir. Quantum Theory Project, 1999—. Dir. J.C. Slater Meml. Computing Lab., 1981-93, Computer and Comm. Resources Coll. Liberal Arts and Scis., 1986-90, exec. dir. info. techs. and svcs. Office of Provost, 1991-96, prof. physics, chmn. physics and engring. physics Tex. Tech. U., Lubbock, 1977-79; cons. Redstone Arsenal Ala., 1972-76; vis. rsch. scholar Mich. Tech. U., 1982-92; vis. scientist IBM Rsch. Ctr., San Jose, Calif., 1975-76; assoc. or dep. dir. Sanibel Symposia; cons. Los Alamos Nat. Lab., 1984—; vis. scientist Max Planck Inst. für Astrophysik, Munich, 1985-94; internat. collaborator Technische U. München Inst. für Theoretische Chemie, 1995—. Contbr. articles to profl. jours. Exec. v.p. U. Fla. chpt. United Faculty of Fla., 1981—83, 2004—. Named Tchr. of Yr. Coll. Arts and Scis. U. Fla., 1973-74. Fellow Am. Phys. Soc.; mem. Am. Assn. Physics Tchrs., Nat. Assn. Hispanic Physicists, Materials Rsch. Soc., Nat. R.R. Hist. Soc., Gulf Atlantic Yacht Club, Organ Hist. Soc., San Juan 21 Class Assn., S.W. R.R. Hist. Soc., Laser 28 Class Assn., Onigaming Yacht Club, Phi Kappa Phi, Sigma Xi, Sigma Pi Sigma. Democrat. Presbyterian. Home: 723 NW 19th St Gainesville FL 32603-1102 Office: Univ Fla Quantum Theory Project PO Box 118435 Gainesville FL 32611-8435 Office Phone: 352-392-1597. E-mail: trickey@ufl.edu.

TRICOLES, GUS PETER, electromagnetic engineer, physicist, consultant; b. San Francisco, Oct. 18, 1931; s. Constantine Peter and Eugenia (Elias) T.; m. Beverly Mildred Ralsky, Dec. 20, 1953 (dec. Dec. 1974); children: Rosanne, Robin; m. Aileen Irma Arenson, Apr. 1, 1980 (div. June 1980). BA in Physics, UCLA, 1955; MS in Applied Math., San Diego State U., 1958; MS in Applied Physics, U. Calif., San Diego, 1962, PhD in Applied Physics, 1971. Engr. Convair divsn. Gen. Dynamics, San Diego, 1955-59, engr. Electronics divsn., 1962-75, engring. mgr. Electronics divsn., 1975-89, sr. engring. staff specialist, 1989-95, Tracor, 1995-99; engr. Smyth Rsch. Assn., San Diego, 1959-61; rsch. asst. Scripps Instn. Oceanography, La Jolla, Calif., 1961-62; sr. engring. staff specialist G.D.E. Systems, Inc., San Diego, 1992—, BAE Sys., 1999—2000; cons. Sci. Applications Internat. Corp., 2003—04. Engring. staff specialist B&M Sys., 2000-2002; cons. Ga. Inst. Tech., Atlanta, 1972, 79-80, Transco Industries, L.A., 1973, Aero Geo Industries, San Antonio, 1980-82, Vantage Assocs., San Diego, 1988, Sci. Application Internat. Corp., 2004; rsch. reviewer NRC, NAS, Boulder, Colo., 1986-88. Author: (with others) Radome Engineering Handbook, 1970, Antenna Handbook, 1988; contbr. articles to profl. jours.; 19 patents in field. With USN, 1952-53. Fellow IEEE (antenna standards com. 1980—, advancement com. 1988), Optical Soc. Am. (local sect. v.p. 1966); mem. Am. Geophys. Union. Avocations: woodworking, photography. Home: 4633 Euclid Ave San Diego CA 92115-3226

TRIECE, ANNE GALLAGHER, magazine publisher; b. Bklyn., July 1, 1955; d. Anthony J. and Mary Ann (Clines) Gallagher; m. David Mark Triece, Nov. 3, 1990; 1 child, Elizabeth Renee. BBA cum laude, CUNY, 1978. Media planner Isidore Lefkowitz Elgort, N.Y.C., 1978-80; sr. media supr. Ted Bates Advt., N.Y.C., 1980-83; account mgr. Prevention mag., N.Y.C., 1983-85; N.Y. mgr. Home mag., N.Y.C., 1985-92; assoc. pub. Met. Home mag., N.Y.C., 1992—. Coord. Arts Program for Homeless, N.Y.C., 1994. Recipient advt. excellence award Knapp Comm., 1985. Mem. Advt. Women N.Y. (commendation 1985). Roman Catholic. Avocations: scuba diving, tennis, skiing.

TRIEN, JAY WILLIAM, accountant; b. Hillside, N.J., May 1, 1940; s. Louis Trien and Beatrice Garfield; m. Ildiko Eva Brayer, Aug. 5, 1973; 1 child, Ooana Louise. BS in Econs., U. Pa., 1962; JD, Rutgers U., 1966; cert. in exec. edn., Harvard U., 1985. Bar: N.J. 1966; CPA, N.Y., N.J., R.I. Prin. Trien & Trien, Newark, N.J., 1968-70; ptnr. Weiner & Co., N.Y.C. and Morristown, N.J., 1970-89; mng. ptnr. Weiner and Co., Morristown, 1986-89; sr. ptnr. Trien, Rosenberg et al, Morristown, 1989—. Sr. mng. dir. Todman & Co., N.Y.C. Pres. United Cerebral Palsy, East Orange, N.J., 1973-75; pres., bd. dirs., treas. The Bridge, Caldwell, N.J., 1975-77; adv. com. mem. Sta. WNET, Newark, 1982-97; bd. govs. Newark Acad., Livingston, N.J., 1980-84. Mem. AICPA, N.J. Soc. CPAs, N.Y. State Soc. CPAs, N.J. Bar Assn. (pres.), Venture Assn. N.J., New Media Assn. N.J., Rothman Inst. Entrepreneurial Studies (bd. dirs.), Morristown Club, Harvard Club, Harvard Bus. Sch. Club NY (bd. dirs.). Avocations: gardening, reading, travel. Home: 112 W 56th St Apt 26N New York NY 10019-3835 Office: Trien Rosenberg et al 177 Madison Ave Morristown NJ 07962-1982 also: Todman & Co CPA PC 120 Broadway New York NY 10271-0002 Office Phone: 973-267-4200 123. E-mail: jay@trienrosenberg.com.

TRIENENS, HOWARD JOSEPH, lawyer; b. Chgo., Sept. 13, 1923; s. Joseph Herman and Myrtle (Wilsberg) T.; m. Paula Miller, Aug. 27, 1946, children: John, Thomas, Nancy. BS, Northwestern U., 1945; JD, 1949. Bar: Ill. 1949, N.Y. 1980, U.S. Dist. Ct. (no. dist.) Ill. 1949, U.S. Dist. Ct. (so. and ea. dists.) N.Y. 1980, U.S. Ct. Appeals (2d, 3d, 7th, 8th, 10th, 11th and D.C. cirs.), U.S. Supreme Ct. 1954. Assoc. firm Sidley, Austin, Burgess & Harper, Chgo., 1949-50; law clk. to Chief Justice Vinson, 1950-52; assoc. Sidley, Austin, Burgess & Smith, Chgo., 1952-56; ptnr. Sidley Austin Brown & Wood, Chgo., 1956—; v.p., gen. counsel AT&T, 1980-86. Trustee Northwestern U., 1967—. With USAAF, 1943 46. Mem. ABA, Ill. Bar Assn., Chgo. Bar Assn., N.Y. State Bar Assn., Am. Coll. Trial Lawyers, Lawyers Club (Chgo.), Chgo. Club, Casino Club (Chgo.), Mid-Day Club, Skokie Country Club, Shoreacres Club, Glen View Club (Golf, Ill.), Met. Club (Washington), Old Elm Club, Sigma Chi. Democrat. Home: 690 Longwood Ave Glencoe IL 60022-1761 Office: Sidley Austin Brown & Wood Apt 605 425 W Surf St Chicago IL 60657-6139 E-mail: htrienens@sidley.com.

TRIER, JERRY STEVEN, gastroenterologist, educator; b. Frankfurt, Germany, Apr. 12, 1933; came to U.S., 1938, naturalized, 1943; s. Kurt J. and Alice L. (Cahn) T.; m. Laurel M. Bryan, June 8, 1957; children: Stanley, Jeryl, Stephen. MD, U. Wash., 1957; MA (hon.), Harvard U., 1973. Diplomate Am. Bd. Internal Medicine. Intern U. Rochester, N.Y., 1957-58, resident in medicine, 1958-59; clin. asso. Nat. Cancer Inst., Bethesda, Md., 1959-61; trainee in gastroenterology U. Wash., Seattle, 1961-63; asst. prof. medicine U. Wis., Madison, 1963-67; asso. prof. U. N.Mex., Albuquerque, 1967-69, Boston U., 1969-73, Harvard U. Med. Sch., Cambridge, Mass., 1973-76, prof., 1976—. Sr. physician Brigham and Women's Hosp.; cons. Dana Farber Cancer Ctr., Nat. Inst. Diabetes and Digestive and Kidney Disease; adv. coun. NIH, 1986-90. Editor: Internal Medicine; mem. editorial bd.; Anatomical Record, 1969-98, Gastroenterology, assoc. editor, 1971-77, mem. editorial bd., 1967-71, 78-83, 93-98, chmn., 1988-93, Am. Jour. Medicine, 1978-87, Current Opinion in Gastroenterology, 1990—; contbr. articles to profl. jours.; contbr. chpts. to books. Served as surgeon USPHS, 1959-61. Recipient Disting. Med. Alumnus award U. Wash., 2004; USPHS/NIH grantee, 1963-94. Mem. Am. Soc. Clin. Investigation, Assn. Am. Physicians, Am. Gastroent. Assn. (pres. 1985-86, Julius Friedenwald medal 1999), Am. Soc. Cell Biology, Am. Fedn. Clin. Research. Office: Brigham and Women's Hosp 75 Francis St Boston MA 02115-6110

TRIGGER, BRUCE GRAHAM, anthropology educator; b. Cambridge (formerly Preston), Ont., Can., June 18, 1937; s. John Wesley and Gertrude Elizabeth (Graham) T.; m. Barbara Marian Welch, Dec. 7, 1968; children: Isabel Marian, Rosalyn Theodora. BA, U. Toronto, 1959; PhD, Yale U., 1964; DSc (hon.), U. N.B., 1987; LittD (hon.), U. Waterloo, 1990; LLD (hon.), U. Western Ont., 1995, McMaster U., 1999, U. Toronto, 2003. Asst. prof. Northwestern U., 1963-64, McGill U., 1964-67, assoc. prof., 1967-69, prof. anthropology, 1969—, chmn. dept., 1970-75, bd. govs., 1996—2001, James McGill prof., 2001—. Mem. bd. govs. McGill-Queen's U. Press, 1988—; Harry Hawthorn Disting. lectr., 1988; Disting. lectr. in archaeology Am. Anthrop. Assn., 1990; Disting. vis. prof. Am. U. in Cairo, 1992; lectr. context and human soc. Boston U., 1997. Author: History and Settlement in Lower Nubia, 1965, Beyond History, 1968, The Huron: Farmers of the North, 1969, 2d edit., 1990, Cartier's Hochelaga, 1972, Nubia Under the Pharaohs, 1976, The Children of Aataentsic, 1976, Time and Traditions, 1978, Gordon Childe: Revolutions in Archaeology, 1980, Natives and Newcomers, 1985, A History of Archaeological Thought, 1989, Early Civilizations, 1993, Sociocultural Evolution, 1998, Artifacts and Ideas, 2003, Understanding Early Civilizations, 2003; vol. editor: Handbook of North American Indians, Vol. 15, 1978; editor Native and Northern Series; co-editor: Cambridge History of the Native Peoples of the Americas, North America Volume, 1996. Recipient Can. Silver Jubilee medal, 1977, Cornplanter medal, 1979, John Porter prize, 1987, Prix Victor-Barbeau Acad. Canadienne-Française, 1991, Prix Leon-Gérin (Prix du Québec), 1991, James R. Wiseman Book award Archaeol. Inst. Am., 1991; Woodrow Wilson fellow, 1959-60, Woodrow Wilson dissertation fellow, 1962-63, Can. Coun. Leave fellow, 1968-69, 76-77, Killam rsch. fellow Can. Coun., 1970-71, 90, 91, leave fellow Social Scis. and Humanities Rsch. Coun. of Can., 1983; named officier, Ordre nat. du Quebec, 2001. Fellow Royal Soc. Can. (Innis-Gerin medal 1985), Soc. Antiquaries of Scotland (hon.); mem. Prehistoric Soc. U.K. (hon.), Huron Great Turtle Clan (adopted), Sigma Xi. Home: Apt 603 3495 rue de la Montagne Montreal QC Canada H3G 2A5 Office: McGill U Dept Anthropology 855 Sherbrooke St W Montreal QC Canada H3A 2T7 Office Phone: 514-398-4288. E-mail: bruce.trigger@mcgill.ca.

TRIGGLE, DAVID JOHN, dean, pharmacist, consultant; b. U.K., Apr. 5, 1935; came to U.S., 1962; s. William John and Maud F. (Henderson) T.; m. Ann M. Jones, Sept. 22, 1959, children: Andrew B., Jocelyn A. BSc in Chemistry, U. Southampton, Eng., 1956; PhD, U. Hull, Eng., 1959. Sch. fellow U. Ottawa, Ont., Can., 1959-61; rsch. fellow U. London, 1961-62; asst. prof. SUNY Sch. of Pharmacy, Buffalo, 1962-65, assoc. prof., 1965-69, prof., 1985-95, chmn. dept., 1971-85, dean, 1985-95, Disting. prof., 1987—, vice-provost for grad. edn., 1995-2001, dean Grad. Sch., 1995-2001, provost, 2000-01, univ. prof., 2000—. Cons. to pharm. industry, 1980—. Author: Chemical Aspects of Autonomic Nervous System, 1965, Neurotransmitter-Receptor Interactions, 1971, Chemical Pharmacology of the Synapse, 1976. Recipient Volwiler Rsch. Achievement award Am. Assn. Colls. Pharmacy, 1988, 89, George Koepf award Biomed. Rsch. Med. Found. Buffalo, 1994. Fellow AAAS; mem. Am. Chem. Soc., Am. Soc. Pharmacology and Therapeutics (Otto Krayer award 1995), Soc. Neurosci., Brit. Pharmacology Soc., Am. Pharm. Assn., Rho Chi (Rho Chi award 1998). Office: SUNY Sch Pharmacy 457 Hochstetter Buffalo NY 14260-0001 Office Phone: 716-645-7315. Business E-Mail: triggle@buffalo.edu.

TRIGIANO, LUCIEN LEWIS, physician; b. Easton, Pa., Feb. 9, 1926; s. Nicholas and Angeline (Lewis) T.; children: Lynn Anita, Glenn Larry, Robert Nicholas. Student, Tex. Christian U., 1944-45, Ohio U., 1943-44, 46-47, Milligan Coll., 1944, Northwestern U., 1945, Temple U., 1948-52. Diplomate Am. Bd. Phys. Medicine & Rehab. Intern Meml. Hosp., Johnstown, Pa., 1952-53; resident Lee Hosp., Johnstown, 1953-54; gen. practice Johnstown, 1953-59; med. dir. Pa. Rehab. Ctr., Johnstown, 1959-62, chief phys. medicine & rehab., 1964-70; fellow phys. medicine & rehab. N.Y. Inst. Phys. Medicine & Rehab., 1962—64; dir. rehab. medicine Lee Hosp., 1964-71, Ralph K. Davies Med. Ctr., San Francisco, 1973-75, St. Joseph's Hosp., San Francisco, 1975-78, St. Francis Meml. Hosp., San Francisco, 1978-83, Rehab. Ctr. Nev., Las Vegas, 1998—2000; pvt. practice Las Vegas, 1998—. Asst. prof. phys. medicine and rehab. Temple U. Sch. Medicine; founder Disability Alert.; bd. adv. Sch. Medicine Temple U., 2003—, bd. visitors, 2003. Served with USNR, 1944-46. Mem. AMA, Am. Coll. Physicians, Pa. Med. Soc., San Francisco County Med. Soc., Am. Acad. Phys. Medicine & Rehab., Am. Congress Phys. Medicine, Calif. Acad. Phys. Medicine, Nat. Rehab. Assn., Babcock Surg. Soc. Home and Office: 1421 Casa Del Rey Ct Las Vegas NV 89117-1538 Personal E-mail: lltmdmd@aol.com.

TRIIPAN, MAIVE, library director; b. Virumaa County, Estonia, Jan. 4, 1942; d. Osvald and Minna (Olesk) Triipan; m. Kalle Dobkevich, Mar. 6, 1971 (div. June 4, 1974); 1 child, Raul. B. of Libr., Tartu U., Tartu, Estonia, 1967. Rsch. mgmt. asst. Libr. of Estonian Acad. Sci., Tallinn, Estonia, 1967-74, asst. dir. rsch. work, 1974-84, dir., 1984—. Mem. State Libr. Coun., Tallinn, 1974-87, State Libr. Coun. at Dept. of Culture and Edn., Tallinn, 1989—, Tech. U. Coun., 1993—, Estonian Nat. Libr. Coun., Tallinn, 1994—; fin. mgr. Merelaug, 1998-99; project mgmt. Scis. Dept. Estonian Inst. Pub. Adminstrn.; project mgmr. Style Wear, Tallinn, 2000-01; specialist further edn. Astangu Vocat. Rehab. Ctr., Tallinn, 2000, head dept. IT and staff tng., 2002-, head dept. pub. relationship, 2003. Editl. bd. Estonian Retrospective, 1975; mng. pub. National Bibliography 1525-1940, 1993. Mem. Estonian Librs. Assn. Avocations: literature, music, art. Business E-Mail: maive.triipan@astangu.ee.

TRILLIN, CALVIN, writer, journalist; b. Kansas City, Mo., Dec. 5, 1935; s. Abe and Edyth T.; m. Alice Stewart, Aug. 13, 1965 (dec.); children: Abigail, Sarah Stewart. BA, Yale U., 1957; DLitt (hon.), Beloit Coll., 1987; LHD (hon.), Albertus Magnus Coll., 1990; LHD hon., U. Mo., 2003; DLitt (hon.), SUNY, 1996, U. N.C., 1998, Susquehanna U., 1999; DLitt. (hon.), Long Island U., 2002. Reporter, writer Time mag., 1960-63; staff writer New Yorker mag., 1963—; columnist Nation mag., 1978-85; syndicated columnist, 1986-95; columnist Time mag., 1996-2001. Trustee N.Y. Pub. Libr. Author: An Education in Georgia, 1964, Barnett Frummer is an Unbloomed Flower, 1969, U.S. Journal, 1971, American Fried, 1974, Runestruck, 1977, Alice, Let's Eat, 1978, Floater, 1980, Uncivil Liberties, 1982, Third Helpings, 1983, Killings, 1984, With All Disrespect, 1985, If You Can't Say Something Nice, 1987, Travels With Alice, 1989, Enough's Enough, 1990, American Stories, 1991, Remembering Denny, 1993, Deadline Poet, 1994, Too Soon to Tell, 1995, Messages From My Father, 1996, Family Man, 1998, Tepper Isn't Going Out, 2002, Feeding A Yen, 2003, Obviously On He Sails, 2004; author, performer one-man show Calvin Trillin's Uncle Sam, Am. Place Theatre, N.Y.C., 1988, Calvin Trillin's Words, No Music, Am. Place Theatre, 1990. Office: care New Yorker 4 Times Sq New York NY 10036-6522 Office Phone: 212-286-5651.

TRILLING, GEORGE HENRY, physicist, researcher; b. Bialystok, Poland, Sept. 18, 1930; came to U.S., 1941; s. Max and Eugenie (Walfisz) T.; m. Madeleine Alice Monic, June 26, 1955; children: Stephen, Yvonne, David. BS, Calif. Inst. Tech., Pasadena, 1951, PhD, 1955. Rsch. fellow Calif. Inst. Tech., Pasadena, 1955-56; Fulbright post-doctoral fellow Ecole Polytechnique, Paris, 1956-57; asst. to assoc. prof. U. Mich., Ann Arbor, 1957-60; assoc. to prof. dept. physics U. Calif., Berkeley, 1960-94, prof. emeritus, 1994—. Fellow Am. Phys. Soc., Am. Acad. Arts and Scis.; mem. NAS. Achievements include research in high energy physics. Office: Lawrence Berkeley Nat Lab Berkeley CA 94720-0001 Office Phone: 510-486-6801.

TRILLING, LEON, aeronautical engineering educator; b. Bialystok, Poland, July 15, 1924; came to U.S., 1940, naturalized, 1946; s. Oswald and Regina (Zakhejm) T.; m. Edna Yuval, Feb. 17, 1946; children: Alex R., Roger S. BS, Calif. Inst. Tech., 1944, MS, 1946, PhD, 1948. Rsch. fellow Calif. Inst. Tech., 1948- 50; Fulbright scholar U. Paris, 1950-51, vis. prof., 1963-64; mem. faculty MIT, Cambridge, 1951—, prof. aerospace and astronautics, 1962-94, prof. emeritus, 1994—, mem. coun. on primary and secondary edn., 1992—. Mem. Program in Sci. Tech. and Soc., Engring. Edn. Mission to Soviet Union, 1958; vis. prof. Delft Tech. U., 1974-75; vis. prof. engring. Carleton Coll., 1987. Pres. Met. Com. Ednl. Opportunity, 1967-70, Coun. for Understanding of Tech. in Human Affairs, 1984—. Guggenheim fellow, 1963-64. Fellow AAAS. Home: 180 Beacon St Boston MA 02116-1408 Office: MIT 77 Massachusetts Ave Cambridge MA 02139-4307 E-mail: trilling@mit.edu.

TRIM, DONALD ROY, consulting engineer; b. Saginaw, Mich., June 23, 1937; s. Roy E. and Agnes (Kontranowski) T.; m. Dorothy Mae Franek, Aug. 11, 1962; children: Jeffrey D., Gregory S., Christopher M. BS in Civic Engring., U. Mich., 1959. Registered profl. engr., Mich., Ohio, Fla.; registered land surveyor, Mich. Engr. Francis Engring., Saginaw, 1959-64, Edwin M. Orr, Inc., Dearborn, Mich., 1964-66; pres. Wade-Trim Group, Plymouth, Mich., 1966-96, CEO, 1996-99, chmn., 1999—. V.p. Plymouth Canton Basketball Assn., 1980-84; bd. govs. Greater Mich. Found., Lansing, 1983-85. Mem. Nat. Soc. Profl. Engrs., Cons. Engrs. Coun. Mich. (dir. 1972-73, Pres. 1983-84), Am. Cons. Engrs. Coun. (v.p. 1986-88, pres. 1998-99), Am. Waterworks Assn. Roman Cath. Office: Wade-Trim Group 400 Monroe St Ste 310 Detroit MI 48226-2962 E-mail: dtrim@wadetrim.com.

TRIMBLE, JAMES T., JR., federal judge; b. Bunkie, La., Sept. 13, 1932; s. James T. Sr. and Mabel (McNabb) T.; m. Murel Elise Biles, Aug. 18, 1956; children: Elise Rumsey, Mary Olive Beacham, Martha McNabb Elliott, Sarah Trimble Moritz. Student, U. La., Lafayette, 1950-52; BA in Law, La. State U., 1955, JD, 1956. Bar: La. 1956. With Gist, Murchison & Gist (now Gist, Methvin, Hughes & Munsterman), 1959-78, Trimble, Percy, Smith, Wilson, Foote, Walker & Honeycutt, 1979-86; U.S. magistrate U.S. Dist. Ct. (we. dist.) La., 1986-91, judge, 1991—. Lt. USAF, 1956-59. Mem. Southwest La. Bar Assn., La. Bar Assn., La. Bar Found. Office: 611 Broad St Ste 237 Lake Charles LA 70601-4380 Office Phone: 337-437-3884.

TRIMBLE, KATHLEEN LOUISE, library director; b. Reading, Pa., Oct. 10, 1949; d. Melvin Blackburn and Ruth Louise (Kreitz) T.; m. Richard Harvey Greenberg, May 20, 1984; children: Max, Jacob. BA, U. Toledo, 1972, MLS, 1979. Librarian II Toledo Blade, 1971-75, librarian I, 1975-78, asst. head librarian, 1976-78, head librarian, 1978-82; mgr. library info. U.S. News and World Report, Washington, 1982-83, library dir., 1983-97, dir. editl. adminstrn., 1997—. Recipient Henebry award News Divsn., 1993. Mem. Spl. Libraries Assn. (dir. newspaper div. 1978-80, sec.-treas. 1979-81). Jewish. Office: US News & World Report Ste 150 1050 Thomas Jefferson St NW Washington DC 20007-3817

TRIMBLE, PRESTON ALBERT, retired judge; b. Salina, Okla., Aug. 27, 1930; s. James Albert and Winnie Louella (Walker) T.; m. Patricia Ann Beadle; children: Todd, Beth, Amy. BA, U. Okla., 1956, LL.B., 1960. Bar: Okla. 1960. Practice law, 1960; asst. county atty., 1960-62; county atty., 1962-67; dist. atty., 1967-79; dist. judge, 1979-91. Spl. instr. S.W. Center Law Enforcement Edn.; cons. prosecution mgmt. Mem. Jud. Council Okla.; chmn. Okla. Corrections Workshop; mem. planning com. Nat. Inst. Crime and Delinquency; mem. com. on multi-agy. problems in criminal justice Appellate Judges Conf. Bd. dirs. Okla. U. Crisis Ctr., 1970—, ARC, Lake Murray Conservation Assn.; trustee Nat. Assn. Pretrial Svc. Agys. Resource Ctr., Sarkeys Found., 1994—. With USNR, 1948-52; col. USAFR. Mem. Okla., Cleveland County bar assns., Nat. Dist. Attys. Assn. (past pres.), Okla. Dist. Attys. Assn. (past pres.), Nat. Coll. Dist. Attys. (bd. regents), Am. Legion, Lions, Amateur Field Trial Clubs Am. (trustee 2002—). Democrat. Methodist. Home: 1886 Trailview Dr Norman OK 73072-6655 Office: 231 S Peters Ave Norman OK 73069-6035 Office Phone: 405-321-8272. *An elected public official must remember that the people own his position and he only holds it in trust for them.*

TRIMBLE, SANDRA ELLINGSON, lawyer; b. Buffalo, Wyo., May 10, 1952; d. Andrew C. and Edna E. Ellingson; children: Samuel James, Stephen Joseph. BA with highest distinction, Colo. State U., 1974; MEd, Sul Ross State U., 1977; JD cum laude, Georgetown U., 1989. Bar: Md. 1989, D.C. 1990. Contract specialist USAF, Pope AFB, N.C., 1979-81; purchasing rep. Damson Oil Corp., Houston, 1982-86; summer assoc. Fried Frank Harris Shriver & Jacobson, Washington, 1988; law clk. Sullivan & Cromwell, Washington, 1988-89; assoc. Cleary Gottlieb Steen & Hamilton, Washington, 1989-97; of counsel Orrick Herrington & Sutcliffe LLP, Washington, 1997—. Assoc. notes editor Georgetown Law Jour., 1988-89. Recipient Disting. Achievement in Advocacy award Internat. Acad. Trial Lawyers, 1989; Nat. Merit scholar, 1970; law fellow Georgetown U. Law Ctr., 1987-88. Mem. ABA, Phi Beta Kappa. Office: Orrick Herrington & Sutcliffe LLP 3050 K St NW Ste 200 Washington DC 20007-5135 E-mail: strimble@orrick.com.

TRIMBLE, STANLEY WAYNE, hydrology and geography educator; b. Columbia, Tenn., Dec. 8, 1940; s. Stanley Drake and Clara Faye (Smith) T.; m. Alice Erle Gunn, Aug. 16, 1964; children: Alicia Anne, Jennifer Lusanne. BS, U. North Ala., 1964; MA, U. Ga., 1970, PhD, 1973. Asst. prof. hydrology and geography U. Wis., Milw., 1972-75; from asst. prof. to prof. UCLA, 1975—. Vis. asst. prof. U. Chgo., 1978, vis. assoc. prof., 1981, vis. prof. environ. geography, 1990—, vis. prof. U. Durham (Eng.), 1998; vis. lectr. U. London, 1985; hydrologist U.S. Geol. Survey, 1974-84; vis. prof. U. Vienna, 1994, 99; Frost lectr. Brit. Geomorphological Rsch. Group, Durham, Eng., 1994; vis. rsch. lectr. Oxford U., 1995; Fulbright scholar in U.K., 1995; vis. fellow Keble Coll., Oxford U., 1995, Hatfield Coll. U. Durham, 1998. Author: Culturally Accelerated Sedimentation on the Middle Georgia Piedmont, 1971, Man-Induced Erosion on the Southern Piedmont, 1700-1970, 1974, Soil Conservation and the Reduction, 1982, Sediment Characteristics of Tennessee Streams, 1984, (with A Ward) Environmental Hydrology, 2004; joint editor-in-chief: Catena, 1995—; editor: Encyclopedia of Water Science, 2003-; contbr. articles to profl. jours. Served to 1st lt. U.S. Army, 1963-65. Grantee U.S. Geol. Survey, Washington, 1974-79, Wis. Dept. Natural Resources, Madison, 1978, 82, 93, 94, 95, NSF, Washington, 1976, Agrl. Rsch. Svc. of USDA, Washington, 1972, Nat. Geographic Soc., 1993. Mem. NAS-NRC (com. on watershed mgmt. 1996-98), Assn. Am. Geographers, Am. Geophys. Union, Soil Conservation Soc. Am., Brit. Geomorphol. Rsch. Group, Sigma Xi. Republican. Avocations: historic houses, documentation and restoration, landscape gardens. Office: UCLA Dept Geography 1255 Bunche Hall Los Angeles CA 90095-1524 Office Phone: 310-825-1071. Business E-Mail: trimble@geog.ucla.edu.

TRIMBLE, THOMAS JAMES, retired utility company executive, lawyer; b. Carters Creek, Tenn., Sept. 3, 1931; s. John Elijah and Mittie (Rountree) T.; m. Glenna Kay Jones, Sept. 3, 1957; children: James Jefferson, Julie Kay. BA, David Lipscomb U., 1953; JD, Vanderbilt U., 1956; LLM, NYU, 1959. Bar: Tenn. 1956, Ariz. 1961, U.S. Dist. Ct. Ariz. 1961, U.S. Dist. Ct. D.C. 1963, U.S. Ct. Appeals (10th cir.) 1971, U.S. Supreme Ct. 1972, U.S. Ct. Appeals (9th cir.) 1975. From assoc. to ptnr. Jennings, Strouss & Salmon, Phoenix, 1960-85, mng. ptnr., 1985-87; sr. v.p., gen. counsel, corp. sec. S.W. Gas Corp., Las Vegas, Nev., 1987-96, gen. counsel, 1987-92; corp. sec. Primerit Bank, 1990-92, pres., 1994-96; exec. v.p. Energy Ins. (Bermuda) Ltd., 1992-94, bd. dirs., 1992-97, pres., 1994—96. Bd. dirs. Energy Ins. Mut. Ltd., 1988-97, vice chmn., 1992-94, chmn., 1994-96. Mem. editorial bd. Vanderbilt U. Law Rev., 1954-56. Mem. Pepperdine U. Bd. Regents, Malibu, Calif., 1981—, sec., 1982-2000, chmn., 2000—, mem. exec. com., 1982-89, 95—; bd. visitors Pepperdine Sch. Law, Malibu; trustee Okla. Christian U., Oklahoma City, 1994—; pres. Big Sisters Ariz., Phoenix, 1975, bd. dirs., 1970-76; chmn. Sunnydale Children's Home, Phoenix, 1966-69, bd. dirs., 1965-75; pres. Clearwater Hills Improvement Assn., Phoenix, 1977-79, bd. dirs., 1975-80; trustee Nev. Sch. of Arts, 1988-92, chmn., 1989-90. 1st lt. JAGC, USAF, 1957-60. Fellow Ariz. Bar Found. (editl. bd. Jour. 1975-80), Am. Gas Assn. (legal sect. mng. com. 1987-96), Order of Coif, Southshore Golf Club (Las Vegas), Kiwanis (pres. Phoenix 1972-73), Phi Delta Phi. Republican. Mem. Ch. Christ. Home: 10 Rue Du Ville Way Henderson NV 89011-2200 E-mail: trimblevegas@llvresort.com.

TRIMBLE, VANCE HENRY, retired newspaper editor; b. Harrison, Ark., July 6, 1913; s. Guy L. and Josephine (Crump) T.; m. Elzene Miller, Jan. 9, 1932; 1 dau., Carol Ann. Student pub. schs., Wewoka, Okla. Cub reporter Okemah (Okla.) Daily Leader, 1928; worked various newspapers in Okmulgee, Muskogee, Tulsa and, Okla.; successively reporter, rewrite man, city editor Houston Press, 1939-50, mng. editor, 1950-55; news editor Scripps-Howard Newspaper Alliance, Washington, 1955-63; editor Ky. Post and Times-Star, Covington, 1963-79. Author: The Uncertain Miracle, 1974, Sam M. Walton, 1990, (biography) E.W. Scripps, 1992, Frederick Smith of Federal Express, 1993, An Empire Undone: Rise and Fall of Chris Whittle, 1995; co-author: Happy Chandler Autobiography, 1989; editor: Scripps-Howard Handbook, 1981. Trustee Scripps-Howard Found., 1974-79. Recipient Pulitzer prize for nat. reporting, 1960, Raymond Clapper award, 1960, Sigma Delta Chi award for disting. Washington correspondence, 1960, Frank Luther Mott award for journalism book rsch. U. Mo., 1993; named to Okla. Journalism Hall of Fame, 1974. Mem. Am. Soc. Newspaper Editors, Nat. Press Club (Washington, Press Club (Houston), Wewoka Country Club. Clubs: Nat. Press (Washington); Press (Houston);Wewoka Country. Baptist. Home: 25 Oakhurst Rd Wewoka OK 74884-3714 Personal E-mail: vhtrimble@aol.com.

TRIMBLE, WILLIAM CATTELL, JR., retired lawyer; b. Buenos Aires, Feb. 7, 1935; s. William Cattell and Nancy Gordon (Carroll) Trimble; m. Barbara Janney, June 19, 1960; children: William C, Margery M Kennelly. AB, Princeton U., 1958; LL.B., U. Md., 1964. Bar: Md 1965. With firm Ober, Grimes & Shriver, Balt., 1965-87, ptnr., 1970-87, mng. ptnr., 1973-77; counsel Semmes, Bowen & Semmes, Balt., 1987—2000; ret., 2000; mem. Gov.'s Commn. to Revise Annotated Code of Md., 1975-83. Hon consul, Netherlands, 1986—2003; pres bd trustees Valley Sch, 1968—73; trustee Garrison Forest Sch, 1975—95, Gilman Sch, 1980—84. Lt USNR, 1958—61. Mem.: ABA, Md Bar Asn, Soc Cincinnati, Greenspring Valley Hunt Club, Colonial Club (Princeton). Episcopalian. E-mail: williamtrimble@msn.com.

TRIMMIER, CHARLES STEPHEN, JR., lawyer; b. Chgo., June 25, 1943; s. Charles Stephen and Lucille E. (Anderson) T.; m. Rae Wade Trimmier, Aug. 19, 1966; children: Charles Stephen, Hallie Wade. BA, U. Ala., Tuscaloosa, 1965, JD, 1968. Bar: Ala. 1968. From assoc. to ptnr. Rives, Peterson, Pettus and Conway, Birmingham, Ala., 1968-77; pres. TrimmierLaw Firm, Birmingham and Mobile, Ala., Tampa, Fla., 1977—. Gen. counsel Nat. Assn. State Chartered Credit Union Suprs., 1983-2001, Ala. Credit Union League, Fla. Credit Union League, La. Credit Union League. Editor-in-chief: Ala. Law Rev., 1968. Mem. ABA (bus. and banking law sect., credit union com.), Ala. Bar Assn., Birmingham Bar Assn., Comml. Law League, Ala. Law Inst., Shades Valley Rotary, Shades Valley Jaycees (sec. 1973). Episcopalian. Home: 3819 River View Cir Birmingham AL 35243-4801 Office: Trimmier Law Firm PO Box 1885 Birmingham AL 35201-1885 E-mail: steve@trimmier.com.

TRINCHERO, AGNES THERESA, social services consultant, administrator, educator; b. Niles, Calif. d. Louis Jacob and Theresa Marie (DeMattei) T. BA, San Jose State U.; MSW, U. Calif., Berkeley; DSW, U. So. Calif., L.A. Lic. clin. social worker Calif. Fulbright lectr. U.S. Dept. of State, Italy; pvt. practice Laguna Beach, Calif., 1993—. Bd. dirs. Calif. Social Welfare Archives, LA. Recipient Silver medallion, YWCA of North Orange County, Child Advocacy award, Child Welfare League Am. Mem. NASW (Daniel Koshland Leadership award Calif. chpt.), Laguna Art Mus., L.A. County Mus. Art, Nat. Cathedral Assn. Democrat. Roman Catholic. Avocations: travel, theater, dance, writing, gardening.

TRINGALE, ANTHONY ROSARIO, insurance executive; b. Syracuse, N.Y., Apr. 20, 1942; s. Anthony and Susan Marie Tringale; children: Anthony William, Michael Paul, Mark David, Amber Marie. BSFS, Georgetown U., 1967. CLU. Office mgr. trainee N.Y. Life Ins. Co. No. Va., 1965-66, office mgr., 1966, field underwriter, 1966-68; mgmt. asst. home office N.Y. Life Ins. Co., N.Y.C., 1973, gen mgr. Pitts., 1973-76; gen. mgr. Acacia Mut. Life Ins. Co., Annandale, Va., 1976-83, fin. and ins. planner, mgmt. and mktg. cons., 1983-86; from field rep. to mktg. com. Acacia Mut. Life, Anandale, Va., 1983-86; prin. Ins. Consulting Group/Benefits-By-Design, Fairfax, Va., 1986—; pres. Acacia Prodn. Clubs, 1984, 86. Lectr. estate and employee and exec. fringe benefit plans and retirement programs, bus. ins. and comm.; mem. steering com. Entrepreneurship Forum, Washington, 1980—2004; founding bd. mem. Commonwealth Va. DEPA Found., 2003-; nat. adv. bd. Entrepreurship Inst., Columbus, Ohio, 1985—; mem. supts. bus. and industry adv. coun. Fairfax County Pub. Schs., 1989—, mem. mktg edn. adv. bd., 1980—, chmn. 1983-84, 90-91. Contbr. articles in field of personal and bus. fin. strategies to Md. Bus. Observer, Washington Bus. Jour., NALU's Life Assoc. News; radio host Basically Bus. Sta. WGMS-FM, Washington, 1988-91. Trustee SME-1 Accreditation Inst. U. Memphis, 1990—99, Syracuse U., 1995—99; past liaison rep. Am. Soc. CLUs, Bryn Mawr, Pa., 1988—98; arbitrator Fairfax County Dept. Consumer Affairs; v.p., sec., bd. dir., exec. com. The Jeane Dixon Children to Children Found.; chmn. VIP panel D.C. and No. Va., 1988—92; pres. VIP panel, D.C. and No. Va., 1992—94, Birch Pond Homeowners Assn., 1998—2000; bd. dir., exec. com., pres. United Cerebral Palsy of D.C. and No. Va., 1985—2004; pres., adv. bd. Fairfax County Corp. of Salvation Army, 1996—2004; pres. United Cerebral Palsy of D.C. and No. Va., 2002; founding vice chmn. Fairfax Orgn. Christians/Jews United in Svc.; lector, extraordinary minister Basilica Nat. Shrine Immaculate Conception, 1980—2003; bd. dirs., v.p. exec. com., chmn. grants com. No. Va. Cmty. Found., 1979—2004; bd. dir. Summer Opera Theater Co., 1996—98, Nat. Cath. Cmty. Found., 1996—97. Recipient 2000 Crystal award No. Va. Cmty. Found. Mem. No. Va. Soc. CLUs (past pres.), Am. Soc. CLUs, No. Va. Assn. Life Underwriters (treas. 1972, nat. com. 1997-99, Pres.' Cup 1991-92), Assn. Advanced Life Underwriting, Sales and Mktg. Execs. Met. Washington (pres. 1979-80, 95-97, treas. 1989-92, bd. dirs. 1990—, sr. v.p. profl. devel. 1993-95, Man of Yr. 2000), Nat. Assn. Life Underwriters (Nat. Mgmt. award Gen. Agts. and Mgrs. Conf. 1976-83, exec. com. 1984-85, life qualifying), No. Va. Estate Planning Coun. (exec. com. 1985-92, pres. 1990-91), Internat. Platform Assn. (trustee, bd. govs. 1990—), No. Va. Gen. Agts. and Mgrs. Assn. (pres. 1980-81, dir. 1982-83), Greater Washington Area Health Underwriters, Fairfax County C. of C. (dir. small bus. 1989-90, dir. membership 1990-91, exec. com. dir. at large 1991-92, Small Bus. Adv. of Yr. award 1990), Nat. Christopher Columbus Quincentary Jubilee Adv. Bd. (dir. at large 1995—), Nat. Italian-Am. Found. Coun. of 1000 and Italian Am. Leaders Com. Venture Clinic (chmn., pres. 1989-94, TV interviewer, host The Venture Game), Million Dollar Round Table (life, qualified), John Carroll Soc. Ins. Club Washington (pres. 1997-98), Birch Pond Homeowners Assn. (pres. bd. dirs. 1998-2000). Office: Ins Cons Group 12813 Dogwood Hills #222 Fairfax VA 22033-3249

TRINKAUS, JOHN WILLIAM, management educator; b. Mt. Vernon, N.Y., July 17, 1925; s. Bernard and Elsie (Kelly) T.; m. Irene Klimowski, July 31, 1954; children: Joanne Trinkaus Dillon, Robert John, John William. BEE, NYU, 1952, PhD, 1976; MBA, CCNY, 1961. Registered profl. engr., Mass. Engr. Bendix Aviation Corp., Teterboro, NJ, 1947-52, Curtis Wright Corp., Carlstadt, NJ, 1952-53, Sperry Corp., Great Neck, NY, 1953-68; prof. CUNY Baruch Coll., NYC, 1968-81, assoc. dean, 1981-93, prof. emeritus, 1993—. Engring. cons. Electronic Industries Assoc., Washington, 1960-68, USAF, Washington, 1965-68; mgmt. cons. Ford Found., NYC, 1980-82, Interracial Coun. Bus. Opportunity, NYC, 1983-93; vis. disting. prof. St. John's U., NYC, 1993-96. Chmn., rsch. comm. Am. Acad. Profl. Law Enforcement, Mineola, NY, 1978-79; cons. NYC Vol. Urban Con. Group, 1979-84. Sgt. US Army, 1945-46. Recipient 1st prize paper Nat. Fedn. Ind. Bus., Washington, 1992, (Ig)Nobel award, 2003. Mem.: Soc. Bus. Ethics, Assn. Pvt. Enterprise Edn., US Assn. Small Bus. Entrepreneurship, Acad. Mgmt., Inst. Supply Mgmt. Home: 1 Linden St New Hyde Park NY 11040-2311 Office: Baruch Coll CUNY 1 Bernard Baruch Way New York NY 10010-5518 Office Phone: 646-312-3693.

TRINKAUS-RANDALL, GREGOR, librarian, archivist, preservation administrator; b. Balt., Jan. 10, 1946; s. John Phillip and Galina Ivanovna (Gorokhoff) Trinkaus; m. Vickery Edith Trinkaus-Randall, May 22, 1976; children: Jennifer Alison, Christopher Erik. BA, U. Wis., 1968, MA, 1973, MLS, 1980. Archival asst./accessioner State Hist. Soc. Wis., Madison, 1977—81; libr., limnology dept. U. Wis., Madison, 1977—80; conservation/preservation intern Yale U. Libr., New Haven, 1981; asst. curator USS Constitution Mus., Boston, 1981—82; archivist Computer Mus., Marlborough, Mass., 1982; libr./archivist Peabody Mus., Salem, Mass., 1983—88; preservation specialist Mass. Bd. of Libr. Commrs., Boston, 1988—. Mem. adv. com. Northeast Document Conservation Ctr., 1989—; preservation adv. com. NELINET, 1991—2000; chmn. task force theft and mutilation State of Mass., 1989—90, chmn. task force permanent paper, 1989—90; cons. in field. Author: Protecting Your Collections: A Manual of Archival Security, 1995; contbr. articles to profl. jours. Mem. Nat. Ski Patrol, 1966—, Devil's Head Ski Patrol, Merrimack, Wis., 1976—81, regional tng. advisor, 1978—81, Noshaba Valley Ski Patrol, Westford, Mass., 1981—, tng. advisor, 1982—; instr. outdoor emergency care, 1988—; trainer/evaluator Sr. Outdoor Emergency Care, 1990—, tng. coord., 1999—2002; trainer/evaluator Sr. Ski and Toboggan, 1995—; tchr. Royal Scottish Country Dance Soc., Boston, 1976—; instr. first aid, CPR ARC, Lowell, Mass.; USSF Grade 7 Referee, USSF D coaching license. Fellow: Soc. Antiquaries of Scotland; mem.: Scottish Dance, Cultural and Edn. Assn. (bd. dirs. 1987—), New Eng. Hist. Geneal. Soc. (mem. preservation com. 1994—2004, libr. com. 1994—2004), Midwest Archives Conf., Soc. Am. Archivists (host com. chair 2003—04), Phi Kappa Phi. Office: Mass Bd Libr Commrs 648 Beacon St Boston MA 02215-2070 Office Phone: 617-267-9400 ext. 236. Business E-Mail: gregor.trinkaus-randall@state.ma.us.

TRIPATHI, RAM KISHORE, physicist, researcher; b. Rae Bareli, India, Jan. 1, 1942; arrived in U.S., 1966; s. Shiva Kumar and Devi Mani Tripathi; m. Pushpa Shukla Tripathi, May 26, 1966; 1 child, Sanjay. BS, U. Lucknow, 1961, MS, 1963; PhD, U. Kans., 1970. Asst. prof. U. Ky., Lexington, 1970-71, prof., 1986-87; scientist Kern Forschungsanlage, Juelich, Germany, 1971-73; sr. faculty fellow U. Sussex, Brighton, England, 1973-75; fellow Tata Inst. Fundamental Rsch., Bombay, 1975-78; assoc. prof. Dept. of Energy/Inst. Physics, Bhubaneswar, India, 1978-85; prof. U. Tuebingen, Germany, 1980-82, U. Liege, Belgium, 1985-86; radiation physicist NASA Langley Rsch. Ctr., Hampton, Va., 1987—. Contbr. numerous articles to profl. jours. Pres. internat. cultural activities U. Kans., Lawrence, 1966-68. Fulbright fellow USIA, Washington, 1966-70, Sr. NRC fellow NAS, Washington, 1999; grantee NASA, Dept. of Def., Dept. of Energy, NSF. Fellow AIAA (assoc.), Am. Phys. Soc. (life), AAAS, Am. Nuc. Soc. (life). Avocations: jogging, travel, anthropology. Home: 13 Natalie Dr Hampton VA 23666-5565 Office: NASA Langley Rsch Ctr Ms 188 B Hampton VA 23681-0001

TRIPI, VINCENT JAMES, physician; b. South Euclid, Ohio, Apr. 19, 1926; m. Cynthia Tripi, 1976; 5 children. BS, Kent State U., 1952; DO, Chgo. Coll. Osteo. Medicine, 1957; MD, U. Calif., 1962. Diplomate Am. Osteo. Bd. Surgery; bd. cert. in gen. surgery Am. Osteo. Bd. Surgery. Intern Forest Hills Hosp., 1957-58; resident in gen. surgery Green Cross Gen. Hosp., 1957-61; chief of staff, chief of surgery Harborside Hosp., Fla., 1984-89. Author: New Approach to Pediatric Internal Surgery, 1964. With U.S. Army, 1944-46, ETO. Recipient award of appreciation Zephyr-Haven Nursing Home, 1999. Mem. DAV, Am. Coll. Osteo. Surgeons, Am. Osteo. Assn., Ohio Osteo. Soc. Surgeons (pres. 1974), Fla. Osteo. Med. Assn. Address: 1521 E Memorial Blvd Lakeland FL 33801-2222

TRIPLEHORN, CHARLES A. entomology educator, insects curator; b. Bluffton, Ohio, Oct. 27, 1927; s. Murray E. and Alice Irene (Lora) T.; m. Wanda Elaine Neiswander, June 12, 1949 (dec. Nov. 1985); children: Bradley Alyn, Bruce Wayne; m. Linda Sue Parsons, July 11, 1987. B.Sc., Ohio State U., 1949, MS, 1952; PhD, Cornell U., 1957. Asst. prof. entomology U. Del., Newark, 1952-54; teaching asst. entomology Cornell U., Ithaca, N.Y., 1954-57; asst. prof. entomology Ohio Agrl. Research and Devel. Ctr., Wooster, Ohio, 1957-61, Ohio State U., Columbus, 1961-62, assoc. prof. entomology, 1962-66, prof. entomology, 1966-92, prof. emeritus, 1992—. Econ. entomologist U.S. AID/Brazil, Piracicaba, Sao Paulo, 1964-66; vis. curator Field Mus. Natural History, Chgo., 1974, Can. Nat. Collection, Ottawa, Ont., 1977, Am. Mus. Natural History, N.Y.C., 1982, U. Mich., 1989, U. Ariz., 1989, Nat. Mus. of Natural History, 1998, Cornell U., 1999, Colo. State U., 2000, Brigham Young U., 2000. Co-author: Introduction to the Study of Insects, 7th edit., 2004. Cubmaster Boy Scouts Am., Wooster, Ohio, 1959-60, scoutmaster, Columbus, 1971-72; football coach Upper Arlington Football Assn., Ohio, 1968-71 Grantee Am. Philos. Soc., 1963, NSF, 1979, 85, 92. Mem. Entomol. Soc. Am. (pres. 1985), Coleopterists Soc. (pres. 1976), Royal Entomol. Soc. London, Entomol. Soc. Washington, Sigma Xi, Gamma Sigma Delta Clubs: Wheaton (pres.). Republican. Methodist. Avocations: sports; music; reading; writing. Home: 3943 Medford Sq Hilliard OH 43026-2219 Office: Mus Biol Diversity Div Insects The Ohio State University 1315 Kinnear Rd Columbus OH 43212-1157 Office Phone: 614-292-6839. Personal E-mail: triplhrn@aol.com.

TRIPLETT, ARLENE ANN, management consultant; b. Portland, Oreg., Jan. 21, 1942; d. Vincent Michael and Lorraine Catherine (Starr) Jakovich; m. William Karrol Triplett, Jan. 27, 1962; children: Stephen Michael, Patricia Ann. BA, U. Calif., Berkeley, 1963. Budgets and reports analyst Cutter Labs., Berkeley, 1963-66; controller Citizens for Reagan, 1975-76; dir. adminstrn. Republican. Nat. Com., 1977-80; asst. sec. Dept. Commerce, Washington, 1981-83; assoc. dir. mgmt. Office Mgmt. and Budget, Exec. Office of Pres., Washington, 1983-85; prin. assoc. McManis Assocs., Inc., 1985-87, v.p., 1987-89, sr. v.p., 1989-93; from v.p. to exec. v.p. Am. Tours Internat., Inc., L.A., 1993-97; prin. McManis Assoc., Manhattan Beach, Calif., 1997-98, IBM, Manhattan Beach, Calif., 1999—2002; fin. mgmt. cons., 2002—. Roman Catholic.

TRIPLETT, E. EUGENE, editor; b. LaJolla, Calif., Mar. 12, 1949; s. Erbin Eugene Triplett and Marjorie Ann (Aldrich) Heath; m. Vannie Carol Crow, July 19, 1968; 1 child, Aaron Eugene. BA in Journalism, Ctrl. State U., 1975. Reporter, columnist The Okla. Jour., Oklahoma City, 1976-80; entertainment editor The Daily Oklahoman, Oklahoma City, 1981-85, asst. city editor, 1985-89, city editor, 1989-99, sr. feature writer, columnist, 1999—. Bd. dirs. Crime Stoppers Oklahoma City; mem. comm. com. Okla. Heart Assn., 1989-92. With U.S. Army, 1969-71, Vietnam. Recipient 1st pl. Feature Writing award Soc. Profl. Journalists, 1987, 97-98, 2d pl., 1999-2000. Mem. AP/Okla. News Exec. (pres.-elect 1994-95, pres. 1995-96, 2nd pl. Feature Writing award 1988, 1st pl. Feature Writing award, 2002, 1st pl. Rev. Writing award 2003). Democrat. Avocations: collecting recorded music, feature films, vintage tv shows. Home: 8116 NW 118th St Oklahoma City OK 73162-1113 Office: The Daily Oklahoman 9000 Broadway Ext Oklahoma City OK 73114-3799 Office Phone: 405-475-4105. E-mail: etriplett@oklahoman.com., geneoat@cox.net.

TRIPLETT, KIRK ALLEN, professional golfer; b. Moses Lake, Wash., Mar. 29, 1962; Named winner, Alberta Open, 1988, Nissan Open, 2000. Office: c/o PGA Tour 112 PGA Tour Blvd Ponte Vedra Beach FL 32082

TRIPLETT, PRESTON, retail food company executive; Sec., treas. Brookshire Grocery, Tyler, Tex., sr. v.p., 1999—. Office: Brookshire Grocery 17498 Hwy 695 Tyler TX 75703

TRIPLETT, WILLIAM CARRYL, physician, researcher; b. St. Marys, W.Va., May 9, 1915; s. Harry Carryl and Glenna Olive (Dotson) T.; m. Jane Dinsmoor, June 11, 1940 (div. 1961); children: William C. II, Jan Frances; m. Josephine Vann (div.); children: Harriett, Amber, Charles; m. Kathleen Quigley. BA, W.Va. U., 1936; MD, U. Md., 1940. Intern Ohio Valley Gen. Hosp., Wheeling, W.Va., 1940; resident in internal medicine Berkley County Meml. Hosp., 1941-42; med. dir. Camp Wood (Tex.) Convalescent Ctr.; pvt. practice Corpus Christi, Tex., 1946-68, 72-88; dir. rsch. TRIAD Assocs. Inc., 1947—, ENA, 1968-92, Intercontinental Cardiac Rsch., 1984-92; dir. pub. health Real County, Tex., 1989—; med. dir. Cedar Hills Geriatric Ctr., Camp Wood, Tex., 2003—. Inventor and patentee in field. Bayfront adv. com. Corpus Christi, 1950 55; bay drilling com. Corpus Christi, 1954-56; environ. com., Tex., 1968-72; assoc. dir. Tex. Mil. Inst. Capt. USCG Aux., 1952-56. Named Man of Yr. Camp Wood/Nueces Canyon C. of C., 1990; 18 awards as editor Costal Bd. Medicine, Corpus Christi. Mem. AMA, Tex. Med. Assn., Corpus Christi Yacht Club (comdr. 1953). Anglican. Avocations: hunting, fishing, yachting, hydroplane racing. Home and Office: TRIAD Assocs Inc PO Box 517 Camp Wood TX 78833-0517

TRIPODES, JAMES G. nuclear safety and environmental regulatory affairs professional; b. San Francisco, Mar. 12, 1954; s. George J. Tripodes and Daisy Natsoulas Pimentel; m. Nham T. Tripodes, Nov. 5, 1983. BS in Environ. Planning and Mgmt., U. Calif., Davis, 1978. Registered hazardous substances profl. Nat. Environ. Health Assn.; registered environ. assessor Calif. EPA. Envir. health/safety technician, cyclotron health physicist U. Calif., Davis, 1972-79, health physics mgr. Irvine, 1979-89, assoc. dir. envir. health/safety for envir. reg. affairs, 1989-2001, acting dir. environ. health and safety, 2001—02; dep. dept. head environ. protection Lawrence Livermore (Calif.) Nat. Lab., 2002—03, scientist, 2003—. Co-founder, oversight chmn. Internat. Conf. on Incineration and Thermal Treatment Techs., 1980-2000; prin. investigator, project mgr. U.S. Dept. Energy and Calif. Dept. Health Svcs., 1982-95. Editor: (book and CD-ROM) Proceedings of International Conferences on Incineration and Thermal Treatment Technologies, 1985-2000; guest editor spl. issue: Health Physics Jour., 1991. Mem. govt. affairs coun. Irvine C. of C., 1995—2002; patron Heritage Found., Washington, 1995—, Commonwealth Club of Calif., 2003-. Fellow Acad. Polit. Sci.; mem. AAAS, ASME, Health Physics Soc. (Elda E. Anderson award 1994), Am. Soc. for Quality, Ctr. for Study of the Presidency, N.Y. Acad. Scis. Republican. Avocations: fine art and music appreciation, public affairs. Office: Lawrence Livermore Nat Lab PO Box 808 L-372 Livermore CA 94551 Office Phone: 925-424-2875. Business E-Mail: tripodes2@llnl.gov.

TRIPODI, TONY, social work educator, author, editor; b. Sacramento, Calif., Nov. 30, 1932; s. Nicola and Christina (Grandinetti); m. Roni Roberts, Oct. 28, 1969 (div. 1986); children: Lee Anna, Anthony, David, Stephen; m. Miriam Potocky-Tripodi, July 25, 1998. AB, U. Calif., Berkeley, 1954, MSW, 1958; D of Social Work, Columbia U., N.Y.C., 1963. Rsch. tech. Calif. Dept. Mental Hygiene, Sacramento, 1958-59; rsch. analyst Calif. Youth Authority, Sacramento, 1959-60; from rsch. asst. to asst. prof. Columbia U., N.Y.C., 1962-65; asst. prof. U. Calif., Berkeley, 1965-66; from assoc. prof. to prof. U. Mich. Sch. Social Work, Ann Arbor, 1966-87; assoc. dean prof. U. Pitts. Sch. Social Work, 1987—92; prof., assoc. dir., & doctoral program head Fla. Internat. U., 1992—95; dean, prof. Coll. Social Work OH State U., 1995—. Rsch. assoc. Bklyn. Coll., 1963-65; editor in chief Social Work Rsch. and Abstracts, N.Y.C., 1980-84; interim assoc. dean U. Mich. Sch. Social Work, Ann Arbor, 1985, 1986, 1987; rsch. cons. Zancan Found., Padova, Italy, 1974-1992, NIMH, Silver Spring, Md., 1989-, Nat. Rsch. Adv. Com., Clinton, Mich., 1988-95; co-editor The Journal of Social Work Research and Evaluation: An International Publication, 1998-. Author: (with others) Clinical Social Judgement, 1966, Requiem for Torchy, 2003, and 19 other books; co-editor: Jour. of Social Work Rsch. and Evaluation: An Internat. Pub., 1998-; contbr. articles to profl. jours. Bd. dirs. Parental Stress Ctr., Pitts., 1987-92, Comm. Rsch. Partners, 2000-, Asian Am. Comm. Svc., 2000-, Coun. Public Reps. Assoc., NIH, 2003-, Nat. Assoc. Deans and Dir. Sch. Social Work, 2001-2004, With USNR, 1954-56. Doctoral rsch. fellow Sage Found., N.Y.C., 1960-63; rsch. grantee NSF, 1965-66; Fulbright Hays scholar U.S. Govt., Italy, 1973-74; invited scholar Tilburg U., the Netherlands, 1977; vis. scholar U. Kent, Canterbury, Eng., 1980. Mem. NASW, Acad. Cert. Social Workers, Coun. Social Work Edn., Pres. Soc. Social Work and Rsch, Internat. Assoc. Sch. Social Work, WHO (World Health Orgn.), Mensa, Phi Kappa Phi. Home: 2705 Charing Rd Columbus OH 43221 Office Phone: 614-292-5300.

TRIPOLI, MASUMI HIROYASU, financial consultant; b. Fukuyama, Japan, Apr. 23, 1956; d. Yoshimi and Suzuko Hiroyasu; 1 child, Mona Lisa Tripoli. BA cum laude, U. Wash., 1978; MA, Sophia U., Tokyo, 1981; postgrad., Sydney U., 1982; MBA, Ecole des Hautes Etudes Comml, Jouy-en-Josas, France, 1983. CFP. Corp. planning mgr. Kowa Corp., Osaka, Japan, 1983-85; internat. bond trader Banque Baribas, Tokyo, 1985-86, Westpac Bank, Tokyo, 1987-88; fin. cons. Masumi Tripoli and Assocs., Irvine, Calif., 1989—; anchor newscaster United TV, L.A., 1989-92. Condr. seminars in field. Contbr. articles to profl. jours. Bd. dirs. L.A. Food Bank, Orange County Jr. Achievement; CEO Masumi Tripoli and Mona Lisa Tripoli Found. Grantee Sophia U., 1979, H.E.C., 1983. Mem. Internat. Bd. Cert. Fin. Planners. E-mail: masumiusa@hotmail.com.

TRIPP, AILI MARI, political science educator; b. Market Harborough, UK, May 24, 1958; came to US, 1974; d. Lloyd William Frederick and Marja-Liisa (Aro) Swantz; m. Warren Earl Tripp, Aug. 28, 1976; children: Lloyd Max, Leila Mari. BA, U. Chgo., 1983, MA, 1985; PhD, Northwestern U., Evanston, Ill., 1990. Assoc. prof. dept. polit. sci. and womens studies program U. Wis., Madison, 1992—2002; dir. Women's Studies Rsch. Ctr., 2000; assoc. dean Internat. studies Northwestern U, Evanston, Ill., 2003—. Author: Changing the Rules: The Politics of Liberalization and the Urban Informal Economy in Tanzania, 2001, Women and Politics in Uganda, 2001. Am. Coun. of Learned Soc. fellow, 1991; grantee Inst. for the Study of World Politics, 1988, John D. and Catherine T. MacArthur Found., 1993, AAUW, 1993, Social Sci. Rsch. Coun., 1995, UN World Inst. for the Study of Devel. Econ. Rsch., 1987, Am. Scandinavian Found., 1999. Mem. Am. Polit. Sci. Assn. (Victoria Schuck award 2001), African Studies Assn.

TRIPP, APRIL, special education services professional; BS, Calif. State U., Fullerton, Calif., 1981; MA with hons., Calif. State U., Long Beach, Calif., 1985; MS, Johns Hopkins U., 1994; PhD with hons., Tex. Woman's U., 1989. 1st coord. adapted physical edn. Balt. County Pub. Schs.; assoc. prof. U. Ill., Urbana-Champaign, Ill. Chmn. adapted physical edn. section Md. AHPERD; mem. Nat. Cert. for Adapted Physical Edn. Standards Com., Spl. Olympics. Recipient Excellence in Edn. award-Spl. Tchr. of Yr. Balt. County, Mabel Lee award Am. Alliance Health, Phys. Edn., Recreation and Dance, 1994; grantee Nat. Handicapped Sports. Mem. Nat. PTA (hon. life award 1993), ARAPCS (mem. adapted physical activity coun. exec. com.) Office: Dept Kinesiology Univ Ill Louise Freer Hall 906 S Goodwin Ave Urbana IL 61801 E-mail: atripp3@uiuc.edu.

TRIPP, FREDERICK GERALD, investment advisor; b. Chgo., Oct. 1, 1936; s. Gerald F. and Kathryn Ann (Siebold) T.; m. Terry Anne Shull, Aug. 26, 1967; children: Mark A., Karin M. Coburn, Tracy L. Clark, Tricia L., Patrick G. BS in Econs., Purdue U., 1958; MBA, Lehigh U., 1964; PhD, The Am. U., 1972. Sr. v.p. CRI, Inc., Rockville, Md., 1979-82, Security Pacific, Inc., Seattle, 1982-83; pres. Frederick G. Tripp & Assocs., Inc., Rockville, 1983—. Instr. Troy State U., 1965-67, Am. U., 1975-77, Indsl. Coll. Armed Forces, 1975-80; mem. pres.'s coun. Investment Mgmt. and Rsch., Inc., 1985-97; chmn. coun. Raymond James Fin. Svcs., Inc., 1998-2003. Pres. Doctoral Assn., The Am. U., 1973. Maj. U.S. Army, 1958-67, Vietnam. Mem. Fin. Planning Assn., Investment Mgmt. Cons. Assn., Sigma Pi. Methodist. Avocations: skiing, boating, racquetball, flying. Office: Frederick G Tripp & Assocs 2400 Research Blvd Ste 300 Rockville MD 20850-3243 Home: 303 Redland Blvd Apt 403 Rockville MD 20850-6031 E-mail: fred.tripp@trippinvest.com.

TRIPP, JAMES E. psychotherapist, educator; b. Inkster, Mich., Aug. 19, 1944; s. Luke Samuel and Dorothy Mae Tripp. BA, Wayne State U., 1967, MSW, 1969; EdD, U. No. Colo., 1975. Psychologist, Southfield/Detroit, Mich., 1982—; asst. clin. prof. Wayne State U., Detroit, 1991—. Author: Social Work Internship Manual, 1971; contbr. articles to profl. jours. Bd. mem. Gospel Against AIDS, Detroit, 1995—. Lt. comdr. USPHS Commn. Corps, 1979—82. Avocations: fishing, boating, bicycling, weightlifting, walking. Home: 29401 Wildbrook Dr Southfield MI 48034

TRIPP, KAREN BRYANT, lawyer; b. Rocky Mount, NC, Sept. 2, 1955; d. Bryant and Katherine Rebecca (Watkins) Tripp; m. Robert Mark Burleson, June 25, 1977 (div. 1997); 1 child, Hamilton Chase Tripp Barnett. BA, U. NC, 1976; JD, U. Ala., 1981. Bar: Tex. 1981, US Dist. Ct. (so. dist.) Tex. 1982, US Ct. Appeals (fed. cir.) 1983, US Dist. Ct. (ea. dist.) Tex. 1991, US Supreme Ct. 1994, US Dist. Ct. (no. dist.) Tex. 1998, US Ct. Appeals (5th and 9th cirs.) 2000, US Ct. Appeals (3d cir.) 2001. Law clk. Tucker, Gray & Espy, Tuscaloosa, Ala., 1978-81; law clk. to presiding justice Ala. Supreme Ct., Montgomery, Ala., summer 1980; atty. Exxon Prodn. Rsch. Co., Houston, 1981-86, coord. tech. transfer, 1986-87; assoc. Arnold, White and Durkee, Houston, 1988-93, shareholder, 1994-98; shareholder, head intellectual property sect. for Houston office Winstead, Sechrest & Minick, Attys. at Law, Houston, 1998; pres. Blake Barnett & Co., 1996—2003; pvt. practice Houston, 1999—. Creator, program planner, master of ceremonies 1st and 2d intellectual property law confs. for women corp. counsels. Editor: Intellectual Property Law Rev., 1995—2004; contbr. articles to profl. jour. Chair U. Houston and Houston intellectual Property Law Assoc. Fall CLE Inst. on Intellectual Property, 2000. Mem. ABA (intellectual property law sect., ethics com. 1992-96), Houston Bar Assn. (interprofl. rels. com. 1988-90), Houston Intellectual Property Law Assn. (outstanding inventor com. 1982-84, chmn. 1994-95, sec. 1987-88, treas. 1991-92, bd. dir. 1992-94, 98-2000, nominations com. 1993, 96, chmn. fall CLE Inst. 2000), Tex. Bar Assn. (antitrust law com. 1984-85, chmn. internat. law com. intellectual property law sect. 1987-88, internat. transfer tech. com. 1983-84, planning com. continuing legal edn. conf. on intellectual property 2003), planning comm. for 2003 CLE Inst. on Intellectual property Law, Tex. Exec. Women, Women's Fin. Exch., Am. Intellectual Property Lawyers Assn. (patent law com. 1995), Intellectual Property Owners Assn. (copyright com.), Women in Tech. (founder), Lil Eli's Club (founder), Phi Alpha Delta. Republican. Episcopalian. Office: PO Box 1301 Houston TX 77251-1301 Office Phone: 713-658-9323. Business E-Mail: ktripp@tripplaw.com.

TRIPP, KEVIN, retail executive; Degree in pharmacy, U. Wyo. Pharmacist Osco, Casper, Wyo.; exec. v.p. drug and gen. mdse. Albertson's, Inc., Boise, 2001—. Office: Albertsons Inc 250 Parkcenter Blvd Boise ID 83726

TRIPP, MARIAN BARLOW LOOFE, retired public relations executive; b. Lodgepole, Nebr., July 26; d. Lewis Rockwell and Cora Dee (Davis) Barlow; m. James Edward Tripp, Feb. 9, 1957; children: Brendan Michael, Kevin Mark. BS, Iowa State U., 1944. Writer Dairy Record, St. Paul, 1944-45; head product promotion divsn., pub. rels. dept. Swift & Co., Chgo., 1945-55; mgmt. supr. pub. rels. J. Walter Thompson Co., N.Y.C. and Chgo., 1956-76, v.p. consumer affairs Chgo., 1974-76; pres. Marian Tripp Communications Inc., Chgo., 1976-94. Mem. Am. Inst. Wine and Food, Confriere de la Chaine des Rotisseriers (officer Chgo. chpt.), Mayflower Soc., Daughters of the Am. Revolution, Les Dames D'Escoffier. Episcopalian. Office: 100 E Bellevue Pl Chicago IL 60611-1157 E-mail: mbtripp@aol.com.

TRIPP, SUSAN GERWE, museum director; b. Balt., Dec. 28, 1945; d. Earl Joseph and Maria Elizabeth (Wise) Gerwe; m. David Enders Tripp, June 9, 1977. BS, U. Md., 1967. Home econs. tchr. Balt. County Pub. Sch. Sys., 1967-74; curator of art Johns Hopkins U., Balt., 1974-76, curator of art, archivist, 1976-78, instr. evening coll., 1978-84, dir. univ. collections, 1979-91; supr., instr. art history Goucher Coll., Notre Dame U., Balt., 1977-86; dir. docent tng. Homewood Mus., Balt., 1987-89; exec. dir. Old Westbury (N.Y.) Gardens, 1992-96; writer Stuyvesant, N.Y., 1996—. Dir. Homewood Restoration Adv. Com., 1983-92, Evergreen Restoration Adv. Com., 1988 92, Advancement Basilica Hist. Trust, Inc., 2000-2001; lectr. in field. Co-author: The Garrett Collection of Japanese Art, 1993 (NEA Grant 1980), Contbr. articles to profl. jours. Bd. dirs. Columbia County Hist. Soc., 1996-2002, 2003—, pres. bd. dirs., 1997-2002, sec., 2003—; trustee Regional and Cmty. Hist. Preservation Benefit Plan, 2002—; chmn. Vanderpoel house restoration Columbia County Hist. Soc., 2002-03; judge Hist. Hudson Preservation Awards, 2000—; bd. trustees Am. Numismatic Soc., 2003—. Recipient Hist. Preservation award Balt. Heritage, Inc., 1988, 91, Rsch. award Am. Soc. Interior Designers, 1991. Fellow Am. Numismatic Soc. (standing com., libr., trustee 2003—); mem. Brit. Mus. Soc., Oriental Ceramic Soc., Balt. Mus. Art, Furniture History Soc., Hist. Hudson, Am. Assn. Mus. Columbia County Hist. Soc. (bd. dirs. 2003—, sec. bd. dirs. 2003—), Omicron Nu. Avocations: architecture, archaeology, chinese ceramics, historical restoration. Office: PO Box G Stuyvesant NY 12173-0009

TRIPP, THOMAS MURRAY, finance educator; s. James W. and Patricia Tripp; m. Jodi Tripp, May 24, 1998; children: Chloe, Charlie. BS, U. of Wash., e; PhD, Northwestern U., Evanston, Ill., 1991. Asst. prof. mgmt. Wash. State U., Richland, 1991—94, asst. prof. of mgmt. Vancouver, 1994—97, assoc. prof. of mgmt., 1997—2004, prof. of mgmt., 2004—, dir. of bus. programs, 2001. Contbr. articles to profl. jours. Named Tchr. of the Yr., Wash. State U., Vancouver campus, 2000; recipient Outstanding Faculty Tchg. award, Wash. State U., 1996, Best Conceptual Paper award, Internat. Assn. of Conflict Mgmt., 1999. Avocations: hiking, bicycling, music, kayaking. Office: Washington State Univ 14204 NE Salmon Creek Ave Vancouver WA 98686 Office Phone: 360-546-9754. E-mail: tripp@vancouver.wsu.edu.

TRIPP, THOMAS NEAL, lawyer, political consultant; b. June 19, 1942; s. Gerald Frederick and Kathryn Ann (Siebold) T.; m. Ellen Marie Larrimer, Apr. 16, 1966; children: David Larrimer, Bradford Douglas, Corinne Catherine. BA cum laude, Mich. State U., 1964; JD, George Washington U., 1967. Bar: Ohio 1967, U.S. Ct. Mil. Appeals 1968, U.S. Supreme Ct. 1968, Wyo. 1991. Pvt. practice, Columbus, Ohio, 1969—, Wilson, Wyo., 1991—. Real estate developer, Columbus, 1969—; chmn. bd. Black Sheep Enterprises, Columbus, 1969—; polit. cons. David A. Keene & Assocs., Washington, 1986-96; vice chmn. bd. Sun Valley-Elkhorn Assn., Idaho, 1983-85, chmn., 1986-91; vice chmn. Sawtooth Sports, Ketchum, Idaho, 1983-85; legal counsel Wallace F. Ackley Co., Columbus, 1973—; vice chmn. Triathlon LLC, 1996-2003; presiding judge Ohio Mock Trial Competition, 1986-94; chmn. bd. dirs. White House, 1996; mem. small bus. adv. coun. FCC, 1993-95; dep. spl. adviser to pres. N.Am. Free Trade Agreement, 1993; polit. columnist. Trustee Americans for Responsible Govt., Washington, GOPAC; mem. Peace Corps Adv. Coun., 1981-85; mem. U.S. Commn. on Trade Policy and Negotiations, 1985-88; campaign mgr., fin. chmn. Charles Rockwell Saxbe, Ohio Ho. of Reps., 1974, 76, 78, 80; campaign mgr. George Bush for Pres., 1980, nat. dep. field dir., nat. dep. polit. dir., 1980; alumni admissions coun. Mich. State U., 1984-2000, George Washington U., 1988-2000; regional co-chmn. Reagan-Bush, 1984, nat. fin. com., 1984; mem. Victory '84 fin. com.; mem. Victory '88 fin. com. Bush-Quayle; co-chmn. Ohio Lawyers for Bush/Quayle, 1988; Rep. candidate 2d U.S. Congl. Dist., Idaho, 1988; candidate U.S. Senate, Wyo., 1996; transition dir. Ohio Sec. of State, 1990-91; bd. trustees Columbus Acad. Pvt. Co-ed Secondary Sch., 1991-94, Prescott (Ariz.) Coll., 1998-2000; chmn. bd. dirs. T.R.E.E. Coalition, 1991—; vice-chmn. Am. Conservative Union Found., 2002—; chmn. FirstPrinciplesvs. Pub. Policy Institute, 2003—. 1st lt. U.S. Army, 1967-69. Fellow Pi Sigma Alpha, Vietnam Vet. Am., Phi Delta Phi. Republican. Home: 5420 Clark State Rd Columbus OH 43230-1956

TRIPPENSEE, GARY ALAN, retired aerospace transportation executive; b. Jefferson City, Mo., May 23, 1940; m. Concha Elvira Perez, Aug. 18, 1981; children: Jena, Darin. BSME, U. Mo., Rolla, 1962; AA in Bus., Antelope Valley Coll., Lancaster, Calif., 1974. Lic. airframe and powerplant mechanic, FAA; single/multi-engine comml. aircraft lic. land & sea, Inst.; cert. flight instr., instrument. Aircraft flight test engr. McDonnell Douglas, St. Louis, 1965-79; project mgr. NASA/Dryden Flight Rsch. Ctr., Edwards, Calif., 1979—2001, project mgr. F14, 1983-84, project mgr. F15, 1984-85, project mgr. X-29, 1985-91, project mgr. X-31, 1991-92, internat. test. orgn. dir. X-31, 1993-95, project mgr. X-33, 1996-2000, project mgr. X-37, 2000-01, ret., 2001. Capt. U.S. Army C.E., 1962-65, Vietnam. Recipient Laurels award for aeronautics/propulsion Aviation Week & Space Tech., 1990, 93, Outstanding Alumni award U. Mo.-Rolla, 2000. Mem. EAA, Acad. Mech. Engrs. Avocations: flying, fishing, r/c models. Home: 3410 Callie Dr Grove OK 74344 Office Phone: 918-791-1917. E-mail: garyatrip@juno.com.

TRIPPI, PETER, museum director; b. 1965; Student, NYU, Courtauld Inst. Art, London. With Balt. Mus. Art; asst. vice dir. devel. Bklyn. Mus. Art, 1998—2000; dir. Dahesh Mus., N.Y.C., 2000—. Author: J.W. Waterhouse, 2002; founder, former exec. dir., mem. editl. bd.: Nineteenth-Century Art Worldwide; contbr. essaysGrand Design. Mem.: Assn. Historians Nineteenth-Century Art (treas.), French-Am. C. of C. (assoc.). Office: 580 Madison Ave New York NY 10022*

TRISCO, ROBERT FREDERICK, church historian, educator; b. Chgo., Nov. 11, 1929; s. Richard E. and Harriet Rose (Hardt) T. BA, St. Mary of Lake Sem., Mundelein, Ill., 1951; STL, Pontifical Gregorian U., Rome, 1955, Hist. Eccl.D., 1962; LHD (hon.), Belmont Abbey Coll., 1992. Ordained priest Roman Catholic Ch., 1954. Faculty Cath. U. Am., Washington, 1959-2000, prof. ch. history, 1975-2000, Kelly-Quinn disting. prof. ch. history, 1999-2000, prof. emeritus ch. history, 2000—. Expert 2d Vatican Coun., 1962-65; pres. Am. subcom. Internat. Commn. Comparative Ch. History, 1978-80, assesseur, 1980—; mem. subcoms. Nat. Conf. Cath. Bishops, 1966-76, 87-92; mem. Pontifical Com. Hist. Scis., 1982—; hon. mem. Accademia di San Carlo (Milan), 1986—; hon. prelate (monsignor), 1992; mem. Internat. Joint Commn. for Theol. Dialogue between Cath. Ch. and Orthodox Ch., 1999—; mem. Anglican-Roman Catholic Consultation in U.S., 2002—; mem. adv. com. Assn. Friends of the Archives of Congregation for Doctrine of the Faith (Holy See), 1999—. Author: The Holy See and Nascent Church in the Middle Western U.S., 1826-1850, 1962, Bishops and Their Priests in the United States, 1988; co-author: A Guide to American Catholic History, 2d edit., 1982; editor: Catholics in America, 1976; editor CAth. Hist. Rev., 1963—; co-editor, contbr.: Studies in Catholic History in Honor of John Tracy Ellis, 1985; contbr. articles to profl. jours. Decorated knight Equestrian Order of the Holy Sepulchre of Jerusalem, 1993, knight comdr., 1998. Mem. Am. Hist. Assn., Am. Soc. Ch. History (coun. 1980-82), Am. Cath. Hist. Assn. (exec. sec. 1961—, sec., treas. 1983—), Can. Cath. Hist. Assn. Office: Cath U Am Mullen Library Rm 320 Washington DC 20064-0001 E-mail: trisco@cua.edu.

TRISTANO, SANDRA, circuit court judge; b. Aug. 30, 1951; d. Elias and Shirley (wood) Snitzer; m. Michael Eugene Tristano, Sept. 29, 1979. BA, Cornell U., 1973; JD, Washington U., St. Louis, 1977. Bar: Ill. 1977, U.S. Dist. Ct. (cen. dist.) Ill. 1977. Staff atty. Ill. Dept. Pub. Aid, Springfield, 1977-80; gen. counsel Ill. Dept. Energy and natural Resources, 1980-90, Pace Suburban Bus Svc., 1992-2000; mem. Ill. Labor Rels. Bd., 2000—02; cir. judge Cook County Cir. Ct., 2002—. Pro bono vol. Vols. for Justice, Springfield, 19835; chmn. ABA Pub. Transp. Com., 1997-99. Mem. ABA, Ill. Bar Assn., Chgo. Bar Assn. Home: 1438 Crown Ln Glenview IL 60025-1227

TRITLE, LAWRENCE ALAN, history educator; b. Glendale, Calif., Oct. 13, 1946; s. Robert Charles Jr. and Dorothy (Brown) T.; m. Margaret Burlington, Jan. 31, 1970. BA, UCLA, 1968; MA, U. S. Fla., 1972; PhD, U. Chgo., 1978. Prof. Loyola Marymount U., L.A., 1978—, Marie Chilton chair humanities, 1988. Vis. prof. Loyola U. Chgo., 1981-82, 90-91, UCLA, 1992. Author: Phocion the Good, 1988, From Melos to My Lai. War & Survival, 2000, The Peloponnesian War, 2004; editor: The Greek World in the Fourth Century BC, 1997, Balkan Currents, 1998, Text and Tradition: Studies in Greek History & Histiography, 1999, Crossroads of History Age of Alexander, 2003. Lt. U.S. Army, 1968-71, Vietnam. NEH fellow U. Pa., 1979. Mem. Am. Philol. Assn. (chair com. ancient history 1997-99), Am. Hist. Assn., Assn. Ancient Historians, Soc. Mayflower Descendants (So. Calif. chpt.). Democrat. Home: 8301 Fordham Rd Los Angeles CA 90045-2559 Office: Loyola Marymount U 1 LMU Dr Los Angeles CA 90045-2699 Office Phone: 310-338-7385. Business E-Mail: ltritle@lmu.edu.

TRITSCH, GEORGE LEOPOLD, biochemist, educator, retired biomedical researcher; b. Vienna, Apr. 8, 1929; arrived in U.S., 1940; s. Robert James and Edith Mary Tritsch; m. Norma Elsie Tritsch, June 16, 1951; children: George L., Margaret Ellen, Douglas Evan. BA, NYU, 1948; MS, U. Md., 1951; PhD, Purdue U., 1954. Rsch. assoc. Cornell Med. Coll., N.Y.C., 1954—56, Rockefeller U., N.Y.C., 1956—59; cancer rsch. scientist Roswell Pk. Cancer Inst., Buffalo, 1959—95, cancer. rsch. sci. emeritus, 1995—; from asst. rsch. prof. to prof. emeritus SUNY, Buffalo, 1961—; prof. biochemistry Niagara U., Niagara Falls, NY, 1961—. Vis. prof. dept. biochemistry Dartmouth Med. Sch., 1968, Purdue Cancer Ctr., W. Lafayette, Ind., 1983; mem. grant rev. panel nat. prostatic cancer project NIH, Bethesda, Md., 1975—85; symposium organizer adenosine deaminase N.Y. Acad. Scis., 1984; invited spkr. in field. Editor, author Axenic Mammalian Cell Reactions, 1969, Adenosine Deaminase, 1985; contbr. articles to profl. jours. Bd. dirs. N.Y. State Health Rsch. Coun., Buffalo, 1975—80. Grantee, USPHS, 1960—90, Am. Cancer Soc., 1961—69. Mem.: Soc. Exptl. Biology, Am. Assn. Cancer Rsch., Am. Soc. Pharmacological and Exptl. Therapeutics, Am. Inst. Nutrition, Am. Soc. Biochemistry and Molecular Biology, Harvey Soc., Sigma Xi, Alpha Chi Sigma, Phi Lambda Upsilon. Avocations: playing piano, water sports. Office: Roswell Pk Cancer Inst 666 Elm St Buffalo NY 14263-0001

TRITT, LINCOLN C. (LINCOLN C. GWICH'IN), writer, educator, musician; b. Salmon River, Alaska, Oct. 18, 1946; s. Isaac Albert and Naomi (Peter) T. Grad., Mt. Edgecombe H.S., 1966; student, U. Alaska, 1972, 84-87; student electricity and electronics, student radioman class A sch., Naval Tng. Ctr., 1967. Exploration worker, driver, driller asst. Kandik Oil Field Parker

Exploration, Fairbanks, Alaska, 1977; negotiator Venetie (Alaska) Tribal Govt., 1980, heavy equipment operator, 1982; phone survey rep. Mental Health Program and U. Alaska, 1984; curriculum developer Yukon Flats (Alaska) Sch. Dist., 1985; laborer Peter Kewitt and sons, Deadhorse, Alaska, 1985; bookkeeper Tanana Chiefs Conf., Inc., on-site supr., 1985; translator fed. Indian law Fed. Indian Law workshop, Venetie, Alaska, 1986; grant contract negotiator with fed. agys., 1987; grant adminstr., overall project dir. Arctic Village Traditional Coun., 1988-89; liaison, coord. U.S. Geophys. Inst./U. Alaska, Fairbanks, 1989; instr. rural coll. U. Alaska, 1990; tribal adminstr. Native Vill. Venetie (Alaska), 1994-95. Carpenter Bur. Indian Affairs Sch., Arctic Vill., Alaska, 1970; postal clk. U.S. Postal Svc., Fairbanks, Alaska, 1971, substitute postmaster, 1984—; tchr. Gwich'in lang., 1974; store mgr. Midnight Sun Native Store, Arctic Village, Alaska, 1975. Author screenplay on Native Am. alcohol experience; contbr. essays, stories to Raven Tells Stories: An Anthology of Alaska Native Writings, Coyote Bark, Alaska Mag., Alaskan Epiphany, All Alaska Weekly, Talking Leaves, Tundra Times, The Turtle Quarterly, The Council, Nimrod; columnist Fairbanks Daily News Miner, Northland News; composer (song) Belief; mem. of cast: Earth and the Great Weather, 1993, 95, 97; performed at Athabascan Old-Time Fiddling Festival, Summer Folk Festival, Fairbanks Folk Festival, Plate and Palate Restaurant, Native Village at Alaskaland; cons. (videos, films) Wisdom of the Elders, Caribou People. Firefighter Dept. Natural Resource, Fairbanks, Alaska, 1984; lobbyist Gwich'in People, 1986-87; mem. restructuring com. Howard Luke Alternative Sch., 1993, 94; Rural Campuses U. Alaska, 1990; coord. first Gwich'in Gathering in Arctic Village, Alaska, 1988; mem. coun. Native Village of Venetie (Alaska) Govt., 1974-86; mem. Arctic Village Traditional Coun., 1973-89, chief, 1987-89; mem. sch. bd. Arctic Village, 1974-76. Served with USN, 1966-70, Vietnam. Mem. Native Writers Circle of Ams., Internat. Conf. Higher Edn. Indigenous People, Internat. Conf. Hunting and Gathering Socs., Alaska Native Viet Nam Vets, Fairbanks Folk Fest. Avocations: music, photography, recording, space science, history. Home: PO Box 22016 Arctic Village AK 99722-0016

TRITTEN, JAMES JOHN, national security educator; s. James Hanley and Jennie (Szucs) Tritten; m. Kathleen Brattesani (div. 1983); children: Kimberly, James John Jr.; m. Jasmine Clark, Dec. 29, 1990. BA in Internat. Studies, Am. U., 1971; MA in Internat. Affairs, Fla. State U., 1978; AM in Internat. Rels., U. So. Calif., 1982, PhD in Internat. Rels., 1984. Commd. officer USN, 1967, advanced through grades to commdr., 1981; joint strategic plans officer Office Chief Naval Ops., Washington, 1984—85; asst. dir. net assessment Office Sec. Def., Washington, 1985—86; chmn. dept. nat. security affairs Naval Postgrad. Sch., Monterey, Calif., 1986—89; ret. USN, 1989; assoc. prof. nat. security affairs Naval Postgrad. Sch., Monterey, 1989—93; spl. asst. comdr. Naval Doctrine Command, Norfolk, Va., 1993—96; chief policy and plan divsn. US Joint Forces Command, Suffolk, Va., 1996—2001, mem. joint doctrine divsn., 2001—02; chief tng. inspections divsn. Def. Threat Reduction Agy., Albuquerque, 2002—, asst. chief staff, 2002—. Cons. Rand Corp., Santa Monica, Calif., 1982—84; with Nat. Security Rsch., Fairfax, Va., 1992, Amerlnd, Alexandria, Va., 1996. Author: (book) Soviet Naval Forces and Nuclear Warfare, 1986, Our New National Security Strategy, 1992 (George Washington Honor medal, 1991), A Doctrine Reader, 1996; contbr. chapters to books, articles to profl. jours. Mem. adv. Bd. on Alcohol Related Problems, Monterey, 1987—90; bd. dirs., officer Leadership Monterey Peninsula, 1989—92, Carmel Valley (Calif.) Property Owners Assn., 1989—91; commr. Airport Land Use Commn., Monterey County, 1990—93. Decorated Def. Superior Svc. medal Sec. Def., Washington, DC, Meritorious Svc. medal Sec. Navy, Navy Civillian Supr. Svc. medal; recipient Joint Meritorious Civilian Svc. award, Chmn. Joint Chiefs Staff, 1998, Alfred Thayer Mahan award literary achievement, Navy League US, 1986. Mem.: Mil. Ops. Rsch. Soc. (v.p. 1990—91), US Naval Inst. (Silver and Bronze medals), Naval Order US, Pi Gamma Mu, Pi Sigma Alpha. Republican. Presbyn. Avocations: hiking, writing. Office: Def Threat Reduction Agy-CST 1680 Texas St SE Kirtland Afb NM 87117 Office Phone: 505-846-8734. Personal E-mail: jtritten121@comcast.net. Business E-Mail: james.tritten@abq.dtra.mil.

TRITTER, DANIEL F. lawyer, writer; b. N.Y.C., Jan. 20, 1934; s. Maurice J. and Hermina (Ronay) T.; m. Rita Frances Shane, June 22, 1958; 1 child, Michael Shane. BA, Williams Coll., 1954; MA, Columbia U., 1957; cert., Inst. on East Cen. Europe, 1957; JD, Benjamin N. Cardozo Sch. Law, 1982. Bar: N.Y. 1984, U.S. Dist. Ct. (so. dist., ea. dist.) 1984, U.S. Supreme Ct. 1987. Writer, exec. Diener & Dorskind, Inc., N.Y.C., 1960-71, M.L. Grant, Inc., N.Y.C., 1971-79; pvt. practice, N.Y.C., 1984—. Adj. prof. Williams Coll., 1984, Touro Law Sch., 1989, Benjamin N. Cardozo Sch. Law, 1999. Contbr. essays to profl. jours. Bd. govs. N.Y. chpt. Arthritis Found., 1985-90. Spl. agt. CIC, U.S. Army, 1957-60. Mem. Assn. Trial Lawyers Am., Law and Humanities Inst. (pres. 1986-91, v.p. 1991—), Williams Club. Democrat. Avocations: classical music, writing, sports. Office: 330 W 42nd St Fl 32 New York NY 10036-6902

TRITTER, RICHARD PAUL, strategic planning, safety and risk management consulting executive; b. Boston, Sept. 30, 1945; s. Herman Louis and Rose (Greenblatt) T.; children: Melissa Rosanne, Matthew Alexander, Rachel Danielle, Adam Levi. AB, Columbia Coll., N.Y.C., 1967; JD, Northea. U., 1976. Bar: Mass. 1977, U.S. Supreme Ct. 1980. Mktg. mgr./cons. Digital Equipment Corp., Merrimack, N.H., 1979-86; pres. Video/Demo Ctrs., Inc., Burlington, Mass., 1986-88; v.p. bus. devel. Info. Resources, Inc., Boston, 1988-91; dir. facilitation consulting svcs. Arthur Andersen LLP, Boston, Chgo., 1991-96; consulting dir. Computer Assocs., Inc., Andover, Mass., 1998—2001; pvt. cons. Israel, 2001—; safety mgr. Nachobonim Dry Storage Base. Panelist MIT Enterprise Forum, Cambridge, 1983-89; ptnr., mng. dir. Horn of Africa Fishing Partnership, 1998. Author: Control Self-Assessment: Experience, Current Thinking and Best Practices, 1996, Control Self Assessment—A Guide to Facilitation-Based Consulting, 2000; creator software application testing svc. in coop. with KPMG Peat Marwick, Compliance Testing and Verification, 1981. UN rep. Jubaland Relief and Rehab. Soc., Somalia; dir. Save Somalia Livestock Campaign, 1993. Recipient Better Govt. award Pioneer Inst. for Pub. Policy Rsch., Boston, Safest Constrn. Site in Israel award Nachobonim Dry Storage Base. Achievements include facilitating meetings between opposing clans in the Juba region of southern Somalia; initiated lobster export project with cooperation of Gen. Omar Jess, Col. Ahmed Hashi and other Somali leaders. E-mail: oleh77@yahoo.com.

TRITTON, THOMAS RICHARD, academic administrator, biologist, educator; b. Lakewood, Ohio, Dec. 20, 1947; s. William Frank and Margie Jean (Galbraith) Tritton; m. Louise Meschter Tritton; children: Lara, Christiana. BA, Ohio Wesleyan U., 1969; PhD, Boston U., 1973. Asst. prof. Yale Med. Sch., New Haven, 1975—80; assoc. prof. Yale U., 1980—85; prof. U. Vt., Burlington, 1985—97, vice provost, 1991—97; pres. Haverford Coll., Pa., 1997—. Mem. NIH Exptl. Therapeutics Study Sect., 1988—92. Editor books; mem. editl. bd.: various profl. jours.; contbr. scientific papers to profl. jours. Mem.: Am. Soc. Biol. Chemists, Am. Assn. Cancer Rsch. (com. mem.). Mem. Soc. Of Friends. Avocations: music, tennis. Office: Haverford Coll 370 Lancaster Ave Haverford PA 19041-1336 Office Phone: 610-896-1021. Business E-Mail: ttritton@haverford.edu.

TRIVEDI, MADHUKAR H. psychiatrist; b. Baroda, India, Sept. 22, 1957; came to U.S., 1986; s. Hariprasad and Jyoti T.; m. Beena Madhukar, Aug. 12, 1990; children: Hersh M., Ashesh M. Student, U. Baroda, 1974-76, MB, BChir, 1980. Diplomate Am. Bd. Psychiatry & Neurology. Intern S.S. Gen. Hosp., Baroda, India, 1980-81; resident in radiology Baroda Med. Coll., 1982, resident in psychiatry U. Gen. Hosp., 1982-85; resident in psychiatry Henry Ford Hosp., Detroit, 1986-90, chief resident, 1989-90; rsch. fellow U. Tex. S.W. Med. Ctr., Dallas, 1990-92, NIMH fellow, 1991-93, instr. depression rsch. clinic, 1992-93, dir. depression and anxiety program, 1993-95. Dir. depression module U. Tex. S.W. Med. Ctr., Dallas, 1996—, assoc. prof., 1998—; depression guideline panel Agy. for Health Care Policy and Rsch.; chmn. World Wide Web Conf., Internat. Psychopharmacology Algorithm Project, 1997. Editor Internat. Depression-Neurosci. Rev. Group, 1996—; mem. editl. bd. Depressive Disorders Index & Reviews; contbr. articles to profl. jours. Recipient Young Investigator award Nat. Alliance for Rsch. on Schizophrenia and Devel., 1992-94, New Investigator award NIMH, 1993, Cert. Excellence award Indo-Am. Soc. Biol. Psychiat., 1994. Mem. Am. Psychiat. Assn., Soc. Nuclear Medicine (program chmn. 1990), World Psychiat. Assn. (com. mem. 1995-97), Neuroimaging Adv. Com., Tex. Soc. Psychiat. Physicians (com. mem. 1995-98). Office: UTSW/St Paul Hosp POB 1 Ste 600 5959 Harry Hines Blvd Dallas TX 75390-9101 E-mail: madhukar.trivedi@utsouthwestern.edu.

TRIVELPIECE, ALVIN WILLIAM, physicist, educator, consultant; b. Stockton, Calif., Mar. 15, 1931; s. Alvin Stevens and Mae (Hughes) Trivelpiece; m. Shirley Ann Ross, Mar. 23, 1953; children: Craig Evan, Steve Edward, Keith Eric. BS, Calif. Poly. Coll., San Luis Obispo, 1953; MS, Calif. Inst. Tech., 1955, PhD, 1958. Fulbright scholar Delft (Netherlands) U., 1958—59; asst. prof., then assoc. prof. U. Calif. at Berkeley, 1959—66; prof. physics U. Md., 1966—76; on leave as asst. dir. for research div. controlled thermonuclear research AEC, Washington, 1973—75; v.p. Maxwell Labs. Inc., San Diego, 1976—78; corp. v.p. Sci. Applications, Inc., La Jolla, Calif., 1978—81; dir. Office of Energy Research, U.S. Dept. Energy, Washington, 1981—87; exec. officer AAAS, Washington, 1987—88; dir. Oak Ridge (Tenn.) Nat. Lab., 1989—2000; v.p. Martin Marietta Energy Systems, 1989—95, Lockheed Martin Energy Systems, 1995; pres. Lockheed Martin Energy Rsch. Corp., 1996—2000; cons. Sandia Nat. Labs., Albuquerque, 2000—. Head del. joint NAS and Soviet Acad. Scis. mtg. and conf. on energy and global ecol. problems USSR, 1989; chmn. math. scis. ednl. bd. NAS, 1990—93; chmn. coordinating coun. for edn. NRC, 1991—93, chmn. com. small innovative firms in Russian nuclear cities, 2001; mem. Commn. on Phys. Scis., Math. and Applications, 1993—96, com. on tech. issues related to the comprehensive test ban treaty NAS, 2000—02, Tenn. Sci. and Tech. Adv. Commn., 1993—96, chmn., 1996—99, adv. com. Fedn. Networking Coun., 1992—96; chmn. and pres. Tenn. Tech. Devel. Corp., 1998—2000; bd. dirs. Environ. Literacy Coun. Author: Slow Wave Propagation in Plasma Wave Guides, 1966, Principles of Plasma Physics, 1973; contbr. articles to profl. jours. Named Disting. Alumnus, Calif. Poly. State U., 1978, Calif. Inst. Tech., Pasadena, 1987; recipient U.S. Sec. of Energy's Gold medal for disting. svc., 1986, Disting. Assoc. award, 2000, Tenn. Outstanding Svc. commendation, Senate Joint Resolution #530, 2000; fellow Guggenheim, 1966. Fellow: IEEE (Outstanding Engr. award region 3 1995), AAAS, Am. Phys. Soc.; mem.: NAE, AAUP, Am. Assn. Physics Tchrs., Am. Nuc. Soc., Nat. Press Club, Capital Hill Club, Tau Beta Pi, Sigma Xi. Achievements include patents in field. Home and Office: 14 Wade Hampton Trail Henderson NV 89052-6635 Office Phone: 702-492-1602.

TRIVELPIECE, CRAIG EVAN, computer electronics executive; b. Pasadena, Calif., Apr. 23, 1957; s. Alvin William and Shirley Ann T. Student, Calif. Inst. Tech., 1974-75; BA in Physics, U. Md., 1979. Scientist Maxwell Labs, San Diego, 1979-81; design engr. Rockwell Internat., Costa Mesa, Calif., 1981-83; mgr. engring. Tex. Instruments, Irvine, Calif., 1983-84; owner, pres. CST Engings Inc., Irvine, 1984-91, Circuit Plus, Inc., 1990-2000, 4 Every Wall, Inc., 1990-92, Transnational Telecom Inc., 1995-98; dir. advanced tech. Encryptix, Inc., 2000—01; sr. product mgr. Day Software, Inc., Newport Beach, Calif., 2001—02; gen. mgr. Questerra, Inc., Aliso Viejo, Calif., 2002—. Cons. Payview Ltd., Hong Kong, 1985-88, Airmedia, Inc., 1996-98. Co-inventor: Video Scrambling System, 1985, home video product with Smart Card Access, 1992, Interactive Video System, 1997, Interactive Video System, 2002. Republican. Avocations: Karate, running. Home: 124 46th St Newport Beach CA 92663-2515 Office: Questerra Inc 95 Enterprise Aliso Viejo CA 92656 E-mail: circuitp@earthlink.net., ctrivelpiece@questerra.com.

TRIVISONNO, NICHOLAS LOUIS, communications company executive, accountant; b. Bklyn., Apr. 10, 1947; BBA in Acctg., St. Francis Coll., Bklyn., 1968. Ptnr. Arthur Andersen & Co., N.Y.C., 1979-85, mng. ptnr, Stamford, Conn., 1985-88; sr. v.p. fin. GTE Corp., Stamford, 1988-95; chmn., CEO, ACNielsen, Stamford, 1996—. Republican. Roman Catholic. Avocation: golf. Office: AC Nielsen 770 Broadway New York NY 10003-9522

TRIX, FRANCES, linguistic anthropologist, consultant; b. Bellefont, Pa., Aug. 17, 1948; d. Herbert Phelps and Gertrude Aileen Trix; 1 child, Ramsay Ilyas' m. John Walbridge, 2004. Student, Middleburg Coll., 1966-68; BA, U. Mich., 1970, MA, 1972, MA, 1976, PhD, 1988. Lectr. U. Mich., Dearborn, 1973-74, vis. asst. prof. linguistics Ann Arbor, 1988-89, vis. asst. rsch. scientist, 1989-90; lectr. Mercy Coll., Detroit, 1976-77; dir. bilingual program Dearborn Pub. Schs., 1977-80; asst. prof. anthropology Wayne State U., Detroit, 1990-97, assoc. prof., 1997—. Cons. U.S. Agy. for Internat. Devel., Yemen, 1978, CMS Energy Corp., Jackson, Mich., 1997, NASA, 2000; rsch. assoc. Ctr. Mid. Ea. and N. African Studies U. Mich., Ann Arbor, 1993—, rsch. assoc. Ctr. Russian and E. European Studies, 1996—, U. Mich. Author: Spiritual Discourse, 1993, Albanians in Michigan, 2001; contbr. articles to profl. jours. Coord. Ann Arbor com. Save Bosnia, 1992—; mem. Commn. Albanian-Am., Taylor, Mich., 1994—; mem. steering com. Interfaith Coun. Peace and Justice, Ann Arbor, 1995-96. Woodrow Wilson Found. fellow U. Mich., 1970-71, Internat. Rsch. and Exch. Bd. fellow IREX, 1987-88, Humanities Ctr. Faculty fellow Wayne State U., Detroit, 1998, NEH fellow, 2003. Mem. Middle East Studies Assn., Turkish Studies Assn., Linguistic Soc. Am., Am. Anthrop. Assn. Avocations: English country dancing, travel. Home: 645 Riverview Dr Ann Arbor MI 48104-1853 Office: Wayne State U 906 W Warren Ave Detroit MI 48202 Office Phone: 313-577-6795.

TROCANO, RUSSELL PETER, lawyer; b. Hackensack, N.J., Sept. 7, 1963; s. Rosario Mario and Barbara Ann (Costa) T. BA, Seton Hall U., 1984; JD, Fordham U., 1987, LLM, 1992. Bar: N.J. 1987, N.Y. 1988. Law clk. to presiding justice County of Middlesex, New Brunswick, N.J., 1987-88; assoc. Sellar Richardson Law Firm, Newark and Roseland, N.J., 1988, Morgan Melhuish Monaghan Law Firm, Livingston, N.J., 1988-89; prin., owner Russell P. Trocano, Ridgewood, N.J., 1989—. Mem. San Guiseppe Societa de Santa Croce de Camerina, Paterson, N.J., 1989—. Fordham U. scholar, 1987. Mem. ABA, N.J. Bar Assn., N.Y. State Bar Assn., Bergen County Bar Assn., Passaic County Bar Assn., Brehon Law Soc., Arthur T. Vanderbilt Inn of Cts., Phi Alpha Theta. Roman Catholic. Avocations: mineral collecting, travel, reading. Home and Office: 60 S Maple Ave Ridgewood NJ 07450-4542 Office Phone: 201-445-0777. E-mail: russell.trocano@verizon.net.

TROFE, JENNIFER, pharmacist, educator; b. Phila., Sept. 12, 1974; d. Thomas and Barbara Trofe. Minor in Classical Music, Phila. Coll. of Pharmacy, 1998; BS, PharmD, Phila. Coll. of Pharmacy and Sci., 1998. Registered Pharmacist Pa. Bd. of Pharmacy, 1997, N.J. Bd. of Pharmacy, 1998, Ohio Bd. of Pharmacy, 2001, cert. Pharmacotherapy Specialist Bd. of Pharm. Specialties, 2000. Rsch. asst. prof. in divsn. of transplantation, dept. of surgery U. of Cin., 2002—, asst. prof., dept. of clin. pharmacy Memphis. Recipient Young Investigators award, Am. Soc. of Transplantation. Office: U of Cin 231 Albert Sabin Way Cincinnati OH 45267-0558

TROFFKIN, HOWARD JULIAN, lawyer, diversified company executive; b. Port Chester, NY, Jan. 30, 1937; s. Irving and Frieda Troffkin; m. Rhea Dorothy, May 12, 1963; children: Stephen, Barbara. BS in Chemistry, St. Lawrence U., 1959; postgrad., Columbia U., 1959-60; JD, Georgetown U., 1970. Bar: Va. 1971, D.C. 1972. Rsch. chemist Am. Cyanamid Co., 1961-66, legal trainee, 1966-67, patent agt., 1967-71; assoc. Pennie, Edmonds, Morton, Taylor & Adams, Washington, 1971-77; patent atty. W.R. Grace & Co., Columbia, Md., 1977-86, sr. patent counsel, 1987-98; pvt. practice, 1998—; sec./counsel Concrete Corrosion Inhibitor Trade Assn. Patentee in chemistry field. Mem. Willerburn Civic Assn., 1971-75. Served with AUS, 1960-61. Mem. ABA, Va. Bar Assn., D.C. Bar Assn., Washington Patent Lawyers Assn., Md. Patent Law Assn. (pres. 1981-83), Am. Intellectual Property Law Assn., Am. Chem. Soc., Concrete Corrosion Inhibitors Assn. (sec./counsel). Jewish. Avocations: woodcrafting, travel. Home and Office: 7808 Ivymount Ter Potomac MD 20854-3218 Personal E-mail: troffkin@aol.com.

TROFIMOVA, IRINA (IRENE) ALEXEEVNA, language educator; b. Alma-Ata, Kazakhstan, Sept. 14, 1943; d. Alexei Ivanovich Semyonov and Vitalia Anatolyevna Chirkova. BA in English, Leningrad Tchrs. U., Russia, 1964, MA in English, 1966; PhD in linguistics, Alma-Ata Tchrs. U., 1974; MA in Western Classical Philosophy, U. Philosophy, Alma-Ata, 1977, MA, 1989. Asst. prof. English and German langs. U. Nat. Economy, Alma-Ata, Kazakhstan, 1966—72; grad. student Tchrs. Tng. U., Alma-Ata, Kazakhstan, 1972—74; assoc. prof. English, phsyics in English, Am. and Brit. lit., bus. English, newspaper English Kazakh State U., Alma-Ata, Kazakhstan, 1974—91; assoc. prof. Russian and German langs., Russian lit. Ouachita Baptist U., Arkadelphia, Ark., 1991—. Cons. Ministry of Fgn. Affairs, Alma-Ata, Kazakhstan, 1979—81; cons., interpreter Ministry of Health, Alma-Ata, Kazakhstan, 1982—83; interpreter Ministry of Edn., Alma-Ata, Kazakhstan, 1989—91. Author: (textbooks) Textbook for Physicists, Part 1, 1987, Textbook for Physicists, Part 2, 1988; contbr. articles to profl. jours. Mem.: Ark. Fgn. Lang. Tchrs. Assn., Ark. Philological Assn., Ctrl. Am. Russian Tchrs. Assn. Baptist. Avocations: interior decorating, reading, poetry. Home: 120 Evonshire Dr Arkadelphia AR 71923 Office: Ouachita Baptist Univ 410 Ouachita St Arkadelphia AR 71998 Office Phone: 870-245-5344. Business E-Mail: trofimovai@obu.edu.

TROGANI, MONICA, ballet dancer; b. Newark, Sept. 2, 1963; m. Jay Brooker, July 3, 1993. Grad. high sch., 1980. Ballet dancer N.J. Ballet, West Orange, 1980-83; field asst., coder Reichman Rsch., Inc., NYC, 1984-86; ballet mistress, prin. dancer Dance Theatre of L.I., Port Washington, N.Y., 1984-88; exec. sec. programming dept. The First N.Y. Internat. Festival of the Arts, NYC, 1987-89; guest regisseur Alta. Ballet, Edmonton, Can., 1988-89, ballet mistress, asst. to artistic dir., 1989-93; guest regisseur Ballet du Nord, Roubaix, France, 1991, Dance Theatre of Harlem, NYC, 1993-94; ballet mistress Les Grands Ballets Canadiens, Montreal, 1994—2003; rehearsal dir. Hubbard Street Dance Chicago, 2003—. Avocation: singing. Office: Hubbard St Dance Chicago 1147 W Jackson Blvd Chicago IL 60607*

TROJACK, JOHN EDWARD, lawyer; b. St. Paul, Mar. 30, 1946; s. Albert G. and Eleanor (Mader) T.; m. Mary Jo LaNasa, Oct. 12, 1979; 4 children. BA, U. Minn., 1968; JD, William Mitchell Coll. Law, St. Paul, 1976. Bar: Minn. 1976, U.S. Dist. Ct. Minn. 1976, U.S. Ct. Appeals (8th cir.) 1980, U.S. Supreme Ct. 1980. Assoc. John E. Daubney, St. Paul, 1976-78; ptnr. Wagner, Rutchick & Trojack, P.A., St. Paul, 1978-83; sole practice St. Paul, 1983—. Conciliation Ct. referee Ramsey County Dist. Ct., St. Paul, 1979—; vol. atty. So. Minn. Regional Legal Svcs. Corp., St. Paul, 1982—; arbitrator Hennepin County Dist. Ct., 1986—. Served with USN, 1968-72, capt. USNR. Mem.: Naval Res. Assn., Ramsey County Bar Assn., Minn. Bar Assn., Nat. Network of Estate Planning Attys., The Harvesters Club, Phi Alpha Delta. Address: 1549 Livingston Ave Ste 101 Saint Paul MN 55118-3415 E-mail: jetlawoffice@aol.com.

TROJANOWSKI, JOHN Q. health facility administrator; MD, PhD. Prof. pathology and lab. medicine U. Pa. Sch. Medicine, 1981—; co-dir. Pa. Ctr. for Neurodegenerative Disease Rsch., 1992—; dir. Pa. Inst. on Aging, 2002—. Mem. med. and adv. bd. Nat. Alzheimer's Assn., NIH's Nat. Adv. Coun. on Aging. Recipient Merit award, NIH, Stanley N. Cohen Biomed. Rsch. award, 2000, Potamkin prize for rsch. in Pick's, Alzheimer's and Related Diseases, 1998. Mem.: Am. Soc. Clin. Investigation, Am. Assn. Neuropathologists (pres. 1997). Office: U Pa Health Sys Dept Pathology and Lab Medicine 3d Fl 36th and Spruce Sts Philadelphia PA 19104-4283

TROLANDER, HARDY WILCOX, engineering executive, consultant; b. Chgo., June 2, 1921; s. Elmer Wilcox and Freda Marie (Zobel) T.; m. Imogen Davenport, July 3, 1946 (dec.); children: Megan, Patricia. BS in Engring., Antioch Coll., 1947. Instr. Antioch Coll., Yellow Springs, Ohio, 1947-48; co-founder, CEO Yellow Springs Instrument Co., Inc., 1948-86. Dir., co-founder Cook Design Ctr., Dartmouth Coll., Hanover, N.H., 1975-88; bd. dirs. Deban Inc., Yellow Springs, Camax Tool co., Arvada, Colo.; mem. evaluation panel Inst. Basic Stds., Nat. Bur. Stds., 1977-79. Contbr. articles to profl. jours.; patentee in field. Co-founder, trustee Yellow Springs Community Found., 1974-83; trustee Antioch Coll., 1968-74, chmn. bd., 1972-74; trustee Engring. and Sci. Found., Dayton, 1982-96, Engrs. Club Dayton Found., 1994—, Engring. and Sci. Hall of Fame, 1994—; mem. adv. bd. Coll. Engring. and Computer Sci. Wright State U., 1993—; bd. dirs. united Way Greater Dayton Area, 1984-92; small bus. innovative rsch. grant panels Nat. Sci. Found., 1988—. 1st lt. USAF, 1943-46. Named Outstanding Engr., Dayton Affiliate Socs., 1967, 89. Fellow Dayton Engrs. Club, Am. Inst. for Med. and Biol. Engring.; mem. ACLU, Nat. Acad. Engring., Am. Inst. Biol. Scis. (bioinstrumentation adv., coun. 1969-75), Internat. Orgn. of Legal Metrology (tech. advisor, sec. 1975-82), Amnesty Internat. Democrat. Achievements include co-development of melting point of gallium which has become recognized as a primary defining point of the International Temperature Scale. Home and Office: 3 Aspen Ct Yellow Springs OH 45387-1326 Office Phone: 937-767-4551.

TROLL, KITTY, actress, writer; b. N.Y.C., Dec. 18, 1950; d. Hans and Lillian Holland (Ellman) T.; m. Douglas Getchell (div.); 1 child, Wyatt Theodore. Student, Cambridge Sch. of Weston; studied with Lee Strasberg, Michael Howard, N.Y.C. Instr. drama Pacific (Calif.) High Sch.; founder Mixed-Media Theatre, Dallas. Appeared in (stage prodns.) A Grape for Seeing, The Night of the Iguana, Blues for Mr. Charlie, A Midsummer Night's Dream, Spoon River Anthology, The Moon is Blue, Day of the Races, Old Wives Tale, Bandits, Survivors, Beggar's Choice, Much Ado About Nothing, (films) Stardust Memories, 1980, The Last to Know, 1981, Sun and Moon, Permanent Wave, 1986, (TV) As the World Turns, All My Children, For Richer, for Poorer, Texas; author (screenplay) Holding the Bag, (teleplay) Malpractice, (book) The Party Book. Mem. Actors' Equity Assn., Screen Actors Guild, AFTRA.

TROLLER, FRED, graphic designer, painter, visual consultant, educator; b. Zurich, Switzerland, Dec. 12, 1930; came to U.S., 1961; s. Albert and Katherina (Iseli) T.; m. Beatrice Stocklin, Nov. 22, 1952; children— Simon, Meret BA in Graphic Design, Kunstgewerbeschule, Zurich, 1950. Art dir. Geigy Corp., Ardsley, N.Y., 1961-66; pres. Fred Troller Assoc., Visual Communications Cons., Rye, N.Y., 1966—; chmn., prof. design div. design Sch. Art and Design N.Y. State Coll. Ceramics at Alfred U., 1991—. Author and illustrator articles. Served to pvt. 1st class Inf. Swiss Army, 1949-60 Mem. Am. Inst. Graphic Arts, Alliance Graphique Internationale, Phi Kappa Phi (Alfred U. chpt.). Home and Office: Fred Troller Assocs 12 Harbor Ln Rye NY 10580-2213

TROMBLEY, EDWARD FRANCIS, III, registrar; b. Oneida, N.Y., Sept. 24, 1964; s. Edward F., Jr. and Sharonlee (Sterling) Trombley. BA, SUNY, Oswego, 1986, MS, 1996. Cert. secondary English tchr. N.Y. Adj. instr. Bryant & Stratton Bus. Inst., Liverpool, NY, 1993-96, gen. studies dept. coord., 1996, evening and weekend coll. coord., 1996-98, assoc. dean instrn., 1998-2000, dean adminstrn., 2000—01; homebound student tutor North Syracuse (N.Y.) Sch. Dist., 1994-96; registrar DeVry U., Arlington, Va., 2001—. Mem. adv. bd. East Syracuse-Minoa Sch. Dist., 1996—97; sch. bus. partnership Cicero-North Syracuse Sch. Dist., 1997; conf. del. Assn. Proprietary Colls., Copperstown, NY, 1997, Saratoga, NY, 98; media cons. Bryant and Stratton Bus. Inst., Liverpool, 1997. Mem.: Va. Assn. Coll. Registrars and Admissions Officers, Am. Assn. Coll. Registrars and Admissions Officers, Trick of the Tail Club (rec. sec. 1995—2001). Office: DeVry U Crystal City Campus 2450 Crystal Dr Arlington VA 22202 Business E-Mail: etrombley@dc.devry.edu.

TROMBLEY, JOSEPH EDWARD, insurance company executive, underwriter; b. Hartford, Conn., Aug. 15, 1935; s. Joseph Lawrence and Helen Agnes (Crowley) T.; m. Claire Marie Jenkins, Sept. 20, 1958; children: Patricia A. Trombley Barone, Kevin C. BS, U. Conn., 1957. CLU; chartered fin. cons. Sales rep. Met. Life & Affiliated Co., Bridgeport, Conn., 1960-63, asst. mgr. Nyack, N.Y., 1963-66, field trainer Albany, N.Y., 1966-68, advance underwriting adviser, 1968-69, mgr. Glens Falls, N.Y., 1969-98. Instr. Successful Money Mgmt. Seminars, Glens Falls, 1987-99. Bd. dirs. Adirondack chpt. ARC, Glens Falls, 1982—; mem. adv. bd. N.Y. State Dept. Ins., Albany, 1985-95. 1st lt. U.S. Army, 1958-60. Mem. Tri-County Life Underwriters (bd. dirs. 1969-96, pres. elect 1990, pres. 1991, Man of Yr. 1983), Am. Soc. CLUs,

Estate Planning Coun. Northeastern N.Y., Rotary (bd. dirs. Glens Falls 1982-85). Avocations: golf, woodworking, antiques, travel. Office: Met Life Ins Co PO Box 788 Glens Falls NY 12801-0788

TROMBOLD, WALTER STEVENSON, supply company executive; b. Chanute, Kans., June 21, 1910; s. George John and Margaret (Stevenson) T.; m. Charlotte Elizabeth Kaufman, Dec. 28, 1941; children: Joan Benjamin, Lynn Oliphant, Walter Steven, David George, Charles Phillip. AA, Iola Jr. Coll., 1930; BS in Bus., U. Kans., 1932; spl. degree Balliol Coll., Oxford U., 1943. Pers. worker with evangelist Billy Sunday, 1928; asst. mgr. S.H. Kress & Co., 1932-38; counsel Penn. Mut. Life Ins. Co., 1938-40; field mgr. Travelers Ins. Co., Kansas City, 1940-41; with Reid Supply Co. Wichita, Kans., Kansas City, Mo., Topeka, 1946-86; pres., chmn. bd. Reid Supply Co., Inc., 1954-86; chmn. bd. Trombold Consultation Svc., 1986—. Bd. dirs., v.p. Nat. Distbrs. Coun.; active amateur photographer, 1924—. Bd. dirs., officer YMCA, 1920—; merit badge councilor Boy Scouts Am.; bd. dirs. Wesley Hosp. Assocs., 1972-82, Camp Fire Girls, Salvation Army, mem. adv. bd., 1988—, Salvation Army Rehab. Ctr., 1988—, life mem. PTA, 1953—, pres., 1952; chmn. pers. adv. bd. City of Wichita, Kans., 1956-86; commr. Gen. Assembly Presbyn. Ch. USA, past deacon, elder, trustee; commr. Synods of Mid-Am., Presbytery of So. Kans.; assoc. chmn. Nat. Laymen's Bible Week, 1972-86; mem. Super Sr. Tennis, 1970-98; area chmn. Neighbor Watch, 1990—; ofcl. photographer U. Kans. Relays. Lt. comdr. USN, 1942-46. Seaman USN World War II 1st Class to lt. comdr; exec. officer, commdg. officer USSLST55; participant in fateful Tiger Exercise and D-day, 1944; v.p. Civic Progress Inc., Sales Mgmt., Inc. Recipient award Nat. Jr. C. of C., Wichita Jr. C. of C., Laundry and Cleaners Allied Trades, Old Timer Club Nat., Nat. Distributors Coun., Sr. Men's Tennis Assn., U. Kans. Relays, Kans. State H.S. Assn., Wichita Swim Club, Am. Athletic Union, YMCA, Salvation Army, Rotary, Boy Scouts. Am., Camp Fire Girls, Sr. Men's Swimming, City of Wichita, 3 Navy Compaign Ribbons, Silver Star. Mem. Textile Allied Trades Assn. (bd. dirs., dist. chmn. Hon. Man 1976), Kans. LST Assn. (charter pres. 1990), Kans. U. Alumni Assn. (life), Kans. C. of C., Wichita C. of C., Sales and Mktg. Execs. (bd. dirs., v.p.), Old Timer Club (sec., treas. 1964-86, Hon. Man of Yr. 1977), Wichita Racquet Club, Knife and Fork Internat. Club (bd. dirs., v.p.), Univ. Club (chmn. bd. dirs., v.p.), Rotary (bd. dirs., ofcl. photographer, historian, Disting. Svc. award 1989, 96), Masons (32 degree), Alpha Tau Omega. Republican. Presbyterian. Home: 1401 W River Blvd #3B Wichita KS 67203-3324

TRONCOSO, SERGIO, writer; BA, Harvard Coll., Cambridge, MA, 1979—83; MA, Yale U., New Haven, CT, 1984—87, MPhil, 1987—92. Instr. fiction Yale U., New Haven, 1993—. Bd. mem. Hudson Valley Writers' Ctr., Sleepy Hollow, NY, 1999—. Author: (short story collection) The Last Tortilla and Other Stories, 1999 (Premio Aztlan and SW Book Award, 2000), (novels) The Nature of Truth, 2003. Recipient Premio Aztlan, Rudolfo and Patricia Anaya, 1999, Alumni Hall of Fame, Hispanic Scholarship Fund, 2003; scholar Fulbright Scholarship, US Govt., 1983. Personal E-mail: stroncoso@aol.com.

TRONGALE, NICHOLAS ALBERT, entrepreneur, researcher; s. Nick and Mary Rose Trongale; m. Mary Kathryn Sullivan, Nov. 30, 1980; children: Daniel Louis, Megan Kathryn. BA, Dominican U., 1978; MA, U.S. Naval Postgraduate Sch., 1986, Stanford U., 1994; EdD, U. San Diego, 2001. Enlisted USN, 1979, advanced through grades to capt., ret., 2001; pres., CEO Pb Solutions, San Diego, 2002—, The Comml. Diving Centre, L.L.C., New Iberia, La., 2003—. Author: (research) Changes in Navy Leadership Theory and Practice: Post-Vietnam, China's Defense Moderization, China's Naval Power, Investment Strategy of Information Operations, Implications of Unmaned Air Vehicles for the Future Shape of the Air Force. Decorated Legion of Merit; named E-2C Hawkeye of Yr., Comdr. Fighter/Airborne Early Warning Wing, Pacific, 1988; recipient Nat. Leadership award, Nat. Rep. Congl. Com., 2003; Adm. Arthur S. Moreau scholar, USN, 1992, Fed. Exec. Rsch. fellow, RAND Corp., 1996—97. Mem.: DAV (life), VFW (life), Assn. Gulf Coast Coml. Diving Educators (pres. 2003—), Kappa Delta Pi (life). Achievements include first to commercial diving school specifically tailored to support the Gulf of Mexico oil industry. Office Phone: 858-414-5167. Personal E-mail: trongale@pbsolutions.us.

TRONTELL, MARIE CELESTINE, dean; Diploma, Rutgers State U., 1969, MD, 1976. Diplomate Am. Bd. Internal Medicine (chief proctor exam 1988, 89, 90, 91), Am. Bd. Pulmonary Diseases. Intern in internal medicine, resident in internal medicine Coll. Medicine and Dentistry of N.J.-Rutgers Med. Sch. Hosp., 1976-79, med. chief resident, 1978-79, fellow in pulmonary disease, 1979-81; asst. chief medicine for tng. Robert Wood Johnson Univ. Hosp., New Brunswick, 1980-96, dir. resident tng., 1982-96, chief inpatient svcs., 1987-96; asst. prof. medicine UMDNJ-Robert Wood Johnson Med. Sch., New Brunswick, 1981-87, program dir. internal medicine residency, 1983-96, acting chief divsn. gen. internal medicine, 1986-87, assoc. prof. medicine, 1987-96, assoc. chmn. dept. medicine, 1991—, prof. clin. medicine, 1996—, assoc. dean acad. affairs Piscataway, 1996—. Mem. editl. adv. bd. Info Trends: Medicine, Law, and Ethics; contbr. articles to profl. jours.; spkr. in field. Fellow ACP (mem. grad. med. edn. com. N.J., mem. career change task force 1994), Am. Coll. Chest Physicians; mem. Am. Thoracic Soc., Assn. Behavioral Scis. and Med. Edn., Assn. Program Dirs. in Internal Medicine (nat. coun. mem., mem. membership svcs. com., mem. program planning com.), N.J. Thoracic Soc., Soc. Gen. Internal Medicine., Phi Beta Kappa, Alpha Omega Alpha. Home: 1111 S Branch Dr Whitehouse Station NJ 08889-3234 Office: 675 Hoes Ln # R-102 Piscataway NJ 08854-5627 also: UMDNJ Robert Wood Johnson Med Sch Dept Acad Affairs 675 Hoes Ln Piscataway NJ 08854-5627

TROOP, PAUL MELVIN, public relations executive, journalist; b. Jersey City, N.J., May 13, 1942; s. Bernard Lazarus and Ruth (Weiss) T.; m. Maxine Rubin, Dec. 6, 1970; 1 child, Wendy. BA, U. State of N.Y., 1980. Reporter L.I. Press, Jamaica, N.Y., 1965-66; political editor Suffolk Sun, Deer Park, N.Y., 1966-67; asst. news dir. L.I. Network News, Freeport, N.Y., 1967; asst. editor Am. Sch. & U., N.Y.C., 1967-68; acct. exec. Ruder & Finn, N.Y.C., 1969-70; mng. editor L.I. Comml. Rev., Syosset, N.Y., 1970; bus. writer Atlanta Jour.-Constn., 1970-78; pres. Fin. Comm. Co., Atlanta, 1978—. Cpl. NJNG, 1965-71. Newspaper Fund scholar, 1961, Banking Sch. of the South fellow, 1975. Office: Fin Comm PO Box 4021 Alpharetta GA 30023-4021

TROOST, BRADLEY TODD, neurologist, educator; b. Mankato, Minn., July 5, 1937; s. Henry Bradley and Elizabeth (Todd) T.; m. Elizabeth Gail Godet, Apr. 17, 1976; children: Elizabeth Claire, Laurie Anne. BS with honors in Biophysics, Yale U., 1959; MD, Harvard U., 1963. Diplomate Am. Bd. Psychiatry and Neurology. Intern, Colo. Gen. Hosp., Denver, 1963-64; resident in neurology U. Colo., Denver, 1966-69; NIH fellow in neuro-ophthalmology U. Calif.-San Francisco, 1969-70; asst. prof. U. Miami (Fla.), 1970-76; assoc. prof. U. Pitts., 1976-80; prof. Case Western Res. U., Cleve., 1980-83; prof., chmn. dept. neurology Wake Forest U. Sch. Medicine, Winston-Salem, N.C., 1983—; chief dept. neurology VA med. ctrs., Pitts., Cleve. Bd. dirs. Greater Miami Epilepsy Found., 1973-76. Served to capt. U.S. Army, 1964-66. Fellow Am. Acad. Neurology; mem. Am. Neurol. Assn., Am. Assn. Univ. Profs. Neurology (pres.-elect), Barany Soc. Republican. Episcopalian. Contbr. numerous articles to profl. publs.

TROP, SANDRA, museum administrator; b. Bklyn. BS, NYU, 1955; cert. in arts adminstrn., Harvard U., 1978. From assoc. dir. to dir. Everson Mus. Art, Syracuse, NY, 1974—95, dir., 1995—. Adminstr. edn. dept. Everson Mus. Art, 1972, adminstr. docent program, 1968-72, advt. copy writer, 1965-68; adj. prof. Syracuse U., 1973-75. Mem. founding bd. dirs. Lowe Art Ctr., Syracuse U., Salt City Playhouse, Folk Art Gallery, Syracuse Landmark Theatre; mem. Internat. Com. for Museums and Collections of Modern Art; mem. Literacy Vols. Am.; appointed to Mayor's Commn. on Fin. Planning for City of Syracuse. Mem. Am. Arts Alliance, Am. Assn. Museums, N.E. Regional Mus. Conf., Internat., Syracuse Fedn. Women's Clubs, Corinthian Found. Office: Everson Museum Art 401 Harrison St Syracuse NY 13202-3091

TROPEZ-SIMS, SUSANNE, pediatrician, educator; b. New Orleans, Apr. 13, 1949; d. Maxwell Sterling and Ethel (Ross) Tropez; m. James Carnell White, Apr. 10, 1971 (div. 1992); children: Lisa, Janifer, James Carnell; m. Michael Milroy Sims, Feb. 18, 1995. BS, Bennett Coll., 1971; MD, U. N.C., 1975, MPH, 1982. Diplomate Am. Bd. Pediatrics. Resident in pediat. N.C. Meml. Hosp., Chapel Hill, 1975-76, 77-79; pediatrician Darnell Army Hosp., Ft. Hood, Tex., 1976-77; acting dir. pediat. day clinic Wake County Med. Ctr., Raleigh, NC, 1979-82; dir. pediatric day clinic, asst. prof. U. N.C., Chapel Hill, 1982-88; assoc. prof. pediat. La. State U. Med. Ctr., New Orleans, 1988-97; dir. divsn. pediat. emergency rm. La. State U., New Orleans, 1988-89, chief divsn. ambulatory care, 1989—97; chmn. dept. pediat. Meharry Med. Coll., Nashville, 1997—; chair Mehary Med. Svc. Found., Nashville, 2000—02; chair curriculum com. Meharry Med. Coll., Nashville, 2003—. Clin. dir. maternal and child health units New Orleans Health Dept., 1992-97, chief divsn. cmty. pediat. and adolescent medicine, 1992-97; pediatrician Shelly Child Devel. Ctr., Raleigh, 1981-88, child med. examiner program, 1979-88; chair sch. health com. local chpt. AAP, 1993-96; mem. Nat. Com. Sch. Health, 1992-99; chair health info. network bd. Nat. Edn. Assn., 2000-02. Contbr. articles to profl. jour. Chair adminstrv. bd. Cornerstone U.M.C., 1993-96, chair edn. com., 1991-92; mem. United Meth. Women, Walnut Terr. Child Devel. Ctr., Raleigh, 1981-83, chmn., 1982-83; chmn. pastor parish com. Longview Ch., Raleigh, 1982-84, 87-88, chmn. membership care com.; chair bd. NEA-Health Info. Network, 2000-02; chair bd. trustees Clark Meml. United Meth. Ch., 2002—. Fellow preventive medicine, 1979-82, Faculty Devel. fellow U. NC Sch. Medicine, 1985-87. Fellow Am. Acad. Pediatrics (mem. sch. health com.); mem. N.C. Pediatric Soc. (com. child abuse and neglect, adolescent pregnancy), La. Pediatric Soc., Ambulatory Pediatric Assn., Adolescent Pregnancy Coalition United Way, Bennett Coll. Alumnae Assn. Democrat. Office Phone: 615-327-6332. Business E-Mail: stsims@mmc.edu.

TROPIN, KENNETH G. fund management executive; b. N.Y.C., Aug. 17, 1953; s. Leonard and Ruth (Safron) Tropin; m. Kathleen Tropin, Aug. 6, 1986; children: Nicholas, Kelly. BA, Goddard Coll., 1974. Fin. cons. Shearson, N.Y.C., 1980-82; sr. v.p. Dean Witter Reynolds, N.Y.C., 1982-89; pres., chief exec. officer John W. Henry & Co., Inc., Westport, Conn., 1989—93; founder, chmn. Graham Capital Mgmt., Rowayton, Conn., 1994—. Mem.: Managed Futures Assn. (chmn. 1991). Avocations: golf, skiing, tennis, sculpture. Office: Graham Capital Mgmt Rockledge Financial Ctr Rowayton CT 06853 Office Phone: 203-899-3400.*

TROPP, RORY, emergency medicine physician; b. Queens, N.Y., May 10, 1958; s. Murray and Elaine (Backerman) T.; m. Shelley Ames, May 25, 1986; children: Lauren, Joshua, Dustin, Jessica. B in Chemistry, Bklyn. Coll., 1979; MD, Downstate Med. Ctr., Bklyn., 1983. Diplomate Am. Coll. Emergency Physicians. Intern, resident Albany (N.Y.) Med. Ctr., 1983-85; resident emergency medicine L.I. Jewish Hosp., New Hyde Park, N.Y., 1987-90; attending ED Saratoga, Saratoga Springs, N.Y., 1985-87; attending chmn. ED and clin. instr. QA Com. L.I. Jewish and Queens Hosp. Ctr., New Hyde Park, N.Y., 1990-92; attending chair of QA St. Elizabeth's Hosp., Utica, N.Y., 1992-93; ED attending interim dir. Rome (N.Y.) Hosp., 1993-96; attending physician emergency medicine Nathan Littauer Hosp., Gloversville, N.Y., 1996—, Basset Healthcare, 1996-98, Nathan Littauer Hosp., 1998—. Fellow Am. Coll. Emergency Physicians; mem. Oneida County Med. Soc. Avocations: white water rafting, snow mobiling, horseback riding, shade tree mechanic, home remodeling.

TROSINO, VINCENT JOSEPH, SR., insurance company executive; b. Upland, Pa., Nov. 19, 1940; s. Sylvester N. and Stella Trosino; m. Patricia Ann Gibney, June 18, 1960; children: Laura, Valerie, Vincent Jr. BS in Psychology, Villanova U., 1962; MS in Psychology, Ill. State U., 1973. Ops. supr. State Farm Mut. Auto Ins. Co., Springfield, Pa., 1962-67, personnel mgr. Bloomington, Ill., 1970-72, dir. personnel, 1972-74, corp. v.p., 1986-87, exec. v.p., 1987—, pres., vice-chmn. bd., COO, 1998—, vice-chmn. bd. dirs. Costa Mesa, Calif., 1995, dep. regional v.p., 1976-80, regional v.p. Wayne, N.J., 1981-85. Bd. dirs. State Farm Fire & Casualty Co., State Farm Life Ins. Co., State Farm Internat. Services, State Farm Investment Mgmt. Corp., all Bloomington; dir., Vulcan Materials Co., Ala., 2003-. Bd. dirs. Chilton Hosp., Pompton Lakes, N.J., 1982-85, Jr. Achievement, McLean County, Ill., 1971, McLean County Law and Justice Com., 1970, McLean County Alcohol and Drug Assistance Corp., 1970-74, The Brookings Inst., Washington, 1996. Mem. N.J. Ins. News Svc. (pres. 1984-85, bd. dirs.), N.J. Joint Underwriting Assn. (bd. dirs. 1982-85), Jud. Inquiry Bd. State of Ill. (apptd. by Gov. Edgar, 1992—), Nat. Italian Am. Found. (bd. mem.). Avocations: trout fishing, tennis, golf. Office: State Farm Ins Cos 1 State Farm Plz Bloomington IL 61710-0001

TROST, BARRY MARTIN, chemist, educator; b. Phila., June 13, 1941; s. Joseph and Esther T.; m. Susan Paula Shapiro, Nov. 25, 1967; children: Aaron David, Carey Daniel. BA cum laude, U. Pa., 1962; PhD, MIT, 1965; D (hon.), U. Claude Bernard, Lyons, France, 1994, Technion, Israel, 1997. Mem. faculty U. Wis., Madison, 1965—, prof., chemistry, 1969—, Evan P. and Marion Helfaer prof. chemistry, from 1976, Vilas rsch. prof. chemistry; prof. chemistry Stanford U., 1987—, Tamaki prof. humanities and scis., 1990, chmn. dept., 1996—2002; Lord Todd vis. prof. Cambridge U., England, 2002—. Cons. Merck, Sharp & Dohme, E.I. duPont de Nemours.; Chem. Soc. centenary lectr., 1982 Author: Problems in Spectroscopy, 1967, Sulfur Ylides, 1975; editor-in-chief Comprehensive Organic Synthesis, 1991—, ChemTracts/Organic Chemistry, 1993—; editor: Structure and Reactivity Concepts in Organic Chemistry series, 1972—; assoc. editor Jour. Am. Chem. Soc., 1974-80; mem. editl. bd. Organic Reactions Series, 1971—, Chemistry A European Jour., 1995—, Sci. of Synthesis, Houben-Weyl Methods of Molecular Transformations, 1995—; contbr. numerous articles to profl. jours. Named Chem. Pioneer, Am. Inst. Chemists, 1983; recipient Dreyfus Found. Tech.-Scholar award, 1970, 1977, Creative Work in Synthetic Organic Chemistry award, 1981, Baekland medal, 1981, Alexander von Humboldt award, 1984, Guenther award, 1990, Janssen prize, 1990, Roger Adams award, Am. Chem. Soc., 1995, Presdl. Green Univ. Challenge award, 1998, Nicholas medal, 2000, Yamada prize, 2001, Yamada Prize, 2001, ACS Nobel Laureate Signature award, Graduate Ed. Chemistry, 2002, John Scott award, City of Phila., 2004; fellow, NSF, 1963—65, Sloan Found., 1967—69, Am. Swiss Found., 1975—, Zencca, 1997; scholar Cope scholar, 1989. Mem.: NAS, AAAS, Chem. Soc. London, Am. Acad. Arts and Scis., Am. Chem. Soc. (award in pure chemistry 1977, Roger Adams award 1995, Herbert C. Brown award for creative rsch. in synthetic methods 1999, Nobel Laureate Signature award for grad. edn. in chemistry 2002, Arthur C. Cope award 2004). Office: Stanford U Dept Chemistry Stanford CA 94305

TROST, CARLISLE ALBERT HERMAN, retired naval officer; b. Valmeyer, Ill., Apr. 24, 1930; s. Elmer Herman and Luella Caroline (Hoffman) T.; m. Pauline Louise Haley, May 1, 1954; children— Carl, Laura Lee, Steven, Kathleen. Student, Washington U., St. Louis, 1948-49; BS, U.S. Naval Acad., 1953; Olmsted scholar, U. Freiburg, W. Ger., 1960-62. Commd. ensign U.S. Navy, 1953, advanced through grades to adm., 1985; exec. officer U.S.S. Scorpion, 1962-63, U.S.S. Von Steuben, 1963-65; mil. asst. to Dep. Sec. Def., 1965-68; comdg. officer U.S.S. Sam Rayburn, 1968-69; staff Comdr. Sub Force Atlantic, 1969-70; exec. asst. to Sec. Navy, 1970-73; comdr. Submarine Group Five, 1973-74; asst. chief Bur. Naval Personnel, 1974-76; dir. systems analysis div. Office Chief Naval Ops., Washington, 1976-78; dep. comdr.-in-chief U.S. Pacific Fleet, 1978-80; comdr. U.S. Seventh Fleet, 1980-81; dir. Navy program planning Office Chief Naval Ops., 1981-85; comdr.-in-chief U.S. Atlantic Fleet, 1985-86, chief naval ops., 1986-90. Bd. dirs. Lockheed Martin Corp., Gen. Pub. Utility Corp., GPU Nuclear Corp., Bird-Johnson Co., Gen. Dynamics Corp., Precision Components Corp.; chmn. Olmsted Fedn. Trustee U.S. Naval Acad. Found. Decorated Def. D.S.M. with cluster, Navy D.S.M. with 2 clusters, Army D.S.M., Air Force D.S.M., Legion of Merit with 2 oak leaf clusters, Navy Achievement medal, Def. Disting. Svc. medal; named Outstanding Young Man of Am. Nat. Jr. C. of C., 1964 Mem. U.S. Naval Inst., U.S. Naval Acad. Alumni Assn. (chmn.). Episcopalian. Home: 11 Compromise St Annapolis MD 21401-1806

TROST, EILEEN BANNON, lawyer; b. Teaneck, N.J., Jan. 9, 1951; d. William Eugene and Marie Thelma (Finlayson) Bannon; m. Lawrence Peter Trost Jr., Aug. 27, 1977; children: Lawrence Peter III, William Patrick, Timothy Alexander. BA with great distinction, Shimer Coll., 1972; JD cum laude, U. Minn., 1976. Bar: Ill. 1976, U.S. Dist. Ct. (no. dist.) Ill. 1976, Minn. 1978, U.S. Tax Ct. 1978, U.S. Supreme Ct. 1981. Assoc. McDermott, Will & Emery, Chgo., 1976-82, ptnr., 1982-93; v.p. No. Trust Bank Ariz. N.A., Phoenix, 1993-95; ptnr. Sonnenschein Nath & Rosenthal, Chgo., 1995—. Mem. Am. Coll. Trust and Estate Coun., Minn. Bar Assn., Internat. Acad. Estate and Trust Law, Chgo. Estate Planning Coun. Roman Catholic. Office: Sonnenschein Nath & Rosenthal 8000 Sears Tower Chicago IL 60606 Office Phone: 312-876-8149. E-mail: etrost@sonnenschein.com.

TROST, LOUIS FREDERICK, JR., banker, financial planner; b. Kansas City, Mo., Dec. 11, 1926; s. Louis Frederick and Roberta Ford (Broadus) T.; m. Ann Horner Tillma, Mar. 23, 1951 (div. Oct. 1978); children: Louis Frederick III, Scott Tillma; m. Charlotte Granville Graham, Nov. 15, 1984. BBA, U. Okla., 1951; postgrad., grad. Bell Sys. Execs. program, Northwestern U., 1960; grad., Sch. Banking of South, Baton Rouge, 1968, Coll. Fin. Planning, Denver, 1989. Cert. fin. planner. Divsn. mgr. South Western Bell Tel Co., Oklahoma City, 1951—64; sr. v.p. Liberty Nat. Bank & Trust Co., Oklahoma City, 1964—91; pres., CEO Lincoln Nat. Bank, Oklahoma City, 1991—95, vice chmn., 1995—2003, CEO, 2002—03. Advisor Bapt. Found. Okla., Oklahoma City, 1994—; bd. rep., exec. com. Coun. Fed. Home Loan Banks, Washington, 1998-2001; mem. gov.'s Cmty. Devel. Capital Formation Task Force, 1998-2003. Pres., bd. dirs. Travelers Aid, Oklahoma City, 1962; treas., bd. dirs. Okla. Symphony Orch., 1983—87; pres., bd. dirs. Mental Health Assn., Oklahoma City, 1996; mem. Cmty. Devel. Adv. Coun. of Fed. Res. Bank of Kansas City, 2002—03. Master sgt. U.S. Army, 1945—46, PTO. Named Outstanding Young Man in Oklahoma City, Oklahoma City Jaycees, 1960; named Ky. Col., Gov. of Ky., 1970; recipient letter of commendation Mental Health Assn., 1996. Mem. Am. Bankers Assn., Ind. Bankers Assn. Am., Okla. Bankers Assn. (sr. mgmt. com. 1995-2003), Oklahoma City Golf and Country Club (bd. dirs. 1989-91), Petroleum Club Oklahoma City (v.p., treas., bd. dirs. 1979-81), The Assocs. (U. Okla.), Faculty Club, Masons, Scottish Rite, Shriners, Royal Order Jesters, Kiwanis (past pres. Oklahoma City), Assn. of the U.S. Army, Phi Gamma Delta (treas., bd. dirs. Ednl. Found. 1989-97, Wall of Fame award 1997). Baptist. Avocations: gardening, reading, travel. Home and Office: 1601 Queenstown Rd Oklahoma City OK 73116-5522

TROTT, STEPHEN SPANGLER, federal judge, musician; b. Glen Ridge, N.J., Dec. 12, 1939; s. David Herman and Virginia (Spangler) Trott; m. Carol C. Trott; children: Christina, Shelley. BA, Wesleyan U., 1962; LLB, Harvard U., 1965; LLD (hon.), Santa Clara U., 1992; LLD (hon.), U. Idaho, 2001. Bar: Calif. 1966, U.S. Dist. Ct. (cen. dist.) Calif. 1966, U.S. Ct. Appeals (9th cir.) 1983, U.S. Supreme Ct. 1984. Guitarist, mem. The Highwaymen, 1958—; dep. dist. atty. L.A. County Dist. Atty.'s Office, L.A., 1966—75, chief dep. dist. atty., 1975—79; U.S. dist. atty. Central Dist. Calif., L.A., 1981—83; asst. atty. gen. criminal divsn. Dept. Justice, Washington, 1983—86; faculty Nat. Coll. Dist. Attys., Houston, 1973; chmn. central dist. Calif. Law Enforcement Coord. Com., Houston, 1981—83; coord. L.A.-Nev. Drug Enforcement Task Force, 1982—83; assoc. atty. gen. Justice Dept., Washington, 1986—88; chmn. U.S. Interpol, 1986—88; judge U.S. Ct. of Appeals (9th cir.), Boise, Idaho, 1988—. Trustee Wesleyan U., 1984—87; adv. council Big Brothers, Big Sisters S.W. Idaho, 2001—; ofcl. photographer World Cup Wrestling Championship, 2003—; bd. dirs., pres. Children's Home Soc., Idaho, 1990—. Recipient Gold record as singer-guitarist for Michael Row the Boat Ashore, 1961, Disting. Faculty award, Nat. Coll. Dist. Attys., 1977. Mem.: Am. Coll. Trial Lawyers, Boise (Idaho) Philharm. Assn. (bd. dirs. 1995—, v.p. 1997—99, pres. 1999—2003, pre-concert lectr. 1997—), Idaho Classic Guitar Soc. (founder, pres. 1989—), Internat. Brotherhood Magicians, Idaho Racing Pigeon Assn., Magic Castle, Brentwood Racing Pigeon Club (pres. 1977—82), Wilderness Fly Fishers Club (pres. 1975—77). Republican. Office: US Ct Appeals 9th Cir 667 US Courthouse 550 W Fort St Boise ID 83724-0101

TROTT, WILLIAM MACNIDER, lawyer; b. Raleigh, N.C., July 30, 1946; s. Graham Foard and Cornelia (McKimmon) T.; m. Holly Wooten, Oct. 17, 1970 (div.); children: Hollister Wooten, James McKimmon; m. Jean Little, Aug. 11, 1984; children: Elizabeth Yost, William MacNider. AB, U. N.C., 1968, JD, 1971; LLM with highest honors, George Washington U., 1971. Bar: N.C. 1971, U.S. Dist. Ct. (ea., mid. and we. dists.) N.C. 1975, U.S. Supreme Ct. 1975. Assoc. Young, Moore and Henderson, Raleigh, 1975-78; ptnr., mem. Young, Moore & Henderson, Raleigh, 1978—. Mem. N.C. Law Rev., 1969-71; lectr., author N.C. Bar Assn., 1984, 85, 87, Am. Law Firm Assn., 1999, 2000, Lorman Ednl. Svcs., 2000, 2001. Pres. Capital Area Soccer League, Raleigh, 1984-85; bd. dirs. N.C. Tennis Assn., Greensboro, 1987-94, N.C. Tennis Found., 1994—, v.p.; mem. Wake County Pks. and Recreation Commn., Raleigh, 1988-97, vice chmn., then chmn.; mem. sch. health adv. commn. Wake County Bd. Edn., 1997-99; sec., v.p. Raleigh Tennis Found., 1996—; bd. of vis., Peace Coll., 2004-; Lt. JAGC, USNR, 1971-75. Morehead scholar U. N.C., 1964-68, Wettach scholar U. N.C. Law Sch., 1968-71; state tennis age group doubles champion, 1963, 64, 98. Mem. ABA, N.C. Bar Assn., Wake County Bar Assn., Execs. Club, Carolina Country Club (bd. dirs. 2001-), Legal Elite Bus. North Carolina, 2003. Episcopalian. Office: Young Moore & Henderson PO Box 31627 Raleigh NC 27622-1627 Office Phone: 919-782-6860.

TROTTA, FRANK P., JR., lawyer; BA, JD, LLM, MBA. Bar: N.Y. U.S. Dist. Ct. (no. and we. dists.) N.Y., U.S. Ct. Mil. Appeals, U.S. Dist. Ct. (so. and ea. dists.) N.Y., U.S. Ct. Internat. Trade, U.S. Tax Ct., U.S. Supreme Ct., U.S. Ct. Appeals (D.C. cir.), U.S. Ct. Customs and Patent Appeals, D.C., Conn., Pa. Assoc. Weil, Gotshal & Manges, N.Y.C.; pvt. practice Washington, N.Y.C., New Rochelle, NY, Greenwich, Conn. Former mem. bd. govs ABA; former mem. faculty Practicing Law Inst.; governing mem. Nat. Jud. Coll., Am. Bar Endowment, ABRA Pension Fund; former chmn. bd. advisors Columbia U. Grad. Sch. Bus., Inst. for Non-for-Profit Mgmt. Former bd. dirs. Boys Town of Italy; former mem. Fund for Justice and Edn.; former chmn. New Rochelle Rep. Party; mem. bd. edn. Greenwich Cath. Sch.

TROTTA, RIC CHARLES, aerospace company executive, consultant; b. N.Y.C., Mar. 7, 1942; s. Sigmund Robert and Anita Dolores (La Penna) T.; m. Carolyn Carey Bealle Trotta, May 29, 1965; children: Bradley Charles, Ric Charles Jr., Lauren Carey. Student in elec. engring., U. Va., 1959-62; BA in Physics, NYU, 1966; MBA in Mktg., Hofstra U., 1977; postgrad., Carnegie Mellon U., 1987. Engr. Grumman Aerospace Corp., Bethpage, NY, 1966-68, asst. to v.p., 1968-70, advanced programs mgr., 1970-78, mgr. technology planning, 1978-81, asst. dir. advanced systems, 1981-83; dir. corp. ind., rsch. and devel. Grumman Corp., 1983-86, dir. corp. devel. and resources, 1986-94; pres. Trotta Assoc., Cons. to Govt. and Industry, Centerport, 1994—. Sr. player global war games U.S. Naval War Coll., Newport, RI, 1985—; mem. resources working group Fed. Emergency Mgmt. Agy., Washington, 1991—; vice-chair nat. adv. coun. Fed. Lab. Consortium, 1999—, vice chmn., 2000, chmn., 01; mem. nomination and award selection com. L.I. Tech. Hall of Fame, 2003—. Author: Industry Independent Rsch. and Devel. Study, 1996, Assessing the Impact of Regulatory and Legislative Changes to the DOD Independent Research and Developement Program, 1997, Maritime Industry Definition and Structure- A Workbook for Assessing Organization Capabilities Versus Industry Needs, 1997; Contbg. author: Public Control of Medical Care, 1978, National Security Assessment of the U.S. Maritime Industry Surveys: Building and Repairing of Ships, Boats and other Marine Platforms, Maritime Research Development and Education, 2000, Nat. Security Assesment of Shipbldg. and Repair Ind., 2001, Assessment of Industry Attitudes on Collaborating with U.S. Department of Defense in Research and Development and Technology Sharing, 2003. Mem. com. on sch. utilization Harborfield Sch. Dist., Greenlawn, 1984; bd. dir. Community Sch., Centerport, NY, 1985. Recipient Community Svc. award Town of Huntington, N.Y., 1985. Mem. Nat. Security Indsl. Assn., Electronic Industries Assn., Mine Warfare Assn. (bd. dirs. 1997), Assn. Nat. Def. and Emergency Resources, Sigma Nu (historian 1961).

Avocations: fishing, tennis, sailing, cooking. Home and Office: 21 Little Bull Ct Centerport NY 11721-1450 Office Phone: 631-424-3700. E-mail: RTrotta@TrottaAssociates.com., RicTrotta@aol.com.

TROTTA, VINCENT JOHN, transportation executive; b. Huntingdon, Pa., May 7, 1965; s. Vincent Paul and Mary Jane (Stanko) T.; m. Melanie Dawn Wood, June 15, 1991. BS, W.Va. U., 1987. Elec. engr. GE Transp. Systems, Erie, Pa., 1987-91, program mgr., 1991-93, mgr. sales/svc., 1993-96; pres., dir. GE Lokomotif Indonesia, Jakarta, Indonesia, 1997; gen. mgr. GE Transp. Systems, Belo Horizonte, Brazil, 1998-2000; master black belt GE Aircraft Engines, Cin., 2000-2001, gen. mgr. global accessories sales, 2001—. Avocations: travel, golf. Office: 1 Neumann Way Cincinnati OH 45215-1915 E-mail: vincent.trotta@ae.ge.com.

TROTTER, CHARLIE, chef; Degree in polit. sci., U. Wis., 1982. Owner, chef Charlie Trotter's, Chgo. Author: Charlie Trotter's, Charlie Trotter's Vegetables, Charlie Trotter's Seafood, Charlie Trotter's Desserts, Charlie Trotter's Meat and Game, Kitchen Sessions with Charlie Trotter, Gourmet Cooking for Dummies; host: (tv series) Kitchen Sessions with Charlie Trotter. Recipient Grand award, Wine Spectator, Best Restaurant in U.S., 2000. Office: 816 W Armitage Ave Chicago IL 60614

TROTTER, F(REDERICK) THOMAS, retired academic administrator; b. L.A., Apr. 17, 1926; s. Fred B. and Hazel (Thomas) T.; m. Gania Demaree, June 27, 1953; children— Ruth Elizabeth, Paula Anne (dec.), Tania, Mary. AB, Occidental Coll., 1950, DD, 1968; STB, Boston U., 1953, PhD, 1958; LHD, Ill. Wesleyan U., 1974, Cornell Coll., 1985, Westmar Coll., 1987; LLD, U. Pacific, 1978, Wesleyan Coll., 1981; EdD, Columbia Coll., 1984; LittD, Alaska Pacific U., 1987. Exec. sec. Boston U. Student Christian Assn., 1951-54; ordained elder Calif.-Pacific, Methodist Ch., 1953; pastor Montclair (Calif.) Meth. Ch., 1956-59; lectr. So. Calif. Sch. Theology at Claremont, 1957-59, instr., 1959-60, asst. prof., 1960-63, assoc. prof., 1963-66, prof., 1966, dean, 1961; prof. religion and arts, dean Sch. Theology Claremont, 1961-73; mem. Bd. Higher Edn. and Ministry, United Meth. Ch., 1972-73, gen. sec., 1973-87; pres. Alaska Pacific U., Anchorage, 1988-95; ret., 1995. Dir. Inst. for Antiquity and Christianity at Claremont. Author: Jesus and the Historian, 1968, Loving God with One's Mind, 1987, God Is with Us, 1997, Politics, Morality, and Higher Education, 1997, weekly column local newspapers; editor-at-large: Christian Century, 1969-84. Trustee Dillard U. Served with USAAF, 1944-46. Kent fellow Soc. for Values in Higher Edn., 1954; Dempster fellow Meth. Ch., 1954 Mem. Rotary Internat. (Anchorage Downtown), Commonwealth North. Home: 75-136 Kiowa Dr Indian Wells CA 92210

TROTTER, HERMAN EAGER, JR., (HERMAN TROTTER), retired music critic; b. Providence, Sept. 25, 1925; s. Herman Eager, Sr. and Shelley Fern (Jones) T.; m. Johanne Marguerite Haberstro, Sept. 22, 1956 (div. Apr. 1996); children: Kim Avery. Holly Anne. Joy Caroline; m. Rosa Spillane Whetzle, July 22, 1996. BA, Yale U., 1946. Pub. utility sec. analyst Mass. Mut. Life Ins. Co., Springfield, 1947-51; sales engr., mgr. Buffalo office B-I-F Industries, Providence, 1951-56; asst. sec. Buffalo Batt and Felt Co, Depew, N.Y., 1956-68; account exec. Harold Warner Advt., Buffalo, N.Y., 1968-77; freelance music critic Buffalo News, 1968-77, staff music critic, 1977—2001, music critic emeritus, 2002. Contbr. articles to profl. and popular jours., and to New Grove Dictionary of Music. Program annotator Buffalo Philharm., 1964-70. Lt. (j.g.) USN, 1943-46, PTO. Mem.: Music Critics Assn. (v.p. 1988—93, sec. 1999—2003). Avocations: travel, record collecting. Home: 107 Oakland Pl Buffalo NY 14222-2047 E-mail: herros72296@aol.com.

TROTTER, LESLIE EARL, operations research educator, consultant; b. Muskogee, Okla., Nov. 17, 1943; s. Leslie Earl and Sylvia Helene (Freeze) T.; m. Jomi Tuggle, July 19, 1968 (div. Dec. 1995); children: Colleen Nicole, Eamonn Scott; m. Jeannine Rouch, July 7, 2000. AB in Math., Princeton U., 1965; MS in Indsl. and Systems Engring., Ga. Inst. Tech., 1971; PhD in Ops. Rsch., Cornell U., 1973. Sci. computer programmer Lockheed-Ga. Co., Marietta, 1965-68; computer applications analyst Control Data Corp., Atlanta, 1968-70; postdoctoral rsch. assoc. Math. Rsch. Ctr., U. Wis., Madison, 1973; asst. prof. Yale U. Sch. Orgn. and Mgmt., New Haven, 1974-75; assoc. prof. ops. rsch. Cornell U. Sch. Ops. Rsch. and Indsl. Engring., Ithaca, NY, 1975-84, dir. of Sch., 1983—87, 1998—99, prof., 1984—; dir. Advanced Computational Optimization Lab. Cornell Theory Ctr., 1995—2001. Vis. prof. Bonn (Germany) U., 1977-79, math. dept. E.P.F.L., Lausanne, Switzerland, 1984-85, 91-92, 2000, Math. Inst., Augsburg (Germany) U., 1987-88; vis. cons. Bell Labs., Holmdel, N.J., 1981. Editor optimization area Jour. Ops. Rsch., 1982-87; contbr. numerous articles to profl. jours. Recipient tchg. excellence awards Cornell U., 1977, 81, 93, 94, 98, sr. U.S. scientist award Alexander von Humboldt Found., Germany, 1988; numerous rsch. grants NSF, 1974—, including High Performance Computing and Comms. Grand Challenge award, 1995—01. Mem. Ops. Rsch. Soc. Am., Math. Programming Soc. (treas. 1988-94), Soc. for Indsl. and Applied Math. Avocations: exercise, hiking, music. Office: Cornell U Sch Ops Rsch Engring Rhodes Hall Ithaca NY 14853 Office Phone: 607-255-5360. E-mail: ltrotter@cs.cornell.edu.

TROTTER, LLOYD G. electric power industry executive; b. Cleveland, Apr. 9, 1945; m. Teri Trotter; 3 children. BBA, Cleve. State U., 1972, PhD in Bus. Adminstrn. (hon.), 2001. Field svc. engr. GE Lighting, 1970; various positions GE, 1970-90; v.p., gen. mgr. mfg. ED&C, 1990-98; sr. v.p. GE, 1998-99; pres., CEO GE Indsl. Sys., 1999—; CEO, consumer & indsl. divsn. GE, 2004—. Started GE African-Am. forum, 1990. Rep. for GE America's Promise. Named 50 Most Important African-Am. in Tech., USBE&IT and Blackmoney.com, 2004. Avocation: collector of Harlem Renaissance Period art and wine. Office: GE Cons & Industrial GE Appliance Park 9500 Williamsburg Plz Louisville KY 40222*

TROTTER, THOMAS ROBERT, lawyer; b. Akron, Ohio, Apr. 11, 1949; s. Fred and Josephine (Daley) Trotter; m. Martha Kaltenbach, 2003. BA, Ohio U., 1971; JD, Tulane U., 1975. Bar: Ohio 1975, D.C. 2000, U.S. Dist. Ct. (no. dist.) Ohio 1975. Assoc. Squire, Sanders & Dempsey, Cleve., 1975-80; shareholder Buckingham, Doolittle & Burroughs, Akron, 1980—. Trustee Cascade Capital Corp., Akron, 1983—; chair taxation and legis. com. Greater Akron C. of C., 1988-95; trustee Akron-Summit Solid Waste Mgmt. Authority, 1994-97 Trustee Akron Symphony Orch., 1984-93, trustee Weathervane Cmty. Playhouse, 1996-2003, pres., 1999-2001. Mem. ABA, Ohio Bar Assn. (chair local govt. law com.), Akron Bar Assn., Nat. Assn. Bond Lawyers, Sigma Alpha Epsilon. Democrat. Home: 180 W Fairlawn Blvd Akron OH 44313 Office: Buckingham Doolittle & Burroughs LLP PO Box 1500 50 S Main St Akron OH 44309-1500 Office Phone: 330-258-6488. E-mail: ttrotter@bdblaw.com.

TROTZ, BARRY, professional hockey coach; Asst. coach U. Manitoba, 1984; head coach, gen. mgr. Dauphin Kings Jr. Hockey Club, 1985-87; head coach U. Manitoba, 1987; chief western scout Washington Capitals, 1988, asst. coach, 1991, head coach, 1992-95, U.S. Team at AM. Hockey League All Star Game, 1996, Nashville Predators Hockey Team, 1997—. Office: Nashville Predators 501 Broadway Nashville TN 37203-3932

TROUNSTINE, PHILIP JOHN, communications consultant, institute administrator; b. Cin., July 30, 1949; s. Henry P. and Amy May (Joseph) Trounstine; children: Jessica, David; m. Deborah Williams, May 1, 1993; children: Amy, Ryan, Patrick Wilkes. Student, U. Vt., 1967-68, Stanford U., 1968-70; BA in Journalism, San Jose State U., 1975. Graphic artist Eric Printing, San Jose, Calif., 1972-75; reporter Indpls. Star, Ind., 1975-78, San Jose Mercury News, Calif., 1978-83, editl. writer, 1983-86, polit. editor, 1986-99; ednl. cons. Teen Recovery Strategies, 1995-99; comms. dir. Gov. Gray Davis, Calif., 1999-2001, comm. cons., 2001—; dir. Survey and Policy Rsch. Inst. at San Jose State U., 2001—. Co-author: Movers & Shakers: The Study of Community Power, 1981. Creator, writer SPJ Gridiron Show, San Jose, 1981-91. Pulliam fellow, 1975, Duke U., 1991, J.S. Knight fellow Stanford U., 1993-94. Mem. Soc. Profl. Journalists (mem. nat. ethics com. 1993-96), Seascape Golf Club. Jewish. Avocations: golf, fishing. Home: 620 Middlefield Dr Aptos CA 95003-3560 E-mail: phil@trounstine.com.

TROUP, GORDON A. health facility administrator; With Am. Hosp. Supply Corp., Cardinal Distbn., 1991—99, exec. v.p. field ops., 1999—2000; pres. pharm. distbn. and splty distbn. bus. Cardinal Health, Inc., 2000—03, exec. v.p., 2003—, pres. nuclear pharmacy svcs., 2003—. Office: Cardinal Health Inc 7000 Cardinal Pl Dublin OH 43017

TROUPE, MARILYN KAY, educational administrator; b. Tulsa, Sept. 30, 1945; d. Ernest Robinson and Lucille (Andrew) T. BA in History, Okla. State U., 1967, MA in History, 1976, EdD, 1993; lic. in cosmetology, Troupe's Beauty Sch., 1970. Cert. tchr. Okla., Tenn. Tchr. social studies Maragret Hudson Prog., Tulsa, 1969-81; tutor Tulsa Indian Youth, 1971-72; instr. cosmetology McLain-Tulsa Pub. Schs., 1982-94; instrnl. devel. specialist Okla. Dept. Vocat. and Tech. Edn., Stillwater, 1987-94; asst. prof., coord. tchr. prep. prog. chair divsn. liberal studies and edn. Lane Coll., Jackson, Tenn., 1995-97; dir. divsn. educator preparation Ky. Edn. Profl. Stds. Bd., Frankfort, 1997—. Vis. lectr. Okla. State U., 1980-81; cons., lectr. cosmetology. Bd. dirs., mem. adv. bd. Stillwater Park and Recreation, Stillwater Cmty. Rels. and Fair Housing, 1991-94; bd. dirs. Adult Day Care Ctr., 1990-94, Early Childhood Profl. Devel. Coun.; v.p. Okla. Recreation and Park Soc., 1994; judge Okla. Sch. Sci. and Math., 1994; mem. Leadership Stillwater, 1990; vol. Spl. Olympics State Games, Meals on Wheels, United Way, Frankfort Soup Kitchen; mem. women's adv. coun. Jackson Regional Hosp.; mem. adv. com. Okla. Task Force: Goals for Tomorrow, Roman Cath. Ch., Tulsa, 1985-86; mem. Ky. Early Childhood Profl. Devel. Coun.; grad. Leadership Ky., 2001; mem. Ky. Literacy Partnership. Recipient numerous awards for profl. and civic contbns. including Woman of the Yr. award Zeta Phi Beta, 1985, Salute award Gov. Okla., 1985, Outstanding Cmty. Svc. cert. WomenFest, 1985. Mem. AAUW, ASCD, Nat. Coun. Accredition Tchr. Edn. (bd. examiners), Okla. Assn. Advancement of Black Ams. in Vocat. Edn. (Golden Torch award 1994), Ky. Assn. Black Sch. Educators, Vocat. Indsl. Clubs Am. (dist. adv. 1985-86, Appreciation award 1985), Am. Vocat. Assn., Okla. Vocat. Assn., Okla. State Beauty Culturalists League (pres. 1979-85, Outstanding Svc. award 1985), Nat. Assn. Bus. and Profl. Women's Club (charter mem., past pres.), Stillwater C. of C. (bd. dirs.), Langston Alumni Assn., Frankfort-Lexington Links, Cath. Daus. Am., Phi Alpha Theta, Theta Nu Sigma, Alpha Kappa Alpha (Soror of the Yr. 1993), Iota Lambda Sigma, Phi Delta Kappa, Alpha Kappa Alpha. Democrat. Avocations: travel, reading, collecting antiques, volunteer work, shopping.

TROUSDALE, STEPHEN RICHARD, newspaper editor; b. L.A., May 29, 1963; s. Richard Gardner Trousdale and Geraldine Barbara Wisdom. AB, Stanford U., 1985. News editor L.A. Daily Commerce, 1986—87; edit. page editor L.A. Daily Jour., 1987—89, mng. editor, 1989—96; bus. editor Copley L.A. Newspapers, 1996—97; dep. bus. editor Contra Costa Times, 1997—2000, bus. editor, 2000—. Mem. Soc. Profl. Journalists (past pres. L.A. chpt.), AP Mng. Editors, Calif. Soc. Newspaper Editors, Soc. Am. Bus. Editors and Writers. Avocations: skiing, Karate. Home: 1820 Virginia St Apt B Berkeley CA 94703-1345 Office: Contra Costa Newspapers 2640 Shadelands Dr Walnut Creek CA 94598-2513 E-mail: strousdale@cctimes.com.

TROUT, CHARLES HATHAWAY, historian, educator; b. Seattle, Nov. 3, 1935; s. Charles Whyron and Elizabeth (Hathaway) T.; m. Margot Stevens, Dec. 30, 1961 (div. 1983); children: Nicholas H., Benjamin C.; m. Katherine Taylor Griffiths, Oct. 6, 1984. BA, Amherst Coll., 1957; MA, Columbia U., 1961, PhD, 1972. History instr. Hill Sch., Pottstown, Pa., 1958-59, Philips Exeter Acad., (N.H.), 1960-69; prof. history Mt. Holyoke Coll., South Hadley, Mass., 1969-80; provost, dean faculty Colgate U., Hamilton, N.Y., 1980-90; pres. Washington Coll., Chestertown, Md., 1990-95; tchr. Tchr. for Africa, Korongoi, Litein, Kenya, 1996-97. Vis. prof. U. Mass. Labor Rels. and Rsch. Ctr., 1974-80; interim pres., Harcum Coll., Bryn Mawr, Pa., 2002-03, pres., 2003—. Author: Boston, The Great Depression, and the New Deal. Chmn. bd. World Edn. Inc.; trustee Sultana Projects, Inc. Columbia U. Pres.'s scholar, 1959-60; NEH rsch. fellow, 1975-76; Charles Warren fellow Harvard U., 1978-79. Democrat. Episcopalian. Home: 211 N Queen St Chestertown MD 21620-1627 Office: Harcum Coll Office of President Bryn Mawr PA 19010 Business E-Mail: ctrout@harcum.edu.

TROUT, LINDA COPPLE, state supreme court chief justice; b. Tokyo, Sept. 1, 1951; BA, U. Idaho, 1973, JD, 1977; LLD (hon.), Albertson Coll. Idaho, 1999. Bar: Idaho 1977. Judge magistrate divsn. Idaho Dist. Ct. (2d jud. divsn.), 1983-90, dist. judge, 1991-92, acting trial ct. adminstr., 1987-91; justice Idaho Supreme Ct., 1992—, chief justice, 1997—. Instr. coll. law U. Idaho, 1983, 88. Mem. Idaho State Bar Assn., Clearwater Bar Assn. (pres. 1980-81).

TROUT, MARGIE MARIE MUELLER, civic worker; b. Apr. 27, 1923; d. Albert Sylvester and Pearl Elizabeth (Jose) Mueller; m. Maurice Elmore Trout, Aug. 24, 1943; children: Richard Willis, Babette Yvonne. Student, Webster Coll., 1944-45. Cert. genealogist Bd. Cert. Genealogy. Sec. offices Robertson Aircraft Corp., St. Louis, 1942; speed lathe and drill press operator Busch-Selzer Diesel Engine Co., St. Louis, 1942-43; Cub Scout den mother Vienna, Austria, 1953-55, Mt. Pleasant, Mich., 1955, London, 1956-57; leader Nat. Capitol coun. Girl Scouts U.S.A., Bethesda, Md., 1963-65; co-chmn. Am. Booth YWCA and Red Cross Ann. Bazaars, Bangkok, 1970-72; worker ARC, Vientiane, Laos, 1959-60, Bangkok, 1970-72; activities co-chmn., exec. bd. mem. Women's Club Armed Forces Staff Coll., Norfolk, Va., 1975-77. Mem. Am. Women's Clubs, Embassy Clubs, Internat. Women's Clubs Vienna, 1952-55, London, 1956-59, Vientiane, 1959-61, Munich, Germany, 1965-69, Bangkok, 1969-72, Norfolk, 1975-77. Crochet articles exhibited Exhbn. of Works of Art by the Corps Diplomatique, London, 1958. Home: 6203 Hardy Dr Mc Lean VA 22101-3114

TROUT, MAURICE ELMORE, diplomat; b. Clifton Hill, Mo., Sept. 17, 1917; s. David McCamel and Charlotte Temple (Woods) T.; m. Margie Marie Mueller, Aug. 24, 1943; children— Richard Willis, Babette Yvonne. BA, Hillsdale Coll., 1939; MA in Pub. Adminstrn, St. Louis U., 1948, PhD in Polit. Sci, 1950. Joined U.S. Fgn. Service, 1950; assigned Paris, 1950-52, Vienna, 1952-55, London, 1955-59, Vientiane, Laos, 1959-61; with Office Exec. Dir. Bur. Far Eastern Affairs, Dept. State, Washington, 1961-65; Am. consulate gen. Munich, 1965-69; 1st sec., consul Am. embassy, Bangkok, 1969—72; dep. office dir. Bur. Politico-Mil. Affairs, Dept. State, Washington, 1972-75; Dept. State advisor Armed Forces Staff Coll., Norfolk, Va., 1975-77. Bd. dirs. Internat. Sch., Bangkok, 1970-72. Served with USCG, 1939-45; capt. USAFR, 1951-55. Recipient Achievement award, Hillsdale Coll., 1962. Mem. Am. Fgn. Service Assn., Diplomatic and Consular Officers Ret., Delta Tau Delta, Delta Theta Phi, Pi Gamma Mu. Home: 6203 Hardy Dr Mc Lean VA 22101-3114

TROUT, MONROE EUGENE, hospital systems executive; b. Harrisburg, Pa., Apr. 5, 1931; s. David Michael and Florence Margaret (Kashner) T.; m. Sandra Louise Lemke, June 11, 1960; children: Monroe Eugene, Timothy William. AB, U. Pa., 1953, MD, 1957; LLB, Dickinson Sch. of Law, 1964, JD, 1969; LLD (hon.), Dickinson Sch. Law, 1996, Bloomfield Coll., 1994, Cumberland Coll., 2003. Intern Great Lakes (Ill.) Naval Hosp., 1957-58; resident in internal medicine Portsmouth (Va.) Naval Hosp., 1959-61; chief med. dept. Harrisburg State Hosp., 1961-64; dir. drug regulatory affairs Pfizer, Inc., N.Y.C., 1964-68; v.p., med. dir. Winthrop Labs., N.Y.C., 1968-70; med. dir. Sterling Drug, Inc., N.Y.C., 1970-74, v.p., dir. med. affairs, 1974-78, sr. v.p., dir. med. affairs, bd. dirs., mem. exec. com., 1978-86; pres., CEO Am. Healthcare Sys., Inc., 1986-95, chmn., 1987-95; also bd. dirs. Am. Healthcare Systems, Inc.; chmn. emeritus Am. Healthcare Sys., Inc., 1995—; interim CEO Cytran Inc., 1996. Bd. dirs. Baxter Internat., SAIC; chmn. bd. dirs. Cytyc Inc., 1998—2002, Ineed MD, Inc., Am. Excess Ins. Ltd., 1990—95; adj. assoc. prof. Bklyn. Coll. Pharmacy; spl. lectr. legal medicine, trustee Dickinson Sch. Law, 1970—73; trustee Ariz. State U. Sch. Health Adminstrn., 1988—91; mem. rsch. bd. Sterling Winthrop, 1977—86; mem. Joint Commn. Prescription Drug Use, 1976—80; sec. Commn. on Med. Malpractice, HEW, 1971—73, cons., 1974; co-chmn. San Diego County Health Commn., 1992—94. Mem. editl. bd. Hosp. Formulary Mgmt., 1969-79, Forensic Sci., 1971—, Jour. Legal Medicine, 1973-79, Reg. Tox. and Pharmac, 1981-87, Med. Malpractice Prevention, 1985—; editl. reviewer Annals of Internal Medicine; contbr. articles to profl. jours. Exec. com. White House Mini Conf. on Aging, 1980; mem. Nat. Health Adv. Bd. AAA; chmn. bd. Am. Coll. Legal Medicine Found., 1983—87; mem. N.Y. State Commn. Substance Abuse, 1978—80, Town Coun., New Canaan, 1978—86, vice chmn., 1985—86; trustee Cleve. Clinic, 1971—87, Albany Med. Coll., 1977—86, St. Vincent DePaul Ctr. for the Homeless, 1987—90, U. Calif.-San Diego Thornton Hosp. and Med. Ctr., 1990—97, San Diego Mus. Art, 1996—98, Bapt. Health Sys. Found., Knoxville, 1999—; trustee, vice chmn. Morehouse Med. Sch., 1980—89; assoc. trustee U. Pa.; bd. visitors U. Pa. Sch. Nursing, 1988—92; pres. bd. trustees U. Calif. San Diego Found., 1994—97; vice chmn. Med. Commn. for Food and Shelter, Inc.; chmn. Internat. B'nai B'rith Dinner, 1989, 1994; Rep. dist. leader New Canaan, 1966—68; bd. dirs. New Canaan Interchurch Svc. Com., 1965—69, Athletes Kidney Found., Cir. in the Sq. Theatre Inc., 1984—86, Knoxville Symphony Soc., 2001—04, Knoxville Opera Co., 2001—04, East Tenn. Hist. Soc. Recipient Alumni award of merit U. Pa., 1953, Disting. Alumni award Dickinson Sch. Law, 1989, Nat. Healthcare award Internat. B'nai B'rith, 1991, Entrepreneur of Yr. award San Diego, 1994, Horatio Alger award, 1995, Salvation Army Tradition of Caring award, 1996, Cívis Universitatus award U. Calif. San Diego, 1997, Gold Medal award, Am. Coll. Legal Medicine, 1999, Bapt. Health Sys. Visionary award, 2002. Fellow Am. Coll. Legal Medicine (v.p., pres., bd. govs.); mem. AMA (Physician's Recognition awards 1969, 72, 76, 82, 85, 88, 92), Med. Execs. (pres. 1975-76), Delta Tau Delta (Alumni Achievement award 1996, Named to 100 Most Influential Delts of Twentieth Century 2000). Lutheran. Office: 2110 Cove View Way Knoxville TN 37919

TROUTMAN, CHARLES HENRY, III, lawyer; b. Wooster, Ohio, Mar. 25, 1944; BA, Wheaton Coll., 1966; JD, Am. U., 1969; M in Comparative Law, So. Meth. U., 1970. Bar: Ill. 1969, D.C. 1969, Guam 1973, U.S. Ct. Appeals (9th cir.) 1973, Trust Territory Pacific Islands 1973, U.S. Supreme Ct. 1976, Commonwealth of No. Mariana Islands 1978. Asst. atty. gen., 1970—74; assoc. Cronin, Trotman & Assocs., 1974—75; atty. gen., 1975—77; counsel Dept. Edn., Guam, 1977—78; compiler of laws Govt. of Guam, Agana, 1978—2004, consumer counsel, 2004—, acting atty. gen., 1987, 2002; mem. counsel Commn. on Self-Determination, 1987—2002. Mem.: ABA, Guam Bar Assn., Christian Legal Soc., Am. Soc. Internat. Law, Fed. Bar Assn. (sec. local chpt.). Presbyterian. Home: PO Box 455 Hagatna GU 96932-0455 Office: Judicial Ctr 2-200E 120 W OBrien Dr Hagatna GU 96910 Office Phone: 671-475-3324. E-mail: ctrout@ite.net.

TROUTMAN, GEORGE WILLIAM, geologist, petroleum geological advisor; b. Aug. 8, 1949; s. George I. and Ellen G. Troutman; m. Marcia Lyn Roseman, Aug. 14, 1971; children: Nancy, Anthony, Janet, David, Barbara, Jonathan. Student, Murray State U., 1967-68; BS in Geology, Western Ky. U., 1974. Lic. prof. geoscientist Tex. Geophys. engr. Birdwell divsn. Seismograph Svc. Corp., Ohio, Pa., W.Va., 1974-77; geologist Consol. Natural Gas, Clarksburg, W.Va., 1977-79; exloration geologist Mountain Fuel Supply Corp., Denver, 1979-80; regional exploration geologist Al-Aquitaine Exploration, Ltd., Denver, 1980-81; sr. staff geologist Resources Investment Corp., Denver, 1981-82; geol. mgr. Petro-Lewis Corp., MCR, Oklahoma City, 1982-84; pres., geologist Troutman Geol. & Assocs., Edmond, Okla., 1984-2000; geol. advisor Devon Energy, Oklahoma City, 2000—03; sr. staff E&P geologist onshore-we. U.S. Dominion Exploration & Prodn., Inc., Oklahoma City, 2003—. With USN, 1968-70. Mem. Am. Assn. Petroleum Geologists (cert.), Soc. Profl. Well Log Analysts, Oklahoma City Geol. Soc. (exec. com. 1985-86, editor Shale Shaker Digest XI 1982-85, treas. 1987-88, v.p. 1988-89, pres.-elect 1996-97, pres. 1997-98), Ardmore Geol. Soc., New Orleans Geol. Soc., Computer Oriented Geol. Soc., Geophys. Soc. of Oklahoma City, East Tex. Geol. Soc., West Tex. Geol. Soc., Kans. Geol. Soc. Republican. Mem. Lds Ch. Office: Dominion Exploration & Prodn Inc Ste 600 14000 Quail Springs Pky Oklahoma City OK 73134 Office Phone: 405-641-6764. E-mail: troutman@geologist.com.

TROUTMAN, J. GREGORY, lawyer; b. Louisville, Dec. 7, 1966; BA in Polit. Sci. cum laude, U. Louisville, 1989, JD, 1992; LLM in Taxation, Boston U., 1993. Bar: Ky. 1992, U.S. Fed. Claims Ct. 1994, U.S. Dist. Ct. (we. dist.) Ky. 1995, U.S. Dist. Ct. (ea. dist.) Ky. 1998, U.S. Ct. Appeals (6th cir.) 1998, U.S. Ct. Appeals (7th cir.) 1999. Pvt. practice, Louisville, 1992-94; assoc. Morris, Garlove, Waterman & Johnson, Louisville, 1994—99, ptnr., 2000—. Mem. ABA, Ky. Bar Assn., Louisville Bar Assn. Office: Morris Garlove Waterman & Johnson 1000 One Riverfront Plaza Louisville KY 40202 Office Phone: 502-589-3200. Fax: 502-589-3219. E-mail: JGT@mgwj.com.

TROUTNER, JOANNE JOHNSON, director, consultant, secondary school educator; b. Muncie, Ind., Sept. 9, 1952; d. Donal Russel and Lois Vivian (Hicks) Johnson; m. Lary William Troutner, May 17, 1975. BA in Media and English, Purdue U., 1974; MS in Edn., 1976. Media spls. Lafayette (Ind.) Sch. Corp., 1974-77, 81-83, computer resource tchr., 1983-84; media splst. Tippecanoe Sch. Corp., Lafayette, 1984-85; ednl. support, 1985-87; coord. instrl. support, 1988-94; tchr. English Minot (N.D.) Pub. Schs., 1978-79, dir. tech. and media, 1994—; media specialist, 1979-81. Vis. prof. continuing edn. U. S.C., Columbia, 1983, U. N.D.; instr. Purdue U., West Lafayette; software selector Elem. Sch. Libr. Collection. Author: The Media Specialist, The Microcomputer and the Curriculum, 1983, World Desk-Classroom Internet Guide, 1998, The Internet: A Curriculum Oriented Guide, 1998, 2003, Using the Internet and Technology to Strengthen Learning in English/Language Arts and Social Studies, 1999, Integrating Technology and the Internet into English and Social Studies Classroom, 2002, Strengthen Your Classroom with Technology, 2004; materials rev. columnist: Sch. Libr., Media Quar., computer literacy columnist: Jour. Computers Math. and Sci. Tchg., computer software columnist: Tchr. Libr., 1989—, internet columnist:, 1995—; editor: Ind. Computer Educators newsletter. Active Greater Lafayette Leadership Acad. Alumni Group, 1983—; bd. dirs. Lafayette Family Svc. Agy., 1987—89, Tippecanoe County Pub. Libr., trustee, 1990—2000, pres., 1994—95; mem. dean's adv. coun. Sch. Edn. Purdue U., 2003—. Recipient Disting. Alumni award, Purdue U. Sch. Edn., 2003. Mem.: ASCD, ALA, Internat. Soc. Tech. Educators, Ind. Computer Educators (bd. dirs. 1986—92, pres. 1990—91), Internat. Coun. Computers in Edn. (interactive video spl. interest group newsletter editor 1986—87), Am. Assn. Sch. Librs. (sec. 1983—84, 2d v.p. 1985—86), Ind. Assn. Media Educators (chmn. computer divns. 1982—84), Phi Beta Kappa, Phi Delta Kappa (v.p. programs 1987—88, v.p. memberships 1988—89, pres. 1989—90), Kappa Delta Gamma. Home: 4001 Penny Packers Mill Rd Lafayette IN 47909-3557 Office: Tippecanoe Sch Corp 21 Elston Rd Lafayette IN 47909-2899 Office Phone: 765-474-2481. Personal E-mail: troutner@mndspring.com.

TROUTT, WILLIAM EARL, academic administrator; b. Bolivar, Tenn., June 13, 1949; s. Jack and Earline (Shearin) Troutt; m. Carole Pearson, Nov. 26, 1970; children: Carole Anne, Jack. BA, Union U., Jackson, Tenn., 1971; MA, U. Louisville, 1972; PhD, Vanderbilt U., 1978. Admissions counselor Union U., 1973—75; asst. dir. Tenn. Higher Edn. Commn., Nashville, 1975—78; sr. assoc. McManis Assocs. Inc., Washington, 1978—80; exec. v.p. Belmont Coll., Nashville, 1981—82, pres., 1982—99, Rhodes Coll., Memphis, 1999—. Active Leadership Nashville, Mayors Com. on Excellence; sec. Tenn. Student Assistance Corp., 1986—. Named one of Nations Most Effective Coll. Pres., Exxon Found. Study, 1986; scholar Luther Rice Scholar, So. Bapt. Theol. Sem., 1971. Mem.: So. Assn. Colls. and Schs. (commnr. comm. colls. 1986—), Tenn. Ind. Colls. Fund (sec.-treas. 1986—), Tenn. Coun. Pvt. Colls. (chmn. 1985—), Nashville Area C. of C. (bd. dirs. 1985—), Rotary. Office: Office of the Pres 2000 N Pkwy Memphis TN 38112-1690

TROUTT POWELL, EVE, historian, educator; m. Timothy Powell; children: Jibreel, Gideon. BA in history and lit., Harvard U., 1983, MS in middle ea. studies, 1988, PhD. in middle ea. studies, 1995. Reporter trainee The N.Y. Times; assoc. prof. of history U. of Ga., Athens, Ga., 1995—. Author: (book) A Different Shade of Colonialism: Egypt, Great Britian and the Mastery of the Sudan, 2003; co-editor: The African Diaspora in the Mediterranean Lands of

Islam, 2001. Fellow, Inst. for advanced Study, Princeton U., 1999, Lilly Tchg. Fellow, U. of Ga., John D. and Catherine T. MacArthur Found., 2003. Office: Univ of Georgia dept of History LeConte Hall Rm 220 Athens GA 30602

TROUTWINE, GAYLE LEONE, lawyer; b. Kansas City, Mo., Feb. 26, 1952; BS, N.W. Mo. State U., 1973; JD with honors, U. Mo., 1978. Bar: Mo. 1978, Oreg. 1983, U.S. Dist. Ct. (we. dist.) Mo., Wash. 1984, U.S. Ct. Appeals (9th cir.), U.S. Dist. Ct. (we. dist.) Wash., U.S. Supreme Ct., Hawaii 1995. Ptnr. Williams & Troutwine, P.C., Portland, Oreg., 1986—; pres., CEO Hula Moons Farm, Maui, Hawaii, 1999—2002, Apricot Rise, Kahului, Hawaii, 1999—2003. Spkr. in field. Contbr. articles to profl. jours. Mem. Jud. Steering com., 1994, Made in Hawaii Coun., 2000—02; bd. mem. Portland Area Women's Polit. Caucus, 1992—95, Oreg. Women's Polit. Caucus, 1996—; steering com. mem. Breast Implant Litig., 1992—, Tobacco Litig. Named Queen of Torts Wall St. Jour., 1996. Mem.: ATLA (bd. govs.), Maui Bd. Realtors, Western Trial Lawyers Assn. (bd. govs. 1992—), Greater Kansas City (sec. 1981—82), Women Lawyers Assn., Wash. Trial Lawyers Assn., Hawaii Trial Lawyers Assn., Calif. Trial Lawyers Assn., Oreg. Trial Lawyers Assn. (bd. govs. 1987—91), Wash. State Bar, Oreg. State Bar (exec. bd. litig. sect. 1984—88, chmn. 1987—88, procedure and practice com. 1985—88, bd. govs. 1990—93), Mo. Bar, Hawaii State Bar. Democrat.

TROVER, ELLEN LLOYD, lawyer, rancher; b. Richmond, Va., Nov. 23, 1947; d. Robert Van Buren and Hazel (Urban) Lloyd; m. Denis William Trover, June 12, 1971; 1 dau., Florence Emma. AB, Vassar Coll., 1969; JD, Coll. William and Mary, 1972. Asst. editor Bancroft-Whitney, San Francisco, 1973-74; owner Ellen Lloyd Trover Atty.-at-Law, Thousand Oaks, Calif., 1974-82; ptnr. Trover & Fisher, Thousand Oaks, Calif., 1982-89; pvt. practice law Thousand Oaks, Calif., 1989-98; mng. ptnr. The Lloyd-Trover Partnership, Thousand Oaks, Calif., 1998—. Editor: Handbooks of State Chronologies, 1972. Trustee Conejo Future Found., Thousand Oaks, 1978—91, trustee emeritus, 1992—, vice chmn., 1982—84, chmn., 1984—88; pres. Zonta Club Conejo Valley Area, 1978—79; trustee Hydro Help for the Handicapped, 1980—85, Atlantis Found., 1994—; pres. Vista Santa Rosa Assn., 2001—. Mem. State Bar Calif., Va. State Bar, Phi Alpha Delta. Democrat. Presbyterian. Home: PO Box 297 Coachella CA 92236 Office: 1107E E Thousand Oaks Blvd Thousand Oaks CA 91362-2816 E-mail: etrover@yahoo.com.

TROVILLION, ALLEN, state legislator, contractor; b. Winter Park, Fla., May 1, 1926; B in Bldg. Constrn., U. Fla., 1950. Mem. Fla. Ho. of Reps., 1994—; chmn. corrections com., 1996-97; mem. edn. K12, transp., ednl. facilities coms., 1996-97; mem. info. tech. resources com., 1996-97. Coach Little League, Pony League; scoutmaster Boy Scouts Am.; pres. United Way; mem. bd. govs. Citrus Club; mem. Econ. Devel. Com. Mid Fla.; pres. Ctrl. Fla. Builders Exch.; pres. U. Ctrl. Fla. Found.; chmn. Winter Park C. of C.; mem. adv. com. to bd.; mem. regional bd. Greater Orlando C. of C.; mem. nominating com. 9th Jud. Cir.; mayor Winter Park, 1962-67; trustee Winter Park Meml. Hosp., 1967-74; bd. dirs. Jr. Achievement, Fla. League Municipalities, Orange County Sch. Found. Named Citizen of Yr., Winter Park C. of C., 1991. Mem. Assocd. Builders and Contractors, Christian Businessmens Com., Jaycees (Winter Park chpt. Man of Yr.), Rotary (pres., Paul Harris fellow), Phi Gamma Delta. Republican. Avocation: golf. Office: Fla Capitol 402 S Monroe St Tallahassee FL 32399-6526 Home: 1360 Palmetto Ave Winter Park FL 32789-4916 E-mail: trovillion.allen@leg.state.fl.us.

TROWBRIDGE, ALEXANDER BUEL, JR., business consultant; b. Englewood, N.J., Dec. 12, 1929; s. Alexander Buel and Julie (Chamberlain) T.; m. Eleanor Hutzler, Apr. 18, 1981; children by previous marriage: Stephen C., Corrin S., Kimberly. Grad., Phillips Acad., Andover, Mass., 1947; AB cum laude, Princeton U., 1951; LLD (hon.), D'Youville Coll., 1967, Hofstra U., 1968, Hobart Coll., William Smith Coll., 1975. With Calif. Tex. Oil Co., 1954-59; ops. mgr. Esso Standard Oil S.A. Ltd., Panama C.Z., 1959-61, div. mgr., 1961-63; pres. Esso Standard Oil Co., P.R., 1963-65; asst. sec. commerce for domestic and internat. bus. U.S., 1965-67; sec. of commerce, 1967-68; pres. Am. Mgmt. Assn., N.Y.C., 1968-70, The Conf. Bd., Inc., N.Y.C., 1970-76; vice chmn. bd. Allied Chem. Corp., 1976-80; bd. dirs. NAM, Washington, 1978—, pres., 1980-90. Mem. Pres.'s Task Force on Pvt. Sector Initiatives, Nat. Commn. on Social Security Reform, 1982; mem. Nat. Commn. on Exec., Legis. and Jud. Salaries, 1985, Nat. Commn. on Pub. Svcs.; mem. Competitiveness Policy Coun., 1991. With USMCR, 1951-53, maj. Res. Decorated Bronze Star with combat V; recipient Arthur Flemming award, 1966, Pres.'s E cert. for export service, 1968, Bryce Harlow award for Bus.-Govt. Rels., 1988. Mem. Coun. Fgn. Rels., Met. Club, Georgetown Club, Univ. Club. Home: 1823 23rd St NW Washington DC 20008-4030 Office: 1317 F St NW Ste 500 Washington DC 20004-1105

TROWBRIDGE, DALE BRIAN, chemistry professor; b. Glendale, Calif., May 17, 1940; s. Dale Beverly and Alison Amelia (Goldsborough) T.; m. Helen Elaine Turner, July 2, 1966; children: Katelin Elizabeth, David Brian. BA, Whittier Coll., 1961; MS, U. Calif., Berkeley, 1964, PhD, 1970. Chemist Aerojet Gen., Azusa, Calif., 1961-62; chemistry tchr. Berkeley H.S., 1964-66; prof., chemistry dept. chmn. Sonoma State U., Rohnert Park, Calif., 1969—; vis. prof. chemistry U. Calif., Berkeley, 1970-74, 88; rsch. assoc. Cambridge U., 1978. Contbr. articles to profl. jours. Mem. AAAS, Am. Chem. Soc., Internat. Platform Assn., Sigma Xi. Home: 6039 Elsa Ave Rohnert Park CA 94928-2246 Office: Sonoma State U 1801 E Cotati Ave Rohnert Park CA 94928-3609 Office Phone: 707-664-2187. Business E-Mail: dale.trowbridge@sonoma.edu.

TROWBRIDGE, JOHN PARKS, physician; b. Dinuba, Calif., Mar. 24, 1947; s. John Parks and Claire Dovie (Noroian) Trowbridge; children: Sharla Tyann, Lyndi Kendyll. AB in Biol. Scis., Stanford U., 1970; MD, Case Western Res. U., 1976; postgrad., Fla. Inst. Tech., 1983-85. Diplomate in Preventive Medicine, Am. Bd. Clin. Metal Toxicology Therapy (examiner for bd. 1987—, protocol coun. 1996-98), Am. Bd. Biologic Reconstructive Therapy (examiner for bd. 1994-97), Am. Bd. Anti-Aging Medicine, 1998, Nat. Bd. Med. Examiners. Intern in gen. surgery Mt. Zion Hosp. & Med. Ctr., San Francisco, 1976-77; resident in urol. surgery U. Tex. Health Sci. Ctr., Houston, 1977-78; pvt. med. practice (health recovery unit, pain relief unit, life long health unit) Life Celebrating Health Assn., Humble, Tex., 1978—. Chief corp. med. cons. Tex. Internat. Airlines, Houston, 1981-83; immunology rsch. asst. Stanford U. Med. Ctr., Stanford, Calif., 1967-70; night lab. supr. Kaiser Found. Hosp., Redwood City, Calif., 1971-72; advisor to bd. dirs. Am. Inst. Med. Preventics, Laguna Hills, Calif., 1988-90; sr. aviation med. examiner FAA, 1983-96; lectr., cons. in field. Co-author: The Yeast Syndrome, 1986, Chelation Therapy, 1985, 2d edit., 1990, Yeast Related Illnesses, 1987, Do What You Want to Do, 1996, The Rumble in Humble: Heart Surgery and All That Jazz, 1997, Living Well Past 50: Rejuvenate Your Heart and Arteries, 1998; contbr. Challenging Orthodoxy: America's Top Medical Preventives Speak Out, 1991; weekly radio show host (KBME-AM): Feeling Better-...Naturally, with Dr. John Trowbridge, Houston, 2003-2004; contbr. articles to profl. jours. Adv. bd. Tex. Chamber Orchestra, Houston, 1979-80; med. dir. Humble unit Am. Cancer Soc., 1980-81; med. cons. personal fitness program Lake Houston YMCA, 1981-83. Nat. Merit scholar, 1965-69, Calif. State scholar, 1967-69; recipient Resolution of Commendation house of dels., 1974 Am. Podiatry Assn., Spl. Profl. Svc. Citation bd. trustees, 1976, Am. Podiatry Students Assn. Fellow: Am. Coll. Advancement in Medicine (v.p. 1987—89, pres.-elect 1989—91), Am. Soc. for Laser Medicine and Surgery; mem.: AMA, Neuro Cranial Restructuring Drs. Assn., Heavy Metal Toxicology Rsch. Inst. (pres. 2003-) (pres. 2002—03, rsch. inst. pres. 2003—), Am. Soc. Life Ext. Physicians (founding), Am. Assn. Nutritional Cons., Am. Acad. Thermology, Nat. Health Fedn. (chmn. bd. govs. 1989), Am. Soc. Gen. Laser Surgery, Am. Acad. Environ. Medicine, Legal and Edn. Found. Am. Preventive Med. Assn. (bd. dirs. 1996—99, charter), Am. Preventive Medicine Assn. (bd. dirs. 1992—99, charter), Am. Coll. Preventive Medicine, Internat. Coll. Integrative Medicine (editor newsletter 2000—01, bd. dirs. 2000—, sec. 2002—), N.Am. Cervicogenic Headache Soc., Royal Soc. Medicine (London, sect. orthop.), Soc. for Orthomolecular Medicine, Great Lakes Coll. Clin. Medicine (bd. dirs. 1991—95, med. rsch. instnl. rev. bd., v.p. 1993—94, pres. 1994—95, program chair Advanced Tng. Seminar in Heavy Metal Toxicology 1996—98, bd. dirs. 1999—2000), Huxley Inst. for Biosocial Rsch., Inst. Health Freedom (bd. dirs. 1997—2001), Arthritis Trust Am. (med. adv. bd. 1995—), Internat. Acad. Bariatric Medicine, N.Y. Acad. Scis., Aerospace Med. Assn., Houston Acad. Medicine, Harris County Med. Soc., Tex. Med. Assn., Am. Acad. Anti-Aging Medicine, Assn. Am. Physicians and Surgeons. Avocations: private piloting, computer applications. Office: Life Celebrating Health Assn 9816 Memorial Blvd Ste 205 Humble TX 77338-4206 Office Phone: 281-540-2329. Personal E-mail: jptlch@earthlink.net. Business E-Mail: info@healthchoicesnow.com.

TROWBRIDGE, THOMAS, JR., mortgage banking company executive; b. Troy, NY, June 28, 1938; s. of Thomas and Elberta (Wood) T.; m. Delinda Bryan, July 3, 1965; children: Elisabeth Tacy, Wendy Bryan. BA, Yale U., 1960; MBA, Harvard U., 1965. V.p. James W. Rouse & Co., Balt., 1965-66, Washington, 1966-68, San Francisco, 1968-73, 76-78; pres. Rouse Investing Co., Columbia, Md., 1973-76, Trowbridge, Kieselhorst & Co., San Francisco, 1978-97, CEO, chmn., 1997-2000; ret., 2000. Bd. dirs. Columbia Assn., 1975-76; trustee, treas. The Head-Royce Sch., Oakland, Calif., 1980-84; trustee, pres. Gen. Alumni Assn. Phillips Exeter Acad., 1984-90. Lt. USNR, 1960-63. Mem. Urban Land Inst., Calif. Mortgage Bankers Assn. (bd. dirs. 1991-98, pres. 1996-97), Mortgage Bankers Assn. Am. (bd. govs. 1993-2000), Naval War Coll. Found., 2000-, Olympic Club, Pacific Union Club, Lambda Alpha Internat. Republican. Presbyterian. Avocation: golf. Home: 4 Ridge Ln Orinda CA 94563-1318

TROXEL, DAVID B. pathologist; b. Elgin, Ill., 1936; MD, Northwestern U., 1962. Intern Chgo. Wesley Meml. Hosp., 1962—63; residency Mayo Clinic Found., Rochester, 1963—64, Presbyn. Hosp., Denver, 1966—68; clinical prof. Divsn. of Health & Med. Sci., U. Calif., Berkeley. Cons., govr. Doctors Ins. Com. Contbr. articles to jours. Mem.: Calif. Soc. of Pathologists (former pres.), Am. Bd. of Pathology (former pres.). Office: U Calif Berkeley 570 Univ Hall Berkeley CA 94720*

TROXEL, RONALD LEWIS, religious studies educator; b. Elmhurst, Ill., Apr. 2, 1951; s. James R. and Rosemary E. Troxel; m. Jacqueline J. Froberg, Mar. 30, 1956; children: Benjamin, Bryan. BA, Bethel Coll., Arden Hills, Minn., 1973; MDiv, Bethel Theol. Sem., Arden Hills, Minn., 1977; MA, U. Wis., Madison, 1986, PhD, 1989. Mem. clergy Spring Green Congl. Ch., Spring Green, Wis., 1980—82; sr. lectr. U. Wis., Madison, Wis., 1991—. Undergrad. advisor U. Wis., Madison, Wis., 2002. Contbr. articles to profl. jours. and bulls. Mem.: Soc. Bibl. Lit., Spring Green Lions (bd. dirs. 2000—02).

TROXELL, LUCY DAVIS, management consultant; b. Cambridge, Mass., Apr. 25, 1932; d. Ellsworth and Mildred (Enneking) Davis; m. Charles DeGroat Bader, June 13, 1952 (div. Aug. 1974); children: Christie P. Walker, Mary Bader Montgomery, Charles D. Bader Jr., David Bradford Bader; m. Victor Daniel Shirer Troxell, Aug. 1974. BA, Smith Coll., Northampton, Mass., 1952; grad., Inst. Paralegal Training, Phila. Cert. employee benefit specialist, assoc. in risk mgmt. Paralegal O'Melveny & Myers, L.A., 1976-77; acct. exec. Olanie Hurst & Hemrich, L.A., 1977 78; asst. to trustee Oxford Ins. Mgmt., L.A., 1978-80; dir. corp. svcs., asst. corp. sec. Consolidated Elec. Distbrs., Inc., Westlake Village, Calif., 1980-93; pres. MONMAK LDT, Westlake Village, 1993—. Vol. Friends of the Westlake Village Libr., 2000—, ARC; clk. St. Mathew's Parish Vestry, Pacific Palisades, Calif., 1988, sr. warden, 1989—90; lic. lay eucharistic min. Episcopal Ch.; sustaining bd. dirs. Jr. League, Hartford, Conn., 1952—58, L.A., 1952—60; bd. dirs. Smith Coll. Club, Hartford, 1952—58, Nat. Charity League, L.A., 1964—68, Theatre Palisades, 1960—74; bd. dirs., treas. HOA Lakeshore Cmty. Assn., 1999—2002. Sophia Smith scholar. Fellow: Risk and Ins. Mgmt. Soc. (program chmn. L.A. chpt. 1985—86), Internat. Soc. Cert. Employee Benefit Specialists (bd. dirs., sec., treas. 1988—89, pres. 1989—90, edn. chmn. L.A. chpt. 1986—88). Republican. Avocations: finance, acting, music, art. Home: 450 Puerto Del Mar Pacific Palisades CA 90272-4233 Office: MONMAK LDT 32001 Viewlake Ln Westlake Village CA 91361

TROXLER, CAROLE WATTERSON, historian, educator; b. LaGrange, Ga., Feb. 22, 1943; d. Eugene Price and Virginia (Knight) W.; m. George Wesley Troxler, Aug. 25, 1967; children: Heidi, Lydia. AB, U. Ga., 1964; MA, U. N.C., 1966, PhD, 1974. Instr. Davidson County C.C., Lexington, N.C., 1966-68; asst. prof. history Elon (N.C.) U. (formerly Elon Coll.), 1970-81, assoc. prof., 1981-87, prof., 1988—. Author: The Loyalist Experience in North Carolina, 1976, Shuttle & Plow: A History of Alamance County, N.C., 1999; (video) Ambush on Cane Creek: The Battle of Lindley's Mill, 1981 (Gertrude Carraway award 1982), Pyle's Defeat: Deception at the Racepath, 2003 (Willie Parker Peace History Book award), (compact disk) Alamance County, NC Transcripts of Census and Tax Records, Vol 1 (Willie Parker Peace History Book award); editor: Deloise C. Browning, Here for a Season, 2002; contbr. chpt. to books: Loyalists and Community in North America, 1994; Moving On: Black Loyalists in the Afro-Atlantic World, 1999; contbr. numerous articles to profl. publs., including Jour. So. History, N.C. Hist. Rev., others. Active Haw River Assembly, Bynum, N.C., 1984—. Recipient H.C. Bradshaw award SAR, 1981; Woodrow Wilson fellow, U. N.C., 1964-65, tchg. fellow Woodrow Wilson Nat. Fellowship Found., 1965-66; faculty devel. program grantee Can. Embassy, 1982, rsch. grantee North Caroliniana Soc., 1992. Fellow Royal Nova Scotia Hist. Soc., Isle of Man Natural History and Antiquarian Soc.; mem. Am. Hist. Assn., N.Am. Conf. British Studies, Assn. Can. Studies in U.S., So. Hist. Assn., Internat. Coun. Can. Studies, Hist. Soc. N.C. (bd. dirs., pres., program chmn. 1986—), N.C. Lit. and Hist. Assn., Trading Path Assn. (bd. dirs. 2001—), So. Conf. British Studies, N.Am. Manx Assn. (life), Manx Heritage (life), Alpha Delta Kappa (v.p., sec. 1982—, rsch. grantee 1982, 99), Phi Alpha Theta (faculty advisor 1979-94), Phi Beta Kappa. Avocation: music of the British Isles and upland south. Home: 2748 Amick Rd Elon NC 27244 E-mail: carole.troxler@elon.edu.

TROY, ANTHONY FRANCIS, lawyer; b. Hartford, Conn., Apr. 16, 1941; children: Anthony John, Francis Gerard II. BA in Govt., St. Michael's Coll., Vt., 1963; LLB, U. Richmond, Richmond, Va., 1966. Bar: Va. 1966, D.C. 1972, U.S. Dist. Ct. (ea. dist.) Va. 1966, U.S. Dist. Ct. (we. dist.) Va. 1967, U.S. Ct. Appeals (4th cir.) 1967, U.S. Supreme Ct. 1969. Asst. atty. gen. Commonwealth of Va., Richmond, 1966-72, atty. gen., 1977-78; assoc. Colson & Shapiro, Washington, 1972-74; ptnr. Troutman, Sanders LLP, Richmond, 1978—. Conard Mattox Disting. adj. prof. chair law U. Richmond Law Sch. Contbr. articles to profl. jours. Trustee Sci. Mus. Va. Fellow Am. Law Found., Va. Law Found. Home: 308 N Lombardy St Richmond VA 23220-3532 Office: Troutman Sanders LLP PO Box 1122 Richmond VA 23218-1122 E-mail: tony.troy@troutmansanders.com.

TROY, FREDERIC ARTHUR, II, medical biochemistry educator; b. Evanston, Ill., Feb. 16, 1937; s. Charles McGregor and Virginia Lane (Minto) T.; m. Linda Ann Price, Mar. 23, 1959; children: Karen M., Janet R. BS, Washington U., St. Louis, 1961; PhD, Purdue U., 1966; postdoctoral, Johns Hopkins U., 1968. Asst. prof. U. Calif. Sch. Medicine, Davis, 1968-74, assoc. prof., 1974-80, prof., 1980—, chmn., 1991-94, 2004—; vis. prof. Karolinska Inst. Med. Sch., Stockholm, 1976-77. Cons. NIH, Bethesda, Md., 1974—, NSF, Washington, 1975—, Damon Runyon Cancer Found., N.Y.C., 1980-81, VA, Washington, 1984-88, U.S. Army Breast Cancer Study Sect., 1999—. Mem. editl. bd. Jour. Biol. Chem., 1988—, Glycobiol., 1990—; contbr. articles to profl. jours. Recipient Research Cancer Devel. award Nat. Cancer Inst., 1975-80; Eleanor Roosevelt Internat. Cancer fellow Am. Cancer Soc., 1976-77. Mem. AAAS, Am. Soc. Biol. Chemistry and Molecular Biology, Am. Assn. Cancer Rsch., Am. Chem. Soc., Am. Soc. Enologists, Biochemistry Soc., Biophysics Soc., Am. Fedn. for Clin. Rsch., N.Y. Acad. Scis., Soc. for Glycobiol. (pres. 1991-92), Am. Med. and Grad. Sch. Dept. Biochem. (pres.-elect 1995—), Sigma Xi. Office: Sch Medicine Dept Biochem and Molecular Medicine U Calif Davis CA 95616

TROY, NANCY J. art history educator; BA magna cum laude with honors in art, Wesleyan U., 1974; MA, Yale U., 1976, PhD, 1979. Gallery asst. Waddington Galleries, London, 1973; rsch. asst. Soc. Anonyme Collection, Yale U., New Haven, 1975, tchg. asst. history of art dept., 1975-76; asst. prof. dept. history of art Johns Hopkins U., Balt., 1979-83; asst. prof. dept. art history Northwestern U., Evanston, Ill., 1983-85, assoc. prof., 1985-92, prof., 1992-93, chmn. dept., 1990-92; vis. prof. UCLA, 1994; vis. prof. art history U. So. Calif., L.A., 1994-95, prof., 1995—, chmn. dept., 1997—. Scholar-in-residence Getty Rsch. Inst. for History Art and Humanities, L.A., 1993-96, organizer Work in Progress lecture series, 1993-98; series co-editor Histories, Culturs, Contexts, Reaktion Book, London; curatorial coord., spl. cons. to Ilya Bolotowsky Retrospective, Solomon R. Guggenheim Mus., N.Y.C., summers 1972-74; asst. to curator French paintings Nat. Gallery Art, Washington, summer 1975, bd. advisors Ctr. for Advanced Study in VisualArts, 1999-2002; guest curator Yale U. Art Gallery, 1979; mem. fine arts accessions com. and com. on collections Balt. Mus. Art, 1979-82; cons. De Stijl: 1917-1931, Visions of Utopia exhbn. Walker Art Ctr., Mpls., Washington, The Netherlands, 1982; cons. amplifying art program Art Inst. Chgo., 1984-85; mem. vis. com. Harvard U. Art Mus., Cambridge, Mass., 1992-98; lectr., chmn., moderator numerous symposia, 1980—; numerous invited lectures, 1975—, including U. Brighton, Eng., U. London, Middlesex U., London, Royal Coll. Art, London, U. Toronto, Mt. Holyoke Coll., Barnard Coll., Columbia U., Newcomb Coll., Tulane U., Los Angeles County Mus. Art, Art Inst. Chgo., Terra Mus. Am. Art, Chgo., N.C. Mus. Art, Raleigh, McGill U., Montreal, Vassar Coll; mus. projects peer rev. panelist NEH, 1991; peer reviewer Woodrow Wilson Ctr., Washington, 1994, 96; external reviewer dept. art history U. Mich., 1987; bd. dirs. Nat. Com. for History Art, 1998—; peer reviewer for promotion and tenure Boston U., Lake Forest Coll., Middlesex U., Occidental Coll., U. Mo., Columbia, U. Va., 1996-98. Author: The De Stijl Environment, 1983, Modernism and the Decorative Arts in France: Art Nouveau to Le Corbusier, 1991, (exhbn. catalog) Mondrian and Neo-Plasticism in America, 1979; editor-in-chief The Art Bull., 1994-97; editor: (with Eve Blau) Architecture and Cubism, 1997; series co-editor Histories, Cultures, Contexts; mem. editl. bd. Art Bull., 1993—, Grey Room, 1998—; contbr. articles and book revs. to profl. jours., including Decorative Arts Soc. Jour., Design Issues, Art Bull., October, Archithese, Arts mag., Portfolio, Design Book Rev., chpts. to books. Mem. Md. Coun. on Arts, 1981-82; trustee Wesleyan U., 1994-97. Recipient Disting. Alumna award Wesleyan U., 1991, postdoctoral tchg. award Lilly Endowment, 1985, Andrew W. Mellon professorship for advanced study in the visual arts Nat. Gallery Art (declined), 2000-02; Fulbright-Hays grantee, The Netherlands, 1977-78, travel grantee Kress Found., summer 1976, spring 1977, grantee Am. Coun. Learned Soc., summers 1981, 91, 98-99; grantee Graham Found. for Advanced Studies in Fine Arts, 1982, publ. grantee, 1989; grantee NEH, 1982-83, Am. Philos. Soc., 1986, Inst. for Advanced Study Sch. Hist. Studies, 1987, Getty Rsch. Inst. for History Art and Humanities, 1989-90, Zumberge Faculty Rsch. and Innovation Fund, U. So. Calif., 1998-99, Guggenheim Found., 1998-99; AT&T rsch. fellow Northwestern U., 1992-93. Mem. Coll. Art Assn. Am. (nominating com. 1990, bd. dirs. 1992-97, ann. meeting local host com. L.A. 1998-99), Soc. Archtl. Historian (sec. Chgo. chpt. 1984-85, peer reviewer Jour. 1996), Nat. Com. for the History of Art (bd. dirs.), Sterling and Francine Clark Art Inst. (mem. fellowship com.). Office: U So Calif Dept Art History University Park 104 Watt MC 0293 Los Angeles CA 90089-0001*

TROY, WILLIAM C. mathematician, educator; b. Rochester, N.Y., July 7, 1947; s. Gerald Troy and Elizabeth Regan. BS, St. John Fisher Coll., Rochester, N.Y., 1969; MA, SUNY, Buffalo, 1970; PhD, SUNY, 1974. Prof. math. U. Pitts., 1974—2002. Author: (book) Spatial Patterns, Higher Order Models in Physics and Mechanics, 2001; contbr. over 90 articles to profl. jours. Recipient Career Devel. award, NIH, 1978—83. Mem.: Soc. for Indsl. and Applied Math.

TROYER, ALVAH FORREST, agriculture executive, plant breeder; b. LaFontaine, Ind., May 30, 1929; s. Alvah Forrest and Lottie (Waggoner) T.; m. Joyce Ann Wigner, Sept. 22, 1950; children: Anne, Barbara, Catherine, Daniel (dec.). BS, Purdue U., 1954; MS, U. Ill., 1956; PhD, U. Minn., 1964. Rsch. assoc. U. Ill., Urbana, 1955-56; rsch. fellow U. Minn., St. Paul, 1956-58; rsch. sta. mgr. Pioneer Hi-Bred Internat., Inc., Mankato, Minn., 1958-65, rsch. coord., 1965-77; dir. R & D, Pfizer Genetics, St. Louis, 1977-81, v.p. and dir. R & D, 1981-82; v.p. R&D, DEKALB Plant Genetics, 1982-93; cons. Hybrid Seed divsn. Cargill, Mpls., 1993-98; adj. prof. crop sci. dept. U. Ill., 1998—. Rschr. corn breeding, econ. botany, crop physiology, increasing genetic diversity, recent corn evolution. Contbr. articles to numerous publs.; developer of popular corn inbred lines and hybrids. Master sgt. U.S. Army, 1951-53, Korea. Recipient Nat. Coun. Comml. Plant Breeders Genetics and Plant Breeding award, 1992, Outstanding Achievement award U. Minn., 1998, nat. award for agrl. excellence Nat. Agrl. Mktg. Assn., 1999. Fellow AAAS, Am. Soc. Agronomy, Crop Sci. Soc. Am.; mem. Am. Genetic Assn., Genetic Soc. Am., N.Y. Acad. Scis., CAST, VFW, Masons, Sigma Xi, Gamma Sigma Delta (Award of Merit 1996), Alpha Zeta, Lambda Chi Alpha, Gamma Alpha. Methodist. Home: 611 Joanne Ln Dekalb IL 60115 Business E-Mail: atroyer@uiuc.edu.

TROYER, JOHN GORDON, philosopher, educator; b. Detroit, Feb. 12, 1943; s. Gordon Ralph and Dorothy Alice Troyer; m. Barbara Sanders Troyer, June 28, 1992; m. Stephanie Fantl Troyer, June 11, 1965 (dec. Nov. 1, 1989); children: Jennifer Laurel, Gwyneth Margaret. BA, Swarthmore Coll., 1965; MA, Harvard U., 1967, PhD, 1971. From instr. to assoc. prof. U. Conn., Storrs, Conn., 1970—77, assoc. prof., 1977—. Editor: Intentionality, Language, and Translation, 1974, In Defense of Radical Empiricism, 1998, The Classical Utilitarians, 2003. Frank Knox Meml. fellow, Harvard U., 1969—70, Younger Humanist fellow, NEH, 1974. Mem.: Am. Philos. Assn., Oxford Bibliographical Soc., Internat. Berkeley Soc., Phi Beta Kappa. Democrat. Home: 840 Mansfield City Rd Storrs Mansfield CT 06268 Office: Dept Philosophy Univ Conn 344 Mansfield Rd Storrs Mansfield CT 06269

TROYER, LEROY SETH, architect; b. Middlebury, Ind., Nov. 23, 1937; s. Seth and Nancy (Miller) T.; m. Phyllis Eigsti, May 24, 1958; children: Terry, Ronald, Donald. BArch, U. Notre Dame, 1971. Founder, pres., CEO LeRoy Troyer and Assocs., South Bend, Ind., 1971; chmn. The Troyer Group, Inc. (formerly LeRoy Troyer and Assocs.), Mishawaka, Ind., 1988—; pres. Southfield, Inc., 1988—. Pres. Lead Devel., Inc. Author numerous documents; contbr. numerous papers and articles to publs. Past pres., chair Environic Found. Internat., Inc.; mem. Mennonite Econ. Devel. Assn. Internat., 1983-94, chmn. bd., 1987-91; bd. dirs. Habitat for Humanity Internat. Americus, Ga., 1987-93 (global leadership coun., 2003—), Coun. of Christian Colls. and Univs., 1991-96, Habitat for Humanity St. Joseph County, Ind., 1992-99, 2001—; bd. dirs. Bethel Coll., 1988-97, 2001—, Mishawaka, CONNECT, HHS, South Bend, 1999-2003; bd. dirs., exec. com., trustee Fourth Freedom Forum Internat., 1996—; bd. dirs. Evangelicals for Social Action, Wynnewood, Pa., 1997-2003; chmn. Miracle of Nazareth Internat. Found., 2000-03. Recipient numerous local, state and nat. awards and honors. Fellow AIA (practice mgmt. com., chmn. 1983-84), Ind. Soc. Archs. Avocations: photography, travel, reading, art, woodworking. Home: 1442 Deerfield Ct South Bend IN 46614-6429 Office: The Troyer Group Inc 550 Union St Mishawaka IN 46544-2346 Office Phone: 574-259-9976. Business E-Mail: leroy@troyergroup.com.

TROYER, THOMAS ALFRED, lawyer; b. Omaha, Aug. 15, 1933; s. Robert Raymond and Dorothy (Darlow) T.; m. Sally Jean Brown, June 28, 1958; children: Kenneth D., Robert C., Virginia D., Thomas C. BA, Harvard U., 1955; JD, U. Mich., 1958. Bar: Colo. 1958, U.S. Ct. Appeals (D.C. cir.) 1967. Assoc. Holme, Roberts, More & Owen, Denver, 1958-61; USAF, Denver, 1961-62; trial atty. U.S. Dept. Justice, Washington, 1962-64; legal staff Asst. Sec. Treasury for Tax Policy, Washington, 1964-66; assoc. tax legis. counsel U.S. Dept. Treasury, Washington, 1966-67; mem. Caplin & Drysdale, Washington, 1967—. Pres. Stern Fund, N.Y.C., 1985—86; bd. dirs. Children's Def. Fund, Washington, 1977—, Mineral Policy Ctr., Washington, 1988—2002; trustee Natural Resources Def. Coun., N.Y.C., 1977—, Carnegie Corp., N.Y.C., 1983—91, Cmty. Found. Nat. Capital Region, 1992—2000; chairperson Charity Lobbying in Pub. Interest, Washington. Contbr. numerous articles to profl. jours. Bd. dirs. Common Cause, Washington, 1980-83; mem. Treasury Adv. Commn. on Pvt. Philanthropy and Pub. Needs, Washington, 1976-77; mem. adv. group to Commr. Internal Rev., Washington, 1978-80; mem. com. of visitors U. Mich. Law Sch., Ann Arbor, 1982—; mem. IRS Commr.'s

Exempt Orgn. Adv. Group, Washington, 1987-90. Fellow Am. Bar Found., Am. Coll. Tax Counsel; mem. ABA (vice chmn. govt. rels. tax sect. 1989-91, commn. on homelessness and poverty 1992-94), Coun. for Excellence in Govt., Am. Law Inst. Democrat. Home: 5514 Cedar Pkwy Chevy Chase MD 20815-3444 Office: Caplin & Drysdale Chartered 1 Thomas Cir NW Ste 1100 Washington DC 20005-5894 Office Phone: 202-862-5025.

TROZZOLO, ANTHONY MARION, chemistry professor; b. Chgo., Jan. 11, 1930; s. Pasquale and Francesca (Vercillo) T.; m. Doris C. Stoffregen, Oct. 8, 1955; children: Thomas, Susan, Patricia, Michael, Lisa, Laura. BS, Ill. Inst. Tech., 1950; MS, U. Chgo., 1957, PhD, 1960. Asst. chemist Chgo. Midway Labs., 1952-53; assoc. chemist Armour Rsch. Found., Chgo., 1953-56; tech. staff Bell Labs., Murray Hill, N.J., 1959-75; Charles L. Huisking prof. chemistry U. Notre Dame, 1975-92, Charles L. Huisking prof. emeritus, 1992—; asst. dean U. Notre Dame Coll. Sci., 1993-98; P.C. Reilly lectr. U. Notre Dame, 1972, Hesburgh Alumni lectr., 1986, Disting. lectr. sci., 1986. Vis. prof. Columbia U., N.Y.C., 1971, U. Colo., 1981, Katholieke U. Leuven, Belgium, 1983, Max Planck Inst. für Strahlenchemie, Mülheim/Ruhr, Fed. Republic Germany, 1990; vis. lectr. Academia Sinica, 1984, 85; Phillips lectr. U. Okla., 1971; C.L. Brown lectr. Rutgers U., 1975; Sigma Xi lectr. Bowling Green U., 1976, Abbott Labs., 1978; M. Faraday lectr. No. Ill. U., 1976; F.O. Butler lectr. S.D. State U., 1978; Chevron lectr. U. Nev., Reno, 1983; J. Crano lectr. U. Akron, 2000; plenary lectr. various internat. confs.; founder, chmn. Gordon Conf. on Organic Photochemistry, 1964; trustee Gordon Rsch. Confs., 1988-92; cons. in field. Assoc. editor Jour. Am. Chem. Soc., 1975-76; editor Chem. Revs., 1977-84; editorial adv. bd. Accounts of Chem. Rsch., 1977-85; cons. editor Encyclopedia of Science and Technology, 1982-92; contbr. articles to profl. jours.; patentee in field. Fellow AEC, 1951, NSF, 1957-59; named Hon. Citizen of Castrolibero, Italy, 1997; recipient Pietro Bucci prize U. Calabria/Italian Chem. Soc., 1997. Fellow: AAAS, Inter-Am. Photochem. Soc., N.Y. Acad. Scis. (chmn. chem. scis. sect. 1969—70, Halpern award in photochemistry 1980), Am. Inst. Chemists (Student award 1950); mem.: Am. Chem. Soc. (lectr., Tex. lectr. 1975, Disting. Svc. award St. Joseph Valley sect. 1979, Coronado lectr. 1980, Pacific Coast lectr. 1981, Coronado lectr. 1993, N.Y. State lectr. 1993, Hoosier lectr. 1995, Ozark lectr. 1995, Coronado lectr. 1998, Osage lectr. 1998, Rocky Mountain lectr. 1996, 2002), Sigma Xi. Roman Catholic. Home: 1329 E Washington St South Bend IN 46617-3340 Office: U Notre Dame Dept Chemistry-Biochemistry Notre Dame IN 46556-5670 Office Phone: 574-631-5768. Business E-Mail: trozzolo.4@nd.edu.

TRPIS, MILAN, vector biologist, scientist, educator; b. Mojsova Lucka, Slovakia, Dec. 20, 1930; came to U.S., 1971, naturalized, 1977; s. Gaspar and Anna (Sevcikova) T.; m. Ludmila Tonkovic, Dec. 15, 1956; children: Martin, Peter, Katarina. MS, Comenius U., Bratislava, 1956; PhD, Charles U., Prague, 1960. Research asst. Slovak Acad. Sci., Bratislava, 1953-56, sci. asst., 1956-60, scientist, 1960-62, ind. scientist, 1962-69; ecologist-entomologist East Africa-Aedes Rsch. Unit WHO, Dar es Salaam, Tanzania, 1969-71; asst. faculty fellow dept. biology U. Notre Dame, 1971-73, assoc. faculty fellow, 1973-74; assoc. prof. med. entomology Johns Hopkins U. Sch. Hygiene and Pub. Health, 1974-78, prof., 1978—, dir. labs. med. entomology. Med. entomology; rsch. assoc. U. Ill., Urbana, 1966-67, Can. Dept. Agr., Lethbridge, Alta., 1967-68; dir. Biol. Rsch. Inst. Am., 1971-79; external dir. rsch. Liberian Inst. Biomed. Rsch., 1981-89; dir. AID project on transmission of river blindness in areas of Liberia, Sierra Leone, and Cote d'Ivoire; dir. WHO rsch. grant; tech. adv. com. AID Vector Biology and Control Project, 1986-91; dir. Johns Hopkins U./Fed. U. Tech. Akure Onchocerciasis Project in Nigeria, 1991-94, Johns Hopkins U./Organisation de Coordination et de Cooperation pour la Lutte les Grandes Endemies-Pierre Richet Inst. Onchocerciasis Project, Bouakè, Ivory Coast, 1993-96; dir. Johns Hopkins U./Pierre Richet Inst./ORSTOM onchocerciasis project in Ivory Coast, 1993-96; prof.-advisor doctoral students, Africa, Asia, Cen. Am., 1979—. Editor: Jour. Biologia, 1956-71, Jour. Entomol. Problems, 1960-72; zool. sect.: Jour. Biol. Works, 1960-71; Contbr. articles to profl. jours. Dir. WHO project on prophylactic drugs for river blindness, Liberia, 1985-87. Recipient Slovak Acad. Sci., 1st prize for research project. Mem. AAUP, AAAS, Am. Inst. Biol. Sci., Am. Mosquito Control Assn., Am. Soc. Parasitologists, Helminthol. Soc. Washington, Am. Soc. Tropical Medicine and Hygiene, Entomol. Soc. Am., Am. Genetic Assn., Soc. of Vector Ecology, N.Y. Acad. Scis., Johns Hopkins U. Tropical Medicine Club, Smithsonian Assocs., Royal Soc. Tropical Medicine and Hygiene, Royal Entomol. Soc. of London, Sigma Xi, Delta Omega (Alpha chpt.). Home: 1504 Ivy Hill Rd Cockeysville MD 21030-1418 Office: Johns Hopkins U 615 N Wolfe St Baltimore MD 21205-2103 Business E-Mail: mtrpis@jhsph.edu.

TRUAN, CARLOS F. insurance agent, state legislator; b. Kingsville, Tex., June 9, 1935; BBA, Tex. A&I U., 1959. Ins. agt. N.Y. Life Ins. Co., 1960—; mem. Tex. Ho. of Reps., 1969-76, Tex. Senate, 1977—, vice chair adminstrn. com., vice chair fin. com., chair internat. rels., trade and tech. com., vice chair natural resources subcom. on water, others. Named Gov.-For-A-Day, Mar. 8, 1986. Democrat. Office: PO Box 12068 Austin TX 78711-2068 also: 4531 Ayers St Ste 402 Corpus Christi TX 78415-1418

TRUANT, ALLAN L. medical educator, laboratory scientist, health science association administrator; b. July 6, 1950; BS, U. Mich., 1971; PhD, U. Oreg., 1977. Fellow Ctrs. for Disease Control, Atlanta, 1977-79; assoc. prof., assoc. dir. Univ. Tex. Med. Br., Galveston, 1979-85; prof., dir. clin. microbiology, immunology and virology lab. Temple U. Hosp. and Sch. Medicine, Phila., 1985—. Inspector Coll. Am. Pathologists, Chgo., 1983—; mem. exam. bd. Am. Bd. Bioanalysis, St. Louis, 1996—. Editor: Manual of Commercial Methods in Clinical Microbiology, 2002. Recipient Rorer award for manuscript excellence Am. Coll. Gastroenterology, 1983. Office: Temple U Hosp and Sch Medicine Broad Ontario Sts Philadelphia PA 19140 Office Phone: 215-707-3210. E-mail: truantal@tuhs.temple.edu.

TRUAX, DENNIS DALE, civil engineer, educator, consultant; b. Hagerstown, Md., July 25, 1953; s. Bernard James and Dorothy Hilda Truax; m. Jeanie Ann Knable, Aug. 20, 1977. BSCE, Va. Poly. Inst. and State U., 1976; MS, Miss. State U., 1978, PhD, 1986. Registered profl. engr., Miss.; diplomate Environ. Engring. Asst. dep. constrn. mgr. Fairfax County, Va., 1972-74; design engr. Washington County, Md., 1976; instr. Miss. State U., Starkville, 1980-86, asst. prof. civil engring., 1986-91, assoc. prof., 1991-96, prof., 1996—. Prin. corp. pres. ASD, LLC, 1997-2000; prin., v.p. engring. ATi, Inc., 2000—; environ. engring. cons. Mem. editl. bd. ASCE/NSPE Profl. Issues Jour., 1999—. Lay leader Aldersgate United Meth. Ch., Starkville, 1982-85, chmn. pastor/parish rels., 1985-86, chmn. coun. on ministries, 1986-90, chmn. adminstrv. bd., 1990-92, chmn. fin. com., 1992-94, 2001-2003, chmn. bd. trustees, 1996-97; adviser Triangle Fraternity, Starkville, Alumni Bd. Dirs. treas., 1989-96; bd. dirs. Meth. Student Ctr., Miss. State U., 1983-90, chmn. pastor/parish rels., 1984-86, v.p. bd., 1986, pres., 1987-89, treas., 1990-91; del. to ann. conf. Miss. Conf. United Meth. Ch., also vice chmn. com. on higher edn.; active Starkville dist. lay coun. Miss. State Herrin-Hess Prof., 1993-94, 94-95, 95-96. Recipient Golden Key Outstanding Faculty award Golden Key Nat. Honor Soc., 1994, Miss. Outstanding Civil Engr. of Yr., ASCE Miss. sect., 1995; named Outstanding Young Man Am., U.S. Jaycees, 1983. Fellow ASCE (chair student svcs. com. 1995-96, vice chair 1996-97, adv. Miss. State chpt. 1981—, chair career guidance com. 1991-92, sec. 1990-91, Miss. sect. pres.-elect 1990-91, pres. 1991-92, chmn. student svc. com. 1995-96, scholarship com. 1998—, chair scholarship com. 2000-01, No. Miss. br. pres. 2000-2001, dist. 14 dir. 2001-, fin. com., com. on diversity and women in civil engring.); mem. NSPE, Am. Water Works Assn. (Ala.-Miss. chpt. scholarship bd. dirs. 1994—, bd. sec.-treas. 1998—), Miss. Engring. Soc. (pres., pres.-elect region 3 v.p., bd. dirs., Tombigbee chpt. pres., chpt. pres.-elect, Engring. educator 1995, Educator of the Yr. award 1995), Water Environ. Fedn. (rsch. com.), Sigma Xi (sec., pres.-elect, pres. Miss. State chpt.), Tau Beta Pi, Chi Epsilon. Democrat. Home: 1054 Southgate Dr Starkville MS 39759-8810 Office: Miss State U PO Box 9546 Mississippi State MS 39762-9546

TRUBETSKOY, VLADIMIR SERGEEVICH, polymer chemist; b. Moscow, Oct. 13, 1957; s. Sergey V. and Nina V. Trubetskoy; m. Olga V. Merzlikine, Feb. 9, 1984; children: Sergey, Vassily, Ivan. M in Chemistry summa cum laude, Moscow State U., 1974, MS, 1979; PhD in Biochemistry, USSR Acad. Med. Scis., Moscow, 1984. Sr. rsch. fellow Inst. Exptl. Cardiology, Moscow, 1984-90; postdoctoral fellow dept. biochemistry U. Tenn., Knoxville, 1990-91; asst. in chemistry Ctr. Imaging and Pharm. Rsch., Mass. Gen. Hosp., Boston, 1991-93; assoc. chemist dept. radiology Med. Sch. Harvard U., Ctr. Imaging and Pharm. Rsch., Mass. Gen. Hosp., Boston, 1993-96; sr. chemist Mirus Corp., Madison, Wis., 1996—. Co-contbr. articles, contbr. rev. to profl. jours. Radiol. Soc. N.Am. Seed grantee, 1996; Small Bus. Innovation rsch. grantee NIH, 1998, 2000; recipient Outstanding Pharm. Paper award Controlled Release Soc., 1993. Mem. Am. Chem. Soc., Am. Soc. for Gene Therapy, Controlled Release Soc. Eastern Orthodox. Office: Quintessence Bioscis Inc 505 S Rosa Rd Madison WI 53719 Fax: 608-441-2849. E-mail: vladimirt@quintbio.com.

TRUBEY, LILLIAN PRISCILLA, secondary education educator, retired; b. Hastings, Mich., Jan. 18, 1917; d. Leon George and Ethel Ada (Harlem) Tolhurst; m. Stanley Roger Trubey, Aug. 12, 1940 (dec. May 1965); children: Roger, Cornelia. BA, U. Mich., 1938, MA, 1942; MEd, Fla. Atlantic Univ., 1967; PhD, Fla. State U., 1972. Tchr. River Rouge (Mich.) H.S., 1938-41, South Broward H.S., Hollywood, Fla., 1951-69; tchr., head Eng. dept. Hollywood Hills H.S., 1969-84; tax preparer H&R Block, Ft. Lauderdale, 1985-92. Tchr. Fla. State U., Tallahassee, 1970-71, Miami Dade Jr. Coll., Miami, Fla. 1971-72. Sec. Women's Rep. Club, Broward Co., 1947-49, v.p., 1950-51; sec. Victoria Park Civic Assn., Ft. Lauderdale, 1975-78; vol. VITA, 1993-2003; pres. Fla. Speech Assn., 1968-69. Mem. Genealogical Soc. Broward Co. (sec. 1991-93, pres. 1993-95, 99, editor IMPRINTS, 1993), Retired Educators Broward Co., Ft. Lauderdale Bridge Club (dir. 1995, 97-99), Guild Miniature Artisans, Delta Kappa Gamma. Episcopalian. Avocations: duplicate bridge, miniatures, genealogy. Home: 1415 NE 4th Pl Fort Lauderdale FL 33301-1371

TRUBO, RICHARD M. writer; b. LA, Calif., Apr. 2, 1946; s. William Trubo, Ida Trubo; m. Donna R. Grodin; children: Melissa, Michael. BA, UCLA, 1967, MS, 1968. Co-host ("Confrontation"), writer KOST-FM, LA, 1968—71; bur. chief / contbg. editor HEI Pub. / Miller Freeman Pub. (Med. World News), San Francisco, 1983—88; med. editor, writer, cons. Feeling Fine Co., LA, 1989—2000; bur. chief/contbg. editor HEI Pub. / Miller Freeman Pub. (Med. world News), Houston. Author: (book) An Act of Mercy, 1975; prodr.: (documentary film) Children of the State, 1977; author: (book) From Victim to Victor, 1987, The H.A.R.T. Program, 1992, Flying Through Hollywood by the Seat of My Pants, 1992, The Mental Edge, 1999, Tapping the Healer Within, 2001, Courage, 2001, Stairway to Heaven, 2002, (books) , (articles (published 1979-2002) (NY Times, LA Times, Harvard Med. Sch. Health Publ. Group, CBS Health Watch, MSNBC, Reader's Digest, Mayo Clinic website, World Book Pub., The Lancet, others); cons.: doc. film Am. Acad. of Pediat., 2002—03, prod.: Website WebMD, 2002—03. Recipient Journalism award of Excellence, Am. Acad. Facial Plastic and Reconstructive Surgery, 1990, Blakeslee award, Am. Heart Assn., 1991. Mem.: Am. Soc. Journalists & Authors, Nat. Assn. Med. Communicators, Am. Med. Writers Assn., Nat. Assn. Sci. Writers.

TRUCANO, MICHAEL, lawyer; b. Washington, May 28, 1945; s. Peter Joseph and Fern Margaret (Bauer) T.; m. Doreen E. Struck, 1969; children: Michael, David. BA, Carleton Coll., 1967; JD, NYU, 1970. Assoc. Dorsey & Whitney, Mpls., 1970-75, ptnr., 1976—, head of office, 2000—03. Office: Dorsey & Whitney LLP Ste 1500 50 S 6th St Minneapolis MN 55402-1498 Office Phone: 612-340-2673. E-mail: trucano.mike@dorsey.com.

TRUCE, WILLIAM EVERETT, chemist, educator; b. Chgo., Sept. 30, 1917; s. Stanley C. and Frances (Novak) T.; m. Eloise Joyce McBroom, June 16, 1940; children: Nancy Jane, Roger William. BS, U. Ill., 1939; PhD, Northwestern U., 1943. Mem. faculty Purdue U., 1946-88, prof. chemistry, 1956-88, prof. chemistry emeritus, 1988—, asst. dean Grad. Sch., 1963-66. Com. mem. numerous univ.; chmn. profl. meetings; exec. officer Nat. Organic Symposium, 1961; chmn. Gordon Rsch. Conf. on Organic Reactions and Processes; cons. in field. Co-author book; contbr. articles to profl. jours., chpts. to books. Guggenheim fellow Oxford U., 1957 Mem. Am. Chem. Soc., Phi Beta Kappa (sec. Purdue chpt.), Sigma Xi (pres. Purdue chpt.). Achievements include research in new methods of synthesis, devel. new kinds of compounds and reactions. Home: 220 Hopi Pl Boulder CO 80303-3533 E-mail: etruce@infionline.net.

TRUCHARD, JAMES J. engineering executive; BS in Physics, MSEE, PhD, U. Tex. Mng. dir. acoustical measurements divsn. Applied Rsch. Labs., U. Tex., Austin, 1963-76; co-founder, pres., chmn. Nat. Instruments Corp., Austin, 1976—, also bd. dirs. Office: Nat Instruments Corp 11500 N Mopac Expwy Austin TX 78759

TRUCKENBRODT, YOLANDA BERNABE, retired air force officer, consultant; b. Manila, June 17, 1952; d. Nestor Leynes and Zenaida Bernabe Javier; m. Edmund Phillip Truckenbrodt, July 27, 1972. BA, Far Ea. U., Manila, 1971; AS, C.C. of the Air Force, 1979; MBA, Angelo State U., 1980; MPA, U. West Fla., 1987; D of Pub. Adminstrn., Nova Southeastern U., 2000; diploma, Air Command and Staff Coll., 1995. Cert. Dept. of Def.'s Acquisition Profl. in Program Mgmt., USAF Software Quality Assurance. Enlisted USAF, 1974, advanced through grades to maj., ret., 1998; program mgr. KC-135 Reengine Dep. for Airlift and Trainer Sys., Wright-Patterson AFB, Ohio, 1980-84; electronic warfare program mgr. Tactical Sys. Divsn., Eglin AFB, Fla., 1985—89; program mgr. Airborne Warning and Control Sys. Elec. Sys. Ctr., Hanscom AFB, Mass., 1989—92; program analyst ballistic missile def. hdqs. Air Force Materiel Command, Wright-Patterson AFB, 1992-94; congl. liaison staff officer Plans and Programs Divsn., Wright-Patterson AFB, 1995-98. Flight comdr. detachment 847 Res. Officers Tng. Corps, San Angelo, Tex., 1978—80; chairperson Asian-Am. Pacific Islander Heritage Com., Eglin AFB, 1986—87; officer-in-charge Air Force Assn. Nat. Acquisiton Symposium, Wright-Patterson AFB, 1993—94; student-in-residence Def. Sys. Mgmt. Coll., Ft. Belvoir, Va., 1994; staff officer Directorate of Plans and Programs, Wright-Patterson AFB, 1995—98; guest spkr. Nat. Bus. and Profl. Assn., San Angelo, 1993. Contbr. articles to profl. jours. Pres. Filipino-Am. Assn., Fort Walton Beach, Fla., 1987; vol. Air Force Mus., Dayton, Ohio, 1995—96; vol. reading tutor Ohio Reads Program, 2002—; vol. Nightingale Ho., Wright-Patterson AFB, 1996—98; vol. income tax preparer Ret. Officers Assn., Wright-Patterson AFB, 1999—; vol. social worker United Way, Dayton, 1982—84; bd. dirs. Filipino-Am. Assn., Ft. Walton Beach, Fla., 1987, Filipino-Am. Coun. N.W. Fla. Nominee Lt. Robert Sullivan Meml. award, Eglin AFB, 1985; named Airman of the Quarter, Air Weather Svc. Comm. Squadron, 1975, Career Woman of Yr., Gayfers Career Club of Okaloosa County, Fla., 1987, Jr. Officer of the Quarter, Airlift and Trainer Sys., Wright-Patterson AFB, 1983, Airborne Warning and Control Systems, Hanscom AFB, 1991, winner, State of Ohio Summer Biathlon Series Championship Cup, 2002, 2d Pl. Overall winner for half-marathon, 4th Internat. Marathon on Great Wall, China, 1999, winner numerous race awards in track and field and Summer Biathlons; named one of Outstanding Young Women of Am., 1983; recipient Appreciation and Recognition award, Dyess AFB Human Rels. Coun., 1976, 1977, Air Force Res. Tng. Corps (ROTC) Leadership award, 1979, Arnold Air Soc. Outstanding Pledge award, 1979, Drill Commandant of Yr. award, 1978; Robert G. Carr scholar, Detachment 847 ROTC, Angelo State U., 1978, 1980. Mem. Women in Mil. Svc. for Am. Meml. (charter), Air Force Women Officers Assoc., Angelo State U. Alumni Assn. (Disting. ROTC Alumnae of Yr. 2002), Ohio River Rd. Runners Club, Sigma Beta Delta (life). Avocations: travel, arts and music, summer biathlons, marathons, photography.

TRUCKER, ALBERT, plastic surgeon; b. St. Joseph, Mich., Aug. 5, 1924; s. Albert and Louise (Goebel) T. BA, Johns Hopkins U., 1951; MD, U. Md., 1956. Diplomate Am. Bd. Plastic Surgery. Intern in gen. surgery U. Calif., San Francisco, 1956-59; resident in plastic surgery Mayo Clinic, Rochester, Minn., 1959-62; pvt. practice Santa Rosa, Calif., 1962—. Mem. Am. Soc. Plastic Surgery, Calif. Soc. Plastic Surgery. Address: PO Box 3722 Santa Rosa CA 95402-3722

TRUCKSIS, THERESA A. retired library director; b. Hubbard, Ohio, Sept. 1, 1924; d. Peter and Carmella (DiSilverio) Pagliasotti; m. Robert C. Trucksis, May 29, 1948 (dec. May 1980); children: M. Laura, Anne, Michele, Patricia, David, Robert, Claire, Peter; m. Philip P. Hickey, Oct. 19, 1985 (dec. May 1993). BS in Edn., Youngstown Coll., 1945; postgrad., Youngstown State U., 1968-71; MLS, Kent State U., 1972. Psychometrist Youngstown (Ohio) Coll., 1946-49; instr. ltd. svc. Youngstown State U., 1968-71; libr. Pub. Libr. Youngstown & Mahoning County, Youngstown, 1972-73, asst. dept. head, 1973-74, asst. dir., 1985-89, dir., 1989-97, NOLA Regional Libr. System, Youngstown, 1974-85. Contbr. articles to profl. jours. Mem. bd. Hubbard Sch. Dist., 1980-85. Mem. ALA, Ohio Libr. Assn. (bd. dirs. 1979-81), Pub. Libr. Assn. Address: 133 Viola Ave Hubbard OH 44425-2062

TRUDEAU, GARRETSON BEEKMAN (GARRY TRUDEAU), cartoonist; b. N.Y.C., 1948; m. Jane Pauley, June 14, 1980; children: Ross and Rachel (twins), Thomas. BA, Yale U., 1970, MFA, 1973, DHL, 1976. Syndicated cartoonist, writer. Creator: comic strip Doonesbury; syndicated nationwide comic strip; author: Still a Few Bugs in the System, 1972, The President is a Lot Smarter Than You Think, 1973, But This War Had Such Promise, 1973, Call Me When You Find America, 1973, Guilty, Guilty, Guilty, 1974, Joanie, 1974, The Doonesbury Chronicles, 1975, What Do We Have for the Witnesses, Johnnie?, 1975, Dare to Be Great, Ms. Caucus, 1975, Wouldn't A Gremlin Have Been More Sensible?, 1975, We'll Take it From Here, Sarge, 1975, Speaking of Inalienable Rights, Amy..., 1976, You're Never Too Old for Nuts and Berries, 1976, An Especially Tricky People, 1977, As the Kid Goes For Broke, 1977, Stalking the Perfect Tan, 1978, Any Grooming Hints for Your Fans, Rollie?, 1978, Doonesbury's Greatest Hits, 1978, But The Pension Fund was Just Sitting There, 1979, We're Not Out of the Woods Yet, 1979, A Tad Overweight, but Violet Eyes to Die For, 1980, And That's My Final Offer!, 1980, The People's Doonesbury, 1981, He's Never Heard of You, Either, 1981, In Search of Reagan's Brain, 1981, Ask for May, Settle for June, 1982, Unfortunately, She Was Also Wired for Sound, 1982, Adjectives Will Cost You Extra, 1982, Gotta Run, My Government is Collapsing, 1982, The Wreck of the Rusty Nail, 1983, You Give Great Meeting, Sid, 1983, Guess Who Fish Face, 1983, It's Supposed to be Yellow Pinhead: Selected Cartoons From Ask For May, Settle For June, Vol. I, 1983, Do All Birders Have Bedrooms, 1983, Farewell to Alms, 1984, Doonesbury Dossier: The Reagan Years, 1984, Doonesbury: A Musical Comedy, 1984, Check Your Egos at the Door, 1985, That's Doctor Sinatra, You Little Bimbo, 1986, Death of a Party Animal, 1986, Doonesbury Deluxe: Selected Glances Askance, 1987, Downtown Doonesbury, 1987, Calling Dr. Whoopee, 1987, The Doonesbury Desk Diary 1988, 1987, Talking Bout My G-G-Generation, 1988, We're Eating More Beets, 1988, Read My Lips, Make My Day, Eat Quiche & Die! A Doonesbury Collection, 1989, Small Collection, 1989, The Doonesbury Stamp Album, 1990, 1990, Recycled Doonesbury: Second Thoughts on a Gilded Age, 1990, You're Smokin' Now, Mr. Butts! A Doonesbury Book, 1990, Welcome to Club Scud: A Doonesbury Book, 1991, Action Figure: The Life and Times of Doonesbury's Uncle Duke, 1992, The Portable Doonesbury, 1993, In Search of Cigarette Holder Man: A Doonesbury Book, 1994, Doonesbury Nation, 1995, Flashbacks: Twenty-five Years of Doonesbury, 1995, The Bundled Doonesbury: A Pre-Millennial Anthology, 1998, Peace Out, Dawg! Tales from Ground Zero, 2002, Got War?, 2003; co-author: Tales From the Margaret Mead Taproom, 1979; plays include: Doonesbury, 1983, Rapmaster Ronnie, A Partisan Review (with Elizabeth Swados), 1984 Pulitzer Prize for Editorial Cartooning, 1975.*

TRUDEAU, JAMES BRIANE, communications executive; s. Benoit Phillippe and Barbara Ann Trudeau; m. Virginia Grace Merrick, June 25, 1983; children: Emily Claire, Anna Sierra. BFA in Design and Prodn., N.C. Sch. Arts, 1978. V.p. entertainment MGM Grand, Las Vegas, 1992—97; entertainment exec. Universal Studios Orlando, 1997—. Prodr.: (live entertainment) EFX (LVRJ award, 1997). Recipient award, Making of MGM, Making of EFX. Achievements include design of world's largest videowall - MGM. Office Phone: 407-363-8750. Personal E-mail: jtrudeau@bigfoot.com.

TRUDEL, MARC J. botanist, educator; PhD, Cornell U. Prof. plant physiology and horticulture Laval U., 1969—, former dean sch. agrl. and food scis., 1983-91, former dir. gen. continuing edn., 1992-97, v.p. devel., 1997—2003. Office: 18 Rue de Liege Saint Jean-Sur-Richelieu PQ Canada J3B 8N4 E-mail: marc.trudel@plg.ulaval.ca.

TRUDELL, CYNTHIA, automotive executive; b. St. John, Can., 1953; married; 2 children. Degree in chemistry, U. Wolfville, Can.; D of Phys. Chemistry, U. Windsor, Ont., Can., 1978. Chem. process engr. Ford Motor Corp., Windsor, Can., 1979-81; sr. engring. supr., supt. mfg. GM, Windsor, Can., 1981-87, engring. mgr. Willow Run transmission complex Ypsilanti, Mich., 1987-89, ops. mgr., 1989-90; chief engr. process techs. Powertrain Advanced Mfg. Systems, St. Catherines, Ont., Can., 1990-92, mgr. engine & foundry ops., 1992-95; plant mgr. Wilmington (Del.) Assembly Ctr., 1995; pres. Saturn, Spring Hill, Tenn., 1995—, chmn., 1997—. Office: Saturn Corp 100 Saturn Pkwy Spring Hill TN 37174-2493

TRUDNAK, STEPHEN JOSEPH, landscape architect; b. Nanticoke, Pa., Feb. 25, 1947; s. Stephen Adam and Marcella (Levulis) T.; m. Arden Batchelder Weill, Sept. 6, 1980. BS in Landscape Arch., Pa. State U., 1970. Jr. landscape arch. Kling Partnership, Phila., 1970-72; mem. landscape arch. firm Keith French Assocs., Washington, 1972-73; head dept. landscape arch. Linganore Ctr. Design, Frederick, Md., 1973-74, Toups and Loiederman, Rockville, Md., 1974-76; project landscape arch. Kaiser Transit Group, So. Calif. Rapid Transit Dist., Dade County Transit Improvement Program, Metro Rail Transit Cons.; v.p. Harry Weese & Assocs., Ltd., Miami, Fla., 1976-84; v.p. landscape arch. Canin Assocs., Orlando, Fla., 1984-87; dir. planning and design Bonita Bay Properties, Inc., Bonita Springs, Fla., 1987-91; prin. Stephen J. Trudnak, P.A. Landscape Arch. and Land Planning, 1991—. Bd. dirs., v.p. Koreshan State Hist. Site, 1989—94; mem. "not for profit" com. Bonita Springs Cmty. Redevel. Agy., 1994—97; v.p. Bonita Springs Mainstreet Program, 1996, 2000, pres., 1997—98; bd. dirs. Bonita Springs YMCA, 1999—, mem. exec. com., 2000—03, chair facilities design task force, 2000—04; del. for Congressman Peter Goss Congl. Small Bus. Summit, 1998, 2000; del. representing Fla. state rep. Carol Green Fla. Small Bus. Summit, 1999. Recipient Alumni Achievement award, Pa. State U., Dept. Landscape Architecture, 2003. Fellow Am. Soc. Landscape Archs. (pres. Fla. chpt. 1983, chpt. adv. bd. 1984-85, elections task force 1986, publs. task force 1987, trustee 1987-89, membership task force, chmn. 1989-90, nat. v.p. chpt. and mem. svcs. 1992-94, non-dues revenue task force 1994-95, ASLA On-Line com. 1997—, chair 1999, specifications task force 1998-99), Nat. Xeriscape Coun. (Fla. steering com.), Nat. Speleol. Soc. SCARAB; mem. Bonita Springs C. of C. (chair beautification com. 1991-92, 94-95, chair awards task force 2000, bd. dirs. 1995-2000, v.p. edn. divsn. 1996-98, vice chmn. cmty. devel. divsn. 1998-99, chmn. tech. com. 2003-, Affiliate of Yr. 1997, Citizen of Yr. 1999, Charter Class Leadership Bonita Grad. 2000). Office: 4261 Bonita Beach Rd Bonita Springs FL 34134 E-mail: strudnak@trudnak.com.

TRUE, ALISON COCHRAN, newspaper editor; b. Detroit, Aug. 10, 1961; d. Thomas Perry and Valery (Martin) T.; m. Frederick Mosher, June 12, 1993; children: Henry Arthur True Mosher. BA, Vassar Coll., 1984. Various positions including mailroom clk., asst. to editor, asst. editor Chgo. Reader, 1984—94, editor, 1994—. Named one of Chgos. 100 Most Influential Women, Crain's Chgo. Bus., 2004. Office: Chgo Reader 11 E Illinois St Chicago IL 60611-5652*

TRUE, JEAN DURLAND, entrepreneur, oil industry executive, gas industry executive; b. Nov. 27, 1915; d. Clyde Earl and Harriet Louise (Brayton) Durland; m. Henry Alfonso True Jr., Mar. 20, 1938; children: Tamma Jean (Mrs. Donald G. Hatten), Henry Alfonso III, Diemer Durland, David Lanmon. Student, Mont. State U., 1935-36. Ptnr. True Drilling Co., Casper, Wyo., 1951—94, True Oil Co., Casper, 1951-94, Eighty-Eight Oil LLC, 1955-94, True Geothermal Energy Co., 1980—, True Ranches, 1981-94. Officer, dir. White Stallion Ranch, Inc., Tucson, Smokey Oil Co., Casper. Mem. steering com. YMCA, Casper, 1954-55, bd. dirs., 1956-68; mem. bd. dirs. Gottsche Rehab. Ctr., Thermopolis, Wyo., 1966-93, mem. exec. bd., 1966-93, v.p.,

1983-90; mem. adv. bd. for adult edn. U. Wyo., 1966-68; mem. Ft. Casper Commn., Casper, 1973-79; bd. dirs. Mus. of Rockies, Bozeman, Mont., 1983-87, mem. Nat. Adv. Bd., 1997 2000; bd. dirs Nicolaysen Art Mus., 1988-93, Nat. Cowboy and We. Heritage Mus., 1997-2002, dir. emeritus, 2002--; mem. Nat. Fedn. Rep. Women's Clubs; dep. Rep. Nat. Conv., 1972; trustee Trooper Found., 1995—. Mem. Casper Area C. of C., Alpha Gamma Delta, Casper Country Club, Petroleum Club. Episcopalian. Office: PO Box 2360 Casper WY 82602-2360

TRUE, KATIE, state legislator; Pa. state rep. Dist. 37, 1993—. Republican. Office: 143 East Wing PO Box 202020 Harrisburg PA 17120-2020

TRUE, RAYMOND STEPHEN, writer, editor, analyst, consultant; b. Lowell, Mass., June 29, 1934; s. Sylvester Raymond and Madeline Rose (Farrell) T.; m. Doreen Therese Jambrosek. BA, U. Chgo., 1961, MBA, 1968, postgrad., 1968—69. Commd. 2nd lt. USAF, 1953, advanced through grades to col., 1980; master navigator U.S. Air Force Res., Chgo., 1957-77; regional cons. U.S. Bur. Census, 1970-71; dir. ops. U.S. Air Force Res., Milw., 1977-80, base civil engr., 1980-87, chief planning analyst, 1987-89; owner Classic Comics Libr., 1990—. Fire marshall Milw. County, 1980-87, chmn. membership Reserve Officers Assn., Wash. 1975-78. Editor Classics Newsletter, 1971-75. Precinct committeeman, Libertyville, Ill., 2000—; pres. ROA chpt. 61, 2000-02; chmn. Rep. Assembly Lake County, 2001-; mem. steering com. Ill. Ctr. Rights Coalition, 2004-; mem. Ill. Rep. State Platform Com., 2004. Mem. Air Force Assn., Grad. Sch. Bus. Exec. Coun. U. Chgo. Roman Catholic. Avocations: stamp collecting/philately, antique books, videophile. Address: 839 Terre Dr Libertyville IL 60048-1649 E-mail: raymon8844@aol.com.

TRUE, ROY JOE, lawyer; b. Shreveport, La., Feb. 20, 1938; s. Collins B. and Lula Mae (Cady) T.; m. Patsy Jean Hudsmith, Aug. 29, 1959; children: Andrea Alane, Alyssa Anne, Ashley Alisbeth. Student, Centenary Coll., 1957; BS, Tex. Christian U., 1961; LLB, So. Meth. U., 1963, postgrad., 1968—69. Bar: Tex. 1963. Pvt. practice, Dallas, 1963—; pres. Invesco Internat. Corp., 1969-70, True & Shackelford and predecessors, 1975—2002; of counsel Shackelford, Melton & McKinley, 2002—. Bus. adviser, counselor Mickey Mantle, 1969-95; dir. The Mickey Mantle Found., 1995-98. Mem. editl. bd. Southwestern Law Jour., 1962-63. Served with AUS, 1956. Mem. ABA, Dallas Bar Assn., Tex. Assn. Bank Counsel, Phi Alpha Delta. Home: 5601 Ursula Ln Dallas TX 75229-6429 Office: 10100 N Central Expy 6th Fl Dallas TX 75231 Office Phone: 972-490-1400. Business E-Mail: rtrue@shacklaw.net.

TRUEB, MARTIN R. toy company executive; Asst. treas. Amway Corp., 1995—97; sr. v.p., treas. Hasbro Inc., 1997—. Office: Hasbro Inc 1027 Newport Ave Pawtucket RI 02862*

TRUEBA, FERNANDO, film director and producer, screenwriter; b. Madrid, Jan. 18, 1955, s. Maximo Rodriguez and Palmira Trueba; m. Cristina Huete, Oct. 8, 1982; 1 child, Jonas-Groucho. Film critic El Pais, newspaper, Madrid, 1976-79; editor, dir. Casablanca, film mag., Madrid, 1981-83; film dir., prodr., screenwriter Creative Artists Agy., Beverly Hills, Calif. Dir., screenwriter Opera Prima, 1980 (Silver Hugo award Chgo. Film Festival 1980), Mientras el Cuerpo Aguante, 1982, Sal Gorda, 1983, Se Infiel y No Mires con Quien, 1985, El Año de Las Luces, 1986 (Silver Bear award Berlin Film Festival 1987), The Mad Monkey, 1989, Belle époque, 1992 (Academy Award, Best Foreign Language Film, 1993), Two Much, 1996; producer, screenwriter A Contratiempo, 1981, De Tripas Corazon, 1984, La Mujer de tu Vida, 1988-89; producer Lulu de Noche, 1985, El Juego Mas Divertido, 1987, Earth Magicians, 1989—, Amo tu cama rica, 1991, Alas de mariposa, 1991 (Concha of Gold award San Sebastian Film Festival 1991), Sublet, 1992, La Buena Vida, 1996; dir. La Nina de Tos Ojos, 1998, also dir. short films. Mem. Acad. Motion Pictures Spain (pres. 1988). Home: Bueso Pineda 29 28043 Madrid Spain Office: Creative Artists Agy c/o Emanuel Nunez 9830 Wilshire Blvd Beverly Hills CA 90212-1804

TRUEBLOOD, EMILY HERRICK, artist, librarian; b. Alexandria, Va., Aug. 13, 1942; d. Lorman Chancellor and Helen Julia (Smith) Trueblood; m. Ernest Theodore Patrikis, Mar. 18, 1972. Student, Beloit (Wis.) Coll., 1960-62; BA, U. Wis., 1965; MS, Columbia U., 1969. Libr. Fed. Res. Bank of N.Y., N.Y.C., 1969—95, chief libr., 1985-95; ret., 1995. One- and two-person shows include Lumen Winter Gallery, New Rochelle Pub. Libr., N.Y., 1996, Old Print Shop, N.Y.C., 2003; exhibited in group shows at Gallery 71, N.Y.C., 1996, Michael Ingbar Gallery, N.Y.C., 1996, 97, 2000, 2001, Old Print Shop, N.Y.C., 1998, 2001, 03, Kanagawa, Japan, 1992, 95, New Pub. Libr., Newark, 1994, III Bienal Internacional de Grabado, Spain, 1995, 97, Xylon 13, Winterthur, Switzerland, 1997-2001, The N.Y. Hist. Soc., N.Y.C., 2001, Internat. Miniature Art Biennial, Quebec, Canada, 2002, NY Transit Mus., 2003. Recipient Purchase prize, Trenton State Coll., 1982, Conn. Graphic Arts Ctr., 2001, Catherine Lorillard Wolfe Huntington bronze medal for pastel/graphics, 2002. Mem.: Salmagundi Club, Audubon Artists (Silver medal of honor for graphics 1999, 2001), Spl. Libr. Assn., Nat. Assn. Women Artists, Nat. Arts Club, Pen and Brush Inc., Soc. Am. Graphic Artists (v.p. 2003—). Avocations: swimming, hiking. Home: 20 E 9th St New York NY 10003-5944

TRUEBLOOD, HARRY ALBERT, JR., oil company executive; b. Wichita Falls, Tex., Aug. 28, 1925; s. Harry A. and Marguerite (Barnhart) T.; m. Lucile Bernard, Jan. 22, 1953; children: Katherine T. Astin, John B. Student, Tex. A&M Coll., 1942-43; BS in Petroleum Engring., U. Tex., 1948. Petroleum engr. Cal. Co., 1948-51; chief engr. McDermott & Barnhart Co., Colo., Tex., 1951-52; cons. petroleum and geol. engr. Denver, 1952-55; pres. Colo. Western Exploration Inc., Denver, 1955-58, Consol. Oil and Gas., Inc., 1958-88, chmn. bd., CEO, 1969-88, Princeville Devel. Corp., 1979-87, pres., 1984-86; chmn. bd., CEO Columbus Energy Corp., 1983-2000; pres., mng. mem. HAT Resources LLC, 2001—. Chmn. bd., CEO, Princeville Airways, Inc., 1979-87; chmn. bd. dirs., pres. CEC Resources, Ltd., 1984-99; bd. dirs. NYTIS Exploration Co. With USNR, 1944-46, ensign, 1949-55. Mem. Soc. Petroleum Engrs., Am. Petroleum Inst., World Pres. Orgn., Chief Execs. Orgn. (bd. dirs.), Ind. Petroleum Assn. Am. (exec. com.), Natural Gas Supply Assn. (exec. com.), Cherry Hills Country Club, One Hundred Club. Roman Catholic. Home: 2800 S University Blvd Apt 82 Denver CO 80210-6056 Office: 1720 S Bellaire St Ste 912 Denver CO 80222-4334 Office Phone: 303-300-6792. E-mail: htrueblood@sprynet.com.

TRUEBLOOD, MAX BLAIR, physicist, educator; b. Chester, Ill., July 24, 1947; s. Carl Harold and Thelma Ellen Trueblood; m. Susan Elaine Spiller, Jan. 7, 1978; children: James Michael, Wesley Earl, Joshua Thomas Holloway. BS, MS, So. Ill. U., 1973. Sr. rsch. aide Cloud and Aerosol Sci Lab., U. Mo., Rolla, 1977—. Pres. Lasea Aerosol Svcs., Ltd, Rolla, 1993—. Staff sgt. USAR, 1971—97. Methodist. Home: 14075 State Rte Y Rolla MO 65401 Office: U Mo Cloud and Aerosol Sci Lab Rolla MO 65409 Personal E-mail: trueblud@rollanet.org. E-mail: trueblud@umr.edu.

TRUEHILL, MARSHALL, JR., minister; b. New Orleans, Sept. 5, 1948; s. Marshall Truehill and Inez Gray Williams; adopted s. Elizabeth (May) T.; m. Mary Ola Williams, Dec. 20, 1969 (div. 1972); m. Valli Maria Dobard, July 22, 1972 (div. 1999); children: Briana Traci, Marshall III, Jessica, Quentin; m. Miranda Sally Farr, Dec. 28, 1999. B in Music Edn., Xavier U., 1973; BTh, Christian Bible Coll., 1979; MDiv, Orleans Bapt. Theol. Sem., 1986; D Ministry, New Orleans Bapt. Theol. Seminary, 1990; postgrad., U. New Orleans; ThD, A.P. Clay Christian Theol. Coll., 2004. Ordained to ministry Bapt. Ch., 1980; cert. tchr., La. Tchr. Orleans Parish Sch. Bd., New Orleans, 1973-78, Delgado Community Coll., 1975-78; pastor Faith in Action Bapt. Ch., 1982—95; founder, pastor First United Bapt. Ch., 1995—. Founder, dir. Faith in Action Evangel. Team, New Orleans, 1977—; lectr. Nat. Bapt. Conv. on Congl. Evangelism, New Orleans, 1977-79; cons. So. Bapt. Conv. Home Mission Bd., La., 1986-1997; CEO TradeWins Ptnrs. LLC, 2001. Bd. dirs. Project New Orleans, 1983-99, New Orleans Jobs Initiatives, vice chmn., 1997-2002; apptd. by mayor to New Orleans City Planning Commn., 1998-2007. Democrat. Avocations: computers, aquariums, interior decorating, aerobics. Office Phone: 504-488-2657. Personal E-mail: mtruejr@aol.com. *The greatest investment one can make in this life is an investment in the life of another person. That is the only investment with eternal value.*

TRUELL, GEORGE FOSTER, management consultant; b. NYC, Oct. 17, 1929; s. George Foster and Elaine (Shattuck) T.; m. Patricia Stitt, June 28, 1952; children: Deborah, Nancy, George. BS in Indsl. and Labor Rels., Cornell U., 1951. Cert. mgmt. cons. Inst. Mgmt. Cons. Pers. asst. DuPont Co., Wilmington, Del., 1951-53; pers. supr. Welch Foods, Inc., Westfield, NY, 1953-59; v.p. indsl. rels. Graphic Controls Corp., Buffalo, 1959-71; pres. George Truell Assocs., Buffalo, 1971—. Author: How to Manage For More Profitable Results, 1974, Building and Maintaining Your Non-Union Organization, 1980, Performance Appraisal-Current Issues and New Directions, 1980, Coaching and Counseling-Key Skills for Managers, 1981, Building and Managing Productive Work Teams, 1984, How To Obtain Cooperation and Agreement From Others, 1987, Helping Employees Cope With Change-A Manager's Guidebook, 1988, Employee Involvement-A Guidebook for Managers, 1991, Coaching and Counseling in Team-Based Organizations, 1996; contbr. articles to profl. jours. Mem.: Am. Mgmt. Assn. Republican. Office: George Truell Assocs 495 N Forest Rd Williamsville NY 14221-5036 Office Phone: 716-634-3491.

TRUEMAN, WILLIAM PETER MAIN, broadcaster, newspaper columnist; b. Sackville, N.B., Can., Dec. 25, 1934; s. Albert William and Jean Alberta (Miller) T.; m. Eleanor Joy Wark, Dec. 22, 1956; children: Anne, Mark, Victoria. Student, U. N.B., 1951-54. UN corr. Montreal Star, 1957-62, Washington corr., 1962 65; parliamentary corr. Toronto Star, Ottawa, Ont., 1965-67; nat. dir. UN Assn. in Can., 1967-68; nat. news writer CBC, Toronto, 1968-69, exec. producer news, head network news, 1969-72; freelance reporter, 1972-73; anchorman Global TV News, Don Mills, Ont., 1974-88; free lance broadcaster, 1988-2000; media critic Toronto Star's Starweek mag., 1988-96; Kingston Whig-Std., 1989-96. Host, mng.editor Canadian Discovery Channel TV series Great Canadian Parks, 1995-2000. Decorated officer Order of Can.; recipient Bowater award for journalism, 1962, Sam Ross award, 1983, Queen's Golden Jubilee Medal, 2002. E-mail: peter.trueman@sympatico.ca.

TRUEMPER, JOHN JAMES, JR., retired architect; b. Helena, Ark., June 18, 1924; s. John James and Mary Ann (Jacob) T.; m. Julia Clare Wood, Nov. 21, 1956; children: Zachary Wood, John James III, Ann Truemper Penick. BS in Arch., U. Ill., 1950; DHL (hon.), Lyon Coll., 1995. With archtl. firm Cromwell, Truemper, Levy, Thompson, Woodsmall Inc. (and predecessors), Little Rock, 1950-94, v.p., 1972-74, pres., 1974-81, chmn. bd., 1980-89; ret., 1994. Mem. Ark. Bd. Architects, 1974-82. Prin. works include Ark. system for edn. and tng. mentally retarded, 1956-78, Winrock Farm, Morrilton, Ark., 1953-58, Ark. State Parks, 1955-75, Ark. Power & Light Co., 1961-89, Lyon Coll., Batesville, 1983-94; author: A Century of Service, 1885-1985, 1985. Pres. Ark. Arts Ctr., 1979, chmn. bd., 1980; mem. Little Rock Bldg. Code Bd. Appeals, 1961-86, chmn., 1971-86; mem. Ark. Hist. Preservtion Rev. Bd., 1987-99; bd. dirs. Little Rock Met. YMCA, 1975-84; mem. Friends of Libr. Bd., U. Ark., Little Rock, 1989-99, pres. 1995-97; bd. dirs. Greater Little Rock C. of C., 1986-88. With USAAF, 1943-46. Recipient Winthrop Rockefeller Meml. award Ark. Arts Center, 1980 Fellow AIA. Roman Catholic. Home: 6502 Cantrell Rd Little Rock AR 72207-4219

TRUESDALE, JOHN CUSHMAN, government executive; b. Grand Rapids, Mich., July 17, 1921; s. John Cushman and Hazel (Christianson) T.; m. Karin A. Nelson, Feb. 10, 1957; children— John Cushman, Charles N., Margaret E., Andrew C. AB, Grinnell Coll., 1942; MS, Cornell U., 1948; JD, Georgetown U., 1972. Bar: Md. bar 1972, D.C. bar 1973. Field examiner NLRB, Buffalo and New Orleans, 1948-52, adminstrv. analyst Washington, 1952-57, assoc. exec. sec., 1963-68, dep. exec. sec., 1968-72, exec. sec., 1972-77, 81-94, mem., 1977-81, 94, 95, chmn., 1998-2001, labor arbitrator, 1996—98, 2001—; mem. Fgn. Svc. Grievance Bd., 1997—2003. Dir. info., dir. World Data Center/Rockets and Satellites, IGY, Nat. Acad. Scis., Washington, 1957-63 Editor-in-chief: How to Take a Case Before the NLRB, 1997-98, 2002--. Served with USCG, 1943—46. Recipient Presdl. award Pres. of U.S., 1988. Mem. ABA, Nat. Acad. Arbitrators, D.C. Bar Assn., Assn. Labor Rels. Agys. (pres. 1992-93), Indsl. Rels. Rsch. Assn. (internat. exec. bd. 2002—). Democrat. Congregationalist.

TRUESDELL, TIMOTHY L. private investor; b. Niles, Mich., Oct. 8, 1951; s. Patrick Daniel and LaVonne Marie (Fries) T. BA, U. Notre Dame, 1974. Asst. to exec. dir. Notre Dame U. Alumni Assn., 1974-77, asst. dir., 1977-79; alumni editor Notre Dame mag., 1979-83; v.p. Truesdell Real Estate Investment, Sacramento, 1983-85; dir. devel. rsch. U. Notre Dame, 1985-99; portfolio mgr. Kamm Partnership, South Bend, Ind., 1999—. Devel. cons. Am. Acad. Neurology, 1991-92, Harvest Devel., Ponte Vedra, Fla., 1999-2003, Hospice of St. Joseph County, South Bend, Ind., 1992-93, U. St. Thomas, Mpls., Xavier U., Cin., 1993-94, Niles Cmty. Libr., 1993-97, St. Joseph Mishawaka (Ind.) Health Svcs., 1995-96, Berrien County ARC, 1996, Advancement Ptnrs., Inc., Columbus, 1996-2003, Little Flower Cath. Ch., South Bend, Ind., 1997-98, No. Ind. Ctr. for History, South Bend, 1998-2000; bd. dirs. Women's Care Ctr., Mishawaka, Ind., 1999-2000. Councilman City of Niles, 1983-91; pres. St. Mary's Sch Bd. Edn., Niles, 1981-82; chmn. S.W. Mich. Cmty. Ambulance, Niles, 1985-89; mem. Rep. Nat. Com.; pres. Fernwood Bot. Garden, Niles, 1997-98. Mem. Am. Assn. Individual Investors, Optimists (sec. 1983-84), Knights of Malta, Notre Dame Club of St. Joseph Valley, Notre Dame Club of Kalamazoo. Republican. Roman Catholic. Avocations: golf, antique collecting. Office: 11185 Elizabeth Dr Three Rivers MI 49093 Office Phone: 269-244-8921. Personal E-mail: timothytruesdell@verizon.net.

TRUESDELL, WALTER GEORGE, minister, librarian; b. N.Y.C., Oct. 22, 1919; s. George Anson and Hattie (Evans) T.; m. Mary Schurok, June 10, 1944; children: Walter George, Susan Hattie. AB, Columbia U. Columbia Coll., 1941; MDiv, Theol. Sem. of the Ref. Episcopal Ch., Phila., 1944; BLS, Pratt Inst., 1950; MA, Columbia U. Tchrs. Coll., 1975; DD (hon.), Cummins Theol. Sem. Reformed Episcopal, Summerville, S.C., 2002. Ordained to ministry Ref. Episcopal Ch., 1944. Asst. min. First Ref. Episcopal Ch., N.Y.C., 1944-54, sr. assoc. min., 1989—; rector Ch. of the Redemption, Bklyn., 1956—; lectr. apologetics and English Bible Theol. Sem. Ref. Episcopal Ch., Phila., 1945-48, libr. Phila. (relocated to Blue Bell, Pa., Sept. 2000), 1964-93, Shelton Coll., 1951-69; libr. Cummins Theol. Sem. Reformed Episcopal, Summerville, SC, 1996—2002. Chmn. com. on state of ch. Ref. Episcopal Ch., 1960-87, mem., 1987-96, mem. gen. com. 1978-96; real estate broker, 1979—. Editor Episcopal Recorder, 1980-90. Mem. ALA (life), Pa. Libr. Assn., Assn. Statisticians Am. Religious Bodies. Home and Office: 306 E 90th St New York NY 10128-5121 *Out of the privilege of a broad educational background and living in the astonishing technology of the 20th century, and yet to be, in the turbulence of war, crime, starvation, and distress of mind and spirit, I am convicted anew of the need to know Christ, who said, "I am the way, the truth, and the life." Therefore, I labor in Christian education to the strengthening of mind, body, and spirit.*

TRUETT, HAROLD JOSEPH, III, (TIM TRUETT), lawyer; b. Alameda, Calif., Feb. 13, 1946; s. Harold Joseph and Lois Lucille (Mellin) T.; 1 child, Harold Joseph IV; m. Anna V. Billante, Oct. 1, 1983 (dec. June 2000); 1 child, James S. Carstensen; m. Patricia Maynord, Mar. 5, 2002. BA, U. San Francisco, 1968, JD, 1975. Bar: Calif. 1975, Hawaii 1987, U.S. Dist. Ct. (ea., so., no., and cen. dists.) Calif. 1976, Hawaii 1987, U.S. Ct. Appeals (9th cir.) 1980, U.S. Supreme Ct. 1988, U.S. Ct. Fed. Claims, 1995. Assoc. Hoberg, Finger et al, San Francisco, 1975-78, Bledsoe, Smith et al, San Francisco, 1979-80, Abramson & Bianco, San Francisco, 1980-83; mem. Ingram & Truett, San Rafael, 1983-90; prin. Winchell & Truett, San Francisco, 1991—. Lectr. trial practice Am. Coll. Legal Medicine, 1989-90, 2003, Calif. Continuing Edn. of the Bar. Bd. dirs. Shining Star Found. 1991—, pres., 2001—, Marin County, Calif.; mem. Marin Dem. Coun., San Rafael, 1983-90, 2002. Lt., aviator USN, 1967-74. Mem. ABA, Hawaii Bar Assn., Calif. Bar Assn. (com. for adminstrn. of justice, conf. of dels.), San Francisco Bar Assn., San Francisco Trial Lawyers Assn., Lawyers Pilots Assn. Roman Catholic. Home: 48 Valley Rd San Anselmo CA 94960 E-mail: tim@truettlaw.com.

TRUETT, LILA FLORY, economics professor; b. Emporia, Kans., June 30, 1947; d. Ulysses Earl and Ursula Mabel (Schwindt) Matile; m. Donald Gene Flory, May 26, 1967 (div. 1973); m. Dale Brian Truett, Apr. 4, 1977; stepchildren: Katherine, Patrick. BA in Math., Kans. State U., 1968; MA in Econs., U. Iowa, 1971, PhD in Econs., 1972. Teaching asst., then part-time instr. U. Iowa, Iowa City, 1969-71; asst. prof. Iowa Wesleyan Coll., Mt. Pleasant, 1971-73, Appalachian State U., Boone, N.C., 1973-75; from asst. prof. to prof. econs. U. Tex., San Antonio, 1975—81, prof. econs., 1981—. Outside reviewer dept. econs., Colo. State U., Colorado Springs, 1988, S.W. Tex. State U., San Marcos, Tex., 2001. Co-author: Intermediate Microeconomics, 1984, Economics, 1987, Managerial Economics, 7th edit., 2001, 8th edit., 2004; contbr. numerous articles to profl. jours. Mem. Fin. Execs. Inst., Fin. Mgmt. Assn., Am. Econ. Assn., So. Econ. Assn., Ea. Fin. Assn., Midwest Fin. Assn., Western Econs. Assn., Ea. Econs. Assn., Omicron Delta Epsilon, Beta Gamma Sigma. Brethren. Avocations: reading, music, travel, gardening. Home: 16402 NW Military Hwy San Antonio TX 78231-1224 Office: U Tex Dept EconS San Antonio TX 78249-0633

TRUEX, DOROTHY ADINE, retired university administrator; b. Sedalia, Mo., Oct. 6, 1915; d. Chester Morrison and Madge (Nicholson) T. AB, William Jewell Coll., 1936; MA, U. Mo., 1937; EdD, Columbia U., 1956. Asst. dean women N.W. Mo. State U., Maryville, 1939-43, dean women, 1943-45, Mercer U., Macon, Ga., 1945-47, U. Okla., Norman, 1947-69, assoc. prof., 1969-72, dir. rsch. and program devel., 1969-74, prof. edn., 1972-74, dir. grad. program in student pers. svcs., 1969 74; vice chancellor for student affairs U. Ark., Little Rock, 1974-83, alumni specialist, 1983-84, acad. adviser, 1984-87. Exec. bd. N. Cen. Assn. Schs. and Colls., 1977-83. Author 7 novels. Mem. Nat. Assn. Women Deans, Adminstrs. and Counselors (pres. 1973-74), So. Coll. Pers. Assn. (pres. 1970), Okla. Coll. Pers. Assn. (pres. 1972-73), William Jewell Coll. Alumni Assn. (pres. 1970-73), WOman's City Club (pres. 2000-2001), Pi Beta Phi, Alpha Lambda Delta, Mortar Bd., Sigma Tau Delta, Cardinal Key, Gamma Alpha Chi, Kappa Delta Pi, Pi Lambda Theta, Alpha Psi Omega, Pi Gamma Mu, Delta Kappa Gamma, Phi Delta Kappa, Phi Kappa Phi. (nat. v.p. 1986-89) Avocation: writing. Home: 14300 Chenal Pkwy Apt 7422 Little Rock AR 72211-5819

TRUGLIA, CHRISTEL, state legislator; b. Germany; m. Anthony D. Truglia (dec.); 3 children. Student, Darien (Conn.) H.S. Mem. Conn. Ho. of Reps., Hartford, 1973-84, 88—, Conn. Senate, Hartford, 1984-87. Mem. appropriations, human svcs., substance abuse prevention coms, L.I. task force, children at risk task force and gray haired caucus; mem. Dem. Leadership Coun., 1991—, Nat. Order of Women Legislators, 1991—, Lower Fairfield County Conf./Exhbn. Authority, 1992—, Com. on Edn. Excellence, 1992—. Vice chmn. Stamford (Conn.) Dem. City Com., 1976-78; bd. dirs. Com. on Tng. and Employment, 1990—; mem. exec. com. Lower Fairfield County Action Against Chem. Dependency, 1991—; active Coun. on Probate Jud. Conduct, 1976-88, Stamford Com. on Aging, 1978-88, Child Care Ctr. of Stamford, Family Re-entry, Inc., 1990—, Aide for Retarded Inc. Aux. Recipient Hannah G. Solomon Cmty. Svc. award Nat. Coun. Jewish Women, 1987, Spl. award Family Re-entry, 1990, Friend of Edn. award Conn. Coun. for Am. Pvt. Edn., 1991, Adv. Leadership award, 1991, Appreciation cert. Conn. Acad. Physicians Assts., 1991, Cmty. Svc. award Coun. Chs. and Synagogues, 1991, Law Day Liberty Bell award Stamford-Norwalk Regional Bar Assn., 1992, United Srs. in Action award Conn. Gen. Assembly, 1992, Child Adv. Legis. Leadership award Conn. Coalition for Children, 1992, Spl. Recognition award Coalition of 100 Black Women of Lower Fairfield County, 1992, Bd. dirs. Jewish Home for Elderly, 1992; named Child Adv. Legislator, State Coalition for Children and State Commn. on Children, 1990, Legis. Advisor of Yr., Conn. Youth Svcs. Assn., 1990. Mem. Rippowan Bus. and Profl. Women's Club (Woman of Yr. 1991). Democrat. Home: 7 Gypsy Moth Landing Stamford CT 06902-7725 Office: Conn Ho of Reps State Capitol Hartford CT 06106-1591

TRUHLAR, DONALD GENE, chemist, educator; b. Chgo., Feb. 27, 1944; s. John Joseph and Lucille Marie (Vancura) T.; m. Jane Teresa Gust, Aug. 28, 1965; children: Sara Elizabeth, Stephanie Marie. BA in Chemistry summa cum laude, St. Mary's Coll., Winona, Minn., 1965; PhD in Chemistry, Calif. Inst. Tech., 1970. Asst. prof. chemistry and chem. physics U. Minn., Mpls., 1969—72, assoc. prof., 1972—76, prof., 1976—93, Inst. of Tech. prof., 1993—98, Inst. of Tech. disting. prof., 1998—, Lloyd H. Reyerson prof., 2002—. Cons. Los Alamos Sci. Lab.; vis. fellow Joint Inst. for Lab. Astrophysics, 1975-76; sci. dir. Minn. Supercomputer Inst., 1987-88, dir., 1988—. Editor Theoretical Chemistry Accounts (Theoretica Chemica Acta), 1985—98, Computer Physics Comms., 1986—, Topics Phys. Chemistry, 1992—99, Understanding Chem. Reactivity, 1990—92, editl. bd. Jour. Chem. Physics, 1978—80, Chem. Physics Letters, 1982—, Jour. Phys. Chemistry, 1985—87, Understanding Chem. Reactivity, 1993—, Advances in Chem. Physics, 1993—, Internat. Jour. Modern Physics C., 1994—, IEEE Computational Sci. and Engring., 1994—98, Internat. Jour. Quantum Chemistry, 1996—2000, Computing in Sci. and Engring., 1999—, Jour. Chemical Theory and Computation, 2004—, editor Theoretical Chemistry Accounts, 1998—2001, chief adv. editor, 2002—. Recipient Minn. award, 2003, Nat. Acad. Scis. award for Sci. Reviewing, 2004; fellow, Alfred P. Sloan Found., 1973—77; grantee, NSF, 1971—, NASA, 1987—95, U.S. Dept. Energy, 1979—, NIST, 1995—98, Dept. of Def., 2001—; scholar, Ruhland Walzer Meml. scholar, 1961—62; John Stauffer fellow, 1965—66, NDEA fellow, 1966—68. Fellow AAAS, Am. Phys. Soc.; mem. Am. Chem. Soc. (sec.-treas. theoretical chemistry subdivsn. 1980-89, councilor 1985-87, assoc. editor jour. 1984—, Award for computers in chem. and pharm. rsch. 2000). Achievements include research, numerous publications in field. Home: 5033 Thomas Ave S Minneapolis MN 55410-2240 Office: U Minn 207 Pleasant St SE Minneapolis MN 55455-0431 E-mail: truhlar@umn.edu.

TRUHLAR, ROBERT J. lawyer; b. Chgo., Apr. 11, 1948; BA, St. Mary's Coll., 1970; JD, U. Denver, 1981. Bar: Colo. 1981, U.S. Dist. Ct. Colo. 1981, U.S. Ct. Appeals (10th cir.) 1981, U.S. Supreme Ct. 1981. Ptnr. Truhlar and Truhlar, LLP, Littleton, Colo. Part-time faculty master program in human resource mgmt. Chapman U., 1990—96; adj. prof. U. Denver Coll. Law, 1992—93. Bus. editor: Denver Law Jour., 1979—80; contbr. chapters to books. Mem.: Coll. Labor and Employment Lawyers, Arapahoe County Bar Assn. (bd. dirs. 1991—93, 1994—2001, officer 1996—2000, pres. 1999—2000), Colo. Bar Assn. (pres.-elect 2002—, v.p. 1997—98, bd. govs. 1997—2001, 2002—, mem. legal fee arbitration com. 1982—83, 1984—, labor law com. 1988—, co-chmn. 1989—92). Office: Colo Bar Assn Ste 900 1900 Grant St Denver CO 80203 also: Truhlar and Truhlar LLP 1901 W Littleton Blvd Littleton CO 80120

TRUITT, ANNE DEAN, artist; b. Balt., Mar. 16, 1921; d. Duncan Witt and Louisa Folsom (Williams) Dean; m. James McConnell Truitt, Sept. 19, 1947 (div.); children— Alexandra, Mary McConnell, Samuel Rogers. BA, Bryn Mawr Coll., 1943; postgrad., Inst. Contemporary Art, Washington, 1948-50. Exhibited in one woman shows at Andre Emmerich Gallery, N.Y.C., 1963, 65, 69, 75, 80, 86, 91, Danese Gallery, N.Y.C., 1998, 2001, Minami Gallery, Tokyo, 1964, 67, Balt. Mus. Art, 1969, 75, 92, Pyramid Galleries, Washington, 1971, 73, 75, 77, Whitney Mus. Am. Art, N.Y.C., 1973-74, Corcoran Gallery, Washington, 1974, Osuna Gallery, Washington, 1979, 81, 86, 89, 91-92, Neuberger Mus., Purchase N.Y., 1986, Georgia O'Keefe Mus., Santa Fe, 2000; exhibited in group shows at Balt. Mus. Art, 1970, 72-73, 82, Whitney Mus. Am. Art, 1970-71, 72, 77, Phillips Collection, Washington, 1971-72, Pyramid Galleries, 1972, 73, Mus. Contemporary Art, Chgo., 1974, 77, Indpls. Mus. Art, 1974, Nat. Gallery Art, Washington, 1974, Corcoran Gallery Art, Washington, 1975, numerous others; translator: (with C.J. Hill) Marcel Proust and Deliverance from Time (Germaine Brée), 1955; author: Daybook: The Journal of an Artist, 1982, Turn: The Journal of an Artist, 1986, Prospect: The Journal of an Artist, 1996. Guggenheim fellow, 1970; Nat. Endowment for Arts fellow, 1971, 77; Australia Council for Arts fellow, 1981 Home: 3506 35th St NW Washington DC 20016-3114

TRUITT, RICHARD BYRON, landscape architect; b. El Paso, Tex., Dec. 25, 1937; s. Charles Lee and Elenia May Truitt; m. Doris Iva House, Feb. 23, 1963; 1 child, Bonnie Leona. Cert. in Hort. and Landscape, Dayton Beach (Fla.) C.C., 1956. Cert. law and ornamental pest control; registered landscape architect, Fla. Pvt. practice, Ormond Beach, Fla., 1956—. Contbr. articles to profl. jours. Pres. Civitan Club, Ormond Beach; vice chair Devel. Rev. Bd., Ormond Beach, 1995-98; chair Beautification Bd., Ormond Beach, 1978-95; bd. dirs., trustee Louitte Manor retirement Ctr., Daytona Beach, 1984-97; charter mem. Bot. Gardens of Volusia County; bd. dirs. Episc. Ch., Diocese of Ctrl. Fla., Orlando, 1979-81; Eucharistic minister Episc. Ch. With Army N.G., 1956-66. Recipient Spl. award City of Ormond Beach for outstanding svcs. as chair and mem. of beautification Bd., 1995. Mem. Ormond Beach C. of C. (pres. 1990, Spl. Award for contbn. and dedication to beautification 1989), Holly Hill C. o C. (pres. 1989), Fla. Nurseryman and growers Assn. (pres. Ctrl. East Coast chpt. 1977). Republican. Episcopalian. Home and Office: 115 Country Club Dr Ormond Beach FL 32176-5415

TRUJILLO, ANGELINA, endocrinologist; b. Long Beach, Calif. BA in Psychology, Chapman Coll., 1974; postgrad., U. Colo., 1974-75, MD, 1979. Resident in internal medicine Kern Med. Ctr., Bakersfield, Calif., 1979-82; fellow in endocrinology UCLA, Sepulveda, Calif., 1982-84, chief resident dept. internal medicine, 1985-86; chief diabetes clinic Sepulveda (Calif.) VA Med. Ctr., 1986-89; physician specialist Olive View Med. Ctr., Sylmar, Calif., 1989; chief divsn. endocrinology U. S.D. Sch. Medicine, Sioux Falls, 1990—2001; ACOS R&D Royal C. Johnson VA Med. Ctr., Sioux Falls, 1998—2001. Adj. instr. UCLA, 1982-84, adj. asst. prof. medicine, 1985-89, clin. asst. prof. family medicine, 1994-2001; asst. prof. U. S.D. Sch. Medicine, 1990-94, assoc. prof., 1994—, assoc. dir. internal medicine residency program, 1992-95; spkr. in field. Pub. spkr. in diabetes, women and heart disease. Grantee NIH, 1986-89, Am. Diabetes Assn., 1985-87, Pfizer, Inc., 1990-91, Nat. Heart, Lung, and Blood Inst., 1994—, Bristol-Myers Squibb, 1994-2001 Mem. ACP, Am. Fedn. Clin. Rsch. (med. sch. rep., endo/metabolism subspecialty coun.), Am. Soc. Hypertension, Am. Diabetes Assn., Assn. Program Dirs. in Internal Medicine, Assn. Clerkship Dirs. in Internal Medicine, S.D. State Med. Assn., Seventh Dist. Med. Soc., Wilderness Med. Soc. (mem. environ. coun.). Office: U SD Sch Med 1400 W 22nd St Sioux Falls SD 57105-1505

TRUJILLO, ROBERT, musician; b. Santa Monica, Calif., Oct. 23, 1964; Band mem. Suicidal Tendencies, Infectious Grooves, Ozzy Osbourne, Metallica, 2003—. Musician (bassist, also prodr.): (albums) (with Infectious Grooves) Plague That Makes Your Booty Move, 1991, Sarsippius' Ark, 1993; musician: (bassist) Groove Family Cyco, 1994, Mas Borracho, 2000, (with Suicidal Tendencies) Art of Rebellion, 1992, Suicidal for Life, 1994, (with Ozzy Osbourne) Down to Earth, 2001, Live at Budokan, 2002, Ozzman Cometh: Greatest Hits, 2002, (with Metallica) St. Anger, 2003 (Grammy award for Best Metal Performance, 2003), (others) Poder Latino, A.N.I-.M.A.L., 1998; musician: (bassist, vocals, prodr., engr., mastering) Twelve Piece Band, Project Tru, 1999; musician: (bassist) Christmas That Almost Wasn't, Various Artists, 2001, Metallic Assault: A Tribute to Metallica, Various Artists, 2001, Problem Child, Cyco Mike, 2001, Revolution, Insolence, 2001, 1919 Eternal, Zakk Wylde's Black Label Society, 2001, Degradation Trip, Jerry Cantrell, Vol. 1 & Vol. 2, 2002, Different Shade of Green: Tribute to Green Day, Various Artists, 2003, Prison Cell, Wirebox, 2003, Immaculate Deception: A Tribute to the Music of Madon, 2004, Stairway to Rock (Not Just) A Led Zepplin Tribute, Various Artists, 2004; performer: (TV soundtrack) Osbourne Family Album, 2002. Office: Elektra Entertainment Group 75 Rockefeller Plaza New York NY 10019-7284*

TRUJILLO, SOLOMON D. telecommunications executive; m. Corine Trujillo; 3 children. BS, MBA, U. Wyo. With US West, Denver, 1974-92, pres., CEO mktg. resources, 1992-95, pres., CEO, 1995-97; CEO Graviton, Inc., San Diego, 1997—. Bd. dirs. Dayton Hudson Corp., Bank of Am., World Econ. Forum; mem. Nat. Security Telecom. Coun.; advisor U.S. govt. on trade policy as appointee Investment and Svcs. Policy Adv. Com., Office of the Pres. Bd. trustees Aspen Inst., chair ann. seminar on Hispanic Ams. and the Bus. Cmty.; bd. dirs. Tomás Rivera Policy Inst.; mem. corp. bd. advisors Nat. Coun. of La Raza; bd. fellows Claremont Grad. U.; chmn. bd. trustees Ctr. for the New West, Denver. Named one of 100 Most Influential Latinos in the Nation by Hispanic Bus. Mag.; recipient Cmty. Svc. award NCCJ, Disting. Svc. award Colo. Civil Rights Commn., Corp. Advocate of the Yr. award U.S. Hispanic C. of C. Office: Graviton Inc 8130 La Mesa Blvd La Mesa CA 91941-6437

TRUJILLO-CUTHRELL, LORETTA MARIE, chemical engineer; b. Santa Fe, N.Mex., May 22, 1959; d. Jose E.F. and Irene D. (Fernandez) Trujillo; m. Robert Blair Cuthrell, May 16, 1987. BSChemE, U. N.Mex., 1988. Process engr. Kerr McGee Chem., Trona, Calif., 1989-91; chem. engr. N.Am. Chem. Co., Trona, 1991-98, quality coord., 1992-98, IMC Chem., Trona, Calif., 1998-2000; lab. supr. GTC, Albuquerque, 2000—01; chemist State of N.Mex. Health Dept. Mem. AIChE (vice chmn. 1995—), Women in Mining.

TRULEAR, HAROLD DEAN, minister, theological educator, social researcher; b. Phila., Oct. 4, 1954; s. Harold Holland and Elizabeth C. (Dean) T.; m. Vickie Lynette Butler, June 27, 1981; children: Harold Butler, Jared Morgan, Frances Elizabeth. BA, Morehouse Coll., 1975; MPhil, Drew U., 1979, PhD, 1983. Club dir. Youth for Christ, Paterson, N.J., 1977-83; assoc. prof. ch. and society Drew U., Madison, N.J., 1978-87; dir. black ch. studies Ea. Bapt. Theol. Sem., Phila., 1987-90; dean 1st profl. programs N.Y. Theol. Sem., N.Y.C., 1990-96, prof. ch. and society, 1990-98; v.p. Pub./Pvt. Ventures, Phila., 1998—. Assoc. pastor Cmty. Bapt. Ch., Paterson, 1981-87, 91-97; pastor Mt. Zion Bapt. Ch., Phila., 1987-90; assoc. min. Zion Bapt. Ch., Ardmore, Pa.; clergy assoc. St. Mary's Episcopal Ch., Ardmore; cons. Christian Coll. Consortium, 1990, Vanderbilt U. Div. Sch., Nashville, 1995; mem. adv. bd. Phila. Project for Youth Ministry, 1995-97; bd. dirs. N.Y. Christian Higher Edn. Consortium, N.Y.C. Guest editor The Pastor Scholar, 1997; contbr. chpts. to books. Bd. dirs. Paterson Clergy Assn., 1977-83, Opportunities Industrialization Ctr., Paterson, 1981-87, Inter Varsity Christian Fellowship, Madison, Wis., 1995—, Inndwelling, World Impact, Chester, Pa. Grantee N.J. Hist. Commn., 1984, Assn. Theol. Schs., 1984, Ford Found., 1994-95. Fellow Partnership for Rsch. on Religion and At Risk Youth; mem. Am. Acad. Religion, Soc. for the Study Black Religion, Soc. for Pentecostal Studies, Bapt. Mins. Conf., Am. Bapt. Chs. N.J. (mins. coun.), Phi Beta Kappa. Republican. Achievements include research on youth, young adults, religion and public policy. Home: 912 Church Ln Yeadon PA 19050-3717 Office: Pub Pvt Ventures 2005 Market St Ste 900 Philadelphia PA 19103-7060

TRULY, RICHARD H. academic administrator, former federal agency administrator, former astronaut; b. Fayette, Miss., Nov. 12, 1937; s. James B. Truly; m. Coleen Hanner; children: Richard Michael, Daniel Bennett, Lee Margaret. B in Aero. Engring., Ga. Inst. Tech., 1959. Commd. ensign USN, 1959; advanced through grades to vice adm.; assigned Fighter Squadron 33; served in U.S.S. Intrepid; served in U.S.S. Enterprise; astronaut Manned Orbiting Lab. Program USAF, 1965—69, NASA, 1969—, comdr. Columbia Flight 2, 1981, Challenger Flight 3, 1983; dir. Space Shuttle program, 1986—89; adminstr. NASA, 1989—92; v.p., dir. Georgia Tech Rsch. Inst., Atlanta, 1992—97; dir. Nat. Renewable Energy Lab., Golden, Colo., 1997—. Recipient Robert H. Goddard Astronautics award, AIAA, 1990. Mem.: NAE. Office: Nat Renewable Energy Lab 1617 Cole Blvd Golden CO 80401-3305

TRUMAN, EDWIN MALCOLM, federal official; b. Albany, N.Y., June 6, 1941; m. Tracy P. T.; children: David, Christine. BA, Amherst Coll., 1963; MA, Yale U., 1964, PhD, 1967; LLD (hon.), Amherst Coll., 1988. Dir. Divsn. of Internat. Finance, 1977-87; staff dir., bd. govs. FRS, 1987-98; asst. Sec. of the Treas. Fed. Govt. Internat. Affairs, Washington, 1998—. Contr. articles toprofl. jours. Office: Internat Affairs Dept of the Treasury 1500 Pennsylvania Ave NW Washington DC 20220-0001 E-mail: tnttruman2@aol.com., ted.truman@do.treas.gov.

TRUMAN, MARGARET, author; b. Independence, Mo., Feb. 17, 1924; d. Harry S (32nd Pres. U.S.) and Bess (Wallace) T.; m. E. Clifton Daniel Jr., Apr. 21, 1956; children: Clifton T., William, Harrison, Thomas. LHD, Wake Forest U., 1972; HHD, Rockhurst Coll., 1976. Concert singer, 1947-54, actess, broadcaster, author, 1954—; author: Souvenir, 1956, White House Pets, 1969, Harry S. Truman, 1973, Women of Courage, 1976, Murder in the White House, 1980, Murder on Capitol Hill, 1981, Letters from Father, 1981, Murder in the Supreme Ct., 1982, Murder in the Smithsonian, 1983, Murder on Embassy Row, 1985, Murder at the FBI, 1985, Murder in Georgetown, 1986, Bess W. Truman, 1986, Murder in the CIA, 1987, Murder at the Kennedy Center, 1989, Murder in the National Cathedral, 1990, Murder at the Pentagon, 1992, Murder on the Potomac, 1994, First Ladies, 1995, Murder in the National Gallery, 1996, Murder in the House, 1997, Murder at the Watergate, 1998, Murder in the Library of Congress, 1999, Murder at Foggy Bottom, 2000, Murder in Havana, 2001, Murder at Ford's Theatre, 2002, The President's House, 2003; editor: Where the Buck Stops: The Personal and Private Writings of Harry S. Truman, 1989. Trustee and v.p. Harry S. Truman Inst.; sec. bd. trustees Harry S. Truman Found.

TRUMBETTA, SUSAN L. psychology educator; d. Daniel and Marjorie C. Trumbetta; m. David John Montanye, June 12, 1983. BA, Mt. Holyoke Coll.; M.Div., Yale U.; PhD, U. of Va., 1995. Asst. prof. rsch. dept. pediat. U. of Louisville, 1997—99; asst. prof. dept. psychology Vassar Coll., Poughkeepsie, NY, 1999—. Office: Vassar Coll Dept of Psychology 124 Raymond Ave Poughkeepsie NY 12604

TRUMBLE, DENNIS ROBERT, biomedical engineer; b. Homestead, Fla., Jan. 25, 1961; s. John Robert Trumble and Yolanda Marie VanEpps; m. Kathleen Ann Simpson, Dec. 27, 1991. BSEE, U. Notre Dame, 1983, MSEE, 1985; MS in Bioengring., Pa. State U., 1987. Rsch. instr. surgery Drexel U., Phila.; biomedical engr., rsch. scientist Allegheny Gen. Hosp., Pitts., 1988—. Contbr. articles to profl. jours. Mem. instl. animal care and use com. Allegheny-Singer Rsch. Inst., Pitts., 1999—2004. Grantee, Whitaker Found., 1993—95, NIH, 1999—2004; scholar, U. Notre Dame, 1984—85, Pa. State U., 1985—87. Mem.: AAAS, Am. Soc. Artificial Internal Organs, Am. Physiol. Soc. Achievements include patents in field; invention of Muscle Energy Converter. Avocations: travel, writing, music, history of science. Office: Allegheny Gen Hosp 320 Et North Ave Pittsburgh PA 15212 Office Phone: 412-359-3660. E-mail: trumble@wpahs.org.

TRUMBULL, DAVID LEWIS KITCHEN, trade association executive; b. Highland Park, Mich. s. Ben Gordon and Lois Virginia (Wilson) Kitchen; m. Mary N. DiZazzo, Sept. 29, 2003. AB, U. Mich., 1991. Rsch. asst. U. Mass., Boston, 1992-93; programmer Commonwealth of Mass., Boston, 1993-94; in charge mem. svcs. Nat. Textile Assn., Boston, 1994—; exec. dir. Am. Flock Assn., Boston, 1994—2001. Chmn. Cambridge (Mass.) Rep. City Com., 1994-2002; asst. sec. NAACP, Cambridge, 1994-96, v.p., 1996-98; chmn. Ward 3, Boston Rep. Com., 2003—. Mem. Textile Club (exec. com. 1996—, treas. 1998—). Episcopalian. Home: 130 Bowdoin St # 1110 Boston MA 02108 Office: Nat Textile Assn 6 Beacon St # 1125 Boston MA 02108 E-mail: trumbulld@earthlink.net.

TRUMBULL, TERRY ALAN, energy and environmental consultant, lawyer; b. Berkeley, Calif., Nov. 5, 1945; s. Larry Edward and Emily Josephine (Grote) Trumbull; m. Patricia Jane Vogel, Aug. 24, 1968; children: Eryn, Morgann. BA, U. Calif., Davis, 1967; JD, Georgetown U., Washington, 1970; LLM, George Washington U., 1973. Bar: DC 1971, Calif. 1973. Mem. legal staff Dept. Interior, Washington, 1970; sr. staff Inst. Inst. Pub. Adminstrn., Washington, 1970—71; legal advisor to dept. asst. adminstr. planning and evaluation EPA, Washington, 1972—73; legis. and regulatory counsel Gen Electric Co., San Jose, Calif., 1973—78; ptnr. Atkinson, Farasyn, Smith, Sherer and Trumbull, Mountain View, Calif., 1978—79; dep. town atty. Town of Woodside, Colo., 1979—. Chmn. Calif. Waste Mgmt. Bd., Sacramento, 1979—84, part time chmn., 1984—85; pres. Edarra, Inc., Palo Alto, Calif., 1983—; environ. law instr. dept. environ. studies San Jose State U., Calif., 1998—. Mem. Calif. Planning Roundtable, 1980—81, Santa Clara County Energy Task Force, Santa Clara County Environ. Task Force, Nat. Commn. on Resource Conservation and Recovery, 1981—, Hazardous Waste Mgmt. Coun., 1982—84, Santa Clara County Planning Commn., Calif., 1976—79, 1996—2002, chmn., 1979, 1998—99; mem. hearing bd. Bay Area Air Quality Mgmt. Dist., 2002. Mem.: Assn. State Solid Waste Ofcls. (chmn.solid waste com., bd. dirs. 1979—84), Calif. Geothermal Energy Coord. Coun., Calif. County Planning Commrs. Assn. (chmn. air quality com. 1976—79), Calif. Bar Assn. Democrat. Office: 1011 Lincoln Ave Palo Alto CA 94301-3046

TRUMBULL, WILLIAM ERNEST, retired surgeon, educator; b. Portland, Oreg., Mar. 16, 1924; MD, NYU, 1951. Bd. cert. in surgery, 1959. Intern L.A. County-Harbor, Torrance, Calif., 1951-52, surg. resident, 1953-58; staff St. John's Hosp.-Health Ctr., Santa Monica, Calif.; asst. clin. prof. UCLA. Fellow ACS; mem. Calif. Med. Assn., L.A. Surg. Soc., Pacific Coast Surg. Assn. Personal E-mail: wtrumbull@earthlink.net.

TRUMKA, RICHARD LOUIS, labor leader, lawyer; b. Nemacolin, Pa., July 24, 1949; s. Frank Richard and Eola Elizabeth (Bertugli) T.; m. Barbara Vidovich, Nov. 27, 1982; 1 child, Richard L. BS, Pa. State U., 1971; JD, Villanova U., 1974. Bar: U.S. Dist. Ct. (D.C.) 1974, U.S. Ct. Appeals (3d, 4th and D.C. cirs.) 1975, U.S. Supreme Ct. 1979. Atty. United Mine Workers Am., Washington, 1974-77, 78-79, internat. pres., 1982-95; miner, operator Jones & Laughlin Steel, Nemacolin, Pa., 1977-78, 79-81; internat. exec. bd. Dist. 4 United Mine Workers Am., Masontown, Pa., 1981-82; sec. treas. AFL-CIO, Washington, 1995—; pres. emeritus United Mine Workers Assn., 1995—. Bd. dirs. Am. Coal Found.; mem. Nat. Coal Council, 1985. Trustee Pa. State U. Recipient Labor Responsibility Award, Martin Luther King Ctr. for Nonviolent Social Change, 1990. Democrat. Roman Catholic. Office: AFL-CIO 815 16th St NW Washington DC 20006-4145

TRUMP, DONALD JOHN, real estate developer; b. N.Y.C., 1946; s. Fred C. and Mary Trump; m. Ivana Zelnicek, 1977 (div. 1991); children: Donald, Jr., Ivanka, Eric; m. Marla Maples, Dec. 30, 1993 (div. 1999); 1 child, Tiffany. BS Economics, U. Pa., Wharton Sch. Fin., 1968. Pres. Trump Orgn., N.Y.C.; owner Trump Tower, Trump Parc, Trump Palace, Trump Bldg. at 40 Wall St., N.Y.C., Trump Internat. Hotel and Tower, N.Y.C., Chgo., Trump Plz. Hotel and Casino, Trump Marina, Trump Taj Mahal, Atlantic City, Trump Casino Riverboat, Buffington Harbor, Ind., Trump 29 Casino, Palm Springs, Calif., W. Side Rail Yards devel. as Trump Pl., N.Y.C., Mansion at Seven Springs, Bedford, NY, Mar-a-Lago Club, Palm Beach, Fla.; ptnr.-owner 610 Park Ave. and Trump World Tower, N.Y.C., Trump Park Ave. (formerly Delmonico Hotel), Trump Grande Ocean Resort and Residences, Miami Beach, Fla., Trump Internat. Hotel and Twr., Chgo.; chmn., pres. Trump Org., N.Y.C. Owner Trump Internat. Golf Club, Palm Beach, Trump Nat. Golf Club, Briarcliff Manor, NY, Ocean Trails Golf Course, Palos Verde, Calif., Trump Nat., Bedminster, NJ, Trump Mgmt. Group Modeling/Talent Agy.; pres. Trump Pageants LP, includes Miss Universe, Miss USA and Miss Teen USA. Author (with Tony Schwartz): The Art of the Deal, 1987; author: (with Charles Leerhsen) Surviving at the Top, 1990; author: (with Kate Bohner) The Art of the Comeback, 1997; author: (with Dave Shiflett) The America We Deserve, 2000; author: (with Meredith McIver) How To Get Rich, 2004; exec. prodr.: (TV series) The Apprentice, 2004—; host (TV series) The Apprentice, 2004—. Com. mem., Celebration of Nations Commemorating 50th Anniversary UN and UNICEF; Co-chmn. N.Y. Vietnam Vets. Meml. Fund; founding mem. constrn. com. Cathedral of St. John the Divine; mem. N.Y. Citizens Tax Coun., Fifth Ave Assn., Realty Found. of N.Y., Met. Mus. of Art's Real Estate Coun.; mem. adv. bd. Lenox Hill Hosp., United Cerebral Palsy; spl. advisor to Pres.'s Coun. on Phys. Fitness and Sports; mem. N.Y. Sportsplex Commn.; chmn. N.Y. citizens com. 78th Ann. NAACP Conv., 1987; grand marshall Nation's Parade, 1995; bd. dirs. Police Athletic League; bd. overseers Wharton Sch.; founding mem. adv. bd. Wharton Real Estate Ctr.; bd. dirs. Fred C. Trump Found.; chmn. Donald J. Trump Found. Named Developer of Yr., Constrn. Mgmt. Assn. Am., 1999, Hotel and Real Estate Visionary of the Century, UTA Fedn., 2000; named to Wharton Hall of Fame, Benefactors bd. dirs., Hist. Soc. Palm Beach County, 2003; recipient Entrepreneur of Yr. award, Wharton Entrepreneurial Club, 1984, Ellis Island Medal of Honor, 1986. Achievements include rebuilding the Wollman Skating Rink in Central Park in three months.

TRUMP, MARTHA LINDLEY BLAINE BEARD, philanthropist; m. Robert Trump, 1984; 1 child, Christopher. Student, U. Tokyo. Clothing line creator Am. Classics by Blaine Trump, QVC, 1999. Fundraiser Am. Ballet Theatre, Meml. Sloan-Kettering Cancer Ctr.; vice-chair God's Love We Deliver. Named one of 50 Most Beautiful People World, People mag., 1998; recipient Marietta Tree award for pub. svc., Citizen's Com. for NYC, 1998. Achievements include all proceeds from clothing line Am. Classics by Blaine Trump go to God's Love We Deliver. Office: God's Love We Deliver 166 Ave of the Americas New York NY 10013

TRUMPBOUR, JOHN, historian, researcher, director; b. Greensboro, NC, Feb. 23, 1959; s. Robert and Virginia Trumpbour. BA, History, Stanford U., Palo Alto, Calif., 1977—82; PhD, History, Harvard U., Cambridge, Mass., 1982—96. Rsch. dir. Harvard Trade Union Program, 1999—, Labor & Worklife Program at Harvard Law Sch., 2002—. Cons. and rschr. African Am. Labor Leaders' Econ. Summit, Cambridge, Mass., 1997—; rschr. and fellowships com. Sci. & Engring. Workforce Project at Nat. Bur. of Econ. Rsch., Cambridge, Mass., 2001—; editl. bd. Labor History, London, 2004—. Author: (book) Selling Hollywood to the World: U.S. and European Struggles for Mastery of the Global Film Industry, 1920-1950, 2002 (Allan Nevins prize for Lit. Excellence.); editor: How Harvard Rules, 1989, The Dividing Rhine: Politics and Society in Contemporary France and Germany, 1989. Bd. of directors Boston Moblzn., 1999—2001; co-chair Samia Tenants Orgn., Boston, 1996—2000; fellowships com., Rhodes and Marshall scholarships Leverett Ho., Harvard U., 1987—. Recipient NAAA Found. prize for best essay on the U.S. and Mid. East, NAAA Found., 1987, James Birdsall Weter Award (for best thesis), Stanford U., Dept. of History, 1982; fellow Sawyer Fellow, Harvard U., Mellon Found., 1996-97, Belgian Am. Edn. Found. Fellow, Brussels, Belgium, Belgian Am. Edn. Found., 1989-1990; grantee Sloan Found. grant for rsch. on sci. workers in India, Sci. & Engring. Workforce Project at NBER, 2002. Mem.: Soc. for Historians of Am. Fgn. Rels. Home: 60 Woodstock Avenue #14 Brighton MA 02135 Office: Labor & Worklife Program Harvard Univ 1350 Massachusetts Avenue #731 Cambridge MA 02138 Personal E-mail: john_trumpbour@harvard.edu. E-mail: john_trumpbour@harvard.edu.

TRUMPENER, KATIE, literature educator; Student, U. Freiburgh, West Germany; BA with honors, U. Alberta, Can.; MA in Eng. and Am. Lit., Harvard U.; PhD in Comparative Lit., Stanford U., 1990. Assoc. prof. germanic studies U. Chgo., 1990—. Author: Bardic Nationalism: The Romantic Novel and the British Empire, 1997 (MLZ prize for a First Book, 1998, British Acad. Rose Mary Crawshay prize, 1998); co-editor: Modern Philology. Office: Univ Chgo Eng Dept Gates-Blake 324 1050 E 59th St Chicago IL 60637 E-mail: ktrumpen@midway.uchicago.edu.

TRUNDLE, W(INFIELD) SCOTT, publishing executive newspaper; b. Maryville, Tenn., Mar. 24, 1939; s. Winfield Scott and Alice (Smith) T.; m. Elizabeth Latshaw, Oct. 14, 1989; children: Stephen, Allison. BA, Vanderbilt U., 1961, JD, 1967. Bar: Tenn. 1967. Spl. agt. U.S. Secret Service, 1963-66; asso. to partner firm Hunter, Smith, Davis & Norris, Kingsport, Tenn., 1967-72; pub. Kingsport (Tenn.) Times-News, 1972-78; pres. Greensboro (N.C.) Daily News, 1978-80; exec. v.p. Jefferson Pilot Publs., Inc., Greensboro and Clearwater, Fla., 1980-82; v.p., bus. mgr. Tampa Tribune (Fla.), 1982-91; sr. v.p. Hillsborough C.C., 1991-93; publisher Ogden (Utah) Standard Examiner, 1993—. Assoc. prof. East Tenn. State U., 1973-77; bd. dirs. Ogden Indsl. Devel. Corp.; bd. dirs. Weber Econ. Devel. Corp.; treas., bd. dirs. Utah Def. Alliance; bd. dirs., vice chmn. Container Recycling Inst., Washington. Trustee Eccles Dinosaur Park and Mus. Found.; chmn. Weber County Legacy Trust. Mem. Tenn. Bar Assn., Weber Ogden C. of C. (bd. dirs.). Methodist. Home: 1580 Maule Dr Ogden UT 84403-0413 Office: Ogden Publ Corp PO Box 12790 Ogden UT 84412-2790 E-mail: strundle@aol.com.

TRUNZO, THOMAS HAROLD, JR., lawyer; b. McKeesport, Pa., Oct. 23, 1948; children: Melissa, Kirsten. BA, Tufts U., 1976; JD, Vt. Law Sch., 1980. Bar: N.H. 1980, Mass. 1981, Vt. 1988. Ptnr. Mullaly & Trunzo Law Offices, West Lebanon, N.H., 1980-87; pvt. practice Lebanon, N.H., 1987—. Active Sch. Bd. Orford (N.H.) Sch. Dist., 1980—87; mem. Orford Planning Bd., 1991—93; moderator Rivendell Sch. Dist., Orford, 1998—2002. Mem. Assn. Trial Lawyers Am., Nat. Lawyers Guild, N.H. Bar Assn. (Pro bono award 1987, 2003), Vt. Bar Assn., Grafton County Bar Assn. Democrat. Home: 797 NH Rte 10 Orford NH 03777 Office: PO Box 825 20 W Park St Ste 415 Lebanon NH 03766-0825 E-mail: ttrunzo@innevi.com.

TRUOG, WILLIAM EDWARD, III, pediatrician, educator, researcher; b. Kansas City, Mo., Feb. 5, 1947; s. William E. and Virginia (Sylvester) Truog; m. Jill D. Jacobson, July 11, 1992. BA cum laude, Carleton Coll., 1969; MD, U. Chgo., 1973. Intern, resident pediat., chief resident Children's Orthop. Hosp.-U. Wash., Seattle, 1973—76, rsch. fellow neonatology, 1976—78; asst. prof., assoc. prof., prof. pediat. U. Wash., Seattle, 1978—93; prof. pediat. Sch. Medicine U. Mo. Kansas City, 1993—. Med. dir. infant ICU Children's Orthop. Hosp., Seattle, 1982—91. Author: Critical Care of the Newborn, 1983, 1988; contbr. articles to profl. jours. Named First Physician Scientist, Children's Mercy Hosp., 1993; recipient Sosland Endowed Chair Neonatal Rsch., 2001; grantee, NIH, 1981, 1984, 1997, 2002. Mem.: Perinatal Rsch. Soc., We. Soc. Pediat. Rsch., Soc. Pediat. Rsch., Am. Pediat. Soc., Am. Thoracic Soc. (grantee 1978). Episcopalian. Office: Children's Mercy Hosp 2401 Gillham Rd Kansas City MO 64108-4619

TRUONG, D. HIEP, lawyer; b. Saigon, Vietnam, May 16, 1972; BBA, U. Calif., Berkeley; JD, Santa Clara U., 1999. Bar: Calif. Law clk. intern Office of US Atty., Ea. Dist., Sacramento, 1998, Office of US Atty., No. Dist., San Jose, Calif., 1999; cert. law clk. LA County Dist. Atty.'s Office, 1999—2000; assoc. Grancell, Lebovitz et al., San Jose, Calif., 2000—01, Manning & Marder et al. LLP, San Francisco, 2001—. Moot ct. judge Stanford (Calif.) U., 2002. Contbr. articles to profl. jours. Recipient Am. Jurisprudence Bancroft-Whitney award, 1999; scholar Chancellor's, Regents scholar, U. Calif.; B.T. Collins scholar. Mem.: ABA. Home: 2504 Stonebrook Dr Modesto CA 95355 Office: Manning & Marder et al LLP 625 Market St 4th Fl San Francisco CA 94105 Personal E-mail: hiep_9@yahoo.com. E-mail: dht@mmker.com.

TRUONG, LONG KHANH, software consultant; b. Nhatrang, South Vietnam, Mar. 1, 1952; s. Nhu Van Truong and Thanh Thi Do; m. Chau Duong Nguyen, Feb. 1, 1961; children: Vy Nguyen-Truong, Christopher, Anthony. BS in Mech. Engring., Pa. State U., 1981; MS in Computer Sci. and Applications, Va. Tech., 1999. Mem. tech. staff Electronic Assocs. Inc., Cherry Hill, N.J., 1981-84; sr. engr.tech. staff McDonnell Douglas, St. Louis, 1984-87; prin. engr. Hughes Aircraft, Herndon, Va., 1987-97; sr. mem. tech. staff MITRE Corp., Reston, Va., 1997-2000, SRA Internat., Inc., Fairfax, Va., 2001—. Lt. Artillery Sch., Duc My, South Vietnam, 1971-75. Office: SRA Internat Inc 4300 Fair Lakes Ct Fairfax VA 22033 Home: 13632 Wildflower Ln Clifton VA 20124-1043 E-mail: long_truong@sra.com.

TRURAN, JAMES WELLINGTON, JR., astrophysicist, educator; b. Brewster, N.Y., July 12, 1940; s. James Wellington and Suzanne (Foglesong) T.; m. Carol Kay Dell'Acy, June 26, 1965; children— Elaina Michelle, Diana Lee, Anastasia Elizabeth. BA in Physics, Cornell U., 1961; MS in Physics, Yale U., 1963, PhD in Physics, 1966. Postdoctoral rsch. assoc. NAS-NRC Goddard Inst. Space Studies, NASA, N.Y.C., 1965-67; asst. prof. physics Belfer Grad. Sch. Sci., Yeshiva U., 1967-70; rsch. fellow in physics Calif. Inst. Tech., 1968-69; assoc. prof. Belfer Grad. Sch. Sci., Yeshiva U., 1970-72, prof., 1972-73; prof. astronomy U. Ill., Urbana, 1973-91; sr. vis. fellow, Guggenheim Meml. Found. fellow Inst. Astronomy, U. Cambridge, Eng., 1979-80; trustee Aspen Ctr. Physics, 1979-85, 91-93, 96-99, v.p., 1985-88; assoc. U. Ill. Ctr. for Advanced Study, 1979-80, 86-87; prof. astronomy astrophysics U. Chgo., 1991—. Alexander von Humboldt-Stiftung sr. scientist Max-Plank Inst., Munich, Germany, 1986-87, 94; Beatrice Tinsley vis. prof. U. Tex.,

Austin, 1999. Contbr. articles to profl. jours.; co-editor: Nucleosynthesis, 1968, Nucleosynthesis— Challenges and New Developments, 1985, Nuclear Astrophysics, 1987, Type Ia Supernovae: Theory and Cosmology, 2000, Cosmic Chemical Evolution, 2002; editor: Physics Letters B, 1974-80. Co-recipient Yale Sci. and Engring. Assn. annual award for advancement basic or applied sci., 1980 Fellow AAAS, Am. Phys. Soc.; mem. Am. Astron. Soc., Am. Phys. Soc., Internat. Astron. Union. Home: 210 Wysteria Dr Olympia Fields IL 60461-1202 Office: U Chgo Dept Astronomy Astrophysics 5640 S Ellis Ave Chicago IL 60637-1433

TRURAN, WILLIAM RICHARD, electrical engineer; b. Franklin, NJ, Feb. 14, 1951; s. Wilfred Hardy and Stella Eva (Hall) Truran; m. Virginia Lynn Johnson, Aug. 18, 1979; children: Michael, Wendy. BSEE, U. Tenn., 1972; MBA, Fairleigh Dickinson U., 1981; MS in Indsl. Engring., Columbia U., 1994; PhD in Tech. Mgmt., Stevens Inst. Tech., 2000. Registered prof engr, NJ, NY, Pa, Calif, prof planner, NJ; cert. project mgmt. profl. Design engr. Gordos Corp., Bloomfield, N.J., 1972-73; project engr. Edwards Engring., Pompton Plains, N.J., 1973-78; sr. engr. Apollo Tech., Whippany, N.J., 1978-81; elec. product mgr. Dodge-Newark, Fairfield, N.J., 1981-96; pres Trupower Engring., Sparta, N.J., 1984—. Pres TEC Corp NJ, Sparta, 1988—; adj prof Stevens Inst Technology; adj. prof. Seton Hall U.; consult in field. Contbr. articles to profl jours. Active foster child orgn Christian Children's Fund; bd. mgrs. Columbia Engring. Sch. Alumni; v.p. bd. mgrs. Columbia Engring. Sch. Alumni Assn., v.p. student rels. Mem.: NSPE (legis action network, minuteman), Acad. of Mgmt., Nta. Assn. Environ. Profls., Sierra Club, Nature Conservancy. Episcopalian. Avocations: skiing, water-skiing, triathalons, marathons, antique Corvettes. Home and Office: 37 Rainbow Trl Sparta NJ 07871-1724 Office Phone: 973-729-1471. Business E-Mail: wrt1@columbia.edu.

TRUSCHKE, EDWARD F. retired medical association administrator; Formerly with Xerox Corp; past exec. dir. BankAm. Found.; past sr. v.p. social policy, chmn. social policy com., sec. pub. policy com. to bd. dirs., head social policy dept. BankAm. Corp.; pres. Alzheimer's Assn., Chgo., 1994—2001.

TRUSCOTT, CARL J. federal agency administrator; b. Augusta, Ga., 1957; BS in Criminal Justice, U. Del., 1979. U.S. Secret Svc. agent, 1981—2004; spl. agent in charge Presdl. Protective Divsn., 2001—03; asst. dir. U.S. Secret Svc. Office Protective Rsch., U.S. Dept. Homeland Security, 2003—04; dir. Bur. Alcohol, Tobacco, Firearms and Explosives, U.S. Dept. Justice, Washington, 2004—. Recipient Dirs. Life Saving award, 1986, Sr. Exec. Svc. Performance award, 2001, 2002, Spl. award for disting. svc. to the Exec. Office of the Pres., 2002, Presdl. Rank award as Meritorious Exec., 2003. Office: Bur Alcohol Tobacco Firearms and Explosives Office Pub and Govtl Affairs 650 Massachusetts Ave NW Rm 8290 Washington DC 20226

TRUSDELL, MARY LOUISE CANTRELL, retired state educational administrator; b. Chandler, Okla., Oct. 24, 1921; d. George Herbert and Lois Elizabeth (Bruce) Cantrell; m. Robert William Trusdell, Jan. 7, 1943; children— Timothy Lee, Laurence Michael. BA, Ga. So. Coll., 1965; MEd, U. Va., 1974. Dir. specific learning disabilities program Savannah Country Day Sch., Ga., 1960-65; learning disabilities tchr. Richmond pub. schs., Va., 1966-73; dir. New Community Sch., Richmond, 1974-75; dir. Fed. Learning Disabilities Project, Dept HEW, Mid. Peninsula, Va., 1975-76; supr. programs for learning disabled Va. Dept. Edn., Richmond, 1976-86; bd. dirs. Learning Disabilities Council, Richmond, Very Spl. Arts- Va., 1986-91; mem. adv. com. Learning Disabilities Research and Devel. Project, Woodrow Wilson Rehab. Ctr., Fisherville, Va., 1983. Co-editor: Understanding Learning Disabilities: A Parent Guide and Workbook, 1989, 3d edit., 2002. Bd. dirs. Savannah Assn. Retarded Children, 1957-60, Meml. Guidance Clinic, Richmond, 1966-69. Named Tchr. of Yr., Learning Disabilities Ctr., Richmond, 1972. Mem. Orton Dyslexia Soc. (pres. capital area br. 1968-70, nat. bd. dirs. 1970-72, Va. br. 1986-91), Alliance for the Mentally Ill. Cen. Va. (pres. 1991-93). Presbyterian. Avocations: travel, theater, reading.

TRUSH, MICHAEL A. medical educator; PhD, W.Va. U., 1978. Prof. toxicological scis. Johns Hopkins U., Balt., dep. dir. NIEHS. Office: Johns Hopkins U NIEHS 615 N Wolfe St Baltimore MD 21205-2103

TRUSKOWSKI, JOHN BUDD, lawyer; b. Chgo., Dec. 3, 1945; s. Casimer T. and Jewell S. (Kirk) T.; m. Karen Lee Sloss, Mar. 21, 1970; children: Philip K., Jennifer B. BS, U. Ill., 1967; JD, U. Chgo., 1970. Bar: Ill. 1970, U.S. Dist. Ct. (no. dist.) Ill. 1970, U.S. Tax Ct. 1977. Assoc. Keck, Mahin & Cate, Chgo., 1970-71, 74-78, ptnr., 1978-97, Lord, Bissell & Brook, Chgo., 1997—. Author, editor Callaghan's Federal Tax Guide, 1987. Lt., USNR, 1971-74. Mem. ABA, Ill. State Bar Assn., Chgo. Bar Assn. Republican. Unitarian. Avocations: model railroading, stamp collecting/philately. Home: 251 Kimberly Ln Lake Forest IL 60045-3862 Office: Lord Bissell & Brook Harris Bank Bldg 115 S Lasalle St Chicago IL 60603-3801 Office Phone: 312-443-0257.

TRUSLOW, DONALD, bank executive; b. Summit, N.J., May 13, 1958; BA in Commerce, U. Va. Joined Wachovia Corp., 1980, treas., comptr., mgr. middle market corp. banking group, chief credit officer S.C. bank, head loan adminstrn. Piedmont Triad Region, loan adminstrn. mgr. internat. group, loan adminstrn. officer, internat. baking and gen. loan adminstr., sr. exec. v.p. chief risk officer, 2001—. Bd. dirs. Risk Mgmt. Assn., Arts and Sci. Coun., Charlotte; bd. visitors Babcock Grad. Sch. Mgmt., Wake Forest U. Mem.: Fin. Svcs. Roundtable. Office: Wachovia Corp Ste 400 301 S College St Charlotte NC 28288

TRUSSELL, CHARLES TAIT, columnist; b. Balt., May 9, 1925; s. Charles Prescott and Beatrice (Tait) T.; m. Woodley Grizzard, Dec. 27, 1953 (div. 1990); children: Galen Tait, Thomas Marshall; m. Nancy Rathbun Billington, Dec. 19, 1990. BA in Journalism, Washington and Lee U., 1949. Reporter St. Petersburg (Fla.) Times, also; writer Congl. Quar. News Features, 1951-54; reporter Wall St. Jour., 1954-56, Washington Evening Star, 1956; asso. editor Nation's Business mag., 1956-64, mng. editor, 1964-69; sr. editor Congressional Quar., Inc., 1969-70; dir. pub. relations and advt. Investment Co. Inst., Washington, 1970-72; free-lance writer, real estate investor, 1972-74; v.p. Am. Forest Inst., Washington, 1974-79, sr. v.p., 1980-81; v.p. Am. Enterprise Inst., 1981-86; dir. comms. Constitution Bicentennial Commn., 1986-88; freelance writer, columnist, 1988—. Nat. corr. Clear Mountain Comms. Producer: documentary record album The Best of Washington Humor, 1963; author: Beating the Competition, 1992; editor: Successful Management, 1964, (with Paul Hencke) Dear NASA Please Send Me a Rocket, 1964, Timeless Truths for Kids, 2002. Served with USNR, 1944-46. Recipient Loeb Spl. Achievement award for mags. U. Conn., 1961, Benjamin Fine Journalism award, 1992. Mem. Washington Assembly (exec. com. 1961-65, chmn. 1965), Rotary Internat. Beta Theta Pi. Home: 2467 Cherry Rd Manistee MI 49660-

TRUSSELL, JAMES, economist, educator, dean; b. Columbus, Ga., Oct. 17, 1949; BS summa cum laude in Maths., Davidson Coll., 1971; BPhil, Oxford U., 1973; PhD in Econs., Princeton U., 1975. From asst. prof. econs. to prof., dean Princeton (N.J.) U., 1975—. Co-author: The Loving Book, 1972, Contraceptive Technology, 1998, 2d edit., 2004; contbr. articles to profl. jours. Mem. Am. Statis. Assn., Am. Pub. Health Assn., Population Assn. Am., Australia Population Assn., Phi Beta Kappa., Assn. Reproductive Health Profls., Internat. Union for the Scientific Study of Population. Office: Princeton U Office of Population Rsch Wallace Hall Princeton NJ 08544-2007 E-mail: trussell@princeton.edu.

TRUSTY, SHARON, state legislator; b. Oregonia, Ohio, Aug. 27, 1945; children: Katherine Doberstein, Jonna Patterson, Jessica Zachary. Mem. Ark. State Senate, 2001—. Bd. dirs. Simmons First Bank. Co-chair Ark. Rep. Party, 1984-86; bd. mem. Ark. Dept. Workforce Edn., 1997-98; staff mem., legis. liason Gov. Mike Huckabel, 1999; commr. Ark. Dept. Econ. Devel.; chair bd. dirs. St. Mary's Regional Med. Ctr. Republican. Baptist. Office: 8 Pine Forest Russellville AR 72801 also: State Capitol Rm 320 Little Rock AR 72201 E-mail: trustys@arkleg.state.ar.us.

TRUTTER, JOHN THOMAS, consulting company executive; b. Springfield, Ill., Apr. 18, 1920; s. Frank Louis and Frances (Mischler) T.; m. Edith English Woods II, June 17, 1950 (dec.); children: Edith English II, Jonathan Woods. BA, U. Ill., 1942; postgrad., Northwestern U., 1947-50, U. Chgo., 1947-50; LHD (hon.), Lincoln Coll., 1986. Various positions Ill. Bell, Chgo., 1946-58, gen. traffic mgr., from asst. v.p. pub. rels. to gen. mgr., 1958-69, v.p. pub. rels., 1969-71, v.p. operator svcs., 1971-80, v.p. community affairs, 1980-85; mem. hdqs. staff AT&T, N.Y.C., 1955-57; pres. John T. Trutter Co., Inc., Chgo., 1985—; pres., CEO Chgo. Conv. and Visitors Bur., 1985-88; pres. Chgo. Tourism Coun., 1988-90; v.p. Profl. Impressions Media Group, Inc., 1998-2000, prof. emeritus, 2001. Mem. adv. bd. The Alford Group, Chgo., 1984—, Bozell-Worldwide, Chgo., 1994-96; chancellor Lincoln Acad. of Ill., 1985-2001. Co-author: Handling Barriers in Communication, 1957, The Governor Takes a Bride, 1977 Past chmn., life trustee Jane Addams Hull House Assn.; chmn. United Cerebral Palsy Assn. Greater Chgo., 1967-95, hon. chmn., 1995—, chmn. Canal Corridor Assn., 1991-99; bd. dirs. Chgo. Crime Commn., Abraham Lincoln Assn., Lyric Opera Chgo.; v.p. English Speaking Union, 1989-91, bd. govs., 1980—; chmn. bd. City Colls. Chgo. Found., 1987-91; past chmn. Children's Home and Aid Soc. Ill.; v.p. City Club Chgo.; treas. Chgo. United, 1970-85; mem. Ill. Econ. Devel. Commn., 1985; past presiding co-chmn. NCCJ; numerous others; bd. govs. Northwestern U. Libr. Coun., 1984—; trustee Lincoln (Ill.) Coll., 1987-90, Mundelein Coll., 1988-91; mem. sch. problems coun. State Ill. Assembly, 1985-91, spl. commn. on adminstrn. of justice in Cook County, 1986-92; founding chmn. adv. coun. Evanston Hist. Soc., 1995-98. Lt. col. U.S. Army, 1945. Decorated Legion of Merit; recipient Laureate award State of Ill., 1980, Outstanding Exec. Leader award Am. Soc. Fundraisers, Humanitarian of Yr. award, Jane Addams award The Hull House Assn., 1991, Nat. Infinitec award for individual leadership in assistive technology for disabled people, 1997, Jack Brickhouse award for outstanding svcs., 2000. Mem. Pub. Rels. Soc. Am., Sangamon County Hist. Soc. (founder, past pres.), Ill. State Hist. Soc. (pres. 1985-87), Coun. on Ill. History (chmn. 1991—), U. Ill. Alumni Assn. (bd. dirs. 1990-94), Tavern Club, Econ. Club, Mid-Am. Club, Alpha Sigma Phi (Nat. Merit Achievement award 1994), Phi Delta Phi. Fax: 847-441-0582.

TRYBAN, ESTHER ELIZABETH, lawyer; b. Chgo., Aug. 14, 1958; d. Chester Joseph and Lottie Elizabeth (Napora) Tryban. AAS with honors, Elgin (Ill.) C.C., 1977, AS with honors, 1982; BS with honors, Roosevelt U., Chgo., 1986; JD, U. Chgo., 1989. Bar: Ill. 1989, U.S. Dist. Ct. (no. dist.) Ill. 1989, U.S. Ct. Appeals (7th cir.) 1990, U.S. Supreme Ct., 1996. Supr. adminstrv. svcs. law dept. Motorola, Inc., Schaumburg, Ill., 1977-86; staff law clk. U.S. Bankruptcy Ct., No. Dist. Ill., Chgo., 1989-90; sr. counsel City of Chgo., 1990—. Mem. ABA, Nat. Lawyers Guild, Assn. Former Bankruptcy Law Clks, Ill. State Bar Assn., Chgo. Bar Assn. (chair govt. svc. com. 1996-97), Advocates Soc. (historian Chgo. chpt. 2004—). Roman Catholic. Avocations: reading, football, travel. Office: City Dept Law 30 N Lasalle St Ste 900 Chicago IL 60602-2503 E-mail: lw00026@cityofchicago.org.

TRYBUL, THEODORE NICHOLAS, engineering educator; b. Chgo., Apr. 12, 1935; s. Theodore and Sophie Trybul; children: Adrienne, Barbie, Cathy, Diane, Elizabeth, Teddy. BS summa cum laude, U. Ill., 1957; MS summa cum laude, U. N.Mex., 1963; DSc summa cum laude, George Washington U., 1976. Registered profl. engr., D.C. Dir. Sr. Exec. Svc., ES-IV Fed. Govt., Washington, 1966-83; prof. George Washington U., Washington, 1983-94, Tex. Grad. Sch., Corpus Christi, Tex., 1994—98; prof., dir. Grad. Sch. Bus. and Tech. Nat. U., Sacramento, 1998—. Cons. NSF, Advanced Rsch. Projects Agy., U.S. Dept. Edn., NIH, Advanced Material Concepts Agy., Surgeon Gen.'s Office, Natl. Acad. Scis., IBM, Intel, Microsoft, GTSI; adv. bd. NSF, NIH, Natl. Acad. Engring., Surgeon Gen.'s Office. Contbr. articles to profl. jours. Col. U.S. Army, 1957. Fellow ASME, Soc. for Computer Simulation, Health Care Execs.; mem. AAUP, Am. Mgmt. Assn., Audubon Soc., Sierra Club, Sir Isaac Walton Soc., Pi Tau Sigma, Phi Beta Kappa, Kappa Mu Epsilon, Sigma Xi. Avocations: golf, tennis, fishing, mountain climbing. Office: Auburn Lake Trails CC 2418 Westville Cool CA 95614 Office Phone: 530-887-9551. Personal E-mail: coolted@infostations.com. Business E-Mail: ttrybul@hotmail.com.

TRYGGVASON, BJARNI V. astronaut; b. Reykjavik, Iceland, Sept. 21, 1945; 2 children. BSc in Engring. Physics, U. Brit. Columbia, 1972; student in Engring., U. We. Ontario. Meteorologist Atmospheric Environ. Svc., Toronto, Canada, 1972—73; rsch. assoc. U. We. Ont., Canada, 1974—78, lectr. applied math., 1979—82; with Nat. Rsch. Coun., Ottawa, Canada, 1982—83; astronaut NASA, Houston, 1983—. Guest rsch. assoc. Kyoto U., Japan, 1978, James Cook U., Townsville, Australia, 1978; lectr. U. Ottawa, Canada, 1982—92, Carleton U., 1982—92; rep. NASA microgravity measurement working group Can. Space Agy.; astronaut space shuttle STS-85, 1997. Mem.: Can. Aeronautics & Space Inst. Avocations: scuba diving, skiing, parachuting. Office: Astronaut Office CB NASA Johnson Space Center Houston TX 77058

TRYGSTAD, LAWRENCE BENSON, lawyer; b. Holton, Mich., Mar. 22, 1937; BA, U. Mich., 1959; JD, U. So. Calif., 1967. Bar: Calif. 1968, U.S. Supreme Ct. 1974. Legal counsel Calif. Tchrs. Assn., United Tchrs. L.A., L.A., 1968-71; ptnr. Trygstad & Odell, L.A., 1971-80; pres. Trygstad Law Corp., L.A., 1980—. Instr., tchr. negotiation U. Calif.-Northridge; panelist TV shows Law and the Teacher. Bd. dirs. George Washington Carver Found., L.A. Mem. ABA, Calif. Bar Assn., L.A. County Bar Assn., Calif. Trial Lawyers Assn., L.A. Trial Lawyers Assn., Nat. Orgn. Lawyers for Edn. Assns., Am. Trial Lawyers Assn., Phi Alpha Delta. Home: 4209 Aleman Dr Tarzana CA 91356-5405 Office: 1880 Century Park E Ste 404 Los Angeles CA 90067-1609 Office Phone: 310-552-0500.

TRYLOFF, ROBIN S. food products executive; BS, U. Mich.; MS, U. Chgo. Exec. dir., cmty. rels. Sara Lee Corp.; exec. dir. Sara Lee Found., pres., 2002—. Chair, bd. dirs. Donors Forum of Chgo., 2004. Office: Sara Lee Found 3 First Nat Plz Chicago IL 60602-4260

TRYTEK, DAVID DOUGLAS, insurance company executive; b. Cleve., Jan. 18, 1955; s. Edmund Trytek and Mary Elaine Salzwedel Blech; m. Lorie Ann Stone, Apr. 10, 1982; children: Dane, Douglas. BS in BA, Bowling Green (Ohio) State U., 1977. Claims adjuster Liberty Mus. Ins. Co., Toledo, 1977-80, claims supr. Milw., 1980-85, spl. claims examiner Boston, 1986-89, claims mgr. Green Bay, Wis., 1989-93; tech. svcs. mgr. Liberty Mut. Ins. Co., Milw., 1993-95; regional field investigations mgr. Liberty Mutual Ins. Co., Milw., 1996—, Wausau Ins. Co., Milw., 2001—. Arbitrator Inter-Co. Arbitration Com., Milw., 1984-85. Coach Toledo Optimists Youth Hockey Assn., 1979-80, Wauwatosa (Wis.) Recreation Dept., 1980-85, YMCA Youth Baseball, 1994; alt. Worker's Compensation divsn. Ins. Adv. Com., Madison, Wis., 1994 youth football coach, Sussex, Wis., 1994-99, youth baseball coach, 1994-99, 2002-2003; bd. dirs. Wis. Street Rod Assn. Mem. Exptl. Aircraft Assn., Warbirds of Am., USA Hockey Inc., Internat. Assn. of Spl. Investigation Units, Wis. Street Rod Assn. (bd. dirs. 1999-2002). Avocations: camping, ice hockey, golf, military aircraft. Office: Liberty Mut Ins Co 11800 W Park Pl Milwaukee WI 53224-3009 Office Phone: 414-577-9605.

TRYTHALL, HARRY GILBERT, music educator, composer; b. Knoxville, Tenn., Oct. 28, 1930; s. Harry Gilbert and Clara Hannah (Akre) T.; m. Jean Marie Slater, Dec. 28, 1951 (div. 1976); children: Linda Marie, Karen Elizabeth; m. Carol King, Sept. 19, 1985. BA, U. Tenn., 1951; MusM, Northwestern U., 1952; DMA, Cornell U., 1960. Asst. prof. music Knox Coll., Galesburg, Ill., 1960-64; prof. music theory and composition George Peabody Coll. Tchrs., Nashville, 1964-75; dean Creative Arts Ctr., 1975-81; prof. music W.Va. U., Morgantown, 1975-96; ret., 1997; pres. Luxikon Music, Pandora-Synthe Records, Westover, W.Va., 1983—. Vis. prof. U. Federal do Espiritu Santo, Vitoria, Brazil, 1999—. Author: Principles and Practice of Electronic Music, 1974, Eighteenth Century Counterpoint, 1993, Sixteenth Century Counterpoint, 1994; past mem. editorial bd. Music Educators Jour.; composer orchestral music, chamber and electronic music. With USAF, 1953-57. Office Phone: 972-407-1081. Personal E-mail: htrythal@yahoo.com.

TRZASKA, JOYCE ANNE, publishing executive; b. Great Falls, Mont., Jan. 4, 1950; d. Wendell Babe and Valerie Hurst; m. Gregory Warren Trzaska, June 27, 1970; children: James Warren, Gena Anne McKinnon, Lori Lynn. Student, Taft Coll., 1968—69. Pub. A Snow Man with Feelings, The Giraffe That Wore A Necklace, Mister Giraffe: Bow Tie & Long Gold Chain!. Mem.: Bakersfield Obedience Tng. Club (assoc.). Republican. Lutheran. Home: 45 Jackson Ln Port Ludlow WA 98365 Personal E-mail: gtrz100160@aol.com.

TRZASKO, JOSEPH ANTHONY, psychologist, educator; b. Jamaica, N.Y., June 4, 1946; s. Joseph Anthony and Lottie Marion (Nadraus) T.; m. Ann Elizabeth Kidd, June 26, 1971; 1 son, Joshua Damon. *Dr. Joseph Trzasko was greatly influenced by the work and education ethic of his parents and grandparents, who were born and immigrated from Poland early 1900's. Maternal Grandparents: Anna Grzmala and Andrew Nadraus. Paternal Grandparents: Mary Laskowska and Anthony Trzasko. Parents, Lottie M. and Joseph A., are retired professional photographers. Dr. Trzasko met and married Ann E. Kidd, while completing his doctoral studies at the University of Vermont. The Kidd family is a well known ski family and reportedly related to Capt. Kidd. Ann and Joseph Trzasko have one son, Joshua D., who graduated cum laude from Cornell University's College of Engineering and presently is majoring in Bio-Medical Engineering at the Mayo Clinic's College of Medicine.* BA cum laude, U. N.H., 1967; MA, U. Vt., 1969, PhD, 1972. Cert. behavioral therapy, 1976, psychologist 1977; diplomate Am. Bd. Psychol. Specialties, 1997, Am. Bd. Forensic Examiners, 1998; cert. profl. qualification in psychology Assn. State and Provincial Psychology Bds. Prof. dep. psychology Mercy Coll., Dobbs Ferry, N.Y., 1969—; postdoctoral internship Ridge State Home and Tng. Sch., Colo. Dept. Insts., 1980; staff psychologist St. Dominic's Intermediate Care Facility for Devel. Disabled, Blauvelt, N.Y., 1980—; cons. psychologist Jewish Guild for Blind, N.Y.C., 1983—2002, Orange County A.H.R.C., Newburgh, N.Y., 1985—; pvt. practice clin. psychology. Chair ednl. psychology test devel. Ednl. Testing Svc., 2000—; neuro-forensic psychologist Supervised Life Styles Behavioral Health Clinic, 2002—. *Following a PhD (Psychology) from the University of Vermont, Dr. Joseph Trzasko has been employed for the past 35 years at Mercy College as Full-Professor, and for the past 24 years at St. Dominic's ICF as psychologist. Dr. Trzasko continues to serve as Consulting Psychologist for the St. Dominic's ICF and for the OC AHRC (15+ years), special education population. In addition to being a NYS Licensed Psychologist, Dr. Trzasko is Board Certified and has received a Certificate of Professional Qualification in Psychology. Dr. Trzasko currently has a private practice with a specialization in Psychological Evaluation.* Contbg. author: Working with Visually Impaired Young Children: A Curriculum Guide for Birth -3 Year Olds, 1992; contbg. author: Working with Visually Impaired Young Students: A Curriculum Guide for 3 to 5 Year Olds, 1998. NDEA fellow U. Vt., 1967-69; NSF faculty rsch. participation grantee Ednl. Commn. States/Nat. Assessment Ednl. Progress, 1976. Mem. AAUP, Am. Psychol. Assn., Am. Coll. Forensic Examiners. Roman Catholic. Home and Office: 30 Lake Dr Somers NY 10589-2420 Office Phone: 914-277-5907. Personal E-mail: jatphd@hotmail.com. Business E-Mail: jtrzasko@mercy.edu.

TRZYNA, CHRIS, physical education educator; b. Chgo. d. Edward and Helen Trzyna. BS, No. Ill. U., 1976, MS, 1983, C.A.S. in Adminstrn. and Supervision, 1991. Cert. tchr. Ill. Tchr., asst. athletic dir. Libertyville HS, 1976—; girls volleyball coach Libertyville HS, 1987—. Recipient Volleyball Coach of the Yr., Libertyville HS, 2000. Mem.: AAHPERD, Ill. Athletic Dirs. Assn., Ill. High Sch. Assn. (soccer adv. com.), Ill. Assn. Health, Phys. Edn. Recreation and Dance, Delta Psi Kappa (v.p. 1975—76). Office: Libertyville High School 708 W Park Ave Libertyville IL 60048-2604 Business E-Mail: chris.trzyna@district128.org.

TSAI, CHIH-LING, management educator; b. Taipei, Republic of China, Jan. 7, 1952; came to U.S., 1976; s. Liang-Chih and Chen-Ling (Lu) T.; m. Ching-Ju Liao, July 23, 1970; children: Wen-Lin, Wen-Ting. BS, Tamkang Univ., Taipei, 1974; MS, Univ. Ill., 1978; PhD, Univ. Minn., 1983. Asst. prof. bus. NYU, N.Y.C., 1983-85; lectr. Univ. Tex., Austin, 1985-86; from assoc. prof. to prof. mgmt. Univ. Calif., Davis, 1988-93, prof. mgmt., 1993—. Contbr. articles to profl. jours. Office: Grad Sch Mgmt Univ Calif Davis Davis CA 95616-8609

TSAI, CHRISTINA W. civil engineer, educator; arrived in U.S., 1995; d. Jin-Yi Tsai and Jau-Jr Chen; m. Shih-Ping Ho, Jan. 4, 2001. BS in Civil Engring., Nat. Taiwan U., Taipei, 1995; MS in Civil Engring., U. Ill., Urbana, 1997, MS in Applied Math., 2000, PhD in Civil Engring., 2001. Rsch. scientist Ill. State Water Survey, Champaign, Ill., 2000—01; asst. prof. SUNY, Buffalo, 2001—. Contbr. articles to profl. jours. Recipient Stout Water Resources Rsch. award, U. of Ill. at Champaign-Urbana, 2000; grantee, SUNY at Buffalo Interdisciplinary Rsch. and Creative Activities Fund, 2002, Environ. Sci. Inst. SUNY at Buffalo, 2003. Mem.: ASCE (assoc. ExCEED tchg. fellow 2003), Am. Soc. of Engring. Edn., Internat. Assn. of Hydraulic Rsch., Internat. Water Resources Assn., Am. Geophys. Union, Am. Soc. of Women Engineers, Phi Kappa Phi. Avocations: reading, travel. Office: SUNY at Buffalo 233 Jarvis Hall Buffalo NY 14260 Office Phone: 716-645-2114 2414. E-mail: ctsai4@eng.buffalo.edu.

TSAI, CYNTHIA EKBERG, entertainment executive; b. Coronado, Calif., Jan. 22, 1956; d. Gerald Von Ekberg and Kathleen (Horrell) Culver; m. Gerald Tsai, Oct. 31, 1987 (div. 1995). Student, U. Miami, 1974—75; BA in Psychology, U. Mo., 1978. V.p. Merrill Lynch, San Diego, 1979-82, Kidder Peabody, San Diego, 1982-85; pres. Nugene Tech., NYC, 1996-97, Health-Expo, NYC, 1995—. Dir. Micro Islet, 2004—; gen. ptnr. MassTech Ventures, 1993—. Chmn. Am. Friends London Symphony Orch., Am. London Symphony Orch. Found. Fellow Fgn. Policy Assn.; mem. World Econ. Forum, 1992-98, NY Econ. Club. Democrat. Roman Catholic. Avocations: walking, travel. Home: 800 5th Ave New York NY 10021-7216 Office: HealthExpo 18 E 41st St New York NY 10017-6222 Office Phone: 212-689-8787.

TSAI, JAMES C. ophthalmologist, researcher; BA in Neurosci., Amherst Coll., 1985; MD, Stanford U., 1989; MBA, Vanderbilt U., 1998. Diplomate Am. Bd. Ophthalmology, Nat. Bd. Med. Examiners. Intern Cedars-Sinai Med. Ctr., LA, 1989—90; resident in ophthalmology U. So. Calif./Doheny Eye Inst., LA, 1990—93; fellow Bascom Palmer Eye Inst., Miami, Fla., 1993—94, Moorfields Eye Hosp., London, 1994—95; asst. prof. ophthalmology and visual scis. Vanderbilt U. Sch. Medicine, Nashville, 1995—2001; dir. glaucoma divsn., assoc. prof. ophthalmology Harkness Eye Inst., Columbia U. Coll. Physicians and Surgeons, N.Y.C., 2001—. Homer McK. Rees Glaucoma scholar, Columbia U., 2001—04. Fellow: ACS, Am. Acad. Ophthalmology (Achievement award). Office: Harkness Eye Inst Columbia Univ 635 West 165th St New York NY 10032

TSAI, JINGPHA (JEFFREY TSAI), computer scientist, educator; b. Cha-I, Taiwan; m. Fuh-Te Tsai; children: Edward, Christina. MS, Northwestern U., 1983, PhD, 1985. Prof. U. Ill., 1997—. Author 5 books; co-editor-in-chief: Artificial Intelligence Tools, 1994; contbr. more than 160 articles to profl. jours. Recipient Univ. scholar award U. Ill., Tech. Achievement award IEEE Computer Soc. Fellow IEEE, AAAS, Soc. for Design and Process Sci. Office: MCI 154 EECS Dept 851 S Morgan St Chicago IL 60607-7042

TSAI, TOM CHUNGHU, chemical engineer; b. Kaohsiung, Taiwan, Oct. 24, 1948; arrived in U.S., 1971, naturalized, 1984; s. Shu and Kwei (Kao) T.; m. Joyce Chionhwa Pai, Dec. 17, 1974; children: Wayne, Jimmy Payne. BS in Chem. Engring., Nat. Taiwan U., Taipei, 1970; MS in Chem. Engring., Purdue U., 1973, PhD in Chem. Engring., 1975. Registered profl. engr., Tex. Sr. process engr. CE-Lummus Co., Bloomfield, N.J., 1975-80; sr. engr. Bechtel Petroleum Inc., Houston, 1980-83; cons. engr. TDS Assocs., Houston, 1983-88; process engring. assoc. Dow Chem. Co., Freeport, Tex., 1988—. Mem. internat. adv. bd. Ency. Chem. Processing and Design, 1995—. Co-author, contbr.: Ethylene-Keystone to the Petrochemical Industry, 1980, Kirk-Othmer Encyclopedia of Chemical Technology, 1980, Pyrolysis: Theory and Industrial Practice, 1983, Refining & Petrochemical Tech. Yearbook, 1987, Encyclopedia of Chemical Processing and Design, 1990, 94, 95, 96, Unit Operations

Handbook, 1992; contbr. articles to profl. jours. Bd. dirs. H.S. for Performing and Visual Arts PTO, Houston, 1993-95. 2d lt. Republic of China Army, 1970-71. Mem.: AIChE, Assn. Chinese Orgns. (Houston) (pres. 2003), Assn. Chinese Am. Profls. (divsn. chmn. 1988—89, v.p. 2000—01, pres.-elect 2001—02, pres. 2002—03). Achievements include patents in field. Home: 1503 Ashford Hollow Ln Houston TX 77077-3903 Office: The Dow Chem Co 400 W Sam Houston Pkwy S Houston TX 77042-1299 Office Phone: 713-978-2324. E-mail: tomctsai@dow.com.

TSAI, WEN-YING, sculptor, painter, engineer; b. Xiamen, Fujian, China, Oct. 13, 1928; came to U.S., 1950, naturalized, 1962; s. Chen-Dak and Ching-Miau (Chen) T.; m. Pei-De Chang, Aug. 7, 1968; children: Lun-Yi and Ming Yi (twins). Student, Ta Tung U., 1947-49; BSME, U. Mich., 1953; postgrad., Art Students League N.Y., 1953-57, Faculty Polit. and Social Sci., New Sch., 1956-58. Cons. engr., 1953-63; project mgr. Cosentini Assocs., 1962-63; project engr. Guy B. Panero, Engrs., 1956-60. Creator cybernetic sculpture based on prin. harmonic motion, stroboscopic effects; one-man shows include, Ruth Sherman Gallery, N.Y.C., 1961, Amel Gallery, N.Y.C., 1964, 65, Howard Wise Gallery, N.Y.C., 1968, Kaiser Wilhelm Mus. Haus Lange, Krefeld, Germany, 1970, Hayden Gallery of MIT, Cambridge, Ont. Sci. Centre, Toronto, Can., 1971, Corcoran Gallery Art, 1972, Denise René Gallery, 1972, 73, Musée d'Art Contemporain, Montreal, 1973, Museo de Arte Contemporáneo, Caracas, 1975, Wildenstein Art Center, Houston, 1978, Museo de Bellas Artes, Caracas, 1978, Hong Kong Mus. Art, 1979, Isetan Mus. Art, Tokyo, 1980, Galerie Denise René, Paris, 1983, Nat. Mus. History, Taipei, Taiwan, 1989, Taiwan Mus. of Art, Taichung, 1990, China Nat. Mus. Fine Arts, Beijing, 1997, Centre Georges Pompidou, 2001; one man show: Galerie Denise René, Paris, 2000, Shanghai Art Mus., 2002; represented maj. internat. exhbns., also numerous group exhbns., in permanent collections, Centre Georges Pompidou, Paris; Tate Gallery, London, Albright-Knox Gallery, Buffalo Mus., Addison Gallery Am. Art, Andover, Mass., Museo de Arte Contemporáneo, Caracas, Museo de Bellas Artes, Caracas, Whitney Mus., Chrysler Art Mus., Orlando Sci. Ctr., MIT, Hayden Gallery, Kaiser Wilhelm Mus., Mus. Modern Art, Israel Mus., Jerusalem, Artware, Kunst und Elektronik, Honnover-Messe, Great Exploration-The Hands on Mus., Taiwan Mus. Art, Saibu Gas Mus., Nagoya City Mus., Mus. fü Holographie, Kanagawa Sci. Pk., Hong Kong Sci. Mus., others; commd. works include: fountain at Land Mark, Hong Kong, 1980,, water sculpture at Shell Tower, Singapore, 1982, cybernetic upward falling fountains (2), Paris; creator spatial dynamic hydro-cybernetic systems for 42d Internat. Exhbn. Art-La Biennale di Venezia, 1986, Digital Visions-Computers and Art, Everson Mus. of Art, 1987, Contemporary Arts Ctr. Cin., 1987, IBM Gallery of Sci. and Art, N.Y.C., 1988, Phenomena Art Expo, Fukuoka, Japan, 1989, Wonderland of Sci.-Art Kanagawa Internat. Art Sci. Exhbn., Kawasaki, Japan, 1989, Vienna Messe-Wiener Festwochen, 1989, Kanagawa Internat. Art & Sci. Exhbn., Kawasaki, Japan, 1989, Artec 91, Internat. Biennale in Nagoya, Japan, 1991 (Artec Grand Prix winner), Homage à Denise Reñe-Cybernetic Arts, Musée Nat. d'art Modern Ctr. Georges Pompidon, 2001, Shanghai Internat. Biennale for Contemporary Arts, Shanghai Art Mus., 2004; developed concept "5 elements," proposal for new modern sculpture park for Oriental Plz., Beijing, 1996-98; creator first CD-ROM version of cybernetic sculpture, 1995, Info-Art Kwang Ju Internat. Biennale Korea, Osaka Triennale, 1995—, Internet Graphics Gallery, 1995; featured: Art for Tomorrow-The 21st Century, CBS-TV, 1969, Video Variation, WGBH-TV, 1971, Science and Art, Japan TV Man Union, 1982, Art and Sci.-Innovation, Sta. WNET-TV, 1988, The World of Wen-Ying Tsai, Taiwan Pub. TV, 1991. Recipient Soc. Merit award U. Mich., 2001; John Hay Whitney fellow, 1963, MacDowell fellow, 1965, fellow Center Advanced Visual Studies, MIT, 1969, 70. Inventor upward falling fountain, computer mural, multiple light computer array, utilizing environ. feedback control system.

TSALIKIAN, EVA, physician, educator; b. Piraeus, Greece, June 22, 1949; came to U.S., 1974; d. Vartan and Arousiak (Kasparian) T.; m. Arthur Bonfield, Apr. 8, 2000. MD, U. Athens, 1973. Rsch. fellow U. Calif., San Francisco, 1974-76; resident in pediats. Children's Hosp., Pitts., 1976-78, fellow in endocrinology, 1978-80; rsch. fellow Mayo Clinic, Rochester, Minn., 1980-83; asst. prof. pediats. U. Iowa, 1983-87, assoc. prof. pediats., 1987—2004, prof. pediats., 2004—, dir. pediat. endocrinology, 1988—, interim head pediats., 2004. Fellow Juvenile Diabetes Found., 1978-80, Heinz Nutrition Found., 1980-81; recipient Young Physician award AMA, 1977. Mem. Am. Diabetes Assn. (mem. bd. mid Am. sect.), Endocrine Soc., Soc. Pediat. Rsch., Lawson Wilkins Soc. for Pediat. Endocrinology, Internat. Soc. Pediat. and Adolescent Diabetes. Home: 206 Mahaska Dr Iowa City IA 52246-1606 Office: U Iowa Dept Pediatrics 2856 JPP Iowa City IA 52242

TSANG, DAVID D. computer company executive; Chmn., CEO, pres. Oak Tech, Sunnyvale, Calif., also bd. dirs. Office: Oak Tech 1390 Kifer Rd Sunnyvale CA 94086-5305

TSANG, RAYMOND, electronics executive; Mng. dir. and strategic bus. dir. for China Nat. Semiconductor Asia, 1987—94; mng. dir. Sunrise Tech. Ltd., 1995—97; v.p. gen. mgr. Pericom Tech., Inc., 1998—2000; CEO Sunrise Tech., Ltd., 2000—01; v.p. and regional dir. Avnet Elec. Mktg. Hong Kong and China Ops., Avent, Inc., 2001—02; v.p. Avnet, Inc., 2002—; pres. Avnet Elec. Mktg. Asia, Avent, Inc., 2002—. Office: Avnet Inc 2211 S 47th St Phoenix AZ 85034

TSAO, GUS, information technology executive; b. Chongqing, China; arrived in U.S., 1968, naturalized, 1989; Mem. staff City of Columbus; head R&D Dept. DennisonTRG Sys.; founder Daybreak Technologies Inc., Evermore Software, Monterey Pk., Calif., 1999—, pres., 1999—, CEO, 1999—. Office: Evermore Software 1101 Northridge Place Monterey Park CA 91754*

TSAO, JENNIE CHING-I, research scientist, educator; d. Jean Huang and James Chih-Ming Tsao; m. Aram Dobalian, June 2, 2002. BA, UCLA, 1981, PhD, 1999; BS, City U., London, Eng., 1994. Cert. clin. psychology Fla. Rsch. asst. City U., London, 1994—94; grad. therapist UCLA Psychology Clinic, 1995—96; project collaborator UCLA Anxiety Disorders Behavioral Program, 1995—97, sr. therapist and assessor, 1996—98, project dir., 1996—99; supr. Cmty. Outreach Prevention and Edn. Svc., UCLA Sch. of Medicine, 1997—98; post-doctoral rsch. coord. UCLA Pediatric Pain Program, Sch. of Medicine, 1999—2000, asst. rsch. psychologist, 2000—01; rsch. asst. prof. NIMH Ctr. for the Study of Emotion and Attention, U. Fla., Gainesville, 2001—03, Nat. Rural Behavioral Health Ctr., U. Fla., Gainesville, 2002—04; rsch. scientist UCLA Pediatric Pain Program, Sch. Medicine, L.A., 2004—. Clin. supr. Fanning Springs Primary Care Clinic, Nat. Rural Behavioral Health Program, U. Fla., 2002—04, Nat. Rural Behavioral Health Program, Gainesville, 2002—04, Fear & Anxiety Disorders Clinic, U. Fla., Gainesville, 2001—04; peer reviewer Jour. Abnormal Psychology, 2000—, Health Psychology, 2000—01, Jour. of Pediatric Psychology, 2000—, Psychosomatic Medicine, 2000—01, Behavior Rsch. and Therapy, 2000—, Jour. of Pain and Symptom Mgmt., 2000—, Jour. Cons. and Clin. Psychol., 2004—. Editor (sr.): Cognitive and Behavioral Practice, 2004—; editor: (assoc.) Journal of Pediatric Psychology, Special Issue: Pain, 2004—; contbr. chapters to books, articles pub. to profl. jour.; author: (jour. article) Pain, Med. Care, Jour. of Nervous and Mental Disease, Jour. of Pediatric Psychology. Recipient Social Sci. prize, KPMG, 1993, Young Investigators Travel award, Am. Pain Soc., 2001, 2003—04; fellow, UCLA Dept. Psychology, 1994—95; grantee, 1995, 1995—97, Nat. Insts. Mental Health, 1996—98, UCLA Dept. Psychology, 1997, Health Resources and Svcs. Adminstrn., 2003—04, Aty. Healthcare Rsch. and Quality, 2003—, Nat. Inst. Drug Abuse, 2004—; Regents scholar, UCLA Coll. Letters and Sci., 1978—81. Mem.: Anxiety Disorders Assn. Am. (Career Devel. Travel award 2003), Am. Pain Soc., Am. Assn. for the Advancement of Behavior Therapy, Phi Beta Kappa. Achievements include Professional Appearance on ABC's 20/20 segment entitled, Don't Panic; Professional Appearance on NBC's Dateline segment entitled, Butterflies are Free; Professional Appearance on Canadian Broadcasting Corporation program The Nature of Things. Office: UCLA Pediatric Pain Rsch Program 10940 Wilshire Blvd Ste 1450 Los Angeles CA 90024 Business E-Mail: jtsao@ufl.edu.

TSAO, VIVIAN J. artist, educator; arrived in US, 1974, naturalized; d. Sheng Fen and Wendy (Hsiung) Tsao; m. Raymond Clyde Coreil, June 5, 1976. BA, Nat. Taiwan Normal U., 1973; MFA Painting, Carnegie Mellon U., Pitts., 1976. Art instr. Nat. Taipei Tchrs. Coll., 1972—74; corr. in US Hsiung Shih Art Monthly, Taiwan, 1980—96; artist Ceres Gallery, N.Y.C., 1984—; artist in residence Asian Am. Arts Ctr., N.Y.C., 1985—86; adj. asst. prof. fine arts Pace U., N.Y.C., 1990—; artist Biddington's Internet Gallery, N.Y.C., 2000—; art commentator in US United Daily News (Chinese), Taiwan, 2003—. Artist presenter on panel China Inst. Gallery, N.Y.C., 1989; program auditor (art reviewer) N. Y. State Coun. Arts, N.Y.C., 1990—96, mem. jury panel, 1996—99. Author: (Chinese) The Mark of Time: Dialogues with Vivian Tsao on Art in New York, 2003; one-woman shows include among 61 solo and group exhbns. Light in the Season, Ceres Gallery, N.Y.C., 2003, Pastel Soc. of Am. Invitational Exhbn., Butler Inst. of Am. Art, Ohio, 2003, Second Curator Series, Nat. Arts Club, N.Y.C., 2003; author: The Mark of Time, 2003; Invitational Exhbn. of Painting & Sculpture, Am. Acad. of Arts and Letters, N.Y.C., 2004. Sponsor student presentations Dyson Coll., Soc. Fellows, Pace U., 1994, 1995, 2000; interpreter internat. symposium Met. Mus. Art, N.Y.C., 1985; judge Employees Art Show N.Y. State Supreme Ct., 1995. Scholarship grantee, Carnegie Mellon U., Pitts., 1975, artist in residence grantee, N.Y. State Coun. Arts . Asian Am. Arts Ctr., 1985—86. Fellow: Soc. Fellows Dyson Coll., Pace U.; mem.: Coll. Art Assn. Am., Pastel Soc. Am. (Cert. Merit 1981). Achievements include Art shows positively reviewed in N.Y. Times and World Jour. (Chinese). invited exhibitor Am. Acad. Arts and Letters, N.Y.C., Bklyn. Mus., Butler Inst. Am. Art, Ohio, Nat. Arts Club., N.Y.C., others. Avocations: films, music, seashell collecting. Home: 17 Fuller Pl Brooklyn NY 11215-6006 Office: Pace U Dept Fine Arts 41 Park Row New York NY 10038 Personal E-mail: viviantsao@earthlink.net.

TSAU, WILLIAM WEN-SHIUNG, civil engineer, consultant, structural engineer; b. Formosa, Taiwan, July 20, 1946; arrived in U.S., 1973, naturalized, 1982; s. Chun Fu and Yu In (Young) Tsau. BSCE, Northeastern U., Boston, 1978; MSCE, U. Wyo., 1981. Registered profl. civil and structural engr., Ill., N.Mex. Civil engr. Nat. Taiwan Power Co., Taipei, Taiwan, 1970—73; grad. scholar, tchg. asst. U. Wyo., 1979—81; project/design/resident engr. Johnson-Fermelia & Crank, Inc., also J.F.C. Enterprises, J.F.C. Internat., Inc., Kemmerer and Rock Springs, Wyo., 1981—85; gen. engr. Corp of Engrs. U.S. Army, 1985—86, civil/structural engr. prin. design and project, 1986—. Cons. ROTC Taiwanese Army Engr. Sch., 1969—70, Army Engr. Res. 2d lt. Taiwanese Army Res., 1970—73. Named to Nat. Profl. Engring. Hall of Fame. Fellow: ASCE; mem.: Am. Concrete Inst., IABSE, Assoc. U.S. Army, Am. Assn. Ret. People, Sigma Xi (life), Tau Beta Pi (life). Achievements include research in optimization of stiffened and unstiffened hybrid girders, large scale structural system of conventional sheet pile cofferdam with computer applications; bridge and bulkhead design inspection rating inland waterway lock and dam periodic inspection and continuing evaluation maintenance repair and rehab; computer aid analysis, design layouts in civil and structural engring.; CASE, concrete lock wall, steel sheet pile; military engineering and construction projects; prepare and review criteria package works for host nation project. Home: 3368 E Kimberly Rd Davenport IA 52807 Address: 1515 9th St Rock Springs WY 82901-6057 Office: Unit 45010 Box 111 Apo AP 96338-5010

TSCHERNISCH, SERGEI P. academic administrator; BA, San Francisco State U.; MFA in Theatre, Stanford U.; student, San Francisco Actors' Workshop, Stanford Repertory Theatre. Founding mem. Calif. Inst. of Arts, 1969, mem. faculty, assoc. dean Sch. Theatre, dir., 1969-80; prof. dept. theatre U. Md., College Park, 1980-82; dir. divsn. performing and visual arts Northeastern U., Boston, 1982-92; dean Coll. of Comm. and Fine Arts Loyola Marymount U., L.A., 1992-94; pres. Cornish Coll. of Arts, Seattle, 1994—. Advisor NEA; mem. com. USIA; cons. to many festivals. Office: Cornish College of the Arts 1000 Lenora St Seattle WA 98121-2718

TSCHERNY, GEORGE, graphic designer; b. Budapest, Hungary, July 12, 1924; s. Mendel and Bella (Heimann) T.; m. Sonia Katz, July 7, 1950; children— Nadia, Carla Student, Pratt Inst., Bklyn., 1947-50. Staff designer Donald Deskey & Assocs., N.Y.C., 1950-53; designer, assoc. George Nelson & Assocs., N.Y.C., 1953-55; pres. George Tscherny, Inc., N.Y.C., 1955—. Instr. Pratt Inst., Bklyn., 1956, bd. advisors, 1979; instr. Sch. Visual Arts, N.Y.C., 1955-64; curriculum cons. Phila. Coll. Art, 1967; Mellon vis. prof. Cooper Union, N.Y., 1978 Retrospective exhbn. Visual Art Mus., N.Y.C., 1992; exhibited in group shows, Germany, 1962-67, Italy, 1974, U.S., 1975; represented in permanent collections Mus. Modern Art, N.Y.C., Cooper Hewitt Mus., N.Y.C., Libr. of Congress, Washington, Bibliotheque nationale de France, Paris, Kunstgewerbeschule der Stadt Zurich; monograph of work George Tscherny, Minimum Means, Maximum Meaning, 2004. Contbr. design svcs. to UN Assn., Sta. WNET Pub. TV, Am. Lung Assn., Peace Corps, Cystic Fibrosis Found., L.I. State Park Commn. With U.S. Army, 1943-46, ETO. Recipient numerous awards, Am. Inst. Graphic Arts medal, 1988, Art Dirs. Club N.Y. (hall of fame 1997), N.Y. Type Dirs. Club, Silver medal Warsaw Biennale, 1976; inducted into Art Dirs. Club Hall of Fame, 1997. Mem. Am. Inst. Graphic Arts (pres. 1966-68), Alliance Graphique Internationale. Office: 238 E 72nd St New York NY 10021-4503 E-mail: gtscherny@aol.com.

TSCHETTER, KRIS, professional golfer; b. Detroit, Dec. 30, 1964; m. Kirk Lucas. BA in Radio, T.V., Film, Tex. Christian U., 1987. Mem. Ladies Pro Golf Assn., 1987—. Tour victories include 1991 J.C. Penney Classic, 1992 Northgate Computer Classic. Office: c/o Ladies Pro Golf Assn 100 International Golf Dr Daytona Beach FL 32124-1082

TSCHINKEL, ANDREW JOSEPH, JR., law librarian; b. Catskill, N.Y., Aug. 8, 1952; s. Andrew Joseph and Marie Frances (O'Connor) Tschinkel; m. Frances K. Quigley, Nov. 4, 1989. BA summa cum laude, St. John's Coll., Jamaica, N.Y., 1975, MLS, 1977; MBA, Fordham U., 1983. Grad. asst. divsn. libr. sci. St. John's U., Jamaica, 1975-77, asst. law libr., 1977-79, adj. law libr., 1983-87; head libr. Christ the King HS, Middle Village, NY, 1979-80; sr. law libr. Bklyn. Supreme Ct., 1980-81; prin. law libr. N.Y. Supreme Ct., Jamaica, 1981—. Named Alumnus of the Yr., Grad. Sch. Arts & Scis. Divsn. Libr. & Info. Sci. St. John's U., 1993; recipient Pub. Svc. award, Queens Borough Pres. and N.Y. Tel. Co., 1986. Mem.: Law Libr. Assn. Greater N.Y. (bd. dirs. 2003—), Am. Assn. Law Librs., Elks, Beta Phi Mu. Republican. Office: NY Supreme Ct Libr 88-11 Sutphin Blvd Jamaica NY 11435-3716 Business E-Mail: atschink@courts.state.ny.us.

TSCHOEPE, THOMAS, retired bishop; b. Pilot Point, Tex., Dec. 17, 1915; s. Louis and Catherine (Sloan) T. Student, St. Thomas Sch. Pilot Point, 1930, Pontifical Coll. Josephinum, Worthington, Ohio, 1943. Ordained priest Roman Cath. Ch., 1943. Asst. pastor, Ft. Worth, 1943—46, Sherman, Tex., 1946—48, Dallas, 1948—53; adminstr. St. Patrick Ch., Dallas, 1953—56; pastor St. Augustine Ch., Dallas, 1956—62, Sacred Heart Cathedral, Dallas, 1962—65; bishop San Angelo, Tex., 1966—69, Dallas, 1969—90; ret. bishop, 1990; asst. pastor St. Joseph Parish, Waxahachie, Tex., 1990—. Home and Office: St Joseph Ch 504 E Marvin Ave Waxahachie TX 75165-3406

TSCHUMI, BERNARD, architect; b. Lausanne, Switzerland, Jan. 25, 1944; BArch, Fed. Inst. Tech., Zurich, Switzerland, 1969. Tchr. Archtl. Assn., London, 1970—80, Inst. Architecture and Urban Studies, N.Y.C., 1976, Princeton U. Sch. Architecture, 1980—81, Cooper Union, 1980—83; dean Columbia U. Grad. Sch. Architecture, Planning & Preservation, N.Y.C., 1988—2003; head firm Bernard Tschumi Architects, Paris, 1983—, NYC, 1988—. Davenport vis. prof. arch. Contbr. The Manhattan Transcripts, 1981, Architecture and Disjunction, 1994, Event Cities, 1994, Bernard Tschumi: Architecture and Event, 1994. Recipient 1st prize for design of new Sch. of Architecture, Paris, 1994, Legion d'Honneur, Ordre des Arts et Lettres, Grand Prix National d'Architecture, 1996. Mem.: College Internat. de Philosophie. Office: Bernard Tschumi Architects 227 W 17th St 2nd Fl New York NY 10011 Office Phone: 212-807-6340. Office Fax: 212-242-3693.*

TSCHUMPER, GREGORY SCOTT, chemist, educator; s. Robert F and Patricia L Tschumper; m. Allison Burkette, Oct. 7, 2000; 1 child, Anne Paige. B.S., Winona State U., Minn., 1995; PhD, U.Ga., Athens, 1999—99. Asst. prof. U. of Miss., University, 2001—. Postdoctoral rschr. Emory U., Atlanta, 2000—01, Swiss Fed. Inst. of Tech., Zurich, Switzerland, 1999—2000. Contbr. scientific papers to profl. meetings and confs. Fellow Faculty Rsch. Fellowship, U. of Miss. Office of Rsch. and Sponsored Programs, 2003; grantee Rsch. Innovation award, Rsch. Corp., 2003-2005. Mem.: Southeastern Theoretical Chemistry Assn. (vice chair 2002—03, chair 2003—04), Am. Chem. Soc. (local sect. chair 2003). Office: Univ Miss Dept Chemistry & Biochemistry University MS 38677

TSE, CHARLES YUNG CHANG, pharmaceutical executive, lawyer; b. Shanghai, Mar. 22, 1926; s. Kung Chao and Say Ying (Chen) T.; m. Vivian Chang, Apr. 25, 1955; 1 dau., Roberta. BA in Econs, St. John's U., Shanghai, 1949; MS in Acctg, U. Ill., 1950; JD, N.Y. Law Sch., 1990. Asst. to controller Am. Internat. Group, N.Y.C., 1950-54, asst. mgr. Singapore-Malaysia, 1955-57; with Warner-Lambert Co., Morris Plains, N.J., 1957-86, area mgr. S.E. Asia, 1966-68, regional dir. S.E. Asia, 1968-69, v.p. Australasia, 1970-71, pres. Western Hemisphere Group, 1971-72, pres. Pan Am. Mgmt. Center, 1972-76, pres. European Mgmt. Center, 1976-78, pres. Internat. Group, 1979-86, sr. v.p. corp., 1980-83, exec. v.p. corp., 1984-85, vice chmn., 1985-86. Dir. Foster Wheeler Corp., Livingston, N.J., 1984-98, Superior Telecom., Inc., 1996—, Com. of 100; mem. faculty bus. adminstrn. dept. Fairleigh Dickinson U., 1961-64; pres. Cancer Rsch. Inst., Inc., N.Y.C., 1991-92. Bd. visitors CCNY, 1974-78; trustee Morristown Meml. Hosp. (N.J.), 1982-86; bd. dirs. Bus. Council for Internat. Understanding, 1984-87. Mem. NAM (dir. 1984-86), Assn. of the Bar of the City of N.Y. (mem. Asian affairs com. 1991-2001). Office: 300 Park Ave Fl 17 New York NY 10022-7402

TSE, EDMUND SZE-WING, insurance company executive; b. Hong Kong, Jan. 2, 1938; m. Peggy Pik-Kin Wai, Dec. 18, 1965; children: Ada Koon-Hang, Elaine Koon-Ming. BA in Math., U. Hong Kong, 1960; diploma mktg. mgmt. program, Stanford U. Grad. Sch. of Bus., 1980; DSS (hon.), U. Hong Kong, 2002. Dep. gen. mgr. Nan Shan Life Ins. Co., Ltd., Taipei, Taiwan, 1970-74, pres., mng. dir., 1975-83, chmn., 1990, hon. chmn., 2003; various positions Am. Internat. Assurance Co., Ltd., Hong Kong, 1961-70, dir., 1983, chmn., CEO, 2000—, dir., 1996; sr. vice chmn. Am. Internat. Group, Inc., 2002—. Bd. dirs., dir., pres. AIA Found., Hong Kong, 1995; bd. dirs. AIG Global Investment Corp. (Hong Kong) Ltd., 1999, AIG Mktg. Corp., 2001, Am. Internat. Data Centre Ltd., Hong Kong, 1984, chmn., Hong Kong, 97; bd. dirs. Project Hope Hong Kong Found. Ltd., 2000; non-exec. dir. Property and Casualty Co. Ltd.; bd. dirs. Seacliff Ltd., Hong Kong, 1994; bd. dirs., vice-chmn. Am. Life Ins. Co., United States, 1992; bd. dirs. C.V. Starr & Co., Inc., United States, 1994, sr. v.p., United States, 98; bd. dirs. China Am. Holding Co., United States, 1993, The Starr Found., 1999, AIG Asian Infrastructure Investment Devel. Corporetum Ltd., Bermuda, 1996; dir. AIG Asian Infrastructure Investment Devel. Co. Ltd., Bermuda, 1994; bd. dirs. AIG Asian Infrastructure Mgmt. Ltd., Bermuda, 1994, AIG Asian Infrastructure Mgmt. II, Ltd., Bermuda, 1997, AIG Global Investment Corp. (Asia) Ltd., Bermuda, 1996, Am. Internat. Assurance Co. (Bermuda) Ltd., 1983, pres., 92; bd. dirs. Am. Internat. Reinsurance Co. Ltd., Bermuda, 1996, C.V. Starr Internat. Investment Mgmt. Co. Ltd., 1999; bd. dirs., pres., voting shareholder Tri Star Enterprises Ltd., Bermuda, 2002; bd. dirs. UGC Holdings Ltd., British Virgin Islands, 1994, Shanghai Jin Jiang-Universal Devel. Co. Ltd., China, 1994; bd. dirs., chmn. & pres. Green Heights, Inc. (The "Lookout"), Panama, 1986; bd. dirs., voting shareholder Starr Internat. Co. Inc., Panama, 1992, Underwriters Adjustment Co., Inc., Panama, 1997; bd. dirs. & vice-chmn. The Philippine Am. Life and Gen. Ins. Co., 1991; v.p. komisaris P.T. Asuransi AIU Indonesia, 1991, pres. komisaris, 97; chmn. bd. suprs. Dana Pensuin Lembaga Keuangan AIA Indonesia, 1997; v.p. commr. P.T. Asuransi AIG Lippo Life, Indonesia, 1999; bd. dirs. Am. Internat. Assurance Co. (Australia) Ltd., 1985, chmn., 97; bd. dirs. AIA Superannuation Co. Ltd., Australia, 1986, chmn., Australia, 97; bd. dirs. AIG Card (Thailand) Co. Ltd., 2001; bd. dirs., chmn. Am. Internat. Assurance Co. (Vietnam) Ltd., 2000. Nat. & area chmn. Hong Kong Pacific Ins. Conf.; mem. The Hong Kong Govt.'s Ins. Adv. Com., 1988—96; mem. exec. com. Bus. and Profls. Fedn. of Hong Kong, China Overseas Friendship Assn.; mem. Hong Kong Forum, Internat. Consultative Forum for the Mayor of Tianjin, China; mem. Hong Kong com. Pacific Basin Econ. Coun.; patron Soc. of Registered Fin. Planners Ltd.; mem. career devel. bd. The Chinese U. of Hong Kong; bd. dirs. The Starr Found.; mem. hon. advisor panel for BSc (Actuarial Sci.) program., dept. stats./actuarial sci. The U. of Hong Kong; founding mem. World Presidents' Orgn. Hong Kong Chapter; chmn. governing bd. Gen. Ins. Coun., 1989—90, dep. chmn. of bd., 1988—89, chmn. legis. sub-com., 1988—89, 1993—94; mem. Hong Kong Ins. Ind. Coalition, 1996—98; chmn. stats./info. subcom. Ins. Coun. of Hong Kong, 1984—88; bd. dirs. Life Ins. Mktg. and Rsch. Assn. (LIMRA), 1994—97; mem. adv. bd. Mandatory Provident Fund, 1996—98; chmn. Asia adv. bd. Project HOPE, USA, 1997—99; mem. selection com. The election of the HKSAR Chief Exec. and Provisional Legis., 1996; mem. election com. The HKSAR Legis. Coun. election, 1998, 2000; trustee ednl. trust The Hong Kong Fedn. of Insurers, 1990—93, mem. election sub-com., 1990—92, dep. chmn., 1991—92, chmn., 1992—93; mem. Working Group on Reinsurance and Captive Ins., 1996—98; trustee The Fudan U., China. Recipient Disting. Businessman of Yr., Taiwan, 1997, Gold Bauhinia Star (GBS), The Hong Kong Spl. Adminstrv. Region, 2001, Ins. Hall of Fame, 2003; hon. fellow, U. Hong Kong, 1998. Mem.: Asia Soc. Hosp. Kong Ctr. (mem. adv. coun. 2004—, 2004), Chinese U. Hong Kong (appointments bd., hon. v.p.), Hong Kong U. Alumni Assn. (hon. v.p. 2003—04). Home: 10C Headland Rd Repulse Bay Hong Kong Office: Am Internat Assurance Co Ltd No 1 Stubbs Rd POB 444 Hong Kong Hong Kong Fax: 852-2572-4695.

TSE, HARLEY Y. immunologist, educator; b. China, July 17, 1947; s. Ton-Cheuk and Hou-Ying (Choy) T.; m. Kwai-Fong Chui, Jan. 13, 1979; children: Kevin Y., Alan C., Leslie W. BS with honors, Calif. Inst. Tech., 1972; PhD, U. Calif., San Diego, 1977; MBA, Rutgers U., 1986. Fellow Arthritis Found., NIH, Bethesda, Md., 1977-80; sr. rsch. immunologist Merck Sharp & Dohme Rsch. Lab., Rahway, N.J., 1980-83, rsch. fellow, 1983-86; adj. asst. prof. Columbia U., 1981-84; assoc. prof. Wayne State U. Sch. Medicine, Detroit, 1986—, grad. officer dept. immunology and microbiology, 2003—. Mem. immunol. sci. study sect. NIH, 1995-99; grad. officer dept. immunology and microbiology Wayne State U. Sch. Medicine, 2003—. Contbr. articles to profl. jours. Bd. dirs. Chinese Social Svc. Ctr., San Diego, 1975. Recipient NIH Rsch. Career Devel. award, 1992-97; Calif. Biochem. Rsch. fellow, 1975; Arthritis Found. fellow, 1977-80; grantee NIH, 1988—, Nat. Multiple Sclerosis Soc., 1988—. Mem. Am. Assn. Immunologists, Chinese Student Assn. (pres. 1974-76), Soc. Chinese Bioscientists in Am., Detroit Immunol. Soc. (pres. 1989-91). Roman Catholic. Home: 5393 Tequesta Dr West Bloomfield MI 48323-2351 Office: Wayne State U Sch Medicine 540 E Canfield St Detroit MI 48201-1928 Office Phone: 313-577-1564. Business E-Mail: htse@wayne.edu.

TSE, MAN-CHUN MARINA, educational association administrator; b. Kai-Ping, China, Dec. 14, 1948; came to U.S., 1972; d. Sun-Poo and Su-ling Cheung. BA in English, U. Chinese Culture, Taipei, Taiwan, 1970; MS in Spl. Edn., U. So. Calif., 1974; leadership program diploma, Harvard U., 2003. Cert. tchr., spl. edn. tchr., Calif. Rsch. asst. lit. U. Chinese Culture, 1970-72; English tchr. Tang-Suede Mid. Sch., Taiwan, 1970-72; instr. Willing Workers, Adult Handicapped Program L.A. Sch. Dist., 1976-77; instr. ESL Evans Adult Sch., L.A., 1977—82; instr. ESL and polit. sci. Lincoln Adult Sch., L.A., 1986—94; spl. edn. tchr. Duarte (Calif.) Unified Sch. Dist., 1977—2000; prin. assoc. under sec. Office of English Lang. Acquisition, Lang. Enhancement and Acad. Achievement for Limited English Proficient Students U.S. Dept. Edn., 2000—. Commr., program co-chair Calif. Spl. Edn. Adv. Commn., Sacramento, 1994-96; mem. Calif. State Bd. Edn., 1996-99; mem. Calif. State Summer Sch. for the Arts, 1998-99; coun. mem. L.A. County Children Planning Coun., 1995—; com. mem. L.A. County Sci. & Engring. Fair Com., 1993—; hon. adv. bd. Asian Youth Ctr., San Gabriel City, Calif., 1992—; exec. bd. Pres. Com. on Employment of People with Disabilities (U.S.), 1997—; com. mem. tchr. devel. project Nat. Assn. State Bd. Edn., 1977—; mem. Calif.

State Supts. Art Task Force, 1997-98; advisor Calif. Coun. Tech., 1996-99; mem. Calif. Rehab. Coun. Appeared on numerous TV and radio programs. Bd. trustee Bruggemeyer Libr., Monterey Park, Calif., 1993-99; pres. L.A. County Coun. Reps., 1994—; mem. Calif. Statewide Focus Group Diversity, Sacramento, 1995-97; chair Chinese Am. Edn. Assn., 1993—; co-chair, co-founder Multi-Cultural Cmty. Assn., 1992—; bd. dirs. Rosemead-Taipei Sister City, 1993—, San Gabriel Valley Charity Night Com., 1992—; chmn. Los Angeles County-Taipei County Friendship Com., 1996—. Recipient Recognition cert. Duarte Edn. Found., 1990, Calif. Legis. Assembly, 1993, cert. Valley View Sch., 1991, award State Calif., 1991, Appreciation award City Rosemead, 1992, Commendation cert. Alhambra Sch. Dist., 1992-93, Edn. award Asian Youth Ctr., 1992, 1992, Commendation cert. City L.A., 1992, commendation County L.A., 1992, award U.S. Congress, 1993, Proclamation City Alhambra, 1993, Chinese Am. PTA award, 1993, John Anson Ford award L.A. County Human Rels. Com., 1993, Appreciation cert. Chinese Consolidated Benevolent Assn., 1994, City Monterey Park, 1995, Recognition cert. Calif. State Senate, 1994, Spl. Achievement award Calif. Spl. Edn. Adv. Commn., 1997, Duarte United Edn. Ctr., 1997, Outstanding Comm. Svc. award City of Duarte, Calif., 1997, Disting. Woman of Yr. award Calif. 24th Dist. Sen.'s Office, 1997, Svc. award Calif. Fedn. Exceptional Children Coun., 1998, Calif. Sanitorial award, 1999, L.A. County Bd. Suprs. Outstanding Svc. award, 1999, Monterey Park City award, 1999. Mem. Calif. Tchr. Assn., Chinese Edn. Assn., Internat. Platform Assn., Nat. Assn. State Bds. Edn. Office: US Dept Edn Mary Switzer Bldg 330 C St SW Rm 5082 Washington DC 20202-6510

TSENG, AMPERE AN-PEI, mechanical engineer, educator, administrator; b. Kiangsi, China, Jan. 21, 1946; came to U.S., 1971, naturalized, 1982; s. Chi-Kung and Ai-Chung; m. Maggie Shih-Ying Yang, Aug. 9, 1975; children: Claire, Karen, Miles. MS, U. Ill, 1974; PhD, Ga. Inst. Tech., 1978. Mech. engr. Taitan (Taiwan) Industries Pty. Ltd., 1968-71; devel. engr. Westinghouse Electric Corp., Tampa, Fla., 1977-79; staff engr. Martin Marietta Labs., Balt., 1979-84; tech. staff, project leader RCA Labs., Princeton, N.J., 1984-85; assoc. prof. Drexel U., Phila., 1985-91, prof., 1991-96; dir. Ctr. for Automation Mfg., 1990-94; prof., dir. Mfg. Inst., Ariz. State U., Tempe, 1996—. Mem. editl. bd. Adv. Mfg. Processes, 1986-88, Jour. Engring. Materials and Tech., 1987-93, Mfg. Rev., 1991-93, Jour. Materials Processing and Mfg. Sci., 1992—, Advances in Polymer Tech., 1995—, Jour. Chinese Mech. Engring., 1997—. Recipient Cert. of Appreciation, Aluminium Assn., 1984, award for superior performance Martin Marietta Labs., 1979-84; grantee NSF, Nat. Inst. Stds. and Tech., Dept. Energy, Dept. Def., 1979-84; Alcoa Found. award, 1987, Nat. Sci. Coun. Professorship, Nat. Chenykung U., 1993, Nat. Taiwan U., 2001, Guest Professorship, Shanghai Jaio Tung U. and Beijing Tsinghua U. Fellow ASME (chair materials divsn.). Home: 4946 E Cheery Lynn Rd Phoenix AZ 85018-6550 Office: Ariz State U Mech Engring PO Box 876106 Tempe AZ 85287-6106

TSENG, GEORGE SHIHCHI, anesthesiologist; b. Kaeshung, Taiwan, June 20, 1967; s. Tony and Helen T. BA, Boston U., MD, 1992. Diplomate Am. Bd. Anesthesiology. Resident U. Hosp., Utah Sch. Medicine, Salt Lake City, 1994-97; critical care specialist, anesthesiologist St. Francis Med. Ctr., Honolulu, 1999-2000; chief profl. svcs. 154th MDS, Hickam AFB, Hawaii, 2000—. Maj. Hawaii Air N.G. Pediatric anesthesiology fellow St. Louis Children's Hosp., 1997-98, critical care fellow The Cleve. Clinic Found., 1998-99. Mem. AMA, Am. Soc. Anesthesiology, Soc. Critical Care Medicine, Soc. Pediatric Anesthesia/ Republican. Avocations: martial arts, violin, physical fitness, photography. Office: St Francis Med Ctr/CCU 2230 Liliha St Honolulu HI 96817 E-mail: gtseng67@aol.com.

TSENG, ROSE, academic administrator; BS, Kansas State U.; MS, PhD Nutrition, U. Calif., Berkeley. Registered dietician. Prof., chair, dir., assoc. dean San Jose State U., 1970—86, dean Coll. Applied Scis. and Arts, 1986—93; chancellor, CEO West Valley-Mission C.C., Calif., 1993—98; chancellor U. Hawaii-Hilo, 1998—. Office: U Hawaii-Hilo 200 W Kawili Hilo HI 96720-4091

TSIEN, RICHARD WINYU, biology professor; b. Tating, Kweichow, People's Republic China, Mar. 3, 1945; s. Hsue-Chu and Yi-Ying (Li) T.; m. Julia Shiang Aug. 29, 1971; children: Sara Shiang-Ming, Gregory Shiang-An, Alexa Tsien-Shiang. BS, MIT, 1965, MS, 1966; DPhil, Oxford U., Eng., 1970. Rsch. student Eaton Peabody Lab. Auditory Physiology, Mass. Eye and Ear Infirmary, 1966; asst. prof. dept. physiology, Yale U. Sch. Medicine, New Haven, 1970-74, assoc. prof., 1974-79, prof., 1979-88; George D. Smith prof. molecular and cellular physiology Stanford (Calif.) U., 1988—, chmn. dept., 1988-94. Established investigator Am. Heart Assn., 1974-79. Author: Electric Current Flow in Excitable Cells, 1975. Recipient Otsuka award Internat. Soc. Heart Rsch., 1985; Rhodes Scholar, 1966; Weir Rsch. fellow, 1966-70 Univ. Coll., Oxford, 1966-70, lecturing fellow Balliol Coll., Oxford, 1969-70 Mem. Soc. Gen. Physiologists (pres. 1988), Biophys. Soc. (Kenneth S. Cole award 1985), Soc. for Neurosci. Democrat. Home: 866 Tolman Dr Palo Alto CA 94305-1026 Office: Stanford U Dept Molecular & Cellular Physiology 300 Pasteur Dr Palo Alto CA 94304-2203

TSIEN, ROGER YONCHIEN, chemist, cell biologist; b. N.Y.C., Feb. 1, 1952; s. Hsue Chu and Yi Ying (Li) T.; m. Wendy M. Globe, July 30, 1982. AB summa cum laude in Chemistry and Physics, Harvard Coll., 1972; PhD in Physiology, U. Cambridge, 1977; D (hon.), Katholieke U., Leuven, Belgium, 1995. Rsch. asst. U. Cambridge, Eng., 1975-78; asst. prof. Dept. Physiology-Anatomy U. Calif., Berkeley, 1981-85, assoc. prof., 1985-87, prof., 1987-89, prof. pharmacology, chemistry and biochemistry San Diego, 1989—; biological investigator Howard Hughes Med. Inst. Rsch. Lab, Calif., 1989—; co-found. Aurora Bioscis. Corp., 1994, Senomyx, Inc., 1998. T.Y. Shen vis. prof. Medicinal Chem., MIT, 1991, Todd vis. prof. Chem., U. Cambridge, 2003. Contbr. chpts. to books, articles to profl. jours. Recipient Herbert Sober Lectureship, Am. Soc. Biochemistry and Molecular Biology, 2000, Pearse Prize, Royal Microscopical Soc., 2000, Am. Chem. Soc. award for Creative Invention, 2002, Anfinsen award, Protein Soc., 2002, Dr. H.P. Heineken Prize for Biochemistry and Biophysics, 2002, Lamport prize N.Y. Acad. Scis., 1986, Javits Neurosci. Investigator award Nat. Inst. Neurol. Disorders and Stroke, 1989—, Young Scientist award Passano Found., 1991, W. Alden Spencer Neurobiology award Columbia U., 1991, Bowditch lectureship Am. Physiol. Soc., 1992, Gairdner Found. Internat. award, 1995, Doctorate honoris causa, Katholieke Universiteit Leuven, Belgium, 1995; Artois-Baillet-Latour Health prize (Belgium), 1995, Basic Rsch. prize Am. Heart Assn., 1995, Faculty Rsch. lectureship U. Calif., San Diego, 1997, Faculty Rsch. Lectureship, Univ. Calif., San Diego, Acad. Senate, 1997, EG&G Wallac award for Innovation in High Throughput Screening Soc. for Biomolecular Screening, 1998, Max Delbrück medal, Max Delbrück Centrum für Molekulare Medizin, Berlin, 2002, Wolf prize in Medicine, Israel, 2004; Comyns Berkeley Rsch. fellow Gonville & Caius Coll., 1977-81; Marshall scholar British Govt., 1972-75, Searle scholar, 1983-86; Hugh Davson Disting. Lecturer, Am. Physiological Soc., 2003, Konrad Bloch Lectureship, Harvard U., 2003, Keith Porter Lectureship, Am.Soc. Cell Biology, 2003. Mem. Amer. Acad. Arts & Sciences, NAS, IOM, Phi Beta Kappa. Achievements development and extensive biological application of molecules to measure and/or manipulate intracellular calcium, sodium, and hydrogen ions, cyclic adenosine-3', 5'-monophosphate, nitric oxide, inositol phosphates, membrane potential, protein trafficking, protein-protein interaction, and gene expression; developed biochemistry and redesign of green fluorescent protein; elucidation fo signal transduction mechanisms in calcium oscillations and synaptic plasticity; inventor new methods for microscopic imaging and pharmaceutical high-throughput screening. Office: Tsien Lab HHMI - UCSD CMM West 310 9500 Gilman Dr La Jolla CA 92093-0647 E-mail: rtsien@ucsd.edu.*

TSIGELNY, IGOR, research scientist; m. Valentina Kouznetsova. PhD, Inst. Physics and Mechanics, Acad. Sci. Ukraine, 1972—78. Asst. scientist U. Calif., San Diego, 1994—99, assoc. scientist, 2000—. Author: (book) Molecular Cybernetics; editor: Protein Structure Prediction: Bioinformatic Approach. Mem.: Biophysical Soc., US Fencing Assn. Achievements include 11 Patents. E-mail: itsigeln@ucsd.edu.

TSIMHONI, OMER, engineering educator; b. Haifa, Israel, June 1, 1965; s. Moshe (Buki) and Daphne Tsimhoni; m. Maya Eibschitz, Aug. 17, 1995; 1 child, Liam Jonathan. BSc, U. Tel Aviv, Israel, 1991—94; MSE, U. Mich., 1996—98, PhD, 1996—2003, PhD, 1998—2004. Rsch. asst. UMTRI, Ann Arbor, Mich., 1997—2003. Author: (technical reports) Study Of In-vehicle Sys. Usage While Driving. Maj. Air Force. Mem.: Human Factors and Ergonomics. Office: Univ Michigan 2901 Baxter Rd Ann Arbor MI 48109-2150

TSIRPANLIS, CONSTANTINE N. theology, philosophy, classics and history educator; b. Kos, Greece, Mar. 18, 1935; came to U.S., 1957; m. Sophia Pappas, July 12, 1975; children: Kalliope-Chrysoula, Nike. BA, STM, lic. in theology magna cum laude, Halke Theol. Sem., Istanbul, Turkey, 1957; ThM, Harvard U., 1962; ThD, Union Theol. Sem., 1963; MA, Columbia U., 1966, PhD, 1970, Fordham U., 1973; DLitt (hon.), World Acad. Arts and Culture, 1993. Instr., organizer Greek-Am. cmtys., 1958-63; founder, chmn., prof. modern Greek studies NYU, 1963-70; prof. world history N.Y. Inst. Tech. N.Y.C. and Delaware County Coll., Media, Pa., 1967-75; disting. prof. theology, sociology, history, ecumenism, Greek studies Union Theol. Sem., Barrytown, NY, 1976-97; chmn., prof. scriptures, patristics, Greek lang. St. Sophia Ukraine Orthodox Theol. Sem. Am., Somerset, NJ, 1999—. Chmn., prof. classics Collegiate Sch., N.Y.C., 1967-69; prof. modern Greek lang. and lit. New Sch. for Social Rsch., N.Y.C., 1968-70; prof. classical mythology Hunter Coll. CUNY, 1968-70. Author numerous books including A Short History of the Greek Language, 1966, rev. edit., 1970, A Modern Greek Reader for Americans, 1967, rev. edit., 1968, A Modern Greek Idiom and Phrase Book, 1978, Mark Eugenicus, 1979, N. Cabasilas, 1979, Greek Patristic Theology, 22 vols.; founder, editor The Patristic and Byzantine Rev., 1981—; pub., editor-in-chief Hellenism In Am., 1969—; contbr. articles to profl. jours. Decorated Medal of Nat. Rebirth 1821 (Greece), medals of Byzantine nobility, including count, baron, G. chevalier, Gt. Prior of N.Am., medal of Accademia Ferdinandea, medals of Diethnés Hetereia Hellenon Logotechnon, also hon. pres. Mem. Am. Soc. Neohellenic Studies (founder, v.p.), Pan Dodecanisian Fedn. U.S., Am. Hist. Assn., Am. Philog. Assn., Am. Acad. Medieval Studies, Internat. Assn. Byzantine Studies, Am. Philos. Assn., N.Am. Patristic Soc., Hellenic Philog. Assn., Am. Soc. Papyrologists, Am. Inst. Patristic-Byzantine Studies (pres., founder), Justinianum Oikoumenikon R.C. (pres., founder), World Acad. Arts and Culture (hon.). Home and Office: 12 Minuet Ln Kingston NY 12401-6955 Fax: 845-331-1002. Office Phone: 845-336-8797.

TSIVIDIS, YANNIS P. electrical engineering educator; b. Piraeus, Greece, Dec. 22, 1946; came to U.S., 1970; s. Pelopidas I. and Maria (Filippa) T. BS, U. Minn., 1972; MS, U. Calif., Berkeley, 1973, PhD, 1976. Asst. prof. elec. engring. Columbia U., N.Y.C., 1976-81, assoc. prof., 1981-84, prof., 1984—, Nat. Tech. U., Athens, Greece, 1992-95; Charles Batchelor chair prof. Columbia U., N.Y.C., 1998—. Cons. AT&T Bell Labs., Murray Hill, N.J., 1977-88. Author: Operation and Modeling of the MOS Transistor, 1987, 2d edit., 1999, Mixed Analog-Digital VLSI Devices and Technology, 1996; co-editor: Design of Mos VLSI Circuits for Telecommunications, 1985, Integrated Continuous-Time Filters, 1993, Design of Analog-Digital VLSI Circuits for Telecommunications and Signal Processing, 1994; contbr. over 100 articles to profl. jours.; patentee in field. Recipient best paper award European Solid State Cirs. Conf., 1986, Great Tchr. award Columbia U., 1991, Disting. Faculty Tchg. award Columbia Engring. Sch. Alumni Assn., 1998, Presdl. award for outstanding tchg. Columbia U., 2003. Fellow IEEE (Baker best paper award 1984, Darlington award 1987, Guillemin-Cauer award 1998, Circuits and Sys. Golden Jubilee 2000, co-recipient L. Winner Outstanding Paper award 2003). Office: Columbia Univ Dept Elec Engring New York NY 10027

TSO, TIEN CHIOH, federal agency official, plant physiologist; b. Hupeh, China, July 25, 1917; came to U.S., 1947, naturalized, 1961; s. Ya Fu and Suhwa (Wang) T.; m. Margaret Lu, Aug. 28, 1949; children: Elizabeth, Paul. BS, Nanking U., China, 1941, MS, 1944; PhD, Pa. State U., 1950; postgrad., Oak Ridge Inst. Nuclear Studies. Supt. exptl. farm Ministry Social Affairs, China, 1944-46; exec. sec. Tobacco Improvement Bur., 1946-47; rsch. chemist Gen. Cigar Rsch. Lab., 1950-51; with USDA, 1952—; prin. plant physiologist crop research div. Agrl. Rsch. Svc./USDA, Beltsville, Md., 1964-66, leader tobacco quality investigations, tobacco and sugar crops research br., 1966-71, chief tobacco lab., 1972-83, sr. exec. service, 1974-83, collaborator, 1984—; exec. dir. Internat. Devel. and Edn. in Agr. and Life Scis., 1984-96, chmn. bd., 1997-2001, hon. chmn. bd., 2001—. Cons. World Bank, Nat. Cancer Inst., Ky. Tobacco Health Rsch. Inst., China Nat. Tobacco Corp., Philippine Tobacco Rsch. Ctr., Philip Morris Tobacco Corp. Author: Physiology and Biochemistry of Tobacco Plants, 1972, Production, Physiology and Biochemistry of Tobacco Plants, 1991, Agriculture in China: 1949-2030, 1998; contbg. author: Ann. Rev. Plant Physiology, Vol. 9, 1958, The Chemistry of Tobacco and Tobacco Smoke, 1972, Toward Less Harmful Cigarettes, 1968, 71, 75, 80; editor: Structural and Functional Aspects of Phytochemistry, 1972, Recent Advances in Tobacco Science, vol. 1, 1975, Agriculture in China: 1949-2030, 1998, also procs. Fellow AAAS, Am. Soc. Agronomy (chmn. colloquium on agr. and life scis. in China 1983, 84, 85, 86, 87, 88-89), Am. Inst. Chemists; mem. Am. Chem. Soc., Am. Soc. Plant Physiologists, Phytochem. Soc. N.Am. (pres. 1971, life mem.), Tobacco Chemists Rsch. Conf. (symposium chmn. 1965, 79, chmn. 1975, 83), World Conf. Smoking and Health (sect. chmn. 1967, 71, 75), Tobacco Workers Conf., N.Y. Acad. Scis., Interagy. Smoking and Health Forum (chmn. 1979-83), Nat. Coordinating Com. on Tobacco-Related Rsch., Sigma Xi, Gamma Sigma Delta. Achievements include research publs. on establishment of loci of alkaloid formation, biosynthetic pathway, interconversion and fate of alkaloids in tobacco plants, chem. composition as affected by macro and micro elements, homogenized leaf curing, health-related factors including mycotoxins and phenolics, potential for agricultural self-sufficiency in China in the next century. Home: 4306 Yates Rd Beltsville MD 20705-2758 Office: Beltsville Agr Rsch Ctr Bldg 005 Beltsville MD 20705 also: Ideals Inc 5010 Sunnyside Ave Beltsville MD 20705-2320 Business E-Mail: tsot@ba.ars.usda.gov. *We are thankful to those fools who dare to dream of something new and seemingly impossible.*

TSOHANTARIDIS, TIMOTHEOS, minister, religion educator; b. Katerini, Greece, Feb. 7, 1954; came to U.S., 1967; s. Ioannis and Parthena (Karipidis) T.; m. Valerie Ann Hoffman, July 11, 1977; children: Demetrius, Thaddeus. BA, Barrington Coll., 1977; MDiv, Gordon-Conwell, 1980; MA, Ashland Theol. Sem., 1985; PhD, U. Am., 2002. Ordained to ministry Evang. Friends Ch., 1986. Ch. planter Ea. region Evang. Friends Ch., North Ridgeville, Ohio, 1980-85; prof. religion, Greek, dir. Christian life, soccer coach George Fox Coll., Newberg, Oreg., 1985—90; prof. Biblical studies and Greek George Fox U., Newberg, 1993—. Author: (in Greek) Greek Evangelicals: Pontus to Katerini, 1985. Mem. Am. Acad. Religion, Soc. Bibl. Lit., Nat. Soccer Coaches Athletic Assn. (soccer coach, Nat. Coach of Yr. 1989). Home: 414 N Meridian St Newberg OR 97132-2625 Office: George Fox Coll 414 N Meridian St Newberg OR 97132-2625

TSOI, EDWARD TZE MING, architect, interior designer, urban planner; b. New Orleans, Aug. 7, 1943; s. Edward Mong Yok and Ruby Liu Wei (Hsia) T.; m. Louise Smoyer, June 15, 1968; children: Laura Li Ling, Alison Li Mei. BArch, MIT, 1966; MArch, M in City Planning, U. Pa., 1968, cert. in urban design, 1969. Registered architect, Mass., La. Assoc. Sert/Jackson & Assocs., Cambridge, Mass., 1969-76; assoc. prin. Skidmore Owings & Merrill, Boston, 1976-83; prin. Tsoi/Kobus & Assocs., Inc., Cambridge, 1983—, pres., 1985-89, 93—. Instr. Sch. Design, Harvard U., Cambridge, 1980-84. Designer Marine Resource Ctr., 1994. Chmn. Arlington (Mass.) Redevel. Bd., 1972—; chmn. 1st parish Unitarian Universalist Ch., Arlington, 1990; pres. bd. dirs. Cambridge Salvation Army, 1990—; mem. Boston Civic Design Commn., 1993—. Recipient Best New Med. Facility award Symposium on Healthcare, 1993, Grand Honor award Assn. Gen. Contractors, 1993, award Lotus Devel. Corp. landscape award Urban Design, 1991, nat. award for renovation Ford Model T plant Urban Land Inst., 1995. Fellow AIA; mem. Boston Soc. Architects (pres. 1993-94). Democrat. Avocations: windsurfing, boating, woodworking, carpentry. Home: 16 Devereaux St Arlington MA 02476-8114 Office: Tsoi/Kobus & Assocs Inc PO Box 9114 Cambridge MA 02238-9114 Office Phone: 617-475-4000. Business E-Mail: etsoi@tka-architects.com.

TSOUCALAS, NICHOLAS, federal judge; b. N.Y.C., Aug. 24, 1926; s. George Michael and Maria (Monogenis) T.; m. Catherine Aravantinos, Nov. 21, 1954; children: Stephanie, Georgia. BSBA, Kent State U., 1949; LLB, N.Y. Law Sch., 1951. Bar: N.Y. 1953. Sole practice, N.Y.C., 1953-55, 59-68; asst. U.S. atty. So. Dist. N.Y., 1955-59; judge Criminal Ct., City of N.Y., 1968-86; acting supreme ct. judge State of N.Y., N.Y.C., 1975-82; judge U.S. Ct. Internat. Trade, N.Y.C., 1986—; now sr. judge. Dist. leader Republican Party N.Y. County, N.Y.C., 1961-68; mem. Rep. Exec. Com., N.Y.C., 1961-68. Served with USN, 1944-46, 51-52. Recipient Proficiency in Constl. Law award N.Y. Law Sch., N.Y.C., 1951, Man of Yr. award St. Paul Soc., N.Y.C., 1971. Mem. ABA, N.Y. County Lawyers Assn., Fed. Bar Assn., Greek Am. Lawyers Assn., Am. Hellenic Edn.l Prog. Assn. Lodges: Parthenon, Masons. Republican. Greek Orthodox. Avocations: basketball, racquetball, stamp collecting/philately, walking, dance. Office: US Ct Internat Trade 1 Federal Plz New York NY 10278-0001

TSOULFANIDIS, NICHOLAS, engineering educator, dean; b. Ioannina, Greece, May 6, 1938; came to U.S., 1963; s. Stephen and Aristea (Ganiou) T.; m. Zizeta Koutsombidou, June 21, 1964; children: Stephen, Lena. BS in Physics, U. Athens, Greece, 1960; MS in Nuclear Engring., U. Ill., 1965, PhD in Nuclear Engring., 1968. Registered profl. engr., Mo. Prof. nuclear engring. U. Mo., Rolla, 1968—, vice chancellor acad. affairs, 1985-86, assoc. dean for rsch. Sch. Mines and Metallurgy, 1989—. Sr. engr. Gen. Atomic Co., San Diego, 1974-75; researcher Cadarache France, 1986-87. Author: Measurement and Detection of Radiation, 1984, 2d edit. 1995; co-author: Nuclear Fuel Analysis and Management, 1990; editor: Nuclear Technology, 1997, 2nd edit., 1999. Mem. Am. Nuclear Soc. (chmn. radiation protection shielding div. 1987-88), Health Physics Soc., Nat. Soc. Profl. Engring., Rotary. Office: U of Mo Rolla Dept Nuc Engring 1870 Miner Cir Dept Nuc Rolla MO 65409-0001

TSU, I-FEI, materials engineer; s. Jung-Chang Tsu and Chiou-Kuei Chang; m. Han-Fang Ying, Jan. 11, 1969. PhD, U. Wis. Madison, 1996. Post doctoral rsch. assoc. Argonne Nat. Lab., Argonne, Ill., 1996—97; sr. staff engr. Seagate Tech., Bloomington, Minn., 1998—. Mem. Materials Rsch. Soc., Pittsburgh, Pa., 1996—. Author: (scientific research) Transmission Electron Microscopy study of Grain Boundary structure of YBCO Bi-Crystals (Outstanding scholar, Am. Soc. of Microscopy, 1996). Mem.: Materials Rsch. Soc. Achievements include patents for increasing the read-back amplitude in magnetic recording heads by adding a nonmagnetic metallic layer in the reader gap. Office: Seagate Tech 7801 Computer Ave Bloomington MN 55435 Office Phone: 952-402-8359. E-mail: itsu@seagate.com.

TSUANG, MING TSO, psychiatrist, educator; b. Tainan, Taiwan, Nov. 16, 1931; came to U.S., 1971; s. Ping Tang and Chhun Kuei (Lin) T.; m. Snow Huei S. Ko, Nov. 24, 1958; children— John, Debby, Grace. MD, Nat. Taiwan U., Taipei, 1957; PhD in Psychiatry, 1965, PhD (Sino-Brit. Fellowship Trust scholar), certs. in epidemiology and stats., population genetics, psychiat. genetics, U. London, 1965; D.Sc. in Psychiat. Genetics and Epidemiology, Faculty of Sci., U. London, 1981. Intern Nat. Taiwan U. Hosp., 1956-57, resident in psychiatry, 1957-61, assoc. prof. psychiatry, staff psychiatrist, 1968-71; collaborating investigator Internat. Pilot Study of Schizophrenia, WHO, 1966-71; vis. assoc. prof. psychiatry Washington U. Sch. Medicine, St. Louis, 1971-72; assoc. prof., staff psychiatrist U. Iowa Coll. Medicine, Iowa City, 1972-75, prof. psychiatry, 1975-82, prof. psychiat. epidemiology, 1978-82; clin. tchr., lectr. to residents, med. students; cons. psychiatrist VA Hosp., Iowa City, 1972-82; prof., vice chmn. sect. of psychiatry and human behavior Brown U., Providence, 1982-85; assoc. med. dir. Butler Hosp., Providence, 1982-85, dir. psychiat. epidemiology research unit, 1982-85; prof. psychiatry Harvard Inst. Psychiat. Epid. and Genetics Harvard U. Med. Sch. and Harvard Sch. Pub. Health; dir. psychiat. epidemiology and genetics Mass. Mental Health Ctr., Boston; chief psychiatry, chmn. Ctr. for Mental Health Brockton-West Roxbury VA Med. Ctr., 1985-94; head and supt. dept. psychiatry Harvard U. at Mass. Mental Health Ctr., 1992—; Stanley Cobb prof. Psychiatry Harvard U., 1993—; dir. Harvard Inst. Psychiatric Epedemiology & Genetics, 1994—. Mem. epidemiol. studies rev. com. NIMH, 1976-79, mem., chmn. rsch. scientist devel. rev. com. NIMH, 1982-86, chmn. epidemiologic studies rev. com., 1989-90; mem. extramural sci. adv. bd. NIMH, 1990—; mem. med. rsch. svc. planning coun. Vets. Health Svcs. and Rsch. Adminstrn., VA Cen. Office, 1990—; vis. prof. psychiatry (Josiah Macy faculty scholar award) Oxford U., Eng., Warneford Hosp., 1979-80; chmn. mental health policy working group, div. health and policy research and edn. Harvard U., 1986—. Author: (with R. Vandermey) Genes and The Mind: Inheritance of Mental Illness, 1980, Schizophrenia: The Facts, 2d edit., 1997, (with S.V. Faraone) The Genetics of Mood Disorders, 1990; co-editor: Schizoaffective Psychoses, 1986, Handbook of Schizophrenia, vol. 3, 1988, Affective and Schizoaffective Disorders, Similarities and Differences, 1990, also monographs.; contbr. chpts. to books, numerous articles to profl. jours. Recipient Clin. Rsch. award Am. Acad. Clin. Psychiatrists, 1983, Rema Lapous award APHA, 1984, Stanley Dean award for rsch. on schizophrenia Am. Coll. Psychiatrists, 1989, Lifetime Achievement award Internat. Soc. Psychiat. Genetics, 1995, Taiwanese-Am. award for Achievement in Sci. and Engring., 1995. Mem. Psychiat. Rsch. Soc., Am. Psychopathol. Assn., Soc. for Life History Rsch. in Psychopathology (steering com. 1989—, Inst. of Medicine/NAAS, Academia Sinica Taiwan, Sigma Xi. Office: 170 Morton St Jamaica Plain MA 02130-3735 *My constant goal is to do the best work I can, to eschew anxiety about the result, to learn from failure, and to build upon success, not for personal honor but for the good of mankind, as God's servant within a serving profession. Helping others is not possible without self-discipline, self-sufficience, and self-sacrifice; at the same time, helping others strengthens the self for its tasks.*

TSUBAKI, ANDREW TAKAHISA, theater director, educator; b. Chiyoda-ku, Tokyo, Japan, Nov. 29, 1931; s. Ken and Yasu (Oyama) T.; m. Lilly Yuri, Aug. 3, 1963; children: Arthur Yuichi, Philip Takeshi. BA in English, Tokyo Gakugei U., Tokyo, Japan, 1954; postgrad. in Drama, U. Saskatchewan, Saskatoon, Canada, 1958-59; MFA in Theatre Arts, Tex. Christian U., 1961; PhD in Speech & Drama, U. Ill., 1967. Tchr. Bunkyo-ku 4th Jr. High Sch., Tokyo, 1954—58; instr., scene designer Bowling Green (Ohio) State U., 1964—68; asst. prof. speech & drama U. Kans., Lawrence, 1968—73, assoc. prof., 1973—79; vis. assoc. prof. Carleton Coll., Northfield, Minn., 1974; lectr. Tsuda U., Tokyo, 1975; vis. assoc. prof. theatre Tel-Aviv (Israel) U., 1975—76; vis. prof. theatre Mo. Repertory Theatre, Kansas City, Mo., 1976, Nat. Sch. Drama, New Delhi, 1983; prof. theatre, film, east Asian Languages and Cultures U. Kans., Lawrence, 1979—2000, prof. emeritus, 2000—. Dir. Internat. Theatre Studies Ctr., U. Kans., Lawrence, 1971-2000, Operation Internat. Classical Theatre, 1988—; Benedict disting. vis. prof. Asian studies Carleton Coll., 1993; area editor Asian Theatre Jour., U. Hawaii, Honolulu, 1982-94; chmn. East Asian Langs. and Cultures, U. Kans., Lawrence, 1983-90; mem. editl. bd. Studies in Am. Drama, Oxford, Miss., 1985-88. Dir. plays Kanjincho, 1973, Rashomon, 1976, 96, King Lear, 1985, Fujito and Shimizu, 1985, Hippolytus, 1990, Busu and the Missing Lamb (Japan) 1992, Suehirogari and Sumidagawa, 1992, 93, Tea, 1995; choreographed Antigone (Greece), 1987, Hamlet (Germany), 1989, The Resistible Rise of Arturo Ui, 1991, Man and the Masses (Germany), 1993, The Children of Fate (Hungary), 1994, The Great Theatre of the World (Germany); editor Theatre Companies of the World, 1986; contbg. author to Indian Theatre: Traditions of Performance, 1990; contbr. 7 entries in Japanese Traditional plays to the Internat. Dictionary of Theatre, vol. 1, 1992, vol. 2, 1994. Recipient World Univ. Svc. Scholarship U. Saskatchewan, 1958-59, University fellow U. Ill., 1961-62, Rsch. fellow The Japan Found., 1974-75, 90, Rsch. Fulbright grantee, 1983. Fellow Coll. Am. Theatre (elected 2002); mem. Am. Theatre Assn., Asian Theatre Program (chair 1976-79), Assn. for Asian Studies, Assn. Kans. Theatres., Assn. Kans. Theatres U/C Div. (chmn. 1980-82), Assn. for Theatre in Higher Edn., Assn. for Asian Performance. Democrat. Buddhist. Avocations: ki-aikido (4th dan), photography, travel. Home: 924 Holiday Dr Lawrence KS 66049-3005 E-mail: atsubaki@ku.edu.

TSUBOUCHI, DAVID H. Canadian provincial official; BA in English, York U.; LLB, Osgoode Hall Law Sch. Ward 5 councillor Town of Markham, 1988-94; sr. ptnr. Tsubouchi & Nichols & Assocs., 1994-95; apptd. Min. of Cmty. and Social Svcs. Ont. Progressive Conservative Govt., 1995-99; solicitor gen. Province of Ont., 1999—; also chair health and social svcs. policy com. Chmn. planning and devel. com., econ. alliance com., indsl. and corp. devel. com. Markham Hist. Mus.; apptd. Min. Consumer & Comml. Affairs Can., 1996; Registrar Gen. Ontario, 1996; chair Cabinet Legis. & Regulations Com., 96; re-elected mem. Provincial Parliament for Markham Ont. Legislature, 1999; apptd. chair Mgmt. Bd. of Cabinet by Premier Mike Harris, 2001. Named Optimist of Yr., 1985-86; recipient Air Can. Heart of Gold award, 1988; granted Coat of Arms, Gov. Gen.'s Office, 1993, award of appreciation, First Nations Chiefs of Police, Ontario Soc. for the Prevention of Cruelty to Animals Mem.: Markham Lions Club. Office: 77 Wellesley St 12th Fl Toronto ON Canada M7A 1N3

TSUI, DANIEL C. electrical engineer, physicist; b. Henan, China, 1939; PhD in Physics, U. Chgo., 1967. Rsch. assoc. U. Chgo., 1967—68; mem. technical staff Bell Labs., Murray Hill, NJ, 1968—82; Arthur LeGrand Doty prof. dept. elec. engring. Princeton (N.J.) U., 1982—. Contbr. articles to profl. jours. Recipient Buckley prize for Condensed Matter Physics, 1984, Benjamin Franklin medal in Physics, 1998, Nobel prize in Physics, 1998. Fellow: AAAS; mem.: NAS, Materials Research Soc., Am. Physical Soc., IEEE, Acad. Sinica. Office: Princeton U Dept Elec Engring Rm B 426 PO Box 5263 Princeton NJ 08544-0001 Fax: 609-258-6279. E-mail: tsui@ee.princeton.edu.

TSUI, FRANK, physicist, educator; s. Yat K Tsui and Yuching Chen; m. Annie Hsu; 1 child, Albert. BS in engring. physics, U. of Calif. at Berkeley, 1984; ME in applied and engring. physics, Cornell U., 1986; MS in physics, PhD in physics, U. of Ill. at Urbana-Champaign, 1992. Rsch. fellow U. of Mich., 1992—95; asst. prof. of physics and materials sci. U. of NC, 1995—2001, assoc. prof. of physics and materials sci., 2001—, asst. chair of dept. of physics and astronomy, 2002—. Recipient Career award, NSF, 1997—2001; IBM fellowship, U. of Ill., 1988—91, Sokol fellowship, U. of Mich., 1993—95. Mem.: Materials Rsch. Soc., Am. Phys. Soc., Tau Beta Bi Engring. Honor Soc., Phi Kappa Phi Nat. Honor Soc. Office: U of NC CB# 3255 Phillips Hall Chapel Hill NC 27599 E-mail: ftsui@physics.unc.edu.

TSUI, LAP-CHEE, molecular genetics educator; b. Shanghai, Dec. 21, 1950; arrived in Can., 1981; s. Jing Lue Hsue and Hui Ching Wang; m. Ellen Lan Fong, Feb. 11, 1977; children: Eugene, Felix. BS, Chinese U. Hong Kong, 1972, MPhil, 1974, DSc (hon.), 1991; PhD, U. Pitts., 1979; DCL (hon.), U. King's Coll., Halifax, N.S., Can., 1991; DSc (hon.), U. N.B., Can., 1991; DLL (hon.), U. St. Francis Xavier, Antigonish, N.S., Can., 1994. Postdoctoral investigator Oak Ridge (Tenn.) Nat. Lab., 1979-80; postdoctoral fellow Hosp. for Sick Children, Toronto, Ont., Can., 1981-83, geneticist-in-chief, 1996—2002; asst. prof. depts. genetics and med. genetics U. Toronto, Ont., Can., 1983-88, assoc. prof., 1988-90, prof., 1990—, univ. prof., 1994—; H.E. Sellers chair in cystic fibrosis, 1998—; head genetics and genomic biology program, 1998—2002. Chmn. chromosome 7 subcom. Human Gene Mapping Workshop, 1986-97; mem. mammalian genetics study sect. NIH, Bethesda, Md., 1988-93; dir. Cystic Fibrosis Rsch. Ctr., Hosp. for Sick Children Spl. Rsch. Ctr., 1994—; scientist Med. Rsch. Coun. Can., 1989—; advisor European Jour. Human Genetics, 1992—, Molecular Medicine Today, 1995—; ajd. prof. U. New Brunswick; vice-chancellor U. Hong Kong. Editor Cytogenetics and Cell Genetics, 1988-92, Internat. Jour. Genome Rsch., 1990—; assoc. editor Am. Jour. Human Genetics, 1990-93, Genomics, 1994—; mem. editl. bd. Mammalian Genome, 1990, Clin. Genetics, 1991—, Human Molecular Genetics, 1991-99; communicating editor Human Mutation, 1995—, Molec. Medicine Today, sr. editor: Physiological Genomics, 2000-01; internat. adv. The Chinese Jour. of Medical Genetics, 2000—; editor Biochimica et Biophysica Acta, 2002—; contbr. over 300 articles to sci. jours.; co-discoverer cystic fibrosis gene, 1989. Trustee Edn. Found., Fedn. Chinese Canadian Profls., Toronto, 1987—. Recipient Paul di Sant Agnese Disting. Achievement award Cystic Fibrosis Found., 1989, Zellers SR. Scientist award, 2001, Gold medal of honor Pharm. Mfrs. Assn. Can., 1989, award of excellence Genetics Soc. Can., 1990, Gairdner Internat. award 1990, Cresson medal Franklin Inst., 1992, E. Mead Johnson award, 1992, Disting. Scientist award The Canadian Soc. Clin. Investigators, 1992, Canadian Conf. medal 1992, Sarstedt Rsch. prize, 1993, Sanremo Internat. award for Genetic Rsch., 1993, J.P. Lecocq prize Inst. de France, 1994, Henry Friesen award The Canadian Soc. for Clin. Investigation and the Royal Coll. of Physicians and Surgeons of Can., 1995, Can. Med. Assn. award of honour, 1996, Jonas Salk award Ontario March of Dimes, 1997, Initiative Cmty. Svc. award Toronto Biotech., 1998, Disting. Scientist award Med. Rsch. Coun., 2000, Killam prize Can. Coun., 2002; named scholar Can. Cystic Fibrosis Found., 1984-86. Fellow Royal Soc. Can., Royal Soc. London, Academia Sinica; pres. Human Genome Orgn., Am. Soc. Human Genetics. Office: Vice-Chancellor's Office U Hong Kong Pokfulam Rd Hong Kong Hong Kong

TSUKAYAMA, DERRICK KAWIKA, police sergeant, consultant; b. Honolulu, Oct. 3, 1954; s. Chomei D. and Elfrieda K. Tsukayama; m. Phyllis K. Chun, Nov. 10, 1988; children: Aran Chun, J.D. BS in Human Svcs., Wayland Bapt. U., 2000. Cert. use of force expert U.S. Dist. Ct. Hawaii; cert. constl. law expert U.S. Dist. Ct. Hawaii; cert. laws of arrest/search and seizure expert U.S. Dist. Ct. Hawaii. Br. mgr. Wackenhut Security Corp. Internat., Maui, Molokai, Hawaii, 1975-77; met. police officer Honolulu Police Dept., 1977-95, met. police sgt., 1995—. Bd. dirs. Honolulu Police Fed. Credit Union, credit com., 1999-2000; cons. Clough/Cameron Cons., Honolulu, 1983-90; instr. Calif. POST Cert., Sacramento, 1992-93. Author: (tng. manual) Constitutional Law for Law Enforcement, 1994, (employee rehab. program) Comprehensive Tactical Intervention Program, 1993 (Unit of the Quarter award 1997). Coord., participant Project Grad., Kailua, Hawaii, 1996-2000. Recipient Disting. Police award MADD, 1993, City and County Officer of Yr., City and County of Honolulu, 1999. Avocations: spending time with family, helping others, outrigger canoe paddling, tennis, deep sea fishing. Office: Honolulu Police Dept Ste 330 715 S King St Honolulu HI 96813 Office Fax: (808) 522-7095.

TSUNG, CHRISTINE CHAI-YI, financial executive; b. Nanking, China, Mar. 23, 1948; came to U.S., 1970; d. Chi-Huang Tsung and Siao-Tuan Huang. BBA, Nat. Taiwan U., Taipei, 1970; postgrad., Washington U., St. Louis, 1970-71; MBA, U. Mo., 1973. Acct. Capital Land Co., St. Louis, 1972-74; chief acct. Servis Equipment Co., Inc., Dallas, 1974-75; acctg. supr. Calif. Microwave, Sunnyale, 1975-76; budget and sales mgr. Columbia Pictures TV Internat., Burbank, Calif., 1976-77; acctg. mgr. Husquarna, San Diego, 1977-82; sr. acct. City of Poway, Calif., 1982-88, fin. mgr., 1988-95; pres., CEO China Airlines, 2000—. Pres., treas. Jade Poly Investment, Beverly Hills, Calif., 1989—; cons. assoc. Metro Properties, San Diego, 1989—; cons. Kaohsiung City, Taiwan, 2000—. Tchr. San Diego North County Chinese Sch., 1985-86; v.p. San Diego Chinese Culture Assn., 1982-86, bd. dirs., 1988-90, 93-94. Mem. Assn. Asian Pacific Airlines, Pacific Asia Travel Assn. (exec. bd.), Govt. Fin. Officers Assn. (Cert. of Achievement 1988-94), Calif. Soc. Mcpl. Fin. Officers (standing com. membership devel., Cert. of Award 1988-94), Mcpl. Treas. Assn. U.S. and Can., Taiwanese C. of C. of N.Am. (bd. dirs. 1994-95). Avocations: travel, swimming, tennis, golf, reading. Office: China Airlines 2F 131 Sec 3 Nanking E Rd Taipei Taiwan Fax: 886-2-2514-5889. E-mail: c_tsung@china.airlines.com.

TSUTAKAWA, EDWARD MASAO, management consultant; b. Seattle, May 15, 1921; s. Jin and Michiko (Oka) T.; m. Hide Kunugi, Aug. 11, 1949; children: Nancy Joyce, Margaret Ann Langston, Mark Edward. Student, U. Wash., 1941, Wash. State U., 1949. Free-lance comml. artist, Spokane, 1943-47; artist Maag & Porter Comml. Printers, Spokane, 1947-54; organizer Litho Art Printers, Inc., Spokane, 1954—, gen. mgr., pres., 1965-80. Charter organizer, dir. Am. Comml. Bank, 1965-80; prin. E.M. Tsutakawa Co., bus. cons. U.S., Japan Trade Negotiator, 1980-89; v.p., operation officer, dir. Mukogawa Ft. Wright Inst.; exec. in residence Whitworth Coll. Grad. Sch., 1999; hon. prof. edn. dept. Wash. State U., 2000. Pres. emeritus Spokane-Nishinomiya Sister City Soc., Sister Cities Assn. of Spokane; mem. Eastern Wash. State Hist. Soc.; bd. dirs. Spokane Regional Internat. Trade Alliance, Leadership Spokane. Recipient Disting. Svc. medal Boy Scouts of Japan, 1967, Cultural medal in Edn., Japan, 1985, Disting. Svc. award City of Nishinomiya, 1971, Disting. Svc. to Expo '74 State of Wash., 1974, Book of Golden Deeds award Exch. Club, 1978, Disting. Cmty. Svc. award UN Assn., 1979, Whitworth Coll., 1987, Svc. to Youth award Spokane YMCA, 1988, Silver Hawk medal Boy Scouts Japan, 1997, Internat. Rels. and Trade Pioneer Recognition, Spokane Area C. of C., 1998; decorated Order of Sacred Treasure medal Govt. of Japan, 1984. Mem. Japanese Am. Citizens League, Japan Am. Soc. Wash. State (pres.'s award 1991), Kiwanis (Spokane). Methodist. Home: 4116 S Madelia St Spokane WA 99203-4229 E-mail: etsutakawa@mfwi.org.

TSYBAKOV, BORIS SOLOMON, information theory and communication networks researcher, educator; b. Moscow, May 14, 1934; s. Solomon Mark and Evdokia Tikhon (Tsybakova) Pinsker; m. Lidia Sergey Tsybakova, Oct. 14, 1956; 1 child, Alexander. D of Sci. in Engring., Moscow Inst. of Physics/Tech. Jr. rschr. Inst. for Radio and Electronic Engring., Moscow, 1958-63, sr. rschr., 1963-77; head of lab. Inst. for Info. Transmission Problems, Moscow, 1977-2000; prin. engr. Qualcomm, Inc., San Diego, 1999—. Prof. Moscow Inst. of Physics and Tech., 1965—93. Mem. editl. bd. Problems of Info. Transmission Jour., 1965—; editor Wireless Personal Comms., An Internat. Jour., 1992—, Jour. Comms. and Networks, 1999—; mem. internat. adv. com. Advanced Electronic Comm. Rsch. & Edn. Jour.; contbr. articles to profl. publ. and lectr. courses on info. theory and commn. sys.; supervisor of 18 grad. in engring. Recipient full prof. title diploma, 1979, Prominent Comm. Profl. of Russia award Pres. of Russia, 1996, Paper award INFOCOM'95 on Math. Analysis of the Self-Similar Traffic, 1995. Mem.: IEEE (Info. Theory Soc. paper award on Invention of the Stable Multiple-Access Algorithm 1981), Russian Acad. Sci. Club. Avocation: lawn tennis. Office: Qualcomm Inc 5775 Morehouse Dr Rm L-529G San Diego CA 92121-1714 Business E-Mail: borist@qualcomm.com.

TSYGAN, LEONID IOSIFOVICH, civil engineer, writer; b. Kiev, Ukraine, Dec. 22, 1938; arrived in U.S., 1979; s. Iosif Haim-Garshevech and Bluma Leybovna Tsygan; m. Emmilia Igorevna Shustova, 1971 (div. 1984); 1 child, Russell; m. Zhanna Iosifovna Polonskaya, 1997; 1 child, Joshua 1 stepchild, Lana Polonskaya. BSCE, Kiev Inst. Hwy. Engring., 1968; computer programmer, Syrit Computer Sch. Sys., N.Y.C., 1983. Sr. engr. State Design Inst. Hwys., Kiev, 1968—78; draftsman King and Gavaris Cons. Engrs. Inc., N.Y.C., 1979—81; designer, draftsman Berger, Lehman Assocs. P.C., Rye, NY, 1982—84; bridge designer E. Pavlo Consulting Engr., N.Y.C., 1984—89; engr. Anuman & Whitney Cons. Engr., N.Y.C., 1990—91; asst. civil engr. N.Y.C. Dept. Transp., N.Y.C., 1992—. Contbr. poetry to anthologies. Alt. del. N.Y.C. Dept. Transp. local 375, chpt. 37, DC 37 AFSCME, AFL-CIO, N.Y.C., 2000—. Co-recipient medal for design of Moscow cable-stay bridge, State Design Inst. Hwys., 1976; named to Poetry's Elite: The Best Poets of 2000. Achievements include test track for road pavement and bridge structure with test material in Willowbrook Park, Staten Island.

TU, CHING-I, humanities educator, researcher; b. Nanking, China, May 13, 1935; s. Show-mei and I-fang Tu; m. Sabrina S. Wang, June 14, 1970; children: Stephen Shih-chung, Sylvia Shih-yun. PhD, U. Wash., Seattle, 1967; BA, Nat. Taiwan U., 1958. Prof., chair Rutgers U., New Brunswick, NJ, 1975—, asst. and assoc. prof., 1966—75. Chair, adv. bd. Asian Studies Rutgers U., New Brunswick, NJ, 1998—; vis. prof. Nat. Taiwan U., Taipei, 1974—75; vis. assoc. prof. U. Hawaii, Honolulu, 1971—72. Author: Poetic Remarks in the Human World, 1970, Anthology of Chinese Literature, 1972, Readings in Chinese Classical Literature, 1981; editor: Tradition and Creativity: Essays on East Asian Civilizations, 1986, Classics and Interpretations: The Hermeneutic Traditions in Chinese Culture, 2000. Grantee Grant for Developing Chinese Studies at Rutgers U., Chiang Ching-kuo Found. for Internat. Scholarly Exch., 1993-1996, Grant for Developing Korean Studies at Rutgers U., The Korea Found., 1995-1998, Grant for Developing Japanese Studies at Rutgers U., The Japan Found., 1992-1995, Grant for Developing Korean Studies at Rutgers U., The Korea Found., 2001-2004. Mem.: Assn. Asian Studies, Am. Assn. for Chinese Studies, Assn. for Fgn. Lang. Dept. Chairs. Avocations: travel, reading, exercise. Office: Asian Studies Rutgers University College Ave New Brunswick NJ 08901-1164

TU, KING-NING, materials scientist, educator; b. Canton, China, Dec. 30, 1937; s. Ying-Chiang and Chan Sau-yuk Tu; m. Chiao Ching Chiao, Sept. 25, 1965; children: Olivia, Stephen. PhD, Harvard, Cambridge, Mass., 1968. Sr. mgr. dept. materials sci. IBM T. J. Watson Rsch. Ctr., Yorktown Heights, NY, 1968—93; prof. and chair Dept. Materiala Sci. and Engring. UCLA, LA, 1993—. Academician Academia Sinica, Nankang, Taipei, Taiwan, 2002. Author: (textbook) Electronic Thin Film Science. Recipient Application to Practice Award, The Metall. Soc., 1988. Fellow: Am. Phys. Soc. Achievements include patents for Device reliability. Home: 11500 Sunset Blvd Los Angeles CA 90049 Office: Univ Calif Los Angeles 405 Hilgard Avenue Los Angeles CA 90095-1595 Business E-Mail: kntu@ucla.edu. E-mail: kntu@ucla.edu.

TU, SUSAN, retired librarian; b. Taipei, Taiwan, June 10, 1923; arrived in U.S., 1961, naturalized, 1976; d. Tsungming Tu and Sonsui Lin; children: Helene Lin, Andy Lin, Jean Lin, Charlyn Lin. Student, Surugadai Girl's Jr. Coll., Tokyo, 1942, Taihoku Imperial U., Taiwan, 1944, U. Calif., Berkeley, 1961; BA, Utah State U., 1965; MA, U. Utah, 1971; MSLS, La. State U., 1973, cert. of med. librarianship, 1975, MEd, 1977, postgrad., 1976-77. Tchr. Taipei (Taiwan) Mcpl. Girls' High Sch., 1958-61; chief libr. Saints Coll., Lexington, Miss., 1974-76; hosp. libr. U.S. Army, Ft. Polk, La., 1977-79; dist. libr. Rock Island (Ill.) dist. U.S. Army Corps Engrs., 1979-83, div. libr. North Atlantic div., 1984-88; dist. libr. N.Y. Dist., N.Y.C., 1988-90. From TIU to NTU- The Reminiscences of Miss Susan Tu, 2002; co-prodr.: (videos, slide prodns., TV program). Mem. adv. bd. The Formosa Chamber Music Soc., Inc. Mem. Spl. Librs. Assn., Chinese-Am. Librs. Assn., Photographic Soc. Am. Avocations: photography, travel, beauty appreciation, literature, music.

TU, WEI-MING, historian, philosopher, writer; b. Kunming, Yunnan, China, Feb. 26, 1940; came to U.S., 1962, naturalized, 1976; s. Shou-tsin (Wellington) and Shu-li (Sonia Ou-yang) T.; m. Helen I-yu Hsiao, Aug. 24, 1963 (div.); 1 son, Eugene L.; m. Rosanne V. Hall, Mar. 17, 1982; children: A. Yalun, Mariana Mei-ling B., Rosa Wen-yun. BA, Tunghai U., 1961; MA, Harvard U., 1963, PhD, 1968. Vis lectr. humanities Tunghai (Taiwan) U., 1966-67; vis. lectr. East Asian studies Princeton U., 1967-68, asst. prof., 1968-71; asst. prof. history U. Calif., Berkeley, 1971-73, assoc. prof., 1973-77, prof., from 1977; vis. prof. Chinese history and philosophy Harvard U., 1981-82, prof. Chinese history and philosophy, 1982—, chmn. com. on study of religion, 1984-87, chmn. dept. East Asian langs. and civilizations, 1991-92, coord. Dialogue of Civilizations, 1990-93. Dir. Inst. Culture and Communication, East-West Ctr., Honolulu, 1990-91; vis. prof. dept. philosophy Peking U., 1985; disting. vis. prof. depts. philosophy and history Taiwan U., 1988; 10th Ch'ien Mu lectr. New Asia Coll., The Chinese U. of Hong Kong, 1989; 1st Henry Chai lectr. Hong Kong U., 1989; vis. prof. Ecole Pratique des Hautes Etudes, U. Paris, 1991; bd. dirs. Inst. Advanced Rsch. in Asian Sci. and Medicine, 1993—; trustee Adironack Work-Study Project, Inc., 1990—; chmn. adv. bd. Inst. Literature and Philosophy, Academia Sinica, 1993—; gov. Inst. East Asian Philosophies, Singapore, 1983-93; pres. Contemporary Mag., Taiwan, 1986-96; acad. adviser Chinese Culture Acad., Beijing; vice-chmn. Internat. Confician Assn., Beijing, 1994, Annual Freeman Lectr. Wesleyan U., 1982; assembly speaker Grinnell Coll., 1983; commencement speaker Grad. Theol. Union at Berkeley, 1990; keynote speaker alumni conf. East-West Ctr., Bangkok, 1990; GET lectr. Bal State U., 1991; panelist 1st World Chinese Enterprises Conv., Singapore, 1991; Paul Desjardins Meml. lectr. Haverford Coll., 1992; baccalaureate speaker Swarthmore Coll., 1993; co-moderator seminar, the Chineses in the Global Community, Aspen Inst., 1994—; nat. lectr. Indian Coun. Philosophy, 1995; guest prof. Wuhan U., Peking U., 1996—, Nanjing U., 1997—, Shandong U., 1998—; Foester lectr. U. Calif. Berkeley, 1996; Green lectr. U. B.C., 1997; Burke lectr. U. Calif. San Diego, 1997; dir. Harvard Yenchnig Inst., 1996—; plenary panelist XXth World Congress Philosophy, Boston, 1998. Author: Neo-Confucian Thought in Action— Wang Yang-ming's Youth, 1976, Centrality and Commonality— An Essay on Chung-Yung, 1976, Humanity and Self-Cultivation— Essays in Confucian Thought, 1980, Confucian Ethics Today: The Singapore Challenge, 1984, Confucian Thought: Selfhood as Creative Transformation, 1985, The Way, Learning, and Politics: Perspective on the Confucian Intellectual, 1988, Toward the "Third Epoch" of Confucian Humanism: Problems and Prospects (in Chinese), 1989, A Reflection on Confucian Self-Consciousness (in Chinese), 1990, The Modern Spirit and the Confucian Tradition (in Chinese), 1993; editor: The Triadic Tension: Confucian Ethics, Max Weber and Industrial East Asia, 1991, The Confucian World Observed, 1992, The Living Tree: Changing Meaning of Being Chinese, 1993, China in Transformation, 1994, Confucian Traditions in East Asian Modernity, 1996; co-editor: Confucianism and Human Rights, 1998; mem. editl. bd. Asian Thought and Soc., 1976—, Harvard Jour. Asiatic Studies, 1983, Philosophy East and West, 1984—, The Twenty-First Century (Chinese); contbr. articles Philosophy East and West, Jour. Asian Studies, Daedalus, The Monist, Chinese lang. jours. and newspapers. Am. Council Learned Socs. fellow, 1968-69; research grantee Center East Asian Studies, Harvard U., 1968-69; research grantee Humanities Council Princeton U., 1970-71; research grantee U. Calif., 1973-74; sr. scholar Com. on Scholarly Communication with People's Republic of China Nat. Acad. Scis., 1980-81; Fulbright-Hays research scholar Peking U., 1985; interviewed by Bill Moyer in World of Ideas, 1991. Fellow Am. Acad. Arts and Scis. (exec com. fundamentalism project 1988-96), Soc. for Study of Value in Higher Edn.; mem. Am. Soc. for the Study Religion, Assn. Asian Studies (dir. 1971-75), Am. Hist. Assn., Soc. Asian and Comparative Philosophy, Am. Acad. Religion, AAAS, Asia Soc. N.Y. Office: Harvard U Dept East Asian Langs and Civilizations Cambridge MA 02138 *As an all-embracing humanist tradition, Confucianism seeks to find integrated and holistic solutions to socio-political problems. One of its core ideas is self-cultivation, signifying that the way to universal peace takes personal knowledge as the point of departure. Learning to be human, in the Confucian perspective, entails an unceasing spiritual transformation. This quest for self-realization involves an ever-expanding circle of human-relatedness. It is not simply a search for one's own inner spirituality but a concern for the establishment of a fiduciary community for humankind as a whole.*

TUAN, KAILIN, management consultant, educator; b. Hefei, China, Sept. 9, 1925; m. Lianba G. Tuan; 1 child, Wayne. BS, Chiao Tung U., Shanghai, 1948; MBA, U. Pa., 1952; PhD, New Sch. for Social Rsch., N.Y.C., 1966. Asst./assoc. prof. Upsala Coll., East Orange, NJ, 1959—74; prof. U. Balt., 1974—77, Temple U., Phila., 1977—93, prof. emeritus, 1993—. Prof., dir. Internat. Ins. Inst., Nankai U., Tianyin, China, 1987—97; hon. prof. various Chinese univs.; lectr. in field; econ. adviser to Taiwan and the Philippines, 1970—73; adviser Ministry of Fin., Taiwan, 1970—90; Far Ea. rep. Internat. Coop. Alliance, 1970; cons. to several maj. U.S. and Brit. ins. and bus. cos., 1970—80. Contbr. articles more than 100 numerous articles to profl. jour. publ. in profl. and academic jour. and bus./ins. mag. USA, UK, Japan, China, Taiwan and other Asian countries; author: Modern Insurance Theory and Edn./Ins. Inst. for Asia and the Pacific, 1972—75, Essays in Risk Management, 1988, The Risk Management Movement, 1999, Studies in the Theory of Risk and Insurance, 1995. Recipient Internat. Friendship award, Chinese Govt., 2000, FLMI Ins. Edn. award, Life Office Mgmt. Assn., 2001, Pres.'s award, Ins. Acctg. and Sys. Assn., 2002. Mem.: U.S. Am.-China C. of C. (founder, bd. dirs.), Am. Risk and Ins. Assn., Internat. Ins. Soc. Avocations: gardening, Go. Office: Temple Univ Dept Risk Mgmt and Ins Philadelphia PA 19122

TUBB, JAMES CLARENCE, lawyer; b. Corsicana, Tex. s. Cullen Louis and Sarah Elmore (Chapman) T.; m. Suzanne Alice Smith, Nov. 25, 1954; children: James Richard, Sara Elizabeth, Daniel Chapman. BA, So. Meth. U., 1951, JD, 1954. Bar: Tex. 1954, U.S. Dist. Ct. (no. dist.) Tex. 1955, U.S. Ct. Appeals (5th cir.) 1959, U.S. Supreme Ct. 1978; cert. comml. real estate specialist, 1983; lic. Tex. real estate broker; cert. mediator Dallas Bar Assn. With legal dept. Schlumberger Well Surveying Corp., Houston, 1954-55; claims atty. Franklin Am. Ins. Co., Dallas, 1957-58; ptnr. Vial, Hamilton, Koch, Tubb & Knox and predecessor firm Akin, Vial, Hamilton, Koch & Tubb, Dallas, 1958-84; dir., ptnr. Winstead, McGuire, Sechrest & Minick, Dallas, 1984-90; pvt. practice Dallas, 1990—. Guest lectr. on real estate broker liability Real Estate Ctr., Tex. A&M U., 1987. Mem. bd. deacons Highland Park Presbyn. Ch., Dallas, 1972—78, ruling elder, 1978—84, 1988—91; mem. permanent jud. commn. Grace Presbytery, 1984—90; bd. dirs. Christian Concern Found., 1965—71, Dallas County affiliate Am. Diabetes Assn., 1991—95. With Tex. Air N.G., 1949—51, 1st lt. JAGC, SAC USAF, 1955—57, 1st lt. USAF, ret. Recipient Outstanding Student award Student Bar Assn., 1954. Fellow Tex. Bar Found.; mem. ABA (chmn. comml. law com. gen. practice sect. 1982-84, real estate probate and trust law sect.), Tex. Bus. Law Found., Tex. Bar Assn., Am. Arbitration Assn. (sec. comml. arbitration panelist), Dallas Country Club, Dallas County Rep. Men's Club (sec. 1978-79). Home and Office: 3407 Haynie Ave Dallas TX 75205-1842 Office Phone: 214-232-8964.

TUBB, LARRY, health facility administrator; b. Memphis, Tenn., Feb. 16, 1948; s. Berniece C. Tubb; children: Robert W., Charles T. MBA, Tex. Christian U., Ft. Worth, 1987. Pres. Cook Children's Home Health, Ft. Worth, 1983—. Office: Cook Children's Home Health 1919 Eighth Ave Fort Worth TX 76110

TUBBS, DAVID EUGENE, mechanical engineer, marketing professional; b. Springfield, Ill., Jan. 12, 1948; s. Eugene Lewellyn and Jacqueline Flo (Jones) T.; m. Linda Alyson Smith, Aug. 2, 1970; children: Corbin David, Cavan Scott. BSME, Ill. Inst. Tech., 1970; postgrad., Okla. State U., 1992. Registered profl. engr., Ill., Okla. Project engr. Sargent & Lundy, Chgo., 1970-82, bus. devel. mgr., 1982-83; mgr. power sales Yuba Heat Transfer Corp., Tulsa, 1983-85; with press products mktg. Nordam, Tulsa, 1985-86; dir. mktg. Brooks Aero. Svc. div. Nordam, Tulsa, 1986-91; mech. dept. mgr. The Benham Group, Tulsa, 1991-93; chief mech. engr. EDECO Engrs./Cons., Tulsa, 1993-94; mktg. support mgr. AGC Tech. Svcs. Inc., Tulsa, 1994-97; lead piping engr. Black & Veatch Pritchard, Overland Park, Kans., 1998—. Mem. ASME, Am. Welding Soc., Ill. Inst. Tech. Alumni Assn. (bd. dirs. 1977-80), Delta Tau Delta, Pi Tau Sigma. Clubs: Toastmasters. Republican. Avocations: bridge, racquetball, ussf soccer referee. Home: 9801 W 118th St Apt 10 Overland Park KS 66210-3167 Office: Black & Veatch Pritchard inc 10905 Grandview St Overland Park KS 66210-1504

TUBBS, EDWARD LANE, banker; b. Delmar, Iowa, Apr. 17, 1920; s. Clifton Marvin and Mary Ellen (Lane) T.; m. Grace Barbara Dyer, Nov. 27, 1941 (dec.); children: Steven, Alan, William; m. Elaine Marshall, Mar. 11, 2000. BS, Iowa State U., 1941; postgrad., U. Wis. Grad. Sch. Banking. With Iowa State U. Agrl. Ext. Svc., Newton, 1942; instr. vets. on-farm DeWitt (Iowa) Schs., 1957-58; v.p., dir. Jackson State Bank, Maquoketa State Bank, 1959-66. Pres., dir. Ohnward Bancshares, Inc.; chmn., dir. 1st Ctrl. State Bank, DeWitt; dir. Tri-County Bank & Trust; pres., dir. Mabsco Agrl. Svcs., Inc., 1982-87; supt. banking State of Iowa, 1987-89; bd. dirs. Iowa Bus. Growth Corp.; lectr. banking schs.; exeh. del. USSR, 1959, 85; banking indsutry del. Baltic Countries, 1993; state dir. Conf. State Bank Supts., 1988-89. Contbr. articles in field. Pres. Elwood (Iowa) Sch. Bd., 1956-62; treas. City of Maquoketa, 1975-81; mem. People to People; trustee Sharar Found., Clinton Coll., 1983-86; v.p., bd. dirs. Timber City Indsl. Devel. Corp.; treas. Maquoketa Cmty. Svcs., 1967-80; trustee Iowa 4-H Found., 1987-91, Hoover Presdl. Libr. Assn. Inc., truatee, 1987—; gov. Iowa State U. Found., 1989—; trustee CCFA Found., 1990-94; elder, moderator United Ch. of Christ. With AUS, 1942-43. Recipient 4-H Club Alumni award, 1962, 2001, Century Farm award Iowa Dept. Agr., 1976, Disting. Pub. Svcs. award Jackson County, 1990, Gold Clover award Iowa 4-H Club, Heart of Gold award, 1996, Iowa Agrl. Ext. Assn. award, 1982, Floyd Andre award, 1985, Cmty. Svc. award Mt. St. Clare Coll., 2002; named Jaycee Boss of Yr., 1970; named to Iowa Agrl. Hall of Fame, 1985, Clinton Fair Hall of Fame, 1999. Mem. Bank Adminstrn. Inst., Am. Bankers Assn. (dir., coun. 1984-86, Ag Bruning award 2000, award for lifetime contbn. to agrl. banking 2000), Iowa Bankers Assn. (treas. 1978-79, pres. 1980-81, James Leach Lifetime Contribution to Banking award 2002), Am. Legion, Isaac Walton League, Iowa State U. Alumni Assn. (dir. 1980-86), Maquoketa C. of C. (dir. 1966-69), Order of Knoll (founders club Iowa State U.), Iowa Friends of Agr. (exec. com. 1987—), Rotary (Paul Harris

fellow), Gamma Sigma Delta (Alumni Achievement award 1989), Alpha Zeta. Home: 1605 Blair Ct Maquoketa IA 52060-3301 Office: 203 N Main St Maquoketa IA 52060 2204 E-mail: edtubbs@caves.net.

TUBESING, RICHARD LEE, library director; b. Kansas City, Mo., Nov. 25, 1937; s. Clarence and Letha (Thacker) T. BA, Yale U., 1959; MA, U. Chgo., 1969; MSL, Western Mich. U., 1972. Asst. to dir. U. Louisville, 1972-73; reference libr. Ga. Tech. Libr., Atlanta, 1973-76; head bus. and sci. Atlanta Pub. Libr., 1976-79; libr. dir. Lewis U., Romeoville, Ill., 1979-81; collection devel. coord. U. Toledo Libr., 1981-86; libr. dir. Coll. of the Southwest, Hobbs, N.Mex., 1986-89; libr. dir., dir. libr. sci. program Glenville (W.Va.) State Coll., 1989-99; ret., 1999. Author: Architectural Preservation, 1978, Architectural Preservation and Urban Renovation, 1982. Program coord. Lea County Archaeol. Soc., Hobbs, 1987-89. Lt. j.g. USNR, 1960-63. Mem. W.Va. Libr. Assn., Lea County Libr. Assn. (v.p. 1987-88, pres. 1988-89). Avocation: collecting primitive and peasant art. Home: 143 E Valley Dr Glenville WV 26351-9416 Fax: 304-462-5671. E-mail: ricktubesing@lycos.com.

TUBMAN, WILLIAM CHARLES, lawyer; b. N.Y.C., Mar. 16, 1932; s. William Thomas and Ellen Veronica (Griffin) T.; m. Dorothy Rita Krug, Aug. 15, 1964; children: William Charles Jr., Thomas Davison, Matthew Griffin. BS, Fordham U., 1953, JD, 1960; postdoctoral, NYU Sch. Law, 1960-61. Bar: N.Y. 1960, U.S. Ct. Appeals (2d cir.) 1966, U.S. Supreme Ct. 1967, U.S. Ct. Customs and Patent Appeals 1971. Auditor Peat, Marwick Mitchell & Co., N.Y.C., 1956-60; sr. counsel Kennecott Corp., N.Y.C., 1960-82, Phelps Dodge Corp., N.Y.C., 1982-85, sec., 1985-95, v.p., 1987 95; pres. Phelps Dodge Found., Phoenix, 1988-95. Author: Legal Status of Minerals Beyond the Continental Shelf, 1966. Mem. scholarship adv. coun. U. Ariz., 1990-92; active Big Bros., Inc., N.Y.C., 1963-73; trustee Phoenix Art Mus., 1989-94; bd. dirs. St. Joseph Hosp. Found., 1994-2003, emeritus, 2003—, chmn., 1994-95; bd. dirs. The Phoenix Symphony, 1994-95. Recipient Disting. Svc. cert. Big Brothers Inc., 1968. Mem.: ABA, N.Y. State Bar Assn. Democrat. Roman Catholic. Home: 8008 N 66th St Paradise Valley AZ 85253-2612

TUCCERI, CLIVE KNOWLES, science writer and educator, consultant; b. Bryn Mawr, Pa., Apr. 20, 1953, d. William Henry and Clive Ellis (Knowles) Hulick; m. Eugene Angelo Tucceri, Sept. 1, 1984 (div. Nov. 1991); 1 child, Clive Edna. BA in Geology, Williams Coll., 1975; MS in Coastal Geology, Boston Coll., 1982. Head sci. dept. Stuart Hall Sch., Staunton, Va., 1975-77; mem. sci. faculty William Penn Charter Sch., Phila., 1977-79, Tower Sch., Marblehead, Mass., 1982-86, Bentley Coll., Waltham, Mass., 1986-88; adminstrv. dir., co-founder Stout Aquatic Libr. Nat. Marine and Aquatic Edn. Resource Ctr., Wakefield, R.I., 1982-89; sci. faculty Mabelle B. Avery Sch., Somers, Conn., 1989—90; faculty, head sci. dept. MacDuffie Sch., Springfield, Mass., 1992—93; sci. faculty East Hampton (Conn.) Middle Sch., 1993—, sci. team leader, 1994—95, sci. chmn. grades K-12, 1995—. Cons. Longmeadow (Mass.) Pub. Schs., 1989-94, Addison-Wesley Pub. Co., Menlo Prk, Calif., 1986-94; cons., freelance writer Prentice-Hall Inc., Needham, Mass., 1991. Co-head class agt. Williams Coll. Alumni Fund, 2000—, vice chair, 2003—; admissions rep. Williams Coll., 2001—; vol. The Bushnell Ctr. for Performing Arts, 2001—; mem. search com. Christ Ch., Middle Haddam, Conn., 2000—01, mem. vestry, 2002—; bd. dirs. People Against Rape, Staunton, 1976—77. Mem.: AAUW (bd. dirs., br. pres.-elect 1975—77, v.p. 1985—86, sec. 1986—87), NEA, NSTA, Cousteau Soc., Conn. Edn. Assn., Conn. Sci Tchrs. Assn., Conn. Sci. Suprs. Assn., Mass. Environ. Edn. Soc. (bd. dirs. 1985—88), Mass. Marine Educators (pres. 1987—89, bd. dirs. 1983—91, editor Flotsam and Jetsam MA Marine Educators newsletter 1991—97), Southeastern New Eng. Marine Educators (publs. chair Nat. Conf. com.), Nat. Mid. Level Sci. Tchrs. Assn., Nat. Marine Edn. Assn. (sec. 1986—87, chpt. rep. 1987 1989), Sigma Xi. Episcopalian. Avocations: renovating old homes, sailing, gardening, reading. Home: 12 Birchwood Dr East Hampton CT 06424-1312

TUCCERI, ELLEN LEE, medical/surgical nurse; b. Boston, Feb. 7, 1945; d. Martin and Natalie (Green) Weiner; m. Anthony Tucceri, June 17, 1988 (dec. Mar. 1993). Student, Boston U. Sch. Edn., 1967-68; BS in Bus. Edn., U. Mich., 1969; postgrad., NYU, 1973-74; MBA in Mktg., Fordham U., 1983; AD in Nursing, U. New Eng., 2003. RN Maine, NH. Circulation mgr. McGraw Hill Publs. Co., NYC, 1973-76; mgr. distbn. rsch. McGraw Hill Info. Sys. Co., NYC, 1976-80, distbn. mgr., 1980-85, mgr. market adminstrn., 1985-87, dir. market adminstrn., 1987-88; owner, operator Golden Pearl, Ogunquit, Maine, 1989-2001; staff nurse Portsmouth (NH) Regional Hosp., 2003—. Cons. Arts and Bus. Coun., NYC, 1979—80, 1984—88; bd. dirs. Fairmont Tenants Corp., 1986—88, Dunelawn Condominium Assn., 1990—97, pres., 1994—97; alt. mem. Appeals Bd. Town of York, 1998—2000, mem., 2000—01; chmn. budget com. Town of Ogunquit, 1989, mem. bd. selectman, 1990—97, chmn. bd. selectman, 1991; mem. adv. bd. York County Tech. Coll., 1996—2001. Mem.: Vis. Nurse Assn. So. Maine (bd. dirs. 1997—, treas. 1999—2000, v.p. 2000—01).

TUCCI, GERALD FRANK, manufacturing executive; b. NYC, Sept. 9, 1926; s. Frank and Mary (Fattizzi) T.; m. Eva G. Gyllander, May 14, 1968; children: Francis Henrik, Michael Fredrik, Amy Christina. Student, Dartmouth Coll., 1944; BSc in Naval Sci., Brown U., 1946, BSME, 1948; MBA with distinction, Harvard U., 1950. Mfg. trainee Am. Can Co., Jersey City, 1950-51; asst. v.p., plant mgr. Artcraft Hosiery Mills, Inc., Darby, Pa., 1951-53; v.p. Leach & Garner, Co., Attleboro, Mass., 1953-63, Gen. Findings, Inc., Attleboro, 1953-63; chmn. Micro Contacts, Inc., Hicksville, NY, 1963—; pres. Micro Pneumatic Logic, Inc., Ft. Lauderdale, Fla., 1973—. Lt. (s.g.) USNR, 1944-47. Mem. ASME, Am. Soc. Mfrs., North Hempstead Country Club, Met. Club (NY), Harvard Bus. Sch. Club NY, Frenchman's Creek Country Club, Beta Theta Pi. Republican. Roman Catholic. Office: 62 Alpha Plz Hicksville NY 11801-2618 E-mail: gerrytucci@aol.com.

TUCCI, JOSEPH M. computer software and services executive; b. 1947; BA, Manhattan Coll.; MBA, Columbia U. With Sperry Corp., 1970-86; pres. U.S. ops. Unisys Corp., 1986-90; exec. v.p. ops. Wang Labs., Inc., 1990-93, chmn. bd., CEO, 1993—99; pres. EMC, Hopkinton, Mass., 2000—, CEO, 2001—. Office: EMC 176 South St Hopkinton MA 01748

TUCCI, MARK A. state agency administrator; b. Trenton, N.J., Dec. 14, 1950; s. William F. and Theresa M. (Miccio) T.; m. Carolyn J. Bilecki, July 10, 1971; children: Nicholas A., Anthony M., Vincent J. BS, Trenton State Coll., 1972, MEd, 1978; cert. pub. mgr., Rutgers U. Cert. N.J. chief sch. adminstr., prin., supr., tchr. of deaf, tchr. of handicapped, N.J.; cert. quality mgr. Am. Soc. Quality. Tchr. Katzenbach Sch. for the Deaf, West Trenton, N.J., 1972-82, spl. asst. to supt., 1982-85; exec. asst. to asst. commr. edn. N.J. Dept. Edn., Trenton, 1985-87; chief of enterprise license bur. N.J. Casino Control Commn., Atlantic City, 1987-91, dir. organizational devel., 1991-99, dir. adminstrn., 1992-93; orgn. devel. leader Dept. Environ. Protection, N.J., 1999—. Adj. faculty Human Resource Devel. Inst., Princeton, N.J., 1996-98; examiner N.J. Quality Achievement Award Program, 1993-94, 96, sr. examiner, 1994, judge, 1997-98; judge N.J. Exemplary State and Local Awards Program, 1994-96, N.J. Quality Achievement Award, 1997—; chmn. N.J. Quality Achievement Award Focus Group, 1994-96; adj. faculty, Ocean Co. Coll., 1999—. Mem. editorial bd. periodical for Trenton chpt. Phi Delta Kappa, 1986-88; columnist Total Quality Management, 1994; contbr. articles to profl. pubs. Chmn. bd. trustees AIDS Support Found., Inc., 1995; cub scout leader Trenton chpt. Boy Scouts Am., 1981-84, dist. com. Jersey Shore Coun., 1995-96; pres. Katzenbach chpt. N.J. State Employees' Assn., 1979; co-chmn. adv. coun. Mercer County Spl. Edn. Assn., 1984; mem. bus. adv. coun. Atlantic C.C., 1990-99; lead judge Gov.'s Award for Performance Excellence, 1998-2000; bd. dirs. Quality New Jersey, Inc. 2004-; leadership planning team, Global Com. on Future of Orgnl. Devel., 2003-. Leader of team that won Nat. Pub. Svc. Excellence award for state govt. and Gov.'s award for performance excellence, 2000, NJ State Profl. Achievement award, 2003, Best Practices in NJ State Govt. anm. workshop series, 2002. Mem. Am. Soc. for Quality Control (sr., cert. quality mgr.), Cert. Pub. Mgrs. Soc. N.J. (fellow trustee), Phi Delta Kappa, Kappa Delta Pi. Roman Catholic. Avocations: reading, journalism, martial arts, photography, songwriting. Home: 273 Neptune Dr Manahawkin NJ 08050-5026 Office: NJ Dept Environ Protection PO Box 420 Trenton NJ 08625-0420 E-mail: mtucci@dep.state.nj.us.

TUCCI, STANLEY, actor; b. N.Y.C., Nov. 11, 1960; BFA, SUNY, Purchase, 1982. Appeared in films Fear Anxiety and Depression, 1990, Men of Respect, 1991, In The Soup, 1992, Beethoven, 1992, Prelude to A Kiss, 1992, Undercover Blues, 1993, The Pelican Brief, 1993, Somebody to Love, 1994, It Could Happen to You, 1994, Mrs. Parker and the Vicious Circle, 1994, Jury Duty, 1995, Kiss of Death, 1995, A Modern Affair, 1995, Captive, 1995, The Daytrippers, 1996, Montana, 1997, Life During Wartime, 1997, The Eighteenth Angel, 1997, Deconstructing Harry, 1997, A Life Less Ordinary, 1997, The Imposters, 1998, A Midsummer Night's Dream, 1999, Joe Gould's Secret, 1999, In Too Deep, 1999, The Whole Shebang, 2000, Bull, 2000, Sidewalks of New York, 2001, America's Sweethearts, 2001, Big Trouble, 2002, Road to Perdition, 2002, Maid in Manhattan, 2002, The Core, 2003, The Life and Death of Peter Sellers, 2004, The Terminal, 2004; (TV series) Murder One, 1995, Winchell, 1998 (Emmy award 1998), (TV film) Conspiracy, 2001 (Golden Globe award 2001); actor, co-dir., co-prodr., (film) Big Night, 1996 (Ind. Spirit award for best 1st screenplay 1996). Office: William Morris Agy c/o David Yocum 151 S El Camino Dr Beverly Hills CA 90212-2775

TUCCI, STEVEN MICHAEL, health facility administrator, physician, recording industry executive; b. N.Y.C., Oct. 5, 1949; s. Louis Alexander and Nina Ida (Cerone) T.; m. Mari E. Koerner, Nov., 1974; children: Alexander, Michael, Lara. BS, Manhattan Coll., 1971; MS, SUNY, Brockport, 1977; PhD, Albany Med. Coll., 1978, MD, 1981. Diplomate Am. Coll. Phys. Medicine and Rehab., Am. Coll. Pain Mgmt.; cert. Nat. Bd. Med. Examiners. Rsch fellow Birth Defects Inst. N.Y. State Dept. Health, 1976-81; instr. anatomy Albany (N.Y) Med. Coll., 1977-78, rsch. assoc. divns. endocrinology, 1978-81, asst. prof. anatomy, 1978-79, rsch. assoc. dept. anatomy, 1979-81; commd. officer student trainee, extern Nat. Inst. Neurol. and Communicative Disorders and Stroke/NIH, 1981; from intern to resident divsn. phys. medicine and rehabilitation George Washington Univ., 1981-84; staff fellowclin. ctr. dept. phys. medicine and rehabilitation NIH, 1983-84; mem. staff dept. medicine Commonwealth Hosp., Fairfax, Va., 1983-84; mem. med. staff Doctor's Hosp., Sarasota, Fla., 1984, med. dir. phys. medicine and rehab., 1989, med. dir., 1994—; founding med. dir. The Ctr. at Manatee Springs, Bradenton, Fla., 1985-86, The Rehab. Inst. Sarasota, Fla., 1986-88; med. dir. Fawcett Meml. Hosp., Port Charlotte, Fla., 1988—; med. dir. phys. medicine and rehab. Charlotte Community Rehab. Ctr., Port Charlotte, 1988; co-founder Sports, Pain and Rehab. Medicine Assocs., Sarasota and Port Charlotte, 1992; med. dir. Manatee Meml. Hosp., Bradenton, 1993—; pres., CEO Groove Tone Records, Sarasota, 1994-96. Writer: (music) Take Me Down to the Ballgame, 1994, Spell on Me, 1994, On the Road to Nowhere, 1994; contbr. articles, papers to profl. jours. Mem. AMA, USTA, Am. Acad. Phys. Medicine and Rehab., Am. Coll. Sprots Medicine, Am. Congress Rehabilitative Medicine, Am. Soc. Pain Mgmt., Fla. Med. Assn., Fla. Soc. Phys. Medicine and Rehab., Major League Baseball Players Alumni Assn., Rep. Presdl. Task Force, Rep. Senatorial Inner Circle. Republican. Roman Catholic. Avocations: musician, tennis, fishing. Office: Sports and Rehab Medicine 7147 Curtiss Ave Sarasota FL 34231-1207

TUCHMAN, STEVEN LESLIE, lawyer, consul; b. Indpls., Sept. 3, 1946; s. Frederick and Lillian (Alper) T. BA, Ind. U., 1968, JD, 1971; cert. internat. law, City Coll. London, 1970. Bar: Ind. 1971, registered: (mediator). Advisor Den Danske Bank, Copenhagen, 1971-73; assoc. Melvin Simon and Assoc., Inc., Indpls., 1973-81; pvt. practice Indpls., 1981-90; critic Sta. WFYI-FM, Indpls., 1987—95, Sta. WTHR-TV, Indpls., 1987-95; ptnr. Lewis & Kappes, Indpls., 1990—, pres., 2001—03. Commr., Ind. Arts Commn., 2000—; adj. prof. real estate law Ind. U. Sch. Bus., 1983-84. Columnist The New Ties, Indpls., 1989; contbr. articles to profl. jours. V.p. Dance Kaleidoscope, Indpls., 1980-81; pres. Festival Dance Theatre, Indpls. and NYC, 1983-84; chmn. task force subcom. Indpls. Pub. Schs. Referendum, 1985; subcom. chmn. exec. com. Internat. Violin Competition Indpls., 1986-89; chmn. real estate com. cmty. adv. coun. Jr. League Indpls., 1987-90; chmn. Indpls. Com. Fgn. Rels., 1990—; bd. dirs. Planned Parenthood Ctrl. Ind., 1987-92, v.p. 1989-91, pres. 1991-92; steering com., affiliate pres.' coun. nat. com. Planned Parenthood Fedn. Am.; active Jewish Cmty. Rels., 1988-90; bd. dirs. Am. Cabaret Theater, 1999—, pres., 2002—, hon. Danish consul, 2003—; commr. Indpls. Historic Preservation Commn., 2003—. Mem. ABA, Ind. State Bar Assn. (ho. dels. 1986—), Indpls. Bar Assn. (com. long range plans 1987-88, Disting. award), Am. Immigration Lawyers Assn. (chmn. Ind. chpt., 1994-96, bd. govs., 1994-96), Ind. Supreme Ct. Disciplinary Commn. (grievance com.), Indpls. Bar Found. Office: 1700 One American Sq PO Box 82053 Indianapolis IN 46282-2053

TUCHMANN, ROBERT, lawyer; b. N.Y.C., July 7, 1946; s. Frederick C. and Hildegard (Jung) Tuchmann; m. Naomi R. Walfish, June 1, 1969; children: David, Paul. AB, Oberlin Coll., 1967; JD, Harvard U., 1971. Bar: Mass. 1971, U.S. Dist. Ct. Mass. 1971. Assoc. Hale and Dorr, Boston, 1971-76, jr. ptnr., 1976-80, sr. ptnr., 1980—2004, Wilmer, Cutler, Pickering, Hale and Dorr, Boston, 2004—. Lectr. Mass. Continuing Legal Edn., 1976—99. Pres. Project Bread-The Walk for Hunger, Boston, 1990—98; chair Ctrl. Artery Environ. Oversight Com., 1992—; mem. New Fed. Courthouse Task Force, 1993—99; bd. overseers Rogerson Cmtys., 1995—; co-chair Mayor's Ctrl. Artery Completion Task Force, 2001—; mem. com. Oberlin Coll., 1990. Mem.: Boston Soc. Archs. (bd. dirs. 2004—), Downtown Boston Transp. Mgmt. Assn. (chmn. 1996—), Mass. Conveyancers Assn. (com. chmn. 1984—89), Boston Bar Assn. (com. chmn. 1977—81), Island Alliance (trustee 1997—2000), Abstract Club. Office: Wilmer Cutler Pickering Hale and Dorr LLP 60 State St Boston MA 02109-1816 Office Phone: 617-526-6920. Business E-Mail: robert.tuchmann@wilmerhale.com.

TUCK, AMY, lieutenant governor; b. Starkville, Miss., July 8, 1963; d. Grady William and Mary (Boykin) Tuck. BA in Polit. Sci., Miss. State U., Starkville, 1985; postgrad., Miss. State U., Miss. State U., Starkville, 1992—; JD, Miss. Coll., 1989. Legal asst. Ben. F. Hilburn Jr., Atty. at Law, Starkville, Miss., 1984-85; grad. asst. dept. polit. sci. Miss. State U., Starkville, 1986-87; law clk. Minor Buchanan, Jackson, Miss., 1987-88, Deposit Guaranty Nat. Bank, Jackson, 1988-89; state senator dist. 15 State of Miss., Jackson, 1990-99, lt. gov., 2000—. Adj. prof. Wood Jr. Coll., Mathiston, Miss., 1990-95. Mem. Oktibbeha County Voter Re-Registration Com., Oktibbeha County Fedn. Dem. Women; bd. dirs. Oktibbeha County Am. Cancer Soc., 1991-92; mem. local rels. com. Children and Family Svcs.; assoc. mem. Nat. Mus. Women in the Arts, 1992-93. Mem. NAFE, Am. Legis. Exch. Com., Am. Soc. Pub. Adminstrs., Nat. Conf. State Legislature, Nat. Order Women Legislators, Miss. State U. Alumni Assn., Starkville Area Bus. and Profl. Women's Club, Oktibbeha County C. of C., Gamma Beta Phi, Pi Sigma Alpha, Omicron Delta Kappa, Phi Delta Phi (vice-magister 1988, historian 1988-89). Democrat. Methodist. Office: Office of the Lt Gov PO Box 1018 Jackson MS 39215-1018

TUCK, EDWARD FENTON, venture capitalist; b. Memphis, July 5, 1931; s. Edward Fenton and Jane Florence (Lewis) T.; m. Janet Allene Barber, July 6, 1957; children: Jean, Ann. BSEE, Mo. Sch. Mines, 1953; elec. engr. (hon.), U. Mo., 1980, D Engring. (hon.), 1997. Registered profl. engr., Calif. Various engring. and mfg. mgmt. positions Lenkurt Elec. Co. divsn. GTE, San Carlos, Calif., 1957-62; v.p., co-founder Kebby Microwave Corp., San Carlos, 1962-64; asst. tech. dir. ITT, 1964-67, v.p., tech. dir. N.Am. Telecomms. Group, 1967-72; gen. mgr., pres. Tel-Tone Corp., Kirkland, Wash., 1972-74; v.p. mktg. and engring. Am. Telecomm. Corp., El Monte, Calif., 1975-79; pres. Edward Tuck & Co. Inc., West Covina, Calif., 1979-86; gen. ptnr. The Boundary Fund, West Covina, 1986-95, Kinship Ptnrs. II, 1990—. Prin. Falcon Fund, 1982—; bd. dirs. TriQuint Semiconductors, Beaverton, Oreg.; chmn. High Tower Software, Aliso Viejo, Calif. Contbr. articles to profl. jours. Trustee U. Mo., Rolla. Named mem. Acad. Elec. Engring. U. Mo. Fellow Instn. Radio, Elec. and Electronic Engrs. Australia; mem. IEEE (sr., 1st prize for article 1962), AAAS, Assn. Profl. Cons. (pres., bd. dirs. 1979-86). Democrat. Office: Kinship Partners II 100 N Barranca St Ste 920 West Covina CA 91791 Business E-Mail: ed@falconfund.com.

TUCK, GRAYSON EDWIN, real estate agent, former natural gas transmission executive; b. Richmond, Va., May 11, 1927; s. Bernard Okly and Erma (Wiltshire) T.; m. Rosalie Scroggs, June 6, 1947; children— Janice Lorrain, Kenneth Edwin, Carol Lynn. BS, U. Richmond, 1950. Payroll clk., cost clk. Gen. Baking Co., Richmond, 1948-51; jr. accountant Commonwealth Natural Gas Corp., Richmond, 1951-55, sr. accountant, 1956-57, accounting supr., 1957-58, asst. treas., 1959-62, asst. sec., asst. treas., 1963-64, treas., asst. sec., 1965-77; treas. Commonwealth Natural Resources, Inc., 1977-81, CNG Transmission Co. subs., 1977-79; sec.-treas. Air Pollution Control Products, Inc., Richmond, 1970-73; asst. treas., asst. sec. Commonwealth Gas Distbn. Corp., Richmond, 1969-79; mgr. taxes and cash mgmt. Commonwealth Gas Pipeline Corp., subs. Columbia Gas System Inc., 1981-86; investor, realtor Bill Eudailey & Co., 1986—. Active Boy Scouts Am., 1965—69; bd. dirs. Henrico Area Mental Health Retardation Svcs., 1983—85; active Elpis Christian Ch., 2001—; deacon Presbyn. Ch., 1958—86, elder, 1986—2001, treas., 1968—70. With USNR, 1945—46. Mem. Nat. Assn. Accts. (assoc. dir. 1963-64) Home: 2923 Oakland Ave Richmond VA 23228-5827 Office: 6401 Mallory Dr Richmond VA 23226-2911

TUCK, JOHN CHATFIELD, former federal agency administrator, public policy advisor; b. Dayton, Ohio, May 28, 1945; m. Jane McDonough, 3 children. BS, Georgetown U., 1967. Various positions as asst. to Rep. leaders Ho. of Reps., Washington, 1974-77, chief Rep. floor ops., 1977-81; asst. sec. to majority U.S. Senate, 1981-86, spl. asst. then dep. asst. to pres. for legis. affairs, 1986-87; dep. asst. to Pres. of U.S. and exec. asst. to chief of staff Office Chief of Staff, The White Ho., 1987-88; asst. to Pres. and dir. Office Chief of Staff, 1988-89; under sec. Dept. Energy, Washington, 1989-92; sr. pub. policy advisor Baker, Donelson, Bearman & Caldwell, Washington, 1992—. With USN, 1968-73, ret. capt. USNR, 1973-94. Republican. Office: Baker Donelson Bearman & Caldwell 801 Pennsylvania Ave NW Ste 800 Washington DC 20004-2616

TUCK, RUSSELL R., JR., former college president; b. June 9, 1934; m. Marjorie Gay Tuck; children: Russell R. III, Catherine Elizabeth. BS in Chemistry, Union U., 1956; MS in Biology, George Peabody Coll. Vanderbilt U., 1957, PhD in Curriculum and Instrn., 1971; studied, Wash. U., 1960—61. Instr. biology, asst. coordinator Korean Tchr. Edn. Program George Peabody Coll. Vanderbilt U., Nashville, 1957-59; tchr. biology, chmn. sci. dept. University City (Mo.) Sr. High Sch., 1960-63, from asst. prin. to prin., 1963-70; prin. Parkway North Sr. High Sch., St. Louis County, Mo., 1971-78; asst. supt. Parkway Sch. Dist., St. Louis County, 1979-81, assoc. supt., 1981-84; pres. Calif. Bapt. Coll., Riverside, 1984-94, pres. emeritus, 1994—. Contbr. articles to profl. jours. Bd. dirs. Opera Assn.; pres. Riverside County chpt. ARC, 1989-90; active Bapt. Ch., local hosp. assn. bd., local edn. com.; World Affairs Coun. Mem. Calif. Bapt. Hist. Soc. (bd. dirs.), Calif. Bapt. Devel. Found. (bd. dirs.), Am. Assn. Sch. Adminstrs., Inland Empire Higher Edn. Coun. (pres. 1987-88), Rotary, Kappa Delta Pi, Phi Delta Kappa. Lodges: Rotary. Home: 14000 Chelmsford Dr Gainesville VA 20155

TUCKER, ALAN CURTISS, mathematics professor; b. Princeton, N.J., July 6, 1943; s. Albert William and Alice Judson (Curtiss) W.; m. Amanda Almira Zeisler, Aug. 31, 1968 (div. 1997); children: Lisa, Kathryn, Edward; m. Ann K. Hong, Feb. 16, 1997. BA, Harvard U., 1965; MS, Stanford U., 1967, PhD, 1969. Asst. prof. applied math. SUNY, Stony Brook, 1970-73, assoc. prof. applied math., 1973-78, prof. applied math., chmn., 1978-89, SUNY Disting. Teaching prof., 1989—. Vis. asst. prof. math. U. Wis., Madison, 1969-70; vis. assoc. prof. computer sci. U. Calif., San Diego, 1976-77; vis. prof. ops. research Stanford U., 1983-84; cons. Sloan Found., 1981-85; acad. cons. 40 colls. and univs. Author: Applied Combinatorics, 1980, Unified Introduction to Linear Algebra, 1987, Linear Algebra, 1993; assoc. editor Math. Monthly, 1996-2001, Applied Maths. Letters, 1986—; contbr. 45 rsch. articles to profl. jours. Ga. U. Consortium Disting. Visitor, 1982; NSF grantee, 1972-86. Mem. Math. Assn. Am. (chmn. publs. 1982-86, editor Studies in Math. series 1979-86, v.p. 1988-90, chmn. ednl. coun. 1990-96, Disting. Tchr. award 1994, Trevor Evans award 1996), U.S. Commn. Math. Instrn., Am. Math. Soc., Ops. Rsch. Soc. Am., Soc. Indsl. Applied Maths., Sigma Xi (chpt. pres. 1987—). Home: 19 Crosby Place Cold Spring Harbor NY 11724-2404 Office: SUNY At Stony Brook Dept Of Applied Math Stony Brook NY 11794-3600 Office Phone: 631-632-8365. E-mail: atucker@notes.sunysb.edu.

TUCKER, ALAN DAVID, publisher; b. Erie, Pa., Mar. 9, 1936; s. Meredith LaDue and Monica (Klocko) Tucker; m. Kiyoko Iizuka, Feb. 8, 1963; 1 child, Kumi. AB, Princeton U., 1957. Lic. real estate salesperson N.Y. Assoc. editor Hawthorn Books, N.Y.C., 1964-66; editor John Day Co., Inc., N.Y.C., 1966-72; mng. editor David McKay Co., Inc., N.Y.C., 1972-75, v.p., 1975-78, exec. v.p., editl. dir., 1978-84; editl. dir. Fodor's Travel Guides, Inc., N.Y.C., 1978-84; prodr. Penguin Travel Guides and other publs., N.Y.C., 1984-91; gen. editor Berlitz Travellers Guides, N.Y.C., 1991-95; consulting sr. analyst Genesis Group Assocs., Montclair, NJ, 1995—2001; v.p. mktg. strategy Oxygen Advt., Inc., N.Y.C., 1996—; consulting sr. analyst Adis Bus. Intelligence, Langhorne, Pa., 2002. Real estate sales assoc. Halstead Property Co., N.Y.C., 1999—. Author: Capitation and Risk Sharing, 1995, Integrated Health Information Systems, 1997, Provider-Sponsored Managed Care, 1998, Convergence in Coordinated Care, 1998; co-author: The Electronic Superhighway 1997-2010: Opportunities for the Healthcare Industry, 1996, Diabetes Disease Management, 1995, 2d edit., 1998, Asthma Disease Management, 1997, 2d edit., 1999, Hypertension Management, 1999, Management of Congestive Heart Failure, 1999, Intelligence Report: Depression, 1999, Intelligence Report: Lung Cancer, 2000, Strategic Audit: Alzheimer's and Parkinson's Diesease, 2000, Strategic Audit: Stroke and Multiple Sclerosis, 2000, Asthma Forum, 2001, Osteoporosis Forum, 2001, Psoriasis Forum, 2001, Congestive Heart Failure Forum, 2001, Obesity Forum, 2002, Allergic Rhinitis Forum, 2002, Pain Management Forum, 2002, Handbook of Healthcare Marketing, 2003. With USNR, 1957—60. Mem.: Real Estate Bd. N.Y., Am. Coll. Healthcare Execs. (regent's adv. coun. N.Y.C. region), N.Y. Travel Writers Assn. (past pres.), Soc. Am. Travel Writers. Office: 186 Riverside Dr New York NY 10024-1007 also: 34 Still Meadow Rd Sharon CT 06069-2133

TUCKER, ALLAN MARC, mastering engineer; b. Bklyn., May 26, 1949; BA, CUNY, 1971. Rec. engr. Bell Sound Studios, N.Y.C., 1971-73, Platinum/Chess Records, Englewood, N.J., 1975-77, Vanguard Records, N.Y.C., 1977-80, Foothill Sound, N.Y.C., 1971-88; pres., chief mastering engr. Foothill Digital, N.Y.C., 1988—. Rec. engr. Malcolm Addey Recorders, N.Y.C., 1972-87; ops. mgr. Nat. Video and Rec. Studios, N.Y.C., 1979-83; freelance studio engr., 1971-88. Mastering engr. over 2,000 albums/CDs. Recipient 2 Visionary awards 3M Corp.; selected Beta/Co-developer by Sonic Solutions, 1988-91; winner Emmy, TEC and Grammy awards. Mem. Nat. Acad. Rec. Arts and Scis., Audio Engring. Soc., Sonic Solutions DVD-Audio Developers Group, Audio Engring. Soc. (chmn. N.Y. sect.). Office: Foothill Digital Inc 215 W 91st St New York NY 10024-1321 Business E-Mail: tucker@foothilldigital.com.

TUCKER, ALVIN LEROY, retired government official; b. Bklyn., Sept. 7, 1938; s. Alvin Leroy Jr. and Alveria (Klune) T.; m. Jacqueline Twiggs, Aug. 27, 1966; children: Hazel, Pluma, Jacqueline, Alvin. BS, U. Md., 1965. CPA, Md.; cert. internal auditor; cert. govt. fin. mgr.; cert. def. fin. mgr. Auditor Dept. Army, Washington, 1965-67; dep. insp. gen. HUD, Washington, 1986-89; auditor Dept. Def., Washington, 1967-72, budget analyst, 1972-79, dir. tng. and edn., 1979-83, dep. asst. insp. gen., 1983-86, dep. comptr., 1989-94, dep. CFO, 1991-97, chmn. concessions com., 1989-97; sr. mgr. Grant Thornton LLP, Alexandria, Va., 1997—. Mem. steering com. Joint Fin. Mgmt. Improvement Program, 1990-93; mem. CFO's Coun., 1989-97, chmn. fin. sys. com., 1989-97; mem. Fed. Acctg. Stds. Adv. Bd., 1991-97; chmn. Cert. Def. Fin. Mgr. Commn., 2004—. With U.S. Army, 1958-61. Recipient Def. medal for disting. civilian svc. with Bronze Palm, meritorious sr. exec. medal. Mem. AICPA, Am. Soc. Mil. Comptrs., Assn. Govt. Accts. (nat. exec. com. 1993-94), Kiwanis (club pres. 1981-82, 86-87). Avocation: genealogy. Office: Grant Thornton 333 John Carlyle St Ste 500 Alexandria VA 22314

TUCKER, ANNE WILKES, curator, photography historian and critic, lecturer; b. Baton Rouge, Oct. 18, 1945; AAS in Photographic Illustration, Rochester Inst. Tech., 1968; BA in Art History, Randolph-Macon Women's Coll.; MFA in Photographic History, SUNY-Buffalo, 1972. Rsch. asst. Internat. Mus. Photography at the George Eastman House, Rochester, NY, 1968—70; rsch. assoc. Gernsheim Collection U. Tex., Austin, 1969, 1979; curatorial intern dept. photography Mus. Modern Art, N.Y.C., 1970—71; photography cons. Creative Artists Pub. Svc. Program, N.Y.C., 1971—72; vis. lectr. New Sch. for Social Rsch., 1973; dir. photography lecture series Cooper Unionn Forum, N.Y.C., 1972—75; lectr. Cooper Union for Advancement of Arts and Sci., 1972—75; vis. lectr. Phila. Coll. Art, 1973—75; affiliate artist U. Houston, 1976—80; curator photography Mus. Fine Arts, Houston, 1976—; Gus and Lyndall Wortham cur., photographic historian and critic, lectr. Trustee Visual Studies Workshop, 1980—2000, Houston Ctr. Photography, 1991—96, Houston Foto Fest, 1988—; visual arts panel The Houston Festival, 1981—83; adv. bd. Randolph-Macon Woman's Coll. Art Gallery, 1982—84; dir. numerous exhbns. and workshops; lectr. in field; mem. numerous juries and panels. Author: (books and catalogues) The Woman's Eye, 1973; author: (with William C. Agee) The Target Collection of American Photography, 1977; author: Target II: 5 American Photographers, 1981, Target III: In Sequence, 1982; author: (with Philip Brookman) Robert Frank: New York to Nova Scotia, 1986; author: (with Maggie Olvey) The Sonia and Kaye Marvins Portrait Collection, 1986, 1995; author: Photo Notes and Filmfront, 1977; author: (with other curators) The Museum of Fine Arts, Houston: A Guide to the Collection, 1981; author: Unknown Territory: Photography by Ray K. Metzker, 1957-83, 1984, Fifth Annual International Fine Art Photography Exposition, 1984; author: (with Andy Grundberg) American Prospects: The Photographs of Joel Slernfeld, 1987, 1994; author: (with Willie Morris) American Classroom: The Photographs of Catherine Wagner, 1988; author: (with Pamela Allara) Crosscurrents/Crosscountry, 1988; author: (with other authors) Money Matters: A Critical Look at Bank Architecture, 1990; author: The Blue Moon: Photographs by Keith Carter, 1990; author: (with Pete Daniel) Carry Me Home: Photographs by Debbie Fleming Caffery, 1990; author: George Krauze, 1991, Tradition and the Unpredictable: The Allan Chasanoff Photographic Collection, 1994, Quest for the Moon, 1995, (exhbns. and catalogues) Brassai: Eye of Paris, 1999, Louis Faurer, 2002, History of Japanese Photography, 2003; co-prodr. (video) Fire in the East: The Portrait of Robert Frank, 1986; editor: (books and catalogues) The Anthony G. Cronin Memorial Collection, 1979, (manual) Susanne Bloom and Ed Hill, 1980, The Photo League, 1987, Czech Modernism 1900-1945, 1990, Paul Strand: Essays on His Life and Work, 1991, George Krause, 1992; contbr. articles to profl. jours. and mags. Recipient Third Ann. Publ. award, Internat. Ctr. Photography, 1987, John Simon Guggenheim Meml. Alumna Achievement award, Randolph-Macon Woman's Coll., 1993; fellow Found. fellow, 1983—84; grantee Nat. Endowment Arts grantee, 1976, 1986, 1989. Mem.: Houston Ctr. for Photography, Art Table, Inc., Coll. Art Assn., Soc. Photographic Edn. (nat. bd. dirs. 1976—80, sec. 1977—79). Office: Mus Fine Arts PO Box 6826 Houston TX 77265

TUCKER, BEVERLY SOWERS, information specialist; b. Trenton, N.J., Dec. 1, 1936; d. Eldon Jones and Verbeda Eleanor (Roberts) Sowers; m. Harvey Richard Tucker, Dec. 27, 1958 (div. Nov. 1983); children: Randall Richard, Brian Alan. BS in Chemistry with distinction, Purdue U., 1958; MS in Geology, No. Ill. U., 1985; MA in Library and Info. Sci., Rosary Coll., 1989. Asst. rsch. librarian CPC Internat., Argo, Ill., 1958-62; chem. patent searcher Chgo., 1962-66; info. specialist C. Berger & Co., Wheaton, Ill., 1986, Amoco Corp., Naperville, Ill., 1987-99, Baxter Healthcare, Round Lake, Ill., 1999—2003; faculty Coll. Du Page, Glen Ellyn, Ill., 1989—; with Baxter Healthcare, Round Lake, Ill., 1999—2003. Mem. Spl. Libraries Assn., Ill. Fedn. Women's Club (treas. 5th dist. 1979-81, Outstanding Jr. Clubwoman award 1979-80), Garden Club Council Wheaton (pres. 1981-82), Wheaton Jr. Woman's Club (pres. 1977-78, Single Parent scholar 1984), Gardens Etc. Club (pres. 1978-79), Alpha Lambda Delta, Delta Rho Kappa, Theta Sigma Phi, Alpha Chi Omega (grantee 1985). Republican. Presbyterian. Avocations: bridge, needlecrafts, gourmet cooking. Home: 1507 Paula Ave Wheaton IL 60187-6135

TUCKER, BOWEN HAYWARD, lawyer; b. Providence, Apr. 13, 1938; s. Stuart Hayward and Ardelle Chase (Drabble) T.; m. Jan Louise Brown, Aug. 26, 1961; children: Stefan Kendric Slade, Catherine Kendra Gordon. AB in Math., Brown U., 1959; JD, U. Mich., 1962. Bar: R.I. 1963, Ill. 1967, U.S. Supreme Ct. 1970. Assoc. Hinckley & Allen, Providence, 1962-66; sr. atty. Caterpillar, Inc., Peoria, Ill., 1966-72; counsel FMC Corp., Chgo., 1972-82, sr. litigation counsel, 1982-95, assoc. gen. counsel, 1995-2000; v.p. eLaw Forum, Washington, 2000—01; owner Strategic Litigation Mgmt., Arlington Heights, Ill., 2000—. Chmn. legal process task force Chgo. Residential Sch. Study Com., 1973-74, mem. Commn. on Children, 1983-85, Ill. Com. on Rights of Minors, 1974-77, Com. on Youth and the Law, 1977-79; mem. White House Conf. on Children, ednl. svcs. subcom., 1979-80; chairperson Youth Employment Task Force, 1982-83; mem. citizens com. on Juvenile Ct. (Cook County), 1978-94, chmn. detention subcom., 1982-92; mem. econ. effects adv. com. Rand Inst. Civil Justice, 1990-92; bd. dirs. Voices Ill. Children, 1998—. 1st lt. U.S. Army, 1962-69. Mem. ABA, Am. Law Inst., Ill. State Bar Assn., R.I. Bar Assn., Chgo. (chmn. com. on juvenile law, 1976-77), Chgo. Lincoln Inn of Ct. (sec., treas. 1996-98), Constrn. Industry Mfrs. Assn. (exec. com. of Lawyers' Coun. 1972, 75-79, vice chmn. 1977, chmn. 1978-79), Mfrs. Alliance (products liability coun. 1974-95, vice chmn. 1981-83, chmn. 1983-85), Product Liability Adv. Coun. (bd. dirs. 1986-2000, exec. com. 1990-97, vice chmn. 1991-93, chmn. 1993-95), ACLU (bd. dirs. Ill. divsn. 1970-79, exec. com. 1973-79, sec. 1975-77), Am. Arbitration Assn. (mem. panel of arbitrators 1985-96), Phi Alpha Delta, Brown Univ. of Chgo. Club (nat. alumni schs. program 1973-85, v.p. 1980-81, pres. 1981-86), Lawyers Club of Chgo. Home: 107 W Noyes St Arlington Heights IL 60005-3747 Office Phone: 312-861-5940.

TUCKER, BRIAN, seismologist; BA, Pomona Coll., 1967; PhD, U. Calif., San Diego, 1975; MA in Pub. Policy, Harvard U., 1991. Founder GeoHazards Internat., 1991—. Cons. prof. dept. civil engring. Stanford U.; bd. dirs. World Seismic Safety Initiative. Mem. editl. bd.: Jour. Earthquake Engring. Fellow MacArthur Found., 2002. Office: GeoHazards Internat 200 Town and Country village Palo Alto CA 94301

TUCKER, CYNTHIA ANNE, journalist; b. Monroeville, Ala., Mar. 13, 1955; d. John Abney and Mary Louise (Marshall) Tucker; m. Michael Pierce, Dec. 26, 1987 (div. 1989). BA, Auburn U., 1976. Reporter The Atlanta Jour., 1976-80, editorial writer, columnist, 1983-86; reporter The Phila. Inquirer, 1980-82; assoc. editorial page editor The Atlanta Constitution, 1986-91, editorial page editor, 1992—. Bd. dirs. ARC, 1989-93, Families First, 1988—, Internat. Women's Media Found., 1994—. Nieman fellow Harvard U., 1988-89; Pullitzer Prize finalist for commentary, 2004. Mem.: Coun. Fgn. Rels., Nat. Assn. Minority Media Execs., Nat. Assn. Black Journalists, Am. Soc. Newspaper Editors (Disting. Writing award 2000). Mem. United Ch. Christ. Office: Atlanta Constitution 72 Marietta St NW Atlanta GA 30303-2804*

TUCKER, CYNTHIA DELORES NOTTAGE (MRS. WILLIAM M. TUCKER), political party official, former state official; b. Phila., Oct. 4, 1927; d. Whitfield and Captilda (Gardiner) Nottage; m. William M. Tucker, July 21, 1951. Student, Temple U., Pa. State U., U. Pa.; student hon. degrees, Villa Maria Coll., Erie, Pa., 1972, Morris Coll., Sumter, S.C., 1976; DHL (hon.), U. D.C. Sec. of state Commonwealth of Pa., Harrisburg, 1971-77; nat. pres. Fedn. Democratic Women, 1979-81; v.p. Pa. chpt. NAACP, nat. v.p. bd. trustees; mem. nat. adv. bd. Nat. Women's Polit. Caucus; now chair Black Caucus Nat. Dem. Com. Mem., vice chair Pa. Black Dem. Com., 1966—; chair Women for Dem. Action, 1967—; nat. chair Nat. Polit. Congress of Black Women, Inc., 1992—; sec., mem. Phila. Zoning Bd. Adjustment, 1968-70; vice chair Pa. Dem. State Com., 1970-76; mem. exec. com. Dem. Nat. Com., 1972-76; Dem. candidate lt. gov., Pa., 1978; v.p. Phila. Tribune Newspaper; del. Dem. Nat. Conv., Pa., 2000. Del. to White Ho. Conf. on Civil Rights; bd. dirs. Phila. YWCA, New Sch. Music, Martin Luther King Ctr. for Social Change; pres., founder Phila. Martin Luther King Assn.; mem. Commonwealth bd. Med. Coll. Pa.; bd. assocs. Messiah Coll.; founder, pres. Bethune-DuBois Fund; bd. mem. Del. Valley Coll.; mem. adv. bd. Parents TV Coun.; spl. contbn. fund trustee NAACP. Recipient Freedom Fund award NAACP, 1961, Svc. and Achievement award NAACP, 1964, Phila. Tribune Charities Ann. award, Cmty. Svc. award Opportunities Industrialization Ctr., Emma V. Kelley Achievement award Nat. Elks, 1971, Thurgood Marshall award, 1982, Lincoln U. Nat. Leadership award, 1993, Cmty. Svc. award Quaker City chpt. B'nai B'rith; named Best Dressed Woman of Yr., Ebony mag., One of 100 Most Influential Black Ams., 1973-77; included in 1996 People mag.'s list of Twenty-Five Most Intriguing People; George Gallup Inst. fellow. Mem. Nat. Assn. Secs. State (v.p.), Pa. Bd. Property, Commn. Interest Coop., Gov. Affirmation Act Coun., Nat. Assn. Real Estate Brokers, Bus. and Profl. Women's Club, Links (dir.), Alpha Kappa Alpha (hon.). Achievements include first to to be an African-American president of the National Federation for Democratic Women. Home: 6700 Lincoln Dr Philadelphia PA 19119-3155

TUCKER, DENNIS STEPHEN, materials scientist; s. Richard Andrew and Dorothy Nell Tucker; m. Dona Kay Etheridge, Aug. 29, 1973; children: Jonathan Christopher, Jennifer Kristen, Jeremy Andrew. BA in Math., LaVerne Coll., Calif., 1977; MS in Ceramic Engring., Ga. Inst. Tech., Atlanta, 1978; PhD in Materials Sci., U. Fla., Gainesville, 1983. Rsch. scientist Atlantic Richfield Co., Chatsworth, Calif., 1983—84; staff Los Alamos Nat. Lab., N.Mex., 1984—85; asst. prof. Ga. Inst. of Tech., Atlanta, 1985—88; sr. rsch. scientist NASA/MSFC, Huntsville, Ala., 1988—. Mem.: Soc. Photoinstrumentation Engrs., Soc. Glass Tech. (assoc.), Soc. Photo Instrumentation Engrs. (assoc.). Achievements include patents pending in field. Avocations: travel, bicycling. E-mail: dr.dennis.tucker@nasa.gov.

TUCKER, DIANE STRAUS, publishing executive; b. N.Y.C., Oct. 23, 1951; d. R. Peter and Ellen (Sulzberger) Straus; m. Carll Tucker, Mar. 20, 1976; children: Peter, Rebecca, David. BA, Yale U., 1973. Pub. Trade Pubs., Westchester, NY, 1985—99; group pub. Manhattan Media, N.Y.C., 2001—. Treas. Yale Alumni Mag.; mem. exec. com. Dean for Am., 2002—03. Home: 37 Pound Ridge Rd Bedford NY 10506 Office: Manhattan Media 63 West 38 New York NY 10018

TUCKER, DON EUGENE, retired lawyer; b. Rockbridge, Ohio, Feb. 3, 1928; s. Beryl Hollis and Ruth (Primmer) T.; m. Elizabeth Jane Parke, Aug. 2, 1950; children: Janet Elizabeth, Kerry Jane, Richard Parke. BA, Aurora Coll., 1951; LL.B., Yale, 1956. Bar: Ohio 1956. Since practiced in, Youngstown, Ohio; asso. Manchester, Bennett, Powers & Ullman, 1956-62, ptnr., 1962-73, of counsel, 1973-87; gen. counsel Comml. Intertech Corp., Youngstown, 1973-75, v.p., gen. counsel, 1975-83, also dir., sr. v.p., gen. counsel, 1983-87, sr. v.p., 1987-93; ret., 1993. Solicitor Village of Poland, Ohio, 1961-63; former chmn. bd., pres., trustee United Cerebral Palsy Assn., Youngstown and Mahoning County; trustee Mahoning County Tb and Health Assn.; former trustee, pres. Indsl. Info. Inst.; former pres., trustee Ea. Ohio Lung Assn.; trustee, former chmn. Cmty. Corp.; trustee, former pres. Butler Inst. Am. Art. With USMCR, 1946-48, 51-53. Mem. Ohio Bar Assn., Mahoning County Bar Assn. (pres. 1972, trustee 1970-73), Youngstown Area C. of C. (chmn. bd. dirs. 1979). Methodist. Home: 6005 Martins Point Rd Kitty Hawk NC 27949-3819

TUCKER, DONALD, assemblyman; b. Mar. 18, 1938; BA in Urban Planning, Goddard Coll. Councilman at large City of Newark, NJ, 1974—; assemblyman N.J. New Gen. Assembly, 1998—; spkr. pro tempore NJ, 2002—. Mem. Passaic Valley Sewerage Commn., 1985—. 2d class airman USAF, 1955—59. Democrat. Office: 329 S Orange Ave Newark NJ 07103 E-mail: AsmTucker@njleg.org.

TUCKER, EDWIN WALLACE, law educator; b. N.Y.C., Feb. 25, 1927; s. Benjamin and May Tucker; m. Gladys Lipschutz, Sept. 14, 1952; children: Sherwin M., Pamela A. BA, NYU, 1948; LLB, Harvard U., 1951; LLM, N.Y. Law Sch., 1963, JSD, 1964; MA, Trinity Coll., Hartford, Conn., 1967. Bar: N.Y. 1955, U.S. Dist. Ct. (ea. and so. dists.) N.Y. 1958, U.S. Ct. Appeals (2d cir.) 1958, U.S. Supreme Ct. 1960. Pvt. practice, N.Y.C., 1955-63; Disting. Alumni prof. and prof. emeritus bus. law U. Conn., Storrs, 1963—, mem. bd. editors occasional paper and monograph series, 1966-70. Author: Adjudication of Social Issues, 1971, 2d edit., 1977, Legal Regulation of the Environment, 1972, Administrative Agencies, Regulation of Enterprise, and Individual Liberties, 1975, CPA Law Review, 1985; co-author: The Legal and Ethical Environment of Business, 1992; book rev. editor Am. Bus. Law Jour., 1964-65, adv. editor, 1974—; co-editor Am. Bus. Jour., 1965-73; mem. editl. bd. Am. Jour. Small Bus., 1979-86; editor Jour. Legal Studies Edn., 1983-85, editor-in-chief, 1985-87, adv. editor, 1987—; mem. bd. editors North Atlantic Regional Bus. Law Rev., 1984—. With USAF, 1951-55. Recipient medal of excellence Am. Bus. Law Assn., 1979. Mem. Acad. Legal Studies in Bus., North Atlantic Regional Bus. Law Assn. Home: 11 Eastwood Rd Storrs Mansfield CT 06268-2401

TUCKER, FRANK HAMMOND, history professor; b. Millville, NJ, Dec. 29, 1923; s. Frank Edmund and Evalyn Godfrey Tucker; m. Kathryn Churchill Libby (dec. Dec. 1994), Aug. 23, 1947; children: Elizabeth T. Gould, Sarah T. Owens, Margaret T. Mitchell. BS, Johns Hopkins U., 1948; MA, Georgetown U., 1950, PhD, 1954. Bassoonist Balt. Symphony Orch., 1941—43; commd. ensign USN, 1943, advanced through grades to lt. comdr., 1954, ret., 1963; lectr. history extension divsn. U. Md., Yokohama, Japan, 1956-57, lectr. history College Park, 1959-63; prof. history Colo. Coll., Colorado Springs, 1963-89, prof. emeritus, 1989—. Author: The White Conscience, 1969, The Frontier Spirit and Progress, 1979, Knights of the Mountain Trails, 2003; contbr. over 35 articles, 40 revs. to profl. jours. Bassoonist Balt. Symphony Orch., 1941-43; bd. mem., Charter Assn., Colorado Springs, 1964-67; pres. Landmarks Preservation Coun., Pike's Peak Region, 1969-73, mem. exec. bd. ARC, 1965-71, head Pike's Peak region Westerners Internat., 1991-92, gov. Pike Bicentennial com., 2004. Fellow Am. Coun. Learned Socs.; mem. Am. Hist. Assn., Rocky Mountain Social Sci. Assn. (bd. mem. 1966-69), Maine Hist. Soc., Gloucester County Hist. Soc., Cumberland County Hist. Soc., Atlantic County Hist. Soc., Rotary (exec. bd. 1971-73). Episcopalian. Avocation: hiking. Home and Office: 1525 Alamo Ave Colorado Springs CO 80907

TUCKER, GARY JAY, psychiatrist, educator; b. Cleve., Mar. 6, 1934; s. Isadore Martin and Blanche Hanna (Luftig) T.; m. Sharon Ruth Pobby, June 10, 1956; children: Adam, Clare. AB, Oberlin Coll., 1956; MD, Case Western Res. U., 1960; postdoctoral fellow, Yale U., 1961-64; MA (hon.), Dartmouth Coll., 1977. Diplomate Am. Bd. Psychiatry and Neurology. Asst. prof. psychiatry Sch. Medicine Yale U., New Haven, 1967-70, assoc. prof. psychiatry, 1970-71; with Dartmouth Med. Sch., Hanover, N.H., 1971-85, prof. psychiatry, 1974-85, chmn. dept., 1978-85; chmn. psychiatry and behavioral scis. Sch. Med. U. Wash., Seattle, 1985-98; prof. psychiatry U. Wash., Seattle, 1985—. Bd. dirs. Am. Bd. Psychiatry and Neurology. Co-author: Rational Hospital Psychiatry, 1974, Behavioral Neurology, 1985; contbr. articles to profl. jours. Lt. Commdr. USN, 1964-67. Fellow Am. Psychiat. Assn.; mem. W. Coast Coll. Biol. Psychiatry, Sigma Xi, Alpha Omega Alpha. Democrat. Jewish. Avocations: photography, motorcycles. Office: U Washington Dept Psychiatry PO Box 356560 Seattle WA 98195-6560

TUCKER, H. RICHARD, oil company executive; b. Streator, Ill., Oct. 2, 1936; s. H.L. and Dorothy A. (Miller) T.; children by previous marriage: Randall R., Brian A.; m. Cheryl L. Kirk, Jan. 14, 1984. BS in Chem. Engring., Purdue U., 1958; MBA, Northwestern U., 1962. Project engr. crude oil supply Amoco Corp., Chgo., 1958-64, specialist product supply, 1965-66, coord. fgn. crude oil supply, 1967-68; coord. orgn. planning Amoco Internat. Corp., Chgo., 1969-70, Amoco Corp., Chgo., 1970-72, mgr. adminstrv. svcs., 1972-84, mgr. real estate svcs., 1984-86, coord. spl. studies, 1986-89, dir. quality mgmt., 1989-92; mgr. cost mgmt., 1992-94. V.p. Amoco Realty Co., 1984-91, Amoco Devel. Co., 1984-91. Mem. adv. com. Sch. Bd. Wheaton, Ill., 1966; mem. Citizen's Nominating Com., Wheaton, 1972; leader Boy Scouts Am., Wheaton, 1979-82; dir. Oak Brook Colony Condominium Assn., 1992-94. Mem. Westhaven Home Owners Assn. (pres. 1965-67), Phi Eta Sigma, Omega Chi Epsilon, Beta Gamma Sigma, Tau Beta Pi. Avocations: tennis, bridge, hiking.

TUCKER, HOWARD MCKELDIN, investment banker, consultant; b. Washington, Apr. 1, 1930; s. Howard Newell and Bessie Draper (McKeldin) T.; m. Julia Spencer Merrell, Feb. 1, 1952 (div. 1975); children: Deborah, Mark, Alexander, H. David; m. Megan Evans, Aug. 17, 1979. BA, U. Va., 1954. CFA. With J.P. Morgan & Co., 1954—61, Mackall & Coe, Washington, 1962—69, Legg Mason Wood Walker & Co., Washington, 1969—79, Govt. Rsch. Corp./Nat. Jour., 1979—82, Potomac Asset Mgmt., 1982—91; ptnr., mng. dir. Capital Insights Group, Washington, 1992—2001; with Skillsmith, LLC, 2002—. Mem. task force balance-of-payments U.S.Treasury Dept., 1967-72; cons. County Natwest (Washinton Analysis Corp.), 1985-90; bd. dirs. Monarch Enterprises, Inc., Uniflight, Inc., Sci. Mgmt. Assocs., Inc., Jeffrey Bigelow Assocs. Author: Literature in Medicine, In Memoriam, Michael Halberstam, M.D., 1984; book reviewer Washington Post; contbr. articles to profl. jours. Dir. Washington Area Coun. Chs., 1962-65; vestryman Christ Episcopal Ch., Georgetown, 1962-65; mem. chpt. Washington Nat. Cathedral, 1966-72; del. Va. Republican Conv., 1968; trustee Nat. Cathedral Sch. for Girls, 1972-78; chmn. Missionary Devel. Fund Episcopal Diocese D.C., 1974; co-dir. Andover-Exeter Washington Intern Program, 1976-86; co-organizer U.S.-Ger. Parliamentary Exchange, 1980-82; observer OECD, 1980-82; spl. overseas visitor Australian Govt., 1982; patron West Europe program Woodrow Wilson Ctr., 1985-86; bd. dirs. Am. Hort. Soc., 1998-. With USNR, 1950-56. Mem.: Fin. Analysts Fedn., Washington Soc. Investment Analysts, Nat. Economists Club, Dumplings, Alexandria Seaport Found., Cogswell Soc., Hist. Alexandria Found., Old Domincon Boat Club, Nat. Press Club, Naval and Mil. Club London, Georgetown Visitation Tennis Club, Saints and Sinners Club, Beta Theta Pi. Home: 4 Potomac Ct Alexandria VA 22314-3821

TUCKER, J. WALTER, JR., steel manufacturing executive; Vice chmn. Keystone Consolidated Industries, Inc., Dallas, chmn., 1987—. Office: 3 Lincoln Ctr 5430 LBJ Fwy Ste 1740 Dallas TX 75240-2697 Fax: 972-458-8108.

TUCKER, JACK WILLIAM ANDREW, writer, film editor, producer, lecturer; b. Portland, Oreg., May 1, 1944; s. Admyrl Foster and Aileen Eloise (McDaniels) T. BA in English, Portland State U., 1964. Film editor MGM TV, Culver City, Calif., 1984-86, Cannon Film Group, Beverly Hills, Calif., 1988, Columbia TV, Burbank, Calif., 1988, Paramount Pictures, Hollywood, Calif., 1990—. Editor: (TV) Winds of War, 1982 (Emmy award nominee 1983), The Fifth Missile, 1986, 240-Robert, 1979, Flatbed Annie and Sweetpie, 1979, (films) Shogun, 1980, Salsa, 1988, They're Playing With Fire, 1983, Viper, 1988, Nightmare on Elm Street IV, 1988, Distortions, 1987, Diplomatic Immunity, 1991, Illusions, 1992, Double-O-Kid, 1993, A Million to Juan, 1994, To the Ends of Time, 1996, Cotton Mary, 1999; prodr.: The Magazine, 1997, Earth Minus Zero, 1998. Sgt. USAF, 1964-68, Vietnam. Mem. NATAS, Am. Cinema Editors (treas. 1993—, editor CINEMEDITOR mag. 1994—).

TUCKER, JAMES RAYMOND, primary education educator; b. Pueblo, Colo., Apr. 18, 1944; s. James George and Pauline F. (Sena) T.; m. Kathie Owens; 1 child, Brittany. BA, U. So. Colo., 1966; MA, U. No. Colo., 1990, postgrad., 1991. Tchr. Sinclair Mid. Sch., Englewood, Colo., 1971-93, Denver Pub. Schs., 1993—. Co-dir. Nick Bolleteri Tennis Acad., Boulder, Colo., 1986; head tennis coach Englewood High Sch., 1971—. Sgt. U.S. Army, 1967-70. Finalist Coach of Yr., Nat. H.S. Coaches Assn., 2001, 2004. Mem. NEA, U.S. Profl. Tennis Assn., U.S. Profl. Tennis Registry, Internat. Platform Assn., Colo. Edn. Assn., Meadow Creek Tennis and Fitness, Colo. H.S. Coaches Assn. (Achievement award 1989, 92, Tchr. of Yr. 1973, 78, 86, Coach of Yr. 1986, 87, 90, 96, 97, Franklin award 1988, 89, Nat. Asst. Coach of Yr., 2002). Home: 8801 W Belleview Ave Unit A207 Littleton CO 80123

TUCKER, JOHN MARK, librarian, educator; s. Paul Marlin and Edith Tucker; m. Barbara Ann Wilson, Mar. 22, 1968. BA, David Lipscomb Coll., 1967; MLS, George Peabody Coll. Tchrs., 1968, specialist in edn., 1972; PhD, U. Ill., 1983. Head libr. Freed-Hardeman Coll., Henderson, Tenn., 1968-71; reference libr. Wabash Coll., Crawfordsville, Ind., 1973-79, Purdue U., West Lafayette, Ind., 1979-82, asst. prof. libr. sci., 1979-85, assoc. prof. libr. sci., 1985-89, sr. reference libr. Humanities, Social Sci. and Edn. Libr., 1982-90, prof. libr. sci., 1989—, libr. Humanities, Social Sci. and Edn. Libr., 1990—2003, prof. emeritus library sci., 2003—; dean libr., info. resources Abilene Christian U., 2003—. Mem. grantee com. instl. coop. NEH, 1991—94. Co-editor: (book) Reference Services and Library Education, 1983, User Instruction in Academic Libraries, 1986, American Library History, 1989; editor: Untold Stories: Civil Rights, Libraries and Black Librarianship, 1998; mem. editl. bd. Dictionary of American Library Biography, 2002; contbr. articles to profl. jours. Thomas S. Wilmeth grantee, 1988, Frederick B. Artz Rsch. grantee, Oberlin Coll. Archives, 1991, Rsch. fellow, Coun. Libr. Resources, 1990. Mem.: SCV, ALA (chair libr. history round table 1993—94), So. Hist. Assn., Soc. Historians Gilded Age and Prog. Era, Disciples of Christ Hist. Soc., Assn. Coll. and Rsch. Librs., Assn. Bibliography History, Friends U. Ill. Libr., Beta Phi Mu, Phi Kappa Phi. Democrat. Mem. Chs. Of Christ. Home: 1687 Bent Tree Dr Abilene TX 79602 Office: Brown Libr Abilene Christian U Box 29208 Abilene TX 79699-9208 Office Phone: 325-674-2387. E-mail: mark.tucker@acu.edu.

TUCKER, JOHN RICHARD, mathematician, educator, writer, researcher; s. Clifford Maltbie and Alice Malitsoff Tucker; m. Robin C. Donaldson, Oct. 1, 1988. BA, Wash. Coll., Chestertown, Md., 1966—70; MPhil, George Wash. U., Washington, DC, 1970—76, PhD, 1976—80. Computer specialist, math. analyst Chi Associates, Inc., Arlington, Va., 1976—80; asst. prof., applied math. Va. Commonwealth U., Richmond, 1980—83; asst. prof., math. Mary Wash. Coll., Fredericksburg, Va., 1983—88; staff officer, math. scis. bd. NAS, Washington, 1989—93, sr. program officer, brd on math scis, 1993—94, dir., math. scis. bd., 1994—99; asst. prof., indsl. & applied math. U. S.C., Aiken, 1999—2001; head, dept. math. Notre Dame Acad., Middleburg, Va., 2001—. Lectr., math. George Wash. U., Washington, 1971—79; dir., post-bacalaureate cert. program in computer sci. Va. Commonwealth U., Richmond, 1982—83; rsch. scientist U.S. Dept. Energy's Savannah River Site, Edgefield, SC, 2000—01. Fellow, NSF, 1970—74. Mem.: Nat. Coun. Teachers Math., Am. Statis. Assn., Am. Math. Soc. Episcopalian. Office: Math Dept Notre Dame Acad 35321 Notre Dame Ln Middleburg VA 20117 Personal E-mail: greyfriar0@mail.lycos.com.

TUCKER, JOSHUA AARON, political scientist; b. New York, NY, Apr. 17, 1971; m. Elisabeth Eva Gordon. BA, Harvard U., 1989—93; M in internat. studies, U. of Birmingham, 1993—94; MA, PhD, Harvard U., 1994—2000. Asst. prof. of politics and internat. affairs Princeton U., 2000—. Exec. bd. mem. Ctr. for the Study of Dem. Politics, Princeton U. Contbr. articles to profl. jours. Recipient Edward M. Chase Dissertation prize, Harvard U., 2001, Westview Press award, Mid-West Polit. Sci. Assn., 1998; grantee Fgn. Lang. and Area Studies fellowship, US Dept. of Edn., 1997—98; East European Dissertation fellowship, Am. Coun. for Learned Societies, 1999—2000, Fgn. Lang. and Area Studies fellowship, US Dept. of Edn., 1995—95. Office: Princeton University 322 Bendheim Hall Princeton NJ 08544

TUCKER, KEITH A. investment company executive; b. 1945; BBA, U. Tex., 1967, JD, 1970. With KPMG Peat Marwick, Dallas, 1970-85, Stephens, Inc., Little Rock, 1985-87, Trivest Inc., Miami, Fla., 1987-91; dir. Waddell & Reed Inc., Shawnee Mission, Kans., 1989—, vice chmn., 1991—, chmn. Office: Waddell & Reed Inc 6300 Lamar Ave Shawnee Mission KS 66202-4200

TUCKER, KELLY H. music educator; b. Columbia, SC, Nov. 16, 1960; d. Lindsey Buchanan and Sandra Elizabeth Hennessee; m. Larry Richard Tucker, Dec. 16, 1990. MS in Ednl. Adminstrn., Capella U., Mpls., Minn., 1999—2000; MA in gifted edn., Converse Coll., Spartanburg, SC, 1994—95;

BME in music edn., Lander U., Greenwood, SC, 1982—84. Cert. Nat. Bd. tchr. NBPTS, 2002. Asst. band dir. Greenwood HS, SC, 1984—87; band dir. Ware Shoals Jr. and Sr. HS, SC, 1987—88. Band dir. St. Andrews Mid., Columbia, 1988—98, Crayton Mid. Sch., Columbia, 1998—2004; lead tchr. Richland Dist. One, Columbia, 1995—2004. Musician performer - Columbia cmty. band, conductor - Berkley All-County Band, performer - Palmetto concert band, performer - Columbia Woodwind Quintet, conductor-Region IV Jr Symphonic Band, Cornerstone Presbyn. Orch., conductor - Sumter Mid. Sch. Honor Band, conductor - Ea. District Honor Band, conductor - US Collegiate Wind Band, conductor - Georgetown All-County. Recipient Citation of Excellence, Nat. Band Assn., 1993, Scroll of Excellence, Women Band Directors Internat., 1993, Outstanding Young Woman of Am., 1986 and 1990. Mem.: S. Band Directors Assn. (assoc.), Music Educators Nat. Conf. (assoc.), Women Band Directors Internat. (assoc.), Nat. Band Assn. (assoc.), Phi Beta Mu, Tau Beta Sigma (life; dist. and nat. del.). Presbyn. Pca. Achievements include Teacher of the Year - St. Andrews 1994. Home: 1425 Kennerly Rd Irmo SC 29063 Office: Busbee Middle Sch 1407 Dunbar Rd Cayce SC 29033 Office Phone: 803-739-3113. Office Fax: 803-739-4133. Personal E-mail: kellytucker@sc.rr.com E-mail: ktucker@lex2.org.

TUCKER, LAUREY DAN, lawyer; b. El Dorado, Ark., Oct. 23, 1936; s. Floyd A. and Harriet Kathleen (Graves) T.; m. Katherine Washburn, June 21, 1958; children: Laurie Tucker Diaz, Dana Tucker Kleine. BSChemE, U. Okla., 1959, LLB, 1962. Bar: Okla. 1962, Tex. 1972. Patent atty. Phillips Petroleum Co., Bartlesville, Okla., 1964-67, Monsanto Co., St. Louis, 1967-70, patent mgr. Texas City, Tex., 1970-74; ptnr. Hubbard. Tucker & Harris, Dallas, 1974-94, Harris, Tucker & Hardin, Dallas, 1994-97, Locke Purnell Rain Harrell, Dallas, 1997-98, Locke Liddell & Sapp LLP, Dallas, 1999—. 1st lt. U.S. Army, 1962-64. Republican. Episcopalian. Avocations: fishing, hunting, travel. Office: Locke Liddell & Sapp LLP 2200 Ross Ave Ste 2200 Dallas TX 75201-6776 Office Phone: 214-740-8730. Business E-Mail: ldtucker@lockeliddell.com.

TUCKER, LAWRENCE C. investment company executive; Gen. ptnr. Brown Bros. Harriman & Co., N.Y.C. Office: Brown Bros Harriman & Co 59 Wall St New York NY 10005-2808

TUCKER, LOUIS LEONARD, retired historical society administrator; b. Rockville, Conn., Dec. 6, 1927; s. Joseph and Dora (Conn) T.; m. Beverley Jones, Mar. 27, 1953; children: Mark T., Lance K.; m. Carolyn woollen, Sept. 14, 1996. BA, U. Wash., 1952, MA, 1954, PhD, 1957. Instr. history U. Calif., Davis, 1958; fellow Inst. Early Am. History and Culture, Williamsburg, Va., 1958-60; instr. history Coll. William and Mary, 1958-60; dir. Cin. Hist. Soc., 1960-66; asst. commr., state historian of N.Y., N.Y. State Edn. Dept., 1966-76; also dir. N.Y. State Bicentennial Commn., 1969-76; dir. Mass. Hist. Soc., Boston, 1977-97. Author: Puritan Protagonist, 1962, Cincinnati During Civil War, 1962, Cincinnati's Citizen Crusaders, 1967, Our Travels, 1968, Cincinnati: Students Guide to Local History, 1969, James Allen, Jr.: From Elkins to Washington, 1969, Connecticut's Seminary of Sedition, Yale College, 1974, Clio's Consort: Jeremy Belknap and the Founding of the Massachusetts Historical Society, 1990, The Massachusetts Historical Society: A Bicentennial History, 1791-1971, 1996, Worthington Chauncey Ford: Scholar and Adventurer, 2001. Dir. Shaker Mus., 1967-74; Am. Heritage Co., 1973-75, Ft. Ticonderoga Assn., 1990-97. Served with AUS, 1946-47. Winston Churchill fellow, 1969 Mem. Am. Assn. State and Local History (pres. 1972-74) Home: 328 Harvard St Cambridge MA 02139-2002

TUCKER, MARC STEPHEN, education policy analyst, author; b. Boston, Nov. 15, 1939; s. David Jones and Natalie (Croman) T.; m. Linda Beth Hepler, Sept 27, 1964 (div. 1973); children: Matthew, Joshua; foster child, Julie Beers. AB, Brown U., 1961; MSS, George Washington U., 1982. Lighting dir., camera Sta. WGBH-TV, Boston, 1962-64, asst. dir. edn. div., 1964-66; asst. to pres. Edn. Devel. Ctr., Newton, Mass., 1966-71; asst. dir. NWREL, Portland, Oreg., 1971-72; assoc. dir. Nat. Inst. Edn., Washington, 1972-81; dir. Project on Info. Tech. and Edn., Washington, 1981-84; exec. dir. Carnegie Forum on Edn. and the Econ., Washington, 1985-87; pres. Nat. Ctr. on Edn. and the Economy, Rochester, N.Y., 1988—; prof. edn. U. Rochester, 1988—. Staff dir., prin. author Carnegie report-A Nation Prepared: Teachers forthe 21st Century, 1986. Chmn., pres. Brass Chamber Music Soc., Annapolis, Md., 1980-81; mem. bd. advisors Apple Edn. Found., 1984-85, bd. visitors Wake Forest U., 1987—, bd. visitors U. Pitts. Sch. of Edn., 1987—, bd. advisors Bank St. Coll. Edn. Ctr. for Children and Tech., 1987—. Democrat. Office: Nat Ctr on Edn and the Economy Ste 700 1 Thomas Cir NW Washington DC 20005-5802

TUCKER, MARCUS OTHELLO, judge; b. Santa Monica, Calif., Nov. 12, 1934; s. Marcus Othello Sr. and Essie Louvonia (McLendon) T.; m. Indira Hale, May 29, 1965; 1 child, Angelique. BA, U. So. Calif., 1956; JD, Howard U., 1960; MA in Criminal Justice, Chapman U., 1997; BS in Liberal Arts, Regents Coll., SUNY, 1999. Bar: Calif. 1962, U.S. Dist. Ct. (cen. dist.) Calif. 1962, U.S. Ct. Appeals (9th cir.) 1965, U.S. Ct. Internat. Trade 1970, U.S. Supreme Ct. 1971. Pvt. practice, Santa Monica, 1962-63, 67-74; dep. atty. City of Santa Monica, 1963-65; asst. atty. U.S. Dist. Ct. (Cen. Dist.) Calif., 1965-67; commr. L.A. Superior Ct., 1974-76; judge mcpl. ct. Long Beach (Calif.) Jud. Dist., 1976-85; judge superior ct. L.A. Jud. Dist., 1985—; supervising judge L.A. County Dependency Ct. L.A. Superior Ct., 1991-92, presiding judge Juvenile divsn., 1993-94. Asst. prof. law Pacific U., Long Beach, 1984, 86; justice pro tem Calif. State Ct. Appeals (2nd cir.), 1981; mem. exec. com. Superior Ct. of L.A. County, 1995-96. Mem. editl. staff Howard U. Law Sch. Jour., 1959-60. Pres. Community Rehab. Industries Found., Long Beach, 1983-86, Legal Aid Found., L.A., 1976-77; bd. dirs. Long Beach coun. Boy Scouts Am., 1978-92. With U.S. Army, 1960-66. Named Judge of Yr. Juvenile Cts. Bar Assn., 1986, Disting. Jurist Long Beach Trial Trauma Coun., 1987, Honoree in Law Handy Cmty. Ctr., L.A., 1987, Bernard S. Jefferson Jurist of Yr. John M. Langston Bar Assn. Black Lawyers, 1990, Judge of Yr. Long Beach Bar Assn., 1993, Judge of Yr., First Ann. Adoption Cong., 1997, Jurist of Yr., Juvenile Cts. Bar Assn., 1997, Daniel O'Connell award Irish-Am. Bar Assn., 1999, named to Nat. Bar Assn. Hall of Fame, 2002; recipient award for Law-Related Edn. Constl. Rights Found./L.A. County Bar Assn., 1992, commendation L.A. County Bd. Suprs., 1994. Fellow Internat. Acad. Trial Judges; mem. ABA, Calif. Judges Assn. (chmn. juvenile law com. 1986-87, Svc. award 2001), Langston Bar Assn. (pres. bd. dirs. 1972-73, named to hall of fame 2001), Calif. Assn. Black Lawyers, Santa Monica Bay Dist. Bar Assn. (treas. 1969-71), Am. Inns of Ct., Selden Soc. Avocations: comparative law, travel. Office: 415 W Ocean Blvd Dept 245 Long Beach CA 90802-4512

TUCKER, MAUREEN ANN, musician; b. Jackson Heights, N.Y., Aug. 26, 1944; d. James Thomas and Margaret Mary (Daly) T.; divorced; children: Kerry, Keith, Austen, Kate, Richard. Grad., Levittown (N.Y.) Meml. H.S., 1962. Drummer Velvet Underground, 1965-71; guitarist, songwriter, singer Moe Tucker Band, 1989—. Recordings include (singer, guitarist, songwriter) Playin Possum, 1981, Life in Exile After Abdication, 1986, (prodr., arranger) I Spent a Week There The Other Night, 1990, Dogs Under Stress, 1993; drummer Lou Reed Band, Japan, 1990, European tours with Velvet Underground, 1993, Moe Tucker Band, 1989—. Tchr. English St. Pauls Hispanic Ministry, Douglas, Ga., 1990—. Inducted into Rock & Roll Hall of Fame, 1996. Roman Catholic. Office: Maureen Tucker Music PO Box 2357 Douglas GA 31534-2357

TUCKER, MELVIN JAY, education educator, researcher; s. Earle Homer and Florence Gertrude Tucker; m. N. Evelyn Rapalus, June 27, 1953; children: Ann Evelyn Jobson, Ellen Marie Tucker-Cohen, Michael Jay. BA, U. Mass., Amherst, Mass., 1953, MA, 1954; PhD, Northwestern U., Evanston, Il., 1962. Instr. Colby Coll., Waterville, Maine, 1959—60, MIT, Cambridge, Mass., 1960—63; assoc. prof. U. Buffalo, Buffalo, 1963—. Dir. grad. studies, history Univ. Buffalo, 1979—85; fellow Medieval Ctr., SUNY, Binghampton, 1970—77. Author: The Life of Thoms Howard, Earl of Surrey and Second Duke of Norfolk, 1443-1524; co-author: Centering: A Guide to Inner Growth, 2nd ed.; contbr. chapters to books; contbg. editor: History of Childhood Quarterly, 1973—76, Journal of Psycho History, 1976—84. 1st lt. USAF, 1954—56, Japan. Recipient Fulbright Award, Fulbright Commn., 1958-1959, Cert. of Merit, Buffalo & Erie County Hist. Soc., 1974, Cert. of Recognition, Career Planning, U. Buffalo, 2002. Mem.: Assn. for the Bibliography of History (coun. mem. 1982—92), Am. Hist. Assn., North Am. Conf. of Brit. Studies. Roman Catholic. Avocations: walking, movies. Office: History Dept Univ Buffalo 580 Pk Hall Buffalo NY 14260 Business E-Mail; mjtucker@acsu.buffalo.edu., mjtucker@acsu.buffalo.edu.

TUCKER, NINA ANGELLA, hospital administrator; b. Miami, Fla., June 6, 1965; d. Joseph John and Diane (Accolla) A.; 1 child, Ryan. BA, Emory U., Atlanta, Ga., 1987; MA in Health Adminstrn., MBA, U. Fla., Gainesville, 1990. Asst. adminstr. Med. City Dallas, 1990-92, Meml. Hosp. West, Pembroke Pines, Fla., 1992-95; adminstr. Joe DiMaggio Children's Hosp. Women's Svcs. at Meml. Regional Hosp., Hollywood, Fla., 1995—. Pres. Meml. Employees Fedl. Credit Union, 1993—. Recipient Regents award Am. Coll. Healthcare Execs., 1996. Roman Catholic. Avocations: walking, water-skiing. Office: Meml Regional Hosp 3501 Johnson St Hollywood FL 33021-5487

TUCKER, PAUL THOMAS, computer company executive; b. Evanston, Ill., Apr. 9, 1948; s. Charles E. Jr. and Francine G. Tucker; m. Carolyn K. Montgomery, 1967 (div. 1981); 1 child, Sean P.; m. Patricia M. Merlie, 1984 (div. 1995). BEE, U. Ill., 1970, MEE, 1971, PhD in elec. engring., 1975. Founder, ptnr., primary design engr. HAL Devices, 1968-71; pres., dir. engring., and chmn. bd. HAL Communications Corp., 1971-83; sr. rsch. engr., assoc. prof. U. Ill. Grad. Coll., 1971-83, 1983-87; sr. v.p. Commodity News Svcs., Inc., subs. Knight-Ridder, Inc., 1983-88; sr. v.p. Bus. Info. Svcs. div. Knight-Ridder, Inc., 1985-90; COO Knight-Ridder Fin., Inc., N.Y.C., 1990-91, pres., CEO, 1991-96; v.p., corp. develop. Computer Sciences Corp., El Segundo, Calif., 1996—. Cons. Magnavox Corp., 1974-78, Control Data Corp., 1978, TDK Corp., Tokyo, Japan, 1976-82, Commodity News Svcs., Inc., 1980-82; tchr. Parkland Jr. Coll., 1980-81; mem. U. Ill. President's Coun., 1978—. Patentee (4) in field. Strategic tech. planning bd. Mercy Hosp. Found., 1978-82; bd. dirs. Urbana C. of C., 1980-82. Office: Computer Sciences Corp 2100 East Grand Ave El Segundo CA 90245 E-mail: ptucker@csc.com.

TUCKER, RICHARD A. airport terminal executive; Exec. dir. Huntsville (Ala.) Internat. Airport, Huntsville, Al., 1995—. Office: Huntsville Internat Airport 1000 Glenn Hearn Blvd Box 20008 Huntsville AL 35824

TUCKER, RICHARD LEE, civil engineer, educator; b. Wichita Falls, Tex., July 19, 1935; s. Floyd Alfred and Zula Florence (Morris) T.; m. Shirley Sue Tucker, Sept. 1, 1956; children: Bryan Alfred, Karen Leigh. BCE, U. Tex., 1958, MCE, 1960, PhDCE, 1963. Registered profl. engr., Tex. Instr. civil engring. U. Tex., 1960-62, from asst. prof. to prof., 1962-74, assoc. dean engring., 1963-74; v.p Luther Hill & Assoc., Inc., Dallas, 1974-76; Joe C. Walter chair in engring. U. Tex., Austin, 1976—, dir. Constrn. Industry Inst., 1983-98, dir. Ctr. Constrn. Industry Studies, 1998—. Pres. Tucker and Tucker Cons., Inc., Austin, 1976—. Contbr. numerous articles and papers to profl. jours. Recipient Erwin C. Perry award, Coll. Engring., U. Tex., 1978, Faculty Excellence award, 1986, Joe J. King Profl. Engring. Achievement award, 1990, Disting. Engring. Grad., 1994; Ronald Reagan award for Individual Initiative, Constrn. Industry Inst., 1991; named Outstanding Young Engr., Tex. Soc. Profl. Engrs., 1965, Outstanding Young Man, City of Arlington, 1967; fellow Inst. for Constructive Capitalism, 1990-91. Fellow ASCE (R.L. Peurifoy award 1986, Thomas Fitch Rowland prize 1987, Tex. sect. award of honor 1990); mem. NSPE (Constrn. Engr. Educator award 1993, Engr. of Yr. 2001), NAE, Soc. Am. Mil. Engrs., The Moles (hon.). Baptist. Office: Univ Tex Coll Engring Constrn Industry Inst ECJ5 2 Austin TX 78712

TUCKER, ROBERT DENNARD, health care products executive; b. Tifton, Ga., July 18, 1933; s. Robert Buck and Ethel Margaret (Dennard) T.; m. Peggy Angelyn Smith, June 23, 1957; children: Robert Barron, Jennifer Lee. BBA, Ga. State U., 1958. With sales and sales mgmt. Johnson & Johnson Inc., New Brunswick, N.J., 1958-68; v.p., gen. mgr. ASR Med. Industries, N.Y.C., 1968-72, Howmedica Suture div. Pfizer Inc., N.Y.C., 1972-75; exec. v.p., chief operating officer R. P. Scherer Corp., Detroit, 1976-79; pres., chief operating officer Scherer Sci. Inc., Atlanta, 1980-95, also bd. dirs; chmn., chief exec. officer Scherer Health Care Inc., Atlanta, 1980-95, also bd. dirs. Bd. dirs., pres., CEO Splty. Surgictrs., Inc., Atlanta, 1997—2002; bd. dirs., chmn., CEO Maximum Benefits Co., Atlanta; chmn., CEO Throwleigh Techs., LLC, 1995—; bd. dirs., mem. exec. com. Horizon Med. Products, 2002—. Pub: Tuckers of Devon, 1983; author, pub.: Descendants of William Tucker of Throwleigh, Devon. Chmn. bd. Health Industries Mfrs. Assn. polit. action com., Washington, 1983-85; trustee, past pres. Ga. Horse Found., Atlanta; trustee Brenau Coll., Gainesville, Ga., 1985—. Served with USN, 1951-54, Korea. Decorated Knight of Malta, Imperial Russian Order of St. John; recipient Disting. Service award Brenau Coll., 1987. Mem. Nat. Assn. Mfrs., Health Industries Mfrs. Assn. (bd. dirs. 1979-86, disting. service recognition 1981, 86), Pharm. Mfrs. Assn., Thoroughbred Owners and Breeders Assn. Ky. and Ga. (Man of Yr. 1984). Clubs: Cherokee (Atlanta); Big Canoe (Ga.). Republican. Methodist. Avocations: scuba diving, tennis, genealogical research. Home: 405 Townsend Pl NW Atlanta GA 30327-3037 Office: Throwleigh Techs PO Box 220 Ball Ground GA 30107

TUCKER, ROBERT PAUL, landscape architect, city planner; b. Little Rock, Ark., July 1, 1958; s. Jack Arthur and Dorothy Jean Tucker. Student, Tex. A&M U., 1981; B in Landscape Arch., U. Ark., 1983; M in Landscape Arch., Ohio State U., 1989. Registered landscape arch., Ill. Landscape arch. Enplanar, Inc., New Orleans, 1983-85, Laubmann-Reed & Assoc., Atlanta, 1986-87; grad. rsch. assoc. Knowlton Sch. Arch. Ohio State U., Columbus, 1987-89, tutor, 1987-89; planner, landscape arch., urban designer Skidmore, Owings & Merrill, Chgo., 1989-91; urban designer, redevel. specialist Dept. Streets and Sanitation, Chgo., 1991-99; greening coord. for program mgmt. of renovations to L.A. Unified Sch. Dist. 3d/Internat., Inc., 2000—. Prin. works include Pritzker Park, 1992, Mich. Ave. Streetscape, State St. Renovation, Chgo., Gross Park, McCormick Pl. Conv. Ctr. Expansion Project, among others. Mem. Bright New Cities: A Forum, Chgo., 1993-96; mem. Friends of Downtown, Chgo., 1996-97. Recipient numerous awards. Mem. Am. Inst. Cert. Planners (cert.), Am. Soc. Landscape Archs., Am. Planning Assn. Avocations: landscape photography, hiking, canoeing, urban studies, travel. Office: 3d/Internat Inc 12100 Wilshire Blvd Los Angeles CA 90025-7120 E-mail: rpt1@pacbell.net.

TUCKER, RUSSELL B. insurance company executive; V.p. Torchmark Corp., Birmingham, Ala., 1997—2001, exec. v.p., chief info. officer, 2001—. Office: Torchmark Corp 2001 3rd Ave S Birmingham AL 35233

TUCKER, SCOTT ARTHUR, music educator; b. Boston, Sept. 17, 1957; MusM, New Eng. Conservatory of Music, Boston, 1986. Choral dir. Milton (Mass.) Acad., 1986—95; asst. condr. Harvard U., Cambridge, 1987—93; dir. choral music Cornell U., Ithaca, NY, 1995—. Composer choral music. Bd. mem. Musicians for World Harmony, 2003. Scholar St. Botolph award, St. Botolph Club, 1985; Presser Scholarship, Theodore Presser Pub. Co., 1980. Mem.: Intercollegiate Men's Choirs (bd. mem. 2000), Am. Choral Dirs. Assn. (life; N.Y. chair of repertoire and stds. 2000). Office: Cornell Univ 233 Lincoln Hall Ithaca NY 14853 Office Phone: 607-255-3423. Office Fax: 607-254-2877. E-mail: sat14@cornell.edu.

TUCKER, SHIRLEY LOIS COTTER, botanist, educator; b. St. Paul, Apr. 4, 1927; d. Ralph U. and Myra C. (Knutson) Cotter; m. Kenneth W. Tucker, Aug. 22, 1953. BA, U. Minn., 1949, MS, 1951; PhD, U. Calif., Davis, 1956. Asst. prof. botany La. State U., Baton Rouge, 1967-71, assoc. prof., 1971-76, prof., 1976-82, Boyd prof., 1982-95, prof. emerita, 1995—. Adj. prof. dept. biology U. Calif., Santa Barbara, 1995—. Co-editor: Aspects of Floral Development, 1988, Advances in Legume Systematics, Vol. 6, 1994; contbr. numerous articles on plant devel. to profl. jours. Recipient, Outstanding Alumni Achievement award U. Minn., 1999; fellow Linnean Soc., London, 1975—, Fulbright fellow Eng., 1952-53. Mem. Bot. Soc. Am. (v.p. 1979, program chmn. 1975-78, pres.-elect 1986-87, pres. 1987-88, Merit award 1989), Am. Bryological and Lichenological Soc., Brit. Lichenological Soc., Am. Inst. Biol. Scis., Am. Soc. Plant Taxonomists (pres.-elect 1994-95, pres. 1995-96), Phi Beta Kappa, Sigma Xi. Home: 3987 Primavera Rd Santa Barbara CA 93110-1467 Office: U Calif Dept Biology EEMB Santa Barbara CA 93106 Business E-Mail: tucker@lifesci.ucsb.edu.

TUCKER, SUSAN CAROL, state legislator; b. Winfield, Kans., Nov. 7, 1944; d. Allen and Jeanne (Lawrence) Shaffer; m. Mike A. Tucker, Dec. 2, 1967; children: Mark, David. Student, U. Nigeria, 1965; BA magna cum laude, Mich. State U., 1966. English tchr. Lexington (Mass.) High Sch., 1966-69; legis. aide Mass. Legislature, Boston, 1980-82; mem. Ho. of Reps. Mass. Great and Gen. Ct., Boston, 1983-92, vice chair edn. com., chair spl. commn. on child abuse, mem enery com., ethics com.; mem. Mass. Senate, Boston, 1998—. Chair Mass. Caucus Women Legislators. V.p. Mass. LWV, Boston, 1977-80. Recipient Environ. Achievement award Environ. Lobby Mass., 1984, Legislator of Yr. for Victim's Rights award, 1990. Mem. Nat. Women's Polit. Caucus. Democrat. Office: Mass Senate R 416-A State House Boston MA 02133

TUCKER, TANYA DENISE, singer; b. Seminole, Tex., Oct. 10, 1958; d. Beau and Juanita Tucker; children: Presley, Beau Grayson. Singer Tanya Tucker Inc., 1959—. Regular on Lew King Show; rec. artist formerly with Columbia Records, MCA Records, Capital Records; albums include Tear Me Apart, Chagnes, Delta Dawn, Dreamlovers, Here's Some Love, TNT, Girls Like Me, Greatest Hits, 1989, Greatest Hits (1972-75), Greatest Hits Encore, 1990, Greatest Country Hits, 1991, Greatest Hits 1990-92, 1993, Love Me Like You Use To, 1987, Strong Enough to Bend, 1988, Tanya Tucker Live, Tennesee Woman, 1990, What Do I Do With Me, 1991, (with Delbert McClinton) Can't Run From Youself, 1997, Soon, 1993, Fire to Fire, 1994, (with T. Graham Brown, Delbert McClinton) Tanya, 1995, Christmas with Tanya Tucker and Suzy Bogguss, 1995, The Best of My Love, 1995, Love Songs, 1996, Complicated, 1997, Little Things, 1997, Super Hits, 1998; TV appearances include A Country Christmas, 1979, The Georgia Peaches, 1980; actress: (mini-series) The Rebels, 1979, (film) Jeremiah Johnson, 1968. Recipient: Country Music Assn. award, 1991, female vocalist of the year; 2 Grammy nominations, 1994. Office: Tanya Tucker Inc 109 Westpark Dr Ste 400 Brentwood TN 37027-5032

TUCKER, THOMAS JAMES, retired investment manager; b. Atlanta, Sept. 5, 1929; s. Thomas Tudor and Carol (Govan) T.; m. Margaret Guerard. BA, U. of the South, 1952. With CIT Corp, N.Y.C., 1957—72; pres., CEO AmSouth Fin. Corp., Birmingham, Ala., 1972—82, chmn. bd., 1982, also dir., 1972—93; exec. v.p. AmSouth Bank N.A., Birmingham, 1982—93, chief credit officer, 1992; prin. Tucker Investments, Birmingham, 1993—2003; ret., 2003. Exec. v.p. AmSouth Bancorp, Birmingham, 1982-93; bd. dirs. Alabanc Properties Corp., Birmingham, chmn., 1991-93; bd. dirs. Birmingham Broadway Series Inc., treas., 1996-97, pres., 1997-99, chmn., 1999-2001; co-founder Garland-Govan Scholarship Fund, U. South. Contbr. articles on credit and leasing to trade jours.; photographer gen. interest mags., 1970—. Bd. dirs. Birmingham Cmty. Devel. Corp.; chmn. bd., 1990-93. 1st lt. USAF, 1952-56. Mem. Vulcan Trail Assn., Birmingham Art Mus. Assn., Birmingham Bot. Soc., Birmingham Canoe Club (bd. dirs. 1990-96), Photography Guild, Shades Valley Camera Club, Cahaba River Soc. (adv. bd. 1991-92, bd. dirs. 1993-98, v.p. orgnl. devel. 1995-98), Ala. Growth Strategies Task Force, Regional Open Space and Trails Alliance, Manigault Soc., Sewanee Devel. Coun., Order of Purple/U. of the South, The Club, Jefferson Club, Silhouettes Club. Episcopalian. Avocations: photography, high altitude hiking, white water canoeing. Home: 4132 Old Leeds Rd Birmingham AL 35213-3210

TUCKER, THOMAS RANDALL, public relations executive; b. Indpls., Aug. 6, 1931; s. Ovie Allen and Oris Aleen (Robertson) T.; m. Evelyn Marie Armuth, Aug. 9, 1953; children: Grant, Roger, Richard. AB, Franklin Coll., 1953. Grad. asst. U. Minn., 1953-54; dir. admissions registrar Franklin Coll., 1954-57; with Cummins Engine Co., Inc., Columbus, Ind., 1957, dir. pub. rels., 1968-88; pub. rels. cons. Mem. sch. bd. trustees Bartholomew County, Ind., 1966-72, pres., 1968-69; mem. Ind. State Bd. Edn., 1977-89; treas. Bartholomew County Rep. Ctrl. Com., 1960-80; sec. Columbus Learning Ctr. Mgmt. Corp.; hon. trustee Franklin Coll.; trustee Ind. State Mus. Mem. Pub. Rels. Soc. Am., Columbus (Ind.) C. of C. (Cmty. Svc. award 1986), Rotary, Sagamore of the Wabash, Kappa Tau Alpha, Phi Delta Theta, Sigma Delta Chi. Lutheran. Home: 4380 N Riverside Dr Columbus IN 47203-1123 Office: PO Box 3005 Columbus IN 47202-3005

TUCKER, THOMAS WILLIAM, mathematics professor; b. Princeton, N.J., July 15, 1945; s. Albert William Tucker and Alice Judson (Curtiss) Beckenbach; m. Mollie Dalton; children: Thomas John, Emily McDonnell. AB magna cum laude, Harvard U., 1967; PhD, Dartmouth Coll., 1971. Instr. Princeton U., 1971-73; from asst. prof. to prof. math. Colgate U., Hamilton, N.Y., 1973-83, prof., 1983—, Charles G. Hetherington prof. math., 1994—, chmn. math. dept., 1982-86, acting dean coll., 1991-92, dir. divsn. nat. sci., 1993-96. Vis. assoc. prof. Dartmouth Coll., Hanover, N.H., 1978-79; cons. Ednl. Testing Svc., 1973—, Inst. for Def. Analyses, Princeton, (summers) 1974, 75, 78, 79, 84, 85; chmn. advanced placement calculus com. Coll. Bd., N.Y.C., 1983-87; pres. Calculus Consortium for Higher Edn., Inc., 1998—. Co-author: Topological Graph Theory, 1987; editor: Priming the Calculus Pump, 1990; contbr. numerous articles to profl. jours. NSF grantee, 1976-77, 80-82, 86-88, 89, 90-97. Mem. Math. Assn. Am. (mem., chmn. many coms., v.p. 1990-92), Am. Math. Soc. Home: 21 Hamilton St Hamilton NY 13346-1329 Office: Colgate U Dept Math Hamilton NY 13346 E-mail: ttucker@mail.colgate.edu.

TUCKER, WATSON BILLOPP, lawyer; b. Dobbs Ferry, N.Y., Nov. 16, 1940; s. Watson Billopp and Mary (Prema) T.; children: Robin, Craig, Christopher, Alexander, John. BS, Northwestern U., Evanston, Ill., 1962; JD magna cum laude, Northwestern U., 1965. Bar: Ill. 1965, U.S. Dist. Ct. (no. dist.) Ill. 1966, U.S. Supreme Ct. 1971, U.S. Dist. Ct. (no. dist.) N.Y. 1976, U.S. Ct. Appeals (2d, 3d, 5th, 6th, 7th, and 9th cirs.). Ptnr. Mayer, Brown, Rowe & Maw, Chgo., 1972-99, Smith Tucker & Brown, DeKalb, Ill., 1999—. Fellow Am. Coll. Trial Lawyers. Office: Smith Tucker & Brown 115 N 1st St Dekalb IL 60115-3201 E-mail: wbtucker@smithtuckerbrown.com.

TUCKER, WILLIAM EDWARD, academic administrator, minister; b. Charlotte, N.C., June 22, 1932; s. Cecil Edward and Ethel Elizabeth (Godley) T.; m. Ruby Jean Jones, Apr. 8, 1955; children: Janet Sue, William Edward, Gordon Vance. BA, Barton Coll., Wilson, N.C., 1953, LLD (hon.), 1978; BD, Tex. Christian U., 1956; MA, Yale U., 1958, PhD, 1960; LHD (hon.), Chapman Univ., 1981; DH (hon.), Bethany Coll., 1982; DD (hon.), Austin Coll., 1985; LHD (hon.), Kentucky Wesleyan Coll., 1989. Ordained to ministry Disciples of Christ Ch., 1956; prof. Barton Coll., 1959-66, chmn. dept. religion and philosophy, 1961-66; mem. faculty Brite Div. Sch., Tex. Christian U., 1966-76, prof. ch. history, 1969-76, dean, 1971-76, chancellor, 1979-98, chancellor emeritus, 1998—. Pres. Bethany (W.Va.) Coll., 1976-79; dir. RadioShack Corp., 1985-2003, Brown and Lupton Found.; mem. gen. bd. Christian Ch. (Disciples of Christ), 1971-74, 75-87, adminstrv. com., 1975-81, chmn. theol. edn. commn., 1972-73, mem. exec. com., chmn. bd. higher edn., 1975-77; dir. Christian Ch. Found., 1980-83; moderator Christian Ch. (Disciples of Christ), 1983-85 Author: J.H. Garrison and Disciples of Christ, 1964, (with others) Journey in Faith: A History of the Christian Church (Disciples of Christ), 1975; also articles. Bd. dirs. Van Cliburn Found., 1981—, Amon Carter Mus., Ft. Worth Symphony Orch. Mem. Exch. Club, Phi Beta Kappa. Home: 2337 Colonial Pky Fort Worth TX 76109-1030 Office: 100 Throckmorton St Ste 416 Fort Worth TX 76102-2870 Business E-Mail: w.tucker@tcu.edu.

TUCKER, WILLIAM P. lawyer, writer; b. Kingston, N.Y., Jan. 26, 1932; s. Philip and Mary (McGowan) T.; m. Dolores F. Beaudoin, June 10, 1961; children: Andrew M., Thomas B., Mary A. BA, Hunter Coll., 1958; JD, St. John's U., 1962. Bar: N.Y. 1962, U.S. Dist. Ct. (ea. dist.) N.Y. 1963, Fla. 1980. Assoc. Mendes & Mount, N.Y.C., 1962-63; ptnr. Cullen and Dykman, Bklyn. and Garden City, N.Y., Washington and Newark, 1963-98, Golden, Wexler & Sarnese, Garden City/Purchase/S.I., 1998-2001; pvt. practice, 2001—. Former

gen. counsel Broadway Nat. Bank, Wartburg Luth. Svcs., Luth. Ctr. for the Aging, Martin Luther Ter. Apts., Inc., Interfaith Med. Ctr., Roosevelt Savs. Bank, Olympian Bank, GreenPoint Bank, Ridgewood Savs. Bank, Atlantic Liberty Savs., F.A., Bethpage Fed. Credit Union, Mcpl. Credit Union, Lincoln Savs. Bank, Bklyn. Savs. Bank, Met. Savs. Bank, Crossland Savs. Bank, Bushwick Savs. Bank, Anchor Savs. Bank; former spl. counsel OCI Mortgage Corp., Bklyn C. of C., Downtown Bklyn. Bus. Assn., Bank of N.Y., Chase Manhattan Bank, Fleet Bank, Kraft Credit Union, Apple Bank for Savs., Barclays Bank of N.Y.; chmn. bd. dirs. Broadway Nat. Bank; co-owner Slaem Keizer Volcanoes N.W. League baseball team, Norwich Navigators Ea. League baseball beam; former v.p., N.W. Profl. Baseball League; bd. dirs., Bklyn. Sportsplex, Inc. Author: DP-or Billy and Jerry in the Promised Land, 1996, Moving Home Plate, 1999, (novels) Excalibur, 2001, With Justice for All, 2003; contbr. articles to profl. jours.; author: (novels) Kingsway 37, 2004. Past mem. Selective Svc. Bd. 33; past pres. St. Vincent Ferrer Home Sch. Assn.; del. Diocesan Union Holy Name Socs.; mem. coun. St. John's U.; mem. coun. of regents St. Francis Coll., Bklyn.; bd. dirs. Faith Home Found., St. Josephs Coll. Served U.S. Army, Korean War. Mem. Am. Coll. Real Estate Lawyers, N.Y. State Bar Assn., Fla. Bar Assn., Savs. Banks Lawyers Assn. Bklyn., Suffolk County Bar Assn., Savs. Bank Assn. N.Y. State (law com.), Bklyn. Mcpl. Club (pres.), Knight of Malta. Home: 23 Bunker Hill Dr Huntington NY 11743-5705 Office: 145 East Main St Huntington NY 11743 E-mail: wptucker@optonline.net.

TUCKMAN, BRUCE WAYNE, educational psychologist, educator, researcher; b. N.Y.C., Nov. 24, 1938; s. Jack Stanley and Sophie Sylvia (Goldberg) T.; children: Blair Z., Bret A. BS, Rensselaer Poly. Inst., 1960; MA, Princeton U., 1962, PhD, 1963. Rsch. assoc. Princeton (N.J.) U., 1963; rsch. psychologist Naval Med. Rsch. Inst., Bethesda, Md., 1963-65; assoc. prof. edn. Rutgers U., New Brunswick, N.J., 1965-70, prof., 1970-78, dir. Bur. R&D, 1975-78; dean Coll. Edn. Baruch Coll., CUNY, 1978-82; sr. rsch. fellow CUNY, 1982-83; dean Coll. Edn. Fla. State U., Tallahassee, 1983-86, prof., 1983—98; prof., dir. W.E. Dennis Learning Ctr., Ohio State U., Columbus, 1998—. Author: Preparing to Teach the Disadvantaged, 1969 (N.J. Assn. Tchrs. of English Author's award 1969), Conducting Educational Research, 1972, 5th rev. edit., 1999 (Phi Delta Kappa Rsch. award 1973), Evaluating Instructional Programs, 1979, 2d rev. edit., 1985, Analyzing and Designing Educational Research, 1979, Effective College Management, 1987, Testing for Teachers, 1988; (novel) Long Road to Boston, 1988, Educational Psychology: From Theory to Application, 1992, 96, 98, 2002, Learning and Motivation Strategies: Your Guide to Success, 2002. Rsch. dir. Task Force on Competency Stds. Trenton, N.J., 1976. N.Y. State Regents scholar, 1956; Kappa Nu grad. scholar, 1960; NIMH predoctoral fellow, 1961, 62; Rutgers U. faculty study fellow, 1974-75 Fellow: APA; mem.: Am. Ednl. Rsch. Assn. Office: 250B Younkin Success Ctr 1640 Neil Ave Columbus OH 43201-2333 Office Phone: 614-688-8284.

TUCKNER, MICHELLE, newscaster; b. Hudson, Wis. BS in Journalism/Broadcast News, U. Kans. Weekend news reporter KTKA, Topeka; anchor/reporter WEAU-TV Channel 13, 2000—. Recipient award, Kans. Assn. Broadcasters, William Randolph Hearst Journalism awards; scholar, Assn. for Women in Sports Media, 1999. Office: WEAU PO Box 47 Eau Claire WI 54702

TUCKSON, REED V. academic administrator; Grad, Howard Univ.; Ph. D., Georgetown Univ. of Medicine. Commr. of pub. health Washington DC, 1986—90; sr v.p. for programs March of Dimes Birth Defects Found., 1990—91; pres. Charles R. Drew U., L.A., 1991—97; sr. v.p. profl. stds. AMA, Chgo., 1998—2000; sr. v.p. of consumer health and med. care advancement United Health Group, 2000—.*

TUCKWELL, BARRY EMMANUEL, musician, music educator; b. Melbourne, Australia, Mar. 5, 1931; s. Charles Robert and Elizabeth (Hill) T.; children: David Michael, Jane Madeleine, Thomas James; m. Susan Levitan, June 21, 1992. Grad., Sydney (Australia) State Conservatorium; DMus (hon.), Sydney U., Australia, 1994. Prof. French horn Royal Acad. Music, 1962-74; mem. mgmt. com. London Symphony Orch. Trust, 1963-68; mem. faculty congregation arts Dartmouth Coll., 1968-69; music educator, condr., musician. Guest prof. Harvard U., Yale U., others With Melbourne, Sydney, Halle, Scottish Nat. and Bournemouth symphony orchs., 1947-55; solo French horn, London Symphony Orch., 1955-68; tchr., soloist and chamber music player, 1968—, mem. Chamber Music Soc. of Lincoln Ctr., N.Y.C., 1974-81, dir. London Symphony Orch. Ltd., 1957-68, chmn., 1961-68, mem. Tuckwell Wind Ensemble, Tuckwell Wind Quintet, Tuckwell Horn Quartet, chief condr. Tasmanian Symphony Orch., 1980, condr., music dir. Md. Symphony Orch., 1982-98, rec. artist for RCA, CRI, Angel, London, Argo.; author: Playing the Horn, 1978, The Horn, 1983; editor: Horn Lit. for G. Schirmer, Inc; leader ann. French horn workshop, Fla. State U., Claremont Music Festival, 1970-71. Decorated Order Brit. Empire; companion Order of Australia; recipient Harriet Cohen Meml. medal for soloists, 1968. Fellow Royal Coll. Music, Royal Soc. arts; mem. Internat. Horn Soc. (hon., pres. 1969-77, 92-94), Royal Acad. Music (hon.), Guildhall Sch. Music (hon.). Address: 13140 Fountain Head Rd Hagerstown MD 21742-2839 Office: Gallo & Giordano 76 W 86th St New York NY 10024-3607

TUDOR, BRENDA S. retail company executive; CPA. Acct. Strand, Skees, Jones & Co., Asheville, N.C.; gen. acctg. mgr. Ingles Markets, Inc., Black Mountain, N.C., 1984-88; controller, sec., 1988-98; v.p., CFO, 1998—; also bd. dirs. Office: Ingles Markets Inc 1560 Hwy 70 E Black Mountain NC 28711

TUDOR, THOMAS RAE, electric power industry executive; b. Albany, Ga., Jan. 20, 1958; s. Willian Winston and Adelaide Agnes Tudor; m. Deborah Ann Hawks, Aug. 1, 1998; children: Jeffrey Alan Hawks Jr., Steven Michael Hawks, Sean Tare Hawks. AS, SUNY, 1988, BS, 1995. Field engr. Tracor, Inc., California, Md., 1982-87; systems engring. br. mgr. CACI, Inc., Great Mills, Md., 1987-88; contract adminstr. So. Md. Elec. Coop., Inc., Hughesville, Md., 1988—. Mem. Md. Photovoltaics Utilities Working Group, Annapolis, 1993—, Utilities Photovoltaic Group, Washington, 1994—. Bd. dirs. So. Md. Resource Conservation & Devel., Inc., Waldorf, 1995—. With USCG, 1977-81. Recipient Solar Park Power award Md. Energy Adminstr. & Interstate Renewable Energy Coun. St. Clements Island State Park, Md., 1997. Independent. Episcopalian. Avocations: american history, foreign coin collecting, photovoltaics. Office: So Md Elec Coop Inc 15035 Burnt Store Rd Hughesville MD 20637-1937

TUDRYN, JOYCE MARIE, professional society administrator; b. Holyoke, Mass., July 27, 1959; d. Edward William and Frances Katherine (Bajor) T.; m. William Wallace Friberger III, Sept. 18, 1982; 1 child, Kristen. BS in Comm., Syracuse U., 1981. Asst. editor Nat. Assn. Broadcasters, Washington, 1981-83; dir. programs Internat. Radio and TV Soc. Found., N.Y.C., 1983-87, assoc. exec. dir., 1988-94; exec. dir. Internat. Radio and TV Soc., N.Y.C., 1994-97, pres., 1997—. Spkr. in field; nat. adv. bd. Alpha Epsilon Rho Broadcasting Soc., 1988-91, 93-94, hon. trustee, 1994-98, officer, 1999-2001; v.p. Corp. for Ednl. Radio and TV, 1988-94; adv. bd. Marist Coll. Sch. Comm., 1999—, Syracuse U. Newhouse Sch. Pub. Comm., 1999—; vice chmn. edn. iEmmy Festival, 1999; guest prof. U. Scranton, 2000. Columnist TV Facts, Figures and Film mag., 1983-88; one-woman photography exhbn. Synchronicity Space, N.Y.C., 1998. Recipient Disting. Edn. Svc. award Broadcast Edn. Assn., 2003; named one of Most Influential Women in Radio, Radio INK Mag., 2003; inducted into Syracuse U. Newhouse Sch. Profl. Wall of Fame Gallery, 2000. Mem. N.Y. Media Roundtable, Gamma Phi Beta. Avocation: photography. Office: Internat Radio and TV Soc Found 420 Lexington Ave Ste 1601 New York NY 10170-1799

TUEBER, WILLIAM, electronics executive; CFO, controller EMC Corp., Hopkinton, Mass., sr. v.p., CFO. Office: EMC Corp PO Box 9103 Hopkinton MA 01748-9103

TUELL, JACK MARVIN, retired bishop; b. Tacoma, Nov. 14, 1923; s. Frank Harry and Anne Helen (Bertelson) T.; m. Marjorie Ida Beadles, June 17, 1946; children— Jacqueline, Cynthia, James. BS, U. Wash., 1947, LL.B., 1948; S.T.B., Boston U., 1955; MA, U. Puget Sound, 1961, DHS, 1990; D.D., Pacific Sch. Religion, 1966; LLD, Alaska Pacific U., 1980. Bar: Wash. 1948; ordained to ministry Meth. Ch., 1955. Practice law with firm Holte & Tuell, Edmonds, Wash., 1948-50; pastor Grace Meth. Ch., Everett, Wash., 1950-52, South Tewksbury Meth. Ch., Tewksbury, Mass., 1952-55, Lakewood Meth. Ch., Tacoma, 1955-61; dist. supt. Puget Sound dist. Meth. Ch., Everett, 1961-67; pastor 1st United Meth. Ch., Vancouver, Wash., 1967-72; bishop United Meth. Ch., Portland, Oreg., 1972-80, Calif.-Pacific Conf., United Meth. Ch., L.A., 1980-92; interim sr. pastor First United Meth. Ch., Boise, Idaho, 1995. Mem. gen. conf. United Meth. Ch., 1964, 66, 68, 70, 72; pres. coun. of Bishops United Meth. Ch., 1989-90. Author: The Organization of the United Methodist Church, 1970, 9th edit. 2002. Pres. Tacoma U.S.O., 1959-61, Vancouver YMCA, 1968; v.p. Ft. Vancouver Seamens Cnt., 1969-72; vice chmn. Vancouver Human Rels. Commn., 1970-72; pres. Oreg. Coun. Alcohol Problems, 1972-76; trustee U. Puget Sound, 1961-73, Vancouver Meml. Hosp., 1967-72, Alaska Meth. U., Anchorage, 1972-80, Willamette U., Salem, Oreg., 1972-80, Willamette View Manor, Portland, 1972-80, Rogue Valley Manor, Medford, Oreg., 1972-76, Sch. Theology at Claremont, Calif., 1980-92, Methodist Hosp., Arcadia, Calif., 1983-92; pres. nat. div. bd. global ministries United Meth. Ch., 1972-76, pres. ecumenical and interreligious concerns div., 1976-80, Commn. on Christian Unity and interreligious concerns, 1980-84, Gen. Bd. of Pensions,1984-92, Calif. Coun. Alcohol Problems, 1985-88. Jacob Sleeper fellow, 1955 Methodist. Home and Office: 816 S 216th St # 637 Des Moines WA 98198-6331

TUELL, STEVEN SHAWN, religious studies educator, minister; b. Est Liverpool, Ohio, Oct. 3, 1956; s. Bernard Earl and Mary Louise Tuell; m. Wendy Louise Rodan, May 30, 1981; children: Sean Michael, Anthony Ryan, Mark Anderson. BA magna cum laude, W.Va. Wesleyan Coll., 1978; MDiv, Princeton Theol. Sem., 1981; PhD, Union Theol. Sem., 1989. Student pastor Siloam and DeBowj United Meth. Chs., Allentown, NJ, 1979—81; pastor Red Hill and Murphytown United Meth. Chs., Parkersburg, W.Va., 1981—85; instr. religious studies Coll. William & Mary, Williamsburg, Va., 1988; asst. prof. Bible and religion Erskine Coll., Due West, SC, 1989—92; asst. prof. religious studies Randolph-Macon Coll., Ashland, Va., 1992—97, assoc. prof. religious studies, 1997—, chmn. religious studies, 2003—. Interim pastor Woodlake United Meth. Ch., Midlothian, Va., 1994. Author: The Law of the Temple in Ezek, 1992, 1 and 2 Chronicles, 2001; musician: (albums) Dumbarton's Drums, 1997. Mem.: Va UM Hist. Soc., Va. UM Bd. Higher Edn. Ministries, S.E. Commn. Study Religion, Soc. Biblical Lit. (mem. steering com. 1981—), Amnesty Internat. Democrat. Meth. Office: Randolph Macon College Ashland VA 23005 Office Phone: 804-752-7280. E-mail: stuell@rmc.edu.

TUER, DAVID A. petroleum industry executive; BSME, U. Calgary. Asst. dep. min. energy Govt. of Alta.; mgr. spl. projects PanCanadian Petroleum, Calgary, Alta., 1988, v.p. spl. projects, v.p. mktg., 1989-94, sr. v.p. mktg., info. sys. and downstream bus. devel., 1989-94, pres., CEO. Mem. Bus. Coun. Nat. Issues; co-chair Climate Change Ctrl.; chmn. bd. govs. Mt. Royal Coll., Calgary.

TUETING, SARAH, professional hockey player; b. Winnetka, Ill., Apr. 26, 1976; Degree in neurobiology, Dartmouth Coll. Goal keeper U.S. Nat. Women's Hockey Team, 1996—. Recipient ice hockey Gold medal Olympic Games, Nagano, Japan, 1998. Avocations: soccer, tennis, playing piano and cello. Office: c/o USA Hockey 1775 Bob Johnson Dr Colorado Springs CO 80906

TUFANO, CHARLES C. paper company executive; b. Rochester, NY, Sept. 29, 1944; BS in Indsl. Engring., Tex. A&M U., 1966. From sales staff to sales mgr. St. Regis, Cleve., 1967—82; gen. mgr. to dir. Packaging, Buffalo, 1982—95; from dir. printing papers to sr. v.p. Paper Distbn., 1995—2001; pres. Unisource, Norcross, Ga., 1999—. Office: Unisource 600 Govewrnors Lake Pkwy Norcross GA 30071

TUFANO, PAUL J, computer company executive; Degree in Econs., ST. John's U.; MBA in Fin., Acctg., Internat. Bus., Columbia U. With IBM, 1984—2001; CFO Maxtor Corp., 1996—, COO, 2001—. Office: 500 McCarthy Blvd Milpitas CA 95035

TUFARO, RICHARD CHASE, lawyer; b. N.Y.C., July 9, 1944; s. Frank P. and Stephania A. (Maida) T.; m. Helen M. Tufaro, June 25, 1977; children: Mary C., Edward F., Paul R., Cynthia M. AB magna cum laude, Dartmouth Coll., 1965; LLB cum laude, Harvard U., 1968. Bar: N.Y. 1969, D.C. 1992, Md. 1994; U.S. Dist. Ct. (so. dist.) N.Y. 1973, U.S. Dist. Ct. (ea. dist.) N.Y. 1978, U.S. Dist Ct. (D.C. dist.), 1994; U.S. Dist. Ct. (Md. dist.), 1996, U.S. Ct. Apls. (2d cir.) 1973, (5th cir.) 1976, (9th cir.) 1979, (6th cir.) 1980, (4th cir.), 1995; U.S. Ct. Claims, 1985, U.S. Ct. Appeals (3d cir.) 1990, U.S. Ct. Appeals (D.C. cir.) 1992; U.S. Sup. Ct., 1975. Law clk. Appellate-Div. N.Y. State, N.Y.C., 1970-71, assoc. Milbank, Tweed, Hadley & McCloy, N.Y.C., 1971-72, adminstrv. asst. White House Domestic Coun., Washington, 1972-73, assoc. Milbank, Tweed, Hadley & McCloy, N.Y.C., 1973-77, ptnr. 1978—. Served to capt. U.S. Army, 1968-70. Decorated Bronze Star with oak leaf cluster. Mem. ABA, Am. Mgmt. Assn., Phi Beta Kappa. Home: 7109 Heathwood Ct Bethesda MD 20817-2915 Office: 1825 I St NW Ste 1100 Washington DC 20006-5417

TUFT, MARY ANN, executive search firm executive; b. Easton, Pa., Oct. 11, 1934; d. Ben and Elizabeth (Reibman) T. BS, West Chester (Pa.) State Coll., 1956; MA, Lehigh U., 1960. Cert. assn. exec. Nat. trainer Girl Scouts U.S.A., N.Y.C., 1965-68; cons. Nat. League for Nursing, N.Y.C., 1968-69; exec. dir. Nat. Student Nurses Assn., N.Y.C., 1970-85; mem. Commn. on Dietetic Registration, Am. Dietetic Assn., 1981-85; pres. Specialized Cons. Ltd., 1983-85; exec. dir. Radiol. Soc. N.Am., Oak Brook, Ill., 1985-88; pres. Tuft & Assocs., Inc., 1989—. Trustee, Found. of the Nat. Student Nurses Assn., 2001—; adv. bd. Cognitive Neurology and Alzheimer's Disease Ctr. of Northwestern Univ./Feinberg Sch. of Medicine. Bd. dirs. Nurses House, Inc., 1981-85, midwest region Am. Friends of Hebrew U., 2000-, coun. trustees, 2004-; mem. exec. com. Chgo. Sinai Cong., 1987-91, v.p., 1988. Recipient Disting. Alumnus award West Chester State Coll., 1979; Mary Ann Tuft Scholarship Fund named in her honor Found. Nat. Student Nurses Assn.; Kepner-Tregoe scholar, 1966. Mem. ALA (pub. mem. com. on accreditation 1993-95), Am. Soc. AAssn. Execs. (bd. dirs. 1980-83, trustee for cert. 1980-83, vice chmn. 1983-84), N.Y. Soc. Assn. Execs. (pres. 1978-79, bd. dirs. 1975-78, 1st Outstanding Exec. award 1982), Continuing Care Accreditation Assn. (bd. dirs. 1983-85), Specialized Cons. in Nursing (faculty). Office Phone: 312-642-8889. Business E-Mail: matuft@tuftassoc.com.

TUFTE, EDWARD ROLF, writer, publisher, statistics educator; b. Kansas City, Mo., Mar. 14, 1942; s. Edward E. and Virginia (James) T.; m. Inge Druckrey BS, Stanford U., 1963, MS, 1964; PhD, Yale U., 1968; HHD (hon.), Cooper Union, 1992, Conn. Coll., 1995, St. Joseph's Coll., 1997, Md. Art Inst., 1999, Mpls. Coll. Art, 2000, Williams Coll., 2000; HHD hon., Univ. of the Arts, 2003. Asst. prof. pub. policy Princeton U., 1967-71, assoc. prof., 1971-74, prof., 1974-77; prof. polit. sci., stats., computer sci. Yale U., New Haven, 1977-99; pres. Graphics Press, Cheshire, 1983—. Author: Quantitative Analysis of Social Problems, 1970, Size and Democracy, 1973, Data Analysis, 1974, Political Control of the Economy, 1978 (Kammerer award 1979, Citation Classic 1989), The Visual Display of Quantitative Information, 1983 (Citation Classic 1992), Envisioning Information, 1990, Visual Explanations, 1997. Pres. Cheshire Neighborhood Assn., 1984-87. Recipient Best Graphic Design award Internat. Design, 1990, Wittenborn award, 1991, Best Book Design award Assn. Ind. Publs., Computer Press Assn. award, 1991, Sci. award Phi Beta Kappa, 1991, AIGA book show, 1998, book award AIA, 1998, book award STC, 1998, book award Internat. Design, 1998, book award Am. Ctr. for Design, 1998; Ctr. for Advanced Study in Behavioral Scis. fellow, 1973-74; Guggenheim fellow, 1977. Fellow Am. Acad. Arts and Scis., Am. Statis. Assn. Office: Graphics Press PO Box 430 Cheshire CT 06410

TUGGLE, CLYDE CEBRON, communications editor, beverage company executive; b. Atlanta, Apr. 9, 1962; s. Arthur Coleman and Nelle (Martin) T. Student, Ludwig-Maxillian U., Munich, 1982-83; completed exec. program, U. VA. Darden Sch. Bus.; BA in German Studies and Econ., Hamilton Coll., Clinton, N.Y., 1984; MDiv, Yale U., 1988. Market analyst Scott, Fitton & Co., New Haven, 1987-88; editor, corp. issues comm. dept. The Coca-Cola Co., Atlanta, 1989—92, mng. editor, 1992, exec. asst. to chmn. and CEO, 1992—98, dir. ops. devel., dep. to div. pres., region mgr. Vienna, 1998—2000, exec. asst. for chmn. and CEO to v.p. Atlanta, 2000—03, dir., Worldwide Comm., 2001—02, sr. v.p., Worldwide Public Affairs and Comm., 2002—, mem., exec. com., 2003. Bd. dirs. Sledco, Inc.; trustee Kennesaw State U., Fox Theatre, Gettysburg Nat. Battlefield Mus. Found.; mem. US Austria C. of C. Bd. dirs. Peachtree Resurgens, Atlanta Hist. Soc., 1990, Odyssey Counseling Ctr., 1990, Sheltering Arms, Southern Center for Internat. Studies, Yale U. Divinity Sch., Atlanta Symphony Orch. Mem.: Shepard Center Adv. Bd., Arthur W. Page Soc., Emory U. (bd. of visitors), Coun. on Foreign Relations. Episcopalian. Office: The Coca-Cola Co PO Box 1734 Atlanta GA 30301-1734

TUGGLE, FRANCIS DOUGLAS, dean, consultant; b. Portsmouth, Va., Jan. 19, 1943; s. Francis Joyner and Florence Eleanor (Dahlgren) T.; m. Mary Ann Tredway, June 3, 1967; children: Wendy Elizabeth, Laura Michelle. SB, MIT, 1964; MS, Carnegie-Mellon U., 1967, PhD, 1971. Prof. bus. adminstrn. and computer sci. U. Kans., Lawrence, 1968-78; Jesse H. Jones prof. mgmt. Rice U., Houston, 1978-90; dean Kogod Coll. Bus. Adminstrn., Am. U., Washington, 1990-96, prof. info. systems and strategic planning, 1996—2002; Robert J. ad Carolyn A. Waltos Jr. dean Argyros Sch. Bus. Econs. Chapman U., Orange, Calif., 2002—. Bd. dirs. Equus II, Inc., Houston, Internat. Expert Sys. Inc., Houston, v.p. mktg. devel.; dir.-at-large Inst. for Ops. Rsch. and Mgmt. Scis., 1995; sr. cons. RWD Techs., Inc.; v.p. Timegate.com. Author: How to Program a Computer, 1975, Organizational Processes, 1978. Com. chmn. United Way Tex. Gulf Coast, Houston, 1985-88. Ford Found. fellowship, 1966. Mem. Inst. for Ops. Rsch. and Mgmt. Scis. (bd. dirs. 1995, v.p. 1992-94), Am. Assn. Artificial Intelligence, Assn. for Computing Machinery, Acad. of Mgmt., Sigma Xi, Beta Gamma Sigma, Alpha Kappa Psi. Episcopalian. Avocations: golf, bicycling, jogging, painting, drawing. Home: 20465 Via Torralba Yorba Linda CA 92887 Office: Argyros Sch Bus Econs Chapman U 1 University Dr Orange CA 92866 Office Phone: 714-997-6537. E-mail: tuggle@chapman.edu.

TUGGLE, MIKE, writer, secondary school educator; b. Tulsa, Okla., Dec. 1, 1938; s. Albert Amos Tuggle and Christine Eppy White; m. Susan Joan Kennedy (div.); children: Melissa, Andrea, Lilah. MA creative Writing, San Francisco State, Calif., 1971. Tchr. CA poets in schs., San Francisco, Marin, Sonoma, Calif., 1975—. Editor (pub.): (anathology) California Oranges, 1981; author: (poetry) Cazadero Poem, 1994; host (open mic) The River Reader Bookstore, Guerneville, 2001—04, (reading series) Gold Coast Coffee Co., Duncan Mills, 2001—04. SP-4 U.S. Army, 1961—63, Ft. Ord., Calif. Recipient Dickens award, 2002, Boswell award in poetry, 1969, 1984; grantee Poetry Grant, Sonoma Cmty. Found., 1992. Democrat. Home: PO Box 421 Cazadero CA 95421

TUGWELL, FRANKLIN, think-tank executive; b. San Juan, P.R. BS, Columbia Coll., 1963; MA in Pub. Law and Govt., Columbia U., 1964, PhD in Polit. Sci., 1969. From instr. to prof. to Avery prof. Govt., chair Dept. Govt. Pomona Coll., Claremont (Calif.) Grad. Sch., 1961-88; sr. analyst for Energy Program, U.S. Office Tech. Assessment, 1979-80; dept. asst. adminstr. AID, 1980-81; sr. cons. for Internat. Projects and Programs, Pacific Gas and Electric Enterprises, 1988-89; dir. Renewable Energy and the Environment, Winrock Internat., Arlington, Va., 1989-92, v.p. for Programs and Global Projects, 1993, pres. Environ. Enterprises Assistance Fund, 1989-93, pres., CEO, 1999—; exec. dir. Heinz Endowments, Pitts., 1993-99. Adj. disting. prof. Heinz Sch. of Carnegie Mellon U.; mem. adv. bd. Forbes Fund, Local Initiative Support Corp. Author: Energy Crisis and Political Economy: Politics and Markets in the Management of Natural Resources, 1988, Energy: Managing the Transition (with John C. Sawhill, Hanns Maull and Seichi Oshima), 1978, The Politics of Oil in Venezuela, 1975; editor, contributor: Search for Alternatives: Public Policy and the Study of the Future, 1973; contbr. articles to profl. jours. Bd. dirs. Environ. Enterprises Assistance Fund (chair), Environ. Ptnrs. Fund (chair), Allegheny Conf. on Cmty. Devel. (audit and fin. com., compensation subcom.), Pitts. Cultural Trust (exec. com.), Pitts. Downtown Partnership, Strategic Investment Fund, Inc., Heinz Ctr. for Sci., Econs. and the Environment, United Way, Pitts. Symphony Soc., Pitts. Partnership for Neighborhood Devel. Internat. Affairs fellow Coun. Fgn. Rels.; recipient (twice) Wig Disting. Professorship award for Excellence in Tchg. Mem. Cosmos Club (Washington), Duquesne Club (Pitts.), Philanthropy Roundtable, Coun. on Founds. (legislation and regulations com.), Social Venture Network, Grantmakers of Western Pa., Pitts. High Tech. Coun. Office: Winrock Internat 1621 N Kent St Ste 1200 Arlington VA 22209 E-mail: ftugwell@winrock.org.

TUINSTRA, JOHN S. music educator, consultant; b. Evergreen Park, Ill., Dec. 8, 1956; s. John S. and Audrey H. Tuinstra; m. Katherine Kay Katibian, Nov. 19, 1964; children: Jessie Alexandra, Hannah Mary. MB in Edn., U. Wis., 1981, MM in Edn., 1989, MusD in Arts, 2003. Prin. tuba Wis. Chamber Orch., Madison, Wis., 1981—; music educator Madison (Wis.) Area Cath. Band Program, 1982—90, Sauk Prairie HS, Sauk City, Wis., 1986—87; music instr. U. Wis., Whitewater, 1991—; prin. tuba Wis. Wind Orch., Waukesha, 1998—; music instr. Carroll Coll., Waukesha, Wis., 1998—. Cons. DEG Music Products, Lake Geneva, Wis., 1996—. Arranger (music for brass) Madrigals by Marenzio, Largo from the New World Symphony for Brass Quintet, Ave Maria by Vittoria for tuba quartet. Mem.: Wis. Sch. Music Assn., Wis. Music Educators Assn., Internat. Tuba Euphonium Assn., Phi Mu Alpha Sinfonia. Office: Univ Wis 800 W Main St Whitewater WI 53190 Office Phone: 262-472-5709. E-mail: tuinstrj@uww.edu.

TUKE, ROBERT DUDLEY, lawyer, educator; b. Rochester, NY, Dec. 5, 1947; s. Theodore Robert and Doris Jean (Smith) T.; m. Susan Devereux Cummins, June 21, 1969; children: Andrew, Sarah. BA with distinction, U. Va., 1969; JD, Vanderbilt U., 1976. Bar: Tenn. 1976, U.S. Dist. Ct. (mid. dist.) Tenn. 1976, U.S. Ct. Appeals (6th cir.) 1976, U.S. Ct. Appeals (4th cir.) 1978, U.S. Ct. Appeals (fed. cir.) 1993, U.S. Supreme Ct. 1986, U.S. Ct. Internat. Trade 1993. Assoc. Farris, Warfield & Kanaday, Nashville, 1976—79, ptnr., 1980—94, Tuke Yopp & Sweeney, Nashville, 1994—99, Trauger, Ney & Tuke, Nashville, 2000—. Adj. prof. law Vanderbilt U. Law Sch., Nashville; faculty PLI, 1995—. Author: (with others) Tennessee Practice, 1992—; editor-in-chief Vanderbilt Law Rev.; contbr. articles to profl. jours. Mem. Tenn. Adoption Law Study Commn., 1993-96, Metro CATV Com. Capt. USMC, 1969-73. Decorated Cross of Gallantry; Patrick Wilson Merit scholar. Mem. ABA, Am. Health Law Assn., Nat. Assn. Bond Lawyers, Am. Acad. Adoption Attys. (past pres.), Tenn. Bar Assn., Nashville Bar Assn., Order of Coif. Democrat. Episcopalian. Avocations: rowing, running, bicycling, hiking, travel. Office: 222 4th Ave N Nashville TN 37219-2115 Office Phone: 615-256-8585. E-mail: rtuke@tntlaw.net.

TUKES, JAMU WAYNE, educational consultant; b. Chgo., Aug. 6, 1949; s. Thomas Benjamin Tukes and Ollie Mae Jackson-Tukes; m. Abena-Tiwaa Tukes, Feb. 11, 1974; children: Ari, Efia, Sidney. BA, George Williams Coll., 1972; MA, Roosevelt U., 1978; PhD, Logos Grad. Sch., 1993. Pers. dir. Inst. for Juvenile Rsch., Chgo., 1972-75; program coord., substance abuse counselor Bobby E. Wright Comprehensive Cmty. Mental Health Ctr., Chgo., 1975-78; profl. employment cons. Gen. Employment Enterprise, Chgo., 1978-79; sr. acad. advisor Columbia Coll., Chgo., 1979—. Bd. dirs. S.P.I.R-I.T.S., S.O.A., Inc., Chgo., 1998—, Stop-Time, Chgo., 1999-2000, Ctr. for Black Music Rsch.; co-founder, owner House of Fragrance, Chgo., 1993-97; bd. advisors Accrediting Coun. for Continuing Edn. and Tng., Richmond, Va., 1998. Author: Fragrance Mystique, 2000. Team leader, grant reader divsn. higher edn. U.S. Dept. Edn., Washington, 1999, 2001; advisor African American Alliance-Columbia, 1989-91; cmty. acvitist, 1987; counselor Better Boys Found., 1979-81. Recipient Plaque African Am. Alliance, 1991, cert.

Fred Hampton Image Award, 1987. Mem. Assn. Black Psychologists. Avocations: visual art, reading, music, gardening, travel. Office: Columbia Coll Chgo 600 S Michigan Ave Chicago IL 60605 E-mail: wtukes@popmail.colum.edu.

TULAFONO, TOGIOLA T.A. governor; b. Aunu'u Island, American Samoa, Feb. 28, 1947; s. Aitu and Silika (Vaatu'itu'i) T.; m. Maryann Taufaasau Mauga, Sept. 17, 1984; children: Puataunofo, Olita, Cherianne, Emema, Timoteo, Rosie. Grad., Honolulu Police Acad., 1967; BA, Chadron State Coll., 1970; JD, Washburn U., 1975. Bar: Kans., Am. Samoa. Police instr. Am. Samoa Police Dept., Pago Pago, 1967; adminstrv. asst. Sec. of Samoan Affairs, Pago Pago, 1970-71; legal asst. Atty. Gen., Pago Pago, 1971-72; assoc. Law Offices of George A. Wray, Pago Pago, 1975-77; v.p. South Pacific Island Airways, Pago Pago, 1977-79; judge Dist. Ct. of Am. Samoa, Pago Pago, 1979-80; chmn. bd. dirs. Am. Samoa Power Authority, Pago Pago, 1978-80; mem. Am. Samoa Senate, Pago Pago, 1981-85, 89—; pres. Nayram Samoa, Ltd., Pago Pago, 1985-88; lt. gov. Am. Samoa Pago Pago, 1997—2003; gov. Am. Samoa, 2003—. Chmn. Senate Investigation Com., 1993—. Chmn. Bd. Higher Edn., Am. Samoa, 1993—; bd. dirs. Am. Samoa Jr. Golfers' Assn.; deacon Sailele Congrl. Ch. Mem. ATLA, Am. Samoa Bar Assn., Kans. Bar Assn., Samoa Profl. Golfer's Assn. (pres. 1985-87), Am. Samoa Golf Assn. (pres.). Democrat. Congregationalist. Office: Office of the Gov Ter of American Samoa Pago Pago AS 96799

TULCHIN, DAVID BRUCE, lawyer; b. N.Y.C., Dec. 2, 1947; s. Philip Tulchin and Mary (Weiner) Black; m. Nora Barrett, Aug. 20, 1972; children: Rachel, Daniel, Laura. BA, U. Rochester, 1970; JD, Harvard U., 1973. Bar: N.Y. 1974, U.S. Dist. Ct. (so. & ea. dists.) N.Y. 1975, U.S. Ct. Appeals (2d cir.) 1975, U.S. Supreme Ct. 1977, U.S. Ct. Appeals (5th cir.) 1978, U.S. Ct. Appeals (1st & 6th cirs.) 1984, U.S. Dist. Ct. (no. dist.) Ohio 1984, U.S. Ct. Appeals (3d, 4th & Fed. cirs.) 1988, U.S. Ct. Appeals (7th cir.) 1991, U.S. Dist. Ct. (we. dist.) N.Y., 1996. Law clk. to Judge Frederick V.P. Bryan U.S. Dist. Ct. So. Dist. N.Y., N.Y.C., 1973-75; assoc. Sullivan & Cromwell, N.Y.C., 1975-82, ptnr., 1982—. Mem. ABA, Assn. Bar of City of N.Y., Fed. Bar Coun., N.Y. State Bar Assn., Fed. Cir. Bar Assn. Office: Sullivan & Cromwell 125 Broad St Fl 28 New York NY 10004-2489

TULCHIN, STANLEY, banker, lecturer, author, business reorganization consultant, credit manager; Founder, chmn. bd. STA Internat., Westbury, NY, 1955—95. Bd. dirs. N.Y. Inst. Credit, Topps Corp.; founder, chmn. Reprise Capital Corp. Prodr.: (plays) Dinner With Friends, 2000 (Pulitzer Prize, 2000), The Unexpected Man, 2000, Fortune's Fool, 2002 (Tony award (2), 2002), Vincent in Brixton, 2003 (Olivier award, 2003), Hitchcock Blonde, 2003. Recipient Leadership in Credit Edn. award N.Y. Inst. Credit, 1990. Mem. Comml. Law League Am. (Pres'. Cup award 1975, past bd. govs., vice-chmn. bd. editors Comml. Law Jour., bd. dirs. Fund for Pub. Edn.), Nat. Assn. Credit Mgmt. Office: STA Internat PO Box 707 Uniondale NY 11553-0707 Office Phone: 516-997-2400.

TULL, THERESA ANNE, retired diplomat; b. Runnemede, N.J., Oct. 2, 1936; d. John James and Anna Cecelia (Paull) T. BA, U. Md., 1972; MA, U. Mich., 1973; postgrad., Nat. War Coll., Washington, 1980. Fgn. svc. officer Dept. State, Washington, 1963, Brussels, 1965-67, Saigon, 1968-70; dep. prin. officer Am. Consulate General, Danang, Vietnam, 1973-75; prin. officer Cebu, Philippines, 1977-79; dir. office human rights, 1980-83; charge d'affaires Am. Embassy, Vientiane, Laos, 1983-86; Dept. State Senior Seminar, 1986-87; ambassador to Guyana, 1987-90; diplomat-in-residence Lincoln U., Pa., 1990-91; dir. office regional affairs, bur. East Asian & Pacific affairs Dept. State, Washington, 1991-93; amb. to Brunei Bandar Seri Begawan, 1993-96. Recipient Civilian Service award Dept. of State, 1970, Superior Honor award, 1977 Mem. Am. Fgn. Svc. Assn., Women's Civic Club. Address: 3500 Boardwalk Apt 726N Sea Isle City NJ 08243

TULL, WILLIS CLAYTON, JR., librarian; b. Crisfield, Md., Feb. 22, 1931; s. Willis Clayton and Agnes Virginia (Milbourne) T.; m. Taeko Itoi, Dec. 18, 1952. Student, U. Balt., 1948, Johns Hopkins U., 1956; BS, Towson (Md.) State Coll., 1957; MLS, Rutgers U., 1962; postgrad., Miami U., Oxford, Ohio, 1979. Editl. clk. 500th Mil. Intelligence Svc. Group, 1952-53; tchr. Hereford Jr.-Sr. H.S., Parkton, Md., 1957-59; aide Enoch Pratt Free Libr., Balt., 1959-61, profl. asst., 1962-64; coord. adult svcs. Washington County Free Libr., Hagerstown, Md., 1964-67; asst. regional libr. Eastern Shore Regional Libr., Salisbury, Md., 1967; br. libr. Balt. County Pub. Libr., Pikesville, Md., 1968-71, asst. area br. libr. Essex, Md., 1971-72, sr. info. specialist Catonsville, Md., 1972-87, on-line supr. Towson, Md., 1988-89, sr. info. specialist Reisterstown, Md., 1989-90; exec. dir. Milbourne and Tull Rsch. Ctr., 1991—2002. Contbr. to profl. and geneal. jours. Mem. Rep. Ctrl. Com. Baltimore County, 1971-72. With U.S. Army, 1949-52. Fellow Nat. Congress Patriotic Orgns.; mem. Freedom To Read Found., Md. Libr. Assn. (chmn. intellectual freedom com. 1969-70), Friends Johns Hopkins U. Librs., Md. Assn. for Adult Edn. (coord. Western Md. region 1965-67), Am. Coun. Trustees and Alumni, Am. Acad. Religion, Ctr. for Theology and the Natural Scis., Metaphys. Soc. Am., Nat. Assn. Scholars, Woodrow Wilson Internat. Ctr. for Scholars, Assn. for Asian Studies, World Future Soc., Freedom House, Internat. Rescue Com., Nature Conservancy, Unitarian Universalist Hist. Soc. Unitarian and Universalist Geneal. Soc. (founder, bd. dirs. 1971-87), Md. Geneal. Soc., Royal Soc. St. George, Sons and Daus. Pilgrims, Descs. Early Quakers, SAR, Soc. War of 1812, Ancient and Hon. Mech. Co. Balt., Rutgers Club, Kappa Delta Pi. Home: 800 Southerly Rd Apt 414 Towson MD 21286-8407

TULLER, HARRY LOUIS, materials science and engineering educator; BS, Columbia U., 1966, MS, 1967, DSc in Engring., 1973. Rsch. assoc. physics Technion, Haifa, Israel, 1974-75; from asst. to assoc. prof. materials sci. and engring. MIT, Cambridge, 1975-81, prof. materials sci. and engring., 1981—; dir. Crystal Physics and Electroceramics Lab., Cambridge, 1985—. Vis. prof. U. Pierre et Marie Curie, Paris, 1990; faculty chair Sumitomo Electric Industries, 1992-98. Co-editor: High Temperature Superconductors, 1988, Electroceramics and Solid State Ionics, 1988, Science and Technology of Fast Ion Conductors, 1989, Sold State Ionics, 1992, Interfacially Controlled Functional Materials: Electrical and Chemical Properties, 2000, Oxygen Ion and Mixed Conductors and Their Technological Applications, 2000; series editor: Electronic Materials: Science and Technology; editor-in-chief Jour. Electroceramics. Fulbright travel grantee, 1990, Alexander von Humboldt fellow, 1997. Fellow Am. Ceramic Soc. (N.E. chair 1983); mem. IEEE, Electrochem. Soc. (co-organizer 1st, 2d and 3d internat. symposium ionic and mixed conducting ceramics 1991, 94, 97, co-organizer 1997 NATO/ASI Oxygen Ion & Mixed Conductors Summer Sch.), Materials Rsch. Soc. Jewish. Avocations: photography, gardening. Office: MIT 77 Massachusetts Ave Rm 13-3126 Cambridge MA 02139-4307

TULLIS, EDWARD LEWIS, retired bishop; b. Cin., Mar. 9, 1917; s. Ashar Spence and Priscilla (Daugherty) T.; m. Mary Jane Talley, Sept. 25, 1937; children: Frank Loyd, Jane Allen (Mrs. William Nelson Offutt IV); m. Katharine Crum Irwin, Sept. 4, 1997. AB, Ky. Wesleyan Coll., 1939, LHD, 1975; BD, Louisville Presbyn. Theol. Sem., 1947; DD, Union Coll., Barbourville, Ky., 1954, Wofford Coll., 1976; LHD, Claflin Coll., 1976, Lambuth Coll., 1984. Ordained to ministry Methodist Ch., 1941; service in chs. Frenchburg, Ky., 1937-39, Lawrenceburg, Ky., 1939-44; asso. pastor 4th Ave. Meth. Ch., Louisville, 1944-47, Irvine, Ky., 1947-49; asso. sec. ch. extension sect. Bd. Missions, Meth. Ch., Louisville, 1949-52; pastor First Meth. Ch., Frankfort, Ky., 1952-61, Ashland, Ky., 1961-72; resident bishop United Meth. Ch., Columbia, S.C., 1972-80, Nashville area, 1980-84, ret., 1984. Instr. Bible Ky. Wesleyan Coll., 1947-48; instr. Louisville Presbyn. Theol. Sem., 1949-52; mem. Meth. Gen. Conf., 1956, 60, 64, 66, 68, 70, 72, Southeastern Jurisdictional Conf., 1952, 56, 60, 64, 68, 72, bd. mgrs. Bd. Missions, 1962-72, mem. bd. discipleship, 1972-80, v.p. Gen. Coun. on Fin. and Adminstrn., 1980-84; Chaplain Ky. Gen. Assembly, 1952-61; chmn. Frankfort Com. Human Rights, 1956-61, Mayor's Adv. Com. Human Rels., Ashland, 1968-72. Author: Shaping the Church from the Mind of Christ, 1984, The Birth of the Book: A Study in the Origin and Growth of the Bible, 1998. Contbr. articles to religious jours. Sec., bd. dirs. Magee Christian Edn. Found.; trustee Emory U., 1973-80, Alaska Meth. U., 1965-70, Ky. Wesleyan Coll., Martin Coll., Lambuth Coll., McKendree Manor, Meth. Hosps., Memphis, Lake Junaluska Assembly, 1966-88; chair adv. bd. Found. for Evangelism, United Meth. Ch., 1991—. Recipient Outstanding Citizen award Frankfort VFW, 1961, Mayor's award for outstanding svc. Ashland, 1971, Heroes, Sts. and Legends award, Wesley Meth. Village Ky., 1997, Chief Junaluska award Lake Junaluska Assembly, 1998, Outstanding Alumnus award Ky. Wesleyan Coll., 2000, Disting. Alumnus award Louisville Presbyn. Sem., 2002; named to Ky. Wesleyan Coll. Hall of Fame, 2004. Mem.: Kiwanis. Methodist. Home: 510 Crum Dr Lake Junaluska NC 28745 E-mail: etullis1@mindspring.com.

TULLMAN, GLEN, management consultant; BA in Anthrop., Oxford (Eng.) U. With CCC Info. Svcs. Group, 1983—94; CEO Enterprise Sys., Inc., 1994—97, Allscripts Healthcare Solutions Inc., Libertyville, Ill., 1997—, chmn. bd. Office: Allscripts Healthcare Solutions Inc 2401 Commerce Ave Libertyville IL 60048*

TULLOCH-REID, ELMA DEEN, nurse, consultant; b. Erie, Pa., June 27, 1938; d. Theodore and Roberta (Hicks) Carlisle; children: Robynne and Stacey (twins). BS, N.C. Agrl. and Tech. State U., 1960; MA, Calif. State U., 1977; Ed.D., Nova U., 1981. Staff nurse Michael Reese Hosp., Chgo., 1960-62; instr. Cook County Sch. Nursing, Chgo., 1962-64; tchr. St. Joseph Convent, Trinidad, West Indies, 1964-66; med./surg. coordinator St. Vincent Coll. Nursing, L.A., 1966-68, med./surg. coord., 1968-69; charge nurse Century City Hosp., L.A., 1971-72; tchr. L.A. Unified Schs., 1972-75; dir. edn. and tng. Imperial Hosp., Inglewood, Calif., 1977-79; pres. Elma Tulloch-Reid Assocs., L.A., 1981—. Asst. prof. dept. continuing edn. Calif. State U., Long Beach, 1977—81, assoc. prof., 1982—; instr. Pilot Program in Health Occupations, Culver City Unified Sch. Dist., 1985—; mem. Citizen Amb. Program to Republic of China, 1995, Citizen Amb. Program to Singapore (World Conf. on Domestic Violence, 1998; DON edn. and rsch. King Drew Med. Ctr., L.A., 1991—95; dir. edn. Daniel Freeman Hosps., Inc., Inglewood, Calif., 1996—2001; dir. edn. svcs. Queen of Angels/Hollywood Presbyn. Med. Ctr., 2001—; clin. performance examiner Regents Coll. NYU. Cmty. instr. certified basic life support L.A. Cardio-Pulmonary Resuscitation Consortium, 1981-82. Recipient commendation City of Los Angeles XXIII Olympiad, 1984. Mem. Nat. Orgn. Mothers of Twins, NAFE, Am. Nurses Found., Am. Coll. Healthcare Execs., N.C. Agrl. and Tech. State U. Alumni Assn., AAUW, Assn. for Psychol. Type, Orgn. Healthcare Educators (sec. 1998-2000, pres. 2001-02), Westside Mothers of Twins Club L.A. (pres. 1971-73), Phi Kappa Phi Home: 1056 S Cochran Ave Los Angeles CA 90019-2857

TULLOCK, GORDON, economics professor; b. Rockford, Ill., Feb. 13, 1922; s. George and Helen T. JD, U. Chgo., 1947. Fgn. svc. officer, China, 1947-56; postdoctoral fellow U. Va., 1958-59; asst. prof. U. S.C., 1959-60, assoc. prof., 1960-62, U. Va., Charlottesville, 1962-67; prof. econs. and polit. sci. Rice U., Houston, 1967-68; prof. econs. and pub. choice Va. Poly. Inst. and State U., Blacksburg, 1968-72, univ. disting. prof. econs. and pub. choice, 1972-83, George Mason U., Fairfax, Va., 1983-87; prof. U. Ariz., Tucson, 1987-99; prof. law and econ. George Mason U., Arlington, Va., 1999—. Editl. dir. Center for Study of Pub. Choice, 1968-90; vis. disting. scholar Baruch U., N.Y.C., spring 1987; dir. DHC, Eldora, Iowa; mem. Jour. Social and Biol. Structure; bd. editors Internat. Jour. Law and Econs., Atlantic Econ. Jour., Bioecons. Soc. Author: (with J.M. Buchanan) The Calculus of Consent, 1962, The Politics of Bureaucracy, 1965, The Organization of Inquiry, 1966, Toward a Mathematics of Politics, 1967, Private Wants, Public Means, 1970, The Logic of the Law, 1971, The Social Dilemma, 1974, (with Richard B. McKenzie) The New World of Economics, 1975, (with Richard B. McKenzie) Modern Political Economy, 1978, Trials on Trial, 1980, Toward a Theory of the Rent-Seeking Society, 1980, Economics of Income Redistribution, 1983, The Economics of Wealth and Poverty, 1986, Autocracy, 1987, The Economics of Special Privilege and Rent Seeking, 1989, Economic Hierarchies, Organization and the Structure of Production, 1992, The New Federalist, 1994, On the Trial of Homo Economicus, 1994, On Voting: A Public Choice Approach, 1998, Government Failure: A Primer in Public Choice, 2002, (with others) The Political Economy of Rent Seeking, 1989. Fellow Am. Econ. Assn.; mem. Am. Acad. Arts and Scis., So. Econ. Assn. (past pres.), Western Econ. Assn. (pres.), Am. Polit. Sci. Assn., Pub. Choice Soc. (sec. 1965-), Assn. for Asian Studies, Inst. Econ. Affairs (coun. mem.), Mont Pelerin Soc., Bioecons Soc. (hon. chmn.). Home: 3800 Fairfax Dr Apt 213 Arlington VA 22203-1759 Office: George Mason U Rm 433A 3401 N Fairfax Dr Arlington VA 22201-4498 Office Phone: 703-993-4908. Business E-Mail: gtulloc1@gmu.edu.

TULLY, DANIEL PATRICK, financial services executive; b. 1932; m. Grace Tully; children: Daniel G., Eileen, Elizabeth, Timothy. BBA, St. Johns U., 1953. With Merrill Lynch, Pierce, Fenner & Smith, N.Y.C., 1955—, mem. acctg. dept., 1955-59, acct. exec. trainee, 1959-63, asst. to mgr. Stamford, Conn. office, 1963-70, mgr., 1970-71, v.p., 1971-79, dir. individual sales, 1976-79, exec. v.p., 1979-82, pres. individual services group, 1982-84, pres. consumer mktg., from 1984; pres., COO Merrill Lynch & Co., Inc., N.Y.C., 1985; former exec. v.p. Merrill Lynch & Co. (parent), N.Y.C., 1979, CEO, 1992-96, chmn., 1993-97, chmn. emeritus. Served U.S. Army, 1953-55. Office: Merrill Lynch & Co Inc 301 Tresser Blvd Fl 12 Stamford CT 06901-3239

TULLY, DARROW, newspaper publisher; b. Charleston, W.Va., Feb. 27, 1932; s. William Albert and Dora (McCann) T.; m. Victoria Lynn Werner; children: Bonnie Tully Paul, Michael Andrew. Student, Purdue U., 1951; BA in Journalism, St. Joseph's Coll., 1972; PhD in Journalism (hon.), Calumet (Ind.) Coll., 1975. V.p., gen. mgr. Stas. WDSM-AM-FM and WDSM-TV, Duluth, Minn., 1956-59; bus. mgr. Duluth Herald & News Tribune, 1960-62; gen. mgr. St. Paul Dispatch & Pioneer Press, 1962-66; pub. Gary (Ind.) Post-Tribune, 1966-73; v.p., pub. Wichita (Kans.) Eagle & Beacon, 1973-75; pres. San Francisco Newspaper Agy., 1975-78; exec. v.p., pub. Ariz. Republic & Phoenix Gazette, 1978-85; editor., pub., chief exec. officer Ojai (Calif.) Valley News, 1987-90; pres., pub., CEO Beacon Comms., Acton, Mass., 1990-92; asst. to pres. newspaper divsn. Chronicle Pub. Co., 1992-94. Author: Minority Representation in the Media, 1968. Trustee Calumet Coll. Recipient Disting. Achievement award Ariz. State U., 1982, Disting. Journalist award No. Ariz. U./AP, 1983, 1st Pl. Editorial Writing award Ariz. Planned Parenthood, 1983. Mem. Am. Soc. Newspaper Editors, Soc. Profl. Journalists. Office: 9862 Bridgeton Dr Tampa FL 33626-1802 Office Phone: 813-926-9709. Personal E-mail: dtully1@tampabay.rr.com.

TULLY, HERBERT BULLARD, chemical manufacturing executive; b. Glen Ridge, N.J., Sept. 3, 1943; s. Richard Golfe and Marie Foster (Towne) T.; m. Nancy Dee Zook, Dec. 22, 1967; children: Kimberly, Christine, Gregory. BS, U. Calif., Berkeley, 1967. Mem. fin. mgmt. staff Gen. Electric Co., San Jose, Calif., 1967-70, mem. corp. audit staff Schenectady, N.J., 1970-73, mgr. acct. dept. San Leandro, Calif., 1973-75; mgr. audit dept. Am. Express Co., Fireman's Fund, San Francisco, 1975-77; asst. controller Fireman's Fund Ins. Co., San Francisco, 1977-81; controller Wilbur-Ellis Co., San Francisco, 1981-86, asst. treas., 1986-89, vp treas., 1989—2000, CEO, pres., 2000—. Bd. dirs. Overseas Cos., San Francisco. Office: Wilbur Ellis 345 California Street Flr 27 San Francisco CA 94104*

TULLY, HUGH MICHAEL, music educator; b. N.Y.C., Sept. 21, 1947; s. Hugh Joseph and Grace Esther (Glynn) T.; children: Andrea Clare, Alexander Clayton. BS, Western Conn. State U., 1969; MS, U. N.H., 1980; EdD, Boston U., 1989. Dir. music Ashford (Conn.) Elem. Sch., 1969-72, Berlin (N.H.) Regional Cath. Sch., 1972-77; band dir. Somersworth (N.H.) H.S., 1977—. Founder, liaison Somersworth Music Boosters, 1980—; spokesperson Consortium Chamber Singers, Brookfield, N.H., 1989-91. Mem. Mensa. Avocation: writing children's stories. Home: 204 Wentworth Rd Brookfield NH 03872-7104 Office: Somersworth HS Memorial Dr Somersworth NH 03878

TULLY, JOHN CHARLES, research chemical physicist; b. N.Y.C., May 17, 1942; s. Harry V. and Pauline (Fischer) T.; m. Mary Ellen Thomsen, Jan. 23, 1971; children: John Thomsen, Elizabeth Anne, Stephen Thomsen. BS, Yale U., 1964; PhD, U. Chgo., 1968. NSF postdoctoral fellow U. Colo. and Yale U., 1968-70; mem. tech. staff AT&T Bell Labs., Murray Hill, NJ, 1970-82, disting. mem. tech. staff, 1982-85, head phys. chemistry rsch. dept., 1985-90, head materials chem. rsch. dept., 1990-96; Kemp prof. dept. chemistry, physics and applied physics Yale U., New Haven, 1996—. Vis. prof. Princeton (N.J.) U., 1981-82, Harvard U., Cambridge, Mass., 1991. Contbr. articles to sci. jours.; author, prodr. movie Dynamics of Gas-Surface Interactions, 1979. NSF predoctoral fellow, 1965-68. Fellow AAAS, Am. Phys. Soc. (chem. physics exec. com. 1983-86), Am. Acad. Arts & Scis.; mem. Am. Chem. Soc. (chmn. theoretical chemistry subdiv. 1991-92, phys. chemistry divsn. 1993-94, Peter Debye award 1995, Madison Marshall award 1999, Theoretical Chemistry award 2004), NAS, Internat. Acad. Quantum Molecular Scis., Conn. Acad. Sci. and Engring., Sigma Xi. Achievements include patent on Method and Apparatus for Surface Characterization Utilizing Radiation from Desorbed Particles; fundamental theoretical contributions towards atomic level understanding of chemical reaction dynamics. Office: Yale Univ Dept Chemistry PO Box 208107 New Haven CT 06520 8107

TULLY, SUSAN BALSLEY, pediatrician, medical educator; b. San Francisco, July 12, 1941; d. Gerard E. Balsley Sr. and Norma Lilla (Hand) Carey; m. William P. Tully, June 19, 1965; children: Michael William, Stephen Gerard. BA in Premed. Studies, UCLA, 1963, MD, 1966. Diplomate Am. Bd. Pediat. with subsplty. in pediatric emergency medicine. Intern L.A. County-U. So. Calif. Med. Ctr., 1966-67, jr. resident pediat., 1967-68; staff pediatrician, part-time Permanente Med. Group, Oakland, Calif., 1968; sr. resident pediat. Kaiser Found. Hosp., Oakland, 1968-69, Bernalillo County Med. Ctr., Albuquerque, 1969-70, chief resident pediatric outpatient dept., 1970; instr. pediat., asst. dir. outpatient dept. U. N.Mex. Sch. Medicine, Albuquerque, 1971-72; asst. prof. pediat., dir. ambulatory pediat. U. Calif., Irvine, 1972-76, asst. prof. clin. pediat., vice chair med. edn., 1977-79; staff pediatrician Ross-Loos Med. Group, Buena Park, Calif., 1976-77; assoc. prof. clin. pediat. and emergency medicine U. So. Calif. Sch. Medicine, 1979-86; dir. pediatric emergency dept. L.A. County/U. So. Calif. Med. Ctr., 1979-87; prof. clin. pediat. and emergency medicine U. So. Calif. Sch. Medicine, 1986-89; dir. ambulatory pediat. L.A. County/U. So. Calif. Med. Ctr., 1987-89; clin. prof. pediat. UCLA, 1989-93, vice chair pediat., 1996-97, prof. clin. pediat., 1993-97, prof. emeritus, 1997—; dir. ambulatory pediat. Olive View-UCLA Med. Ctr., 1989-96, chief pediat., 1996-97, cons. pediatrician, 1997—. Mem. survey team pediatric emergency svcs. L.A. Pediatric Soc., 1984—86; mem. adv. bd. preventive health project univ. affiliated program Children's Hosp. L.A., 1981—83; lectr. nursing pediat. nurse practitioner program Calif. State U., L.A., 1997—; pediat. toxicology cons. L.A. County Regional Poison Control Ctr. Med. Adv. Bd., 1981—97; clin. faculty rep. pediatric advancement and promotion com. UCLA Sch. Medicine, 1992—93; pediatric liaison dept. emergency medicine Olive View/UCLA Med. Ctr., 1989—96, dir. lead poisoning clinic, 1993—99; mem. quality assurance com. Los Angeles County Cmty. Health Plan, 1986—89. Author: (with K.E. Zenk) Pediatric Nurse Practitioner Formulary, 1979; (book chpt. with W.A. Wingert) Pediatric Emergency Medicine: Concepts and Clinical Practice, 1992, 2d edit., 1997; (with others) Educational Guidelines for Ambulatory/General Pediatrics Fellowship Training, 1992, Physician's Resource Guide for Water Safety Education, 1994; reviewer Pediatrics, 1985-89; editl. cons. Advanced Pediatric Life Support Course and Manual, 1988-89, Archives of Pediatrics and Adolescent Medicine, 1996-2001; dept. editor Pediatric Pearls Jour. Am. Acad. Physician Assts., 1989-94; tech. cons., reviewer Healthlink TV Am. Acad. Pediatrics, 1991; reviewer Pediatric Emergency Care, 1992—; question writer sub-bd. pediatric emergency medicine Am. Bd. Pediatrics, 1993-98; assoc. editor: Curriculum for the Training of General Pediatricians, 1996; cons. to lay media NBC Nightly News, Woman's Day, Sesame Street Parents, Parenting, Los Angeles Times; author numerous abstracts; contbr. articles to profl. jours. Cons. spl. edn. programs Orange County Bd. Edn., 1972-79; mem. Orange County Health Planning Coun., 1973-79; co-chairperson Orange County Child Health and Disability Prevention Program Bd., 1975-76; mem. Orange County Child Abuse Consultation Team, 1977-79; mem. project adv. bd. Family Focussed "Buckle Up" Project, Safety Belt Safe, U.S.A., 1989-96. Fellow Am. Acad. Pediat. (life, active numerous sects. and coms., active Calif. chpt.); mem. APHA, Ambulatory Pediatric Assn., L.A. Pediatric Soc. (life). Democrat. Avocations: art needlework, reading. Office: Olive View UCLA Med Ctr Pediatrics 3A108 14445 Olive View Dr Sylmar CA 91342-1495

TULLY, THOMAS ALOIS, building materials executive, consultant, educator; b. Dubuque, Iowa, Nov. 11, 1940; s. Thomas Aloysius and Marjorie Mae (Fosselman) T.; m. Joan Vonnetta Dubay, Nov. 30, 1963; children: Thomas Paul, Maureen Elizabeth. BA, Loras Coll., 1962; postgrad., Georgetown U., 1963-66; MPA, Harvard U., 1968. Mgmt. trainee Office of Sec. Def., Washington, 1962-63, fgn. affairs officer, 1963-70; v.p. Dubuque Lumber Co., 1970-84, pres., 1984-91, Tully's, 1991-92, LBM Mktg. Assocs., Inc., 1992—. Adj. instr. Divine Word Coll., 1971, Loras Coll., 1972; adj. instr. Clarke Coll., 1987-89, instr., 1989-91, asst. prof., 1992-97, chmn. dept. acctg. and bus., 1993-97, dir. small bus. inst., 1994-97; dir. MBA program U. Dubuque, 1997-2000; founder, exec. dir. Dubuque Area Com. on Fgn. Rels., 2001—, pres., 2002—; pres. Hills and Dales Child Devel. Ctr., Inc., 1992-96; trustee Alverno Apts., 1995-2001, pres., 1999-2001. Mem. Dubuque Human Rights Commn., 1974—75, chmn., 1975, Iowa State Com. for Employer Support of Guard and Res. Forces, 1988—, area chmn., 2000—, Iowa state coord., 2004—; city councilman Dubuque, 1975—79; bd. dirs. League Iowa Municipalities, 1977—79; mayor City of Dubuque, 1978; vice chmn. Iowa Temporary State Land Preservation Policy Com., 1978—79; pres. N.E. Iowa Regional Coordinating Coun., 1985—93, East Ctrl. Intergovtl. Assn. Bus. Growth, Inc., 1987—2002, chmn., 1993—2002; bd. dirs. Pvt. Industry Coun. of Dubuque and Delaware Counties, Inc., 1983—86; trustee Divine Word Coll., 1989—97; pres. Barn Cmty. Theatre, 1988—89; chmn. bd. trustees United Way Svcs. of Dubuque, 1990, campaign chmn., 1991, bd. mem., 1980—94; trustee Carnegie-Stout Pub. Libr., 2001—, pres., 2003—04. Recipient Meritorious Civilian Svc. award Sec. of Def., 1970, Gov.'s Vol. award, 1989. Mem. Nat. Lumber and Bldg. Material Dealers Assn. (exec. com. 1988 90), Iowa Lumbermen's Assn. (pres. 1984, chmn. legis. com. 1985-90), Northwestern Lumbermens Assn. (bd. dirs. 1984-87, 2d v.p. 1988, 1st v.p. 1989-90, pres. 1990-91). Democrat. Roman Catholic. Home: 838 Stone Ridge Pl Dubuque IA 52001-1362 Office: LBM Mktg Assocs 838 Stone Ridge Pl Dubuque IA 52001 Office Phone: 515-252-4192. E-mail: tully.thomas@alumni.ksg.harvard.edu.

TULLY, WILLIAM P. civil engineer, academic administrator; b. 1940; BCE, MCE, Northeastern U.; PhD in Civil Engring., Syracuse U. Registered profl. engr., N.Y. Former engr. E.H. Porter Co., Peabody, Mass.; former structural engr. LeMessurier Assocs., Boston; with SUNY Coll. Environ. Sci. and Forestry, Syracuse, N.Y., 1966—, v.p. program affairs, provost, former dept. chmn. civil engring., 1987—, former v.p. academic affairs, now v.p. program affairs, provost. Office: SUNY Coll of Environ Sci Office VP Program Affairs/Provost 1 Forestry Dr Syracuse NY 13210-2712

TUMAY, MEHMET TANER, geotechnical consultant, educator, research administrator; b. Feb. 2, 1937; came to U.S., 1959; s. Bedrettin and Muhterem (Uybadin) T.; m. Karen Nuttycombe, June 15, 1962; children: Peri, Suna. BSCE, Robert Coll. Sch. Engring., Istanbul, Turkey, 1959; MSCE, U. Va., 1961; postgrad., UCLA, 1963—64; PhD, Tech. U. Istanbul, 1971. Lic. civil engr., La., Ga., S.C., Turkish Chamber of Civil Engring. Instr. civil engring. U. Va., Charlottesville, 1961-62; asst. prof. civil engring. U. Louisville, 1962-63; tchg. fellow UCLA, 1963-64; asst. prof. civil engring. Robert Coll. Sch. Engring., Istanbul, 1966-71; assoc. prof. dept. civil engring. Bogazici U., Istanbul, 1971-75; Ga. Gulf disting. prof. La. State U., Baton Rouge, 1976—; Fugro-Cesco postdoctoral rsch. fellow U. Fla., Gainesville, 1975-76. Adv. prof. U. Vicosa, Minas Gerais, Brazil, 1991—, Tongji U., Shanghai, 1991—; dir. geomechanics program NSF, Washington, 1990-94; dir. rsch. La. Transp. Rsch. Ctr., Baton Rouge, 1994-97; assoc. dean rsch. and grad. studies Coll. Engring., La. State U., 1997—; maitre de conferences Ecole Nationale des Ponts et Chaussees, Paris, 1980-94; geotech. cons. Sauti, Spa, Cons. Engrs., Italy, 1969-72, SOFRETU-RATP, Paris, 1972-73, D.E.A., Cons. Engrs., Istanbul, 1974-75, BOTEK, Ltd., Istanbul, 1975—, Senler-Campbell Assocs., Louisville, 1979-90, Fugro Gulf-Geogulf, Houston, 1980-83; cons. UN Devel. Program, 1982-84, 87; cons. in field. Contbr. articles to profl. jours. AID

scholar, 1975-76, French Ministry External Rels. scholar, 1982. Fellow: ASCE; mem.: ASTM, Transp. Rsch. Bd. of the Nat. Acads, (emeritus), Internat. Soc. Soil Mechanics and Found. Engring., Turkish Chamber Civil Engrs., Turkish Soil Mechanics Group, La. Engring. Soc., Am. Soc. Engring. Edn., Tau Beta Pi, Chi Epsilon, Sigma Xi. Home: 2217 Dove Hollow Dr Baton Rouge LA 70809-1275 Office: La State U Coll Engring Baton Rouge LA 70803-0001 Office Phone: 225-578-9165. Business E-Mail: mtumay@eng.lsu.edu.

TUMBLESON, STEPHAN NORMAN, music educator; b. Cin., Ohio, July 21, 1970; s. Lawrence Daniel and Donna Mae Tumbleson; m. Andrea Lynn Kranz, June 29, 1996. BSc in music edn., U. of Cin. Coll. Conservatory, 1992; M in music edn., Miami U., 2000. Lifetime tchg. cert. in Tex., provisional tchg. cert. Ohio. Specialist E-4 USAR, 1988—92. Mem.: Ohio Educators Assn., Internat. Assn. of Jazz Educators, Ohio Music Educators Assn., Pi Kappa Lambda. Avocations: fly fishing, home remodeling. Office: Fairfield City Schools 5050 Dixie Hwy Fairfield OH 45014

TUMOLO, MICHAEL L. corporate lawyer; V.p., counsel Toys 'R' Us, Paramus, N.J., 1981—. E-mail: tumolom@toysrus.com.

TUNE, BRUCE MALCOLM, pediatrics educator, renal toxicologist; b. N.Y.C., Aug. 26, 1939; s. Buford M. and Sylvia Tune; m. Nancy Carter Doolittle, Sept. 13, 1969; children: Sara E., Steven M. AB, Stanford U., 1963, MD, 1965. Diplomate Am. Bd. Pediat., Am. Bd. Pediatric Nephrology, Nat. Bd. Med. Examiners. Intern in medicine and pediatrics Strong Meml. Hosp., Rochester, NY, 1965—66; rsch. assoc. Lab. Kidney and Electrolyte Metabolism, Nat. Heart Inst., NIH, Bethesda, Md., 1967—69, clin. assoc., 1968—69; resident in pediat. Stanford (Calif.) U. Sch. Medicine, 1966—67, chief resident, 1969—70, fellow in pediatric renal and metabolic disease, 1970—71, asst. prof. pediat., 1971—77, assoc. prof., 1977—83, prof., 1983—, acting chmn. dept., 1991—93, dir. pediatric nephrology, 1971—97, prof. pediat. divsn. pediatric nephrology, 1998—, now emeritus prof. pediat. divsn. pediatric nephrology. Attending physician, chief pediatric renal svcs. Stanford U. Hosp., Palo Alto, Calif., 1971—76, Children's Hosp. at Stanford, Palo Alto, 1971—91; cons. physician Santa Clara Valley Med. Ctr., San Jose, Calif., 1973—; attending physician, chief pediatric renal svcs. Lucile Salter Packard Children's Hosp. at Stanford, 1991—98, acting chief pediatric medicine, 1991—93, attending physician, 1997; mem. rev. panel internat. study kidney diseases in children N.Y.C. NIH, 1973—74; polycystic kidney disease study group, Albuquerque, 1984; mem. spl. study sect. on genetics and kidney maturation, Bethesda, Md., 92; cons. Lilly Rsch. Labs., Indpls., 1980, Merck Sharp and Dohme Labs., Rahway, NJ, 1980, Bristol Labs., Syracuse, NY, 1982, ICI Pharms., Cheshire, England, 1992, Gilead Scis., Foster City, Calif., 1993, Zeneca Pharms., Mereside, England, 1994—; organizing mem., chmn. session on antibiotics NIH and EPA Conf. on Nephrotoxicity of Drugs and Environ. Toxicants, Pinehurst, NC, 1981; co-dir. Coop. Study Therapy of Steroid-Resistant Focal Glomerulosclerosis in Children, 1988—; mem. rsch. grant rev. panel Ont. (Can.) Ministry Health, 1992—, Wellcome Trust, London, 1994—; reviewer bd. environ. studies and toxicology NRC, 1994. Editl. bd. Am. Jour. Kidney Diseases, 1981—94, guest editor Contemporary Issues in Nephrology, 1984, Jour. Am. Soc. Nephrology, 1991; contbr. articles to med. jours. Grantee NIH, 1974—77, 1979—83, 1985—89, 1990—95. Mem.: Am. Soc. Pharmacology and Exptl. Therapeutics, Am. Heart Assn. (coun. on kidney diseases, grantee 1985—88, 1989—92), Western Soc. for Pediatric Rsch., Internat. Pediatric Nephrology Assn., Am. Soc. Pediatric Nephrology (coun. 1978—82, rsch. subcom. 1993—), Internat. Soc. Nephrology, Am. Soc. Nephrology, Alpha Omega Alpha, Phi Beta Kappa. Office: Stanford U Sch Medicine Dept Pediatrics 300 Pasteur Dr Rm G306 Palo Alto CA 94304-2203*

TUNE, JAMES FULCHER, lawyer; b. Danville, Va., May 13, 1942; s. William Orrin and Susan Agnes (Fulcher) T.; m. Katherine Del Mickey, Aug. 2, 1969; children: Katherine Winslow, Jeffrey Bricker. BA, U. Va., 1964; MA, Stanford U., 1970, JD, 1974. Bar: Wash. 1974, U.S. Dist. Ct. (we. dist.) Wash. 1974. Assoc. Bogle & Gates, Seattle, 1974-79, ptnr., 1980-99, head comml./banking dept., 1985-93, mng. ptnr., 1986-93, chmn., 1994-99; ptnr. Dorsey & Whitney LLP, Seattle, 1999-2001, Stoel Rives LLP, Seattle, 2001—, Seattle mng. ptnr., 2002—. Bd. dirs. Keynetics Inc., Boise, Idaho, Nichirei U.S.A., Inc., Seattle, Tengu Co., Santa Fe Springs, Calif.; chmn. Seattle-King City Econ. Devel. Coun., 1992. Chmn. Seattle Repertory Theatre, 1995, Corp. Coun. for the Arts, 2001—02, United Way King County, 2004. Lt. USN, 1964—69, Vietnam. Woodrow Wilson fellow, 1964, Danforth Found. fellow, 1964. Mem. ABA, Wash. State Bar Assn. (lectr. CLE 1976, 78, 84, 99, 02), Seattle C. of C. (vice chmn. City Budget Task Force 1980-82), Ranier Club, Seattle Tennis Club, Phi Beta Kappa. Presbyterian. Office: Stoel Rives LLP 600 University St Ste 3600 Seattle WA 98101-3197 E-mail: jftune@stoel.com.

TUNG, KO-YUNG, lawyer; b. Peking, China, Feb. 20, 1947; came to U.S., 1964; s. Tien-chung and Hung-Fang (Wong) T.; m. Alison Heydt, Feb. 2, 1975; children: Vanessa, Adrian, Cameron, Gregory. BA, Harvard U., 1969; JD, U. Tokyo, 1971. Bar: N.Y., 1973. Assoc. Debevoise & Plimpton, N.Y.C., 1973-76; ptnr. Tung, Drabkin & Boynton, N.Y.C., 1976-84, O'Melveny & Myers, N.Y.C., 1985-99; v.p., gen. counsel The World Bank, Washington, 1999—; sec.-gen. Internat. Ctr. for Settlement of Investment Disputes, Washington, 2000—. Adj. assoc. prof. sch. law NYU, 1974-88. Mem. Coun. on Fgn. Rels., N.Y.C., 1986—, The Brookings Inst., 1990, Overseas Devel. Coun., Washington, 1990-99, The Japan Soc., 1990, Asia Soc., 1994—, Presl. Commn. U.S. Pacific Trade Investment Policy, 1996-97, Trilateral Commn., N.Y.C., 1990-97; chmn., bd. govs. East West Ctr., Honolulu, 1990-99; U.S. Nat. Commn. for Pacific Econ. Cooperation, 1991—; bd. dirs. Asian Am. Legal Def. and Edn. Fund, 1990—; vice chmn. adv. coun. Human Rights Watch/Asia, 1997-99, Am. Law Inst., 1997—. Law Faculty fellow Harvard U., 1993. Mem. Am. Law Inst., Am. Arbitration Assn., Internat. Panel Arbitrators, Phi Beta Kappa. Office: The World Bank 1818 H St NW Washington DC 20433-0001 E-mail: Ktung@worldbank.org.

TUNG, PRABHAS, plastic surgeon; b. Ubol, Thailand, Apr. 3, 1944; s. Sathee and Seng (Ngium) T.; m. Patarin C. Sinjin; children: Tony, Tommy. MD, Mahidol U., Bangkok, 1968. Diplomate Am. Bd. Plastic Surgery. Plastic surgeon pvt. practice, Flint, Mich., 1980-82, Sacramento, Calif., 1982—. Office: 2801 K St Ste 200 Sacramento CA 95816-5118

TUNG, ROSALIE LAM, business educator, consultant; came to U.S., 1975; d. Andrew Yan-Fu and Pauline Wai-Kam Lam; m. Byron Poon-Yang Tung; 1 chlid, Michele Christine. BA, York U., 1972; MBA, U. B.C., 1974, PhD in Bus. Adminstrn., 1977. Lectr. diploma divsn. U. B.C., 1975, lectr. exec. devel. program, 1975; asst. prof. mgmt. Grad. Sch. Mgmt., U. Oreg., Eugene, 1977-80; assoc. prof. U. Pa., Phila., 1981-86; prof., dir. internat. bus. ctr. U. Wis., Milw., 1986-90; endowed chaired prof. Simon Fraser U., 1991—. Fgn. expert Fgn. Investment Commn., China; vis. scholar U. Manchester (Eng.) Sci. and Tech., 1980; vis. prof. UCLA, 1981, Harvard U., 1988, Copenhagen Bus. Sch., 1995, 97, Chinese U. Hong Kong, 1997, Peking U., 2001, China Europe Internat. Bus. Sch., 2002-03; Wis. disting. prof. U. Wis. Sys., 1988-90, Ming and Stella Wong chair in internat. bus., 1991—. Author: Management Practices in China, 1980, U.S.-China Trade Negotiations, 1982, Chinese Industrial Society After Mao, 1982, Business Negotiations with the Japanese, 1984, Key to Japan's Economic Strength: Human Power, 1984, The New Expatriates: Managing Human Resources Abroad, 1988; editor: Strategic Management in the U.S. and Japan, 1987, International Management in International Library of Business and Management Series, 1994, Internat. Ency. Bus. and Mgmt., 1996, IEBM Handbook of International Business, 1998, Learning from World Class Companies, 2001. Recipient Leonore Rowe Williams award U. Pa., 1990, U. B.C. Alumni 75th Anniversary award, 1990, Advanced Global Competitiveness Rsch. award, 1997, Woman of Distinction in the Professions, Mgmt. and Trades award YWCA, Vancouver, 1998; York U. scholar, 1972; Univ. fellow, Seagram Bus. fellow, H.R. MacMillan Family fellow; Oppenheimer Bros. Found. fellow, 1973-74, U. B.C. fellow, 1974-75, H.R. Macmillan Found. fellow, 1975-77. Fellow Royal Soc. Can., Acad. Mgmt. (bd. govs. 1987-89, v.p. 2001-02, pres. 2003—), Internat. Acad. Cultural Rsch. (founding), Acad. Internat. Bus. (mem. exec. bd., treas. 1985-86); mem. Internat. Assn. Applied Psychology, Am. Arbitration Assn. (comml. panel arbitrators). Roman Catholic. Avocation: creative writing. Office: Simon Fraser U Faculty Bus Adminstrn Burnaby BC Canada V5A 1S6 Office Phone: 604-291-3083.

TUNGATE, DAVID E. lawyer, educator; b. Columbus, Ohio, Apr. 22, 1945; s. Ernest O. and Diantha (Woltz) T.; m. Mary Ann V. Montaleone, Jan. 27, 1968; children: David, Melissa. BA, U. Ill., Champaign, 1967, JD, 1970. Bar: U.S. Dist. Ct. (we. dist.) Pa. 1970, Superior Ct. Pa., 1971, Supreme Ct. Pa., 1971, U.S. Ct. Appeals (3d cir.) 1973, U.S. Ct. Claims 1987, U.S. Dist. Ct (ea. dist.) Wis. 1989, U.S. Ct. Appeals (fed. cir.) 1990. Assoc. Eckert, Seamans, Cherin & Mellott, Pitts., 1976-75, ptnr., 1976—. Adj. prof. Carnegie Mellon U., Pitts., 1991—, U. Pitts. Sch. of Law, 1996—. Contbr. articles to profl. jours.; author bus. book revs. Pitts. Post-Gazette, 1986—. Chmn. Zoning Hearing Bd. Upper St. Clair, 1991—. Mem. ABA, Penn. Bar Assn., Allegheny County Bar Assn. Office: Eckert Seamans Cherin & Mellott 42d Fl USX Tower 600 Grant St Pittsburgh PA 15219-2702

TUNGATE, JAMES LESTER, lawyer; b. Sept. 27, 1947; s. Ernest O. Jr. and Diantha (Woltz) T.; m. Susan Sumner, Aug. 25, 1973; children: Edward Ernest, James Aaron. BS, Ill. Wesleyan U., 1969; MA, Northwestern U.-Ill., 1970, PhD, 1972; JD, U. Ill.-Urbana, 1979; hon. DHL, London Sch. (Eng.), 1972. Bar: Ill. 1979, U.S. Supreme Ct. 1985. Spl. instr. Northwestern U., Evanston, Ill., 1971; prof., chmn. Loyola U., New Orleans, 1971-76; state dir. News Election Svc., New Orleans, 1972-74; dir. Inst. Religious Communications, New Orleans, 1974-76; asst. to state's atty. Iroquois County, Watseka, Ill., 1978; ptnr. Tungate & Tungate, Watseka, Ill., 1979-98; pres. Tungate Law Offices, Ltd., Watseka, Ill., 1998—. Media cons. Inst. Politics, New Orleans, 1973-76; legal cons., lectr. Iroquois Mental Health Ctr., Watseka, 1980—; lectr. law Kankakee Community Coll., Ill., 1982; instr. law, Purdue U., 2000; dir. Iroquois Mental Health Ctr., 1980—; chmn. Iroquois County chpt. ARC, 1982-84, 85—; dir. Iroquois Republican Council, 1983— . Author: Romantic Images in Popular Songs, 1972; Readings in Broadcast law, 1975. Recipient Internat. Radio and TV Found. award; Harnow scholar U. Ill., 1976. Mem. Ill. Bar Assn. (elected assembly mem. 2004), Iroquois County Bar Assn. (Law Day chmn., pres. 1998—), Chgo. Bar Assn., AASR (elected mem. supreme coun. of Ancient Accepted Scottish Rite, 2001, chmn jurisprudence, Internat. DeMolay Legion of Honor award 2002), Masons (master 1982-83), Scottish Rite (most wise master 1997-98, 33-degree 1999), Mohammed Shrine, Pi Alpha Delta. Republican. Methodist. Home: 146 W Hislop Dr Cissna Park IL 60924-8718 Office: Tungate Law Offices 744 E Walnut St PO Box 337 Watseka IL 60970-0337

TUNHEIM, JERALD ARDEN, academic administrator, physicist, educator; b. Claremont, S.D., Sept. 3, 1940; s. Johannes and Annie Tunheim; children: Jon, Angie, Alec. BS in Engring. Physics, S.D. State U., 1962, MS in Physics, 1964; PhD in Physics, Okla. State U., 1968. Vis. scientist Sandia Corp., Albuquerque, 1970-71, Ames (Iowa) AEC Labs., 1972; asst. prof. S.D. State U., Brookings, 1968-73, assoc. prof., 1973-78, prof., 1978-80, prof., head physics dept., 1980-85; dean Ea. Wash. U., Cheney, 1985-87; pres. Dakota State U., Madison, S.D., 1987—. Bd. dirs. Nat. Skill Stds. Bd., 1998—. Co-author: Elementary Particles and Unitary Symmetry, 1966, Quantum Field Theory, 1966; contbr. articles to profl.jours. Bd. dirs. Lake Area Improvement Corp. Grantee USDA, 1987-88, S.D. Govt. Office Edn. Devel., 1988-89, U.S. Dept. Edn., Eisenhower Program, 1985-86, 87-90, 92-93, 95-96, U.S. Dept. Edn. Math. and Sci. Program, 1989-92; named Tchr. of Yr. S.D. State U., 1972. Mem. NSPE, Am. Phys. Soc., Am. Assn. Physics Tchrs., Madison C. of C. (bd. dirs. 1990—), Rotary. Republican. Lutheran. E-mail: Jerald.Tunheim@dsu.edu.

TUNHEIM, KATHRYN H. public relations executive; b. Sacred Heart, Minn., 1956; BA in Polit. Sci., U. Minn., 1979. Staff asst. U.S. Senator Wendell Anderson, 1977-79; mgr., bus. planning NCR Comten, 1979-81; corp. pub. rels. mgr. Honeywell, 1981-84, dir. corp. pub. rels., 1985-86; v.p. pub. rels. and internal comm. Honeywell Inc., 1987-90; pres., CEO Tunheim Santrizos, Mpls., 1990—. Office: Tunheim Santrizos 1100 Riverview Tower 8009 34th Ave S Minneapolis MN 55425-1608

TUNICK, LARAINE DONISI, publishing executive; b. Oyster Bay, N.Y., Jan. 18, 1958; m. Lee M. Tunick, May 18, 1991; children: Benjamin, Allison. BS, N.C. State U., 1980. Advtg. coord. CMP Publications, Inc., Manhasset, N.Y., 1982-85, rsch. analyst, 1985-87, sr. rsch. mgr., 1991-95, rsch. dir., 1995-97, sr. rsch. mgr., 1998—; mkt. rsch. mgr. Cahners Pub. Co., N.Y.C., 1987-89; sr. rsch. mgr. Ziff-Davis Pub. Co., N.Y.C., 1989-91. Home: 7 Wainer Ct Centerport NY 11721-1557

TUNINSKAYA, GALINA M. chemist, consultant; b. Lutsk, Volinskiy, Ukraine; came to U.S., 1993; d. Michael and Faina (Metushanska) T.; m. Mark Rokhfeld, Dec. 30, 1979; children: Marianna, Dmitriy. BS, Leningrad Inst. Chem. Engring., Russia, 1975, MS, 1977. Engr., chemist Linen Mfg., Zhitomir, Ukraine, 1977-80; from. prof. to rsch. chemist Pedagogical Inst., Zhitomir, Ukraine, 1980-93; from rsch. chemist to chief chemist Applied Consumer Svcs., Miami, 1993-97, v.p., 1997—. Active Russian Outreach Program, Miami, 1995—. Mem. AAAS, Am. Chem. Soc., Am. Soc. for Quality. Office: Applied Consumers Svcs 11890 NW 87th Ct Unit 8 Hialeah Gardens FL 33018 E-mail: acsgalina@aol.com.

TUNISON, ELIZABETH LAMB, education educator; b. Portadown, Northern Ireland, Jan. 7, 1922; came to U.S., 1923; d. Richard Ernest and Ruby (Hill) Lamb; m. Ralph W. Tunison, Jan. 24, 1947 (dec. Apr. 1984); children: Eric Arthur, Christine Wait, Dana Paul. BA, Whittier Coll., 1943, MEd, 1963. Tchr. East Whittier (Calif.) Schs., 1943-59; tchr. T.V. TV Channels 13 and 28, So. Calif. Counties, 1960-75; dir. curriculum Bassett (Calif.) Schs., 1962-65; elem. sch. prin. Rowland Unified Schs., Rowland Heights, Calif., 1965-68; assoc. prof. edn. Calif. State Poly. U., Pomona, 1968-71; prof. Whittier Coll., 1968-88, prof. emerita, 1988—. Bd. dirs. Restless Legs Syndrome Found., mem. adv. coun.; facilitator So. Calif. Orgn. Bd. dirs. Presbyn. Intercmty. Hosp. Found.; founder Restless Legs Support Group (chmn. 1995-2003), Restless Leg Syndrome, nat. adv. com., 2003-. Recipient Whittier Coll. Alumni Achievement award 1975; Helen Hefernan scholar 1963. Mem. AAUP, Assn. Calif. Sch. Adminstrs. (state bd., chmn. higher edn. com. 1983-86, region pres. 1981-83, Wilson Grace award 1983), PEO (pres. 1990-92), Assistance League of Whittier (v.p. 1994-96), Delta Kappa Gamma (v.p. 1996-97, Woman of Yr. 2001). Home: 900 E Harrison Ave F-10 Pomona CA 91767

TUNNER, WILLIAM SAMS, urological surgeon; b. San Antonio, Nov. 14, 1933; s. William Henry and Sarah Margaret (Sams) T.; m. Sallie Berry Woodul, Dec. 4, 1965; children: William Woodul, Jonathan Sams. Student, Washington and Lee U., 1952-55; MD, U. Va., 1960. Diplomate Am. Bd. Urology. Intern in surgery, then asst. surg. resident Duke Hosp., 1960-62; fellow cancer surgery Cancer Inst. NIH, Bethesda, Md., 1962-64; resident in urol. surgery Cornell-N.Y. Hosp., 1964-68, fellow transplantation, dialysis and biochemistry, instr., 1968-70; asst. prof. urol. surgery U. Tex. Med. Sch., San Antonio, 1970-72; pvt. practice Richmond, Va., 1972—. Mem. staff Henrico County St. Marys Hosp., Chippenham, Johnston-Willis hosps.; asst. clin. prof. urology Med. Coll. Va., 1972—. Contbr. articles to med. jours., films. Fellow: ACS (past pres. Va. chpt., past gov. at large), Am. Acad. Pediatrics (affiliate); mem.: SR (pres. for State of Va. 2001—), AMA, Am. Nephrology Assn., Am. Urol. Assn., Soc. Pediatric Urology, Transplantation Soc., Soc. Internat. Irologie, Va. Soc. Sons of Revolution (pres.), Country Club Va., Beta Theta Pi, Alpha Epsilon Delta. Episcopalian. Avocation: equestrian activities. Home: Braedon Farm 1240 Shallow Well Rd Manakin Sabot VA 23103-2300 Office: St Mary's Hosp Profl Bldg 5855 Bremo Rd Richmond VA 23226-1926

TUNNICLIFF, DAVID GEORGE, civil engineer, consultant; b. Ord, Nebr., Sept. 18, 1931; s. George Thomas and Ada Ellen (Ward) Tunnicliff; m. Elaine Jean Interrante, Oct. 17, 1959 (div.); children: Martha Allison Tunnicliff Loeb, Vivian Jean; m. Joan Elizabeth Duchesneau, Oct. 25, 1975. BS, U. Nebr., 1954; MS, Cornell U., 1958; PhD, U. Mich., 1972. Registered profl. engr., Nebr., Mass. Engr. Nebr. Dept. Rds., Lincoln, 1954-60; from asst. prof. to assoc. prof. Wayne State U., Detroit, 1960-67; chief tech. svcs. Warren Bros. Co., Cambridge, Mass., 1967-79; prin., cons. engr. D.G. Tunnicliff, Cons. Engr., Omaha, 1979—. Contbr. articles to profl. jours. Rep. precinct del., Detroit, 1965—66. With U.S. Army, 1955—56. Mem.: ASCE, ASTM, Transp. Rsch. Bd. (com. chair 1983—89), Assn. Asphalt Paving Tech. (bd. dirs. 1976—78). Mem. Evangel. Convenant Ch. Home and Office: DG Tunnicliff Cons Engr 9624 Larimore Ave Omaha NE 68134-3038 Office Phone: 402-572-9431.

TUNSTALL, DOROTHY FIEBRICH, early childhood educator; b. Elizabeth City, Va., Sept. 18, 1939; d. Louie Ludwig and Nancy Julia (Drafts) Fiebrich; m. Frank S. Clark Jr., June 11, 1961 (div. 1970); children: Sherri Ann D'Alessio, Debra Sue Pate, Frank S. Clark III; m. Jim Tunstall, June 1987 (div. 1995). BA in Elem. Edn., Stetson U., 1961, MA in Edn., 1963; Ed. Spec. in Edn. Adminstrn., U. S.C., 1991, PhD in Early Childhood, 1993. Cert. tchr. Fla., S.C. Substitute tchr. Broward County Schs., Ft. Lauderdale, Fla., 1963-70, EABE tchr., 1972-80; title I, tchr. for fed. govt. South Fla. State Hosp., Pembroke Pines, Fla., 1970-72; tchr. spl. edn. Richland Sch. Dist. #2, Columbia, S.C., 1980-81; COBOL programmer Comptr. Gen.'s Office, Columbia, 1982-85; tchr. spl. edn. Calhoun County Schs., St. Matthews, S.C., 1985-88; tchr. kindergarten Fairfield County Schs., Winnsboro, S.C., 1989-92; dir. St. Paul's Child Care Ministry, Columbia, SC, 1997—2000, Good Shepherd Day Sch., Columbia, 2001—. Adj. prof. U. S.C., Columbia, 1994—. Active Lexington County Adolescent Pregnancy Prevention Bd., 1999—, Lexington County First Steps Bd., 2001—03; v.p. unit 7 Am. Legion Aux., 2000—02, pres. unit 7, 2002—. Mem.: AAUW (pres. 1998—2002), Mental Health Assn. in Mid-Carolina (v.p. 1992—93, bd. dirs., Pres. award 1993), Lexington County Arts Assn. (pres. 1992—93, Newcomer's award 1981), Wildlife Action Inc. (pres. 1991—93), Beta Sigma Phi (Girl of Yr. 1967). Avocations: reading, gardening. Home: 159 Corley Mill Rd Lexington SC 29072-7600 Office: Good Shepherd Day Sch 3909 Forest Dr Columbia SC 29204 Office Phone: 803-787-4148. E-mail: directorgsds@aol.com., gsdsdir@sc.rr.com.

TUNUGUNTLA, HARI SIVA GURUNADHA RAO, urologist; s. Arjuna Rao and Sundara Suseela Tunuguntla; m. Renuka Tunuguntla. Bachelor of Medicine & Bachelor of Surgery, Guntur Med. Coll., Andhra Pradesh, India, 1984; MS in Gen. Surgery, All India Inst. of Med. Scis., New Delhi, 1987; Master Chirurgie in Urology, Postgraduate Inst. of Med. Edn. And Rsch., Chandigarh, India, 1995. Lic. Andhra Pradesh Med. Coun., Hyderabad, India, 1984, Tamil Nadu Med. Coun., Chennai (previously, Madras), India, 1993, cert. Ednl. Commn. for Fgn. Med. Grads., 1996, indefinite cert. Ednl. Commn. for Fgn. Med. Grads., 2002, application status letter Med. Bd. of Calif., 2002, temporary lic. for resident tng. program Commonwealth of Va., Bd. of Medicine, 2002, tng. lic. Fla. Bd. Medicine, 2003. Rotating intern Govt. Gen. Hosp. and Guntur Med. Coll., India, 1982—83; jr. resident in gen. surgery All India Inst. of Med. Scis., New Delhi, 1984—87; sr. resident and tchg. fellow, dept. of surgery, gastrointestinal surgery and liver transplantation All India Inst. Of Med. Scis., New Delhi, 1987—89; registrar, divsn. of surgery Kugler's Hosp., Guntur, India, 1990—92; registrar, dept. of urology and renal transplantation Christian Med. Coll. and Christian Med. Coll. Hosp., Vellore, India, 1993; sr. resident, dept. of urology Postgraduate Inst. of Med. Edn. and Rsch., Chandigarh, India, 1993—95; sr. resident, tchg. fellow dept. of urology and renal transplantation SRI Venkateswara Inst. of Med. Scis., Tirupati, India, 1995—96, asst. prof., dept. urology and renal transplantation, 1997, Sanjay Gandhi Postgrad. Inst. of Med. Scis., Lucknow, India, 1997—99; rsch. fellow North Fla. Rsch. Inst., Gainesville, 2000—01; clin. fellow dept. of urology U. of Calif., Davis Sch. of Medicine, Sacramento, 2001—02; clin. fellow dept. urology U. Miami, Sch. Medicine, Fla., 2003—. Mem. editl. asst. Indian Jour. of Urology; reviewer: Indian Jour. Med. Scis., 2003; mem. working com. Nat. Med. Jour. of India, mem. internat. reviewers panel Med. Sci. Monitor;, co-author chpts. in 10 textbooks; contbr. articles to profl. jours. Mem., hosp. computerization com. Sanjay Gandhi Postgraduate Inst. of Med. Scis., Lucknow, India, 1997—99, mem., hosp. mortality com., 1999. Grantee Chakroborti Fellowship in Urology, U. of Calif., 1999; scholar In Urology, PFIZER, 2002; Intramural Rsch. Grant, Sanjay Gandhi Postgraduate Inst. of Med. Scis., India, Hargoving Meml. Traveling Fellowship, Urological Soc. of India, 1993. Mem.: AMA, Am. Coll. Surgeons, Soc. Internat. Urology, European Assn. Of Urology, Am. Urol. Assn. (corr.), North Zone Chpt. Of The Urol. Soc. Of India (life), Indian Soc. Of Organ Transplantation (life), Urolithiasis Soc. Of India (life Young Sci. Medallion award 1993), Urol. Soc. Of India (life), Alumni Assn. Of Guntur Med. Coll., India. Achievements include research in Etiopathogenesis of recurrent calcium oxalate urolithiasis; Clinical mgmt. of upper gastrointestinal hemorrhage in a tropical country; Role of ultrasound vs. lithoclast (pneumolithotripsy) in ureteroscopic lithotripsy for ureteral calculi; development of Endoscopic injection sclerotherapy for radiation-induced hemorrhagic cystitis; research in Role of holmium laser in mgmt. of calcified ureteral stents; Clinicopathologic and molecular correlations in prostate cancer; research in Urodynamic evaluation of patients with chronic non-bacterial prostatitis; Determination of optimal frequency of self-calibration of urethra to prevent recurrence of urethral strictures in men; Long-term outcomes following open pyeloplasty for congenital ureteropelvic junction obstruction; Metabolic and urodynamic evaluation of bowel segments incorporated in the urinary tract; Metabolic abnormalities in patients with congenital ureteropelvic junction obstruction and ipsilateral renal calculi; Duplex dopper ultrasonography vs. Mag-3 diuretic renogram vs. whitaker test in evaluation of equivocal ureteropelvic junction and ureterovesical junction obstruction; Experimental induction and study of portal hypertension in rabbits; Immunoglobulin abnormalities in oral cancer; Work on kidney stones, a study of pattern of citrate excretion in normal healthy controls and calcium stone patients and the effect of potassium citrate treatment; Interstim sacral neuromodulation for lower urinary tract dysfunction; Sling surgery for female urinary incontinence; Urethroplasty for male urethral strictures; Urolithiasas urodynamics; Urinary diversions. Home: 753 Classon Ave Apt 9K Brooklyn NY 11238-4698

TUOHEY, CONRAD GRAVIER, lawyer; b. Bklyn., Dec. 27, 1933; s. James L. and Rose Gravier Tuohey; m. Judith Octavia Jeeves, July 7, 1956; children: Octavia Jeeves, Heather Gravier, Meighan Judith, Caragh Rose. BA, George Washington U., 1957; JD, U. Mich., 1960. Bar: Calif. 1962, N.Y. 1980, D.C. 1980. Dir. Fed. Home Loan Bank, San Francisco, 1980—83; legal cons., counsel Calif. State Senate, 1981—87; counsel Senate Select com. Pacific Rim, 1986—87. Mem. Citizens adv. bd. Orange County Transit com., 1966—68; pres. Friends of Calif. State U., Fullerton, 1969—71, Calif. Alliance Ptnrs. Progress, 1969—72; mem. InterAm. bd. Ptnrs. Alliance Progress, 1969—72; mem. nat. bd. dirs., 1970—72. Contbr. articles to profl. jours. With U.S. Army, 1951—54, leader rifle squad. Decorated Combat Infantryman's badge, Korean Svc. medal with 3 battle stars. Mem.: N.Y. Bar Assn., D.C. Bar Assn., State Bar Calif., Phi Sigma Kappa, Phi Delta Phi. Home and Office: 23391 Rockrose Mission Mission Viejo CA 92692-1686 E-mail: tuohey@lawyer.com.

TUOHEY, MARK HENRY, III, lawyer; b. Rochester, N.Y., Sept. 27, 1946; s. Mark Henry Tuohey; m. Martha Tuohey; children: Brendan, Sean, Devin. BA in History, St. Bonaventure U., 1968; JD, Fordham U., 1973. Bar: D.C. 1973, U.S. Supreme Ct. 1980, U.S. Ct. Appeals (D.C. cir.) 1974, U.S. Dist. Ct. D.C. 1974, N.Y. 1984. Asst. U.S. atty. U.S. Atty.'s Office, Washington, 1973-77; spl. trial counsel U.S. Dept. Justice, Washington, 1977-79; spl. counsel to U.S. Atty. Gen. Washington, 1979; co-adminstrv. ptnr. Washington office Vinson & Elkins, Washington; dep. ind. counsel Whitewater Investigation, 1994-95; spl. counsel D.C. City Coun. Investigation of Met. Police Dept., 1998. Trustee Cath. U. Am., 2002—, Washington Jesuit Acad., 1999—. Served to 1st lt. U.S. Army, 1970—71. Master: Wm. Bryant Inn. of Ct.; fellow: Am. Bar Found. (bd. dirs. 1980—85), Am. Law Inst., Am. Coll. Trial Lawyers; mem.: ABA (chair standing com. on continuing edn. bar 1980—85, litig. sect. coun. 1980—90, mem. Am. Law Inst./ABA com. continuing profl. edn. 1983—), Bar Assn. D.C. (Lawyer of the Yr. 2001), Jud. Conf. US Ct. Appeals (DC cir.), DC Bar Found. (chair 1998—), DC Bar (bd. govs. 1988—94, pres. 1993—94), DC Sports and Entertainment Commission (chair 2003—). Home:

1655 Kalmia Rd NW Washington DC 20012-1125 Office: Vinson & Elkins The Willard Office Bldg 1455 Pennsylvania Ave NW Fl 7 Washington DC 20004-1013 Office Phone: 202-639-6660. Business E-Mail: mtuohey@velaw.com.

TUPA, RON, state senator; b. Harbor Beach, Mich., Aug. 25, 1966; BA in Philosophy, U. Tex., 1989; Tchg. Cert. in Secondary Edn., U. Colo., 1994; grad., Darden Sch. Polit. Leadership, 1996. Dockworker, 1991-94; tchr. social studies, 1994—; Dem. rep. dist. 14 Colo. State Ho. of Reps., 1994-2000; Dem. senator dist. 18 Colo. State Senate, 2000—. Mem. state, vets. and mil. affairs coms. Colo. Ho. of Reps.; mem. edn. and legis. audit coms. Colo. State Senate, vice chmn. vets. and mil. affairs and transp. coms. Mem. Dem. Party Com., 1992-95; mem. Boulder County Exec. Com., 1992-96; pres. Colo. Young Dems., 1993 95. Mem. U. Colo. Alumni Assn., U. Tex., TX-Exes Alumni Assn. Office: Colo State Senate State Capitol 200 E Colfax Rm 271 Denver CO 80203 also: 5438 Glendale Gulch Cir Boulder CO 80301-3501 E-mail: tuparep14@aol.com., rtupa@sni.net.

TUPPER, LEON F. manufacturing executive; BS in Indsl. Psychology, Wayne State U.; MS in Indsl. Psychology, U. Mich.; postgrad., Dartmouth U. Tng. mgr. Am. Motors Corp., Detroit, 1972-77, buyer/procurement specialist, 1977-83, sr. buyer interior trim group, 1983-86, purchasing mgr. interior trim group, 1986-88; sales mgr. steering divsn. Sheller-Globe Corp., Toledo, Ohio, 1984-88; dir. sales and engring. Gilreath Mfg., Inc., Howell, Mich., 1988-91, pres., CEO, owner, 1991—. Trustee Cleary Coll., Ypsilanti, Mich.; treas., trustee High/Scope Edn. Rsch. Found.; bd. trustees Rehab. Inst. of Mich., Detroit Med. Ctr., bus. sch. bd. exec. advisors Wayne State U.; mem. friends of the Detroit Area Pre-Coll. Engring. Program, Nat. Conf. for Cmty. Justice, 100 Black Men of Detroit. Office: Gilreath Manufacturing Inc 15565 Northland Dr W Ste 812 Southfield MI 48075-5325 also: PO Box 408 Howell MI 48844-0408 Fax: 248-728-1753.

TUPPER, RON, public health, policy, and management educator; b. Natick, Mass., Aug. 25, 1945; s. Ralph and Madeline (Boyde) Moore-Tupper; m. Malinda McGilvray, July 28, 1987; children: Michelle, Melissa, Madeline Marie. BA in Psychology, U. Nebr., 1969; MSc in Health Mgmt./Health Edn., S W Tex. State U., 1975. Asst. dir.-unit mgmt. Bexar County Hosp., San Antonio, Tex., 1971-72; assoc. dir. adminstrv. svcs. Robert B. Green Hosp., San Antonio, 1972-74; hosp. adminstr. Maverick County (Tex.) Hosp., 1975-78, Hosp. Affiliates, Internat., Nashville, Tenn., 1978-82; divsn. mgr. Mgmt. Recruiters Internat., Irving, Tex., 1983-88; v.p. adminstrn. Stores, Inc., McAllen, Tex., 1990—; exec. dir. Area Health Edn. Ctr., Weslaco, Tex., 1995-99; dir. South Tex. Ctr. for Rural Pub. Health Tex. A&M U. Sys. Health Sci. Ctr., McAllen, 1999—; prof., dir. Sch. Rural Pub. Health Tex. A&M U. System Health Sci. Ctr., College Station, 2001—; faculty prof., dir. McAllen br. campus Tex. A&M U. Sys. Health Sci. Ctr. Sch. Rural Pub. Health, College Station. Founder, bd. chair Cmty. Health Mgmt. Corp.-El Milagro Indigent Clinic, McAllen, 1996—, U. Tex. Med. Br. at Galveston Indigent Cancer Clinic. Chair, health and health edn. adv. com. State of Tex. Senator Appt., Tex./Mex., 1996, mem. South Tex. health adv. com., Lower Rio Grande Valley, 1996; mem. steering com. Tex. A&M U. Sch. of Rural Public Health, Rio Grande Valley rep., 1997—; mem. Tex. Dept. of Health U. Tex. Mobile Health Van com., 1996—. Staff sgt. USAF, 1964-70. Decorated Vietnam Svc. medal, Air Force conduct medal. Mem. Tex./Mex. Border Assn., Midwest Migrant Health Com. Avocations: writing, carpentry, community development. Office: South Tex Ctr for Rural Pub Health Tex A&M Uni Sys Hlth Sci 3700 N 10th St Ste 210 Mcallen TX 78501-1775 E-mail: Tupper@medicine.tamu.edu.

TURANO, DAVID A. lawyer; b. Ashtabula, Ohio, Sept. 9, 1946; s. Egidio A. and Mary Agnes (Bartko) T.; m. Karen J. Emmel, Aug. 29, 1970; children: Aaron, Thad, Bethen, Kyle. BS, Kent State U., 1968; JD, Ohio State U., 1971. Bar: Ohio 1971. Staff atty. The Pub. Utilities Commn. Ohio, Columbus, 1971-72; assoc., then ptnr. George, Greek, King, McMahon and McConnaughey, Columbus, 1972-79; ptnr. Baker & Hostetler, Columbus, 1979-96, Harris, Carter, Mahota, Turano & Mazza, Columbus, 1996-97, Harris, Turano & Mazza, Columbus, 1997—2003; of counsel Shoemaker, Howarth & Taylor, LLP, Columbus, 2003—. Mem. ABA, Ohio State Bar Assn., Columbus Bar Assn., Transp. Lawyers Assn. Roman Catholic. Office: Shoemaker Howarth & Taylor LLP 471 E Broad St Ste 2001 Columbus OH 43215 Office Phone: 614-232-0426.

TURBIDY, JOHN BERRY, investor, management consultant; b. Rome, Ga., Oct. 18, 1928; s. Joseph Leo and Louyse (Berry) T.; m. Joan Marsales, Dec. 19, 1958 (dec.); children: John Berry, Trevor Martin; m. Jaquelin Lamond Schulter, June 8, 1995. Grad., Darlington Sch., 1945; BA, Duke U., 1950; postgrad., NYU, 1952, Emory U., 1954-56. Various positions Lockheed Aircraft, Marietta, Ga., 1951-56; gen. mgmt. cons. McKinsey & Co., N.Y.C. and London, 1956-63; v.p. adminstrn. ITT Europe, Inc., Brussels, 1963, v.p., group exec. European consumer products, 1964-65, v.p., group exec. for No. Europe, 1965-67; corp. v.p. adminstrn. Celanese Corp., N.Y.C., 1967-68; pres., mng. dir. SIACE, SP.A. subs., Milan, 1968-69; chmn. bd., pres. Vecta Group, Kalamazoo, 1970-74; sr. v.p. corp. devel. IU Internat. Corp., Phila., 1974-78, exec. v.p., 1978-83; pres., chief exec. officer Pitcairn Fin. Mgmt. Group, Jenkintown, Pa., 1984-90; chmn. Office John Turbidy, 1990-95; mng. dir. Friedman, Turbidy & Co., Inc., N.Y.C., 1995—2000. Bd. dirs. Statute of Liberty Ellis Island Found. Served with USNR, 1952. Mem. Sea Island Club, Sea Bright Beach Club. Address: 113 Biltmore Saint Simons Island GA 31522 E-mail: jbturb@hotmail.com.

TURBIN, RICHARD, lawyer; b. N.Y.C., Dec. 25, 1944; s. William and Ruth (Fiedler) T.; m. Rai Saint Chu-Turbin, June 12, 1976; children: Laurel Mei, Derek Andrew. BA magna cum laude, Cornell U., 1966; JD, Harvard U., 1969. Bar: Hawaii 1971, U.S. Dist. Ct. Hawaii 1971. Asst. atty. gen., Western Samoa, Apia, 1969-70; dep. pub. defender Pub. Defender's Office, Honolulu, 1970-74; dir. Legal Aid Soc. Hawaii, Kaneohe, 1974-75; sr. atty., pres. Law Offices Richard Turbin, Honolulu, 1975—. Legal counsel Hawaii Crime Commn., 1980-81. Co-author: Pacific; author: Medical Malpractice, Handling Emergency Medical Cases, 1991; editor Harvard Civil Rights-Civil Liberties Law Rev., 1969. Legal counsel Dem. Party, Honolulu County, 1981-82; elected Neighborhood Bd., 1985, elected chair, 1990-97; bd. dirs. Hawaii chpt. ACLU, 1974-78, East-West Ctr. grantee, 1971, 72. Mem. ATLA, ABA (chair internat. torts and ins. law and practice com., mem. governing coun., chair tort and ins. practice sect. 1999-2000, 1999-2000), Hawaii Bar Assn., Hawaii Trial Lawyers Assn. (pres. 2002), Hawaii Jaycees (legal counsel 1981-82), Chinese Jaycees Honolulu (legal counsel 1980-81), Honolulu Tennis League (undefeated player 1983), Hawaii Harlequin Rugby Club (sec., legal counsel 1978-82), Pacific Club, Outrigger Canoe Club.' Jewish. Home: 4817 Kahala Ave Honolulu HI 96816-5231

TURCHI, PETER JOHN, aerospace and electrical engineer, physicist, educator; b. N.Y.C., Dec. 30, 1946; s. Charles Orlando and Fay Florence Turchi; m. Judith Ann Radogna, June 13, 1967; children: Janita Nicole, Rebecca Lenore. BSE in Aerospace and Mech. Sci./Physics, Princeton U., 1967, MA, 1969, PhD, 1970. Rsch. assoc. Plasma Propulsion Lab., Princeton (N.J.) U., 1963—70; plasma physicist Air Force Weapons Lab., Kirtland AFB, N.Mex., 1970—72; rsch. physicist Naval Rsch. Lab., Washington, 1972—77, chief Plasma Tech. br., 1977—80; scientist R&D Assocs., Arlington, Va., 1980—81; dir. RDA Washington Rsch. Lab., Alexandria, Va., 1981—89; prof. aerospace engring. Ohio State U., Columbus, 1989—99; leader hydrodynamics and pulsed power sci. Los Alamos (N.Mex.) Nat. Lab., 1999—2002; sr. scientist for high power microwaves and pulsed power Air Force Rsch. Lab., Kirtland AFB, N.Mex., 2002—. Chmn. Megagauss Inst., Inc., Alexandria, 1979—89, bd. dirs.; chmn. mech. and aero. engring. adv. coun. Princeton U., 1988—92, mem. engring. sch. adv. coun., 1988—92, dean's leadership coun., 1992—93; resident/collateral faculty Ohio Aerospace Inst., 1989—95; lab. cons. Los Alamos (N.Mex.) Nat. Lab., 1989—99; intergovtl. sr. rsch. scientist USAF Phillips Lab. and Air Force Rsch. Lab., Kirtland AFB, 1990—2002; vis. chief scientist Advanced Weapons and Survivability, 1996—97; lectr. George Washington U., 1987—89, Air Forced Pulsed Power Lecture Program, 1979—81, Internat. Space U., 1998; cons. on pulsed power tech.; chmn. 2d Internat. Conf. on Megagauss Fields, Arlington, 1979, Spl. Conf. on Prime-Power for High Energy Space Systems, Norfolk, Va., 1982; co-chmn. Directed Energy Profl. Soc. High Power Microwave Conf., Albuquerque, 2004, NASA Conf. on Fusion Space Propulsion, Huntsville, Ala., 2000; mem. internat. organizing com. Megagauss Magnetic Field Confs., 1979—; adj. prof. aerospace engring. Ohio State U., Columbus, 1988, 1999—2002. Editor: Space Propulsion, Propulsion Techniques: Action and Reaction, 1998, Megagauss Physics and Tech., 1980; assoc. editor Jour. Propulsion and Power, 1990-93; guest editor IEEE Transactions on Plasma Sci., 1997-98; contbr. chpts. to books and articles to profl. jours.; patentee in field. Pres. Collingwood (Va.) Civic Assn., 1980-81; rep. Mt. Vernon (Va.) Coun., Mt. Vernon Dist., Fairfax County; pres. Pulsed Power Conf. Inc., Albuquerque, 1985-87, bd. dirs., 1983—; bd. dirs. Vista Encantada Neighborhood Assn., 2002—. 1st lt. USAF, 1970-72. NSF Grad. fellow, 1967-70; recipient Invention award USAF, 1972, Rsch. Publ. award Naval Rsch. Lab., 1976, USN and Air Force Invention awards, 1978-83. Fellow: IEEE (tech. program chmn. 5th and gen. chmn. 6th pulsed power confs. 1985—87, plasma sci. and applications exec. com. 1987—89, pulsed power sci. and tech. standing com. 1995—, chmn. 2000—02, Erwin Marx award for pulsed power tech. 1999), AIAA (assoc.; tech. com. plasmadynamics and lasers 1983—86, internat. chmn. 18th, 19th, 21st and 22d elec. propulsion confs. 1985—91, elec. propulsion tech. com. 1987—93, chmn. 1991—93, standing com. acad. affairs 1997—2003, elec. propulsion tech. com. 1997—, editl. adv. bd. 1998—2004, Nat. Student award 1967); mem.: Elec. Rocket Propulsion Soc. (pres. 1994—), Am. Phys. Soc., Princeton Campus, Tau Beta Pi, Sigma Xi. Achievements include research in electromagnetic implosion soft x-ray source, high energy x-ray generation by ultrahigh speed plasma flows, plasma flow switch for magnetic energy delivery above 10 megamperes; stabilized liner implosion system for controlled thermonuclear fusion. E-mail: Peter.Turchi@kirtland.af.mil.

TURCO, LEWIS PUTNAM, English educator; b. Buffalo, N.Y., May 2, 1934; s. Luigi and May Laura (Putnam) T.; m. Jean Cate Houdlette, May 29, 1934; children: Melora Ann, Christopher Cameron. BA, U. Conn., 1959; MA, U. Iowa, 1962; LHD (hon.), Ashland U., 2000. Instr. Cleve. State U., 1960-64; asst. prof. Hillsdale (Mich.) Coll., 1964-65; asst. prof. to full prof. SUNY, Oswego, 1965-96, poet-in-residence, 1995, prof. emeritus, 1996. Grad. asst. English, U. Conn., 1959; editorial asst. Writer's Workshop, U. Iowa, 1959-60; vis. prof. SUNY, Potsdam, 1968 69; Bingham Poet in Residence, U. Louisville, 1982; Writer in Residence, Ashland U., 1991; founding dir. Cleve. State U. Poetry Ctr., 1962, program in writing arts, SUNY Oswego, 1968. Author: First Poems, 1960, Awaken, Bells Falling: Poems 1959-67, 1968, The Inhabitant, 1970, Pocoangelini: A Fantography and Other Poems, 1971, American Still Lifes, 1981, numerous other poetry books including The Shifting Web: New and Selected Poems, 1989, The Green Maces of Autumn, Voices in an Old Maine House, 2002, The Collected Lyrics of Lewis Turco/Wesli Court, 2004; author numerous non-fiction books including The Book of Forms: A Handbook of Poetics, 1968, 3d edit., 2000, Visions and Revisions of American Poetry, 1986, Dialogue, 1989, Emily Dickinson, Woman of Letters, 1993, The Book of Literary Terms, 1999, The Book of Dialogue, 2004, A Sheaf of Leaves: Literary Memoirs, 2004, others; editor: The Life and Poetry of Manoah Bodman, 1999; contbr. articles to profl. jours. Sec. City of Oswego Charter Revision Commn., 1990-91; active Oswego Opera Theater Chorus, Oswego Festival Chorus, 1986—. With USN, 1952-56. Recipient scholarship Meriden Record-Jour. Pub. Co., U. Conn., 1957-58, 58-59, Disting. Alumnus award, 1992, Melville Cane award Poetry Soc. Am., 1986, Bordighera Bilingual Poetry prize Sonia Raiziss-Giop Charitable Found., 1997, John Ciardi award for lifetime achievement in poetry Italian-Am., Found. Am., 1999, others; resident fellowships Yaddo Found., 1959, 77, Faculty fellowships Rsch. Found. of SUNY, 1966-67, 69, 71, 73, 78; grant-in-aid, 1969; inducted into Meriden Hall of Fame, 1993. Home: PO Box 161 Dresden ME 04342-0161 E-mail: mathom@gwi.net.

TURCOTTE, DONALD LAWSON, geophysical sciences educator; b. Bellingham, Wash., Apr. 22, 1932; s. Lawson Phillip and Eva (Pearson) Turcotte; m. Joan Meredith Luecke, May 17, 1957; children: Phillip Lawson, Stephen Bradford. BS, Calif. Inst. Tech., 1954, PhD, 1958; M in Aero. Engring., Cornell U., 1955. Asst. prof. aero. engring. U.S. Naval Postgrad. Sch., Monterey, Calif., 1958-59; asst. prof. aero. engring. Cornell U., Ithaca, N.Y., 1959-63, assoc. prof., 1963-67, prof., 1967-73, prof. geol. scis., 1973-85, Maxwell Upson prof., 1985—2002, chmn., 1981-90; disting. prof. geology U. Calif. Davis, 2003—. Author (with others): Statistical Thermodynamics, 1963, Space Propulsion, 1965, Geodynamics, 1982, Fractals and Chaos in Geology and Geophysics, 1992, Mantle Convection, 2001. Trustee U. Space Rsch. Assn., 1975—79. Recipient Wegener medal, European Union Geosci., 1991, Disting. Alumni award, Calif. Inst. Tech., 1999; sr. postdoctoral rsch. fellow, NSF, 1965—66, Guggenheim fellow, 1972—73. Mem.: NAS, Am. Acad. Arts and Scis., Seismol. Soc. Am., Geol. Soc. Am. (Day medal 1982), Am. Geophys. Union (Charles A. Whitten medal 1995, William Bowie Medal 2003), El Macero Country Club. Home: 27104 Middle Golf Dr El Macero CA 95618 Office: Univ Calif Dept Geology Davis CA 95616 Office Phone: 530-572-6808. Business E-Mail: turcotte@geology.ucdavis.edu.

TURCOTTE, GLENN W. electrical products company executive; b. 1941; With Katy Industries, Inc., Englewood, Colo., 1981—, exec. v.p., 1993—, dir., 1995—, COO, 1998—, COO, exec. v.p., dir., 2000—; pres., CEO Glit, Inc., Wrens, Ga., Microtron Abrasives, Pineville, N.C., Moldan Corp., Pineville; chmn. bd. Duckback Products, Chico, Calif. Office: Katy Industries Inc PO Box 360 Middlebury CT 06762-0360 Fax: (303) 290-9344.

TURCOTTE, JEAN-CLAUDE CARDINAL, archbishop; b. Montreal, Que., Can., June 26, 1936; s. Paul-Émile and Rita (Gravel) Turcotte. Student, U. Cath., Lille, France; DD (hon.), McGill U.; lic. theology, Grand Seminaire Montreal. Ordained priest Roman Catholic Ch., 1959, consecrated bishop. Aux. bishop Diocese of Montreal, Canada, 1982—90, archbishop, 1990—. Mem.: Coun. of Social Commn., Congregation of Causes of Saints. Roman Catholic. Office: 2000 Sherbrooke Ouest Montreal PQ Canada H3H 1G4

TURCOTTE, JOHN ARTHUR, JR., lawyer; b. Lowell, Mass., Mar. 27, 1950; s. John A. and Dorothy J. (Gillette) Turcotte; m. Mary Catherine Willett, Nov. 12, 1976; 1 child, Sarah Hamilton. BS, Boston Coll., 1972; JD, St. Louis U., 1976. Bar: Mo. 1977, U.S. Dist. Ct. (ea. dist.) Mo. 1979, U.S. Ct. Appeals (8th cir.) 1981. Law clk. to presiding justice Mo. Ct. Appeals (ea. dist.), St. Louis, 1976—78; assoc. Lashly, Caruthers, Baer & Hamel, 1978—81, ptnr., 1981—83, Diekemper, Hammond, Shiners, Turcotte & Larrew, 1983—. Fellow: Am. Acad. Matrimonial Lawyers; mem.: ABA, Bar Assn. Met. St. Louis (chmn. com. on cts., Merit award 1983), Mo. Assn. Trial Attys., Assn. Trial Lawyers Am. Democrat. Roman Catholic. Home: 139 Wildwood Ln Saint Louis MO 63122-5135 Office: Diekemper Hammond Shinners Turcotte & Larrew 7730 Carondelet Ave Ste 200 Saint Louis MO 63105-3326 Office Phone: 314-727-1015. Personal E-mail: jturx@aol.com. Business E-Mail: jturcotte@dhstl.com.

TURCOTTE, MARGARET JANE, retired nurse; b. Stow, Ohio, May 17, 1927; d. Edward Carlton and Florence Margaret (Hanson) McCauley; m. Rene George Joseph, Nov. 24, 1961 (div. June 1967); 1 child, Michael Lawrence. RN, Ohio. Nurse St. Thomas Hosp., 1949-50; pvt. duty nurse, 1950-57; polio nurse Akron Children's Hosp., 1953-54; mem. nursing staff Robinson Meml. Hosp., Ravenna, Ohio, 1958-67, head ctrl. svc., 1963-67; supr. ctrl. svc. Brentwood Hosp., Warrensville Heights, Ohio, 1967-93, infections control nurse, 1982-91; emergency med. technician. Mem. aux. Robinson Meml. Hosp.; vol. Portage County Vis. Nurse Svc. and Hospice; active RSVP. Mem. St. Thomas Hosp. Alumni Assn. Democrat. Mem. Christian Ch. (Disciples Of Christ). Home: 714 Woodgate Blvd Apt 201 Ravenna OH 44266-2548

TURCOTTE, MATHIEU, Olympic athlete; b. Sherbrooke, Que., Can., Feb. 8, 1977; Profl. speed skater, Canada, 1998—. Recipient Gold medal, World Team Championships, 1998, 2000, 2001, 2003, Gold medal 5000m short track men's relay, 2002 Olympic Games, Bronze medal 1000m. Avocation: movies. Office: Speed Skating Can 2781 Lancaster Rd Ste 402 Ottawa ON K1B 1A7 Canada

TUREK, PAUL JOHN, III, construction executive; b. Columbia, SC, Feb. 10, 1964; s. Paul John Jr. and Patricia Veronica (Saluta) T.; m. Emma Lactao, Dec. 24, 1995; children: Samantha Claire, Paul John, Isabella. BS in Civil Engring., Northwestern U., 1986. Registered civil engr., Calif. Constrn. mgr. Brown & Root Inc., Houston, 1990-94; sr. project mgr. Shorenstein Co., San Francisco, 1994-98; v.p. Thompson Brooks, Inc., San Francisco, 1998-2000; pres. Summa III, Inc., San Francisco, 2000—04; sr. assoc. Marx Okubo, San Francisco, 2004—. Active Walnut Creek Masters Swim Team. 1st lt. USMC, 1986-90. Avocations: fly fishing, swimming. Home: 2121 Cerro Rd Walnut Creek CA 94596-5714 Office: Marx Okubo 444 Spear St # 205 San Francisco CA 94105 E-mail: turekp@msn.com.

TUREK, ROMAN, professional hockey player; b. Pisek, Czech Republic, May 21, 1970; Profl. hockey player Dallas Stars, 1996—99, St. Louis Blues, 1999—2001, Calgary Flames, 2001—. Played in NHL All-Star game, 2000. Recipient William M. Jennings Trophy, 1998 99, 1999—2000. Office: Calgary Flames Canadien Airlines Saddledome PO Box 1540 Station M Calgary AB Canada T2P 3B9

TUREK, SONIA FAY, journalist; b. NYC, Aug. 2, 1949; d. Louis and Julia (Liebson) T.; m. Gilbert Curtis, June 18, 1995. BA in English, CCNY, 1970; MSLS, Drexel U., 1972; MS in Journalism, Boston U., 1979. Children's libr. Wissahickon Valley Pub. Libr., Ambler, Pa., 1973; supr. children's svcs. Somerville Pub. Libr., Somerville, Mass., 1973-78; stringer The Watertown (Mass.) Sun, 1979, The Bedford (Mass.) Minuteman, 1979; reporter The Middlesex News, Framingham, Mass., 1979-83, The Boston Herald, 1983, asst. city editor, city editor, 1983-86, asst. mng. editor features, 1986-89, asst. mng. editor Sunday, 1989-93, dep. mng. editor, arts and features, 1993-99, wine columnist, 1984—. Tchr. Cambridge (Mass.) Ctr for Adult Edn., 1982, 83; adj. prof. Boston U., 1986; travel writer The Boston Herald, 1984—. Avocations: wine and food, travel, sailing. Personal E-mail: sfturek@aol.com.

TUREKIAN, KARL KAREKIN, geochemistry educator; b. NYC, Oct. 25, 1927; s. Vaughan Thomas and Victoria (Guleserian) T.; m. Arax Roxanne Hagopian, Apr. 22, 1962; children: Karla Ann, Vaughan Charles. AB, Wheaton (Ill.) Coll., 1949; MA, Columbia U., 1951, PhD, 1955; DSc (hon.), SUNY, Stony Brook, 1989. Lectr. geology Columbia U., 1953-54, rsch. assoc. Lamont-Doherty Earth Obs., 1954-56; asst. prof. Yale U., 1956-61, assoc. prof., 1961-65, prof. geology and geophysics, 1965 72, Henry Barnard Davis prof. geology and geophysics, 1972-85, Benjamin Silliman prof., 1985—2003, Sterling prof., 2003—, chmn. dept., 1982-88; curator meteorites and planetary sci. Peabody Mus., archaeology coun., dir. Yale U. Ctr. for the Study of Global Change; chmn. studies in the environment, 1992-93; dir. Yale Inst. for Biospheric Studies, 1999—2003. Cons. Pres.'s Commn. Marine Sci. Engring. and Resources, 1967-68; oceanography panel NSF, 1968-70; NASA exobiology panel Am. Inst. Biol. Scientists, 1966-69; mem. NAS-NRC, climate rsch. bd., 1977-80, ocean sci. bd., 1979-82, ocean studies bd., 1989-92, 98-2000, bd. on global change, 1992-95, Commn. Phys. Scis., Math. Resources, 1986-90, Commn. Geoscis., Environment and Resources, 1990-92, Com. Global Change Rsch., 1994-98; mem. com. on techs. for cleanup of subsurface contamination DOE Weapons Complex, 1997-98; mem. group experts sci. aspects Marine Pollution UN, 1971-73; mem. Water Sci. and Tech. Bd., 2003—. Author: Oceans, 1968, 2d edit., 1976, Chemistry of the Earth, 1972, (with B.J. Skinner) Man and the Ocean, 1973, (with C.L. Drake, J. Imbrie and J.A. Knauss) Oceanography, 1978, Global Environmental Change, 1996; editor: (with J. Steele and S. Thorpe) Encyclopedia of Ocean Sciences, 2001, (with H.D. Holland) Treatise on Geochemistry, 2003; editor Jour. Geophys. Resource, 1969-75, Earth and Planetary Sci. Letters, 1975-89, Global Biogeochemical Cycles, 1990-95, Geochim. Cosmochim. Acta, 1997-99. Served with USNR, 1945-46. Guggenheim fellow Cambridge U., 1962-63; Fairchild Disting. scholar Calif. Inst. Tech., 1988; recipient Wollaston medal, The Geol. Soc. London, 1998. Fellow AAAS, Geol. Soc. Am., Meteoritical Soc., Am. Geophys. Union (Maurice Ewing medal 1997), Am. Acad. Arts and Scis.; mem. NAS, Am. Chem. Soc., Geochem. Soc. (pres. 1975-76, V.M. Goldschmidt medal 1989), Sigma Xi (pres. Yale chpt. 1961-62). Home: 555 Skiff St North Haven CT 06473-3013 Office: Yale U Dept Geology and Geophysics PO Box 208109 New Haven CT 06520-8109 E-mail: karl.turekian@yale.edu.

TURGEON, PAUL R. computer program manager; b. Lewiston, Maine, June 18, 1957; s. Roger Marcel and Jeannine Turgeon. BSEE, Rensselaer Poly. Inst., 1979; M, George Washington U., 1996. Design engr. IBM, Kingston, N.Y., 1979-87, engring. mgr., mainframe developer, 1987-90, from engring. mgr., mainframe developer to mgr. e-server I/O hardware devel. Poughkeepsie, NY, 1990—2001, program mgr. z-series, hardware devel., 2002—. Contbr. articles to profl. jours.; patentee in field. Mem. Project Mgmt. Inst. (founder Mid-Hudson Valley chpt. 1996—). Avocations: hiking, camping, bass fishing, high end audio, record collecting. Office: IBM 2455 South Rd Poughkeepsie NY 12601 Home: 8 River Cliff DR Marlboro NY 12542-5318 E-mail: turgeon@us.ibm.com.

TURGEON, PIERRE, professional hockey player; b. Rouyn, Quebec, Aug. 29, 1969; With N.Y. Islanders, 1992-95, Montreal Canadiens NHL, 1995-97, St. Louis Blues NHL, 1997—2001, Dallas Stars, 2001—. Played in NHL All-Star Game, 1990, 93, 94. Recipient Michel Bergeron Trophy, 1985-86, Michael Bossy Trophy, 1986-87, Lady Byng Meml. Trophy, 1992-93. Mailing: c/o Dallas Stars Reunion Arena 777 Sports St Dallas TX 75207

TURI, LOUIS, publishing executive; b. Pont Saint Esprit, French Riviera, France (incl. Monaco), Feb. 26, 1950; s. Marie Angela Di-Rollo, Joseph DiCaprio Turi. CEP - FPA, College de Pont St Esprit, Pont Saint Esprit, 1956—73. Cert. FPA -ASME section 9 welding 1973. Recording artist Phillips -Phonogram, Paris, 1975—83; pres. Startheme Pubs. LTD, Phoenix, 1991—. Lectr. in field. Author: Astropsychologist -Futuristic Stock Market. Recipient Distinction Cup Musicianship, Royal Sch. of Music, 1976, Writer's Digest award for 3 books, 2001. Mem.: Am. Assn. of Astrologers (Phoenix 1998—2002, AFA Conv. Fla. 1998). Republican. Christian. Avocation: travel. Home and Office: Startheme Publications Inc 4411 N 23rd St Phoenix AZ 85016-5515 E-mail: dr.turi@cox.net.

TURILLO, MICHAEL JOSEPH, JR., management consultant; b. Hartford, Conn., Aug. 22, 1947; s. Michael Joseph and Alice (Vargas) T.; m. Deborah Sherburne; children: Stephanie, Christopher. BS, Providence Coll., 1969; MBA, Syracuse U., 1972; MS, U. Mass., 1973. Cons. Peat, Marwick, Mitchell & Co. (now KPMG LLP), Boston, 1974-77, mgr., 1977-82, ptnr., 1982—, nat. cons. practice dir. for fin. svc. cos., 1985-91. Chmn. Internat. . Mgmt. Cons. Practice Com. on Banking and Fin., 1986—98; nat. ptnr.-in-charge Fin. Svcs.-Specialized Cons., 1990—93, Capital Strategies, 1995—97; nat. lead ptnr. in charge Global Capital Group, 1993—94; nat. ptnr. in charge fin. svcs. Knowledge Mgmt., 1997—98, global chief officer, 1998—2001; with IBM Practice Exec. Collaborative Commerce, 2001—. Com. mem. United Way, Boston, 1981-83; trustee Elliot Montessori, South Natick, Mass., 1984-85; dir. Greater Boston coun. Boy Scouts Am., 1988—; adv. bd. Lesley Coll. Capt. U.S. Army, 1969-71, Vietnam. Decorated Bronze Star Mem. Bank Mktg. Assn., Assn. Planning Execs., Assn. Corp. Planners, Beta Gamma Sigma. Roman Catholic. Avocations: tennis, photography, travel, golf. Home: 47 South St Natick MA 01760-5526 Office: IBM Global Svcs 404 Wyman St Waltham MA 02454 E-mail: mturillo@us.ibm.com.

TURINO, GERARD MICHAEL, physician, medical scientist, educator; b. N.Y.C., May 16, 1924; s. Michael and Lucy (Arciero) T.; m. Dorothy Estes, Aug. 25, 1951; children: Peter, Phillip, James. AB, Princeton U., 1945; MD, Columbia U., 1948. Diplomate: Am. Bd. Internal Medicine. Intern Columbia U., Bellevue Hosp., 1948-49, asst. resident in medicine, 1949-50; resident in medicine New Haven Hosp., 1950-51; chief resident in medicine Columbia U. div. Bellevue Hosp., 1953-54; sr. fellow N.Y. Heart Assn., 1956-60; career investigator Health Research Council City of N.Y., 1961-71; asst. prof. medicine Columbia U., 1960-67, assoc. prof., 1967-72, prof. medicine, 1973-83, John H. Keating prof. medicine, 1983—; mem. staff Presbyn. Hosp., N.Y.C., 1960—, attending physician, 1983—; dir. med. svcs. St. Lukes-Roosevelt Hosp., N.Y.C., 1983-92; dir. St. Lukes-Roosevelt Hosp. James P.

Mara Ctr, 1997. Cons. on sci. affairs Am. Thoracic Soc., 1992—; mem. sci. adv. com. Nat. Heart, Lung, and Blood Inst., Am. Lung Assn., Am. Heart Assn., N.Y. Lung Assn., N.Y. Heart Assn.; mem. staff divsn. med. sci. Nat. Rsch. Coun., Washington;mem. Sci. Adv. Coun. Alpha, Antitrypsin Found. cons. VA Hosp., East Orange, N.J., 1962-67; cons. in medicine Englewood (N.J.) Hosp., Hackensack (N.J.) Hosp., pres.-elect Am. Bur. Med. Advancement in China, 1994, pres., 1994-2001, chmn., 2001-. Contbr. articles to med. jours. Mem. Bd. Edn., Alpine, N.J., 1960-67. Served to capt. USAF, 1951-53. Recipient Joseph Mather Smith prize Columbia U., 1965, Alumni medal, 1983, Silver medal Alumni Assn. Coll. Physicians and Surgeons Columbia U., 1979, gold medal, 1986, Edward Livingston Trudeau medal Am. Lung Assn., 2003, Fellow AAAS; mem. Assn. Am. Physicians, Am. Soc. Clin. Investigation, Harvey Soc., Am. Thoracic Soc. (pres. 1987-88, Edward Livingston Trudeau prize 2003), Am. Fedn. Clin. Rsch., Am. Physiol. Soc. (chmn. steering com. respiration sect.), Am. Heart Assn. (award of merit 1980, Disting. Achievement award 1989, bd. dirs.), N.Y. Heart Assn. (pres. 1981-83, dir.), N.Y. Lung Assn. (dir.), N.Y. Med.-Surg. Soc. (pres. 1995), N.Y. Clin. Soc., Princeton Club (N.Y.C.), Maidstone Club, Devon Yacht Club, Century Assn. Club. Home: 66 E 79th St New York NY 10021-0244 Office: St Lukes Roosevelt Hosp 1000 10th Ave New York NY 10019-1192 E-mail: GMT1@Columbia.edu.

TURINSKY, PAUL JOSEF, nuclear engineer, educator; b. Hoboken, N.J., Oct. 20, 1944; s. Paul J. and Wilma A. (Budig) T.; m. Karen Ann DeLuca, Aug. 29, 1966; children: Grant Dean, Beth Noelle. BS, U. R.I., 1966; MSE, U. Mich., 1967, PhD, 1970; MBA, U. Pitts., 1979. Asst. prof. Rensselaer Poly. Inst., Troy, N.Y., 1971-73; engr., mgr. nuclear design Westinghouse Elec. Corp., Pitts., 1973-78, mgr. core devel., 1978-80; head dept. nuclear engring. N.C. State U., Raleigh, 1980-88, 99—, prof., 1980—, dir. Electric Power Rsch. Ctr., 1989—; pres. Nuclear Fuel Mgmt. Assocs., 1994—. Bd. dirs. Quantum Rsch. Svcs.; cons. Electric Power Rsch. Inst., Palo Alto, Calif., 1980-98, Sci. Applications Internat. Corp., 1990-92, U.S. Dept. of Energy, 1993; tech. specialist Internat. Atomic Energy Agy., Vienna, Austria, 1982—; mem. nuclear safety rev. bd. Duke Power Co., Charlotte, N.C., 1986-2001; cons. Can. Nuc. Safety Commn., 2000-. Author: (with others) CRC Handbook of Nuclear Reactor Calculations, 1986; contbr. more than 100 articles to tech. jours. Recipient Outstanding Tchr. award, N.C. State U., 1985, Supercomputer award, IBM, 1991, Alcoa Disting. Rschr. award, 1993, E.O. Lawrence award in nuc. tech., U.S. Dept. Energy, 2002, Merit award, Alumni Soc. U. Mich., 2003. Fellow: Am. Nuc. Soc. (chmn. reactor physics divsn. 1987—88, chmn. math. and computer divsn. 1995—96, bd. dirs. 1990—93, Mark Mills award 1971, Eugene E. Wigner Reactor Physics award 2003, Arthur Holly Compton award 2004); mem.: AAAS (math. com.), Soc. Indsl. and Applied Math., Edison Electric Inst. (Power Engring. Educator award 1992), Am. Soc. Engring. Educators (chmn. nuc. engring. divsn. 1984—85, Glenn Murphy award 1990), IEEE Computer Soc. Office: NC State U Dept Nuclear Engring PO Box 7909 Raleigh NC 27695-7909 Business E-Mail: turinsky@ncsu.edu.

TURK, AUSTIN THEODORE, sociology educator; b. Gainesville, Ga., May 28, 1934; s. Hollis Theodore and Ruth (Vandiver) T.; m. Janet Stuart Irving, Oct. 4, 1957 (div. 1977); children: Catherine, Jennifer; m. Ruth-Ellen Marie Grimes, July 27, 1985. BA cum laude, U. Ga., 1956; MA, U. Ky., 1959; PhD, U. Wis., 1962. Acting instr. sociology U. Wis., Madison, 1961-62; from instr. to prof. sociology Ind. U., Bloomington, 1962-74; prof. U. Toronto, Can., 1974-88, U. Calif., Riverside, 1988—, chmn. dept. sociology, 1989-94; interim dir. Robert B. Presley Ctr. for Crime and Justice Studies, 1994-95. Author: Criminality and Legal Order, 1969, Political Criminality, 1982; gen. editor crime and justice series SUNY Press, Albany, 1990—; contbr. articles to jours. in field. Mem. Calif. Mus. Photography, 1988—, Citizens Univ. Com., 1990—. Recipient Paul Tappan award Western Soc. Criminology, 1989. Fellow Am. Soc. Criminology (pres. 1984-85); mem. Am. Sociol. Assn. (chair criminology sect. 1975-76), Law and Soc. Assn. (trustee 1982-85), Acad. Criminal Justice Scis. Democrat. Avocations: gardening, reading, swimming, tennis. Office: Dept Sociology U Calif Riverside Riverside CA 92521-0001 E-mail: austin.turk@ucr.edu.

TURK, ELIZABETH ANN, music educator; b. N.Y.C., July 10, 1957; d. William Robert Turk, Elizabeth Ann Brittingham. BA in Music and History, Dowling Coll.; MA in German Lang. and Lit., Hofstra U.; MA in European History, SUNY Stony Brook; MA in Music Libr. Sci., Columbia U. Tchg. asst SUNY, Stony Brook, 1986—88; lectr. music Dowling Coll., Oakdale, NY, 1988—91; tchr. music Amityville Pub. Schs., Amityville, NY, 1991—; dir. theater arts, dir. choral music Miller Pl. H.S.; music dir. Amityville H.S., Commack H.S. South, Carriage House Players, Kids for Kids Theater, Inc. Tchr. vocal music Miller Place Pub. Sch., Miller Place, NY, Hewlett Woodmere Pub. Sch., Hewlett, NY; pvt. tchr. and vocal coach, Massapequa, NY. Singer (soloist): Rome Opera Festival, 1989, 1990; performer: Tchaikovsky Competition, 1978, 1982, 1986, Minn. Opera, 1979, 1980, 1981, L.I. Youth Orch. Summer Tours; dir.: Sleeping Beauty, Sound of Music, Fiddler on the Roof, Little Shop of Horrors, Cinderella, Oliver, numerous others; choreographer Fiddler on the Roof, Sound of Music, Little Shop of Horrors, Oliver, Grease. Recipient award for further study, Met. Opera, 1981—90, Herald award for choreography and music dir. Mem.: Suffolk County Music Educator's Assn., Music Educators Nat. Conf., Suffolk County Wrestling Assn. (tournament dir. league V 1974—, numerous awards), White Star Triangle (Beloved Queen 1973—74), Order Ea. Star (various offices, assoc. condr.). Home: 90 Clock Blvd Massapequa NY 11758

TURK, JAMES CLINTON, federal judge; b. Roanoke, Va., May 3, 1923; s. James Alexander and Geneva (Richardson) T.; m. Barbara Duncan, Aug. 21, 1954; children— Ramona Leah, James Clinton, Robert Malcolm Duncan, Mary Elizabeth, David Michael. AB, Roanoke Coll., 1949; L.L.B., Washington and Lee U., 1952. Bar: Va. bar 1952. Assoc. Dalton & Poff, Radford, Va., 1952-53; ptnr. Dalton, Poff & Turk, Radford, 1953-72; state senator from Va., 1959-72; judge U.S. Dist. Ct. (we. dist.) Va., Roanoke, 1972-73, chief judge, 1973—. Dir. 1st & Mchts. Nat. Bank of Radford Mem. Va. Senate, from 1959, minority leader.; Trustee Radford Community Hosp., 1959— . Served with AUS, 1943-46. Mem. Order of Coif, Phi Beta Kappa, Omicron Delta Kappa. Baptist (deacon). Home: 1002 Walker Dr Radford VA 24141-3018 Office: US Dist Ct 246 Franklin Rd SW # 220 Roanoke VA 24011-2214 Fax: (540) 857-5123. Office Phone: 703-857-5122. Business E-Mail: jamest@vawd.u.s.courts.gov.

TURK, JAMES CLINTON, JR., lawyer; b. Radford, Va, Oct. 27, 1956; s. James Clinton and Barbara (Duncan) T.; m. Allison Blanding, Oct. 16, 1993; children: Lindsey Leigh, Katherine Alexandra, Alana Rae. BA in Econs., Roanoke Coll., 1979; JD, Samford U., 1984. Bar: Va. 1984, U.S. Dist. Ct. (ea. and we. dists.) Va. 1984, U.S. Bankruptcy Ct. 1985, U.S. Ct. Appeals (4th cir.) 1985, U.S. Supreme Ct. 1988; cert. specialist in civil and criminal trial advocacy Nat. Bd. Trial Advocacy; AV rated Martindale Hubbell. Ptnr. Stone, Harrison & Turk, Radford, 1985—. Adj. prof. criminal justice dept. Radford U.; bd. dirs. New River brs. SunTrust Bank. Sec. Radford Rep. Com., 1984—; fundraising chmn. Am. Heart Assn., Radford, 1986—; bd. dir. New River Valley Workshop, Inc., v.p., 1990-92, pres., 1992-93; bd. dirs. new River C.C. Ednl. Found.; apptd. chmn. and dir. Va. Student Assistance Authorities by Gov. George Allen, 1994—; escheator City of Radford and Pulaski County; rep. western dist. CJA Panel Atty., Va.; mem. 4th Cir. Jud. Conf., 2000-01. Recipient Bill Geimer Capital Defender award, Va. Capital Care Clearinghouse, 2000—01. Mem. ATLA (sustaining, fellow Coll. of Advocacy), Ted Dalton Am. Inn Courts (barrister), ABA, Am. Bd. Trial Adv., Am. Coll. Barristers, Va. Bar Assn. (civil litig. sect. coun. 1991—, criminal litig. sect. coun. 1994—), Nat. Assn. Criminal Def. Lawyers (life; death penalty com. and indigent def. com.), Va. Trial Lawyers Assn., Inn of Cts., Jaycees, Am. Inn of Ct., Rotary. Republican. Roman Catholic. Avocations: weightlifting, golf, travel, flying, scuba diving. Home: 460 Quailwood Dr Blacksburg VA 24060-6724 Office: Stone Harrison Turk PC PO Box 2968 Radford VA 24143-2968 Office Phone: 540-639-9056 x6.

TURK, JOHN COBB, architect, educator; b. Buffalo, Oct. 16, 1930; s. Roswell Lester and Alice Knoche (Cobb) Turk; m. Joanna D. Paulat, 1959 (dec. Apr. 1966); 1 child, Christine Paulat; m. Sandra Miriam Baruch, Mar. 18, 1967 (dec. June 1986); m. Mary Jean Raftery, June 25, 1988. BA, Colgate U., 1952. Registered arch., S.C. Apprentice Frank Lloyd Wright's Taliesin Fellowship, Spring Green, Wis., Scottsdale, Ariz., 1955—57; archtl. draftsman various archs., Buffalo, 1959-72; instr. archtl. engring. tech. Midlands Tech. Coll., Columbia, SC, 1972-77, head dept. archtl. engring. tech., 1977-79, head constrn. tech. dept., 1979-84; arch. Carlisle Assocs., Columbia, 1984-87; arch., dir. engring. and housing Ft. Jackson, Columbia, 1987-88; arch., head design and estimating dept. Facilities Mgmt. Office U. S.C., Columbia, 1988-2000, arch., 2001—04; owner Architecture Light, Columbia, 2004—. Dir. Lake Murray Assn., 2001—02. With C.E. U.S. Army, 1953—55. Mem.: Constrn. Specifications Inst. (bd. dirs. Columbia chpt. 1996—98, v.p. 1998—99, pres.-elect 1999—2000, pres. 2000—01, dir. 2001—, constrn. documents technician), Intertel, Mensa (v.p. Columbia chpt. 1978, sec. 1998—2001). Republican. Unitarian Universalist. Avocation: boating. Home and Office: 112 Schooner Ln Columbia SC 29212-8032 Office Phone: 803-781-2859. Personal E-mail: jct@att.net.

TURK, RICHARD ERRINGTON, retired psychiatrist; b. Staten Island, N.Y., Oct. 6, 1925; s. Richard Jason and Marian (Errington) T.; m. Dec. 30, 1948 (widowed Dec. 23, 1978); children: Stephanie, Jeffrey, Alan. BS, Dartmouth Coll., 1945; MD, Johns Hopkins Med. Sch., 1948. Diplomate Am. Bd. Psychiatry. Intern Highland-Alameda County Hosp., Oakland, Calif., 1948-49; resident Herrick Meml. Hosp., Berkeley, Calif., 1949-50; fellow psychiatry Harvard Med. Sch., Boston, 1950-51, 53-54; clin. instr. UCLA Med. Sch., 1954-70; pvt. practice psychiatry Berkeley, 1954-85. Pvt. practice, Walnut Creek, Calif., 1972-88; staff Herrick Meml. Hosp., 1954-85, Walnut Creek Hosp., 1972-88, John Muir Meml. Hosp., Walnut Creek, 1972-88. Capt. USAF Res., 1951—53, Korea. Mem. AMA, Am. Psychiat. Assn., No. Calif. Psychiat. Assn., Calif. Med. Assn., Alameda-Contra Costa County Med. Assn. Avocations: travel, bicycling, boating, car camping.

TURK, THOMAS LIEBIG, cultural organization administrator; b. Indpls., July 4, 1936; s. Laurel Herbert and Esther Lucille (Liebig) T.; m. Judith Ann Prochnow, July 26, 1969; children: Martisha Emily, Benjamin Edward. AB, DePauw U., 1958; MA, Mich. State U., 1960; cert., Harvard U., 1973. Promotion and publicity dir. Sta. WMSB-TV Mich. State U., East Lansing, 1961, asst. editor news bur., 1962-63, fine arts assoc. producer Sta. WKAR-TV, 1963-68, fine arts producer Sta. WKAR-TV, 1969-81; acting dir. publicity DePauw U., Greencastle, Ind., 1961-62; exec. dir. Cultural Activities Ctr., Temple, Tex., 1981-91; mng. dir. Texarkana (Tex.) Regional Arts & Humanities Coun., 1991-93; exec. dir. Met. Nashville Arts Commn., 1993—2003, Tennesseans for the Arts, 2003—. Pres. Met. Lansing (Mich.) Fine Arts Coun., 1975-77, Mich. Assn. Comm. Arts Agys., East Lansing, 1979-81; Gov. apptd. mem. Mich. Coun. for Arts, 1979-81; chmn. Mich. Arts Forum, 1980-81; pres. U.S. Urban Arts Fedn., 1999-2000. Producer, co-producer: 400 programs for local, nat. and internat. distbn. on pub. TV, 1963-81. With USAF, 1960. Mem. Nat. Assembly Local Arts Agys. (bd. dirs. 1979-85), Tennesseans for the Arts (bd. dirs. 2000-03), Rotary, Sigma Chi. Episcopalian. Home and Office: 105 Harpeth Trace Ct Nashville TN 37221-3105 Office Phone: 615-353-5056. Personal E-mail: turktj@comcast.net.

TURKEL, BRUCE, advertising executive; Prin., creative dir. Turkel Advt., Coconut Grove, Fla., 1983-95, Turkel Advt. (merged with Schwartz & Kaplan Advt.), Coconut Grove, Fla., 1995; exec. creative dir. Turkel, Schwartz & Ptnrs., Coconut Grove, 1995—. Office: Turkel Schwartz & Ptnrs 2871 Oak Ave Coconut Grove FL 33133-5207

TURKEL, STANLEY, hotel consultant, management executive; b. N.Y.C., Sept. 2, 1925; s. Nathan and Mollie (Kurtzman) Turkeltaub; m. Barbara Bell, June 12, 1955 (div. Apr. 1971); children: Marc Alexander, Allison Lee; m. Rima Sokoloff, Apr. 26, 1971; stepchildren: Joshua Bernard Forrest, Benay Debra Forrest. BS, NYU, 1947; MBA, St. Johns U., Jamaica, N.Y., 1980. Laundry cons. Victor Kramer Co. Inc., N.Y.C., 1952-59; v.p., space planner Michael Saphier Assocs., N.Y.C., 1959-62; with spl. hotel svcs. Loews Hotel Corp., N.Y.C., 1962-63; res. mgr. Americana Hotel, N.Y.C., 1963-64; gen. mgr. Drake Hotel, N.Y.C., 1964-66; mng. dir. Summit Hotel, N.Y.C., 1966-67; product line mgr. hotels ITT, N.Y.C., 1968—75; prin., owner Stanley Turkel Co., Hotel Cons., Kew Gardens Hills, NY, 1976—. Mem. faculty NYU Ctr. Hospitality, Tourism and Sports Mgmt. Contbr. articles to N.Y. Times, Wall St. Jour., N.Y. Newsday, Washington Post, Smithsonian Mag., N.Y. Post, N.Y. Daily News, Hotel and Motel Mgmt., Cornell Quar., Lodging Hospitality, The Bottomline, Nat. Real Estate Investor, Hotel Interactive. Mem. ACLU. With USAAF, 1943-45. Mem.: Civic Affairs Forum (chmn. 1987—93), Internat. Soc. Hospitality Cons. (cert.), Am. Hotel and Lodging Assn. (MHS cert.), City Club NY (trustee 1964—97, pres. 1966—68, chmn. 1977—88, chmn. exec. com. 1988—91). Avocations: Reconstruction period of Am. history, civic affairs, autograph collecting, tennis. Office Phone: 917-628-8549. Personal E-mail: stanturkel@aol.com. *As a lifelong civic activist, I cherish the godless constitution and especially the first amendment which provides protection for unpopular speech and creates a wall of separation between church and state.*

TURKNETT, JAMES C. minister; b. Dallas, May 8, 1967; s. Jerry Claid and Frances Ann Turknett; m. Kay Frances Turknett, July 31, 1992. DMin, Tex. Christian Bible Inst., Fort Worth, 1997. Master driver U.S. Army, Republic of Korea, 1987—91, equal opportunity officer, 1988—94, drill sgt., 1992—94; ins. agt. Atlanta Life Ins., Tex., 1995—96; fin. svc. regional mgr. Primerica/So. Security, Tex., 1996—98; minister Faith and Power Ministry Ch., Tex., 1994—; CEO Life Changers Enterprise, Tex., 2003—. Author: (books) How To Be a Paymaster, 2003, How To On Radio, 2003, How To Start a Business, 2003. Mem. Dallas C. of C., 2002—. Decorated 7 Achievement Medals U.S. Army. Democrat. Avocations: basketball, football, soccer, track, ping pong/table tennis. Office: Faith and Power Ministry Ch 2120 N St Augustine #126 Dallas TX 75227 Office Phone: 972-329-1358. Business E-Mail: takingthecity@sbcglobal.net.

TURKOVA, HELGA, library director; b. Prague, Czech, Apr. 20, 1942; d. Johann Turek and Anna (Kusbachová) Turková. Grad., Charles U., Prague, Czech, 1964, PhD, 1969. Diploma in librarianship. Libr. Czechoslovak Acad. of Scis., Prague, Czech, 1964-65, Prague Info. Svc., Prague, Czech, 1965-67; ind. spez. libr. Dept. of Hist. Castles Libr. Nat. Mus. Libr., Prague, Czech, 1967-90, dir., 1990—. Co-author: (book) Rilke and Kraus and Vrchotovy J., 1985, (catalogue) Catalog incunabula in Castle Libraries, 1992, 2001; editor: Sborník Národního muzea-řada C-literární historie, 1990—. Mem coun Friends Old Prague, 1963—, Soc R M Rilke, 1992—. Mem.: Literary Sci Soc Sci Acad Czech Republic, Spolecnost Národního muzea, Asn Librarians. Roman Catholic. Avocations: history of Prague, history, art. Office: Knihovna Národni muzeum Václavské náměsti 68 115 79 Prague 1 Czech Republic Office Phone: 00420-224497368. E-mail: helga.turkova@nm.cz.

TURKS, HILDEGARD MARIA (HILDEGARD MARIA CHRONIS), retired security investigator, writer; b. Bruckander Mur, Austria, Nov. 10, 1949; arrived in U.S., 1962; d. Karl Franz Ignaz Popetschnigg and Margarete Galfuss; m. Ray Turks Jr., Apr. 16, 1970 (div. Apr. 20, 1971); 1 child, Joana Margarete Lee; m. James Chronis, Dec. 6, 1975 (dec. Aug. 6, 1994). Various civilian duties USAF, Baumholder and Zweibrucken, Germany, 1964—71; restaurant mgr. Jackson Heights, NY, 1976—84; bartender N.Y.C., 1976—84; undercover investigator, security pers., 1978—85. Author: Little Snapple, 1992. Recipient Golden Globe award, World of Poetry, 1987—89, Editor's Choice award, Internat. Libr. Poetry, 2001—03. Avocations: art, writing, walking, travel, helping others. Home: 3300 Hobbs Rd Apt 123 Amarillo TX 79109-3251

TURLEY, J. WILLIAM, lawyer; b. Van Nuys, Calif., Jan. 11, 1948; s. Billy Brown and Kathryn Ann Turley; children: Timothy Jay, Damon Andrew, William Ross. BA, U. Mo., 1970, JD, 1974. Bar: Mo. 1974, U.S. Dist. Ct. (we. dist.) Mo. 1974. Stockholder Wesner, Turley & Kempton, Inc., Sedalia, Mo., 1975-84; ptnr. Carnahan, Carnahan & Turley, Rolla, Mo., 1984-87, ptnr. Williams, Robinson, Turley, Crump & White, 1987-96; sr. counsel Shelter Ins. Cos., 1996—. Author: Trial Handbook for Missouri Lawyers, 1984; contbr. articles to profl. jours.; v.p. Mo. Lawyer's Trust Acct. Found., 1990. Mem. Mo. Bar Assn. (bd. govs. 1986-96, exec. com. 1989-90), Assn. Trial Lawyers Am. (bd. govs. 1985-89), Mo. Assn. Trial Attys. (pres. 1985). Home: 2626 Huntleigh Pl Jefferson City MO 65109 Office: Shelter Ins Cos 1817 W Broadway Columbia MO 65218 Office Phone: 573-214-4110. Business E-Mail: bturley@shelterinsurance.com.

TURLEY, JAMES S. corporate financial executive; BS, Rice U., 1976, MBA, 1978. With Ernst & Young, Houston, 1977—79, St. Louis, 1979—87, U.S. nat. dir. client svcs. and bus. devel. N.Y.C., 1987—90, coord. ptnr. St. Louis, 1991—93, area dir. entrepreneurial svcs., 1993—94, mng. ptnr. upper midwest area, 1994—98, metro. N.Y. area mng. ptnr. N.Y.C., 1998—2000; dep. global chair Ernst & Young Internat., N.Y.C., 2000—01, global chair, 2001—, global CEO, 2003—. Office: 787 Seventh Ave New York NY 10019*

TURLEY, STEWART, retired retail company executive; b. Mt. Sterling, Ky., July 20, 1934; s. R. Joe and Mavis S. Turley; children from previous marriage: Carol Cohen, Karen Shockley; m. Linda A. Mulholland; stepchildren: Kathleen Smiley, Kristine Johnson. Student, Rollins Coll., 1952-53, U. Ky., 1953-55. Plant mgr. Crown Cork & Seal Co., Orlando (Fla.), Phila., 1955-66; mgr. non-drug ops., dir. corporate employee rels. and spl. svcs. Eckerd Corp. (formerly Jack Eckerd Corp.), Clearwater, Fla., 1966-68; v.p. Eckerd Corp., Clearwater, Fla., 1968-71, sr. v.p., 1971-74, dir., 1971-97, pres., chief exec. officer, 1974-96, chmn. bd., 1975-97. Bd. dirs. WCI Cmtys., Inc. Past chmn. U.S. Ski Team Found.; bd. dirs. Vilar Ctr. Found., Vail Valley Found., Steadman-Hawkins Sports Medicine Found. Mem. Nat. Assn. Chain Drug Stores (bd. dirs., chmn. bd. 1978-79, 88-89), Fla. Coun. 100 (past chmn.), Chief Execs. Orgn., Carlouel Yacht Club, Belleair Country Club, Eagle Springs Golf Club, Kappa Alpha. Office: 1465 S Fort Harrison Ave Clearwater FL 33756-2505

TURLIK, IWONA, communication executive; b. Poznan, Poland, May 18, 1951; d. Mieczyslaw and Anna (Rymaszewska) Lemanczyk; m. Marian Turlik, Aug. 25, 1973; 1 child, Daniel. MSEE, Tech. U. Wroclaw, 1973, PhD, 1977. Faculty Tech. U. Wroclaw, Poland, 1977-81; from tech. staff to program mgr. Bell No. Rsch., Research Triangle Park, N.C., 1981-89; prof. U. N.C., Charlotte, 1990-94; v.p., dir. Motorola Advanced Technology Ctr., Tech. Acquisition Office, Schaumburg, Ill., 1994—. Author: Multichip Module Handbook, 1997, Multichip Module Technology Handbook, 1997. Fellow IEEE. Office: Motorola Advanced Technology Ctr 1301 E Algonquin Rd Schaumburg IL 60196-1078

TURLINGTON, CHRISTY, model; b. Walnut Creek, Calif., Jan. 2, 1969; d. Dwain and Elizabeth Turlington; m. Ed Burns, June 7, 2003; 1 child. With Ford Models, Inc., 1985; model Calvin Klein, 1986, Calvin Klein's Eternity Fragrance, 1988; with Maybelline Cosmetics, 1992; co-creator, skin care line Sundari, 2000—. Beauty spread with Vogue, 1987; has worked with Herb Ritts, Patrick Demarchelier, Steven Meisel; has worked for Anne Klein, Michael Kors, Chanel, Perry Ellis; appeared in George Michael's "Freedom" video. Author: Living Yoga. Spokesperson for anti-smoking CDC. Office: United Talent Agy 9560 Wilshire Blvd Ste 500 Beverly Hills CA 90212-2427 also: 344 E 59th St New York NY 10022-1513

TURLO, GEORGE JERZY, architect, city planner, artist; b. Wilno, Poland, Mar. 13, 1934; came to U.S., 1966; s. Michael and Olga Turlo; m. Stephanie W. Turlo, 1957 (div. 1980); children: Peter A., Ralph C.; m. Christine B. Turlo, Feb. 14, 1981. M.Engring. and Arch., Gdansk (Poland) Poly. Inst., 1958; postgrad., Brown U., 1967, Providence Coll., 1967-69. Sr. city planner Dept. Arch. and Bldg. Inspection, Koszalin, Poland, 1958-60; architect Miastoprojekt Kosalin, 1960-61; dir. dept. City of Kotobrzeg, Poland, 1961-62; planning dir. City of Stupsk, Poland, 1962-66; supr. current planning Dept. Planning City of Providence, 1966-2000; ret., 2000. One-man show Turlo Art Gallery, Providence, 1997-2000; exhibited in group shows R.I. Watercolor Soc., Providence Art Club, Wickford Art Assn.; represented in permanent collection Providence Biltmore Hotel, Providence Washington Ins., Mayor's Office, Providence City Hall, Coastal Credit Union, also numerous pvt. collections; author: Noble Hearts, 2004. Recipient Providence Art Club award, 1998. Mem. R.I. Watercolor Soc., Fla. Suncoast Watercolor Soc., Art League Manatee County, Wickford Art Assn. Avocations: fine art, writing, bicycling, swimming. Home: 8718 28th Ave E Palmetto FL 34221 E-mail: turlo@msn.com.

TURNAGE, JEAN ALLEN, retired state supreme court chief justice; b. St. Ignatius, Mont., Mar. 10, 1926; JD, Mont. State U., 1951; D of Laws and Letters (hon.), U. Mont., 1995. Bar: Mont. 1951, US Supreme Ct. 1963. Former ptnr. Turnage, McNeil & Mercer, Polson, Mont.; former Mont. State senator from 13th Dist.; pres. Mont. State Senate, 1981—85; chief justice Supreme Ct. Mont., 1985-2001. Mem. Mont. State Bar Assn., Nat. Conf. Chief Justices (past pres.), Nat. Ctr. State Courts (past chair). Office: Turnage & Mercer PO Box 460 Polson MT 59860 Office Phone: 406-883-5367.

TURNBACH, ANN, publishing executive; V.p. human resources Houston Chronicle. Office: Houston Chronicle PO Box 4260 Houston TX 77210-4260

TURNBAUGH, ROY CARROLL, archivist; b. Peoria, Ill., Oct. 16, 1945; s. Roy Carroll and Zora (Alexander) T.; m. Donna Marie Chase, Mar. 28, 1970; children: Andrew, Peter. BA, Aurora Coll., 1969; AM, U. Ill., 1973, PhD, 1977. Asst. prof. U. Ill., Urbana, 1977-78; archivist Ill. State Archives, Springfield, 1978-85; dir. Oreg. State Archives, Salem, 1985—. Mem. Nat. Hist. Publs. and Records Commn., 2000—. Mem. Nat. Assn. Govt. Archives Records Adminstrs. (pres. 1998-2000), Soc. Am. Archivists (C.F.W. Coker prize 1984, Fellows Posner prize 1999). Office: Oreg State Archives 800 Summer St NE Salem OR 97310-1347 E-mail: roy.c.turnbaugh@state.or.us.

TURNBAUGH, WILLIAM ARTHUR, archaeologist, educator; b. Williamsport, Pa., June 1, 1948; s. William Hugh and Louise Elizabeth (Muller) Turnbaugh; m. Sarah Ropes Peabody, Oct. 12, 1974. BA in History summa cum laude, Lycoming Coll., 1970; PhD in Anthropology, Harvard U., 1973. Accredited mem. Register Profl. Archaeologists. Curator of archaeology Lycoming County Mus., Williamsport, 1968-70; tchg. fellow, dept. anthropology Harvard U., Cambridge, Mass., 1971-72, asst. to dir. Peabody Mus., 1973-74; asst. prof. anthropology U. R.I., Kingston, 1974-78, assoc. prof. anthropology, 1978-83, prof. anthropology, 1983—. Ind. contracting archaeologist ea. U.S. and Can., 1968—74; dir. U. R.I. Mus., 1975—77; adv. bd. Inst. Conservation Archaeology, Cambridge, 1976—83. Author: Man, Land and Time, 1975, Material Culture of RI-1000, 1984; co-author: Indian Baskets, 1986, rev. edit., 2004, R.F.D. Country!, 1988, Indian Jewelry of the American Southwest, 1988, rev. edit., 1997, Basket Tales of the Grandmothers, 1999, Understanding Physical Anthropology & Archaeology, 8th edit., 2002; assoc. editor: Historical Archaeology, 1986—; contbr. articles to profl. jours., chapters to books. V.p., acting pres. Lycoming County Hist. Soc., Williamsport, 1968—70; designed ofcl. flag Lycoming County, Pa., 1970. Recipient Archie award, Soc. Pa. Archaeology, 1967, Disting. Alumni citation, Lycoming Coll., 1987, J. Alden Mason award, Soc. Pa. Archaeology, 1988; fellow NSF, 1970—73, Woodrow Wilson Found., 1970—71. Fellow: Explorers Club; mem.: Soc. Hist. Archaeology, Soc. Am. Archaeology, Sigma Xi, Phi Alpha Theta, Phi Kappa Phi. Unitarian Universalist. Avocations: travel, geology, American history. Office: Univ RI Dept Sociol and Anthropol Kingston RI 02881 Business E-Mail: wtu4496u@postoffice.uri.edu.

TURNBULL, ANN PATTERSON, special educator, consultant, research director; b. Tuscaloosa, Ala., Oct. 19, 1947; d. H. F. and Mary (Boone) Patterson; m. H. Rutherford Turnbull III, Mar. 23, 1974; children: Jay, Amy, Kate. BS in Edn., U. Ga., 1968; MEd, Auburn U., 1971; EdD, U. Ala., 1972. Asst. prof. U. N.C., Chapel Hill, 1972-80; prof., co-dir. Beach Ctr. U. Kans., Lawrence, 1980—. Author: Free Appropriate Public Education, 2000, Families, Professionals and Exceptionality, 2001, Exceptional Lives: Special Education in Today's Schools, 2004. Recipient Rose Kennedy Internat. Leadership award, Kennedy Found., 1990, 20th Century award in Mental Retardation, 1999; Joseph P. Kennedy Jr. Found. fellow, 1987-88. Mem.: Internat. League Socs. for Persons with Mental Handicaps (com. chair

1986—90), The Arc-U.S. (named Educator of Yr. 1982), Am. Assn. on Mental Retardation (bd. dirs. 1986—88, v.p. 2001, pres.-elect 2002, pres. 2003—04). Democrat. Avocations: travel, exercise. Home: 1636 Alvamar Dr Lawrence KS 66047-1714 Office: Univ Kans Beach Ctr 3136 1200 Sunnyside Dr Lawrence KS 66045-7534 Office Phone: 785-864-7608. E-mail: turnbull@ku.edu.

TURNBULL, CHARLES W. governor; b. St. Thomas, V.I., Feb. 5, 1935; BS, Hampton U., 1958, MS, 1959; PhD, U. Minn., 1976. Elem., sec. sch. tchr., asst. prin. various pub. schs.; prin. Charlotte Amalie H.S.; asst. commr. to commr. Dept. Edn.; prof. history U. V.I.; gov. U.S. V.I., St. Thomas, 1999—. Chair V.I. Bd. Edn.; bd. dirs. U. V.I., Roy Lester Schneider Hosp.; chmn., Public Fin. Authority. Democrat. Methodist. Office: Office of the Governor Government House 21-22 Kongens Gade Saint Thomas VI 00802

TURNBULL, DAVID JOHN (CHIEF PIERCING EYES-PENN), cultural association executive; b. Hornell, N.Y., May 18, 1930; s. Gerald and Dorothy Esther (Badgley) T.; m. Martha Lillian Crouse, Aug. 12, 1949 (div. 1960); children: Garry David, Mary Jane Stuhr, Dorothy Grace Houde; m. Frances Early Spring Vickery, May 4, 1985; adopted children: Donna, Ashley, Jessica. Degree in ministry, Elim Bible Coll., 1964. Dir. pub. rels. Elim Bible Inst., Lima, N.Y., 1960-61; pastor Eagle Harbor (N.Y.) Ch., 1962-65, South Lima (N.Y.) Gospel Ch., 1962-66; ind. ins. agent, 1965-82; chief, counselor, performer weddings and funerals Pan-Am. Indian Assn., Nocatee, Fla., 1980—, pub. Pan.-Am. Indian Assn. News, 1984—. Mem. Ministerial Assn. Mem. Nocatee Ch. of God. Avocation: investigative reporter on children's issues. Home and Office: 2902 Airport Rd SE PO Box 244 Nocatee FL 34268-0244

TURNBULL, GORDON KEITH, metal company executive, metallurgical engineer; b. Cleve., Nov. 10, 1935; s. Gordon Gideon and Florence May (Felton) T.; m. Sally Ann Ewing, June 15, 1957; children: Kenneth Scott, Stephen James, Lynne Ann, June Patricia, James Robert. BS in Metall. Engring., Case Western Res. U., 1957, MS in Metall. Engring., 1959, PhD in Phys. Metallurgy, 1962. Engr. then sr. engr. casting and forgings div., Cleve. Research ALCOA, 1962-67, sr. metallurgist quality assurance, Cleve. Forge Plant, 1967-68; group leader fabricating metallurgy div. ALCOA Tech. Ctr., Pitts., 1968-71, sect. head, mgr. ingot casting div., 1971-78, mgr. fabricating metallurgy div., 1978-79, asst. dir. finishes engring. properties and design, 1979-80; mgr. bus. planning services, corp. planning dept. ALCOA, Pitts., 1980-82, dir. tech. planning, 1982-86, v.p. tech. planning, 1986-91, exec. v.p. strategic analysis/planning and info., 1991-97; exec. v.p. bus. system AICOA, Pitts., 1997—. Patentee method of not compacting titanium powder. Governing bd. Allegheny Ctr. Christian & Missionary Alliance Ch., Pitts. Mem. AIME, ASM, Nat. Acad. Engring., Am. Foundrymen's Soc., Rsch. Bd., Sigma Xi. Avocation: hockey. Home: 550 Fairview Rd Pittsburgh PA 15238-1745 Office: Aluminum Co Am 201 Isabella St Pittsburgh PA 15212-5859

TURNBULL, H. RUTHERFORD, III, law educator, lawyer; b. NYC, Sept. 22, 1937; s. Henry R. and Ruth (White) T.; m. Mary M. Slingluff, Apr. 4, 1964 (div. 1972); m. Ann Patterson, Mar. 23, 1974; children: Jay, Amy, Katherine. Grad., Kent (Conn.) Sch., 1955; BA, Johns Hopkins U., 1959; LLB with honors, U. Md., 1964; LLM, Harvard U., 1969. Bar: Md., N.C. Law clk. to Hon. Emory H. Niles Supreme Bench Balt. City, 1959-60; law clk. to Hon. Roszel C. Thomsen U.S. Dist. Ct. Md., 1962-63; assoc. Piper & Marbury (now Piper Rudnick), Balt., 1964-67; prof. Sch. Govt. U. N.C., Chapel Hill, 1969—80, U. Kans., Lawrence, 1980—. Prof. spl. edn., courtesy prof. law U. Kans. Editor-in-chief Md. Law Rev. Cons., author, lectr., co-founder, co-dir. Beach Ctr. on Disability, U. Kans.; pres. Full Citizenship Inc., Lawrence, 1987-93; spl. staff-fellow U.S. Senate subcom. on disability policy, Washington, 1987-88; bd. dirs. Camphill Assn. N.Am., Inc., 1985-87; trustee Judge David L. Bazelon Ctr. Mental Health Law, 1993—, chmn., 2000—. With U.S. Army, 1960-65. Recipient Nat. Leadership award Nat. Assn. Pvt. Residential Resources, 1988, Internat. Coun. for Exceptional Children, 1996, Am. Assn. on Mental Retardation, 1997, Century award Nat. Trust for Hist. Preservation in Mental Retardation, 1999, Nat. Adv. award Am. Music Therapy Assn., 2002, Leadership award Camphill Assn. N.Am., 2004, Leadership award The Arc of the U.S., 2004; named Nat. Educator of Yr., The Arc of the U.S., 1982; Pub. Policy fellow Joseph P. Kennedy, Jr. Found., 1987-88. Fellow Am. Assn. on Mental Retardation (pres. 1985-86, bd. dirs. 1980-86); mem. ABA (chmn. disability law commn. 1991-95), U.S.A. Assn. for Retarded Citizens (sec. and dir. 1981-83), Assn. for Persons with Severe Handicaps (treas. 1988, bd. dirs. 1987-90), Nat. Assn. Rehab. Rsch. and Tng. Ctrs. (chair govt. affairs com. 1990-93), Internat. Assn. Sci. Study of Mental Deficiency, Internat. League of Assns. for Persons with Mental Handicaps, Johns Hopkins U. Alumni Assn. (pres. N.C. chpt. 1977-79). Democrat. Episcopalian. Home: 1636 Alvamar Dr Lawrence KS 66047-1714 Office: U Kans 3111 Haworth Hall 1200 Sunnyside Ave Lawrence KS 66045-7534 Office Phone: 785-864-7610. Business E-Mail: Rud@ku.edu.

TURNBULL, JOHN CAMERON, retired pharmacist, consultant; b. Regina, Sask., Can., Sept. 5, 1923; s. Cameron Joseph and Lillian Irene (Pentz) T.; m. Hazel Evelyn Rockwell, July 31, 1948; children— Lillian Elizabeth, John Rockwell, Jocelyn Hazel. BS in Pharmacy, U. Sask., 1949. Pharmacist with village and city pharmacies, 1945-50; supr. pharm. services Dept. Pub. Health, Province of Sask., 1950-52; ops. mgr. Nat. Drugs, Ltd., Winnipeg, and Saskatoon, 1953; exec. dir. Can. Pharm. Assn., Toronto, Ont., 1953-78; ret. Sec.-treas., mng. dir. Canadian Pharm. Realty Co. Ltd.; mem. provisional bd. Pharmacare Ltd.; registrar-treas. Pharmacy Examining Bd. of Can., 1963-68, mem. bd., 1963-78; pharmacy cons., dir. drug service Ministry of Health, Barbados, 1979-84; staff assoc. Mgmt. Scis. for Health, Boston, 1984-85; cons. logistics and pharms. USAID, East Caribbean, PanAm. Health Orgn./WHO (Belize, Cen. Am.), 1985—. Chmn. Govt.'s Spl. Com. on Acetylsalicylic Poisonings, 1967; mem. Emergency Health Svcs. Adv. Com.; gen. chmn. Allied Air Forces Reunion, 1995, 96. Served to squadron leader RCAF, 1941-45. Decorated D.F.C., Order of Can., 1975; recipient Can. Centennial medal, 1967, Queen's Jubilee medal, 1977, Can. 125th Anniversary medal, 1992, John C. Turnbull rsch. ann. award in socio-econs. pharmacy established in his honor Can. Pharm. Assn., 1990. Mem. Fedn. Internationale Pharmaceutique (v.p.), Inst. of Assn. Execs. (hon. life), Conf. of Pharmacy Registrars of Can. (sec.), Commonwealth Pharm. Assn. (coun. 1969-78); hon. mem. Am., Canadian, Saskatchewan, B.C., Alta., Ont., Man., N.S. Pharm. Assns., Sask. Pharm. Assn., Ont. Pharmacists Assn., Canadian Soc. Hosp. Pharmacists, Rho Pi Phi. Mem. United Ch. of Canada. Club: Bayview Country (past dir.). Home: 40 Banstock Dr North York Toronto ON Canada M2K 2H6 Personal E-mail: jc.turnbull@sympatico.ca.

TURNBULL, MARJORIE REITZ, foundation executive, former state legislator; b. Madison, Wis., July 4, 1940; d. J. Wayne anf Frances H. (Millikan) R.; m. Augustus Bacon Turnbull, Nov. 26, 1965 (dec. Nov. 1991). Student, Agnes Scott Coll., 1958-60; BA, U. Fla., 1962; MA, U. Ga., 1968. Legis. analyst Fla. Ho. of Reps., Tallahassee, 1973-85, staff dir. com. on health and rehab. svcs., 1975-78, exec. asst. to speaker, 1978-80; asst. dir. Devel. Svc. Program Office, Tallahassee, 1980-82; dep. asst. sec. Health Planning State Fla., 1982-84; ind. cons. legis. mgmt. and planning, Tallahassee, 1984-95, state rep., 1994-2000; exec. dir. Tallahassee C.C. Found., 1995—. County commr. Leon County, Tallahassee, 1988-94; bd. dirs. Fla. Assn. Counties, Tallahassee, 1993-94, Tallahassee Symphony Orch., 1992—, Apalachee coun. Girl Scouts U.S., Tallahassee, 1988—. Recipient Outstanding Svc. in Govt. award Delta Kappa Omega, Tallahassee, 1996; named Woman of Yr., AAUW, Tallahassee, 1991, County Champion in the Legislature, Fla. Assn. Counties, 1995, Legislator of Yr., Fla. Assn. Sch. Supts., 1999; recipient Girl Scout Woman of Distinction award, 1999, Disting. Svc. award Fla. Student Assn., 2000, Disting. Citizens award Boy Scout Coun., 2000, Meritorious Achievement award Fla. A&M U., 2000, Legis. Advocacy award Fla. Coalition Against Domestic Violence, 2000, Freedom from Violence Leadership award, 2000, Model of Achievement award Tallahassee C.C., 2001. Mem. Rotary (program com. 1992—), Zonta Internat., Fla. Blue Key. Democrat. Presbyterian. Avocations: scuba diving, travel, cultural activities. Home: 3221 E Lakeshore Dr Tallahassee FL 32312-2062 Office: Tallahassee C C 444 Appleyard Dr Tallahassee FL 32304 E-mail: turnbulm@tcc.fl.edu.

TURNBULL, ROBERT SCOTT, retired manufacturing executive; b. North Dumfries, Ont., Can., Dec. 19, 1929; s. Leslie William and Marjorie Clara (Scott) T.; m. Dawna Rose Sinclair, Feb. 17, 1956 Sr. Matriculation, Galt U., Ont., 1950; M.T.C., U. Western Ont., 1975. Cert. mgmt. acct. Credit mgr Can. Gen. Tower, Cambridge, Ont., 1951-53, gen. acct., 1953-62, comptroller, 1962-68, v.p. mktg., 1968-78, v.p., gen. mgr., 1978-96, pres., 1996-99, dir., sr. officer; ret., 2001. Mem. Chem. Fabrics and Films Assn. (bd. dirs.), Soc. Plastics Industry (mem. Automotive Coun.), Japan Soc. (bd. dirs.), Soc. Mgmt. Accts. Home: 26 Lansdowne Rd S Cambridge ON Canada N1S 2T3

TURNBULL, VERNONA HARMSEN, retired residence counselor, education educator; b. Teeds Grove, Iowa, Dec. 6, 1916; d. Henry Ferdinand and Ida Amelia (Dohrmann) Harmsen; m. Alexander Turnbull, Oct. 12, 1961. BA, Cornell Coll., Mt. Vernon, Iowa, 1939; MEd, U. Colo., Boulder, 1947, profl. cert. edn., 1955. Cert. secondary and h.s. tchr. Tchr. English, Latin and phys. edn. Winslow (Ill.) H.S., 1939-45; dir. women's activities, instr. Trinidad (Colo.) State Jr. Coll., 1947-53; counselor women, assoc. prof. edn. Western State Coll., Gunnison, Colo., 1953-54; instr., residence counselor Stephens Coll., Columbia, Mo., 1955-61; ret., 1961. Active Salvation Army Aux. Mem. AAUW, Am. Assn. Ret. Persons (corr. sec. 1986-87), Kena Kampers Camping Club. Avocations: photography, camping, art, dance, baking.

TURNDORF, HERMAN, anesthesiologist, educator; b. Paterson, N.J., Dec. 22, 1930; s. Charles R. and Ruth (Blumberg) T.; m. Sietske Huisman, Nov. 24, 1957; children: David, Michael Pieter. AB, Oberlin Coll., 1952; MD, U. Pa., 1956. Diplomate Am. Bd. Anesthesiology. Instr. anesthesiology U. Pa. Hosp., 1957-59; asst. anesthetist med. sch. Harvard U., Mass. Gen. Hosp., Boston, 1961-63; assoc. attending anesthesiologist, asst. dir. dept. anesthesiology Mt. Sinai Hosp., N.Y.C., 1963-70, clin. prof. anesthesiology, 1966-70; prof., chmn. dept. anesthesiology W.Va. U. Sch. Medicine and Med. Ctr., Morgantown, 1970-74, NYU Sch. Medicine, 1974—2000; dir. anesthesiology NYU Tisch Hosp., Bellevue Hosp. Ctr., 1974—2000; pres. med. bd., med. dir. Bellevue Hosp. Med. Ctr., 1990—91, 1997; ret., 2000. Co-author: Anesthesia and Neurosurgery, 2nd edit., 1986, Trauma, Anesthesia and Intensive Care, 1990; contbr. over 200 articles to profl. jours. Lt. M.C., USNR, 1959-61. Fellow Am. Coll. Chest Physicians, Am. Coll. Anesthesiologists (mem. bd. govs. 1977-85, chmn. bd. govs. 1984), N.Y. Acad. Medicine; mem. AMA, Am. Soc. Anesthesiologists, Assn. Univ. Anesthetists, Internat. Soc. Study of Pain, Soc. Acad. Anesthesia Chairmen, Soc. Critical Care Medicine, Soc. Neurosurg. Anesthesia and Neurologic Supportive Care, N.Y. Acad. Scis., N.Y. State Soc. Anesthesiologists. Home: PO Box 412 East Boothbay ME 04544-0412

TURNER, ALICE KENNEDY, editor; b. Mukden, Manchuria; d. William Taylor and Florence Bell (Green) T. BA, Bryn Mawr Coll., 1962. Sr. editor Holiday mag., N.Y.C., 1969-70; assoc. editor Publishers Weekly, N.Y.C., 1972-74; sr. editor Ballantine Books, N.Y.C., 1974-76, New York mag., N.Y.C., 1976-80; fiction editor Playboy mag., Chgo., N.Y.C., 1980—2001. Author: Yoga for Beginners, 1973, The History of Hell, 1993; co-author: The New York Woman's guide, 1975; editor: Playboy Stories, 1993, The Playboy Book of Science Fiction, 1996; co-editor: Snake's-hands: The Fiction of John Crowley, 2002. Home: 2 Charlton St New York NY 10014-4909

TURNER, ALMON RICHARD, retired art historian, educator; b. New Bedford, Mass., July 28, 1932; s. Louis Alexander and Margaret (Mather) T.; m. Jane Beebe; children: Louis Hamilton, David Alexander. AB, Princeton U., 1955, MFA, 1958, PhD, 1959. Instr. in fine arts U. Mich., Ann Arbor, Mich., 1959-60; from instr. to prof. art and archaeology Princeton U., NJ, 1960-68; prof. fine arts Middlebury Coll., Vt., 1968-74, dean faculty, 1970-74; prof. fine arts, pres. Grinnell Coll., Iowa, 1975-79; prof., dir. Inst. Fine Arts NYU, NYC, 1979-82, dean faculty arts and scis., 1982-85, prof. dept. fine arts, 1985-2000, dir. N.Y. Inst. Humanities, 1986-93, Paulette Goddard prof. in arts and humanities, 1994—2000, prof. emeritus, 2000—. Author: Vision of Landscape in Renaissance Italy, 1966, 73, (With G. Andres and J. Hunisak) Art of Florence (L'Art de Florence), 1988 (prix 1989), Inventing Leonardo, 1993, Renaissance Florence: The Invention of a New Art, 1997, La Pietra: Florence, a Family, and a Villa, 2002 Mem. Coll. Art Assn., Century Assn., NJ Aubudon Soc. (1st v.p. 1990-93, pres. 1993-96), Phi Beta Kappa. Democrat. Unitarian Universalist. Avocations: birding, photography. Home: PO Box 2322 Cape May NJ 08204-7322

TURNER, ANDREW L. healthcare management company executive; BA, Ohio State Univ. Adminstr skilled nursing facility, Springfield, Ohio, 1970-75; mgr. regional nursing home chain; sr. v.p. ops. Hillhaven Corp.; co-founder Horizon Healthcare Corp., 1986-89; founder, chmn.,CEO Sun Healthcare Group, Albuquerque, 1989—2000; chmn. Ballantrae Healthcare, 2000—; founder, chmn. Endura Care, 2000—, Code Blue Staffing Solutions, 2001—; mem. bd. of directors Sports Clubs/L.A., Watson Pharmaceuticals. Office: Ballantrae Healthcare 1128 Pennsylvania St NE Albuquerque NM 87110

TURNER, BARBARA A. former dance company executive; b. Louisville; BA, U. Ky.; MA, U. Louisville. Dir. devel. Ballet Internat., Indpls., now mng. dir. Office: Ballet Internat 502 N Capitol Ave Ste B Indianapolis IN 46204-1204

TURNER, BERT S. construction executive; b. Elizabeth, La, Nov. 2, 1921; m. Suzanne Wilbert; 5 children. B in Mech. Engring., La. State U., 1943; MBA, Harvard U., 1949; DSc (hon.), La. State U., 1996. With Esso Standard Oil Co., 1946-57, Nichols Constrn. Inc., Baton Rouge, 1957-61, Nichols Constrn. Corp., Baton Rouge, 1961—; founder, chief exec. officer Turner Industries Ltd., Baton Rouge, chmn. emeritus. Bd. dirs. La. State U. Found., Pennington Biomedical Rsch. Mem. Jr. Achievement of Greater Baton Rouge, Baton Rouge C. of C., Baton Rouge Jaycees; bd. dir. La. State Mus.; chmn. bd. supervisors La. State U., pres.; Indsl. Contractors Assn.; mem. La. Polit. Action Coun., Friends of Angio-Am. Art Mus., Baton Rouge Green, Challenger Learning Ctr., Lindy Boggs Space Station, Mission Control Com., La. State U. Alumni Assn. Hall of Distinction, La. State U. Engring. Hall of Distinction, T. Harry Williams Ctr. Develop. Coun. Office: Turner Inds Ltd 8687 United Plz Blvd Ste 500 PO Box 2750-70821 Baton Rouge LA 70809 Office Phone: 225-922-5050. Office Fax: 225-922-5055. Business E-Mail: tturner@turner-industries.com.*

TURNER, BILLIE LEE, botanist, educator; b. Yoakum, Tex., Feb. 22, 1925; s. James Madison and Julia Irene (Harper) T.; m. Virginia Ruth Mathis, Sept. 27, 1944 (div. Feb. 1968); children: Billie Lee, Matt Warnock; m. Pauline Henderson, Oct. 22, 1969 (div. Jan. 1975); m. Gayle Langford, Apr. 18, 1980; children (adopted): Roy P., Robert L. BS, Sul Ross State Coll., 1949; MS, So. Meth. U., 1950; PhD, Wash. State U., 1953. Teaching asst. botany dept. Wash. State U., 1951-53; instr. botany dept. U. Tex., Austin, 1953, asst. prof., 1954-58, assoc. prof., 1958-61, prof., 1961-2000, now S.F. Blake prof. botany, chmn., 1967-75, dir. Plant Resources Ctr., 1957—, emeritus prof., 2000—. Asso. investigator ecol. study vegetation of, Africa, U. Ariz., Office Naval Research, 1956-57; vis. prof. U. Mont., summers 1971, 73, U. Mass., 1974 Author: Vegetational Changes in Africa Over a Third of a Century, 1959, Leguminosae of Texas, 1960, Biochemical Systematics, 1963, Chemotaxonomy of Leguminosae, 1972, Biology and Chemistry of Compositae, 1977, Plant Chemosystematics, 1984; assoc. editor: Southwestern Naturalist, 1959—. Served to 1st lt. USAAF, 1943-47. NSF postdoctoral fellow U. Liverpool, 1965-66. Mem. Bot. Soc. Am. (sec. 1958-59, 60-64, v.p. 1969), Tex. Acad. Sci., Southwestern Assn. Naturalists (pres. 1967, gov.), Am. Soc. Plant Taxonomists (Asa Gray award 1991), Internat. Assn. Plant Taxonomists, Soc. Study Evolution, Phi Beta Kappa, Sigma Xi. Office: U Tex Plant Resources Ctr Main Bldg 228 Austin TX 78712

TURNER, BILLIE LEE, II, geography educator; b. Texas City, Tex., Dec. 22, 1945; s. Billie Lee and Virginia Ruth (Mathis) T.; m. Linda Lee Van Zandt, June 6, 1968; children: Billie Lee III, Victoria Kelly. BA in Geography, U. Tex., 1968, MA in Geography, 1969; PhD, U. Wis., Madison, 1974. Asst. prof. geography U. Md., Catonsville, 1974-76, U. Okla., Norman, 1976-79, Clark U., Worcester, Mass., 1980-81, assoc. prof., 1981-85, prof., 1985—, dir. grad. sch. geography, 1983-88, 97-98; dir. George Perkins Marsh Inst., 1991-97. The Higgins prof. environment and soc., 1996—. Author: Once Beneath the Forest, 1983; author: (with T.M. Whitmore) Cultivated Landscapes of Native Middle America on the Eve of Conquest, 2001; author: (with W. Steffen et al.) Global Change and the Earth System: A Planet Under Pressure, 2004; editor: Pre-Hispanic Maya Agriculture, 1978, Pulltrouser Swamp, 1983, Comparative Farming Systems, 1987, The Earth as Transformed by Human Action, 1990, Population Growth and Agriculture of Change in Africa, 1993, Changes in Land Use and Land Cover: A Perspective from the Columbian Encounter, 1995, Regions at Risk: Comparisons of Threatened Environments, 1995, Integrated Land-Change Science and Tropical Deforestation in Southern Yucatan: Final Frontiers, 2004; contbr. articles to profl. publs. Served with U.S. Army, 1969—71. Rsch. grantee NSF, 1978-82, 84-85, 89-90, 93-96, Nat. Geog. Soc., 1984-85, NEH, 1987-89, A.W. Mellon, 1987-90, Rockefeller Bros., 1988, NASA, 1992-94, 97—, SSRC, 1993, Centenary medal Royal Scottish Geog. Soc., 1996; Guggenheim fellow, 1981-82; sr. fellow Green Ctr. for Sci. and Soc., 1994; fellow Ctr. for Advanced Studies in the Behavioral Scis., 1994-95. Fellow AAAS; mem. NAS, Am. Acad. Arts and Scis., Assn. Am. Geographers (rsch. honors 1995), Soc. Am. Archeology. Home: 19 Farnum St Worcester MA 01602-2101 Office: Grad Sch Geography Clark U Worcester MA 01610 Office Phone: 508-793-7325. Business E-Mail: bturner@clarku.edu.

TURNER, BRACHA, Naive Landscape painter; b. Jerusalem; Exhbns. include 55 solo exhbns. and numerous juried exhbns.: J.F. Kennedy Art Gallery, Montreal, New Eng. Fine Arts Inst., Boston, Internat. Women in the Arts Conf., Beijing; permanent display of paintings include Hadassah Hdqtrs., N.Y., ZOA House, Tel-Aviv, Nat. Coun. of Jewish Women, N.Y., Ichilov Hosp., Tel-Aviv, Office of the Mayor of Jerusalem, Israel, The Bible Mus. Tel Aviv, Office of the Mayor N.Y.C., Rambam Hosp., Haifa, Israel, others; painting reproduced on cards by Hadassah; contbr. drawings to Sara's Daughters Sing, 1989.

TURNER, BRENDA GALE, librarian, educator; d. Fred Owen White and Ruth Ann Dillon-White; m. David Presnell Turner, Aug. 31, 1984. AA in Secretarial Sci., Ohio Valley Coll., 1977, AA, 1978; BS, U. Rio Grande, 1986; MLS, Ind. U., 1988; postgrad., Fla. State U., 2001. Circulation libr., tng. coord. Purdue U. Libraries, West Lafayette, Ind., 1988—91; pub. services libr. Lexington C.C., Ky., 1991—93; dir. librs. Faulkner U., Montgomery, Ala., 1993— . Author: (scholarly work) Outsourcing: The In Thing (Alabma Libr. Associations Blackwell North America's Rsch. Promise award, 2001). Mem. Perry Hill Rd. Ch. of Christ, Montgomery, 1993. Mem.: ALA, Ala. Assn. Coll. and Rsch. Librs. (pub. rels. officer 1999—2001), Christian Coll. Librs. (pres. 2002—04), Ala. Libr. Assn. (pub. rels. officer 2001—02). Conservative. Avocations: travel, exercise, cooking. Office Phone: 334-386-7299.

TURNER, BRENDA KAYE, state legislator; b. Oak Ridge, Mar. 14, 1948; d. James Bookie and Virginia (Sivley) T. BA, U. Tenn., Chattanooga, 1974; MA, U. Ala., Tuscaloosa, 1977. Asst. to clk. Ala. Ho. of Reps., Montgomery; pub. info. specialist Tuscaloosa Park and Recreation Authority; resource tchr. spl. edn. Catoosa County, Ga.; mem. Tenn. Ho. of Reps., Nashville. Mem. AAUW, Epilepsy Found., Chattanooga C. of C. Address: 3425 Audubon Dr Chattanooga TN 37411-4402

TURNER, BRIAN ALLEN, sport management director, educator; b. Waco, Tex., Oct. 6, 1965; m. Gretchen Marie Treptow, June 1, 1996; 1 child, Briana Marie. BS in Edn., Baylor U., Waco, Tex., 1988; MEd, Tarleton State U., Stephenville, Tex., 1997; PhD, The Ohio State U., Columbus, 2001. Lic. secondary phys. edn. tchr. Tex. Edn. Agy., 1988, secondary computer sci. tchr. Tex. Edn. Agy., 1988, secondary maths. tchr. Tex. Edn. Agy., 1991. Tchr., coach Waco (Tex.) Ind. Sch. Dist., 1988—98; grad. tchg. asst. The Ohio State U., Columbus, Ohio, 1998—2000; asst. prof., dir. sport mgmt. DeSales U., Center Valley, Pa., 2001—. Math. Curriculum Fellow, Tex. Assn. Supervision Curriculum, 1991, Delbert Oberteuffer scholarship, Coll. of Edn. at The Ohio State U., 2000. Mem.: North Am. Soc. Sport Mgmt., Phi Kappa Phi. Home: 3162 Watermill Dr Macungie PA 18062 Office: DeSales U 2755 Station Ave Center Valley PA 18034 Personal E-mail: brian.turner@desales.edu.

TURNER, BRUCE EDWARD, lawyer; b. Wichita Falls, Tex., Oct. 31, 1947; s. Charles William and Marie Jeanne (Masson) T.; m. Barbara Lu Oakes, Oct. 8, 1982; children: Gradie, Anna Marie, Kelly. BA, Tex. Tech U., 1970, JD, 1973; LLM, NYU, 1974. Bar: Tex. 1974, U.S. Dist. Ct. (so. dist.) Tex. 1975, U.S. Tax Ct. 1975, U.S. Ct. Appeals (8th cir.) 1979, U.S. Dist. Ct. (no. dist.) Tex. 1988; bd. cert. comml. real estate. Assoc. Dillingham, Schleider & Marquelette, Houston, 1974-76, Johnston & Feather, Dallas, 1976-80; tax counsel Atlantic Richfield Co., Dallas, 1980-81; corp. counsel Lehndorff, Dallas, 1981—; owner Turner & Assocs., Dallas, 1983—. Spkr., contbg. writer Advanced Real Estate Seminar, 1994. Mem. Tex. Bar Assn., Dallas Bar Assn., ICC Practitioners. Clubs: Downtown Mens (Dallas). Republican. Methodist. Home: 3708 Southwestern Blvd Dallas TX 75225-7220 Office: Ste 1150 4120 International Pkwy Carrollton TX 75007-1959

TURNER, CAL, JR., discount stores executive; married. BA cum laude, Vanderbilt U., 1962. With Dollar Gen. Corp., Scottsville, Ky., 1965—, v.p., 1966-67, exec. v.p., 1967-77, pres., 1977-88, chief exec. officer, 1988—2002, chmn., 1989—, also bd. dirs. Bd. dirs. First Am. Nat. Bank, Nashville, Thomas Nelson Pub. Co., Ky. Coun. on Econ. Edn. Trustee Lindsey Wilson Coll., Columbia, Ky.; chmn., Canderbilt U. Med. Ctr., NAshville; mem. adv. bd. Easter Seal Soc. of Tenn., Inc.; chmn. United Way Mid. Tenn. Literacy Task Force, 1989-90; chmn. bd. dirs. Nashville Read, chief exec. officer forum bd. Mem. Nashville Area C. of C. (bd. dirs.), NCCJ (bd. dirs.). Office: Dollar Gen Corp 104 Woodmont Blvd Ste 500 Nashville TN 37205-2285

TURNER, CARLTON EDGAR, pharmacist, presidential advisor; b. Choctaw County, Ala., Sept. 13, 1940; s. Edgar and Opel Estelle (Emmons) Turner Kelly; m. Mary Ann DuPuy, June 24, 1973; children: Anne Marie, Catherine Elizabeth. BS, U. So. Miss., 1966, MS in Chemistry, 1969, PhD in Chemistry, 1970; postdoctoral in Pharmacy, U. Miss., 1971. Dir. Marijuana Rsch. Project U. Miss., Oxford, 1971-81, assoc. dir. Rsch. Inst., 1972-80, dir. Rsch. Inst., 1980-81; dir. White House Drug Abuse Policy, Washington, 1981-83, spl. asst. to Pres. for drug abuse policy, 1983-87; exec. v.p. scientific affairs Carrington Labs., Inc., Irving, Tex., 1994—, COO, 1994—, pres. & CEO. Cons. UN Narcotics Lab., Geneva, 1974-81, Lemery Pharms., Mexico City, 1977-81 Author over 100 sci. papers, publs., books; patentee in field. Mem. Peoples Republic of China Med. Exchange Tour, 1979. Served in AUS, 1958-61. Armstrong lectr. Aerospace Med. Assn., 1982; recipient Parent Resources Inst. Drug Edn. award, 1982, Nat. Fedn. Parents for Drug Free Youth award, 1983, Internat. Pres. award Lions Club, 1983 Mem. Am. Soc. Pharmacognosy, Am. Council Marijuana (sci. advisor), Sigma Xi, Kappa Psi, Rho Chi Lodges: Lions. Republican. Methodist. Office: Carrington Labs Inc PO Box 168128 Irving TX 75016-8128

TURNER, CHRISTOPHER EDWARD, cell biology educator; b. Birmingham, Eng., Sept. 17, 1961; came to U.S., 1987; s. Frank and Brenda Turner; m. Susan Benoit, Sept. 2, 1989. BSc, Sheffield (Eng.) U., 1983; DPhil, Oxford (Eng.) U., 1986. Postdoctoral fellow U. N.C., Chapel Hill, 1987-91; asst. prof. cell biology SUNY Health Sci. Ctr., Syracuse, 1991—. Contbr. articles to Jour. Cell Biology, Jour. Cell Sci., Jour. Biol. Chemistry. Rsch. grantee NIH, 1991—, Muscular Dystrophy Assn., 1992—; established investigator Am. Heart Assn., 1995-2000. Mem. AAAS, Am. Soc. for Cell Biology, Brit. Soc. for Cell Biology. Avocations: hiking, biking, golf. Office: SUNY Health Sci Ctr Dept Anatomy/Cell Biology 750 E Adams St Syracuse NY 13210-1834

TURNER, DAVID G. information technology executive; married; 1 child. B in Computer Sci. and Math., Del. State U., 1986; MS, Fairleigh Dickinson U.; exec. MBA program, Dartmouth Coll. Various sales and mktg. positions AT&T, 1986—2000; sr. v.p. sales and mktg. Gateway, Poway, Calif., 2000—. Named Small Bus. Adv. of Yr., U.S. Dept. Commerce Small Bus. Adminstrn., 1996; recipient Nat. Salute to Achievers in Industry award, YMCA, 1999, Cmty. Svc. award, Inst. for Student Achievement, 2000. Office: Gateway 14303 Gateway Pl Poway CA 92064

TURNER, DAVID LOWERY, system safety engineer; b. Atlanta, Feb. 2, 1936; s. Albert Olson and Ella May (Waldrop) Turner; m. Jeanette Smith, Mar. 25, 1962 (div. 1968); m. Sharon Kay Brewer, May 26, 1972 (div. 1978); m. Rita M. Robertson, Aug. 25, 1993 (div. 2001); children: Angela Kay, Jacqueline Kay. Student, Samford U., 1958-60, U. Ala., 1960-62, U. Houston, 1977-79; BS in Safety Engring., Kennedy-Western U., 1991. Registered profl. safety engr.; lic. claims adjuster, Tex., real estate agt., Tex. Safety engr. USF&G, Birmingham, Ala., 1963-69, Parker Bros. Co. Inc., Houston, 1969-80; safety dir. MGF Oil Corp./MGF Drilling Co., Houston, 1980-84; safety mgr. Creole Prodn. Svcs. Inc., Houston, 1985-86; safety div. mgr. Mason Chamberlain Inc., Stennis Space Center, Miss., 1986-91; sys. safety engr. Raytheon Engrs. and Constructors, A Raytheon Co., Johnston Island, 1991—2001, Washington Group Internat., 2001—. Cons. Fullbright and Jaworski Law Firm, Houston, 1980-81. Vol. West Meml. Vol. Fire Dept., Katy, Tex., 1979-80. With USAF, 1954-58. Mem. Am. Soc. Safety Engrs. (profl.), Nat. Safety Coun., Sys. Safety Soc., Tex. Safety Assn., Nat. Ready Mix Concrete Assn., Internat. Assn. Drilling Contractors, NASA Safety Coun., Gulf Coast Safety Coun., MCI Exec. Safety Coun. (co-chmn. 1986-91). Republican. Baptist. Avocations: hunting, fishing, golf, tennis, bowling. Office: Washington Group Internat Johnston Island Apo AP 96558 Home: PO Box 215 Daleville AL 36322 E-mail: dTurner@jacads.com.

TURNER, DAVID REUBEN, publisher, author; b. N.Y.C., Dec. 9, 1915; s. Charles and Eva (Turner) Moskowitz; m. Ann Louise Perkins, Apr. 29, 1946 (div. 1976); children— Eve (Mrs. William Watters), Ruth. BS, Coll. City N.Y., 1936, MS in Edn, 1937. Co-founder Arco Pub. Co., N.Y.C., 1937, pub., dir., 1937-78; v.p. parent co. Prentice-Hall, Inc., 1979-80; pres. Turner Pub., 1980-92. Pub. cons. under Ford Found. contract Burma Translation Soc., Rangoon, 1959-60 Author: more than 300 books on tests and testing, including High School Equivalency Diploma Tests, 1951, 75, How to Win a Scholarship, 1955, Scoring High On College Entrance Tests, 1969, 71, Food Service Supervisor, 1968, Bank Examiner, 1968, Accountant-Auditor, 1960, 77, Officer Candidate Tests, 1978, Professional-Administrative Career Exams, 1979, English Grammar and Usage for Test-Takers, 1976, College Level Examination Program, 1979. Adviser bd. publs. Union Am. Hebrew Congregations. Home and Office: 13 Glengary Rd Croton On Hudson NY 10520-2139

TURNER, DOUGLAS LAIRD, writer, editor, columnist; b. Buffalo, N.Y., Jan. 5, 1932; s. Henry Albert and Effie Donna (McIndoo) T.; m. Mary Joan Hassett, July 7, 1962; children: Christopher Henry, Mary Julia, Albert William. BA, Brown U., 1954; postgrad., Stanford U., 1968. Reporter Buffalo (N.Y.) Courier-Express, 1957-60, state capital corr., 1960-64, fin. editor, 1964, city editor, 1964-70, exec. editor, 1971-80, Washington bur. chief, 1981-82; Washington corr. Buffalo (N.Y.) Evening News, 1982, Washington columnist, 1983, Washington bur. chief, 1989—. Adj. asst. prof. journalism Canisius Coll., 1999, N.Y. State Commn. on Pub. Access to Records, 1976-81; founder, dir. Friends of Williamsburg Rowing Inc., 1993—. Mem. U.S. Olympic Rowing Team, 1956. With U.S. Army Counter Intelligence Corps, 1956-57. Nation champion four-oared shell with cox, 1956; winner Hanlan Trophy, Royal Can. Henley Regatta, 1956; recipient numerous awards Am. Newspaper Guild, N.Y. State Associated Press Assn., personal citations Erie County Legislature, N.Y. State Assembly, Buffalo Common Coun. Mem. Nat. Press Club (former gov. 1988), Potomac Boat Club, Gridiron Club (Wash.). Roman Catholic. Home: 7923 Saint George Ct Springfield VA 22153-2741 Office: Buffalo News Washington Bur 1141 National Press Building Washington DC 20045-2101

TURNER, E. DEANE, lawyer; b. Auburn, N.Y., Aug. 4, 1928; s. Alfred Edward and Bertha (Deane) T. AB summa cum laude, Princeton U., 1950; LLB cum laude, Harvard U., 1953. Bar: NY 1953. Assoc. Dewey Ballantine LLP and predecessor firms, N.Y.C., 1953-63, ptnr., 1963—, of counsel, 1991—. Treas. Harvard Law Sch. Assn., N.Y.C., 1964-83; elder, trustee Brick Presbyn. Ch., N.Y.C., 1976—, pres. bd. trustees, 1988-90; trustee Presbytery N.Y.C., 1993-98, pres. bd. trustees, 1995-98; com. to adminstr. James N. Jarvie Endowment, 1993-2000. Fellow Am. Coll. Investment Counsel (emeritus); mem. Soc. Mayflower Descendants, Soc. Colonial Wars, Union Club, John's Island Club, Phi Beta Kappa. Republican. Home: 1120 5th Ave New York NY 10128-0144 also: 381 Llwyds Ln Johns Island Vero Beach FL 32963 Office: Dewey Ballantine LLP 1301 Avenue Of The Americas New York NY 10019-6022

TURNER, ELAINE S. allergist, immunologist; b. Glen Cove, N.Y., 1947; MD, Med. Coll. Pa., 1974. Diplomate Am. Bd. Allergy & Immunology, Am. Bd. Internal Medicine. Intern Michael Reese Hosp., Chgo., 1974-75; resident in internal medicine Cleve. Clinic, 1976-78; fellow in allergy & immunology Northwestern U., Chgo., 1978-80; with St. Mary's Hosp., Va., Henrico Drs. Hosp., Va. Mem. ACP, Am. Acad. Allergy, Asthma and Immunology, Va. Allergy Soc., Richmond Acad. Medicine. Office: Va Adult & Pediat Allergy & Allergy Ste 103 7605 Forest Ave Richmond VA 23229-4936

TURNER, ELIZABETH ADAMS NOBLE (BETTY TURNER), real estate company executive; b. Yonkers, N.Y., May 18, 1931; d. James Kendrick and Orrel (Baldwin) Noble; m. Jack Rice Turner, July 11, 1953; children: Jay Kendrick, Randall Ray. BA, Vassar Coll., 1953; MA, Tex. A&I U., 1964. Ednl. cons., Tex. sales mgr. Noble & Noble Pub. Co., N.Y.C., 1956-67; psychometrist Corpus Christi Guidance Ctr., 1967-70; psychologist Corpus Christi State Sch., 1970-72, dir. programs, asst. supt., 1972, dir. devel. and vol. svc., 1972-76, dir. rsch. and tng., 1977-79; psychologist Tex. Mental Health and Mental Retardation, 1970-79, program cons., 1979-85; pres. Turner Co., 1975-82; mayor pro tem Corpus Christi, 1981-85; mayor, 1987-91; CEO, pres. Corpus Christi C. of C., 1991-94; pres. Betty Turner Real Estate, 1999—. V.p. bus. and govt. rels. ctrl. and south Tex. divsns. Columbia Healthcare Corp., 1994—99. Dir. alumni Corpus Christi State U., 1976-77; coord. vols. Summer Head Start Program, Corpus Christi, 1967; chmn. spl. gifts com. United Way, Corpus Christi, 1970; mem. Corpus Christi City Coun., 1979-91; family co-founded Barnes and Noble, N.Y.C.; founder Com. of 100 and Goals for Corpus Christi; pres. USO; bd. dirs. Coastal Bend Coun. Govts., Corpus Christi Mus., Harbor Playhouse, Cmtys. in Schs., YWCA, Y-Teen Sponsor, Del Mar Coll. Found., Tex. A&M at Corpus Christi Pres.' Coun., Food Bank, Hispanic C. of C., TAMACC Corp. Ptnrs., Salvation Army, Jr. League, Coun. Deaf Silent Found.; bd. Southside Cmty. Hosp., 1987-93, Gulfway Nat. Bank, 1985-92; strategic planning com. Meml. Hosp., 1992, Tex. Capital Network Bd., 1992-95, Humana Hosp., Physician Relocation and Condo Sales, Rehab. Hosp., dir. of vols., South Tex., Admiral Tex. Navy; bd. dirs. Pacific Southwest Bank, 1997-2000, St. David's/Austin and Medth. Healthcare Sys., San Antonio, 1997-99; apptd. Gov.'s Commn. for Women, 1984-85, Leadership Tex. Class I, Corpus Christi, Class II; founder Goals for Corpus Christi, Bay Area Sports Assn., Assn. Coastal Bend Mayor's Alliance; founder Mayor's Commn. on the Disabled, Mayor's Task Force on the Homeless; active Port Aransas Cmty. Ch., U. Tex. Sch. Nursing Adv. Coun., 1998-99; bd. dirs. Del Mar Coll. Found., 1998—, Am. Heart Assn., 1999-2000, Bethune Day Care Nursery, 1999—, Jr. League Cmty. Adv. Coun., 1999-2000, Strategic Planning Com., 2000—, Silent Found., 2001—, 21st Century Charter Sch., 2001-02, Boys and Girls Club of Corpus Christi, 2002—, Nat. AARP, 2002-04; pres.-elect Food Bank, 2002—; elder Cmty. Presbyn. Ch. Named Corpus Christi Newsmaker of Yr., 1987; recipient Love award, YWCA, 1970, Y's Women and Men in Careers award, 1988, Recognition award, Rotary, 1991, Comdr.'s award for pub. svc., U.S. Army, Scroll of Honor award, Navy League, award, Tex. Hwy Dept., Road Hand award, Tex. Hwy. Commn., Women of Distinction award, Girl Scouts Tex. Mem. NAACP (life), Tex. Psychol. Assn. (pres., mem. exec. bd.), Psychol. Assn. (pres., founder), Tex. Mcpl. League (bd. dirs.), Jr. League Corpus Christi, Tex. Bookman's Assn., Tex. Assn. Realtors, Corpus Christi Town Club, Corpus Christi Yacht Club, Jr. Cotillion Club, Kappa Kappa Gamma. Home: 403 Blue Heron Dr Port Aransas TX 78373 Office Phone: 361-877-1111. E-mail: bettytyrner@centurytel.net.

TURNER, ELVIN L. retired educational administrator; b. Springfield, Ohio, Jan. 9, 1938; s. Willie and Jinada (Lawson) T.; m. Betty Jo Breckinridge, June 11, 1966 (div. Jan. 1972); 1 child, Anthony; m. Carrie Johnson, Aug. 3, 1972; 1 child, Brenetta Bell. BS in Biology and Chemistry, Knoxville (Tenn.) Coll., 1962; MEd, U. Cin., 1968; postgrad., Nova U., Ft. Lauderdale, Fla., 1973, Kensington U., Glendale, Calif., 1993—. Cert. secondary prin., tchr., Ohio. Spl. edn. tchr. Cin. Pub. Schs., 1965-69, coord. spl. edn., 1969-72, asst. prin., 1972-78, prin., 1978-90, asst. prin., 1990-93. Part-time adj. prof. Mt. St. Joseph (Ohio) Coll., 1987—88; mem. adv. com. Millcreek Psychiat. Ctr. for Children, Cin., 1988—89; bus driver Bristol Village Retirement Cmty., 1997—99; ombudsman Pro-Srs., Cin., 1993—96, Waverly, Ohio, 1997—; vol. ombudsman rep. Area Agy. on Aging Dist. Seven, Inc., Portsmouth, Ohio; sec. Bristol Village Residents Assn., 1997. Vol. Ohio Dept Aging, Columbus, 2002—; asst. feeding program Visiting The Sick Ministries; master of ceremonies Black History Month Soul Food Luncheon; elected sec. exec. adv. coun. Bristol Village Nat. Ch. Residencies, Waverly, 1997; mem. bd. deacons New Hope Bapt. Ch., Hamilton, Ohio, 1993; Sunday sch. tchr. Bethel AME Ch., Lebanon, Ohio, 1996; active Pilgrim Missionary Bapt. Ch., Columbus, Ohio, 2000—; chmn. sick com. Usher Bd.; mem. Templeaire Choir; Bible study course instr. Asbury North United Meth. Ch., Columbus, 2000—01, instr. Vacation Bible Sch., 2000; bd. dirs. Big Bros./Big Sisters, Cin., 1973. Recipient plaques and grants, including plaque for statewide outstanding sr. vol. radio, TV and newspaper coverage, Independence, Ohio, 2001. Mem. Nat. Assn. for Secondary Sch. Prins., Prins. Assn. Secondary Sch. Adminstrs., Knoxville Coll. Alumni Assn., Phi Delta Kappa, Alpha Phi Alpha. Avocations: bowling, golf, reading, travel. Home: PO Box 13617 Columbus OH 43213-0617 Office: 923 Findlay St Portsmouth OH 45662

TURNER, EUGENE ANDREW, manufacturing executive; b. Bridgeton, N.J., Aug. 7, 1928; s. Benjamin Homer and Pearl Irene (Wolbert) T.; m. Paula Ann Webb, 1987; children: Mary Ann, John-Reed. BA, Rutgers U., 1956; student, Columbia U., 1980. With Owens Ill., 1950-73, regional mgr. West Coast, 1970-73; v.p. adminstrn. Midland Glass Co., Cliffwood, N.J., 1973-76, pres., chief operating officer, 1981-82, also bd. dirs.; v.p., gen. mgr. Anchor Hocking Corp., Lancaster, Ohio, 1976-81; dir. ops. Theo Chem. Labs., Tampa, Fla., 1988-90, Profit Counselors Inc, Sarasota, Fla., 1990-94; pres. Profit Sys. Inc., Oklahoma City, 1994—. Mng. cons. 1987-88; trustee Glass Packaging Inst. Mem. Harbor Island Club, Seaview Country Club, Navesink Country Club. Home: 1103 Tedford Way Oklahoma City OK 73116-6006 Office Phone: 405-209-1103. Personal E-mail: gene227@juno.com. *Take time to learn the chosen business then develop credibility by doing what you say you will do.*

TURNER, EVAN HOPKINS, retired art museum director; b. Orono, Maine, Nov. 8, 1927; s. Albert Morton and Percie Trowbridge (Hopkins) T.; m. Brenda Winthrop Bowman, May 12, 1956; children: John, Jennifer. AB cum laude, Harvard U., 1949, MA, 1950, PhD, 1954; hon. degree, Swarthmore Coll., Sir George Williams U., Cleve. State U.; Case Western Res. U., 2001. Head docent svc. Fogg Mus., Cambridge, Mass., 1950-51; curator Robbins Art Collection of Prints, Arlington, Mass., 1951; teaching fellow fine arts Harvard U., 1951-52; lectr., research asst. Frick Collection, N.Y.C., 1953-56; gen. curator, asst. dir. Wadsworth Atheneum, Hartford, Conn., 1956-59; dir. Montreal Mus. Fine Arts, Que., Can., 1959-64, Phila. Mus. Art, 1964-77, Ackland Art Mus., 1978-83, Cleve. Mus. Art, 1983-93. Adj. prof. art history U. Pa., U. N.C., Chapel Hill, 1978-83; disting. vis. prof. Oberlin Coll., 1993-95. Author: Ray K. Metzker: Photographs, 2001. Recipient Chevalier L'Ordre Arts Lettres. Mem. Assn. Art Mus. Dirs., Coll. Art Assn. Am., Am. Mus. Assn., Century Assn. Club. Home: 2125 Cypress St Philadelphia PA 19103-6507

TURNER, FLORENCE FRANCES, ceramist; b. Detroit, Mar. 9, 1926; d. Paul Pokrywka and Catherine Gagal; m. Dwight Robert Turner, Oct. 23, 1948; children: Thomas Michael, Nancy Louise, Richard Scott, Garry Robert. Student, Oakland C.C., Royal Oak, Mich., 1975-85, U. Ariz., Yuma, 1985, U. Las Vegas, 1989—. Pres., founder Nev. Clay Guild, Henderson, 1990-94, mem. adv. bd., 1994-2000, v.p., 2000—02. Workshop leader Greenfield Village, Dearborn, Mich., 1977-78, Plymouth (Mich.) Hist. Soc., 1979, Las Vegas Sch. System, 1989-90, Detroit Met. area, 1977-85. Bd. dirs. Las Vegas Art Mus., 1987-91; corr. sec. So. Nev. Creative Art Ctr., Las Vegas, 1990-94. Mem.: Nev. Camera Club, Las Vegas Gem Club, So. Nev. Rock Art Enthusiasts, Phi Kappa Phi. Avocations: photography, collecting gems, travel.

TURNER, FRED, JR., soil scientist, consultant; b. Paris Crossing, Ind., Jan. 13, 1920; s. Fred and Laura Evangeline (Click) T.; m. Marilyn Carr Cantelou, July 24, 1942 (dec. 1975); 1 child, Fred Lynwood; m. Lillian Irene Clark, Dec. 31, 1975 (dec. 1996); m. Gloria E. Lopez, Feb. 10, 1998; 1 child, Venny Jean. BS, U. Ariz., 1948; MS, Washington State U., 1951; PhD, Mich. State U., 1958. Cert. profl. in agronomy, crops and soils Am. Registry of Cert. Profls. Soil scientist USDA, Mandan, N.D., 1953-54; from asst. prof. soil sci. to emeritus U. Ariz., Tucson, 1957-83, emeritus soil scientist, 1983—. Adv. USAID and U. Ariz., Fortaleza, Brazil, 1966-68; specialist USAID World Bank, Yemen, Arab Rep., 1979, 81; head agrl. dept. Sutanate of Oman, 1983-85; prof., head dept. soils and water Sultan Qaboos U., Muscat, Oman, 1988-94. Contbr. articles to profl. jours. Pres. Copper Coun. Boy Scouts Am., Safford, Ariz., 1976-78, Rotary Club, Safford, 1978; chmn. Am. Red Cross, Safford, 1968-80. Col. USAF, 1940-46 (Asiatic-Pacific), 51-54, Korea. Recipient Appreciation award U. Ariz. Alumni Assn., 1966, Pub. Svc. award Nat. Weather Svc., Washington, 1976, Silver Beaver award Boy Scouts Am., Phoenix, 1976. Mem. Internat. Soc. Soil Sci., Am. Soc. Agonomy, Soil Sci. Am., Sigma Xi. Republican. Methodist. Avocations: photography, golf, fishing. Home and Office: #509 3045 Alanapuaa Pl Honolulu HI 96818-2792 E-mail: fredngloria@hotmail.com.

TURNER, FRED L. retired fast food company executive; b. 1933; married. BS, Drake U., 1954. With McDonald's Corp., Oak Brook, Ill., 1956—2004, exec. v.p., 1967—68, pres., chief adminstrv. officer, 1968—73, CEO, 1973—87, chmn., 1977—90, sr. chmn., 1990—2004. Bd. dirs. Baxter Internat. Inc. With U.S. Army, 1954-56. Office: McDonald's Corp One Kroc Dr Oak Brook IL 60523

TURNER, FREDERICK CLAIR, JR., education educator; b. Cambridge, Mass., Apr. 4, 1961; s. Frederick Clair Turner and Caroline Nielsen; m. Anne Whitmore Fischer, June 3, 1990; 1 child, Althea Whitmore. BA, Brown Univ., Providence, R.I., 1984; MA, Columbia Univ., N.Y., 1985; PhD, Univ. Calif., San Diego, Calif., 2002. Freelance journalist, Boston, 1986—96; lectr. Mass. Inst. Tech., Cambridge, Mass., 1999—2002; asst. prof. Stanford Univ., Stanford, Calif., 2003—. Author: Echoes of Combat, 1996. Mem.: Soc. for the Social Studies of Sci., Nat. Book Critics Cir., Internat. Comm. Assoc. Office: Dept Comm Stanford Univ Bldg 120 Stanford CA 94305

TURNER, GEORGE MASON, lawyer; b. Butte, Mont., Sept. 2, 1935; s. William Dale and Bernice (Ownby) T.; m. Angela Gloria Aparicio, Oct. 14, 1995; children: Esther, Lesley, Allyson, Aaron, Alexander. BS in Polit. Sci., Brigham Young U., 1959, MS in Polit. Sci., 1960; JD, UCLA, 1968. Bar: Calif. 1969, U.S. Dist. Ct. Calif. 1969, U.S. Supreme Ct. 1976, U.S. Ct. Claims 1981, U.S. Tax Ct. 1981. Assoc. Munns & Kofford, Pasadena, Calif., 1969-72; ptnr. Turner & Smart, Pasadena, 1972-85, The Law Offices of George M. Turner, Pasadena, 1985—; pvt. practice, 1972—. Instr. estate tax law Am. Coll. Bryn Mawr, Pa., 1976; monitor Continuing Edn. of Bar, Calif., 1985. Author: Revocable Trusts, 5th edit., 2003, Irrevocable Trusts, 3d edit., 1997, Revocable Trusts-The Centerpiece of Estate Planning, 1998. V.p. San Gabriel Valley Boy Scouts Am., Pasadena, 1976-78; pres. San Gabriel Valley Estate Planning Co., Pasadena, 1979-80; bd. dirs., chmn. bd. Calif. Family Study Ctr., North Hollywood, 1975-92, Ettie Lee Homes, Los Angeles, 1984-90. Recipient Silver Beaver award Boy Scout Am., 1979. Mem. ABA, Calif. Bar Assn., Los Angeles Bar Assn., Pi Sigma Alpha. Republican. Mem. Lds Ch. Avocation: photography. Office Phone: 626-795-8491. E-mail: turnerlaw@attglobal.net.

TURNER, GEORGE PEARCE, consulting company executive; b. Dallas, Aug. 22, 1915; s. Fred Horatio and Florence (Phillips) T.; m. June Lori Haney, Feb. 4, 1943 (div. 1976); children: Bruce Haney, Brian Phillips, Mark Richardson; m. Kathryn Blank Hauf, June 1976. Student, U. Tex., 1932-33, 35-36, 40-41, So. Methodist U., 1934; BA in Internat. Rels. cum laude, U. So. Calif., 1962, MS in Internat. Pub. Adminstrn. summa cum laude, 1966; PhD in Econs. and Internat. Rels., Columbia Pacific U., 1982, PhD in Pub. Adminstrn. and Internat. Rels., 1985. Archtl. designer, L.A., 1946-48; prin. Lieburg & Turner (cons. engrs.), Pasadena, Calif., 1947-48; pres. Radiant Heat Engring., Inc., Pasadena, 1948-53; exec. asst. to dir. fgn. subsidiaries S.Am. Fluor Corp. Ltd., L.A., 1953-54; mem. exec. staff Coast Fed. Savs. & Loan Assn., 1954-55; exec. staff Holmes & Narver, Inc., L.A., 1955-61; mgr. project devel. S.Am. ops. Southwestern Engrng. Co., L.A., 1962; pres. Haney Devel. Corp., 1964-90, Fomento e Inversiones Quisqueyanos C. por A., Santo Domingo de Guzman, Dominican Republic, 1967-98; gen. mgr. for Venezuelan ops. Hale Internat. Inc., Caracas, 1970-71; dir., mgr. Consortium Lomas de La Lagunita, Caracas, 1970, Consortium Desarrollos Urbanos, Valencia, Venezuela, 1970; pres. Haney Investment Corp. (HANCO), 1974-90, Casa FOMIQ, 1978-98, Caribbean Vagabond Ltd., Grand Cayman Island, B.W.I., 1981-90, Kay Pearce & Turner, Ltd., Newtown Square, Pa., 1981-98; sec. Integrated Industries of Atlantic County, N.J.; gen. ptnr. N.Y. Ave. Parking Assocs., Atlantic City, 1980-91. Adviser, provisional pres., Dominican Republic, 1965-66, constl. pres. of republic, 1966-68; projects programmer Nat. Planning Inst. Peru Tri-Partite Mission, 1962-65; ofcl. OAS adviser Nat. Office Tourism Dominican Republic, 1966-67, Nat. Office Cultural Patrimony, Liga Mcpl. Dominicana, 1967-68; cons., dir. projects, programming, tech. matters Mission Recovery and Rehab., Dominican Republic, 1965-67; dep. dir. Tech. Assistance Mission Dominican Republic, 1967-68; cons. assignments for program assistance Inter-Am. Tng. Ctr., Fed. U. Ceara, Brazil; OAS adviser on tech. assistance to Chile, Argentina, Uruguay, Peru, Brazil, 1962-68; cons. Wildwood Ocean Towers, N.J., 1969-70, Capital Investment Devel. Corp., Downing Ctr., Downingtown, Pa., 1971-77; dir. for Project Monitor and owners agt., hosp. tower Hahnemann Med. U. and Hosp., Phila., 1975-78; pres. Urban Planning and Devel. Corp., Exton, Pa., 1978-79; cons., corp. sec., v.p. Constrn. Devel. and Properties Mgmt. Group, Integrated Industries Inc., Exton, 1978-80; ltd. ptnr. Marsh Creek Assocs. Two, 1985-98; apptd. to faculty Columbia Pacific U., 1987; cons. internat. consortium for multi-billion dollar econ. devel. program with projects in countries of Pacific Rim and Ea. Europe, 1993-95; established Casa FOMIQ awards program, 1995. Author: An Analysis of the Economy of El Salvador, 1961, The Alliance for Progress: Concept Versus Structure, 1966, Some Observations on the Decade of the 1960s - U.S. vis-a-vis Latin America, 1982, Latin American Odyssey, 1985, Third Generation, 1990, Growing Up Male in America: With the Prince Charming Mystique, 1993; pub., editor Fountain of Age, The Jour. of Casa FOMIQ, 1995; contbr. articles to profl. publs., including Archtl. Record, S.W. Builder and Contractor, House & Garden, Wood, Artistic Homes, Perfect Home mag., Ranch and Modern Homes. With USAF, 1941-45. Decorated OAS Medal of Honor; recipient Citation for Valiant Svc. in Dominican Republic, 1965-66, Ofcl. OAS Commendation for Program Contbns., Peru, Dominican Republic, Brazil, Venezuela, 1969. Mem. Delta Phi Epsilon, Alpha Sigma Lambda. Home and Office: PO Box 997 Truckee CA 96160 Office Phone: 530-587-4928.

TURNER, HARRY EDWARD, lawyer; b. Mt. Vernon, Ohio, Dec. 25, 1927; s. Paul Hamilton and Harriett (Krafft) T.; m. Shirley Marilyn Eggert, July 8, 1950; children: Harry Edward, Thomas Frederick (dec. Mar. 1995). BA, Baldwin Wallace Coll., 1951; JD, Ohio No. U., 1954. Bar: Ohio 1954, U.S. Supreme Ct. 1966. Practice in Mt. Vernon, 1954—; state rep. Ohio Gen. Assembly, 1973-85; solicitor Mt. Vernon, 1958-62. Prosecutor Mt. Vernon Municipal Ct., 1955-58 Mem. Mt. Vernon City Sch. Bd., 1964-70, pres., 1965-70; trustee Ohio Sch. Bd. Assn., 1968-70, Hannah Browning Home, 1987-2001, Sta. Break/Commn. on Planning Svcs., 1989-95; mem. Knox County Pub. Defender Commn., 1987-91. With USN, 1946-47. Mem. Ohio State Bar Assn., Knox County Bar Assn. (pres. 1970), Alpha Sigma Phi, Sigma Delta Kappa. Republican. Lutheran. Home: 1575 Yauger Rd Apt 15 Mount Vernon OH 43050-8299 Office: 118 E High St Mount Vernon OH 43050-3443

TURNER, HARRY WOODRUFF, lawyer; b. Blairsville, Pa., May 2, 1939; s. James McKinnie and Dorothy Elizabeth (Tittle) Turner; m. Mary Elizabeth Phelan, Dec. 30, 1972; children: James William, David Woodruff. AB, U. Pitts., 1961; JD, Harvard U., 1964. Bar: Pa. 1965, U.S. Supreme Ct. 1979. Assoc. Kirkpatrick & Lockhart, LLP, Pitts., 1964-71; ptnr. Kirkpatrick & Lockhart, Pitts., 1971—. Bd. vis. Coll. Arts & Scis. U. Pitts., 1988—2003, chair bd. vis. Sch. Info. Scis., 1994—2002, trustee, 1995—2003, bd. vis. Med. Sch., 1995—2002; mem. Fed. Jud. Selection Comm., Pa., 1995—, chair, Pa., 1997—. Trustee Pitts. Opera, 1993—, pres., 2001—; trustee, v.p. Torrance (Pa.) State Hosp., 1969—73; chair distbn. com. William L. Benz Found., 1985—; bd. dirs. Am. Heart Assn., Pitts., 1993—2002; alt. del. Rep. Nat. Conv., Miami, 1968, Houston, 1992, Phila., 2000, Rep. State Com., 1996—; trustee U. Pitts., 1995—2003, Wilson Coll., Chambersburg, Pa., 1978—89, Pitts. Cultural Trust, 2002—. Mem.: SAR (pres. 1995—96), ABA, Allegheny County Acad. Trial Lawyers, Allegheny County Bar Assn., Internat. Acad. Trial Lawyers, Am. Law Inst., Pa. Bar Assn., U. Pitts. Alumni Assn. (pres. 1991—92), Duquesne Club, Fox Chapel Golf Club. Presbyterian. Office: Kirkpatrick & Lockhart 1500 Oliver Building Pittsburgh PA 15222-2312 Office Phone: 412-355-6478. Business E-Mail: wturner@kl.com.

TURNER, HENRY BROWN, finance executive; b. N.Y.C., Sept. 3, 1936; s. Henry Brown III and Gertrude (Adams) T.; m. Sarah Jean Thomas, June 7, 1958 (div.); children: Laura Eleanor, Steven Bristow, Nancy Carolyn. AB, Duke U., 1958; MBA, Harvard U., 1962. Controller Fin. Corp. of Ariz., Phoenix, 1962-64; treas., dir. corporate planning Star-Kist Foods, Terminal Island, Calif., 1964-67; dir., 1st v.p. Mitchum, Jones & Templeton, Los Angeles, 1967-73; asst. sec. Dept. Commerce, Washington, 1973-74; v.p. fin. N-Ren Corp., Cin., 1975-76; v.p. Oppenheimer & Co., N.Y.C., 1976-78; exec. v.p., mng. dir. corporate fin. Shearson Hayden Stone Inc., N.Y.C., 1978-79; sr. mng. dir. Ardshiel Inc., 1980-81, pres., 1981-93, chmn. emeritus, 1994—. Vis. lectr. U. Va. Sch. of Bus.; bd. dirs. MacDonald & Co., Pembrook Mgmt., Inc., Golden State Vintners, Inc., Cellu-Tissue Corp., Wrangler Four Peaks Ranch, Rio Verde, Ariz. Sponsor Jr. Achievement, 1964-67. Served to lt. USNR, 1958-60. Coll. Men's Club scholar Westfield, N.J., 1954-55 Mem. Fed. Govt. Accountants Assn. (hon.), Duke Washington Club, Omicron Delta Kappa.

TURNER, HUGH JOSEPH, JR., lawyer; b. Paterson, NJ, Oct. 5, 1945; s. Hugh Joseph and Louise (Sullivan) T.; m. Charlene Chiappetta, Feb. 11, 1983. BS, Boston U., 1967; JD, U. Miami, Coral Gables, Fla., 1975. Bar: Fla. 1975, U.S. Dist. Ct. (so., no. and mid. dists.) Fla. 1975, U.S. Ct. Appeals (11th cir.) 1981, U.S. Supreme Ct. 1984. Tchr. Browne & Nichols, Cambridge, Mass., 1968-72; ptnr. Smathers & Thompson, Miami, Fla., 1981-87, Kelley Drye & Warren, Miami, 1987-93, English, McCaughan & O'Bryan, Ft. Lauderdale, 1993—2001, Redgrave & Turner LLP, Boca Raton, Fla., 2001—03, Akerman Senterfitt, Ft. Lauderdale, 2003—. Chmn. Fla. Bar internat. law sect., 1988-89. Contbg. author book on internat. dispute resolution Fla. Bar, 1989; contbr. articles to profl. jours. Bd. dirs. Japan Soc. South Fla., Miami, 1989-97; mem. Sea Ranch Lakes Village Coun., 1997-2000; mayor Sea Ranch Lakes, 2000-02. Mem.: ABA, Def. Rsch. Inst. Avocation: running. Office: Akerman Senterfitt Ste 1600 350 E Las Olas Blvd Fort Lauderdale FL 33301-2229 Office Phone: 954-463-2700. Business E-Mail: hturner@akerman.com.

TURNER, I. BRUCE, archivist; b. Monmouth, Ill., July 4, 1946; s. Lynn W. and Vera A. Turner; m. Sue Ann Steck, June 14, 1980; children: Jessica L., Kristen M., Kathryn E. BA, Otterbein Coll., 1967; MA, U. Ill., 1968, PhD, 1977; MSLS, U. Ky., 1977. Cert. Acad. of Cert. Archivists. Head spl. collections SUNY, Oswego, NY, 1977—82; head of archives and spl. collections U. La., Lafayette, 1983—. Co-author: (book) Jefferson Davis Parish: An Oral History, 2000; co-editor: Guide to Manuscript Repositories in La., 1998. Mem. La. State Hist. Records Adv. Bd., 1998—. Recipient Friends of the Edith Garland Dupre' Libr. Endowed Prof. of Libr. Sci. award, U. of La., Lafayette, 1998—. Mem.: La. Hist. Assn., La. Archives and Manuscripts Assn. (pres. 1993—94), Soc. SW Archivists (pres. 2000—01), Soc. Am. Archivists (chmn. archival history roundtable 1995—2000, chmn. acquisitions and appraisal sect. 1986—87, 2000—01), Beta Phi Mu, Phi Alpha Theta. Presbyterian. Home: 100 Normandy Rd Lafayette LA 70503 Office: U Louisiana at Lafayette PO Box 40199 Lafayette LA 70504 E-mail: bturner@louisiana.edu.

TURNER, JACKSON PARKS, financial company executive; b. Oct. 28, 1924; Pres. Cabin Crafts, Inc., Dalton, Ga., 1946-70; chmn. bd. First Nat. Bank, Dalton, 1970-80, Ga. Ports Authority, Savannah, 1976-86, CC Fin., Inc., Dalton, 1975—, Alliance Nat. Bank, Dalton, 1999—. Office: 210-214 W Morris St PO Box 607 Dalton GA 30722-0607

TURNER, JAMES, congressman; b. Feb. 6, 1946; m. Ginny; 2 children. BBA, U. Tex., 1968, MBA, JD, U. Tex., 1971. Lawyer; state govt. official; mem. 105-108th Congresses from 2nd Tex. dist., 1997—; mem. govt. oversight com.; former mem. nat. security com.; ranking mem. House Select Com. on Homeland Security. Mem. Econ. Growth, Natural Resources, and Regulatory Affairs subcom., Nat. Security, Internat. Affairs, and Criminal Justice subcom. House Govt. Reform and Oversight Com., Mil. Rsch. and Devel. subcom., Mil. Procurement subcom. House Nat. Security Com. Democrat. Baptist. Office: Ho of Reps 330 Cannon Hob Washington DC 20515-4302 also: Rm 201 701 N 1st St Ste 201 Lufkin TX 75901-2804 Fax: 409-632-8588; 202-225-2401. E-mail: tx02wyr@mail.house.gov.

TURNER, JAMES A. architecture educator; BS, U. Mich., 1971, MArch, 1973. Tchg. asst. U. Mich. Sch. Arch., Ann Arbor, 1971—73, instr., 1976—79, asst. prof., 1979—85, assoc. prof., 1985—92; prof. arch. U. Mich. Taubman Coll. Arch. and Urban Planning, Ann Arbor, 1992—, assoc. chair arch., 1992—; assoc. rsch. scientist U. Mich. Sch. Arch., Ann Arbor, 1985—92; mem. computer policy com. U. Mich. Coll. Arch. and Urban Planning. Author: Architectural Acoustic Teaching Software, 1997. Mem.: Assn. Computer-Aided Design in Arch. Office: Univ Mich Taubman Coll Arch and Urban Planning 2000 Bonisteel Blvd Ann Arbor MI 48109-2069*

TURNER, JAMES LEE, lawyer; b. Muncie, Ind., Aug. 20, 1959; s. Jack Edwin and Nancy Kathleen (Marvin) T.; m. Leah Wakeland, Dec. 26, 1981; children: Selena Katherine, Shannon Leigh. BS, Ball State U., 1981; JD, Ind. U., 1984. Bar: Ind. 1984, U.S. Dist. Ct. (so. dist.) Ind. 1984. Assoc. Bingham, Summers, Welsh & Spilman, Indpls., 1984—. Bd. dirs., sec. Near Eastside Community Fed. Credit Union, 1984-87; mem. Marion County Recycling Commn. Mem. ABA, (environ. law com., Tort & Ins. Practice Sect.), Ind. State Bar Assn., Indpls. Bar Assn. Def. Research Inst. Clubs: Sierra (Hoosier chtp. Indpls.). Democrat. Home: 6501 Bracken Ridge Ave Cincinnati OH 45213-1003 Office: Bingham Summers Welsh & Spilman 2700 One Ind Sq Indianapolis IN 46204

TURNER, JAMES THOMAS, judge; b. Clifton Forge, Va., Mar. 12, 1938; s. James Thomas and Ruth (Greene) T.; m. Patricia Sue Renfrow, July 8, 1962; 1 child, James Thomas. BA, Wake Forest Coll., 1960; JD, U. Va., 1965. Bar: Va. 1965, U.S. Ct. Appeals (4th and fed. cirs.), U.S. Supreme Ct. Assoc. Williams, Worrell, Kelly & Greer, Norfolk, Va., 1965, ptnr., 1971-79; U.S. magistrate U.S. Dist. Ct. (ea. dist.) Va., Norfolk, 1979-87; judge U.S. Ct. Fed. Claims, 1987—. Mem. ABA, Fed. Bar Assn., Va. Bar Assn., Norfolk and Portsmouth Bar Assn. (sec. 1975-79). Office: 717 Madison Pl NW Washington DC 20439-0002

TURNER, JANET SULLIVAN, painter, sculptor; b. Gardiner, Maine, Nov. 15, 1935; d. Clayton Jefferson and Frances (Leighton) Sullivan; m. Terry Turner, Oct. 6, 1956; children: Lisa Turner Reid, Michael Ross, Jonathan Brett. BA cum laude, Mich. State U., 1956. Rep. Am. Women in Art, UN World Conf. on Women, Nairobi, Kenya, 1985. One-woman shows include San Diego Art Inst., 1971, St. Joseph U., Phila., 1981, Villanova (Pa.) U. Gallery, 1982, Pa. State U., Middletown (Pa.), 1985, Temple U. (Pa.), 1986, Widener U. Art Mus., Chester, Pa., 1987, 94, Rosemont Coll., Pa., 1995, Sande Webster Gallery, Phila., 1998, 2000; exhibited in group shows at Del. Art Mus., Wilmington, 1978, Woodmere Art Mus., Phila., 1980, 2000, Port of History Mus., Phila., 1984, Allentown Art Mus., 1984, Trenton (NJ) City Mus. Ellarslie Open VIII, 1989, Ammo Gallery, Bklyn., 1989, Pa. State Mus., Harrisburg, 1990-94, Galeria Mesa, Ariz., 1991, Del. Ctr. for Contemporary Arts, Wilmington, 1992, Holter Mus., Helena, Mont., 1992, S.W. Tex. State U., San Marcos, 1993, Fla. State U. Mus., Tallahassee, 1993, Newark Mus., 1993, U. Del., 1994, 1st St. Gallery, NYC, 1994, Noyes Mus., NJ, 1995, Sande Webster Gallery, Phila. 1995-2003, Phila. Art Mus., 1997, Krasdale Gallery, White Plains, NY, 2001, Moore Coll. of Art, Phila. Sculptors, Phila. Pa., 2002; represented in permanent collections Nat. Mus. Women in Arts, "American Album", Wash. D.C., Kresge Art Mus., East Lansing, Mich, ARA Svc. Inc., Phila., Blue Cross/Blue Shield, Phila., Am. Nat. Bank and Trust co., Rockford, Ill., Burroughs Corp., Lisle, Ill., State Mus. Pa., Harrisburg, Bryn Mawr (Pa.) Coll., Rosemont Coll., Villanova (Pa.) Coll., LaSalle U. Art Mus., Phila., Noyes Mus., NJ, Nat. Liberty Mus., Phila., Kimmel Ctr., Phila. Bd. dirs. Rittenhouse Sq. Fine Arts Ann., Phila., 1984—86. Recipient 2d pl. award San Diego Art Inst. 19th Ann. Exhbn., 1971, award of merit Pavilion Gallery, Mt. Holly, N.J., 1991, 3d pl. Katonah Mus. of Art, N.Y., 1992, purchase award State Mus. of Pa., Harrisburg, 1992. Mem. Artists Equity (pres. 1987-88), Nat. League of Am. Pen Woman, Phila. Watercolor Club, Delta Phi Delta. Republican. Roman Catholic. Home: 88 Cambridge Dr Glen Mills PA 19342-1545

TURNER, JIM L. bottler manufacturing executive; b. Houston, 1945; BA, Baylor U. Chmn., CEO Dr Pepper/Seven Up Bottling Group Inc, Dallas, 1985—. Named Beverage Industry Man of Yr., 1990; recipient Horatio Alger award Haratio Alger Assn. Dist. Ams., 1998. Office: Dr Pepper/Seven-Up Bottling Group Inc 5950 Sherry Ln Dallas TX 75225

TURNER, JOAN DALE, elementary school educator; b. Milw., Aug. 21, 1933; s. Dale Curry and Lucile Curtis Shockley; m. Willard David Turner, Aug. 18, 1956 (dec. Mar. 1992); children: Nancy Joan Katz, Susan Ellen Vogt, David Dale. BA in Edn., Principia Coll., 1955; postgrad., Tex. Women's U., 1969; Montessori Edn. degree, Xavier U., 1994; postgrad., Wright State U., 1999. Tchr. kindergarten Elmhurst Pub. Schs., 1955—56, Milw. Pub. Schs., 1956—59; tchr. HeadStart, Dallas, 1969; with Dallas Pub. Schs., 1969; tchr. grade 2 Lake Forest Country Day, Ill., 1971—72, tchr. kindergarten, 1972—76; tchr. grade 4 Lake Forest Pub. Schs., 1976—77; tchr. grades 3 and 4 Elizabeth Forward Sch. Dist., Pa., 1990—92; tchr. Montessori presch. age 3-6 Dayton Pub. Schs., Ohio, 1993—2003. Substitute tchr. Elizabeth Forward Sch. Dist., 1988—90. Vol. Hilltop Sanatorium, Lake Bluff, Ill., 1977—78, nurses aide, 1978—86; Sunday sch. tchr. First Ch. of Christ, Scientist, Lake Forest, Ill. Mem.: NEA, Mariemont Preservation Found., Principia Alumni Assn. of Cin., State Tchrs. Ret. Assn., Ohio Ret. Tchrs. Assn. Mem. First Ch. Of Christ, Scientist. Avocations: gardening, hiking. Home: 4 Denny Pl Cincinnati OH 45227

TURNER, JOHN ANDREW, economist; b. Chgo., July 9, 1949; s. Henry Andrew and Mary Margaret (Tilton) T.; m. Kathleen King Peery, June 21, 1975; 1 child, Sarah. BA, Pomona Coll., Claremont, Calif., 1971; MA, Stanford U., 1972; PhD, U. Chgo., 1977. Rsch. econ. SSA, Washington, 1976-80, U.S. Dept. Labor, Washington, 1980-96, ILO, Geneva, 1996-98; rsch. econ. Office of Sec. U.S. Dept. Labor, 1999-2000, Pub. Policy Inst., AARP, 2000—. Cons. OECD, Paris, 1989, IMF, 1995, AFL-CIO, 1996; chmn. Internat. Pension Conf., U.S. Dept. Labor, Washington, 1990; adj. prof. George Washington U., 1994-96. Author: Pension Policy for a Mobile Labor Force, 1993; editor: Trends in Pensions, 1989 (transl. into Japanese 1991), Pension Policy: An International Perspective, 1991, Trends in Health Benefits, 1993, Private Pension Policies in Industrialized Countries, 1995, Securing Employer-Based Pensions, 1996, Social Security: Development and Reform, 2000. Fulbright scholar Institut de Recherches Economiques et Sociales, France, 1994. Mem. Am. Econ. Assn., Nat. Acad. Social Ins. Methodist. Avocation: tennis. Home: 3713 Chesapeake St NW Washington DC 20016-1813 Office: AARP 601 E St NW Washington DC 20049 E-mail: jturner@aarp.org.

TURNER, JOHN FREELAND, federal agency administrator; b. Jackson, Wyo., Mar. 3, 1942; s. John Charles and Mary Louise (Mapes) T.; m. Mary Kay Brady, 1969; children: John Francis, Kathy Mapes, Mark Freeland. BS in Biology, U. Notre Dame, 1964; postgrad., U. Innsbruck, 1964-65, U. Utah, 1965-66; MS in Ecology, U. Mich., 1968. Rancher, outfitter Triangle X Ranch, Moose, Wyo.; chmn. bd. dirs. Bank of Jackson Hole, 1985-89; photojournalist; mem. Wyo. Ho. of Reps., 1970-74, Wyo. Senate, 1974-89, pres., 1987-89; dir. Fish and Wildlife Svc. Dept. Interior, Washington, 1989-93; pres. Conservation Fund, Arlington, Va., 1993—2001; asst. sec. for oceans, int. environ., and scientific affairs U.S. Dept. State, Washington, 2001—. Chmn. bd. dirs. Inst. Environ. and Natural Resources, U. Wyo., Laramie; exec. adv. Hancock Timber Resource Group, 1993—2001; chmn. rev. com. Argonne Nat. Lab.-West, U. Chgo., 1999—2001; bd. dirs. Land Trust Alliance, 1994—2000, vice-chmn.; bd. dirs. N.E. Utilities, 1995—2001; mem. Nat. Coal Coun., 1995—, Teton Sci. Sch. Bd., Nat. Wetland Forum, 1983, 87; mem. exec. com. Coun. of State Govts.; chmn. Pride in Jackson Hole Campaign, 1986; chmn. steering com. UN Conv. on Wetlands of Internat. Importance, 1990—93; head U.S. delegation Conv. on Internat. Trade Endangered Species. Author: The Magnificent Bald Eagle: Our National Bird, 1971. Named Citizen of Yr. County of Teton, 1984; recipient Nat. Conservation Achievement award Nat. Wildlife Fedn., 1984, Sheldon Coleman Great Outdoors award, 1990, Pres.'s Pub. Svc. award The Nature Conservatory, 1990, Stewardship award Audubon Soc., 1992, Nat. Wetland Achievement award Ducks Unlimited, 1993, Chevron/Times Mirror Nat. Conservation Leadership award, 1995. Mem. Nat. Wildlife Refuge Assn. (bd. dirs.), Boone and Crocket Club (profl. mem.). Republican. Roman Catholic. Office: US Dept State Oceans, Int Environ & Scientific Affairs 2201 C St NW Washington DC 20520

TURNER, JOHN GOSNEY, insurance company executive, director; b. Springfield, Mass., Oct. 3, 1939; s. John William and Clarence Oma (Gosney) T.; m. Leslie Corrigan, June 23, 1962; children: John Fredric, Mary Leslie, James Gosney, Andrew William. BA, Amherst Coll., 1961; student, Advanced Mgmt. Program, Harvard U., 1980. Assoc. actuary Monarch Life Ins. Co., Springfield, Mass., 1961-67; group actuary Northwestern Nat. Life Ins. Co., Mpls., 1967-75, sr. v.p. group, 1975-79, sr. v.p., chief actuary, 1979-81, exec. v.p., chief actuary, 1981-83, pres., chief operating officer, 1983—; chmn., CEO Northwestern Nat. Life Ins. Co. (now ReliaStar Fin. Corp.), Mpls., 1993—. Dir. NWNL Reins. Co., NWNL Gen. No. Life, North Atlantic Life Ins. Co. N.Y. Trustee Abbott-Northwestern Hosps., Evans Sch. Found.; chmn. Minn. Trustees of the Evans Scholars Found. Fellow Soc. Actuaries; mem. Am. Acad. Actuaries, Western Golf Assn. (dir.), Minn. Golf Assn. Clubs: Minikahda (Mpls.). Home: 301 Kenwood Pkwy Apt 502 Minneapolis MN 55403-1165

TURNER, JOHN NAPIER, former prime minister of Canada, legislator; b. Richmond, Eng., June 7, 1929; s. Leonard and Phyllis (Gregory) T.; m. Geills McCrae Kilgour, May 11, 1963; children: Elizabeth, Michael, David, Andrew. BA with honors in Polit. Sci., U. B.C., Can., 1949; BA, Oxford U., Eng., 1951, BCL, 1952; MA, Oxford U., 1957; postgrad., U. Paris, 1952-53; LLD (hon.), U.N.B., 1968, York U., Toronto, 1969, U. B.C., 1986, U. Toronto, 1996, Assumption U., Windsor, 2002; D. of Civil Law (hon.), Mt. Allison U., N.B., 1980. Bar: Eng. 1953, Que. 1954, Ont. 1968, B.C. 1969, Y.T. 1969, N.W.T. 1969, Barbados 1969, Trinidad 1969. With Stikeman, Elliot, Tamaki, Mercier and Turner, Montreal, Que., 1953-65, McMillan Binch, Toronto, 1976-84; M.P. for St. Lawrence-St. George Montreal, 1962-68, Ottawa-Carleton, 1968-76; parliamentary sec. to Minister of Northern Affairs and Nat. Resources, 1963-65; minister without portfolio, 1965-67; registrar-gen. Govt. of Can., 1967-68, minister of consumer and corp. affairs, 1968, solicitor-gen., 1968, minister of justice and atty.-gen. of Can., 1968-72, minister of fin., 1972-75, prime minister of Can., 1984; leader Liberal Party Can., 1984-90; mem. parliament Vancouver Quadra, 1984-93; with Miller Thomson, Toronto, 1990—. Created Queen's Counsel, Ontario and Quebec, 1968. Author: Senate of Canada, 1961, Politics of Purpose, 1968. Can. Track Field Champion, 1948; mem. English Track and Field Team, 1950-51. Appointed Companion of Order of Can., 1995. Mem. Eng. Bar Assn., Grey's Inn London, Bar. Assns. of Ont., Que., B.C., Barbados, Trinidad, Mt. Royal Club, Montreal Racquet Club, Badminton and Racquet Club, York Club, The Vancouver Club, Nat. Club. Liberal. Roman Catholic. Avocations: tennis, canoeing, skiing. Home: 59 Oriole Rd Toronto ON Canada M4V 2E9 Office: Miller Thomson LLP 2500 20 Queen St W Toronto ON Canada M5H 3S1 E-mail: jturner@millerthomson.ca.

TURNER, JOHN SIDNEY, JR., retired otolaryngologist, educator; b. Bainbridge, Ga., July 25, 1930; s. John Sidney and Rose Lee (Rogers) T.; m. Betty Jane Tigner, June 5, 1955 (dec.); children: Elizabeth, Rebecca, Jan Marie; m. Nina Jones, June 16, 1999. BS, Emory U., 1952, MD, 1955. Diplomate Am. Bd. Otolaryngology. Intern U. Va. Hosp., 1955-56; resident in otolaryngology Duke U. Med. Ctr., 1958-61; prof. otolaryngology Emory U., Atlanta, 1961-95, chmn. divsn., 1961—95; ret. Ear specialist, chief otolaryngology Emory Clinic, 1961-95; area cons. in field U.S. 3d Army, 1962-69; assoc. dir. heart disease control program Fla. Bd. Health, 1956-58; Ga. state chmn. Deafness Rsch. Found., 1968-95; v.p. Clifton Casualty Ins. Co., Atlanta, 1975-95. Mem. internat. editl. bd. Drugs Jour., 1982—, Ethicals in Med. Progress, 1982—, Dialogue Jour., 1988-95; mem. editl. bd. Otolaryngology—Head and Neck Surgery, 1991; contbr. chpts. to books, articles to profl. jours. With USPHS, 1956-58. Recipient Appreciation award Children of Fulton County and Fulton County Health Dept., 1975, Citation for Disting. Svc., Fla. divsn. Am. Cancer Soc., 1957, Lester A. Brown award Ga. Soc. Otolaryngology*Head and Neck Surgery, 1995. Mem. AMA, So. Med. Assn. (chmn. otolaryngology sect. 1974, cert. of appreciation 1974), Am. Acad. Otolaryngology--Head and Neck Surgery (Honor award 1994), Triological Soc. (v.p., chmn. so. sect. 1991—), Am. Acad. Otolaryngic Allergy, Ga. Soc. Otolaryngology (pres. 1973), Med. Assn. Ga., Med. Assn. Atlanta, Assn. Acad. Depts. Otolaryngology, Optimists (pres. Atlanta 1975), Alpha Omega Alpha. Democrat. Methodist. Home: 3451 Marina Crest Dr Gainesville GA 30506-1061

TURNER, KATHLEEN, actress; b. Springfield, Mo., June 19, 1954; m. Jay Weiss, 1984; 1 child, Rachel Ann. Student, Cen. Sch. of Speech and Drama, London, Southwest Mo. State U.; BFA, U. Md. Various theater roles, Broadway debut: Gemini, 1978, Cat on a Hot Tin Roof, 1990, Indiscretions, 1995; appeared in TV series The Doctors, 1977, Style and Substance, 1996; TV movies inlcude Friends At Last, 1995, Moonlight and Valentino, 1995; films include Body Heat, 1981, A Breed Apart, 1982, The Man With Two Brains, 1983, Crimes of Passion, 1984, Romancing the Stone, 1984, Prizzi's Honor (Golden Globe award for best actress), 1985, The Jewel of the Nile, 1985, Peggy Sue Got Married, (D.W. Griffith award for best actress, Oscar nomination for best actress) 1986, Julia and Julia, 1988, Switching Channels, 1988, Who Framed Roger Rabbit, 1988, Accidental Tourist, 1988, The War of the Roses, 1989. V.I. Warshawski, 1991, Undercover Blues, 1993, House of Cards, 1993, Serial Mom, 1994, Naked in New York, 1994, A Simple Wish, 1997, (TV movie) Love in the Ancient World, 1997, (TV movie) Legalese, 1998, The Real Blonde, 1998, The Virgin Suicides, 1999, Prince of Central Park, 1999, Love and Action in Chicago, 1999, Baby Geniuses, 1999; dir. (Showtime Cable movie) Leslie's Folly, 1994; also performed in radio shows with the BBC, 1992, 93; voice: Bad Baby, 1997, Beautiful, 2000. Office: ICM care Chris Andrews 8942 Wilshire Blvd Beverly Hills CA 90211-1934

TURNER, KATHLEEN J. communications educator, consultant; d. Josiah Shelden Turner and Anne A. Alexander; m. Raymond Sprague. BA in Comm. and English, U. Kans., 1974; MA in Comm., Purdue U., 1976, PhD in Comm., 1978. Asst. prof. comm. Denison U., Granville, Ohio, 1978—79, U. Notre Dame, Ind., 1979—85; assoc. prof. comm. U. Tulsa, Okla., 1985—86, Tulane U., New Orleans, 1986—2000; prof. comm. Queens U. Charlotte, NC, 2000—04, Knight-Crane prof. comm., 2001—04; prof. comm. studies Davidson Coll., 2004—. Media/pub. rels. cons. La. Vocal Arts Chorale, New Orleans, 1993—99. Mem.: Pub. Rels. Soc. Am., Popular Culture Assn., So. States Comm. Assn., Ctrl. States Comm. Assn. (life Fedn. prize 1985), Nat. Comm. Assn. (life), Phi Beta Kappa. Achievements include research in Lyndon Johnson's Dual War: Vietnam and the Press (University of Chicago Press, 1985); Doing Rhetorical History: Concepts and Cases (edited; University of Alabama Press, 1998); Musical and Visual Invention in Miami Vice in Vande Berg and Wenner, Television Criticism (with Raymond Sprague, 1990); Diary of a Generation: The Rhetoric of Sixties Protest Music in Savage and Nimmo, Politics in Familiar Contexts (with Raymond Sprague, 1990); Ego Defense and Media Access: Conflicting Rhetorical Needs of a Contemporary Social Movement, Central States Speech Journal (1980); Comic Strips: A Rhetorical Perspective, Central States Speech Journal (1977). Office: Davidson Coll Comm Studies Box 7066 Davidson NC 28035-7066 Office Phone: 704-894-2528. E-mail: kturner@davidson.edu.

TURNER, KATHRYN CLAIRE, medical educator, writer; d. Jay Walter man; m. Steve Charles Turner, Feb. 17, 1968; 1 child, Teresa Lynn Anders. Tchg. cert., Sacramento State Univ., Calif. Cert. tchr., chiropractic asst., EMT Calif. Chiropractic asst. instr. Sacramento County Office of Edn., 1990—; chiropractic cons. Unlimited Chiropractic Services. Lectr. Calif. Chiropractic Assn., Sacramento. Author: (text book) The Chiropractic Assistant. Mem.: Calif. Teachers Assn., Sacramento County Office of Edn. (assoc.; grievance chairperson 2003), Calif. Chiropractic Assn. (assoc.). Achievements include development of State of Calif. curriculum for the Chiropractic Assistant Training Program. Office: Sacramento County Office of Education 9738 Lincoln Village Drive Sacramento CT 95827 E-mail: kturner@scoe.net.

TURNER, KELLEY BAILEY, non-profit consultant, volunteer program administrator; b. Houston, Mar. 17, 1962; d. Myron Edgar Bailey and Georgia Numsen (Reynolds) White; m. Mark Edward Turner, May 21, 1994. BA in Art History and Comms. cum laude, U. St. Thomas, 1993. Lic. FCC. Coord. sch. svcs., asst dir. vis. svcs. Houston Mus. Natural Sci., Edn. Sch. Svcs., Houston, 1991-94; coord. vol. svcs. and comty. partnerships Hermann Hosp., Houston, 1996-98; adminstr. Vols. in Pub. Schs. Cmty. Partnerships Houston Ind. Sch. Dist., 1998-2001; prin. Cmty. Devel. Resources, Houston, 2001—; dir. vol. svcs. and cmty. outreach Bering Omega Cmty. Svcs., Houston, 2002—03. Presenter Internat. Conf. on Vol. Adminstrn., Chgo., 1999—; instr. Vol. Mgmt. Acad., Houston C.C.; cons. Susan G. Komen Breast Cancer Found. Mem. Jr. League of Houston, Inc., 1990-94; floor presenter Mus. Natural Sci., 1991-94; vol. Houston SPCA; mem. adv. bd. Houston Internat. Festival, 1992-93, chmn. curriculum guide, 1992-93, chmn. curriculum guide com.; bd. dirs. country selection com. Chrysalis Repertory Dance Co., 1995-97; bd. dirs., membership chair Houston Assn. Vol. Adminstrs., 1998-2000, bd. dirs. 2002—; mem. adv. coun. Ret. Srs. vol. Program, Interfaith Ministries of Greater Houston, 1999-2000; vol. team capt. Houston Mayor's Summit on Women, 1999; mem. com. Internat. Yr. of Vols., 2000—; mem. bd. advocates Planned Parenthood Houston and Southeast Tex., 2000-01. Named Vol. of Yr. Jr. League Houston, 1991. Home and Office: 1923 Vassar St Houston TX 77098-5429 Fax: 713-526-9256. Office Phone: 713-522-2831. Business E-Mail: communitydr@pdq.net.

TURNER, KEVIN, retail executive; m. Shelly Turner. BS, E. Ctrl. U., 1987. Cashier Wal-Mart Stores, Inc., Ada, Okla., 1985—88, with internal audit dept., 1988—89, bus. analyst info. sys. div., strategy mgr. info. sys. div., dir. info. sys. div., v.p. and asst. chief info. officer info. sys. div., chief info. officer info. sys. div., 2000—03, exec. v.p., 2000, pres. and CEO Sam's Club div., 2002—. Office: Wal-Mart Stores Inc 702 SW Eighth St Bentonville AR 72716

TURNER, KEVIN PAUL, music educator; s. Ervin and Remitha Turner; m. Yolanda G. Turner, Nov. 21, 1993; m. Vivian Ann Hardy-Turner, June 19, 1982 (div. Jan. 31, 1983); children: Kevin P. Turner, Jr., Kristi Nichole-Rachelle, Jeffery D., David, Stasha L. Core, Timesha L. Sampson, Erica Jordan. Ordained Elder Pentecostal Fellowship Ch., 2001. Svc. ctr. adminstr. ARC, Birmingham, Ala., 1992—2000; instr. music U. Ala., Birmingham, Ala., 1995—. Asst. min. music First Bapt. Ch. - Kingston, Birmingham, Ala., 1995—; choral dir. Sixth Ave. Bapt. Ch., Birmingham, Ala., 1996—2001; v.p. Pentecostal Fellowship Ch., Inc., Sylacauga, Ala., 1998—. Composer: UAB Gospel Choir Lessons for Life CD; dir.: Black Gospel Music in America (Finalist - The Ellen Greg Ingalls/UAB Nat. Alumni Wards, 2001). Faculty adv. Student Challenge, Birminham, Ala., 2000—02; vice chair Powerfest, Alabaster, Ala., 1999—2003; v.p., legal com., conv. coord. Pentecostal Fellowship Churches, Inc, Sylacauga, Ala., 1998—2003. Mem.: Ch. Tax Assn. (assoc.; lay mem. 2003—03). Home: PO Box 55502 Birmingham AL 35255-5502 Office: U Ala at Birmingham HB 401 - 1530 Third Ave S Birmingham AL 35294-1260 Office Phone: 205-934-6155. Office Fax: 205-975-1931. Personal E-mail: holyharvest@kevinturner.org. E-mail: kturner@uab.edu.

TURNER, LARAINE ELIZABETH, elementary school educator; b. Ft. Wayne, Ind., June 16, 1955; d. Robert Edward Bauer and Marjorie Therese Landolfi; m. Tony Turner, Nov. 16, 1994; children: Deontray, Kimberly McIvor, Tony III, Xavier Scott. BA in Journalism and Comm., Pacific Union Coll., 1981; BA in Elem. Edn., Calif. State U., Long Beach, 1995; postgrad., Seminaire-du-Saleve, Collonges, France, 1978—79. Profl. clear multiple subject tchg. credential Calif. Tchr. Los Nietos Unified Sch. Dist., Whittier, Calif., 1995—2000, Downey (Calif.) Unified Sch. Dist., 1996—2000, ABC Unified Sch. Dist., Cerritos, Calif., 1997—2000; elem. tchr. Neuva Vista Elem. Sch./L.A. Unified Sch. Dist., Calif., 2000—, magnet drama tchr., dir., 2000—. Author: The Rise and Fall of the Witch on the Bayou, 2000, The Little Rosebud, 2001; composer: (songs) Little Rosebud, The Thorns of the Rose, The River of Life, Song of the Bayou (Chanson du Bayou), Love is Not Defied, Poor Li'l Baby. With USAR, 1985—92. Recipient Cert. of Appreciation, Alhambra Sch. Dists. Author Festival, 2002—03. Mem.: Calif. Authors, Soc. Children's Book Writers and Illustrators', Christ Temple Ch., Sacred Holy Ghost Temple Ch., Am. Legion. Democrat. Avocations: dance, travel, singing. Office: Nueva Vista Elem/Magnet Sch 4412 Randolph St Bell CA 90201 Office Phone: 323-869-4698.

TURNER, LEE, travel company executive; b. 1952; BS, Worcester Polytechnic Inst., 1974; MBA, Dartmouth, 1976. With Baxter Healthcare, Deerfield, Ill., 1976-79, 82-87, Southeastern Pub. Svc. Co., Miami Beach, Fla., 1979-82; exec. v.p. BTI Ams., Inc., Northbrook, Ill., 1987-98; CFO WorldTravel Ptnrs., Northbrook, 1998—. Office: World Travel Ptnrs 2700 Patriot Blvd Ste 200 Glenview IL 60025-8064

TURNER, LEE IRWIN, lawyer; b. Cleve., May 2, 1944; s. Louis and Harriet (Keizer) T.; married; children: Brooke, Brett, Brittany, Breanne, Brenna. B.S., Ohio State U., 1966, J.D. cum laude, 1969. Bar: Mich. 1969, Ohio, 1969, U.S. Dist. Ct. (no. dist.) Ohio 1971, U.S. Dist. (ea. dist.) Mich. 1971, U.S. Ct. Appeals (6th cir.) 1984. Assoc., Sommer, Schwartz, Silver, Schwartz, Detroit, 1969-73; ptnr. Turner & Turner, P.C., Southfield, Mich., 1973— . Mem. Assn. Trial Lawyers Am., Mich. Trial Lawyers Assn., Detroit Bar Assn., Southfield Bar Assn., Oakland County Bar Assn. Democrat. Jewish. Office: 26000 W 12 Mile Rd Southfield MI 48034-1783

TURNER, LELAND, architectural firm executive; 2 children. BArch, Tex. Tech U., 1972. Dir. design mgmt. Marriott Corp.; dir. hospitality FKP Arch., 2002—. Mem. editl. adv. bd. Penton's Designing Mag. Mem.: Nat. Coun. Archtl. Registration Bds. Avocation: drag racing. Office: 8 Greenway Plz Ste 300 Houston TX 77046-0899

TURNER, LETITIA RHODES, artist; b. Media, Pa., Aug. 17, 1923; d. Samuel Noblit and Letitia (Eves) Rhodes; m. Ellwood Jackson Turner Jr., Aug. 1, 1942; children: Rue Baronsky, Letitia Mayo, Elizabeth Rorke. Diploma, Cowanova Sch. Dancing, 1941. Dance instr. Cowanova Sch. Dancing, 1939—41; sec., treas. Rose Tree Realty Inc., Media, Pa., 1961-81. Dance tchr., 1939, 40, 41. Portrait painter (Portrait of Mary 3d pl. 1990, Portrait of Brett 2d pl. 1987); painter portrait commns., 1977-95. Pres. Am. Legion Aux., Media, 1991-2002, photographer, 1992, sec., 1993—; sec. Del. County Am. Legion Aux., 1994, historian, 1995; 1st v.p. Woman's Aux. Media Presbyn. Ch., Media, 1963; mem. D.A.R.E., Media, 1983-91, 92, 93—. Mem. Artist Guild Delaware County, Art League Delaware County, Artist Guild of Riddle Village, Am. Legion Aux. (sec. Del. County 1993, historian 1994). Republican. Avocations: needlepoint, holiday spa, art design for ch. bulletin covers. Home and Office: Riddle Village L-302 Media PA 19063

TURNER, LISA HILL, county official; b. Rexburg, Idaho, Sept. 11, 1959; d. Dale A. and Betty Jean (Owens) Hill; m. Rick I. Turner, June 10, 1979; 1 child, Keith D. Staff mem. Fremont County Herald-Chronicle, St. Anthony, Idaho, 1977-93, editor, 1985-93; chief dep. treas. Fremont County, St. Anthony,

Idaho, 1994-95, info. sys. adminstr., 1995—. Bd. dirs. Foster Grandparents, Fremont Gen. Hosp. Found.; sec. fisherman's breakfast com., v.p. pub. affairs Pioneer Days Com., St. Anthony, Idaho, 2001, 2002. Named Most Respected Citizen, Free Fisherman's Breakfast, 1991, Hon. Chef, 1987; recipient Cert. of Appreciation, Idaho Gov. Cecil Andrus, 1990. Mem. So. Fremont C. of C. (sec. 1985-88, dir. 1986-89). Mem. Lds Ch. Avocations: golf, horseback riding, camping, snowmobiling.

TURNER, LISA PHILLIPS, human resources executive; b. Waltham, Mass., Apr. 10, 1951; d. James Sinclair and Virginia Turner. BA in Edn. and Philosophy magna cum laude, Washington Coll., Chestertown, Md., 1974; AS in Electronics Tech., AA in Engring., Palm Beach Jr. Coll., 1982; MBA, Nova U., 1986, DSc, 1989; PhD, Kennedy Western U., 1990. Cert. Sr. Profl. in Human Resources, quality engr.; lic. USCG capt.; lic. pvt. pilot FAA. Founder, pres. Turner's Bicycle Svc., Inc., Delray Beach, Fla., 1975-80; electronics engr., quality engr. Audio Engring. and Video Arts, Boca Raton, Fla., 1980-81; tech. writing instr. Palm Beach Jr. Coll., Lake Worth, Fla., 1981-82; adminstr. tng. and devel. Mitel Inc., Boca Raton, 1982-88; mgr. comm. and employee rels. Modular Computer Systems, Inc., Ft. Lauderdale, Fla., 1988-89; U.S. mktg. project mgr. Mitel, Inc., Boca Raton, 1990-91; v.p. human resources Connectronics, Inc., Ft. Lauderdale, 1991-93; sr. mgr. human resources Sensormatic Electronics Corp., Boca Raton, 1993-98, dir. human resources, 1998—2001; chief tng. officer, dir. human resources Tyco Fire and Security Svcs., Inc., Boca Raton, 2001—. Contbg. author Kitplanes Mag. With USCG Aux. Recipient Human Resources Profl. Excellence award, Soc. Human Resource Mgmt., 1999. Mem. Soc. for Human Resource Mgmt., Internat. Assn. Quality Cirs., Am. Soc. Quality Control, Fla. Employment Mgmt. Assn., Am. Acad. Mgmt., Employment Assn. Fla., Am. Capts. Assn., Citizens Police Acad., Aircraft Owners and Pilot's Assn., Exptl. Aircraft Assn., Fla. Aero. Club. Achievements include being the first female to construct, complete and fly a pulsar XP aircraft. Home: 1358 Fairfax Cir E Boynton Beach FL 33436-8612 Office: Tyco 1 Town Center Rd Boca Raton FL 33436-1010 Office Phone: 561-989-7979. Personal E-mail: lisaturner@prodigy.net. Business E-Mail: lisaturner@tycoint.com.

TURNER, LYLE C. biotechnology company executive; BA in Chemistry, U. Calif., San Diego. With Syntro Corp., 1981—85, mgr. bus. devel.; tech. sales specialist Beohringer Mannheim Corp., 1985—87; dir. sales and mktg. Stratagene, 1987—88; founder, pres., CEO and dir. Invitrogen Corp., Carlsbad, Calif., 1988—. Office: Invitrogen Corp 1600 Faraday Ave Carlsbad CA 92008-7313

TURNER, MALCOLM ELIJAH, biomathematician, educator; b. Atlanta, May 27, 1929; s. Malcolm Elijah and Margaret (Parker) T.; m. Ann Clay Bowers, Sept. 16, 1948; children: Malcolm Elijah IV, Allison Ann, Clay Shumate, Margaret Jean; m. Rachel Patricia Farmer, Feb. 1, 1968; children: Aleta van Riper, Leila Samantha, Alexis St. John, Walter McCamy. Student, Emory U., 1947-48; BA, Duke U., 1952; M.Exptl. Stats., N.C. State U., 1955, PhD, 1959. Analytical statistician Communicable Disease Center, USPHS, Atlanta, 1953; rsch. assoc. U. Cin., 1955, asst. prof., 1955-58; asst. statistician N.C. State U., Raleigh, 1957-58; assoc. prof. Med. Coll. Va., Richmond, 1958-63, chmn. div. biometry, 1959-63; prof., chmn. dept. statistics and biometry Emory U., Atlanta, 1963-69; chmn. dept. biomath., prof. biostats. and biomath. U. Ala., Birmingham, 1970-82, prof. biostats. and biomath., 1982—, prof. emeritus biostats., 1998—. Instr. summers Yale U., 1966, U. Calif. at Berkeley, 1971, Vanderbilt U., 1975; prof. U. Kans., 1968-69; vis. prof. Atlanta U., 1969; cons. to industry. Mem. editorial bd. So. Med. Jour., 1990—; contbr. articles to profl. jours. Fellow Ala. Acad. Sci., Am. Statis. Assn. (hon.), AAAS (hon.); mem. AAUP, AMA (affiliate), Biometrics Soc. (mng. editor Biometrics 1962-69), Soc. for Indsl. and Applied Math., Mensa, Sigma Xi, Phi Kappa Phi, Phi Delta Theta, Phi Sigma. Home: 1734 Tecumseh Trl Pelham AL 35124-1012 Personal E-mail: malcolmt@scientist.com. *The logic of induction is the quest.*

TURNER, MARGUERITE ROSE COWLES, library administrator; b. June 21, 1941; d. John Clinton and Marguerite Eileen (Slaybaugh) Cowles; 1 son, Jeffrey Jason. BA, U. New Orleans, 1963; MLS, La. State U., 1966; MA in History, U. So. Miss., 1970. Reference libr. Pascagoula (Miss.) Jr. H.S., 1970-71, Irwin County H.S., Ocilla, Ga., 1971-72; dir. Fitzgerald (Ga.) Carnegie Libr., 1974-80; adminstrv. librarian Assumption Parish Libr., Napoleonville, La., 1980-83; dir. Jacob S. Mauney meml. Libr., Kings Mountain, NC, 1983—2004; ret., 2004. Author poems, short stories; writer weekly column Kings Mountain Herald, Shelby Star: contbr. articles to profl. jours. Sunday sch. tchr., First Baptist Ch., librarian, 1975—, Fitzgerald, 1978-80, Napoleonville, 1980-83. Mem. ALA, N.C. Libr. Assn., Broad River Libr. Assn. Republican.

TURNER, MARTA JONES, public affairs professional; V.p. pub. affairs Flowers Industries, Inc., Thomasville, Ga., 1998—. Office: Flowers Industries Inc 1919 Flowers Cir Thomasville GA 31757-1137

TURNER, MARVIN LESERE, musician; b. Eutaw, Ala., May 1, 1961; s. Allen and Emma Lou Turner; m. Patricia A. Jeffery, June 20, 1992; children: Trishana, Marvin Jr., Karl. BS, Ala. State U., Montgomery, 1979—84. Band dir. Greene County H.S., Eutaw, Ala. Mem.: Capitol Lodge #39, Omega Psi Phi, Phi Mu Alpha. Avocation: saxophone. Home: Rte 1 Box 57-N Boligee AL 35443 Office: Greene County HS PO Box 658 Eutaw AL 35462 Office Phone: 205-372-3789.

TURNER, MARY JANE, educational administrator; b. Colorado Springs, Colo., June 1, 1923; d. David Edward and Ina Mabel (Campbell) Nickelson; m. Harold Adair Turner, Feb. 15, 1945 (dec.); children: Mary Ann, Harold Adair III. BA in Polit. Sci., U. Colo., 1947, MPA in Pub. Adminstrn., 1968, PhD in Polit. Sci., 1978. Secondary tchr. Canon City (Colo.) Sch. Dist., 1950-53; tchr. assoc. in polit. sci. U. Colo., Denver, 1968-70, Boulder, 1970-71; rsch. asst. Social Sci. Edn. Consortium, Boulder, 1971, staff assoc., 1972-77; dir. Colo. Legal Edn. Program, Boulder, 1977-84; assoc. dir. Ctr. for Civic Edn., Calabasas, Calif., 1984-88; dir. Close Up Found., Alexandria, Va., 1988-92, sr. edn. advisor Arlington, Va., 1992—. Author: Political Science in the New Social Studies, 1972; co-author: American Government: Principles and Practices, 1983, 4th edit., 1996, Law in the Classroom, 1984, Civics: Citizens in Action, 1986, 2d edit., 1991, U.S. Government Resource Book, 1989; contbg. author: Internat. Ency. Dictionary of Edn., 2000. Chair curriculum com. Idaho State Bar Found., 2000—. Recipient Isadore Starr award for spl. achievement in law-related edn. ABA, 1997. Mem. Nat. Coun. for Social Studies (chair nominations 1983-84, chair bicentennial com. 1986), Social Sci. Edn. Consortium (pres. 1986-87, bd. dirs. 1984-87, 99—), Pi Lambda Theta, Pi Sigma Alpha. Democrat. Presbyterian. Office: Close Up Found 44 Canal Center Plz Alexandria VA 22314-1592 E-mail: turnermj@my180.net.

TURNER, MEGAN WHALEN, author; b. Fort Sill, Okla., Nov. 21, 1965; d. Donald Peyton and Nora Courtenay (Green) Whalen; m. Mark Bernard Turner. BA in English Lang. and Lit. with honors, U. Chgo., 1987. Buyer children's books Harper Court Bookstore, Chgo., 1988-89, Bick's Books, Washington, 1991-92. Author: Instead of Three Wishes, 1995, The Thief, 1996 (Newbery Honor award 1997), The Queen of Attolia, 2000. Mem. Authors' Guild. Address: care Greenwillow Books 1350 Ave of the Ams New York NY 10019

TURNER, MICHAEL, congressman; b. Dayton, Ohio, Jan. 11, 1960; married; m. Lori Turner; 2 children. BA, Ohio No. U.; JD, Case Western U.; MBA, U. Dayton. Mayor City of Dayton, Ohio, 1994—2002; mem. U.S. Ho. Reps. from 3rd Ohio dist., 2003—. Republican. Office: 1740 Longworth House Office Bldg Washington DC 20515

TURNER, MICHAEL STANLEY, astrophysics educator, researcher; b. L.A., July 29, 1949; s. Paul Joseph and Janet Mary (Lindholm) T.; m. Terri Lee Shields, Aug. 1978 (div. Sept. 1980); m. Barbara Lynn Ahlberg, Sept. 10, 1988; children: Rachel Mary, Joseph Lucien. BS in Physics, Calif. Inst. Tech., 1971; MS in Physics, Stanford U., 1973, PhD in Physics, 1978. Enrico Fermi fellow U. Chgo., 1978-80, from asst. to assoc. prof. physics and astronomy and astrophysics, 1980-85, prof., 1985—, chmn. dept. astronomy and astrophysics, 1997—2003, Bruce V. and Diana M. Rauner Disting. Svc. prof., 1998—; scientist Fermi Nat. Accelerator Lab., Batavia, Ill., 1983—2003; asst. dir. U.S. Nat.Sci. Found., 2003—. Trustee Aspen (Colo.) Ctr. Physics, 1984—97, 2002—, pres., 1989—93, hon. trustee, 2002—; Halley lectr. Oxford U., 1994; Klopsteg lectr. Am. Assn. Physics Tchrs., 1999; Neils Bohr lectr. Copenhagen U., 2001; Marker lectr. Pa. State U., 2002; Paul fellow Bonn U., 2000; Houston lectr. Rice U., 2003; Herzfield lectr. Cath. U., 2004; Buhl lectr. Carnegie Mellon U., 2004. Author: (with E.W. Kolb) The Early Universe, 1990; contbr. over 200 articles to profl. jours. Bd. trustees Ill. Math. Sci. Acad., 1998-2003, Project Exploration, Ill., 2002-03. Sloan fellow A.P. Sloan Found., 1983-88, W. Paul fellow Bonn U., 2000. Fellow Am. Acad. Arts and Scis., Am. Phys. Soc. (mem. exec. bd. 1992-94, chmn. publ. oversight com. 1993-94, chmn. nominating com. 1999-2000, Lilienfeld prize 1997, Primakoff lectr., 2003), Phi Beta Kappa (nat. lectr. 2002-2003); mem. NAS (NRC astronomy astrophysics survey com. 1998-2000, chair NRC com. Physics of Universe, 2000-02), AAAS (chair physics sect. 2003), Am. Astron. Soc. (Helen B. Warner prize 1984), Internat. Astron. Union, Sigma Xi. Office: U Chgo Astron & Astrophysics Ctr 5640 S Ellis Ave Chicago IL 60637-1433 Office Phone: mturner@nsf.gov., 703-292-8809.

TURNER, NANCY DELANE, nutritionist, educator, researcher; b. Atlanta, Nov. 8, 1956; d. Pheron Oclesia and Dicie Ethel Turner. Student, Emory U., 1974-75; BS, Tex. A&M U., 1978, MS, 1984, PhD, 1995. Cert. nutrition specialist. Student tech. Tex. A&M U., College Station, 1980-84, rsch. assoc., 1984-95, asst. rsch. scientist, 1996-98, rsch. asst. prof., 1998—2003, assoc. prof., 2003—. Freelance cons., manuscript editor, College Station, 1986—; ptnr. O.O.C. Cons.; assoc. mem. Interdisciplinary Fac. Nutrition, 1996—, exec. coun., 2001—, assoc. head, 2002--, Interdisciplinary Fac. Toxicology, 2001—. Contbr. chpts. to books, abstracts and articles to refereed publs.; mem. editl. bd. Jour. Animal Sci., 1999-2002; ad hoc reviewer Bioresource Tech., 1995-2002, Jour. Nutrition, 1997—, Jour. Animal Sci., 1998-99, Am. Jour. Clin. Nutrition, 2000—, Nutrition and Cancer, 2000—, Alcohol, 2002—, Biochimica et Biophysica Acta, 2002—, Cancer Letters, 2002-03; assoc. editor Am. Soc. Nutrition Scis. Nutrition Notes. Judge Brazos Valley Sci. Fair, 1998—; mem. pub. rels. com. Bryan/College Sta. chpt. Habitat for Humanity, 1998—2002. Recipient Ethel Ashworth-Tsutsui Meml. award for mentoring, 1998; Dan. F. Jones Meml. scholar Tex. A&M U., 1990. Mem. AAAS, Am. Soc. Animal Sci., Am. Assn. Cereal Chemists, N.Y. Acad. Scis., Soc. Exptl. Biology and Medicine, Am. Physiol. Soc., Am. Assn. for Cancer Rsch., Sigma Xi, Gamma Sigma Delta. Achievements include definition of phys. mechanism whereby structure modifications in response to new ammonia treatment increases digestibility of fibrous material and grain for ruminants; rsch. in defining physiol. mechanisms of altered tissue and bone growth patterns in transgenic mice; the role of fiber, fat and phytochemicals in colon cancer etiology. Office: Tex A&M U Dept Animal Sci Human Nutrition Sect 212 Kleberg 2471 Tamu College Station TX 77843-2471 E-mail: nancy-turner@ansc.tamu.edu.

TURNER, NORV, professional football coach; m. Nancy Turner; 3 children. Asst. coach Univ. of So. Calif., 1976—84; receivers coach Los Angeles Rams, 1985—90; offensive coord. Dallas Cowboys, 1991—93; head coach Washington Redskins, 1994—2000; offensive coord. San Diego Chargers, 2001, Miami Dolphines, 2002—03; head coach Oakland Raiders, 2004—. Office: c/o The Oakland Raiders 1220 Harbor BayParkway Alameda CA 94502

TURNER, PAMELA, psychologist; b. Glen Ridge, N.J., Aug. 29, 1952; d. Warren H. and Lucille M. Turner. BS in Math., Bucknell U., 1974; MS in Computer Sci., Rutgers U., 1978; MA in Psychology, Columbia U., 1986, EdD in Psychology, 1992. Lic. psychologist, N.J. Sr. tech. assoc. Bell Labs., Holmdel-West Long Branch, N.J., 1974-80, mem. tech. staff West Long Branch, 1981-83, Bell Comm. Rsch., Piscataway and Red Bank, N.J., 1984-88, orgnl. devel. specialist Morristown, N.J., 1989-90; intern U. Ga. Counseling and Testing Ctr., Athens, 1990-91; psychotherapist Advanced Psychol. Svcs., Freehold, NJ, 1993-96; staff psychologist Kimball Med. Ctr.-St. Barnabas Behavioral Health, Toms River, NJ, 1996—2002; psychologist in pvt. practice Jackson, NJ, 1996—. Adj. asst. prof. Columbia U. Tchrs. Coll., N.Y.C., 1994-95 Singer: Monmouth Civic Chorus, 1975—97; soloist: Brookdale C.C. Opera, 1986, Athens (Ga.) Choral Soc., 1990—91; singer: Met. Singers/Greek Choral Soc., 1989—97, Jackson Summer Theater, 2000, Jackson Civic Chorus, 1999—, Jackson Civic Chamber Ensemble, 2000—. Cmty. lectr. Monmouth and Ocean Counties, NJ, 1993—; mem. drug and alcohol abuse adv. com. Jackson Twp. Bd. Edn., 1997; mem. Jackson Twp. Mcpl. Alliance for Prevention of Alcohol and Drug Abuse, 1996—98; mem. Jackson Twp. Youth Adv. Bd., 1997—98; mem. founding bd. Jackson (NJ) Coun. for Arts, 1998—, chair, 2002—. Mem.: APA, N.J. Psychol. Assn., East Coast Regional Dressage Assn. (newsletter editor 1997—). Avocations: singing, horses, desktop publishing. Office: Jackson Psychology and Wellness Ctr PO Box 752 Jackson NJ 08527 E-mail: jpwc@monmouth.com.

TURNER, PATRICK NOEL WADDINGTON, fund manager; b. Burnham, Eng., Mar. 31, 1960; came to U.S., 1981; s. Noel Walter and Shirley (Vaughn) T.; m. Hilary Jennifer Cosell, Sept. 18, 1982 (div. Dec. 1989); 1 child, Payton; m. Amber Lea Bohmfalk, Feb. 2, 1991; children: Benton, Lily. BA with honours, Oxford (Eng.) U., 1981, MA with honours, 1982; MBA in Fin., NYU, 1988. Asst. treas. Bankers Trust Co., N.Y.C., 1981-84; v.p. Marine Midland Bank, N.Y.C., 1984-89; dir. Barclays Bank PLL, N.Y.C., 1989-95; mng. ptnr. Canterbury Mezzanine Capital LP, N.Y.C., 1995—. Chmn. Rutland Plastics, Inc., N.C. Treas., trustee Manhattan Sch. Music, N.Y.C., 1998—. Mem. Racquet and Tennis Club, Creek Club, Field Club. Episcopalian. Avocations: music, golf, skiing, tennis, charities. Office: Canterbury Mezzanine Capital 600 Fifth Ave 23d Fl New York NY 10020

TURNER, PETER MERRICK, retired manufacturing company executive; b. Toronto, Ont., Can., July 4, 1931; s. William Ian MacKenzie and Marjorie (Merrick) T.; m. Beverley Brophey, Sept. 13, 1958 (dec.); children: Peter Merrick, Christopher Harold, David MacKenzie; m. Alix Johanna Houston, Aug. 17, 1991 (div. 1999). BASc, U. Toronto, 1954; MBA, Harvard U., 1956. Staff asst. controllers dept. Bridgeport Brass Co., Conn., 1956-57; sec. treas. Perkins Paper Products Co., Montreal, Que., Can., 1957-58; with Texaco Can. Ltd., Montreal, 1958-68, treas., 1966-68; dir. budgeting and planning, corp. devel. Molson Breweries Ltd., Montreal, 1968—; v.p. planning Molson Breweries Can. Ltd., 1968-70; v.p. corp. devel. Molson Industries Ltd., Toronto, 1970-72; exec. v.p. Bennett Pump Inc., Muskegon, Mich., 1972-73, pres., chief exec. officer, 1973-78; v.p. corp. planning and devel. Sealed Power Corp., Muskegon, 1978-83, group v.p. internat., 1981-83, group v.p. Gen. Products Group, 1984-89; v.p. bus. devel. SPX Corp., Muskegon, 1989-91, v.p. ops., 1991-92, v.p. corp. planning and devel., 1992-94; ret., 1994; vice chmn. Bennett Pump Co., 1998—. Lectr. extension dept. McGill U., 1960-67, Grand Valley State Coll., 1979 Gen. chmn. red shield appeal Montreal Salvation Army, 1969-70; chmn. McGill Assocs., Montreal, 1969-70; bd. dirs. Hackley Hosp., 1975-94, West Shore Symphony Orch., 1976-94; bd. dirs. Muskegon C.C. Found., 1976-94. Mem. Mount Royal Club, Granite Club, Lake O'Hara Trail Club, Zeta Psi. Episcopalian. Home: 4292 E Glen Ct Muskegon MI 49441-4587

TURNER, RALPH HERBERT, sociologist, educator; b. Effingham, Ill., Dec. 15, 1919; s. Herbert Turner and Hilda Pearl (Bohn) T.; m. Christine Elizabeth Hanks, Nov. 2, 1943; children: Lowell Ralph, Cheryl Christine. BA, U So. Calif., 1941, MA, 1942; postgrad., U. Wis., 1942-43; PhD, U. Chgo., 1948. Rsch. assoc. Am. Coun. Race Relations, 1947-48; faculty UCLA, 1948—, prof. sociology and anthropology, 1959-90, prof. emeritus, 1990—, chmn. dept. sociology, 1963-68; chmn. Acad. Senate U. Calif. System, 1983-84. Vis. summer prof. U. Wash., 1960, U. Hawaii, 1962; vis. scholar Australian Nat. U., 1972; vis. prof. U. Ga., 1975, Ben Gurion U., Israel, 1983; vis. fellow Nuffield Coll. Oxford U., 1980; disting. vis. prof. Am. U., Cairo, Egypt, 1983; adj. prof. China Acad. Social Scis., Beijing, People's Republic China, 1986. Author: (with L. Killian) Collective Behavior, 1957, 2d edit., 1972, 3d edit., 1987, The Social Context of Ambition, 1964, Robert Park on Social Control and Collective Behavior, 1967, Family Interaction, 1970, Earthquake Prediction and Public Policy, 1975, (with J. Nigg, D. Paz, B. Young) Community Response to Earthquake Threat in So. Calif., 1980, (with J. Nigg and D. Paz) Waiting for Disaster, 1986; editl. cons., 1959-62; editor: Sociometry, 1962-64; acting editor: Ann. Rev. of Sociology, 1977-78; assoc. editor, 1978-79, editor, 1980-86; adv. editor: Am. Jour. Sociology, 1954-56, Sociology and Social Rsch., 1961-74; editl. staff: Am. Sociol. Rev., 1955-56; assoc. editor: Social Problems, 1959-62, 67-69; cons. editor: Sociol. Inquiry, 1968-73, Western Sociol. Rev., 1975-79; mem. editl. bd. Mass Emergencies, 1975-79, Internat. Jour. Crit. Sociology, 1974-76, Symbolic Interaction, 1977-90, 95—. Mobilization, 1996—. Mem. behavioral scis. study sect. NIH, 1961-66, chmn., 1963-64; dir.-at-large Social Sci. Rsch. Coun., 1965-66; chmn. panel on pub. policy implications of earthquake predictions Nat. Acad. Scis., 1974-75, also mem. earthquake study del. to Peoples Republic of China, 1976; mem. policy adv. bd. So. Calif. Earthquake Preparedness program, 1987-92, mem. com. social edn. and action L.A. Presbytery, 1954-56. Served to lt. (j.g.) USNR, 1943-46. Recipient Faculty prize Coll. Letters and Scis. UCLA, 1985; Faculty Rsch. fellow Social Sci. Rsch. Coun., 1953-56; Sr. Fulbright scholar U.K., 1956-57; Guggenheim fellow, U.K., 1964-65; Faculty Rsch. lectr. UCLA, 1987, UCLA Emeritus of Yr., 1997. Mem. AAAS (exch. del. to China 1988), AAUP, Am. Sociol. Assn. (coun. 1959-64, chmn. social psychology sect. 1960-61, pres. 1968-69, chmn. sect. theoretical sociology 1973-74, chmn. collective behavior and social movements sect. 1983-84, Cooley-Mead award 1987), Pacific Sociol. Assn. (pres. 1957), Internat. Sociol. Assn. (coun. 1974-82, v.p. 1978-82), Soc. Study Social Problems (exec. com. 1962-63), Soc. for Study Symbolic Interaction (pres. 1982-83, Charles Horton Cooley award 1978, George Herbert Mead award 1990), Sociol. Rsch. Assn. (pres. 1989-90), Am. Coun. of Learned Soc. (exec. com. of coun. 1990-93), UCLA Emeriti Assn. (coun., pres. 1992-93), U. of Calif. Emeriti Assns. (chair-elect 1996-97, chair 1997-98, Panunzio award 2002). Home: 1126 Chautauqua Blvd Pacific Palisades CA 90272-3808 Office: UCLA 405 Hilgard Ave Los Angeles CA 90095-9000

TURNER, RALPH JAMES, obstetrician, gynecologist; b. Waco, Tex., 1952; BS, McMurry U., 1974, BA, 1976; MD, U. Tex. Southwestern, Dallas, 1978. Cert. in med. mgmt. Am. Coll. Physician Exec., Tulane U., 1996, diplomate Am. Coll. Physician Execs.; diplomate Am. Bd. Ob-Gyn. Intern Tripler Army Med. Ctr., Honolulu, 1978-79, resident ob-gyn., 1979-82; ob-gyn. Darnall U.S. Army Cmty. Hosp., Ft. Hood, Tex., 1982-86, Presbyn. Hosp., Dallas, 1986—. Trustee Genesis Physicians Group, 1992—, chmn. 1997-2002; ob-gyn. Columbia Med. Ctr., Plano, Tex., 1994—, Presbyn. Hosp., Plano, 1994—; med. adminstr., interim med. dir. Sys. Health Providers Inc., 1995-97, 99-2001; presenter in field. Contbr. articles to profl. jours. Trustee Found. of Am. Assn. Gynecol. Laparoscopists, 1996—2001, exec. dir., 2001—. Mem. ACOG, Am. Assn. Gynecol. Laparoscopists (bd. trustees 2000—), Am. Coll. Physician Execs., Am. Inst. Ultrasound in Medicine, Am. Soc. for Reproductive Medicine. Methodist. Office: 8160 Walnut Hill Ln Ste 324 Dallas TX 75231-4391 also: Ste 101 1600 Colt Rd Plano TX 75075

TURNER, RAYMOND EDWARD, science educator, researcher, administrator; b. Portsmouth, Va., Dec. 13, 1948; s. Vernon and Kate Alicia (Ely) T.; m. Merlene Jeanette Blackett, Aug. 12, 1972 (div. June 1982); 1 child, Ebony Elysia; m. Margaret Elizabeth Alleyne, May 25, 1985. BS in Chemistry, Bklyn. Coll., 1974; MS, Fordham U., 1982; MS, PhD, Poly. U., Bklyn., 1986; postgrad., Harvard U., 1997. Rsch. technician Cornell U. Med. Sch., 1974-79; rsch. worker Columbia U. Med. Sch., 1979-81; postdoctoral fellow Sch. of Pub. Health Harvard U., Boston, 1987-88; prof. math. and chemistry Roxbury C.C., Boston, 1987-94, assoc. dean math., sci. and tech., 1995-98, exec. dean of sci., media and info. technology, 1999—. Author: (textbook) Developing Concepts in Science, 1991, rev. 2d edit., 1994. Major MSC, USAR, Vietnam. Vis. scholar Harvard U., 1997—. Mem. Am. Chem. Soc., Sigma Xi. Methodist. Achievements include research on the solution properties of hyaluronic acid oligosaccharides. Office: Roxbury Cmty Coll 1234 Columbus Ave Boston MA 02120-3423

TURNER, REGINALD MAURICE, JR., lawyer; b. Detroit, Feb. 25, 1960; s. Reginald and Anne Laura (Mims) T.; m. Marcia Holland, June 10, 1989. BS in Indsl. Psychology, Wayne State U., 1982; JD, U. Mich., 1987. Bar: Mich. With UPS, Livonia, Mich., 1977-83, Profl. Pers. Svc. div. B.P.A. Enterprises, Detroit, 1983-84; summer assoc. Office of the Gen. Counsel GM Corp., Detroit, 1985, 86; law clk. Sachs, Nunn, Kates, Kadushin, O'Hare, Helveston & Waldman, Detroit, 1987; jud. law clk. to Hon. Dennis W. Archer Mich. Supreme Ct., Detroit, 1987-89; ptnr. Sachs, Waldman, O'Hare, Helveston, Hodges & Barnes, P.C., Detroit, 1989—; atty. Clark Hill PLC, Detroit, 2000—. Vice chair Detroit Police Found. White House fellow, 1996-97; recipient Irving Stenn Jr. award U. Mich. Law Sch., 1987; named Barrister of the Yr., Outstanding Young Lawyer State Bar Mich., 1995. Mem. ABA, ACLU, NAACP, Fed. Bar Assn., Nat. Bar Assn., State Bar Mich. (commn., pres. 2002-03), Wolverine Bar Assn. (past pres.), Alpha Phi Alpha. Office: Clark Hill PLC 500 Woodward Ave Ste 3500 Detroit MI 48226-3435 E-mail: rturner@clarkhill.com.

TURNER, ROBERT COMRIE, composer; b. Montreal, Que., Can., June 6, 1920; s. William Thomson and Myrtle Wellsteed (Snowdon) T.; m. Sara Nan Scott, June 30, 1949; children: Alden, Martin, Carolyn. BM, McGill U., 1943, MusD, 1953; postgrad., Royal Coll. Music, 1947-48; MusM, George Peabody Coll. Tchrs., 1950. Sr. music producer Canadian Broadcasting Corp., Vancouver, B.C., 1952-68; lectr. music U. B.C., Vancouver, 1955-57; asst. prof. music Acadia U., Wolfville, N.S., Can., 1968-69; prof. composition U. Manitoba, Winnipeg, 1969-85, prof. emeritus, 1985—. Composer-in-residence MacDowell Colony, Peterborough, N.H., 1987. Over 70 compositions including Opening Night: A Theatre Overture, 1955, The Third Day (Easter Cantata), 1962, Symphony for Strings, 1960, Capriccio Concertante, 1975, Third String Quartet, 1975, opera The Brideship, 1967, Trio (transition) for Violin Cello and Piano, 1969, The Phoenix and the Turtle, 1964, Concerto for Two Pianos and Orchestra, 1971, Johann's Gift to Christmas, 1972, Eidolons, 1972, Variations on The Prairie Settler's Song, 1974, From a Different Country, 1976, Lament for Linos, 1978, Amoroso Canto, 1978, Shadow Pieces (after Joseph Cornell), 1981, opera Vile Shadows, 1983, Symphony in One Movement, 1983, Encounters I-IX, 1984, Time for Three, 1985, Playhouse Music, 1986, Concerto for Viola and Orchestra, 1987, Shades of Autumn, 1987, Manitoba Memoir, 1989, Third Symphony, 1990, a Group of Seven, 1991, The River of Time, 1994, House of Shadows, 1994, Four "Last Songs", 1995, Festival Dance, 1997, Diverti-Memento for Chamber Orch., 1997; All-Turner concert, 1989, Canada House, London; com. mem. Vancouver Internat. Festival; adjudicator Met. and San Francisco Opera auditions; Bramwell Tovey and The Winnipeg Symphony Orch. premiered The River of Time for SATB chorus and orch. in celebration of Robert Turner's 75th yr., 1996. Served with Royal Can. Air Force, 1943-45. Recipient Commemorative medal for 125th Anniversary of Confedn. of Can., 1993, Queen's Golden Jubilee medal, 2003; overseas scholar Royal Coll. Music, 1947-48; fellow Can. Coun., 1966-67; grantee Man. Arts Coun., 1982-83, 85, Can. Coun. Artists, 1990-92. Mem. Soc. Composers, Authors and Music Pubrs. of Can., Can. League Composers, Can. Music Ctr., Order of Can., MacDowell Colony. Home: 1725 Beach Dr Apt 405 Victoria BC Canada V8R 6H9 E-mail: robert-comrie-turner@hotmail.com.

TURNER, ROBERT EDWARD, psychiatrist, educator; b. Hamilton, Ont., Can., June 8, 1926; s. Robert William and Alice May T.; m. Gene Anne Stewart, Sept. 27, 1952; children: Margaret, John, Robert, Richard. BA with honors in Zoology and Chemistry, McMaster U., 1948; MD, U. Toronto, 1952. Intern Hamilton Gen. Hosp., 1952-53; resident Bristol (Eng.) Mental Hosps. Group, 1953-55; practice medicine specializing in psychiatry Toronto, Ont.; dir. Forensic Clinic Toronto Psychiat. Hosp., 1958-66; sr. psychiatrist forensic service Clarke Inst. Psychiatry, Toronto, 1966, chief forensic service, 1967-69, med. dir., 1969-76; asst. prof. dept. psychiatry U. Toronto, 1964-68, prof., 1973-77, prof. forensic psychiatry, 1977-91, prof. emeritus, 1991—. Cons. in psychiatry Law Reform Commn. Can., 1972-85; staff psychiatrist, 1987—; dir. Met. Toronto Forensic Service, 1977-87; hon. cons. Clarke Inst. Psychiatry, 1991—. Author: Pedophilia and Exhibitionism, 1964; contbr. articles on psychiatry and law to profl. jours. Pres. Kenneth G. Gray Found., 1971—; mem. legal task force Com. on Mental Health Svcs. for Ont., Ont. Coun.

Health, 1978-79; dep. warden Cathedral Ch. of St. James, Toronto, 1978-79, 92-94, rector's warden, 1994-96; bd. dirs. Clin. Inst. Addiction Rsch. foun. Ont., 1973-86, chmn., 1985-86; bd. dirs. Addiction Rsch. Found., 1982-86. Recipient Queen's Commemorative Jubilee medal, 2002. Fellow Royal Coll. Physicians and Surgeons Can., Am. Psychiat. Assn. (disting. life fellow), Can. Psychiat. Assn. (life, bd. dirs. 1974-77), Ont. Psychiat. Assn. (life, pres. 1975-76), Can. Med. Assn., Ont. Med. Assn., Med.-Legal Soc. Toronto (coun. 1979-82). Home: 301 1387 Bayview Ave Toronto ON Canada M4G 3A5 Office: Clarke Inst Psychiatry 250 College St Toronto ON Canada M5T 1R8 Office Phone: 416-979-6831. Business E-Mail: dr_turner@rogers.com.

TURNER, ROBERT FOSTER, law educator, writer; b. Atlanta, Feb. 14, 1944; s. Edwin Witcher and Martha Frances (Williams) T. AB, Ind. U., Bloomington, 1968; postgrad., Stanford U., 1972-73; JD, U. Va., 1981, SJD, 1996. Bar: Va. 1982, U.S. Supreme Ct. 1986. Rsch. assoc., pub. affairs fellow Hoover Instn. on War, Revolution and Peace, Stanford U., 1971-74; spl. asst., legis. asst. U.S. Sen. Robert P. Griffin, 1974-79; assoc. dir. Ctr. for Nat. Security Law U. Va., Charlottesville, 1981, 87—; sr. fellow, 1985-86; spl. asst. undersec. for policy Dept. Def., 1981-82; counsel Pres.'s Intelligence Oversight Bd., White House, 1982-84; prin. dep. asst. sec. for legis. and intergovtl. affairs Dept. State, 1984-85; pres. U.S. Inst. Peace, Washington, 1986-87; lectr. in law and in govt. and fgn. affairs U. Va., Charlottesville, 1988-93, assoc. prof., 1993-97, prof., 1997—; Charles H. Stockton prof. internat. law Naval War Coll., 1994-95. Disting. lectr. U.S. Mil. Acad., West Point, 1995. Author: Myths of the Vietnam War: The Pentagon Papers Reconsidered, 1972, Vietnamese Communism: Its Origins and Development, 1975, The War Powers Resolution: Its Implementation in Theory and Practice, 1983, Nicaragua v. United States: A Look at the Facts, 1987, Repealing the War Powers Resolution: Restoring the Rule of Law in U.S. Foreign Policy, 1991, The ABM Treaty and the Senate: Issues of International and Constitutional Law, 1999, The Real Lessons of the Vietnam War, 2002, The Jefferson-Hemings Controversy, 2004, (with John Norton Moore) The Legal Structure of Defense Organization, 1986, International Law and the Brezhnev Doctrine, 1987, Readings on International Law, 1995, (with John Norton Moore and Frederick Tipson) National Security Law, 1990, (with John Norton Moore and Guy B. Roberts) National Security Law Documents, 1995; contbr. articles to profl. jours. and newspapers. Pres. Endowment of U.S. Inst. Peace, 1986-87; trustee Intercollegiate Studies Inst., 1986-92; bd. dirs. Thomas Jefferson Inst. for Pub. Policy, 1997—; chmn. scholars commn. on Jefferson-Hemings matter Thomas Jefferson Heritage Soc., 2000-01. Grantee Hoover Press, 1972, Earhart Found., 1980, 1989-90, Inst. Ednl. Affairs, 1980, Carthage Found., 1980. Mem. ABA (chmn. com. on exec.-congl. rels., sec. internat. law and practice 1983-86, adv. com. on law and nat. security 1984-86, standing com. on law and nat. security 1986-92, chmn. 1989-92, editor ABA Nat. Security Law Report 1992-99), Federalist Soc. (chmn. subcom. on nat. security law 1998—), Bd. Rsch. Cons., Inst. Fgn. Policy Analysis, Mensa, Am. Soc. Internat. Law, Nat. Eagle Scout Assn., Coun. on Fgn. Rels., Acad. of Polit. Sci. Office: Univ Va Sch of Law Ctr for Nat Security Law 580 Massie Rd Charlottesville VA 22903-1738 Office Phone: 434-924-4083. Business E-Mail: bobturner@virginia.edu.

TURNER, ROBERT GERALD, university president; b. Atlanta, Tex., Nov. 25, 1945; s. Robert B. and Oreta Lois (Porter) T.; m. Gail Oliver, Dec. 21, 1968; children: Angela Jan, Jessica Diane AA, Lubbock Christian Coll., 1966, LLD (hon.), 1985, Pepperdine U., 1989; BS, Abilene Christian U., 1968; MA, U. Tex., 1970, PhD, 1975. Tchr. Weatherford High Sch., Tex., 1968-69; tchr. Lanier High Sch., Austin, Tex., 1969-70; instr. psychology San Antonio Coll., 1970-72; instr. Prairie View A & M U., Tex., 1973-75; asst. prof. psychology Pepperdine U., Malibu, Calif., 1975-78, assoc. prof. psychology, 1978-79, dir. testing, 1975-76, chmn. social sci. div., 1976-78, assoc. v.p. univ. affairs, 1979; assoc. prof. psychology U. Okla., Norman, 1979-84, exec. asst. to pres., 1979-81, acting provost, 1982, v.p. exec. affairs, 1981-84; chancellor U. Miss., University, 1984-95; pres. So. Meth. U., Dallas, 1995—. Pres. Southeastern Conf., 1985-87; trustee Pepperdine U., 1994-95; mem. Pres.'s Commn., NCAA, 1989-92, chmn., 1991-92; mem. Knight Commn. on Intercollegiate Athletics, 1991-2004; chmn. pres. coun. Miss. Assn. Colls., 1985-86; mem. def. adv. com. Svc. Acad. Athletic Programs, 1992—; bd. dirs. J.C. Penney, Am. Advantage Funds. Author: (with L. Willerman) Readings About Individual and Group Differences, 1979. Contbr. articles to profl. jours. Recipient Outstanding Alumni award Abilene Christian U., 1989; inducted New Boston H.S. Athletic Hall of Fame, 1993. Mem. Young Pres. Orgn., Sigma Xi, Beta Alpha Psi, Phi Theta Kappa, Alpha Chi, Phi Kappa Phi. Mem. Ch. of Christ. Avocations: reading, tennis, golf, travel. Office: So Meth Univ Office Of The Pres Dallas TX 75275-0001

TURNER, ROBERT I. finance company executive; b. 1953; BA, SUNY, Binghamton, 1973; MSBA, U. Mass., 1976. CPA. With Price Waterhouse, 1979-81; with treas. and investment banking divsn. Citicorp, 1982-87; corp. v.p. PaineWebber Inc., 1988-95; CFO Knight Securities; mem. adv. bd. Roundtable Ptnrs., LLC, 1996; exec. v.p., CFO, treas., dir. Knight Trading Group, Inc. (formerly Knight/Trimark Group), Jersey City; CFO Knight Securities. Office: 23d Fl 525 Washington Blvd Jersey City NJ 07310

TURNER, ROBERT LLOYD, state legislator; b. Columbus, Miss., Sept. 14, 1947; s. Roosevelt and Beatrice (Hargrove) T.; m. Gloria Harrell; children: Roosevelt, Robert, Ryan. BS, U. Wis., Racine, 1976. Mgr. French Quarter Restaurant, Racine, 1989; legislator Wis. State Assembly, Madison, 1990—, mem. transp. com. bldg. commn., mem. ways and means com., labor com., fin. institutions com., minority vice chmn. caucus, highway com., chmn. Dem. Caucus. Br. sales mgr. ETG Temporaries, Inc., Racine, 1989—; pub. Communicator News, Racine, 1989—; v.p. Racine Raider Football Team. State chmn. Dem. Black Polit. Caucus, Madison; pres. Bd. Health, Racine; chmn. Wis. State Elections Bd., Madison, 1990; alderman Racine City Coun., 1976—; chair Econ. Devel. Com., Racine; regional dir. Badger State Games, Racine; active Pvt. Industry Coun. Southeastern Wis., 1988-89, bd. dirs. Racine County Youth Sports Assn.; active Racine Juneteenth Day Com., bd. advisors Big Bros./Big Sisters. Sgt. USAF, 1967-71, Vietnam. Decorated Commendation medal; named Man of Yr. 2d Missionary Bapt. Ch., 1983. Mem. Dem. Caucus (chmn., 2003), Urban League (pres. bd. dirs.), NAACP (2d v.p.), VFW, Vietnam Vets. Am. (life mem.), Am. Legion, Masons (supreme coun. 33rd degree), Shriners. Democrat. Home: 36 Mckinley Ave Racine WI 53404-3414 Office: Wis Assembly PO Box 8953 Madison WI 53708-8953

TURNER, RONALD L. information services executive; BS in Aerospace Engrng., U. Tenn.; MS in Engrng., U. Fla.; MS in Mgmt., MIT. Sys. command USAF, 1968—73; with Martin Marietta, 1973—87; pres., CEO GEC Marconi Electronic Sys., 1987—93; chmn., pres., CEO Ceridian Corp., Mpls., 1993—. Bd. dir. Ceridian Corp., FLIR Sys., Inc., Minn. Bus. Partnership, Minn. Mtg.; v.chmn. Electronic Industries Alliance. Office: Ceridian Corp 3311 E Old Shakopee Rd Minneapolis MN 55425-1640

TURNER, ROSS JAMES, investment corporation executive; b. Winnipeg, Man., Can., May 1, 1930; permanent U.S. resident, 1980; s. James Valentine and Gretta H. (Ross) T.; children: Ralph, Rick, Tracy., U. Man. Extension, 1951, Banff Sch. Advanced Mgmt., 1956. Chmn./pres., CEO Genstar Corp., San Francisco, 1976-86, also bd. dirs.; chmn. Genstar Investment Corp., San Francisco, 1987—. Fellow Soc. Mgmt. Accts. Can.; mem. Pacific Union Club, Rancho Santa Fe Golf Club, Peninsula Golf and Country Club. Office: Genstar Investment Corp Four Embarcadero Ctr Ste 1900 San Francisco CA 94111-4191 E-mail: dcordell@gencap.com.

TURNER, SHARON P. dean, dental educator, dentist; b. Charleston, W.Va., Aug. 8, 1950; d. George Brock and Anna Hopkins Pullen; m. Aubrey Williams Turner, Jr., Feb. 26, 1972; children: Brock Leslie Turner, Martin Gresham Turner, Karen Anna Turner. BA in Biology, Winthrop U., 1971; DDS, U. N.C., 1979; JD, N.C. Ctrl U., 1995. Lic.: N.C. (atty.); dentist N.C., Oreg., diplomate Am. Acad. Pain Mgmt. Pvt. dental practitioner Dengler & Turner, Raleigh, N.C., 1985-86; asst. prof. of diagnostic scis. U. N.C. Sch. of Dentistry, Chapel Hill, 1986-94, assoc. prof. of diagnostic scis., 1994-98, dir. patient admissions and emergency svcs., 1986-94, dir. dental faculty practice, 1989-98, assoc. dean for adminstrn. planning, 1994-98; dean, prof. dentistry Oreg. Health and Sci. U. Sch. Dentistry, Portland, 1998—2003; dean U. Ky. Coll. Dentistry, Lexington, 2003—. Cons. VA Hosp., Durham, N.C., 1999. Contbg. author: Oral Surgery, 1999. Youth group leader Eno River Unitarian Universalist, Durham, 1996-97, Sunday Sch. tchr., 1997-98; girl scout leader Pines of Carolina Coun., Girl Scouts U.S., Durham, N.C., 1990-94. Named one of Top 25 Visionary Leaders in Dentistry, Am. Student Dental Assn., 1999. Fellow Internat. Coll. Dentists, Am. Coll. Dentists, Am. Coll. Legal Medicine; mem. ADA, Am. Dental Edn. Assn., Am. Acad. Pain Mgmt., Internat. Assn. Dental Rsch., Intenat. Assn. for Study of Pain, Soc. for Exec. Leadership in Academic Medicine (v.p. 1999-2000, pres. 2000-01), Acad. General Dentistry. Avocations: swimming, hiking, singing. Office: U Ky Coll Dentistry Chandler Med Ctr 800 Rose St Lexington KY 40536-9707*

TURNER, STAFFORD, education educator, baritone; s. Eunice Turner; m. Rebecca Byerley, Sept. 9, 1961. AA, Truett-McConnell Coll., Cleve., GA, 1981; MusB, Shorter Coll., Rome, GA, 1983; MusM, U. N.Tex., Denton, TX, 1987; Mus D, Coll. Conservatory of Music-Univ. of Cin., Cin., OH, 2000. Instr. of music Shorter Coll., Rome, Ga., 1987—92; asst. prof. of voice, voice area head Hardin-Simmons U., Abilene, Tex., 2000—04; assoc. prof. music in voice Shenandoah Conservatory of Shenandoah U., Winchester, Va., 2004—. Singer: (Operas) (oratorio, recital) various (Abilene Cultural Affairs Vol. of the Yr., 2002, Wash. Internat. Voice Competition, 1992, Met. Opera Nat. Coun. Auditions-Regional Finalist, 1990, Met. Opera Nat. Coun. Auditions-2nd Pl. Winner, SE Region, 1983). Musician First Ctrl. Presbyn. Ch., Abilene, Tex., 2000—03. Fellow Tchg. Asst., U. Cin., 1995-1997, Study/Performance, Tanglewood Music Festival, 1996, Tchg. Asst., U. of North Tex., 1984-1986; scholar Study in Bayreuth, Germany, Wagner Soc. of Bremen, Germany, 1994, Study in Graz, Austria, Am. Inst. of Musical Studies, 1992, Study in Salzburg, Austria (Mozarteum), Pro Mozart Soc., Atlanta, GA, 1990. Mem.: Nat. Assn. of Teachers of Singing, Coll. Music Soc., Phi Theta Kappa, Pi Kappa Lambda, Phi Mu Alpha. Office: Shenandoah U Conservatory of Music 1460 University Dr Abilene TX 22601

TURNER, STANSFIELD, former government official, lecturer, writer, teacher; b. Chgo., Dec. 1, 1923; s. Oliver Stansfield and Wilhelmina Josephine (Wagner) T.; m. Eli Karin Gilbert, Mar. 16. 1985 (dec. Jan. 2000). Student, Amherst Coll., 1941-43, DCL, 1975; BS, U.S. Naval Acad., 1946; MA (Rhodes scholar), Oxford U., 1950, LIID, Sierra Nev. Coll., 1984; HumD, Roger Williams Coll., 1975; DSc in Edn, Bryant Coll., 1977; LLD, Salve Regina Coll., 1977, The Citadel, 1980, Pace U., 1980. Ensign USN, 1946, advanced through grades to adm., 1975, ret., 1979; served primarily in destroyers; commd. U.S.S. Horne, guided missile cruiser, 1967-68; aide to Sec. Navy; comdr. carrier task group 6th Fleet, 1970-71; dir. systems analysis div. Office Chief Naval Ops., Navy Dept., Washington, 1971-72; pres. Naval War Coll., Newport, R.I., 1972-74; comdr. U.S. Second Fleet, 1974-75; comdr.-in-chief Allied Forces So. Europe, NATO, 1975-77; dir. CIA, Washington, 1977-81; John M. Olin Disting. prof. nat. security U.S. Mil. Acad., West Point, 1989-90; prof. U. Md. Grad. Sch. Pub. Affairs, 1991—. Sr. rsch. fellow Norwegian Nobel Inst., Oslo, Norway, 1995-96; mem. bd. visitors U.S. Naval Acad., 1996—. Author: Secrecy and Democracy, 1985, Terrorism and Democracy, 1991, Caging the Nuclear Genie, 1997, Caging the Genies: A Workable Plan for Chemical, Biological and Nuclear Weapons. Decorated Nat. Security medal, Legion of Merit, Bronze Star. Home and Office: PO Box 2117 Springfield VA 22152-0117

TURNER, STEPHEN MILLER, lawyer, oil company executive; b. Omaha, Mar. 13, 1939; s. Clinton Heron and Margaret Elizabeth (Miller) T.; m. Claudine Mengin, Aug. 10, 1968; children; Marshall C., Scott M. BA, William Jewell Coll., 1961; JD, U. Iowa, 1964; LLM, U. Chgo., 1966. Bar: Ohio 1969, D.C. 1975, N.Y. 1982. Asst. U.S. atty. U.S. Dept. Justice, Sioux City, Iowa, 1966-67; U.S. atty. No. Dist. of Iowa, Sioux City, 1967-68; assoc. Squire, Sanders & Dempsey, Cleve., 1968-74, mng. ptnr. Brussels, 1975-82, ptnr. N.Y.C., 1982-89; sr. staff assoc. Pres.'s Counsel on Exec. Reorgn., Washington, 1969-70; sr. v.p., gen. counsel Texaco Inc., White Plains, N.Y., 1989-99. Ohio Bar Assn., N.Y. State Bar Assn., D.C. Bar Assn., Burning Tree Country Club (Greenwich). Republican. Presbyterian. Home: 67 Londonderry Dr Greenwich CT 06830-3509 Office: Texaco Inc 2000 Westchester Ave Greenwich CT 06830

TURNER, STEPHEN PARK, philosopher, sociologist, educator; b. Chgo., Ill., Mar. 1, 1951; s. Lawrence Lynn and Natalie (Stephens) Turner; m. Kimberly Anne Wills, Apr. 21, 1990; children: Evan Wills, Douglas Carrera. AB, AM in Sociology, U. Mo., Columbia, 1971, AM in Philosophy, 1972, PhD in Sociology, 1975. Asst. prof. U. South Fla., 1975—80, assoc. prof., 1980—84; vis. prof. Va. Poly. Inst. and State U., Blacksburg, 1982, U. Notre Dame, Notre Dame, Ind., 1985; prof., dept. of sociology U. South Fla., 1984—87; vis. prof. Boston U., Boston, 1987; grad. rsch. prof., dept. of sociology U. South Fla., 1987—89, grad. rsch. prof., dept. of philosophy Tampa, Fla., 1989—; dir. Ctr. Social and Polit. Thought, 1994—. Author: (book) Sociological Explanation as Translation, 1980, The Search for a Methodology of Social Science: Durkheim, Weber, and the 19th Century Problem of Cause, Probability, and Action, 1986, The Social Theory of Practices, Brains/Practices/Relativism: Social Theory after Cognitive Science, Liberal Democracy 3.0: Civil Society in an Age of Experts; co-author: (with F. Weed): Conflict in Organizations, 1983; co-author: (with R. Factor) Max Weber and the Dispute Over Reason and Value: A Study in Philosophy, Ethics, and Politics, 1984; co-author: (with Jonathan Turner) The Impossible Science: An Institutional Analysis of American Sociology, 1990; co-author: (with Dirl Käsler) Sociology Responds to Fascism, 1992; co-author: (with Regis A. Factor) Max Weber: The Lawyer as Social Thinker, 1994; co-editor (with M. Wardell): Sociological Theory in Transition, 1986; editor: (collection) The Cambridge Companion to Weber, (book) Émile Durkheim: Sociologist and Moralist, 1993, The Social Theory of Practices: Tradition, Tacit Knowledge, and Presuppositions, 1994; contbg. editor: (jour.) Sociological Theory, 1985—88, Social Studies of Science, 1986—, History of the Human Sciences, 1986—; contbr. Named Simon Hon. Prof., U. Manchester, 1996-1997; fellow Fellowships for U. Profs., NEH, 1991-1992, Fellowship, Swedish Collegium for Advanced Study in Social Scis., 1992, 1998. Mem.: Soc. Social Studies Sci., So. Sociol. Soc., Am. Sociol. Assn., Am. Philos. Assn., St. Petersburg Yacht Club, Prairie Club. Home: 103 2nd Ave Saint Petersburg FL 33706-4303 Office: Univ S Fla Dept Philosophy Tampa FL 33620

TURNER, TED (ROBERT EDWARD TURNER), former television executive, philanthropist; b. Cin., Nov. 19, 1938; s. Robert Edward and Florence (Rooney) Turner; m. Judy Nye (div.); children: Laura Lee, Robert Edward IV; m. Jane Shirley Smith, June 1965 (div. 1988); children: Beau, Rhett, Jennie; m. Jane Fonda, Dec. 21, 1991 (div. 2001). Grad. in classics, Brown U.; DSc in Commerce (hon.), Drexel U., 1982; LLD (hon.), Samford U., 1982, Atlanta U., 1984; D Entrepreneurial Sci. (hon.), Cen. New Eng. Coll. Tech., 1983; D in Pub. Adminstrn. (hon.), Mass. Maritime Acad., 1984; D in Bus. Adminstrn. (hon.), U. Charleston, 1985. Account exec. Turner Advt. Co., Atlanta, 1961—63, pres., COO, 1963—70; pres., chmn. bd. Turner Broadcasting Sys., Inc., Atlanta, 1970—96; vice chmn. Time Warner Inc. (merger Turner Broadcasting Sys.), 1996—2000; bd. dirs. Atlanta Hawks; owner Atlanta Braves. Co-founder Nuclear Threat Initiative, DC, 2001—; bd. dirs. Martin Luther King Ctr., Atlanta. Named Yachtsman of Yr. 4 times; named to Hall of Fame, Promotion and Mktg. Assn., 1980, Nat. Assn. for Sport and Phys. Edn. Hall of Fame, 1986; recipient Outstanding Entrepreneur of Yr. award, Sales Mktg. and Mgmt. Mag., 1979, Salesman of Yr. award, Sales and Mktg. Execs., 1980, Pvt. Enterprise Exemplar medal, Freedoms Found. at Valley Forge, 1980, Communicator of Yr. award, Pub. Rels. Soc. Am., 1981, N.Y. Broadcasters, 1981, Internat. Communicator of Yr. award, Sales and Mktg. Execs., 1981, Nat. News Media award, VFW, 1981, Disting. Svc. in Telecomm. award, Ohio U. Coll. Communication, 1982, Carr Van Anda award, Ohio Sch. Journalism, 1982, Spl. award, Edinburgh Internat. TV Festival, Scotland, 1982, Media Awareness award, United Vietnam Vets. Orgn., 1983, Bd. Govs. award, Atlanta chpt. NATAS, 1982, Spl. Olympics award, Spl. Olympics Com., 1983, Dinner of Champions award, Ga. chpt. Multiple Sclerosis Soc., 1983, Praca Spl. Merit award, N.Y. Puerto Rican Assn. for Cmty. Affairs, 1983, World Telecomm. Pioneer award, N.Y. State Broadcasters Assn., 1984, Golden Plate award, Am. Acad. Achievement, 1984, Outstanding Supporter Boy Scouting award, Nat. Boy Scout Coun., 1984, Silver Satellite award, Am. Women in Radio and TV, Lifetime Achievement award, N.Y. Internat. Film and TV Festival, 1984, Corp. Star of Yr. award, Nat. Leukemia Soc., 1985, Disting. Achievement award, U. Ga., 1985, Tree of Life award, Jewish Nat. Fund, 1985, Bus. Exec. of Yr. award, Ga. Security Dealers Assn., 1985, Life Achievement award, Popular Culture Assn., 1986, George Washington Disting. Patriot award, SAR, 1986, Mo. Honor medal, Sch. Journalism, U. Mo., 1987, Golden Ace award, Nat. Cable TV Acad., 1987, Sol Taishoff award, Nat. Press Found., 1988, Citizen Diplomat award, Ctr. for Soviet-Am. Dialogue, 1988, Chmn.'s award, Cable Advt. Bur., 1988, Directorate award, NATAS, 1989, Paul White award, Radio and TV News Dirs. Assn., 1989, Bus. Marketer of Yr. award, Am. Mktg. Assn., 1989, Disting. Svc. award, Simon Wiesenthal Ctr., 1990, Glasnost award, Vols. Am. and Soviet Life mag., 1990, Time Mag. Man of the Year, 1991, Cable & Broadcasting's Man of the Century, 1999, Carnegie Medal of Philanthropy, 2001, numerous others; won America's Cup in his yacht Courageous, 1977. Mem.: NAACP (life; bd. dirs. Atlanta chpt.), Nat. Cable TV Assn. (Pres.'s award 1979, 1989, Regional Employer of Yr. award 1976), Cousteau Soc., Nat. Audubon Soc., Bay Area Cable Club (hon.). Avocations: sailing, fishing. Office: Nuclear Threat Initiative 1747 Pennsylvania Ave NW 7th Flr Washington DC 20006

TURNER, THOMAS MARSHALL, telecommunications executive, consultant; b. Cumberland, Md., Aug. 17, 1951; s. James Richard and Laura Roselie (Durst) T. BS in Indsl. Tech. and Mgmt., U. Md., 1973, MA in Indsl. Tech. and Mgmt., 1980. Grad. asst U. Md., College Park, 1975-76; sales assoc., gen. mgr. Equity Trades Reality, Riverdale, Md., 1976-83; account exec. RCA Corp., Greenbelt, Md., 1983; sr. telecomm. cons. CMC, Inc., Washington, 1984 86, ORS Assoc., McLean, Va., 1986-87; owner, pres. T-1 Comm., Boca Raton, Fla., 1987—, Optimum Reconciliation Svc., Inc., Pompano Beach, Fla., 1996—. Cons. Marriott Corp., Bethesda, Md., 1990-99, Group Health, Inc., N.Y.C., 1991-92, Colgate-Palmolive Co., 1993-94, State of Md., 1993, Trump Corp., 1993, Martin-Marietta, 1994, Matsushita, 1994, Montgomery Wards, 1994, Nabisco Foods, 1994, Harris Corp., 1995-99, Urban League, 1995-99, EDS, 1995-99, Chem. Bank, 1996-99, Chase Manhattan Bank, 1997-99, Arnold & Porter, 2001, Bechtel, 2001—, Booz, Allen & Hamilton, 2002, Comsat, 2001—, Fairchild, 2001—, GEICO, 2001—, Howard Hughes Med. Inst., 2001—, IBM, 2001—, State Farm Ins., 2001—, Swales Aerospace, 2002—, Wells Fargo, 2001—; grad. asst. instr. Dale Carnegie Inst., 1992. Contbr. articles to profl. jours. Vol. ARC, Riverdale, Md., 1977-80; instr. Jr. Achievement Bus. Co-op, Rockville, Md., 1979-82. Recipient Highest Achievment award Dale Carnegie Inst., 1989. Mem. ASTD, Telecomm. Mgrs. Assn. of Capital Area, Toastmasters, Sigma Alpha Epsilon Alumni Assn.

TURNER, TIMOTHY THOMAS, music educator, musician; b. Steubenville, Ohio, Oct. 30, 1975; s. Robin Stilwell and Ouanita Dixie Turner; m. Mica Hope Kale, Dec. 15, 1998; children: Kirsten Cheyene, Kody Austin. BA in Music Edn., West Liberty State Coll., W.Va., 1999. Registered EMT Nat. Registry and Ohio Cert., 2000, cert. CPR instr. Am. Heart Assn., 2002; music edn. K-12 tchr. Ohio, W.Va., and Pa., 2003. Clk. Hills Dept. Store, Steubenville, Ohio, 1994—99, ch. organist Brilliant Christian Ch., Ohio, 1999—; band dir. Buckeye Local H.S., Rayland, Ohio, 1999—2000; gen. music tchr. Switzerland of Ohio Sch. Dist., Beallsville, 2000—01; choir dir. Indian Creek Jr. High, Mingo Junction, Ohio, 2001—02; band dir. Wellsburg Mid. Sch., W.Va., 2002—. Substitute condr. Wash. Symphony Orch., 2003—04; piano tuner private; mem. Island Saxophone Quartet. Mem.: Nat. Assn. of Music Edn. (licentiate; collegiet pres. 1997—98), Mingo Sportsman's Club. Democrat-Npl. Church Of Jesus Christ Of Latter-Day Saints. Office: Wellsburg Mid Sch Band 1447 Main St Wellsburg WV 26070 Personal E-mail: turner@musician.org.

TURNER, TINA (ANNA MAE BULLOCK), singer; b. Brownsville, Tenn., Nov. 26, 1939; m. Ike Turner, 1956; children: Craig, Ike Jr., Michael, Ronald. Singer (with): Ike Turner Kings of Rhythm, and Ike and Tina Turner Revue; appeared in (films) Gimme Shelter, 1970, Soul to Soul, 1971, Tommy, 1975, Sgt. Pepper's Lonely Hearts Club Band, 1978, Mad Max Beyond Thunderdome, 1985, Break Every Rule, 1986, Last Action Hero, 1993, concert tours of Europe, 1966, Japan and Africa, 1971, Showtime TV concert Wildest Dreams, albums with Ike Turner Hunter, 1970, Ike and Tina Show II, Ike and Tina Show, 1966, Ike and Tina Turner, Bad Dreams, 1973, Ike and Tina Turner Greatest Hits, vol. 1.2 and 3, 1989, Greatest Hits, 1990, Proud Mary, 1991, The Ike and Tina Turner Collection, 1993, solo albums Let Me Touch Your Mind, 1972, Tina Turns the Country On, 1974, Acid Queen, 1975, Love Explosion, 1977, Rough, 1978, Airwaves, 1979, Private Dancer, 1984, Break Every Rule, 1986, Tina Live In Europe, 1988, Foreign Affair, 1989, Simply the Best, 1991, What's Love Got to Do With It? (soundtrack), 1993, recordings Sixties to Nineties, with others, 1994, Wildest Dreams, 1996, Twenty Four Seven, 2000; performer (with USA): for Africa on song We are The World, 1985; author: (autobiography) I, Tina, 1985. Nominee Grammy (Best Pop Female Vocal) for "I Don't Wanna Fight", 1994; named to Rock and Roll Hall of Fame, 1991; recipient Grammy award, 1972, 1985, 1986.

TURNER, TOM, writer, editor; b. Oakland, Calif., 1942; m. Mary Jorgensen; children: Bret and Kathryn (twins). BA in Polit. Sci., U. Calif., 1965. Vol. Peace Corps, Turkey, 1965-67; grant analyst Head Start, 1968; editor, adminstrv. asst. Sierra Club, 1968-69; various positions including exec. dir. Friends of the Earth, 1969-86, also editor Not Man Apart; staff writer, dir. publs., sr. editor Earthjustice, 1986—. Author: Wild By Law: the Sierra Club Legal Defense Fund and the Places It Has Saved, 1990, Sierra Club: 100 Years of Protecting Nature, 1991, Justice on Earth, Earthjustice and the People It Has Served, 2002; contbr. to The Ency. of the Environment, 1994, also chpts. to books; contbr. articles to Sierra, Defenders, Wilderness, San Francisco Chronicle, San Francisco Examiner, L.A. Times, Oakland Tribune, Washington Post, Mother Earth News, Outside, others. Office: Earthjustice 426 17th St 6th Fl Oakland CA 94612 Office Phone: 510-550-6700. Business E-mail: tturner@earthjustice.org.

TURNER, W. BRUCE, computer company executive; B, U.S. Mil. Acad.; MBA, U. Tampa, 1989. Dir. leisure equity rsch. Raymond James, 1989-94; mng. dir. equity rsch. Salomon Smith Barney, 1994-99; chmn. GTECH Holdings Corp., West Greenwich, R.I., 2000—. Office: GTech Corp 55 Technology Way West Greenwich RI 02817-1717 Fax: 401-392-1000.

TURNER, WALTER W. manufacturing executive; Grad., Glenville State Coll. Various positions Koppers Industries, Pitts., 1969—, pres., CEO, 1998—. Chmn. bd. Tarconard S.D., Nyborg, Denmark. Office: Koppers Industries 436 7th Ave Ste 2026 Pittsburgh PA 15219-1800

TURNER, WARREN AUSTIN, state legislator; b. Berkeley, Calif., Dec. 21, 1926; s. Warren Mortimer and Rebecca Oline (Noer) T.; m. Beverly Daune Mackay, Mar. 29, 1952; children: Daune Scott, Warren Adair, Alan Corey. BA, U. Calif., Berkeley, 1950, BS, 1952, MPH, 1958. Pub. acct. Price Waterhouse, San Francisco, 1951-52, AW Blackman, Las Vegas, Nev., 1952-56; asst. adminstr. Marin Gen. Hosp., San Rafael, Calif., 1958-60; assoc. dir. UCLA Hosp., 1960-68; founding adminstr. Walter O. Boswell Meml. Hosp., Sun City, Ariz., 1968-81; pres. Sun Health Corp., 1981-89; mem. Ariz. Senate, Phoenix, 1993-97, chmn. rules com., vice chair health com., mem. appropriations, family svcs. and transp. com., 1995-97. Chmn. appropriation subcom., K-12, C.C.'s and natural resources. With USN, 1944-46. Mem.: Ariz. Acad. Republican. Avocations: breeding and showing siamese cats, fishing, mining. Home: 18432 W Glendale Ave Waddell AZ 85355-9737

TURNER, WESLEY R. publishing executive; m. Shirley; children: Sara, Leslie. Grad., U. Tex. With Ft. Worth Press, 1973-75; from advtsg. sales rep. to v.p. advtsg. Ft. Worth Star-Telegram, 1975-86, pres., publ., 1997—; exec. v.p., gen. mgr. Kansas City Star, 1990-97; pres. Sutton Industries, 1987-90. Office: Knight Ridder Inc Fort Worth Star-Telegram 400 W 7th St Fort Worth TX 76102-4701

TURNER, WILLIAM COCHRANE, international management consultant; b. Red Oak, Iowa, May 27, 1929; s. James Lyman and Josephine (Cochrane) T.; m. Cynthia Dunbar, July 16, 1955; children: Scott Christopher, Craig Dunbar, Douglas Gordon. BS, Northwestern U., 1952; LLD (hon.), Thunderbird Am. Grad. Sch. Internat. Mgmt., 1993. Pres., chmn. bd. dirs. Western Mgmt. Cons., Inc., Phoenix, 1955-74, Western Mgmt. Cons. Europe, S.A., Brussels, 1968-74; U.S. amb., permanent rep. OECD, Paris, 1974-77, vice chmn. exec. com., 1976-77, U.S. rep. Energy Policy Com., 1976-77, mem. U.S. dels. internat. meetings, 1974-77; chmn., CEO Argyle Atlantic Corp., Phoenix, 1977—. Mem. western internat. trade group U.S. Dept. Commerce, 1972-74; U.S. Rep. Consultative Group parent orgn. Coord. Com. (COCOM) Multilateral Export Controls Communist Nations, Paris, 1974-77; chmn. European adv. coun., 1981-88, Asia Pacific adv. coun. AT&T Internat., 1981-88; mem. U.S.-Japan Bus. Coun., Washington, 1987-93, European adv. coun. IBM World Trade Europe/Mid. East/Africa Corp., 1977-80; Asia Pacific adv. coun. Am. Can Co., Greenwich, Conn., 1981-85, GE of Brazil adv. coun. GE Co., Coral Gables, Fla., 1979-81, Caterpillar of Brazil adv. coun. Caterpillar Tractor Co., Peoria, Ill., 1979-84, Caterpillar Asia Pacific Adv. Coun., 1984-90, U.S. adv. com. Trade Negotiations, 1982-84; chmn., dir. WorldWideTalk, Inc., Melbourne, Fla., 1999—; founding mem. Pacific Coun. Internat. Policy, L.A., 1995—; chmn. internat. adv. coun. Avon Products, Inc., N.Y.C., 1985-98; adv. coun. Spencer Stuart and Assocs., N.Y.C., 1984-90; chmn., internat. adv. coun. Advanced Semiconductor Materials Internat. NV, Bilthoven, The Netherlands, 1985-88; co-chmn. internat. adv. bd. Univ. of Nations, Lausanne, Switzerland and Kona, Hawaii, 1985—; bd. govs. Joseph H. Lauder Inst. Mgmt. and Internat. Studies, U. Pa., 1983-2001; trustee Heard Mus., Phoenix, 1983-86, nat. adv. bd., 1986-93; chmn. adv. bd. One Touch, Encinitas, Calif., 2002—, Significant Ventures, Inc., Solano Beach, Calif., 2002—. Bd. dirs. Rural Metro Corp., Phoenix, 1993—; mem. vestry Am. Cathedral, Paris, 1976—77; nat. trustee Phoenix Country Day Sch., 1971—74; bd. govs. Atlantic Inst. Internat. Affairs, Paris, 1977—88; dir. Atlantic Inst. Found., Inc., N.Y.C., 1984—90; active European Cmty.-U.S. Businessmen's Coun., 1978—79; nat. trustee Nat. Symphony Orch. Assn., Washington, 1973—83, Am. Sch., Paris, 1976—77, Orme Sch., Mayer, Ariz., 1970—74; nat. coun. Salk Inst., 1978—82; mem. U.S. Adv. Com. Internat. Edn. and Cultural Affairs, 1969—74; nat. rev. bd. Ctr. Cultural and Tech. Interchange Between East and West, 1970—74; trade and environ. com. Nat. Adv. Coun. for Environ. Policy and Tech.-U.S. EPA, Washington, 1991—95; chmn. Internat. Adv. Coun. Plasma Tech., Inc., Santa Fe, 1992—97; trustee Thunderbird Am. Grad Sch. Internat. Mgmt., 1972—, chmn. bd. trustees, 1987—89; adv. bd. Ctr. Strategic and Internat. Studies, Georgetown U., 1977—81; bd. govs. Am. Hosp. of Paris, 1974—77; pres., bd. dirs. Phoenix Symphony Assn., 1969—70; chmn. Ariz. Joint Econ. Devel. Com., 1967—68; exec. com., bd. dirs. Ariz. Dept. Econ. Planning and Devel., 1968—70; chmn. bd. Ariz. Crippled Children's Svcs., 1964—65; treas. Ariz. Rep. Com., 1956—57; chmn. Ariz. Young Rep. League, 1955—56; founding chmn. bd. Mercy Ships Internat., Inc., Lindale, Tex., 1985—2000, bd. dirs., 2000—; dir. exec. com., chmn. internat. com. Ariz. Econ. Coun., Phoenix, 1989—93; dir. exec. com. Orgn. for Free Trade and Devel., Phoenix, 1991—93; bd. dirs. World Wildlife Fund/US, 1983—85, World Wildlife Fund/The Conservation Found., 1985—89, Nat. Coun., 1989—2002. Recipient East-West Ctr. Disting. Svc. award, 1977. Mem. U.S. Coun. Internat. Bus. (trustee, exec. com.), Coun. Fgn. Rels., Coun. Am. Ambs. (vice chmn. bd.), Nat. Adv. Coun. on Bus. Edn., Met. Club (N.Y.C.), Paradise Valley (Ariz.) Country Club, Bohemian Club (San Francisco), Metropolitan Club, NYC. Fax: 480-948-4674. Office Phone: 480-998-1890. E-mail: wct-aac@cox.net.

TURNER, WILLIAM WEYAND, writer; b. Buffalo, N.Y., Apr. 14, 1927; s. William Peter and Magdalen (Weyand) T.; m. Margaret Peiffer, Sept. 12, 1964; children: Mark Peter, Lori Ann. BS, Canisius Coll., 1949. Spl. agt. in various field offices FBI, 1951-61; free-lance writer Calif., 1963—; sr. editor Ramparts Mag., San Francisco, 1967—. Investigator and cons. Nat. Wiretap Commn., 1975; U.S. del. J.F.K. Internat. Seminar, Rio de Janeiro, 1995. Author: The Police Establishment, 1968, Invisible Witness: The Use and Abuse of the New Technology of Crime Investigation, 1968, Hoover's F.B.I.: The Men and the Myth, 1970, Power on the Right, 1971, (with Warren Hinckle and Eliot Asinof) The Ten Second Jailbreak, 1973, (with John Christian) The Assassination of Robert F. Kennedy, 1978, (with Warren Hinckle) The Fish is Red: The Story of the Secret War Against Castro, 1981, updated, expanded, retitled as Deadly Secrets: The CIA-Mafia War Against Castro and the Assassination of JFK, 1992, Rearview Mirror: Looking Back at the FBI, the CIA and Other Tails, 2001; contbg. author: Investigating the FBI, 1973; contbr. articles to popular mags.; book reviewer L.A. Times. Dem. candidate for U.S. Congress, 1968. Served with USN, 1945-46. Mem. Authors Guild, Internat. Platform Assn., Press Club of San Francisco. Roman Catholic. Avocation: tennis. Home and Office: 163 Mark Twain Ave San Rafael CA 94903-2820

TURNER-SILVIA, JOANN, writer, vocalist, actress, music producer; b. Berkeley, Calif., July 6, 1952; d. Willie Turner and Bessie Lee Allen-Turner; m. William Louis Silvia, Apr. 16, 1996 (div. Apr. 17, 2000); 1 child, Anthon Julien Smith. Cert., Burbank (Calif.) Film Workshop, 1973; AA, Modesto (Calif.) Jr. Coll., 2001. Singer, prodr. JoAnn Turner Inc., Las Vegas, 1970—75, CEO, 1974—75; peace officer Dept. of Corrections, San Rafael, Calif., 1983—86; entertainment promoter Turner Prodns., Alameda, Calif., 1986—; actress Nancy Hayes Casting, San Francisco, 1990—; writer Jats Visions, Modesto, 1999—. Spkr. in field. Author: (screenplays) Mahogany, 1973, (plays) Just Another Day in Oakland, 1999, others; actor: (plays) Boundary Line, 1994. Mem. adv. bd. Mandela Ho., Oakland, Calif., 1985—; co-founder Nat. Coalition of Oppression, Seattle, 1970. Named Miss Congeniality, Beauty Pageant of Am., San Francisco, 1977. Mem.: NAACP. Avocations: walking, movies, reading, golf. Home: PO Box 582902 Modesto CA 95358-0050

TURNER VANLYDEGRAF, CLAUDIA BETH, writer, researcher; b. Salinas, Calif., Mar. 19, 1945; d. Prentiss Dixon Hill and Barbara Clayborne, Leonard Francis Balch (Stepfather); m. Robert Michael Turner, May 21, 1966 (div. Aug. 14, 1972); children: David Michael Reinhardt, Jeffrey Warren Gregory, Amber Beth Turner. Student, El Camino Coll., 1969—72. Cert. Nev. State Ins. Bd., 1999; Nev. Real Estate Divsn., 1979. Cost/manpower budget analyst Hughes Aircraft Co., Culver City, Calif., 1972—77; auditor No. Nev. Health & Welfare & Pension Plans Adminstrv. Office, Reno, 1980—81; co-owner TV Signal Corp, Cold Springs, Nev., 1981—86; flagger, laborer Laborers Local 169, Reno, 1989—94; jewelry sales assoc. SuperPawn/Camco, Reno, 1994—96; sales - loan assoc. Pioneer Jewelry & Loan, Reno, 1996—97; owner - document rsch. firm Coyote Svcs., Cold Springs, 1998—; pub./owner Coyote News, Cold Springs, 1998—2002. Author: Notes from Nobody, 2001. Citizens adv. bd. Washoe County Commn., Cold Springs, 1999—2001; adv. - reporter Cold Springs Cmty. Assoc, 1998—2003; lobbyist Nev. Mem.: UnNamed Writers Group, Ea. Star. Independent. Avocations: genealogy, gemology, antiques, history, art. Home: 17890 Fantail Circle Cold Springs NV 89506 Office: Coyote Services 17890 Fantail Circle Cold Springs NV 89506 Office Phone: 775-972-6530. Personal E-mail: cltvcoyote@aol.com.

TURNEY, JAMES EDWARD, computer scientist; b. Greensburg, Pa., May 14, 1933; s. James Edward and Mary Elizabeth (Koch) T.; m. Joan Lois Sweeney, Sept. 1, 1957 (dec. Jan. 1982); m. Audra Varnagy, Mar. 27, 1982; children: Audrey, Jennifer, Jill, Joy. BS in Indsl. Engring., Northeastern U., 1961; MS in Indsl. Mgmt., MIT, 1964; PhD in Mgmt., Calif. Coast U., 1993. Sr. cons. Peat Marwick Mitchell Co., L.A., 1965-68; gen. mgr. Technicolor, Inc., Hollywood, Calif., 1968-70; dir. Intercontinental Computing, Inc., Kansas City, Mo., 1970-72; v.p. Insight Systems, Ltd., Des Moines, 1972-76; pres. Pro Data Sys., Inc., Austin, Tex., 1976—. Prof. computer sci. Park U., Austin, 1997-2003; online instr. Park U., Austin, 2001-2003, U. Phoenix, Austin, 2002-03, Austin C. C., 2001-, Learning Tree U., 2003—, DeVry U., 2003—. Bd. dirs. Luth. Ch., Wayland, Mass., 1964-66, Palos Verdes, Calif., 1967-71, Overland Pk., Kans., 1973-76, San Jose, Calif., 1991-92, Corpus Christi, Tex., 1993-95. Sgt. U.S. Army, 1953-56. Mem. ASTD (v.p. fin. 1998—), Am. Inst. Indsl. Engrs. (pres. 1966-67), Mensa (local sec. 1994-97), Tex. Jazz Festival Soc. (pres. 1995-97), Austin Runners Club (mem. coord. 1999), Project Mgmt. Inst. Republican. Avocations: sailing, music, photography, writing, running. Home and Office: Pro Data Systems Inc 6508 Convict Hill Rd Austin TX 78749-1770 E-mail: drjet@austin.rr.com.

TURNEY, SHARON JESTER, retail executive; b. 1958; BA in Bus. Edn., U. Okla. With Foley's, 1979—88, Neiman Marcus, 1989—2000, sr. v.p. gen., mgr. gen. merchandise, 1997—98, exec. v.p. merchandising, creative prodn., advt. and pub. rels., 1998; pres., CEO Neiman Marcus Direct, 1999—2000; CEO, pres. Victoria's Secret Catalogue, 2000—. Office: Victorias Sectret Direct LLC 3425 Morse Crossing Columbus OH 43219

TURNIPSEED, BARNWELL RHETT, III, journalist, public relations consultant; b. Apr. 6, 1929; s. Barnwell Rhett and L. (Rogers) T.; m. Jane Whitley, June 12, 1982. BA in Journalism, U. Ga., 1950, MA in Journalism, 1960. With Sta. WGGA, Gainesville, Ga., 1943-46; prodn. mgr. Sta WGGA, Gainesville, Ga., 1958-60; with Sta. WRFC, Athens, Ga., 1947-50; program dir. Sta. WKYW, Louisville, 1953, Sta. WGBA, Columbus, Ga., 1953-55; sr. corr., sci. editor Voice of Am. Worldwide English, 1960-72; coord. radio-TV pub. affairs HEW, 1972-73; mem. staff Ga. Congressman Phil Landrum, 1974-75; dir. solar energy tech. info. Dept. Energy, Washington, 1975-77, spl. asst., 1977-81; pvt. practice, 1981-88, 94—; instr. West Ga. Coll., Carrollton, 1988-89, 90-94; asst. prof. Brenau Coll., Gainesville, Ga., 1989-90; mgr. WWGC-FM, Carrollton, Ga., 1990-94. Dir. Ga. Broadcasters Annual Awards, 1998—. Author: History of Georgia Broadcasting, 1972; prin. corr. Voice of Am. (Peabody award winning space exploration broadcasts, 1969). Symphony Guild rep. Louisville, Columbus, Ga. Jaycees; active symphony and arts devel. Sgt. U.S. Army, 1950-52. Named to Ga. Broadcasters Hall of Fame, 2003; recipient Two Meritorious Svc. awards, USIA. Mem. Nat. Assn. Sci. Writers (life), Aircraft Owners and Pilots Assn., Sigma Delta Chi. Democrat. Methodist. Home and Office: 295 Greenfield Cir Fayetteville GA 30215-2622

TURNLEY, DAVID CARL, photojournalist; b. Fort Wayne, Ind., June 22, 1955; s. William Loyd and Elizabeth Ann (Protsman) Turnley; m. Karin Nicolette, Apr. 15, 1989. BA in French, U. Mich., 1977; student, Sorbonne, Paris, 1975; DMus (hon.), Keele (Eng.) U., 1991. Staff photogapher Sliger Home Newspapers, Northville, Mich., 1978—80, Detroit Free Press, 1980—99; European based photographic corr. Detroit Free Press/Black Star Paris, 1988—99; Neiman fellow Harvard U., Boston, 1997—98; internat. exec. prodr. Corbis Sygma, N.Y.C., 1999—. Author: Why Are They Weeping? South Africans under Aparthied, 1988, Beijing Spring, 1989, Moments of Revolution: Eastern Europe, 1990; London Decca Records. Recipient Canon essay award for S. African coverage, 1985, World Press Picture of Yr. award for Earthquake in Armenia, 1988, Robert Capa Gold medal for China, Romania coverage, 1990, Pulitizer Prize for China, E. Europe coverage, 1990.

TURNLUND, JUDITH RAE, nutritionist; b. St. Paul, Sept. 28, 1936; d. Victor Emanuel and Vida Mae (Priddy) Hanson; m. Richard Wayne Turnlund, Nov. 9, 1957; children: Michael Wayne, Mark Richard, Todd Hanson. BS in Chemistry and Psychology, Gustavus Adolphus Coll., 1958; PhD in Nutrition, U. Calif., Berkeley, 1978. Registered dietitian. Postdoctoral fellow U. Calif., Berkeley, 1978-80, lectr., 1984-92, adj. assoc. prof., 1989-97; rsch. nutrition scientist Western Regional Rsch. Ctr./Western Human Nutrition Ctr., USDA, San Francisco, Albany, and Davis, Calif., 1980—; rsch. leader Western Human Nutrition Ctr. USDA, San Francisco, 1993-96; adj. prof. nutrition U. Calif., Davis, 2000—. Vis. asst. prof. Am. U. Beirut, Lebanon, 1979, 80. Editor: Stable Isotopes in Nutrition, 1984; contbr. articles to profl. jours. Recipient Cert. of Merit, USDA/ARS, 1984, 93, 98, Disting. Alumni citation Gustavus Adolphus Coll., 1988, Am. Inst. Nutrition's Lederle award in Human Nutrition, 1996; USDA grantee, Nat. Dairy Coun. grantee. Fellow Am. Soc. Nutritional Scis.; mem. Am. Soc. Clin. Nutrition, Am. Dietetic Assn. Home: 2276 Great Hwy San Francisco CA 94116-1555 Office: U Calif USDA/ARS Western Human Nutrition Rsch One Shields Ave Davis CA 95616 E-mail: jturnlun@whnrc.usda.gov.

TURNOVSKY, STEPHEN JOHN, economics professor; b. Wellington, New Zealand, Apr. 5, 1941; came to U.S., 1981; s. Frederick and Liselotte Felicitas (Wodak) T.; m. Michelle Henriette Louise Roos, Jan. 21, 1967; children: Geoffrey George, Jacqueline Liselotte. BA, Victoria U., Wellington, 1962, MA with honors, 1963; PhD, Harvard U., 1968. Asst. prof. econs. U. Pa., Phila., 1968-71; assoc. prof. U. Toronto, Ont., Can., 1971-72; prof. Australian Nat. U., Canberra, 1972-82; IBE disting. prof. econs. U. Ill., Champaign, 1982-87; prof. econs. U. Wash., Seattle, 1987—, chmn. dept., 1990-95; Castor prof., 1993—. Rsch. assoc. Nat. Bur. Econ. Rsch., Cambridge, Mass., 1983-93. Author: Macroeconomic Analysis and Stabilization Policy, 1977, International Macroeconomic Stabilization Policy, 1990, Methods of Macroeconomic Dynamics, 1995, 2d edit., 2000, International Macroeconomic Dynamics, 1997; mem. editl. bd. several jours.; contbr. articles to profl. jours. Fellow Econometric Soc., Acad. Social Scis. in Australia; mem. Soc. Econ. Dynamics and Control (pres. 1982-84, editor Jour. Econ. Dynamics and Control 1981-87, 95-2001). Avocations: skiing, hiking, music. Home: 6053 NE Kelden Pl Seattle WA 98105-2045 Office: Dept Econs U Wash Box 353330 Seattle WA 98195-3330 Office Phone: 206-685-8028. E-mail: sturn@u.washington.edu.

TURNQUIST, JERRY L. teacher, journalist; b. Elgin, Ill., Mar. 5, 1949; s. Ralph C. and Frances B. T.; m. Kathleen A. Turnquist, Dec. 29, 1984; adopted children: Dennis, Eric. AA, Elgin C.C., 1969; BS, No. Ill. U., 1971, MS, 1979. Tchr. history and sci. Sch. Dist. U. - 46, Elgin, Ill., 1972—; tax preparer H&R Block Premium, Elgin, 1977—. Columnist Daily Herald, Elgin, 1995—; co-host: (local radio show) Elgin 100 Years Ago, Sta. WRMN, 1995—. Trustee Gail Borden Pub. Libr., Elgin, 1995—; bd. dirs. Ill. State Hist. Soc., Elgin, Springfield, 1998-2000; chmn. Elgin Heritage Commn., 1986-91, others. Named Disting. Alumnus Elgin C.C., 1989, Keyman of the Yr., Elgin Jaycees, 1981; recipient Outstanding Svc. award Elgin Heritage Commn., 1995. Mem. Elgin Area Hist. Soc. (bd. dirs. 1986-98). Home: 619 Canyon Ln Elgin IL 60123-5219 E-mail: ibemrt@aol.com.

TUROCK, BETTY JANE, library and information science educator; b. Scranton, Pa., June 12; d. David and Ruth Carolyn (Sweetser) Argust; m. Frank M. Turock, June 16, 1956; children: David L., B. Drew. BA magna cum laude (Charles Weston scholar), Syracuse U., 1955; postgrad. (scholar), U. Pa., 1956; MLS, Rutgers U., 1970, PhD, 1981. Library and materials coordinator Holmdel (N.J.) Public Schs., 1963-65; story-teller Wheaton (Ill.) Public Library, 1965-67; ednl. media specialist Alhambra Public Sch., Phoenix, 1967-70; br. librarian, area librarian, head extension service Forsyth County Public Library System, Winston-Salem, NC, 1970—73; asst. dir., dir. Montclair (N.J.) Public Library, 1973—76; asst. dir. Monroe County Library System, Rochester, N.Y., 1978-81; asst. prof. Rutgers U. Sch. Comms., Info. and Libr. Studies, 1981-87; assoc. prof. Rutgers U. Sch. Comm. Info and Libr. Studies, 1987-93, prof., 1994—, dept. chair, 1989-95, dir. MLS program, 1990-95, assoc. dean, 2002—04, prof., dean emeritus, 2004—; pres. Rock Info. Assocs., 2004—. Vis. prof. Rutgers U. Grad. Sch. Library and Info. Studies, 1980-81; adviser U.S. Dept. Edn. Office of Libr. Programs, 1988-89. Author: Serving Older Adults, 1983, Creating a Financial Plan, 1992; editor: The Bottom Line, 1984-90; contbr. articles to profl. jours. Trustee Raritan Twp. (N.J.) Pub. Libr., 1961—62, Keystone Coll., 1991—, Freedom to Read Found., 1994—97, Librs. for the Future, 1994—97, Fund for Am.'s Librs., 1995, Trejo Found., 1995—; trustee Bd. Am. Libr., Paris, 1999—; mem. Bd. Edn. Raritan Twp., 1962—66; ALA coord. Task Force on Women, 1978—80; mem. action coun.; treas. Social Responsibilities Round Table, 1978—82. Charles Weston scholar Syracuse U., 1955; recipient N.J. Libr. Leadership award, 1994; named Woman of Yr. Raritan-Holmdel Woman's Club, 1975. Mem. AAUP, Am. Soc. Info. Sci., Assn. Libr. and Info. Sci Edn., Am. Libr. Assn. (pres. 1995-96, pres.-elect 1994-95, exec. bd. 1991-97, coun. 1988-97, equality award 1998), Rutgers U. Grad. Sch. Library and Info. Studies Alumni Assn. (pres. 1977-78, Disting. Alumni award 1994, Extraordinary Libr. Advocate of 20th Century award 2000), Phi Theta Kappa, Psi Chi, Beta Phi Mu, Pi Beta Phi. Unitarian Universalist. Home: 39 Highwood Rd Somerset NJ 08873-1834 Office: Rutgers U 4 Huntington St New Brunswick NJ 08901-1071 Office Phone: 732-864-0130. E-mail: bturock@scils.rutgers.edu.

TUROCK, JANE PARSICK, nutritionist; b. Peckville, Pa., Apr. 15, 1947; d. Paul Charles and Elizabeth Dorothy (Mistysyn) Parsick; m. Michael John, July 12, 1968; children: Eric Matthew, Nathan Andrew, J. Seth, Melanie Kay. BS, Marywood Coll., Scranton, 1969; MS, Marywood Coll., 1982. Registered dietitian; cert. nutrition specialist. Registered dietitian Jane P. Turock, Scranton, Pa., 1985—; founder and chief dietitian Gastric Bubble, Scranton, Pa., 1986—; prof. Penn State Coll., Scranton, Pa., 1987—; dietitian & presenter WNEP TV Healthwatch, Avoca, Pa., 1988—; dir. & chief dietitian Vascular Inst. of Northeast Pa., Pa., 1989—; owner, mgr. Nutrition...Plus/Fitness Unlimited, Scranton, Pa., 1991—. Cons. Home Health Care Assn., Clarks Summit, 1985—; dietitian Clarks Summit, 1985—; founder Nat. Nutrition Month Bakeoff; dir. Camp Jane. Treas. Lackawanna County Med. Soc. Aux., 1974-76, pres., 1979-80, bd. dirs., 1980-81; allocations com. United Way Lackawanna County, 1990—; mem. bd. dirs. Lupus Found., 1995, St. Francis of Assissi Kitchen, 1995. Mem. Am. Dietic Assn., Northeast Dist. Pa. Dietic Diet Therapy, Consulting Nutritionists in Pvt. Practice, Am. Diabetic Assn., Northeast Womens Network, Allied Wedding Firm. Republican. Roman Catholic. Avocations: skiing, tennis, gourmet cooking, jogging, swimming. Office: Nutrition Plus/Lady Jane Fitness 375 N 9th Ave Scranton PA 18504-2005 also: Abington Family Svcs 211 N State St Clarks Summit PA 18411-1087 also: Lady Jane Inc dba The Ski Habit Union Dale PA 18470 also: Nate's Outdoor Sports Ctr 611 State St Clarks Summit PA 18411 also: Jane P Turock MSRD 397 N 9th Ave Scranton PA 18504-2005 E-mail: janeturock@excite.com.

TUROCY, CATHERINE, performing company executive; BFA magna cum laude, Ohio State U., 1974. Tchr. Baroque dance STEPS Dance Studio, N.Y.C., 1991—95; tchr. The Baroque Ballet Workshop, Calif., 1995—, Baroque Dance Workshops, 1996—; dancer Cleve. Ballet Co., 1967—70, Modern Dance Troupe, Ohio State U., 1971—74, The Baroque Dance Ensemble, 1972—80, The Auk Mime and Dance Troupe, 1974—75, The Max Co., 1976—77, The Mitchell Rose Dance Co., 1977—78, Court Dance Co. N.Y., 1977—79; dancer, artistic dir. The N.Y. Baroque Dance Co., 1976—. Guest choreographer; vis. lectr.; vis. artist. Creator (video) The Art of Dancing: An Introduction to Baroque Dance, 1979 (Dance Film award, 1979); author: Moving History/Dancing Cultures: A Dance History Reader, 2001, Dance Masters: Roseman, Janet Lynn, 2001; dancer numerous videos, TV, plays, stage, choreographer numerous musicals, modern dance, stage. Named Chevalier in Order of Arts and Letters, French Govt., 1995; recipient N.Y. Dance and Performance award, 2001, Jerome Found. award for choreographic creation, 1985; fellow, Nat. Endowment for Arts, 1980—81, 1987, N.Y. Found. for Arts, 1990, Nat. Endowment for Arts Choreography, 1980, 83, 84, 86-88, 90, 94-96, 96-97; grantee, Nat. Endowment for Arts Heritage and Preservation, 1997—98; scholar, Getty, 1997. Mem.: Alpha Lambda Delta. Home: 6901 Gaston Ave Dallas TX 75214

TUROK, PAUL HARRIS, composer, music reviewer; b. N.Y.C., Dec. 3, 1929; s. Joseph and Esther (Pashman) T.; m. Susan Kay Frucht, Mar. 24, 1967. BA, Queens Coll., N.Y.C., 1950; MA, U. Calif., Berkeley, 1951; MS, Baruch Coll., 1986. Music dir. Sta. KPFA, Berkeley, 1955-56; lectr. CCNY, 1959-63; vis. prof. Williams Coll., Williamstown, Mass., 1963-64; music critic New York Herald-Tribune, 1964-65; critic, columnist Music Jour., New York, 1964-79, Ovation mag., New York, 1980—; critic, contbr. New York Times, 1984—, Sta. WQXR, First Hearing, New York, 1985—. Pub. Turok's Choice, 1990—. Composer musical compositions, premiered Indpls. Symphony, 1971, Louisville Orch., 1973, Cleve. Orch., 1973, Phila Orch., 1976; opera Richard III, 1975, Sousa Overture, 1976, Lanier Songs, 1978, English Horn Quintet, 1982, Cello Sonata, 1984, Organ Toccata, 1984, Tourist Music, 1985, String Quartet No. 4, 1986, Rhapsody for Band, 1987, Piano Dance, 1988, Violin Sonata, 1989, From Sholem Aleichem, 1990, Abac for trumpet and organ, 1990, Partita for three winds, 1991, Concerto for two violins and orchestra, 1991, Piano Trio, 1992, C.C. 6 for bassoon and orchestra, 1992, Fantasy for 4 flutes and piano, 4 hands, 1994, Clap, Cluck, Count: Three Interactive Proverbs for Chidren and Orchestra, 1995, Sonata No. 2 for Cello and Piano, 1996, Concerto for Piano and Orch., 1997, Canzone Concertante No. 7 for viola, percussion and strings, 1998, Reeling in the Y2K, 1999, Flute Sonata, 2000, Behold, Thou Art Fair, 2001, Sextet for piano and winds, Partita No.3 for English horn, 2002, Variations on a theme by Grieg for 8 trombones, Elegy in Memory of Nathan Schwartz, 2002, C.C. No. 8 for Violin and Orch., String Quartet No. 5, 2003, C.C. No. 9 for Trumpet and Strings, 2003, Caprice d'Octobre for 3 violins, 2004, Brass Quintet No. 2, 2004. Served with U.S. Army, 1953-55. Hertz travelling scholar, U. Calif., 1956-58; Grammy nominee 1992, 93. Jewish. Avocations: world travel, computing.

TUROV, DANIEL, financial writer, investment executive; b. Bklyn., Jan. 15, 1947; m. Rosalyn B. Kalishock, Aug. 25, 1968 (dec.); children: Joshua Nathaniel, Steven Russell; m. Tasanee Boonchert, Mar. 15, 2000. Registered investment advisor. Account exec. Walston & Co., 1969-72, Thomson McKinnon Securities, 1972-75; sr. v.p. Faulkner Dawkins & Sullivan, 1975-77, Cowen & Co., N.Y.C., 1977-80; dir. Turov Investment Group divsn. Moore & Schley, Cameron & Co., N.Y.C., 1980-82; v.p. Dean Witter Reynolds, Inc., N.Y.C., 1982-83, sr. v.p., 1983-84; pres. Just Right Comm., 1992—2002; pres., CEO, Turov Investment Group Inc., 1999—. Chmn. Philtrum Advt. Corp., 1982-84; mem. faculty N.Y. Inst. Fin., New Sch. Social Rsch.; mem. panel The Wall St. Transcript's Option Roundtable; interviewer to CNN, 2000; spkr. in field. Author: (monthly) Turov on Investments and Hedging, 1972-80; monthly investment column Best Buys Mag., 1982-83; editor New Innovations Pub. Corp., 1979-86, Turov on Timing, 1993—; contbr. articles to profl. jours. and newspapers; interviewed on CNN, 2000. Recipient Supertrader of Yr. award Stock Traders Almanac, 1994, 2001. Mem. Nat. Futures Assn. (registered commodity trading advisor). Office: Turov Investment Group Inc 9070 Togan Ave San Diego CA 92129 Office Phone: 858-484-5100.

TUROW, SCOTT F. lawyer, writer; b. Chgo., Apr. 12, 1949; s. David D. and Rita (Pastron) Turow; m. Annette Weisberg, Apr. 4, 1971; 3 children. BA magna cum laude, Amherst Coll., 1970; MA, Stanford U., 1974; JD cum laude, Harvard U., 1978. Bar: Ill. 1978, U.S. Dist. Ct. (no. dist.) Ill. 1978, U.S. Ct. Appeals (7th cir.) 1979. Asst. U.S. atty. U.S. Ct. Appeals (7th dist.), Chgo., 1978—86; ptnr. Sonnenschein Nath & Rosenthal, Chgo., 1986—. E.H. Jones lectr. Stanford U., 1972—75. Author: One L.: An Inside Account of Life in the First Year at Harvard Law School, 1977, Presumed Innocent, 1987, The Burden of Proof, 1990, Pleading Guilty, 1993, The Laws of Our Fathers, 1996, Personal Injuries, 1999, Reversible Errors, 2002, Ultimate Punishment: A Lawyer's Reflections on Dealing With the Death Penalty, 2003; contbr. articles to profl. jours. Mem.: Chgo. Coun. Lawyers, Chgo. Bar Assn. Office: Sonnenschein Nath Rosenthal 233 S Wacker Dr Ste 8000 Chicago IL 60606-6491

TURPENING, PATRICIA EILEEN KELLER, law librarian; b. Columbus, Ohio, Mar. 1, 1952; d. William Waite and Eileen Catherine (Miller) Keller; m. Richard Whitley Denham, Oct. 10, 1981 (div. Mar. 1986); 1 child, Michael Richard; m. Glen Thomas Turpening, Apr. 16, 1997. BS, Findlay Coll., 1974; MSLS, U. Ky., 1978. Cert. in preservation mgmt. Sch. Communication, Info. and Libr. Studies, Rutgers U., 1999. Acquisitions libr. Supreme Ct. Ohio Law Libr., Columbus, 1974-76, Robert S. Marx Law Libr., U. Cin., 1978-88, head preservation and archives, 1988—. Libr. Rendigs, Fry, Kiely & Dennis, Cin., 1979-85. Editor Tech. Svcs. Law Libr., 1990-94, The Abbey Newsletter: Preservation of Library and Archival Materials, 2004; contbr. articles to profl. jours. Mem. ALA, LWV, AAUW, NOW, AAUP, Am. Assn. Law Librs. (travel grantee 1984, preservation cons., coord. of library programs, Renee D. Chapman Meml. award for Outstanding Contbns. in Tech. Svcs. Law Librarianship 2004), Soc. Am. Archivists, Ohio Preservation Coun., Ohio Regional Assn. Law Librs. Episcopalian. Office: U Cin Robert S Marx Law Libr PO Box 210142 Cincinnati OH 45221-0142 E-mail: pat.turpening@law.uc.edu.

TURPIN, CALVIN COOLIDGE, retired university administrator, educator; b. Granite City, Ill., Nov. 8, 1924; s. Golden and Gertrude (West) T.; m. Eudell Coody, June 29, 1944; children: Susan Turpin Jones, John Thomas. BA, Baylor U., 1949, MA, 1952; BD, So. Bapt. Theol. Sem., 1955, M of Religious Edn., 1958; MA, Vanderbilt U., 1962; MDiv, So. Bapt. Theol. Sem., 1973;

DSc in Theology, Golden Gate Bapt. Theol. Sem., 1967. Prof. history and Greek Jacksonville Coll., Tex., 1950-52; prof. religion Belmont Coll., Nashville, 1955-56, Austin-Peay State U., Clarksville, Tenn., 1956-57; assoc. libr. Inst. of Old Testament Golden Gate Bapt. Theol. Sem., Mill Valley, Calif., 1961-66; dir. libRs., prof. libr. sci. Minot (N.D.) State Coll., 1966-67; dir. libRs., prof. religion Judson Coll., Marion, Ala., 1967-70; prof. religion, dir. libRs. Hardin-Simmons U., Abilene, Tex., 1970-77. Vis. prof. Tex. Woman's U., Denton, 1974-75. Author: Beyond My Dreams: Memories and Interpretations, 1992, Writings and a Selected Bibliography of Calvin C. Turpin, 1995, 50 Years of Ministry: Challenges and Changes, 1997; co-author: Rupert N. Richardson: The Man and His Works, 1971, History of the First Baptist Church, Gilroy, California, 1995; contbr. numerous articles to profl. publs. Nat. dep. chief chaplains CAP-USAF Aux., 1990-92; Calif. dept. chaplain Am. Legion, San Francisco, 1990-92, 94-95; nat. chaplain, Am. Legion, Indpls., 2000-01; vets. pk. commr. San Benito County, Hollister, Calif., 1990 92; rent control commr. City of Hollister, 1993-95. Brigadier gen. USSC, 1992—. Named San Benito County LULAC Vet. of the Yr., 2001; named to, Ark. Boys State Hall of Fame, 2001; Lilly Endowment scholar, Lilly Found., 1962. Mem. Rotary Club, Lions Club, Beta Phi Mu, Phi Delta Kappa, Gamma Iota. Republican. Baptist. Avocations: volunteer chaplaincy, writing, authentic cowboy cooking. Home: 188 Elm Dr Hollister CA 95023-3430 E-mail: ccturpin@hollinet.com.

TURPIN, DAVID HOWARD, biologist, educator; b. Duncan, B.C., Can., July 14, 1956; s. George Howard and Marilyn Elizabeth (Jones) T.; m. S. Laurene Clark, Oct. 4, 1985; children: Chantal, Joshua. BSc in Biology, U. B.C., 1977, PhD in Botany and Oceanography, 1980. Postdoctoral rsch. fellow Natural Scis. Engring. Coun., 1980-81; rsch. assoc. Simon Fraser U., 1980; v.p. Sigma Resource Cons., Vancouver, 1980-81; from asst. prof. to assoc. prof. Queen's U., Kingston, Canada, 1981-90, prof. biology, 1990-91, dean arts & sci., 1993-95, vice prin. acad., 1995-2000; prof., head botany U. B.C., 1991-93; pres., vice-chancellor U. Victoria, 2000—. Invited spkr. profl. meetings univs. worldwide. Co-editor: Plant Physiology, Biochemistry and Molecular Biology, 1990, 2d edit., 1996; mem. editl. bd. Jour. Phycology, 1992-96, Plant Physiology, 1988-92, Plant Cell and Environ., 1994-96, Jour. Exptl. Botany, 1995-98; contbr. chpts. in books; author numerous articles, conf. procs. V.p. Great Lakes Tomorrow, 1986-90; mem. program com. Great Lakes Course Ont. Sci. Ctr., 1988; Kingston City rep. Cataraqui Regional Conservation Authority, 1984-86. Recipient Excellence in Tchg. Alumni award Queen's U., 1989, Outstanding Alumni award U. B.C., 1990, Darbaker prize in phycology Am. Bot. Assn., 1991; Natural Sci. and Engring. Rsch. Can. E.W.R. Stacie Meml. fellow, 1989-90; Capt. T.S. Byrne Meml. scholar U. B.C., 1980; postgrad. scholar Natural Scis. and Engring. Rsch. Coun., 1979-81, Edith Ashton Meml. scholar U. B.C., 1979, NRC scholar, 1978-79; Natural Scis. and Engring. Rsch. Coun. grantee, 1982—. Fellow Royal Soc. Can.; mem. Phycological Soc. Am., Am. Soc. Limnology and Oceanography, Can. Soc. Plant Physiologists (C.D. Nelson award 1989), Am. Soc. Plant Physiologists (cert. recognition 1992). Office: Office of the Pres U Victoria Bus and Econ Bldg Rm 454 Victoria BC Canada V8W 2Y2 Business E-Mail: pres@uvic.ca.

TURPIN, JOSEPH OVILA, counselor, educator; b. Rockford, Ill., July 11, 1943; s. D. John and Mona Belle (Albright) T.; m. Hester R. Thompson, June 26, 1969; children: Matthew, Michael. AB in Sociology, Ind. U., 1965, MS in Mental Retardation, 1966, postgrad., 1966-67; PhD in Rehab. Psychology, U. Wis., 1986. Rsch. assoc. Ind. U., Bloomington, 1966-67; instr. U. Wis. Parkside Ext., Kenosha, 1967-71; tchr. Kenosha Unified Sch. Dist., 1967-71; coord. Racine area Gov.'s Com. on Spl. Learning State of Wis. Dept. Adminstrn., 1971-73; dir. Racine County Comprehensive Mental Health, Mental Retardation, Alcohol and Other Drug Abuse Svc. Bd, 1973-78; vocat. cons., counselor supr. Industrial Injury Clinic, Neenah, Wis., 1978-83; owner, vocat. expert Vocat. Counseling Svc., Inc., Madison, Wis., 1983-88; teaching intern, counseling supr., student tchr. supr. U. Wis., Madison, 1983-86; asst. prof. rehab. counselor edn. Ohio U., Athens, 1986-89; assoc. prof. rehab. counseling program Calif. State U., San Bernardino, 1989-94, prof. rehab. counseling program, 1994—, coord. rehab. counseling program, 1990-94, 2000—. Mem. sch. psychologist exam. com. Dept. Edn. State of Ohio, 1989; rschr., presenter, cons. in field. Contbr. articles to profl. publs. Bd. dir. United Cerebral Palsy of Racine County, 1969-73, Children's House, Inc., Racine, 1971-73, Ctrl. Ohio Regional Coun. on Alcoholism, 1987-89, Ctr. for Cmty. Counseling and Edn., 1993-99, pres., 1998; bd. dir. Inland Caregivers Resource Ctr., 1993-99, Health and Hosp. Planning Com. of Racine County, 1976; treas. Cub Scout Pack # 68, Boy Scouts Am., Neenah, 1981-83, Whitcomb Village Assn., Inc., 1984; bd. dir. Aquinas HS, 1992-94, pres. 1994; HS liaison West Point Parents Club of Inland Empire, 1992-94; budget rev. com. United Fund Racine County, 1975. Grantee Rehab. Svcs. Adminstrn., 1985-88, Ohio U., 1987-88, Ohio U. Coll. Osteo. Medicine and Coll. Edn., 1989, Office Spl. Edn. and Rehab., 1989-92, Inland Reg. Ctr., 1999. Mem. ACA (pub. policy and legis. com. 1992-94, various subcoms.), APA, Assn. Counselor Educators and Supr. (we. region legis. chair 1996-98), Am. Rehab. Counseling Assn. (exec. coun. 1992-94, ethics com. 1990-91, chair coun. on profl. preparation and stds. 1992-94), Nat. Rehab. Counseling Assn. (bd. dirs. 1993-94, chmn. grievance com., pres. 1997), Nat. Rehab. Assn. (bd. dir. 1998), Nat. Rehab. Assoc. Pacific Region, (Bd. dir., 2002; pres-elect. 2002) Alliance Rehab. Counseling (bd. dir. 1996-98, co-chair 1998). Office: Calif State U 5500 University Pkwy San Bernardino CA 92407-2318 Business E-Mail: jturpin@csusb.edu. E-mail: rx300xx@aol.com.

TURPIN, RICHARD E. sales executive; b. Hamilton, Ohio, Aug. 10, 1950; 1 child, Vincent Paul Huntington Turpin. Degree, UCLA, 1972. Dir. sales Pepsico, Hamilton; dir. mktg. Tri-State, Inc., Columbus, Ohio; dir. sales CMR, Inc., Columbus, Ohio, 1985-96; self-employed cons. Turpin Assocs., Cin., 1996—; former v.p. U.S. Plywood/Champion Papers; sr. exec. Arch Wireless, 1996—. Vol. Children's Svcs., Columbus, 1994—, Old English Sheepdog Rescue. Recipient Citizenship award Chgo., 1970, Rosa Pards Wall of Tolerance award, 2004—, Rosa Parks Humanitarian award, 2004. Mem. ARch Pres. Club, Columbus C. of C. (com. chmn. 1993-94), Columbus Exec. Sales Assn., Dayton Realtors, Dayton C. of C., Pres.'s Club. Jewish. Home: 4535 Bonita Dr Unit 180 Middletown OH 45044-6788 E-mail: rturpin@cinci.rr.com.

TURQUETTE, ATWELL RUFUS, logician; b. Texarkana, Tex., July 14, 1914; s. Rufus Watson and Dale Cook (Warmack) Turquette; m. Lucille Case Le Roy, June 2, 1937 (dec. Feb. 1956); m. Maxine Harriet Kennedy, Apr. 2, 1958 (dec. Aug. 1992); m. Frances D. Bond, Dec. 27, 1998. BA, U. Ark., 1936; MA, Duke U., 1937; PhD, Cornell U., 1943. Asst. prof. Fla. So. Coll., Lakeland, 1937-38; fellow U. Chgo., 1938-39; assoc. prof. Fla. So. Coll., Lakeland, 1939-40; assistantship, fellow Cornell U., Ithaca, N.Y., 1940-43, instr., 1943-45; asst. prof. U. Ill., Champaign-Urbana, 1945-48, assoc. prof., 1948-52, prof., 1952-75, prof. emeritus, 1975—. Co-author: Many-valued Logics, 1952; contbg. author: Les 265 communications, Congrès International des Mathématiciens, Nice, 1970; editor: Jour. of Symbolic Logic, 1950-68; patentee in field. Duke U. scholar, 1936; U. Chgo. fellow, 1938; grantee NSF, 1968-70, Rockefeller Gen. Edn. Bd., 1954. Mem. Am. Math. Soc., Soc. Indsl. and Appl. Math., Symbolic Logic Assn., London Math. Soc., Calcutta Math. Soc., AAAS, N.Y. Acad. Scis., Am Phil. Assn. Achievements include design for multi-valued circuits, functional completeness and incompleteness results for many-valued logics; minimal axiomatizations for many-valued logics; relating Pascal triangles to Post sets; deciphering Peirce's triadic logic. Home: 914 W Clark St Champaign IL 61821-3328 E-mail: aturquette1@iopener.net.

TURQUETTE, FRANCES BOND, editor; b. Atlanta, Sept. 25, 1931; d. Sewell Hinton and Lavonia DeLay Dixon; m. Charles Eugene Bond, Sept. 12, 1952 (div. Jan. 1969); children: Turner D., Laura S., L. Irene, Cynthia D., Nelson K.; m. Atwell Rufus Turquette, Dec. 27, 1998. Student, Wesleyan Coll., 1948—50; BA in Journalism, U. Ga., 1952; MA in Art History, U. Ill., 1971. Editl. asst. Meth. Pub. Ho., Nashville, 1952-53, Rsch. Press, Champaign, Ill., 1972-73; editing supr. McGraw-Hill Book Co., N.Y.C., 1974-80; publs. editor pub. affairs U. Ill., Urbana, 1974, 80-88; editor Nat. Ctr. for Supercomputing Applications, Champaign, 1988-96. Vis. faculty, editor Coll. of Commerce, U. Ill. Urbana, 1972-74; ref. com., Editorial and Composition Standards McGraw Hill Book Co., N.Y.C., 1975-77; editor, writer access, 1988-96. Mem. program chair, liaison, bd. govs. Channing Murray Found., Urbana, 1982-92; mem. adv. bd. to freeze nuclear weapons 15th Congrl. Dist., 1982-87; co-pres. SANE/Freeze, Champaign County, 1992-94. Mem. Nat. Assn. Sci. Writers, Art Inst. Chgo. (nat. assoc.), Lyric Opera Chgo., Theta Sigma Phi. Unitarian Universalist. Avocations: travel, writing, gardening, photography. Home: 914 W Clark St Champaign IL 61821-3328 E-mail: aturquette1@iopener.net.

TURRELL, RICHARD HORTON, SR., banker; b. Kingston, Pa., Apr. 9, 1925; s. George Henry and Margaret (Clark) T.; m. Sally Wolfe, May 28, 1955; children: Richard H. Jr., David C., Douglas W. (dec.). Student, Cornell U., 1943; BS in Commerce, Washington and Lee U., 1949. Rep. sales Del. Lackawanna and Western Coal Co., Phila., 1949-51; asst. to pres. N.Y.C., 1951 58; broker Auchincloss Parker & Redpath, N.Y.C., 1958-61; mgr. investments Fiduciary Trust Co. Internat., N.Y.C., 1961-94, v.p., 1965-94, sr. v.p., 1968-94, sec., 1971-84. Asst. sec. Blue Coal Corp., N.Y.C., 1953-58; v.p., bd. dirs. Pine Raleigh (N.C.) Corp., 1966-93. Trustee, overseer Simon's Rock of Bard Coll., Gt. Barrington, Mass., 1968-93; trustee Monmouth Univ., West Long Branch, N.J., 1980—, chmn. bd. trustees, 1989-92; chmn. Millburn-Short Hills (N.J.) Rep. Com., 1973-78; trustee Children's Specialized Hosp. Found., Mountainside, N.J., 1989-95; bd. dirs. ARC Martin County, Fla., 2000. With Signal Corps, U.S. Army, 1943-46, PTO. Named Disting. Alumnus, Washington and Lee U., 1986. Mem. Baltusrol Golf Club (Springfield, N.J., gov. 1977), Capitol Hill Club (Washington), Turtle Creek Club (Tequesta, Fla.), Masons, Irem Temple Aaonms, Phi Beta Kappa, Phi Eta Sigma, Alpha Kappa Psi, Omicron Delta Kappa (hon.), Beta Gamma Sigma, Phi Delta Theta. Presbyterian. Avocations: golf, history, education. Home: 114 Turtle Creek Dr Tequesta FL 33469-1547

TURRENTINE, HOWARD BOYD, federal judge; b. Escondido, Calif., Jan. 22, 1914; s. Howard and Veda Lillian (Maxfield) T.; m. Virginia Jacobsen, May 13, 1965 (dec.); children: Howard Robert, Terry Beverly; m. Marlene Lipsey, Nov. 1, 1991. AB, San Diego State Coll., 1936; LLB, U. So. Calif., 1939. Bar: Calif. 1939. Practiced in San Diego, 1939-68; judge Superior Ct. County of San Diego, 1968-70, U.S. Dist. Ct. (so. dist.) Calif., Calif., sr. judge, 1970—. Served with USNR, 1941-45. Mem. ABA, Fed. Bar Assn., Am. Judicature Soc. Office: US Dist Ct 940 Front St San Diego CA 92101-8994

TURRI, JOSEPH A. lawyer; b. Seneca Falls, N.Y., July 24, 1943; s. Louis Arthur and Assunta (Faiola) T.; m. Susan Ruth Testa, Dec. 29, 1975 (dec.); 1 child, Michael James. BA, SUNY, Buffalo, 1965; JD, Cornell U., 1970. Bar: N.Y. 1971, U.S. Dist Ct. (we. dist.) N.Y. 1971, U.S. Supreme Ct. 1974, U.S. Dist. Ct. (so. dist.) N.Y. 1996, U.S. Ct. Appeals (2d cir.) 1996. Ptnr. Harris Beach LLP, Rochester, N.Y., 1970—, mgmt. ptnrs. com., 1991-97, chmn. constrn. law dept., 1992-98, 2002—, chmn. litigation dept., 1994-96, pres., 1999—2002. Bd. dirs. Thousand Island Park Corp., N.Y.; v.p. Castle Bay Ltd., Rochester, N.Y.; arbitrator Am. Arbitration Assn., Syracuse, 1985—. Bd. dirs. Rochester Downtown Devel. Corp., 1992-97. Mem. N.Y. State Bar Assn., Monroe County Bar Assn., Assn. Gen. Contractors, Met. Forum (trustee). Avocations: horseback riding, antique wooden boats. Home: 21 Evergreen Ln Rochester NY 14618-4719 Office: Harris Beach LLP 99 Garnsey Rd Pittsford NY 14534

TURRILL, FRED LOVEJOY, surgeon; b. Redlands, Calif., Sept. 14, 1922; s. Gardner Stilson and Virginia Marie (Johnson) T.; m. Edith Mae Brown, Mar. 17, 1951; children: Brian Casey, Kevin Michael, Ann Louise, Mark. AS, Glendale Coll., 1942; BSE, U. Mich., 1944; MD, U. So. Calif., 1950. Diplomate Am. Bd. Surgery. Intern L.A. County/U. So. Calif. Med. Ctr., 1950-52, resident surgery, 1952-56; surgeon Turrill, Shader & Myles, Glendale, Calif., 1956—. Prof. surgery U. So. Calif., L.A., 1974—. Contbr. articles to profl. jours. With U.S. Army, 1942-46. Grantee USPS, 1956-57. Mem. ACS (gov. 1977-84), Collegium Internat. Chirurgiae, Pacific Coast Surg. Assn. (councillor 1980-83), We. Surg. Assn., Soc. Grad. Surgeons (life hon., pres. 1970-71), L.A. Surg. Soc. (pres. 1975). Republican. Avocations: fishing, boating, hunting, travel.

TURRO, NICHOLAS JOHN, chemistry professor; b. Middletown, Conn., May 18, 1938; s. Nicholas John and Philomena (Russo) T.; m. Sandra Jean Misenti, Aug. 6, 1960; children: Cynthia Suzanne, Claire Melinda. BA, Wesleyan U., 1960, DSc (hon.), 1984; PhD, Calif. Inst. Tech., 1963. Instr. chemistry Columbia U., N.Y.C., 1964-65, asst. prof., 1965-67, assoc. prof., 1967-69, prof. chemistry, 1969—, William P. Schweitzer prof. chemistry, 1982—, chmn. chemistry dept., 1981-84, co-chmn. dept. chem. engring. and applied chemistry, 1997-2000, prof. earth and environ. engring., 1998—. Author: Molecular Photochemistry, 1965; author: (with A.A. Lamola) Energy Transfer and Organic Photochemistry, 1971; author: Modern Molecular Photochemistry, 1978; mem. editl. bd.: Jour. Reactive Intermediates, Langmuir and Proceedings of Nat. Acad. Scis., 2004. Recipient Eastman Kodak award for excellence in grad. rsch. pure chemistry, 1973, award, E.O. Lawrence U.S. Dept. Energy, 1983, Porter medal, European Photochem. Soc., Inter-Am. Photochem. Soc., 1994, Havinga medal, Leiden, The Netherlands, 1994, Disting. Alumnus award, Calif. Inst. Tech., 1996, Strahlenchemie preis, Max-Planck-Inst., Mülheim, Germany, 1998, Dir's. award for Tchr.-Scholar, NSF, 2002; fellow NSF, Alfred P. Sloan Found., Guggenheim fellow, Oxford U., 1985. Mem.: AAAS, NAS (editl. bd. Procs. NAS 2002—), European Photo-Chem. Assn. (Porter medal), Inter-Am. Photochemistry Soc. (award 1991, 1994), N.Y. Acad. Scis. (Freda and Gregory Halpern award in photochemistry 1977), Am. Chem. Soc. (mem. editl. bd. jour. 1984—87, Fresenius award 1973, award for pure chemistry 1974, Harrison Howe award Rochester, N.Y. sect. 1986, Arthur C. Cope award 1986, James Flack Norris award 1987, award in colloid and surface chemistry 1999, Gibbs medal award Chgo. sect. 2000, George C. Pimentel award 2004), Sigma Xi, Phi Beta Kappa. Office: Columbia U 3000 Broadway New York NY 10027-6941

TURSO, VITO ANTHONY, government and public affairs executive; b. N.Y.C., N.Y., Jan. 3, 1948; s. Vito Anthony and Helen (Smanko) T.; m. MaryAnn Ponzo, July 12, 1980; children: Lisa Lynn, Laura Mae, Nicole Vita. Student, Queens Coll., Flushing, N.Y., 1965-69. Reporter L.I. Press, Jamaica, N.Y., 1966-77; asst. Metro editor The Trib, N.Y.C., 1977-78; dir. pub. affairs N.Y.C. Dept. Sanitation, 1978-90; dep. commr. for pub. affairs N.Y.C. Dept. Correction, 1990 94; dep. commr for pub. affairs and community svcs. N.Y.C. Dept. of Environ. Protection, 1994-95; exec. v.p. Dan Klores Comms. Pub. Rels., 1995—2002; dep. commr. pub. info and cmty. affairs N.Y.C. Dept. Sanitation, 2002—. Guest lectr. N.Y.U., 1998, New Sch. for Social Rsch., N.Y.C., 1988, Pace U., 1990. Host pub. affairs shows on TV and radio, 1981, 88; contbr. articles to pop. mags. Bd. dirs. Ozone Tudor Civic Assn., Ozone Park, N.Y., 1982-90. Recipient Bronze medal Internat. Film and TV Festival N.Y., 1985, Page One award N.Y. Newspaper Guild, 1976. Mem. Pub. Rels. Officers Soc. N.Y. (pres. 1983-85), Pub. Rels. Soc. Am. (bd. dirs. 1987-88), Am. Diabetes Assn. (bd. dirs. N.Y. chpt. 1989-91), Bklyn. Tech. H.S. Alumni Assn. (bd. dirs. 1984—), N.Y. Press Club, Inc. (bd. dirs. 1978). Roman Catholic. Avocations: golf, music. Home: 133-33 84th St Ozone Park NY 11417-1919 Office: 125 Worth St New York NY 10013

TURTELL, NEAL TIMOTHY, librarian; b. N.Y.C., Nov. 1, 1949; s. Richard Roland and Ann Grace (Glover) T. AB, Fordham U., 1971; MLS, Pratt Inst., 1975. Cataloger-libr. Ford Found., N.Y.C., 1972-75, U.S. Dept. Transp., Washington, 1975-77; spl. projects libr. Smithsonian Instn., Washington, 1977-81, chief catalogue records, 1981-82; asst. dir. tech. svcs. U. Wis., Oshkosh, 1982-83, asst. prof. libr. sci., 1982-83; asst. chief libr. Nat. Gallery of Art, Washington, 1983-87, exec. libr., 1987—. Contbr. to book revs. Libr. Jour., 1972-75, exhbn. catalogue. Bd. trustees Pyramid Atlantic Ctr. for Printmaking and the Art of the Book, Riverdale, Md., 1988—, v.p. bd. trustees, 1991—. Mem. Art Librs. Soc. N.Am., Rsch. Librs. Group (steering com. for art and architecture 1988-89), Grolier Club. Home: 1631-B S Hayes St Arlington VA 22202-2713 Office: Nat Gallery of Art 4th & Constitution Ave NW Washington DC 20565-0001

TURTURRO, AIDA, actress; b. NYC, Sept. 25, 1962; Grad., State U. NY, New Paltz, 1984. Actor: (films) Life with Mikey, 1993, Money Train, 1995, Sleepers, 1996, Fallen, 1998, Celebrity, 1998, Deep Blue Sea, 1999, Mickey Blue Eyes, 1999, Bringing Out the Dead, 1999, Play It to the Bone, 1999, Crocodile Dundee in Los Angeles, 2001; (TV series) As the World Turns, 1998, The Soprano's, 2000—; (Broadway plays) A Streetcar Named Desire, 1992, (guest appearance): (TV series) Law and Order, 1990. Office: 1100 Ave of the Americas New York NY 10036

TURTURRO, JOHN, actor; b. Brooklyn, Feb. 28, 1957; s. Nicholas and Katherine Turturro; m. Katherine Borowitz; children: Amedeo, Diego. Grad., SUNY (New Paltz), 1978; student, Yale Drama Sch. Worked in regional theater and off-Broadway prodns.: Danny and the Deep Blue Sea; Men Without Dates; Tooth of the Crime; La Puta Vida; Chaos and Hard Times; The Bald Soprano; Of Mice and Men; The Resistable Rise of Arturo Ui, 1991; Waiting for Godot; appeared in Broadway prodn.: Death of a Salesman, 1984; appeared in films: Raging Bull, 1980; The Flamingo Kid, 1984; To Live and Die in L.A., 1985; Desperately Seeking Susan, 1985; Hannah and Her Sisters, 1986; Gung Ho, 1986; Offbeat, 1986; The Color of Money, 1986; The Sicilian, 1987; Five Corners, 1988; Do the Right Thing, 1989; Miller's Crossing, 1990; Men of Respect; Mo Better Blues, 1990; Jungle Fever, 1991; Barton Fink, 1991; Backtrack, 1991; Brain Donors, 1992; Fearless, 1993; Festival, 1991; Being Human, 1994; Quiz Show, 1994; Grace of My Heart, 1994; Search and Destroy, 1995; Unstrung Heroes, 1995; Clockers, 1995; Box of Moonlight, 1996; Girl 6, 1996; The Big Lebowski, 1997; Animals, 1997; The Truce, 1998; Lesser Prophets, 1998; Rounders, 1998; He Got Game, 1998; The Source, 1999; The Cradle Will Rock, 1999; Company Man, 1999; Two Thousand and None, 1999; Oh Brother, Where Art Thou?, 1999; The Man Who Cried, 1999; The Luzhin Defense, 1999; Anger Management, 2003; appeared in films Collateral Damage, 2000, Mr. Deeds, 2002, Secret Passage, 2002, Secret Window, 2004; actor: (TV films) Monday Night Mayhem, 2002; dir.: (films, debut) Mac; (films) Illuminata, 1998, Thirteen Conversations About One Thing, 2000. Office: care ICM 40 W 57th St New York NY 10019-4001 also: 16 N Oak St 2 A Ventura CA 93001-5620*

TURTURRO, NICHOLAS, actor; b. N.Y.C., Jan. 29, 1962; m. Jamie Biunno, 1984 (div. 1985) 1 child; m. Lissa Espinosa, 1986; 1 child. Actor films including: Mo' Better Blues, 1990, Men of Respect, 1991, Jungle Fever, 1991, Mac, 1992, Malcolm X, 1992, Men Lie, 1994, Cosmic Slop, 1994, Federal Hill, 1995, The Search for One-eye Jimmy, 1996, Shadow Conspiracy, 1997, Excess Baggage, 1997, (tv series) NYPD Blue, 1993-99, Hercules, 1998, (tv movies) Mob Justice, 1995, In the Line of Duty: Hunt for Justice, 1995, Falling from the Sky: Flight 174, 1995, Mercenary II: Thick & Thin, 1997, Witness to the Mob, 1998, Hellraiser 5: Inferno, 2000, Recess: School's Out, 2001, Purgatory Flats, 2002, The Biz, 2002, The Hollow, 2004; tv guest appearances include: Law & Order, 1990, L.A. Law, 1986, Drew Carey Show, 1995. Office: United Talent Agy 9560 Wilshire Blvd Ste 500 Beverly Hills CA 90212-2427*

TURTZ, MARILYN JOAN, artist, painter, educator; b. Bklyn., Jan. 23, 1955; d. Isidore and Elsie (Shapiro) Turtz; m. Jonathan Block Friedman, July 1, 1982; children: Charles Michael, David Lawrence. Student, SUNY, Stony Brook, 1973—74; BFA in Painting, Pratt Inst., 1978; MFA in Painting, Bklyn. Coll., 1985. Cert. tchr. NY. Mus. educator Bklyn. Mus., 1977—79; art tchr. Bklyn. Friends Sch., 1978—87, 1990—91; dir. BAC's By and for Youth Mus. Bklyn. Arts Coun., 1998—2001, dir., artist, educator, 2000—. Cons. in field. One-woman shows include Home Grown Gallery, Cold Spring Harbor, NY, 1992, West Harbor Gallery, Oyster Bay, NY, 1994, First Story Gallery, Louisville, 1994, Discovery Gallery, Sea Cliff, NY, 1994, 1997—98, Gallery North, Setauket, NY, 1997, Matera, Italy, 1997, NY Inst. Tech., Central Islip, NY, 1999, Gallery Emanuel, Great Neck, NY, 2000, Heckscher Mus. Art Bryant Libr., Roslyn, NY, 2001, Dolan Gallery, Locust Valley, NY, 2003, exhibited in group shows at Heckscher Mus., Huntington, NY, 1990, 1998, Guild Hall, Easthampton, NY, 1989, Charles A. Wustum Mus. Fine Art, Racine, Wis., 1991, Home Grown Gallery, Cold Spring Harbor, NY, 1992, Bowery Gallery, NYC, 1993, Lizan Tops Gallery, East Hampton, NY, 1996, Bridgewater/Lustberg Gallery, NYC, 1997, Gallery North, Setauket, NY, 1997—2003, Nat. Acad. Design, NYC, 1998, 2000, Parrish Art Mus., Southhampton, NY, 1998—99, Sidney Mishkin Gallery, NYC, 1999, Cold Spring Harbor (NY) Labs., 2000, LI Mus., Stony Brook, NY, 2001—02, Hubert Gallery, NYC, 2002, OK Harris Gallery, 2003, represented in numerous pub. and pvt. collections; contbr. articles to profl. jours.; Exhibited in group shows at The Dennis and Phillip Ratner Mus., MD, 2004. Active Artists Against Hunger, Sea Cliff, NY, 1996—2000, Visual AIDS, NYC, 1998—; instr. Glen Cove Citizens Com. Against Substance Abuse, 1988—90. Recipient 1st pl. in tile art, Mus. Stony Brook, NY, Excellence award, L.I. Devel. Corp., Artist in Residence Weir Farm Trust, Conn., 2004; Arts for Transit grant, Met. Transit Authority, NYC, 1992, Centennial Celebration grant, Cold Spring Harbor Lab., 1999. Avocations: art, music, hiking. Home: 6 Sunset Ave Glen Cove NY 11542 Office: Bklyn Arts Coun 195 Cadman Plz W Brooklyn NY Personal E-mail: mturtz@aol.com.

TUSCHMAN, JAMES MARSHALL, lawyer; b. Nov. 28, 1941; s. Chester and Harriet (Harris) T.; m. Ina S. Cheloff, Sept. 2, 1967; children: Chad Michael, Jon Stephen, Sari Anne. BS in Bus., Miami U., Oxford, Ohio, 1963; JD, Ohio State U., 1966. Bar: Ohio 1966, U.S. Ct. Appeals (6th and 7th cirs.), U.S. Supreme Ct. Assoc. Shumaker, Loop & Kendrick, Toledo, 1966—84, ptnr., 1970—84; co-founder, chmn. ops. com. Jacobson Maynard Tuschman & Kalur, Toledo, 1985—97; COO Ohio Ferrous Group Omnisource Corp., Toledo, 1998—99, dir. bus. devel. No. Ohio group, 1999—2001; of counsel Barkan & Robon Ltd., Maumee, Ohio, 2002—. Chmn. bd., sec. Tuschman Steel Co., Toledo, 1969-76, Toledo Steel Supply Co., 1969-86; vice-chmn. bd. Kripke Tuschman Industries, Inc., 1977-85; ptnr. Starr Ave. Co., Toledo, 1969-86. Past trustee, chmn. bd. trustees U. Toledo; past trustee, chmn. fin. com., past treas. Maumee Valley Country Day Sch.; past trustee, v.p., treas. Temple B'nai Israel, 1984-88; mem. nat. alumni coun. Ohio State U. Coll. Law; mem., co-chmn. subcom. on structure, governance and fin. Gov.'s Commn. on Higher. Fellow Internat. Soc. Barristers; mem. ATLA, Am. Bd. Trial Advocates, Ohio Bar Assn., Toledo Bar Assn., Ohio Trial Lawyers Assn., Million Dollar Advocates Forum, Toledo Club, Inverness Country Club, Zeta Beta Tau, Phi Delta Phi. Home: 2579 Olde Brookside Rd Toledo OH 43615-2233 Office: Barkan & Robon Ltd 1701 Woodlands Dr Maumee OH 43537-4092 Office Phone: 419-897-6500. Business E-Mail: jmt.barrob@buckeye-express.com.

TUSHMAN, J. LAWRENCE, wholesale distribution executive; Ptnr., mgr. Sherwood Food Distbrs., Detroit. Office: Sherwood Food Distributors 18615 Sherwood St Detroit MI 48234-2813

TUSIANI, JOSEPH, foreign language educator, author; b. Foggia, Italy, Jan. 14, 1924; came to U.S., 1947, naturalized, 1956; s. Michael and Maria (Pisone) T. Dottore in Lettere summa cum laude, U. Naples, 1947, LittD, 1971; Dottore (hon.), U. Foggia, 2004. Lectr. in Italian lit. Hunter Coll., 1950-62; chmn. Italian dept. Coll. Mt. St. Vincent, 1948-71. Vis. assoc. prof. NYU, 1956-64, CUNY, 1971-83; prof. Herbert H. Lehman Coll., 1971-83; NDEA vis. prof. Italian Conn. State Coll., 1962. Author: Dante in Licenza, 1952, Two Critical Essays on Emily Dickinson, 1952, Poesia Missionaria in Inghilterra ed America, 1953, Sonettisti Americani, 1954, Melos Cordis: Poems in Latin, 1955, Lo Speco Celeste, 1956, Odi Sacre; poems, 1958, The Complete Poems of Michelangelo, 1960, Rind and All, 1962, Lust and Liberty (The Poems of Machiavelli), 1963, The Fifth Season, 1963, (novels) Envoy from Heaven, 1965, Tasso's Jerusalem Delivered, 1970, Boccaccio's Nymphs of Fiesole, 1971, Gente Mia and Other Poems, 1978, (poems in Latin) In Exilio Rerum, 1985, (autobiography) La Parola Difficile, vol. I, 1988, (poems in Latin) Confinia Lucis et Umbrae: La Parola Nuova, vol. II, 1991, La Parola Antica, vol. III, 1992, (poems in Italian) Il Ritorno, 1992, Bronx America, 1992, Annemale Parlante, 1994, Carmina Latina, 1994, La Poceide, 1996, Carmina Latina, vol. 11, 1998, Li Quatte Staggione, 1998, Lu Deddú, 1999, Maste Peppe Cantarine, 2000, Lu Ponte de Sôla, 2001, In Quattro Lingue, 2001, Dante's Divine Comedy (As told for young people), 2001, L'ore de Gesu Bambine (a Christmas play in verse), 2001, La Prima Cumpagnia, 2002,

(in Apulian dialect) La Tomba de Patre Pí, 2003, (plays) (in verse) La Cunte de Pasqua, 2003, La Padula (in Apulian dialect, 2004; translator: Pulci's Morgante, 1998. Recipient Greenwood prize for poetry in England, 1956, Outstanding Tchr. award, 1969, cavaliere ufficiale Italian Republic, 1973, Leonardo Covello's educator award, 1980, Leone di San Marco award, 1982, Avis award, 1983, Joseph Tusiani scholarship fund established in his honor at Lehman Coll., 1983, Congl. medal merit, 1984, Progresso medal liberty, 1986, Gold plaque City Hall San Marco, 1986, Outstanding tchr. award Am. Assn. Tchrs. Italian, 1986, Renoir literary award, 1988, Joseph Tusiani, Poet, Translator, Humanist (An Internat. Homage), 1995, Enrico Fermi award, 1995, Fiorello La Guardia award, 1998; Melvin Jones fellow, 1995, Gov.'s award for excellence, 1999, Apulia prize of Regione Puglia, 1999, Gold medal at Rome's Capitol, 2004, Gold medal Gov. of Regione Puglia, 2004, prize Italiani nel Mondo, 2004; Joseph Tusiani Found. established at U. Lecce, 1998, Nat. Endowment for the Haminities, 1998. Mem. Poetry Soc. Am. (v.p.), Cath. Poetry Soc. Am. (dir. 1958, Spirit gold medal 1968) Home: 308 E 72nd St New York NY 10021-4727 *Strange how this continually re-edited Who's Who forces one to work and achieve.*

TUSKA, JON, author, publisher; b. South Milwaukee, Wis., Apr. 30, 1942; s. Andrew and Florence Catherine (Tommet) T.; m. Vicki Piekarski, May 24, 1980; 1 child, Jennifer Lee. BA, Marquette U., 1965. Owner Pers. Cons., Milw., 1969-74; editor, pub. Views & Revs. mag., 1969-75; freelance writer, 1975--91; co-owner, agt. Golden West Literary Agy., Portland, Oreg., 1992—. Mem. adj. faculty MA and tchg. program and undergrads. Lewis and Clark Coll., 1979-88' staff music critic Ovation mag., 1987-89, Fanfare mag., 1989-95; spl. film. cons. Images of Indians, PBS, 1980, Images of Appalachia, PBS, 1984, Mommy, Who's Winning Now? The Cold War in America, Turner, 1986, Say It with Music: Irving Berlin's America, PBS, 1986, Broadway's Eternal Romantics: Lerner and Loewe, PBS, 1988, John Wayne: Standing Tall, PBS, 1989, Big Guns Talk, Turner, 1997; prodr. classical music programs, art and news features and interviews with musicians and motion picture personalities, and film revs. for radio stas. Oreg. Pub. Broadcasting. Author: Philo Vance: The Life and Times of S.S. Van Dine, 1973, The Films of Mae West, 1973, The Filming of the West, 1976, The Detective in Hollywood, 1978, The Vanishing Legion: A History of Mascot Pictures 1927-35, 1982, 2d edit., 1986, Billy the Kid: A Bio/Bibliography, 1983, Dark Cinema: American Film Noir in Cultural Perspective, 1984, The American West in Film: Critical Approaches to the Western, 1985, In Manors and Alleys: A Case-Book on the American Detective Film, 1988, A Variable Harvest: Essays and Reviews in Literature and Film, 1989, Encounters with Filmmakers: Eight Career Studies, 1991, The Complete Films of Mae West, 1992, Billy the Kid: His Life and Legend, 1994, (with Vicki Piekarski) The Frontier Experience: A Reader's Guide to the Life and Literature of the American West, 1984; editor-in-chief (with Piekarski) Ency. of Frontier and Western Fiction, 1983; editor: The Western Story: A Chronological Treasury 1894-1994, 1994, Shadow of the Lariat, 1995, Star Western: Twenty-Two Western Stories from the Golden Age, 1995, The Big Book of Western Action Stories, 1995, (with Piekarski) The Morrow Anthology of Great Western Short Stories, 1997, The First Five Star Western Corral, 2000, Five Star Westerns, 2000, Stories of the Golden West, Book One, 2000, Book Two, 2001, Book Three, 2002, Book Four, 2003, Odyssey to the North: Northwestern Stories, 2003. Avocations: reading, classical music, film history, book collecting. Home and Office: 2327 SE Salmon St Portland OR 97214-3943 Office Phone: 503-232-0238. Personal E-mail: jtuska@qwest.net.

TUSZYNSKI, MARK H. neurologist; b. Halifax, N.S., Canada, Feb. 27, 1959; came to U.S., 1959; s. Alfons and Jadwiga (Allman) T.; m. Karen R. Dobkins, July 15, 1995; 1 child, Matthew. BS, U. Minn., 1979, MD, 1983; PhD, U. Calif., 1991. Resident Cornell U./ NYU, 1984—87; asst. prof. U. Calif. San Diego, 1991—96, assoc. prof., 1996—2002, prof., 2002—, dir. Ctr. Neural Repair. Mem., editorial bd. Experimental Neurology, 1997—, Frontiers in Bioscience, 1997—, Neurobiology of Disease, 2000—, Neurological Disease and Therapy section, 2000—; mem., scientific advisory bd. The Paralysis Project, 1997—, Comitato Promotore Telethon, 1997—, The Christopher Reeve Paralysis Found., 1999—, Can. & Amer. Spinal Rsch. Org., 2000—. Author: CNS Regeneration, 1997. Nat. Rsch. Service award, 1987, Physician Scientist award, 1988, Silvio O. Conte Physician -Scientist award, Amer. Academy of Neurology, 1995, Bernard Sanberg Memorial award for Brain Repair, Amer. Society for Neural Transplantation & Repair, 2000, C.U. Ariens Kappers award, Netherlands Inst. for Brain Rsch., 2001. Mem., Amer. Neurological Found., 1998; Fellow, Amer. Society for Neural Transplantation & Repair, 1998. Office: Dept Neurosciences 0626 Sch Med U Calif San Diego La Jolla CA 92093

TUTASHINDA, KWELI (BRIAN P. ALTHEIMER), chiropractic physician, educator; b. Wynne, Ark., May 14, 1956; s. Joe Porché and Lura Ella (Darden) Altheimer; divorced; 1 child, Chinyere R.; m. Leonor Quiñonez, June 13, 1987; children Xihuanel, Rukiya, Jomoké. BA in Philosophy summa cum laude, U. Ark., 1978; D of Chiropractic cum laude, Life Chiropractic Coll. West, San Lorenzo, Calif., 1989. Tchr. English Oakland (Calif.) Pub. Schs., 1984-86; tchr. spl. programs U. Calif., Berkeley, 1984-92, 94-95, 98-00; instr. phys. diagnosis and chiropractic tech. Life Chiropractic Coll. West, Haywood, Calif., 1989—99; pvt. practice Berkeley, 1989—; owner Imhotep Chiropractic & Wellness Clinic; dir. Imhotep Wellness Workshops & Seminars. Developer rehab. tng. Editor, pub. Foresight Mag., 1982-84; author, pub. Toward a Holistic Worldview, 1985, Therapeutic Exercises for the Spine, 1999; developer rehab. tng.; contbr. articles to Chiropractic History. Recipient 1st degree Black Belt Tae Kwon Do, 1976. Mem. Sufi Order of the West, Naqshbandi Sufi Order. Islam. Avocations: yoga, martial arts, writing, reading, jogging. Office: 3358 Adeline St Berkeley CA 94703-2737 E-mail: tutateam@awol.

TUTEN, JAMES H. educational association administrator, educator; b. Varnville, S.C., Oct. 12, 1968; s. Henry M. and Annette B. Tuten; m. Belle Tuten, Jan. 11, 1992; 1 child, Tom. BA, Coll. of Charleston, 1990; MA, Wake Forest U., N.C., 1992; PhD, Emory Universtity, Atlanta, 2003. Interlibrary loan dir. Emory Med. Sch., Atlanta, 1996—97; lectr. Juniata Coll., Huntingdon, Pa., 1998—2001, asst. provost, 2001—. Cons. Hist. Climate Investigators, Williamsburg, Va., 2000—01; chair 125th anniversary com. Juniata Coll., 2000—01, coord. vis. speakers, 2000—; editl. bd. Juniata Voices, Huntingdon, Pa., 2001—. Contbr. nonfiction book Before the New Deal, 1999, Dictionary of American History, 2002, American National Biography, 1999, book reviews South Carolina Hist. Mag., Ency. Gilded Age and Progresive Era. State level judge Nat. History Day, Winston-Salem, NC, 1991, vol. Huntingdon, Pa., 1998—2004; bd. mem. Huntingdon County Hist. Soc., Pa., 2002—04; judge We The People Contest, Carlisle, Pa., 2003—04; bd. mem. Stone Ch. of Brethren, Huntingdon, Pa., chair bd. dirs., 2003, mem. strategic planning team, 2000—01. Fellow History Dept. Fellowship, Emory U., 1996—97; scholar Wake Forest Grad. Sch., Wake Forest U., 1990—92; Fine Arts Scholar, Coll. of Charleston, 1986—90. Mem.: Nat. Assn. of Fellowships Advisors, S.C. Hist. Soc., Orgn. of Am. Historians, So. Hist. Assn., Phi Alpha Theta, Omicron Delta Kappa. Democrat. Avocations: birdwatching, travel, ship modeling, stamp collecting/philately, music. Office: Juniata Coll Moore St Huntingdon PA 16652 Personal E-mail: tutenj@juniata.edu.

TUTHILL, JAY DEAN, II, investment executive; b. Wilmington, Del., Dec. 10, 1953; s. Jay Dean Tuthill and Annabelle (Carney) Kressman; m. Laura Ann Behr, Nov. 23, 1972 (div. May 1981); 1 child, Elizabeth; m. Assunta Sera, Oct. 10, 1991; children: Lori, Michael, Mark. BSChemE, U. Del., 1981; MBA with honors, U. Mich., 1988. Engr. Exxon, Detroit, 1981-86; mgr. bus. planning Am. Cyanamid, Wayne, NJ, 1988-94; portfolio mgr. Am. Express, Paramus, NJ, 1994-95; pres. Buckingham Fin., Ridgewood, NJ, 1995—; CFO Prismatic Corp., Newburgh, NY, 1997—; mng. dir. Tuthill & Merker LLC, Ridgewood, NJ, 1999—. Mem. Assn. Investment Mgmt. and Rsch., N.Y. Soc. Security Analysts (vice chair comms. and mktg. com. 1994—, Vol. of Yr. award 1995), Inst. Chartered Fin. Analysts (chartered CFA), Ridgewood C. of C. (profl. com. 1996), Beta Gamma Sigma, Tau Beta Pi. Republican. Roman Catholic. Avocations: golf, piano. Home: 530 Valley Rd Apt 1M Montclair NJ 07043-2714 Office: Tuthill & Merker LLC 1250 E Ridgewood Ave Ste 18 Ridgewood NJ 07450-3930

TUTHILL, WALTER WARREN, financial executive, international business consultant; b. Madison, N.J., Nov. 28, 1941; s. Walter Warren and Elizabeth Emma (Kniskern) T.; m. Barbara Ann Stephens, Apr. 22, 1967. BSBA, U. N.C., 1964. CPA Calif., N.Y., N.J., N.C.; cert. info. systems auditor. Sr. mgr. Price Waterhouse, N.Y.C., 1964-77; dir. internal audit Carter Hawley Hale Stores Inc., L.A., 1977-82, gen. auditor, 1982-85, v.p., 1985-93; sr. v.p. retail control Broadway Stores, Inc., L.A., 1993-96; v.p. retail control Federated Dept. Stores, Inc., L.A., 1996-97; COO Gelfand, Rennert & Feldman divsn. PricewaterhouseCoopers LLP, L.A., 1997-2001; dir. cons. WongHolland LLP, CPAs, Woodland Hills, Calif., 2001—. Lectr. in field. Contbr. articles to profl. jours. Mem. AICPA, N.Y. Soc. CPAs, Am. Acctg. Assn., Nat. Retail Mchts. Assn. (chmn. bd. internal audit group 1982-84, bd. dirs.), Info. Sys. Audit and Control Assn. Avocations: international travel, computers, classical music, photography, philanthropy. Office: Wong Holland LLP CPA 4919 Topanga Canyon Blvd Woodland Hills CA 91364-3113 Office Phone: 818-999-5273. Personal E-mail: wwtuthill@earthlink.net. *Life is what happens when we're planning something else.*

TUTINO, THOMAS JAMES, theater educator, set designer; b. Milw., Wis., Oct. 5, 1958; s. Henry John and Jacqueline Marie Tutino; m. Susan Lagelle Helmering, Nov. 17, 1984; children: Jessica Lagelle, Anthony Henry. AB in Theatre, Western Ky. U., Bowling Green, 1980; MFA in Scenic Design, Boston U., 1983. Prof. dept. of theatre and dance Western Ky. U., Bowling Green, 1990—. Scenic designer Jemima Boone, Nine: The Musical, Frankenstein, Camelot, Into the Woods, Ben Franklin's Apprentice, The Diary of Anne Frank, Noises Off, over 80 others. Mem.: Theatre Comm. Group, Southeastern Theatre Conf., U.S. Inst. for Theatre Tech. (SE Sect.) (chair 1998—2000, Founder's award 2003), U.S. Inst. for Theatre Tech, United Scenic Artists (USA-829). Avocations: instrumental rock guitar, historic home restoration. Home: 1242 College St Bowling Green KY 42101-2621 Office: WKU Dept Theatre & Dance 1 Big Red Way Bowling Green KY 42101 Office Phone: 270-745-5878. E-mail: tom.tutino@wku.edu.

TUTINS, ANTONS, electronics and audio engineer; b. Ludza, Latvia, May 2, 1933; s. Francis and Veronika (Seipulniks) Tutins; came to U.S., 1950, naturalized, 1963; student U. Minn., 1951-55; BS in Elec. Engring., Ill. Inst. Tech., 1970; MBA, U. Chgo., 1974; m. Raita Snebergs, July 8, 1961; 1 child, Robert. With Motorola Communications div., Chgo., 1964-73; product engring. mgr. Knowles Electronics, Inc., Franklin Park, Ill., 1973-81; dir. quality assurance and mfg. engring. Perma Power Electronics Inc., Chgo., 1982-95; pres. AT Systems, Des Plaines, Ill., 1995—; tech. cons. Accord, Inc., Westchester, Ill., 1995—. Bd. dirs. Spl. Interest Group of Object Oriented Tech., 1995—. With USN, 1955-57. Mem. IEEE, Acoustical Soc. Am., Chgo. Acoustical and Audio Group (pres. 1977-78), Audio Engring. Soc, Midwest Acoustics Conf. (exec. com., pres. 1980), Latvian Cath. Student Assn. Dzintars (pres. 1979-81), Am. Latvian Cath. Assn. (registered agt. 1978—, v.p. 1985), Baltic Info. Exch. (v.p. 1991—), Motorola Engring. Club (pres. 1970-71). Roman Catholic. Home: 1338 Briar Ct Des Plaines IL 60018-2146 Office: 10301 W Roosevelt Rd Westchester IL 60154-2575

TUTOR, RONALD N. construction company executive; b. Oct. 13, 1940; BS in Finance, U. So. Calif., 1963. Pres., CEO Tutor-Saliba Corp.; COO, also dir. Perini Corp., Framingham, Mass. Bd. dirs. Southdown Corp.; mem. adv. com. U. So. Calif. Sch. Engring. Recipient L.A. Conservancy Preservation award, 1994, Greater L.A. African-Am. C. of C. Contractor of yr. award, 1994, U.S. Army C.E. L.A. Dist. Contractor of Yr. award, 1994, NCCJ Real Estate and Constrn. Industry Humanitarian award, 1992. Mem. Am. Concrete Inst.

TUTTLE, ASHLEY, dancer; b. Columbia, SC; Student, Sch. Am. Ballet. Mem. Am. Ballet Theatre, N.Y.C., 1987—, soloist, 1992—, prin. ballerina, 1997—. Roles include Mathilda Kchessinska in Anastasia, Callipe and Polyhymnia in Apollo, Nikiya in La Bayadere, mother/sweathear in Billy the Kid, Cinderella and the Spring Fairy in Cinderella, Prayer in Copellia, Gulnare and the pas de deux in Le Cosaire, the Queen of the Driads, Amour and flower girl in Don Quixote, others, featured roles in Ballet Imperial, Cruel World, Drink to Me Only With Thine Eyes, The Leaves are Falling, leading roles in Brahms-Haydn Variations, The Elements, Jump Start, Piece D'Occasion. Office: Am Ballet Theatre 890 Broadway New York NY 10003

TUTTLE, BYNUM R., JR., brokerage house executive; b. Burlington, N.C., Jan. 7, 1950; s. Bynum R. Sr. and Ruby B. T.; m. (div.); children: Andrew Scott, Anna Katherine. MS, Mars Hill Coll., 1973; MEd, U. N.C., 1978. Tchr. Greensboro (N.C.) City Schs., 1973-78; group sales Pilot Life Ins. Co., Greensboro, 1978-84; sales mgr. The Ins. Ctr. N.C., Greensboro, 1984-87; pres., cons. Employee Benefit Designs, Denton, 1987—; mng. ptnr. Triune Tech., LLC, Denton, N.C., 1998—. Agt. adv. com. Ptnrs. Nat. Health Plan, Winston-Salem, N.C., 1999—. N.C. Dept. Ins., Raleigh, N.C., 1997-98, Lincoln Nat. Life, Ft. Wayne, Ind., 1986; com. mem. Citizens for Bus. & Industry, Raleigh, 1992. Adv. com. Energy United Electric Membership, Lexington, N.C., 1996—; bd. dirs. Family Affair Care Group, Gibsonville, N.C., 1992—, J.E. Rogers Meml. Scholarship Fund, Denton, 1995—, Greensboro Jaycees, 1980; coun. mem. Summerville Bapt. Ch. Recipient Ten Key Men award Jaycees, 1979. Mem. Nat. Assn. Health Underwriters (v.p. 1999, nat. legis. chmn. 1997), N.C. Assn. Health Underwriters (pres. 1996-97, Frederick W. Joyner Disting. Svc. award 1998, Honor Coun. award 1993, 95-99), Triad Assn. Health Underwriters (pres. 1994-95). Avocations: water sports, golf, reading, travel. Home: 706 Mountain Shore Dr Denton NC 27239 Office: Employee Benefit Designs Inc PO Box 1110 Denton NC 27239-1110

TUTTLE, JEREMY BALLOU, neurobiologist; b. N.Y.C., Oct. 9, 1947; s. John Bauman and Charlotte Marion (Root) T.; m. Sara Jane Stasko, Mar. 23, 1971. AB, U. Rochester, 1969; PhD, Johns Hopkins U., 1977. Postdoctoral fellow U. Conn., Storrs, 1976-79, vis. asst. prof., 1980, asst. prof. in residence, 1981-84; asst. prof. physiology U. Va., Charlottesville, 1984-87, asst. prof. neuroscience, 1987-90, rsch. asst. prof., 1990-93, assoc. prof. urology neuroscience, 1993-98, prof., 1998—. Contbr. articles to Devel. Biology, Science, Jour. Neuroscience, others. Chmn. mem. Common Area Planning Commn., 1984-87; pres. bd. Earlysville Forest Homeowner's Assn., 1986-89, Earlysville, Va.; chmn. urology spl. emphasis panel NIH, 1996-2001; chmn. spl. emphasis panel on female pelvic floor disorders Nat. Inst. Child Health and Human Devel., 1999. U. Rochester Hon. scholar, 1965-69, Regent's scholar for Medicine, 1969, NIH predoctoral fellow, 1971-75, Nat. Rsch. Svc. fellow, 1976-79, Nat. Spinal Cord Injury Found. rsch. fellow, 1979-80; recipient Rsch. Career Devel. award Nat. Inst. Neurol. Disease/NIH, Muscular Dystrophy Assn. Rsch. award, 1990—; Am. Heart Assn. grantee, 1987-89, 90—, fellowship, Fogarty Internat. Ctr. for Rsch. NIH, Japan, 1997. Achievements include research on NGF dynamics in hypertrophic disease, carbon dioxide transport and chemosensitivity, molecular mechanisms of quantal synaptic transmission, nerve growth factor synthesis by vascular smooth muscle, trophic regulation of motor neurons, neurodegenerative diseases. Office: U Va Med Sch PO Box 801392 Charlottesville VA 22908-1392 Office Phone: 434-924-5634. Business E-Mail: tuttle@virginia.edu.

TUTTLE, JERRY OWEN, retired naval officer, business executive; b. Hatfield, Ind., Dec. 18, 1934; s. Charles Merritt and Wenonah Hathaway (Parker) T.; m. Barbara Ann Bonifay, Dec. 31, 1956; children: Michael Charles, Vicky Ann, Mark Jerreld, Stephen Scott, Monique Therese. Grad., Devry Tech. Inst., 1954; BS, Naval Postgrad. Sch., 1962; MA in Internat. Relations, George Washington U., 1969; postgrad., Naval War Coll., 1968-69. Enlisted U.S. Navy, 1955, commd. ensign, 1956, advanced through grades to vice adm., 1987; aide and flag lt. to comdr-in-chief Pacific Fleet, 1969-70; exec. officer Attack Squadron 174, 1970-71, Attack Squadron 81, comdg. officer, 1971-73; mem. staff comdr. U.S. Naval Air Forces, Atlantic Fleet, 1973-74; comdr. Attack Carrier Air Win 3, 1974-75; comdg. officer USS Kalamazoo, 1975-76, comnavairlant, 1976-77; comdg. officer USS John F. Kennedy, 1977-78, 78-79; spl. asst. to chief of naval ops. Dir. Intelligence Agy., Washington, 1979, dir. for plans and policy div., 1979-81; comdr. Carrier Group 8, Norfolk, Va., 1981-83, Carrier Group 2/Battle Force 6th Fleet, Naples, Italy, 1983-84; naval insp. gen. Washington, 1984-85; dep., chief of staff U.S. Atlantic Fleet/Chief of Staff, U.S. Atlantic Command, 1985-86; dir. for command, control, communication systems Office of Joint Chiefs of Staff, 1987-89, dir. space & electronic warfare, 1989-93; ret. USN, 1993; v.p. bus. devel. Oracle Corp., 1994-96; pres. ManTech Sys. Engring. Corp., 1996-2000, SAVANTAGE (formerly Reltek Sys. and Design, Inc.), 2000—02; pres., CEO J.O.T. Enterprises, LLC, 2002—. Decorated Def. Superior Svc. medal, Legion of Merit (4), Meritorious Svc. medal (2), D.F.C. (3), Air medal (23), Def. Disting. Svc. medal, Disting. Svc. medal; comdr. Nat. Order of Merit (France); recipient John Paul Jones awd for inspirational leadership Navy League, 1978; listed in Fed. Computer Week's 1991, 92 Federal 100 for his impact on govt. computer systems. Mem. AIAA (Control, Com. and Intelligence award for contbn. to overall effectiveness of C3I Systems 1991), AFCEA (contbn. award 1989, Jon Boyce award 1992), Assn. Naval Aviators (Gold Eagle). Office Phone: 703-385-7522. Office Fax: 703-385-7733. Business E-Mail: jt@sseusa.com. *Drive yourself to lead others; to think only of the best; to work only for the best and expect only the best; to be just as enthusiastic about the success of others as you are about your own.*

TUTTLE, KENNETH LEWIS, engineering educator, consultant; b. Toledo, Oreg., Apr. 4, 1944; s. Martin Lewis and Norma Corinne (Nichols) T.; m. Susanna Anna Maria Woodworth, June 24, 1967; children: Stephanie, Meghan, Lewis. BS, U.S. Naval Acad., 1967; MS, Oreg. State U., 1974, PhD, 1978. Registered profl. engr., Oreg. (environ. branch added in 1995). Commd. ensign USN, 1967, advanced through grades to lt., 1971, line officer, 1967-69, intelligence officer Tan An, Vietnam, 1970-71; grad. asst. Oreg. State U., Corvallis, 1972-76; rsch. engr. Weyerhaeuser Co., Tacoma, 1977-81; pvt. practice Federal Way, Wash., 1982-83; assoc. prof. mech. engring. U.S. Naval Acad., Annapolis, Md., 1983—2004, dir. marine propulsion labs., 1984—90, ret.; rschr. and cons. in field. Dir. Ocean and Marine Engring. Divsn., Am. Soc. for Engring. Edn., Washington, 1989-91; mem. com. on shipboard pollution control, Nat. Rsch. Coun., Washington, 1994-96; chmn. environ. panel Soc. Naval Arch. and Marine Engrs., Jersey City, 1993-2000; prin. cons. Solid Fuel Rsch., Annapolis, 1984—. Author: Combustion Mechanisms in Wood Fired Boilers, 1978, Review of Biomass Gasification in Progress in Biomass Conversion, 1984, Thermodynamics: A Computer-Based Approach, 2001, 2003; contbr. articles to profl. jours. Mem. Combustion Inst., George C. Marshall Inst. Achievements include patent for method for combustion of wood fuels in spreader-stoker boilers; discovery of the effects of underfire air on emissions; aided in development of pulverized wood burner and fixed-bed wood gasifier. Home: 25609 Dog Creek Rd John Day OR 97845

TUTTLE, MARV, finance association executive; b. 1955; BA in journalism, Drake U. CEO Fin. Planning Assn., 2004—, assoc. exec. dir., pub., editor Jour. Fin. Planning. Mem.: Am. Soc. Assn. Exec. (ASAE) (cert. assn. exec. (CAE) 1996, Most Improved Mag./Jour. for Jour. Fin. Planning), Colo. Soc. Assn. Exec. (pres.). Office: 1615 L St NW Ste 650 Washington DC 20036-5606 Office Phone: 800-322-4237. Office Fax: 404-845-3660.

TUTTLE, ROGER LEWIS, lawyer, educator; b. Wyandotte County, Kans., Nov. 9, 1930; s. Emmett Joseph and Freda Alberta (Lewis) T.; m. Beverly Jean Campbell, Aug. 3, 1957; children— Pamela Anne, Deborah Jean Tuttle Edwards. B.A., U. Kans., 1952; J.D., U. Miss., 1958. Bar: Miss. 1958, U.S. Dist. Ct. (so. dist.) Miss. 1958, U.S. Dist. Ct. (no. dist.) Miss. 1959, U.S. Dist. Ct. (ea. dist.) La. 1963, U.S. Ct. Appeals (4th cir.) 1964, Va. 1965, U.S. Dist. Ct. (ea. dist.) Va. 1971, U.S. Supreme Ct. 1971, U.S. Dist. Ct. (we. dist.) Va. 1976, Okla. 1982, U.S. Dist. Ct. (no. dist.) Okla. 1983, U.S. Ct. Appeals (10th cir.) 1983. Assoc. Neill, Clark & Townsend, Indianola, Miss., 1958-61, Heidelberg, Woodliff & Franks, Jackson, Miss., 1961-62; area atty. Exxon, New Orleans and Charlotte, N.C., 1962-65; asst. counsel Lawyers Title Ins. Corp., Richmond, Va., 1965-71; gen. atty. A.H. Robins Co., Richmond, 1971-76; asst. gen. counsel Dan River Inc., 1976-82; prof. law Oral Roberts U., Tulsa, 1982-85, dean, 1985-87, clin. prof. med. jurisprudence, 1987-88; chief legal officer, corp. sec. Oral Roberts Ministries, 1986-88; of counsel Freed & Haskins, Richmond, 1988-89, Conner & Edwards, Richmond, 1989, Davis & Tuttle, 1989-90, pvt. practice, 1990—. Mem. Spl. Adv. Counsel to Mayor, Richmond, 1971-76; mem. Richmond Air Pollution Control Bd., 1972-73; bd. dirs. Richmond Met. Authority, 1973-76. Served to lt. col. M.I., USAR, 1952-73. Decorated Mil. Cross (Belgium), Bronze Star, Army Commendation Medal with oak leaf cluster; named Prof. of Yr., Oral Roberts U., 1984-85. Mem. Va. Bar Assn., Miss. Bar Assn., Okla. Bar Assn. (civil procedure com., mem. continuing legal edn. com.), Assn. Trial Lawyers Am., Am. Coll. Legal Medicine, Assn. Former Intelligence Officers, Army CIC Vets. Assn., Phi Alpha Delta, Pi Kappa Alpha. Republican. Presbyn. Clubs: Masons, Scottish Rite, Shriners. Contbr. articles to legal publs. Office: 13624 Northwich Dr Midlothian VA 23112-4932 Office Phone: 804-744-5654.

TUTTLE, WILLIAM G(ILBERT) T(OWNSEND), JR., research executive, retired military officer; b. Portsmouth, Va., Nov. 26, 1935; s. William Gilbert and Edith Inez (Ritter) Tuttle; m. Helen Lynn Warren, Dec. 27, 1959; children: Lynn, Robert, Jonathan. BS, U.S. Mil. Acad., 1958; MBA, Harvard U., 1963. Commd. 2d lt. U.S. Army, 1958, advanced through grades to gen., 1989; dir. combat service support Office Combat Devels., Hdqrs. Tng. and Doctrine Command, Ft. Monroe, Va., 1976-77; comdr. 3d Armored Divsn. Support Command Frankfurt, Germany, 1977-79; comdr. Mil. Traffic Mgmt. Command Eastern Area Bayonne, NJ, 1979-81; dir. force mgmt. Hdqrs. Dept. Army, Washington, 1981-82; chief policy and programs br. Supreme Hdqrs. Allied Powers Europe, 1982-84; comdr. U.S. Army Operational Test and Evaluation Agy., 1984-86; dep. commdg. gen. Logistics, Tng. and Doctrine Command and commdg. gen. U.S. Army Logistics Ctr., Ft. Lee, Va., 1986-89; commdg. gen. U.S. Army Material Command, Alexandria, Va., 1989-92; pres., CEO Logistics Mgmt. Inst., McLean, Va., 1993—2001; ret., 2001; cons., author, trustee Logistics Mgmt. Inst., McLean, 2002—. U.S. Army Kermit Roosevelt lectr., 1991; bd. visitors Def. Acquisition U., 2003—; chmn. Procurement Round Table, 2003; exec. fellow Inst. for Def. and Bus. U. NC Kenan-Flagler Sch. Bus., 2004; cons. Def. Sci. Bd., 1994—98, 2004; chmn. Def. Sci. Bd. Task Force on Mobility; cons. NRC, 2000—01; prof. logistics Coll. Bus. and Pub. Policy U. Alaska, 2004—; bd. dirs. Xybernaut Corp. Decorated Def. D.S.M., D.S.M. Navy and Air Force, D.S.M. (3) U.S. Army. Mem.: U.S. Army Transp. Corps Regtl. Assn. (pres. 2003—), Assn. U.S. Army (Pres.'s award 1992), Nat. Def. Indsl. Assn. (Logistics Emeritus award 1998), Nat. Def. Transp. Assn. Lutheran. Personal E-mail: btuttle3@cox.net.

TUTTLE, WILLIAM MCCULLOUGH, JR., history professor; b. Detroit, Oct. 7, 1937; s. William McCullough and Geneva (Duvall) T.; m. Linda Lee Stumpp, Dec. 12, 1959 (div.); children: William McCullough III, Catharine D., Andrew S.; m. Kathryn Nemeth, May 6, 1995. BA, Denison U., 1959; MA, U. Wis., 1964, PhD, 1967. Faculty mem. U. Kans., Lawrence, 1967—, prof. history, 1975-2000, intra-univ. prof., 1982-83; sr. fellow in So. and Negro history Johns Hopkins U., 1969-70; Charles Warren fellow Harvard U., Cambridge, Mass., 1972-73; vis. prof. U. So. Columbia, 1980; assoc. fellow Stanford Humanities Ctr., 1983-84; rsch. assoc. U. Calif., Berkeley, 1986-88; prof. Am. Studies U. Kans., Lawrence, 2000—. Vis. scholar Radcliffe Coll., 1993-94. Author: Race Riot: Chicago in the Red Summer of 1919, 1970, 2d edit., 1996, W.E.B. Du Bois, 1973, (with David M. Katzman) Plain Folk, 1982, (with others) A People and A Nation, 1982, 6th edit., 2001, "Daddy's Gone to War": The Second World War in the Lives of America's Children, 1993; contbr. chpts. to books, numerous articles to profl. jours. Dem. precinct committeeman, Lawrence, 1980-90. Lt. USAF, 1959-62. Recipient Merit award Am. Assn. for State and Local History, 1972, Balfour S. Jeffrey award Humanities and Social Scis., 2004; Younger Humanist fellow NEH, 1972-73, Guggenheim fellow, 1975-76, NEH fellow, 1983-84, rsch. fellow Hall Ctr., 1990, Kemper fellow for tchg. excellence, 1998; grantee Evans, 1975-76, Beveridge, 1982, NEH, 1986-89. Mem. Soc. Am. Historians (elected), Am. Hist. Assn., Orgn. Am. Historians, Am. Studies Assn., Assn. for Study of African Am. Life and History, Lawrence Trout Club, Golden Key (hon.), Omicron Delta Kappa, Phi Beta Delta, Phi Gamma Delta. Home: 713 Louisiana St Lawrence KS 66044-2339 Office: U Kans Dept Am Studies Lawrence KS 66045-0001 Office Phone: 785-864-9476. E-mail: tuttle@ku.edu.

TUTU, DESMOND MPILO, archbishop emeritus; b. Klerksdorp, Republic of South Africa, Oct. 7, 1931; m. Leah Nomalizo Shenxane; children: Trevor Thamsanqa, Theresa Thandeka, Naomi Nontombi, Mpho Andrea. Diploma in

teaching, Pretoria (Republic of South Africa) Bantu Normal Coll., 1953; BA, U. South Africa, 1954; licentiate in theology, St. Peter's Theol. Coll., Republic of South Africa, 1960; postgrad, King's Coll., U. London; DD (hon.), Gen. Theol. Sem., N.Y., 1978, Aberdeen U., Scotland, 1984, Trinity Luth. Sem., 1985, Trinity Coll., Hartford, Conn., 1986, Chgo. Theol. Sem., 1986, U. West Indies, Trinidad and Tobago, 1986, Oberlin Coll., 1986, U. of the South, 1988, Emory U., 1988, Wesleyan U., 1990, Lincoln U., Pa., 1990, Oxford U., Eng., 1990; DCL (hon.), Kent (Eng.) U., 1978; LLD (hon.), Harvard U., 1979, Claremont Grad. Sch., 1984, Temple U., 1985, 86, Mt. Allison U., Sackville, N.B., Can., 1988, Northeastern U., 1988; ThD (hon.), Ruhr U., 1981; STD (hon.), Columbia U., 1982, Dickinson Coll., 1984; LHD (hon.), St. Paul's Coll., 1984, Howard U., 1984, Morehouse Coll., 1986, Cen. U., 1986, CUNY, 1986; HHD (hon.), Wilberforce U., 1985; PhD (hon.), U. Rio, Rio de Janiero, 1986; hon. doctorate, U. Strasbourg, France, 1988, Wesleyan U., 1990, Lincoln U., 1990, U. Mo., 1990, U. New Rochelle, 1990,, 1990, Brown U., 1990, Seton Hall U., 1990, U. P.R., 1990, others. Ordained priest Anglican Ch., 1961. Schoolmaster, 1954-57; parish priest, 1960—; lectr. Fed. Theol. Sem., 1967-69, UBLS Roma, Lesotho, 1970-72; assoc. dir. theol. edn. fund World Coun. Chs., Bromley, England, 1972-75; dean of Johannesburg South Africa, 1975-76; bishop of Lesotho, 1976-78; bishop of Johannesburg, 1985-86; archbishop of Cape Town, 1986-96; archbishop emeritus City of Capetown, 1996—; chairperson Truth and Reconciliation Commn., 1996—; vis. prof. The Episcopal Div. Sch., Cambridge, 2002. Sec.-gen. South African Council Chs., 1978-85; vis. prof. Anglican Studies, N.Y. Gen. Theol. Sem., 1984; pres. All Africa Conf. of Chs., 1987-97; chancellor U. Western Cape, Republic of South Africa, 1988—. Author: (collections of sermons and addresses) Crying in the Wilderness, 1982, Hope and Suffering, 1983, The Rainbow People of God: The Making of a Peaceful Revolution, 1994, An African Prayer Book, 1995, No Future Without Forgiveness, 1999. Vice chmn. Internat. Alert, 1986; mem. disbursements adv. com. Fund for Edn. in South Africa, N.Y.C., 1988; mem. com. of honor for meml. to Imre Nagy and companions Hungarian Human Rights League, 1988; mem. hon. com. Spl. Fund for Health in Africa, 1990. Recipient Prix d'Athene Onassis Found., 1980, Family of Man gold medallion, 1983, Martin Luther King Jr. Humanitarian award Ann. Black Am. Hero and Heroines Day, 1984; Nobel prize for peace, 1984, Martin Luther King Jr. Peace award, 1986, Internat. Integrity award John-Roger Found., 1986, Pres. award Glassboro State Coll., 1986, World Pub. Forum award City of San Rafael, Calif., 1986, Order of So. Cross Govt. of Brazil, 1987, Order of Merit Govt. of Brazil, 1987, Pacem in Terris award Quad Cities, 1987, Albert Schweitzer Humanitarian award Emmanuel Coll., 1988, Freedom of the City Florence, Italy, 1985, Methyr Tydfil, U.K., 1986, Durham, Eng., 1987, Hull, Eng., 1988, Disting. Peace Leadership award Nuclear Age Peace Found., 1990, Pres.'s medal Claremont Grad. Sch., U.S., 1990, Freedom of the Borough of Lewisham, U.K., 1990, Freedom of the City of Kinshasa, 1990, Grand Officier de la Légion d'Honneur, Pres. Chirac of France, 1998, Lifetime Achievement award CARE USA, 1999, Vision 2000 award Cath. Charities USA, 1999, award Ho. of Commons, Can., 1999, The Wilberforce medallion Lord Mayor and City Coun. Kingston upon Hull, 1999, Pres. meda. Georgetown U., Washington, 2001, Humanitarian award N.Y.C. Office Comptr., 2002; co-recipient Third World prize, 1989; King's Coll. fellow, 1978. Mem. NAACP (life), World Council Global Co-operation. Anglican. Office: The Desmond Tutu Peace Ctr PO Box 1092 Milnerton 7435 Cape Town South Africa

TUTWILER, MARGARET DEBARDELEBEN, stock exchange executive, former federal agency administrator; b. Birmingham, Ala., Dec. 28, 1950; d. Temple Wilson and Margaret (DeBardeleben) Tutwiler, II. Student, Finch Coll., 1969-71; BA, U. Ala., 1973. Sec. Ala. Rep. Party, Birmingham, 1974; scheduler Pres. Ford Com., Birmingham, 1975-78; exec. dir. Pres. Ford Com. Ala., Birmingham, 1976; pub. rels. rep. Nat. Assn. Mfrs. for Ala. and Miss., Birmingham and Washington, 1977-78; dir. scheduling George Bush for Pres. Com., Houston and Washington, 1978-80; spl. asst. to Pres. Reagan and exec. to Chief of Staff The White House, Washington, 1981-85; asst. sec., pub. affairs & public liaison U.S. Dept. Treasury, 1985-88; sr. advisor transition team U.S. Dept. State, Washington, 1988-89, asst. sec. pub. affairs, spokesman, 1989-92, U.S. amb. to Morocco Rabat, 2001—03, under sec., pub. diplomacy & pub. affairs Washington, 2003—04; ptnr. Fitzwater & Tutwiler, Inc., Washington, 1993—2001; exec. v.p., comm. & govt. relations NY Stock Exchange Inc., NYC, 2004—. Dep. chmn. Bush-Quayle '88, Washington, 1988. Recipient Woman of Yr. award Wake Forest U., 1986, Alexander Hamilton award, 1988, Am. Ctr. for Internat. Leadership's Marshall award for outstanding leadership Birmingham Sothern's GALA 10, 1991. Republican. Episcopalian. Office: NY Stock Exchange 11 Wall St New York NY 10005

TUUL, JOHANNES, physics educator, researcher; b. Tarvastu, Viljandi, Estonia, May 23, 1922; came to U.S., 1956, naturalized, 1962; s. Johan and Emilie (Tulf) T.; m. Marjatta Murtoniemi, July 14, 1957 (div. Aug. 1971); children: Melinda, Melissa; m. Sonia Esmeralda Manosalva, Sept. 15, 1976; 1 child, Johannes. Elem. Tchg. Credential, Tartu Normal Sch., Estonia, 1941; diploma in Elec. Engring., Stockholm Tech. Inst., 1947; BS, U. Stockholm, 1955, MA, 1956; ScM, Brown U., 1957, PhD, 1960. Tchr. Valuste Elem. Sch., 1941-43; escaped to Finland December, 1943; after Finland surrendered to Russia escaped to Sweden, 1944; instr. Stockholm Tech. Inst., 1947-49; lab. engr. Electrical Prospecting Co., Stockholm, 1949-53; elec. engr. LM Ericsson Telephone Co., Stockholm, 1954-55; rsch. physicist Am. Cyanamid Co., Stamford, Conn., 1960-62; sr. rsch. physicist Bell & Howell Rsch. Ctr., Pasadena, Calif., 1962-65; from asst. to assoc. prof. Calif. State Poly. U., Pomona, 1965-68, chmn. physics and earth scis. dept., 1971-75, prof. physics, 1975-91; prof. emeritus, 1992—. Vis. prof. Pahlavi U., Shiraz, Iran, 1968-70; cons. Bell & Howell Rsch. Ctr., Pasadena, Calif., 1965, Teledyne Co., Pasadena, Calif., 1968; guest researcher Naval Weapons Ctr., China Lake, Calif., 1967, 72; resident dir. Calif. State U. Internat. Programs in Sweden and Denmark, 1977-78. Author: Physics Made Easy, 1974; contbr. articles to profl. jours. Pres. Group Against Smoking Pollution, Pomona Valley, Calif., 1976; foster parent Foster Parents Plan, Inc., Warwick, R.I., 1964-2003; block capt. Neighborhood Watch, West Covina, Calif., 1982-84; citizen amb. People to People Internat., 1990—; mem. Physics Edn. Del. to Peoples Rep. China, 1990; mem. Baltic Assist Delegation, 1992; mem. Industry and Sci. Initiative 1 Delegation to Cuba, 2000; mem. Mission in Understanding to Iceland and Greenland, 2002; mem. Global Peace Initiative to Egypt, 2003. Fellow Brown U., 1957-58; rsch. grantee U. Namur (Belgium), 1978, Ctr. Nat. Recherche Scientifique, France, 1979; recipient Humanitarian Fellowship award Save the Children Fedn., 1968, spl. award Travelers' Century Club, 1998. Mem. AAAS (life), N.Y. Acad. Scis., Am. Phys. Soc. Republican. Roman Catholic. Achievements include research in energy conservation and new energy technologies. E-mail: tuuljohannes@hotmail.com.

TUZCU, ERTUGRUL, retail executive; b. Skopje, Sirbia, Yugoslavia, Mar. 8, 1953; came to U.S., 1976; s. Enver and Nigar Tuzcu; m. Karen Agnes Owen, May 17, 1986. BSME, Bosphorous U., Istanbul, Turkey, 1976; MS in Indls. Engring., U. Minn., 1978. Sr. analyst indsl. engring. Dayton Hudson Corp. (now Target Corp.), Mpls., 1978-81, mgr. indsl. engring, selling cost, 1981-83, mgr. indsl. engring., selling cost, accounts payable, 1983-84, mgr. mdse. fin. services, 1984-85, mgr. inventory control, payroll, 1985-87, mgr. expense control, 1987, sr. v.p., merchandise planning, 1995—96, exec. v.p., store ops., dept. store divsn., 1996; exec. v.p., store ops., Marshall Field's Target Corp. Adj. faculty U. Minn., Mpls, 1978-82. Recipient Energy Saver's Award of Excellence Minn. Energy Agy. and Natural Gas Council, 1980. Mem. Am. Inst. of Indsl. Engrs., Minn. Soc. Indsl. Engrs. (Young Engr. of Yr. 1980, 81), Am. Mgmt. Assn., Minn. Turkish Am. Assn. (auditor 1987). Office: Marshall Fields 700 On The Mall Minneapolis MN 55478-0001

TUZEE, MICHELLE, newscaster; m. Craig Tuzee; 2 children. BA in journalism, U. So. Calif. Prodr., anchor, reporter KJCT-TV, Grand Junction, Colo.; reporter WBAY-TV, Wis.; anchor, reporter WFTX-TV, Fort Myers, Fla.; co-anchor, Today in Florida, 7 News at Noon WSVN, Miami; co-anchor, Eyewitness News at 4, 6 and 11pm KABC 7, Los Angeles, 1997—. Office: ABC7 Broadcast Ctr 500 Circle Seven Dr Glendale CA 91201

TUZEL, TULIN, food service executive; b. Istanbul, Turkey, Jan. 26, 1950; came to the U.S., 1967; m. Turhan Tuzel; children: Erin, Sasha, Armand. BSChemE, CCNY; MSChemE, N.Y. Poly. Inst.; MBA, U. Conn. Rsch. engr. Olin Corp., La.; rschr. Nestle, N.J.; v.p. R&D Sara Lee Corp., Chgo.; sr. v.p. R&D, chief tech. officer Burger King Corp., Miami, Fla. Avocation: tennis. Office: Burger King Corp PO Box 020783 17777 Old Cutler Rd Miami FL 33157-6347

TUZIL, TERESA JORDAN, clinical social worker, psychotherapist; b. N.Y.C., May 13, 1948; d. Lester Francis and Kathleen Geraldine (Brady) Jordan; m. Joseph Stephen Tuzil, Jan. 15, 1972; children: Joseph IV, Brian Joseph; BA, St. John's U., 1970; MSW, Hunter Coll., 1973. Cert. in gerontology; credentialed alcoholism counselor, alcoholism and substance abuse counselor; cert. sch. social work specialist, N.Y., Diplomate in Clin. Social Work N.Y., Social worker Salvation Army Foster Care and Adoption Services, N.Y.C., 1971-72; sr. caseworker Jewish Assn. for Services to the Aged, N.Y.C., 1973-78; program cons. Cmty. Coun. of Greater N.Y., N.Y.C., 1978-79; pvt. practice individual and family psychotherapy, Seaford, N.Y., 1976-; caseworker Nassau County Dept. Social Services Children's Protective Service, 1983-90, Pennsula Counseling Ctr. Outpatient Alcoholism Treatment Ctr., 1996-99; sch. social work specialist Deer Park (N.Y.) Unified Sch. Dist.; adj. clin. instr. Hunter Grad. Sch. Social Work, 1975-78; field instr. Grad. Sch. Social Work, Rutgers U., 1975-77; program cons. Assn. for Services to Aged, Bklyn., 1981-90. Mem. Nat. Assn. Social Workers, Acad. Cert. Social Workers, Nat. Assn. Addiction Counselors, Mem. NY State Soc. Clin. Social Workers. Editor: Jour. of Gerontological Social Work, 1977-; contbr. articles to profl. publs. in field. Home and Office: 3859 Tiana St Seaford NY 11783-3508 E mail: TJT3378751@aol.com.

TUZLA, KEMAL, mechanical engineer, scientist; b. Adapazari, Sakarya, Turkey, Feb. 23, 1943; came to U.S., 1974; s. Hayrettin and Muberra (Horozlu) T.; m. Asuman Fatma Cokmez. MME, Istanbul (Turkey) Tech. U., 1966, PhD in Mech. Engring., 1972. Instr. Istanbul Tech. U., 1966-72, asst. prof., 1974, assoc. prof., 1978-81; instr. Air Force Coll., Istanbul, 1973-74; rsch. asst. prof. U. Wash., Seattle, 1974-78; sr. rsch. scientist Lehigh U., Bethlehem, Pa., 1981—2002, assoc. chair, dept. chem. engring., 2003. Mem. organizing com. 2d Thermal Sci. Conf., Istanbul; 1979, 3d Conf., Trabzon, Turkey, 1981; cons. Goodyear Tire & Rubber Co., Akron, Ohio, 1984-86, Exxon Nuclear, Richland, Wash., 1985-88. Editor Proc. 2d Thermal Sci. Conf., 1979; contbr. articles in area of thermal scis. to profl. jours. Co-founder Turkish Am. Cultural Assn., Seattle, 1977. Grantee rsch. grantee, Los Alamos (N.Mex.) Nat. Lab, 1989—91, Ben Franklin Tech. Ctr., Bethlehem, 1989—2001, Gas Rsch. Inst., 1987—91, Elec. Power Rsch. Inst., 1991—94;, Goodyear Tire & Rubber Co., 1985—86. Mem. ASHRAE, AIChE, Sigma Xi. Achievements include research in heat transfer in two-phase flows, boiling, fluidized beds, electronic components and nuclear safety. Home: 96 Valley Park S Bethlehem PA 18018-1335 Office: Lehigh U Chem Engring Iacocca Hall 111 Research Dr Bethlehem PA 18015-4732

TVILDIANI, DIMITRY, cardiologist; b. Tbilisi, Georgia, June 30, 1956; s. David Tvildiani and Juliana Zubiashvili; m. Khatuna Chkheidze; children: Tamar, Gegi, Michael. MD, State Med. U., Tbilisi, 1978; PhD, State Inst. Transplantology, Moscow, 1980. Chief scientist diagnostic dept. State Inst. Cardiology, Tbilisi, 1980—89; dean AIETI Med. Sch., Tbilisi, 1989—99; gen. mgr. Dimas Radiology, N.Y.C., 1999. Achievements include patents for noninvasive index of cardiac contractility; noninvasive method of renal blood flow assesmnet. Office: Image Pro LLC 101-18 Queens Blvd.Forest Hills NY 11375 Personal E-mail: tvildianid@aol.com.

TWACHTMAN-CULLEN, DIANE, communication disorders and autism specialist; b. Hartford, Conn. d. Peter and Olga Margaret (DeSarro) DeMaio; m. Walter A. Twachtman, Jr.; children: Jennifer Leigh, Erich Todd; m. James T. Cullen. BA, MA in Speech-Lang. Pathology, U. Conn., diploma in early chilhood spl. edn., 1002, PhD, 1994. Lic. speech lang. pathologist, Conn. Pvt. practice autism cons.; exec. dir. Autism and Devel. Disabilities Consultation Ctr., Higganum, Conn., 1991—. Former instr., clin. supr. U. Conn.; adj. faculty mem. Ctrl. Conn. State U.; mem. profl. adv. bd. Boston Higashi Sch. Author: A Passion to Believe, Trevor Trevor, How to Be A Para Pro: A Comprehensive Traiing Manual for Paraprofessionals. Mem. Am. Speech-Lang.-Hearing Assn., Conn. Speech-Lang.-Hearing Assn., Autism Soc. Am. (bd. profl. advisors), Autism Soc. Ohio, Autism Soc. Conn. (past pres. 2 terms, mem. profl. adv. bd.), Asperger's Assn. New Eng., Greater Hartford Autism Soc. (founding). Address: 61 Landing Rd Higganum CT 06441-4140

TWAGILIMANA, AIMABLE, English educator, writer; b. Muyira, Butare, Rwanda, Dec. 4, 1961; arrived in U.S., 1992; s. Louis Mudugu and Belancila Nyiragakinga; m. Marie-Rose Nkundimfura, Dec. 26, 1987; children: Leandre Munyana, Raissa Umwari. BA in English, Nat. U. of Rwanda, Butare, 1984, MA in English, 1986; MA in Applied Linguistics, U. of Reading, Berkshire, Eng., 1989; PhD in English, SUNY, Buffalo, 1995. Cert. tchr. h.s. Nat. U. of Rwanda. Lectr. Nat. U. of Rwanda, Ruhengeri, 1986—92; asst. prof. SUNY, Buffalo, 1995—2000, assoc. prof. English, 2000—. Dir. of studies faculty of letters Nat. U. of Rwanda, Ruhengeri, 1991—92. Author: (novel) Manifold Annihilation, 1996, (book) Race and Gender in the Making of an African American Literary Tradition, 1997, In Their Own Voices: Rwandan Refugees Speak Out, 1997, Hutu and Tutsi (The Heritage Library of African People series), 1998, The Debris of Ham: Ethnicity, Regionalism and the 1994 Rwandan Genocide, 2003. Fellow, NEH, 1999, 2003; scholar, Fulbright Found., 1992—95, Brit. Coun., 1988—89. Mem.: MLA, Assn. of Am. Transls., Nat. Coun. of Tchrs. of English, Nat. Assn. of Lit. Critics. Roman Catholic. Home: 68 Fairchild Pl Buffalo NY 14216 Office: SUNY 1300 Elmwood Avenue Buffalo NY 14222 Personal E-mail: twagila12@hotmail.com. E-mail: twagila@bscmail.buffalostate.edu.

TWAIN, SHANIA (EILLEEN REGINA EDWARDS), country musician; b. Windsor, Ontario, Can., Aug. 28, 1965; d. Sharon and Jerry Twain(Stepfather), Clarence Edwards; m. Robert John Lange, Dec. 28, 1993; 1 child, Eja. Recs. Beginnings, 1989—90, 1999, Shania Twain, 1993, The Woman in Me, 1995 (Acad. Country Music Assn. Award for Album of Yr., 1995, ABC Radio Networks Country Music Award for Female Video Artist of Yr., 1995, Billboard Music Award for Country Album of Yr., 1996, Grammy award for Best Country Album, 1996), These Blues are Mine, 1996, Come on Over, 1997, Star Profile, 1999, Maximum Shania, 2000, Complete Limelight Sessions, 2001, Up!, 2002 (Can. Country Music Assn. Award for Album of Yr., 2003, Billboard Music Award for Country Album of Yr., 2003). Recipient Country Music TV (Europe) Rising Star award, 1993, Am. Music Award for Favorite New Country Artist, 1995, Can. Country Music Assn. Award for female vocalist of yr., 1995, Acad. of Country Music Award for Top New Female Vocalist, 1995, Best Country Album Grammy award, 1995, Blockbuster Entertainment Award for Favorite New Country Artist, 1996, Country Music TV (Europe) award for Female Artist of Yr., 1996, Juno Award for Country Female Vocalist of Yr., 1996, Juno Award for Entertainer of Yr., 1996, World Music Award for World's Best Selling Country Artist, 1996, Favorite New Artist award, Am. Music Awards, 1996, Am. Music Award for Best Female Country Artist, 1997, Juno Award for Country Female Vocalist of Yr., 1997, Juno Award for Internat. Achievement, 1997, Am. Music Award for Favorite Female Country Artist, 1998, Billboard Music Award for Female Artist of Yr., 1998, Country Music Assn. Award for Entertainer of Yr., 1999, Acad. Country Music Award for Entertainer of Yr., 1999, Am. Music Award for Favorite Female Country Artist, 1999, Am. Music Award for Favorite Female Pop/Rock Artist, 1999, Blockbuster Entertainment Award for Favorite Overall Single, 1999, Juno Award for Country Female Vocalist of Yr., 1999, Grammy Award for Best Female Country Vocal Performance (You're Still The One), 1999, Grammy Award for Best Country Song (You're Still The One), 1999, Juno Award for Best Songwriter, 2000, Juno Award for Best Country Female Artist, 2000, Grammy Award for Best Female Vocal Country Performance (Man!I Feel Like A Woman), 2000, Grammy Award for Best Country Song (Come On Over), 2000, Acad. Country Music Award for Entertainer of Yr., 2000, Billboard Music Award for Top County Artist of Yr., 2003, Billboard Music Award for Country Album Artist of Yr., 2003, Juno Fan Choice Award, 2003, Juno Award for Artist of Yr., 2003, Juno Award for Country Rec. Yr. (I'm Gonna Getcha Good), 2003, Can. Country Music Assn. Award for Video of Yr. (I'm Gonna Getcha Good), 2003, Can. Country Music Assn. Award for Female Artist of Yr., 2003. Office: Mercury Records 66 Music Sq W Nashville TN 37203-4315 Address: Shore Fire Media c/o Georgette Pascale 32 Court St Fl 16 Brooklyn NY 11201-4404*

TWARDOWICZ, STANLEY JAN, artist, photographer; b. Detroit, July 8, 1917; s. Joseph and Anna Ligenski; m. Lillian Dodson, Mar. 15, 1971. Student, Meinzinger Art Sch., Detroit, 1940-44, Skowhegan (Maine) Sch. Painting and Sculpture, summer 1946. Instr. Ohio State U., 1946-51; prof. Hofstra U., 1965-87. Exhibited paintings Mus. Modern Art, Guggenheim Mus., Whitney Mus., Art Inst. Chgo., Carnegie Internat., Pa. Acad. Fine Arts, Am. Acad. Arts and Letters, Houston Mus., Milw. Art Ctr., Peridot Gallery, N.Y.C., others; retrospective exhbns. Hecksher Mus., Huntington, N.Y., 1974, Emily Lowe Gallery, Hempstead, N.Y., 1979, 40 Yr. Retrospective of Paintings Firehouse Gallery, Garden City, N.Y.; exhibited photographs Images Gallery, N.Y.C., one man show: Odeon Gallery, Sag Harbor, N.Y., 1993, Ursala Lanning Gallery, Columbus, Ohio, 1995, Mitchell Algus Gallery, N.Y.C., 1996-2000, Phoenix Art Mus., 2001-02; represented in permanent collections Mus. Modern Art, L.A. County Mus., Newark Mus., Milw. Art Ctr., Ball State Tchrs. Coll., Harvard U., Vassar Coll., Hirshhorn Mus. and Sculpture Garden, others. Guggenheim fellow, 1956 Home: 133 Crooked Hill Rd Huntington NY 11743-3811

TWARJAN, COLLEEN ANN, dental hygienist; b. Manchester, N.H., Jan. 1, 1956; d. Robert Francis and Josephine Margaret (O'Brien) H.; m. John Paul Twarjan Jr., Oct. 9, 1982; children; Jesse, Max, Sam. AA, N.H. Tech. Inst., Concord, 1977. Dental hygienst Dr. Steven Christenson, Concord, N.H., 1977-78, Dr. Joseph Maroun, Salem, N.H., 1978-83, Dr. Christos Giotopoulos, Manchester, 1978-84, Lindner Dental Assocs., Bedford, 1997—. Mem. Smyth Rd. PTO, Manchester, N.H., 1988—, treas. 1989-96, v.p., 1996, pres., 1997-99; v.p. Hillside PTO, 1999-2000, pres. 1997-98. Roman Catholic. Avocation: gardening. Office: Lindner Dental Assocs Bedford NH 03110

TWEEDY, ROBERT HUGH, equipment company executive; b. Mt. Pleasant, Iowa, Mar. 24, 1928; s. Robert and Olatha (Miller) T.; B.S. in Agrl. Engring., Iowa State U., 1952; m. Genevieve Strauss, Aug. 15, 1969; children— Bruce, Mark; 1 stepdau., Mary Ellen Francis. Sr. engr. John Deere Waterloo Tractor Works, Waterloo, Iowa, 1953-64; mktg. rep. U.S. Steel Corp., Pitts., 1964-68; mgr. product planning agrl. equipment div. Allis-Chalmers Corp., Milw., 1969-76, mgr. strategic bus. planning Agrl. Equipment Co., 1976-85; mgr. strategic bus. planning Deutz-Allis Corp., 1985-89; project mgr. AGCO Corp., Batavia, Ill., 1989-94; retired, 1994; chmn. agrl. research com. Farm and Indsl. Equipment Inst., Chgo., 1974-76, mem. safety policy adv. com., 1972-89; mem. farm conf. Nat. Safety Council, Chgo., 1973-89; mem. industry sector adv. com. No. 16, U.S. Dept. Commerce, 1982-85; bd. dirs. C.V. Riley Meml. Found. Recipient citation in engring. Iowa State U., 1983. Fellow Am. Soc. Agrl. Engrs. (v.p. 1974-78, pres. 1981-82, gen. chmn. hdqrs. bldg. project 1968-70; chmn. Found. Trustees 1983-88, Wis. Engr. of Year award 1980, McCormick-Case Gold medal 1989), Masons. Patentee in field. Home: 3301 Alt 19 Lot 172 Dunedin FL 34698-1524

TWERSKI, ABRAHAM JOSHUA, psychiatrist; b. 1930; MD, Marquette U., 1959. Bd. cert. psychiatry; ordained rabbi. Psychiat. resident U. Pitts. Western Psychiat. Inst.; clin. dir. dept. psychiatry St. Francis Hosp., Pitts.; assoc. prof. psychiatry U. Pitts. Sch. Medicine; founder, med. dir. emeritus Gateway Rehab. Ctr., Aliquippa, Pa. Author 32 books. Office: Gateway Rehab Ctr 100 Moffett Run Rd Aliquippa PA 15001-9152

TWICHELL, CHASE, poet; b. New Haven, Conn., Aug. 20, 1950; d. Charles P. and Ann (Chase) T. BA, Trinity Coll., Hartford, 1973; MFA, U. Iowa, 1976. Editor Pennyroyal Pr., W. Hatfield, Mass., 1976-84; assoc. prof. English U. Ala., 1984-88; mem. MFA Program in Creative Writing, Warren Wilson Coll., 1999—; editor Ausable Press, 1999—. Asst. prof. Hampshire Coll., 1983-84; co-editor Alabama Poetry Series, 1984-88; lectr. Princeton U., 1990-98; faculty MFA program in creative writing Goddard Coll., 1997-99. Author: (poetry) Northern Spy, 1981, The Odds, 1986, Perdido, 1991, The Ghost of Eden, 1995; editor: The Practice of Poetry, 1992, The Snow Watcher, 1998. Recipient Acad. award in lit. Am. Acad. Arts and Letters, 1994; Nat. Endowment for Arts fellow, 1987, 93, Guggenheim fellow, 1990.

TWIFORD, JIM, former state legislator; b. Wheaton, Wy., Nov. 17, 1942; m. Jenne Lee Twiford. Pres. senate Wy. Ho. of Reps., 1999—2000; dir. of transp. and physical plant Converse County School District #1, Douglas, Wyo., 2001. Roman Catholic. Office: 615 Hamilton Street Douglas WY 82633 Fax: 307-358-3515. E-mail: jim@twiford.org.

TWIGG, NANCY L. nursing association administrator; Exec. dir. State of N.Mex. Bd. Nursing, Albuquerque. Office: State NMex Bd Nursing 4206 Louisiana Blvd NE Ste A Albuquerque NM 87109-1841

TWIGGS, DENNIS GLENN, psychologist, writer; b. Marion, N.C., Feb. 5, 1946; s. James Glenn and Velra Ledford Twiggs; m. Tamara Jean Hatley, July 13, 1969; 1 child, Jason Scott. BS, Appalachian State U., 1965—69, Masters, 1972—73; PhD, Tulane U., 1973—77. Lic. psychologist NC, 1979, Tex., 1978. Counselor US Army Green Beret, Fort Bragg, NC, 1972; therapist Mt. Vernon Clinic, Wilmington, NC, 1972; tchg. asst. Tulane U., New Orleans, 1974—77; staff psychologist Mexia State Sch., Mexia, Tex., 1978; dir. adjunctive therapy San Antonio State Sch., 1978; lic. psychologist pvt. practice, Winston Salem, NC, 1979—. Cons. Cardiac Rehab., NC, 1980—85; bd. psychologists Vocat. Rehab., NC, 1980—2000; adj. faculty High Pt. U., High Point, NC, 1983—90. Author: (book) Psychological and Spiritual Evolution, 1995, Integrational Psychology, 1996, Psyche, Soul, and Spirit, 1998. Co-founder Soc. Reform Mental Health, 2002, bd., 2002, Assn. Mentally Handicapped, Winston Salem, 1981, pres., 1982; bd. Piedmont Handicapped Assn., Winston Salem, 1983. 1st lt. Army Green Beret USAR, 1969—72, various. Recipient Nat. Hon. Rsch. Soc., Sigma Xi, 1978, Disting. Svc. Award, NC Rehab. Assn., 1982; grantee Grant for Delayed Stress, Veterans Admin., 1982. Achievements include discovery of Integrational Psychology; In media: Science, 1979, Age and Environ. Interaction in Recovery of loss of Brain Function; Journ. Am. Phys. Assn., 1981, Use of biofeedback in tng. Mentally Handicapped; In press: Sci. Found. Neurotic and Psychotic Reactions. Avocations: book reviewer lib. journ and others, classical guitar, reading, study of physics and cosmology, hiking. Home: 3664 Heathrow Dr Winston Salem NC 27127 Office: Pvt Practice PO Box 25881 Winston Salem NC 27114 E-mail: twiggsmanny@aol.com.

TWIGG-SMITH, THURSTON, newspaper publisher; b. Honolulu, Aug. 17, 1921; s. William and Margaret Carter (Thurston) Twigg-S.; m. Bessie Bell, June 9, 1942 (div. Feb. 1983); children: Elizabeth, Thurston, William, Margaret, Evelyn; m. Laila Roster, Feb. 22, 1983 (div. Dec. 1994); m. Sharon Smith, Feb. 28, 1996. B.Engring., Yale U., 1942. With Honolulu Advertiser, 1946-2000, mng. editor, 1954-60, asst. bus. mgr., 1960-61, pub., 1961-86; pres., dir., chief exec. officer Honolulu Advertiser, Inc., 1962-93, chmn., 1993-2000. Chmn., dir., CEO Persis Corp., 1962-2002, chmn. Twigg-Smith Group LLC, 2002—. Trustee Honolulu Acad. Arts, The Contemporary Mus., Hawaii, The Skowhegan Sch., Maine, Yale Art Gallery, New Haven. Maj. AUS, 1942-46. Mem. Waialae Country Club, Pacific Club, Oahu Country Club, Outrigger Canoe Club. Personal E-mail: ttwiggsmith@aol.com.

TWILLEY, JOSHUA MARION, lawyer; b. Dover, Del., Mar. 23, 1928; s. Joshua Marion and Alice Hunn (Dunn) T.; m. Rebecca Jane Buchanan, Dec. 27, 1952; children: Stephanie, Jeffrey, Linda, Edgar, Joshua; m. Rosemary Miller, Dec. 1, 1972. BA cum laude, Harvard U., 1950, JD, 1953. Bar: Del. 1953, U.S. Dist. Ct. Del. 1960, U.S. Supreme Ct. 1976. Pvt. practice, Dover, 1955-72; sr. ptnr. Twilley, Jones & Feliceangeli, Dover, 1972-88, Twilley, Street & Braverman, Dover, 1988-95, Twilley & Street, Dover, 1995—. Pres. Del. Indsl. Enterprises, Inc.; chmn. Incorporating Svcs. Ltd., Del. Incorporating Svcs. Ltd.; bd. dirs. 1st Nat. Bank Wyo.; sec. Sunshine Builders, Inc. mem. Del. Pub. Svc. Commn., 1975—, vice chmn. 1995—; pres. Kent County Levy

Ct., 1970-75. Mem. exec. com. Del. Dem. Com., 1970-93; pres. Elizabeth Murphey Sch., 1957—. With U.S. Army, 1953-55. Mem ABA, Del. Bar Assn., Kent County Bar Assn. Democrat. Lutheran. Avocations: gardening, landscape architecture. Home: 124 Meadow Glen Dr Dover DE 19901-5544 Office: 426 S State St Dover DE 19901-6724 E-mail: rtwilley@erols.com.

TWILLMAN, ROBERT KEITH, psychologist; b. Boonville, Mo. s. Ralph W. and Doris L. T.; m. Nancy A. Thompson, July 23, 1983; 1 child, Talia. AB, U. Chgo., 1983; PhD, UCLA, 1989. Lic. psychologist. Staff psychologist Pitts. Cancer Inst., 1990-92; clin. asst. prof. psychiatry U. Kans., Kansas City, 1992-2001; dir. psychosocial svcs. U. Kans. Cancer Ctr., Kansas City, 1992—2001; clin. assoc. prof. psychiatry U. Kans., Kansas City, 2001—; pain mgmt. program dir. U. Kans. Hosp., 2001—. Mem. Am. Psycho-Oncology Soc. (dir. 1995-2003), Am. Alliance Cancer Pain Initiatives (dir. 1996—, pres.-elect 2002-2003, pres. 2003—), Kans. Cancer Pain Initiative (pres. 1997—). Office: U Kans Med Ctr 3901 Rainbow Blvd Kansas City KS 66160-3026 Office Fax: 913-588-8005. Business E-Mail: rtwillma@kumc.edu.

TWINAME, JOHN DEAN, minister, human services administrator; b. Mt. Kisco, N.Y., Dec. 27, 1931; s. C. G. and Constance Jean (Ulmer) Twiname; m. Carolyn Anderson, Aug. 6, 1955; children: Karen, Jeanne, Julia. AB, Cornell U., 1953; MBA, Harvard U., 1957; MDiv, Union Theol. Sem., 1983. Ordained to ministry Presbyn. Ch., 1983. Sales rep. Am. Hosp. Supply Corp., Evanston, Ill., 1957-60, dir. product research, 1961, sales mgr., 1962, asst. to div. pres., 1963, product mgr., 1964, mktg. mgr., 1965-67, mktg. v.p., 1968-69; dep. adminstr. Social and Rehab. Svc., HEW, Washington, 1969-70, adminstr., 1970-73; adminstr. Office Health Office Health, Cost of Living Coun., 1973-74; pvt. cons. Mott-McDonald Assocs., Inc., Washington, 1974-76, pres., 1976-78; exec. v.p. Am. Health Found., N.Y.C., 1978-81; co-pres. HealthCare Chaplaincy, Inc., N.Y.C., 1983-93, co-chair exec. com., 1993-94, life trustee, 1995—, exec. v.p., 1999—2000. Cons. exec. Coll. Chaplains, 1997; acting sr. min. Green's Farms Ch., Westport, Conn., 2001—03, pastoral assoc., 2003—. Treas. U.S. com. Internat. Coun. Social Welfare, 1977—80; mem. pres. coun. United Hosp. Fund, 1991—99; voting mem. Empire Blue Cross/Blue Shield, 1994; chmn. bd. dirs. Bauman Bible Telecasts, Inc., 1976—80; sec. bd. dirs. U.S. Coun. Internat. Yr. of Disabled Persons, 1979—81; founding bd. dirs. Am. Paralysis Assn. (formerly Paralysis Cure Rsch.), 1976—83; bd. dirs. Epilepsy Found. Am., 1978—85; chmn. bd. dirs. Chgo. Bus.-Indsl. Project, 1967—68, People to People Com. for Handicapped, 1976—78; bd. dirs. N.Y. Regional Transplant Program, 1988—92, Beck Mack & Oliver Ptnrs. Fund, 2000—. 1st lt. AUS, 1953—55. Recipient Disting. Svc. award, Coll. Chaplains, 1992, Wholeness of Life award, The Health Care Chaplaincy, Inc., 2003, Disting. Alumnus award, Union Theol. Sem., 2004; Baker scholar, Bus. Sch. Harvard U. Home: 60 East End Ave New York NY 10028 Office: HealthCare Chaplaincy Inc 315 E 62d St New York NY 10021-7767 Office Phone: 203-237-2728.

TWINING, LYNNE DIANNE, clinical psychologist and psychoanalyst, professional society administrator, educator, writer; b. Midland, Mich., Aug. 14, 1951; d. James and Dorothy Twining; m. Alan Howard Mass; 1 child, Allegra Liliane Twining-Mass. BA in Psychology, Oakland U., 1974; MSW, Wayne State U., 1977; MA in Psychology, Yeshiva U., 1993, D in Psychology, 1995. Cert. Bklyn. Inst. Psychotherapy and Psychoanalysis. Social work supr. non-profit orgn., Detroit, 1977-83; co-founder, co-dir. Women Psychotherapists Bklyn., 1986-95, dir., 1995—; co-dir. Affiliated Psychotherapists of Greater N.Y.C. and Phila., 1996—; pvt. practice Bklyn., N.Y., 1987—; psychotherapy rschr. Beth Israel Med. Ctr., N.Y.C., 1992-94; fac. Bklyn. Inst. Psychotherapy and Psychoanalysis, 2003—. Author: (with other) Metro Detroit Guide, 1975; contbg. editor: Detroit Guide, 1983; asst. prodr. docudrama Home; columnist Bklyn. Woman; contbr. articles to profl. jours. Bd. dirs. Progressive Artists and Educators Coalition, Detroit, 1977-79. Fellow Am. Orthopsychiat. Assn.; ACLU (sec. exec. bd. Mich. chpt. 1982-83), APA, Am. Mental Health Alliance (charter), Internat. Fedn. Psychoanalytical Edn., N.Y. State Psychol. Assn., N.Y. Acad. Scis., Soc. for Psychotherapy Rsch., Nat. Trust for Hist. Preservation, Tng. Inst. Nat. Assn. Advancement Psychoanalysis (affiliate), Women Psychotherapists Bklyn. (founding mem.), Amnesty Internat. (freedom writer), Bklyn. Inst. Psychotherapy and Psychoanalysis Soc. (bd. dirs. 2003-), Families With Children From China. Avocations: jazz, travel, piano, reading, contemporary art. Office: 55 Eastern Pky Ste 3H Brooklyn NY 11238-5913 also: 5 E 22nd St New York NY 10010

TWISDALE, HAROLD WINFRED, dentist; b. Roanoke Rapids, N.C., Apr. 28, 1933; s. James Robert and Elma (Smith) T.; m. Barbara Ann Edmonds, Aug. 2, 1958 (div. Apr. 1974); children: Harold Winfred, Leigh Ann.; m. Frances Jean Winstead, July 1983. BS in Dentistry, U. N.C., 1955, D.D.S., 1958. Individual practice dentistry, Charlotte, N.C., 1961—; head, dept. dental prosthetics Meml. Hosp., 1964-66; lectr. dental subjects.; pres., gen. mgr. WCTU-TV, Charlotte Telecasters, Inc., 1967-69, WATU-TV, Augusta, Ga., Augusta Telecasters, Inc., 1968-69, Television Presentations, Inc., Charlotte, 1967-69; partner Twisdale and Steel Assos., Charlotte, 1965-70; propr. Twisdale Enterprises, Charlotte, 1965-70. Pres. Memphis Telecasters, Inc., 1966-76, Va. Telecasters, Inc., Richmond, 1966—, Durham-Raleigh Telecasters, Inc., Durham, N.C., 1966-70, Gentil Elite, Inc., 1979— Transp. chmn. Miss N.C. Pageant, 1965; v.p. N.C. Jaycees, 1963-64; Trustee Boys Home, Lake Waccomaw, N.C., 1966-67. Served to capt. USAF, 1958-60. Recipient various awards Charlotte Jaycees, 1962-66. Fellow Acad. Dentistry Internat.; mem. ADA, N.C. Dental Found., N.C. Dental Soc., Charlotte Dental Soc. (chmn. various coms. 1961—), Am. Analgesia Soc., Internat. Analgesic Soc. (dir. 1980-85), N.C. Dental Soc. Anesthesiology (v.p. 1983-84), Charlotte Analgesia Study Club (co-founder 1970), N.C. 2d Dist. Dental Soc., Metrolina Dental Soc. (founder 1994, pres. 1994-95), U. N.C. Dental Alumni Assn., Southeastern Analgesia Soc. (founder 1972, pres. 1972-74), Lambda Chi Alpha, Delta Sigma Delta. Republican. Methodist. Home: 2221 Streatley Ln Matthews NC 28105-6648 Office: 6623 Executive Circle #110 PO Box 25528 Charlotte NC 28229-5528 *I must give the full credit for any achievement I might have accomplished in life to my mother and father. They not only provided me the means and direction one needs to make even the slightest accomplishment in our mortal life, but most of all, they gave me love, understanding, and a sense of values. These values have never deserted me, nor have they been compromised, even in the darkest hours of depression or during the brightest times of accomplishment. They have been my steady companions.*

TWIST, PAUL FRANCIS, JR., neonatologist; b. Buffalo, Nov. 6, 1946; s. Paul Francis and Hazel Mary (Schoetz) T.; m. Angela Margaret McNerney, Aug. 7, 1970; children: Patrick, Michael, Brendan. BS in Pharmacy, St. John's U., Jamaica, N.Y., 1969; DO, U. Osteo. Medicine, Des Moines, 1973. Lic. physician Ohio, Ill., N.Y.; lic. pharmacist, Iowa. Resident in pediatrics Good Samaritan Hosp., Cin., 1973-75, fellow in neonatology, 1975-76, Loyola Med. Ctr., Maywood, Ill., 1976-77; dir. neonatology and newborn medicine Winthrop-Univ. Hosp., Mineola, N.Y., 1977—, attending physician dept. pediatrics and obstetrics, 1978—; assoc. clin. prof. sch. nursing Adelphi U., Garden City, N.Y., 1985—; asst. prof. pediatrics N.Y. Coll. Osteo. Medicine, Westbury, 1980-85, assoc. prof. pediatrics, 1985—. Attending physician Mercy Hosp., Rockville Centre, N.Y., 1978—, Nassau County Med. Ctr., East Meadow, N.Y., 1980—; cons. Glen Cove (N.Y.) Community Hosp., 1980—, St. Francis Hosp., Roslyn, N.Y., 1983—; lectr. in field. Contbr. articles to profl. jours. Bd. dirs. Little Village Sch., Garden City, 1980—; mem. internal rev. bd. St. John's U., Jamaica, 1981—; pres. St. Pius X Sch. Bd., Plainview, N.Y.; treas. Sch. of the Holy Child Fathers Club, Old Westbury, N.Y. Mem. Am. Pharm. Assn., N.Y. State Med. Soc., Nassau County Pediatric Soc. (rep. dist. II 1987-90), Am. Osteo. Assn., N.Y. State Osteo. Soc., Am. Acad. Pediatrics, Nat. Perinatal Assn. (com. on fetus and newborn 1979, chpt. 2 dist. II, N.Y.), N.Y. State Perinatal Soc., Assn. of N.Y. State Regional Perinatal Ctr., Am. Soc. for Parenteral and Enteral Nutrition. Roman Catholic. Home: 1 Equestrian Ct Huntington NY 11743-6637 Office: Winthrop-Univ Hosp 259 1st St Mineola NY 11501-3987

TWIST-RUDOLPH, DONNA JOY, neurophysiology and neuropsychology researcher; b. Cape May, N.J., Dec. 3, 1955; d. Donald and Mary Ann (Johnson) Twist; m. Daniel Jay Rudolph, Jan. 10, 1981; children: Andrew, Adam, Matthew. BS, Boston U., 1978; MA, SUNY, Stony Brook, 1984; PhD, SUNY, 1986. Licensed phys. therapist, N.Y., Conn. Postdoctoral fellow, rsch. scientist N.Y. U. Med. Ctr., Rusk Inst. Rehab. Medicine, N.Y.C., 1986-87; dir. rsch. and edn. Norwalk (Conn.) Hosp., 1987-98, dir. rsch., dir. rehab. svcs., 1994—; dir. devel. Bridgeport Hosp. Found., Yale New Haven Health, Bridgeport, Conn., 2002—. State bd. examiner N.Y. State Phys. Therapy Licensing Exam. Profl. Svcs., Albany, 1986—; adj. asst. prof. Mt. Sinai Sch. Med., N.Y.C., 1990—. Exec. prodr.: All the King's Horses, All the King's Men: How to Prevent Head Injury in Our Children (Gold award Houston Internat. Film Festival, 1992, 1997), Save Me a Dance (Silver award Charleston Internat. Film Festival, 1997). Named one of Outstanding Young Woman Am., 1981, 83; grantee Easter Seal Rsch. Found., 1985-87, Rehab. Svcs. Adminstr. Dept. Edn., 1991, U.S. Dept. Edn., Pfizer Inc.; recipient Therapeutic Techs. Ins. award, 1989, Sci. Rsch. award Sigma Xi. Mem. Am. Phys. Therapy Assn., Am. Congress Rehab. Medicine, N.Y. Acad. Scis. Home: 371 Midlock Rd Fairfield CT 06430-1857 Office: Bridgeport Hosp 267 Grant St Bridgeport CT 06611

TWITCHELL, KENT, artist; b. Lansing, Mich., Aug. 17, 1942; s. Robert E. and Wilma Doris (Berry) Twitchell; m. Susan Catherine Fessler, Dec. 27, 1975 (div. 1986); m. Pandora Seaton, Feb. 23, 1990; children: Rory, Artie. AA, East L.A. Coll., 1969; BA, Calif. State U., 1972; MFA, Otis Art Inst., 1977; DA (hon.), Biola U., 1989; DFA (hon.), Otis Coll. Art and Design, 1996. Illustrator USAF, 1960-65; display artist J. C. Penney Co., Atlanta, 1965-66; abstract artist, painter L.A., 1968-70; mural artist, 1971—. Instr. L.A. County HS Arts, L.A., 1987—90, Otis/Parsons Art Inst., L.A., 1980—83. Exterior mural, Steve McQueen monument, Union at 12th St., L.A., 1971, The Freeway Lady, Hollywood Fwy., L.A., 1974, Edward Ruscha monument, Hill St. at Olympic, 1987, L.A. Marathon mural, 405 Fwy., Inglewood, Calif., 1988, Dr. J monument, 1234 Ridge Ave., Phila., 1989, L.A. Chamber Orch., Harbor Fwy. Downtown L.A., 1991—93, Will Rogers monument, Calif. Theater, San Bernardino, Calif., 1998—99, Hillside Meml. Pk., Culver City, Calif., 2001—04, Centinela Ave., Carnegie Libr., Iowa, 2004—, one-man shows include L.A. Mcpl. Art Gallery, 1980, Loyola Marymount U., L.A., 1985, Thinking Eye Gallery, 1986, Valparaiso (Ind.) U. Art Mus., 1987, Westmont Coll. Art Gallery, Santa Barbara, 1987, Biola U. Art Gallery, La Miranda, Calif., 1987, Vincent Price Gallery-East L.A. Coll., 1990, Lizardi-Harp Gallery, Pasadena, Calif., 1991, U. Redlands Art Gallery, 1997, Koplin Gallery, L.A., 1998, AIA, 2002, exhibited in group shows at L.A. Mcpl. Art Gallery, 1977, 1981, 1994, 1996, Calif. Polytech. U., Pomona, 1978, Santa Monica Coll., 1978, L.A.C.E. Gallery, 1981, Otis/Parsons Art Inst., L.A., 1987, Mayer Schwarz Gallery, Beverly Hills, 1988, 1990, Principia Coll., Elsah, Ill., 1989, Koplin Gallery, Santa Monica, 1992, 1995, 1998, L.A. County Mus. Art, 1992, Robert Berman Gallery, Santa Monica, 1995, Art Ctr./Coll. Design, Pasadena, 1996, Riverside (Calif.) Art Mus., 1996, represented by, Koplin Del Rio Gallery, L.A. Mem. adv. bd. Artists Equity Assn., 1980—88, Mural Conservancy L.A., 1988—. Grantee, Calif. Arts Coun., 1978, Nat. Endowment Arts, 1986. Avocation: theology. Home: 9505 Main St PO Box 145 Upper Lake CA 95485-0145 Office Phone: 707-275-2726. E-mail: artkent@saber.net.

TWITCHELL, THOMAS EVANS, neurologist, educator; b. Springfield, Ohio, Sept. 4, 1923; s. Ernst Albert and Charlotte Marie (Schelling) T.; m. Patricia Ann O'Brien, Nov. 18, 1956; children: Carol, Susan, Mauyra, Evelyn. MD, U. Mich., 1946. Rsch. fellow in neurophysiology Yale U., New Haven, 1947; intern in neurology Boston City Hosp., 1947-48, rsch. fellow in neurology, 1948-49; USPHS rsch. fellow in neurophysiology Yale U., 1949-51; asst. resident in medicine New Eng. Med. Ctr., Boston, 1954, chief resident in neurology, 1954-55, neurologist, 1955-88; instr. neurology Tufts U. Sch. Medicine, Boston, 1955-56, asst. prof. neurology, 1956-62, assoc. prof. neurology, 1963-83, prof., 1983-88, prof. neurology, 1983-88, prof. emeritus, 1988—. Rsch. assoc. in psychology MIT, Cambridge, 1963-77. Served to capt. USAF, 1952-54. Mem. Am. Acad. Neurology, Am. Neurol. Assn. (sr.), Mass. Med. Soc. Avocations: music, philosophy, physics, literature. Home: 54 Longfellow Rd Wellesley MA 02481-5221

TWOMBLY, CY (EDWIN PARKER TWOMBLY JR.), artist; b. Lexington, Va., Apr. 25, 1928; Student, Boston Mus. Sch. Fine Arts, 1948-49, Washington and Lee U., 1950, Art Students League, 1951; studied with, Frank Kline and Robert Motherwell, Black Mountain Coll., 1952. Head dept. art So. Sem. and Jr. Coll., Buena Vista, Va., 1955-56. One man shows include: Milw., 1968, Nicholas Wilder Gallery, 1969, Herron Inst. Art, Indpls., 1969, Guggenheim Mus., N.Y.C., 1976, Mus. Modern Art, N.Y.C., 1976, Vancouver Art Gallery, 1982, Mus. Hans Lange, Krefeld, W.Ger., 1982, Santa Barbara Contemporary Arts Forum, 1984; retrospective exhbn. Whitney Mus. Art, N.Y.C., 1979; group exhbns. include N.Y.U., 1967, Whitney Mus. Am. Art Annual, 1967, Royal Acad. Arts, 1981, Larry Gagosian Gallery, Los Angeles, 1982, Young Hoffman Gallery, Chgo., 1982, Blum Gallery, N.Y.C., 1982; large-scale masterworks include: The Age of Alexander, 1959—60, Triumph of Galatea, 1961, Untitled (Say Goodbye Catallus, to the Shores of Asia Minor), 1994; represented in permanent collections R.I. Sch. Design, Whitney Mus. Am. Art, Mus. Modern Art, N.Y.C., Ludwig Collection, Aachen, Thomas Segal Gallery, Tavelli Gallery, Adler Gallery, also pvt. collections N.Y.C., Chgo., Washington and Europe. Va. Mus. Fine Arts fellow 1952-53. Fellow Am. Acad. Arts and Letters. Office: Cy Twombly Gallery 1511 Branard Houston TX 77006*

TWOMBLY, JEAN SAWYER, musician, educator; b. Bethlehem, Pa., Feb. 12, 1946; d. Edwin A. and Elizabeth (Stempel) Sawyer; m. Stephen Doane Twombly, Dec. 29, 1979. BS in Music Edn. magna cum laude, Susquehanna U., 1968; MMus in Early Music Performance, Longy Sch. Music, Cambridge, Mass., 1994. Artistic dir. Ensemble Soleil, N.H., 1995—. Adj. asst. prof. Colby-Sawyer Coll., New London, N.H., 1986—; pvt. music tchr., New London, 1983—. Grantee N.H. Humanities Coun., 1997-99, N.H. State Coun. on Arts, 1998, 99. Mem. Boston Musician's Assn., Early Music Am., Viola da Gamba Soc. New Eng. (bd. dirs. 1999—). Avocations: stained glass, poetry, skiing, sailing. Office: Ensemble Soleil PO Box 933 New London NH 03257-0933

TWOMBLY, STEPHEN DOANE, magazine publisher; b. Summit, N.J., July 26, 1953; s. Doane and Betty (Bowers) T.; m. Jean Sawyer. BA summa cum laude, Drew U., 1976. Dist. mgr. McGraw-Hill Publs. Co., N.Y.C., 1978-83; dir. advt. IDG Communications, Peterborough, N.H., 1983-84, pub. RUN, 1984-87, pub. AmigaWorld, 1985—; group pub. Consumer/Home Mag., Special Products, 1987-88; v.p. IDG Communications/Peterborough, 1988-89, exec. v.p., 1989—90; pub. dir. PC Resource, 1988; exec. v.p., pub. dir. PCResource IDG Communications/Peterborough, 1989—90, Cahners Pubs. Co., Newton, Mass., 1990—97; nat. sales mgr. Datanation, 1990—92, assoc. pub., 1993—94; pub. Digital News & Rev., 1994—95, Reseller Mgmt., 1995—97; v.p. sales IDG Channel Svcs. Corp., Framingham, Mass., 1997—98; v.p., pub. New Age Jour & Body & Soul, 1998—2001; pub. dir. Weider Pubs. Natural Health mag., 2001—03; group pub. Advanstar Comm. Sensors & Frontline Solutions, 2003—04; pub. CMO mag. Internat. Data Group, 2004—. Spkr. in field. Mem. Sigma Phi. Avocations: composing, painting, outdoor sports. Home: PO Box 1365 New London NH 03257 Office: CXOMedia Inc 492 Connecticut Path Rd Framingham MA 01701 Office Phone: 508-988-7962. E-mail: stwombly@cxo.com.

TWOMEY, ELIZABETH ANN MOLLOY, education educator; b. Lynn, Mass.; d. Hugh E. and Theresa A. (Callahan) Molloy; children: Ann, Paula, Charles. AB, Emmanuel Coll., 1959; MEd, Mass. State Coll., 1964; EdD, Boston Coll., 1982; LLB (hon.), Notre Dame, Manchester, N.H., 1984; LHL (hon.), Emmanuel Coll., 1998. Elem. sch. tchr. Lynn (Mass.) Pub. Schs., 1959-63; English tchr. Reading (Mass.) Pub. Schs., 1973-75, prin., 1975-81, vice prin., 1981-82; supt. Lincoln (Mass.) Pub. Schs., 1982-88; assoc. commr. Dept. Edn., Quincy, Mass., 1988-92, dep. commr. Concord, N.H., 1992-94, commr., 1994—2000. Adj. prof. Lynch Sch. Edn. Boston Coll., 2000—. Trustee Emmanuel Coll., Boston, 1975-85, U. N.H., Durham, 1994—. Recipient Disting. Alumni award Emmanuel Coll., 1984. Avocations: walking, reading, gardening. Office: Lynch Sch Education Boston Coll Concord NH 02467

TWOMEY, JOHN HUMPHREY, JR., language educator; b. Springfield, Mass., July 10, 1945; s. John H. and Honor M. Twomey; children: Lisa, Allison. BA, So. Conn. State, 1967; PhD, St. Louis U., 1973. Chancellor prof., chair Fgn. Langs. and Lit. dept. U. Mass. Dartmouth, Dartmouth, 1972—. Office: Univ Mass Dartmouth Old Westport Rd North Dartmouth MA 02747

TWOMEY, KEVIN, pharmaceutical executive; BA in econ. and acctg., St. John's U. Various positions Deloitte & Touche, 1972—89, Fleming Companies, Inc., 1989—2000, sr. v.p., fin. and contr., 1999—2000, dir., planning and analysis, promoted to ops. contr., then, v.p. and contr., 1995—99; sr. v.p., chief acctg. officer Rite Aid Corp., 2000—. Office: Rite Aid Corp 30 Hunter Lane Camp Hill PA 17011

TWOMEY, THOMAS A., JR., lawyer, educator; b. N.Y.C., Dec. 8, 1945; s. Thomas A. and Mary (Maloney) T.; m. Judith Hope Twomey, Dec. 15, 1979; stepchildren: Erling Hope, Nisse Hope. BA, Manhattan Coll., 1967; postgrad., U.Va., 1967-68; JD, Columbia U., 1970. Bar: N.Y. 1972, U.S. Tax Ct. 1974. Asst. town atty. Town of Southampton N.Y., 1973-74; spl. asst. dist. atty. Suffolk County, N.Y., 1973-74; pvt. practice law Riverhead, N.Y., 1974-75; ptnr. Hubbard & Twomey, Riverhead, 1976-79, Twomey, Latham, Shea & Kelley, Riverhead, 1980—. Chair N.Y. State East End Econ. and Environ. Task Force, 1993; mem. deans coun. Stonybrook Sch. Medicine, 1991—; adj. prof. environ. law Southampton Coll., 1977-78. Bd. dirs. East End Arts Coun., Riverhead, 1983, Guild Hall East Hampton, 1993—; bd. dirs. East Hampton Libr., 1994—, pres., 1998—; trustee L.I. Power Authority, 1989-94; town historian, Town of East Hampton, 1999, vice chair East Hampton Town 350th Anniversary com., 1998, editor East Hampton Histor. Collection; historian N.Y. State Dem. Com., 2000-01; chair East Hampton 350th lecture series, 1998. Recipient Environ. award, U.S. EPA, 1980, Citizen of Yr. award L.I. Farm Bur., 2002. Mem. ABA, Suffolk County Bar Assn., State Energy Coun., N.Y. State Fresh Water Wetlands Appeals Bd. Democrat. Home: #9 Two Holes of Water Rd East Hampton NY 11937

TWOMEY, TIMOTHY, architect; Grad., U. So. Calif.; MArch, Harvard U.; JD, UCLA. Prin. Shelpley Bulfinch Richardson & Abbott, Boston, 1993, prin. chief adminstrv. officer, in-house counsel, 1993—. Past mem. bldg. design and constrn. faculty Northeastern U.; lectr. in field; constrn. dispute mediator, arbitrator, ct. apptd. master. Contbr. articles to profl. jours. Chair local cmty. planning commn. and sch. com. Mem.: AIA, Boston Soc. Archs. Office: Shepley Bulfinch Richardson & Abbott 40 Broad St Boston MA 02109-4306*

TYBOUT, RICHARD ALTON, economics professor; b. Phila., Sept. 28, 1920; s. Richard Raymond and Lillian (Alton) T.; m. Rita Holloway, Sept. 7, 1946; children: Alice Marie, James Richard, Robert Maxwell. BChemE, U. Del., 1943; MSChemE, U. Mich., 1946, MA in Econs., 1947, PhD in Econs., 1952. Instr. U. Mich., Ann Arbor, 1952-54; asst. prof. Ohio State U., Columbus, 1954-57, assoc. prof., 1957-62, prof., 1962-88, prof. emeritus, 1988—. Editor: Economics of Research and Development, 1965, Environmental Quality and Society, 1975; author: Government Contracting in Atomic Energy, 1956, The Reactor Supply Industry, 1960, Atomic Power and Energy Resource Planning, 1958; co-author: The Columbus Area Economy, 1966. Named Ford Faculty Study Fellow, Ford Foun., 1959-60, Phoenix Predoctoral Fellow, U. Mich., 1949-51. Mem. Am. Econ. Assn., Sierra Club (chmn. econs. com. 1975-85), Toastmasters Internat. (pres. Worthington chpt., 2002-03), Tau Beta Pi, Phi Kappa Phi, Beta Gamma Sigma. Avocations: construction, swimming, sailing. Home: 324 Pingree Dr Columbus OH 43085-3158 Office: Ohio State U Dept Econs 1945 N High St Columbus OH 43210-1120

TYCHAN, TERRENCE J. grants and acquisitions administrator; BA in Liberal Arts, Ohio State U.; M in Fin. Mgmt., George Washington U.; postgrad., Harvard U. Contract ops. Army Electronics Command, Ft. Monmouth, N.J.; instr. in math. Zanesville, Ohio; dep. asst. sec. Office of Grants and Acquisition Mgmt. Dept. HHS, Washington. Office: Dept of HHS Grants and Acquisitions Rm 517-D/HH Bldg 200 Independence Ave SW Washington DC 20201-0004

TYDINGCO-GATEWOOD, FRANCES MARIE, judge; b. Oahu, Hawaii, Jan. 21, 1958; d. Daniel J. and Francesca S. Tydingco; m. Robert Gatewood; children: Daniel Gatewood, Michael Gatewood, Stephen Gatewood. BA in Polit. Sci., Marquette U., 1980; JD, U. Mo., Kansas City, 1983. Law clk. to Hon. Forest W. Hanna Jackson County Cir. Ct., Kansas City, 1983—84; asst. atty. gen. Govt. of Guam, 1984—88, chief prosecutor, 1990—94; asst. prosecutor Jackson County Prosecutor's Office, Mo., 1988—90; trial judge Superior Ct. Guam, 1994—2002; assoc. judge Supreme Ct. Guam, 2002—. Profl. Tech. scholar, Govt. of Guam. Office: Supreme Ct Guam Guam Jud Ctr Ste 300 120 W O'Brien Dr Hagatna GU 96910 Home: 222 Chalan Santo Papa Ste 222 Hagatna GU 96910 Business E-Mail: ftgate@guamsupremecourt.com.

TYER, TRAVIS EARL, library consultant; b. Lorenzo, Tex., Oct. 23, 1930; s. Charlie Earl and Juanita (Travis) T.; m. Alma Lois Davis, Nov. 6, 1951; children: Alan Ross, Juanita Linn. BS, Abilene Christian U., 1952; BLS, U. North Tex., 1959; AdM in LS, Fla. State U., 1969, postgrad., 1969-71. Librarian, tchr. pub. schs., Gail, Lubbock, and Seminole, Tex., 1952-61; with Dallas Pub. Library, 1961-66, coordinator young adult services, 1962-66; library dir. Lubbock Pub. Library, 1966, Lubbock City-County Libraries, 1967-68; grad. library sch. faculty-state personnel coordinator Emporia (Kans.) State U., 1971-72; sr. cons. profl. devel. Ill. State Library, Springfield, 1972-80; exec. dir. Great River Libr. Sys., Quincy, Ill., 1980-94; cons. pub. rels. and comm. Alliance Libr. Sys., Quincy, 1994-97; ind. libr. cons., 1997—. Lectr. summer workshops Tex. Woman's U., U. Okla., U. Utah, Fla. State U., U. North Tex.; adj. faculty U. Mo., 1986-89; cons. in field; mem. adv. com. Ill. State Libr., 1984-87, 93-96; pres. Resource Sharing Alliance West Ctrl. Ill., Inc., 1981-94, sec., 1994-97; pres. Ill. Libr. System Dirs. Orgn., 1992-94. Contbr. articles to library jours. Inductee U. North Tex. Libr. and Info. Sci. Hall of Fame, 1990. Mem. ALA, Ill. Libr. Assn., Ill. Ctr. for the Book, Friends of Librs. U.S.A., U. North Tex. Sch. Libr. and Info. Sci. (life), Friends Lubbock City-County Librs. (life), Ill. Sch. Libr. MEdia Assn. Democrat. Mem. Ch. of Christ. Home and Office: 2008 S Arrowood Ct Quincy IL 62305-8961 Office Phone: 217-223-5024.

TYGRETT, HOWARD VOLNEY, JR., judge, lawyer; b. Lake Charles, La., Jan. 12, 1940; s. Howard Volney and Hazel (Wheeler) T.; m. Linda Lee; children: Carroll Diane, Howard V. III. BA, Williams Coll., 1961; LLB, So. Methodist U., 1964. Bar: Tex. 1964. Gen. atty. SEC, 1964-65; law clk. to chief judge U.S. Dist. Ct. No. Dist. Tex., 1965-67; ptnr. Tygrett & Walker and predecessors, Dallas, 1968-98; state dist. judge, 86th dist. Kaufman County, Tex., 2003—. Bd. dirs. Routh St. Center, 1976-83, Theatre Three, 1974-75, Shakespeare Festival, 1978-81, Suicide and Crisis Ctr., 1983-8; chmn. Terrell Hist. Preservation Commn., 2000-2003. Mem. Tex. Bar Assn., Civitan (lt. gov. Tex. dist. 1976-77, gov. 1979-80), Terrell Heritage Soc. (v.p. 1999—), Delta Phi, Delta Theta Phi. Episcopalian. Home: 505 Pacific Ave Terrell TX 75160-2073 Office: Kaufman County Courthouse 100 W Mulberry Kaufman TX 75142 Office Phone: 972-932-4331 ext. 127.

TYKESON, DONALD ERWIN, broadcast executive; b. Portland, Oreg., Apr. 11, 1927; s. O. Ansel and Hillie Martha (Haveman) T.; m. Rilda Margaret Steigleder, July 1, 1950; children: Ellen, Amy, Eric. BS, U. Oreg., 1951. V.p., dir. Liberty Comm., Inc., Eugene, Oreg., 1963-67, pres., CEO, dir., 1967-83; mng. ptnr. Tykeson/Assocs. Enterprises, 1983—; chmn. bd. Bend Cable Comm., LLC, 1983—2002, vice chmn., 2002—; chmn. bd. Ctrl. Oreg. Cable Advt., LLC, 1992—. Mem. coun. pub. reps. NIH, 2002—; pres. Tykeson Found., 1995—; mem. Hoover Instn. bd. overseers Stanford U., 2002-. Bd. dirs. Nat. Multiple Sclerosis Soc., 1987—2003, Nat. Coalition Rsch. in Neurol. and Communicative Disorders, 1984—89, Sacred Heart Med. Ctr.

Found., 1995—; chmn. pub. and gov. info. com. Nat. Coaltion in Rsch., C-SPAN, 1980—89; vice-chmn. we. area Nat. Multiple Sclerosis Soc., 1983—2002; trustee U. Oreg. Found., 1996—, Eugene Art Found., 1980—85, Oreg. Health Scis. U. Found., 1988—91; vice-chmn., 1988—92; mem. bus. adv. coun. U. Oreg. Coll. Bus. Adminstrn., 1973—, mem. steering com., 1997—2001, dean search com., 1998—; mem. Oreg. Investment Coun. State of Oreg., vice chmn., 1988—92. Mem. Nat. Assn. Broadcasters, Nat. Cable TV Assn. (dir. 1976-83), Chief Execs. Orgn., Vintage Club (bd. dirs. 1996-99, chmn. fin. com., treas. 1996-99, pres. Custom Lot Assn. 1992-97), Country Club Eugene (dir. 1975-77, sec. 1976, v.p. 1977), Multnomah Athletic Club, Arlington Club, Rotary, Alexis de Tocqueville Soc., Confrérie Chevaliers du Tastevin Sous Commanderie de Coachella Valley. Home: 447 Spyglass Dr Eugene OR 97401-2091 Office: Tykeson Assocs Enterprises PO Box 70006 Eugene OR 97401-0101 Office Phone: 541-683-4511.

TYKOCINSKI, MARK L. molecular immunologist, gene therapist; b. Lakewood, N.J., Nov. 26, 1952; married, 1978; 4 children. BA, Yale U., 1974; MD, N.Y. U., 1978. Resident in internal medicine Columbia-Presbyn. Med. Ctr., 1978-79; resident in anatomy pathology N.Y. U. Med. Ctr., 1979-81; med. staff fellow immunogenetics Nat. Inst. Allergy & Infectious Diseases/NIH, 1981-83; prof. pathology Sch. Medicine Case Western Reserve U., 1973-98; staff physician U. Hosps., Cleve., 1983-98; Simon Flexner prof., chair dept. pathology and lab. medicine U. Pa., 1998—. Recipient Warner-Lambert/Parke-Davis award Am. Soc. for Investigative Pathology, 1995. Mem. Am. Assn. Pathologists, Am. Assn. Cancer Rsch. Achievements include research in genetically engring. proteins for immunotherapy protein factors.

TYKSINSKI, EUGENE KORY, broadcast executive; b. Rome, N.Y., Jan. 14, 1935; s. Kostyn Stanley and Mary Jenny (Farraggio) T.; m. Ann Elizabeth Percival, June 21, 1965 (div. Sept. 1981); children: Cory, Stephen, Mary Beth; m. Elizabeth Salter Roetter, Aug. 15, 1987; 1 child, Matthew. Student, Utica Coll., 1952-54; BS, Lemoyne Coll., 1959. Budget analyst N.Y. State Divsn. Budget, Albany, 1963-67; prin. analyst N.Y. Senate Fin. Com., Albany, 1967-83, sec., 1983-93; exec.dir. Assn. Pub. Broadcasting Sta. N.Y., Albany, 1993—. Co-author: Criminal Justice Process of New York, 1965. Capt. USMC, 1959-63. Recipient Pub. Svc. award Rockefeller Inst. Pub. Adminstrn., Albany, 1992. Fellow State Acad. Pub. Adminstrn (bd. dirs. 1995—); mem. Am. Soc. Pub. Adminstrn. (past pres.), Fort ORange Club. Avocations: sailing, golf, reading. Home: 830 Creek Ct Slingerlands NY 12159-3007 Office: Assoc of Public Broadcasting 33 Elk St #200 Albany NY 12207-1062

TYL, NOEL JAN, baritone, astrologer, writer; b. West Chester, Pa., Dec. 31, 1936; BA, Harvard U., 1958. Bus. mgr. Houston Grand Opera Assn., 1958-60; account exec. Ruder and Finn Pub. Rels., N.Y.C., 1960-62; profl. astrologer, 1970—; editor Astrology Now mag., 1974-79. Pres. Tyl Assocs., Inc. pub. rels. and advt., 1980-89; media spokesman; internat. lectr., locations including U.S., Moscow, London, Oslo, Copenhagen, Berlin, Amsterdam, The Netherlands, Toronto, Ont., Tel Aviv, Bologna. Winner Am. Opera Auditions, 1964; opera singer U.S. and Europe, 1964-80; Wagner specialist; appearances include Vienna State Opera, Düsseldorf, Rome, Milan, Barcelona, N.Y.C. Opera, also throughout U.S.; author: Principles and Practice of Astrology, 12 vols., 1973-75, Teaching and Study Guide, 1976, The Horoscope as Identity, 1974, Holistic Astrology, 1980, Prediction in Astrology, 1991, Synthesis and Counseling in Astrology, 1994, Astrology of the Famed, 1995, Predictions for a New Millennium, 1996, Astrological Timing of Critical Illness, 1998, Creative Astrologer, 1999, Solar Arcs, 2001, Intimacy, Sexuality, and Relationship, 2001. Mem. Astrology's World Orgn./AFAN (presiding officer 1982-98). Home: 17005 E Player Ct Fountain Hills AZ 85268-5721

TYLER, ANNE (MRS. TAGHI M. MODARRESSI), writer; b. Mpls., Oct. 25, 1941; d. Lloyd Parry and Phyllis (Mahon) T.; m. Taghi M. Modarressi, May 3, 1963 (dec. Apr. 1997); children: Tezh, Mitra. BA, Duke U., 1961; postgrad., Columbia U., 1962. Author: If Morning Ever Comes, 1964, The Tin Can Tree, 1965, A Slipping-Down Life, 1970, The Clock Winder, 1972, Celestial Navigation, 1974, Searching for Caleb, 1976, Earthly Possessions, 1977, Morgan's Passing, 1980, Dinner at the Homesick Restaurant, 1982, The Accidental Tourist, 1985, Breathing Lessons, 1988 (Pulitzer Prize for fiction 1989), Saint Maybe, 1991, (juvenile) Tumble Tower, 1993, Ladder of Years, 1995, A Patchwork Planet, 1998, Back When We Were Grownups, 2001, The Amateur Marriage, 2004; contbr. short stories to nat. mags. Home: 222 Tunbridge Rd Baltimore MD 21212-3422

TYLER, BRIAN JOSEPH, lawyer; b. Hanover, Pa., Mar. 22, 1966; s. Joseph Glenn and Rose Marie (Neiderer) T. BA, Gettysburg U., 1991; JD, Widener U., 1996. Dep. clk. U.S. Bankruptcy Ct., Harrisburg, Pa., 1991-92; program adminstr. Chpt. 13 Trustee Office, Harrisburg, 1992-96; ptnr. Purcell, Krug & Haller, Harrisburg, 1996—. Lectr., faculty Pa. Bar Inst., Mechanicsburg, 1997—2004; mediator U.S. Bankruptcy Ct., Harrisburg, 1998. Mem. Leadership Harrisburg Area; bd. dirs. Harrisburg Cmty. Theatre, 1997—2001, chmn. bd., 2001—02. With USAF, 1984—88. Office: Purcell Krug & Haller 1719 N Front St Harrisburg PA 17102-2392 Office Phone: 717-234-4178. E-mail: btyler@pkh.com.

TYLER, CARL WALTER, JR., retired physician, health research administrator; b. Washington, Aug. 22, 1933; s. Carl Walter and Elva Louise (Harlan) T.; m. Elma Hermione Matthias, June 23, 1956 (dec. Dec. 1991); children: Virginia Louise, Laureen, Jeffrey Alan, Cynthia T. Crenshaw. AB, Oberlin Coll., 1955; MD, Case-Western Res. U., 1959. Diplomate Am. Bd. Ob-Gyn. Rotating intern Univ. Hosps. of Cleve., 1959-60, resident in ob-gyn, 1960-64; med. officer USPHS, 1964; obstetrician-gynecologist USPHS Indian Health Service, Tahlequah, Okla., 1964-66; epidemic intelligence service officer Bur. Epidemiology, Ctrs. for Disease Control, Atlanta, 1966-67, dir. family planning evaluation div., 1967-80, asst. dir. for sci., 1980-82, acting dir. Ctr. for Health Promotion and Edn., 1982, dir. epidemiology program office, 1982-88, med. epidemiologist Office of Dir., 1988-90, asst. dir. for acad. programs, pub. health practice program office, 1990-97; clin. assoc. prof. ob.-gyn. Emory U. Sch. Medicine, Atlanta, 1997-98. Clin. asst. prof. ob-gyn Emory U. Sch. Medicine, Atlanta, 1966-80, clin. assoc. prof., 1980—, also clin. assoc. prof. preventive medicine and community health, adj. assoc. prof. sociology Coll. Arts and Scis., 1977-90; adj. assoc. prof. pub. health Sch. Pub. Health, 1990—; clin. prof. pub. health and community medicine Morehouse Sch. Medicine, Atlanta, 1990—; mem. Nat. Sleep Disorders Rsch. Commn., 1990—; mem. adv. com. on oral contrapection WHO, Geneva, 1974-77, mem. adv. com. maternal and child health, 1982-88; lectr. in field Editor: (monograph) Venereal Infections; assoc. editor: Maxcy-Rosenau Textbook of Public Health and Preventive Medicine, 13th edit., 1992; contbr. articles to profl. jours. Chmn. Dekalb County Schs. com. on instruction programs, subcom. on health, phys. edn. and safety, (Ga.), 1967-68; active Ga. State Soccer Coaches Assn., Atlanta, 1973-79, DeKalb County YMCA Josiah Macy Found. fellow, 1956-58; NIH grantee, 1961-64; recipient Superior Service award, 1974, Meritorious Service medal USPHS, 1984, Disting. Service medal, 1988; Carl S. Shultz Population award APHA, 1976, medal of Excellence Ctrs. for Disease Control, 1984. Fellow Am. Coll. Ob-Gyn (chmn. community health com. 1974-77), Am. Coll. Preventive Medicine, Am. Coll. Epidemiol.; mem. Am. Epidemiologic Soc., Internat. Epidemiologic Assn., Assn. Tchrs, Preventive Medicine (bd. dirs. 1988-89), Am. Pub. Health Assn. (governing council 1976-78), Assn. Planned Parenthood Profls., Population Assn. Am., Sierra Club Avocations: photography, camping.

TYLER, DANA, anchor; b. Columbus, Ohio; BA in Mktg. and Broadcast Journalism, Boston U. Intern WBNS-TV, Columbus, gen. assignment reporter, 1981—83, co-anchor weekday newscasts, 1983—90; weekend co-anchor/corr. WCBS-TV, N.Y.C., 1990—. Lectr. in field. Vol. N.Y.C. Sch. Vol. Programs. Honored by Harlem YMCA, Y of Greater N.Y.; recipient Emmy award for outstanding anchor, 1987, Emmy award for outstanding newscast, 1996, Emmy award for coverage of NYC Blackout, 2004. Office: WCBS-TV/CBS Corp 524 W 57th St New York NY 10019-2924

TYLER, DARLENE JASMER, retired dietitian; b. Watford City, N.D., Jan. 26, 1939; d. Edwin Arthur and Leola Irene (Walker) Jasmer; m. Richard G. Tyler, Aut. 26, 1977 (dec.); children: Ronald, Eric, Scott. BS, Oreg. State U., 1961. Registered dietitian. Clin. dietitian Salem (Oreg.) Hosp., 1965-73; sales supr. Sysco Northwest, Tigard, Oreg., 1975 77; clin. dietitian Physicians & Surgeons Hosp., Portland, Oreg., 1977-79; food svc. dir. Meridian Park Hosp., Tualatin, Oreg., 1979-2000; ret., 2000. Mem. Am. Soc. Hosp. Food Svc. Adminstrs., Am. Dietetic Assn., Oreg. Dietetic Assn., Portland Dietetic Assn. Episcopalian. Home: 4314 Botticelli Lake Oswego OR 97035 E-mail: darlenejtyler@aol.com.

TYLER, DAVID EARL, veterinary medical educator; b. Carlisle, Iowa, July 12, 1928; s. Guy Earl and Beatrice Virginia (Slack) T.; m. Alice LaVon Smith, Sept. 6, 1952; children: John William, Anne Elizabeth. BS, Iowa State U., 1953, D.V.M., 1957, PhD, 1963; MS, Purdue U., 1960. Instr. dept. vet. sci. Purdue U., 1957-60; asst. prof. dept. pathology Coll. Vet. Medicine, Iowa State U., 1960-63, asso. prof., 1963-66; prof., head dept. pathology and parasitology Coll. Vet. Medicine, U. Ga., 1966-71, head dept. pathology, 1971-79, prof., 1971-91, prof. emeritus, 1991—, ret., 1991. Co-founder internat. vet. pathology slide bank, 1984, co-dir., 1984-98; apptd. discussant Charles L. Davis Found. for Advancement Vet. Pathology, 1977-91. Cub Scout master, 1967-69, scout com. chmn., 1970-72; elder Disciples of Christ Ch., 1968—, chmn. ch. bd., 1973-74, 92-94; mem. citizens com. to County Bd. Edn., 1968-70; bd. dirs. Christian Coll., Ga., 1974-77. With AUS, 1946-48. Recipient Borden award Gail Borden Co., 1956, Norden Disting. Teaching award Norden Labs., 1964, 69, 81, 85, 91, Prof. of Yr. award Coll. Vet. Medicine, Iowa State U., 1965, Outstanding Prof. award Coll. Vet. Medicine, U. Ga., 1970, 76, 80-81, 83, 86, 87-88, 90, Joshia Meigs Teaching award, 1985, Stange award Coll. Vet. Med., Iowa State U., 1987, Phi Zeta Teaching award, 1985, N.Am. Outstanding Tchr. award, 1991, Omicron Delta Kappa Outstanding Prof. award U. Ga., 1981, Harold W. Casey award C.L. Davis Found., 1995. Mem. AVMA, Farm House, Am. Coll. Vet. Pathologists (mem. council 1975-77, exam. com. 1982-85), Am. Assn. Vet. Med. Colls. (chmn. com. teaching-learning materials 1975-77), Nat. Program for Instructional Devel. in Vet. Pathology (adv. com. 1976-77), Aghon, Sigma Xi, Phi Eta Sigma, Alpha Zeta, Gamma Sigma Delta, Phi Kappa Phi, Phi Zeta (chpt. sec.-treas. 1982-84), Omega Tau Sigma. Home: 160 Sunny Brook Dr Athens GA 30605-3348

TYLER, DIANE LAZZELLE, elementary school educator; b. Morgantown, W.Va., Feb. 5, 1941; d. Frank Glen DeVille and Mary Jeanne Lazzelle; m. Karl A. Henry, July 23, 1962 (div. Apr. 1987); 1 child, Karoline Louise Henry; m. James L. Tyler, Apr. 10, 1992. BS in Elem. Edn., W.Va. U., 1962; MS in Elem. Edn., SUNY, Fredonia, 1987. Elem. tchr. Pitts. Pub. Schs., 1962—63, Rochester (N.Y.) City Schs., 1963—67, Hamburg (N.Y.) Cen., 1967—98, mentor, 1994, social studies coord., 1995—96, N.Y. state stds. coord., 1996—98; adj. prof. Canisius Coll., 1992—2002. Coop. learning trainer South Town Tchrs. Ctr., Hamburg, NY, 1990—98; bd. rep. Erie County Mental Health, Buffalo, 1984—87. Pres. Sweet Adelines, Hamburg, 1971—73; co-chmn. Hamburgh Holidays, Hamburg, 1973—75. Recipient Tchr. of Excellence, Western N.Y. Women Adminstrs., 1997. Mem.: Writers by the Sea (leader 1999—2002), Newcomers at Beaches (bd. dirs. 2001—02), Young Reps. Club (pres. 1972—74), Phi Delta Kappa. Republican. Episcopalian. Home: 315 S Ocean Grande Dr PH-1 Ponte Vedra Beach FL 32082 E-mail: songster41@aol.com.

TYLER, DONALD EARL, urologist; b. Ontario, Oreg., Oct. 3, 1926; s. Charles Maurice and Iva (Hess) T.; 1 child, Paul Donald. MD, U. Oreg., 1950; JD, U. Denver, 1967. Diplomate Am. Bd. Urology, Am. Coll. Legal Medicine. Fellow in gen. surgery, urology The Mayo Found., Rochester, Minn., 1952, 55-58; clin. instr. in urology U. Utah Med. Sch., Salt Lake City, 1959-64. Author: A New and Simple Theory of Gravity, 1970, Origin of Life from Volcanoes and Petroleum, 1983, Earliest Man of Am. in Oreg., USA: With Photographs of Paleolithic Artifacts, 1986, Crooked Judges, Lawyers and Ins. Companies, 1990, The Other Guy's Sperm: The Cause of Cancer and Other Diseases, 1994, Homo Americanus: An Original American Species, 1998, American Paleolithic: Boat Building Eight Million Years Ago, 1999, Foreign Sperm: The cause of sexually transmitted diseases, cancers, autoimmune diseases, Alzheimer's, Schizophrenia, and Kuru, 2004. Lt. USNR, 1944-45, 52-54, WWII, Korea. Mem.: Phi Eta Sigma, Alpha Omega Alpha. Avocations: archaeology, anthropology, geology, skiing, swimming. Home: 1092 SW 2d Ave Ontario OR 97914-2121

TYLER, ERIC OWEN, pediatrician; b. Columbia, Tenn., Oct. 18, 1955; s. Harry Everett and Elizabeth (Lawrence) T.; m. Fran Till Tyler, July 29, 1978; children: Emily, Mallory, Mollie. BS, Harding U., 1977; MD, U. Tenn., 1981. Intern, resident U. Ala., Birmingham, 1984; pediatrician Pediat. Assocs. Alexander City, Ala., 1985—. Bd. dirs. ARC, Tallapoosa County, 1998—. Fellow: Am. Acad. Pediats., Am. Coll. Pediats.; mem.: Am. Coll. Physician Execs. Avocations: reading, gardening. Office: Pediat Assocs of Alex City PO Box 1269 1962 Cherokee Rd Alexander City AL 35010-3437

TYLER, GAIL MADELEINE, nurse; b. Dhahran, Saudi Arabia, Nov. 21, 1953; (parents Am. citizens); d. Louis Rogers and Nona Jean (Henderson) T.; m. Alan J. Moore, Sept. 29, 1990; 1 child, Sean James. AS, Front Range C.C., Westminster, Colo., 1979; BSN, U. Wyo., 1989. RN, Colo. Ward sec. Valley View Hosp., Thornton, Colo., 1975-79; nurse Scott and White Hosp., Temple, Tex., 1979-83, Meml. Hosp. Laramie County, Cheyenne, Who., 1983-89; dir. DePaul Home Health, 1989-91; field staff nurse Poudre Valley Hosp. Home Care/Poudre Care Connection, 1991-98, Rehab. and Vis. Nurses Assn., Fort Collins, Colo., 1999—2003; resource pool nurse Poudre Valley Hosp., Fort Collins, Colo., 2003—. Parish nurse Rocky Mountain Parish Health Ministry Orgn., pres., 2004 05. Avocations: doll collecting, sewing, reading, travel. Office: Poudre Valley Hosp 1024 S Lemay Ave Fort Collins CO 80524

TYLER, H. RICHARD, physician, educator; b. Bklyn., Oct. 16, 1927; s. Max M. and Beatrice F. T.; m. Joyce Colby, June 17, 1951; children— Kenneth, Karen, Douglas, Lori. AB, Syracuse U., 1947; BS in Medicine, MD, Washington U., 1951; MA (hon.), Harvard U., 1989. Diplomate Am. Bd. Neurology and Psychiatry. Intern Peter Bent Brigham Hosp., Boston, 1951-52; resident in neurology Boston City Hosp., 1952-54; public health fellow Neurol. Inst., Queen's Sq., London, Salpêtrière, Paris, 1954-55; asst. in pediatrics and neurology Johns Hopkins Hosp., Balt., 1955-56; neurologist Peter Bent Brigham Hosp., Boston, 1956-74; asst. in neurology Harvard Med. Sch., Boston, 1956-59, assoc. in neurology, 1959-61, instr., 1961-64, asst. prof., 1964-68, assoc. prof., 1968-73, prof., 1974-98, prof. emeritus, 1999—. Sr. physician Brigham and Women's Hosp., Boston, 1974—, dir. neurol. svc., 1979-88. Co-editor: Current Neurology I and II, 1979, 80; mem. editorial bd.: Jour. Neurology, 1979-84, Classics on Neurology and Neurosurgery Libr., 1983—; contbr. articles in field to profl. jours. Trustee Brookline Pub. Libr., 1970-2001, chmn. bd. trustees, 1985-86, 90-91. Served with U.S. Army, 1946-47. Mem. Am. Neurol. Assn., Am. Acad. Neurology (hon.), Mass. Med. Soc. Office: 1 Brookline Pl Ste 503 Brookline MA 02445-7224 Office Phone: 617-735-8720. E-mail: HTyler1798@aol.com.

TYLER, JEFF WAYNE, veterinarian, researcher; b. Ft.Dodge, Iowa, May 31, 1957; s. Robert Reginald and Bobbi Lee Tyler; m. Carolyn Jean Henry, Mar. 21, 1991; children: Morgan Lee, Wayne Cody, Trevor Charles, Reginald James, Sydney Suzanne, Quinn Michelle. DVM, U. Minn., St.Paul/Minneapolis, 1977—81; MPVM, U. of Calif., Davis, 1984—85, PhD, 1986—89. Large Animal Internal Medicine Am. Coll. of Vet. Internal Medicine, 1992. Asst. prof. Auburn U., Auburn University, Ala., 1989—2003; assoc. prof. Wash. State U., Pullman, Wash., 1993—97; prof. U. Mo., Columbia, 1997—, dir. clin. rsch. Contbr. over 170 articles to profl. jours. Recipient Am. Vet. Med. Assn./Am. Feed Industry award, 2003. Fellow: Am. Coll. of Vet. Internal Medicine. Achievements include research in neonatal health and disease susceptibility in livestock. Office: Dept Vet Medicine 379 ECampus Dr Columbia MO 65211

TYLER, JOHN DUKE, psychologist, educator; b. Nashville, Nov. 30, 1943; s. John Duke and Eleanora (Hammond) Tyler; m. Shirley Kay Montgomery; 1 child, Wade McLeod. BA, Vanderbilt U., 1965; PhD, U. Tex., Austin, 1970. Bd. cert. diplomate Am. Bd. Profl. Psychology. Prof. psychology U. ND, Grand Forks, 1970—; dir. Family Inst., Grand Forks, 1980—. Dir., Psychol. Svcs. Ctr. U. ND, Grand Forks, 1979—98. Contbr. articles to profl. jours. Fellow: Acad. Clin. Psychology; mem.: APA, ND Psychol. Assn. (pres. 1982—83). Office: U ND Psychology Dept Grand Forks ND 58202

TYLER, JOHN EDWARD, III, lawyer; b. Kansas City, Mo. BA, U. Notre Dame, 1986, JD, 1989. From assoc. to ptnr. Lathrop & Gage L.C., Kansas City, 1989-99; sr. v.p., gen. counsel, sec. Ewing Marion Kauffman Found., Kansas City, 1999—. Adj. prof. Rockhurst U., Kansas City, 2000—; bd. advisors Nat. Ctr. Philanthropy and Law, NYU, 2003-. Contbr. articles to profl. jours. Pres. Genesis Sch., Kansas City, 1995-97; pres. Archbishop O'Hara H.S., Kansas City, 1994-97, bd. dirs.; pres. Sch. Bd. Diocese of Kansas City-St. Joseph, 2002—; chmn. tax increment fin. commn. city of Raytown, Mo., 1997-99; bd. dirs. Ctr. for Mgmt. Assistance, Kansas City, pres., 1999-2001. Named Man of Yr. Leukemia Soc., Kansas City, 1998, Bernie Hoffman award Cmty. Svc, Awards Found., 1997. Mem. ABA, Mo. Bar Assn. (Thomas D. Cochran award for cmty. svc. 1995), Kans. Bar Assn., Kansas City Met. Bar Assn. (Young Lawyer of Yr. 1998). Home: 2420 SW Wintercreek Ct Lees Summit MO 64081-4085 Office: Ewing Marion Kauffman Found 4801 Rockhill Rd Kansas City MO 64110-2046

TYLER, KENNETH LAURENCE, neurologist, researcher; b. Boston, May 6, 1953; s. H. Richard and Joyce (Colby) T.; m. Lisa Johnson, Oct. 27, 1979; children: Maxwell Johnson, Eric Johnson. AB magna cum laude, Harvard U., 1974; MD, Johns Hopkin's U., 1978. Diplomate Am. Bd. Internal Medicine, Am. Bd. Psychiatry and Neurology. Resident in medicine Brigham and Women's Hosp., Boston, 1978-80; resident in neurology Mass. Gen. Hosp., Boston, 1980-83; rsch. fellow Med. Sch. Harvard U., Boston, 1983-84, instr. Med. Sch., 1984-86, asst. prof. Med. Sch., 1986-91; assoc. prof. med. sch. U. Colo., Denver, 1991-95, prof. med. sch., 1995—, vice-chmn. neurology dept. med. sch., 1998-2000, Reuler-Lewin Family prof. neurology, 2001—. Chief neurology svc. Denver VA Med. Ctr., 1994—; mem. med. rsch. adv. group Dept. VA. Mem. editl. bd. Microbial Pathogenesis, 1990—, Jour. Neurol. Scis., 1990-97, Jour. Virology, 1991-98, Jour. Hist. Neurosci., 1993-96, Archives of Neurology, 1997—, Jour. Neurovirology, 1995 , Apoptosis, 2002—, Exptl. Neurology, 2003—, Neurology, 2003—, Jour. Infectious Disease, 2003—; editor: Infections in the Central Nervous Systems; contbr. articles to profl. jours. Alfred P. Sloan Found. fellow, 1988-90. Fellow ACP, Am. Acad. Neurology (bd. dirs., chair membership com., past pres. history sect. program com., S. Weir Mitchell award, Lawrence McHenry award 2000), Infectious Disease Soc. Am.; mem. Am. Soc. Neurol. investigation (past pres., sec., treas.), Am. Soc. Clin. Investigation, Am. Soc. Virology, Soc. for Exptl. Neuropathology (coun.), Am. Neurol. Assn., Soc. Neurosci. Home: 788 Milwaukee St Denver CO 80206-3902 Office: U Colo Hlth Sci Ctr 4200 E 9th Ave B-182 Neurology Denver CO 80262-0001

TYLER, LIV, actress; b. Portland, Maine, Jan. 7, 1977; d. Steven Tyler (lead singer: Aerosmith) and Bebe Buell. Motion picture actress and print model. Actress (films): Silent Fall, 1994, Empire Records, 1995, Stealing Beauty, 1996, Inventing the Abbotts, 1997, Armageddon, 1998, Onegin, 1999, The Little Black Book, 1999, Cookie's Fortune, 1999, Plunkett & MaCleane, 1999, One Night at McCool's, 2001, Lord of the Rings: The Fellowship of the Ring, 2001, The Lord of the Rings: The Two Towers, 2002, The Lord of the Rings: The Return of the King, 2003, Jersey Girl, 2004.; appeared in Aerosmith's music video, Crazy, 1994. Office: c/o CAA 9830 Wilshire Blvd Beverly Hills CA 90212-1804

TYLER, LLOYD JOHN, retired lawyer; b. Aurora, Ill., May 28, 1924; s. Lloyd J. and Dorothy M. (Curtis) T.; m. Inez Chappell Busener, Feb. 25, 1970; children by previous marriage: Barbara Tyler Miller, John R., Benjamin C., Robert B., Amy C. Tomas. BA, Beloit Coll., 1948; JD, U. Mich., 1951. Bar: Ill., Mich. bars 1951. Mem. firm Sears, Streit, Tyler and Dreyer and (predecessors), Aurora, Ill., 1951-62, Tyler and Hughes (P.A.), Aurora, 1962-99; ret. Lectr., speaker on profl. subjects, 1964— Contbr. chpts. to profl. books, articles to profl. jours. Democratic precinct committeeman, 1954-59; mem. Batavia (Ill.) Sch. Bd., 1959-62. Served with USAAF, 1943-46. Fellow Am. Bar Found.; mem. Am. Bar Assn. (Ho. of Dels. 1975-79), Ill. Bar Assn. (gov. 1970-78, pres. 1978-79, chmn. legislative com. 1980, task force on alternative forms of legal service 1981-82, long range planning com. 1982-88, fed. judiciary appointment com. 1984-90, spl. com. on merit selection 1987—), Ill. Bar Found. (pres. 1972-75), Ill. Inst. Continuing Legal Edn. (dir. 1971-75, 77-79), Ill. Lawyers Polit. Action Com. (trustee 1982—, chmn. 1987-88), Soc. Trial Lawyers Ill., Appellate Lawyers Assn., Phi Beta Kappa, Omicron Delta Kappa. Presbyterian. Home: 701 Fargo Blvd Geneva IL 60134-3227

TYLER, RICHARD JAMES, personal and professional development educator; b. Warwick, R.I., June 16, 1957; s. Virginia (Campanella) Tyler. Gen. mgr. Gem Exch., Charlotte, N.C., 1977; nat. sales mgr. So. Merchandising, Charlotte, 1978; pres. Direct Import Distributing, New Orleans, 1981; nat. territorty dir. TV Fanfare Pub., 1982; v.p. ARC Pub., New Orleans, 1983; exec. v.p., gen. mgr. Superior Bedrooms, Inc., 1984; CEO Richard Tyler Internat., Inc., Houston, Internat. Bus. Inst., Inc., Houston, Tyler Internat. Rsch. Inst., Inc., Houston, Shopportunities, Houston, Richard Tyler Investments Ltd., 2000. Mem. adv. bd. Sales and Mktg. Mag., N.Y.C., 1991—; founder Leadership of Tomorrow program; profl. speaker, cons. in field. Author: Creating Excellence in Quality and Service, 1991, The Science and Art of Excellent Selling, 1993, Richard Tyler's Guide to Entrepreneurial Excellence, 1993, Richard Tyler's Smart Business Strategies: The Guide to Small Business Marketing Excellence, 1996, The Power of Professional Selling Program, 2002; pub. newsletter Richard Tyler's Excellence Edge, 1992, Entrepreneur Cover Story, 1999; contbr. articles to profl. publs. Mem. Rep.-Senatorial Inner Cir., Washington, 1991; mem. presdl. victory team Rep. Nat. Com., 2002, Tex. rep. pres. club, 2002; bd. dirs. Be An Angel Fund Charity, 2002. Mem. ASTD, Soc. Human Resource Mgmt., Nat. Speakers Assn., Internat. Platform Assn., Internat. Assn. Entrepreneurs. Avocations: sports, theater, deep sea fishing, amateur wrestling. E-mail: richardtyler@richardtyler.com.

TYLER, ROBERT R. psychologist, consultant; s. Roy E. and Betty J. Tyler; m. Carol J. Albrecht, Mar. 8, 1968; children: Robert R. Tyler, Jr., M. Suzanne McGann. BS in Bus., Chaminade Coll., 1974; MS in Safety, U. So. Calif., 1981; PhD in Psychology, U. Ctrl. Fla., 1997. Cert. comml. pilot FAA, 1970, modeling and simulation profl. Nat. Tng. Systems Assn., Arlington, VA, 2002. Commd. 2d lt. USMC, 1967, advanced through grades to col., 1993; exec. officer / ops. officer Marine Wing Support Group 17, Marine Corps Base Camp Butler, Japan, 1986—87; commdg. officer Marine Aerial Refueling Transport Tng. Squadron 253, Marine Corps Air Station, Cherry Point, NC, 1987—89; dir. aviation safety Hdqs., USMC, Washington, 1990—93; dir. marine corps programs Naval Tng. Systems Ctr., Orlando, 1993—97; ret. USMC, 1997; chief adminstr., nat. aviation & transp. ctr. Dowling Coll., Oakdale, Long Island, NY, 1998—98; human factors advisor to the faa Advancia Corp., Washington, 1998—99; chief scientist Crown Consulting, Inc., 1999—2001; prin. human factors advisor Trios Associates, 2001—02; divsn. mgr., simulation tech. svcs. MTS Technologies, Arlington, Va., 2002—. Co-chmn. Internat. / Industry Tng. Simulation and Edn. Conf., Orlando, 1993—97; assoc. editor Marine Corps Gazette, Marine Corps Base Quantico, Va., 1990—93; adj. prof. Embry-Riddle Aero. U., Andrews AFB, 1999—. Co-pres. Potomac H.S. Crew Booster Club, Dumfries, Va., 1984—86; congl. pres. Holy Trinity Luth. Ch., Falls Church, 2000—02; congregational pres. St. Timothy Luth. Ch., Havelock, NC, 1989—99. Decorated 32 Strike Flight Air Medals, Meritorious Svc. medal,, Legion of Merit, . Mem.: APA, Marine Corps Aviation Assn., Human Factors and Ergonomic Soc., Aircraft Owners and Pilots Assn., Phi Kappa Phi. Home: 9322 Branchside Lane Fairfax VA 22031-6017 Office: MTS Technologies Inc 2800 Shirlington Road Suite 1000 Arlington VA 22206 Office Phone: 703-575-2954. Personal E-mail: robttyler@msn.com. E-mail: tylerr@mtstech.com.

TYLER, RONNIE CURTIS, historian; b. Temple, Tex., Dec. 29, 1941; s. Jasper J. and Melba Curtis (James) T.; m. Paula Eyrich, Aug. 24, 1974. BSE, Abilene (Tex.) Christian Coll., 1964; MA, Tex. Christian U., 1966, PhD (Univ. fellow), 1968; DHL, Austin Coll., 1986. Instr. history Austin Coll., Sherman, Tex., 1967-68, asst. prof., 1968-69; asst. dir. collections and programs Amon Carter Mus., Ft. Worth, 1969-86; dir. Tex. State Hist. Assn., 1986—; prof. history U. Tex., Austin, 1986—. Adj. prof. history Tex. Christian U., 1971-72; cons. visual materials Western. Am. art. Author: Santiago Vidaurri and the Confederacy, 1973, The Big Bend: The Last Texas Frontier, 1975, The Image of America in Caricature and Cartoon, 1975, The Cowboy, 1975, The Mexican War: A Lithographic Record, 1974, The Rodeo Photographs of John Addison Stryker, 1978, Visions of America: Pioneer Artists in a New Land, 1983, Views of Texas: The Watercolors of Sarah Ann Hardinge, 1852-56, 1988, Nature's Classics: John James Audubon's Birds and Animals, 1992, Audubon's Great National Work: The Royal Octavo Edition of the Birds of America, 1993, Prints of the West, 1994, Alfred Jacob Miller: Artist as Explorer, 1999; (with Paula Eyrich Tyler) Texas Museums: A Guidebook, 1983; editor: (with Lawrence R. Murphy) The Slave Narratives of Texas, 1974, Posada's Mexico, 1979, Alfred Jacob Miller: Artist on the Oregon, 1982, Wanderings in the Southwest in 1855 (J.D.B. Stillman), 1990, Prints and Printmakers of Texas, 1997. Pres. Tarrant County (Tex.) Hist. Soc., 1975-77. Good Neighbor Commn. scholar Instituto Tecnologico Monterrey, Mex., 1967; Am. Philos. Soc. grantee, 1970-71; recipient H. Bailey Carroll award, 1974; Coral H. Tullis award, 1976 Mem. Am. Antiquarian Soc., Tex. Inst. Letters (Friends of Dallas Pub. Libr. award), Philos. Soc. Tex. (sec. 1990—), Phi Beta Kappa. Home: 4400 Balcones Dr Austin TX 78731-5710 Office: Ctr Studies Tex Hist 2/306 Richardson Hall University Tex Austin TX 78712 E-mail: rtyler@mail.utexas.edu.

TYLER, W(ILLIAM) ED, finance company executive; b. Cleve., Nov. 3, 1952; s. Ralph Tyler and Edith (Green) Kauer; m. Vickie Sue Boggs, Feb. 7, 1976; children: Stacia Leigh, Adam William. BS in Elec. Engring., Ind. Inst. Tech., 1974; MBA, Ind. U., 1977; postgrad., Harvard U., 1981; postgrad. in bus., Baruch U., 1988. From electronic engr. to exec. v.p. R.R. Donnelley & Sons Co., Warsaw, Ind., 1974—95, exec. v.p. & chief tech. officer, 1995—98; CEO, pres. Moore Corp. Ltd., 1998—2001, Willoughby Capitol, Lake Forest, Ill., 2001; CEO Ideapoint Ventures, 2002—. Personal E-mail: edtyler1@aol.com.

TYLER, WILLIAM HOWARD, JR., advertising executive, educator; b. Elizabethton, Tenn., May 21, 1932; s. William Howard and Ethel Margaret (Schueler) T.; m. Margery Moss, Aug. 31, 1957; children: William James, Daniel Moss. Student, Iowa State U., 1950-52, U. Iowa, 1952; AB in Lit., BJ in Advt., U. Mo., 1958, MA in Journalism, 1966. Advt. mgr. Rolla (Mo.) Daily News, 1958-59; instr. sch. journalism U. Mo., Columbia, 1959-61; copy writer, then v.p. copy dir. D'Arcy Advt. Agy., St. Louis, 1961-67; writer, producer, creative supr. Gardner Advt. Co., St. Louis, 1967-69; sr. v.p., creative dir. D'Arcy, McManus, Masius, St. Louis, 1969-77; exec. v.p., creative dir. Larson Bateman Advt. Agy., Santa Barbara, Calif., 1977-80; v.p. advt. Pizza Hut, Inc., Wichita, Kans., 1980-82; v.p., creative dir. Frye-Sills/Y&R, Denver, 1980; exec. v.p., creative dir. Gardner Advt. Co., St. Louis, 1982-88; exec. v.p., ptnr., creative dir. Parker Group, St. Louis, 1988-91; pres. Tylertoo Prodns., St. Louis, 1991—. Assoc. prof. St. Louis U., 1993-2003, prof., 2003—. Mng. editor St. Louis Advt. Mag., 1992-95. Trustee Blackburn Coll., Carlinville, Ill., 1983—84; bd. advisors U. Mo. Journalism Sch., 1986—91. Named AAF 9th Dist. Educator of Yr., 1998. Mem. U. Mo. Alumni Assn. (bd. dirs. 1969-70), Advt. Club Greater St. Louis, Golden Key (hon.), Mensa, Kappa Tau Alpha (hon.). Episcopalian. Office: Saint Louis U Dept Comm Xavier 300 3733 W Pine Blvd Saint Louis MO 63108-3305 Office Phone: 314-977-3190. E-mail: tylerwh@slu.edu.

TYLEVICH, ALEXANDER V. sculptor, architect, educator; b. Minsk, Belarus, Sept. 12, 1947; arrived in U.S., 1989; s. Wulf Tylevich and Asia Klebanova; m. Poline M. Dvorkin, Jan. 22, 1981; children: Alexei, Katherine. BA in Arch., Minsk Archtl. Inst., 1965; MA in Arch., Byelorussian Poly. Inst., Minsk, 1971. Prin., sr. arch. Minskprojekt, 1971-84; artist, arch. Fine Arts Found., Minsk, 1984-89; sculptor-arch. Tylevich Arts, St. Paul, 1989—. Prin. works include Vincentian Letter, DePaul U., Chgo., Letterdance, Minn. State U., Mankato, St. Francis de Sales, Morgantown, W.Va., Thomas More Chapel, U. St. Thomas, Mpls., Blue Springs.Net, Blue Springs, Mo., Letters of Creation, Wayzata, Minn., Montessori's Vision: Through the Eyes of a Child, Lake Country Sch., Mpls., Tree of Life, U. Minn., Mpls., Sculpture Anoka Ramsey C.C., Coon Rapids, Minn., Resurrection, Ch. of St. Stephen, Anoka, Minn., Madonna and Child, The Ch. of St. Mary, Alexandria, Minn., Gateway to Belief/Point of Belief, St. Mary's U., Winona, Minn., Thomas Becket, Cath. Cmty. of Thomas Becket, Eagan, Minn., Tribute to Erich Mendelsohn, FORECAST Pub. Artwork, St. Paul, Zenon Possis, North Meml. Hosp., Mpls., Winona Tech. Coll. Aviation Facility, St. Francis de Sales Cath. Ch., Morgantown, W.Va., North Shore Synagogue, Syosset, N.Y., Mt. Zion Temple, St. Paul, St. Paul Sem., St. Joseph Abbey, St. Benedict, La., Mepkin Abbey, S.C., Immaculate Conception Cath. Ch., Durham, N.C., Ctr. of Minsk, Minsk City Govt. Bldg., Subway Sta., pvt. collections, exhibited in group shows at Monumental Art of Byelorussia, Minsk, 1989, Nat. Jewish Mus., Washington, 1993, Harvard U. Grad. Sch. Design New Eng., 1993, St. John's U., Collegeville, Minn. Grantee Minn. Met. Regional Arts Coun., 1991, Howard B. Brin Arts Endowment, 1991, FORECAST Pub. Artworks, 1993. Fellow Archtl. Assn. USSR. Home: 1937 Highland Pkwy Saint Paul MN 55116-1350 E-mail: tyleart@aol.com.

TYLLIA, FRANK MICHAEL, university official, educator; b. Rossland, B.C., Can., Dec. 1, 1942; came to U.S., 1942; s. Alex J. and Lenora M. (Janni) T.; m. Kathryn A. McWalter, Mar. 21, 1970. BBA, Gonzaga U., 1965, BA in Edn., 1967; MA in Edn., Seattle U., 1972. Tchr. pub. schs., Seattle, 1967-72, prin., 1972-78, Edmonds Sch. Dist., Lynnwood, Wash., 1978-97; field supr. M Tchg. City U., Bellevue, Wash., 1997—, field supr. edn. leadership, 1999—. Adj. prof. Seattle Pacific U., 1990—, Mont. State U., 1999—. Active alumni mentoring program Gonzaga U., Seattle, 1993—; mem. Kirkland Cmty. Accountability Bd.; active King County Juvenile Justice, 1997—; mem. King County Diversion Adv. Bd., 1998—. Mem. ASCD, Assn. Wash. Sch. Prins. (various coms.), Washington Athletic Club, Phi Delta Kappa. Home and Office: 4527 103d Ln NE Kirkland WA 98033-7639

TYMAS-JONES, RAYMOND, dean; s. Raymond Jones, Sr. and Burnetta Tymas Jones; m. Shirley Diane Romeo, June 22, 1968 (div. Sept. 19, 1982); children: Chrishaun Jones, Raymond Jones. MusB, Howard U., 1977—77; MusM, Wash. U., 1979; PhD, Wash. U., St. Louis, 1988. Assoc. prof. music Buffalo State Coll., 1983—93, assoc. dean, asst. to dean, 1990—93; assoc. prof. music U. No. Iowa, Cedar Falls, 1993—97, dir. of the sch. of music, 1993—98, prof. of music, 1997; prof. music Ohio U., Athens, 1998—, dean, coll. fine arts, 1998—. Music dir. World Student Games, Buffalo, 1991; music director, chorus director Univ. Games, Buffalo, 1993; panelist Ohio Arts Coun., Columbus, Ohio, 2001—. Bd. dirs. Southwestern Ohio Cultural Arts Ctr., Athens, 2000; ex-officio bd. dirs. Ohio Valley Summer Theatre, Athens, 2000; v.p. Athena Cinemas Co./Athena Cinema Theater, Athens, Ohio, 2001. Grantee Rsch. Multiculturalism Music Edn., SUNY, 1991, Cmty. Enrichment, Rouse Corp., 1994, Ohio Arts Coun., 2002, Ohio U., 2002. Mem.: Coun. Coll. Arts Sci. (assoc.; presenter 2001), Ohio Arts Coun. (assoc.; support panel 2001), Internat. Coun. Fine Arts Deans (assoc.; bd. dirs. 1999). Avocations: wine, reading, cooking. Office: College of Fine Arts Ohio University 54 E Union St Jennings House Athens OH 45701 Office Phone: 740-593-1809. Personal E-mail: tymas-jo@ohio.edu., rtymasjones2@msn.com.

TYMES, NATHANIEL, JR., statistician, educator; b. Montgomery, Ala., Feb. 10, 1959; s. Nathaniel Tymes, Sr. and Annie Jean Tymes. BS, U. Ala., Tuscaloosa, 1981; MDiv, United Theol. Sem., Dayton, Ohio, 1985; MS, Air Force Inst. Tech., Dayton, 1987; MA, U. N.Mex, 1995, PhD, 2002. Commd. 2d lt. USAF, 1981, advanced through grades to maj., 1994; space systems performance analyst Nat. Aerospace Intelligence Ctr., Wright-Patterson AFB, Ohio, 1981—85; air-to-air vulnerability analyst Aero. Sys. Divsn., Eglin, AFB, Fla., 1987—91; operational effectivenss test mgr. HQ Air Force Operational Test and Evaluation Ctr., Kirtland AFB, N.Mex., 1991—94; sr. weapon systems analyst Office Aerospace Studies, Kirtland AFB, N.Mex., 1994—97; ret. USAF, 1997; asst. prof. stats. Ferris State U., Big Rapids, Mich., 2002—. Part time instr. Okaloosa-Walton C.C., Niceville, Fla., 1988—91; adj. instr. math and religion St. Leo Coll., Hurlburt FLD, Fla., 1989—91; instr. math and quantitative methods Troy State U. - Fla. Region, Hurlburt FLD, Fla., 1990—91; part-time instr. math. Albuquerque Tech.-Vocat. Inst., 1996—2002; tchg. asst. U. N.Mex, Albuquerque, 1997—2002. Tutor Wesley Cmty. Ctr., Dayton, Ohio, 1982—87; vol. mentor Partness In Success, Dayton, 1983—2000; asst. to pastor Home Ave First Ch. of God, Dayton, 1983—87. Named Vol. of the Yr., Wesley Cmty. Ctr., 1983, Partners In Success, 1984—85. Mem.: Soc. for Indsl. and Applied Math., Interface Found. N.Am., Inst. Ops. Rsch. and Mgmt. Sci., Am. Statis. Assn., Am. Math. Soc., Kappa Mu Epsilon. Libertarian. Achievements include research in attrition at the Air Force Academy; use of multiwavelets in signal denoising. Home: 223 Hunters Ln NE Rockford MI 49341 Office: Ferris State Univ 119 South St Big Rapids MI 49307 Personal E-mail: tymesn@ameritech.net. E-mail: tymesn@ferris.edu.

TYMESON, JODI, state official; b. Boone, Iowa, June 27, 1955; BA, U. No. Iowa; MPA, Drake U. Tchr.; state rep., 2001—. Mem. edn. com.; mem. human resources com.; mem. oversight and comms. com.; vice chair appropriations com.; mem. ways and means com. Inspector gen. Iowa N.G. Republican. Office: State Capital E 12th and Grand Des Moines IA 50319

TYMKOVICH, TIMOTHY MICHAEL, federal judge; b. Denver, Co., Nov. 2, 1956; married; 2 children. BA, Co. Coll., 1979; JD, Univ. of Co. Sch. of Law, 1982. Clk. Co. Supreme Ct., 1982—83; assoc. Davis, Graham, & Stubbs, 1983—89; of Counsel Bradley Campbel Carney & Madsen, 1990—91; solicitor gen. Office of the Co. Atty. Gen., 1991—96; ptnr. Hale Hackstaff Tymkovich & ErkenBrack, 1996—2003; judge US Ct. of Appeals (10th cir), 2003—. Mem.: ABA, Internat. Soc. of Barristers, Colo. Bar Found., Am. Law Inst. Office: Byron White US Courthouse 1823 Stout St Denver CO 80257

TYMOCHKO, JOHN ALAN, financial services executive; b. Sharon, Pa., May 25, 1950; s. John and Betty Jane (Bennett) T.; m. Lorraine Anne Mitchell, May 22, 1982 (div. Jan. 1986). BA, U. Pitts., 1971, MA, 1972. V.p. Prudential Ins. Co., Newark, 1972—. Home: 500 E 77th St Apt 1020 New York NY 10162-0004 Office: Prudential Ins Co 2 Prudential Plaza Newark NJ 07101

TYNDALL, DAVID GORDON, business educator; b. Bangalore, India, Nov. 19, 1919; s. Joseph and Annie E. (Parsons) T.; m. Margaret Patricia Davies, Apr. 4, 1942; children: Caroline Lee, David Gordon, Benjamin. BComm, U. Toronto, 1940, MA, 1941; PhD, U. Calif., 1948. Asst. prof. bus. adminstrn. Cornell U., Ithaca, N.Y., 1947-49; assoc. prof. Carnegie-Mellon U., Pitts., 1949-53; assoc. prof., dir. analytical studies U. Calif., Berkeley, 1955-67, lectr., 1979-82. V.p. fin. and adminstrn., investment officer U. Alta., Edmonton, 1967-74; prof. fin., 1974-79; investment adv. Berkeley, 1979-96. Served with Royal Can. Air Force and Army, 1942—45. Fulbright fellow, 1952 Unitarian-Buddhist. Home: 88 Clarewood Ln Oakland CA 94618-2243 E-mail: gtyndall@pacbell.net.

TYNDALL, GAYE LYNN, secondary school educator; b. Reno, Apr. 21, 1953; d. Chris H. and Ellen (Hutchinson) Gansberg; m. Dave Tyndall, Mar. 17, 1973; children: Jody, Dave. BS, U. Nev., Reno, 1987, postgrad. Cert. secondary tchr. Tchr. math, sci. Douglas High Sch., Minden, Nev., 1987—. Treas. Nev. Sci. Project, Reno, 1990—; presenter Reading and Writing in the Math Classroom Internat. Reading Assn., Nat. Sci. Tchrs., Assn., 1990-92. Recipient Nev. State Tchr. of Yr. award Nev. Bd. Edn., 1993. Mem. Nat. Coun. Tchrs. Math., Calif. Math Coun. Avocations: momming, rodeo, family activities. Office: Douglas High Sch PO Box 1888 Minden NV 89423-1888

TYNE, MICHAEL D. architectural firm executive; Founding mem. Ross Planning Assocs., 1968—77; joined Karlsberger Cos., Columbus, Ohio, 1977, COO, exec. v.p., pres., CEO, 1987—, chmn., 1994—. Former pres. Simon Kenton Coun., Ohio. Office: Karlsberger Cos 99 E Main St Columbus OH 43215-5189*

TYNER, HOWARD A. publishing executive, newspaper editor, journalist; b. Milw., May 30, 1943; s. Howard Arthur and Katharine Elizabeth Tyner; m. Elizabeth Jane Adams, May 3, 1969; children: Sophie Elizabeth, Ian Adams. BA, Carleton Coll., 1965; MSJ, Northwestern U., 1967. Sports editor Chippewa Herald-Telegram, Chippewa Falls, Wis., 1965—66; fgn. corr. UPI, 1967—77; with Chgo. Tribune, Chgo., 1977—2001, fgn. corr. Moscow, 1982—85, fgn. editor Chgo., 1985—88, asst. mng. editor, 1988—90, dep. mng. editor, 1990—92, assoc. editor, 1992—93, v.p., editor, 1993—2001; v.p./editorial Tribune Pub. Co., 2001—. Mem. adv. bd. Alfred Friendly Press Fellowships, Washington, 1988—; mem. exec. bd. World Press Inst., 1994—. Mem.: Found. for Am. Comms. (adv. bd. 1997—), Am. Press Inst. (bd. dirs. 1997—), Am. Soc. Newspaper Editors (mem. found. bd. 1994—). Home: 2700 Park Pl Evanston IL 60201-1337 Office: Chgo Tribune Co 435 N Michigan Ave Chicago IL 60611-4066

TYNER, LEE REICHELDERFER, lawyer; b. Annapolis, Md., Mar. 12, 1946; d. Thomas Elmer and Eleanor Frances (Leland) Reichelderfer; m. Carl Frederick Tyner, Aug. 31, 1968; children: Michael Frederick, Rachel Christine, Elizabeth Frances. BA, St. John's Coll., 1968; MS, U. Wash., 1970; JD, George Washington U., 1975. Bar: Wash., D.C., U.S. Dist. Ct. (D.C.), U.S. Ct. Appeals (4th cir., 1st cir., 9th cir., D.C. cir., 5th cir., 8th cir., 11th cir., 10th cir.), U.S. Ct. Claims, U.S. Supreme Ct. Profl. staff U.S. Senate Commerce Com., Washington, 1970-72; trial atty. Land and Natural Resources div. U.S. Dept. Justice, Washington, 1975-85; atty. Office of Gen. Counsel U.S. EPA, Washington, 1985—. Bd. dirs. Grace Episcopal Day Sch., Silver Spring, Md., 1987-89, vestry Grace Episcopal Ch., 1997—2003; den leader, cubmaster Boy Scouts Am., Silver Spring, 1987-91. Recipient Bronze medals, U.S. EPA, 1988, 1992, 2002, 2003. Mem. Order of the Coif. Episcopalian. Home: 1416 Geranium St NW Washington DC 20012-1518 Office: US EPA 2366A 1200 Pennsylvania Ave NW Washington DC 20460 E-mail: skildpadde@aol.com., tyner.lee@epa.gov.

TYNER, MCCOY (ALFRED MCCOY SULAIMON SAUD TYNER), jazz pianist, composer; b. Phila., Dec. 11, 1938; Mem. Art Farmer and Benny Golson's Jazztet, 1959, John Coltrane Quartet, 1960-65; ind. pianist, 1965—. Rec. artist (with John Coltrane) A Love Supreme, Live at the Village Vanguard, Coltrane, Meditations, solo (albums) Reaching Fourth, The Real McCoy, Time for Tyner, Extensions, Asante, Tender Moments, rec. (with Jackie McLean albums) It's About Time, Echoes of a Friend, Enlightenment, Atlantis, Passion Dance, Together, 4 x 4, 13th House, Dimensions, discography Just Feelin', Hancock/Jarrett, Key of Soul, McCoy Tyner: The Earthly Trios, Vol. 6, Great Moments with McCoy Tyner, Reevaluations: the Impulse Years, Today and Tomorrow, Live at Newport, McCoy Tyner Live at Newport, 1963, McCoy Tyner Plays Ellington, 1964, Jazz Profile, 1967, Expansions, 1968, Cosmos, 1969, Extensions, 1970, Echoes of a Friend, Song for My Lady, Sahara, Reflections: A Retrospective (1972-1975), 1972, Atlantis, Sama Layuca, 1974, Trident, 1975, Focal Point, Fly with the Wind, 1976, Supertrios, Inner Voices, 1977, Together, The Greeting, Passion Dance, 1978, Horizon, 1979, 4 X 4, 1980, 13th House, 1981, Looking Out, 1982, Dimensions, 1983, Paris Bossa, 1984, Double Trios, 1986, Blues for Coltrane, Tribute to John Coltrane, It's About Time, Live at the Musicians Exchange Cafe,What's New, Bon Voyage, 1987, Uptown/Downtown, Inception/Nights of Ballads of Blues, Revelations, The Real McCoy, 1988, Solar/McCoy Tyner Trio Live at Sweet Basil, Live at Sweet Basil, Vol. 1, Vol. 2, Things Ain't What They Used To Be, 1989, Remembering John, Double Exposure, 44th Street Suite, Turning Point, Blue Bossa, Soliloquy, New York Reunion, 1991, The Turning Point, 1992, Manhattan Moods, Hot Licks: Giant Steps, Four Times Four, Journey, 1993, Prelude and Sonata, McCoy Tyner, 1994, Infinity, Live in Warsaw, Jazz Classics, Live at Sweet Basil, 1995, The Best of McCoy Tyner: The Blue Note Years, Best Of-Blue Note Years, 1996, What the World Needs Now: The Music of Burt Bacharach, Autumn Mood, Nights of Ballads and Blues, Inception, Plays Duke Ellington (Remastered Feat. Garrison/Jones), Jazz Profile (Jazz Profile Series), 1997, Priceless Jazz, Reaching Fourth, Asante, La Leyenda De La Hora, Priceless Jazz (Priceless Jazz Collection), 1998. Recipient Grammy award Best Jazz Instrumental Performance, Individual or Group, 1996.

TYNER, NEAL EDWARD, retired insurance company executive; b. Grand Island, Nebr., Jan. 30, 1930; s. Edward Raymond and Lydia Dorothea (Kruse) T.; children: Karen Tyner Redrow, Morgan. BBA, U. Nebr., 1956. Jr. analyst Bankers Life Nebr., Lincoln, 1956-62, asst. v.p. securities, 1962-67, v.p. securities, treas., 1967-69, fin. v.p., treas., 1970-72, sr. v.p. fin., treas., 1972-83, pres., chief exec. officer, 1983-87, chmn., pres., chief exec. officer, 1987-88, chmn., CEO, 1988-95; pres. Net Cons., Paradise Valley, Ariz., 1995—. Bd. dirs. Union Bank & Trust Co. Trustee U. Nebr. Found., Lincoln Found. Capt. USMC, 1950-54, Korea. Fellow: CFAs; mem.: Omaha/Lincoln Soc. Fin. Analysts, Mountain Shadows Golf Club. Lutheran. Avocations: tennis, computers. Office: 8225 N Golf Dr Scottsdale AZ 85253-2716

TYNG, ANNE GRISWOLD, architect; b. Kuling, Kiangsi, China, July 14, 1920; d. Walworth and Ethel Atkinson (Arens) T.; 1 child, Alexandra Stevens. AB, Radcliffe Coll., 1942; M of Architecture, Harvard U., 1944; PhD, U. Pa., 1975. Assoc. Stonorov & Kahn, Architects, 1945-47; assoc. Louis I. Kahn Architect, 1947-73; pvt. practice architecture Phila., 1973—; adj. assoc. prof. architecture U. Pa. Grad. Sch. Fine Arts, 1968-96. Assoc. cons. architect Phila. Planning Commn. and Phila. Redevel. Plan, 1954; vis. disting. prof. Pratt Inst., 1979-81, vis. critic architecture, 1969; vis. critic architecture Rensselaer Poly. Inst., 1969, 78, Carnegie Mellon U., 1970, Drexel U., 1972-73, Cooper Union, 1974-75, U. Tex., Austin, 1976; lectr. Archtl. Assn., London, Xian U., China, Bath U., Eng., Mexico City, Hong Kong U., 1989, Baltic Summer Sch., Architecture and Planning, Tallinn, Estonia, Parnu, Estonia, 1993, Alicante U., Spain, 1997, Barcelona U., Spain, 1997; panel spkr. Nat. Conv. Am. Inst. Architects, N.Y.C., 1988, also numerous univs., throughout U.S. and Can.; asst. leader People to People Archtl. del. to China, 1983; vis. artist Am. Acad., Rome, 1995. Subject of films Anne G. Tyng at Parsons Sch. of Design, 1972, Anne G. Tyng at U. of Minn., 1974, Connecting, 1976, Forming the Future, 1977; work included in Smithsonian Travelling Exhbn., 1979-81, 82, Louis I. Kahn: In the Realm of Architecture, 1990-94, Mus. Contemporary Art Travelling Exhbn., L.A., 1998—; author, editor: Louis Kahn to Anne Tyng, The Rome Letters 1953-1954, 1997; contbr. articles to profl. publs.; prin. works include Walworth Tyng Farmhouse (Hon. mention award Phila. chpt. AIA 1953); builder (with G. Yanchenko) Probability Pyramid, 1984. Fellow Graham Found. for Advanced Study in Fine Arts, 1965, 79-81. Fellow AIA (Brunner grantee N.Y. chpt. 1964, 83, dir., mem. exec. bd. dirs. Phila. chpt. 1976-78, John Harbeson Disting. Svc. award Phila. chpt. 1991); mem. Nat. Acad. Design (nat. academician), C.G. Jung Ctr. Phila. (planning com. 1979-97), Form Forum (co-founder, planning com. 1978-85). Democrat. Episcopalian. E-mail: agtyng@aol.com.

TYREE, ALAN DEAN, clergyman; b. Kansas City, Mo., Dec. 14, 1929; s. Clarence Tillman and Avis Ora (Gross) T.; m. Gladys Louise Omohundro, Nov. 23, 1951; children: Lawrence Wayne, Jonathan Tama, Sharon Avis. BA, U. Iowa, 1950; postgrad., U. Mo.-Columbia, 1956-58, U. Mo.-Kansas City, 1961-62. Ordained to ministry Cmty. of Christ, 1947. Appointee min., Lawrence, Kans., 1950-52; mission adminstr. (Mission Sanito), French Polynesia, 1953-64; regional adminstr. Denver, 1964-66; mem. Council Twelve Apostles, Independence, Mo., 1966-82, sec., 1980-82, mem. First Presidency, 1982-92; ret. First Presidency, 1992; pastor East 39th Street Congregation Cmty. of Christ, Independence, 2000—02. Mem. Joint Coun. and Bd. Appropriations, 1966-92; originator music appreciation broadcasts Radio Tahiti, 1962-64, Mission Sanito Radio Ministry, 1960-64; instr. Music/Arts Inst., 1992—, Met. C.C.'s, 1994—. Editor: Cantiques des Saints French-Tahitian hymnal, 1965, Exploring the Faith: A Study of Basic Christian Beliefs, 1987; mem. editing com.: Hymns of the Saints, 1981; author: The Gospel Graced by a People: A Biography of Persons in Tahiti, 1993, Evan Fry: Proclaimer of Good News, 1995, Priesthood: For Other's Sake, 1996, God: Getting to Know the Unknown, 1998. Bd. dirs. Outreach Internat. Found., 1979-82, mem. corp. body, 1982-92; mem. corp. body Independence Regional Health Ctr., 1982-92, v.p., 1983-92, bd. dirs., 1984-93; mem. bd. publs. Herald House, 1984-92; mem. corp. body Restoration Trail Found., 1982-92; chmn. Temple Art Com., 1988-94; bd. dirs. Independence Symphony Orch., 1992-96, pres., 1995-96; mem. human rels. commn. city of Independence, 1995-97, chmn., 1996-97. Recipient Elbert A. Smith Meml. award for publ. articles, 1968, 72 Mem. Phi Beta Kappa, Phi Eta Sigma. Home and Office: 3408 S Trail Ridge Dr Independence MO 64055 Office Phone: 816-373-8151. E-mail: tyree@mail.com.

TYREE, DONALD ANDREW, financial educator; b. St. Louis, Nov. 19, 1930; s. Wesley F. and Dena (Krieter) T.; m. Sherry Johnson, Nov. 18, 1978; 1 son, Paul H. (dec.); children by previous marriage: Wesley G., Thomas A. BS, BA, Washington U., St. Louis, 1953, MBA, 1956; PhD in Finance, U. Tex. at Austin, 1959. Research asso. Washington U., 1953; lectr. U. Tex., 1956-59; mem. faculty St. Louis U., 1959—2000, prof. finance, 1969—2000, chmn. dept., 1968—80, 1983—95, assoc. dean Sch. Bus. Adminstrn., 1973-74. Cons. in field. Mem. St. Louis County Ins. Com., 1962-68 Author: Small Loan Industry in Texas, 1960, School Insurance Administration, 1975, Urban Residential Mortgage Financing: Lending Practices in St. Louis, 1979. Served with AUS, 1953-55. Wienhiemer fellow, 1955-56; Tex. Savs. and Loan Assn. fellow, 1956-59 Home: 14 Huntleigh Woods Saint Louis MO 63131-4818

TYREE, JAMES C. insurance company executive; b. 1957; Grad., Ill. State U., 1979. With Mesirow Ins. Svcs. Inc., Chgo., 1980—, CEO, chmn., CEO, 1994—. Mem. Juv. Diabetes Rsch. Found. Internat.; bd trustee Roosevelt Univ. Mem.: Exec. Club, Econ. Club. Office: Mesirow Ins Svcs Inc 350 N Clark St Chicago IL 60610-4712*

TYREE, LEWIS, JR., retired compressed gas company executive, inventor, technical consultant; b. Lexington, Va., July 25, 1922; s. Lewis Sr. and Winifred (West) T.; m. Dorothy A. Hinchcliff, Aug. 21, 1948; children: Elizabeth Hinchcliff, Lewis III, Dorothy Scott. Student, Washington & Lee U., 1939-40; BS, MIT, 1947. Cryogenic engr. Joy Mfg. Co., Michigan City, Ind., 1947-49; v.p. Hinchcliff Motor Service, Chgo., 1949-53; cons. engr. Cryogenic Products, Chgo., 1953-76, Liquid Carbonic Corp., Chgo., 1960-76; exec. v.p. Liquid Carbonic Industries, Chgo., 1976-87. Bd. dirs. Liquid Carbonic Industries, Chgo., Worldwide Cryogenics (MVE), New Prague, Minn. Patentee in cryogenics. Served to 1st lt. U.S. Army, 1943-46, PTO. Mem. Soc. Cin., ASME, Am. Soc. Heating, Refrigeration, and Air Conditioning Engring., Hinsdale Golf Club, Lexington Golf and Country Club. Republican. Episcopalian. Home: 250 Pantops Mountain RD Apt 5104 Charlottesville VA 22911-8701

TYRITY, KATHY MILICA, reporter, editor; b. Akron, Ohio, Dec. 19, 1953; d. Zirovko Chirich and Ada Fay Tyrity; m. Robert Laird Brockruoy, Oct. 12, 1974 (div. Dec. 19, 1977); 1 child, Sara Bays. BS, Butler U., Indianapolis, IN; Diploma (hon.), Silva. Reporter Sarasota (Fla.) Herald Tribune, 1978—83; city editor Sarasota Times, 1983—89; corr. reporter Akron Beacon Jour., Akron, Ohio, 1991—94; city editor Coshocton Tribune, Coshocton, Ohio, 1994—95; sec. Estate of Don Quist, Hudson, Ohio, 1995—2000; corr. reporter Sun Newspaper, Medina, Ohio, 1999—2002; asst. tchr. Akron(Ohio) Pub. Schools, 2001—02. Author: three books. Active Republicans of Sarasota Club, Sarasota, Fla., 1977—89; psychic Akron Psychic Fairs, Cleveland, Akron, Canton, Ohio; healer Akron Theosophy Soc., Akron, Ohio. Recipient Second Pl., Nat. Associated Collegiate Press, 1976, Mark Distinciton as Photo Editor, 1976, Most Coop., Journalism Award, Kenmore H.S., 1971. Mem.: Grand Cross, Rainbow Order (advisor 1970—74), Internat. Theosophy Club, Sigma Delta Chi (hon.; journalist 1976—). Achievements include research in Notable findings in medical research on psychics. Avocations: drawing, sketching, painting, doing healings, giving readings.

TYRL, PAUL, mathematics educator, researcher, consultant; b. Prague, Czech Rep., Dec. 24, 1951; came to U.S., 1970, naturalized, 1978; s. Vladimir Tyrl and Marta Kocian. BA with honors, N.J. City U., 1977, MA, 1980; EdD,

Rutgers U., 1987. Cert. tchr. secondary edn., higher edn. N.J. quality controller Agfa-Perutz, Munich, 1969-70; technician AT&T, Kearny, N.J., 1970-73; acquisition librarian N.J. City U., 1973-74, post office supr., 1974-76, dir. math. lab., instr. math., 1976-80; instr. math. Hudson County C.C., N.J., 1980-82, assoc. prof. coord. math., 1982-84; prof., chmn. math., acad. coord., curriculum dir. Sch. New Resources-New Rochelle Coll., N.Y.C., 1984—. Rschr. Rutgers U., New Brunswick, N.J., 1980—; cons. Jersey City Bd. Edn., N.J., 1982—. Contbr. articles to profl. jours. Recipient Commemorative medal of honor, 1986. Mem. AAAS, ASCD, Nat. Coun. Tchrs. Math. (reviewer and referee), N.Y. Acad. Scis., Am. Ednl. Rsch. Assn., Math. Assn. Am., Am. Math. Assn. 2-Yr. Colls., Am. Math. Soc., Am. Mus. Natural History, Nat. Geog. Soc., Nat. Wildlife Fedn., Smithsonian Instn. Roman Catholic. Achievements include research in math. anxiety and math. problem solving.

TYROCH, ROXANNE MARIE, internist, educator; b. Phoenix, Ariz., Nov. 5, 1964; d. Donald Bernard Richards and Bertha Chavez; m. Alan Tyroch, Dec. 5, 1992; children: Christian, Moriah. BSc in Nursing, Ariz. State U., 1987; MD, U. Ariz., 1991. Cert. ABIM. Intern Good Samaritan Regional Med. Ctr., 1991—92, resident, 1992—94; chief resident internal medicine Phoenix (Ariz.) VAMC, 1994—95; physician Linder-Quann Med. Group, Fresno, Calif., 1995—97; asst. assoc. prof. Tex. Tech. U. Health, El Paso, 1997—2002, assoc. prof., 2002—. Mem. faculty exec. com. Tex. Tech. Health Sci. Ctr., El Paso, 1998—2001; cons. Tex. Cancer, Austin, Tex., 2000—01. Editor: (CD Rom) Tyroch Angels, 2002, (website) Colorectal Cancer Screening, 2002, (brochure) Cancer Screening, 2002. Team mgr. Destination Imagination, El Paso, 2000—02; coun. vol. Boy Scouts Am., El Paso, 2000—, cubmaster, 2003—04, mem. Praise and Worship Ensemble, St. Mark's United Meth. Ch., El Paso, 1998—. Grantee, Tex. Cancer Coun., 1999—2002, Rio Grande Cancer Found., 2000—03, Ctr. Border Health Rsch., 2000—03. Mem.: ACP, Am. Cancer Soc. (bd. dir. Tex. Coun. Divsn. 2000—04), Soc. Gen. Internal Medicine, Assn. Tchrs. Preventive Medicine. Avocations: guitar, Kendo. Home: 201 Cactus Pointe Ct El Paso TX 79912 Office: Tex Tech Univ Health Sci Ctr 4800 Alberta Ave El Paso TX 79905

TYROLER, HERMAN ALFRED, epidemiologist; Grad., NYU Sch. medicine. Lic. to practice, N.C. Prof., now alumni disting. prof. dept. epidemiology U. N.C. Mem. Inst. of Medicine, Nat. Acad. Scis. Office: U NC Dept Epidemiology 137 E Franklin St Ste 306 Chapel Hill NC 27599-0001

TYRRELL, D. LORNE J. university dean; Dean U. Alberta Faculty Medicine and Dentistry, Edmonton, Canada, 1994—; dir. Glaxo Heritage Research Institute. Officer of the Order of Canada Govt. of Canada, 2002. Recipient ASTech award for innovation and science, Kaplan award for excellence in research, Prix Galien Canada medal for research, Gold medal, The Canadian Liver Foundation, 2000, Alberta Order of Excellence, Province of Alberta, 2000. Office: U Alta Fac Med & Dentistry 2J2 00 WMC Edmonton AB Canada T6G 2R7

TYRRELL, GERALD GETTYS, banker; b. Canton, China, Dec. 27, 1938; came to U.S., 1940. s. Gerald Fraser and Virginia Lee (Gettys) T.; m. Jane Haldeman, June 1961 (div. Aug. 1975); children: Gerald F., Jane N., Robert M.; m. Elizabeth Ann Drautman, Mar. 31, 1978. BA, Yale U., 1960; MA, Rutgers U., 1971. Cert. real estate financier. With 1st Nat. Bank of Louisville, 1961—89, sr. v.p., 1975—81, exec. v.p., 1981—89; pres., chmn. Churchill Mortgage Corp., 1975—77; chief fin. cons. City of Louisville Office of Downtown Devel., 1989—2000; exec. v.p. Univ. Group, Consultants for Bus., Prospect, 2000—. Vice chmn. bd. dirs. Porcelain Metals Corp., 2001—, bd. dirs. Author: A Positive Approach to Financing Black Business, 1972 Trustee, treas. Patton Mus., Ft. Knox, Ky., 1970—96; treas. Soc. Colonial Wars in Commonwealth of Ky., 1970—89, sec., 1996—99, gov., 2000—; treas. gen. Gen. Soc. Colonial Wars, 2004—; mem. exec. bd. Boy Scouts Am., 1983—; bd. dirs. The Louisville Orch., 1984—90, Crane Ho., The Asia Inst., 1988—, pres., 1995—97; bd. dirs., chmn. fin. com. Glassworks Found., Inc., 2001—03; bd. dirs. Thomas Merton Found., 2003—. Served to capt. U.S. Army, 1960—68. Recipient Disting. Service Ribbon Ky. Nat. Guard, 1966 Mem. Robert Morris Assocs., Nat. Soc. Real Estate Fin. (bd. govs), Louisville Country Club, Pendennis Club. Democrat. Avocations: fine wines, tennis. E-mail: betsyandgerald@aol.com.

TYRRELL, LILIAN, craftsperson, artist; b. London, 1944; One-woman shows include Akron (Ohio) Art Mus., 1984, 1991, Coll. Wooster (Ohio) Art Mus., 1986, Massillion (Ohio) Mus., 1989, Ctr. for Tapestry Arts, N.Y.C., 1990, U. Mo., St. Louis, 1991, St. Mary's Coll., Notre Dame, Ind., 1992, Mus. for Textile, Toronto, 1992, Richmond (Ind.) Art Mus., 1993, Va. Ctr. Craft Arts, Richmond, 1993, Cleve. Mus. Art, 1994, Ins. Devel. Co., Columbus, Ohio, Pepper Pike Place Assocs., Cleve., Jacob, Visconsi and Jacob. Named 1st visual artist of yr., Cleve. Arts, 1993; individual artists fellow, Ohio Arts Coun., 1982—83, 1985—86, 1988—89, 1990—91, 1992—93, regional visual arts fellow, Arts Midwest/NEA, 1989—90, visual arts fellow, NEA, 1994—95.

TYRRELL, ROBERT EMMETT, JR., periodical editor, writer; b. Chgo., Dec. 14, 1943; s. R. Emmett and Patricia (Rogers) T.; m. Judy Mathews Tyrrell, Feb. 12, 1972 (div. Dec. 1989); children: Patrick, Kathryn, Anne; m. Jeanne Hauch Tyrrell, May 23, 1998. BA, Ind. U., 1965, MA, 1967. Founder, editor-in-chief The Am. Spectator, Arlington, Va., 1967—. Chmn. Am. Alternative Found., Inc., Arlington, Va., 1967—; adj. fellow Hudson Inst. Author: Public Nuisances, 1979, The Liberal Crack-Up, 1984, The Conservative Crack-up, 1992, Boy Clinton: The Political Biography, 1996, (with anonymous author) The Impeachment of William Jefferson Clinton, 1997, Madame Hillary: The Dark Road to the White House, 2004; editor: Network News Treatment of the 1972 Democratic Presidential Candidates, 1972, The Future That Doesn't Work, 1977, Orthodoxy, 1987; writer nationally syndicated polit. column; contbg. editor: The New York Sun. Recipient Am. Eagle award Invest in Am. Coun., 1977; named Greatest Pub. Svc. Performed by an American 35 Years or Under award Am. Inst. for Pub. Svc., 1977, Ten Most Outstanding Young Men in Am., Jaycees, 1978. Roman Catholic. Avocations: handball, fishing, listening to classical music, reading. Office: The American Spectator 1611 N Kent St Arlington VA 22201

TYRRELL, THOMAS NEIL, former metal processing executive; b. Valdosta, Ga., Feb. 5, 1945; s. Thomas W. and Marilynn (Bowler) T.; children from previous marriage: Tracey, Torrey, Taryn; m. Diane Montague, 1995. BA in Bus. Adminstra., Elmhurst Coll., 1967; LLD (hon.), Baldwin-Wallace Coll., 1992. Sales loop trainee Bethlehem (Penn.) Steel Corp., 1967; gen. product sales person Bethlehem Steel Sales Office, Greensboro, N.C., 1968-73; product specialist Bethlehem Steel Corp., 1973-78; v.p. mktg. Raritan River Steel, Perth Amboy, N.J., 1978-86; CEO Am. Steel & Wire Corp., Cuyahoga Hgts., Ohio, 1986-94; vice chmn., CAO Birmingham (Ala.) Steel Corp., 1994-96; pres., ceo Bar Technologies, Inc., 1996-98; ceo Republic Engineered Steels, Akron, Ohio, 1998-99; ceo. Republic Technologies Intl.(merger USS/KOBE, Bar Technologies & Republic Engineered Steels), Akron, Ohio, 1999-00. Bd. dirs. Birmingham Steel Corp. Contbr. articles to profl. jours. Vol. Leadership Cleve., 1987, Baldwin Wallace Coll., 1989—, Elmhurst Coll., 1990—, Ohio Valley Corridor Commn. emeritus, 1990—. Named Entrepreneur of Yr. Northeast Ohio, Venture Inc. mag., 1988; recipient Register award for Bus. and Commerce, Esquire mag., 1988. Mem. Wire Assn. Internat., Cold Finished Bar Inst., Am. Wire Producers Assn., Indsl. Fastener Inst., Concrete Reinforced Steel Inst., Am. Inst. Steel Engrs., Summit Club (Birmingham), Old Overton C. of C. Roman Catholic. Avocations: running, fishing, scuba diving, weight training. Office: Republic Technologies Intl 3770 Embassy Pkwy Akron OH 44333-8367

TYSOE, RONALD W. retail executive; b. Vancouver, British Columbia; married; 4 children. Degree in commerce, U. of British Columbia1, 1976; degree in law, University of British Columbia, 1978. Sr. dir. of adminstrn. to sr. dir. corp. adminstrn. to sr. dir. of fin. to v.p. corp. develop., 1981—86; v.p., treas., prin. fin. officer Allied Stores Corp., 1986—88; exec. v.p. of corp. develop. Campeau Corp., 1987—90; pres. Campeau U.S., 1988—90; CFO Federated Dept. Stores, 1990—97, vice chair, fin. and real estate, 1990—. Mem. bd. dirs. Federated Dept. Stores, 1988—, E.W. Scripps Co., 1996—, Gt. Am. Fin. Resources, Inc. Office: Federated Dept Stores 7 W 7th St Cincinnati OH 45202

TYSON, CICELY, actress; b. N.Y.C., Dec. 19, 1933; d. William and Theodosia Tyson; m. Miles Davis, 1981 (div.). Student, N.Y. U., Actors Studio; hon. doctorates, Atlanta U., Loyola U., Lincoln U. Former sec., model. Co-founder Dance Theatre of Harlem; bd. dirs. Urban Gateways Tage appearances include: The Blacks, 1961-63, off-Broadway, Moon on a Rainbow Shawl, 1962-63, Tiger, Tiger, Burning Bright, Broadway; films include: Twelve Angry Men, 1957, Odds Against Tomorrow, 1959, The Last Angry Man, 1959, A Man Called Adam, 1966, The Comedians, 1967, The Heart is a Lonely Hunter, 1968, Sounder, 1972 (Best Actress, Atlanta Film Festival, Nat. Soc. Film Critics, Acad. award nominee, Best Actress, Emmy award, Best Actress in a spl., 1973), The Blue Bird, 1976, The River Niger, 1976, A Hero Ain't Nothin' but a Sandwich, 1978, The Concorde-Airport 79, 1979, Bustin' Loose, 1981, Fried Green Tomatoes, 1991, Jefferson in Paris, 1995, The Grass Harp, 1996, Aftershock, 1999; TV appearances include: (series) East Side, West Side, 1963, Sweet Justice, 1994-95, Road to Galveston, 1996; (films) Marriage: Year One, 1971, The Autobiography of Miss Jane Pittman, 1974, Just an Old Sweet Song, 1976, Wilma, 1977, Roots, 1977, A Woman Called Moses, 1978, King, 1978, The Marva Collins Story, 1981, Benny's Place, 1982, Playing With Fire, 1985, Samaritan: The Mitch Snyder Story, 1986, Acceptable Risks, 1986, Intimate Encounters, 1986, The Women of Brewster Place, 1989, Heat Wave, 1990 (Cable Ace award 1991), Winner Takes All, 1990, The Kid Who Loved Christmas, 1990, When No One Would Listen, 1992, Duplicates, 1993, House of Secrets, 1993, Oldest Living Confederate Widow Tells All, 1994 (Emmy Awd., Best Supporting Actress - Miniseries), Mama's Flora Family, 1998 (Image award 1999), Always Outnumbered, 1998, Ms. Scrooge, 1997, The Price of Heaven, 1997, Riot, 1997, Bridge of Time, 1997, A Century of Women, 1994,; other appearances include: Wednesday Night Out, 1972, Marlo Thomas and Friends in Free to Be...You and Me, 1974, CBS: On the Air, 1978, Liberty Weekend, 1986, The Blessings of Liberty, 1987, Without Borders, 1989, Visions of Freedom: A Time Television Special, 1990, Clippers, 1991, A Century of Women, 1994 Trustee Human Family Inst.; trustee Am. Film Inst. Recipient Vernon Price award, 1962; also awards NAACP Nat. Council Negro Women; Capitol Press award. Office: More/Medavoy Mgmt Dirs Guild of Am Bldg 7920 W Sunset Blvd Ste 401 Los Angeles CA 90046-3300

TYSON, CYNTHIA HALDENBY, academic administrator; b. Scunthorpe, Lincolnshire, Eng., July 2, 1937; came to U.S., 1959; d. Frederick and Florence Edna (Stacey) Haldenby; children: Marcus James, Alexandra Elizabeth. BA, U. Leeds, Eng., 1958, MA, 1959, PhD, 1971; DHL (hon.), Mary Baldwin Coll., 2003. Lectr. Brit. Council, Leeds, 1959; faculty U. Tenn., Knoxville, 1959-60, Seton Hall U., South Orange, N.J., 1963-69; faculty, v.p. Queens Coll., Charlotte, N.C., 1969-85; pres. Mary Baldwin Coll., Staunton, Va., 1985—2003, pres. emerita, 2003—; pres. Robert Haywood Morrison Found., 2002—. Contbr. articles to profl. jours. Mem. Va. Internat. Trade Commn., Richmond, 1987; trustee Am. Frontier Culture Mus., Va.; mem. Va. Lottery Bd., 1987-94; chair selection com. State of Va. Rhodes Scholarship Competition, 1993-97; bd. dirs. Cmty. Found. Staunton, Augusta County and Waynesboro, 1993-98. Fulbright scholar, 1959; Ford Found. grantee Harvard U., 1981; Shell Oil scholar Harvard U., 1982. Mem.: Assn. Presbyn. Colls. and Univs. (bd. dirs. 1998), So. Assn. Colls. and Schs. (vice chair 1998, pres.-elect 2001, pres. 2002), Assn. Va. Colls. and Univs. (pres. 1997—98), So. Assn. Colls. for Women (pres. 1980—81), Mary Baldwin Coll. (hon.), Phi Beta Kappa. Republican. Office: Robert Haywood Morrison Found 1373 East Morehead St Ste 2 Charlotte NC 28204-2979

TYSON, DAVID T. academic administrator; b. Gary, Ind., 1948; Postgrad in sociology & theology, U. Notre Dame; EdD, Ind. U., 1980. Prof. mgmt. U. Notre Dame, v.p. student affairs; pres. U. Portland, Oreg., 1990—. Trustee St. Mary's Coll., Ind.; bd. mem. Assn. Catholic Colls. & Univs. (ACCU); trustee U. Notre Dame; bd. mem. USAF's Air U. Office: U Portland Office Pres 5000 N Willamette Blvd Portland OR 97203-5743

TYSON, DONALD JOHN, food company executive; b. Olathe, Kans., Apr. 21, 1930; s. John W. and Mildred (Ernst) T.; m. Twilla Jean Womochil, Aug. 24, 1952; children: John H., Cheryl J., Carla A. Student, U. Ark. Plant mgr. Tyson Foods, Inc., Springdale, Ark., 1951-55, pres., 1955-67, chmn., chief exec. officer, 1967-95, sr. chmn., 1995—. Mem.: Elks. Home: 2210 W Oaklawn Dr Springdale AR 72762-6900 Office: Tyson Foods Inc PO Box 2020 Springdale AR 72765-2020

TYSON, H. MICHAEL, retired bank executive; b. Houston, Aug. 16, 1938; s. Howard Ellis and Myrle (Daunoy) T.; m. Judith O. Gilbert, June 24, 1960; children: H. Michael II, Michelle Lee. BBA cum laude, U. Tex., 1962; postgrad., Stonier Grad Sch. Banking, Rutgers U., 1974. Personnel mgr. Foods div. Anderson Clayton Co., Dallas, 1962-70; exec. v.p. adminstrn. Tex. Commerce Bancshares, Houston, 1970-79; v.p. fin. and adminstrn., chief fin. officer, dir. Houston Chronicle Pub. Co., 1979-87; vice chmn., dir. Tex. Commerce Bank-Houston; exec. v.p., exec. trust officer Tex. Commerce Bancshares, 1987-95. Dir. Paranet Inc., Assoc. Bldg. Svcs., MCG/Dulworth Inc. Bd. dirs. Sam Houston coun. Boy Scouts Am., Houston Livestock Show & Rodeo, Houston Festival Found.; trustee McCullough Found., W.A. Smith Found.; chmn. The Houston Parks Bd. Served with USMCR, 1961-67. Mem. Houston C. of C. (com. chmn.), Pers. Round Table, Am. Newspaper Pub. Assn., Houston Indsl. Rels. Group, Fin. Execs. Inst. (bd. dirs.), Internat. Newspaper Fin. Execs., Houston Club (dir., pres.), River Oaks Country Club (dir.), Houston Yacht Club (dir.). Methodist. E-mail: hmtyson@sbcglobal.net.

TYSON, JOHN H. food products executive; b. Springdale, Ark., Sept. 5, 1953; s. Don and Jean Tyson; m. Kimberly McCoy; children: John Randal, Olivia Laine. BBA, So. Meth. U., 1975. Complex mgr. N.C. area Tyson Foods, Inc., Springdale, v.p. mktg. corp. accounts, purchasing mgr., retail sales mgr. N.E. states, pres. beef and pork divsn.; pres., chmn. Tyson Foods Inc., Springdale, 1998-00, pres., chmn., CEO, 2000—01, chmn., CEO. Polit. liaison to Washington and Little Rock Tyson Foods, Inc. Bd. dirs. Area United Way; supporter Farm Aid; vol. activities for well-being and edn. of Ark. children. Named Man of Yr., Ark. Poultry Industry, 1994. Mem.: Ark. Poultry Fedn. (past pres.), Am. Meat Inst., Nat. Assn. Mfrs. Avocations: deep sea fishing, music, golf. Office: Tyson Foods Inc 2210 W Oaklawn Dr Springdale AR 72762-6999*

TYSON, KIRK W. M. management consultant; b. Jackson, Mich., July 2, 1952; s. George Carlton and Wilma Marion (Barnes) Tyson; m. Terri Lynn Long, Mar. 25, 2000; 1 child, Gabriel 1 stepchild, Robert. BBA, Western Mich. U., 1974; MBA, DePaul U., Chgo., 1982. CPA, Ill.; cert. mgmt. cons. Bus. cons. Arthur Andersen & Co., Chgo., 1974-84; v.p. cons. First Chgo. Corp., 1984; chmn. Kirk Tyson Internat., 1984-2000; pres. The Perpetual Strategist, Chgo., 2001—. Author: Business Planning, 1982, Business Intelligence: Putting It All Together, 1986, Competitor Intelligence: Manual and Guide, 1990, Competition in the 21st Century, 1996, The Complete Guide to Competitive Intelligence, 1998 2d rev. edit. 2002, The Perpetual Strategist, 2004. Pres., Chgo. Jr. Assn. Commerce and Industry Found., 1977-79; active Easter Seals Soc., 1977, Am. Blind Skiing Found., 1977-78, Jr. Achievement, 1976-77, United Way Met. Chgo., 1979-80, Urban Gateways, 1975; Rep. precinct committeeman Downers Grove Twp., 1985-88; treas. St. Charles H.S. Football Booster club, 1994-95. Fellow Soc. Competitive Intelligence Profls.; mem. Rotary Club of Chgo., Alpha Kappa Psi (Disting. Alumni Svc. award 1974-86, named Alumnus of Yr. 2003). Office: The Perpetual Strategist 30 S Wacker Dr Ste 2200 Chicago IL 60606-7456 E-mail: kirk.tyson@kirktyson.com.

TYSON, LAURA D'ANDREA, dean, economist, educator; b. Bayonne, N.J., June 28, 1947; BA, Smith Coll., 1969; PhD, MIT, 1974. Prof. econ. and bus. adminstrn. U. Calif., Berkeley, 1978-98, BankAmerica dean Haas Sch. Bus., 1998—; chmn. Pres.'s Coun. Econ. Advisors, Washington, 1993-95; nat. econ. advisor to Pres. U.S. Nat. Econ. Coun., Washington, 1995-96. Prin. Law and Econs. Consulting Group; bd. trustees Asia Found.; mem. adv. bd. Barter Trust, Epiphany, Shorenstein Co. LP, G7 Group, Inc. Editor: (with John Zysman) American Industry in International Competition, 1983, (with Ellen Comisso) Power, Purpose and Collective Choice: Economic Strategy in Socialist States, 1986, (with William Dickens and John Zysman) The Dynamics of Trade and Employment, 1988, (with Chalmers Johnson and John Zysman) Politics and Productivity: The Real Story of How Japan Works, 1989, Who's Bashing Whom? Trade Conflict in High Technology Industries, 1992; mem. adv. bd.: Jour. Econ. Perspectives; mem. bd. editors: Am. Prospect and Calif. Mgmt. Rev.; econ. viewpoint columnist: Bus. Week mag.; commentator: Nightly Bus. Report; author domestic and internat. econ. policy matters in Washington Post, N.Y. Times, and other nat. and internat. syndicated newspapers and mags. Mem. Nat. Bipartisan Commn. Future Medicare, 1997—99. Mem.: Trilateral Commn., New Am. Found., Morgan Stanley, Dean Witter, Discover & Co., Inst. Internat. Econs., Human Genome Scis., Inc., Healtheon Corp., Fox Entertainment Group, Inc., Eastman Kodak Co., Coun. Fgn. Rels., Ameritech Corp. Office: Haas Sch Bus 545 Student Srvs # 1900 Berkeley CA 94720-0001

TYSON, LISA N. food products executive; Assoc. atty. corp. securities group Winstead, Sechrest & Minick, 1991—98; v.p., asst. gen. counsel Suiza Foods, 1998—2002; sr. v.p., dep. gen. counsel, asst. sec. Dean Foods, 2002—. Office: Dean Foods 2515 McKinney Ave Ste 1200 Dallas TX 75201-1945

TYSON, MIKE G. boxer; b. N.Y.C., June 30, 1966; s. John Kilpatrick and Lorna Tyson; m. Robin Givens, Feb. 7, 1988 (div. Feb. 1989). Defeated Trevor Berbick to win World Boxing Coun. Heavyweight Title, Nov. 1986; defeated James Smith to win World Boxing Assn. Heavyweight Title, 1987; defeated Tony Tucker to win Internat. Boxing Fedn. Heavyweight Title, Aug. 1987; defeated Michael Spinks to win Internat. Boxing Fedn. Heavyweight Title, June 1988; undisputed heavyweight champion 1988-90 (defeated by James "Buster" Douglas); defeated Frank Bruno to win WBC Heavyweight Title, 1996; defeated by Evander Holyfield, 1996; won over Frans Botha, 1998. Commentator for Showtime. Hon. sports chmn. Cystic Fibrosis Assn. N.Y., 1987—, Young Adult Inst., N.Y.C., 1987—. Achievements include being the youngest heavyweight champion in history.*

TYSON, NEIL DEGRASSE, museum director; BA in Physics, Harvard U., 1980; MA in Astronomy, U. Tex., Austin, 1983; PhD in Astrophysics, Columbia U., 1991; DS (hon.), CUNY, 1997, Ramapo Coll., 2000, Dominican Coll., 2000, U. Richmond, 2001, Bloomfield Coll., 2002. Postdoctoral rsch. assoc. dept. astrophysics Princeton U., 1991—94; staff scientist Am. Mus.-Hayden Planetarium, N.Y.C., 1994—95, acting dir., 1995—96; chair dept. astrophysics Am. Mus. Natural History, N.Y.C., 1997—99, Frederick P. Rose dir. Hayden Planetarium, 1999—. Contbr. articles to profl. jours. Named Sexiest Astrophysicist Alive, People Mag., 2000; named one of 40 under 40, Craines Mag., 1996; recipient Medal of Honor, Columbia U., 2001. Fellow: N.Y. Acad. Scis.; mem.: Nat. Soc. Black Physicists, Internat. Planetarium Soc., Astron. Soc. Pacific, Am. Phys. Soc., Am. Astron. Soc. Office: Dept Astrophysics Am Mus Natural History Central Park W at 79th St New York NY 10024

TYSON, TERRI LYNN, television programming producer, consultant; b. Dayton, Ohio, May 11, 1962; d. Charles Albert Long and Patsy Arlene Fox; m. Kirk W.M. Tyson, Mar. 25, 2000. AA, Miami-Dade C.C., 1983; BA in Theater, Fla. State U., 1985; postgrad., United Theol. Sem., 2003—. Singer, actress, 1985-91; dir. devel. Chgo. Christian Indsl. League, Chgo., 1993-95; dir. comm. Greater Chgo. Food Depository, Chgo., 1995-97; ptnr. Horizons Comms. Group, Chgo., 1997-99; pres. Piper Prodns., Inc., Chgo., 1999-2001, Tyson Chgo., 2001—. Pres.: (TV documentaries) The Corner Pub, 1997 (Emmy nomination 1997, Telly award 2000), The Long Way Home, 1998 (Emmy nomination 1998, Telly award 2000), The Hunger Heroes, 2000 (Emmy nomination 2000, Gracie Allen award 2000). Democrat. United Methodist. Office: Tyson Chgo 980 N Michigan Ave Ste 1400 Chicago IL 60611 E-mail: piperpro@aol.com.

TYSOR, RONALD W. retail executive; CFO Federated Dept. Stores, Inc., Cin., federated vice chmn. fin., real estate, 1990—. Mem. Federated Direct; pres., COO Campeau Corp., 1989. Office: Federated Dept Stores 7 W 7th St Cincinnati OH 45202

TYSZKOWSKI, ROBERT, business executive; b. Boston, May 25, 1961; s. Walter and Nora Francis (Lange) T.; m. Patricia Anne McArdle, Dec. 30, 1995. Sci. diploma, Riverside Mil. Acad., 1979; grad., U.S. Army ROTC Program, 1979; BA, U. Mass., 1983; BS, U. N.H., 1985; postgrad., Harvard U., 1985-87, 90-93. Lic. cons. Mass. Dept. Pub. Health; cert. instr. Mass. State Police. Rsch. asst. Ritzman Rsch. Lab., Durham, N.H., 1984-85; clin. pathology intern Brigham & Women's Hosp., Harvard Med. Sch., Boston, 1985-87; clin. rschr., cell biologist Mass. Gen. Hosp., Harvard Med. Sch., Boston, 1987—; CEO Lange Internat., Boston, 1987—; dir. ops. Renal Rsch. Unit, Boston, 1989—, radiation safety officer, 1990-96; exec. dir. Radiation Safety Svcs., Inc., Boston, 1996—; sr. ptnr. P.M.T. Assoc., Inc., Boston, 1996—; sr. v.p. Evidaunt Investigations, Inc., N.Y.C., 1997-99, CFO, 1999—; sr. ptnr. Back Bay Assocs., Boston, 2001—. Vice-chmn. bd. Evidaunt Investigations, Inc., Boston, 1997—; chmn. bd. Ea. Equine Assocs., Inc., Hamilton, Mass., 1985—, Lange Internat., Boston, 1987—, Radiation Safety Svcs., Inc., Boston, 1996—, Armser Corp., 1999—; mem. adv. com. U.S. Combined Tng. Assn., 1986-90, Ptnrs. Healthcare Sys., 1997—; mem. adv. bd. P.M.T. Assocs. Inc., Boston, 1996—, Middlesex County Dep. Sheriff's Assn., 2000—, Mass. Assn. Italian-Am. Police Officers, 2000—. Author: Why Children Fail, 1982, Battle in the North Georgia Hills, 1983, The Judges, Part I and II, 1987, Brief History of the Union Club of Boston, 1997, Biography of Pastor G.B. Dangers, 2000; editor, contbg. author The Centurion, 2000—, The Guardian, 2000—; contbr. numerous articles to profl. jours. Co-chmn. organizing com. Harvard-Yale Benefit Polo, Hamilton, 1990, U. N.H. Fund Raising Event, Boston, 1991; mem. organizing com. U. N.H. Equestrian Events, 1983-85, Ledyard Three-day Event, Wenham, Mass., 1987-88, 90, U. Mass. Fund Raising Drive, Amherst, 1980-81. Dana fellow, 1981-82, fellow Harvard U., 1987-89. Mem. AAAS, Am. Coll. Forensic Examiners, Am. Nuc. Soc., Admiral Nimitz Found., N.Y. Acad. Scis., Am. Soc. Notaries, Assn. of Offcl. Analytical Chemists Internat., Boston Athenaeum (life), Health Physics Soc., Inst. of Early Am. History and Culture (inst. assoc.), New Eng. Hist. Geneal. Soc., Nat. Assn. Investigative Specialists, Mus. Fine Arts/Boston, Redwood Libr. and Athenaeum, Nimitz Mus. Pacific War, Tex. State Archives, Manhattan C. of C., U.S. Ct. Tennis Assn., U.S. Golf Assn., U.S. Polo Assn., Faculty Club, Nat. Tennis Club (Newport, R.I.), Myopia Polo Club, Tennis and Racquet Club, Union Club, Univ. Club. Republican. Episcopalian. Avocations: equestrian sports, royal tennis. Office: Lange Internat PO Box 5669 Boston MA 02114-0011 also: Armser Corp 100 Park Ave Fl 16 New York NY 10017 also: Evidaunt Investigations Inc 60 State St Ste 700 Boston MA 02109-1803 E-mail: armser@aol.com.

TYTELL, JOHN, humanities educator, writer; b. Antwerp, Belgium, May 17, 1939; came to U.S., 1941; s. Charles and Lena (Gano) T.; m. Mellon Gregori, May 28, 1967. BA, CCNY, 1961; MA, NYU, 1963, PhD, 1968. Grad. reader NYU, 1963-67; lectr. Queens Coll., N.Y.C., 1963-68, assoc. prof., 1968-73, 1973-76, prof. English, 1977—; exec. editor Am. Book Rev., 1979—; vis. prof. Rutgers U., 1980, U. Paris, 1983; cons. Nat. Humanities Faculty, Ga., 1978—. Author: The American Experience, 1970, Naked Angels, 1976, Ezra Pound: The Solitary Volcano, 1987, reissued 2004, Passionate Lives, 1991, The Living Theatre: Art, Exile and Outrage, 1995, Paradise Outlaws: Remembering the Beats, 1999, Reading New York., 2003; contbr. articles to mags. including Am. Scholar, Partisan Rev., Vanity Fair, Fame. NEH fellow, 1974 Home: 69 Perry St New York NY 10014-3297 Office: Queens Coll Flushing NY 11367 Office Phone: 718-997-4654.

TYUS-SHAW, TINA, newscaster; Grad., Tenn. State U. Reporter, Macon, Ga.; anchor WSAV-TV, Savannah, Ga., 1992—, field anchor, 1995, co-anchor, lead Healthwatch corr. Recipient torchbearer, Olympic Torch Run (Ga.), 1996. Office: WSAV-TV3 1430 E Victory Dr Savannah GA 31404

TZAGOURNIS, MANUEL, endocrinologist, educator, retired dean, academic administrator; b. Youngstown, Ohio, Oct. 20, 1934; s. Adam and Argiro T.; m. Madeline Jean Kalos, Aug. 30, 1958; children: Adam, Alice, Ellen, Jack, George. BS, Ohio State U., 1956, MD, 1960, MS, 1967. Intern Phila. Gen. Hosp., 1960-61; resident Ohio State U., Columbus, 1961-63, chief med. resident, 1966-67, instr., 1967-68, asst. prof., 1968-70, assoc. prof., 1970-74, prof., 1974—, asst. dean Coll. Medicine, 1973-75, assoc. dean, med. dirs. hosps., 1975-80, v.p. health svcs., dean of medicine, 1981-95, v.p. health scis., 1995-99; pvt. practice endocrinology Columbus, 1967—; dean emeritus Coll. medicine Ohio State U., Columbus, v.p. health scis. emeritus, 2001—; mem. staff Ohio State U. Hosps./James Cancer Hosp. & Rsch. Ctr. Contbg. author: textbook Endocrinology, 1974, Clinical Diabetes: Modern Management, 1980; co-author: Diabetes Mellitus, 1983, 88; contbr. chpts. to books. Citation Ohio State Senate Resolution No. 984, 1989. Capt. U.S. Army, 1962-64; bd. trustees Hellenic Coll./Holy Cross. Recipient Homeric Order of Ahepa Cleve. chpt., 1976, Phys. of Yr. award Hellenic Med. Soc. N.Y., 1989; citations Ohio State Senate and Ho. of Reps., 1975, 83 Mem. AMA, Am. Red Cross (past chair, bd. dirs. ctrl. Ohio 1996—), Assn. Am. Med. Colls., Columbus Med. Assn., Deans' Coun. Mem. Greek Orthodox Ch. Home: 4335 Sawmill Rd Columbus OH 43220-2243 Office: Ohio State U Coll Medicine 1024 Cramblett Hall 456 W 10th Ave Columbus OH 43210-1238

TZAKIS, ANDREAS GERASIMOS, surgeon, educator, research scientist; MD, U. Athens, Greece, 1974; PhD, Nat. U. Athens, 1999. Intern Mt. Sinai Hosp., N.Y.C., 1977—78, resident surgery, 1978—79, SUNY at Stony Brook, Long Island, NY, 1979—82, chief resident surgery, 1982—83; fellow in transplantation surgery U. Pitts., 1983—85; asst. prof. surgery U. Pitts. Sch. Medicine, 1985—89, assoc. prof. surgery, 1989—94, prof. surgery, 1994, U. Miami (Fla.) Sch. Medicine, 1994. Mem. adv. bd. Archives of Gastroenterohepatology, 1997; presenter, panelist, lectr. in field. Mem. editl. bd.: Clin. Tranplantation, 1993, Transplantation, 1994, Pediat. Transplantation, 1997, Jour. Investigative Surgery, 1997, Graft, 1998, Annals Gastroenterology, 1999, Liver Transplantation, 1999; contbr. numerous articles to profl. jours. 2nd lt. Med. Corp Greek Air Force, 1974—77. Mem.: ACS, AMA, Internat. Pediat. Transplant Assn., Inc., Xenotransplantation Assn., Am. Surg. Assn., Am. Assn. for the Study of Liver Diseases, Internat. Coll. Surgeons, Am. Coll. Angiology, Internat. Pancreas and Islet Transplant Assn., Hellenic Tranplantation Soc., Soc. Internat. Surgery, Soc. U. Surgeons, Assn. for Acad. Surgery, Acad. Surg. Rsch., The Transplantation Soc., Am. Soc. Transplant Surgeons. Office: 1801 NW 9th Ave Ste 511 Miami FL 33136 E-mail: atzakis@med.miami.edu.

TZIMAS, NICHOLAS ACHILLES, orthopedic surgeon, educator; b. Greece, Apr. 18, 1928; arrived in U.S.A., 1955, naturalized, 1960. s. Archilles Nicholas and Evanthia B. (Exarchou) T.; m. Helen J. (Papastylopoulos), Apr. 22, 1958; children: Yvonne and Christina. MD, U. Athens, Greece, 1952. Intern St. Mary's Hosp., Hoboken, NJ, 1955—86; resident in gen. surgery Misericordia Hosp., N.Y.C.; resident in orthopedic surgery Bellevue Hosp., N.Y.C., NY, 1957—60; instr. orthopedic surgery N.Y. U. Sch. Medicine, 1961—63, asst. clin. prof., 1963—65, asso. clin. prof., 1965—71, clin. prof., 1971—. Mem. staff Univ. and Bellevue Hosp.; chief children's orthopedics, 1966; orthopedic cons. Inst. Rehab. Medicine, N.Y. U., 1966, St. Agnes Hosp., White Plains, N.Y., 1972; advisory com. Bur. Handicapped Children, N.Y.C., 1975; spl. invitations for tchg., Osaka, Japan, 1970, Jerusalem, 1974, São Paolo, Brazil, 1976, Taranto, Italy, 1977, Bari, Italy, 1978, Barquisimeto, Venezuela, 1979, Bogotá, Colombia, 1983, Buenos Aires, Argentina, 1983. Author of articles on spina bifida child mgmt. Served with M.C. Greek Army, 1952-55. Named Ofcl. Knight of Italian Republic, 1979 Fellow Am., Internat. Coll. Surgeons; mem. N.Y. Acad. Medicine, N.Y. State, N.Y. County Med. Soc., Am. Acad. Orthopedic Surgeons, Am. Congress Rehab. Medicine, Am. Acad. Cerebral Palsy. Mem. Greek Orthodox Ch.; Archon of the Ecumenical Patriarchate of Constantinople. Home: 33 Edgewood St Tenafly NJ 07670-2909 Office: 530 1st Ave New York NY 10016-6402 Office Phone: 212-263-7278. Personal E-mail: ntzimas@aol.com. Business E-Mail: nicholasotzimas@med.nyu.edu.

TZIMOPOULOS, NICHOLAS D. educational administrator; b. Eptachorion, Greece, Feb. 19, 1941; came to U.S., 1956; s. Demetrius and Soultana (Davos) T. BA in Chemistry and Math., U. N.H., 1965; MS in Analytical Chemistry, Boston Coll., 1967, PhD in Phys. Chemistry, 1971. Dir. rsch. So. N.H. Services, Manchester, 1978-80; prof. phys. chemistry U. Northern Fla., Jacksonville, 1981-82; chmn. math and sci. The Bartram Sch., Jacksonville, Fla., 1980-83; prof. chemistry Valencia C.C., Orlando, Fla., 1983-84; dir. sci. edn. Schs. of the Tarrytowns, North Tarrytown, N.Y., 1984-91; dir. sci., math. and tech. Lexington (Mass.) Pub. Schs., 1989—2002; pres. Omega Pub., 2002—. Adj. prof. sci. edn. Boston U., 1993—; nat. acad. advisor The Tesseract Group, Inc., 1997—. Author: Modified Null-Point Potentiometry, 1967, Irreversible Processes, 1971, mathematics-Science Curricula, 1982, Modern Chemistry, 1990, 93, Life, Earth, Physical Sciences, 1987, 90, General Sciences Books 1 and 2, 1987, 90, The Next Generation: Teachers Resources Curriculum Guide, 1993, The Stuff of Dreams: Teachers Resource Curriculum Guide, 1993. N.H. rep. N.E. Metric Action Council, 1978-80; Tufts U. del. New Eng. Energy Congress, 1978; liaison Kiwanis Regional Sci. and Engring. Fair, Jacksonville, 1983; founder N.H. Legis. Acad. Sci. and Tech., Concord, 1980; mem. operating com. Mass. Sci. Fair, 1990—. Recipient Outstanding commendations in sci. achievement Internat. Sci. and Engring. Fair, 1986, CMA Catalyst award, 1987, N.Y. State Presdl. award for excellence in sci. and math., 1989. Fellow: Signa Xi (exec. bd. Harvard U. chpt. 1998); mem.: NSTA (coordination and superision sci. edn. com. 2001—), ASCD, AAAS, Nat. Sci. Tchrs. Assn., Fla. Acad. Sci., N.Y. Acad. Sci., Am. Chem. Soc. (Fla. congl. del. 1984, treas. Fla. sect. 1983, 1984, chmn. Jacksonville sect. 1982—83, dir. Westchester County, N.Y. sub-sect. 1986—, high sch. esams. com. 1982—86, Outstanding Chem. Tchr. Fla. 1982, S F U.S. 1983, Nichols award 1986), Greek Orthodox Youth Assn. (pres. Manchester, N.H. 1963—65), Rotary Internat. Democrat. Avocations: photography, classical music, guitar, travel, soccer.

TZITSIKAS, HELENE, retired Hispanic literature educator; b. Athens, Greece, Apr. 2, 1926; came to U.S., 1944; d. Christos Jean and Evangelia (Chouases) T. BA, Lake Forest (Ill.) Coll., 1952; MA, Northwestern U., 1954, PhD, 1963. Instr. Rockford (Ill.) Coll., 1962-63, asst. prof., 1963-65; assoc. prof. Hispanic lit. Mich. State U., East Lansing, 1965-71, prof., 1971-91, prof. emerita, 1991—. Author: Santiago Ramón y Cajal-Obra Literaria, 1965, El Persaniento Español 1898-1899, 1967, Fernando Santiván - Humanista y Literato, 1971, 2d edit., 1985, Dos Revistas Chilenas: Los Diez y Artes y Letras, 1973, El sentimiento Ecológico, 1977, La supervivencia existencial de la mujer, 1982, El Quijotismo y la raza en la Generacion de 1898, 1988, Los exiliados argentinos en Montevideo durante la éoca de Rosas, 1991. Recipient Diana award YWCA, Lansing, Mich., 1988, cert. of employee recognition, 1988. Mem. MLA, AAUP, MLA Am., Am. Assn. Tchrs. Spanish and Portuguese, Univ. Club Mich. State U., Daus. Penelope. Greek Orthodox. Avocations: theater, music, painting, gardening, literary research. Office: Mich State U Dept Romance and Classical Langs East Lansing MI 48824

TZOU, ROBERT DA, engineering educator; b. Koashong, Taiwan, Sept. 3, 1955; s. Tze-Shing and Moo-Lang T.; m. Na Li Tzou; children: Patricia, Andy. BSME, Nat. Cheng-Kung U., Taiwan, 1979; PhD in Applied Mechanics, Lehigh U., Bethlehem, Pa., 1987. Asst. prof. dept. mech. engring. U. N.Mex., Albuquerque, 1988-92, assoc. prof. dept. mech. engring., 1992-96; prof. dept. mech. and aerospace engring. U. Mo., Columbia, 1996-97, prof., chmn. dept. mech. and aerospace engring., 1997—. Keynote lectr. 1997 Brazilian Congress of Mech. Engring., Macro-to Microscale Heat Transfer: The Lagging Behavior; invited spkr. SPIE 44th Annual Meeting and Exhbn., Ultrafast Heat Transport: The Lagging Behavior, 1999. Author: Annual Review of Heat Transfer, Vol. IV, 1992, Macro-to Microscale Heat Transfer: The Lagging Behavior, 1997. Recipient Rsch. Excellence award U. N.Mex., Albuquerque, 1994, Teaching Excellence award U. N.Mex., Albuquerque, 1991. Fellow ASME; mem. Sigma Xi Soc. Scientific Rsch., Tau Beta Pi Nat. Soc. Engring. Sci., Pi Tau Sigma Nat. Soc. Mech. Engring. Office: Dept Mech & Aerospace Engr University Of Missouri Columbia MO 65211-0001 Fax: 573-884-5090. E-mail: TzourR@missouri.edu.

UBALDI, MICHAEL VINCENT, lawyer; b. Stockton, Calif., May 2, 1948; s. Ben Raymond and Audrey Grace (Smalley) U.; m. Terryanne Ubaldi (div. Apr. 1990); children: Jennifer N., Justin M.; m. Linda A. Ubaldi, Feb. 14, 1991. BA, Calif. State U., Sacramento, 1971; JD, U. Calif., San Francisco, 1974. Bar: Calif. 1974. Assoc. Bullen, McKone & McKinley, Sacramento, 1974-81; ptnr. Duncan, Ball, Evans & Ubaldi, Sacramento, 1981—. Bd. dirs. Sutter Hosps. Found., Sacramento, 1985-92, Make-A-Wish Found., Sacramento, 1990-98, Mercy Hosps. Found., Sacramento, 1993—; mem. bus. adv. bd. Sch. Bus. Calif. State U., Sacramento, 1999—. Mem. No. Calif. Assn. Def. Counsel (bd. dirs. 1998—). Avocations: golf, art, travel. Office: Duncan Ball Evans & Ubaldi 641 Fulton Ave Fl 2D Sacramento CA 95825-4800

UBELL, EARL, writer, consultant; b. Bklyn., June 21, 1926; s. Charles and Hilda (Kramer) U.; m. Shirley Leitman, Feb. 12, 1949; children— Lori Ellen, Michael Charles. BS, CCNY, 1948; DSc (hon.), N.Y. Tech., 2001. With N.Y. Herald Tribune, 1943-66, successively messenger, asst. sec. to mng. editor, reporter, 1943-53, sci. editor, 1953-66, syndicated columnist, 1956-66; sci. commentator MBS, 1958-59; spl. sci. editor WNEW, N.Y., 1962; health and sci. editor WCBS-TV, N.Y.C., 1966-72, 78-95; health editor PARADE mag., 1983-97, contbg. editor, 1997—. Dir. TV news NBC News, N.Y.C., 1972-76; producer spl. broadcasts TV news, 1976-78; producer documentaries Medicine in America, 1977, Escape from Madness, 1977; author: The World of Push and Pull, 1964, The World of The Living, 1965, The World of Candle and Color, 1969, How to Save Your Life, 1972, (with Carol C. Flax) Mother/Father/You, 1980, (with Randi Londer) Parade Family Health Companion, 1996. Pres. Council Advancement Sci. Writing, Inc., 1960-66, bd. dirs., 1960-96, founder, 1996—; chmn. Center Modern Dance Edn., Inc., 1962-82; pres. North Jersey Cultural Coun., 1966-72; bd. dirs. Dance Notation Bur., 1968—, chmn. bd., 1975-94; bd. dirs. Sex Info. and Edn. Council U.S., 1967-69, YMHA, Bergen County, 1968-73, Nat. Center Health Edn., 1977. Served as aviation radioman USNR, 1944-46 . Recipient Mental Health Bell award N.Y. State Soc. Mental Health, 1957, Albert Lasker med. journalism award, 1958, Nat. Assn. Mental Health award for radio program, 1962, Sci. Writers award Am. Psychol. Found., 1965, Westinghouse award AAAS, 1960, Empire State award, 1963, TV Reporting award N.Y. Assoc. Press, 1969, 71, N.Y. Emmy award, 1971, Samuelson award N.Y. League for Hard of Hearing, Legal-Med. award Milton Helpern Library of Legal Medicine, Spl. Achievement award Deadline Club, 1982, Disting. Contbn. award, 1983, Nat. Media award Am. Diabetes Assn., 1985, N.Y. State Mental Health Council award, 1987, Ann. Svc. award Dance Notation Bur., 1990. Mem. Nat. Assn. Sci. Writers (pres. 1960-61), Nuclear Energy Writers Assn. (pres. 1965-66), Phi Beta Kappa (pres. Gamma chpt. 1976-77). *I learn something new, in depth, every 5 years—x-ray crystallography, French, statistics, polling, stock market—I am refreshed.*

UBELL, ROBERT NEIL, editor, publisher, educator, consultant; b. Bklyn., Sept. 14, 1938; s. Charles and Hilda (Kramer) U.; m. Rosalyn Deutsche, Sept. 24, 1976; children: Jennifer Hayslett-Ubell, Elizabeth Miller. BA, Bklyn. Coll., 1961; postgrad., Acad. Fine Arts, Rome, Italy, 1959-60, CUNY, 1961-62, Pratt Graphic Arts Workshop, N.Y.C., 1972-73. Assoc. editor Nuclear Industry, Atomic Indsl. Forum, 1962-64; from editor to sr. editor Plenum Pub. Corp., N.Y.C., 1965-70, v.p., editor in chief, 1970-76; editor The Sciences, N.Y. Acad. Scis., N.Y.C., 1976-79; Am. pub. Nature, N.Y.C., 1979-83; founding pub. Nature Biotechnology, 1983; pres. Robert Ubell Assocs., N.Y.C., 1983-97, BioMedNet, Ltd., 1996-97; exec. v.p. Marcel Dekker, Inc., N.Y.C., 1997-99; dir. web-based distance learning Stevens Inst. Tech., Hoboken, NJ, 1999—2001, dean online learning, 2001—03, dean sch. profl. edn., 2004—. Instr. MIT, 1987, Columbia U. Coll. Physicians and Surgeons, 1987; mem. editl. com. The Scientist, 1987-90; mem. Book Industry Study Group, Inc., 1992; vis. com. Nat. Acad. Press, NRC, NAS, 1986; books subcom. Am. Inst. Physics, 1985-91; awards com. Am. Inst. Physics-U.S. Steel Sci. Writing Awards, 1982-83; publs. com. Am. Inst. Biol. Scis., 1994, N.Y. Acad. Scis., 1976-97; cons. Lotus Devel. Corp., 1987-89, Coalition for Networked Info., 1995-98, Am. Soc. Addiction Medicine, 2003—; pub. info. com. Nat. Acad. Engring., 1989—; program com. Soc. Scholarly Pub., 1989-91; rev. panel NSF, 2000, 03, Nat. Sci., Math. and Tech. Edn. Digital Libr., 2000, Internat. Opportunities Scientists and Engrs., 2003, Reform Undergrad. Engring. Edn., 2003; distance learning observer Middle States Commn. on Higher Edn., 2000—; chair Sloan Found. Greater N.Y.C. ALN Conf., N.Y.C., 2002; mem. planning com. Breakthrough Thinking in Online Bus. Edn., 2002-03; mem. adv. panel Nat. Rsch Inst. on Wireless Tech. in Edn. and Industry, 2002; mem. adv. coun. Alliance Expanded Tchr. Preparation Cmty. Colls.; co-host Stevens Views Radio, 2002—; adv. bd. comm. industry network N.J. Tech. Coun., 2002—, Sloan Found. Corp. e-Learning, 2003—; prin. investigator Sloan Greater N.Y.C. Online Learning Ctr., 2003-; co-chair Sloan Edn. Corp. U. Online Learning Bd. Dirs., 2003—, Slaon Workshop Corp.-Acad. Online Learning, 2004; cons. in field. Author: (with Marvin Leiner) Children Are the Revolution, 1974; (with Mark Tesoriero) Negotiating Networked Licensing Agreements, 1995, Cost Centers and Measures in the Networked Information Value Chain, 1997, The R&D Economics in the Digital Environment, 1998; editor Nature Directory of Biologicals, 1981, Physics Today Buyer's Guide, 1984-89; exec. editor: Linguistics: The Cambridge Survey, 1987-88, Pre-Med Handbook, 1986, International Encyclopedia of the Social Sciences, Vol. 19, 1991, Encyclopedia of Astronomy and Astrophysics, 1991, Sci. Am. Triumph of Discovery, 1995, Oxford Encyclopedia of Climate and Weather, 1996; cons. editor ISI Press, 1985-87, Am. Inst. of Physics Book Program, 1986-96; Am. Chem. Soc. Book Program, 1989; cons. pub. Computers in Physics, 1987-91; series editor Masters of Modern Physics, 1991-96, Creators of Modern Chemistry, 1994-95, Sci. Am. Focus, 1995-96; mem. editl. bd. ISI Press, 1986-90, Grants Mag., 1981-85, Nonprofit Mgmt. and Fin., 1980-85; editl. dir. Nutrition Advisor, 1998-99; mem. editl. bd. Innovations in End of Life Care, 1999-2003; editl. advisor Cancer Practice, Am. Cancer Soc., 1997-98; contbr. articles to profl. jours. Chmn. bd. Woodword Sch., 1971-74; adv. com. Children's TV Workshop, 1980; bd. dirs. Parkinson's Walk Found., 2001—, Hekate, 2003-04. Mem. AAAS, ASTD, N.Y. Acad. Scis. (mem. publs. com. 1976-97), Nat. Assn. Sci. Writers. Office: Stevens Inst Tech WebCampusStevens Castle Point Hudson Hoboken NJ 07030 Business E-Mail: rubell@stevens.edu.

UBERALL, HERBERT MICHAEL STEFAN, physicist, researcher; b. Neunkirchen, Austria, Oct. 14, 1931; arrived in U.S., 1953, naturalized, 1963; s. Michael and Stefanie U.; m. Reyna Tosta, 1981; children by previous marriage: Bernadette Chauvallon, Bertrand. PhD, U. Vienna, Austria, 1953, Cornell U., 1956; PhD (honoris causa), U. Le Havre, France, 1987. Staff mem. Signal Corps Labs., Ft. Monmouth, N.J., 1953-54; research asst. Cornell U., 1954-56; research fellow Nuclear Physics Research Lab., U. Liverpool, Eng., 1956-57; Ford Found. fellow CERN, Geneva, Switzerland, 1957-58; research physicist Carnegie Inst. Tech., Pitts., 1958-60; asst. prof. U. Mich., Ann Arbor, 1960-64; assoc. prof. Cath. U. Am., Washington, 1964-65, prof. physics, 1965-94, prof. emeritus, 1994—. Vis. prof. U. Paris VII Jussieu, 1984-85, U. Le Havre, 1990, 92, 94, 96, U. Bordeaux, 1993, 95, U. Aix-Marseille II and Lab. Mech. Acoustics, 1995, Ecole Centrale de Lille, 1997, Tech. U. Denmark, 1998; cons. Naval Rsch. Lab., Washington, 1966-92. Author: Electron Scattering from Complex Nuclei, 1971; co-author: Giant Resonance Phenomena, 1980, Nuclear Pion Photoproduction, 1991; editor: Acoustic Resonance Scattering, 1992; co-editor: Long Distance Neutrino Detection, 1979, Classical and Quantum Dynamics, 1991, Coherent Radiation Sources, 1985, Coherent Radiation Processes in Strong Fields, 1991, Radar Target Imaging, 1994; contbr. 300 articles to profl. jours. Recipient Fgn. medal French Soc. Acoustics, 1996. Fellow IEEE, Am. Phys. Soc., Acoustical Soc. Am., Washington Acad. Scis. (Achievement award 1984); mem. AAUP, ASEE, Am. Acad. Mech., Electromagnetics Acad., Internat. Union Radio Sci. Office: Catholic U Dept Physics Washington DC 20064-0001 Home: 2500 G St NW #519 Washington DC 20007-4364 E-mail: uberallh@msn.com.

UBEROI, MAHINDER SINGH, aerospace engineer, researcher; b. Delhi, India, Mar. 13, 1924; arrived in U.S., 1945, naturalized, 1960; s. Kirpal Singh and Sulaksha (Kochar) Uberoi. BS, Punjab U., Lahore, India, 1944; MS, Calif. Inst. Tech., 1946; DEng, Johns Hopkins U., 1952. Registered profl. engr. Mem. faculty U. Mich., Ann Arbor, 1953-63, prof. aerospace engring., 1959-63, vis. prof., 1963—64; prof. U. Colo., Boulder, 1963—2000, chmn. dept. aerospace engring., 1963-75; fellow F. Joint Inst. Lab. Astrophysics, Boulder, 1963-74; rschr., 2004—. Exch. scientist Soviet Acad. Scis., 1966, U.S. Nat. Acad. Scis.; invited prof. U. Que., Canada, 1972—74; vis. scientist Max Planck Inst. Astrophysics, Munich, 1974; hon. rsch. fellow Harvard U., 1975—76. Contbr. articles to profl. jours.; editor: Cosmic Gas Dynamics, 1974. Coun. mem. Ednl. TV Channel 6, Inc., Denver, 1963—66. Guggenheim fellow, Royal Inst. Tech., Sweden, 1958. Mem.: Am. Phys. Soc., Tau Beta Pi. Home: 819 6th St Boulder CO 80302-7418

UBINGER, JOHN W., JR., lawyer; b. Pitts., Jan. 31, 1949; BBA cum laude, Ohio U., 1970; JD, U. Notre Dame, 1973. Bar: Pa. 1973. Ptnr. Jones Day, Pitts. Instr. environ. dispute resolution Duquesne U. Bd. dirs. Pa. Environ. Coun., chmn. task force on reuse of indsl. sites, 1994-95; bd. dirs. Allegheny Land Trust, 1993-2003; adv. com. Allegheny County Dept. Air Pollution Control, 1992-95, Allegheny County Contaminated Sites Redevel. Study, 1994-95. Fellow: Air and Waste Mgmt. Assn. (chmn. Western Pa. sect. 1989—90); mem.: ABA (natural resources, energy, environ. law and alternative dispute resolution sects.), Assn. Conflict Resolution (practitioner/educator/rschr. membership), Allegheny County Bar Assn. (chmn. environ. law sect. 1991), Environ. Law Inst. (assoc.), Pa. Bar Assn. (chmn. environ., mineral and natural resources law sect. 1990—91). Office: Jones Day 1 Mellon Ctr 500 Grant St Pittsburgh PA 15219-2502 Office Phone: 412-394-7908. E-mail: jwunbinger@jonesday.com.

UBUKA, TOSHIHIKO, biochemist, educator, academic administrator; b. Kagaminocho, Okayama, Japan, Jan. 31, 1934; s. Yoshio and Shigeko (Hashimoto) U.; m. Satoko Iwamiya, Oct. 18, 1960; children: Takayoshi, Hiromi, Atsue. MD, Okayama U., 1959, PhD, 1964. Rsch. assoc. Med. Coll. Cornell U., NYC, 1968—71; with Okayama U., 1964-73, asst. prof., 1973-80, assoc. prof. Med. Sch., 1980-81, prof. Med. Sch., 1981-99, dean Med. Sch., 1997-99, prof. emeritus, 1999—; prof., dean Kawasaki U. of Med. Welfare, 1999—2001, prof., v.p., 2001—. Co-author: Methods in Enzymology, vol. 143, 1987; editor Acta Med. Okayama, 1980-99, Physiol. Chem. Phys. and Med. NMR, 1982—, Amino Acids, 1991—; chief editor Acta Med. Okayama, 1987-90. Fellow Japanese Biochem. Soc., Japanese Soc. Nutrition and Food Sci.; mem. AAAS, NY Acad. Scis., Internat. Soc. Amino Acid Rsch., Soc. Study Inborn Errors Metabolism, The Protein Soc. Achievements include research in sulfur biochemistry, sulfur nutrition, cysteine metabolism in mammals, protein modification with mixed disulfides; inborn errors of cysteine metabolism, analysis of sulfur compounds. Avocation: Kendo (Japanese fencing). Home: 527-1 Nishikarakawa Okayama 701-1213 Japan Office: Kawasaki U Med Welfare De Clin Nutrition 288 Matsushima Kurashiki Okayama 701-0193 Japan

UCCIARDO, FRANK JOSEPH, television journalist, reporter; b. N.Y.C. s. Joseph J. and Jeanne Barraca Ucciardo. BFA in Comms., MA in Comms., N.Y. Inst. Tech. UN corr. Mut. Radio Network, N.Y.C.; corr. Newsday, Melville, N.Y., CNN Cable News Network, N.Y.C.; anchorman Fin. News Network, N.Y.C.; corr. NBC Radio Network, N.Y.C.; bur. chief UPI Radio, N.Y.C.; reporter NEWS 12, L.I., N.Y.; TV journalist, investigative reporter Sta. WPIX-TV, N.Y.C.; film cameraman, editor Channel 67, Action News, Long Island, N.Y.; dir., prodr. All Points Broadcasting, N.Y.C.; reporter Sta. WOR-Radio 710, N.Y.C.; corr., anchorman Sta. WLIW-TV PBS, Garden City, N.Y.; anchor, reporter Sta. WATR-TV, Channel 20, Waterbury, Conn.; reporter Sta. WNEW Radio, N.Y.C.; TV journalist, investigative reporter UPN 9 News, Secaucus, N.J., 2000—. Writer, dir., prodr.: (documentary) The Berlin Candy Bomber, 1998 (Deadline Club News Feature award Soc. Profl. Journalists 1999). Folio award for investigative reporting L.I. Coalition for Fair Broadcasting, 1996, (2), 2000, award for investigative journalism Silaurian Soc. N.Y.; RIAS fellow in econs. and politics. Mem. UN Corrs. Assn. (broadcasting chmn. UN hdqs. 1996), Soc. Profl. Journalists (treas. Deadline club, Deadline Club News Feature award 1999), Am. Fedn. Radio & T.V. Artists, NATAS (N.Y. chpt., Emmy award N.Y. chpt. 1997), N.Y. Press Club (emeritus mem.), Drama Desk of N.Y., Press Club L.I. Avocations: travel, cinema, dance, boating, theater. E-mail: unca42@usa.net.

UCHIDA, KINYA, consumer products company executive; Joined Canon, Inc., 1963, with camera export divsn.; joined Canan L.Am., Panama, 1969; pres. Canon, Inc., Brazil, Canon, Inc., L.Am., Inc., 1979, Canon, Inc., Singapore, 1986, Canon France S.A., 1995; pres., CEO Canon USA, Inc., Lake Success, NY, 1999—, also bd. dirs., sr. mng. dir. bd. dirs., 2004. Office: Canon USA Inc One Canon Plaza Lake Success NY 11042*

UCHIDA, MITSUKO, pianist; b. Dec. 20, 1948; d. Fujio and Yasuko Uchida. Student, Hochschule für Musik, Vienna, Austria. Artist-in-residence Cleve. Orch., 2001—. Performer: performs regularly with Berlin Philharm., Vienna Philharm., Cleve. Orch., L.A. Philharm., Chgo. Symphony Orch., others, recs. include complete piano sonatas and concertos of Mozart, Beethoven's piano concertos, Debussy's Etudes, Schubert Sonatas and Impromptus, Schoenberg Piano Concerto, Carnegie Hall recital series Mitsuko Uchida: Vienna Revisited, 2002—. Recipient Gramophone award, 2001, Instrumental Award, Royal Philharm. Soc., 2004. Avocation: music. Address: Van Walsum Mgmt Ltd 4 Addison Bridge Pl London W14 8XP England E-mail: chouse@vanwalsum.com.

UCHIDA, PRENTISS SUSUMU, entrepreneur, management executive; b. Nov. 30, 1940; s. Fred Toshio and Elise Chiyoye (Kurasaki) U.; m. Patrica Ann White, Oct. 17, 1981; children: S. Akemi, Toshio C., K. Kansai P. BA, San Jose State U., 1963; postgrad., Santa Clara U. Bus. Sch., 1965, Stanford U. Exec. Inst., 1975. Programmer Lockheed Missiles & Space Co., Sunnyvale, Calif., 1963-66, Adage Inc., L.A., 1966-69; founder, pres., chmn. Vector Gen. Inc., Woodland Hills, Calif., 1969-79; pres. InnerGame Corp., L.A., 1979-83; chmn. bd., CEO Secom Gen. Corp., Calabasas, Calif., 1984-86; pres. Rice Sys. Co., Calabasas, 1981-89. Bd. dirs. chmn. bd. dirs. Potter Electronics, Inc., Yanceyville, N.C., 1984-86, Secom Communications Co., Southfield, Mich., 1984-86, Nickel Equipment Co., Grand Rapids, Mich., 1985-86; mgmt. cons., Agoura, Calif., 1986-87; real estate developer, Palm Beach County, Fla., 1987-91, Futurestrader, Jupiter, Fla., 1989-91, Clear Resource Corp., Agoura Hills, Calif., 1989—; nat. mktg. dir. and ind. distbr. Nat. Safety Assocs., Memphis, 1990-97, pres. VanderBolt Co., 1995-98, Getbetter, Inc., Comm. and Mktg., Agoura Hills, Calif., 1998—, InKahootz, Inc., San Francisco, 2001-2003. Mem. adv. com. Stanford U. Exec. Inst., 1975—76; bd. dirs. United Crusade/United Way, 1977—79. Mem. Assn. Computer Machinery, Am. Mgmt. Assn., Aircraft Owners and Pilots Assn., Jupiter C. of C., Thousand Lakes/Westlake Village C. of C., Calabasas C. of C.

UCHIN, ROBERT ALLEN, dean, endodontist; b. Phila., Apr. 19, 1933; s. Harry and Doris (Goodman) U.; m. Marlene Florence Neiman; children: Andrew, Richard, Carol. Student, Franklin and Marshall Coll., 1951-53; DDS, Temple U., 1957. Diplomate Am. Bd. Endodontics. Fellow research teaching. dept. endodontics Temple U., Phila., 1959-60, instr. Sch. of Dentistry, 1960-69; co-chmn. endodontic sect. Dade County (Fla.) Dental Research Clinic, 1961-75; founding v.p., chmn. Endodontic sect. Broward County (Fla.) Dental Research Clinic, 1974-79; clin. assoc. Sch. of Dentistry U. Fla., Gainsville, 1970; practice dentistry specializing in endodontics Ft. Lauderdale, Fla., 1960—; assoc. dean, dir. extramural programs Coll. Dental Medicine, Nova Southeastern U., Ft. Lauderdale, Fla., 1996—2002, dean, 2002—. Chmn. Endodontic sect. Atlantic Coast Research Clinic, 1971-75; vis. lectr. Emory U., 1965, U.N.C., 1970, 72, U. Wash., 1972, U. Pitts., 1974, U. Pa., 1973—; cons. VA Hosp., Miami, 1968-86, Cen. Office, 1972-84, dir. endodontic residency, 1972-79; bd. dirs., founding chmn. Gold Coast Savs. and Loan Assn. of Fla., 1984—, Commonwealth Savs. and Loan of Fla., Ft. Lauderdale, 1979-84; adv. dir. Landmark First Nat. Bank, Ft. Lauderdale, 1974-81. Assoc. editor Jour. Endodontics and Traumatology, 1981-89; contbr. numerous articles to profl. jours. Pres., Temple Emanu-El Reform Congrega-

tion, Ft. Lauderdale, 1967-69; trustee, Vanguard Sch., Haverford, Pa., 1971-77; bd. dirs., Vanguard Sch., Ft. Lauderdale, 1970-73, Performing Arts Found., Broward County, Fla., 1986—. Served to capt. USAF, 1957-59. Fellow Am. Assn. Endodontists (pres. 1976); mem. Fla. Dental Assn. (past pres.), Broward County Dental Assn. (pres. 1982), Rotary (pres. Ft. Lauderdale 1969-70). Republican. Jewish. Avocations: fly fishing, stamp collecting/philately, orchids. Office: Coll Dental Medicine Nova Southeastern U 3200 S Univ Dr Fort Lauderdale FL 33328*

UCHITELLE, LOUIS, journalist; b. N.Y.C., Mar. 21, 1932; s. Abraham and Alice Lee (Cronbach) U.; m. Joan Eva Shapiro, Oct. 7, 1966; children: Isabel Anne, Jennifer Emily. BA, U. Mich., 1954. Reporter Mt. Vernon (N.Y.) Daily Argus, 1955-57; with AP, 1957-80, fgn. corr. and bur. chief, 1964-67, Buenos Aires, 1967-73; supervising editor AP Newsfeatures, N.Y.C., 1974-76; bus. news editor AP, 1977-80; asst. bus. and fin. editor N.Y. Times, 1980-87, econ. writer, 1987—. Instr. journalism Sch. Gen. Studies, Columbia U., 1976-89. Home: 11 Ridgecrest W Scarsdale NY 10583-2046 Office: NY Times 229 W 43rd St New York NY 10036-3959 Office Phone: 212-556-1705. Business E-Mail: louisu@nytimes.com.

UCHUPI, ELAZAR, geologist, researcher; b. N.Y.C., Oct. 31, 1928; parents Alfonso and Carmen (Urbizu) U. BS, CCNY, 1952; MS, U. So. Calif., 1954, PhD, 1962. Rsch. asst. U. So. Calif., L.A., 1955-62, Woods Hole (Mass.) Oceanographic Inst., 1962-64, assoc. scientist, 1964-79; sr. scientist Woods Hole (Mass.) Oceanog. Inst., 1979-93, sr. scientist emeritus, 1993—. J. Seward Johnson chmn. oceanography, 1989-93. Mem. Gulf of Mexico panel Joint Oceanog. Instns. Deep Earth Sampling, 1972-74; mem. Sci. Com. for Oceanic Rsch. Working Group 41, 1973-74; mem. steering com. U.S. Oceanog. Office Relief Map Worlds' Oceans; mem. site survey panel Joint Oceanog. Instns., 1978-85; compiler geol. maps on ocean margin drilling; adj. rschr. Inst. Exploration, Mystic, Conn., 1997—. Mem. editl. staff Offshore Mag., 1972-74, Marine Geology, 1971-75; co-author 4 books North Atlantic, geology of Atlantic Ocean, and morphology of rocky mems. of Solar Sys. Recipient cert. of recognition Nat. Assn. Geology Tchrs., Inc., and its Crustal evolution Edn. project, 1979, medal editl. adv. bd. Offshore Mag., 1974, Frances P. Shepard award, 1991. Mem. Am. Geophys. Union, Archeol. Inst. Am., Sociedad Geologica de Espana. Achievements include research in seismic reflection, magnetic and gravity profiles of the eastern Atlantic continental margin and adjacent deep seafloor, Caribbean, Bahamas, Iberian Margins, New England margin, Branefield Trough, South Scotia Ridge, Canary Islands, Red Sea, Persian Gulf, Gulf of Oman, Black Sea, Egyptian Margin, Western Mediterranean, East Pacific Rise, Mohns Ridge, suspended matter and other properities of surface waters of the northeastern Atlantic Ocean, the continental margin off western Africa: Angola to Sierra Leone, Senegal to Portugal, sediments of 3 bays of Baja, Calif.: Sebastian Viscaino, San Cristobal and Todos Santos, characteristics of sediments of the mainland shelf of southern Calif., submarine geology of the Santa Rosa-Cortes Ridge, sediments on the continental margin off eastern U.S., the continental slope between San Francisco and Cedrow Island, Mex., sediments of the Palos Verdes shelf, sediments and topography of Kane Basin, statistical parameters of Cape Cod Beach and eolian sands, basins of Gulf of Mex., structure of Georges Bank, and the continental margin of the Atlantic coast of the U.S. and off west Africa, topography and structure of Northeast Channel, Gulf of Mex., and Cashes Ledge, Gulf of Maine, distribution and geologic structure of Triassic rocks in the Bay of Fundy and the northeastern part of the Gulf of Maine, microrelief of the continental margin south of Cape Lookout, N.C., shallow structure of the Straits of Fla., sub-surface morphology of L.I., Block Island, Rhode Island sounds, and Buzzards Bay, bathymetry of the Gulf of Mex., slumping on the continental margin southeast of L.I., N.Y., woody debris on the mainland shelf off Ventura, southern Calif., the continental margin south of Cape Hatteras, N.C., the Atlantic continental shelf and slope of the U.S., geological structure of the continental margin off Gulf Coast of the U.S., and more. Office: Woods Hole Oceanographic Inst Dept Geology Geophysic Woods Hole MA 02543

UCKO, DAVID ALAN, museum consultant; b. N.Y.C., July 9, 1948; s. Lawrence L. and Helen H. Ucko; m. Barbara Alice Clark, Aug. 13, 1977; 1 child, Aaron. BA, Columbia Coll., N.Y.C., 1969; PhD, MIT, 1972. Asst. prof. chemistry Hostos C.C., CUNY, Bronx, 1972-76, Antioch Coll., Yellow Springs, Ohio, 1976-79, assoc. prof. chemistry, 1979; rsch. coord. Mus. Sci. and Industry, Chgo., 1979-80, dir. sci., 1981-87, v.p., 1986-87; dep. dir. Calif. Mus. Sci. and Industry, L.A., 1987-90; pres. Kansas City (Mo.) Mus., 1990-2000, Sci. City at Union Sta., 1999-2000; exec. dir. Koshland Sci. Mus. and Sci. Outreach, NAS, Washington, 2001—02; pres. Mus. + More LLC, 2002—; program dir. Informal Sci. Edn. NSF, 2003—; guest faculty mus. mgmt. program U. Colo., Boulder, Colo., 2001. Rsch. assoc., assoc. prof. dept. edn. U. Chgo., 1982—87; adj. staff scientist C. F. Kettering Rsch. Lab., Yellow Springs, 1977—79. Author: (book) Basics for Chemistry, 1982, Living Chemistry, 2d edit., 1986; contbr. articles to profl. jours.; host, prodr. (radio program) Science Alive!, 1983—87, developer numerous mus. exhibits. Apptd. Nat. Mus. Svcs. Bd., 1996—2003; trustee Mus. Without Walls, 1996—2000, Sci. Pioneers, 2000. Recipient Up and Comers award, Jr. Achievement Mid.-Am., 1992; fellow Woodrow Wilson, 1969, NIH postdoctoral, 1972; grantee, NSF, NEH, U.S. Dept. Edn., Ill. Humanities Coun., 1976—88. Fellow: AAAS (at large sect. Y 1987—93); mem.: Am. Assn. Museums (mus. assessment program adv. com. 2000—03), Assn. Sci. Tech. Ctrs. (publs. com. 1984—94, chmn. 1988—94, ethics com. 1994—95, legis. com., chmn. 1996—2000), Phi Lambda Upsilon, Sigma Xi, Alpha Sigma Nu (hon.). Home: 2528 Queen Anne's Ln NW Washington DC 20037-2148

UCKO, FRANZ, research scientist, consultant, writer; b. Kattowitz, Silesia, Germany, Sept. 28, 1919; naturalized, 1946; s. Arthur and Else Ucko; m. Betty Jean Eshelman, Mar. 20, 1948 (div. Feb. 1993); children: John Arthur (dec.), Marianne Elizabeth; m. Ruth Helene Holmes, July 1, 1997 (dec. Oct. 16, 2002). Degree in mech. engring., Technische Hochschule, Berlin, Germany, 1939. Dir. R&D Buckbee-Mears Co., St. Paul, 1949-59; mgr. microlithography Motorola Semiconductors, Phoenix, 1960-63; sr. rsch. scientist Control Data Corp., Mpls., 1964-86. Rsch. cons. Cross Tech., Mpls., 1987-90. Author: A New Beginning, 1993, The Story of the Photomask, Love One Another: A Story of the Extermination of an Indigenous People; patentee in field; contbr. articles to profl. jours. Chair citizens adv coun. Hubbs Ctr. for Continuing Learning, St. Paul, 1999. With U.S. Army, 1945-47, lt., 1947-48, PTO. Recipient Outstanding Svc. award St. Paul Cmty. Edn. Adv. Coun., 2001. Presbyterian. Avocations: writing, lithographic jewelry making. Congregationalist. Home: 664 Sextant Ave W Roseville MN 55113-3425

UDAGAWA, TAKESHI, physicist, researcher; b. Tokyo, May 3, 1932; arrived in U.S., 1970; s. Saheiji Udagawa and Teruko (Yamazaki) Urayama; m. Yukiko Amano, Mar. 20, 1960 (dec. Oct. 1989); children: Yoichi, Taturo; m. Mami Eto, Apr. 15, 1991. BS, Tokyo Inst. Sci., 1957; MS, Tokyo U. of Edn., 1959, PhD, 1962. Instr. Tokyo Inst. Tech., 1962-64; rsch. assoc. Fla. State U., Tallahassee, 1964-66; rsch. fellow Niels Bohn Inst., Copenhagen, 1966-68; assoc. prof. Kyoto (Japan) U., 1968-70; prof. dept. physics U. Tex., Austin, 1970—. Rsch. fellow Kernforschungsanlage, Juelich, Germany, 1981—95. Contbr. articles to profl. jours. Recipient Fgn. Mins. commendation in Commemoration of 150th Anniversary Japan/U.S. Relationship, 2004; Rsch. grantee, Dept. Energy, Washington, 1970—96. Mem.: Japanese Phys. Soc., Am. Phys. Soc. Achievements include contributions to various aspects of nuclear reaction theories. Home: 4018 Amy Cir Austin TX 78759-8146 Office: U Tex Dept Physics Austin TX 78712 Office Phone: 512-471-1984. Business E-Mail: udagawa@physics.utexas.edu.

UDALL, CALVIN HUNT, lawyer; b. St. Johns, Ariz., Oct. 23, 1923; s. Grover C. and Dora (Sherwood) U.; m. Doris Fuss, Dec. 11, 1943; children: Fredric, Margaret Udall Moses, Julie (Mrs. Blair M. Nash), Lucinda Udall Romney, Tina Udall Rodriguez. LL.B., U. Ariz., 1948. Bar: Ariz. 1948. Ptnr. Fennemore Craig, 1953—. Ariz. spl. counsel Arizona v. California, 1954-62; mem. Coun. on Legal Edn. Opportunity, 1983-93. Mem. cast, Phoenix Mus. Theatre, 1959-65. Fellow Am. Coll. Trial Lawyers, Am. Bar Found. (bd. dirs. 1986-89, fellows chmn. 1988-89), Ariz. Bar Found. (Disting. Svc. award 1993); mem. ABA (ho. dels. 1962-92, bd. govs. 1981-84, exec. com. 1983-84, chmn. task force on minorities 1984-86), Maricopa County Bar Assn. (pres. 1957, Disting. Pub. Svc. award 1986), State Bar Ariz. (bd. govs. 1960-65), Ariz. Law Coll. Assn. (bd. dirs. 1967-80, pres. 1978-79, U. Ariz. Disting. Citizen award 1984, bd. visitors 1991—) Office: Fennemore Craig 3003 N Central Ave Ste 2600 Phoenix AZ 85012-2913

UDALL, JOHN NICHOLAS, JR., pediatric gastroenterologist; b. Washington, Dec. 30, 1940; BS, Brigham Young U., 1965; MD, Temple U., 1969; PhD, MIT, 1980. Diplomate Nat. Bd. Med. Examiners, Am. Bd. Pediatrics, Sub-bd. Pediatric Gastroenterology, Am. Bd. Nutrition; lic. physician Calif., Mass., Ariz., La. Rotating intern L.A. County/U. So. Calif. Med. Ctr., L.A., 1969-70, resident in pediat., 1972-74; postdoctoral rsch. fellow in pediatric gastroenterology Baylor Coll. Medicine, Houston, 1974-76; postdoctoral rsch. fellow pediatric pharmacology neonatology U. Ariz. Health Scis. Ctr., Tucson, 1976-77; postdoctoral rsch. fellow in clin. nutrition Children's Hosp., Harvard Med. Sch., Boston, 1977-79; instr. pediat., asst. prof. pediat. Harvard Med. Sch., Boston, 1979-81, 81-86; lectr. dept. nutrition/food sci., asst. dir. clin. rsch. ctr MIT, Cambridge, Mass., 1980-85; sci. staff, dir. pediatric rsch. Shriners Burn Inst., Boston, 1981-86, 85-86; assoc. prof. pediat. U. Ariz. Coll. Medicine, Tucson, 1986-92; prof. pediat. La. State U. Health Scis. Ctr., New Orleans, 1992—, Richard E.L. Fowler prof. pediat., 1999—; chief sect. pediatric gastroenterology and nutrition New Orleans Children's Hosp., 1992—; clin. prof. pediat. Sch. Medicine Tulane U., New Orleans, 1992—. Resident physician Clin. Rsch. Ctr., MIT, 1977-80, prin. investigator, 1980-85; assoc. staff physician Mass. Rehab. Hosp., Boston, 1978-85; asst. in pediatrics Mass. Gen. Hosp., Boston, 1979-86; dir. nutrition support svc. Children's Hosp., Boston, 1983-85, assoc. in medicine/gastroenterology, 1983-86; dir. sect. pediatric gastroenterology U. Ariz. Health Scis. Ctr., Tucson, 1986-92. Contbr. numerous articles to profl. jours., chpts. to books; editorial bd. Mass. Gen. Hosp. Dietary Manual, 1982, Seminars in Pediatric Gastroenterology and Nutrition, 1990—, Healthy Kids: The Magazine for Parents, 1990—, Jour. Pediatric Gastroenterology and Nutrition, 1991—, Nutrition: The Internat. Jour. of Applied and Basic Nutrition Scis., 1993—; editorial adv. bd. Snyder Comms., Rockville, Md., 1990-92; book rev. editor Jour. Pediatric Gastroenterology and Nutrition, 1983-90. With USPHS, 1970-72. Grantee NIH, 1978-80, 81-83, 83-86, 84-89, 86-89, 1993, Shriners Hosp., 1986-89, Ariz. Disease Control Rsch. Commn., 1988-90, U. Ariz. Small Grants Project, 1988-89, Joseph and Mary Cacioppo Found., 1988-89. Fellow Am. Acad. Pediatrics; mem. Internat. Soc. Supramolecular Biology, N.Am. Soc. for Pediatric Gastroenterology, Soc. for Pediatric Rsch., Am. Burn Assn., AAAS, Am. Soc. Clin. Nutrition (nomination com. 1993), Am. Inst. Nutrition, Western Soc. Pediatric Rsch., Am. Gastroenterol. Assn., Nat. Ileitis and Colitis Found., Am. Soc. Parenteral and Enteral Nutrition, Pima County Pediatric Soc. (sec. 1988), Ariz. Pediatric Soc., Am. Pediatric Soc., Tucson Area Soc. Parenteral and Enteral Nutrition Office: Children's Hosp Pediatric Gastroenterology 200 Henry Clay Ave New Orleans LA 70118-5720

UDALL, MARK, congressman; b. Tucson, July 18, 1950; m. Maggie Fox; children: Jed, Tess. B.Am. Civilization, Williams Coll., 1972. Course dir., educator Colo. Outward Bound Sch., 1975-85, exec. dir., 1985-95; mem. dist. 13 Colo. Ho. of Reps., 1997-99; mem. U.S. Congress from 2d Colo. dist., Washington, 1999—; Dem. dep. regional whip for western U.S.; mem. resources com., small bus. com., sci. com. Democrat. Avocation: mountain climbing. also: 1333 W 120th Ave Ste 210 Westminster CO 80234-2710 Office: US House of Representitives 115 Cannon HOuse Office Building Washington DC 20515

UDALL, THOMAS (TOM UDALL), congressman; b. Tucson, May 18, 1948; s. Stewart and Lee Udall; m. Jill Z. Cooper; 1 child, Amanda Cooper. BA, Prescott Coll., 1970; LLB, Cambridge (Eng.) U., 1975; JD, U. N.Mex., 1977. Law clk. to Hon. Oliver Seth U.S. Ct. Appeals (10th cir.), Santa Fe, 1977-78; asst. U.S. atty. U.S. Atty.'s Office, 1978-81; pvt. practice Santa Fe, 1981-83; chief counsel N.Mex. Health & Environ. Dept., 1983-84; ptnr. Miller, Stratvert, Togerson & Schlenker, P.A., Albuquerque, 1985-90; atty. gen. State of N.Mex., 1991-98; mem. 106th Congress from N.Mex., 3d dist., 1999—, mem. small bus. com., mem. resources com., mem. vets.' affairs com. Past pres. Rio Chama Preservation Trust; mem. N.Mex. Environ. Improvement Bd., 1986—87; past bd. dirs. La Compania de Teatro de Albuquerque, Santa Fe Chamber Music Festival; bd. dirs. Law Fund, 1991—98. Mem. Nat. Assn. Attys. Gen. (pres. 1996), Kiwanis. Democrat. Office: US Ho Reps 1414 Longworth HOB Washington DC 20515-3103

UDALL, VESTA HAMMOND, special education educator; b. Jacksonville, Fla., Dec. 8, 1942; d. Vesta Shields and Gladys Wilcox Hammond; m. John Scriven Udall, July 18, 1964 (div. Feb. 27, 1973); children: Adrien Evelyn, Peter John. BA, Winthrop U., 1964; MEd, U. Phoenix, 1997; postgrad., U. Fla., No. Ariz. U., Ariz. State U. Cert. tchr. Ariz. Various elem. and H.S. tchg. positions Duval County Schs., Jacksonville, 1964—68; tchr. Flagstaff (Ariz.) Jr. H.S., 1974—76, Fickett Jr. H.S., Tucson, 1976—78, Devereux Sch., Scottsdale, Ariz., 1978—80, East Valley H.S., Maricopa County Regional Sch. Dist., Phoenix, 1989—97, Madison Jail and Maricopa County Sheriff's Office, Phoenix, 1997—2000; prof. Phoenix Coll., 1998—; spl. edn. tchr. Westwood H.S., Mesa (Ariz.) Sch. Dist., 2000—. Presenter in field; developer spl. edn. programs. Precinct committeeman Rep. Party, Mesa, 1985—. Named Educator of Yr., Phoenix Sun, 1995. Mem.: Nat. Edn. Assn., Mesa Edn. Assn. Ariz. Republican. Mem. Lds Ch. Avocations: hiking, river running, birdwatching, biking. Home: 2264 E Fairfield St Mesa AZ 85213 Office: Phoenix Coll 1100 W Thomas Rd Phoenix AZ 85013 Personal E-mail: vhudall@aol.com.

UDDIN, NASIM, civil engineer, educator; b. Chittagong, Bangladesh, Jan. 3, 1963; came to U.S., 1988; s. Jalal Ahmed and Jainab Begam; m. Jamina Jabeen, Mar. 20, 1994. BSCE, Bangladesh U. Engring. and Tech., Bangladesh, 1986; MSCE, U. Okla., 1989; PhD, SUNY, Buffalo, 1992. Registered prof. engr., Ind., N.Y. Lectr. civil engring. Bangladesh U. Engring. and Tech., Bangladesh, 1986-88; staff engr. Acres Internat., Buffalo, 1992-97; asst. prof. U. Evansville, Ind., 1997—; assoc. prof. U. Ala., Birmingham, 2001—; assoc. scientist Ctr. Disaster Preparedness, 2001—. Contbr. articles to profl. jours. Coord. HAZUS Program, Evansville, 1997—; exec. com. Disaster Resistant Cmty., Evansville, 1997—. Mem.: ABET (assessment coord. 2001—), Internat. Com. Large Dams, Internat. Soc. Computational Engring., Am. Soc. Engring. Edn., ASCE (mem. nat. com. engring. mgmt. and bus. practices 2001—), Islamic Soc. Evansville (gen. sec. 1998—). Avocations: jogging, weightlifting, gardening. Office: U Ala Dept Civil and Environ Engring Birmingham AL 35294-4440 Home: 5206 Stonehedge Dr Evansville IN 47715-5960 E-mail: nuddin@uab.edu.

UDELL, BUDD ALLEN, music educator; b. Grand Rapids, Mich., Apr. 4, 1934; s. Vor Loren and Bonnie K. Udell; m. Marlene Jean Doolittle, June 23, 1957; children: Shelley, Sherri. MusB, Ind. U., 1957, MusM, 1965; Mus D, U. Cinn., 1972. Composer, arranger US Navy Band, Wash., DC, 1958—61; dir. of bands W. Va. U., Morgantown, W.Va., 1963—70; asst. dean U. Cin., Cin., 1972—74; exec. dir. Music Tchrs. Nat. Assn., Cin., 1974—77; chmn. U. Fla., Music Dept., Gainesville, Fla., 1977—85; music prof. U. Fla., 1985—2001; ret., 2001. Adj., clinician MusicFest Orlando, Orlando, Fla., 1994—; music dir., condr. Gainesville Civic Chorus, 1981—2004. Composer various music compositions and arrangements. Chair, pub. rels. Gainesville Comm. Min., Gainesville, 2004—. With USN, 1958—61. Named Outstanding Composer, ASCAP. Mem.: Fla. State Music Tchrs. Assn. (pres. 1985—87). Avocations: golf, fishing, woodworking.

UDELL, HOWARD R. pharmaceutical executive; Grad., CUNY; LLB, NYU. Bar: N.Y., Conn., U.S. Supreme Ct. Former ptnr. Millard, Greene & Udell, Stamford, Conn.; gen. counsel Purdue Pharma, Stamford, Conn., 1977—89, group v.p., gen. counsel, 1989—99, exec. v.p., gen. counsel, 1999—2003, exec. v.p., chief legal officer, 2003—. Office: Purdue Pharma 1 Stamford Forum Stamford CT 06901

UDEN, DAVID ELLIOTT, cardiologist, educator; b. Montreal, Sept. 7, 1936; s. Reginald and Elsie Ada (Elliott) U.; children: Thomas Elliott, Linda Ann, Christopher Elliott. BSc, McGill U., 1958; MD, McGill U., Quebec, Can., 1962. Diplomate Am. Bd. Internal Medicine; cert. cardiovascular disease, cert. interventional cardiology. Attending cardiologist Toronto Western Hosp., 1972-93, The Wellesley Hosp., Toronto, 1990-93; asst. prof. medicine U. Toronto, 1975-93; chief of cardiology Oconee Meml. Hosp., Seneca, SC, 1993-97, chief of medicine, 1994—96, 2000—02; elected mem. S.C. Med. Discipline Commn., 1996-98, 2000—; apptd. Discipline Commn., 2000—. Contbr. articles to profl. jours. With RCAF, 1963-66. Fellow Am. Coll. Cardiology, Am. Heart Assn. Coun. on Clin. Cardiology, Soc. for Cardiac Angiography and Intervention. Avocations: travel, photography. Office: Oconee Cardiology Assocs 109 A Omni Dr Seneca SC 29672 Office Phone: 864-882-0847.

UDEVITZ, NORMAN, publishing executive; b. Cheyenne, Wyo., Jan. 22, 1929; s. Jay and Edith (Stienberg) U.; m. Marsha Rae Dinner, Dec. 17, 1960; children: Jane, Kathryn, Andrew. Student, U. Colo., 1946-49. With Cheyenne Newspapers Inc. Cheyenne, 1949-54; editor-pub. Wyo. Buffalo, Cheyenne, 1954-63; account supr. Tilds & Cantz Advt. Agy., L.A., 1963-66; exec. v.p. Fitzgerald, Maahs & Miller, L.A., 1966-71; staff writer The Denver Post, 1971-88; dir. pubs. Am. Water Works Assn., Denver, 1988-97; ret., 1997. Sgt. USNG, 1950-53. Named Colo.'s Outstanding Journalist, U. Colo., 1977; recipient Pulitzer Prize Gold medal Columbia U., 1986. Mem. Investigative Reporters and Editors Inc., (bd. dirs. 1978-80, 81-83), The Newspaper Guild (McWilliams award 1976, 77). Jewish. Home: 4677 E Euclid Ave Littleton CO 80121-3224

UDLER, RUBIN YAKOVLEVICH, linguist; b. Braila, Muntenia, Romania, Sept. 27, 1925; came to U.S., 1992; s. Yakov Aronovich and Dina Vladimirovna (Gleizer) U.; m. Malka Il'inichna Alexenberg, July 8, 1956; children: Arthur, Angela. B in Philol. Sci., U. Chernovtsy, Ukraine, 1951; M in Philol. Sci., USSR Acad. Scis., Moscow, 1961; D in Philol. Sci., USSR Acad. Scis., Leningrad, 1974. Dep. chmn. fgn. langs. dept. Chernovtsy State Pedagogical Inst., 1951-56; jr. sci. rschr. dialectology sect. Moldavian br. USSR Acad. Scis., Kishinev, Moldova, 1956-61; chief dialectology and exptl. phonetics sect. Moldavian Acad. Scis., 1961-80, chief dialectology and history of lang. sect., 1980-86, chief dialectology and linguistic geography dept., 1986-92, dep. of academician-sec. of social studies dept., 1989-92; ctr. assoc. U. Ctr. for Internat. Studies U. Pitts., 1994—. Translator Soviet Bucovina newspaper, Chernovtsy, 1951-52; mem. editl. bd. Moldavian Lang. and Lit., 1961-91, Jour. Linguistics and Study of Lit., 1991-92; sr. sci. rschr. All-Union Cert. Com., Moscow, 1963; presenter at cong., confs., and symposiums. Author: Moldavian Dialects of the Chernovtsy Area Consonantism, 1964, Dialectological Division of the Moldavian Language, Parts 1 and 2, 1976, The Cursed Years, 2003; co-author: The Moldavian Linguistic Atlas, 4 parts, 1968-73, Dialectological Dictionary, 5 vols., 1985-86, Dialectological Texts, 6 parts, 1969-87, The Historical Grammar of the Moldavian Language, 1964, Notes on Modern Moldavian Literary Language, 1967, Moldavian Dialectology, 1976, The Carpathian Dialectological Atlas, 6 vols., 1987-98; author more than 235 pub. works with total volume of more than 455 editl. sheets; mng. editor, co-editor approximately 60 monographs, dictionaries, atlases, collection of dialectological texts, collections of articles, theses, brochures with total volume of more than 1275 editl. sheets. Corr. mem. Moldavian Acad. Scis. Presidium of Moldavian Acad. Scis.; mem. Holocaust Ctr. United Jewish Fedn. Greater Pitts. Jewish. Avocations: collecting old books, coins, travel. Home: 1535 Shady Ave Pittsburgh PA 15217-1455 Office: Univ Ctr Internat Studies U Pitts 41 G40 Forbes Quadrangle Pittsburgh PA 15260

UDOFF, ERIC JOEL, diagnostic radiologist; b. Balt., Oct. 8, 1948; s. Melvin Jerome and Esther (Fisher) U.; m. Ronni Ann Chapin, June 7, 1980; children: Brian Evan, Jonathan Andrew. AB, Washington U., 1969; MD, U. Rochester, 1973. Intern, resident in diagnostic radiology U. Chgo., 1973-77; instr. in cardiovasc. radiology Johns Hopkins U., Balt., 1977-79; radiologist Sinai Hosp., Balt., 1979-86, Mt. Sinai Med. Ctr., Milw., 1986-88, Sinai Hosp., Balt., 1988-90; asst. prof. radiology Johns Hopkins U. Hosp., 1990-91; radiologist North Fulton Regional Hosp., Roswell, Ga., 1991-97; instr. thoracoabdominal imaging U. Va., 1997-98, Radiologist, Diagnostic Imaging Specialists, Atlanta, 1998—. Mem. AMA, Am. Roentgen Ray Soc., Am. Coll. Radiology, Radiol. Soc. N.Am., Ga. Radiol. Soc., Phi Beta Kappa. Avocations: reading, tennis. Office: 6000 Lake Forrest Dr Ste 475 Atlanta GA 30328 E-mail: esurad@aol.com.

UDVAR-HAZY, STEVEN F. leasing company financial executive; b. Budapest, Hungary, Feb. 23, 1946; came to U.S., 1958. m. Christine L. Henneman, June 7, 1980; 3 children. BA, UCLA, 1968; HHD (hon.), U. Utah (Dixie Coll.), 1990. Cert. airline transp. jet pilot. Pres. Internat. Lease Fin. Corp., Beverly Hills, Calif., 1973—. Bd. dirs. Sky West Inc., St. George, Utah. Mem. Wings Club (Achievement to Aviation award 1989). Office: Internat Lease Fin Corp Ste 3900 1999 Avenue Of The Stars Los Angeles CA 90067-6032

UDVARHELYI, GEORGE BELA, neurosurgery educator emeritus, cultural affairs administrator; b. Budapest, Hungary, May 14, 1920; came to U.S., 1955; s. Bela and Margaret (Bakacs) U.; m. Elspeth Mary Campbell, July 24, 1956; children: Ian Steven, Susan Margaret, Jane Elizabeth. BS, St. Stephen Coll., 1938; MD, U. Budapest, 1944, U. Buenos Aires, 1952; D honoris causa, Semmelweis Med. Sch., Budapest, 1988, Western Md. Coll., 1997. Diplomate Am. Bd. Neurol. Surgery. Intern resident in surgery Red Cross Hosp./11th Mil. Hosp., Budapest, 1942-44; asst. resident Neurol. Univ. Clinic, Budapest, 1944-46; postdoctoral fellow U. Vienna, Austria, 1946-47; fgn. asst. Psychiat. Clinic, U. Berne, Switzerland, 1947-48; asst. resident in neurosurgery Hosp. Espanol, Cordoba, Argentina, 1948-50; resident neurosurgeon Inst. Neurosurgery, U. Buenos Aires, 1950-53; asst. Neurolsurgical Clinic, U. Cologne, Fed. Republic Germany, 1953-54; registrar Royal Infirmary, Edinburgh, Scotland, 1954-55; from fellow to full prof. Johns Hopkins U., Balt., 1955-84, prof. emeritus, dir. cultural affairs, 1984-92, assoc. prof. radiology, 1963-84, Phi Beta Kappa lectr., 1980. Neurosurg. cons. Social Security Adminstrn., Balt., 1962-89, Disability Determination Svc., Balt., 1991-93; vis. prof., guest lectr. U. Va., Charlottesville, 1977, Children's Hosp. Ea. Ont., Ottawa, Can., 1977, U. Salzburg, Austria, 1981, U. Vienna, Austria, 1983, Mayo Clinic, Rochester, Minn., 1983, U. Cape Town, Republic of South Africa, 1984, U. Porto, Portugal, 1985; vis. prof. Temple U., Phila., 1979, U. Vt., Burlington, 1980, Aukland (New Zealand) Gen. Hosp., 1989, George Washington U., 1991, U. Mainz, Fed. Republic Germany, 1991, numerous others; lectr. in field. Contbr. numerous articles to profl. jours., book chpts. Mem. program com. Balt. Symphony Orch., 1972-80, edn. com. Walters Art Gallery, Balt., 1985-88. Recipient Lincoln award Am. Hungarian Found., 1980, Eisenberg award Humanities, 1996; Humanities grantee NEH, 1984-91. Fellow ACS; mem. AAUP, Am. Assn. Neurol. Surgeons (life, Humanitarian award 1991), Congress Neurol. Surgeons (sr.), Am. Assn. Neuropathologists, Pan-Am. Med. Assn., Soc. Brit. Neurol. Surgeons (corr.), Pavlovian Soc. N.Am., German Neurol. Soc. (corr.), Internat. Soc. Pediatric Neurosurgery (founding), Hungarian Neurosurg. Soc. (corr.), Argentine Acad. Sci. (corr.), Am. Soc. for Laser Medicine and Surgery (charter), Johns Hopkins Med. Assn., Johns Hopkins Faculty Club, 14 West Hamilton Club (chair steering com. 1977-83), Cosmos Club (chair program subcom. 1991—), Landsdowne Club (London), Alpha Omega Alpha. Roman Catholic. Avocations: music, literature, travel, chess.

UDWADIA, FIRDAUS ERACH, engineering educator, consultant; b. Bombay, Aug. 28, 1947; came to U.S., 1968. s. Erach Rustam and Perin P. (Lentin) U.; m. Farida Gagrat, Jan. 6, 1977; children: Shanaira, Zubin. BS, Indian Inst. Tech., Bombay, 1968; MS, Calif. Inst. Tech., 1969, PhD, 1972; MBA, U. So. Calif., 1985. Mem. faculty Calif. Inst. Tech., Pasadena, 1972-74; asst. prof. engring. U. So. Calif., Los Angeles, 1974-77, assoc. prof. mech., civil, and aerospace engring. and bus. adminstrn., 1977-83, prof. aerospace and mech. engring., civil engring. and bus. adminstrn., 1983-86, prof. engring, bus. adminstrn., math., 1986—, prof. engring., bus. adminstrn., math., 1999—; also bd. dirs. Structural Identification Computing Facility, U. So. Calif. Cons. Jet Propulsion Lab., Pasadena, 1978—, Argonne Nat. Lab., 1982-83, Air Force Rocket Lab., Edwards AFB. Calif., 1984—, Air Firce Rsch. Lab., 1990—; vis. prof. applied mechanics and mech. engring. Calif. Inst. Tech., Pasadena, 1993. Author: Analytical Dynamics, A New Approach, 1996; editor (assoc.): (jour.) Applied Math. and Computation, Discrete Dynamics in Nature and Soc., Jour. Optimization Theory and Applications, Jour. Franklin Inst., Jour. Differential

Equations and Dynamical Sys., Nonlinear Studies, Jour. Math. Analysis and Applications, Jour. Math. Problems in Engring.; editor: Jour. of Aerospace Engring.; mem. adv. bd.: jour. Jour. Tech. Forecasting and Social Change; editor: Advances in Dynamics and Control, 2000, Dynamical Systems and Control, 2004; contbr. articles to profl. jours. Bd. dirs. Crisis Mgmt. Ctr., U. So. Calif. NSF grantee, 1976—; recipient Golden Poet award, 1990. Mem. AIAA, ASCE, ASME, Am. Acad. Mechanics, Soc. Indsl. and Applied Math., Seismological Soc. Am., Sigma Xi (Earthquake Engring. Research Inst., 1971, 74, 84). Achievements include patents for in field. Avocations: poetry, piano, chess. Home: 2100 S Santa Anita Ave Arcadia CA 91006-4611 Office: U So Calif 430K Olin Hall University Park Los Angeles CA 90007 Office Phone: 213-740-0495. Business E-Mail: fudwadia@usc.edu.

UDY, RAE, columnist, writer; b. Ogden, Utah, Mar. 24, 1950; d. Verl Nish Udy and Elizabeth Jones White; m. Steven James Weese, Apr. 9, 1971; children: Nation Verl Weese, Luke Ray Weese. B, Weber State U., 1968. Columnist Longview News Jour., Longview, Tex., 1989—; lifestyle editor Marshall News Messenger, Marshall, Tex., 1999—2000. Mem. and past v.p. East Tex. Writers Assn., 1987—. Author: (book) Countdown Cooking, 1993. Mem.: Ladies Aux. of Frat. of Eagles. Democrat. Christian. Avocations: gardening, travel, camping. Office: Rae Udy P O Box 5965 Longview TX 75608 Office Phone: 903-777-2723. Personal E-mail: raeudy@msn.com.

UEBERROTH, PETER VICTOR, former baseball commissioner; b. Evanston, Ill., Sept. 2, 1937; s. Victor and Laura (Larson) U.; m. Virginia Nicolaus, Sept. 1959; children— Vicky, Heidi, Keri, Joe BS in Bus., San Jose State Coll., 1959. Ops. mgr. then v.p. Trans Internat., 1959-62; founder, chmn. Transp. Cons. Internat., 1963-79; pres., mng. dir. Los Angeles Olympic Organizing Com., 1979-84; commr., chief exec. officer of major league baseball N.Y.C., 1984-89; co-chmn. Doubletree Hotels Corp., Phoenix, 1993—; chmn. U.S. Olympic Comm., 2004—. Former chmn. Ask Mr. Foster Travel Service; chmn. Colony Hotels, Intercontinental Tours, Inc., First Travel Corp; mem. bd. dirs. California Angels. Author: Made in America, 1985 Named Man of Yr., Time mag. and Sporting News, 1984; recipient Scopus award Am. Friends of Hebrew U., Jerusalem, 1985 Office: Ambassadors Intl Inc 110 S Ferrall St Spokane WA 99202*

UECKER, BOB, actor, radio announcer, former baseball player, television personality; b. Milw., Jan. 26, 1935; m. Judy Uecker, 1976 (div. 2001); 4 children. Major league baseball player Milw. Braves, Nat. League, 1962, 63; major league baseball player St. Louis Cardinals, 1964, 65, Phila. Phillies, 1966-67, Atlanta Braves, 1967; radio-TV announcer Milw. Brewers, 1971—; commentator ABC Monday Night Baseball, 1976-82; commentator playoff and world series NBC Baseball, 1994-98. Host War of the Start, Bob Ueckers Wacky World of Sports, Saturday Night Live; guest Tim Conway show, Who's the Boss, Peter Marshall Show; appeared in Fatal Instinct. Co-star TV series Mr. Belvedere, ABC-TV, 1985-1990; guest TV appearances include Late Night with David Letterman, The Tonight Show, Midnight Special, LateLine, 1998; also numerous commls.; author: Catcher in the Wry, 1985; films include: Major League, 1989, Major League 2, 1994, (voice over) Homeward Bound II: Lost in San Francisco, 1996, Major League: Back to the Minors, 1998, Andre the Giant: Larger Than Life, 1999. Recipient Big B.A.T. award Baseball Assistance Team, 1995; inducted Wis. Performing Artists Hall of Fame, 1993, Wis. Broadcasters Assn. Hall of Fame, 1994, Wis. Sports Hall of Fame, 1998. Office: Milw Brewers Baseball Club Milw County Stadium 1 Brewers Way Milwaukee WI 53214-3651

UEDA, REED TAKASHI, historian, educator; b. Honolulu, Sept. 14, 1949; s. Goro and Mildred (Yoshimoto) Ueda; m. Peggy Lynn Rubin; children: Katya, Alyona. BA, UCLA, 1970; MA, U. Chgo., 1973, Harvard U., 1976, PhD, 1981. Rsch. editor Harvard Ency. Am. Ethnic Grups, Cambridge, Mass., 1977-79; instr. Harvard U., Cambridge, 1980-81, assoc. Ctr. Am. Polit. Studies; prof. Tufts U., Medford, Mass., 1981—. Vis. prof. Brandeis U., Waltham, Mass., 1986, Harvard U., 1987—89, 1996; mem. steering group com. on internat. migration MIT, 1996—; mem. Boston History Collaborative, 1998—2000; staff historian Dreams Freedom Immigration Mus., Boston, 1999—2003; mem. rev. panel nat. stds. in history Coun. Basic Edn., 1995; mem. nat. assessment ednl. progress U.S. Dept. Edn., 1991—92, mem. planning com. nat. adv. com. U.S. history framework, 1992—94, mem. nat. adv. com. nat. stds. in civics and govt., 1994—95, mem. nat. adv. com. nat. stds. profl. tchg., 1994—95. Author: (book) Avenues to Adulthood, 1987, Postwar Immigration America, 1994; assoc. editor: Jour. Interdisciplinary History, 1996—; mem. editl. bd. Harvard Ednl. Rev., 1977—78, Am. Quar., 1993, Mass. Hist. Rev., 2000—. Mem. Gov.'s Edn. Reform Rev. Commn., 1994—2002; mem. coun. fgn. rels. Boston (Mass.) Working Group Nat. Interest, 1995; mem. coun. for basic edn. Review Panel for Nat. Standards in Hist., 1995; mem. US Dept. Edn., Nat. Assessment of Ednl. Progress, 1991—92, US Dept. Edn., Nat. Adv. Planning Com. for US Hist. Framework, 1992—94, US Dept. Edn., Nat. Standards in Civics and Gov., 1994—95, US Dept. Edn., Nat. Standards in Profl. Tchg. Fellow, Am. Coun. Learned Soc., Woodrow Wilson Internat. Ctr., NEH, Charles Warren Ctr. Fellow: Mass. Hist. Soc. (mem. planning com. immigration and urban history sem. 1999—); mem.: Immigration and Ethnic Hist. Soc. (exec. bd.). Office: Tufts U Dept History Medford MA 02155 Business E-Mail: reed.ueda@tufts.edu.

UEHLEIN, E(DWARD) CARL, JR., lawyer; b. Boston, May 7, 1941; s. Edward Carl and Elizabeth (Thatcher) U.; m. Judith Taylor, June 16, 1962; children: Christine, Sara. Student, Bowdoin Coll., Brunswick, Maine, 1958-59; BA, Swarthmore Coll., 1962; LLB, Boston Coll., 1965. Bar: Mass. 1965, D.C. 1968. Atty. Nat. Labor Relations Bd., Atlanta, 1965-68; assoc. Morgan, Lewis & Bockius, Washington, 1968-71; exec. asst. to sec. U.S. Dept. Labor, Washington, 1971-73; ptnr. Morgan Lewis & Bockius, Washington, 1973—2001, counsel, 2001—. Sec.-treas. Carlou Corp., Wilmington, Del., 1969-71. Fellow Ford Found., 1961. Mem. ABA, FBA, D.C. Bar Assn., Belle Haven Country Club, Ballybunion Golf Club, Royal Dornoch Golf Club. Avocations: travel, golf, reading. Office: Morgan Lewis & Bockius 1111 Pennsylvania Ave Washington DC 20004 Office Phone: 202-739-5075. Business E-Mail: ecuehlein@morganlewis.com.

UEHLING, BARBARA STANER, educational administrator; b. Wichita, Kans., June 12, 1932; d. Roy W. and Mary Elizabeth (Hilt) Staner; children: Jeffrey Steven, David Edward. BA, U. Wichita, 1954; MA, Northwestern U., 1956, PhD, 1958; degree (hon.), Drury Coll., 1978; LLD (hon.), Ohio State U., 1980. Mem. psychology faculty Oglethorpe U., Atlanta, 1959-64, Emory U., Atlanta, 1966-69; adj. prof. U. R.I., Kingston, 1970-72; dean Roger Williams Coll., Bristol, RI, 1972-74; dean arts scis. Ill. State U., Normal, 1974-76; provost U. Okla., Norman, 1976-78; chancellor U. Mo.-Columbia, 1978-86, U. Calif., Santa Barbara, 1987-94; mem. Pacific Rim Pub. U. Pres. Conf., 1990-92; exec. dir. Bus. and Higher Edn. Forum, Washington, 1995-97. Cons. North Ctr. Accreditation Assn., 1974-86; mem. nat. educator adv. com. to Comptr. Gen. of U.S., 1978-79; mem. Commn. on Mil.-Higher Edn. Rels., 1978-79, Am. Coun. on Edn., bd. dirs. 1979-83, treas., 1982-83, mem. Bus.-Higher Edn. Forum, 1980-94, exec. com. 1991-94; sr. vis. fellow Am. Coun. Edn., 1987; mem. Commn. on Internat. Edn., 1992-94, vice chair 1993; bd. dirs. Coun. of Postsecondary Edn., 1986-87, 90-93, Meredith Corp., 1980-99; mem. Transatlantic Dialogue, PEW Found., 1991-93; mem. West Coast adv. bd. Inst. Internat. Edn., 2004—. Author: Women in Academe: Steps to Greater Equality, 1979; mem. editl. bd. Jour. Higher Edn. Mgmt., 1986-95; contbr. articles to profl. jours. Bd. dirs., chmn. Nat. Ctr. Higher Edn. Mgmt. Sys., 1977-80; trustee Carnegie Found. for Advancement of Tchg., 1980-86, Santa Barbara Med. Found. Clinic, 1989-94; bd. dirs. Resources for the Future, 1985-94; mem. select com. on athletics NCAA, 1983-84, also mem. presdl. commn.; mem. Nat. Coun. on Edn. Rsch., 1980-82. Social Sci. Rsch. Coun. fellow, 1954-55; NSF fellow, 1956-57; NIMH postdoctoral rsch. fellow, 1964-67; named one of 100 Young Leaders of Acad. Change Mag. and ACE, 1978; recipient Alumni Achievement award Wichita State U., 1978, Alumnae award Northwestern U., 1985, Excellence in Edn. award Pi Lambda Theta, 1989. Mem. Am. Assn. Higher Edn. (bd. dirs. 1974-77, pres. 1977-78), Western Coll. Assn. (pres.-elect 1988-89, pres. 1990-92), West Coast Adv. Bd., Inst. Internat. Edn., Golden Key, Sigma Xi. Personal E-mail: bcharlton3@hotmail.com.

UELAND, SIGURD, JR., retired lawyer; b. Mpls., June 1, 1937; s. Sigurd and Harriet (Scofield) U.; m. Harriet Moulton, Dec. 27, 1963; children: Scott, Leif, Tora, Sigurd III. BA, Yale U., 1959; LL.B., U. Minn., 1962. Bar: Minn. 1963. Asso. firm Neville, Johnson & Thompson, Mpls., 1963-67; corp. atty. Whirlpool Corp., Benton Harbor, Mich., 1968-69, Honeywell Inc., Mpls., 1969-97, sec., 1977-97, asst. gen. counsel, 1980-93, v.p., 1983-97. Mem. Am. Soc. Corp. Secs. (chmn. 1996-97). Congregationalist.

UFFELMAN, MALCOLM RUCJ, electronics company executive, electrical engineer; b. Clarksville, Tenn., Oct. 22, 1935; s. Malcolm C. and Margaret Lillian (Davidson) U.; m. Sarah White Barksdale, June 11, 1957; children: Malcolm Rucj Jr., Katharina White, Davidson Barksdale, Jefferson Churchill. BS, Vanderbilt U., 1957; MS, George Washington U., 1963. Engr. Melpar, Inc., Falls Church, Va., 1957-60; v.p. Scope, Inc., Reston, Va., 1960-73; sr. cons. MRI, Inc., McLean, Va., 1973-78; v.p. Racal Communications Inc., Rockville, Md., 1978-80; sr. cons. MRJ, Inc., Fairfax, Va., 1980-82; v.p., gen. mgr., Ctr. Advanced Planning and Analysis E-Systems Inc., Fairfax, 1982-96; v.p. Constellation Comm., Inc., Fairfax, 1996-99; patent agt., 1999—2000; exec. v.p. Contact Corp., 2000—. Contbr. numerous articles to profl. jours.; holder 7 patents in field. Scoutmaster Troop 183 Boy Scouts Am., Oakton, Va., 1973-79; bd. dirs. Camco Fund, 2002—. Capt. USAR, 1957-69. Fellow IEEE; mem. Cosmos Club (Washington), Internat. Brotherhood Magicians. Republican. Episcopalian. Avocations: sailing, reading, travel, magic, fly fishing.

UFFNER, MICHAEL S. automotive executive; b. Phila., July 18, 1945; s. Ray and Shirley A. (Block) Uffner; m. Marilyn A. Ursomarso; 1 child, Lauren R. BA, U. Pa., 1971, MA, 1971. V.p. Union Park Pontiac, BMW, Honda, Wilmington, Del., 1972-82; pres. Del. Motor Sales Inc., Auto Team Del., Wilmington, 1982—. Mem. manpower tng. adv. com. GM, pres. dealer adv. coun., 1985, mem. dealer policy bd., 1990—91; trustee Christiana Health Care Sys., 2002—. Mem. Wilmington Police Bus. Adv. Coun., 1991—; bd. dirs., mem. exec. com. BBB Del., 1992—, chmn., 1998—2000; mem. New Castle County Small Bus. Commn., 1993—. Recipient Quality Dealer award, Time Mag., 1997, numerous other awards. Mem.: Del. Automobile and Truck Dealers Assn. (bd. dirs., v.p. 1992—93, pres. 1994—95), Am. Econ. Assn., Cadillac Motor Car Divsn. Nat. Dealers Coun. (vice chmn. 1989—90, chmn. 1990—91, chmn. DeVille brand com. 1995—97), Tavistock Civic Assn. (pres. 1976—77), U.S. C. of C. (bd. dirs. 1998—2004, chmn. pub. affairs com. 2001—04), Del. C. of C. (chmn. small bus. com. 1991—95, bd. dirs. 1993—, chmn. small bus. alliance 1995—96, mem. exec. com. 1995—, vice chmn. bd. dirs. 1996—99, chmn. bd. dirs. 2000—02), Am. Heart Assn. (bd. dirs. Del. chpt. 1981—98, pres. 1985—86, chmn. 1986—87, v.p., bd. dirs. Nat. Ctr. 1987—90), U. Pa. Alumni Assn. (v.p. Del. chpt. 1978—80, pres. 1980—81), Univ. Whist Club, Ocean City Yacht Club, Hidden Creek Golf Club, Fieldstone Golf Club. Office: 1606 Pennsylvania Ave Wilmington DE 19806-4018

UFFORD, CHARLES WILBUR, JR., lawyer; b. Princeton, N.J., July 8, 1931; m. Isabel Letitia Wheeler, May 20, 1961; children: Eleanor Morris Ufford Léger, Catherine Latourette Ufford-Chase, Alison Wistar Ufford Salem. BA cum laude (Francis H. Burr scholar), Harvard U., 1953, LLB, 1959; postgrad. (Lionel de Jersey Harvard studentship), Cambridge U., Eng., 1953-54. Bar: N.Y. 1961, U.S. Tax Ct. 1963. Assoc. Riggs, Ferris & Geer, N.Y.C., 1959-61; from assoc. to ptnr. Jackson, Nash, Brophy, Barringer & Brooks, 1961-78; ptnr. Skadden, Arps, Slate, Meagher & Flom, N.Y.C., 1978-92, of counsel, 1993-96. Contbr. articles to legal jours. Trustee Nat. Squash Racquets Ednl. Found., N.Y.C., 1972-81; mem. Princeton Monthly Meeting, Soc. of Friends, clk., 1986-88, 99; mem. exec. com. Friends Com. on Nat. Legislation, 1997-98; bd. dirs. Pennswood Village, 1998—, Friends Fiduciary Corp., 1999—. Nat. Intercollegiate Squash Racquets champion, 1952-53; mem. NCAA All-Am. Soccer Ist team, 1952. Fellow Am. Coll. Trust and Estate Counsel (transfer tax study com. 1990-93); mem. ABA, N.Y. Bar Assn. (chmn. trusts and estates law sect. 1984), Assn. Bar City N.Y., N.Y. State Office of Ct. Adminstrn. (Surrogates Ct. Adv. Com., 1994-96), U.S. Squash Racquets Assn. (hon. life; trustee endowment fund 1984-96), Internat. Lawn Tennis Club U.S.A. (dir. 1982—). Office: 150 Mercer St Princeton NJ 08540-6827 Office Phone: 609-921-8085. E-mail: cuffordl@aol.com. *Integrity, perseverance, compassion and humor are all very well--but the key is to be blessed by a Divine Improvidence.*

UFIMTSEV, PYOTR YAKOVLEVICH, physicist, electrical engineer, educator; b. Ust'-Charyshskaya Pristan', Altai Region, Russia, July 8, 1931; s. Yakov Fedorovich and Vasilisa Vasil'evna (Toropchina) U.; m. Tatiana Vladimirovna Sinelschikova; children: Galina, Ivan, Vladimir. Grad., Odessa State U., Russia, 1954; PhD, Ctrl. Rsch. Inst. of Radio Industry, Moscow, 1959; DSc, St. Petersburg State U., Russia, 1970. Engr., sr. engr., sr. scientist Ctrl. Rsch. Inst. of Radio Industry, Moscow, 1954-73; sr. scientist, head scientist Inst. Radio Engring. & Electronics Acad. Scis., Moscow, 1973-90; prin. engr. Northrop Grumman Corp., 1995—2000; prof. U. Calif., Irvine, 2003—. Vis. prof., adj. prof. UCLA, 1990—2003; mem. sci. bd. radio waves Acad. Scis., Moscow, 1960—90. Author: Method of Edge Waves in the Physical Theory of Diffraction, 1962, Theory of Edge Diffraction in Electromagnetics, 2003; contbr. articles to profl. jours. Recipient USSR State Prize, Moscow, 1990, Leroy Randle Grumman medal for outstanding sci. achievement, N.Y.C., 1991, 20th Century Achievement medal, Cambridge, 1996, Hall of Fame medal, Cambridge, 1996. Fellow IEEE; assoc. fellow AIAA; mem. Electromagnetics Acad. (U.S.), A.S. Popov Sci. Tech. Soc. Radio Engring., Electronics & Telecommunication (Russia). Achievements include origination of the Physical Theory of Diffraction, used for design of American stealth aircrafts and ships; for radar-cross-section calculation, and antenna design. Office: U Calif Irvine Dept Mech and Aerospace 5251 California Ave Irvine CA 92612

UGGAMS, LESLIE, entertainer; b. N.Y.C., May 25, 1943; d. Harolde Coyden and Juanita Ernestine (Smith) Uggams; m. Grahame John Kelvin-Pratt, Oct. 16, 1965; children: Danielle Nicole Pratt, Justice Harolde John Kelvin-Pratt. Student, Juillard Sch. Music, 1961-63; degree (hon.), Jarvis Coll., Tyler, Tex., Wilberforce (Ohio) U. Appeared on (TV series) Beulah, 1949, featured on Sing Along with Mitch, 1961—64, starred in (Broadway plays) Hallelujah Baby, 1967 (Tony award, 1968), Her First Roman Broadway Musical, 1968, star of (weekly TV variety show) The Leslie Uggams Show, 1969, appearances in nightclubs top TV mus. variety shows, appeared in films Two Weeks in Another Town, Black Girl, 1962, Skyjacked, 1972, Poor Pretty Eddie, 1973, appeared in (TV miniseries) Roots, ABC-TV, 1977 (Critics Choice award as best supporting actress, 1977), (TV films) Sizzle, 1981, Harlem, 1993, Star (Broadway musicals) Blues in the Night, 1982, (Broadway musical) Jerry's Girls, 1985, Anything Goes, 1987, star (off-Broadway) The Old Settler, 1999 (Audelco award as best actress), (dramatic play), 1999; appeared in: Thoroughly Modern Millie, 2004; star (musical play) King Hedley II, 2001 (nominated Tony award best actress, 2001), Thunder Knocking on the Door, 2002 (Audelco award best actress, 2002), (TV miniseries) Backstairs at the White House, 1979, co-host (TV series) Fantasy TV, 1982—83 (Emmy award 1983, 1983); author: The Leslie Uggams Beauty Book, 1966. Founding mem. BRAVO chpt. City of Hope, Los Angeles, 1969, treas., 1969—79. Named best singer on TV, 1962—63; recipient Drama Critics award, Newspaper and TV critics, 1968, Tony award, 1968, Emmy award, 1993. Mem.: SAG, NARAS, AFTRA, Actors' Equity Assn. Democrat. Presbyterian. Avocations: needlepoint, knitting, tennis, squash, exercising. Office: The Gage Group Inc care Phillip Adelman 315 W 57th St Frnt 4H New York NY 10019-3158 E-mail: leslie@leslieuggams.com.

UGHETTA, WILLIAM CASPER, lawyer, manufacturing executive, director; b. N.Y.C., Feb. 8, 1933; s. Casper and Frieda (Bohland) U.; m. Mary L. Lusk, Aug. 10, 1957; children: William C., Robert L., Edward F., Mark R. AB, Princeton U, 1954; LLB, Harvard U., 1959. Bar: N.Y. 1959. Assoc. Shearman & Sterling, N.Y.C., 1959-67; asst. sec. Corning Glass Works, N.Y., 1968-70, sec., counsel, 1971-72, v.p., gen. counsel, 1972-82, sr. v.p., gen. counsel, 1983-98. Bd. dirs. Chemung Canal Trust Co., Covance Inc. Bd. dirs. Steuben Area coun. Boy Scouts Am.; trustee Corning C.C. Lt. (j.g.) USN, 1954-56. Mem. Assn. of Bar of City of N.Y., ABA, N.Y. State Bar Assn., Am. Corp. Counsel Assn. (trustee 1982-85), Princeton Club (N.Y.C.), Univ. Club (N.Y.C.), Corning Country Club. Home: 10519 North Rd Corning NY 14830-3235

UGURLU, OZAN, research scientist; b. Ankara, Turkey, Mar. 16, 1979; s. Sitki and Belma Ugurlu. BS, METU, Ankara, 1997—2001; PhD (hon.), Iowa State U., 2003; MS (hon.), Alfred U., 2003. Rsch. asst. Alfred U., NY, 2001—03, Iowa State U./Ames Lab., Iowa, 2003—. V.p. ISU Turkish Student Assn., Ames, 2003—04. Achievements include research in characterization of magnetocaloric Gd-Si-Ge samples using SEM/TEM; characterization and optimization of slurries for selective gelation printing (SGP). Home: 5910 WLincoln Way Apt #308 Ames IA 50014 Office: Ames Lab 206 Wilhelm Hall Ames IA 50011 Personal E-mail: ozan@iastate.edu.

UH, DAVID KEUN, civil engineer; b. Korea, Jan. 28, 1935; s. Kwang Sun and Hyo Sook (Lee) Uh; came to U.S., 1956, naturalized, 1968; student Barclay Coll., 1956, So. Nazarene U., 1956-57; B.S. in Engring., U. Mich., 1961; M.S., Columbia U., 1968; m. Meong Jae Kim, June 4, 1966; children— Benjamin, Steven. Design engr. Allied Chem. Corp., 1963-66; sr. design engr. Frederick Snare Corp., 1966-68; project engr. Edwards & Hjorth, 1968-70; sr. engr. Soros Assocs., Inc., 1970-73; assoc. cons. engr., corp. engring. and cons. engring. dept. Ebasco Services Inc., 1973-92 (all N.Y.C.); prin. David Uh Cons. Engr., 1992–; cons. on offshore nuc. power plant, hydro, fossile, co-gen, nuc. power plants, highrise comml. bldgs., offshore coal handling, and new ch. constrn. Mem. governing bd. dirs., sec. Korean Cultural Ctr., 1969-72, 74-80, editor News Bull., 1970-72, chmn. edn. com., 1986; chmn. bd. trustees L.I. Central Korean Ch., 1981-82, pres. Korean Inst., 1981-87; mem. L.I. Presbyn. Ch., chmn., sec. edn. com., 1990, chmn. fin. com., treas., 1991-92, 2000—, governing elder, 1991—. Registered profl. engr., N.Y., N.J., Guam, Republic of Korea. Mem. ASCE, Kyunggi Alumni Assn. Am. (exec. dir. 1971-91), Kyunggi Alumni Assn. N.Y. (pres. 1969-72), Korean Student Assn. N.Y. (pres. 1962-63), U. Mich. Alumni Assn. (life), Columbia U. Engring. Alumni Assn. Republican. Club: The U. Mich. L.I. (bd. govs. 1986-88). Home: 24 Woodbine St Coram NY 11727-1138 Office: 24 Woodbine St Coram NY 11727-1138 Personal E-mail: daviduh@optonline.net.

UHDE, THOMAS WHITLEY, psychiatry educator, psychiatrist; b. Louisville, Jan. 6, 1948; s. George Irwin and Maurine U.; m. Marlene Ann Kraus, Oct. 22, 1977; children: Miles August, Katherine Kraus. BS, Duke U., 1971; MD, U. Louisville, 1975. Postdoctoral fellow Yale U., New Haven, 1975-79, chief resident clin. rsch. unit, 1979; rsch. fellow NIMH, 1979-81; pvt. practice in psychiatry Bethesda, Md., 1979-93; clin. adminstr. sect. psychobiology BPB, NIMH, ADAMHA, Bethesda, Md., 1979-80, chief unit on anxiety and affective disorders, 1982-89, chief 3-West clin. rsch. unit, 1980-90, chief sect. on anxiety and affective disorders, 1989-93; asst. clin. prof. Uniformed Svcs. U. Health Scis., Bethesda, Md., 1982-85, assoc. clin. prof. uniformed svcs., 1985-91; attending staff Clin. Ctr. NIH, Bethesda, Md., 1982-93; chmn. dept. psychiatry Detroit Receiving Hosp. and Harper Hosp., 1994-98; psychiatrist in chief Detroit Med. Ctr., 1993—2001; clin. prof. Uniformed Svcs. U. Health Scis. Sch. Medicine, Bethesda, 1991—; chmn. dept. psychiatry and behavioral neuroscis. Wayne State U. Sch. Medicine, Detroit, 1993—2001; prof. dept. pharmacology Wayne State U. Sch. of Medicine, Detroit, 1993—2003; prof., chair dept. psychiatry Penn State Coll., Hershey, Pa., 2004—, dir. ctrl. Pa. Psychiatric Inst., 2004—, dir. neurosci. rsch. inst., 2004—. Prof., psychiatry and behavioral neuroscis. dept., Wayne State U. Sch. Medicine, 1993-2003, assoc. dean rsch. and grad. programs, 1999-2001; asst. dean neuroscis., 2001-03; mem. sci. adv. com. Bethesda, Md., 1990; cons. Rsch. Scientist Devel. Rev. Com., HHS, ADAMHA, 1983, Career Devel. Program Awards Com., VA, Washington, 1986, Primary Care Rsch. Program, ADAMHA, 1988; exec. bd. Anxiety Disorders Assn. Am., 1991-93, 99-, chair sci. adv. bd., Rockville, Md., 1991-93. Editor-in-chief (jour.) Anxiety; editor-in-chief Depression and Anxiety; mem. editl. bd. Actualities Medicales Internationales en Psychiatrie, 1983, Jour. Affective Disorders, 1986, Jour. Anxiety Disorders, 1987-95, Biol. Psychiatry, 1998—2001; contbr. more than 300 sci. articles to profl. jours. Capt. USPHS, 1979-93. Recipient The Ackerly award, 1975, Nat. Rsch. Svc. award, 1979, A.E. Bennet Neuropsychiat. Rsch. Found. award, Brain, Body & Mind award USPHS, Recognition award ADAA; Am. Coll. Neuropsychopharmacology travel fellow. Mem. Am. Coll. Neuropsychopharmacolgoy, Am. Coll. Psychiatry, Am. Soc. of Clin. Psychopharmacology, Internat. Brain Rsch. Orgn., Sleep Rsch. Soc. Office: Penn State Coll Medicine Dept Psychiatry PO Box 850 500 University Dr Hershey PA 17033-0850 Office Phone: 717-531-8515. E-mail: tuhde@psu.edu.

UHL, GEORGE R. science administrator; b. Balt., Oct. 24, 1951; BA, Johns Hopkins U., 1973, PhD in Pharmacology and Exptl. Therapeutics, 1978, MD, 1979. Diplomate Am. Bd. Psychiatry and Neurology. Intern internal medicine Stanford (Calif.) U. Sch. Medicine, 1979—80; resident dept. neurology Johns Hopkins Hosp., Balt., 1980—83; asst. prof. dept. neurology and neurosci. Johns Hopkins U. Sch. Medicine, 1983—85; instr. neurology Harvard Med. Sch., 1983—84, asst. prof. neurology, 1984—88, asst. prof. program in neurosci., 1986—88; chief molecular neurobiology Addiction Rsch. Ctr. Nat. Inst. on Drug Abuse, 1988—92, acting sci. dir. Intramural Rsch. Program, 1994—96; chief divsn. intramural rsch. molecular biology br. Nat. Inst. on Drug Abuse, NIH, Balt., 1993—. Neurologist Johns Hopkins Hosp., Balt., 1983—85, Balt., 1988—93, Mass. Gen. Hosp., Boston, 1983—88; assoc. investigator Howard Hughes Med. Inst., 1984—88; neurologist Johns Hopkins Bayview Med. Ctr., Balt., 1988—; mem. program com. Coll. on Problems of Drug Dependence; mem. program and exec. coms. Internat. Narcotics Rsch. Conv.; mem. policy adv. com. Nat. Neurologic Rsch. Bank; mem. sci. adv. bd. Nat. Intramural Sequencing Ctr., NHGRI; mem. instnl. rev. bd. NIDA; mem. com. for clin. rsch. NIH; grant reviewer for multiple agys. Mem. editl. bd.: Jour. Neurochemistry, 1997—2001, Neuropsychopharmacology, 1997—2001, asst. editor: Addiction Biology, 1997—2001; contbr. articles to profl. jours. Recipient Michael Shanoff Rsch. award, Mathilde Solowey Rsch. award, Troy Daniels Lectureship award; Sloan Found. scholar in neurosci., McKnight Found. scholar in neurosci., Md. Senatorial scholar, Nat. Merit scholar. Mem.: AAAS, Restless Leg Found. (sci. adv. bd.), Am. Parkinson's Disease Assn. (sci. adv. bd.), Movement Disorders Soc., Am. Coll. Neuropharmacology, Soc. for Neurosci. (mem. program com.), Am. Soc. for Human Genetics, Am. Acad. Neurology, Am. Neurol. Assn. Achievements include research in molecular neuropharmacology and molecular genetics, especially of drug abuse, pain and Parkinsonism; complex genetics of human disorders, especially drug abuse and neurodegenerations; neurodegenerative disorders, especially Parkinson's disease; drug-gene interactions in brain. Office: 5500 Nathan Shock Dr Baltimore MD 21224 Home: 1620 Dogwood Hill Rd Baltimore MD 21286

UHL, HENRY STEPHEN MAGRAW, internist, educator; b. Wilkes-Barre, Pa., July 23, 1921; s. John Hamilton and Rebecca Ursula (Magraw) Uhl; m. Louise Powell Butler, Nov. 30, 1946 (div. 1979); 1 child, Meredith Louise Conley; m. Nancy Hyde Easley, Feb. 16, 1980 (dec. Jan. 29, 1998); m. Bernice Mallard Everett, June 25, 1999. AB, Princeton U., 1943; MD, Harvard U., 1947; MA Adeundem hon., Brown U., 1967. Diplomate: Am. Bd. Internal Medicine. Intern in pathology John Hopkins Hosp., Balt., 1947-48; asst. resident Johns Hopkins Hosp., Balt., 1948, asst. dept. medicine, 1949; asst. in pathology Johns Hopkins Med. Sch., 1947-48, instr. anatomy and pathology, 1948-49; intern med. service Henry Ford Hosp., Detroit, 1949-50; Mich. Heart Assn. research fellow Wayne State U. Coll. Medicine and Detroit Receiving Hosp., 1950-51, sr. asst. resident med. service and asst. in medicine, 1951-52, instr. medicine and research assoc., 1952-53; dir. med. edn. Worcester City Hosp. (Mass.) and Bay State Med. Ctr., Springfield, Mass., 1953-60; mem. faculty, adminstrn. Albany Med. Coll., N.Y., 1960-66; prof. med. sci. Brown U, Providence, 1966-71; dir., prof. medicine U. N.C., Mountain Area Health Edn. Ctr., 1973-78; prof. medicine Creighton U., Omaha, 1978-86, Bowman Gray Sch Medicine, Wake Forest U., Winston-Salem, N.C., 1986—; cons. NIH, also hosps., N.Y., R.I., N.C., 1960-78. Contbr. articles to profl. jours. Served to ensign M.C. USNR, 1942-45. Recipient Disting. Service award Mountain Area Health Edn. Found., Asheville, N.C., 1978 Mem. ACP, Alliance Continuing Med. Edn., Am. Soc. Internal Medicine, Assn. Hosp. Med. Edn. (pres. 1958-60, John C. Leonard Meml. award 1984), Soc. Health

and Human Values Clubs: Princeton (N.Y.C.); Press (Omaha); Fontenelle Hills Country (Bellevue, Nebr.). Achievements include research in Uhl's anomaly. Home: 2800 Monticello Dr Winston Salem NC 27106

UHL, PHILIP EDWARD, artist, photographer, cinematographer; b. Toledo, Aug. 19, 1949; s. Philip Edward and Betty Jean U. Student, Dayton Art Inst., 1967-68, Art Students League, 1974. Creative dir. Ctr. for Civic Initiative, Milw., 1969-71; VISTA vol. Office Econ. Opportunity, 1969-71; artist, photographer Assn. Honolulu Artists, 1974-77; pres. Uhl Enterprises div. Makai Photography, Honolulu, 1977—, Videoscapes div. Channel Sea TV, Honolulu, 1977—. Cons. Pan Am. Airways, N.Y.C., Honolulu, 1979-84, ITTC Travel Ctr., Honolulu, 1982-83, Royal Hawaiian Ocean Racing Club, Honolulu, 1984—, Sail Am.-Am's Cup Challenge, Honolulu, 1985-86, Am. 3 Found., Am. Cup Def., San Diego, 1991-92, Am. 3 Found. Womens Team, 1994-95, UHL Studios, Hawaii, 2000—. Co-prodr. video documentary White on Water, 1984 (Emmy 1984), Racing the Winds of Paradise (Golden Monitor award Internat. TV Assn. 1989); prodr.: Joy of Life (Golden Monitor award Internat. TV Assn. 1988), Sailors on the Sea, 1990, Teamwork, Talent, Technology (Tele award 1993); cameraman, prodr.: Pan Am. Clipper Cup 1980, 82, 84, Kenwood Cup, 1986, 88, 90, 92, 94, 96, 98, 2000 (2 Tele awards 1994), ESPN Kenwood Cup, 1990, 92, 94, ESPN Am.'s Cup, 1991-92, 94-95, Transpac, 1991, 93, 95, 97, 99 (video documentary) Rocking the Boat, 1994-95, Dateline NBC Setting Sail 1994-95, numerous spls., reports on ABC-TV, NBC-TV, CBS-TV, PBS, NHK, BBC, TFI, F1, TVNZ and numerous other major worldwide broadcast networks; prodr. At the Helm, America' Cup 2000 TVNZ; photographer, dir. graphic design/photography (video documentary) Transpac 100 years across the Pacific, 2001: (book) Nautical Quar. (Soc. Pub. Designer award 1984); contbr. numerous articles, photos to yachting publs., numerous exhbns. fine/digital art; exhibited in group shows in Honolulu, Tokyo, Hong Kong, Syndey, Isle of Wight, Las Vegas, N.V., San Diego, San Francisco, L.A., N.Y.C., Osterville, Mass.; represented in permanent collections City & County of Honolulu, Hawaii Maritime Mus., UCLA Med. Ctr., others. Mem. Am. Print Alliance, Am. Soc. Marine Artists, Soc. Internat. Nautical Scribes, Internat. Yacht Restoration Sch., Honolulu Printmakers, Digital Art Soc. Hawaii, Assn. Hawaii Artists, U.S. Sailing Assn., Royal Hawaiian Ocean Racing Club, Tutukaka South Pacific Yacht Club, Waikiki Yacht Club. Office: UHL Enterprises 1750 Kalakaua Ave Ste 3-757 Honolulu HI 96826-3766 E-mail: uhl@aol.com.

UHL, SCOTT MARK, state agency administrator; b. Balt., July 6, 1950; s. Edward George and Maurine Barbara (Keleher) Uhl; m. Charlene Hughins, Feb. 29, 1988. BA, Lehigh U., 1972. Cmty. systems developer Md. Mental Hygiene Adminstrn., Balt., 1979-82, chief, housing and cmty. support, 1982-89; adminstr., cmty. programs, dep. secretariat pub. health Md. Health and Mental Hygiene, Balt., 1989-95; dep. dir. Md. Devel. Disabilities Adminstrn., Balt., 1995—. Pres. Waterfields Press, Inc., 1994—; mem. CARE adv. bd. Md. Dept. Human Resources, Balt., 1987—94; prin. staff Md. Gov.'s Task Force Long Term Fin. Planning for Individuals with Disabilities, 1991—92. Mem. State Adv. Coun. Adminstrv. Hearings, 1993—97. Recipient Gov's Citation, 1992. Republican. Home: 2004 Sleepy Hollow Dr Woodbine MD 21797 Office: Md Health & Mental Hygiene 201 W Preston St Baltimore MD 21201-2323

UHLENBECK, KAREN KESKULLA, mathematician, educator; b. Cleve., Aug. 24, 1942; d. Arnold Edward and Carolyn Elizabeth (Windeler) Keskulla; m. Olke Cornelis, June 12, 1965 (div.) BS in Math., U. Mich., 1964; PhD in Math., Brandeis U., 1968. Instr. math. MIT, Cambridge, 1968-69; lectr. U. Calif., Berkeley, 1969-71; asst. prof., then assoc. prof. U. Ill., Urbana, 1971-76, assoc. prof., then prof. Chgo., 1977-83; prof. U. Chgo., 1983-88; Sid W. Richardson Found. Regents' Chair in Math. U. Tex., 1988—. Spkr. plenary address Internat. Conress Maths., 1990; mem. com. women on sci. and engring. NRC, 1992-94; mem. steering com., dir. mentoring program for women Inst. for Advanced Study/Park City Math. Inst. Author: Instantons and Four Manifolds, 1984. Contbr. articles to profl. jours. Recipient Common Wealth award for Sci. and Invention, PNC Bank, 1995; NSF grad. fellow, 1964-68, Sloan Found. fellow, 1974-76, MacArthur Found. fellow, 1983-88. Mem. AAAS, NAS, Alumni Assn. U. Mich. (Alumnae of Yr. 1984), Am. Math. Soc., Assn. Women in Math., Phi Beta Kappa. Avocations: gardening, canoeing, hiking. Office: U Tex Dept Math Austin TX 78712

UHLENBRUCK, NIKOLAUS THEODOR, finance educator; m. Leslie Arlene Hilton, Apr. 9, 1988; children: Benjamin Johannnes Hilton, Stephanie Marie, Timothy Theodor. Diplom Kaufman, U. of Cologne, Germany, 1986; PhD, U. of Colo., 1995. Asst. prof. of mgmt. Calif. State U. San Marcos, San Marcos, 1996—99, Tex. A&M U., College Station, 1999—2004, U. Mont., 2004—, dir. Small Bus. Inst., 2004—. Cons. Freedom Chem. Co., Phila., 1995, Prudential Relocation Svcs., Boulder, Colo., 1991—96, Chinese Petroleum Co., Taipei, Taiwan, 2002. Author: (book) The Innovative Potential of Services for Manufacturing Firms; contbr. articles to profl. jours. Grantee, Shell Oil Co. Found. grantee, 2002. Office: U Mont Sch Bus Admin Missoula MT 59812 Office Phone: 979-845-1445. Office Fax: 406-243-6191.

UHLENHUTH, EBERHARD HENRY, psychiatrist, educator; b. Balt., Sept. 15, 1927; s. Eduard Carl Adolph and Elisabeth (Baier) Uhlenhuth; m. Helen Virginia Lyman, June 20, 1952; children: Kim Lyman, Karen Jane, Eric Rolf. BS in Chemistry, Yale U., 1947; MD, Johns Hopkins U., 1951. Intern Harborview Hosp., Seattle, 1951-52; resident in psychiatry Johns Hopkins Hosp., Balt., 1952-56, asst. psychiatrist in charge outpatient dept., 1956-61, psychiatrist in charge, 1961-62; chief adult psychiatry clinic U. Chgo. Hosps. Clinics, 1968-76; instr. psychiatry Johns Hopkins U., 1956-59, asst. prof., 1959-67, assoc. prof., 1967-68, U. Chgo., 1968-73, prof., 1973-85, acting chmn., 1983-85; prof. psychiatry U. N.Mex., Albuquerque, 1985-97, prof. emeritus, 1997—, vice chmn. for edn., 1991-94. Cons. in field; mem. clin. psychopharmacology rsch. rev. com. NIMH, 1968-72, mem. treatment devel. and assessment rsch. rev. com., 1987-88; mem. psychopharmacology adv. com. FDA, 1974-78; mem. adv. group to Treatment of Depression Collaborative Rsch. Program, NIMH, 1978-92; mem. study rev. com. Xanax Discontinuation Program, The UpJohn Co., 1988-92, Nat. Adv. Coun. on Drug Abuse, NIDA, 1989-92, Coop. Studies Evaluation Com., VA, 1989-92. Mem. editl. bd. Jour. Affective Disorders, 1978—, Psychiatry Rsch., 1979-96, Behavioral Medicine, 1982—, Neuropsychopharmacology, 1992-95, Exptl. and Clin. Psychopharmacology, 1992-99, Anxiety, 1992—; contbr. articles to profl. jours. Recipient Rsch. Career Devel. award USPHS, 1962-68, Rsch. Scientist award, 1976-81. Fellow Am. Coll. Neuropsychopharmacology (pres. 1986), Am. Psychiat. Assn., Am. Psychopath. Assn.; mem. Balt.-Washington Soc. for Psychoanalysis, Collegium Internat. Neuro-Psychopharmacologicum, Psychiat. Rsch. Soc. Office: U NMex Dept Psychiatry MSC09 5030 1 Univ New Mex Albuquerque NM 87131-0001 Office Phone: 505-272-8876. Business E-Mail: uhli@unm.edu.

UHLER, WALTER CHARLES, government official, writer; b. Lebanon, Pa., Feb. 23, 1948; s. Victor Cornelius and Barbara Jean (Malin) U.; m. Judy Ann Sherk, Aug. 7, 1967 (div. 1984); children: Terry Allen, Matthew David. Life partner: Carol A. DePrisco. BA in Polit. Sci. cum laude, BA in Russian cum laude, cert. Russian area, Pa. State U., 1973, MPA, 1992. Tchg. asst. Pa. State U., University Park, 1975-76; procurement agt. Naval Aviation Supply Office, Phila., 1976-80; contracts adminstr. GSA, Phila., 1980-81; contracting officer Def. Logistics Agy., Phila., 1981-86, corp. contracting officer, 1986-94; chief fin. svcs., 1993—2001; chief of ops. Def. Contract Mgmt. Agy., Lockheed Martin Delaware Valley, 2001—; regional cons. Def. Logistics Agy., L.A., 1985-86, nat. cons. Cameron Station, Va., 1989-90, leader Testing Agy., 1994, Privatization Assessment Team Ft. Belvoir, Va., 1997-98. Participant Air Force Intelligence Conf. on Soviet Affairs, Arlington, Va., 1988, Venona Conf., Washington, 1996, Ballistic Missile Def. Conf., Washington, 1998, AP/Harriman Inst. Conf., N.Y.C., 1999, State of the World Forum, N.Y.C., 2000; testified against nat. missile def., Vt. Ho. of Reps., 2002; gave radio interviews on nat. missile def., Vt., Calif., Wis., Radio Free Europe/Radio Liberty, 2002; presenter, 11th ann. Russia-Am. Conf., St. Petersburg, Russia, 2002; spkr. on contracts DOD Conf., Cleve., 1988, on restructuring costs, Memphis, 1994; chmn. Ann. Nat. Conf. Contracting Officers and Auditors, 1987-93; mem. Citizen Amb. Archivists' Del. to Russia and Poland, 1995, Citizen Amb. Del. to China, 1996, Russia and Finland, 1998; prodr., interviewer (with George Enteen) Sergei Vasilievich Utechin's Oral Reminiscences, 1997—; pres, Russian-American Internat. Studies Assn, 2004-. Contbr. articles to profl. jours. Baseball coach Valley Athletic Assn., Bensalem, Pa., 1979-88, basketball coach, 1980-85, coord., 1981; tutor Ctr. for Literacy, Phila., 1991-93, Project GIVE, Phila., 1995-98. Recipient Comdrs. Excellence award Defense Contract Mgmt. Area Ops., 1993. Mem. Am. Assn. for Advancement Slavic Studies, Soc. for Mil. History, Acad. Polit. Sci., Nat. Book Critics Cir., Am. Acad. of Polit. and Social Scis., Friends of the Free Libr. of Phila., Am. Hist. Assn. Democrat. Avocations: history, literature, Pa. State U. football. Office: DCMA LMDV L-3 Bldg 1 Federal St Camden NJ 08102 E-mail: waltuhler@aol.com.

UHLIG, FRANK, JR., editor, writer; b. N.Y.C., June 15, 1927; s. Franklin R. Uhlig and Elisabeth (Lazenby) Sutherland; m. Inna Winocour, 1957; children: Valerie, Melissa. BA in History, Kenyon Coll., 1951. Head book dept. U.S. Naval Inst., Annapolis, Md., 1960-62, editor Naval Rev., 1962-81, sr. editor U.S. Naval Inst., 1969-81; editor Naval War Coll. Rev. Naval War Coll., Newport, R.I., 1981-93, wargame commentator, 1982-99, head advanced rsch., 1984-88, emeritus, sponsored rsch. scholar, 1993—, Writer, spkr., tchr. Naval War Coll., and other orgns., 1970—; spkr. on naval matters, WWII, Vietnam, 1970—. Author: How Navies Fight, 1994; editor: Vietnam: The Naval Story, 1986; contbr. more than 50 articles to profl. publs. Mem. Mystic Seaport Mus. With USN, 1945-47. Recipient A.T. Mahan award for lit. achievement Navy League of U.S., 1970. Mem. N.Am. Soc. Oceanic History, U.S. Naval Inst., Soc. for Mil. History, Naval War Coll. Found. Episcopalian. Avocations: politicial issues, military, maritime and technological developments. Home: 60 Boulevard Ter Middletown RI 02842 4908 Office: Naval War Coll Code 3 686 Cushing Rd Newport RI 02841-1213

UHLIR, ARTHUR, JR., electrical engineer, university administrator; b. Chgo., Feb. 2, 1926; s. Arthur and Helene (Houghteling) U.; m. Ingeborg Williams, July 24, 1954; children: Steven, Donald, David. BS, Ill. Inst. Tech., 1945, MSChemE, 1948; SM in Physics, U. Chgo., 1950, PhD in Physics, 1952. Process analyst Douglas Aircraft, Chgo., 1945; asst. engr. Armour Rsch. Found., Chgo., 1945-48; tech. staff Bell Telephone Labs., Murray Hill, N.J., 1951-58; dir. semi- condr. research and devel., mgr. semicondr. div., group v.p. engring. Microwave Assos., Inc., Burlington, Mass., 1958-69; dir. rsch. Computer Metrics, Rochelle Park, N.J., 1969-73; prof. elec. engring. Tufts U., Medford, Mass., 1970-94, chmn. dept. elec. engring., 1970-75, dean of engring., 1973-80. AEC fellow, 1949-51 Fellow IEEE, AAAS; mem. Am. Phys. Soc., Sigma Xi. Home: 45 Kendal Common Rd Weston MA 02493-2159 Office: Tufts Univ Dept Elec Engring & Computer Sci Medford MA 02155 Personal E-mail: auhlir@mailaps.org.

UHLMANN, ELENORE ARLENE, interior designer, writer; b. Ada., Mich., July 18, 1922; d. Arthur Benjamin and Arla Mary (Kriedler) Hale; m. Robert Carl Uhlmann, Jan. 14, 1939 (dec. Jan. 5, 1995); children: J. Louise Uhlmann Zielke, Nancy Jean Uhlmann. Student, U. Mich., 1939, 68, Kendall Sch. Design, 1940, Heaneys Bus. Coll., 1941. Designer, sales rep. Mfr.'s Showroom, Grand Rapids, Mich., 1966-71; designer, decorator Regent Interiors, Clearwater, Fla., 1971, Chandlers, Dunedin, Fla., 1972-76, Square Yard, Dunedin, Fla., 1976-80; instr. Palm Harbor (Fla.) Libr., 1997-98. Presentor at numerous workshops and clubs. Contbr. articles and essays to mags. Mem. Jr. League, 1972-89. Avocations: writing, painting, travel. Mailing: 7711 N 51st Ave 1080 Glendale AZ 85301

UHLMANN, FREDERICK GODFREY, commodity and securities broker; b. Chgo, Dec. 31, 1929; s. Richard F. and Rosamond G. (Goldman) U.; m. Virginia Lee Strauss, July 24, 1951; children: Richard, Thomas, Virginia, Karen, Elizabeth. BA, Washington and Lee U., 1951. Ptnr. Uhlmann Grain Co., Chgo., 1951-61; v.p. Uhlmann & Co., Inc., Chgo., 1961-65; sr. v.p. H. Hentz & Co., Chgo., 1965-73, Drexel Burnham Lambert Inc., Chgo., 1973-84; exec. v.p., dir. bus. futures Dean Witter Reynolds Inc., Chgo., 1984-85; sr. v.p., mgr. commodity dept. Bear, Stearns & Co., Inc., Chgo., 1985-88; exec. v.p. Rodman & Renshaw, Inc., 1988-95; sr. v.p. LIT-Divsn. of First Options Inc., Chgo., 1995-98; chmn. Chgo Bd. Trade, Ill., 1973-74; sr. v.p., exec. dir. MAN Financial, 1998—. Ptnr. Uhlmann Investments, LLC. Trustee Highland Pk. Hosp., Ill.; bd. dir. Dist. 113 H.S. Found., 1990—, Mt. Sanai Hosp. Inst., Chgo., 1999—. Mem. Nat. Futures Assoc. (dir. 1981-2000, vice chair 1998-2000), Futures Industry Assn. (bd. dir., chmn. 1975-76), Futures Industry Inst. (bd. dir.). Home: 783 Whiteoaks Ln Highland Park IL 60035-3656 E-mail: fgu73@aol.com.

UHR, JONATHAN WILLIAM, immunologist, educator, researcher; b. N.Y.C., Sept. 8, 1927; s. Jacques Stanley Uhr and Mary Wetsman; m. Roberta Joy Klibanoff (div.); children: Jacqueline, Sarita. AB, Cornell U., 1948; MD, NYU, 1952. Diplomate Am. Bd. Internal Medicine. Dazian fellow dept. microbiology NYU Med. Ctr., 1955-56; chief resident in medicine Mt. Sinai Hosp., N.Y.C., 1956-57; instr. dept. microbiology NYU Sch. Medicine, 1957-58, asst. prof. medicine, 1958-62, assoc. prof., 1962-68, prof., 1968-72; prof. dept. microbiology and internal medicine U. Tex. Southwestern Med. Ctr. & Cancer Immunobiology Ctr., Dallas, 1972—; chair dept. microbiology U. Tex. Southwestern Med. Ctr., Dallas, 1972-97. Dir. Irvington House Inst. for Rheumatic Fever and Allied Diseases, N.Y.C., 1962-72; vis. prof. microbiology Yale U., 1970-72; assoc. attending physician Univ. Hosp., N.Y.C., 1963-72; assoc. vis. physician Bellevue Hosp., N.Y.C., 1959-72; cons. internal medicine Manhattan Vet.'s Hosp., 1964-74. Contbr. articles to profl. publs. With USN, 1945-46. Recipient Newcomb Cleveland prize AAAS, 1963, Squibb award Infectious Diseases Soc. Am., 1971, NAS award, 1984, Faculty medal Med. Sch. Montpellier, France, 1984, Abbott-ASM Lifetime Achievement award, 1999; Commonwealth fellow Walter and Eliza Hall Inst. Med. Rsch., 1961-62. Mem. Am. Assn. Immunologists (pres. 1989—), Am. Assn. Pathologists, Am. Soc. Clin. Investigation, Transplantation Soc., Assn. Am. Physicians. Office: U Tex Southwestern Med Ctr Dept Cancer Immunobiology 5323 Harry Hines Blvd Dallas TX 75390-8576 E-mail: Jonathan.Uhr@southwesternmed.edu.

UHRIG, JENNIFER DEE, researcher; b. East Stroudsburg, Pa., July 18, 1973; d. William Anthony and Sandra Suzanne Uhrig; m. Lester William Dimmick III, Oct. 14, 2000. BBA, Wilkes U., Wilkes-Barre, Pa, 1997; MHA, Wilkes U., Wilkes-Barre, Pa., 1997; PhD, Pa. State U., Univ. State Pk., Pa, 2001. Grad. asst. Wilkes U., Wilkes-Barre, Pa., 1995—97; rsch./tchg. asst. Pa. State U., Univ. Pk., Pa., 1997—2000; summer rsch. assoc. RAND, Santa Monica, Calif., 1999—99; health sevcs. rsch. RTI Internat., Rsch. Triangle Pk., NC, 2001—. Recipient RTI Internat. President's Award, RTI Internat., 2003, Dissertation Rsch. Award, Pa. State U., Coll. of Health and Human Devel., 1999-2000, Outstanding Achievement Award in Health Adminstrn., Wilkes U., Sch. of Bus., Soc. and Pub. Policy, 1997, Outstanding Student Award in Bus. Adminstrn., 1995; grantee Dissertation Grant Award, Agy. for Healthcare Rsch. and Quality, 2000-2001. Mem.: AcademyHealth. Office: RTI Internat 3040 Cornwallis Rd PO Box 12194 Research Triangle Park NC 27709

UHRIG, ROBERT EUGENE, nuclear engineer, educator; b. Raymond, Ill., Aug. 6, 1928; s. John Matthew and Anna LaDonna (Fireman) U.; m. Paula Margaret Schnepf, Nov. 27, 1954; children: Robert John, Joseph Charles, Mary Catherine, Charles William, Jean Marie, Thomas Paul, Fredrick James. BS with honors, U. Ill., 1948; MS, Iowa State U., 1950, PhD, 1954; grad. Advanced Mgmt. Program, Harvard U., 1976. Registered profl. engr., Iowa, Fla. Instr. engring. mechanics Iowa State U., 1948-51; assoc. engr., rsch. asst. Inst. Atomic Rsch. (at univ.), 1951-54, assoc. prof. engring. mechanics and nuc. engring., also group leader, 1956-60; prof. nuc. engring., chmn. dept. U. Fla., Gainesville, 1960-68, on leave, 1967-68, dean Coll. Engring., 1968-73, dean emeritus, 1989—; dep. asst. dir. rsch. Dept. Def., Washington, 1967-68; dir. nuc. affairs Fla. Power & Light Co., Miami, 1973-74, v.p. for nuc. affairs, 1974-75, v.p. nuc. and gen. engring., 1976-78, v.p. advanced systems and tech., 1978-86; disting. prof. engring. U. Tenn., Knoxville, 1986—2002, disting. prof. engring. emeritus, 2003—; disting. scientist Oak Ridge Nat. Lab., 1986—2002, disting. scientist emeritus, 2003—. Instr. engring. mechanics U.S. Mil. Acad., 1954-56; rep. Dept. Def. to com. on acad. sci. and engring. Fed. Coun. Sci. and Tech., 1967; chmn. engring. adv. com. NSF, 1972-73; bd. dirs. Engring. Coun. Profl. Devel., 1968-72; mem. commn. edn. for engring. profession Nat. Assn. State Univs. and Land Grant Colls., 1969-72; apptd. mem. adv. com. on reactor safeguards U.S. Nuc. Regulatory Commn., 1997-2001. Author: Random Noise Techniques in Nuclear Reactor Systems, 1970, trans. into Russian, 1974; co-author: (with Lefteri H. Tsoukalas) Fuzzy and Neural Approaches in Engineering, 1997—. Served to 1st lt. USAF. Recipient Sec. of Def. Civilian Svc. award, 1968, Outstanding Alumni award U. Ill. Coll. Engring., 1970, Alumni Profl. Achievement award Iowa State U., 1972, President's medallion U. Fla., 1973; Disting. Achievement citation Iowa State U. Alumni Assn., 1980, Glenn Murphy award Am. Soc. for Engring. Edn., 1992. Fellow ASME (life, Richards Meml. award 1969), AAAS, Am. Nuc. Soc. (chmn. edn. com. 1962-64, chmn. tech. group for edn. 1964-66, bd. dirs. 1965-68, exec. com. bd. 1966-68); mem. Am. Soc. Engring. Edn. (pres. S.E. sect. 1972-73, chmn. nuc. engring. divsn. 1966-67, 88-89, rsch. award S.E. sect. 1962, Glenn Murphy award as Outstanding Educator 1992), John Henry Newman Honor Soc., Sigma Xi, Tau Beta Pi, Phi Mu Epsilon, Pi Tau Sigma, Phi Kappa Phi (Disting. Mem. award 1997). Home: 5221 NW 44th Pl Gainesville FL 32606-4328 Office: U Tenn Pasqua Nuc Engring Bldg Knoxville TN 37996-2300 Office Phone: 352-974-3110. Business E-Mail: ruhrig@utk.edu.

UHRIK, CARL THOMAS, computer scientist, educator; b. Cedar Rapids, Iowa, Dec. 9, 1957; s. Richard Lee and Shirley Marie Uhrik; m. Michael W. Burkart, Sept. 1, 1999. BSEE, Tex. A&M U., 1980, MS in Computer Sci., 1981; MS, U. Ill., 1985, PhD, 1991. Asst. lab. mgr. Lab. for Informatic Engring. U. Trento, Italy, 1990-95; speech recognition engr. Berdy Med. Sys., Boulder, Colo., 1996-99; prof. U. Phoenix, Denver, 1996—; internationalization engr. Intl.com/Lionbridge, Boulder, 1999—. Fulbright scholar, 1986-87. Roman Catholic. Avocations: vegan vegetarian cooking, reading, films, outdoors, biking. Home: 3725 Birchwood Dr Apt 23 Boulder CO 80304-1421 E-mail: uhrik@hotmail.com.

UHRIK, STEVEN BRIAN, clinical social worker, psychotherapist, employee assistance professional, behavioral science consultant; b. Chgo., June 30, 1949; s. George Stephen and Elizabeth Gertrude Beisse (Will) U.; m. Mee Phon C. Uhrik. BA, No. Ill. U., 1973; MSW, U. Ill., 1980; Cert. Study, Loyola U., Chgo. Lic. clin. social worker; cert. conflict mediation. Vocat. coord. O.H. Industries divsn. Opportunity House, Inc., Sycamore, Ill., 1970-79; clin. social worker, family counselor Rockford (Ill.) Meml. Hosp., 1979-81, co-dir. devel. chronic pain program, 1979-80; social worker West Suburban Kidney Ctr., S.C., Oak Park, Ill., 1981-87; behavioral sci. cons. Continental Health Care, Ltd., Oak Park, 1981-87; mgr. employee assistance Grant Hosp. Chgo., 1987-89; regional mgr. employee assistance Motorola, Inc., 1989-95, global mgr. GECS ops. and drug alcohol program, 1995—; pres. Personal Consultation Counseling and Psychotherapy, Carol Stream, Ill., 1983-89. Profl. spkr. Recipient award Dekalb-Sycamore Human Rels. Commn., 1974; developed patient edn. program for dialysis patients and family members Nat. Kidney Found. of Ill. Mem. NASW, Acad. Cert. Social Workers, Soc. for Human Resource Mgmt. (workplace health, safety and security com., Nat. Assn. Watch and Clock Collectors. Avocations: antique automobiles, photography, collecting restoration watches and clocks. Office: Motorola Inc Rm 110 EAP 1301 E Algonquin Rd CRC Schaumburg IL 60196-1077 E-mail: SUhrik@worldnet.att.net.

UHRY, ALFRED FOX, playwright; b. Atlanta, Dec. 3, 1936; s. Ralph Kahn and Alene (Fox) Uhry; m. Joanna Kellogg; children: Emily Uhry Rhea, Elizabeth Uhry MacCurrach, Katharine, Nell. BA, Brown U., 1958. Playwriter Flora Roberts Inc. Worked with composer Frank Loesser, 1960—63; instr. Eng. drama Calhoun High Sch., 1963—80; instr. lyric writing NYU, 1985—88. Author: (plays) Driving Miss Daisy, 1987 (Drama Desk award nomination for best play, 1987, ulitzer Prize for drama, 1988, L.A. Drama Critics Circle award for best play, 1989), (musicals) Chapeau, 1977, (adapter) Little Johnny Jones, 1982, Follow Thru, 1984, (lyrics) Here's Where I Belong, 1968, Swing, 1980, (lyrics, libretto) The Robber Bridegroom, 1978 (Drama Desk award nomination for best play, 1975, Tony award nomination for best book of a musical, 1976), America's Sweetheart, 1985, (screenplays) Mystic Pizza, 1988, Driving Miss Daisy, 1989 (Academy award for best adapted screenplay, 1989, WGA award, 1989), Rich in Love, 1993, Last Night Of Ballyhoo, 1996 (Tony award for Best Play, 1997). Mem.: Dramatists Guild (coun. 1989—, Elizabeth Martow prize 1987). Office: care Flora Roberts Inc 157 W 57th St Ph A New York NY 10019-2210

UICKER, JOSEPH BERNARD, retired engineering company executive; b. Mar. 29, 1940; s. John Joseph and Elizabeth Josephine (Flint) U.; m. Mary Catherine Howze, June 5, 1965 (div. Oct. 1971); children: Patricia, Suzzane; m. Janet Ann Ballman, Sept. 22, 1973. BSME, U. Detroit, 1963, MS, 1965. Registered profl. engr., Mich. Engr. Smith Hinchman & Grylls, Detroit, 1964-72, chief mech. engr. health facilities, 1972-73, asst. dir. health facilities, 1973-75, v.p., dir. mech. engring., 1975-82, v.p., dir. profl. staff, 1983-2000; also bd. dirs.; ret., 2000. Dir. Smith Group, Detroit, 1984-2000. Capt. U.S. Army, 1966—67. Mem. NSPE, ASME, ASHRAE, Soc. Am. Mil. Engrs., Engring. Soc., Athletic Club. Avocations: golf, photography, gardening. Home: 15250 Knolson St Livonia MI 48154-4736 E-mail: juicker@ameritech.net.

UILKEMA, JOHN K. lawyer; BSE in Mech. Engring., U. Mich., 1957; JD, George Washington U., 1961. Bar: D.C. 1962, Calif. 1963, U.S. Patent and Trademark Office, U.S. Dist. Ct. (all dists.) Calif., U.S. Ct. Appeals (Calif.), U.S. Dist. Ct. (all dists.) D.C., U.S. Ct. Appeals (D.C.), U.S. Ct. Appeals (fed. cir.). Ptnr. Thelen Reid & Priest LLP, San Francisco. Mem.: ABA (bd. govs. sect. intellectual property 2002—). Office: Thelen Reid & Priest LLP Ste 1800 101 Second St San Francisco CA 94105

UJIFUSA, GRANT MASASHI, editor; b. Worland, Wyo., Jan. 4, 1944; s. Tom Mamoru and Mary Takayo (Okugawa) U.; m. Katherine Adams Glover, June 23, 1969 (div. June 1974); m. Amy Jane Brooks, Sept. 9, 1978; children: Steven, Andrew. BA, Harvard U., 1965; MA, Brandeis U., Waltham, Mass., 1967; postgrad., Brown U., Providence, 1969. Book editor Houghton Mifflin, Boston, 1974-77, Random House, N.Y.C., 1977-84, Macmillan, N.Y.C., 1984-88; mag. editor Reader's Digest, Pleasantville, N.Y., 1988-98; founder, CEO Best Am. Minds, Pubs., 2000—. Founding editor, co-author: The Almanac of American Politics, 1972—. Chief strategist Japanese-Am. Redress Effort, Japanese Am. Citizen's League, 1982-92; hon. mem. Co. K, 442d Regtl. Combat Team; bd. dirs. Japanese Am. Nat. Mus., Nat. Japanese Am. Meml. Found. Recipient Spl. award Japanese Am. Citizens League, San Francisco, 1988, Excellence 2000 award Outstanding Asian Am., 1992. Mem. U.S. Pan Asian C. of C. Home: 9 Greenridge Dr Chappaqua NY 10514-1303 E-mail: Captain129@aol.com.

UJIOKA, TAKESHI, endocrinologist; b. Kumamoto, Japan, Apr. 21, 1963; s. Irei and Fumiko U.; m. Akiko Sakata, Nov. 16, 1996; 1 child, Hirotaka. MD, Miyazaki Med. Coll., 1991; PhD, Kumamoto U., 1998. Cert. physician, Japan. Resident Kumamoto Univ. Hosp., Japan, 1991-94; rsch. scientist Trinity U., San Antonio, Tex., 1998—. Contbr. articles to profl. jours. Grantee The Lalor Found., Providence, R.I., 1999. Mem. Japan Soc. Ob/Gyn, Japan Endocrine Soc., Japan Soc. Fertility and Sterility. Avocations: political science, Asian history. Office: Trinity Univ/Dept Biology 715 Stadium Dr San Antonio TX 78212-3104 E-mail: tujioka@trinity.edu.

UKE, ALAN KURT, company executive; b. L.A., Nov. 24, 1952; s. Mustafa Tugrul Uke and Gladys Jean Hunnicott; m. Lisa Joyce Katter, 1975 (div.); 1 child, Gregory; m. Diane Christiansen, Jan. 12, 1985; children: Leslie, John. Student, Dartmouth Coll., 1971. Univ. Calif., San Diego, 1975. Prin., owner Underwater Kinetics, Powag, Calif., 1971—; pres. UK Corp., Del Mar, Calif., 1980—. Patentee, inventor in field. Pres. San Diego Aircraft Carrier Mus., 1993—, San Diego Taxpayers Assn. Found., 1996-98, North County Coun. Aging, Vista, Calif., 1998-2000; chmn. learning for life divsn. Boy Scouts Am., 1999-2000. Recipient Entrepreneur of Yr. award San Diego County,

1997, Headliner of Yr. award San Diego Press Club, 1997. Mem.: World Pres.'s Assn. Republican. Lutheran. Avocations: travel, reading, astronomy. Office: Underwater Kinetics 13400 Danielson St Poway CA 92064 E-mail: auke@uwkinetics.com.

UKROP, JAMES E. retail executive; b. 1937; Vice chmn., CEO Ukrop's Super Markets Inc., 1958—, chmn. Office: Ukrop's Super Markets Inc 600 Southlake Blvd Richmond VA 23236-3922

UKROPINA, JAMES R. lawyer; b. Fresno, Calif., Sept. 10, 1937; s. Robert J. and Persida (Angelich) Ukropina. AB, Stanford U., 1959, MBA, 1961; LL.B., U. So. Calif., 1965. Bar: Calif. 1966. Assoc. firm O'Melveny & Myers, Los Angeles, 1965-72, ptnr., 1972—80, 1992—2000, of counsel, 2001—; exec. v.p., gen. counsel Santa Fe Internat. Corp., Alhambra, Calif., 1980-84, dir., 1981-86; exec. v.p., gen. counsel Pacific Enterprises, Los Angeles, 1984-86, pres. and dir., 1986-89, chmn. bd. and chief exec. officer, 1989-91. Bd. dirs. Lockheed Martin Corp., Pacific Life Ins. Co., Trust Co. of the West, Ctrl. Natural Resources., Indymac Bancorp, Keck Found. Editor in chief So. Calif. Law Rev, 1964-65. Trustee Stanford U., 1991-2000 Mem. ABA, Calif. Bar Assn., Los Angeles County Bar Assn., Annandale Golf Club, Calif. Club, Beta Theta Pi. Office: O'Melveny & Myers 400 S Hope St Los Angeles CA 90071-2899

ULAKOVICH, RONALD STEPHEN, real estate developer; b. Youngstown, Ohio, Nov. 17, 1942; s. Stephen G. and Anne (Petretich) U. BS, Indsl. Engring. Coll., 1967; MS, Method Engring., Ill. Inst. Tech., 1969. Methods engr. Supreme Products, Chgo., 1964-66; pres. Contract Chair, 1966-70; v.p. sales Amrep Corp., Rosemont, Ill., 1970-73; pres. Condo Assoc., Ltd., Arlington Heights, Ill., 1973—, Am. Resorts Internat. Ltd., 1983. Named Employee of Yr., 1965; recipient Nat. Home Builders Grand award, 1977, Million Dollar Cir. award Chgo. Tribune, 1978, Cert. of Recognition award Congl. Com., 1982, Cert. of Merit award Pres. Reagan's Task Force, 1984; named to Ky. Col., State of Ky., 1982. Mem. Am. Assn. Investors, Apt. Owners Assn., Real Estate Soc. of Syndicators and Investors, Am. Resort and Residential Devel. Assn. Roman Catholic. Avocations: auto racing, golf. Home: 510 Van Buren Dundee IL 60118 Office Phone: 815-874-4737. E-mail: RSGU@cometlink.com.

ULANOFF, STANLEY M. communications executive; b. Bklyn., May 30, 1922; s. Samuel H. and Minnie (Druss) U.; m. Bernice Mayer, June 15, 1947; children: Roger, Amy Ulanoff Christie, Lisa M. Ulanoff, Dory Ulanoff Kennedy. BA in Journalism, U. Iowa, 1943; MBA in Mktg., Hofstra U., 1955; PhD in Comm., NYU, 1968. Copywriter promotions dept. N.Y. Times, 1946—49; asst. to pres. SUNY, Stony Brook, 1962-64; prof. mktg., head advt., sales promotion & pub. rels. divsn. Baruch Coll. (CUNY), NY, 1964—86; pres. Viewmark Prodns. Inc. d.b.a. Advisions, 1986—. Cons. U.S. Dept. Def., Grosset & Dunlap pubs., Siebel/Mohr, U.S. Postal Svc.; cons, asst. to pres. Compton Advt.; arbitrator N.Y. Stock Exch., Nat. Assn. Securities Dealers; cons. Hasbro Toys. Author or editor 34 books including Handbook of Sales Promotion, also mags., newspaper articles, rsch. papers; prodr. over 200 video documentaries. 2nd lt. U.S. Army, 1945; Brig. gen. USAR, Mil. Svc., 1942-84. Decorated Chevalier dans l'Ordre des Palmes Academique, Republic of France, Legion of Merit, Meritorious Svc. medal, Army Commendation medal, Army Achievement medal, U.S. Army, Silver Conspicuous Svc. Cross, Merit medal State of N.Y., 1st prize award Am. Assn. Advt. Agys.; named VIP (Very Important Prof.) Splty. Adv. Assn. Internat. (2); Am. Assn. Advt. Agys. fellow, Eastman-Kodak fellow in film prodn.; Lewis Kleid Direct Mail Advt. scholar. Mem. Mil. Intelligence Res. Soc. (pres.), Res. Officers Assn. (pres.); disting. alumnus, Hofstra Univ. Office: 17 The Serpentine Roslyn NY 11576-1736 Fax: 516-484-2930.

ULBRECHT, JAROMIR JOSEF, chemical engineer; b. Ostrava, Czechoslovakia, Dec. 16, 1928; s. Josef and Leopolda U.; m. Vera Krafneter, July 10, 1952; children: Jan Stanislav, Magdalena Vera. Ing., Czech Inst. Tech., Prague, 1952, PhD, 1958. Dept. head rsch. divsn. synthetic rubber co., Zlin, Czechoslovakia, 1958-63; head lab. engring. rheology Czechoslovak Acad. Scis., Prague, 1963-68; prof. chem. engring. U. Salford, Eng., 1968-78; prof., chmn. dept. chem. engring. SUNY, Buffalo, 1978-83; chief divsn. chem. process metrology Nat. Bur. Standards, Washington, 1984-88; dep. dir. office tech. evaluation and assessment Nat. Inst. Standards and Tech. (formerly Nat. Bur. Standards), Washington, 1989-90, dir. tech. programs, tech. svcs., 1991-94; pres. OFI Tech Svcs., Rockville, Md., 1994—. Author: Non-Newtonian Liquids, 1967, Mixing of Liquids by Mechanical Agitation, 1985, Process Sensing and Diagnostics, 1989, Competitiveness of the U.S. Chemical Industry in International Markets, 1990; editor: Chemical Engineering Communications, 1976-86; contbr. numerous articles to profl. jours. Recipient Outstanding Scholarship award Czech Acad. Scis., 1965, 67, Purkyne medal Czech Acad. Scis., 1999, Meml. Hybl medal Czech Tech. U., 2002; Alexander von Humboldt fellow, 1967 Fellow Am. Inst. Chem. Engrs.; mem. Soc. Rheology, Am. Chem. Soc., Czech Acad. Engring. (hon. fgn.), Sigma Xi. Office: OFI Tech Svcs Inc 311 High Gables Dr #308 Gaithersburg MD 20878 E-mail: jjulbrecht@aol.com.

ULE, GUY MAXWELL, JR., stockbroker; b. Chgo., Jan. 2, 1940; s. Guy Maxwell and Margaret (Karahuta) U.; m. Angela Joanne Genelli, Nov. 17, 1975. BA, Harvard U., 1961, MBA, 1967. Analyst, phys. distbn. specialist TWA, N.Y.C. and Phila., 1967-69, supr. comml. passenger sales N.Y.C., 1969-71; pvt. practice cons. N.Y.C., 1971-72; mgr. sales mktg. Source Equities, N.Y.C., 1972; ptnr., N.Y.C. office mgr. Daley, Coolidge & Co., 1972-77; v.p., divsn. mgr. Rosenkrantz, Ehrenkrantz, Lyon & Ross Inc., 1977-85, Ingham Becker & Co., Inc., 1985-87; v.p., asst. sec. Meyers, Pollock, Robbins Inc., 1987-89; v.p., Max Ule divsn. Herzog Heine Geduld Inc., 1989-2000; v.p. investments Shields & Co., Inc., 2000—. Pres. Max Ule & Co., Inc., N.Y.C., 1977-2004, Max Ule Advt. & Mktg., Inc., N.Y.C., 1980—; brokerage info. cons. Internet World Wide Web, 1995. Creator first discount brokerage system on computer, 1980. Chmn., pres. Assn. in Manhattan for Autistic Children, 1985-86. Lt. USN, 1962-65. Mem.: Racquet Club Phila., Knickerbocker Club, Racquet and Tennis Club. Republican. Episcopalian. Avocations: photography, court tennis, overseas travel. Home: 8 Gramercy Park S Apt 5B New York NY 10003-1721 Office: Shields and Co 140 Broadway 44th Fl New York NY 10005 Office Phone: 212-809-1160. E-mail: maxule@aol.com.

ULEAU, THOMAS F. corporate executive; CEO, pres. Sweetheart Holdings, Owing Mills, Md. Office: Sweetheart Holdings 10100 Reisterstown Rd Owings Mills MD 21117-3815

ULEN, GENE ELDRIDGE, elementary school educator; b. Detroit, June 13, 1939; d. James Swan and Dorothy Benson Eldridge; m. Ian Paul Ulen, Aug. 10, 1933; children: Heather Jean, Lori Dorothy. BA in Edn., Mich. State U., 1960, MA in Edn., 1961; adminstrv. credential, Point Loma U., 1987. 2nd grade tchr. San Diego Unified Schs., San Diego, 1962—70; 6th grade tchr. Crown Pointe Elem. Sch., San Diego, 1971—86; 4th-5th gifted class tchr. Cadman Elem. Sch., San Diego, 1987—2000; substitute tchr. All Saints Sch., San Diego, 2000—. Active San Diego Nat. Women Polit. Group, 1995—2000; sec. LaJolla (Calif.) Dem. Club, 2000—02. Mem.: LWV, LaJolla Book Club, Phi Delta Kappa (bd. mem. 1986—2000). Episcopalian. Avocations: roses, sailing, bridge, tennis. Home: 5840 Cozzens St San Diego CA 92122

ULEVICH, NEAL HIRSH, photojournalist; b. Milw., June 18, 1946; s. Ben and Lea Jean (Klitsner) U.; m. Maureen Ann Vaughan, Sept. 25, 1974; children: Jacob Vaughan, Sarah Beatrice. BA in Journalism, U. Wis., 1968. Reporter A.P., 1968-69, photographer, photo editor, 1971-78, Asia photo editor, 1978-83. Freelance writer, Vietnam, Hong Kong, 1969-71; fellow in journalism U. Wis.-Madison, 1971-72 Recipient Pulitzer prize for news photography, 1977. Jewish. Home: Apt E101 8135 S Poplar Way Centennial CO 80112

ULITIN, VLADIMIR GREGOR, retired Russian language and literature educator; b. Kamensk, Russia, Sept. 29, 1908; came to U.S., 1949; s. Gregory Anton and Taisiya Alexandra (Dubovskaya); m. Helen Sawa, Nov. 20, 1958 (div. 1968); m. Sophia Gregor Kishkovsky, Fev. 2, 1969; 1 child, Leonid. Student, Robert Coll., Istanbul, Turkey, 1924-28; BS, U. Belgrade, Yugoslavia, 1932; BA, Pomona Coll., 1968. Civil engr. Austrian firm, Yugoslavia, Austria, Poland, 1932-45; social worker, dir. refugee children UNRRA, Austria, 1945-49; dir. refugee pr. Am. Friends Svc. Com., Pasadena, Calif., 1950-57; instr. Russian, Calif. Inst. Tech., Pasadena, 1957-61, Pasadena City Coll., 1957-61, U. Calif., Riverside, 1960-61; asst. prof. Russian lang. and lit. Pomona Coll., Claremont, Calif., 1960-64, assoc. prof., 1964-74, disting. prof., 1968-74, prof. emeritus, 1974—. Editor Vestnik jour., 1961-70; contbr. articles to mags. Mem. Congress Russian-Ams. (So. Calif. rep.), Claremont Univ. Club (hon.). Russian Orthodox. Avocations: gardening, roses, sports. Home: 841 Miami Ct Claremont CA 91711-2531

ULLAH, AMAN, economist, educator; b. Varanasi, India, July 30, 1946; arrived in U.S., 1972; s. Ata Ullah Khan and Razia Begum; m. Shobha Ullah, Apr. 16, 1951; 1 child, Sushana. BA in Stats., Econs., Math., Lucknow U., 1964, MS in Math. Stats., 1966; PhD in Econs., Delhi U., 1971. Post-doctoral fellow So. Meth. U., 1972—73, asst. prof., 1973—75; assoc. prof. U. Western Ont., Canada, 1975—82, prof., 1982—89, U. Calif., Riverside, 1989—. Visitor Australian Nat. U., 1976, Netherlands Sch. Econometrics, 1978, Ctr. for Ops. Rsch. and Econometrics, Belgium, 1980—81, Indian Statis. Inst., 1983—84, 1984, U. NSW, Australia, 1986; visitor dept. econometrics and ops. rsch. Monash U., Australia, 1980; visitor Ctr. for Multivariate Analysis U. Pitts., 1982—83; Disting. Erskine fellow U. Canterbury, New Zealand, 1986; vis. prof. U. Ill., 1987, Tillburg U., Netherlands, 1994, U. Dortmund, Germany, 1995, Bilkent U., Turkey, 1998, U. Victoria, Canada, 1998, City U., Hong Kong, 1999, FGV, Brazil, 1999, Jawahar Lal Nehru U. and Delhi Sch. Econs., 2000, Lahore U. Mgmt. Scis., 2000, Bilkeut U., Turkey, 2000, U. Ca Froscari di Venezia, Italy; vis. scholar Stanford U., 1988; disting. visitor York U., Canada, 1990, Tinbergen Inst. Econometrics, Netherlands, 1994; lectr. in field; presenter in field. Author: Recent Advances in Regression Methods, 1981, Econometrics: A Varying Coefficients Approach, 1981, Semi Parametric and Nonparametric Econometrics, 1988, Contributions to Econometric Theory and Applications, 1990, Handbook of Applied Economic Statistics, 1998, Nonparametric Econometrics, 1999, Handbook of Applied Econometrics and Statistical Inference, 2002, Finite Sample Econometrics, 2003; contbr. articles to profl. jours.; co-editor: Econometric Revs., 1989—2002, Econometric Revs., vol. 14, 1995, Econometric Revs., vol. 15, 1996; assoc. editor: Econometrics Revs., Jour. Quantitative Econs., Pakistan Jour. Applied Econs., Jour. Nonparametric Stats., Empirical Econs., Sankhya, The Middle Eastern: Bus. and Econ. Rev. Fellow, NAS, 1996; grantee, Nat. Scis. and Engring. Rsch. Coun., 1982—85, 1985—88, 1989—90, Social Sci. and Humanities Rsch. Coun. Can., 1982—83, 1994—97, Acad. Devel. Fund, U. Western Ont., 1984—86; Rsch. grantee, Can. Coun., 1977—78, Nat. Scis. and Engring. Rsch. Coun., 1978—79, 1979—80, 1980—81, Social Sci. and Humanities Rsch. Coun. Can., 1987—90, Learve fellow, 1980—81. Mem.: Econometric Soc. Achievements include research in nonparametric econometrics; finite sample econometrics. Home: 1269 Golden Vale Dr Riverside CA 92506 Office: Dept Econs Univ Calif Riverside CA 92521-0203

ULLAS, YVONNE LEE, primary school educator; AA, Yakima Valley C.C., 1979; BA in Edn., Ctrl. Wash. U., 1981, postgrad., 1991, Antioch U., 1992; MEd, Heritage Coll., 1995. Parent educator Yakima Sch. Dist., 1975-79; camp dir. Yakima Parks and Recreation, 1979-86; tchr. St. Joseph's Grade Sch., Yakima, 1981-86, Naches Primary Sch., 1988—. Commr. Gov.'s commn. on Early Learning, 1998-2000; bd. dirs. Gov.'s Profl. Educator Standards bd. Named Tchr. of Month, KAPP TV, 1993, US West Washington State Outstanding Tchr., 1994, Wash. State Tchr. of Yr., 1998; recipient Christa McAuliffe Excellence in Edn. award, 2000; grantee Share 105 Tech., 1997. Mem. NEA, Wash. Edn. Assn., Naches Edn. Assn. (dist. del.), Naches Edn. Assn. (bldg. rep.), Yakima Valley C.C. Alumni Assn., Ctrl. Washington U. Alumni Assn., Heritage Coll. Alumni Assn., Retired Tchrs. Assn., N.W. Regional Ednl. Lab., Nat. State Tchr. of Yr. Assn., Parent, Tchr., Student Assn. Office: Naches Valley Primary Sch 2700 Old Naches Hwy Yakima WA 98908-8900 Home: 1615 S 13th Ave Yakima WA 98902

ULLBERG, KENT JEAN, sculptor; b. Gothenburg, Sweden, July 15, 1945; arrived in US, 1974; s. Jean Wilgot and Kerstin Aina (Axelson) U.; m. Veerle Rufina Vermeir, May 5, 1978; children: Robert, Gerald. Diploma in sculpture, Swedish State Sch. Art, 1966. Cert. conservator German Assn. Museology. Curator Nat. Mus. and Art Gallery, Botswana, Africa, 1971-74; curator III Mus. Natural History, Denver, 1974-75. Principle works include Lincoln Ctr. Eagle, Dallas, 1981, Wind in the Sails, Corpus Christi, Tex., 1983, Genesee Eagle, Mumford, N.Y., 1984, Deinonychus Dinosaurs, Phila., 1987, Whooping Cranes Fountain, Washington, 1989, Swordfish Monument, IGFA Hdqs., Dania, Fla., 1999, Broward Conv. Ctr., Fountain, Ft. Lauderdale, Fla., Rudor Monument, Stockholm, 1991, Monumental Triptych Art Mus. South Tex., 1993, Bird Mountain Telecom. Hdqs., Stockholm, 1994, Christ Monument, Corpus Christi, 1995, Grizzly Bear Monument, Nat. Mus. Wildlife Art, Jackson, Wyo., 1994, King Penguin Monument, Mystic Marine Life Aquarium, Conn., 1997, R.T. Peterson Meml., Mystic Sealife Aquarium, Conn., 1997, Cougar Monument San Antonio Zoo, 1998, Otters Monument St. Louis Zoo, 1998, Tex. State Aquarium, 1998, Swordfish Monument, Dania Beach, Fla., 1998, Spanish Bull Monument, Johnson C. Smith U., Charlotte, N.C., 1999, Ram Monum, U. N.C., Chapel Hill, 2001, First Nat. Bank Omaha Can. Geese Monument, 2002. Recipient Gold medal Tex. Rangers Hall of Fame, 1980, Rungius award Nat. Mus. Wildlife Art, 1996, Prix de West award Nat. Cowboy Hall of Fame, 1998, award for wildlife Autry Nat. Ctr., 2004; named Master Wildlife Artist, 1987. Fellow: NAD (academician 1990, Barnett prize 1995, Speyer prize 1995), Am. Soc. Marine Artists, Nat. Acad. Western Art (gold medal 1981, 1982, 1988, 1995, 1999), Nat. Sculpture Soc. (Percival Dietsch award 1979, gold medal 1983, Hering award 1993, Silver medal and John Cavanaugh Meml. prize 2002); mem.: Soc. for Wildlife Art of Nations, Allied Artists of Am. (N.Y. Silver medal 1989), Soc. Animal Artists (medal merit 1979, 1980, 1982, 1987, 1996, 2001, E. Haller award 2001, Sponsor award 2002), Explorers Club N.Y.C. Office Phone: 361-851-1600. E-mail: ullberg@kentullberg.com.

ULLESTAD, MERWIN ALLAN, tax services executive; b. Hampton, Iowa, June 29, 1949; s. Allan L. and Georgia E. (Simms) U.; m. Crystal R. (Kleppinger), Sept. 17, 1977. BS, Iowa State U., 1971. CPA, PFS, Iowa, Tenn.; lic. capt. inland waters USCG. Ptnr. Coopers and Lybrand, Des Moines, 1971-83; ptnr. in charge, tax svcs. Touche Ross and Co., Nashville, 1983-89; ptnr. tax svcs. Deloitte & Touche, LLP, Nashville, 1989—2002; mem.-in-charge tax svcs. Kraft Bros, Esstman, Paton & Harrell PLLC, Nashville, 2002—. Adj. tax prof. Simpson Coll., 1981-82; spkr. prof. acct. seminar Lipscomb U., 1990-2001. Editor: Abingdon Clergy Income Tax Guide, 1989-98. Sustaining membership capt. Mid. Tenn. coun. Boy Scouts Am., 1985—88; mem. Econ. Devel. Com., 1988—90; mem. ednl. adv. com. Nashville Health Care Coun., 1998—2002; bd. dirs., mem. exec. com., treas. United Way Mid. Tenn., 1990—96, mem. allocations panel, 1983—89; bd. dirs., mem. exec. com. Am. Cancer Soc., Des Moines, 1977—83, Nashville City Ballet, 1983—85; bd. dirs., chmn. fin. com. Watkins Coll. Art and Design, 1996—2001; bd. dirs. Gilda's Club, Nashville, treas., 1996—2002; trustee, program chmn., sec. Tenn. Fed. Tax Inst., 2001—; bd. dirs. Tenn. chpt. Arthritis Found., 2003—. Mem. AICPA (cert. Pers. Fin. Specialist), Tenn. Soc. CPAs, Iowa Soc. CPAs, Internat. Assn. for Fin. Planning (pres., bd. dirs. Nashville chpt. 1987-90), Nashville Estate Planning Coun. (pres. 1996-97, dir.), Nashville Songwriters Assn. Internat. (fin. cons. to bd. dirs. 1990-97), Nashville C. of C. (employment coun. 1999-2002, editor HR notes 2000-01), Seven Seas Cruising Assn., Old Hickory Country Club, Nashville City Club, Commonwealth Yacht Club, Niue Yacht Club, Sint Maarten Yacht Club. Avocations: sailing, hiking, music. Office: 555 Great Circle Rd #200 Nashville TN 37228-1310 E-mail: mullestad@kraftcpas.com.

ULLIAN, ELAINE S. health facility administrator; b. Jan. 3, 1948; MPH, U. Mich., 1973; BA, Tufts U., 1969. Pres., CEO Faulkner Corp./Faulkner Hosp., 1987-94; v.p. clinical ops New England Med Ctr, 1984-86; dir. strategic planning consult. FinReport Systems/Amherst Assoc., 1982-84; dir of planning assist. admin. Boston U. Med Ctr Hosp, Boston, 1976-82; dir. Hill Burton Prog. Mass. Dept of Health, Boston, 1974-76; advocate planner, comm. organizer Eastern Middlesex Opportunities Council, 1969-72; assoc. prof. Boston U. Sch of Public Health, Boston, 1994—; lecturer Harvard Sch of Public Health, 1987—; vice chair Conference of Boston Tching Hosp., 1993—; pres. ceo Boston Med Ctr, Boston, 1996—. Recipient: Maimonides award for Outstanding Leadership in Health Care of the Anti-Defamation League, 1989; Abigail Adams award for Political Leadership of the Mass. Women's Political Caucus, 1992; Mass. Health Council award for Outstanding Leadership in Public Health, 1994; The Boston Club Achievement award, 1995; Fifth Anniversary Community Service award, Bostonian Club, 1995. Bd of dirs.: Greater Boston Chamber of Commerce, Corp. Advisory Bd Pine Manor Junior Coll.; mem., Governor's Council on Economic Growth and Tech., Mayor's Special Advisory Comm. on Health Care, 1994-95, chair, Health, Family, Youth servs comm., Menino Transition Team, 1993-94, Health and Human Servs comm., Weld Transition Team, 1990, chair, Metropolitan Boston Hosp. Council, 1988-90, bd mem. Mass. Hosp. Assoc., 1988-90, mem., Regional Policy Board, Amer. Hosp Assoc., 1990-93, Tufts Associated Health Plan, 1987-94, Celebrate Discovery Inc., Mass. Taxpayers Found., 1992-, Mass. Health Research Inst., 1987-94. Office: Boston Med Ctr Exec Ofc Talbot 1 1 Boston Medical Ctr Pl Boston MA 02118-2908

ULLMAN, BETH ROBIN, vocalist, voice educator; b. Bluffton, Ind., Nov. 21, 1954; d. Joseph Charles Ullman and Patricia Lee Chalfant. Bachelor of Music, U. Tex., 1987. Freelance vocalist and pianist, Austin, Tex., 1987—; instr. voice McLennan C.C., Waco, Tex., 1994—; singer, arranger and prodr. The Beat Divas, Austin, 1999—. Music dir. Unity Ch. of the Hills, Austin, 1995—99. Musician and songwriter: CD Aren't We the Lucky Ones, 1990, Go Within, 1998 (Favorite CD, KUT Radio, 1998), The Beat Divas--Live, 2003, studio session singer: Walt Disney Films, 1999, 2000, prodr., writer, performer: jazz concert Dyin' to Swing, 1994. Named Best Jazz Vocalist, Austin Critics Poll, 1993; recipient Beth Ullman/Rich Harney Day, Austin City Coun., 1996. Mem.: Tex. Commn. on Arts. Avocations: weightlifting, walking, gardening, water sports. Office: McLennan CC 1400 College Dr Waco TX 76708 Home: 4212 Village Oak Dr Waco TX 76710-1428

ULLMAN, EDWIN FISHER, biotechnology consultant; b. Chgo., July 19, 1930; s. Harold P. and Jane F. Ullman; m. Elizabeth J. Finlay, June 26, 1954; children: Becky L., Linda J. BA, Reed Coll., 1952; MA, Harvard U., 1954, PhD, 1956. Research chemist Lederle Labs., Am. Cyanamid, Pearl River, N.Y., 1955-60; group leader central research div. Am. Cyanamid, Stamford, Conn., 1960-66; sci. dir. Synvar Research Inst., Palo Alto, Calif., 1966-70; v.p., dir. research Syva Co., Palo Alto, 1970-95; v.p., dir. rsch. Behring Diagnostics Inc., San Jose, Calif., 1995-97; scientific cons., 1997—; chief sci. officer Thau MDx, LLC, Santa Barbara, Calif., 2001—02, Genomics Discov-rRx, Corp., Fremont, Calif., 2002—03. Mem. various sci. adv. bds.; mem. adv. bd. San Francisco State U. Coll. of Sci. and Engring., 1994-96. Mem. editl. bd. Jour. Organic Chemistry, 1969-74, Jour. Immunoassay, 1979—, Jour. Clin. Lab., Analysis, 1986-87, Jour. Clin. Ligand Assay Soc., 1999—; contbr. articles to sci. jours.; patentee in field. NSF predoctoral fellow, 1952-53; U.S. Rubber Co. fellow, 1954-55. Recipient Clin. Ligand Assay Soc. Mallinckrodt award, 1981, Can. Soc. Clin. Chemists Health Group award, 1982, Inventor of Yr. award Peninsula Patent Law Assn., 1987. Fellow AAAS; mem. Am. Chem. Soc., Am. Assn. Clin. Chemistry (Van Slyke award N.Y. sect. 1984, No. Calif. sect. award 1991, Outstanding Contbns. to Clin. Chemistry in Selected Area of Rsch. award 1997, Ann. Edwin F. Ullman award established 1998), Phi Beta Kappa.

ULLMAN, JEFFREY DAVID, computer scientist, educator; b. N.Y.C., Nov. 22, 1942; s. Seymour and Nedra L. (Hart) Ullman; m. Holly E. Ullman, Nov. 19, 1967; children: Peter, Scott, Jonathan. BS, Columbia U., 1963; PhD, Princeton U., 1966, U. Brussels, 1975, U. Paris-Dauphine, 1992. Mem. tech. staff Bell Labs., Murray Hill, NJ, 1966-69, cons., 1969-89; prof. elec. engring., computer sci. Princeton (N.J.) U., 1969-79; prof. computer sci. Stanford (Calif.) U., 1979—2003, prof. emeritus, 2003—; CEO, Gradiance Corp., 2004—. Mem. computer sci. adv. panel NSF, 1974—77, mem. info., robotics and intelligent sys. adv. panel, 1986—88; mem. exam. com. computer sci. grad. record exam. Endl. Testing Svc., 1978—86; chmn. doctoral rating com. computer sci. N.Y. State Regents, 1989—93, 1998—99; mem. tech. adv. bd. Google, 1998—, Viquity, 1999—2002, Surromed, 1999—, Whizbang Labs, 1999—2002, Quiq, 1999—2002; adv. bd. World Wide Web Consortium, 1998—99; bd. dirs. Junglee, 1996—98, Kirusa, 2001—03, Enosys software, 2000—01, 2002—03. Author: (book) Principles of Database and Knowledge-Base Systems, 1988, 1989; author: (with A. V. Aho and J. E. Hopcroft) Data Structures and Algorithms, 1983; author: (with A. V. Aho and R. Sethi) Compilers: Principles, Techniques and Tools, 1986; author: (with A. V. Aho) Foundations of Computer Science, 1992, Elements of ML Programming, 1994, 1998; author: (with J. Widom) A First Course in Database Systems, 1997, 2002; author: (with J. E. Hopcroft and R. Motwani) Intro. to Automata, Languages, and Computation, 2001; author: (with H. Garcia-Molina and J. Widom) The Complete Book of Database Systems, 2002. Fellow Guggenheim, 1989. Fellow: Assn. Computing Machinery (coun. 1978—80, Spl. Interest Group Mgmt. Data Contbns. award 1996, Outstanding Educator award 1998, Knuth prize 2000); mem.: NAE, Spl. Interest Group Mgmt. Data (vice chmn. 1983—95), Computing Rsch. Assn. (bd. dirs. 1994—2001), Spl. Interest Group Automata and Computability Theory (sec.-treas. 1973—75). Home: 1023 Cathcart Way Palo Alto CA 94305-1048 Office: Stanford U Dept Computer Sci 433 Gates Hall 4A-Wing Stanford CA 94305-9040 E-mail: Ullman@cs.stanford.edu.

ULLMAN, JOEL CLARKE, obstetrician/gynecologist; b. N.Y.C., 1937; s. Daniel and Sylvia (Miller) U.; m. Evelyn Janet Fuast, June 11, 1961; children: Carin, Steven, Randie. BA, U. Vt., 1969; MD, NYU, 1963. Diplomate Am. Bd. Ob/gyn. Intern Beth Israel Hosp., N.Y.C., 1963-64, resident, 1964-66, 68-69; staff New Rochelle (N.Y.) Hosp. Medicine, Beth Israel Med. Ctr., N.Y.C.; asst. clin. prof. ob/gyn. Albert Einstein Med. Coll.; dir. gynecol. endoscopic surgery Sound Shore Med. Ctr. Bd. dirs. Planned Parenthood, Westchester, N.Y. Fellow Am. Coll. Obstetricians/Gynecologists.

ULLMAN, LEO SOLOMON, lawyer; b. Amsterdam, The Netherlands, July 14, 1939; s. Frank Leo and Emily (Konijn) U.; m. Katharine Laura Marbut, Aug. 27, 1960; chldren: Laura, Susan, Valerie, Frank. AB, Harvard U., 1961; JD, MBA, Columbia U., 1964. Bar: N.Y. 1966, U.S. Ct. Claims 1966, U.S. Tax Ct. 1969, U.S. Customs Ct. 1970. Assoc. Sullivan & Cromwell, N.Y.C., 1965-68; pres., mem. Ullman, Miller & Wrubel and predecessors, N.Y.C., 1970-81; mem. Reid & Priest, 1984-91, of counsel, 1991-92, Schnader, Harrison, Segal & Lewis, N.Y.C., 1993-99; chmn., CEO Cedar Shopping Ctrs., Inc. (NYSE). Adj. prof. internat. bus. NYU, 1972-77; lectr., panelist profl. organs. programs. Co-author: Investeringen in Onroerend Goed in de Verenigde Staten, 1982; editor: European Taxation, Internat. Bur. Documentation, Amsterdan, 1964-65; founding editor: Taxation of Private Investment Income in Europe; contbr. articles to profl. publs. Mem. Port Washington (N.Y.) Bd. Edn., 1970-73, pres., 1972-73; bd. dirs. Found. for Jewish Hist. Mus. in Amsterdam, Inc.; bd. dirs. Anne Frank Ctr., U.S.A., chmn., 1994-2000; bd. dirs. Cmty. Chest of Port Washington. Served with USMCR, 1959-65. Co-recipient Cmty. Svc. award, Port Washington, 1981, Citizen of Yr. award, Cmty. Chest, Port Washington, 2003; Harlan Fiske Stone scholar Columbia Law Sch., 1963. Mem. ABA (tax sect. com. U.S. taxation of fgn. persons), N.Y. State Bar Assn. (tax sect. com. internat. trade and investment), Harvard Club, Netherlands Club. Home: Seacoast Ln Sands Point NY 11050-1230 Office: 44 S Bayles Ave Port Washington NY 11050 E-mail: leoullman@aol.com.

ULLMAN, MYRON EDWARD, III, retail executive; b. Youngstown, Ohio, Nov. 26, 1946; s. Myron Edward Jr. and June (Cunningham) U.; m. Cathy Emmons, June 20, 1969; children: Myron Cayce, Denver Tryan, Peter Brynt, Benjamin Kyrk, Kathryn Kwynn, Madylin Ming Yan. BS in Indsl. Mgmt., U. Cin., 1969; postgrad. Inst. Ednl. Mgmt., Harvard U., 1977. Internat. account mgr. IBM Corp., Cin., 1969-76; v.p. bus. affairs U. Cin., 1976-81; White House fellow The White House, Washington, 1981-82; exec. v.p. Sanger

Harris div. Federated Stores, Dallas, 1982-86; mgr. dir., chief oper. officer Wharf Holdings Ltd., Hong Kong, 1986-88; chmn., CEO, dir. R.H. Macy & Co. Inc., N.Y.C., 1988 95; dir., deputy chmn. Federated Dept. Stores, Inc.; chmn., CEO DFS Group Ltd., San Francisco, 1995-98, group chmn., 1999-2000; also bd. dirs.; dir. gen., group mng. dir. LVMH, Louis Vuitton Moet Hennessy, Paris, 1999—2002. Mng. dir. Lane Crawford Ltd., Hong Kong, 1986-88; bd. advisors Gt. Traditions Corp., Cin.; chmn. Omni Hotels, Hampton, N.H., 1988; co-chmn. Global Crossing, Ltd., 2002-04; chmn. bd. dirs. Mercy Ships Internat., 1992-; bd. dirs. Starbuck's Coffee Co., Segway LLC, Polo Ralph Lauren, Taubman Ctrs., Kendall Jackson Wine Estates, Lucille Packard Found. for Children's Health, Stanford U. Children's Med. Ctr. Internat. v.p. U. Cin. Alumni Assn., 1980—; bd. dirs. Nat. Multiple Sclerosis Soc., N.Y.C.; bd. dirs. Brunswick Sch., Greenwich, Conn., U. Cin. Found., Lincoln Ctr. Devel., Deafness Rsch. Found., 1997-2001; chmn. exec. coun. U. Calif. Med. Ctr. Found., San Francisco, 2002—, bd. dirs., 1998—. Mem. White House Fellow Alumni Assn., Econ. Club N.Y.C. (bd. dirs., exec. com.), Nat. Retail Fedn. (vice chmn., bd. dirs., exec. com. 1993—), Delta Tau Delta (treas. 1967-68). Republican. Office: c/o Jackson Hole Group Ste 935 100 Spear St San Francisco CA 94105 Business E-Mail: mike@meullman.com.

ULLMAN, TRACEY, actress, singer; b. Slough, Eng., Dec. 30, 1959; m. Allan McKeown, 1984; children: Mabel Ellen, John Albert Victor. Student, Itaia Conti Stage Sch., London. Appeared in plays Gigi, Elvis, Grease, The Rocky Horror Show, Four in a Million, 1981 (London Theatre Critics award), The Taming of the Shrew, 1990, The Big Love, (one-woman stage show) 1991; films include The Young Visitors, 1984, Give My Regards to Broad Street, 1984, Plenty, 1985, Jumpin' Jack Flash, 1986, I Love You To Death, 1990, Household Saints, 1993, I'll Do Anything, 1994, Bullets over Broadway, 1994, Ready to Wear (Prêt-à-Porter), 1994, Everybody Says I Love You, 1996; Brit. TV shows include Three of a Kind, A Kick Up the Eighties, Girls on Top; actress TV series: The Tracey Ullman Show, from 1987-90 (Emmy award Best Performance, Outstanding Writing, 1990, Golden Globe award Best Actress, 1987), Tracey Takes On, 1996— (four Emmys including Outstanding Music, Comedy and Variety Show 1997, Cable Ace award for best comedy variety series 1996); album You Broke My Heart in Seventeen Places (Gold album). Recipient Brit. Acad. award, 1983, Am. Comedy award, 1988, 90, 91, Emmy award for Best Performance in a Variety/Music Series for "Tracey Ullman Takes on New York", 1994. Office: IFA Talent Agy 8730 W Sunset Blvd Ste 490 Los Angeles CA 90069-2248

ULLMANN, OWEN, journalist; b. Neptune, NJ, Nov. 16, 1947; s. Marcel Andre Ullmann and Jane Horowitz; m. Lois M. Kietur, Aug. 6, 1977; children: Cara L., Daniel E. BA, Rutgers U., 1969; MA, U. Wis., 1973. Reporter Daily Jour., Elizabeth, NJ, 1969—71, State Jour., Madison, Wis., 1972; automotive reporter AP, Detroit, 1973—77, labor, econs. reporter Washington, 1977—83; econs., White House, State Dept. reporter Knight-Ridder Newspapers, Washington, 1983—93; econs. corr., news editor Bus. Week, Washington, 1993—99; reporter, editor USA Today, 1999—. Author: (biography) Stockman: The Man, The Myth, The Future, 1986, exec. editor Internat. Economy, 2000—; contbg. editor: Washingtonian, 1987—. Recipient Merriman Smith award, White House Corrs. Assn., 1988, Aldo Beckman award, 1989, Disting. Journalist award, U. Wis. Journalism Sch., Madison, 1999. Office: USA Today 7950 Jones Branch Dr Mc Lean VA 22102

ULLRICH, ROBERT ALBERT, academic administrator; b. Port Jefferson, N.Y., Mar. 25, 1939; s. Albert Herman and Marie Kathryn (Miller) U.; m. Portia M. Little; children: Karl Albert, Eleanor Marie. BS, U.S. Mcht. Marine Acad., 1960; MBA, Tulane U., 1964; D in Bus. Adminstrn., Washington U., 1968. Marine engr. Lykes Bros. Steamship Co., New Orleans, 1960-62; trainee IBM Corp., New Orleans, 1964-65; sr. rsch. officer London Sch. Econs., 1968-69; prof. Vanderbilt U., Nashville, 1969-88; dean Clark U., Worcester, Mass., 1988-96, prof., 1996-98; dean Ithaca (N.Y.) Coll., 1998—. Author: Motivation Methods, 1981, Robotics Primer, 1983; co-author: Organization Theory and Design, 1980; editor: The American Work Force, 1984. Lt. j.g. USNR, 1960-66. Mem. Beta Gamma Sigma. Office: Sch Business Ithaca College Ithaca NY 14850-7170 Office Phone: 607-274-3341. E-mail: rullrich@ithaca.edu.

ULMAN, LOUIS JAY, lawyer; b. Balt., Mar. 24, 1946; s. Erwin Ira And Rose (Clayman) U.; m. Diana Lynn Milford, Aug. 17, 1969; children: Kenneth, Douglas. BA, Dickinson Coll., 1967; JD, Am. U., 1970. Bar: Md. 1970. Assoc. Ulman & Cohan, Balt., 1970-75; ptnr. Ulman & Ulman, Balt., 1975-80, Weinberg & Green, Columbia, Md., 1980-92; prin. Hodes, Ulman, Pessin & Katz, Columbia, 1992—. Adj. prof. law Washington Coll. of Law, Am. U., 1997-98; vice chmn. Md. Pub. Broadcasting Commn.; chmn. Md. Racing Commn. Pres. Santa Claus Anonymous, Balt., 1975; mem. Howard County Bd. Social Svc., Ellicott City, Md., 1990. Mem. Md. State Bar Assn. (com. on rels. with fin. profls. 1985-92), Howard County Bar Assn., Internat. Assn. for Fin. Planning. Democrat. Jewish. Office: 10500 Little Patuxent Pkwy Columbia MD 21044-3585

ULMER, DAVID, information technology executive; V.p. sales and mktg. 3-D Visions, Redondo Beach, Calif., 1988—95; pres., CEO Earjam.com, San Jose, Calif. Mem.: Digital Media Assn. (bd. dirs.), Optical Storage Tech. Assn. (bd. dirs.), Secure digital Music Initiative (founding rep.). Office: Earjam.com 55 Almaden Blvd 425 San Jose CA 95113-1608

ULMER, EVONNE GAIL, health science facility executive; b. Bagley, Minn., Sept. 12, 1947; d. John Ferdinand and Elsie Mabel (McCollum) Lundmark; m. G. Bryan Ulmer, Jan. 11, 1969; 1 child, G. Bryan. Diploma, St. Luke's Hosp., Duluth, Minn., 1968; BS, St. Joseph's Coll., N. Windam, Maine, 1981; MHA, U. Minn., 1984; JD, T.M. Cooley Law Sch., Lansing, Mich., 1997. Bar: Mich. 1997. Staff nurse Baton Rouge Gen., 196970, St. Luke's Hosp., Duluth, Minn., 1968-69, 71-72; asst. adminstr. Hickory Heights Care Ctr., Metarie, La., 1972-73; asst. head nurse Eisenhower Hosp., Colorado Springs, Colo., 1973-74; dir. pt. care svcs. St. Vincent's Gen. Hosp., Leadville, Colo., 1974-78; insvc., quality assurance dir. Watsatch Hosp., Heber City, Utah, 1979; adminstr. Prospect Park Living Ctr., Estes Park, Colo., 1982-84; asst. adminstr. Estes Park Med. Ctr., Colo., 1979-84; CEO Weston Co. Hosp. and Manor, Newcastle, Wyo., 1984-92, Ionia (Mich.) County Meml. Hosp., 1992—; pres. Ionia County Health Sys., 1995—. *Evonne Ulmer lectures in areas of rural health, Emtala, and employment labor law. She serves as loyal council (pro-bono) to Ionia area Chamber of Commerce and Enrich. She is a member of the American Bar Association section on Healthcare, Labor, and Litigation, the American Health Lawyers Association, and Michigan Bar Association Labor and Health Law sections. She is a member of the Healthcare Financial Management Association and a fellow in the American College of Healthcare Executives.* Mem. Am. Hosp. Assn. Chgo. (trustee 1998-01, past tech. small and rural governing coun., past del. region and policy bd., past chair small and rural governing com., leadership com.), Medicare Geog. Reclassification Rev. Bd., Mich. Health and Hosp. Assn. (past bd. dirs., vice-chair smaller hops. coun.), ASHRM (editl. adv. bd.). Republican. Lutheran. Home: 536 Skyview Dr Ionia MI 48846-9776 Office: Ionia County Meml Hosp Ionia MI 48846 Office Phone: 616-527-4200. Personal E-mail: evonneulmer@hotmail.com.

ULMER, FRANCES ANN, former lieutenant governor; b. Madison, Wis., Feb. 1, 1947; m. Bill Council; children: Amy, Louis. BA in Econs. and Polit. Sci., U. Wis.; JD with honors, Wis. Sch. Law. Polit. advisor Gov. Jay Hammond, Alaska, 1975-81; former mayor City of Juneau, Alaska; mem. Alaska Ho. of Reps., 1986-94, minority leader, 1992-94; lt. gov. State of Alaska, 1995—2002; U.S. rep. to North Pacific Anadramous Fish Commn., 1994—; disting. prof. U. Alaska, Anchorage, 2003—. Democrat. E-mail: affau@uaa.alaska.ed.*

ULMER, JEANNE WILDE, judge; b. Nanticoke, Pa., Sept. 17, 1925; d. Charles Gordon and Ethel M. (Jones) Wilde; m. Herbert T. Ulmer Jr., Oct. 26, 1945; children: Carol, H. Thomas III, Joanne, Deborah. Student, Hood Coll., 1944. Bar: SC (municipal judge). Woman's page editor Times and Democrat, Orangeburg, SC, 1954—58; spl. corr. News and Courier, Charleston, SC, 1958—59; dir. Calhoun County Mus., St. Matthews, SC, 1959—83; mcpl. judge Cameron Mcpl. Ct., Cameron, SC, 1989—95. Pres. Calhoun County Health and TD Assn., St. Matthews, SC, 1963; mem. SC Tricentennial Comm., SC, 1968—70. Author: The Ulmers of South Carolina, Billets-Doux, 2000, (poetry) The Rebuttal and Rebound Thoughts, 2000. Chmn. March of Dimes, 1950—60; leader, coun. chmn. Girl Scouts USA, 1954—65; chmn. Cameron Election Comm., Cameron, 1984—88. Recipient Prof. Svc. award, SC Confederation of Mus., 1993. Mem.: Calhoun County Friends of Mus., Nat. Jud. Coll. Almuni Chpt. of SC, Nat. Welsh - Am. Found., Welsh Soc. of Phila. Home and Office: 106 Old Orangeburg Rd Cameron SC 29030-9518

ULMER, MELVILLE PAUL, physics and astronomy educator; b. Washington, Mar. 12, 1943; s. Melville Jack and Naomi Louise (Zinkin) U.; m. Patricia Elifson, Dec. 28, 1968; children: Andrew Todd, Jeremy John, Rachel Ann. BA, Johns Hopkins U., 1965; PhD, U. Wis., 1970. Asst. research U. Calif., San Diego, 1970-74; astrophysicist Harvard Smithsonian Ctr. for Astrophysics, Cambridge, Mass., 1974-76; asst. prof. Dept. Physics and Astronomy, Northwestern U., Evanston, Ill., 1976-82, assoc. prof., 1982-87, dir. astrophysics program, 1982—, prof., 1987—; dir. Lindheimer and Dearborn Obs. Northwestern U., 1982—. Co-investigator on Gamma Ray Ob. experiment and Orbiting Solar Ob. 7. Contbr. articles to profl. jours. Fellow Am. Phys. Soc.; mem. Am. Astron. Soc., Soc. Photo-optical Instrumentation Engrs., Internat. Astron. Union. Home: 2021 Noyes St Evanston IL 60201-2556 Office: Northwestern U Dearborn Obs 2131 Sheridan Rd Evanston IL 60208-0832

ULMER, WALTER FRANCIS, JR., consultant, former army officer; b. Bangor, Maine, Apr. 2, 1929; married; 3 children BS in Engring., U.S. Mil. Acad., 1952; M of Regional Planning, Pa. State U., 1973. Commd. 2d lt. U.S. Army, 1952, advanced through grades to lt. gen., 1982; dep. comdr. U.S. Army Armor Ctr., Ft. Knox, Ky., 1974-75; commandant-of cadets U.S. Mil. Acad., West Point, N.Y., 1975-77; dir. human resources devel. U.S. Army, Washington, 1978-79; comdr. 3d Armored Div., Frankfurt, Germany, 1979-82; comdg. gen. III Corps and Ft. Hood, Tex., 1982-85, ret., 1985; pres., CEO Ctr. for Creative Leadership, Greensboro, N.C., 1985-94; ind. cons., 1995—. Lectr. in field Contbr. articles to profl. jours. Home: 250 Riverbay Dr Moneta VA 24121-3138 E-mail: riverbay6@aol.com.

ULRICH, LARS, drummer; b. Gentofte, Denmark, Dec. 26, 1963; Drummer Metallica, 1981—. Albums Kill 'em All, 1983, Ride the Lightning, 1984, Master of Puppets, 1986, ...And Justice for All, 1988, Metallica, 1991, Live Sh*t: Binge and Purge, 1993, Garage Days Re-visited, Load, 1996, Kill 'Em All, 1995; albums Garage Inc., 1999; albums S&M, 1999, St. Anger, 2003; actor: (video) A Year in the Half in the Life of Metallica, Freddie Mercury Tribute Concert, 1992, Metallica: Cunning Stunts, 1998. Recipient Grammy award, 1989, 1990, 1991, 1998, 1999, 2000. Office: care Metallica Elektra Records 75 Rockefeller Plz New York NY 10019-6908

ULRICH, LAUREL THATCHER, historian, educator; b. Sugar City, Idaho, July 11, 1938; d. John Kenneth and Alice (Siddoway) Thatcher; m. Gael Dennis Ulrich, Sept. 22, 1958; children: Karl, Melinda, Nathan, Thatcher, Amy. BA in English, U. Utah, 1960; MA in English, Simmons Coll., 1971; PhD in History, U. N.H., 1980. Asst. prof. humanities U. N.H., Durham, 1980-84, asst. prof. history, 1985-88, assoc. prof., 1988-91, prof., 1991-95; prof. history and women's studies Harvard U., Cambridge, Mass., 1995—, James Duncan Phillips prof. early Am. history, 1997—, dir. Charles Warren Ctr., 1997—. Audiocourse cons. Annenberg Found.; cons., participating humanist numerous exhibits, pub. programs, other projects; project humanist Warner (N.H.) Women's Oral History Project; bd. editors William & Mary Quar., 1989-91, Winterthur Portfolio, 1991—. Author: Good Wives: Image and Reality in the Lives of Women in Northern New England, 1650-1750, 1982, A Midwife's Tale: The Life of Martha Ballard Based on Her Diary, 1785-1812, 1990 (Pulitzer Prize for history 1991), The Age of Homespun: Objects and Stories in the creation of an American Myth, 2001; contbr. articles, abstracts, essays and revs. to profl. publs. Coun. mem. Inst. Early Am. History and Culture, 1989-91; trustee Strawberry Banke Mus., 1987-93. NEH fellow, 1982, 84-85, MacArthur Fellowship award, 1992-97, John Simon Guggenheim fellow, 1991-92; women's studies rsch. grantee Woodrow Wilson Fellowship Found., 1979; co-recipient Best Book award Berkshire Conf. Women's Historians, 1990; recipient Best Book award Soc. for History of Early Republic, 1990, John S. Dunning prize and Joan Kelly Meml. prize Am. Hist. Assn., 1990, Bancroft Prize for Am. History, 1991. Mem. Orgn. Am. Historians (nominating com. 1992—, ABC-Clio award com. 1989), Am. Hist. Assn. (rsch. coun. 1993-96). Office: Harvard U Charles Warren Ctr Emerson Hall 4th Fl Cambridge MA 02138*

ULRICH, PAUL GRAHAM, lawyer, writer, editor; b. Spokane, Wash., Nov. 29, 1938; s. Donald Gunn and Kathryn (Vandercook) U.; m. Kathleen Nelson Smith, July 30, 1982; children: Kathleen Elizabeth Pennington, Marilee Rae McCracken, Michael Graham Ulrich. BA with high honors, U. Mont., 1961; JD, Stanford U., 1964. Bar: Calif. 1965, Ariz. 1966, U.S. Ct. Appeals (9th cir.) 1965, U.S. Supreme Ct. 1969. Law clk. judge U.S. Ct. Appeals, 9th Circuit, San Francisco, 1964-65; assoc. Lewis and Roca, Phoenix, 1965-70, ptnr., 1970-85; pres. Paul G. Ulrich P.C., Phoenix, 1985-92, Ulrich, Thompson & Kessler, P.C., Phoenix, 1992-94, Ulrich & Kessler, P.C., Phoenix, 1994-95, Ulrich, Kessler & Anger, P.C., Phoenix, 1995-2000, Ulrich & Anger, P.C., Phoenix, 2000—03, Paul G. Ulrich P.C., 2003—; owner Pathway Enterprises, 1985-91. Judge pro tem divsn. 1, Ariz. Ct. Appeals, Phoenix, 1986; instr. Thunderbird Grad. Sch. Internat. Mgmt., 1968-69, Ariz. State U. Coll. Law, 1970-73, 78, Scottsdale C.C., 1975-77, also continuing legal edn. seminars. Author and pub.: Applying Management and Motivation Concepts to Law Offices, 1985; editor: Arizona Appellate Handbook, 1978 2000, Working With Legal Assistants, 1980, 81, Future Directions for Law Office Management, 1982, People in the Law Office, 1985-86; co-author, pub.: Arizona Healthcare Professional Liability Handbook, 1992, supplement, 1994, Arizona Healthcare Professional Liability Defense Manual, 1995, Arizona Healthcare Professional Liability Update Newsletter, 1992-99; co-author, editor: Federal Appellate Practice: Ninth Circuit, 1994, 2d edit., 1999, supp. 2004; contbg. editor Law Office Econs. and Mgmt., 1984-97, Life, Law and the Pursuit of Balance, 1996, 2d edit., 1997. Mem. Ariz. Supreme Ct. Task Force on Ct. Orgn. and Adminstrn., 1988-89; mem. com. on appellate cts. Ariz. Supreme Ct., 1990-91; bd. visitors Stanford U. Law Sch., 1974-77; adv. com. legal assisting program Phoenix Coll., 1985-95; atty. rep. 9th Cir. Jud. Conf., 1997-2000. With U.S. Army, 1956. Recipient continuing legal edn. award State Bar Ariz., 1978, 86, 90, Harrison Tweed spl. merit award Am. Law Inst./ABA, 1987. Fellow Ariz. Bar Found. (founding 1985—); mem. ABA (chmn. selection and utilization of staff pers. com., econs. of law sect. 1979-81, mem. standing com. legal assts. 1982-86, co-chmn. joint project on appellate handbooks 1983-85, co-chmn. fed. appellate handbook project 1985-88, chmn. com. on liaison with non-lawyers orgns. Econs. of Law Practice sect. 1985-86), Am. Acad. Appellate Lawyers, Am. Law Inst. (life), Am. Judicature Soc. (Spl. Merit citation 1987), Ariz. Bar Assn. (chmn. econs. of law practice com. 1980-81, co-chmn. lower ct. improvement com. 1982-85, co-chmn. Ariz. appellate handbook project 1976-2000), Coll. Law Practice Mgmt., Maricopa County Bar Assn. (bd. dirs. 1994-96), Calif. Bar Assn., Phi Kappa Phi, Phi Alpha Delta, Sigma Phi Epsilon. Democrat. Home and Office: 2223 E Shea Blvd Phoenix AZ 85028-3113 Office Phone: 602-248-9465. Personal E-mail: ulrichpc@aol.com.

ULRICH, RICHARD WILLIAM, finance executive; b. Toledo, Oct. 30, 1950; s. Richard William Josef and Vera (Bender) U.; m. Pamela Ann Momenee, Apr. 19, 1974; 1 child, Nathanial Richard James. BBA, U. Toledo, 1973; postgrad., Stanford U., 1987. CPA, Ill. Sr. acct. Assocs. Mgmt. Co., South Bend, Ind., 1973-76; acquisition analyst Assocs. Fin. Svcs., South Bend, 1975-76; sr. v.p., contr. Assocs. Comml. Corp., Chgo., 1976-87; sr. v.p. corp. fin. Assocs. Corp. N.Am., Dallas, 1987-97; group pes. FirstPlus Fin. Corp., 1997—. Mem. AICPA, Ill. CPA Soc. Office: 250 Carpenter Frwy PO Box 660237 Dallas TX 75266-0237

ULRICH, ROBERT GARDNER, retail food chain executive, lawyer; b. Evanston, Ill., May 6, 1935; s. Charles Clemens and Nell Clare (Stanley) U.; m. Diane Mary Granzin, June 6, 1964; children— Robert Jeffrey, Laura Elizabeth, Meredith Christine. LL.B. (Law Rev. key), Marquette U., Milw., 1960. Bar: Wis. 1960, Ill. 1960, N.Y. 1981. Law clk. to fed. dist. judge, Milw., 1961-62; atty. S.C. Johnson & Son, Inc., Racine, Wis., 1962-65, Motorola, Inc., Franklin Park, Ill., 1965-68; atty., then asst. gen. counsel Jewel Cos., Inc., Melrose Park, Ill., 1968-75; v.p., gen. counsel Gt. Atlantic & Pacific Tea Co., Inc., Montvale, N.J., 1975-81, sr. v.p., gen. counsel, sec., 1981—. Mem. Am. Bar Assn., N.Y. State Bar Assn. Home: 500 Weymouth Dr Wyckoff NJ 07481-1217 Office: Gt Atlantic & Pacific Tea Co Box 418 2 Paragon Dr Montvale NJ 07645-1718

ULRICH, ROBERT J. retail executive; b. 1944; Grad., U. Minn., 1967, Stanford U., 1978. Chmn., chief exec. officer, dir. Dayton Hudson Corp.; with Dayton Hudson Corp. (now Target Corp.), Mpls., 1967—, exec. v.p. dept. stores divsn., 1981-84, pres. dept. stores divsn., 1984-87, chmn., CEO Target stores divsn., 1987-93, dir., 1993—; chmn, CEO Target Corp. (formerly Dayton Hudson Corp.), Mpls., 1994—. Bd. dirs. Yum Brands!, Inc. Office: Target Corp 1000 Nicollet Mall Minneapolis MN 55403-2467*

ULRICH, THEODORE ALBERT, lawyer; b. Spokane, Wash., Jan. 1, 1943; s. Herbert Roy and Martha (Hoffman) Ulrich; m. Nancy Allison, May 30, 1966; children: Donald Wayne, Frederick Albert. BS cum laude, U.S. Mcht. Marine Acad., 1965; JD cum laude, Fordham U., 1970; LLM, NYU, 1974. Bar: NY 1971, U.S. Ct. Appeals (2d cir.) 1971, U.S. Supreme Ct. 1974, U.S. Ct. Claims 1977, U.S. Customs Ct. 1978, U.S. Ct. Internat. Trade 1981, U.S. Ct. Appeals (5th cir.) 1988, U.S. Ct. Appeals (DC cir.) 1992, Colo. 1993, U.S. Ct. Appeals (10th cir.) 1994. Mng. clk. U.S. Dept. Justice, NYC, 1968 69, law clk. to fed. dist. judge, 1969-70; assoc. Cadwalader, Wickersham & Taft, NYC, 1970—94, ptnr., 1980-94, Popham, Haik, Schnobrich & Kaufman, Ltd., Denver, 1994-96; pvt. practice law Denver, 1996—. Author: Arbitration of Construction Contracts, V, 1991; co-author: Encyclopedia of International Commercial Litigation, 1991; contbg. author: Marine Engineering Economics and Cost Analysis, 1995; author, editor Fordham Law Rev., 1969. Leader Boy Scouts Am., Nassau County, NY, 1984-94, Denver, 1994—. Capt. USCGR, 1965-86. Mem. ABA, Colo. Bar, Denver Bar, Maritime Law Assn., Am. Soc. Internat. Law, Soc. Naval Archs. and Marine Engrs., U.S. Naval Inst., Am. Arbitration Assn. Home and Office: 4300 E 6th Ave Denver CO 80220-4940 E-mail: tnulrich@gte.net.

ULRICH, WERNER, patent lawyer; b. Munich, Mar. 12, 1931; came to U.S., 1940, naturalized, 1945; s. Karl Justus and Grete (Rosenthal) U.; m. Ursula Wolff, June 28, 1959; children— Greta, Kenneth. BS, Columbia U., 1952, MS (NSF fellow 1952-53), 1953, Dr.Engring. Sci., 1957; MBA, U. Chgo., 1975; JD, Loyola U., Chgo, 1985. Bar: Ill., 1985. With AT&T Bell Labs, Naperville, Ill., 1953-95; head electronic switching dept. AT&T Bell Labs., Naperville, Ill., 1964-68; dir. Advanced Switching Tech., Naperville, 1968-77, head maintenance architecture dept., 1977-81; sr. atty. Intellectual Property Law Orgn., Naperville, 1981-95; pvt. practice Glen Ellyn, Ill., 1995—. Vis. lectr. U. Calif., Berkeley, 1966-67 Inventor of over 20 telecommunications inventions; patentee electronic switching systems, Fellow IEEE; mem. ABA, Ill. State Bar Assn., Am. Intellectual Property Law Assn., Tau Beta Pi, Beta Gamma Sigma. Office: 434 Maple St Glen Ellyn IL 60137-3826

ULRICH, WERNER RICHARD, union education administrator; b. NYC, Sept. 26, 1941; s. Werner and Erna (Schreiner) U.; m. Marie Sciacca, July 18, 1965; children: Kenneth, Clifford, Richard. AAS, Voorhees Tech. Inst., 1969; BA, SUNY, Old Westbury, 1985; MS, N.Y. Inst. Tech., 1990. Mechanic "A" Con Edison of N.Y., N.Y.C., 1963-68; apprentice steamfitter Steamfitters', Local Union # 638, Long Island City, N.Y., 1968-73, journeyman steamfitter, 1973-85; dir. edn. Steamfitters' Edn. Fund, N.Y.C., 1985—. Blood dr. coord. Steamfitters', Local Union # 638, Long Island City, 1987—; usher, capt. Holy Name of Mary Roman Cath. Ch., 1984—; mem. steering coun. L.I. Women's Coun., 1992—; skilled worker emeritus N.Y. State Tng. Partnership Coun., 1993—; mem. S.I. Job Svc. Employer Com., 1993—. With U.S. Army, 1959-62. Recipient John J. Theobald award N.Y. Inst. Tech., 1989, Commr.'s award N.Y. State Dept. Labor, 1991, L.I. Women's award L.I. Women's Coun., 1991, N.Y. State Gov.'s cert. of Appreciation, 1994, Donald Grabowski Outstanding Apprenticeship Program award, N.Y. State Commnr. Labor, 2001. Mem. ASME, Nat. Fire Protection Assn., U.S. Apprenticeship Assn., Am. Legion, KC. Avocation: horticulture.

ULSTROM, ROBERT A. retired pediatrician; b. Mpls., Feb. 23, 1923; m. Mary Janet McGrath, 1946 (dec. 1981); 3 children; m. Betty Bernard, 1982 (div. 1985). BS, U. Minn., 1944, MD, 1946; postgrad., Strong Meml. Hosp. Lic. physician, Minn., Calif.; diplomate Am. Bd. Pediatrics with subspecialty in endocrinology (bd. dirs. 1980-86, v.p. 1985, chmn. rsch. and devel. com. 1980-86, tech. adv. com. for devel. of computerized examinations 1983-86), Am. Bd. Emergency Medicine (bd. dirs. 1982-86). Intern, resident in pediats. U. Rochester, 1946-48; instr., asst. prof. U. Minn., Mpls., 1950-53, assoc. prof., 1956-61, prof. pediatrics, 1961-64, 66-90, prof. emeritus, 1990—, acting head dept. pediats., 1961—62, assoc. dean Coll. Med. Scis., 1967-70; asst. prof. UCLA, 1953-56, prof., 1964-67, chmn. dept. pediatrics, 1964-67; vis. prof. medicine U. So. Calif., 1982-83, ret. Chief pediats. 97th Gen. Hosp., 1949-50; cons. in pediats. Harbor Gen. Hosp., L.A., 1953-56, 64-67, Mpls. Gen. Hosp., 1956-64, Hennepin County Gen. Hosp., 1967-90, hon. staff, 1990—; Well Child Clinic cons. City of L.A., 1953-56; track physician Donneybrooke Racetrack, Brainerd, Minn., 1968-73; dir. Reg. Ctr. for Metabolic Defects, 1975-79; cons. Ellwood & Assocs., 1986-87; med. legal cons. various plantiffs, 1985-95; mem. med. adv. bd. Group Health, Inc., 1967-90, Diabetes Detection and Edn. Ctr., 1969-71; mem. grants review com. Human Growth Inc., 1974-78; mem. tech. adv. com. on human genetics Minn. State Bd. Health, 1976-90; mem. pers. selection com. NIH, 1979, mem. gen. medicine study sect. NIH, 1964-68; mem. divsn. med. scis. NRC, 1961-64; oral examiner Am. Bd. Pediats., 1970-89; expert witness for prosecution U.S. Fed. Dist. Ct., Mpls., 1994-95; instr. computer course for beginners Elder Learning Inst., Coll. Continuing Edn., U. Minn., 1995—, bd. dirs., 1996-2000, webmaster, author, 1997-2002, v.p., 1998-99, mentor undergraduate students Coll. Liberal Arts, 1992—. Mem. editl. bd. Jour. Pediats., 1962-65; contbr. articles to profl. jours. Sec.-treas. Minn. Med. Found., 1967-68. With M.C., U.S. Army, 1948-50. Markle scholar in med. scis., 1954-59; Pew Found. fellow, 1985-86; recipient Wyeth award for med. rsch., 1963. Mem. AAAS, Am. Pediat. Soc., Am. Soc. Clin. Investigation, Ctrl. Soc. for Clin. Rsch., Endocrine Soc., Lawson-Wilkins Pediat. Endocrine Soc. (founding mem., membership com. 1971-75, chmn. 1975), Midwestern Pediat. rsch. Soc. (coun. 1961-64), Soc. for Pediat. Rsch. (NRC rep. 1961-64), Western Soc. for Clin. rsch., Western Soc. for Pediat. Rsch., Alpha Omega Alpha, Phi Rho Sigma. Home: 4616 Sunset Rdg Minneapolis MN 55416-3335 Personal E-mail: ulstr001@tc.umn.edu.

ULTAN, LLOYD, historian, educator; b. Bronx, N.Y., Feb. 16, 1938; s. Louis and Sophie U. BA cum laude, Hunter Coll., 1959; MA, Columbia U., 1960. Assoc. Edward Williams Coll., Fairleigh Dickinson U., Hackensack, NJ, 1964-74, asst. prof. history, 1974-75, assoc. prof., 1975-83, prof., 1983—. Cons. in field. Editor Bronx County Hist. Soc. Jour., 1964—, Bronx County Hist. Soc. Press, 1981—; author: The Beautiful Bronx, 1920-50, 1979, Legacy of the Revolution: The Valentine-Varian House, 1983, The Bronx in the Innocent Years, 1890-1925, 1985, The Presidents of the United States, 1989, The Bronx in the Frontier Era: From the Beginning to 1696, 1993, The Bronx: It Was Only Yesterday, 1935-65, 1993, Roots of the Republic, Vol. VI, 1996, The Bronx Cookbook, 1997, Bronx Accent: A Literary and Pictorial History of the Borough, 2000, The Birth of The Bronx, 1609-1900, 2000; contbr. Ency. N.Y. City, 1995. Gen. sec. Bronx Civic League, 1964—67; v.p. bd. trustees Bronx County Hist. Soc., 1965—67, 1977—84, curator, 1968—71, pres., 1971—76, historian, 1986—; founding mem., bd. dirs. Bronx Coun. on Arts, 1968—71; chmn. Bronx County Bicentennial Commn., 1973—76, Bronx Borough Pres.'s Bicentennial Adv. Com., 1974—76; vice chmn. Commn. Celebrating 350 Yrs. of the Bronx, 1989; mem. program guidelines com. N.Y.C. Dept. Cultural Affairs, 1976—77; mem. N.Y.C. Com. on Cultural Concerns, 1982—88, N.Y.C. Mayor's Task Force on Spontaneous Memls.,

2002; bd. sponsors Historic Preservation com. St. Ann's Ch. Morrisania, 1987—; ofcl. historian Bronx Borough, NY, 1996—; bd. dirs. Nat. Shrine Bill of Rights, Mt. Vernon, NY, 1983—, 91 Van Cortlandt Owners Corp., 1986—. Recipient Fairleigh Dickinson U. 15-Yr. award, 1979, 20-Yr. award, 1984, 25-Yr. award, 1989, 30-Yr. award, 1994, 35-Yr. award, 1999, Outstanding Tchr. of Yr. award, 1994; named N.Y.C. Centennial Historian, 1999, N.Y.C. Book award for borough history N.Y. Soc. Libr., 2001; named to Hunter Coll. Alumni Hall of Fame, 1974; N.Y. State Regents Coll. tchg. fellow, 1959. Mem.: AAUP (v.p. Teaneck chpt. 1992—93, sec. coun. of FDU chpts. 1992—93), N.Y. Hist. Soc., Am. Hist. Assn., Sigma Lambda, Alpha Chi Alpha, Phi Alpha Theta. Home and Office: 91 Van Cortlandt Ave W Bronx NY 10463-2712 *Transmitting the heritage of the past to the youth and to the mature adult, either through the spoken or written word, not only ensures that the civilization we inherited will be passed on, it will also warn people about earlier mistakes that should now be shunned and will, hopefully, inspire them to add their own positive contribution. I believe I am continuing to perform this service.*

ULVILA, JACOB WALTER, management consultant; b. Chgo., May 13, 1950; s. Toivo Einor and Belle Evelyn (Vanderbilt) U.; m. LouAnna Notargiacomo, Aug. 7, 1976; 1 child, Alexander Michael. BSEE, U. Ill., 1972; MBA, U. Mich., 1974; DBA, Harvard U., Boston, 1979. Decision analyst Decisions & Designs, Inc., McLean, Va., 1974-77, 79-80; vis. assoc. prof bus. adminstrn. U. Va., Colgate Darden Grad. Sch. Bus. Adminstrn., Charlottesville, Va., 1982-83; exec. v.p., also dir. Decision Sci. Consortium, Inc., Reston, Va., 1980-91; founder, prin. Decision Sci. Assocs., Inc., Vienna, Va., 1991—. Contbr. articles to profl. jours., chpts. to books. Recipient Franz Edelman award for mgmt. sci. achievemednt, Inst. Mgmt. Sci., 1987. Mem. Inst. Ops. Rsch. Mgmt. Sci., Maserati Club Am., Lamborghini Owners Club, Lamborghini Club Am., Maserati Club Internat. Avocation: exotic italian automobiles. Office: Decision Sci Assocs Inc PO Box 969 Vienna VA 22183

UMANS, ALVIN ROBERT, manufacturing executive; b. N.Y.C., Mar. 11, 1927; s. Louis and Ethel (Banner) U.; m. Nancy Jo Zadek, June 28, 1953 (div.); children: Kathi Lee Umans Lind, Craig Joseph; m. Madeleine Sayer, Sept. 21, 1985; 1 child, Valentine Brett. Student, U. Rochester, 1945. Sales mgr. Textile Mills Co., Chgo., 1954-56; regional sales mgr. Reflector Hardware Corp., Melrose Park, Ill., 1956-58, nat. sales mgr., 1959-62, v.p., 1962-65, pres., treas., dir., 1965-92; pres., CEO RHC/Spacemaster Corp., Melrose Park, 1992-97, chmn., CEO, 1997—. Chmn., bd. dirs. Goer Mfg. Co., Inc., Charleston, SC; chmn., dir. Morgan Marshall Industries, Inc., Ill., Capitol Hardware, Inc., Ill., Spartan Showcase Inc., Mo.; v.p., dir. Adams Comm., Chgo.; bd. dirs. Monroe Comm., Chgo.; chmn., treas., dir. Spacemaster Corp., Del. Trustee Mt. Sinai Hosp. Med. Ctr., Chgo., 1970—, chmn. bd., 1987-89; trustee Schwab Rehab. Hosp., Chgo., 1987—, chmn. bd., 1987-89; trustee Sinai Health Sys., Chgo., 1993—, chmn., 1995-97; mem. Cook County Bur. Adv. Com., 1994—; trustee Driehaus Mutual Funds, 1996—; bd. dirs. Milton & Rose Zadek Fund, 1965-78; governing bd. mem. Cinema/Chgo., 1988-89. Served with AUS, 1945-46. Mem. Nat. Assn. Store Fixture Mfrs. (dir. 1969-70), World Pres.'s Orgn., Chgo. Pres.'s Orgn. Clubs: Standard (Chgo.). Home: 132 E Delaware Pl Chicago IL 60611-1445 Office: RHC/Spacemaster Corp 1400 N 25th Ave Melrose Park IL 60160-3001 E-mail: arumans@rhcspacemaster.com.

UMANSKY, DIANE, publishing executive; B in journalism, U. RI. Corr. Bergen Record; writer various teen publs. including Scholastic; mng. editor Nickelodeon; sr. editor First for Women; editor-in-chief MediZine Guidebook, 1995—. Freelance writer First for Women, SELF, Family Circle, American, Harper's Bazaar, Working Mother, Good Housekeeping, Weight Watchers. Office: MediZine 298 Fifth Ave 2nd Fl New York NY 10001

UMBEHOCKER, KENNETH SHELDON, priest; b. Mpls., Sept. 23, 1934; s. Kenneth and Mildred Adeline (Johnson) U. BA, Vanderbilt U., 1956; MDiv, Seabury-Western, Evanston, Ill., 1959, 2000; M Mgmt., U. Ga., 1974. Ordained to ministry Episcopal Ch., 1959. Priest-in-charge St. John's Ch., Hallock, Minn., 1959-62; rector St. Paul's Ch., Virginia, Minn., 1962-67; priest-in-charge Emmanuel Ch., Rushford, Minn., 1968-74; asst. to dean Gethsemane Cathedral, Fargo, N.D., 1974-86; priest-in-charge St. Peter's Ch., Warroad, Minn., 1986-90; rector Ch. of the Good Shepherd, Windom, Minn., 1990-94, St. John's by the Lake, Worthington, Minn., 1990-94, Holy Trinity, Luverne, Minn., 1990-94, Episcopal Parish of St. Mark and St. John, Jim Thorpe, Pa., 1995—. Community developer, 1968-86; trustee Episcopal Diocese of Minn., Mpls., 1987-90, coun. mem., 1980-94; mem. standing com. Diocese of Bethlehem, 1998—. Field rep. Am. Cancer Soc., Mpls., 1965-67; dept. mgr. Rochester (Minn.) Area C. of C., 1967-74; exec. dir. Fargo Parking Authority and Downtown Assn., 1974-86. Seabury fellow Seabury-Western Sem., 1980; named Young Man of Yr. Rochester Jaycees, 1970; recipient Order of Purple Cross, York Rite Coll. North Am., 1988; Canterbury scholar Canterbury Cathedral of Canterbury, Eng., 1996. Mem. Am. Acad. Parish Clergy, Am. C. of C. Execs., Nat. Parking Assn. (v.p. 1983-86, Disting. Svc. award 1985), Union League Phila., Knights Templar (grand comdr. N.D. club 1985-86), Masons (grand chaplain Minn. club 1994), Seven Continents Club, Rotary Internat. Home: 32 Race St Jim Thorpe PA 18229-2004 E-mail: markjohn@ptd.net. *Working in the secular world as well as in the sacred makes a person more attuned to the needs and wants of the people in the pew and I find that that has enhanced my life tremendously.*

UMBERSON, MARILYN KAY, music educator; d. Lester V. Zobac and Agnes M. Drahos Zobac; m. George E. Umberson, Oct. 22, 1933; children: Brad D. Smith, James A. Smith, Rhonda Murray, Janna Hosmer, Alicia Kassenbrock. BA, BA in Music, Clarke Coll., 1968; MusM in Edn., No. Ariz. U., 1986. Cert. tchr. basic elem. and music Ariz., 1975, tchr. Am. Orff Schulwerk Assn., 1983, Kodaly, 2000, educator early child/mid. child music Nat. Bd. Profl. Tchg. Standards, 2002. Tchr. music and classroom St. Thomas the Apostle Sch., Phoenix, 1976—79; educator music and strings Creighton Sch. Dist., Phoenix, 1980—84; tchr. music Kyrene Sch. Dist., Tempe, Ariz., 1985—. Presenter in field. Contbr. articles to mags.; performer: USO, 1964—65. People to people ambassador, Russia, 2004. Recipient A. Sullivan Music award, Clarke Coll., 1968. Mem.: Ariz. Music Educators Assn., Am. Orff Schulwerk Assn. (tchr. tnr. 1993—99), Music Educators Nat. Conf. Roman Catholic. Avocations: golf, skiing, brain and music research, composing, travel.

UMBREIT, WAYNE WILLIAM, bacteriologist, educator; b. Markesan, Wis., May 1, 1913; s. William Traugott and Augusta (Abendroth) U.; m. Doris McQuade, July 31, 1937; children: Dorayne Loreda, Jay Nicholas, Thomas Hayden. BA, U. Wis., 1934, MS, 1936, PhD, 1939. Instr. soil microbiology Rutgers U., 1937-38; faculty U. Wis., Madison, 1938-44, asst. prof. bacteriology and chemistry, 1941-44; faculty Cornell U., 1944-47, prof. bacteriology, 1946-47; head dept. enzyme chemistry Merck Inst., Rahway, N.J., 1947-58; asso. dir., 1958; chmn. dept. bacteriology Rutgers U., New Brunswick, N.J., 1958-75, prof. microbiology, dir. grad. programs, 1969-83, prof. emeritus microbiology, 1983—; dir. labs. So. Br. Watershed Assn., 1983-89. Author: (with Burris, Stauffer) Manometric Techniques, 1945, 5th edit., 1972, (with Oginsky) An Introduction to Bacterial Physiology, 1954, Metabolic Maps, 1960, Modern Microbiology, 1962, Essentials of Bacterial Physiology, 1976; Editor: Advances in Applied Microbiology, vols. 1-10, 1959-68; Contbr. articles to profl. jours. Recipient Biochem. Congress Symposium medal Paris, France, 1952 Fellow Am. Acad. Microbiology, NY Acad. Sci., AAAS; mem. Am. Soc. for Microbiology (Eli Lilly award 1947, Carski Found. award 1968), Soc. Biol. Chemists, Am. Chem. Soc., Theobald Smith Soc. (Waksman award 1957, past pres.), AAUP, Sigma Xi. Home: 812 Covered Bridge Rd Holland PA 18966 Personal E-mail: wumbreit@aol.com.

UMEH, MARIE ARLENE, English language educator; b. Bklyn., Aug. 29, 1947; d. Rudolph Vasper and Erma Eunice (Hinds) Linton; m. Davidson C. Umeh, Jan. 7, 1976; children: Ikechukwu, Uchenna, Chizoba, Ugochukwu. BA, St. John's U., Jamaica, N.Y., 1970; MS, Syracuse U., 1972; MPS, Cornell U., 1977; MA, U. Wis., 1980, PhD, 1981. Instr. SUNY, Brockport, 1972-74, Oneonta, 1974-75; asst. instr. Cornell U., Ithaca, N.Y., 1976-77; prin. lectr. Anambra State Coll., Awka, Nigeria, 1982-89; substitute assoc. prof. Medgar Evers Coll., CUNY, Bklyn., 1989; adj. prof. Hostos C.C., CUNY, Bronx, 1990—2003, Queens Coll., CUNY, Flushing, N.Y., 1990; assoc. prof. English John Jay Coll., CUNY, 1990—, faculty advisor, 1989—. Adj. prof. SUNY, Stony Brook, 2000—. Editor: Flora Nwapa, 1998, Buchi Emecheta, 1996; editor Rsch. in African Lit., 1995, Who's Who Among American Teachers, 1998; contbg. editor: Who's Who in Contemporary Women's Writing, 2001. Recipient Africademic award, John Jay Coll. African Students Assn., 1996, Dominican Students award, 1993, PSC-CUNY award, 1998, 1999, Gender Studies award, John Jay Coll.,CUNY, 2001; fellow Summer Tchrs. Workshop, NEH, 2003. Mem.: AAUW, MLA (African Lit. Divsn. exec. 1999—2001), Virginia Woolf Soc., N.Y. African Studies Assn., African Lit. Assn. Avocations: reading, writing, aerobics, jazz. Office: CUNY John Jay Coll Criminal Justice Dept English 445 W 59th St New York NY 10019-1104 Office Phone: 212-237-8726. E-mail: msumeh@aol.com.

UMEMOTO, TERUO, chemist, researcher, chemicals executive; b. Hikari, Yamaguchi, Japan, Jan. 11, 1949; s. Katsuichi Ikeda and Masa (Nakahara) U.; m. Toshiko Kanamori, Mar. 26, 1978; children: Yukio, Makiko. BS, Okayama (Japan) U., 1971; MS, Osaka (Japan) U., 1973, DSc, 1976. Rschr. Sagami Chem. Rsch. Ctr., Sagamihara, Japan, 1976-81, sub-chief rschr., 1981-88, chief rschr., 1988-90; sr. rschr. MEC Lab., Daikin Industries, Ltd., Tsukuba, Japan, 1990-93, mgr., 1993-98; chief rschr. Fuji Chem. Industry Co. Ltd., Toyama, Japan, 1998; pres. IM&T Rsch., Inc., Denver, 1999—. Lectr. Sci. U. Tokyo, 1992-93, Kyushu U., Fukuoka, Japan, 1993, Chiba (Japan) U., 1993, Gifu U., Japan, 1998; vis. rschr. Nagoya Indsl. Inst. Japanese Govt., 1995. Inventor Jour. Am. Chem. Soc., 1990, 93, Jour. Organic Chemistry, 1994. Mem. Am. Chem. Soc., Chem. Soc. Japan (Progress award 1983), The Soc. of Synthetic Organic Chemistry (Japan), Japanese Assn. Fluorine Chemists.

UMFLEET, RANDY GENE, minister, music educator; b. Olney, Ill., May 6, 1961; s. Gene Elden and Phyllis Joann Umfleet; m. Ruth Naomi Logan, Sept. 1, 1990; children: Arianne Alexus, Landon Taylor. MusB in Edn., Ea. Ill. U., Charleston, IL, 1983. Cert. sacred music and Christian edn. Moody Bible Inst., Chgo., 1984, lic. Clergy State of Mich., 1999. Dir. of music Calvary Ref. Ch., Orland Park, Ill., 1983—87; asst. dir. alumni rels. Moody Bible Inst., Chgo., 1984—88; dir. music and youth Fellowship Ref. Ch., Lombard, Ill., 1987—89; dir. fine arts Sunshine Cmty. Ch., Grand Rapids, Mich., 1989—99; pastor worship ministries South Bapt. Ch., Lansing, Mich., 1999—. Dir. programming John Guest Evangelistic Crusades, Grand Rapids, Mich., 1989—94; dir. contemporary ensemble Ref. Bible Coll., Grand Rapids, Mich., 1994—97; musician Back to God Hour; contr. Reformed Worship mag.; actor summer stock theater. Chmn. sch. leadership coun. Windemere Pk. Charter Acad., Lansing, Mich., 2000. Avocations: cooking, camping, travel. Office: South Baptist Ch 5250 Cornerstone Dr Lansing MI 48917 Office Phone: 517-322-2000 121. Personal E-mail: rumfleet@southlife.com. E-mail: rumfleet@southlife.com.

UMHOLTZ, CLYDE ALLAN, financial analyst; b. Du Quoin, Ill., Dec. 20, 1947; s. Frederick Louis and Opal Kathleen (Beard) U. BS, U. Ill., 1969; MS, U. Miss., 1972; MBA, Memphis State U., 1983, PhD, 1986; Dr of Higher Learning (hon.), London Sch. Econs., 2002. CFA; cert. systems profl., tax practitioner; registered profl. engr.; cert. data processor. Supr. quality control Champion Internat. Corp., Oxford, Miss., 1971-72; mgr. divsn. quality control Cook Industries, Memphis, 1973; engring. planner Northwest Industries and subs., Memphis, 1974-75; long range planning and analysis W.R. Grace and Co. and subs., Memphis, 1975-78; mgr. planning and analysis Ctr. Nuc. Studies Memphis State U., 1979-83; data processing mgr. Shelby County (Tenn.) Govt., 1983-87, dep. adminstr., 1987—, spl. asst. to county exec., 1989—. Adj. prof. U. Tenn., Memphis, 1985—; ptnr. Custom Data Systems Inc., Memphis, 1987—, Western Techs. Inc., Memphis, 1988—; bd. dirs. Am. Tech. Inst., Memphis, Am. Info. Cons., Atlanta, Eastgate Corp., Anaheim, Calif., CIPCO Corp., Chgo., Sanford Cons. Group, London, Paris; bd. underwriters Lloyd's of London; diplomate editl. adv. bd. Brent's Peerage, London, Memphis-Amsterdam Gateway Com., Holland, 1997; Goodwill Amb. Am. Ukrainian Trade Alliance, Kiev, 1997—, Asian Econ. Recovery Coun., Tokyo, 1998—; elected to U.S. China Bd. of Trade, 2002; adv. bd. Fed. Res. Bank, Memphis, 1998—; mem. Am./Japanese Tire Safety Adv. Bd., 2000, Tenn. Commn. on Homeland Security, 2002—; diplomate Multi-Country Healthcare Exch., 2003, Medicare Nat. Study Com., 2003; oversight com. Internat. Energy Prodn. Alliance, 2003; adv. com. OPEC Price Stblzn. Coop., 2004; cons. in field. Author: Prototyping of Computerized Financial Systems, 3rd edit., 1997, Context Analysis in System Design, 2nd edit., 1999, The Family Partnership-An Estate Planning Model, 3rd edit., 2000, The Use of Chemical Molecules as Computer Switches, 2002; contbr. articles to profl. jours.; inventor angle trisector. Active presdl. election campaigns, 1968-72, 80-2004; del. Rep. Nat. Conv., 1996-2004; mem. Rep. Nat. Com., 2002—; active mayoral campaign, Memphis, 1975, 83, 87, 91, Shelby County, 1990, 94, sheriff's campaign Shelby County, 1990, 94, Mid-South Billy Graham Crusade, 1978; del. So. Govs.' Conf., 1992-93; gov. staff State of Tenn., 1993-94; mem. Mayor's Adv. Com., Memphis, 1991; steering com. Future Memphis, 1992, Arena Football League, Memphis, 1994; mem. Houston Oilers Relocation Com., 1996; adv. coun. Kordes' Gardens, Hamburg, Germany; study com. Nat. Electoral Coll., 2001; co-chmn. 27th Ann. Pres.'s Dinner, 2002; oversight com. Fin. Acctg. Stds. Bd., 2002-. Recipient Oratorical award Optimist Club, 1963, Leadership and Human Rels. award Dale Carnegie Inst., 1977, Disting. Svc. award State of Tenn., 1991; NSF fellow, 1970-72. Fellow NAS, Australian Acad. Scis., NY Acad. Scis., Am. Acad. Info. Tech.; mem. AAAS, AIChE, Am. Mgmt. Assn., Fin. Execs. Inst., Am. Chem. Soc., Assn. MBA Execs., Data Processing Mgmt. Assn., Planning Execs. Inst., Am. Assn. Investment Advisors, U. Ill. Alumni Assn., U. Miss. Alumni Assn., Memphis State U. Alumni Assn., Am. Rose Soc. (accredited life rose judge 1990), Am. Iris Soc., Am. Hemerocallis Soc., Elvis Presley Meml. Soc., Am. Hort. Soc., Internat. Platform Assn., Gt. Am. Pyramid Boosters Memphis, Mensa, Admirals Club, Oxford Club, London Club, Exec. Club Memphis, Petroleum Club Memphis, Olympic Soc. Atlanta, Order of De Molay. Baptist. Home: 3580 Hanna Dr Memphis TN 38128-3451 Office Phone: 901-388-3997.

UMMER, JAMES WALTER, lawyer; b. Pitts., July 16, 1945; s. Walter B. and Rose P. (Gerhardt) U.; m. Janet Sue Young, Dec. 21, 1968; children: James Bradley, Benjamin F. BA, Thiel Coll., 1967; JD, Duke U., 1972. Bar: Pa. 1972. Trust officer Pitts. Nat. Bank, 1972-75; tax atty., shareholder Buchanan Ingersoll P.C., Pitts., 1975-92; prin. Hirtle, Callaghan & Co., Pitts., 1992-93; shareholder Babst, Calland, Clements and Zomnir, Pitts., 1993-99; ptnr. Reed, Smith, Shaw & McClay, Pitts., 2000—03, Rothman Gordon, P.C., Pitts., 2003—. Golf course cons., Orlando, Fla. Trustee Thiel Coll., Greenville, Pa., 1984—, The Childrens' Inst., Pitts., 1984—; mem. bd. visitors Duke U. Div. Sch., 1999—. Fellow Am. Coll. Probate Counsel, Am. Coll. Trust and Estate Counsel; mem. Estate Planning Coun. Western Pa. (pres. 1986-87), Tax Club (Pitts.), Duquesne Club, Rolling Rock Club, Oakmont Country Club. Republican. Presbyterian. Home: 200 Woodland Farms Rd Pittsburgh PA 15238-2024 Office: Rothman Gordon PC 3d Fl Grant Bldg Grant St Pittsburgh PA 15219 Office Phone: 412-338-1105. E-mail: jwummer@rothmangordon.com.

UMMINGER, BRUCE LYNN, government official, scientist, educator; b. Dayton, Ohio, Apr. 10, 1941; s. Frederick William and Elnora Mae Umminger; m. Judith Lackey Bryant, Dec. 17, 1966; children: Alison Grace, April Lynn. BS in Biology magna cum laude with honors, Yale U., 1963, MS, 1966, MPhil, 1968, PhD, 1969; postgrad., U. Calif., Berkeley, 1963—64; cert. univ. adminstrv./mgmt. tng. program, U. Cin., 1975; cert., Fed. Exec. Inst., 1984. Asst. prof. dept. biol. scis. U. Cin., 1969-73, assoc. prof. dept. biol. scis., 1973-75, acting head dept. biol. scis., 1973-75, prof. dept. biol. scis., 1975-81, dir. grad. affairs, 1978-79; program dir. regulatory biology program NSF, Washington, 1979-84, dept. dir. cellular bioscis. divsn., 1984-89, mem. sr. exec. svc., 1984—, acting divsn. dir., 1985-87, 88-89, divsn. dir. cellular bioscis. divsn., 1989-91, divsn. dir. integrative biology and neurosci., 1991—99, sr. scientist office integrative activities, office of dir., 1999—; sr. advisor on health policy Office of Internat. Health Policy Dept. State, Washington, 1988; sr. advisor on biodiversity Smithsonian Instn., 1993-94. Exec. sec. Nat. Sci. Bd. Com. on Ctrs. and Individual Investigator Awards, 1986-88; mem. NSF rev. panel Exptl. Program to Stimulate Competitive Rsch., 1989, Rsch. Improvement in Minority Instns., 1986, 87, U.S.-India Coop. Rsch. Program, 1981-82, U.S.-India Exch. of Scholars Program, 1979-81; vice chmn. biotech. rsch. subcom. Fed. Coord. Coun. on Sci. Engring. and Tech., Office Sci. and Tech. Policy, 1991-94; exec. sec. subcom. biodiversity and ecosystem dynamics, com. on environment and natural resources Nat. Sci. and Tech. Coun., 1994, mem. interagy. working group on rsch. misconduct policy implementation, 2000-; mem. group nat. experts on safety in biotech., OECD, 1988-89; mem. sr. exec. panel Exec. Potential Program, Office Pers. Mgmt., 1988-89; mem. space shuttle proposal rev. panel in life scis. NASA, 1978, rsch. assocs. in space biology award com., 1985-91, chmn. cell and devel. biology discipline working group, space biology program, 1990-91, chmn. gravitational biology panel, NASA Specialized Ctrs. Rsch. and Tng., 1990, chmn. NASA specialized ctrs. rsch. and tng. peer rev. panel, 1995, mem. exec. steering com. in life scis., 1991, mem. gravitational biology facility sci. working group, 1992-95, mem. space sta. biol. rsch. project sci. working group, 1995-96, mem. NASA neurolab. steering com., 1993; mem. panel study biol. diversity, Bd. Sci. and Tech. Internat. Devel. NRC, 1989; exec. sec. adv. planning bd. Nat. Biodiversity Info. Ctr., Smithsonian Instn., 1993-94; mem. adv. screening com. in life scis. Coun. for Internat. Exch. of Scholars, 1978-81; liaison rep. nat. heart, lung and blood adv. coun. NIH, 1979-87, nat. adv. child health and human devel. coun., 1990-99; recombinant DNA adv. com., 1988; liaison rep. agrl. biotech. Rsch. Adv. com., USDA, 1989-94; mem. Interagy. Rsch. animal com., 1984-88; Interagy. working group on Internat. Biotech., 1988-94; chmn. proposal panel in biology Sci. Found. Ireland, 2002, Human Proteomics Site Visit, 2003. Author book chpts. and contbr. articles to profl. jours.; assoc. editor Jour. Exptl. Zoology, 1977-79; editl. adv. bd. Gen. and Comparative Endocrinology, 1982. Mem. world mission com. Ch. of the Redeemer, New Haven, 1967-68; Sunday Sch. steering com. Calvary Episcopal Ch., Cin., 1972-73, sr. acolyte, 1972-77, adult edn. com., 1975-76; deacon Faith Presbyn. Ch., Springfield, Va., 1996-99; adv. com. mem. Wakefield H.S., 1991-92, PTA exec. bd., 1991-92; sci. adv. com. Arlington Pub. Schs., 1987-92, adv. coun. on instrn., 1991-92; adv. bd. mem. Campbell Comml. Coll., Cin., 1977-79. Recipient George Rieveschl, Jr. Rsch. award U. Cin., 1973, Presdl. Rank Meritorious Exec. award NSF, 1992; U. Cin. Grad. Sch. fellow 1977—, NSF fellow 1964; rsch. grantee NSF 1971-79. Fellow AAAS (coun. 1980-83, 89-90, mem. program com. for 1989 ann. meeting 1988, chairperson-elect sect. G-Biol. Scis. 1987-88, chairperson 1988-89, ret. 1989-90), N.Y. Acad. Scis.; mem. Am. Soc. Zoologists (sec., mem. exec. com. 1979-81, chmn. nominating com. 1981, sec. divsn. of comparative physiology and biochemistry 1976-77, chmn. Congl. Sci. Fellow Program com. 1986-89, mem. 1991-93), Am. Physiol. Soc. (program adv. com. 1978-81, program exec. com., 1983-86, mem. steering com., comparative physiology sect. 1978-81, sec. Am. Physiol. Soc.-Am. Soc. Zoologists Task Force on Comparative Physiology 1977-78), Am. Inst. Biol. Scis. (chmn. selection com., congl. sci. fellow zool. scis. 1987, mem. congl. fellow liaisons com. 1991), Sr. Execs. Assn., Assn. of Yale Alumni (del. 1990-93), Mory's Assn., Yale Club (Washington), Sigma Xi (Disting. Rsch. award U. Cin. chpt. 1973, pres. U. Cin. chpt. 1977-79), Mensa. Home: 4087B S Four Mile Run Dr Arlington VA 22204-5604 Office: NSF Ofc Integrative Activities 4201 Wilson Blvd Rm 1270 Arlington VA 22230-0001 E-mail: bumminge@nsf.gov.

UMPHENOUR, RUSSELL V., JR., food services executive; Pres., CEO RTM Restaurant Group, Atlanta. Office: RTM Restaurant Group 5995 Barfield Rd NE Atlanta GA 30328-4411

UMPIERRE, LUZ MARIA, women studies educator, foreign language educator; b. Santurce, P.R., Oct. 15, 1947; d. Eduardo Umpierre-Pulzoni and Providencia (Herrera) Umpierre. BA, Sagrado Corazón, Santurce, 1970; MA, Bryn Mawr Coll., 1976, PhD, 1978; postgrad., U. Kans., 1981-82, New Sch. for Social Rsch., 1995-96. Asst. prof. Rutgers U., New Brunswick, N.j., 1978-84, assoc. prof., 1984-89; prof., head dept. Western Ky. U., Bowling Green, 1989-91; prof., chair dept. SUNY, Brockport, 1991-94, sr. lectr. Cortland, 1996-97. Vis. asst. prof. Ithaca (N.Y.) Coll., 1997-98; assoc. prof. Bates Coll., Maine, 1998-2000, spkr. Latino Promotions, 2000-. Author: (poems) In Wonderland, 1982, ...And Other Misfortunes, 1985, The Margarita Poems, 1987, For Christine, 1995; mem. editl. bd. Third Woman Press, 1990—, The Américas Rev., 1989-94. Guest spkr. AIDS Mass., Boston, 1990; sec. N.J. Voters for Civil Liberty, 1984. Recipient Order of Merit, U.S. Congress, 2003; named Woman of Yr. Western Ky. U., 1990, Outstanding Woman of Maine U.S. Congress Proclamation, 2002; recipient Lifetime Achievement award Coalition of Gay & Lesbian Orgn. in N.J., 1990; Ford Found. fellow, 1981. Mem. MLA (del. 1978), Melus, Feministas Unidas. Avocations: writing, reading, lobbying. Home: PO Box 568 Auburn ME 04212-0568 E-mail: LUmpierre@aol.com.

UMPLEBY, STUART ANSPACH, management consultant, educator; b. Tulsa, Mar. 5, 1944; s. Joseph Gray and Mary Carolyn (Woerheide) U.; m. Gertraud Maria Zangl, Mar. 7, 1986; children: Oliver Gray, Nicholas Anspach. BS in Engring., BA in Polit. Sci., U. Ill., 1967, MA in Polit. Sci., 1969, PhD in Comm., 1975. Engr. Westinghouse Electric Corp., Pitts., 1966, Machinen Fabrik Froriep, Dusseldorf, Germany, 1967; instr. U. Ill., Urbana, 1968—70; prof. George Washington U., Washington, 1975—, dir. rsch. prog. in social and orgnl. learning, 1993—. Cons. U.S. AID, Washington, 1979, IBM Intertrade, Vienna, 1990, Bled, Yugoslavia, 1990, World Bank, 2000; lectr. Hitachi Ltd., Tokyo, 1970, Inst. for Systems Studies, Soviet Acad. of Scis., Moscow, 1983, 87, 91, Union of Scientists, Sofia, Bulgaria, 1988; guest scholar U. Pa., Phila., 1983, Internat. Inst. for Applied Systems Analysis, Vienna, 1984, U. Maribor, Slovenia, 1998; guest prof. U. Vienna, 1990, Inst. for Adv. Studies, Vienna, summer 1997; faculty facilitator Quality and Innovation Initiative GW Sch. of Bus. and Pub. Mgmt., 1994-97. Author: (with others) Adequate Modeling of Systems, 1983, Power, Autonomy, Utopia: New Approaches toward Complex Systems, 1986, Managers and National Culture, 1993, A Science of Goal Formulation: American and Soviet Discussions of Cybernetics and Systems Theory, 1991, also editor (with Vadim N. Sadovsky), Cybernetics of National Development, 1991, also editor (with Robert Trappl); contbr. articles to Cybernetics and Systems, Futures, Population and Environ., Systems Practice, Telecommunications Policy, Soc., Bus. and Soc. Rev., Ekistics, Policy Scis., Jour. Aesthetic Edn., others. Vol. human devel. projects Inst. of Cultural Affairs, Washington, 1976-82. Rsch. grantee NSF, U. Ill., 1972-73, George Washington U., 1977-80, C.F. Kettering Found., U. Ill., 1973, Charles Stewart Mott Found., George Washington U., 1995, Nathan Cummings Found., George Washington U., 1999, U.S. Dept. State Bur. Ednl. and Cultural Affairs, George Washington U., 1994--. Mem. Am. Soc. for Cybernetics (pres. 1980-82), Austrian Soc. for Cybernetic Studies (assoc. editor jour. 1990—). Office: George Washington U Dept Mgmt Sci Washington DC 20052-0001

UNAKAR, NALIN JAYANTILAL, biological sciences educator; b. Karachi, Sindh, Pakistan, Mar. 26, 1935; came to U.S., 1961; s. Jayantilal Virshankar and Malati Jaswantrai (Buch) U.; m. Nita Shantilal Mankad; children: Rita, Rupa. BS, Gujerat U., Bhavnagar, India, 1955; MSc, Bombay U., 1961; PhD, Brown U., 1965. Research asst. Indian Cancer Research Ctr., Bombay, 1955-61; USPHS trainee in biology Brown U., Providence, 1961-65; research assoc. in pathology U. Toronto, Ont., Can., 1965-66; asst. prof. biology Oakland U., Rochester, Mich., 1966-69, assoc. prof., 1969-74, prof., chmn. biology dept., 1974-87, prof., 1974-2000, prof. emeritus, 2000—, adj. prof. biomed. scis., 1984—. Mem. coop. cataract research group Nat. Eye Inst., Bethesda, Md., 1977—; mem. visual scis. study sect. NIH, Bethesda, 1982-86, mem. cataract panel, 1980—. Mem. vis. bd. Lehigh U., Bethlehem, Pa., 1986-89. Grantee Nat. Cancer Inst., NIH, 1967-70, Nat. Eye Inst., NIH, 1976-97. Mem. AAAS, Am. Soc. Cell Biology, Assn. Rsch. in Vision and Ophthalmology, Sigma Xi. Home: 2822 Rhineberry Rd Rochester Hills MI 48309-1912

UNAN, GEORGE VINCENT, adult education educator; b. Bell Island, Newfoundland, Can., July 19, 1920; arrived in U.S., 1958; s. Samuel S. Unan and Ellen A. Kennedy-Unan; m. Myra Lanza Unan, Apr. 3, 1948 (div. July 1974); children: Veronica Gonzalez, Vivien Irving, Valerie Kitto, Venessa Mangione, Vernon A.; m. Gahyle Rich Unan, July 26, 1975; 1 child, Diane Baer. BS, Calif. State U., Long Beach, 1965, MBA, 1967. Cost estimator Hydro Electric Power Commn., Toronto, Canada, 1950—58; chief acct. Darco

Industries, El Segundo, Calif., 1959—62; contr., sec./dir. State Industries, L.A., Calif., 1962—68; contr. Direct Image Corp., Monterey Park, Calif., 1968—70, Harrington Indsl. Plastics, L.A., 1970—83; CFO Long Beach Conv. Ctr., 1984—86; educator Anaheim (Calif.) Adult H.S. Dist., 1997—. Seminar instr. in field; educator, exploratory seminars U. Sydney, Australia, 1987—96, Nat. U. Buenos Aires, Argentina, 1993, Charles U., Prague, Czech Republic, 1996. Author: Anecdotes and Quintessences From The Holy Bible, 1999. Adv. bd. Orange County, Santa Ana, Calif., 1984—97; mem. oversight com. Orange County Transp. Authority, Santa Ana, 1997—99; chmn., mem. Citizens Adv. Commn., Cypress, Calif., 1985—96. Home: 6424 Anguilla Ave Cypress CA 90630-5308 Office: Anaheim Adult High Sch Dist 1800 Ball Rd Anaheim CA 92804 Office Phone: 714-999-5616.

UNANUE, EMIL RAPHAEL, immunopathologist; b. Havana, Cuba, Sept. 13, 1934; married, 1965; 3 children. B.Sc., Inst. Secondary Edn., 1952; MD, U. Havana Sch. Medicine, Cuba, 1960; MA, Harvard U., 1974. Assoc. exptl. pathology Scripps Clin. and Research Found., 1960-70; intern in pathology Presbyn. Univ. Hosp., Pitts., 1961-62; research fellow in exptl. pathology Scripps Clin. and Research Found., 1962-65; research fellow immunology Nat. Inst. Med. Research, London, 1966-68; from asst. prof. to assoc. prof. pathology Harvard U. Med. Sch., Boston, 1971-74, prof., 1974-77, Mallinckrodt prof. immunopathology, 1977—; prof., chmn. dept. pathology Washington U. Sch. Medicine, St. Louis, 1988—. Recipient T. Duckett Jones award, Helen Hay Whitney Found., 1968, Park-Davis award, Am. Soc. Exptl. Pathology, 1973, Albert Lasker award for Basic Med. Rsch., Lasker Found., 1995. Office: Washington U Sch Medicine Dept Pathology and Immunology Box 8118 Saint Louis MO 63110-1093*

UNCAPHER, MARK ELSON, lawyer, trade association administrator; b. Buffalo, Aug. 4, 1953; s. Mark Elson Uncapher Jr. and Joan (Willard) Gruen; m. Robin Nixon, Aug. 27, 1977; children: Peter McLane, Elizabeth Cameron. BA, George Washington U., 1975; JD, N.Y. Law Sch., 1978. Bar: N.Y., 1979, D.C. 1998. Asst. counsel Comptr. State of N.Y., N.Y.C., 1978-83; sales exec. Sta. WZFM-FM, Pleasantville, N.Y., 1983-86; sales exec. Sta. WPAT Park Comm., Inc., N.Y.C., 1986-94; nat. pres. The Ripon Soc., Washington, 1987-90; co-owner Sta. WWCO, Waterbury, Conn., 1994-97; dir. audit svcs. N.Y.C. Dept. Homeless Svcs., 1994-95; counsel House Subcom. on Govt. Mgmt., Info. and Tech., 1995-98; v.p. and counsel divsn. internet commerce and comm. Info. Tech. Assn. Am., Arlington, Va., 1998—2002, sr. v.p. and counsel, 2002—. Chmn. Ripon Ednl. Fund, 1982-89, bd. dirs., 1982-97; mng. dir. Signal Properties, Brooklyn Heights, N.Y., 1987-95; ptnr. McLane Farms, LaPorte, Inc., 1980-95; U.S. chmn. 5th Transatlantic Conf., London and Cambridge, Eng., 1988. Contbr. articles to profl. jours. including Broadcast Fin. Jour., Ripon Forum. Chmn. Mark O. Hatfield Scholarship Com., Washington, 1985-97; del. candidate for George Bush 14th Congl. Dist., Bklyn., 1980; fin. chmn. Kings County Rep. Com., 1993-94, Montgomery County (Md.) Rep. Com., 2000; mem. Pres.-elect Bush's Transition Team for the FCC, 2000-01. Mem. ABA, Fed. Comm. Bar Assn., Computer Law Assn., Capitol Hill Club (Washington), Men's Rep. Club of Montgomery County. Republican. Congregationalist. Home: 6210 Greentree Rd Bethesda MD 20817 3362 Office: Info Tech Assn Am 1401 Wilson Blvd Ste 1100 Arlington VA 22209-3101 E-mail: muncapher@ITAA.Org.

UNDAR, AKIF, research scientist, biomedical engineer, educator; b. Istanbul, Turkey, Aug. 3, 1963; arrived in U.S., 1987; s. Fikret and H. Neriman Undar; m. F. Pinar Albayrak; children: Damla, Akifcan. BS, Yildiz U., Istanbul, 1986; MS, S.W. Tex. State U., 1992; MSE, U. Tex., 1994, PhD, 1996. Asst. instr., dir. surg. rsch. U. Tex. Health Sci. Ctr., San Antonio, 1996—97; instr. Baylor Coll. Medicine, Houston, 1997—99, asst. prof. surgery, 1999—2002, assoc. prof., 2002—03; assoc. prof. pediat., surgery and bioengring. Pa. State Coll. Medicine, Hershey, 2003—. Tchg. asst. U. Tex., Austin, 1994—96; dir. perfusion rsch. Tex. Children's Hosp., Houston, 1997—2001, dir. rsch., 2001—03; presenter, lectr. in field. Mem. editl. bd. Artificial Organ, 2003—, ASAIO Jour., 2004—; contbr. articles to profl. jours. Rsch. grantee, AHA Tex. affiliate, 1998-2000, Tanox, Inc., 1999-2001, NIH, 2000, NHLBI, 2004—, Pa. Health Dept., 2004—. Mem.: ASAIO, AHA (cert. 2000), Internat. Soc. Rotary Blood Pumps, Biomedical Engring. Soc., Internat. Soc. Artificial Organs. Office: Pa State Milton S Hershey Med Ctr Pa State Children's Hosp Dept Pediat 500 University Dr P Box 850 Hershey PA 17033 Business E-Mail: aundar@psu.edu.

UNDERBERG, MARK ALAN, lawyer; b. Niagara Falls, N.Y., July 9, 1955; s. Alan Jack and Joyce Love (Wisbaum) U.; m. Diane Englander, Mar. 22, 1986; children: Andrew Englander, James Englander. BA, Cornell U., 1977, JD, 1981. Bar: N.Y. 1981. Law clk. to chief judge U.S. Ct. Appeals (3d cir.), Wilmington, Del., 1981-82; assoc. Debevoise & Plimpton, N.Y.C., 1982-87; mng. dir., dep. gen. counsel Henley Group, Inc., N.Y.C., 1987-90, mng. dir., gen. counsel, 1990-92; v.p., gen. counsel Abex Inc., Hampton, N.H., 1992-95. V.p., gen. counsel Fisher Sci. Internat. Inc., Hampton, N.H., 1991-97, cons. 1997-98; counsel Paul, Weiss, Rifkind, Wharton & Garrison, N.Y.C., 1998-99, ptnr., 2000—. Editor-in-chief Cornell Law Rev., 1980-81. Mem. ABA, Assn. of Bar of City of N.Y., Genesee Valley Club, University Club. Office: Paul Weiss Rifkind Wharton & Garrison 1285 Avenue Of The Americas New York NY 10019-6065 Office Phone: 212-373-3368. Business E-Mail: munderberg@paulweiss.com.

UNDERDOWN, DAVID EDWARD, historian, educator; b. Wells, Eng., Aug. 19, 1925; s. John Percival and Ethel Mary (Gell) U. BA, U. Oxford, 1950, MA, 1951, Yale U., 1952; B.Litt., U. Oxford, 1953; D.Litt. hon., U. of South, 1981. Asst. prof. U. of South, Sewanee, Tenn., 1953-58, assoc. prof., 1958-62; then assoc. prof. U. Va., Charlottesville, 1962-68; prof. Brown U., Providence, 1968-85, Munro-Goodwin Wilkinson prof., 1978-85; vis. prof. Yale U., New Haven, 1979, prof., 1986-94, George Burton Adams prof., 1994-96, emeritus, 1996—. Dir. Yale Ctr. Parliamentary History, 1985-96; vis. Mellon prof. Inst. for Advanced Study, 1988-89; vis. fellow All Souls Coll., Oxford, 1992; Ford's lectr. Oxford U., 1992. Author: Royalist Conspiracy in England, 1960, Pride's Purge, 1971, Somerset in the Civil War and Interregnum, 1973, Revel, Riot and Rebellion, 1985, Fire from Heaven, 1992, A Freeborn People, 1996, Start of Play, 2000. Guggenheim fellow, 1964-65, 91-92, fellow Am. Coun. Learned Socs., 1973-74, NEH fellow, 1980-81. Fellow Royal Hist. Soc., Brit. Acad. (corrs.); mem. Am. Hist. Assn., Conf. Brit. Studies. Office: Yale U Dept History New Haven CT 06520 Business E-Mail: david.underdown@yale.edu.

UNDERHILL, JACOB BERRY, III, retired insurance company executive; b. N.Y.C., Oct. 25, 1926; s. Jacob Berry, Jr. and Dorothy Louise (Quinn) U.; m. Cynthia Jane Lovejoy, Sept. 9, 1950 (div. Sept. 1962); children: David Lovejoy, Kate Howell Underhill Kerwin, Benedict Quinn; m. Lois Beachy, Nov. 2, 1963 (div. July 1987); m. Betsy F. Ashton, Oct. 17, 1987. Grad., Phillips Exeter Acad., 1944; AB, Princeton U., 1950. Editor Courier & Freeman, Potsdam, N.Y., 1950-53; reporter Democrat & Chronicle, Rochester, N.Y., 1953-56; chief editorial writer St. Petersburg (Fla.) Times, 1956-59; asso. editor McGraw Hill Pub. Co., N.Y.C., 1959-61, Newsweek, N.Y.C., 1961-63; asst. press sec. to Gov. N.Y., 1963-67; dep. supt., 1st dep. supt. State N.Y. Ins. Dept., 1967-72; v.p., sr. v.p., exec. v.p., dir., vice chmn. bd., pres. N.Y. Life Ins. Co., N.Y.C., 1972-86. Hon. chmn. bd. dirs. Manhattan Eye, Ear and Throat Hosp.; trustee emeritus Nat. Trust for Hist. Preservation. With USNR, 1944-46. Mem. Players Club, Links Club, Piping Rock Club (Locust Valley, N.Y.). Home: 410 E 57th St New York NY 10022-3059

UNDERHILL, ROBERT ALAN, consumer products company executive; b. Columbus, Ohio, June 9, 1944; s. Robert Alan and Grace Ruth (Smith) U.; m. Lynn Louise Stentz, Oct. 18, 1963 (dec. Dec. 1997); children: Robert Alan III, Richard Louis; m. Lynn Carol Riviere, July 4, 1998. Student, Case Western Res. U., 1962—64, Ohio State U., 1965. With tech. svc. dept. Gen. Tire & Rubber Co., Akron, Ohio, 1966-69; quality control engr. Edmont-Wilson Co., Canton, Ohio, 1969-70; mgr. quality assurance Pharmaseal Labs., Massillon, Ohio, 1970-72; mgr. R & D Internat. Playtex Corp., Paramus, NJ, 1972-78; from mgr. to dir. R & D Kimberly-Clark Corp., Neenah, Wis., 1978-83, v.p. R & D, 1983-93, sr. v.p. R & D, sr. tech. officer, 1994-99; trustee United Health Group, 1994-99, exec. com., vice-chmn., 1997-99, chmn. compensation com., 1994-99; pres. Tech. Solutions, Inc., Appleton, Wis., 1999—. Trustee Novus Health Group, 1993—94; bd. dirs. Appleton (Wis.) Med. Ctr., 1993—96; trustee Thedacare, 1999—2002, chmn., 2000—01. Patentee (U.S. and fgn.) med. device; mem. editl. bd. Revs. in Process Chemistry and Engring. jour. Exec. bd. Bay Lakes coun. Boy Scouts Am., 1988-92, bd. dirs. Outagamie County (Wis.) chpt. ARC, 1993-99, chmn. nominations com., 1993-99, exec. com., 1994-99, sec., 1994-99; bd. dirs. Cmty. Blood Ctr., Appleton, Wis., 1996-2001, 2003—, chmn., 1999-2000; bd. dirs. Cmty. Found. Fox Valley Region, 1997-2003, vice-chmn. 1998-2003; bd. dirs. Silver Lake Coll., Manitowoc, Wis., 1998-2000; corp. bd. dirs. U. Wis. Med. Sch. Fox Valley Family Practice Residency Program, 1998—; rsch. adv. com. Inst. Paper Sci. and Tech., 1998-99; trustee Lawrence U., 1998-2001; bd. dirs. Appleton Med. Ctr. Found., 1999-2004, United Way Fox Cities, 2000-03, Goodwill of North Ctrl. Wis., Inc., 2000-03, Cmty. Hospice Found., 2001—; active 1st Congl. Ch., Appleton; dean's adv. coun. U. Mo. Coll. Engring., Columbia, 1999-2001; pres.'s coun. Children's Hosp. of Wis., 2003—, bd. dirs., 2004—. Mem. AAAS, NY Acad. Scis., Am. Assn. Blood Banks (stds. com. 1997-99), Svc. Corps. Ret. Execs., Rotary Internat., Riverview Country Club (bd. dirs. 2002-03, v.p. 2003), Appleton Rotary Club (sec. 2001-03, v.p. 2003-04, pres. 2004-), Pi Delta Epsilon. Republican. Avocations: stock market investment analysis, travel. Home and Office: 2525 W Prospect Ave Appleton WI 54914-8718 E-mail: rau@athenet.net.

UNDERWEISER, IRWIN PHILIP, mining executive, lawyer; b. NYC, Jan. 3, 1929; s. Harry and Edith (Gladstein) U.; m. Beatrice J. Kortchmar, Aug. 17, 1959; children: Rosanne, Marian, Jeffrey. BA, CCNY, 1950; LL.D., Fordham U., 1954; LL.M., NYU, 1961. Bar: N.Y. 1954. With firm Scribner & Miller, N.Y.C., 1951-54, 56-62; partner firm Feuerstein & Underweiser, 1962-73, Underweiser & Fuchs, 1973-77, Underweiser & Underweiser, 1977—. V.p., sec. Sunshine Mining Co., Kellogg, Idaho, 1965-70, chmn. bd., 1970-78, pres., 1971-74, 77, v.p., 1977-83; vice chmn., dir. Underwriters Bank and Trust Co., N.Y.C., 1969-73; sec., dir. Bus. Consortium Fund, 1994—, Triad Capital Corp. N.Y., 1994—; dir. Anchor Post Products, Inc. Bd. dirs. Silver Inst. Inc., vice chmn., 1998-2001; bd. dirs. Bronx Mus. of the Arts, 1993-2001, Sheltering the Homeless is Our Responsibility, 1993-2001, 02—; gen. counsel, mem. bus. council Friends City Center Music and Drama, N.Y.C., 1966-67; pres. W. Quaker Ridge Assn., 1969-70; treas. Scarsdale Neighborhood Assn. Presidents, 1970-71. Served with AUS, 1954-56. Mem. Am., N.Y. State bar assns., Bar Assn. City N.Y., Phi Beta Kappa, Phi Alpha Theta. Home: 7 Rural Dr Scarsdale NY 10583-7701 Office: 1 Water St White Plains NY 10601

UNDERWOOD, ANTHONY PAUL, lawyer; b. Atlanta, June 25, 1955; s. Paul L and Charlene B. (Snider) U.; children: Andrew Ryan, Elizabeth Kaitlin, Caroline MacKenzie. BA, U. North Ala., 1977; MA, JD, Samford U., 1980; MS, Johns Hopkins U., 1983; LLM, Judge Adv. Gen.'s Sch., 1994. Bar: Ala. 1980, U.S. Claims Ct. 1982, U.S. Ct. Mil. Appeals 1982. Trial atty. U.S. Army, various locations, 1980-87; sr. assoc. Doke & Riley, Dallas, 1987-89; legal counsel, dir. contracts Hughes Aircraft Co., Torrence, Calif., 1989-93; mgr., contracts Hughes Missile Systems Co., Tucson, 1993-95; dir., contracts & licensing Lockheed Martin Internat. Launch Svcs., San Diego, 1995—2000; prof. bus. Piedmont Coll., Demorest, Ga., 2000—01; chief bus. counsel U.S. Army Space Command, Colorado Springs, Colo., 2001—02; dir. contracts and export compliance Ball Aerospace and Tech. Corp., Boulder, Colo., 2002—. Author: A Progressive History of the Young Men's Business Club of Birmingham, Ala.: 1946-70, 1980. Lt. col. USAR, 1980-2002 Mem. ABA (vice chair various coms., pub. contract law sect). Republican. Avocations: travel, running, reading, skiing. Mailing: 906 Hover Ridge Cir Longmont CO 80501 Office: Ball Aerospace & Tech Corp 1600 Commerce St Boulder CO 80306 Office Phone: 303-939-4222. E-mail: gunderwo@ball.com.

UNDERWOOD, BLAIR, actor, director; b. Tacoma, Aug. 25, 1964; s. Frank and Marilyn Underwood; m. Desiree Da Costa, Sept. 17, 1994; 3 children. Student, Carnegie-Mellon U. TV debut The Cosby Show, 1985; actor (films) Krush Groove, 1985, The Second Coming, 1992, Posse, 1993, Just Cause, 1995, Set it Off, 1996, Gattaca, 1997, Deep Impact, 1998, Asunder, 1998, The Wishing Tree, 1999, Rules of Engagement, 2000 (NAACP Image award for sup. actor, 2001), G, 2002, Full Frontal, 2002, Malibu's Most Wanted, 2003, (TV series) One Life to Live, 1985-86, Downtown, 1986, LA Law, 1987-94, High Incident, 1996, City of Angels, 2000 (NAACP Image award for lead actor, 2001), Fatherhood, 2004, LAX, 2004, (TV movies) The Cover Girl and the Cop, 1989, Murder in Mississippi, 1990, Heat Wave, 1990, Father and Son: Dangerous Relations, 1993, Soul of the Game, 1996, Mistrial, 1996, Mama Flora's Family, 1998; theater credits include Measure for Measure, 1993, El Negro en Peru, The Game of Love and Chance, and Love Letters. Co-founder Artists for a New South Africa, 1989. Named Artist of the Year, Harvard Found., Harvard U., 2002; recipient Humanitarian Award, Muscular Dystrophy Assoc., LA, 1993. Office: William Morris Agency 151 El Camino Dr Beverly Hills CA 90212*

UNDERWOOD, CECIL H. former governor, company executive; b. Josephs Mills, W.Va., Nov. 5, 1922; s. Silas and Della (Forrester) U.; m. Hovah Hall, July 25, 1948; children: Cecilia A., Craig Hall, Sharon. AB, Salem (W.Va.) Coll., 1943; AM, W.Va. U., 1952; rsch. fellow, Amelia Earhart Found., Ann Arbor, Mich., 1954-56; LLD, Marietta (Ohio) Coll., 1957, Bethany (W.Va.) Coll., 1957, W.Va. U., 1957, W.Va. Inst. Tech., 1957, W.Va. State Coll., 1961, Concord Coll., 1960; D of Humanics, Salem Coll., 1957; Dr. Pub. Adminstrn., W.Va. Wesleyan Coll., 1958; LHD (hon.), Shepherd Coll., 1964; LittD, Western New Eng. Coll., 1969; LHD, Marshall U., 1997; D in Pub. Svc., Alderson Broaddus Coll., 1997; DSc (hon.), W. Va. Sch. Osteopathic Med., 1998; hon. degree, Davis and Elkins Coll., 1998, Fairmont State Coll., 1999. Tchr. high sch., 1943-46; staff Marietta Coll., 1946-50; v.p. Salem Coll., 1950-56; gov. State of W.Va., 1957—61, 1997—2001; v.p. Island Creek Coal Co., 1961-64; dir. civic affairs Monsanto Co., 1965-67, v.p., 1967; pres. Cecil H. Underwood Assocs., 1965-80, Franswood Corp., 1968-75, Bethany (W.Va.) Coll., 1972-75, Princess Coals, Inc., Huntington, 1978-81, Morgantown (W.Va.) Indsl. Park, Inc., 1983-96, Software Valley, 1989-92, Mon View Heights of W.Va., 1993-96; field underwriter N.Y. Life Ins. Co., 1976-78; chmn. bd. Princess Coals, Inc., Huntington, 1981-83. Sec. bd. dirs. Huntington Fed. Savs. and Loan Assn., 1961-96; pres. Huntington Found.; chair Cecil H. Underwood Inst. Mem. W.Va. Ho. Dels., 1944-56, minority floor leader, 1949, 51, 53, 55; Mem. exec. com. Gov.'s Conf., 1959; chmn. So. Regional Edn. Bd., 1959-60, 1999-2000; Pres. Young Republican League of W.Va., 1946-50; parliamentarian Young Rep. Nat. Conv., Boston, 1951; del.-at-large Rep. Nat. Conv., 1960, 64, 72, 76, 80, 84, 88, 2000, temporary chmn., 1960; Chmn. bd. dirs. W.Va. Found. Ind. Colls., Appalachian Regional Hosps.; chmn. bd. dirs. W.Va. div. Am. Cancer Soc., nat. bd. dirs., chmn. nat. crusade com., 1976-77, chmn. com. on legacies and planned giving, 1979; chmn. bd. dirs. Salem Coll., 1978-89, Salem Internat. U., 1989—; bd. dirs. Higher Edn. Loan Program of W.Va., 1980-94; chair W.Va. Coun. on Vocat. Edn., 1982-96, W.Va. State Coll. System, 1991, Nat. Edn. Goals Panel, 1998-99; regional vice chmn. Boy Scouts Am., 1961-67; dir. Fed. Home Loan Bank of Pitts. Mem. Nat. Assn. State Coun. Vocat. Edn. (pres. 1994-96), Masons, Shriners, Elks, Rotary, Sigma Phi Epsilon, Pi Kappa Delta. Republican. Methodist.

UNDERWOOD, EVELYN B. elementary and secondary educator, consultant, counselor; b. Hernando, Miss., Jan. 6, 1943; d. Herbert Miller and Sallie Bell Campbell; children from previous marriage: James Lee, Theodore, Timothy, Angela Renee, Herbert Dwayne; m. King James Underwood, May 28, 1977. BA BOG, Ea. Ill. U., 1983, MS in Edn., 1988, EdS, 1993; JD, Ind. U., 1987; PhD, U. Ill., 2000; DHL (hon.), Faith Grant Coll., Birmingham, Ala., 1995. Cert. tchr. h.s. and upper elem. guidance, Ill.; cert. in adminstrn., Ill.; ordained elder (minister) Free Will Bapt. Ch. Asst. to mgr. Shelton Laundry, Urbana, Ill., 1961-63; sec. U. Ill., Urbana, 1964-68, asst. to exec. dir. Afro Am. Studies Commn., 1969-71, asst. to dir. minority student affairs, 1971-84, 87-89; educator, counselor Urbana Sch. Dist. 116, 1983-93, counselor, 1993—. Elected. mem., sec. Urbana Bd. Edn., 1968-80; cert. legal intern to fed. judge, legal svcs., atty. gen., Indpls., Bloomington, Ind., Champaign, Ill., 1986-87; founder Evelyn Burnett Underwood Instrumental Music Student Assistance Program, Urbana Sch. Dist. 116, 1994—. Contbr. articles and papers to profl. publs. Mem. exec. com. Concerned Citizens Com., Champaign, 1963-85; overseer U. Ill. YWCA Endowment Com., Champaign, 1994—; v.p. Mnisterial Alliance of Champaign-Urbana and Vicinity, 1999—. Recipient Outstanding Achievement to Nat. Sch. Bd. Assn. Black Caucus, 1976; fellow U. Ill., 1990. Mem. AAUW, Ill. Assn. Multicultural Counseling (pres.-elect 2000), Ill. Edn. Assn. (region 9 rep. 1999—), Ill. Counseling Assn., Urbana Edn. Assn. of NEA/Ill. Edn. Assn. (v.p. 1994-98), Ill. Career Devel. Assn., Ill. Sch. Counselors Assn., Optimist Club Internat. Democrat. Avocations: missionary work, tutoring and counseling youth.

UNDERWOOD, JANE HAINLINE HAMMONS, anthropologist, educator; b. Ft. Bliss, Tex., Oct. 30, 1931; d. Frank and Lydia (Williams) Hammons; m. Van K. Hainline, Oct. 20, 1947 (div. 1966); children: Michael K., Susan J.; m. John W. Underwood, July 4, 1968; 1 dau., Anne K. AA, Imperial Valley Coll., 1957; BA, U. Calif., Riverside, 1960; MA, UCLA, 1962, PhD, 1964. Asst. prof. U. Calif., Riverside, 1963-68; research anthropology Yap Islands, 1964, 65-66; prof. anthropology U. Ariz., Tucson, 1968-99, prof. emeritus, 1999—, assoc. dean Grad. Coll., 1979-80, asst. provost for grad. studies, 1980-82, acting dir. Sch. Health Related Professions, 1980-82, asst. v.p. research, assoc. dean Grad. Coll., 1982-87; assoc. Micronesian Area Rsch. Ctr., 1987—. Contbr. articles to profl. jours. Woodrow Wilson fellow, 1960-61; UCR Jr. Faculty fellow, 1968 Fellow AAAS; mem. Am. Assn. Phys. Anthropologists (v.p. 1980-82), Assn. Study Human Biology, Pacific Sci. Assn. (life), Assn. for Study Social Biology (bd. dirs. 1996-99), Sigma Xi (pres. U. Ariz. chpt. 1991-92). Home: 2228 E 4th St Tucson AZ 85719-5118 E-mail: kammagar@prodigy.net.

UNDERWOOD, MARK FOREST, lawyer; b. Ft. Campbell, Ky., Feb. 14, 1964; s. Harry Wayne and Alicia Elkins Underwood; m. Cynthia Jean Walker, Sept. 13, 2003. BBA, Marshall U., 1986; JD, Pepperdine U., 1989; grad., Nat. Inst. Trial Advocacy, 1992, Am. Trial Lawyers Ultimate Advocacy Coll., 2002; diplomate, Gerry Spence Trial Lawyers Coll., 2002. Bar: Calif. 89, W.Va. 96, D.C. 97, U.S. Ct. Appeals (4th cir.) 99. Assoc. Hagenbaugh & Murphy, L.A., 1989—92, Crosby, Healey, Roach & May, L.A., 1992—94; ptnr. Fredeking & Fredeking, Huntington, W.Va., 1994—96; pvt. practice Underwood Law Offices, Huntington, 1997—. Mem. W.Va. State Legis., 1997—98. Recipient Frasure Singleton Legis. fellowship, W.Va. Legislature, 1985. Mem.: ATLA, Nat. Coll. DUI Defense. Democrat. Presbyterian. Home: 910 Fourth Ave Ste 1111 Huntington WV 25701 Office: Underwood Law Offices 910 4th Ave Huntington WV 25701 E-mail: markunderwood@markunderwood.com.

UNDERWOOD, PAUL BENJAMIN, gynecologist, oncologist, educator; b. Greer, S.C., Aug. 8, 1934; s. Paul Benjamin and Gladys (Guest) U.; m. Peggy Joyce Outen, July 7, 1957; children: Paul Benjamin III, Mary Barton. MD, Med. U. S.C., 1959. Diplomate Am. Bd. Ob-gyn., Am. Bd. Gynecol. Oncology. Intern Med. U. S.C., Charleston, 1959-60, resident, 1960-64; fellow M.D. Anderson Hosp. and Tumor Inst., Houston, 1966-67; asst. prof. U. S.C., 1967-70, assoc. prof., 1970-74, prof., 1974-79; chmn. dept. ob-gyn. U. Va. Sch. Medicine, Charlottesville, 1979-99; staff, dir. gynecology, assoc. dean admissions Med. U. S.C., Charleston, 1999—, dir. divsn. gynecol. oncology, 2002. Contbr. numerous articles to med. jours. With USN, 1964-66. Recipient Alumni of Yr. award Med. U. S.C., 1989. Mem. Am. Coll. Ob-gyn., Soc. Gynecol. Oncologists (coun. 1972-75, v.p. 1977-78, pres. 1983), Am. Assn. Ob-gyn. (sec. 1992-95, pres. 1999—), Felix Rutledge Soc. (pres. 1977), Am. Gynecol. Club (pres. 1996), So. Med. Soc., Charlottesville Med. Soc., S.C. Ob-gyn. Soc., Thegos Soc., Alpha Omega Alpha. Office: 171 Ashley Ave Charleston SC 29425-0001 Office Phone: 843-792-4026. Business E-Mail: underwp@musc.edu.

UNDERWOOD, PAUL LESTER, cardiologist; b. Knoxville, Tenn., Mar. 23, 1960; MD, Mayo Med. Sch., 1984. Diplomate Am. Bd. Cardiovascular Disease. Intern Henry Ford Hosp., Detroit, 1984-85; resident in internal medicine Mayo Grad. Sch. Medicine, Rochester, Minn., 1985-87; fellow in cardiology Cleve. Clinic, 1990-93; fellow in interventional cardiology Iowa Heart Ctr., Des Moines, 1993; dir. emergency medicine, dir. ICU St. Croix Hosp., U.S. V.I., 1987-90; staff North Phoenix (Ariz.) Heart Ctr., 2001—. Mem. AMA, Nat. Med. Assn., Assn. Black Cardiologists (pres.), Am. Coll. Cardiology (councilor), Am. Heart Assn. (bd. dirs. Ariz. affiliate), Soc. for Cardiac Angiography and Interventions. Office: North Phoenix Heart Ctr 9100 N 2d St Ste 321 Phoenix AZ 85020 E-mail: drundrwd@aol.com.

UNDERWOOD, RICHARD ALLAN, English language educator; b. Plymouth, Mich., Mar. 28, 1933; s. Harold Raymond and Yvonne Clara (Foster) U.; m. Sandra Jane Hayes, Nov. 17, 1962; 1 child, Eric Michael. BA, U. Mich., 1955, MA, 1967, PhD, 1970. Asst. prof. Clemson (S.C.) U., 1970-77, assoc. prof., 1977-84, prof. English, 1984—. Author: A Little Bit of Love, 1963, Shakespeare's "The Phoenix and Turtle": A Survey of Scholarship, 1974, Shakespeare on Love: The Poems and the Plays, 1985, The Two Noble Kinsmen and Its Beginnings, 1993; translator: En Smula Karlek, 1969, 81; editor: Phoenix with a Bayonet: A Journalist's Interim Report on the Greek Revolution (by Bayard Stockton), 1971. 1st lt. U.S. Army, 1955-57. Fellow Bread Loaf Writers Conf., 1963; vis. scholar Rackham Sch. Grad. Studies, U. Mich., 1983-85, 90-91, 91-92, 92-93, 93-94. Avocation: piano music. Home: 111 Lakeview Cir Clemson SC 29631-1019 Office: Clemson U 809 Strode Clemson SC 29631-1436

UNDERWOOD, ROBERT ANACLETUS, former congressman, university official; b. Tamuning, Guam, July 13, 1948; m. Lorraine Aguilar; 5 children. BA with honors in History, Calif. State U., 1969, MA in History, 1971; cert. edn. adminstrn., U. Guam, 1976; DEd, U. So. Calif., 1987. Loader, sorter United Parcel Svc., L.A., 1966-72; tchr. George Washington High Sch., 1972-74; asst. prin. for bus. and student pers. George Washington H.S., 1974-76; asst. and acting prin. Inarajan Jr. H.S., 1976; instr., dir. bilingual bicultural tng. program U. Guam, 1976-81, asst. prof., 1981-83, dir. bilingual edn. assistance for Micronesia project, 1983-88, dean Coll. Edn., 1988-90, acad. v.p., 1990—; mem. del. 103d-107th Congress from Guam, Washington, 1993—2003. Mem. House resources com., armed svcs.; chmn. Asian Pacific Caucus 106th Congress; part-time curriculum writer Guam Bilingual Edn. Project, 1973-76; chmn. Chamorro Lang. Commn., 1979-90. Named Citizen of Yr., Nat. Assn. Bilingual Edn., 1996, Alumnus of Yr. Calif. State U., 1999. Roman Catholic. Office: US Ho Reps 2418 Rayburn Ho Office Bldg Washington DC 20515-0001 E-mail: guamtodc@mail.house.gov.

UNDERWOOD, ROBERT LEIGH, venture capitalist; b. Paducah, Ky., Dec. 31, 1944; s. Robert Humphreys and Nancy Wells (Jessup) Underwood; m. Susan Lynn Doscher, May 22, 1976; children: Elizabeth Leigh, Dana Whitney, George Gregory. BS with great distinction, Stanford U., 1965, MS, 1966, PhD, 1968; MBA, Santa Clara U., 1970. Rsch. scientist, project leader Lockheed Missiles & Space Co., Sunnyvale, Calif., 1967—71; spl. asst. for engring. scis. Office Sec., Dept. Transp., Washington, 1971—73; sr. mgmt. assoc. Office Mgmt. and Budget, Exec. Office Pres., 1973; with TRW Inc., L.A., 1973—79, dir. retail nat. accts., 1977—78, dir. product planning and devel., 1978—79; pres., CEO OMEX, Santa Clara, Calif., 1980—82; v.p. Heizer Corp., Chgo., 1979—85; pres. No. Capital Corp., Chgo., 1985—86; mng. ptnr. ISSS Ventures, 1986—88; founding ptnr. N.Am. Bus. Devel. Co., Chgo., 1988—; pres., CEO Polymer Corp., Rockland, Mass., 2003—. Trustee Burridge Mut. Funds, 1996—98; dir. various pvt. and pub. portfolio cos., 1979—. Contbr. articles to profl. jours. Mem. sch. bd. Avoca Dist. 37, 1990—99, v.p., 1996—99; mem. adv. bd. Leavy Sch. Bus. and Adminstrn. Santa Clara U., 1995—; mem. adv. com. on indsl. innovation NSF, 1982—96; trustee Kenilworth Union Ch., 2003—; elder Presbyn. Ch., 1978—79. Fellow, NASA, NSF; scholar, Alcoa. Mem.: IEEE, Indian Hill Club (Winnetka, Ill.), Chgo. Club, Union League Chgo., Beta Gamma Sigma, Tau Beta Pi, Phi Beta Kappa, Sigma Xi. Home: 59 Woodley Rd Winnetka IL 60093-3748 Office: 135 S La Salle St Chicago IL 60603-4159

UNDERWOOD, STEVEN CLARK, publishing executive; b. Arlington Heights, Ill., Dec. 1, 1960; s. Donald William and Mary Frances (Clark) U. BBA, U. Tex., 1982, MBA, 1987; JD, So. Meth. U., 1985. Bar: Tex. 1985. Sr. fin. analyst CBS, Inc., N.Y.C., 1987-89; assoc. bus. mgr. Supplementary Edn. Group Simon & Schuster, Englewood Cliffs, N.J., 1989-90, bus. mgr. Fearon/Janus/Quercus divsn. Belmont, Calif., 1990-92, pres.

Fearon/Janus/Quercus divsn., 1992-93, pres. Globe Fearon divsn. Upper Saddle River, NJ, 1993-96; v.p., dir. of bus. devel. Secondary Edn. Group, Simon and Schuster, Upper Saddle River, NJ, 1996-97; v.p. bus. devel. Simon and Schuster, Upper Saddle River, NJ, 1997-98; v.p. sch. markets Troll Comms., Mahwah, NJ, 1998—2001; v.p., contr. Current Med. Directions divsn, MediMedia USA, Inc., N.Y.C., 2002—. Mem. ABA, Am. Mgmt. Assn. (pres.'s assn.), Assn. Am. Pubs., Nat. Eagle Scout Assn., Coll. Bus. Adminstrn. Students' Assn., Tex. Bar Assn., Tex. Alumni Assn., U. Tex. Century Club, Alpha Phi Omega, Beta Gamma Sigma, Phi Kappa Phi, Phi Eta Sigma, Golden Key. Republican. Methodist. Avocations: sailing, scuba diving, Karate, camping, rafting. Home: 902 Somerset Ct Ramsey NJ 07446-2919 Office Phone: 212-771-9842.

UNDERWOOD, THOMAS WOODBROOK, communications company executive; b. Royal Oak, Mich., Nov. 29, 1930; s. Elmer and Della Marie (Zimmer) U.; m. Louise Virginia, May 24, 1953 (dec. Feb. 1979); children: Ann Marie Underwood Shuman, Dan and Dave (twins). BAS in Elec. Engring., Milw. Sch. Engring., 1957, MS in Comms., 1995, PhD in Comms., 1998. Service analyst, writer ITT Gillfillan, Los Angeles, 1958-60; sr. tech. editor, writer Smithkline Beckman, Fullerton, Calif., 1960-78, tech. com. mgr. Brea, Calif., 1978-85; pres. Tranwood Communications, Santa Ana, Calif., 1985—. Tech. editor, writer manuals for manned space flights to Mars and the moon. Served to staff sgt. USAF, 1950-54, Korea. Fellow Soc. Tech. Comms. (Orange County chpt., assoc., pres. 1992, 93, treas. 1966, 88), Am. Med. Writers Assn, U.S. C. of C., Santa Ana C. of C. Democrat. Home and Office: Tranwood Comm PO Box 1852 Palm Springs CA 92263-1852

UNDERWOOD, VERNON O., JR., grocery stores executive; b. 1940; children: Jeff, Chris. BBA, U. So. Calif. With Young's Market Co., L.A., 1955—, pres., 1975—97, CEO, chmn. bd., 1990—. Avocations: golf, bird hunting, travel, smoking Marlboros. Office: Young's Market Co 2164 N Batavia St Orange CA 92865-3109

UNGAR, ERIC EDWARD, mechanical engineer; b. Vienna, Nov. 12, 1926; came to U.S. 1939; s. Irwin Isidor and Sabina (Schlesinger) U.; m. Goldie Edna Becker, July 1, 1951; children: Judith Fishman, Susan Green, Ellen Borgenicht, Sharon Ungar Lane. BSME, Washington U., St. Louis, 1951; MS, U. N.Mex., 1954; DSc in Engring., NYU, 1957. Aero-ordnance engr. Sandia Corp., Albuquerque, 1951-53; rsch. scientist, asst. prof. NYU, 1953-58; chief cons. engr. Bolt Beranek & Newman, Inc., Cambridge, Mass., 1958-96. Chief engring. scientist Acentech Inc., Cambridge, 1993—. Co-author: Structure-Borne Sound, 1973, 2nd edit. 1988; contbr. articles to profl. jours., chpts. to books. 1st lt. U.S. Army, 1945-48, ETO. Recipient Per Bruel Gold Medal for Noise Control and Acoustics ASME, 1994. Fellow ASME (life; chmn. design engring. divsn. 1978-80, Centennial medallion 1981, Per Bruel Gold medal for noise control and acoustics 1994), AIAA (assoc.), Acoustical Soc. Am. (pres. 1991-92, Trent-Crede Silver medal 1983); mem. Inst. for Noise Control and Engring. (bd. cert., pres. 1985, Disting. Noise Control Engr. award 2004). Home: 15 Considine Rd Newton MA 02459-3603 Office: Acentech Inc 33 Moulton St Cambridge MA 02138-1118 Office Phone: 617-499-8022. E-mail: eungar@acentech.com.

UNGARETTI, RICHARD ANTHONY, lawyer; b. Chgo., May 25, 1942; s. Dino Carl and Antoinette (Calvetti) U.; children: Joy A., Paul R. BS, DePaul U., 1964, JD, 1970. Bar: Ill. 1970, U.S. Dist. Ct. (no. dist.) Ill. 1970, U.S. Supreme Ct. 1980. Assoc. Kirkland & Ellis, Chgo., 1970-74; ptnr. Ungaretti & Harris, Chgo., 1974—. Mem. adv. coun. DePaul Coll. Law, Chgo., 1988. Mem. ABA, Chgo. Bar Assn., Ill. State Bar Assn., Internat. Coun. Shopping Ctrs., Am. Coll. Real Estate Lawyers, Justinian Soc., Urban Land Inst. (assoc.), Lamda Alpha Avocations: golf, fishing, hunting. Office: Ungaretti & Harris 3500 Three First Nat Plz Chicago IL 60602 E-mail: raungaretti@uhlaw.com.

UNGARO, EMANUEL MATTEOTTI, fashion designer; b. Aix-en-Provence, France, Feb. 13, 1933; s. Cosimo and Concetta (Casalino) U.; m. Laura; 1 dau. Student, Lycée, Aix-en-Provence, 1943-50. Worked with father as tailor, Aix-en-Provence, 1951-54; then for Camps Paris, 1955-57. With Cristobal Balenciaga, Paris, 1957-64, dir. Balenciaga br., Madrid, 1958-60; worked for André Courréges, Paris, 1964; ind. couturier, Paris, 1965. Designer of both couture and ready-to-wear men's and women's fashions; also fragrance designer since 1977. Office: 2 Ave Montaigne F 75008 Paris France

UNGARO, JOSEPH MICHAEL, newspaper publishing executive, consultant; b. Providence, Nov. 4, 1930; s. Rocco and Lucy (Motta) U.; m. Evelyn Short, Apr. 15, 1961; children: Elizabeth Anne, Joseph Michael, Ellen Lucia. BA, Providence Coll., 1952; MS in Journalism, Columbia, 1953. With Providence Jour.-Bull., 1951-73, mng. editor Evening Bull., 1967-72; mng. editor Eve. Bull., also dir. planning and devel. Providence Jour. and Bull., 1972-73; mng. editor Westchester-Rockland Newspapers, White Plains, N.Y., 1974-75, v.p., exec. editor, 1975-84, pres., gen. mgr., 1984-86, pres., publisher, 1986-90; pres., chief exec. officer Detroit Newspaper Agy., 1990-91; cons., 1991—. Mem. Am. Newspaper Pubs. Assn. (past chmn. research inst., conv. program com.), Am. Soc. Newspaper Editors, AP Mng. Editors Assn. (past pres.) Home: 379 Pond Shore Dr Charlestown RI 02813-2007 Office Phone: 401-364-6032. Personal E-mail: joeungaro@aol.com.

UNGARO, SUSAN KELLIHER, magazine editor; married; 3 children. BA, MA, William Patterson Coll. From mem. staff to editor-in-chief Family Circle mag., NYC, 1976—94, editor-in-chief, 1994—. Bd. dirs. Brazelton Found., Nat. Marrow Found., H.E.L.P. (Housing Enterprise for the Less Privileged). Named named Top Businessperson of Yr., Irish America magazine; recipient President's Award, New Jersey Press Women's Assn., 1995, William Paterson University Legacy Award, 1998, Muriel Fox communications award for professional excellence and commitment to advocacy journalism, NOW Legal Defense Fund, 1998. Mem.: Am. Soc. Mag. Editors (bd. dir. 1998—, pres. 2003—). Office: Gruner & Jahr 375 Lexington Ave New York NY 10017-5514

UNGARO-BENAGES, URSULA MANCUSI, federal judge; b. Miami Beach, Fla., Jan. 29, 1951; d. Ludivico Mancusi-Ungaro and Ursula Berliner; m. Michael A. Benages, Mar., 1988. Student, Smith Coll., 1968-70; BA in English Lit., U. Miami, 1973; JD, U. Fla., 1975. Bar: Fla. 1975. Assoc. Frates, Floyd, Pearson et al, Miami, 1976-78, Blackwell, Walker, Gray et al, Miami, 1978-80, Finley, Kumble, Heine et al, Miami, 1980-85, Sparber, Shevin, Shapo et al, Miami, 1985-87; cir. judge State of Fla., Miami, 1987-92; U.S. dist. judge U.S. Dist. Ct., Miami, 1992—. Mem. Fla. Supreme Ct. Race & Ethnic & Racial Bias Study Commn., Fla., 1989-92, St. Thomas U. Inns of Ct., Miami, 1991-92; mem. Jud. Resources Com. Jud. Conf. U.S.; chmn. Ct. Svcs. Com. So. Dist. Fla., chmn. Magistrate Judge Com.; mem. personnel com. 11th Cir. Jud. Coun. U.S. Bd. dirs. United Family & Children's Svcs., Miami, 1981-82; mem. City of Miami Task Force, 1991-92. Mem. ABA, Fed. Judges Assn., Fla. Assn. Women Lawyers, Dade County Bar Assn., Eugene Spellman Inns of Ct. U. Miami. Office: US Dist Ct 301 N Miami Ave Fl 11 Miami FL 33128-7702 Office Phone: 305-523-5550.

UNGER, BARBARA, poet, retired educator; b. N.Y.C., Oct. 2, 1932; d. David and Florence (Schuchalter) Frankel; m. Bernard Unger, 1954 (div. 1976); m. Theodore Sakano, 1987; children: Deborah, Suzanne. BA, CCNY, 1955, MA, 1957; advanced cert., NYU, 1970. Grad. asst. Yeshiva U., 1962-63; edn. editor County Citizen, Rockland County, NY, 1960-63; tchr. English N.Y.C. Pub. Schs., 1955-58, Nyack (N.Y.) H.S., 1963-67; guidance counselor Ardsley (N.Y.) H.S., 1967-69; prof. English Rockland C.C., Suffern, NY, 1969—95, ret., 1995. Poetry fellow Squaw Valley Cmty. of Writers, 1980; writer-in-residence Rockland Ctr. for Arts, 1986. Author: (poetry) Basement, 1975, Learning to Fox Trot, 1989, The Man Who Burned Money, 1980, Inside the Wind, 1986, Blue Depression Glass in Troika One, 1991, (fiction) Dying for Uncle Ray, 1990; co-author (with Lloyd Ultan): (non-fiction) Bronx Accent: A Literary and Pictorial History of the Borough, 2001 (N.Y. Soc. Libr. Book award for borough history, 2001, J.M. Kaplan Furthermore grant); contbr. Anthology Mag. Verse, Yearbook Am. Poetry, 1984, Anthology Mag. Verse, Yearbook Am. Poetry, 1989, poetry and fiction to more than 75 lit. mags. Ragdale Found. fellow, 1985, 86, 89, SUNY Creative Writing fellow, 1981-82, Edna St. Vincent Millay Colony fellow, 1984, Djerassi Found. fellow, 1991, Hambidge Ctr. for Creative Arts and Scis. fellow, 1988; NEH grantee, 1975; recipient Goodman Poetry award, 1989, Anna Davidson Rosenberg award Judah Magnes Mus., 1989, Roberts Writing award, 1990, New Letters Lit. awards, 1990; finalist Am. Fiction Competition, 1982, John Williams Narrative Poetry Competition, 1992; honorable mention Chester Jones Nat. Poetry Contest. Mem.: PEN, Authors' Guild, Acad. Am. Poets, Poets and Writers. Office Phone: 845-357-1683.

UNGER, GARY ALLEN, recording industry executive, singer, lyricist, composer, music publisher; b. Clinton, Iowa, Aug. 14, 1947; s. Charles Elmer Unger and Lois Grace Haack. Grad. high sch., Ill., 1967. Internat. import-export mgr. G & U Enterprises, Clinton, 1968—; mgr., pres. Groove Song Music, Clinton, 1968—, Narrowroad Music, Clinton, 1980—96; mgr., v.p. ACI, Clinton, 1978-79; mgr., pres. ECI Internat. Records, Clinton, 1980-96, GTM, Clinton, 1973, Nashville, 1976—; pres. Sugarvine Music (BMI). On Art Bell Radio Talk Show, Radio Network, 1996-97. Lyricist: songs I Will Always Love You Part I and II, I Like It, I Love It, Thinkin About You, Give Them All to Jesus, My White Rabbi6, 1995, My Coloring Book, 1955, In My Life, 0158, I Knew You When, 1958, A Stranger In My House, 1959, Birthday, 1959, God Bless the Service, Please! Don't Tell Me No More Lies, The Wink, Lord I Lift Your Name on High, 1961, Jesus Oh! Jesus, Oh!, The Shake, 1961, You and Me, 1961, The Closer You Get, 1961, Home, 1961, You Light Up My Life, 1968, Don't Tell Me No Lies, 1963, Check Yes or No, Country Sunshine, 1965, Tennessee River, 1965, Blue, 1965, One Day At a Time, 1965, Dancin Shaggin on the Boulevard, 1965, Carving Your Love With Me, 1965, If Your Not In It for Love I'm Out of Here, 1966, Lyricist (with G. Russen): songs The Love in Her Soul, Lyricist: songs Heart to Heart, 1968, Fool for Your Love, God Bless You Jesus, 1967, God Bless the Service, Born in This U.S.A., 1967, No Doubt, Parts I, II, and III, I've Never Been to England, Real Love, Hey June and Darline, I Got Jesus on My Mind, God Bless the Service, Parts I and II, Heaven O Sweet Angel, Please Remember Me, Oh! Country Doll, Oh! Baby Doll, You Win My Love, Lyricist (with G.A. Unger and J. Ward): songs Oh! Sweet Honey, 1997, Lyricist: songs Girl, I Love You, Love is Like a Butterfly, Let Us Pray Together, Lost in the 50's Tonight, Kentucky Rain, Blue I'm So Blue, All I Want is a Life with You Jesus, On the 4th of July, Boot Scootin Boogie, Love Is, Lyricist (with Joan Brothers): songs Almost Like a Song, Lyricist: songs Why Can't Every Day Be Like Christmas, Moody Blues, Third Rock From the Sun, God Bless Texas Too, Maybe You Can Drive My Car, Oh, My, My, Those Rock N Years, My Achin Breakin Heart, Born to Love You, We Were Meant for Each Other, Jesus OH! Jesus I Love You, Don't Worry Be Happy Like Happy, Lyricist): songs Please Don't Bump the Jukebox, Lyricist: songs Hey It's a Small Town, God Bless the U.S.A. (Born in the USA), The Happiest Guy in the Whole USA, God Writes the Songs, When You Walked In, You Better Think Twice Again, My Coloring Book, Independence Day, Together With Our Heartfelt Love, She's Gone Country, You Light Up My Life, Give Them All to Jesus, Chasing That Neon Rainbow, 1963, Touched By a Holy Angel?, Almost Everywhere, No One Else on Earth, Praise the Lord, On American Bandstand, Love Is, If Tomorrow Never Comes, In My Life, The Long and Winding Roads, Please! Remember Me, Hello-Good-Buy, Oh! Country Doll, Creator of the Stars, Our Heart Felt Love, 1997, Lyricist (with Joan Brothers): songs Sweet Country Girl, 2001, Lyricist (with G.A. Unger and W. Cochran): songs God Bless the American Veterans, 2001, Lyricist: songs Tennessee Love In America, lyricist: songs The Power of His Love, God Bless the U.S.A. and Those Who Were Born in the U.S.A. Mem. RIAA, GNACMAI, Nat. Assn. Songwriters Internat., Nat. Music Found. Fax: 563-243-1334.

UNGER, GERE NATHAN, emergency physician, lawyer; b. Monticello, N.Y., May 15, 1949; s. Jessie Aaron and Shirley (Rosenstein) Unger; m. Alice J. McGowan, July 21, 1990; children: Elijah, Breena, Ari, Sasha, Arlen. JD, Bernadean U., 1979; MD, Inst. Polytecnico, Mexico City, 1986; D Phys. Medicine, Met. U., Mexico City, 1987; postgrad., Boston U., 1993, Harvard Law Sch., 1994-96; LLM in Med. Law, U. Glasgow, 2001. Diplomate Am. Bd. Forensic Examiners, Am. Bd. Med. Legal Analysis Medicine and Surgery, Am. Bd. Forensic Medicine, Am. Bd. Risk Mgmt., Am. Bd. Disability Analysts. Med. dir. Vietnam Vets. Post-Traumatic Stress Disorder Program, 1988-90; emergency rm. physician, cons. in medicaid fraud Bronx (N.Y.)-Lebanon Hosp., 1990—; clin. legal medicine Paladin Profl. Group, P.A., Palm Beach, Fla., 1992-98; pres. Albany Law Jour. Co., Inc., 1998—; jurisconsult Office of Gere Unger, M.D., J.D., 1999—. Mem. surg. critical care com. Am. Soc. Critical Care Medicine, 1992; mem. peer rev. com. Nat. Inst. Disability and Rehab. Rsch., Office Spl. Edn., U.S. Dept. Edn., 1993; mediator, arbitrator, negotiator World Intellectual Property Orgn., 1994; mem. clin. ethics com. Inst. Medecine Legale et de Medecine Sociale, Strasbourg, France, 1994; mediator, arbitrator World Bank, 2000—. Mem. editl. bd. Am. Bd. Forensic Examiners, 1993, Jour. Neurol. and Orthopaedic Medicine and Surgery, 1993. Comdt. Broward County Marine Corps League, 1995—. With USMC, 1968—72. Fellow: The Cognitive Sci. Soc., Exec. Practice Mgmt., Am. Coll. Forensic Examiners, Internat. Coll. Surgeons (mem. ethics com. 1994, mem. emergency response program eastern region 1994), Am. Acad. Neurol. and Orthopedic Surgeons, Am. Coll. Legal Medicine; mem.: FBA (mem. health com., rep. ABA 1994, chmn. med. malpractice/tort com., liaison to AMA), ATLA (N.Y. state capt. 1992), ABA, N.Y. State Defenders Assn., Nat. Am. Indian Ct. Judges Assn., N.W. Indian Bar Assn., Internat. Assn. Prosecutors, Am. Soc. Investigative Pathology, Internat. Criminal Law Network (The Hague), Internat. Assn. Prosecutors, Internat. Royal Soc. Medicine (London), Nat. Assn. Forensic Econs., Am. Soc. Laser Medicine and Surgery, Kennedy Inst. Ethics, Am. Coll. Physician Execs. (chair forum law and med. mgmt. 1995), Internat. Bar Assn., Nat. Coll. Advocacy. Avocations: flying, boating. Office: PO Box 2765 Concord NH 03302 Office Phone: 978-089-0963. E-mail: fsi@justice.com.

UNGER, HOWARD ALBERT, artist, photographer, educator; b. Mt. Vernon, N.Y., Oct. 13, 1944; s. Howard Albert and Florence A. (Peterson) U.; m. Anrita Abelow, Aug. 25, 1972; 1 son, Christopher Howard. Student, Art Students League, N.Y.C., 1960-61, Sch. Visual Arts, 1975-76, N.Y. Inst. Holography, 1976; BFA, Kent State U., 1966, MA, 1968; MEd, Columbia U., 1972, EdD, 1975; MA, N.Y. Inst. Tech., 1994. Cert. open water diver, 1988, advanced scuba diver, 1989. Grad. tchg. fellow in photo-journalism Kent State U., 1966-67, instr. in art, 1966-67, grad. teaching fellow in art, 1967-68; head program in art, tchr. art Kew-Forest Prep. Sch., Kew Gardens, N.Y., 1968-69; technician TV sta. Tchrs. Coll., Columbia U., 1971-72, instr. art and edn., 1972-75, instr. curriculum and tchg., 1976-82, instr. dept. comm., computing and tech. in edn., 1982—; asst. prof. visual comm. tech. dept. humanities Ocean County Coll., 1972-78, assoc. prof., 1979-82, prof., 1982—, gallery coord. Fine Arts Ctr., 1972—. Part-time grad. instr. comm. arts N.Y. Inst. Tech., N.Y.C., 1994-95; instr. comm. and edn. Sch. Edn. NYU, 1973-74; design and photograph coord. RCA Records, N.Y.C., 1969-70; freelance designer, 1965— Exhibitor photography in one-man shows, Photographis Societas Photographis, Columbia U., 1971, Ziegfeld Gallery, N.Y.C., 1972; group shows, Kent State U., 1965-68, Ocean County Coll., 1973-83, 14 Sculptor Gallery, N.Y.C., 1995; permanent collections, Internat. Ctr. Photography, N.Y.C., Mus. Holography, N.Y.C., Kent State U., Ocean County Coll., Tchrs. Coll., Columbia U., pvt. collections; lectr. in photography; co-author: (with William Maxwell) photog. illustrator Printmaking: A Beginner's Handbook, 1977; photog. illustrator: The Fourth R. Stewart Kranz, 1971; contbg. author: A Tour Through The Realm of Science Plus Art, 1974; photography critic: Village Voice, 1976-77; photography columnist Soho Weekly News, 1977-78. Recipient 1st place award Am. Greeting Card Competition, 1966; recipient honorarium dept. curriculum and teaching Tchrs. Coll., Columbia U., 1973 Mem. Soc. Photography Educators, NEA, Mus. Modern Art, N.J. Edn. Assn., Met. Mus. Art, Am. Mus. Natural History, Profl. Assn. Diving Instrs. (lic. advanced scuba diver), Nat. Assn. Underwater Instrs. (lic. advanced scuba diver). Republican. Home: 515 E 79th St New York NY 10021-0705 Office: Ocean County Coll College Dr Toms River NJ 08754-2001

UNGER, IRWIN, historian, educator; b. Bklyn., May 2, 1927; s. Elias C. and Mary (Roth) U.; m. Bernate Myra Spaet, Feb. 1956 (div.); children: Brooke David, Miles Jeremy, Paul Joshua; m. Debi Irene Weisstein, May 11, 1970; stepchildren: Anthony Allen, Elizabeth Sarah. B in Social Scis., CCNY, 1948; MA, Columbia U., 1949, PhD, 1958; student, U. Wash., 1949—51. Instr. Columbia U., 1956-58; asst. prof. Long Beach (Calif.) State Coll., 1959-62; assoc. prof. U. Calif., Davis, 1962-66; prof. history NYU, NYC, 1966—2000, prof. emeritus, 2000—. Vis. lectr. U. PR, 1958—59. Author: The Greenback Era: A Social and Political History of American Finance: 1865-1879, 1964, The Movement: A History of the American New Left, 1974, (with Debi Unger) The Vulnerable Years: The United States, 1896-1917, Turning Point: 1968, 1988, The Best of Intentions: The Rise and Fall of the Great Society Programs, 1996, (with Debi Unger) LBJ: A Life, 1999. Served with AUS, 1952-54. Recipient Pulitzer prize for history, 1965; Guggenheim fellow, 1972-73, Rockefeller humanities fellow, 1980-81, Harry Frank Guggenheim fellow, 1987-88. Home: 473 W End Ave New York NY 10024-4934 E-mail: ungerclio@aol.com.

UNGER, KAREN VIRGINIA, director; d. Gunnar Fredrick Unger and Florence Mae Tawyea; m. John Anton Geisen, Aug. 23, 1964 (div.); 1 child, Rebecca Lynn Geisen. MEd, Calif. State Poly. U., 1969; M in Counseling Psychology, Chapman Coll., 1974; MSW, Ariz. State U., 1976; EdD, Boston U., 1987. Dir. Phoenix Alternative H.S., Westwood, Mass., 1978—81; dir. supported edn. svcs. Ctr. Psychiat. Rehab., Boston U., Boston, 1981—93; dir. rsch. and tng. Vinfen Corp., 1993—94; rsch. assoc. prof. U. Ariz., Tucson, 1995—98; pres. Rehab. Through Edn., Portland, 1995—. Vice chmn., bd. dirs. Outside In, Portland, 1998—2001, Garlington; mental health adv. bd. Dept. Mental Health, Salem, Oreg., 1999—2002. Author: Handbook of Supported Education: Providing Services for People With Psychiatric Disabilities; contbg. author: Readings in Psychiatric Rehabilitation, Psychiatric Rehabilitation: Putting Theory into Practice; co-author: New Directions for Mental Health Services Sourcebook; editor (guest editor): Spl. Edit. Supported Edn., Jour.Psychiatric Rehab., Spl. Edit. Supported Edn. The Jour. Calif. Allianee Mentally Ill; contbr. articles to profl. jours.; prodr.: (video) It Can Happen Here. Recipient Mertious Svc. award, Mass. Alliance Mentally Ill, 1987, Recognition award, Assn. Higher Edn. and Disability, 1997; fellow, NIMH, 1976—77; grantee, Dept. Edn., 1988—91, U.S. Dept. Edn., 1995—98; scholar, Sears and Roebucks, 1960, N.D. State U., 1960, Boston U., 1976. Democrat. Achievements include development of Supported Education, Exemplary Practice in Psychiatric Rehabilitation. Avocations: yoga, reading. Office: Rehabilitaion Through Education PO Box 82176 Portland OR 97282 Personal E-mail: kvunger@easystreet.com. Business E-Mail: kvunger@easystreet.com.

UNGER, LAURA SIMONE, lawyer, commissioner; b. N.Y.C., Jan. 8, 1961; d. Raymond and Susan Marie (Vopata) Simone; m. Peter Van Buren Unger, June 29, 1991. BA in Rhetoric, U. Calif., Berkeley, 1983; JD, N.Y. Law Sch., 1987. Bar: Conn. 1987, N.Y. 1988. Staff atty. divsn. enforcement SEC, 1988-90; legis. counsel to Sen. Alfonse M. D'Amato, 1990-91; minority counsel Senate com. banking, housing and urban affairs, 1991-95, counsel, 1995-97; commr. U.S. SEC, Washington, 1997—, acting chmn., 2001. Bd. dirs. MBNA Corp., 2004—. Recipient Performance award SEC, N.Y., 1988, D.C., 1989. Mem. ABA (subcom. on civil litigation and SEC enforcement matters and subcom. on SEC adminstrn., budget and legislation of the ABA bus. law sect. com. on federal regulation of securities), Fed. Bar Assn., Jr. League Washington, Decade Soc., Women in Housing and Fin. Roman Catholic. Avocations: tennis, jogging, movies, concerts, music. Office: US SEC 450 5th St NW Ms 6/8 Washington DC 20549-0001

UNGER, PAUL A. packaging and international affairs specialist; b. San Diego, Sept. 10, 1914; s. Louis A. and Ray (Seidman) U.; m. Sonja Franz, Jan. 2, 1947; children: Alan, Gerald, Tamara Unger-Hyman. AB, Harvard U., 1936. With pub. rels. dept. Works Progress Adminstrn., Washington, 1936-39; with community rels. Dept. U.S. Housing Authority, Washington, 1939-44; relief adminstr. UN Relief and Rehab. Adminstrn., Egypt and Yugoslavia, 1944-47; deputy asst. sec. U.S. Dept. of Interior, Washington, 1947-50, internat. specialist, 1950-53; devel. mgr. The Unger Co., Cleve., 1953-57, pres., 1957-62, 64-88, chmn., 1988-93; sr. advisor, 1994—, The Unger Co., Cleve., 1994—; dep. adminstr. U.S. Dept. Commerce, Washington, 1962-63. Mem. U.S. com. Internat.Coun. on Social Welfare; organizer, leader tours to Yugoslavia, Hungary, Austria, Czechoslovakia, East Germany, Poland, USSR, China; leader trade mission to Australia and New Zealand U.S. Dept. of Commerce; mem. U.S. Trade Agreements Com.; U.S. del. GATT Trade Negotiations Confs. Pres. Coun. Internat. Programs; chmn. Cleve. adv. subcom. U.S. Commn. on Civil Rights; chmn. Mayor's Urban Renewal Task Force, Presdl. Campaign Coms. for No. Ohio (chmn.), Gov.'s Internat. Trade Coun.; chmn. Unger Croatia Inst. Pub. Adminstrn. Kennedy Sch. Govt., Harvard U., The Unger Croatia Ctr., Cleve. State U. Recipient Recognition award Rotary, 1974, Neighborhood Ctrs. Assn., 1978, Internat. Exch. award Coun. Internat. Programs, 1985, Outstanding Citizen Achievement award U.S. AID, 2004; inductee Hall of Fame City Club of Cleve., 1995, Cleveland Heights H.S. Hall of Fame, 1997. Mem. City Club (trustee 1972-75, v.p. 1975), Forum Found. (pres. 1988-91), Cleve. Coun. on World Affairs (program chmn., v.p., mem. exec. com.), English Speaking Union (past pres. Cleve. br., nat. v.p.), Cleve. Skating Club, Cleve. Playhouse Club, Cleve. Blue Book. Home: 13515 Shaker Blvd Apt 2 A Cleveland OH 44120-1506 Office: 3530 Warrensville Center Rd Shaker Heights OH 44122 Office Phone: 216-491-0040. E-mail: punger@ecaddress.com.

UNGER, PAUL WALTER, retired soil scientist; b. Winchester, Tex., Sept. 10, 1931; s. Edwin Herman and Elsie Anna (Schmidt) U.; m. Barbara Charlene Dutton, Sept. 13, 1960; children: Gary Robert, Paula Dianne. BS, Tex. A&M U., 1961; MS, Colo. State U., 1963, PhD, 1966. Soil scientist USDA Agrl. Rsch. Svc., Bushland, Tex., 1965-81, soil scientist/rsch. leader, 1981-87, supervisory soil scientist/rsch. leader, 1987-93, soil scientist, 1993-2000; ret., 2000. Cons. Food and Agrl. Orgn. UN, Rome, 1986. Author or co-author bulls. and articles; co-editor conf. proc.; editor book. With U.S. Army, 1952-55. Recipient Disting. Svc. award Great Plains Agrl. Coun., 1984; named Scientist of Yr., USDA-Agrl. Rsch. Svc., So. Plains Area, 1987. Fellow Am. Soc. Agronomy (emeritus, selection com. 1988-89), Soil Sci. Soc. Am. (emeritus, assoc. editor 1977-82, divsn. chmn. 1986, mem. selection com. 1994-95, Applied Rsch. award 1991), Soil and Water Conservation Soc. (various local and state offices, photography awards 1990-92); mem. Internat. Soil Tillage Rsch. Orgn., World Assn. Soil and Water Conservation. Lutheran. Avocations: photography, gardening, woodworking. Personal E-mail: pwunger@cox.net.

UNGER, PETER KENNETH, philosophy educator; b. N.Y.C., Apr. 25, 1942; s. Sidney and Naomi (Fein) U.; m. Susan Gill, June 2, 1977; 1 child, Andrew. BA, Swarthmore Coll., 1962 DPhil, Oxford U., Eng., 1966. Instr. U. Wis., Madison, 1965-66, asst. prof., 1966-70, assoc. prof., 1970-72; assoc. prof. NYU, N.Y.C., 1972-75, prof., 1975—. Author: Ignorance, 1975, 2d edit., 2002, Philosophical Relativity, 1984, 2d edition, 2002, Identity, Consciousness and Value, 1990, Living High and Letting Die, 1996; contbr. articles to profl. jours. Guggenheim fellow, 1974, NEH fellow, 1993. Mem. Am. Philos. Assn. Democrat. Home: 100 Bleecker St New York NY 10012-2202 Office: Dept Philosophy NYU 503 Main Bldg Washington Sq New York NY 10003 Office Phone: 212-998-8321.

UNGER, RICHARD WATSON, history professor; b. Huntington, W.Va., Dec. 23, 1942; s. Abraham I. and Marion Patterson U.; 1 child, Emily Patterson. BA, Haverford Coll., Pa., 1963; AM, U. Chgo., 1965; MA, Yale U., 1967, MPhil, 1969, PhD, 1971. Prof. dept. history U. B.C., Vancouver, Canada, 1969—. Author: Dutch Shipbuilding Before 1800, 1978, The Ship in the Medieval Economy, 600-1600, 1980, The Art of Medieval Technology: The Image of Noah the Shipbuilder, 1991, Ships and Shipping in the North Sea and Atlantic, 1400-1600, 1997, A History of Brewing in Holland, 900-1900, Economy, Technology and the State, 2001, Beer in the Middle Ages and the Renaissance, 2004; editor: Cogs, Caravels and Galleons, 1994; co-editor: War at Sea in the Middle Ages and the Renaissance, 2003, Studies in Medieval and Renaissance History, 1978-95; contbr. articles to profl. jours. Trustee Vancouver Maritime Mus., 1979-83, 97-98. Mem. Medieval Assn. Pacific (pres. 1994-96), Econ. History Soc., Soc. Nautical Rsch., Soc. Hist. Tech. Office: U BC Dept History 1297-1873 East Mall Vancouver BC Canada V6T 1Z1 E-mail: richard.unger@ubc.ca.

UNGER, ROBERTA, architect; BArch, Kent State U. Registered Ga. Prin. Arch. Group, Atlanta, 1991—. Adv. bd. So. Poly. Inst., 1999—2000; commr. Dekalb County Historic Preservation Commn.; bd. dirs. North Ga. Arch. Found. Fellow: AIA (dir. 1987—89, sec. 1990, v.p. 1991, pres. 1993, bd. dirs. 1994, Ivan Allen award 1995, Bronze medal 1995, Svc. to Profession award 1994); mem.: Dekalb C. of C. Office: 381 Venable St Atlanta GA 30313

UNGER, ROGER HAROLD, physician, scientist; b. N.Y.C., Mar. 7, 1924; s. Lester and Beatrice (Raphael) Unger; m. Barbara Latz, June 28, 1946; children: Christine, Craig, Jimmy; m. Marlise Mantel, Dec. 16, 1981; 1 child, Romy-Michelle. BS, Yale U., 1944; MD, Columbia U., 1947; MD (hon.), U. Geneva, 1976, U. Liège, Belgium, 1980. Diplomate Am. Bd. Internal Medicine. Asst. prof. internal medicine U. Tex. Med. Sch., Dallas, 1959—64, assoc. prof., 1964—69, prof., 1969—; dir. Ctr. for Diabetes Rsch., U. Tex. Health Sci. Ctr., Dallas, 1985—, Touchstone/West Disting. chair diabetes rsch., 1989—. Sr. med. investigator VA Med. Ctr., Dallas, 1979—99; mem. Nat. Diabetes Adv. Bd., Bethesda, Md., 1985—; mem. adv. coun. Nat. Inst. Diabetes, Digestive and Kidney Diseases, 1990—94. Editor: Glucagon, 1972, Glucagon Physiology etc., 1981; assoc. editor (jour.) Diabetes, 1979—84, mem. editl. bd., 1975—79, Endocrinology, 1976—81; author: 64 chpts. in textbooks; contbr.: over 360 articles to sci. jours. With U.S. Army, 1946—48, with USPHS, 1950—52. Recipient Lilly award, Am. Diabetes Assn., 1964, Banting medal, 1975, David Rumbough award, Juvenile Diabetes Assn., 1975, Joslin medal, Harvard U., 1979, Claude Bernard award, European Assn. for Study of Diabetes, 1979, Fred Conrad Koch award, Endocrine Soc., 1983, Maurice Derot prize, Jour. Diabetique, Paris. Mem.: Am. Soc. for Clin. Investigation (emeritus), Assn. Am. Physicians, Am. Acad. Arts and Scis., NAS. Office: Ctr for Diabetes Research 5323 Harry Hines Blvd Dallas TX 75390-7208

UNGERLEIDER, LESLIE G. neuroscientist; b. N.Y.C., Apr. 17, 1946; d. Albert and Frieda (Mandel) Cohen; m. Robert Desimone, Sept. 6, 1982; 1 child, Matthew David. BA magna cum laude, SUNY, Binghamton, 1966; PhD, NYU, 1970. Asst. prof. psychology Okla. State U., Oklahoma City, 1970-72; postdoctoral fellow Dept. Psychology Stanford (Calif.) U., 1972-75, Neuropsychology Lab. NIMH, Bethesda, Md., 1975-78, staff fellow, 1978-80, sr. staff fellow, 1980-85, rsch. psychologist, 1985-91, chief sect. neurocircuitry, 1992—95, chief lab brain and congnition, 1995—. Mem. editorial bd. Neuropsychologia, 1990—, J. Neurosci, 1996—, Cerebrol Cortex, 1998—, Human Brain Mapping, 1993—; contbr. articles to profl. jours. Fellow AAAS, APA, Am. Psychol. Soc.; mem. Soc. Neurosci., NAS Inst. Medicine. Achievements include basic research on nonhuman primates revealing neural mechanisms and cortical circuitry underlying visual perception and memory. Office: NIH Bldg 10 / Rm 4C104 10 Center Dr Bethesda MD 20892-0001

UNGLESBY, LEWIS O. lawyer; b. New Orleans, July 6, 1949; s. Lewis Huber and Mary Jane (Holloway) U.; m. Gail Hoy, Aug. 15, 1970; children: Lewis, Lance, Blake. BS, U. Miss., 1971; JD, La. State U., 1974. Bar: La. 1974, U.S. Dist. Ct. (ea., mid., and we dists.) La. 1974, U.S. Ct. Appeals (5th cir.) 1974, U.S. Supreme Ct. 1980; bd. cert. criminal and civil trial adv. Nat. Bd. Trial Advocacy. With Unglesby & Marrineaux Law Firm; mem. judge's benchbook com. La. Supreme Ct., 1982—. Spl. counsel La. State Senate, 1991-98, Gov. La., 1996-98; lectr. La. Assn. Criminal Def. Lawyers, 1987-91. Editor criminal law sect. La. Trial Lawyers Brief, 1988—. Fellow Am. Bd. Criminal Lawyers; mem. ABA, La. Bar Assn. (ho. of dels. 1979-87, lectr.), NACDL, ATLA (criminal law com. 1989-90), La. Trial Lawyers Assn. (chmn. criminal law sect. 1983-85, bd. govs. 1983-94, exec. com. 1991-2002, lectr.). Home: 14415 Highland Rd Baton Rouge LA 70810-5312 Office: 246 Napoleon St Baton Rouge LA 70802-5937

UNHJEM, MICHAEL BRUCE, lawyer; b. Fargo, ND, Aug. 22, 1953; s. Kalmer Joseph and Lorelei Mae (Myhra) U.; m. Mary Ruth Burges, June 19, 1976; children: Kaia Mary, David Burges, Kirsten Elizabeth. BA magna cum laude, Jamestown Coll., 1975; JD with distinction, U. N.D., 1978. Bar: N.D. 1978. Pvt. practice, Jamestown, N.D., 1978-86; compliance officer Norwest Bank, Jamestown, N.D., 1981-84; planned giving officer Jamestown Coll., Anne Carlsen Sch., Jamestown, 1984-86; asst. to pres., gen. counsel Blue Cross Blue Shield of N.D., Fargo, 1986-91, pres., chief exec. officer, 1991—, Pioneer Mutual Life Ins. Co., Fargo, 1997—99. Chmn. bd. dirs. Lincoln Mut. Life & Casualty Ins. Co., Fargo, Noridian Adminstr. Svc., LLC, Fargo, Noridian Ins. Svc., Inc., Fargo; bd. dirs. TriWest HC All, Prime Ther, Jamestown Coll., Cass Clay United Way Western Conf. Prepaid Health Plans. State rep. N.D. Legis. Assembly, Bismarck, 1974-86; mem. Nat. Conf. Commrs. on Uniform State Laws, Chgo., 1981—, chmn., Bismarck, 1982-86; co-chmn. Bush for Pres. Com., 1980, 88, 92; presdl. appointee Nat. Coun. on Disability, Washington, 1990. Named Outstanding Young North Dakotan, N.D. Jaycees, 1983; recipient Nat. Excellence in Leadership award State of N.D., 1988, Disting. Leadership award N.D. Psychol. Assn., 1988, Spl. Presdl. Commendation award Am. Psychiatric Assn., 1989, Toastmaster Internat. Comm. and Leadership award, 1992. Mem. ABA, N.D. Bar Assn., Cass County Bar Assn., Kiwanis, Elks, Masons, Shriners. Republican. Lutheran. Office: Blue Cross Blue Shield 4510 13th Ave S Fargo ND 58121-0002

UNIS, RICHARD L. judge; b. Portland, Oreg., June 11, 1928; BS, JD, U. Oreg. Bar: Oreg. 1954, U.S. Dist. Ct. Oreg. 1957, U.S. Ct. Appeals (9th cir.) 1960, U.S. Supreme Ct. 1965. Judge Portland Mcpl. Ct., 1968-71, Multnomah County Dist. Ct., 1972-76, presiding judge, 1972-74; former judge Oreg. Cir. Ct. 4th Judicial Dist., 1977-90; former sr. dep. city atty. City of Portland; assoc. justice Oreg. Supreme Ct., Portland, 1990-96; spl. master U.S. Dist. Ct. House, Portland, 1996—. Adj. prof. of local govt. law and evidence Lewis & Clark Coll. Northwestern Sch. Law, 1969-76, 77-96; spl. master supr. La.-Pacific Inner-Seal Siding nationwide class action litig.; faculty mem. The Nat. Judicial Coll., 1971-2000, former faculty mem. Am. Acad. Judicial Edn. Author: Procedure and Instructions in Traffic Court Cases, 1970, 101 Questions and Answers on Preliminary Hearings, 1974. Bd. dirs. Oreg. Free from Drug Abuse; mem. Oreg. Adv. Com. on Evidence Law Revision, chmn. subcom., 1974-79. Maj. USAFR, JAGC, ret. Recipient Meritorius Svc. award U. Oregon sch. Law, 1988; named Legal Citizen of Yr. Oreg. Law Related Edn., 1987; inducted into The Nat. Judicial Coll. Hall of Honor, 1988. Mem. Am. Judicature Soc. (bd. dirs. 1975, Herbert Harley Nat. award 1999), Am. Judges Assn., Multnomah Bar Found., Oregon Judicial Conf. (chmn. Oreg. Judicial Coll. 1973-80, legis. com. 1976—, exec. com. of judicial edn. com., judicial conduct com.), N.Am. Judges Assn. (tenure, selection and compensation judges com.), Dist. Ct. Judges of Oreg. (v.p., chmn. edn. com.), Nat. Conf. Spl. Ct. Judges (exec. com.), Oreg. State Bar (judicial adminstrn. com., sec. local govt. com., com. on continuing certification, uniform jury instrn. com., exec. com. criminal law sect., trial practice sect. standards and certification com., past chmn., among others), Oreg. Trial Lawyers Assn. (named Judge of Yr. 1984). Office: US Dist Ct House 1000 SW 3rd Ave Portland OR 97204-2930 Office Phone: 503-669-7286.

UNISON-PACE, WENDY JANE, nursing educator; b. Mar. 20, 1964; d. Harvey Charles and Bette Adele (Aimone) U. BS, No. Ill. U., 1988; BSN, Concordia U. and West Suburban Coll. Nursing, 1995; MS in Nursing Adminstrn., Va. Commonwealth U., 2002. Cert. Trauma Nurse Core Course, ACLS. Mem. faculty Coll. at W.Va., 1996-97; emergency rm./trauma ctr. nurse, clin. nurse Charleston Area Med. Ctr., Charleston, W.Va., 1997-98; emergency rm./trauma ctr. nurse, clin. nurse, quality assurance coord., newsletter editor Med. Coll. Va. Hosps./Va. Commonwealth U. Health Sys., Richmond, 1998—2002; asst. Office of Health Policy, dir. nursing emergency svcs. Va. Commonwealth U. Health Sys., Richmond, 2002—03; dir. nursing emergency svcs. Cooley-Dickenson Hosp./Dartmouth-Hitchcock Health Alliance, 2003—04; mgr. emergency and trauma svcs. and pediat. ctr. Suburban Hosp., Bethesda, Md., 2004—; assoc. prof. nursing No. Va. C.C. Med. Scis. Campus, 2004—. Instr. ARC, Lombard, Ill., 1986-98. Recipient 1st pl. Award of Hon., Addison Cultural Arts Devel. Commn., 1982, Vol. Educator Excellence awards ARC, 1987-91, Cmty. Health Edn. & Safety Svcs. award, ARC, 1988, Cert. Appreciation, 1992, Dr. Alma J. Labuski Leadership award Student Nurses Assn. Ill., 1994, Pres. Svc. award West Suburban Coll. of Nursing, 1995. Mem.: ANA, Nat. Assn. for Healthcare Quality, Emergency Nurses Assn., Nat. League Nursing, Student Nurses Assn. Ill. (hon.; v.p. 1994—95, programs com. chair 1994—95), Sigma Theta Tau, Sigma Lambda Sigma (v.p. 1985—86, pres. 1986—87). Home: PO Box 5693 Fredericksburg VA 22403 E mail: wjanen@aol.com.

UNITHAN, DOLLY, visual artist; b. Kelantan, Malaysia; arrived in US, 1976; Postgrad., Brit. Coun. Fine Arts Exch., 1974, Ecole Nationale des Beaux Arts de Nancy, France, 1974; BFA, Hornsey Coll. Art, 1975; MFA, Pratt Inst., 1978. Summer intern Guggenheim Mus, NYC, 1976; panelist, artist in residence Asian Am. Arts Ctr., 1993; lectr. in field. One-person shows include Internat. Art Ctr., London, 1975, Am. Assn. State Colls. and Univs., Orlando, Fla., 1977, Sloan Gallery, Lock Haven State Coll., Pa., 1978, Permanent Mission of Malaysia to UN, NYC, 1987, Kerr Gallery, NYC, 1987, Lyman Allyn Art Mus., New London, Conn., 1990, UN Secretariat, NYC, 1991, Gracie Mansion, NYC, 1994, Angel Orensanz Found., NYC, 1995, Cathedral of St. John the Divine, NYC St. Boniface Chapel Gallery, 1996; exhibited in group shows including Palace of Westminster, Hos. of Parliament, London, 1978, City Mus. and Art Gallery, Gloucester, Eng., 1978, Mus. Art, Hove, Eng., 1978, Contemporary Gallery, Warsaw, Poland, 1978, BWA Gallery, Wroclaw and Szczecin, Poland, 1978, Arts Coun. Gallery, Belfast, No. Ireland, 1978, Parrish Art Mus., Southampton, NY, 1979, Modern Art Ctr., Guadalajara, Mex., 1979, Alternative Mus., NYC, 1981, Nat. Mus. Fine Arts, Havana, Cuba, 1986, Hillwood Art Mus., Brookville, NY, 1988, PS 1 Mus., NYC, 1990, Nat. Art Gallery, Kuala Lumpur, 1991-92, League of Nations Archives, Palais des Nations, Geneva, 1993, Jewish Mus., Vienna, Austria, 1993, Peace Mus., Remagen, Germany, Westbeth Galleries, NYC, Tweed Courthouse Gallery, NYC, 1994, China Art Mus., Beijing, 1995, Raiffeisenkasse, Ulrich bei Steyr, Peace parish, Austria, 1996, Ctrl. Children's and Youth Arts Palace, Samarkand, Uzbekistan, 1997, Palais des Nations, United Nations Office, Geneva, 1998, Firehouse, NYC, 1999, Cathedral of St. John the Divine Synod Hall, NYC, 2002, Asian Am. Arts Ctr., NYC, 2002, Royal Castle, Warsaw, Poland, 2003; represented in permanent collections including Lock Haven State Coll., Pa., Alternative Mus., NYC, Am. Assn. State Colls. and Univs., Washington, Permanent Mission of Malaysia to UN, Wilfredo Lam Ctr., Havana, Malaysian Embassy, Washington, Spirit Found., NYC, Asian Am. Arts Ctr., NYC, World Bank, Washington, Libr. Congress, 2001; artwork included in (jours.) Multicultural Edn., 1994, Artspiral, 1994, (book) Sculpture, Technique, Form, Content, Imagine Strawberry Fields. Named grad. scholar, Mara, Malaysia, 1976—78, Archives of Contemporary Arts, Venice Biennale, 1990; recipient Artist award, Rainbow Art Found., NYC, 1985, Art award ArtQuest '88, Internat. Art Competition, Calif., 1988; grantee, Lee Found., Singapore, 1972, 1976, Pollock-Krasner Found., 1991—92. Avocation: collecting antiques. Personal E-mail: dollyunithan@yahoo.com.

UNPINGCO, JOHN WALTER SABLAN, federal judge; b. 1950; BA, St. Louis U., 1972; MBA, JD, NYU, 1976; LLM, Georgetown U., 1983. Bar: Guam 1977, D.C. 1983, Calif. 1992. Atty. Ferenz, Bramhall, Williams & Gruskin, Guam, 1976-77; atty. Office Staff Judge Advocate USAF, 1977-85, civilian atty., Office Staff Judge Advocate, 1985-87; counsel U.S. Naval Air Warfare Ctr., China Lake, Calif., 1987-92; fed. judge U.S. Dist. Ct. (Guam dist.), 1992—. Part-time instr. U. Md. Far East divsn., Yokota Air Base, Tokyo, 1983-87, European divsn., RAF Mildenhall, Suffolk, U.K., 1979-82, U. Guam, 1994-99. Pres. Guam Swim League, 2000; pres. parish coun. Our Lady of Hope Parish, 2000-. Mem. ABA, State Bar Calif., Guam Bar Assn., Internat. Legal Soc. Japan, D.C. Bar Assn., NWC Community Fed. Credit Union (bd. dirs. 1991-92). Office: US Dist Ct 4th Fl US Courthouse 520 W Soledad Ave Hagatna GU 96910

UNRUH, ERIC W. music educator, academic administrator; s. Cecil A. and Maurine Unruh; m. Gayle A. Christenson, Aug. 23, 1980; children: D. Alexander, Michael, Christopher. BA, Bethany Coll., 1979; MusM, Northwestern U., Evanston, Ill., 1981, Mus D, 1989. Chmn. dept. music Casper Coll., Casper, Wyo., 1991—. Commr. cmty./jr. coll. accreditation Nat. Assn. Schs. Music, Reston, Va., 1998—. Composer: (music composition) Magnificat, 2000 (Rosenthal Outstanding Educator award, 1998). Named Educator of Yr., Wyo. Music Educators Assn., 2002—; grantee, Wyo. Cmty. Found., 1999. Mem.: Music Educator's Nat. Conf. Home: 4440 S David Casper WY 82601 Office: Casper Coll 125 College Dr Casper WY 82601 E-mail: unruh@caspercollege.edu.

UNRUH, HOWARD K., JR., military officer, university administrator; b. Balt. m. Diane R. Caslow; three children: Meredith, Allison, H. Kirk III. AB, Princeton U., 1970; MEd, Harvard U.; MA in Am. Studies, U. Hawaii. Commd. ensign USN, 1970, advanced through ranks to rear adm.; various assignments to Dep. Comdr. Naval Surface Force, U.S. Atlantic Fleet, 1995—; comdr. Readiness Command Midwest. Dir. devel. rels., sec. Princeton U.; trustee or bd. dirs. several civic orgns. Decorated Legion of Merit (2), Meritorious Svc. medal (2), Navy Commendation medal (4), Nat. Def. medal with Bronze Star, Republic of Vietnam Svc. medal with Bronze Star, others. Mem. Naval Res. Assn., Surface Navy Assn., Univ. Cottage Club, Princeton Club N.Y.C. Office: Princeton Univ Recording Sec 330 Alexander St Princeton NJ 08540-7123

UNRUH, JAMES ARLEN, bank executive; b. Goodrich, N.D., Mar. 22, 1941; m. Candice Leigh Voight, Apr. 28, 1984. BSBA, Jamestown Coll., 1963; MBA, U. Denver, 1964. Dir. corp. planning and analysis Fairchild Camera & Instrument, Calif., 1974-76, v.p. treasury and corp. devel., 1976-79, v.p. fin., 1979-80, Memorex Corp., Santa Clara, Calif., 1980-82, Burroughs Corp. (now known as Unisys Corp.), Detroit, 1982-84, sr. v.p. fin., 1984-86, exec. v.p. fin., 1986, exec. v.p., 1986-89, pres., COO, 1989-90, pres., CEO, 1990-91, chmn. bd. dirs., CEO, 1991-97; founding prin. Alerion Capital Group L.L.C., Scottsdale, Ariz., 1998—. Bd. dirs. Prudential Fin. Corp., Tenet Healthcare Corp., Apex Microtech. Corp., LumenIQ Corp., BioVigilant Corp. Trustee Jamestown Coll., N.D. Home: 5426 E Morrison Ln Paradise Valley AZ 85253 Office Phone: 480-367-0900. E-mail: jimunruh@alerion.com.

UNRUH, RICHARD GREENWOOD, III, artist; b. Bryn Mawr, Pa., May 29, 1964; s. Richard Greenwood Jr. and Deborah Crittenden Unruh; m. Hollis McLellan Unruh; 1 child, Campbell James. BA, Conn. Coll., 1986. Investment trainee Kidder Peabody & Co., Paris, 1986; internat. equities position trader Jefferies & Co., N.Y.C., 1987-88; equity sales trader Lazard Freres & Co., LLC, N.Y.C., 1988-95; fine artist N.Y.C., 1995—; comml. artist, 1997—. Fine art dealer Greenwood Fine Art, LLC, 2003—; bd. dirs. Lyman Allyn Mus. Illustrator: Blinker, The Little Star That Learned To Shine, 2000; solo exhbns. New London Art Soc. Gallery, New London, Conn., 1999, Bruce Hurley Gallery, SoHo, N.Y., 1998; nat. group exhbns. Old Slave Mart Mus., Charleston, S.C., 1999, Art Ctr. of Northern N.J., Milford, 1997 (2d prize High Achievement award), Silvermine Arts Guild Ctr., New Canaan, Conn., 1996, Mystic (Conn.) Art Assn., 1995; featured in American Showcase, 2000, 2001, Illustrators and Designers, Vols. 23, 24. Mem.: Stonington Village Improvement Assn. (v.p. bd. dirs. 2001—04). Home: 17 Elm St Stonington CT 06378-1272 Office: 395 Broadway Apt 3A New York NY 10013-3540

UNSAL-TUNAY, NURAN, geological engineer, researcher; b. Igdir, Turkey, Dec. 26, 1956; came to U.S., 1995; d. Kamil and Feride (Gunay) Tunay; m. Ilhan Unsal, Oct. 28, 1979; 1 child, Volkan. Diploma in Geol. Engring., Earth Sci. Geol. Engring., Turkey, 1982; cert. in Civil Engring., Min. of Pub. Works, Ankara, Turkey, 1985. Geol. engr. Gen. Directorate of Bank of Provinces, Konya-Ankara, Turkey, 1982-84, Gen. Directorate of Hwy., Kayseri-Ankara, Turkey, 1984-89, Adminstrn. Pub. Works, Manisa, Turkey, 1989-95. Cons. Pub. Works, Manisa, Turkey, 1989-95; adv. bds. Pub. Works, Municipality, Civil Cts., Manisa, Turkey, 1992-94. Inventor: Adaptation of Stabilized Hydrated Lime, Publication of the Chamber of Geol. Engring. of Turkey, 1993. Recipient of presentations 46th Congress of Geology of Turkey, Ankara, 1993. Fellow Geol. Assn. Can.; mem. Geol. Soc. Am., Chamber of Geol. Engrs. of Turkey. Achievements include the soil improvement with hydrated lime stabilization; applied in the area of Manisa Teachers House Buildings, was one of the first applications in Turkey. Home: 30-69 Hobart St Apt 1N Woodside NY 11377

UNSELL, LLOYD NEAL, energy organization executive, former journalist; b. Henryetta, Okla., May 12, 1922; s. John William and Rhoda Elizabeth (Martinez) U.; m. Nettie Marie Rogers, Sept. 24, 1944 (dec.); children: Lloyd Neal, Jonna Kay Unsell Wilhelm, James Allan (dec.). Student, U. Ill., Kalamazoo Coll., 1942-43. Mem. editorial staff Tulsa Daily World, 1947-48; successively staff writer, dir. communications, v.p. pub. affairs, exec. v.p., pres. and chief exec. officer Ind. Petroleum Assn. Am., Washington, 1948-87. Chmn. selection com. for Milburn Petty award Am. Petroleum Inst.-Assn. Petroleum Writers, 1972-86 Author reports and articles in field. Co-chmn. corp. adv. com. Vietnam Vets. Meml., 1981-82. Served with U.S. Army, 1942-46, ETO, PTO. Recipient Spl. award as outstanding petroleum industry communicator Assn. Petroleum Writers, 1960, Russell B. Brown Meml. award, 1981, Robert J. Enright award Am. Petroleum Inst./Assn. Petroleum Writers, 1986, Disting. Service award Nat. Energy Resources Orgn., 1987, Lloyd N. Unsell award established in his honor Ind. Petroleum Assn. Am., 1993; named Hon. Chief Roughneck U.S. petroleum industry, 1986. Mem. Nat. Press Club, Rocky Mountain Oil and Gas Assn. (hon. life), The Jefferson Energy Found. (co-founder 1987). Clubs: Washington Golf and Country. Republican. Baptist. Home: 38335 Point Breeze Rd Coltons Point MD 20626 Office: Ste 300 1201 15th St NW Washington DC 20005 Personal E-mail: lunsell@erols.com.

UNSER, ALFRED, JR., race car driver; b. Apr. 19, 1962; s. Al Unser Sr.; m. Shelley Unser (div.); children: Al, Cody, Shannon. Named winner, SCCA Super VEE Champion, 1981, 24 Hours of Daytona, 1986, 1988, IROC Champion, 1987, 1988, Indy Car Champion, 1990, 1994, Indpls. 500, 1992, 1994, Driver of Yr., 1990, Athlete of Yr., ABC's Wide World of Sports, 1991; recipient ESPY award Auto Racing Performer of Yr., ESPN, 1994. Achievements include winner 8 out of 16 Indy car races; 31 care career victories and 7 career poles. Office: Team Penske 366 Penske Plaza Reading PA 19603 Address: PO Box 56696 Albuquerque NM 87187-6696

UNSWORTH, RICHARD PRESTON, minister, educator, school administrator; b. Vineland, N.J., Feb. 7, 1927; s. Joseph Lewis and Laura (MacMillan) U.; m. Joy Merritt, Aug. 20, 1949; children: Sarah, John, Mary, Lucy. BA, Princeton U., 1948; BD, Yale U., 1954; ThM, Harvard U., 1963; STD, Dickinson Coll., 1971; LHD, Washington and Jefferson Coll., 1971; LLD, Smith Coll., 1992. Ordained to ministry Presbyn. Ch., 1953. Tchr. Bible and English Mt. Hermon Sch., 1948-50; asst. chaplain Yale U., New Haven, 1950-54; chaplain, assoc. prof. Smith Coll., Northampton, Mass., 1954-64, chaplain, prof. religion, 1967-80; dean William Jewett Tucker Found. and prof. religion Dartmouth (N.H.) Coll., 1963-67; headmaster Northfield (Mass.) Mt. Hermon Sch., 1980-88, pres., 1989-91, headmaster emeritus, 1991—; headmaster Berkshire Sch., Sheffield, Mass., 1991-96; dean of the chapel Smith Coll., 1996-98, lectr. religion, 1996—99, sr. fellow Kahn Inst., 1998—. Pres. Critical Langs. and Area Studies Consortium, 1987-97; cons. Ednl. Assocs., Inc., 1967-69, U.S. Office Edn., 1969-77. Author: Sexuality and the Human Community, 1970, Dignity and Exploitation: Christian Reflections on Images of Sex in the 1970s, 1974, A Century of Religion at Smith College, 1975; (with Arnold Kenseth) Prayers for Worship Leaders, 1978; contbg. author; Sex Edn. and the Schs., 1967; editor: Rethinking Childhood, 2004. Leader Operation Crossroads Africa unit, Nigeria, 1961, mem. adv. bd., 1961-66; mem. adminstrv. com. Student Christian Movement New Eng., 1964; mem. Mass. unit So. Christian Leadership conf., 1968; trustee Conf. on Religion in Ind. Schs., 1961-63; pres. Am. Friends of Coll. Cevenol, France, 1957-63, 90-94, Am. rep., 1958-82; trustee Mt. Holyoke Coll., 1982-89, chair, 1984-89, chmn. emeritus, 1989—, Am. Sch. Tangier, Morocco, 1982-87, Eaglebrook Sch., 1992-98, Acad. Music, Northampton, 1998-99, Mus. Sci., Boston, 1993-95; bd. dirs. Family Planning Coun. Western Mass., 1972-81; bd. dirs. Ind. Schs. Assn. Mass., 1992-96. Mem. AAUP, Nat. Assn. Coll. and Univ. Chaplains, Am. Acad. Religion, Assn. Ind. Schs. New Eng. (pres. 1993-96), Headmasters Assn., Nat. Commn. on Asia in Schs., Asia Soc. N.Y.C., U. Club. Home: Apt 2603 500 Crestwood Dr Charlottesville VA 22903-4884

UNTERBECK, AXEL JOACHIM, pharmaceutical executive, director; b. Leipzig, Germany, Nov. 10, 1953; came to U.S., 1986; s. Joachim and Brigitte (Noack) U.; m. Anett Maria Sartor-Unterbeck, Aug. 29, 1987. Abitur, Gymnasium, Bergneustadt, Germany, 1973; MS in molecular biology, U. Bonn., Germany, 1982; PhD, U. Cologne, Germany, 1986. Rsch. assoc. U. Cologne, 1982-86; sr. rsch. scientist Bayer AG, West Haven, Conn., 1986-89, assoc. dir. Wuppertal, Germany, 1989-92; dir. Bayer Corp., West Haven, 1992—97; pres., chief science officer Memory Pharm. Corp., 1998—. Cons. Software House, Cologne, 1978-86; adv. bd. Dahlem Confs., Berlin, 1990-91; rev. com. mem. NIH, Bethesda, Md., 1988-92. Author: Molecular Biology of Aging, 1989; inventor in field. Mem., trainer Life Rescue, Germany, 1973-75; trainer German Air Force, 1973-75. Sgt. German Air Force, 1973-75. Mem. N.Y. Acad. Scis., Swimming Club, Yacht Club. Avocations: photography, sailing, travel, swimming, music. Office: Memory Pharmaceuticals Corp 100 Philips Pkwy Montvale NJ 07645*

UNTERBERGER, BETTY MILLER, history educator, writer; b. Glasgow, Scotland, Dec. 27, 1923; d. Joseph C. and Leah Miller; m. Robert Ruppe, July 29, 1944; children: Glen, Gail, Gregg. BA, Syracuse U., 1943; MA, Harvard U., 1946; PhD, Duke U., 1950. Asst. prof. E. Carolina U., Greenville, 1948-50; assoc. prof., dir. liberal arts ctr. Whittier Coll., Calif., 1954-61; assoc. prof. Calif. State U.-Fullerton, 1961-65, prof., chmn. grad. studies, 1965-68; prof. history Tex. A&M U., College Station, 1968—. Vis. prof. U. Hawaii, Honolulu, summer 1967, Peking U., Beijing, 1988; vis. disting. prof. U. Calif., Irvine, 1987—, Patricia and Bookman Peters prof. history, 1991—; vis. prof. Charles U., Prague, Czechoslovakia, summer 1992, Regents prof., 2000—; mem. adv. com. fgn. rels. U.S. Dept. State, 1977-81, chair, 1981; mem. hist. adv. com. U.S. Dept. Army, 1980-82, USN, 1991—; mem. Nat. Hist. Publs. and Records Commn., 1980-84; mem. history rev. panel to Dir. of CIA, 1999—. Author: America's Siberian Expedition 1918-1920: A Study of National Policy, 1956, 69 (Pacific Coast award Am. Hist. Assn. 1956); editor: American Intervention in the Russian Civil War, 1969, Intervention Against Communism: Did the U.S. Try to Overthrow the Soviet Government, 1918-20, 1986, The United States, Revolutionary Russia and the Rise of Czechoslovakia, 1989, paperback edit. with a 2000 yr. perspective, 2000; contbr.: Woodrow Wilson and Revolutionary World, 1982, The Liberal Persuasion, 1997, The United States and the Russian Civil War, microfilm edit., 25 reels, 2001; mem. editl. adv. bd. The Papers of Woodrow Wilson, Princeton U., 1982-92, Internt. History, 1999—; bd. editors: Diplomatic History, 1981-84, Red River Valley Hist. Rev., 1975-84. Trustee Am. Inst. Pakistan Studies, Villanova U., Pa., 1981—, sec., 1989-92; mem. League of Women Voters. Woodrow Wilson Found. fellow, 1979; recipient Disting. Univ. Tchr. award State of Calif. Legislature, 1966. Mem. LWV, NOW, AAUW, Am. Hist. Assn. (chair 1982-83, nominating com. 1980-83), Orgn. Am. Historians (govt. relations com.), Soc. Historians of Am. Fgn. Relations (exec. council 1978-81, 86-89, govt. relations com. 1982-84, v.p. 1985, pres. 1986, co-winner Myrna F. Bernath prize 1991), Am. Soc. for Advancement Slavic Studies, Coordinating Com. on Women in Hist. Profession, Rocky Mountain Assn. Slavic Studies (program chair 1973, v.p. 1973-74), So. Hist. Assn., Asian Studies Assn., Assn. Third World Studies, Czechoslovak Soc. Arts and Scis., Czechoslovak History Conf., Women in Nat. Security, Women's Fgn. Policy Coun., Beyond War, Peace History Soc., Sierra Club, Phi Beta Kappa, Phi Beta Delta. Office: Tex A&M U Dept History College Station TX 77843-0001 Business E-Mail: bettymu@tamu.edu.

UNTERMAN, THOMAS, venture capitalist, lawyer; b. Newport, R.I., Oct. 23, 1944; s. Martin D. and Ruth (Marcus) U.; m. Janet M. Mead, Sept. 27, 1980; children: Rebecca, Amy. AB, Princeton U., 1966; JD, U. Chgo., 1969. Bar: Calif. 1970. Assoc. Orrick, Herrington & Sutcliffe, San Francisco, 1969-75, ptnr., 1975-86, Morrison & Foerster, San Francisco, 1986-92; sr. v.p., gen. counsel The Times Mirror Co., L.A., 1992-95, sr. v.p., CFO, 1995—, exec. v.p., CFO, 1998-99; mng. ptnr. Rustic Canyon Ventures, Santa Monica, Calif., 2000—. Democrat. Jewish. Office: Rustic Canyon Ventures 2425 Olympic Blvd Ste 6050W Santa Monica CA 90404-4030

UNTERMEYER, CHARLES GRAVES (CHASE UNTERMEYER), ambassador, diplomat; b. Long Branch, N.J., Mar. 7, 1946; s. Dewitt Edward and Marguerite Alonza (Graves) U.; m. Diana Cumming Kendrick, Oct. 6, 1990; 1 child, Ellyson Chase. AB, Harvard Coll., 1968. Polit. reporter Houston Chronicle, 1971-74; exec. asst. County Judge of Harris County, Houston, 1974-76; state rep. Tex. Ho. of Reps., Austin, 1977-81; exec. asst. V.P. George H.W. Bush, Washington, 1981-83; dep. asst. sec. installations & facilities Navy Dept., Washington, 1983—84, asst. sec. manpower & reserve affairs, 1984—88; asst. to the pres. White House, Washington, 1989-91; dir. Voice of Am., Washington, 1991-93; dir. govt. affairs Compaq Computer Corp., Houston, 1993—2002; v.p. prof. pub. policy U. Tex. Health Sci. Ctr., Houston, 2002—04; U.S. amb. to Qatar US Dept. State, 2004—. Bd. visitors U.S. Naval Acad., Annapolis, Md., 1993-96, chmn., 1995; mem. Tex. State Bd. Edn., 1999-2003, chmn., 1999-2001. Author: Houston Survival Handbook, 1980. Commnr. Port of Houston, 1995-98; bd. dirs. Nat. Pub. Radio, 1996-98. Lt. USNR, 1968-70. Inst. Politics fellow Harvard U., 1980; recipient George Washington Honor medal Freedoms Found., 1969. Republican. Episcopalian. Home and Office: Am Embassy Arcent-9A Box 520 Apo AE 09898

UNVERFERTH, BARBARA PATTEN, small business owner; b. Hartford, Conn., Sept. 27, 1945; d. Leslie A. and Mildred B. (Owen) Patten; m. Robert L. Gerbig, June 1968 (div. 1977); children: Patricia G. Toohey, R. Braden Gerbig, Jo Ann Gerbig; m. Donald Unverferth, Dec. 29, 1978 (deceased); children: Katherine J. Unverferth, Megan M. Unverferth. BA cum laude, Ohio Wesleyan U., 1967; MS in Zoology, Ohio U., 1969; MS in Pathology, Ohio State U., 1980. Rsch. asst. Scripts Inst., LaJolla, Calif., 1969-70; tchr. biology Mariemont H.S., Cin., 1970-71; rschr. dept. cardiology Ohio State U., Columbus, 1980-84; gen. ptnr. Art Access, Columbus, 1993—. Founder, pres. Unverferth House Inc., Columbus, 1988—; mem. dirs. cir. Wexner Ctr., Columbus, 1995—. Author (book chpt.) Dilated Cardiomyopathy, 1985. Corr. sec. Jr. League, Columbus, 1974; corr. sec., mem. exec. bd. Childhood League, Columbus, 1980-85; sec. womens bd. Mus. of Art, Columbus, 1992-93; mem. Columbus AIDS Task Force, 1998. NSF grantee, 1966, NSF fellow, 1968; named Woman of Yr. Rotary Club Upper Arlington, Ohio, 1993. Mem. Kappa Alpha Theta (pres. alumni club 1976). Avocations: tennis, skiing. Office: Art Access 540 S Drexel Ave Bexley OH 43209 E-mail: unvi@aol.com.

UNWIN, GEOFF, consulting company executive; With Hoskyns; vice-chmn., CEO Cap Gemini Ernest & Young. Office: Cap Gemini Ernst & Young 11 rue de Tilsitt 75017 Paris France

UOTILA, URHO ANTTI KALEVI, engineering educator; b. Pöytyä, Finland, Feb. 22, 1923; came to U.S., 1951, naturalized, 1957; s. Antti Samuli and Vera Justina (Kyto) U.; m. Helena Vanhakartano, Aug. 6, 1949; children: Heidi, Kirsi, Elizabeth, Julie, Trina, Caroline. BS, Finland's Inst. Tech., 1946, MS, 1949; PhD, Ohio State U., 1959. Surveyor, geodesist Finnish Govt., 1944-46, 46-51; geodesist Swedish Govt., 1946; research asst. Ohio State U., 1952-53, research assoc., 1953-58, research supr., 1959-88, lectr. in geodesy, 1955-57, asst. prof., 1959-62, assoc. prof., 1962-65, chmn. dept. geodetic sci., 1964-84, prof., 1965-89, chmn., prof. emeritus, 1989—. Mem. Solar Eclipse Expdn. to Greenland, 1954; Mem. adv. panel on geodesy U.S. Coast and Geodetic Survey, Nat. Acad. Sci., 1964-66; mem. geodesy and cartography working group, space sci. steering com. NASA, 1965-67, mem. geodesy/cartography working group, summer conf. lunar exploration and sci., 1965, mem. geodesy and cartography adv. subcom., 1967-72; mem. ad hoc com. on N.Am. datum div. earth scis. Nat. Acad. Scis.-N.A.E., 1968-70; bd. dirs. Internat. Gravity Bur., France, 1975-83; mem. com. on geodesy Nat. Acad. Scis., 1975-78 Mem. editorial adv. com.: Advances in Geophysics, 1968-77; Contbr. articles to profl. jours., encys. Served with Finnish Army, 1942-44. Recipient Kaarina and W.A. Heiskanen award, 1962, Apollo Achievement award NASA, 1969, Disting. Svc. award Surveyor's Inst. Sri Lanka, Earle J. Fennell award Am. Congress on Surveying and Mapping, 1989. Fellow Am. Geophys. Union (v.p. geodesy sect. 1964-68, pres. 1968-70), Am. Congress Surveying and Mapping (nat. dir. 1970-73, 2d v.p. 1977-78, pres.-elect 1978-79, pres. 1979-80), Internat. Assn. Geodesy (pres. spl. study group 5.30 1967-71, pres. sect. V 1971-75, exec. com. 1971-79); mem. Am. Assn. Geodetic Surveying (pres. 1984-86), Am. Soc. Photogrammetry, Can. Inst. Surveying, Univs. Space Research Assn. (trustee 1973-75), Finnish Nat. Acad. Scis. (fgn.), Profl. Land Surveyors Ohio (hon.), Ala. Soc. Profl. Land Surveyors (hon.), Tenn. Assn. Profl. Surveyors (hon.) Achievements include: research in geometric geodesy, phys. geodesy and statis. analysis of data. Home: 4329 Shelbourne Ln Columbus OH 43220-4243 Office: Ohio State U 2070 Neil Ave Columbus OH 43210-1226

UPADHIAYA, UMESH CHANDRA, engineer, consultant; b. Dabha, India, July 11, 1927; arrived in US, 1977; s. Bhagwati Prashad and Shri (Devi) Upadhiaya; m. Susila Devi, Nov. 7, 1954; children: Anita, Amit. Diploma in Elec. and Mech. Engring., Tech. Coll., Dayalbagh, India, 1948; MSME, Fla. Internat. U., 1990. Registered profl. engr., Fla. Asst. engr. Hindusthan Sugar, Gola, India, 1954—60; mech. engr. Bagpat Sugar, India, 1960—61; erection engr. Dhampur Sugar, India, 1961—62; cons. Mehta Group, Uganda, 1962—73; project mgr. KCP Ltd., Madras, India, 1973—74; design engr. Joint Sugar Project Unit, Surabaya, Indonesia, 1974—77; cons. engr. Tate & Lyle Enterprises Inc., Miami, Fla., 1977—85, ATV Projects, Bombay, 1990—93; ind. cons. Davie, Fla., 1993—. Contbr. articles to profl. jours. Home: 6510 Sedgewyck Cir W Davie FL 33331-3455 Office Phone: 954-434-5265. E-mail: ravaY2K@bellsouth.net.

UPADHYAY, YOGENDRA NATH, physician, educator; b. Gorakhpur, India, Dec. 21, 1938; arrived in U.S., 1963; s. Murlidhar and Vansraji (Pande) U.; m. Cecile R. Yonish; children: Abha, Sameer, Sanjay. MB, BS, All India Inst. Med. Scis., New Delhi, 1962. Diplomate Am. Bd. Psychiatry and Neurology, Am. Bd. Pediatrics. Instr. in pediatrics Johns Hopkins U. Sch. Medicine, Balt., 1969-71; fellow in child psychiatry Johns Hopkins Hosp./Johns Hopkins U., Balt., 1971-72; resident, then sr. resident in psychiatry Albert Einstein Coll. Medicine/Bronx Mcpl. Hosp. Ctr., 1972-74, fellow in child psychiatry, 1974-75; chief, partial hosp. program for children, dept. psychiatry Brookdale Hosp., Bklyn., 1976-77; med. dir. West Nassau Mental Health Ctr., Franklin Sq., N.Y., 1977-80; asst. prof. clin. psychiatry SUNY, Stony Brook, 1978-92; dir. child and adolescent psychiatry Nassau County Med. Ctr., East Meadow, N.Y., 1980-92; sr. psychiatrist South Oaks Hosp., Amityville, N.Y., 1992—, pres. med. staff, 1995-97, svc. med. dir. child and adolescent psychiatry, 1995-97, med. dir., 1997—; sr. v.p., Medical Affairs South Oak Hosp. and Broadlawn Nursing Home, 2001—. Sr. v.p. med. affairs LI Home, Amityville, NY, 2001—. Fellow Am. Psychiat. Assn. (cons. task force treatments psychiat. disorders 1989—, disting. fellow 2003), Am. Acad. Child and Adolescent Psychiatry, Allmsonians of Am. (founding pres. 1982-86). Office: S Oaks Hosp 400 Sunrise Hwy Amityville NY 11701-2508 Office Phone: 631-264-4000.

UPATNIEKS, JURIS, retired optical engineer; b. Riga, Latvia, May 7, 1936; arrived in U.S., 1951; s. Karlis and Eleonora (Jegers) Upatnieks; m. Ilze Induss, July 13, 1968; children: Ivars, Ansis. BSEE, U. Akron, Ohio, 1960; MSEE, U. Mich., 1965. Rsch. asst., then rsch. assoc. Willow Run Labs. U. Mich., Ann Arbor, 1960-69; rsch. engr. Inst. Sci. and Tech., U. Mich., Ann Arbor, 1969-72, Environ. Rsch. Inst. Mich., Ann Arbor, 1973-93; sr. engr. Applied Optics, Ann Arbor, 1993—2001; ret., 2001. Lectr. elec. engring. dept. U. Mich., 1971—73, adj. assoc. prof. elec. engring. and computer sci. dept., 1974—2001, adj. rsch. scientist dept. mech. engring. and applied mechanics, 1996—2001. Contbr. articles to profl. jours. 2d lt. U.S. Army, 1961—62. Recipient Holley medal, ASME, 1976, Inventor of the Yr. award, Assn. Advancement Invention and Innovation, 1976. Fellow: Latvian Acad. Sci. (Grand medal 1999), Acad. Soc. Austrums, Soc. Photographic Instrumentation Engrs. (Robert Gordon award 1965), Optical Soc. Am. (R. W. Wood prize 1975), Am. Latvian Assn. Achievements include patents in field. Avocations: camping, gardening, hiking. E-mail: upatnks@netrek.net.

UPBIN, HAL J. consumer products executive; b. Bronx, N.Y., Jan. 15, 1939; s. David and Evelyn (Sloan) U.; m. Shari Kiesler, May 29, 1960; children: Edward, Elyse, Danielle. BBA, Pace Coll., 1961. CPA, N.Y. Tax sr. Peat, Marwick, Mitchell & Co., N.Y.C., 1961-65; tax mgr. Price Waterhouse & Co., N.Y.C., 1965-71; dir. taxes Wheelabrator-Frye Inc., N.Y.C., 1971-72, treas., 1972-74; pres. Wheelabrator Fin. Corp., N.Y.C., 1974-75; v.p., chief fin. officer Chase Manhattan Mortgage and Realty Trust (became Triton Group Ltd. 1980), N.Y.C., 1975-76, pres., 1976-78, pres., chmn., 1978-83, also dir.; chmn., pres., dir. Isomedics, 1983-85; chmn., pres. Fifth Ave. Cards, Inc., Fifth Retail Corp., Ashley's Stores, Ashley's Outlet Stores, 1984-88; bd. dirs. Stacy Industries, 1984-88; vice chmn. Am. Recreation Products, St. Louis, 1985-88, vice chmn., pres., 1988—, chmn., 1992—; v.p. corp. devel., chmn. acquistion com. Kellwood Co., Chesterfield, Mo., 1990—, exec. v.p. corp. devel., chmn. acquisition com., 1992—, pres., COO, 1994—, pres., COO, dir., 1995-97, pres., CEO, 1997—, also bd. dirs., chmn. Bd. dirs. First Banks, Inc., Regional Bus. Coun., Coun. Nat. Trustees, Nat. Jewish Med. and Rsch. Ctr., Nat. Coun. Wash. U. Olin Sch. Bus., Brown Shoe Co.; trustee Pace U. Past pres. Jewish Temple. Mem. AICPA, N.Y. State Soc. CPA's, Franklin Jaycees (v.p.). Home: 625 S Skinker Blvd Saint Louis MO 63105-2301 Office: Kellwood Co PO Box 14374 Saint Louis MO 63178-4374 E-mail: HJU@kellwood.com.

UPBIN, SHARI, theatrical producer, director, agent, educator; b. N.Y.C. children: Edward, Elyse, Danielle. Master tap instr. Talent mgr. Goldstar Talent Mgmt., Inc., N.Y.C., 1989-91. Faculty Nat. Shakespeare Conservatory, N.Y. Asst. dir.: (plays, 1st Black-Hispanic Shakespeare prodn.) Julius Ceasar, 1979; dir.(choreographer): (plays) Matter of Opinion, 1980, Side by Side, 1981; prodr.(dir.): Vincent, The Passions of Can Gogh, 1981,; (Broadway plays) Bojangles, TheLife of Bill Robinson, 1984; dir.: Captain America, 1996; (plays) Fiddler of the Roof, Cabaret, Life with Father, Roar of the Grease Paint, 1979—82, Feminist Movements, 1997; co-prodr.: One Mo' Time; prodr., dir.: Flypaper, 1991—92; Women on Their Own, Things My Mother Never Told Me; How Could Cupid Be So Stupid!, 1999; Timeless Divas, 2003; prodr.: 20th Ann. One Mo' Time, 2000, Vintage 2001, Timeless Divas! Salute to Women in Cabaret, Broadway Over 40, Timeless Divas! Musical Stars of The Silver Screen, 2004. Founder Queens Playhouse, N.Y., Children's Theatre, Flushing, N.Y.; mem. Willy Mays' Found. Drug Abused Children. Recipient Jaycees Svc. award Jr. Miss Pageants Franklin Twp., N.J., 1976. Mem. League Profl. Theatre Women (past pres.), Soc. Stage Dirs. and Choreographers, Coalition of Women in Arts & Media (bd. dirs.), Actors Equity Assn., Villagers Barn Theatre (1st woman pres.), N.Y. Womens Agenda (bd. dirs.). E-mail: shariupbin@earthlink.net.

UPDIKE, HELEN HILL, investment manager, financial advisor; b. N.Y.C., Mar. 27, 1941; d. Benjamin Harvey and Helen (Gray) Hill; m. Charles Bruce Updike, Sept. 7, 1963 (div. 1989); m. Asa Rountree, Oct. 10, 1998. BA, Hood Coll., 1962; PhD, SUNY, Stony Brook, 1978; postgrad., Harvard U., 1986. Lectr. SUNY, Stony Brook, 1969-75; asst. prof. U. Mass., Boston, 1975-77, Hofstra U., Hempstead, NY, 1978-85, assoc. prof., 1985-90, chmn. dept. econs. and geography, 1981-84, assoc. dean Hofstra Coll., 1984-87; pres. Interfid Capital Corp., 1987—2001; prin. Bridgewater Advisors, N.Y.C., 2001—. Cons. econ. policy, 1973—; vis. asst. prof. SUNY, Stony Brook, 1977—78; commentator WNYC Radio, 1997—; bd. dirs. Faberge, McCrory Corp. Author: (book) The National Banks and American Economic Development, 1870-1900, 1985. Trustee Madeira Sch., Greenway, Va., 1984—88, Literacy, Inc., 1997—2002; mem. nat. adv. bd. Outward Bound, 1986—92; trustee, v.p. L.I. Forum Tech., 1979—85; trustee Outward Bound, 1988—97. Mem.: AAAS. Office: Bridgewater Advisors 452 Fifth Ave New York NY 10018

UPDIKE, JOHN HOYER, writer; b. Shillington, Pa., Mar. 18, 1932; s. Wesley R. and Linda G. (Hoyer) U.; m. Mary E. Pennington, June 26, 1953 (div. 1976); children: Elizabeth, David, Michael, Miranda; m. Martha Bernhard, Sept. 30, 1977. AB, Harvard U., 1954; student, Ruskin Sch. Drawing and Fine Art, 1954-55. With New Yorker mag., N.Y.C., 1955-57. Author: (fiction) The Poorhouse Fair, 1959 (Richard and Hinda Rosenthal Found. award Am. Acad. and Nat. Inst. Arts and Letters 1960), The Same Door, 1959, Rabbit, Run, 1960, Pigeon Feathers, 1962, The Centaur, 1963 (Nat. Book award for fiction 1963, Prix Medicis Etranger 1966), Olinger Stories, 1964, Of the Farm, 1965, The Music School, 1966, Couples, 1968, Bech: A Book, 1970, Rabbit Redux, 1971, Museums and Women, 1972, Warm Wine, 1973, A Month of Sundays, 1975, Marry Me, 1976, Couples, 1976, The Coup, 1978, From the Journal of a Leper, 1978, Problems, 1979, Too Far to Go: The Maples Stories, 1979 (Am. Book award nomination 1980), Three Illuminations in the Life of an American Author, 1979, Your Lover Just Called: Stories of Joan and Richard Maple, 1980, The Chaste Planet, 1980, Rabbit Is Rich, 1981 (Pulitzer prize for fiction 1982, Nat. Book Critics Circle award 1982, Am. Book award 1982), Invasion of the Book Envelopes, 1981, Bech Is Back, 1982, The Beloved, 1982, The Witches of Eastwick, 1984, Confessions of a Wild Bore, 1984, Roger's Version, 1986 (Nat. Book Critics Circle award nomination 1986), Trust Me, 1987, More Stately Mansions, 1987, S., 1988, Rabbit at Rest, 1990 (Pulitzer prize for fiction 1991, Nat. Book Critics Circle award 1991), Memories of the Ford Administration, 1992, Brazil, 1994, The Afterlife, 1994, In the Beauty of the Lilies, 1996, Toward the End of Time, 1997, Bech at Bay, 1998, Gertrude and Claudius, 2000, Licks of Love: Short Stories and a Sequel, Rabbit Remembered, 2000, The Complete Henry Bech, 2001, Seek My Face, 2002, The Early Stories 1953-75, 2003 (PEN/Faulkner award 2004), Villages, 2004; (poetry) The Carpentered Hen and Other Tame Creatures, 1958, Telephone Poles, 1963, A Child's Calendar, 1965, The Angels, 1968, Bath after Sailing, 1968, Midpoint, 1969, Seventy Poems, 1972, Six Poems, 1973, Tossing and Turning, 1977, Sixteen Sonnets, 1979, Five Poems, 1980, Spring Trio, 1982, Jester's Dozen, 1984, Facing Nature, 1985, Collected Poems 1953-1993, 1993, A Helpful Alphabet of Friendly Objects, 1995, In the Cemetery High Above Shillington, 1996, Radiators, 1998, Americana, 2001, Not Cancelled Yet, 2003, (plays) Three Texts from Early Ipswich, 1968, Buchanan Dying, 1974, (non-fiction) Assorted Prose, 1965, On Meeting Authors, 1968, A Good Place, 1973, Picked-Up Pieces, 1975, Hub Fans Bid Kid Adieu, 1977, Talk from the Fifties, 1979, Ego and Art in Walt Whitman, 1980, Hawthorne's Creed, 1981, Hugging the Shore, 1983 (Nat. Book Critics Circle award 1984), Emersonianism, 1984, Just Looking, 1989, Self-Consciousness, 1989, Odd Jobs, 1991, Golf Dreams, 1996, More Matter, 1999, On Literary Biography, 1999; adapter: (librettos) The Magic Flute, 1962, The Ring, 1964, (plays) Bottom's Dream, 1969; author words and music: (with Gunther Schuller) The Fisherman and His Wife, 1970; editor: Pens and Needles, 1970, (with S. Ravenel) The Best American Short Stories 1984, 1984, A Century of Arts and Letters, 1998, (with K. Kenison) The Best Am. Short Stories of the Century, 1999, Karl Shapiro: Selected Poems, 2003.. Recipient O. Henry First Short Story award, 1966, 91, MacDowell medal for literature, 1981, Medal of Honor for literature Nat. Arts Club, 1984, PEN/Malamud Meml. prize PEN/Faulker award Found., 1988, Nat. Medal of Arts, 1989, Harvard Arts medal, 1998, Nat. Book Found. award Lifetime Achievement, 1998, Nat. Humanities medal, 2003; Guggenheim fellow, 1959. Mem. AAAL, Am. Acad. Arts. and Scis. Democrat. Episcopalian.

UPGREN, ARTHUR REINHOLD, JR., astronomer, educator, writer; b. Mpls., Feb. 21, 1933; s. Arthur Reinhold and Marion (Andrews) U.; m. Joan Koswoski, Jan. 7, 1967; 1 child, Amy Joan. BA, U. Minn., 1955; MS, U. Mich., 1958; PhD, Case Western Res. U., 1961. Research assoc. Swarthmore Coll., Pa., 1961-63; astronomer U.S. Naval Obs., Washington, 1963-66; asst. prof. Wesleyan U., Middletown, Conn., 1966-73, assoc. prof., 1973-81, dir. Van Vleck Obs., 1973-93, John Monroe Van Vleck prof., 1981—, chmn. dept. astronomy, 1968-86, 90-93; v.p. Fund Astrophys. Research, N.Y.C., 1973—, chmn. grants com., 1985—. Vis. lectr. U. Md., 1964-66, George Washington U., 1965-66, Thames Sci. Ctr., New London, Conn., 1990, 92; vis. prof. Yale U., 1979-80, sr. rsch. scientist, 1997—; adj. prof. U. Fla., 1984-99; outdoor lighting cons. Wesleyan U., 1991—, Vt. State Agy. Natural Resources, 1993-94; dir. Internat. Dark-Sky Assn., 1997—; reviewer books in astronomy, meteorology, classical music and urban demographics. Author: Night Has a Thousand Eyes: A Naked-Eye Guide to the Sky, its Science and Lore, 1998; co-author (with Jurgen Stock): Weather: How it Works and Why It Matters, 2000, The Turtle and The Stars: Observations of an Earthbound Astronomer, 2002, Many Skies: Alternative Histories of the Sun, Moon, Planets, and Stars, 2004; editor: The Nearby Stars and the Stellar Luminosity Function, 1983, Mapping the Sky-Past Heritage and Future Directions, 1988, Star Catalogues: A Centennial Tribute to A.N. Vyssotsky, 1989, Fundamentals of Astronomy, 1990, Precision Photometry: Astrophysics of the Galaxy, 1991, Objective Prism and Other Surveys, 1991, Databases for Galactic Structure, 1993, Hot Stars in the Halo, 1994, New Developments in Array Technology and Applications, 1995, Anni Mirables: A Symposium Celebrating the 90th Birthday of Dorrit Hoffleit, 1997. Conn. state chair New Eng. Light Pollution Adv. Group, 1994—. Grantee NSF, 1967-99; fellow Wesleyan Ctr. for Humanities, 1996. Fellow Royal Astron. Soc.; mem. Internat. Astron. Union (commn. v.p. 1982-85, pres. commn. 24 1985-88), Am. Astron. Soc. (Harlow Shapley lectr. 1977—, vice-chmn. dynamical astronomy div. 1988-89, chmn. 1989-90, chmn. AAS com. on light pollution 2000—), Astron. Soc. Pacific, Illumniating Engring. Soc. N.Am., Internat. Dark Sky Assn. (bd. dirs. 1997—).

UPHAM, STEADMAN, academic administrator, anthropologist, educator; b. Denver, Apr. 4, 1949; s. Albert Tyler and Jane Catherine (Steadman) U; m. Margaret Anne Cooper, Aug. 21, 1971; children: Erin Cooper, Nathan Steadman. BA, U. Redlands, 1971; MA, Ariz. State U., 1977, PhD, 1980. Dist. sales mgr. Ind. News Co. Inc., Los Angeles, 1971-72; regional sales mgr. Petersen Pub. Co, Los Angeles, 1972-74; archeologist, researcher Bur. Land Mgmt., Phoenix, 1979; research asst. Ariz. State U., Tempe, 1979-80; chief archeologist Soil Sytems Inc., Phoenix, 1980-81, N.Mex. State U., Las Cruces, N.Mex., 1981-85, asst. prof. to assoc. prof., 1982-87, assoc. dean, 1987-90; prof. anthropology, vice provost for rsch., grad. dean U. Oreg., Eugene, 1990—. Inerim dir. Cultural Resources Mgmt. divsn. N.Mex. State U., Las Cruces, 1988; mem. exec. com. Assn. Grad. Schs., 1994—; bd. dirs. Coun. Grad. Schs., 1995—. Author: Polities and Power, 1982, A Hopi Social History, 1992; editor: Computer Graphics in Archaeology, 1979, Mogollon Variability, 1986, The Sociopolitical Structure of Prehistoric Southwest Societies, 1989, The Evolution of Political Systems, 1990; also articles. Advanced seminar grantee Sch. of Am. Research, 1987, research grantee NSF, 1979, 1984-85, Hist. Preservation grantee State of N.Mex., 1982-84, 1991, 92, Ford Found. 1991-92, U.S. Dept. Edn. 1991-93. Fellow Am. Anthropol. Assn.; mem. Nat. Phys. Sci. Consortium (pres. 1992-95), We. Assn. Grad. Schs. (pres. 1994-95), Assn. Grad. Schs. (exec. com. 1995—), Coun. Grad. Schs. (bd. dirs. 1995—). Office: U Oreg Office Acad Affairs 207 Johnson Hall Eugene OR 97403

UPHOFF, CHARLES MAYNARD, news correspondent, writer; b. Madison, Wis., May 9, 1944; s. Walter Henry and Mary Josephine Uphoff; m. Louise Joan Backer, Apr. 2, 1970; children: James, Jennifer Uphoff-Gray, Sarah. Student, U. Colo., U. Minn., 1962—63; BA in Polit. Sci., U. Colo., 1967; student, New Sch. Social Rsch., 1969. Tchr. cert. 1967. Dir. Head Start Ctr. Colo. Migrant Coun. Ctr., Colo., 1967—68; edn. action organizer Bedford-Stuyvesant Youth-In-Action, Bklyn., 1968—70; dir. youth devel. program Dane County Cmty. Action Commn., Madison, 1970—73, dir. adult edn. and tng., 1973—75, employment specialist work experience program, 1975—77, assoc. dir., resource developer, 1986—92; exec. dir. Madison Justice Ctr., Am. Friends Svc. Com., 1977—79; coord. Wis. Gov.'s Conf. Children and Families-Bur. Children Youth and Families, Madison, 1979—81; employment specialist Op. Fresh Start, Madison, 1981—86; computer sys. cons. MicroAge, Madison, 1992—94; tech. support specialist Sitel Tech. Svcs., Madison, 1994—2000; exec. dir. Family Enhancement, Madison, 2000—02; corr., freelance writer Oreg. Observer, Fitchburg Star, Oreg., Wis., 2002—04. Chair Wis. Del. 1980 White Ho. Conf. Families, Mpls., 1980; del. ICA Global Devel. Conf., Chgo., 1980. Poet (poem) Garage Sale (Nat. Poetry Libr. award, 2003); author: (musical) A Dress Rehearsal. Vol. field organizer Presdl. Campaign Senator Eugene McCarthy, Wis., Ind., Oreg., Calif., N.Y., Kans., 1968; alderperson, pres. city coun. City of Fitchburg, Wis., 1983—89; mem. bd. Dane County Ethic Bd., Madison, 1989—93, Wis. Coun. Family Rels., 1989—93; mem. sch. bd. Oreg. Sch. Dist., Oreg., Wis., 1993—2002; mem. bd. Madison Theatre Guild, 2002—04. Home: 2475 Lalor Rd Oregon WI 53575

UPHOFF, JAMES KENT, education educator; b. Hebron, Nebr., Sept. 1, 1937; s. Ernest John and Alice Marie (Dutcher) U.; m. Harriet Lucille Martin, Aug. 6, 1962; 1 child, Nicholas James. BA, Hastings Coll., 1959; MEd, U. Nebr., 1962, EdD, 1967. Tchr. Walnut Jr. H.S., Grand Island, Nebr., 1959-65, dept. chmn., 1962-65; instr. dept. edn. U. Nebr., Lincoln, 1965-66; curriculum intern Bellevue (Nebr.) Pub. Schs., 1966-67; asst. prof. edn. Wright State U., Dayton, Ohio, 1967-70, assoc. prof., 1970-75, prof. edn., 1975—, co-dir. pub. edn. religion studies ctr., 1972-75, dean br. campuses, 1974-79, dir. lab. experiences, 1982-91, chmn. dept. tchr. edn., 1994-97, dir. coll. student svcs., 1994-97, dir. profl. field experiences, prof. emeritus, 1997—, assoc. dir. Ctr. for Tchg. and Learning, 1999—. Vis. prof. U. Dayton, 1968—69, 1998, 99; adj. prof. Antioch McGregor, 2003—; mem. educator stds. bd. State of Ohio, 2004—. Author: (with others) Summer Children: Ready or Not for School, 4th edit., 1986, School Readiness and Transition Programs: Real Facts from Real Schools, 1990, 2d edit., 1995; editor: Dialogues on Development Curriculum K and I, 1987, Changing to a Developmentally Appropriate Curriculum-Successfully: 4 Case Studies, 1989; bi-weekly columnist Oakwood Register newspapers; weekly commentator on edn. WYSO-FM Pub. Radio. Bd. dirs. pub. edn. fund Dayton Found., 1985-97; mem. Luth. Ch. coun., 1987-90, chair, 1988-90; mem. Oakwood City Schs. Bd. Edn., 1989—, v.p., 1994, 95, 2004, pres., 1996, 97, 2004. Phi Delta Kappa scholar, 1969; Malone fellow in Arab Islamic studies, 1989; U. Nebr. Alumni award, 2002. Mem. ASCD (dir. 1974-79, editor early childhood network 1989-98, editor and facilitator pub. edn. and religion network 1992—), Western Ohio Edn. Assn. (pres. 1974-75, exec. com. 1979-85), Ohio Assn. Supervision and Curriculum Devel. (v.p. 1972-73), Nat. Coun. Social Studies, Ohio Coun. Social Studies, Ohio Sch. Bds. Assn. (chair rules com. 1993-94, mem. policy and legislation com. 1994—, Achievement award 1995, 96, 98, 2000, 04, Master Boardsman award, 2004, trustee 1996-2002, exec. com. 1998-99, pres.-elect 2000, pres. 2001), Nat. Assn. Edn. Young Children, Dayton Area Coun. Social Studies (pres. 1970-71, 85-87), Ohio Assn. Edn. Young Children (com. chair 1992-95), Dayton Assn. for Young Children (exec. bd. 1988-94), LWV Greater Dayton (edn. dir. 1981-85), Ohio Coun. Chs. (edn. com. 1973-75), Nat. Sch. Bd. Assoc. (policy and rels. com., 2003), Ohio Dept. Edn. (gifted edn. adv. coun., 2001)Optimists Club (pres. 1983-85, sec.-treas. 1988-99), Phi Delta Kappa (chpt. pres. 1983-84, 98—, chpt. advisor 1988-94, area coord. 2001—03, chpt./mem. liaison 2004—), Kappa Delta Pi. Republican. Home: 150 Spirea Dr Dayton OH 45419-3409 Office: Wright State U CTL 023 Library Dayton OH 45435 Office Phone: 937-775-3651. Business E-Mail: james.uphoff@wright.edu.

UPMEYER, LINDA, state official; b. July 1952; married. Bachelor's degree, U. Iowa, 1997; M in Nursing, Drake U., 1999. Family nurse practitioner; state rep., 2003—. Mem., vice-chair edn. appropriation subcom.; mem. human resources standing com.; mem. environ. protection standing com.; mem. appropriations standing com. Mem.: Iowa Nursing Assn. (chair polit. action com.), Sigma Theta Tau (mem. Gamma chpt.). Office: State Capitol E 12th and Grand Des Moines IA 50319

UPPMAN, THEODOR, concert and opera singer, voice educator; b. San Jose, Calif., Jan. 12, 1920; s. John August and Hulda Maria (Thörnström) U.; m. Jean Seward, Jan. 31, 1943; children: Margot, Michael. Student, Coll. of Pacific, 1938-39, Curtis Inst. Music, 1939-41, Stanford U., 1941-42, U. So. Calif., 1948-50. Mem. profl. com. regional auditions Met. Opera; voice faculty Mannes Coll. Music, 1977—, Manhattan Sch. Music, 1988—; tchr. master classes Britten-Pears Sch. Advanced Mus. Studies, 1985—, Glimmerglass Opera, Cooperstown, N.Y., 1990, 93, Opera Theatre of St. Louis, 1993, Steans Inst. at Ravinia Festival, 1995; dir. vocal dept. Music Acad. of the West, Santa Barbara, Calif., 1988. Profl. debut as baritone, No. Calif. Symphony, 1941, appeared in Pelléas et Mélisande, San Francisco Symphony, 1947; performed in: Pelleas et Melisande, City Ctr. Opera Co., N.Y., 1948; debut, San Francisco Opera Co., 1948, N.Y. recital, Times Hall, 1950; appeared: title role Billy Budd opera premiere, Royal Opera House, London, Eng., 1951, Theatre des Champs Elysees, Paris, France, 1952; performed in: Billy Budd, NBC-TV Opera Theatre, 1952; Met. Opera Co. prodsn. including Pelleas et Melisande, 1953-62, Magic Flute, 1956-77, La Perichole, 1956-71, Don Giovanni, 1957-73, Madam Butterfly, 1961-78, Cosi fan Tutte, 1962-71, L'Italiana in Algeri, 1973-75; Britten's Gloriana, Cin. May Festival, 1956 (U.S. premiere); world premieres of Floyd's The Passion of Jonathan Wade, N.Y.C. Opera, 1962, Villa Lobos' Yerma, Santa Fe Opera, 1971, Pasatieri's Black Widow, Seattle Opera, 1972, Barab's Philip Marshall, Chautauqua, 1974; Aix en

Provence Festival, summer 1964, Aldeburgh Festival, summer 1975, Chgo. Lyric Opera debut, 1964, War Requiem by Britten, Dallas, Cleve., Cin. orchs., 1965, Damnation of Faust, N.Y. Philharmonic, 1966; Am. premiere: Billy Budd, Chgo. Lyric Opera, 1970, Death in Venice (Britten), Geneva Opera, 1983; World premiere: A Quiet Place (Bernstein), Houston Opera, 1983, A Quiet Place, LaScala, 1984, A Quiet Place, Vienna Staatsoper, 1986; recordings include world premiere broadcast Billy Budd, 1951, Fauré Requiem, 1951, The Art of Theodor Uppman, 1954-57; concert opera symphony appearances throughout, U.S., also radio, TV. Hon. dir. Britten-Pears Sch. for Advanced Mus. Studies, 1987—. With U.S. Army, 1943-46, World War II. Recipient 1st prize Atwater Kent Found. Auditions, Gainsborough Found. award, 1947. Address: 201 W 86th St New York NY 10024-3328

U'PRICHARD, DAVID C. pharmaceutical executive; BS in Pharmacology with 1st class honors, U. Glasgow, Scotland; PhD in Pharmacology, U. Kans. Postdoctoral fellow Johns Hopkins U., Balt., 1975—78; assoc. prof. Northwestern U. Med. Sch., 1978—83; with Nova Pharms., 1983; exec. v.p. ICI/Zeneca, 1986—97, internat. rsch. dir., 1994—97; pres. R&D SmithKline Beecham, 1997—99; CEO 3-Dimensional Pharms., Inc., Yardley, Pa., 1999—, also bd. dirs. Hon. prof. U. Glasgow; instr. U. Pa., Phila.; bd. dirs. Lynx Therapuetics, Inc. Co-editor: Molecular Neurobiology, Epinephrine; contbr. articles to profl. jours. Office: 3D Pharms Inc 3 Lower Makefield Corp Ctr 1020 Stony Hill Rd Yardley PA 19067

UPRIGHT, DIANE WARNER, art dealer; b. Cleve. d. Rodney Upright and Shirley (Warner) Lavine. Student, Wellesley Coll., 1965-67; BA, U. Pitts., 1969; MA, U. Mich., 1973, PhD, 1976. Asst. prof. U. Va., Charlottesville, 1976-78; assoc. prof. Harvard U., Cambridge, Mass., 1978-83; sr. curator Ft. Worth Art Mus., 1984-86; dir. Jan Krugier Gallery, N.Y.C., 1986-90; sr. v.p., head contemporary art dept. Christie's, N.Y.C., 1990-95; pres. Diane Upright Fine Arts, N.Y.C., 1995—. Author: Morris Louis: The Complete Paintings, 1979, Ellsworth Kelly: Works on Paper, 1987, various exhbn. catalogues; contbr. articles to art jours. Mem. Art Table, Inc. Office: Diane Upright Fine Arts 188 E 76th St New York NY 10021-2826

UPRIGHT, KIRBY GRANT, lawyer; b. South Canaan, Pa., Sept. 12, 1946; s. Lyle Lee and Ellen May (Kirby) U.; m. Joyce Ann Keyasko, Oct. 4, 1975; children: Chad, Scott. BS, Pa. State U., 1970; JD, U. Akron, 1973; LLM in Taxation, Temple U., 1977. Bar: Pa. 1973, U.S. Dist. Ct. (mid. dist.) Pa. 1978, U.S. Ct. Appeals (3d cir.) 1981, U.S. Tax Ct. 1979; CPA, Pa. Staff acct. Peat, Marwick, Mitchell, Phila., 1973-77; assoc. Henkleman, Kreder, O'Connell & Brooks, Scranton, Pa., 1977-82; ptnr. Young, Upright, Catina & Parker, Stroudsburg, Pa., 1982—2003; mem. King, Spry, Herman, Freund & Faul, LLC, Bethleham, Pa., 2004—. With U.S. Army, 1964-67, Vietnam. Fellow Am. Coll. Trust and Estate Counsel; mem. Pa. Bar Assn. (chmn. Real Property, Probate, and trust divsn.), Pa. State U. Alumni Assn., Pocono Mountain Club (Stroudsburg, pres. 1982-85), Masons, Rotary (v.p.), Penn State Planned Giving Adv. Coun. Home: 53 Wyndham Hills Cresco PA 18326-0053 Office: PO Box 443 East Stroudsburg PA 18301-0443 Office Phone: 610-332-0390. E-mail: kupright@kingspry.com.

UPSHAW, GENE, sports association executive; b. Robstown, Tex., Aug. 15, 1945; s. Eugene and Cora (Riley) U.; 1 son, Eugene; m. Teresa Buich, 1986; children: Justin, Daniel. BS, Tex. A&I U., 1968; postgrad., Calif. State U., 1969, Golden Gate U., 1980. Player Oakland Raiders, 1967-82; player rep.-alt. NFL Players Assn., Oakland, Calif., 1970-76, mem. exec. com., 1976-80, pres., 1980-83, exec. dir., 1983—; ptnr. Gene Upshaw & Assocs., Mgmt. Cons. Firm, Oakland, Calif., 1970-78. Chmn. bd. NFL Players Inc., or Players Inc. Mem. Calif. Gov.'s Council Wellness and Phys. Fitness; mem. Calif. Bd. Govs. for Community Colls.; former planning commr. Alameda County, Calif., coordinator voter registration and fund raising. Served with U.S. Army, 1967-73. Named Offensive Lineman of Yr., Am. Football Conf., 1973, 74, 77, Lineman of Yr., NFL, 1977, Pro Bowl selection 6 times, All Pro selection Sporting News, 1967-77, All Pro selection UPI, 1967-77, All Pro selection AP, 1967-77, All Pro selection TV Guide, 1967-77, All Pro selection Profl. Football Writers, 1967-77; mem. NFL Championship Team, 1976, 1980; recipient Byron (Whizzer) White Humanitarian award NFL Players Assn., 1980, A. Philip Randolph A. Philip Randolph Inst., 1982; listed 13th in Top 100 Most Powerful People in Sports, Sporting News, 1993. Mem. Alpha Phi Alpha Democrat. Baptist. Office: NFL Players Assn 2021 L St NW Fl 6 Washington DC 20036-4909

UPSHAW, HARRY STEPHAN, psychology educator; b. Birmingham, Ala., July 10, 1926; s. N.H. and Florence (Arnold) U.; m. Paula Binyon, June 18, 1950; children: Alan Binyon, Phyllis, David Arnold, Stephan Lipner. Student, U. Ala., 1946-47; AB, U. Chgo., 1949; MA, Northwestern U., 1951; PhD, U. N.C., 1956. Asst prof. psychology U. Ala., 1954-57; spl. instr. psychology Simmons Coll., Boston, 1957-58; research asso. Ednl. Research Corp., Cambridge, Mass., 1957-58; asst. prof., then assoc. prof. pub. health U. N.C., 1958-61, lectr., assoc. prof. psychology, 1958-64, rsch. prof. psychology, 1991-97; assoc. prof. Bryn Mawr (Pa.) Coll., 1964-65; assoc. prof., then prof. emeritus psychology U. Ill., Chgo., 1965-91, prof. emeritus, 1991—, dept. head, 1968-72; assoc. dir. Office of Social Sci. Rsch., 1981-87. Guest prof. U. Mannheim, Germany, 1975, Fulbright scholar Technische Universitaet Berlin, 1978-79; vis. scholar Inst. for Rsch. in Social Sci., U. N.C., 1991-92; del. to South Africa, People to People Amb. Program, 2004. Editorial cons., Jour. Exptl. Social Psychology, Research in Personality, Jour. Applied Social Psychology, Jour. Personality Social Psychology; Contbr. articles to profl. jours. Served with AUS, 1944-46. Fellow Am. Psychol. Assn., Soc. Exptl. Social Psychol. Home: 155 N Harbor Dr Apt 1303 Chicago IL 60601-7397 Office Phone: 312-819-0408. Personal E-mail: hupshaw@uic.edu.

UPSHUR, CAROLE CHRISTOFK, psychologist, educator; b. Des Moines, Oct. 18, 1948; d. Robert Richard and Margaret (Davis) Chistofk; 1 child, Emily. AB, U. So. Calif., 1969; EdM, Harvard U., 1970, EdD, 1975. Lic. psychologist, Mass. Planner Mass. Com. on Criminal Justice, Boston, 1970-73; licensing specialist, planner, policy specialist Mass. Office for Children, Boston, 1973-76; asst. prof. Coll. Pub. and Cmty. Svc. U. Mass., Boston, 1976-81, assoc. prof., 1982-93, prof., 1993-2001, chmn. Ctr. for Cmty. Planning, 1979—81, 1984—86, 1995—96; prof., interim assoc. dean family medicine and cmty. health Grad. Sch. Biomed. Scis. U. Mass. Med. Sch., Boston, 2004—. Sr. rsch. fellow Maurice Gaston Inst. Latino Pub. Policy, 1993—, Ctr. Social Devel. & Edn., 1991-2001, Gerontology Inst., 1996-2001, McCormack Inst. for Pub. Affairs, dir. PhD in Pub. Policy program, 1995-2001; cons. to govt. and cmty. agys.; assoc. in pediat., sr. rsch. assoc. U. Mass. Med. Sch., 1983-94; adj. prof. Heller Sch. Social Welfare, Brandeis U., 1985-98; prof. family medicine and cmty. health U. Mass. Med. Sch. and Meml. Health Care, 2004-; interim assoc. dean, Clin. and Population Health Rsch. Grad. Sch., U. Mass. Med. Sch., 2004—. Contbr. articles to profl. jours. Mem. Brookline Human Rels.-Youth Resources Commn., 1988-91, Gov.'s Commn. on Facility Consolidation, 1991-92, Mass. Healthcare Adv. Com., 1993—. Fellow Mass. Psychol. Assn.; mem. APA, APHA, Soc. Tchrs. of Family Medicine. Office: U Mass Med Sch Dept Family Med 55 Lake Ave N Worcester MA 01655

UPSON, DONALD V. retired corporate financial executive; b. Hutchinson, Kans., Feb. 8, 1934; s. William Ernest and Luella Beatrice (Hutchison) U.; m. Janis Carol Anderson, Sept. 16, 1956; children: Mark Steven, Brent William. BS, Kans. State U., 1956. C.P.A. With Peat, Marwick, Mitchell & Co., 1956, 60-81, ptnr., 1974-81; exec. v.p., dir. internal audit Del E. Webb Corp., Phoenix, 1981-85; mgr. info. systems Tiernay Turbines Inc., Phoenix, 1986; chief fin. officer Schomac Corp., Tucson, 1986-88; adminstr. U. Ariz., Tucson, 1988-90; pres., chief exec. officer Ariz. Commerce Bank, Tucson, 1990-91; chief fin. officer O'Connor, Cavanagh, Anderson, Westover, Killingsworth & Beshears, P.A., Phoenix, 1991-94; fin. cons., 1995-97; ret., 1997. Pres. Community Orgn. for Drug Abuse, Alcohol and Mental Health Services, Inc., 1977-78; bd. dis. Phoenix council Boy Scouts Am., elder Presbyterian Ch. Served to lt. USAF, 1956-59. Mem. Am. Inst. C.P.A.s, Ariz. Soc. C.P.A.s, Beta Theta Pi (pres. 1955-56) Republican. Home and office: 1313 E Sheena Dr Phoenix AZ 85022-4485 E-mail: DVUPSON@aol.com.

UPSON, STUART BARNARD, advertising agency executive; b. Cin., Apr. 14, 1925; s. Mark and Alice (Barnard) U.; m. Barbara Jussen, Nov. 2, 1946; children: Marguerite Nichols, Anne Marcus, Stuart Barnard. BS, Yale U., 1945. With Dancer, Fitzgerald, Sample, Inc., N.Y.C., 1946-86, sr. v.p., 1963-66, exec. v.p., 1966-67, pres., 1967-74, chmn., 1974-86, DFS-Dorland, N.Y.C., 1986-87; dir. Saatchi & Saatchi Inc., N.Y.C., 1987—. Bd. dirs. Fresh Air Fund, N.Y., Advt. Coun. With USNR, 1943-46. Mem. St. Elmo Soc. Clubs: Wee Burn Country (Darien); Sky (N.Y.C.); Blind Brook, Pine Valley Golf, Ocean Forest Golf. Home: 16 Wrenfield Ln Darien CT 06820-2201 Office: Saatchi & Saatchi Inc 375 Hudson St New York NY 10014-3658

UPSON, THOMAS FISHER, judge, former state senator, lawyer; b. Waterbury, Conn., Sept. 30, 1941; s. J. Warren and Grace (Fisher) U.; m. Barbara Secor (div. Jan. 1979); children: Secor, Chauncey Julius; m. Katherine Wolff, June 1, 1996. BA in History, Washington and Jefferson Coll., 1963; LLB, U. Conn., 1968; postgrad., Trinity Coll., 1969—72, Georgetown U., 1971—72. Bar: Conn., 1969, U.S. Dist. Ct. (2d dist.) 1969, U.S. Supreme Ct. 1973. Lawyer Upson & Secor, Waterbury, 1969—70, 1974—76; lawyer, spl. asst. U.S. Dept. Commerce, Washington, 1970—72; lawyer, spl. asst. to adminstr. GSA, Washington, 1973—74, dir. admissions St. Margaret's McTernan Sch., Waterbury, 1977—78; with divsn. spl. revenue State of Conn., Hartford, 1978—82; assoc. Moynahan & Ruskin, Waterbury, 1979—81; ptnr. Upson & Daly, Waterbury, 1981—2001; mem. Conn. Senate, Hartford, 1985—2001, chmn. gen. law com., vice-chmn. jud. com., majority whip, 1985—86, asst. minority leader, 1987-88, 89-90, minority leader protempore, 1991-92, dep. minority leader, 1993-94, dep. majority leader, chmn. jud. com., 1995-96, dep., then asst. minority leader, ranking mem. jud. com., 1997-2000; judge Superior Ct. State of Conn., Hartford, 2001—. Moderator 1st Congl. Ch., Waterbury, 1986-91; bd. dirs. Easter Seals United Way, Waterbury, 1984-88; Rep. candidate for Congress, 6th Dist. Conn., 1976; mem. Conn. Rep. Ctrl. com., 1983-91; mem. Waterbury Rep. Town Com., 1980-85; dir. Mattatuck Mus., 1993-2003; former dir. Waterbury Symphony Orch.; former sec. and dir. First Ch. Housing, Inc.; pres. Naugatuck Valley Devel. Corp., 1975-76. Mem. ABA, Conn. Bar Assn., Waterbury Bar Assn., SAR, Soc. Colonial Wars, Soc. of the Founders of the Hartford, Phi Gamma Delta, Univ. Club (Waterbury). Lodges: Kiwanis (former pres., lt. gov. SW New Eng. dist.), Elks. Republican. Congregationalist. Avocations: hiking, music, history. Home: 210 Southwest Rd Waterbury CT 06708-3214 Office: Ansonia/Milford Jud Dist 14 W River St Milford CT 06460-3396

UPTIGROVE, KENNETH R. library administrator; b. Flint, Mich., Oct. 6, 1943; s. Kenneth R. and Ilah L. (Horton) U.; m. Suzanne C. Glass, Apr. 6, 1968; children: Chad K., Kathy S. BA, U. Mich., 1967, MLS, 1969. Br. rsch. libr. Genesee County Libr., Flint, 1963-69; sch. libr. Kearsley Community Schs., Flint, 1969-70; dir. Owosso (Mich.) Pub. Libr., 1970—94, Shiawassee Dist. Libr., Owosso, 1994—. Contbr. articles to mags. Mem. ALA, Mich. Library Assn. (Pub. library div. sec.-treas. 1981-82, chmn. coop. caucus 1986-87, mgmt. and adminstrn. caucus, sec.-treas. 1988-89), Flint Area Library Assn. (pres. 1970), Ruffed Grouse Soc. (pres. Lansing chpt. 1979-81, treas. Mich. coun. 1983-89, pres. 1989—), Owosso Circulators (pres. 1987-88), Kiwanis (Chmn. coms. 1980—, pres. 1999-2000, sec. 2001-02). Congregationalist. Office: Shiawassee Dist Libr 502 W Main St Owosso MI 48867-2687

UPTON, ARTHUR CANFIELD, experimental pathologist, educator; b. Ann Arbor, Mich., Feb. 27, 1923; s. Herbert Hawkes and Ellen (Canfield) Upton; m. Elizabeth Bache Perry, Mar. 1, 1946; children: Rebecca A., Melissa P., Bradley C. Grad., Phillips Acad., Andover, Mass., 1941; BA, U. Mich., 1944, MD, 1946. Intern Univ. Hosp., Ann Arbor, 1947, resident, 1948—49; instr. pathology U. Mich. Med. Sch., 1950—51; pathologist Oak Ridge (Tenn.) Nat. Lab., 1951—54, chief pathology-physiology sect., 1954—69; prof. pathology SUNY Med. Sch. at Stony Brook, 1969—77, chmn. dept. pathology, 1969—70, dean Sch. Basic Health Scis., 1970—75; dir. Nat. Cancer Inst., Bethesda, Md., 1977—79; prof., chmn. dept. environ. medicine NYU Med. Sch., N.Y.C., 1980—92, prof. emeritus, 1993—; clin. prof. radiology U. N.Mex. Sch. Medicine, 1993—95, clin. prof. pathology, 1992—95; clin. prof. environ. and cmty. medicine U. Medicine and Dentistry N.J.-Robert Wood Johnson Med. Sch., 1995—. Attending pathologist Brookhaven Nat. Lab., 1969—77; dir. Inst. Environ. Medicine, Med. Sch., NYU, 1980—92; mem. various coms. nat. and internat. orgns.; lectr. in field; mem. adv. bd. GM Cancer Rsch. Found. Assoc. editor Cancer Rsch., mem. editl. bd. Internat. Union Against Cancer. Served with U.S. Army, 1943—46. Named nat. lectr., Sigma Xi, 1989—91; recipient Ernest Orlando Lawrence award for atomic field, 1965, Claude M. Fuess award, 1980, Sarah L. Poilley award for pub. health, 1983, CHUMS Physician of Yr. award, 1985, Basic Cell Rsch. in Cytology Lectureship award, 1985, Fred W. Stewart award, 1986, Ramazzini award, 1986, Lovelace Med. Found. award, 1993. Fellow: N.Y. Acad. Sci., Soc. Risk Analysis (Outstanding Achievement award 1997); mem.: AAAS, Ramazzini Inst. (pres. 1992—2003), Assn. Univ. Environ. Health Sci. Ctrs. (pres. 1982—90), Internat. Assn. Radiation Rsch., N.Y. State Health Rsch. Coun. (chmn. 1982—90), Soc. Exptl. Biology and Medicine, Sci. Rsch. Soc. Am., Gerontol. Soc., Peruvian Oncology Soc. (hon.), Japan Cancer Assn. (hon.), Am. Soc. Exptl. Pathology (pres. 1967—68), Am. Assn. Cancer Rsch. (pres. 1963—64), Internat. Assn. Radiation Rsch. (pres. 1983—87, 1983—87), Radiation Rsch. Soc. (councilor 1963—64, pres. 1965—66), Inst. Medicine of NAS (Comfort-Crookshank award for cancer rsch. 1979), Internat. Acad. Pathology, Am. Assn. Pathologists and Bacteriologists, Sigma Xi, Nu Sigma Nu, Alpha Omega Alpha, Phi Gamma Delta, Phi Beta Kappa. Achievements include research in on pathology of radiation injury and endocrine glands, on cancer, on carcinogenesis, on experimental leukemia on aging. Office: Robert Wood Johnson Med Sch Rm N-112 675 Hoe's Ln Piscataway NJ 08854 Home: 250 E Alameda Apt 636 Santa Fe NM 87501 Office Phone: 732-235-3460. Business E-Mail: acupton@eohsi.rutgers.edu.

UPTON, CHRIS L. publishing executive; b. Tazewell, Tenn., Sept. 19, 1971; s. Lee Roy Upton and Elbra L. Davis. Dep. sheriff, jailor Union County Sheriff's Dept., Maynardville, Tenn., 1989—98; publ. Union News Leader, 1990—; dep. sheriff, jailor Claiboine County Sheriff's Dept., Tazewell, 1998—2000; police officer City of Maynardville, 1990—; jail adminstr., dep. Union County Sheriff's Dept., 2002—. Advisor Union County Sheriff's Explorers, Maynardville, 1990—, Sharps Chapel Fire Explorers, 1996—. Firefighter Sharps Chapel Vol. Fire Dept., fire chief, 1996—; mem. Sharps Chapel Cmty. Park, v.p., 1998—2000; mem. sch. bd. Union County Bd. Edn., Maynardville, 2002—. Home: 2783 Sharps Chapel Rd Sharps Chapel TN 37866 Office: Union News Leader PO Box 866 Maynardville Hwy Maynardville TN 37807 E-mail: enewspaper@aol.com.

UPTON, FREDERICK STEPHEN, congressman; b. St. Joseph, Mich., Apr. 23, 1953; s. Stephen E. and Elizabeth Brooks (Vial) U.; m. Amey Richmond Rulon-Miller, Nov. 5, 1983; 2 children. BA in Journalism, U. Mich., 1975. Staff asst. to Congressman David A. Stockman, Washington, 1976-81; legis. asst. Office Mgmt. and Budget, Washington, 1981-83, dep. dir. legis. affairs, 1983-84, dir. legis. affairs, 1984-85; mem. U.S. Congress from 6th Mich. dist., Washington, 1987—; mem. edn. and the workforce com., energy and commerce com. Field mgr. Stockman for Congress, St. Joseph, 1975; campaign mgr. Globensky for Congress, St. Joseph, 1981. Republican. Office: US House of Reps 2161 Rayburn HOB Washington DC 20515-2206 also: 157 S Kalamazoo Mall Ste 180 Kalamazoo MI 49006

UPTON, HOWARD B., JR., writer, lawyer; b. Tahlequah, Okla., May 17, 1922; s. Howard B. and Marjorie (Ross) U.; m. Jean Devereaux, June 14, 1945; children— Pamela, Barbara, Martha, Brian BA, U. Okla., 1943, LLB, 1948. Cert. assn. exec. Dir. indsl. relations Western Petroleum Refiners Assn., Tulsa, 1948-51; exec. v.p. Petroleum Equipment Inst., Tulsa, 1951-87; dir. Telex Corp., Tulsa, 1972-88; mgmt. columnist Inflight Mag. of Southwest Airlines, 1988-93. Lectr. dept. engring. profl. devel. U. Wis., 1988-97, U. Alaska, Fairbanks, 1991-93. Frequent contbr. to Wall St. Jour.; columnist Petroleum Equipment and Tech. Mag.; book rev. Tulsa World, 1999--. Dir. Tulsa Zoo Friends, Inc., 1993-97. Mem. Am. Soc. Assn. Execs. (bd. dirs. 1964-68, Gold Circle award 1977, 82), Okla. Bar Assn. Democrat. Home: 5133 E 25th Ct Tulsa OK 74114-3749

UPTON, RICHARD THOMAS, artist; b. Hartford, Conn., May 27, 1931; s. Ray Granville and Helen Marie (Colla) U.; 1 son, Richard Thomas, II. BFA, U. Conn., 1960; MFA, Ind. U., 1963. Artist-in-residence Artists for the Environ., Del. Water Gap, 1972, UGA Program Abroad, Cortona, Italy, 1982-85. Numerous exhibns. including most recently, exhibitions include Condeso/Lawler Gallery, N.Y.C., 1995, Nat. Acad. of Design, 1996, The Language of Landscape, 1997, Sordoni Art Gallery, 1997, The Drawings of Richard Upton: Ireland & Italy, List Art Gallery, Swarthmore, Ben Shahn Art Galleries, 1998, Landscape and Memory: The Paintings and Drawings of Richard Upton, 1982-1999, Houghton Gallery, The Cooper Union for the Advancement of Sci. and Art, N.Y.C., 1999, Represented in permanent collections Zimmerli Art Mus., Nat. Mus. of Am. Art, Smithsonian Instn., Mus. Modern Art, N.Y.C., Victoria and Albert Mus., London, Bibliot Nat., Paris, Montreal Mus. Fine Arts, Rose Art Mus. Brandeis, Mus. Fine Art, Houston, Nat. Acad. Design, N.Y.C., Met. Mus. Art, The Tang Tchg. Mus. and Art Gallery, Skidmore Coll.; artist (commns. include) Eros Thanatos Suite (German poem and woodcuts), Interlaken Corp., Providence, 1967, Salamovka Poster, Okla. Art Ctr., 1974, artist (with poems by Stanley Kunitz) River Road Suite, 1976, suite of drawing Robert Lowell at 66, 1977, suite of drawings Salmagundi mag. for humanities, The Anxious Landscape, paintings, drawings Bellarmine Coll., Louisville, 1989. With USNR, 1950-54. Recipient designer award Interlaken Corp., 1967; subject of monographs: Richard Upton and the Rhetoric of Landscape, Paul Hayes Tucker, U. Mass., U. Wash. Press, 1991, The Tuscan Landscapes of Richard Upton, Stanley C. Grand, Sordoni Art Gallery & Fred Licht, curator, Collezione Peggy Guggenheim, Venice, Wilkes U., 1997, The Drawings of Richard Upton, David Shapiro, Salmagundi, Skidmore Coll., 1997, Landscape & Memory: The Paintings & Drawings of Richard Upton, 1982-98, The Irwin S. Chanin Sch. Architecture of Cooper Union, 1999, A Table of Green Fields: Richard Upton's Cortona Landscapes, Richard Howard, 1999, List Gallery, Ben Shahn Galleries About Painting; Tang Teaching Mus. Art Gallery, 2004; fellow Fulbright Found., 1964, Ballinglen Arts Found., Ireland, 1994; grantee Nat. Endowment for Arts/Artists for Environ., 1972, Richard Florsheim Fund, 1992; elected to Nat. Acad. of Design, 1995, Tang Teaching Mus. and Art Gallery, 2004. Home: 1 North Ln Saratoga Springs NY 12866-4369

UPTON PUCCINELLI, NANCY MARIE, education educator, researcher; b. Walnut Creek, Calif., Apr. 27, 1971; d. Eugene Frank and Helen Louise Puccinelli; m. David Mark Upton, July 27, 2002. BA, U. of Calif., 1993; MA, Harvard Grad. Sch. of Arts and Scis., 2000; PhD, Harvard Grad. Sch. of Arts and Scis., Mass., 2000. Intern Am. Heart Assn., West Covina, Calif., 1993; tchg. asst. Harvard Grad. Sch. of Arts and Scis., Cambridge, 1995—99, rsch. asst., 1996—99; post-doctoral fellow Harvard Bus. Sch., Boston, 1999—2001; lectr. Boston U. Grad. Sch. of Mgmt., 2000; asst. prof. Emerson Coll., Boston, 2001—03; asst. prof. Sawyer Sch. of Mgmt. Suffolk Univ., 2003—; post-doctoral fellowship Harvard Bus. Sch. Cons. Coca-Cola, Germany, 2000, Procter & Gamble, Cin., 2000, Mind of the Market Lab, Harvard Bus. Sch., Boston, 2000—01. Author: (journal article) Jour. of Nonverbal Behavior, Occupl. Therapy Jour. of Rsch., (conf. paper) Easter Psychol. Assn., Assn. of Consumer Rsch., Am. Psychol. Soc. (Am. Psychol. Soc. Student Rsch. Caucus Student Rsch. Competition, 1996), (conf. special session) Soc. for Consumer Psychology, Harvard Bus. Sch. Case, (conf. paper) Soc. for Consumer Psychology. Nominee Outstanding Tchg. award, Melaine and Stanley Miller; fellow Grad. Fellowship, Kappa Kappa Gamma Found., 1995—98; grantee U. Honors Program Rsch. Grant, Am. Honda Found., 1992, Mini-Grant, U. of Calif. Riverside, 1992, Elsie Hopestill Stimson Meml. Fund, Harvard U., 1994—95, Rsch. Travel Grant, Harvard Grad. Student Coun., 1996, Barbara Ditmars Bequest, Harvard U., 1997, John B. Knox Bequest, 1997, Maria E. McMaster Bequest, 1997, Grant, Am. Psychol. Soc. Student Caucus, 1997, Faculty Advancement Fund Grant, Emerson Coll., 2001, 2002, Summer Rsch. Grant, 2002, Travel Grant, 2002, 2003. Mem.: Soc. for Consumer Psychology, Assn. of Consumer Rsch. Avocation: internat. travel. Office: Suffolk Univ 8 Ashburton Pl Boston MA 02108-2770 Personal E-mail: nancy@upton.com.

URAHN, SUSAN K. foundation administrator; BA in Sociology, D of Policy & Adminstrn., U. Minn. With rsch. dept. Minn. Ho. Reps.; dir. planning & evaluation Pew Charitable Trusts, Phila., 1994—. Rschr. in field. Contbr. tech. reports to profl. pubs. Office: Pew Charitable Trusts 2005 Market St Ste 1700 Philadelphia PA 19103-7017

URAKAMI, AKIO, manufacturing company executive; b. Tokyo, Apr. 17, 1942; came to U.S., 1991; s. Yutaka and Tomiko (Nagai) U.; m. Keiko Tanaka, Feb. 7, 1971; children: Yuji, Masako, Kota. BS, Tokyo Inst. Tech., 1965; MS, Northwestern U., 1967, PhD, 1970. Rsch. engr. Ryobi Ltd., Hiroshima, Japan, 1970-72, corp. planning mgr., 1972-76, v.p. internat., 1976-84, exec. v.p., 1984-91; chmn., pres. Ryobi N.Am., Inc., Easly Anderson, S.C., 1991—. Mem. pres.'s adv. coun. Clemson (S.C.) u., 1992—. Trustee The Urakami Found., Hiroshima, 1978—; bd. dirs. Japan Am. Assn. of We. S.C., Greenville, 1992—. Mem. Keizai Doyu Kai. Office: Ryobi NAm Inc PO Box 1207 Anderson SC 29622-1207

URAL, ERDEM A. engineering executive, educator; PhD, U. Mich. Pres. Loss Prevention Sci. and Technologies, Inc., Stoughton, Mass., 2001—; adj. prof. fire protection engring. Worcester (Mass.) Poly. Inst., 2001—. Mem. Aviation Rulemaking Adv. Com. Fuel Tank Inerting Harmonization Working Group. Contbr. articles to profl. publs., chpt. to handbook. Safety and health divsn. AIChE, New York, NY, 2002—; pres, adv. bd. Literacy Volunteers of Am., MML, Norwood, Mass., 2001. Recipient Outstanding Achievement award, FM Global; fellow, NATO, 1976—79, Rackham Sch. Grad. Studies, U.S. Dept. Energy. Mem.: NFPA (mem. phys. and chm. data consistency adv. bd. 2002—), AIChE (mem. editl. bd. Process Savety Progress), ASTM (chmn. com. 1999), Tau Beta Pi. Achievements include research in gas and dust explosions; fire/explosion protection and incident investigations; quantification of thermal environments produced by fire, heat and smoke detection; smoke transport-aging-deposition processes. Office: Loss Prevention Sci and Tech 659 Pearl St Stoughton MA 02072

URAL, OKTAY, civil engineering educator; BA in Math., Trinity U., 1956; BS in Civil Engring., Tex. A&M U.; MSCE, U. Tenn., 1959; PhD in Civil Engring., N.C. State U., 1964; BSCE, 1958. Asst. prof. U. Mo., Rolla, 1967-69, assoc. prof., 1969-73, prof., 1973, founding dir. Inst. for Interdisciplinary Housing Studies; prof. Fla. Internat. U., Miami, 1973—, founding dir. constrn. div. Coll. Engring. and Applied Scis., dir. Inst. Housing and Bldg. Lectr. various univs.; chmn., dir., 30 nat. and internat. confs.; bd. dirs. Internat. Found. Earth Constrn., Internat. Coun. Bldg. Rsch. Studies and Documentation, Rotterdam, The Netherlands, 1978-80; mem. sci. adv. panel UN Disaster Relief Orgn.; pres. Turkish Housing Authorit, advisor to prime min. Turkish Republic, 1990-92. Author: Matrix Operations and Use of Computers in Structural Engineering, 1971, Finite Element Method: Basic Concepts and Applications, 1973, A Systematic Approach to Basic Utilities in Developing Countries, 1974, Construction of Lower-Cost Housing, 1980; editor-in-chief Internat. Jour. Housing Sci. and Its Applications, 1977—; editor 22 vols. of sci. congress procs.; contbr. articles to profl. jours. Grantee HUD, Washington, Com. on Banking and Currency, U.S. Ho. of Reps., NSF, Fla. Power and Light Co., Fla. Internat. U. Found., Inc., Dept. Edn., State Fla.; recipient Medail de Vermeil for Experts, Govt. France. Fellow ASCE (chmn. structures com. on electronic computation edn. com., urban planning and devel. div. housing com., control group, Harland Bartholomew award); mem. Internat. Assn. Housing Sci. (pres.), Am. Soc. Engring. Edn. (internat. com.), Sigma Xi, Tau Beta Pi, Phi Kappa Phi, Chi Epsilon. Home: 3608 Anderson Rd Coral Gables FL 33134 Office: Fla Internat U Inst Housing & Bldg Dept Civil Engring Miami FL 33199-0001 E-mail: ural@itu.edu.tr.

URAM, GERALD ROBERT, lawyer; b. Newark, July 11, 1941; s. Arthur George and Mildred (Stein) U.; m. Melissa Gordon, May 27, 1995; children: Michael, Alison, Carolyn Gordon Lewis. BA, Dartmouth Coll., 1963; LLB, Yale U., 1967. Bar: NY 1967. Assoc. Paul, Weiss, Rifkind, Wharton & Garrison, NYC, 1967-74; v.p., corp. counsel Prudential Bldg. Maintenance Corp., NYC, 1974; ptnr. Davis & Gilbert, NYC, 1974—. Lectr. NY Law Sch.

Contbr. to profl. publs. Bd. dirs. St. Francis Friends of Poor, Inc. Mem. ABA, NY State Bar Assn., Assn. Bar City of NY. Office: 1740 Broadway Fl 3 New York NY 10019-4315 Office Phone: 212-468-4815. Business E-Mail: guram@dglaw.com.

URANGA, JEAN R. lawyer; b. West Point, N.Y., Sept. 30, 1949; BA, Western Wash. U., 1971; JD, Willamette U., 1975. Bar: Idaho 1975, U.S. Dist. Ct. Idaho 1975, U.S. Ct. Appeals (9th cir.) 1980. Atty. Uranga & Uranga, Boise, Idaho. Mem.: Idaho State Bar (continuing legal edn. com. 1987—90, discipline hearing com. 1983—86, Supreme Ct. com. on child custody mediation 1989—, bankruptcy and family law sects., bar commr. 1990—93, pres. 1992). Office: Uranga and Uranga PO Box 1678 714 N Fifth St Boise ID 83701-1678

URATO, BARBRA CASALE, entrepreneur; b. Newark, Oct. 10, 1941; d. Dominick Anthony and Concetta (Castrichini) Casale; m. John Joseph Urato, June 20, 1965; children: Concetta U. Graves, Gina E., Joseph D. Student, Seton Hall U., 1961-63. File clk. Martin Gelber Esquire, Newark, 1956-58; policy typist Aetna Casualty Ins., Newark, 1959-61; sec. to dean Seton Hall U., South Orange, N.J., 1961-63; paralegal sec. Judge Robert A. McKinley, Newark, 1963-65, Joseph Garrubbo, Esquire, Newark, 1965-66; office mgr. Valiant I.M.C., Hackensack, N.J., 1971-73; asst. pers. mgr. Degussa Inc., Teterboro, N.J., 1975-78; night mgr. The Ferryboat Restaurant, River Edge, N.J., 1976-78; mgr. Fratello's and Ventilini's, Hilton Head, S.C., 1978-80; day mgr. Ramada Inn Restaurant, Paramus, N.J., 1980-81; mgr. Gottlieb's Bakery, Hilton Head, 1982-83; asst. mgr. closing dept. Hilton Head Mortgage Co., 1983-84; owner, mgr. All Cleaning Svc., Hilton Head, 1984—; owner Hilton Head Investigations, 1990-93, 1990-92, Aaction Investigators, 1992-94. Mem. NAFE, Profl. Women of Hilton Head, Assn. for Rsch. and Enlightenment, Rosicrucian Order. Roman Catholic. Avocations: metaphysics, music, gardening, learning.

URBACH, MICHAEL H. utilities/energy executive; CPA. Ptnr. Urbach, Kahn and Werlin, P.C.; commr. N.Y. State Taxation and Fin., 1995-99; sr. v.p., CFO N.Y. Power Authority, White Plains, 1999—. Chair State Employees Federated Appeal, 1996-97. Bd. mem. Russell Sage Coll.; past pres. Coun. Cmty. Svcs., Equinox, Inc., Albany Jewish Cmty. Ctr., Colonie Country Club; past chmn. St. Peter's Hosp. Assocs.; officer, bd. mem. United Way Northeastern N.Y., Albany Boys Club, Albany Jewish Cmty. Coun., Hospitality House, Sr. Svcs. Albany, Jr. Achievement of the Capital Dist. Mem. AICPA, N.Y. State Soc. CPAs (Outstanding CPA in Govt. award 1997). Office: NY Power Authority 123 Main St White Plains NY 10601

URBAN, ALAN GENE, painter, art executive; b. Chgo., Apr. 12, 1948; s. Ernest Frank and Jean Barbara (Jenicek) U.; m. Katherine Ann Taylor, Apr. 17, 1982; children: Jennifer, Alexander. AA, Miami-Dade C.C., 1968; BA, U. South Fla., 1971. Art dir. St. Petersburg (Fla.) Times Pub. Co., 1972-75; pres., creative dir. Urban, Taylor and Assocs., Miami, 1975—; sr. ptnr. Fiddler and Urban, Inc., Miami, 1982—. Cons. El Norte Pub. Co., Monterey, Mex., 1979-80, Columbus (Ohio) Dispatch Pub. Co., 1980-81, El Diaria De Nuevo Laredo (Mex.), 1982-84, Zocalo Pub. Co., Piedras Negras, Mex., 1985—, Ctr. for Fine Arts, Miami, 1993-95. Exhibited in group shows at Soc. Four Arts, 1979, 99, Nat. All Media Competition, Ridge Art Assn., 2000, Art 2000, Nathan D. Rosen Mus. Gallery, 2D/3D All Fla. Exhbn., Ft. Myers Alliance for the Arts, 2000, Spin-Nat. Theme Show (1st place award), Alan Urban, Paintings and Graphic Design (two-person show), Pensacola Jr. Coll. Gallery, 1999, All-Fla. Juried Competition and Exhbn. (Merit award), 1999, 2000, Print Regional Design Annual show, 1986 (2 certs. of excellecnce), Graphic Design: USA, 1986 (2 Desi awards), Printing Industry Am. show, 1986 (Best of Category award), Pensacola Jr. Coll. Art Gallery, 1999, Boca Raton Mus. Art, 2000; published in art and design mags. including Typograph 13 (Merit award) How Mag., Publish Mag., Design Ann. (2 Best in Category awards), Graphic Design Inspirations and Innovations, Prints Regional Design Anns., 90-92 (5 merit awards); patentee antenna device. Sustaining mem. Sta. WPBT Pub. Television, Miami, 1979; mem. Met. Mus. and Art Ctr., Miami, 1987. Recipient IMMY award Info. Industry Assn., 1985, Award of Merit, Boca Raton Mus., 1999; 9 awards of merit, Am. Inst. Graphic Arts, 1990, 11 awards of merit, 1992, award of merit, Graphis Design, 1993. Mem. Am. Adv. Fedn. (ADDY awards 1985—), Am. Inst. Graphic Artists, Graphic Arts Guild, Soc. Publ. Designers (Award of Merit 1985), Soc. Newspaper Design, Ft. Lauderdale Mus. of Art, Boca Raton Mus. of Art, Bakehouse Art Complex, Art Ctr./S. Fla., Lowe Art Mus., Mus. of Contemporary Art. Republican. Presbyterian. Office: Urban Taylor and Assocs 12250 SW 131st Ave Miami FL 33186-6402

URBAN, AMANDA (BINKY URBAN), literary agent; m. Ken Auletta, 1977; 1 child. BA in English, Wheaton Coll., Mass. Gen. mgr. N.Y. mag.; editl. mgr. Esquire mag.; literary agent Internat. Creative Mgmt., N.Y.C., v.p., co-dir. lit. dept., 1988—98, co-head, 1999—. Office: Internat Creative Mgmt 40 W 57th St New York NY 10019*

URBAN, FRANK HENRY, retired dermatologist, state legislator; b. St. Louis, May 24, 1930; s. Frank and Helen Gertrude (Zingsheim) U.; m. Lois Elaine Thurwachter, June 18, 1954 (dec. 1991); children: James, Barbara, Michael, Mark, David, Bruce, John; m. Kathryn Calvert Bloomberg, Nov. 28, 1992. BS in Med. Sci., U. Wis., 1951, MD, 1954; MS, U. Minn., 1960. Diplomate Am. Bd. Dermatology. Intern Beaumont Army Hosp., El Paso, 1954-55; resident Mayo Clinic, Rochester, Minn., 1957-60; pvt. practice dermatology Wauwatosa, Wis., 1960-93; asst. clin. prof. Med. Coll. Wis., Wauwatosa, 1964—; mem. Wis. State Assembly, Madison, 1989—. Trustee Village Bd. of Elm Grove, Wis., 1985-87, pres., 1987-89; bd. dirs. ARC of Greater Milw.; pres. Friends U. Wis.-Milw. Sch. Edn., 1995—, bd. dirs.; hon. mem. Potawatomi coun. Boy Scouts Am., pres., 1974-76. Recipient Silver Beaver award East Cen. Region Boy Scouts Am., 1972, Silver Antelope award, 1979, Civic Leadership award State Med. Soc. Wis., 1990, Disting. Svc. award U. Wis. Med. Sch. Alumni Assn., 1991. Fellow Am. Acad. Dermatology; mem. Wis. Dermatol. Soc. (pres. 1969-70), Wis. State Med. Soc. (dir. 1987-92, 93—), Milw. County Med. Soc. (caucus chmn. 1987-92, pres.-elect 1992-93, pres. 1993-94), Brookfield C. of C. (Outstanding Mem. award 1992). Republican. Roman Catholic. Avocations: walking, photography, toy trains, music. Office: State Capitol PO Box 8953 Madison WI 53708-8953

URBAN, GLEN L. management educator; b. Wausau, Wis., Apr. 15, 1940; BSME, U. Wis., 1963, MBA, 1964; PhD, Northwestern U., 1966. Asst. prof. MIT, Cambridge, Mass., 1966-70, assoc. prof., 1970-77, prof. mktg. and mgmt. sci., 1977—, Dai-Ichi Kangyo Bank prof. mgmt., 1987-93, dep. dean Sloan Sch. Mgmt., 1987-91, co-dir. Internat. Ctr. for Rsch. on Mgmt. of Tech., 1992-93, dean Sloan Sch. Mgmt., 1993-98, prof. mgmt., 1998—. Co-founder Mgmt. Decision Systems, Inc., 1970, Mgmt. Sci. for Health, Inc., 1972, Mktg. Tech. Interface, Inc., 1991, InSite Mktg., 1997. Author: (with D.B. Montgomery) Management Science in Marketing, 1969, (with J.R. Hauser and N. Dholakia) Essentials of New Product Development, 1987, (with Steven H. Star) Advanced Marketing Stragety: Phenomena, Analysis and Decisions, 1991, Design and Marketing of New Products, 2d edit., 1993; mem. editl. bd. Mktg. Sci.; reviewer for Mgmt. Sci. (Best Paper award 1986), Jour. Mktg. Rsch. (O'Dell award 1983, 88), Ops. Rsch., Jour. Mktg. (Best Paper award 1996); contbr. over 30 articles to profl. jours. Recipient Best Paper award Jour. of Mktg., 1996. Mem. Inst. Mgmt. Sci., Ops. Rsch. Soc. Am., Am. Mktg. Assn. (Converse award for Lifetime Achievements in Mktg. 1996). Office: MIT Sloan Sch Mgmt 38 Memorial Dr # E56-332 Cambridge MA 02142-1347 E-mail: glurban@mit.edu.

URBAN, HENRY ZELLER, newspaperman; b. Buffalo, July 11, 1920; s. George Pennock and Florence Lenhard (Zeller) U.; m. Ruth deMoss Wickwire, Apr. 28, 1948; children: Ruth Robinson Urban Smith, Florence de Moss Urban Hunn, Henry Zeller, Ward Wickwire. Grad., Hotchkiss Sch., 1939; BS, Yale U., 1943. Treas. George Urban Milling Co., 1946-53; with Buffalo Eve. News, 1953—, asst. bus. mgr., 1957-62, bus. mgr., 1962-71, treas., dir., 1971-74, pres., pub., 1974-83. Bd. dirs. Travelers Aid Soc., 1953-59, Buffalo Fine Arts Acad., 1960-63, 73-76, 82-89, YMCA, 1955-68; trustee Elmwood-Franklin Sch., 1967-70; trustee Canisius Coll., 1977-83, bd. regents, 1972-78; adv. bd. Medaille Coll., 1968-83; chmn. parents council Hamilton Coll., 1977. Lt. USNR, 1942-46. Mem. Buffalo C. of C., N.Y. State Pubs. Assn. (dir. 1970-73, 76-79) Clubs: Mid-day (Buffalo), Tennis and Squash (Buffalo), Buffalo (Buffalo), Buffalo Country (Buffalo), Saturn (Buffalo), Pack (Buffalo); Sankaty Head (Nantucket); Nantucket Yacht. Home: 57 Tudor Pl Buffalo NY 14222-1615 Office: 1 News Plz Buffalo NY 14203-2930

URBAN, JOSEPH JAROSLAV, engineer, consultant; b. Chocen, Czechoslovakia, Mar. 11, 1922; came to U.S., 1955; s. Josef and Ludmila (Moravcova) U.; children: H.U. Heinicke, R. Bruce. Diploma in engring., U. Prague, Czechoslovakia, 1948; postgrad., U. Toronto, 1952-55. Registered profl. engr. Mgr. Urban Mfg., Chocen, 1942-48; prof. Masaryk U., Nuernberg, Fed. Republic Germany, 1950; designer C.A. Meadows Cons. Engrs., Toronto, 1952-55, Rondo Devel. Corp., Stamford, Conn., 1955-58; designer, chief engr., v.p. Huck Co. Inc. Engrs., Montvale, N.J., 1958-72, also bd. dirs.; pvt. practive cons. engr. Pleasantville, N.Y., 1972—. Exec. cons. Crown Cork and Seal Co. Inc., Phila., 1972=94. Designer various types of machines for U.S. govt. and U.S. industries-printing presses, book binding and can mfg. equipment, pinsetter, computers, glass machines; writer tech. books; patentee in field. Recipient World War II decoration Field Marshall Alexander, 1945., Outstanding Person 20th Century. Mem. Acad. Art and Sci., Moose, K.C. Roman Catholic. Avocations: protection of wildlife, naturalist, painting, classical music, fine art collector. Home and Office: 71 Bacon Hill Rd Pleasantville NY 10570-3501

URBAN, KEITH, country singer, songwriter; b. New Zealand, Oct. 26, 1967; Former band mem. (with Peter Clarke) The Ranch, Nashville, 1997; signed record deal with Capital Nashville, 1997; signed mgmt. contract with I.R.S., Tenn., 1997. Singer: (albums) "1991", 1997, Ranch, 1997, Keith Urban, 1999, Golden Road, 2002, In the Ranch, 2004, (singles) Raining on Sunday, 2003; singer, prodr.: singles "Somebody Like You", How To Lose A Guy In 10 Days (Original Soundtrack), 2003. Recipient Grammy award nomination for best country instrumental performance for "Rollercoaster", ARIA award for outstanding acheivement, Australian Record Industry Assn., 2001. Mailing: Capital Records 3322 W End Ave Nashville TN 37203 Office Phone: 615-269-2000.*

URBAN, MISTY RAE, research scientist; b. Wisconsin Rapids, Wis., July 6, 1975; d. Roy John and Mary Urban. BBA, U. Wus, Whitewater, 1997; MA, Fla. State U., 2003. Cons. Accenture, Milw., 1997—2000; dept. mgr. Barnes & Noble, Inc., Madison, Wis., 2000—01; grad. tchg. asst. Fla. State U., Tallahassee, 2001—03; grad. rschr. Cornell U., Ithaca, NY, 2003—. Tutor in English. Mem. selection com. Traci D. Urban Meml. Scholarship, Wisconsin Rapids, Wis., 1997—2003. Sage fellow, Cornell U., 2003—04. Mem.: SE Medieval Assn.

URBAN, NICOLE D. biostatistician; b. Trenton, NJ, Aug. 16, 1946; d. James Ross Stewart and Patricia Bryant Urban; m. Lee Emery Edlefsen (div.); children: Kerstin Lara Edlefsen, Paul Thatcher Edlefsen. BA in English lit., Simmons Coll., 1970; MS in biostatistics, Harvard Sch. of Pub. Health, 1973, DSc, 1978. Prin. investigator, Specialized Program of Rsch. Excellence grant in ovarian cancer NIH/Nat. Cancer Inst., Seattle, 1999—; sci. dir. Marsha Rivkin Ctr. for Ovarian Cancer Rsch., Seattle, 1996—; mem., cancer prevention rsch. program, divsn. of pub. health sciences Fred Hutchinson Cancer Rsch. Ctr., Seattle, 1998—; rsch. prof., dept. of health services, sch. of pub. health and cmty. medicine U. of Wash., Seattle, 2000—; program head, gynecologic cancer rsch. program Fred Hutchinson Cancer Rsch. Ctr., Seattle, 2001—. Mem., p30/p50 working group Nat. Cancer Adv. Bd., 2002—; participant, strategic planning project meeting, applied cancer screening rsch. br. Nat. Cancer Inst., 2001—; mem., external adv. com., specialized program of rsch. excellence in breast cancer Vanderbilt U., 2001—; mem., med. adv. bd. Nat. Ovarian Cancer Coalition, 2001—; chair, external adv. com., specialized program of rsch. excellence in ovarian cancer U. of Tex., 2000—; co-chair, gynecologic cancers progress rev. group Nat. Cancer Inst., 2000—; mem., wash. state cancer registry adv. coun. Wash. State Dept. of Health, 1996—, mem., breast and cervical early detection exec. com., 1994—. Contbr. articles to profl. jours. Grant, Nat. Institutes of Health/Nat. Cancer Inst., 1999—, US Dept. of Def., 2002—, Nat. Institutes of Health/Nat. Cancer Inst., 1997—2002, 1997—2002, US Dept. of Def./United States Army Med. Rsch. and Materiel Command (Ovarian Cancer Rsch. Program), 1998—2001. Mem.: Am. Assn. for Cancer Rsch., South West Oncology Group, Assn. for Health Services Rsch., Am. Soc. of Preventive Oncology, Soc. for Clin. Trials. Office: Fred Hutchinson Cancer Rsch Ctr PO Box 19024 Seattle WA 98109-1024

URBANAS, ALBAN WILLIAM, estate planner; b. Balt., Jan. 5, 1952; s. William Peter and Anna Mary (Danaitis) U.; m. Elizabeth Iza Davis, Nov. 18, 1995. BA, U. Paris-Sorbonne, 1976, PhD, 1982; MBA, George Mason U., 1994. Instr. ESL The Paris-Am. Acad., Paris, 1977-78; coord. French & English programs Marubeni-France, Paris, 1978-81; adj. asst. prof. English U. Paris, 1978-81; coord. French and English programs CACI Lang. Ctr., Arlington, Va., 1983-85; adj. asst. prof. philosophy Georgetown U., Washington, 1983-84; vis. asst. prof. French George Washington U., Washington, 1985, adj. asst. prof. philosophy, 1985-86; asst. prof. philosophy & French Franklin Coll., Lugano, Switzerland, 1986-89; vis. asst. prof. philosophy Colby Coll., Waterville, Maine, 1989-90; vis. asst. prof. French NYU, Paris, 1990; assoc. prof. philosophy and French Wesley Coll., Dover, Del., 1990-97; vis. assoc. prof. philosophy Washington Coll., Chestertown, Md., 1997-98; estate planner, 1998—. Moderator Aspen Inst., 1997—. Author: La notion d'accident chez Aristote, 1988; contbr. articles to profl. jours. Bd. dirs. Dover Arts Coun., 1993-96, Del. Ballet, 1994-95; bd. dirs., v.p. Alliance Française of Wilmington, Del., 1993-96. Recipient Lithuanian Lang. Inst. Title grant USSR Ministry Culture, 1986; NEH grantee U. Ill., 1991; French Cultural Svcs. scholar, Strasbourg, 1992; Jesse Ball duPont Found. fellow, 1992, 96. Mem. Am. Philos. Assn., Am. Mgmt. Assn., Internat. Assn. Mgmt., Balt. Coun. Fgn. Rels. Avocations: marathon running, investment theory, international travel, hiking, skiing. Office: Sagemark Cons Inc 2070 Chain Bridge Rd Ste 300 Vienna VA 22182-2596

URBANETTI, JOHN SUTHERLAND, internist, consultant; b. Mineola, N.Y., Aug. 14, 1943; s. Anthony Joseph and Mildred S. U.; children: Andrew, Alexis. AB, Johns Hopkins U., 1964, MD, 1967. Diplomate Am. Bd. Internal Medicine and Pulmonary Diseases. Internal medicine intern Johns Hopkins Hosp., Balt., 1967-68, internal medicine resident, 1968-69; fellow in pulmonary cardiology McGill U., Montreal, Can., 1971-74; asst. prof. medicine and dir. pulmonary lab. Tufts New Eng. Med. Ctr. Hosp., Boston, 1974-80; asst. prof. clin. medicine and pulmonary diseases Yale U., New Haven, Conn., 1980—. Cons. toxic inhalation US Surgeon Gen., U.S. Army, USN, USAF, 1974—; cons. biochem. terrorism Dept. of Def., Dept. Justice, 1974—, Dept. State, 1999—. Author: Carbon Monoxide Poisoning, 1980, Pulmonary Management of Surgical Patients, 1982, Battlefield Chemical Inhalation, 1988, Chemical and Biological Warfare, 1997; contbr. articles to profl. jours. Capt. USAF, 1969-71. Recipient Commdr's award for pub. svc. U.S. Army, 1990. Fellow Royal Coll. Physicians and Surgeons (Can.), Am. Coll. Physicians, Am. Coll. Chest Physicians; mem. Am. Thoracic Soc., Aerospace Medicine Soc. Avocation: swimming. Office: Southeastern Pulmonary Assocs 155 Montauk Ave New London CT 06320-4842 Office Phone: 860-444-2223. Business E-Mail: jsu@jhu.edu.

URBANIK, THOMAS, II, civil engineering educator, researcher; b. Oceanside, N.Y., Feb. 15, 1946; s. John George and Helen Rita (Waterhouse) U.; m. Cynthia Ellen Myers, Feb. 23, 1948; children: Michael T., Steven J. BS, N.Y. State Coll. Forestry, 1968; BSCE, Syracuse U., 1969; MSCE, Purdue U., 1971; PhD, Tex. A&M U., 1982. Registered profl. engr., Mich., Tex., Tenn. Traffic engr. City of Ann Arbor (Mich.), 1971-76; rsch. engr. Tex. A&M U., College Station, 1977—2001; prof., Goodrich chair of excellence in transp. U. Tenn., Knoxville, 2001—. Cons. Battelle Pacific N.W. Labs., Richland, Wash., Fed. Hwy. Adminstrn., Washington, Kittelson and Assocs., Portland, Oreg., Entergy, Buchanan, NY. Mem. ASCE, Inst. Transp. Engrs., Transp. Rsch. Bd. (assoc.). Republican. Lutheran. Office Phone: 865-974-7709. E-mail: turbanik@utk.edu.

URBANO, JUAN ANTONIO, broadcast executive, television producer, television director; b. Havana, Cuba, Jan. 5, 1968; s. Antonio and Nereyda (Perez) Urbano; m. Veronica Delgado; 1 child, John Anthony. AS in Film Prodn., Miami Dade C.C. Creative svcs. editor WSVN Channel 7, Miami Beach, Fla., 1988—94; prodr., editor Visionline, Inc., Miami, Fla., 1994—2004; sr. prodr., sr. editor MGM Networks L.Am. LLC, Miami, Fla., 1999—, promotions mgr., 2002—03, promotions and opers. mgr., 2003—. Recipient Suncoast Regional Emmy, NATAS, 1997, 1998. Mem.: Nat. Acad. of Arts and Scis. Roman Catholic. Avocations: scuba diving, camping, travel. Office Phone: 308-934-2740. Personal E-mail: urbanob@bellsouth.net. E-mail: juanurbano@bellsouth.net.

URBANOWSKI, FRANK, publishing company executive; b. Balt., Mar. 5, 1936; s. Frank and Tofilla (Jakubik) U.; m. Julia Blocksma; children: Alexandra, Tasha. BS in Ceramic Engring., Va. Poly. Inst.; postgrad., Columbia U. Rep. Ronald Press, 1960-61; editor coll. dept. Macmillan Co., 1961-66; editorial dir. Glencoe Press, 1966-68, v.p., 1968-72, pub., 1972-73; dir. market devel. Ednl. Testing Service, 1973-75; dir. Mass. Inst. Tech. Press, Cambridge, 1975—2003. Chmn. exec. coun. Profl. Scholarly Publs. divsn., 1979-81; bd. dirs. Cambridge Insight Meditation Ctr., 1985—; bd. dirs. Wisdom Press, U. Calif. Press., Transaction Press, U. Press NE; trustee MCLE. Mem. Am. Assn. Pubs. (dir. 1979-81), Assn. Am. Univ. Press (dir. 1979-81, pres. 1990-91), Cambridge Boat Club. Home: 915 Snake Mountain Rd Middlebury VT 05753-9220 Office: MIT Press 5 Cambridge Ctr Cambridge MA 02142-1407 E-mail: furb@mit.edu.

URBIK, JEROME ANTHONY, financial consultant; b. Chgo., Oct. 30, 1929; s. Anthony Frank and Sophie Elizabeth Urbik; m. Barbara Jean Chamernik, Sept. 1956; children: Laura M. Kern, Michael A., Anthony J., Mary King Gil, John T., Maria T. BA in Philosophy, St. Mary's Coll., Techny, Ill., 1953; CLU degree, Am. Coll., 1970, ChFC degree, 1979. Chartered fin. cons. Field underwriter MONY Fin. Svcs., Chgo., 1955-59, merchandising specialist N.Y.C., 1959; pvt. practice brokerage cons. Northfield, Ill., 1960-64; CEO Hinsdale (Ill.) Assocs. Fin. Svcs. Corp., 1964-90, CEO emeritus, 1990—. V.p. Interstate Coll. Personology, San Diego, 1982-87; pres. Gen. Agts. Mgrs. Conf., 1967-68. Mem. publ. com. Crisis mag., Washington, 1989—; contbr. articles on industry to profl. jours.; mem. editl. bd. Leaders mag., 1981-90. Mem. adv. coun. Congressman Henry Hyde, Nat. Rep. Com., Washington; mem. Small Bus. Devel. Ctr. exec. bd. advisors Lewis U., Lockport, Ill., 1987-90; exec. coord. Legatus of Chgo., 1990-91 (Cath. CEO); bd. dirs. United Rep. Fund, 1987-92; bd. advisors Am. Life League, Washington, 1990-98, Cath. Citizens Ill., 1997—; bd. dirs. Nat. Rep. Coalition for Life, 1990—. Named Small Bus. Acct. of Yr. for State of Ill. SBA, 1987. Mem. Am. Soc. CLUs, Chgo. Orchestral Assn., Chgo. Lyric Opera, Latin Liturgy Assn. (v.p. Chgo. chpt. 1997—). Roman Catholic. Avocations: reading, writing, power boating, classical music. Home: 474 South St Elmhurst IL 60126-4120 Office: Hinsdale Assoc Fin Svc Corp 15 Spinning Wheel Rd Ste 414 Hinsdale IL 60521-2987 Office Phone: 630-325-7100. E-mail: jaurbik@comcast.net.

URBINA, FEBE GLORIA, elementary school principal; b. Nuevo Laredo, Tamaulipas, Mexico, Aug. 25, 1942; came to U.S., 1947; d. Manuel Urbina and Irene Salce de Urbina. BA, Howard Payne Coll., 1965; MEd, U. Houston, 1975. Cert. tchr., adminstr., biling. educator, spcl. edn., mid mgmt., ednl. diagnostician, Tex. Cashier Weingarten Grocery, Houston, 1960-64; social worker Neighborhood Ctrs. Assn., Houston, 1965-68; elem. sch. tchr. Houston Ind. Sch. Dist., 1968-70, curriculum coord., 1970-2000, prin., 1973—. Adj. instr. Adult Edn. Houston C.C., 1965-71; mem. Legal United L.Am. Citizens Ednl. Adv. Bd., Houston, 1975-76; adj. English tchr. Harris County C.C., Pasadena, Tex., 1986-88; mem. supt.'s adv. bd. Houston Ind. Sch. Dist., 1990-97; presenter Conv. of Excellence, 1988, 90, 95, 98, Conv. Sch. External Funds, 1998, Lightspan Conv., 1998. Co-author: (book) Strategies for Bilingual/ESL Teachers, 1968. Sunday Sch. Tchr. Southmain Bapt. Ch., Houston, 1970-76; ch. pianist Heights Bapt. Temple, Houston, 1976-86; mem. Meadowbrook Civic Club, Houston, 1987-98. Recipient Mary Hill Davis award Home Mission Bd., Atlanta, 1961; named Hispanic Principal of Yr., Houston Ind. Sch. Dist. 1975, Principal of Yr. 1994. Mem. ASCD, Houston Assn. for Sch. Adminstrs. Avocations: travel, music, mission trips, translating, reading. Home: 899 Old Genoa Red Bluff Rd Houston TX 77034-4010 Office: Bonner Elem Sch 8100 Elrod St Houston TX 77017-5216

URBINA, MANUEL, II, legal research historian, history educator; b. Rodriguez, Nuevo Leon, Mex., Sept. 23, 1939; came to U.S., 1947; s. Manuel and Irene (Salce) de Urbina. BA, Howard Payne Coll., 1962; postgrad., Nat. Autonoma U. Mex., Mexico City, 1963-64; MA, U. Tex., 1967, PhD, 1976; postgrad., Cambridge (Eng.) U., 1982; JD, U. Houston, 1983. Prof. Latin Am. history Coll. of the Mainland, Texas City, Tex., 1967—. Founder, curator Urbina Mus. History of Mex., Houston, 1990—; chmn., legal counsel Urbina Found., Houston, 1985—; chmn., CEO Urbina Pub. Co. Inc., Houston and Mexico City, 1985—. Author: (TV Series) The Mexican Side of the Texas Revolution, 1985, The Mexican Side of the Mexican War, 1985, The Battle of San Jacinto-A Mexican Viewpoint, 1985, The Battle of the Alamo-A Mexican Viewpoint, 1986, Relations Between the United States and Mexico, 1987, General Emiliano Zapata in North American Historiography, 1989, The Mexican War in International Law, 1995, The Mexican War in United States Constitutional Law, 1996, Efectos De La Independencia De Texas Sobre El Gobierno, La Política, Y La Sociedad De México, 1996, Bilingual Dollars of the Bank of Texas (1835) in the Context of the Separation of Texas From Mexico, 1998, General Pancho Villa in International Law, 1999; editor, interviewer history videos, oral history interviews with participants in the Mexican Revolution; contbr. articles to newspapers and mags. including Houston Chronicle, Mexico City Novedades, San Antonio Light, Boletin Del Archivo General Del Estado de Nuevo León, Boletin de la Sociedad Numismatica de Mexico. Founder Cinco de Mayo Assn., Galveston County, Tex., 1976; founder, faculty sponsor Mex. Am. Student Assn., Coll. of Mainlan, 1974—. Named Hispanic of Yr. Galveston County League of United Latin Am. Citizens, 1982; NEH grantee, 1971-72; U.S. Dept. State scholar diplomat, 1979. Mem. League of United Latin Am. Citizens, Tex. State Hist. Assn., Howard Payne U. Alumni Assn., U. Houston Law Alumni Assn., U. Tex. Alumni Assn., Interam. C. of C., Soc. Numismatica Mex. Democrat. Baptist. Avocations: reading, research, travel, trumpet playing, volunteer work. Home: 887 Old Genoa Red Bluff Rd Houston TX 77034-4010

URBINA, RICARDO MANUEL, judge; b. 1946; BA, Georgetown U., 1967, JD, 1970. Trial atty. Pub. Defender Svc. for D.C., 1970-72; prin. Urbina & Libby, Washington, 1972-73, Law Office of Ricardo M. Urbina, Washington, 1973-74; prof. law, dir. criminal justice program Howard U., Washington, 1974-81; assoc. judge D.C. Superior Ct., 1981-94; judge U.S. Dist. Ct. D.C., 1994—. Adj. prof. Antioch Sch. Law, 1976, Georgetown U. Law Ctr., Washington, 1982, George Washington U. Nat. Law Ctr., Washington, 1993—; instr. Nat. Inst. Trial Advocacy, 1976, 78; vis. instr. trial advocacy Howard Law Sch., 1996—. Recipient VIDA award lifetime recognition cmty. svc.; All-Am. track and field NCAA 880 Champion, 1966; named Georgetown U. Athletic Hall of Fame. Mem. ABA, D.C. Hispanic Bar Assn., Nat. Bar Assn., Hispanic Nat. Bar Assn., Washington Bar Assn., D.C. Bar Assn., Women's Bar Assn., Fahy Inns of Ct. (emeritus), Counsellors of Washington D.C., Coun. for Ct. Excellence, Nat. Coun. La Raza, Phi Delta Phi. Office: US Dist Ct DC US Courthouse Rm 4311 333 Constitution Ave NW Washington DC 20001-2802

URBINA, SUSANA PATRICIA, psychology educator, consultant; came to U.S., 1962; d. Fernando Alfredo and Patricia Urbina. BA magna cum laude, Mary Manse Coll., Toledo, 1966; MA, Fordham U., 1968, PhD, 1972. Lic psychologist, Fla. Asst. prof. psychology Marywood Coll., Scranton, Pa., 1972-73, Mary Manse Coll., Toledo, 1973-75; dir. YWCA Women's Ctr., Toledo, 1975; lectr. in psychology U. Md. European Divsn., Germany, 1975-76; adviser, asst. prof. psychology U. North Fla., Jacksonville, 1976-80, assoc. prof., 1980-98, prof., 1998—. Field supr. Psychol. Corp., N.Y.C., 1979; pvt. practice psychol. assessment, 1978-92. Author books, reports and jour. articles in field. Bd. dirs. Hubbard House, Jacksonville, 1983-86. Fellow APA (vol. abstractor 1977-81, com. profl. practice and standards 1992-94, chair

1994, com. psychol. tests and assessment 1998-2000, chair 1999, continuing profl. edn. com., 2004-06), Soc. for Personality Assessment; mem. Southeastern Psychol. Assn., Jacksonville Women's Network, Sigma Xi, Kappa Gamma Pi. Democrat. Avocations: bicycling, swimming, reading, movies. Office: U North Fla Dept Psychology 4567 Saint Johns Bluff Rd S Jacksonville FL 32224-2646

URBOM, WARREN KEITH, federal judge; b. Atlanta, Nebr., Dec. 17, 1925; s. Clarence Andrew and Anna Myrl (Irelan) U.; m. Joyce Marie Crawford, Aug. 19, 1951; children: Kim Marie, Randall Crawford, Allison Lee, Joy Renee. AB with highest distinction, Nebr. Wesleyan U., 1950, LLD (hon.), 1984; JD with distinction, U. Mich., 1953. Bar: Nebr. 1953. Mem. firm Baylor, Evnen, Baylor, Urbom, & Curtiss, Lincoln, Nebr., 1953-70; judge U.S. Dist. Ct. Nebr., 1970—; chief judge U.S. Dist. Ct. Dist. Nebr., 1972-86, sr. judge, 1991—. Mem. com. on practice and procedure Nebr. Supreme Ct., 1965-95; mem. subcom. on fed. jurisdiction Jud. Conf. U.S., 1975-83; adj. instr. trial advocacy U. Nebr. Coll. Law, 1979-90; bd. dirs. Fed. Jud. Ctr., 1982-86; chmn. com. on orientation newly apptd. dist. judges Fed. Jud. Ctr., 1986-89; mem. 8th Cir. Com. on Model Criminal and Civil Jury Instrns., 1983—; mem. adv. com. on alternative sentences U.S. Sentencing Com., 1989-91. Contbr. articles to profl. jours. Trustee St. Paul Sch. Theology, Kansas City, Mo., 1986-89; active United Methodist Ch. (bd. mgrs., bd. global ministries 1972-76, gen. com. on status and role of women, 1988-96, gen. conf. 1972, 76, 80, 88, 92, 96, 2000); pres. Lincoln YMCA, 1965-67; bd. govs. Nebr. Wesleyan U., chmn. 1975-80. With AUS, 1944-46. Recipient Medal of Honor, Nebr. Wesleyan U. Alumni Assn., 1983. Fellow Am. Coll. Trial Lawyers; mem. ABA, Nebr. Bar Assn. (ho. of dels. 1966-70, Outstanding Legal Educator award 1990), Lincoln Bar Assn. (Liberty Bell award 1993, pres. 1968-69), Kiwanis (Disting. Svc. award 1993), Masons (33 deg., Grand Master's Humanitarian award 2003), Am. Inns of Ct. (Lewis F. Powell Jr. award for Professionalism and Ethics 1995), Robert Van Pelt Am. Inn of Ct. (Lifetime Mentor award, 2002). Methodist. Home: 4421 Ridgeview Dr Lincoln NE 68516-1516 Office: US Dist Ct 586 Fed Bldg 100 Centennial Mall N Lincoln NE 68508-3859 E-mail: urbom1@aol.com.

URCIOLO, JOHN RAPHAEL, II, real estate developer, real estate and finance educator; b. Washington, June 29, 1947; s. Joseph John and Phillie Marie (Petrone) U.; m. Jean Marie Manning, Jan. 2, 1972 (dec. Jan. 1990); m. Andrea Zedalis, Mar. 9, 2002. BBA, Am. U., 1969, MS in real estate, 1971. Cert. real estate broker, appraiser. Rschr. Homer Hoyt Inst., Washington, 1967-69; econ. Nat. Assn. Home Builders, Washington, 1971-75; lectr., assoc. prof. Montgomery Coll., Rockville, Md., 1971-72; assoc. prof. U. Md., College Park, 1972-79; property mgr. Urciolo Realty Co., Washington, 1976-79; comml. broker Urciolo & Urciolo, Washington, 1980-82; real estate developer Urciolo Properties, LLC, Takoma Park, Md., 1982—. Cons. Nat. Ski Area Assn., Hartford, 1978-79, Montgomery County Govt., Rockville, 1980-81; adj. prof. Am. U., Washington, 1980-91; court expert Superior Ct. for D.C., Civil and Criminal divsns.; lectr. to various orgns. Author: Real Estate Manual, 1976; co-author: The White Book of Ski Areas (U.S. and Can.), 1977-79, Industry Edition-The White Book, 1978, The Housing Fact Book, 1976, Housing Component Costs, 1975, 2d edit., 1976, Material Usage in Housing, 1970; co-editor: Labor Wage Rate Bulletin, 1976. Co-chair bd. dirs. Liz Lerman Dance Exch., Takoma Park, Md., 1997—; chmn. facade adv. bd. and Econ. Devel. Com., City of Takoma Park; chmn. bd. Lido Civic Club of Washington. Fellow Urban Mass Transp. Assn., 1969, Am. U., 1970; Soc. Real Estate Appraisers scholar, 1968. Mem. Cert. Real Estate Appraisers, Am. Planning Assn., Am. Univ. Real Estate Assn. (charter, v.p. edn., v.p. award 1983), Rho Epsilon (editor newsletter 1969). Republican. Roman Catholic. Avocations: skiing, golf. Office: Urciolo & Urciolo 6935 Laurel Ave Ste 100 Takoma Park MD 20912-4413 Office Phone: 301-270-4442. E-mail: jurciolo@comcast.net.

URCIUOLI, J. ARTHUR, investment executive; b. Syracuse, N.Y., Nov. 13, 1937; s. Joseph R. and Nicoletta Anne (Phillips) U.; m. Margaret Jane Forelli, Aug. 13, 1966; children: Caryn Sloan Jacoby, Christian J.A. BS, St. Lawrence U., 1959; JD, Georgetown U., 1966; grad. Advanced Mgmt. Program, Harvard Bus. Sch., 1982. Bar: N.Y. 1966. Atty. Brown, Wood, Fuller, Caldwell & Ivey, N.Y.C., 1966-69; internat. investment banker, dir. internat. fin. Merrill Lynch, N.Y.C., Paris, 1970-78; pres. Merrill Lynch Internat., 1978-82; chmn. Merrill Lynch Internat. Bank, London; dir. banking div. Merrill Lynch Capital Markets, 1980-84; dir. Merrill Lynch Bus. Fin. Services, Merrill Lynch Co., 1984-93; dir. mktg. group Merrill Lynch Pvt. Client, 1993-97, chmn. Internat. Pvt. Client Group, 1997-99, ret., 1999; chmn. Archer Group, 1999—. Bd. dirs. Kroll Inc., Family Capital Growth Ptnrs., L.P. Contbr. articles to profl. jours. Trustee St. Lawrence U., 1976-89, Bruce Mus., Greenwich, Conn., 1990-94; bd. dirs. United Way, Greenwich, 1978-81. Capt. USMC, 1959-63. Mem. Securities Assn. (chmn. sales and mktg. com. 1987-89), Forum for Investor Advice (chmn. 1996-98), River Club (N.Y.C.), N.Y. Yacht Club, Riverside (Conn.) Yacht Club, The Oaks Club (Sarasota, Fla.). Republican. Congregationalist. Office Phone: 941-966-4941. E-mail: archie22@comcast.net., archercorp@home.com., archergroup@comcast.net.

URDANG, ALEXANDRA, book publishing executive; b. N.Y.C., June 29, 1956; d. Laurence Urdang and Irena (Ehrlich) Urdang de Tour. BA in English Lit., U. Conn., 1977. Customer svc. and fulfillment mgr. Universe Books, N.Y.C., 1978-79, sales mgr., assoc. mktg. mgr., 1980-82; asst. v.p., dir. spl. sales Macmillan Pub. Co., N.Y.C., 1982-88; v.p. new markets Warner Books, Inc., N.Y.C., 1988-97. Avocations: architecture, art, antiques. Office: Apt 2A 201 E 69th St New York NY 10021-5472

URDANG, LAURENCE, lexicographer, publisher; b. N.Y.C., Mar. 21, 1927; s. Harry Rudman and Annabel (Schafran) U.; m. Irena B. Ehrlich vel Sluszny, May 23, 1952 (div.); children: Nicole Severyn, Alexandra Stefanie. BS, Columbia U., 1954, postgrad., 1954-58. Lectr. gen. linguistics NYU, 1956-61; assoc. editor dictionary dept. Funk & Wagnalls, Inc., N.Y.C., 1957; reference editor Random House, Inc., N.Y.C., 1957-61, dir. reference dept., 1962-69; pres. Laurence Urdang, Inc., Old Lyme, Conn. and Aylesbury, Eng., 1969—; chmn. bd. Laurence Urdang Assocs., Ltd., Aylesbury, 1969-78; editor Verbatim Books, Old Lyme and Aylesbury, 1974—. Compiler, editor, author numerous books; mng. editor: Random House Unabridged Dictionary, 1966; editor in chief: Random House College Dictionary, 1968, Random House Dictionary of Synonyms and Antonyms, 1960, N.Y. Times Everyday Reader's Dictionary of Misunderstood, Misused, Mispronounced Words, 1972, 2d edit., 1985, Editor, Verbatim, The Language Quar., 1974-97, Dictionary of Advertising Terms, 1977, Official Associated Press Almanac, 1976, Hammond Almanac, 1977, Picturesque Expressions, 1980, 2d edit., 1985, Illustrated Children's Dictionary, 1979, Basic Dictionary of Synonyms and Antonyms, 1979, 2d edit., 1986, The Synonym Finder, 1979, Collins English Dictionary, 1979, Verbatim: Vols. I, II, 1978, Vols. III, IV, V, VI and Index, 1981, -Ologies & -Isms, 1978, 81, 86, Twentieth Century American Nicknames, 1979, A Treasury of Biblical Quotations, 1980, The Timetables of American History, 1981, 3d edit., 2001, Mosby's Medical and Nursing Dictionary, 1983, Allusions, 1982, 86, Modifiers, 1982, Suffixes, 1982, Prefixes, 1984, Holidays and Anniversaries, 1985, Slogans, 1985, Mottoes, 1986, Numerical Allusions, 1986, Names and Nicknames of Places and Things, 1987, Loanwords Dictionary, 1987, The Whole Ball of Wax, 1988, The Dictionary of Confusable Words, 1988, A Fine Kettle of Fish, 1990, The Oxford Thesaurus, 1992, 2nd edit., 1997, The Oxford Desk Dictionary, 1995, The Oxford Desk Thesaurus, 1995, The New Century Dictionary, 1996, The New Century Thesaurus, 1996, The Compact Oxford Thesaurus, 1997. Served with USNR, 1944-45. Fellow Dictionary Soc. N.Am. (hon.); mem. Linguistic Soc. Am. (hon.), Am. Name Soc., Am. Dialect Soc., Soc. Indexers, Euralex, Naval Club (London). Office Phone: 860-434-2104. E-mail: urdang@sbcglobal.com.

U'REN, MARIE RITA, travel company executive, pre-school educator; b. Ft. Monmouth, NJ, Jan. 12, 1940; d. Paul Robert and Ray Rita Tyler; m. William Francis Henry U'Ren, Jr., Jan. 31, 1959; children: William Tyler, Christine Marie. Tchr. Calvary Luth. Nursery Sch., Millbrae, Calif., 1967—82; group sales Bulanti Travel, Redwood City, Calif., 1980—82; ptnr., dir. of group sales Custom Travel Consultants, Woodside, Calif., 1982—94. Fashion show co-chmn. Festival of Trees, Easton, Md., 2000—01, ho. tour co-chmn., 1999—2003; co-chmn. arts marketplace Acad. Art Mus., Easton, Md., 1998—2001, arts marketplace preview party chmn., 2002; shut down the town day steering com. Easton Bus. Mgmt. Assn./Main St. Easton, Easton, Md., 2000—01; Christmas wreath co-chmn. Main St. Easton, 1995—2004; vol. duck stamp booth Waterfowl Festival, Easton, Md., 1996—2004; chair of numerous committees Parent Tchr. Associations, Belmont, Calif., 1972—84; chmn., libr. com. Acad. Art Mus., Easton, Md., 2002—04; chmn. promotions com. Easton Main St., Inc., Easton, Md., 2000—04; co-chmn. Olde Tyme Holiday Parade, Easton, Md., 1995—2004; treas. chairty antiques show Mental Health Assn. in Talbot County, Easton, Md., 2004; chmn. Heritage award com., auditorium com., fin. com. Hist. Soc. Talbot County, Easton, Md., 2002—04; sec. Acad. Art Mus., Easton, Md., 2002—04; treas. Talbot County Am. Heart Assn., Easton, Md., 1998—2002; sec., mem. agy. rev. com. United Fund of Talbot County, Easton, Md., 2001—04; welcome ctr. liason, gala fundraising com. The Avalon Found., Easton, Md., 2001—04; grant writer Cmty. Alliance for the Performing Arts, Easton, Md., 2000—03; mem. Dance Harrison St., Easton, Md., 2001—04; sec. Friends of Hospice, Easton, Md., 2001—02, mem., 2001—04; parenttalk chmn. Mental Health Assn. in Talbot County, Easton, Md., 1998—2001, bd. dirs., 2003—04; registrar, reunion com. 1st Bn. 7th Marines Vietnam, Washington, 2000—02, Las Vegas, 2004; co-chair preview party, charity antiques show Mental Health Assn. in Talbot County, Easton, Md., 2003; costumer Cricket Theatre, Easton, Md., 2000—04; costume com. Habitat for Humanity Follies, Easton, Md., 1996—99; vol. asst. mgr., tharpe antiques Hist. Soc. of Talbot County, Easton, Md., 1996—2004; chmn. or co-chairman, Talbot county antiques show and sale Talbot County Am. Heart Assn., Easton, Md., 1997—2001; pres. Bay Area Aux., Myasthenia Gravis Found., San Mateo, Calif., 1976—78. Recipient Vol. Svc. award, Benjamin Fox Elem. Sch. PTA, 1977, Silver Hon. Svc. award, Ralson Mid. Sch. PTA, 1980, Hon. Svc. award, Carlmont H.S. PTSA, 1984, Vol. of the Yr., Dickens of a Christmas and Easton Bus. Mgmt. Authority, 1995, Cert. of Appreciation, Talbot County Am. Heart Assn., 1996, Vol. Excellence, First Night Talbot, 1997, Cert. of Appreciation, Talbot County Am. Heart Assn., 1997, Vol. Recognition award, Easton Bus. Mgmt. Authority, 2000, Talbot County and State of Md., 2002. Home: 127 S Harrison St Easton MD 21601 Personal E-mail: muren@bluecrab.org.

URENA, ALEX, chef; Apprentice chef El Bulli, Spain; chef Bouley, N.Y.C.; co-chef, co-owner Blue Hill, N.Y.C. Office: Blue Hill 75 Washington Pl New York NY 10011

URHAUSEN, JAMES NICHOLAS, real estate developer, construction executive; b. Berwyn, Ill., Oct. 6, 1943; s. Jack Nicholas and Florence Frances (Stalzer) U.; m. Philomena Anne Malizia, July 16, 1966 (div. 1980); children: Kristen Anne, James Nicholas III; m. Anne Siegert, July 22, 1983; children: Bradley James, Samantha Elise. BA, St. Procopius Coll., Lisle, Ill., 1965. High sch. tchr. Nazareth Acad., LaGrange Park, Ill., 1965-66; asst. village mgr. Village of Hinsdale, Ill., 1966-69; village mgr. Village of Oak Brook, Ill., 1969-73; v.p., sec.-treas. Collins Devel. Corp., St. Charles, Ill., 1973-80; exec. v.p. Westway Constrn. Corp., St. Charles, Ill., 1980-84, pres., chief exec. officer, 1984—. Guest lectr. No. Ill. U., Dekalb, 1976—; expert witness Ill. Dept. of Transp., Chgo., 1976—; dir. Harris Bank/St. Charles, Ill., 1992—. Chmn. Hotel Baker Bd. Gov.'s St. Charles, 1982-84, Bd. of Fire and Police Commmrs., St. Charles, 1986—; mem. 708 Comty. Mental Health Bd., St. Charles, 1986—, Kane County Selective Svc. Sys. Bd., St. Charles, 1981—, Kane County Solid Waste Adv. Com., Geneva, 1990—, Metra Citizen's Adv. Bd., 1993—; bd. dirs. Neighborhood Improvement Assn., St. Charles Twp., 1992—, pres., 1996—; bd. dirs. Delnor Cmty. Health Sys., 1993—, Glenwood Sch. for Boys, 1996—; chair tech. adv. com. Kane County Stormwater Mgmt. Com., 1996—. Mem. Home Bldrs. Assn. Greater Chgo. (dir. 1989—), Nat. Assn. Home Bldrs., No. Ill. Home Bldrs. Assn., Fox Valley Polit. Action Group, St. Charles C. of C. (amb. 1988, Community Devel. award 1989, Charlemagne award 1993, Sam Walton Bus. Leadership award 1996). Republican. Roman Catholic. Avocations: golf, rail photography, power boating, model trains. Office: Westway Constrn Corp 440 S 3rd St Saint Charles IL 60174-2854 Home: 5N143 Maple Ct Denton KS 66017-6259

URIAS, JOHN M. military officer, government agency administrator; b. Vandenberg AFB, Calif. BS, U. Calif., Davis; MS in Elec. Engring., Naval Postgrad. Sch.; MA in Nat. Security and Strategic Studies, Naval War Coll.; grad., Air War Coll., Def. Systems Mgmt. Coll., Coll. of Naval Command and Staff. Commd. 2d lt. U.S. Army, 1975, advanced through grades to maj. gen.; dep. for systems acquisition U.S. Army Tank-Automotive and Armaments Command, 1998—99; project mgr. Warfighter Info. Network-Terrestrial PEO Command, Control and Comm., Ft. Monmouth, NJ; platoon leader, exec. officer Battery C, 2nd Bn.,1st Air Def. Arty., Germany; adj. 4th Supply and Transport Bn., Ft. Carson, Colo.; battery comdr., ops. officer and exec. officer 4th Bn., 61st Air Def. Arty., Ft. Carson, Colo.; comdr. 2nd B. 44th Air Def. Arty. 101st Airborne Divsn., Ft. Campbell, Ky.; R&D coord. U.S. Army Missile and Space Intelligence Ctr., Redstone Arsenal, Ala.; exec. asst. to the sci. and tech. advisor comdr.-in-chief USCINCPAC, chief R&D br. strategic planning and policy directorate; asst. project mgr. for command, control, comm. and intelligence Army Tactical Missile Sys.; asst. project mgr. for army airspace command and control Air Def. Command and Control Systems; program exec. officer for air, space, and missile def. and dep. commdg. gen. for rsch., devel. and acquisition U.S. Army Space and Missile Def. Command, Huntsville, Ala., 1999—. Office: USArmy Space and Missile Defense Command PO Box 1500 Huntsville AL 35807-3801

URIBE, JAVIER MIGUEL, investment executive; b. Baranquilla, Colombia, Sept. 4, 1941; s. Jose and Ofelia (Diaz-Granados) U.; m. Dena Rue Whitaker, Apr. 1, 1963 (div. Sept. 1987); children: Sandra J., Joseph J., Cristina; m. Diana L. Anglada, Dec. 4, 1987. BS in Indsl. Mgmt., Purdue U., 1967. With Citibank, N.A., 1967, resident v.p., 1975-76, v.p. Port of Spain, Trinidad, 1976-78, N.Y.C., 1978-80, San Juan, P.R., 1980-85; pres. Citicorp Fin. Svcs. Corp., San Juan, P.R., 1980-85; chmn., chief exec. officer Merrill Lynch Govt. Securities, San Juan, 1985-88; pres. San Juan Capital Corp., 1988—. Advisor exec. program Ind. U., Bloomington, 1978-80; chmn. Trinfinance Leasing, Port of Spain, Trinidad, 1976-78, Met. Mortgage Co., San Juan, 1989—; trustee Ashford Presbyn. Community Hosp., San Juan, 1990-96. Bd. dirs. Maracaibo (Venezuela) Botannical Gardens Found., 1974-75. Mem. Securities Industry Assn. of P.R. (founder, treas. 1985-86), N.Am. Assn. (bd. dirs. Caracas, Venezuela chpt. 1973-74), Dorado Beach Golf Club, Centro Ecuestre de P.R. (pres. 1989-91), Equestrian Fedn. (v.p. 1989-91), Ingenio Polo Club. Roman Catholic. Avocation: golf. Home and Office: San Juan Capital Corp PO Box 9023462 San Juan PR 00902-3462 Office Phone: 787-278-1250. E-mail: javier.uribe@sanjuancapitalcorp.com.

URIE, JOHN JAMES, lawyer, retired Canadian federal judge; b. Guelph, Ont., Can., Jan. 2, 1920; s. G. Norman and Jane A. U.; m. Dorothy Elizabeth James.; children: David, Janet, Alison. B.Commerce, Queen's U.; LL.B., Osgoode Hall Law Sch. Bar: Ont. 1948. Ptnr. firm Burke-Robertson, Urie, Weller & Chadwick, Ottawa, Ont., 1948-73; judge Fed. Ct. Can., Ottawa, 1973-90; counsel Scott and Aylen, Ottawa, 1991-2000, Borden, Ladner, Gervais, Ottawa, 2000—. Gen. counsel to Joint Com. of Senate and House of Commons on Consumer Credit; chmn. planning com. First Nat. Conf. on Law, Ottawa, 1972; judge Ct. Martial Appeal Ct., 1973-90. Past pres. County of Carleton Law Assn.; past v.p. Children's Aid Soc.; past pres. Eastern Profl. Hockey League. Served with Cameron Highlanders of Ottawa Can. Army, 1942-45. Mem. Royal Can. Mil. Inst., Phi Delta Phi. Mem. United Ch. of Canada. Clubs: Cameron Highlanders of Ottawa Assoc. (Ottawa), Ottawa Hunt and Golf (Ottawa), Rideau (Ottawa). Office: Borden Ladner Gervais 100 Queen St Ottawa ON Canada K1P1J9

URION, DAVID KIMBALL, pediatric neurologist, researcher, educator; b. Cin., Aug. 4, 1954; s. Phillip Allen and Lenore (Barrow) U.; m. Kerrie Eileen Flynn, Mar. 6, 1982 (div. Oct. 1986); 1 child, Kara Flynn; m. Deborah Choate, Sept. 27, 1987; 1 child, Rufus Walker Choate. AB, Dartmouth Coll., 1976; MD, Stanford U., 1980. Diplomate Am. Bd. Psychiatry and Neurology. Intern Peter Bent Brigham Hosp., Boston, 1980-81; resident, neurology Longwood Area Neurology Program, Boston, 1981-82; resident, pediatrics Children's Hosp., Boston, 1982-83; resident, child neurology Longwood Area Neurology Program, Boston, 1983-84, chief resident, child neurology, 1984-85; instr. neurology Med. Sch., Harvard U., Boston, 1985-87, asst. prof., 1987-2000; assoc. prof., 2000—; mem. faculty Sch. Edn. Harvard U., Cambridge, Mass., 1985—; asst. in neurology Children's Hosp., Boston, 1985-88; assoc. in neurology, 2000—; dir. learning disabilities-behavioral neurology program Children's Hosp., Boston, 1985—, dir. neurology clinics, 1987-91. Treas. Children's Hosp. Neurology Found., 1986—, v.p., 1992—99, clerk, 1999—. Author: Pediatric Neurology for the House Officer, 1988; translator: The Brain Machine (Jeannerod), 1985; contbr. articles to med. jours., chpts. to books. Mem.: Internat. Child Neurology Assn., Child Neurology Soc., Am. Acad. Neurology. Democratic Socialist. Episcopalian. Office: Children's Hosp Neurology 300 Longwood Ave Boston MA 02115-5724 E-mail: david.urion@tch.harvard.edu.

URIS, PATRICIA FIRME, health science association administrator; b. Muskegon, Mich. BSN, U. Colo., 1974, MS in Psychiatric/Mental Health Nursing, 1978, PhD in Nursing, 1993. Staff nurse Colo. Mental Health Inst., Denver, 1984-76; on-call staff Bethesda PsycHealth Sys., Denver, 1977; clin. specialist Pk. E. Comprehensive Cmty. Mental Health Ctr., Denver, 1978; asst. exec. dir. Colo. Nurses Assn., Denver, 1979-80; project co-dir. Western Interstate Commn. Higher Edn., Boulder, Colo., 1980-85; project dir. Western Inst. Nursing/Western Soc. Rsch. Nursing, Boulder, 1987-90, assoc. dir., 1987-90, spl. cons., 1990-94; program devel., mgmt. cons. Arvada, Colo., 1994-95; asst. prof. U. Colo. Health Scis. Ctr., Denver, 1995-99; program adminstr. Bd. Nursing Colo. Dept. Regulatory Agys., Denver, 1999—. Guest lectr. U. Colo. Health Scis. Ctr., 1979-82, 80-83, 94-97, Metro. State Coll., 1979-82; cons. U. Alaska, 1982, Wyo. Dept. Health and Social Svcs., 1982, Utah Dept. Health, 1982; reviewer Appleton-Century-Crofts Pub. Co., 1985, Colo. Dept. Health and Environment, 1996, 97, Nat. Assn. Sch. Nurses, Inc., 1997, HHS, 1997, 98, 99. Cons. Rocky Mountain Ctr. Healthcare Ethics; mem. clin. adv. bd. ONEDAY/The Family AIDS Project, Denver; mem. stds. based edn. com. Arvada W. Sch. Improvement Leadership Team, Jefferson County, Colo. Recipient NIH stipend, 1976-78; Calloway scholar U. Colo. Health Scis. Ctr. Mem. ANA, Am. Psychiatric Nurses Assn., Assn. Child and Adolescent Psychiatric Nurses, Soc. Edn. and Rsch. Psychiatric-Mental Health Nursing, Nat. Assn. Sch. Nurses, Colo. Nurses Assn. (ANA del. 1982, 84, mem. commn. social and legis. concerns 1981-85, chair 1983-84, Virginia S. Paulson award 1981), Colo. Mental Health Assn. (pro bono vol.), Sigma Theta Tau (chpt. bd. dirs. 1993-96, mem. rsch. com. 1995-99, chmn. 1995-96, Henrietta Loughran scholar 1993).

URKIEL, WILLIAM STANLEY, diversified company executive; BA in History, Marist Coll., 1967; MBA, Iona Coll., 1969. With IBM, 27 yrs, contr. entry sys. divsn., dir. fin. info. sys. comm. group, v.p. ops. real estate and constrn. divsn., contr. personal sys. product line, v.p. Personal Computer Co., CFO, sr. mng. dir. IBM-Japan, until 1995; mgr. corp. control. responsibilities AMP, Inc., Harrisburg, Pa., from 1995, corp. v.p. fin., CFO in charge global fin. mgmt., 1998-99; CFO & sr. v.p. IKON Office Solutions, Inc., Malvern, Pa., 1999—. Mem. Mfrs. Alliance, Fin. Exec. Inst. Office: AMP Inc 470 Friendship Rd Harrisburg PA 17111-1203 Mailing: IKON Office Solutions Inc 70 Valley Stream Pkwy Malvern PA 19355

URKOWITZ, MICHAEL, banker; b. Bronx, N.Y., June 18, 1943; s. David and Esther (Levy) U.; m. Eleanor Naomi Dreazen, July 2, 1966; children—Brian, Denise. B.Engring., CCNY, 1965, M.M.E., 1967. Project engr. Lunar Module program Grumman Corp., Bethpage, N.Y., 1964-72; asst. to dep. commr. for housing code compliance, project mgr. City of N.Y., 1972-74; 2d v.p. Chase Manhattan Bank, N.Y.C., 1974-77, v.p. group exec. ops. dept., 1977-80, sr. v.p., 1980-85, exec. v.p., corp. ops. and sys. exec., 1985-87; sector exec. Chase InfoServ Internat., N.Y.C., 1987-95, exec. consumer products integration and tech., 1995-96, Chase credit card bus. exec., 1996-2000, ret. N.Y.C., 2000; sr. adv. Deloitte Cons., N.Y.C. Bd. dirs. CEDEL, Luxembourg, Master Card U.S., Depository Trust Co., N.Y.C., 1992-95, Bank Leumi, U.S.; lectr. CCNY, 1967-68. Contbg. author: Thermal Control and Radiation, 1972. Mem. adv. bd. N.Y. C. chpt. Salvation Army, 1989—2001. Mem. Tau Beta Pi, Pi Tau Sigma. Office: Deloitte Cons 2 World Fin Ctr New York NY 10281-1414 Personal E-mail: murkowitz@optonline.net. *Working against my own standards as opposed to the standards set by others, provides the greater challenge but yields greater satisfaction.*

URLACHER, HERBERT, state legislator; b. New England, N.D., Dec. 30, 1931; m. Claire Urlacher; 5 children. Farmer, rancher; mem. N.D. State Ho. of Reps., Bismarck, 1989-91, N.D. Senate from 36th dist., Bismarck, 1992—. Pres. Stark County Sch. Officers, N.D. Water Users, West River Joint Water Resource Bd.; past pres. ch. coun. St. Mary's Ch.; bd. dirs. Water Resources Bd. N.D.; mem. Stark County Water Resource Bd.; mem. adv. bd. State Water Commn. Mem. KC, Elks. Office: ND State Capitol 600 E Boulevard Ave Bismarck ND 58505-0660 also: 3320 94th Ave SW Taylor ND 58656-9643

URMAN, JEFFREY DAVID, physician, educator; b. N.Y.C., May 23, 1944; s. Julius and Rose Claire Urman; m. Marian K. Kleinfeld, June 28, 1970; children: Jamie David, Daniel Jay. BS, U. Conn., 1967; MD, Cornell U., 1972. Diplomate Am. Bd. Internal Medicine and Rheumatology. Int. Wash. Hosp. Ctr., Wash., D.C., 1972-73, res., 1973-75; fellshp. in rheumatology Univ. Conn. Health Ctr., Farmington, CT, 1975-77; physician Redwood Med. Clinic, Redwood City, Calif., 1977-90; clin. prof. medicine Stanford (Calif.) U. Med. Ctr., 1977—; physician Permanente Med. Group, Mountain View, Calif., 1990—, physician-in-charge, 1995—. Contbr. articles to profl. jours. Fellow: ACP, Am. Coll. Rheumatology. Office: 555 Castro St Mountain View CA 94041-2060

URMY, NORMAN B. hospital administrator; b. Ft. Smith, Ark., June 26, 1944; married. BA, Williams Coll., 1966; MA, U. Chgo., 1969. Various positions Mass. Gen. Hosp., Boston, 1966-67; adminstrv. resident NYU Med. Ctr., 1968, adminstrv. asst., 1969-70, asst. adminstr., 1970-76, assoc. adminstr., 1976-79, adminstr., v.p. ops., 1979-82; exec. dir. Vanderbilt Univ. Hosp. & Clinic, Nashville, 1985-98; exec. v.p. clin. affairs Vanderbilt Univ. Med. Ctr., Nashville, 1998—; exec. dir. and CEO Vanderbilt U. Hosp. and Clinic, 2002—. Mem. ACHE. Office: D-3300 MCN Vanderbilt U 1161 21st Ave Nashville TN 37232-2104*

URNESS, KENT D. insurance company executive; b. 1948; With The St. Paul Co., Inc., 1971, v.p. comml. ins., 1985—90, sr. v.p. global splty. practices, 1999—2001, exec. v.p. internat., 2001—; sr. v.p. agy. broker svcs. St. Paul Fire and Marine Ins. Co., 1991—92; pres. St. Paul Internat. Ins. Co. Ltd., 1993—. Office: The St Paul Cos, Inc 385 Washington St Saint Paul MN 55102

UROWSKY, RICHARD J. lawyer; b. N.Y.C., June 28, 1946; s. Jacob and Anne (Granick) Urowsky. BA, Yale U., 1967, JD, 1972; BPhil, Oxford U., Eng., 1970. Bar: N.Y. 1973, U.S. Dist. Ct. (so. dist.) N.Y. 1973, U.S. Ct. Appeals (2d cir.) 1973, U.S. Supreme Ct. 1977. Law clk. to Justice Reed U.S. Supreme Ct., Washington, 1972—73; assoc. Sullivan & Cromwell LLP, N.Y.C., 1973—80, ptnr., 1980—. Mem. ABA, Assn. of the Bar of the City of N.Y., Fed. Bar Coun., N.Y. County Lawyers Assn., Yale Club, Links Club, India House Club, Lyford Cay Club. Office: Sullivan & Cromwell LLP 125 Broad St New York NY 10004-2498 Business E-Mail: urowskyr@sullcrom.com.

URQUHART, JOHN, medical researcher, educator; b. Pitts., Apr. 24, 1934; s. John and Wilma Nelda (Martin) U.; m. Joan Cooley, Dec. 28, 1957; children: Elizabeth Urquhart Vdovjak, John Christopher (dec. 1965), Robert Malcolm, Thomas Jubal. BA with honors, Rice U., 1955; MD with honors, Harvard U., 1959; D honoris causa, U. Utrecht, 1997. Lic. physician, Calif. Walter B. Cannon fellow in physiology Harvard Med. Sch., Boston, 1956, Josiah Macy, Jr. fellow, 1956-58, 59-61; intern in surgery Mass. Gen. Hosp., 1959-60, asst. resident, 1960-61; investigator Nat. Heart Inst., NIH, Bethesda, Md., 1961-63; asst. prof. physiology U. Pitts. Sch. Medicine, 1963-66, assoc. prof., 1966-68, prof., 1968-70; prof. biomed. engring. U. So. Calif., LA, 1970-71; prin. scientist ALZA Corp., Palo Alto, Calif., 1970-86, dir. biol. scis., 1971-74, pres. rsch. divsn., 1974-78, dir., 1976-78, chief scientist, 1978-82, sr.

v.p., 1978-85. Co-founder APREX Corp., Fremont, Calif., pres., 1986-88, dir., 1986-95, chmn., 1988-91, chief scientist, 1988-95; co-founder, chief scientist AARDEX Ltd., Zug, Switzerland, 1995-; vis. prof. pharmacology U. Limburg Sch. Medicine (now Maastricht U.), Maastricht, Netherlands, 1984-85, vis. prof. pharmacology, epidemiology, 1986-91, prof. pharmacology, epidemiology, 1991-2004, prof. emeritus, 2004; adj. prof. biopharm. scis. U. Calif.-San Francisco, 1984-; mem. dir.'s adv. com. NIH, 1986-88; Boerhaave lectr. U. Leiden, Netherlands, 1991, 94, 95, 97; bd. dirs. HBM BioVentures Ltd., Cayman Islands; bd. dirs. Inveresk Rsch. Group, Inc., Cary, NC, vice-chmn. 2002—. Co-author: Risk Watch, 1984; contbr. numerous articles to sci. jours.; patentee therapeutic systems for controlled drug delivery and regimen compliance monitoring (43). Trustee Kettering U. (formerly GMI Engring. and Mgmt. Inst.), Flint, Mich., 1983—. Served with USPHS, 1961-63. NIH grantee, 1963-70; Bowditch lectr. Am. Physiol. Soc., 1969; recipient Disting. Alumni award, Rice U., 2002. Fellow AAAS, Royal Coll. Physicians of Edinburgh, Royal Soc. Edinburgh (corr.), Internat Soc. for Pharmacoepidemiology; mem. Biomed. Engring. Soc. (pres. 1976), Boyleston Med. Soc., Internat. Soc. Pharmaco-epidemiology, Am. Soc. Clin. Pharmacology and Therapeutics, Soc. for Clin. Trials, Endocrine Soc., Saturday Morning Club Palo Alto, Am. Physiol. Soc., Soc. Risk Analysis, Calif. Acad. Medicine. Home and Office: 975 Hamilton Ave Palo Alto CA 94301-2213 E-mail: urquhart@ix.netcom.com.

URQUHART, KARIN MAY, foundation administrator, environmentalist; b. Oakland, Calif., Feb. 2, 1935; d. Charlotte Muriel Hively and Alfred Jonathon Alstrom; m. G. Donald Urquhart, Oct. 6, 1956; children: Gaylene Urquhart, Steve Hart, Cindy McDonell, Shelly Urquhart, Laurie Swisher, Scott Urquhart, James Urquhart. Exec. dir. Marin Conservation League, San Rafael, Calif., 1980-95; trustee Marin Cmty. Found., Larkspur, Calif., 1995—; exec. dir. Digital Village Found., Novato, Calif., 1996-97. Founding chair Marin Conservation Corps, San Rafael, 1982-87; mem. citizens adv. com. Citizen's Energy Impact Program, San Rafael, 1979-83; pres. Environ. Forum Marin, Kentfield, Calif., 1974-76, Marconi Conf. Ctr., Marshall, Calif., 1995—; mem. adv. com. Marin Resource Recovery Com., San Rafael, 1974-76; com. mem. Marin County Visitor Svcs. Com., San Rafael, 1995-96; mem. Marin County Waste Mgmt. Adv. Com., San Rafael, 1987-92; commr., pres. Marin County Parks Recreation and Open Space Commn., San Rafael, 1975-95; bd. dirs. Marin Agrl. Land Trust, Point Reyes, Calif.; spkr. in field. Illustrator (children's book) Mr. Buckeye Nut, 1970; contbr. numerous articles to newspapers and mags. Active steering com. Marin Women's Hall of Fame, San Rafael, 1994-96; mem. Marin County Trails Com., San Rafael, 1975-95; pesticide safety instr. U. Calif. Statewide Integrated Pest Mgmt. Project, Davis, 1994; mem. environ. sci. adv. bd. Dominican Coll., San Rafael, 1994-96; chair com. to appoint Marin Cmty. Found. trustees Marin Coun. Agencies, San Rafael, 1994; trustee Marin Cmty. Found., 1995, mem. cmty. partnership com., 1995, mem. earth day every day com., 1996; mem. Wed. Morning Dialogue, San Rafael, 1994-99; mem. adv. coun. Calif. Dept. Transp., Dist. IV, San Francisco, 1991-92; founding chair, bd. dirs. Marin Environ. Alliance, San Rafael, 1988-96; dir. Marin County Fair, San Rafael, 1985-2000; chair Marin County Open Space Com., San Rafael, 1973-95; bd. dirs. Marin Agrl. Land Trust, 1995; bd. dirs., pres. Marconi Conf. Ctr., 1995; vice-chair Lake Almanor Cmty. Found. Recipient Women Making History 11 annual award Senator Barbara Boxer, 1983, First Women of Achievement award AAUW, 1987, Exec. Dir. of Yr. award for excellence in developing cmty. partnerships Marin Coun. Agencies, 1989, Vol. award Environ. Fedn. Calif., 1989, Cert. of Recognition for recycling leadership Californians Against Waste, 1989, Conservation award DAR, 1995, inclusion award Congrl. Record of U.S., 1995; named Marin County's Outstanding Cmty. Vol., Calif. Dept. Parks and Recreation, 1995; named to Marin Women's Hall of Fame, 1993. Mem.: Marin County C. of C. (mem. govtl. affairs com. 1989—90), Marin Soc. Artists. Avocations: travel, gardening, painting, swimming, cooking. Home: 383 Cascade Dr Fairfax CA 94930 Fax: 415-460-0260. E-mail: Karinur@comcast.net.

URQUHART, TONY, artist, educator; b. Niagara Falls, Ont., Can., Apr. 9, 1934; s. Archer Marsh and Maryon Louise (Morse) U.; m. Madeline Mary Jennings, July 1958 (div. 1976); children: Allyson, Robin, Marsh, Aidan; m. Mary Jane Carter Keele, May 1976; 1 dau., Emily. B.F.A., U. Buffalo, 1958. Artist-in-residence U. Western Ont., London, 1960-63, 64-65, asst. prof. fine arts, 1967-70, assoc. prof., 1970-72; prof. fine art U. Waterloo, Ont., 1972-99, chmn. dept., 1977-79, 82-85, 94-96, ret., 1999; lectr. McMaster U., Hamilton, Ont., 1966-67. One-man shows Winnipeg Art Gallery, 1959, Walker Art Gallery, Mpls., 1960, Richard Demarco Gallery, Edinburgh, Scotland, 1975, Power of Invention: Drawings from seven decades, Nat. Gallery Can., 2003; group shows, Pitts. Biennial, 1958, Guggenheim Internat., N.Y.C., 1958, Art of the Ams. and Spain, Madrid, Barcelona, Rome, Paris, 1964, Nat. Gallery Can., Toronto, 1972, Mus. Modern Art, Paris, 1976; represented permanent collections, Nat. Gallery Can., Art Gallery, Ont., Fed. Art Bank of Ottawa, Montreal Mus., Vancouver Art Gallery, Mus. Modern Art, Victoria and Albert Mus., London, Museo Civico, Lugano, Switzerland, Hirshhorn Mus., Washington, Bibliotec Nat., Paris; chmn., Jack Chambers Meml. Found., 1978-85; resident artist, Kitchener-Waterloo Art Gallery, Kitchener, Ont., 1981-83; illustrator: The Broken Ark: A Book of Beasts, 1969, I Am Walking in the Garden of His Imaginary Palace by Jane Urquhart, 1982, False Shuffles by Jane Urquhart, 1982, (50 drawings) Cells of Ourselves (text G.M. Dault), 1989, Memories of a Governor General's Daughter, 1990, Warbrain: poems by Stuart MacKinnon, 1994, Walking to the Saints, by Anne McPherson, 2000. Decorated Order of Can.; recipient Edits, I Arts Coun., Ont., 1974, Kilchener Waterloo Visual Arts award, 1994; winner Nat. Outdoor Sculpture Competition MacDonald Stewart Art Ctr., 1987, Outdoor Sculpture competition, Rim Park, Waterloo, 2002; grantee Can. Coun. award, 1963, 79, travel grantee, 1967, 69, 70, 74, 75, 76, 88, 91, project cost grantee, 1981, 82, short-term grantee, 1991, All Can. Coun. Mem. Can. Artists Representation (1 of 3 founding mem.'s, sec. 1968-71, life 1999), Nat. Gallery of Can. (life), Art Gallery of Ont. (life), London Reginal Art Gallery (life), MacDonald Stewart Art Centre Gallery Stratford (life). Office: Dept Fine Arts U Waterloo Waterloo ON Canada N2L 3G1

URROZ-RAPOLD, PATRICIA JULIA S. retired diplomat, writer; b. Key West, Fla., Feb. 16, 1949; children: Jean Sebastien Bodin Rapold, Nicolas Richard Rapold. BA in Polit. Sci., Boston U., 1971. Consul ad-honorem Nicaragua Boston Ministerio de Relaciones Exteriores, Managua, Nicaragua, 1969—74; social security disability examimer Mass. Rehab. Commn., Boston, 1971—72. Author, pub., poet: Seasonal Living In The Catskills Windham High Peak And Trails, 1994 (Internat. Poet Of Merit award, 1996). Hospitality coord. for fgn. visitors Internat. Ctr., N.Y.C., 1991—93. Recipient Appreciation award for vols., Internat. Ctr., N.Y.C., 1993. Mem.: AAUW (member). Roman Catholic. Avocations: hiking, swimming, reading, collecting. Home: Meadow Winds Rt 52 211 Sara Ln Newburgh NY 12550 Office: Worldstar Corp 245 E 93d St Apt 29 C New York NY Personal E-mail: Rapold@aol.com. Business E-Mail: LordSeb@aol.com.

URRY, GRANT WAYNE, retired chemistry educator; b. Salt Lake City, Mar. 12, 1926; s. Herbert William and Emma (Swanner) U.; m. Lillian Alibertini, Sept. 4, 1946; children— Lisa, Claudia, Serena, Anthony. SB, U. Chgo., 1947, PhD, 1953. Research asst., then research assoc. U. Chgo., 1949-53, research assoc., asst. prof., 1954-55; asst. prof. Washington U., St. Louis, 1955-58; assoc. prof. Purdue U., Lafayette, Ind., 1958-64, prof., 1964-68; prof. chemistry Tufts U., Medford, Mass., 1968-92, Robinson prof. chemistry, 1970-92, chmn. dept., 1968-73, Robinson prof. emeritus chemistry, 1992—. Alfred P. Sloan fellow, 1956-58 Fellow N.Y. Acad. Scis., Am. Inst. Chemists, AAAS; mem. Am. Chem. Soc., Am. Soc. Sci. Glassblowers, Fedn. Am. Scientists, Sigma Xi, Phi Lambda Upsilon. Personal E-mail: gurry@comcast.net.

URSANO, ROBERT JOSEPH, psychiatrist; b. Heidelberg, Ger., May 26, 1947; s. James Joseph and Neoma Faye (Summers) U.; m. Diane T. Ursano; children: Amy, Anna. BS magna cum laude, U. Notre Dame, 1969; MD, Yale U., 1973; grad., Washington Psychoanalystic Ins, 1986. Diplomate Nat. Bd. Med. Examiners, Am. Bd. Psychiatry and Neurology; lic. physician N.Y., Tex., Md. Resident in psychiatry Wilford Hall USAF Med. Ctr., 1973-75; postdoctoral fellow in psychiatry Yale U./Yale Psychiat. Inst., 1975-77; staff psychiatrist USAF Sch. Aerospace Medicine, Brooks AFB, Tex., 1977-79; clin. asst. prof. U. Tex. Health Sci. Ctr., San Antonio, 1977-79; asst. prof. and dir. third yr. clerkships dept. psychiatry Uniformed Svcs. U. Health Scis., Bethesda, Md., 1979-81, assoc prof. and dir. 3rd yr. clerkships, 1981-83, assoc. prof. and assoc. chmn. dept. psychiatry, 1983-86, prof. and assoc. chmn. dept. psychiatry, 1987-92, prof., chair dept. psychiatry, dir.Ctr. for the Study of Traumatic Stress, 1992—. Examiner Am. Bd. Psychiatry and Neurology, 1984—; asst. prof. Nat. Naval Med. Ctr Dept. Psychiatry, Georgetown U. Sch. Medicine, Washington, 1980-84, assoc. prof., 1984-88, prof., 1988—. Author: Concise Guide to Psychodynamic Psychotherapy, 1990, Concise Guide to Principles and Practice of Psychodynamic Psychotherapy in the Era of Managed Care, 1998; editor: Individual and Community Responses to Trauma and Disaster: The Structure of Human Chaos, 1994, Emotional Aftermath of The Persian Gulf War: Veterans, Families, Communities and Nations, 1996, Acute and Chronic PTSD, 1997, Trauma and Disaster: Responses and Management, 2003, Terrorism and Disaster: Individual and Community Mental Health Interventions, 2004, Bioterrorism: Indivduals and the Public's Health, 2004; reviewer Am. Jour. Psychiatry, Jour. Nervous and Mental Disease, Psychosomatics, Psychiatry, Jour. Applied Social Psychology, Archives of Gen. Psychiatry, Hosp. and Community Psychiatry, all 1986—, Jour. Neuropsychiatry and Clin. Neurosci., 1988—, Jour. Traumatic Stress, 1989—; editor-in-chief Psychiatry, 1999—; mem. editl. bd. Mil. Medicine; contbr. articles to profl. jours., chpts. to books. Decorated Air Force Commendation medal; recipient Dept. Def. Humanitarian Svc. medal, Dept. Def. Superior Svc. award, William C. Porter award Assn. Mil. Surgeons of U.S.; recipient Disting. Tchg. award Am. Soc. Psychoanalyst Physicians, Life Time Achievement award Internat. Soc. Traumatic Stress Studies. Fellow Am. Psychiat. Assn., Am. Coll. Psychiatrists, Am. Coll. Psychoanalysts; mem. Am. Psychoanalytic Assn., Internat. Psychoanalytic Assn., Am. Psychosomatic Soc., Washington Psychiat. Soc., Washington Psychoanalytic Soc., Acad. Medicine Washington DC, Soc. USAF Psychiatrists (v.p. 1981-82), Assn. for Acad. Psychiatry, Alpha Epsilon Delta, Phi Beta Kappa. Home: 3900 Cleveland St Kensington MD 20895-3804 Office: Uniformed Svcs U Health Sci 4301 Jones Bridge Rd Bethesda MD 20814-4712

URSHAN, NATHANIEL ANDREW, minister, church administrator; b. St. Paul, Aug. 29, 1920; s. Andrew David and Mildred (Hammergren) U.; m. Jean Louise Habig, Oct. 1, 1941; children: Sharon, Annette, Nathaniel, Andrew. Student, Columbia U., 1936-39; DTh (hon.), Gateway Coll. Evangelism, 1976. Ordained to ministry United Pentecostal Ch. Internat. Evangelist, 1941-44; assoc. pastor, 1944-46, N.Y.C., 1947-48, Indpls., 1948-49; pastor Calvary Tabernacle, Indpls., 1949-78; presbyter Ind. Dist. United Pentecostal Chs., 1950-77; asst. gen. supt. United Pentecostal Ch. Internat., 1971-77, gen. supt., 1978—; chancellor Urshan Grad. Sch. of Theology, Florissant, Mo., 2002. Host radio show Harvestime, 1961-78, 81—; chaplain Ind. Ho. of Reps., 1972. Author: Consider Him, 1962, These Men Are Not Drunk, 1964, Book of Sermons of the Baptism of the Holy Spirit, 1968, Major Bible Prophecy, 1971. Mem. internat. com. YMCA, 1958-79, bd. dirs. Indpls. chpt. 1961-79, world service chmn. Region L., 1969-71; chmn. Heart Fund Campaign, 1968-69; mem. screening com. Marion County Reps., Ind., 1973-74; chmn. Ministerial Com. of Richard Lugar for May of Indpls., 1968, William Hudnut for Mayor, 1975; bd. dirs. Little Red Door, Cancer Soc. Indpls., 1974-77. Recipient gold and brass medallion Heart Fund., Indpls., 1968-69; Nathaniel A. Urshan Day named in his honor, Nov. 3, 1979, Mayor Hudnut, Indpls. Mem. Indpls. Ministerial Assn. Mem. United Pentecostal Ch. Office: United Pentecostal Ch Internat 8855 Dunn Rd Hazelwood MO 63042-2212

URSTADT, CHARLES DEANE, real estate executive; b. N.Y.C., June 13, 1959; s. Charles Jordan and Elinor McClure Urstadt. BA cum laude, NYU, 1982. Mng. agt. Sulzberger-Rolfe, Inc., 1982-83; v.p., mem. exec. com., dir. residential sales Urstadt Property Co. (was Pearce, Urstadt, Mayer & Greer), Bronxville, N.Y., 1984-86, exec. v.p., 1986-97, pres., 1997—; pub., editor-in-chief N.Y. Constrn. News, N.Y.C., 1984-92; assoc. broker Brown Harris Stevens Inc., N.Y.C., 1992-96, exec. dir., 1996-97, sr. v.p., sales dir., 1997—. Bd. dirs. 61 E 86th St Owners Corp., 1987-89, 90-95, sec., 1990-95; bd. dirs. 18 East 81st St Tenants Corp., 1996-2001. Bd. dirs. The Ensemble Studio Theater, 1988-91, The Friends of 13 Inc., 1992—, East Side Assn., 1988-97, v.p., 1990-95, pres., 1995-97; mem. bd. dirs. Urstadt Biddle Properties, Inc. (formerly HRE Properties), 1991—, Preservation League N.Y., 2001—; mem. N.Y. State Bd. Hist. Preservation, 1996—. Mem. N.Y. Bldg. Congress (bd. dirs. 1988-91), treas. 1989-91). Office: 2112 Broadway New York NY 10023-2142 also: 2 Park Pl Ofc 3 Bronxville NY 10708-4107 Home: 10 Venetian Way Apt 2105 Miami Beach FL 33139-8834

URSTADT, CHARLES J. real estate executive; b. Oct. 27, 1928; s. Charles G. and Claire C. (Jordan) U.; m. Elinor McClure Funk, Mar. 23, 1957; children: Charles Deane, Catherine Urstadt Biddle. BA, Dartmouth Coll., 1949, MBA, 1951; LLB, Cornell U., 1953; LLD with honors, Pace U., 1990. Bar: N.Y. Assoc. Nevius Brett & Kellogg, N.Y.C., 1953-58; asst. sec. Webb & Knapp, Inc., N.Y.C., 1958-63; v.p., sec., counsel Alcoa Residences, Inc., N.Y.C., 1963-67; commr. N.Y. State Divsn. Housing and comty. Renewal, N.Y.C., 1967-73; chmn. Battery Park City Authority, N.Y.C., 1968-78, Urstadt Property Co. Inc., 1979—. Chmn. Urstadt Biddle Properties, 1986—; trustee Tchrs. Ins. and Annuity Corp., 1985-97; N.Y. Trustee Pace U., 1973— Hist. Hudson Valley, 1997—; mem. fin. com. N.Y. Rep. State Com., 1981—, del. Rep. Nat. Conv., 1988; mem. Gov.'s Task Force on N.Y. Housing, 1988-90; bd. dirs. N.Y.C. Partnership, Inc., 1984-93; chmn. Realty Found. of N.Y., 1989—, N.Y. State Statue of Liberty Celebration Found., 1983-84, N.Y. State Housing Fin. Agy., 1969, Tri-State Regional Planning Commn., 1969-70; vice-chmn. Battery Park City Authority, 1997—; mem. Pres.'s Commn. on Housing, 1981-82, others. Lt. USNR, 1954-56. Office: Urstadt Biddle Properties 321 Railroad Ave Greenwich CT 06830-6306

URVAL, KRISHNA RAJ, health facility administrator, educator; b. Mangalore, India, July 3, 1955; came to U.S., 1984; s. Rajgopal Rao and Bhoomi Devi (Kanemar) U.; m. Purnima K. Hebbar, May 23, 1985; children: Nikita, Nikhil. MBBS, MD, Govt. Med. Coll., Mysore City, India, 1979; DCH, U. West Indies, Kingston, Jamaica, 1985. Bd. cert. pediatrics, allergy/immunology. Resident pediats. U. West Indies, Jamaica, 1980—85, Interfaith Med. Ctr., Bklyn., 1985—88, chief resident, 1987—88; fellow immunology U. South Fla., St. Petersburg, 1988—90; assoc. Wyo. Chest and Allergy Clinic, Casper, 1990—91; med. dir. Ohio Valley Allergy Inst., Wheeling, W.Va., 1991—; clin. assoc. prof. W.Va. U., Morgantown, 1991—. Bd. dirs. W.Va. Am. Lung Assn., Charleston. Bd. dirs. Child Care Resource Ctr., Wheeling, 1992—; med. dir. Asthma Support Group, Wheeling, 1992—. Fellow Am. Acad. Pediatrics; mem. AMA, Am. Coll. Allergy/Immunology, Am. Acad. Allergy/Immunology. Democrat. Hindu. Avocations: tennis, ping pong/table tennis, shuttle badmitton. Office: Ohio Valley Allergy Inst 2101 Jacob St Ste 601 Wheeling WV 26003-3844

USABIAGA ARROYO, JAVIER, secretary of agriculture, livestock and rural development for Mexico; b. Celaya, Guanajuato, Mex., Aug. 20, 1939; Studied pub. acctg., Escuela Bancaria y Comercial, Mexico City. With Hays Farms Ltd., Ont.; collaborator various cos. including Covemenxx, Empacadora Gen. Agrícola del Bajío, Equipos y Tractores del Bajío, Alimentos Deshidratados del Bajío; sec. agrl. and rural devel. State of Guanajuato, 1995—2000; mem. Fed. Chamber of Deps.; sec. agriculture, livestock and rural devel. Govt. of Mex., 2000—. Vice-chmn. bd. cons. Banamex-Accival Fin. Group. Mem.: Asociación Mexicana Secs. Desarrollo Agropecuario A.C. (hon.), Assn. Garlic Prodrs. Ctrl. Mex. (hon.; chmn.), Assn. Breeders Holstein Frieslan Mex. (hon.; chmn.). Office: Ave Insurgentes Sur 476 Col Roma Sur Deleg Cuahtemoc Mexico City Mexico

USCHEEK, DAVID PETROVICH, retired chemist; b. University Heights, Ohio, July 9, 1937; s. Peter Ivanovich and Marie (Ocasek) U. BS, Case Western Res. U., 1959; PhD in Chem. Engring., LaSalle U., 1998. Chemist The Glidden Co., Cleve., 1963-67, Mobil Chem. Co., Cleve., 1967-71, Limbacher Coatings, Cleve., 1971-72; tech. dir. Continental Products, Euclid, Ohio, 1972-80; chemist Body Bros. Paint Corp., Bedford, Ohio, 1980-83, Harrison Paint Corp., Canton, Ohio, 1983-88, Akron (Ohio) Paint and Varnish, 1988-95, Ritrama Duramark, 1995-98, Mahoning Paint Corp., 1999-2000; ret., 2000—. Cons. The Analyst, Chardon, Ohio, 1991—. Mem. Am. Chem. Soc., Internat. Union of Pure and Applied Chemists, N.Y. Acad. Scis. Home: 8602 Auburn Rd Chardon OH 44024-8711 Fax: 440-392-9728.

USDIN, GENE LEONARD, psychiatrist; b. N.Y.C., Jan. 31, 1922; s. I. L. and Eva (Miller) U.; m. Cecile Weil, Nov. 8, 1947; children: Cecile Catherine Burka, Linda Ann, Steven William, Thomas Michael. Student, U. N.C., 1939—40, U. Fla., 1940—41; BS, Tulane U., 1943, MD, 1946. Diplomate Am. Bd. Psychiatry and Neurology (asst. examiner, 1956-80), Am. Bd. Legal Medicine. Intern Touro Infirmary, New Orleans, 1946—47; resident psychiatry Cin. Gen. Hosp., 1949—51; fellow psychiatry Tulane Sch. Medicine, 1951—52; pvt. practice psychiatry New Orleans, 1952—86; pvt practice psychiatry, 1996—; asst. prof. clin. psychiatry Tulane U., 1959—62, assoc. clin. prof., 1962—67, La. State U., 1967—71, clin. prof., 1971—96, clin. prof. emeritus, 1996—; sr. psychiatrist Ochsner Clinic, 1986-96, sr. psychiatrist emeritus, 1996—; prof. Notre Dame Sem., 1969-75; chief divsn. neurology and psychiatry Touro Infirmary, New Orleans, 1962—66, dir. psychiat. svcs., 1966—71. McLaughlin-Gallie vis. prof. Royal Coll. Physicians and Surgeons of Can., 1983; Robert O. Jones lectr. Atlantic Maritime Provinces Psychiat. Assn. (Can.), 1976; sr. psychiatrist DePaul and Charity Hosps.; sr. psychiat. cons. Ochsner Med. Found., New Orleans, 1980-85, Timberlawn Psychiat. Hosp., Dallas, 1979-93; chmn. psychiat. cons. com. Am. Bar Found., 1970-73; mem. nat. psychiat. adv. bd. Achievement and Guidance Ctrs. Am., Inc., 1991-92. Editor-in-chief Psychiatry Digest, 1964-71, 75-79, Psychiatry Digest (Europe), 1981-92, ACP-Psychiat. Update, 1980-94, 1995-96, 2000-, co-editor 1994-95; editor Medilex Digest of Psychiatry, 1980—; mem. editl. bd. Acad. Psychiatry, 1989-92, Mental Hygiene, 1969-76, Clin. Medicine, 1965-71, 75-88, Med. Digest, 1965-71, Jour. Hosp. and Cmty. Psychiatry, 1975, chmn., 1980-81, Jour. Psychiat. Edn., 1975-89, Am. Jour. Family Therapy, 1978—, Am. Jour. Social Psychiatry, 1981-87, Swiss Med. Digest, Psychiatry, 1981—, Extracta Medica Practica Psychiatrie, 1981-, Behavioral Scis. and the Law, 1982-92, Dynamic Psychotherapy, 1982-90, Psychiat. Medicine, 1982-88, Advances in Therapy, 1983-96, Clin. Psychiatry News, 1983-92, Contemporary Psychiatry, 1984-93, Health Disease, 1986—, The Psychiat. Times, 1985— (book rev. editor 1988-2002), Clin. Advances in the Treatment of Psychiat. Disorders, 1987—, Jour. Ottawa Med. Sch, 1976-90, Psychiatry Bookshelf, 1976-78, Women's Psychiat. Health, 1992—; mem. internat. adv. bd. Jour. Psicopatologia, Madrid, 1989-94; editor: Psychoneurosis and Schizophrenia, 1966, Practical Lectures in Psychiatry for the Medical Practitioner, 1966, Adolescence: Care and Counseling, 1967, Perspectives on Violence, 1972, (with Peter A. Martin and A.W. Swipe) A Physician in the General Practice of Psychiatry, 1970, The Psychiatric Forum, 1973, Sleep Research and Clinical Practice, 1973, Psychiatry: Education and Image, 1973, Overview of the Psychotherapies, 1975, Schizophrenia: Biological and Psychological Perspective, 1976, Depression: Clinical, Biological and Psychological Perspectives, 1977, Psychiatric Medicine, 1977, (with Charles K. Hofling) Aging: The Process and the People, 1978, (with Jerry M. Lewis, II) Psychiatry in General Medical Practice, 1979, (with David R. Hawkins) The Office Guide to Sleep Disorders, 1980, (with Jerry M. Lewis) Treatment Planning in Psychiatry, 1982; contbr. articles to profl. jours. Bd. trustees United Fund Greater New Orleans, 1966-70. Served to lt. (j.g.) USNR, 1947-49. Recipient Physician of Yr. award Orleans Parish Med. Soc., 1984, Outstanding Alumni Lectr. award Tulane U. Sch. Medicine, 1986, Seymour Pollack Disting. Svc. award Am. Acad. Psychiatry and the Law, 1988, Outstanding Contbrn. to Social Psychiatry award Am. Assn. for Social Psychiatry, 1993, Lifetime Achievement awards Tulane Med. Alumni Assn., 1996, Fla. Hosp. Ctr. for Psychiatry, 1996, La. State U. Sch. Medicine Dept. Psychiatry Chmn.'s award, 1998-99, Champion of Pub. Health award Tulane U. Sch. Pub. Health and Tropical Medicine, 2001; named Psychiatrist of Yr., La. Psychiat. Med. Assn., 1994, Psychiat. Times, 1997. Fellow Am. Psychiat. Assn. (chmn. com. on psychiatry and law 1964-68, mem. com. on ethics 1970-74, com. on membership 1970-74, com. on evaluation svcs. bd. 1974-77, com. on pub. affairs 1976-78, chmn. ad hoc com. on election procedures, 1980-81, trustee at large 1978-81, coun. on internat. affairs 1986-91, sec. gen. Interamerican Coun. of Psychiat. Orgns. 1988-91, recipient 3d ann. Certificate of Recognition for Excellence in Med. Student Edn. 1993, Warren Williams award, 1995, Spl. Presdl. commendation 1998), So. Psychiat. Assn. (bd. regents 1969-72, chmn. 1971-72, pres. 1973-74), La. Psychiat. Assn. (past pres.), Am. Coll. Psychiatrists (bd. regents 1967-70, pres. 1978-79, E.B. Bowis award for Outstanding Contbns. 1973, Disting. Svc. award for Oustanding Contbns. in Am. Psychiatry 1980), Acad. Psychosomatic Medicine (mem. exec. coun. 1974-76), New Orleans Soc. Psychiatry and Neurology (past pres.), Group Advancement Psychiatry (bd. dirs. 1970-77, treas. 1973-77), Am. Assn. Social Psychiatry (pres. 1986-88), World Assn. for Social Psychiatry (exec. coun. 1988-90); mem. La. Med. Soc. (chmn. com. on mental health 1966-70), Orleans Parish Med. Soc., Nat. Assn. Mental Health (mem. profl. adv. coun. 1968-75), Inst. of Mental Hygiene (pres. 1978-79). Home and Office: 3 Newcomb Blvd New Orleans LA 70118-5527 Office Phone: 504-866-5405. Personal E-mail: GUsdin3333@aol.com.

USELTON, BILL W. secondary school educator; b. Oklahoma City, Dec. 14, 1959; s. Jerry Max and Minnie Jewel Uselton; m. Cathy Sue Uselton, Oct. 16, 1982; children: Kelly Irene, Jennifer Elaine. A in Fine Arts, Oscar Rose Jr. Coll., Midwest City, Okla., 1980; BFA, Ctrl. State U., Edmund, Okla., 1982. Cert. secondary sch. tchr. Constract substitute Choctaw (Okla.) Pub. Schs., 1982-84; tchr. Choctaw Jr. H.S., 1984-86, Choctaw H.S., 1986—. Author: Triad of Evil, 1993. Mem. World Jewish Congress; tour guide S.W. Radio Ch., Oklahoma City, 1982; chmn. Confederate Meml., Choctaw, 1996—. Republican. Baptist. Home: 1024 S Anderson Rd Choctaw OK 73020

USERA, VINCENT L. state agency administrator; Asst. atty. gen. Alaska Dept. Law, Comml. Sec., 1991—99; acting dir. Dept. Cmty. and Econ. Devel., 1999—. Office: PO Box 110807 Juneau AK 99811-0807

USHAKOV, YURI VIKTOROVICH, diplomat; b. Moscow, Mar. 13, 1947; married; 1 daughter. Grad., Moscow State Inst. Internat. Relations, 1970; PhD in History, Diplomatic Acad. With Soviet Embassy in Denmark Ministry Fgn. Affairs of the USSR, 1970-75, with, 1975-86; dep. chief mission, min.-counsellor Embassy of the USSR/Russian Fedn., Denmark, 1986-92; dir. Dept. of All-European Coop. Ministry Fgn. Affairs Russian Fedn., 1992—96; amb., permanent rep. Russian Fedn. to the Orgn. Security and Coop. Europe, Vienna, 1996-98; dep. min. fgn. affairs Govt. Russian Fedn., 1998-99, amb. to the U.S., 1999—. Office: Embassy of the Russian Fedn 2650 Wisconsin Ave NW Washington DC 20007-4600 Fax: 202-298-5749.

USHENKO, AUDREY ANDREYEVNA, painter, art historian, educator; b. Princeton, July 28, 1945; d. Andrew Pavlevitch and Fay (Hampton) U.; m. S.M. Harcaj; 1 child, Emily. Student, Sch. of Art Inst., 1963-64; BA, Ind. U., 1965; MA, Northwestern U., Evanston, Ill., 1967, PhD, 1979. Instr. Valparaiso (Ind.) U., 1968-73, asst. prof., 1978-79; instr. Alan R. Hite Inst. U. Louisville, 1973-74; asst. prof. Northwestern U., Evanston, Ill., 1974-75; vis. faculty Columbia Coll., 1980-88; assoc. prof. Ind.-Purdue U., Ft. Wayne, Ind., 1988—. Gallery artist Gruen Gallery, Chgo., 1983—, Denise Bibro Gallery, N.Y.C., 1993—, Yvonne Rapp Gallery, Louisville, 1989—; artist oil paintings Bacchus & Ariadne III, 1987 (NAD Clark prize), Social Security, 1987 (Purchase prize 1989), Chgo. Art Expo, 1996, Marriage Project-Travelling Exhbn., 1996, Conviviality, 1997 (NAD Isidor Medal 1997), Fort Wayne Mus. of Art, 1998; curator exhbn., N.Y.C., 1998-99. Mem. AAUP (sec. local chpt. 1990—), NAD. Democrat. Orthodox. Avocations: reading, music. Home: 2519 East Dr Fort Wayne IN 46805-3612

USHER, CHARLES LINDSEY, social work educator, public policy analyst; b. Portsmouth, Va., Aug. 12, 1949; s. Henry George and Lottie Frances (Dickens) U.; m. Janan Bailey, Aug. 14, 1971; children: Lindsay Erin, Ellen Ashley. BA in Polit. Sci., Old Dominion U., 1971, M in Urban Studies, 1974; postgrad., U. Mich., 1975; PhD in Polit. Sci., Emory U., 1976. Asst. prof. polit. sci. Miami U. of Ohio, Oxford, 1976-78, U. N.C., Charlotte, 1978-80; policy analyst, sr. policy analyst Rsch. Triangle Inst., Rsch. Triangle Park, N.C., 1980-84, dir. Ctr. for Policy Studies, 1985-92; exec. dir. Northeastern N.C. Tomorrow, Inc., Elizabeth City, 1984-85; Wallace H. Kuralt Sr. prof. pub.

welfare policy/adminstrn. U. N.C., Chapel Hill, 1993—. Presenter in field. Assoc. editor Evaluation Rev., 1987-89; contbr. articles to profl. jours. Grantee Annie E. Casey Found., 1992—, Edna McConnel Clark Found., 1995-96, Casey Family Program, 1999-2002. Mem.: Am. Evaluation Assn. Home: 4215 Swarthmore Rd Durham NC 27707-5389 Office: U NC Sch Social Work 301 Pittsboro St Chapel Hill NC 27599-3550

USHER, NANCY SPEAR, retired language arts educator; b. Malden, Mass., Mar. 13, 1938; d. George Alonzo and Mary Elizabeth (York) Spear; m. Walter Lansley Whitlock, June 13, 1959 (div. Oct. 1961); m. Frederic Laurence Usher, Apr. 19, 1970 (dec. April 1998). BS in Edn., U. So. Maine, 1960; postgrad., Boston U., Salem State Coll., 1964-68. 5th grade tchr. Melrose (Mass.) Sch Dept., 1961-63, 7th grade English tchr., 1963-65, 71-97, 7th grade spl. needs tchr., 1965-70; ret., 1997. Freshman girls' basketball coach Melrose High Athletic Dept., 1973-77. Mem. U. So. Maine Alumni Assn. Avocations: golf, boating, reading. E-mail: nusher38@aol.com.

USHER, THOMAS JAMES, steel executive, energy executive; b. Reading, Pa., Sept. 11, 1942; s. Paul T. and Mary (Leonard) Usher; m. Sandra L. Mort, Aug. 14, 1965; children: Leanne, Jimmy, Lauren. BS in Indsl. Engring., U. Pitts., 1964, MS in Ops. and Rsch., 1965, PhD in Systems Engring., 1971. Indsl. engr. U. S. Steel Corp., Pitts., 1966—76, asst. gen. supt., 1975—78, asst. div. supt. Gary, Ind., 1978—81, asst. to pres., mng. dir. facility planning and engring. Pitts., 1982—83, v.p. engring., 1982—83, pres., 1991, U.S. Steel Mining Co., Inc., Pitts., 1983—84, v.p. engring. steel, 1984—, sr. v.p. steel ops., 1984—, exec. v.p. heavy products steel divsn., 1986—89, pres. steel divsn., 1990; pres., COO USX Corp., Pitts., 1994—95, chmn., CEO, 1995—. Bd. dirs. PNC Bank, PPG Industries, UPMC Health Sys. Mem. Leadership Pitts., 1984; trustee Multiple Sclerosis, Pitts., 1985; chmn. Allegheny Trails coun. Boy Scouts Am., Pitts, 1985, United Way, Pitts., 1985, U.S.-Korea Bus. Coun., 1993—; U.S.-Japan Bus. Coun.; trustee U. Pitts., 1994—, The Bus. Roundtable Nat. Found., 1995; vice chmn. Internat. Iron and Steel Inst. Bus. Coun., 1997. Mem.: Am. Iron and Steel Engrs. (bd. dirs. 1984—85), Dinamo/Ovia (bd. dirs. 1985), Am. Iron and Steel Inst., The Club at Nevillewood, Augusta Nat. Golf Club, Burning Tree Club, Oakmont Club, Dougle Eagle Club, Laurel Valley Club, Duquesne Club, Rolling Rock Club. Avocations: golf, tennis, racquetball, scuba diving, swimming. Office: USX Corp Room 6100 600 Grant St Ste 6100 Pittsburgh PA 15219-2805

USHER, See RAYMOND, USHER

USIP, EBENGE ETEFIA, economics professor; b. Ikot Obiokoi, Akwa Ibom, Nigeria, Oct. 22, 1948; arrived in USA, 1970, permanent resident, 1987; s. Etefia Essiet and Mary Unwaedo Usip; m. Sharon Elaine Lord, May 27, 1984; children: Nsikan, Ebenge Jr., Kufre, Unyime. BS, SUNY, Albany, NY, 1974, MA, 1976; PhD, U of Conn., Storrs, Conn., 1984. Asst. prof. Youngstown State U, Youngstown, Ohio, 1985—89, assoc. prof., 1990—98, prof., 1999—. Author: (Teaching Home Page) The Ctr. for Web-Based Ed. in Quantitative Econ., 1996 (creativity on Intergrating New Tech. in the tchg. of Undergrad. Econ., 1998), (jour. publication) Coll. Student Jour., 1998, Soc. Sci. Computer Rev., 1998, The Ohio Jour. of Econ. and Politics, 1998, Jour. of Econ. Ed. (JEE), 1999, (book) Learning Econ. and Bus. Stats. with SPSS/win, 4th edit., 2003. Recipient Perseverance in Application of External Funding, The Graduate School/OH, 2002; grantee CCLI-Ed. Material Develop. NSF Grant #0127362, Nat. Sci. Found. (NSF)/DC, 2001. Mem.: Ea. Econ. Assoc. (assoc.), Am. Statis. Assoc. (assoc.), Am. Econ. Assoc. (assoc.). Methodist. Avocations: soccer, tennis, photography, video games, travel. Home: 1202 Will-O-Wood Dr Hubbard OH 44425 Office: Youngstown State Univ 1 University Plaza Youngstown OH 44555

USTAYEV, RAKHIM, psychologist; b. Kirki, Turkmenistan, Sept. 10, 1910; came to U.S., 1981:; s. Ephraim and Balur (Ustozodayev) U.; m. Sipora Ustayev, Nov. 22, 1938; children: Efrem, Istam, Svetlana, Mikhail, David, Maria, Rubin. MS in Psychology, Pedag. Inst., Dushanbe, Tajikistan, 1939; Candidate Sci. in Psychology, Baku (Azerbajan) Pedagogic Inst., 1973. Tchr. Pedagogic Sch., Kurgan-Tube, Tajikistan, 1939-40, Pub. Sch., Dushanbe, Tajikistan, 1943-53; prof. psychology Dushanbe Pedagogic Inst., 1953-81. Author: Thinkers of the Ancient East, 1992, Thinkers About Spiritual Life, 1994, Thinkers About Perconal Psychology, 1997, Chosen Psychology, 1999. Lt. Soviet Army, 1940-43. Mem. N.Y. Acad. Scis. Jewish. Home: 105-40 62d Rd Apt 2S Forest Hills NY 11375

USTIAN, DANIEL C. trucking executive; With Navistar Internat. Corp., 1973—, group v.p., gen. mgr. engine group, 1990—99, pres., 1999—, COO, 2002—03, CEO, 2003—, chmn., 2004—. Office: Navistar International Corp PO Box 1488 4201 Winfield Rd Warrenville IL 60555 Office Phone: 630-753-5000.

USUI, LESLIE RAYMOND, retired clothing executive; b. Wahiawa, Hawaii, Feb. 2, 1946; s. Raymond Isao and Joyce Mitsuyo (Muramoto) U.; m. Annie On Nor Hom, Oct. 23, 1980; 1 child, Atisha. BA in Zool., U. Hawaii, 1969, MA in Edn., 1972. Cert. tchr. Hawaii. Flight steward United Airlines, Honolulu, 1970; spl. tutor Dept. Edn., 1971-73; v.p. Satyuga, Inc., Honolulu, 1974-80, pres., 1980-97; also bd. dirs.; ret., 1997. Cons. Hawaii Fashion Guild, 1978-79. Composer: Song to Chenrayzee, Song to Karmapa. Co-founder, Kagyu Thegchen Ling Meditation Ctr., 1974-03; bd. dir. Maitreya Inst., 1983-86, Palpung Found., 1984—; mem. US Senatorial Bus. Adv. Bd., Wash., 1988; charter mem. Citizens Against Govt. Waste, 1988—, Citizens for Sound Economy, 1987-91, Nat. Tax Limitation Com., 1988-89. Mem. Am. Biog. Inst. (life, bd. govs. 1990), Internat. Biog. Centre (life), World Inst. Achievement (life), Cousteau Soc., Nature Conservancy, Waikiki Aquarium. Republican. Buddhist. Avocations: oriental gardening, music. Home: PO Box 161257 Honolulu HI 96816-0926 Office: Satyuga Inc PO Box 161257 Honolulu HI 96816-0926

UT, HUYNH CONG, photojournalist; b. Saigon, Vietnam; Photojournalist AP, Saigon, 1966—77, LA, 1977—. Named one of 100 best U.S. journalists 20th Century, NYU Dept. Journalism and Mass Comm.; recipient Pulitzer prize, 1973, World Press Photo award, 1973, Sigma Delta Chi award, George Pol Meml. award, Overseas Club award. Office: AP Photo Dept 221 S Figueroa St Los Angeles CA 90012

UTEGULOV, ZHANDOS N. research scientist; b. Almaty, Kazakhstan, Jan. 16, 1973; arrived in US, 1996; s. Nurpeis Imangalievich Utegulov and Iren Khairullovna Muldagalieva; m. Diana Nurdauletkyzy Akysh, July 20, 2002; 1 child, Amir Zhandosuly. BS in physics and English, Kazakh nat. U., Kazakhstan, 1996; MS in photonics, Okla. State U., 1999, PhD in physics, 2003. Rsch. engr. Optoelectronics Lab, Kazakh Nat. U., Almaty, Kazakhstan, 1994—96; grad. tchg. asst. Okla. State U., Physics Dept., Stillwater, Okla., 1996—97; grad. rsch. asst. Okla. State U., Ctr. for Laser & Photonics Rsch., Stillwater, 1997—2003; postdoctoral rsch. scientist U. Cin., Cin., 2004—. Cons. UES, Inc., Dayton, Ohio, 2003—04. Contbr. articles various profl. jours. Judge Sci. Fair Contest, Tulsa, Okla., 2003; treas. Ctrl. Asian Student Assn., Okla. State U., Stillwater, Okla., 2000. Lt. Anti-Aircraft Defense, 1993—95, Kazakhstan. Mem.: Optical Soc. of Am., Am. Physical Soc. Avocations: music, history, soccer, downhill skiing, fgn. lang. Office: U Cin 345 Coll Ct Cincinnati OH 45221 Office Phone: 513-325-5389.

UTELL, MARK JEFFREY, medical educator; b. N.Y.C., July 25, 1946; m. Lois Brooks; 1 child, Michael Jon. BA cum laude, Dartmouth Coll., 1968; MD, Tufts U., 1972. Diplomate Am. Bd. Internal Medicine. Intern St. Elizabeth's Hosp., Boston, 1972-73, resident in internal medicine, 1973-75; from instr. to prof. sch. medicine U. Rochester, N.Y., 1975-92, prof. Sch. Medicine, 1992—, prof. medicine and environ. medicine Sch. Medicine. Dir. respiratory and med. ICUs Strong Meml. Hosp., Rochester, 1977-89, mem. intensive care com., 1977-87; co-dir. pulmonary and critical care sch. medicine U. Rochester, 1984-91, dir. pulmonary and critical care, 1991—; occupl. medicine program, 1988—, assoc. chmn. clin. affairs dept. environ. medicine, 1992—, dir. occupl. and environ. medicine divsn., 1992—, acting chair dept. medicine, 1998-99; cons. VA, 1977—, EPA, 1980—, mem. clean air sci. adv. com., 1988-94; chmn. Environ. health Com., 1998—; mem. exec. com. EPA Sci. adv. bd.; reviewer site visit com. NIH, 1982, outside reviewer respiratory and applied physiology sect. NHLBI, 1982; mem. rev. study sect. Nat. Inst. Environ. Health Scis., 1990-94, mem. task force for rsch. planning; mem. health rsch. com. Health Effects Inst., 1985-94, chair, 2000—; mem. N.Y. State Commr.'s Panel on Tuberculosis, Syracuse, 1988; mem. commn. life scis. NRC, NAS, 1989; mem. panel airborne particulate matter in spacecraft NASA, 1987, mem. environ. health scis. working group, 1993-94. Co-author: Inhalation Toxicology of Air Pollution: Clinical Research Considerations, 1985, Susceptibility to Inhaled Pollutants, 1989; co-editor: Advances in Controlled Clinical Inhalation Studies, 1993; mem. editl. bd. Jour. Aerosol Medicine, Annals of Internal Medicine, 1997-99, Inhalation Tech., Environ. Health Perspectives, Inhalation Toxicology, 1989-2001; guest reviewer various jours.; contbr. over 100 articles to profl. jours. Bd. dirs. Am. Lung Assn. N.Y. State, 1986-88. Grantee Nat. Inst. Environ. Health Scis., Nat. Heart Lung and Blood Inst., EPA, Elec. Power Rsch. Inst., Dow Corning Corp. Fellow AAAS, ACP, Am. Coll. Chest Physicians (mem. steering com. sect. environ. occupl. health 1983-87, assessment asthma in workplace com. 1994); mem. Am. Physiol. Soc., Am. Thoracic Soc. (chmn. scientific assembly on environ. and occupl. health 1987, mem. planning com., 1992-94, respiratory protective guidelines com., 1993-95, other coms.), Am. Coll. Occupl. Environ. Medicine, N.Y. Trudeau Soc. (pres. 1986). Home: 16 Framingham Ln Pittsford NY 14534-1048 Office: U Rochester Sch Medicine Dept Medicine Pulmonary 601 Elmwood Ave Dept Medicine Rochester NY 14642-0001

UTERMOHLEN, HERBERT GEORG, dermatologist; b. Göttingen, Germany, Nov. 27, 1948; came to U.S., 1990, permanent resident; s. Paul Ernst and Gertrud (Quentin) U.; 1 child, Christian. MD, U. Göttingen, 1976. Specialist in dermatology and allergy U. Hosps. Göttingen, 1980-84; pvt. practice Hamburg, Germany, 1986-89, Scarsdale, N.Y., 1990—. With German Armed Forces, 1977-79. Mem. AMA, AAAS, N.Y. Acad. Scis., Deutsche Gesellschaft Für Psychiat. and Nervenheilkunde, Deutsche Dermatology Gesellschaft. Home: 923 Saw Mill River Rd Ste 263 Ardsley NY 10502-1106

UTIAN, WULF HESSEL, gynecologist, endocrinologist; b. Johannesburg, Sept. 28, 1939; came to U.S., 1976; s. Harry and Ethel Utian; m. Moira Mervis, Oct. 4, 1964; children: Brett David, Lara Peta. MBBCh, Witwatersrand U., Johannesburg, S.Africa, 1962; PhD, U. Cape Town, S. Africa, 1970. Cons. ob-gyn Groote Schuur Hosp., Cape Town, 1967-76; dir. reprodn. endocrinology Univ. Hosps., Cleve., 1976-80; dir. ob-gyn Mt. Sinai Med. Ctr., Cleve., 1980-89; pres. U. Ob-Gyn. Specialties, Inc., 1980-99; dir. Cleve. Menopause Clinic, 1986-2000; prof., chmn. dept. reproductive biology Case Western Reserve U., Cleve., 1989-99; dir. ob-gyn. U. Hosps. of Cleve., 1989-99. Cons. Internat. Health Found., Geneva, 1976-92; cons. women's health Cleve. Clinic Found., 2000—; cons. women's midlife health to nat. media, pharm. industry and health providers; assoc. prof. Case Western Res. U., Cleve., 1976-89, prof. reproductive biology, 1989-99, prof. emeritus reproductive biology and ob-gyn., 2000—; pres. Rapid Med. Rsch., 1996—. Author: Menopause in Modern Perspective, 1980, Your Middle Years, 1980, The Menopause and Hormonal Rplacement Therapy--Facts and Controversies, 1991, Managing Your Menopause, 1992; editor: Maturitas, 1980-93, Premenstrual Syndrome, 1981, Menopause Management, 1988—, Menopause, 1993—. Named one of Top Ten Rschrs. in Women's Health, Ladies Home Jour., 1999. Fellow ACOG, Royal Coll. Ob-Gyn. (Am. rep. to com. 1994-2000, honored for menopause rsch. and tchg. 2000), Internat. Coll. Surgeons (v.p. 1983-89); mem. Internat. Menopause Soc. (exec. com. 1981-96, pres. 1993-96, sec. Coun. Affiliated Menopause Socs. 1996-99, chmn. 1999—), N.Am. Menopause Soc. (exec. dir., hon. founding pres. 1989—). Avocations: sailing, hiking. Home: Point East P-7 27500 Cedar Rd Beachwood OH 44122-8105 Office: RMR Inc 29001 Cedar Rd Ste 202 Cleveland OH 44124-4041 E-mail: utian@menopause.org.

UTKIN, VADIM I. electrical engineer, educator; b. Moscow, Oct. 30, 1937; arrived in U.S., 1994; s. Ivan V. Utkin and Liya B. Kovelman; 1 child, Alexi. BS, Moscow Power Inst., 1960; PhD, Inst. Control Scis., Moscow, 1964, DS, 1971; degree (hon.), U. Sarajevo, Yugoslavia, 1978. Engr., rschr., sr. rschr., head lab. Inst. Control Scis., 1960—94; prof. Ohio State U., Columbus, 1994—. Author: Sliding Mode in Variable Structure System (in Russian), 1974, Sliding Mode in Control and Optimization, 1978; co-author: Sliding Mode Control in Electromolecular Systems, 1999; assoc. editor: Automatica, 1972—2000, Internat. Jour. Control, 1980—. Recipient Lenin prize, Govt. of USSR, 1971. Fellow: IEEE (chmn. tech. com. on sliding mode control, mem. adminstrv. com.); mem.: ASME (Oldenburger medal). Avocations: tennis, skiing, skating. Office: Ohio State U Elec Engring Dept 2015 Neil Ave Columbus OH 43210 Business E-Mail: utkin.2@osu.edu.

UTLAUT, WILLIAM FREDERICK, electrical engineer; b. Sterling, Colo., July 26, 1922; s. Frederick Ernst and Francis Ruth Hanna U.; m. Jeanne Elizabeth Pomeroy, Aug. 4, 1946; children— Mark William, Niles Frederick, Paige Elizabeth. Utlaut Moore. BSE.E., U. Colo., 1944, MSE.E., 1950, PhD in Elec. Engring, 1966; diploma, Naval Radar Sch., 1945. Engr. Gen. Electric Co., Schenectady, 1946-48, Nat. Bur. Standards, Boulder, Colo., 1952-53; instr. U. Colo., 1948-52, 53-54; dir. Inst. for Telecommunications Scis., U.S. Dept. Commerce, Boulder, 1954-99; assoc. adminstr. Nat. Telecom and Info. Adminstrn., Boulder, 1980-99. Chmn. U.S. study group 1, Internat. Radio Consultative Com., 1975-99, mem. U.S. nat. com., 1970-81; mem. electromagnetic wave propagation panel, adv. group aerospace research and devel. NATO, 1978-81, adv. com. Nat. Research Council, 1986—; chmn. ANSI-ECSA tech. com. on Integrated Services Digital Network, 1984-99, U.S. nat. com. Internat. Consultative Com. on Telegraph and Telephone Joint Working Party, 1986-99. Guest co-editor spl. joint issue: IEEE Trans. on Spectrum Mgmt, 1981, IEEE Trans. on Communications, 1975; guest editor spl. issue: Radio Sci, 1974; contbr. numerous articles to profl. jours. Bd. dirs. YMCA, 1955—; mem. bd. mgmt. 1st Congl. Ch., 1960-66, 78—; mem. engring. devel. council U. Colo., 1969-81. Served in USN, 1943-46. Recipient Gold medal U.S. Dept. Commerce, 1971, 95, Disting. Engring. Alumnus award U. Colo., 1973. Fellow IEEE (Harry Dimond Meml. award leadership radio sci. and engring. 1989, Presdl. Rank award 1990, 96, policy bd. Comm. Soc.), Internat. Sci. Radio Union, Am. Nat. Stds. Inst., Exch. Carriers Stds. Assn.

UTLEY, F. KNOWLTON, library director, educator; b. Northampton, Mass., May 4, 1935; s. Frederick K. and Florence E. (Moore) Utley; m. Faith E. Green, July 2, 1960; children: Richard F., Stephen R., David E. BS, Castleton State Coll., 1960; MA, U. Conn., 1967; EdD, Boston U., 1979; MLS, U. Ala., 1993. Tchr. indsl. arts Montpelier (Vt.) High Sch., 1960-61, Southwick (Mass.) H.S., 1961-63; tchr., drafting instr. Putnam (Conn.) H.S., 1963-68; media specialist Ctrl. Conn. State U., New Britain, 1968-69, dir. media svcs., 1969-72; doctoral tchg. fellow Boston U., 1972-73; dir. libr., media svcs. Manchester (Mass.) Pub. Schs., 1973-79; assoc. prof. libr. scis. U. Maine, Farmington, 1979-80; dir. grad. program libr. media Livingston (Ala.) U., 1980-83; dir. libr. media svcs. Am. Internat. Coll., Springfield, Mass., 1983—. Pres. C/W Mars-Ctrl. and We. Mass. Auto Res., 1987—88; chmn. bd. dirs. Cooperating Librs. of Great Springfield, 1988—89, We. Mass. Media Coun., 1991—93; founder, headmaster Hampshire Christian Acad., South Hadley, Mass., 1996—2002. Mem. Belchertown Housing Authority, 2000—; trustee Clapp Meml. Libr., Belchertown, Mass., 2003—. Mem.: ALA, Belchertown Hist. Commn., Mass. Libr. Assn., New Eng. Libr. Assn., Assn. Edn. Comm. and Tech., Am. Christian Schs. Internat., Phi Delta Kappa. Home: 11 Canal Dr Belchertown MA 01007-9224 Office: Am Internat Coll 1000 State St Springfield MA 01109-3151 Office Phone: 413-205-3225. Business E-Mail: kutley@cwmars.org.

UTLEY, JON BASIL, think-tank executive, journalist; b. Moscow, Mar. 10, 1934; came to U.S., 1939, naturalized, 1952; s. Arcadi and Freda (Utley) Berdichevsky; m. Ana Maria Hijar, 1968. Student, U. Munich, 1952, Alliance Française, Paris, 1956; BS, Georgetown U., 1956. Mgr. Am. Internat. Underwriters, Cali, Colombia, 1959-60; editor, pub. Bogotá Bull., 1960-61; v.p. Universal Investors Svcs., Nassau, 1962-67; real estate developer Washington, 1968—; mng. gen. ptnr. Kimwill Oil Assocs., Warren, Pa., 1978-86; pres. Ocean McLean Corp., 1989-97, Needle in a Haystack, Washington, 1990-98, Needle Express, 1993-98; fgn. corr. Jour. Commerce, Internat. Reports, S. Am., 1969-74; columnist Times of the Ams., 1974-92, assoc. editor, 1981-92; columnist Washington Inquirer, 1981-90, Washington Times, 1981-82; contbg. editor Conservative Digest, 1984-89; mem. editl. adv. bd. Internat. Reports, 1981-91. Lectr. Accuracy in Media, treas., Ukraine, 1997, Cyprus, 99, Freedoms Found. Valley Forge; commentator Voice of Am., 1985—2003; Jamestown Found. observer Russian elections, 2000. Contbr. articles to Washington Post, Harvard Bus. Rev., Nat. Rev., Human Events, Miami Herald, Lincoln Rev., N.Y.C. Tribune, Am. Legion mag., El Salvador Gazette, The World and I, Antiwar.com, Lima Times, others. Observer Guatemalan elections Georgetown U. Ctr. Strategic Studies, 1985, Romanian elections, 1990; trustee Ctr. Internat. Rels., adv. com. Solidarity Endowment; co-founder Com. to Avert a Mideast Holocaust, 1990-94. Assoc. scholar Competitive Enterprise Inst., 1995-98; Robert A. Taft fellow Ludwig Von Mises Inst., 1998—. Fellow: Atlas Econ. Rsch. Found. (sr.; dir. Russian projects 2000—); mem.: Coun. Nat. Policy, Ams. Against Bombing/Ams. Against World Empire (chmn. 1998—), Hispanic Am. Ctr. Econ. Rsch. (bd. dirs. 1997—), World English Lang. Newspaper Assn. (pres. 1996), United Srs. Assn. (bd. dirs. 1993—2001, v.p. Amcham Cuba 2003—), Coun. Inter-Am. Security (bd. dirs. 1988—93), Phila. Soc., Nat. Press Club. Office: 910 17th St NW Ste 422 Washington DC 20006-2605 Personal E-mail: Jutly@aol.com.

UTRATA, CARL IGNATIUS, corporate counsel, corporate executive; b. Trnava, Slovak Republic, Sept. 23, 1940; came to U.S., 1949, naturalized, 1955; s. Joseph and Irma Mary Utrata; m. Mary Ann M. Nypaver, June 17, 1972; children: Edward Joseph, Stephanie Ann. BS in Fgn. Service, Georgetown U., 1963; JD, Case Western Res. U., 1971. Bar: Ohio 1972, U.S. Dist. Ct. (no. dist.) Ohio 1983, U.S. Ct. Appeals (6th cir.) 1987. Indsl. rels. staff asst. Republic Steel Corp., Buffalo, 1967-68, safety-labor supr. Cleve., 1969-84, coord., mgr. equal employment opportunity, 1972-79, corp. dir. equal employment opportunity, 1979-84; pvt. practice, 1985-91; corp. counsel ISK Bioscls. Corp., Mentor, Ohio, 1991-98; pvt. practice Cleve., 1998—. Dean legal studies, instr. Acad. Ct. Reporting, Cleve.; lectr. paralegal studies program Cuyahoga C.C., Cleve., 2003—. Pres. Lakewood Neighbors Assn., Ohio, 1974, libr. levy chmn., 1975, mem. zoning initiative com., 1976-78; trustee Coun. on Human Rels., Cleve., 1982-88, pres., 1985-88; assoc. v.p. United Way Svcs., Cleve., 1984-85; trustee legal Aid Soc. Cleve., 1986-88; co-founder, pres. bus., industry and edn. con. Urban League Cleve., 1978-79. With U.S. Army, 1963-65, ETO. Mem. ABA (pesticide subcom. 1995-98), Am. Crop Protection Assn. (law com. 1995-98), Cleve. Employers Equal Opportunity Assn. (co-founder, chmn. 1982, pres.' cup 1983). Home and Office: 1506 Arthur Ave Cleveland OH 44107-3804 E-mail: ciutrata@hotmail.com.

UTSEY, GLENDA FRAVEL, architecture educator; BArch, U. Oreg., 1971, MLA, 1977. Assoc. head for student affairs dept. arch. U. Oreg., Eugene. Office: Dept Arch 210 Lawrence Hall 1206 Univ Oreg Eugene OR 97403-1206*

UTT, GLENN S., JR., medical products executive; b. Neodesha, Kans., Aug. 7, 1926; s. Glenn S. and Reba Pauline (White) U.; m. Mary Lou Ford, Aug. 8, 1948; 1 child, Jan A. BSEE, BSBA, Kans. State U., 1949; MBA, Harvard U., 1951. Salesman Drexel Furniture Co., N.C., 1951-55; v.p. Booz Allen & Hamilton, Chgo. and Zurich, Switzerland, 1955-62; exec. v.p. Abbott Labs., North Chicago, Ill., 1962-83, also dir., ret., 1983. Chmn. bd. U.P. Hotel Group Inc., Houghton, Mich.; ret. dir. Synergen, Selectide and Sugen biotech cos. Co-author: Lalique Perfume Bottles, 1990. Alderman City of Lake Forest, Ill., 1972-76, chmn. recreational bd., 1975-78; mem. exec. com. Lake County Republican Fedn., Waukegan, Ill., 1974-83. With USN, 1944-46, USAF (res.), 1948-53. Mem.: Beta Theta Pi. Avocations: antiques, objects of art. Home: PO Box 810 Houghton MI 49931 Personal E-mail: mlbud@webtv.net.

UTTAL, SUSAN, legal administrator; b. N.Y.C., Oct. 8, 1954; d. Sheldon and Jane Louise (Kaufmann) Uttal. BA, Clark U., 1976; cert. paralegal, Inst. Paralegal Tng., Phila., 1978. Legal asst. Winthrop, Stimson, Putnam & Roberts, N.Y.C., 1978-80; legal coord. Schroder Real Estate Corp., N.Y.C., 1980-83; legal asst. supr. real estate svcs. dept. Cravath, Swaine & Moore, N.Y.C., 1983-89; sr. legal asst. real estate dept. Rackemann, Sawyer & Brewster, Boston, 1989-90; sr. legal asst. leasing and real estate depts. Goulston & Storrs, Boston, 1990-97; contracts adminstr. Cabletron Systems, Inc., Rochester, N.H., 1997-99; v.p. ops. Nonpareil Software, New Durham, N.H., 1999—. Mem. Clark U. N.Y. Young Alumni Assn. (steering com.). Democrat. Jewish. Avocations: pottery, piano, photography, bicycling, gourmet cooking. Office: Nonpareil Software Inc 39 N Shore Rd New Durham NH 03855-2113 E-mail: skosko@panaceapottery.com.

UTTAL, WILLIAM R(EICHENSTEIN), psychology and engineering educator, research scientist; b. Mineola, N.Y., Mar. 24, 1931; s. Joseph and Claire (Reichenstein) U.; m. Michiye Nishimura, Dec. 20, 1954; children: Taneil, Lynet, Lisa. Student, Miami U. Oxford, Ohio, 1947-48; BS in Physics, U. Cin., 1951; PhD in Exptl. Psychology and Biophysics, Ohio State U., 1957. Staff Psychologist, mgr. behavioral sci. group IBM Rsch. Ctr., Yorktown Heights, NY, 1957-63; assoc. prof. U. Mich., Ann Arbor, 1963-68, prof. psychology, 1968-86, rsch. scientist, 1963-86, prof. emeritus, 1986—; grad. affiliate faculty dept. psychology U. Hawaii, 1986-88; rsch. scientist Naval Ocean Systems Ctr.-Hawaii Lab., Kailua, 1985-88; prof., chmn. dept. psychology Ariz. State U., Tempe, 1988—90, prof. dept. indsl. engring., 1992—99, affiliated prof., Dept. of Computer Sci. and Engring., 1993-98, prof. emeritus, 1999—. Vis. prof. Kyoto (Japan) Prefectural Med. U., 1965-66, Sensory Sci. Lab., U. Hawaii, 1968, 73, 2003, U. Western Australia, 1970-71, U. Hawaii, 1978-79, 80-81, U. Auckland, 1996, U. Freiburg, 1997, U. Sydney, 1999; pres. Nat. Conf. on On-Line Uses Computers in Psychology, 1974. Author: Real Time Computers: Techniques and Applications in the Psychological Sciences, 1968, Generative Computer Assisted Instruction in Analytic Geometry, 1972, The Psychobiology of Sensory Coding, 1973, Cellular Neurophysiology and Integration: An Interpretive Introduction, 1975, An Autocorrelation Theory of Visual Form Detection, 1975, The Psychobiology of Mind, 1978, A Taxonomy of Visual Processes, 1981, Visual Form Detection in Three Dimensional Space, 1983, Principles of Psychobiology, 1983, The Detection of Nonplanar Surfaces in Visual Space, 1985, The Perception of Dotted Forms, 1987, On Seeing Forms, 1988, The Swimmer: A Computational Model of a Perceptual Motor System, 1992, Toward a New Behaviorism: The Case Against Perceptual Reductionism, 1998, A Computational Model of Vision: The Role of Combination, 1999, The War Between Mentalism and Behaviorism, 2000, The New Phrenology: Limits on the Localization of Cognitive Processes in the Brain, 2001, A Behaviorist Looks at Form Recognition, 2002, Psychomythics, 2003, Dualism, 2004; editor: Readings in Sensory Coding, 1972; assoc. editor Readings in Sensory Coding, 1972, Behavioral Rsch. Method and Instrn., 1968—90, Computing: Archives for Electronic Computing, 1963—75, Jour. Exptl. Psychology, Perception and Performance, 1974—79, cons. editor Jour. Exptl. Psychology: Applied, 1994—97; contbr. articles to profl. jours. Served to 2d lt. USAF, 1951-53. USPHS spl. postdoctoral fellow, 1965-66; NIMH research scientist award, 1971-76 Fellow AAAS, Am. Psychol. Assn., Am. Psychol. Soc. (charter), Soc. Exptl. Psychologists (chmn. 1994-95); mem. Psychonomics Soc. Achievements include patents in field. Office: Ariz State U Dept Indsl Engring Tempe AZ 85287-1104 Office Phone: 480-965-8634. E-mail: aowru@asu.edu.

UTTER, DONALD L. music educator; b. Poughkeepsie, N.Y., Apr. 18, 1951; s. Clarence and Marion (Cobb) U. BS, Susquehanna U., 1974; MusM, Ind. U., 1979. Cert. tchr. music K-12 N.Y. Music educator Webutuck Ctrl. Sch., Anenia, N.Y., 1979-84, Pawling (N.Y.) High Sch., 1984—. Rep. N.Y. State Sch. Music, Pawling, 1995-98; solo festival judge N.Y., 1990—; past v.p. Tchrs. Assn., 1993-94. Bd. dirs. Pawling (N.Y.) Concert Series, 1988—, County Farm Bur., Millbrook, N.Y., 1991-95; bd. dirs. Rep. Party, Pawling, 1993, chmn., 2000-03; varsity golf coach Pawling H.S. Named Coach of the Yr., Pawling High Sch., 1994. Mem. Dutchess County Music Educators (chmn. All-County Music Festival 1993-95), Music Educators Nat. Conf., Am. Fedn. Musicians Local 85. Republican. Methodist. Avocations: golf, skiing, reading. Home: 93 Harmony Rd Pawling NY 12564-0089 Office: Pawling HS Reservoir Rd Pawling NY 12564

UTTER, ROBERT FRENCH, retired judge; b. Seattle, June 19, 1930; s. John and Besse (French) Utter; m. Elizabeth J. Stevenson, Dec. 28, 1953; children: Kimberly, Kirk, John. BS, U. Wash., 1952; LLB, 1954. Bar: Wash. 1954. Pros. atty., King County, Wash., 1955-57; individual practice law Seattle, 1957-59; ct. commr. King County Superior Ct., 1959-64, judge, 1964-69, Wash. State Ct. Appeals, 1969-71, Wash. State Supreme Ct., 1971-95, chief justice, 1979-81; ret., 1995; lectr. Ctrl. and Eastern European Legal Inst., Prague, Czech Republic, 2000, 01, 2002, dean faculty, 2001—. Lectr. in field; leader comparative law tour, China, 1986, China, 87, China, 88, China, 91, Russia, 89, South Africa, 97, Ukraine, 98, Hungary, 98, Czech Republic, 98; adj. prof. constl. law U. Puget Sound, 1987—94; cons. CEELI, 1991, 1993—, USIA, 1992; visitor to Kyrgystan Judiciary, Kazakhstan, 1993—96, Mongolia, 1997; lectr. Albanian Judiciary, 1994, 95, 2000—, Georgian Judiciary, 1999, Serbian Judiciary, 2001—02; commentator on Moldovan constitution, 2003. Editor: books on real property and appellate practice; author: books on state consl. law. Pres., founder Big Brother Assn., Seattle, 1955—67, Job Therapy Inc., 1963—71; mem. exec. com. Conf. Chief Justices, 1979—80, 1981—86; pres. Thurston County Big Bros./Big Sisters, 1984; lectr Soviet Acad. Moscow, 1991; USIA visitor to comment on jud. sys. Latvia, 1992, 1993—94; trustee Linfield Coll. Named Alumnus of the Yr., Linfield Coll., 1973, Judge of the Yr., Wash. State Trial Lawyers, 1989, Outstanding Judge, Wash. State Bar Assn., 1990, Seattle-King County Bar Assn., 1992, Conder-Faulkner lectr., U. Wash. Sch. Law, 1995, Disting. Alumnus, Sch. Law U. Wash., 1995; recipient Henry Jackson Disting. Pub. Svc. award, Nat. Wash. Sch. Law, 2000, Warren E. Burger award, Nat. Ctr. for State Cts., 2003, Vol. award, ABA-CEELI Program, 2003; Disting. Jud. scholar, U. Ind., 1987. Fellow: Chartered Inst. Arbitrators; mem.: ABA (commentator on proposed constns. of Albania, Bulgaria, Romania, Russia, Lithuania, Azerbaijan, Uzbekistan, Byelarus, Kazakhstan, and Ukraine), Am. Judicature Soc. (sec. 1987—, chmn. bd. dirs., mem. exec. com., Herbert Harley award 1983, Justice award 1998), Order of Coif. Baptist.

UTTERBACK, BETTY HARRIS, writer; b. Coalmont, Ind., July 30; d. Earl Daniel and Esther Jane (Bosley) Harris; student in journalism Ind. U., 1945-47; BA in Cultural Studies, Empire State Coll., 1988; m. Max Gene Utterback, Aug. 10, 1947 (dec.); children: Pamela Kim Utterback Tyminski, Max Andrew. Pub. relations ofcl. Purdue U., 1947-50; free lance writer, 1950-69, 84—; with Gannett Rochester (N.Y.) Newspapers, 1969-84, TV editor, 1973-80, feature writer, 1980-84, columnist Gannett News Service, 1973-80. Co-author: (with John Robertson) Suddenly Single, 1986. Bd. dirs. Literacy Vols. Am., Rochester, 1984-87. Recipient 1st prize for feature N.Y. State AP, 1977. Republican. Presbyterian. Home: 103 Stoutenburgh Lane Pittsford NY 14534

UTTERBACK, WILL HAY, JR., retired labor union administrator, genealogist; b. Amarillo, Tex., Mar. 10, 1947; s. Will Hay and Marie (Willey) U.; m. Margaret Jane Smith, July 31, 1982. JD (hon.), Pacific Northwestern U., 1980. Cert. Genealogical Record Splist. Pres. BillCo Enterprises, Amarillo, Tex., 1974-86, Comm. Workers Am. Local 6128, Amarillo, 1988—2003; ret., 2003. Audiovisual cons. Franklin D. Roosevelt Libr., Hyde Park, N.Y., 1971—; cons. Smithsonian Instn., Washington, 1983; lectr. Ind. Scholar Network, Amarillo, 1982—; spl. cons. Ednl. Video Group, Greenwood, Ind., 1989—. Contbr. articles to profl. publs.; reconstructor newsreel film, 1974—. Bd. dirs. Panhandle Tech-Prep Consortium; mem. citizens budget com. United Way. Named Ky. Col., 2001. Mem. Am. Hist. Assn., Nat. Hist. Soc., Ctr. for Study of Presidency, Assn. Profl. Genealogists. Mem. Ch. of Christ. Home: PO Box 51796 Amarillo TX 79159-1796

UTZ, SARAH WINIFRED, nursing educator; b. San Diego; d. Frederick R. and Margaret M. (Gibbons) U.; BS, U. Portland, 1943, EdM, 1958; MS, UCLA, 1970; PhD, U. So. Calif., 1979. Clin. instr. Providence Sch. Nursing, Portland, Oreg., 1946-50, edn. dir., 1950-62; edn. dir. Sacred Heart Sch. Nursing, Eugene, Oreg., 1963-67; asst. prof. nursing Calif. State U., L.A., 1969-74, assoc. prof., 1974-81, prof., 1981—, assoc. chmn. dept. nursing, 1982—; cons. in nursing curriculum, 1978—; healthcare cons., 1991—; past chmn. ednl. adminstrs., cons., tchrs. sect. Oreg. Nurses Assn., past pres. Oreg. State Bd. Nursing; mem. rsch. program Western Interstate Commn. on Higher Edn. in Nursing; chmn. liaison com. nursing edn. Articulation Coun. Calif. Author articles and lab manuals. Served with Nurse Corps, USN, 1944-46. HEW grantee, 1970-74, Kellogg Found. grantee, 1974-76, USDHHS grantee, 1987—; R.N., Calif., Oreg. Mem. Am. Nurses Assn., Calif. Nurses Assn. (edn. commr. region 6 1987—, chair edn. interest group region 6, 1987—), Am. Ednl. Rsch. Assn., AAUP, Phi Delta Kappa, Sigma Theta Tau. Formerly editor Oreg. Nurse; reviewer Western Jour. Nursing Rsch. Home: 1409 Midvale Ave Los Angeles CA 90024-5454 Office: 5151 State University Dr Los Angeles CA 90032-4226

UVENA, FRANK JOHN, retired printing company executive, lawyer; b. Ernest, Pa., Feb. 2, 1934; AB, Ohio U., Athens, 1959; LLB, Ohio State U., Columbus, 1963. Bar: Ill. 1963. Assoc. firm McDermott, Will & Emery, Chgo., 1963-68; atty. R.R. Donnelley & Sons, Chgo., 1968-75, v.p., gen. counsel, 1975-84, sr. v.p. law and corp. staffs, 1984-95. Bd. dirs. Am. Liver Found., Ill., 1996, national, 2001, Parents/Friends Elizabeth Ludeman Devel. Ctr., 1986. With AUS, 1954-56. Mem. ABA, Ill. Bar Assn., Chgo. Bar Assn.

UVILLER, DAPHNE RACHEL, journalist; b. N.Y.C., Nov. 2, 1971; d. H. Richard and Rena (Katz) Uviller; m. Sacha Henry Spector, Sept. 9, 2001. BA, Yale U., 1993. Investigation asst. Spl. Commr. Investigation, N.Y.C., 1994—97; contbg. writer/editor Time Out New York, N.Y.C., 1997—; contbr. Newsday, N.Y.C., 1998—. Freelance screenwriter, 2001—. Contbr. articles to mags. Mem.: P73 Prodns. (bd. dirs. 2001—), Yale Dramatic Alumni Assocs. (sec. 1994—).

UYEDA, SEIYA, geophysics educator; b. Tokyo, Nov. 28, 1929; s. Seiichi and Hatsuo (Okino) U.; m. Mutsuko Kosaka, July 6, 1952; children: Taro, Makiko, Naoko. BS, U. Tokyo, 1952, DSc, 1958; DSc (hon.), U. Athens, Greece, 1996. Rsch. assoc. Earthquake Rsch. Inst. U. Tokyo, 1957-64, assoc. prof. Geophys. Inst., 1964-69, prof. Earthquake Rsch. Inst., 1969-90; prof. dept. marine sci. and tech. Tokai U., Shimizu, Japan, 1990-94, dir. earthquake prediction rsch. ctr., 1995-96; prof. Tex. A&M U., College Station, 1990-95. Dir. Internat. Frontier Program on Earthquake Rsch. Riken, 1996—2002. Author: Debate About the Earth, 1966, Island Arcs, 1973, The New View of the Earth, 1978. Recipient Tanakadate prize Soc. Terrestrial Magnetism and Electricity, 1955, G.P. Woollard award Geol. Soc. Am., 1989, Matsumae Prize for Academic Accomplishment, Tokai Univ., 1992. Fellow AAAS (hon.), Nat. Acad. Sci. (fgn. assoc., A Agassiz medal 1972), Russian Acad. Scis. (fgn.), Geol. Soc. London (hon.), European Union Geoscis. (hon.), Am. Geophys. Union (Walter Bucher medal 1991); mem. Am. Acad. Arts and Scis. (fgn.), Soc. Geology France (assoc.), Japan Acad. (Acad. prize 1987). Home: 2-39-6 Daizawa Setagaya-ku Tokyo 155-0032 Japan Office: Tokai U 3-20-1 Orido Shimizu 424 8610 Japan Office Phone: +81-543-36-2862. E-mail: suyeda@st.rim.or.jp.

UYEHARA, OTTO ARTHUR, mechanical engineering educator emeritus, consultant; b. Hanford, Calif., Sept. 9, 1916; s. Rikichi and Umi (Nakayama) U.; m. Chisako Suda, Aug. 12, 1945; children: Otto Kenneth, Susan Joy Uyehara Schultheiss, Emi Ryu Uyehara-Stewart. BS, U. Wis., 1942, MS, 1943, PhD, 1946. Postdoctoral fellow U. Wis., Madison, 1945-46, rsch. assoc., 1946-47, asst. prof., then assoc. prof., 1949-57, prof., 1957-82, prof. emeritus, 1982—; pvt. practice cons. Anaheim, Calif., 1985—. Mem. sci. adv. com. Echlin Corp., Branford, Conn., 1980—. Recipient Sci. Achievement award Japan Soc. Automotive Engrs, Internal Combustion Engine award ASME, 1994. FEllow Soc. Automotive Engrs.; mem. ASME (internal combustion divsn., Internal Combustion award 1994), Japan Soc. Mech. Engrs. (hon.). Home: Apt 303 380 S Anaheim Hills Rd Anaheim CA 92807-4062

UYS, JURGEN PETER BRINKER, securities analyst; came to U.S., 1955; s. Johannes Marthinus and Reinette McKay (Weidemann) U. BS, U. Pa., 1974; MBA, Columbia U., 1977. CFA. Securities analyst Equibank, N.A., Pitts., 1974-76; fin. analyst Amax Inc., Greenwich, Conn., 1978-80; v.p. Equitable Investment Mgmt., N.Y.C., 1980-85; securities analyst Swiss Am. Securities, N.Y.C., 1986-91; gen. ptnr. Peter Uys Partnership, Ltd., N.Y.C., 1991—. Mem. Huguenot Soc. Am. (treas. 1991-92), Assn. for Investment Mgmt. and Rsch., Psi Upsilon. Episcopalian. Personal E-mail: jpbu@msn.com.

UYSAL, MUZAFFER SHAMIL, management educator; s. Samil and Ifakat Uysal; m. Nese Kirimker, July 28, 1970; 1 child, Deylin Shamil. BS, Anakara Acad. Econs. and Comml. Scis., 1976; MBA, U. New Haven, 1980; PhD, Tex. A&M U., 1983. Asst. prof. Dokuz Eylul U., Izmir, Turkey, 1984—85, Clemson U., SC, 1985—88, assoc. prof., 1988—91, Va. Tech, Blacksburg, 1992—, prof. Contbr. articles to profl. jours. Fellow: Internat. Acad. Study Tourism, Phi Beta Delta (hon.; treas. 2000—02); mem.: Internat. Soc. Quality-of-Life Studies (bd. mem. 1999—2002), Internat. Travel and Tourism Rsch. Assn. (conf. program reviewer 1988—93). Home: 303 Seminole Dr Blacksburg VA 24060 Office: Virginia Tech HTM 355 Wallace Hall Blacksburg VA 24061-04 Personal E-mail: samil@vt.edu. E-mail: samil@vt.edu.

UZAN, BERNARD, artistic director; b. Tunis, Tunisia, Dec. 5, 1944; arrived in Can., 1988; s. Henri and Elise Gabrielle (Pansieri) Uzan; m. Diana Soviero, Nov. 9, 1984. PhD, Paris U., 1968. Gen. & artistic dir. Théâtre français d'Amérique, Boston, 1973-83, Tulsa Opera, 1987-88, L'Opéra de Montreal, 1988—2001; stage dir. Palm Beach Opera, Fla., 2003—. Adminstr., exec. dir. Alliance français de Boston, 1974—83; stage dir. U.S., San Francisco, Fla., Phila., New Orleans, Portland, Dallas; stage dir. Can., Montreal, Toronto, Vancouver, Quebec City, Edmonton, Calgary; stage dir. europe, Monte-Carlo, Zurich, Palermo, Turin; stage dir. in charge internat. affairs Eurolyrica, 1997—; bd. dirs. Opera Am. Address: PO Box 8143 Englewood NJ 07631 Office: Palm Beach Opera 415 S Olive Ave West Palm Beach FL 33401 E-mail: odm@total.net.

UZMAN, BETTY BEN GEREN, retired pathologist; b. Fort Smith, Ark., Nov. 17, 1922; d. Benton Asbury and Myra Estelle (Petty) Geren; m. L. Lahut Uzman, Dec. 17, 1955 (dec.); 1 dau., Betty Tuba. Student, Fort Smith Jr. Coll., 1939-40; BS, U. Ark., 1942; MD, Washington U., 1945; postgrad., M.I.T., 1948-50; MA (hon.), Harvard U., 1967. Intern Childrens Hosp., Boston, 1945-46; resident in pathology Barnes Hosp., St. Louis, 1946-48; Am. Cancer Soc. research fellow MIT, Cambridge, Mass., 1948-50; chief biol. ultrastructure and exptl. pathology Children's Cancer Research Found., Boston, 1950-71; instr. Harvard Med. Sch., Boston, 1949-53, assoc., 1953-56, research assoc., 1956-67, assoc. prof., 1967-71, prof., 1971-72; head research dept. Sparks Regional Med. Center, Fort Smith, 1972-74; prof. pathology La. State U., Shreveport, 1974-77, U. Tenn., Memphis, 1978-89, retired. Assoc. chief staff rsch. VA, Shreveport, 1974-77; staff pathologist VA, Memphis, 1978-89, chief lab. svc., 1986-87; chief field ops., spl. asst. to dir. VA Central Office, Washington, 1978-79, dir. med. rsch. svcs., 1979-80; chmn. pathology A Study sect. NIH, 1973-76; cons. to sci. dir. Children's Cancer Rsch. Found., Boston, 1971-73; mem. adv. com. on prevention, diagnosis and treatment Am. Cancer Soc., 1970-73, 77-80; mem. adv. bd. Office Regeneration Rsch., VA, 1985-89; disting. vis. investigator Inst. Venezolano Investigation Cientificas, Caracas, 1972-74 Decorated Order of Andres Bello 1st class Venezuela; recipient Weinstein award United Cerebral Palsy, 1964; Am. Cancer Soc. research fellow, 1948-50 Mem. AAAS (emerita), Am. Soc. Cell Biology, Soc. Devel. Biology, Am. Acad. Neurology (assoc.), Am. Soc. Neurochemistry, Microscopy Soc. Am. (Diatome poster award 1985), Internat. Acad. Pathology, Am. Assn. Neuropathology (assoc.), Soc. Neurosci., Am. Assn. Cancer Rsch. Home and Office: Geren Farm 16048 E State Highway 197 Scranton AR 72863-0048 Personal E-mail: bguzman@aol.com.

UZZELL-BAGGETT, KARON LYNETTE, career officer; b. Goldsboro, N.C., Apr. 28, 1964; d. Jesse Lee and Ernestine Smith Uzzell; m. Ronald Walter Baggett, July 26, 1990; 1 child, Kathleen; stepchildren: Christina, Brian, Adam. BS, U. N.C., 1986; postgrad., U. Md., 1993-96. Commd. 2nd lt. USAF, 1986, advanced through grades to lt. col., 1990, exec. officer 6ACCS, 1986-88, ops. tng. officer 7393MUNSS Murted AFD, Turkey, 1988-89, command and control officer 52FW Spangdahlem AB, Germany, 1989-92, SENEX mission dir. 89AW Andrews AFB, Md., 1992-95, dep. chief classified control Office Sec. Def., 1995-97, chief classified control Office Sec. Def., 1998-99, flight comdr., dir. ops. 82TRSS Sheppard AFB, Tex., 1999—2001; detachment comdr. USAFE MSS, Vicenza, Italy, 2001—02; comdr. 78MSS, Robins AFB, Ga., 2002—04, 416EMSS, Karshi-Khanabad, Uzbekistan, 2003—04. Emergency med. technician Orange County Rescue Squad, Hillsborough, N.C., 1985-86; treas. Melwood PTA, Upper Marlboro, Md., 1994-97; meml. vol. Women in Mil. Svc., Washington, 1993—; entitlements vol. Whitman Walker Clinic, Washington, 1993-98; dir. pers. Air U., Maxwell AFB, Ala., 2004—. Mem. Women in Mil. Svc. for Am., So. Poverty Law Ctr. Democrat. Baptist. Avocations: running, weightlifting, sewing, cross stitching, gardening. Home: 2319 Walbash Dr Montgomery AL 36116

VACANTI, JOSEPH PHILIP, pediatric surgeon, transplant surgeon; b. Omaha, Oct. 31, 1948; BS summa cum laude, Creighton U., 1970; MD with high distinction, U. Nebr., 1974. Diplomate in gen. surgery and pediatric surgery Am. Bd. Surgery. Clin. fellow in surgery Harvard Med. Sch., Boston, 1979-83; asst. in surgery Children's Hosp., Boston, 1983-90, sr. assoc. in surgery, 1990-98, dir. organ transplant, 1990-98, dir. lab. for transplant and tissue engring., 1990—; asst. prof. surgery Harvard Med. Sch., Boston, 1983-90, assoc. prof., 1990-97, prof., 1997—; John Homans prof. surgery Harvard Med. Sch./Mass. Gen. Hosp., 1998—; dir. Lab. Tissue Engring. and Organ Fabrication Mass. Gen. Hosp., 1998—, dir. Pediat. Transplant, 1998—, chief Dept. Pediat. Surgery, 2003—; surgeon-in-chief Mass. Gen. Hosp. Children, 2003—. Rsch. affiliate MIT, Cambridge, 1988—. Author some 30 book chpts. and more than 150 sci. articles; co-founder, sr. editor Tissue Engring.; mem. editl. bd. Cell Transplantation; mem. editl. adv. bd. Tissue Engring. Intelligence Unit, R.G. Landes. Recipient Sidney Farber award Children's Hosp., 1983, Spl. Recognition award Am. Liver Found., 1987. Fellow ACS; mem. Tissue Engring. Soc. (co-founder, pres.), Am. Soc. Transplant Surgeons, Transplantation Soc., Am. Pediat. Surg. Assn., Soc. Univ. Surgeons, Inst. Medicine. Office: Mass Gen Hosp 55 Fruit St Boston MA 02114-2696 Office Phone: 617-724-1725. Business E-Mail: jvacanti@parthners.org.

VACAR, RICHARD M. airport executive; BS, MBA, Calif. State U.; JD, Loyola Marymount U. Dir. Dept. Aviation Houston Airport Sys.; also dir. aviation Ellington Field, Bush Intercontinental Airport (Houston), William P. Hobby Airport. Office: Houston Airport Sys 16930 JFK Blvd Houston TX 77032

VACCA, JOHN JOSEPH, JR., television executive; b. Chgo., Apr. 7, 1922; s. John Joseph and Caroline (Bain) V.; m. Alice Isabel Ure, May 2, 1944; children: John Joseph, Dawn Susan, Kim Frances. Student, Northwestern U., 1940-42, Internat. Corr. Schs., 1950-54, Harvard U., 1966. Editor, Midwest Times, Chgo., 1940-41; with prodn. dept. NBC Radio, 1946-47; news dir. sta. KECK, Odessa, Tex., 1947-49, chief announcer, 1948-49; program mgr. KOSA-Radio, Odessa, 1949-55; sta. mgr. KOSA-TV, 1955-61, gen. mgr., 1962-72; v.p., dir. Trigg Vaughn Stas., Inc., Odessa, 1962-67; sec. Odessa Broadcasting Co., 1950-72; asst. sec. Doubleday Broadcasting Co., 1967-77, v.p., 1967-75, sr. v.p., 1975-77; gen. mgr. KDTV, Dallas, 1972-73; TV cons. Dallas, 1978—; v.p., dir., gen. mgr. Heart O'Texas Broadcasting, Waco, Tex., 1978-83; v.p. Dunn Prodns., Inc., Dallas, 1984-88, pres., 1989-92; ind. TV producer Dallas, 1992—. Author: Seven Keys to Success, 1981. Bd. dirs. Odessa Community Chest, 1964-72, Better Bus. Bur., 1956-72; campaign maj. ARC, 1951-72; publicity adviser Ector County chpt. Nat. Found. for Infantile Paralysis, 1949-72; campaign coordinator Civic Music Assn., 1950-72; sponsor, adviser Permian Playhouse, 1959-72, v.p., bd. dirs., 1971-72, City councilman, Odessa, 1962-64; Bd. dirs. Am. Cancer Soc. Served with USAAF, 1942-46. Recipient Zeus award Epsilon Sigma Alpha, 1971 Mem. Nat., Tex. assns. broadcasters, Tex. AP Broadcasters Assn., Advt. Club Odessa (pres. 1960-61, dir. 1960-63), C. of C. (publicity adviser 1950-72), Holy Name Soc. Clubs: K.C. (sec. Odessa 1950-51). Roman Catholic. Home and Office: 646 Harvest Hill Ln Lewisville TX 75067-3588 *A philosophy of service, personal and through broadcasting, coupled with a sincere approach to excellent Human Relations have formed the keystone of my career. Consistent honesty and a constant effort to give and produce much more than required have always been guiding principles. My goals have been set with flexible policies to implement them, ever mindful that 'change' is an integral part of life and progress.*

VACCARO, ALEXANDER R. orthopedist, surgeon; b. White Plains, N.Y., Sept. 25, 1961; s. Alexander Richard and Sue Francis (Schmitz) V.; m. Marjorie Lynne Rheinheimer, June 26, 1993; children: Maxwell, Alexander, Juliana. BS, Boston Coll., 1983; MD, Georgetown U., 1987. Diplomate Am. Bd. Orthopedic Surgery. Prof. Orthop. Surgery Thomas Jefferson U. Hosp., Phila., 1993—96; attending orthop. surgeon Rothman Inst., Phila., 1996—. Co-dir. Spine Fellowship Program Thomas Jefferson U. Hosp., Phila., 1997—; co-dir. Reconstructive Spine Svc. Rothman Inst., Phila., 1997—. Contbr. chpts. in books, numerous articles to profl. jours. Recipient Outstanding Basic Sci. Paper award, Cervical Spine Rsch. Soc., 1996, Best Poster Exhibit, 2001, award, Jeffrey Lance Spinal Cord Injury Found., 2001, Econ. and Cultural Achievement award, Italian Accademia Europea per le Relasioni Economiche e Culturali, 2002;, Japanese Orthop. fellow, 2000, Scoliosis Rsch. Soc. fellow, 2003. Mem. AMA, Phila. Orthopedic Soc., Jefferson Orthopedic Soc., Phila. Orthopedic Soc., Pa. Orthopedic Soc. Roman Catholic. Avocations: Marathon runner, Eucharistic minister, illustrator. Home: 1645 Waverly Rd Gadwyne PA 19035 Office: Rothman Inst 925 Chestnut St 5th Fl Philadelphia PA 19107

VACCARO, BRENDA, actress; b. Bklyn., Nov. 18, 1939; d. Mario and Christine (Pavia) V. Student, Neighborhood Playhouse, 1958-60. Appeared in Broadway plays: Everybody Loves Opal, 1961, The Affair, 1962, Tunnel of Love, 1962, Children from Their Games, 1963, Cactus Flower, 1965 (Tony award best supporting actress), The Natural Look, 1967, How Now Dow Jones, 1968 (Tony nomination best actress in mus. comedy), The Goodbye People, 1968 (Tony nomination for best actress in drama), Father's Day, 1971, California Suite with Neil Simon, The Odd Couple, 1985 with Sally Struthers, Jake's Women, 1992 with Alan Alda-A Neil Simon Play, Full Gallop (one woman show), 1998; motion pictures include: House by the Lake, 1977, Midnite Cowboy, 1969, Where It's At, 1969, I Love My Wife, 1970, Summer Tree, 1971, Going Home, 1971, Once Is Not Enough, 1975, Airport '77, 1977, Fast Charlie, 1977, Capricorn One, 1978, First Deadly Sin, 1980, Zorro, The Gay Blade, Supergirl, 1984, Water, 1986, Heart of Midnight, 1988, Cookie, 1988, Ten Little Indians, 1988, Masque of the Red Death, 1989, Love Affair, 1994, The Mirror Has Two Faces, 1996; TV appearances in The Greatest Show on Earth, 1963, Fugitive, 1963, Defenders, 1965, Doctors and Nurses, 1965, Coronet Blue, 1967, Naked City, The FBI, 1969, The Psychiatrist, 1971, Name of the Game, 1971, Marcus Welby, M.D, 1972, Banacek, 1972, McCloud, 1972, McCoy, Streets of San Francisco, Sara, 1976 (Emmy nomination for best dramatic actress), Paper Dolls, Dear Detective, 1979, The Pride of Jesse Hallam, 1980, A Long Way Home, 1981, Star Maker, 1981, Deceptions, 1985, St. Elsewhere, Murder She Wrote, 1990, Trials of Rosie O'Neil, 1991, Civil Wars, 1991, Flesh and Blood, 1991, The King of Queens, 1998, Ally McBeal, 1998, Friends, 1996; TV movie appearances in Travis Logan, D.A, 1971, What's A Nice Girl Like You, 1971, Honor Thy Father, 1973, Sunshine, 1973, The Big Ripoff, 1975, Julius and Ethel Rosenberg, 1978, Guyana Tragedy: The Story of Jim Jones, 1980, Paper Dolls, Dear Detective, 1989, Stolen: One Husband, Columbo, 1990, Once Is Not Enough (Academy award, Golden Globe award, People's Choice award), The Shape of Things (Emmy award for supporting actress), Golden Girls Ebbs Tide Revenge (Emmy award 1991), Red Shoe Diaries, 1991, Following Her Heart, 1994, Sing Me the Blues Lena, 1995, Touched by an Angel, 1996, Stolen One Husband, 1997, Johnny Bravo Show (voice over series animation), 1993-2000, When Husbands Cheat, 1998, Fat Girl (voice over series animation), 2001. Recipient Theatre World award, 1961-62, 3 Tony nominations, 2 Hollywood Fgn. Press Assn. nominations.

VACCARO, JEROME VINCENT, psychiatrist, educator, healthcare executive; b. Bklyn., Apr. 17, 1955; BS, CUNY, 1977; MD, Albert Einstein U., 1981. Diplomate Am. Bd. Psychiatry. Chief resident Albert Einstein U., Bronx, N.Y., 1984-85; assoc. prof. U. Hawaii, Honolulu, 1985-89, UCLA, 1989—. Med. dir. PacifiCare Behavioral Health, 1996-2001, pres., CEO, 2001--; pres., CEO PacifiCare Dental/Vision, 2001-. Editor: Community Psychiatry, 1995; contbr. articles to med. jours. including Hosp. and Comty. Psychiatry, Comty. Mental Health Jour. Mem. Am. Psychiat. Assn., Am. Assn. Comty. Psychiatrists (editor jour. 1984-93). Office: Pacificare Behavioral Health PO Box 25186 Santa Ana CA 92799-5186

VACCARO, RALPH FRANCIS, marine biologist; b. West Somerville, Mass., Apr. 30, 1919; s. Angelo Ralph and Adelaide (Alberlini) V.; m. Martha Ann Walsh, Apr. 19, 1955; children: Christopher Ralph, Adelaide Marie, John Michael, Mark Joseph, Thomas James (dec.), Peter Anthony. BS, Tufts U., 1941; M.P.H., MIT, 1943. Sanitary engring. aide Commonwealth of Mass., Boston, 1946-47; pub. health bacteriologist Assn. Am. Railroads, Balt., 1947-48; sr. rsch. scientist Woods Hole Oceanographic Inst. (Mass.), 1948-86, chmn. dept. biol., 1984-85; cons. environ. quality; assoc. math.-sci. staff Falmouth (Mass.) High Sch., 1989—. Patentee in field. Served with USPHS, 1956—; served with U.S. Army, 1943-46. Mem. Am. Soc. Limnology and Oceanography, AAAS Republican. Roman Catholic. Home: PO Box 245 West Falmouth MA 02574-0245

VACCHELLI, ROBERT FRANCIS, lawyer; b. Hartford, Conn., Jan. 29, 1951; s. Frank P. and Helen (DeRobertis) V.; m. Cathy Kinnane; 1 child. AB, Coll. of the Holy Cross, Worcester, Mass., 1973; JD, Suffolk U., 1977. Bar: Conn. 1977, U.S. Dist. Ct. Conn. 1978, U.S. Ct. Appeals 1979, U.S. Supreme Ct. 1981, Calif. 1983. Assoc. Stoner, Gross & Chorches, Hartford, 1977-78; asst. atty. gen. Conn. Atty. Gen.'s Office, Hartford, 1978—. Tutor Sch. Law U. Conn., 1997-98; contbr. seminar U.S. Bur. Alcohol, Tobacco & Firearms, 1984; spkr. various seminars, 1986—; argued before U.S. Supreme Ct., 1989; advisor Conn. Gen. Assembly Law Revision Commn., 1992; state coord. Internat. Extraditions, 1998—. Author: Liquor Licensing in Connecticut, 1987. Commr. Glastonbury, Conn. Pub. Bldg. commn., 1986, Glastonbury Wetlands Authority, 1987; mem. Dem. Town Com., Glastonbury, 1986-91; vice chmn. bd. dirs. Glastonbury ABC, 1989-94; elected mem. Glastonbury Conn. Bd. Assessment Appeals, 2003—. Recipient Am. Jurisprudence Book prize Lawyer's Co-op. Publ. Co., 1976, proclamation Glastonbury Conservation Commn., 1988, Merit award State of Conn., 1986, 91, 92, 95, 97, 98, 2004. Mem. ABA, ATLA, Conn. Bar Assn. (chmn. adminstrv. law exec. com., specialization certification subcom. 1982-89, mcpl. law com. 1982-87), U.S. Supreme Ct. Hist. Soc., Conn. Bot. Soc., Wadsworth Atheneum. Avocation: astronomy. Office: Office of the Atty Gen Mackenzie Hall 110 Sherman St Hartford CT 06105-2267

VACCHI, STEVE, music educator; b. Fall River, Mass., Oct. 20, 1968; s. Donald Vacchi and Patricia Sullivan. Mus B (high distinction), Eastman Sch. of Music, Rochester, N.Y., 1990; Mus M, The Hartt Sch., West Hartford, Conn., 1993; Mus D, La. State U., 1997. Bd. regents fellow La. State U., Baton Rouge, 1993—96; asst. prof. bassoon Wichita State U. Sch. of Music, Kans., 1996—2000; assoc. prof. bassoon U. of Oreg. Sch. of Music, Eugene, 2000—. Assoc. prin., second bassoonist Baton Rouge Symphony Orch., 1993—96; prin. bassoonist Acadiana Symphony Orch., Lafayette, La., 1994—96; guest prin. bassoonist Shanghai Symphony Orch., 1995; prin. bassoonist Wichita Symphony Orch., Kans., 1996—2000; faculty mem. Brevard Music Ctr., NC, 2000—01; prin. bassoonist Eugene Opera Orch., Oreg., 2000—, Oreg. Festival of Am. Music, Eugene, 2001—, Oreg. Mozart Players, Eugene, 2002—; bassoonist Oreg. Bach Festival Orch., Eugene, Oreg., 2002—; performer with profl. orchestra across U.S. and 23 countries. Musician: (cd recording) Eastman Wind Ensemble: Live in Osaka, 1990, American-Soviet Youth Orchestra: Dvorak, Symphony No. 9, 1992, International Symphony Orchestra: Music by the Red Sea, 1993, New World Symphony: Music of Ingolf Dahl, 1995, Chorus Civitas Chamber Orchestra: Music of Ralph Vaughan Williams, 1995, Baton Rouge Symphony: A Holiday Symphony, 1995, The Yeni Makam Series of Edward Hines, 1999, Trio 335/Bach: The Art of the Fugue, 2002, Chamber music of Tomas Svoboda, 2003. Grantee The Fund for U.S. Artists, Arts Internat. of N.Y., 2000. Mem.:

The Coll. Music Soc., Am. Fedn. of Musicians, Internat. Double Reed Soc., Pi Kappa Lambda, Phi Kappa Phi. Avocations: travel, languages, hiking. Office: Sch of Music 1225 U of Oreg Eugene OR 97403-1225 Office Phone: 541-346-3748.

VACCHIANO, JULIE CATHERINE, special education educator; b. Neptune, N.J., Oct. 16, 1948; d. James and Rose (Infanto) V. BS in Edn., Trenton State Coll., 1972; MS in Edn., Monmouth Coll., 1979, MS in Edn. in Spl. Edn., 1988. Remedial asst. Holmdel (N.J.) Bd. Edn., 1972-73; classroom tchr. St. Benedict Sch., Holmdel, 1973-85; founder/dir. acad. support svcs. students with learning disabilites Monmouth Coll., West Long Branch, NJ, 1981-94, reading coord., 1980—90; learning disabilities tchr., cons. Jackson (N.J.) Bd. Edn., 1995—. Adj. prof. Brookdale C.C., Lincroft, N.J., 1975-85; adj. prof. ednl. dept. Monmouth Coll., West Long Branch, 1988-94. Contbr. articles to manuals; presenter ednl. issues statewide, 1988—. Mem. N.J. Learning Cons. Assn., Kappa Delta Pi. Office: Jackson Bd Edn 101 Don Donnor Blvd Jackson NJ 08527-5019

VACCO, DENNIS C. lawyer; b. Buffalo, Aug. 16, 1952; s. Carmen A. and Mildred V.; m. Kelly McIlroy; children: Alex, Connor. BA, Colgate U., 1974; JD, SUNY, Buffalo, 1978. Bar: N.Y. 1978, Fed. Ct. 1978, 82. Asst. dist. atty. Office of Erie County Dist. Atty., Buffalo, 1978-82, chief G.J. bureau, 1982-88; U.S. Atty. We. Dist. N.Y. Buffalo, 1988-93; atty. gen. State of New York, Albany, 1993-98; v.p. for govtl. affairs Waste Mgmt. Inc., 1998-99; pres. Waste Mgmt. N.Y. LLC, 1999—2003; pvt. practice atty. Boston, 2003—. Chmn. Atty. Gen.'s Environ. Subcom., Atty. Gen.'s Subcom. on Organized Crime and Violent Crime; mem. Nat. Environ. Enforcement Coun. Co-chair Erie County Community Commn. on Alcohol and Substance Abuse; bd. dirs. United Way of Erie County. Recipient Environ. Enforcement Leadership award Atty. Gen. Dept. of Justice, Washington, 1991. Mem. N.Y. State Bar Assn., Erie County Bar Assn., Nat. Dist. Attys. Assn., N.Y. State Dist. Attys. Assn., NCCJ, Hamburg Devel. Corp., 100 Club of Buffalo, U. Buffalo Law Alumni Assn. (bd. dirs.). Republican. Roman Catholic. Avocations: travel, sports. Office Phone: 716-713-1679.

VACHER, CLIVE GRAHAM, aerospace executive; b. Oxford, Eng., Mar. 25, 1970; s. Peter John and Polly Mary Anne (King) V. BA with honors, London Sch. Econs., 1992, MBA, MIT, 1998. Sgt. Lancashire Police, Preston, Eng., 1992-96; gen. mgr. Conn. airfoil repair ops. United Techs. Pratt and Whitney Aircraft Engines, East Hartford, Conn., 1998—. Home: 465 Buckland Hills Dr Apt 29111 Manchester CT 06040-9122 Office: Pratt & Whitney Aircraft 400 Main St East Hartford CT 06108-0968

VACHHER, PREHLAD SINGH, psychiatrist; b. Rawalpindi, Punjab, Pakistan, Nov. 30, 1933; came to U.S., 1960; s. Thakar Singh and Harbans Kaur (Ghai) V.; m. Margaret Mary Begley, Oct. 9, 1963; children: Paul, Sheila, Mary Ann, Eileen, Mark. Grad., Khalsa Coll., India, 1950; MD, Panjab U., Amritsar, India, 1956. Diplomate Am. Bd. Psychiatry. Staff N.J. State Hosp., Trenton, 1965-66, Wayne County Gen. Hosp., Eloise, Mich., 1966-68; pvt. practice Livonia, Mich., 1966-75, Woodstock, Va., 1991-96; pres. Vachher Psychiat. Cu., P.C., Livonia, 1975-91. Dir. community psychiatry Northville (Mich.) State Hosp., 1968-71; cons. staff Kingswood Hosp., Ferndale, Mich., 1967-72, Annapolis Hosp., Wayne, 1967-88, St. Joseph Mercy Hosp., Ann Arbor, 1970-89; westland staff Margaret Montgomery Hosp., 1988-91; bd. dirs. Oakland Rental Housing Assn., 1990-91; med. dir. mental health unit Shenandoan County Meml. Hosp., Woodstock, Va., 1991-94. Mem. Am. Psychiat. Assn., Va. Psychiat. Soc., Sikh Physicians in Mich. (bd. dirs. 1987), Canton C. of C. (pres. 1975), Sikh Bus. Profl. Coun. (pres. 1988—), Rotary (Canton and Plymouth, Mich., Woodstock).

VACHON, LOUIS, psychiatrist, educator; b. Montreal, June 15, 1932; m. Monique Blain, June 25, 1960. BA, U. Montreal, 1952, MD, 1958. Diplomate Am. Bd. Psychiatry and Neurology. Intern Hotel Dieu de Montreal, Que., 1957-58, resident in psychiatry, 1958-61; psychiat. resident Instiut Albert Prevost, Montreal, 1958-61; sr. physician Medfield (Mass.) State Hosp., 1961-62; rsch. assoc., then instr. Boston U. Med. Sch., 1962-68, asst. prof., then assoc. prof., 1968-87, interim chmn. div. psychiatry, 1985-87, prof., chmn. div. psychiatry, 1987-96. Dir. psychiatry outpatient svc. Univ. Hosp., Boston, 1978-85, interim psychiatrist-in-chief, 1985-87, psychiatrist-in-chief, 1987-96, vis. physician in psychiatry, 1987—. Contbg. author: Comprehensive Textbook of Psychiatry, 1989. Fellow Am. Psychiat. Assn.; mem. Boston Psychoanalytic Soc. Inst., Am. Psychoanalytic Assn., Internat. Psychoanalytic Assn., Mass. Psychiat. Soc., Am. Psychosomatic Soc., Mass. Med. Soc. Boston. Office: Boston U Sch Medicine 85 E Newton St # M957 Boston MA 02118-2340

VACHON, LOUIS-ALBERT CARDINAL, archbishop; b. St. Frederic, Que., Can., Feb. 4, 1912; s. Napoleon and Alexandrine (Gilbert) Vachon. DPh. Laval U., 1947, degree (hon.), 1982; DTh, St. Thomas Aquinas U., Rome, 1949; degree (hon.), U. Montreal, McGill and Victoria, 1964, Guelph U., 1966, Moncton U., 1967, Bishop's, Queen's and Strasbourg U., 1968, U. Notre Dame, 1971, Carleton U., 1972, Laval U., 1982. Superior Grand Seminaire Qué., Québec, 1955—59; superior gen. Le Séminaire de Qué., 1960—77; prof. philosophy Laval U., 1941—47, prof. theology, 1949—55, vice-rector, 1959—60, rector, 1960—72; protonotary apostolic, 1963—77; aux. bishop of Que., 1977—81; archbishop of Que. and primate of Can., 1981—90; apptd. Cardinal with title St. Paul of the Cross, 1985. Past pres. Corp. Laval U. Med. Ctr.; mem. Sacred Congregation for Clergy, Vatican, 1986—; adminstrv. bd. Nat. Order Qué., 1985—, Can. Conf. Cath. Bishops, 1981—; pres. Conf. Rectors and Prins. Que. Univs., 1965—68. Author: Espérance et Présomption, 1958, Verité et Liberte, 1962, Unité de l'universite, 1962, Apostolat de l'universitaire Catholique, 1963, Memorial, 1963, Communauté universitaire, 1963, Progres de l'universite et Consentement Populaire, 1964, Responsabilite collective des universitaires, 1964, Les humanites aujourd'hui, 1966, Excellence et loyauté des universitaires, 1969; editor: Pastoral Letters, 1981—. Assoc. bd. dirs. Que. Symphony Orch.; hon. pres. La Soc. des etudes Grecques et Latines Qué; bd. govs. Laval U. Found. Decorated officier Ordre de la Fidelite (France), companion Order of Can., du Conseil de langue (France), Ordre nat. du Qué., officier Legion of Honor (France). Fellow: Royal Soc. Can.; mem.: Internat. Fedn. Cath. Univs. (adminstrv. bd. 1963—70), Assn. Univ. Partiellement ou Entierement Langue Française (adminstrv. bd. 1961—69), Internat. Assn. Univs. (dep. mem. adminstrv. bd. 1965—70), Assn. Univs. and Colls. Can. (pres. 1965—66), Canadian Assn. French Lang. Educators (pres. 1970—72), Ordre des Francophones d'Amérique. Roman Catholic.

VACHON, MARILYN ANN, retired insurance company executive; b. Fort Wayne, Ind., Dec. 12, 1924; d. Robert J. and Maude (Shaffer) V. Asst. treas Lincoln Nat. Life Ins. Co., Fort Wayne, Ind., 1961-87, asst. v.p., 1973-87, sec., 1980-87; asst. sec. Lincoln Nat. Corp., Fort Wayne, 1977-80, asst. treas., 1977-87, sec., 1980-87. Home: 1825 Cortland Ave Fort Wayne IN 46808-2446

VACHON, REGINALD IRENEE, mechanical engineer; b. Norfolk, Va, Jan. 29, 1937; s. Rene Albert Vachon and Regina (Galvin) Radcliffe; m. Mary Eleanor Grigg, Jan. 16, 1960; children: Reginald Irenee, Eleanor Marie. Student, U.S. Naval Acad., 1954-55; BME, Auburn U., 1958, MS, 1960; PhD, Okla. State U., 1963; LLB, Jones Law Sch., 1969. Bar: Ala. 1971; registered profl. engr., Ala., Ga., Miss., La., Wis., Tex.; chartered engr. U.K.; cert. d'Iugenieur Mecanicien, France. Engr. Hayes Internat., 1958; instr., rsch. asst. Auburn U., 1958-60, rsch. assoc., 1961, assoc., prof., 1963-78; R&D engr. E.I. DuPont, 1960; aerospace engr., technologist NASA Marshall Space Flight Ctr., summers, 1964, 65; pres. Vachon Nix & Assoc., 1977—, VNA Sys. Inc., 1982—. Chmn. bd. dir. Optimal Systems Internat., Inc., 1969-95; COO, Thacker Constrn. Co., Thacker Orgn. Inc., 1981-90, United Info. Techs., Inc., Global Interated Techs. Inc.; pres., CEO, Compris Tech., Inc., 1991-92; chmn., Global Risk Mngr., Inc., 1992—, Direct Measurements, Inc., 2002—; prin. Gipco Holdings Internat., Ltd., 1994—; mem. sci. tech. adv. com. U.S. Dept. Homeland Security. Contbr. articles to profl. jours.; patentee in field. With U.S. Army, 1960—61. Fellow AIAA (assoc.), Inst. Mech. Engrs.; mem. ABA, NSPE, ASME (hon., pres. 2003-04), Ala. Bar Assn., Soc. Frances des Mecaniciens, The Phoenix Soc. of Atlanta, Pan American Acad. Engring. (charter mem.); Cosmos Club, NY Yacht Club, Peachtree Racket Club. Roman Catholic. Home: 1414 Epping Forest Dr NE Atlanta GA 30319-2539 Office: PO Box 190093 Atlanta GA 31119-0093 E-mail: vachonr@asme.org.

VACHSS, ANDREW HENRY, lawyer, writer, juvenile justice and child abuse consultant; b. N.Y.C., Oct. 19, 1942; s. Bernard and Geraldine (Mattus) V. BA, Case Western Res. U., 1965; JD magna cum laude, New Engl. Sch. Law, 1975. Bar: N.Y. 1976, U.S. Dist. Ct. (so. and ea. dists.) N.Y. 1976. Program rep. USPHS, Ohio, 1965-66; unit supr N.Y.C. Dept. Social Svcs., 1966-69; urban coord. Community Devel. Found., Norwalk, Conn., 1969-70; dir. Uptown Community Orgn., Chgo., 1970-71; dep. dir. Medfield (Mass.)-Norfolk Prison Project, 1971-72; dir. intensive treatment unit ANDROS II, Roslindale, Mass., 1972-73; project dir. Mass. Dept. Youth Svcs., Boston, 1972-73; dir. Juvenile Justice Planning Project, N.Y.C., 1975-85; pvt. practice N.Y.C., 1976—. Organizer, coord. Calumet (Ind.) Community Congress, 1970; bd. dirs. Libra Inc., Cambridge, Mass., Advocacy Assocs., N.Y. and N.J.; adj. prof. Coll. New Resources, N.Y.C., 1980-81; lectr. trainer, speaker to numerous orgns.; cons. on juvenile justice and child abuse to numerous orgns., 1971—. Author: The Life-Style Violent Juvenile: The Secure Treatment Approach, 1979, (novels) Flood, 1985, Strega, 1987, Blue Belle, 1988, Hard Candy, 1989, Blossom, 1990, Sacrifice, 1991, Shella, 1993, Another Chance to Get it Right, 1995, 2003, Down in the Zero, 1994, Footsteps of the Hawk, 1995, Batman: The Ultimate Evil, 1995, False Allegations, 1996, Safe House, 1998, Choice of Evil, 1999, Dead and Gone, 2000, Pain Management, 2001, Only Child, 2002, The Getaway Man, 2003, Down Here, 2004, (graphic novels) Predator: Race War, 1995, Hard Looks, 2002, (audiobook) Proving It, 2001, (short stories) Born Bad, 1994, Everybody Pays, 1999; editor-in-chief: New Eng. Law Rev., 1974—75, contbg. editor: Parade; contbr. articles. Bd. of counselors Childtrauma Acad., Baylor Coll. of Medicine; bd. adv. Protect PAC; mem. expert adv. panel on catastrophic child abuse N.Y. State Office of Mental Health. Recipient Grand Prix de Lit. Policiére, 1988, Falcon award Maltese Falcon Soc. Japan, 1988, Deutschen Krimi Preis, Die Jury des Bochumer Krimi Archivs, 1989, Raymond Chandler award Giuria a Noir Festival, 2000, 1st Annual Harvey R. Houck Award (Justice for Children) for Child Advocacy, 2003. Indsl. Area Found. Tng. Inst. fellow, 1970-71, John Hay Whitney Found. fellow, 1976-77. Mem. PEN, Writers Guild of Am. Office: Ste 2860 420 Lexington Ave New York NY 10170-2899

VACKETTA, CARL LEE, lawyer, educator; b. Danville, Ill., Aug. 3, 1941; s. Peter G. and Julia M. (Columbus) V. BS, U. Ill., 1963, JD, 1965. Bar: Ill. 1965, D.C. 1968, U.S.Dist. Ct. D.C. 1968, U.S. Ct. Fed. Claims 1968, U.S. Supreme Ct. 1970. Tax lawyer GM, Detroit, 1965-66; ptnr. Sellers, Conner & Cuneo, Washington, 1968-74, Pettit & Martin, 1974-95, Piper & Marbury, 1995-99, Piper Rudnick LLP, 1999—. Adj. prof. law Georgetown U., 1971—. Co-author: Government Contract Default Termination, 1991, 93, 95, 97, 99; co-editor Extraordinary Contractual Relief Reporter, 1974—. Capt. U.S. Army, 1966—68. Fellow ABA (sec. pub. contract law sect. 1978-79, coun. 1979-82, pub. contract law sect., editor in chief Pub. Contract Law Jour. 1994—), Nat. Contract Mgmt. Assn.; mem. Fed. Bar Assn., D.C. Bar Assn., Nat. Assn. Purchasing Mgrs., University Club (Washington). Roman Catholic. Office: Piper Rudnick LLP 1200 19th St NW Fl 7 Washington DC 20036-2430 Office Phone: 202-861-6460. E-mail: carl.vacketta@piperrudnick.com.

VADAPARTY, KUMAR VENKATA, finance company executive, director; b. Visakhapatnam, Andhra Pradesh, India, June 1, 1961; s. Jagannadha Rao and Bhavani Vadaparty; m. Dawn Cohen. Degree in electronics engring., Andhra U.; M Computer Sci., Indian Inst. Tech., Kanpur; PhD, Rutgers U., 1992. Cert. java architect Microsoft, 1999. Asst. prof. Case Western Res. U., Cleve., 1992—96; sr. rschr. Bell Comm. Rsch., Morristown, NJ, 1995—96; dir. mgmt. dept. Merrill Lynch. Cons. Bell Comm. Rsch., 1987—95. Translator: A Modern View of Telugu Prosody, 2001. Recipient Gold Medal award, Andhra U., 1983, Young Investigator award, NSF, 1993; fellow, Elai Lilly Pharm. Co., 1993. Mem.: Internat. Exec. Guild (life). Achievements include first to architected a major system that enables Merrill Lynch accept customer orders at substantially lower cost of ownership. E-mail: kumar_vadaparty@ml.com., vadaparty@yahoo.com.

VADHAN, SALIL PRAVIN, computer scientist, educator; s. Pravin and Vimla Vadhan; m. Jennifer Sun. AB summa cum laude, Harvard U., 1995; CAS with hons., Cambridge (Eng.) U., 1996; PhD, MIT, 1999. Postdoctoral fellow Lab. Computer Sci., MIT, Cambridge, Mass., 1999—2000; asst. prof. computer Sci. Harvard U., Cambridge, 2001—; fellow Radcliffe Inst. Advanced Study, Cambridge, 2003. Vis. prof. Inst. Advanced Study, Princeton, NJ, 2000—01. Recipient Career Devel. award, NSF, 2001; Sloan Rsch. fellow, Alfred P. Sloan Found., 2002. Office: Division of Engineering and Applies Scis 33 Oxford Street Cambridge MA 02138

VADLAMANI, SUCHITA, newscaster; Degree, U. Chgo. Overnight anchor KSDK-TV, St. Louis; bus. anchor, corr. CNBC India, Mumbai, India, CNBC Today; anchor, co-prodr. Asian Working Woman CNBC Asia, Singapore; anchor Sta. WAGA-TV, Atlanta, 2002—. Recipient award, Indian Profl. Network, 2003. Office: WAGA TV 1551 Briarcliff Rd NE Atlanta GA 30306*

VADNAL, JOHN LOUIS, dean, mathematician, educator; s. John Edward and Constance Louise (Spehek) Vadnal; m. Tina Marie Smith, July 22, 1989; 1 child, Joshua David Creed. BS in Civil Engring., U. Fla., 1977; MS in Mechanics and Hydraulics, MS in Applied Math., PhD in Mechanics and Hydraulics, U. Iowa, 1984; diploma, Kyoto (Japan) U., 1984; Summer program, Von Karman Inst. for Fluid Dynamics, Brussels, Belgium, 1979—79. Lic. profl. engr., Tenn. Mech. engr. TVA, Norris, Tenn., 1985—89; asst. prof. engring. U. Evansville, Ind., 1989—91, cross country coach, 1989—91; design engr. Duke Power Co., Charlotte, NC, 1991—96; adj. prof. math U. NC, Charlotte, NC, 1994—96; chair dept. sci. and math Tenn. Temple U., Chattanooga, 1996—99; hydraulic engr. US Army Corps Engrs., Jacksonville, Fla., 2000—01; dean Trinity Bapt. Coll., Jacksonville, Fla., 1999—, prof. math., 1999—. Editor Am. Soc. Civl Engrs., Knoxville, Tenn., 1987—89. Tchr. Sunday sch. Trinity Bapt. Ch., Jacksonville, Fla., 1999—. Recipient Terrell award, Am. Soc. Civil Engrs., 1986. Mem.: Math. Assn. Am., Phi Kappa Phi, Tau Beta Pi. Democrat. Avocation: running. Office: Trinity Baptist College 800 Hammond Boulevard Jacksonville FL 32221 Office Phone: 904-596-2449. E-mail: jvadnal@tbc.edu.

VADUS, GLORIA A. scientific document examiner; b. Forrestville, Pa. Diploma, Cole Sch. Graphology, Calif., 1978; BA in Psychology Counseling, Columbia Pacific U., 1981, MA in Psychology, 1982; diploma handwriting expert, Edith Eisenberg, Bethesda, Md., 1991. Diplomate Am. Bd. Forensic Examiners; cert. Am. Acad. Graphology, Washington, 1978, ct. qualified document examiner. registered graphologist 1978, cert. behavioral profiling and cert. questioned documents Am. Bd. Forensic Examiners, CHS Am. Bd. Homeland Security, 2004. Pres., owner Graphinc, Inc., 1985—. Accredited instr. graphology Montgomery County Schs., Md., 1978—79; instr. Psychogram Centre, 1978—85, Coun. Graphol. Socs., 1980; testifier superior and probate cts.; pub. forum panelist, lectr., rschr., script therapist pers. selection specialist; writer in field; cons. graphologist; developed Trilogy base for rsch. Am. Handwriting Analysis Found. Author: numerous studies and papers in field, also environ. papers. Chmn. Letter of Hope for POWs; vol. Montgomery County, 1987—88; bd. dirs., cmty. affairs chair East Gate I Civic Assn., Potomac, Md., 1985—87. Named one of 500 Leaders World Influence; recipient Spl. award, US/Japan Marine Facilities Panel Valuable Contbr. Japanese Panel UJNR/MFP, 1978—94, Gold Nib Analyst of Yr. award, Am. Handwriting Analysis Fedn., 1982, Dancing Fan award, Marine Tech. Soc., Tokyo chpt., 1991, Profound Contbr. to Soc. to the Yr., 2000, Internat. Peace prize, United Cultural Conv. of USA, 2003, Am. Bronze medal of Honor for contbns. to handwriting, ABI, 2001, medal of Honor, 2004, Order of Excellence, IBC, 2004, Gold medal of Honor, 2004. Fellow: Am. Bd. Forensic Examiners (life; awards chair 1993—94, Meritorious award 1994, Outstanding Contbn. cert.); mem.: Coun. Graphical Socs. (bd. dirs. 1982—84), Soc. Francaise de Graphologie for Am. Handwriting Analysis Found., Nat. Assn Document Examiners (bd. dirs. 1985—92, ethics hearing bd. 1986, chmn. nominations com. 1987—88, ethics chmn. 1988, parliamentarian 1988—92), Nat. Forensic Ctr., Am. Handwriting Analysis Found. (life; chmn. rsch. com., chmn. adv. bd. 1981—87, bd. dirs. 1981—91, pres. 1982—84, chmn. nominations com. 1985—86, officiator 1986, policy planning and ethics com. 1986—91, ethics chmn. 1989—91, chmn., past pres. adv. bd. 1989—91, hon. profl. women's adv. bd. 1999, cert.), Nature Conservancy, Charles F. Menninger Soc., IEEE-Distaff (internat. chmn. bd. dirs. 1969—72, fashion show chair 1969—72), Internat. Platform Assn., Nat. Wildlife Fedn., Nat. Capitol Jaguar Owners Club (judge 1975—78), Sierra Club, Henry Hicks Garden Club of the Westburys, N.Y. (v.p., pres. elect, judge, chair flower shows, bd. dirs. 1967—71), Soroptomist Internat. (internat. chair, v.p., Bethesda chpt. Montgomery County, bd. dirs. 1987—92), Nat. Writers Club. Home: 8500 Timber Hill Ln Potomac MD 20854-4237 E-mail: fvadus@ieee.org.

VAFA, CUMRUN, education educator; b. Tehran, Iran, Aug. 1, 1960; BS in physics and math., Mass. Inst. of Tech., 1981; PhD, Princeton U., 1985. Assoc. prof. Harvard U., 1988—90, prof., 1990—. Recipient Pres. Young Investigators award, Nat. Sci. Found., 1989, Alfred P. Sloan award, Alfred P. Sloan Found., 1989, Packard Found. award, Packard Found., 1989. Office: Jefferson Lab of Physics Harvard U 17 Oxford St Room v467 Cambridge MA 02138

VAGELOS, PINDAROS ROY, pharmaceutical executive, researcher; b. Westfield, N.J., Oct. 8, 1929; s. Roy John and Marianthi (Lambrinides) V.; m. Diana Touliatos, July 10, 1955; children: Randall, Cynthia, Andrew, Ellen. AB, U. Pa., 1950; MD, Columbia U., 1954; DSc (hon.), Washington U., 1980, Brown U., 1982, U. Medicine and Dentistry of N.J., 1984, NYU, 1989, Columbia U., 1990; LLD (hon.), Princeton U., 1990; LHD (hon.), Rutgers U., 1991; DSc (hon.), N.J. Inst. Tech., 1992, SUNY, 1994, Mt. Sinai Med. Sch., 1997, U. B.C., 1998, U. Pa., 1999. Intern medicine Mass. Gen. Hosp., 1954-55, asst. resident medicine, 1955-56; surgeon Lab. Cellular Physiology, NIH, 1956-59, Lab. Biochemistry, 1959-64, head sect. comparative biochemistry, 1964-66; prof. biochemistry, chmn. dept. biol. chemistry Washington U. Sch. Medicine, St. Louis, 1966-75, dir. divsn. biology and biomed. scis., 1973-75; sr. v.p. research Merck, Sharp & Dohme Research Labs., Rahway, N.J., 1975-76, pres., 1976-84; corp. sr. v.p. Merck & Co., Inc., Rahway, N.J., 1982-84, exec. v.p., 1984-85, CEO, 1985-86, chmn., CEO, 1986-94, ret. chmn., CEO, 1994; chmn. Regeneron Pharms., Inc., Tarrytown, NY, 1995—. Mem. Inst. Medicine, NAS, 1974—; chmn. sci. adv. bd. Ctr. for Advanced Biotech. and Medicine, 1985-94; bd. dirs. Prudential Ins. Co., 1989-2001. Trustee U. Pa., 1988-99, chmn. bd., 1994-99; trustee Rockefeller U., 1976-94, Danforth Found., 1978—; mem. President's Commn. on Environ. Quality, 1991-93, Adv. Com. Trade Policy and Negotiations, 1992-94, Bus. Coun., 1987-95; bd. mng. dirs. Met. Opera Assn., Inc., 1989-95; bd. dirs. N.J. Performing Arts Ctr., 1989-99, co-chmn, 1992. Recipient award for chemistry in svc. to soc., NAS, 1995, Pupin medal, 1995. Mem. Am. Chem. Soc. (Enzyme Chemistry award 1967), Am. Soc. Biol. Chemists, Nat. Acad. Scis., Am. Acad. Arts and Scis., Am. Philosophical Soc., Bus. Roundtable (policy com. 1987-94). Achievements include discovery of acyl-carrier protein. Avocations: jogging, tennis. Office: Regeneron 777 Old Saw Mill River Rd Tarrytown NY 10591

VAGET, HANS RUDOLF, language professional, educator; b. Marienbad, Czechoslovakia, Feb. 2, 1938; came to U.S., 1964; s. Hans Ernst and Berta (Isop) V.; m. Ann Leone; children: Melanie Claudine, Erec Alexander. MA, U. Tübingen, Fed. Republic Germany, 1964; PhD, Columbia U., 1969. Instr. Columbia U., N.Y.C., 1964-67; from instr. to prof. Smith Coll., Northampton, Mass., 1967—. Vis. prof. U. Calif., Irvine, 1979, Columbia U., 1985, Princeton U., 1986-87, Yale U., 1991, U. Hamburg, 1992. Author: Dilettantismus bei Goethe, 1971, Goethe. Der Mann von 60 Jahren, 1982, Thomas-Mann Kommentar, 1984; author, editor: Briefwechsel T. Mann-Agnes Meyer, 1992, J.W. Goethe: Erotic Poems, 1996, Im Schatten Wagners, 1999; contbr. articles to profl. and ednl. publs. Recipient Thomas Mann-Medaille, 1994; grantee NEH, 1985, Am. Coun. Learned Socs., 1986. Mem. MLA, German Studies Assn., Assn. Tchrs. of German, Deutsche Schillergesellschaft, Thomas-Mann-Gesellschaft, Goethe Soc. N.Am. (co-founder), Wagner Soc., Am. Musicol. Soc. Office: Smith Coll Dept German Northampton MA 01063-0001

VAGNINI, LIVIO LEE, chemist, forensic consultant; b. North Bergen, NJ, Apr. 26, 1917; s. Frank S. and Margaret (Avondo) V.; m. Daniele Hogge, Sept. 29, 1949; children: Frank, Stephen, Eric. BS in Chemistry, Fordham U., 1938; postgrad., U. Md. Med. Sch., 1938-39. Diplomate Am. Bd. Forensic Examiners. Chemist H.A. Wilson Co. div. Englehard Industries, Inc., 1940-42; chief chemist U.S. Army Graves Registration, Liege, Belgium, 1946-48; chief forensic chemist U.S. Army Criminal Investigation Lab., Frankfurt, Fed. Republic Germany, 1948-60; sr. chemist FDA, Washington, 1960-62, CIA, Washington, 1963-73; project engr. Mitre Corp., McLean, Va., 1973-75; staff scientist Planning Research Corp., McLean, 1975-77; program dir. L. Miranda Assocs., Washington, 1978-81; forensic cons. Carmel, Calif., 1981—. Contbr. articles to profl. publs. Active Ft. Ord (Calif.) Retiree Coun., 1988—; treas. Alliance Francaise Monterey Peninsula; adv. commn. Monterey County Commn. Vets. Svcs., 1990-92; Assn. Former Intelligence Officers, 1973—. With U.S. Army, 1942-46, lt. col. ret., 1975. Decorated Bronze Star; named Vet. of Yr. in Monterey County, 2000. Fellow Am. Inst. Chemists, Am. Acad. Forensic Scis., Am. Chem. Soc.; mem. Nat. Assn. for Uniformd Svcs. (Monterey chpt.)Internat. Soc. Blood Transfusion, Internat. Soc. Forensic Toxicology, Ret. Officers Assn. (pres. Monterey County chpt. 1985), Sons in Retirement (pres. Pebble Beach br. 1986), Am.-Scandinavian Soc. (pres. 1989, program dir. Monterey County 1989), Internat. Assn. of Forensic Sci., Am. Coll. of Forensic Examiners (diplomate). Roman Catholic. Home: 26069 Mesa Dr Carmel CA 93923-8952 E-mail: liviaki@aol.com.

VAGO, ANTHONY SCOTT, investment representative; b. Albuquerque, Jan. 4, 1975; s. Robert Nicholas and Rita V.; m. Kelly Erica Florence, Aug. 26, 2000; children: Austin, Alexander. B of Liberal Studies, So. Ill. U., 1999, M Pub. Adminstrn., 2000; postgrad., Webster U., 2000—. Respiratory care practitioner II St. Elizabeth's Hosp., Belleville, Ill., 1995-2000; sr. bus. analyst The Boeing Co., St. Louis, 2000—01; investment rep. Edward Jones Co., 2001—, First Collinsville Bank, 2003—. Mem. Sigma Phi Epsilon. Avocations: travel, exercising, boating.

VAGT, ROBERT F. academic administrator; m. Ruth Anne Vagt, 1968; children: Ashley, Lindsey. BA in Psychology, Davidson Coll., 1969; MDiv, Duke U. Ordained to ministry Presbyn. Ch. Dir. clin. programs N.W. Ala. Mental Health Ctr.; exec. dir. Mcpl. Assistance Corp., N.Y.C., 1979—80; chmn., pres., COO Seagull Energy Corp.; pres. Davidson Coll., 1997—. Bd. dirs. Cornell Cos., Inc. Bd. vis. Davidson Coll., 1992—, mem. Ultra Soc., nat. leader Ann. Fund, 1993—95. Recipient Alumni Svc. award, Davidson Coll., 1996. Office: Pres's Office Davidson Coll PO Box 1719 Davidson NC 28036-1719

VAGTS, DETLEV FREDERICK, law educator; b. Washington, Feb. 13, 1929; s. Alfred and Miriam (Beard) Vagts; m. Dorothy Larkin, Dec. 11, 1954; children: Karen, Lydia. Grad., Taft Sch., 1945; AB, Harvard U., 1948, LLB, 1951. Bar: Mass. 1961. Assoc. Cahill, Gordon, Reindel & Ohl, N.Y.C., 1951-53, 56-59; asst. prof. law Harvard U. Law Sch., Cambridge, Mass., 1959-62, prof., 1962—, Eli Goldston prof., 1981-84, Bemis prof., 1984—, dir. internat. tax program, 1998-2000. Counselor internat. law Dept. of State, 1976—77. Author (with others): Transnational Legal Problems, 1968, 4th edit., 1994, Basic Corporation Law, 1973, 3d edit., 1989, Transnational Business Problems, 3d edit., 2003; editor: Secured Transactions Under the Uniform Commercial Code, 1963—64; assoc. reporter (with others): Restatement of Foreign Relations Law, book rev. editor: Am. Jour. Internat. Law, 1986—93, co-editor-in-chief:, 1993—98. 1st lt. USAF, 1953—56. Recipient Max Planck Rsch. award, 1991. Mem.: ABA, Coun. Fgn. Rels., Am. Soc. Internat. Law, Phi Beta Kappa. Home: 29 Follen St Cambridge MA 02138-3502 Office: Sch Law Harvard U Cambridge MA 02138 Business E-Mail: vagts@law.harvard.edu.

VAHAVIOLOS, SOTIRIOS JOHN, electrical engineer, researcher, engineering executive; b. Mistra, Greece, Apr. 16, 1946; s. John Apostolos and Athanasia (Pavlakos) Vahaviolos; m. Aspasia Felice Nessas, June 1, 1969; children: Athanasia, Athena, Kristy. BSEE, Fairleigh Dickinson U., 1970; MSEE, Columbia U., 1972, M in Philosophy, 1975, PhDEE, 1976. Mem. tech. staff Bell Tel. Labs., Princeton, NJ, 1970-75, supr., 1975-76, dept. head, 1976-78; founder, pres., CEO Phys. Acoustics Corp., Princeton, 1978—, MISTRAS Holdings Corp., Princeton, 1984-94, chmn. quality svcs. labs., 2000—. Adviser Greece Ministry Def., Athens, 1986—88; bd. dirs. Orthosonics, Inc., N.Y.C.; chmn. policy com. Internat. Com. Nondestructive Testing. Contbr. scientific papers to profl. publs. Chmn. Princeton sect. United Fund, 1976—78; adv. bd. Trenton State Coll., 1983—; chmn. Greek Independence Parade, N.Y.C., 2002; v.p. Fedn. Greek Soc. in Greater N.Y.; bd. dirs. Holy Cross Greek Orthodox Sch. Theology, Boston, 1989—; pres. bd. trustees St. George Greek Orthodox Cmty., Trenton, NJ. Recipient Spartan Merit award, Spartan World Soc., 1987, Entrepreneur of the Yr. award, Arthur Young/Inc. Mag., 1989. Fellow: IEEE (Centennial Medal award 1984, Mittlemen Achievement award 1993), Acoustic Emission Working Group, Am. Soc. Nondestructive Testing (bus. and fin. com. 1984—87, 1988—, bd. dirs. 1985, sec. 1989, treas. 1990, v.p. 1991, pres. 1992, chmn. bd. 1993, chmn. internat. com. nondestructive testing 1994—, editor handbook on acoustic emission 1988, Lester Honor award 1998, Gold medal 2001); mem.: ASTM, Internat. Fund Advancement Nondestructive Testing (v.p.), N.Y. Acad. Scis., IEEE Indsl. Electronics Soc. (sr. mem. adminstv. com. 1988, founder, v.p. conf. 1974—78, editor Trans. on Indsl. Electronics 1976—82, 2d prize Student Paper Constest 1970, Outstanding Young Engr. award 1984). Greek Orthodox. Achievements include 13 U.S. patents; 7 fgn. patents. Avocations: bird hunting, soccer, technical writing, gardening. Home: 7 Ridgeview Rd Princeton NJ 08540-7601 Office: Phys Acoustics Corp PO Box 3135 Princeton NJ 08543-3135 Personal E-mail: sotirios@pacnett.com.

VAIDYANATHAN, RAMACHANDRAN, computer engineer, educator; s. L. V. and Visalakshi Ramachandran; m. Janaki Vaidyanathan; children: Shruti, Deepti. B, Indian Inst. of Tech., India, 1983; M, Indian Inst. of Tech., 1985; PhD, Syracuse U., 1990. Asst. prof. to assoc. prof. La. State U., Baton Rouge, 1990—. Co-author: Dynamic Reconfiguration: Architectures and Algorithms; contbr. articles to profl. jours. Mem.: IEEE. Achievements include patents for optical slab waveguide for high-speed interconnects. Office: La State U Elecl Computer Engring Dept Baton Rouge LA 70803-5901 Office Phone: 225-578-5238.

VAIL, CHARLES DANIEL, veterinarian, consultant; b. Denver, June 11, 1936; s. Allan Paden and Katherine Marie (Phillips) V.; m. Jean Williams Ebsen, June 15, 1963; children: Ellen Marie, David Elston. BS, Colorado A&M, 1958; DVM, Colo. State. U., 1960. Asst. veterinarian Colo. Racing Commn., Littleton, 1958-60; equine practitioner Littleton Large Animal Clinic, 1960—; track veterinarian Centennial Race Track, Littleton, 1962-63. Editor in chief Equine Practice, 1986-2000; contbr. articles to profl. jours. Mem. selection com. Outstanding Biology Tchr. award Colo., 1978-80, 88—, Arapahoe Fair Assn., Littleton, 1965-84, gallery disting. grads. Colo. State U. Coll. Vet. Medicine, 1989; chmn. Littleton Rotary Western Heritage Art Fair; bd. dirs. Animal Assistance Found. Denver, 1991-2004, v.p., 1995-96, pres., 1996-97, Western Vet. Conf., 1997-2000, v.p., 2001, pres. elect, 2002, pres., 2003, Friends Littleton Pub. Libr./Mus., 2000-04, Rocky Mountain Stroke Assn., Araphoe C.C. Found., 2004—; mem. devel. coun. Colo. State U., 2002—. Recipient Honor Alumni award Coll. Vet. Medicine, Colo. State U., 1991. Mem. AVMA (publs. com. 1981-87), Am. Assn. Equine Practitioners (pres. 1985), Colo. Vet. Medicine Assn. (pres. 1980, Veterinarian of Yr. award 1987), Denver Area Vet. Medicine Soc. (pres. 1975), Arapahoe Town and Gown Soc. (v.p. 1999, pres. 2000), Colo. State U. Alumni Assn. (pres. 2001-02), Nottingham Club, Rotary (pres. Littleton 1992-93), Sigma Alpha Epsilon, Omicron Delta Kappa. Home: 5921 S Cherrywood Cir Littleton CO 80121-2465 Office: Littleton Large Animal Clinic 8025 S Santa Fe Dr Littleton CO 80120-4305 Office Fax: 303-794-9466.

VAIL, IRIS JENNINGS, civic worker; b. N.Y.C., July 2, 1928; d. Lawrence K. and Beatrice (Black) Jennings; grad. Miss Porters Sch., Farmington, Conn.; m. Thomas V.H. Vail, Sept. 15, 1951; children: Siri J., Thomas V.H. Jr., Lawrence J.W. Mem. exec. com. Garden Club Cleve., 1962—83; mem. women's coun. Western Res. Hist. Soc., 1960—, Cleve. Mus. Art, 1953—. Chmn. Childrens Garden Fair, 1966-75, Public Square Dinner, 1975; bd. dirs. Garden Center Greater Cleve., 1963-77; trustee Cleve. Zool. Soc., 1971-98, life trustee 1998—; mem. Ohio Arts Coun., 1974-76, pub. sq. com. Greater Cleve. Growth Assn., 1976-93, pub. sq. preservation and maintenance com. Cleve. Found., 1989-93, chmn. pub. sq. planting com., 1993. Hon. trustee Cleve. Bot. Garden, 2001. Recipient Amy Angell Collier Montague medal Garden Club Am., 1976, Ohio Gov.'s award, 1977. Mem. Chagrin Valley Hunt Club, Cypress Point Club, Kirtland Country Club, Colony Club, Women's City of Cleve. Club (Margaret A. Ireland award). Home: 14950 County Line Rd Chagrin Falls OH 44022-6800

VAIL, MARY BARBARA, publicist; b. Kingsville, Tex., Apr. 24, 1956; d. Fred G. and Nora J. (Smith) Leon; m. David L. Vail, Mar. 30, 1980; children: Sean Kristofer, Ashley Noel. Student, Tex. A&I U.; BS, U. Hawaii, 1982; postgrad., Hawaii Pacific U., 1991-92. Display specialist Linda's, Kingsville, 1986-87; mktg./membership dir. Malibu (Calif.) Riding and Tennis Club, 1990-91; mktg. dir. Pacific Aerospace Mus., Honolulu, 1991-93; pres. Vail Media, Inc. (Scarlett Mktg. & Promotions), Aiea, Hawaii, 1993-95; owner, sole propr. Mary B. Vail Publicist. Vol. fundraiser AOWC, Point Mugu, Calif., 1990-91; vol. Laguna Vista Elem. Sch., Camarillo, Calif., 1990, Barbers Point (Hawaii) Elem. Sch., 1992—; vol., mil. liaison 1st Night Honolulu, 1991; co-chmn. Aloha Family Festival, Pearl Harbor, Hawaii, 1991, Fly Thru Time, 1992, 93, 94, Mugu Air Show, Chinese C. of C. Fashion Show, 1994, Narcissus Festival;, Ho'Okipa Aloha, HIA Hospitality Tng. Coun.; vol. numerous orgns. including Salvation Army, Spl. Olympics, Honolulu C. of C., Am. Diabetes Assn., Am. Diabetes Found., Japanese C. of C., Muscular Dystrophy Assn., Juvenile Diabetes Assn., Make-A-Wish Metro N.Y., Children's Miracle Network, Susan G. Komen Breast Cancer Found., Las Vegas C. of C., Profl. Black Women's Alliance, Hadassah Jewish Women's Orgn., Maddux Found., Candlelighters for Childhood Cancer, USA mag. Make A Difference Day, Shade Tree, women and children's shelter, Sunrise Children's Hosp. Make A Wish Found., Leukemia an Lymphomia Soc., Leukemia Soc., Andre Agassi Grand Slam for Children, Andre Agassi Holiday Party for At-Risk Youths, Fox-5, Children's Miracle Network Telethon, Cystic Fibrosis,, St. Jude Children's Hosp., Clark County Heritage Mus., Girl Scouts Am. Decorated knight Dynastic Mil. Constantinian Order St. George; recipient Nev. Womens Role Model award Nev. State Atty. Gen., 2001; named Female Humanitarian, Las Vegas C. of C., 2000, Nev. Womens Role Model Nev. Atty. Gen., 2001. Mem. NAFE, Pub. Rels. Soc. Am., Pub. Rels. Soc. Hawaii, U. Hawaii Alumni Assn., Food Science and Numan Nutrition Alumni Assn., So. Nev. Homebuilders Assn. Avocations: jogging, crafts, sewing, landscaping, decorating. E-mail: davidvail@earthlink.net.

VAIL, THOMAS VAN HUSEN, retired newspaper publisher and editor; b. Cleve., June 23, 1926; s. Herman Lansing and Delia (White) V.; m. Iris W. Jennings, Sept. 15, 1951; children: Siri Jennings Burki, Thomas Van Husen, Jr. AB in Politics cum laude, Princeton U., 1948; HHD (hon.), Wilberforce U., 1964; LHD, Kenyon Coll., 1969, Cleve. State U., 1973. Reporter Cleve. News, 1949-53, polit. editor, 1953-57; with Cleve. Plain Dealer, 1957-91, v.p., 1961-63, pub., editor, 1963-91, pres., 1970-91; dir. AP, 1968-74; ret., 1991. Bd. dirs. Greater Cleve. Growth Assn.; bd. dirs., past pres. Cleve. Conv. and Visitors Bur.; mem. Nat. Adv. Commn. on Health Manpower; presdl. apptd. to U.S. Adv. Commn. on Info., Pres.'s Commn. for Observance 25th Anniversary UN; trustee No. Ohio region NCCJ, Nat. Brotherhood Week chmn., 1969; trustee Cleve. Coun. World Affairs; fellow Cleve. Clinic Found.; former mem. Downtown Cleve. Corp.; former mem. distbn. com. Cleve. Found.; chmn., founder New Cleve. Campaign; trustee, founder Cleve. Tomorrow; former trustee Com. Econ. Devel.; former mem. Pres.'s Adv. Coun. on Pvt. Sector Initiatives. With USNR, 1944-46, lt. (j.g.), 1950. Recipient Nat. Human Rels. award, 1970, Cleve. Man of Year award Sales and Mktg. Execs. Cleve., 1976, Ohio Gov.'s award, 1982, Downtown Bus. Coun. recognition award Greater Cleve. Growth Assn., 1983, award NCCJ, 1970, award Mt. Vernon Adv. Com., 1994. Mem. Nat. Assn. Profl. Journalists (Lifetime Hall of Fame), Am. Newspaper Pubs. Assn., Am. Soc. Newspaper Editors, Soc. Profl. Journalists, Kirtland Country Club (Willoughby, Ohio), Sand Ridge Golf Club (Chardon, Ohio), Cypress Point Club (Pebble Beach, Calif.), Bohemian Club (San Francisco), Chagrin Valley Hunt Club (Gates Mills, Ohio), Links Club (NYC). Episcopalian. Home: L'Ecurie 14950 County Line Rd Hunting Valley Chagrin Falls OH 44022 Office: 29225 Chagrin Blvd Ste 200 Pepper Pike OH 44122-4632

VAIL, VAN HORN, German language educator; b. Buffalo, Dec. 23, 1934; s. Curtis Churchill and Faith Newbrook (Ely) V.; m. Michele Juliette Edelstein, May 5, 1969; 1 son, Mark Curtis. BA, U. Wash., 1956; MA, Princeton U., 1961, PhD, 1964. Instr. Princeton U., 1962-65, asst. prof., 1965-66; asst. prof. German Middlebury (Vt.) Coll., 1966-69, assoc. prof., 1969-75, prof., 1975—; chmn. dept. Middlebury Coll., Vt., 1970-73, 87-88, dir. studies Middlebury Sch. in Germany, 1967-68, 70-71, 74-75, 85-86, 88-89, 92-93, 95-96. Mem. nat. screening com. Fulbright Scholarships, 1979-81. Author: German in Review, 1967, 4th edit., 2004, Der Weg zum Lesen, 1967, 4th edit., 2004, Modern German, 1971, 3d edit., 1992, Tonio Kröger als Weg zur Literatur, 1974, Workbook for Modern German, 1992, Student Manual for 3d edit. of German in Review, 2000, Classroom Manual for 4th Edit. of German in Review, 2004. Served to 1st lt. M.I., U.S. Army, 1956-58. Fulbright scholar U. Heidelberg, 1958-59 Mem. MLA Home: 352 Cider Mill Rd Middlebury VT 05753-9407 Office: Middlebury Coll Middlebury VT 05753 E-mail: vail@middlebury.edu.

VAILLANCOURT, ALLISON M, human resources specialist; b. Atlanta, Ga., July 1, 1962; d. Rod K McEwen and Patricia L McHenry; children: Kaitlin, Grace. BA, U.Wis., 1984; MA, U. Wis., 1990; PhD, U. Colo., 1995. Spl. asst. to chancellor U. Colo., 1994—96, spl. asst. to the pres., 1996; assoc. dir. U. Ariz., 1996—2002, exec. dir., 2002—03, asst. v.p., human resources, 2003—. Mem.: Soc. for Human Resource Mgmt. of Greater Tuscon (bd. mem.), Southwestern Regoin of Profl. Assn. for Human Resources (bd. mem.), Coll. and Univ. Profl. Assn. for Human Resources (bd.mem.). Office: Univ of Ariz P O Box 21058 888 N Euclid Tucson AZ 85721 Business E-Mail: vaillana@email.arizona.edu.

VAILLANCOURT, JEAN-GUY, sociology researcher and educator; b. Chelmsford, Ont., Can., May 24, 1937; s. Royal A. and Marie (Lavallée) V.; m. Pauline Hansen, June 6, 1966 (div. 1983); 1 child, Véronique. BA magna cum laude, Laurentian U., Sudbury, Ont., 1957; licenciate in Philosophy, Faculté des Jésuites, Montreal, Que., Can., 1961; licentiate in Sociology, Gregorian U., Rome, 1964; PhD in Sociology, U. Calif., Berkeley, 1975. Lectr. St. Boniface (Man.) Coll., Can., 1964-65; asst. prof. U. de Montréal, Que., Can., 1969-76, assoc. prof., 1976-83, prof. sociology, 1983—, chmn. dept., 1984-87. Adminstr., 1998; mem. consultative com. Can. amb. for disarmament, Ottawa, Ont., 1984-91, consultative com. on environ. Hydro-Que., 1984-90. Author: Papal Power, 1980, Essais d'écosociologie, 1982; co-editor: Le processus électoral au Québec, 1976, Roots of Peace, 1986, Environnement et développement Problèmes socio-politiques, 1991, Gestion de l'environnement, éthique et société, 1992, Instituer le développement durable, 1994, Aspects sociaux des précipitations acides au Québec, 1994, La recherche sociale en environnement, Nouveaux paradigmes, 1996, L'énergie au Québec, Quels sont nos choix? Montréal, Ecosocieté, 1998, Les sciences sociales de l'environnement, 1999, La gestion écologique des déchets, 2000, Développement durable et participation publique, 2003; editor-in-chief Sociologie et Sociétés, 1978-87. Mem. coun. City of Dunham, Que., 1976-80; bd. dirs. Oxfam-Que., 1976-79, Can. Inst. Internat. Peace and Security, Ottawa, Ont., 1986-89, European Univ. Ctr. for Peace Studies, Burg Schlaining, Burgenland, Austria, 1989-93, Groupement forestier du Haut-Yamaska, 1993—, Club 2/3, 1995—. Grantee Conseil de Recherche en sci. sociale du Canada, 1982, FCAR, 1989-95, 96—, Social Sci. Rsch. Coun., 1983-86, 90—, Can. Inst. Internat. Peace and Security, 1985, 91; fellow Can. Coun., 1965-68. Mem. Internat. Sociol. Assn., Assn. Can. des sociologues et anthropologues de langue française, Sci. for Peace, Pugwash, Group 78. Roman Catholic. Avocations: tree farming, travel. Home: 953 Cherrier Apt 3 Montréal QC Canada H2L 1J2 Office: U Montréal Dept Sociology Montreal QC Canada H3C 3J7 Office Phone: 514-343-5959. E-mail: jean.guy.vaillancourt@umontreal.ca.

VAINDER, MELANIE, speech pathology/audiology services professional, educator; b. N.Y.C. d. Louis Aaron and Pauline Vainder; m. Andrew Balmuth, May 28, 1979. BA, MA, Herbert H. Lehman Coll., 1977. Lic. speech pathologist NY, cert. ASHA 1978. Prof., dir. gen. edn./assessment SUNY, Farmingdale, 1998—, chmn. mid. states steering com., 2002—, dir. assessment grant/info. mgmt. pilot program, 2003—. Dir. assessment grant/info. mgmt. pilot program SUNY, 2002, Provost System Adminstrn. gen. edn. assessment rev. coun., mem., mem. adv. coun. on gen. edn., adv. coun. for honors prog., mem., NY; presenter in field. Recipient Tchr. of Excellence award for Speaking/Listening, NYS English Coun., 1987, Chancellor's Award for Excellence in Tchg., SUNY, 1996. Mem.: Am. Assn. Higher Edn., Am. Speech and Lang. Assn. (cert.). Avocations: boating, travel. Office: SUNY 2350 Broadhollow Rd Farmingdale NY 11735 Office Phone: 631-420-2776. Office Fax: 631-271-2661. Business E-Mail: Melanie.Vainder@farmingdale.edu.

VAINSCHTEIN, ARKADY, physics educator; b. Novokuznetsk, Russia, Feb. 24, 1942; MS in Physics, Novosibrisk U., 1964; Budker U., 1968. Prof. physics Novosibirsk, 1983-89; dir. theoretical physics inst. U. Minn., 1993-96, mem. theoretical physics inst., 1990—, Gloria Lubkin prof. physics, 1990—. Vis. prof. U. Minn., 1989-90. Mem. Am. Phys. Soc. Office: U Minn Sch Physics & Astronomy 116 Church St SE Minneapolis MN 55455-0149

VAIRA, PETER FRANCIS, lawyer; b. McKeesport, Pa., Mar. 5, 1937; s. Peter Francis and Mary Louise (Bedogne) V.; m. Mary Hohler, 1981. BA, Duquesne U., 1959, JD, 1962. Bar: Pa. 1963, D.C. 1968, Ill. 1984, U.S. Ct. Appeals (D.C. cir.) 1964, Ill. Supreme Ct. Ill. 1984, U.S. Dist. Ct. (no. dist.) Ill., U.S. Dist. Ct. (ea. dist.) Pa. Atty. Chgo. Strike Force, Justice Dept., 1968-72; atty. in charge Phila. Strike Force, 1972-73, Chgo. Strike Force on Organized Crime, 1973-78; U.S. atty. Ea. Dist. Pa., Phila., 1978—83; ptnr. Lord Bissel & Brook, Chgo., 1983-86, Fox, Rothschild, O'Brien & Frankel, Phila., 1986-90, Buchanan Ingersoll, Phila., 1990-92, Vaira & Assocs., Phila., 1992-93, Vaira & Riley, Phila., 1993—. Exec. dir. Pres.'s Commn. on Organized Crime, 1983; ind. hearing officer Laborers Internat. Union N.Am., 1995—; panelist, seminar, controlling internat. organized crime, Rome, Sorrento, Italy, June 1994; panelist, Internat. Conf. on Trial by Jury, Buenos Aires, Oct. 1996. Author: Eastern District Practice Rules Annotated, 2004, Corporate Responses to Grand Jury Investigations, 2004; contbr. articles to profl. jours. Mem. Mayor's Search Com. for Police Commr., Phila., 1992; corruption task force Phila. Police, 1997; press officer women's amateur championship U.S. Golf Assn., 2003. Lt. USNR, 1963-68. Recipient Spl. Commendation award Justice Dept., 1976 Fellow Am. Coll. Trial Lawyers (chmn. criminal procedure com. 1995-98, mem. comms. com.), Chartered Inst. Arbitrators; mem. ABA (mem. criminal justice coun. 1986), Am. Law Inst. (mem. editl. bd. The Legal Intelligence, The Phila. Lawyer), Union League (Chgo.), Phila. Country Club. Office: Vaira & Riley 1600 Market St Ste 2650 Philadelphia PA 19103-7226 Office Phone: 215-751-2700. Personal E-mail: p.vaira@vairariley.com.

VAIRO, ROBERT JOHN, insurance company executive; b. Bklyn., Sept. 27, 1930; s. John and Antonietta (DeRose) V.; m. Carol P. Andross, Apr. 8, 1951 (div. Feb. 1979); children: Robert J., Gregory J.; m. Inge R. Buhlbecker, Feb. 20, 1979. Student, Coll. Ins., N.Y.C., 1953-62; Exec. Program in Bus. Adminstrn., Columbia U., 1973. CPCU. Under asst. mgr. Atlantic Cos., N.Y.C., 1952-62; underwriter mgr., v.p. Fireman's Fund Ins. Co., N.Y.C., 1962-75; v.p., sr. v.p. underwriting C & F Ins. Cos., Morristown, N.J., 1975-79; exec. v.p., pres. U.S. Ins. Group, Morristown, N.J., 1979-82; chmn., chief exec. officer C & F Underwriters Group and The North River Ins. Co., Morristown, N.J., 1982-86; pres., chief oper. officer Crum and Forster, Inc., Morristown, 1987-88, pres., chief exec. officer, 1988-90, chmn., pres., chief exec. officer, 1990-92, also bd. dirs. Chmn. Ins. Services Office, N.Y.C., 1983, Am. Ins. Assn., Washington, 1990. Pres. Lincoln Park City Council, N.J., 1971-76. Served with USMC, 1951-53. Mem. Soc. CPCUs, Am. Inst. for Chartered Property Casualty Underwriters (dir., chmn. 1991-92), Desert Highlands Golf Club (pres. 1997-99), Coalition Pinnacle Peak, Inc. (pres. 1998—). Roman Catholic. Home: # 451 10040 E Happy Valley Rd Scottsdale AZ 85255-2388 E-mail: sonoran@aol.com.

VAISEY, DAVID GEORGE, librarian, archivist; b. Tetbury, Eng., Mar. 15, 1935; s. William Thomas and Minnie (Payne) V.; m. Maureen Anne Mansell, Aug. 7, 1965; children: Katharine, Elizabeth. BA, Oxford U., Eng., 1959, MA, 1962. Archivist Staffordshire County Council, Stafford, Eng., 1960-63; from asst. librarian to sr. asst. librarian Bodleian Library, Oxford, Eng., 1963-75, keeper of western manuscripts, 1975-86, Bodley's librarian, 1986-96, Bodley's librarian emeritus, 1997—. Dep. keeper Oxford U. Archives, 1966-75, keeper, 1995-2000; vis. prof. dept. library studies UCLA, 1985; commr. Royal Commn. Hist. Manuscripts, 1987-98; founding chmn. Nat. Coun. Archives, 1988-91. Served to 2d lt. Brit. Army, 1954-56. Decorated encomienda Order of Isabel la Catolica (Spain), comdr. Order Brit. Empire; fellow Exeter Coll., Oxford, 1975, emeritus fellow, 2000; hon. rsch. fellow, Univ. Coll., London, 1987, hon. fellow Kellogg Coll., Oxford, 1996. Fellow: Soc. Antiquaries, Royal Hist. Soc.; mem.: Soc. Archivists (pres. 1999—2002), Brit. Records Assn. (v.p. 1998—). Office: Bodleian Libr Broad St Oxford OX1 3BG England E-mail: david.vaisey@bodley.ox.ac.uk.

VAJK, HUGO, manufacturing executive; b. Ljubljana, Slovenia, Mar. 26, 1928; emigrated to Can., 1947, naturalized, 1953; s. Hugo and Magda (Slatnar) V.; m. Barbara Lois Hallin, June 13, 1953; children: Tanja Astrid, Hugo Anthony, Madeleine Louise, Anita Marie, Nicolette Cecile, Moira Suzanne. Student, Inst. Poly., Grenoble, France, 1947; B.Eng. with honors, McGill U., Montreal, Que., Can., 1951; MS, Carnegie Mellon U., 1953. Product mgr. Joy Mfg. Co., Buffalo, 1957-59, dir. gen. Paris, 1960-63; with Massey-Ferguson, Ltd., 1964-78; pres. Moteurs Perkins S.A., Paris, 1964-65, Massey-Ferguson Ltd., Paris, 1966-69, v.p. logistics parent co. Toronto, 1970-72, exec. v.p., 1973-78; dir. GEC Inc., subs. Gen. Electric Co., Eng., 1979; chmn. English Electric Corp., Elmsford, N.Y., 1979; with Garret Corp. div. Signal Cos., 1980-84; v.p. Garrett Automotive Products; pres. Garrett Automotive Group, Allied-Signal, Inc., 1985—90; chmn. Inovatek Advisors, Inc., New Port Richey, Fla., 1988—; pres. ATM Communications Internat., Inc., Wilmington, Del., 1991—. Mem.: ASME, Assn. Profls. Engrs. Ont., Yacht Club de France (Paris), Royal Can. Yacht Club (Toronto), Univ. Club of Toronto. Home and Office: PO Box 1115 New Port Richey FL 34656-1115 Personal E-mail: hugovajk@aol.com. E-mail: atmcomm@cardpay.com.

VAKANAS, GEORGE P. process engineer, research scientist, consultant, entrepreneur; s. Petros and Maria (Loizou) Vakanas. BS in Physics, BSME, U. Ariz., 1990; MS, Stanford U., 1995; PhD, Ariz. State U., 2002. Rsch. engr. Cyprus Neuroscience & Tech. Inst., Nicosia, Cyprus, 1990—93; prodn. mgr. The Multimedia Factory, Nicosia, Cyprus, 1993—95; curriculum engr. and cons. Cybernet Institutes, Nicosia, Cyprus, 1995—98; sr. process engr. Intel Corp., Santa Clara, Calif., 2001—. Author: (tng. materials and curriculum) Multi-lingual Computer Curriculum for Children (INPEX'95 Silver Medal in Ednl. Tech., 1995). Mem.: US-EU Initiative for Gender Ednl. Infrastructure (co-founder 1999—2000), Stanford Alumni Assn. (life). Achievements include patents pending for Laser Fabrication Method for Subsurface Microstructures; A Repair Capability for thermofluidic Micro-electromechanical Systems (MEMS). Office: Intel Corp IMO/SC2-12 2200 Mission Blvd Santa Clara CA 94052 Personal E-mail: vakanas@stanfordalumni.org. E-mail: george.p.vakanas@intel.com.

VAKERICS, THOMAS VINCENT, lawyer; b. Lorain, Ohio, Mar. 26, 1944; s. Paul Peter and Margaret Theresa (Dobos) V.; m. Kathryn Ida Rogers, Aug. 7,1965; children: Meredith Vakerics Ehler, Mitchell Thomas. BA, Bowling Green State U., 1965; JD with honors, George Washington U., 1968. Bar: U.S. Dist. Ct. D.C. 1968, U.S. Ct. Appeals (D.C. cir.) 1969, U.S. Supreme Ct. 1974, U.S. Ct. Internat. Trade 1982, U.S. Ct. Appeals (Fed. cir.) 1982. Antitrust trial atty. FTC, Washington, 1969—73; assoc. Gore, Cladouhos & Brashares, Washington, 1973—75; ptnr. O'Connor & Hannan, Washington, 1975—84, Bayh, Tabbert & Capehart, Washington, 1984—86, Morgan, Lewis & Bockius, Washington, 1986—88, Winthrop, Stimson, Putnam & Roberts, Washington, 1988—94, Perkins Coie, 1994—2004, Sandler, Travis & Rosenberg, P.A., Washington, 2004—. Vis. prof. Nihon U., Tokyo, 1981-88. Author: Antitrust Basics, 1985, Antidumping, Countervailing Duty and Other Trade Actions, 1987; contbr. articles to profl. jours. Mem. ABA (vice chmn. internat. antitrust law com. sect. internat. law and practice 1992-95), Internat. Bar Assn., D.C. Bar Assn., Solar Energy Rsch. Inst. (editl. adv. bd. Solar Energy Law Reporter 1979-82), Order of Coif, Phi Delta Phi, Pi Sigma Alpha, Phi Alpha Delta, Sigma Chi. Democrat. Roman Catholic. Office: Sandler Travis & Rosenberg PA 1300 Pennsylvania Ave NW Ste 400 Washington DC 20004 Office Phone: 202-216-9307. Office Fax: 202-842-2247. Business E-Mail: tvakerics@strtade.com.

VALACHOVIC, RICHARD W. medical association administrator; Former assoc. prof. oral medicine Harvard U., former chief of dentistry, Health Svcs.; exec. dir. Am. Assn. Dental Schs., Washington, 1997—. Fellow: Am. Coll. Dentists, Am. Acad. Pediat. Dentistry. Office: Am Assn Dental Schs Ste 600 1625 Massachusetts Ave NW Washington DC 20036-2244

VALADE, GARY C. automobile company executive; b. Detroit, Oct. 13, 1942; BSEE, Mich. State U., 1966, MBA, 1968. Mgmt. trainee, budget and profit analyst Chrysler Corp., Auburn Hills, Mich., 1968-74, budget and acctg. supr. Huber Avenue Foundry, 1974-76, fin. specialist enging and casting divsn., 1976-78, contr. Jefferson and Hamtramck assemblies, 1978-80, mgr. product analysis and cost planning, 1980-84, asst. contr. corp. fin. control, 1984-90, v.p., corp. contr., 1990-91, v.p. corp. pers., 1992-93, exec. v.p., CFO, 1993—; exec. v.p. global procurement and supply Daimler Chrysler Corp., Auburn Hills, Mich. Trustee Henry Ford Health Sys., Adrian Coll., Chrysler Corp. Fund; mem. corp. coun. Interlochen Ctr. for Arts; chmn. Mich. Colls. Found. Mem. Mich. State U. Eli Broad Coll. Bus. Alumni Assn. (bd. dirs.). Office: Daimler Chrysler Corp 1000 Chrysler Dr Auburn Hills MI 48326-2766

VALADEZ, RUDOLPH ANTONIO, security firm executive, consultant, writer, artist; b. Elmertownship, Mich., July 30, 1942; s. Aldofo Valadez and Catalina Gamez; m. Jo Ann Gomez; children: John L. children: Rudolph A., Monique M., Emilio Alejandro. BS, Am. U., 1971; postgrad., St. Thomas U., 1990, Pacific West Coll., 1995. Spl. agt.-mgr., chief Soviet CounterIntelligence, Chief of Counter Internat. Terrorism FBI, Washington, 1967—92; adminstr.-commr. Western Regional U.S. Immigration & Naturalization Svc., Laguna Niguel, Calif., 1992—93; TV and radio commentator Spanish Channel 52, KTNQ, L.A., 1993—95; security cons. Valadez Assocs. Internat., Inc., L.A., 1994—. Author: (Book) Uncommon Common Sense: The Anatomy of Peril, 2001, Instant Philosopher, 2002, Emilio Kosterlitzky, 2002; exhibitions include Global Art Gallery, Seattle, 2002, Cambria (Calif.) Art Gallery, 2002. Bd. dirs. Basic Adult Spanish Edn. for Spanish Illiteracy, L.A., 1986—90. Recipient Pub. Svc. Recognition, Calif. State Senate, 1992, Outstanding Pub. Svc. award, L.A. County Bd. Suprs., 1992, Cold War Svc. Recognition award, U.S. Dept. Def., 2001. Mem.: Am. Soc. Indsl. Security. Roman Catholic. Achievements include patents for handcuff holster; self recharging battery; automobile third rear light to indicate driver activity and pending action. Avocations: painting, flying, woodworking, travel. Office: Valadez Assocs Internat Inc Ste 2 4353 Teesdale Ave Studio City CA 91604 Home: 12582 Navel Ct Riverside CA 92503-7056 Personal E-mail: r.valadez@attworldnet.com. Business E-Mail: r.valadez@mai_assoc.com.

VALAKIS, M. LOIS, retired elementary school educator; b. Phila., Jan. 25, 1939; d. John Demosthenes and Blanche Antoinette Marquis Valakis. BS in Edn., Framingham (Mass.) State Tchrs. Coll., 1959. Elem. edn. tchr. Town of Framingham, 1959—98. Mem. ESEA Title III project, Framingham, 1969—70. Avocations: reading, music, photography. Home: 2 Concord Ter Framingham MA 01702

VALANCE, MARSHA JEANNE, library director, story teller; b. Evanston, Ill., Aug. 2, 1946; Children's libr. trainee N.Y. Pub. Libr., N.Y.C., 1968-69; ref. libr. Acton (Mass.) Meml. Pub. Libr., 1969-70; mgr. The Footnote, Cedar Rapids, Iowa, 1976-78; assoc. editor William C. Brown, Dubuque, Iowa, 1978-79; dir. Dubuque County Libr., 1979-81, G.B. Dedrick Pub. Libr., Geneseo, Ill., 1981-84, Grand Rapids (Minn.) pub. Libr., 1984-89; mgmt. libr. Wis. Regional Libr. for Blind and Physically Handicapped, 1989—. Workshop coord., participant, sect. chmn. profl. confs.; LSCA grant reviewer Dept. Edn., 1989-95. Author: (with others) Mystery, Value and Awareness, 1979, Pluralism, Similarities and Contrast, 1979; contbr. articles and book revs. to publs. Troop leader Miss. Valley Coun. Girl Scouts USA, Cedar Rapids, 1976-78; mem. liturgy com. St. Malachy's Roman Cath. Ch., Geneseo, 1983; com. judging clinic 4-H, Moline, Ill., 1984; trustee KAXE No. Cmty. Radio, 1986-89, ICTV, 1988-90; sec. Grand Rapids Cmty. Even. Coun., 1986; coach Itasca County 4-H Horse Bowl Team, 1987; dir. Grand Rapids Storyfest, 1987-89; program chmn. Spotlight on Books Conf., 1989; bd. dirs., trustee Vols. in Svc. to the Visually Handicapped, 1989—; audio describer Artreach, Mllw., 1991-98. Nat. merit scholar, 1964-68; recipient Weavers award Telephone Pioneers, 1992, outstanding svc. award Badger Assn., 1999; grantee Iowa Humanities Bd. 1981, Minn. Libr. Found., 1985, 86, 87, Blandin Found., 1986, Arrowhead Regional Arts Coun., 1987, 89, Ms. Soc., 1989, Sunrise Found., 2000. Mem. ALA, Wis. Libr. Assn., Iowa Librs. Medium Size (sec. 1981), Northlands Storytelling Network (bd. dirs. 1988-94, v.p. 1989, pres. 1990, editor Grapevine 1991-94), Nat. Storytelling Assn., Alliance Info. and Referral Svcs., DAR (constn. chmn. 1983-84), Miss. Valley Morgan Horse Club, Wis. Morgan Horse Club (newsletter editor 1994-95, sec. 1995), Western Working Family Morgan Horse Club, Am. Morgan Horse Assn., Geneseo Jr. Women's Club (internat. chmn. 1983-84), UCLA Club Wis. (pres. 1990-91), Alpha Gamma Delta. Home: 343 N 62d St Milwaukee WI 53213-4130 Office: Wis Regional Libr Blind & Physically Handicapped 813 W Wells St Milwaukee WI 53233-1436 Office Phone: 414-286-3010. E-mail: mvalan@mpl.org

VALANIS, KIRK CHRISTIAN, theoretical mechanics researcher, educator; b. Lefkara, Larnaca, Cyprus, Mar. 6, 1930; came to U.S., 1961; s. Christakis and Panayota Valanis; m. Lilian E. Salisbury, Sept. 10, 1955 (div.); children: Christina, Paul, Catherine; m. Barbara G. Geesey, Sept. 11, 1978. BS with honors, Imperial Coll., London, 1955, MSc, 1957; PhD, Purdue U., 1963. Prof. Iowa State U., Ames, 1964-68; prof., head U. Iowa, Iowa City, 1968-78; dean engring. U. Cin., 1978-83, prof., 1983-86; rsch. prof. U. Portland, Oreg., 1998—; pres. Endochronics Inc., Vancouver, Wash., 1986-96; owner Endochronics Co., Vancouver, 1996—. Cons. S-Cubed, La Jolla, 1976-92, Jet Propulsion Lab., Pasadena, Calif., 1966-92; bd. dirs. U. Crete, 1978-86. Author: Irreversible Thermodynamics, 1977; editor, author: Constitutive Equations, 1976; contbr. articles to profl. jours. Rsch. grantee NSF, 1978, Amy Rsch. Office, 1984, AF Office of Scientific Rsch., 1969, Waterways Experiment Sta., 1992. Fellow ASME; mem. Soc. of Engring. Sci., Math. Assn. of Am., Acad. of Mechanics, Hellenic Soc. Rheology (hon.). Greek Orthodox. Avocations: bridge, chess, tennis, hiking, stamp collecting/philately. Home: 544 NW View Ridge Way Camas WA 98607-9380

VALASQUEZ, JOSEPH LOUIS, industrial engineer; b. Balt., Apr. 15, 1955; s. Jose Louis and Edith Rosabel (Saunders) V.; m. Nicole Diane Feldser, Sept. 4, 1983; children: Alexandra Nicole, Joseph Jr. AA, Essex Coll., 1977; BS in Indsl. Engring., U. Ariz., 1982; MBA in Fin., So. Ill. U., 1985. Registered profl. engr., Fla.; cert. quality engr.; cert. quality auditor; cert. quality mgr.; cert. project mgmt. profl.; cert. integrated resource mgmt.; pvt. pilots license. Machinist Bausch & Lomb, Balt., 1974-77; indsl. engr. IBM Corp., Tucson, 1980-81; sr. indsl. engr. Gen. Dynamics, San Diego, 1981-83; supr. engring. Avco Corp., Nashville, 1983-84; mgr. engring. Burroughs Corp., Coral Springs, Fla., 1984-85; dir. total quality mgmt. Lambda Novatronics, Inc., Pompano Beach, Fla., 1984-94; champoint of continuous improvement Allied Signal, 1994-97, Sensormatic Corp., 1997-98; v.p. corp. quality Sunbeam Corp., Delray Beach, Fla., 1998-2001; quality/productivity exec. Bank Am., Charlotte, N.C., 2001—. Computer cons., Margate, Fla., 1987; founder, owner E.P.I. Cons., Pompano Beach. Mem. Am. Inst. Indsl. Engrs., Fla. Engring. Soc. Republican. Roman Catholic. Avocations: real estate management, computer programming, mountain climbing, canoeing, private pilot. Home: PO Box 49616 Charlotte NC 28277-0082 E-mail: joe.l.valasquez@bankofamerica.com.

VALBUENA, VIVIAN, brokerage house executive; b. Wilmington, Del., Sept. 29, 1965; d. Julian Valbuena-Briones and Barbara Hobart Valbuena; m. David Wiliam Buxbaum, Nov. 22, 1996. BA, U. of Del., Newark, 1988. Sr. editor Banco Santander, N.Y.C., 1996—99; mg editor, emerging mkts. BNP Paribas, N.Y.C., 1999—2001; assoc. dir., fixed income Barclays Capital, N.Y.C., 2001—. Contbr. articles to profl. jours. Budget com. Episc. Diocese of NY, N.Y.C., 2000—03; bd. dirs. China Barrett Assn., Carmel, NY, 2003. Avocations: tennis, travel, food, theater, mysteries. Office: Barclays Capital 200 Park Ave New York NY 10016 Office Phone: 212-412-1339. Office Fax: 212-412-7335. Personal E-mail: vivian.valbuena@mindspring.com.

VALDES, JACQUELINE CHEHEBAR, psychologist, consultant, researcher; b. Bklyn., Sept. 17, 1962; d. Gabriel and Rosy (Mosseri) Chehebar; m. Manuel Valdes, June 3, 1990; children: Raquel Elena Valdes, Michael Aaron Valdes. BA, U. Conn., 1983; cert. in substance abuse studies, Nova U., 1987, MS, 1988; PhD, Nova U., Ft. Lauderdale, 1992. Diplomate Am. Coll. Forensic Examiners, Am. Coll. Psychol. Specialties in Neuropsychology. Children's outpatient coord. Jewish Family Svc., Miami Beach, Fla., 1988-89; neuropsychology apprentice Robert A. Levitt, Ph.D., PA, Miami Beach, Fla., 1989-90; intern Columbia Presbyn. Med. Ctr., N.Y.C., 1990-91; fellow and resident Robert A. Levitt, PhD, PA, Ft. Lauderdale, 1991-93; pvt. practice, Hollywood, Fla., 1993—; dir. neuropsychology svcs. Meml. Regional Hosp., Hollywood, 1995-99; cons. neuropsychology Devel. and Early Intervention Clinic Joe DiMaggio Children's Hosp., 2000—. Psychology supr., educator Sunrise (Fla.) Rehab. Hosp., 1992-93; rschr. North Broward Med. Ctr., 1992-93, asst. dir. internship, 1993-94, Memory Disorders Ctr. Neurolog. Inst., Pompano, Fla., 1992-98, dir., 1994-98; neuropsychologist Neurologic Cons., Fort Lauderdale, Fla., 1992-98, Neurol. Cons. Hollywood, Fla., 1992-97; neuropsychology cons. Sunrise (Fla.) Rehab. Hosp., 1992-94; chairperson minority affairs Broward County Psych. Assn., 1997-98. Contbr. articles to profl. jours. Sec. Spanish Speaking Neuropsychology Interest Group, L.A., 1993-94; apptd. Child Sexual Abuse Svc. Provider Task Force, 1989. Mem. APA, Internat. Neuropsychol. Soc., Nat. Acad. Neuropsychologists, Am. Acad. Neurology, Brain Injury Assn., Fla. Psychol. Assn. Democrat. Jewish. Home: 520 E Mt Vernon Dr Plantation FL 33325-3600 Office: 2214 Hollywood Blvd Hollywood FL 33020-6605 Office Phone: 954-927-9555. E-mail: jcvaldesphd@aol.com.

VALDES, JUAN CARLOS, marketing executive; b. Santiago de las Vegas, Habana, Cuba; came to U.S., 1966; s. Hidalgo Valdes and Angela Teresa Valdes Montes de Oca. AA, Miami Dade C.C., Miami, Fla., 1976; student, Fla. Internat. U., 1977-78, Internat. Coll. Naples, Fla., 1988-89. Purchasing coord. Barnett Bank, Miami, 1975-76; internat. purchasing v.p. Mid-East Caribbean Trading Co., Miami and London, 1976-80; internat. mktg. devel. Mid-East Caribbean Petroleum Co., London, 1978-80; exec. v.p. internat., COO Rysell Internat., various locations, 1980—. Cons. Rysell Internat. Mktg. Devel. Group, St. Domingo, Dominican Republic, 1984—, Forest Internat. Group, Manaus, Brazil, 1988—; comptr. Rancho Santa Barbara, Clemiston, Fla., 1986-90; COO Juan Valdes & Son Cigar Co., Dominican Republic and Miami, 1988—; exec. v.p., COO, Amazon Trade Devel. Corp., Miami and Manaus, 1988—; bd. dirs. A Place Called Hope. Roman Catholic. Avocation: travel. Office: ATDC 13876 SW 56th St Miami FL 33175-6021 E-mail: jcv1357@aol.com.

VALDÉS, KAREN W. art gallery director, educator; b. L.A., May 25, 1945; d. Richard Victor and Eleanor M. (Tomte) V.; m. Thomas E. Schwarz, Oct. 14, 1989. BFA, U. Calif., Irvine, 1968; MFA, Fla. State U., 1974. Dir. cultural events Fla. State U., Tallahassee, 1973-75; curator exhbn. Art Mus. So. Tex., Corpus Christi, 1975-76; assoc. prof., dir. gallery Miami (Fla.)-Dade Community Coll., 1976-84; dir. Gloria Luria Gallery, Miami, 1985; curator exhbn. Mus. Art, Ft. Lauderdale, Fla., 1985-89; assoc. prof., dir. univ. galleries U. Fla., Gainesville, 1989-95; gallery curator Arts Ctr. Galleries, Okaloosa-Walton C.C., Niceville, Fla., 1995—. Panelist NEA, Ft. Lauderdale, 1978-80, Dade County Art in Pub. Places, Miami, 1980-83, GSA Commn., 1982, Arts in State Bldgs., Gainesville, 1989—. Mem. Am. Assn. Mus., Coll. Art Assn., U. Fla. Hispanic Faculty Assn. Democrat. Avocation: sailing. Office: Arts Ctr Galleries Okaloosa-Walton CC 100 College Blvd E Niceville FL 32578-1347

VALDEZ, ARNOLD, dentist, lawyer; b. Mojave, Calif., June 27, 1954; s. Stephen Monarez Jr. and Mary Lou (Esparza) V.; m. Brandy Radovich, Dec. 31, 1994; children: Bayleigh, Briton, Barrington, Brennan. BS in Biol. Sci., Calif. State U., Hayward, 1976; BS in Dental Sci. and DDS, U. Calif., San Francisco, 1982; MBA, Calif. State Poly. U., 1985; BS and JD cum laude, Pacific West Coll. Law, 1995. Bar: Mex., 1996; diplomate Am. Bd. Forensic Medicine, Am. Bd. Forensic Examiners, Am. Bd. Forensic Dentistry, World Clin. Laser Inst., 2004; cert. ind. med. examiner, qualified med. examiner, Calif. Pvt. practice emphasizing in temporomandibular joint and Myofascial Pain Dysfunction Disorders, Pomona, Calif., 1982—90; pvt. practice emphasizing temporomandibular joint and Myofascial Pain Dysfunction Disorders Claremont, Calif., 1982—; CEO, Valcom, 1994—96; assoc. Marin, O'Connell & Meché, 1996. CEO, Valcom-A Telecom. Corp.; network adminstr. Amiga and IBM compatibles; mem. adv. com. dental assisting program Chaffey Coll., Rancho Cucamonga, Calif., 1982—, Citrus Coll. Azuza, Calif., 2003—; mem. staff Pomona Valley Hosp. Med. Ctr.; ptnr. Marin, O'Connell & Meché; mem. digital adv. group Soredex, 2000—. Vol. dentist San Antonio Hosp. Dental Clinic, Rancho Cucamonga, 1984—, Pomona Valley Assistance League Dental Clinic, 1986—; bd. dirs. Pacific West Coll. Law, 1993—, v.p. fgn. devel., 1996—, v.p. curriculum, 1998—; founding bd. dirs. World Clin. Laser Inst. Fellow, World Clin. Laser Inst., 2004, Pierre Fall Chard Acad., 2004. Fellow Am. Coll. Forensic Examiners (life), Acad. Gen. Dentistry (mastership 1994), World Congres of Mimimally Invavsive Dentistry (diplomate), ADA (life); mem. Am. Equilibration Soc., The Cranial Acad., Newport Harbor Acad. Dentistry, Calif. Dental Assn. (table clinic judge 1998), Tri-County Dental Soc. (co-chmn. mktg. 1986, chmn. sch. screening 1987, Golden Grin award), Acad. Gen. Dentistry, Acad. Osseo Integratiion, Acad. Computerized Dentistry of N. Am., U. Calif.-San Francisco Alumni Assn., U. So. Calif. Sch. Dentistry Golden Century Club, Toastmasters, Psi Omega, Delta Theta Phi. Democrat. Roman Catholic. Avocations: skiing, gymnastics, kenpo karate (3d degree black belt), racquet sports, dance. Home: 515 Seaward Rd Corona Del Mar CA 92625-2600 Office: 410 W Baseline Rd Claremont CA 91711-1607 E-mail: dentski@adelphia.net. *Personal philosophy: Life is a journey, not a destination!.*

VALDEZ, DENISE, newscaster; BA in TV broadcasting, Pepperdine U. Reporter KMIR-TV, Palm Springs, 1992; weekend anchor, reporter KCCN-TV, Monterey, Calif., 1992—93; co-anchor, reporter KSAT-TV, San Antonio, 1994—2001; weekend anchor, reporter KXAS-TV (NBC), Dallas/Ft. Worth, 2001—02; co-anchor, Channel 4 News with Furnell Chatman NBC4, Los Angeles, 2002—, interim co-anchor, Today in LA. Mem.: Nat. Assn. of Hispanic Journalists. Office: NBC 4 3000 W Alameda Ave Burbank CA 91523

VALDEZ, JOSE CARBAJAL, JR., poet, lyricist; b. Solano, Nueva Vizcaya, Philippines, Jan. 8, 1932; arrived in U.S., 1969; s. Jose Abella Valdez, Sr. and Laureana Cabato (Carbajal) Valdez; m. Clavel Garduque Corrales-Valdez, July 26, 1956; children: Fred, Lorna, Jose III, Walter, Meha. AA, Luna Colls., Tayug, Pangasinan, The Philippines, 1952; BS in Edn., Adventist-U. of the Philippines, Cavite, Silang, 1954. Cert. sr. tchr. civil svc. eligibility Civil Svc. Commn. Tchr. Polillo Acad., Quezon, Philippines, 1955—56, Namuac Acad., Sanchez Mira, Philippines, 1960—67, Thoburn Meml. Acad., Sanchez Mira, Philippines, 1967—69, San Diego City Schs., 1977—78; med. technician Paradise Valley Hosp., National City, Calif., 1970—95; writer Internat. Soc. Poets, Owings Mills, Mo., 1997—; lyricist Hilltop Records, Hollywood, Calif., 2000—. Author: (book) Golden Treasures, 1999. Recipient Editor's award, Internat. Libr. Poetry, 2000, Merit award, Internat. Soc. Poets, 2000, 2002. Republican. Seventh-Day Adventist. Achievements include experimentation and research on plant propagation: hybridization or cross-breeding of plants (fruit trees); produced the most-grafted lemon tree with 40 varieties in one tree; cross-bred guava from Thailand and Philippine guavas. Avocations: gardening, reading, painting, fishing, walking. Home: 1440 Lorenz Ave San Diego CA 92114 E-mail: joseclavelvaldez@aol.com.

VALDEZ DEL ALAMO, ELIZABETH, art historian, educator; d. Elizabeth Pyle Valdez Wirsching and Earl Henry Hornbostel, Norbert Rolf Wirsching (Stepfather); m. Constancio del Alamo. BA, Sarah Lawrence Coll., 1968; MAT, Yale U., 1969; PhD, Columbia U., 1986. Assoc. prof. art history Montclair State U., NJ, 1990—. Bd. dirs. Internat. Ctr. of Medieval Art, N.Y.C., 2002—, advisor to bd. dirs., 2001—02. Editor (with Stephen Lamia): Decorations for the Holy Dead: Visual Embellishments on Tombs and Shrines of Saints, International Medieval Research, vol. 8, 2002; editor: (with Carol Pendergast) Memory and the Medieval Tomb, Aldershot: Ashgate (The Samuel H. Kress Found.: subvention, 1999); contbr. (exhibition catalogues) Maravillas de la España medieval: Tesoro Sagrado y Monarquía, 2 vols., 2001, The Art of Medieval Spain: 500-1200 A.D., Met. Mus. of Art, 1993, contbr. with Constancio del Alamo De Limoges a Silos, Madrid: Sociedad Estatal para la Acción Cultural Exterior, 2001, contbr. The Cloisters. Studies in Honor of the Fiftieth Anniversary., Met. Mus. of Art, 1992; mem. editl. bd.: Medieval Rev. Fellow, Samuel H. Kress Found., 1981—82, J. Paul Getty Found. for Arts, 1988—89, Howard Found., 2001—02; grantee 1988, Comité Conjunto Hispano-Norteamericano para la Cooperación Cultural y Educativa, 1988, NJ. Com. for Humanities, 1992, The Program for Cultural Cooperation Between Spain's Ministry of Culture and U.S. Univ., 1997, Nat. Endowment forHumanities, 1997; Chester Dale & Andrew W. Mellon fellow, Met. Mus. of Art, 1981—83. Mem.: Am. Soc. Hispanic Art Hist. Studies, Coll. Art Assn., Internat. Ctr. Medieval Art (bd. of directors 2002—), Medieval Acad. Am. (life). Achievements include research in convincingly redating and interpreting the later Romanesque sculpture of Santo Domingo de Silos; first study applying reception theory to a medieval Spanish monument. Office: Montclair State Univ Dept Art and Design Upper Montclair NJ 07043

VALDEZ-FLORES, CIRIACO, risk assessment consultant; b. San Carlos, Tamaulipas, Mex., Nov. 22, 1957; s. Ciriaco Valdez-Guevara and Maria Concepcion Flores de Valdez; m. Nancy Esther Vivas-Rodriguez, Dec. 20, 1985; children: Martin Roberto Valdez-Vivas, Natalia Isabel Valdez Vivas. BS, Inst. Tecnologico de Cd. Victoria, Victoria, Tamaulipas, Mex., 1980; MS in Engring., Tex. A&M U., 1983; PhD, Tex. A & M U., 1987. Registered profl. engr., Tex., 1990. Prof. Inst. Tecnologico de Cd. Victoria, 1980—88; sr. risk assessment cons. Sielken & Associates Consulting, Inc., Bryan, Tex., 1987—. Tchg. asst. Tex. A&M U., Coll. Sta., Tex., 1983—86, vis. asst. prof., 1989—92, master thesis adviser, 1989—92. Contbr. articles to profl. jours. Tchr. St. Thomas Aquinas Cath. Ch., Coll. Sta., 2002—03; tchr. religious edn. for adults St. Mary's Cath. Ch., Coll. Sta., 1999—99, marriage preparation sponsor, 1996—2003. Scholar, CONACyT (Mex.), 1980—85. Mem.: The Inst. for Ops. Rsch. and Mgmt. Scis., Alpha Pi Mu. Achievements include development of software system to infer distribution of contaminant concentrations in individual items collected in composites; general simulation software for risk assessment; general curve-fitting of probability distributions for censored and uncensored observations. Office: Sielken & Associates Consulting Inc 3833 Texas Avenue Suite 230 Bryan TX 77802

VALDIVIA, HECTOR HORACIO, medical educator; b. Loreto, Mex., Aug. 23, 1958; married. MD, Nat U. Mex., 1982, PhD, 1987. Teaching asst. Nat. U. Mex. Sch. Medicine, Mexico City, 1980-86; rsch. assoc. Baylor Coll. Medicine, Houston, 1986-89; assoc. scientist U. Wis. Sch. Medicine, Madison, 1989-92; rsch. asst. prof. U. Md. Med. Sch., Bapt., 1992-94; asst. prof. dept. physiology U. Wis. Med. Sch., Madison, 1994-99, assoc. prof. dept. physiology, 1999—. Lectr. and researcher in field. Contbr. articles to profl. jours., chpts. to books. Cystic Fibrosis Found. fellow, 1989-91. Mem. Am. Heart Assn. (scintific coun. 1995—), Biophys. Soc. U.S.A. Office: U Wis Med Sch Dept Physiology 1300 University Ave Madison WI 53706-1510

VALDMAN, ALBERT, language and linguistics educator; b. Paris, Feb. 15, 1931; came to U.S., 1944, naturalized, 1953; s. Jacques and Rose (Standman) V.; m. Hilde Wieners, Aug. 19, 1960; 1 child, Bertrand André. AB, U. Pa., 1953; AM, Cornell U., 1955, PhD, 1960; Doctorate honoris causa, U. Neuschâtel, 1991. Linguistic scientist Fgn. Service Inst., 1957-59; asst. prof. Romance langs. Pa. State U., 1959-60; mem. faculty Ind. U., Bloomington, 1960—, prof. French, Italian and linguistics, 1966—, chmn. dept. linguistics, 1963-68, Rudy prof., 1986—; vis. prof. Harvard, summer 1965. Vis. lectr. U. West Indies, 1965-66; Fulbright lectr. U. Nice, France, 1971-72, 75-76, 83-85, 86, 87, 89; cons. in field, 1959— Author: Applied Linguistics-French, 1960, Drillbook of French Pronunciation, 1964, 70, Trends in Language Teaching, 1966, College French in the New Key, 1965, Saint-Lucian Creole Basic Course, 1969, Basic Course in Haitian Creole, 1970, First and Second Level High School French, 1972, 2d edit., 1977, Langue et Culture, 1975, Introduction to French Phonology and Morphology, 1976, Le Creole: Structure, Statut et Origine, 1978, Haitian Creole English Dictionary, 1982; co-author: En Route—Introduction au français et au monde francophone, 1986; editor: Pidgin and Creole Linguistics, 1977, Le Francais hors de France, 1979; co-editor: Theoretical Orientations in Creole Studies, 1980, Historicity and Variation in Creole Studies, 1981, Issues in International Bilingual Education, 1982, Haiti Today and Tomorrow: An Interdisciplinary Study, 1984, The Evaluation of Foreign Language Proficiency, 1987, Ann pale Kreyol: Learning Haitian Creole, 1987, Dis-Moi!, Viens Voir!, C'est Ça!, 1989, Bien Entendu! Introduction á la prononciation française, 1993, Learners' Dictionary of Haitian Creole, 1996, French and Creole in Louisiana, 1997, Chez Nous, 1997, Dictionary of Louisiana Creole, 1998. Decorated comdr. dans l'Ordre dans Palmes Académiques; recipient Florence Steiner prize, Am. Coun. Tchg. Fgn. Langs., 1998; Guggenheim fellow, 1968, Fulbright fellow, 1985. Mem. Internat. Assn. Applied Linguistics (sec.-gen. 1984-87, pres. 1987-94), Am. Assn. Tchrs. of French (v.p. 1990-94, pres. 1995-98), Comité Internat. des Créolistes (v.p. 1996—), Phi Beta Kappa. Office: Ind U CREDLI BH 604 Bloomington IN 47405 Office Phone: 812-855-0098. E-mail: valdman@indiana.edu.

VALDMAN, BERTRAND A. utilities executive; With JP Morgan Securities, Inc., 1987—2003, former mng. dir. natural resources group; sr. v.p., CFO Puget Sound Energy, Bellevue, Wash., 2004—. Office: Puget Sound Energy 10885 NE 4th St PO Box 97034 Bellevue WA 98009*

VALDOVINO, LUIS HECTOR, art educator; b. Bahía Blanca, Argentina, June 7, 1961; s. Héctor Clemente Valdovino and Nelly Isabel Baquedano. BFA, Ohio U., 1985; MFA, U. of Ill., 1987. Asst. prof. Fine Arts Dept., U. of Colo., Boulder, 1993—2000, assoc. prof., 2000—; vis. asst. prof. Carnegie-Mellon U., Pitts. Video art work, The World of Dance, Truco, Cocteau Cento, Día de los Muertos (The Last of the 20th Century), A Refutation of Time, Una Historia/A History (Broadcasts: Deep Dish TV, N.Y., 1992), Work in Progress, Tierra Nueva, Themes, Standards, Eat Like a Winner, Patagonia, Another World of Dance. Recipient award, Ctr. for New TV/John D. and Catherine T. MacArthur Found., 1991; fellow Regional Fellowship, Ctr. for New TV, 1987, 1988, 1990, Individual Artist Fellowship, Ill. Arts Coun., 1992, Nat. Endowment for the Arts, 1994, Western States Regional Media Arts Fellowship, Nat. Endowment for the Arts/Am. Film Inst., 1994; grantee Travel Grant Pilot, Nat. Endowment for the Arts/Arts Internat., 1992, Ind. Film/Video Grant, Am. Film Inst., 1993. Mem.: Assn. of Ind. Film/Video (assoc.), U. Film/Video Assn. (assoc.), Soc. for Photographic Edn. (assoc.), Film Arts Found. (assoc.), Coll. Art Assn. (assoc.). Office: U of Col Fine Arts Dept Boulder CO 80309 Office Phone: 303-492-5482.

VALE, MARGO ROSE, physician; b. Balt., June 16, 1950; d. Henry and Pauline Esther (Koplow) Hausdorff; m. Michael Allen Vale, Aug. 22, 1971; children: Edward, Judith. BA magna cum laude, Brandeis U., 1971; MD, Albert Einstein Coll. Medicine, 1975. Diplomate Am. Bd. Dermatology. Resident in internal medicine and dermatology NYU, N.Y.C., 1975-79, Bellevue Hosp., N.Y.C., 1975-79, VA Hosp., N.Y.C., 1975-79; staff physician HIP Greater N.Y., Bay Shore, 1979-81; pvt. practice medicine Huntington, N.Y., 1981—. Cons. in dermatology Huntington Hosp., 1981—, Gurwin Jewish Geriatric Ctr., Commack, N.Y., 1990—. Contbr. articles to profl. jours. Mem. Am. Acad. Dermatology, Med. Soc. State N.Y., Long Island Dermatology Soc., Suffolk County Med. Soc., Suffolk Dermatology Soc. (pres. 1990-92), Phi Beta Kappa. Avocations: cooking, photography, sketching, music. Office: 205 E Main St Huntington NY 11743-2923

VALE, WYLIE W. biochemist; BS, Rice U., 1964; PhD in Physiology & Biochemistry, Baylor U., 1968. Biochemist The Salk Inst., La Jolla, Calif., 1970-78, Clayton Found. Lab. Peptide Biology br. The Salk Inst., La Jolla, 1978—. Elected mem. Inst. of Medicine, 2000. Recipient Fred Conrad Koch award Endocrine Soc., 1997. Office: Clayton Found Lab Peptide Biology The Salk Inst 10010 N Torrey Pines Rd La Jolla CA 92037-1002

VALENCIA, MARGARITA, Spanish language educator; b. Bogotá, Colombia, Nov. 28, 1952; arrived in U.S., 1973; BA, MA in Polit. Sci., U. Calif., Santa Barbara. Profl. clear single subject tchg. credential in Spanish; cert. eligibility for Calif. prelim. adminstrv. svcs. credential. Tchr. Spanish Manual Arts H.S. L.A. Unified Sch. Dist., 1994—. Mem.: Acad. Polit. Sci. N.Y., L.A. World Affairs Coun., Sierra Club. Office Phone: 562-428-3874.

VALENCIA, ROGELIO PASCO, electronics engineer; b. Paombong, Bulacan, The Philippines, Mar. 18, 1939; came to U.S., 1959; s. Silvino Carlos and Basilia Galang (Pasco) V.; m. Amelia Almendarez Gomez, May 31, 1965; children: Zenaida Leticia, Lucinda Amelia, Rogelio Pasco II. Student mech. engring., Mapua Inst. Tech., Manila, 1955-59; student English and math., Coll. William and Mary, 1963-64, numerous USCG tng. schs. Enlisted man USCG, 1959, advanced through grades to chief warrant officer; with USCG cutter Rush, Vietnam, 1970-71; sr. tech. officer USCG Loran Sta., Hokkaido, Japan, 1977-78, exec. officer Dana, Ind., 1978-79; ret., 1979; computer analyst Wyman & Gordon Co., Danville, Ill., 1979-80; precision measurement electronics lab. technician USAF, Rantoul, Ill., 1980-88, digital computer engr., 1988—. Achievements include designing synchronous Loran clock, field telephone monitor. Home: 1303 Bradford Cir Saint Joseph IL 61873-9625 Office Phone: 217-766-4131. Personal E-mail: rpvalencia@insight.com.

VALENSTEIN, SUZANNE GEBHART, art historian; b. Balt., July 17, 1928; d. Jerome J. and Lonnie Cooper Gebhart; m. Murray A. Valenstein, Mar. 31, 1951. With dept. Asian Art Met. Mus. Art, N.Y.C., 1965—. Rsch. curator Asian Art. Author: Ming Porcelains: A Retrospective, 1970, A Handbook of Chinese Ceramics, 1975, rev. and enlarged, 1989, Highlights of Chinese Ceramics, 1975, (with others) Oriental Ceramics: The World's Great Collections: The Metropolitan Museum, 1977, rev., 1983, The Herzman Collection of Chinese Ceramics, 1992. Mem. Oriental Ceramic Soc. (London), Oriental Ceramic Soc. (Hong Kong). Office: Met Mus Art Dept Asian Art Fifth Ave at 82nd St New York NY 10028

VALENTE, LOUIS PATRICK (DAN VALENTE), business and financial executive; b. Somerville, Mass., July 26, 1930; s. Luigi and Mary Constance (Fedele) V.; m. Jeanne Barbara Peters, Oct. 3, 1992; children: Louis, Marianne, Steven, Diane, Richard, Carol, Susan. CPA, Bentley Coll., Boston, 1955. Cost acct. Cambridge Corp., Lowell, Mass., 1953-55; sr. acct. Flaherty, Bliss & Co., CPAs, Boston, 1956-61; fin. analyst Sanders Assocs., Nashua, N.H., 1961-62; contract audit adminstr. Dept. Def. Audit Agy., Boston, 1962-66, DOE, Las Vegas, 1966-68; asst. controller EG&G, Inc., Wellesley, Mass., 1968-71, asst. v.p., treas., 1971-74, dir. fin., 1974-79, officer, corp. treas., 1979-83, v.p. bus. devel., 1985-91, sr. v.p. mergers, acquisitons and investments, 1991-95; bus. and fin. cons., 1995-97; chmn., CEO Palomar Med. Tech., Inc., Burlington, Mass., 1997—. Bd. dirs. Meditech Inc., Westwood, Mass., Patient Care Tech., Atlanta, MKS Instruments, Inc., Andover, Mass., Palomar Med. Tech. Inc., Burlington, SurgiLight, Inc., Orlando, Fla. Selectman Town of Burlington, 1970-73, 76-79, chmn., 1972-79; trustee, mem. fin. com. Choate-Symmes Hosp., Woburn, Mass., 1972-80; pres.'s adv. coun.

Bentley Coll. With USAF, 1951-53. Mem. AICPA, Fin. Execs. Inst., Mass. Soc. CPAs, Bentley Coll. Alumni Assn., New Eng. Coun., KC Lodge. Roman Catholic. Home: 44 Concord Rd Weston MA 02493-1223

VALENTE, LUIZ FERNANDO, Portuguese and Brazilian studies and comparative literature educator; b. Rio de Janeiro, Mar. 16, 1950; came to U.S., 1969; naturalized, 1994; Diploma in French studies, U. Nancy, 1968; AB summa cum laude in French lit., Bowdoin Coll., 1971; PhD in Comparative Lit., Brown U., 1983. Teaching fellow Portuguese Brown U., Providence, 1982-83, vis. lectr. Brazilian lang. and lit., 1983-86, lectr. Portuguese and Brazilian studies, 1986-89, asst. prof., 1989-93, assoc. prof. Portuguese-Brazilian studies, comparative lit., 1993—; instr. Portuguese Providence Coll., 1976-77, instr. Portuguese, French, 1977-80, asst. prof. Portuguese and French, 1980-82. Vis. prof. comparative lit., grad. program in linguistics and lit. Pontificia U. Cath. do Rio Grande do Sul, Porto Alegre, Brazil, 1988, 93; chair conf. sessions and panels; vis. examiner in Portuguese, self-instrnl. program in Less-Commonly-Taught Langs., Bates Coll., 1974-83; state examiner in Portuguest R.I. Dept. Edn., State Portuguese Proficiency Exam., 1977-82. Assoc. editor Brasil/Brazil: A Jour. of Brazilian Lit.; cons. editor Latin Am. Lit., The Explicator; reader Modern Lang. Studies, PMLA, Comparative Studies in Society and History; contbr. articles to profl. jours. and encys., chpts. to books. Portuguese Govt. fellow, 1981. Mem. Modern Lang. Assn. Am., Am. Assn. Tchrs. Spanish and Portuguese (bd. dirs. R.I. chpt. 1990-92), Northeastern Assn. Brazilianists (v.p. 1985-87, pres. 1987-89, sec-treas. 1989—), Internat. Comparative Lit. Assn., Am. Comparative Lit. Assn., Can. Comparative Lit. Assn., So. Comparative Lit. Assn., N.E. Modern Lang. Assn., New Eng. Coun. Latin Am. Studies, Latin Am. Studies Assn., Soc. Study Narrative Lit., Brazilian Assn. Comparative Lit., Internat. Inst. Iberoamericana, Phi Beta Kappa. Office: Brown U Dept Portuguese and Brazilian Studies PO Box 0 Providence RI 02912

VALENTE, PETER CHARLES, lawyer; b. NYC, July 3, 1940; s. Francis Louis and Aurelia Emily (Cella) V.; m. Judith Kay Nemeroff, Feb. 19, 1966; children: Susan Lynn, David Marc. BA, Bowdoin Coll., 1962; LLB, Columbia U., 1966; LLM, NYU, 1971. Bar: N.Y. 1967. Assoc. Blank Rome LLP (formerly Tenzer Greenblatt LLP), N.Y.C., 1967-73, ptnr., 1973—, practice group leader pvt. client practice group, 2003—. Co-author column on wills, estates and surrogates's practice N.Y. Law Jour. Fellow Am. Coll. Trust and Estate Counsel; mem. ABA, N.Y. State Bar Assn. (lectr. on wills, trusts and estates), Assn. of Bar of City of N.Y., N.Y. County Lawyers' Assn. (former bd. dirs. and chmn. com. on surrogates' ct., lectr. on wills, trusts and estates), Phi Beta Kappa. Office: Blank Rome 405 Lexington Ave New York NY 10174-0002 E-mail: pvalente@blankrome.com.

VALENTI, JACK JOSEPH, former motion picture executive; b. Houston, Sept. 5, 1921; m. Mary Margaret Wiley, June 1, 1962; children: Courtenay Lynda, John Lyndon, Alexandra Alice. BA, U. Houston, 1946; MBA, Harvard U., 1948. Co-founder, formerly exec. v.p. Weekley and Valenti, Inc. (advt.), 1952-63; spl. asst. to Pres. Lyndon Johnson The White House, 1963-66; chmn., CEO Motion Picture Assn. Am., Inc., 1966—2004. Adj. prof. govt. and pub. adminstrn. Am. U., 1977; bd. dirs. Riggs Nat. Corp. Washington. Author: Bitter Taste of Glory, 1971, A Very Human President, 1976, Speak Up With Confidence: How To Prepare, Learn and Deliver an Effective Speech, 1982, Protect and Defend, 1992, Speak Up With Confidence, 2002; contbr. articles to mags. Trustee, bd. dirs. Am. Film Inst. Served with USAAF, 1942-45. Decorated D.F.C., Air medal with five oak leaf clusters, Disting. Unit Citation with cluster, European Theater Ribbon with 4 battle stars, Chevalier de la Legion d'honneur (France).

VALENTINE, ALAN DARRELL, symphony orchestra executive; b. San Antonio, July 18, 1958; s. Lonnie Darrell Jr. and Marjorie (Childs) V.; m. Jari Ann Ruhl, Aug. 10, 1979 (div. 1987); children: Brandon Darrell, Chelsea Michelle; m. Karen Kay Bingham, Oct. 21, 1989 (div. 2001); 1 child, Nathan Lee; m. Connie Linsler, July 21, 2002. MusB, U. Houston, 1981. Orch. mgr. U. Houston Symphony, 1977-81; gen. mgr. Mid-Columbia Symphony Soc., Richland, Wash., 1981-83, Greensboro (N.C.) Symphony Soc., 1983-85; orch. mgr. Symphony Soc. San Antonio, 1985-87; mng. dir. Chattanooga Symphony and Opera, 1987-88; exec. dir. Okla. Philharm. Soc., Oklahoma City, 1988-98, Nashville Symphony, 1998—. Mem. adj. faculty Arts Administrn., Oklahoma City U., 1992— Recs. include Best of Greensboro Symphony Orchestra Silver Season, 1983, A Christmas Festival-San Antonio Symphony, 1986, A Time of Healing-Oklahoma City Philharmonic, 1995; (CD) Howard Hanson The Nashville Symphony, 2000, Charles Ives The Nashville Symphony, 2000, George Whitefield Chadwick-Nashville Symphony, 2002, Bernetein's West Side Story, Nashville Symphonyh, 2002, Amy Beach Gaelic Symphony, Nashville Symphony, 2003; TV prodns. include Music of the Americas-Placido Domingo with San Antonio Symphony, 1986, Perry Como Christmas Special-San Antonio Symphony, 1986, Sagebrush Symphony-Oklahoma City Philharmonic with Michael Martin Murphey, 1996, Kathie Lee: Just In Time for Christmas-Okla. City Philharmonic & Guests, 1996, Martina McBride Christmas Special Nashville, Symphony and Guests, 1998. Bd. dirs. Classen Sch. for Artistically and Academically Gifted, 1995-98, Arts Festival Okla., 1991-. Mem. NARAS (bd. dirs. 2002-), Am. Symphony Orch. League (bd. dirs. Cmty. and Urban Symphony Orch. divsn. 1981-83, policy com. A 1995-98, chmn. group III mgrs. 1996-98, vice chmn. group III mgr. 2003), Rotary, Phi Mu Alpha. Presbyterian. Avocations: computers, racquetball, reading. Office: Nashville Symphony 2000 Glen Echo Ste 204 Nashville TN 37215 E-mail: alandv@aol.com.

VALENTINE, ANNA MAE, retired nurse; b. Owosso, Mich., July 26, 1926; d. Robert Harry and Della Jane (Gander) Thompson; m. Manley Lavern Nixon, Aug. 3, 1946 (div. 1961); children: Terry Lee, Douglas Kent, LaVerna Ann, Norma Jean; m. Donald F. Clewley, Aug. 27, 1961 (dec. 1973); m. Heinz Weidenbruch, 1984 (dec. 1999); m. Roland J. Valentine, Nov. 1, 2003. ADN, Lansing (Mich.) C.C., 1983; BS in Health Studies, Western Mich. U., Kalamazoo, 1993. RN, Mich. Staff nurse Sparrow Hosp., Lansing, 1958-62, Ingham Med. Hosp., Lansing, 1962-64, Lansing Gen. Hosp., 1964-66, 77-88, Hazel I. Findlay Country Manor, St. Johns, Mich., 1987-89, Staff Builders, Okemos, Mich., 1990-96; ret., 1996. Democrat. Avocations: knitting, crocheting, embroidery, travel, dance. Home: 9855 E Irvington Rd Unit 189 Tucson AZ 85730-5234 E-mail: aweidenbruch@msn.com., annaw@voyager.net.

VALENTINE, BRIAN, information technology executive; BS in Computer Sci., Ea. Washington U. Software engr. Intel Corp.; with Microsoft, 1987—, gen. mgr., server application div., 1998, sr. v.p. windows core operating systems divsn., 1998—. Office: One Microsoft Way Redmond WA 98052-6399*

VALENTINE, DEAN, film producer; AB, U. Chicago, 1976. Pres. Walt Disney TV/Touchstone TV; pres., CEO United Paramount Network, Los Angeles, 1997—2002; with Europlay Capital Advisors, LLC, 2002—03; pres. First Family Entertainment, Beverly Hills, 2004. Office: First Family Entertaninment LLC 9595 Wilshire Blvd Ste 407 Beverly Hills CA 90212*

VALENTINE, DEBRA A. lawyer; b. Cleve., Apr. 16, 1953; AB magna cum laude in History, Princeton U., 1976; JD, Yale U. Law School, 1980. Bar: D.C., U.S. Dist. Ct. D.C., U.S. Ct. Appeals (D.C. Cir., 3d Cir., 11th Cir.), U.S. Supreme Ct. Law clk. Judge Arlin M. Adams, U.S. Ct. Appeals, 3d Cir., Phila., 1980-81; atty./advisor Office of Legal Counsel, Dept. of Justice, Washington, 1981-85; assoc. O'Melveny & Myers, Washington, 1985-91, ptnr., 1991-95; dep. dir. policy planning FTC, Washington, 1995-96, asst. dir. for internat. antitrust, 1996-97, gen. counsel, 1997-2001; ptnr., co-chair antitrust practice group O'Melveny & Myers, Washington, 2001—. Cons. Sec. of State's Adv. Com. South Africa. Bd. editors BNA Antitrust & Trade Regulation Reporter; contbr. articles to profl. jours. Adv. mem. bd. dirs. The Washington Ballet. Fulbright scholar, 1976-77. Mem. ABA, Internat. Bar Assn., Am. Law Inst., D.C. Bar, Coun. on Fgn. Rels., Phi Beta Kappa. Home: 2853 Ontario Rd NW Apt 605 Washington DC 20009-2246 Office: O'Melveny & Myers 1625 I St NW Washington DC 20006-4001 E-mail: dvalentine@omm.com.

VALENTINE, FOY DAN, clergyman; b. Edgewood, Tex., July 3, 1923; s. John Hardy and Josie (Johnson) V.; m. Mary Louise Valentine, May 6, 1947; children: Mary Jean, Carol Elizabeth, Susan Foy. BA, Baylor U., 1944, LLD (hon.), 1979; ThM, Southwestern Baptist Theol. Sem., 1947, ThD, 1949; DD, William Jewell Coll., 1966, Louisiana Coll., 1989. Ordained to ministry Bapt. Ch., 1942. Dir. Bapt. student activities colls. in Houston, 1949-50; pastor First Bapt. Ch., Gonzales, Tex., 1950-53; dir. Christian life commn. Bapt. Gen. Conv. Tex., 1953-60; exec. dir., treas. Christian life commn. So. Bapt. Conv., 1960-87, exec. officer for devel., 1987-88; chmn. So. Bapt. inter-agy. council, 1965-67. Willson lectr. applied Christianity Wayland Bapt. Coll., 1963; Christian ethics lectr. Bapt. Theol. Sem., Ruschlikon-Zurich, Switzerland, 1966; Layne lectr. New Orleans Bapt. Theol. Sem., 1974; Jones lectr. Union U., 1976; Staley Disting. Christian scholar/lectr. La. Coll., 1981; Simpson lectr. Acadia Divinity Coll., Nova Scotia, 1982; H.I. Hester lectr. on preaching Midwestern Bapt. Theol. Sem., 1984; Belote lectr. Christian ethics Hong Kong Bapt. Theol. Sem., 1990; co-chmn. commn. religious liberty and human rights Bapt. World Alliance, 1966-75, chmn. commn. Christian ethics, 1976-80, mem. gen. coun., 1976-80; mem. Nashville Met. Human Rels. Commn., 1966-78, Pres.'s Commn. for Nat. Agenda for the Eighties, 1980; guest columnist USA Today; lectr. on Christian ethics Bible Inst. for Evangelism and Missions, St. Petersburg, USSR, 1991; co-chmn. Baylor U. Heritage Club, 2000-01. Author: Believe and Behave, 1964, Citizenship for Christians, 1965, The Cross in the Marketplace, 1966, Where the Action Is, 1969, A Historical Study of Southern Baptists and Race Relations 1917-1947, 1980, What Do You Do After You Say Amen?, 1980, Hebrews, James, 1 and 2 Peter: Layman's Bible Book Commentary, 1981, Whatsoever Things Are Lovely, 2004; editor: Christian Faith in Action, 1956, Peace, Peace, 1967, Christian Ethics Today, 1995-2000; contbr. to numerous anthologies, articles to profl. jours. Pres. Ctr. for Christian Ethics, 1990-2000; trustee Interfaith Alliance, 1994—, Ams. United for Separation of Ch. and State, 1960-93, pres., 1989-93; bd. dirs. Bapt. Joint Com. Pub. Affairs, 1960-87, Chs. Ctr. Theology and Pub. Policy, 1976-87, T.B. Maston Found., Texans Against Gambling; mem. bd. fellows Interpreter's House, 1967-78, Ctr. for Dialogue and Devel., 1987-96. Recipient Disting. Alumnus award Southwestern Bapt. Theol. Sem., 1970, Brooks Hays Meml. Christian Citizenship award, 1983, Disting. Alumni award Baylor U., 1987. Mem. Am. Soc. Christian Ethics. Democrat. Home and Office: 12527 Matisse Ln Dallas TX 75230-1741

VALENTINE, GENE C. securities dealer; b. Washington, Pa., June 19, 1950; s. John N. and Jane S. Valentine. BS in Psychology, Bethany Coll., 1972; student, U. Vienna, Austria, 1971-72. Commd. ensign USN, 1972, advanced through grades to lt., 1987, hon. discharged, 1978; owner Horizon Realty, San Francisco, 1978-82; dir. land acquisitions Windfarms Ltd. subs. Chevron, U.S.A., San Francisco, 1980-82; v.p. mktg. Christopher Weil & Co., Sherman Oaks, Calif., 1982-85; chmn., CEO Pacific Asset Group Inc. (name now Fin. West Group, Inc.), Westlake Village, Calif., 1985—. Bd. dirs. Fin. West Group, Inc., Paradox Holdings; founder, chmn., dir. Second Byte Found.; founder, chmn. Peace Point Farms Equestrian Facility, LLC and Found., Bethany, W.Va. Trustee Bethany Coll., W.Va., 1998—; mem. Rep. Party, L.A. Mem. NASD, Internat. Assn. Fin. Planning (bd. dirs. L.A. chpt. 1982-87). Episcopalian. Avocations: equestrian, sailing, tennis, golf, running. Office: Fin West Group Inc 2663 Townsgate Rd Westlake Village CA 91361-2702 Fax: 805-495-9935. E-mail: gturner@fwg.com.

VALENTINE, GORDON CARLTON, retired secondary school educator; b. Norwich, N.Y., Nov. 18, 1946; s. Carlton Everett and Helen Janet (Thompson) V.; m. Deborah Lee Preston, Oct. 15, 1977; children: Heather, Megan, Matthew. BA, SUNY, Cortland, 1968, MS in Edn., 1970. Cert. tchr., N.Y. Tchr. Sherburne-Earlville Ctrl. Sch., Sherburne, N.Y., 1968-70, Marathon (N.Y.) Ctrl. Sch., 1970-87; social welfare examiner Dept. Social Svcs., Cortland, 1988; tchr. Homer (N.Y.) Ctrl. Sch., 1989—2003; ret., 2003—. Adj. instr. Tompkins-Cortland C.C., Dryden, N.Y., 1982—; mem. profl. staff devel. and supportive supervision model Homer Ctrl. Sch., 1989-92, asst. varsity cross country coach, jr. high track coach, varsity track coach, 1972-87, jr. high soccer coach, 1972-86, jr. varsity girls' soccer coach, 1989-90. Recipient Christa McAliffe Tchr.'s award, 1991, Yearbook Dedication, 1983. Mem. ASCD, Homer Tchrs. Assn., NYSUT, AFT, Challenger Ctr. of NASA, Ctrl. N.Y. State Coun. for Social Studies, Nat. Coun. Social Studies, SUNY Cortland Alumni Assn. (bd. dirs. 1993—, mem. admissions com., mem. mktg. com., mem. rsch. devel. com., nom. and by-law com., young alumni com., exec. com., rec. sec. 1998-2002, asst. treas. 2002-03). Democrat. Avocations: running, reading, volunteer coaching. Home: 4024 Collegeview Dr Cortland NY 13045-1501

VALENTINE, H. JEFFREY, legal association executive; b. Phila., Sept. 28, 1945; s. Joshua Morton and Olga W. (Wilson) V.; 1 child, Karyn. BS, St. Louis U., 1964, postgrad., 1966-68. Programmer, systems analyst Honeywell Electronic Data Processing, Wellesley Hills, Mass., 1964-66; account exec. Semiconductor div. Tex. Instruments, New Eng., 1966-68; New Eng. sales exec., Mid-Atlantic regional mgr. Electronic Instrumentation Co., 1968-70; pres. Nat. Free Lance Photographers Assn., Doylestown, Pa., 1970-89; pres., dir. Towne Print & Copy Ctrs. Inc.; v.p., exec. dir. Nat. Paralegal Assn., 1982—; pres. Paralegal Assocs., Inc., 1982—; chief operating officer Doylestown Parking Corp., 1977-88. Bd. dirs. Law Enforcement Supply Co., Solebury, Valtronics Supply Co., Towne Print & Copy Centers Inc., Solebury, Doylestown Stationery and Office Supply, Energy Mktg. Assocs., Inc., Solebury, Paralegal Placement Network; pres. Paralegal Pub. Corp., 1983-90; pub. Paralegal Jour.; pres. Valco Enterprises Inc., 1986—, Paralegal Employment Sys., Inc., 1988, Solebury Press, Inc., 1989—; ptnr. J&S Gen. Contractors, 1993—, J&S Landscaping Tree Svc., 1993—, J&S Estate and Property Mgmt., 2001--; owner Specialized Computer Consulting, 1992—. Author: Photographers Bookkeeping System, 1973, rev. edit., 1978, Photographers Pricing Guides, 1971, 72, 74, 75, Available Markets Director's - 4 Vols., 1973-77, National Model Sources Directory, Nat. Paralegal Salary and Employment Survey, 1985-86, 88, 90-92, 93-94; also articles, bulls. and pamphlets. Exec. sec. Doylestown Bus. Assn., 1972-78, pres., 1979, 83, v.p., 1981. Recipient Internat. Men of Achievement award, 1988; named Personalities of the Am., 1988. Mem. London Coll. Applied Scis., Nat. Fedn. Paralegal Assns., Photog. Industry Coun., Nat. Assn. Legal Assts., Am. Soc Assn. Execs., Soc. Assn. Mgrs., Nat. Fedn. Ind. Business (mem. action coun. com.), Nat. Parking Assn., Nat. Office Products Assn., Graphic Arts Assn. Delaware Valley, Nat. Assn. Federally Licensed Firearms Dealers, Nat. Compostition Assn., Internat. Platform Assn. Office: PO Box 406 Solebury PA 18963-0406

VALENTINE, JAMES WILLIAM, paleobiology educator, writer; b. LA, Nov. 10, 1926; s. Adelbert Cuthbert and Isabel (Davis) V.; m. Grace Evelyn Whysner, Dec. 21, 1957 (div. 1972); children: Anita, Ian; m. Cathryn Alice Campbell, Sept. 10, 1978 (div. 1986); 1 child, Geoffrey; m. Diane Mondragon, Mar. 16, 1987. BA, Phillips U., 1951; MA, UCLA, 1954, PhD, 1958. From asst. prof. to assoc. prof. U. Mo., Columbia, 1958-64; from assoc. prof. to prof. U. Calif., Davis, 1964-77, prof. geol. scis. Santa Barbara, 1977-90, prof. integrative biology Berkeley, 1990-93, prof. emeritus, 1993—. Author: Evolutionary Paleoecology of the Marine Biosphere, 1973, On the Origin of Phyla, 2004; editor: Phanerozoic Diversity, 1985; co-author: Evolution, 1977, Evolving, 1979; contbr. articles to profl. jours. Served with USNR, 1944-46, PTO. Fulbright rsch. scholar, Australia, 1962-63; Guggenheim fellow Yale U., Oxford U., Eng., 1968-69; Rockefeller Found. scholar in residence, Bellagio, Italy, summer 1974; grantee NSF, NASA. Fellow Am. Acad. Arts and Scis., Geol. Soc. Am.; mem. NAS, AAAS, Paleontol. Soc. (pres. 1974-75, medal 1996, Lapworth medal 2004). Avocation: collecting works of Charles Darwin. Home: 1351 Glendale Ave Berkeley CA 94708-2025 Office: U Calif Dept Integrative Biology Berkeley CA 94720-0001 E-mail: jwvsossi@socrates.berkeley.edu.

VALENTINE, JOHN LESTER, state legislator, lawyer; b. Fullerton, Calif., Apr. 26, 1949; s. Robert Lester and Pauline C. V.; m. Karen Marie Thorpe, June 1, 1972; children: John Robert, Jeremy Reid, Staci Marie, Jeffrey Mark., David Emerson, Patricia Ann. BS in Acctg. and Econs., Brigham Young U., 1973, JD, 1976. Bar: Utah 1976, U.S. Dist. Ct. Utah, U.S. Ct. Appeals (10th cir.), U.S. Tax Ct., U.S. Supreme Ct. 2002; CPA. Atty. Howard, Lewis & Petersen, Provo, Utah, 1976—; mem. Utah Ho. Reps., 1988-98, Utah Senate, Dist. 14, Salt Lake City, 1999—. Instr. probate and estates Utah Valley State Coll.; instr. fin. planning., adj. prof. law Brigham Young U.; chmn. revenue and taxation com. Utah Senate, 1999-2000, vice chmn. exec. appropriations com., judiciary com., pub. edn. subcom., majority whip 2001—; mem. exec offices, cts., corrections and legis. appropriations subcom., Utah Ho. of Reps., 1988-90, capital facilities subcom., 1988-90, retirement com., 1988-90, judiciary com., 1988-92, strategic planning steering com., 1988-90, interim appropriations com., 1988-94, tax. review commn., 1989-98, ethics com., 1990-92, human svcs. and health appropriations subcom., 1990-92, revenue and taxation com., 1988-98, vice chmn. 1990-92; vice chmn. exec. appropriations, 1990-92; chmn. exec. appropriations com., 1992-94, chmn. rules com., 1994-96, higher edn. appropriations com. 1994-96, asst. majority whip, 1996-98; apptd. to state senate, 1998, elected, 2000, majority whip, 2000—. Mem. adv. bd. Internat. Sr. Games, 1988—; active Blue Ribbon Task Force on Local Govt. Funding, Utah League Cities and Towns, 1990-94, Criminal Sentencing Guidelines Task Force, Utah Judicial Coun., 1990-92, Access to Health Care Task Force, 1990-92, Utah County Sheriff Search and Rescue, Orem Met. Water Bd., Alpine Sch. Dist. Boundary Line Com., 1986-90, Boy Scouts Am.; bd. regents Legis. Adv. Com. UVCC.; mem. exec. bd. Utah Nat. Parks Coun.; mem. adv. coun. Orchard Elem. Sch., Mountainlands Com. an Aging; bd. trustees Utah Opera Co.; judge nat. and local competitions Moot Ct.; voting dist. chmn.; state, county del.; lt. incident command sys. Utah County Sheriff. Recipient Silver Beaver award Boy Scouts Am., Taxpayer Advocate award Utah Taxpayer Assn. Mem. ABA (tax sect.), Utah State Bar, CPA Com., Tax Sect. Specialization Com., Bicentennial Com. Republican. Mem. Lds Ch. Avocation: mountain climbing. Office: Howard Lewis & Petersen 120 E 300 N Provo UT 84606-2907

VALENTINE, MARK CONRAD, dermatologist; b. Parkersburg, W.Va., Sept. 26, 1948; s. Sestel and Margaret Elaine (Sabolo) V.; m. Elizabeth Michelle Monezis, Apr. 21, 1975; children: Perry Martin, Owen Mark. BA, W.Va. U., 1970; MD, Johns Hopkins U., 1974. Intern, resident U. Hosps. Cleve., 1974-76, resident, 1976-79; dermatologist pvt. practice, Everett, Wash., 1979—. Clin. prof. U. Wash., Seattle, 1979—; active med. staff Providence Gen. Med. Ctr., Everett, 1979—. Editl. bd. Jour. of Am. Acad. Dermatology, 1998—. Bd. dirs., sec. City Libr. Bd., Mukilteo, Wash., 1994-99; bd. dirs., v.p. Everett Symphony Bd., 1982-85, 2001—; bd. dirs. Book Arts Guild, Seattle, 1988-90. Nat. Merit scholar, 1966. Mem. AMA, Am. Acad. Dermatology (adv. coun. 1983-86), Wash. State Dermatological Assn. (pres.-elect 1996, pres. 1996-97), Seattle Dermatology Soc. (pres. 1985-86), Snohomish County Med. Soc. (bd. dir. 2001—), Rotary (Everett), Phi Beta Kappa. Avocations: book collecting, book binding, guitar, piano. Office: 3327 Colby Ave Everett WA 98201-6403 Office Phone: 425-258-6767. E-mail: mark1105@aol.com.

VALENTINE, NANCY MARIE, nursing administrator, educator; b. Phila. BSN, Rutgers State U., 1969; MSN, U. Pa., 1972; MPH, Harvard U., 1978; PhD in Econs. and Health Policy, Brandeis U., 1991. Child care worker Ea. State Sch. and Hosp. for Emotionally Disturbed Children, Trevose, Pa., 1968; staff nurse Abington (Pa.) Meml. Hosp., 1969-70; pub. health nurse Cmty. Nursing Svcs., Phila., 1970; camp nurse Camp Spruce Hill, Tolland, Mass., 1971; staff nurse student health ctr. Temple U., Phila., 1970-72; group co-therapist McLean Hosp., Belmont, Mass., 1974-76, 1970-72, clin. nursing supr., 1973-78; nurse therapist Expansion, Inc., Bedford, Mass., 1977-78; project dir. Boston State Coll., Mass., 1978-80; fellow HHS, Washington, 1980-81; DON Boston City Hosp., 1981-83; co-founder, cons. Nightingale, 1982-89; adminstr. for nursing McLean Hosp., Belmont, Mass., 1983-93; asst. chief med. dir. nursing programs Dept. VA, Washington, 1993—. Mem. implementation com. Inst. Mass. Gen. Hosp., Boston, 1989, assoc. prof., 1991-94; adj. instr. U. Mass., Boston, 1991—; adj. prof. Northea. U., Boston, 1990—, Cath. U., 1993—, Georgetown U., 1995; assoc. in psychiatry Med. Sch. Harvard U., 1992—; instr. psychiat. nursing Newton Jr. Coll., Newtonville, Mass., 1975; project coord. NIMH, 1974-76; clin. instr. Boston Coll., Chestnut Hill, 1979-80; lectr. Mass. Nurses Assn., 1984, 86, 91; editl. referee Jour. Studies on Alcohol; cons. N.E. Ga. Med. Ctr., 1991, 92, 93, Charter Hosp. Long Beach, Calif., 1989; mem. nursing practice adv. com. Mass. Bd. Registration in Nursing, 1991; mem. adv. bd. dept. nursing Middlesex C.C., Bedford, Mass., 1983-88; mem. interdisciplinary med. adv. com. Blue Cross/Blue Shield Mass., 1989; mem. coordinating com. house staff monitoring and clin. tng. conditions Boston U. Med. Ctr., 1989-90; cons., presenter in field. Mem. editl. bd. Nat. Nurses Soc. on Addictions, Jour. Psychosocial Nursing and Mental Health Svcs., Am. Psychiat. Nurses Assn.; mem. editl. adv. bd. Adminstrn. and Policy in Mental Health; field editor Jour. Mental Health Adminstrn.; contbr. articles to profl. jours. Mem. adv. bd. Project Task Force to Determine Feasibility of Continuing LPN Tng. Program, Youville Hosp., Cambridge, Mass., 1985-86; mem. orgn. health profls. U. Calif. San Francisco Med. Ctr., 1980-81. Capt. U.S. Army Nurse Corp Res. Grantee Robert Wood Johnson Found., 1988, McLean Hosp., 1988, Mass. State Coll. System, 1979; recipient Brandeis U., 1983-85, Phila. Bd. Edn. scholarship, 1965; Harvard U. fellow, 1977-78; recipient Outstanding Alumni award Rutgers U. Coll. Nursing, 1987, Malcolm Alderfer Schweiker award, Outstanding Alumni award U. Pa., 1987, Minkoff prize Brandeis U., 1991. Fellow Am. Acad. Nursing; mem. ANA (task force on assistive personnel 1991), Am. Orgn. Nurse Execs., Soc. for the Edn. and Rsch. of Psychiatric Nurses, Am. Coll. Mental Health Adminstrn., APHA, Nat. Nurses Soc. Addictions, Mass. Nurses Assn. (task force on nurses with substance abuse problems, chairperson task force on nurses' aides, coun. on nursing svc. adminstrn., rep. task force on nursing assts. Mass. Bd. Registration in Nursing 1989-90, liaison with Mass. Med. Soc. 1988-92, Human Need Svcs. award 1985), Mass. Orgn. Nurse Execs., Nursing Honor Soc., Mass. Pub. Health Assn., Nurses United for Reimbursement Svcs., New Eng. Orgn. for Nurses, Am. Psychiatric Nurses Assn., Brandeis U. Florence Heller Sch. of Social Welfare Policy Alumni Assn., Harvard U. Sch. of Pub. Health Alumni Assn., U. Pa. Sch. Nursing Alumni Assn., Rutgers U. Coll. Nursing Alumni Assn., Sigma Theta Tau. Office: Dept VA Nursing Program 810 Vermont Ave NW # 18 Washington DC 20420-0001

VALENTINE, RALPH SCHUYLER, chemical engineer, research director; b. Seattle, Nov. 3, 1932; s. John Campbell and Elizabeth Florence (Patterson) V.; m. Jeanne Marie Belanger, June 15, 1957; children: Susan Diana, Jacqueline Leigh, John Campbell. BSChemE, U. Wash., 1955, PhDChemE, 1963; MSChemE, U. Ill., 1956. Registered profl. engr., Calif., Va., Wash. Rsch. engr. Chevron Rsch. Corp., Richmond, Calif., 1956-61; instr. U. Wash., Seattle, 1961-63; mgr. fluid dynamics Aerojet-Gen., Sacramento, 1963-69; mgr. chem. tech. Atlantic Rsch. Corp., Alexandria, Va., 1969-79; mgr. rsch. United Techs. Chem. Systems, San Jose, Calif., 1979-91; gen. mgr. Greater Pocatello Sr. Citizens, Inc., 2001—. Lectr. U.S. Naval Postgrad. Sch., Monterey, Calif., 1968, UCLA Modern Devels. in Propulsion, L.A., 1967-68, USAF Astronautics Labs., Lancaster, Calif., 1967, U.S. Army R & D Unit, Sacramento, 1966. Contbr. 23 tech. articles to profl. jours.; patentee in field. Recipient NASA commendation for Apollo work, Houston, 1969, 1st prize Ceramographic Exhbn. Am. Ceramics Soc., 1974. Mem. Am. Inst. Chem. Engrs. (life). Republican. Home: 1515 Satterfield Dr Pocatello ID 83201-8002 E-mail: ralph_s_valentine@yahoo.com.

VALENTINE, ROBERT JOHN (BOBBY VALENTINE), former professional baseball manager; b. Stamford, CT, May 13, 1950; m. Mary Branca, Jan. 8, 1977; 1 child, Robert John Jr. Student, U. Southern California, Arizona State U. Player Pioneer League, Ogdon, 1968, Pacific Coast League, Spokane, WA, 1969-71, Los Angeles Dodgers, Los Angeles, CA, 1971-72, California Angels, CA, 1973-75, International League, Charleston, WV, 1975, Pacific Coast League, Salt Lake City, 1975, Hawaii, HI, 1976, San Diego Padres, San Diego, 1975-77, New York Mets, NY, 1977-78, Seattle Mariners, Seattle, 1979; scout, infield instr. San Diego Padres, San Diego, 1981; minor league infield instr. New York Mets, 1982, third base coach, 1983-85; mgr. Texas Rangers, Arlington, TX, 1985-96, N.Y. Mets, 1996—2002; commentator, Baseball Tonight ESPN, 2003—. Owner Bobby Valentine's Sports Gallery Cafe, Conn., Tex., and R.I. Named Am. League Mgr. of Yr. UPI, 1986;

recipient William A. Shea Disting. Little League Grad. award, 1987; inductee Italian Am. Sports Hall Fame, 1990. Office: Bobby Valentine's Sports Gallery Cafe 225 Main St Stamford CT 06903

VALENTINE, STEVEN RICHARDS, lawyer; b. Memphis, Jan. 30, 1956; s. William Robert and Lenita Joanne (Nelms) V.; m. Susan Marie Burke, Jan. 14, 1984; children: Christina Michele, William Robert II, Steven Richards Jr., Thomas Burke, Diana Elizabeth. Grad., Capitol Page Sch., Washington, 1974; student, Earlham Coll., 1974-77; B of Gen. Studies with distinction, Ind. U., 1979, JD, 1982. Bar: Ill. 1983, D.C. 1985, U.S. Ct. Appeals (D.C. cir.) 1986, U.S. Supreme Ct. 1986, U.S. Ct. Appeals (9th cir.) 1989. Chief investigator consumer protection divsn. Office Atty. Gen., State of Ind., 1980-82; exec. dir. Ams. United for Life Legal Def. Fund, Chgo., 1982-83; chief counsel subcom. on separation of powers U.S. Senate, Washington, 1983-85, chief counsel subcom. on cts., 1985; adminstrv. asst. U.S. Senator John P. East, Washington, 1985-86; dir. Office of Policy Devel. and Comm. Legal Svcs. Corp., Washington, 1986-87; counselor to asst. atty. gen. civil divsn. U.S. Dept. Justice, Washington, 1987-88; dep. asst. atty. gen. civil divsn. U.S. Justice Dept., Washington, 1988-93, gen. counsel to U.S. Senator Robert C. Smith, 1993-99; legis. dir. to U.S. Senator Robert C. Smith, 1996-99; of counsel Preston Gates Ellis & Rouvelas Meeds LLP, Washington, 1999—2002, ptnr., 2002—. Mem. exec. com., bd. dirs. Deluxe West, Inc.; bd. dirs. The Preston Project, Inc.; sr. fellow John C. Stennis Ctr. for Pub. Svc. Author: Each Time A Man, 1978, All Shall Live, 1980, (with others) Abortion and the Constitution, 1987, Principle Over Politics, 2004; contbr. articles to profl. jours. Recipient spl. commendation U.S. Atty. Gen., 1993; John C. Stennis Congl. staff fellow, 1995-96. Mem. SAR, Rep. Nat. Lawyers Assn., Federalist Soc., Capitol Hill Club. Republican. Roman Catholic. Avocations: history, baseball. Home: 6487 Warwick Cir Alexandria VA 22315-5045 Office: 1735 New York Ave NW Ste 500 Washington DC 20006-5209 E-mail: rickv@prestongates.com., rsv1984@aol.com.

VALENTINE, WILLIAM EDSON, architect; b. Winston-Salem, N.C., Sept. 3, 1937; s. Howard Leon and Sally (Cunningham) V.; m. Jane Dorward, Aug. 13, 1939; children: Anne, Karen, William. BArch, N.C. State U., 1960; MArch, Harvard U., 1962. Co-chmn. Hellmuth, Obata & Kassabaum Inc., San Francisco, 1962—. Chmn. Hellmuth, Obata & Kassabaum Design Bd., also bd. dirs. Served to 1st lt. U.S. Army, 1960-61. Fellow AIA. Clubs: Harvard. Office: Hellmuth Obata Kassabaum 1 Bush St Ste 200 San Francisco CA 94104-4404

VALENTINE, WILLIAM NEWTON, physician, educator; b. Kansas City, Mo., Sept. 29, 1917; s. Herbert S. and Mabel W. Valentine; m. Martha Hickman Winfree; children: William, James, Edward. Student, U. Mich., Ann Arbor, 1934—36, U. Mo., Columbia, 1936—37; MD, Tulane U., New Orleans, 1942. Diplomate Am. Bd. Internal Medicine. Intern Strong Meml. Hosp., Rochester, NY, 1942—43, asst. resident in medicine, 1943, chief resident in medicine, 1943—44; specialist, attending physician in internal medicine Wadsworth Hosp., L.A., 1949—88, VA Ctr., L.A., 1949—88; specialist, attending physician in internal medicine Ctr. Health Scis. UCLA, 1949—, prof. medicine, 1957—88, chmn. dept., 1963—71, prof. emeritus medicine, 1988—. Contbr. articles to profl. jours. Capt. MC AUS, 1944—47. Recipient Mayo Soley award for excellence in rsch., Western Soc. Clin. Rsch., 1978, 53d Annual UCLA faculty rsch. lectr., 1978. Master: ACP (John Phillips Meml. award for disting. achievements in internal medicine 1979); fellow: Am. Soc. Hematology (Henry Stratton lectr. 1978), Internat. Soc. Hematology (v.p. U.S. 1976—80); mem.: NAS, Am. Acad. Arts and Scis., Western Soc. Clin. Rsch., Western Assn. Physicians (pres. 1969—70), Assn. Am. Physicians, Am. Soc. Clin. Investigation (v.p. 1962), Am. Bd. Internal Medicine. Republican.

VALENZUELA, JULIO SAMUEL, sociologist, educator; b. Concepción, Chile, Mar. 30, 1948; came to U.S., 1970; s. Raimundo Arms and Dorothy Dueul (Bowie) V.; m. Erika Fresia Maza, Mar. 22, 1969. Licenciatura, Universidad de Concepcion, 1970; PhD, Columbia U., 1979. Asst. prof. Yale U., New Haven, 1977-80, Harvard U., Cambridge, Mass., 1980-85, assoc. prof., 1986, U. Notre Dame, Ind., 1987-89, prof., dept. chairperson, 1989-92, fellow Kellogg Inst., 1987—. Sr. assoc. fellow St. Antony's Coll., Oxford U., 1992-93, 96—; campaign adv. presidl. election, Chile, 1999; cons. labor policy Chilean Govt., 2000, 01. Author: Democratizacion via Reforma, 1986; co-author: Chile, A Country Study; co-editor: Chile: Politics And Society, 1976, Military Rule In Chile, 1986, Issues In Democratic Consolidation, 1992; contbr. chpts. to books, articles to profl. jours. Fellow NEH ind. scholarship rsch. 1983-84, conf. grant 1987; John Simon Guggenheim fellow, 1996. Mem. Am. Sociol. Assn., Internat. Sociol. Assn. (v.p. rsch. com. #44 1990—), Latin Am. Studies Assn. (nominating com. 1987-88), Am. Polit. Sci. Assn., New Eng. Coun. Latin Am. Studies (pres. 1984-85). Methodist. Office: U Notre Dame Kellogg Inst Notre Dame IN 46556 Office Phone: 574-631-6410. E-mail: valenzuela1@nd.edu.

VALERA, EVE MARIE, neuroscientist; d. Ernest and Arlene Valera; m. Kevin Mark Spencer, Nov. 4, 2001. BA Summa Cum Laude, Siena Coll., 1992; AM, U. Ill., 1996, PhD, 1999. Postdoctoral fellow Harvard Med. Sch., Mass Gen. Hosp., Charlestown, Mass., 2000—03; postdoctoral fellow in clin. neuropsychology Mass. Mental Health Ctr. and Beth-Israel Deaconess Ctr., Boston, 2000—02; instr., asst. in rsch. Harvard Med. Sch., Mass Gen. Hosp., Charlestown, Mass., 2003—. Postdoctoral fellow Mass Mental Health Ctr., Beth Israel Deaconess Ctr., Boston, 2000—01. Contbr. articles to profl. jours. Recipient Lilly Fellowship award, Eli Lilly and Co., 2003, Herman-Eisen award for Profl. Contbn. to Psychology, U. of Ill., 1998; fellow Grad. Coll. fellow, 1993; grantee Grad. Coll. Thesis Project Grant, U. Ill., 1996, Nat. Rsch. Svc. award, NIH, 2002-2003, Nat. Rsch. Svc. Award, 1998-1999, Women's Studies Funding for Feminist Scholarship, U. of Ill., 1996; scholar FMRI Tng. Course Scholarship, APA, 2001. Mem.: Internat. Soc. for Traumatic Stress Studies, Internat. Neuropsychological Soc., Cognitive Neuroscience Soc. Office: Mass Gen Hosp 149 13th St Rm 2651 Charlestown MA 02129 Office Phone: 617-724-0307. E-mail: eve_valera@hms.harvard.edu.

VALERI, LAURA E. writer, educator; arrived in U.S., 1978; d. Valerio Valeri and Anna Cateni Valeri; m. Enrique Contreras, Aug. 8, 1989 (div. Aug. 1998). BA, NYU; MFA, Fla. Internat. U., 2000, U. Iowa, 2002. Tutor Fla. Internat. U., North Miami, 1998—99, lab. dir., 1999, Nova Southeastern U., Davie, 2001; tchr. asst. dept. rehtoric U. Iowa, Iowa City, 2001—02. Adj. prof. dept. English Fla. Atlantic U., Boca Raton, 2002, Broward C.C., Davie, 2002—03, Fla. Internat. U., 2002—03, adj. lectr., tchg. asst., 1998—2000. Author: The Kind of Things Saints Do, of poems. Recipient John Gardner Fiction award, Binghamton U., 2003, John Simmons Short Fiction award, 2002, Josephine Friedman Short Fiction award; fellow, Iowa Writers Workshop.

VALERI, TONY, Canadian government official; m. Terri Boswell; 2 children. Degree in econs., McMaster U. M.P. for Lincoln House of Commons, 1993-97, parliamentary sec. to Min. Fin. Jean Chretien, 1997—99, mem. standing com. on fin., vice chair standing com. on industry, chair standing com. on govt. ops., m.p., 1997—99; min. transport Govt. of Canada, Ottawa, 2003—. Former instr. Mohawk Coll.; chair Nat. Liberal Caucus Task Force on Jobs and Small Bus. Mem. Ind. Ins. Brokers Assn. Can. (bd. dirs.), Hamilton and Dist. Sub-Contractors Assn. (v.p.). Office: Transport Canada 330 Sparks St K1A 0N5 Ottawa ON Canada

VALERIANI, RICHARD GERARD, news broadcaster; b. Camden, N.J., Aug. 29, 1932; s. Nicholas and Christine (Camerota) V.; m. Kathie Berlin, Apr. 20, 1980; 1 child, Kimberly. BA, Yale U., 1953; postgrad., U. Pavia, Italy, 1953-54, U. Barcelona, Spain, 1954. Reporter The Trentonian, Trenton, 1957; with AP, 1957-61, corr., 1959-61; with NBC-TV News, 1961—, corr., 1964-83, nat. corr. N.Y.C., 1983-88; free-lance journalist and media cons., 1988—. Participant 2d Carter-Ford debate, 1976. Author: Travels With Henry, 1979; actor: (feature film) Crimson Tide, 1995. With AUS, 1955-56. Recipient Overseas Press Club award for best radio reporting, 1965 Mem. Elihu Soc. Home: 23 Island View Dr Sherman CT 06784-2036 E-mail: rvaleriani@aol.com.

VALERIO, JOSEPH MASTRO, architectural firm executive, educator; b. Dec. 26, 1947; m. Linda A. Searl; children: Joseph Jr., Anthony. BArch, U. Mich., 1970; MArch, UCLA, 1972. Registered architect, Wis., Ill., Ind., Mo., Calif., Tex., Ariz., Minn., Ala., Iowa, Ind., Md., Mich., Okla., Ga., Mass., N.J., N.Y., N.C., Va., Utah, D.C., Wash., Oreg., cert. Nat. Coun. Archtl. Registration Bds. Pres. Chrysalis Corp. Architects, 1970-85; assoc. prof. U. Wis., 1973-86; design dir. Swanke Hayden Connell Architects, 1985-86; v.p. architecture A. Epstein and Sons, Inc., 1986-88; pres. Valerio-Assocs. Inc., 1988-94; prin. Valerio Dewalt Train Assocs., Inc., Chgo., 1994—. Mem. nat. bd. peer reviewers GSA; spkr. Ariz. State U., UCLA, U. Ariz., U. Cin., others; cons. USG Interiors, Formica Corp., AAAS, NAS, NEA; vis. critic and lectr. in field. Prin. works include corp., high-tech. indsl., retail, health and residential bldgs.; author: Movie Palaces, 1983; (monograph) Joe Valerio, 1999; editor: Architectural Fabric Structures, 1985; featured in Inside Architecture, Domestic Interiors, 1997, New Am. Apt., 1997, Internat. Interiors, 1997, Lofts/Living and Working Spaces, 1999. Mem. exec. bd. men's coun. Mus. Contemporary Art, 1989-91; mem. exec. bd. Contemporary Arts Coun., 1994-96 (pres. 1999). Recipient Honor awards Wis. Soc. Architects, 1975, 81, 84, 85, Gov.'s Award for Design Excellence, State of Mich., 1979, Gold medal Inst. Bus. Designers, 1988, Design award Progressive Architecture, 1991, Architectural Record Interiors award 1993, 95, 96, Disting. Interior award Inst. Bus. Designers, Chgo., 1993; honored by Emerging Voices series Archtl. League N.Y., 1984, Met. Home mag., Interiors mag. Fellow AIA (programs chmn. design com. Chgo. chpt. 1990, long range planning com. 1992, chair nat. com. on design 1997, Nat. Honor award 1981, 93, Interiors award Chgo. chpt. 1988, 90, 92, 95-97, 99-2002, 04, Disting. Bldg. award 1991, 93, 2004, Nat. Interior Honor award 1993, 96, 2003, Divine Detail award 1999, 2001), Chgo. Architecture Club (pres. 1994). Office: Valerio Dewalt Train Assocs 500 N Dearborn St Fl 9 Chicago IL 60610-4900 Office Phone: 312-332-0363. Business E-Mail: jvalerio@buildardie.com.

VALERIO, MATTHEW F. lawyer; b. Lawrence, Mass., Sept. 28, 1963; s. Fred Ernest Jr. Valerio and Carole Elaine (Closson) Mimeault; m. Joanne F. Stockton, Aug. 6, 1988. BA, St. Michael's Coll., 1985; JD, Western New Eng. Coll., 1988. Bar: Mass. 1989, Vt. 1989, U.S. Dist. Ct. Mass. 1989, U.S. Dist. Ct. Vt. 1989, U.S. Ct. Appeals (2d cir.) 1998. Pvt. practice, Springfield, Mass., 1989; assoc. Abatiell & Wysolmerski, Rutland, Vt., 1989-94; ptnr. Abatiell & Valerio, Rutland, Vt., 1994—2001, defender gen. State of Vt., 2001—. Adj. prof. Coll. St. Joseph, Rutland, 1993-99. Fin. chmn. Rutland County Rep. Com., 1991-93. Mem. ABA (young lawyers divsn. dist. rep. Vt., Maine 1994-96, Vt. state membership chair 1995—), New Eng. Bar Assn. (bd. mem. 1997—, pres. 1999-2000), Vt. Trial Lawyers Assn., Vt. Bar Assn. (treas., exec. com. young lawyers sect. 1990-92, chmn.-elect exec. com. 1992, chmn. 1993-94, bd. bar mgr. 1992-2003, pres.-elect 2000-01, pres. 2001-02), Vt. Criminal Def. Lawyers Assn. (bd. dirs. 1993-96), Assn. Trial Lawyers Am., Kiwanis (bd. dirs. Rutland chpt. 1990-96, v.p. 1991-92, pres. 1993-94, pres. Rutland area mentor program 1994-96, disting. svc. award 1989-92, N.E. dis disting. pres. award 1993-94). Avocations: baseball, wrestling, blues. Office: Office Defender Gen 14-16 Baldwin St Montpelier VT 05633-3301 Office Phone: 802-828-3168.

VALERIO, MICHAEL ANTHONY, diversified financial services company executive; b. Detroit, Sept. 20, 1953; s. Anthony Rudolph and Victoria (Popoff) V.; m. Barbara Ann Nabozny, Oct. 8, 1983. BA, U. Mich., Dearborn, 1975. CPA, Mich. Jr. acct. Carabell, Bocknek CPA's, Southfield, Mich., 1975-76; sr. acct. Purdy, Donovan & Beal, CPA's, Detroit, 1976-77; mgr. Buctynck & Co., CPA's, Southfield, 1978-79; controller Transcontinental Travel, Harper Woods, Mich., 1979-80; exec. v.p. Holland Cons., Inc., Detroit, 1980-85; controller, CFO SLC Recycling Industries, Inc., Warren, Mich., 1985-98; owner Pinnacle Fin. Consulting, PLLC, Livonia, Mich., 1994—. Owner Pinnacle Prof. Planning, LLC, 2002—. Mem. AICPA, Mich. Soc. CPAs, Acctg. Rsch. Found. Roman Catholic. Office: Pinnacle Fin Consulting PLLC 33300 Five Mile Rd Ste 102 Livonia MI 48154-3074

VALERIO BARRAD, CATHERINE M. lawyer; BA, U. Calif., San Diego, 1982; MBA, UCLA, 1984; JD magna cum laude, Northwestern U., 1993. Ba: Calif. 1993, U.S. Ct. Appeals (9th cir.) 1994. Law clk. to Hon. Douglas H. Ginsburg, U.S. Dt. Appeals for D.C. Circuit, Washington, 1993-94; assoc. Sidley & Austin, L.A., 1994—. Contbg. author: Federal Appellate Practice Guide, Ninth Circuit, 1994; articles editor Northwestern U. Law Rev., 1992-93; contbr. articles to legal publs. Mem. Order of Coif. Office: Sidley & Austin 555 W 5th St Los Angeles CA 90013-1010 Fax: 213-896-6688. E-mail: cbarrad@sidley.com.

VALERO, DORON, real estate executive; b. 1957; BSE, Nova U., 1986. Pres., CEO Global Fund Investments, Inc., 1988-94; sr. v.p., COO Equity One, Miami Beach, 1994-00, pres., COO, 2000—. Mem. ICSC, NAREIT. Office: Equity One Ste 200 1696 NE Miami Gardens Dr North Miami Beach FL 33179

VALERO, RENÉ ARNOLD, clergyman; b. N.Y.C., Aug. 15, 1930; s. Caesar J. and Maria Luisa (Cordova) Valero; B.A. in Liberal Arts, Immaculate Conception-Cathedral Coll., 1952; M.S.W., Fordham U., 1962. Ordained to ministry Roman Cath. Ch., 1956; asso. pastor St. Michael-St. Edward, Bklyn., 1956-57, St. Agatha, Bklyn., 1957-60; dir. Bklyn. Cath. Charities Family Service, 1960-69; dir. Bklyn. Diocesan Office for Aging, 1969-74; coordinator Bklyn. Diocesan Hispanic Apostolate, 1974-79; pastor Blessed Sacrament, Jackson Heights, N.Y., 1979-82; aux. bishop Diocese of Bklyn., 1980—; vicar for immigrants and refugees Diocese of Bklyn., 1983-90; regional bishop Queens, 1990-94, Queens North, 1994—. Home: 34-43 93rd St Jackson Heights NY 11372-3743 Office: Immaculate Conception Ctr 7200 Douglaston Pky Douglaston NY 11362-1941 Office Phone: 718-229-8001 x710.

VALESKIE-HAMNER, GAIL YVONNE, information systems specialist; b. San Francisco, May 16, 1953; d. John Benjamin and Vera Caroline (Granstrand) Valeskie; m. David Bryan Hamner, May 21, 1983. Student, Music Conservatory, Valencia, Spain, 1973, U. Valencia, 1973; BA magna cum laude, Lone Mountain Coll., 1973, MA, 1976. Fgn. exchange broker trainee Fgn. Exchange Ltd., San Francisco, 1978-79; fgn. exchange remittance supr. Security Pacific Nat. Bank, San Francisco, 1979-81; exec. sec. Bank of Am., San Francisco, 1981-83, fgn. exchange ops. supr., 1983-84; word processing specialist Wolborg-Michelson, San Francisco, 1984-86; office mgr. U.S. Leasing Corp., San Francisco, 1986-88; cons. Valeskie Data/Word Processing, San Francisco, 1987-89, pres., 1989—. Sec. Schm., mem. mission edn. com. Luth. Women's Missionary League, Vallejo, Calif., 1986-94; vol. Luth. Braille Workers, Vallejo, 1987; organist Shepherd of Hills Luth. Ch., San Francisco, 1988—. Mem. NAFE, Profl. Assn. Secretarial Svcs. (pres. 1993—), Am. Guild Organists, Am. Choral Dirs. Assn. Avocations: singing, ceramics, piano, needlecrafts, writing. Home and Office: 1396 Geneva Ave San Francisco CA 94112-3835

VALETTE, JEAN PAUL, writer; b. Paris, Oct. 21, 1937; s. Jean and Monique (Lavie) V.; m. Rebecca M. Valette, Aug. 6, 1959; children: Jean-Michel, Nathalie, Pierre. Baccalaureat, U. Poitiers, France, 1954; Diplome, Hautes Etudes Commls. de Paris, 1959; PhD, U. Colo., 1962. Acct. Arthur Andersen, 1964-66; rsch. economist Charles River Assocs., 1966-69. Author: Lisons, 1968, The Role of Transportation in Regional Economic Development, 1971, France, A Cultural Review Grammar, 1973, C'est comme ça, 1978, 1986, Spanish for Mastery, 1980, 1984, 1988, 1996, French for Mastery, 1975, 1981, 1986, 1989, 1990, Contacts: langue et culture françaises, 1976, 1982, 1985, 1989, 1994, 1997, 2001, French for Fluency, 1985, Rencontres, 1985, Situaciones, 1988, 1994, Discovering French, 1993, 1994, 1995, 1997, 2000, Discover French, 2004, Discovering French Interactive, 1994, A votre tour, 1995, Ventanas, 1998, Europak, 2000, Weaving the Dance, Navajo Yeibichai Textiles (1910-1950), 2000. Decorated Palmes Académiques (France). Mem. Am. Assn. Tchrs. French, Am. Coun. on Tchg. of Langs. Address: 16 Mount Alvernia Rd Chestnut Hill MA 02467-1019

VALETTE, REBECCA MARIANNE, Romance languages educator; b. N.Y.C., Dec. 21, 1938; d. Gerhard and Ruth Adelgunde (Bischoff) Loose; m. Jean-Paul Valette, Aug. 6, 1959; children: Jean-Michel, Nathalie, Pierre. BA, Mt. Holyoke Coll., 1959, LHD (hon.), 1974; PhD, U. Colo., 1963. Instr., examiner in French and German U. So. Fla., 1961-63; instr. NATO Def. Coll., Paris, 1963-64, Wellesley Coll., 1964-65; asst. prof. Romance Langs. Boston Coll., 1965-68, assoc., 1968-73, prof., 1973—2003, prof. emeritus, 2003—. Lectr., cons. fgn. lang. pedagogy; Fulbright sr. lectr., Germany, 1974; Am. Coun. on Edn. fellow in acad. adminstrn., 1976-77. Author: Modern Language Testing, 1967, rev. edit., 1977, French for Mastery, 1975, rev. edit., 1988, Contacts, 1976, rev. edit., 1993, 97, 2001, C'est Comme Ça, 1978, rev. edit., 1986, Spanish for Mastery, 1980, rev. edit., 1989, 94, Album: Cuentos del Mundo Hispanico, 1984, rev. edit., 1992, French for Fluency, 1985, Situaciones, 1988, rev. edit., 1994, Discovering French, 1994, 97, 2001, A votre tour, 1995, Ventanas Uno, 1998, Images 1, 2, 3, 1999, Reflections on the Connolly Book of Hours, 1999, Weaving the Dance, 2000, Discovering French Nouveau, 2004; contbr. articles to fgn. lang. pedagogy and Native Am. art publs. Decorated officer Palmes Académiques, chevalier Ordre Nat. du Mérite (France). Mem. MLA (chmn. divsn. on tchg. of lang. 1980-81), Am. Coun. on Tchg. Fgn. Langs., Am. Assn. Tchrs. French (v.p. 1980-86, pres. 1992-94), Alliance Francaise of Boston and Cambridge (pres. 2002—), Phi Beta Kappa, Alpha Sigma Nu, Pi Delta Phi. Home: 16 Mount Alvernia Rd Chestnut Hill MA 02467-1019 Office: Boston Coll Lyons 304 Chestnut Hill MA 02467-3804 E-mail: valette@bc.edu.

VALGEMAE, MARDI, English educator; b. Viljandi, Estonia, Nov. 10, 1935; came to U.S., 1949; s. Parfeni and Ella (Peterson) V.; m. Mare M. Kivijarv, Dec. 28, 1957; children: Monika L., Sven M. BA, Rutgers U., 1957; PhD, UCLA, 1964. Asst. prof. English UCLA, L.A., 1964-68; assoc. prof. English Lehman Coll., CUNY, Bronx, 1968-74; prof. English Lehman Coll. CUNY, Bronx, 1975—; dir. city and humanities program Lehman Coll., CUNY, 1984-88, chmn. English dept., 1988-97. Vis. asst. profl. lectr., George Washington U., Washington, 1968. Author: Accelerated Grimace, 1972, Ikka Teatrist Moteldes, 1990, Linn ja Teater, 1995, Kaugekone, 1999, Eelarvamusi, 2003; co-editor: Baltic Literature and Linguistics, 1973. 1st lt. U.S. Army. 1958-60. ACLS European Travel grantee, 1970, 81; Woodrow Wilson fellow, 1960. Mem. Modern Lang. Assn. Am., Assn. Advancement Baltic Studies, PEN. Office: CUNY Lehman Coll Dept English Bronx NY 10468 E-mail: mardival@mindspring.com.

VALIA, HARDARSHAN S. research scientist; b. Khurda, Orisa, India, June 15, 1945; arrived in U.S., 1969; s. Santokh Singh and Harbans Kaur; m. Bhupinder Kaur Valia, Jan. 10, 1982; children: Vikram Singh, Anu Kaur. MS, Nagpur (India) U., 1968; MA, Bryn Mawr Coll., 1971; PhD, Boston U., 1976. Asst. prof. Case Western U., Cleve., 1978, Oberlin (Ohio) Coll., 1978—79; staff scientist Inland Steel, East Chicago, Ind., 1979—. Mem. tech. com. Am. Iron and Steel Inst., Washington, 1995—2001. Contbg. author Kirk-Othmer Encyclopedia, 1993, Making, Shaping, and Treating of Steel, 1999, (website) Am. Iron and Steel Inst. Recipient J.B.T. gold medal, Nagpur U., 1965, medal, Am. Iron and Steel Inst., 1989. Mem.: Soc. for Organic Petrology, Iron and Steel Soc. (program com. 1995—, chmn. J. Becker award 2001—, Joseph Becker award 1999). Office: Ispat Inland Steel 3001 E Columbus Dr East Chicago IN 46312

VALIANT, LESLIE GABRIEL, computer scientist, educator; b. Mar. 28, 1949; s. Leslie and Eva Julia (Ujlaki) V.; m. Gayle Lynne Dyckoff, 1977; children: Paul A., Gregory J. BA, Kings Coll., Cambridge, U.K., 1970; DIC, Imperial Coll., London, 1973; PhD, U. Warwick, U.K., 1974. Vis. asst. prof. Carnegie-Mellon U., Pitts., 1973-74; lectr. U. Leeds, Eng., 1974-76; lectr., reader U. Edinburgh, Scotland, 1977-82; vis. prof. Harvard U., 1982, Gordon McKay prof. computer sci. and applied math., 1982-2001, T. Jefferson Coolidge prof. computer sci. and applied math., 2001—. Guggenheim fellow, 1985-86; recipient Nevanlinna prize Internat. Math. Union, 1986, Knuth prize, 1997. Fellow Royal Soc., Am. Assn. for Artificial Intelligence; mem. NAS. Office: Harvard U 33 Oxford St Cambridge MA 02138-1903

VALK, ROBERT EARL, corporate executive; b. Muskegon, Mich., Aug. 21, 1914; s. Allen and Lulu (Schuler) V.; m. Ann Parker, August 9, 1941 (div. July 1959); children: James A., Sara C.; m. Alice Melick, Dec. 29, 1960 (dec. 1999); children: Marie, Susan. BS in Mech. Engring, U. Mich., 1938. With Nat. Supply Co., 1938-55, plant mgr., 1945-48, works mgr. Toledo, Houston and Gainesville, Tex., 1949-55; asst. v.p. prodn. Electric Auto-Lite Co., Toledo, 1956, v.p., group exec. gen. products, 1956-60; gen. mgr. mfg. automotive div. Essex Internat., Inc., 1960-66, v.p. corp., gen. mgr. automotive div., 1966-74; pres. ITT Automotive Elec. Products Div., 1974-80; v.p. ITT N.Am. Automotive Ops. Worldwide, 1980-86; chmn. Chamberlin, Davis, Rutan & Valk, 1986—. Trustee Henry Ford Health Care Sys., Detroit. Mem. Am. Soc. Naval Engrs., Soc. Automotive Engrs., Am. Ordnance Assn., Am. Mgmt. Assn., Air Force Assn., Am. Mfrs. Assn., Wire Assn., Nat. Elec. Mfrs. Assn., Engring. Soc. Detroit, Country Club (Detroit), Renaissance Club, Yondotega Club, Econs. Club (Detroit), Grosse Pointe Club, Bay View Yacht Club, Question Club. Republican. Episcopalian. Home: 80 Renaud Rd Grosse Pointe Shores MI 48236-1742 Office: 21 Kercheval Ave Ste 270 Grosse Pointe Farms MI 48236-3633 Office Phone: 313-886-8000.

VALLADO, DAVID ANTHONY, aerospace engineer; b. Winchester, Mass., May 14, 1958; s. Anthony C. and Rebecca B. Vallado; m. Laura Ann Vallado, Mar. 18, 1984; children: Simone, Kathleen, Samuel. BS in Astrodynamic Engring., USAF Acad., 1980; MS in Sys. Mgmt., U. So. Calif., 1982; MS in Astrodynamic Engring., AF Inst. Tech., Wright-Patterson AFB, Ohio, 1984. Commd. 2d lt. USAF, Norton AFB, Calif., 1980, advanced through grades to lt. col., 1997; MX stage I project officer Ballistic Missile Office, Norton AFB, 1980-83; trajectory applications engr. 544th Strategic Intelligence Wing, Offutt AFB, Nebr., 1985-88; asst. prof. USAF Acad., Colo., 1988-92; dep. chief astrodynamics AF Rsch. Lab., Kirtland AFB, N.Mex., 1992-98; orbital analyst U.S. Space Command, Peterson AFB, Colo., 1998-2000; prin. engr. Raytheon, Aurora, Colo., 2000—03; tech. program mgr. Analytical Graphics, Inc., Colorado Springs, Colo., 2004—. Mem. adj. faculty Colo. Tech. U., Colorado Springs, 1990—92. Co-author: Systems Engineering Design, 1993; author: Fundamentals of Astrodynamics and Applications, 1997, 2d edit., 2004; contbr. articles to profl. jours. Named an Outstanding Young Men of Am., 1998; recipient Raytheon Distinguished Excellence in Technology, 2001. Mem.: AIAA (mem. com. stds.), Am. Astronautical Soc. (mem. space flight mech. com.). Lutheran. Avocations: classical piano, woodworking, stained glass, hiking, bicycling. Office: Analytical Graphics Inc 7150 Campus Dr Ste 260 Colorado Springs CO 80920-6522 Office Phone: 719-573-2600. Personal E-mail: valladod1@worldnet.att.net. Business E-Mail: dvallado@agi.com.

VALLARTA, JOSEFINA M. retired child neurologist; b. Manila, Philippines, June 23, 1935; came to U.S., 1966; d. Salvador Del Mundo and Josefa Gotauco; m. Leopoldo Vallarta, May 28, 1959; children: Jocelyn Devita, Vivien Temperani, Maria Vallarta, Paula Jurion. AA, U. Santo Tomas, Manila, 1953, MD magna cum laude, 1958; MSc in Neurology, McGill U., Montreal, Can., 1963. Diplomate Am. Bd. Pediatrics, Am. Bd. Psychiatry and Neurology. Resident, fellow Montreal Children's Hosp., 1959-62; fellow in neuropathology Montreal Neurol. Inst., 1962-63; child neurologist Rainier Sch., buckey, Wash., 1967-75, Children's Orthopedic Hosp., Seattle, 1967-75, Marybridge Children's Hosp., Tacoma, 1974-93, Neurology and Neurosurgery Assocs., Tacoma, 1975-90, Child Devel. and Mental Retardation Ctr., U. Wash., Seattle, 1976-89; pres. med. staff Marybridge Children's Hosp., Tacoma, 1980, med. dir. neurodevel. program, 1979-93; clin. instr., assoc. prof. pediatrics and neurology U. Wash., 1967—; ret., 1994. Examiner Am. Bd. Neurology, San Diego, L.A. and Seattle, 1982, 85, 90, 91; bd. dirs. Am. Bd. Neurology; presenter in field; mem. pediat. ICU Marybridge Children's Hosp., 1976-90; mem. med. bd. Wash. Elks therapy Program, 1981-93. Author: Caring for Our Special Children Early: Intervention Services, 1996; contbr. articles to med. jours. Winthrop scholar, 1957-58. Mem. Wash. State Med. Assn., Child Neurology Soc., S.W. Wash. Pediatric Soc., N.w. Pacific Soc. Neurology and Psychiatry, Soc. Devel. and Behavioral Pediatrics, Med. Soc.

Pierce County (pub. sch. health com. 1981-83, ethics com. 1980-93). Avocations: travel, jazzercise, hiking, dance, quilting. Home: 10408 SW 268th St Vashon WA 98070-8424 also: 22607 N Via De La Caballa Sun City West AZ 85375-2215

VALLBONA, CARLOS, physician; b. Granollers, Barcelona, Spain, July 29, 1927; came to U.S., 1953, naturalized, 1967; s. José and Dolores (Calbó) V.; m. Rima Gretel Rothe, Dec. 26, 1956; children— Rima Nuria, Carlos Fernando, María Teresa, Marisa. BA, BS, U. de Barcelona, 1944, MD, 1950. Diplomate Am. Bd. Pediatrics. Child health physician Escuela de Puericultura, Barcelona, 1952, Stagier Etranger Hôpital des Enfants Malades, Paris, 1952-53; intern, resident U. Louisville, 1953-55; resident Baylor Coll. Medicine, Houston, 1955-56, prof. rehab. medicine, 1967—, assoc. prof. physiology and pediatrics, 1962-69, prof., chmn. dept. community medicine, 1969-95, prof. family medicine, 1980-95, Disting. Svc. prof. family and cmty. medicine, 1995—. Adj. prof. U. Tex. Sch. Pub. Health, U. Tex. Health Sci. Ctr., Houston; chief community medicine service Harris County Hosp. Dist.; staff gen. med. service Tex. Children's Hosp.; staff The Inst. Rehab. and Research; staff St. Luke's Episcopal Hosp., con. staff VA Med. Ctr., Houston; Fulbright vis. prof., 1967; cons. WHO, NIH, Nat. Center Health Stats. Pan Am. Health Orgn., Nat. Center Health Service Research; advisor Conseller Sanitat, Catalunya. Author numerous articles in field; editorial bd. several Sci. jours. French Ministry of Edn. fellow, 1952; Children's Internat. Center fellow, 1953; co-recipient Gold medal 6th Internat. Congress Phys. Medicine, 1972; Public Citizen of Yr. San Jacinto chpt. Nat. Assn. Social Workers, 1974; Outstanding Tchr. award Baylor Coll. Medicine Class of 1980, 83, 85, 87, 88; decorated officer Order of Civil Merit (Spain), Medalla Narcis Monturiol (Catalunya). Mem. Am. Acad. Family Physicians, Am. Coll. Med. Informatics (founding mem. 1984), Nat. Acad. Practice (disting. practitioner 1984), Soc. Pediatric Research (emeritus), AMA, Tex. Med. Assn., Am. Coll. Chest Physicians, Am. Pub. Health Assn. (chmn. elect med. care sect. 1989-90), Am. Coll. Preventive Medicine, U.S.-Mex. Border Health Assn., AAAS, Am. Congress Rehab. Medicine, Catalan Soc. Pediatrics (hon.), Argentinian Soc. Internal Medicine (hon. 1986), Argentinian Med. Soc. (hon. 1986), Spanish Acad. Pediatrics (ambulatory pediatrics sect. hon. 1987), Assn. Tchrs. Preventive Medicine, Spanish Profls. Am. (pres. 1988), Soc. Catalana Hipertensio (hon. pres.), Sigma Xi, Alpha Omega Alpha. Roman Catholic. Home: 2001 Holcombe Blvd Houston TX 77030-4222 Office: Baylor Coll Medicine One Baylor Plz Rm 650E Houston TX 77030-3404

VALLBONA, RIMA-GRETEL ROTHE, retired foreign language educator, writer; b. San Jose, Costa Rica, Mar. 15, 1931; d. Ferdinand Hermann and Emilia (Strassburger) Rothe; m. Carlos Vallbona, Dec. 26, 1956; children: Rima-Nuri, Carlos-Fernando, Maria-Teresa, Maria-Luisa. BA/BS, Colegio Superior de Senoritas, San Jose, Costa Rica, 1948; diploma, U. Paris, 1953; diploma in Spanish Philology, U. Salamanca, Spain, 1954; MA, U. Costa Rica, 1962; D in Modern Langs., Middlebury Coll., 1981. Tchr. Liceo J.J. Vargas Calvo, Costa Rica, 1955-56; faculty U. St. Thomas, Houston, 1964-95, prof. Spanish, 1978-95, Cullen Found. prof. Spanish, 1989, head Spanish dept., 1966-71, chmn. dept. modern fgn. lang., 1978-80, prof. emeritus, 1995—, ret. Vis. prof. U. Houston, 1975-76, Rice U., 1974, 80-83, 95, U. St. Thomas, Argentina, 1972; vis. prof. U. St. Thomas, Merida program, 1987-95. Author: Noche en Vela, 1968, Yolanda Oreamuno, 1972, La Obra en Prosa de Eunice Odio, 1981, Baraja de Soledades, Las Sombras que Perseguimos, 1983, Polvo del Camino, 1972, La Salamandra Rosada, 1979, Mujeres y Agonias, 1982, Cosecha de Pecadores, 1988, El arcangel del perdon, 1990, Mundo, demonio y mujer, 1991, Los infiernos de la mujer y algo mas, 1992, (crit. edit.) Vida i sucesos de la Monja Alferez, 1992, Flowering Inferno-Tales of Sinking Hearts, 1994, La narrativa de Yolanda Oreamuno, 1996, Tormy, la Prodigiosa Gata de Donaldito, 1997, Tejedoras de sueños versus realidad, 2003; mem. (editl. bd.) Letras Femeninas, 1984—98, Alba de America, U.S., sec. (culture) Inst. Literario y Cultural Hispanico; co-dir.: Foro Literario, 1987—89; contbg. editor: The Americas Rev., 1989—95; contbr. numerous articles and short stories to lit. mags. Mem. scholarship com. Inst. Hispanic Culture, 1978, 79, 88, 91, chmn., 1979, bd. dirs., 1974-76, 88-89, 91-92, chmn. cultural activities, 1979, 80, 85, 88-89; bd. dirs. Houstoh Pub. Libr., 1984-86; bd. dirs. Cultural Arts Coun. Houston, 1991-92. Recipient Aquileo J. Echeverria Novel prize, 1968, Jorge Luis Borges Short Story prize, Argentina, 1977, Agripina Montes del Valle Novel prize, 1978, Constantin Found. grant for rsch., U. St. Thomas, 1981, Lit. award, S.W. Conf. Latin Am. Studies, 1982, Ancora Lit. award, Costa Rica, 1984, Civil Merit award, King Juan Carlos I of Spain, 1989, Children's Book award, Bay Area Writers League, 2003. Mem.: Nat. Writers Assn., Inst. Lit. y Cultural Hispanico, Casa Argentina de Houston, Inst. Hispanic Culture Houston, Latin Am. Writers Assn. Costa Rica, Inst. Internat. de Lit. Iberoam., Latin Am. Studies Assn., Academia Norteamericana de la Lengua Espanola (elected), S.W. Conf. Orgn. Latin Am Studies, South Ctrl. MLA, Houston Area Tchrs. Fgn. Lang., Houston Area Tchrs. Spanish and Portuguese, Am. Assn. Tchrs. Spanish and Portuguese, Sigma Delta Pi, Phi Sigma Iota. Roman Catholic. Home: 3706 Lake St Houston TX 77098-5522 E-mail: rvallbona@aol.com.

VALLE, RAFAEL F. obstetrician-gynecologist; b. Mendoza, VE, Mex., Sept. 6, 1935; came to U.S., 1966; MD, Madrid U., 1965. Diplomate Am. Bd. Ob-Gyn. Intern Mt. Sinai Hosp., Mpls., 1966-67, resident in surgery, 1967-69; resident in ob-gyn. U. Minn., Mpls., 1969-72; attending physician Hennepin County Med. Ctr. and U. Minn. Hosps., 1972—75, Northwestern U. Hosp., Chgo., 1975—, practice in ob-gyn., 1975—. Prof. OB-GYN Northwestern U. Med. Sch. Mem. ACOG, Assn. Prof. Obs. Gynecol., Am. Assn. Gynecol. Laparoscopists, Am. Fertility Soc., Chgo. Gynecol. Soc., Internat. Soc. Gynecol. Endoscopy, European Soc. Human Reprodn. and Embryology. Office: Northwestern U Med Sch 680 N Lake Shore Dr Ste 1015 Chicago IL 60611 Office Phone: 312-695-0651. Business E-Mail: rvalle@nmff.org.

VALLEE, JACQUES FABRICE, venture capitalist; b. Pontoise, France, Sept. 24, 1939; arrived in US, 1962; s. Gabriel and Madeleine (Passavant) V.; m. Janine M. Saley, Oct. 19, 1960; children: Olivier, Catherine. BS in Math., U. Paris Sorbonne, 1959; MS in Astrophysics, U. Lille, France, 1961; PhD in Computer Sci., Northwestern U., 1967. Sr. software specialist RCA Corp., Cherry Hill, N.J., 1969-70; mgr. infosystems Stanford U., Palo Alto, Calif., 1970-71; rsch. engr. SRI Internat., Menlo Park, Calif., 1971-72; sr. rsch. fellow Inst. for Future, Menlo Park, 1972-76; chmn. Infomedia Corp., Palo Alto, 1976-81; v.p. Sofinnova, Inc., San Francisco, 1982-86; gen. ptnr. Euro-Am. Ventures, 1987—; pres. EUROCAL Venture Mgmt.; gen. ptnr. Sigefi, Burnette & Vallee, LLP, 2000—. Bd. dirs. Triformix, Inc., Santa Rosa, Calif., Chaos Telecom, San Diego. Author: Computer Message Systems, 1984, Dimensions, 1988, Confrontations, 1990, Revelations, 1991, Forbidden Science, 1992, FastWalker, 1996, The Four Elements of Financial Alchemy, 2000, The Heart of the Internet, 2003. Trustee Inst. for the Future, Menlo Park. Recipient Jules Verne prize, Paris, 1961. E-mail: jacques@sbvpartners.com.

VALLEE, JUDITH DELANEY, environmentalist, writer, fundraiser; b. NYC, Mar. 14, 1948; d. Victor and Sally Hammer; m. John Delaney, Apr. 9, 1974 (div. 1978); m. Henry Richard Vallee, May 15, 1987. BA, CUNY, 1976. Exec. dir. Save the Manatee Club, Maitland, Fla., 1985—. Apptd. U.S. Manatee Recovery Plan Team, Jacksonville, Fla., 1988-97, Fla. Manatee Tech. Adv. Coun., Tallahassee, 1989-2002, Save the Manatee Com., Orlando, Fla., 1985-92, World Conservation Union/Sirenia Specialist Group, Switzerland, 1996; advisor Save the Wildlife Inc., Chuluota, Fla., 1992-93; bd. dirs. Environ. Fund for Fla. Lobbyist Save the Manatee Club, 1989; vol. Broward County Audubon Soc., Ft. Lauderdale, 1983-84, Wild Bird Care Ctr., Ft. Lauderdale, 1984. Recipient Refuge Support award Chassahowitzka Nat. Wildlife Refuge, 1989. Democrat. Avocations: creative writing, antiques, wildlife observation, canoeing. Office: Save the Manatee Club Inc 500 N Maitland Ave Ste 210 Maitland FL 32751-4458 Office Phone: 407-539-0990. Personal E-mail: jvallee100@aol.com. Business E-Mail: jvallee@savethemanatee.org.

VALLEE, ROY, electronics company executive; b. Southbridge, Mass. married; 2 children. AS in electronics tech., Don Bosco Tech. Inst., 1971. Electronics tech. radio products Don Bosco Tech. Inst., 1971—77; field sales rep. Avnet, Inc., Great Neck, NY, 1977—92, from sys. bus. mgr., gen. sales mgr. to vice-chmn., pres., COO, 1992—98, chmn., CEO, Phoenix, 1998—, bd. dirs., 1991—. Bd. dirs. Teradyne, Synopsys, Inc.; exec. com. Global Tech. Distbn. Coun. Mem. Govs. Coun. of Innovation and Tech. Named to Hot 25 Execs., Electronic Buyer's News, 1997, 1999, 2000. Office: Avnet Inc 2211 S 47th St Phoenix AZ 85034-6403

VALLENTYNE, PETER LLOYD, philosophy educator; b. New Haven, Mar. 25, 1952; s. John Ruben and Ann Vera (Tracy) V.; m. Marie Helene Pastides, June 26, 1981. BA, McGill U., Montreal, Que., Can., 1978; MA, U. Pitts., 1981, PhD, 1984. Actuarial supr. Great West Life Assurance Co., Winnipeg, Man., Can., 1973-75; asst. prof. U. Western Ont., London, 1984-88, Va. Commonwealth U., Richmond, 1988-90, assoc. prof. philosophy, 1990-2000, prof. philosophy, 2000—03. Editor: Contractarianism and Rational Choice: Essays on Gauthier, 1991, The Origin of Left-Libertarianism, 2000, Left-Libertarianism and Its Critics, 2000; assoc. editor: Politics, Philosophy and Economics, 2000, Desert and Justice, 6 vols., 2003; mem. editl. bd. Utilitas, 1994—, Econs. and Philosophy, 1998-2003, editor, 2003—. Ethics, 2003—. Mem. Am. Philos. Assn., Can. Philos. Assn., So. Soc. Philosophy and Psychology, Va. Philos. Assn. (pres. 1994-95). Avocations: piano, ballroom dance, art films. Office: Dept Philosophy U Missouri Columbia Columbia MO 65211 Office Phone: 573-882-3192. Business E-Mail: vallentynep@missouri.edu.

VALLERAND, PHILIPPE GEORGES, sales executive; b. Montreal, Que., Can., June 12, 1954; arrived in U.S., 1982; s. Louis Philippe and Beatrice (Goupil) V.; m. Laura Jean Frombach, Sept. 25, 1979; children: Harmonie May, Jeremy Thomas, Emilie Rose. Student, U. Montreal, 1974, U. Sherbrooke, 1975, U. Que., 1976, White Mgmt. Sch., London, 1981. Cert. mktg. and sales Internat. Orgn. for Standardization, 2002. Dir. resort Club Mediterranee Inc., Bahamas, Switzerland, Africa, Guadaloupe, West Indies, 1978—80; v.p. Franglo/Sunsaver Inc., London and Hyeres, France, 1980-82; v.p. sales Source Northwest, Inc., Woodinville, Wash., 1982—93; pres., CEO The PGV Group, Inc. Sr. comdr. Royal Rangers Boys Club, Monroe, Wash., 1988-96; bd. dirs. Christian Faith Ctr., Monroe, 1988-94; mem. Rep. Nat. Com.; co-chmn. Rep. Bus. Adv. Coun.; bd. trustees Northwest Coll.; pres. leadership coun., Trinity Western U. Recipient Disting. Sales & Mktg. Exec. award Internat. Orgn. Sales & Mktg. Execs., 1993, 96; named Rep. of Yr., Wash. State, 2000-03; named to 500 Inc. Mag., 1983, 89. Mem. Am. Mktg. Assn. (adv. bd.), Sales and Mktg. Execs. Internat. Avocations: skiing, world travel. Business E-Mail: pvallerand@prime1.com.

VALLES, JUDITH, mayor, former academic administrator; b. San Bernardino, Calif., Dec. 14, 1933; d. Gonzalo and Jovita (Lopez-Torices) V.; m. Chad Bradbury, Sept. 30, 1956 (dec. Sept. 1969); children: Edith Renella, Nohemi Renella, Chad; m. Harry Carl Smith, Oct. 13, 1985. BA in English, Redlands (Calif.) U., 1956; MA in Spanish Lit., U. Calif., Riverside, 1966; doctorate (hon.), U. Redlands, 2000. Instr. Spanish San Bernardino (Calif.) Valley Coll., 1963-84, head dept. fgn. lang., 1971-76, chair div. humanities, 1976-81, dean extended day, 1981-83, adminstrv. dean acad. affairs, 1983-87, exec. v.p. acad. and student affairs, 1987-88; pres. Golden West Coll., Huntington Beach, Calif., 1988—; mayor San Bernardino, 1998—. Mem. adv. com. Police Officers Standards and Tng. Commn., Sacramento, 1991—. Author fgn. lang. annals and sociol. abstracts. Speaker statewide edn. and community orgns., 1988—; bd. dirs. exec. coun. and chief exec. officers Calif. Community Colls., 1990—. Recipient Bishops award for diocese, Outstanding Pub. Svc. award NALEO, 2001; named One of Outstanding Women Orange County YWCA, 1990, Citizen of Achievement LWV, 1989, Woman of Distinction Bus. Press, 1998, Influential Latina of the Yr. Hispanic Lifestyle, 1998, State of Calif. Woman of the Yr., 1999, Humanitarian Yr. Cath. charities, 1999, Citizen Yr. Boy Scouts Am., 1999, Empire Woman Yr. State Assembly, 1999, Outstanding Cmty. Leader, Cmty. Found., 2002, Woman of Yr., State Senate, 2003; inducted into Hall of Fame, San Bernardino Valley Coll. Mem. Women's Roundtable Orange County, Conf. and Visitors Bur., C. of C. (Vanguard), Kiwanis, Charter 100. Avocations: opera, theater, reading, running. Office: Conf Mayors 300 N D St San Bernardino CA 92418-0001

VALLETTA, AMBER, model; b. Tulsa, Feb. 9, 1973; m. Hervé Le Bihan. With Boss Models, N.Y.C.; Elite Models, N.Y.C., 1996—. Office: Fl 2 300 Park Ave S New York NY 10010-5313

VALLEY, JOHN WILLIAMS, geology educator, researcher; b. Winchester, Mass., Feb. 28, 1948; s. George Edward Valley Jr. and Louisa (Williams) Valley; m. Andrée Taylor, Aug. 12, 1972; children: Matthew Taylor, David Taylor. AB, Dartmouth Coll., 1970; MS, U. Mich., 1977, PhD, 1980. Asst. prof. Rice U., 1980—83, U. Wis., Madison, 1983—85, assoc. prof., 1985—89, prof., 1989—, chair dept. geology and geophysics, 1996—99. Editor: Stable Isotopes in High Temperature Geological Processes, 1986, Stable Isotope Geohemistry, 2001; assoc. editor: Jour. Geophys. Rsch., 1992, Am. Jour. Sci., 1996—; contbr. over 500 articles to profl. jours. Recipient N.L. Bowen award, Am. Geophys. Union, 2003; grantee Postdoctoral fellowship, NSF, 1980; Fulbright scholar, 1989—90. Fellow: Mineral Soc. Am. (councilor 1993—96), Geol. Soc. Am. (assoc. editor GSA Bull. 1985—91). Achievements include first calibration of the calcite-graphite geothermometer; discovery of new minerals, fluorphlogopite and fluortremolite; new applications of stable oxygen, carbon, hydrogen and sulfur isotope ratios to the study of metamorphic, igneous, and sedimentary processes; development of techniques to analyze stable isotope ratios in situ in microscopic samples; first demonstration of diffusive exchange of oxygen in metamorphic minerals; originator, Cool Early Earth Hypothesis. Avocation: Appalachian Mountain Club. Office: Univ Wis Dept Geology and Geophysics 1215 W Dayton St Madison WI 53706-1600 Office Phone: 608-263-5659. Business E-Mail: valley@geology.wisc.edu.

VALLI, FRANKIE (FRANCIS CASTELLUCCIO), singer; b. Newark, May 3, 1937; Student pub. schs., Newark. With vocal group Four Lovers, 1956—61, The Four Seasons, 1962—77, albums (with The Four Seasons) Sherry, Greetings, Big Girls Don't Cry, Ain't That A Shame, 1963, Stay, Golden Hits, We Love Girls, Live On Stage, Dawn, Born To Wander, Rag Doll, 1964, Sing Big Hits, Entertain You, Gold Vault Hits, Working My Way Back To You, 1965, Christmas Album, Genuine Imitation, Life Gazette, Seasoned Hits, 1968, Edizione D'oro, 1969, Big Ones, 1971, Chameleon, 1972, Gold, Our Day Will Come, Close To You, Fallen Angel, Who Loves You, Helicon, 1975, The Four Seasons Story, 1976, Reunited, 1981, Hope and Glory, 1992, (as solo artist) Solo, 1967, Timeless, 1968, Inside You, Closeup, Our Day Will Come, 1975, Valli, 1977, Frankie Valli Is The Word, 1978, Grease (original soundtrack), 1978, The Very Best of Frankie Valli, 1979, Heaven Above Me, 1980, Frankie Valli: Hits from the 60's, 1983; actor: (films) Beach Ball, 1965, All This and World War II, Ebony, Ivory and Jade, 1976, Grease, Sergeant Pepper's Lonely Hearts Club Band, 1978, Dirty Laundry, 1987, Eternity, 1989, Modern Love, 1990, Opposite Corners, 1995; (TV films) Witness to the Mob, 1998; (TV series) The Sopranos, 2004—. Named to Rock 'n' Roll Hall of Fame (with The Four Seasons), 1990.*

VALLIERE, FLORA LEE, law firm official; b. Neptune, N.J., Dec. 4, 1950; d. Joseph Sidney and Anna (Warar) Rosenthal; m. Lewis Ira Weinstein (div. 1976); m. Robrt John Valliere (div. 1986); children: Stuart Glenn, Gillian Melissa. AA, Miami-Dade Jr. Coll., 1972; student, Fla. Internat. U., 1973-74; grad. in cosmetology, Norwood Beauty Sch., North Miamia, Fla., 1975; student, Nova Southeastern U., Davie, Fla., 1996. Notary pub., Fla. Waitress Windmill Restuarant, West End, N.J., 1966-72; artist, antique dealer, 1972-75; hairdresser Century Plaza Salon, Deerfield Beach, Fla., 1976-80; saleswoman Fedco Drugs, Ft. Lauderdale, Fla., 1986-93; cashier, pharmacy technician Winn-Dixie Supermarkets, Ft. Lauderdale, 1994-96; receptionist, sec. Law Firm Lonergan, Murawski, Vizcarrondo & Usan, Ft. Lauderdale, 1996-99. Vol. Coop. Feeding Program, Ft. Lauderdale, 1996, 99, Arnold Abbot's Love Thy Neighbor Feeding Program for Homeless, 1999. Democrat. Jewish. Avocations: frequenting art shows, beach, collecting antiques, music, reading. Address: 3047 Perry Ave Greenacres FL 33463-2060

VALLIERE, ROLAND EDWARD, performing company executive; b. Pawtucket, R.I., Oct. 3, 1954; s. Roland Edgar and Anita Alice (Dubois) V.; m. Stacey Lyn Rein, June 3, 1984 (separated). MusB, New England Conservatory, 1978; MFA, Brandeis U., 1984. Regional mgr. Syracuse (N.Y.) Symphony, 1984-86; gen. mgr. N.H. Symphony, Manchester, 1986-89; exec. dir. Hudson Valley Philharmonic, Poughkeepsie, N.Y., 1989-92, Omaha Symphony, Nebr., 1992-95, Kansas City Symphony, Mo., 1995—2002, dir. tech, 2002—. Presenter Am. Symphony Orchestra League, Washington, 1987, 90. Office: PO Box 22534 Kansas City MO 64113-0534

VALLNER, JOSEPH J. medical products executive; BS in Pharmacy, MS in Phys. Chemistry, PhD in Pharmaceutics, U. Wis. Former assoc. prof. pharmaceutics U. Ga.; formerly with G.D. Searle and Co., Syntex Corp., Sequus Pharms.; exec. v.p., COO Cell Genesys, Inc., Foster City, Calif., 1999—2001, pres., COO, 2001—.

VALVASSORI, GALDINO E. physician; b. Milan, 1926; MD, U. Milan, 1950. Diplomate Am. Bd. Radiology. Intern Columbus Hosp., Chgo., 1957; resident Meml. Ctr.-Cornell, 1954-56; fellow Columbus Hosp., Chgo., 1958-59; mem. staff U. Ill. Hosp., Chgo., 1966—; prof. radiology and otolaryngology U. Ill., 1966—; prof. U. Chgo., 1960-65; cons. dept. radiology St. Francis Hosp., Evanston, Ill., 2001—. Mem. AMA, Am. Coll. Radiology, Am. Roentgen Ray Soc., Roentgen Soc. N.Am., Am. Soc. Neuroradiology, Am. Soc. Head and Neck Radiology. Office: Univ Ill Outpatients Care Ctr 1801 W Taylor Chicago IL 60612 Office Phone: 312-996-1999. Business E-Mail: gvalvassor@ameritech.net.

VALVO, BARBARA-ANN, lawyer, surgeon; b. Elizabeth, N.J., June 7, 1949; d. Robert Richad and Vera (Kovach) V. BA in Biology, Hofsta U., 1971; MD, Pa. State U., 1975; JD, Loyola Sch. Law, 1993. Bar: La. 1993; diplomate Am. Bd. Surgery. Surg. intern Nassau County Med. Ctr., East Meadow, NY, 1975-76; resident gen. surgery Allentown (Pa.)-Sacred Heart Med. Ctr., 1976-80; asst. chief surgery USPHS, New Orleans, 1980-81; pvt. practice gen. surgery New Orleans, 1981-89; pvt. practice med. malpractice law, 1995—. Upjohn scholar, 1975. Fellow ACS; mem. ABA, Fed. Bar Assn., La. Bar Assn., La. Trial Lawyers Assn. Republican. Avocations: computers, raising animals. Office: 4130 Loire Dr Ste A Kenner LA 70065 Office Phone: 504-467-8762. Personal E-mail: bavalvo@att.net.

VALYI-NAGY, TIBOR G. neuropathologist, virologist; b. Debrecen, Hungary, Jan. 7, 1958; arrived in U.S., 1988; s. Tibor Valyi-Nagy and Ilona Gonczol; m. Klara Peto, Sept. 11, 1982; children: Tibor, Zsofia. MD, Debrecen U., 1982; PhD, Hungarian Acad. Scis., Budapest, 1994. Cert. anatomic and neuropathology Am. Bd. Pathology, 2003, med. microbiology Hungarian Bd. Med. Microbiology, 1988. Rsch. assoc. Nat. Inst. Dermatology, Budapest, 1982—88; rsch. fellow U. Tex. Med. Br., Galveston, 1984—86; rsch. assoc. The Wistar Inst., Phila., 1988—95; resident physician in anatomic and neuropathology Vanderbilt U. Med. Ctr., Nashville, 1995—2000; instr. and attending neuropathologist Vanderbilt U. Sch. Medicine, Nashville, 2000—02; dir. neuropathology, asst. prof. U. Ill., Chgo., 2002—. Home: 597 Glen Ellyn Pl Glen Ellyn IL 60137 Office: Univ Illinois at Chicago 1819 W Polk St Rm 446 (MC847) Chicago IL 60612-7335 Office Phone: 312-996-1772. Personal E-mail: valyint@aol.com. E-mail: tiborv@uic.edu.

VAN, FRITZ See **VAN DUYSE, FRANCIS**

VAN, GEORGE PAUL, international money management consultant; b. Isle Maligne, Que., Can., Feb. 12, 1940; s. Raymond Murdoch and Germaine Marie (Brassard) V.; m. Janine Marie Irene Therese Yvette Boily, Sept. 15, 1962; children: John, Robert, Caroline. BA, McGill U., 1961; DHA, U. Toronto, 1963. Sr. cons. Agnew Peckham and Assocs., Toronto, 1963-65; CEO, exec. dir. Misericordia Corp., Edmonton, Alta., Can., 1965-68; Chief operating officer, exec. v.p. Texpack, Ltd., Brantford, Ont., 1968-70, also bd. dirs.; group v.p. Will Ross, Inc., Milw., 1970-73; exec. v.p. Nortek, Inc., Cranston, R.I., 1973-77, also bd. dirs.; pres., chief operating officer Hosp. Affiliates Internat., Incs. (subs. INA Corp.), Nashville, 1977-80, also bd. dirs.; chmn., pres., CEO Health Group, Inc., Nashville, 1977-80; chmn., CEO Columbia Corp. (formerly Franklin Corp.), Nashville, 1984-88; pres. Grinders Switch Farms, Grinders Shooting Club, Centerville, Tenn., 1990—; chmn. Van Hedge Fund Advisors, Inc., Nashville, 1992—, Van Hedge Fund Advisors Internat., Inc., Van Fund Mgmt. II, 1996—, Van Fund Mgmt. I, Inc., Van Money Mgr. Rsch., Inc., 1997—, chmn., CEO Project W, 2000—. Contbr. articles to profl. jours. Bd. dirs. Tulane U. Med. Ctr., 1977-80, Nashville Inst. for the Arts, 1987-88, Nashville Symphony, 1987-88, Fedn. Internat. de Tir aux Armes Sportives de Chasse, Paris, 1990-92; mem. Internat. Tech. Commn. for Sporting Clays, Paris, 1990; bd. overseers U. Pa. Sch. of Nursing, 1979-82, 84-88, assoc. trustee U. Pa., 1979-82, 84-88; chmn. internat. com. U.S. Sporting Clays Assn., 1989-92; active pres.'s coun. Andrew Jackson Inst., 1993-94; adv. bd. Fin. Mktg. Rsch. Ctr. Vanderbilt U. Recipient several scholarships. Mem. Westside Club, Grinders Switch Club. Home and Office: 2025 Sunset Hills Ter Nashville TN 37215

VAN, PETER, lawyer; b. Boston, Sept. 7, 1936; s. Frank Lewis and Ruth (Spevack) V.; m. Faye Anne Zinck, 1991; children: Jami Lynne, Robert Charles. BA, Dartmouth, 1958; LLD, Boston Coll., 1961. Bar: Mass. 1962. Assoc. Brown, Rudnick, Freed and Gesmer, Boston, 1961-63; assoc. Fine and Ambrogne, Boston, 1963-65, ptnr., 1966-73, sr. ptnr., 1973—, mng. ptnr., chmn. exec. com., 1988-90; ptnr., mem. exec. com. Mintz, Levin, Cohn, Ferris, Glovsky and Popeo, P.C., Boston, 1990-97; ptnr. Bingham, McCutchen LLP, Boston, 1997—. Mem. fin. com., overseer Beth Israel Hosp. Boston. Mem. Masons. Office: Bingham McCutchen LLP 150 Federal St Boston MA 02110-1713 Office Phone: 617-951-8676. E-mail: peter.van@bingham.com.

VANAGAS, RIMANTAS ANDRIUS (RAY VANAGAS), entrepreneur; b. Chgo., Jan. 10, 1958; s. Liudas and Birute A. (Bielskis) Vanagas. Student, Northwestern U., 1980-81; BA in Physics, Econs. and Polit. Sci., Lake Forest (Ill.) Coll., 1982. Prof. basketball player European divsn., Munich, 1982; ski instr., capt. race team Breckenridge (Colo.) Ski Sch., 1979-80; chmn. bd. dirs. Vancher Corp., Wheeling, Ill., 1980-84; sales exec. Chgo. HMO, 1984-85; exec. dir. Physique, Inc., Highland Park, Ill., 1985; pres., CEO Sports Life, Inc., Highland Park, 1985-88; sr. v.p. JPC Consulting, Chgo., 1988-91; pres., CEO Printing Advisors, Inc., Naperville, Ill., 1990-94; sr. exec. George S. May Internat. Consulting Co., Park Ridge, Ill., 1994-95; pres., CEO Cafe Alexander, Naperville, 1995—2002; pres. Movie Magic Workshops, 2002—; founder, real estate investor, devel. RBML Real Estate Inc., 2002—. Cons. Nautilus Exercise Ctrs., Inc., Wheeling, 1979—83, G. Ross Comm., Lake Bluff, Ill., 1986; mng. dir. Ford Model Mgmt., Chgo., 2000—; pres., CEO Alexander Talent Mgmt., 2001—. Actor:, 1981—; prodr., 1981—; actor: (films) Shut-Eye, 2001; prodr.: numerous music videos, commls., inds. and corp. films. Leader Lithuanian Air Scouts, 1976—80; campaign asst. Ronald Reagan Re-Election Campaign, Ill., 1983; active Baltic Nations Athletic Olympiad; vol. coach basketball, baseball, 1984—87. Roman Catholic. Avocations: collecting coins and stamps, travel, skiing, golf, tennis. Home: 1680 Greene Ridge Dr Naperville IL 60565-6753 Office Phone: 630-202-3898. E-mail: rayvanagas@aol.com.

VAN AKEN, JOHN HENRY, retired marine surveyor, engineer, consultant; b. Haarlem, The Netherlands, Sept. 26, 1922; arrived in U.S., 1952; s. Antony and Maria Petronella (Renzen) van Aken; m. Hendrika A. Bonneur, Sept. 25, 1947 (div. Feb. 1960); 1 child, Antony Laurens; m. Helen Jemison, July 17, 1962 (dec. Feb. 1978); m. Marilyn McDaniel, July 13, 1980 (dec. Sept. 2001). Marine Engr., Acad. Tech. Sci. and Arts, of Design, Rotterdam, 1940. Asst. mgr. repair dept. Wilton-Feyenoord Dockyards, Schiedam, The Netherlands, 1945-52; supt. machinery Ala. Dry Dock & Shipbldg. Co., Mobile, 1958-60; project mgr. Kerr-McGee Oil Industries, Oklahoma City, 1954-58, 60-63; insp. George Sharp Co., Naval Architects, Newport News, Va., 1960; pres. John H. van Aken Co. Inc., Marine Surveyors and Cons. Inc., Mobile, 1963-99; ret., 2002. Non-exclusive surveyor Panama Bur. Shipping, Internat. Cargo Gear Bur., Registr. Italiano Navale, Lloyd's Register of Shipping. Named hon. consul gen. Republic of South Africa; decorated comdr. Order Good Hope,

South Africa; Paul Harris fellow Rotary. Mem. Soc. Naval Architects and Marine Engrs., Nat. Assn. Marine Surveyors, Netherlands Soc. Marine Technologists, Athelstan Club, Fairhope Yacht Club, Mobile Rotary. Home: 500 Spanish Ft Blvd #52 Spanish Fort AL 36527-5004 Personal E-mail: jhvanaken@aol.com.

VAN AKEN, NORMAN, chef; Chef, owner Norman's Restaurant, Coral Gables, Fla. Author: Feast of Sunlight, 1988, The Great Exotic Fruit Book, 1995, Norman Van Aken's New World Cuisine, 1997, New World Cuisine=Latin America, 2001. Recipient James Beard award, Robert Mondavi award, Food Arts Silver Spoon award. Office: 21 Almeria Ave Coral Gables FL 33134

VAN AKEN, WILLIAM J. construction executive; b. 1954; Grad. South Utah State Coll., 1984, Case Western Res. U., Cleve., 1990. Pvt. practice as contractor, Cedar City, Utah, 1976-83; with Sam W. Emerson Co., Cleve., 1983—, pres., treas., 1990—. Office: Sam W Emerson Co 3365 Richmond Rd Ste 200 Cleveland OH 44122-4178

VAN AKKEREN, LORRAINE SUE, research assistant; b. Balt., July 22, 1943; d. Gordon David and Ida (Rackoff) Goldstein; children: Adrienne Dawn Mandeville, Joel Rackoff. BA, Monmouth Coll., 1965. Chief art and photography depts. Nat. Biomed. Rsch. Found., Washington, 1965-74; prodn. control asst. Optimum Sys., Inc., Rockville, Md., 1974-76; sr. assoc. Computer Documentation & Tng., Kensington, Md., 1976-91; mem. svcs. rep., survey asst. Group Health Assn., Washington, 1989; sr. rsch. asst. Am. Assn. of Colls. of Osteo. Medicine, Chevy Chase, 1989—; chair osteo. medicine Ed. Leadership Task Force, AACOM, 2000—02. Vice-chair Rockville mem. adv. coun. Group Health Assn., 1992-94, vice-chair cen. mem. adv. com., Washington, 1992-94, mem. claims appeals com., Washington, 1993-94, mem. complaints com., Washington, 1992-94, mem. benefits com., 1989-92, mem. mental health task force, 1988-90. Artist: (book covers) Atlas of Protein Sequence and Structure, 1966-74 (1st prize Comml. Illustration Silver Spring Showcase of Md. 1968), Engineering Analysis of Dental Forces: Theory and Application, 1970, (jour. cover) Pattern Recognition, 1969. Carpool chair Charles E. Smith Jewish Day Sch., Rockville, 1982-96, gift cert. fundraiser, 1991-94, chair subcom. on arts, 1983-85; Sunday sch. and faculty records Luth. Ch. St. Andrew Sunday Sch., Wheaton, Md., 1983-94; mem. Bethesda Jewish Congregation Choir; advisor Montgomery County 1st Aid unit Boy Scout Explorer Post 521 (formerly Montgomery County ARC 1st Aid unit), 1995—; rep. ctrl. mem. adv. panel Humana Group Health Plan, Inc., mem. Rockville, chair Montgomery County, mem. adv. panel, 1994-97; mem. New Beginnings, Inc., 1996-2004-2004; active mobile adoption unit Montgomery County Humane Soc. foster dog program, 2000—. Avocations: crossword puzzles, swimming, needlecrafts, volunteer work, cooking. Home: 3814 Delano St Wheaton MD 20902-1031 Office: Am Assn Colls Osteo Med 5550 Friendship Blvd #310 Chevy Chase MD 20815-7231 E-mail: dachsielover@verizon.net., lorries@aacom.org.

VAN ALFEN, NEAL K. plant pathologist; b. Ogden, Utah, July 17, 1943; s. Gerrit Johan and Marguerite (Noorda) Van A. BS, Brigham Young U., 1968, MS, 1969; PhD, U. Calif., Davis, 1972. Asst. plant pathologist Conn. Agr. Exp. Sta., New Haven, Conn., 1972-75; asst. prof. biology Utah State U., Logan, 1975-78, extension plant pathologist, 1975-78, assoc. prof. of biology, 1978-82, prof. of biology and molecular biology/biochem., 1982-90; prof. and head/dept. of plant pathology/microbiology Tex. A&M U., College Station, Tex., 1990-99; dean agrl. and environ. scis. U. Calif., Davis, 1999—. Fellow AAAS, Am. Phytopathol. Soc.; mem. Am. Phytopathol. Soc. (councilor-at-large 1994-97, v.p., pres. 1997-2000), Am. Soc. for Microbiology. Office: U Calif-Davis Coll Agrl and Environ Scis 1 Shields Ave Davis CA 95616-5270 Office Phone: 530-752-1605. E-mail: nkvanalfen@ucdavis.edu.

VAN ALLEN, BARBARA MARTZ, marketing professional; d. Walter Atlee and Barbara Jean (Winebrenner) Martz; m. Peter Cushing Van Allen, Sept. 3, 1983; children: Caroline Kent, Peter Cushing Jr. BA with honors, U. N.C., 1976; MA, George Washington U., 1983; MBA, NYU, 1993. Legis. asst. U.S. Ho. of Reps., Washington, 1976-81, legis. dir., 1981-83; dir. ITT Corp., N.Y.C., 1984-90; pres. Van Allen Assocs., N.Y.C., 1990-93, 2000—; mng. dir. Cushman & Wakefield, Inc., N.Y.C., 1994-2000. Bd. dirs. Washington Nat. Cathedral Coll. Preachers, 2000—. Mem. N.Y.C. Jr. League, 1986—; mem. econ. devel. task force N.Y.C. Mayoral Campaign and Transition Team, 1994—95; bd. dirs. 801 West End Avenue Corp., N.Y.C., 1995—99. Recipient Star awards for print campaign and internal comm. Bus. Mktg. Assn., 1996, nat. pro-comm. profl. excellence award for radio, 1996, Pro Com. award, 1997, Impact award, 1998. Mem. NAFE, Internat. Assn. Bus. Communicators (Iris Merit award 1996, Ace Merit award 1996, Ace award of excellence for pub. 1997, Ace award of merit for Reporter's Handguide 1997, N.Y. Fest. award, BMA Pro Comm. award for Direct Mail: Soup to Nuts, 1998, APEX award for Real Estatements publ., 1998), Bus. and Profl. Women's Club, YWCA Acad. Women Achievers. Home: 4407 Hadfield Ln NW Washington DC 20007-2034

VAN ALLEN, JAMES ALFRED, physicist, researcher; b. Mt. Pleasant, Iowa, Sept. 7, 1914; s. Alfred Morris and Alma E. (Olney) Van A.; m. Abigail Fithian Halsey, Oct. 13, 1945; children: Cynthia Schaffner, Margot Cairns, Sarah Trimble, Thomas, Peter. BS, Iowa Wesleyan Coll., 1935; MS, U. Iowa, 1936, PhD, 1939; ScD (hon.), Iowa Wesleyan Coll., 1951, Grinnell Coll., 1957, Coe Coll., 1958, Cornell Coll., Mt. Vernon, Iowa, 1959, U. Dubuque, 1960, U. Mich., 1961, Northwestern U., 1961, Ill. Coll., 1963, Butler U., 1966, Boston Coll., 1966, Southampton Coll., 1967, Augustana Coll., 1969, St. Ambrose Coll., 1982, U. Bridgeport, 1987; DHL (hon.), Johns Hopkins U., 1999. Rsch. fellow, physicist dept. terrestial magnetism Carnegie Instn., Washington, 1939-42; physicist, group and unit supr. applied physics lab. Johns Hopkins U., 1942, 46-50, organizer, leader sci. expdns. study cosmic radiation Peru, 1949, 1950, 1952, 57, 1957; prof. physics, head dept. U. Iowa, Iowa City, 1951-85, Carver prof. physics, emeritus, 1989-92, Regent disting. prof., 1992—; now prof. emeritus. Rsch. assoc. Princeton U., 1953-54; mem. devel. group radio proximity fuze Nat. Def. Rsch. Coun., OSRD; regents fellow Smithsonian Instn., 1981; pioneer high attitude rsch. with rockets, satellites and space probes. Author: Origins of Magnetospheric Physics, 1983, First to Jupiter, Saturn and Beyond, 1981; 924 Elementary Problems and Answers in Solar System Astronomy, 1993; contbg. author: Physics and Medicine of Upper Atmosphere, 1952, Rocket Exploration of the Upper Atmosphere; editor: Scientific Uses of Earth Satellites, 1956, Cosmic Rays, the Sun, and Geomagnetism: The Works of Scott E. Forbush, 1993; acting editor Jour. Geophys. Rsch.-Space Physics, 1991-92; contbr. numerous articles to profl. jours. * Lt. comdr. USNR, 1942-46, ordnance and gunnery specialist, combat observer. Recipient Physics award Washington Acad. Sci., 1949, Space Flight award Am. Astronautical Soc., 1958, Louis W. Hill Space Transp. award Inst. Aero. Scis., 1959, Elliot Cresson medal Franklin Inst., 1961, Golden Omega award Elec. Insulation Conf., 1963, Iowa Broadcasters Assn. award, 1964, Fellows award of merit Am. Cons. Engrs. Coun., 1978, Nat. Medal of Sci., 1987, Nansen award and prize Norwegian Acad. Sci. and Letters, 1990, Vannevar Bush award NSF, 1991, Gerard P. Kuiper prize Am. Astron. Soc. 1994; named comdr. Order du Merit Pour la Recherche et l'Invention, 1964; Guggenheim Found. rsch. fellow, 1951. Fellow Am. Rocket Soc. (C.N. Hickman medal devel. Aerobee rocket 1949), IEEE, Am. Phys. Soc., Am. Geophys. Union (pres. 1982-84, John A. Fleming award 1963, William Bowie medal 1977); mem. NAS, AAAS (Abelson prize 1986), Iowa Acad. Sci., Internat. Acad. Astronautics (founding), Am. Philos. Soc., Am. Astron. Soc., Royal Astron. Soc. U.K. (Gold medal 1978), Royal Swedish Acad. Sci. (Crafoord prize 1989), Am. Acad. Arts and Scis., Cosmos Club, Sigma Xi (Procter prize 1987), Gamma Alpha. Presbyterian. Achievements include discovery of radiation belts (now named the Van Allen belts) around earth in 1958 with satellite missions Explorer I and Explorer III. Office: Univ Iowa Dept Physics and Astronomy 701 Van Allen Hall Iowa City IA 52242-1403 E-mail: james-vanallen@uiowa.edu.

VAN ALLEN, VERONICA ELAINE, marketing and public relations professional; b. Jamaica, N.Y., May 6, 1936; d. William James and Florence Veronica (Lester) Van Allen; children: Veronica E. Davis, Valerie E. Boyd; m. Ian Helsby, July 4, 1998. BEd, U. Miami, 1963; cert., U.S. Chamber Inst. Orgn. Mgmt., Boulder, Colo., 1984—88. Cert. tchr., Fla. English, phys. edn. tchr. Dade County Sch. Sys., Miami, Fla., 1963-67; founder, coach girls' track team Acad. of the Holy Names, Tampa, Fla., 1972—74; exec. dir. Royal Palm Festival Inc., West Palm Beach, Fla., 1978-82; exec. v.p. No. Palm Beaches C. of C., Palm Beach Gardens, Fla., 1982-88; dir. mktg., pub. rels. Operation Explore, Palm Beach Gardens, Fla., 1993—. Exec. dir. World Trade Coun., 1983-86. Editor (newspaper supplement) Royal Palm Festival, 1978-82 (Advt. Club aw ard 1980), video pub., 1981 (Internat. Festival Assn. award 1981); editor (ann. chamber mag.) Guide to No. Palm Beaches, 1984-88, Air Show mag., 1987. Vice chmn. Tourist Devel. Coun. Palm Beach County, 1987, mem., 1983—88; vice chmn. Leadership Palm Beach County, 1985—86, bd. dirs., 1984—89; mem. mil. acad. screening com. Congressman Tom Lewis, Palm Beach Gardens, 1986—94; bd. dirs. Sun Fest, 1982—84; mem. Internat. Coun. Air Shows, 1981—86, Alumni Assn.LPBC, 1987—; coord. religious instrn. St. Paul of the Cross, North Palm Beach, Fla., 1977—80. Mem. U. Miami Alumni Assn., Internat. Festival Assn., Am. C. of C. Execs. Republican. Roman Catholic. Avocations: reading, skiing, theater, tennis, aerobics. Home: 170 Esperanza Way Palm Beach Gardens FL 33418 Office Phone: 561-694-0822. E-mail: ronnieandian@aol.com.

VAN ALLEN, WILLIAM KENT, lawyer; b. Albion, N.Y., July 30, 1914; s. Everett Kent and Georgia (Roberts) Van A.; m. Sally Schall, Nov. 11, 1944; children: William Kent, Jr., George Humphrey, Peter Cushing. AB, Hamilton Coll., 1935; LL.B., Harvard U., 1938. Bar: N.Y. 1938, D.C. 1939, N.C. 1951, U.S. Dist. Ct. (we. dist.) N.C. 1951, U.S. Dist. Ct. (mid. dist.) N.C. 1953, U.S. Ct. Appeals (4th cir.) 1951, U.S. Ct. Claims 1946, U.S. Tax Ct. 1940, FCC 1939, ICC 1940, U.S. Supreme Ct. 1946. With Hanson, Lovett & Dale, Washington, 1938-41, 46-50; ptnr. Lassiter, Moore and Van Allen and Moore and Van Allen, Charlotte, N.C., 1951-87; of counsel Moore & Van Allen, Charlotte, 1988—. Permanent mem. Jud. Conf. 4th Jud. Circuit. Vestryman Episc. Ch., 1957-60, 66-69; mem. Mecklenburg County Bd. Public Welfare, 1954-59, chmn. 1957-59; bd. dirs. N.C. Found. Commerce and Industry, 1965-73, Found. U. N.C. at Charlotte, 1979-89, Charlotte Symphony Orch., 1981-82, Mercy Health Svcs., 1983-88; chmn. Charlotte Area adv. coun. Am. Arbitration Assn., 1967-76; bd. dirs. United Community Svcs., 1972-77, v.p., 1972; bd. mgrs. Charlotte Country Day Sch., 1956-61, chmn., 1959-61, bd. visitors, 1978-2004, chmn., 1987-88; bd. advisers U. N.C.-Charlotte, 1983-84; trustee Spastics Hosp., 1951-60, Mint Mus. Art, 1976-79, Surtman Found., 1955-90, Mercy Hosp. Found., 1979-84; bd. visitors Johnson C. Smith U., 1978-89; pres. Charlotte Symphony League, 1980-81, Friends of U. N.C. at Charlotte, 1990-91. Served with USNR, 1941-45, commdg. officer destroyer escort ATO and PTO; released to inactive duty as lt. comdr. Mem. ABA, Charlotte C. of C. (bd. dirs. 1971-75, v.p. 1972-75). Mil. Order of Carabao, Holland Soc. N.Y., Charlotte Country Club, Charlotte City Club, Chevy Chase Club (Md.), Mullett Lake Country Club (Mich.), Mill Reef Club, Phi Beta Kappa, Chi Psi. Office: Moore & Van Allen Ste 4700 100 N Tryon St Charlotte NC 28202-4003 Office Phone: 704-331-1021.

VAN ALLSBURG, CHRIS, author, artist; b. Grand Rapids, Mich., June 18, 1949; s. Richard Allen and Doris Marie (Christiansen) Van A.; m. Lisa Carol Morrison, Aug. 17, 1976. BFA, U. Mich., 1972; MFA, R.I. Sch. Design, 1975. Tchr. R.I. Sch. Design, Providence. Author, illustrator: The Garden of Abdul Gasazi, 1979 (Caldecott Honor Book 1980, Irma Simonton Black award Bank St. Coll. Edn. 1980, Boston Globe/Horn Book award 1980), Jumanji, 1981 (Caldecott medal 1982, Boston Globe/Horn Book award 1982, Children's Choice award Internat. Reading Assn. 1982, Am. Book award, 1982, Ky. Bluegrass award No. Ky. U. 1983, Buckeye Children's Book award Ohio State Libr. 1983, Wash. Children's Choice Picture Book award Wash. Libr. Media Assn. 1984, W. Va. Children's Book award 1985), Ben's Dream, 1982 (Parents Choice award for illustration Parents' Choice Found. 1982), Wreck of the Zephyr, 1983 (Silver medal Soc. Illustrators 1983), The Mysteries of Harris Burdick, 1984 (Parents Choice award for illustration Parents' Choice Found. 1984, Irma Simonton Black award Bank St. Coll. Edn. 1985, Boston Globe/Horn Book award 1985, World Fantasy award 1985), The Polar Express, 1985 (Parents Choice award for illustration Parents' Choice Found. 1985, Caldecott medal 1986, Boston Globe/Horn Book award 1986, Ky. Bluegrass award No. Ky. U. 1987), The Stranger, 1986 (Parents Choice award for illustration Parents' Choice Found. 1986), The Z Was Zapped: A Play in Twenty-Six Acts, 1987, Two Bad Ants, 1988, Just A Dream, 1990, The Wretched Stone, 1991, The Widow's Broom, 1992, The Sweetest Fig, 1993, The Two Figs, 1993, Bad Day at River Bend, 1995, Zathura, 2002; illustrator: Swan Lake, 1989; exhibited works at Whitney Mus. Art, N.Y.C., Mus. Modern Art, N.Y.C., Alan Stone Gallery, N.Y.C., Grand Rapids (Mich.) Art Mus., Port Washington (N.Y.) Pub. Libr.; permanent collections include Kerlan Collection at U. Minn. Recipient Hans Christian Andersen award nomination, 1985. Jewish. Office: Houghton Miffin Co 222 Berkeley St Boston MA 02116-3748

VAN ALSTYNE, VANCE BROWNELL, arbitration management consultant; b. Rochester, N.Y., Feb. 3, 1924; s. Guy and Jessie Van Alstyne; m. Jane Van Alstyne, Aug. 12, 1950; children: Cary B., Stacey E. BA, U. Rochester, 1948; LLB, Blackstone Coll. Law, 1964. Rsch. asst. Gilbert Assoc, Inc., NYC, 1950-56; corp. sec., v.p., dir. R.C. Simpson & Staff Inc., Newark and Ridgewood, NJ, 1956-74; pres., dir. R.C. Simpson, Inc., Charlotte, NC, 1975—, Ridgewood, NJ, 1975—91, Charlotte, NC, 1991—. 2d lt., navigator 12th Air Force USAF, 1943—45. Mem.: Indsl. Rels. Rsch. Assn., Am. Arbitration Assn., Atlantic Salmon Fedn. Office: RC Simpson Inc South Trust Plaza 5950 Fairview Rd Ste 604 Charlotte NC 28210-3178 E-mail: van.fsh@att.net.

VAN ALSTYNE, W. SCOTT, JR., lawyer, educator; b. East Syracuse, N.Y., Sept. 21, 1922; s. Walter Scott and Cecil Edna (Folmsbee) Van A.; m. Margaret Reed Hudson, June 23, 1949 (div.); children: Gretchen Anne, Hunter Scott; m. Marion Graham Walker, May 3, 1980. BA, U. Buffalo, 1948; MA, U. Wis., 1950, LL.B., 1953, S.JD, 1954. Bar: Wis. 1953. Assoc. Shea & Hoyt, Milw., 1954-56; asst. prof. law U. Nebr., 1956-58; pvt. practice Madison, Wis., 1958-72; prof. law U. Fla., 1973-90, prof. emeritus, 1990—; lectr. law U. Wis., 1958-72; lectr. Cambridge-Warsaw Trade Program Cambridge U. (Eng.), 1976. Vis. prof. law Cornell U., 1977, U. Leiden, The Netherlands, 1988, 91; spl. lectr. U. Utrecht, The Netherlands, 1991; vis. prof. Wake Forest U., 1997; spl. counsel Gov. of Wis., 1966-70; bd. dirs. non-resident divsn. State Bar Wis., 1981-96, pres., 1988-90, bd. govs. 1988-90. Prin. author: Goals and Missions of Law Schools, 1990; contbr. articles to profl. jours. Mem. Gov.'s Commn. on Edn., Wis., 1969-71; cons. Wis. Commn. on Legal Edn., 1995-96. Served with AUS, 1942-45, 61-62; col. Res., ret. Decorated Legion of Merit. Fellow: Wis. Bar Found. (life); mem.: Holland Soc., Sons of Revolution, Netherland Club (N.Y.C.), Madison (Wis.) Club, Ft. Rensselaer Club (N.Y.), Phi Beta Kappa, Order of Coif, Phi Delta Phi, Omicron Delta Kappa. Republican. Presbyterian. Office: U Fla Holland Law Ctr Gainesville FL 32611

VAN ANDEL, JAY, direct selling company executive; b. Grand Rapids, Mich., June 3, 1924; s. James and Nella (Vanderwoude) Van A.; m. Betty J. Hoekstra, Aug. 16, 1952 (dec. Jan. 18, 2004); children: Nan, Stephen, David, Barbara. Student, Pratt Jr. Coll., 1945, Calvin Coll., 1942, 46, Yale, 1943-44; DBA (hon.), No. Mich. U., 1976, Western Mich. U., 1979, Grand Valley State U., 1992; LLD (hon.), Ferris State Coll., 1977, Mich. State U., 1997. Co-founder, sr. chmn., owner Amway Corp. (now a subsidiary of Ada-based Alticor Inc.), Ada, Mich.; founder Van Andel Edn. and Med. Rsch., Grand Rapids, Mich. U.S. amb., commr. gen. Genoa Expo '92, 1992 World's Fair marking 500th Anniversary of Columbus Journey to Am.; chmn. bd. Amway Internat., Amway Hotel Corp., Amway Environ. Found., Nutrilite Products, Inc.; chmn. Ja-Ri Corp., Ada, Mich.; mem. adv. coun. Am. Private Edn. Participant White Ho. Conf. Indsl. World Ahead, 1972; chmn. Mich. Rep. fin. com., 1975-81; Founding chmn. Right Place Com., Grand Rapids, Mich.; mem. adv. council Nat. 4H Found.; trustee Hillsdale (Mich.) Coll., Citizens Rsch. Coun. Mich., Hudson Inst., Indpls. and Washington; dir. Jamestown Found., Gerald R. Ford Found.; bd. dirs., trustee, treas. Washington, Heritage Found., Washington; pres. Van Andel Found.; co-chmn. Mich. Botanic Garden Capital Campaign; founding chmn. Citizen's Choice, Washington; former bd. dirs. BIPAC, Washington, former chmn. Netherlands-Am. Bicentennial Commn; former mem. bd. govs. USO World. Served to 1st lt. USAAF, 1943-46; mem. U.S.O. World of Governors. Knighted Grand Officer of Orange-Nassau, The Netherlands; recipient Disting. Alumni award Calvin Coll., 1976, Golden Plate award Am. Acad. Achievement, Gt. Living Am. award and Bus. and Profl. Leader of the Yr. award Religious Heritage Am., George Washington medal of Honor Freedom Found., Gold medals Netherland Soc. of Phila. and NYC, Disting. Citizen award Northwood Inst., Patron award Mich. Found. for Arts, 1982, Achievement award UN Environment Programme, 1989, UN Environment Programme Achievement award Amway, 1989, Adam Smith Free Enterprise award Am. Legis. Exchange Coun., 1993, Disting. Svc. award Rotary Grand Rapids, Gold Medal Netherlands Soc. NY, Edison Achievement award Am. Mktg. Assn., 1994, named Bus. Person Yr. Econ. Club Grand Rapids, 1990, Clare Booth Luce award, Heritage Found., 1998, Jr. Ach. Nat. Bus. Hall of Fame, 1998, Donald Porter Humanitarian award YMCA Heritage Club, 1999; named to Grand Rapids Bus. Hall of Fame; World fellow Duke of Edinburgh's award. Mem. Sales and Mktg. Execs. Internat. Acad. Achievement (charter), Direct Selling Assn. (bd. dirs., hall of fame), U.S. C. of C. (past chmn. bd.), Right Place Com. (founding chmn.), de Tocqueville Soc. (former chmn.), Nat. Chamber Found. (dir.), Mensa Soc. USA, Peninsular Club, Cascade Hills Country Club, Lotus Club, Capitol Hill Club (Washington), Macatawa Bay Yacht Club (Holland, Mich.), Le Mirador Country Club (Switzerland), Econ. Club (Grand Rapids), Omicron Delta Kappa (hon.) Mem. Christian Reformed Ch. (elder). Home: 7186 Windy Hill Dr SE Grand Rapids MI 49546-9745 Office: Amway Corp 7575 Fulton St E Ada MI 49355-0001*

VAN ANDEL, STEVE ALAN, consumer products company executive; b. Ada, Mich., Oct. 9, 1955; BLS in Econs. and Bus., Hillsdale Coll., 1978; MBA in MKtg., Miami U., Oxford, Ohio, 1979. V.p. mktg. Amway Corp., Worldwide, chmn. exec. com. policy bd.; vice chmn. Amway Japan Ltd.; chmn. Amway Asia Pacific Ltd., Amway Corp., Ada, 1995—, CEO, 1995—. Dir. Met. Found., Operation Enterprise-AMA; bd. dirs. Met. Hosp. Found., Mich. Nat. Bank Corp., Ctr. for Internat. Pvt. Enterprises, Gerald Ford Found., Std. Fed. Bank, Grand Rapids John Ball Zoo Soc., Borgess Metro Health Alliance, Met. Health Corp.; mem. dean's adv. bd. Seidman Sch. of Bus.; co-CEO, Alticor Inc. Bd. dirs. Grand Rapids John Ball Soc., Amway Environmental Found. Mem. U.S. C. of C. (chmn. 2002). Office: Amway Corp 7575 Fulton St E Ada MI 49355-0001

VAN ANTWERPEN, FRANKLIN STUART, federal judge; b. Passaic, NJ, Oct. 23, 1941; s. Franklin John and Dorothy Van Antwerpen; m. Kathleen Veronica O'Brien, Sept. 12, 1970; children: Joy, Franklin W., Virginia. BS in Engring. Physics, U. Maine, 1964; JD, Temple U., 1967; postgrad., Nat. Jud. Coll., 1980. Bar: Pa. 1969, U.S. Dist. Ct. (ea. dist.) Pa. 1971, U.S. Ct. Appeals (3d cir.) 1971, U.S. Supreme Ct. 1972. Corp. counsel Hazeltine, Corp., N.Y.C., 1967-70; chief counsel Northampton County Legal Aid Soc., Easton, Pa., 1970-71; assoc. Hemstreet & Smith, Easton, 1971-73; ptnr. Hemstreet & VanAntwerpen, Easton, 1973-79; judge Ct. Common Pleas of Northampton County, Pa., 1979-87, U.S. Dist. Ct. (ea. dist.) Pa., Phila., 1987—2004, U.S. Ct. Appeals (3rd. cir.), 2004—. Apptd. to US Sentencing Commn. Jud. Working Group, 1992-93; apptd. to US Jud. Conf. Com. on Defender Svcs., 1997, chmn. subcom. on fed. defender funding, 2000-01; trial judge US vs. Scarfo, 1988-89; adj. prof. Northampton County Area CC, 1976-81; solicitor Palmer Twp., 1971-79; gen. counsel Fairview Savs. and Loan Assn., Easton, 1973-79; lectr. on law of evidence Pa. Bar Inst., 1985-92. Contbr. articles to Cardozo Law Rev., 1967. Recipient Booster award Bus. Indsl. and Profl. Assn., 1979, George Palmer award Palmer Twp., 1980, Citizen of Yr. award, 1981, Law Enforcement Commendation medal Nat. Soc. SAR, 1990, Disting. Alumni Achievement award Newark Acad., 2001, Law Day award Temple Law Sch. Alumni Assn., 2004; named an Alumnus Who Has Made a Difference in the World, U. Maine, 1991. Mem. ABA (com. on jud. edn.), Fed. Bar Assn. (hon.), Fed. Cir. Bar Assn., Pa. Bar Assn., Northampton County Bar Assn., Am. Judicature Soc., Fed. Judges Assn., Pomfret Club, Union League Club, Pa. Soc. Club, Sigma Pi Sigma. Office: US Courthouse 601 Market St Philadelphia PA 19106-1790 Office Phone: 610-252-6522.

VAN APPLEDORN, MARY JEANNE, composer, music educator, pianist; b. Holland, Mich., Oct. 2, 1927; d. John and Elizabeth (Rinck) van A. MusB with distinction, Eastman Sch. Music, 1948, MusM, 1950, PhD in Music, 1966; postgrad., MIT, 1982. Chmn. music theory and music composition Tex. Tech. Univ., Lubbock, 1950—, chmn., founder symposium of contemporary music, 1951-82, chmn. grad. studies in music, 1970-81, Paul Whitfield Horn prof., 1989—. Author: Keyboard Singing and Dictation Manual, 1968; composer: Suite for Carillon, 1980 (1st prize World Carillon Fedn., 1980), Set of Seven, 1988, Festival a Kerkrade, Cantata: Rising Night After Night, 1990, 7th World Congress Women in Music, 1991, Passages (Brit. Trombone Assn. award, 1996); composer: (for band) Lux: Legend of Sankta Lucia, 1982, Cacophony (Va. Coll. Band Dirs. Nat. Assn. award, 1981); composer: (for saxophone and tape) Liquid Gold, 1986 (Premio Ancona award, 1986); composer: (for viola and cello) Four Duos, 1987 (1st prize Tex. Composers Guild); composer: (for clarinet and piano) Sonatine, 1988; composer: (for trumpet and band) Concerto, 1990; composer: (for symphonic band) Opus One CD177: Cycles of Moons and Tides, 1995; composer: (for concert band) Cycles of Moons and Tides, 1995; composer: (for violin and orch.) Rhapsody, 1997; composer: (for unaccompanied SATB choir) Les hommes vides, 1996; composer: (for Native Am. flute, strings and percussion) Music of Enchantment, 1997; composer: (for violin and piano with string orch.) Terrestrial Music, 1997; composer: (for clarinet quartet) Gestures, 1999; composer: (for 2 coloratura sopranos and piano) Songs without Words, 2000; composer: (for percussion orchestra) Symphony, 2000; composer: (for trombone quartet) Miniatures, 2000; composer: (for orchestra) Meliora, 2000, A Symphony of Celebration, 2003; composer: (for bassoon and strings) Soundscapes, 2002; composer: (for clarinet, violoncello and piano) Passages III, 2003; composer: (for trombone and piano) Musique, 2003; composer: (for solo guitar) Sonata, 2003; composer: (for piano) Fantasia, 2004; composer: (for clarinet, cello, and piano) Mirrors, 2004; Octet for Bassoons, 2004. Commd. for carillon work Skybells Crystal Cath. Carillon, 1991. Recipient Internat. Trumpet Guild Brass Trio Competition award for Trio Italiano, 1996, Rhapsody for Violin and Orch., 1996, Incantations for Oboe and Piano, 1998, Five Psalms for Trumpet, Tenor Voice and Piano, 1998, Galilean Galaxies for Flute, Bassoon and Piano, 1998, Symphony for Percussion Orch., 2000, Festive Fanfare and Postlude for Trumpets, Snare Drums and Cymbals, 2000, A Symphony of Celebration, 2002, Meliora Symphony for Winds and Percussion, 2003; faculty rsch. grantee Tex. Tech. U., 1982, MIT, 1982. Mem. ASCAP (mem. ann. std. panel awards 1980-2004), Soc. Composers Inc., Internat. League Women Composers, Delta Kappa Gamma (internat. scholar 1959-60), Mu Phi Epsilon, Alpha Chi Omega, Kappa Kappa Psi, Tau Beta Sigma. Home: 1629 16th St Apt 216 Lubbock TX 79401-4703 Office: Tex Tech U PO Box 42033 Lubbock TX 79409-2033 Office Phone: 806-742-2270 ext. 230. Business E-Mail: mvanappl@ttacs.ttu.edu.

VAN ARK, JOAN, actress; d. Carroll and Dorothy Jean (Hemenway) Van A.; m. John Marshall, Feb. 1, 1966; 1 child, Vanessa Jeanne. Student, Yale Sch. Drama. Appeared at Tyrone Guthrie Theatre, Washington Arena Stage, in London, on Broadway; performances include: (stage) Barefoot in the Park, 1965, School for Wives, 1971, Rules of the Game, 1974, Cyrano de Bergerac, Ring Round the Moon, A Little Night Music, 1994, Three Tall Women, 1995, Vagina Monologues, L.A., Denver, Colo., San Diego, Calif. 2001-2002, The Exonerated, N.Y.C. 2002, (TV series) Temperatures Rising, 1972-73, We've Got Each Other, 1977-78, Dallas, 1978-81, Knots Landing, 1979-92 (also dir. episodes Letting Go, Hints and Evasions), (voice) Santa Bogito, 1995; (TV movies) The Judge and Jake Wyler, 1972, Big Rose, 1974, Shell Game, 1975, The Last Dinosaur, 1977, Red Flag, 1981, Shakedown on the Sunset Strip, 1988, My First Love, 1989, Murder at the PTA, 1990, To Cast a Shadow, 1990, Always Remember I Love You, 1990, Grand Central Murders, 1992, Tainted Blood, 1992, Someone's Watching, 1993, When the Darkman Calls, 1994, Loyal Opposition: Terror in the White House, 1998, Intimate Portrait: Michele Lee, 1999, Intimate Portrait, Joan Van Ark, 2002. Tornado Warning, 2002; (TV miniseries) Testimony of Two Men, 1978, Knots Landing: Back to the Cul-de-Sac, 1997; dir., star ABC-TV Afterschool Spl. Boys Will Be Boys, 1993; films, Frogs, 1970 Held for Ransom, 2000, UP Michigan,2001, The

Icemakers, 2002. Recipient Theatre World award, 1970-71, L.A. Drama Critics Cir. award, 1973, Outstanding Actress award Soap Opera Digest, 1986, 89. Mem. AFTRA, SAG, Actors Equity Assn., Dir. Guild of Am. Address: care William Morris Agy Inc c/o Sam Haskell 151 S El Camino Dr Beverly Hills CA 90212-2704

VAN ARNAM, MARK STEPHEN, manufacturing executive; b. Erie, Pa., Oct. 27, 1949; s. George Mark and Patricia Anne (Dunne) Van Arnam; m. Lisa Osborne; children: Emerald Scout, Mark Stephen Jr. Student, Geneseo State U., 1967-68, Daytona Beach Community Coll., 1971-73. EMT, Fla. Dir. ops. Emergency Med. Svcs., Daytona Beach, Fla., 1972-81; v.p. Wheeled Coach Industries, Orlando, Fla., 1982-91; pres. and CEO Am. Emergency Vehicles, Jefferson, N.C., 1991—, Am. Emergency VEH, 1991—, INTERFLEET, 1995—; exec. v.p. Halcore Group, 1998—. Bd. dirs. Vann Data Systems, Daytona Beach; mem. risk adv. bd. Azstar Casualty Co., Scottsdale, Ariz., 1989-92. With USN, 1967-71, Vietnam. Mem. Nat. Ambulance Mfrs. Assn. (pres. 1987-90), Am. Ambulance Assn., Calif. Ambulance Assn. Methodist. Avocation: travel. Office: Am Emergency Vehicles 165 American Way Jefferson NC 28640

VANARSDALE, DIANA CORT, social worker; b. N.Y.C., Oct. 27, 1934; d. Arthur and Augusta Deutsch; m. Leonard VanArsdale, Sept. 17, 1978; children by previous marriage: Hayley, Daniel. BS, NYU, 1955; MSW, Colmbia U., 1957. Clinician Payne Whitney Clinic, N.Y. Hosp., N.Y.C., 1957-59; clinician psychiat. clinic Jewish Bd. Guardians, N.Y.C., 1959-61; founder, pres. Bix Six Towers Nursery Sch., N.Y.C., 1962-67; dir. intake and social svc. L.I. Consultation Ctr., Forest Hills, N.Y., 1966-84, clin. dir., coord. clin. svcs., 1984-86; supr. faculty mem. L.I. Inst. Mental Health, 1981-87; dir. Srs. Option Svc., Allendale, NJ, 1980—90. Author: Transitions: A Woman's Guide To successful Retirement, 1991. Mem. NASW, N.Y. Soc. Clin. Social Workers. Home: 47-30 61st St 18C Woodside NY 11377-5763

VAN ARSDALEN, KEITH NORMAN, urologist; b. Plainfield, N.J., Sept. 26, 1951; s. Norman Charles and Thelma Marie Svendsen Van Arsdalen; children: Bryce, Leigh, Jill, Kyle. BS, Muhlenberg Coll., 1973; MMS, CMDNJ, 1975; MD, Med. Coll. Va., 1977. Intern, resident U.Md., Balt., 1977-79; resident Med. Coll. Va., Richmond, 1979-82; asst. prof. surgery, urology U. Pa., Phila., 1983-89, asst. prof. surgery, urology, radiology, 1989-97, prof. surgery, urology, radiology, 1997—. Dir. male fertility sect. U. Pa. Sch. Medicine Divsn. Urology, 1983—, dir. shock wave lithotripsy svcs., 1985—; attending urologist Children's Hosp. Phila., 1989—; chief urology sect. Phila. V.A. Med. Ctr., 1990—2001; expert adv. panel U.S. Pharm. Conv., Rockville, Md., 1990—95; mem. scientific bd. Nat. Kidney Found., N.Y.C., 1992—98. Asst. editor Jour. Endourology, 1987-2003; contbr. articles to profl. jours., chpts. to books. Recipient Paul Rodin Leberman Teaching award Urology Residents, Phila. 1993, 98, Alumni Star award Va. Commonwealth U., 1993, John Morgan Soc. award, 1998; U. Pa. NKF-AUA rsch. fellow, 1982-83. Fellow: ACS (program com. 1992); mem.: AAAS, Urodynamics Soc., Soc. Univ. Urologists, Soc. Study Male Reproduction, Soc. Study Impotence, Soc. Reproductive Surgeons, Soc. Minimally Invasive Therapy, Soc. Laparoendoscopic Surgeons, Soc. Basic Urologic Rsch., Internat. Soc. Urology, Phila. Urol. Soc. (sec.-treas. 1992—98, pres.-elect 1998—99, pres. 1999—2000), Urol. Assn. Pa., Assn. Acad. Surgery, Am. Soc. Reproductive Medicine, Am. Soc. Andrology, Am. Assn. Clin. Urologists, Am. Urol. Assn., Coll. Physicians Phila. (mid-Atlantic sect. edn. com. 1989—90, rsch. com. rep. 1990—94, local arrangements com. 1991—94, chmn. 1992—93, program com. 1996—97, rsch. com. rep. 1999—2002). Avocations: fishing, skiing, swimming, reading, house restoration. Office: Urology 9 Penn Tower 3400 Spruce St Philadelphia PA 19104-4206 Office Phone: 215-662-2891.

VAN ARSDALL, ROBERT ARMES, engineer, retired air force officer; b. Omaha, Oct. 5, 1925; s. Samuel Peter and Althea (Armes) Van A.; m. Margaret Cooper Kiersted, June 9, 1948; children— Robert Armes, Janet Althea, Susan DeBaun, Kathryn Ann. BS, U.S. Mil. Acad., 1948; postgrad., U. Colo., spring 1961; MS, George Washington U., 1968. Commd. 2d lt. USAF, 1948, advanced through grades to col., 1968; grad. Randolph AFB, Tex., 1949; assigned 5th Air Rescue Group, Westover AFB, Mass., 1949-51; student USAF Squadron Officer Sch., Maxwell AFB, Ala., 1950; pilot, ops. officer 9th Air Rescue Group, Burton-Wood, Manston and Bushy Park, Eng., 1951-55; ops. officer Hdqrs. Air Rescue Service, Orlando AFB, Fla., 1955-57; plans officer Hdqrs. Air R & D Command, Balt., also Andrews AFB, Md., 1957-60; grad. USAF jet qualification course, Randolph AFB, 1959; tng.-with-industry Air Force Inst. Tech., Martin Co., Denver, 1960-61; chief plans div. Hdqrs. Space Systems Div., L.A., 1961-63; exec. officer Office Space Systems, Office Sec. Air Force, 1963-67; assoc. Air War Coll. program, Washington, 1964-66; student Naval War Coll., 1967-68; dep. dir. Dept. Def. Manned Space Flight Support Office, Patrick AFB, Fla., 1968-69; dir. range engring., 1969-70; dir. range ops. Air Force Eastern Test Range, 1970-72; comdr. USAF Satellite Test Ctr., Sunnyvale, Calif., 1972-73; vice comdr. USAF Satellite Control Facility, L.A., 1973-74, comdr., 1974-76; staff engr. Pan Am. World Airways, Cocoa Beach, Fla., 1976-78, project dir., 1978-79, program mgr., 1980-85, dir. internat. projects, 1985-88; program dir. Diego Garcia, 1989, ret., 1989. Decorated Air Force Commendation medal with two oak leaf clusters, Legion of Merit with oak leaf cluster. Life mem. Assn. Grads. U.S. Mil. Acad.; charter mem. Nat. Soujourners, USAF Acad. Athletic Assn. Clubs: Mason, Burton-wood Air Force (gov.), Bushy Park Air Force (gov.), Orlando Air Force (gov.), Andrews Air Force (gov.), Space Systems Division Air Force (gov.). Republican. Methodist. Home: 660 Cinnamon Ct Satellite Beach FL 32937-4301 Personal E-mail: rvanarsdall@cfl.rr.com.

VANARSDALL, ROBERT LEE, JR., orthodontist, educator; b. Crewe, Va., Feb. 7, 1940; s. Robert Lee Sr. and Margie Mae (Jenkins) V.; m. Sandra E. Hoffman, Aug. 11, 1962; children: Robert Lee III, Lesley, Ashley. BA in Econs., Coll. William and Mary, 1962; DDS, Med. Coll. Va., 1970; cert. Orthodontics and Periodontics, U. Pa., 1973. Diplomate Am. Acad. Periodontology, Am. Bd. Orthodontics. Staff Children's Hosp., Phila., 1973—; prof. orthodontics, chmn. dept. orthodontics U. Pa., Phila., 1981—; prof. dentistry, chmn. Med. Coll. Pa., Phila., 1989—. K.G. prof. orthodontics U. Sydney, Australia, 2001; bd. dir. Nat. Dental Ins. Co., Denver. Editor: Internat. Jour. Adult Orthodontics and Orthognathic Surgery, 1986-2003, Orthodontoics: Current Principles and Techniques, 2d edit., 1994, 3d edit., 2000; editl. bd. profl. jours.; contbr. articles to profl. jours. Bd. dirs. Phila. Soc. William and Mary Alumni Assn. Lt. USNR, 1962-65. Fellow Coll. Physicians of Phila. 1978, Am. Coll. Dentistry 1980. Mem. ADA, Am. Assn. Orthodontists, Stomatological Club Phila., Angle Soc. Orthodontists (v.p. ea. component, pres. 2004—), Phila. Soc. Orthodontists (pres. 1989, chmn. sci. affairs coun. 1990—), Internat. Coll. of Dentists. Roman Catholic. Avocations: antiques, architecture. Home: 208 Ashwood Rd Villanova PA 19085-1504 Office: Penn Dental 34th and Market St Philadelphia PA 19104 Office Fax: 215-898-0998.

VANARSDEL, ROSEMARY THORSTENSON, English studies educator; b. Seattle, Sept. 1, 1926; d. Odin and Helen Catherine (McGregor) Thorstenson; m. Paul P. VanArsdel Jr., July 7, 1950 (dec. Jan. 1994); children: Mary M., Andrew P. BA, U. Wash., 1947, MA, 1948; PhD, Columbia U., 1961. Grad. tchg. asst. Columbia U., N.Y.C., 1948-50; acting instr. U. Wash., Seattle, 1961-63; asst. prof. U. Puget Sound, Tacoma, Wash., 1967-69, assoc. prof., 1970-77, prof. English, 1977-87, disting. prof. emeritus, 1987—, dir. Writing Inst., 1976-86, dir. semester abroad, 1977, dir. Legal English program Sch. Law, 1973-77. Vis. prof. Gonzaga U., Pacific Luth. U., Whitman Coll., Willamette U., 1977. Author: Victorian Periodicals: A Guide to Research, Vol. I, 1978, Vol. II, 1989, George Eliot: A Centenary Tribute, 1982, Victorian Periodicals and Victorian Society, 1994, Periodicals of Queen Victoria's Empire, An Exploration, 1996, Florence Fenwick Miller: Victorian Feminist, Journalist, Educator, 2001; mem. editl. bd. Wellesley Index to Victorian Periodicals, 1824-1900, 1968-88, A Union List of Victorian Serials, 1979-85, Victorian Rev., 1990—; contbr. articles to profl. jours. Recipient Doris Bronson Morrill award Kappa Kappa Gamma, 1982, Disting. Alumnae award Broadway H.S., Seattle, 1991. Fellow Royal Soc. Lit.; mem. MLA, Oxford Bibliog. Soc., Nat. Coun. Tchrs. English (Achievement awards, dir. 1974-77), Rsch. Soc. for Victorian Periodicals (pres. 1981-83). Home: 5051 50th Ave NE Apt 48 Seattle WA 98105-2863

VANARSDEL, THOMAS PAUL, architect, engineering consultant; b. Phila., July 7, 1923; s. William Campbell and Mabel Elizabeth V.; m. Carolyn Jean Beall; children: Thomas II, Peter Roland, Carolyn Sue, Richard, Kathryn Jean (dec.). BS in Sci., Purdue U., 1948; degree in Elec. Engring., U.S. Army, 1944; JD cum laude, Bernadean U., 1983. Registered profl. engr., Ind., Ohio, Miss.; registered architect, Ohio. Chief structural engr. Fanning and Howey, Celina, Ohio, 1968-74; dir. pipeline safety divsn. Pub. Svc. Commn. State of Ind., Indpls., 1976-87; engr. Rundell-Ernstberger, Muncie, Ind., 1987-97; arch. City of Fortville, Ind., 1997; pvt. practice architect, engr. Fortville, 1997—. Patentee in field; expert witness in Mich., Ohio, Ind., 1987-99. World record holder Sr. Masters Divsn. 220# class bench press competition Mem. AAAS, AIA, Nat. Soc. Profl. Engrs., Bldg. Officials Code Adminstrs. Internat., Indpls. Scientific and Engring. Found. (chmn. of ops. com.), N.Y. Acad. Scis., Indpls. Scientech. Club, Scottish Rite Mason, Murat Shrine. Home and Office: PO Box 4 Fortville IN 46040-0004

VANASEK, JAMES GEORGE, commercial banker; b. Chgo., Jan. 20, 1944; s. James Harold and Virginia Edna (Von Asch) V.; m. Deborah Ann Zaccagnini, Nov. 28, 1975. AB, Ind. U., 1966; MBA, Penn State U., 1968. Sr. v.p. Pitts. Nat. Bank, 1968-79, Banc Ohio Nat. Bank, Columbus, 1979-84; exec. v.p. First Interstate Bank of Ariz., Phoenix; chief credit officer Norwest Bank; sr. v.p., chief credit risk officer Washington Mutual Inc., 1999—2001, exec. v.p. chief credit risk officer, 2001—04, chief enterprise risk officer, 2004—. Bd. dirs. Robert Morris Assocs., Phoenix, Assn. for Corporate Growth, Phoenix. Sgt. U.S. Army Res., 1968-74. Mem. Phi Beta Kappa. Republican. Home: 20547 NE 27th Pl Redmond WA 98074-4351 Office: Washington Mutual Inc 1201 3rd Ave Seattle WA 98101

VANASKIE, THOMAS IGNATIUS, judge; b. Shamokin, Pa., Nov. 11, 1953; s. John Anthony and Delores (Wesoloski) V.; m. Dorothy Grace Williams, Aug. 12, 1978; children: Diane, Laura, Thomas. BA magna cum laude, Lycoming Coll., 1975; JD cum laude, Dickinson U., Carlisle, Pa., 1978. Bar: Pa. 1978, U.S. Dist. Ct. (mid. dist.) Pa. 1980, U.S. Ct. Appeals (3rd cir.) 1982, U.S. Supreme Ct. 1983. Law clk. to chief judge U.S. Dist. Ct. (mid. dist.) Pa., Scranton, 1978-80; assoc. Dilworth, Paxson, Kalish & Kauffman, Scranton, 1980-85, ptnr., 1986-92; prin. mem. Elliott, Vanaskie & Riley, 1992-94; dist. judge U.S. Dist. Ct. (mid. dist.) Pa., 1994—99, chief judge, 1999—. Counsel Gov. Robert P. Casey Com., Harrisburg, Pa., 1987-92; mem. Jud. Copnf. of U.S., 2003—; mem. Jud. Conf. Com. Info. Tech.; mem. Third Cir. Jud. Coun.; chair automation and tech. com. U.S. Cir. Ct. 3d cir., 2004, co-chair 3d cir. task force on info. resources, 1998—; lectr. in field. Contbr. articles to profl. jours. Mem. Scranton Waste Mgmt. Com., 1989; trustee Scranton Prep. Sch., 1997—. Recipient James A. Finnegan award Finnegan Found. Mem. Judicature, Pa. Bar Assn., Fed. Judges Assn. (bd. dirs. 1998). Democrat. Avocations: golf, reading. Office: William J Nealon Fed Bldg & US Courthouse PO Box 913 235 N Washington Ave Scranton PA 18501

VANATTA, CHESTER B. retired business executive, educator; b. Bartlesville, Oklahoma, Sept. 3, 1935; s. Benjamin Franklin and Iona Ruth (Hayes) V.; m. Patsy Lou (Straub), May 29, 1958; children: Tracy Ann, Christopher B., John Scott BS in Mktg., U. Kans., Lawrence, 1959, MS in Acctg., 1962; Advanced Mgmt. Program, Harvard U., Cambridge, Mass., 1972. Mem. staff Arthur Young and Co., Kans. City, Mo., 1962—69, regional dir, Dallas, 1969—72, ptnr., 1969—85, mng. ptnr. Chgo., 1972—76, dir., 1973—85, mng. ptnr., vice chmn. ops. N.Y.C., 1976—81, mng. ptnr., vice chmn. S.W. Region Dallas, 1981—85; exec. in residence, Paul J. Adam Disting. lectr. U. Kans. Sch. Bus., Lawrence, Mo., 1985—90; pres. Exec. Cons. Group, Lawrence, Kans., 1985—96. Bd. dir. Atlantis Plastics, Inc., Miami., Fla. Trustee Kans. U. Endowment Fund, 1983-; bd. dir. Kans. Alumni Assn., 1984-91, pres., 1986-87. Mem. AICPA, Shangri La Country Club. Democrat. Avocations: golf, seminary, travel, auctioneering, photography. Home: 29990 S 567 Rd Monkey Island OK 74331-8180 Personal E-mail: chet@aboutvanatta.com.

VAN ATTA, DAVID MURRAY, lawyer; b. Berkeley, Calif., Oct. 20, 1944; s. Chester Murray and Rosalind (Eisenstein) Van A.; m. Jo Ann Masaoka; 1 child, Lauren Rachel. BA, U. Calif., Berkeley, 1966; JD, U. Calif., Hastings, 1969. Bar: Calif. 1970. Asst. gen. counsel Boise Cascade Corp., Palo Alto, Calif., 1970-73; ptnr. Miller, Starr & Regalia, San Francisco, 1973-87, Graham & James, San Francisco, 1987-93, Hanna & Van Atta, Palo Alto, 1993—. Instr. Golden Gate U., San Francisco, 1984-85; U. Calif., Berkeley, 1976-84. Author: (with Hanna) California Common Interest Developments Law and Practice, 1999. Mem. ABA, Am. Coll. Real Estate Lawyers (bd. govs., sec.), Calif. Bar Assn. (vice chmn. exec. com. real property law sect. 1982-85, chmn. condominium and subdivsn. com. real property law sect. 1981-83), Cmty. Assn. Inst., Urban Land Inst., Anglo-Am. Real Property Inst., Rotary Club Palo Alto, Lambda Alpha Internat. Soc. Avocations: skiing, tennis, painting. Office: Hanna & Van Atta 525 University Ave Ste 705 Palo Alto CA 94301-1921

VANATTA, JOHN CROTHERS, III, physiologist, physician, educator; b. Lafayette, Ind., Apr. 22, 1919; s. John Crothers and Ida Lahr (Raub) V.; m. Carol Lee Geisler, July 30, 1944; children: Lynn Ellen, Paul Richard. BA, Ind. U., 1941, MD, 1944. Intern Wayne County Gen. Hosp., Eloise, Mich., 1944-45, resident in internal medicine, 1946-47; fellow in physiology, pharmacology Southwestern Med. Coll., Dallas, 1947-48, fellow in exptl. and internal medicine, 1948-49; instr. physiology U. Tex. Southwestern Med. Sch., 1949-50, asst. prof., 1950-53, assoc. prof., 1953-57, prof. physiology, 1957—, Robert W. Lackey prof. physiology, 1987-89; prof. physiology So. Meth. U. Dallas, Dallas, 1969-80, Baylor Coll. Dentistry, Dallas, 1992—; mem. staff Parkland Meml. Hosp., Dallas, 1953-57, VA Hosp., Dallas, McKinney, Tex., 1956-58. Cons. div. nuclear edn. tng. AEC, 1964-67 Author: Oxygen Transport, Hypoxia and Cyanosis, 1974, Fluid Balance - A Clinical Manual, 1988; contbr. articles to profl. jours. Scouter, Circle 10 Coun. Boy Scouts Am., Dallas, 1963-78; v.p. Luth. Health Care Coun. N. Tex., 1975-80, pres., 1980-81. Served as lt. (j.g.) M.C., USNR, 1945-46, PTO. Mem. AMA, AAAS, Am. Physiol. Soc., Soc. Exptl. Biology and Medicine, Phi Beta Pi, Sigma Xi, Delta Tau Delta. Lutheran (councilman 1951-91, v.p. 1974-75). Home: 10416 Remington Ln Dallas TX 75229-5262 Office Phone: 214-648-3328. Business E-Mail: john.vanatta@utsouthwestern.edu.

VANAUKEN, ALAN BRADLEY, management consultant; b. Rochester, N.Y., June 13, 1957; s. Richard Arnold and Roberta May (Ketchell) Vanauken. BS, Rensselaer Poly. Inst., 1979; MBA, Harvard U., 1984. Asst. product mgr. Hallmark Cards, Inc., Kansas City, Mo., 1984-86, project mgr., 1986-87, product devel. mgr., 1987-88, sr. new bus. strategist, 1988-90, bus. mktg. mgr., 1990-92, mktg. mgr., food team, 1992-95, dir. brand mgmt. and mktg., 1995-98; pres. Brand Forward Inc., 1999—. Ptnr., co-founder Nadier Assocs., Troy, NY, 1978—79; staff cons. Arthur Anderson & Co., N.Y.C., 1979—81, sr. cons., 1981—82; mem. adv. coun. Kellog Gradh. Sch. Mgmt., Kansas City, 1988—96; v.p. mktg. Element K, 2000—02. Author: (book) The Brand Managment Checklist, 2002, Brand Aid, 2003. Mem. adv. com. Arts Ptnrs., Kansas City, 1987—88; dist. activities chmn. Boy Scouts Am., 1995—96, coun. exec. bd., 1997—2000, coun. membership chmn., 1996—2000; mem. United Way Chmn.'s Club, 1992—; mem. com. Rochester Area Cmty. Found., 2002—; mem. exec. com., bd. dirs. Young Audiences, Inc., Kansas City, 1987—90; chmn. RPI Alumni Admissions Com., Kansas City, 1984—2000, mem. alumni addmissions steering com., 1988—94, 1998—99, vice chmn., 1990—92, chmn., 1992—94, 1998—99; bd. dirs. Advt. Coun. Rochester, 2000—. Named Product champion new products, Birthday Times, 1986, Anniversary Times, 1987; named to Top 25 (Kansas City) Up and Comers, 1997; recipient James E. West Fellowship award, 1994, various awards, Boy Scouts Am., Lantern award, Adv. Coun. Rochester, 2004. Mem.: Renesselaer Alumni Assn. (bd. dirs. 1990—99, v.p. 1994—98, Dir.'s award 1989, Alumni Key award 1994, Alumni Admissions Recognition of Excellence award 1994), Harvard Bus. Sch. Club of Rochester (bd. dirs. 2003—, v.p. 2004), Harvard Club. Presbyterian. Avocations: skiing, sailing, swimming, music, reading. Home and Office: 145 Pond Rd Honeoye Falls NY 14472-9352 Office Phone: 585-624-2043. E-mail: vanauken@brandforward.com.

VAN BAALEN, DONNA GALE, artist, retired pharmacist; b. Sterling, Colo., Jan. 29, 1930; d. Felix Thomas and Edna (Burgess) Ems; m. Chase Van Baalen, June 20, 1954 (dec. Jan. 1986); children: Patricia, Aaron, Julie. Mem.: Corpus Christi Art Guild, Art Ctr. Corpus Christi, World Fedn. Miniaturists, Hilliard Soc. Miniaturists, Miniature Art Soc. Fla., Miniature Artists Am. Home: 116 N 11 PO Box 417 Port Aransas TX 78373 E-mail: dvanbd@netscape.net.

VAN BEBBER, DAVID L. food products executive; b. Hiawatha, Kans., May 10, 1956; m. Sue Van Bebber; 4 children. BA, U. Ark., 1978, JD, 1981. Bar: Ark. 1982. Sr. v.p., dir. legal svcs. Tyson Foods Inc., Springdale, Ark., 1998—. Active Ark. Bd. Edn., Springdale, St. Thomas Episcopal Ch., Springdale. Mem.: ABA, Ark. Bar Assn. Office: Tyson Foods Inc 2210 W Oakland Dr Springdale AR 72762-6999

VANBEBBER, GEORGE THOMAS, federal judge; b. Troy, Kans., Oct. 21, 1931; s. Roy Vest and Anne (Wenner) V.; m. Alleen Sara Castellani. AB, U. Kans., 1953, LLB, 1955. Bar: Kans. 1955, US Dist. Ct. Kans. 1955, US Ct. Appeals (10th cir.) 1961, US Supreme Ct., 2003. Pvt. practice, Troy, 1955-58, 1961-82; asst. U.S. atty. Topeka, Kansas City, Kans., 1958-61; county atty. Doniphan County, Troy, 1963-69; mem. Kans. House of Reps., 1973-75; chmn. Kans. Corp. Commn., Topeka, 1975-79; U.S. magistrate Topeka, 1982-89; judge U.S. Dist. Ct., Kansas City, Kans., 1989-95, chief judge, 1995-2001. Mem. ABA, Kas. Bar Assn. Episcopalian. Office: US Dist Ct 529 US Courthouse 500 State Ave Kansas City KS 66101-2403

VAN BEEK, ALLEN LESTER, plastic surgeon; b. Westfield, N.D., Jan. 21, 1943; m. Sharon Van Beek; children: Gregory, Troy, Jeremy. MD, U. Minn., 1968. Cert. Am. Bd. Plastic Surgery, 1979. Intern Brooke Army Gen. Hosp., San Antonio, 1968—69; resident, gen. surgery Ind. U. Sch. Medicine, Indpls., 1971—75; resident, plastic surgery So. Ill. U., Springfield, 1976—78; fellow U. Louisville, 1975; clin. assoc. prof., dept. surgery U. Minn. Med. Sch., Mpls.; pres. Plastic Surgery Ednl. Found., 2003—. Flight surgeon U.S. Army, 1969—71, Vietnam. Mem.: Am. Soc. Plastic Surgeons, Am. Cleft Palate-Craniofacial Assn., Am. Coll. Surgeons, Am. Assn. Hand Surgery. Office: 7373 France Ave S Ste 510 Edina MN 55435*

VAN BELLINGHEN III, JULIAN, composer, writer, actor, film company executive; b. N.Y.C., Dec. 28, 1967; s. Carolyn Ann Zalackas. BA, SUNY, 1992. Pres. Blackstaar Entertainment, LLC, N.Y.C., 1999—. Former profl. athlete hockey. Author plays, composer. Office: Blackstaar Entertainment LLC New York NY 10001 Office Phone: 917-414-9168. Personal E-mail: blackstaarent@hotmail.com. Business E-Mail: staarfilms@hotmail.com.

VANBIESBROUCK, JOHN, professional hockey player; b. Detroit, Sept. 4, 1963; m. Rosalinde V. Vanbiesbrouck. With N.Y. Rangers, 1981—83, Vancouver Canucks, Canada, 1993, Florida Panthers, 1993—97, Phila. Flyers, 1998—. Mem. NHL All-Star Team, 1985—86; player NHL All-Star Game, 1994. Named NHL All-Star, 1985—86, Sporting News NHL All-Star, 1985—86, 1993—94; recipient Vezina Trophy (NHL Outstanding Goaltender), 1985, 1986, Terry Sawchuk Trophy, 1983—89, Tommy Ivan Trophy, 1983—84. Office: Philadelphia Flyers 3601 S Broad St One CoreStates Complex Philadelphia PA 19148

VAN BOCKSTAELE, ELISABETH JEANNE, neuroscientist, researcher; b. Paris, Jan. 4, 1965; d. Pierre Georges and Kathleen Mary (Garrish) Van B.; m. Erol Veznedaroglu, June 27, 1993; children: Lauren Kincal, Alec Tristan. BA, Sarah Lawrence Coll., Bronxville, N.Y., 1985; MS, N.Y.U., 1989; PhD, 1991. Grad. student N.Y.U., 1986-91; postdoctoral fellow Cornell U. Med. Coll., N.Y.C., 1991-93, instr. in Neuroscience, 1993-94, asst. prof. Neuroscience, 1994-96; asst. prof. Thomas Jefferson U., Phila., 1996-98, assoc. prof., 1998—. Author: Central Neural Mechanisms in Cardiovascular Regulation, 1991; contbr. articles to profl. jours. Named NARSAD Young Investigator Nat. Alliance for Rsch. on Schizophrenia and Depression, 1994-96; recipient NIDA First award Nat. Inst. on Drug Abuse, 1994-99, Established Investigatorship award Am. Heart Assn., 1996, a.e. Bennett award Soc. Biol. Psychiatry, 1999. Mem. Soc. for Neuroscience. Office: Thomas Jefferson Univ Dept Pathology & Cell Biol 1020 Locust St Rm 520 Philadelphia PA 19107-6731

VAN BOKKELEN, JOSEPH SCOTT, prosecutor; b. Chgo., June 7, 1943; s. Robert W. and W. Louise (Reynolds) Van B.; m. Sally Wardall Huey, Aug. 14, 1971; children— Brian, Kate. B.A., U. Ind., 1966, J.D., 1969. Bar: Ind. 1969, U.S. Dist. Ct. (so. dist.) Ind. 1969, U.S. Dist. Ct. (no. dist.) Ind. 1973, U.S. Ct. Appeals (7th cir.) 1973, U.S. Supreme Ct. 1973. Dep. atty. gen. State of Ind., Indpls., 1969-71, asst. atty. gen., 1971-72; asst. U.S. atty. No. Dist. Ind., Hammond, 1972-75; ptnr. Goldsmith, Goodman, Ball & Van Bokkelen, Highland, Ind., 1975—2001; U.S. atty. Ind. No. Dist., 2001-. Recipient Outstanding Asst. U.S. Atty. award U.S. Dept. Justice, 1974. Mem. ABA, Fed. Bar Assn., Ind. Bar Assn., Criminal Def. Lawyers Assn. Office: 1001 Main St Ste A Dyer IN 46311-1234 Home: 1744 Poplar Ln Munster IN 46321-3849

VAN BORTEL, MARY CATHERINE, sales executive; d. Howard Van B. Sales mgr. John Holtz Mercedes Banz-BMW, until 1985; used car sales, 1985-91; owner Can Bortel Subaru, 1991—. Office: Van Bortel Motorcar Inc 6327 Rte 96 Victor NY 14564

VANBRODE, DERRICK BRENT, IV, trade association administrator; b. Elgin, Ill., Sept. 3, 1940; Grad., N.Y. Inst. Criminology, 1963. Sr. v.p. Am. Fraternal Programmers, Inc., North Miami, Fla., 1977—. Mgmt. cons. Am. Fedn. Police, Am. Law Enforcement Officers Assn., Nat. Assn. Chiefs of Police, Am. Police Acad. Editor: Who's Who in American Law Enforcement, 1976-93, Crime Watch mag, 1981—, Police Times/Command, 1975—. Pres. Greater Miami Assn. Licensed Beverage Owners, 1973— . Decorated Grand Cross Knights of St. Michael; comdr. Royal Knights of Justice. Mem. Greater North Port Fla. C. of C. (founder, pres.) Clubs: Miami Millionaires (founder, past pres.), Millionaires Internat. (pres. 1983—), Miami Shores Country, Racquet. Office: 6350 Horizon Dr Titusville FL 32780 Home: 3547 S Washington Ave Titusville FL 32780-5613

VAN BROEKHOVEN, ROLLIN ADRIAN, federal judge; b. Dallas, June 3, 1940; s. Harold and Loraine (Chafer) Van B.; m. Diana Gullett, Oct. 6, 1962; children: Gretchen, Heidi. BS, Wheaton Coll., 1962; JD cum laude, Baylor U., 1968; LLM, George Washington U., 1975; DPhil, Oxford U., 1991, DLitt, 1993; DPS (hon.), Gordon Coll., 1997. Bar: Tex. 1968, U.S. Ct. Mil. Appeals 1970, U.S. Ct. Claims 1970, U.S. Supreme Ct. 1975. Commd. 2d lt. U.S. Army, 1962, advanced through grades to maj., 1969; trial atty. Ft. Hood, Tex., 1968-70, Heidelberg, West Germany, 1970-71; gen. counsel U.S. Army Procurement Agy., Frankfurt, West Germany, 1971-74; asst. gen. counsel Dept. Army, Washington, 1975-77, resigned, 1977; dep. counsel NAVSUP, Dept. Navy, Washington, 1977-80; judge Armed Svcs. Bd. Contract Appeals, Washington, 1980—. Editor-in-chief Baylor Law Rev., 1968; contbg. author textbooks; contbr. articles to legal jours. Pres. PTA, Frankfurt, 1972-74; mem. Frankfurt Cmty. Adv. Coun., 1972-74; mem. Child Abuse Coun., Killeen, Tex., 1968-69; elder, chmn. Evang. Free Ch., Manassas, Va., 1980-84; bd. dirs. Trinity Sem., Deerfield, Ill., 1982-88; trustee Outreach, Inc., Grand Rapids, Mich., 1977-95; mem. gen. bd. Evang. Free Ch. of Am., 1982-88, mem. stds. com. Evans Coun. for Fin. Accountability, 1982—; bd. regents, bd. incorp mems Dallas Theol. Seminary, 1988—; chmn. stds. com., bd. dirs. Evang. Coun. Fin. Accountability, 1982—. Recipient Spl. Recognition award Mariano Galvez U., Guatemala, 1984; decorated in svc. Mem. ABA, FBA, Tex. Bar Assn., Contract Appeals Judges Assn. (bd. dirs.), Oxford Soc. Scholars (chmn.). Republican. Home: 8026 Whitting Dr Manassas VA 20112-4705

VAN BRUNT, ARTHUR HOFFMAN (PETER), economist, educator; b. Orange, Nj, May 27, 1942; s. Arthur Hoffman Van Brunt, Jr. and Mary Emily Van Brunt; m. Debi Sue Stec, Oct. 10, 1999; children: Justin, Kristina Elena. BA in Econs., Tufts Univ., 1965; MBA, Wharton Sch., 1967. Coop. vol. Peace Corps, Barquisimito, Venezuela, 1967—69; tng. ctr. dir. BASICO, Inc., San Jose, Costa Rica, 1970—75; asst. v.p. Manufacturer's Hanover Trust Co.,

NYC, 1976—80; dir., strategic planning Save the Children Fedn., Westport, Conn., 1980—84; regional manager-latin am. CARE, Inc., NYC, 1984—89; assoc. prof. SUNY, Delhi, 1990 . Cons. CARE, Inc., NYC, 1991, Save the Children Fedn., Westport, 1992—93, Lawyers in Delaware County, NY, 1991—. Contbr. articles to profl. jours. Treas., v.p., pres., adv. bd. mem. Habitat for Humanity, Delaware County, NY, 1990; treas., v.p., exec. bd. United U. Professors of Delhi, Delhi, 2000. Mem.: Nat. Bus. Edn. Assn., Tchrs. of Acctg. at Two Yr. Colls. Avocations: reading, bicycling, chess, tennis. Home: 28 Main St Apt 7 Delhi NY 13753 Office: SUNY Sanford Hall Delhi NY 13753 E-mail: vanbruap@delhi.edu.

VAN BRUNT, EDMUND EWING, physician; b. Oakland, Calif., Apr. 28, 1926; s. Adrian W. and Kathryn Anne (Shattuck) Van B.; m. Claire Monod, Feb. 28, 1949; children: Karin, Deryk, Jahn. BA in Biophysics, U. Calif., Berkeley, 1952; MD, U. Calif., San Francisco, 1959; ScD (hon.), U. Toulouse, France, 1978. Postdoctoral fellow NIH, 1961-63; rsch. assoc. U. Calif., San Francisco, 1963-67; staff physician Kaiser Permanente Med. Ctr., San Francisco, 1964-91; dir. div. rsch. Kaiser Permanente Med. Program, Oakland, Calif., 1979-91; assoc. dir. Kaiser Found. Rsch. Inst., Oakland, 1985-91, sr. cons., 1991—; Kaiser Permanente Med. Program No. Calif. region. Adj. prof. U. Calif., San Francisco, 1975-92; chmn. instnl. rev. bd. Kaiser Permanente No. Calif. region, 1986—; pres. bd. trustees French Found. Med. Rsch. and Edn., San Francisco, 1994-98. Contbr. articles to profl. books and jours. With U.S. Army, 1944-46; mem. bd. dirs Almaeda County Meals on Wheels, 2004—. Fellow ACP, Am. Coll. Med. Informatics; mem. Calif. Med. Assn., U. Calif. San Francisco Emeritus Faculty Assn. Avocations: flying, photography, swimming. E-mail: e.vanbrunt@comcast.net.

VAN BRUNT, GARY T. consumer products company executive; Asst mgr. to mgr., 2d Phoenix store Discount Tire, Scottsdale, Ariz., 1970—77, asst. v.p. Ariz. region, 1977—80, v.p. purchasing, We. region, 1980—85, sr. v.p. purchasing, all regions, 1985—97, exec. v.p. co. ops., 1997—99, CEO, 1999—. Office: Discount Tire 14631 N Scottsdale Rd Scottsdale AZ 85254

VAN BRUNT, WILLIAM A. lawyer, business executive; m. Gail Van Brunt; 3 children. Grad. with honors, Pa. State U.; grad., MIT, Boston U., Harvard U. Sr. v.p., gen. counsel Carlson Cos., Minnetonka, Minn., 2000—. Office: Carlson Cos 701 Carlson Pkwy Minnetonka MN 55305

VAN BRUNT-BARTHOLOMEW, MARCIA ADELE, retired social worker; b. Chgo., Oct. 21, 1937; d. Dean Frederick and Faye Lila (Greim) Slauson; m. Orris E. Bartholomew; children: Suzanne, Christine, David. Student, Moline (Ill.) Pub. Hosp. Sch. Nursing, 1955—57; BA with disting. scholastic record, U. Wis., Madison, 1972, MSW, 1973. Social worker divsn. cmty. svcs. Wis. Dept. Health Social Svcs., Rheinlander, 1973, regional adoption coord., 1973—79, chief adoption and permanent planning no. region, 1979—83, asst. chief direct svcs. and regulation no. region, 1983—84; adminstr., clin. social worker No. Family Svcs., Inc., 1984—2003; ret. Counselor, psychotherapist, pub. spkr., cons. in field of clin. social work. Fed. tng. grantee, U. Wis., Madison, 1973. Home: 5264 Forest Ln Rhinelander WI 54501-7900 E-mail: barmar@charter.com. *The greatest and most immediate resource a person has to use is herself. Learning how to be a resource to yourself and others is a constant process. When there are setbacks in life, allow time to react and regroup. Then find a way to change the setback into a move forward by using it as an impetus to make a positive change in life.*

VANBRUNT-KRAMER, KAREN, business administration educator; b. Milw., May 1, 1934; D. Roy Charles and Viola Marguerita (Yerges) VanBrunt; m. Allen Lloyd Weitermann (div. 1963); 1 child, Tera Lee Johnson; m. Keith Kramer (div. 1979); children: Holden Jon, Stafford James. BS, U. Wis., 1956; MA, NYU, 1976; PhD, Ohio State U., 1992. Owner Design By Karen Lee, Larchmont, N.Y., 1975-82; interior designer Maurice Vallency Design, N.Y.C., 1976-79; grad. rsch. assoc. Ctr. on Edn. and Tng. for Employment, Columbus, Ohio, 1987-92; assoc. prof. bus. adminstrn. St. Joseph Coll., West Hartford, Conn., 1992-99. Lectr. and curriculum developer entrepreneurship state vocat. schs., high schs., colls., and univs. throughout U.S. and Ea. Europe, 1987-92; instr. Berkeley Sch., White Plains, N.Y., 1968-82; adj. prof. N.Y.C. C.C., 1979-83, Milw. Area Tech. Coll., 1983-85, Columbus (Ohio) State C.C., 1986-90, Capital U., Columbus, 1998, U. Wis. Milw., Mt. Mary Coll., Milw.; participant Women in Soc. Citizen Amb. Program to China, 1997, leader Women in Exec. Mgmt. Bus., 1998; mem. Inst. World Affairs, U. Wis., Milw., 1999—. Mem. Wadsworth Atheneum, Hartford, 1992—99, West Hartford Art League, 1993—99; vol. U. Conn. Health Ctr., Farmington, Little Sisters of the Poor, St. Joseph Residence, Enfield, Conn., 1989—92, Milw. Art Mus.; docent Columbus Symphony Orch., 1986—92; mem. women's guild First Cmty. Ch., Columbus, 1985—92. Mem. AAUP (membership chair 1993-97), AAUW (past social chair Wis. br.), NAFE, World Affairs Coun., Am. Vocat. Assn., Ohio Vocat. Assn., Coalition for Effective Orgns., Am. Mktg. Assn., Am. Mgmt. Assn., Nat. Edn. Ctr. for Women in Bus., World Federalist Assn. (Milw. sec./treas. 2001—), Phi Beta Kappa, Phi Kappa Phi, Phi Lambda Theta, Phi Delta Kappa, Delta Pi Epsilon, Omicron Tau Theta. Avocations: theater, art, music, photography, ice dancing. Home: 125 N University Dr Unit 322S West Bend WI 53095-2954

VAN BUITEN, ROBERT D. aerospace engineer; b. Paterson, NJ, Feb. 18, 1927; s. Jerrien and Nellie Ruhling (Bogert) Van Buiten; m. Phyllis Nerine Stoutenburgh, Oct. 14, 1950; children: Lauren, Gregory, Suzanne, Christopher. Degree in mech. engring., Stevens Inst. Tech., 1949. Rocket test engr. Curtiss-Wright Corp., Caldwell, NJ, 1949—51; subcontract engr. Goodyear Aircraft Corp., Glenn L. Martin Co., Hamilton Std. UTC, Engring. Rsch. Corp., 1951—57; advanced engring. mgr. Martin Marietta Corp., Balt., 1957—65; spacecraft program mgr. IBM Corp., Bethesda, Md., 1965—70, divsn. planner Gaithersburg, Md., 1965—70; owner, cons. Van Buiten & Assocs., Columbia, Md., 1971—. Editor: NAS, 1961; author: These Had Thrones, 1972, 2001, Keepin Up Kulchur: John Adams and Sidney Canier Build Pound's Cantos, 2001, 2004, Edward Coke's Impact on the Cantos, 2002; editor: (report) Nat. Acad. Scis. With USN, 1943—46, PTO. Mem.: AIAA, Am. Rocket Soc. Achievements include design of USAF X24-a manned research aircraft, precursor to current NASA space shuttle; high temperature brittle materials; advanced engineering managment of GEMNI 2 man spacecraft rocket launcher, precursor to history's first manned moon landings; research in individual midlife optimization or change in careers (50+ clients) in technology industries; specialize in successful college graduates with previous successes, needing to enrich future careers. Avocations: architecture, sailing, music, history. Home: 10752 Faulkner Ridge Cir Columbia MD 21044

VAN BULCK, HENDRIKUS EUGENIUS, accountant; b. Beek en Donk, The Netherlands, Dec. 13, 1950; came to U.S., 1972; s. Marcellus Maria and Josephina Theodora (Koelman) Van B.; m. Margaret West, Aug. 7, 1976; children: Marcel Allen, Sydney Josette. Grad., Nijenrode, The Netherlands, 1972; MBA, U. Ga., 1974, PhD in Bus. Adminstrn., 1979. CPA, S.C. Instr. U. S.C., Sumter, 1975-77; asst. prof. Clemson (S.C.) U., 1977-80; chmn. dept., assoc. prof. St. Andrew's Presbyn. Coll., Laurinburg, N.C., 1980-83; staff acct. L. Allen West, CPA, Sumter, 1983-84; ptnr. West & Van Bulck, CPAs, Sumter, 1984-88, Van Bulck & Co., Sumter, 1989—. Part time instr. U. S.C., Sumter, 1983-85; cons. med. practice mgmt./bus. valuations. Contbr. articles to profl. jours. Chmn. Make-a-Wish Found., Midlands, S.C., 1983-90; asst. scout master and dist. com. chmn. Boy Scouts Am.; treas. YMCA, Sumter, S.C.; mem. exec. com. Pee Dee Area Coun. Recipient Mktg. award Netherlands Ctr. of Dirs., 1972. Mem. AICPA (accredited in bus. valuation 1999), S.C. Assn. CPAs, Ga. Soc. CPAs, Physicians Viewpoint Network, Kiwanis (pres. Sumter chpt. 1996-97), Med. Group Mgmt. Assn., Beta Gamma Sigma. Presbyterian. Avocations: sailing, photography. Home: 234 Haynsworth PO Box 1327 Sumter SC 29151-1327 Office: Van Bulck & Co CPAs 15 Broad St Sumter SC 29150-4224 Office Phone: 803-775-3000. Business E-Mail: hennie@vanbulckCPAs.com.

VAN BUREN, ABIGAIL (JEANNE PHILLIPS), columnist, lecturer; b. Mpls., Apr. 10, 1942; d. Morton and Pauline (Friedman) Phillips, (the founder of the Dear Abby advice column in 1956). Student, U. Colo., 1960—62. Writer Dear Abby Radio Show, CBS, 1965—71; columnist Dear Abby, 1987—. Bd. mem. Planned Parenthood of Los Angeles, 1989—90; life-time cons. Group for Advancement of Psychiatry, 1995—; bd. adv. Alzheimers Assn. of Los Angeles, 1996—; bd. mem. Rose and Jay Phillips Found., 1991—, ACLU of So. Calif. Found., 1998—; adv. bd. L.A. Internat. Women's Media Found. Courage in Journalism, 2000—; bd. adv. UCLA Med. Ctr., Ctr. for Rsch. and Training in Humane and Ethical Med. Care (CHEC), 2000—. Lifetime cons. Group for Advancement of Psychiatry, 1995—; bd. advisors Alzheimer's Assn. of L.A., 1996—; adv. bd. L.A. Internat. Women's Media Found. Courage in Journalism, 2000—; bd. advisors UCLA Med. Ctr., Ctr. for Rsch. and Tng. in Humane and Ethical Care (CHEC), 2000—; mem. nat. adv. coun. Alzheimer's Assn., 2004—; bd. dirs. Planned Parenthood of L.A., 1989—90, Rose and Jay Phillips Found., 1991—, ACLU of So. Calif. Found., 1998—, MADD, 2003—, Children's Rights Coun., 2003—. Recipient Generations of Choice award, Planned Parenthood of L.A., 1999, Minority Organ/Tissue Transplant Edn. Program (MOTTEP) Key of Life award, Howard U., Wash. D.C., 2000, Award of Appreciation, U.S. Gen. Svcs. Adminstrn. Fed. Consumer Info. Ctr., 2000, Star on Hollywood Walk of Fame for Dear Abby Radio Show, 2001, Recognition by the Office of Nat. Drug Control Policy (ONDCP), award from the White House and Substance Abuse and Mental Health Svcs. Adminstrn. for help in launching Nat. Inhalants and Poisons Awareness Week, 2001, Erasing the Stigma Leadership award, Didi Hirsch Mental Health Ctr., 2001, MOTTEP Award of Excellence, 2001, Commendation for Operation Dear Abby and OperationDearAbby.net, Dept. Navy and USMC, 2002, Appreciation for support of the military svc. mems. of the U.S. for Operation Dear Abby and OperationDearAbby.net, Space and Naval Warfare Sys. Ctr. (SPAWAR), 2002, Alzheimer's Assn. Maureen Reagan Advocacy Award, 2003, Appreciation award, Overeaters Anonymous, 2003, Advocacy award, Alzheimer's Assn. L.A., 2003, award of Appreciation, U.S. GSA Fed. Citizen Info. Ctr., 2004. Mem.: Nat. Adv. Counc., Alzheimers Assn., 2004-, Nat. Planned Parenthood bd. Syndicated in the U.S., Brazil, Mex., Japan, Philippines, Fed. Republic Germany, India, Holland, Denmark, Can., Korea, Thailand, Italy, Hong Kong, Taiwan, Ireland, Saudi Arabia, Greece, France, Dominican Republic, P.R., Costa Rica, U.S. Virgin Islands, Bermuda, and Guam; published on the Internet at DearAbby.com and OperationDearAbby.net for messages to the military. Office: Philips-Van Buren Inc Ste 2710 1900 Ave of the Stars Los Angeles CA 90067

VANBUREN, DENISE DORING, corporate communications executive; b. Troy, N.Y., May 15, 1961; d. James L. and Eunice A. (Myers) Doring; m. Steven Paul VanBuren, Apr. 1, 1989; children: Schuyler Paul, Troy James Doring, Brett Steven VanBuren. BA in Mass Comm. magna cum laude, St. Bonaventure U., 1983; MBA, Mount St. Mary Coll., 1997. Reporter, news anchor Sta. WGNY-AM-FM, Newburgh, NY, 1984; news dir., anchor News-Ctr. 6, Dutchess County, NY, 1985-90; dir. media rels. Ctrl. Hudson Gas & Electric, Poughkeepsie, NY, 1993—, mgr. corp. comms., 1998-99, asst. v.p. corp. comm., 1999-2000, v.p. corp. comm. and cmty. rels., 2000—. Adj. prof. Marist Coll., Poughkeepsie, NY. Co-author: Historic Beacon, 1998, Beacon Revisited, 2003. Councilwoman City of Beacon, 1992-93, chmn. 85th anniversary celebration; pres. Beacon Hist. Soc., 1989-94; bd. dirs. Locust Grove Hist. Site, Stony Kill Found., Inc. Recipient Salute to Women in Bus. & Industry award D.C. YWCA, 1990, 97, Outstanding Chpt. Regent award N.Y. State orgn. DAR, 1999; named Vol. of Yr. award, City of Beacon, 1999. Mem.: DAR (vice regent Melzingah chpt. 1990—98, regent 1998—2001, chmn. state historian com. NY state 1998—2001, nat. chmn. PR 1999—2004, editor-in-chief, Am. Spirit mag.), Greater So. Dutchess C. of C. (bd. dirs.), Nat. Soc. Daus. of Union Vets. of the Civil War, Exch. Club of So. Dutchess (bd. dirs.). Republican. Roman Catholic. Avocations: genealogy, needlecrafts. Office: CH Energy Group Inc 284 South Ave Poughkeepsie NY 12601-4838

VANBUREN, MICHAEL PAUL, music educator; b. Oswego, N.Y., Feb. 20, 1976; s. Keith Glenn VanBuren and Dawn Marie Whitney; m. Beth Haughey, Sept. 4, 1999. BA in Music Edn., Syracuse U., 1998; M in Music Edn., U. Mass., 2003. Cert. music tchr. Pa. Music tchr. Lawrence (Mass.) Pub. Schs., 1998—2001, Centennial Sch. Dist., Warminster, Pa., 2001—. Mem.: Music Educators Nat. Conf. Democrat. Avocations: bicycling, genealogy. Home: 209 Yellowstone Rd Plymouth Meeting PA 19462 Office: Centennial Sch Dist 433 Centennial Rd Warminster PA 18974 Personal E-mail: mvanburen@hotmail.com.

VAN BUREN, WILLIAM BENJAMIN, III, retired pharmaceutical company executive; b. Bklyn., Mar. 25, 1922; s. William Benjamin and Dorothy Marjorie (Way) Van B.; m. Joan Cottrell Whitford, Sept. 11, 1948 (dec. June 1997); children— Susan (dec.), Patricia, William S., Richard W.; m. Norma A. Sutton, Mar. 6, 1999. BA, Washington and Lee U., 1944; LLB, Yale U., 1949. Bar: N.Y. 1950. V.p., sec. Merck & Co., Inc., 1976-86; pres. Merck & Co. Found., 1982-86. Served with USNR, 1943-46. Mem. Phi Beta Kappa. Home: 600 Furlong Dr Austin TX 78746-4126

VAN BURKLEO, BILL BEN, osteopath, emergency physician; b. Tulsa, Nov. 21, 1942; s. Walter Russell and Joan Vera (Brimm) Van B.; m. Paula Mae Brinkley, Mar. 5, 1965 (div. Feb. 1974); children: Baron, Kristy and Kelly (twins). BS, U. Tulsa, 1965; DO, Okla. State U., 1981. Diplomate Nat. Bd. Osteo. Examiners. Defensive back, quarterback, punter Can. Football League, Ottawa, Calgary, 1966-73; dir. sports and spl. events Tulsa Cable TV, 1974-78; rotating intern Corpus Christi (Tex.) Osteo. Hosp., 1981-82; family physician Antlers (Okla.) Med. Clinic, 1982-90, Colbert (Okla.) Med. Clinic, 1989-90; dir. dept. emergency Valley View Regional Hosp., Ada, Okla., 1990-97; regional med. dir. Okla., N.Mex., Ariz., Calif. Okla. Spectrum Emergency Care, Inc., 1994-97; dir. emergency dept. Carl Albert Hosp., AOA, Ada, Okla., 1997—. Mem. clin. faculty Coll. Osteo. Medicine, Okla. State U.; dir. emergency svcs. Chickasaw Indian Nation, 1997-99; v.p. med. affairs Annashne Corp., 1999—; lectr. U. Hefei MEd. Sch., China. Author newspaper column, several computer programs. Mem. Rep. Senatorial Inner Ctr., Washington, 1990-99 (medal of Freedom 1994, 99); affiliate faculty Am. Heart Assn. Named to Alltime Greats of Okla., Jim Thorpe Award Com., 1975. Fellow Assn. Emergency Physicians; mem. Am. Assn. Physician Specialists, Am. Osteo. Assn., Am. Coll. Family Practice, Okla. Osteo. Assn., S.W. Okla. Osteo. Assn. (pres. 1990-91). Avocations: tennis, flying, sailing. Home: PO Box 181199 Corpus Christi TX 78480-1199 E-mail: vanb@brightok.net.

VAN BUSKIRK, JAMES EDWARD, librarian, writer; b. L.A., Aug. 29, 1952; s. Edward Riley Van Buskirk and Anne Marie Van Buskirk (nee Burns). BA in Sociology, U. Calif., 1977, MLS, 1981. Program mgr., James C. Hormel Gay & Lesbian Ctr. San Francisco Pub. Libr., 1992—. Co-author: Gay by the Bay: A History of Queer Culture in the San Francisco Bay Area (Lambda Lit. award nominee, 1997); contbr.: San Francisco Almanac, Best of San Francisco, Knopf Guide California, Contemporary Gay American Poets and Playwrights, anthology Liberating Minds: The Stories and Professional Lives of Gay, Lesbian, and Bisexual Librarians and their Advocates, bibliography Bibliography of Gay and Lesbian Art, anthology Dangerous Families: Queer Writers on Surviving. Office: San Francisco Pub Libr 100 Larkin St San Francisco CA 94102 E-mail: jvanbuskirk@sfpl.org.

VAN BUSKIRK, WILLIAM CHARLES, engineering educator; b. Mayfield, Utah, Mar. 11, 1942; s. Ellis Cornelius Van Buskirk and Edith Whitlock; m. Joyous Ann Moore, June 4, 1964; children: William Charles Van Buskirk, Jr., Christopher Todd. BS, U.S. Mil. Acad., West Point, N.Y., 1964; MS, Stanford U., Calif., 1966; PhD, Stanford U., 1970. Registered profl. engr., La., 1972. Prof. and head of biomed. engring. Tulane U., New Orleans, 1977—91, dean of engring., 1991—98; provost N.J. Inst. of Tech., Newark, 1998—2004, disting. prof., 2004—. Fellow: Am. Inst. of Med. and Biol. Engring., ASME. Home: 94 Washington Ave Carteret NJ 07008 Office: New Jersey Institute of Technology Department of Biomedical Engineering Newark NJ 07102 Office Phone: 973-596-8380. Personal E-mail: vanb@comcast.net. E-mail: vanbuskirk@njit.edu.

VANBUTSEL, MICHAEL R. real estate broker, builder and developer; b. Alma, Nebr., Dec. 7, 1952; s. Julius and Margaret (McCorkle) VanB.; m. Susan VanButsel; children: Vanessa, Stephanie, Jamie, Krysta, Alexis. BArch, U. Nebr., 1975. Lic. real estate broker, Fla. Asst. to v.p. constrn. cen. adminstrn. U. Nebr., Lincoln, 1975-76; architect Consol. Architects Engrs., Omaha, 1976-77; archtl. project mgr. Dana, Larson, Roubal Architects, Phoenix, 1977-79; mktg. dir. Dick, Fritsche Architects, Phoenix, 1979-81; mktg. mgr. Lendrum Design Group, Phoenix, San Diego, 1982-85; owner Developers Mgmt. Group, Phoenix, 1985-86; contracts mgr. Turner Constrn., Phoenix, 1986-87; v.p. devel. The Bay Plaza Co., C.J.C. Nichols Co., St. Petersburg, Fla., 1987-96; COO, exec. v.p. Internat. Care Mgmt., Inc., St. Petersburg, 1996-98; pres. North Star Devel., St. Petersburg, 1998—; real estate mgr., v.p., designated broker Mida Group, Danka, Corp. Real Estate Svcs., St. Petersburg, 1998-99; v.p., group environ. dir. Skanska USA Bldg. Co., Tampa, Fla., 1999—2004; project exec. Bovis Lend Lease, Inc., 2004—. Vice chair Environ. Devel. Commn., St. Petersburg, 2002-03, chair, 2003—; chair cmty. advancement coun. U. So. Fla., St. Petersburg, 1998—2004. Commr. Housing Commn., City of Phoenix; mem. Paradise Valley Planning Com.; bd. dirs. Am. Stage Theater, Cmty. Water Leadership Program; chmn. facilities and strategic planning com. U. South Fla., St. Petersburg, 1999—2002, chmn. acad. planning com.; bd. dirs. Pinellas Econ. Devel. Coun.; vice-chair environ. adv. com. S.W. Fla. Water Mgmt. Dist., 2002—; Pinellas adv. bd. ARC; allocations com. United Way, 1998—2000; mem. Real Estate Investment Coun., St. Petersburg USA and Russia Birthday Commemoration, 2002—03, Pinellas County Transp. Task Force, Pinellas Redevel. Task Force; mem. pres. search com. U. South Fla., St. Petersburg; chair legis. affairs com. devel. coun. All Children's Hosp.; pres. Mariners for Sen. John McCain, Ariz.; surrogate spkr. for Congressman Eldon Rudd; mem. Senate roundtable Sen. Connie Mack, Fla.; Westside campaign chair Rick Baker for Mayor, 2001; mem. Ivory Club Pinellas County Rep. Party, 2001—, Pinellas County Assembly, 2002; bd. dirs. Gran Prix St. Petersburg 2003 Found.; mem. Gulf Coast Museum of Art. Mem. Fla. Gulfcoast Comml. Assn. Realtors, Pinellas Leadership (mem. selection com. 2003), Leadership Tampa Bay, St. Petersburg C. of C. (chair environ. com., chair transp. com.), Valley Leadership (Phoenix)., Nat. Assn. Office and Indsl. Parks. Republican. Avocations: gourmet cooking, geo-political books, tai chi. Office: Bovis Lend Lease Inc 4510 Oak Fair Blvd Ste 210 Tampa FL 33710 Office Phone: 813-621-1628. Home Fax: 941-776-5670; Office Fax: 813-621-1506. Personal E-mail: michaelvb4@yahoo.com. Business E-Mail: michael.vanbutsel@bovislendlease.com.

VAN CAMP, BRIAN RALPH, judge; b. Halstead, Kans., Aug. 23, 1940; s. Ralph A. and Mary Margaret (Bragg) Van C.; m. Diane D. Miller, 1992; children: M. Megan, Laurie E. AB, U. Calif., Berkeley, 1962, LLB, 1965. Bar: Calif. 1966. Dep. atty. gen., State Calif., 1965-67; agy. atty. Redevel. Agy., City of Sacramento, 1967-70; asst./acting sec. Bus. and Trans. Agy., State of Calif., 1970-71; commr. of corps. State of Calif., Sacramento, 1971-74; partner firm Diepenbrock, Wulff, Plant & Hannegan, Sacramento, 1975-77, Van Camp & Johnson, Sacramento, 1978-90; sr. ptnr. Downey, Brand, Seymour & Rohwer, 1990-97; judge Superior Ct., Sacramento County, 1997—. Lectr. Continuing Edn. Bar, Practicing Law Inst., Calif. CPA Soc., Calif. Jud. Edn. Rsch. Contbr. articles to profl. jours. Mem. Rep. State Ctrl. Com. Calif., 1974-78; mem. electoral coll. Presdl. Elector for State of Calif., 1976; mem. Calif. Health Facilities Fin. Authority, 1985-89; mem. Capital Area Devel. Authority, 1989-97, chmn., 1990-97; mem. Calif. Jud. Coun. Task Force on Quality of Justice, 1998-99, Jud. Coun. Adv. Com. on Civil and Small Claims Law, 2002—; bd. dirs. Sacramento Symphony Assn., 1973-85, Sacramento Symphony Found., 1993-2003, Sacramento Area Commerce and Trade Orgn., pres. 1986-87, Sacramento Valley Venture Capital Forum, 1986-90, League to Save Lake Tahoe, 1988-95, Valley Vision, Inc., 1993-97; elder Fremont Presbyn. Ch., 1967-. Recipient Sumner-Mering Meml. award Sacramento U. Calif. Alumni Assn., 1962, Thos. Jefferson award Am. Inst. Pub. Svc., 1994, Excellence in Achievement award Calif. Alumni Assn., 1997; named Outstanding Young Man of Yr., Sacramento Jaycees, 1970, Internat. Young Man of Yr., Active 20-30 Club Internat., 1973, Judge of Yr., Sacramento Consumers Attys., 2003. Mem. Boalt Hall Alumni Assn. (bd. dirs. 1991-94), Lincoln Club Sacramento Valley (bd. dirs. 1975-90, pres. 1984-86), U. Calif Men's Club (pres. 1968), Sutter Club, Kanadhar Ski Club, Rotary Club Sacramento (pres. 1993-94, Paul Harris Fellow award 1995), Comstock Club (pres. 1976-77). Republican. Presbyterian. Office: 720 9th St Sacramento CA 95814-1302 Office Phone: 916-874-8030. E-mail: vancamp@saccourt.com.

VAN CAMP, DIANA J. music educator; b. Washington, Oct. 24, 1946; d. Gordon Ashley and Gabrielle Marie-Anne Van Camp. B in Music Edn., Ind. U., 1969; MusM, Fla. State U., 1976; PhD in Music Edn., Ohio State U., 1989. Cert. tchr. music K-12 Ohio. Orch. tchr. Gainesville (Fla.) City Schs., 1969—72; orch. tchr., profl. violinist Memphis Symphony and Schs., 1975—79; music edn. and orch. tchr. Otterbein Coll., Westerville, Ohio, 1979—82; tchg. assoc. music edn. Ohio State U., Columbus, 1982—85; orch. dir. Bexley (Ohio) City Schs., 1985—86, Newark (Ohio) City Schs., 1987—. Pvt. violin studio, Newark, 1990—. Violinist: Southea. Ohio Symphony, 1992—, Welsh Hills Symphony, 1990—, Land of Legend Philharmonic, 1995—, Ctrl. Ohio Symphony, 2000—. Grantee, Nat. Endowment for the Arts, 1975—79. Mem.: Ohio Music Educators Assn., Music Educators Nat. Conf., Sigma Alpha Iota. Avocations: walking, hiking, swimming, church work. Home: 125 Beechtree Rd Whitehall OH 43213 Personal E-mail: musicalmate@prodigy.net.

VAN CAMPEN, STEPHEN BERNARD, executive recruiter, consultant; b. East Stroudsburg, Pa., Oct. 1, 1941; s. Bernard Allen and Marion (Van Whye) Van C.; m. Ellen Baars, July 22, 1989; children: Brendon, Regan, Meghan, Taylor, Hannah. BS in Sci. and Pre-Veterinary Med., Pa. State U., 1959-64; postgrad. in indsl. rels., George Washington U. Grad. Sch, 1965-68; law student, U. Balt., 1966-68. With FDA, Balt., Washington, 1964-66; indsl. rels. officer Joseph E. Seagrams & Sons, Balt., N.Y.C., San Francisco, 1966-72; worldwide dir. exec. staffing RCA/Hertz Corp., N.Y.C., 1972-74; dir. internat. indsl. rels. Revlon Internat., N.Y.C., 1974; pres., owner, cons. Gilbert & Van Campen Exec. Search, Internat. (subs.: J.B. Gilbert Assocs., Inc., Amtrade Assocs., Internat., GVC Fin. Svcs.), N.Y.C., 1974—; past owner, pres. Lillagaard Hotel Corp., Ocean Grove, NJ, 1992—; owner N.J. Profl. Meeting Planners Group; chmn. No. Shore Region Convention and Vis. Bur., Encore Svcs., Hackettstown, NJ, 1999—; pres. spl. investigations and verificatiuons divsn. Van Campen Assoc. Internat., 2003—. Appointed to N.J. Gov.'s Commn. on Internat. Trade, 1992; Bush White House nominee to Nat. Parks Adv. Commn., Dept. Interior; chmn. internat. trade subcom. ad hoc N.J. Assembly Small Bus. Adv. Coun.; bd. dirs. N.J. SBDC, N.J. Shore Region Tourism Coun.; named to Commerce and Econ. Devel. Transition Team for Gov.-elect Christine Todd Whitman; chmn. Econ. Devel. Task Force, Warren County, N.J., 1994; participant in meetings. with Pres. Castro 1st U.S.-Cuba Bus. Summit, Havanna, 1998. Rep. fundraiser; active N.J. Rep. Gov.'s Club, N.J. State Fin. Com.; appointed to Congressman Zimmer's Warren County N.J. Fed. Adv. Com., Warren County Econ. Adv. Coun., N.J. Gov.'s appointee 1988— and chmn. fed. enacted Del. Water Gap Nat. Recreation Area citizens adv. com., Gov.-elect Christie Todd Whitman Transition Team-Commerce and Econ. Devel. and Tourism; elected to Warren County Rep. Com.; chmn. adv. bd. Warren Presdl. Correctional Facility; chmn. Calno Cemetery Assn.; chmn. Warner County Econ. Devel. Blue Ribbon Task Force; vice chmn. bd. trustees Warren County C.C., 1983—, chmn. found. bd., presdl. search com. 2003, ops. com. 2003, ambassador N.Y. Coun. Cmty. Colls.; exec. bd. Tri-County Washington coun. and George Washington coun. Boy Scouts Am.; bd. dirs. N.J. Shore Regional Tourism Coun., N.Y. dir. SBDC, N.J. Juvenile Justice Adv. Bd.; mem. 1st N.J. Trade Del. Soviet Union; mem. commerce and econ. devel. transition team Gov.-elect Christie Whitman, N.J., 1994; chmn. N.J. assembly bus. retention com. of Task Force for Bus. Rentention, Attraction, Expansion and Internat. Trade; chmn. N.J. Gov.'s Conf. Travel and Tourism, Allaire City, 1994; chmn. N.J. No. Shore Region CUB Allaire Airport Conv. Ctr.; pres.-elect Warren County Econ. Partnership. Recipient Medal of Honor, Ellis Island, 1994, Disting. Citizen award Boy Scouts Am., 1992. Mem. ASTD, Am. Mgmt. Assns., Am. Coun. on Germany, U.S. C. of C., Nat. Fgn. Trade Coun., World Trade Inst., U.S.-USSR Trade and Econ. Coun., N.Y. C. of C. and Industry, N.J. C. of C., Commerce and Industry Assn. N.J., Am. C.

of C.s and U.S. Bus. Couns. Abroad, Soc. Human Resource Mgmt., Nat. Assn. Corp. and Profl. Recruiters, Employment Mgmt. Assn., N.J. Hotel/Motel Assn. (bd. dirs., mem. exec. bd.), N.J. Travel Industry Assn. (bd. dirs., v.p. exec. bd.), N.Y. Pers. Mgmt. Assn., Soc. Plastics Engrs., Soc. Cosmetic Chemists, Small Bus. Adv. Coun., Ocean Grove C. of C. (vice chmn.). Republican. Methodist. Home: 37 Petersburg Rd Hackettstown NJ 07840-4903 Office: Gilbert & Van Campen Intl 108 High St Ste 2 Hackettstown NJ 07840

VANCE, ANDREW ANDERSON, JR., humanities educator; b. Statesville, N.C., Jan. 26, 1941; s. Andrew Anderson and Pauline (Chaffin) Vance; m. Sara Frances McGee, Aug. 24, 1968; children: Sara Claudia, Caroline Maxwell. AB, Davidson Co., 1962; MA, La. State U., 1965, PhD, 1973; JD, Wake Forest U., 1976. Bar: N.C. 1976. Asst. in English Lycée Alain Chartier, Bayeux, France, 1962—63; asst. prof. French Lyon Coll. (formerly Ark. Coll.), Batesville, 1965—66, Catawba Coll., Salisbury, NC, 1966—76, assoc. prof. French and bus. law, 1977—82, prof. French and bus. law, 1982—, William Weaver Prof. Humanities, 2001—, chair, dept. modern fgn. langs., 1993—96, 2002—. Mem.: Am. Assn. Tchrs. French. Presbyterian. Avocation: cattle farming. Office: Catawba Coll 2300 West Innes St Salisbury NC 28144 E-mail: avance@catawba.edu.

VANCE, CHRISTOPHER, political organization worker; b. Seattle, 1962; m. Annmarie Vance; children: Adam, Natalie. BA in Polit. Sci., We. Wash. U., 1984. Staff Congressman Rod Chandler; rsch. analyst Wash. State Senate; state rep., dist. 31 Wash. Ho. of Reps., 1991—93; councilman, dist. 13 King County Coun., 1994—2001; chmn. Wash. State Rep. Party, 2001—. Office: 16400 S Center Pkwy Ste 200 Seattle WA 98188

VANCE, ELBRIDGE PUTNAM, mathematics educator; b. Cin., Feb. 7, 1915; s. Selby Frame and Jeannie (Putnam) V.; m. Margaret Gertrude Stoffel, Aug. 5, 1939 (div. 1975); children: Susan (Mrs. Timothy Griffin), Peter Selby, Douglas Putnam, Emily (Mrs. Charles Harold Beynon III); m. Jean Haigh, Jan. 1975. Student, Haverford Coll., 1932-33; AB, Coll. Wooster, 1936; MA, U. Mich., 1937, PhD, 1939. Asst. U. Mich., 1937-39; instr. U. Nev., 1939-41, asst. prof., 1941-43; vis. lectr. Oberlin (Ohio) Coll., 1943-46, asst. prof., 1946-50, asso. prof., 1950-54, prof., 1954-83, prof. emeritus, 1983—, chmn. dept., 1948-77, acting dean Coll. Arts and Scis., 2d semester, 1965-66, 1st semester, 1970-71. Chmn. advanced placement com. Coll. Entrance Exam. Bd., 1961-65, chief reader, 1956-61; chmn. com. examiners math. Comprehensive Coll. Tests, Ednl. Testing Service, 1965-67 Author: Trigonometry, 2d edit, 1969, Unified Algebra and Trigonometry, 1955, Fundamentals of Mathematics, 1960, Modern College Algebra, 3d edit, 1973, Modern Algebra and Trigonometry, 3d edit, 1973, An Introduction to Modern Mathematics, 2d edit, 1968, Mathematics 12, 1968, Solution Manual for Mathematics 12, 1968; Book review editor: Am. Math. Monthly, 1949-57; asso. editor, 1964-67. Mem. Oberlin Sch. Bd., 1952-60, pres., 1957-60. NSF Faculty fellow, 1960-61 Mem. Math. Assn. Am., Nat. Council Tchrs. of Math., Am. Math. Soc., Phi Beta Kappa, Sigma Xi, Phi Kappa Phi. Home: 315 Yorktown Pl Apt D4 Vermilion OH 44089-2104

VANCE, JIMIE A. dentist; b. Lansing, Mich., Feb. 9, 1921; s. Arby Franklin and Grace Emma (Scott) V.; divorced, 1979; children: Jimie A., Fred Arthur, Anita Jean Kadzierski. BS, Concord Coll., Athens, W.Va., 1947; DMD, U. Louisville, 1954; PhD, Wheeling Coll., 1980. Dentist, Kent, Ohio, 1955-64, Miami, 1964-95, Melbourne, Fla., 1995—. Pres., dir., officer Dade County Dental Rsch. Clinic, Miami and Melbourne, 1964—; lectr., various profl. meetings, Clin. Hypnosis, Acad. Therapists and Councillors. Contbr. articles to profl. jours. Mem. bd., Kent Meth. Ch., 1955-64, Kuedall Meth. Ch. (Miami), 1964-72, Olympia Heights Meth. Ch. (Miami), 1987-85, deacon Assemblies of God Ch. (Miami, liturgist, mem. bldg. com., 1972-87, mem. choir Bowe Gardens Bapt. Ch, Melbourne, 1995—. With USN, 1941-46, PTO, USAFR, 1952-54. Named top dentist in Am. 2001, Consumers Rsch. Coun. Am. Mem. ADA, Fla. Dental Assn., Ctrl. Dist. Dental Soc., Brevard County Dental Soc., Acad. Gen. Dentistry (officer), Fla. Acad. Gen. Dentistry (officer, editor newsletter 1962-65), Southeast Fla. Acad. Gen. Dentistry (founder 1952), Dental Study Club (Melbourne), Am. Legion (post 163), Moose Lodge (Melbourne), Masons, Shriners, Delta Sigma Delta. Methodist. Republican. Avocations: travel, photography. Office: 1121 S Wickham Rd West Melbourne FL 32904

VANCE, LESLIE EDWIN, information technology educator; b. Richland Center, Wis., Sept. 28, 1949; s. Leslie William Vance and Beata Ann (Harris) Elliott. BA, U. Wis., 1979, MA, 1981; PhD, Pa. State U., 1986. Announcer Sta. WRCO, Richland Ctr., Wis., 1966—68, Sta. WCOW, Sparta, 1968—69; news dir. Sta. WRJC, Mauston, 1969—72; photographer Richland Ctr., 1972—76; rsch. asst. Ctr. for Comm. Rsch., Madison, 1979—81; mgr. instrnl. support ctr. Pa. State U., State College, 1981—86; ednl. technologist Princeton (N.J.) Ctr. Edn., 1986—87; tech. architect Accenture, St. Charles, Ill., 1987—2001; info. tech. coord. S.W. Wis. Tech. Coll., Fennimore, 2001—02; artist, photographer, video prodr. Richland Ctr., 2002—; assoc. prof. Herzing Coll., Madison, 2002—03; program coord. Western Gov.'s U., Salt Lake City, 2003—. Cons. Rite Aid Corp., Camp Hill, Pa., Electronic Pub. Task Force, Motorola U., Schaumberg, Ill., U. Wis., Madison, Learning and Evaluation Assocs. Inc., State College, Pa.; exec. adv. bd., The Journal of Management Executive. Contbr. chpts. to books, articles to profl. jours.; presenter in field; prodr. (ednl. video) The Wisconsin Sesquicentennial Coach Run, Dressage Schooling for the Horse and Rider; designer (courses) Object Technology Starter Kit, 1995, Spreadsheets for Educators, 1984; designer, co-designer computer programs on instrnl. devel. Avocations: carriage driving, equine photography. Home: PO Box 17791 Holladay UT 84117-0791

VANCE, MARY LEE, academic administrator; b. Seoul, Korea, Nov. 16, 1957; d. Irwin F. and Mae Hoeft; m. Eric J. Vance. BA, U. Wis., 1979, MA, 1983; PhD, Mich. State U., 1993. From advisor to coord, Mich. State U., East Lansing, 1984-93; coord. Holmes Scholars Holmes Group, East Lansing, 1993-94; dir. edn. student svcs. Iowa State U., Ames, 1994-97; dir. acad. support and advising svcs. George Mason U., Fairfax, Va., 1997—. Adj. asst. prof. Iowa State U., 1994-97; cons. Southeastern Assn. Edn. Opportunity Program Personnel, Memphis, 1993-94. Contbr. articles to jours. Mem. strategic planning steering com. Ames Cmty. Sch. Dist., 1995-96; mem. Leadership Ames, 1995; bd. dirs. YWCA, Ames, 1996; mem. Make A Wish, 1998—. Recipient Outstanding Asian Pacific Am. Faculty/Staff awards, 1985-93, All U. Diversity Photo award, 1992, Outstanding Grad. Woman Spl. Merit award, 1992, Appreciation, Southeastern Assn. Ednl. Opportunity Program Pers., 1992, 93, 94, Office Supportive Svcs., 1993, Holmes Scholars, 1994, Holmes Group, 1994, Cert. of Achievement, Leadership Ames, 1995, Cert. Recognition, Univ. Disability Group, 2000, Cert. Appreciation, Korean Quar., 2003, Woman of Color, UW Superior, 2003. Mem. Nat. Orgn. Acad. Advising Assn., Assn. Higher Edn. and Disability, Nat. Orientation Dirs. Assn., Asian Pacific Am. Women's Leadership Inst., Acad, Affairs Adminstrs., Nat. Assn. Colls. and Employers (chair acad. staff senate). Bapt. Avocations: reading, gourmet cooking, eating, movies, writing book reviews. Office: Wis Pub Liberal Arts Coll Univ Wisconsin 134 Old Main,Belknap&Catlin,PO Box2000 Superior WI 54880-4500 Office Phone: 715-394-8515. E-mail: mvance@uwsuper.edu.

VANCE, MICHAEL CHARLES, lawyer; b. Marshalltown, Iowa, May 31, 1951; s. Randall Scott and Irma Vance; m. Bonnie K. Becker, Jan. 1, 1995; children: Thomas Randall, Patrick Michael. BA in Polit. Sci. and Econs., U. Iowa, 1973, JD with distinction, 1976. Bar: Iowa 1976, U.S. Dist. Ct. (so. dist.) Iowa 1976, U.S. Tax Ct. 1991. Sole practice, Mt. Pleasant, Iowa, 1976—. Atty. City of Wayland, Iowa, 1976—; instr. bus. law Iowa Wesleyan Coll., Mt. Pleasant, 1977-78; asst. county atty. Henry County, Mt. Pleasant, 1979-97, jud. magistrate, 1997—; mem. Iowa Supreme Ct. Commn. on Unauthorized Practice of Law, 2002. Bd. dirs. Cmty. Mental Health of Henry, Louisa and Jefferson Counties, Mt. Pleasant, 1977-82; chairperson Henry County Dems., Mt. Pleasant, 1978-83; pres. Mt. Pleasant Sesquicentennial Assn., 1984-86; mem. St. Alphonsus Ch. Parish Coun. pres., 1983-85; trustee Mt. Pleasant, 1985—. Mem. ABA, Iowa Bar Assn. (bd. govs. 1996-2002, jud. adminstrn. com. 2002, scope and correlations 2003-), Henry County Bar Assn. (sec.-treas. 1977-78, v.p. 1978-79, pres. 1979-80, 88-91), Iowa Trial Lawyers Assn., Iowa Conf. Bar Assn. Presidents (bd. dirs. 1979-81), Iowa Assn. Jud. Magistrates (bd. dirs. 1998-2002), Mt. Pleasant C. of C. (bd. dirs. 1991-93, named Citizen of Yr. 1985), Mt. Pleasant Jaycees (bd. dirs. 1978-83), Rotary, KC, Omicron Delta Kappa, Omicron Delta Epsilon. Roman Catholic. Home: 2005 Bittersweet Cir Mount Pleasant IA 52641-8301 Office: PO Box 469 101 N Jefferson St Mount Pleasant IA 52641-2039

VANCE, PATRICIA H. state legislator; b. Williamsport, Pa., Mar. 19, 1936; m. Charles D. Vance. RN, Harrisburg Hosp. Sch. Nursing, 1957. Mem. Pa. Ho. of Reps., Harrisburg. Home: 3806 Market St Camp Hill PA 17011-4327 Office: Pa Ho of Reps B-16 Main Capitol PO Box 202020 Harrisburg PA 17120-2020

VANCE, RALPH BROOKS, SR., oncologist, educator; b. Jackson, Miss., Dec. 4, 1945; s. Brooks C. and Chrystine G. (Gober) V.; m. Mary Douglas Allen, June 18, 1979; children: Brooks, Barrett. BA in Biology and German, U. Miss., 1968, MD, 1972. Asst. prof. medicine U. Miss., Jackson, 1978—86, assoc. prof. medicine, 1986—93, prof. medicine, 1993—. Chief of staff U. Miss. Hosp. and Clinics, Jackson, 1989-90; pres. faculty senate Univ. Med. Ctr., Jackson, 1986-87, univ. clin. assoc., pres., 1987-89. Author (with others) Development in Molecular Virology: Herpes Virus DNA, 1982; contbr. numerous articles and abstracts to profl. jours. Nat. pres. Am. Cancer Soc., 2003—, bd. dirs., nat. pres., exec. com.; bd. dirs. ARC, Jackson; bd. Blue Cross/Blue Shield Miss., Jackson, 1989—92. Named to Hall of Fame, U. Miss., 1968. Fellow ACP; mem. Am. Assn. for Cancer Edn., Am. Fedn. for Clin. Rsch., Am. Soc. Clin. Oncology, Am. Assn. for Cancer Rsch., Miss. Acad. Scis., S.W. Oncology Group, Sigma Xi. Office: U Miss Sch Medicine 2500 N State St Jackson MS 39216-4505 Office Phone: 601-984-5590. Business E-Mail: rvance@medicine.umsmed.edu.

VANCE, ROBERT PATRICK, lawyer; b. Feb. 12, 1948; s. James Robert and Lucy Juanita (McMath) V.; m. Sarah Elizabeth Savoia, June 11, 1971; 1 child, Robert Patrick, Jr. BA with honors, La. State U., 1970, JD, 1975. Bar: La. 1975, U.S. Dist. Ct. (ea. dist.) La. 1975, U.S. Dist. Ct. (mid. dist.) La. 1978, U.S. Dist. Ct. (we. dist.) La. 1979, U.S. Ct. Appeals (5th cir.) 1975, U.S. Ct. Appeals (11th cir.) 1981, U.S. Supreme Ct. 1981. Assoc. Jones, Walker, Waechter, Poitevent, Carrere & Denegre, New Orleans, 1975-80, ptnr., 1980—, exec. com., 1991—95, 1997—2002, mng. ptnr., 1994—95, 1999—2000, 2004—, chmn. litigation, 2003—. Contbr. articles to profl. jours. Fellow Am. Coll. Bankruptcy, Nat. Bankruptcy Conf. (mem. exec. com.); mem. ABA (past chair bankruptcy litigation com.), Am. Law Inst., La. State Bar Assn. (past chair consumer and bankruptcy law sect., chmn. continuing legal edn. com.), New Orleans Bar Assn., La. Bankers Assn. (chmn. bank counsel com. 1992-93), Pi Sigma Alpha, Phi Beta Kappa (Faculty Group award), Phi Kappa Phi. Democrat. Roman Catholic. Home: 1821 State St New Orleans LA 70118-6219 Office: Jones Walker Waechter Poitevent Carrere & Denegre 201 Saint Charles Ave Ste 5200 New Orleans LA 70170-5100 Office Phone: 504-582-8194. E-mail: pvance@joneswalker.com.

VANCE, VERNE WIDNEY, JR., retired lawyer; b. Omaha, Mar. 10, 1932; s. Verne Widney and June Caroline (Henckler) V.; m. Anita Paine, June 27, 1970; children: Lisa J. Castleton, Charles Hebard Paine, Virginia Caroline. AB, Harvard U., 1954, JD, 1957. Bar: D.C. 1957, Mass. 1964. Law clk. U.S. Dist. Judge, Mass., 1957-58; assoc. Covington & Burling, Washington, 1958-60; atty. adv. Devel. Loan Fund, Washington, 1960-61; legal counsel US AID, Washington, 1961-63; assoc. Foley, Hoag & Eliot LLP, Boston, 1963-67, ptnr., 1967-2000; ret., 2000. Lectr. law Boston U., 1964-66; corp. clk. S.S. Pierce Co., 1971-72. Pres. UN Assn. Greater Boston, 1964-66, 77-78, treas., 1974-77; mem. Mass. Adv. Council on Edn., 1969-75, chmn., 1975; mem. Dem. City Com., Newton, Mass., 1972—, Gov.'s Local Govt. Adv. Commn., 1986-90; alderman City of Newton, 1982-91; pres. Newton Bd. of Aldermen, 1988-91; mem. Newton Sch. Com., 1994-2001, chair 2000-01; trustee Judge Baker Children's Ctr., 1994—, clk., 2002--; trustee Mass. Bay C.C., 1987-98, vice chmn., 1989-91, chmn. 1991-97; pres. Mass. C.C. Assn., 1996-97. Mem. Boston Bar Assn. (bd. editors bar jour. 1986-90), Longwood Cricket Club. Home: 101 Old Orchard Rd Chestnut Hill MA 02467-1202 Office: Foley Hoag LLP 155 Seaport Blvd Boston MA 02109-2106 E-mail: vvance@fhe.com.

VANCE SIEBRASSE, KATHY ANN, legislative staff member; b. Kansas City, Kans., Oct. 28, 1954; d. Donald Herbert Vance and Barbara June (Boris) Vance-Young; m. Charles Richard Siebrasse, Mar. 8, 1980; 1 stepson, Michael (dec.); 1 son, Bradley. BS in Journalism, No. Ill. U., 1976. Reporter Des Plaines (Ill.) Suburban Times and Park Ridge Herald, 1974-75, DeKalb (Ill.) Daily Chronicle, 1976-78; stringer Rockford (Ill.) Register Star, 1978; editor The MidWeek Newspaper, DeKalb, 1978-81, owner and pub., 1982—2001; legis. aide Ill. State Senator J. Bradley Burzynski, Sycamore, 2001—. Part-time journalist The Midweek, DeKalb, 2004—. Active No. Ill. U. Found., 1992-99, mem. exec. bd., 1994-99, chair bus. and industry for No. Ill. U. campaign, 1993-94; pres. DeKalb Athletic Barb Boosters, 1995-97; chair Kishwaukee Hosp. Health Coun., Comm. Com., 1984-92, DeKalb County Partnership for a Substance Abuse Free Environment, 1990-2001; bd. dirs. DeKalb Edn. Found., sec., 1987-89, pres., 1989-93, active, 1987-94; sponsor Big Bros./Big Sisters Bowl-a-Thon, food drive Salvation Army, 1990-2002; bd. mem. Am. Heart Assn., 2000—; active Relay for Life, Am. Cancer Soc., 1999-2001, Heart Walk, Am. Heart Assn., 2000—; chair capital campaign Tails Humane Soc., 2002; pres.-elect, publicity chair Joseph F. Glidden Homestead Found.; bd. dirs., chair fundraising campaign Suicide Prevention Svcs., Batavia, 2002—. Recipient Comty. Svc. award Nat. Assn. of Advt. Pubs., 1980, Athena award Oldsmobile, DeKalb C. of C., 1990, Bus. of Yr., 1994, Heritage award Kishwaukee Cmty. Hosp., 2003. Mem. Soc. Profl. Journalists, Ill. Press Assn., No. Ill. Newspaper Assn., Ind. Free Papers Am. (Cmty. Svc. award 1992-93, 2nd pl. nat. gen. excellence award 1996), DeKalb County Farm Bur., DeKalb and Sycamore C. of C. (editor Sycamore newsletter 1994-96, mem. DeKalb Athena award com., bd. dirs., v.p. DeKalb 1996, chair 1997, Sam Walton Bus. Leader of Yr. De Kalb chamber 1999). Avocations: photography, reading, swimming, skiing, sailing. Office: State Sen J Bradley Burzynski 505 DeKalb Ave Sycamore IL 60178

VANCIL, BERNARD K. research and development company executive, physicist; b. Portland, Oreg., Oct. 19, 1946; s. Kenneth Theodore and Lois Eleanor Vancil; m. Karen Waugh, Apr. 11, 1970 (div. Dec. 0, 2000); children: Kathryn Myers, Elizabeth Peters, Allen, Cynthia, Deborah. BA in Physics, U. Calif., Berkeley, 1969; MA in Physics, UCLA, Calif., 1975. Tech. staff Hughes Aircraft Co., Torrance, Calif., 1975—77, Tektronix, Inc., Beaverton, Oreg., 1977—81; consulting engr. self-employed, 1981—85; pres. FDE Associates, FDE, Inc., 1998—2002, E-beam, Inc., 2002—. Head U.S. del. Internat. Vacuum Electron Sources Conf., 2002. Author technical conference presentations; contbr. articles to technical jours. 1st lt. U.S. Army, 1969—71, Vietnam. Recipient cert. of Recognition, NASA, 1999; grantee Small Bus. Innovation Rsch., NASA Glenn Rsch. Ctr., 1996, 1998, 2001, 2000, Small Bus. Innovation Rsch. Grant, 1992. Mem.: IEEE, Soc. For Info. Display. Achievements include patents in field; patents pending in field. Avocations: camping, writing, economics, literature, music. Office: E-Beam Inc 21070 SW Tile Flat Rd Beaverton OR 97007 E-mail: bernie@fdeassc.com.

VAN CLEAVE, WILLIAM ROBERT, international relations educator; b. Kansas City, Mo., Aug. 27, 1935; s. Earl Jr. and Georgiana (Offutt) Van C.; children: William Robert II, Cynthia Kay. BA in Polit. Sci. summa cum laude, Calif. State U., Long Beach, 1962; MA in Govt. and Internat. Rels., Claremont (Calif.) Grad. Sch., 1964, PhD, 1966. Political scientist Stanford U., 1964-67; mem. faculty U. So. Calif., 1967-87, prof. internat. rels., 1974-87, dir. def. and strategic studies ctr., 1971-87; prof., dept. head, dir. Ctr. for Def. and Strategic Studies Southwest Mo. State U., 1987—; sr. rsch. fellow Hoover Instn. Stanford U., 1981-97. Chmn. Strategic Alternatives Team, 1977-90; acting chmn. Pres.'s Gen. Adv. Com. on Arms Control, 1981-82; spl. asst. Office Sec. Def., mem. Strategic Arms Limitation Talks (SALT) delegation, 1969-71; mem. B team on Nat. Intelligence Estimates, 1976; mem. exec. panel, bd. dirs. Com. Present Danger, 1980-93; dir. transition team Dept. Def., 1980-81; sr. nat. security advisor to Ronald Reagan, 1979-80; mem. nat. security affairs adv. council Republican Nat. Com., 1979-89; research council Fgn. Policy Research Inst., Inst. Fgn. Policy Analysis; co-dir. Ann. Internat. Security Summer Seminar, Fed. Republic Germany, 1981-98; trustee Am. com. Internat. Inst. Strategic Studies, 1980—; vis. prof. U.S. Army Advanced Russian Inst., Garmisch, Fed. Republic Germany, 1978-79; chmn. adv. bd. Internat. Security Coun., 1991-96; cons. in field, mem. numerous govt. adv. coms. Co-author: Strategic Options for the Early Eighties: What Can Be Done?, 1979, Tactical Nuclear Weapons, 1978, Nuclear Weapons, Policies, and the Test Ban Issue, 1987, Strategy and International Politics, 2000; author: Fortress USSR, 1986; mem. bd. editors Global Affairs. Co-chmn. Scholars for Reagan, 1984; mem. exec. coun., dir. NCAA rels. Haka Bowl, NCAA Postseason Football Bowl. With USMC, 1953-61. Recipient Freedom Found. award, 1976, Outstanding Contbn. award Air War Coll., 1979, award teaching excellence U. So. Calif., 1980, 86; named Outstanding Prof. U. So. Calif., 1977, Disting. Alumnus Claremont Colls., 1978; Woodrow Wilson fellow, 1962, NDEA fellow, 1963-65. Mem. Internat. Inst. Strategic Studies (U.S. com., bd. trustees). Home: 8226 E Panther Hollow Ln Rogersville MO 65742-8386 Office: Dept Def and Strategic Studies Southwest Mo State U Springfield MO 65804-0095

VAN CLEVE, ROBERT BALDWIN, cardiologist; b. St. Louis, Dec. 1, 1931; s. William T. and Catherine Cornelia (Moore) Van C.; m. Sarah Agnes Towers, July 9, 1955; children: Sarah Elizabeth Weldon, Catherine Moore Bauman, Mary Agnes Miller, Robert B. Jr. AB, Princeton U., 1954; MD, Columbia U., 1958. Diplomate Am. Bd. Internal Medicine, Am. Bd. Cardiovasc. Disease. Intern, resident U. of Va. Hosp., Charlottesville, 1958-61; ward resident Barnes Hosp., St. Louis, 1962; Harvard Med. Sch. fellow Mass. Gen. Hosp., 1965; cardiologist Riverside Clinic, Jacksonville, Fla., 1965-98, Jacksonville Cardiology Clinic, 1998—. Cardiology cons. USN Hosp., Jacksonville, 1965-72; clin. prof. medicine U. Fla., 1977-88; chief of staff Riverside Hosp., Jacksonville, 1983-84, chief cardiology, 1985-90; chmn. hosp. authority U. Hosp.; v.p. attending staff Found. Duval County Interns and Residents. Contbr. articles to profl. jours., including Circulation, Jour. Am. Med Assn., Jour. Fla. Med. Assn. Chmn. recreation adv. bd. City of Jacksonville; bd. dirs. Salvation Army, Jacksonville; elder 1st Presbyn. Ch. Lt. comdr. USN, 1962-64. Fellow: ACP, Am. Coll. Cardiology. Republican. Avocations: tennis, scuba diving, golf, gardening. Home: 3500 Richmond St Jacksonville FL 32205-9422 Office: 3900 University Blvd S Jacksonville FL 32216-4313 Fax: 904-82805508.

VAN CLEVE, RUTH GILL, retired lawyer, government official; b. Mpls., July 28, 1925; d. Raymond S. and Ruth (Sevon) Gill; m. Harry R. Van Cleve, Jr., May 16, 1952 (dec. Oct. 2001); children: John Gill, Elizabeth Webster, David Hamilton Livingston. Student, U. Minn., 1943; AB magna cum laude, Mt. Holyoke Coll., 1946, LLD, 1976; LLB, Yale U., 1950. Bar: D.C. 1950, Minn. 1950. Intern Nat. Inst. Pub. Affairs, 1946-47; atty. Dept. Interior, 1950-54, asst. solicitor, 1954-64; dir. Office Territorial Affairs, 1964-69, 1977-80, dep. asst. sec., 1980-81, acting asst. sec., 1993; atty. Solicitor's Office, 1981-93, FPC, 1969-75, asst. gen. counsel, 1975-77. Author: The Office of Territorial Affairs, 1974, The Application of Federal Laws to the Territories, 1993. Mem. Guam War Claims Rev. Commn., 2003—04. Recipient Fed. Woman's award, 1966, Disting. Svc. award Dept. Interior, 1968, Presdl. Rank award, Pres. U.S., 1989. Mem. Phi Beta Kappa. Unitarian. Home: 4400 Emory St Alexandria VA 22312-1321

VANCLIEF, LYLE, former Canadian government official; b. Prince Edward County, Can. m. Sharon Hall; children: Kurt, Vanessa. Student, Belleville Coll. Inst.; BS in Agr., U. Guelph, 1966. Mem. family-owned bus. Willowlee Farms Ltd., Prince Edward County; mem. parliament House of Commons, Prince Edward-Hastings, 1988—, min. agrl. and agri-food, 1997—2003. Parliamentary sec. to Minister of Agr. and Agri-food, 1993; mem. standing com. on Agr.; co-critic for agr., assoc. critic for pub. works, House of Commons, 1988-93; mem. Ont. Task Force Health and Safety in Agr., 1983-85; mem., chmn. several coms. for Minister of Agr.; speaker in field of agrl. econs. and politics. Past twp. councillor, chmn. planning bd. Prince Edward Hastings; mem. bd. edn. Prince Edward County, chmn. bd. dirs., chmn. salary negotiating com.; active United Ch., past chmn. bd. dirs. Rednersville Pastoral Charge. Mem. Ont. Inst. Agrologists, Agrl. Inst. of Can. Office: 59 S Front St Belleville ON Canada K8N 5P4 also: House of Commons 207 Confederation Bldg Ottawa ON Canada K1A 0A6

VANCO, JOHN L. art museum director; b. Erie, Pa., Aug. 21, 1945; s. John Jr. and Alice (Crozier) V.; m. Kathleen Merski, 1971; children: John H., Jesse L. BA, Allegheny Coll., 1967. Dir. Erie (Pa.) Art Mus., 1968—. Mem. adv. panels Pa. Coun. on the Arts, Harrisburg, 1974—, Mid Atlantic Arts Found., Balt., 1992, 2002, Nat. Endowment for Arts, 2000; curator Contemporary Music Series, 1982—, Erie Art Mus. Blues and Jazz Festival, 1992—. Photographer miscellaneous exhbns.; curator miscellaneous exhbns. including A Peculiar Vision: The Work of George Ohr, The Mad Potter of Biloxi, From Mickey to the Grinch: Art of the Animated Film, Poems in Clay: Arthur Osborne's Plastic Sketches for the Low Art Tile Works, Teco: Art Pottery of the Prairie Sch., In Harmony with the Earth; author: A Roycroft Desktop: Musings on Elbert Hubbard and the Roycroft Shops, 1994, Loud & Clear: Resonator Guitars and the Dopyera Brothers' Legacy to American Music, 1998, Structured Color: Kiyokatsu Matsymiya, 2003. Chief adminstrv. officer Discovery Square, Erie, 1991-92; bd. dirs. Pa. Humanities Coun., 2001—. Office: Erie Art Mus 411 State St Erie PA 16501-1106 Office Phone: 814-459-5477.

VAN CURA, JOYCE BENNETT, librarian; b. Madison, Wis., Mar. 25, 1944; d. Ralph Eugene and Florence Marie (Cramer) Bennett; m. E. Jay Van Cura, July 5, 1986. BA in Liberal Arts (scholar), Bradley U., 1966; MLS, U. Ill., 1971. Libr. asst. Rsch. Libr. Caterpillar Tractor Co., Peoria, Ill., 1966-67; ref. libr., instr. libr. tech. Ill. Ctrl. Coll., East Peoria, Ill., 1967-73; asst. prof. Sangamon State U. (U. Ill.-Springfield), Springfield, Ill., 1973-80, assoc. prof., 1980-86; head libr. ref. and info. svcs. dept. Ill. Inst. Tech., 1987-90; dir. Learning Resources Ctr. Morton Coll., 1990—2003. Reviewer Libr. Jour., Am. Ref. Books Ann.; convenor Coun. II, Ill. Clearinghouse for Acad. Libr. Instrn., 1978; presentor 7th Ann. Conf. Acad. Libr. Instrn., 1977, Nat. Women's Studies Assn., 1983, others; participant Gt. Lakes Women's Studies Summer Inst., 1981, Nat. Inst. Leadership Devel. seminar, 1995. Contbr. articles to profl. jours. Pres. Springfield chpt. NOW, 1978—79; invited Susan B. Anthony luncheon, 1978, 1979; mem. adv. bd. Suburban Libr. Sys., 1992—94, Nat. Commn. Learning Resources; v.p. membership Riverside chpt. Lyric Opera Chgo., 1994—96, 1999—; active Riverside Arts Ctr.; Dem. precinct Committeewoman, 1982—85; vice-moderator Fourth Presbyn. Women, 1989—90; elder Riverside (Ill.) Presbyn. Ch., 1992—, mem. session, 1993—96, 2000—01, mem. adminstrn. com., 1993—2003, chmn. adminstrn. com., 1993—96, 1999, 2000—01, mem. endowment com., 1996—98; bd. dirs. Berwyn-Cicero Coun. on Aging. Ill. state scholar, 1962-66; recipient Citizenship award Am. Legion, 1962, Cert. of Recognition Ill. Bicentennial Commn., 1974. Mem.: AAUW (bd. dirs. Riverside br. 1992—94, 1997—99, chmn. standing com. on women Springfield br., com. on women Ill. state divsn.), ALA, Lyric Opera Chgo. Riverside Chpt. (v.p. 1995—), Ill. Libr. Assn. (presenter 1984), Nat. Assn. Women in C.C., Springfield Art Assn., No. Ill. Learning Resources Coop. (del. 1990—2003, steering com. West Suburban postsecondary consortium 1996—2000), Nat. Women's Studies Assn. (presenter 1983, 1984, 1995), Women in Mgmt., Am. Mgmt. Assn., No. Ill. Learning Resources Consortium Bd., Spl. Librs. Assn., Ill. Assn. Coll. and Rsch. Librs. (bibliog. instrn. com.), Libr. Info. and Tech. Assn., Libr. Adminstr. and Mgmt. Assn. (ref. and adult svcs. divsn.), Assn. Coll. and Rsch. Librs., Am. Opera Soc. of Chgo., Nat. Trust Hist. Preservation, Musicians Club of Women Chgo., Beta Phi Mu. Home: 181 Scottswood Rd Riverside IL 60546-2221

VAN DALEN, GORDON JOHN, physicist, educator; b. Tokyo, Sept. 19, 1951; came to the U.S., 1952; s. John and Ruth Margaret (Payne) Van D.; m. Carolyn Margaret Boutin, Apr. 8, 1978; children: John Edward, Stephen Michael. BS, U. Calif., Riverside, 1973, MS, 1975, PhD, 1978. From rsch. asst. to assoc. prof. U. Calif., Riverside, 1975-89, prof., 1990—2003; ret., 2003. Assoc. dean U. Calif., Riverside, 1990-93, dept. chmn., 1994-95; rsch.

prof. Embry-Riddle Aeronautical U., 2003—. Contbr. articles to profl. jours. Mem. AAAS, Am. Phys. Soc., Am. Assn. Physics Tchrs., Phi Beta Kappa. Achievements include rsch. in experimental particles. E-mail: gordonvandalen@aol.com.

VAN DAM, HEIMAN, psychoanalyst; b. Leiden, Netherlands; s. Machiel and Rika van D.; m. Barbara C. Strona, Oct. 6, 1945; children: Machiel, Claire Ilena, Rika Rosemary. AB, U. So. Calif., 1942, MD, 1945. Fellow in child psychiatry Pasadena (Calif.) Child Guidance Clinic, 1950; gen. practice psychiatry and psychoanalysis L.A., 1951—; instr. L.A. Psychoanalytic Inst., 1959—, co-chmn. com. on child psychoanalysis, 1960-67, tng. and supervising psychoanalyst, 1972—; supr. child and adolescent psychoanalysis So. Calif. Psychoanalytic Inst., 1986—. Cons. Reiss Davis Child Study Center, 1955-76, Neighborhood Youth Assn., L.A., 1964-69; assoc. clin. prof. psychiatry and pediats. UCLA Sch. Medicine, 1960-96, clin. prof. psychiatry and pediats., 1996—; vis. supr. child psychoanalysis San Francisco Psychoanalytic Inst., 1969-79, 2002—, Denver Psychoanalytic Inst., 1972-74; adv. bd. Western State U. Coll. Law, Fullerton, Calif., 1965-83. Corr. editor Arbeits Hefte Kinderanalyse, 1985—; contbr. articles to profl. jours. Trustee, edn. com. Center for Early Edn., 1964-92, v.p., 1978-79; bd. dirs. Child Devel. and Psychotherapy Tng. Program, L.A., 1975-80, pres., 1975-77; bd. dirs. L.A. Child Devel. Center, 1977-86, treas., 1978-80; mem. cult clinic Jewish Family Service, L.A., 1978-86; bd. dirs. Lake Arrowhead Crest Estates, 1990-99. Served to capt. M.C. AUS, 1946-48. Mem. Am. Psychoanalytic Assn. (com. on ethics 1977-80), Assn. Child Psychoanalysis (councillor 1966-69, sec. 1977-74, mem. nominating com. 1978 84, membership com. 1988—, Marianne Kris lectr. 1995), Internat. Assn. Infant Psychiatry (co chmn. program com. 1980-83), Internat. Soc. Adolescent Psychiatry (sci. adv. com. 1988—), Phi Beta Kappa. Office: 2864 McConnell Dr Los Angeles CA 90064-4658 Office Phone: 310-208-4888.

VANDAME, JEAN-MARIE RICHARD, diversified financial services company executive; b. Gien, France, Oct. 30, 1960; s. Marc and Antoinette (Dumouchel de Premare) V.; m. Chantal Marie de Blocquel de Croix de Wismes, Sept. 3, 1983; children: Thomas, Camille, Clemence, Alix. MS, Inst. Super. Electronique, Paris, 1982; MBA, Inst. Adminstrn. Entreprises, Paris, 1984. Product mktg. engr. Tex Instruments, Paris, 1983-84, field sales engr. Rennes, France, 1984-86; sr. mgr. Ernst & Young, Paris, 1986—92, assoc. ptnr., 1995—96, internat. ptnr., 1996—2000, ptnr., 2004—; pres. KnowledgeWare, Brussels, 1992—95; ptnr. CG Ernst & Young, Chgo., 2000—03. Office: Ernst & Young 92037 Paris France Home: 24 Avenue Theophile Gautier 75016 Paris France Office Phone: +33 146 93 44 03. E-mail: vandame6@hotmail.com.

VANDAMENT, WILLIAM EUGENE, retired academic administrator; b. Hannibal, Mo., Sept. 6, 1931; s. Alva E. and Ruth Alice (Mahood) V.; m. Margery Vandament, Feb. 2, 1952; children: Jane Louise, Lisa Ann. BA, Quincy Coll., 1952; MS, So. Ill. U., 1953; MS in Psychology, U. Mass., 1963, PhD, 1964; LittD, No. Mich. U., 1997. Psychologist Bacon Clinic, Racine, Wis., 1954-61; NDEA fellow U. Mass., Amherst, 1961-64; asst. prof. SUNY, Binghamton, 1964-69, univ. examiner and dir. instl. research, 1969-73, asst. v.p. planning, instl. research, 1972-76; exec. asst. to pres., dir. budget and resources Ohio State U., Columbus, 1976-79, v.p. fin. and planning, 1979-81; sr. v.p. adminstrn. NYU, N.Y.C., 1981-83; provost, vice chancellor acad. affairs Calif. State U. System, Long Beach, 1983-87; Trustees prof. Calif. State U., Fullerton, 1987-92; pres. No. Mich. U., 1991-97, ret., 1997. Contbr. articles to psychol. jours. and books on higher edn. Office: 2662 E 20th St Apt 310 Signal Hill CA 90755 E-mail: vandament@aol.com.

VAN DE BOVENKAMP, SUE ERPF, charitable organization executive; b. N.Y.C.; d. George Norton and Bettina Lions (Hearst) Mortimore; student Gardner Sch., Art Students League, Cooper Union; m. Armand Grover Erpf, 1965 (dec.); children: Cornelia Aurelia, Armand Bartholomew; m. Gerrit Pieter Van de Bovenkamp, Aug. 11, 1973 (div.). Pres. Armand G. Erpf Fund, N.Y.C., 1971—; founder, hon. chmn. Erpf Catskill Cultural Ctr., 1972—. Bd. advisors, founder N.Y. Zool. Soc., 1971—, 1001 Nature Trust, 1973, William Beebe fellow, 1983—; fellow in perpetuity Met. Mus. Art, 1977; life fellow Pierpont Morgan Libr., 1974—; mem. coun.of friends Whitney Mus. Am. Art, 1971-77; mem. Whitney Circle, 1978-93; bd. dirs. Catskill Ctr. for Conservation and Devel., 1983-86; mem. adv. coun., dept. art history and archaeology Columbia U., 1972—, established univ. seminar on uses of oceans, 1977, mem. adv. coun. Translation Ctr., 1986; life conservator N.Y. Pub. Libr., 1980; fellow Frick Collection; 1971—, Whitney fellow, 2994—; mem. coun. Agribus. Coun., Inc., 1979-87; founder, life mem. World Wildlife Fund, 1973—, bd. dirs., 1984-89; mem. pres.'s coun. Columbia U., 1973-78; life mem. Mus. City N.Y., 1972—, mem. pres.'s coun., 1971—. Mem. N.Y. Acad. Scis., The Planetary Soc., Mus. Natural History (life), Asia Soc. (pres.'s coun.), Wildlife Fedn. (adv.), African Wildlife Found. (pres.'s cir.). mem. Mus. of Natural Hist. pres., coun. of the Asia Soc. Office: The Armand G Erpf Fund 640 Park Ave New York NY 10021-6126

VANDEBUNTE, EILEEN J. health facility administrator; b. Sioux Falls, S.D., July 8, 1945; BA, Central Coll., 1967; MPA, Fairleigh Dickinson, 1998. Office: Monmouth Med Ctr 300 Second Ave Long Branch NJ 07740

VANDE CREEK, DREW EVAN, historian, educator; b. Topeka, July 2, 1964; s. Larry Ray and Celia Vander Ark Vande Creek; m. Leanne Marie Lauer, Aug. 31, 2002. BA, Coll. Wooster, 1986; MA, U. Va., 1990, PhD, 1996. Dir. digital projects No. Ill. U. Librs., DeKalb, 1998—. Digitization cons. The Field Mus., Chgo., 2002—. Grantee, NEH, 2000, 2001, 2002, 2004. Home: 584 Carriage Dr Batavia IL 60510 Office: No Ill Univ Libr Dekalb IL 60115

VANDE HEY, JAMES MICHAEL, corporate executive, former air force officer; b. Maribel, Wis., Mar. 15, 1916; s. William Henry and Anna (Zimmerman) VandeH.; m. Jean Margretta Schilleman, June 23, 1944; children: James Todd, Dale Michael, Dean Clark. Student, U. Wis., 1947-49; BA, U. Philippines, 1955; postgrad., Air War Coll., Maxwell AFB, Montgomery, Ala., 1956-57. Commd. 2d lt. USAAF, 1941; advanced through grades to brig. gen. USAF, 1967; fighter pilot PTO, 1941-45; including Hawaii, Dec. 7, 1941; duty in command and USAF level including duty in Europe (NATO) and Philippines, 1945-69; dep. chief of staff Hdqrs. USMACV, Saigon, Vietnam, 1969-71; assigned Hdqrs. Tactical Air Command, 1971—; mem. faculty Air War Coll., 1957-59, dep. for acads., dean of faculty, 1959-61; ret., 1971; pres. Vanson Inc., 1971—, Vande Hey Inc., 1976—. Decorated D.S.M., Legion of Merit with two oak leaf clusters, D.F.C. with two oak leaf clusters, Bronze Star, Air medal with 7 oak leaf clusters, decorations from Philippine, Vietnamese and Korean govts. Mem. USAF Hist. Found., Air Force Assn., Pearl Harbor Survivors Assn., Iwo Jima Survivors Assn. Roman Catholic. Home: 3374 S El Dorado Austin TX 78734-5232

VAN DE KAMP, JOHN KALAR, lawyer; b. Pasadena, Calif., Feb. 7, 1936; s. Harry and Georgie (Kalar) Van de K.; m. Andrea Fisher, Mar. 11, 1978; 1 child, Diana. BA, Dartmouth Coll., 1956; JD, Stanford U., 1959. Bar: Calif. 1960. Asst. U.S. atty., L.A., 1960-66; U.S. atty., 1966-67; dep. dir. Exec. Office for U.S. Attys., Washington, 1967-68, dir., 1968-69; spl. asst. Pres.'s Commn. on Campus Unrest, 1970; fed. pub. defender L.A., 1971-75; dist. atty. Los Angeles County, 1975-83; atty. gen. State of Calif., 1983-91; ptnr. Dewey Ballantine, L.A., 1991-96, of counsel, 1996—; pres. Thoroughbred Owners, Calif., 1996—2004. Mem. Calif. Dist. Attys. Assn. (pres. 1975-83), Nat. Dist. Attys. Assn. (v.p. 1975-83), Peace Officers Assn. L.A. County (past pres.), Nat. Assn. Attys. Gen. (exec. com. 1983-91), Conf. Western Attys. Gen. (pres. 1986), State Bar Calif. (bd. govs. 2001-04, pres-elect 2004—). Office: Dewey Ballantine LLP 333 So Grand Ave Ste 2600 Los Angeles CA 90071-1530 Office Phone: 213-621-6511. Business E-Mail: jvandekamp@deweyballantine.com.

VANDELL, KERRY DEAN, real estate and urban economics educator; b. Biloxi, Miss., Jan. 8, 1947; s. Benedict Sandy and Eleanor Ruby (Lenhart) V.; m. Deborah Ann Lowe, May 16, 1970; children: Colin Buckner, Ashley Elizabeth. BA, MME, Rice U., 1970; M City Planning, Harvard U., 1973; PhD, MIT, 1977. Assoc. engr. Exxon Co., USA, Houston, 1970-71; asst. prof. So. Meth. U., Dallas, 1976-80, assoc. prof., 1980-86, prof., chmn. dept., 1986-89; prof. real estate and urban land econs., chm. dept. U. Wis., Madison, 1989-93, dir. Ctr. for Urban Land Econs. Rsch., 1991—2004, Tiefenthaler chairholder, 1996—; exec. dir. Bolz Ctr. Arts Adminstrn., Madison, 2000—. Vis. assoc. prof. Harvard U., Cambridge, Mass., 1985-86; vis. prof. U. Calif., Berkeley, 1988-89, U. Hong Kong, 1997; bd. dirs. Park Bank, Madison, U. Rsch. Pk., Chrisken Realty Trust. Mem. editl. bd. Jour. Real Estate Fin. and Econs., 1989—, Land Econs., 1989—, Jour. Property Rsch., 1989-94, Real Estate Econs., 1980—, Internat. Real Estate Rev., 2002—; contbr. numerous articles on mortgage default risk, neighborhood dynamics, econs. of architecture, and appraisal theory to profl. jours. Fellow Homer Hoyt Advanced Studies Inst. (faculty 1989—, bd. dirs.); mem. Urban Land Inst., Am. Real Estate and Urban Econs. Assn. (2nd v.p. 1989, 1st v.p. 1990, pres. 1991, co-editor jour. 1991-96), Asian Real Estate Soc. (bd. dirs. 2002), Am. Real Estate Soc. Episcopalian. Home: 3301 Topping Rd Madison WI 53705-1436 Office: U Wis Sch Bus 975 University Ave Madison WI 53706-1324 Office Phone: 608-262-5800. Business E-Mail: kvandell@bus.wisc.edu.

VANDEMARK, MICHELLE VOLIN, critical care, neuroscience nurse; b. Sioux Falls, S.D., Feb. 14, 1962; d. Verlynne V. and Suzanne (Cronin) Volin; m. Richard E. VanDemark, June 5, 1982; children: Andrew Porter, Hannah Elizabeth. BA in Biology, Lake Forest (Ill.) Coll., 1984; BSN, Northwestern U., Chgo., 1986; MS in Nursing, Loyola U., Chgo., 1990. RN, Ill., S.D.; cert. neurosci. nursing, CNRN, ACLS. Staff nurse neurosci. unit Evanston Hosp., Ill., 1986-90, staff nurse intensive care unit, 1990-93; neurosci. clin. nurse specialist Sioux Valley Hosp., Sioux Falls, S.D., 1995—. Mem. Am. Assn. Neurosci. Nurses (pres. Gt. Plains chpt. 1995-96, bd. dirs. 2000 03), Sigma Theta Tau, Alpha Sigma Nu. Home: 321 E 27th St Sioux Falls SD 57105-3032

VANDEMARK, ROBERT GOODYEAR, retired retail company executive; b. Youngstown, Ohio, Sept. 1, 1921; s. Arthur Glenn and Lola (Goodyear) V.; m. Jean Chapman, Sept. 19, 1943; children: Ann (Mrs. William K. Butler), Peggy Lynn (Mrs. Michael Murray). BSc, Ohio U., 1943. Dept. mgr. F. & R. Lazarus, Columbus, Ohio, 1947-54; asst. controller Boston Store, Milw., 1954-57; v.p., treas. Cleland Simpson Co., Scranton, Pa., 1957-65; asst. to exec. v.p. Bergdorf Goodman, N.Y.C., 1965-68; treas. Garfinckel, Brooks Bros., Miller & Rhoads, Inc., Washington, 1968-69, v.p., 1969-73, exec. v.p., 1973-79, vice chmn., 1979-83; chmn., chief exec. officer Garfinckel's, 1983-87. Head dept. and specialty stores div. United Fund, Scranton, Pa., 1960-65; bd. dirs. Goodwill Industries, 1964-65; treas. Washington Nat. Cathedral. Served to 1st lt. AUS, 1943-46; col. Res. Decorated Bronze Star with V and cluster, Mil. Order of Wilheim. Mem. Fin. Execs. Inst., Nat. Retail Mchts. Assn. (sec., treas., 1st v.p., pres., dir., mem. exec. com. fin. exec. divsn.), Delta Tau Delta, City Club Washington, Washington Golf and Country Club, Army-Navy Club, Burning Tree Golf Club, Laurel Oak Country Club (Fla.), Masons (32d degree), Kiwanis (Fla.). Home: 933 Woburn Ct Mc Lean VA 22102-2132 also: 3362 Charles MacDonald Dr Sarasota FL 34240

VAN DEMARK, RUTH ELAINE, lawyer; b. Santa Fe, May 16, 1944; d. Robert Eugene and Bertha Marie (Thompson) Van D.; m. Leland Wilkinson, June 23, 1967; children: Anne Marie, Caroline Cook. AB, Vassar Coll., 1966; MTS, Harvard U., 1969; JD with honors, U. Conn., 1976; MDiv, Luth. Sch. Theology, Chgo., 1999. Bar: Conn. 1976, Ill. 1977, U.S. Dist. Ct. Conn. 1976, U.S. Dist. Ct. (no. dist.) Ill., U.S. Ct. Appeals (7th cir.) 1984, U.S. Supreme Ct. 1983; ordained to ministry, Luth Ch., 1999. Instr. legal rsch. and writing Loyola U. Sch. Law, Chgo., 1976-79; assoc. Wildman, Harrold, Allen & Dixon, Chgo., 1977-84, ptnr., 1985-94; prin. Law Offices of Ruth E. Van Demark, Chgo., 1995—2003; pastor Wicker Park Luth. Ch., Chgo., 1999—. Mem. rules com. Ill. Supreme Ct., 1999-2002, chair appellate rules subcom., 1996-2002; mem. dist. ct. fund adv. com. U.S. Dist. Ct. (no. dist.) Ill., 1997—. Assoc. editor Conn. Law Rev., 1975-76. Bd. dirs. Lutheran Soc. Svcs. Ill., 1998—, sec., 2000—02, chmn., 2002-; mem. adv. bd. Horizon Hospice, Chgo., 1978—, YWCA Battered Women's Shelter, Evanston, Ill., 1982-86; del.-at-large White House Conf. on Families, L.A., 1980; mem. alumni coun. Harvard Divinity Sch., 1988-91; vol. atty. Pro Bono Advs. Chgo., 1982-92, bd. dirs., 1993-99, chair devel. com., 1993; bd. dirs. Friends of Pro Bono Advs. Orgn., 1987-89, New Voice Prodns., 1984-86, Byrne Piven Theater Workshop, 1987-90, Luth. Social Svcs. Ill. (sec., 2000—), 1998—; founder, bd. dirs. Friends of Battered Women and Their Children, 1986-87; chair 175th Reunion Fund Harvard U. Div. Sch., 1992; dean Ctrl. Conf. Met. Chgo. Synod ELCA. Mem. ABA, Ill. Bar Assn., Conn. Bar Assn., Chgo. Bar Assn., Appellate Lawyers Assn. Ill. (bd. dirs. 1985-87, treas. 1989-90, sec. 1990-91, v.p. 1991-92, pres. 1992-93), Women's Bar Assn. Ill., Jr. League Evanston (chair State Pub. Affairs Com. 1987-88, Vol. of Yr. 1983-84), Chgo. Vassar Club (pres. 1979-81), Cosmopolitan Club (N.Y.C.). Home: 2046 W Pierce Ave Chicago IL 60622-1946 E-mail: revwplc@earthlink.net.

VANDEN, HARRY EDWIN, political science educator; b. Wilmington, Del., Sept. 29, 1943; s. Harry Edwin Sr. and Rena Baker (Van Zandt) V.; m. Vera Esther Ballin, Sept. 3, 1967 (div. Feb. 1995); children: David Jeffrey, Jonathan Harry. Diploma, U. Madrid, 1965; BA, Albright Coll., 1966; MA, Cert. in L.Am. Studies, Syracuse U., 1969; PhD, New Sch. Social Rsch., 1976. Field rsch. coord. Nat. Opinion Rsch. Ctr., N.Y.C., 1969-70; adj. asst. prof. Richmond Coll., CUNY, N.Y.C., 1971; Fulbright scholar U.S. Govt., Lima, Peru, 1973-74; tech. expert Inst. Nacional Administración Pública, Lima, 1974-75; from asst. prof. to prof. U. South Fla., Tampa, 1975—, dir. Caribbean and L.Am. Ctr., 1993-97. Author: Mariátegui: influencias en su formación ideológica, 1975, National Marxism in Latin America, 1986, A Bibliography of Latin American Marxism, 1991; co-author: Democracy and Socialism in Sandinista Nicaragua, 1993, Latin America: The Power Game, 2002; co-editor: The Undermining of the Sandinista Revolution, 1997; contbr. articles to profl. jours., chpts. to books. V.p. bd. dirs. WMNF Cmty. Radio, Tampa, 1990-96; bd. dirs. Hispanic Svcs. Coun., Tampa, 1996-2003; internat. election observer with Jimmy Carter/Carter Ctr., Venezuela, 1998, Nicaragua, 2001. NEH grantee, 1980. Mem. Soc. for Iberian and L.Am. Thought (pres. 1983-85), Southeastern Coun. on L.Am. Studies (pres. 1988-89), L.Am. Studies Assn. (co-chair Ctrl. Am. sect. 1997-2000), Am. Polit. Sci. Assn., Am. Soc. Internat Law. Democrat. Avocations: Judo, swimming, sailing. Office: U South Fla Dept Govt 4202 E Fowler Ave Tampa FL 33620-8100 E-mail: vanden@chuma1.cas.usf.edu.

VAN DEN BERG, EGERTON, airport executive; m. Caroline Merritt; 7 children. Legal counsel Orlando Exec., Orlando Internat. Airport, 1967—76, 1980—95; exec. dir. Orlando Internat. Airport, Orlando, Fla., 1997—. Office: Orlando Internat Airport One Airport Blvd Orlando FL 32827

VANDENBERG, JOKA MARIA, physicist, researcher; b. Heemstede, The Netherlands, Jan. 24, 1938; came to the U.S., 1968; d. Antonius Vandenberg and Maria Elisabeth Van Amerongen; m. Rudolf Johannes Voorhoeve, May 11, 1968 (div. Aug. 1975); children: Lucy, Niels; m. James Charles Phillips, Mar. 1, 1996. B in Physics, State U., Leiden, The Netherlands, 1959, M in Phys. Chemistry, 1962, PhD in Solid State Physics, 1964. Tchg. asst. Lab. Inorganic Chemistry, Leiden, 1959-60; rsch. asst. Lab. Crystallography, Amsterdam, 1962-64; rschr. Royal Dutch Shell Lab., Amsterdam, The Netherlands, 1964-68; postdoctoral staff Bell Labs., Murray Hill, N.J., 1968-69, cons., 1972; mem. tech. staff Lucent Techs., Murray Hill, 1973-2001. Mem. affirmative action com. Bell Labs., Murray Hill, 1990-91. Mem. IEEE, Am. Phys. Soc., Royal Dutch Acad. Scis. (corr.). Achievements include patent for super conducting films. Home: 204 Springfield Ave Summit NJ 07901 E-mail: joka_berg@comcast.net.

VANDENBERG, PETER RAY, publishing executive; b. Geneva, Ill., Sept. 8, 1939; s. Don George and Isabel (Frank) Vandenberg; m. Kathryn Stock, June 1973 (div. Apr. 1977). BBA, Miami U., 1962. Creative adminstr. E.F. McDonald Incentive Co., Dayton, Ohio, [illegible]-73; mfrs.' rep. Denver, 1974-75; mgr. Homestake Condominiums, Vail, Colo., 1975-76; desk clk. Vail Run Resort, 1976-77; sales rep. Colo. West Advt., Vail, 1977-79, pres., 1980-83, Colo. West Publ., Vail, 1983—, casa-sol.com Mexican Vacation Rentals, Puerto Vallarta, Mexico, 1999—. With U.S. Army, 1963—66. Mem.: Sigma Chi. Avocations: sports, music, reading. Business E-Mail: coloradowestpub@yahoo.com.

VANDENBERG, SARA E. secondary school educator; d. Donald and Erma J. Vandenberg; m. Johnny Bohnen, Mar. 17, 1990 (div. Feb. 23, 2004); children: Gray S. Bohnen, Ginger C. Bohnen. BA, U. of Chgo., 1990, MA, 1992. Cert. secondary English tchr. ESL endorsement Colo. Dept. of Edn. Paralegal Jenner & Block Attys. at Law, Chgo., 1986—91; tchr., vol. coord. Travelers and Immigrants Aid, Chgo., 1992—95; tchr. Harold Wash. City Coll., Chgo., 1992—92; nat. workplace literacy grant tchr. Coll. of Lake County, Ill., 1995—96; tchr. Erie Neighborhood Ho., Chgo., 1995—98, Skills for Tomorrow, Oak Park, Ill., 1996—98, Dist. 11 Adult and Family Edn., Colorado Springs, 1998—2000; tchr. mil. programs Pikes Peak C.C., Colorado Springs, 1999; ELA coord. Cheyenne Mountain Sch. Dist., Colorado Springs, 2000—; tchr. Cheyenne Mountain H.S., Colorado Springs, 2000—, Cheyenne Mountain Jr. High, Colorado Springs, 2000—; regional trainer English Lang. Acquisition Unit of Colo. Dept. of Edn., Colorado Springs, 2003—. Adj. faculty Regis U., Colorado Springs, 1999—2001; tchr.-in-resident U. Colo., Pikes Peak, 2002; item writer Mountain West Consortium, Colo., 2003—, bias and sensitivity reviewer, Colo., 2003; task force mem. Pikes Peak Literacy Strategies Group, Colorado Springs, 2003—; sheltered instrn. observational protocal trainer Bilingual and English Lang. Devel. Program U. of Denver, Denver and Colorado Springs, 2003—; elem. summer sch. tchr. Cheyenne Mountain Sch. Dist., Colorado Springs, 2003, sponsor Heritage Lang. Club, 2003—. Author, rschr.: tchr. resource manual Pikes Peak Literacy Strategies Project, author: (naturalization and English textbook) Chicago Latino Citizen Coalition. Recipient Secondary English Lang. Acquisition, Heritage Lang. Club funding grant, Broadmoor Hotel/Cheyenne Mountain Sch. Dist. Partnership in Edn., 2002, 2003. Mem.: ASCD, Internat. Reading Assn., Colo. Tchrs. of English to Spkrs. of Other Langs. Avocations: hiking, backpacking, photography, travel, archaeology. Office: Cheyenne Mountain Sch Dist 1118 W Cheyenne Rd Colorado Springs CO 80906 E-mail: vandenberg@cmsd.k12.co.us.

VAN DEN BERG, SARA JANE, English educator; b. St. Paul, May 19, 1942; d. Henry John and Edith Ann (Hutchins) Streich; m. Kent Talbot van den Berg, June 11, 1976; 1 child, David Talbot. BA summa cum laude, U. Minn., 1964; MA, Yale U., 1965, PhD, 1969. Instr. Fordham U., N.Y.C., 1968-70; asst. prof. Fairfield (Conn.) U., 1970-73, Occidental Coll., L.A., 1973-76, Ohio State U., Columbus, 1976-80, U. Wash., Seattle, 1980-87, assoc. prof. English, 1987—2000, chmn. curricular policy bd., 1996-98; prof. English St. Louis U., 2000—, chmn. English dept., 2000—. Mem. editl. bd. Modern Lang. Quar., 1995-2000, The Ben Jonson Jour., 1995—, Psyart: The Jour., 1997—; author: The Action of Ben Jonson's Poetry, 1987. Huntington Libr. fellow, 1987, NEH fellow, summer 1987, 2003. Mem. MLA (divsn. lit. and psychology 1990-94, chmn. 1992-93), Renaissance Soc. Am., Milton Soc. Am., Pacific Ancient and Modern Lang. Assn. (exec. com. 1997-99). Office: St Louis U Dept English 3800 Lindell Blvd Saint Louis MO 63108 Office Phone: 314-977-3010. E-mail: vandens@slu.edu.

VAN DEN BERGH, SIDNEY, astronomer; b. Wassenaar, Netherlands, May 20, 1929; emigrated to U.S., 1948; s. Sidney J. and Mieke (van den Berg) vandenB.; m. Paulette Brown; children by previous marriage: Peter, Mieke, Sabine. Student, Leiden (The Netherlands) U., 1947-48; AB, Princeton U., 1950; M.Sc., Ohio State U., 1952; Dr. rer. nat., Goettingen U., 1956, DSc (honoris causa), 1995, DSc (honoris causa), 2001. Asst. prof. Perkins Obs., Ohio State U., Columbus, 1956-58; research assoc. Mt. Wilson Obs., Palomar Obs., Pasadena, Calif., 1968-69; prof. astronomy David Dunlap Obs., U. Toronto, Ont., Can., 1958-77; dir. Dominion Astrophys. Obs., Victoria, B.C., 1977-86; prin. rsch. officer NRC Can., 1977-98, rschr. emeritus, 1998—. Adj. prof. U. Victoria, 1977—. Decorated officer Order of Can. Fellow Royal Soc. London; mem. Am., Royal Astron. Soc. (assoc.), Canadian Astronomy Soc. (sr. v.p. 1988-90, pres. 1990-92). Home: 418 Lands End Rd Sidney BC Canada V8L 5L9 Office Phone: 250-363-0006. E-mail: sidney.vandenbergh@nrc.ca.

VAN DEN BERGHE, PIERRE LOUIS, sociologist; b. Lubumbashi, Congo, Jan. 30, 1933; s. Louis and Denise (Caullery) van den B.; m. Irmgard C. Niehuis, Jan. 21, 1956; children: Eric, Oliver, Marc. BA, Stanford U., 1952, MA, 1953; PhD, Harvard U., 1960. Asst. prof. sociology Wesleyan U., Middletown, Conn., 1962-63; asso. prof. sociology SUNY, Buffalo, 1963-65; prof. sociology and anthropology U. Wash., Seattle, 1965-98, prof. emeritus, 1998—. Vis. prof. U. Natal, South Africa, 1960-61, Sorbonne, Paris, 1962, U. Nairobi, Kenya, 1967-68, U. Ibadan, Nigeria, 1968-69, U. Haifa, Israel, 1976, U. New South Wales, Australia, 1982, U. Strasbourg, France, 1985, U. Tuebingen, Fed. Republic Germany, 1986, Tel Aviv U., 1988, U. Cape Town, South Africa, 1989; fellow Advanced Study in Behavioral Scis., Stanford, Calif., 1984-85. Author: 22 books including South Africa, A Study in Conflict, 1965, Race and Racism, 1967, Academic Gamesmanship, 1970, Man in Society, 1978, Human Family Systems, 1979, The Ethnic Phenomenon, 1981, Stranger in Their Midst, 1989, State Violence and Ethnicity, 1990, The Quest for the Other, 1994. Served with M.C. U.S. Army, 1954-56. Mem. Am. Sociol. Assn., Am. Anthrop. Assn., Sociol. Rsch. Assn., Human Behavior and Evolution Soc. Home: 2006 19th Ave E Seattle WA 98112-2902 Office: U Wash Dept Sociology 353340 Seattle WA 98195-3340 E-mail: plvdb@u.washington.edu.

VAN DEN BLINK, NELSON MOOERS, light industrial manufacturing executive; Chmn., CEO Hiliard Corp., Elmira, N.Y., 1982—. Office: Hilliard Corp 100 W 4th St Elmira NY 14901-2190

VANDENBOS, GARY ROGER, psychologist, publisher; b. Grand Rapids, Mich., Dec. 16, 1943; s. Paul Martin and Irene (Dorenbos) V.; m. Jane Annunziata, Dec. 16, 1983; 1 child, Bret. BS, Mich. State U., 1967, MA, 1969; PhD, U. Detroit, 1973. Dir. Howell (Mich.) Area Community Mental Health Ctr., 1973-77; dir. nat. policy studies Am. Psychol. Assn., Washington, 1977-82, exec. dir. for publs., 1984—; prof. U. Bergen, Norway, 1982-84. Project cons. Rand Corp., Santa Monica, Calif., 1984-89; bd. dirs. Am. Biodyne Found., San Francisco; newspaper pub. APA Monitor, 1985—. Author: Psychotherapy with Schizophrenic, 1981; editor Pscyhology and National Health Insurance, 1979; assoc. editor Am. Psychologist Jour. Office: Am Psychol Assn 750 1st St NE Washington DC 20002-4241

VANDEN BOUT, PAUL ADRIAN, astronomer, physicist, educator; b. Grand Rapids, Mich., June 16, 1939; s. Adrian and Cornelia (Peterson) Vanden B.; m. Rachel Ann Eggebeen, Sept. 1, 1961; children: Thomas Adrian, David Anton AB, Calvin Coll., 1961; PhD, U. Calif.-Berkeley, 1966. Postdoctoral fellow U. Calif., Berkeley, 1966-67; postdoctoral fellow Columbia U., N.Y.C., 1967-68, instr., 1968-69, asst. prof., 1969-70, U. Tex., Austin, 1970-74, assoc. prof., 1974-79, prof., 1979-84; dir. Nat. Radio Astronomy Obs., Charlottesville, Va., 1985—2002, sr. scientist, 2003—; dir. Atacama Large Millimeter Array, Charlottesville, Va., 2002—03. Sr. scientist Nat. Radio Astronomy Obs., 2003—; cons. NSF, NASA. Fellow Fulbright Found., Heidelberg, Fed. Republic Germany, 1961-62, Leiden, Netherlands, 1977 Fellow AAAS, Am. Phys. Soc.; mem. Am. Astron. Soc., Internat. Astron. Union, Internat. Radio Sci. Union. Office: Nat Radio Astronomy Obs 520 Edgemont Rd Charlottesville VA 22903-2454 Office Phone: 434-296-0231. Business E-Mail: pvandenb@nrao.edu.

VAN DEN DAELE, LELAND DOUGLAS, psychology educator, psychological measurement company executive; s. Leopold Francis van den Daele and Dorothy Catherine Krolik; m. Lee Ling Tham, June 9, 2000; children: Alphonse Francis children: Leopold Augustine. *Leland's great grandparents left Brussels, Belgium in 1895. Great grandfather, Alphonse, was a real estate investor. Grandfather Frank was Los Angeles Middle Weight Golden Gloves Champion and a life-long chief railroad engineer for Union Pacific. Father, Leopold was the US 1932 Junior Olympic Champion in gymnastics. Leland practices yoga and meditates. Sons Leopold and Alphonse are toddlers with the world before them. Wife Lee Ling Tham, BA Hon 1989, M. App Psych*

1992, Murdoch U Western Australia, fluent in 5 languages, is a member of the Hong Kong Psychological Society in private practice. She taught for Ohio University in public and private sectors. BA in Psychology, U. of San Francisco, 1962; MS, Purdue U., 1964, PhD, 1967. Lic. psychoanalysis Am. Inst. of Psychoanalysis, psychologist Bd. of Psychology, Calif., diplomate clin. psychology Am. Bd. of Profl. Psychology, Washington, cert. stress mgmt. Inst. for Personality and Ability Testing, lic. psychologist SUNY, N.J.; cert. Yoga instr. Internat. Sivananda Yoga Vendanta Ctr. Asst. prof. of psychology U. of Ill., Urbana, Ill., 1966—72; vis. assoc. prof. Tchrs. Coll., Columbia U., N.Y.C., 1973—75; lectr. in psychology Rutgers U., New Brunswick, NJ, 1976—81; faculty Am. Inst. of Psychoanalysis, N.Y.C., 1979—85, supervising psychoanalyst, 1983—85; assoc. prof. Calif. Sch. of Profl. Psychology, San Diego, 1985—94; prof. of psychology Calif. Inst. of Integral Studies, San Francisco, 1994—, divsn. dir. of psychology, 1996—97, dean of profl. psychology, 1998—2002; pres. faculty senate Calif. Inst. Integral Studies, San Francisco, 1996—97; CEO Psychodiagnostics Press, San Francisco, 2001—. Dir. of psychol. rsch. Oceana, Ltd., San Francisco, 1994—96; cons. Ctr. for Moral Judgment, Harvard U., Cambridge, Mass., 1976—87; rsch. cons. Inst. for Pedagogical Studies, Tchrs. Coll., Columbia U., N.Y.C., 1970—74; head bio-psychological investigation, internat. biol. program Milton Olive Found., Brown County, Miss., 1968—72; statistician Inst. for Rsch. on Exceptional Children, U. of Ill., Urbana, 1968—70; editl. bd. Am. Jour. of Psychoanalysis, N.Y.C., 1978—. *Pioneer psychoanalyst among first non-medical graduates of the American Institute of Psychoanalysis, New York City. Engaged in private practice and academic research and teaching for 37 years. Member of the Editorial Board of the American Journal of Psychoanalysis for 25 years. Developed new methods for assessment of dreams, cognition, and personality. Served as Dean of the School of Professional Psychology at the California Institute of Integral Studies, coordinated programs and clinics, new initiatives, supervised faculty and administered budget with 4.5 million annual revenue. Current president of Psychodiagnostics that develops innovative approaches to assessment and publishes tests for mental professionals.* Author: (monograph) A Developmental Study of the Ego Ideal; editor: (spl. jour. issue) Symposium on Narcissism: Differing Psychoanalytic Perspectives; author: (chpt.) Lifespan Developmental Psychology: Normative Life Crises, Organization and Transformation, Dialectical Psychology, Procedings of the First International Conference on Jung's Psychology and Chinese Culture; contbr. articles to profl. jours. Pres. Assn. for Psychoanalytic Edn. and Tng., La Jolla, Calif., 1987—89; chair pro tem Princeton Soc. for Psychology and Psychoanalysis, Princeton, 1981—82. Named Lawra Hansen Meml. Lectr., Iowa State U., 1970; recipient David Ross fellowship, Purdue U., 1965—66, Sr. postdoctoral fellowship, NIMH, 1970—72, postdoctoral fellowship, Internat. Inst. for Humanistic Studies, 1978. Fellow: Am. Acad. of Clin. Psychology; mem.: APA, Internat. Soc. for the Study of Neuropsychoanalysis, Am. Assn. for Advancement of Psychoanalysis (counselor, mem. exec. com. 1982—85). Green Party. Buddhist Anglican. Achievements include development of Music Apperception Test; Life Span Theory of Preference; first to Direct Interpretation of Dreams; New Program in Preschool Education; Contributions to Neuro-Psychoanalysis. Avocations: nutrition and food preparation, mountain climbing, meditation, art collection, bicycling. Office: Calif Inst Integral Sudies 1453 Mission St San Francisco CA 94103 Home: 10 Mohave Ct Corte Madera CA 94925 Personal E-mail: lvandendaele@ciis.edu. E-mail: lvandendaele@ciis.edu.

VANDEN EYNDEN, CHARLES LAWRENCE, mathematician, educator; b. Cin., June 25, 1936; s. Lawrence Norbert George and Sophia (Koester) Vanden Eynden; m. Joan Brody, Aug. 3, 1967; children: Lisa, Jennifer. BS, U. Cin., 1958; MA, U. Oreg., 1960, PhD, 1962. NSF fellow U. Mich., Ann Arbor, 1962-63; asst. prof. U. Ariz., Tucson, 1963-65, Miami U., Oxford, Ohio, 1965-67; vis. asst. prof. Pa. State U., State College, 1967-68; asst. prof. Ohio U., Athens, 1968-69; from assoc. prof. to prof. math. Ill. State U., Normal, 1969—2002; ret., 2002. Author: Elementary Number Theory, 1987, 2001; co-author: Discrete Mathematics, 1987, 93, 97, 2002, Elementary Abstract Algebra, 1993. Office: Ill State U Dept Math Normal IL 61761 E-mail: cve@ilstu.edu.

VAN DEN HENDE, FRED J(OSEPH), human resources executive; b. Chgo., Sept. 28, 1953; s. Maurice Everett and Alice Helen (Davey) Van Den H.; m. Sharon Joyce Kucharski, Oct. 4, 1975; children: John Michael, Karen Michelle. BA, DePaul U., 1975; grad., U. Wash. Sch. Exec. Dev., 1981; MS, Nat. Louis U., 1998. Cert. sr. profl. human resources. Asst. v.p. human resources Land of Lincoln Savs. and Loan, Berwyn, Ill., 1977-84; v.p. human resources Uptown Fed. Bank FSB, Niles, Ill., 1984-88; dir. human resources Archdiocese of Chgo., 1988—. Mem. Savs. Assn. Pers. Adminstrn., Berwyn, 1977-84; part-time instr. Inst. Fin. Edn., Chgo., 1984-90, Moraine Valley C.C., Palos Hills, Ill., 1984-90; adj. faculty Coll. Mgmt. and Bus., nat. Louis U., 1998—. Sch. bd. treas. St. Rene Sch., Chgo., 1981; sch. bd. mem. St. Daniel the Prophet Sch., Chgo., 1986-88, 93-95, sch. bd. chmn., 1988-89; boy scout leader St. Daniel Parish, Chgo., 1987-94. Recipient Oustanding Achievement in the Field of Athletics award St. Rita H.S. Alumni Assn., Chgo., 1991; Athletic scholar DePaul U., Chgo., 1971-75. Mem. Nat. Assn. Ch. Pers. Adminstrs., Soc. for Human Resource Mgmt. (mem. sch.-to-work com. 1998-2000), Ill. State C. of C. (human resources com. 1979-2003, healthcare com. 1998-2003), Inst. Internat. Human Resources, Am. Mgmt. Assn. (Chicago Area Tng. Coun. 2001—), Soc. for Human Resource Profls. (edn. adv. com. 2002—). Roman Catholic. Avocations: camping, fishing, coaching youth sports teams, horseback riding. Home: 5130 S Mulligan Ave Chicago IL 60638-1316 Office: Archdiocese of Chgo 155 E Superior St Chicago IL 60611-2911 E-mail: fvandenhende@archchicago.org.

VANDEN HEUVEL, KATRINA, magazine editor; b. N.Y.C., Oct. 7, 1959; d. William Jacobus and Jean Babette (Stein) Vanden H.; m. Stephen F. Cohen, Dec. 4, 1988; 1 child, Nicola Anna. BA summa cum laude in Politics, Princeton U., 1982. Prodn. assoc. ABC Closeup Documentaries, 1982-83; asst. editor The Nation, N.Y.C., 1984-89, editor-at-large, 1989-93, acting editor-in-chief, 1994-95, editor-in-chief, 1995—. Vis. journalist Moscow News, 1989; Moscow coord. Conf. Investigative Journalism After the Cold War, 1992; co-founder, co-editor Vyi i Myi, 1990—. Editor: The Nation, 1865-1990; The Best of the Nation, 1990-2000: Selections from the Independent Magazine of Politics and Culture, 2001, A Just Response: The Nation on Terrorism, Democracy and September 11, 2001, 2002; co-editor: Voices of Glasnost: Interviews with Gorbachev's Reformers, 1989, Taking Back America, 2004; contbr. articles to newspapers. Recipient Maggie award Planned Parenthood Fedn. Am., 1994. Mem. Correctional Assn. N.Y. (dir.), Inst. for Women's Policy Rsch. (bd. dirs.), Coun. Fgn. Rels., Inst. Policy Studies (trustee), Network of East-West Women (bd. advisors), Franklin and Eleanor Roosevelt Inst. (trustee), Moscow Ctr. for Gender Studies (mem. adv. com.), Century Assn. Office: The Nation 33 Irving Pl Fl 8 New York NY 10003-2332

VAN-DEN-NOORT, STANLEY, neurologist, educator; b. Lynn, Mass., Sept. 8, 1930; s. Judokus and Hazel G. (Van Blarcom) van den N.; m. June Le Clere, Apr. 17, 1954; children: Susanne, Eric, Peter, Katherine, Elizabeth. AB, Dartmouth, 1951; MD, Harvard, 1954. Intern then resident Boston City Hosp., 1954-56, resident neurology, 1958-60; rsch. fellow neurochemistry Harvard U., 1960—62; instr. medicine Case Western Res. U., Cleve., 1962-66, asst. prof., 1966-69, assoc. prof., 1969-70; prof. neurology U. Calif., Irvine, 1970—, chief dept. neurology, 1970—72, chair dept. neurology, 1986—98, assoc. dean Coll. Medicine, 1972-73, dean, 1973-85. Mem. cons. staff U. Calif., Irvine (Calif.) Med. Ctr., Long Beach (Calif.) VA Hosp.; mem. revision com. U.S. Pharmacopoeial Conv., 1990-95. Mem. med. adv. bds., Nat. Multiple Scierosis Soc./Myasthenia Gravis, 1971—, Orange County chpt. Nat. Multiple Sclerosis Soc., 1971—, Orange County Health Planning Coun., 1971-85, Nat. Com. Rsch. in Neurol. Disease, 1982-87. Lt. M.C. USNR, 1956-58. Fellow ACP, Am. Acad. Neurol.; mem. AMA, Am. Neurol. Assn., Nat. Multiple Sclerosis Soc. (chief med. officer 1997-2002), Orange County Med. Assn., Calif. Med. Assn. Home: 17592 Orange Tree Ln Tustin CA 92780-2353 Office: U Calif Dept Neurology Pottscholk Med Plaza Irvine CA 92697-4275 Office Phone: 849-824-6486. Business E-mail: svandenn@uci.edu.

VANDEN WYNGAARD, JULIANNE MARGUERITE, music educator; b. Grand Rapids, Mich., Apr. 22, 1938; d. Theodore Arthur and Edith Marguerite Rambeau; m. Turner Graham Washington Jr., Feb. 9, 1958 (div. Apr. 1962); 1 child, Marguerite; m. Joe Nicolaas Vanden Wyngaard, Apr. 2, 1966. BFA, U. Wis., Milw., 1983; diploma, Netherlands Carillon Sch., Amersfoort, The Netherlands, 2000. From instr. to assoc. prof. Grand Valley State U., Allendale, Mich., 1965—2003, prof., 2003—. Carillonneur Grand Valley State U., Allendale, 1997—. Named Tchr. of Yr., Mich. Music Tchrs. Assn., 1986. Mem.: Guild Carillonneurs in N.Am., Mu Phi Epsilon (4th v.p. 1995—2003). Avocation: needlecrafts. Office: Grand Valley State Univ 1 Campus Dr Allendale MI 49401

VAN DE PUTTE, LETICIA, pharmacist, state senator; b. Tacoma, Dec. 6, 1954; d. Daniel and Isabel (Aguilar) San Miguel; m. Henry P. Van de Putte, Jr., Oct. 223, 1977; children: Nichole, Vanessa, Henry, Gregory, Isabella, Paul. Student, St. Mary's U., San Antonio, 1973-74, U. Houston, 1975, 76-77, U. Tex., 1979; cert. JFK sch. exec. program, Harvard U., 1993. Registered pharmacist, Tex. Pharmacist in charge Botica Guadalupana, San Antonio, 1982-85; owner Loma Park Pharmacy; State Senator Dist. 26, Tex., 1999—. Mem. Tex. State Hispanic Caucus, vice-chair, 2000—01, chair, 2001—03; mem. Veteran Affairs and Military Installations Com., chair, 2003—; mem. Adminstrn. Com., 2003, Bus. & Commerce Com., 2003, Edn. Sub-com. on Higher Edn., 2003; pres. Nat. Hispanic Caucus State Legislatures, 2003—; vice-pres. Nat. Conf. State Legislatures, 2004—. Bd. mem. Santa Rosa Children's Hosp. Found., 2003—; steering com. Milbank Mem. Fund. Recipient Legis. Excellence Award, ACLU, 2001, Session Player 77th Legis. Session, Tex. Monthly Mag., 2001, Best of 77th Legis., Hispanic Jour. Mag., 2001, Pub. Policy Award, Am. Lung Assn., Tex., 2001, Champion for Diabetes Recognition Award, Am. Diabetes Assn., 2003, Pub. Servant of Yr., Am. with Disabilities Act, 2003, Women of Yr., Mex. Am. Bus. Profl. Women, 2003, Legis. Champion Award, Tex. Dept. Pub. Safety Officer's Assn., 2004, Children's Championship Award, United Way of San Antonio, 2004, Appreciation Award, SAISD-Fine Arts Edn. Coalition, San Antonio, 2004. Democrat. Office: 3718 Blanco Rd Ste 2 San Antonio TX 78212-1330 E-mail: leticia.vandeputte@senate.state.tx.us.

VAN DER BEEK, JAMES, actor; b. Chesire, Conn., Mar. 8, 1977; s. James and Melinda Van Der Beek; m. Heather McComb, 2003. Appeared in films Angus, 1995, I Love You, I Love You Not, 1996, Varsity Blues, 1999, Harvest, 1999, Scary Movie, 1999, Jay and Silent Bob Strike Back, 2001, Texas Rangers, 2001, The Rules of Attraction, 2002; Dawson's Creek (TV series), 1998-2003. Scholar, Drew Univ. Office: J Michael Bloom & Assocs 9255 W Sunset Blvd Fl 7 Los Angeles CA 90069-3309

VANDERBEEK, JEFFREY, diversified financial services company executive; BS, Bloomfield Coll. With Donaldson Lufkin & Jenrette; mng. dir., COO, fixed income ctrl. funding dept. Lehman Brothers Holdings Inc., 1984—93, COO, fixed income govt. dept., 1993—96, COO, fixed income derivative dept., 1993—96, head, global fixed income divsn., 1996—2000, head, capital markets divsn., 2000—02, head, global risk mgmt., pvt. equity and strategy, 2002—. V. chmn., bd. mem. Dorothy Rodbell Cohen Found.; mem. exec. com. Boston Coll. Wall St. Coun. Office: Lehman Brothers Holdings Inc 745 Seventh Ave New York NY 10019

VANDERBEKE, PATRICIA K. architect; b. Detroit, Apr. 3, 1963; d. B. H. and Dolores I. VanderBeke. BS in Architecture, U. Mich., 1985, MArch, 1987. Registered arch., Ill. Archtl. intern Hobbs & Black, Assocs., Ann Arbor, Mich., 1984-86, Fry Assocs., Ann Arbor, 1988; arch. Decker & Kemp Architecture/Urban Design, Chgo., 1989-92; prin., founder P. K. VanderBeke, Arch., Chgo., 1992—. Mem. adv. com. dept. arch., Triton Coll. Contbr. photographs and articles to Inland Arch. mag.; contbr. photographs to AIA calendar. Chair recycling com. Lake Point Tower Condo. Assn., Chgo., 1990—, chair. ops. com., 1993; mem. benefit com. The Renaissance Soc., U. Chgo., Redmoon Theater, Chgo. George S. Booth travelling fellow, 1992. Mem. AIA (participant 1st ann. leadership inst. 1997, 1st place nat. photog. contest award 1992, hon. mention 1994, membership com. Chgo. chpt.), Chgo. Archl. Club, hon. mention 2000 Burnham Prize Competition, The Cliff Dwellers (mem. arts com.). Office: 155 W Burton Pl Apt 16 Chicago IL 60610-1326

VANDERBILT, ARTHUR T., II, lawyer; b. Summit, NJ, Feb. 20, 1950; s. William Runyon and Jean (White) V. *Grandfather and namesake, Arthur T. Vanderbilt, was Chief Justice of the Supreme Court of New Jersey (1948-1957), Dean of NYU School of Law (1943-1947), and President of the American Bar Association (1937-1938). The main building at NYU School of Law bears his name.* BA, Wesleyan U., Middletown, Conn., 1972; JD, U. Va., 1975. Bar: N.J. 1975, U.S. Dist. Ct. N.J. 1975, U.S. Supreme Ct. 1978. Jud. clk. to presiding justice N.J. Superior Ct., 1975-76, dep. atty. gen., 1976-78, asst. counsel to gov., 1978-79; ptnr. Carella, Byrne, Bain & Gilfillan, Roseland, N.J., 1979—. Chmn. Supreme Ct. Ethics Com.; mem. Supreme Ct. Adv. Com. Profl. Ethics. Author: Changing Law 1976, Jersey Justice, 1978, Law School, 1981, Treasure Wreck, 1986, Fortune's Children, 1989 (Book of the Month Club, Readers Digest and fgn. edits.), New Jersey's Judicial Revolution, 1997, Golden Days, 1998 (fgn. edits.), Jersey Jurists, 1998, The Making of a Bestseller, 1999, Gardening in Eden, 2003. Trustee Elizabeth (NJ) Presbytery. Named to N.J. Literary Hall of Fame. Fellow: ABA Found.; mem.: ABA (Scribes award 1976), Nat. Writers Union, The Authors Guild, Inc., Nat. Assn. Bond Lawyers, Am. Judicature Soc., N.J. Bar Assn., Capitol Hill Club, Hyannis Yacht Club. Republican. Presbyterian. Avocation: writing. Office: Carella Byrne Bain & Gilfillan 5 Becker Farm Rd Roseland NJ 07068-1735 Office Phone: 973-994-1700.

VANDERBILT, GLORIA MORGAN, artist, actress, fashion designer; b. N.Y.C., Feb. 20, 1924; d. Reginald Claypoole and Gloria (Morgan) V.; m. Pasquale di Cicco (div.); m. Leopold Stokowski, 1945 (div. 1955); children—Stanislaus, Christopher; m. Sidney Lumet, 1956 (div.); m. Wyatt Emory Cooper, 1963; children— Carter V. (dec.), Anderson H. Attended, Mary C. Wheeler, Miss Porter's schs.; studied acting with, dir. Sanford Meisner, beginning 1955. Exhibited in one-man shows at Rabun Studio, N.Y.C., 1948, Bertha Shaeffer Gallery, N.Y.C., 1954, Juster Gallery, N.Y.C., 1956, Hammer Gallery, N.Y.C., 1966, 68, Cord Gallery, N.Y.C., 1966, Washington Gallery Art, 1968, Neiman-Marcus, Dallas, 1968, Vestart Gallery, N.Y.C., 1969, Parish Museum, Southampton, N.Y., also in Nantucket, Mass., Houston, Reading, Pa., Monterey, Calif., Nashville; exhibited in group shows, Washington Gallery Art, 1967, Hoover Gallery, San Francisco, 1971, stage career; acted in summer stock prodn. The Swan; made Broadway debut in The Time of Your Life, 1955; other stage appearances include Picnic, 1955, The Spa, 1956, Peter Pan, 1958, The Green Hat; made TV debut in Tonight At 8:30; other TV appearances include Colgate Comedy Hour, 1955, Flint and Fire on U.S. Steel Hour, 1958, Family Happiness on U.S. Steel Hour, 1959, Very Important People; appeared in film Johnny Concho, 1955; dir. design film, Riegel Textile Corp., N.Y.C., from 1970; designer stationary and greeting cards, Hallmark Co., fabrics, Bloomcraft Co., bed linens, Martex Co., table linens, Peacock Co., Gloria Vanderbilt jeans; also china, glassware, scarves. Recipient Sylvania award 1959, Fashion award Neiman-Marcus 1969. Author: Love Poems, 1955, (with Alfred Allen Lewis) Gloria Vanderbilt Book of Collage, 1970, Woman to Woman, 1979, Once Upon a Time: A True Story, 1985, novel Never Say Good-Bye, 1989, The Memory Book of Starr Faithfull, 1994; author: (with Alfred Allen Lewis) play Three by Two, early 1960's, Black White, White Knight, 1987; poems and short stories. Mem. Actors Equity, Screen Actors Guild, AFTRA, Authors League Am., Am. Fedn. Arts.

VANDERBILT, KERMIT, English language educator; b. Decorah, Iowa, Sept. 1, 1925; s. Lester and Ella (Qualley) V.; m. Vivian Osmundson, Nov. 15, 1947; 1 dau., Karen Paige. BA, Luther Coll., Decorah, 1947, Litt. D. (hon.), 1977; MA, U. Minn., 1949, PhD, 1956. Instr. English U. Minn., 1954-57; instr. U. Wash., 1958-60, asst. prof. English, 1960-62; asst. prof. San Diego State U., 1962-65, assoc. prof., 1965-68, prof., 1968-90, prof. emeritus, 1990—. Vis. prof. Am. lit. U. B.C., Can., Vancouver, summer 1963; vis. prof. U. Oreg., summer 1968 Author: Charles Eliot Norton: Apostle of Culture in a Democracy, 1959, The Achievement of William Dean Howells: A Reinterpretation, 1968, American Literature and the Academy: The Roots, Growth and Maturity of a Profession, 1986 (Choice award for outstanding acad. books), Theodore Roethke in A Literary History of the American West, 1987; editor: (with others) American Social Thought, 1972, April Hopes (W.D. Howells), 1975, The Rise of Silas Lapham, 1983, spl. issue Am. Literary Realism, winter 1989, La Litterature Americaine, 1991, 3d edit., 1997, The Beautiful and Damned (F. Scott Fitzgerald), 1998; mem. edit. bd. U. Wash. Press, 1960-62, Twentieth Century Lit., 1969-2002; contbr. numerous articles to profl. jours. Served with USNR, 1943-46. Outstanding Prof. San Diego State U., 1976; Guggenheim fellow, 1978-79; Huntington Library fellow, 1980; Am. Philos. Soc. grantee, 1964, Am. Council Learned Socs. grantee, 1972, Nat. Endowment for Humanities grantee, 1986. Mem. Am. Studies Assn. (exec. council 1968-69), So. Calif. Am. Studies Assn. (pres. 1968-69), Philol. Assn. Pacific Coast (chmn. sect. Am. lit. 1968), MLA, Internat. Mark Twain Soc. (hon.), United Profs. of Calif. (Disting. prof. 1978) Home: 6937 Coleshill Dr San Diego CA 92119-1920

VANDERBURG, PAUL STACEY, insurance executive, consultant; b. Detroit, Apr. 13, 1941; s. Harold Stacey and Alice Bertha (Lyle) V. Cert. in plastics tech., Oakland U., 1966; AS in Bus., C.S. Mott C.C., 1971; Casualty Claims Law Assoc., Am. Ednl. Inst., 1986; BA in Bus. Adminstrn. and Mgmt., Columbia Pacific U., 1990; cert. in human resource devel., U. South Fla., 1992; fraud claims law assoc., Am. Ednl. Inst., 1995; grad., FBI Citizens Acad., Tampa, 2003. Lic. ins. adjuster Mich., Fla.; cert. cir. civil mediator U. South Fla. Mediation Inst., 2001, cert. county court mediator State Fla. Supreme Ct., 2002. Ins. field claims adjuster Underwriters Adjusting Co., Pontiac, Mich., 1972-76; pres., CEO Sun Cycle, Inc., Drayton Plains, Mich., 1975-77; sr. ins. claims adjuster Kemper Ins. Group, Tampa, Fla., 1979-80; ins. field claims adjuster Auto-Owners Ins. Co., Lakeland, Fla., 1981-82; sr. recovery specialist CIGNA Corp., Tampa, 1984-85; ins. field claims adjuster Seaboard Adjustment Bur., Lakeland, 1985-87; sr. field claims ins. adjuster Hallmark Ins. Adjusters, Clearwater, Fla., 1987-88; pvt. practice Tampa, 1988—. Author: Insurance Subrogation Management, 1991. Apptd. law enforcement rep. Hillsborough County (Fla.) Human Rels. Bd., 1999—. Staff sgt. U.S. Army, 1963-69. Mem.: Assn. Property and Casualty Claims Profls., Soc. of Claims Law Assocs., Assn. of Workers' Compensation Claims Profls., Fla. Acad. Profl. Mediators, Ctr. for Internat. Security Studies, Fla. Sheriffs Assn., Am. Security Coun. (nat. adv. bd.), FBI Citizens Acad. Alumni Assn. (bd. dirs.), Am. Legion. Republican. Avocations: boating, fishing, photography. Home and Office: 5448 Circle Dr (WWG) Spring Hill FL 34607-1407 Office Phone: 813-886-9669. Office Fax: 352-592-2191. Personal E-mail: chum2828@aol.com.

VANDERHEIDEN, GREGG C. engineering educator, research scientist; b. Norway, Mich., Oct. 27, 1949; s. Paul H. and Marion A. Vanderheiden; m. Katherine R. Donaho, Sept. 20, 1985; 1 child, James A. BSEE magna cum laude, U. Wis., 1972, MS in Biomed. Engring., 1974, PhD in Tech. in Comm. Rehab. and Child Devel., 1984. Dir. Trace R&D Ctr., Madison, 1972—; clin. staff dept. rehab. medicine Comm. Aids and Sys. Clinic U. Wis. Hosp. and Clinics, Madison, 1979—92; faculty human factors program dept. indsl. engring. U. Wis., Madison, 1986—, faculty dept. biomed. engring., 1998—. Prin. investigator over 150 grants and projects, 1971—; cons. in field; presenter in field; mem. exec. com. biomed. engring. program U. Wis., Madison, 1997—; mem. exec. com. and bd. dirs. Rehab. Engring. Soc. N.Am., 1981—96, past pres., 1993—94; field peer reviewer NSF, U.S. Office Spl. Edn. Programs, Nat. Inst. Disability and Rehab. Rsch.; mem. grant rev. panel Internat. Bus. Machines Corp., 1987; mem. sci. rev. and evaluation bd. VA Dept. Medicine and Surgery, Rehab. Engring. R&D Svc., 1979—; co-chair Industry-Govt. Com. on Access to Computers and Info. Sys. for Disabled Persons, 1983—88; founding mem. Internat. Com. on Accessible Documentation for People with Print Disabilities. Mem. editl. bd.: Jour. Rehab. Rsch., 1983—2000, Jour. Computers and Human Svcs., 1984—, Assistive Tech., 1988—99, Internat. Jour. Universal Access in the Info. Soc., 2001; contbr. chapters to books; mem. editl. bd.: Internat. Jour. Tech. and Aging, 1989—; contbr. articles to profl. jours. Fellow: Am. Inst. Med. and Biol. Engring.; mem.: Internat. Soc. for Alternative and Augmentative Comm. (mem. founding com.), Assn. for Computing Machinery, Inst. Indsl. Engrs. (sr.), Human Factors and Ergonomics Soc. Achievements include patents for touchscreen for the vision impaired; control panel for individual with disabilities; flexible access system for touchscreen devices; long-range optical pointing for vide screens; automonitoring communication devices for handicapped persons; development of Universal Remote Console Communication (URCC) protocol; SET Standard for Electrical Interconnections for Augmentative Communication and Control Aids; KEI Standard for Keyboard Emulating Interfaces; GIDEI Standard for General Input Device Emulating Interfaces; Serial Control Standard for Electronic Control of Power Wheelchairs. Office: Trace R&D Ctr Engring Ctrs Bldg 1550 Engineering Dr Madison WI 53706 Office Phone: 608-262-6966. Business E-Mail: gv@trace.wisc.edu.

VANDERHEYDEN, MARC A. academic administrator; b. Belgium; m. Diana. M, D, Cath. U. V.p. acad. affairs Cedar Crest Coll., dean faculty; pres. St. Michael's Coll., 1993—. Office: St Michael's Coll 1 Winooski Park Colchester VT 05439-0001

VANDERHOEF, LARRY NEIL, academic administrator; b. Perham, Minn., Mar. 20, 1941; s. Wilmar James and Ida Lucille (Wothe) Vanderhoef; m. Rosalie Suzanne Slifka, Aug. 31, 1963; children: Susan Marie, Jonathan Lee. BS, U. Wis., Milw., 1964, MS, 1965; PhD, Purdue U., 1969, Doctorate (hon.), 2000, Inje U. Korea, 2002. Postdoctorate U. Wis., Madison, 1969—70; asst. prof. biology U. Ill., Urbana, 1970-74, assoc. prof., 1974—77, prof., 1977—80, head dept. plant biology, 1977—80; provost Agrl. and Life Scis., U. Md., College Park, 1980—84; exec. vice chancellor U. Calif., Davis, 1984—91, exec. vice chancellor, provost, 1991—94; chancellor, 1994—. Rsch. assoc. U. Wis., 1970—72; vis. investigator Carnegie Inst., 1976—77, Edinburgh (Scotland) U., 1978; cons. in field. Fellow, NRC, 1969—70, Eisenhower fellow, 1987; grantee Dimond Travel grantee, 1975, NSF, 1972, 1974, 1976—79, NATO, 1980. Mem.: AAAS, Nat. Assn. State Univ. and Land Grant Colls. (exec. com. 2000—), Am. Soc. Plant Physiology (bd. editors 1977—82, trustee, exec. com., treas. 1982—88, chmn. bd. trustees 1994—97). Home: 16 College Park Davis CA 95616-3607 Office: U Calif Davis Office Chancellor Davis CA 95616

VAN DER HOEK, SHERRY A. counselor; b. Chgo., July 20, 1956; d. John Albert and Stella Rose (dec.) Troike; m. Herman Vanderhoek (dec.); stepchildren: Michiel, Martin. AAS, Prairie State Coll., 1992; BA, Govs. State U., 1994, MA, 1997. Lic. profl. counselor, Ill.; cert. counselor Nat. Bd. Cert. Counselors. Counselor South Suburban Coun. on Alcoholism, East Hazel Crest, Ill., 1990-93, South Suburban Family Shelter, Hazel Crest, Ill., 1996-97; facilitator Aunt Martha's Youth Svcs. Ctr., Inc., Park Forest, Ill., 1991-92; grad. asst. Govs. State U., University Park, Ill., 1995-97; pvt. practice counselor Matteson, Ill., 1998—. Mem.: ACA, Ill. Alcoholism and Drug Dependence Assn., Assn. Counselor Edn. and Supervision (Outstanding Grad. Student Scholarship award 1997), Internat. Assn. Addiction and Offender Counselors, Ill. Counselor Educators and Suprs. (Outstanding Grad. Student award 1996), Ill. Alcohol and Other Drug Profl. Cert. Assn., Ill. Counseling Assn. (founder Govs. State Chpt., pres. 1996, regional gov. 1997—2000), Chi Sigma Iota (chpt. sec. 1995), Psi Chi (chpt. founder, pres. 1997). Avocations: stained glass, cross-stitch, cooking. Home and Office: 3761 W 216th Pl Matteson IL 60443

VANDERHOOFT, ROB, investment company executive; b. Winnipeg; Grad., U. Manitoba, Can., 1987. Equity analyst Great West Life Assurance Co.; with Greystone Managed Investments Inc., Regina, Canada, 1991—, pres., chief investment officer, 1995—. Office: Greystone Managed Investments 300 Park Ctr 1230 Blackfoot Dr Regina SK Canada

VANDER HORST, KATHLEEN PURCELL, nonprofit association administrator; b. Glen Rock, NJ, Jan. 15, 1945; d. Thomas Ralph and Elizabeth Jeanne (Burnett) Purcell; m. John Vander Horst Jr., Feb. 12, 1972 (div. Oct. 1993). Dir. devel. svcs. Johns Hopkins U., Balt., 1968-71; dir. devel. Union of Colls. of Art, Kansas City, Mo., 1971-72; dir. pub. rels. Md. Ballet and Ctr.

Stage, Balt., 1973-76; dir. program devel. Joint Ctr. for Polit. and Econ. Studies, Washington, 1976-90, v.p. program devel., 1990—2000, cons., 2001—. Dir., Roland Park Cmty. Found., Balt., 1990-2000, vice-chmn., 1998-99, chmn., 2000-02; dir., chair program com. Centro de la Comunidad, Balt., 1997-2001. Office Phone: 410-448-5233.

VANDERKOLK, MARY DEDECKER, nursing educator; b. Highland Park, Mich., Feb. 7, 1951; d. Frank Joseph and Jean Marie (Halmich) DeDecker; m. Michael Homer VanderKolk, June 18, 1977; children: Lauren, Christopher, Nicole, Allison. BS in Psychology, Mich. State U., 1972, BSN, 1975; MSN, Wayne State U., 1980, postgrad., 1989—; MBA, Lake Superior State U., 1993. Nurse externe E.W. Sparrow Hosp., Lansing, Mich., 1974-75, charge nurse gen. surgery unit, 1975-76, staff nurse ICU, 1976-77; staff nurse SICU Catherine McCauley Health Ctr., Ann Arbor, Mich., 1977-81, summer 1982; asst. prof. Ea. Mich. U., Ypsilanti, 1981-84; mem. contingency staff ICU Munson Med. Ctr., Traverse City, Mich., 1984-85; lead instr. advanced med./surg. nursing Northwestern Mich. Coll., Traverse City, 1985-87, dept. head nursing, 1987-98, nursing prof., 1998— Defendant nurse expert witness, 1989-94, 96, 97-98; mem. adj. fculty MSN program Grand Valley State U., Grand Rapids, Mich., 1991; com. mem. devel. coun. Munson Med. Ctr., 1992-93; sec./treas. Rural Emergency Med. Edn. Consortium, Traverse City, 1993-95, bd. dirs., 1993-99; bd. dirs., sec. Twin Bays Skating Club, 2000—. Co-author: Adoption Without Fear, 1989; co-author, co-prodr. (video) Tracheostomy Care and Suctioning Techniques, 1984. Coord. health edn. team Immaculate Conception Ch., Traverse City, 1994-95, mem. adv. com. health ministry, 1994—; mem. course devel. team Nursing Virtual C.C. Collaborative of Mich., 2000-01. Recipient Excellence in Teaching award Nat. Inst. Staff & Orgnl. Devel., 1993. Mem. ANA, Nat. League Nursing, Mich. Nurses Assn. (mem. cabinet adminstrn. and edn., rep. at large bd. dirs. 1987-89, 89-91, rec. sec. 1988-89), Mich. Coun. Nursing Edn. Adminstrs. (corr. sec. bd. dirs. 1988-89, 89-90, v.p./pres. elect 1990-91, pres. 1991-92, immediate past pres. 1992-93), Mich. League Nursing (dir. area V 1994-96), King. Internat. Nursing Soc. (founding mem. 1996—), County Med. Soc. Aux., Sigma Theta Tau. Avocations: travel, water sports, downhill skiing, figure skating. Office: Northwestern Mich Coll 1701 E Front St Traverse City MI 49686-3016

VANDER LAAN, MARK ALAN, lawyer; b. Akron, Ohio, Sept. 14, 1948; s. Robert H. and Isabel R. (Bishop) Vander L.; m. Barbara Ann Ryzenga, Aug. 25, 1970; children: Aaron, Matthew. AB, Hope Coll., 1970; JD, U. Mich., 1972. Bar: Ohio 1973, U.S. Dist. Ct. (so. dist.) Ohio 1973, U.S. Ct. Appeals (6th cir.) 1978, U.S. Supreme Ct. 1981. Assoc. Dinsmore, Shohl, Coates & Deupree, Cin., 1972-79; ptnr. Dinsmore & Shohl, Cin., 1979—. Chair litig. dept., 2001—; spl. counsel Ohio Atty. Gen.'s Office, 1983—; spl. prosecutor State of Ohio, 1985-94; city solicitor City of Blue Ash, Ohio, 1987—, City of Silverton, Ohio, 1999—; trustee Cin. So. Railway, 1994—, pres., 1999—; trustee, chair Grassroots Leadership Acad., 1997—. Mem. Cin. Human Rels. Commn., 1980-86; mem. Leadership Cin. Class XIII, 1989-90; trustee Legal Aid Soc. of Cin., 1981-94, pres., 1988-90; trustee Volunteer Lawyers for the Poor Found., pres., 2003— Mem. ABA, Ohio Bar Assn., Cin. Bar Assn. (ethics com. 1983—), Sixth Cir. Jud. Conf. (life), Potter Stewart Am. Inn of Ct. (master), Queen City Club. Office: Dinsmore & Shohl 1900 Chemed Ct 255 E 5th St Cincinnati OH 45202-4700 Office Phone: 513-977-8238. E-mail: mark.vanderlaan@dinslaw.com.

VANDERLINDEN, CAMILLA DENICE DUNN, telecommunications industry executive; b. Dayton, July 21, 1950; d. Joseph Stanley and Virginia Danley (Martin) Dunn; m. David Henry VanderLinden; Oct. 10, 1980; 1 child, Michael Christopher. Student, U. de Valencia, Spain, 1969; BA in Spanish and Secondary Edn. cum laude, U. Utah, 1972, MS in Human Resource Econs., 1985. Asst. dir. Davis County Community Action Program, Farmington, Utah, 1973-76; dir. South County Community Action, Midvale, Utah, 1976-79; supr. customer service Ideal Nat. Life Ins. Co., Salt Lake City, 1979-80; mgr. customer service Utah Farm Bur. Mutual Ins., Salt Lake City, 1980-82; quality assurance analyst Am. Express Co., Salt Lake City, 1983-86, quality assurance and human resource specialist, 1986-88, mgr. quality assurance and engring. Denver, 1988-91; mgr. customer svc. Tel. Express Co., Colorado Springs, Colo., 1991-97; dir. Call Ctr. United Membership Mktg. Group, Lakewood, Colo., 1997-98; telesvcs. industry mgr. Piton Found., Denver, 1998—; customer care and tng. dir. SafeRent, 2000—; pvt. call ctr. cons., 2000—; dir. quality assurance Tele-Servicing Innovations, 2000—02; ops. mgr. Bayaud Industries, 2002—. Mem. adj. faculty Westminster Coll., Salt Lake City, 1987-88. mem. adj. faculty, mem. quality adv. bd. Red Rocks C.C., 1990-91. Vol. translator Latin Am. community; vol. naturalist Roxborough State Park; internat. exch. coord. EF Fgn. Exch. Program. Mem. Internat. Customer Svc. Orgn. (officer call ctr. chpt.), Colo. Springs Customer Svc. Assn. (officer). Christian. Avocations: swimming, hosting foreign exchange students. Home: 10857 Snow Cloud Trail Littleton CO 80125-9211 Office Phone: 303-946-1235. Personal E-mail: camillavan@usa.net.

VAN DER LINDEN, FRANK MORRIS, historian; b. Hendersonville, N.C., Mar. 8, 1919; s. William Harrison and Floride Bowden (Morris) van der L.; m. Georgia Kathlyn Huddle, Feb. 11, 1951; children: Frank Robert, Margaret Lyn, Anne Morris. AB, Lenoir-Rhyne Coll., 1939. Reporter, editl. writer Hickory N.C. Daily Record, 1939-42; mng. editor Hickory Daily Record, 1942-45; reporter Cottrell News Bur., Washington, 1945-52; Washington bur. chief Nashville Tenn. Banner, 1952-86; White House corr. Sacramento Calif. Union, 1979-89; columnist United Feature Syndicate, N.Y., 1971-76. Guest panelist NBC-TV Meet the Press, 1956-75. Author: Dark Horse, 1944, The Turning Point: Jefferson's Battle for the Presidency, 1962, Nixon's Quest for Peace, 1972, The Real Reagan, 1981, Lincoln: The Road to War, 1998. Mem. The Lincoln Commn., Washington, 1989-98. Mem. U.S. Capitol Hist. Soc. (oral history program dir. 1976-94), The Cosmos Club (editl. bd. 1988—). Presbyterian. Avocation: historical research. Home and Office: 5301 Westbard Cir Apt 247 Bethesda MD 20816-1430

VANDERLIP, ELIN BREKKE, philanthropic executive; b. Oslo, June 7, 1919; came to the U.S., 1934; m. Kelvin Cox, Nov., 1946 (dec. 1956); children: Kelvin Jr., Narcissa, Henrik and Katrina (twins). With Norwegian Embassy, Washington, Norwegian Fgn. Ministry, London, 1941-44, Red Cross, Calcutta, India; pres. Friends of French Art, Portuguese Bend, Calif. Sponsor of charity art conservation fundraising events Friends of French Art; tour leader Ile de France, Anjou, Bordelais, Provence-Cote d'Azur, Alsace, Dordogne, Lyonnais-Isere, Brittany, Burgundy, Normandy, Languedoc, Loire, Gascony, Le Nord, Charente, Champagne, Eure et Loir, 1978-96, Route de Berry, Auvergne and Toulouse. Decorated Comdr. Order of Arts and Letters (France) Chevalier of the Legion of Honor. Home and Office: Villa Narcissa 100 Vanderlip Dr Palos Verdes Peninsula CA 90275-5920 Fax: (310) 377-4584. E-mail: VillaCissa@aol.com.

VAN DER MARCK, JAN, art historian; b. Roermond, The Netherlands, Aug. 19, 1929; arrived in U.S., 1957; s. Everard and Anny (Finken) van der Marck; m. Ingeborg Lachmann, Apr. 27, 1961 (dec. 1988); m. Sheila Stamell, May 24, 1990. BA, U. Nijmegen, The Netherlands, 1952, MA, 1954, PhD in Art History, 1956; postgrad., U. Utrecht, The Netherlands, 1956-57, Columbia U., 1957-59. Curator Gemeentemuseum, Arnhem, Netherlands, 1959-61; asst. dir. fine arts Seattle World's Fair, 1961-62; curator Walker Art Center, Mpls., 1963-67; dir. Mus. Contemporary Art, Chgo., 1967-70; assoc. prof. art history U. Wash., Seattle, 1972-74; dir. Dartmouth Coll. Mus. and Galleries, 1974-80, Center for Fine Arts, Miami, 1980-85; curator 20th century art, chief curator Detroit Inst. Arts, 1986-95, consultative curator, 1998—2003. Author: (book) Romantische Boekillustratie in Belgie, 1956, George Segal, 1975, Arman, 1984, Bernar Venet, 1988, The Art of Contemporary Bookbinding, 1997, Art and the American Experience, 1998, Lucio Pozzi, 2001; contbr. articles to art jours., essays to catalogues. Decorated officer Order Arts and Letters, knight Order of Orange Nassau; fellow Netherlands Orgn. Pure Rsch., 1954—55, Rockefeller Found., 1957—59, Aspen Inst., 1974, 1994, Ctr. Advanced Study in Visual Arts, Nat. Gallery, Washington, 1986. Fellow: Pierpont Morgan Libr.; mem.: Les Amis de la Reliure Originale, Assn. Internat. Bibliophilie, Internat. Art Critics Assn., Grolier Club.

VAN DER MEER, SIMON, physicist; b. The Hague, The Netherlands, Nov. 24, 1925; s. Pieter and Jetske (Groeneveld) van der M.; m. Catharina M. Koopman, Apr. 26, 1966; children: Esther, Mathijs. Engring. degree in physics, Poly U., Delft, The Netherlands, 1952; Dr. (hon.), U. Geneva, 1983, U. Amsterdam, The Netherlands, 1984, U. Genoa, Italy, 1985. Research engr. Philips Physics Lab., Eihdhoven, The Netherlands, 1952-55; sr. engr. CERN European Orgn. Nuclear Research, Geneva, 1956-90; ret., 1990. Co-recipient Nobel prize for physics, 1984. Mem. AAAS (fgn., hon.), Royal Netherlands Acad. Scis. (corr.).

VAN DER MEULEN, JOSEPH PIERRE, neurologist; b. Boston, Aug. 22, 1929; s. Edward Lawrence and Sarah Jane (Robertson) VanDer M.; m. Ann Irene Yadeno, June 18, 1960; children: Elisabeth, Suzanne, Janet. AB, Boston Coll., 1950; MD, Boston U., 1954. Diplomate Am. Bd. Psychiatry and Neurology. Intern Cornell Med. div. Bellevue Hosp., N.Y.C., 1954-55, resident, 1955-56, Harvard U., Boston City Hosp., 1958-60, instr., fellow, 1962-66; assoc. Case Western Res. U., Cleve., 1966-67, asst. prof., 1967-69, assoc. prof. neurology and biomed. engring., 1969-71; prof. neurology U. So. Calif., L.A., 1971—; also dir. dept. neurology Los Angeles County/U. So. Calif. Med. Center; chmn. dept. U. So. Calif., 1971-78, v.p. for health affairs, 1977—, dean Sch. Medicine, 1985-86, 95-97, vice dean med. affairs, 1995-97; dir. Ind. Health Professions, L.A., 1991—. Vis. prof. Autonomous U. Guadalajara, Mex., 1974; pres. Norris Cancer Hosp. and Research Inst., 1983-98, chmn. 2004. Contbr. articles to profl. jours. Mem. med. adv. bd. Calif. chpt. Myasthenia Gravis Found., 1971-75, chmn., 1974-75, 77-78; med. adv. bd. Amyotrophic Lateral Sclerosis Found., Calif., 1973-75, chmn., 1974-75; mem. Com. to Combat Huntington's Disease, 1973—; bd. dirs. Calif. Hosp. Med. Ctr., Good Hope Med. Found., House Ear Inst., L.A. Hosp. Good Samaritan, Children's Hosp. of L.A., Barlow Respiratory Hosp., U. So. Calif. Univ. Hosp., chmn., 1991—; bd. dirs. Assn. Acad. Health Ctrs., chmn., 1991-92; pres. Scott Newman Ctr., 1987-89. Served to lt. M.C. USNR, 1956-58. Nobel Inst. fellow Karolinska Inst., Stockholm, 1960-62; NIH grantee, 1968-71 Mem. AMA, Am. Neurol. Assn., Am. Acad. Neurology, L.A. Soc. Neurology and Psychiatry (pres. 1977-78), L.A. Med. Assn., Calif. Med. Soc., L.A. Acad. Medicine, Alpha Omega Alpha (councillor 1992—), Phi Kappa Phi. Home: 39 Club View Ln Palos Verdes Peninsula CA 90274-4208 Office: U So Calif 1540 Alcazar St CHP 100 Los Angeles CA 90089-9001 Office Phone: 323-442-1307. Business E-Mail: vanderme@usc.edu.

VANDERMEUSE, DAVID C. music educator; b. Algoma, Wis., Apr. 8, 1954; s. Julius Cletus and Mae Jane Vandermeuse; m. Catherine Jane McDermott, May 7, 1977; children: David P., Matthew R., Amy M., Scott J. BS Agrl. Edn., BME, U. Wis., River Falls, 1979; Master's Agrl. Industries, U. Wis.-Platteville, 1987. Vocat. agrl. tchr. Dodgeland HS, Juneau, Wis., 1979—80, Hartford Union HS, Wis., 1980—85, spec. edn. tchr., 1986—87, music tchr., 1988—. Music dir. Hartford City Band, 1998—; dir. of referees Hartford Soccer Club, 1996—2002. Mem.: Internat. Tubar-Euphonium Assn., Nat. Assn. Sports Officials, Music Educators Nat. Conf. Achievements include performing in a brass quintet. Avocation: gardening. Home: 1042 Cedar Street Hartford WI 53027 Office: Hartfod Union High School 805 Cedar Street Hartford WI 53027

VANDER MOLEN, JACK JACOBUS, engineering executive, industrial facility planner, consultant; b. Assen, Drenthe, Netherlands, May 28, 1916; came to U.S., 1947, naturalized 1952; s. Evert Moll and Victorina Sweelssen; m. Ina Mary Auerbach, 1946 (dec. Jan. 1991); 1 child, Diona Rosemary Kirsch-Vander Molen; m. Alishia McMillan, Apr. 7, 1992. ME, M.T.S., Haarlem, 1940; postgrad. computer program specialist, Ariz. Tech., 1982. Lic. real estate sales profl., Ariz. Draftsman, designer Fokker Aircraft, Amsterdam, Netherlands, 1939-40; asst. plant mgr. Bruynzeel's Deuren Fabriek, Zaandam, Netherlands, 1941-44; civilian mgr. Allied Hdqrs. Rest Ctrs., Maastricht, Amsterdam, Netherlands, 1944-45; cen. staff tech. efficiency and orgn. Philips Radio, Eindhoven, Holland, 1945-47; indsl. engr. N.Am. Philips, Dobbs Ferry, N.Y., 1947-48; supr. methods and standards Otis Elevator Co., Yonkers, N.Y., 1948-51; staff engr., material handling and distbn., cons. Drake, Startzman, Sheahan & Barclay, N.Y.C., 1951-55; mgr. material handling engring. Crane Co., Chgo., 1955-60; assoc., cons. A.T. Kearney & Co., Inc., Chgo., 1960-67; pres., cons. J.J. Vander Molen & Co., Internat., Oak Park, Ill. and Sun City, Ariz., 1967—; real estate agt. Del E. Webb Devel. Co., Sun City, Ariz., 1976-86; ret. Jack J. Vander Molen & Co., 1997. Real estate sales, Del E. Webb Devel. Co., Sun City, Ariz., 1976-86. Conceptual developer of plants, warehouses and terminals, computerized conversion of inventory into building and equipment requirements for major food chains such as Migros, Switzerland, Great Atlantic & Pacific Tea Co., U.S., Tengelmann, Germany, Hema, The Netherlands. With Dutch resistance, U.S. and Can. Armed Forces, 1940-45 Mem. ASME (life), Internat. Materials Handling Soc. (nat. dir. 1960, pres. Chgo. chpt. 1959), Engrs. Club of the Sun Cities Area. Avocations: swimming, music, reading, walking, sketching. Home: 17630 N Foothills Dr Sun City AZ 85373-2158

VANDER MOLEN, THOMAS DALE, lawyer; b. Ann Arbor, Mich., Oct. 30, 1950; s. John and Eleanor Ruth (Driesens) Vander M.; m. Judith P. Wrahlstad, June 16, 2001; children from previous marriage: Laura, David, Eric. BA, Calvin Coll., 1972; JD magna cum laude, Harvard U., 1975. Bar: Minn. 1976, U.S. Dist. Ct. Minn. 1981, U.S. Claims Ct. 1983, U.S. Tax Ct. 1977, U.S. Ct. Appeals Fed. Cir., 1988. Law clk. to judge U.S. Ct. Appeals-First Cir., Boston, 1975-76; assoc. Dorsey & Whitney, Mpls., 1976-81; ptnr. Dorsey & Whitney LLP, Mpls., 1982—, gen. counsel, 1993—2001. Mem. editorial bd. Harvard Law Rev., 1973-75. Presbyterian. Office: Dorsey & Whitney LLP 50 South 6th St Minneapolis MN 55402-1498

VANDER MYDE, PHILIP LOUIS, architectural design firm executive; b. Whiteside County, Ill., Apr. 4, 1931; s. Louis John and Ann Marie (Pals) Vander; m. Martha T. Grier, Mar. 15, 1969; children: Jane Gray, John Philip, Martha Maslin. Student, Central Coll., 1949-50; BA in Arch., U. Minn., 1958. Registered architect, Va., Md., D.C., N.C., Tenn., Pa., Mich., N.J., Ill., W.Va., Del. Architect Vosbeck-Ward & Assocs., Alexandria, Va., 1962-64; assoc. ptnr. Vosbeck Vosbeck & Assocs., Alexandria, Va., 1966; ptnr. VVKR Partnership, Alexandria, 1967-70, mng. ptnr., 1967-70, mng. ptnr. Md. office University Park, 1970-80; prin. VVKR, Inc., Alexandria, 1980-83; mng. ptnr. for architecture Dewberry & Davis, Fairfax, Va., 1983-87; mng. ptnr. Senseman/VanderMyde, Alexandria, 1987-89; prin. ADD, Inc., Washington, 1989-92; pres., CEO Additions, Inc., Va., 1992—. Prin. works include Prince Georges Hosp. Ctr., 1977, U. Md. LawLibr., 1978, Frederick County Courthouse, 1979, Md. Dept. Agr. Hdqrs., 1980, Belle Haven Country Club, 1988, First Am. Bank Va., North Tower, 1989, Naval Res. Assn., Hdqrs., 1998, Fine Arts Ctr. & Theatre, St. Mary's Ryken H.S., 1999. Capt. USNR, 1959-61. Recipient Honor award Bicentennial Design awards, AIA; 17 design awards, 1970-86; Paul Harris fellow, 1992. Mem. AIA (pres. Potomac Valley chpt. 1977-78, fed. Liaison Task Force 1991-93), Vauxlceuse Citizens Assn. (past pres.), Minn. Alumni Assn., Belle Haven Country Club, Potomac Soc., Rotary (pres. 1994-95, Disting. Rotarian award 1998), First Flight Mil. Officers Assn. (pres. 2003—), The Priory St. King Charles the Martyr, Sovereign Mil. Order of Temple of Jerusalem, Knight of Order (Grand Cross), Sigma Alpha Epsilon (past pres.). Republican. Presbyterian. Avocations: golf, fishing, boating, photography. Home: 261 N Dogwood Trail Southern Shores NC 27949-3138 Office Phone: 252-261-6402. E-mail: additions@charter.net.

VANDER NAALD EGENES, JOAN ELIZABETH, small business owner, educator; b. Des Moines, Feb. 13, 1936; d. Bert and Cathryn Alice (Bunger) Vander Naald; m. David Iddings Grant, July 25, 1959 (div. Oct. 1984); children: Jeffrey, Pamela, Elizabeth, Jennifer. BA, U. Iowa, 1958. Cert. profl. in edn., Iowa, Colo.; cert. travel agt., Iowa. Instr. St. Katherine's Sch., Davenport, Iowa, 1958-59, Iowa Ctrl. C.C., Fort Dodge, 1959-61; city councilwoman Boone, Iowa, 1980-86; instr. Des Moines Area C.C., Boone Campus, 1983; founder, owner, importer Global Ednl. Svcs., Des Moines, 1992-97; receptionist, sec. Automobile Club of So. Calif., West Los Angeles, 1997-2001. Bd. mem. Iowa Psychology Bd. Examiners, Des Moines, 1984-93; rsch. interviewer Iowa State U., Ames, 1984; resource tchr., workshop presenter about Russia, 1988-94; freelance photographer, 1988—. Lifetime mem. Rep. Senatorial Inner Circle, Washington, 1987—; pres. Iowa 4th Dist. Rep. Women, 1990-91, Polk County (Iowa) Rep. Women, 1994; precinct chair 12, ward 01, Des Moines, 1995-97; pres. Des Moines Metro Opera Guild, 1996-97, coun. sec., 1995-97; extensive vol. activities, including various fundraising chairs. Recipient 1st prize Youth Projects, Iowa Devel. Commn., 1983, Women Helping Women award for volunteerism, Boone, 1983; named Entrepreneur of Yr. in Iowa award GE, 1993. Republican. Avocation: swimming. Home: 36047 Palomino Way Palm Desert CA 92211

VANDERPLOEG, JAMES M. preventive medicine physician; b. Upland, Calif., Nov. 22, 1950; BA, U. Iowa, 1975. Cert. Aerospace Medicine and Occupational Medicine. Intern U. Hosp./U. Calif., San Diego, 1975-76; resident in otolaryngoloty U. Iowa Hosps., Iowa City, 1978-79; resident in occupational medicine U. Tex. Sch. Pub. Health, Houston, 1980-82, assoc. prof. occupational health; mem. staff St. John Hosp., Nassau Bay, Tex.; pres., partner Ctr. Aerospace & Occupl. Medicine, Houston. Bd. mem. Am. Bd. Preventive Medicine, Schiller Park, Ill., 1993-98, exec. dir., 1998—. Mem. Am. Coll. Occupational Medicine, ACPrM-AerosMA. Office: Ctr for Aerospace & Occupl Medicine 700 Gemini St Ste 110 Houston TX 77058-2735*

VANDERPOOL, WARD MELVIN, management and marketing consultant; b. Oakland, Mo., Jan. 20, 1918; s. Oscar B. and Clara (McGuire) V.; m. Lee Kendall, July 7, 1939. MEE, Tulane U. V.p. charge sales Van Lang Brokerage, Los Angeles, 1934-38; mgr. agrl. div. Dayton Rubber Co., Chgo., 1939-48; pres., gen. mgr. Vee Mac Co., Rockford, Ill., 1948—; pres., dir. Zipout, Inc., Rockford, 1951—, Wife Saver Products, Inc., 1959—. Chmn. bd. Zipout Internat., Kenvan Inc., 1952—, Shevan Corp., 1951—, Atlas Internat. Corp.; pres. Global Enterprises Ltd., Global Assocs. Ltd.; chmn. bd. dirs. Am. Atlas Corp., Atlas Chem. Corp., Merzat Industries Ltd.; trustee Ice Crafter Trust, 1949—; bd. dirs. Atlas Chem. Internat. Ltd., Kenlee Internat., Ltd., Shrimp Tool Internat. Ltd.; mem. Toronto Bd. Trade; chmn. bd. dirs. Am. Atlas Corp., Am. Packaging Corp. Mem. adv. bd. Nat. Security Council, congl. adv. com. Heritage Found.; mem. Rep. Nat. Com., Presdl. Task Force, Congrl. Adv. Com. Hon. mem. Internat. Swimming Hall of Fame. Mem. Nat. (dir. at large), Rock River (past pres.), sales execs., Sales and Mktg. Execs. Internat. (dir.), Am. Mgmt. Assn., Rockford Engring. Soc., Am. Tool Engrs., Internat. Acad. Aquatic Art (dir.), Am. Inst. Mgmt. (pres. council), Am. Ordnance Assn., Internat. Platform Assn., Heritage Found., Ill. C. of C., Jesters Club, IAA Swim Club, Elmcrest Country Club, Pyramid Club, Dolphin Club, Marlin Club, Univ. Club, Athletic Club, Oxford Club, Masons (consistory), Shriners, Elks. Home: 374 Parkland Dr SE Cedar Rapids IA 52403-2031 also: 40 Richview Rd # 308 Toronto ON Canada M9A 5C1 also: 704 Park Center Dr Santa Ana CA 92705-3563 Office: PO Box 1972 Cedar Rapids IA 52406-1972

VANDERRYN, JACK, philanthropic foundation administrator; b. Groningen, The Netherlands, Apr. 14, 1930; came to U.S., 1939; s. Herman Gabriel and Henrietta S.E. (Hartog) V.; m. Margrit Wolfes, Mar. 18, 1956; children: David, Judith, Amy, Daniel. BA, Lehigh U., 1951, MS, 1952, PhD, 1955. Rsch. and grad. teaching asst. Lehigh U., Bethlehem, Pa., 1952-55; asst. prof. chemistry Va. Poly. Inst., Blacksburg, 1955-58; rsch. participant Oak Ridge (Tenn.) Nat. Lab., 1957; chemist AEC, Oak Ridge, 1958-62, tech. adviser to asst. gen. mgr. R & D, Washington, 1962 67, asst. to gen. mgr., 1971-72, tech. asst. to dir. div. applied tech., 1972-73, chief energy tech. br., div. applied tech., 1973-75; acting dir. div. energy storage Energy Rsch. and Devel. Adminstrn., Washington, 1975, dir. Office Internat. R & D Programs, 1975-77; dir. Office Internat. Programs Dept. Energy, Washington, 1977-82; dir. energy and natural resources AID, Washington, 1982-91; program dir. environment Moriah Fund, Washington, 1991—2003; sr. fellow, environ. and devel. Moriah Fund., 2003—. Sr. sci. adviser U.S. Mission to Internat. Atomic Energy Agy., Dept. State, Vienna, Austria, 1967-71; lectr. Brookings Instn., 1965-66. Mem., dep. pres., exec. bd. Am. Internat. Sch., Vienna, 1968-71; v.p. Oak Ridge Civic Music Assn., 1959-60; pres. Washington Print Club, 1986-91; pres. Consultative Group on Biodiversity, 1997-2000. Home: 8112 Whittier Blvd Bethesda MD 20817-3123 Office: Moriah Fund Ste 1000 1634 I St NW Washington DC 20006-4003 Office Phone: 202-783-8488. E-mail: jvanderryn@moriahfund.org.

VANDERSLICE, THOMAS AQUINAS, electronics executive; b. Phila., Jan. 8, 1932; s. Joseph R. and Mae (Daly) V.; m. Margaret Hurley, June 9, 1956; children: Thomas Aquinas, Paul Thomas Aquinas, John Thomas Aquinas, Peter Thomas Aquinas. BS in Chemistry and Philosophy, Boston Coll., 1953; PhD in Chemistry and Physics, Cath. U. Am., 1956. With GE, Fairfield, Conn., from 1956, gen. mgr. electronic components bus. div., 1970-72, v.p., 1970, group exec. spl. systems and products group, 1972-77, sr. v.p., sector exec. Power System Sector, 1977-79, exec. v.p., sector exec. Power System Sector, 1979-84; pres., chief oper. officer, dir. Gen. Tel. & Electronics Corp., Stamford, Conn., 1979-83; chmn., CEO, Apollo Computer, Inc., Chelmsford, Mass., 1984-89, M/A COM, Inc., Lowell, Mass., 1989-95. Bd. dirs. Texaco, Inc. Patentee low pressure gas measurements and analysis, gas surface interactions and elec. discharges; co-author: Ultra High Vacuum and Its Applications, 1963; reviser: Scientific Foundations of Vacuum Technique, 1960; contbr. to profl. jours. Trustee Boston Coll., past chmn., past trustee Comm. Econ. Devel. Recipient Bicentennial medal Boston Coll., 1976; Fulbright scholar, 1953-56. Mem. NAE, ASTM, Am. Vacuum Soc., Am. Chem. Soc., Am. Inst. Physics, Royal Poinciana Golf Club (Naples, Fla.), Oyster Harbors Club, Sigma Xi, Tau Beta Pi, Alpha Sigma Nu, Sigma Pi Sigma. Office: LeRivage Unit 10N 4351 Gulf Shore Blvd N Naples FL 34103-2697

VANDERSLIDE, JAMES T. computer company executive; PhD in Physics. Various positiosn including staff engr. fed. systems Divsn. IBM, Gaithersburg, Md., 1966-99, sr. mng. dir. Asia Pacific Group Tokyo, 1988-91; vice chmn. Dell Computer Corp., Round Rock, Tex., 1999—. Bd. dirs. Unitrode Corp. Office: Dell Computer Co 1 Dell Way Round Rock TX 78682-0001 also: 1807 W Braker Ln Bldg C Austin TX 78758-3605

VAN DER SPIEGEL, JAN, engineering educator; b. Aalst, Belgium, Apr. 12, 1951; arrived in U.S., 1980; BSEE, U. Leuven, 1971, MSEE, 1974, PhD in Elec. Engring., 1979; M of Arts and Sci., U. Pa., 1988. 2d lt. Belgian Air Force, 1979—80; asst. prof. elec. engring. U. Pa., Phila., 1981-87, assoc. prof., 1987-95, prof. elec. engring., 1995—, dir. Ctr. Sensor Tech., 1989-98, chmn. dep. elec. engring., 1998—2002, interim chmn. dept. elec. and sys. engring., 2002—. Patentee integ. ambient sensing, radiation sens. retina sens., gen prupost neural comp., novel ferroelectric sensors, background calibration for pipelined analog-digital converters; editor Sensors and Actuators, 1986—. Postdoctoral fellow U. Pa., 1980-81; named Presdl. Young Investigator The White House, 1984. Fellow IEEE; mem. Neural Network Soc., Tau Beta Pi. Office: U Pa Ctr Sensor Techs Moore Sch Elec Engring 200 S 33d St Rm 203 Philadelphia PA 19104-6314

VANDERSTAPPEN, HARRIE ALBERT, Far Eastern art educator; b. Heesch, The Netherlands, Jan. 21, 1921; arrived in US, 1959; s. Johannes and Johanna (van de Poel) V. Student, Theol. Sch., Helvoirt and Teteringen, The Netherlands, 1939-45, Chinese Lang. Sch., Peking, People's Republic of China, 1946-48; PhD in Far Eastern Art, U. Chgo., 1955. Ordained priest Roman Catholic Ch., 1945. Student lang., also tchr., writer, Tokyo, 1955-57; tchr. Nanzan U., Nagoya, Japan, 1957-59; prof. Far Eastern art U. Chgo., 1959-92, chmn. dept. art, 1964-69, prof. emeritus dept. art, 1991—. Author: The T.L. Yuan Bibliography of Chinese Art and Archaeology, 1975; author, editor: Ritual and Reverence, 1989; assoc. editor Monumenta Serica, 1955—; contbr. articles to profl. jours. Recipient Teaching of Art History award Nat. Coll. Art Assn. Am., 1985; Harrie A. Vanderstappen Disting. Chair established at U. Chgo., 1995. Mem. Asia Soc., Assn. Asian Arts Home: 1901 Waukegan Rd Techny IL 60082-6000 E-mail: hvanderstappen@aol.com.

VANDERVEEN, JOHN E. nutritionist, federal agency administrator; b. Prospect Park, N.J., May 13, 1934; m. Ernestine Neuhardt, June 3, 1967; children: Keith Bradley, Kimetha Leigh. BS, Rutgers U., 1956; PhD, U. N.H., 1961. Nutritionist USAF, 1961-75; dir. divsn. nutrition FDA, Washington,

1975-92, dir. office plant & dairy foods and beverages, 1992-98. Served to 1st lt. USAF, 1961-64. Office: FDA Ctr Food Safety and Applied Nutrition 5100 Paint Branch Parkway College Park MD 20740-3335 E-mail: jvanderv@cfsan.fda.gov.

VAN DERVEER, TARA, university athletic coach; b. Niagara Falls, N.Y., June 26, 1953; Grad., Indiana U., 1975. Coach women's basketball Stanford U. Cardinals, 1985—, U.S. Nat. Women's Team, 1995-96. Coach gold medalist Women's Olympic Team, 1996. Achievements include champions NCAA Divsn. 1 A, 1990, 92. Office: Stanford U Womens Basketball Dept Athletics Stanford CA 94305

VANDERVELD, JOHN, JR., international business development specialist; b. Chgo., Oct. 24, 1926; s. John J. and Rose (Renkema) V. Pres. Nat. Disposal Contractors, Barrington, Ill., 1952-71; sr. v.p., dir. Browning Ferris Industries, Houston, 1971-78; pres. Pioneer Equities, Inc., 1975-90, C.J.V. Corp., Dallas, 1990-92; sr. corp. advisor Vector Environmental Techs., Inc., 1993-96. Dir. Am. Far East, Inc., Dallas and Tokyo; adv. bd. Southwestern Legal Found., 1975-1998. Bd. dirs. Internat. Bible Soc., mem. exec.com., 1982-98; bd. dirs. Global Action; chmn. Brookshire Capital Corp., 2000—. Mem. Nat. Solid Waste Mgmt. Assn. (former chmn. govt. industry coordinating council, mem. environ. research com.) Home: 7031 Brookshire Dr Dallas TX 75230-4248 Office Phone: 214-692-8995. E-mail: jv-brookshire@sbcglobal.net.

VANDER VELDE, WALLACE EARL, aeronautical and astronautical educator; b. Jamestown, Mich., June 4, 1929; s. Peter Nelson and Janet (Keizer) Vander V.; m. Winifred Helen Bunai, Aug. 29, 1954; children: Susan Jane, Peter Russell. BS in Aero Engring, Purdue U., 1951; Sc.D., Mass. Inst. Tech., 1956. Dir. applications engring. GPS Instrument Co., Inc., Newton, Mass., 1956-57; mem. faculty Mass. Inst. Tech., 1957—, prof. aero. and astronautics, 1965—. Cons. to industry, 1958— Author: Flight Vehicle Control Systems, Part VII of Space Navigation, Guidance and Control, 1966, (with Arthur Gelb) Multiple-Input Describing Functions, 1968; also papers. Served to 1st lt. USAF, 1951-53. Recipient Edn. award Am. Automatic Control Coun., 1988. Fellow AIAA; mem. IEEE. Home: 50 High St Winchester MA 01890-3314 Office: MIT Rm 9-335 Dept Aero and Astronautics Cambridge MA 02139

VANDERVER, TIMOTHY ARTHUR, JR., lawyer; b. Birmingham, Ala., Jan. 25, 1944; s. Timothy Arthur and Jeanette (Grimes) V.; m. Virginia Cassandra Nye, Oct. 1, 1966 (dec. July 2001); m. Susan Elliotte McVay, Mar. 20, 2003; children: Timothy A. III, Glenn Bruce, Benjamin Richard. BA, Washington and Lee U., 1965; BA in Law, Oxford (Eng.) U., 1967, MA, 1983; JD, Harvard U., 1969. Bar: D.C., U.S. Ct. Appeals (D.C. cir.) 1969, U.S. Ct. Appeals (5th cir.) 1984, U.S. Ct. Appeals (3d and 11th cirs.) 1989, U.S. Supreme Ct. 1978. Assoc. Covington & Burling, Washington, 1969-72, Dept. of Interior, Washington, 1972-76; ptnr. Patton Boggs L.L.P., Washington, 1976—. Editor: Clean Air Law and Regulation, 1992, Environmental Law Handbook, 1994. Capt. U.S. Army, 1970-71. Presbyterian. Home: 9000 Congressional Ct Potomac MD 20854-4608 Office: Patton Boggs LLP 2550 M St NW Ste 500 Washington DC 20037-1350 Office Phone: 202-457-6074.

VAN DER VEUR, PAUL W. humanities educator; b. Medan, Indonesia, Aug. 28, 1921; came to U.S., 1947; s. Wilhelmus Marius and Johanna (Guldemond) van der Veur; m. Karol Anne Kaiser, July 21, 1951 (div. Aug. 1971); children: Julia, Paul Roscoe; m. Barbara Walker, Sept., 1973; children: Anne, Mark. BA, Swarthmore Coll., 1949; MA, U. Minn., 1950; PhD, Cornell U., 1955. Instr. Yale U., New Haven, 1954-56; asst. prof. U. Hawaii, Honolulu, 1956-59, assoc. prof., 1959-61; sr. rsch. fellow Australian Nat. U., Canberra, 1961-66; prof. No. Ill. U., DeKalb, 1966-67, Ohio U., Athens, 1967-91, prof. emeritus, 1991—, dir. S.E. Asia studies, 1967-73, 77, 1981-85, 88-90. Cons. Veriation Films, Menlo Park, Calif., 1984-85. Co-editor and author: Papua-New Guinea Elections, 1965, Toward a Glorious Indonesia, 1987; author: New Guinea Boundaries 2 vols., 1966, The Lion and the Gadfly, 2004. Mem. Athens County Soil and Conservation Agy., 1967-91. With Royal Netherlands Indies Army, 1941-47 (POW, Japan, 1942-45). Fulbright fellow U.S. Fulbright Assn., 1980-81. Mem. Assn. for Asian Studies. Democrat. Avocation: tree planting and management. Home: 3600 Galt Ocean Dr # 2-C Fort Lauderdale FL 33308

VAN DER VOO, ROB, geophysicist; b. Zeist, The Netherlands, Aug. 4, 1940; arrived in U.S., 1970; s. Maximiliaan and Johanna Hendrika (Baggerman) Van der V.; m. Tatiana M. C. Graafland, Mar. 26, 1966; children: Serge Nicolas, Bjorn Alexander. BS, U. Utrecht, Netherlands, 1961, MS, 1965, PhD, 1969. Rsch. asst. U. Utrecht, 1964-65, rsch. assoc., 1965-69, sr. rsch. assoc., 1969-70; vis. asst. prof. U. Mich., Ann Arbor, 1970-72, asst. prof., 1972-75, assoc. prof., 1975-79, prof. geophysics, 1979—, chmn., 1981-88, 91-95, Arthur F. Thurnau prof., 1994-97, dir. honors program Coll. Lit., Sci. and the Arts, 1998—2003. Guest prof. ETH, Zurich, Switzerland, 1978, Kuwait U., 1979, Utrecht U. and Delft U. Tech., 1997-98. Author: Paleomagnetism of the Atlantic, Tethys and Iapetus Oceans, 1993; contbr. articles to profl. jours. Recipient Russell award, U. Mich., 1976, Disting. Faculty Achievement award, 1990, Benjamin Franklin medal in Earth Scis., 2001. Mem. Geol. Soc. Am. (pres. 2004), Am. Geophys. Union, Geologische Vereinigung (Germany), Royal Acad. Scis. (Netherlands), Royal Norwegian Soc. Scis. and Letters, Sigma Xi, Phi Kappa Phi. Home: 2305 Devonshire Rd Ann Arbor MI 48104-2703 Office: U Mich 4534 CC Little Bldg Ann Arbor MI 48109-1063 Office Phone: 734-764-8322. E-mail: voo@umich.edu.

VANDER VOORT, DALE GILBERT, textile company executive; b. Paterson, N.J., Feb. 7, 1924; s. Gilbert H. and Lillian (Hatton) Vander V.; m. Florine E. Storey, Aug. 6, 1944 (dec.); children: Lydia Ann, Dale Gilbert, Roy Lee. B.M.E., Clemson U., 1944. Gen. mgr., dir. Stevens Linen Assos., Webster, Mass., 1954-56; gen. mgr. Montreal Cottons Ltd., Valleyfield, Que., Can., 1951-54; supt. Mill 4 Dan River Mills, Danville, Va., 1946-51; sr. v.p. United Merchants & Mfrs. Inc., N.Y.C., 1972-77; chmn. bd. Asso. Textiles Can. Ltd., 1969-77; pres., chief exec. officer Arnold Print Works, Inc., Adams, Mass., 1977-83, Alton Fabrics, Allentown, Pa., 1983-85; pres. Asheville Dye & Finishing, Swannanoa, N.C., 1985-87; pres., chief exec. officer River Dyeing and Finishing Co., Asheville, N.C., 1988—. Dir. Northwestern Bank, Asheville, N.C., Western Carolina Industries Inc., Brit. Silk Dyeing Co., Valchem Australia, Profile Sports Corp., West Lebanon, N.H. Mem. coun. Luth. Ch., 1962—. Lt. AUS, 1943-46. Decorated Bronze Star, Purple Heart. Mem. ASME, Am. Assn. Textile Chemists and Colorists, Can. Textile Inst. (dir.), Soc. Advancement of Mgmt. (nat. gov. 1961-62), Can. Club (N.Y.), Asheville Country Club. Home: 214 Stratford Rd Asheville NC 28804-1440 also: 131 Riverside Dr Asheville NC 28801-3136 E-mail: riverdye@aol.com.

VANDERWALKER, DIANE MARY, materials scientist; b. Springfield, Mass., Nov. 1, 1955; BS, Boston Coll., 1977; PhD, MIT, 1981. NATO fellow U. Oxford, Eng., 1981-82; asst. prof. SUNY, Stony Brook, 1983-85; materials rsch. engr. Army Rsch. Lab. (formerly U.S. Army Materials Tech. Lab.), Watertown, Mass., 1986-94. Cons. IBM, Yorktown Heights, N.Y. Contbr. articles to profl. publs. Mem. N.Y. Acad. Scis. Roman Catholic.

VANDER WEIDE, CHERI DEVOS, sports team executive, marketing professional; b. Grand Rapids, Mich., Feb. 3, 1961; m. Robert A. Vander Weide. BA in Bus. Adminstrn., Hope Coll. Dir. health and beauty mktg. Amway Corp., Ada, Mich., v.p. corp. affairs, mem. policy bd.; exec. vice-chmn. gov. bd. Orlando Magic Basketball. Trustee United Arts of Ctrl. Fla.; chmn. children's hosp. com. Butterworth Hosp. Office: Orlando Magic 2 Magic Place 8701 Maitland Summit Blvd Orlando FL 32810-5915

VANDERWILT, JEFFREY T. theology studies educator; Ph.D., U. of Notre Dame, South Bend, Ind., 1990—96. Asst. prof. Loyola Marymount U., Los Angeles, 1998—. Author: (book) Communion with Non-Catholic Christians: Risks, Challenges, and Opportunities, A Church without Borders: The Eucharist and the Church in Ecumenical Perspective. Office: Loyola Marymount University 1 LMU Dr Ste 3700 Los Angeles CA 90045-2659 E-mail: jvanderw@lmu.edu.

VAN DER WYST, GEON, dancer; b. Melbourne, Australia; Student, Australian Ballet Sch., 1989—90, St. Francis Xavier's Coll., 1987—88. Mem. Australian Ballet, 1991—95, soloist, 1995—96, sr. artist, 1996—2001; prin. dancer Nat. Ballet Can., Toronto, Canada, 2001—. Dancer (ballets) The Sleeping Beauty, Romeo and Juliet, Cinderella, Onegin, Manon, Apollo, The Competition, Madam Butterfly, Anna Karenina, The Merry Widow, Don Quixote, Songs of a Wayfarer, Theme and Variations, The Taming of the Shrew, Etudes, In the Night, Divergence, Jardi Tancat, Gemini, Three of Us, Fall River Legend, Por vos Muero, Rites, Equus. Office: Walter Carsen Ctr Nat Ballet Can 470 Queens Quay West Toronto ON Canada M5V 3K4 Home: 155 Dalhousie St # 1048 Toronto Canada M5B 2P7

VANDEUSEN, BRUCE DUDLEY, educational association administrator; b. Lorain, Ohio, Aug. 20, 1931; s. Clarence Elmer and Margaret (Richards) VanD.; m. Ann Marie Groves, Aug. 17, 1957; children: David Bruce, Elizabeth Ann. Janet Marie. BA, Ohio Wesleyan U., 1952; MS, U. Mich., 1958, PhD, 1971; MAE., Chrysler Inst. Engring., Highland Park, Mich., 1958. Registered profl. engr., Mich. Fellow Ohio State U., Columbus, 1953-54; student engr. Chrysler Corp., Highland Park, 1956-58, sr. research scientist, 1958-67; chief engr. Chrysler Def., Inc., Center Line, Mich., 1967-79, mgr. advanced devel., 1979-82; dir. advanced devel. Gen. Dynamics, Warren, Mich., 1982-87, program dir., 1987-93; pres. Edn. Svcs., Birmingham, Mich., 1994—. Contbr. numerous articles to profl. publs.; patentee electronic cirs. Trustee Birmingham Bd. Edn., Mich., 1976-88, pres., 1979-84, 87-88; trustee Birmingham Community House, 1981-87. Mem. Soc. Automotive Engrs. (chmn. sci. engring. activity 1967-69, Arch T. Colwell award 1968). Republican. Methodist. Home: 4173 Chatfield Ln Troy MI 48098-4327 Office: Edn Svcs PO Box 170 Birmingham MI 48012-0170 Office Phone: 248-269-9598. E-mail: Vandeus@yahoo.com. *Accept, embrace and instigate change, not for the sake of change but for the sake of improvement.*

VANDE VELDE, VIVIAN LORRAINE, writer; b. N.Y., June 18, 1951; d. Pasquale and Marcelle Laura Brucato; m. James Gerrard Vande Velde, Apr. 20, 1974; 1 child, Elizabeth Lynn. Author: (novels) A Hidden Magic, Alison Who Went Away, Heir Apparent, Never Trust a Dead Man (Edgar award (Mystery Writers of Am.), 2000). Recipient Anne Spencer Lindbergh Prize in Children's Lit., Charles A. and Anne Morrow Lindbergh Found., 2001/2002, Black-Eyed Susan Award, Md. Ednl. Media Orgn., 2002, Vol. State Book Award, Tenn. Libr. Assn., 2002, Nev. Young Readers' Award, Nev. Libr. Assn., 1998, Best Books for Young Adults, Quick Pick for Reluctant Young Adult Readers, YALSA Popular Paperback for Young Adults, ALA. Mem.: Rochester Area Childrens Writers & Illustrators, Soc. of Children's Book Writers & Illustrators. Roman Catholic. E-mail: marketing@holidayhouse.com.

VAN DEVENDER, J. PACE, physical scientist, management consultant; b. Jackson, Miss., Sept. 12, 1947; m. Nancy Jane Manning, 1971; 3 children. BA in Physics, Vanderbilt U., 1969; MA in Physics, Dartmouth Coll., 1971; PhD in Physics, U. London, 1974. Physicist diagnostics devel. Lawrence Livermore Lab., 1969; mem. tech. staff pulsed power rsch. and devel. Sandia Nat. Labs., Albuquerque, 1974-78, divsn. supr. pulsed power rsch. divsn., 1978-82, dept. mgr. fusion rsch., 1982-84, dir. pulsed power scis., 1984-93, dir. corp. comm., 1993, dir. Nat. Indsl. Alliances Ctr., 1993-95; pres. Prosperity Inst., 1995-98; dir. strategic scis. ctr. Sandia Nat. Labs., Albuquerque, 1998—, Chief info. officer, 1998—, dir. exec. staff, 2002. Mem. bd. trust Vanderbilt U., 1969-73. With U.S. Army, 1969-71. Recipient Ernest Orlando Lawrence Meml. award US Dept. Energy, 1991; named one of 100 Most Promising Scientists Under 40, Sci. Digest, 1984; Marshal scholar U. London, 1971-74. Fellow Am. Phys. Soc.; Phi Beta Kappa, Omicron Delta Kappa, Sigma Xi. Office: Sandia Nat Labs MS 0103 PO Box 5800 Albuquerque NM 87185-0103

VANDEVENDER, ROBERT LEE, II, nuclear engineering consultant; b. Muncie, Ind., Nov. 16, 1958; s. Robert Lee and Evelyn June (Matthews) V.; m. Laura Jo Longfellow, June 11, 1977 (div. July 1990); children: Holly Suzanne, Robert Lee III, Bryan Matthew; m. Deborah Ann Kieffer, Sept. 26, 1992. Grad., Naval Nuc. Power Sch., Orlando, Fla., Nuc. Power Tng. Unit, West Milton, N.Y., 1979, Naval Engring. Lab. Technician Sch., West Milton, 1979; AS, Mohegan C.C., Norwich, Conn., 1983; grad., GE Thermodynamics, Heat Transfer and Fluid Flow Sch., 1986; cert. achievement, Joliet Jr. Coll., 1986; grad., GE Sr. Reactor Operator Sch., 1986; BS in Nuc. Tech., Excelsior Coll., 2003. Lead engring. lab. technician, staff instr. Knolls Atomic Power Lab. U.S. Dept. Def., West Milton, 1979-81; sr. reactor operator, simulator instr. GE Nuc. Tng. Svcs., Morris, Ill., 1985-87; sr. lead engr., nuc. engring. cons. ABB Impell Corp., Melville, NY, 1991-93; nuc. engring. cons. Megan Corp., Allentown, Pa., 1993-94, Primera Engrs., Inc., Chgo., 1994-95, Estes Corp., Joliet, Ill., 1995-2001; co-founder V-Team, Inc., Channahon, Ill., 1997-98; co-founder, co-owner, pres. Am. Paper Connection, Inc., Joliet, 1998—, GDS Assocs., Downers Grove, Ill., 1999; nuc. engring. cons. Ferg & Assocs., 2001—. Adminstrv. coord., cons. Davis Besse Nuc. Power Sta. Toledo Edison, 1987—88; adminstrv. cons., supr. ops. support Nine Mile Pt. Nuc. Sta. Niagara Mohawk Power Corp., Oswego, NY, 1988—90; lead engring. cons. design baseline compilation Phila. Electric Co., King of Prussia, Pa., 1991; engring. cons. final safety analysis Zion (Ill.) Nuc. Sta. Commonwealth Edison Co., 1991, lead engr. dual unit outage fire protection sentry procedure devel., 93; engring. cons. Quad Cities Nuc. Power Sta., Cordova, Ill., 1994, Dresden Nuc. Power Sta., Morris, Ill., 1994—96; project mgr. Dresden Sta. Dept. Nuc. Safety, 1997; engring. cons. tech. specification upgrade project Zion Sta., 1996, supr. ops. procedures group, 1997—98; lead writer, condensate prfilter mod. project LaSalle (Ill.) Nuc. Sta., 2000; tech. cons., ops. supr. fuel transfer project Yankee Rowe (Mass.) Nuc. Power Sta., 2001—03; ops. supr. NAC Internat., 2001—03; nuc. oversight cons. Conn. Yankee Atomic Power Co., 2003—. Author: The Vandevender, Wilson, McAshlan, Silvers and Kimmel Families, 1990, (with Robert Friedberg) Paper Money of the United States, 13th and 14th edits., (with John Schwartz) Standard Guide to Small Size U.S. Paper Money, 1994, (with Gene Hessler) Comprehensive Catalog of U.S. Paper Money, 1997. Vol. examiner FCC, Gettysburg, 1985—; merit badge counselor Boy Scouts Am., Muncie, 1983. With USN, 1977-85, Ind. Guard Res., 1975-76, USNR, 1976-77, 85-87. Recipient radiosport diploma for operating achievement Internat. Amateur Radio Union, 1984, 85. Mem. Am. Legion (life), Am. Nuc. Soc. (life), Am. Radio Relay League (life, asst. tech. coord. 1985-87), Internat. Platform Assn., Am. Numismatic Assn. (life), VFW (life), Masons (life), Scottish Rite (life), Odd Fellows (grand ruler Ind. 1975-76, pres. region X 1975-76, rep. to UN Pilgrimage for Youth 1976), NRA (life), Soc. Paper Money Collectors (life), Profl. Currency Dealers Assn. Republican. Avocations: genealogy, amateur radio, coin collecting/numismatics. Home: PO Box 1010 Plainfield IL 60544-1010 Office: Am Paper Connection Inc PO Box 2816 Joliet IL 60434-2816

VANDEVER, JUDITH ANN, county official; b. Hemstead, N.Y., Aug. 6, 1941; d. John Anthony Klym and Kathryn M. (Lane) Trexler; children: Garret, Kimberlee Vandever Johnson. Dep. recorder Clark County Recorder, Las Vegas, Nev., 1979-91, chief dep. recorder, 1991-93, asst. recorder, 1993-94, county recorder, 1995—. State chair Nev. Young Woman of the Yr., 1991; mem. S.M.A.R.T. Team Clark County Sch. Dist., 1994—95; mem. ctrl. com. State/County Dem. Ctrl. Com., 1988—; state dir. Women Ofcls. Nat. Assn. Counties, 1997—. Recipient Leadership Dedication award Amigos De HIP, 1996, Women Elected Ofcls. Spotlight award Women's Dem. Club, 1996. Mem. ASPA, Nat. Assn. County Recorders and Clks. (bd. dirs. 1999—), Nat. Assn. County Recorders, Election Ofcls. and Clks. (bd. dirs. 1999-02), Assn. of Profl. Mortage Women,Assn. of Recorders Mgrs. and Adminstrs., U. Nev.-Las Vegas Jean Nidetch Women's Ctr. (original founder), Leadership Las Vegas Alumni Assoc., Las Vegas C. of C. (bd. of trustees, cmty. coun. 1995-98). Office: Clark County Recorder 500 S Grand Central Pkwy Las Vegas NV 89106-4506

VANDEVER, WILLIAM DIRK, lawyer; b. Chgo., Aug. 1, 1949; s. Lester J. and Elizabeth J. V.; m. Kathi J. Zellmer, Aug. 26, 1983; children: Barton Dirk, Brooke Shelby. BS, U. Mo., Kansas City, 1971, JD with distinction, 1974. Bar: Mo. 1975, U.S. Dist. Ct. (we. dist.) Mo. 1975. Dir. Popham Law Firm, Kansas City, Mo., 1975—. Lectr. in field, Kansas City Mo., 1979—. Issue editor U. Mo.-Kansas City Law Rev., 1974. Bd. govts. IOLTA, 1989—91. Fellow Am. Bd. Trial Advs. (Best Lawyers in Am.-tort law); mem. ABA, ATLA, Mo. Assn. Trial Attys., Kansas City Met. Bar Assn. (treas., sec., pres., elected to 16th Jud. Commn. 1988-94), Kansas City Bar Found. (treas. 1992, sec. 1994, pres. 1996-98, pres. award domestic violence 1999), Interest on Lawyer Trust Accts. of Mo. (bd. govs.), Kansas City Mem. Svcs. (pres. 1988—, commr. 16th jud. cir. selection com.), U. Mo. Kansas City Found. (fin. com. 1998), Phi Delta Phi, Beta Theta Pi. Avocations: tennis, skiing, running, reading. Home: 11380 W 121st Ter Shawnee Mission KS 66213-1978 Office: Popham Law Firm 1300 Commerce Trust Bldg Kansas City MO 64106

VAN DE VYVER, SISTER MARY FRANCILENE, academic administrator; b. Detroit, Sept. 6, 1941; d. Hector Joseph and Irene Cecilia (Zygailo) V. BA, Madonna Coll., 1965; MEd, Wayne State U., 1970, PhD, 1977. Joined Sisters of St. Felix of Cantalice, Roman Cath. Ch., 1959. Tchr. Ladywood High Sch., 1967-71, Gabriel Richard H.S., 1971-74; adminstrv. asst. to pres. Madonna Coll., Livonia, Mich., 1974-75, acad. dean, 1975-76; now pres. Madonna U., Livonia, Mich. Office: Madonna U Office of President 36600 Schoolcraft Rd Livonia MI 48150-1176

VANDEWALLE, GERALD WAYNE, state supreme court chief justice; b. Noonan, N.D., Aug. 15, 1933; s. Jules C. and Blanche Marie (Gits) VandeW. BSc, U. N.D., 1955, JD, 1958. Bar: N.D., U.S. Dist. Ct. N.D. 1959. Spl. asst. atty. gen. State of N.D., Bismarck, 1958-75, 1st asst. atty. gen., 1975-78; justice N.D. Supreme Ct., 1978-92, chief justice, 1993—. Mem. faculty Bismarck Jr. Coll., 1972-76; mem. Nat. Ctr. for State Cts. Rsch. adv. coun.; mem. fed.-state jurisdiction com. Jud. Conf. of the U.S. Editor-in-chief N.D. Law Rev, 1957-58. Active Bismarck Meals on Wheels Recipient Sioux award U. N.D., 1992, Ednl. Law award N.D. Coun. Sch. Attys., 1987, Love Without Fear award Abused Adult Resource Ctr., 1995, N. Dakota State Bar Assoc. Dist. Service Award, 1998. Mem. ABA (co-chmn. bar admissions com. 1991-99, mem. coun. sect. legal edn. and admissions, chmn. coun. sect. legal edn. and admissions), State Bar Assn. N.D., Burleigh County Bar Assn., Conf. of Chief Justices (past pres., bd. dirs. 1996-98, chmn. fed.-state tribal rels. com.), Am. Contract Bridge League, Order of Coif, N.D. Jud. Conf. (exec. com.), Elks, KC, Phi Eta Sigma, Beta Alpha Psi (Outstanding Alumnus award Zeta chpt. 1995), Beta Gamma Sigma, Phi Alpha Delta. Roman Catholic. Office: ND Supreme Ct State Capitol 600 E Boulevard Ave Bismarck ND 58505-0530 E-mail: gvandewalle@ndcourts.com.

VAN DE WATER, MARK E. investment company executive; b. Dec. 17, 1963; BA in Polit. Sci. and Econs., St. Lawrence U., 1986; MA in Internat. Devel., George Washington U., 1998. Legis. asst. Congressman Les AuCoin; ptnr. VanFleet, Metzner & Meredith; profl. staff mem. Senate Com. on Appropriations, 1991-94, dep. staff dir., 1994-96; v.p. investment devel. dept. Overseas Pvt. Investment Corp., 1996—; now sr. v.p. bus. devel. Intellibridge, Washington, 1996-2000. Presdl. scholar; John C. Stennis fellow John C. Stennis Ctr. for Pub. Svc., 1995. Office: NW #100B 1101 30TH St Washington DC 20007-3706

VAN DE WATER, SUSAN D. physiatrist; BA in Biology, Oberlin Coll., 1974; PhD, U. Rochester, 1979; MD, U. Tex., San Antonio, 1986. Diplomate Am. Bd. Physical Medicine and Rehabilitation. Postdoctoral fellow U. Tex. Med. Br., Galveston, 1979-81; resident Rehab. Inst. Chgo., 1986-90; med. dir. Meml. Rehab. Hosp., Midland, Tex., 1990-94; physiatrist, assoc. med. dir. Health South Rehab. Hosp., Midland, 1994—. Chmn. phys. medicine and rehab. com. Meml. Hosp. and Med. Ctr., Midland, 1991-92, 93-94, Med. Ctr. Hosp., Odessa, Tex., 1990-92; mem. med. adv. bd. Tex. Rehab. Commn., 1994—. Contbr. articles to profl. jours. Louise Barekman Meml. scholar Tex. Med. Assn., 1985, Bowen-Vogt Med. scholar, 1984, J. Belcher Trust scholar, 1983, So. Med. Assn. scholar 1982; Grad. fellow NSF, 1974-77, Rush Rhees Grad. fellow U. Rochester, 1974-77. Fellow Am. Acad. Phys. Medicine and Rehab.; mem. AMA, Assn. Acad. Physiatrists, Tex. Soc. Phys. Medicine and Rehab., Tex. Med. Assn., Midland County Med. Assn., U. Tex. San Antonio Alumni Assn., Alpha Omega Alpha, Phi Beta Kappa. Office: PO Box 4766 Midland TX 79704-4766

VANDE WOUDE, GEORGE FRANKLIN, molecular biologist, cancer researcher; b. Brooklyn, N.Y., Dec. 25, 1935; s. George Franklin Sr. and Alice Beatrice (Leudesdorff) V.W.; m. Dorothy Helen Stapel, Apr. 5, 1959; children: Susan Joan, Gail Louise, Cynthia Irene, Alice Helene. Student, Hope Coll., 1953-54; BA, Hofstra U., 1959; MS, Rutgers U., 1962, PhD, 1964. Postdoctoral rsch. assoc. USDA Plum Island, Greenport, N.Y., 1964-65, rsch. scientist, 1965-72; chief virus tumor biochemistry Nat. Cancer Inst. NIH, Bethesda, Md., 1972-81, chief lab. molecular oncology, 1981-83; dir. basic rsch. program Nat. Cancer Inst.-Frederick (Md.) Cancer R & D Ctr., 1983—98; dir. Van Andel Rsch. Inst., Grand Rapids, Mich., 1999—. Contbr. over 100 articles and sci. papers to profl. publs., 35 book chpts. Recipient Robert J. and Claire Pasarow Found. award, 1989. Mem. AAAS, Am. Soc. for Microbiology, Am. Assn. for Cancer Rsch. Achievements include research in fields of biology and cancer. Office: Van Andel Inst 333 Bostwick NE Grand Rapids MI 49503

VAN DE ZILVER, PETER A.L. economist, business executive; b. June 26, 1949; MA in Econs., U. So. Calif., 1979. CFA, Calif. MIS mgr. Sunnyglen Corp., Newport Beach, Calif., 1984-92; v.p., quantitative analyst PIMCO, Newport Beach, 1992—. E-mail: zilver@pimco.com.

VAN DIJK, FRITS, food products executive; b. Jakarta, Indonesia, Oct. 6, 1947; married; 2 children. B in Econs., U. Rotterdam, The Netherlands; grad. program for exec. devel., Internat. Inst. Mgmt. Devel., Lausanne, Switzerland. Sales rep. Nestlé U.K., 1970—71; asst. to mng. dir. Nestlé India, 1972—74; product mgr. (milks) Nestlé Philippines, 1975—78, mktg. dir., 1985—86; mktg. beverage divsn. Nestlé, Vevey, Switzerland, 1979—81; mktg. mgr. Nestlé Sri Lanka, 1982—84; COO Nestlé Malaysia, 1987—88, market head, 1988—94, Nestlé Japan, 1995—99; chmn., CEO Nestlé Waters, 2000—; dep. exec. v.p. Nestlé S.A., 2002, exec. v.p., 2003—. Office: Nestle Waters NAm Holdings Inc 777 W Putnam Ave Greenwich CT 06830

VAN DINE, ALAN CHARLES, advertising agency executive, writer; b. Ford City, Pa., Jan. 12, 1933; s. Albert and Helen (Remaley) Van D.; m. Joan Anne Hodges, Jan. 29, 1955 (div. Jan. 1971); children: Lynn, Mark, Barbara, Michael; m. Holly Long Shefler, Apr. 23, 1977. BA, Duquesne U., 1955; postgrad., U. Pitts., 1968—71. Editor Mt. Lebanon News, Pa., 1956-58; editorial dir. Pitts. Suburban Newspapers, 1958-61; writer and assoc. creative dir. Batten, Barton, Durstine & Osborne, Pitts., 1961-70; pres., creative dir. Van Dine, Horton, McNamara, Manges, Inc., Pitts., 1970-89; chmn. Van Dine, Humphrey, Inc., Pitts., 1989-95; cons. in field, 1996—. Mem. adv. coun. Internat. Poetry Forum, Pitts., 1969-80. Author: Can You Imagine?, 1967, Unconventional Builders, 1977, revised edit., 2001, (humor) The Encyclopedia of Advertising, 1987, Clyde Hare's Pittsburgh, 1994, Light Verse for a Heavy Universe, 2004; columnist Pitts. mag., 1977-78, Pa. Illustrated, 1979-81; contbr. articles, essays, short stories, and poems to mags. 1st lt. USAF, 1956. Recipient numerous awards Art Dirs. Club N.Y., 1964—, Bus. and Profl. Advt. Assn., 1964—, Am. Advt. Fedn., 1999. Mem. Chartiers Country Club. Avocations: golf, tennis, darkroom photography, cartooning, computer programming. Personal E-mail: AVDZZZ@bellatlantic.net.

VAN DINE, HAROLD FORSTER, JR., architect, artist; b. New Haven, Aug. 28, 1930; s. Harold Forster and Marguerite Anna (Eichstedt) Van D.; m. Maureen Kallick, Mar. 1, 1983; children by previous marriage: Rebecca Van Dine, Stephanie Van Dine Natale, Gretchen Van Dine Natale. BA, Yale Coll., 1952; MArch, Yale Sch. Arch., 1958. Registered architect. Designer Minoru Yamasaki & Assocs., Detroit, 1958-60; chief designer Gunnar Birkerts & Assocs., Detroit, 1960-67; prin. Straub, Van Dine & Assocs., Troy, Mich., 1967-80; chief architecture and design officer Harley Ellington Design, Southfield, Mich., 1980-95; archtl. cons. Birmingham, Mich., 1995—. V.p. Fields, Devereaux, HEPY, L.A., 1984-95. Prin. works include Mcpl. Libr., Troy, Mich., campuses for Oakland (Mich.) Community Coll., North Hills Ch., Troy, First Ctr. Office Plaza, chemistry bldgs at U. Mich. and Ind. U., G.M.F. Robotics Hdqrs., Flint Ink Rsch. and Devel. Ctr., Comerica Bank Ops. Ctr., Christ the King Mausoleum, Chgo., Resurrection Mausoleum, Staten Island, Mich. Biotech Inst., Ford Sci. Rsch. Labs, Fetzer Inst. Hdqrs. and

Retreat Ctr., Cen. Mich. U. Music Sch., Oakland U. Sci. Techs. Bldg., Corning (N.Y.) Credit Union. Bd. dirs. Cultural Coun. Birmingham/Bloomfield, 1990-99. Served to lt. (j.g.) USN, 1952-55 Recipient Book award AIA, 1958, Excellence in Architecture Silver medal AIA, 1958, Gold medal Detroit chpt. AIA, 1987, Mich. Soc. of Architects gold medal, 1991, over 50 major design awards; William Wirt Winchester travelling fellowship Yale U. Sch. Architecture, 1958; elect. to AIA Coll. Fellows, 1979. Mem.: Pewabic Soc. (bd. dirs. 1983—2002). Home: 1000 Stratford Ln Bloomfield Hills MI 48304-2930 E-mail: mvandhv@aol.com.

VAN DINE, VANCE, investment banker; b. San Francisco, July 2, 1925; s. Melvin Everett and Grace Winifred (Harris) Van D.; m. Isabel Erskine Brewster, Sept. 8, 1956 (dec.); 1 dau., Rose M. (dec.). BA, Yale U., 1949; LLB, NYU, 1955. Assoc. Morgan Stanley & Co., N.Y.C., 1953 59, 61 63, ptnr., 1963-75; mng. dir. Morgan Stanley & Co., Inc., N.Y.C., 1970-83; adv. dir. Morgan Stanley & Co., N.Y.C., 1983—. Cons. Internat. Bank for Reconstn. and Devel., 1959-61; chmn. Doane Western Co. Author: The Role of the Investment Banker in International Transactions, 1970, The U.S. Market After Controls, 1974. Bd. dirs. Yale U. Alumni Fund, Combined Health Appeal of Greater N.Y., Rec. for Blind, Inc., N.Y.C., 1979-89; trustee Cancer Rsch. Inst., N.Y.C., Nassau County Art Mus., L.I. U., 1979-91; gov. dir. Fgn. Policy Assn., 1980-89. With USN, 1943-46. Recipient Yale Class of 1949 Disting. Service award, 1983. Mem. The Pilgrims of the U.S., Union Club, Piping Rock Club, N.Y. Yacht Club, Seawanhaka Corinthian Yacht Club, Church Club, Yale Club (N.Y.C.), Met. Opera Club. Republican. Episcopalian. Office: Morgan Stanley & Co Ste C2E 1221 Avenue Of The Americas New York NY 10020-1008 Home: 515 E 72nd St Apt 36F New York NY 10021-4074 E-mail: vancevandine@msdw.com.

VANDIVER, DONNA, public relations executive; BJ, MBA in Mgmt. Pres. Vandiver Group, St. Louis, 1993—. Bd. dirs. Am. Heart Assn.; mem. adv. bd. Pky. Edn. Found. Named Small Bus. Person of the Yr. SBA, 1998; recipient Quest award Nat. Fedn. Press Women, 1999. Mem. Nat. Assn. Women Bus. Owners (Bd. dirs. St. Louis chpt., Disting Women Bus. Owner of the Yr. award 1999), Assn. Corp. Growth, St. Louis Press Club, Downtown St. Louis Partnership, St. Louis Regional Commerce and Growth Assn., Media Club. Office: Vandiver Group 10411 Clayton Rd Saint Louis MO 63131-2928

VANDIVER, FRANK EVERSON, institute administrator, former university president, author, educator; b. Austin, Tex., Dec. 9, 1925; s. Harry Shultz and Maude Folmsbee (Everson) V.; m. Carol Sue Smith, Apr. 19, 1952 (dec. 1979); children: Nita, Nancy, Frank Alexander; m. Renée Aubry, Mar. 21, 1980. Rockefeller fellow in humanities, U. Tex., 1946-47, Rockefeller fellow in Am. Studies, 1947-48, MA, 1949; PhD, Tulane U., 1951; MA (by decree), Oxford (Eng.) U., 1963; HHD (hon.), Austin Coll., 1977; DHL (hon.), Lincoln Coll., 1989, BA (hon.), 1994. Apptd. historian Army Service Forces Depot, Civil Service, San Antonio, 1944-45, Air U., 1951; prof. history La. State U., summers 1953-57; asst. prof. history Washington U., St. Louis, 1952-55, Rice U., Houston, 1955-56, assoc. prof., 1956-58, prof., 1958-65, Harris Masterson Jr. prof. history, 1965-79, chmn. dept. history and polit. sci., 1962-63, dept. history, 1968-69, acting pres., 1969-70, provost, 1970-79, v.p., 1975-79; pres., chancellor N. Tex. State U., Denton and Tex. Coll. Osteo. Medicine, 1979-81; pres. Tex. A&M U., College Station, 1981-88, pres. emeritus, disting. U. prof., 1988—; founding pres. Acad. Marshall Plan, 1992; Sara and John Lindsey chair in humanities, 1988. Harmsworth prof. Am. history Oxford U., 1963-64; vis. prof. history U. Ariz., summer 1961; master Margarett Root Brown Coll., Rice U., 1964-66; Harmon lectr. Air Force Acad., 1963; Keese lectr. U. Chattanooga, 1967; Fortenbaugh lectr. Gettysburg Coll., 1974; Phi Beta Kappa assoc. lectr., 1970—; vis. prof. mil. history U.S. Mil. Acad., 1973-74; hon. pres. Occidental U., St. Louis, 1975-80; chmn. bd. Am. U. Cairo, 1992-97, acting pres., 1997-98. Editor: The Civil War Diary of General Josiah Gorgas, 1947, Confederate Blockade Running Through Bermuda, 1861-65: Letters and Cargo Manifests, 1947, Proceedings of First Confederate Congress, 4th Session, 1953, Proceedings of Second Confederate Congress, 1959, A Collection of Louisiana Confederate Letters; new edit., J.E. Johnston's Narrative of Military Operations; new edit., J.A. Early's Civil War Memoirs, The Idea of the South, 1964, Battlefields and Landmarks of the Civil War, 1996; author: Ploughshares Into Swords: Josiah Gorgas and Confederate Ordnance, 1952, Rebel Brass: the Confederate Command System, 1956, Mighty Stonewall, 1957, Fields of Glory, (with W.H. Nelson), 1960, Jubal's Raid, 1960, Basic History of the Confederacy, 1962, Jefferson Davis and the Confederate State, 1964, Their Tattered Flags: The Epic of the Confederacy, 1970, The Southwest: South or West?, 1975, Black Jack: The Life and Times of John J. Pershing, 1977 (Nat. Book Award finalist 1978), (address) The Long Loom of Lincoln, 1986, Blood Brothers: A Short History of the Civil War, 1992, Shadows of Vietnam: Lyndon Johnson's Wars, 1997, 1001 Things Everyone Should Know About the Civil War, 1999, 1001 Things Everyone Should Know About World War II, 2002; also hist. articles, mem. bd. editors: U.S. Grant Papers, 1973—. Mem. bd. trustees Am. U. in Cairo, 1988, chmn., 1992-97. Recipient Laureate Lincoln Acad., Ill., 1973, Carr P. Collins prize Tex. Inst. Letters, 1958, Harry S. Truman award Kansas City Civil War Round Table, Jefferson Davis award Confederate Meml. Lit. Soc., 1970, Fletcher Pratt award N.Y. Civil War Round Table, 1970, Outstanding Civilian Svc. medal Dept. Army, 1974, Nevins-Freeman award Chgo. Civil War Round Table, 1982, T. Harry Williams Meml. award, 1985, Pres. medal Am. U. in Cairo, 1999; named Hon. Knight San Jacinto, 1993, Hon. Mem. Sons of Republic of Tex., 1986; rsch. grantee Am. Philos. Soc., 1953, 54, 60, Huntington Libr. rsch. grantee, 1961; Guggenheim fellow, 1955-56. Fellow Tex. Hist. Assn.; mem. Am. Hist. Assn., So. Hist. Assn. (assoc. editor jour. 1959-62, pres. 1975-76), Tex. Inst. Letters (past pres.), Jefferson Davis Assn. (pres., chmn. adv. bd. editors of papers), Soc. Am. Historians (councillor), Tex. Philos. Soc. (pres. 1978), Civil War Round Table (Houston), Orgn. Am. Historians, Phi Beta Kappa. Clubs: Cosmos, Army and Navy (Washington); Briarcrest Country (College Station). Achievements include originating idea of Coll. space grant program. Office: The Mosher Inst for Internat Policy Studies Texas A&M U 2400 TAMU Blocker Bldg College Station TX 77843-2400 E-mail: smaxwell@tamu.edu.

VANDIVER, RENEE LILLIAN AUBRY, interior designer, architectural preservator; b. New Iberia, La., Nov. 7, 1929; d. Harold George and Josephine Fortier (Brown) Aubry; m. Arthur Roderick Carmody, Jr., Jan. 1952 (div. 1979); children: Helen Bragg Carmody Stroud, Renee Josephine Carmody Mathews, Arthur Roderick III, Patrick Gerard, Timothy H.A., Mary Joellyn, Virginia Caroline, Joseph Barry; m. Frank Everson Vandiver, Mar. 21, 1980. BFA, Sophie Newcomb Coll. Tulane U., 1951; postgrad., U. Paris, 1951-52, Centinary Coll., 1966-68, La. State U., Shreveport, 1978. Designer, supt. art New Iberia Parish Elementary Schs., 1951; archtl. drafter and designer Perry L. Brown, Inc., Baton Rouge, 1950-52; tchr. art St. Joseph's Elem. Sch., Shreveport, 1960-69; designer, illustrator, saleswoman Stierwalt Interiors, Shreveport, 1974-78; design cons. for president's homes and gardens North Tex. State U., Tex. A&M U., Denton, College Station, 1980-88; design cons., planner, saleswoman, pres. Renee Aubry Vandiver Interiors, College Station, Tex., 1980—; design cons. Am. U. in Cairo, 1997—; proofreader, editor, rschr., asst. Office of Frank E. Vandiver, College Station, 1998—. Interior design and house constrn. cons. Heritage Antiques and Interiors, New Iberia, 1972—; interior design cons., Tenn., La., S.C., 1980—; invited student Middle Eastern master painter Sabri Raghab; involved with consultations and contruction large new campus, pres.'s home grounds Am. U., Cairo. Editl. and illustrations collaborator works on gen. mil. history with Frank E. Vandiver, 1990—; works include design constrn. of new Pres.'s Home on campus of Am. U. of Cairo, 2004. Mem. NAFE, DAR, Constrn. Specifications Inst., Dallas Market Ctr., Houston Market Ctcr., Jr. League, Textile Mus., Mus. Women in Arts, Tex. A&M U. Women's Club (hon. pres. 1981—), Fedn. Tex. A&M U. Mother's Club. Avocations: painting, playing piano, gardening, travel, reading. Home: PO Box 10600 College Station TX 77842-0600

VANDO, GLORIA, poet, publishing executive; d. Anita Velez-Mitchell and Erasmo Vando; m. William Harrison Hickok; m. Maurice Peress, July 5, 1955 (div. Sept. 1, 1980); children: Lorca Peress, Paul Peress, Anika Peress. BA, Tex. A&I-Corpus Christi, 1975. Pub. / editor Helicon Nine Edits., Kansas City, Mo., 1990—; founding pub. / editor Helicon Nine Mag., Kansas City, Mo., 1977—90. Co-founder The Writers Pl., Kansas City, Mo., 1992—. Writer (poetry book) Shadows & Supposes, 2002 (Poetry Soc. America's Alice Fay Di Castagnola Award, 1998, Latino Poetry Book award Latino Hall Fame, 2003), Promesas: Geography of the Impossible, 1993 (Thorpe Menn Book Award, 1994), (poem) HE2-104: A Planetary Nebula in the Making (Billee Murray Denny Prize, 1991), poetry (Kans. Arts Commn. Poetry Fellowship, 1989); editor Helicon Nine Jour. V.p. Midwest Ctr. for the Lit. Arts, Inc., Kansas City, Mo., 1992—2002; adv. bd. mem. BkMk Press, Kansas City, Mo., 1998—2002. Mem.: Beyond Baroque, Poets Ho., PEN Internat., Poetry Soc. Am., Acad. Am. Poets. Avocations: photography, dance. Office: Helicon Nine Editions 3607 Pennsylvania Kansas City MO 64111 Personal E-mail: helicon9@aol.com. E-mail: helicon9@aol.com.

VAN DOKKUM, JAN, manufacturing executive; m. Lynn van Dokkum; 3 children. B of Elec. Engrng., M of Elec. Engring., Inst. Tech. Regional v.p. sales Seimens Transmission and Distbn.; pres., COO Seimans Power Transmission & Distbn., Inc., 1997—2002; pres. United Techs. Corp., South Windsor, Conn., 2002—. Office: United Techs Corp UTC Power 195 Govs Hwy South Windsor CT 06074

VAN DOMELEN, JOHN FRANCIS, academic administrator; b. Havana, Cuba, Oct. 19, 1942; s. Floyd and Sara (Molina) Van D.; m. Naomi Ruth Kittlesen. BS in Applied Physics, Mich. Tech. U., 1964; MS in Water Res. Mgmt., U. Wis., Madison, 1972; PhD in Civil Engring., U. Wis., 1974. Commd. 2nd lt. USAF, 1964, advanced through grades to col., 1988; mgr. engring. Charmin Paper Products Co., Green Bay, Wis., 1969-70; asst. prof. Norwich U., Northfield, Vt., 1974 79, head engring. and tech. dept., 1979-83, head engring. and tech. div., 1983-85, v.p. acad. affairs, dean of faculty, 1985-90; pres. Wentworth Inst. Tech., Boston, 1990—. Mem. Engring. Workforce Commn. Contbr. articles to profl. jours. Trustee New Eng. Assn. Schs. and Colls., 2003—. Decorated Cross of Gallantry (Vietnam); recipient Centennial medal IEEE, 1984. Mem. ASCE, Am. Soc. Engring. Edn., Sci. Rsch. Soc. N.Am. Avocations: golf, science fiction. Office: Wentworth Inst Tech 550 Huntington Ave Boston MA 02115-5998 Business E-Mail: vandomelenj@wit.edu.

VAN DOREN, EMERSON BARCLAY, mediator; b. Rahway, N.J., Dec. 30, 1940; s. Emerson Maynard and Jaqueline Pendleton (Hicks) Van D.; m. Janet Elisabeth Bumbarger, Dec. 28, 1963; children: Pendleton Barclay, Virginia Cary. BA, Harvard U., 1962; JD, U. Mich., 1965; postgrad. degree (hon.), Air War Coll., Maxwell AF Base, Ala., 1985. Bar: Ky. 1965, N.H. 1971, U.S. Dist. Ct. (we. dist.) Ky. 1966, U.S. Dist. Ct. N.H. 1972. Assoc. Brown, Ardery, Todd & Dudley, Louisville, 1965-66; judge adv. USAF, 1966-71, 72-76; pvt. practice N. Conway, N.H., 1971-72; sr. procurement atty. U.S. Dept. Energy, Washington, 1976-81, dep. asst. gen. counsel for procurement, 1981-85; adminstrv. judge, mediator U.S. Energy Bd. Contract Appeals, Arlington, Va., 1985, chmn., chief adminstrv. judge, 1985—2001. Chmn. U.S. Energy Fin. Assistance Appeals Bd., U.S. Energy Invention Licensing Appeals Bd., U.S. Energy Patent Compensation Bd.; mediator. Capt. USAF, 1966-76, col. USAFR, command mobilization asst. to staff judge adv., 1988-90, ret., 1990. Decorated Meritorious Svc. medal with one oak leaf cluster, Commendation medal with one oak leaf cluster, Legion of Merit award; Leckie fellow, Resident fellow U. Mich.; named Outstanding Young Judge Adv., AF Systems Command, 1975. Mem. ABA, FBA, Sr. Execs. Assn. (chpt. pres. 1993-96), Bd. Contract Appeals Bar Assn. (co-chair practices and policy com.), N.H. Bar Assn., Ky. Bar Assn. Avocations: surf and fly fishing, mountain hiking. Home and Office: 92 Pronghorn Trail # 30 Cameron MT 59720

VAN DOREN, SHAUN CLARK, chemist, former mayer, city official; b. Somerville, NJ, July 21, 1970; s. John Miller Van Doren Jr. and Barbara Elizabeth Van Doren. AS in chemistry, Raritan Valley Cmty. Coll., Somerville, NJ, 1991; BS in chemistry, Trenton (NJ)State Coll., 1993; MA in mgmt., Stevens Inst. Tech., Hoboken, NJ, 0201. Notary pub. Instrumentation specialist AT&T Bell Labs., 1992—96; EH&S project specialist Lucent Techs., Murray Hill, NJ, 1996—. Pres. Tewksbury Hist. Soc., 1999—2003; mem. Tewksbury (NJ) Rep. Club, 1990—; mayor Twp. of Tewksbury NJ, 2001, twp. committeeman, 1997—, historian, 1994—. Recipient Young Citizen of the Yr., Senator Bill Bradley, 1990, Citizen of the Yr., Twp. of Tewksbury NJ, 1990. Mem.: Am. Chem. Soc., Tewksbury (NJ) Foot Bassets. Republican. Lutheran. Avocations: gardening, local history, reading. Home: PO Box 132 Oldwick NJ 08858

VAN DOVER, ROBERT BRUCE, physicist; b. Eatontown, N.J., Apr. 30, 1952; BS, Princeton U., 1974; MS, Stanford U., 1975, PhD, 1980. Disting. mem. tech. staff Bell Labs., Lucent Techs., Murray Hill, N.J., 1980-2000; dist. mem. tech. staff Agere Systems, Murray Hill, 2000—. Patentee in field. Fellow Am. Phys. Soc. (sec.-treas. topical group on magnetism and its applications); mem. IEEE (sr.), IEEE Magnetics Soc., AAAS, Materials Rsch. Soc. Office: Agere Systems 600 Mountain Ave Rm It-106 New Providence NJ 07974

VAN DRESER, MERTON LAWRENCE, ceramics engineer; b. Des Moines, June 5, 1929; s. Joseph Jerome and Victoria (Love) Van D.; m. Evelyn Lenore Manny, July 12, 1952; children: Peter, Jennifer Sue. BS in Ceramic Engring., Iowa State U., 1951. Tech. supt. Owens-Corning Fiberglas Corp., Kansas City, Mo., 1954-57; rsch. engr. Kaiser Aluminum & Chem. Corp., Milpitas, Calif., 1957-60, rsch. sect. head, 1960-63, lab. mgr., 1963-65, assoc. dir. rsch., 1965-69, dir. refractories rsch. Pleasanton, Calif., 1969-72, dir. non-metallic materials rsch., 1972-83, v.p., dir. rsch. Indsl. Chem. div. and Harshaw/Filtrol Partnership, 1983-85, dir. bus. devel. Pleasanton, 1985-88, cons., 1988—2003. Mem. adv. bd. dept. ceramic engring. U. Ill., 1974-78; chmn. tech. adv. com. Refractories Inst., 1980-84; mem. nat. materials adv. bd. Nat. Acad. Sci.; mem. Indsl. Rsch. Inst. Contbr. articles to sci. jours.; patentee in field. Sustaining membership chmn. local dist. Boy Scouts Am., 1980; pres. PTA, 1967-68; vol. exec. Pakistan Internat. Exec. Svc. Corps, 1990-91. Aviator C.E., U.S. Army, 1951-54. Recipient Profl. Achievement citation Iowa State U., 1978; named to Lambda Chi Alpha hall of fame, 1996. Fellow: Am. Ceramic Soc. (v.p. 1973—74); mem.: AIME, ASTM (hon.), Metall. Soc., Nat. Inst. Ceramic Engrs., Brit. Ceramic Soc., Masons, Rotary (pres. Pleasanton Club 2002—03, pres. Club Found. 2003—04, Paul Harris fellow), Keramos (pres. 1976—78, herald 1980—84, Greaves Walker Roll of Honor award). Avocation: comml. pilot. Home and Office: 40 Castledown Rd Pleasanton CA 94566-9749 E-mail: m_evandreser@msn.com.

VANDROSS, LUTHER, singer; b. N.Y., Apr. 20, 1951; s. Luther Sr. and Mary Ida Vandross. Student, Western Mich. U. Albums include: Never Too Much, 1981, Busy Body, 1983, Forever, For Always, For Love, 1982, The Night I Fell In Love, 1985, Give Me The Reason, 1986, Any Love, 1988, The Best of Luther Vandross...The Best of Love, 1989 (Grammy award: Best R&B Male Vocal Performance for "Here and Now" 1990), The Power of Love, 1991 (2 Grammy awards: Best R&B Song, Best R&B Male Vocal Performance for "The Power of Love"), Never Let Me Go, 1993 (Grammy nomination: Best Rhythym & Blues Male Vocal for "How Deep Is Your Love"), Luther, 1993, Songs, 1994, This is Christmas, 1995, Your Secret Love, 1996, One Night With You, The Best of Love, 1997, Always & Forever -- The Classics, 1998, Greatest Hits, 1999, Superstar Christmas, 1997, I Know, 1998, Best Of, 1999, Luther Vandross, 2001, The Ultimate Luther Vandross, 2001, Home for Christmas, 2002, Stop to Love, 2002, Dancing With My Father, 2003 (Grammy awards: Best Song, Best R&B Album, Best Male R&B Performance, Best R&B Performance by a Duo or Group with Vocals for "The Closer I Get to You"), Live 2003 at Radio City Music Hall, 2003; formed R&B band Luther, 1975; 1st hit song Everybody Rejoice (A Brand New Day), 1972; co-host Soul Train Music awards; duet with Janet Jackson "Best Things In Life are Free," (Grammy nomination: Best R&B Performance by a Duo or Group with Vocal). Office: J Records 745 5th Ave New York NY 10151*

VAN DUSEN, ALBERT CLARENCE, university official; b. Tampa, Fla., Aug. 30, 1915; s. Charles H. and Maude E. (Green) Van D.; m. Margaret Davis, Jan. 3, 1943; children: Margaret Van Dusen Pysh, Jane Katherine, Sara Elizabeth (Mrs. Frank J. Matyskiela). BS, U. Fla., 1937, AM, 1938; PhD, Northwestern, 1942; LittD, U. Tampa, 1959; L.H.D., Duquesne U., 1967. Instr., asst. prof. dept. psychology U. Fla., 1938-41; asso. prof. psychology Northwestern U., 1946, dir. summer session, 1948-52, v.p. pub. relations, 1952-56; prof. psychology, bus. adminstrn. and edn. U. Pitts., 1956-85, asst. chancellor for planning and devel., 1956-59, vice chancellor the professions, 1959-67, vice chancellor program devel. and pub. affairs, 1967-71, vice chancellor, sec. univ., 1971-80, vice chancellor emeritus, spl. asst. for pub. affairs, 1980-85, vice chancellor emeritus, prof. emeritus psychology, bus. adminstrn. and edn., 1985—, ctr. assoc. univ. ctr. for internat. studies, 1986—. Bd. dirs. Dollar Bank, Pitts. Editor: Proc. Am. Coll. Personnel Assn; contbr. articles to profl. jours. Bd. govs. Pinchot Inst. Conservation Studies; vice chmn., bd. dirs. The Buhl Found., World Affairs Coun. Pitts., vice chmn. bd. dirs. Duquesne U., acting chmn., 1987-88; bd. dirs. Pitts. YMCA, ACTION Housing, Inc., Assn. Am.'s Pub. TV Stas., QED Communications Inc., chmn. 1981-88; bd. dirs. Japan-Am. Soc. Pa.; mem. Pa. Pub. TV Network Commn.; chmn., bd. trustees Pitts. History and Landmarks Found.; pres. bd. trustees H.C. Frick Ednl. Commn., United Way Pa.; dir. South Hills Child Guidance Ctr.; chmn. selfcare study Health Edn. Ctr., Pitts., 1979-80; mem. Walter Reed Hovey Fellowship com. Pitts. Found. Lt. USNR, 1942-46. Fulbright sr. scholar Australian-Am. Ednl. Found., 1980 Fellow Am. Psychol. Assn., Am. Psychol. Soc., Pa. Psychol. Assn., Internat. Found. Social Econ. Deve.; mem. Internat. Assn. Schs. Insts. Adminstrn., C. of C. (dir. 1953-55), Am. Coll. Pub. Rels. Assn. (v.p. 1956-58), Assn. Deans and Dirs. Summer Sessions (sec. 1950-51), Profl. Schs. and World Affairs Com. (chmn. edn. and world affairs 1965-67), Am. Pers. and Guidance Assn., Midwest Psychol. Assn., Ea. Psychol. Assn., Pitts. Psychol. Assn., Internat. Assn. Applied Psychology, Western Pa. Coun. Econ. Edn., Internat. Assn. Schs. and Insts. Adminstrn., Friends of Art for Pitts. Schs. (charter mem.), Phi Beta Kappa, Sigma Xi, Beta Theta Pi, Beta Gamma Sigma. Clubs: Univ. (Pitts.), Duquesne (Pitts.), St. Clair Country (Pitts.). Home: 1290 Boyce Rd Apt C333 Pittsburgh PA 15241-3958

VAN DUSEN, BLANCHE BAKER, actress, sculptor; b. N.Y.C., Dec. 20, 1956; d. Jack and Carroll (Baker) Garfein; m. R. Bruce Vandusen; children: Zane, Dara, Wynn. Student, Wellesley Coll. Sculpture rep. by River Gallery, Irvington, N.Y., Sculpture Showcase, New Hope, Pa. Appeared in films The Handmaid's Tale, Shakedown, Raw Deal, Sixteen Candles, Cold Feet, The Seduction of Joe Tynan, TV program Holocaust (Emmy award for Best Supporting Actress); sculpture exhibited in shows at Nat. Arts Club, N.Y.C., Pen and Brush Club, N.Y.C., Salmagundi Club, N.Y.C., Cropsey-Newington Found., N.Y., Perry House Galleries, Alexandria, Va., Balch Inst., Phila., Alexandria Mus. Art, La., Coos Art Mus., Coos Bay, Oreg., Pound Ridge (N.Y.) Mus., Farmington Mus., N.Mex., Nat. Sculpture Soc., N.Y.C.; solo show Grants Pass Mus. Art, Eugene, Oreg., 2000. Named Anti-defamation League Woman of Achievement, 1979; recipient Philip Isenberg award Pen and Brush Club, 1995, Leonard Meiselman award Salmagundi Club, 1998, Agop Agopoff Meml. award Salmagundi Club, 1998, 2000, Leonard Meiselman award The Pen and Brush Club, 1999, Agop Agopoff Meml. award Newington Cropsey Found., 1998, H.A. Fahdli award Salmagundi Club, 1996, Pietro Montana award HVA Newington Cropsey Found., 1997, 98, Helen Beling award Coos Art Mus., 1998; winner Manhattan Artists Showcase Manhattan Arts Internat., 1996-98; named Best in Show Pound Ridge Mus., 1998.

VAN DUSEN, GLENN T. business executive; b. Houston, Dec. 25, 1944; s. Glenn Thornton Van Dusen and Barbara L. (Folse) Hanna; m. Jeanette Bearden Nosky, Feb. 14, 1976; children: Cheryl C., Kimberly D. BBA in Acctg., U. Tex., 1972. Store controller Montgomery Ward, Brownsville, Tex., 1972-78; acctg. mgr. Norton Co., Brownsville, 1978-83; owner Photo Finish, Missouri City, Tex., 1984-85; corp. controller Basic Sys., Inc., Houston, 1985-87, Backlog Group, Houston, 1988-95, Staff Force, Inc., Houston, 1995—. Treas. PTA, Katy, Tex., 1987-89, Homeowner's Assn., Katy, 1994-96. With U.S. Army, 1967-71, Germany. Mem. Inst. Mgmt. Accts., Tex. Assn. Staffing. Republican. Avocations: golf, genealogy, travel, rare coins. Office: Staff Force Inc 15915 Katy Fwy Ste 160 Houston TX 77094-1707 E-mail: gvandusen@staff-force.com.

VAN DUSEN, WILSON M. writer, psychologist; b. San Francisco, Sept. 11, 1923; s. Wilson M. and Martha Alice (Ebert) Van Dusen; m. Marjorie Lee Monroe, June 24, 1947; children: Joann, Rebekah. AB, U. Calif., Berkely, 1948, MA, 1949; PhD, U. Ottawa, Can., 1952; LittD, Am. Apostolic U., Seattle, Wash., 2001. Cert. Psychologist Calif., Master Unlimited Panama. Clin. psychologist US Army, Ft. Ord., Calif., 1949—50, Mendocino State Hosp., Talmage, Calif., 1952—68, chief psychologist, 1953—; assoc. dir. Awareness House, Oakland, Calif., 1968—73; pres. Philemon Found., Ukiah, Calif., 1973—. Hon. prof. Pacific Sch. of Religion, Berkeley, Calif., 2002—. Contbr. over 350 articles to profl. jours.; author: The Presence of Other Worlds, 1974, Beauty, Wonder, and the Mystical Mind, 1999, The Design of Existence, 2001, Just Beyond the Physical World, 2002. Ret. USCG Auxiliary, 1984—99; Regent Nat. Eagle Scout Assoc., 1981. Lt. USNR, 1945—61. Decorated knight Grand Cross Order of St. Michael, Knight Bachelor (Sir) King Peter II Jugoslavia; recipient Life Mem., Swedenborg Found. & Soc./ NYC, London, 1960. Mem.: Noble Co. of the Rose. Achievements include discovery of the 5th, 6th, & 7th dimensions of space. Avocations: writing, reading, navigation. Home: 705 Willow Ave Ukiah CA 95482-4244

VAN DUYN, MONA JANE, poet, educator; b. Waterloo, Iowa, May 9, 1921; d. Earl George and Lora G. (Kramer) Van D.; m. Jarvis A. Thurston, Aug. 31, 1943. BA, U. No. Iowa, 1942; MA, U. Iowa, 1943; D.Litt. (hon.), Washington U., St. Louis, 1971, Cornell Coll., Iowa, 1972, U. No. Iowa, 1991, U. of the South, Sewanee, Tenn., 1993, George Wash. U., 1993; LHD, Georgetown U., 1993. Instr. in English U. Iowa, Iowa City, 1943-46; instr. in English U. Louisville, 1946-50; lectr. English Univ. Coll., Washington U., 1950-67; poetry editor, co-pub. Perspective, A Quar. of Lit., 1947-67. Lectr. Salzburg (Austria) Seminar Am. Studies, 1973; adj. prof. poetry workshop Washington U., Spring 1983; vis. Hurst prof., 1987; poet-in-residence Sewanee Writers Conf., 1990, Breadloaf Writing Conf., Mass., 1974. Author: Valentines to the Wide World, 1959, A Time of Bees, 1964, To See, To Take, 1970, Bedtime Stories, 1972, Merciful Disguises, 1973, Letters from a Father and Other Poems, 1983, Near Changes, 1990 (Pulitzer Prize for poetry 1991), Firefall, 1993, If It Be Not I, 1993, Selected Poems, 2002. Recipient Eunice Tietjens award, 1956, Helen Bullis prize, 1964, 76, Harriet Monroe award, 1968, Hart Crane Meml. award, 1968, Borestone Mountains 1st prize, 1968, Bollingen prize, 1970, Nat. Book award, 1971, Sandburg prize Cornell Coll., 1982, Shelley Meml. prize Poetry Soc. Am., 1987, Lilly prize for poetry, 1989, Mo. Arts award, 1990, Golden Plate award Am. Acad. Achievement, 1992, Arts and Edn. Coun. St. Louis award, 1994; grantee Nat. Coun. Arts, 1967, NEA, 1985; Guggenheim fellow, 1972. Fellow Acad. Am. Poets (chancellor 1985-99); mem. NAAS, Nat. Acad. Arts and Letters (Loines prize 1976), Acad. Arts Scis. Achievements include first woman to be named United States poet laureate, 1992.

VAN DUYSE, FRANCIS DONALD (FRITZ VAN), publisher; b. Sturgeon Bay, Wis., May 2, 1926; s. Francis Lewis and Gertrude (Simon) Van D.; m. Dorothy Marie Walden, May 15, 1953 (div. Feb. 1978); children: Susan, Rebecca, Francis Roy, Sarah. BBA, Spencerian Coll., 1949. Baseball announcer Albany (Ga.) Cardinals, 1953-54, Waycross (Ga.) Bears, 1955, Valdosta (Ga.) Tigers, 1956; pub., editor Wis. All-Sports, Green Bay, 1958-68, Wis. Playground, Green Bay, 1958—68, Pro Football Exclusive, 1969—72; sports dir. WLUK-TV, Channel 11, Green Bay, 1962-63; CEO, announcer Gemini Broadcasting Co., Appleton, Wis., 1980-82; pres., CEO MegaPrint Internat., Sturgeon Bay, Wis., 1986—2000; pub., editor Fritz Van Newsletter, 2002—04, Pro Sportsletter, 2003—. Freelance sports announcer, 2003—. Author: History of the Green Bay Packers, 1965; pub., editor (yearbooks) Salute to the Packers 1961-68. With USN, 1944-46. Avocations: chess, exercise, writing. Home: 1811 Michigan St Apt 1E Sturgeon Bay WI 54235-3704

VAN DYCK, NICHOLAS BOORAEM, minister, foundation official; b. Pasadena, Calif., Aug. 10, 1933; s. David Bevier and Anna Booraem (Richardson) Van D.; m. Marcia Perera, June 14, 1958; children: Karen Rhoads, Jennifer Bevier, Sarah Paxson, Rebecca Booraem. BA, Rutgers U., 1959; BD, Union Theol. Sem., N.Y.C., 1962; PhD, U. St. Andrews, 1965.

Ordained to ministry Presbyn. Ch., 1962. Pastor Palisades (N.Y.) Presbyn. Ch., 1964-68; tchr., adminstr. Princeton (N.J.) Theol. Sem., 1968-76; exec. dir. Action Research Corp., Princeton, 1976-77; exec. dir., founder Nat. Council for Children & TV, Princeton, N.Y.C. and Los Angeles, 1977-82; pres. Nat. Council for Families and TV, Princeton, N.Y.C. and Los Angeles, 1982-87; pres., chief exec. officer Religion In Am. Life, Princeton, Phila, N.Y.C., 1988-2000. Chmn. Assn. for Theol. Field Edn., U.S. and Can., 1975-76. Pub., editor TV and Families, 1982-87; contbr. articles to profl. jours. Bd. dirs. ARC, Princeton, 1984-89, Princeton Youth Fund, 1983-89, YMCA, Princeton, 1986-89, George H. Gallup Internat. Inst., 1990-2000. Lt. USNR, 1954-58. Scholar-in-residence Aspen (Colo.) Inst. for Humanistic Studies, 1985. Mem. Soc. for Psychol. Study Social Issues, Ind. Sector, Princeton Club, Nassau Club, Rotary (pres. Princeton club 1981-82, bd. dirs. found. 1985-95). Avocation: collecting antique autos.

VAN DYCK, PETER CUYLER, health services administrator, pediatrics educator; b. Dec. 9, 1939; married; 3 children. BA in Physiology, U. Ill., 1962; MS in Physiology, MD, U. Ill., Chgo., 1966; MPH in Maternal and Child Health, U. Calif., Berkeley, 1973. Diplomate Nat. Bd. Med. Examiners. Intern, then resident in pediatrics Children's Meml. Hosp., Chgo., 1966-68, chief resident, 1968-89; instr. Med. Sch. Northwestern U., Chgo., 1968-89; chief pediatrics Health Clinic U.S. Army, Frankfurt, Germany, 1969-71, primary nursery physician 97th Gen. Hosp., 1971-72; pediatric cons. Internat. Red Cross, Amman, Jordan, 1973; dir. maternal and child health Utah State Div. Health, Salt Lake City, 1973-74, dir. div. family health svcs., 1974-92, acting exec. dir., 1984-85, acting dir. div. health care financing (Medicaid), 1986-87; sr. med. advisor to adminstr. HRSA, 1992-93; asst. prof. Med. Ctr. U. Utah, Salt Lake City, 1976-82, prof. Med. Ctr., 1991—; sr. med. advisor to dir. Maternal and Child Health Bur., 1993-94; dir. Office of State and Com. Health Maternal and Child Health Bur., 1994—, Maternal and Health Bur., Dept. HHS, 1989—; acting assoc. adminstr. for maternal & child health, Health Resources & Svcs. Adminstrn. U.S. Dept. HHS, 1998—99, assoc. adminstr. for maternal & child health, Health Resources & Svcs. Adminstrn., 1999—. Adj. assoc. prof. health Univ. Utah, Salt Lake City, 1975—, adj. asst. prof. Coll. Nursing, 1976—; mem. adv. com. U. Utah Coll. Nursing, 1976-80, Albert Einstein Coll. Medicine, Ctr. for Disease Control, 1983-86, John F. Kennedy Child Devel. Ctr., Denver, 1979-82; faculty coord. Crippled Children's Svcs. Advanced Inst., Children's Hosp., Columbus, Ohio, 1983—; mem. maternal and child health/Medicaid tech. assistance group Health Care Financing Adminstrn., 1987-93; mem. planning com., faculty Surgeon Gens. Conf., 1987; mem. various coms. and task forces; presenter, cons., reviewer in field; cons. Interagy. Efforts Children Spl. Health Needs Federated States Micronesia, 1991, Third Pacific Basin Interagy Conf. Individuals Spl. Health Care Needs No. Marianas Islands, 1992; faculty mem. Med. Ctr. Georgetown U., Washington, 1993; chief party U.S. Del. Third Regional Follow-up Meeting World Summit Children, Antigua, Guatemala, 1995. Contbr. articles to profl. jours. Co-chmn. sch. health com. Utah State Bd. Edn., Utah Dept. Health, 1974-92, statewide immunization action com. Awareness Com., 1977-78; project dir. Sudden Infant Death Syndrome Regional Ctr., Utah, 1975-80; chmn. Govs. Adv. Coun. for Developmentally Disabled Children, 1976-78; mem. task force on svcs. to presch. handicapped children Utah State Legis., 1984, tech. adv. coun. Utah Children, 1985-88, adv. bd. Jr. League, 1985-88; bd. dirs. Exceptional Child Ctr., Utah, 1975-80. Recipient Nat. Leadership award Dept. Health and Human Svcs., 1989, Nat. Achievement award Healthy Mothers, Healthy Babies, 1991; named one of 500 Most Influential Healty Policymakers Health Care 500, 1992; grantee U.S. Dept. Health and Human Svcs., Ctrs. for Disease Control., Devel. Diabetes Coun., Bur. Edn. for the Handicapped, Bur. Community Health Svcs.; WHO fellow, 1995. Mem. APHA (mem. various coms., chmn. maternal and child health sect. 1988—, Ross award 1977), Nat. Acad. for State Health Policy (mem. steering com. 1987-95), Nat. Found. March of Dimes (chmn. med. adv. bd. 1975-93, Plaque for Outstanding Svc. 1977-78), Nat. Early Childhood Tech. Assistance System (mem. nat. adv. com. 1988-90), Am. Acad. Pediatrics (mem. various coms.), Nat. Assn. of State Bds. Edn. (mem. task force on adolescent pregnancy 1979-80), Nat. Assn. State and Territorial Maternal and Child Health and Crippled Children Dirs. (pres. 1978-80), March of Dimes Birth Defect Found. (mem. nat. chpt. grants rev. com. 1988-92), Intermountain Pediatrics Soc. (mem. legis. and child abuse coms. 1974-76), Utah Pub. Health Assn. (mem. various coms., pres. 1984-86, mem. editorial bd. 1976-77, Beaty award 1985). Office: Maternal & Child Health Bur Parklawn Bldg Rm 18-31 5600 Fishers Ln Rockville MD 20852-1750

VAN DYCK, WENDY, dancer; b. Tokyo; Student, San Francisco Ballet Sch.; BA in Performing Arts, St. Mary's Coll., 2003. With San Francisco Ballet, 1979—96, prin. dancer, 1987—96, instr., tchr., 1996; co-dir. Lawrence Pech Dance, San Francisco, 1996—. Performances include Forgotten Land, The Sons of Horus, The Wanderer Fantasy, Romeo and Juliet, The Sleeping Beauty, Swan Lake, Concerto in d: Poulenc, Handel-a Celebration, Menuetto, Intimate Voices, Hamlet and Ophelia pas de deux, Connotations, Sunset, Rodin, In the Night, The Dream: pas de deux, La Sylphide, Beauty and the Beast, Variations de Ballet, Nutcracker, The Comfort Zone, Dreams of Harmony, Rodeo, Duo Concertant, Who Cares; performed at Reykjavik Arts Festival, Iceland, 1990, The 88th Conf. of the Internat. Olympic Com., LA, 1984, with Kozlov and Co. Concord Pavilion; guest artist performing role Swan Lake (Act II), San Antonio Ballet, 1985, Giselle, Shreveport (La.) Met. Ballet, 1994; featured in the TV broadcast of Suite by Smuin. Mailing: PO Box 1 Littleriver CA 95456 Office Phone: 415-308-5881. E-mail: wvandyck7@earthlink.net.

VAN DYK, FREDERICK THEODORE, political scientist, writer; b. Bellingham, Wash., Oct. 6, 1934; s. Ted and June Ellen (Williams) Van Dyk; m. Julia Jean Covacevich, Nov. 22, 1957 (dec. 1996); children: Theodore, Robert, Terry Jean, Sue Ellen. BA, U. Wash., 1955; MS, Columbia U., 1956. Reporter, editor Seattle Times, 1956-57; advt. public relations exec. Boston and N.Y.C., 1958-62; acting dir. European Community Info. Service, Washington, 1962-64; asst. to Hubert Humphrey, Vice Pres. of U.S., 1964-68; v.p. Columbia U., N.Y.C., 1968-69; pres. Van Dyk Assocs., Washington, 1969-76; asst. adminstr. AID, Washington, 1977; v.p. Weyerhaeuser Co., Tacoma, 1978—80; pres. Center for Nat. Policy, Washington, 1981-85, Van Dyk Assocs., 1985-98; exec. v.p. Milken Inst., Santa Monica, Calif., 1998-99; vis. scholar Claremont (Calif.) Grad. U., 1999-2000; sr. fellow UCLA Sch. Pub. Policy and Social Rsch., 1999-2000; columnist Seattle Post-Intelligencer, 2001—. Contbr. essays to gen. publs. Mem. Coun. Fgn. Rels., Presdl. Commn. Fgn. Assistance, Pacific Coun. Internat. Policy; bd. dirs. Com. Study Am. Electorate, Franklin and Eleanor Roosevelt Inst., Jean Monnet Coun., Humphrey Inst. With M.I. U.S. Army, 1957, with M.I. U.S. Army, 1961—62. Mem.: Rainier Club (Seattle), Delta Upsilon. Personal E-mail: t_van_dyk@hotmail.com.

VAN DYK, TINA KANGAS, microbiologist, researcher; d. Donald Arne and Sirkka Liisa Kangas; m. Drew Emerson Van Dyk, Sept. 25, 1982; children: Peter Joel, Lisa Anne. S.B., MIT, 1978, S.M., 1981; Ph.D., U. Del., 1998. Sr. rsch. biologist DuPont Co., Wilmington, Del., 1981—. Contbr. over 52 articles to profl. jours. Grad. fellow, NSF, 1978—81. Mem.: Am. Soc. Microbiology (conf. organizer, editl. bd. Applied and Environ. Microbiology 1999—). Orthodox Presbyterian. Achievements include 5 issued US patents in the field of bioluminescence applications; development of LuxArray technology. Office: DuPont Co Exptl Sta Rte 141 Wilmington DE 19880-0173

VAN DYKE, CLIFFORD CRAIG, retired bank executive; b. Ft. Madison, Iowa, June 23, 1929; s. Charles Clifford and Frances Mary (Butterwick) Van D.; m. Edith Ellicott Powers, Aug. 4, 1951 (dec. Oct. 1980); children: Carol Elizabeth, Deborah Ellicott, Jill Anne, Lisa Ellicott. BA, Knox Coll., 1951; MBA, Harvard U., 1955. Asst. v.p. Nat. Bank of Detroit, 1962-65, v.p., 1965-76; pres. Peoples Nat. Bank & Trust Co. of Bay City, Mich., 1976-78, chmn. bd., pres., 1979-86; chmn. bd., pres., chief exec. officer New Ctr. Bank Corp., Bay City, Mich., 1986; chmn. First of Am. Bank-Bay City, N.A., 1987-89; sr. v.p. First of Am. Bank-Mid Mich. N.A., 1990-94; ret., 1994. Trustee Kantzler Found., Bay City, 1979—; chmn. bd., pres. Bay County Growth Alliance, 1987—. 1st lt. U.S. Army, 1951-53, Korea. Mem. Bay City Country Club, Saginaw Valley Torch Club, Rotary. Independent. Unitarian Universalist. Office: Bay County Growth Alliance PO Box 369 Bay City MI 48707-0369 Office Phone: 989-893-5596. E-mail: bcga@concentric.net.

VAN DYKE, CRAIG, psychiatrist, director; b. Detroit, Oct. 4, 1941; married; two children. BS, U. Wash., 1963, MD, 1967. Asst. prof. psychiatry Yale U., New Haven, Conn., 1974-78; from assoc. to prof. psychiatry U. Calif., San Francisco, 1979-86, prof., chmn. dept. psychiatry, 1994—. Mem. Am. Psychosom. Soc., Internat. Coll. Psychosom. Medicine, Soc. Neurosci., Internat. Neuropsychol. Soc. Office: U Cal San Francisco Langley Porter Psychiatric Inst 401 Parnassus Ave San Francisco CA 94143-9911 E-mail: cvd@lppi.ucsf.edu.

VAN DYKE, DANIEL L. geneticist; b. Paterson, N.J., Mar. 1, 1947; PhD, Ind. U., 1976. Cert. med. genetics and clin. cytogenetics Am. Bd. Med. Genetics. Divsn. head genetics labs. Henry Ford Hosp., Detroit, 1975—; faculty U. Mich. Med. Sch., Detroit, 1978-94, Case Western Res. U., Cleve., 1994—. Mem.: Am. Bd. Med. Genetics (pres. 1998—2000, chair dept. med. genetics 1999—). Address: Henry Ford Hospital Cytogenetics Lab 2799 W Grand Blvd Detroit MI 48202-2608*

VAN DYKE, DICK, actor, comedian; b. West Plains, Mo., Dec. 13, 1925; m. Marjorie Willett, Feb. 12, 1948 (div. May 1984); children: Christian, Barry, Stacey, Carrie Beth. Ed. high sch. With Wayne Williams, founded advt. agy., Danville, Ill., 1946. Chmn. Nick at Nite, 1992—. Appeared school plays, civic theatre prodns.; appeared with Philip Erickson in pantomine act The Merry Mutes, Eric and Van, 1947-53; TV master ceremonies The Music Shop, Atlanta, Morning Show, CBS, 1955, Cartoon Show, 1956; TV variety show Dick Van Dyke Show, New Orleans; guest appearances TV shows, 1958, Golden Girls, 1985 (Emmy nominee), Jake and the Fatman, 1987, Coach, 1989, Sabrina the Teenage Witch, 1996, Becker, 1998; TV host Flair, ABC, 1960; Broadway debut in The Girls Against the Boys, 1959, Van Dyke and Company, 1976, The Van Dyke Show, CBS, 1988; performed in Broadway musical Bye Bye Birdie, 1960-61 (also motion picture version); (TV) Dick Van Dyke Show, CBS, 1961-66, New Dick Van Dyke Show, 1971-74; performer weekly comedy program Carol Burnett Show; (TV series) Diagnosis Murder, 1993-2002; (TV movies) Daughters of Privilege, 1991, The House on Sycamore Street, 1992, Diagnosis of Murder, 1992, A Twist of the Knife, 1993, The Dick Van Dyke Show Remembered, 1994; star, exec. prodr. Without Warning, 2002, Town Without Pity, 2002; performed in motion pictures including What a Way To Go, 1964, Mary Poppins, 1965, Divorce American Style, 1967, Chitty, Chitty, Bang, Bang, 1968, The Comic, 1969, Some Kind of Nut, 1969, Cold Turkey, 1971, The Morning After, 1974, The Runner Stumbles, 1979, Drop-Out Father, 1982, Found Money, 1983, Dick Tracy, 1990; Author: Faith, Hope, and Hilarity, 1970. With USAAC, World War II. Recipient Theater World award 1960, Antoinette Perry award for best mus. comedy actor 1961, Emmy award for comedy NATAS, 1962, 64, 65, 77, Life Career award Acad. Sci. Fiction, Fantasy and Horror Films, 2000, Lifetime Achievement award in comedy, 1994. Office: William Morris Agy Inc care Sol Leon 151 S El Camino Dr Beverly Hills CA 90212-2775

VAN DYKE, DONALD LEE, systems engineer, consultant; b. Portsmouth, Ohio, Oct. 2, 1947; arrived in South Africa, 1973; s. Donald Kenneth and Marion (Grimmer) Benk; m. Karin Frylinck, May 18, 1985; 1 child, Bradley. BS in Aeronautical Enging., Embry-Riddle Aero. U., 1995. Cert. aero. engr., airline transport pilot, flight instr., South Africa. Project engr. Sierra Rsch. Corp., 1970-73; mng. dir. Dynamic Tech./Command Airways, South Africa, 1973—82; cons./pilot Magnum Airlines, South Africa, 1982-84; head safety, pilot Comair, South Africa, 1984—96; chief exec. Advanced Mgmt. Concepts, Bonaero Park, South Africa, 1996—98; dir. ops. Internat. Air Transport Assn., Montreal, Canada, 1998—. Radar cons. South Africa Coun. for Sci. and Indsl. Rsch., 1973—74; sr. cons. Sun Air, South Africa, 1996; mem. ops. panel, flight crew licensing and tng. panel Internat. Civil Aviation Orgn. Inventor radar range normalization unit; patentee in field of light detection; developer (software) Flitebase Airline Info. Mgmt. Sys. Fellow: Royal Aero. Soc.; mem.: AIAA (sr.), N.Y. Acad. Scis., IEEE Computer Soc. Republican. Roman Catholic. Home: 429 Concord Dr Beaconsfield QC Canada H9W 5T1 Office: Internat Air Transport Assn 800 Pl Victoria, PO Box 113 Montreal QC Canada H4Z 1M1

VAN DYKE, GENE, oil company executive; b. Normal, Ill, Nov. 5, 1926; BS in Geol. Engring., U. Okla., 1950. Geologist Kerr-McGee, Oklahoma City, 1950; chief geologist S.D. Johnson Co., Wichita Falls, Tex., 1950-51; ind. geologist, oil operator, 1951-58; ptnr. Van Dyke and Mejlaender, Houston, 1958-62; owner, pres. Van Dyke Oil Co. (now Vanco Energy Co.), Houston, 1962—, also bd. dir. Bd. dir. Van Dyke Netherlands, Inc.; Vanco Energy Company is active in deepwater west Africa and is currently the largest license holder with over 25 million acres in depths between 1,000 and 10,000 feet. Compiler index of geol. articles to South La. With AC US Army, 1945. Named Living Legend in Wildcatting, Houston Geol. Soc., 2000; named to Hall of Fame, Dutch Am. Heritage Soc., 2001. Mem.: Am. Assn. Petroleum Geologists, Ind. Petroleum Assn., Houstonian Club, Houston Petroleum Club, Houston Club. Republican. Episcopalian. Office: Vanco Energy Co 3 Greenway Plz 12th Fl Houston TX 77046 E-mail: info@vancoenergy.com.

VAN DYKE, MILTON DENMAN, aeronautical engineering educator; b. Chgo., Aug. 1, 1922; s. James Richard and Ruth (Barr) Van D.; m. Sylvia Jean Agard Adams, June 16, 1962; children: Russell B., Eric J., Nina A., Brooke A. and Byron J. and Christopher M. (triplets). BS, Harvard U., 1943; MS, Calif. Inst. Tech., 1947, PhD, 1949. Research engr. NACA, 1943-46, 50-54, 55-58; vis. prof. U. Paris, France, 1958- 59; prof. aero. Stanford, 1959—; prof. emeritus, 1992—. Pres. Parabolic Press. Author: Perturbation Methods in Fluid Mechanics, 1964, An Album of Fluid Motion, 1982; editor: Ann. Rev. Fluid Mechanics, 1969-99. Trustee Soc. For Promotion of Sci. and Scholarship, Inc. Served with USNR, 1944-46. Guggenheim and Fulbright fellow, 1954-55 Mem. Am. Acad. Arts and Scis., Nat. Acad. Engring., Am. Phys. Soc., Phi Beta Kappa, Sigma Xi, Sierra Club. Office: Stanford U Div Mechs & Computation Stanford CA 94305-4040

VAN DYKE, THOMAS WESLEY, lawyer; b. Kansas City, Mo., May 12, 1938; s. Harold Thomas and Elizabeth Louise (Barritt) Van D.; m. Sharon Edgar, Jan. 30, 1960; children: Jennifer Van Dyke Winters, Jeffrey. BA, U. Kans., 1960; JD, U. Mich., 1963. Bar: Mo. 1963, Kans. 1983. Atty. SEC, Washington, 1963-64; legal asst. to commr. Hamer E. Budge, Washington, 1964-65; from assoc. to ptnr. Linde Thomson Langworthy Kohn & Van Dyke, P.C., Overland Park, Kans., 1965-91. Co-chmn. ALI-ABA Tax and Bus. Planning Seminar, 1987-96; mem. securities adv. panel Sec. of State of Mo., 1984-89. Mem. ABA (fed. regulation securities com. bus. law sect. 1982-2004, negotatiated acquisitions com. 1989-2004), Kans. Bar Assn., Mo. Bar Assn. (corp. banking and bus. law com., chmn. full com. 1983-84, past chmn. securities law subcom.), Carriage Club (bd. dirs. 1986-89). Republican. Avocations: tennis, golf, reading. Office: Bryan Cave LLP 3500 One Kansas City Pl 1200 Main St Kansas City MO 64105 Office Phone: 816-374-3201. E-mail: twvandyke@bryancave.com.

VAN DYKE, WILLIAM GRANT, manufacturing executive; b. Mpls., June 30, 1945; s. Russell Lawrence and Carolyn (Grant) Van D.; m. Karin Van Dyke; children: Carolyn Julie, Colin Grant, Alexander Grant, Stephanie Joyce. BA in Econs., U. Minn., 1967, MBA, 1972. V.p., CFO Northland Aluminum Co., Mpls., 1977-78; controller Donaldson Co., Inc., Mpls., 1978-80, v.p. controller, 1980-82, v.p., CFO, 1982-84, v.p., gen. mgr. indsl. group, 1984-94, pres., COO, 1994-96, pres., CEO, 1996—2004, chmn., 1996—, also bd. dirs. Bd. dirs. Graco Inc., Alliant Techsystems. Lt. U.S. Army, 1968-70, Vietnam. Mem. Kappa Sigma Alumni Assn. Avocations: running; bicycling. Office: Donaldson Co Inc 1400 W 94th St Minneapolis MN 55431-2370*

VAN DYKE-COOPER, ANNY MARION, retired financial company executive; b. Howard, Ont., Can., Sept. 30, 1928; d. Anthony and Anna (Koolen) Van D.; m. John Arnold Cooper, Apr. 9, 1983. BA, Concordia U., 1959. CFA. Tchr. Lanoraie Sch. Bd., 1946-47; sec, Can. Nat. Rys., Montreal, Que., 1947-51; sec. Sorel (Que.) Industries Ltd., 1952-53; with Bell Investment Mgmt. Corp. and BIMCOR, Inc. subs. Bell Can., Montreal, 1953-83; portfolio mgr. U.S. Equities, 1971-83; chmn., dir. Cooper, Van Dyke Assocs. Inc., Bloomfield Hills, Mich., 1983-96; ret. Mem. Inst. Chartered Fin. Analysts (trustee 1979-80), Assn. Investment Mgmt. and Rsch. (treas. 1977-78, vice-chmn. 1978-79, chmn. 1979-80), Fin. Analysts Soc. Detroit, Montreal Soc. Fin. Analysts (program chmn., pres. 1974-75), Can. Coun. Fin. Analysts (vice-chmn. 1976-77). Home: 2425 Gulf of Mexico Dr Unit 13B Longboat Key FL 34228-3215 E-mail: marionvdc@hotmail.com.

VAN DYKEN, AMY, Olympic athlete; b. Engelwood, Colo., Feb. 15, 1973; d. Don and Becky Van Dyken; m. Alan McDaniel, Oct. 1995. Student, Colo. State U. Swimmer U.S. Nat. Resident Team, Colorado Springs, Colo., 1994, U.S. Olympic Team, Atlanta, 1996, Sydney, 2000; ret. Named Female NCAA Swimmer of Yr., 1994, Assoc. Press Female Athlete of the Yr., 1996, USOC Sports Woman of the Yr., 1996, Woman's Sports Found. Woman of the Yr., 1996, USA Swimming Swimmer of the Yr., 1996, Phillips Performance of the Yr. award, 1996; named one of Glamour's Top Ten Women of the Yr., 1996; recipient Bronze medal, World Championships, 1994, Triple Gold medals, Pan Am. Games, 1995, Silver medal, 1995, Gold medal 50 meter freestyle, Atlanta Olympic Games, 1996, Gold medal 100 meter butterfly, 1996, Gold medal 4x400 meter freestyle relay, 1996, Gold medal 4x100 meter medley relay, 1996, Gold medal 4x400 freestyle, Sydney Olympic Games, 2000, ESPY award, best female athlete, 1997. Achievements include 1st American women to win 4 gold medals in any event during a single Olympic game.*

VANE, DENA, magazine editor-in-chief; Editor-in-chief First for Women, Englewood Cliffs, NJ. Office: First for Women Bauer Pub Co 270 Sylvan Ave Englewood Cliffs NJ 07632-2521

VANE, JOHN ROBERT, pharmacologist; b. Worcestershire, Eng., Mar. 29, 1927; s. Maurice and Frances Florence Vane; m. Elizabeth Daphne Page, Apr. 4, 1948; children: Nicola, Miranda. BSc in Chemistry, U. Birmingham, 1946; MSc in Pharmacology, Oxford U., 1949, D Phil., 1953, DSc, 1970; MD (hon.), U. Cracow, Poland, 1977, Copernicus Acad. Medicine, Cracow; doctorate (hon.), Rene Descartes U., Paris, 1978; DSc (hon.), CUNY, 1980, Aberdeen U., 1983, N.Y. Med. Coll., Birmingham U., U. Surrey, 1984, Camerino U., Italy, 1984, Louvain, 1986, Buenos Aires, 1986; DHC in Medicine and Surgery (hon.), U. Florence; DSc (hon.), U. London, 1995, U. Verona, 1997. Fellow Therapeutic Rsch. Coun., Oxford U., 1946—48; rsch. worker Sheffield U., 1948-49; rschr. worker Nuffield Inst. Med. Rsch., Oxford U., 1949—51; Stothert rsch. fellow Royal Soc., 1951—53; instr., then asst. prof. pharmacology Yale U. Med. Sch., 1953—55; mem. faculty Inst. Basic Med. Scis., Royal Coll. Surgeons Eng., 1955—73, prof. exptl. pharmacology, 1966—73; group R & D dir. Wellcome Found. Ltd., Beckenham, 1973—85; dir.-gen. William Harvey Rsch. Inst. St. Bartholomew's/Royal London Sch. of Medicine/Dentistry, Queen Mary/Westfield Coll., U. London, 1986—97, hon. life pres. William Harvey Rsch. Inst., 1997—. Bd. dirs. De Code Genetics Inc., Iceland. Co-editor: Adrenergic Mechanisms, 1960, Prostaglandin Synthetase Inhibitors, 1974, Metabolic Functions of the Lung, 1977, Handbook of Experimental Pharmacology, 1978, Prostacyclin, 1979, Interaction Between Platelets and Vessel Walls, 1981, Endothelin, 1989, 1991, 1993, 1995, 1998, New Targets in Inflammation, 1996, Therapeutic Roles of Selective Cox-2 Inhibitors, 1998, Selective Cox-2 Inhibitors, 2001; contbr. numerous articles to profl. jours. Freeman City of Scranton (Pa.), 1988, City of Taipei (Taiwan), 1989, City of New Orleans, 1995; hon. life pres. William Harvey Rsch. Found., 2000—. Decorated knight bachelor; recipient Baly medal, Royal Coll. physicians, Albert Lasker Basic Med. Rsch. award, Peter Debye prize, Nuffield Gold medal, Ciba Geigy Drew medal, Soc. Endocrinology, 1981, Nobel prize in physiology or medicine, 1982, Galen medal, Worshipful Soc. Apothecaries, 1983, Louis Pasteur Found. prize, Santa Monica, Calif., 1984, Nat. Headache Found. award, 1988, Hamburg Gold medal, Royal Pharm. Soc. Gt. Britain, 1996. Fellow: ACP (hon.), Royal Soc. (Royal medal 1989), Inst. Biology, Royal Coll. Physicians London (hon.), Royal Coll. Pathologists (hon.), Royal Coll. Surgeons of Eng. (hon.), Brit. Pharm. Soc. (hon.), Royal Nat. Acad. Medicine (hon.); mem.: NAS (fgn. assoc.), Soc. Drug Rsch., Am. Acad. Arts and Scis. (fgn. hon.), Physiol. Soc. (hon.), Polish Pharm. Soc. (hon.), Polish Acad. Scis. (fgn.), Royal Netherlands Acad. Arts and Scis., Royal Acad. Medicine Belgium, Alpha Omega Alpha (hon.). Office: William Harvey Research Inst Charterhouse Sq London EC1M 6BQ England E-mail: vanedvanel@fsnet.co.uk.*

VANE, SYLVIA BRAKKE, anthropologist, writer, publishing executive, researcher; b. Fillmore County, Minn., Feb. 28, 1918; d. John T. and Hulda Christina Brakke.; m. Arthur Bayard Vane, May 17, 1942; children: Ronald Arthur, Linda, Laura Vane Ames. AA, Rochester Jr. Coll., 1937; BS with distinction, U. Minn., 1939; postgrad, Radcliffe Coll., 1944; MA, Calif. State U., Hayward, 1975. Med. technologist Dr. Frost and Hodapp, Willmar, Minn., 1939-41; head labs. Corvallis (Oreg.) Gen. Hosp., 1941-42; dir. lab. Cambridge (Mass.) Gen. Hosp., 1942-43; staff Peninsula Clinic, Redwood City, Calif., 1947-49; vice pres. Cultural Systems Rsch. Inc., Menlo Park, Calif., 1978—; pres. Ballena Press, 1981—. Cons. cultural resource mgmt. So. Calif. Edison Co., Rosemead, 1978-81, San Diego Gas and Elec. Co., 1980-83, Pacific Gas and Elec. Co., San Francisco, 1982-83, Wender, Murase & White, Washington, 1983-87, Yosemite Indians, Mariposa, Calif., 1982-91, San Luis Rey Band of Mission Indians, Escondido, Calif., 1986-89, U.S. Ecology, Newport Beach, Calif., 1986-89, Riverside County Flood Control and Water Conservation Dist., 1985-95, Infotec, Inc., 1989-91, Alexander & Karshmer, Berkeley, Calif., 1989-92, Desert Water Agy., Palm Springs, Calif., 1989-90, Met. Water Dist., 1992-2001, Nat. Park Svc., 1992-2001, Applied Earthworks, Inc., 1997-2001, N.W Econ. Assocs., 2002-2004, County of Riverside, 2002-03, Aqua Calinte Cultural Mus., 2003—. Author: (with L.J. Bean), California Indians, Primary Resources, 1977, rev. edit., 1990, The Cahuilla and the Santa Rosa Mountains, 1981, The Cahuilla Landscape, 1991, Ethnology of the Alta California Indians, vol. I Pre Contact, vol. II POst Contact, 1992, Spanish Borderlands Sourcebooks, vols. 3, 4; contbr. chpts. to several books. Bd. dirs. Sequoia Area coun. Girl Scouts U.S., 1954-61; bd. dirs., v.p., pres. LWV, South San Mateo County, Calif., 1960-65. Fellow Soc. Applied Anthropology, Am. Anthropology Assn.; mem. Southwestern Anthropology Assn. (prog. chmn. 1976-78, newsletter editor 1976-79), Soc. for Am. Archaeology, Soc. Calif. Archaeology (Martin A. Baumhoff Spl. Achievement award 1998). Mem. United Ch. of Christ. Office: Ballena Press 823 Valparaiso Ave Menlo Park CA 94025-4206

VANE, TERENCE G., JR., finance company executive, lawyer; b. Elgin, Ill., Jan. 17, 1942; s. Terence Gregory and Velma Mary (Mersman) V.; m. Patricia Bryant, Aug. 29, 1964; children: Terence Gregory III, Lourdene DeLynne, Christopher Theodore. BA, Ind. U., 1964, JD, 1967. Bar: Ind. 1967, Tex. 1977, N.C. 1992, Fla. 2002. Staff atty. Assocs. Discount Corp., South Bend, Ind., 1967-69; asst. gen. counsel Assocs. Mgmt. Corp., South Bend, 1969-74, Assocs. Comml. Corp., South Bend, 1974-76, Assocs. Ins. Group, Inc., Dallas, 1976-77; gen. counsel, v.p. ins. ops. Assocs. Corp. N.Am., Dallas, 1977-80, gen. counsel, sr. v.p. ins. ops., 1981-82, gen. counsel, sr. v.p. consumer fin. and ins. ops., 1982-86, gen. counsel, sr. v.p. diversified consumer fin. svcs. and credit card ops., 1986-88; exec. v.p., gen. counsel, sec., dir. Barclays Am. Corp., Charlotte, NC, 1988-91; pres. Vector Fin. Svcs., Inc., Charlotte, 1991-95, bd. dirs.; sr. v.p., assoc. gen. counsel EquiCredit Corp., Jacksonville, Fla., 1996-97; sr. v.p., gen. counsel, sec. First Street Mortgage Corp., Jacksonville, 1997-98, Home Alliance Mortgage Co., Jacksonville, 1998-2000, Alliance Capital Ptnrs. Group, Jacksonville, 2000—02, Slott & Barker, Jacksonville, 2002—. Chmn. bd. dirs., sec. Youth Concert Found. for Promotion Creative Arts, 1981—; bd. dirs. N.C. Bus. Com. Edn., 1988-91. Mem. ABA (com. on consumer fin. svcs. law), Fla. Bar Assn., Ind. Bar Assn., Tex. Bar Assn., N.C. Bar Assn., Nat. Assn. Ind. Insurers (laws com. 1978-86), Consumer Credit Ins. Assn. (chmn. property ins. legis. com. 1979-85), Am. Fin. Svcs. Assn. (law com., chmn. environ. law subcom.), Conf. Consumer Fin. Law (governing com.), Chmn. Home Equity Mortgage Assn., Lawyers Round Table, Safari Club Internat. (pres.-elect, dir. North Fla. chpt.). Home: 13802 Fiddlers Point Dr Jacksonville FL 32225-5427 Office: 334 East Duval Street Jacksonville FL 32202-2718

VAN EMBURGH, JOANNE, lawyer; b. Palmyra, N.J., Nov. 18, 1953; d. Earl Henry and Clare (Kemmerle) Van E.; m. Samuel Michael Surloff, July 6, 1993. BA summa cum laude, Catholic U., 1975; JD cum laude, Harvard Law Sch., 1978. Bar: Calif. 1978. Assoc. atty. Agnew Miller & Carlson, L.A., 1978-82; ptnr. Sachs & Phelps, L.A., 1982-91, Heller, Ehrman, White & McAuliffe, L.A., 1991-93; mng. council Toyota Motor Sales, USA, Inc., Torrance, 1993—, asst. gen. coun., 2000—. Mem. ABA. Avocations: reading, cooking, sports. Office: Toyota Motor Sales USA Inc 19001 S Western Ave Torrance CA 90501-1106

VAN ENGEN, THOMAS LEE, state legislator; b. Sioux Center, Iowa, Mar. 28, 1953; s. Leo Herman and Dolores (Nelma) Van E.; m. Rosalyn Faye Vander Plaats, 1979; children: Matthew Thomas, David James, Jeremy Lee. BA, Dordt Coll., Sioux Center, 1979. Chair dist. 15 Minn. Ho. of Reps., St. Paul, 1992-94, mem., 1994—96; life and health ins. agt. Am. United Life Ins. Co. and Blue Cross Blue Shield Minn., St. Paul, 1997-98; devel. cons. Terwisscha Construction, Willmar, 1998—. Del. Rep. dist. and state convs., 1984-94, Minn. Rep. Ctrl. Com., 1989-94; chmn. Pipestone County Com., Minn., 1988-89, Kandiyohi County Com., 1991-93; co-chmn. dist. 15 Minn. Senate, 1990-92, chmn., 1992-94; candidate for Minn. Ho. of Reps., 1992, 2002; chmn. edn. com. Cmty. Christian Sch. Bd., 1990-94; elder Christian Reformed Ch., 1985-88, 96-99, 2001—, handicapped children and adults, 1978-82, chem. dependency counselor, 1982-94. With U.S. Army, 1972-74. Mem. CAP (mission pilot 1996—, moral leadership officer 2000—, squadron comdr. 2000—), Am. Legion, Kiwanis. Republican. E-mail: tve@tds.net.

VAN ETTEN, JAMES, plant pathologist, educator; BA in Biology, Carleton Coll., 1960; MS in Plant Pathology, U. Ill., 1963, PhD in Plant Pathology, 1965. NSF postdoctoral fellow dept. genetics U. Pavia, Italy, 1965—66; from asst. to assoc. prof. dept. plant pathology U. Nebr., Lincoln, 1969—74, prof. dept. plant pathology, 1974—86, William Allington prof. plant pathology, 1986—93, William Allington disting. prof. plant pathology, 1993—. Coord. plant sci. initiative U. Nebr., Lincoln, 1997—99; co-chmn. Gordon Conf. on Fungal Metabolism, 1984; com. mem. study sect. on microbial physiology NIH, 1978, 81, 1984—87; com. mem. grants panel plant pathology and weeds USDA, 1991, 92. Assoc. editor: Exptl. Mycology, 1976—96, Virology, 1989—; mem. edit. bd. Phytopathology, 1974—77, Jour. Bacteriology, 1980—85, Molecular and Cellular Biology, 1981—85, Molecular Plant Pathology, 1999—; contbr. articles to profl. jours. Fellow: AAAS, Am. Acad. Microbiology, Am. Phytopathological Soc.; mem.: NAS, Sigma Xi. Office: U Nebr-Lincoln Dept Plant Pathology 406 Plant Sciences Hall Lincoln NE 68583-0722

VAN ETTEN, PETER WALBRIDGE, foundation executive; b. Boston, May 10, 1946; s. Royal Cornelius Van Etten and Peggy June (Walbridge) Hutchins; m. Mary Peters French, Sept. 5, 1968; children: Molly, Clarissa, Ellen. BA, Columbia U., 1968; MBA, Harvard U., 1973. Br. mgr. BayBanks, Brookline, Mass., 1968-71; loan officer Bank of Boston, 1973-76; CFO Univ. Hosp., Boston, 1976-79; exec. v.p., CFO New Eng. Med. Ctr., Boston, 1979-89; pres., CEO Transition Systems, Boston, 1986-89; dep. chancellor U. Mass. Med. Ctr., Worcester, 1989-91; CFO Stanford (Calif.) U., 1991-94, pres., CEO Stanford Univ. Hosp., 1994-97; CEO UCSF Stanford Health Care, 1997-99; exec. com. U. Healthsystem Consortium, 1997-99, vice chmn., 1998-99; dir. Calif. Healthcare Assn., 1998-99, IDX Sys., Inc., 1999-2001; pres., CEO Juvenile Diabetes Found. Internat., N.Y.C., 2000—. Dir. Transition Sys., Inc., 1996—98, Duke U. Health Sys., 2003—. Chair campaign United Way San Francisco, 1998. Office: Juvenile Diabetes Found 120 Wall St New York NY 10005-3904 Office Phone: 212-479-7515. Business E-Mail: pvanetten@jdf.org.

VAN EXEL, NICKEY MAXWELL, professional basketball player; b. Kenosha, Wis., Nov. 27, 1971; s. Nickey Maxwell and Joyce Van Exel; 1 child, Nickey Maxwell III. Attended, Trinity Valley C.C., 1989-91, U. Cin., 1993. Guard L.A. Lakers, 1993-98, Denver Nuggets, 1998—2002, Dallas Mavericks, 2002—03, Golden State Warriors, 2003—04, Portland Trailblazers, 2004—. Named to NBA All-Rookie 2d team, 1994. Office: c/o Portland Trailblazers 1 Cneter Court ste 200 Portland OR 97227*

VAN EYS, JAN, retired pediatrician, educator, administrator; b. Hilversum, The Netherlands, Jan. 25, 1929; came to U.S., 1951; s. Jan and Geertruida (Floor) van E.; m. Catherine Travis; children: Jan Peter, D. Catherine. PhD in Biochemistry, Vanderbilt U., 1955; MD, U. Wash., 1966. Diplomate Nat. Bd. Med. Examiners, Am. Bd. Pediatrics, Am. Bd. Pediatric Hematology/Oncology. Postdoctoral fellow McCollum Pratt Inst., Johns Hopkins U., Balt., 1955-57; asst. prof. biochemistry Vanderbilt U., Nashville, 1957-62, assoc. prof., 1962-71, prof., 1971-73; intern, resident in pediatrics Vanderbilt U. Hosps., Nashville, 1966-69; pediatrician M.D. Anderson Hosp. U. Tex., Houston, 1973-94, prof. pediatrics, 1973-94, Mosbacher prof. pediatrics, 1979-87, Mosbacher chair, 1988-90, chmn. dept., 1983-88, head div., 1983-90, chmn. dept. exptl. pediatrics, 1983-90; David R. Park prof. pediatrics U. Tex. Med. Sch., Houston, 1990-94, chmn. dept., 1987-94; clin. prof. pediat. Sch. Medicine, Vanderbilt U., Nashville, 1994—. Cons. Cancer Info. Svcs. for Code Ethics and Pediatric Cancers, 1986-89. Author: (with T.S. Carter and C. Jordan) The Howell Kindred, 1979, Humanity and Personhood: Personal Reactions to a World in Which Children Can Die, 1981, (with M. Weiner) Nicotinic Acid, Drug, Nutrient and Cofactor, 1983; contbr. numerous articles, abstracts, papers, book chpts., and revs. to profl. publs.; editor: (with J.T. Truman and C. Pochedly) Human Values in Pediatric Hematology/Oncology, 1986, (with R.A. Dowell and D. Copeland) The Child With Cancer in the Community, 1988, Cancer in the Very Young, 1989; chief editor pediatric sect. Year Book of Cancer, 1978-87, cons. editor, 1974-78; assoc. editor Nutrition and Cancer, 1978-95, Jour. Pediatric Hematology/Oncology, 1982-92, Houston Med. Jour., 1986-93, Cancer Prevention Internat., 1993—, The Pharos, 1994—; also editor/co-editor proc. of workshops, clin. and mental health confs., ann. symposiums, etc. Pres. bd. trustees Inst. Religion, Houston, 1989-94; mem. adminstrv. bd. Westbury United Meth. Ch., Houston, 1989-94; bd. dirs. McKendree Sr. Care Corp., Nashville, 1996—, Alive Hospice, Nashville, 1998—, Tenn. Hemophilia and Bleeding Disorder Found., 1995-2001, 2003—, Nat. Hemophilia Found., 1997-2003, Vanderbilt U. Wesley Found.; chmn. health and welfare Tenn. Ann. Conf. United Metho. Ch., 1996-2004. Fellow Am. Acad. Pediatrics, Am. Coll. Nutrition; mem. Am. Pediatric Soc., Am. Soc. Hematology, Am. Soc. Clin. Oncology, Am. Med. Writers Assn., Am. Soc. for Parenteral and Enteral Nutrition, So. Med. Assn., World Fedn. for Hemophilia, Tex. Pediatric Soc., Houston Pediatric Soc. (pres. 1981-82), Houston Acad. Medicine, Harris County Med. Assn., U. Tex. M.D. Anderson Cancer Ctr. Assocs., Nashville Acad. Medicine, Davidson County Pediat. Soc., Sigma Xi, Alpha Omega Alpha. Home and Office: 3504 Ruland Pl Nashville TN 37215-1812 E-mail: jan.van.eys@vanderbilt.edu., janvaneys@cs.com.

VAN FAASEN, WILLIAM C. health insurance company executive; Past sr. v.p. operational svcs. Blue Cross Blue Shield Mich.; exec. v.p., COO Blue Cross/Blue Shield Mass., Boston, 1990-92, pres., CEO, 1992—2002, chmn., pres., CEO, 2002—04, chmn., CEO, 2004—. Bd. dirs. IMS Health, Inc., Liberty Mut. Group, NSTAR. Office: Blue Cross/Blue Shield MA Landmark Ctr 401 Park Dr Boston MA 02215-5000

VAN FLEET, DAVID DOMINIC, educator; b. Binghamton, N.Y., Nov. 27, 1940; s. Walter Anthony Van Fleet, Sr. and Katherine Elizabeth Van Fleet; m. Ella Webb, Aug. 27, 1966; children: Marijke, Dirk. BS, U. Tenn., 1962, PhD, 1969. Instr. U. Tenn., Knoxville, 1963—67, Kingsport Grad. Study Program, Kingsport, Tenn., 1967—70; asst. prof. U. Akron, Akron, 1970—73; from asst. prof. to prof. Tex. A&M U., College Station, 1973—89; prof. Ariz. State U. W., Phoenix, 1989—, MBA dir., 1999—2004. Prin. lectr. A. Frank Smith Jr. Lectureship series Southwestern U., 2000. Author: (book) Military Leadership: An Organizational Behavior Perspective, 1986, Organizational Behavior: A Managerial Viewpoint, 1983, Contemporary Management (3rd. edition), 1994, Contemporary Management (2nd edition), 1991, Contemporary Management (1st edition), 1991, Behavior in Organizations, 1991; contbr. numerous articles to profl. jours., chpts. to books; editor: N-File Newsletter, 1976—78, Acad. of Mgmt. Newsletter, 1979—82, Jour. of Mgmt., 1987—89. Recipient Faculty Achievement Award in Rsch., Scholarship, and Creative Activity, Ariz. State U. W., 2001, Outstanding Svc. award, Coll. Bus. Adminstrn., Tex. A&M U., 1985. Fellow: Acad. Mgmt. (chmn. mgmt. history divsn. 1980—81, dep. dean 1996—99), So. Mgmt. Assn. (pres. 1995); mem.: Southwestern Fedn. of Adminstrv. Disciplines (bd. dirs. 1985—87), Allied So. Bus. Assn. (pres. 1995), S.W. Acad. of Mgmt. (pres. 1986—87). Home: 4849 E Altadena Ave Scottsdale AZ 85254 Office: Arizona State University West PO Box 37100 Phoenix AZ 85069-7100 Personal E-mail: ddvf@asu.edu. Business E-Mail: mbaininfo@asu.edu.

VAN FLEET, GEORGE ALLAN, lawyer; b. Monterey, Calif., Jan. 20, 1953; s. George Lawson and Wilma Ruth (Williams) Van F.; m. Laurie Elise Koch, July 20, 1975; children: Katia Elaine, Alexander Lawson. BA summa cum laude, Rice U., 1976; JD summa cum laude, Columbia U., 1977. Bar: Tex. 1978, U.S. Dist. Ct. (so. dist.) Tex. 1978, U.S. Dist. Ct. (we. dist.) Tex. 1987, U.S. Dist. Ct. (no. dist.) Tex. 1988, U.S. Dist. Ct. (ea. dist.) Tex. 1991, U.S. Tax Ct., 1984, U.S. Ct. Appeals (5th cir.) 1978, U.S. Ct. Appeals (11th cir.) 1981, U.S. Ct. Appeals (D.C. cir.) 1982, U.S. Ct. Appeals (fed. cir.) 1993, U.S. Supreme Ct. 1981. Law clk. U.S. Ct. Appeals (2d cir.), N.Y.C., 1977; assoc. Vinson & Elkins, Houston, 1977-84, ptnr., 1984—. Co-chmn. Antitrust Practice Group. Co-author: Federal Civil Procedure Before Trial--Firth Circuit, 1997, The Competition Laws of NAFTA, Canada, Mexico and the United States, 1997, Business and Commercial Litigation in Federal Courts, 1998, supplement, 2003; editor: Annual Review of Antitrust Law Developments, 2000; co-author: Am. Legal Ethics Libr., 2002, Doing Business in Texas, 2003, State Antitrust Practice and Statutes, 2004, Inside the Minds: Leading Lawyers on unfair Competition, Trade Regulation and Litig., 2003; contbr. articles to profl. jour. Mem. bd. visitors Columbia U., 1992—; mem. City of Houston Ethics Com., 1992—98, chmn., 1995—98, bd. dirs. Nat. Appleseed Found., 2002—, Tex. Appleseed Ctr., 1998—, vice chmn., 1999—2002, chmn., 2002—04. Recipient Ordroneaux prize Columbia U., 1977, W. Frank Newton award for outstanding contbns. in provision of access to legal svcs. to the poor State Bar Tex., 2002; James Kent scholar Columbia U., 1974-77. Fellow Tex. Bar Found., Am. Bar Found.; mem. ABA (com. chmn. 1987-95, mem. coun. 1996-99, com. chmn. 2000-02, mem. ho. dels. 2002-, mem. nominating com., 2003-, sect. officer 2002-),State Bar Tex. (mem. coun. 2000-), Houston Bar Assn. (sect. chair 1991-93), Tex.-Mex. Bar Assn. (pres. 1998-2000), Phi Beta Kappa. Democrat. Jewish. Home: 3430 S Parkwood Dr Houston TX 77021-1238 Office: Vinson & Elkins LLP 1001 Fannin St Ste 2300 Houston TX 77002-6760 Office Phone: 713-758-2006. E-mail: avanfleet@velaw.com.

VANG, TIMOTHY TENG, religious organization administrator; b. Xieng Khouang, Laos, May 10, 1956; came to U.S., 1976; s. Nao Chai and Mai (Yang) V.; m. Chee Yang, Jan. 1, 1974 (dec. June 1975); m. Lydia Joua Xiong, July 7, 1979; children: Jennifer P., Nathan K., Victor C., Richard M., Tiffany P., Jasmine M. BS in Missions, Cin. Bible Coll., 1984; MDiv in Ch. Ministries, Can. Theol. Sem., Regina, Sask., 1991; DMin in Ch. Leadership, Fuller Theol. Sem., Pasadena, Calif., 1999. Ordained to ministry Ch. of Christ, 1984, Christian and Missionary Alliance, 1986. Machine operator Pellet Co., Green Bay, Wis., 1977-78; mental health worker Inst. Human Design, Oshkosh, Wis., 1978-80; ch. planter Ch. of Christ, Eau Claire, Wis., 1984-86; pastor Boulder (Colo.) Hmong Alliance Ch., 1986-87; dir. Christian edn. Hmong dist. Christian and Missionary Alliance, Brighton, Colo., 1986-87, dist. supt., 1991-96; sr. pastor Sacramento Hmong Alliance, 1997—. Mem. bd. mgrs. Christian and Missionary Alliance, 1994-97; trustee Crown Coll., 1992-96. Organizer Fox Valley Lao/Hmong Assn., Appleton, Wis., 1979. Lt. U.S./Hmong Allied Army, 1971-75. Mem. Christian And Missionary Alliance Ch. Avocations: reading, writing, walking. Office: Sacramento Hmong Alliance Ch 9131 Locust St Elk Grove CA 95624-2017 E-mail: tmtvang@aol.com.

VAN GELDER, MARC CHRISTIAAN, retail executive; b. Amsterdam, The Netherlands, May 21, 1961; s. Bob Frits and Maria Johanna (Van Teeseling) Van G.; m. Karah L. Henry, July 7, 1990; children: Alexander F., Robert H. M of Econs., Erasmus U., Rottendam, The Netherlands, 1986; MBA, Wharton Sch., U. Pa., 1990. Asst. v.p. Drexel-Burnham Lambert, N.Y.C., 1986-88; sr. mgr. McKinsey & Co., Amsterdam, 1990-96; dir. bus. devel. Ahold, Netherlands, 1996—98; v.p. supply chain mgnt. The Stop & Shop Supermarket Company, 1998—99, sr. v.p., logistics & supply chain mgnt., 1999-2000; pres. & CEO Peapod Inc., Skokie, IL, 2000—. Author: Venture Capital Market, 1985. Mem. Wharton Alumni Club The Netherlands (pres. 1991-98), Netherlands Am. C. of C. (bd. dirs.). Avocations: skiing, horseback riding, arts. Office: Peapod Inc 9933 Woods Dr Ste 375 Skokie IL 60077-1057 Office Phone: 847-583-6323.

VAN GELDER, RUDOLPH, sound recording engineer; b. Jersey City; s. Louis and Henrietta Van G.; m. Elva Myrow (dec. 1979); m. Janet R. Herrmann, May 11, 1982 (dec. Feb. 2002). OD, Pa. State Coll. Practiced optometry, Teaneck, N.J., 1960; owner, operator Van Gelder Rec. Studio, Inc., Englewood Cliffs, N.J., 1960—. Mem. Audio Engring. Soc., Nature Conservancy. Avocation: wildlife photogrphy. Office: 445 State Route 9 W Englewood Cliffs NJ 07632-2703

VANGER, MILTON ISADORE, history educator; b. N.Y.C., Apr. 11, 1925; s. Max Manuel and Rose (Rothstein) V.; m. Elsa M. Oribe, Sept. 10, 1956; children: John, Mark, Rachel. AB, Princeton U., 1948; MA, Harvard U., 1950, PhD, 1958. Teaching fellow history Harvard U., 1952-56; instr. Okla. State U., 1956-58; asst. prof. history Sacramento State Coll., 1958-62; mem. faculty Brandeis U., Waltham, Mass., 1962—, prof. history, 1973-84, prof. emeritus, 1984—. Chmn. com. Latin Am. studies, 1971-81; invited lectr. 50th anniversary conf. commemorating death of Batlle y Ordoñez of Uruguay, 1979; invitee to inauguration of pres. Sanguinetti, Uruguay, 1985; Barnette Miller vis. prof. history, Wellesley Coll., 1990. Author: José Batlle y Ordoñez of Uruguay: The Creator of His Times, 1902-1907, 1963, 2d edit., 1980, Spanish transl., 1968, 2d edit., 1992, The Model Country: José Batlle y Ordoñez of Uruguay, 1907-1915, 1980, Spanish transl., 1983, 2d edit., 1991, Reforma o Revolución La Polémica Batlle-Mibelli, 1917, 1989; outside reviewer NEH, Radcliffe Inst.; contbr. articles to profl. jours. Juror for Lindahl Prize, Inst. Latin Am. Studies, Stockholm. With AUS, 1943-45. Doherty Found. fellow, 1950-52; grantee Am. Philos. Soc., 1966; recipient Hermes prize for best history pub. in Uruguay, 1983. Mem. New Eng. Council Latin Am. Studies (sec.-treas. 1970-72), Am. Hist. Assn., Conf. on Latin Am. History, Amnesty Internat., Phi Beta Kappa. Democrat. Jewish. Address: 931 Massachusetts Ave Ste 503 Cambridge MA 02139

VAN GESTEL, ALLAN, judge; b. Boston, Dec. 3, 1935; BA, Colby Coll., 1957; LLB, Boston U., 1961; MA (hon.), Colby Coll., 1999. Bar: Mass. 1961, U.S. Dist. Ct. Mass. 1963, U.S. Ct. Appeals (1st cir.) 1969, U.S. Supreme Ct. 1972, U.S. Ct. Claims 1979, U.S. Ct. Appeals (2d cir.) 1980, U.S. Dist. Ct. (no. dist.) N.Y. 1980, U.S. Dist. Ct. (we. dist.) N.Y. 1993, U.S. Ct. Appeals (3d cir.) 1993, U.S. Ct. Appeals (5th cir.) 1995. Assoc. firm Goodwin, Procter & Hoar, Boston, 1961-70, ptnr., 1970-96; assoc. justice Superior Ct. Mass., 1996—; presiding justice Suffolk County Bus. Litigation Session, 2000—. Spl. counsel Boston Fin. Commn., 1974; spl. counsel to Mass. Commn. on Jud. Conduct, 1986; mem. Scituate (Mass.) Bd. Zoning Appeals, 1970, Scituate Planning Bd., 1972; spl. counsel Gov. of N.Y. on Indian Land Claims, 1985-96; spl. counsel to Gov. and Atty. Gen. of Vt. on Indian Claims, 1987-90; chmn. standing adv. com. Mass. Rules Civil Procedure, 1986-93; overseer Colby Coll., 1990-99, trustee, 1999—. Contbr. numerous articles on Eastern Indian land claims, ct. adminstrn., capital punishment to profl. jours. Fellow Am. Coll. Trial Lawyers; mem. ABA, Mass. Bar Assn., Boston Bar Assn. (chmn., task force on drugs and the cts.), Supreme Jud. Ct. Hist. Soc. (chmn. bd. overseers 1993-96), Mass. Hist. Soc.

VAN GILDER, JOHN CORLEY, neurosurgeon, educator; b. Huntington, W.Va., Aug. 14, 1935; s. John Ray and Sarah Pool (Corley) Van G.; m. Kerstin Margarita Olesson, Mar., 1965; children: Sarah, John, Rachel, David. BA, W.Va. U., 1957, BS, 1959; MD, U. Pitts., 1961. Diplomate Am. Bd. Neurol. Surgery. (examiner 1976, 79, 84). Intern Pa. Hosp., Phila., 1961, asst. resident in surgery, 1964-65, Wilkes-Barre (Pa.) Hosp., 1962; asst. resident neurosurgery Barnes Hosp., St. Louis, 1966-68, sr. resident, 1968-69; instr. neurosurgery Yale U. Sch. Medicine, New Haven, 1970, asst. prof., 1970-73, assoc. prof., 1973-76; prof. neurosurgery U. Iowa, Iowa City, 1976—, chmn. div. neurosurgery, 1976—, exec. com. dept. surgery, 1978-81. Fellow neurosurgery Wash. U. Sch. Medicine, St. Louis, 1965-66, instr., 1966; attending neurosurgeon VA Hosp., New Haven, 1970-73, cons. 1973-76; assoc. to attending neurosurgeon Yale-New Haven Med. Ctr., 1970-76; cons. VA Hosp., Iowa City, 1976—; neurol. surg. cons. Vets. Affairs Hdqrs., Washington; mem. clin. coordinating com. U. Iowa Cancer Ctr., 1979—; presenter numerous papers at profl. meetings., confs., symposia; vis. prof. U. Tenn., 1984, Tufts U. Med. Ctr., Boston, 1986, U. Tex., San Antonio, 1987, U. Mich., Ann Arbor, 1988, People's Republic China at Hunan Med. Coll., Beijing Neurol. Inst., Tianjin Med. Coll. Hosp., Tiantan Xili, Xian Gen. Hosp., 2d Mil. Coll., Shanghai, Suzhou Med. Coll. Shanghai, 1985, USSR at Burdenk Inst., Kiev Neurol. Inst., Leningrad Neurol. Soc., 1989, Western Reserve U., Cleve., 1993, Yale U., New Haven, Conn., 1994, U. Wash., Seattle, 1997, Mayo Clinic, 1998, U. Calif., San Francisco, 1998, Ind. U., 1999; mem. ad. hoc rev. bd. Surg. Neurology, 2001—, Spine, 2000—. Author: (with others): Principles of Surgery, 2d edit., 1973, Brief Textbook of Surgery, 1976, Aneurysmal Subarachnoid Hemorrhage, 1981, Operative Neurosurgical Techniques, Indications, Methods, and Results, 1982, Sports Medicine, 1982, Neurosurgery, 1982, Clinical Neurosurgery, 1982, Operative Neurosurgical Technique, Vol. II, 1982, 88, Vol. III, 1995, Current Therapy in Neurosurgical Surgery, 1985, 2d edit., 1987, Craniovertebral Junction Abnormalities, 1987, Decision Making in Neurological Surgery, 1987, Neurological Surgery, 3d edit., 1988, Anterior Cervical Spine Surgery, 1993, Brain Surgery: Complication Avoidance and Management, 1993, Neurosurgical Emergencies, 1994, Techniques of Spinal Fusion and Instrumation, 1995, Somatic Gene Therapy, 1995, Infections in Neurological Surgery, 1999; contbr. numerous articles and abstracts to profl. jours.; co-author teaching films; mem. editorial bd. Neurosurgery jour., 1978-84. Capt. USAF, 1962-64. Grantee NIH, 1973-78, Nat. Cancer Inst., 1980-88. Fellow: ACS (membership com. Iowa dist. #1 1983—); mem.: AMA, Am. Bd. Neurol. Surgery (dir. 1992—98, chmn. 1997—98, residency rev. com.-neurol. surgery 1995—2001, neurosurgery chmn. 1999—2001), Am. Acad. Neurol. Surgery (v.p. 1995—), Midwest Surg. Assn., Soc. Neurol. Surgeons (chmn. membership com. 1986—87, treas. 1991—, pres 1997—98, treas. 1991—96, pres. 1997, Disting. Svc. award 2004), Iowa-Midwest Neurosurg. Soc. (pres. 1978—79), Johnson County Med. Soc. (program com. 1984—88, chmn. 1985—86), Iowa Med. Soc., Neurol. Soc. Am. (long range planning com. 1984—, v.p. 1985, pres. 1998—99), Rsch. Soc. Neurol. Surgeons, Am. Assn. Neurol. Surgeons (awards com. 1986—87, bd. dirs. 1986—90, chmn. 1987—88), Congress Neurol. Surgeons (resident placement com. 1970), Am. Physiol. Soc., Ga. Neurosurg. Soc. (hon.), Sigma Xi. Home: 330 S Summit St Iowa City IA 52240-3220 Office: U Iowa Hosps & Clinics Dept Neurosurgery 200 Hawkins Dr Iowa City IA 52242-1009 Office Phone: 319-356-2772.

VAN GINKEL, BLANCHE LEMCO, architect, educator; b. London, 1923; d. Myer and Claire Lemco; m. H. P. Daniel van Ginkel, 1956; children: Brenda Renee, Marc Ian. B.Arch., McGill U., 1945; M.C.P., Harvard U., 1950. Tech. asst. Nat. Film Bd. Can., 1943-44; mgr. City Planning Office, Regina, Sask., Can., 1946; architect Atelier Le Corbusier, Paris, 1948; asst. prof. architecture U. Pa., 1951-57; ptnr. van Ginkel Assocs., Montreal, Que., Can., also Toronto, Ont., Can., 1957—; prof. architecture U. Toronto, 1977—92, dir. Sch. Architecture, 1977-80, dean faculty architecture and landscape architecture, 1980-82. Vis. critic Harvard U., 1958, 70; adj. prof. U. Montreal, McGill U., others; curator exhbns. RCA, U. Toronto, others. Contbr. articles to profl. jours. Mem. Nat. Capital Planning Com., Ottawa, Art Adv. Com., Ottawa; mem. adv. com. Nat. Mus.'s Corp.; mem. Que. Provincial Planning Commn.; founder, v.p. Corp. of Urbanists of Que., 1963-65; bd. dirs. Montreal Internat. Film Festival, 1961-66. Decorated Order of Can.; recipient Internat. Fedn. Housing and Planning Grand Prix award, 1956, Massey medal for arch., 1962, Mademoiselle Mag. award, 1957, Queen's Silver Jubilee medal, 1977, Citizenship citation Can. Govt., 1991, Queen's Golden Jubilee medal, 2002, award of Order of Urbanists of Que., 2003. Fellow AIA (hon.), Royal Archtl. Inst. Can. (exec. com. 1971-74), Toronto Soc. Arch.; mem. Can. Inst. Planners (bd. dirs. 1961-64), Assn. Collegiate Schs. Architecture (bd. dirs. 1981-84, v.p. 1985-86, pres. 1986-87, Disting. Prof. award 1989), Royal Can. Acad. Art (bd. dirs. 1992—2000), Internat. Archive of Women Architects (bd. dirs. 1985-2001), Ont. Assn. Arch. (life), Order of Can. Office: 38 Summerhill Gardens Toronto ON Canada M4T 1B4

VAN GINKEL, JOHANNES AUGUSTE, geographer, educator; b. Kota-Radjah, Indonesia, June 22, 1940; arrived in the Netherlands, 1950; s. Gysbert and Sipkje W. (Westra) van G.; m. Anna Maria E. Teepen, Aug. 25, 1965; children: Auke Gysbert Heino, Mapje Ank Marit. MS in Geography and History cum laude, Utrecht (Netherlands) U., 1966, PhD in Social Scis. cum laude, 1979; Doctorate (hon.), Babes-Bolyai U., Cluj-Napoca, 1996, State U. Calif., Sacramento, 2003. Prof. geography and history Thomas à Kempis Coll., Arnhem, Netherlands, 1965-68; assoc. prof. geography Utrecht U., 1968-80, full prof. human geography and planning, 1980—, dean of faculty, 1981-85, mem. bd. govs., 1985-97, rector magnificus, 1986-97; rector UN U., Tokyo, 1997—. Chmn. Netherlands Trilateral Adv. Coun. Sci. Policy, 1991-97; bd. dirs. European Assn. Univs., 1989-98, v.p. 1994-98; mem. coun. UN U., 1992-97, v.p., 1995-97; bd. dirs. Internat. Assn. Univs., 1990-95, v.p., 1995-2000, pres., 2000—; mem. European Sci. and Tech. Assembly, 1994-97; mem. adv. group higher edn. UNESCO, 1995—; steering group World Conf. on Higher Edn., Paris, 1996-98; vice chair bd. trustees Asian Inst. Tech., 1997—; chmn. organizing com. 28th Internat. Geog. Congress: Land, Sea and the Human Effort, The Hague, The Netherlands, 1996. Author: a.o. Zicht op de Stad, 1977, Die Randstad Holland, 1979, Suburbanisatie en Recente Woonmilieus, 1979, Algemene Sociale Geografie, 1984, Nederland in Delen, 1989, University 2050: the Organization of Creativity and Innovation, 1994, Networks and Strategic Alliances within and between Universities and with the Private Sector, 1999, In Quest of Human Security, 2000, Citizens Participation and Informed Consent in Urban Environmental Management, 2000, Variety and Impact: Differences that Matter. Some Thoughts on the Variety of University Governance Systems and their impact on University Policies and Strategies, 2001, Reflections on Human Development and the Environment, 2002, What Does Globalization Mean for Higher Education?, 2003; editor: Geografisch Tijdschrift, 1970-79. Chmn. Regional Conf. of Municipalities, Utrecht, 1988-93; treas. Netherlands' Univs. Found. for Internat. Cooperation, Nuffic, 1986-97. Decorated knight Netherlands Lion; hon. fellow Internat. Tng. Ctr. for Aerospace Survey and Earth Scis. Mem. Royal Netherlands Acad. Arts and Scis. (social scis. coun.), Academia Europea, Found. for Fundamental Rsch. in Geog. and Environ. Scis. (chmn. 1982-91), Netherlands Interdisciplinary Demographic Inst. (chmn. sci. com. 1986-95, bd. govs. 1996—, chmn. 1996-2000), Internat. Tng. Ctr. for Aerospace Survey and Earth Scis. (bd. dirs. 1986-94, chmn. 1994-98), Internat. Geog. Union (chmn. Netherlands br. 1988-92), Royal Netherlands Geog. Soc., Netherlands' Inst. for Urban and Regional Planning and Pub. Housing, Rotary, Sports Coun. Hoevelaken Municipality (chmn., 1969-73), Hockey Club Amersfoort (mem. tech. com. 1970-75), Sports Club Kampong, Utrecht (chmn. youth divsn. 1976-82). Avocations: sports, travel. Home: Park Arenberg 63 De Bilt NL3731EP Netherlands Office: UNU 5-53-70 Jingumae, Shibuya-ku Tokyo 150-8925 Japan

VAN GORDER, JAN REID, lawyer, insurance company executive; b. Endicott, N.Y., Dec. 28, 1947; s. George Austin and Elizabeth Anne (Brown) Van G.; m. Linda Susan Massarelli, July 31, 1976; children: Austin Reid, Lewis Evan, Thomas Drew, Elizabeth Marie. BA, U. Pa., 1970; JD, Temple U., 1975. Assoc. gen. counsel Phila. Life Ins. Co., 1975-78, Harleysville (Pa.) Ins. Co., 1978-81; v.p., sec., gen. counsel Erie (Pa.) Ins. Group, 1981-82, sr. v.p., sec., gen. counsel, 1983-90, exec. v.p., sec., gen. counsel, 1990—. Bd. dirs. Pa. Assigned Claims Plan, Erie Indemnity Co., Erie Ins. Co., Erie Family Life Ins. Co. Bd. dirs. Erie Art Mus., Hamot Med. Ctr., Erie. Mem. ABA, Pa. Bar Assn., Erie County Bar Assn., Nat. Assn. Ind. Insurers (legis. com.), Ins. Fedn. Pa. (legis. com.), Newcomen Soc. U.S., Pa. Client Security Fund, Kahkwa Club, Erie Club, Union League Phila. Republican. Episcopalian. Avocations: hunting, fishing, skiing, golf. Office: Erie Ins Group 100 Erie Insurance Pl Erie PA 16530-0001

VAN GORDER, JOHN FREDERIC, lawyer; b. Jacksonville, Fla., Mar. 22, 1943; s. Harold Burton and Charlotte Louise Van G.; m. Sandra Joan Hagen, June 4, 1977 (div. June 1995); children: Alyssa Jane, Kathryn Ann; m. Ann Michele Brancato, Oct. 7, 1995. Grad., Dover (Eng.) Coll., 1961; AB, Dartmouth Coll., 1965; postgrad., Air Force Inst. Tech., 1967-68; MS in Adminstrn., George Washington U., 1973; postgrad., U. Va., Coll. William and Mary, Cath. U. Am., Northeastern U., Babson Coll., U. South; JD, Fordham U., 1981. Bar: N.J. 1981, U.S. Dist. Ct. N.J. 1981, N.Y. 1983, U.S. Supreme Ct. 1989. Commd. 2d lt. USAF, 1965, advanced through grades to capt., 1968; weapons contr. Aerospace Def. Commd., Ft. Lee, Va., 1965-67; buyer electronics sys. divsn. Air Force Sys. Commd., Bedford, Mass., 1968-69; project mgr. rsch. and devel. Hdqrs. USAF, Washington, 1969-73, br. chief pers., 1973-74; presdl. social aide The White House, Washington, 1971-74; assoc. Louis C. Kramp & Assocs., Washington, 1975; program officer J.M. Found., N.Y.C., 1975-81; assoc. Winne, Banta & Rizzi Esqs., Hackensack, N.J., 1981-83; asst. sec., program adminstr. Glenmede Trust Co., Phila., 1983—86; exec. dir., asst. sec. Leon Lowenstein Found., 1986—. Atty. Rent Leveling Bd., Borough of Bergenfield, N.J., 1983; pres. Vanguard Corp., Massapequa, N.Y., 1996-2001; adj. prof. Grad. Sch. Edn., Fordham U., N.Y.C., 1997—, mem. adv. com. N.Y.C. Pub. Schs. Supts.' Network, 1998--, judge Nat. Sch. Change awards, 2001--, mem. program devel. adv. com. Grad. Sch. Edn., 2000--. Chmn. N.Y.C. steering com. Nat. Congress on Volunteerism and Citizenship, 1976; mem. exec. com. Mayor's Vol. Action Coun., 1977-78; bd. govs. N.Y. Jaycees Found., 1978-79; bd. govs., 4th v.p. First Assembly Dist. Rep. Club, 1977-82; vestryman All Saints Episc. Ch., Bergenfield, 1982-83; mem. Tabernacle Twp. Planning Bd., 1985-88, Tabernacle Bd. Edn., 1988-91, Tabernacle Rep. Club, 1983-93; jr. warden, 1987-88, sr. warden, 1989-90, vestryman, lay reader St. Peter's Episc. Ch., Medford, N.J., 1985-93; program adv. com. Toshiba Am. Found., 1993-99; trustee, dir. Support Ctr. of N.Y., N.Y.C., 1995-97, Robert A. Taft Inst. Govt., N.Y.C., 1994-97; bd. dirs. N.Y. C. Pub./Pvt. Initiatives, Inc., 1996-2000, bd. dirs. NY Regional Assn. Grantmakers, 1998—; bd. trustees Calvin K. Kazanjian Econs. Found., 2002—; mem. adv. com. Ctr. for Advancement of Children's Mental Health, Columbia U., N.Y.C., 2003—. Col. USAFR, ret., serving brother, Priory in U.S.A., Order of St. John, 2003-. Named Outstanding Young Man of VA., 1975, USAF Res. Officer of Yr., 1985. Mem. Internat. (senator; v.p. 1975; rep. to UN 1976), U.S. (nat. v.p. 1973-74), D.C. (pres. 1972-73), N.Y.C. (bd. govs. 1978-79) Jaycees, SAR, Soc. Mayflower Descs., ABA, N.Y. Bar Assn., Student Bar Assn. (class pres. 1978-81), Toastmasters (local pres. 1969-70, area gov. 1970-71), Lions (pres. Medford Twp. club 1985-86, co-chmn. Charity Ball 1987), Masons, Alpha Delta Phi. Republican. Episcopalian. Address: 7 E Bayview St Massapequa NY 11758-7602

VAN GRAAFEILAND, ELLSWORTH ALFRED, federal judge; b. Rochester, N.Y., May 11, 1915; s. Ivan and (Gohr) Van Graafeiland; m. Rosemary Vaeth, May 26, 1945; children: Gary, Suzanne, Joan, John, Anne. AB, U. Rochester, 1937; LLB, Cornell U., 1940. Bar: N.Y. 1940. Practiced in, Rochester; judge U.S. Ct. Appeals (2nd cir), Rochester, NY, 1974—85; sr. judge U.S. Ct. Appeals (2d cir.), 1985--. Fellow: N.Y. Bar Found., Am. Bar Found.; mem.: ABA (ho. dels. 1973—75), Am. Coll. Trial Lawyers., Monroe County Bar Assn. (past pres.), N.Y. State Bar Assn. (v.p. 1972—73, pres. 1973—74, chmn. negligence compensation and ins. sect. 1968—69), Oak Hill Country Club, Kent Club, Masons. Home: 1 Tiffany Ct Pittsford NY 14534-1067 Office: Fed Bldg 100 State St Ste 423 Rochester NY 14614-1309

VAN GRAAFEILAND, GARY P. lawyer; BA, Union Coll., 1968; JD, Cornell U., 1972. Bar: N.Y. 1973. Asst. gen. counsel Eastman Kodak, Rochester, N.Y., 1989-92, sr. v.p., gen. counsel, sec., 1992—. Office: Eastman Kodak Co 343 State St Rochester NY 14650-0001

VAN GRACK, STEVEN, lawyer; b. Memphis, Oct. 6, 1948; s. Irving and Edna (Schwartz) Van Grack; m. Gail Beverly Lang, Nov. 18, 1972 (div.); children: Adam, Ryan, Brandon, Allison; m. Susan M Freeland, May 21, 1993. BA, U. Md., 1970, JD, 1974. Bar: 1974 (Md), DC 1976, US Dist Ct Md 1976, US Dist Ct DC 1976, US Ct Appeals (4th cir) 1977, US Supreme Ct 1978. Law clk. to presiding justice Montgomery County Cir. Ct., Rockville, Md., 1974-75; assoc. Joseph Roesser Law Offices, Silver Springs, Md., 1975-78; ptnr. Ebert & Bowytz, Washington, 1978-80; mng. ptnr. Van Grack, Axelson & Williamowsky, Rockville, 1980—. Instr, lectr Montgomery Col, Germantown, Md., 1983—85. Cubmaster packs 1343 and 1449 Boy Scouts of Am.; coach Rockville Baseball Assn.; trustee Shady Grove Adventist Hosp. Found.; co-chmn. Montgomery County March of Dimes WalkAmerica Com., 1998—2003; pres. Md. Inst. for Continuing Profl. Edn. of Lawyers, 2003—; chmn. Md. Real Estate Commn., 2001—; gen. counsel Montgomery County Dem. Ctrl. Com., Kensington, Md., 1978—82; campaign mgr. Com. to Elect the Sitting Judges, Rockville, Md., 1982; mayor City of Rockville, Md., 1985—87; Dem. candidate 8th Congl. Dist. Md., 1994; bd. dirs. Washington Met. Coun. Govts. With USAR, 1970—71. Named one of Oustanding Young Men Am, Jaycees, 1978, 1981; recipient Fifth Ann Pro Bono Serv Award, Montgomery County Bar Found, 1998, Extraordinary Commitment to the Delivery of Legal Servs Award, 1999, Nancy Dworkin Award, Montgomery County Comn Children and Youth, 2001, Pro Bono Svc. award, Women's Bar Assn. Md., 2003. Fellow: Md Bar Found (Profl. Legal Excellence award 2002); mem.: ATLA, ABA, Rockville CofC (bd dirs), Montgomery County Bar Asn (Outstanding Comt Chair of the Yr Award 2001), Md Trial Lawyers Asn, Md Bar Asn. Jewish. Avocations: running, swimming, exercising, coin collecting/numismatics, political button collecting. Home: 808 Fordham St Rockville MD 20850-1018 Office: Van Grack Axelson & Williamowsky 401 N Washington St Rockville MD 20850-2223 Office Phone: 301-738-7671. E-mail: sug@vawlaw.com.

VAN GRUNSVEN, PAUL ROBERT, lawyer; b. Green Bay, Wis., Mar. 11, 1961; s. David Edward and Carol Ann (Janssen) Van G. BS, Marquette U., 1983, JD, 1986; LLM in Health Law, De Paul U., 1995. Bar: Wis. 1986, U.S. Dist. Ct. (ea. dist.) Wis. 1986. Mem. Techmeier & Van Grunsven, S.C., Milw., 1986-89, shareholder, 1989-2001; chair health law dept. Kasdorf, Lewis & Swietlik, S.C., 2001—. Adj. prof. Marquette U. Law Sch., Milw., 1995—. Recipient Am. Jurisprudence award Lawyer's Coop. Pub. Co., 1986. Mem. ATLA, Wis. Trial Lawyers for Public Justice, Wis. Acad. Trial Lawyers (bd. dirs., co-editor The Verdict), Wis. Bar Assn., Milw. Bar Assn. (co-chair health law sect.). Roman Catholic. Avocations: golf, football, baseball, basketball. Office: Kasdorf Lewis & Swietlik SC 11270 W Park Pl Ste 500 Milwaukee WI 53224- Office Phone: 414-577-4000. Business E-Mail: pvangrunsven@kasdorf.com.

VAN GUNDY, GREGORY FRANK, retired lawyer; b. Columbus, Ohio, Oct. 24, 1945; s. Paul Arden and Edna Marie (Sanders) Van G.; m. Lisa Tamara Langer. BA, Ohio State U., Columbus, 1966, JD, 1969. Bar: N.Y. 1971. Assoc. atty. firm Willkie Farr & Gallagher, N.Y.C., 1970-74; v.p. legal, sec. Marsh & McLennan Cos., Inc., N.Y.C., 1974-79, v.p., sec., gen. counsel, 1979-2000, sec., 2000—03, retired, 2003. Mem. Phi Beta Kappa. Roman Catholic. Home: 232 Fox Meadow Rd Scarsdale NY 10583-1640 Personal E-mail: vgfam@aol.com.

VAN GUNDY, JEFF, professional basketball coach; b. Hernet, Calif., Jan. 19, 1962; married. Graduate cum laude, Nazareth Coll. Head coach McQuaid Jesuit H.S., Rochester, N.Y., 1985-86; grad. asst., asst. coach Providence Coll., 1986-88; asst. coach Rutgers U., N.J., 1988-89, N.Y. Knicks, N.Y.C., 1989-96, head coach, 1996—2001, Houston Rockets, 2003—. Office: c/o Houston Rockets Two Greenway Plz Ste 400 Houston TX 77046

VAN GUNDY, SEYMOUR DEAN, nematologist, plant pathologist, educator; b. Feb. 24, 1931; s. Robert C. and Margaret (Holloway) Van G.; m. Wilma C. Fanning, June 12, 1954; children: Sue Ann, Richard L. BA, Bowling Green State U., 1953; PhD, U. Wis., 1957. Asst. nematologist U. Calif., Riverside, 1957-63, assoc. prof., 1963-68, prof. nematology and plant pathology, 1968-73, assoc. dean rsch., 1968-70, vice chancellor rsch., 1970-72, chmn. dept. nematology, 1972-84; prof. nematology and plant pathology, assoc. dean rsch. Coll. Natural and Agrl. Scis., 1985-88, acting dean, 1986, interim dean, 1988-90, dean, 1990-93, emeritus dean, prof., 1993—. Former mem. editl. bd. Rev. de Nematologie, Jour. Nematology and Plant Disease; contbr. numerous articles to profl. jours. NSF fellow, Australia, 1965-66; grantee Rockefeller Found., Cancer Rsch., NSF, USDA. Fellow AAAS, Am. Phytopathol. Soc., Soc. Nematologists (editor-in-chief 1968-72, v.p. 1972-73, pres. 1973-74, hon. mem. 1997). Home: 1188 Pastern Rd Riverside CA 92506-5619 Office: U Calif Dept Nematology Riverside CA 92521-0001 E-mail: vangundy@hotmail.com.

VANHAECKE, ERWIN S. F. pharmaceutical executive; b. Brugge, Belgium, Oct. 10, 1960; s. Robert and Liliane (Boghmans) V.; m. Kathleen Van Den Haesevelde, Sept. 10, 1988; children: Laurens, Liselotte. Pharmacist, State U., Ghent, Belgium, 1983, indsl. pharmacist, 1985, PhD in Pharmacy, 1989; postgrad. bus. mgmt., Vlaamse Ekonomische Hoge Sch., Brussels, 1989. Rsch. asst. State U., Ghent, 1983-89, lectr., 1987-89; quality assurance mgr. Alcon-Couvreur, Puurs, Belgium, 1990-98, quality assurance and regulatory affairs mgr., 1999-2000; group dir. quality assurance Pharmaceuticals Alcon, Ft. Worth, 2000—01; v.p. corp. quality assurance Pharmaceuticals/Consumer Products, 2001—04. Contbr. numerous articles to profl. jours. Lt. Belgian M.C., 1985-86. Mem. Parenteral Drug Assn., Regulatory Affairs Profl. Soc., EyeCare Industries, Ophthalmic Spl. Interest Group (chmn. 1997-99). Home: 1350 Claiborne Ln Aledo TX 76008 Office: 6201 South Freeway Fort Worth TX 76134 E-mail: erwin.vanhaecke@alconlabs.com.

VAN HALEN, EDDIE, guitarist, rock musician; b. Nijmegan, The Netherlands, Jan. 26, 1957; arrived in U.S., 1967; s. Jan and Eugenia Van Halen; m. Valerie Bertinelli, Apr. 1981. Student, Pasadena City Coll.; studied piano. Formed group with brother Alex: Broken Combs (name changed later to Mammoth); musician (leader group): Van Halen, 1974—; musician: (albums), 1978, Van Halen II, 1979, Women and Children First, 1990, Fair Warning, 1981, Diver Down, 1982, 1984, (1984), 5150, 1986, OU812, 1988, For Unlawful Carnal Knowledge, 1991, Van Halen Live: Right Here Right Now, 1993, Balance (with lead singer Nino Bettancourt), 1995, Best of Van Halen, Vol. 1, 1996, Van Halen III, 1998. Office: Warner Bros Records 75 Rockefeller Plz New York NY 10019-6908

VAN HANDEL, MICHAEL J. staffing company executive; Dir., internal audit Manpower, Inc., Milw., 1989, v.p., internat. acctg., 1993—95, chief acctg. officer, treas., 1995—98, sr. v.p., 1998—2002, CFO, 1998—, exec. v.p., 2002—. Office: Manpower Inc 5301 N Ironwood Rd Milwaukee WI 53217-4982

VAN HAREN, PETER, lawyer; b. 1945; BA, LLB, U. Ariz. Bar: Ariz. 1973. Asst. city atty. City of Phoenix, 1976—78, city atty., 2000—, City of Prescott, Ariz., 1978—84, City of Glendale, Ariz., 1984—2000. Town mgr. City of Paradise Valley, Ariz. Office: City Hall 200 W Washington St Ste 1300 Phoenix AZ 85003 Business E-Mail: peter.vanharen@phoenix.gov.

VAN HAREN, W(ILLIAM) MICHAEL, lawyer; b. Grand Rapids, Mich., Feb. 15, 1948; s. Adrian William and Donna Bell (Burkett) Van H.; m. Kathryn Mary Desmet, Aug. 7, 1971; children: Ryan C., Amy K., Andrew M., Megan E. BS, U. Mich., 1970; JD magna cum laude, U. Detroit, 1975. Bar: Mich. 1975, U.S. Dist. Ct. (we. dist.) Mich. 1975. Assoc. Warner, Norcross & Judd, Grand Rapids, 1975-81, ptnr., 1981—. Adj. prof. taxation Seidman Sch. Bus., Grand Valley State U., Grand Rapids, 1983-85. Assoc. editor U. Detroit Sch. Law Jour. Urban Law, 1974-75; co-editor (handbook) Probate Practice in Decedents Estates, 1985. Co-chmn. profl. divsn. Kent County United Way, Grand Rapids, 1983, 84; pres. Garfield Pk. Nature Ctr., Grand Rapids, 1977, Garfield Pk. Neighborhhod Assn., Grand Rapids, 1979; bd. dirs. Western Mich. Estate Planning Coun., 1986-89, Cath. Social Svcs., 1997-2002, Goodwill Found., 2002—; mem. fin. com. St. Robert's Ch., Ada, Mich., 1997-2002. Fellow Am. Coll. Trust and Estate Coun.; mem. Mich. Bar Assn. (probate and estate planning coun. 1981-93, treas. 1987-88, sec. 1989-90, vice chmn. 1990-91, chair 1992-93, exec. officer 1993—), Mich. Bar Found., Univ. Club. Republican. Roman Catholic. Avocations: squash, golf, hunting. Home: 9007 Conservation St NE Ada MI 49301-9797 Office: Warner Norcross & Judd 900 Fifth Third Ctr 111 Lyon St NW Ste 900 Grand Rapids MI 49503-2487 Office Phone: 616-752-2125.

VAN HEERTUM, RONALD LANNY, physician; b. Englewood, N.J., Nov. 23, 1940; s. Arnold and Irene Gladys (Ostheimer) V.; children: Richard Jonathan, Beth Jennifer; m. Jacqueline Carol Brunetti, Sept. 7, 1980; children: Jonathan Jason, Kristin Ashley. BA, Gettysburg Coll., 1962; MD, N.J. Med. Sch., 1966. Diplomate Nat. Bd. Med. Examiners, 1967, Am. Bd. Radiology, 1971, Am. Bd. Nuclear Medicine, 1973. Intern Hackensack (N.J.) Hosp., 1966-67; resident in radiology St. Vincent's Hosp. & Med. Ctr. N.Y., 1967-69, fellow in radiology and nuclear medicine, 1970-71, clin. asst. dept radiology, 1971; asst. chief nuclear medicine svc. Tripler Army Med. Ctr., Honolulu, 1972, chief nuclear medicine svc., 1972-74; adj. prof. Sch. Pharmacy U. Pacific, Stockton, Calif., 1973-74; fellow in nuclear medicine SUNY, 1974-75; asst. chief nuclear medicine sect., asst. attending radiologist St. Vincent's Hosp. and Med. Ctr. N.Y., 1975-76; clin. asst. prof. of radiology Sch. Medicine NYU, 1977-83; chief nuclear medicine sect. St. Vincent's Hosp. & Med. Ctr. of N.Y., 1977-91, assoc. attending physician depts. radiology and medicine, 1977-78, attending physician depts. radiology and medicine, 1978-91, dir. Nuclear Radiology Residency Tng. Program, 1980-88, 80-91, asst. dir. dept. radiology, 1981-91, med. dir. Sch. Nuclear Medicine Tech., 1982-91; assoc. prof. clin. radiology N.Y. Med. Coll., Valhalla, 1983-88, prof. clin. radiology, 1988-91; dir. mini-fellowship program St. Vincent's Hosp. Cerebral SPECT Lng. Ctr., 1991—; prof. clin. radiology Coll. Physicians & Surgeons of Columbia U., N.Y., 1991—; attending physician dept. radiology Columbia-Prsbyn. Med. Ctr., 1991—, dir. Nuclear Medicine Residency Tng. Program, 1991—; attending physician dept brain imaging N.Y. Psychiatric Inst., 1993—; vice chmn. dept. radiology Coll. Physicians and Surgeons Columbia U., 1993—. Cons. nuclear medicine Catholic Med. Ctr. of Bklyn. and Queens, 1979-88, The Long Island Coll. Hosp., 1980-88, dept. radiology St. Vincent's Hosp. and Med. Ctr. of N.Y., 1991—, biological studies unit N.Y. Psychiat. Inst., 1993—, The Oxford Project to Investigate Memory and Aging, The John Radcliffe Infirmary and Dept. of Clin. Pharmacology Oxford U., 1993—; alt. del. Am. Coll. Nuclear Physics, 1980-82; core mem. DOE Sponsored Consensus Panel Brain SPECT Perfusion Imaging: Optimizing Image Aquisition & Processing, 1991; vis. prof. Brooke Army Med. Ctr., San Antonio, 1978, Howard U. Med. Coll., Washington, 1980, South Hills Health Systems, Pitts., 1981, St. Barnabas Med. Ctr., Livingston, N.J., 1989, Eastern Va. Med. Sch. Norfolk Gen. Hosp., 1990, U. Puerto Rico Med. Ctr., VA Med. Ctr., 1993, U. Wash. Med. Ctr., Seattle, 1994. Contbr. articles to profl. jours. Major USAR, 1971-74. Recipient Physician Recognition award AMA, 1974-93; numerous rsch. grants in field. Fellow Am. Coll. Radiology (N.Y. State Chpt.), N.Y. Acad. Medicine (sec. nuclear medicine sect. 1993—); mem. Am. Coll. Nuclear Physics, Am. Roentgen Ray Soc., Radiological Soc. N. Am., N.Y. Roentgen Soc., N.Y. Med. Soc., N.Y. County Med. Soc., Soc. Nuclear Medicine (mem. bd. govs. greater N.Y. chpt. 1982-84, 86-89, mem. acad. coun. 1988, mem. brain imaging coun. 1988—, sub-chmn. gastroenterology scientific program com. 1989-90, pres. elect brain imaging coun. 1990-92, pres. 1992-94, sub.-chmn. psychiatry-clin. sci. program com. 1993-94), Soc. Thoracic Radiology (sr. mem.). Presbyterian.

VAN HELDEN, PETE, food products executive; Pres. Albertson's Inc., Melrose Park, Ill., 1999—; sr. v.p. of oper. Jewel-Osco, Melrose Park, Ill. Office: Albertsons Inc Jewel-Osco 1955 W North Ave Melrose Park IL 60160-1181

VAN HENGEL, MAARTEN, banker; b. Amsterdam, The Netherlands, Mar. 29, 1927; came to U.S., 1950, naturalized, 1957; s. Adrianus J. and Helena (Gips) van H.; m. Drusilla Drake Riley, Dec. 1, 1951; children: Maarten, Virginia, Hugh, Drusilla. Student, Kennemer Lyceum, Bloemendaal, Holland, 1939-45. With tng. programs of Amsterdamsche Bank, N.V., Amsterdam, Lazard Bros. & Co. Ltd., London and Canadian Bank of Commerce, Montreal, Que., Can., 1945-49; with Brown Bros. Harriman & Co., 1950—, ptnr., 1968—. Bd. dirs. Netherlands-Am. Found. Served with AUS, 1951-53. Mem.: India House, Netherland (N.Y.C.); Fishers Island Country, Hay Harbor (Fishers Island); Sleepy Hollow Country (Scarborough, N.Y.). Home: 350 River Rd Briarcliff Manor NY 10510-2418 Office: Brown Bros Harriman & Co 140 Broadway New York NY 10005

VAN HOESEN, BETH MARIE, artist, printmaker; b. Boise, Idaho, June 27, 1926; d. Enderse G. and Freda Marie (Soulen) Van H.; m. Mark Adams, Sept. 12, 1953. Student, Escuela Esmaralda, Mexico City, 1945, San Francisco Art Inst., 1946, 47, 51, 52, Fontainbleau (France) Ecole des Arts, Acad. Julian and Acad., 5Grande Chaumier, Paris, 1948-51; BA, Stanford U., 1948; postgrad., San Francisco State U., 1957-58. One-Woman shows include, De Young Mus., San Francisco, 1959, Achenbach Found., Calif. Palace Legion of Honor, San Francisco, 1961, 74, Santa Barbara (Calif.) Mus., 1963, 74, 76, Oakland (Calif.) Mus., 1980, John Berggruen Gallery, San Francisco, 1981, 83, 85, 88, 91; traveling exhibit Am. Mus. Assn., 1983-85; group shows include, Calif. State Fair, Sacramento, 1951 (award), Library of Congress, Washington, 1956, 57, San Francisco Mus. Modern Art, 70 (award), Boston Mus. Fine Arts, 1959, 60, 62, Pa. Acad. Fine Arts, Phila., 1959, 61, 63, 65, Achenbach Found., 1961 (award), Bklyn. Mus., 1962, 66, 68, 77, Continuing Am. Graphics, Osaka, Japan, 1970, Hawaii Nat. Print. Exhbn., Honolulu, 1980 (award), Oakland Mus., 1975 (award); represented in permanent collections, including, Achenbach Found., San Francisco, Fine Arts Mus., Bklyn. Mus., Mus. Modern Art, N.Y.C., Oakland Mus., San Francisco Mus. Modern Art, Victoria and Albert Mus., (London), Chgo. Art Inst., Cin. Mus., Portland (Oreg.) Art Mus. (Recipient award of Honor, San Francisco Art Commn. 1981); author: Collection of Wonderful Things, 1972, Beth Van Hoesen Creatures, 1987, Beth Van Hoesen: Works on Paper, 1995, Beth Van Hoesen Teddy Bears, 2000. Mem. Calif. Soc. Printmakers (award 1993), San Francisco Women Artists. Office: c/o John Berggruen 228 Grant Ave Fl 3D San Francisco CA 94108-4612

VAN HOFTEN, JAMES DOUGAL ADRIANUS, business executive, former astronaut; b. Fresno, Calif., June 11, 1944; s. Adriaan and Beverly (McCurdy) van H.; m. Vallarie Davis, May 31, 1975; children: Jennifer Lyn, Jamie Juliana, Victoria Jane. BS, U. Calif.-Berkeley, 1966; MS, Colo. State U., 1968, PhD, 1976. Asst. prof. U. Houston, 1976-78; astronaut NASA, Houston, 1978-86; sr. v.p., mgr. advanced systems line Bechtel Nat., Inc., San Francisco, 1986-93; project mgr. Hong Kong New Airport projects, 1993-96; sr. v.p., mgr. N.E. Asia, gen. mgr. Bechtel Civil Co., Hong Kong, 1996-98; sr. v.p., mgr. N.Am. projects Bechtel Infrastructure, San Francisco, 1998-99; program mgr. New Scottish Air Traffic Control Ctr., London, 1999-2000; dir. programmes Nat. Air Traffic Svcs., 2000—02; mng. dir. aviation Bechtel Corp., 2002—. Served with USN, 1969-74; lt. col. Air N.G. 1984-88. Recipient Disting. Service award Colo. State U., 1984; Disting. Citizen award Fresno Council Boy Scouts Am., 1984; Disting. Achievement award Pi Kappa Alpha, 1984 Fellow AIAA; mem. ASCE (Aerospace Sci. and Tech. Application award 1984). Republican.

VAN HOLDE, KENSAL EDWARD, biochemistry educator; b. Eau Claire, Wis., May 14, 1928; s. Leonard John and Nettie (Hart) Van H.; m. Barbara Jean Watson, Apr. 11, 1950; children: Patricia, Mary, Stephen, David. BS, U. Wis., 1949, PhD, 1952. Research chemist E.I. du Pont de Nemours & Co., 1952-55; research assoc. U. Wis., 1955-56; asst. prof. U. Wis. at Milw., 1956-57; mem. faculty U. Ill., Urbana, 1957-67; prof. dept. biochemistry and biophysics Oreg. State U., Corvallis, 1967; Am. Cancer Soc. rsch. prof., 1977-93; disting. prof., 1988-93; disting. prof. emeritus, 1993—; instr.-in-charge physiology course Marine Biol. Lab., Woods Hole, Mass., 1977-80; mem. research staff Centre des Recherches sur les Macromolecules, Strasbourg, France, 1964-65; mem. study sect. USPHS, 1966-69, 91—; staff Weizmann Inst., Israel, 1981, Lab. Léon Bnillouin, Saclay, France, 1989-90. Author: Physical Biochemistry, 1971, Chromatin, 1988; (with C. Mathews) Biochemistry, 1989, 2nd edit., 1995, 3d edit, 2000, Principles of Physical Biochemistry, 1998; editor: Biochmica Biophysica Acta, 1966-68; mem. editl. bd. jours. Biol. Chemistry, 1968-75, 81-87, 91-92, assoc. editor, 1992—, Biochemistry, 1973-76, 82-89; contbr. profl. jours. Trustee Marine Biol. Lab., Woods Hole, 1979-82, 84-92. NSF sr. postdoctoral fellow, 1964-65; Guggenheim fellow, 1973-74; European Molecular Biology Orgn. fellow, 1975; Humbolt fellow, 2000-01. Fellow AAAS; mem. NAS, Am. Soc. Biochemistry and Molecular Biology, Biophys. Soc., Am. Acad. Arts and Scis. Home: 229 NW 32nd St Corvallis OR 97330-5020 Office: Oreg State U Dept Biochemistry Corvallis OR 97331 Office Phone: 541-737-4155. Business E-Mail: vanholdk@onid.orst.edu.

VANHOLE, WILLIAM REMI, lawyer; b. Denver, June 25, 1948; s. Joseph and Mildred VanHole; m. Gemma VanHole, Feb. 7, 1971. BS, Colo. State U., 1970; JD, U. Idaho, 1976. Bar: Idaho 1976, U.S. Dist. Ct. Idaho 1976, U.S. Dist. Ct. (ea. dist.) Wis. 1998, U.S. Ct. Appeals (9th cir.) 1983, U.S. Supreme Ct., 2003. Law clk. to judge U.S. Dist. Ct. Idaho, Boise, 1976-78; assoc. Quane, Smith, Howard & Hull, Boise, 1978-81, Langroise, Sullivan & Smylie, Boise, 1981-83; asst. U.S. atty. U.S. Dept. of Justice, Boise, 1983-87; U.S. atty. Dist. of Idaho, 1984-85; assoc. gen. counsel Boise Cascade Corp., 1987—. Served with U.S. Army, 1970-72 Mem. ABA, Fed. Bar Assn., Idaho Bar Assn., Idaho Assn. Def. Counsel, Def. Rsch. Inst., Am. Judicature Soc. Republican. Avocations: skiing, fishing, golf. Office: Boise Cascade Corp PO Box 50 Boise ID 83728-0050

VAN HOLLEN, CHRISTOPHER, JR., congressman; b. Karachi, Pakistan, Jan. 10, 1959; s. Christopher and Eliza (Farnsworth) Van H.; m. Katherine A. Wilkens; children: Anna, Nicholas, Alexander. BA, Swarthmore Coll., 1982; MPP, Harvard U., 1985; JD cum laude, Georgetown U., 1989. Legis. asst. for def. and fgn. policy Office of Senator Charles McC. Mathias, Md., 1985-87; profl. staff mem. U.S. Senate Fgn. Rels. Com., Washington, 1987-89; sr. legis. advisor Washington office Md. Gov. William D. Schaefer, 1989-91; assoc. Arent, Fox, Kintner, Plotkin & Kahn, Washington, 1991—; mem. Md. Ho. of Dels., Annapolis, 1991-94; mem. dist. 18 Md. Senate, Annapolis, 1995—2001; mem. U.S. Ho. Reps. 8th Md. dist., Washington, 2003—. Chair Hlth./Human Svcs. subcom., 2000—. Councillor Atlantic Coun. U.S.; mem. Kensington Citizens Assn. Recipient Resolution of Excellence U.S. Senate Fgn. Rels. Com. Democrat. Office: 1419 Longworth House Off Bldg Washington DC 20515-2008

VAN HOLLEN, J.B. lawyer; Grad., St. Olaf's Coll., U. Wis. Asst. U.S. atty. We. Dist. Wis., 1991—93; atty. Bayfield County, 1993—; U.S. atty. We. Dist. Wis., 2002—. Office: PO Box 1585 Madison WI 53701

VAN HOOMISSEN, GEORGE ALBERT, state supreme court justice; b. Portland, Oreg., Mar. 7, 1930; s. Fred J. and Helen F. (Flanagan) Van H.; m. Ruth Madeleine Niedermeyer, June 4, 1960; children: Geroge T., Ruth Anne, Madeleine, Matthew. BBA, U. Portland, 1951; JD, Georgetown U., 1955, LLM in Labor Law, 1957; LLM in Jud. Adminstrn., U. Va., 1986. Bar: D.C. 1955, Oreg. 1956, Tex. 1971, U.S. Dist. Ct. Oreg. 1956, U.S. Ct. Mil. Appeals 1955, U.S. Ct. Customs and Patent Appeals 1955, U.S. Ct. Claims 1955, U.S. Ct. Appeals (9th cir.) 1956, U.S. Ct. Appeals (D.C. cir.) 1955, U.S. Supreme Ct. 1960. Law clk. for Chief Justice Harold J. Warner Oreg. Supreme Ct., 1955-56; Keigwin teaching fellow Georgetown Law Sch., 1956-57; dep. dist. atty. Multnomah County, Portland, 1957-59; pvt. practice Portland, 1959-62; dist. atty. Multnomah County, 1962-71; dean nat. coll. dist. attys., prof. law U. Houston, 1971-73; judge Cir. Ct., Portland, 1973-81, Oreg. Ct. Appeals, Salem, 1981-88; justice Oreg. Supreme Ct., Salem, 1988—2001. Adj. prof. Northwestern Sch. Law, Portland, Willamette U. Sch. Law, Portland State U.; mem. faculty Am. Acad. Judicial Edn., Nat. Judicial Coll.; Keigwin Teaching fellow Georgetown U. Law Sch. Mem. Oreg. Ho. of Reps., Salem, 1959-62, chmn. house jud. com. With USMC, 1951-53; col. USMCR (ret.). Recipient Disting. Alumnus award U. Portland, 1972. Master Owen M. Panner Am. Inn of Ct.; mem. ABA, Oreg. State Bar, Bar Assn., Oreg. Law Inst. (bd. dirs.), Arlington Club, Multnomah Athletic Club, Univ. Club. Roman Catholic. Office: Oreg Supreme Ct 2105 SW Elm St Portland OR 97201 E-mail: gavanhoomissen@qwest.net.

VAN HOOSER, DAVID, retired manufacturing executive; CFO, sr. v.p. Owens-Illinois Inc., Toledo. Office: Owens Ill Inc One Seagate Toledo OH 43666

VAN HOOSER, PATRICIA LOU SCOTT, art educator; b. Springfield, Mo., Oct. 4, 1934; d. Arthur Irving and Isoline Elizabeth (Jones) Scott; m. Buckley Blaine Van Hooser, Mar. 28, 1956 (div.); children: Buckley Blaine II, Craig Alan. BA, Drury U., 1956; MS in Art, Pittsburg (Kans.) State U., 1968. Society writer Springfield News & Leader & Press, 1955—56; hostess radio program Sta. KSEK, Pittsburg, Kans., 1962—63; tchr. art and home econs. Hurley (Mo.) HS, 1956—57; art supr. elem. sch. Mountain Grove, Mo., 1960; tchr. art Hickory Hills Sch., Springfield, 1960—61; tchr art and English jr. and sr. schs., Baxter Springs, Kans., 1965—75; art coord. Joplin (Mo.) Elem. Sch. Dist., 1975—. Lectr. in field; chmn. for S.W. Mo., Nat. Youth Art Month. Bd. dirs. Spiva Art Ctr.; sec. Parents without Ptnrs., CV & FE Credit Union; bd. recorder S.W. Mo. Credit Unions. Mem.: ASCD, NEA, AAUW (2d v.p. Joplin br.), Epsilon Sigma Alpha, Pittsburg State U. Alumni Assn. (sec., pres. Joplin br.), Joplin Cmty. Concert Assn., S.W. Mo. Mus. Assn., Mo. Edn. Assn., S.W. Mo. Dist. Art Tchrs., Mo. Art Edn. Assn., Nat. Art Edn. Assn., Assn. Childhood Edn. Internat. (pres. Joplin br., pres. Mo. state), Writers of Six Bulls, Joplin Writer's Guild, Cafe au Lait Club. Methodist. E-mail: Pvanhooser6@cs.com.

VAN HORN, HUGH M. physicist, astronomer, educator; b. Williamsport, Pa., Mar. 5, 1938; s. Robert Dix and Virginia Elizabeth (Moody) Van H.; m. Mary Susan Boon, Sept. 17, 1960; children: Kathleen Susan, Mary Margaret, Michael Hugh George. BSc, Case Inst. Tech., 1960; PhD, Cornell U., 1965. NASA predoctoral traninee Cornell U., Ithaca, 1963-65; rsch. assoc. U. Rochester, 1965-67, asst. prof., 1967-73, assoc. prof., 1973-77, prof., 1977-96, chmn. dept. physics and astronomy, 1980-86, acting assoc. dean Coll. Arts and Scis., 1987-89, acting chmn. dept. physics and astronomy, 1992-93; Shapley lectr. Am. Astron. Soc., 1981-95; dir. divsn. astron. sci. NSF, Arlington, Va., 1993-2000, sr. sci. advisor Directorate Math. Phys. Sci., 2000—02, dir. nat. facilities divsn. materialsrsch., 2002—. Vis. fellow Joint Inst. Lab. Astrophysics, 1973—74; sr. scientist Lab. Laser Energetics, 1985—96; vis. prof. U. Tex., 1987; vis. investigator dept. terr. magnetism Carnegie Inst. Washington, 2000—02; prin. investigator NASA and NSF grants; adj. prof. U. Rochester, 1996—. Editor: (with V. Weidemann) White Dwarfs and Variable Degenerate Stars, 1979, (with S. Ichimaru) Strongly Coupled Plasma Physics, 1993; contbr. articles on white dwarfs, neutron stars and dense matter to profl. jours. Fellow AAAS; mem. Am. Astron. Soc., Internat. Astron. Union. Office: NSF Divsn Materials Rsch 4201 Wilson Blvd Arlington VA 22230-0001 E-mail: hvanhorn@nsf.gov.

VAN HORN, KEITH, professional basketball player; b. Oct. 23, 1975; m. Amy Van Horn; children: Sabrina, Nicholas. Grad., U. Utah, 1997. Basketball player N.J. Nets, East Rutherford, NJ, 1997—2001, Phila. 76ers, 2002—03, New York Knicks, 2003—04, Milwaukee Bucks, 2004—. Named first team All-Am., U. Utah, 1997. Achievements include being the top scorer U. Utah and Western Athletic conf. hist; 3 time Western Athletic Conf. Player of Yr. 1995-97. Office: c/o Milwaukee Bucks 1001 N 4th st Milwaukee WI 53203*

VAN HORN, O. FRANK, retired counselor, consultant; b. Grand Junction, Colo., Apr. 16, 1926; s. Oertel F. and Alta Maude (Lynch) Van H.; m. Dixie Jeanne MacGregor, Feb. 1, 1947 (dec. Nov. 1994); m. Evelyn Anne Carroll, Mar. 22,1998; children: Evelyn (dec.), Dorothy. AA, Mesa Coll., 1961; BA, Western State Colo., 1963; MEd, Oreg. State U., 1969. Counselor, mgr. State of Oreg.-Employment, Portland and St. Helens, 1964-88; pvt. practice counselor and cons. St. Helens, 1988-96. Chair Task Force on Aging, Columbia County, 1977-79; advisor Western Interstate Commn. on Higher Edn., Portland, 1971, Concentrated Employment and Tng., St. Helens, 1977, County Planning Bd., Columbia County, Oreg., 1977-80, City Planning Bd., St. Helens, 1978, Youth Employment Coun., St. Helens, 1978, Task Force on Disadvantaged Youth, St. Helens, 1980; counselor Career Mgmt. Specialists Internat.; instr. Portland C.C. Mem. ACA, Oreg. Counseling Assn., Internat. Assn. Pers. in Employment Svc. (Outstanding Achievement award 1975), Nat. Employment Counselors Assn. Democrat. Home: 464 Leelo Ct Florence OR 97439-7632

VAN HORNE, JAMES CARTER, economist, educator; b. South Bend, Ind., Aug. 6, 1935; s. Ralph and Helen (McCarter) Van H.; m. Mary A. Roth, Aug. 27, 1960; children: Drew, Stuart, Stephen. AB, De Pauw U., 1957, DSc (hon.), 1986; MBA, Northwestern U., 1961, PhD, 1964. Comml. lending rep. Continental Ill. Nat. Bank, Chgo., 1958-62; prof. fin. Stanford U. Grad. Sch. Bus., 1965-75, A.P. Giannini prof. fin., 1976—, assoc. dean, 1973-75, 76-80; dep. asst. sec. Dept. Treasury, 1975-76. Bd. dirs. BB&K Fund Group, Suntron Corp., Montgomery St. Income Securities; commr. workers compensation Rate Making Study Commn., State of Calif., 1990-92. Author: Function and Analysis of Capital Market Rates, 1970, Financial Market Rates and Flows; co-author: Fundamentals of Financial Management, 2001, Financial Management and Policy, 2002; assoc. editor Jour. fin. and Quantitative Analysis, 1969-85, Jour. Fin., 1971-73, Jour. Fixed Income, 1990—. Mem. bd. trustees DePauw U., 1989-96. With AUS, 1957. Mem. Am. Fin. Assn. (past pres., dir.), Western Fin. Assn. (past pres., dir.), Fin. Mgmt. Assn. Home: 2000 Webster St Palo Alto CA 94301-4049 Office: Stanford U Grad Sch Bus Stanford CA 94305

VAN HORNE, R. RICHARD, oil company executive; b. Milw., June 7, 1931; s. Ralph Rupert and Edna (Benson) Van H.; m. Elizabeth Whitaker Dixon, July 3, 1954; children— Ann Van Horne Arms, R. Ross, Margaret Van Horne Shuya BBA, U. Wis., 1953. Various positions Anaconda Am. Brass Co., Milw. and Kenosha, Wis., 1955-72, pres., chief exec. officer Waterbury, Conn., 1972-74, Anaconda Aluminum Co., Louisville, 1974-82; sr. v.p. pub. affairs Atlantic Richfield Co., Los Angeles, 1982-85. Bd. visitors Sch. Bus., U. Wis., Madison; mem. U. Wis. Found.; trustee Louisville Cmty. Found. 1st lt. U.S. Army, 1953-55 Sr. fellow Bellarmine Coll. Mem. Mchts. and Mfrs. Assn. (bd. dirs. 1983-85), Am. Petroleum Inst., Nat. Planning Assn. (com. on new Am. realities 1982-84), Bascom Hill Soc., Minocqua Country Club, Sara Bay Country Club. Republican. Episcopalian. Avocations: golf, reading, gardening. Home: Unit 261 3040 Grand Bay Blvd Longboat Key FL 34228-4401 Office: Atlantic Richfield Co 515 S Flower St Ste 3700 Los Angeles CA 90071-2201

VAN HOUSEN, THOMAS CORWIN, III, retired architect; b. Oak Park, Ill., Jan. 2, 1927; s. Thomas Corwin and Dorothea (Saunders) Van H.; children: Deborah, Victoria, Constance. BA, Lawrence U., 1951; BArch, U. Minn., Mpls., 1954; MArch in Urban Design, Harvard U., 1962. Registered architect, Minn., Wis. With Ellerbe Assocs., Inc., St. Paul, 1951-61; architect, prin. Progressive Design Assocs., Inc., St. Paul, 1961-71; architect, developer, v.p. Landmark Devel. Corp./Appletree Enterprises, Inc., Bloomington, Minn., 1971-85; architect, developer Mortenson Devel. Co., Mpls., 1985-88; architect, design, bldg. dir. D&B Collaborative, Inc., Mpls., 1989—99. Bldg. official City of North Oaks, Minn., 1964-78; mem. Minn. League of Municipalities-Metro, St. Paul, 1970-72, Gov.'s Open Space Adv. Com., St. Paul, 1972-74. With U.S. Air Force, 1945-47, ETO. Recipient Outstanding House award St. Paul Jaycees, 1958, 62; named finalist (team mem.) Archtl. competition Boston City Hall, 1962. Fellow AIA (nat. bd. dirs. 1985-88, v.p., pres.-elect Minn. chpt. 1994-95, pres. 1995, spl. award 1981, Presdl. citation 1988, 90, 2000); mem. N.W. YMCA. Republican. Lutheran. Avocations: tennis, swimming, music.

VAN HOUTEN, FRANKLYN BOSWORTH, geologist, educator; b. N.Y.C., July 14, 1914; s. Charles Nicholas and Hessie Osborne (Bosworth) Van H.; m. Jean Oliver Sholes, Feb. 18, 1943 (dec. Sept. 23, 1997); children: Jean S., F. Bosworth, David Gordon. BS, Rutgers U., 1936; PhD, Princeton U., 1941. Instr. dept. geology Williams Coll., 1939-42; asst. prof. Princeton U., 1946-51, assoc. prof., 1951-55, prof., 1955-85, prof. emeritus, 1985—; vis. prof. geology UCLA, 1964, State U. N.Y. at Binghamton, 1971; geologist U.S. Geol. Survey, 1948-67. Temporary geologist Geol. Survey Can., 1953, Yukon Expdn., geol. expdns. to Morocco, Tunisia, Libya, Egypt, Madagascar Author reports and articles on geology. Served as lt. USN, 1942-46. Fellow Geol. Soc. Am.; mem. Am. Assn. Petroleum Geologists, Soc. Econ. Paleontologists and Mineralogists (hon. mem., Twenhofel medal), Internat. Assn. Sedimentologists, Colombia Geol. Soc. (hon.), Delta Upsilon. Home: 168 Fitzrandolph Rd Princeton NJ 08540 7224

VAN HOUTEN, G. DAVID, food service executive; b. Waco, Tex. m. Carol Van Houten; children: Tara, Brant, Blaine. Mgmt. degree, Tex. A&M U. Various positions Coca-Cola Bottling Bus., 1972—86; pres., gen. mgr. Coca-Cola Bottling Co. of N. Tex., 1986—96; sr. v.p., pres., Ctrl. N.Am. Group Coca-Cola Enterprises, 1996—2000, sr. v.p., pres., Western N.Am. Group, 2000—01, exec. v.p., pres., N.Am. Group, 2001—. Office: Coca-Cola Enterprises 2500 Windy Ridge Pkwy Atlanta GA 30339

VAN HOUTEN, JAMES FORESTER, retired insurance company executive, educator, consultant; b. Fullerton, Calif., Jan. 13, 1942; s. James Forester and Lois Evangeline (Trout) V.H.; m. Mary Ann Nelson; children: Kimberly Evangeline, Lori Lynn. BA in English Lit., St. Mary's U.; MBA, Ill. State U. CPCU, CLU. Sales mgr. for Can. Motors Ins. Corp. divsn. GM, Detroit, 1963-74; v.p. sales Volkswagen Group, St. Louis, 1974-78; v.p. personal lines mktg. Wausau Ins. Cos., St. Louis, 1978-80, v.p., chief mktg. officer life and health, 1980-84; v.p., chief mktg. and strategic planning officer Country Cos., Bloomington, Ill., 1984-89; pres., CEO Mut. Svc. Ins. Cos., St. Paul, 1989—2002. Prof. strategic mgmt. MBA program U. Minn., 1990—, Metro State U., 2002—; bd. dirs. Strategic Mgmt. Rsch. Ctr., U. Minn., Credit Dept., Inc., EMPO Corp., J.J. Hill Bus. Ref. Libr.; lead instr. mktg. Hubert Humphrey Inst. Pub. Affairs, 2004—. Program leader Youth Black Achievers, St. Paul; exec. bd. Arrowhead coun. Boy Scouts Am., Minn. Assn. Scholars; active Minn. Acad. Stds. Com., Minn. Acad. Excellence Found-Friends. Mem. Ins. Fedn. Minn. (past chmn. bd.), Minn. Assn. Mutual Ins. Cos. (past pres.), Nat. Coop. Bus. Assn. (bd. dirs. and exec. com., chair fin. com.), Minn. Bus. Partnership (bd. dirs., Minn. K-12 edn. com .), Ctr. Am. Experiment Think Tank (bd. dirs., ex com., chair fin. and audit com.).

VAN HOUTEN, JANET E. music educator; b. Hillsboro, Kans., Apr. 1, 1943; d. Chester H. and Elfreda Fast; m. Diether H. van Houten, Oct. 3, 1970; children: Mark, Douglas. BS with highest honors, Tabor Coll., Hillsboro, Kans., 1965. 6th grade tchr. Topeka Schs., 1965—67; 4th grade tchr. Am. Sch., Cali, Colombia, 1967—69; 5th grade tchr. Aurora Sch., Aurora, Colo., 1969—70; 5th and 6th grade tchr. Omaha, 1973; pvt. piano tchr. van Houten Music Studio, various locations, 1978—. Mem. Sheridan Arts Coun., Sheridan, Wyo., 1996—99, YMCA, Sheridan, 1989—; pianist First Bapt. Ch., Sheridan, 1989—. Mem.: Music Tchrs. Nat. Assn., Wyo. Music Tchrs. Assn. (editor 1999—2004), Sheridan Music Tchrs. Assn. (pres. 1992—2004). Republican. Baptist. Avocation: house plants. Home: 1832 Edwards Dr Sheridan WY 82801

VAN HOY, PHILIP MARSHALL, lawyer; b. Washington, Nov. 8, 1947; s. Joe Milton and Helen Virginia (Spangler) V.; m. Sylvia Kathryn Smith, Dec. 30, 1972; children: Marshall, Travis. AB, Duke U., 1970, JD, U. N.C., 1973. Bar: N.C. 1973, U.S. Dist. Ct. (ea., we. and mid. dists.) N.C. 1974, U.S. Ct. Appeals (4th cir.) 1974, U.S. Supreme Ct. 1978. Labor counsel Duke Power Co., Charlotte, NC, 1973—80; assoc. Siegel, O'Connor & Kainen, Charlotte, 1980—83; ptnr. Mullins & Van Hoy, Charlotte, 1983—89, Van Hoy, Rentlinger, Adams & Dunn, Charlotte, 1989—. Mem. N.C. OSHA Rev. Bd., 1985-92, Mecklenburg County, N.C. Personnel Commn., 1985-92, N.C. Leadership Coun. Co-state chmn. Gardner for Lt. Gov., 1988, alt. del. Rep. Nat. Conv., Detroit, 1980; chmn. Mecklenburg County Young Rep. Com., 1979, vice chmn., 1980-83; Duke U. Athletics Coun., 1999-02. 1st lt. U.S. Army, 1973-81. Named top employment lawyer N.C., Bus. N.C. Mag., 2002; named to Best Lawyers in Am., 2001—, Outstanding Lawyers of Am., 2003. Mem. N.C. Bar Assn. (councillor labor and employment law sect. 1985-88, chmn. EEOC com. 1983-92), N.C. State Bar, 4th Cir. Jud. Conf., Rotary, Charlotte Cotillion Club (pres. 1979-80), City Club, Myers Park Country Club (dir. 1994-96, 2000-03). Republican. Methodist. Home: 2615 Hampton Ave Charlotte NC 28207-2521 Office: Van Hoy Reutlinger Adams & Dunn 737 East Blvd Charlotte NC 28203-5113 Office Phone: 704-375-6022.

VANIER, JACQUES, physicist; b. Dorion, Que., Can., Jan. 4, 1934; s. Henri and Emma (Boileau) V.; m. Lucie Beaudet, 1961; children: Lyne, Pierre. BA, U. Montreal, 1955, BSc, 1958; MSc, McGill U., 1960, PhD, 1963. Lectr. U. Montreal, 1961-63, McGill U., 1960-63; physicist Varian Assocs., Beverly, Mass., 1963-67, Hewlett Packard Co., Beverly, 1967; prof. elec. enging. U. Laval, Que., 1967-83; physicist Nat. Rsch. Coun., Ottawa, 1983-94, head elec. and time standards, 1984-86, dir. Lab. Basic Standards, 1986-90, dir. gen. Inst. for Nat. Measurement Standards, 1990-93; prof. physics U. de Montreal, 1995—. Cons. Comm. Components Corp., Costa Mesa, Calif., 1974-76, EGG Co., Salem, Mass., 1979-82, Kernco, Danvers, Mass., 1995—; chmn. com. A URSI, 1990-93; chmn. exec. com. CPEM, 1990-94; mem. Internat. Com. Weights and Measures, 1992-96; guest worker IEN, Torino, Italy, 1996-97. Author: Basic Theory of Lasers and Masers, 1971, (with C. Audoin) The Quantum Physics of Atomic Frequency Standards, 1989; contbr. articles to profl. jours.; patentee (4) in field. Recipient Disting. Precision Time & Time Interval Svc. award PTTI Organizing Com., 1998. Fellow IEEE (Centennial medal 1984, I.I. Rabi award 1994, Instrument & Measurement Soc. award 1999), Royal Soc. Can., Am. Phys. Soc. Office Phone: 514-425-5055. Business E-Mail: jac.vanier@sympatico.ca.

VANIER, JERRE LYNN, art director; b. Phoenix, June 11, 1957; i. Jerry Dale Barber and Betty Jane (Brady) Barber Hughes; m. Kent Douglas Wick, May 4, 1979 (div. June 1994); 1 child, Jared Kent Wick; m. Jay David Vanier, June 6, 1994; 1 child, Jolie Jacqueline. BA in Art History magna cum laude, Ariz. State U., 1978, MA in Humanities. Chmn., vice chmn. Internat. Friends of Art, Scottsdale, Ariz., 1990-96; dir. 19th and 20th century art Joy Tash Gallery, Scottsdale, 1996-97; dir. estate art Vanier Fine Art, Ltd., Scottsdale, 1997-98, dir., 1998—, Vanier Galleries on Marshall, Scottsdale, 1999—. Mem. pub. art collection adv. bd. Scottsdale Cultural Coun., 1990—, Phoenix Jr. League, Art Renaissance Initiative Faces of Ariz. Mem. DAR (Ariz. page continental congress 1993, Ariz. vice chmn. Jr. Am. Citizen com. 1998, 3d vice regent Camelback chpt. 1993), Colonial Dames Am., Daus. Republic of Tex. (non-resident), Nat. Soc. Arts and Letters (Valley of Sun chpt. bd. dirs. 1988-92, art chmn. 1988-90, membership chmn. 1990-92), Jr. League Phoenix, Alpha Delta Pi, Phi Kappa Phi. Republican. Avocations: genealogy, collecting contemporary art. Office: 7106 E Main St Scottsdale AZ 85251-4316

VAN INWAGEN, PETER JAN, philosophy educator; b. Rochester, N.Y., Sept. 21, 1942; s. George Butler and Mildred Gloria (Knudson) van I; m. Margery Bedford Naylor, Mar. 31, 1967 (div. Apr. 1988); 1 child, Elizabeth Core; m. Elisabeth Marie Bolduc, June 3, 1989. BS, Rensselaer Poly. Inst., 1965; PhD, U. Rochester, 1969. Vis. asst. prof. U. Rochester, N.Y., 1971-72; asst. prof. Syracuse U., N.Y., 1972-74, assoc. prof., 1974-80, prof. philosophy, 1980-95; John Cardinal O'Hara prof. of philosophy U. Notre Dame, South Bend, Ind., 1995—. Vis. prof. U. Ariz., Tucson, 1981; lectr. U. of St. Andrews, 2003, Oxford U., 2000, U. London, 1998. Author: An Essay on Free Will, 1983, Material Beings, 1990, Metaphysics, 1993, God, Knowledge and Mystery, 1995, The Possibility of Resurrection, 1997, Ontology, Identity, and Modality, 2001; editor: Time and Cause, 1980, Alvin Plantinga, 1985, Metaphysics: The Big Questions, 1998; mem. editl. bd. Jour. Faith and Philosophy, Philos. Perspectives, Nous, Philos. Studies, Jour. of Ethics, Philosophy and Phenomenological Rsch.; contbr. articles to profl. jours. Served to capt. U.S. Army, 1969-71 NEH grantee, 1983-84, 89-90. Mem. Am. Philos. Assn., Soc. Christian Philosophers. Democrat. Episcopalian. Home: 52145 Farmington Square Rd Granger IN 46530-6403 Office: U Notre Dame Dept Philosophy South Bend IN 46556-4619 Office Phone: 574-631-5910. E-mail: peter.vaninwagen.1@nd.edu.

VAN KALDEKERKEN, ROLF, retail executive; With Inmac; country mgr. Viking, 1994—98, v.p., country mgr. Germany, Benelux and Austria, 1998—2000, exec. v.p. European ops., 2000; pres. European ops. Office Depot, Inc., Delray Beach, Fla., 2000—. Office: Office Depot Inc 2200 Old Germantown Rd Delray Beach FL 33445

VANKATESAN, THIRUMALAI, engineering educator; BS with honors, Indian Inst. Tech., Kanpur, India, 1969, MS, 1971; PhD, CUNY, 1977. Grad. rsch. asst., mem. tech. staff Bell Labs., Murray Hill, NJ, 1974—84; mem. tech. staff, head surface group Bellcore, Red Bank, NJ, 1984—90; founder, dir. Surface Modifications Ctr. Rutgers U., New Brunswick, NJ, 1986—88; chmn. bd., founder, chief tech. officer Neocera Inc., Beltsville, Md., 1989—; prof. physics and ceramics Rutgers U., New Brunswick, NJ, 1990; prof. physics and elec. engring. U. Md., College Park, Md., 1990—. Vis. scientist applied physics dept. Calif. Inst. Tech., Pasadena, 1984; external adv. mem. Nuclear Sci. Ctr. Fellow: Am. Phys. Soc. (mem. adv. bd. Indsl. Physicist, mem. physics policy com.). Achievements include research in physics and applications of thin film and heterostructures of multi-component oxides and other inorganic compounds; synthesis of materials with special emphasis on high temperature superconducting cuprates, colossal magnetoresistive manganites. Office: U Md Ctr for Superconductivity Rsch Dept Phys 1364 Physics College Park MD 20742

VAN KIRK, DONALD JOHN, forensic specialist, engineering executive, consultant, writer; b. Detroit, Jan. 6, 1935; s. Kenneth John and Helen Van Kirk; m. Wyva A. Moore, Apr. 28, 1956; 1 child, Cheryl Ann; m. David W. Cyrus. AS, Henry Ford CC, 1961; BSEE, Wayne State U., 1964, MS in Engring. Mechanics, 1969; MBA, U. Mich., 1975. TV technician Sta. WXYZ-TV, Detroit, 1959—60, Sta. WTVS-TV, Detroit, 1960—64; product design engr. Ford Motor Co., Dearborn, Mich., 1964—66, rsch. engr., 1969—73, sr. design engr., 1973—84; pres. D. J. Van Kirk P.E. & Assocs., Inc., 1985—98, Creations & Innovations Unlimited, Inc., 1998—2002, Van Kirk Enterprises, 2002—. Instr. Henry Ford CC, Ford continuing edn. programs; mgmt. cons. Author: Accident Investigation & Reconstruction, 2000; contbr. articles to profl. jours. Vol. Consumer Product Safety Com., Washington, 1977; chmn. Consumer Affairs Com., Dearborn, 1977—79; vol. traffic safety com. Dearborn Police Dept., 1979; cert. advanced master gardener Mich. State U. Extension Svc.; chmn. bldg. and plans com. Dearborn Hills Home Owners Assn., 1973—75. With USN, 1955—59. Recipient Editors award, Internat. Shrine Clown Assn. mag. Fellow: Am. Acad. Forensic Scis.; mem.: ASTM, Mich. Soc. Profl. Engrs. (past pres.), Oakland County Traffic Safety Assn., Soc. Automotive Engrs., Nat. Soc. Profl. Engrs., Am. Coll. Forensic Examiners (diplomate), Am. Bd. Forensic Examiners, Toastmasters Internat. (pres. Masters of the Goose and Gridiron Club), Dearborn Exch. Club (Outstanding Svc. award 1974, Man of the Yr. award 1975), Scottish Rite, Shriners, Masons (grand master 1996—97, 33 degree). Presbyterian. Achievements include patents for cold weather diesel starting aid. Home: 731 Ridgemont Ave Dearborn MI 48124-1220

VAN KIRK, JAYE FRANCES, psychology educator; d. Joseph Francis and Rowena Jang; m. Timothy Mark Van Kirk, Aug. 3, 1991. BA in Psychology, San Francisco State U., 1973—77; MA in Exptl. Psychology, Calif. State U., Fullerton, 1979—84; ABD in Psychobiology, Ohio State U., 1983—90. Prof. of psychology San Diego Mesa Coll., 1990—. Presenter in field. Mem. editl. adv. bd.: Annual Edits. Biopsychology, 1998—99, Our Sexuality, 7th edit., 1999, Annual Editions Biopsychology, 2000—01; co-editor: Asian Am. Psychol. Assn. Newsletter, 2000—; contbr. chapters to books, articles to profl. jours. Recipient Va. Staudt Sexton Nat. Faculty Advisor award, Psi Beta, 1998, 1999; fellowship, Ohio State U., 1983-1987. Mem.: APA, Western Psychol. Assn. (coun. reps. 2001—), Asian Am. Psychol. Soc., Am. Psychol. Soc., Psi Beta (chmn. com. Diversity Project 2000 and Beyond 2000, v.p. Western/Rocky Mountain region 2000—04, pres.-elect 2003—04, pres. 2004—). Avocations: cooking, photography. Office: San Diego Mesa College 7250 Mesa College Drive G-100 San Diego CA 92111 Office Phone: 619-388-2290.

VAN KIRK, JOHN ELLSWORTH, retired cardiologist; b. Dayton, Ohio, Jan. 13, 1942; s. Herman Corwin and Dorothy Louise (Shafer) Van K.; m. Patricia L. Davis, June 19, 1966 (div. Dec. 1982); 1 child, Linnea Gray. BA cum laude, DePauw U., Greencastle, Ind., 1963; BS, Northwestern U., Chgo., 1964, MD with distinction, 1967. Diplomate Am. Bd. Internal Medicine, Am. Bd. Internal Medicine subspecialty in cardiovasc. disease; cert. Nat. Bd. Med. Examiners. Intern Evanston (Ill.) Hosp., 1967-68; staff assoc. Nat. Inst. of Allergy & Infectious Diseases., Bethesda, Md., 1968-70; resident internal medicine U. Mich. Med. Ctr., Ann Arbor, 1970-72, fellow in cardiology, 1972-74, instr. internal medicine, 1973-74; staff cardiologist Mills Meml. Hosp., San Mateo, Calif., 1974—2001, vice-chief medicine, 1977-78, dir. critical care, 1978-96, critical care utilizaton rev., 1988-99, dir. pacemaker clinic, 1976-99; staff cardiologist Mills-Peninsula Hosp., Burlingame, Calif., 1996-99; ret., 1999. Dir. transitional care, 1996—99; mem. courtesy staff Sequoia Hosp., 1984—2001, ret., 1999. Contbr. rsch. articles to profl. jours. Recipient 1st prize in landscaping Residential Estates, State of Calif., 1977. Fellow Am. Coll. Cardiology; mem. AMA (Physician's Recognition award 1968, 72, 75, 77, 80, 82, 85, 87, 89, 93, 97, 2000), Calif. Med. Assn., San Mateo County Med. Soc., Am. Heart Assn., San Mateo County Heart Assn. (bd. dirs. 1975-78, mem. bay area rsch. com. 1975-76, mem. edn. com. 1975-77, pres.-elect 1976-77, pres. 1977-79), Alpha Omega Alpha. Republican. Mem. United Brethren Ch. Avocations: gardening, computer science, tennis, woodworking, electronics, amateur radio. Home: 235 Amherst Ave San Mateo CA 94402-2201 Personal E-mail: John_VanKirk@msn.com.

VAN KIRK, ROBERT JOHN, nursing case manager, educator; b. Jersey City, Sept. 18, 1944; s. Robert and Doris V.; m. Marjorie Ann Carroll, Mar. 23, 1968 (div. Nov. 30, 1993); children: Walter, Michael, Robert Jr., Peggy; m. Nancy A. Fix, Aug. 31, 1996. BA cum laude, U. Conn., 1974; MEd, Kent State U., 1983; D of Nursing, Case Western Res. U., 1986. RN Ohio. Sales mgr. Nutmeg Home Protection, Middlebury, Conn., 1972-74; theater mgr. SBC Mgmt. Corp., Boston, 1974; dist. supr. Selected Theatres Mgmt. Corp., Lyndhurst, Ohio, 1974-86; nat. sales mgr. ZBS Video, Inc., Lyndhurst, 1981-82; staff nurse Cleve. Clinic Found., 1986-87, clin. instr., 1987-88, head nurse, 1988-93, case mgr., 1993—, diabetes educator, 2002—; asst. clin. prof. Case Western Res. U., Frances Payne Bolton Sch. Nursing, Cleve., 1990—; case mgr. Cleve. Clin. Home Care, 1993—2002; CEO Lifelong Learning, Inc., Chagrin Falls, Ohio, 2002—. Health officer Lake County (Ohio) Bd. Alcohol, Drug Addiction and Mental Health Svcs., 1991—; co-chmn. United Way, Cleve., 1991-93. Staff sgt. U.S. Army, 1964—71, Vietnam. Recipient Achievement award Greater Cleve. Nurses Assn., 1986. Mem. AACN, Am. Assn. Tchrs. German, Am. Assn. Tchrs. Portuguese and Spanish, Assn. Specialists in Aging, Frances Payne Bolton Sch. Nursing Alumni Assn. (pres. 1992-93), Kappa Delta Pi, Sigma Theta Tau. Avocations: pocket billards, furniture making. Home: 495 Bell Rd Chagrin Falls OH 44022-4160 Office: Cleve Clinic Found 6801 Brecksville Rd Ste 10 Independence OH 44131 also: Lifelong Learning Inc PMB 132 46 Shopping Plz Chagrin Falls OH 44022-3022 E-mail: drbobvankirk@adelphia.net.

VAN KIRK, THOMAS L. lawyer; b. Pa., June 25, 1945; s. Theodore and Mary Jane (Young) Van K.; children: Thomas Jr., Christopher. BA, Bucknell U., 1967; JD cum laude, Dickinson U., 1970. Bar: Pa., U.S. Dist. Ct. (we. and ea. dists.) Pa. 1971, U.S. Ct. Appeals (3d cir.) 1972, U.S. Supreme Ct. 1976. Clk. Pa. Superior Ct., 1970-71; assoc. Buchanan Ingersoll, Pitts., 1971-77, ptnr., 1978—, chief oper. officer, 1985—. Bd. dirs. Buchanan Ingersoll P.C.; v.p. State Pa. Economy League; bd. dirs. Western Pa. Economy League, chair, 1998. Chmn. Pitts. Downtown Partnership, 1995-97; bd. dirs. Capital divsn. Pa. Economy League, sec./treas., 1995; bd. dirs. Pitts. Cultural Trust, 1998, Catalyst Connection, PEG, U. Pitts. Cancer Inst., Doyle Ctr. for Mfg. Tech. Mem.: ABA, Allegheny County Bar Assn., The Club at Nevillewood, Rivers Club, Duquesne Club. Democrat. Lutheran. Home: 1010 Osage Rd Pittsburgh PA 15243-1014 Office: Buchanan Ingersoll PC 301 Grant St Fl 20 Pittsburgh PA 15219-1410

VAN LARE, WENDELL JOHN, lawyer; b. Newark, N.Y., Mar. 1, 1945; s. Julian J. and Doris Elizabeth (Lacknor) Van L.; m. Sheila Gilbert, Aug. 20, 1967 (div. Apr. 1987); children: Jonathan S., Allison R.; m. L. Karen Stack, May 7, 1987. BS, SUNY, New Paltz, 1967; JD, Union U., 1972. Bar: N.Y. 1973, U.S. Supreme Ct., 1980. Assoc. Harter, Secrest & Emery, Rochester, N.Y., 1972-77; asst. dir. labor rels. Gannett Co., Inc., Rochester, 1977-80, dir. labor rels. Rochester and Arlington, 1980-93, v.p., labor counsel Arlington, 1993-94, v.p., sr. labor counsel, 1994—. Comments editor Albany Law Rev., 1971-72. Pres. Opera Theatre of Rochester, N.Y., 1983-85. Lt. (j.g.) USNR, 1968-70. Mem. ABA, N.Y. Bar Assn., Va. Bar Assn., River Bend Golf and Country Club. Avocation: genealogy. Office: Gannett Co Inc 7950 Jones Branch Dr Mc Lean VA 22102

VAN LIEROP, JOHN HENRY, JR., music educator; b. St. Louis, Oct. 3, 1947; s. John Henry and Mary Frances Van Lierop. BA in Music Edn., Seattle Pacific U., 1969; postgrad., U. Wash., 1976—78. Cert. tchr. Wash. 6th grade tchr. Seattle Christian Sch., Seattle, 1969—74; 3d grade tchr. Clark County Christian Sch., Vancouver, Wash., 1974—75; 2d grade tchr. Mountlake Christian Sch., Mountlake Terrace, Wash., 1975—76; pvt. piano instr. West Seattle Piano Studio, Seattle, 1976—. Organist, pianist Mount Baker Park Presbyn. Ch., Seattle, 1976—80, Tibbetts United Meth. Ch., Seattle, 1981—; piano adjudicator Am. Coll. Musicians, Austin, Tex., 1987—, Nat. Fedn. Music Clubs, Indpls., 1988—. Contbr. articles to profl. publs. Named Tchr. of Yr., Western Assn. Christian Schs., 1976; named to Hall of Fame, Am. Coll. Musicians, 1992. Mem.: Seattle Music Tchrs. (pres. 1984—86), Nat. Guild Piano Tchrs., Nat. Fedn. Music Clubs (treas. 1988—). Republican. Methodist. Avocations: hiking, trains, cats. Home and Office: 6552 40th Ave SW Seattle WA 98136 E-mail: musicman@nwlink.com.

VAN LINT, VICTOR ANTON JACOBUS, physicist; b. Samarinda, Indonesia, May 10, 1928; came to U.S., 1937; s. Victor J. and Margaret (DeJager) Van L.; m. M. June Woolhouse, June 10, 1950; children: Lawrence, Kenneth, Linda, Karen. BS, Calif. Inst. Tech., Pasadena, 1950, PhD, 1954. Instr. Princeton (N.J.) U., 1954-55; staff mem. Gen. Atomic, San Diego, 1957-74; physics cons. San Diego, 1974-75; staff mem. Mission Research Corp., San Diego, 1975-82, 83-91; cons., 1991—; spl. asst. to dep. dir. sci. and tech. Def. Nuclear Agy., Washington, 1982-83. Author, editor: Radiation Effects in Electronic Materials, 1976; contbr. articles to profl. jours. Served with U.S. Army, 1955-57. Recipient Pub. Service award NASA, 1981. Fellow IEEE. Republican. Mem. United Ch. of Christ. Home and Office: 1032 Skylark Dr La Jolla CA 92037-7733 Office Phone: 858-459-9554.

VAN LOKEREN, MARY ANN KREY, beer wholesaler executive; b. St. Louis, June 17, 1947; d. Frederick Curtis and Phyllis M. (Terry) R.; m. John F. Krey III (dec. Nov. 1986); 1 child, Laura Christine; m. Michael Van Lokeren, Apr. 15, 1994. BA, Washington U., St. Louis, 1969, MBA, 1988. Sec. Krey Distbg., St. Charles, Mo., 1978-80, v.p., 1980-86, pres., chief exec. officer, 1986—. Bd. dirs. Laclede Gas Co., St. Louis, Commerce Bancshares, Inc., Kansas City, Mo., Masco Corp. Mem. Mo. Clean Water Commn., Jefferson City, 1988—; bd. dirs. Arts and Edn. Coun. St. Louis, St. Louis Art Mus., Kids Under Twenty-One, World Affairs Coun., Variety Club, SBA Region VII, St. Louis Children's Hosp.; bd. dirs., trustee Washington U. Recipient Leadership award YWCA, 1993; named Mo. Anheuser-Buscher wholesaler, 1989, Woman of Yr. Variety Club, 1994. Mem. Young Pres. Orgn., Regional Commerce and Growth Assn. (bd. dirs. 1990—), Jr. League St. Louis. Office: Krey Distbg 150 Turner Blvd Saint Peters MO 63376-1078

VAN LOUCKS, MARK LOUIS, venture capitalist, business advisor; b. Tampa, Fla., June 19, 1946; s. Charles Perry and Lenn (Bragg) Van L.; children: Brandon, Charlie; m. Lee Ann Rose, Oct. 1, 1998. BA in Comm. and Pub. Policy, U. Calif., Berkeley, 1969. Sr. v.p. mktg., programming and corp. devel. United Cable TV Corp., Denver, 1970-81, advisor, 1983-89; sr. v.p., office of chmn. Rockefeller Ctr. TV Corp., N.Y.C., 1981-83; advisor United Artists Commun. Corp., Englewood, 1989-91; investor, business advisor in pvt. practice Englewood, 1983—; founder, prin. owner Glory Hole Saloon & Gaming Hall, Central City, Colo., 1990—, The Canyon Casino, Black Hawk, Colo., 1990—; chmn., CEO Bask Internat., Englewood, 1990—. Bd. dirs. Wild West Devel. Corp., Denver; sr. v.p., bd. dirs. GSI Cable TV Assocs., Inc., San Francisco, 1984-90; guest lectr. on cable TV bus., 1985-91; cons. Telecommunications, Inc., Denver, 1989-93. Producer HBO spl. Green Chili Showdown, 1985; producer TV spl. 3 Days for Earth, 1987; producer, commd. artist nuclear war armament pieces; contbr. articles to profl. jours. Chmn. Cops in Crisis, Denver, 1990—; bd. dirs. the NOAH Found., Denver, 1976—; founding dir. Project for Responsible Advt., Denver, 1991-92; chmn. mayor's mktg. adv. bd., Central City, Colo. Named hon. capt. Denver Police Dept., 1991—, fin. advisor L. Rose Co., 1995—. Mem. Casino Owners Assn. (founding dir. 1989—), Colo. Gaming Assn. (dir. 1990—), recipient S'nnaeel Evol award, 1995), Glenmoor Country Club, The Village Club. Republican. Jewish. Avocations: music, woodworking, philanthropy, vintage autos. Office: MLVL Inc 333 W Hampden Ave Ste 1005 Englewood CO 80110-2340

VAN LUVEN, WILLIAM ROBERT, management consultant; b. Toledo, Feb. 15, 1931; s. Harold Calvin and Ruth Frick (Routson) Van L.; m. Lyda Marie Buchanan Jones, Nov. 15, 1956 (div. Sept. 1960); children: Lynn Chase, Michael Frick; m. Barbara Wilson Ehni, Aug. 17, 1968; children: Eric Finley, Jay Palmer. BBA, U. Toledo, 1957; postgrad., U. Va., 1979. Group gen. mgr. Union Camp Corp., Wayne, N.J., 1961-73, 1979-82; pres.container & carton divs. Clevepak Corp., White Plains, N.Y., 1973-79; v.p., gen. mgr. Jefferson Smurfit Corp., Clayton, Mo., 1982-84; pres. Wm. R. Van Luven & Assocs. Inc., St. Louis, 1984—; exec. dir. Exec. Svcs. Corps of St. Louis. Bd. dirs. Smurfit Industries, Alton, Ill., 1982-84, O'Connor Pharm. Corp., Detroit, 1982-84; pres. Mo. Clippers, Inc. (Great Clips for Hair Franchise), 1988—. Cons. United Way of Greater St. Louis, 1987—; chair United Way Mgmt. Assistance Ctr., 1988-90; dir. Combined Health Appeal, Sherwood Forst Camp, Places for People, Inc., Christian Svc. Ctr. With USN, 1951-53. Recipient Keyman award Toledo C. of C., 1956. Mem. Fibre Box Assn., Composite Can & Tube Inst. (pres. 1979), Paperboard Packaging Council, U.S. Brewers Assn., Racquet Club (St. Louis), Univ. Club (St. Louis), Shriner, Sigma Nu. Republican. Episcopalian. Avocations: running, skiing, biking. Home: 2 Portland Ct Saint Louis MO 63108-1291 Office Phone: 314-277-7949. Personal E-mail: wrvl@aol.com.

VANMARCKE, ERIK HECTOR, civil engineer, educator; b. Menen, Belgium, Aug. 6, 1941; arrived in U.S., 1965, naturalized, 1976; s. Louis Eugene and Rachel Louisa (van Hollebeke) Vanmarcke; m. Margaret Marie Delesie, May 25, 1965 (div. Feb. 22, 1999); children: Lieven Vanmarcke, Ann Vanmarcke Forzani, Kristien Vanmarcke Webber; m. Marilyn Durkee, July 14, 2001. BS, U. Leuven, Belgium, 1965; MS, U. Del., 1967; PhD in Civil Engring, MIT, 1970. From instr. to prof. civil engring. MIT, Cambridge, 1969-85, Gilbert W. Winslow Career Devel. prof., 1974-77, dir. civil engring. sys. group, 1976-80; prof. civil engring. and ops. rsch. Princeton (N.J.) U., 1985—, affiliated faculty mem. Bendheim Ctr. Fin., 1998—, dir. grad. studies civil engring. and ops. rsch., 1990—94. Cons. Office Sci. and Tech. Policy, 1978—80, Nat. Inst. Stds. and Tech., 2003, various govt. agys. and engring. firms; vis. scholar in engring. Harvard U., 1984—85; Shimizu Corp. vis. prof. Stanford U., 1991; mem. exec. com. Princeton (N.J.) Materials Inst., 1991—93; mem. Princeton (N.J.) Environ. Inst., 1996—; mem. com. vulnerability critical infrastructure Nat. Res. Coun., 1999—2001; mem. com. program on robotics and intelligent sys. Princeton (N.J.) U., 1999—. Author: (book) Random Fields: Analysis and Synthesis, 1983, Quantum Origins of Cosmic Structure, 1997; editor: Internat. Jour. Structural Safety, 1981—91. Named Disting. Probabilistic Methods Educator, Soc. Automotive Engrs., 2002; recipient Sr. Scientist award, Japan Soc. Promotion Sci., 1991, Disting. Engring. Alumnus award, U. Del., 1994. Mem.: ASCE (chair com. risk assessment and mgmt. Geo-Inst. 1996—2000, chair com. risk and vulnerability Coun. Natural Disaster Reduction 1998—2003, chair exec. com. coun. disaster risk mgmt. 2003—, Raymond C. Reese Rsch. award 1975, Walter L. Huber Rsch. prize 1984), Royal Acad. Arts and Scis. Belgium (fgn.), Internat. Soc. Soil Mechanics and Geotech. Engring. (chair com. TC32 risk assessment and mgmt. 1998—2001), Seismol. Soc. Am., Am. Geophys. Union. Home: 578 Province Line Rd Hopewell NJ 08525-3104 Office Phone: 609-258-5896. Business E-Mail: evm@princeton.edu.

VAN MASON, RAYMOND, dancer, choreographer; Prin. dancer Ballet West, Salt Lake City; ballet master, choreographer Ballet Pacifica, Irvine, Calif., 1999—; artistic dir. Eccles Sch. of Ballet Theatre Arts, Utah; founder Imagine Ballet Theatre, Utah. Dance performances include Swan Lake, Gisells, Sleeping Beauty, Romeo & Juliet, Anna Karenina, The Nutcracker, Carmina Burana, White Mourning, Ophelia; choreographer: Requiem: A Liturgical Ballet, 1990, A Pilgrimage: A Liturgical Ballet, 1992, Lady Guinevere, Chameleon, Carmina Burana, Symphony # 7, 1992, others. Office: Eccles Sch of Ballet Theatre Arts 2580 Jefferson Ave Ogden UT 84401*

VANMEER, MARY ANN, publisher, writer, researcher, webmaster; b. Mt. Clemens, Mich., Nov. 22, 1947; d. Leo Harold and Rose Emma (Gulden) VanM. Student, Micha. State U., 1965-66, 67-68, U. Sorbonne, Paris, summer 1968; BA in Edn., U. Fla., 1968-70. Pres. VanMeer Tutoring and Translating, N.Y.C., 1970-72; freelance writer, 1973-79; pres. VanMeer Publs., Inc., Clearwater, Fla., 1980-88, VanMeer Media Advt., Inc., Clearwater, 1987-88; exec. dir., founder Nat. Ctrs. for Health and Med. Info., Inc., Palm Beach, Fla., 1990-93; pres., CEO ThriftyTraveling.com, Inc. (formerly Traveling Free Pubs.,), 1993—. Author: Traveling with Your Dog, U.S.A., 1976, How to Set Up a Home Typing Business, 1978, Freelance Photographer's Handbook, 1979, See America Free, 1981, Free Campgrounds, U.S.A., 1982, Free Attractions, U.S.A., 1982, VanMeer's Guide to Free Attractions U.S.A., 1984, VanMeer's Guide to Free Campgrounds, 1984, The How to Get Publicity for Your Business Handbook, 1987, Asthma: The Ultimate Treatment Guide, 1991, Allergies: The Ultimate Treatment Guide, 1992, Thrifty Traveling, 1995, 2d edit., 1996; pub. Nat. Health and Med. Trends Mag., 1986-88, ThriftyTraveling.com Newsletter and website, 1993—, online and hard-copy edits., 1999—, Over 50 Thrifty Traveler Newsletter, 1997-98, Net News for the Thrifty Traveler Newsletter, 1997-98, LuxuryTraveling.com newsletter and website, 2001—; webmaster ThriftyTraveling.com, ThriftyTravelPortal.com, 2003—, LuxuryTraveling.com and VanMeer.com websites. Pub. info. chairperson, bd. dirs. Pinellas County chpt. Am. Cancer Soc., Clearwater, 1983-84, 86-88; mem. fin. devel. com. ARC, Palm Beach County, 1990-92. Mem. Am. Booksellers Assn., Soc. Am. Travel Writers. Office: ThriftyTraveling.com Inc PO Box 8168 Clearwater FL 33758-8168 E-mail: editor@thriftytraveling.com.

VAN METER, ABRAM DEBOIS, lawyer, retired banker; b. Springfield, Ill., May 16, 1922; s. A.D. and Edith (Graham) Van M.; m. Margaret Schlipf, Dec. 1, 1956; children: Andy, Alice, Ann. BS, Kings Point Coll., 1946; JD, Northwestern U., 1948. Bar: Ill. 1949. Ptnr. Van Meter, Oxtoby & Funk, Springfield, 1949—2001; adminstrv. asst. to treas. State of Ill., Springfield, 1963; v.p. Ill. Nat. Bank, Springfield, 1964-65, pres., 1965-88, chmn. bd. dirs., 1988-90, also bd. dirs.; chmn. bd. dirs. Nat. City, Springfield, 1990-93, dir. emeritus, 1993—. Chmn. bd. dirs. Ill. Housing Devel. Authority, 1977-2003; chmn. bd. trustees So. Ill. U., 1989-2001; bd. dirs., mem. exec. com. Meml. Med. Ctr. (emeritus). Mem. ABA, Ill. Bar Assn., Sangamon Bar Assn., Chgo. Club, Chgo. Athletic Club, Sangamo Club, Island Bay Yacht Club, Home: 6 Fair Oaks St Springfield IL 62704-3222 Office: Nat City 1 N Old State Capitol Plz Springfield IL 62701-1323

VANMETER, VANDELIA L. retired director; b. Seibert, Colo., July 17, 1934; d. G.W. and A. Pearl Klockenteger; m. Victor M. VanMeter, Jan. 21, 1954; children: Allison C., Kristopher C. BA, Kansas Wesleyan U., 1957; MLS, Emporia State U., 1970; PhD, Tex. Woman's U., 1986. Cert. libr. media specialist. Tchr. Ottawa County Rural Sch., Kans., 1954-55; social scis. tchr. McClave (Colo.) High Sch., 1957-58, Ellsworth (Kans.) Jr. High Sch., 1959-68; libr., media specialist Ellsworth (Kans.) High Sch., 1968-84; asst. prof. libr. sci. U. So. Miss., Hattiesburg, 1986-90; chair dept. libr./info. sci. Spalding U., Louisville, 1990-96, libr. dir., 1991-99, prof., 1991—99. Cons. to sch., pub. and spl. librs., Kans., Miss., Ky., 1970-99; mem. Ky. NCATE Bd. Examiners. Author: American History for Children and Young Adults, 1990, World History for Children and Young Adults, 1992, America in Historical Fiction, 1997; editor: Mississippi Library Media Specialist Staff Development Modules, 1988, Library Lane Newsletter, 1991-99; contbr. chpts. to books; contbr. articles to profl. jours. Active City Coun., Ellsworth, Kans., 1975-79, Park Bd., Ellsworth, 1975-79; bd. dirs. Robbins Meml. Libr., 1977-79. Grantee Kans. Demonstration Sch. Libr., 1970-72, Miss. Power Found., 1989, Project Technology Enhances Curriculur Instrn., 1996-97; named Women of Yr. Bus. and Profl. Women of Ellsworth, Kans., 1976. Mem. ALA, Assn. Coll. and Rsch. Librs., Ky. Libr. Assn., Assn. for Libr. and Info. Sci. Educators.

VAN METER, WOODFORD SPEARS, ophthalmologist, surgeon; b. Paris, Ky., June 30, 1953; s. Robert Hardin and Mary Spears Van Meter; m. Dorothy Clark Van Meter, Sept. 5, 1987; children: Mary Miller, Wood. BS, Davidson Coll., N.C., 1975; MD, Vanderbilt Med. Sch., 1979. Lic. Ky., 1984. Ophthalmology resident Mayo Clinic, Rochester, Minn., 1979—83; fellowship Emory U., Atlanta, 1983—84; chief ophthalmology Ctrl. Bapt. Hosp., Lexington, 1992—; prof. ophthalmology Univ. Ky., Lexington, 2000—. Assoc. examiner Am. Bd. Ophthalmology, 2000—; cons., ophthalmic devices panel CDRH, FDA, Md., 1996—; chair accreditation bd. Eye Bank Assn. of Am., Washington. Contbr. 40 jour. articles, 12 book chpts., 60 presentations. Mem. Good Shepherd Episcopal Ch., Lexington, 1987—; bd. dirs. Hist. Paris Bourbon Co., Ky., 1986—, Ky. Chpt. Nature Conservancy, Lexington, 1985—96, Univ. of Ky. Libr. Assocs., Lexington, 1987—; dir. Nat. City Bank, Lexington, 1992—2003, Ky. Bank, Paris, 2003—. Fellow: Am. Acad. Ophthalmology (Sr. Achievement award 2002, Honor award 1993), Am. Coll. Surgeons. Avocations: golf, tennis, running, white-water canoeing, antiques. Office: Woodford S Van Meter MD 1760 Nicholasville Rd Ste 203 Lexington KY 40503 Office Phone: 859-275-4001.

VAN METRE, LAUREN, foundation administrator; M of Russian Studies, Georgetown U.; postgrad., Johns Hopkins U. Mem. policy planning staff Office Internat. Security Affairs, Pentagon, Washington; program officer rsch. & studies U.S. Inst. Peace, Washington. Contbr. articles to profl. jours. Office: US Inst Peace 1200 17th St NW Ste 200 Washington DC 20036-3011

VAN METRE, MARGARET CHERYL, artistic director, dance educator; b. Maryville, Tenn., Nov. 24, 1938; d. Robert Fillers and Margaret Elizabeth (Goddard) Raulston; m. Mitchell Robert Van Metre II, Aug. 25, 1956; 1 child, Mitchell Robert. Elem., intermediate and advanced tchg. certs. Dir. Van Metre Sch. of Dance, Maryville, 1958-96; artistic dir. Appalachian Ballet Co., Maryville Coll., 1972-96; founding dir. Appalachian Ballet Co., 1972; dir. Van Metre Arts Mgmt., S.C., 1996—. Chmn. dance panel Tenn. Arts Commn., 1973-74; chmn. Bicentennial Ballet Project, Tenn., 1975-76; mem. Nat. Bd. Regional Dance Am., 1997-2003; owner Van Metre Arts Mgmt., Edisto Island, S.C., 1996—. Choreographer ballets: Delusion, 1965, Hill Heritage Suite, 1972, Dancing Princesses, 1983. Mem. Tenn. Assn. of Dance (pres. 1972), Southeast Regional Ballet Assn. (pres. 1996, 97, 98, 99, 2003-04). Democrat. Episcopalian. Home: 2103 Myrtle St Edisto Island SC 29438-3437

VAN MIDDLESWORTH, LESTER, physiology, biophysics and medicine educator; b. Washington, Jan. 13, 1919; s. Lester and Hazel Lucile (Brandt) VanM.; m. Nellie Rue Franklin, June 29, 1948; children: Linda V. Anderson, Jane V. Norman, Frank L., Paul E. BS in Chemistry, U. Va., 1940, MS in Chemistry, 1942, MS in Physiology, 1944; PhD in Physiology, U. Calif., Berkeley, 1946; MD, U. Tenn., 1951. Teaching asst. dept. physiology U. Va., 1944, U. Calif., Berkeley, 1944—45; instr. U. Tenn. Med. Units, Memphis, 1946—52, instr. in medicine, 1953—57, asst. prof. physiology, 1952—54, assoc. prof., 1954—59, prof., 1959—89, prof. emeritus physiology and biophysics, 1989—, asst. prof. medicine, 1957—61, assoc. prof., 1961—72, prof. medicine, 1972—89, prof. medicine emeritus, 1989, Disting. prof. physiology and medicine, 1986—. Rotating intern City of Memphis Hosps., 1951-52; cons. chief chemist Piedmont Apple Products Corp., Charlottesville, Va., 1940-46, Crocker Radiation Lab., U. Calif., Berkeley, 1946-47, Oak Ridge Inst. Nuclear Studies, 1950-54; guest co-investigator Endocrine Labs. Tufts Med. Coll., Boston, summers 1954, 55, 56, 59, 61, 64, 66, 69, Scripps Clinic and Rsch. Found., La Jolla, Calif., 1957; guest investigator in endocrinology Harbor Gen. Hosp., UCLA, 1971, Frederick Joliot Hosp., Orsay, France, 1972, Lawrence Livermore Radiation Lab. U. Calif., 1970; staff mem. clinic for med. thyroid disease patients, City of Memphis and U., Tenn., 1951—; mem. internat. com., 1990-2002. Author 145 publs. in profl. jours., 186 abstracts and oral presentations; work on permanent display Smithsonian Nat. Mus. Am. History, Washington, D.C. Recipient Disting. Svc. award, 1985, Disting. Alumnus award U. Tenn. Coll. Medicine, 1989; USPHS career rsch. grantee, 1962-89. Mem. Am. Chem. Soc., Am. Physiol. Soc., AAAS, Soc. Exptl. Biology and Medicine, Am. Soc. Clin. Investigation, So. Soc. Clin. Investigation, Health Physics Soc., Endocrine Soc., Am. Thyroid Assn. (Disting. Svc. award 1988), Sigma Xi (rsch. award 1944, 86, nat. lectr. 1989-91), Alpha Chi Sigma Achievements include research in audiogenic siezures and worldwide radioiodine fallout. Home: 1950 Lyndale Ave Memphis TN 38107-5109 Office: U Tenn Health Sci Ctr 894 Union Ave Memphis TN 38163-3514

VAN MILLIGEN, JAMES M. health care administrator; b. Chgo., Feb. 12, 1949; s. Alferd C. and H. Patricia Van M.; m. Jane Standley, May 5, 1971. B of Health Sci., Wichita State U., 1977, M of Health Sci., 1984. Physician asst. Wichita Osteo. Clinic, 1977-84; data mgr. Preferred Health Care, 1984-85; dir. network devel. Equicor, 1986-87; chief oper officer WPAA, Inc., 1987—, WPPA-HMO, Inc., 1995-2000. Mem. Wichita Traffic Commn., 1980-86, pres. 1985; pres. Wichita Ind. Neighborhoods, 1994-95, bd. dirs., 1995-98; pres. Fairmount Neighborhood Assn., Wichita, 1986-95, v.p., 1985, 2004; advisor United Sch. Dist. #249 Bus. & Tech. Com., Wichita, 1993-94, Mayor's Adv. Coun., Wichita, 1989-92; bd. dirs. Cmty. Housing Svcs., 2000—, v.p., 2000-01. With U.S. Army, 1970-73, Vietnam. Mem. Nat. Assn. Health Underwriters (Journalism award 1991), Am. Assn. Health Plans (PPO coun. 1998—), Kans. Assn. Health Underwriters (bd. dirs. 1994-95), Ctrl. Kans. Assn. Health Underwriters (bd. dirs. 1990-95, pres. 1994, Med. Soc. Sedgewick County (assoc. exec. dir. 1987—), Wichita Area C. of C. Avocations: historic restoration, farming. Home: 1717 Fairmount St Wichita KS 67208-1919 Office: WPPA Inc 1102 S Hillside St Wichita KS 67211-4004 Office Phone: 316-683-4111. Business E-Mail: van@wppainc.com.

VAN MOL, LOUIS JOHN, JR., public relations executive; b. Knoxville, Tenn., Oct. 7, 1943; s. Louis John and Evelyn (Ramsay) Van M.; m. Deborah Ruth Boyd, Nov. 1, 1969; children: Derek, Millicent. BS, U. Tenn., 1966. Staff writer, editor AP, Knoxville and Nashville, 1963-66, 69; account exec. to exec. v.p. Holder, Kennedy & Co., Nashville, 1970-74, exec. v.p., 1978-79; dir. info. TVA, Knoxville, 1974-78; co-founder, ptnr. Dye, Van Mol & Lawrence, Nashville, 1980—. Bd. dirs. East Tenn. Children's Hosp., Knoxville, 1977-78, Martha O'Bryan Ctr., Nashville, 1985-87, United Way Comm. Com., 1987-91, Am. Heart Assn. Mid. Tenn., Nashville, 1991-92, Leadership Nashville, 1992-93, Crime Stoppers Nashville, 1986-92, Alcohol and Drug Coun. Mid. Tenn., Nashville, 1991-93, Martha O'Bryan Found., 1998-2000, Pencil Found., 2003—, Nashville Songwriters Found., 2004—; chmn. bd. dirs. Nashville Downtown Partnership, 1999-2000; bd. govs., exec. com. Nashville C. of C., 1999-2000; chmn. Goodwill Industries Mid. Tenn., 1996-97, mem. exec. com., 1996- . Lt. U.S. Army, 1966-68. Decorated Bronze Star. Mem. Richland Country Club (bd. dirs. 1997-99, pres. 1999), Cumberland Club, Sigma Delta Chi. Presbyterian. Home: 2836 Wellesley Trace Nashville TN 37215-1049 Office: Dye Van Mol & Lawrence Pub Rels 209 7th Ave N Nashville TN 37219-1802

VAN MOLS, BRIAN, publishing executive; b. L.A., July 1, 1931; s. Pierre Matthias and Frieda Carthyll (MacArthur) M.; m. Barbara Jane Rose, Oct. 1, 1953 (dec. 1968); children— Cynthia Lee, Matthew Howard, Brian; m. Nancy Joan Martell, June 11, 1977; children— Thomas Bentley, Cynthia Bentley, Kristi AB in English, Miami U., Oxford, Ohio, 1953. Media supr. McCann-Erickson Inc., 1955-58; salesman Kelly Smith Co., 1959; with sales Million Market Newspaper Inc., 1959-63; sales mgr. Autoproducts Mag., 1964; sr. salesman True Mag., 1965-68, Look Mag., 1969-70; regional advt. dir. Petersen Pub. Co., Los Angeles, 1971-74; pub. Motor Trend, 1982-84; nat. automotive mktg. mgr. Playboy Enterprises, Inc., N.Y.C., 1984-85, nat. sales mgr., 1985—; western advt. dir. Playboy mag., 1985-86; assoc. pub., advt. dir. Cycle World CBS, Inc., Newport Beach, Calif., 1974-81, pub., 1981; v.p., advt. dir. Four Wheeler Mag., Canoga Pk., Calif., 1986-88; v.p., dir. advt. western div. Gen. Media, Inc., 1988-91; v.p., dir. new bus. devel. Paisano Pub., Inc., Agoura Hills, Calif., 1991-92; dir. mktg. Crown Publs., 1993-94; exec. v.p. Voice Mktg. Inc., Thousand Oaks, Calif., 1994, DMR The Reis Co., Tustin, Calif., 1995-96; COO Mesa Exhaust Products, Inc., Costa Mesa, Calif., 1996-97. Mktg. dir. McMullen Argus Pub., Inc., Anaheim, Calif., 1998-2001. Served with U.S. Army, 1953-55 Mem. Los Angeles Advt. Club, Adcraft Club Detroit, Advt. Sportsmen of N.Y. Republican. Episcopalian. Home: 57 St Andrews Cir Durango CO 81301 E-mail: bvanmols@frontier.net.

VANN, JOHN DANIEL, III, library consultant, historian; b. Raleigh, N.C., June 14, 1935; s. John Daniel Jr. and Sybil Dean (Wilson) V.; m. Ellen Jane Rogers, June 21, 1969; children: John Daniel IV, Justin Fitz Patrick. BA with honors, U. N.C., 1957; MA, Yale U., 1959, PhD, 1965; M in Librarianship, Emory U., 1971; postgrad., Columbia U., 1962-63, Stanford U., 1977-78. Ordained deacon, elder Presbyn. Ch., commd. temporary supply preacher Northumberland Presbytery. Assoc. prof. history Campbell Coll., Buie's Creek, N.C., 1961-63; bibliographer European history and lit. Newberry Libr., Chgo., 1963-65, asst. reference librarian, 1963-65; prof. history Calif. Bapt. Coll., Riverside, 1965-66; dir. libr., prof. history Bapt. Coll. at Charleston, S.C., 1966-69; libr. Keuka Coll., Keuka Park, N.Y., 1969-71; chief libr., prof. libr., chmn. libr. dept. S.I. Community Coll. CUNY, 1971-76; prof. libr. Coll. S.I. CUNY, 1976-79; head libr. Lockwood Libr./SUNY, Buffalo, 1979-80; asst. dir. for planning, univ. librs. SUNY, Buffalo, 1980-81; exec. dir. librs. and learning resources, prof. U. Wis., Oshkosh, 1981-87; dir. libr. svcs. Bloomsburg U. Pa., 1987-89, dean libr. svcs., 1989-98; spl. asst. to vice chancellor for info. technology Pa. State Sys. Higher Edn., 1999; prin. J. Daniel Vann Consulting, 2000—; interim dir., adj. prof. of bibliography Union Theol. Sem. and Presbyn. Sch. of Christian Edn., 2003—. Resident planner, cons. on libr. bldgs. and collection devel.; bd. dirs. Coun. Wis. Librs., 1983-86, Susquehanna Libr. Coop., 1987-98, sec./treas., 1993-95. Mem. internat. editl. bd. Libr. Times Internat., 1984—; contbr. chpts. to books, articles to profl. jours. Trustee Maplewood (N.J.) Meml. Libr., 1977-79, v.p., 1979; bd. dirs. Coun. Wis. Librs., 1983-86, Midwest Rotary Multi-Dist. Short Term Internat. Youth Exch., 1987, Oshkosh (Wis.) Symphony Assn., 1986-87, Protestant campus ministry Bloomsburg U., 1999—2002, United Cerebral Palsy of Winnebagoland, Oshkosh, 1986-87; active coms. Winnebago Presbytery, Presbyn. Ch., 1984-87; com. on min. Northumberland Prsbytery, Presbyn. Ch., 1992-96, com. on preparation for ministry, 1996—2002, coun., 1999—2002; commr. Synod of Trinity Presbyn. Ch. (USA), 1999—2003, exec. com., 2002—2003. Acad. Libr. Mgmt. intern Coun. on Libr. Resources Stanford U., 1977-78. Mem. ALA (com. mem.), Am. Hist. Assn., Archons of Colophon, Assn. for Libr. Collections and Tech. Svcs., Assn. Coll. and Rsch. Librs. (com. chmn., sec. chmn. 1977-78, editl. bd., bd. dirs. 1976-78), Bibliog. Soc. Am., Libr. Adminstrn. and Mgmt. Assn. (com. mem.), Libr. and Info. Tech. Assn., Reference and User Svcs. Assn., Medieval Acad. Am., Pa. Libr. Assn. (coun., sect. dir., mem. coun., Round Table chair), Bloomsburg Rotary Club (Paul Harris fellow), Beta Phi Mu, Phi Alpha Theta. Republican. Home: 810 E 2nd St Bloomsburg PA 17815-2011 also: 1216 Rennie Ave Richmond VA 23227-4723

VAN NAARDEN BRAUN, KIM, epidemiologist; d. Robert and Renee Van Naarden; m. Joshua Braun, Nov. 28, 1971. BA, U. Pa., Phila., 1991—95; PhD, Columbia U., NY, 1999—2004. Epidemiologist Ctrs. Disease Control and Prevention, Atlanta, 1997—. Recipient Carl Tyler award, Excellence Pub. Health Practice; fellow Pierre Decoufle Fellowship, Excellence Devel. Disabilities Epidemiology.

VAN NESS, JAMES EDWARD, electrical engineering educator; b. Omaha, June 24, 1926; s. Hubert James and Jean (Woodruff) Van N.; m. Mary Ellen Dolvin, Dec. 28, 1948; children: Rebecca Ellen, Barbara Jean, Margaret Ann, Julie Lynn. BS, Iowa State U., 1949; MS, Northwestern U., 1951, PhD, 1954.

Faculty elec. engring. dept. Northwestern U., 1952—, prof. emeritus, chmn. dept., 1969-72; dir. Computer Center, 1962-65; vis. assoc. prof. U. Calif., Berkeley, 1958-59. Vis. prof. MIT, 1973-74. Ariz. State U., winter 1984 Contbr. Articles to profl. jours. Served with USNR, 1944-46. Fellow: IEEE; mem.: NAE (elected). Home: 2333 Central St Unit 404 Evanston IL 60201 E-mail: vanness@northwestern.edu.

VAN NESS, JOHN RALPH, university official, educator; b. Columbus, Ohio, Oct. 22, 1939; s. Ralph Taylor and Norma Gertrude (Thorp) Van N.; children: Heather Thorpe, Hilary Clark; m. Sandra M. Martinez, Jan. 1999; 1 stepchild, Alejandro. BA, The Colo. Coll., Colo. Springs, 1965; MA, U. Pa., 1969, PhD, 1979. Instr. West Chester (Pa.) U., 1969-70, Knox Coll., Galesburg, Ill., 1970-73, Fort Lewis Coll., Durango, Colo., 1974-76; cons. fund raising pvt. practice Phila., 1977-79; capital campaign son. John F. Rich Co., Phila., 1979-84; v.p. for coll. rels., adj. prof. anthropology Ursinus Coll., Collegeville, Pa., 1984-89; exec. v.p., prof. Moore Coll. Art and Design, Phila., 1989-90, pres., 1990-92, Mus. N.Mex. Found., Santa Fe, 1992-93, N.Mex. State U. Found., 1995-97; asst. v.p. Lehigh U., 1997-98, assoc. v.p., 1998—. Bd. dirs. Ctr. for Land Grant Studies, Santa Fe, 1978-94; editl. bd. Jour. of the West, Manhattan, Kans., 1980-88. Co-author: Cañones: Values, Crisis and Survival in a Northern New Mexico Village, 1981; author: Hispanos in Northern New Mexico, 1991; co-editor: Spanish and Mexican Land Grants in New Mexico and Colorado, 1980, Land, Water and Culture, 1987; editor: New Mexico Land Grant Series, vols. 1-5, 1983, 84, 87, 89, 94. Recipient Teaching Fellowship U. Pa.; grantee Ford Found., Nat. Sci. Found. Mem. Am. Anthrop. Assn., Am. Assn. Museums, Coun. for Advance and Support Edn., Nat. Soc. Fund Raising Execs., Pi Gamma Mu, Phi Delta Theta. Democrat. Avocations: architecture, art, sports. Fax: 610- 868-6560. E-mail: jrv3@lehigh.edu.

VAN NESS, PATRICIA CATHELINE, composer, violinist; b. Seattle, June 25, 1951; d. C. Charles and Marjorie Mae (Dexter) Van N.; m. Peter Charles Marks. Student, Wheaton (Ill.) Coll., 1969-70, Gordon Coll., 1972. Composer: ballet score for Beth Soll, 1985, 87, 94, for Monica Levy, 1988, for Boston Ballet, 1988, 90, for Charleston Ballet Theatre, 1994; text and music for voices and early instruments with text translated into Latin for Evensong, 1991, Five Meditations, 1993, Cor Mei Cordis, 1994, Arcanae, 1995, Ego sum Custos Angels, 1995, Tu Risa, 1996, The Nine Orders of the Angels, 1996; various scores, 1985-2004; rec. violinist A&M Records, Private Lightning, 1980, Telarc Internat. Arcanae and Ego sum Custos Angela, 1996, Telarc Internat. Michael and Thronorum, 1999, Telarc Internat. The Fourth River, 1999, Sapphire Night, 2003; composer-in-residence First Church in Cambridge (Mass.), Congregational, 1996—, Coro Allegro, 1998, The Boston Athenaeum, 2002-03, Boston Landmarks Orch., 2003. Grantee Mass. Cultural Coun., 1993, 96, New Eng. Biolabs. Founds., 1989, Mass. Arts Lottery Coun., 1988, Meet the Composer, 1997, 98; recipient Spl. Recognition award Barlow Internat. Composition for Evensong, 1993, 1st prize His Majestie's Clerkes Choral Competition, 1997. Mem.: ASCAP (Std. award 1996—2004), Alliance Women in Music, Am. Music Ctr., Am. Composers Forum. Avocation: major league baseball.

VAN NESS, PATRICIA WOOD, religious studies educator, consultant, author; b. Peterborough, NH, Sept. 12, 1925; d. Leslie Townsend and Bernice E. (Coburn) Wood; m. John Hasbrouck Van Ness, June 13, 1953; children: Peter Wood, Stephen Hasbrouck, Timothy Coburn. BA, U. Wash., 1947; MA, Inst. Transpersonal Psychology, Palo Alto, Calif., 1993. Leader various workshops and retreats, 1979—; records mgr. dept. pub. rels. Std. Oil Co., NJ, (now Exxon Corp., NYC), 1948-50, sec. pub. rels. dept., 1951—53; sec. law dept. Johnson & Johnson, New Brunswick, NJ, 1953-54; reporter Hudson Valley Newspapers, Highland, NY, 1972-74; acting assoc. dir. office of pub. rels. SUNY, New Paltz, 1974; ednl. cons. Ulster County Assn. for Mental Health, Kingston, NY, 1973-76; Christian educator Meth. Ch., New Paltz, NY, 1976—78, White Plains Presbyn. Ch., NY, 1978—81; adminstrv. asst. Ctr. for Cont. Edn. Calif. Econ., Palo Alto, Calif., 1983-84; profl. rep. pvt. practice Palo Alto, 1984; adminstrv. asst. Inventory Transfer Systems Inc., Palo Alto, 1984-85; Christian Educator Bedford Presbyn. Ch., NH, 1986—88; coord. pub. rels., adminstrv. asst. Inst. Transpersonal Psychology, Menlo Pk., NJ, 1981-83. Workshop leader and cons. Author: Transforming Bible Study with Children, 1991; assoc. editor and writer Bible Workbench, 1993—; contbr. numerous articles to profl. jours. Trustee Peterborough (NH) Players, 1998—2001. Mem. Assn. Presbyn. Ch. Educators. Avocations: swimming, reading, contra dancing, theater. Home: 11 Jaquith Rd Jaffrey NH 03452-6406 E-mail: pwvn@monad.net.

VAN NESS, PAUL C. neurologist, educator; b. LA, Aug. 27, 1956; BS, U. Calif., Riverside, 1978; MD, UCLA, 1981. Cert. neurology Am. Bd. of Psychiatry and Neurology, 1987, clin. neurophysiology Am. Bd. of Psychiatry and Neurology, 1992, electroencephalography and evoked potentials Am. Bd. of Clin. Neurophysiology, 1987. Adj. asst. prof. of neurology UCLA, 1985—88; staff neurolgist Cleve. Clinic Found., 1988—95; assoc. prof. of neurology U. Tex. Southwestern Med. Ctr., Dallas, 1995—. Dir. U. Tex. Southwestern Epilepsy Ctr., Dallas, 1995—. Mem.: Am. Acad. of Neurology, Am. Clin. Neurophysiology Soc., Am. Epilepsy Soc. Office: UT Southwestern Med Center J3126 Neurology 5323 Harry Hines Blvd Dallas TX 75235-9036 E-mail: paul.van_ness@utsouthwestern.edu.

VAN NEVEL, J. PAUL, communications executive; b. New Richmond, Wis., Apr. 26, 1938; m. Lois E. Anderson, Apr. 14, 1962; two children. BS, U. Wis., 1961. Dir. pub. info. U. Wis. Med. Ctr., 1961-62, 64-68, assoc. dir., 1968-69; dir. pub. rels. Johns Hopkins Med. Instsn., Balt., 1969-73; dep. assoc. dir. for cancer comm. Nat. Cancer Inst. NIH HHS, 1973-74, assoc. dir. cancer comm., 1974—99; pres. Van Nevel Comms. (biomed. rsch. comm. firm), Potomac, Md., 2000—. Cons. Howard Hughes Med. Inst., 1987—. Mem. editl. bd. Jour. Nat. Cancer Inst., 1988—2001. Bd. dirs. Leadership Montgomery, 2004—. Montgomery Vol. Dental Clinic. With U.S. Army, 1962—64. Recipeint Outstanding Svc. award Cancer Care Inc., 1996, Presdl. award meritorious exec., U.S. Sr. Exec. Svc., 1999, Disting. Svc. award, U. Wis., Madison, 1999. Mem. Assn. Am. Med. Colls. (mem. group on pub. affairs. 1964-95, chair group on pub. affairs 1971), Am. Cancer Soc. (liaison nat. comm. com. 1974-1999), NIH Alumni Assn. (pres. 2004-). E-mail: pvn@vannevel.com.

VANNI, ROBERT JOHN, lawyer; b. Richmond, Va. s. Anthony J. and Jeanette V. BSBA, Babson Coll., 1966; JD, NYU, 1969; cert., U. Catholique L'Ouest, Angers, France, 1971; MBA, Columbia U., 1977. Bar: N.Y. 1969. Asst. econ. affairs officer UN Secretariat, N.Y.C., 1969—72; assoc. Shearman & Sterling, N.Y.C., 1972—79; gen. counsel N.Y.C. Dept. Cultural Affairs, N.Y.C., 1979—86; v.p., gen. counsel, sec. N.Y. Pub. Libr., Astor Lenox and Tilden Founds., N.Y.C., 1986—. Bd. dirs. Nonprofit Coordinating Com., 2001—; chair, of counsel N.Y.C. cultural instns., 1987—; bd. advisors Nat. Ctr. Philanthropy and the Law, 1997-2000. Bd. dirs. Afghanistan Relief Com., N.Y.C., 1980-86, Am.-Italy Soc., N.Y.C., 1983-95, Jazz Found. Am., N.Y.C., 1990-95; trustee Louis Armstrong Edn. Found., 1997—. Named one of Outstanding Young Men in Am. Mem. Nat. Assn. Coll. and Univ. Attys. (co-chair com. on museums and librs. 1996-2000), N.Y.C. Bar Assn. (chair com. on internat. trade 1983-87, mem. long range planning com., nonprofit orgn. com., art law com. 2000-03). Office: N Y Pub Libr 5th Ave and 42d St New York NY 10018*

VANNIASINGHAM, SAMUEL KANAGASABAPATHY, accountant; b. Singapore, Oct. 16, 1950; arrived in U.K., 1974; s. Nathan Kesagar and Mabel Gnanaratnam (Subramaniam) V.; m. Heather Christine Clark, August 5, 1981; children: Daniel James, David Joseph. Diploma in Acctg., Stamford Ctr., Singapore, 1972; degree Profl. Acctg., Chartered Assn. Cert. Accts., London, 1979. Articled clk. Peat, Marwick, Mitchell, Singapore, 1974-75; part-time tchr. Adult Edn. Bd., Singapore, 1972-75; mgmt. trainee E. Russell Ltd., London, 1977-79, accounts mgr., 1980-85; mgmt. acct. MAT Transport Internat. Ltd., London, 1985-86, group mgmt. acct., 1986-87, group acct., 1988; group fin. contr. and co. sec. C & S Group, 1989; mgr. fin. acct. Channel Four TV, London, 1989-92; pvt. practice Sam Vann & Co., Chartered Cert. Accts., London, 1992. Staff sgt. in nat. svc. Police dept., Singapore, 1968-75. Recipient Bravery commendation medal Police Force, Singapore, 1974. Fellow Chartered Assn. Cert. Accts.; mem. Brit. Inst. Mgmt., Singapore Cricket Assn. (test cricketer 1971-75), North London Enterprise Club (dir. 1994-2001), North London C. of C. (co-opted dir. 1999-2001), Hazelwood Squash Club (North London). Methodist. Avocations: squash, cricket. Home: 17 Hyde Way Edmonton London N9 9RU England Office: Sam Vann & Co Lee Valley Technopark London N14 5HN England

VANNICE, M. ALBERT, chemical engineering educator, researcher; b. Broken Bow, Nebr., Jan. 11, 1943; s. Duane M. and Eugenia R. (Farmer) Vannice; m. Bette Ann Clark, Jan. 2, 1971. BSChemE, Mich. State Univ., 1964; MS, Stanford Univ., 1966, PhD, 1970. Engr. Dow Chem. Co., Midland, Mich., 1966, Sun Oil Co., Marcus Hook, Pa., 1970; sr. rsch. engr. Esso Rsch. & Engr. Co., Linden, NJ, 1971—76; assoc. prof. Pa. State Univ., State College, 1976—80, prof., 1980—, disting. prof., 1991—2002, M.R. Fenske prof. chem. engring., 1996—2002, W.H. Joyce chair in chem. engring., 2002—. Cons. Eastman Chem. Co., Kingsport, Tenn., 1980—2000; mem. adv. bd. Absorption Sci. and Tech., 1982—95. Contbr. articles to profl. jours. Recipient award, N.Y. Catalysis Soc., 1985, P.H. Emmett award, 1987, award, Pa.-Cleve. Catalysis Soc., 1988, Humboldt Rsch. award, 1990, Fulbright award, 1996. Mem.: AIChE (profl. Progress award 1986), N.Am. Catalysis Soc. (pres. 1997—2001), Am. Chem. Soc. Achievements include patents in field; research in effects of strong metal-support interactions on catalytic behavior; studies of CO hydrogenation; studies NOx reduction; catalyst characterization. Office: Pa State Univ 107 Fenske Lab University Park PA 16802-4400 E-mail: mavche@engr.psu.edu.

VAN NOORD, DIANE C. artist, educator; b. Muskegon, Mich., Dec. 12, 1950; d. Ernest Raymond and Judith Ann (Olsen); m. Calvin G. Van Noord, Sept. 26, 1981; children: Tawn Star, Brian Calvin, Timothy John. BA, Hope Coll., 1991; MA, Western Mich. U., 1994. Artist, Holland, Mich., 1996—99; pvt. art tchr., 2000—. Guest lectr. Counterpart Assn., Grand Haven, Mich., 1997, Lakeland Painters, Grand Haven, 1997, Traverse City (Mich.) Art Assn., 1997, Holland Christian Schs., 1998, 99, 2000. Exhbns. include Neville Pub. Mus., Green Bay, Wis., 1994, Carillon Gallery, Ft. Worth, 1995, 97, Sedona (Ariz.) Arts Ctr., 1995, 96, 99, Holland Area Arts Coun., 1995, Pitts. Ctr. for the Arts, 1995, Miss. Mus. Art, Jackson, 1995, Unitarian Universalist Ch., Phoenix, 1996, Lakeland Painters, Grand Haven, Mich., 1996, Sun Cities Mus. Art, Sun City, Ariz., 1997, Art Inst. Phoenix, 1998, Hill Country Arts Found., Ingram, Tex., 1998, Mus. Tex. Tech. U., Lubbock, 1998, Dunton Gallery, Arlington Heights, Ill., 2000, Internat. Mus. Art, El Paso, 2000; one-woman shows include Gallery Upstairs, Grand Haven, 1996, Moynihan Gallery, Holland, 1997, Trinity Presbyn. Ch., Denton, 1997, Show Sabbatical, 1998, 99, Freedom Village, Holland, 2000, Acad. Artists Assn., Springfield, Mass., 2001, Hilton Head Art League, 2001, Oil Painters Am., Chgo., 2002, Audubon Artists N.Y., 2002, Magnum Opus XIV, Sacramento, 2002, Am. Artists Profl. League, N.Y.C., 2002, Celebration of Western Art, San Francisco, 2002, Hilton Head Art League, 2003, 2004, Oil Painters Am., Taos, N.Mex., 2003, Scottsdale Artists Sch, 2004, Nat. Watercolor Soc., 2004, Rocky Mountain Plein Air Painters, 2004; permanent collections in Fla., Ariz., Mich., Nebr., Ind.; contbr. articles to profl. jours. Recipient Merchant's award Lakeland Painters, 1996, No. Ariz. Watercolor Soc., Sedona Arts Ctr., 1999, Diane Parssinen Meml. award No. Ariz. Watercolor Soc., 2001, 2d prize Internat. Artist Mag., 2002, Honorable Mention, Artists Mag., 2002, 2004. Mem. Ariz. Watercolor Assn., No. Ariz. Watercolor Assn., Oil Painters Am. (assoc.), Nat. Watercolor Soc. (assoc.), Allied Artists (assoc.), Am. Women Artists (assoc.). Republican. Home: 6418 Oakridge Dr Holland MI 49423-8999 E-mail: dvn@dianevannoord.com.

VAN NORMAN, WILLIS ROGER, retired computer systems researcher, consultant; b. Windom, Minn., June 17, 1938; s. Ralph Peter and Thelma Pearl (Bare) Van N.; m. Irena Anne Penner, Sept. 7, 1959; children: Eric Jon, Brian Mathew, Karin Ruth. AA, Worthington Jr. Coll., 1958; BS, Mankato State Coll., 1960; MS, St. Thomas U., 1991. Tchr. chemistry, St. Peter, Minn., 1961, Byron, Minn., 1962; tchr. spl. edn. Rochester, Minn., 1963-65; instr. Pilots Ground Sch., Rochester Jr. Coll., 1968-69; with Mayo Clin., Rochester, 1962-88; developer biomed. computer sys., 1974—; staff analyst Analyst Internat., 1988—2002. Instr. Gopher Aviation, 1968-71; founder, mgr. Van Norman's Flying V Ranch, 1972—, Van Norman Airport, St. Charles, 1977—. Woodland advisor, 1995—; founding mem. Zumbro Valley Woodland Coun., 1996; treas. United Meth. Ch. Named Olmstead County Conservation Farmer of Yr., 1992; recipient River Friendly Farmer award, 1997. Mem. NEA, Minn. Edn. Assn., Mankato State Alumni Assn. (dir.), Minn. Flying Farmers (v.p., pres.), Internat. Flying Farmers (dir.), Am. Radio Relay League (mgr. Minn. sec. traffic net), Rochester Amateur Radio Club (pres.). Home: 19230 26th St NE Saint Charles MN 55972-2016 Personal E-mail: wrvn@aol.com.

VAN NOSTRAND, C. ALEXANDRA, finance educator, consultant; d. Bunnie Zimba and Bruce Rich. BA in Polit. Sci., SUNY, Albany, 1973—77; MA in Orgn. Devel., Fielding Inst., Santa Barbara, Calif., 1990—91, PhD in Human and Orgnl. Sys., 1991—93. Asst. prof., bus. Wayland Bapt. U., Lubbock, Tex., 1993—94; assoc. prof., mgmt. Hardin-Simmons U., Abilene, Tex., 1995—97; assoc. prof., internat. mgmt. Franklin Coll., Lugano, Switzerland, 1997—2001; assoc. prof., internat. bus. Palm Beach Atlantic U., West Palm Beach, Fla., 2001—. Cons. in pvt. practice, Glendale, Ariz., 1993—95, Abilene, Tex., 1995—97, Lugano, Switzerland, 1997—2001, West Palm Beach, Fla., 2001—. Mem. The Jr. League of the Palm Beaches, West Palm Beach, Fla., 2004. Mem.: Acad. Internat. Bus. Lutheran. Avocation: travel.

VAN NOSTRAND, CATHARINE MARIE HERR, consultant, speaker, educator, writer; b. Dubuque, Iowa, June 17, 1937; d. King George and Julia Marie (Hansen) Herr; m. David Michael Van Nostrand, July 16, 1960; children: Laura Susan Van Nostrand Caviani, Catharine Louise, Maren Thyra. Student, Grinnell Coll., 1955-57; BA in Music Edn., U. Iowa, 1959; MA in Human Devel., St. Mary's U. of Minn., Winona, 1989. Music specialist, Bound Brook, N.J. and Brookline, Mass., 1959 62; coord. music and worship First United Meth. Ch., St. Cloud, Minn., 1970-75; founder, prin. cons. Catharine Van Nostrand & Assocs., St. Cloud, 1975—2003. Guest lectr., author-in-residence nat. colls. and univs., regional, statewide, nat. and internat. acad. symposia, 1975—2003; tng. and devel. cons. numerous bus., govt., health and ednl. orgns.; keynote spkr. and workshop facilitator regional and nat. confs. and convs., 1987—2003; cons./featured spkr. on Equal Opportunity for European Union countries, 1995; cofounder, leader Music and Worship Camp Koinonia Retreat Ctr., Annandale, Minn., 1973; cofounder, leader Women's Fitness Camp, YMCA Camp Olson, Longville, Minn., 1970s. Author: Gender-Responsible Leadership: Detecting Bias, Implementing Interventions, 1993; contbr. articles to profl. jours. Capt. prof. div. fundraising for area family YMCA, St. Cloud, 1975; founding bd. dirs. St. Cloud Civic Orch.; vol. radio interviewer Minn. Pub. Radio and WJON Radio, Collegeville/St. Cloud, 1976-77; bd. dirs. Minn. Orch., Coll. St. Benedict, 2002— Mem. AAUW. Democrat. Methodist. Avocations: bicycle touring, reading, gardening, cultural events. Home: 2854 Winnebago Rd Sartell MN 56377-2373

VAN NOSTRAND, RICHARD CHARLES, lawyer; b. Johnstown, N.Y., Sept. 20, 1955; s. Charles F. and Delores M. (Trajlinek) Van N.; m. Deborah A. Genovese, Aug. 6, 1977; children: Emily Kate, Kelsey Lynn. BA in History, Binghamton U., Binghamton, 1977; JD, Duke U., 1980. Bar: Mass. 1980, U.S. Dist. Ct. Mass. 1981, U.S. Ct. Appeals (1st cir.) 1983, U.S. Ct. Claims 1983, U.S. Supreme Ct. 2003. Assoc. Bloom and Schwartz, Westborough, Mass., 1980-83, Bloom and Van Nostrand, Westborough, 1983-84; pvt. practice Westborough, 1984; assoc. Mirick, O'Connell, DeMallie and Lougee, Worcester, Mass., 1984-87, ptnr., 1988—. Atty. Vol. Lawyers Svc., Worcester, 1981—; legal counsel Mass. Jaycees, 1985—86; bd. dirs. Legal Assistance Corp. of Cen. Mass., treas., 1996—99; chmn. Northborough Pers. Bd., 1994—97; trustee Mass. Legal Assistance Corp., 2001—; mem. Joint Bar on Judicial Appointments, 2001—, chair, 2001—02. Bd. dirs. United Way of Cen. Mass., 1991—99, chmn. allocations divsn., 1991—93. Named one of Outstanding Young Men Am., 1985, Outstanding Young Leader of Worcester, 1995. Mem.: ABA (nat. conf. bar pres. 1995—96, del. 2003—), New England Bar Assn. (v.p. 2003—), Mass. Continuing Legal Edn., Inc. (trustee 1997—), Worcester County Bar Assn. (chmn. trial practice sect. 1988—90, chmn. Superior Ct. com. 1990—91, exec. com. 1991—97, pres. 1995—96, Pres. award 1990, 1995, 1997), Mass. Bar Assn. (bd. dels. 1995—96, budget and fin. com. 1997—, v.p. 2001—02, pres.-elect 2002—03, pres. 2003—), Worcester County Bar Found. (life; pres. 1996—97), Worcester Jaycees (pres. 1984—85). Democrat. Lutheran. Home: 109 Madison Rd Northborough MA 01532-2280 Office: Mirick OConnell 100 Front St Worcester MA 01608-1477 Office Phone: 508-791-8500. Business E-Mail: rvannostrand@modl.com.

VAN NOY, TERRY WILLARD, health care executive; b. Alhambra, Calif., Aug. 31, 1947; s. Barney Willard and Cora Ellen (Simms) V.; m. Betsy Helen Pothen, Dec. 27, 1968; children: Bryan, Mark. BS in Bus. Mgmt., Calif. State Poly. U., 1970; MBA, Pepperdine U., 1991. CLU. Group sales rep. Mutual of Omaha, Atlanta, 1970-74, dist. mgr., 1974-77, regional mgr. Dallas, 1977-82, nat. sales mgr. Omaha, Neb., 1982-83, v.p. group mktg., 1983-87, div. dir. Orange, Calif., 1987-95; pres., CEO, Amil Internat., Las Vegas, 1995-98; prin. Van Noy Consulting Group, Henderson, Nev., 1998—. Vice-chmn. State Nev. Reinsurance Bd., mem. divsn. ins. health adv. com.; presenter in field. Vice-chmn. Morning Star Luth. Ch., Omaha, 1987; adv. bd. Chapman U. Sch. Bus.; exc. com. ABL Orgn.; chmn. bd. trustees Desert Rsch. Inst. Found. Mem. Am. Soc. CLU, Orange County Employee Benefit Coun., We. Pension and Benefits Conf., Las Vegas Valley Soaring Assn. (v.p.), Internat. Found. Employee Benefit Plans. Republican. Avocations: skiing, scuba diving, soaring. Home and Office: 2312 Prometheus Ct Henderson NV 89074-5324 Office Phone: 702-433-9677.

VAN OOSTENBURG, PAUL GARY, lawyer; b. Ridgewood, NJ, Sept. 19, 1956; s. Gordon Lee and Mildred Elizabeth Van Oostenburg; children: Max, Dana. BA magna cum laude in psychology, Hope Coll., 1974; JD, Wayne State U., 1978. Bar: Mich. 1982. Atty. Smith Haughey Rice & Roegge, Grand Rapids, Mich., 1982—. Author: A Cuban Misconception, 1994 (1st place arts festival, 1994). Basketball coach EGR Recreational Dept., East Grand Rapids, Mich., 1999—2003; deacon West Min. Presbyn. Ch., Grand Rapids, Mich., 1991. Democrat. Presbyn. Avocations: travel, fishing, writing, coaching, hiking. Home: 330 Rosewood SE Grand Rapids MI 49506 Office: Smith Haughey Rice and Roegge 250 Monroe Ave NW Grand Rapids MI 49503 Office Phone: 616-458-9462. Office Fax: 616-774-2461. E-mail: pvanoostenburg@shrr.com.

VAN OPPEN, PETER H. information technology executive; BA, Whitman Coll.; MBA, Harvard U. Cons. mgr. Bain & Co., PriceWaterhouse LLP; CEO ADIC, 1994—, chmn. bd., 1984—; with Interpoint Corp., 1985—96. Dir. W. Wireless Corp., Seattle Br. of Fed. Res. Bank, San Francisco; trustee Whitman Coll. Scholar Baker Scholar, Harvard Bus. Sch. Office: ADIC PO Box 97057 Redmond WA 98073-9757 also: ADIC 11431 Willows Rd NE Redmond WA 98052

VANORA, JEROME PATRICK, lawyer; b. Dec. 18, 1941; s. Jerome Anthony and Mary (Fitzpatrick) V.; m. Marianne Elizabeth Hartmann, Oct. 12, 1968; children: Judith, Kimberly. BA, Queens Coll., 1963; JD, St. John's U., 1966. Bar: N.Y. 1967. Atty. N.Y. Dept. of State Corp. Bur., Albany, 1967-70; sr. atty. divsn. human rights N.Y.C., 1970-81; assoc. atty. divsn. housing cmty. renewal, 1981—2002. Dir. hearings unit (chief adminstrv. law judge) office of rent adminstrn., divsn. housing and cmty. renewal, N.Y.C., 1984—99; asst. counsel Nassau County Rent Guidelines Bd., 1982—86; lectr. (twice yearly) L.I. U., Greenvale, NY, 1984—85; per diem adminstrv. law judge N.Y. State Divsn. Human Rights, 2002—. Contbr. articles to profl. jours. Mem.: N.Y. State Bar Assn., Nat. Assn. Adminstrv. Law Judges, Phi Beta Kappa. Republican. Roman Catholic. Home: 1100 Delmar Ave Franklin Square NY 11010-2703

VAN ORDEN, PHYLLIS JEANNE, librarian, educator; b. Adrian, Mich., July 7, 1932; d. Warren Philip and Mabel A. Nancy (Russell) Van O. BS, Ea. Mich. U., 1954; AMLS, U. Mich., 1958; EdD, Wayne State U., 1970. Sch. librarian East Detroit (Mich.) Pub. Schs., 1954-57; librarian San Diego Pub. Library, 1958-60; media specialist Royal Oak (Mich.) Pub. Schs., 1960-64; librarian Oakland U., Rochester, Mich., 1964-66; instr. Wayne State U., Detroit, 1966-70; asst. prof. Rutgers U., New Brunswick, N.J., 1970-76; prof. library science Fla. State U., Tallahassee, 1977-91, assoc. dean for instrn., 1988-91; prof. libr. sci. program Wayne State U., Detroit, 1991-93; dir. Grad. Sch. of Libr. and Info. Sci. U. Wash., Seattle, 1993-96; cons. in field, 1996—. Editor: Elementary School Library Collection, 1974-77; author: Collection Program in Schools, 2001, Library Service to Children, 1992, Selecting Books for the Elementary School Library Media Center, 2000. Fla. State Libr. grantee, 1984, 86, 88; Lillian Bradshaw scholar Tex. Woman's U., 1993. Mem.: ALA (libr. resources and tech. svcs. divsn., Blackwell/N.Am. scholarship award 1983), Assn. for Libr. and Info. Sci. Edn. (pres. 1990, Svc. award 1997), Assn. Libr. Svc. to Children (past pres., Dist. Svc. award 2002), Pi Lambda Theta. Avocations: music, knitting, physical fitness, cooking, travel. E-mail: vanordp@u.washington.edu.

VAN OSS, STEPHEN A. electronics executive; CPA. Auditor Price Waterhouse; with acctg., investor rels., ops. Reliance Electric; dir. info. sys. WESCO, Pitts., 1997—2000, v.p., CFO, 2000—. Office: WESCO Four Station Sq Commerce Ct Ste 700 Pittsburgh PA 15219

VAN PATTEN, JAMES JEFFERS, education educator; b. North Rose, N.Y., Sept. 8, 1925; s. Earl F. and Dorothy (Jeffers) Van P.; married. BA, Syracuse U., 1949; ME, Tex. Western Coll., 1959; PhD, U. Tex., Austin, 1962. Asst. prof. philosophy and edn. Central Mo. State U., Warrensburg, 1962-64, assoc. prof., 1964-69; assoc. prof. fis. overseas U. Okla., Norman, 1969-71; prof. edn. U. Ark., Fayetteville, 1971-99, prof. emeritus, 1999—. Visiting scholar, U. Mich., 1981, UCLA, 1987, U. Tex., Austin, 1987; vis. prof./scholar U. Fla., Gainesville, 1994; adj. Fla. Atlantic U., 2000-03. Editor: Conflict, Permanency and Change in Education, 1976, Philosophy, Social Science and Education, 1989, College Teaching and Higher Education Leadership, 1990, Social-Cultural Foundations of Educational Policy in the U.S., 1991, Watersheds in Higher Education, 1997, Challenges and Opportunities For a New Millennium, 1998, Challenges and Opportunities for Education in the 21st Century, 1999, Higher Education Culture, Case Studies For A New Century, 2000, A New Century In Retrospect and Prospect, 2000; Author: Academic Profiles in Higher Education, 1992, The Many Faces of the Culture of Higher Education, 1993, The Culture of Higher Education: A Case Study Approach, 1996, What's Really Happening in Education: A Case Study Approach, 1997; Co-author: (with G. Chen and George C. Stone) Individual and Collective Contributions to Humaneness In Our Time, 1997, (with John Pulliam) History of Education in America, 8th edit., 2003, (with Timothy J. Bergen) A Case Study Approach to a Multi-Cultural Mosaic for Education, 2003; contbr. articles to profl. jours. including Futures Rsch. Quar.; founder Jour. of Thought, Educational Systems for the 21st Century, Futures Rsch. Quarterly, summer 2000. Served with inf. U.S. Army, 1944-45. Decorated Purple Heart. Mem. Am. Ednl. Studies Assn., Southern Future Soc., World Future Soc., Am. Philosophy Assn., Southwestern Philosophy of Edn. Soc. (pres. 1970), Am. Ednl. Rsch. Assn., Edn. Law Assn., Nat. Assn. Legal Assts., Kiwanis, Phi Delta Kappa (pres. chpt. U. Ark. 1976-77). Home: 434 W Hawthorn St Fayetteville AR 72701-1934 E-mail: jvanpatt@aol.com.

VAN PELT, ROBERT IRVING, retired firefighter; b. Chgo., May 4, 1931; s. Irving Henry and Lillian Christene (Balder) Van P.; m. Donna Arlene Bengtson, Feb. 3, 1962; children: Robert Scott, Barbara Gail, James Arthur. Grad. H.S., Chgo. Fire dept. capt. Chgo. Fire Dept., 1954-89, ret., 1989. Dir. Edgebrook Cmty. Assn., Chgo., 1974-95, U. Ill. Dad's Assn., 1988-92; dist. vice-chmn. programs Chgo. Area coun. Boy Scouts Am., 1985-93; scouting coord. Edgebrook Luth. Ch., Chgo., 1971—; active PTA Edgebrook Sch., Taft H.S. With U.S. Naval Air Res., 1949-65. Decorated Combat Air Crew Wings, 1951, Armed Svcs. medal; recipient Merit award Boy Scouts Am., 1982, Silver Beaver award, 1987, Svc. award VFW, 1987, Lamb award Luth. Ch., 2000; named to Chgo. Sr. Citizen Hall of Fame, 2000; PTA scholar, 1956. Mem. Naval Air Mus. (founding life), Exptl. Aviation Assn., War Birds Am., E.A.A. War Bird Squadron 4, Am. Legion, Order of Arrow, Liberator (San

Diego), U.S. Navy Meml. Washington (plank), Patrol Bomber Y Consolidated MFG (PBY) Catalina Assn. (life). Avocations: photography, woodworking, model making. Home: 6317 N Hiawatha Ave Chicago IL 60646-4219

VAN PRAAG, HERMAN MEIR, psychiatrist, educator, researcher; b. Schiedam, The Netherlands, Oct. 17, 1929; s. Marinus Maurits and Charlotte Frederique (Leverpoll) V.P.; m. Cornelia Eikens; children: Marinus, Gido, Charlotte, Bart. MD, Leiden U., The Netherlands, 1956; PhD in Neurobiology, U. Utrecht, The Netherlands, 1962. Chief of staff dept. psychiatry Dijkzigt Hosp., Rotterdam, The Netherlands, 1963-66; founder, prof., head dept. biol. psychiatry Psychiat. Univ. Clinic State U., Groningen, Netherlands, 1966-77; prof., head dept. psychiatry Acad. Hosp. State U., Utrecht, 1977-82, Albert Einstein Coll. Medicine, Bronx, NY, 1982-92; prof., head dept. psychiatry and neuropsychiatry Acad. Hosp. U. Maastricht, Netherlands, 1992—99, sci. advisor dept. psychiarty and neuropsychology, 1999—. Emeritus prof. Albert Einstein Coll. Medicine, 1992—; psychiatrist-in-chief Montefiore Med. Ctr., Bronx, 1982—92; Lady Davis vis. prof. Hebrew U. Hadassah U. Hosp., Jerusalem, 1976—77; head WHO Nat. Ref. Ctr. for Study of Psychotropic Drugs, 1969, WHO Collaborating Ctr. for Rsch. and Tng. in Biol. Psychiatry, 1974; founder Found. for Psychiatry and Religion; guest lectr. numerous univs. around the world. Editor: Psychiatria Neurologia Neurochirurgia, 1968-70, Advances in Biological Psychiatry, 1978—; editor-in-chief Psychiatria Neurologia Neurochirurgia, 1971-74, Biology of Behavior, 1975-82, Handbook of Biological Psychiatry, 1975-81, Einstein Monograph Series in Experimental and Clinical Psychiatry, 1988—; European chief-editor Progress in Neuro-Psychopharmacology, 1993—; mem. editl. bd. numerous publs. in field; reviewer Am. Jour. Psychiatry, Archives of Gen. Psychiatry, Jour. Nervous and Mental Disease; mem. internat. scientific commn. Jour. Brazilian Psychiat. Assn. Decorated knight Order of the Dutch Lion, Order Beatrix of The Netherlands; recipient numerous awards and honors. Fellow Am. Coll. Neuropsychopharmacology, Am. Psychiat. Assn.; mem. Royal Acad. Scis. of The Netherlands, Soc. Biol. Psychiatry, Collegium Internationale Neuro-Psychopharmacologicum, Assn. for Advancement of Psychotherapy, Internat. Group for Study of Affective Disorders, Internat. Soc. Psychoneuroendocrinology, European Brain and Behavior Soc., Internat. Assn. for Suicide Prevention, Brit. Pharmacol. Soc., European Soc. for Clin. Investigation, Bataafsch Genootschap der Proefondervindelijke Wijsbegeerte, Am. Coll. Neuropharmacology, Deutsche Gesellschaft fur Psychiatrie und Nervenheilkunde, Israel Med. Assn., Psychiat. Rsch. Soc., N.Y. Acad. Medicine, Am. Psychopathol. Assn., Internat. Coll. Neurobiology, Biol. Psychiatry and Psychopharmacology, Serotonin Club, Internat. Soc. for Rsch. on Emotion, Internat. Soc. Psychoneuroendocrinology, Arbeitsgemeinschaft fur Neuropsychpharmakologie und Pharmakopsychiatrie, World Psychiat. Assn. (chmn. sec. religion, spirituality and psychiatry). Office: Acad Hosp Maastricht PO Box 5800 6202 AZ Maastricht Netherlands E-mail: h.m.van.praag@vanpraag.com.

VAN PUTTEN, MARK, environmentalist; b. Mich. 3 children. Grad. magna cum laude, U. Mich. Founding dir. Great Lakes Natural Resource Ctr., Ann Arbor, Mich., 1982—96; pres., CEO Nat. Wildlife Fedn., Reston, Va., 1996—. Avocation: fishing, hiking. Office: Nat Wildlife Fedn 11100 Wildlife Ctr Dr Reston VA 20190-6000

VAN RAALTE, POLLY ANN, reading and writing specialist, photojournalist; b. N.Y.C., Sept. 22, 1951; d. Byron Emmanuel and Enid (Godnick) Van R. Student, U. London, 1972; BA, Beaver Coll., 1973; MS in Edn., U. Pa., 1974, EdD, 1994, West Chester State Coll., 1977. Title I reading tchr. Oakview Sch., West Deptford Twp. Sch. Dist., Woodbury, N.J., 1974-75, title I reading supr., 1975 summer; lang. arts coord. Main Line Day Sch., Mitchell Sch., Haverford, Pa., 1975-76; reading supr. Salvation Army, Phila., summer 1976; reading Huntingdon Jr. H.S., Abington (Pa.) Sch. Dist., 1976-78; reading specialist No. 2 Sch., Lawrence Pub. Sch., Inwood, N.Y., 1978-87; high sch. reading specialist Cedarhurst, N.Y., 1988-93, Lawrence (N.Y.) H.S., 1988-93; elem. reading specialist No. 5 Sch., 1992—; reading specialist Hewlett (N.Y.) Elem. Sch., Hewlett-Woodmere Pub. Sch., 1987-88, Lawrence Mid. Sch., 1993-95; instr. reading and spl. edn. dept. Adelphi U., 1979—. Columnist South Shore Record, featured columnist, 1992—; columnist Boulevard Mag., 1995-97; photojournalist Manhattan Reports, 1997-2002; feature columnist www.15minutesmagazine.com. Bd. dirs., mem. exec. bd. Five Towns Cmty. Ctr., 1991-93, co-chmn. ednl. youth svcs. edn. com., 1991-93; cons. to sch. dists.; advisor Am. Biog. Inst., Inc.; coord. Five Towns Young Voter Registration, Hewlett, N.Y., summer 1971; chmn. class fund Beaver Coll., also mem. internat. rels. com. U. Pa. scholar, 1977-78; mem. assoc. divsn. Jewish Guild for Blind; mem. N.Y. City Sports Commn.; co-chair youth svcs. com. Mem. Internat. Reading Assn., Wis. Reading Assn., Nat. Coun. Tchrs. English, Nassau Reading Coun., N.Y. Reading Assn., Coun. Exceptional Children, Coun. for a Beautiful Israel, Nat. Assn. Gifted Children, Am. Assn. of the Gifted, Nat./State Leadership Tng. Inst. on the Gifted and Talented, Children's Lit. Assembly, N.Y. State English Coun., Assn. Curriculum Devel., Am. Israel Pub. Affairs Com., New Leadership Com. of Jewish Nat. Fund, State of Israel Bonds New Leadership, Simon Wiesenthal New Leadership Soc., Nat. Polit. Action Com., Am. Friends of Hebrew U. (torch com.), Technion Soc., Am. Friends David Yellin Tchr.'s Coll., Am. Friends Israel Philharm., Am. Friends of Tel Aviv U., Am. Israel Cultural Found., Hadassah, Film Soc. Lincoln Ctr., U.S. Olympic Soc., Friends of N.Y.C. Sports Commn., Cooper-Hewitt Mus., Mus. Modern Art, Met. Mus. Art, Whitney Mus., Phila. Mus. Art, Smithsonian Inst., Friends of Carnegie-Hall, Friends of Am. Ballet Theatre, Friends of Am. Theatre Wing, Women's Am. Orgn. for Rehab. Through Tng. (citi women divsn. N.Y.C.), U. Pa. Alumni Assn. N.Y.C., Dorot Soc., Human Rels. Club (sec.), Actors'Fund, Pi Lambda Theta, Kappa Delta Pi (sec., Internat. Tennis Hall of Fame). Home: 26 Meadow Ln Lawrence NY 11559-1828 Office: #5 Sch Cedarhurst Ave Cedarhurst NY 11516

VAN REES, CORNELIUS S. lawyer; b. N.Y.C., May 29, 1929; s. Cornelius Richard and Beatrice Martin (Shreve) Van R.; m. Virginia Vandewater, Mar. 15, 1953 (div. 1984); children: Pamela Millet Van Rees Lundquist, Claire Katherine; m. Alix McIvor, Jan. 2, 1985. BA, Denison U., 1951; JD, Columbia U., 1954. Bar: N.Y. 1956, U.S. Dist. Ct. (so. dist.) N.Y. 1956, Conn. 1994. Assoc. Thacher Proffitt & Wood, N.Y.C., 1956-62, ptnr., 1963-93, of counsel, 1994—. Mem. exec. com., officer, bd. dirs. Graham Corp.; lectr. in field. Writer in field. Trustee, sec. Williston Northhampton Sch.; mem. senate, honors and prizes com. Columbia U. Harlem Fisk Stone scholar Columbia U., 1954. Mem. ABA (coms. on internat. fin. trans., maritime fin. and devel. in bus. fin.), Alumni Fedn. Columbia U., Inc. (Alumni medal 1984, pres. 1979-81). Avocation: sailing. Home and Office: 35 Cove Side Ln Stonington CT 06378-2902

VAN REGENMORTER, WILLIAM, state legislator; m. Cheryl; four children. Mich. jud. com., econ. devel. com., energy com.; chmn. House Rep. Caucus, 84-90. Commr. Ottawa County Bd. Commrs., 1980-82; mem. Mich. Ho. of Reps., 1982-90, Mich. Senate from 22nd dist., Lansing, 1990—. Named legis. of yr. 1985 Mich. Sheriff's Assn., Mich. Assn. Police, 1988, Police Officer's Assn. Mich., 1989; recipient Santarelli award Nat. Orgn. for Victim Assistance, 1985, justice award Found. for Improvement of Justice, 1986, leadership award Nat. Sheriff's Assn., 1987. Office: Mich Senate State Capitol PO Box 30036 Lansing MI 48909-7536 Home: 5965 16th Avenue Hudsonville MI 49426

VAN RIPER, PAUL PRITCHARD, political science educator; b. Laporte, Ind., July 29, 1916; s. Paul and Margaret (Pritchard) Van R.; m. Dorothy Ann Dodd Samuelson, May 11, 1964; 1 child, Michael Scott Samuelson. AB, DePauw U., 1938; PhD, U. Chgo., 1947. Instr. Northwestern U., 1947-49, asst. prof. polit. sci., 1949-51; mgmt. analyst Office Comptroller Dept. Army, 1951-52; mem. faculty Cornell U., 1952-70, prof., 1957-70; chmn. gov. bd., exec. com. Cornell Social Sci. Research Center, 1956-58; prof., head dept. polit. sci. Tex. A&M U., 1970-77, prof., 1977-81, prof. emeritus, 1981—, coordinator M.P.A. program, 1979-81, named prof. Bush Sch. Govt. and Pub. Svc., 1997—. Vis. prof. U. Chgo., 1958, Ind. U., 1961, U. Strathclyde, Scotland, 1964, U. Mich., 1965, U. Okla., 1969-97, U. Utah, 1979. Author: History of the United States Civil Service, 1958, Some Educational and Social Aspects of Fraternity Life, 1961, (with others) The American Federal Executive, 1963, Handbook of Practical Politics, 3d edit., 1967; editor and co-author: the Wilson Influence on Public Administration, 1990. Mem. exec. com. Civil Svc. Reform Assn., N.Y., 1960-64, hist. adv. com. NASA, 1964-66; bd. dirs. Brazos Valley Cmty. Action Agy., 1975-79, Brazos County Hist. Commn., 1976—; charter mem. Brazos Heritage Soc., pres. 1977-79. Maj. AUS, 1942-46; lt. col. USAR ret. Decorated Croix de Guerre (France). Mem. Am. Polit. Sci. Assn., So. Polit. Sci. Assn., S.W. Polit. Sci. Assn. (exec.com. 1975-77), Am. Soc. Pub. Adminstrn. (nat adv. com. 1957-60, Dimock award 1984, Waldo award 1990, Van Riper award created in his honor 2002), Internat. Personnel Mgmt. Assn., Rotary (pres. Bryan club 1991-92), Phi Beta Kappa, Beta Theta Pi (v.p. 1962, gen. sec. 1963-65), Pi Alpha Alpha, Pi Sigma Alpha, Phi Kappa Phi, Sigma Delta Chi. Republican. Baptist. Home: 713 E 30th St Bryan TX 77803-4789 Office: Tex A and M Univ Dept Polit Sci College Station TX 77843-4348 Office Phone: 979-845-2511.

VAN RIPER, ROBERT AUSTIN, writer, retired public relations executive; b. Mt. Vernon, N.Y., June 18, 1921; s. Austin Millard and Gladys Brownell Van R.; m. Barbara Jean Jacobs, Dec. 2, 1944; children: Alexandra, Tracy. BA, Oberlin Coll., 1943. Acct. exec. Edward L. Bernays Pub. Rels., N.Y.C., 1946-50, N.W. Ayer & Son, Inc., N.Y.C., 1950-54, acct. supr. Phila., 1954-61, v.p. N.Y.C., 1961-67, sr. v.p., 1967-73; pub. rels. counsel Fin. Acctg. Standards Bd., Norwalk, Conn., 1973-91, ret., 1991. Author: (novels) A Really Sincere Guy, 1958, The Governor, 1970, (nonfiction) Setting Standards for Financial Reporting: FASB and the Struggle for Control of a Critical Process, 1994, A Life Divided: George Peabody, Pivotal Figure in Anglo-American Finance, Philanthropy and Diplomacy, 2000; contbr. articles to profl. jours. Bd. dirs., exec. com. United Fund, Phila., 1956-61; trustee Lawrence Hosp., Westchester County, 1966-73, v.p., 1971-73. Lt. (j.g.) USN, 1943-46. Mem. Pub. Rels. Soc. Am. (pres. Phila. chpt. 1960-61), Fairfield County Pub. Rels. Assn. (bd. dirs. 1987-89), Holland Soc., Bronxville Field Club (N.Y.). Presbyterian. Avocations: tennis, music. Home: 4100 N Charles St Apt 810 Baltimore MD 21218

VANRYCKEGHEM, MARTINE, speech pathology/audiology services professional, educator; b. Gent, East Flanders, Belgium, Aug. 14, 1955; arrived in U.S., 1989; d. Roger Vanryckeghem and Juliette Vleeshouwers; m. Gene J. Brutten, Oct. 8, 1993. Grad. in Logopedics, Higher Inst. of Paramed. Professions, Gent, 1977; MS, So. Ill. U., 1991, PhD, 1994. Speech-lang. pathologist Clin. Ctr., Gent, 1977—89; univ. prof. U. of Cen. Fla., Orlando, 1994—. Cons. U. of Zagreb, Croatia, 1998—, Arteveldе Hogeschool, Gent, 1994—, U. of Gent, 1994—. Author: (book) Behavior Assessment Battery: A multi-dimensional and Evidence-based Approach to Diagnostic and Therapeutic Decision Making for Children who Stutter, 2003, Behavior Assessment Battery: A Multi-Dimensional and Evidence-based Approach to Diagnostic and Therapeutic Decision Making for Adults who Stutter, 2003; managing editor: Jour. Fluency Disorders, 1990—2000; contbr. articles to profl. jours. Recipient award. Mem.: Orgn. for Integration of Handicapped People (sci. bd. mem. 1995—), Internat. Fluency Assn., Am. Speech-Lang.-Hearing Assn. (clin. competence in speech-lang. pathology, fluency specialist, fluency mentor). Achievements include research in Behavior Assessment Battery for Adults; Behavior Assessment Battery for Children; The KiddyCAT: A test investigating speech-associated attitude in preschoolers. Avocations: travel, cooking, hiking. Office: U Ctrl Fla HPA-2 Ste 101 4000 Central Blvd Orlando FL 32816-2215

VAN SANT, GUS, JR., director, screenwriter; b. Louisville, 1952; BA in Filmmaking, RISD, 1975. Dir., screenwriter William Morris Agy., Inc., Beverly Hills, Calif. Films include Mala Noche, 1985 (L.A. Film Critics award 1987), Drugstore Cowboy, 1989 (with Daniel Yost: Nat. Soc. Film Critics Best Dir. award 1990, Best Screenplay award 1990, N.Y. Film Critics Best Screenplay award 1990, L.A. Film Critics Best Screenplay award 1989), Internat. PEN Literary award for Screenplay Adaptation (with Daniel Yost 1989), My Own Private Idaho, 1991 (Best Screenplay 1992, Best Film 1992), Even Cowgirls Get the Blues, 1993, To Die For, 1995, Kids, 1995, Ballad of the Skeletons, 1996, Good Will Hunting, 1997. Office: William Morris Agency Inc 151 S El Camino Dr Beverly Hills CA 90212-2775

VAN SAUN, BRUCE, bank executive; married; 3 children. Degree, Bucknell U.; MBA, U. N.C. Various sr. positions Kidder Peabody & Co., Inc.; COO, CFO, Wasserstein Perlla Group, Inc., 1990-94; mng. dir. Deutsche Bank N.Am., 1994-98; exec. v.p., CFO, The Bank of N.Y., N.Y.C., 1998—. Office: The Bank of New York 1 Wall St New York NY 10286

VAN SCHILFGAARDE, JAN, retired agricultural engineer, government agricultural research service administrator; b. The Hague, Netherlands, Feb. 7, 1929; came to U.S., 1946, naturalized, 1957; married; 3 children. BS, Iowa State Coll., 1949, MS, 1950, PhD in Agrl. Engring. and Soil Physics, 1954. Instr., assoc. agrl. engr. Iowa State Coll., 1949-54; asst. prof. agrl. engring. N.C. State Coll., 1954-57, assoc. prof., 1957-62, prof., 1962-64; drainage engr. Agrl. Rsch. Svc. USDA, Raleigh, N.C., 1954-64, from chief water mgmt. engr. soil/water conservation rsch. divsn. to dir. Beltsville, Md., 1964—72, dir. Salinity Lab. Riverside, Calif., 1972-84, dir. Mountain States Area Agrl. Rsch. Svc. Ft. Collins, Colo., 1984-86, assoc. dir. no. plains area Agrl. Rsch. Svc., 1986-91, assoc. dep. adminstr. for natural resources Agrl. Rsch. Svc. Beltsville, Md., 1991-96, dir. Pacific West area, 1996-97; ret., 1997. Vis. prof. Ohio State U., 1962 Mem. ASCE, NAE, Am. Soc. Agrl. Engrs., Soil Sci. Soc., Soil Conservation Soc. Am. E-mail: j.-r.vanschilfgaarde@worldnet.att.net.

VAN SCHOIK, D. RICK, think-tank executive; BS in Oceanography and Engring., U.S. Naval Acad.; MS in Biology, San Diego State U.; postgrad., Harvard U., Tufts U., Natural Resources Leadership Inst., N.C. Environ. fellow Surdna Found., N.Y.C.; environ. cons. S.W. Rsch. Assocs., Inc., Calif.; aquatic conservation biologist The Natural Conservancy, NY, Naval Ocean Sys. Ctr., Calif.; CEO Partnership for the Sounds, NC; mng. dir. S.W. Ctr. for Environ. Rsch. and Policy, San Diego, 1998—. Adj. prof. U. Calif., San Diego, U. Redlands, Palomar C.C., Nassau County Coll. Co-chair Binational Environ. Edn. Coun. of the Californias, City of Encinitas Blue Ribbon Environment Com. With USN. Office: SW Ctr for Environ Rsch and Policy 5250 Campanile Dr San Diego CA 92182-1913 Office Phone: 619-594-0568.

VANSELOW, NEAL ARTHUR, academic administrator, internist; b. Milw., Mar. 18, 1932; s. Arthur Frederick and Mildred (Hoffmann) Vanselow; m. Mary Ellen McKenzie, June 20, 1958; children: Julie Ann, Richard Arthur. AB, U. Mich., 1954, MD, 1958, MS, 1963. Diplomate Am. Bd. Internal Medicine, Am. Bd. Allergy and Immunology. Intern Mpls. Gen. Hosp., 1958—59; resident Univ. Hosp., Ann Arbor, Mich., 1959—63; instr. medicine U. Mich., 1963—64, asst. prof., 1964—68, assoc. prof., 1968—72, prof., chmn. dept. postgrad. medicine and health professions edn., 1972—74; dean Coll. Medicine U. Ariz., Tucson, 1974—77; chancellor med. ctr. U. Nebr., Omaha, 1977—82, v.p., 1977—82; v.p. health scis. U. Minn., 1982—89, prof. internal medicine, 1982—89; chancellor Tulane U. Med. Ctr., New Orleans, 1989—94, chancellor emeritus, 1997—; prof. internal medicine Tulane U., New Orleans, 1989—97, prof. internal medicine emeritus, 1997—. Adj. prof. health sys. mgmt. Tulane U., New Orleans, 1993—99, prof. emeritus, 1999—; chmn. Joint Bd. Osteo. and Med. Examiners Ariz., 1974—77; chmn. coun. on Grad. Med. Edn. Dept. Health and Human Svcs., 1986—91; mem. com. on educating dentists for future Inst. Medicine NAS, 1993—95, chairperson com. on future of primary care, 1994—96, co-chairperson com. on U.S. physician supply, 1995—96, scholar in residence, 1994—95, mem. com. to assess occupl. health and safety tng. needs, 1999—2000, chmn. com. on introducing social and behavioral sci. into med. sch. curriculum, 2002—04; chairperson continuing eval. panel Am. Internat. Health Alliance, 2000—01; mem. adv. com. Medschool.com, 2000—01; adj. prof. Sch. Health Adminstrn. and Policy Ariz. State U., 2000—. Panel on interdisciplinary health profl. edn. Nat. League Nursing, 1996—97; exec. com. United Way Midlands, 1980—82, vice-chmn. 1981 campaign; mem. Commn. on Health Professions Pew Charitable Trusts, 1990—92, 1997—99, Commn. on the Future of Med. Edn. U. Calif, 1996—97; mktg. mgmt. governing coun. U. Hosp. Consortium, 1993—95; trustee Meharry Med. Coll., 1996—; pres., chmn. bd. Am. Friends London Sch. Hygiene and Tropical Medicine, 1998—2002; com. on relationships between medicine and nursing Josiah Macy Jr. Found., 1999—2000; mem. Gov.'s Pan Am. Commn., La., 1991—92; bd. dirs. Devel. Authority for Tucson's Economy, 1975—77, Minn. High Tech. Coun., 1983—86, Minn. Coalition for Health Care Costs, 1983—87, La. Health Care Authority, 1989—90, United Way Greater New Orleans Area, 1992—97; bd. dirs., exec. com. Health Planning Coun. Midlands, Omaha, 1978—82, v.p., 1981—82. Fellow: ACP (workgroup on physician workforce and financing med. edn. 1996), Am. Coll. Physician Execs., Am. Acad. Allergy; mem.: Inst. Med. NAS, Soc. Med. Adminstrs., Assn. Acad. Health Ctrs. (bd. dirs. 1983—89, chmn. bd. dirs. 1988), Rio Verde (Ariz.) Cmty. Assn. (bd. dirs. 2000—04), Phi Beta Kappa, Nu Sigma Nu, Beta Theta Pi, Alpha Omega Alpha, Sigma Xi. Office: Tulane U 18942 E Mountainaire Dr Rio Verde AZ 85263-7093

VAN SETERS, JOHN, retired biblical literature educator; b. Hamilton, Ont., Can., May 2, 1935; s. Hugo and Anne (Hubert) Van S.; m. Elizabeth Marie Malmberg, June 11, 1960; children: Peter John, Deborah Elizabeth. BA, U. Toronto, 1958; MA, Yale U., 1959, PhD, 1965; BD, Princeton Theol. Sem., 1962; ThD (hon.), U. Lausanne, Switzerland, 1999. Asst. prof. dept. Near Eastern studies Waterloo Luth. U., 1965-67; assoc. prof. Old Testament Andover Newton Theol. Sch., 1967-70; assoc. prof. dept. Near Eastern studies U. Toronto, 1970-76, prof., 1976-77; James A. Gray prof. Bibl. lit., dept. religion U. N.C., Chapel Hill, 1977-2000, chmn. dept. religious studies, 1980-88, 93-95, prof. emeritus, 2000—. Adj. prof. dept. religion and culture Wilfrid Laurier U., 2000—. Author: The Hyksos: A New Investigation, 1966, Abraham in History and Tradition, 1975, In Search of History, 1983, Der Jahwist als Historiker, 1987, Prologue to History, 1992, The Life of Moses, 1994, The Pentateuch, 1999, A Law Book for the Diaspora, 2003. Recipient James Henry Breasted prize Am. Hist. Assn., 1985, Book award Am. Acad. Religion, 1986, R.B.Y. Scott Book award Can. Soc. Bibl. Studies, 2004; Woodrow Wilson fellow, 1958; J.J. Obermann fellow, 1962-64; Guggenheim fellow, 1979-80; NEH fellow, 1985-86, Am. Coun. Learned Socs. fellow, 1991-92, sr. rsch. fellow Cath. U. Leuven, Belgium, 1998, Fgn. Rsch. fellow Nat. Rsch. Fund S.Africa, 2002. Mem. Soc. Bibl. Lit., Am. Schs. Oriental Rsch., Soc. Study of Egyptian Antiquities, Am. Oriental Soc., Soc. for Old Testament Study, Cath. Bibl. Assn., Can. Soc. Bibl. Studies (pres. 1999-2000). Home: 600 Maple Forest Pl Waterloo ON Canada N2T 2S8 E-mail: john.vanseters@sympatico.ca.

VAN SICKLE, BRUCE MARION, federal judge; b. Minot, N.D., Feb. 13, 1917; s. Guy Robin and Hilda Alice (Rosenquist) Van S.; m. Dorothy Alfreda Hermann, May 26, 1943; children: Susan Van Sickle Cooper, John Allan, Craig Bruce, David Max. BSL, JD, U. Minn., 1941. Bar: Minn. 1941, N.D. 1946. Pvt. practice law, Minot, 1947-71; judge U.S. Dist. Ct. N.D., 1971-85, sr. judge, 1985—. Mem. N.D. Ho. of Reps., 1957, 59. Served with USMCR, 1941-46. Mem. ABA, N.D. Bar Assn., N.W. Bar Assn., Ward County Bar Assn., Am. Trial Lawyers Assn., Am. Coll. Probate Counsel, Am. Judicature Soc., Bruce M. Van Sickle Inns of Ct., Masons, Shriners, Elks, Delta Theta Phi. Office: US Dist Ct US Courthouse Rm 428 PO Box 670 Bismarck ND 58502-0670

VAN SICKLE, FREDERICK L. federal judge; b. 1943; m. Jane Bloomquist. BS, U. Wis., 1965; JD, U. Wash., 1968. Ptnr. Clark & Van Sickle, 1970-75; prosecuting atty. Douglas County, Waterville, Wash., 1971-75; judge State of Wash. Superior Ct., Grant and Douglas counties, 1975-79, 1979-91, U.S. Dist. Ct. (ea. dist.) Wash., Spokane, 1991—. Co-chair rural ct. com. Nat. Conf. State Trial Judges, 1987-91. 1st lt. U.S. Army, 1968-70. Mem. Am. Adjudicature Soc., Wash. State Bar Assn., Masons (pres. Badger mountain lodge 1982-83), Scottish Rite, Spokane Rotary, Shriners. Office: US Dist Cts US Courthouse PO Box 2209 920 W Riverside Ave Rm 914 Spokane WA 99201-1010

VANSICKLE, SHARON DEE, public relations executive; b. Portland, Oreg., Nov. 10, 1955; BA in Mktg. and Journalism, U. Portland, 1976, postgrad., 1977-79. Reporter Willamette Week, Portland, 1976-77; dir. pub. rels. Tektronix, Portland, 1977-83; prin. pub. rels. KVD Pub. Rels., Portland, 1983-98; CEO KVO Pub. Rslc., Portland, 1999—. Chmn. Pinnacle Worldwide, bd. dirs. pub. rels. coun. Vice chair Portland Met. Area Reg. Arts and Culture Coun.; bd. dirs. CPRF, The Oreg. Entrepreneur's Forum, Pres.'s Coun. on Arts & Sci., U. Portland. Mem. Pub. Rels. Soc. Am. (pres. Portland chpt. 1994-95, chair-elect N. Pac. dist., mem. counsilor's acad., bd. mem. and chair tech. com. 1999 Spring conf.). Office: KVO Pub Rels 200 SW Market St Ste 1400 Portland OR 97201-5741

VANSKA, OSMO, music director; D(hon.), U. Glasgow. Prin. chair Turku Philharm., 1971—76; co-prin. chair Helsinki Philharm., 1977—82; music dir. Lahti Symphony Orch., 1988—96; chief condr. BBC Scottish Symphony Orch. of Glasgow, 1996—2002; music dir. Minn. Orch., 2002—. Guest condr. Boston Symphony Orch., 2002. Condr. numerous recordings with the Lahti Symphony Orch. (Gramophone award, 1996, Cannes Classical award, 2002), (recording) The Tempest (1993 Prix Academie Charles Cros.). Nominee Grammy award for Best Orchestral Performance for a recording with the BBC Scottish Symphony; recipient First prize, Besancon Internat. Young Conductor's Competition, Royal Philharm. Soc. award, 2002. Avocations: sports, motorcycling. Office: Minnesota Orchestra Orchestra Hall 1111 Nicollet mall Minneapolis MN 55403

VAN SLOOTEN, RONALD HENRY JOSEPH, dentist; b. Paterson, NJ, July 12, 1937; s. Henry and Edythe (De Marco) Van S.; m. Joyce Elenor Mandel, 1962 (div. 1969); children: Ronald Henry Jr., Timothy Jay, Lauren; m. Barbara Rose Durante, July 1, 1979; children: Jonathan Henry, Brian Joseph. DDS, Fairleigh Dickinson U., 1962; FAGD, Acad. Gen. Dentistry, 1986. Dentist pvt. practice, Paterson, 1965-76, Ridgewood, NJ, 1969-78, Ho Ho Kus, NJ, 1978—; staff mem. Bainert Meml. Hosp., Paterson, 1966-75, Ridgewood Valley Hosp., 1975—; assoc. prof. Fairleigh Dickinson Dental Sch., Hackensack, NJ, 1973-90; pres. Van Slooten Harbour Marina Inc., Port Henry, NY, 1989—. Cons. NJ Mfrs. Ins. Co., Trenton, 1966—. Pres. Fairleigh Dickinson Sch. Dentistry Alumni Assn., 1976-77. Lt. comdr. USN, 1962-65. Fellow Acad. Gen. Dentistry, Acad. Dentistry Internat.; mem. ADA, Internat. Dental Health Found., NJ Dental Soc., Bergen County Dental Soc. (chmn. Nat. Dental Health Week citation 1970), Moriah C. of C., Ho-Ho-Kus C. of C. Republican. Roman Catholic. Avocations: racquetball, fishing, boating. Office: Ho Ho Kus Profl Bldg 110 Warren Ave Ho Ho Kus NJ 07423-1561 Office Phone: 201-447-1116.

VAN STAVOREN, WILLIAM DAVID, consultant, retired government official; b. Lunenburg, Va., Mar. 14, 1936; s. James Eugene and Marion Estelle (Boyer) Van S.; m. Rosa Kouyoundjian, Dec. 29, 1962; children: John, Christopher, Diane. BS, Va. Poly. Inst., 1960, MS, 1966; Sr. Mgt. in Govt. degree, Harvard U., 1980. Budget analyst U.S. Treasury Dept., Washington, 1963-68; fin. mgr. AID, Washington, 1968-69, U.S. Dept. Justice, Washington, 1969-74, dep. asst. atty. gen., 1977-84, dep. assoc. atty. gen., 1984-85; mgmt. cons., 1985—; pvt. practice cons., 1986—. Mgmt. advisor Va. Commn. on State Govt. Mgmt., Richmond, 1974-76. Served with U.S. Army, 1954-56. Methodist. Office: 2526 E Meredith Dr Vienna VA 22181-4038

VAN STEENWYK, JOHN JOSEPH, health care plan consultant, educator; b. Mpls., July 25, 1931; s. Elmer Arnold and Marion Ione (Thompson) van S.; m. Janice Kevin Sharp, July 11, 1959; children: Jennifer Lee, Edward Arnold, Julie Ann. AB, Oberlin Coll., 1953; MBA, U. Pa., 1955. V.p., cons. The Segal Co., N.Y.C., 1957—81; pres. Health Econs., Inc., Spring House, Pa., 1982—. Clin. asst. prof. cmty. and preventive medicine N.Y. Med. Coll., Valhalla, NY, 1980—2002. With USN, 1955-57. Mem.: APHA, Am. Assn. Health Plans, Health Ins. Assn. Am., Acad. Health (formerly Assn. for Health Svs. Rsch.). Episcopalian. Avocation: gardening. Home: 921 Tennis Ave Ambler PA 19002-2312 Office: Health Economics Inc 768 N Bethlehem Pike PO Box 710 Spring House PA 19477 E-mail: healtheconomics@compuserve.com.

VAN STONE, WILLIAM WEBB, psychiatrist; b. Denver, Mar. 14, 1929; s. Wilfred Douglas and Cora Coleman (Kampf) Van S.; m. Joan Kay Kinnear, Nov. 27, 1958; children: Lisa Kay, Kathryn Louise, David William. BA, Swarthmore Coll., 1951; MD, Cornell U., 1955. Intern Mary Hitchcock Meml. Hosp., Hanover, N.H., 1955-56; resident Menninger Sch. Psychiatry, Topeka, 1958-61; unit chief Topeka VA Hosp., 1963-67; asst. chief of staff Palo Alto (Calif.) VA Med. Ctr., 1967-89, chief treatment svcs., 1989-2000; assoc. chief

for psychiatry VA Central Office, Washington, 2001—. Clin. assoc. prof. psychiatry emeritus Stanford (Calif.) U. Med. Sch., 1968—; mem. faculty Menninger Sch. Psychiatry, 1963-67. Contbr. 30 articles to profl. jours., chpts. to books. Chmn. bd. Miramonte Mental Health Assn., Palo Alto, 1976; pres. No. Calif. Psychiat. Soc., San Francisco, 1986-87, bd. dirs. Cmty. Sch. Music and Arts, Mountain View, Calif., 1969-75, Parents Family and Friends of Lesbians and Gays, 1996-2003. Capt. USNR, 1956-79. Postdoctoral fellow C.F. Menninger Meml. Hosp., 1961-63. Fellow Am. Psychiat. Assn. (disting. life); mem. Am. Assn. Geriatric Psychiatrists, Washington Psychiat. Assn., Group Advancement Psychiatry (com chmn.). E-mail: wvsdc@aol.com.

VAN SUSTEREN, GRETA CONWAY, news anchor, lawyer; b. Appleton, Wis., June 11, 1954; d. Urban Peter and Margery (Conway) Van Susteren; m. John Purcell Coale, Oct. 12, 1987. BA in Econs, U. Wis., 1976; JD, Georgetown U., 1979, LLM, 1982. Bar: D.C. 1979, U.S. Supreme Ct. 1982, Md. 1985, Wis. 1987, U.S. Ct. Appeals (D.C., 2d and 4th cirs.). Ptnr. Milliken, VanSusteren & Canan, Washington, 1982—; with CNN, 1991—2002, co-host Burden of Proof, legal cons. The World Today; host On the Record With Greta Van Susteren Fox News, 2002—. Adj. prof. Georgetown Law Ctr., Washington, 1985—; lectr., panelist Jud. Conf., Washington, 1986. Bd. dirs. Stuart Stiller Found., Washington, 1982—. Stiller fellow, Georgetown Law Ctr., 1980. Mem.: ATLA (lectr. conf. 1986—), ABA, D.C. Bar Assn.

VAN TASSEL, JAMES HENRY, retired electronics executive; b. LaCrosse, Wis., Feb. 15, 1929; s. John Henry and Agnes Cecilia (Anderson) Van T.; m. Mary Louise Carman, Dec. 23, 1961; children: John Peter, James George. BS, U. Wis.-LaCrosse, 1951; MS, Tex. Tech. Coll., 1957, PhD, 1959. Postdoctoral fellow Princeton U., N.J., 1959-60; mem. tech. staff, mgr. Tex. Instruments Co., Dallas, 1960-80; v.p. microelectronics div. NCR Corp., Dayton, Ohio, 1980-91; ret., 1991. Cons. in field; mem. adv. group on electron devices DOD, 1992-97; bd. dirs. Chartered Semiconductor, Singapore, 1994—. Contbr. articles to profl. jours.; patentee in field; co-inventor of hand-held caculator Bd. dirs. Dayton Philharm. Orch., 1983-89, Miamisburg (Ohio) Mound Cmty. Improvement Corp., 1993—. Recipient Florilege d'Or Am Ecia, Paris, 1976, Disting. Alumnus award U. Wis.-LaCrosse, 1979, Holley medal ASME, 1989. Episcopalian.

VAN TASSEL, LOWELL THOMAS, mathematics professor; b. Mpls., Jan. 31, 1932; s. Evan Thomas Van Tassel and Sophia Anna Huebner; m. Diane Laura Diedrich, June 14, 1953; children: Thomas, Laurie, Karin. BS, U. Minn., 1952, MA, 1962. Cert. secondary tchr. Calif. Rsch. asst. U. Minn., Mpls., 1954-56; math. tchr. San Diego Unified Sch. Dist., 1956-65; prof. math. San Diego C.C. Dist., 1965-92, prof. emeritus of math., 1992—. Dept. chmn. math. dept. San Diego City Coll., 1971-72, 74-75; math/physics instr. Naval Tgn. Ctr., San Diego, 1962-66; proctor profl. engring. exams State of Calif. License Bd., Sacramento, 1957-65. Contbr. articles to profl. jours. V.p. Am. Fedn. of Tchrs., San Diego, 1971-72; faculty advisor Ind. Dems. for Action San Diego City Coll., 1967-71; mem. Clairemont Dem. Club, San Diego, 1966-76; juror, criminal trial Superior Ct., San Diego, 1990; elder Holy Cross Luth. Ch., San Diego, 1972-74, 92-94. With USMC, 1951-54; USMCR, 1954-71, maj., 1966-71. Mem. Math. Assn. Am., Calif. Retired Tchrs. Assn., Marine Corps Mus., U. Minn. Alumni Assn. (life.), Nat. Coun. of Tchrs. of Math., Am. Fedn. of Tchrs. (retiree mem.), Phi Delta Kappa, Psi Chi. Lutheran. Avocations: travel, reading, word puzzles, games, bridge. Home: 5550 Lodi St San Diego CA 92117-1138 E-mail: lowellv@webtv.net.

VAN TATENHOVE, GREGORY F. prosecutor; JD, U. Ky. Aide to U.S. Senator Mitch McConnell, Ky.; law clerk U.S. Dist. Ct., Ky.; trial atty. Justice Dept., Ky.; chief of staff to 2nd dist. U.S. rep. Ron Lewis, Ky.; U.S. atty. ea. dist. U.S. Dept. of Justice, Ky., 2001—. Office: 110 W Vine St Ste 400 Lexington KY 40507-1671

VAN TIL, JON, sociology educator; b. Columbus, Ohio, May 15, 1939; m. Trudy Heller, Jan. 2, 1976; children: Ross, Claire. B.A., Swarthmore Coll., 1961; M.A., U.N.C., 1963; Ph.D., U. Calif.-Berkeley, 1970. Instr. sociology Purdue U., West Lafayette, Ind., 1965-66; instr. Swarthmore (Pa.) Coll., 1966-69, asst. prof., 1969-72; rsch. assoc. Brookings Inst., Washington, 1970-71; exec. dir. Pa. Law and Justice Inst., Phila., 1972-74; prof. dept. urban studies and community devel. Rutgers U., Camden, N.J., 1974—; Fulbright disting. prof. U. Ulster, 2004; receipent Career award for Disting. Rsch. and Svc., Nonprofit Orgn. and Vol. Action, 1994. Carlson disting. vis. chair W.Va. U., 2004. Author: Mapping the Third Sector, 1988, Critical Issues in American Philanthropy, 1990, Growing Civil Society, 2000; contbr. articles to profl. jours.; editor-in-chief: Nonprofit and Voluntary Sector Quarterly, 1979-92. Mem. Phi Beta Kappa. Office: Rutgers U Urban Studies Camden NJ 08102

VAN TIL, WILLIAM, education educator, writer; b. Corona, NY, Jan. 8, 1911; s. William Joseph and Florence Alberta (MacLean) Van T.; m. Beatrice Barbara Blaha, Aug. 24, 1935; children: Jon, Barbara, Roy. BA, Columbia U., 1933; MA, Tchrs. Coll., 1935; PhD, Ohio State U., 1946. Tchr. N.Y. State Tng. Sch. for Boys, 1933-34; instr. dept. univ. schs. Coll. Edn., Ohio State U., 1934-36, asst. prof., 1936-43, on leave, 1943-45; researchist, writer Consumer Edn. Study NEA, 1943-44; dir. learning materials Bur. Intercultural Edn., 1944-47; prof. edn. U. Ill., 1947-51; prof. edn., chmn. div. curriculum and teaching George Peabody Coll. Tchrs., Nashville, 1951-57; prof. edn., chmn. dept. secondary edn. N.Y. U., 1957-66, head div. secondary and higher edn., 1966-67; Coffman disting. prof. edn. Ind. State U., Terre Haute, 1967-77, prof. emeritus, 1977; dir. univ. workshops Writing for Profl. Publs., 1978—; founder Lake Lure Press, 1983. Author: The Danube Flows Through Fascism, Economic Roads for American Democracy, The Making of a Modern Educator, Modern Education for the Junior High School Years, The Year 2000: Teacher Education, One Way of Looking At It, Education: A Beginning, Another Way of Looking At It, Van Til on Education, Secondary Education: School and Community, Writing for Professional Publication, rev., 1986; autobiography My Way of Looking At It, 1983, expanded 2d edit., 1996; Sketches, 1989, Admonitions and Challenges, 2002; editor: Forces Affecting American Education, Curriculum: Quest for Relevance, ASCD in Retrospect, 1986, Critique on Work Teaching Education, 1993; author: Teachers and Mentors: Profiles of Distinguished Twentieth Century Professors of Education, 1996, U. S.C. dissertation, William Van Til: Pub. Intellectual, 2002; co-editor: Democratic Human Relations, Intercultural Attitudes in the Making, Education in American Life; adv. editor Houghton Mifflin, 1964-70; interviewed in Social Education, 1989, Preface to the Eight Year Study Revisited, 1998; contbr. articles to profl. jours., popular mags. including Saturday Rev., Woman's Day, Parents; columnist: Ednl. Leadership, Contemporary Edn., Kappan; adv. bd. Profl. Educator, 1984-95. Mem. Ill. Interracial Commn., 1949-51; moderator Nashville Sch. desegregation meetings, 1955-57; mem. adv. bd. Jour. Tchr. Edn., 1956-59; co-organizer Nashville Community Rels. Conf., 1956; cons. Phelps-Stokes Fund project, 1958-62; mem. staff P.R. Edn. Survey, 1958-59, Iran Tchr. Edn. Survey, 1962, V.I. Edn. Survey, 1964; lectr. abroad, 1974; mem. staff U. Ind. Phi Delta Kappa Inst., 1984-90; 1st Ann. Van Til lectr. Ind. State U., 1989. Recipient Centennial Achievement award, Ohio State U., 1970; awards N.J. Collegiate Press Assn., 1962; N.J. Assn. Tchrs. English, 1962; named to Edn. Hall of Fame, Ohio State U., 1989; Annual Van Til Lectr. Series, Ind. State U., est. 1989, est. Annual Van Til Writing award, 1989, award of recognition Spring conf., 1999. Mem. John Dewey Soc. (v.p. 1957-60, acting pres. 1958-59, pres. 1964-66, award 1977, 86, Outstanding Achievement award 1991), Assn. Supervision and Curriculum Devel. (dir. 1951-54, 57-60, pres. 1961-62, chmn. rev. council 1972-73, resolutions com. 1982-85), United Educators (chmn. bd. educators 1969-77), Nat. Soc. Coll. Tchrs. Edn. (pres. 1967-68), Am. Edn. Studies Assn. (editorial bd. 1970-77), Asso. Orgn. Tchr. Edn. (adv. council 1967-73, chmn. issues tchr. edn. 1972-73), Nat. Soc. Study Edn. (editor Yearbook Issues in Secondary Edn. 1976), Kappa Delta Pi (laureate 1980—, chmn. book-of-yr. com. 1984-86, contbr. Honor in Teaching Reflections 1990). Home: 1120 E Davis Dr Terre Haute IN 47802-4065 *As an educator and writer, I believe that mankind's best hope is education which meets individual needs, illuminates social realities, fosters democratic values and utilizes relevant knowledge.*

VAN TINE, KIRK KELSO, federal agency administrator; b. Syracuse, N.Y., Aug. 30, 1948; s. George Kelso and Hariot (Van Alst) V.; m. Barbara Ann Byers, Aug. 14, 1971; children: Lindsay, Meredith. BS in Fgn. Affairs, U.S. Naval Acad., 1970; JD, U. Va., 1978. Bar: D.C. 1978, U.S. Ct. Appeals (D.C. crct.) 1979, U.S. Ct. Appeals (5th crct.) 1980, U.S. Ct. Appeals (8th crct.) 1992, U.S. Ct. Appeals (9th crct.) 1992, U.S. Ct. Appeals (10th crct.) 1993, U.S. Supreme Ct., 1982, U.S. Dist. Ct. D.C. 1979. Commd. ensign USN, 1970, advanced through grades to lt., 1974, resigned, 1975; assoc. Baker & Botts, Washington, 1978-86, ptnr., 1986—2001; gen. counsel U.S. Dept. Transp., Washington, 2001—03, acting dep. sec., 2003—04, dep. sec., 2004—. Mem.: Order of Coif, D.C. Bar Assn. (co-chair litig. and law practice mgmt. sect., chair election bd.). Office: US Dept Transp 400 Seventh St SW Rm 10200 Washington DC 20590 E-mail: kirk.vantine@ost.dot.gov.*

VAN TINE, MATTHEW ERIC, lawyer; b. Tomahawk, Wis., June 21, 1958; s. Kenneth G. and Louise (Olson) Van T.; m. Rena Marie David, Apr. 30, 1988; 1 child, Kristen. AB cum laude, Harvard Coll., 1980; JD magna cum laude, Boston U., 1983. Bar: Ill. 1983, Mass. 1983, U.S. Dist. Ct. Mass. 1984, U.S. Dist. Ct. (no. dist.) Ill. 1986, Seventh Cir., 2001. Law clk. to Hon. Raymond J. Pettine U.S. Dist. Ct. R.I., Providence, 1983-84; assoc. Palmer & Dodge, Boston, 1984-85, Schiff, Hardin & Waite, Chgo., 1985-88; asst. corp. counsel City of Chgo., 1988-92; assoc. to ptnr. Saunders & Monroe, Chgo., 1993-99; of counsel Miller Faucher and Cafferty, Chgo., 2000—. Exec. editor: Boston University Law Rev., 1982-83. Mem. ABA, Chgo. Bar Assn., Inns of Ct. Office: Miller Faucher and Cafferty 30 N Lasalle St Ste 3200 Chicago IL 60602-2506 E-mail: mvantine@millerfaucher.com.

VAN TOL, JENIFER, music educator, musician; b. Little Rock, June 23, 1947; d. Charles F. and Christine O. Edwards; m. Willem C. van Tol, Dec. 14, 1991; children: Stephan Russ, Christiana Russ, John Russ, Erik. BS, Ind. U., 1968; cert. violin tchr., Hamburg (Germany) Conservatory, 1971. Lic. tchr. Tenn. Tchr. English and music Hamburg Gymnasium, 1972—81; profl. violinist Knoxville Symphony, 1982—87; tchr. string orch. Oak Ridge (Tenn.) City Schs., 1987—. Pvt. violin tchr., Hamburg, 1970—81, Oak Ridge, 1981—. Mem.: ASTA (Tenn. pres.-elect 2004—), Music Educators Nat. Conf. Episcopalian. Avocations: reading, knitting, walking. Home: 809 Gulfwood Rd Knoxville TN 37923 Office: Oak Ridge HS 127 Providence Rd Oak Ridge TN 37830

VAN TREASE, SANDRA ANN, insurance company executive; b. St. Louis, Dec. 11, 1960; m. Virgil Van Trease; children: Shawna, Erin. BSBA, U. Mo., St. Louis, 1982; MBA, Washington U., St. Louis, 1992. CPA, Mo.; cert. mgmt. acct., Mo. Sr. mgr. audit divsn. Price Waterhouse, St. Louis, 1982-94; v.p. fin. rep. and investor rels. Alliance Blue Cross/Blue Shield, St. Louis, 1994-95, sr. v.p., CFO, 1995-97, exec. v.p., COO, CFO, 1997—. Author practice cases, 1988, 90. Treas. Art-St. Louis, 1992-94, St. Louis County Fair and Air Show, 1993-94; chmn. adminstrn. Fair St. Louis, 1994-96; bd. dirs. Nat. Multiple Sclerosis Soc., 1997-98, Caring Program for Children, 1998—. Mem. AICPA, Fin. Execs. Inst., Inst. Mgmt. Accts., Mo. Soc. CPA's. Office: Alliance Blue Cross/Blue Shield 1831 Chestnut St Saint Louis MO 63103-2231

VAN TUYL, CECIL L. investment company executive; Chmn., pres., CEO VT Inc., Merriam, Kans. Office: V T Inc PO Box 795 Shawnee Mission KS 66201-0795

VAN TUYLE, GREGORY JAY, nuclear engineer; b. Chgo., Feb. 19, 1953; s. Willard D. and Mary E. (Kershner) Van Tuyle; m. Frances E. Weinstein, Aug. 16, 1994; 1 child, William Steven. BSE magna cum laude, U. Mich., 1975, MSE, 1976, PhD of Nuclear Engring., 1978. From dep. divsn. head to program mgr. Brookhaven Nat. Lab., Upton, NY, 1978-97; program mgr. Los Alamos (N.Mex.) Nat. Lab., 1997—; assoc. dir. Ctr. Homeland Security, 2004—. Contbr. articles to profl. jours. Mem.: Am. Nuc. Soc. (reactor safety divsn. program com. sec. to vice-chmn. 1991—96, chmn. 1996—97, past pres., v.p., treas. L.I. chpt. 1979—97, founder, chair accelerator applications divsn. 1996—98), Brookhaven Nat. Lab. Toastmasters (pres., v.p. 1990—95, award 1991, 1992, 1994). Achievements include performing computer simulation of Chernobyl-4 accident based on Soviet explanation prior to release of Soviet analyses, confirming similarities and evaluating differences. Office: Los Alamos Nat Lab PO Box 1663 Mail Stop K488 Los Alamos NM 87544-0600

VAN TYNE, ARTHUR MORRIS, geologist; b. Syracuse, NY, Aug. 12, 1925; s. Roy Hanford and Isabelle Marguerite (Hoag) Van T.; m. Patricia Wilson Boyd, July 13, 1946; children: Judith, Cynthia, Mark, Peter. AB, Syracuse U., 1951, MS, 1958. Cert. petroleum geologist; lic. geologist, Pa., 1994. Field asst. Syracuse U. Rsch. Inst., 1951-53; geologist Shell Oil Co., Rockies, Gulf Coast, 1953-57; sr. geologist-in-charge NY State Geol. Survey-Oil and Gas Rsch. Office, Wellsville and Alfred, NY, 1958-81; geol. cons. Van Tyne Cons., Wellsville, NYC, NY, 1981—. Gov. appointee mem. NY State Oil, Gas, and Solution Mining Adv. Bd., 1996. Contbr. articles to profl. jours. Dep. mayor Village of Wellsville, 1992—2004; mem. Allegany County Econ. Devel. Com.; committeeman Rep. Party, 1962—77, 1998—2000; bd. dir. Jones Meml. Hosp., Wellsville, 1973—2001, bd. chmn., 1986—95; bd. dir. Wellsville United Way, 1968—80, pres., 1974—75; bd. mem. Drake Well Found. Recipient Cert. of Appreciation Am. Petroleum Inst., 1975, 80, Award of Merit Internat. Oil Scouts Assn. and Appalachian Sect., 1961, 66, 88. Mem.: Syracuse U. Geol. Devel. Coun., Geol. Soc. Am., No. Appalachian Geol. Soc. (pres. 1966—68), Ind. Oil and gas Assn. NY (pres. 1985—88), N.Y. State Oil Prodrs. Assn. (exec. com. 1980—, dir., Svc. award 1981, Oilman of Yr. award 2001), Russian Assn. Oil and Gas Geologists, Am. Assn. Petroleum Geologists (sec., dir. 1989—91, nat. and ea. sect. hon. mem., Nat. and Ea. Disting. Svc. award 1987, 1994, John T. Galey Meml. award ea. sect. 1997, Ho. of Dels. long svc. award 2001), N.Y. Acad. Sci., Rotary (pres. Wellsville 1979—80, Paul Harris fellow). Achievements include discovery of gas production from Queenston formation in NY; Bass Islands thrust structure, a major oil and gas producer in N.Y. and Pa.; contributed for N.Y. State to Appalachian Gas Atlas. Home: 24 Oak St Wellsville NY 14895-1026 Office: Van Tyne Cons PO Box 326 159 1/2 N Main St Wellsville NY 14895-0326 Office Phone: 585-593-6650. Personal E-mail: avantyne@yahoo.com.

VAN UMMERSEN, CLAIRE A(NN), academic administrator, biologist, educator; b. Chelsea, Mass., July 28, 1935; d. George and Catherine (Courtovich); m. Frank Van Ummersen, June 7, 1958; children: Lynn, Scott. BS, Tufts U., 1957, MS, 1960, PhD, 1963; DSc (hon.), U. Mass., 1988, U. Maine, 1991. Rsch. asst. Tufts U., 1957-60, 60-67, grad. asst. in embryology, 1962, postdoctoral tchg. asst., 1963-66, lectr. in biology, 1967-68; asst. prof. biology U. Mass., Boston, 1968-74, assoc. prof., 1974—86, assoc. dean acad. affairs, 1975-76, assoc. vice chancellor acad. affairs, 1976-78, chancellor, 1978-79, dir. Environ. Sci. Ctr., 1980-82; assoc. vice chancellor acad. affairs Mass. Bd. Regents for Higher Edn., 1982-85, vice chancellor for mgmt. systems and telecom., 1985-86; chancellor Univ. System N.H., Durham, 1986-92; sr. fellow New Eng. Bd. Higher Edn., 1992-93; sr. fellow New Eng. Resource Ctr. Higher Edn. U. Mass., 1992-93; pres. Cleve. State U., 1993—2001; v.p., dir. Office of Women Am. Coun. Edn., 2001—. Cons. Mass. Bd. Regents, 1981-82, AGB, 1992—, Kuwait U., 1992-93; asst. Lancaster Course in Ophthalmology, Mass. Eye and Ear Infirmary, 1962-69, lectr., 1970-93, also coord.; reviewer HEW; mem. rsch. team which established safety stds. for exposure to microwave radiation, 1958-65; participant Leadership Am. program, 1992-93; bd. dirs. Nat. Coun. Sci. Environment, 1998—, mem. subcom. for future and fin. Active N.H. Ct. Systems Rev. Task Force, 1989-90, Leadership Cleve. Class '95, Gov.'s Coun. on Sci. and Tech., 1996-98, Strategy Coun. Cleve. Pub. Schs., 1996-98, Cleve. Sports Commn., 1999-2001, Cleve. Mcpl. Sch. Dist. Bd., 1999-2001; New Eng. Bd. Higher Edn., 1986-92, exec. com., 1989-92, N.H. adv. coun., 1990-92; chair Rhodes Scholarship Selection Com., 1986-91; bd. dirs. N.H. Bus. and Industry Assn., 1987-93; governing bd. N.H. Math. Coalition, 1991-92; exec. com. 21st Century Learning Cmty., 1992-93; state panelist N.H. Women in Higher Edn., 1986-93; bd. dirs. Urban League Greater Cleve., 1993-2001, strategic planning com., chair edn. com., 1996-99, sec., exec. com., 1997-99; bd. dirs. Great Lakes Sci. and Tech. Ctr., 1993-2001, edn. com., 1995-2001; bd. dirs. Greater Cleve. Growth Assn., 1994-2001, Civic Vision 2000 and Beyond, Cleve., 1997-98; bd. dirs., exec. com. Sci. and Tech. Coun. Cleve. Tomorrow, 1998-99; rep. N.E. Ohio Tech. Coalition, 1999-2001; trustee Ohio Aerospace Inst., 1993-2001, exec. com., 1996-2001; strategic planning com. United Way, 1996-2000, chair environ. scan subcom. 1996-2001; leadership devel. com. ACE, 1995-98, women's commn., 1999-2001; bd. dirs. United Way, 1995-2001; co-chair Pub. Sector Campaign, 1997-98; bd. dirs. NCAA, divsn. 1, exec. com., 1999-2001; mem. AGB Ctr. for Pub. Higher Edn. Trusteeship and Goverance, 2001-03, Assn. Liaison Officers Adv. Com., 1998-2001. Recipient Disting. Svc. medal U. Mass., 1979, Woman of the Yr. Achievement award YWCA, 1998; Am. Cancer Soc. grantee Tufts U., 1960. Mem. Am. Coun. on Edn. (com. on self-regulation 1987-91), Nat. Conf. Cmty. and Justice (program com. 1996-2001), Nat. Coun. for Sci. and the Environment (bd. dirs. 1999-, fin. and futures coms.), State Higher Exec. Officers (fed. rels. com., 1986-92, cost accountability task force, exec. com. 1990-92), ACE (com. leadership devel.), Nat. Assn. Sys. Heads (exec. com. 1990-92), Nat. Ctr. for Edn. Stats. (network adv. com. 1989-92), New Eng. Assn. Schs. and Colls. (commn. on higher edn. 1990-93), North Ctrl. Assn. Schs. and Colls. (evaluator 1993-2001, chair accreditation teams 1986-90), Greater Cleve. Round Table (bd. dirs. 1993-2001, exec. com. 1995-2001), Cleve. Playhouse (trustee 1994-2001), Nat. Assn. State Univs. and Land Grant Colls. (exec. com. on urban agenda, mem. commn. tech. transfer, state rep.), Am. Assn. State Colls. and Univs. (commn. on urban agenda 1996-2001, bd. dirs. 1996-99, mem. emerging issues task force 1996-98), Phi Beta Kappa, Sigma Xi. Office: American Coun on Edn One DuPont Cir NW Washington DC 20036-1193 Office Phone: 202-939-9390. Business E-Mail: claire_van_ummersen@ace.nche.edu.

VAN VACTOR, MYRA FLORENDO, school librarian, director; d. Tomas Baltazar and Luz Valencia Florendo; m. Lloyd Van Vactor, Apr. 2, 1981. M in Libr. Sci., Columbia U., N.Y.C., 1983. Cert. libr. Wash., 1992. Supr. access services Columbia U. Libraries, N.Y.C., 1981—83; systems analyst Fed. Res. Bank of N.Y., N.Y.C., 1983—90, asst. chief law libr., 1990—92; dir., libr. media ctr. Bellevue CC, Wash., 1995—. Mem.: ALA. Home: 17665 NE 129th Pl Redmond WA 98052 Office: Bellevue CC 3000 Landerholm Circ SE Bellevue WA 98007

VAN VALER, JOE NED, lawyer, land developer; b. Gas City, Ind., Mar. 13, 1935; s. Richard Carl and Wilma Amy (Kelly) Van V.; m. Constance Joy Richardson, June 25, 1960; children: Kimberly Joy, Kelli June, Lynn Louise, Joseph Jeffrey. AB, Franklin Coll., 1959; LLB, Ind. U., 1963. Bar: Ind. 1963, U.S. Dist. Ct. (so. dist.) Ind. 1963. Assoc. Van Valer Law Firm and predecessor firms, 1963-65, ptnr., 1965-75, sr. ptnr., 1975—. Pres. Home Owners Warranty Corp. of Central Ind., Indpls., 1984-91, chmn. bd. dirs. 1991-95; cons. bd. Nat. City Bank Greenwood; chmn. adv. group Home Owners Warranty Corp., Washington, 1988-90, 92-94 also bd. dirs.; pros. atty. 8th Jud. Dist., Franklin, Ind., 1967-74; chmn. Johnson County, Ind., Contractors' Listing Bd.; chmn. bd. Bldg. Industry Svc. Corp., 1995-2000. With AUS, 1957-58. Recipient Alumnus Citation award Franklin Coll., 1996. Mem. ABA, Indpls. Bar Assn., 8th Jud. Cir. Bar Assn., Nat. Assn. Home Builders (bd. dirs.), Ind. Home Builders Assn., Builders Assn. Greater Indpls. (dir.), Indpls. Soc. Republican. Methodist. Office: Van Valer Law Firm 299 W Main St Greenwood IN 46142-3129 E-mail: Joe@vanvalerlaw.com.

VAN VALKENBURG, EDGAR WALTER, lawyer; b. Seattle, Jan. 8, 1953; s. Edgar Walter and Margaret Catherine (McKenna) Van V.; m. Turid L. Owren, Sept. 29, 1990; children: Ingrid Catherine, Andrew Owren. BA, U. Wash., 1975; JD summa cum laude, Willamette Coll. of Law, 1978; LLM, Columbia U., 1984. Bar: Oreg. 1978, U.S. Dist. Ct. Oreg. 1979, U.S. Ct. Appeals (9th cir.) 1980. Law clk. to assoc. justice Oreg. Supreme Ct., Salem, 1978-79; assoc. Stoel, Rives, Boley, Fraser & Wyse, Portland, Oreg., 1979-82, 84-86; ptnr. Stoel Rives LLP, Portland, Oreg., 1986—; instr. Columbia U., N.Y.C., 1982-84. Bd. dirs. Oreg. Sports Authority; chair Oreg. Econ. and Cmty. Devel. Commn., 2003—. Editor-in-chief: Willamette Law Jour. 1977-78. Bd. dirs., chmn. Multnomah County Legal Aid, 1997-98; bd. dirs. Portland Ctr. Stage, 2004—. Mem. ACLU (pres. Oreg. chpt. 1991-93), Oreg. State Bar (chmn. antitrust sect. 1989-90, mem. Ho. of Dels. 1996-98). Office: Stoel Rives LLP 900 SW 5th Ave Ste 2300 Portland OR 97204-1229 E-mail: wvanvalkenburg@stoel.com.

VAN VLECK, FRED SCOTT, mathematician, educator, researcher; b. Clearwater, Nebr., Dec. 12, 1934; s. Harold F. Van Vleck and Patricia A. Scott; m. Charlotte T. Allen, June 18, 1960; children: Erik S., Paul F., Karl J., Kristina M., Teresa A. BS, U. Nebr., 1956, MA, 1957; PhD, U. Minn., 1960. Instr. math. MIT, Cambridge, Mass., 1960—62; asst. prof. math. U. Kans., Lawrence, 1962—65, assoc. prof. math., 1965—68, prof. math., 1968—2004, prof. emeritus, 2004—. Chancellors Club tchg. prof. math. U. Kans., Lawrence, 1985. Co-author: (rsch. monograph) Linear Systems over Commutative Rings, 1986; contbr. articles to profl. jours. Mem.: Math. Assn. Am., Soc. for Indsl. and Applied Math., Am. Math. Soc. Avocations: genealogy, running. Office: Univ Kans Dept Math Jayhawk Blvd Lawrence KS 66045 E-mail: vanvleck@math.ukans.edu.

VAN VLEET, WILLIAM BENJAMIN, retired lawyer, life insurance company executive; b. Milw., Dec. 4, 1924; s. William Benjamin and Irene (Peppey) Van V.; m. Marilyn Nilles, Dec. 26, 1946; children: Terese Van Vleet Svetich, Susan Van Vleet Waldo, William Benjamin III, Monica Van Vleet McCarthy, Mark. Student, Marquette U., 1942-43, Lawrence Coll., Appleton, Wis., 1943-44; LLB, JD, Marquette U., 1948. Bar: Wis. 1948, Ill. 1950. Gen. counsel George Rogers Clark Mut. Casualty Co., Rockford, Ill., 1948-59, Pioneer Life Ins. Co. Ill., Rockford, 1950-68, 81-94, v.p., 1959-91, gen. counsel, 1968-91, exec. v.p., 1981-95, also bd. dirs.; exec. v.p., gen. counsel Pioneer Fin. Svcs., Inc., Rockford, 1985-95, gen. counsel emeritus, dir., 1995-97; pres. Nat. Group Life Ins. Co., Rockford, 1992-93, exec. v.p., gen. counsel, 1993-94, also bd. dirs. Pres. Western Life Ins. Co. Am., Rockford, 1981-82, Health & Life Ins. Co. Am., Rockford, 1984-92, exec. v.p., gen. counsel, 1993-94; pres. Manhattan Nat. Life Ins. Co., Cin., 1990-92, exec. v.p., gen. counsel, 1993-94, also bd. dirs.; exec. v.p., gen. counsel Continental Life and Accident Co., Boise, Idaho, 1993-94, also bd. dirs.; bd. dirs. Nat. Health Svcs. Milw. Mem. adminstrn. Boylan Ctrl. Cath. H.S., Rockford, 1965-72; pres. Diocesan Bd. Edn., Rockford, 1970-78; v.p., pres. Nat. Assn. Bds. Edn., 1972-78; mem. bd. advisors Marion Coll., 1976-79; mem. adv. bd. St. Anthony's Hosp., Rockford, 1978-91; bd. dirs. Crimestoppers, Rockford, 1982-90; co-chmn. United Cerebral Palsy Telethon, Rockford, 1985-95. Mem. Ill. Bar Assn., Winnebago County Bar Assn.

VAN VLIET, CAROLYNE MARINA, physicist, researcher; b. Dordrecht, Netherlands, Dec. 27, 1929; arrived in U.S., 1960, naturalized, 1967; d. Marinus and Jacoba (de Lange) Van V. BS, Free U. Amsterdam, Netherlands, 1949, MA, 1953, PhD in Physics, 1956. Rsch. fellow Free U. Amsterdam, 1950-54, rsch. assoc., 1954-56, asst. dir., 1958-60; postdoctoral fellow U. Minn., Mpls., 1956-57, faculty, 1957-58, 60-70, prof. elec. engring. and physics, 1965-70; prof. theoretical physics U. Montreal, Que., Can., 1969-95, sr. rschr. math. rsch. ctr., 1969-2000, prof. emerita, 1998—. Vis. prof. U. Fla., 1974, 78-88; prof. elec. and computer engring. Fla. Internat. U., 1992-2000; adj. prof. physics U. Miami, 2001—. Contbg. author: Fluctuation Phenomena in Solids, 1965; contbr. articles to profl. jours. Rsch. grantee NSF, Air Force OSR, Nat. Sci. and Engring. Rsch. Coun., Ottawa. Fellow IEEE (life); mem. Am. Phys. Soc., N.Y. Acad. Scis. Office: U Miami James L Knight Physics Bldg 1320 Campo Sano Dr Coral Gables FL 33146 Office Phone: 305-284-2323. E-mail: vanvliet@physics.miami.edu. *The purpose of life is to honor God and to serve mankind.*

VAN VLIET, CLAIRE, artist; b. Ottawa, Ont., Can., Aug. 9, 1933; d. Wilbur Dennison and Audrey Ilene (Wallace) Van V. AB, San Diego State Coll., 1952; MFA, Claremont Grad. Sch., 1954; DFA (hon.), U. of the Arts, Phila., 1993, San Diego State U., 2002. Instr. printmaking Phila. Coll. Art, 1959-65; owner The Janus Press, 1954—; vis. lectr. printmaking U. Wis.-Madison, 1965-66. Mem. bd. advisors Hand Papermaking. One-man exhbns. include Print Club Phila., 1963, 66, 73, 77, Wiggin Gallery, Boston Pub. Libr., 1977, Rutgers U. Art Gallery, 1978, AAA Gallery, Phila., 1980, Dolan/Maxwell Gallery, Phila., 1984, 91, Mary Ryan Gallery, N.Y.C., 1986, Mills Coll., 1986, U. of the Arts, Phila., 1989, Victoria and Albert Mus., London, 1994, Ottawa Sch. of Art

Gallery, Can., 1994, Bates Coll. Mus. of Art, Lewiston, Maine, 1994, 99, N.D. Mus. Art, 1999, Rosenwald Wolf Gallery Univ. Arts.Phila, 2001; group exhbns. include Bklyn. Nat., Phila. Arts Festival, Kunst zu Kafka, Germany, Paper as Medium, Smithsonian Instn., Washington, Paper Now, Cleve. Mus. Art, 1986, Boyle Arts Festival, Ireland, 1993, Libr. Congress, 1997—, N.D. Mus. Art, 1999; represented in permanent collections Nat. Gallery Art, Phila. Mus. Art, Boston Pub. Libr., Libr. of Congress, Cleve. Mus. Art, Montreal Mus. Fine Arts, Victoria and Albert Mus. London, Tate Gallery, London. NEA grantee, 1976-80, Ingram-Merrill Found. grantee, 1989; MacArthur fellow, 1989-94. Mem. NAD, Soc. Printers Boston, Vt. Arts and Scis. Address: 101 Schoolhouse Rd Newark VT 05871-9773 Office Phone: 802-467-3335.

VAN VOORST, ROBERT E. theology educator, minister; b. Holland, Mich, June 5, 1952; s. Robert Eugene and Donna Mae (Boeve) Van V.; m. Mary Lind Bos, June 15, 1974; children: Richard William, Nicholas John. BA, Hope Coll., 1974; MDiv, Western Sem., 1977; PhD, Union Sem., N.Y., 1988. Ordained to ministry Classis of Holland Reformed Ch. in Am., 1977. Pastor Rochester Reformed Ch., Accord, NY, 1977-89; prof. religion Lycoming Coll., Williamsport, Pa., 1989-99, dept. chair, 1997-99; prof. New Testament Western Theol. Sem., Holland, Mich., 1999—. Adj. prof. Susquehanna U., Selinsgrove, Pa., 1991, Bucknell U., Lewisburg, Pa., 1993; vis. prof. Westminster Coll., Oxford, Eng., 1997; N.T. seminar lectr. Oxford U., 2000; interim pastor Lycoming Presbyn. Ch., Williamsport, 1997-99. Author: Ascents of James, 1989, Building New Testament Vocabulary, 1990, 3d edit., 2001, Anthology of World Scriptures, 1994, 4th edit., 2002, Readings in Christianity, 1996, 2d edit., 2000, Anthology of Asian Scriptures, 1999, Jesus Outside the New Testament, 2000, Italian edit., 2004, Reading the New Testament Today, 2004; co-author: Death of Jesus in Early Christianity, 1998; editor Reformed Rev., 2000--; contbr. articles Eerdmans Dictionary of the Bible, 2001, Ency. of Jesus in History, Culture and Thought, 2003, Eerdmans Bible Commentary, 2003; contbr. numerous articles to profl. jour. Mem. Phi Beta Kappa, Phi Kappa Phi, Eta Sigma Phi, Phi Sigma Iota. Avocations: golf, cooking. Home: 1114 Post Ave Holland MI 49424-2550 Office: Western Theol Sem 101 E 13th St Holland MI 49423-3622 Business E-Mail: bob.vanvoorst@westernsem.edu.

VAN WACHEM, LODEWIJK CHRISTIAAN, petroleum company executive; b. Pangkalan Brandan, Indonesia, July 31, 1931; m. Elisabeth G. Cristofoli, June 10, 1958; 3 children. Degree Mech. Engring., Delft U., Delft, The Netherlands., 1953. With Bataafsche Petroleum Maatschappij, The Hague, The Netherlands, 1953; pres. Royal Dutch Petroleum Co., The Hague, The Netherlands, 1982-92; chmn. com. mng. dir. Royal Dutch/Shell Group, The Hague, The Netherlands, 1985-92; chmn. supr. bd. Royal Dutch Petroleum Co., The Hague, Netherlands, 1992—2002. Chmn. bd. dirs. Shell Oil Co. USA, 1982—92; supervisory bd. De Nederlandsche Bank N.V., 1987—92; non. exec. dir. IBM Corp., Armonk, 1992—2002, Credit Suisse Holding, Zurich, 1992—96, Atco Ltd., Calgary, 1993—, AAB Area Brown Boveri Ltd, Zurich, 1996—99; supervisory bd. AKZO Nobel n.v., Arnhem, 1992—2002, Philips Electronics n.v., Amsterdam, 1993—, BMW A.G., Munich, 1994—2002, Bayer A.G., Leverkusen, 1997—2002; chmn. bd. dirs. Zurich Fin. Svcs., 2002—, Globa. Crossing Ltd., 2004—. Decorated C.B.E. (hon.), Knight Brit. Empire (hon.), Comdr. Order of Oranje Nassau, Knight Order Netherlands Lion, Pub. Svc. Star (Singapore). Office: Zurich Financial Svcs Muzenstraat 31 PO Box 16999 2500 BZ The Hague Netherlands Office Phone: 31 70 418 4798.

VAN WAGENEN, JEFFREY ANTHONY, prosecutor, consultant; b. Downey, Calif., June 27, 1972; s. Jeffrey Anthony and Cheryl Ann Van Wagenen; m. Dawn Nicole Osti, May 31, 1997; children: Tyler Anthony children: Brittany Nicole. JD, U. Calif., Hastings, 1997; BA, U. So. Calif., 1994. Sole propr. Law Offices of Jeffrey A. Van Wagenen, Riverside, Calif., 2000—; dep. dist. atty. Riverside County, Riverside, Calif., 1997—2000; apprentice investigator Mc Mackin Investigations, San Francisco, 1995—97; polit. cons. Eddie Mahe Co., Wahington, DC, 1992; congl. intern Congressman Robert K. Dornan, Garden Grove, Calif., 1991—92. Chmn. of criminal law sect. Riverside County Bar Assn., Riverside, 2002—, jud. liason bd. mem., Calif., 2002—; adv. bd. mem. Vols. in Parole, Riverside, Calif., 2000—. Recipient Employee of the Month, Riverside County Dist. Attorney's Office, 1998, 1999. Mem.: Calif. Attorneys Criminal Justice, Nat. Assn. Criminal Def. Lawyers, Leo Deegan Inn of Ct. (assoc. 2000). R-Consevative. Roman Catholic. Office: Law Offices of Jeffrey Van Wagenen Jr 4129 Main St Ste 207 Riverside CA 92501

VAN WAGNER, ELLEN, lawyer, law educator; b. Chgo., Dec. 10, 1942; d. Paul David and Eleanor (Sullivan) Van W.; m. Burton Neal Genda, Mar. 27, 1964 (div.); children: Kevin Paul, Kelly Elan. BA, U. Ariz., 1964; MA, Calif. State U., L.A., 1971; JD, U. La Verne, 1984. Bar: Calif. 1984, U.S. Dist. Ct. (cen. dist.) Calif. 1985, U.S. Ct. Appeals (9th cir.) 1985. Tchr., adminstr. Baldwin Park (Calif.) Sch. Dist., 1965-81; ptnr. Rose, Klein & Marias, Pomona, Calif., 1985-94. Prof. U. La Verne (Calif.) Coll. Law, 1987—. Writer, asst. editor U. La Verne Law Rev., 1981-83, editor-in-chief, 1983-84. Chmn. youth activities commn. City of Baldwin Park, 1971-81. Recipient Humanitarian and Svc. awards L.A. Human Rels. Commn., 1976, 77. Mem. Calif. Bar Assn., L.A. County Bar Assn., Ea. County Bar Assn., Phi Delta Theta. Avocations: travel, sports. Home: PO Box 351 Blue Jay CA 92317-0351 Office: Law Offices Ellen Van Wagner 12474 Central Ave Ste B Chino CA 91710-2664

VAN WART, HAROLD E. biotechnology company executive; BA, SUNY, Binghamton; MS, PhD, Cornell U. Faculty Fla. State U., 1978—92; v.p., dir. Inst. Biochemistry and Cell Biology Syntex, 1992—99; v.p., therapy area head for arthritis and fibrosis diseases Roche Biosci., 1999—2000; v.p. R&D Metabolex Inc., Hayward, Calif., 2000—01, pres., COO, 2001—. Faculty Stanford U., Calif., Harvard Med. Sch., Boston. Contbr. over 100 articles to profl. jours. Office: Metabolex Inc 3876 Bay Center Pl Hayward CA 94545

VAN WAY, CHARLES WARD, III, surgery educator, research scientist; b. Ft. Jay, N.Y., May 1, 1939; s. Charles Ward and Hazel (Shattuck) Van W.; children: Craig Brandon, Brian Ward; m. Gail E. Wilson, Sept. 12, 1987; 1 child, Whitney Elizabeth. BA, Yale U., 1960; MD, Johns Hopkins U., 1964. Diplomate Am. Bd. Surgery-Surg. Critical Care, Am. Bd. Thoracic and Cardiovascular Surgery. Resident in surgery Vanderbilt U., Nashville, 1964-72; prof., dir. surg. nutrition U. Colo. Sch. Medicine, Denver, 1985-88; fellow in clin. pharmacology Vanderbilt U., Nashville, 1967-69; asst. prof. surgery U. Colo. Sch. Medicine, Denver, 1974-78, assoc. prof., 1978-85; chief surgery Denver Gen. Hosp., 1978-85; prof. surgery U. Mo., Kansas City, 1988—, vice-chmn., 1995—2000, chmn., 2000—. Program dir. surgery St. Luke's Hosp., Kansas City, Mo., 1988—95, U. Mo., Kansas City, 2000—02, Kansas City, 2003—, dir. shock-trauma rsch. ctr., 2002—. Author: Surgical Skills in Patient Care, 1978, Pocket Manual of Basic Surgical Skills, 1988; editor: Critical Decisions in Trauma, 1984, Handbook of Surgical Nutrition, 1991, Nutritional Secrets, 1998, 2004; editor-in-chief: Nutrition in Clinical Practice, 2001—02, Jour. Parenteral Enteral Nutrition, 2002—, Med. Bull. Greater Kansas City, 1995—. Scoutmaster Cub Scouts, Denver, 1974-80; vice chmn. Cherry Creek Village Homeowners Assn., Denver, 1975-78; commr. Greenwood Village Planning and Zoning Commn., Denver, 1981-83. Maj. U.S. Army, 1972-74, col. USAR, 1986-2003, ret., 2003. Fellow ACS (Mo. chpt. pres. 1995-96), Am. Coll. Chest Physicians, Am. Coll. Critical Care Medicine; mem. AMA, Am. Soc. Clin. Nutrition, Am. Soc. Nutritional Scis., H. William Scott Jr. Soc., Colo. Trudeau Soc. (pres. 1980-81), Cen. Surg. Assn., Am. Soc. Parenteral and Enteral Nutrition (bd. dirs. 1987-89), Colo. Soc. Parenteral and Enteral Nutrition (pres. 1986-87), Internat. Cardiovascular Soc., Southwestern Surg. Congress, Am. Med. Info. Assn., Assn. for Computing Machinery, Am. Coll. Physician Execs., Kans. City Surg. Soc., Mo. Med. Assn. (mem. coun. 1998—), Met. Med. Assn. (bd. dirs. 1991—, pres.-elect 1997, pres. 1998), Rocky Mountain Vascular Soc., Colo. Vascular Surg. Soc., Am. Assn. Thoracic Surgery, Soc. Internat. de Chirurgerie, Western Vascular Soc., Western Surg. Assn., Soc. Critical Care Medicine, Assn. Surg. Edn., Assn. Program Dirs. in Surgery, Shock Soc. Episcopalian. Avocations: photography, skiing, hiking, writing. Office: 2301 Holmes St Kansas City MO 64108-2640 Office Phone: 816-404-5364. E-mail: charles.vanway@tmcmed.org.

VAN WEELDEN, THOMAS H. waste industry company executive; b. 1955; With Waste Mgmt.; co-owner hauling co. and 3 landfills, nr. Chgo.; exec. v.p. Allied Waste Industries, Inc., Houston, 1997-97, pres., COO Phoenix, 1992-97, CEO, pres. Scottsdale, Ariz., 1997—, chmn., 1998—, also bd. dirs. Bd. dirs. Reid Plastics, Inc. Office: Allied Waste Industries Inc Ste 100 15880 N Greenway Hayden Loop Scottsdale AZ 85260-1649

VAN WESTERING, JAMES FRANCIS, management consultant, educator; b. Bklyn., Dec. 7, 1940; s. Frederick Joseph and Agnes Teresa (Powell) Van W.; m. Karen Lyn Almy, Aug. 27, 1966. BA, Bklyn. Coll., 1963; MBA, Baruch Coll., 1972. Spl. asst. Fed. Res. Bank, N.Y.C., 1967-76; sr. cons. Coopers & Lybrand, N.Y.C., 1976-77; 2nd v.p. Chase Manhattan Bank, N.Y.C., 1977-78; pres. Internat. Comml. Sys., Inc., Forest Hills, N.Y., 1978—; dir. Nat. Data Corp., Atlanta, 1981-82. Adj. asst. prof. Mgmt. Inst., N.Y.U., 1992—. Bd. dirs. Forest Hills (N.Y.) Gardens Corp., 1987-90; pres. N.Y. Forum on Ea. Europe, N.Y.C., 1991—; mem. exec. bd. Sister City program City of N.Y. and Budapest, Hungary, 1995. Served USMCR, 1959-60. Mem. Am. Econs. Assn., Electronic Banking Econs. Soc., Slovak-Am. C. of C. (mem. adv. bd. 1994—). Avocation: historic preservation. Home: 17 Ingram St Forest Hills NY 11375-6828 Office: Internat Comml Sys Inc PO Box 4176 Parkside Sta Forest Hills NY 11375

VAN WIE, PAUL DAVID, secondary school educator, historian; b. Manhasset, N.Y., Sept. 29, 1956; s. Joseph Paul and Florence Elizabeth (Wagner) van W.; m. Ellen Mary van Wie, June 25, 1983; children: Mary Ellen, Elisabeth, Paul David, Joseph. BA, C.W. Post Coll., 1978, MA, 1987; PhD, CUNY, 1989. Cert. secondary edn. Tchr. Spackenkill High Sch., Poughkeepsie, N.Y., 1981-82, Schreiber High Sch., Port Washington, N.Y., 1982-84, Wheatley Sch., Old Westbury, N.Y., 1984—; adj. prof. N.Y. Inst. Tech., Old Westbury, 1987-92, Hofstra U., Hempstead, N.Y., 1992—. Mem. dean's adv. com. L.I. U., Old Brookville, N.Y., 1992-96. Author: The Way it Was, 1994, Image, History and Politics, 1998. Historian Village of Franklin Square, N.Y., 1979—, libr. trustee, 1989—; landmarks commr. Town of Hempstead, 1989—; pres. Franklin Square Hist. Soc.; v.p. Franklin Square Cmty. League, 1990-96. Nat. Humanities fellow U.S. Govt., 1988, Fulbright scholar U.S. Govt., 1990, Coun. Basic Edn. fellow, 1996; recipient Leadership award Nat. Soc. Daughters of Am. Revolution, 1982, N.Y. State Tchr. of Yr. award N.Y. Dept. Edn., 1992. Mem. Am. Hist. Assn., L.I. Coun. Social Studies, Franklin Square Hist. Soc. (pres.). Office: The Wheatley Sch 11 Bacon Rd Old Westbury NY 11568-1502

VAN WINKLE, EDGAR WALLING, retired electrical engineer, computer consultant; b. Rutherford, N.J., Oct. 12, 1913; s. Winant and Jessie Walcott (Mucklow) Van W.; m. Jessie Stetler, Apr. 23, 1938 (dec. July 1992); children: Barbara Van Winkle Clifton (dec. Mar. 2000), Catrina Van Winkle Poindexter, Cornelia Van Winkle Schloss; m. Martha Polyé, May 22, 1993. BEE, Rutgers U., 1936; MS in Indsl. Engring., Columbia U., 1943, PE in Indsl. Engring., 1966. Registered profl. engr., N.J. Elec. engr. A.B. Dumont Labs., Passaic, N.J., 1943-48; chief engr. Facsimile Electronics, 1948-52; cons. Bur. Ships, Washington, 1952; asst. sr. staff scientist Bendix Corp., Teterboro, NJ, 1952-67; sr. staff scientist Conrac Corp., West Caldwell, 1967-78; pres. Empac, Inc., Rutherford, 1979-2001; ret., 2001. Contbr. articles to profl. jours.; patentee in field. Ruling elder Presbyterian Ch., Rutherford, 1984-91, chmn. endowment com., 1984—. Mem. IEEE (life, treas. artificial intelligence sect. North N.J. Chpt. 1982-84), Bendix Mgmt. Club (life), North N.J. Automatic Control Group (chmn. 1967-68), Met. Engring. Mgmt. (chmn. 1966-67), Mensa, Holland Soc., Green Pond Yacht Club (past commodore), Upper Montclair Country Club, Delta Pi. Republican. Achievements include work in artificial intelligence, with subspecialty in mathematical software. Home (Summer): 154 Lake End Rd Newfoundland NJ 07435-1207 Office Phone: 201-729-0848. Personal E-mail: empacem@aol.com.

VAN WINKLE, HANS A. military officer; BS, U.S. Mil. Acad., 1971; MS in Pub. Policy, U. Calif., Berkeley, 1976. Registered profl. engr., Va., 1980. Commd. C.E. U.S. Army, 1971, advanced through grades to maj. gen.; comdr. Co. A, 10th Combat Engr. Bn., 3d Inf. Divsn. U.S. Army Europe, Germany, 1977—79, comdr. 10th Combat Engr. Bn., 3d Inf. Divsn.; asst. prof. econs. U.S. Mil. Acad., West Point, NY, 1979—82; exchange officer Royal Sch. Mil. Engring., England, 1983—85; exec. officer 82d Engr. Bn. U.S. Army Europe, Germany, 1985—87, ops. officer 7th Engr. Brigade, 1987—89; comdr. 8th Engr. Bn., 1st Cavalry Divsn. U.S. Army, Ft. Hood, Tex., 1989—91, comdr. Divsn. Engr. Brigade, 4th Inf. Divsn. Ft. Carson, Colo., 1992—94; dir. tng. U.S. Army Engr. Sch., Ft. Leonard Wood, Mo., 1994—95; dep. chief of staff, engr. U.S. Army Europe and 7th Army, Heidelberg, Germany, 1995—97; comdr., divsn. engr. Great Lakes and Ohio River Divsn. U.S. Army C.E., Cin. and Chgo., 1997—99, dep. commanding gen. Washington, 1999—. Decorated Legion of Merit, Bronze Star medal, Army Commendation medal (3), Meritorious Svc. medal (3), many others. Office: US Army Corps of Engineers 441 G St NW Washington DC 20314-1000

VANWINKLE, JOHN RAGAN, lawyer; b. Ft. Knox, Ky., Dec. 18, 1951; s. John Lloyd and Kate (Morris) VanW.; m. Cathy M. VanWinkle, Dec. 9, 1983; stepchildren: William Gabriel Gammons, Virginia Leigh Gammons. BS, State Coll. Ark., Conway, 1974; JD, U. Ark., 1980. Bar: Ark. 1980, U.S. Ct. Appeals 1981, U.S. Supreme Ct. 1989. Caseworker Mental Retardation Devel. Disabilities Svc., Ft. Smith, Ark., 1974-77; dep. pros. atty. Pros. Atty.-12th Dist., Ft. Smith, 1980-81; ptnr. Person & VanWinkle, Ft. Smith, 1982-86, Sexton, Kirkpatrick, Nolan, VanWinkle & Caddell, Ft. Smith, 1986-89, Hewett, Shock & VanWinkle, Ft. Smith, 1989-91; chancery judge 12th Jud. Cir., Ft. Smith, 1991-92; ptnr. Rose & VanWinkle, Fayetteville, Ark., 1993—, Rose, VanWinkle & Woods, Fayetteville, 1998-2000; pvt. practice Fayetteville, 2000—. Bd. dirs. Family Support Svcs., 1995—, N.W. Ark. Regional Indsl. Devel. Corp., 1996—; v.p. Habitat for Humanity, 1996—; Dem. nominee for Congress 3d Congl. Dist.-Ark., Ft. Smith, 1992; chmn. Sebastian County Dem. Ctr. Com., Ft. Smith, 1989-91; del. Dem. Nat. Conv., 1988. Mem. ATLA, Ark. Trial Lawyers Assn. Methodist. Avocations: golf, reading. Office: Law Offices of John R VanWinkle 2526 E Mission Blvd Fayetteville AR 72703 Office Phone: 479-571-3000. E-mail: john@vanwinkle.com.

VAN WINKLE, WILLIAM, financial planner; b. Englewood, N.J., July 3, 1934; s. Marshall Jr. and Helen (Wescott) V.; m. Beverly Elsie Peterson, Sept. 9, 1956; children: Stuart Wilson, Ainsley Ann Hilfiker, Carrie Van Winkle White. BS in Mech. Engring. and Bus. Adminstrn., Lehigh U., 1957; MS in Fin. Svcs., The Am. Coll., Bryn Mawr, Pa., 1996. Cert. fin. planner. With Procter and Gamble, 1957-67, Sheffield Chem. div. Kraftco, Union, N.J., 1967-71, C.R. Bard, Inc., Murray Hill, N.J., 1971-74; v.p. mfg. Estey Corp., Eatontown, N.J., 1974-79; pres. Van Winkle Assocs., Tinton Falls, N.J., 1979—. Host, prodr. (cable TV program) Financial Matters, 1980. Past pres., trustee Brookdale C.C. Found., Lincroft, N.J. Mem. Million Dollar Round Table (v.p. 1994-95), Past Commodore Shrewsbury Sailing and Yacht Club, N.J. Yacht Racing Assn., Navesink Country Club (Middletown, N.J.), Seabright (N.J.) Beach Club, Holland Soc. N.Y. (pres. 2002—), Useppa Island Club, others. Republican. Episcopalian. Avocations: sailing, walking, reading. Home: 41 Breezy Pt Little Silver NJ 07739-1703 Office: Van Winkle Assocs 776 Shrewsbury Ave Tinton Falls NJ 07724-3006 Office Phone: 732-741-4046.

VANWOERKOM, JACK, retail executive, lawyer; Chief legal counsel, v.p. devel., mng. dir. Europe A.W. Chesterton, 1994—97; gen. counsel Teradyne, Inc., 1998—99; sr. v.p., gen. counsel, sec. Staples, Inc., Framingham, Mass., 1999—. Office: Staples Inc 500 Staples Dr Framingham MA 01702

VAN WORMER, WILLIAM M. music educator, realtor; b. Toledo, Ohio, Oct. 31, 1958; s. Melvin Grant and Mary Angela Van Wormer; m. Julie Kristine Vogt, June 28, 1997; children: Jacob William, Anna Kristine, Rachel Elise. Student, Adrian Coll., 1976—78; MusB in Edn., U. Toledo, 1982, MusM in Edn., 1995; student in Real Estate, Stauzenberger Coll., 2000. Band dir. Toledo (Ohio) Pub. Schs., 1982—; realtor Flex Realty, Toledo, 2000—. Mem.: Toledo (Ohio) Bd. Realtors, Ohio Music Edn. Assn. (Superior Rating 1994—), Toledo (Ohio) Fedn. Tchrs. Avocations: hunting, fishing.

VAN WYCK, GEORGE RICHARD, insurance company executive; b. Wilmington, Vt., Feb. 6, 1928; s. Harold Wait Van Wyck and Ruth Anna Learnard; m. Jeanne Mildred Anderson, Apr. 17, 1948; children: Diana Lee Van Wyck Jenkins, Beryl Jeanne. BS in Math. cum laude, St. Lawrence U., 1953. Actuarial clk. Aetna Life Ins. Co., Hartford, Conn., 1953-55; with Am. Bankers Ins. Group, Miami, Fla., 1955-91, sec., bd. dirs., 1983-89, ret., 1991. Bd. dirs. Jr. Achievement of Greater Miami, 1966-83, pres., 1975-76; bd. dirs. Epworth Village Retirement Complex, Miami, 1966-2000, v.p., 1998-99, chmn. investment com. 1995-99; founding dir., pres. Brickel Children's Ctr., Miami, 1980-82; mem. pers. adv. bd., vice chmn. Dade County, Miami, 1987-89. With USAF, 1946-49. Fellow Life Office Mgmt. Inst.; mem. 1st United Meth. Ch. So. Miami, Phi Beta Kappa. Democrat. Methodist. Avocations: photography, golf, bridge, writing. Home: 8455 SW 44th St Miami FL 33155-4126 Personal E-mail: gvanwyck@cs.com.

VAN WYLEN, GORDON JOHN, former college president; b. Grant, Mich., Feb. 6, 1920; s. John and Effa (Bierema) Van W.; m. Margaret E. DeWitt, Dec. 29, 1951; children— Elizabeth Ann Van Wylen Rudenga, Stephen John, Ruth Margaret Van Wylen Jasperse, David Gordon, Emily Jane Van Wylen Overway. AB, Calvin Coll., 1942; BSE., U. Mich., 1942, MS, 1947; Sc.D., MIT, 1951. Indsl. engr. duPont Co., 1942-43; instr. mech. engring. Pa. State U., 1946-48; asst. prof. mech. engring. U. Mich., 1951-55, assoc. prof., 1955-57, prof., 1957-72, chmn. dept., 1958-65, dean Coll. Engring., 1965-72; pres. Hope Coll., Holland, Mich., 1972-87, pres. emeritus, 1987—. Author: Thermodynamics, 1959; author: (with R.E. Sonntag) Fundamentals of Classical Thermodynamics, 1965; author: 6th edit., 2003, Fundamentals of Statistical Thermodynamics, 1966, Introduction to Thermodynamics, 1971, 3d edit., 1991, Encounter at Sea, 1994; contbr. articles to profl. jours. Trustee Van Andel Edn. Inst. Lt. USNR, 1943-46. Fellow ASME, AAAS; mem. Phi Beta Kappa (hon.), Sigma Xi, Tau Beta Pi, Phi Kappa Phi. Mem. Reform Ch. Am. Home: Apt 600 145 Columbia Ave Holland MI 49423-2980

VAN ZANDT, DAVID E. dean; b. Princeton, N.J., Feb. 17, 1953; m. Lisa A. Huestis; children: Caroline, Nicholas. AB summa cum laude, Princeton U., 1975; JD, Yale U., 1981; PhD in Sociology, U. London, 1985. Bar: Ill. Clk. to Hon. Pierre N. Leval U.S. Dist. Ct. (so. dist.) N.Y., 1981-82; clk. to Hon. Harry A. Blackmun U.S. Supreme Ct., Washington, 1982-83; atty. Davis, Polk & Wardwell, 1984-85; mem. faculty Northwestern U. Law Sch., Chgo., 1985—, dean, 1995—. Mem. planning com. Northwestern U. Corporate Counsel Inst., Northwestern U. Corp. Counsel Ctr. Author: Living in the Children of God, 1991; mng. editor Yale Law Jour., 1980-81; contbr. articles to profl. jours. Office: Northwestern U Sch Law Office of Dean 357 E Chicago Ave Chicago IL 60611-3059

VAN ZANDT, STEVEN, actor, musician, radio personality; b. Winthrop, Mass., Nov. 22, 1950; m. Maureen Santoro. Guitarist E-Street Band, 1975—84, 1999—; host/D.J. Little Steven's Underground Garage, Syndicated Radio, 2002—. Actor: (TV series) The Soprano's, 1999—; musician, composer: albums Men Without Women, 1982, Voices of America, 1984, Sun City, 1985, Freedom - No Compromise, 1987, Revolution, 1989, Born Again Savage, 1999. Office: c/o The Endeavor Agy 10th Fl 9601 Wilshire Blvd Beverly Hills CA 90212*

VANZANT, IYANLA, writer; b. Bklyn., 1953; married; 3 children. BS summa cum laude, Medgar Evers Coll., 1983; JD, Queens Coll. Law Sch., 1988. Host Iyanla (TV talk show), 2001; founder, exec. dir. Inner Visions Worldwide Network, Inc., Silver Spring, Md.; lawyer; ordained minister; inspirational spkr. Author: Tapping the Power Within: A Path to Self-Empowerment for Black Women, 1992, Acts of Faith: Daily Meditations for People of Color, 1993 (BlackBoard Book Yr., 1994), The Value in the Valley: A Black Woman's Guide Through Life's Dilemmas, 1995 (BlackBoard Book Yr., 1995), Interiors: A Black Woman's Healing in Progress, 1995, Faith in the Valley: Lessons for Women on the Journey to Peace, 1996 (BlackBoard Book Yr., 1996), The Spirit of a Man: A Vision of Transformation of Black Men and the Women Who Love Them, 1997, The Big Book of Faith, 1997, Success Gems: Your Personal Motivation Success guide, 1997, In the Meantime: Finding Yourself and the Love You Want, 1998, One Day My Soul Just Opened Up: Forty Days and Forty Nights Toward Spiritual Strength and Personal Growth, 1998, Yesterday I Cried: Celebrating the Lessons of Living and Loving, 1999, Don't Give It Away: A Work Book of Self Awareness and Self Affirmation, 1999, The Good Company: A Woman's Journal for Spiritual Reflection, 1999, Daily Ghetto Mediations: Affirmations for the Ghetto in You, 1999, Until Today!: Daily Devotions for Spiritual Balance and Peace of Mind, 2001, Up from Here: Reclaiming the Male Spirit, 2002, Every Day I Pray, 2001, Living Through the Meantime, 2001. Nat. spokesperson Literacy Vol. Am. Recipient Alumni Yr., Nat. Assn. Equal Opportunity Edn., 1994, Oni award, Internat. Congress Black Women. Mailing: Inner Visions Worldwide Network Inc 926 Phila Ave Silver Spring MD 20910 Office Phone: 301-608-8750. Office Fax: 301-608-3813.

VAN ZANT, SUSAN LUCILLE, principal; b. Torrance, Calif., Apr. 29, 1942; d. Paul McHenry and Lucille Eileen (McQuarrie) Mansfield; m. Jerry Brian Van Zant, Oct. 27, 1960; children: Steven Brian, Karen Daphne Van Zant Hosaka. BA in History and Social Sci., Calif. State U., Long Beach, 1966; MA in Curriculum, No. Ariz. U., 1974; EdD in Adminstrn., U.S. Internat. U., 1982. Cert. elem. tchr., kindergarten and secondary sch. adminstr., Calif. Tchr. Borrego Springs (Calif.) Unified Sch., 1967-69, Poway (Calif.) Unified Sch. Dist., 1969-76, prin., 1976—. Instr. community rels., law and fin. Nat. U., San Diego, 1987-92. Author: (with others) The Principal as Chief Executive, 1991; contbr. articles to profl. jours. Named Calif. Educator of Yr. Calif. State Dept. of Edn./Milken Found., 1989, Blue Ribbon Sch., U.S. Dept. of Edn., 1994; recipient Educator's award Freedom's Found., 1990. Mem. Nat. Assn. Elem. Sch. Prins. (bd. dirs., state leader, Disting. Prin. award 1988), Calif. Alliance for Edn. (coord.), Assn. Calif. Sch. Adminstrs. (chair elem. adminstrn.), Poway Assn. Sch. Mgrs. (pres. 1982), San Diego/Imperial County Adminstrs. (pres. 1993-94), Delta Kappa Gamma (pres. 1990-92). Baptist. Home: 16204 Quail Rock Rd Ramona CA 92065-7214 E-mail: suvanzant@aol.com.

VAN ZANTE, SHIRLEY M(AE), magazine editor; b. Elma, Iowa; d. Vernon E. and Georgene (Woodmansee) Borland; m. Dirk C. Van Zante. AA, Grandview Coll., 1950; BA, Drake U., 1952. Assoc. editor Mchts. Trade Jour., Des Moines, 1952-55; copywriter Meredith Pub. Co., Des Moines, 1955-60, book editor, 1960-67; home furnishings editor Better Homes and Gardens Spl. Interest Publs., Meredith Corp., 1967-74; home furnishing and design editor Better Homes and Gardens mag., 1974-89; writer, editl. cons., 1989-98. Named Advt. Woman of Yr. in Des Moines, 1961; recipient Dorothy Dawe award, 1971, 73, 75, 76, 77, Dallas Market Ctr. award, 1983, So. Furniture Market Writer's award, 1984. Mem. Alpha Xi Delta. Address: 1905 74th St Des Moines IA 50322-5701

VAN ZANTEN, FRANK VELDHUYZEN, retired library system director; b. Heemstede, The Netherlands, Oct. 21, 1932; came to U.S., 1946, naturalized, 1953; s. Adrian V. and Cornelia (Van Eesteren) Van Z.; m. Lois Ruth Holkeboer, June 17, 1961; children— Kiki Maria, Lili Roxanne, Amy Suzanne. AB, Calvin Coll., Mich., 1959; postgrad., U. Wash., 1960; MA in L.S, U. Mich., 1961. Cataloger, extension project asst. Mich. State Library, Lansing, 1961-62; dir. Dickinson County (Mich.) Library, 1962-65, Mid-Peninsula Library Fedn., Iron Mountain, Mich., 1963-65, St. Clair County (Mich.) Library, 1965-68, Tucson Pub. Library, 1968-73; library cons. Ill. State Library, Springfield, 1973-75, asso. dir. for library devel., 1975-78; dir. Mid-Hudson Library System, Poughkeepsie, N.Y., 1978-95; ret., 1996. Served with AUS, 1953-55. Mem. ALA, N.Y. Libr. Assn. Home: 138 Wilbur Blvd Poughkeepsie NY 12603-4635 E-mail: FVZcolors@aol.com., fvanzanten@hvc.rr.com.

VAN ZELST, THEODORE WILLIAM, civil engineer, engineering company executive; b. Chgo., May 11, 1923; s. Theodore Walter and Wilhelmina (Oomens) Van Z.; m. Louann Hurter, Dec. 29, 1951; children: Anne, Jean, David. BS, U. Calif., Berkeley, 1944; BS in Naval Sci., Northwestern U.,

1944, BAS., 1945, MS in Civil Engring., 1948. Registered profl. engr., Ill. Pres., Soil Testing Services, Inc., Chgo., 1948-52; pres. Soiltest, Inc., Chgo., 1948-78, chmn. bd., 1978-80; sec., dir. Exploration Data Cons., Inc., 1980-82; exec. v.p. Cenco Inc., Chgo., 1962-77, vice chmn., 1973-77, also dir., 1962-77. Bd. dirs. Minann, Inc., Testing Sci., Inc., Van Zelst, Inc., Rsch. Park, Inc., Northwestern U., 1992-95, chmn. bd. dirs. Envirotech Svcs., Inc., 1983-85; sec., bd. dirs. Van Zelst, Inc. Wadsworth, Ill., 1983—; pres., bd. dirs. Geneva-Pacific Corp., 1969-83, Geneva Resources, Inc., 1983-91. Treas. Internat. Road Fedn., 1961-64, sec., 1964-79, dir., 1973-88, vice chmn., 1980-87; pres. Internat. Road Edn. Found., 1978-80, 87-88, hon. life bd. dirs., 1988—; bd. dirs. Chgo. Acad. Scis., 1983-86, v.p., 1985-86, hon. dir., 1986—; bd. dirs. Pres.'s Assn., Chgo., 1985-86, Friends of Mitchell Mus., 2003—; mem. adv. bd. Mitchell Indian Mus., Kendall Coll., 1977-94, 2004—; mem. Asian art coun. Art Inst. Chgo., 2004—. Lt. (j.g.) USNR, 1942-45. Ensign USNR, 1944—46, lt. j.g. USNR, 1946. Recipient Service award Northwestern U., 1970, Merit award, 1974, Alumni medal, 1989, Svc. award U. Wis., 1971, La Sallian award, 1975; named Disting. Engring. Alumnus, U. Calif., Berkeley, 2002. Mem. ASCE (Chgo. Civil Engr. of Yr., 1988), Nat. Soc. Profl. Engrs., Western Soc. Engrs., Evanston C. of C. (v.p. 1969-73), Ovid Esbach Soc. (pres. 1968-80), Northwestern U. Alumni Assn., Tau Beta Pi, Sigma Xi. Clubs: Economic, North Shore. Achievements include invention of engring. testing equipment for soil, rock, concrete and asphalt; co-invention of Swing-wing for supersonic aircraft. Home: 1213 Wagner Rd Glenview IL 60025-3297 Office: PO Box 582 Glenview IL 60025-0582 E-mail: trz@earthlink.net.

VAN ZILE, PHILIP TAYLOR, III, lawyer, educator; b. Detroit, Feb. 17, 1945; s. Philip Taylor II and Ruth (Butzel) Van Z.; m. Susan Jones, Sept. 12, 1981; children: Caroline Sage, Philip Taylor IV. BA, Oberlin Coll., 1968; MDiv, Union Theol. Sem., 1971; JD, Mich. State U., 1975. Bar: Mich. 1976, D.C. 1976, U.S. Dist. Ct. (ea. dist.) Mich. 1976, U.S. Ct. Appeals (6th cir.) 1976, U.S. Supreme Ct. 1977, Pa. 1981. Law clk. Mich. Ct. Appeals, Detroit, 1976-78, Mich. Supreme Ct., Detroit and Lansing, Mich., 1978-80; asst. corp. counsel Office of Corp. Counsel, Washington, 1980-87; assoc. Killian & Gephart, Harrisburg, Pa., 1987-89; prin. Law Office of Philip T. Van Zile, Harrisburg, 1989-91; assoc. coun. Office Chief Coun. Pa. Dept. Conservation and Natural Resources, Harrisburg, 1991—; assoc. realtor M.C. Walker Realty, Mechanicsburg, Pa., 1997—. Teaching fellow Detroit Coll. Law, 1976-80; teaching asst. Detroit Gen. Hosp., 1978-80; teaching assoc. Acad. Med. Arts and Bus., Harrisburg, 1990-91. Contbr. articles to profl. jours. Ordained elder Mechanicsburg Presbyn. Ch., 1995—, chmn. vol. ministries, 1995, chmn. peacemaking, 1996, chmn. staff, 1997—. Mem. ABA, Kenwood Club (Chevy Chase, Md.). Office: Pa Dept Conservation/Natural Resources Office Chief Counsel 400 Market St Harrisburg PA 17101-2301

VARANI, FLAVIO, musician, music educator; s. Jose Varani and Eleonor Pastore. Diploma, Ecole de Piano Magada Tagliaterro, Paris, 1968; MusB, Manhattan Sch. Music, 1970, MusM, 1972. Prof. Oakland U., Rochester, Mich., 1972—. Artistic dir. Internat. Chamber Music Acad., Munich, 1993—2002; mem. Galia Trio, Paris, 2000—. Musician: (soloist) Detroit Symphony, (CD) Cartas a Posteridade, The Music of Villa Lobos, Poulenc Nocturnes. Named Outstanding Instrumentalist, Detroit Music Awards, 2001; recipient 1st prize, Internat. Chopin Competition, Majorca, Spain, 1960, Most Outstanding Classical CD award, Detroit Music Awards, 1999. Home: 1207 Smith Ave Birmingham MI 48009 Office: Oakland Univ Rochester MI 48309

VARAT, JONATHAN D. dean, law educator; b. 1945; BA, U. Pa., Phila., 1967, JD, 1972. Law clk. to judge Walter Mansfield U.S. Ct. Appeals (2d cir.), N.Y.C., 1972-73; law clk. to justice Byron White U.S. Supreme Ct., Washington, 1973-74; assoc. O'Melveny & Myers, Los Angeles, 1974-76; acting prof. UCLA, 1976-81, prof., 1981—, assoc. dean, 1982-83, 91-92; dean UCLA Sch. Law, 1998—. Office: UCLA Sch Law PO Box 951476 Los Angeles CA 90095-1476

VARCHMIN, THOMAS EDWARD, environmental health administrator; b. Chgo., Dec. 5, 1947; s. Arthur William and Laurie Eileen (Allen) V.; m. Beth Virginia Plank, Dec. 16, 1972; children: Jeffrey Thomas, Brian Arthur, Jennifer Beth, Matthew James. BA, St. Mary's Coll., Winona, Minn., 1969; MS, Western Ill. U., Macomb, 1977. Registered sanitarian, Wis. Virologist, microbiologist Chgo. Dept. Health, 1974-78; environ. health and safety mgr. Great Atlantic & Pacific Tea Co., Chgo., 1978-79; adminstr. occupational safety and environ. health Nat. Safety Council, Chgo., 1979-80; mgr. environ. health Lake County Health Dept., Waukegan, Ill., 1980-84, mgr. environ. health and pub. relations, 1984-87; mgr. environ. health Cook County Dept. Pub. Health, Oak Park, Ill., 1987-89, asst. dir. environ. health, mgr. intergovtl. rels., 1989-98, dir. environ. health, 1998—. Co-chmn. West Nile Virus Com. for Cook Country, Ill., 2001-03; environ. health cons. Author: Final Report of West Nile Virus Committee for Cork County, 2002—03; editor: Food and Beverage Newsletter, Hospital and Health Care Newsletter, Trades and Services Newsletter, 1979—80. NSF grantee, 1968-69 Mem. Nat. Environ. Health Assn. (registered environ. health specialist), Ill. Environ. Health Assn. (lic. environ. health practitioner), Nat. Safety Coun., Am. Soc. Microbiology, Anvil Club of Ill., Phi Mu Alpha, Delta Epsilon Sigma. Achievements include research on autumn food habits of game fish, behavioral and phys. devel. of barred owl nestlings in Ill. Office: Cook County Dept Pub Health 1010 Lake St Ste 300 Oak Park IL 60301-1133

VARDALOS, NIA, actress, screenwriter; b. Winnipeg, Can., Sept. 24, 1962; d. Constantine and Doreen Vardalos; m. Ian Gomez, 1993. Attended, Ryerson U. Actor: (films) No Experience Necessary, 1996, Men Seeking Women, 1997, Short Cinema, 1998, Meet Prince Charming, 1999, (also writer) My Big Fat Greek Wedding, 2002, (also writer, exec. prodr.) Connie and Carla, 2004, (voice): (TV series) Team Knight Rider, 1997, (guest appearance): High Incident, 1996, Common Law, 1996, The Drew Carey Show, 1997, Boy Meets World, 1998, It's Like, You Know, 1999, Two Guys, a Girl, and a Pizza Place, 1999, Curb Your Enthusiasm, 2000. Office: c/o Brillstein Grey Mgmt 9150 Wilshire Blvd Ste 350 Beverly Hills CA 90212

VARDAN, SUMAN, medical educator; b. Monghyr, Bihar, India, July 25, 1937; came to U.S., 1970; s. Damodar and Sarojini Prasad; m. Asha Vardan, Feb. 25, 1965; children: Sandeep, Swati. MB BS, Bihar U., Laheraisari, 1959, MD, 1964; diploma in tropicae medicine and hygiene, Bihar U., 1965. Diplomate Am. Bd. Internal Medicine, Am. Bd. Clin. Hypertension, Am. Soc. Hypertension, Am. Bd. Cardiovascular Disease. Med. resident Brown U., Providence, 1972—73, cardiology fellow, 1973—75; asst. prof. medicine SUNY, Syracuse, 1975—83, assoc. prof. medicine, 1983—93, prof. medicine, 1993—; dir. hypertension clinic VA Med. Ctr., 1980—, dir. cardiac rehab. program, 2000—, staff physician cardiology and gen. medicine, 1975—2000, staff cardiologist, 2001—. Fellow ACP, ACC; mem. Am. Assn. Physician from India (patron), Am. Soc. Hypertension, Indian Med. Assn. (life). Home: 6292 Danbury Dr Jamesville NY 13078-8737 Office: VA Med Ctr 800 Irving Ave Syracuse NY 13210-2716 E-mail: suman.vardan@med.va.gov.

VARDIN, PATRICIA ANNE, education educator; b. Chgo. d. William and Catherine Vardin; m. Thomas W. Vris; 1 child, Elizabeth Vardin Newman. BS, U. Wis.; Doctorate, M, Columbia U. Tchr's. Coll., 1984. Adj. assoc. prof. Columbia U. Tchr's Coll., NYC, 1983—84; assoc. prof. St Francis Coll., Dept Edn., Bklyn. Heights, NY, 1992—99, Manhattanville Coll., Purchase, NY, 2002—, chmn. early childhood edn., 2002—. Editor: Children's Rights: Contemporary Perspectives, 1979; author: Internat. Encyclopedia of Education, 1984, Montessori Life, 2003. Founder, bd chair New Amsterdam Sympony Orchestra, NYC, 1976—80; bd. chair New Amsterdam Symphony Orchestra, NYC, 2004—; mem. Norwalk Hosp., Norwalk, Conn., 2001—; ednl. coord. Armstrong Chamber Concerts Music Enrichment Program; co-chair MEP Gala. Mem.: Westchester Assn. for the Edn. of Young Children (bd. dirs.), Nat. Assn. Edn. of Young Children. Episcopal. Avocations: swimming, sailing, violin, cmty. vol. Office: Manhattanville Coll 2900 Purchase St Purchase NY 10577 E-mail: vardinvrisp@mville.edn.

VARELA, FERNANDO, anesthesiologist; b. Madrid, Aug. 8, 1936; MD, Madrid U., 1962. Diplomate Am. Bd. Anesthesiology. Fellow Am. Coll. Anesthesiologist; intern Flower Hosp., Toledo, Ohio, 1968-69; resident anesthesiologist Phila. Gen. Hosp., 1969-70; resident in anesthesiology U. Chgo. Hosps., 1970-72; asst. prof. anes. Med. Coll. Ga., Augusta, 1972-73; hosp. staff mem. Trinity Med. Ctr., Moline, Ill., 1973—. Mem. AMA, Am. Soc. of Anesthesiologists, Ill. Med. Soc., Ill. Soc. Anesthesiologists, Rock Island County Med. Soc. Office: 550 30th Ave Ste 7 Moline IL 61265-5975 Home: Apt 1810 988 Boulevard Of The Arts Sarasota FL 34236-4849 E-mail: fervalop@aol.com.

VARELA, VICKI, state official; b. Aurora, Colo. m. Brett J. DelPorto: 2 children. Student, U. Colo., 1976; BA in English, Brigham Young U., 1978. Reporter Associated Press, Denver, Cheyenne, N.Y.C., 1978-79, Deseret News, Salt Lake City, 1979-83, edn. editor, 1983-86; asst. commr. higher edn. for pub. affairs Utah Higher Education Commn., Salt Lake City, 1986-92; dep. chief of staff to gov. State of Utah, Salt Lake City, 1992—. Exec. dir. Olympics Referendum Campaign, Salt Lake City, 1989. Vol. worker with Republican Inst. to train political candidates and campaign mgrs. in developing democracies (helped conduct seminar in Veronezh, Russia, 1995); mem. cmty adv. com. First Presbyn. Ch. Restoration/ Preservation Project; active in European Comty. Visitors' Program, 1996; studied in Germany, Spain, Brussels and Great Britain. Office: Office Gov 210 State Capitol Salt Lake City UT 84114

VARELLA, HAZEL L. education educator, historian; b. Beverly, Mass., Dec. 17, 1932; d. John Luke and Olivia McDonald Luke; m. M David Varella, June 24, 1961; children: John David, James Robert. BS, Bridgewater State Coll., 1954, MEd, 1956; MA, Boston U., 1962. Chmn. social studies Easton (Mass.) Sch. Sys., 1956—97; adj. faculty Bridgewater State Coll., Mass., 1998—; sr. lectr. Curry Coll., Milton, Mass., 1988—. Adv. placement cons. Coll. Bd., Princeton, 1988—. Author: (book) History of Easton V II, 1972, (pamphlets) Growing Up at Sheep Pasture, 1976. Trustee North Easton Savings Bank, 1996—; dir. Ames Free Libr., Easton, 1989—. Recipient Hon. Grand Marshall, Town of Easton, Mass., 2000, Ind. Study Scholar, NEH, Washington, DC, 1984, Outstanding Svc. award, Easton Lions Club, 1997. Mem.: Easton Hist. Soc. (sec., pres. 1969—71, 1990—94). Episc. Avocations: reading, travel. Home: 121 Center St North Easton MA 02356

VARELLAS, SANDRA MOTTE, judge; b. Anderson, S.C., Oct. 17, 1946; d. James E. and Helen Lucille (Gilliam) Motte; m. James John Varellas, July 3, 1971; children: James John III, David Todd. BA, Winthrop U., 1968; MA, U. Ky., 1970, JD, 1975. Bar: Ky. 1975, Fla. 1976, U.S. Dist. Ct. (ea. dist.) Ky. 1975, U.S. Ct. Appeals (6th cir.) 1976, U.S. Supreme Ct. 1978. Instr. Midway Coll., Ky., 1970-72; adj. prof. U. Ky. Coll. Law, Lexington, 1976-78; instr. dept. bus. adminstrn. U. Ky., Lexington, 1976-78; ptnr. Varellas, Pratt & Cooley, Lexington, 1975-93, Varellas & Pratt, Lexington, 1993-97, Varellas & Varellas, Lexington, 1998—. Fayette County judge exec., Ky., 1980—; hearing officer Ky. Natural Resources and Environ. Protection Cabinet, Frankfort, 1984-88; bd. trustees Lexington Network 1994-98, 2002—, sec., 1994-98. Committeewoman Ky. Young Dems., Frankfort, 1977-80; pres. Fayette County Young Dems., Lexington, 1977; bd. dirs. Ky. Dem. Women's Club, Frankfort, 1980-84, bd. dirs., Bluegrass Estate Planning Coun., 1995-98; grad. Leadership Lexington, 1981; chairwoman Profl. Women's Forum, Lexington, Ky., 1985-86, bd. dirs., 1984-87, Aequum award com., 1989-92; mem. devel. coun. Midway Coll., 1990-92; co-chair Gift Club Com., 1992. Named Outstanding Young Dem. Woman, Ky. Young Dems., Frankfort, 1977, Outstanding Former Young Dem., Ky. Young Dems., 1983. Mem. Ky. Bar Assn. (treas. young lawyers divsn. 1978-79, long range planning com. 1988-89), Fla. Bar, Fayette County Bar Assn. (treas. 1977-78, bd. govs. 1978-80), LWV (nominating com. 1984-85), Greater Lexington C. of C. (legis. affairs com. 1994-95, bd.d irs. coun. smaller enterprises 1992-95), The Lexington Forum (bd. dirs. 1996-99), Lexington Philharm. Guild (bd. dirs. 1979-81, 86—), Nat. Assn. Women Bus. Owners (chmn. cmty. liaison/govtl. affairs com. 1992-93). Office: Varellas & Varellas 167 W Main St Ste 1310 Lexington KY 40507-1398

VARESE, FEDERICO, political science educator; b. Italy, Nov. 12, 1965; m. Galia Kravtchenko. Laurea, Bologna (Italy) U., 1990; PhM, Cambridge (Eng.) U., 1991; PhD, Oxford (Eng.) U., 1997. Rsch. fellow Oxford U., 1996-2000; William H. Orrick asst. vis. prof. Yale U., New Haven, 2000—02; asst. prof. Williams Coll., Williamstown, 2002—; univ. sr. lctr. in Criminology Ctr. for Criminological Rsch., Univ. Oxford, England, 2003. Author: The Russian Mafia, 2001. Cpl. maj. paratrooper Italian armed forces, 1992-93. Grantee Internat. Consortium for Polit. and Social Rsch., 1997; Nuffield Coll. studentship, 1991; Lester B. Pearson scholar Ministry of Fgn. Affairs, 1982; receipient Ed. A. Hewett Book Prize, Am. Assoc. for the Advancement of Slavic Studies, in conj. with Nat. Coun. for Eurasian and East European Rsch., 2002. Mem. Am. Polit. Sci. Assn. Office: 1 Warnborough Rd Oxford OX26HZ England E-mail: fvarese@williams.edu.

VARET, MICHAEL A. lawyer; b. N.Y.C., Mar. 9, 1942; s. Guster V. and Frances B. (Goldberg) V.; m. Elizabeth R. Varet, June 3, 1973; 3 children. BS in Econs., U. Pa., 1962; LLB, Yale U., 1965. Bar: N.Y. 1966, U.S. Supreme Ct. 1975, U.S. Dist. Ct. (ea. and so. dists.) N.Y. 1975, U.S. Tax Ct. 1975, U.S. Claims Ct. 1975, U.S. Ct. Appeals (2d cir.) 1975. Mem., chmn. Varet & Fink P.C. (formerly Milgrim Thomajan & Lee P.C.), N.Y.C., 1982-95; mem. firm Piper Rudnick LLP, N.Y.C., 1995—. Bd dir., exec. com., audit com., compensation com., Salisbury Bank and Trust Co., Lakeville, Conn., Salisbury Bancorp, Inc., Lakeville. Trustee Montefiore Med. Ctr., Bronx, N.Y., 1980-92, mem. exec. com., 1985-92; bd. dirs. Sem. Libr. Corp. Jewish Theol. Sem., N.Y.C., 1983-87, United Jewish Appeal-Fedn. Jewish Philanthropies of Greater N.Y., Inc., 1979-86, mem. coun. of overseers, 1986-95; bd. dirs. Mosholu Preservation Corp., Bronx, 1982-88, Yale Law Sch. Fund, 2000—; bd. overseers Jewish Theol. Sem., 1982-90, Jewish Publ. Soc. of Am., 1986-96, exec. com., 1989-94, 95-96; mem. exec. com. Yale Law Sch. Assn., 1990-93; bd. dirs. B. de Rothschild Found. for Advancement Sci. in Israel, 1986—, Piatigorsky Found., 1990—, Scenic Hudson, Inc., 2003—; v.p., sec., bd. dirs. Am. Found. for Basic Rsch. in Israel, 1990—; dir. Plz. Jewish Cmty. Chapel, 2001—; bd. dirs. Am. and Internat. Friends of Victoria and Albert Mus., Inc., 1997-99, treas., 1997-99. Mem. ABA, N.Y. State Bar Assn., Assn. of Bar of City of N.Y. (bd. dirs., exec. com. 1971-75), Internat. Fiscal Assn., Internat. Tax Planning Assn., Yale Club of N.Y.C., Lotos Club. Democrat. Office: Piper Rudnick LLP 1251 Ave of Americas New York NY 10020-1104 Office Phone: 212-835-6000. E-mail: mav@varet.com., michael.varet@piperrudnick.com.

VARGA, DEBORAH TRIGG, music educator, entertainment company owner; b. Dayton, Ohio, Dec. 15, 1955; d. Ernest Cushman and Phyllis Ann (Martz) Trigg; m. Ali M. Abadi, Dec. 30, 1980 (div. July 1987); 1 child, Darren Vincent; m. Richard Charles Varga, June 25, 1994; 1 child, Kathryn Lenore. B of Music Edn. in Violin Performance, Converse Coll., Spartanburg, S.C., 1977. Music educator Seminole County Sch. Bd., Sanford, Fla., 1978-92, Howard County Pub. Schs., Ellicott City, Md., 1993—. Co-founder, co-owner Gold Star Entertainement, Inc., Orlando, Fla., 1984-86, Ctr. Stage Entertainment, Inc., Maitland, Fla., 1986-92; owner Varga Music Entertainement, Highland, Md., 1993—, Composer children's songs, 1990—, Martin Luther King Tribute, Human Rights Commn., Howard County, 1997-00. Mem. Am. Fedn. Musicians, Music Educators Nat. Conf., Am. String. Tchrs. Assn., Nat. Orch. Assn. Avocations: waterskiing, whitewater rafting, tennis, golf, reading. Home: 13464 Allnutt Ln Highland MD 20777-9743

VARGA, JEANNE-MARIE, women's healthcare company executive; BS in Med. Tech., Towson State U.; MA in Mgmt. and Supervision, Ctrl. Mich. U. Sr. sci. reviewer Ctr. for Devices and Radiol. Health, FDA, 1980-83; mgr. U.S. regulatory affairs Sorin Biomedica S.P.A., 1983-87; dir. quality assurance and regulatory affairs Baxter Diagnostics, Inc., 1987-92; v.p. worldwide regulatory and quality Sanofi Diagnostics Pasteur, Inc., 1992-98; v.p. regulatory affairs and quality sys. Women First HealthCare, Inc., San Diego, 1998—. Fax: 619-509-1353.

VARGA, NICHOLAS, historian, archivist, retired educator; b. Elizabeth, N.J., Sept. 13, 1925; s. Joseph and Anna (Buchko) V.; m. Margaret Joan Skinner, Sept. 8, 1951; children: Deidre Kayne, Damian Guy, Colin Piere. BS cum laude, Boston Coll., Chestnut Hill, Mass., 1951, MA, 1952; PhD with honors, Fordham U., 1960. Instr. history Loyola Coll., Balt., 1955-59, asst. prof., 1959-62, assoc. prof., 1962-66, prof., 1966-92, chmn. dept., 1964-68, prof. emeritus, 1992—, coll. archivist, 1976—. Author: Baltimore's Loyola, 1990. Advisor Jo Tydings Election Campaign, Balt., 1964, 70; bd. dirs. UN Assn. Md., Balt., 1966-70; pres. Woodbourne Sch. PTA, Balt., 1967-68; mem. Howard County Bicentennial Com., Ellicott City, Md., 1974-77. Publ. grantee Md. Hist. Soc., 1989. Mem. AAUP (founder, pres. Loyola Coll. chpt. 1966-69), Am. Hist. Assn. (interviewer Cate report 1966), Am. Cath. Hist. Assn. (nominating com. 1975-78), Soc. Am. Archivists, Mid-Atlantic Region Archivists Conf., Alpha Sigma Nu (hon.). Democrat. Byzantine Catholic. Office: Loyola Coll 4501 N Charles St Baltimore MD 21210-2601

VARGA, RICHARD STEVEN, mathematics professor; b. Cleve., Oct. 9, 1928; s. Steven and Ella (Krejcs) V.; m. Esther Marie Pfister, Sept. 22, 1951; 1 dau., Gretchen Marie. BS, Case Inst. Tech. (merged with Case Western Res. U.), 1950; AM, Harvard U., 1951, PhD, 1954; hon. doctorate, U. Karlsruhe, 1991, U. Lille, 1993. With Bettis Atomic Power Lab., Westinghouse Electric Co., 1954-60, adv. mathematician, 1959-60; full prof. math. Case Inst. Tech. (now Case We. Res. U.), 1960-69; Univ. Prof. math. Kent (Ohio) State U., 1969—, dir. rsch. Inst. for Computational Math. Cons. to govt. and industry. Author: Matrix Iterative Analysis, 1962, Functional Analysis and Approximation Theory in Numerical Analysis, 1971, Topics in Polynomial and Rational Interpolation and Approximation, 1982, Zeros of Sections of Power Series, 1983, Scientific Computation on Mathematical Problems and Conjectures, 1990, Matrix Iterative Analysis, 2d revised and expanded edit., 2000, Geršgorin and his Circles, 2004; editor: Numerical Solution of Field Problems in Continuum Physics, 1970, Padé and Rational Approximations: Theory and Applications, 1977, Rational Approximations and Interpolation, 1984, Computational Methods and Function Theory, 1990, Numerical Linear Algebra, 1993; editor-in-chief. Numerische Math., 1988-2002, Electronic Transactions Numerical Analysis; mem. editl. bd. Linear Algebra and Applications, Constructive Approximation, Computational Mathematics (China), Numerical Algorithms, Analysis, Electronic Jour. Linear Algebra, Comms. in Applied Analysis. Recipient Rsch. award Sigma Xi, 1965, von Humboldt prize, 1982, Pres.' medal Kent State U., 1981; Guggenheim fellow, 1963; Fairchild scholar, 1974. Home: 7065 Arcadia Dr Cleveland OH 44129-6065 Office: Kent State U Inst Computational Mat Kent OH 44242-0001 E-mail: varga@math.kent.edu.

VARGA, STEVEN CARL, human resources professional; b. Columbus, Ohio, Jan. 19, 1952; s. Stephen Thomas and Eva Jeney Varga; m. Michelle L. Auld, Nov. 17, 1973; children: Zachary Steven, Joshua Lewis. BA in Psychology and Philosophy magna cum laude, Carthage Coll., 1977; MSA with honors, Ctrl. Mich. U., 1986. Svc. mgr. Chem-Law Corp., Columbus, 1972-75; respiratory therapist St. Catherine's Hosp., Kenosha, Wis., 1975-77; policy analyst Nationwide Ins. Cos., Columbus, 1978-79, asst. mgr. Corp. Tng. Ctr., 1979-86; dir. ednl. tng. Sullivan Payne Co., Seattle, 1986-88, asst. v.p. human resource devel., 1989-93; v.p. Reinsurance Solutions, Inc., Seattle, 1994-95; sr. v.p. Unltd. Potential, Inc., 1995-99; chief human resources officer Columbus Distbg. Co., 2000—. Mem. adv. bd. Nationwide Ins. Co.; W.I.L. bd. mem. Anheuser-Busch Corp. Mem. civic action program com., 1979-86, Nat. Mental Health Assn., 1972-79; mem. occupl. adv. coun. Bellevue C.C., 1989—; v.p. Kenosha County chpt., 1975-77; mem. Franklin County (Ohio) Mental Health Assn., 1978-86. Rhodes scholar, 1976-77. Mem. APA, ASTD, Soc. Broadcast Engrs., Ins. Inst. Am. (contbg. author Principles of Reinsurance, vol. I and II, nat. adv. com. assoc. in reinsurance program), Brokers and Reinsurers Markets Assn. (edn. and tng. co-chair), Am. Mgmt. Assn., Soc. Ins. Trainers and Educators (chmn. regional area planning com.), Carthage Coll. Alumni Assn., Phi Beta Kappa, Psi Chi. Office: Columbus Distbg Co 4949 Freeway Dr E Columbus OH 43229-5401

VARGAS, ARIONEL P. dancer; b. Cuba; Student, Centro Pro Danza, Havana, Cuba. Mem. Royal Winnipeg Ballet, 1996—2000, prin. dancer, 2000—. Dancer (ballets) Dracula, Royal Winnipeg Ballet, Allegro Brillante, Ballo Della Regina, Nutcracker, La Bayadere, Act II, The Leaves are Fading, A Touch of Strauss, 5 Tangos, Creaturehood, Miroirs, The Rite of Spring, Galina Yordanova, Nutcracker, Butterfly, As Above, So Below. Recipient Gold medal, Brazil's Internat. Ballet Competition, 1995, Bronze medal, N.Y. Internat. Ballet Competition, 1996. Office: Royal Winnipeg Ballet 380 Graham Ave Winnipeg MB Canada R3C 4K2

VARGAS, DIANA LISA, television station executive; BA in Mass Media, Hunter Coll., 1983. Acct. exec. Sta. KTTV, L.A., 1988-90, sales, 1990-91, local sales mgr., 1991-94, v.p. gen. sales mgr., 1994-97, v.p. gen. mgr., 1997—. Office: Sta KTTV 1999 S Bundy Dr Los Angeles CA 90025-5203

VARGAS, MARTHA, government liaison; b. Bogota, Columbia; arrived in U.S. 1981. AA in bus. adminstrn., Miami-Dade Cmty. Coll. Asst. to pres. Cafecol Trading Corp., 1985; mktg. asst. Capitol/EMI Records, Miami, 1989; U.N. liasion Together Found., N.Y.C., 1991—. Mem. exec. com. UN DPI/NGO; bd. dirs. Soc. Internat. Devel., N.Y. chap. Office: Together Found 55 E 75th St New York NY 10021-2736 Fax: 212-628-4265.

VARGAS LEGASPI, JUAN, manufacturing executive; b. Aguascalientes, Mex., Feb. 25, 1953; s. Juan Medina and Maria Legaspi De La Luz; m. Martha Perez Carreño; children: Juan, Abraham, Christopher. Bookkeeper, UNAM, Mexico City, 1974-78; diploma in taxes and fin., Inst. of Specialization, Mexico City, 1987; diploma human resources, U. Iberoam., Mexico City, 1979; diploma in fin. analysis, Dun & Bradstreet Inc., 1980; diploma in Econs., Inst. Integration Ibero Am., Mexico City; MBA in Mgmt., Grad. Coll., Mexico City, 1992. Dir. Guantes Vargas, S.Am., 1977—. Chmn. bd. Colegio de Graduados en Alta Direccion, 1995-2000, Centro de Investigaciones sobre la Libre Empresa, A.C., 1990-2000; CEO Grupo Banacci, 1996-2000; fin. cons. in field. Contbr. articles to profl. publs. Cesar Gaviria's bus. assessor Am. States Orgn., 1994-98. Roman Catholic. Avocations: writing, speaking, Karate, soccer. Home: Col Indsl Calz de Guadalupe 392 07800 Mexico City Mexico Office: Guantes Vargas SAm Calzada de Guadalupe 392 Col Industrial 07800 Mexico City Mexico

VARGO, MERRY ELIZABETH, secondary school educator; b. Lorain, Ohio, Mar. 26, 1944; d. Warren L and Marjorie I Meilander; m. Edward L Vargo, June 30, 2000; m. Harry R Stewart, Dec. 30, 1971 (dec. Nov. 1983). BA, Wittenburg U., 1966; MA, Kent State U., 1973. Social studies tchr. Parma Sr. High, Parma, Ohio, 1966—96. Author: (book) I, Terrorist, 2002. Mem.: Writers Guild, Herb Soc., Hist. Soc., Sierra Club, Secular Franciscan Order, Red Hat Soc. Democrat. Roman Catholic. Avocations: reading, gardening, travel.

VARIAN, HAL RONALD, economics professor; b. Wooster, Ohio, Mar. 18, 1947; s. Max Ronald and Elaine Catherine (Shultzman) V.; m. Carol Johnston, Nov. 1986. S.B., MIT, 1969; MA, PhD (NSF fellow), U. Calif.-Berkeley, 1973. Asst. prof. econs. MIT, 1973-77; prof. U. Mich., 1977-95, prof. fin., 1983-95, Reuben Kempf prof. econs., 1984-95; prof. sch. bus., dean sch. info. mgmt. and sys. U. Calif., Berkeley, 1995—, Class of 1944 prof., 1996—. Siena chair in econs., U. Siena, Italy, 1990. Author: Microeconomic Analysis, 1978, Intermediate Microeconomics, 1987, Information Rules, 1998; co-editor Am. Econ. Rev., 1987-90. Guggenheim fellow, 1979-80; Fulbright scholar, 1990 Fellow AAAS, Econometric Soc.; mem. Am. Econ. Soc. Home: 1198 Estates Dr Lafayette CA 94549-2749 Office: U Calif Sims 102 South Hl Berkeley CA 94720-0001

VARIN, ROGER ROBERT, textile executive; b. Bern, Switzerland, Feb. 15, 1925; came to U.S., 1951; s. Robert Francois and Anna (Martz) V.; m. Annemarie Louis, May 24, 1951; children: Roger R.R., Edward C.H., Viviane A.H. BBA, Mcpl. Coll., Bern, 1944; PhD in Chemistry, U. Bern, 1951. Rsch. fellow Harvard U., Cambridge, Mass., 1951-52; rsch. assoc. E.I. DuPont De

Nemours, Wilmington, Del., 1952-62; dir. rsch. Riegel Textile Corp., Ware Shoals, S.C., 1962-71; founder, chief exec. officer Varinit Corp., Greenville, S.C., 1971—. Pres. Greenville Sister City Internat., 1993; bd. dirs. Greenville Symphony Assn., 1997-2000; trustee Brevard Music Ctr., 2000—. Mem. Am. Chem. Soc., Fiber Soc., Soc. Advanced Materials and Process Engring., Rotary (pres. Greenville chpt. 1979-80), Sigma Xi. Office: Varinit Corp PO Box 6602 Greenville SC 29606-6602

VARKEY, PRATHIBHA, preventive medicine physician, medical educator; b. N.Y., Apr. 12, 1974; MD, Christian Med. Coll., Dr. M.G.R. Med. U., Vellore, Tamil Nadu, India, 1995; MPH in Health Care Mgmt., Harvard Sch. Pub. Health, 2001. Resident internal medicine Hosp. St. Raphael, New Haven, 1997—2000; fellow gen. preventive medicine and pub. health Mayo Clinic, Rochester, 2001—03, asst. prof. preventive medicine and internal medicine, dir. assoc. program preventive medicine fellowship. Mem.: AMA Found. (Excellence in Medicine Leadership award 2004). Office: Mayo Clinic 200 First St SW Rochester MN 55905

VARKONYI, ANNA, cultural organization administrator, management consultant, educator; b. Budapest, Hungary, Dec. 18, 1946; d. Geza and Gézáné (Bozzai) V.; m. Tamas Revesz, Jan. 31, 1970; children: Judit, Andras. MS, Tech. U. Budapest, 1970, PhD in Environ. Economy, 1996. Rsch. worker Hungarian Acad. Scis., Budapest, 1970-78; editor Buvar Mag., Budapest, 1978-89; exec. Herald Agy., Budapest, 1991—; pres. Ecovision LLC, Rockaway, NJ, 1996—. Cons. Tetra Pak, Budapest, 1994—2000, European Union, Budapest, Budapest, 1992—96; global virtual faculty Fairleigh Dickinson U., Teaneck, NJ, 2001—. Mem Environ. Mgmt. and Law Assn. (bd. dirs. 1994—), Danube Circle (founder), Soc. Environ. Journalists, Assn. of Hungarian Chemists. Jewish. Avocations: cooking, nature hiking. Office: Herald Pub House Bimbó út 64 1022 Budapest Hungary Home: 1300 Carter Dr Rockaway NJ 07866-5911 Office Phone: 973-978-9249. Personal E-mail: avarkonyi@hptmail.com.

VARLEY, HERBERT PAUL, Japanese language and cultural history educator; b. Paterson, N.J., Feb. 8, 1931; s. Herbert Paul and Katharine L. (Norcross) V.; m. Betty Jane Geiskopf, Dec. 24, 1960 BS, Lehigh U., 1952; MA, Columbia U., 1961, PhD, 1964; DHL (hon.), Lehigh U., 1988. Asst. prof. U. Hawaii, Honolulu, 1964-65; asst. prof. dept. East Asian Langs. and Cultures Columbia U., N.Y.C., 1965-69, assoc. prof., 1969-75, prof., 1975-94, prof. emeritus Japanese history, 1994—, chmn. dept. East Asian Langs. and Cultures, 1983-89. Sen Soshitsu XV prof. Japanese Cultural History U. Hawaii, spring 1991-93, 94—. Author: The Onin War, 1967, The Samurai, 1970, Imperial Restoration in Medieval Japan, 1971, Japanese Culture, 1973, 4th edit., 2000, A Chronicle of Gods and Sovereigns, 1980, Tea in Japan: Essays on the History of Chanoyu, 1989, Warriors of Japan, As Portrayed in the War Tales, 1994; co-editor Sources of Japanese Tradition, Vol. 1, 2d edit., 2001. Bd. govs. Japanese Cultural Ctr. of Hawaii. Served with U.S. Army, 1952-54, Japan Recipient Imperial Decoration Govt. Japan, Order of Rising Sun, Gold Rays With Rosette Mem. Assn. Asian Studies, Japan Soc., Soc. Am. Magicians (pres. local chpt. 1983-84) Avocations: sleight of hand magic; piano. Home: 38 S Judd St Apt 15B Honolulu HI 96817-2609 Office: U Hawaii History Dept Sakamaki Hall A 203 2530 Dole St Honolulu HI 96822-2303 E-mail: pvarley@hawaii.edu.

VARMA, ARUP, finance educator, consultant; b. Allahabad, India, July 31, 1960; s. Leela W. Varma. PhD, Rutgers U., 1996. Dir., assoc. prof. HRIR/GSB Loyola U., Chgo., 1996—. Mem.: Acad. Mgmt. Office: Loyola U HRIR/GSB 820 N Michigan Ave Chicago IL 60657 Office Phone: 312-915-6664. Office Fax: 312-915-6231. E-mail: avarma@luc.edu.

VARMA, ARVIND, chemical engineering educator, researcher; b. Ferozabad, India, Oct. 13, 1947; s. Hans Raj and Vijay L. (Jhanjhee) V.; m. Karen K. Guse, Aug. 7, 1971; children: Anita, Sophia. BS ChemE, Panjab U., 1966; MS ChemE, U. N.B., Fredericton, Can., 1968; PhD ChemE, U. Minn., 1972. Asst. prof. U. Minn., Mpls., 1972-73; sr. research engr. Union Carbide Corp., Tarrytown, N.Y., 1973-75; asst. prof. chem. engring. U. Notre Dame, Ind., 1975-77, assoc. prof., 1977-80, prof., 1980-88, Arthur J. Schmitt prof., 1988—2003, chmn. dept., 1983-88; dir. Ctr. for Molecularly Engineered Materials, 2000—03; R. Games Slayter Disting. prof. and head Sch. of Chemical Engring, Purdue U., 2004—. Vis. prof. U. Wis., Madison, 1981; Chevron vis. prof. Calif. Inst. Tech., Pasadena, 1982; vis. prof. Ind. Inst. Tech.-Kanpur, 1989, U. Cagliari, Italy, 1989, 92; vis. fellow Princeton U., 1996; Piercy vis. prof. U. Minn., 2001. Co-author: Mathematical Methods in Chemical Engineering, 1997, Parametric Sensitivity in Chemical Systems, 1999, Catalyst Design, 2001; editor: (with others) The Mathematical Understanding of Chemical Engineering Systems, 1980, Chemical Reaction and Reactor Engineering, 1987; series editor: Cambridge Series in Chemical Engineering, 1996—; contbr. numerous articles to profl. jours. Recipient Tchr. of Yr. award Coll. Engring. U. Notre Dame, 1991, Spl. Presdl. award 1992, R.H. Wilhelm award AIChE, 1993, Burns Grad. Sch. award 1997, E.W. Thiele award AIChE, 1998, Chem. Engring. Lectureship award, ASEE, 2000, Rsch. Achievement award U. Notre Dame, 2001; Fulbright scholar; Indo-Am. fellow, 1988-89. Office: Purdue U Sch Chem Engring West Lafayette IN 47907

VARMA, BAIDYA NATH, sociologist, broadcaster, poet; b. India; m. Savitri Devi. PhD, Columbia U., 1958. Radio broadcaster to India UN; Asian News Moderator Nat. Edn. TV Network, N.Y.C.; prof. emeritus sociology CUNY. Prodr. radio dramas Voice of Am.; wrote, narrated over 200 documentary films, News of the Day; lectr. numerous univs. U.S., Can., Eng., India; chair Plenary Sessions World Congress of Sociology, Internat. Congress Anthrop. and Enthnological Scis; cons. Nat. Endowment Humanities, Ctr. Migration Studies, Dept. Energy, Wenner-Gren Found. Anthrop. Rsch. in U.S., Can. Coun., Indian Law Inst.; chair faculty seminars Columbia U.; presided Centenary Celebrations Indian Writers, N.Y.C.; vis. prof. Columbia U., other U.S., Indian Univs.; chair panel on religions and sexuality Parliament of World's Religions, 1993. Author: The Sociology and Politics of Development: A Theoretical Study, 1980, Social Science and Indian Society, 1985, New Directions in Theory and Methodology, 1993, Contemporary India (cert. of merit German Govt.), Love Feast, 1995, Spring of Civilization, 1995, Love and Life, 1999, India from Civilization to Nation, 1999; author, editor others; contbr. articles Ency. Americana, profl. jours.; edit. adv. nat., internat. sociol. jours.; author numerous poems. Assoc. trustee Wordsworth Trust; trustee Taraknath Das Found.; bd. scholars Buddhist Cultural Inst., U.S.; judge Permanent People's Tribunal Indsl. and Environ. Hazards and Human Rights, Rome; established Varma Found.; chmn. Sravi Found.; founding mems. Lincoln Ctr. for Performing Arts, N.Y.C.; chmn. bd. trustees Soc. for Restoration of Ancient Vidyadhams of India; trustee Internat. Found. for Vedic Edn., U.S., U.S. Capitol Hist. Soc.; mem. BC Millenium Time Capsule Commn. Sr. faculty fellow Am. Inst. Indian Studies, 1964-65, 84-85; elected to Am. Film Inst.; guest fellow Oxford U., The Sorbonne, Inst. Advanced Study, Simla, India; named Hon. Citizen, Colonial Williamsburg; recipient Cert. of Merit, City Coun. Pres. Yonkers; named Disting. Poet of 1996, Internat. Soc. Poets; elected patron of Am. Acad. Poetry, 1996; inducted Internat. Poetry Hall of Fame, 1996; named Outstanding Scientists of the 20th Century, 500 Leaders of Influence for the Next Millenium, 100 Founding Mem. Libr. of Congress, U.S. Mem. N.Y. Acad. Scis., South Asian Sociols. (1st pres.), Soc. Indian Acads. in Am. (exec. com.), Global Orgn. People of Indian Origin (life), U.S. Capitol Hist. Soc. (trustee). Home: 62 Belvedere Dr Yonkers NY 10705-2814

VARMA, DATLA G.K. radiologist, researcher; b. Bobbili, Andhra, India, June 2, 1951; came to U.S., 1976; now naturalized; s. Datla V. Raju and Datla Satyavathi; m. Siva Kumari, Dec. 20, 1980; children: Datla Kirti, Datla Vivek. MBBS, Andhra Med. Coll., 1975. Diplomate Am. Bd. Radiology, Am. Bd. Nuclear Medicine. Intern King George Hosp., Visakha Patnam, India, 1974-75; resident in anat. pathology Good Samaritan Hosp., Cin., 1977-78; resident in nuclear medicine Univ. Hosp., Cin., 1978-80, resident in radiology, 1980-83; asst. prof. radiology Tulane U., New Orleans, 1983-88, med. dir. diagnostic svcs./radiology dept., 1987-89, assoc. prof. radiology, 1988-89, sect. chief body CT, 1983-89, sect. chief body MRI, 1988-89; assoc. prof. radiology U. Tex./M.D. Anderson Cancer Ctr., Houston, 1989-99, acting sect. chief MRI, 1991-99, prof. radiology, 1999—. Contbr. articles to profl. jours., chpts. to books. Avocations: sports, travel, reading. Home: 3915 Marlowe St Houston TX 77005-2045 Office: Md Anderson Cancer Ctr PO Box 57 Houston TX 77001-0057 E-mail: dvarma@di.mdacc.tmc.edu.

VARMA, RANBIR, economics professor; b. Nov. 29, 1928; BA, Patna U., 1949; MA, Columbia U., 1952; PhD, New Sch. for Social Rsch., 1957. Lectr. Columbia U., 1955-57; asst. prof. L.I. U., 1959-63, assoc. prof., 1963-66, prof. econs., 1966—2003, chmn. econs. dept., 1963—76, 1985—2003, prof. emeritus, 2003. Bd. dirs. L.I. U.-Chung-and U. Program, 1963-64; chmn. commn. I, Bklyn. Ctr., 1964, chmn. dean's selection com., 1969-70; assoc. Columbia U. Faculty Seminar; cons. USIA, 1953-66; session chairperson devel. funds vs. needs, 8th World Conf., Soc. for Internat. Devel., 1966; session chairperson Montclair State Coll., 1977; conf. chairperson Eastern Econ. Assn., Washington, 1978. Author: (with others) Contemporary India, 1964, Goals Priorities and Dollars-The Next Decade, 1966, The Yearbook of the American Philosophical Society, 1968; contbr. articles to profl. jours; mem. editorial bd. Internat. Jour. of Devel. Planning Literature. Sidney Hillman fellowship, 1953-54; grantee Am. Philos. Soc., 1968. Mem. Am. Econ. Assn., Met. Econ. Assn., Soc. for Internat. Devel. Home: 565 W End Ave New York NY 10024-2705 Office: Long Island U Dept Econs University Pla Brooklyn NY 11201

VARMA, SURENDRA K. pediatrician, educator; b. Lucknow, India, Dec. 10, 1939; arrived in U.S., 1968; s. Raghubir P. and Leela Varma; m. Kamlesh Varma, Feb. 25, 1967; children: Rishi Anand, Ritu. MB, BChir, King George Med. Sch., Lucknow, 1962, MD, 1968. Diplomate Am. Bd. Pediat., Am. Subboard Pediat. Endocrinology. Rsch. assoc. MIT, Cambridge, Mass., 1972—74; asst. prof. Tex. Tech. U. Health Sci. Ctr., Lubbock, 1974—78, assoc. prof., 1978—83, prof., 1983—98, univ. dist. prof., 1998—. Instr. Harvard Med. Sch., Boston, 1973—76; vice chair resident rev. com. pediat. Accreditation Coun. Grad. Med. Edn., Chgo., 1997—; presenter in field. Contbr. articles to profl. jours. Lt. col. U.S. Army, 1990—91. Fellow: Am. Coll. Clin. Endocrinology, Am. Acad. Pediat.; mem.: Alpha Omega Alpha. Home: 4617 5th St Lubbock TX 79416 Office: Tex Tech Univ Health Scis Ctr 3601 4th St Lubbock TX 79430 Office Phone: 806-743-2244.

VARMUS, HAROLD ELIOT, former health science association administrator, research scientist, health facility executive, educator; b. Oceanside, NY, Dec. 18, 1939; s. Frank and Beatrice (Barasch) V.; m. Constance Louise Casey, Oct. 25, 1969; children: Jacob Carey, Christopher Isaac. BA, Amherst Coll., 1961; MA, Literature, Harvard U., 1962; MD, Columbia U. Med. Sch., 1966. Intern, resident Presbyn. Hosp., NYC, 1966-68; lectr. dept. microbiology U. Calif., San Francisco, 1970-72, asst. prof., 1972-74, assoc. prof., 1974-79, prof. depts. microbiology and immunology, biochemistry and biophysics, 1979—93, Am. Cancer Soc. research prof., 1984—93; clin. assoc. NIH, Bethesda, Md., 1968-70, dir., 1993—99; pres., CEO Meml. Sloan-Kettering Cancer Ctr., NYC, 2000—. Chmn. bd. on biology NRC, 1991—93; served on WHO Commn on Macroeconomics and Health; bd. dirs. Pub. Libr. Sci.; sci. bd. Grand Challenges in Global Health. Co-recipient Scientist of Yr. award, Calif. Acad. Sci., 1982, Lasker Found. award, 1982, Passano Found. award, 1983, Armand Hammer Cancer prize, GM Alfred Sloan award, Shubitz Cancer prize, 1984, Internat. award, Gardner Found., 1984, Nobel Prize in Physiology or Medicine, 1989; recipient Nat. Medal of Sci., 2002, Vannevar Bush award, NSF, 2001. Mem. NAS, Inst. Medicine, Am. Soc. Virology, Am. Soc. Microbiology, Am. Soc. Cell Biology, Am. Acad. Arts and Scis., Am. Soc. for Biochemistry and Molecular Biology. Democrat. Achievements include research (with J. Michael Bishop) on the the cellular origin of retroviral oncogenes. Office: Meml Sloan-Kettering Cancer Ctr 1275 York Ave New York NY 10021-6094 Office Phone: 212-639-6561.

VARNER, BRUCE H., JR., fire department official, educator; b. Washington, June 21, 1946; s. Bruce H. Varner and Rose A. (Parrish) Lewis; m. Elaine L. Nelson (div. 1974); 1 child, Paul A.; m. Susan A. Nungesser, Oct. 7, 1989 (div. 2000). AA in Fire Protection, Phoenix Coll., 1972; student, Ariz. State U., 1973-77. Firefighter Phoenix Fire Dept., 1967-72, fire engr., 1972-77, fire capt., 1977-83, div. chief, 1983-85, dep. chief, 1985-92; fire chief Carrollton (Tex.) Fire Dept., 1992—. Mem. Nat. Fire Protection Assn. (tech. corr. com. fire svc. protective clothing and equipment), Internat. Assn. Fire Chiefs, Dallas County Fire Chiefs (pres. 2001), S.W. Fire Chiefs, Denton County Fire Chiefs, North Tex. Fire Chiefs Assn. (pres. 1996), Internat. Soc. Fire Svc. Instrn., Hon. Order Ky. Cols., Career Fire Chief of Yr. Fire Chief Mag., 2001; U.S./U.K. Chief Fire Officers Symposium, Wingspread IV Conf., 1996. Avocations: sailing, travel, photography, raquetball. Office: Carrollton Fire Dept 1945 Jackson PO Box 110535 Carrollton TX 75011-0535 E-mail: brucevarner@cityofcarrollton.com.

VARNER, CHARLEEN LAVERNE MCCLANAHAN, nutritionist, educator, administrator, dietitian; b. Alba, Mo., Aug. 28, 1931; d. Roy Calvin and Lela Ruhama (Smith) McClanahan; student Joplin (Mo.) Jr. Coll., 1949-51; BS in Edn., Kans. State Coll. Pittsburg, 1953; MS, U. Ark., 1958; PhD, Tex. Woman's U. 1966; postgrad. Mich. State U., 1955, U. Mo., 1962; m. Robert Bernard Varner, July 4, 1953. Apprentice county home agt. U. Mo., 1952; tchr. Ferry Pass Sch., Escambia County, Fla., 1953-54; tchr. biology, home econs. Joplin Sr. H.S., 1954-59; instr. home econs. Kans. State Coll., Pittsburg, 1959-63; lectr. foods, nutrition Coll. Household Arts and Scis., Tex. Woman's U., 1963-64, rsch. asst. NASA grant, 1964-66; assoc. prof. home econs. Central Mo. State U., Warrensburg, 1966-70, adviser to Colhecon, 1966-70, adviser to Alpha Sigma Alpha, 1967-70, 72, bd. adv. Honors Group, 1967-70; prof., head dept. home econs. Kans. State Tchrs. Coll., Emporia, 1970-73; prof., chmn. dept. home econs. Benedictine Coll., Atchison, Kans., 1973-74; prof., chmn. dept. home econs. Baker U., Baldwin City, Kans., 1974-75; owner, operator Diet-Con Dietary Cons. Enterprises, cons. dietitian, 1973—, Home-Con Cons. Enterprises; adj. prof. Highland (Kans.) CC, 2004—. Active Joplin Little Theater, 1956-60. Mem. NEA, AAUW, AAUP, Mo. State Tchr. Assn., Kans. State Tchr. Assn., Am. Dietetic Assn., Mo. Dietetic Assn., Kans. Dietetic Assn., Am. Home Econs. Assn., Mo. Home Econs. Assn., Kans. Home Econs. Assn., Mo. Acad. Scis., U. Ark. Alumni Assn., Alumni Assn. Kans. State Coll. of Pittsburg, Am. Vocat. Assn., Assn. Edn. Young Children, Sigma Xi, Beta Sigma Phi, Beta Beta Beta, Alpha Sigma Alpha, Delta Kappa Gamma, Kappa Kappa Iota, Phi Upsilon Omicron, Theta Alpha Pi, Kappa Phi. Methodist (organist). Home: PO Box 1009 Topeka KS 66601-1009

VARNER, CHILTON DAVIS, lawyer; b. Opelika, Ala., Mar. 12, 1943; d. William Cole and Frances (Thornton) Davis; m. K. Morgan Varner III, June 19, 1965; 1 child, Ashley Elizabeth. AB with distinction, Smith Coll., 1965; JD with distinction, Emory U., 1976. Assoc. King & Spalding, Atlanta, 1976-83, ptnr., 1983—. Trustee Emory U., Atlanta, 1995—; bd. dirs. Wesley Woods Healthcare, 11th Cir. Ct. Appeals Hist. Soc.; bd. trustees Product Liability Adv. Coun. Found., 1996—. Author: Appellate Handbook for Georgia Lawyers, 1995. Mem. Leadership Atlanta, 1984-85; asst. clk., elder, bd. elders Trinity Presbyn. Ch., Atlanta, 1985-88; exec. com. Ate Arts Alliance, Atlanta, 1981-85; mem. Atlanta Symphony Chorus, 1970-74. Recipient Disting. Alumna award Emory U. Law Sch., 1998. Fellow Am. Coll. Trial Lawyers; mem. ABA, Ga. Bar Assn., Atlanta Bar Assn., Order of Coif, Phi Beta Kappa. Office: King & Spalding 191 Peachtree St NE Ste 4900 Atlanta GA 30303-1740

VARNER, DAVID EUGENE, lawyer; b. Dallas, Oct. 9, 1937; s. E.C. and D. Evelyn (Bauguss) V.; m. Joan Paula Oransky, Aug. 13, 1962; children: Michael A., Kevin E., Cheryl L. BA, So. Meth. U., Dallas, 1958, JD, 1961. Bar: Tex. 1961, Fla. 1974, Okla., 1977, U.S. Supreme Ct. 1978. Assoc. Eldridge, Goggans, Davidson & Silverberg, Dallas, 1962-65; atty., asst. sec. Redman Industries, Inc., Dallas, 1965-66; assoc. gen. atty. Tex. Instruments, Inc., Dallas, 1966-73; sr. atty., asst. sec. Fla. Gas Co., Winter Park, 1973-76; v.p., gen. counsel, sec. Facet Enterprises, Inc., Tulsa, 1976-78, Summa Corp., Las Vegas, Nev., 1978-82; sr. v.p., gen. counsel, sec. Transco Energy Co., Houston, 1982-95; pres. The MKC Group, Houston, 1995—. Mem. royalty mgmt. adv. com. Minority Mgmt. Svc., 1985—87. Mng. editor Southwestern Law Jour., 1960-61 Mem.: Fla. Bar Assn., Tex. Bar Assn. Office: PO Box 79571 Houston TX 77279-9571 Personal E-mail: devarner@msn.com.

VARNER, JOYCE EHRHARDT, retired librarian; b. Quincy, Ill., Sept. 13, 1938; d. Wilbur John and Florence Elizabeth (Mast) Ehrhardt; m. Donald Giles Varner, Sept. 12, 1959; children: Amy, Janice, Christian, Matthew, Nadine. BA, Northeastern Okla. State U., 1980; MLS, U. Okla., 1984. Lab. analyst Gardner Denver Co., Quincy, 1956-60; sales rep. Morrisonville, Ill., 1963-69; libr. clk. U. Ill., Urbana, 1973-75; libr. tech. asst. Northeastern Okla. State U., Tahlequah, 1976-86; asst. reference libr. Muskogee (Okla.) Pub. Libr., 1986-90; libr. Jess Dunn Correctional Ctr., Taft, Okla., 1990-98; ret., 1998; field office supr. Census 2000 Dept. of Commerce, Welling, Okla., 1998. Editor Indian Nations Audubon Nature Notes, 1977-81, 96—; contbr. articles to newspaper. Vol. Lake-Wood coun. Girl Scouts U.S.A., 1975-98, bd. dirs. 1992-98, pres., 1995-96; sec.-treas. Cherokee County Rural Water Dist. 7, 1987—; edn. chmn. Indian Nations chpt. Nat. Audubon Soc., 1989-2000, pres., 2000-04; project dir. Tahlequah Friends of the Libr., 2002-04, pres. 2004—. Recipient Thanks Badge, Lake-Wood coun. Girl Scouts U.S.A., 1990. Mem. AAUW (chair diversity com. 2000), Okla. Libr. Assn. (nominating com. 1989), Okla. Acad. Sci., Okla. Ornithol. Soc. (chmn. libr. com. 1978-88, Award of Merit 1990, pres.-elect 1994, pres. 1995-96), Alpha Chi, Beta Beta Beta, Phi Delta Kappa (Found. rep. 1984-86, historian 1992—). Avocations: nature study, needlecrafts, square dancing, genealogy. Home: 20582 S Welling Rd Welling OK 74471-2001

VARNER, ROBERT BERNARD, counselor, educator; b. Ellsworth, Kans., May 31, 1930; s. Bernard Lafayette and Leota (Campbell) V.; B.S., Kans. State U., Pittsburg, 1952; M.S., U. Ark., 1959; postgrad. Mich. State U., summer 1955, U. Mo., summer 1962, (grantee) U. Kans., 1972-73; m. Charleen LaVerne McClanahan, July 4, 1953. Athletic coach, social sci. tchr. Joplin (Mo.) Sr. High Sch., 1956-63; head social sci. dept. R.L. Turner High Sch., Carrollton, Tex., 1963-66; asst. athletic coach, jr. high sch. social sci. tchr. Warrensburg, Mo., 1966-70; coach, social sci. tchr., Emporia, Kans., 1970-72; asst. cottage dir., counselor Topeka Youth Ctr., 1973—; substitute tchr. Topeka Pub. Schs., 1974— . Recreation dir. Carrollton-Farmers Branch (Tex.) Recreation Center, 1964-66; city recreation dir., Warrensburg, Mo., 1966-68. Served with USN, 1953-54. Mem. NEA, Kans. State U.-Pittsburg Alumni Assn., U. Ark. Alumni Assn., Phi Delta Kappa, Sigma Tau Gamma. Democrat. Methodist. Club: Elks. Address: PO Box 1009 Topeka KS 66601-1009

VARNER, STERLING VERL, retired oil company executive; b. Ranger, Tex., Dec. 20, 1919; s. George Virgle and Christina Ellen (Shafer) V.; m. Paula Jean Kennedy, Nov. 17, 1945; children: Jane Ann, Richard Alan. Student, Murray State Sch. Agr., 1940, Wichita State U., 1949. With Kerr-McGee, Inc., 1941-45; with Koch Industries, Inc., Wichita, Kans., 1945-90, pres., chief operating officer, 1974-86, vice chmn., 1987-90, chmn. bd. dirs., 1990, now bd. dirs.; ret. Owner Shadow Valley Ranch; bd. dirs. Koch Industries Inc. Mem. Wichita Country Club, Crestview Country Club. Mem. Ch. of Christ. Home: 1515 N Linden Ct Wichita KS 67206-3312 Office: Koch Industries Inc PO Box 2256 411 E 37th St N Wichita KS 67219

VARNEY, CARLETON BATES, JR., interior designer, columnist, educator; b. Lynn, Mass., Jan. 23, 1937; s. Carleton Bates and Julia (Raczkowskos) V.; divorced; children: Nicholas, Seamus, Sebastian. BA, Oberlin Coll., 1958; student, U. Madrid, 1957; MA, NYU, 1969; LHD (hon.), U. Charleston, 1987. Sch. tchr., 1958-59; asst. to pres. Dorothy Draper & Co., Inc., 1959-63, exec. v.p., 1963-66, pres., 1966—; dean Carleton Varney Sch. of Art & Design, U. Charleston, W.Va. Designer: Varney and Sons Furniture Collection Kindel Furniture Co., Carleton Varney by-the-yard decorative fabrics, dinnerware and china, crystal glassware, table and bed linen, lamps and light fixtures, ready to wear resort collection Cruzanwear, 1987, mens' wear furnishings for Rawlinson & Marking, London, 1987; Ready to wear resort coll., "A Perfect Day in Paradise", 1998, Colours Resort Collection, 2000; interior designer: Dromoland Castle, Ireland, 1963, 88, Westbury Hotel, Belgium, 1964, NY World's Fair, 1965, Clare Inn, Ireland, 1968, Greenbrier Hotel, White Sulphur Springs, W.Va., 1968-, Westbury Hotel, San Francisco, 1973, Copley Plaza Hotel, Boston, 1976,1996, Amway Grand Plaza Hotel, Grand Rapids, Mich., 1980, The Grand Hotel, Mackinac Island, Mich., 1978-, Equinox House, Manchester, Vt., 1984, Brazilian Ct. Hotel, Palm Beach, Fla., 1985, Waldorf Towers, NYC, 1985, Dawn Beach Hotel, St. Maarten, 1985, Christian Broadcasting Conv. Ctr., 1986, Met. Opera House boutique, NYC, 1985, (cruise ship) World Discoverer, 1984, Arrowwood Conv. Ctr., Purchase, NY, 1987, Boca Raton Hotel and Club, Fla., 1987, Speedway Club, Charlotte, NC, 1987, Coccoloba Plantation, Anguilla, Brit. Virgin Islands, 1987, Villa Madeleine, St. Croix, VI, 1987, Ashford Castle, Ireland, 1988, Adare Manor, Ireland, 1988, The Breakers, Palm Beach, Fla., 1989, Jackson Lake Lodge, Wyo., 1989, V.P.'s Residence, Washington, 1989, Cormorant Cove, St. Croix, VI, 1990, The Buccaneer Hotel, St. Croix, 1991, Dromoland Castle, Internat. Ctr., Ireland, 1991, West Village Golf Resort, Tokyo, 1993, Half Moon Bay Club, Jamaica, The Plaza, NY, 1997, The Hibiscus Restaurant, Palm Beach, Fla., 1999, North Shore Country Club, LI, NY, 2002, Mount Wash. Hotel and Resort, N.H., 2003, Lago Mar Resort and Club, Ft. Lauderdale, Fla., 2003-04; numerous pvt. residences; designer: White House party for celebration Israel-Egypt Peace Treaty, 1979; Palm Beach Cares fashion benefit for Am. Found. for AIDS Research, 1988, log home for Pres. and Mrs. Carter, Ellijay, Ga., 1983; color cons. Carter Presdl. Library, 1986; trustee and curator: former presdl. yacht U.S.S. Sequoia, 1982; retail store: Carleton Varney Rose Cottage, Newmarket-on-Fergus, Ireland, 1991; author: numerous books including You and Your Apartment, 1960, The Family Decorates a Home, 1962 Carleton Varney Decorates Windows, 1975, Be Your Own Decorator, 1979, There's No Place Like Home, 1980, Down Home, 1981, Carleton Varney's ABC's of Decorating, 1983, Staying in Shape: An Insider's Guide to the Great Spas, 1983, Room by Room Decorating, 1984, Color Magic, 1985, The Draper Touch, 1988, Kiss the Hibiscus Goodnight, 1992, The Decorator, 1999; syndicated columnist: Your Family Decorator, 1968—; decorating column Familyclick.com, 2000, Inside Design column N.Y. Post, 2001; contbg. editor Good Housekeeping Mag., 1993-95; contbg. design editor Social and Personal Mag. (Ireland) 1996-; style editor Men's Style mag.; editor-at-large Hamptons Mag., 2000—. Recipient Shelby Williams award for design achievement, 1967, Tommy design award for Covington's Heraldry collection, 1989, Interior Design Hall of Fame award, 1990. Mem. Indsl. Designers Soc. Am., NY State Bd. for Interior Design. Clubs: NY Athletic; Shannon Rowing (Ireland); Millbrook Golf and Tennis (NY). Office: Dorothy Draper & Co Inc 60 E 56th St New York NY 10022-3204 also: Rose Cottage Newmarket-on-Fergus County Clare Ireland also: Carleton Varney by the Yard 2239 15th St # B&C Sarasota FL 34237-2828 Office Phone: 212-758-2810. Personal E-mail: dorothydraper1@aol.com. E-mail: dorothydraper1@aol.com. *My success, I believe, is due to an ability to understand and use vibrant color appropriately, and to strive for perfection of detail in all my designs as details separate the excellent from the ordinary.*

VARNEY, GLENN HERBERT, management educator; b. Jefferson, Ohio, Dec. 1, 1926; s. Herbert Henry and Edna (Schwartz) V.; m. Ruth Constance Park, June 30, 1951; children: Janice McKnight, Kenneth. BSc in Bus. Adminstrn., Ohio State U., 1949, MBA, 1951; PhD, Case Western Res. U., 1971. Cert. sr.profl. in human rels. Pers. mgr. Glidden Co., Cleve., 1951-55; mgr. recruitment and mgmt. devel. Diamond Shamrock, Dallas, 1955-65; dir. human resources Harshaw Chems., Cleve., 1965-68; asst. to dean Case Western Res. U., Cleve., 1968-70; dir. Mgmt. Ctr. Bowling Green (Ohio) State U., 1970-83, prof. mgmt. emeritus, 1970—; pres. Mgmt. Adv. Assocs., Bowling Green, 1968—. Bd. dirs. Self-Directed Resource Ctr., Bowling Green, 1992—, Inst. for Orgnl. Effectiveness, 1979-96; cons. numerous U.S., internat. orgns. Author: Building Productive Teams, 1990, Management by Objectives, 1969, 3 other books; co-author (with Robert Golembiewski) Cases in Organizational Development, 1999 edition, 2003, edition, Bibliography of Organization Devel. and Change Literature pub. by Bowling Green State U.; contbr. over 100 articles to profl. jours. Vol. work with non-profit orgns.; mem. various ch. and cmty. related coms. and projects. Recipient Disting. Svc. award, Acad. Mgmt. Orgn., 2001. Mem. ASTD (nat. v.p. 1980-81, award for leadership 1992, award for excellence 1993, Disting. Svc. award 2001); Soc.

for Human Resources (life accreditation), Acad. Mgmt. (Disting. Svc. award 2001), Beta Gamma Sigma, Omicron Delta Kappa. Republican. Avocations: farm managment, jogging. Home: 546 Hillcrest Dr Bowling Green OH 43402-3616 Fax: 419-354-8781. E-mail: gvarney@bgnct.bgsu.edu.

VARNEY, RICHARD ALAN, health facility administrator; b. Concord, NH, July 8, 1950; s. John Berry and Hattie Elizabeth (Harrington) V.; m. Cheryl Suzanne Glaab, Dec. 31, 1983; stepchildren: Alysen Suzanne, Craig Judson. BS in Phys. Edn., U. N.H., 1972; MHA in Healthcare Adminstrn., Baylor U., 1984; diploma, Command and Gen. Staff Coll., 1986. Commd. 2d lt. U.S. Army, 1973, advanced through grades to lt. col., 1991; dep. asst. CEO Cutler Army Hosp., Ft. Devens, Mass., 1973—76; field med. asst. 38th ADA Bde., Osan Air Base, Republic of Korea, 1977—78; dep. asst. CEO 15th Med. Battalion, Ft. Hood, Tex., 1979—81; adminstrv. resident Ireland Army Hosp., Ft. Knox, Ky., 1982—83; COO, exec. officer U.S. Army Dental Activity, Ft. Knox, 1983—86; grad. instr. Army-Baylor Healthcare Program, San Antonio, 1986—90; project mgr. Office of the Army Surgeon Gen., Washington, 1990—93; ret. U.S. Army, 1993; office mgr. Aebi, Ginty, Romaker & Sprouse MD's, Inc., Lancaster, Ohio, 1993—2000; dir. gen. internal medicine program The Ohio State U. Med. Ctr., Columbus, 2000—. Mem. Source Selection Evaluation Bd.-Champus Reform, Arlington, Va., 1987; mem. adv. com. for assoc. degree program in med. assisting Ohio U., Lancaster, 1998-2000. Adult leader Boy Scouts Am., Tex., Va. and Ohio, 1988-97; mem. Lancaster City Bd. of Health, 1996-2001, pres. pro tem, 1999-2001; mem. Fairfield County Combined Gen. Health Dist. Bd., 2002--. Decorated Legion of Merit, Order of Mil. Med. Merit award, Expert Field Med. badge; named to Hon. Order Ky. Cols., 1989, Outstanding Young Man of Am., 1982. Fellow Am. Coll. Healthcare Execs.; mem. Cul. Ohio Health Adminstrs. Assn., Ohio Med. Group Mgmt. Assn., Mid-Ohio Med. Mgmt. Assn., Profl. Assn. Med. Mgrs., Am. Assn. Procedural Coders, Lancaster Area Soc. for Human Resource Mrmt. (legis. rep. 1998-99, membership chair 1999—), Am. Hosp. Assn., Nat. Eagle Scout Assn., The Ret. Officers Assn., Am. Legion, Fraternal Order of Eagles, Alpha Phi Omega. Avocations: home improvement, music. Home: 1025 E 5th Ave Lancaster OH 43130-3276 Office Phone: 614-293-7901. Personal E-mail: richvarneyosu@yahoo.com. Business E-Mail: varney-1@medctr.osu.edu.

VARNEY, ROBERT NATHAN, retired physicist, researcher; b. San Francisco, Nov. 7, 1910; s. Frank Hastings Sr. and Emily Patricia (Rhine) V.; m. Astrid Margareta Riffolt, June 19, 1948; children: Nils Roberts, Natalie Rhine. AB in Physics with highest honors, U. Calif., Berkeley, 1931, MA, 1932, PhD, 1935; DSc (hon.), Leopold Franzens U., Innsbruck, Austria, 1983. Instr. NYU, 1936-38; asst. prof., assoc. prof., prof. Washington U., St. Louis, 1938-64; mem. rsch. lab. Bell Labs., Murray Hill, NJ, 1951-52; sr. mem. rsch. lab., sr. sci. cons. Lockheed Missiles & Space Co., Palo Alto, Calif., 1964-75; ret., 1975. Mem. Mo. Gov.'s Sci. Adv. Com., St. Louis, 1960-64; guest prof. Leopold Franzens U., 1977-78. Author: Engineering Physics, 1948; (with others) Methods of Experimental Physics, 1968, Introduction to ... Atmospheric Pollution, 1972, Brain Injury without Head Injury, 1999; contbg. author textbook; contbr. over 80 articles to scholarly and profl. jours. Comdr. USNR, 1931-57. Fulbright fellow Leopold Franzens U., Innsbruck, 1971-72, 76-77, NSF sr. postdoctoral fellow Inst. Tech., Stockholm, 1958-59, NRC sr. postdoctoral fellow U.S. Army Ballistic Rsch. Lab., Aberdeen, Md., 1975-76; recipient Cross of Honor 1st Class Austrian Govt., 1981. Fellow Am. Phys. Soc.; mem. Am. Assn. Physics Tchrs., Phi Beta Kappa, Sigma Xi, Tau Beta Pi, Omicron Delta Kappa. Episcopalian. Achievements include research in electron swarms and atmospheric pollutants; studies of closed head brain injuries. Home: 4156 Maybell Way Palo Alto CA 94306-3820 E-mail: riffolt@batnet.com.

VARNEY, ROBERT W. government agency administrator; Bachelor's, U. NH; Master's, Mich. State U. Commr. Dept. Environ. Svcs., NH, 1989—2001; adminstr. region 1 US EPA, Boston, 2001—. Pres. Environ. Coun. of States; chiar Gulf of Maine Coun.; chair Ozone Transport Commn.; chair com. New England Gov.'s Conf. Environment; chair New England Interstate Water Pollution Control Commn. Office: EPA New England Region 1 1 Congress St Boston MA 02114-2023

VARNUM, JAMES WILLIAM, hospital administrator; b. Grand Rapids, Mich., May 29, 1940; s. Robert Otto and Jeannette (Badger) V.; m. Lucinda Hotchkiss, June 6, 1964; children: Kenneth James, Susan Lucinda. AB, Dartmouth Coll., 1962; M.Hosp. Adminstrn. with honors, U. Mich., 1964. Adminstrv. asst. U. Wis. Hosps., Madison, 1963-64, asst. supt., 1964-68, assoc. supt., 1968-69, supt., 1969-73; hosp. adminstr. U. Wash. Hosp., Seattle, 1973-78; pres. Mary Hitchcock Meml. Hosp., Lebanon, N.H., 1978—; prof. Med. Sch., Dartmouth Coll., 1978—. Bd. dirs. Ledyard Nat. Bank, Hanover, NH, VHA, Inc., Irving, Tex., Vt. Inst. Natural Scis., N.H. Charitable Found.; pres. Dartmouth-Hitchcock Alliance, 1983—. Mem.: Am. Hosp. Assn. (trustee 1994—97). Office: Mary Hitchcock Meml Hosp 1 Medical Center Dr Lebanon NH 03756-0001

VARRO, BARBARA JOAN, retired editor; b. East Chicago, Ind., Jan. 25, 1938; d. Alexander R. and Lottie R. (Bess) V. BA, Duquesne U., 1959. Feature reporter, asst. fashion editor Chgo. Sun-Times, 1959-64, fashion editor, 1964-76, feature writer, 1976-84; v.p. pub. rels. Daniel J. Edelman Inc., Chgo., 1984-85; v.p. PRB/Needham Porter Novelli, Chgo., 1985-86; editor Am. Hosp. Assn. News, Chgo., 1987-94; editor spl. sects. Chgo. Tribune, 1995-2000; ret. Recipient awards for feature writing Ill. AP, 1978, 79, 80 Mem.: PEO.

VARSHAVSKY, ALEXANDER JACOB, molecular biologist; b. Moscow, Nov. 8, 1946; came to U.S., 1977; s. Jacob M. and Mary B. (Zeitlin) V.; m. Vera Bingham, Aug. 30, 1990; children: Roman, Anna, Victoria. BS in Chemistry, Moscow State U., 1970; PhD in Biochemistry, Inst. of Molecular Biology, Moscow, 1973. Rsch. fellow Inst. Molecular Biology, Moscow, 1973—76; asst. prof. dept. biology MIT, Cambridge, 1977-80, assoc. prof. dept. biology, 1980-86, prof. dept. biology, 1986-92; Howard and Gwen Laurie Smits prof. cell biology, divsn. biology Calif. Inst. Tech., Pasadena, 1992—. Vis. fellow Internat. Inst. for Advanced Studies, Kyoto; mem. molecular cytology study sect. NIH. Author more than 150 articles in the field of genetics and biochemistry; holder 14 patents. Recipient Novartis-Drew award Novartis, 1998, Merit award NIH, 1998, Gairdner Internat. award (Can.), 1999, Shubitz prize U. Chgo., 2000, Hoppe-Seyler award (Germany), 2000, Alfred P.Sloan Jr. prize GM Cancer Rsch. Found., 2000, Lasker award in Basic Medical Rsch., Albert and Mary Lasker Found, 2000, Shubitz prize in Cancer Rsch., U. Chgo., 2000, Hoppe-Seyler award Soc. for Biochemistry and Molecular Biology, Germany, 2000, Merck award Am. Soc. Biochemistry and Molecular Biology, 2001, Pasarow award in Cancer Rsch., Pascrow Found., 2001, Wolf prize in medicine Wolf Found., Israel, 2001, Massry prize, Massry Found., 2001, Max Planck Rsch. prize, Germany, 2001, Horwitz prize Columbia U., 2001, Wilson medal Am. Soc. Cell Biology, 2002, Stein & Moore award Protein Soc., 2005. Fellow AAAS, Am. Acad. Microbiology, Am. Acad. Arts and Scis.; mem. NAS, Am. Philos. Soc., European Molecular Biology Orgn. (assoc.). Achievements include discoveries in the fields of DNA replication, chromosome structure, ubiquitin system, and intracellular protein turnover. Office: Calif Inst Tech Divsn Biology 1200 East California Blvd Pasadena CA 91125-0001 Office Phone: 626-395-3785. Office Fax: 626-440-9821.

VARZEGAR, MINOO, literature educator, reading specialist; b. Kerman, Iran; d. Abdolrahim and Amjad (Vali) Varzegar; m. Saeid Fatemi, May 8; children: Delaram, Arezou. BA in English, U. Tehran, 1966; MA in Tchg. English, U. Tchr. Edn., 1967; MA in Psychology, U. Tehran, 1969; MA in Tchg. English as a Second Lang., U. Ill., 1971, PhD in Tchg. English as a Second Lang., 1975, postgrad., 1994. Cert. tchr. English, cert. high acad. adminstrn. Asst. prof. U. Tehran, 1979-84, assoc. prof., 1984-94, prof. dept. English, 1984-97, head Dept. English of Evening Classes, 1975-83, dir. Lang. Lab., 1975-80, dir. lang. ctr., 1981-83, head dept. English, 1983-97. Vis. prof. U. Ill., Champaign-Urbana, 1997-99, rsch. scholar, 1997-99; assoc. faculty Columbia U., N.Y.C., 1999-2001; faculty mem. English dept. Rutgers U., Newark, 1999—, William Paterson U., Wayne, N.J., 1999-2001; dir. Ctr. testing and Psychometrics, Min. of Culture and Higher Edn., Tehran, 1975-77; mem. rsch. adv. bd. ABI, 2003. Author: Children's English series, 1990-95, Reading Through Reading (Best Acad. Book), 1992, Testing and Measurement (Best Acad. Book), 1993, A Comprehensive Grammar of English, 1996, Testing TEFL, 1997; author/editor: Issues in Teaching English as a Second Language, 1990, English for the Students of Medicine, 1989; co-author: English for Medical Students, 1974; editor: English for the Students of Medicine (II), 1993, Novin English-Persian Dictionary, vols. I and II, 1993; co-editor: Yadvareh Persian-English Dictionary, vols. I, II, III, 1991, Yadvareh English-Persian Dictionary, vols. I and II, 1991, Yadvareh Unabridged English-Persian Dictionary, 1993, others; contbr. numerous articles to profl. jours. Mem. com. Ctr. Studying and Compiling Univ Books in Humanities Min. Culture and Higher Edn., 1984—97, mem. com. curriculum devel., 1984—97, com. for testing, 1977—79; mem. com. lang. testing Lang. Ctr., 1979—81. Recipient Award for creating an Innovative Model of Reading Comprehension, U. Ill., 1975, Cert. of Appreciation for best adminstrn. U. Mich., 1998, award for extraordinary ability INS, 1998, Disting. Prof. award, 2000, Disting. Rschr. award, 2000, Woman of Achievement award BBC, 2002; U. Ill. grantee, 1975; Fulbright scholar, 1970-75, Profl. Deveol. scholar TESOL, 1999; fellow in rsch. U. Ill., 1973-75; named one of One Thousand Intellectuals, BBC, 2002; named Contemporary Woman of the World, 2003, Outstanding Woman Banou Women's Org., 2003. Mem. Tchrs. of English to the Speakers of Other Langs., U. Ill. Alumni Assn., Am. Assn. for Applied Linguistics, Nat. Coun. Tchrs. English, Internat. Reading Assn. Avocations: computers, reading, painting, tennis, swimming. Home: 290 Anderson St # 6K Hackensack NJ 07601 Office: Rutgers Univ Dept English 5241 Hill Hall 320 Dr Martin Luther King Blvd Newark NJ 07102-1811 E-mail: varzegar@aol.com.

VASCHE, MARK, newspaper editor; Exec. editor Modesto (Calif.) Bee, 1997—. Office: Modesto Bee PO Box 5256 Modesto CA 95352-5256

VASERSTEIN, LUDMILA, music educator; b. Odessa, Ukraine, Sept. 21, 1949; arrived in USA, 1987; d. Peter and Rozalia Ruvinsky; m. Vladimir Vassershteyn, July 8, 1972; 1 child, Gabriel. MusB, Nicolaev (Ukraine) Coll. Music, 1969; MusM, Odessa State Conservatory, Odessa, Ukraine, 1974. Piano tchr. Sch. of Music, Odessa, Ukraine, 1974—87, MDCC, Miami, Fla., 1987—96; music and piano tchr. Montessoir Sch. of Miami Beach, No. Bay Village, Fla., 1988—2003, Gulfstream Montessoir Sch., Inc., Hallandale, Fla., 2003—. Mem.: Nat. Guild of Piano Tchr. (Nat. Honor Roll 2001—03), Music Tchr. Nat. Assoc., Suzuki Assoc. of Am. Republican. Judaism. Avocations: jogging, reading. Home: 251 174th St #1202 Miami Beach FL 33160 Office: Gulfstream Montessori Sch 750 Hallandale Beach Blvd Hallandale FL 33009

VASHOLZ, LOTHAR ALFRED, retired insurance company executive; b. Milw., Feb. 20, 1930; s. Alfred and Charlotte Vasholz; m. Marji Cartwright, Dec. 26, 1954; children: Julie, Ann, Eric. BS, U. Colo., 1952; M of Pub. Svc. (hon.), U. Rio Grande, Ohio. ChFC. Sr. cons. Life Ins. Mktg. & Rsch., Hartford, Conn., 1966-70; v.p. N.Am. Life, Chgo., 1970-73; sr. v.p. Bankers Mut., Freeport, Ill., 1973-75; sales dir. Security Life of Denver, 1975-81; v.p. Union Ctrl. Life Ins. Co., Cin., 1981-85, sr. v.p., 1985-86, mgr. Columbus, Ohio, 1986-87, sr. v.p., chief mktg. officer Cin., 1987-91, exec. v.p., corp. mktg. officer, 1991-95; chmn. Carillon Investments, 1991-95; cons. on mktg. and sales to life ins. industry, 1995—; co-founder, pres. The Stewardship Co., 2001—. Trustee U. Rio Grande, Ohio; mem. trauma program Coachella Valley Orgn. Social Venture Ptnrs. Fellow Life Mgmt. Inst.; mem. Phi Delta Theta (past internat. pres.). Republican. Office Phone: 888-593-3933.

VASILIAUSKAS, EDMUND, retired chemistry professor; b. Lithuania, June 18, 1938; came to the U.S., 1957; s. Vincent and Elena V.; m. Jura B. Gelazius, Jan. 24, 1970 (dec. 1991); children: Eric, Lora, Paul, Thomas; m. Maria Miksiunas, Aug. 4, 1995. BS, Rochester Inst. Tech., 1963; PhD, Loyola U. Chgo., 1970. Chemist Olin Corp., Rochester, N.Y., 1964-65, Witco Corp., Chgo., 1970-71; prof. Moraine Valley Coll., Palos Hills, Ill., 1971—, ret., 2002, prof. emeritus, 2002—. Mem. Am. Chem. Soc. Avocations: travel, music, gardening. Home: 8512 Johnston Rd Burr Ridge IL 60527-7076

VASILJEV, ALEXANDER VALERJOVICH, metallurgical engineer, economist; b. Kuragata, Kazakhstan, June 21, 1955; s. Valery Alexandrovich and Olga Vladimirovna Vasiljev; m. Marina Genadievna Tuzovskaya, Dec. 31, 1985; children: Olga, Nataliya. Diplomate of engring., Metall. Inst., 1977; Candidate Scis., Inst. Engring., Moscow, 1982; postgrad., Inst. Sociology Acad. Scis., Moscow, 1992; PhD in Econs., Acad. Mgmt. Russia, Moscow, 1993. Jr., then sr. scis. employee Inst. Mariupol, Ukraine, 1980-84, mgr. rsch. lab. socioecon. problems., 1985-87; mgr. socially econ. lab. Inst. Labour of Ukraine, Mariupol, 1987-90; mgr. sect. social econ. problems of port's indsl. cities Inst. Econ.-Law Rsch., Nat. Acad. Scis. Ukraine, Mariupol, 1993-98, organizer Mariupol br., 1995-97; chmn. sci. coun. Inst. Econ. and Social/Cultural Rsch., Mariupol, 1989—. Prof. PriAzov State Tech. U., Mariupol, 1993-98, Taganrog's Inst. Mgmt. and Econs., Russia, 2001-02; prod., dep. acad. mgr. staff Mariupol, Ukraine, 2003-2004; vice chmn. Azov, Ukrainian Dept., Acad. Econ., Scis. and Entrepreneurship, Mariupol, 1999—, Civil Internat. Com., Tanais Reg., 2001-; rep. Azov Ukrainian Econ. Dept. Acad. Econ., Sci. and Entrepreneurship in West Europe and Am., Warsaw, 2000—; chief br. mgr. Dep. Acad. Mgr. Staff, Mariupol, Ukraine, 2003-04. Author: Theoretical and Methodological Basis of Concepts of Transformation and Preservation of Labor, 1998, Methodological Fundamentals of Stabilization Socially of Economic Development, 2004, Management of Foreign Trade Activities in Light of Law of Preservation of Labor and Law of Non destroy of Intelligently Spiritual Labor, 2004; contbr. articles to profl. jours. Scholar Acad. Russia, 1991-92 Probationer Inst. IBMER Poland, 2000-2001; recipient cert. Frederick P. Furth Found., 1990, medal "Met. Gotey & Cafa, St. Ignatia", 1999. Mem. AAAS, N.Y. Acad. Scis., 1817 Heritage Soc. N.Y. Acad. Scis., Union Econ. Ukraine, Acad. Econ. Scis. and Entrepreneurship (hon.). Avocations: tennis, windsurfing, travel. Home: Fl 41 Zelinsky 1 St 87534 Mariupol Ukraine Office: Inst Econ/Social/Cult Rsch Stroiteley 39 Ave Box 7 87534 Mariupol Ukraine Office Phone: 380 (0629) 37-39-79. E-mail: vasiljev2003@mail.ru., vasiljev@cic-wsc.org.

VASILY, JOHN TIMOTHY, information systems executive, state government official; b. Everett, Mass., Feb. 5, 1961; s. Andrew and Catherine Agnes (Coyne) V. BA, U. Mass., 1983; MBA, Suffolk U., 1992. Data analyst Higher Edn. Coord. Coun., Boston, 1984-92; sr. programmer, analyst Babson Coll., Babson Park, Mass., 1992-96; dir. new sys. devel. Mass. Dept. Youth Svcs., Boston, 1996-2000; chief info. officer Mass. Dept. Mental Retardation, Boston, 2000—. Adj. instr. Newbury Coll., Brookline, Mass., 1992—, Suffolk U., Boston, 2001—. Co-author: Massachusetts Integrated Post Secondary Education Data System, 1990; author: 1986-87 Completions Supplement, 1989. Recipient Citation for Outstanding Performance Commonwealth of Mass., 1998. Mem. IEEE, Delta Mu Delta, Omicron Delta Epsilon. Avocations: bowling, fishing, hiking, golf, photography. E-mail: John.Vasily@dmr.state.ma.us.

VASKEVITCH, DAVID, information technology executive; 3 children. BS in Math., Computer Sci., Philosophy, M in Computer Sci., U. Toronto. Owner PlanDesign; with 3Com Corp.; dir. U.S. mktg. Microsoft, 1986, gen. mgr. enterprise computing, chief architect, 1998—99, sr. v.p. Bus. Applications Divsn., 2000—01, sr. v.p., chief tech. officer Bus. Platform, 2001—. Author: Client/Server Strategies: A Survival Guide for Corporate Re-engineers, 1993. Avocations: photography, horseback riding. Office: Microsoft One Microsoft Way Redmond WA 98052-6399*

VASKO, PETER THEODORE FREDERICK, priest; b. Bklyn., Nov. 28, 1943; s. Theodore Frederick and Catherine (Buday) V. BA in Philosophy, Cath. U. Am., 1966, BD in Theology, 1969; postgrad., Duke U., 1972-73, Franciscan Studium Biblicum, Jerusalem, 1985-86. Ordained priest Roman Cath. Ch., 1987. Pub. rels. asst. Holiday Inn/Oak Grove, Durham, N.C., 1972-74; dir. devel. NAA, Charlotte, N.C., 1974-76; dir. CETA, New Orleans, 1976-78; v.p. sales Peachtree Corners Corp. Travel, Atlanta, 1978-81; bd. dirs. Franciscan Custody, Jerusalem, 1992—; pres. The Holy Land Found., Jerusalem, 1994—. Editor photo essay See the Holy Land, 1993, The Holy Land and the Millennium, 2000; editor The Holy Land Mag., 1993-95; writer, narrator video On the Road of Christ, 1994; narrator video The Life of Jesus: Scriptural Journey, 1997; guest on Mother Angelica Live, 1996, 97, 98, 2002, Pat Robertson 700 Club, 1996, others; co-prodr. documentary Crisis in the Holy Land, 1994. Bd. dirs. St. Ives Soc., Jerusalem, 1992-94; guide White House Via U.S. Embassy, Jerusalem, 1992—; chaplain U.S. Marines/U.S. Consulate, Jerusalem, 1988—. Recipient Achievement in Pub. Rels. award Pub. Rels. Soc., Raleigh, 1975, Marine Security Guard Bn. Co. B Cert. of Appreciation, 1995, 99, U.S. Marine Security Detachment Comdr. Commendation award, 1999, State of Tex. Commn.:Theodore Peter F. Vasko commd. as Honorary Texax. given by Gov. R. Perry, 2002, Cert. of Flag Presentation of USS Arizona given by Rear Adm. Robert T. Conway, Jr., USN, Comdr., Navy Region, Hawaii, 2002, Cert. of Appreciation for Good Conduct, 2002-03, by UNMC-MSG Detacment of Jerusalem, Cert. of Appreciation by MSG Det for Outstanding Svc. as Det. Chaplain, 2003; named Jaycee of Yr., N.C. chpt., 1973; decorated mem. Equestrial Order of the Holy Sepulchre, 1992. Mem.: Marine Embassy Guard Assn. (mem. 2003).

VASLEF, IRENE, historian, librarian; b. Budapest, Hungary, Mar. 23, 1934; came to U.S., 1956, naturalized, 1960; d. Imre and Ilona (Selyebi-Kovats) Szabo; m. Nicholas P. Vaslef, Sept. 22, 1956; children— Suzanne, Steven. BA, San Jose (Calif.) State U., 1960; MS, Simmons Grad. Sch. Library Sci., Boston, 1963; postgrad., Columbia U., 1968, U. Colo., 1961-62, U. Munich, 1967-68; PhD, Catholic U. Am., 1984. Librarian, Cambridge, Mass., 1962-64; librarian Colorado Springs (Colo.) Sch. System, 1964-67; head catalog librarian Colo. Coll., Colorado Springs, 1968-72; librarian Dumbarton Oaks Rsch. Libr., Trustees for Harvard U., 1972—. Editor/compiler Am. Byzantine Bibliography in Byzantine studies/Etudes Byzantines, 1979—, Classica et Mediaevalia, 1986, Leyden: Brill, 1986; contbr. articles to profl. jours. Mem. Spl. Libraries Assn., Art Libraries Assn. N.Am., Phi Gamma Mu. Home: 4131 N River St Mc Lean VA 22101-5819 Office: Harvard U Dumbarton Oaks Rsch Libr 1703 32nd St NW Washington DC 20007-2934

VASLEF, STEVEN NICHOLAS, surgeon; b. Colorado Springs, Colo., Aug. 16, 1958; s. Nicholas P. and Irene I. (Koncz) V.; m. Maria E. Vaslef, July 11, 1988. BS, MIT, 1980; MD, U. Va., 1984; PhD, Northwestern U., 1990. Diplomate Am. Bd. Surgery with subspecialty in surg. critical care. Intern U. Ill., Chgo., 1984-85, resident in gen. surgery, 1985-92; mem. staff Evanston/Glenbrook Hosps., 1992-94; asst. prof. surgery, asst. pro. bio-med. engring. Northwestern U. Med. Sch., Chgo., 1992-94; asst. prof. surgery Duke U. Med. Ctr., Durham, N.C., 1994-2000, assoc. prof., 2000—, asst. prof. bio-med. engring., 1994—, asst. prof. anesthesiology, 1996—. Mem. ACS; mem. Soc. Critical Care Medicine, Am. Soc. Artificial Internal Organs, Soc. for Surgery of Alimentary Tract, Am. Assn. Surgery of Trauma, Ea. Assn. for Surgery of Trauma. Office: Duke Univ Med Ctr Dept Surgery PO Box 2601 Durham NC 27715-2601 E-mail: vasle001@mc.duke.edu.

VASMATZIDIS, IOANNIS, systems engineer; s. Prodromos and Anna Vasmatzidis; m. Hyesik Choi, Dec. 1, 1995; 1 child, AnnaMaria Choi. Diploma in mech. engring., Aristotle U. of Thessaloniki, Greece, 1988; MS in indsl. engring., U. Okla., 1990, PhD in indsl. engring., 1995. Usability engr. Pershing LLC, Jersey City, 1996—; ergonomics, project engr. BCAM Internat. Inc., Melville, NY, 1995—96; vice pres., group mgr. Pershing LLC, Jersey City, 2001—. Co-author: The Occupational Ergonomics Handbook; contbr. articles numerous profl. jours. Adv. bd. mem. Usability Profl. Group of India. Cleo-Cross Internat. Student award, U. Okla., 1993. Mem.: Usability Profl. Assn., Human Factors and Ergonomics Soc., Alpha Pi Mu Engring. Achievements include research in effects of heat strees on cognitive performance; design of designed the user interface for the marketspeed(TM) windows product of harrisdirect; responsible for overseeing the User interface design of the online brokerage website www.harrisdirect.com. Home: 74 Gerdes Ave Verona NJ 07044 Afghanistan Office: Pershing LLC A BNY Securities Group Co One Pershing Plaza Jersey City NJ 07311 Personal E-mail: vasmas@aol.com. E-mail: ivasmatzidis@pershing.com.

VASQUES, GARY, retail executive, marketing professional; b. 1947; With Gertz Dept. Stores, L.I., NY, 1973—75; buyer domestics, blankets and bedspreads Burdines, Miami, Fla., 1975—79, divisional merchandise mgr. home textiles, 1979—83, v.p., gen. merchandise mgr. decorative home, 1983, sr. v.p., gen. merchandise mgr. domestics, home textiles and decorative home accessories, 1984, sr. v.p., gen. merchandise mgr. home store, 1985—88, group sr. v.p., 1989—90; sr. v.p., gen. mdse. mgr. Montgomery Ward, 1990—92; sr. v.p. mktg. Caldor, 1992—95; exec. v.p. mktg. Kohl's, 1995—. Office: Kohls Corp N56 W17000 Ridgewood Dr Menomonee Falls WI 53051-5660

VASQUES, VICTORIA L. federal agency administrator; m. Fabrice Vasques; 1 child, Alex. BS, Calif. State U., Fullerton; tchg. credentials, U. Calif., Irvine. Dir., Indian Edn. US Dept. Edn., Wash., 2002—; dir., Indian affairs US Dept. Energy, Wash.; edn. program spec. Off Indian Edn., Indian Reservation Econ., Wash., Pres. Commn. HIV Epidemic, Wash.; tech. asst. spec. Nat. Congress of Am. Indians; tribal liaison Com. for 50th Pres. Inaugural. Named Am. Indian Woman of Yr., 1986. Mem.: Decade Soc. Office: US Dept Edn Indian Edn 400 Maryland Ave SW FOB-6 Rm 3W205 Washington DC 20202 E-mail: victoria.vasques@ed.gov.

VASQUEZ, GADDI, federal agency administrator; b. Carrizo Springs, Tex., Jan. 22, 1955; m. Elaine Vasquez; 1 child, Jason. AA in Criminal Justice, Rancho Santiago C.C., 1972; BA in Pub. Svc. Mgmt., U. Redlands, 1980. Police officer City of Orange, Calif., 1975-79; coord. community rels., mgr.'s office City of Riverside, Calif., 1979-81; exec. asst. Orange County Bd. Suprs., 3d Dist., Calif., 1981-85, mem., 1987—95; area mgr. So. Calif. Edison Co., 1985; hispanic liaison Office of Gov. George Deukmejian, Calif., 1985, from dep. appointments sec. to chief dep. appointments sec., 1985-87; dir. Peace Corps, Washington, 2002—. Mem. Transp. Corridor Agys. Bd., 1987—, chmn. 1990-91; local agy. formation commn., 1988-93, chmn. 1990-91; mem. Calif. Film Commn., 1988-91, Calif. Coun. Criminal Justice, 1989—; founder, co-chair, Orange County Health Care Task Force, 1990—; with White House Fellowships Commn., 1990-91; co-chmn. Orange County Congestion Mgmt. Policy Task Force, 1990—; bd. dirs. Orange County Transp. Authority, 1991—, exec. com. 1992—, vice chmn. 1993—; regional advisory and planning coun., 1991—, vice chmn. 1992, chmn. 1993; official observer Armenian Independence elections, 1991. Bd. dirs. Future Leaders Am., Southwest Voter Rsch. Inst., calif. First Amendment Coalition, Orange County Boy Scout Coun., So. Area Foster Care Effort, Orange County Performing Arts Ctr., Opera Pacific; trustee Am. Coun. Young Polit. Leaders; adv. bd. Pediatric Cancer Rsch. Found, Orange County Juvenile Connection Project, Calif. Office Traffic Safety, The Salvation Army Orange County, Project AERO, Constitutional Rights Found. Orange County; community coun. Prentice Day Sch.; hon. adv. bd. Adam Walsh Ctr.; hon. bd. govs. Bower Mus.; leadership coun. Orange County Points Light. Named Officer of Yr., Am. Legion, 1977. Outstanding Young Man of Am. U.S. C.of C., 1985, One of 100 Most Influential Hispanics in U.S. Hispanic Bus. Mag., 1986-87, 88-89, 91-92, 92-93, 2002-03, Govt. Hispanic Bus. Advocate of Yr. U.S. Hispanic Champer Region I, 1991; recipient Alumni Achievement award Santa Ana Coll., 1988, Alumni of Yr.award U. Redlands, 1989, Humanitarian award NCCJ, 1989, award State Child Devel. Adv. Com., 1990, Tree of Life award Jewish Nat. Fund, 1991, Ralph E. Hudson Open Space award Landscape Architects Found., 1992, Outstanding Alumni award Am. Assn. C.C.s, 2003. Office: Peace Corps Off of the Dir 1111 20th St NW Washington DC 20536-0001

VASQUEZ, WILLIAM LEROY, business educator, consultant; b. Austin, Tex., Mar. 9, 1944; s. Eliseo M. and Janie (Garcia) V. BS with distinction, Nova Southeastern U., 1983, MBA, 1985, DBA, 1992. Cert. Inst. Cert. Profl. Mgrs., 1990, Inst. Cert. Computing Profls., 1993. Svc. mgr. Data Gen. Corp., various, Latin Am., 1972-80; product mgr. Gould, Inc., Ft. Lauderdale, Fla., 1980—84, Tektronix Inc., Portland, Oreg., 1984—86, Racal-Milgo, Ft. Lauderdale, 1988—90, Citibank Internat., Ft. Lauderdale, 1991—2001; ret., 2001. Instr. City U., Portland campus, 1987-88; Maryhurst Coll., 1985-88, Nova Southeastern U. (domestic and internat.), 1988—, pres. internat. alumni

assn.; instr. St. Thomas U., 1989—, Fla. Atlantic U., 1993—. Mem. VFW, Nat. Bus. Edn. Assn., U.S. Submarine Vets., Inc., Mensa. Republican. Presbyterian. Avocations: guitar, model trains, fine arts. Home: 9788 NW 18th St Coral Springs FL 33071-5824 Office: Fla Met Univ Grad Sch Business 225 N Federal Hwy Pompano Beach FL 33062

VASS, JOAN, apparel designer; b. N.Y.C., May 19, 1925; d. Max S. and Rose L.; children: Richard, Sara, Jason. Student, Vassar Coll., 1941; BA, U. Wis., 1946. Pres. Joan Vass, Inc., N.Y.C., 1977—, Vass-Ludacer, N.Y.C., 1993—. Recipient Prize de Cashet, Prince Machiabelli, 1980, Coty award, 1979, Disting. Woman in Fashion award Smithsonian Instn., 1980. Office: Joan Vass Inc 36 E 31st St New York NY 10016-6821 also: 214 W 39th St New York NY 10018-6850 E-mail: joanvass@worldnet.att.net.

VASSALLE, MARIO, physiologist; b. Viareggio, Lucca, Italy, May 26, 1928; came to U.S., 1958; s. Giuseppe and Antonietta (Vassalle) V.; m. Anna Maria Petrucci; children: Andrew G., Alessandra A., Massimo B., Roberto M., Francesca A. MD cum laude, U. Pisa, Italy, 1953, specialization in cardiology cum laude, 1955; doctorate honoris causa, U. Ferrara, Italy, 1990. Med. diplomate. Intern Istituto di Medicine and Cardiology U. Pisa, 1953-55, asst. Istituto di Patologia Medica, 1956-58; acting chief resident in medicine French Hosp., N.Y.C., 1958-59; trainee cardiovascular rsch. & tng. program dept. physiology Med. Coll. Ga., Augusta, 1959-60; postdoctoral fellow dept. physiology SUNY-Downstate Med. Ctr., Bklyn., 1960-61, N.Y. Heart Assn. fellow dept. physiology, 1961-62, instr., 1962, vis. asst. prof., 1964-65, asst. prof., 1965-66, assoc. prof., 1966-71, prof., 1971—; NIH fellow Physiologisches Institut U. Bern, Switzerland, 1962-64. Vis. prof. U. Ferrara, 1971, U. Vt., Burlington, 1978, Cath. Univ. Gemelli, Rome, 1984-85, SUNY at Stony Brook, 1994; assoc. editor Am. Jour. Physiology: Heart and Circulatory Physiology, 1976-80; mem. editorial bd. Circulation Rsch., 1974-80, European Jour. Pharmacology, 1985-90, Jour. Electrocardiology, 1985—; mem. editorial bd. New Trends in Arrhythmias, 1985-96, assoc. editor, 1991-96; editorial cons. Am. Jour. Physiology, Circulation, Science, Jour. Molecular Cell Cardiology, Cardiovascular Rsch; cons. NIH; mem. NIH Cardiopulmonary Study Sect., 1981-85, ad hoc mem., 1988; invited participant numerous confs., symposiums and workshops. Author (editor): Research in Phusiology, 1971, Cardiac Physiology for the Clinician, 1976, Excitation and Neural Control of the Heart, 1982; author: Diario di un Fisiologo del Cuore, 1992, Lost Emotions, 1994, The Riddle of the Mind, 1996, The Reality of the Self, 2000; editor: Chanderl McCuskey Brooks: The Scientist and the Man, 1990; author: Dunes, 2001, Twilights, 2003, Not Always, 2004, numerous papers, revs., chpts. and abstracts. Fulbright travel grantee, 1958-62; recipient A. and A. Sinsheimer Fund award, 1966-71, N.Y. Health Rsch. Coun. award, 1972-75. Mem. AAAS, Am. Physiol. Soc., Am. Heart Assn. (coun. on basic scis. 1969—), N.Y. Heart Assn. (bd. dirs. 1978-84), N.Y. Acad. Scis., Cardiac Muscle Soc., Cardiac Electrophysiol. Group (pres. 1972-73), Internat. Study Group for Rsch. in Cardiac Metabolism, Harvey Soc., Mex. Soc. Cardiology (hon.), Sigma Xi (pres. Downstate Med. Ctr. chpt. 1984). Roman Catholic. Home: 104 Huntington Rd Port Washington NY 11050-3511 Office: SUNY Downstate Med Ctr Box 31 450 Clarkson Ave Brooklyn NY 11203-2056 Business E-Mail: mario.vassalle@downstate.edu.

VASSALLO, EDWARD E. lawyer; b. N.Y.C., Aug. 12, 1943; BS, Columbia U., 1965, MS, 1967; JD cum laude, Fordham U., 1973. Bar: N.Y. 1974. Ptnr. Fitzpatrick, Cella, Harper & Scinto, N.Y.C. Mem.: ABA, N.Y.C. Bar Assn., N.Y. Intellectual Property Law Assn. (pres.-elect), Fed. Cir. Bar Assn., Internat. Trademark Assn., Am. Intellectual Property Law Assn. Office: Fitzpatrick Cella Harper & Scinto 30 Rockefeller Plz Fl 38 New York NY 10112-3800

VASSALLUZZO, JOSEPH S. retail company executive; BA, Pa. State U.; MBA, Temple U. Exec. v.p. growth and support svcs. Staples, Inc., Framingham, Mass., 1993, exec. v.p. growth and devel., 1993—96, pres. realty and devel. divsn., 1997—99, vice chmn., 1999—. Worked in real estate Mobil Oil Amerada Hess Corp., Am. Stores Co. Office: Staples Inc PO Box 9265 Framingham MA 01701-9265

VASSAR, RICHARD HOLT, aerospace engineer; b. Dallas, Mar. 27, 1955; s. Clarence Oliver and Barbara (Henderson) Vassar; m. Janet Lynn Odenwaldt, May 29, 1977; 1 child, Rachel Louise. BS in Aerospace Engring., Va. Tech., 1977; MS in Aeronautics and Astronautics, Stanford U., 1978, PhD, 1982. Tech. staff TRW, Redondo Beach, Calif., 1981—84; from staff scientist to FAME program mgr. Lockheed Martin ATC, Palo Alto, Calif., 1984—2002, NIRCam program mgr., 2002—. W.E. Wine scholar, Va. Tech., 1973—77, Engring. fellow, Stanford U., 1977—78. Fellow: AIAA (Engr. of Yr. 1993). Democrat. Achievements include research in end-to-end error analysis for Gravity Probe-B, formation keeping for a pair of satellites in a circular orbit, fast steering mirrors in optical control sys. Avocations: piano, bicycling, hiking, mountain climbing, photography. Office: Lockheed Martin Advanced Tech Ctr 3251 Hanover St Palo Alto CA 94304 Business E-Mail: richard.vassar@lmco.com.

VASSEL, LEE HYLTON, urbanist, social services administrator, writer; b. Port Maria, Jamaica, May 30, 1939; s. Lester L. and Isamenda (Beckford) V.; m. Daisy Mae Eaddy, July 22, 1972 (dec. Sept. 1991); 1 child, Faye Maria; m. Svetlana Tchoubova, Oct. 22, 1997. Cert., U. Cambridge, 1956; BA in English magna cum laude, Queens Coll.-CUNY, 1974; MA in Creative Writing, City Coll.-CUNY, 1976; MS in Urban Affairs, Hunter Coll.-CUNY, 1979. Adj. lectr. Hunter Coll.-CUNY, 1978-80; instr., grad. asst. doctor of arts program in English SUNY, Albany, 1980-83; adj. lectr. Hostos C.C., N.Y.C., 1984-85; case worker N.Y.C. Dept. Social Svcs., 1986-87, ct. liaison, 1988-89; dist. atty. liaison Adminstrn. for Children's Svcs., Bronx, N.Y.C., 1990—, ct. liaison supr., 1995—. Author: In the Black of Us, 1976; contbr. creative writings to lit. publs. (Golden prize Queens Coll./CUNY 1973, 74). Mem. Seton Falls Neighborhood Assn., Bronx, 1989—, Bronx Dist. Atty. Multidisciplinary Team on child phys. and sexual abuse. Mem. MLA, Internat. Soc. Arts, Sci. & Tech., Urban Affairs Assn., Ea. Evaluation Rsch. Soc., Alpha Sigma Lambda. Episcopalian. Avocations: walking, reading, creative writing, classical and reggae music, study. Home: 2029 Strang Ave Bronx NY 10466-2339 Office: Bronx Family Ct 900 Sheridan Ave Bronx NY 10451-3306

VASSELL, GREGORY S. electric utility consultant; b. Moscow, Dec. 24, 1921; came to U.S., 1951, naturalized, 1957; s. Gregory M. and Eugenia M. Wasiljeff; m. Martha Elizabeth Williams, Apr. 26, 1957; children: Laura Kay, Thomas Gregory. Dipl. Ing. in Elec. Engring, Tech. U. Berlin, 1951; MBA in Corp. Fin., NYU, 1954. With Am. Electric Power Svc. Corp., Columbus, Ohio, 1951-88, v.p. system planning, 1973-76, dir., 1973-88, sr. v.p. system planning, 1976-88; electric utility cons. Upper Arlington, Ohio, 1988—. Bd. dirs. Columbus & Southern Ohio Electric Co., 1981-88, Cardinal Operating Co.; mem. tech. adv. com. transmission FPC, 1968-70, FERC Task Force on Power Pooling, 1980-81; mem. U.S. com. World Energy Coun. Contbr. articles to profl. jours. Fellow IEEE (life); mem. NAE, Internat. Conf. Large High Voltage Electric Systems, Athletic Club of Columbus. Home and Office: 2247 Pinebrook Rd Columbus OH 43220-4327

VASSER, JIMMY, professional race car driver; b. Canoga Park, Calif. Grad., Jim Russell Driving Sch., 1983. Race car driver Jim Hayhoe team, 1992—95, Target/Chip Ganassi Racing Team, 1995—. Achievements include race car driver SCCA Formula Ford series, 5 wins in 1984, 5 wins in 1985, 7 wins and nat. championship in 1986; with Formula Atlantic, 1987-89; with Can. Formula 2000 tour, 1989-90, with 5 wins, also win in SCCA Pro Sports 2000, Mesa Martin, Calif; with Formula Atlantic 1991-92, CART series 1992—, individual driving champion, 1996; winner 4 races, 1st champion to complete every race on schedule, leader all drivers in laps completed. Office: c/o Target/Ganassi Racing 3821 Industrial Blvd Indianapolis IN 46254-2507 and: Jimmy Vasser Chevrolet-Toyota 583 Soscol Ave Napa CA 94559-3405

VASSIL, JOHN CHARLES, lawyer; b. Youngstown, Ohio, Mar. 3, 1930; s. Callias and Anastasia (Kyriakides) V.; m. Anita Devlin, Nov. 28, 1965; 1 son, Russell. BS in Chem. Engring., Carnegie Inst. Tech., 1952; JD, George Washington U., 1958. Bar: N.Y. 1960, U.S. Dist. Cts. (so. and ea. dists.) N.Y. 1961, U.S. Ct. Appeals (2d cir.) 1965, U.S. Ct. Appeals (fed. cir.) 1982, U.S. Supreme Ct. 1961. Patent examiner U.S. Patent Office, 1955-58; ptnr. Morgan & Finnegan, LLP, N.Y.C., 1961—2001, counsel, 2002—. Lectr. in field. Served with C.E., U.S. Army, 1953-55. Mem. ABA, Assn. Bar City N.Y., N.Y. Patent Law Assn., Am. Patent Law Assn., Am. Arbitration Assn. Home: 420 E 54th St # 36H New York NY 10022-5179 Office: 345 Park Ave New York NY 10154-0004 E-mail: jcvassil@morganfinnegan.com.

VASSILOPOULOU-SELLIN, RENA, clinician investigator; b. Dec. 29, 1949; MD, Albert Einstein Coll. Medicine, 1974. Resident Montefiore Hosp., Bronx, 1974-77; fellow Northwestern U., Chgo., 1977-80; prof. Univ. Tex., Houston, 1980—. Fellow ACP, Am. Assn. Clin. Endocrinol.; mem. AAAS, AMA, Am. Soc. Bone and Mineral Rsch., Am. Diabetes Assn., Am. Soc. Clin. Oncology, Endo Soc. Office: Anderson Cancer Ctr 1515 Holcombe Blvd # 15 Houston TX 77030-4009

VASSILYADI, MICHAEL, pediatric neurosurgeon; b. Istanbul, Turkey, Nov. 25, 1961; s. Irakli and Cristal Vassilyadi; m. Anastasia Lyras, Aug. 23, 1986; children: Frank Photios, Christal, Anthony Irakli. BSc, McGill U., 1980—83, MSc, 1984—86, MD, CM, 1986—90. Med. staff Children's Hosp. of Ea. Ont., Ottawa, Canada, 1996—. Asst. prof. of surgery U. of Ottawa, 1996—2003; assoc. prof. surgery and pediat. U. Ottawa, 2003—. Contbr. articles to profl. jours.; mem. editl. bd. Pediat. Neurosurgery. Recipient Matching Travel award, Children's Hosp. of Ea. Ont. Rsch. Inst., 1998, 2003, 2004, Best sci. posters, Neurol. Sciences of Que., 1995; Farquharson Rsch. scholarship, Med. Rsch. of Can., 1987, Dr. James Douglas Rsch. fellowship in Pathology, McGill U., 1985. Fellow: ACS, Am. Acad. Pediat., Am. Bd. of Pediatric Neurol. Surgery, Am. Bd. of Neurol. Surgery, Royal Coll. of Physicians and Surgeons of Can.; mem.: Am. Soc. Pediatric Neurosurgeons, Coll. of Physicians and Surgeons of Ont., Coll. des Medecins du Que., Can. Med. Assn., Can. Congress of Neurol. Sciences, Am. Epilepsy Soc., Am. Assn. of Neurol. Surgeons, Ont. Med. Assn., Joint Sect. on Pediatric Neurol. Surgery (AANS/CNS), Internat. Soc. of Pediatric Neurosurgery, Congress of Neurol. Sciences. Greek Orthodox. Achievements include research in Negative-pressure hydrocephalus. Office: Children's Hosp of Eastern Ontario 401 Smyth Rd Ottawa ON Canada K1H 8L1 Office Phone: (613) 737-2316., 613-738-3985. Office Fax: (613) 738-4293. E-mail: vassilyadi@cheo.on.ca.

VASSOLER-FROELIGH, IVANI, education educator, journalist; b. Sapaulo, Brazil, Oct. 31, 1954; arrived in U.S., 1991; d. Walter and Irma Caprera Vassoler; m. Lad Maleniecki Froeligh, Apr. 18, 1991. BA, Soc. Commn., Sao Paulo, Brazil, 1979; MA, Univ. San Diego, Calif., 1995; PhD, Univ. Md., Md., 2002. Journalist Oglobo Newspaper, Sao Paulo, Brazil, 1979—85; fgn. corr. Oestado De Spaulo, Mex. City, 1985—91; journalist Am. Econ. Mag., Calif., 1991—95, Eldorado News, Washington, 1995—2003; instr. polit. sci. Univ. Md., Md., 2003; asst. prof. SUNY, Fredonia, NY, 2003—. Cons. World Bank, Washington, 2001—; comentator/analyst Eldorado News, Brazil. Mem.: Mid. Atlantic Coun. of Latin Am. Studies (James St. Prize 2003), Latin Am. Studies Assn., Am. Polit. Sci. Assn. Roman Cath. Avocations: swimming, reading, movies. Home: 706 Wash Ave Dunkirk NY 14048 Office: State Univ N Y E 368 Thompson Hall Fredonia NY 14063

VASTA, EDWARD, humanities educator; b. Forest Park, Ill., Jan. 18, 1928; s. Joseph and Josephine (Mallimaci) V.; m. Geraldine Stocco, Nov. 28, 1953; children: John, Paula, Joseph, Catherine, Barbara, Salvatore. BA in English, U. Notre Dame, 1952; MA in English Lang. and Lit., U. Mich., 1954; PhD in English and Humanities, Stanford U., 1963. Tchg. intern, acting instr. Stanford U., Palo Alto, Calif., 1956-58; instr. U. Notre Dame, Ind., 1958-61, asst. prof., 1961-66, assoc. prof., 1966-69, fellow Medieval Inst., 1993-97, prof., 1969-97, prof. emeritus, 1998—. Author: The Spiritual Basis of Piers Plowman, 1965, Tales from the Hidden Apple, 2002, Novellas Back and Forth, 2002, Family Passions, 2003, Love and Redemption, 2003, Mud Pie Mysteries: Fables About Children in God's World, 2004; editor: Middle English Survey, 1965, Interpretations of Piers Plowman, 1968: co-editor: Chaucerian Problems and Perspectives, 1979; co-translator: Dante Alighieri, Vita Nuova, 1995, translator: G.A. Mallimaci, For She Distinguished Herself, First Among All, 2003. With USN, 1946-48. Fulbright scholar, 1952-53; Grad. Honors fellow Stanford U., 1958, 59; Danforth grantee, 1961; Creative Writing fellow Nat. Endowment for Arts, 1979. Democrat. Roman Catholic. Home: 52140 Harvest Dr South Bend IN 46637-2923 Business E-Mail: evasta@nd.edu.

VASTAGH, GEORGE FREDERICK, physician; b. Budapest, Jan. 11, 1936; s. Alajos Gusztaf and Ilona Kuthan Vastagh; m. Ann Beam Devos, Mar. 12, 1976 (div. Aug. 1987); children: Andrew, Victoria, Joseph, Vincent. MS, U. Budapest, 1954; MD, U. Graz, 1959; DSc (hon.), U. Budapest, 1963; JD (hon.), U. Minn., 1971. Prof. medicine U. Tex., Dallas, 1962-72; assoc. med. dir. Abbott Labs., North Chicago, Ill., 1972-82; med. dir. Schering-Plough Co., Memphis, 1982-87; pres. G.F. Vastagh, Memphis, 1987—. Legal med. cons. Tenn. Bar Assn., Memphis, 1987-91. Author: Muscle Metabolism, 1971; patentee in field; contbr. articles to profl. jours. Maj. U.S. Army, 1960-62. Fellow Rockefeller Inst.; mem. Pilots Assn., Hungarian Univ. Students in Exile (pres. 1960). Roman Catholic. Avocations: woodworking, flight instructor, gourmet cooking. Home and Office: 2427 Redbud Trail Dr Germantown TN 38139-6427 E-mail: Gvastagh@aol.com.

VASTERLING, PAUL, artistic director; B in Dance and Theater magna cum laude, Loyola U., New Orleans. Profl. dancer Nashville Ballet, Ohio Ballet, Ballet Austin; dancer, faculty mem., ballet master, resident choreographer Nashville Ballet, artistic dir., 1998—. Participant Carlisle Project, Oreg. Ballet Theatre's Am. Choreographers Showcase, Pacifica Choreographic Workshop, New Choreographers on Point program, N.Y.; creator Pub. Libr. Collaboration, Westminster Sch. Program, Oasis Ctr.; lectr. in field. Choreographer Nashville Ballet, Ballet Pacifica, Milw. Ballet, Oreg. Ballet Theatre; prin. works include Firebird, This Heart, Robin Hood, Pop, Messiah, Night of the Iguana, Romeo and Juliet, Seasons, Dracula. Recipient Tenn. Individual Artists Fellowship for Choreography, 1995. Office: Nashville Ballet 3630 Redmon Dr Nashville TN 37209-4827

VASUDEVAN, SRIRAM, risk management professional; b. Bombay, June 7, 1970; arrived in U.S., 1991; s. R. and Rama Vasudevan; m. Archana Ramaswamy, Feb. 2, 1998. BTech in Mech. Engring., Indian Inst. Tech., 1991; MS in Mech. Engring., U. Calif., Santa Barbara, 1992; PhD in Aerospace Engring., Ga. Inst. Tech., 1998. Air resources engr. Calif. Air Resources Bd., El Monte, 1992-93; grad. rschr. Computational Modelling Ctr. Ga. Inst. Tech., Atlanta, 1993-97; devel. engr. Schlumberger Tech. Corp., Sugarland, Tex., 1997—2001; mgr. Quantitative Analysis Sempra Energy Solutions, 2002—. Contbr. article to profl. jour. Vol., organizer South Asian task force Nat. Marrow Donor Program, LA and Atlanta, 1993—. Recipient Best Student Presentation award AIAA, 1997. Mem. ASME (assoc.), Soc. Petroleum Engrs., Sigma Xi. Hindu. Achievements include co-invention of post closure anlaysis in hyudraulic fracturing; development of systematic risk management strategies for end-users of gas and power. Office: 101 Ash St HQ 09 San Diego CA 92108 Home: # 304 10041 Rio San Diego Dr San Diego CA 92108-5632

VATANDOOST, NOSSI MALEK, art school administrator; b. May 22, 1935; d. Adullah Goodar and Mahtaban (Goodar) Malek; m. Ira Varandoost, May 30, 1964; children: Debbie, Cyrus. BA, Western Ky. U., 1970. Art tchr. Met.-Davidson County Sch. Sys., Nashville, 1970-71; dir., owner Nossi Coll. Art, Goodlettsville, Tenn., 1973—. Dir Tenn. Proprietary Bus. Sch. Assn., Inc., pres. Crimson Corp.; treas. Malek & Assos. Inc., 1976; dir. EXCEL Edn. Corp., 1980-86; vis. lectr., cons. EXCEL Bus. Inst., 1980-86. Active mem. Nat. Trust for Hist. Preservation. Mem.: NAFE, Internat. Coun. Design Schs. (pres. 1997—98), Art Inst. Nashville (founder, CEO), Career Coll. Assn., Art Resources of Tenn. (pres. 2000—01), Nat. Assn. of Schs. of Art and Design, Nat. Mus. Women in the Arts (charter), Hendersonville Art Guild, Hendersonville Art Coun. (com. chmn.). Club: Soroptimists (Upper Cumberland Valley, Tenn.). Home: 104 Whirlaway Ct Hendersonville TN 37075 Office: 907 Rivergate Pkwy # E6 Goodlettsville TN 37072

VATAVUK, WILLIAM MICHAEL, chemical engineer, writer; b. Sharon, Pa., Jan. 30, 1947; s. William James and Amelia Agnes (Lenarcic) V.; m. Betsy Ann Chandler, Oct. 27, 1973; 1 child, William Chandler. B in Engring., Youngstown State U., Ohio, 1969. Registered profl. engr., NC. Chem. engr. E.I. DuPont de Nemours, Richmond, Va., 1969-70; sr. chem. engr. U.S. EPA, Durham, NC, 1970-99; pres. Vatavuk Engring., 1999—. Author: Dawn of Peace, 1989 (Pulitzer nomination 1990), Estimating Costs of Air Pollution Control, 1990, Marketing Yourself with Technical Writing, 1992; mem. publs. com. Oilfield Jour.; inventor Vatavuk Air Pollution Control Cost Indexes; contbr. articles to profl. jour. Bd. dir. Bennett Pl. Hist. Site Support Fund, Inc., Durham, 1992—; publicity chmn. Hist. Preservation Soc. Durham, 1989-90; bd. dir. NC 4-H Devel. Fund, Raleigh, NC, 1990-93; tchr., Sunday sch. CCD, 1993. Capt. USPHS, 1970-99. Mem. NC Farm Bur., Mercer County Hist. Soc. (life mem.), USPHS Commd. Officers Assn. (pres. NC br. 1975-76, 84-85), Mil. Officers Assn. of Am. (life). Democrat. Roman Catholic. Avocations: reading, writing, jogging, gardening, solving puzzles. Office: 3512 Angus Rd Durham NC 27705-5404 Office Phone: 919-489-8810. Personal E-mail: william.vatavuk@verizon.net.

VATCHER, JAMES GORDON, retired physician; b. Long Beach, Calif., June 14, 1925; s. Marshall James and Elise Ione (McElhinney) V.; m. Helen Stockwell (div.); children: Michael Gordon, Howard Peter, Donald Alan, Mary Helen, Kimberly Ann; m. Dorothy Caswell, June 1978. BA, Leland Stanford Jr. U., 1950; MD, Stanford U., 1954. Intern in surgery Stanford (Calif.) U. Hosp., 1953-54; resident Stanislaus County Hosp., Calif., 1954-56; physician surgeon Calif. Instn. for Women Dept. Corrections, Frontera, Calif., 1982-97; ret. Bsn Mate III USN CB, 1943-46. Democrat. Avocations: complementary medicine, nutrition, anti oxidant molecular/functional medicine, communication. Home: 872 S Cedarwood St Orange CA 92869-5301

VATER, CHARLES J. lawyer; b. Pitts., Feb. 8, 1950; s. Joseph A. and Helen M. (Genellie) V.; m. Diane E. Vater, June 10, 1972; children: Allison D., Elizabeth A. BA, U. Notre Dame, 1971; JD, U. Pitts., 1975. Bar: Pa. 1975, U.S. Dist. Ct. (we. dist.) Pa. 1975, U.S. Ct. Appeals (3d cir.) 1979. Assoc. Tucker Arensberg, P.C., Pitts., 1975-80, ptnr., shareholder, 1980—. Contbr. articles to profl. jours. Mem.: Estate Planning Coun. Pitts. (bd. dirs. 1988—90, 1995—97, past pres.), Allegheny County Bar Assn. (probate coun. 1988—98, 1999—2000, sec. 2003—), Phi Beta Kappa, Order of Coif. Home: 1615 Trolist Dr Pittsburgh PA 15241-2650 Office: Tucker Arensberg 1 Ppg Pl Ste 1500 Pittsburgh PA 15222-5413 E-mail: cvater@tuckerlaw.com.

VATNER, STEPHEN F. physiologist, researcher, research scientist; m. Dorothy E. Vatner, Aug. 22, 1944; children: Jonathan, Daniel, Ralph. BA, Grinnell Coll., Grinnell, Iowa, 1957—61; MD, NYU, New York, NY, 1961—65; Intern,Residence, U of Va., Charlottesville,VA, 1966—67; Postdoctoral fellow, U of WA, Seattle, WA, 1969. Cardiology. Asst. rsch. physiologist U of CA, San Diego, 1969—70, asst. prof. of medicine, 1971—72, Harvard Med. Sch., Boston, 1972—74; assoc. prof. of medicine Peter Bent Brigham Hosp.-Harvard Med. Schoolm, Boston, 1974—90; prof. of medicine Harvard Med. Sch., Boston, 1990—97; George J. Magovern prof. and dir., cardiovasc. and pulmonary rsch. inst. Allegheny U. of the Health Sciences, Pitts., 1997—99; dir. Weis Ctr. for Rsch., Henry Hood Rsch. Program, Charles B. Degenstein Prof., Penn State Coll. of Medicine, Danville, Pa., 1999—2000; u. prof. of medicine and dir. Cardiovasc. Rsch. Inst., U. of Medicine and Dentistry-New Jersey Med. Sch., Newark, 2000—01; chair, dept. of cell biology and molecular medicine UMDNJ-New Jersey Med. Sch., Newark, 2001—. Editor: (editor-in-chief) Circulation Rsch.; author (contributing author): (manuscript publications) Sci. articles in peer-reviewed jour. Recipient Established Investigatorship, AHA, 1974 -1979, Thomas L. O'Donohue Meml. Lecture in Neuropharmacology, Washington,D.C., 1997, Invited Lecture in Honor of Emeritus Prof. Andre Charlier, Unit of Cardiovasc. Physiology, Universite Catholique De Louvain, Brussels,Belgium, 1997, Hon. Prof., The fourth Mil. Med. U., Xian, China, 1998, George E. Brown Lecture, AHA, 1986, Hawthorne Lecture, Howard U., 1990, Hon. MD Degree, Kagawa Med. Sch., Kagawa,Japan, 1992, Welcome Vis. Prof., U of Nebr., 1993, Wiggers Award, Am. Physiology Soc., 1995, Fouad A. Bashour Disting. physiologist Lectr., U. of TX, S.W. Med. Ctr., 1996, Konrad Witzig Meml. Lectr., The Cardiovasc. Sys. Dynamics Soc., 1996, J.R. Neely Lectr., Geisinger Clinic, Danville, PA, 1997; fellow Fellowship, The Internat. Soc. for Heart Rsch.; grantee Myocardial Hypertrophy and Heart Failure (Program Project)-Project 1 Cardiac Control in gsAlpha and 403 Mice, Nih/nhlbi (Po1 Hl59139-01), 09/15/97 - 08/31/02, Myocardial Hypertrophy and Heart Failure (Program Project) - Core A Adminstrn. of PPG, 09/15/97 - 08/31/02, Myocardial Hypertrophy and Heart Failure (Program Project) - Core B Transgenic Mouse Models for PPG, 09/15/97 - 08/31/02, Effects of Aging on Cardiovasc. Function in Primates, NIH/Aging (7RO1 AG14121-01), 08/01/97 - 07/31/02, Mechanisms of Myocardial Ischemia and Reperfusion (Program Project) - Project 2, Nih/nhlbi (1 Po1 Hl69020-01), 09/30/01 - 08/31/06, (PENDING) Integrative Mechanism in Cardiovasc. Disease (Instl. Tng. Grant), Nhi/nhlbi (1T32 Hl69752-01), 07/01/02 - 06-30-07. Mem.: AHA (executive,credentials,program and nominating committees 1968), Jour. of Molecular and Cellular Cardiology (consulting editor 2000), Circulation Rsch. (consulting editor 1999), Circulation (editl. bd. mem. 1999), Circulation Rsch. (editor-in-chief 1991—99), Am. Jour. of Physiology: Heart and Circulatory Sect. (bd. of med. editors 1998), Hypertension (editl. bd. mem. 1983—89), Procs. of The Soc. for Exptl. Biology and Medicine (editl. bd. mem. 1981—87), Circulation Rsch. (editl. bd. mem. 1981—87), Am. Jour. of Physiology (editl. bd. mem. 1985—90), Am. Jour. of Physiology (editl. bd. mem. 1979—81), AHA (mem. 1968), Am. Assn. of Physicians (assoc.), AHA, Keystone, CO (assoc.; co-director, sci. sessions of councils on sci. and circ. 1986), AHA, Keystone, CO (assoc.; co-director, sci. sessions of councils on sci. and circ.), Coun. on Circulation, AHA (assoc.; chmn., program com. 1982—85), Am. Soc. for Pharmacology and Exptl. Therapeutics (assoc.), Am. Soc. for Clin. Investigation (assoc.), Am. Physiol. Soc. (assoc.), Am. Fedn. for Clin. Rsch. (assoc.), Biophysical Soc. (assoc.), AHA (assoc.; bd. of directors, allegheny county 1997), AHA (assoc.; chmn., nominating com., coun. on circulation 1997—99), Am. Assn. for Accreditation of Lab. Animal Care Bd. of Trustees (assoc.), AHA, Mass. Affiliate (assoc.; v.p. 1990—92), AHA (assoc.; chmn., coun. on circulation 1990—92), AHA (assoc.; vice chmn., coun. on circulation 1988—90). Achievements include research in American Heart Association Research Achievement Award; American Heart Association, Scientific Councils Distinguished Achievment Award; National Institute of Health Merit Award. Office: UMDNJ-NJ Medical School 185 So Orange Ave - Ste G609 PO Box 1709 Newark NJ 07101-1709 Personal E-mail: vatnersf@umdnj.edu.

VATTER, PAUL AUGUST, business administration educator, dean; b. Boston, Sept. 14, 1924; s. August John and Elizabeth Emelia (Kunstler) V.; m. Josette Roman, July 23, 1966; children: Joel Paul, Katherine Alexandra. BA, Holy Cross Coll., 1944; MA, U. Pa., 1947, PhD, 1953; MA (hon.), Harvard U., 1970. Instr. U. Pa., Phila., 1945-53, asst. prof., 1953-58, vice dean of men, 1953-58; asst. dean Harvard U. Bus. Sch., Boston, 1958-62, assoc. prof. bus. adminstrn., 1962-70, prof., 1970-95, Lawrence E. Fouraker prof. bus. adminstrn., sr. assoc. dean, 1989-91, Lawrence E. Fouraken prof. bus. adminstrn. emeritus, 1995—; assoc. fellow Templeton Coll. Oxford (Eng.) U. Author: Quantitative Methods in Management, 1978, The Structure of Retail Trade by Size of Store, 1979, also video tapes. Home: 244 Clifton St Belmont MA 02478-2647 Office: Harvard U Bus Sch Soldiers Fld Boston MA 02163-1317

VATTILANA, JOSEPH WILLIAM, retired chief state safety inspector; b. Wilmington, Del., Mar. 22, 1928; s. Andrew and Elizabeth (Castiglione) V.; (div. 1974); children: Joseph W., Joy Ann; m. Gladys Mary Spence, Nov. 18, 1978. Student, Del. Tech. Community Coll., 1966-70, 89—, Pa. State U., 1976-80. Cert. field instr., instr. for radiation control, work zone safety supr., dir. fleet maintenance, flagger instr. Heavy equipment mechanic Dept. Hwys. and Transp., Bear, Del., 1963-70, equipment supt., 1970-79, hwy. safety engr., 1979-84, chief safety inspector, 1984—. Instr. Flagger-Nat. Safety Coun., 1997; safety cons. for pvt. engring. co., 1994—; speaker and instr. in field. Author: Safety Manual Pass the Word, 1987, Equipment Certification Manuel, 1987, Do Something-Traffic Controls for Emergency Personnel, 1999. Dep. chief, asst. chief-chief driver, bd. dirs., capt. of rescue, sec. Talleyville (Del.)

Vol. Fire Co., 1946-98; instr. ARC Del. chpt., Wilmington, 1956—; hon. life mem. Wilmington Manor Vol. Fire Co., 1985—. Combat medic U.S. Army, 1946, army sgt. 1st class inf. U.S. Army, 1950. Recipient disting. svc. award State of Del., 1986, Lammot duPont Jr. meml. award Del. chpt. ARC, 1989, nat. safety award Am. Traffic Safety Svcs., 1992, Outstanding Vol. of Yr. award Del. Safety Coun., 1996; named man of yr. 1994 Am. Soc. Hwy. Engrs., hon. staff officer Del. State Police, 1994; recipient spl. recognition safety award Federal Hwy. Adminstrn., 1994. Mem. Am. Soc. Hwy. Engrs. (exec. dir. 1st State chpt. 1997, mem. 1st State Hwy. Hall of Fame 2001), New Castle County Fire Chiefs Assn. (pres. 1985-86), New Castle County Vol. Firemans Assn. (pres. 1986-87), Del. State Fire Chiefs Assn. (pres. 1993-94), Del. Hwy. Engrs. (1st and 2nd v.p. 1987-89), Soc. Hwy Engrs. (pres. 1st state chpt. 1988-90), Del. State Fire Police Assn. (hon. life), Del. Safety Engrs. (pres. 1986-87), Am. Legion (life), VFW (life). Roman Catholic. Avocations: woodworking, gardening, fishing. Home: 3333 Silverside Rd Wilmington DE 19810-4804

VAUDRY, J. WILLIAM, JR., lawyer; b. Jacksonville, Fla., Jan. 18, 1941; BBA, Tulane U., 1962, LLB, 1967. Bar: La. 1967. Mem. Lemle & Kelleher, LLP, New Orleans. Bd. editors Tulane Law Rev., 1965-67. Lt. (j.g.) USN, 1962-64. Mem. ABA, La. State Bar Assn., Order of Coif, Phi Delta Phi. Address: Lemle & Kelleher LLP Pan Am Life Ctr 21st flr 601 Poydras St New Orleans LA 70130-6029 Office Phone: 504-584-9408.

VAUGHAN, ALDEN TRUE, history professor; b. Providence, Jan. 23, 1929; s. Dana Prescott and Muriel Louise (True) V.; m. Lauraine A. Freethy, June 1, 1956 (div. 1981); children: Jeffrey Alden, Lynn Elizabeth; m. Virginia Mason Carr, July 16, 1983. BA, Amherst Coll., 1950; MEd, Columbia U., 1956, MA in History, 1958, PhD, 1964. Tchr. Hackley Sch., Tarrytown, N.Y., 1950-51, A.B. Davis High Sch., Mt. Vernon, N.Y., 1956-60; From history instr. to prof. Columbia U., N.Y.C., 1961—, prof. emeritus, 1994. Editor Polit. Sci. Quar., N.Y., 1970-71; gen. editor Early Am. Indian Documents, Univ. Pubs. of Am., 1977—; assoc. editor Ency. of the N.Am. Colonies, Scribners, N.Y., 1993; vis. adj. prof. CUNY, Lehman Coll., N.Y.C., 1971; vis. prof. Clark U., Worcester, Mass., 1987. Author: New England Frontier, 1965, rev. edit., 1979, 3d edit., 1995, American Genesis, 1975, Shakespeare's Caliban, 1991, Roots of American Racism, 1995, others; co-editor: Arden Shakespeare's The Tempest, 1999; contbr. articles to Am. Heritage, Am. Hist. Rev., New Eng. Quar., others Lt. (j.g.) USNR, 1951-55. Recipient fellowship Guggenheim Found., 1973, Sr. fellowship Folger Shakespeare Libr., 1977, 89, Sr. fellowship Am. Antiquarian Soc., 1983. Mem. Am. Antiquarian Soc. (sr. fellowship), Am. Soc. for Ethnohistory, Shakespeare Assn. Am., Soc. Am. Historians (exec. sec., treas. 1965-70), Orgn. Am. Historians (program chmn. 1976), Inst. Early Am. History and Culture (coun. mem. 1985-87), Colonial Soc. Mass., Mass. Hist. Soc. Home: 50 Howland Ter Worcester MA 01602-2631

VAUGHAN, BRAD, engineering and design company executive; With Black & Veatch, Overland Park, Kans., 1974—, dir. devel. TransAmerica Generation Grid project, COO, BV Solutions Group, gen. ptnr., mgr. office ops. energy engring. and constrn. divsn., chief info. officer, 2003—. Office: Black & Veatch 11401 Lamar Overland Park KS 66211

VAUGHAN, DAVID JOHN, corporate financial executive; b. Detroit, July 17, 1924; s. David Evans and Erma Mildred V.; divorced; children: David John, Melissa Ann, Julia Crawford McLaughlin; m. Anne McKeown Miles, Aug. 21, 1975. AB, U. Ill., 1950. Chemist Midland Electric Colleries, Galesburg, Ill., 1950-52; pres. Varrco Distbg. Co., Peoria, 1953—, David Vaughan Investments, Inc., Peoria, 1970—. Adv. bd. Charles Schwab Inc. Trustee Eureka Coll., chmn. bd. trustees; trustee Opera Ill. Lt. USAAF, 1942-46, USAF, 1951-52, Korea. Mem. Peoria Country Club, Northport Point Club (Mich.), Peoria Skeet Club, Racquet Club, Naples Club (Fla.), Naples Bath & Tennis Club, Royal Poinciana Country Club (Naples), Masons, Shriners, Alpha Tau Omega, Phi Eta Sigma, Phi Alpha Delta. Republican. Presbyterian. Office: 5823 N Forest Park Dr Peoria IL 61614-3559 also: 824 N Birchwood Dr Northport MI 49670-9761 also: Office Comstock Bldg Winter Park FL 32789 Home: 861 Swallow Pointe Naples FL 33942 also: 4413 Grandview Dr Peoria IL 61614 E-mail: dvaughan@dviequity.com.

VAUGHAN, EDWIN DARRACOTT, JR., urologist, surgeon; b. Richmond, Va., May 13, 1939; s. Edwin Darracott and Blanche V. (Bashaw) V.; m. Virginia Anne Lloyd, June 30, 1962; children: Edwin Darracott III, Barbara Anderson. BS, Washington and Lee U., 1961; MD, U. Va., 1965, MS, 1969; DSc, Washington and Lee U., 1982. Diplomate Am. Bd. Urology (trustee, v.p. 1988, pres. 1989). Intern Vanderbilt U., 1965-66, asst. resident, 1966-67; chief resident in urology U. Va., 1970-71, asst. prof. urology, 1973-75, assoc. prof., 1975-78, prof., 1978; clin. rsch. fellow Columbia U., 1971-72, rsch. assoc. dept. medicine, 1972-73; James J. Colt prof. urology, chmn. dept. urology Cornell U. Med. Coll., N.Y.C.; attending urologist-in-chief N.Y. Hosp., N.Y.C., 1978—; sr. assoc. dean clin. affairs Cornell U. Med. Coll., N.Y.C., 1993-2001, chmn. dept. urology, 1993-2001. Chief med. officer Cornell Physician Orgn., 1997—; sci. adv. bd. Nat. Kidney Found., 1977-81; sec.-treas. Urology Coun., 1977-80, chmn., 1980-81; med. adv. bd. Coun. High Blood Pressure, 1977; acting co-chief exec. officer Columbia-Cornell Care, L.L.C., 1997; adv. coun. Nat. Diabetes and Digestive and Kidney Diseases, 2002—; bd. visitors U. Va. Editor: Seminars in Urology, 1983-95; assoc. editor Investigative Urology, 1977-78, mem. editl. bd., 1978-94, Brit. Jour. Urology, 2004; editor Campbell's Urology; assoc. editor Brit. Jour. Urology, 2004; contbr. articles to profl. jours. Mem. adv. coun. Nat. Diabetes and Digestive and Kidney Diseases, 2002—; bd. visitors U. Va., 2002. Recipient Rsch. Career Devel. award NIH, 1976-78, Russell and Mary Hugh Scott award Am. Found. Urol. Disease, 1998, J.K. Latimer award N.Y.-N.J. Kidney Found., 1999, Valentine medal N.Y. Acad. Medicine, 2000, Maurice R. Greenberg Disting. Svc. award, 2002, Good Scout award, BSA, 2002, Presdl. award Soc. Basic Sci. Rsch., 2004; NIH tng. grantee, 1967-68; USPHS grantee, 1971-77; Am. Heart Assn. grantee, 1976-79 Mem. ACS, AAAS, Internat. Soc. Urology, N.Y. Acad. Scis., Soc. Univ. Urologists, Am. Urol. Assn. (hon., chmn. rsch. com. 1980-91, treas. N.Y. sect. 1985, v.p. N.Y. sect. 1986, pres. N.Y. sect. 1987, bd. dirs. 1992-97, pres.-elect 2000, pres. 2001, immediate past pres. 2002, Golden Cystoscope award 1981, Disting. Contbn. award 1992, Hugh Hampton Young award 2000), Urol. Soc. Australasia (hon.), Soc. Exptl. Biology and Medicine, Soc. Univ. Surgeons, Soc. Internat. Urology (chmn. bd. 1997—), Am. Found. Urol. Disease (pres. 1987-92, Presdl. Founder award 2004), Soc. Basic Urol. Rsch. (Pres. award 2004), Nat. Kidney and Urol. Disease Adv. Bd. (dep. chmn.), Intersoc. for Kidney and Urol. Disease Rsch. (chmn. 1987), Am. Assn. Genito-Urinary Surgeons (Barringer medal 1993), Am. Surg. Assn., Brit. Assn. Urol. Surgeons (hon., St. Paul's medal), Japanese Urol. Soc. (hon.), Clin. Soc. Genitourinary Surgeons (v.p. 2004), Sigma Chi (Significant Sig award 2000), Alpha Omega Alpha (award 1976), Omicron Delta Kappa (award 1981). Home: 1165 Park Ave Apt 6A New York NY 10128-1210 Office: 525 E 68th St New York NY 10021-4870 Office Phone: 212-746-5480. Business E-mail: evaughan@med.cornell.edu.

VAUGHAN, EUGENE H. investment company executive; b. Brownsville, Tenn., Oct. 5, 1933; s. Eugene H. Sr. and Margaret (Musgrave) V.; m. Susan Bolinger Westbrook, May 11, 1963; children: Margaret Corbin, Richard Bolinger. BA, Vanderbilt U., 1955; MBA, Harvard U., 1961. CFA, 1967. Security analyst Putnam Mgmt. Co., Boston, 1961-64; dir., dir. rsch. Underwood, Neuhaus & Co., Inc., Houston, 1964-70; pres., chief exec. officer Vaughan, Nelson & Boston, Inc., Houston, 1970-77, Vaughan, Nelson, Scarborough & McCullough, L.P., Houston, 1970—. Chmn. bd. dirs. Dreyfus Founders Asset Mgmt. Co., Denver, 1970—. Chair Fin. Analyst Fedn., N.Y.C., 1973-74, bd. dirs., 1969-76; dir. U. Tex. Health Sci. Ctr., Houston, 2002—; pres. Houston Soc. Fin. Analysts, 1967-68; trustee exec. com. Vanderbilt U., Nashville, 1972—, St. John's Sch., Houston, 1980-85, Goodwill Industries, Houston, 1978—, United Way of Tex. Gulf Coast, 1994—; elder First Presbyn. Ch., 1976—; founding chmn., trustee Presbyn. Sch., Houston, 1986-90. Lt. USN, 1955-58. Recipient Disting. Svc. award Fin. Analyst Fedn., 1978, Humanitarian award Am. Jewish Com., 1993, Bus. Leader of Yr. award U. St. Thomas, 1996. Mem. Inst. Chartered Fin. Analysts (trustee 1986-93, chmn. 1989), Assn. for Investment Mgmt. and Rsch. (founding chmn. 1990-91, gov. 1990-93), Greater Houston Partnership (bd. dirs. 1990—, exec. com. 1993—, chair Ctr. Houston's Future 1999—), Houston Club (pres. 1983-84, bd. dirs. 1979-85, chair centennial celebration, 1992-94), Houston Country Club, Coronado Club (Houston), Houston Forum (pres. 1991-92, chmn. 1992-93), Harvard U. Bus. Sch. Club Houston (pres. 1968-69, bd. dirs. 1966-71, 86-90), Vanderbilt Club Houston (chmn. 1984—, pres. 1966 68, Disting. Svc. award 1994), Conferie des Chevaliers du Tastevin, Belle Meade Country Club (Nashville). Republican. Avocations: travel, sailing. Home: 3465 Inwood Dr Houston TX 77019-3129 Office: Vaughan Nelson Scarborough & McCullough 600 Travis Ste 6300 Houston TX 77002

VAUGHAN, HERBERT WILEY, retired lawyer; b. Brookline, Mass., June 1, 1920; s. David D. and Elzie G. (Wiley) Vaughan; m. Ann Graustein, June 28, 1941 (dec. June 2002). Student, U. Chgo., 1937-38; BS cum laude, Harvard U., 1941, LLB, 1948. Bar: Mass. 1948. Assoc. Hale and Dorr, Boston, 1948-54, jr. ptnr., 1954-56, sr. ptnr., 1956-89, co-mng. ptnr., 1976-80, of counsel, 1990—2004, Wilmer Cutler and Pickering Hale and Dorr LLP, Boston, 2004—. Bd. dirs., fin. com. Boston and Maine R.R., 1961—64; vis. fellow New Coll., Oxford U., 1985. Mem. standing com. Trustees of Reservations, 1986—98, chmn., 1988—92, sec., 1992—98, asst. sec., mem. adv. coun., 1998—; mem. bd. trustees Am. Friends New Coll. (Oxford U.); mem. adv. coun. James Madison Program in Am. Ideals and Instns., Princeton U. Fellow: Mass. Hist. Soc., Am. Bar Found. (life); mem.: ABA, Am. Coun. Trustees and Alumni (mem. alumni leadership coun.), Am. Coll. Real Estate Lawyers, Am. Law Inst., Boston Bar Assn., Mass. Bar Assn., Longwood Cricket Club (Brookline), Boston Econ. Club, Union Club (Boston), Badminton and Tennis Club. Office: Wilmer Cutler Pickering Hale and Dorr LLP 60 State St Boston MA 02109-1816 Office Phone: 617-526-6718. E-mail: herbert.vaughan@haledorr.com.

VAUGHAN, JOHN CHARLES, III, horticultural products executive; b. N.Y.C., July 30, 1934; s. John Charles II and Lucille Grace (Dixon) V.; m. Ruth Darden MacLeod, Mar. 4, 1962; children: Elizabeth, John IV, George. AB in Econs., Cornell U., 1956; MBA, Northwestern U., 1962. Salesman Hall & Ellis, Chgo., 1959-62; br. mgr. Vaughan's Seed Co., Downers Grove, Ill., 1963-74, exec. v.p., 1974-76, pres., 1976-84, chmn. bd., 1985-93, ret., 1993. Regional v.p. Am. Seed Trade Assn., Washington, 1985-88; pres. Atlantic Seedsmen's Assn., N.Y.C., 1968; dir. McHutchison LLC. Bd. dirs. George Williams Coll., Downers Grove, 1982-92. 1st Lt. USMCR, 1956-59. Mem. Downers Grove C. of C. (chmn. 1989). E-mail: jvaug5668@aol.com.

VAUGHAN, JOSEPH LEE, JR., education educator, consultant; b. Charlottesville, Va., Dec. 31, 1942; s. Joseph Lee and Ann (Doner) V.; m. Linda Marie De Silva; children: Leigh Ann, Kelley, Stephen, Kathleen. BA, U. Va., 1964, MEd, 1968, EdD, 1974. Tchr. Madison (Va.) High Sch., 1965-67, Darlington Sch., Rome, Ga., 1967-69, Woodberry Forest (Va.) Sch., 1969-74; asst. prof. edn. U. Ariz., Tucson, 1974-80; prof. Tex. A&M U.-Commerce, Mesquite, 1980—, dir. programs in reading edn., 1980-86, 91-92. Dir. programs in reading edn. East Tex. State U., 1980—86; dir. Tex. Ctr. Learning Styles, 1989—95; exec. dir. Children's Inst. of Literacy Devel., Inc., 1995—2004, The Learning Champions, Inc., 2004—. Co-author: Reading and Learning in Content Classrooms, 1978, 2d rev. edit., 1985, Reading and Reasoning Beyond The Primary Grades, 1986. Bd. govs. Sancta Sophia Sem., 1991-98. Mem. ASCD, Nat. Reading Conf., Internat. Reading Assn., Soc. Effective Affective Learning. Unitarian Universalist. Avocations: golf, travel, reading, antiques. Home: 447 Ridgemont Dr Heath TX 75126 Office: Tex A&M U-Commerce 2600 Motley Dr Mesquite TX 75150-3840

VAUGHAN, KENNETH EDWARD, application developer; b. Richmond, Va., 1965; s. Lewis Edward and Jalna Vaughan. BA in history, Va. Tech., 1983-87; MS in information mgmt., Marymount U., 1996. Dir. libr. and rcds. mgmt. Cassidy & Assocs., Inc., Washington, 1988—98; sr. project mgr. Fannie Mae, Washington, 1998—. Mem. Brotherhood of St. Andrew, Lorton, Va., Operations Friends. Mem. Am. Indian Sci. and Engring. Soc., Delta Mu Delta, Delta Epsilon Sigma. Avocations: fishing, softball, reading, computers, cooking. Office: Fannie Mae 3900 Wisconsin Ave NW Washington DC 20016-2892 Home: 25276 Oribi Pl Aldie VA 20105-3406

VAUGHAN, LINDA, publishing executive; Pub. Soap Opera Digest, N.Y.C., 1993—, Soap Opera Weekly, N.Y.C., 1993—. Office: 110 Fifth Ave 4th Fl New York NY 10011

VAUGHAN, MARTHA, biochemist, educator; b. Dodgeville, Wis., Aug. 4, 1926; d. John Anthony and Luciel (Ellingen) V.; m. Jack Orloff, Aug. 4, 1951 (dec. Dec. 1988); children: Jonathan Michael, David Geoffrey, Gregory Joshua. Ph.B., U. Chgo., 1944; MD, Yale U., 1949. Intern New Haven Hosp., Conn., 1950-51; research fellow U. Pa., Phila., 1951-52, Nat. Heart Inst., Bethesda, Md., 1952-54, mem. research staff, 1954-68; head metabolism sect. Nat. Heart and Lung Inst., Bethesda, 1968-74; acting chief molecular disease br. Nat. Heart, Lung and Blood Inst., Bethesda, 1974-76, chief cell metabolism lab., 1974-94; dep. chief pulmonary and critical care medicine br. Nat. Heart, Lung, and Blood Inst., Bethesda, 1994—. Mem. metabolism study sect. NIH, 1965-68; mem. bd. sci. counselors Nat. Inst. Alcohol Abuse and Alcoholism, 1988-91. Mem. editl. bd. Jour. Biol. Chemistry, 1971-76, 80-83, 88-90, assoc. editor, 1992—; editl. adv. bd. Molecular Pharmacology, 1972-80, Biochemistry, 1989-94; editor: Biochemistry and Biophysics Rsch. Comms., 1990-91; contbr. articles to profl. jours., chpts. to books. Bd. dirs. Found. Advanced Edn. in Scis., Inc., Bethesda, 1979-92, exec. com., 1980-92, treas., 1984-86, v.p., 1986-88, pres., 1988-90; mem. Yale U. Coun. com. med. affairs, New Haven, 1974-80. Recipient Meritorious Svc. medal HEW, 1974, Disting. Svc. medal HEW, 1979, Commd. Officer award USPHS, 1982, Superior Svc. award USPHS, 1993. Mem. NAS, Am. Acad. Arts and Scis., Am. Soc. Biol. Chemists (chmn. pub. com. 1984-86), Assn. Am. Physicians, Am. Soc. Clin. Investigation. Home: 11608 W Hill Dr Rockville MD 20852-3751 Office: Nat Heart Lung & Blood Inst Nih Bldg 10 Rm 5N 307 Bethesda MD 20892-0001 E-mail: vaughanm@nih.gov.

VAUGHAN, MICHAEL RICHARD, lawyer; b. Chgo., Aug. 27, 1936; s. Michael Ambrose and Loretta M. (Parks) Vaughan; m. Therese Marie Perri, Aug. 6, 1960; children: Charles Thomas, Susan Enger. Student, U. Ill., 1954-59; LLB, U. Wis., 1962. Bar: Wis. 1962. Chief atty. bill drafting sect. Wis. Legislature, Madison, 1962-68, dir. legis. attys., 1968-72; assoc. Murphy Desmond, and predecessor, Madison, 1972-73, ptnr., 1974—. Mem. Commn. Uniform State Laws, 1966—72; cons. Nat. Commn. Marijuana and Drug Abuse, 1971—73; lectr. CLE seminars. Contbr. articles to profl. jours. Warden, vestryman St. Dunstan's Episcopal Ch., 1973—78, 1980—87; mem. Wis. Episcopal Conf., 1972—76. Mem.: ABA, Dane County Bar Assn., State Bar Wis. (dir. govtl. and adminstrv. law sect. 1971—78, mem. interprofl. and bus. rels. com. 1976—89), Nakoma Golf Club, Madison Club, U. Wis. Law Sch. Bencher Soc., Delta Kappa Epsilon. Home: 4714 Lafayette Dr Madison WI 53705-4865 Office: 2 E Mifflin St Ste 800 Madison WI 53701-2038 Office Phone: 608-257-7181. E-mail: mvaughan@murphydesmond.com.

VAUGHAN, OTHA H., JR., retired aerospace engineer; b. Anderson, SC, July 1, 1929; s. Otha H. and Ethel (Mayfield) Vaughan; m. Betty Frances McCoy; children: Thera Virginia, Leslie, Frances. BSME, Clemson U., 1951, MSME, 1959; postgrad., U. Tenn. Space Inst., Tullahoma, 1975-81, U. Ala., Huntsville, 1974-75. Registered profl. engr., Ala. Commd. 2nd lt. USAF, 1951, advanced through grades to lt. col., 1972; mem. Von Braun R&D group Army Ballistic Missile Agy. (ABMA), Redstone Arsenal, Ala., 1956-60; retired USAF, 1979; rsch. engr., charter mem. NASA Marshall Space Flight Ctr., Huntsville, 1960-99; ret., 1999. Contbr. articles to profl. jours. Named to Thomas Green Clemson Acad. Engrs. and Scientists, Clemson U., 2001. Fellow: AIAA (assoc. Herman Oberth award Ala.-Miss. sect. 1999 1999); mem.: SAR, Res. Officers Assn. (life), Air Force Assn. (life; past v.p. Huntsville chpt.), Exptl. Aircraft Assn., Antique Aircraft Assn. (life), Blackbirds Assn., Minute Man Soc. Ala., Interplanetary Free Floaters (zero-gravity flights in NASA KC-135 aircraft), 8th Air Force Hist. Soc., Nat. Space Club, Shriners, Masons, Aviation Hall of Fame (chartered mem.). Achievements include patents for lunar communications receiver and transmitter for lunar surface missions; participation in design of rocket and space vehicle systems; development of Redstone, Jupiter, Jupiter C, Juno, Saturn I, Saturn IB, and Saturn V, Skylab and Apollo program, and the Space Shuttle launch vehicle systems; design of design criteria for lunar surface operations and mobility for lunar rover program; research in environmental design criteria for lunar and planetary exploration vehicles; zero-g atomospheric cloud physics; atmosphere electricity. Home: 10102 Westleigh Dr SE Huntsville AL 35803-1647 E-mail: skeetv@knology.net.

VAUGHAN, RICHARD C. insurance company executive; CFO Lincoln National Corp., Fort Wayne, Ind. Office: Lincoln National Corp West Tower 39th Fl 1500 Market St Philadelphia PA 19102

VAUGHAN, SAMUEL SNELL, editor, author, publisher; b. Phila., Aug. 3, 1928; s. Joseph and Anna Catherine (Alexander) Vaughan; m. Jo LoBiondo Vaughan, Oct. 22, 1949; children: Jeffrey Marc, Leslie Jane, Dana Alexander, David Samuel. BA, Pa. State U., 1951. Deskman King Features Syndicate, N.Y.C., 1951; asst. mgr. Doubleday Syndicate, 1952—54; advt. mgr. Doubleday, N.Y.C., 1954—56; sales mgr., 1956—58; sr. editor, 1958—68; exec. editor Doubleday, 1969—70; pub., pres. pub. div. Doubleday & Co., Inc., 1970—82, v.p. parent co., 1970—86, editor in chief, 1982—86; sr. v.p. and editor Random House, Inc., 1986—90, editor-at-large, 1990—2004. Mem. faculty, Columbia U., 1978-88; bd. dirs. Ch. Pub. Co.-Seabury Press; lectr. in field. Author: (juveniles) Whoever Heard of Kangaroo Eggs? 1957, New Shoes, 1961, The Two-Thirty Bird, 1965, (history) The Little Church, 1969, Medium Rare: A Look at the Book and Its People, 1977, (humor) Little Red Hood, 1979, The Accidental Profession, 1979, The Community of the Book, 1983, The State of the Heart, 1985; editor: Buckley: The Right Word, 1996; contbr. to N.Y. Times, Sunday Times of London, Daedalus, Am. Heritage, others. Served with USMC, 1946 48. Named Disting. Alumnus Pa. State U., 1977, Alumni fellow, 1981 Mem. Tenafly Tennis Club, Quantuck Beach Club (Westhampton, N.Y.), Century Assn. Episcopalian. E-mail: samuelsvaughan@aol.com.

VAUGHAN, THERESE MICHELE, insurance commissioner; b. Blair, Nebr., June 12, 1956; d. Emmett John and Lonne Kay (Smith) V.; m. Robert Allen Carber, Aug. 15, 1993; 1 child, Kevin Leo Vaughan-Carber. BBA, U. Iowa, 1979; PhD, U. Pa., 1985. CPCU, ASA, ACAS. Asst. prof. Baruch Coll., CUNY, 1986-87; cons. Tillinghast, N.Y.C., 1987-88; dir. ins. ctr. Drake U., Des Moines, 1988-94; ins. commr. State of Iowa, Des Moines, 1994—, dir. dept. commerce, 1996-98. Dir. EMC Ins. Group, Des Moines, 1992—94; trustee Am. Inst. for CPCU, Malvern, Pa., 1996—2002. Chair Jour. of Ins. Regulation Bd., Kansas City, Mo., 1995-99; co-author: Fundamentals of Risk and Insurance, 1996, 99, 2003, Essentials of Insurance: A Risk Management Approach, 1995, 2001; contbr. articles to profl. jours. S.S. Huebner fellow U. Pa., 1979-82; recipient Outstanding Young Alumnus award U. Iowa, 1996; named to Iowa Ins. Hall of Fame, 2003. Mem. Nat. Assn. Ins. Commrs. (pres. 2002, v.p. 2001, sec.-treas. 2000, chair Midwest Zone 1996-99), Am. Acad. Actuaries, Soc. Actuaries, Casualty Actuarial Soc., Soc. CPCU, Am. Risk and Ins. Assn., Beta Gamma Sigma, Omicron Delta Epsilon. Avocations: hiking, biking, reading. Home: 4632 Elm St West Des Moines IA 50265-2993 Office: Iowa Ins Divsn 330 Maple St Des Moines IA 50319-0065

VAUGHAN, WILLIAM WALTON, atmospheric scientist; b. Clearwater, Fla., Sept. 7, 1930; s. William Walton and Ella Vermelle (Warr) Vaughan; m. Wilma Geraldine Stapleton, Dec. 23, 1951; children: Stephen W., David A., William D., Robert T. BS with honors, U. Fla., 1951; grad. cert., USAF Inst. Tech./Fla. State U., 1952; PhD, U. Tenn., 1976. Sci. asst. Air Force Armament Ctr., Eglin AFB, Fla., 1955-58, Army Ballistic Missile Agy., Huntsville, Ala., 1958-60; chief aerospace environ. div. Marshall Space Flight Center, NASA, Huntsville, 1960-76, chief atmospheric scis. div., 1976-86; rsch. prof. atmospheric sci. U. Ala., Huntsville, 1986—, dir. Rsch. Inst., 1986-94; ret., 1994. Cons. atmospheric sci. and tech. stds.; mem. adv. com. NASA. Reviewer:; contbr. articles to profl. jours. Served to capt. USAF, 1951—55. Recipient Exceptional Svc. medal, NASA, 1971. Fellow: AIAA (assoc. Losey Atmospheric Scis. award 1980, Excellence in Aerospace Stds. award 2003), Am. Meteorol. Soc.; mem.: AAAS, Am. Geophys. Union, Stds. Engring. Soc., Sigma Xi. Office: Univ Ala Atmospheric Sci Dept Huntsville AL 35899-0001

VAUGHAN, WORTH EDWARD, chemistry professor; b. N.Y.C., Feb. 1, 1936; s. Royal Worth and Sylvia Marie (Fernholz) V.; m. Diane Marilyn Mayer, Aug. 9, 1969; 1 child, Wayne John BA, Oberlin Coll., 1957; MA, Princeton U., 1959, PhD, 1960. Asst. prof. chemistry U. Wis.-Madison, 1961-66, assoc. prof., 1967-76, prof., 1977—2002, prof. emeritus, 2002—. Mem. bd. advisors Am. Exchange Bank West Br., Madison, 1983-87. Author: Dielectric Properties and Molecular Behavior, 1969; editor: Digest of Literature on Dielectrics, 1974; translation editor: Dipole Moments of Organic Compounds, 1970; contbr. articles to profl. jours. Mem. Am. Chem. Soc. (pres. Wis. sect. 1968, 1998), Phi Beta Kappa, Alpha Chi Sigma Avocations: canoeing, contract bridge. Home: 501 Ozark Trl Madison WI 53705-2538 Office: Univ Wis 1101 University Ave Madison WI 53706-1322 E-mail: vaughan@chem.wisc.edu.

VAUGHN, ANN MARIE, art educator, artist; b. Newton, Mass., Jan. 20, 1941; d. James Charles and Eugenia Marie (Gillis) Murphy; m. Kenneth W. Vaughn Jr., 1964 (div. 1989); children: Kenneth W. III, James Duncan, Catherine Ellen; m. Louis Frederick Roensch, 1996. BA, Regis Coll., 1963; MA, Case We. Res., 1989, Cleve. Inst. Art, 1989. Cert. tchr., visual art specialist. Art tchr. Linn Benton C.C., Albany, Oreg., 1984-87, Bainbridge (Ohio) H.S., 1989-90; owner, operator Woodcrest Studio, Aurora, Oreg., 1992-94, art tchr. Richmond, Va., 1994—. Mem. Shokoe Bottom Arts Ctr., Richmond, 1993—97, Womens Caucus Art, Richmond, 1995—99, NOVA, 1991, Cleve. Ctr. Contemporary Art, 1991; represented U.S. in Brussels Belgium World's Fair, 1959. River St. Gallery, Chagrin Falls, Ohio, 1991—92, one-woman shows include Albany Libr., 1984, Rocky Neck Art Colony, Gloucester, Mass., 1965, Creative Arts Guild Gallery, Albany, 1985, Albany Gen. Hosp., 1985, Corvallis Country Club, 1986, Wickendon Gallery, 1989, Case Western Res. U., Cleve., 1989, Fairmont Gallery, Novelty, Ohio, 1991, Woodburn Art Assn., Oreg., 1992, Cedarfield Gallery, Richmond, 1997, Henry Clay Inn, Ashland, Va., 1998, St. Mary's Hosp. Gallery, Richmond, 1998, two persons shows, VA Eye Ctr., 1998, also many art fairs and festivals. Mem. Rep. Womans Club, Albany, New Virginians, Richmond, Va. Mus. Art. Recipient Judges Choice award, Belgrade Art Show, 1997, others. Mem.: PEO, AAUW (v.p.), Nat. League Am. Pen Women, Richmond, Bon Air Artists Assn. (v.p. 1996—98), Richmond Watercolor Assn., Va. Watercolor Assn., USTA W. Banc Investment Club, Raintree Swim and Racquet Club. Roman Catholic. Avocations: tennis, bridge, cooking, ballet, opera. Home: 213 W Brook Run Dr Richmond VA 23233 Office: Woodcrest Studio PO Box 29121 Richmond VA 23242 E-mail: annartist@msn.com.

VAUGHN, BETTY JEAN, obstetrician/gynecologist; b. Birmingham, Ala., 1932; MD, U. Ala. Sch. Medicine, 1956. Cert. ob/gyn 1967. Intern Mt. Sinai Hosp., Miami Beach, Fla., 1956-57; resident og/gyn Jackson Meml. Hosp., Miami, 1957-60; instr. ob-gyn. Sch. Medicine U. Miami, 1960-63, clin. asst. prof. ob-gyn., 1964-71; pvt. practice Coral Gables, Fla., 1960-66; project dir. Maternity Care and Family Planning Project Dade County Dept. Health, Fla., 1971-80; dep. dir. Orange County Dept. Health, 1980-86, state cons. quality assurance, 1987-90, ret., 1990. Mem. Am. Coll. Ob-Gyn., Orange County Ob-Gyn. Home: 3523 Paige Ct Gainesville GA 30504

VAUGHN, DONALD C. engineering executive; BS in Civil Engring., Va. Poly. Inst. Registered profl. engr. Tex. Constrn. field engr. M.W. Kellogg Co., 1958, various field mgmt. positions; pres. M.W. Kellogg Constructors, Inc. subs. M.W. Kellogg Co., 1980-82; chmn., CEO, pres. M.W. Kellogg Co., Houston, 1983-88; exec. v.p. Rust Internat.; sr. v.p. ops. Dresser Industries, Inc., 1992-95, exec. v.p. petroleum products and svcs., engring. svcs., 1995, pres., COO, dir.; vice chmn., mem. exec. com. Halliburton Co., Dallas, 1998—. Bd. dirs. Dresser-Rand Co., Ingersoll-Dresser Pump Co., Bredero-Shaw; mem. outside bd. dirs. Houston Exploration Co.; past chmn. U.S. sect. Turkish-U.S. Bus. Coun. Commd. officer U.S. Army Corps Engrs. Recogni-

tion Disting. Engring. Alumnus Va. Poly. Inst. Mem. Nat. Constrn. Assn., Tex. Profl. Engring. Soc., 25-Yr. Petroleum Industry, Va. Poly Inst. Com. Excellence, Va. Tech 100 Club. Office: Halliburton Company 4100 Clinton Dr Houston TX 77020-6299

VAUGHN, DONNA BECKER, retired social worker; b. Chgo., June 17, 1939; d. Charles Samuel and Helen Mae Becker; m. John Walter Vaughn, July 30, 1962; children: John Walter, Margaret Vaughn Valentine, Barbara Vaughn Marucco. AB, Ind. U., Bloomington, Indiana, 1957—61. Social worker Alameda County Welfare Dept., Oakland, Calif., 1962—72; social work supr. Roper, Mamaroneck, NY, 1984—94; ret., 1994. Transcriber (book) Dear Catharine, Dear Taylor. Grassroots chmn. LWV of Calif., Sacramento, Calif., 1998; charter pres. LWV of Alameda, Alameda, Calif., 1977—79; copresident PTA Coun., Alameda, Calif., 1984—85, AAUW, Alameda, Calif., 1997—98; pres. Friends of the Alameda Free Libr., Alameda, Calif., 2000—01; mem. of bd. of directors Bay Area Women Against Rape, Oakland, Calif., 1985—89. Democrat. Home: 400 Harbor Light Rd Alameda CA 94501-5933 Personal E-mail: dbvaughn@comcast.net.

VAUGHN, EULALIA COBB, retired science educator, mathematician; b. Smithville, Tenn., Aug. 1, 1926; d. Luther Leonidas Fuson and Allie Pearl Redmon; m. Lewis Latane Cobb, Aug. 14, 1944 (dec. 1980); children: Carl Cobb, Luther Fuson Cobb, Lewis Cobb Jr., James Cobb, David R. Cobb, John Winston Cobb; m. Floyce Vaughn, 1983. BS, Mid. Tenn. State U., 1946, MEd, 1980. Tchr. Secondary Sch., Tulahoma, Tenn., 1946, sci. and math. tchr., 1947, 1948, Pine Bluff, Ark., 1959, Birmingham, Ala., 1965, Nashville, 1965—91; ret. Chair dept. various schs., Tenn., 1967—91; pres. Dekalb County Ret. Tchrs. Assn., 1992—98; tchr. mission sch., 1996—; sponsor Sci. Olympiad Glencliff H.S., Nashville (state winner). Author: Poetry Book, 2001; contbr. articles to Nashville Tennesean. Voter registration Dem. Party, Smithville, 1995—2001; mem. steering com.; women's leader United Meth. Women, Cookeville, Tenn., 1991—2001, sec. comm., dist. pres., 1992—. Mem.: Family Cmty. Edn. (pres.). Democrat. Methodist. Avocation: family. Home: PO Box 132 1161 S Mountain St Smithville TN 37166

VAUGHN, GLORIA C. state representative; b. Corpus Christi, Tex., June 25, 1936; m. James M. Vaughn; children: James, Melodie. Student, Del Mar Jr. Coll., Salvation Army Coll., N.Mex. State U. State rep. dist. 51 N.Mex. State Legis., Santa Fe, 1996—. Mem. Bus. and Industry com. N.Mex. State Legis., Santa Fe, mem. Energy and Natural Resources com. Mem.: FEMA (bd. dirs.), LVA (bd. dirs.), ARC (sec.), Salvation Army, Salvation Army (pres.), Am. Cancer Bd., Boy Scouts Am., Habitat for Humanity (bd. dirs.), Alamogordo Women's Club. Republican. Home: 503 E 16th St Alamogordo NM 88310 Office: New Mexico State Capitol Rm 203 ICN Santa Fe NM 87503

VAUGHN, GREGORY LAMONT, professional baseball player; b. Sacramento, July 3, 1965; Student, Sacramento City Coll., Miami Coll. Player Milw. Brewers, 1989—96, San Diego Padres, 1996-98; outfielder Cincinnati Reds, 1999, Tampa Bay Devil Rays, St. Petersburg, 2000—. Mem. Am. League All-Star Team, 1993, 96. Named Midwest co-MVP, 1987, Am. Assn. MVP, 1989. Office: Tampa Bay Devil Rays One Tropicana Dr Saint Petersburg FL 33705

VAUGHN, JAMES ENGLISH, JR., neurobiologist; b. Kansas City, Mo., Sept. 17, 1939; s. James English and Sue Katherine (Vaughn); m. Christine Singleton, June 18, 1961; children: Stephanie, Stacey. BA, Westminster Coll., 1961; PhD, UCLA, 1965. Postdoctoral rsch. fellow in brain rsch. U. Edinburgh, Scotland, 1965-66; asst. prof. Boston U. Sch. Medicine, 1966-70; head sect. molecular neuromorphology Beckman Rsch. Inst., City of Hope, Duarte, Calif., 1970—, pres. rsch. staff, 1986, chmn. divsn. neurosci., 1987—2001. Editor (assoc. editor): (Jour.) Jour. Neurocytology, 1978—86; contbr. articles to profl. jours.; mem. editl. bd. (Jour.) Synapse, 1986—, reviewer for Jour. Comparative Neurology, 1974—, Brain Research, 1976—. Recipient Alumni Achievement award, Westminster Coll., 2003; fellow Neurosci. Rsch. Program, 1969; grantee, NSF, 1983—87; rsch. grantee, NIH, 1969—99. Mem.: AAAS, N.Y. Acad. Scis., Internat. Brain Rsch. Orgn., Soc. for Neurosci. (chmn. short course 1977), Am. Assn. Anatomists, Am. Soc. Cell Biology, Sigma Xi. Office: City of Hope Beckman Rsch Inst 1450 Duarte Rd Duarte CA 91010-3011

VAUGHN, JOHN CARROLL, minister, educator; b. Louisville, Sept. 22, 1948; s. Harold D. and Morel (Johnson) Vaughn; m. Brenda Joyce Lyttle, June 17, 1968; children: Deborah, John, Rebecca, Daniel, Joseph. BA, Bob Jones U., 1977, MMin, 1991, DD, 1989. Ordained to ministry Bapt. Ch., 1978. Sr. pastor Faith Baptist Ch., Greenville, SC, 1977—; founder/adminstr. Hidden Treasure Christian Sch., Greenville, 1980-84; founder Iglesia Bautista de la Fe, Greenville, 1981-93. Founder, dir. Hidden Treasure Ministries, Greenville, 1981—; exec. bd. Associated Gospel Chs., Hopewell, Va., 1987—93; chaplain Greenville Police Dept., 1987—. Editor: (instrnl. video) Sufficient Grace, 1987, Frontline Mag., 1997—; author: Special Education: A Biblical Approach, 1991, More Precious than Gold, 1994. Chmn. Greenville County Human Rels. Commn., 1986—89; counselor Greenville County Crisis Response Team, 1987—91; co-chmn. Greenville County Sex Edn. Adv. Com., 1988—91; mem. exec. bd. dirs. Fundamental Bapt. Fellowship Internat., 1988—98, exec. dir., 1997—98, exec. v.p., 1998—2003, pres., 2003—; mem. exec. bd. dirs. Internat. Bapt. Missions, 1993—, Christians for Religious Freedom, 1993—98, The Wilds, 1992—; cooperating bd. Bob Jones U., 2003. Mem.: SAR, S.C. Assn. Christian Schs. (pres. 1988—), Am. Assn. Christian Schs. (exec. bd. dirs. 1992—98), Internat. Conf. Police Chaplains, ACFT Owners and Pilots Assn., Am. Legion. Republican. Avocations: flying, golf, gardening, reading, history. Home: 117 Frontline Dr Taylors SC 29687-2675 Office: Faith Bapt Ch 500 W Lee Rd Taylors SC 29687-2513 Office Phone: 864-322-0700. Personal E-mail: pvchaplan@aol.com.

VAUGHN, JOHN ROLLAND, auditor; b. Iola, Kans., Aug. 4, 1938; s. Ralph H. and Alice (Dille) V.; m. Doris K. Black, Sept. 4, 1960; children: Lisa Ann, Brian Douglas. BS in Bus., Emporia State U., 1960. Sr. auditor Arthur Andersen & Co., Kansas City, Mo., 1961-66; gen. auditor First Nat. Bank Kansas City, 1966-69, Commerce Bancshares, Inc., 1969-73; sr. v.p. adminstrv. svcs. divsn. Peoples Trust Bank, Ft. Wayne, Ind., 1973-77; dep. gen. auditor, v.p. Crocker Nat. Bank, San Francisco, 1978-79; v.p., gen. auditor S.W. Bancshares, Houston, 1980-83; sr. v.p., gen. auditor MCorp., Houston, 1984-87, mng. dir., 1988-89; audit dir. Banc One Corp., Dallas, 1990-92; v.p., gen. auditor St. Paul Cos., St. Paul, 1992-97; dir. internal audit Conseco Fin., St. Paul, 1998—2001; v.p., chief audit officer Calif. State Automobile Assn., 2001—02, v.p., chief risk officer, 2002—. Treas. Overland Park (Kans.) Jr. C. of C., 1965—66; outside dir. Overland Park Credit Union; contr. Ft. Wayne Bicentennial Commn., 1974—77; mem. chmns. cabinet Indianhead coun. Boy Scouts Am., 2000—01. Mem. Inst. Internal Auditors (1st v.p. Kansas City 1969-70, pres. 1970-71, midwest regional v.p. 1971-72, Twin Cities chpt. gov. 1993-97, pres. 1994-95, internat. profl. conf. com. 1995-98, internat. ednl. products com. 1999-2002, chpt. gov. 2004—), Fin. Execs. Inst. (dir. Ft. Wayne 1976-77), Risk and Ins. Mgmt. Soc., Hartsmen, Soc. Preservation and Encouragement Barber Shop Quartet Singing in Am., Vocal Majority Chorus, Gt. No. Union Chorus, Sigma Tau Gamma. Home: 5 Henry Ranch Dr San Ramon CA 94583

VAUGHN, KATHY, municipal official; Pres. bd. commrs. Pub. Utility Dist., Everett, Wash. Home: PO Box 1107 Everett WA 98206-1107 Office: Office Bd Commrs Pub Utility Dist 2320 California St Everett WA 98201-3750

VAUGHN, MICHAEL S. law educator; s. Harley (Bud) Dewitt and Judith Ann Vaughn; m. Tzu-Hsiu Nancy Vaughn, Dec. 2, 1989; 1 child, Reid. PhD in Criminal Justice, Sam Houston State U., Huntsville, Tex., 1990—93. Assoc. prof. Ga. State U., Atlanta, 1993—, chmn. dept. criminal justice, 2002—. Book rev. editor, Jour. Criminal Justice Edn. Acad. Criminal Justice Scis., Greenbelt, Md., 1993—96, editor, police forum police sect., 1996—2001; editor, criminal justice rev. and internat. criminal justice rev. Ga. State U., Atlanta, 2001—; contbr., correctional health care report Civic Rsch. Inst., N.Y.C., 1999—. Contbr. articles to profl. jours. and publs. Named Outstanding Alumnus, Coll. of Criminal Justice, Sam Houston State U., 2002; recipient Outstanding Service award, Police Section, Acad. of Criminal Justice Sciences, 1998, Outstanding Paper, Acad. of Criminal Justice Scis., 1996. Mem.: Am. Assn. Univ. Profs., Am. Judicature Soc., Am. Psychology-Law Soc., Am. Soc. Criminology, Acad. Criminal Justice Scis. Avocation: reading. Office: Ga State Univ Criminal Justice PO Box 4018 Atlanta GA 30302-4018 Office Phone: 404-651-3688.

VAUGHN, MO (MAURICE SAMUEL VAUGHN), professional baseball player; b. Norwalk, Conn., Dec. 15, 1967; Student, Seton Hall U., 1987—89. Infielder Boston Red Sox, 1989—98, Anaheim Angels, Calif., 1998—. Active cmty. svc. Youth Groups, Boston. Named Most Valuable Player, Baseball Writers' Assn., 1995; named to Silver Slugger team, Sporting News, 1995, All-Star Team, Am. League, 1995. Office: New York Mets Shea Stadium 123-01 Roosevelt Avenue Flushing NY 11368-1699

VAUGHN, NOEL WYANDT, lawyer; b. Chgo., Dec. 15, 1937; d. Owen Heaton and Harriet Christy (Smith) Wyandt; m. David Victor Koch, July 18, 1959 (div.); 1 child, John David; m. Charles George Vaughn, July 9, 1971. BA, DePauw U., 1959; MA, So. Ill. U., 1963; JD, U. Dayton, 1979. Bar: Ohio 1979, U.S. Dist. Ct. (so. dist.) Ohio 1979, U.S. Cir. Ct. (6th cir.) 1987. Lectr. Wright State U., Dayton, 1965-67; communications specialist Charles F. Kettering Found., Dayton, 1968-71; tchr. English Miami Valley Sch., Dayton, 1971-76; law clk. to judge Dayton Mcpl. Ct., 1978-79; coordinator Montgomery County Fair Housing Ctr., Dayton, 1979-81, 85-89; atty. Henley Vaughn Becker & Wald, Dayton, 1981-90; pvt. practice Noel W. Vaughn Law Offices, Dayton, 1990—. Chmn. Dayton Playhouse, Inc., 1981—92; pres. Freedom of Choice Miami Valley, 1980—83, 1986—87; com. mem. Battered Woman Project-YWCA, 1983—84; pres. Legal Aid Soc., 1983—84; chmn. Artemis House, Inc., 1985—88, bd. dirs., 1988—97, ACLU, 1982—86, Miami Valley Arts Coun., 1985—86, AIDS Found., 1988—90, Miami Valley Fair Housing Ctr., Inc., 1992—94, Human Race Theatre Co., 1995—2000, Housing Justice Fund, 1979—, Dayton Sister City Com., 2001—02. Recipient Order of Barristers award U. Dayton, 1979. Mem.: ABA, Ohio FAIR Plan Underwriting Assn. (bd. govs. 1986—92), Dayton Bar Assn. (chmn. delivery legal svcs. com. 1983—84, family law com. 1991—, chmn. juvenile law com. 2001—03). Office: 1205 Talbott Tower 131 N Ludlow St Dayton OH 45402-1110 Office Phone: 937-222-6635.

VAUGHN, ROBERT CANDLER, JR., lawyer; b. Winston Salem, NC, Sept. 6, 1931; s. Robert Candler and Douglas Arthur V.; m. Carolyn (Hartford), May 2, 1959; children: Patricia Anne, Robert Candler III. BS in Bus. Adminstrn., U. N.C., 1953, JD, 1955. Bar: N.C., 1955, U.S. Dist. Ct. (mid. dist.), 1959, U.S. Tax Ct., 1981. Assoc. Petree, Stockton, Robinson, and predecessor firms, Winston Salem, 1959-65, ptnr., 1965-2000. Bd. dirs. Forsyth Bank & Trust Co., Winston-Salem. Pres., United Way Forsyth County, Winston Salem, 1970-71; chmn. Winston Salem Coliseum and Conv. Ctr. Commn., 1974-78; mem. bd. adisors U. N.C. Tax Inst., Chapel Hill; bd. dirs. Leadership Winston Salem; chmn. Winston Salem Found., 2003, Forsyth Med. Ctr. Found., 1999-2001. Lt. USN, 1955-58. Fellow Am. Bar Found., Am. Coll. Trusts and Estates Counsel (N.C.chmn. 1990-1995); mem. N.C. Bar Assn. (pres. 1985-86, bd. dirs.), U. N.C. Law Alumni Assn. (pres. 1974-75), Am. Coll. Tax Counsel, Old Town Club, Piedmont Club, Rotary. Republican. Methodist. Home: 2575 Club Park Rd Winston Salem NC 27104-2009 Office: Vaughn Perkinson Ehlinger Moxley & Stogner PO Box 25715 Winston Salem NC 27114 Office Phone: 336-794-6001. E-mail: bob.vaughn@vpems.com.

VAUGHN, ROBERT GENE, law educator; b. Chickasha, Okla., Mar. 10, 1944; s. Owen and Ola Mae (Davis) V.; m. Nancy Gaye Breeden, June 28, 1969; children: Amanda Joy, Abigail Jane, Carolyn Elizabeth. BA, U. Okla., 1966, JD, 1969; LLM, Harvard U., 1970. Bar: Okla. 1969, D.C. 1971. Assoc. atty. Pub. Interest Rsch. Group, Washington, 1970-72; asst. prof. law Am. U., 1972-74, assoc. prof., 1974-77, prof., 1977-82, A. Allen King scholar and prof. law, 1982—, acting dep. dean, 1984-85. Author: The Spoiled System: A Call for Civil Service Reform, 1975, Principles of Civil Service Law, 1976, Conflict of Interest Regulation in the Federal Executive Branch, 1979, Merit Systems Protection Board: Rights and Remedies, 1984, South American Consumer Protection Laws, 1996, A Documentary Companion to A Civil Action, 1999, Freedom of Information, 2000. Recipient award for outstanding tchg. Washington Coll. Law, Am. U., United Meth. Ch. Bd. Higher Edn., 1983. Democrat. Episcopalian. Office: Am U Washington Coll Law 4801 Massachusetts Ave NW Washington DC 20016-8181 Business E-Mail: vaughn@wcl.american.edu.

VAUGHN, ROSALYN MAE, educational association administrator; d. Emmet and Rosie Mae Smith; children: Sherolyn Yvonne Spencer, Sonja Annette King, Rosa Leoma. BS in Elem. Edn., So. Ill. U., 1968; MA in Ednl. Leadership, Western Mich. U., 1974; PhD in Workforce Edn. Devel. and Adminstrn., So. Ill. U., 1996. Educator St. Clair County Pub. Schs., Cayseyville, Ill., 1968—69, University City (Mo.) Pub. Schs., 1970—71, Calhoun County Pub. Schs., Battle Creek, Mich., 1971—72; pers. rep., trainer Ralston-Purina Co., Battle Creek, Mich., 1972—74; pub. affairs specialist Kellogg Co., Battle Creek, Mich., 1974—76; MIOSHA dir. Mich. Dept. Labor, Lansing, 1976—80; educator Escambia County Pub. Schools, Pensacola, 1980—83; mgr. Combined Ins. Co. Am., New Orleans, 1983—87; instr., rschr. Pensacola (Fla.) Jr. Coll., 1990—91; grad. internist La. Dept. Labor, Metarie, La., 1993—93; assoc. dean Jones Coll., Jacksonville, Fla., 1996—97; human resources mgr. Dynamic Ednl. Sys., Inc., Jacksonville, Fla., 1997—99; asst. prof. Barry U., Miami Shores, Fla., 1999—, adminstr. human resources devel. and adminstrn. Orlando, Fla., 2000—03; site adminstr. higher edn. leadership doctoral program Nova Southeastern U., Orlando, 2004—. Rev. panelist Family Transition Program, Fla. Dept. Health and Rehab. Svcs., Jacksonville, 1997—99; adminstrv. vol. Polk County Adult Edn. Program, Davenport, Fla., 2002—03; chairperson Mich. Commn. Employment Handicap Persons, Lansing, Mich., 1976—80; steering com., exec. bd. Ctrl. Fla. Higher Edn. Alliance, Orlando, 1999—; mem. Fla. Hosp. Diabetes Ctr., Orlando, 2000—. Recipient Diana award, Mich. Safety Conf., 1978; fellow Ill. Consortium Ednl. Opportunity Program fellow, State Ill. Dept. Edn., 1994—96; scholar State Tchrs.' scholar, 1964—68. Mem.: Ctrl. Fla. Higher Edn. Alliance (mem.-at-large 2001—), Assn. Career Tech. Educators (exec. bd. 2001—), Fla. Exec. Women (assoc.). Achievements include development of Employment Law Certification Program. Home: 409 Riggs Circle Davenport FL 33897 Personal E-mail: rvmshrda@aol.com.

VAUGHN, STEVEN D. veterinary administrator; DVM, U. Ga., 1978. Dir. Office of New Animal Drug Evaluation Ctr. for Vet. Medicine, FDA, 2002—; vet. med. officer divsn. surveillance FDA Ctr. for Vet. Medicine, 1987, chief antiparasitic and physiol. drugs br. divsn. therapeutic drugs for food animals Office of New Animal Drug Evaluation, 1991, dir. divsn. therapeutic drugs for food animals Office of New Animal Drug Evaluation, 1992. Office: FDA Ctr for Vet Medicine Comms Staff 7519 Standish Pl HFV-12 Derwood MD 20855

VAUGHN, THOMAS JOSEPH, earth science educator, administrator; b. Lawrence, Mass., Dec. 23, 1944; s. Thomas Wilbur and Dorothy Agnes (Mallon) V.; m. Priscilla Margaret Bastian, June 30, 1973; children: Matthew Thomas, Judith Diane. BA in History/Geography, Mt. Carmel Coll., Niagara Falls, Ont., Can., 1968; AM in Geography, Boston U., 1972; MEd in Secondary Ednl. Adminstrn., U. Lowell, Mass., 1977; CAGS in Computers in Edn., Lesley U., Cambridge, Mass., 1985. Cert. tchr. earth sci., geography, history, cert. gen. supr., jr.-sr. h.s. prin., Mass. Tchr. earth sci. DeSales H.S., Louisville, 1968-69; tchg. fellow Boston U., 1969-71; liberal arts prof. Bryant-McIntosh Jr. Coll., Lawrence, 1971-72; earth sci. tchr., lead sci. tchr. Arlington H.S., 1972—; adult edn. instr. Arlington (Mass.) Pub. Schs., 1985-90; asst. dir. project ESTEEM Harvard-Smithsonian, Cambridge, Mass., 1993; instr. earth sci. Northeastern U., Boston, 1997—. Telecom. moderator Harvard U. Sci. Tchr. Network, Cambridge, 1986-89; chair study groups for sci. edn. reform Mass. Dept. Edn., Malden, 1995—, sci. tchr. leader, 1998. Co-author: Integrating Computers in Your Classroom: Middle and Secondary Science, 1994, Harvard Smithsonian Project IMAGE, 1997; presenter in field. Lector St. Theresa's Ch., Billerica, Mass., 1975—; trustee Billerica Pub. Libr., 1993—; mem. Billerica Friends of the Libr., 1995—; bd. dirs. Tchr. Leadership Acad. Mass. Recipient Pathfinder award in tech. Mass. Dept. Edn., 1991, Sci. Educator of Yr. award for Middlesex County, Mass. Assn. Sci. Tchrs., 1998, Presdl. award for excellence in tchg. math. and sci. NSF, 2000; Disting. Alumni award U. Mass., Lowell, 2000, Boston U., 2002; Tandy Tech. scholar, 1996, Disting. Alumnia award Boston U., 2002; inducted into Mass. Sci. Educators Hall of Fame, 1992. Fellow Tchr. Leadership Acad. Mass. (bd. dirs.); mem. Nat. Assn. Geosci. Tchrs. (regional pres.), NSTA, Nat. Geog. Soc., Mass. Assn. Scis. Tchrs. (award sect.), Mass. Assn. Sci. Suprs. (pres. 2004—), Alpha Omega Alpha, Gamma Theta Upsilon (local pres.). Democrat. Roman Catholic. Avocations: computers, telecommunications and internet, reading journals and books, walking. Office: Arlington HS 869 Massachusetts Ave Arlington MA 02476-4701 Office Phone: 781-316-3574. Business E-Mail: tvaughn@arlington.k12.ma.us.

VAUGHN, VINCE, actor; b. Mpls., Mar. 28, 1970; s. Vernon and Sharon Vaughn. Actor: (films) For the Boys, 1991, Rudy, 1993, At Risk, 1994, Swingers, 1996, Just Your Luck, 1996, The Lost World: Jurassic Park, 1997, The Locusts, 1997, A Cool, Dry Place, 1998, Return to Paradise, 1998, Clay Pigeons, 1998, Psycho, 1998, South of Heaven, West of Hell, 2000, The Cell, 2000, The Prime Gig, 2000, Zoolander, 2001, Domestic Disturbance, 2001, Dust: An Extraordinary Correspondence, 2002, Old School, 2003, I Love Your Work, 2003, Blackball, 2003, Starsky & Hutch, 2004, Dodgeball: A True Underdog Story, 2004; actor, prodr.: (films) Made, 2001; actor: (TV films) Lies of the Heart, 1991, Sex and the Matrix, 2000; (TV series) Doogie Howser, M.D., 1989, China Beach, 1989, 21 Jump Street, 1989, Hercules, 1998, Mr. Show, 1998, The Larry Sanders Show, 1998, Sex and the City, 2000, Dinner for Five, 2001. Address: United Talent Agy Ste 500 9560 Wilshire Blvd Beverly Hills CA 90212*

VAUGHN, WILLIAM PRESTON, historian, educator; b. East Chicago, Ind., May 28, 1933; s. James Carl and Georgiana (Preston) V.; m. Virginia Lee Meyer, June 10, 1961; 1 child, Rhonda Louise Horton. AB, U. Mo., Columbia, 1955; MA, Ohio State U., 1956, PhD, 1961. Instr. in history U. So. Calif., 1961-62; asst. prof. history U. N. Tex., Denton, 1962-65, assoc. prof., 1965-69, prof., 1969-91. Instr. Tex. Project, Malaysia, 1986, 88. Author: Schools for All: The Blacks and Public Education in the South, 1865-77, 1974, The Antimasonic Party in the United States, 1826-43, 1983, Masonic Home and School of Texas, 2002; editor Transactions Tex. Lodge of Rsch., 1988—; contbr. articles to profl. jours. With arty. U.S. Army, 1956-57 Mem. SAR, SCV, So. Hist. Assn. (life), Historians Early Am. Republic, Blue Friars, Masons, Phi Beta Kappa, Phi Alpha Theta (manuscript competition winner 1972). Republican. Episcopalian. Home: 205 Silver Leaf St Mount Pleasant TX 75455-7405

VAUGHN, WILLIAM T, corporate financial executive; b. 1947; BSc, U. of Ark. CPA. Audit mgr. Arthur Young & Co., 1974—81; contr. Marion Corp., 1981—83, Devon Energy Corp., 1983—87; v.p. fin. Devon Energy, 1987—99, sr. v.p. fin., 1999—. Mem.: Am. Inst. Cert. Pub. Accountants. Office: Devon Energy Corp 20 N Broadway Oklahoma City OK 73102

VAUGHN, WILLIAM WEAVER, retired lawyer; b. Los Angeles, Aug. 29, 1930; s. William Weaver and Josephine (Sweigert) V.; m. Claire Louise M'Closkey, June 2, 1962; children: Robert, Gregory, Elizabeth, Anthony, Christina, James. BA, Stanford U., 1952; LLB, UCLA, 1955. Bar: Calif. 1956. With O'Melveny & Myers, L.A., 1955-56, 57—, ptnr., 1964-96, of counsel, 1996—2002; ret., 2002. Served with U.S. Army, 1956-57. Recipient Learned Hand award Am. Jewish Com., 1991, Joseph A. Ball award for outstanding advocacy Brennan Ctr. for Justice, 1998. Fellow Am. Coll. Trial Lawyers (bd. regents 1992-95); mem. L.A. County Bar Assn. (trustee 1976-78, 80-82), L.A. County Bar Found. (bd. dirs. 1991-95), Assn. Bus. Trial Lawyers (bd. govs. 1980-82), Order of Coif, Calif. Club, Chancery Club I(pres. 1997-98). Office: O'Melveny & Myers 400 S Hope St Los Angeles CA 90071-2899

VAUGHT, RICHARD LOREN, urologist; b. Ind., Oct. 28, 1933; s. Loren Judson and Bernice Rose (Bridges) V.; widowed, July 1987; children: Megan, Niles, Barbara, Mary; m. Nancy Lee Gusa, Aug. 1992. AB in Anatomy and Physiology, Ind. U., 1955; MD, Ind. U., Indpls., 1958. Diplomate Am. Bd. Urology. Intern, then resident in gen. surgery U.S. Naval Hosp., St. Albans, N.Y., 1958-60, resident in urology, 1960-63; spl. fellow Sloan Kettering Meml. Hosp. for Cancer and Allied Diseases, N.Y.C., 1962; pediatric urology observer Babies Hosp., Columbia-Presbyn. Med. Ctr., N.Y.C., 1962; head urology U.S. Naval Hosp., Beaufort, S.C., 1963-65, asst. chief urology, head pediatric urology San Diego, 1965-68; pvt. practice Plaza Urol., Sioux City; med. dir. dept. hyperbaric medicine St. Luke's Regional Med. Ctr., Sioux City, 1988-95. Pres., chmn. bd. dirs. Care Choices of Siouxland, Sioux City, 1987-94; med. dir. Male Impotence Clinic, Marian Health Ctr., Sioux City, 1995-97, Diagnostic Ctr. for Men of S.C., 1997-99. Organizer telecommunications system for deaf, Siouxland, 1983. Lt. comdr. USN, 1958-68. Fellow ACS, Internat. Soc. Cryosurgery, Am. Acad. Pediat.; mem. Am. Urol. Assn., Soc. Pediatric Urology, European Soc. Pediatric Urology (corr.), Undersea and Hyperbaric Medicine Soc., Am. Coll. Hyperbaric Medicine, Am. Soc. Laser Medicine and Surgery, Am. Lithotripsy Soc., Woodbury County Med. Soc. (pres.), Am. Confedn. Urologia, Am. Acad. Male Sexual Health, Sertoma (Sertoman of Yr. award 1983). Home: 111 Bushberry Way Greer SC 29650-2976 E-mail: rvaught100@aol.com.

VAUSE, EDWIN HAMILTON, research foundation administrator; b. Chgo., Mar. 30, 1923; s. Harry Russell and Sylvia Clair (Webster) V.; m. Harriet Evelyn Oestmann, June 30, 1951; children— Karen L., Russell E., Kurt H., Dirk C., Luke E. BS, U. Ill., 1947, MS, 1948; MBA, U. Chgo., 1952; D.Sc. (hon.), U. Evansville, 1977. Registered profl. engr., Ill., Ind. Engr., research dept. Standard Oil Co., Ind., 1948-52, asst. gen. foreman mfg. dept., 1952-57; dir. research adminstrn. Mead Johnson & Co., Evansville, Ind., 1957-60; v.p. Charles F. Kettering Found., Dayton, Ohio, 1960-66, v.p., adminstrn. dir., 1966-67, exec. v.p., 1967-71, v.p. for sci. and tech., 1971-88. Trustee The Found. Center, 1967-73; mem. adv. com. Acad. Forum, Nat. Acad. Scis. Vice-pres. Washington Twp. Bd. Edn., 1963-67; mem. Centerville-Washington Twp. Joint Planning Commn., 1967-68; mem. adv. bd. Center for Students Rights, Dayton, 1966-70; active Boy Scouts Am. Mem. Am. Inst. Chem. Engrs. (past chmn. Chgo. sect.), N.Y. Acad. Scis., Agrl. Research Inst., Nat. Industry State Agrl. Research Council. Clubs: Elks, Kiwanis (past pres.), Masons. Republican. Lutheran. Home: 11834 Calle Parral San Diego CA 92128-4534

VAVALA, DOMENIC ANTHONY, medical scientist, retired military officer; b. Providence, Feb. 1, 1925; s. Salvatore and Maria (Grenci) V. Certificate basic engring., Yale U. Army Specialized Training Program, 1944; BA, Brown U., 1947; MS, U. R.I., 1950; MA, Trinity U., San Antonio, 1954; PhD in Physiology, Accademia di Studi Superiori "Minerva", Italy, 1957; MEd, U. Houston, 1958; DSc (hon.), Nobile Accademia di Santa Teodora Imperatrice, Rome, 1966, DMS (hon.), 1970; DPH (hon.), Nobile Accademia di Santa Teodora Imperatrice, 1983; D Pedagogy (hon.), Studiorum Universitas Constantiniana of Sovrano Ordine Constantiniano di San Giorgio, Rome, 1966; EdD (hon.), Imperiale Accademia di San Cirillo, Pomezia, Italy, 1977; LittD, Univ. Internazionale Sveva "Frederick II", Bergamo, Italy, 1979; D Health Scis. (hon.), Johnson & Wales U., 1993; LLD (hon.), Fridericus II U., Capua, Italy, 1997; MD (hon.), Frederick II U., Providence, Rhode Island, 1999. Research asst. tumor research U. R.I., also asst. entomol. research, 1950; research asst. pharmacology Boston U. Sch. Medicine, 1950-51; commd. 2d lt. med. service USAF, 1951, advanced through grades to lt. col., 1968; physiologist cold injury research team Army Med. Research Lab., Osaka (Japan) Army Hosp., 1951-52; research aviation physiologist USAF Sch. Aviation Medicine, Randolph AFB, Tex., 1952-54, 3605th USAF Hosp., Ellington AFB, Tex., 1955-57, chief physiol. tng., 1957; cons. aviation physiology, film prodn. dept. U. Houston, 1956; research aviation physiologist, head acad. sect. dept. physiol. tng. USAF Hosp., Lackland AFB, Tex., 1957-58; vis. prof. physiology Incarnate Word Coll., San Antonio, 1958; research aviation physiologist, chief physiol. tng. comdr. 832d Physiol. Tng. Flight, 832d Tactical Hosp., Cannon AFB, N.Mex., 1958-65; adj. faculty mem. Eastern N.Mex. U., Portales, 1959-64; instr. adult edn. divsn. Clovis (N.Mex.) mcpl. schs., 1960; research aviation physiologist, comdr. 15th Physiol. Tng.

Flight, 824th USAF Dispensary, Kadena Air Base, Okinawa, 1965-66; research scientist, directorate fgn. tech., aerospace med. div. Brooks AFB, Tex., 1966-68; chief R & D support and interface div., dep. dir. for fgn. tech., 1968-70; adj. instr. Johnson & Wales U., Providence, 1973-74; instr. humanities Johnson and Wales U., Providence, 1974-75, asst. prof. humanities, 1975-77, prof. health scis. and nutrition, 1977-93, prof. emeritus, 1993—, coord. biomed. and behavioral scis. Day Coll. divsn., 1973-75, psychology coord. vets. div. Coll. Continuing Edn., 1974-76, assoc. dean adj. faculty, 1975, dean faculty, 1975-77, coord. acad. devel., 1977-78, dir. mus. series, 1990—, curator Chapel Empress St. Theodora, 1992—. Pres. corp., chmn. bd. dirs. Sovereign Constantinian Order of St. George, Inc., R.I., 1986—; pres. corp., chmn. bd. dirs. The Noble Acad. of Empress St. Theodora of R.I., Inc., 1988—; instr. anatomy, physiology and med. terminology R.I. Hosp., Providence, R.I., 1987-90. Writer, producer: (TV Series) Your Body in Flight, Sta. KUHT, Houston, 1956; (TV series) Highway to Health, Okinawa, 1965; editor-in-chief: NADUS Jour., 1963-85; compiled and edited: Fifty Years of Progress of Soviet Medicine, 1917-67; abstractor, translator in medicine Chem. Abstracts Svc., Am. Chem. Soc., Ohio State U., 1963-74, editor: (Cath parish newspaper) The Logos, Kadena Air Base, Okinawa, 1965-66 (1st pl. 5th Air Force chapel printed news contest); contbr. articles to profl. jours. Trustee, Gov. Ctr. Sch., Providence, 1979-85; mem. scholarship com. St. Sahag and, St. Mesrob Armenian Apostolic Ch., Providence; choir master, music dir. Cannon AFB, N.Mex. Cath. Parish, 1958-65. Served with AUS, 1943-44. Recipient Disting. Svc. award Clovis (N.Mex.) Jaycees, 1959, Acad. Palms Gold medal Accademia Studi Superiori "Minerva", 1960, citation, chief chaplains USAF, 1970, commendation medal USAF, 1970, chief biomed. scientist insignia, biomed. scis. corps USAF Med. Svc., 1970, spl. faculty citation Johnson and Wales U., 1981, contbn. awd. doctoral program ednl. leadership Alan Feinstein Grad. Sch., Johnson and Wales U., Providence, RI, 1999; academician divsn. scis. Accademia di Studi Superiori "Minerva", 1960; Min. Plenipotentiary for U.S. of Nobile Accademia di Santa Teodora Imperatrice, Rome, 1967, rector pro tempore, 1980; decorated knight grand officer Merit Class, Sovereign Constantinian Order St. George, Rome, 1969, Knight of Grand Cross with Constantinian neckchain, Justice Class, Sovereign Constantinian Order St. George, 1969, Knight of Grand Cross Justice Class, Order St. John of Jerusalem, Knights of Malta, Bari, Italy, 1984, Knight of Grand Cross Justice Class, Order St. John of Jerusalem, Knights of Cyprus, Rhodes and Malta, Bari, 1984, Knight of Grand Cordon Justice Class, Order Teutonic Knights, Sao Paulo, 1986, Knight of Grand Cross Justice Class, Mil. Order St. Gereon, Sao Paulo, 1986, Knight of Grand Cross Justice Class, Mil. and Hospitalier Order St Jean d'Acre and St. Thomas, Capua, Italy, 1987, Knight of Grand Cross Justice Class, Mil. and Hospitalier Order St. Mary of Bethlehem, Capua, 1987; recipient Ednl. Professionalism award Domei Toastmasters Internat., 1965; named Magnificent Rector and Pres., The Constantinian U. (Studiorum Universitas Constantiniana), Italy, 1970, Marquis of Royal Throne of Swabia of Hohenstaufen Dynasty, Prince Jean von Schwaben, Bergamo, Italy, 1984, Duke of the New Rome of Imperial Dynasty of Amorium by His Imperial Highness Prince Don Francesco Amoroso d'Aragona, Capua, 2000. Fellow AAAS (emeritus), Tex. Acad. Sci., Royal Soc. Health (London; emeritus), Am. Inst. Chemists (emeritus); mem. Assn. Mil. Surgeons U.S. (life), Nat. Assn. Doctors U.S. (founder 1958, sec.-treas. 1958-85, editor-in-chief The NADUS Jour. 1963-68), Accademia di San Cirillo Italy (hon.), N.Y. Acad. Scis., Phi Sigma, Kappa Delta Pi, Phi Kappa Phi, Alpha Beta Kappa (charter mem., pres. R.I. Alpha chpt. Johnson & Wales U. 1984-92). Home: 30 Oaklawn Ave Apt 219 Cranston RI 02920-9319

VAYDA, ANDREW P. human ecology and anthropology educator; b. Budapest, Hungary, Dec. 7, 1931; came to U.S., 1939; s. Sándor Vajda and Zelma Szentgyörgyi; m. Cherry Lowman, June 19, 1962 (div. April 1976); m. Indah Setyawati, July 10, 1991 (div. July 1997). BA, Columbia U., 1952, PhD, 1956. From asst. prof. to prof. Columbia U., N.Y.C., 1960—72, prof., 1968-72, Rutgers U., New Brunswick, N.J., 1972—. Cons. World Wide Fund for Nature, Jakarta, Indonesia, 1992, 93, 98, Ford Found., Jakarta, 1981-84; sr. rsch. assoc. Ctr. for Internat. Forestry Rsch., Bogor, Indonesia, 2002—. Author: (book) War in Ecological Perspective, 1976, (booklets) Bugis Settlers in East Kalimantan, 1996, Methods and Explanations in the Study of Human Actions and Their Environmental Effects, 1996, Finding Causes of the 1997-98 Indonesian Forest Fires, 1999; editor-in-chief: (periodical) Human Ecology, 1971-77. Recipient Disting. Vis. Scholar award Ctr. for Internat. Forestry Rsch., 1996, Fulbright Lectr./Rsch. award USIA, 1989-90; vis. scholar grantee Ford Found., 1998; rsch. grantee NOAA, 2000—. Fellow AAAS, Am. Anthropol. Assn., Borneo Rsch. Coun., Inst. Human Ecology. Avocations: food, travel, playing squash. Office: Rutgers U Dept Human Ecology New Brunswick NJ 08901 E-mail: vayda@aesop.rutgers.edu.

VAYO, DAVID JOSEPH, composer, music educator; b. New Haven, Mar. 28, 1957; s. Harold Edward and Joan Virginia (Cassidy) V.; m. Marie-Susanne Langille, 2002; children; Rebecca Lynn, Gordon Francis. MusB, Ind. U., 1980, MusM, 1982; D of Musical Arts, U. Mich., 1990. Prof. Nat. U., Heredia, Costa Rica, 1982-84, Nat. Symphony Youth Sch., San Jose, Costa Rica, 1982-84; asst. prof. music Conn. Coll., New London, 1988-91, Ill. Wesleyan U. Sch. Music, Bloomington, 1991-95, assoc. prof., 1995-2000, prof., 2000—. Resident artist Banff Ctr. for Arts, 1992, 94, Va. Ctr. for Creative Arts, 1994, Centrum, Port Townsend, Wash., 1996; participating composer Internat. Soc. Contemporary Music-World Music Days, Yokohama, 2001, Mexico City, 1993, Internat. Double Reed Festival, Rotterdam, The Netherlands, 1995, Internat. Trombone Festival, 1997. Composer chamber composition Signals, 1997 (commd. by Koussevitzky Music Found. and Orkest de Volharding), Symphony: Blossoms and Awakenings, 1990 (performer St. Louis Symphony, Leonard Slatkin condr. 1993), Mosaics and Webs, 2003 (commd. by Nat. Assn. Coll. Wind and Percussion Instrs.), Eight Poems of William Carlos Williams for solo trombonist, 1994 (commd. by St. Louis Symphony), piano trio Awakening of the Heart (commd. Barlow Endowment for Music Composition), 1998; works pub. by So.Music, Internat. Trombone Assn. Press and A.M. Percussion Publs. John Simon Guggenheim Meml. Found. fellow, 2001; Ill. Arts Coun. fellow, 2000. Mem. ASCAP (awards 1988—), Am. Music Ctr. (copying assistance grantee 1992), Coll. Music Soc. (presenter nat. conf. 1990, 94, 96), Soc. for Electro-Acoustic Music in U.S. (presenter nat. conf. 1989), Soc. Composers (membership chmn. 1990-2000, presenter nat. conf. 1990, 92, 95, 97, 98), Am. Composers Forum. Avocations: athletics, popular music, travel, reading, cooking. Office: Ill Wesleyan U Sch Music PO Box 2900 Bloomington IL 61702-2900 Office Phone: 309-556-3068. E-mail: dvayo@titan.iwu.edu.

VAZIRANI-FALES, HEEA, legislative staff member, lawyer; b. Calcutta, India, Apr. 1, 1938; d. Sunder J. Vazirani; m. John Fales Jr., 1978; children: Deepika, Reetika, Ashish, Monika, Jyotika, Denise. AB, Guilford Coll., 1959; JD, Howard U., 1979. Staff/legis. dir. Montgomery County Del, Gen. Assembly of Md., 1981-87; legis. counsel to Congresswoman Constance A. Morella, US Ho. of Reps., Washington, 1987-94, counsel subcom. on postal svc. com. govt. reform, 1995—2000, dep. staff dir. and counsel subcom. on DC govt. reform, 2000—02, counsel subcom. on civil svc., 2003—. Mem. staff Vols. for Visually Handicapped, 1973-79, bd. dirs., 1979-81; bd. dirs. Manipal Edn. and Med. Found., 1970-92. Mem. Phi Delta Phi. Office: Subcom on Civil Svc B-373A Rayburn Bldg Washington DC 20515

VAZIRI, NOSRATOLA DABIR, internist, educator, nephrologist; b. Tehran, Iran, Oct. 13, 1939; came to U.S., 1969, naturalized, 1977; s. Abbas and Tahera Vaziri. MD, Tehran U., 1966. Diplomate Am. Bd. Internal Medicine, Am. Bd. Nephrology; cert. hypertension specialist Am. Soc. Hypertension. Intern Cook County Hosp., Chgo., 1969-70; resident Berkshire Med. Ctr., Pittsfield, Mass., 1970-71, Wadsworth VA Med. Ctr., L.A., 1971-72, UCLA Med. Ctr., 1972-74; prof. medicine U. Calif.-Irvine, 1979—, prof. physiology and biophysics, 2001—, chief nephrology and hypertension divsn., 1977—, dir. hemodialysis unit, 1977-94, vice chmn. dept. medicine, 1982-94, chmn. dept. medicine, 1994-98, chair faculty Coll. Medicine, 1998—2002. Sr. assoc. editor Jour. Spinal Cord Medicine; mem. editl. bd. Kidney Internat., Am. Jour. Nephrology, 1999-2002, Nephron, 1999-2002, Advances in Renal Replacement Therapies, Internat. Jour. Artificial Organs, Spinal Cord Medicine, Jour. Renal Nutrition; contbr. numerous articles to med. jours. Mem. sci. adv. coun. Nat. Kidney Found., 1977—. Recipient Golden Apple award, 1977, Spirit of Nephrology award, Nat. Kidney Found., 2002. Master: ACP; fellow: Am. Heart Assn. (fellow coun. high blood pressure rsch.); mem.: Assn. Profs. Medicine, Western Assn. Physicians (councilor 2003—), Am. Paraplegia Soc. (pres. 1992—94, Donald Munro award 2002), Am. Physiol. Soc., Am. Soc. Nephrology, Alpha Omega Alpha. Home: 66 Balboa Cv Newport Beach CA 92663-3226 Office: U Calif Irvine Med Ctr Div Nephrology Dept Medicine 101 The City Dr Orange CA 92868-3201 Office Phone: 714-456-5142. Business E-Mail: ndvaziri@uci.edu.

VAZQUEZ, DEBRA ALLEN, literature educator; d. Lee Woodson and Patricia Bransford Allen; m. Jose Vazquez, Sept. 16, 1972 (div.); children: Patricia Kina, Stephen Lee, Jose Rafael. BA, U. Fla., 1990, MA in English, 1992. Staff mem. U. P.R., Utuado, 1982—85; prof. Ctrl. Fla. C.C., Ocala, 1992—, Attie Branan chair comm., 1997—2000. Advisor coll. lit. mag. Ctrl. Fla. C.C., 1995—, mem. steering com. Tchg. Learning Ctr., 1997—2000. Author: (poetry book) Language of Mortals, 1999, poetry. Grantee, Ocala Mcpl. Arts Commn., Fla. Humanities Coun., Am. Assn. C.C., Conf. on Am. Pluralism and Identity. Mem.: Fla. C.C. Activities Assn., Fla. Assn. C.C. Avocations: travel, reading, cooking. Office: Ctrl Fla CC 3001 SW College Rd Ocala FL 34474 Home: 4212 SW 6 Sve Ocala FL 34474

VAZQUEZ, GILBERT FALCON, lawyer; b. Eagle Pass, Tex., Oct. 29, 1952; s. Catalina (Falcon) Vazquez. AB in Polit. Sci., Yale U., 1975; JD, Harvard U., 1978. Bar: Tex. 1978, U.S. Dist. Ct. (we. dist.) Tex. 1980, U.S. Ct. Appeals (5th and 11th cirs.) 1981. Ptnr. Matthews & Branscomb, San Antonio, 1978-85, Akin, Gump, Strauss, Hauer & Feld, LLP, San Antonio, 1985—2003, Holland & Knight LLP, San Antonio, 2003—. Co-chmn. issues com. H. Cisneros Mayoral Campaign, San Antonio, 1981; bd. dirs. Bexar County-San Antonio United Way, 1982-87, 91—, San Antonio World Affairs Coun., 1993-96, San Antonio Mus. Assn., 1993-95; mem. exec. com. Mayor's Target 90 Commn., San Antonio, 1985-89, vice chmn., 1987-89; chmn. City of San Antonio Charter Rev. Com., 1991-93, State of Tex. Pension Rev. Bd., 1991-96, vice-chmn., 1994, chair, 1995; bd. dirs. San Antonio Zool. Soc., 1988—, mem. exec. com.(1st v.p.), 2002-; bd. dirs. Harvard Law Sch. Alumni Assn., 2002—; mem. The Pro Bono Coll. of the State Bar of Tex., 2002—. Named Outstanding Young San Antonian, U.S. Jaycees, 1985, Outstanding Vol., J.C. Penny Co., 1984. Mem. ABA (internat. law sect., assoc. editor newsletter 1985-87), Nat. Assn. Bond Lawyers, Tex. Bar Assn. (governing coun. internat. law sect. 1985-88), San Antonio Bar Assn., San Antonio Young Lawyers Assn. (Outstanding Young Lawyer 1987), Hispanic Nat. Bar Assn. (regional pres. 1987-88, nat. sec. 1988-89, v.p. 1989-90), San Antonio World Trade Assn. (bd. dirs. 1987-90), Mexican C. of C. (bd. dirs. 1984-85), Greater San Antonio C. of C. (bd. dirs. 1992-95), Yale Club South Tex. (pres. 1982-85). Democrat. Roman Catholic. Avocations: community redevelopment, music, reading. Office: Holland & Knight LLP 112 E Pecan St Ste 2700 San Antonio TX 78205 Office Phone: 210-229-3000. Business E-Mail: gilbert.vazquez@hklaw.com.

VAZQUEZ, LUIS, electronics engineer; b. N.Y.C., Oct. 22, 1955; s. Luis Angel Vazquez and Petra Rivera; m. Adriana Babiak, Dec. 2, 1995. AS, Univ. P.R., 1976, BSEE, 1979; MA in Humanities, U. Houston-Clear Lake, 2003. Elecs. engr. U.S. Army Aberdeen Proving Ground, Md., 1982—85, NASA Johnson Space Ctr., Houston, 1985—. Author: (short stories) Marrow, From the Asylum, Master thesis: The Molding of Subjugated Peoples. Mem.: Internat. Coun. Systems Engring., U. Houston-Clear Lake Lit. Club. Roman Catholic. Achievements include design of Gun-and-Transducer Simulator; Space Shuttle In-Flight Maintenance Breakout Box; research in Paper: Line-of-Sight (LOS) Blockage and Radio Frequency (RF) Coverage Analysis for the International Space Station (ISS) MiniAERCam Project, 2nd. author. Avocations: reading, writing, travel. Office: NASA Johnson Space Center 2101 NASA Road 1 Houston TX 77058-3607 Office Phone: 281-483-7478. E-mail: luis.vazquez-1@nasa.gov.

VAZQUEZ, MARTHA ALICIA, judge; b. Santa Barbara, Calif., Feb. 21, 1953; d. Remigio and Consuelo Medina Vazquez. BA in Govt., U. Notre Dame, 1975, JD, 1978. Bar: N.Mex. 1979, U.S. Dist. Ct. (we. dist.) N.Mex. 1979. Atty. Pub. Defender's Office, Santa Fe, 1979-81; ptnr. Jones, Snead, Wertheim, Rodriguez & Wentworth, Santa Fe, 1981-93; judge U.S. Dist. Ct. N.Mex., Santa Fe, 1993—. Democrat. Roman Catholic. Office: US Courthouse PO Box 2710 Santa Fe NM 87504-2710 Office Phone: 505-988-6330.

VAZQUEZ, RICHARD MICHAEL, surgeon; b. Chgo., Dec. 24, 1944; MD, U. Ill., 1969. Diplomate Am. Bd. Surgery. Intern Presbyn.-St. Luke's Hosp., Chgo., 1969-70, resident, 1970-74; attending surgeon Northwestern Meml. Hosp., Chgo.; asst. clin. prof. surgery Northwestern U. Med. Sch., 1981—. Cons. Ill. State Police, 1988-2002. Mem. ACS, Soc. Am. Gastrointestinal Endoscopic Surgery, Am. Coll. Phlebology (mem. website veincare com.) Office: 201 E Huron St Ste 11-250 Chicago IL 60611-2968 Office Phone: 312-649-6562. E-mail: drv@veincare.com., drv@gensurg.com.

VAZQUEZ-AZPIRI, A. JAMES, lawyer; b. Madrid, May 3, 1962; s. Hector Tomas and Iris Belinda Mary Vazquez-Azpiri; m. Yanira E. Molina, July 22, 2002; 1 child, Virginia M. MA, U. St. Andrews, Scotland, 1985, Princeton U., 1987; JD, NYU, 1992; LLM, Harvard U., 1995. Bar: Calif. 1992. Adj. atty. U.S. Commn. on Immigration Reform, Washington, 1996—97; atty. Morrison & Foerster, San Francisco, 1992—97; ptnr. Cooley Godward LLP, San Francisco, 1997—. Contbr. articles to profl. jours. Recipient C. Arthur Friedrich award, Internat. Human Rights Law Group, 1993, Wiley M. Manuel award, State Bar of Calif., 1998, Armstrong prize, Princeton U., 1997. Mem.: MLA, Hispanic Bar Assn., Bar Assn. San Francisco, Am. Immigration Lawyers Assn., Princeton Alumni Assn., Harvard Club, Sigma Delta Pi, Phi Eta Sigma, Phi Delta Theta. Avocations: hiking, scuba diving, travel, literature. Home: 672 Sky Hy Cir Lafayette CA 94549 Office: Cooley Godward LLP One Maritime Plz San Francisco CA 94549 E-mail: vazquezaj@cooley.com.

VAZQUEZ MOTA, JOSEFINA, secretary of social development for Mexico; b. Mexico City, Jan. 20, 1951; Degree in Econs., Ibero-Am. U.; diploma studies, Pan-Am. Inst. Top-Level Co. Mgmt. Fed. dep. LVIII Legis., vice-coord. econ. policy; sec. social devel. Govt. of Mex., 2000—. Founder COMEX Integral Devel. Ctr. (CEDIC) for productivity and tng. COMEX Paints; lectr. on social topics, Argentina, Peru, Colombia. Author: books on social topics in Lat. Am.; contbr. articles on social topics in Lat. Am. Mem.: Nat. Polit. Assn. (pres. women's secretariat citizen coord.). Office: Ave Constituyentes 947 Edificio B PA 01110 Mexico City Mexico

VAZZANO, FRANK PAUL, historian, educator; b. Lorain, Ohio, July 31, 1941; s. Anthony Joseph and Dorothy Marie Vazzano; m. Charlotte Louise Schmidt, Aug. 17, 1963; children: Frank Jr., Kristen, Ann-Marie. BS, Bowling Green (Ohio) State U., 1964, MA, 1965; PhD, Kent (Ohio) State U., 1972. Prof. Walsh U., North Canton, Ohio, 1971—. Adj. prof. Kent State U., Stark Campus, Canton, Ohio, 1990—2001. Contbr. articles to profl. jours. Mem.: Am. Italian Hist. Assn., Ohio Acad. History, Orgn. Am. Historians. Roman Catholic. Avocations: writing, gardening, sports. Home: 1043 Liberty Ln NW North Canton OH 44720 Office: Walsh U 2020 Easton St NW North Canton OH 44720 Office Phone: 330-499-7090. Business E-Mail: fvazzano@walsh.edu.

VEACH, ROBERT RAYMOND, JR., lawyer; b. Charleston, S.C., Nov. 28, 1950; s. Robert Raymond and Evelyn Ardell (Vegter) V.; m. Lori Sue Erickson, May 27, 1989. Student, St. Olaf Coll., 1968-70; BS in Acctg., Ariz. State U., 1972; JD, So. Meth. U., 1975. Bar: Tex. 1975, Nebr. 1975, U.S. Dist. Ct. Nebr. 1975, U.S. Dist. Ct. (no. dist.) Tex. 1975, Temporary Emergency Ct. Appeals 1975. Acctg. instr. Sch. Bus. So. Meth. U., Dallas, 1973-74; law clk. to Hon. Joe E. Estes U.S. Dist. Ct. No. Dist. Tex.-Temp. Emergency Ct. Appeals, Dallas, 1975-76; assoc. Locke Purnell Boren Laney & Neely, Dallas, 1976-80; v.p. The Lomas & Nettleton Co., Dallas, 1980-83, Rauscher Pierce Refsnes, Inc., Dallas, 1983-87; pres. RPR Mortgage Fin. Corp., Dallas, 1985-87; sr. shareholder Locke Purnell Rain Harrell, Dallas, 1987-97; exec. v.p. Precision Imaging Solutions, Inc., Dallas, 1998—; pvt. practice Dallas, 1998—. Allied mem. N.Y. Stock Exch., 1985-87; lectr. securities and banking confs.; bd. dirs. pvt. corps.; trustee Correctional Properties Trust (NYSE-CPV), chmn. audit and finance com., 1998-2002, chmn. bd., 2002—. Author legal articles. Dir. North Tex. affiliate Am. Diabetes Assn., Dallas, 1978-81; mem. Gov.'s Task Force Wash. State Housing Commn., 1982-83. Mem. ABA, State Bar of Tex., Nebr. State Bar Assn., Fed. Bar Assn., Dallas Bar Assn. Republican. Methodist. Avocations: golf, antique American firearms. Home: 4223 Brookview Dr Dallas TX 75220-3801 Office: 2911 Turtle Creek Blvd Ste 1240 Dallas TX 75219-6277 Office Phone: 214-520-7544. Business E-Mail: bob@veachlaw.com.

VEACO, KRISTINA, lawyer; b. Sacramento, Mar. 4, 1948; d. Robert Glenn and Lelia (McCain) V.; 1 child, Nina Katherine. BA, U. Calif., Davis, 1978; JD, Hastings Coll. Law, 1981. Legal adv. to commr. William T. Bagley Calif. Pub. Utilities Commn., San Francisco, 1981-86; sr. counsel Pacific Telesis Group, San Francisco, 1986-94; sr. counsel corp. and securities and pol. law AirTouch Comms., San Francisco, 1994-98; asst. gen. counsel, asst. sec. McKesson Corp., San Francisco, 1999—. Mem.: ABA, Am. Soc. Corp. Secs. (pres. San Francisco chpt. 2001—02, mem. adv. com. San Francisco chpt., nat. bd. dirs.), San Francisco Bar Assn., Phi Beta Kappa. Office: McKesson Corp 1 Post St Fl 33 San Francisco CA 94104-5233 Office Phone: 415-983-9154. E-mail: Kristina.veaco@mckesson.com.

VEALE, JOHN EDMOND (JACK VEALE), business executive; b. Winchester, Mass., July 12, 1954; s. Edmond John and Margaret Louise Veale; m. Laurie Jean Howard, Apr. 29, 1978; children: Alex, Jason. BSBA, Norwich U., 1976; MBA, Boise State U., 1987. With S.W. Hide Co., Boise, Idaho, 1976-88, acct., 1977-78, office mgr. corp. office, 1978-79, corp. contr., 1979-81, CFO, 1981-87; divsn. pres. N.W. Mgmt. Assocs., Gt. West Data Sys., 1981-84, CFO, 1984-88; v.p. Spicer Gas Co., Groton, Conn., 1988-90; mgr. Coastal Oil Corp., Revere, Mass., Hasbrouk Heights, N.J., 1990-92; pres. PTCFO, Inc., Conn., 1992—. Mem. bd. advisors Jackson Lumber and Millwork. Mem. Nat. Assn. Corp. Dirs. (chpt. pres.), Am. Soc. for Quality, Turnaround Mgmt. Assn. (bd. dirs.), Rotary Club Internat., Family Firm Inst., Nat. Ski Patrol, Norwich U. Alumni Assn. (bd. dirs.), Alpha Kappa Psi. Republican. Home: 48 Walkley Rd West Hartford CT 06119-1345 Office: PTCFO Inc 48 Walkley Rd Hartford CT 06119-1345

VEALE, TINKHAM, II, former chemical company executive, engineer; b. Topeka, Dec. 26, 1914; s. George W. and Grace Elizabeth (Walworth) V.; m. Harriett Alice Ernst, Sept. 6, 1941; children: Harriett Elizabeth Veale Leedy, Tinkham III, Helen Ernst Veale Gelbach. BS in Mech. Engring., Case Inst. Tech., 1937; LLD, Kenyon Coll., 1981. Registered profl. engr. With Gen. Motors Corp., 1937-38, Avery Engring. Co., 1939, Reliance Electric Co., 1940-41; asst. to pres. Ohio Crankshaft Co., 1942-46; gen. mgr. Tocco Co., 1947-51; pres. Ric Wil Corp., 1952-53, Alco Chem. Corp., 1954-56, dir., 1954-86. Spl. ptnr. Ball Burge & Kraus, investment bankers, 1957-60; chmn. bd. V. and V. Cos., Inc. and subs., Cleve., 1960-65, Alco Standard Corp. and subs., Valley Forge, Pa., 1965-86, Horsehead Industries, Inc. and subs., N.Y.C., 1981—2001, HTV Industries Inc. and subs., Cleve., 1978—; ptnr. Fair Elm Farm, 1948-2000, Kennedy Veale Stable, 1954-2000. Trustee Veale Charitable Found., 1966—. Recipient Silver Bowl award Case Inst. Tech., 1980; recipient Gold Medal Case Inst. Tech., 1982, Univ. medal Case W. Res. U., 2003. Mem. Cleve. Engring. Soc., Nat. Soc. Registered Profl. Engrs., Newcomen Soc., Phi Kappa Psi. Home: PO Box 39 Gates Mills OH 44040-0039 Office: HTV Industries Inc PO Box 295 Gates Mills OH 44040-0295 Office Phone: 440-423-4473.

VEASEY, BYRON KEITH, information systems consultant; b. Washington, Mar. 17, 1957; s. Columbus Jr. and Joan Marie (Ingram) V. BS in Indsl. and Sys. Engring., U. So. Calif., 1979; MBA, Ball State U., 1982; M Mgmt. in Info. Sys., U. Dallas, 1989. Cert. quality analyst Quality Assurance Inst., computing profl. Inst. for Certification of Computer Profls. CIM engr. Mason & Hanger, Amarillo, Tex., 1983-87; bus. sys. analyst E-Sys., Garland, Tex., 1987-89; consulting mgr. Deloitte & Touche, Dallas, 1989-93; sr. cons. CSC, Dallas, 1993-96; solutions mgr. AT&T, Chantilly, Va., 1996-97, Information Advantage, Vienna, Va., 1997; info. sys. cons. DMR Consulting Group, Inc., Atlanta, 1997—99, KPMG, Tampa, Fla., 1999—2000, Arthur Anderson, Dallas, 2000—01, Advance PS, Richardson, Tex., 2001—02, U. Ill., Champaign, 2002—. Mem. Dallas Heart Ball, 1991-92; mem. PM League Dallas Mus. of Art, 1992-93; bd. dirs. Dallas Wind Symphony, 1992; pres. Inst. of Indsl. Engrs., Dallas, 1992-93; v.p. programs Assn. for Sys. Mgmt., Dallas, 1991-93. Capt. USAF, 1979-82. Mem. Am. Legion. Republican. Avocations: theater, saxophone, chess, computers, travel. Office: Decision Support 1816 S Oak St Champaign IL 61820 Home: 1532 Seven Pines Rd Apt K Springfield IL 62704-6606

VEASEY, EUGENE NORMAN, lawyer, retired state supreme court chief justice; b. Wilmington, Del., Jan. 9, 1933; s. Eugene E. and Elizabeth B. (Norman) V.; m. Suzanne Johnson, Aug. 4, 1956; children: Andrew Scott, Dluglas Ross, E. Norman Jr., Marian Elizabeth. AB, Dartmouth Coll., 1954; LLB, U. Pa., 1957. Bar: Del. 158, U.S. Supreme Ct. 1963. Dep. atty. gen. State of Del., 1961-62; chief dep., 1962-63; ptnr. Richards, Layton & Finger, Wilmington, Del., 1963-92; chief justice Del. Supreme Ct., 1992—2004; sr. ptnr. Weil, Gotshal, & Manges, NYC, 2004—. Contbr. articles to profl. jours. Bd. advisors U. Pa. Inst. for Law and Econs. Capt. Del. Air N.G., 1957-63. Fellow Am. Bar Found., Am. Coll. Trial Lawyers, Am. Intellectual Property Law Assn.; mem. Del. Bd. Bar Examiners (chmn. 1973-80), Del. Bar Assn. (pres. 1982-83, chmn. corp. law com. 1969-74, chmn. rules com. Del. Supreme Ct. 1974-80), ABA (chair bus. law sect. 1994-95, chair spl. com. on ethics 2000 1997—), Am. Law Inst. (bd. dirs. conf. chief justice 1994-96, chair professionalism com. 1994-98, 1st v.p. 1998, pres.-elect 1998-99, pres. 1999-00), Nat. Ctr. State Cts. (chair bd. dirs. 1999-00). Republican. Episcopalian. Office: Weil Gotshal & Manges 767 Fifth Ave New York NY 10153

VEATCH, ELIZABETH WILSON, educational administrator; b. Bloomington, Ind., July 26, 1946; d. Henry Babcock and Mary Jane (Wilson) V. BA, Ind. U., 1968; MS, Georgetown U., 1970. Researcher Inter-Am. Found., Arlington, Va., 1971-73, program officer, 1973-86; asst. dir. Office of Fellowships and Grants, Smithsonian Instn., Washington, 1986-96; dir. Nat. Security Edn. Fellowship Program, Acad. Ednl. Devel., Washington, 1996—. Cons. Ford Found., N.Y.C., 1986-88, Inter-Am. Dialogue, Washington, 1990. Bd. dirs. Life Skills Ctr., Washington, 1988-96, Arlington County Community Found., 1991, fundraising com. Mem. Nat. Trust for Historic Preservation, Nat., Dem. Women's Club, Latin Am. Studies Assn. Democrat. Episcopalian. Office: NSEP/AED 1825 Connecticut Ave NW Washington DC 20009-5708 E-mail: eveatch@aed.org.

VEATCH, ROBERT MARLIN, philosophy educator, medical ethics researcher; b. Utica, N.Y., Jan. 22, 1939; s. Cecil Ross and Regina (Braddock) V.; m. Laurelyn Kay Lovett, June 17, 1961 (div. Oct. 1986); children: Paul Martin, Carlton Elliot; m. Ann Bender Pastore, May 23, 1987. BS, Purdue U., 1961; MS, U. Calif. at San Francisco, 1962; BD, Harvard U., 1964, MA, 1970, PhD, 1971; D Humanities (hon.), Creighton U., 1999. Teaching fellow Harvard U., 1968-70; research assoc. in medicine Coll. Physicians and Surgeons, Columbia U., 1971-72; assoc. for med. ethics Inst. of Society, Ethics and Life Scis., Hastings-on-Hudson, N.Y., 1970-75, sr. assoc., 1975-79; prof. med. ethics Kennedy Inst. Ethics Georgetown U., 1979—, prof. philosophy, 1981—, dir., 1989-96; adj. prof. depts. community and family medicine and ob/gyn, 1984—. Mem. vis. faculty various colls. and univs.; mem. gov. bd. Washington Regional Transplant Consortium, 1988—; bd. dirs. Hospice Care D.C., 1989-96, 97-99, pres., 1993-95; active United Network Organ Sharing Ethics Com., 1989-95. Author: Value-Freedom in Science and Technology, 1976, Death, Dying and the Biological Revolution, 1976, rev. edit., 1989, Case Studies in Medical Ethics, 1977, A Theory of Medical Ethics, 1981, The Foundations of Justice, 1987, The Patient as Partner, 1987; (with Sarah T. Fry) Case Studies in Nursing Ethics, 1987, rev. edit., 2000, The Patient-Physician Relationship: The Patient as Partner, Part 2, 1991; (with James T. Rule) Ethical Questions in Dentistry, 1993, 2nd edit., 2004, (with Harley Flack) Case Studies in Allied Health Ethics, 1997, (with Paul DeVries and Lisa Newton) Ethics Applied, 2d. edit., 1999, (with Amy Haddad) Case Studies in Pharmacy

Ethics, 1999, The Basics of Bioethics, 2000, 2d edit., 2003, Transplantation Ethics, 2000; editor or co-editor: Bibliography of Society, Ethics and the Life Sciences, 1973, rev. edit., 1978, The Teaching of Medical Ethics, 1973, Death Inside Out, 1975, Ethics and Health Policy, 1976, Teaching of Bioethics, 1976, Population Policy and Ethics, 1977, Life Span: Values and Life Extending Technologies, 1979, Cases in Bioethics From the Hastings Center Report, 1982, Medical Ethics, 1989, 2d edit., 1997, Cross Cultural Perspectives in Medical Ethics, 1989, rev. edit., 2000; (with Edmund D. Pellegrino and John P. Langan) Ethics, Trust, and the Professions, 1991; (with Tom L. Beauchamp) Ethical Issues in Death and Dying, 1996, (with Hans-Martin Sass and Rihito Kimura) Advance Directives and Surrogate Decision Making in Health Care: United States, Germany, and Japan, 1998, (with Albert R. Jonsen and LeRoy Walters) Source Book in Bioethics: A Documentary History, 1998; assoc. editor Encyclopedia of Bioethics, 1998; editl. bd. Jour. AMA, 1976-86, Jour. Medicine and Philosophy, 1980—, Harvard Theol. Rev., 1975—, Jour. Religious Ethics, 1981—; editl. adv. bd. Forum on Medicine, 1977-81; contbg. editor Hosp. Physician, 1975-85, Am. Jour. Hosp. Pharmacy, 1989-99; sr. editor Kennedy Inst. Ethics Jour., 1991—; contbr. articles to profl. jours. Mem. Soc. Christian Ethics. Office: Georgetown U Kennedy Inst Of Ethics Washington DC 20057-0001 Office Phone: 202-687-6771. Business E-Mail: veatchr@georgetown.edu.

VEBLEN, THOMAS CLAYTON, management consultant; b. Hallock, Minn., Dec. 17, 1929; s. Edgar R. and Hattie (Lundgren) V.; m. Susan Alma Beaver, Sept. 1, 1950 (div. 1971); children: Kari Christen, Erik Rodli, Mark Andrew, Sara Catherine; m. Linda Joyce Eaton, Aug. 30, 1975; 1 child, Kristen Kirby. Student, U. Calif., Santa Barbara, 1950—51; BS, Calif. Poly. U., 1953; MS, Oreg. State U., 1955. Corp. v.p. Cargill, Inc., Wayzata, Minn., 1955-75; spl. asst. Sec. Interior, Washington, 1965; dir. food and agr. SRI Internat., Menlo Park, Calif., 1975-80; pres. Food Sys. Assocs., Inc., Washington, 1980-94; also bd. dirs. Food System Assocs., Inc., Washington; chmn. Enterprise Cons. and Devel., Inc., Mpls., 1990—; dir. Georgetown Cons., Inc., 1993-95; convener The Superior Bus. Firm Roundtable, 1993—; chmn. Kirby Ventures LLC, Mpls., 1997—, Wyatt Ventures, LLC, Mpls., 1999—, Northshore, LLC, Mpls., 2000—. Mem. CMC Inst. Mgmt. Cons., 1988—97, pres. Washington chpt., 1991—93. Co-author: (with M. Nichols) The U.S. Food System, 1978; (with M. Abel) Creating a Superior National Food System, 1992; author: The Way of Business, 2000; editor Food System Update, 1986-95. Treas., bd. dirs. White House Fellows Assn., Washington, 1985; trustee Freedom from Hunger Found., Davis, Calif., 1980-99, chmn., 1986-89; bd. dirs. Patterson Sch., U. Ky., Lexington, 1976-99, Am. Near East Refugee Aid, 1994-. Recipient Presdl. Appointment White House Fellows Program, Washington, 1965. Mem. Coun. on Fgn. Rels., Cato Inst., Cosmos Club. Episcopalian. Avocations: canoeing, gardening. Office: Enterprise Cons and Devel Inc 3105 Bloomington Ave South Minneapolis MN 55407 E-mail: superbizrt@aol.com.

VECCHIO, ROBERT PETER, business management educator; b. Chgo., June 29, 1950; s. Dominick C. and Angeline V.; m. Betty Ann Vecchio; Aug. 21, 1974; children: Julie, Mark. BS summa cum laude, DePaul U., 1972; MA, U. Ill., 1974, PhD, 1976. Instr. U. Ill., Urbana, 1973-76; mem. faculty dept. mgmt. U. Notre Dame, 1976—, dept. chmn., 1983-90, Franklin D. Schurz Prof. Mgmt., 1986—. Editor Jour. of Mgmt., 1995-2000. Fellow: APA, Am. Psychol. Soc., Soc. for Indsl. and Orgnl. Psychology; mem.: Midwest Psychol. Assn., Midwest Acad. Mgmt., Acad. of Mgmt., Phi Eta Sigma, Delta Epsilon Sigma, Phi Kappa Phi. Home: 16856 Hampton Dr Granger IN 46530-6907 Office: U Notre Dame Dept Mgmt Notre Dame IN 46556

VECCHIOTTI, ROBERT ANTHONY, management and organizational consultant; b. N.Y.C., May 21, 1941; s. R. Lucien and Louise Victoria V.; m. Dorothea Irene Hoban, Oct. 12, 1963; children: John Robert, Rachel Irene, Sara Christine. BS, St. Peter's Coll., 1962; MA, Fordham U., 1964; PhD, St. Louis U., 1973. Lic. psychologist, Mo. Psychologist Testing and Advisement Ctr., NYU, Washington Sq. campus, 1964-65; group psychologist McDonnell Douglas, St. Louis, 1967-76, sr. bus. analyst, 1976-77, mgr. bus. planning, 1977-79; pres. Orgnl. Cons. Svcs., Inc., St. Louis, 1980—. Adj. assoc. prof. mgmt. Maryville Coll., St. Louis, 1975-81. Bd. dirs. Cath. Charities of St. Louis, 1981-86, Cath. Family Svc., 1986-2000, Mental Health Assn. St. Louis, 1989—, Sta. KWMU-FM, 1989-94; trustee St. Patrick;s Ctr., 2001—. With U.S. Army, 1965-67. Mem. APA, Strategic Leadership Forum, Mo. Athletic Club, Rotary (past pres.). Office: Organizational Consulting Svcs Inc 230 S Bemiston Ave Ste 1107 Clayton MO 63105-1907 Office Phone: 314-863-1200.

VECCI, RAYMOND JOSEPH, airline industry consultant; b. N.Y.C., Jan. 22, 1943; s. Romeo John and Mary (Fabretti) V.; m. Helen Cecelia Clampett, Sept. 3, 1967; children: Brian John, Damon Jay. BBA, CCNY, 1965; MBA, NYU, 1967. Adminstrv. asst. Internat. Air Transport Assn., N.Y.C., 1961-66; econ. analyst United Airlines, Chgo., 1967-74; asst. v.p. planning and regulatory affairs Alaska Airlines Inc., Seattle, 1975-76, staff v.p. planning and regulatory affairs, 1976-79, staff v.p. planning, 1979, v.p. planning, 1979-85, exec. v.p., chief operating officer, 1986-90, pres., chief exec. officer, 1990-95, chmn., dir., 1991-95; also chmn., pres., chief exec. officer, dir. Alaska Air Group Inc.; pres. Carnival Airlines, Dania, Fla., 1997; exec. v.p. customer svc. Northwest Airlines, pres. Mich. ops. Served with U.S. Army, 1968-69, Vietnam. Decorated Bronze Star. Roman Catholic.

VECELLIO, LEO ARTHUR, JR., construction company executive; b. Beckley, W.Va., Oct. 26, 1946; s. Leo Arthur and Evelyn (Pais) V.; m. Kathryn Grace Cottrill, Nov. 29, 1975; children: Christopher Scott, Michael Andrew. BCE, Va. Poly. Inst. and State U., 1968; MCE, Ga. Inst. Tech., 1969; LLD, Northwood U., 1992. Sr. v.p. Vecellio & Grogan, Inc., Beckley, W.Va., 1973-96, pres., CEO, chmn. bd. dirs., 1996—; mng. ptnr. Deerfield Property Assocs., Beckley, W.Va., 1988—, Vecellio Realty Co., Beckley, W.Va., 1990—; pres. Vecellio Realty Inc., Beckley, W.Va., 1997—; mng. ptnr. Orlando Property Assn. Ltd., 1997—, WRQ Property Assn. Ltd., 1997—; chmn., pres., CEO The Vecellio Group-Holding Co., West Palm Beach, Fla., 2002—. Pres. Vecellio Contracting Corp. and subs. (Ranger Constrn. Industries, West Palm Beach, dba Rauger Const., South, Deerfield Beach, White Rock Quarries, Miami 1990—), Fla., 1982—; founder, past dir. Gulf Nat. Bank, Sophia, W.Va., Nat. Bankers Trust, Beckley; bank dir. Raleigh County Nat. Bank (now United Nat. Bank), W.Va., 1975-87, mem. adv. bd. Sun Trust Banks. Chmn. bd. dirs. Econ. Coun. Palm Beach County, Fla., 1985—, chmn.-elect, 1987, chmn., 1989; gov. Northwood U., West Palm Beach, 1985—; organizer, trustee Beckley Area Found., 1985; v.p., trustee Vecellio Family Found., Beckley, 1972-96, pres., trustee, 1996—; active Mini-Grace Commn., Fla. Coun. 100, 1989—, vice-chmn., 1991—; commn. dir., v.p. Criminal Justice Commn.; chmn. Budget Rev. Task Force, Budget Oversight Task Force; bd. dirs. Palm Beach County Cultural Coun. and Art Sch. Task Force, Fla. Coun. 100, Floridians for Better Transp., exec. com.; corporator Schepens Eye Rsch. Inst., Harvard U., 1993—; mem. engrng. coun. 100 Va. Tech.; mem. pres.'s adv. bd. Ga. Inst. Tech., 2000—; trustee Va. Tech. Found., 2001—. Capt USAF, 1969-73. Recipient Free Enterprise medal, Palm Beac h Atlantic U., 1988, Disting. Engring. Alumni award, Ga. Tech., 2002. Mem. Am. Rd. and Transp. Builders Assn. (dir. 2000, regional vice chmn. 2002), Flexible Pavements Assn. (found, bd. dirs. 1979—), Contractors Assn. W. (bd. dirs. 1975—). Clubs: Mayacoo Lakes Country (West Palm Beach), Adios Golf (Coconut Creek, Fla.), Jupiter Hills (Fla.), Everglade Club, Club Colette. Republican. Roman Catholic. Avocations: golf, boating, skiing. Home: 210 Via Del Mar Palm Beach FL 33480 Office: Vecellio Group Inc PO Box 15065 West Palm Beach FL 33416-5065

VEDDER, EDDIE, singer; b. Evanston, Ill., Dec. 23, 1965; m. Beth Liebling, June 3, 1994. Lead singer (band) Pearl Jam, 1991—, albums Ten, 1991—, Vs., 1993—, Vitalogy, 1994—, No Code, 1996—, Binaural, 2000, Save You, 2002, Riot Act, 2002, contbr. vocals album Temple of the Dog, 1991, Mother Love Bone, 1992, Bob Dylan Thirtieth-Anniversary Tribute, Sweet Relief: A Tribute to Victoria Williams, Shame, Judgement Night Soundtrack, 1993, Yield, 1998, Pearl Jam Live, 1999, appearances (films) Singles, 1992, Dead Man Walking, 1995. Office: care Epic Records 550 Madison Ave New York NY 10022-3211

VEDDER, RICHARD KENT, economics professor; b. Urbana, Ill., Nov. 5, 1940; s. Byron C. and Kathleen (Fry) V.; m. Karen Pirosko, June 18, 1968; children: Virin, Vanette. BA, Northwestern U., Evanston, Ill., 1962; MA, U. Ill., 1963, PhD, 1965. Asst. prof. econs. Ohio U., Athens, 1965-69, assoc. prof. econs., 1969-74, prof. econs., 1974-85; economist Joint Econ. Com. of Congress, Washington, 1981-82; Dist. Prof. of econs. Ohio U., Athens, 1985—. Vis. prof. Claremont (Calif.) McKenna Coll., 1979-80, Econs. Inst. U. Colo., Boulder, 1979, 80, Washington U., St. Louis, 1995, 96; adj. fellow Am. Enterprise Inst., 2003. Author: American Economy in Historical Perspective, 1976, Can Teachers Own Their Own Schools?, 2000; co-author: (monograph) Poverty, Income Distribution, The Family and Public Policy, 1986, Out of Work: Unemployment and Government in Twentieth-Century America, 1993, rev. edit., 1997. Mem. Athens Bd. Edn., 1987-91; bd. dirs. Athens Community Music Sch., 1987-92. Recipient rsch. grants Earhart Found., 1970, 90, Rockefeller Found., 1974, Nat. Chamber Found., 1990, fellowship Inst. for Humane Studies, Palo Alto, Calif., 1983. Mem. Am. Econ. Assn., Econ. History Assn., Rotary. Republican. Presbyterian. Home: 7464 Ridgeview Cir Athens OH 45701-9005 Office: Ohio Univ Dept Econs Bentley Hall Athens OH 45701

VEDDER, ROBERT ALLEN, publishing executive; b. Urbana, Ill., Feb. 10, 1944; s. Byron Thomas and Kathleen Vedder; m. Susan Kay Smith; children: Charles Todd, Robert Scott. BA, DePauw U., Greencastle, Ind., 1962—66. Asst. prodn. mgr. Dow Jones, Silver Spring, Md., 1966—67, Chicepee, Mass., 1968—69, Highland, Fla., 1969, prodn. mgr. Dallas, 1970—71, nat. prodn. mgr. South Brunswick, NJ, 1971—76; gen. mgr. The Trib, N.Y.C., 1977; v.p., gen. mgr., publisher Sun Coast Media, Venice, Fla., 1979—2003. Adv. bd. mem. Boys & Girls Club of Venice; founder, pres. bd. Rotary Futures Com.; hon. chmn., libr. expansion campaign Friends of Jacaranda Pub. Libr.; Relay for Life com. mem. Am. Cancer Soc. 2d class USN, 1967—72. Named Vol. of Yr., Sarasota Schs., 1993, 1996, Grand Marshall, Sun Fiesta Parade, 2003; recipient Disting. Cmty. Svc. Award, S. Venice Rotary, 1993, Sam Walton Cmty. Leader Award, 1998, Elks Club Citizen of Yr., 1998, Lifetime Achievement Award, Venice Little League, 2003. Mem.: Fla. Press Assn., Sertoma Club of Venice, Linebacker Club, Kiwanis. Avocations: gardening, golf.

VEDERNIKOV, YURI P. pharmacologist, educator; b. Tomsk, Russia, Aug. 3, 1937; arrived in U.S., 1991; s. Pavel D. Vedernikov and Tatjana P. Vedernikova; m. Valentina G. Budkina, Mar. 2, 1960 (dec.); 1 child, Alexander Y. Veder. MD, PhD, Sverdlovsk (Russia) Med. Inst., 1963. Cert. medicine pharmacology Med. Inst., Sverdlovsk. Asst. prof. dept. pharmacology Med. Inst., Sverdlovsk, 1963—69; rschr. Inst. Plant and Animal Ecology Ural's Sci. Ctr., USSR Acad. Scis., Sverdlovsk, 1969—73; sr. rschr. All-Union Inst. Med. Info. USSR Health Ministry, Moscow, 1973—74; sr. rschr. Brain Rsch. Inst. Acad. Med. Scis., Moscow, 1974—78, sr. rschr. Cardiology Rsch. Ctr., 1978—91; rsch. instr. dept. medicine Coll. Medicine Baylor U., Houston, 1991—93, asst. prof. dept. anesthesiology and ob-gyn., 1993—95; asst. prof. U. Tex. Med. Br., Galveston, 1995—2000, assoc. prof., 2000—. Contbr. scientific papers to profl. jours. Mem.: Nitric Oxide Soc., Acad. Problems Hypoxy (academician). Achievements include patents for device for the study of mechanical properties of the vessels. Home: 21 Back Bay Cir Galveston TX 77551 Office: U Tex Med Br 301 University Blvd Galveston TX 77555-1062 Business E-Mail: yvederni@utmb.edu.

VEDROS, NEYLAN ANTHONY, microbiologist, educator; b. New Orleans, Oct. 6, 1929; s. Phillip John and Solange Agnes (Melancon) V.; m. Elizabeth Corbett, Apr. 9, 1955; children: Sally Ann, Philippa Jane. BS in Chemistry, La. State U., 1951, MS in Microbiology, 1957; PhD, U. Colo., 1960. Postdoctoral fellow Nat. Inst. Allergy and Infectious Diseases, U. Oreg., Portland, 1960-62; microbiologist Naval Med. Research Inst., Bethesda, Md., 1962-66; research microbiologist Naval Biosci. Lab., Oakland, Calif., 1966-67; assoc. prof. med. microbiology and immunology U. Calif., Berkeley, 1967-72, prof., 1972-91, prof. emeritus, 1991—. Dir. Naval Biosci. Lab., 1968-81; mem. expert panel on bacteriology WHO, 1972-91. Bd. trustees Alameda (Calif.) Library, 1973-78. Served to comdr. M.S.C. USNR, 1952-55, 62-67. Mem.: Internat. Assn. Aquatic Animal Medicine, Internat. Assn. Microbiol. Sci., Am. Soc. Microbiology. Home: 209 Almond Way Healdsburg CA 95448 E-mail: nvedros@earthlink.net.

VEECH, LYNDA ANNE, musician, educator; b. Montclair, N.J., July 19, 1969; d. Robert Gerald, Sr. and Josephine Veech. B in Music Edn., Rutgers U., New Brunswick, 1991, MA in Music History, 1995; MusM in Piano Performance and Pedagogy, Westminster Choir Coll., Princeton, N.J., 1998. Cert. tchr. N.J. Faculty mem. Westminster Conservatory, Princeton, 1995—2000; pvt. studio dir. Studio of Lynda A. Veech, Verona, NJ, 1995—; faculty mem. Essex County Coll., Woodbridge, NJ, 1996—98, Caldwell (N.J.) Coll., 2000—01; choral dir. Caldwell and West Caldwell Pub. Schs., 2000—02; music tchr. Bartle Elem. Sch., Highland Park, NJ, 2002—03, Morris Cath. HS, Denville, NJ, 2003—. Cons. freelance work, Verona, NJ, 1995—2002; participant Hands Across the Water Internat. Tchr. Exch. Program, Australia, 2002. Performer Ameropa Internat. Music Festival, Prague, Czech Republic, 2001. Bd. dirs. Music and More Booster Club, Caldwell, NJ, 2001—02; dir. musician 1st Bapt. Ch., Montclair, 2000—01; organist, choir dir. Calvary Luth. Ch., 2003—; vocalist Canticle AIDS Benefit Ensemble, NJ, 1999—2000. Grantee, Rutgers U., 1991—95, Westminster Choir Coll., 1995—97. Mem.: Music Edn. Assn. (co-founder 2000—), Nat. Conf. Piano Pedagogy, Piano Tchrs. Guild, N.J. Edn. Assn., Am. Choral Dir.'s Assn., Music Educator's Nat. Conf. (treas. 1987, v.p. 1991). Roman Catholic. Avocations: reading, swimming, ballet, poetry, playing music in sacred and secular settings. Home: 124 Sunset Ave Verona NJ 07044 Office: Morris Cath High Sch 200 Morris Ave Denville NJ 07834-1360 Personal E-mail: notenut@aol.com.

VEECH, RICHARD LEWIS, medical researcher, physician; b. Decatur, Ill., Sept. 19, 1935; s. G. Lewis and Jennie Edwards Veech; children: Jennifer Lally, Andrew, Thomas, George. BA, Harvard U., 1957, MD magna cum laude, 1962. USPHS fellow Harvard Med. Sch., Boston, 1962; intern, resident N.Y. Hosp./Cornell Med. Ctr., N.Y.C., 1962-64; clin. assoc. NIMH, Washington, 1964-66, med. officer, rschr., 1969-73; USPHS fellow dept. biochemistry Oxford (Eng.) U., 1966-69; chief lab. alcohol rsch. NIAAA, Washington, 1974-76; chief lab. of metabolism and molecular biology NIH/NIAAA, Rockville, Md., 1976-95, chief unit on metabolic control, 1995—. Mem. editl. bd. Jour. Biol. Chemistry, Bethesda, Md., 1975-80; cons. BTG Internat., London, 1995—. Contbr. over 250 articles to profl. jours., over 10 chpts. to texts and references. Trustee Found. for Advanced Rsch. in Med. Scis., Easton, Md., 1995—. Lt. comdr. USPHS, 1964-66. Recipient N.H. Hero's medal Manchester Union Leader, 1969, Rsch. medal Bly Found., 1974; John Douglas French Alzheimer's Found. grantee. Mem. Cosmos Club. Home: 712 Brent Rd Rockville MD 20850 Office: NIH/NIAAA 12501 Washington Ave Rockville MD 20852 Fax: (301) 443-0930.

VEEDER, PETER GREIG, lawyer; b. Pitts., Aug. 13, 1941; AB, Princeton U., 1963; JD, U. Pitts., 1966. Bar: Pa. 1966, D.C. 1976. Lawyer Thorp Reed & Armstrong, Pitts., 1970-99; of counsel Thorp, Reed & Armstrong LLP, Pitts., 1999—. Office: Thorp Reed & Armstrong LLP 1 Oxford Ctr 301 Grant St Fl 14 Pittsburgh PA 15219-1425

VEGA, BENJAMIN URBIZO, retired judge, television producer; b. La Ceiba, Honduras, Jan. 18, 1916; m. Janie Lou Smith, Oct. 12, 1989; AB, U. So. Calif., 1938, postgrad., 1939-40; LLB, Pacific Coast U. Law, 1941, postgrad.Washington & Lee U., 1943. Bar: Calif. 1947, U.S. Dist. Ct. (so. dist.) Calif. 1947, U.S. Supreme Ct. 1958. Assoc. Anderson, McPharlin & Connors, L.A., 1947-48, Newman & Newman, L.A., 1948-51; dep. dist. atty. County of L.A., 1951-66; judge L.A., County Mcpl. Ct., East L.A. Jud. Dist., 1966-86, retired, 1986; leader faculty seminar Calif. Jud. Coll. at Earl Warren Legal Inst., U. Calif-Berkeley, 1978. Mem. Calif. Gov.'s Adv. Com. on Children and Youth, 1968; del. Commn. of the Califs., 1978; bd. dirs. Los Angeles-Mexico City Sister City Com.; pres. Argentine Cultural Found., 1983. Recipient award for outstanding services from Mayor of L.A., 1973, City of Commerce, City of Montebello, Calif. Assembly, Southwestern Sch. Law, Disting. Pub. Service award Dist. Atty. L.A. Mem. Conf. Calif. Judges, Mcpl. Ct. Judges' Assn. (award for Outstanding Services), Beverly Hills Bar Assn., Navy League, L.A. County, Am. Judicature Soc., World Affairs Council, Rotary (hon.), Pi Sigma Alpha. Home: 101 California Ave Apt 1207 Santa Monica CA 90403-3525

VEGA, CARLOS B. language educator, writer; b. Barcelona, Sept. 22, 1938; arrived in U.S., 1960, naturalized, 1980; s. Carrlos Vega Lopez and Emilia Vega Bellido; m. Dagmar Vega, Aug. 21, 1967; children: Carlos F., Isabel. MA, Ind. U., Bloomington, 1966. Spanish tchr. Seneca H.S., Louisville, Saint Xavier H.S., Louisville; asst. prof., Spanish Edgecliff Coll., Cin.; co-founder Hispanic Inst. Culture; lectr. CUNY, Fairleigh Dickinson U.; Spanish & Portuguese mng. editor Southwestern Pub. Group, Cin., Holt, Rinehart & Winston, N.Y.C., CBS Pub. Group, N.Y.C.; prof., Spanish Montclair State U., NJ, 1998—. Translator: Am.'s Charters of Freedom, U.S. Consitution, Declaration of Independence, the Gettysburg Address, 1986; author: The Truth Must Be Told: How Spain and Hispanics Helped Build the United States, 2002, Conquistadoras, 2003. Spl. asst. to mayor of West New York, N.J., U.S. Congressman Frank Guarini, Hudson County Exec. Office: Montclair State Univ One University Ave Upper Montclair NJ 07043 Home: 6050 Kennedy Blvd E Apt 2E West New York NJ 07093-3939

VEGA, FRANK J. newspaper publishing executive; Pres., CEO Detroit Newspapers. Office: 615 W Lafayette Blvd Detroit MI 48226-3124

VEGA, JOSE GUADALUPE, neuropsychologist, clinical professional; b. June 4, 1953; s. Jose Guadalupe and Bertha (Saenz) V.; children: Lilian Anna, Jose Guadalupe III; m. Alberta L. Valdez, Oct. 5, 1990. BA, Pan. Am. U., Edinburg, Tex., 1975; MA, U. Denver, 1976, PhD, 1979. Lic. psychologist, Colo., profl. counselor, Tex.; diplomate Am. Bd. Med. Psychotherapists, Am. Bd. Vocat. Neuropsychology, Am. Bd. Profl. Disability Cons., Am. Bd. Forensic Examiners, Am. Bd. Psychol. Specialties (forensic neuropsychology), Am. Bd. Profl. Neuropsychology; cert. adminstrn. Halstead-Reitan Neuropsychology test batteries. With Oasis of Chandala, Denver, 1978—79, Maytag-Emrick Clinic, Aurora, Colo., 1979; psychologist Spanish Peaks Mental Health Ctr., Pueblo, Colo., 1980—85; pvt. practice Assocs. for Psychotherapy and Edn., Inc., 1985—86; co-owner Affiliates in Counseling, Psychol. Assessment & Cons., Inc., Pueblo, 1986—87; psychologist Parkview Psychol. Testing Clinic, Pueblo, 1987—93, Colo. Dept. Corrections, 1994—96; pvt. practice Pueblo, 1993—; neuropsychologist Colo. Mental Health Inst., Pueblo, Colo., 2002—. State grievance bd. Psychology Augment Panel, 1988-95. Active Colo. Inst. Chicano Mental Health, Cmty. Youth Orgn., Boys Club Pueblo; mem. health and human svcs. com. City of Pueblo. Mem.: ACA, APA, Hispanic Neuropsychol. Soc., Nat. Hispanic Psychol. Assn., Colo. Psychol. Assn. (bd. dirs. non-metro rep. 1995—2000, pres.-elect 2000, pres. 2001—02, past pres. 2002—03), Reitan Soc. (charter; v.p. 2000—02, pres. 2002—), Colo. Neuropsychol. Soc. (charter), Internat. Neuropsychol. Soc., Nat. Acad. Neuropsychology, Kappa Delta Pi, Phi Delta Kappa. Democrat. Roman Catholic. Office: 1301 W 17th St Pueblo CO 81003-1915 Office Phone: 719-544-8530. E-mail: drvega@aculink.net.

VEGA, MANUEL THOMAS, medical/surgical nurse; b. Ft. Riley, Kans., July 25, 1950; s. Manuel Torres and Bonnie Vega; m. Marie Angela Bettinazzi, Dec. 19, 1947; children: Melanie Kovacevic, Jonathan, Joel, Aaron. MA, Ashland Thoelogical Sem., 1977; BA, U. Toledo, 1980. RN Ohio. Nurse cardiac ICU The Toledo Hosp., 1981—84; nurse geriactic psychiat. Richland Hosp., Mansfield, 1987—90; corrections nurse Richland County Sheriff's Dept., 1990—93; nurse emergency psychiat. svcs. Ctr. Individual and Family Svcs., Manfield, 1993—94; mental health officer Richland County Mental Health Bd., 1995—97; nurse counselor Cleve. Clinic Found., 1997—. Author: Model for Spirituality in Recovery. Lay min. Cath. Ch., Euclid, Ohio, 2002—04. With U.S. Army, 1968—71. Decorated Army Commendation medal U.S. Army. Conservative. Roman Catholic. Avocations: furniture making, music, fishing, writing. Office: Cleveland Clinic Foundation 9500 Euclid Ave Cleveland OH 44195 Office Phone: 216-444-4836.

VEGA, MARYLOIS PURDY, journalist; b. Chgo., Nov. 4, 1914; d. William Thomas and Mary Helene (Buggy) Purdy; m. Carlos Juan Vega, Sept. 4, 1965. BA, U. Wis., Madison, 1935. With Time mag., N.Y.C., 1942-84; chief Letters to the Editor, 1951-67, chief editl. rsch., 1967-76, assoc. editor, 1976-84. Mem.: Overseas Press. Roman Catholic. Home: 303 Birchwood Southbury CT 06488-1378

VEGA, MATIAS ALFONSO, lawyer; b. Paris, Feb. 2, 1952; s. Matias Guillermo and Colette (Lafosse) V.; m. Carmella Margarita Kurczewski, Nov. 20, 1982; 1 child, Alexandra Lafosse. AB, Yale U., 1974; JD, Harvard U., 1977. Bar: N.Y. 1978, U.S. Dist. Ct. (so. and ea. dists.) N.Y. 1979, U.S. Supreme Ct. 1984, U.S. Ct. Appeals (6th and 9th cirs.) 1985, U.S. Dist. Ct. (no. dist.) Calif. 1985. Assoc. Curtis, Mallet-Prevost, Colt & Mosle, N.Y.C., 1977-85, ptnr., 1986—. Contbr. articles to profl. jours. Mem. ABA, Am. Soc. Internat. Law, N.Y. State Bar Assn. (chmn. com. Latin Am. law, internat. law and practice sect. 1987-90), Yale Club. Republican. Roman Catholic. Home: 8 Cerf Ln Mount Kisco NY 10549 Office: Curtis Mallet-Prevost Colt 101 Park Ave Fl 34 New York NY 10178-0061 Office Phone: 212-696-6929. Personal E-mail: matvega@optonline.net. Business E-Mail: mvega@cm-p.com.

VEGA, STEVE, poet; b. NYC, Nov. 13, 1949; s. Exio Ocasio Vega; children: Katherine, James-Paul Christian, Diamond Zhane. Cert. in Bus. Mgmt., Marion Bus. Coll., 1973; cert., John Marshall Law Sch., 1977; cert. in corrections and probations svcs., Chgo. Loop Coll., 1986; BA, Coll. of Comml. Sci., 1995, M in Comml. Svc., 1996, postgrad., 1997; PhD, Lord Baden-Powell Coll., Lake Geneva, Wis., 1998, Fellow of Scouting degree, 2003; wilderness survival course, with APO wardogs, 1988; winter camping survival course, OKPIK, Woodstock, Ill., 1996; sea badge course, Great Lakes Navy Base, 1998. Adult probation officer Cook County, Ill., 1979-93; pub. safety officer, police-fireman aide Morton Grove (Ill.) emergency Svcs. and Disaster Agy., 1998—, police aide, fire rescue mem.; CEO pvt. practice, 2002—. Union chief steward Cook County Adult Probation Dept., AFSCME, 1989—91; 1st v.p. AFSCME local 3486 APD officers, Chgo., 1991—92; cons. Chgo. Police Dept., FBI, U.S. Secret Svc.; dep. dir. Internat. Biog. Ctr., Cambridge, England, 2000. Author: numerous poems; actor: (films) Music Box, Only the Lonely, Gladiator, Hero, Mo Money, Hoffa, Natural Born Killers, Mad Dog and Glory, Eye for and Eye (The Shadow of a Killer), Curly Sue, others; composer, rec. artist: The President Is Crying-September 11, 2001, 2001. Asst. coun. commn. Boy Scouts Am., Chgo., 1997, mem. ctrl. region com. Sea Scouting, 1998; vol., mem. com. City of Chgo. Health Sys. Agy., 1981—85. With USAF, 1970, with mil. aircraft command, mil. honor guard. Decorated Commendation medal USAF, knigth comdr. European Order Knighthood (Italy), 443d Svs. Squadron and Honor Guard USAF Mil. Aircraft Command; named World Poet, 1987—; named one of World's Great Living Poets, 1991; named to Hall of Fame, Lord Baden-Powell U., 2001, 2001; recipient Presdl. commendation, Pres. Ronald Reagan, 1987, 1988, Pres. George Bush, 1990, Arrowhead award, Boy Scouts Am., 1994. Mem.: ASCAP (composer, writer), Fraternal Order Police (officer 1988, sgt.-at-arms), Sovereign Mil. and Hospitaller Order St. George in Karinthia (titular head). Roman Catholic. Avocations: singing, composing, guitar, motorcycling, chess. Address: PO Box 221 Morton Grove IL 60053-0221 E-mail: steve_vega_records@yahoo.com., stevevegaworldpoet@yahoo.com., stevevegapoetamundial@yahoo.com.

VEGA GARCIA, GERARDO CLEMENTE R. Mexico Secretary of Defense; b. Ciudad de Puebla, Puebla, Mex., Mar. 28, 1940; B in Mil. Adminstrn., Superior War Coll.; M in Security and Nat. Def., Nat. Def. Coll.; postgrad., Secretariat of Pub. Edn., Iberoam. U. With Mexican Army, advanced through grades to gen., subaltern officer 32nd infantry bn., subaltern officer 55th bn., capt. 13th infantry bn., capt. 15th cavalry regiment Sarabia, Mexico, officer in command instrn. 13th infantry bn., comdr. 11th infantry bn., 17th bn., comdr. 5th mil. zones, comdr. 34th mil. zone, comdr. 1st mil. region, chief 1st sect. 26th mil. zone, 34d sect. tng., 5th sect. strategic plans Gen. Staff Nat. Def., chief pedagogical inspection com., chief of staff 19th mil. zone,

chief of staff 8th mil. region, mil. attaché to Soviet Union, Poland and East Germany; prof. Heroic Mil. Coll., Superior War Coll.; asst. dir., dir. Nat. Def. Coll.; pres. U. Army and Air Force; sec. def. Govt. of Mex., 2000—. Office: Avila Camacho e Industria Militar Lomas de Sotelo 11640 Mexico City Mexico

VEGHTE, BILL, information technology executive; married; 1 child. BA with hon. in East Asian Studies, Harvard U. From product mgr. to corp. v.p. Microsoft, Redmond, Wash., 1990, corp. v.p. windows server group. Avocations: backcountry skiing, climbing, fishing. Office: One Microsoft Way Redmond WA 98052-6399

VEIGA, JENNIFER, state representative; b. Long Beach, Calif., Oct. 10, 1962; BS, U. Colo., Boulder, 1987; JD with honors, George Washington U., 1987. Assoc. Hall & Evans, LLC, Denver; state rep. dist. 3 Colo. Ho. of Reps., Denver, 1996—, mem. joint com. on legis. con. Nat. del. Am. Coun. Young Polit. Leaders; student coord. Hart campaign U. Colo., 1984. Mem.: AB A, Colo. Women's Bar Assn. (co-chair task force on gender bias, chair pub. policy com.), Colo. Bar Assn., Denver Bar Assn. Democrat. Roman Catholic. Avocations: reading, golf, travel, basketball. Office: Hall & Evans LLC Ste 1700 1200 17th St Denver CO 80202 also: State Capitol # 222 200 E Colfax Ave Denver CO 80203

VEIGEL, JON MICHAEL, science administrator; b. Mankato, Minn., Nov. 10, 1938; s. Walter Thomas and Thelma Geraldine (Lein) V.; m. Carol June Bradley, Aug. 10, 1962. BS, U. Washington, 1960; PhD, UCLA, 1965. Program mgr., congl. sci. fellow Office of Tech. Assessment, U.S. Congress, Washington, 1974-75; div. mgr. Calif. Energy Commn., Sacramento, 1975-78; asst. dir. Solar Energy Rsch. Inst., Golden, Colo., 1978-81; pres. Alt. Energy Corp., Rsch. Triangle Park, N.C., 1981-88, Oak Ridge (Tenn.) Associated Univs., 1988-96. Bd. dirs. Am. Coun. Energy Efficient Economy, Washington, Pacific Internat. Ctr. for High Tech. Rsch., Honolulu; cons. Sunhunner Assocs., LLC, 1996—. Contbr. articles to jours. Trustee Maryville Coll., 1990-96, Mendeleyev U., Moscow, Russia. 1st lt. USAF, 1965-68. Mem. AAAS (past mem. com. on sci. and engring. pub. policy, past chair). Avocation: photography. Office: SunRunner Assocs LLC 16259 W Spring Canyon Way Surprise AZ 85374-4961

VEILLE, JEAN-CLAUDE, maternal-fetal medicine physician, educator; b. France; came to U.S., 1982; m. Ann Veille; children: Olivier, Xavier, Patrique, Robert. BS, McGill U., 1971; MD, U. Montpellier, France, 1977. Fellow in maternal-fetal medicine Oreg. Health Scis., Portland, 1982-84; from asst. prof. to assoc. prof. Case Western Res. U., Cleve., 1984-90; chief maternal, fetal medicine Case Western Reserve U., Cleve., 1989-90; assoc. prof., dir. maternal-fetal med. fellowship program Wake Forest U. Sch. Medicine, Winston-Salem, N.C., 1990-95, prof., 1995—, chief maternal-fetal medicine sect., 1997—2002; chmn. dept. ob-gyn. Albany (N.Y.) Med. Ctr., 2002—. Contbr. articles to profl. jours. Grantee NIH, 1991-2002. Office: 47 New Scotland Ave Albany NY E-mail: veillej@mail.amc.edu.

VEIT, GAE, construction executive; CEO, owner Shingobee Builders, Loretto, Minn., 1980—. Recipient Contractor Yr., Am. Public Works Assn., 1994, Supplier Yr., Alliant Techsystems, 1993, Nat. Female Entrepreneur Yr., Dept. Commerce, 1991. Office: Shingobee Builders PO Box 8 Loretto MN 55357-0008 Fax: 612-479-3267.

VEIT, KENNETH, dean, educator; DO, Phila. Coll. Osteo. Medicine, 1976. Med. dir. So. Huntington Co. Med. Ctr., 1977—79; med. coord. Nat. Health Svc. Corp., Region III (USPHS), 1980—81; chief clin. consultation br. U.S. Pub. Health Svc., 1980—81; interim dean, asst. dean. gad. med. edn., dir. med. edn., chmn. divsn. cmty. medicine, dir. health care ctrs. Phila. Coll. Osteo. Medicine, dean, v.p. acad. affairs, 2002—. Lectr. in field; served numerous cmty. and govt. appts.; mem. several rev. bds. Recipient Humanitarian medal, USPHS, 1981. Office: 4170 City Ave Philadelphia PA 19131

VEITCH, BOYER LEWIS, printing company executive; b. Phila., Oct. 20, 1930; s. Samuel Lewis and Agnes Mae (Bell) V.; m. Emmeline Barbara Smith, Nov. 22, 1952 (dec. Dec. 1994); children: William S., Nancy B., Thomas C.; m. Mary Chisholm Kiehn, Feb. 21, 1998. AB, Lafayette Coll., 1953; postgrad. Wharton Evening Sch., Acctg. and Fin., U. Pa., 1957-59. Advt. dir. Ware Bros. Co., Phila., 1956-62, v.p., 1962-69; salesman Zabel Bros. Co., Phila., 1969-75; chmn. Veitch Printing Corp., Lancaster, Pa., 1975—. Trustee Printers Disability Trust. Trustee Lafayette Coll., Easton, Pa., 1981-86, 87—, vice chmn. coll. rels. com., chmn. ann. fund, 1982-86, mem. fin. com., 1987-92, chmn. athletics and student affairs comn., 1992-97, mem. emeritus exec. com., 1997; mem. gen. adv. com. Lancaster County Career and Tech. Sch. System, 1996—; bd. dirs. Boys and Girls Club, Lancaster, 1980—, pres., 1990-92; dir. Boy's Club Lancaster Found., 1989—, pres., 1992—, elected to Boys and Girls Hall of Fame, 1999; dir. Gt. Valley Civic Assn., 1969-79; trustee Fulton Opera House Found., 1985-91, treas., 1987-89; bd. dirs. North Mus., 1992-94, Lancaster Airport Authority, 1994—, treas., 1994—; trustee PIA Disability Trust, 1994—; chmn. citizens for Schulze Com., Pa. 5th Congressional Dist., 1972-78; vestryman, sr. warden St. Peter's Ch. of Gt. Valley, 1972-78. Served with CIC, U.S. Army, 1954-56. Recipient Bronze Hope Chest award Nat. Multiple Sclerosis Soc., 1982, Nat. Svc. to Youth award Boys and Girls Clubs Am., 1992; named Small Bus. Person of Yr. Lancaster Co., 1991; named to Boys and Girls Club of Lancaster Alumni Hall of Fame, 1999, Graphic Arts Assn. Person of Yr., 2001; named Graphic Arts Assn. Person of Yr, 2001. Mem. SAR, Printing Industries Am. (dir. 1993-98), Graphic Arts Assn. (dir. 1980-98, chmn. 1990-92, Man of Yr. 2001), Lancaster C. of C. and Industry (dir. 1990-93), Lafayette Coll. Alumni Assn. (dir. 1974-78, pres. 1978-80), Pa. Economy League, Nat. Fedn. Ind. Bus., Phi Kappa Psi (past pres. and dir. chpt. alumni assn.), Ash Khan Soc. (hon.). Clubs: Hamilton (bd. dirs. 1995—), Wash Day, Lancaster Country, Avalon Yacht, Lancaster Aero., Lancaster Pirates (first mate 2001-2003, chief 2003-), Susquehanna Litho (dir. 1976-80, pres. 1979-80). Lodges: Rotary (Paul Harris fellow). Republican. Episcopalian. Home: 1044 Sylvan Rd Lancaster PA 17601-1933 also: 65 17th St E Avalon NJ 08202-2234 Office: Veitch Printing Corp 1740 Hempstead Rd Lancaster PA 17601-5889 E-mail: boygin@aol.com.

VEIZER, JAN, geology educator; b. Pobedim, Slovakia, June 22, 1941; arrived in Can., 1973; s. Viktor and Brigita (Brandstetter) Veizer; m. Elena Ondrus, July 30, 1966; children: Robert, Andrew Douglas. Prom. Geol., Comenius U., Bratislava, Slovakia, 1964; RNDr, Comenius U., Bratislava, Slovak Republic, 1968; CSc, Slovak Acad. Sci., Bratislava, Slovakia, 1968; PhD, Australian Nat. U., Canberra, 1971. Asst. lectr. Comenius U., 1963-66; research scientist Slovak Acad. Sci., 1966-71; vis. asst. prof. UCLA, 1972; vis. rsch. scientist U. Göttingen, Fed. Republic Germany, 1972-73; rsch. scientist U. Tübingen, Fed. Republic Germany, 1973; from asst. prof. to full prof. U. Ottawa, Ont., Can., 1973—, rsch. chair NSERC/Noranda/Can. Inst. Advanced Rsch., 1997—; prof. Ruhr U., Bochum, Germany, 1988—; Disting. Univ. prof. U. Ottawa, 2001—. Cons. NASA, Houston, 1983—86; vis. prof., scholar Northwestern U., Evanston, Ill., 1983—87; vis. fellow Australian Nat. U., 1979; vis. prof. U. Tübingen, 1974; Lady Davis professorship Hebrew U., Jerusalem, 1987. Contbr. articles to profl. jours., chapters to books. Served to jr. lt. Med., 1965—66. Named Rsch. Prof. of Yr., 1987; recipient W. Leibniz prize, German Rsch. Found., 1992; fellow Humboldt, 1980, Killam Rsch., Can. Coun., 1986—88. Fellow: Geochem. Soc. Am., Geol. Soc. Am., Geol. Survey Slovak Rep. (Gold medal 2000), Geol. Soc. Can. (Past Pres. medal 1987, Logan medal 1995), Royal Soc. Can. (Willet G. Miller medal 1991, Bancroft medal 2000); mem.: Ski Club. Roman Catholic. Avocations: reading, hiking, skiing, history. Office: Dept Earth Scis U Ottawa Ottawa ON Canada K1N 6N5 also: Ruhr U Inst Geol Mineral Geophys Lehrstuhl Sedimentgeologie 44780 Bochum Germany E-mail: veizer@science.uottawa.ca.

VELA, JOEL E. college president; b. Kerrville, Tex. BA in Social Studies, MA in Edn. and History, EdD. Pres. Palo Alto Coll., San Antonio, Mt. Hood C.C., Gresham, Oreg., 1996—2001; v.p. Rio Grande Coll. Sul Ross State U., Uvalde, Tex., 2001—. Various positions North Lake Coll., Dallas County C.C. Dist., Irving, Tex., Penn Valley C.C., Kansas City, Mo.; initiator Agribus. Inst., Mariachi Curriculum with Campanas de America. Bd. dirs. Mt. Hood Festival of Jazz, United Way; active Workforce Devel. Bd., Cath. Charities, Region 2 Workforce Quality Com. Mem. Hispanic Met. C. of C., Gresham C. of C., Rotary. Office: Mt Hood Cmty Coll 26000 SE Stark St Gresham OR 97030-3300

VELA, MARCELO FERNANDO, gastroenterologist; b. Guatemala City, Guatemala, May 28, 1970; arrived in U.S., 1997; s. Victor Augusto Vela and Lillian del Carmen Aquino de Vela; m. Stacie A. F., Apr. 5, 2003. BSc, U. Francisco Marroquin, Guatemala City, 1992, MD, 1997. Diplomate Am. Bd. of Internal Medicine. Intern Grad. Hosp. MCP Hahnemann Sch. Medicine, Phila., 1997—98, internal medicine resident, 1998—2000, clin. rsch. fellow, 2000—01; gastroenterology fellow Cleve. Clinic Found., 2001—04; asst. prof. medicine Med. U. S.C., 2004—. Contbr. articles to profl. jours., chpts. to books. Recipient Clin. Scholar award, World Congress of Gastroenterology, 2002; grantee, Am. Coll. of Gastroenterology, 2002—03; Gastroenterology fellow, Wyeth-Ayerst, 2001, sr. fellow, Astra-Zeneca, 2001. Mem.: Am. Gastroent. Assn. (clin. practice com. 2002—, young gastroenterologist and trainee com. 2002—). Achievements include research in effect of baclofen and omeprazole on acid and non acid gastroesophageal reflux measured using combined multichannel intraluminal impedance and pH (MII/pH). Avocations: travel, literature. Office: Gastroenterology Med U SC Ste 210 96 Jonathan Lucas St Charleston SC 29424 E-mail: marcevela@aol.com.

VELASQUEZ, ARTHUR, food products executive; m. Joanne Velasquez; 6 children. BSEE, Notre Dame U., 1960; MBA, U. Chgo., 1967. Former pres., prin. CID Broadcasting, Inc., Chgo., Crescent Comm, Calif.; founder, pres. Azteca Corn Products Corp., Chgo., 1970—87, pres. Azteca Food Inc. (formerly Azteca Corn Products), Chgo., 1989—. Bd. dirs. LaSalle Nat. Bank, Peoples Energy Corp., Arvin Industries, Chgo. Metro Bd. Jr. Achievement, Maryville City Youth, Mus. Sci. and Industry; trustee U. Notre Dame, Lincoln Acad. Ill.; commr. Chgo. Econ. Devel. Commn.; mem. bus. adv. coun. U. Ill., Chgo.; mem. adv. coun. U. Chgo. Grad. Sch. Bus.; mem. bd. advisors Cath. Charities, The Big Shoulders Fund, Exec. Svc. Corps. Chgo. Office: Azteca Foods Inc 5005 S Nagle Ave Chicago IL 60638*

VELASQUEZ, EDUARDO A, education educator; BA, U. Calif. at Santa Barbara, 1986; MA, U. Chgo., 1988, PhD, 1994. Vis. instr. Lake Forest Coll., 1989; preceptor Com. on Internat. Rels., U. Chgo., 1990—92; asst. prof. polit. Washington and Lee U., 1994—2000, assoc. prof. polit., 2000—. Vis. scholar Liberty Fund, 2002—03; vis. fellow U. Coll., Oxford U., 2000; president's adv. com. Washington and Lee U., 2004—, student affairs com., 2001, 2003—, univ. libr. com., 2003—, faculty rev. com., 2001—, Oxford U.-Washington Lee exchange com., 2000—, grad. fellowships com., 1999—2003, student faculty hearing bd., 1999—2002, strategic plan adv. com., 1999—2000, fulbright program adv., 1999—2000, adv. sys. rev. com., 1999—2000; facilities com. Williams Sch. of Commerce, Washington and Lee U., 1996; Henry R. Luce professorship in ethics of poverty Washington and Lee U., 1995. Cons. editor Washington and Lee U. Political Review, 1997—2002, manuscript reviewer Perspectives on Political Science, 2001, The Journal of Politics, 2001, Political Theory: An International Journal of Political Philosophy, 2000, American Journal of Political Science, 2000; contbg. editor: Love and Friendship: Rethinking Politics and Affection in Modern Times, 2003, Nature, Woman, and the Art of Politics, 2000; contbr. articles, chapters to books; author: (essays) Democratic Sensibilities, Liberal Education, and the Tyranny of Eros, 1999, On the Liberality and Artifice of Liberal Arts, 1998, conference papers; lectr. Charles A. Culpepper Found. grant, Rockefeller Brothers Fund, 2002, Rsch./Travel grant, Washington and Lee U., 1998—99, Fellowship Rsch. grant, Earhart Found., 1998, John M. Glenn grant-in-aid program, Washington and Lee U., 1996—98, Nat. Endowment for the Humanities, 1995. Office: Williams Sch of Commerce Washington and Lee Univ Lexington VA 24450

VELAYO, RICHARD SORIANO, psychologist, educator, researcher; s. Rodolfo Ratliff Velayo and Teresita Makasiar Soriano. BA in Psychology and Behavioral Scis., De La Salle U., Manila, The Philippines, 1985; MA in Applied Behavior Analysis, U. Pacific, 1988; PhD in Psychology and Edn., U. Mich., 1993. Lectr. De La Salle U., Manila, 1985; grad. tchg. instr., rsch. assoc. U. Pacific, Stockton, Calif., 1986-88; grad. rsch. assoc. U. Mich., Ann Arbor, 1988-89, grad. tchg. instr., 1989-92; adj. asst. prof. Mont. State U., Bozeman, 1993-94; computer coord., assoc. prof. Dept. Psychology, Pace U., N.Y.C., 1994—; coord., MA in Psychology program Pace U., N.Y.C. Mem. editl. bd. Internat. Jour. Instructional Media, 1994—; editor-in-chief Psych-Eye newsletter, 1996—. Pace U. scholar, 1995, 1997. Mem. APA (pres-elect internat. psychology divsn. 2003, Distinction in Rsch. award 1993), Am. Psychol. Soc., Am. Ednl. Rsch. Assn., N.Y. State Psychol. Assn., Coun. of Tchrs. of Undergrad. Psychology, Ea. Psychol. Assn., N.Y. Acad. Scis., Sigma Xi. Office: Pace Univ Dept Psychology 41 Park Row Rm 1324 New York NY 10038-1508 E-mail: rvelayo@pace.edu.

VELAZQUEZ, NYDIA M. congresswoman; b. Yabucoa, P.R., Mar. 28, 1953; Grad., U. P.R.; MA, NYU, 1976. Mem. 103rd-108th Congress from 12th N.Y. dist., Washington, 1992—; mem. banking and fin. svcs. com. 105th-108th Congress from 12th N.Y. dist., dem. mem. small bus. com. Ranking Dem. mem. of the Com. on Sml. Bus., 106th Congress. Democrat. Office: US Ho of Reps 2241 Rayburn HOB Washington DC 20515-0001

VELDEY, BONNIE, special education educator; b. Mpls., Jan. 24, 1960; d. George Joseph III and Ethel Annette Acko; m. Steve Douglas Veldey, June 13, 1991; 1 child, Tyler George. AA, Inver Grove C.C., Inver Grove Heights, Minn., 1989; BA, Coll. St. Catherine, 1991; MA in Spl. Edn., U. St. Thomas, 1998. Sci. tchr. Roma (Tex.) Ind. Sch. Dist., 1991-92; spl. edn. tchr. Clark County Sch. Dist., Las Vegas, Nev., 1996-99; pvt. practice spl. edn. tchr. Mpls., 1999—2001; tchr. spl. edn. Mpls. (Minn.) Pub. Schs., 2001—. Democrat. Roman Catholic. Home: 4331 Minnehaha Ave Minneapolis MN 55406-3908

VELEV, ORLIN D. chemical engineer, educator; b. Plovdiv, Bulgaria, Nov. 3, 1963; m. Anka Veleva; 1 child, Orlin Jr. MS in Chemistry, U. Sofia, Bulgaria; PhD, U. Sofia and Bulgarian Acad. Scis., 1996. Rsch. scientist Japanese Exploratory Rsch. for Advanced Tech. program, Tsukuba, Japan, 1994—95; postdoctoral fellow dept. chem. engring. U. Del., Newark, 1996—98, rsch. asst. prof. dept. chem. engring., 1998—2001; asst. prof. N.C. State U., Raleigh, 2001—. Spkr. in field. Reviewer (numerous jours.); contbr. articles to profl. jours. Recipient Gold medal (first pl. winner), Bulgarian Nat. Chemistry Olympiad, 1982, Bronze medal, Internat. Chemistry Olympiad, Stockholm, 1982, Govtl. awards for excellence, Ministry of Sci. and High Edn. and Ministry of Chem. and Biochemical Industry, Bulgaria, 1989, Camille and Henry Dreyfus New Faculty award, Camille and Henry Dreyfus Found., 2001, Ralph E. Powe award, Oak Ridge Associated Univs., 2002, Career award, NSF, 2003. Mem.: AIChE, Am. Crystallographic Assn., Materials Rsch. Soc., Am. Chem. Soc., Sigma Xi. Achievements include discovery of new types of self-assembling nanostructures, including new classes of microwires and microparticles; first to synthesize inverse opals, one of the most widely studied photonic materials today; patents for research; first to assemble 2D colloidal crystals and novel supraparticles. Office: North Carolina State University Dept Chemical Engineering Raleigh NC 27695-7905 Office Phone: 919-513-4318.

VELEZ, DIANA, historian, educator; b. N.Y.C., Mar. 11, 1949; d. Ismael Velez Rodriguez and Adoracion Pineiro Wiscovitch Velez. BA, CUNY, 1971; MA, PhD, Princeton U., 1977. Assoc. dir. Ctr. Latin Am. Studies U. Pitts., 1984-87; sr. program officer Tinker Found., N.Y.C., 1987-90; asst. dean arts & scis. U. Ctrl. Fla., Orlando, 1991-95, history faculty, 1995—. Doctoral fellowship Ford Found., 1971. Mem. Am. Hist. Assn., Soc. Spanish and Portuguese History, Conf. on Latin Am. History. Office: U Ctrl Fla History Dept PO Box 161350 Orlando FL 32816-1350 E-mail: velez@pegasus.cc.ucf.edu.

VELEZ SILVA, XENIA, Puerto Rican government official; Sec. of treasury Puerto Rico, 1999—. Office: Dept of Treasury PO Box 9024140 San Juan PR 00902-4140

VELICER, JANET SCHAFBUCH, retired elementary school educator; b. Cedar Rapids, Iowa, Aug. 27, 1941; d. Allan J. and Geraldine Frances (Stuart) Schafbuch; m. Leland Frank Velicer, Aug. 17, 1963 (dec. Dec. 2000); children: Mark Allan, Gregory Jon, Daniel James. BS, Iowa State U., 1963, MS, 1966; cert. Elem. Edn., Mich. State U., 1976. Tchr. chemistry Prendergast High Sch., Upper Darby, Pa., 1964-65; tchr. home econs. Cardinal O'Hara High Sch., Springfield, Pa., 1965-66; substitute tchr. Pa., Mich., 1967-76; elem. tchr. Winans Elem. Sch., Waverly, Mich., 1976-78, Wardcliff Elem. Sch., Okemos, Mich., 1978-94; tchr. gifted and talented alternative program grades 4 and 5 Hiawatha Elem. Sch., Okemos, 1994-95; tchr. grade 4 Wardcliff Elem. Sch., 1995-2001; ret., 2001. Computer coord., Great Books coord.; dist. com. mem. math, computer, substance abuse, cable TV, evaluation revision Okemos Pub. Schs., Instrnl. Coun.; del. Mich. Edn. Exch. Opportunity Program, Germany, 1999. Author: (video) Wardcliff School Documentary, 1982, The Integrated Arts Program of the Okemos Elementary Schools, 1983. Citizens adv. com. to develop a five-yr. plan, 1982-83, bldg. utilization adv. com., 1983-84, cmty. use of schs. adv. com., 1984-85, strategic planning steering com., 1989-90, taking our schs. into tomorrow com., 1990-91, bonding election steering com., 1991; chmn. wellness com. Okemos Pub. Schs., 1993-95; bd. dirs. Okemos Music Patrons, 1981-86, pres., 1984-86; faculty rep. PTO; leadership coun. Nat. Inst. Clin. Application Behavioral Medicine, 1998—; chaperone Okemos HS German Club Exch., 1987, Benton Cmty. HS Spanish Club Exch., Mex., 1995, Costa Rica, 1999, Spain, 2001, 03. Recipient Classrooms of Tomorrow Tchr. award Mich. Dept. Edn., 1990. Mem. NEA, NAFE, AARP, Nat. Ret. Tchrs. Assn., Mich. Edn. Assn., Okemos Edn. Assn. (exec. coun.), Mich. Coun. Tchrs. Math., Lansing Woman's Club, Phi Kappa Phi, Omicron Nu, Iota Sigma Pi. Democrat. Avocations: swimming, reading, hiking, travel, cultural events. Home: 2678 Blue Haven Ct East Lansing MI 48823-3804 E-mail: jvelicer@msu.edu.

VELICK, SIDNEY FREDERICK, research biochemist, educator; b. Detroit, May 3, 1913; s. Harry Alexander and Ella (Stocker) V.; m. Bernadette Stemler, Sept. 5, 1941; children: William Frederick, Martha Elizabeth. BS, Wayne State U., 1935; PhD, U. Mich., 1938. Rsch. fellow parasitology Johns Hopkins U., Balt., 1939-40; rsch. assoc. chemistry Yale U., New Haven, 1941-45; mem. biol. chemistry dept. Washington U. Sch. Medicine, St. Louis, 1946-63, prof. biol. chemistry, 1958-64; prof., head dept. biol. chemistry U. Utah Coll. Medicine, 1964-79, prof. emeritus, 1988—. Mem. biochemistry study sect. NIH. Assoc. editor: Archives Biochemistry and Biophysics; editl. bd.: Jour. Biol. Chemistry; contbr. papers on enzyme chemistry to tech. lit. Co-founder, pres. Alliance for the Mentally Ill Utah, 1980-85. Mem. NAS, AAAS, Am. Soc. Biol. Chemists, Am. Chem. Soc., Sigma Xi. Home: 2514 S Elizabeth St # 6 Salt Lake City UT 84106

VELICK, STEPHEN H. medical facility administrator; BS, Wayne State U., 1970, MS, 1980. Mgr. billing Henry Ford Hosp., Detroit, 1970-72, 72-74, mgr. patient svcs., 1974-75, asst. dir. bus., 1975-76, dir. bus. office, 1976-78, assoc. adminstr., 1978-83; exec. dir. Greenfield Health Sys. Corp., Detroit, 1983-86; chief adminstrv. officer Henry Ford Med. Group, Detroit, 1986-90; group v.p., COO Henry Ford Hosp., Detroit, 1990-95, CEO, 1995—. Adv. bd., bd. dirs. various healthcare orgns. Mem. adv. bd. Wayne State U. Coll. Pharmacy & Allied Health; active various cmty. orgns. Mem. Am. Coll. Healthcare Execs. (assoc.), Am. Hosp. Assn. Office: HFH Sys 2799 W Grand Blvd Detroit MI 48202-2608

VELLA, FRED JOHN, social studies educator; b. Steubenville, Ohio, Sept. 14, 1961; s. John Jerry and Catherine Mary Vella; m. Patricia Louise Wetzel, Apr. 27, 1996; 1 child, Fred Patrick. BA in polit. sci., U. Steubenville, 1983. Cert. tchg. social studies Fla., 2002. Congl. LBJ intern US House of Rep., Wash., DC, 1988; social studies tchr. Palm Beach County Schs., W. Palm Beach, Fla., 1997—2001, St. marks Sch., Boynton Beach, Fla., 2002—. City councilman City of Mingo Jct., Ohio, 1986—91. Photographer (exhibitions) Palm Beach Photographic Ctr., 1999, Palm Beach Governors Club, 2003, Artist Showcase of the Palm Beaches, 2004, Hibel Mus. of Art, 2004. Bd. mem. Ohio Mid Ea. Gov. Assn., Cambridge, Ohio, 1986—91, Brooke, Hancock, Jefferson, Metro. Planning Comm., Weirton, W.Va., 1986—94, Jefferson County Beautification Bd. Exec. Com., Steubenville, 1986—96; local chmn. Bicentennial of the US Constn. and NW Ordinance, Mingo Jct., 1987; chmn. Mingo Jct. Comm. Days, 1988—96; sec. Jefferson County Regional Planning Comm., Steubenville, 1991—96; adv. bd. mem. Lake Worth W. Dem. Club, Fla., 1996—; com. mem. Dem. Exec. Com., W. Palm Beach, 1996—, Palm Beach County Schs., W. Palm Beach, 1997—, adv. bd. mem., 1999—; pres. Young Democrats, W. Palm Beach, 2002; bd. mem. Am. Heart Assn., W. Palm Beach, 2002—. Recipient Econ. Forces in US Hist. award, Found. for Tchg. Econ., 2000. Mem.: Profl. Tchrs. Assn. Democrat. Catholic. Achievements include acquired $2.5M Fed. grant for new water plant for City of Mingo Jct. Avocations: photography, gardening, culinary arts, stamps. Home: 6103 Mahogany Dr Boynton Beach FL 33436

VELLACCIO, FRANK, academic administrator; m. Cathy Vellaccio; 4 children. BS, Fordham U.; PhD in Organic Chemistry, MIT, 1974. From mem. faculty to sr. v.p. Coll. of the Holy Cross, Worcester, Mass., 1974—2003, sr. v.p., 2003—. Author (with D.S. Kemp): Organic Chemistry, 1980; contbr. articles to profl. jours. Mem.: Phi Beta Kappa. Office: Coll of the Holy Cross Office of Sr VP 1 College St Worcester MA 01610

VELLACOTT, MAURICE, member of parliament; b. Wadena, Can., Sept. 29, 1955; married; 4 children. B, Briercrest Sch.; M, Can. Theol. Sem.; D, Trinity Internat. U. Elected mem. Saskatoon Dist. Health Bd.; mem. House of Commons, Ottawa, Canada, 1997—, vice chair standing com. human resources develop. Can., dep. critic com. human resources develop. Can., mem. sub. com. status of persons with disabilities, dep. critic health, dep. critic aboriginal affairs, vice chair com. aboriginal affairs and natural resources, co-chair all-party pro-life caucus. Mem. Can. Alliance Family Caucus. Mem.: Sask. Landlord Assn., Sask. Taxpayers Assn., Saskatoon C. of C., Toastmasters, Can. Club Saskatoon. Conservative Party Can. Office: House of Commons Justice Bldg Ste 610 Ottawa ON Canada K1A 0A6 Address: Unit 3-844 51st St Saskatoon SK S7K 5C7 Canada E-mail: vellacott.m@parl.gc.ca.

VELLEMAN, DANIEL JON, mathematics professor; b. Manhasset, N.Y., Aug. 10, 1954; s. Mortiz and Ruth V.; m. Shelley Lynne Jeffery, June 9, 1979. BA, Dartmouth Coll., 1976; PhD, U. Wis., 1980. Instr. U. Tex., Austin, 1980-83; asst. prof. Amherst (Mass.) Coll., 1983-87, assoc. prof., 1987-92, prof., 1992—. Author: How to Prove it, 1994, Which Way Did the Bicycle Go?, 1996, Philosophies of Mathematics, 2002; mem. editl. bd. Am. Math. Monthly, 1997—; editor: Dolciani Mathematical Expositions, 1999—; contbr. articles to profl. jours. Recipient grant NSF, 1982-83, 84-86, 86-87. Mem. Math. Assn. Am. (Lester R. Ford award 1994, Carl B. Allendoerfer Award 1996), Am. Math. Soc., Assn. Symbolic Logic. Office: Amherst Coll Dept Maths and Comp Sci Amherst MA 01002

VELLENGA, KATHLEEN OSBORNE, retired state legislator; b. Alliance, Nebr., Aug. 5, 1938; d. Howard Benson and Marjorie (Menke) Osborne; m. James Alan Vellenga, Aug. 9, 1959; children: Thomas, Charlotte Vellenga Landreau, Carolyn Vellenga Berman. BA, Macalester Coll., 1959. Tchr. St. Paul Pub. Schs., 1959-60, Children's Ctr. Montessori, St. Paul, 1973-74, Children's Ho. Montessori, St. Paul, 1974-79; mem. Minn. Ho. of Reps., St. Paul, 1980-94, mem. tax. com. and rules com., 1991—94, chmn. St. Paul del., 1987—90, chmn. criminal justice div., 1987—90, mem. Dem. steering com., 1981—94, chmn. judiciary, 1991, 92, chmn. edn. fin., 1993—94. Mem. St. Paul Family Svcs. Bd., 1994-95; exec. dir. St. Paul/Ramsey County Children's Initiative, 1994-2000. Chmn. Healthstart, St. Paul, 1987-91; mem. Children, Youth and Families Consortium, 1995-99, Macalester Coll. Alumni, 1995-2001; chair Minn. Higher Edn. Svcs. Coun., 2000-, mem. 1995-; mem. Citizens League Bd., Minn., 1999-2002, State Commn. Cmty. Svc., 2000-04;

bd. dirs. Sexual Violence Ctr., 2004-; mem. U. Minn. Out of School Time Commn., 2004. Mem. LWV (v.p. St. Paul chpt. 1979), Minn. Women Elected Ofcls. (vice chair 1994). Democrat. Presbyterian.

VELMANS, LOET ABRAHAM, retired public relations executive; b. Amsterdam, Netherlands, Mar. 18, 1923; s. Joseph and Anna (Cohen) V.; m. Pauline Edith Van Hessen, Mar. 29, 1949; children: Marianne and Hester (twins), Jessica. Grad., U. Amsterdam, 1947. Info. officer Dutch Govt. in, Singapore, 1945-47; with Hill & Knowlton, Inc., 1953-86; v.p. Hill Knowlton Internat., Geneva, 1959-69, pres., 1960-74, vice chmn., 1969-76, pres. N.Y.C., 1976-86, chmn. bd., chief exec. officer, 1980-86. Contbr. articles on multinat. corps. to profl. jours. Bd. dirs. Lincoln Ctr. Inst., Bennington Coll., Boston Symphony Orch. Decorated Grande Ufficiale Order of Merit, Italy, 1989. Mem. Mid-Atlantic Club of N.Y. Inc. (pres. emeritus). Home: PO Box 178 Sheffield MA 01257-0178

VELO, ANI PIRO, mathematician, educator; b. Tirana, Albania, July 11, 1970; arrived in U.S., 1994; d. Piro and Geti Velo. Diploma, U. Siegen, Germany, 1992; diploma in math. (hon.), U. Tirana, Albania, 1993; PhD, Worcester Poly. Inst., 2000. Asst. prof., Davies fellow dept. math. scis. U.S. Mil. Acad. and Army Rsch. Lab., West Point, NY, 2000—02; asst. prof. dept. math. and computer sci. U. San Diego, 2002—. Rsch. consultant Eastman Kodak Rsch. Labs, West Point, NY, 1997, Gen. Tech. Svcs., L.L.C., NJ, 2001—02; judge Siemens Westinghouse sci. and tech. competition Siemens Found., NJ, 2001—; panelist Nat. Rsch. Coun./Associateship Programs, Washington, 2003—. Vol. Feed the Children; vol. income tax asst. IRS and the Staff Judge Adv. Office, NY, 2002; co. counselor U.S. Mil. Acad., West Point. Recipient Davies fellowship, NRC, 2000—02, Tempus Project scholarship, European Cmty., 1992, Commander's Award for Public Service, US Dept. of Army, 2002. Mem.: Math. Assn. of Am. (Project NExT (New Experience in Tchg.) fellowship 2001—02), Soc. for Indsl. and Applied Math., Soc. for Computer Simulation Internat., Inst. for Ops. Rsch. and Mgmt. Scis. Roman Catholic. Achievements include research in Structural optimization in problems involving elliptic and hyperbolic differential equations. Avocations: walking on the beach and watching the sunset, music, dance, volleyball, cooking. Office: U of San Diego 5998 Alcala Park San Diego CA 92110 Home: 6855 Deer Hollow Pl San Diego CA 92120 Office Phone: 619-260-7846. E-mail: avelo@sandiego.edu.

VELSHI, ALI, news correspondent; b. Kenya; B in Religion, Queens U., Can., 1994. Host The Bus. News; anchor Report on Bus. TV, Canada, 1999, Your Money and the Money Gang, CNNfn, 2001—; bus. anchor Cable Pulse 24, CITY TV, Canada. Recipient fellowship to Congress, Am. Polit. Sciences Assn. Office: CNNfn 5 Penn Plaza Fl 20 New York NY 10010-1810

VELTMAN, MARTINUS J.G. retired physics educator; b. Waalwijk, The Netherlands, June 27, 1931; BS in math and physics, U. Utrecht, The Netherlands, 1953, MS in theoretical physics, 1956, PhD in theoretical physics, 1963. Mem. FOM, Utrecht, Netherlands, 1959—61; fellow CERN, Geneva, 1961—63, staff mem., 1963—66, cons., 1966—72, sci. assoc., 1972—73, mem. sci. policy com., 1976—81, sci. assoc., 1996—97; prof. U. Utrecht, Netherlands, 1966—81; vis. prof. U. Mich., Ann Arbor, 1980, John D. McArthur prof. of physics, 1981—97, emeritus John D. McArthur prof. of physics, 1997—; prof. U. Autonoma de Madrid, 1988—96; Lorentz prof. of physics U. Leiden, Netherlands, 1989; Humboldt scientist Max Planck Inst., Munich, 1989—90, DESY, Hamburg, Germany, 1989—90. Postdoctoral SLAC, Stanford, Calif., 1963—64, Brookhaven Nat. Lab., L.I., NY, 1966; vis. prof. U. Paris, Orsay, France, 1968—69. Recipient High Energy and Particle Physics prize, European Physics Soc., 1993, P.A.M. Dirac Medal and Prize, Internat. Ctr. for Theoretical Physics, 1996, Nobel prize in Physics, 1999. Office: U Mich Dept Physics Randall Lab 500 E University Ave Ann Arbor MI 48109-1120

VELTRI, SANDRA KAY, finance educator; d. Alex Watson and Gloria Boyer, Stephen Boyer (Stepfather); m. George John Veltri, July 14, 1984; children: Kevin Andrew, Megan Noel. EdM, Colo. State U., 1993, PhD, 2003. Prof. Trinidad (Colo.) State Jr. Coll., 1990—. Office: Trinidad State Jr Coll 600 Prospect St Trinidad CO 81082

VELU, YOGESHWAR KARUNAKARAN, industrial engineer, researcher; s. Karunakaran Arcot MohanaVelu and PankajaSelvi Karunakaran; m. Vijayalakshmi Yogeshwar Nithyanandam, Dec. 9, 1969; 1 child, Dhananjay Narayan. BS, Bangalore U., 1991; MS, Clemson U., 1995, Ga. Inst. Tech., 1998; PhD in Fiber and Polymer Sci., N.C. State U., 2003—03. Asst. quality control mgr. Birla Synthetics, Birlapur, 1991—92; rsch. engr. Ga. Inst. Tech., Atlanta, 1997—98; process engr. Nonwovens Coop. Rsch. Ctr., Raleigh, NC, 2002—03; nonwovens engr. Fleetguard, Inc, Cookeville, Tenn., 2003—. Bd. dirs. Sri Venkateswara Temple, Cary, NC, 2001—02. Fellow: Textile Inst.; mem.: ASME, Fiber Soc. Office: P O Box 6001 108 Audrey Plc Cookeville TN 38506 Office Phone: 931-372-9851.

VELUCHAMY, PETHINAIDU, marketing executive; m. Parameswari Veluchamy; 2 children. BS in Chem. Engring., Oreg. State U.; PhD in Chem. Engring., U. Ill. Owner, chmn., CEO Creative Automation Co., 1969—. Office: Veluchamy Cos 1213 Butterfield Rd Downers Grove IL 60515*

VELZ, JOHN WILLIAM, literature educator; b. Englewood, NJ, Aug. 5, 1930; s. Clarence Joseph and Harriet Josephine (O'Brien) Velz; m. Judith M. Palmer, Jan. 22, 1953 (div. Aug. 1967); m. Sarah Elizabeth Campbell, Oct. 18, 1967 (div. Apr. 2001); children: Sue Marie, Gwendolyn Anne, Jennifer Germaine, Jody, Emily. BA in English with high distinction and honors, U. Mich., 1953, MA in English and French, 1954; PhD in English and Classical Tradition, U. Minn., 1963. Instr. Coll. St. Thomas, St. Paul, 1958-60; asst. prof. English Rice U., Houston, 1963-69; prof. U. Tex., Austin, 1969-96, prof. emeritus, 1996—. Vis. prof. U. Paul Valery, Montpelier, France, 1977-78, Julius Maximillians U., Wuerzburg, West Germany, 1981-82, 85-86; asst. dir., lit. adv. Odessa Shakespeare Festival, 1977; faculty mem. Oreg. Shakespeare Festival, 1979; lectr. tour Cen. and Ea. Europe univs., 1993; dir. acad. prodns. of Shakespeare and medieval drama; mem. Acad. Adv. Coun. Globe Theatre Ctr., 1981—; mem. U.S. Com. for Shakespeare's Globe, 1990—; presenter over 100 papers and lectures to learned socs.; reviewer over 50 books and theatrical prodns. Author: Shakespeare and the Classical Tradition, 1968, electronic edit., 2000 (ALA citation, Assn. Coll. and Rsch. Librs. citation); editor: Julius Caesar in MLA's New Variorum Shakespeare, 1966-95, (N.Am.) Cahiers Elisabethains, 1979-81; Shakespeare's English Histories: A Quest for Form and Genre, 1996; co-editor: Collected Papers of James G. McManaway, 1969, One Touch of Shakespeare: Letters of Joseph Crosby to Joseph Parker Norris 1875-1878, 1986, Pegasus Bibliography of Shakespeare's Roman Works, 2003; contbr. over 60 scholarly, interpretive articles, mainly on Shakespeare and on medieval drama, to profl. jours.; mem. editl. bd. Shakespeare Quar., 1975-98, Classical and Modern Lit., 1981-85, Tex. Studies in Lit. and Lang., 1969-92, Shakespeare and the Classroom, 1993—; mem. editl. adv. bd. Complete Works of Shakespeare, 3d edit., 1980, 4th edit., 1992, 5th edit., 1997, 6th edit., 2003; cons. editor South Ctrl. Rev., 1989-92; mem. cons. com. Internat. Studies in Shakespeare and His Contemporaries, 1990—. Recipient Fulbright award, 1977-78, 81-82; recipient Oreon E. Scott award U. Mich., 1953; NEH fellow, 1967-68; Folger Library fellow, 1968 Mem. MLA (life), Assn. Lit. Scholars and Critics, Internat. Shakespeare Assn. (charter), Shakespeare Assn. Am., Malone Soc., Renaissance English Text Soc., Medieval and Renaissance Drama Soc., Marlowe Soc. of Am., H.W. Fowler Soc. (charter), Internat. Soc. Classical Tradition, Phi Beta Kappa, Phi Kappa Phi, Phi Eta Sigma. Home: 809 W 32d St Austin TX 78705-2115 Business E-Mail: jvelz@ccwf.cc.utexas.edu. *Academic life is predicated on the obligation to teach as generously as we have been taught, to serve others as we have been served. This sense of mutuality has been a rationale for my professional life, though it would be impossible to pay all I owe.*

VEMUGANTI, RAMAKRISHAN R. business educator; b. Guntur, India, June 23, 1939; s. Narasimha Rao and Radha Vemuganti; m. Linda Vemuganti, 1984; children: Monica Hinds, Christina Thacker. BA, Sri Raja Rangayya Apparao and Chunduri Venkata Reddi Coll., Vijayawada, India, 1958; MA, Andhra U., Waltair, India, 1960; M in Stats., Indian Statis. Inst., Calcutta, 1962; PhD, Johns Hopkins U., 1971. Rsch. fellow Indian Inst. Mgmt., Calcutta, 1962—67; asst. prof. Johns Hopkins U., Balt., 1971—74; prof. mgmt. sci., chair faculty Merrick Sch. Bus. U. Balt., Balt., 1974—. Contbr. articles to profl. jours. Office: U Balt 1420 N Charles St Baltimore MD 21201 E-mail: rvemuganti@ubalt.edu.

VENDELA, model; b. Sweden; With Ford Models, Inc., N.Y., 1986, Elizabeth Arden, 1988. Appeared on cover of Sports Illustrated Swimsuit Edition, 1993. Office: Ford Models Inc 344 E 59th St New York NY 10022-1513

VENDITTI, CLELIA ROSE See PALMER, CHRISTINE

VENDLER, HELEN HENNESSY, literature educator, poetry critic; b. Boston, Mass., Apr. 30, 1933; d. George and Helen (Conway) Hennessy; 1 son, David. AB, Emmanuel Coll., 1954; PhD, Harvard U., 1960, U. Oslo, 1981; DLitt (hon.), Smith Coll., 1980, Kenyon Coll., 1982, U. Hartford, 1985, Union Coll., 1986, Columbia U., 1987, Washington U., 1991, Marlboro Coll., 1989, Yale U., 2000; DHL (hon.), Fitchburg State U., 1990, Dartmouth Coll., 1992, U. Mass., 1992, Bates Coll., 1992, U. Toronto, Ont., Can., 1992, Trinity Coll., Dublin, Ireland, 1993, U. Cambridge, 1997, Nat. U., Ireland, 1998, Wabash Coll., 1998, U. Mass, Dartmouth, 2000, Yale U., 2000, U. Aberdeen, 2000, Tufts U., 2001, Amherst Coll., 2002, Colby Coll., 2003. Instr. Cornell U., Ithaca, NY, 1960-63; lectr. Swarthmore (Pa.) Coll. and Haverford (Pa.) Coll., 1963-64; asst. prof. Smith Coll., Northampton, Mass., 1964-66; assoc. prof. Boston U., 1966-68, prof., 1968-85. Fulbright lectr. U. Bordeaux, France, 1968-69; vis. prof. Harvard U., 1981-85, Kenan prof., 1985—, Porter U. prof., 1990—, assoc. acad. dean, 1987-92, sr. fellow Harvard Soc. Fellows, 1981-93; poetry critic New Yorker, 1978-99; mem. ednl. adv. bd. Guggenheim Found., 1991-2001, Pulitzer Prize Bd., 1991-99. Author: Yeats's Vision and the Later Plays, 1963, On Extended Wings: Wallace Stevens' Longer Poems, 1969, The Poetry of George Herbert, 1975, Part of Nature, Part of Us, 1980, The Odes of John Keats, 1983, Wallace Stevens: Words Chosen Out of Desire, 1984; editor: Harvard Book of Contemporary American Poetry, 1985, Voices and Visions: The Poet in America, 1987, The Music of What Happens, 1988, Soul Says, 1995, The Given and the Made, 1995, The Breaking of Style, 1995, Poems, Poets, Poetry, 1995, The Art of Shakespeare's Sonnets, 1997, Seamus Heaney, 1998; Coming of Age as a Poet, 2003. Bd. dirs. Nat. Humanities Ctr., 1989—93. Recipient Lowell prize, 1969, Explicator prize, 1969, award Nat. Inst. Arts and Letters, 1975, Radcliffe Grad. Soc. medal, 1978, Nat. Book Critics award, 1980, Keats-Shelley Assn. award, 1994, Truman Capote award, 1996; Fulbright fellow, 1954, AAUW fellow, 1959, Guggenheim fellow, 1971-72, Am. Coun. Learned Socs. fellow, 1971-72, NEH fellow, 1980, 85, 94, Overseas fellow Churchill Coll., Cambridge, 1980, Charles Stewart Parnell fellow Magdalene Coll., Cambridge, 1996, hon. fellow, 1996—. Mem. MLA (exec. coun. 1972-75, pres. 1980), AAAL, English Inst. (trustee 1977-85), Am. Acad. Arts and Scis. (v.p. 1992-95), Norwegian Acad. Letters and Sci., Am. Philos. Soc. (Jefferson medal 2000, lectr. 2004), Phi Beta Kappa. Home: 54 Trowbridge St # 2 Cambridge MA 02138-4113 Office: Harvard U Dept English Barker Center Cambridge MA 02138-3929 Office Phone: 617-496-6028.

VENEMAN, ANN M. secretary of agriculture; b. Modesto, Calif., June 29, 1949; d. John G. and Nita D. (Bomberger) V. BA in polit. sci., U. Calif., Davis, 1970; M in pub. policy, U. Calif., Berkeley, 1971; JD, U. Calif., 1976. Bar: Calif. 1976, U.S. Supreme Ct. 1981. Atty. San Francisco Bay Area Rapid Transit Dist., 1976-78; dep. pub. defender City of Modesto, 1978-80; ptnr. Damrell, Damrell & Nelson, Modesto, 1980-86; asst. to adminstr. Fgn. Agrl. Svc., 1986-87, assoc. adminstr., 1987-89; dep. under-sec. Internat. Affairs and Commodity Programs, 1989-91; dep. sec. U.S. Dept. Agriculture, Washington, 1991-93; sec. Calif. Dept. Food and Agr., 1995—99, U.S. Dept. Agriculture, Washington, 2001—. Bd. dir. Close Up Found. Office: USDA Office Sec 14th & Independence Ave SW Washington DC 20250-0001

VENERABLE, SHIRLEY MARIE, gifted education educator; b. Washington, Nov. 12, 1931; d. John Henry and Jessie Josephine (Young) Washington; m. Wendell Grant Venerable, Feb. 15, 1959; children: Angela Elizabeth Maria Venerable-Joyner, Wendell Mark. PhB, Northwestern U., 1963; MA, Roosevelt U., 1976, postgrad., 1985. Cert. in diagnostic and prescriptive reading, gifted edn., finger math., fine arts, Ill. Tchr. Lewis Champlin Sch., 1963-74, John Hay Acad., Chgo., 1975-87, Leslie Lewis Elem. Sch., Chgo., 1988-99, Robert Emmet Sch., Chgo., 1999—; self employed tutorial programs, 1999—. Sponsor Reading Marathon Club, Chgo., 1991—; co-creator Project SMART-Stimulating Math. and Reading Techniques John Hay Acad., Chgo., 1987-90, curriculum coord., 1985-87; creative dance student, tchr. Kathryn Duham Sch., N.Y.C., 1955-56; creative dance tchr. Doris Patterson Dance Sch., Washington, 1953-55; recorder evening divsn. Northwestern U., Chgo., 1956-62; exch. student tchr. Conservatory Dance Movements, Chgo., 1958-59; art cons. Chgo. Pub. Sch., 1967. Author primary activities Let's Act and Chat, 1991-94, Teaching Black History Through Classroom Tours, 1989-90. Solicitor, vol. United Negro Coll. Fund, Chgo., 1994; sponsor Ward Reading Assn. Marathon, Chgo., 1991-94, 99; active St. Giles Coun. Cath. Women, 1985-96; vol. REAC Ctr. Programs Books, Info., Literacy and Learning, 1997-98. Recipient Meritorious award United Negro Coll. Fund, 1990, 94, Recognition award Alderman Percy Giles, Chgo., 1993. Mem.: ASCD (assoc. Recognition of Svcs. award 1989), Internat. Reading Assn., Nat. Women of Achievement Assn. (Chgo. chpt.), Phi Delta Kappa, Sigma Gamma Rho (Delta Sigma grad. chpt. 1963—93, Sigma chpt. 1992, Eta Xi Sigma chpt.), Eta Xi Sigma (Pearl award for excellence in edn. 1997). Roman Catholic. Home: 1108 N Euclid Ave Oak Park IL 60302-1219

VENETSANOPOULOS, ANASTASIOS NICOLAOS, electrical engineer, educator; b. Athens, Greece, June 19, 1941; arrived in Can., 1968; s. Nicolaos Anastasios and Elli (Papacondilis) Venetsanopoulos. Diploma, Athens Coll., 1960; B Elec. and Mech. Engring., Nat. Tech. U., Athens, 1965, hon. doctorate, 1994; MS, Yale U., 1966, MPhil, 1968, PhD, 1969. Registered profl. engr., Greece, Ont. Asst. in instrn. engring. and applied sci. Yale U., 1966-68, research asst., 1968-69; lectr. U. Toronto, Ont., Can., 1968-69, asst. prof. elec. engring., 1970-73, assoc. prof., 1973-81, prof., 1981—, chmn. communications group dept. elec. engring., 1974-78, 81-86, assoc. chmn. elec. and computer engring., 1978-79, 97—, mem. elec. and computer engring. exec. com., 1981-86, 97—, acting chmn. elec. and computer engring., 1998—99, dean applied sci. and engring., 2001—. Acad. visitor Imperial Coll. Arts and Tech. U. London, 1979—80; vis. prof. Nat. Tech. U. Athens, 1979—80, Fed. U. Tech. Lausanne, Switzerland, 1986—87, Switzerland, 1993—94, U. Florence, Italy, 1987; cons. elec. engring. Consociates Ltd.; chmn. multimedia Bell-Can., 1999—. Editor: Can. Elec. Engring. Jour., 1981—83; contbr. articles to profl. jours., chapters to books. Mem. allocations and agy. rels. com. United Cmty. Fund, Toronto, 1971—74; pres. Hellenic-Can. Cultural Soc., 1972—75; sec. gen. Greek Cmty. Met. Toronto, 1973—75. Recipient Excellence in Innovation award, Info. Tech. Rsch. Ctr., 1996; grantee Fulbright Travel, U.S., 1965, Def. Rsch. Bd. Can., 1972—75, UN, NSF, J. P. Bickell Found., Natural Scis. and Engring. Rsch. Coun. Can. Fellow: IEEE (fin. chmn. internat. symposium on circuit theroy 1973, tech. program chmn. internat. conf. comm. 1978, 1986, vice-chmn. Toronto sect. 1976—77, chmn. 1977—79, assoc. editor Transactions on circuits and sys. 1985—87, guest editor spl. 1987, tech. prgram chmn. internat. conf. on acoustics speech and signal proc 1991, Millenium medal 2001—), Can. Acad. Engring., Engring. Inst. Can.; mem.: Intercultural Coun. (chmn. ednl. com. 1971—80, sr. v.p. 1977—80), Am.-Hellenic Ednl. Progress Assn. (v.p. Toronto sect. 1973—75, pres. 1975—77), N.Y. Acad. Scis., Yale Sci. and Engring. Assn., Can. Soc. Elec. Engring. (chmn. Toronto sect. 1975—77, nat. dir. 1976—88, pres. 1983—86), Assn. Profl. Mech. Engrs. Greece, Assn. Profl. Elec. Engrs. Greece, Assn. Profl. Engrs. Ont., Tech. Chamber Greece, Sigma Xi. Office: U Toronto Fac Applied Sci and Engring Toronto ON Canada M5S 1A4

VENEZIA, WILLIAM THOMAS, school system administrator, counseling consultant; b. Jersey City, Mar. 20, 1952; s. Thomas Michael and Carmela (Crocamo) V. BA in History, St. Peter's Coll., 1974, postgrad., 1978-79, MA in Adminstrn./Supervision, 1984; postgrad., Jersey City State Coll., 1988-90. Cert. tchr., prin., supt., N.J.; cert. in student personnel svcs., N.J. Tchr. various schs. Jersey City Bd. Edn., 1976-92; guidance counselor P.S. # 27/Dickinson High Sch., Jersey City, 1990-92; counselor Montclair (N.J.) State Coll., 1991-92; asst. prin. Frelinghuysen Sch., Morristown, NJ, 1992-97; prin. Alexander Hamilton Sch., Morristown, 1997—2002; dir. guidance Morris Sch. Dist., 2001—02; prin. Thomas Jefferson Sch., Morristown, 2002—. Asst. football coach various schs., 1975-89; instr., adminstr. G.E.D. and A.B.E. programs Jersey City Bd. Edn., 1977-82; interim bd. sec., bus. adminstr. Weehawken Bd. Edn., 1984; mem. adv. bd. Cornerstone Sch., Jersey City, 1988-91; counselor Coll. Bound program Jersey City State Coll., 1989-90; pre-coll. counselor UPWARD Bound project Montclair State Coll., 1991; cons. N.J. Devils hockey team, East Rutherford, 1992, D.A.R.E. program Hudson County Prosecutor, Jersey City, 1992. Vol. counselor Giant Steps adolescent substance abuse treatment facility; active Dante Alighieri Soc., Jersey City, 1993, Jersey City Parents' Coun. Mem. ASCD, NEA, Am. Football Coaches Assn., N.J. Edn. Assn., Assn. Adult Edn. in N.J., N.J. Assn. Sch. Bus. Officials, Hudson County Personnel and Guidance Assn., Morris Pub. Schs. Adminstrv. Coun., Iron Bound Execs. Assn., St. Peter's Coll. Grad. Edn. Assn., Hoboken Elks. Avocations: basketball, travel, antiques. Home: 1 Hickory St Clark NJ 07066-1924 Office: Thomas Jefferson Sch 101 James St Morristown NJ 07960

VENEZKY, RICHARD LAWRENCE, English language educator; b. Pitts., Apr. 16, 1938; s. Bernard Jacob and Isabel (Zeisel) V.; m. Karen F. Gauz, Aug. 2, 1964; children: Dina Yael, Elie Michael. BEE, Cornell U., 1961, MA, 1962; postgrad., U. Calif., Berkeley, 1962-63; PhD, Stanford U., 1965. Sys. programmer, tech. writer Control Data Corp., Palo Alto, Calif., 1962-65; asst. prof. English and computer scis. U. Wis., Madison, 1965-69, assoc. prof. computer scis., 1969-74, prof., 1974-77, chmn. dept., 1975-77; Unidel prof. ednl. studies, prof. computer and info. sci., prof. linguistics U. Del., Newark, 1977—; Benton fellow in literacy U. Chgo., 1994-95. Vis. rsch. assoc. Tel Aviv U., 1969-70, rsch. fellow, 1973; cons. Oxford English Dictionary Supplement; dir. computing Dictionary of Old English, 1971— co-dir. for R & D Nat. Ctr. on Adult Literacy, 1990-95; scholar in residence U.S. Dept. Edn., 1997-98; sr. rschr/ OECD, 1999-01. Author: The Structure of English Orthography, 1970, Testing in Reading, 1974, Random House Spelling Across the Curriculum, 1988, The American Way of Spelling, 1999; co-author: A Microfiche Concordance to Old English, 1981, Letter and Word Perception, 1980, PRS-Pre-Reading Skills Program, 1985, The Subtle Danger, 1987, World of Reading, 1989, The Intelligent Design of Computer-Assisted Instruction, 1991; co-editor: Orthography, Reading and Dyslexia, 1980, Toward Defining Literacy, 1990, Literacy: An International Handbook, 1999; contbr. articles to profl. jours., chpts. to books. Chmn. edn. commn Madison Jewish Community Coun., 1973-77; v.p. Jewish Fedn. Del., 1986-89; regional chmn. Am. Profs. for Peace in Mid. East, 1968-73. Recipient Disting. Faculty award Sch. Edn., U. Del., 2003; grantee Office of Edn., 1964-66, NSF, 1966-74, Nat. Inst. Edn., 1973-77, NEH, 1978-89, Office of Ednl. Rsch. and Improvement, Dept. Edn., 1990-95, Pew Charitable Trusts, 1995-97, Joyce Found., 1996-99, NICHD, 2002-. Fellow Am. Psychol. Soc.; mem. Am. Edn. Rsch. Assn., Internat. Reading Assn., Reading Hall of Fame (pres. 1996-97), Assn. Computing Machinery (Soc. Sci. Study of Reading, Disting. Fellow award, 1999). Democrat. Jewish. Home: 206 Hullihen Dr Newark DE 19711-3651 Office: U Del Room 211 Willard Hall Bldg Newark DE 19716-2999 E-mail: venezky@udel.edu.

VENHAUS, THOMAS J. physicist; b. Grand Island, Nebr., June 15, 1968; s. Rita A. and George J. Venhaus; m. Dawn M. Guilmet, Oct. 12, 1996; children: Greyson W., Elannah N. BS in Physics, Hastings Coll., Nebr., 1992; MS in Applied Sci., The Coll. of William and Mary, Williamsburg, Va., 1994, PhD in Applied Sci., 2000. Postdoctoral Sandia Nat. Lab., Livermore, Calif., 1998—2001; lead project scientist Los Alamos Nat. Lab., N.Mex., 2001—. Cons. Staib Instruments, Williamsburg, Va., 1996—98; vis. scientist Forschungszentrum Karlsruhe, Germany, 1999—99, Princeton Plasma Physics Lab., NJ, 2000. Rsch. grant, The Coll. of William and Mary, 1992—98. Independent. Avocations: woodworking, beer brewing, guitar, bicycling, hiking. Home: 140 Aragon Ave White Rock NM 87544 Office: Los Alamos Nat Lab PO Box 1663 MS C348 Los Alamos NM 87545 Personal E-mail: venhaus@earthlink.net. E-mail: venhaus@lanl.gov.

VENINGA, JAMES FRANK, humanities educator, editor, author; b. Milw., Aug. 26, 1944; s. Frank and Otila Ann (Mauch) V.; m. Catherine M. Williams, Apr. 5, 1969; 1 child, Jennifer Elisa. BA, Baylor U., 1966; MTheol Studies, Harvard U., 1968; MA, Rice U., 1973, PhD, 1974. Instr. U. St. Thomas, Houston, 1971-73, asst. prof., 1974; asst. dir. Tex. Coun. for Humanities, Austin, 1975, exec. dir., 1976-97; pres., dir. Inst. for the Humanities at Salado, 1997-2000; CEO, campus dean U. Wis.-Marathon County, Wausau, 2000—. Dir. Nat. Fedn. State Humanities Couns., Washington, 1980-83; trustee Inst. for Humanities at Salado, Tex., 1980-85; vis. prof. Am. studies U. Tex., Austin, 1984, sr. lectr. Am. studies, 1986; vis. prof. Am. studies Baylor U., 1999. Author: The Humanities and Civic Imagination, 1999; editor: The Biographer's Gift, 1983, Vietnam in Remission, 1985, Standing with the Public, 1997; editor-in-chief Tex. Jour. Ideas, History and Culture, 1982-97. Recipient Baylor Man of Merit award Baylor U., 1985. Home: 309 Country Club Rd Schofield WI 54476 Office: U Wis 518 S 7th Ave Wausau WI 54401-5362 Personal E-mail: j.veninga@verizon.net. Business E-Mail: jveninga@uwc.edu.

VENIT, WILLIAM BENNETT, electrical products company executive, consultant; b. Chgo., May 28, 1931; s. George Bernard and Ida (Schaffel) V.; m. Nancy Jean Carlson, Jan. 28, 1956; children: Steven Louis, Aprilann. Student, U. Ill., Champaign, 1949. Sales mgr. Coronet, Inc., Chgo., 1952-63, pres., chmn. bd. dirs., 1963-74, Roma Wire Inc., Chgo., 1971-74; chmn. bd. dirs. Swing Time #2, Chgo., 1988-89; pres. Wm. Allen Inc., Chgo., 1972-74; pres., chmn. bd. dirs. Wraprama Inc., 1988-95, Swag Lite, Inc., 1989—92. Pres. William Lamp Co., Inc., 1993, 97, William Wire Co., Inc., 1974-76; chmn. bd. dirs. MSWV, Inc., 1978—, pres. bd. dirs. 1985—; pres. Trio Steel Inc., Chgo., 1987-90; chmn. bd. Chgo. Lamp Works LLB, 1995, 98, chair 1996, 98; CEO Chgo. Chair Works, 1998, 2000, 2001; spl. cons. Roto Products, 1998-2002, DMSI Inc., 2002; cons. Nu Style Lamp Shade, 2002—. Patentee Printed-Cir., 1964. With QMC AUS, 1949-52. Avocations: bicycling, golf. Home and Office: 323 Suwanee Ave Sarasota FL 34243-1930 Office Phone: 941-351-5265. Personal E-mail: LampBill@aol.com.

VENKATESAN, RAGURAMAN, computer engineer; b. Sindri, Bihar, India, May 5, 1976; s. Venkatesan Subramaniam and Saraswathy Venkatesan. B.Tech in Elec. Engring., Indian Inst.Tech., Bombay, India, 1998; MS in Elec. and Computer Engring., Ga. Inst.Tech., Atlanta, 2000, PhD in Elec. and Computer Engring., 2003. Sr. cad engr. Intel Corp., Hillsboro, Oreg., 2003—. Tech. reviewer 5 IEEE jours. and confs., 1998—; industry liasion/mentor for Ga. Tech. Semuconductor Rsch. Corp./Ctr. ADvances Interconnect Sci. and Tech., 2003—. Co-author: (Book) Interconnect Technology and Design Issues for Gigascale Integration.; contbr. articles to rsch. publs. Recipient Aryabhatta Sci. Prize, Aryabhatta Sci. Olympiad Com., 1992, Ramanujam Math. Prize, Ramanujam Math. Olympiad Com., 1992, 1994; fellow Intel PhD Fellowship, Intel Corp., 2001; scholar Nat. Talent Sci. Scholarship, Govt. of India/Nat. Coun. of Edn., Rsch. and Tng., 1992-1998, All India Talent Scholarship, Children's Ednl. Trust of India/World Buddha Found., 1993, Mahindra Scholarship for Higher Studies Abroad, Mahindra & Mahindra Corp. Trust, 1998-2003. Mem.: IEEE, Ctr. Advanced Interconnect Sci and Tech., Semiconductor Rsch. Corp. Office: Intel Corp 5200 NE Elam Young Pkwy MS RA3-256 Hillsboro OR 97124 Office Phone: 971-214-9945. E-mail: ragu.venkatesan@intel.com.

VENKATESWARAN, PRAMILA, literature educator; arrived in U.S., 1982; PhD, George Washington U., 1988. Asst. prof. creative writing, women's studies, Am., South Asian and English lit. Nassau C.C., Garden City, NY, 1990—. Author: Thirtha, 2002, (poem) Haze, 1999. Office: Nassau Cmty Coll 1 Education Dr Setaukey NY 11530

VENNAM, VENKATA SURYA PRAKASH, engineering educator, researcher; b. Guntur, India, Jan. 7, 1970; arrived in US, 2000; s. Chalapathi Rao and Aruna Vennam; m. Sowjanya Pamidi, Dec. 9, 1995. B of Tech., Nagarjuna U., Vijayawada, India, 1991; M of Tech., Indian Inst. Tech., Kharagpur, India, 1993; PhD, Indian Inst. Sci., Bangalore, 2000. Scientist Def. R & D Orgn., Bangalore, 1993—2000; rschr. Pa. State U., University Park, 2000—02, vis. asst. prof., 2002—. Cons. in field. Mem. rev. bd. Microwave & Optical Tech. Letters, 2002—. Recipient Young Engr. award, Indian Nat. Acad. Engring., 1999. Mem.: IEEE (sr.; mem. editl. bd. 2002—), Instn. Elect. & Telecomm. Engrs. Achievements include development of fast solvers; design of airborne ultra-low side lobe antenna. Avocations: stamp collecting/philately, chess, music, art. Office: Pa State Univ 121 Electrical Engring E University Park PA 16802-2705 Business E-Mail: vvp2@psu.edu.

VENNAT, MICHEL, former bank executive, lawyer; b. Sept. 17, 1941; m. Marie-Anne Tawil; children: Catherine, Charles-Alexandre, Frédéric-André, Michèle-Anne, Philippe-Olivier. BA magna cum laude, Coll. Jean-de-Brébeuf, Montreal, Que., Can., 1960; LL.L., U. Montreal, 1963; MA, Oxford U., Eng., 1965. Bar: Que. 1966, Paris 1995; apptd. Queen's Counsel 1983. Officer of the Order of Can., 1995. Fgn. affairs officer Dept. External Affairs, Ottawa, Ont., Can., 1965; spl. asst. to Min. Fin., 1966-68; spl. asst. to Hon. Pierre E. Trudeau, Prime Min. of Can., 1968-70, spl. counsel, 1977; chmn. Can. Film Devel. Corp., Montreal, 1976-81; sr. ptnr. Stikeman, Elliott, Montreal, 1970-90; pres. Dumez Investments Inc., 1986-87, Westburne Internat. Industries Ltd., 1987; vice chmn. United Westburne Inc., 1990, vice chmn., CEO, 1991-93, chmn., CEO, 1993-94, also bd. dirs.; pres. Bastos du Canada Limitée, 1987—2000, also bd. dirs.; sr. ptnr. Stikeman Elliot, Montreal, 1994-2000; pres., CEO bus. devel. Bank Canada, 2000—04. Chmn. Moody Industries Inc., 1998—2000; chmn. bd. dirs. Bus. Devel. Bank of Can.; lectr. in constl. law U. Montreal, 1970. Rhodes scholar, 1963-65. Mem. Barreau du Que., Barreau de Paris, Can. C. of C., French C. of C. (Can. bd. dirs.), Mt. Bruno Country Club, Hillside Tennis Club, Mt. Royal Club, Hermitage Club, Knowlton Golf Club, St. John Salmon Club, Montreal Badminton & Squash Club. Avocations: golf, tennis, skiing, fishing, hunting.

VENNERI, SAMUEL L. federal agency administrator; BS in Aerospace Engring., Pa. State U., 1969; MS in Engring. Sci., George Washington, 1975; postgrad., George Washington U. Prin. engr. Fairchild Space Electronics; aerospace asst. cons. Swales and Assocs.; program mgr. materials and structures divdn. Office Aeronautics and Space Tech. NASA, Washington, dir. spacecraft sys. divdn. Office Space Access and Tech., chief technologist, 1996—2000, assoc. adminstr. aerospace tech., 2000—. Office: NASA Hdqrs Mail Code R 300 E St SW Washington DC 20546

VENNING, ROBERT STANLEY, lawyer; b. Boise, Idaho, July 24, 1943; s. William Lucas and Corey Elizabeth (Brown) V.; m. Sandra Macdonald, May 9, 1966 (div. 1976); 1 child, Rachel Elizabeth; m. Laura Siegel, Mar. 24, 1979; 1 child, Daniel Rockhill Siegel. AB, Harvard U., 1965; MA, U. Chgo., 1966; LLB, Yale U., 1970. Bar: Calif., U.S. Dist. Ct. (no. dist.) Calif., 1971, U.S. Dist. Ct. (cen. dist.) Calif. 1973, U.S. Ct. Appeals (9th cir.) 1977, U.S. Supreme Ct. 1977, U.S. Ct. Appeals (fed. cir.) 1986, U.S. Ct. Appeals (D.C. cir.) 1987, U.S. Ct. Fed. Claims 1996. Assoc. Heller Ehrman White & McAuliffe, San Francisco, 1970-73, 73-76, ptnr., 1977—, mem. exec. com., 1991-94. Vis. lectr. U. Wash., Seattle, 1973, Boalt Hall Sch. Law, U. Calif., Berkeley, 1982-85, 89, Sch. Bus., Stanford U., 1986-87. Editor Yale Law Jour., 1969-70. Early neutral evaluator U.S. Dist. Ct. (no. dist.) Calif., 1987—. Fellow Am. Bar Found. (life); mem. ABA, San Francisco Bar Assn. (past chair judiciary com.), CPR Inst. for Dispute Resolution, Olympic Club. Office: Heller White & McAuliffe LLP 333 Bush St San Francisco CA 94104-2878 Office Phone: 415-772-6158.

VENO, RONALD JAMES, JR., travel industry executive; b. Malden, Mass., Feb. 3, 1963; s. Ronald James and Jeanne (Greer) V.; m. Michele Carmelina Sipala, Aug. 12, 1989; children: Erica Joan, Ronald James III. BS, Westfield State Coll., 1985; MBA, Boston Coll., Chestnut Hill, Mass., 1993. Sales rep. Quikrete Co., Everett, Mass., 1987-88; area mgr. Sunoco, Providence, 1988-94; product mgr. Collette Tours, Pawtucket, R.I., 1994-96; dir. sales and mktg. Abercrombie and Kent Overseas, Oak Brook, Ill., 1996-98, v.p. sales and mktg., 1998—. Roman Catholic. Avocations: drawing, painting, fishing. Home: 14130 S Longview Ln Plainfield IL 60544-6010 Office: Abercrombie and Kent Overseas 1520 Kensington Rd Ste 212 Oak Brook IL 60523-2156

VENOSDEL, DANIEL PAUL, agricultural association administrator; b. Pittsfield, Ill., July 19, 1969; s. Danny Boy and Helen Jo Venosdel; m. Cynthia Kay Hallock, July 18, 1997. BS in Agrl. Bus., Calif. State U., Fresno, 1992. Com. mem. USDA, Sacramento, 1998; dir. Calif. Farm Bur. Fedn., Sacramento, 1995—. Polit. cons. ezgov.com, Atlanta, 2000; cons. Natural Resources Edn. Found., Elk Grove, Calif., 2000. Mem. Blood Ctr. Sacramento, 1995-2001; mem. Sacramento County Farm Bur., 1996-2001. Recipient Appreciation for Dedication to Govt. award USDA-Farm Svc. Agy., 1998. Mem. Sigma Alpha Epsilon. Avocations: sports, travel, outdoor activities, legislative process. Office: Calif Farm Bur Fedn 2300 River Plaza Dr Sacramento CA 95833 Office Fax: 916-561-5693. E-mail: pvenosdel@cfbf.com.

VENTENILLA, AURORA CURAMEN, psychiatrist; b. San Jose, The Philippines, Nov. 7, 1939; came to U.S., 1968; d. Tereso and Petra (Patricio) Curamen; m. Doroteo Olba Ventenilla, Oct. 22, 1966; children: Anna, Enrique. MD, Manila Ctrl. U., 1963. Diplomate Am. Bd. Psychiatry and Neurology. Staff psychiatrist Cleve. VA Med. Ctr., 1974—96; contract psychiatrist COMPHEALTH, Salt Lake City, 1996—; staff psychiatrist Windsor Hosp., Chagrin Falls, Ohio, 1999—2001, Fremont (Ohio) Meml. Hosp., 2000—, Ctr. for Families and Children, Parma, Ohio, 1999—. Chief of psychiatry 256 Gen. Hosp. U.S. Army Res., Parma, Ohio, 1986-92. Lt. col. U.S. Army Res., 1982-92. Decorated Army Commendation medal Operation Desert Storm, 1991. Mem. Am. Profl. Practice Assn., Assn. Philippine Physicians in Am., Assn. Philippine Physicians in Ohio. Home: 9826 Tamarack Trl Brecksville OH 44141-4109

VENTER, J. CRAIG, science foundation director, geneticist; m. Claire Fraser. BS in Biochemistry, U. Calif., San Diego, 1972, PhD in Physiology and Pharmacology, 1975. Prof. SUNY, Buffalo; with Roswell Pk. Meml. Inst.; sect. and lab chief Nat. Inst. Neurol. Disorders and Stroke NIH, Bethesda, Md., 1984—92; co-founder, chair, chief scientist The Inst. for Genomic Rsch., 1992—98; co-founder, CEO, pres., chief sci. officer Celera Genomics Corp., Rockville, Md., 1998—2002; chmn. sci. adv. bd. Applera Corp., Norwalk, Conn.; chmn., co-founder, pres. The J. Craig Venter Sci. Found. Joint Tech. Ctr., 2003—; co-founder, pres. Ctr. for the Advancement Genomics, 2003—, Inst. for Biol. Energy Alternatives, 2003—. Bd. dirs. High Tech. Coun. Md.; mem. sci. adv. bd. ValiGene; chmn., bd. trustees The Inst. for Genomic Rsch. Contbr. more than 160 articles to profl. jours. Recipient Beckman award, 1999, Chiron Corp. Biotech. Rsch. award, 1999. Fellow: AAAS, Am. Acad. Microbiology. Achievements include development of extensive rsch. in functional and comparative analysis of genome and gene products in viruses, eubacteria, pathogenic bacteria, archea and eukaryotes, both plant and animal including humans; first to fully sequence seven organisms; pioneered the use of automated gene sequencers; developed expressed sequence tags (ESTs); helped discover more than half of all human genes. Office: The Inst for Genomic Rsch 9712 Medical Center Dr Rockville MD 20850 also: J Craig Venture Sci Found 5 Research Pl Rockville MD 20850*

VENTO, M. THÉRÈSE, lawyer; b. N.Y.C., June 30, 1951; d. Anthony Joseph and Margaret (Stechert) V.; m. Peter Michael MacNamara, Dec. 23, 1977; children: David Miles, Elyse Anne. BS, U. Fla., 1974, JD, 1976. Bar: Fla. 1977, U.S. Dist. Ct. (so. and mid. dists.) Fla. 1982, U.S. Ct. Appeals (5th and 11th cirs.) 1981, U.S. Supreme Ct. 1985. Clk. to presiding justice U.S. Dist. Ct. (so. dist.) Fla., Miami, 1976-78; assoc. Mahoney, Hadlow & Adams, 1978-79, Shutts & Bowen, 1979-84, ptnr., 1985-95; founding ptnr. Gallwey Gillman Curtis & Vento, P.A., 1995—2004; ptnr. Shutts & Bowen, LLP, 2004—. Trustee Miami Art Mus., 1988—, v.p., 1999—; trustee The Beacon Coun., 1995-97, Law Sch. Alumni Coun., U. Fla., 1994—. Fellow Am. Bar Found.; mem. Dade County Bar Assn. (dir. young lawyers sect. 1978-83, editor newsletter 1981-83), Fla. Assn. for Women Lawyers, Fla. Bar Assn. (bd. govs., young lawyers div. 1983-85, civil procedure rules com. 1983-90, exec. coun. trial lawyers sect. 1996—), The Miami Forum (v.p. 1987-88, bd. dirs. 1989-91, co-pres. 2001-2002). Home: 3908 Main Hwy Miami FL 33133-6513 Office: Shutters & Bower LLP 201 S. Biscayne Blvd Ste1500 Miami FL 33131 E-mail: TVento@shutts-law.com.

VENTRES, JUDITH MARTIN, lawyer; b. Ann Arbor, Mich., Feb. 10, 1943; d. D. Lawrence and Donna E. (Webb) Moran; children: Laura M. Buford, Paul M. Martin, A. Lindsay McGill; m. Daniel B. Ventres Jr., Dec. 27, 1984. BA, U. Mich., 1963; postgrad., U. Jean Moulin, Inst. du Droit, Lyon, France, 1981; JD, U. Minn., 1982. Bar: Minn. 1982, Fla. 1991, Colo. 1994, U.S. Tax Ct. 1989, U.S. Dist. Ct. Minn. 1989, U.S. Ct. Appeals (8th cir.) 1989. Tax supr., dir. fin. planning, asst. nat. dir. Coopers & Lybrand, Mpls., 1981-84; dir. fin. planning Investors Diversified Services subs. Am. Express, Mpls. and N.Y.C., 1984-85; sr. tax mgr., dir. fin. planning KPMG Peat Marwick Main & Co., Mpls., 1985-89; prin. Gray Plant Mooty Mooty & Bennett, P.A., Mpls., 2000—02, owner, mng. ptnr. Martin & Assoc. PA, Mpls., 1989—2000, 2002—. Faculty Minn. CLE, 1994; adv. bd. Nicollet/Ebenezer, 1996. Mem. Mpls. C. of C. Campaign, Downtown Coun. Coms., Mpls., 1982-84, Metro Tax Planning Group, 1984-86, Mpls. Estate Planning Coun., 1985-99, Planned Giving Coun.; class chmn. fundraising campaign U. Minn. Law Sch., Mpls., 1985, 98; bd. dirs. Ensemble Capriccio, chmn. fundraising com., 1998-2002; usher Christ Presbyn. Ch., Edina, Minn., 1983—; mem. adv. coun. on planned giving ARC. Mem. ABA (task force on legal fin. planning), Minn. Bar Assn., Hennepin County Bar Assn., Fla. Bar Assn., Colo. Bar Assn., Minn. Soc. CPAs (instr. continuing legal edn. 1983-84, continuing profl. edn. 1982-86, individual, trust and estate provisions Tax Reform Act 1986, continuing legal edn. -estate planning 1994), Minn. Planned Giving Coun., Am. Assn. Ind. Investors (speaker), Am. Soc. CLUs, Minn. Soc. CLUs, Minn. Women Lawyers, Fla. Women Lawyers, Lex Alumnae, U. Mich. Alumni Assn. (coun. govs. 1989—, scholarship chmn.), U. Minn. Alumni Club (bd. dirs. 1996, coun. govs. 1988-96, pres., treas. mem. com.), Interlachen Club, Athletic Club, Lafayette Club, Montana Club, U. Minn. Alumni Assn. (mem. univ. issues com., nat. bd. dirs. 1996-99), The Woman's Club Mpls. Home: 1355 Vine Pl Mound MN 55364-9635 Office: Martin & Assoc PA 3800 American Blvd W #270 Minneapolis MN 55431 Office Phone: 952-857-2424. Business E-Mail: judith@martinandassociates.com.

VENTURA, JESSE (JAMES JANOS), former governor; b. Mpls., July 15, 1951; s. George and Bernice Janos; m. Terry Ventura; children: Tyrel, Jade. Student, North Hennepin C.C. Profl. wrestler, 1973-84; ret.; gov. State of Minn., St. Paul, 1998—2003; host The Jesse Ventura Show, 2003—. Actor starring in several films including Predator; radio talk show host. Mayor City of Brooklyn Park, Minn., 1990-95; bd. advisors Make a Wish of Minn.; vol. football coach Champlin Park H.S. Served with USN, USNR. Mem. Am. Fedn. of TV and radio Announcers, Screen Actors Guild. Independent. Home: 100 Apple Orchard Rd Dellwood MN 55110-1241

VENTURA, ROBIN MARK, professional baseball player; b. Santa Maria, Calif., July 14, 1967; Student, Okla. State U. Mem. U.S. Olympic Baseball Team, Seoul, Republic of Korea, 1988; with Chgo. White Sox, 1988—99; infielder N.Y. Mets, 1999—. Named Coll. Player of Yr., Sporting News, 1987—88, Third Baseman All-Am. Team, 1987—88; named to All-Star Team, Am. League, 1992; recipient Golden Spikes award, USA Baseball, 1988, Golden Glove award, 1991—93, 1996, 1999. Office: New York Yankees Yankee Stafium 161st Street and River Avenue Bronx NY 10451

VENTURI, ROBERT, architect; b. Phila., June 25, 1925; s. Robert C. and Vanna (Lanzetta) Venturi; m. Denise Lakofski, July 23, 1967; 1 child, James Charles. Grad., Episcopal Acad., 1943; AB summa cum laude, Princeton U., 1947, MFA, 1950, DFA (hon.), 1983, Oberlin Coll., 1977, Yale U., 1979, U. Pa., 1980; Laurea Honoris Causa in Architecture, U. Rome "La Sapienza", 1994. Designer firms of Oskar Stonorov, Eero Saarinen and Assos., Louis I. Kahn, 1950—58; ptnr. firm Venturi, Cope & Lippincott, Phila., 1958—61, Venturi and Short, Phila., 1961—64, Venturi and Rauch, Phila., 1964—80, Venturi, Rauch & Scott Brown, Phila., 1980—89, Venturi, Scott Brown and Assocs., Inc., 1989—; from asst. to assoc. prof. architecture U. Pa., 1957—65; Charlotte Shepherd Davenport prof. architecture Yale, 1966—70. With Payette Assocs., Yale U., 1998. Author: Complexity and Contradiction in Architecture, 1966, Complexity and Contradiction in Architecture, 2d edit., 1977, Iconography and Electronics upon a Generic Architecture, 1996; co-author (with Denise Scott Brown and Steven Izenour): Learning from Las Vegas, 1972, Learning from Las Vegas, 2d edit., 1977; co-author: (with Denise Scott Brown) A View from the Campidoglio, Selected Essays, 1953-84, Architecture as Signs and Systems for a Mannerist Time, 2004, author (others, also articles); prin. works include Vanna Venturi House, Phila., 1961, Guild House, 1961, Humanities Bldg., SUNY, 1972, Franklin Ct., Phila., 1972, addition to Allen Meml. Art Mus., Oberlin Coll., 1973, Inst. for Sci. Info. Corp. Hdqs., Phila., 1978, Gordon Wu Hall, Princeton U., 1980, Seattle Art Mus., 1984, The Nat. Gallery, Sainsbury Wing, London, 1986, Fisher and Bendheim Halls, Princeton U., 1986, Gordon and Virginia MacDonald Med. Rsch. Labs. (with Payette Assocs.), UCLA, 1986, Charles P. Stevenson Jr. Libr., Bard Coll., 1989, Roy and Diana Vagelos Labs. IAST (with Payette Assocs.), U. Pa., 1990, Regional Govt. Bldg., Toulouse, France, 1992, Kirifuri Resort Facilities, Nikko, Japan, 1992, Trabant U. Ctr., U. Del., Newark, 1992, Meml. Hall Restoration and Addition, Harvard U., 1992, The Barnes Found. Restoration and Renovation, Merion, Pa., 1993, Disney Celebration (Fla.) Bank, 1993, Gonda (Goldschmied) Neuroscience and Genetics Rsch. Ctr. (with Lee, Burkhart, Liu Inc.), UCLA, 1993, Princeton Campus Ctr., Princeton U., 1996, Anlyan Ctr. for Med. Rsch. and Edn., Yale U. Sch. Medicine, 1998, (with Payette Assocs.) Master Plan and Buildings for U. Mich., 1997—, Baker/Berry Libr., Dartmouth Coll., 1996, Woodmere Art Mus. addition, 2000, Biomed. Rsch. Bldg., U. Ky., 2000, Dumbarton Oaks Libr. Expansion, Washington, D.C., 2001, Stuart Country Day School Theater/Auditorium/Sanctuary, Princeton, N.J., 2001. Trustee Am. Acad. Rome, 1966—71. Decorated comdr. Order Arts and Letters (France); recipient Nat. Medal of Arts, 1992, Pritzker Architecture prize, 1991, Benjamin Franklin medal, The Royal Soc. for Encouragement of Arts, Mfrs. and Commerce, 1993, Vincent J. Scully prize, 2002; fellow Rome Prize Am. Acad., Rome, 1954—56. Fellow: AIA (award 1974, 1977, 1978), Accademia Nazionale di San Luca, Am. Acad. Arts and Scis., Am. Acad. of Arts and Letters, Am. Acad. in Rome, Royal Incorp. Architects of Scotland (hon.), Royal Inst. of Brit. Architects (hon.); mem.: Phi Beta Kappa. Office: Venturi Scott Brown & Assocs Inc 4236 Main St Philadelphia PA 19127-1603 Office Phone: 215-487-0400. E-mail: venturi@vsba.com.

VENTURINI, TISHA LEA, professional soccer player; b. Modesto, Calif., Mar. 3, 1973; Degree in phys. edn., U. N.C. Mem. U.S. Women's Nat. Soccer Team. Mem. championship team CONCACAF, Montreal, 1994. Recipient Gold medal Centennial Olympic Games, 1996, Silver medal world Univ. Games, 1993, Hermann trophy, 1994; mem. championship team CONCACAF, Montreal, 1994; named Player of Yr. Mo. Athletic Club, 1994. Office: c/o US Soccer Fedn 1801 S Prairie Ave # 1811 Chicago IL 60616-1319

VENZAGO, MARIO, conductor; b. Zurich, Switzerland, 1948; m. Marianne Venzago; children: Mario, Gabriel. Studied with, Hans Swarowsky, Vienna, 1973. Music dir. Basel Symphony Orch., 1995—2003, Heidelberg Opera, 1986—89, Deutsche Kammerphilharmonie, 1989—92, Graz Opera Ho., 1990—95, Euskadi Nat. Opera, Spain, 1998—2001, Ind. Symphony Orch., 2002—, Swedish Nat. Orch., 2003—. Guest conductor Berlin Philharmonic, Leipzig Gewandhaus Orchester, London Philharmonic, City of Birmingham Symphony, Orchestre de la Suisse Romande, Phila. Orch., Tonhalle Orchestra Zurich, Tokyo's NHK Symphony, Berlin's Komische Oper, Salzburg Festival, Hannover Radio-Philharmonie, invited by Kurt Masur, Leipzig, Am. debut Hollywood Bowl, 1988, appeared N.J. Symphony, Ind. Symphony, Fla. Philharmonic, 1988; dir.: Balt. Symphony, 1995 (named artistic dir. symphony's summer festival, 2000); prin. conductor Winterthur City Orch., Lucerne Opera Ho., Orchestre de la Suisse Romande. Recipient award, Diapason d'or, awards, Grand Prix du Disque, Edison prize. Office: Ind Symphony Orch 32 E Washington St Ste 600 Indianapolis IN 46204-2919 Business E-Mail: mvenvago@IndianapolisSymphony.org.

VÉR, ISTVAN LASZLO, acoustical engineer, consultant; b. Tápiószecsö, Hungary, Dec. 22, 1934; came to U.S., 1965; s. Istvan and Erzsebet G. (Darázs) V.; 1 child, Kristina M. BSEE, Tech. U., Budapest, 1956; MSEE, Tech. U., Aachen, Germany, 1960; PhD in Acoustics, Tech. U., Munich, 1963. R&D engr. Rohde and Schwarz, Munich, 1960-65; prin. cons. BBN Techs., Cambridge, Mass., 1965—. Author, editor: Noise & Vibration Control Engineering, 1992; holder patents. Recipient U.S. Sr. Scientist award Alexander von Humboldt Found., Germany, 1978, Best Paper award Am. Soc. Heating and Refrigeration Engring., 1979. Fellow Acoustical Soc. Am.; mem. Inst. Noise Control Engring. USA (dir. 1976-77), European Acoustics Assn. Avocations: literature, philosophy, travel, tennis. Office Phone: 978-568-0556.

VERA, ENRIQUE, psychiatrist; b. Buenos Aires, Dec. 3, 1939; came to U.S., 1964; s. Enrique and Nella (Pupulin) V.; m. Sara Grosso, June 13, 1964; children: Sylvia, Nancy, Henry. Grad. in edn., U. Buenos Aires, 1956, MD, 1964. Diplomate Am. Bd. Psychiatry and Neurology. Intern Detroit Meml. Hosp., 1964-65; resident U. Mo., 1968-71; dir. partial hospitalization and crisis unit Western Mo. Mental Health Ctr., Kansas City, 1971-76, dir. screening clinic, 1973-90, dir. psychotherapy unit, 1984-90, dir. forensic unit, 1986-88; grad. Topeka Inst. for Psychoanalysis, 1991; chief med. dir. Ctrl. Kansas City Mental Health Ctr., 1993-94; chief mental health clinic VA Outpatient Clinic, Ft. Myers, Fla., 1994-2000. Assoc. clin. prof. dept. psychiatry U. Mo., Kansas City. Author: Clinical responses to Disaster, 1989. Recipient award for crisis counseling HHS-USPHS, 1993. Fellow Am. Psychiat. Assn.; mem. Fla. Psychiat. Soc., Jackson County Med. Soc. Office: VA Outpatient Clinic 3033 Winkler Ext Fort Myers FL 33916-9413 E-mail: enrique.vera@med.va.gov.

VERAMALLAY, ASHTON ISARDATT, economist, educator; b. Albion Estate, Guyana, Mar. 2, 1940; s. Bonus David and Doris V.; m. Norma Surojni, Apr. 15, 1967; children: Stasia Ashmala, Shayne Ravin. BS in Econs., Sociology, U. Wis., La Crosse, 1970; MS in Econs., Iowa State U., 1972, PhD in Econs., 1976. Sr. master Belvedere Govt. Secondary Sch., Albion, 1963-67; asst. prof. W.Va. State Coll., Institute, 1976-77; from asst. prof. to prof. Ind. Univ. East, Richmond, 1977-90, prof., dir. Ctr. Econ. Edn., 1990—, chair bus. divsn., 1994—2001. Rsch. asst. Iowa State U., Ames, 1972-74, rschr., 1974-76; adv. bd. Small Bus. Devel. Ctr., Richmond, 1994—. Contbg. author: Encyclopedia of Keynesian Economics, 1997; contbr. articles to profl. publs. Mem. adv. bd. Richmond Hosp. Authority, 1995—; pres. ARC, Richmond, 1990; bd. dirs. Habitat for Humanity Greater Richmond, 1990—. Recipient Outstanding Svc. award Ind. Coun. Econ. Educators, 1979, Nat. Coun. Econ. Educators, 1983, 88, Sagamore of the Wabash award State of Ind., 1998. Mem. Internat. Atlantic Econ. Soc., Internat. Assn. Children's Social Econ. Edn. (editl. bd.), Am. Acon. Assn., Nat. Assn. Econ. Educators (mem. com. 1994—), Ea. Econ. Assn. (area rep.), Midwest Econ. Assn., Ind. Acad. Social Sci. (pres. 1992), AAUP, Kiwanis, Richmond C. of C. (edn. com. 1978-92, Dedicated Svc. and Leadership award 1993), Delta Mu Delta (nat. exec. coun.). Avocations: gardening, bicycling, reading, volleyball, cricket. Office: Indiana Univ E 2325 Chester Blvd Richmond IN 47374

VERA NEGRON, SANDRA, literature educator, translator; d. Luis Norberto Vera Nieves and Fredeswinda Negron Cruz. BA in English/Lit., Inter Am. U. P.R., 1993, MA in English/TESL, 1998. Translator, copywriter, proofreader Cmty. Rels. & Press Office U. P.R.-Rio Piedras Campus, 1991—93; tchr. elem. sch. ESL San Juan 3 Sch. Dist., 1995—98; instr. English E.D.P. Coll. Hato Rey Campus, 1998; lectr. English Universidad del Este, Carolina, PR, 1998—2003; instr. English Universidad Metropolitana, Cupey Campus, 1999, InterAm. U. P.R., Metropolitan Campus, 1999—2004, U. P.R., Carolina, 2000—02, Caribbean U., Carolina Campus, 2002, Universidad del Este, Carolina, PR, 2002—. Asst. translator Universidad del Este, Carolina, 2000—. Mem.: NOW, MLA, Witches Against Religious Discrimination, Internat. Fund for Animal Welfare, Am. Anti-Vivisection Soc., People for the Ethical Treatment Animals. Wicca. Avocations: internet and traditional research, literature, animal welfare, women's rights. E-mail: saqqaea@prtc.net.

VERANO, ANTHONY FRANK, retired banker; b. West Harrison, N.Y., Jan. 4, 1931; s. Frank and Rose (Viscomi) Verano; m. Clara Cosentino, July 8, 1951; children: Rosemarie, Diana Lynn. Student, Am. Inst. Banking, 1956-60, Bank Adminstrn. Inst., U. Wis., 1962-64, RCA Programmers Sch., 1965, Burroughs Programmers Sch., 1965, N.J. Bankers Data Processing Sch., 1966-68. With County Trust Co., White Plains, N.Y., 1949-61, sr. auditor, 1960-61; with State Nat. Bank Conn., Bridgeport, 1961—, auditor, 1962-79, exec. auditor, 1979—, Conn. Bank & Trust Co., 1983—; from v.p., auditor to sr. v.p., auditor Gateway Bank, Newtown, Conn., 1987-94, ret., 1996. Tchr. bank auditing Am. Inst. Banking, 1976-78. Mem. adv. bd. Norwalk Community Coll., 1968— . Served with USN, 1951-52. Mem. Bank Adminstrn. Inst. (dir. Stamford chpt. 1967-68, sec. Western Conn. chpt. 1968-69, treas. 1969-70, v.p. 1970-71, pres. 1971-72), Am. Acctg. Assn., Inst. Internal Auditors (cert. bank auditor, cert. bank compliance officer, cert. fin. svcs. auditor). Home: 224 Columbus Ave West Harrison NY 10604-2614 *It is difficult to define the elements of success. There are those who say success is achieved through drive and ambition only. However, those who have achieved their goals in life using only these two principles have probably destroyed more than they have created. Success, I feel, is achieved when drive and ambition are tempered with honesty, fairness, and respect for others. An individual must have a sense of dedication not only to his work and for those with whom he works but, most importantly, for those who work for him. This has been my philosophy in achieving my success.*

VERANT, WILLIAM J. state agency administrator; b. Washington, Dec. 19, 1941; m. Donna M. Verant; children: Bill Jr., Sharon. BSBA, Am. U. V.p. Fed. Home Mortgage Corp., Calif.; recruited by the Fed. Home Loan Bank Bd. to manage various savings & loan instns. during savings & loan crisis in 1980s; dept head comml. and multifamily real estate loans/assets Resolution Trust Corp., Newport Beach, Calif.; dir. fin. instns. divsn., regulation and licensing dept. State of N.Mex., Santa Fe, 1995—, acting dir. securities divsn. Avocation: restoring old cars. Office: State NMex PO Box 25101 725 Saint Michaels Dr Santa Fe NM 87504-7605*

VERBA, SIDNEY, political scientist, educator; b. Bklyn., May 26, 1932; s. Morris Harold and Recci (Salman) V.; m. E. Cynthia Winston, June 17, 1955; children— Margaret Lynn, Ericka Kim, Martina Claire. BA, Harvard U., 1953; MA, Princeton U., 1955, PhD, 1959. Asst. prof. polit. sci. Princeton U., 1960-63, assoc. prof., 1963-64; prof. Stanford U., 1964-68, U. Chgo., 1968-72; prof. govt. Harvard U., 1972—, now Carl H. Pforzheimer prof., dir. univ. library, chmn. dept. govt., 1976-80, assoc. dean Faculty Arts and Scis., 1981—; dir. Harvard U. Library. Chmn. bd. dirs. Harvard U. Press, 1991—; chmn. policy com. Social Sci. Rsch. Coun., 1980-86; mem. Commn. on Behavioral and Social Scis., NRC, 1986-91; Commn. on Preservation and Access, chair com. on internat. conflict and cooperation, NRC, 1991-93; vis. com. MIT Polit. Sci. Dept.; bd. dirs. Social Sci. Rsch. Coun.; Tanner Lectr., Oxford, 1998. Author: Small Groups and Political Behavior, 1961, The Civic Culture, 1963, Caste, Race and Politics, 1969, Participation in America, 1972, Vietnam and the Silent Majority, 1972, The Changing American Voter, 1976, Participation and Political Equality, 1978, Injury to Insult, 1979, Introduction to American Government, 1983, Equality in America, 1985, Elites and the Idea of Equality, 1987, Designing Social Inquiry, 1994, Voice and Equality, 1995, The Private Roots of Public Action, 2001. Guggenheim fellow, 1980-81 Fellow Am. Acad. Arts and Scis.; mem. NAS (chair social and polit. sci. sect. 2002-), Am. Philos. Soc., Am. Polit. Sci. Assn. (exec. coun. 1971-74, v.p. 1979-81, pres.-elect 1993-94, pres. 1994-95, Gladys Kammerer award 1972, Woodrow Wilson Found. award 1976, James Madison award 1993, Warren Miller award 2000), Internat. Studies Assn. (v.p. 1971-72, John Skytte prize 2002). Jewish. Home: 142 Summit Ave Brookline MA 02446-2358 Office: Harvard U Library Dir Cambridge MA 02138

VERBOV, LEV FALKOVICH, metallurgical engineer, writer, translator; b. Leningrad, Russia, Jan. 10, 1937; came to U.S., 1977; s. Falka Shevelevich and Elka Abramovna Verbova; m. Larisa Ivanovna Fedkushova, Nov. 26, 1990; 1 child, Kristina Kulbe. MS in Metall. Engring., Tech. U., St. Petersburg, Russia, 1962. Sr. engr. All-Union Inst. Aluminum, Magnesium and Electrode Industry, St. Petersburg, 1962-77; engr.-scientist Aluminum Co. of Am., New Kensington, Pa., 1979-82; asst. editor Chem. Abstracts Svcs., Columbus, Ohio, 1985-87; cons. R&D scientist ECC Am., Inc., Sandersville, Ga., 1988-90; clk., team mem. Local Census Ctr., Bklyn., 1999-2000; freelance writer Bklyn., 1966—; freelance translator, 1982—. Author: (books) Commercial Star, 1999, Swan Song of Ugly Duckling, 2000; composer: Solemn Melody, 1999; patentee in field. Personal E-mail: lverbov@aol.com.

VERBURG, EDWIN ARNOLD, management consultant; b. Lakehurst, NJ, Oct. 6, 1945; s. Edwin Donald Verburg and Dorothy (Orrell) Hoodless; m. Joyce Elaine Majack, Sept. 14, 1968; children: Adelle Kristine, Wendi Elizabeth. BS, Calif. Poly. U., 1968; M in City Planning, U. Calif., Berkeley, 1970; D in Pub. Adminstrn., George Washington U., 1975. Asst. planner City of Inglewood, Calif., 1970-71; planner City of Glendale, Calif., 1971-72; grad. assoc. U.S. Army Corps Engrs., Washington, 1974-75; mgr. fiscal analysis Met. Washington Coun. Govt., 1975-77; sr. program analyst U.S. Fish and Wildlife Svc., Washington, 1977-79, asst. divsn. chief, 1979-80, divsn. chief, 1980-82, asst. dir. planning and budget, 1982-86, dep. asst. dir. policy budget and adminstrn., 1986-87; dir. office of fin. U.S. Dept. Treas., Washington, 1987-88, dir. fin. svc. directorate, 1988-91, dir. fin. svcs. directorate, dep. CFO, 1991-95; assoc. adminstr. adminstrn. FAA, 1995-98; prin. ptnr. Avant Mgmt. Group, Inc., 1998-99; prin., fedn. govt. svc. Kelly, Anderson & Assocs., 1999—2002, v.p., 2003—. Author: Local State and Federal Fiscal Flows, 5 Vols., 1976; contbr. articles to fed. jours. Recipient Disting. Pub. Svc. award George Washington U., Sch. Bus. and Pub. Mgmt., 1994, Sec. of Treasury Disting Svc. award, 1995, Fin. Mgmt. Svc. Commr. award, 1996. Mem. Am. Inst. Cert. Planners, Am. Planning Assn. (cert. govt. fin. mgr., Merit award Calif. chpt. 1973, First award Nat. Capital area chpt. 1980, Peer award for pub. svc. Dept. of Treasury 1990, sec. of treas. cert. appreciation 1991, Pres.'s Meritorious Svc. award 1991, Commr. Citation Fin. Mgmt. Svc. 1996, Pres. award Combined Fed. Campaign 1997), Arlington Kiwanis (bd. dirs. 1999-2001, v.p. 2001-02, pres.-elect 2002-03, pres. 2003-04). Home: 538 N Oakland St Arlington VA 22203-2219 Office: Kelly Andersen & Assocs Inc 424 N Washington St Alexandria VA 22314-2312

VERCAMMEN, KENNETH ALBERT, lawyer, prosecutor; b. Edison, N.J., Aug. 7, 1959; s. Albert Peter and Carol Ann (Rasche) V.; m. Cynthia Ann Bachenski, July 9, 1989. BS, U. Scranton, 1981; JD, Univ. Del. Law Sch., 1985. Bar: N.J., Pa. 1985, N.Y. 1986, D.C. 1987; cert. mediator N.J. Superior Ct., 1997-. Mng. atty., Cranbury, NJ, 1990—; prosecutor Township of Cranbury, Middlesex County, NJ, 1991—99; spl. acting prosecutor Delaware County, Pa. District Office, Middlesex County Probation Dept., Scranton Dist. Magistrate Office, Woodbridge, East Brunswick, Metuchen, South Brunswick, Clark, Berkeley; acting assoc. prosecutor Carteret Mcpl. Ct., Middlesex County, NJ, 2000. Adj. prof. Middlesex County Coll., Edison, 1990-91, 2001; instr. criminal law and procedure and bus. law; mem. com. mcpl. ct. edn. N.J. Supreme Ct., 1990-97; spkr. litig. engagements, wills, elder law and probate. Author 132 separate law rev. and legal periodicals articles to profl. jours. including N.J. Law Jour., ABA Barrister, N.J. Lawyer, ABA Law Practice Mgmt., Dictum; editor N.J. Municipal Ct. Law Review, 1993-; author, DWI & Drug Cases, 2002. Winner of the N.J. State Bar Gen. Practitioner of the Yr. award, 2002, N.J. Bar Assoc. Svc. to Bar award, N.J. State Bar Assn. YLD award, 1993. Mem.: N.J. State Bar Assn. (chair mcpl. ct. sect.), Middlesex Mcpl. Prosecutor's Assn. (co-chmn. mcpl. ct. practice com. 1997—, mem. bd. trustees 2000—). Avocations: cross-country running, soccer. Office: 2053 Woodbridge Ave Edison NJ 08817

VERCELLOTTI, JOHN RAYMOND, research chemist; b. Joliet, Ill., May 2, 1933; s. Joseph Francis and Mary Teresa (Walowski) V.; m. Sharon Cecile Vergez, Sept. 3, 1966; children: Ellen Theresa, Paul Auguste. BA, St. Bonaventure U., 1955; MS, Marquette U., 1960; PhD, Ohio State U., 1963. Lectr., rsch. assoc. Ohio State U., Columbus, 1963-64; asst. prof. Marquette U., Milw., 1964-67; assoc. prof. U. Tenn., Knoxville, 1967-70; prof. Va. Poly. Inst. & State U., Blacksburg, 1970-79; vis. prof. Inst. G. Ronzoni, Milan, 1977-78; sr. scientist Gulf South Res. Inst., New Orleans, 1980-85; rsch. chemist, rsch. leader So. Regional Rsch. Ctr. USDA, New Orleans, 1985-96, collaborator, 1996—. V.p. and sr. chemist V-Labs Inc., Covington, La., 1980-85, 96—; sr. rsch. advisor Sugar Processing Rsch. Inst., Inc., New Orleans, 1996-99, 2001—; adj. prof. chemistry and physics S.E. La. U., Hammond, 1986—. Contbr. more than 200 articles to Elsevier & Am. Chem. Soc. Symposium Series; author, co-author numerous book chpts., 1960—; contbr. numerous articles to profl. jours. U. Tenn. minority colls. grantee, 1968-70, NSF grantee, 1964—. Fellow Sigma Xi; mem. Am. Chem. Soc. (sec. 1968-90, Melville L. Wolfrom award 1994), Inst. Food Technologists. Democrat. Roman Catholic. Achievements include research on food flavor quality and agricultural commodity utilization, origin of flavor from carbohydrates, lipid oxidation products, and peptides. Home: 113 E 25th Ave Covington LA 70433-2819 Office: V-Labs Inc 423 N Theard St Covington LA 70433-2837 Office Phone: 985-893-0533. Business E-Mail: v-labs@v-labs.com.

VERDERBER, JOSEPH ANTHONY, capital equipment company executive; b. Nov. 30, 1938; s. Joseph Arthur and Dorothy Louise (Buchta) V.; m. Anita Barto, Sept. 10, 1960; children: Joseph Anthony, Lisa C., Paul A. BS in Mech. Engring., MIT, 1960, MS in Mech. Engring., 1961. Registered profl. engr., Ohio. Mgr. rsch. AM Internat., Cleve., 1964-70; dir. engring. Varityper div., East Hanover, N.J., 1971-73, product mgr., 1973-77, v.p. advanced bus. devel. multigraphics div. Mt. Prospect, Ill., 1977-81, gen. mgr. imaging systems group Bedford, Mass., 1981, pres. East Hanover, N.J., 1982-88; corp. v.p. bus. devel. AM Internat., Inc., Chgo., 1988-89; pres. Am. Splty. Products, Dayton, Ohio, 1989-90, Barco Graphics, Inc., Dayton, Ohio, 1990; v.p., gen. mgr. Gen. Scanning, Laser Sys. Divsn., Somerville, Mass., 1991-99; ret., 2000; CEO IBEX Process Tech., 2000. Lectr. Cleve. State U., 1962-67; chmn., SEMI New Eng. Forum, 1994-99; dir. Virtek Vision Internat., Toronto, Can. Recipient Karl Taylor Compton prize MIT, 1960; NSF fellow, 1961; named Inventor of Yr., AM Internat., Chgo., 1980. Mem. ASME, Nat. Printing Equipment and Supply Assn. (bd. dirs. 1986-88). E-mail: javerderber@yahoo.com.

VERDERY, DAVID NORWOOD, broadcast programming executive; b. Waco, Tex., Dec. 12, 1943; s. David Paul and Ruthe (McCawley) V.; m. Randy Lee Mahan, June 6, 1968 (div. 1970); 1 child, David Roderick. Student, Baylor U., 1961-64. Announcer KEFC, Waco, 1962-64; announcer, producer KHFI, Austin, Tex., 1964-65; announcer, prodn. dir. KIXL, Dallas, 1965-66; program dir. KVIL, Dallas, 1967, KABL, San Francisco, 1968-69; nat. program coord. The McLendon Co., Dallas, 1969-73; v.p. programming TM Programming, Dallas, 1973-80, Bonneville Broadcasting Sys., Northbrook, Ill., 1980-86; music dir. KBIG, L.A., 1985-95, asst. program dir., music dir., 1996-97, program dir., 1997; ret., 1998. Mem. Project Angel Food, L.A., 1992-94; mem. Permanent Charities Com., L.A., 1995-97, mem. Reading for the Blind, L.A., 1996-97; bd. dirs. Waco Civic Theatre, 1999-2001, v.p., 2000-01; bd. dirs. Met. Cmty. Ch., 2001—; emperor X Royal Sovereign and Imperial Ct. of Ctrl. Tex. Empire, 2003-04. Named Adult Contemporary Music Dir. of Yr., The Gavin Report, 1992, 93. Avocations: gourmet cooking, theater, travel, musical composing and arranging, magic. E-mail: wacodave@hot.rr.com.

VERDIER, DAVID D'OOGE, ophthalmologist, educator; b. Grand Rapids, Mich., Jan. 22, 1949; s. Leonard D'Ooge and Anita Beatrice (Carvalho) V.; m. Beverly Deane Johnson; children: Renée Leigh, Travis D'Ooge, Eric Leonard, Nora Claire. BA in Polit. Sci., U. Mich., 1971; MD, U. Mich. Med. Sch., 1977. Resident in family practice Med. U. S.C., Charleston, 1977-80; resident in ophthalmology Pitts. Eye and Ear, U. Pitts., 1980-83; corneal and external eye fellowship U. Iowa, Iowa City, 1983-84; pvt. practice med. and surg. ophthalmology Verdier Eye Ctr. P.C., Grand Rapids, Mich., 1984—; assoc. clin. prof. Mich. State U. Coll. Medicine, East Lansing, 1986—. Med. dir. Mich. Tissue Bank, Lansing, Mich., 1995-98, SEECOM, Mich., 1995—; mem. med. adv. bd. Eye Bank Assn. Am., 2003—; bd. dirs. Cape Elethra Found. Contbr. articles to profl. jours. and textbook chpts. Bd. dirs. East Grand Rapids (Mich.) Sch. Found., 1992-2000, Macatawa Bay Yacht Club, Holland, Mich., 1988-90, 94-95, Grand Rapids Art Mus., 1995-2001; bd. dirs. Macatawa Park Cottagers Assn., Holland, 1993-99, pres., 1993-98. Named to Galens Hon. Med. Soc., 1975-77. Mem. Mich. Ophthalmologic Soc (bd. dirs. 1994-2000), Mich. State Med. Soc. (del. 1993-2000). Home: 3043 Mary St SE Grand Rapids MI 49506-3150 Office: Verdier Eye Center PC 1000 E Paris Ave SE Ste 130 Grand Rapids MI 49546-3680

VERDIER, QUENTIN ROOSEVELT, human resources consultant; b. Mancelona, Mich., Mar. 19, 1921; s. John Walter and Louise (Hills) V.; m. Margaret Elizabeth Wells, Nov. 13, 1943 (dec. 1999); children: Margaret Louise, Quentin Wells, Nanette Marie Bloom. AB in Pub. Adminstrn., Kalamazoo Coll., 1943, MA in Pub. Adminstrn., 1947; postgrad., Am. U., 1948-51; PhD in Human Resource Devel., Columbia Pacific U., 1985. Diplomate Am. Bd. Forensic Medicine; bd. cert. forensic examiner; cert. employment cons., pers. cons., forensic examiner, forensic vocat. expert; registered employment agt., Wis. Asst. pers. officer U.S. Savs. Bonds div. U.S. Treasury Dept., Washington, 1951-58; div. chief office of pers. Internat. Coop. Adminstrn./Agy. for Internat. Devel., Washington, 1959-63; dep. chief pub. adminstrn. div. U.S. Ops. Mission/Agy. for Internat. Devel., Saigon, South Vietnam, 1963-65; asst. dir. tng. Inst. Govt. Affairs U. Wis. Extension, Madison, 1966-67; pres. AvailAbility of Madison, Inc., 1967—77. Mem. adv. panel Nat. Forensic Ctr., Princeton, 1983—; intern Group XIV, Nat. Inst. Pub. Affairs, 1948-49. Author City Employee Handbook-Better Pub. Service, 1947; editor hist. pamphlet series Understanding Backgrounds, 1964; contbr. articles to profl. jours. Bd. dirs. Friendship Force of Wis., 1991-95, West Side Sr. Ctr., Madison, Westside Coalition for Older Adults, 1992-93, Fitchburg Commn. Aging, 1997-98; pres. Zor Shrine Clown Unit, 1992-93; mem. Madison Symphony Chorus. With U.S. Army Air Corps, 1943-46. Decorated Republic of Vietnam Merit medal 1st class, 1965; recipient Wm G. Howard prize in polit. sci., 1946, Suggestion awards U.S. Treasury Dept., 1949; Upjohn fellow Kalamazoo Coll., 1946-47. Fellow Am. Coll. Forensic Examiners; mem. Am. Arbitration Assn. (arbitrator mem. panel Chgo. regional office), Am. Assn. Retired Persons, Nat. Forensic Ctr., Wis. Acad. Scis., Arts and Letters (life), Wis. Regional Writers Assn., Nat. Geographic Soc., Smithsonian Instn., Nat. Assn. Retired Credit Union People, Nat. Wildlife Assn., World Future Soc., Internat. Exec. Svc. Corps, Plato, Friendship Force, Internat. Shrine Clown Assn., Sun Valley Health Club, Toastmasters (dist. 36 gov.), Masons (32 degree), Shriners, Rotary (bd. dirs. Madison-WestTown-Middleton club 1988-92), Plato (Madison). Avocations: choral singing, genealogy, clowning, writing, poetry.

VERDILE, VINCENT PAUL, dean, emergency physician; b. Troy, N.Y., Aug. 13, 1955; s. Raphael Mario and Frances (Marinucci) V.; m. Louise Ann Wickware, Aug. 30, 1985. BS, Union U., 1977, MS, 1980; MD, Albany Med. Coll., 1984. Intern U. Pitts., 1984-85, resident in emergency medicine, 1985-87; assoc. med. dir. dept. pub. safety City of Pitts., 1985—93; flight physician Ctr. for Emergency Medicine, Pitts., 1988—93; chair. dept. of emergency med. Albany Med. Coll., 1993—2000, interim dean, 2000, dean, 2001—. Mem. adj. staff dept. emergency medicine Mercy Hosp., Pitts, 1987—93; med. dir., emergency med. technician Community Coll. Allegheny Coll., 1987—93; attending physician emergency dept. Presbyn.-Univ. Hosp., 1987—93; assoc. program dir. residency in emergency medicine Univ. of Pitts., 1987—93, asst. prof. medicine, 1987—93. Contbr. numerous articles to profl. jours. Mem. Soc. Acad. Emergency Medicine, Nat. Assn. Emergency Med. Svcs. Physicians (chmn. membership com. 1988—), Am. Coll. Emergency Physicians, Pa. chpt. Am. Coll. Emergency Physicians, Pa. State Med. Soc., Allegheny County Med. Soc., Am. Assn. Poison Control Ctrs. Roman Catholic. Office: Albany Med Coll 47 New Scotland Ave Albany NY 12208

VERDINE, GREGORY LAWRENCE, chemist, educator; b. Somers Point, NJ, June 10, 1959; s. Richard Daniel and Therese Mary (Delaney) V.; m. Kasumi Koseki, Dec. 1, 1987; children: Vanessa Kaori, Lauren Arika, Erika Rose. BS, St. Joseph's U., Phila., 1982; MA, Columbia U., 1983, PhD, 1986; AB (hon.), Harvard U., 1995. Postdoctoral fellow MIT, Cambridge, Mass., 1986, 87. Harvard Med. Sch., Boston, 1987, 8; asst. prof. chemistry Faculty Arts and Scis. Harvard U., Cambridge, 1988-92, Thomas D. Cabot assoc. prof. chemistry, 1992-94, prof., 1994—2002, Erving prof. chemistry, 2002—. Founder Enanta Pharm., Watertown, Mass., Renegade Therapeutics, Cambridge; bd. sci. counselors Nat. Cancer Inst. Assoc. editor Chemistry and Biology, 1994—; contbr. numerous articles to profl. jours. Recipient Excellence in Chemistry award Zeneca Pharms., 1994; DuPont Young Faculty fellow, 1988, Searle scholar, 1990, Eli Lilly grantee, 1990, Alfred P. Sloan fellow, 1991, NSF Presdl. Young Investigator award, 1991, others. Mem. AAAS, Am. Chem. Soc. (Arthur C. Cope Scholar award 1994, Eli Lilly award 1995). Achievements include research in chemical genetics: the propagation, preservation and expression of genetic information. Office: Harvard U Dept Chemistry/Chem Bio 12 Oxford St Cambridge MA 02138-2902

VERDOL, JOSEPH ARTHUR, chemist; b. Chgo., Oct. 30, 1927; s. Joseph and Molly (Pangerl) Vrdolak; m. Elaine C. Glenn, July 7, 1973; children: David A., Lori. BS in Chemistry cum laude, U. Ill., 1951; PhD in Chemistry, Cornell U., 1955. Dir. polymer rsch. Sinclair Rsch., Harvey, Ill., 1963-68, v.p. N.Y.C., 1968-69; sr. v.p. Arco Tech. Inc., Phila., 1970-86; v.p. Arco Chem. Asia Pacific, Tokyo, 1980-86; pres. Chem. Tech. Worldwide Cons., N.Y.C., 1986—, Tasco Chem. USA. Former lectr. East-West trade Harvard U. Patentee in field of petrochemicals in Canada, Japan and Europe; Contbr. numerous articles to Ency. Polymer Sci. & Tech., Jour. Am. Chem. Soc., Oil & Gas Jour., Rubber Age, Rubber World, Harvard Revs. Lt. USMC, 1945-46, U.S. Army, 1950-51. Fellow Am. Inst. Chemists; mem. Am. Chem. Soc., AAAS. Roman Catholic. Achievements include patents in Petroleum, Polymer and Petrochemical fields, Methyl tertiarybutyl ether; invention of processes and new polymers which are used in petroleum refining, petrochemicals and chemical industry. Office: Chem Tech Worldwide 1641 3rd Ave Ste 16-he New York NY 10128-3623

VERDOORN, D.R. (SID), food service executive; b. Albert Lea, Minn., Feb. 11, 1939; s. Cornelius Emery and Gwen (Pickell) V.; m. Carol Joyce Hoekstra, July 3, 1959; children: Jay Richard, Jeffrey Lee, James Dale. Student, Cen. Coll., Pella, Iowa. With sales C.H. Robinson Co., Mpls., 1963-66, mgr. San Francisco, 1966-71, pers. dir. Mpls., 1971-75, v.p., 1975-77, pres., 1977-2000, CEO, 1977—. Bd. dirs. Produce Mktg. Assocs., Newark, United Fruit and Produce, Washington. With U.S. Army, 1959-61. Republican. Avocations: hiking, water sports. Home: 28210 Woodside Rd Excelsior MN 55331-7950 Office: C H Robinson Co Inc 8100 Mitchell Rd Ste 200 Eden Prairie MN 55344-2178

VERDU, SERGIO, engineering educator; b. Barcelona, Aug. 15, 1958; arrived in U.S., 1980; s. Tomas Verdu and Visitacion Lucas; m. Mercedes Paratje, Jan. 19, 1982; 1 child, Ariana. Diploma in telecom. engring., Poly. U. Barcelona, 1980; MS, U. Ill., 1982, PhD, 1984. Asst. prof. Princeton (NJ) U., 1984-89, assoc. prof., 1989-92, prof., 1993—. Prin. investigator U.S. Office Naval Rsch., NJ Dept. Higher Edn., U.S. Army Rsch. Office, NJ Commn. Sci. and Tech., NSF, U.S.-Israel Binational Sci. Found.; vis. prof. U. Calif., Berkeley, 1998; vis. rsch. prof. Math. Sci. Rsch. Inst., 2002. Author: Multiuser Detection, 1998, Information Theory: Fifty Years of Discovery, 1999; mem. editl. bd. Transactions on Info. Theory, 1990-94;; editor-in-chief Foundations and Trends in Comm. and Info. Theory, 2003—; contbr. numerous articles to profl. jours, chpts. to books. Recipient Nat. U. prize Ministry Edn., Spain, 1982, Presdl. Young Investigator award NSF, 1988, Frederick E. Terman award Am. Soc. Engring. Edn., 2000. Fellow: IEEE (Outstanding Paper award 1998, Millennium medal 2000); mem.: Info. Theory Soc. (bd. govs. 1989—99, v.p. 1995, pres. 1997, Golden Jubilee Paper award 1998, Leonard G. Abraham Paper award 2002). Office: Princeton U Dept Elec Engring Princeton NJ 08544-0001 E-mail: verdu@princeton.edu.

VER DUIN, D'ARLENE K. research scientist; b. Grand Rapids, Mich., Sept. 19, 1952; m. O. Lynn Sims, Mar. 15, 1996. BA in Sociology, U. North Tex., 1995, MPA, 1998. Rsch. scientist U. North Tex., Denton, 1999—. Mem. Ft. Worth Civic Orch. Mem. Am. Sociol. Assn., Pi Alpha Alpha (life). Democrat. Avocations: genealogy, needle arts, viola. Office: Univ North Tex Survey Rsch Ctr PO Box 310637 Denton TX 76203 Business E-Mail: dverduin@scs.unt.edu.

VEREEN, ROBERT CHARLES, retired trade association executive; b. Stillwater, Minn., Sept. 8, 1924; s. George and Leona Lucille (Made) Wihren; m. Rose Catherine Blair, Nov. 5, 1945; children: Robin, Stacy, Kim. Grad. high sch. Mng. editor Comml. West Mag., Mpls., 1946-50, Bruce Pub. Co., St. Paul, 1950-53, Nat. Retail Hardware Assn., Indpls., 1953-59; mng. dir. Liberty Distbrs., Phila., 1959-63; editor Hardware Retailing, Indpls., 1963-80; assoc. pub., dir. communications Nat. Retail Hardware Assn., 1980-84, sr. v.p., 1984-87; Vereen & Assocs., Mgmt., Mktg. Cons., 1987—. Lectr. mgmt. insts.; guest lectr. on distbn. pub.; co-founder U.S.A. Direct; co-founder, ptnr. Eurotrade Mktg., 1988—; ptnr. Hardlines Pers. Finders, 1987—. Author: (with Paul M. Doane) Hunting for Profit, 1965, The Computer Age in Merchandising, 1968, Perpetuating the Family-Owned Business, 1970, The How-To of Merchandising, 1975, The How-To of Store Operations, 1976, A Guide to Financial Management, 1976, Productivity: A Crisis for Management, 1978, Hardlines Rep Report Newsletter, 1984-94, Guidelines to Improve the Rep/Factory Relationships, 1992. Served with AUS, 1943-46. Mem. Am. Soc. Bus. Press Editors (dir., v.p. 1966-70), Soc. Nat. Assn. Publs. (dir., pres. 1970-75, chmn. journalism edn. liaison com. 1976-79), Toastmasters (v.p., treas., sec. 1955-59), Am. Hardware Mfrs. Assn. (co-founder, sec.-treas. Young Execs. Club 1958-,59, 63-65), Hardware-Housewares Packaging Expn. (founder 1960, chmn. com. packaging 1960-62, chmn. judging com. Hardware-Packaging Expn. 1975-78), Packaging Inst., Household Consumer Products Export Coun. (chmn. 1981-83), World-Wide DIY Coun. (exec. sec. 1981-99, dir. emeritus 1999—). Home and Office: 10769 Oriole Ct Indianapolis IN 46231-1006 Office Phone: 317-838-7632.

VEREEN, WILLIAM JEROME, uniform manufacturing company executive; s. William Coachman and Mary Elizabeth V.; m. Lula Evelyn King; children: Elizabeth King, William Coachman. BS in Indsl. Mgmt, Ga. Inst. Tech., 1963. With Riverside Mfg. Co., Moultrie, 1967—, from v.p. to exec. v.p., 1970-77, pres., 1977-84, pres., treas., CEO, 1984—; v.p., dir. Moultrie Cotton Mills, 1969—; exec. v.p. Riverside Industries, Inc., Moultrie, 1973-77, pres., 1977-84, CEO, 1984—, also dir. V.p. Riverside Uniform Rentals, Inc., Moultrie, 1971-80, pres., 1980-84, CEO, bd. dirs.; pres. Riverside Mfg. Co. (Ireland) Ltd., 1977—, Right Image Corp., Riverside Mfg. Co. GmbH, Germany, 1979—, also CEO, dir., 1984; pres., treas., CEO G.A. Rivers Corp., Riverside Mfg. Co. (U.K.) Ltd.; pres., treas. CEO, bd. dirs. Textile Clothing Tech. Corp.; chairholder Tyner eminent scholars, prof. coll. human scis. Fla. State U., 1993-94, mem. coll. human scis. devel. bd.; bd. dirs. Ga. Power Co., Gerber Sci., Inc., Blue Cross/Blue Shield Ga., Cerulean Cos., Inc., Trade and Tourism, Ga. Rsch. Alliance, Ga. Corp. Indsl. Devel.; mem. trilateral commn. apparel labeling NAFTA; so. regional adv. dir. Bank of Am. (GA) (formerly Nations Bank, N.A.); advisor textile and apparel tariffs and quotas U.S. Dept. State Bd.; mem. World Econ. Forum, Davos, Switzerland. Bd. dirs. Moultrie-Colquitt County (Ga.) Devel. Authority, 1973-77, Moultrie-Colquitt County United Givers, 1968-75, Moultrie YMCA, 1968-75, Colquitt County Cancer Soc., 1969-73; trustee Cmty. Welfare Assn. Moultrie, 1970—, Pineland Sch., Moultrie, 1971-75, Leadership Ga., 1972—, Ga. Coun. Econ. Edn.; trustee Am. Apparel Edn. Found.; adv. bd. Ga. Tech. sch. of textile and fiber engring.; elder 1st Presbyterian Ch. Capt. USMCR, 1963-67. Decorated Bronze Star with combat V, Purple Heart. Mem. Internat. Apparel Fedn. (2d v.p., 1st v.p., bd. dirs., exec. com., chmn. 1991-92), Am. Apparel Mfrs. Assn. (bd. dirs., exec. com., edn. found. com., 2d vice chmn., chmn. 1990-91), Nat. Assn. Uniform Mfrs. and Distbrs. (bd. dirs. 1988-91), Am. Apparel Edn. Found. (v.p., trustee), Capital City Club (Atlanta), Commerce Club (Atlanta), World Econ. Forum, Sunset Country Club, Ga. C. of C., Elks, Kiwanis, Sigma Alpha Epsilon. Office: PO Box 460 Moultrie GA 31776-0460

VERE HODGE, RICHARD ANTHONY, pharmaceutical executive, consultant; b. Burnham-on-Sea, Somerset, Eng., Dec. 27, 1943; s. Francis and Eleanor Mary Vere Hodge; married; 3 children. BA, Trinity Coll., Dublin, 1966; DPhil, Worcester Coll., Oxford, Eng., 1969. With Beecham Pharms. (then SmithKline Beecham Pharms., now GlaxoSmithKline), England, 1969-96, project mgr. human interferon project, 1974-76, chief biochemist antiviral chemotherapy project, 1981—92; loaned expert on famciclovir to World-wide Strategic Product Devel., 1993—96, assoc. dir., 1995—96; dir. Vere Hodge Antivirals Ltd., Reigate, Surrey, Eng., 1996—. Cons. Pharmasset, Inc., Atlanta, 2000—. Contbr. articles in profl. jours., chpts. to books; patent for treatment of latent infection of herpesvirus, 1999. Founding mem. Ch. Roof Fund Com., Leigh, Reigate, Surrey, England, 1998—99. Mem. Royal Soc. Chemistry, Am. Soc. Microbiology, Internat. Soc. Antiviral Rsch., The Chromatography Soc. Avocations: bell-ringing, gardening, hill walking. Office: Vere Hodge Antivirals Ltd Leigh Reigate Surrey RH2 8RD England E-mail: averehodge@aol.com.

VERES, BOB, editor; b. 1952; Editor, pub. Inside Info.; editor-at-large Dow Jones Investment Advisor; editor MorningstarAdvisor.com, 2000—. Cons. TIAA-CREF, Am. Express Fin. Svc., J.P. Morgan, Inc. Author: The Cutting Edge in Financial Services, 2003. Office: Morningstar Inc 225 W Wacker Dr Chicago IL 60606

VERFAILLIE, HENDRIK A. food products company executive; b. 1945; Joined Monsanto, St. Louis, 1976, pres. former agrl. group, corp. v.p., 1993, exec. v.p., 1995, pres., CEO, 1999—2002, also bd. dirs.

VERFAILLIE, ROLAND BRUCE, mental health professional; b. Woodbury, N.J., Feb. 27, 1949; s. Roland Bird and Patricia Barbara Verfaillie; m. Donna L. Sessa, May 30, 1980; children: Loren, Eric. PhD, Trinity Coll., 2000. Pre-trial intervention specialist Fla. Dept. Corrections, West Palm Beach, 1973-76; forensic psychologist Lantana Correctional Inst., Dept. Corrections, Lantana, Fla., 1976—79; ctr. dir. the Counseling Ctr., Delray Beach, Fla., 1978-79; dir. cmty. mental health ctr. U.S. Dept. Def., Bad Hersfeld, Germany, 1980—83, supr. psychologist cmty. counseling svcs. Augsburg, Germany, 1983—84, dir. cmty. & family activities Augsburg mil. cmty., 1984—89; unit supr. adolescent substance abuse treatment program Savannas Hosp., Port St. Lucie, Fla., 1989—92; co-founder, exec. dir. Recovery Assics, Inc., Port St. Lucie, 1992—. Adj. prof. Indian River C.C., Ft. Pierce, Fla., 1991—93, Fla. Atlantic U., Boca Raton, Fla., 1978, City Coll., Chgo., 1983—85, U. Md., 1985—88; spkr. in field; cons. Drug Free Workplace Programs, Treasure Coast, Fla., 1992—2001. Author: The Ashley Dancers, 1998, The Lie, 2000, Fast Track, 2001. Employee assistance provider Treasure Coast EAP, 1992—2001; chmn. task force Batterers Intervention Project, Treasure Coast, Fla., 1999—2001. Mem. ACA, Am. Assn. Marriage and Family Counselors, Nat. Assn. Alcoholism and Drug Abuse Counselors, Fla. Alcohol and Drug Abuse Assn. (Bus. Man of Yr. for Fla. 2003). Avocations: running, kayaking, hunting, writing. Home: 672 Cleveland Ave Stuart FL 34994 Office: Recovery Assocs Inc 8000 S US #1 Ste 202 Port Saint Lucie FL 34952 Personal E-mail: versessa@bellsouth.net.

VERGARA, CAMILO JOSÉ, photographer; BA in Sociology, U. Notre Dame, 1968; MA in Sociology, Columbia U., 1977, postgrad. Co-author: Silent Cities: The Evolution of the American Cemetery, 1989; author: The New American Ghetto, 1995 (Robert E. Park award Am. Sociol. Assn., 1997), American Ruins, 1999, Unexpected Chicagoland, 2001, Twin Towers Remembered, 2001. Fellow Revson fellow, Columbia U., 1986—87, MacArthur Found. fellow, 2002.

VERGARE, MICHAEL J. psychiatrist, department chairman; b. Phila., 1945; MD, Hahnemann U., 1971. Bd. cert. gen. psychiatry, bd. cert. geriatric psychiatry. Intern Hahnemann U., Phila., 1971—72, resident psychiatry, 1972—75; assoc. v.p. Belmont Behavioral Health; prof. psychiatry Temple U. Sch. Medicine; chair dept. psychiatry Albert Einstein Med. Ctr.; med. dir. Jefferson Behavioral Health Network; chmn. dept. psychiatry Thomas Jefferson U. and Med. Coll., Phila. Founding mem. Phila. Coalition for the Responsible Closing of Phila. State Hosp.; active Consumer Satisfaction

Team, Phila.; mem. nat. adv. coun. Substance Abuse and Mental Health Svcs. Adminstrn., Ctr. for Mental Health Svcs. Contbr. chapters to books, articles to profl. jours. Recipient Edward Lawlor award, Phila. Psychiat. Soc., 2000, Sr. Citizen Judicare Project Med. Svcs. award, 2001. Mem.: AMA, Am. Psychiat. Assn. Office: Thomas Jefferson Med Coll Dept Psychiatry Ste 210 833 Chestnut E Philadelphia PA 19107

VERGE, PIERRE, legal educator; b. Quebec City, Can., Jan. 9, 1936; s. Francis and Regina (Roy) V.; m. Colette Habel, June 29, 1963; children—Marc, Caroline, Louis. BA, Laval U., 1956, LL.L., 1959, LL.D., 1971; MA, McGill U., 1962, Cambridge U., 1977; LL.M., U. Toronto, 1968; 1971. Bar: Que. 1961, Queen's Counsel 1976. Pvt. practice law, Quebec City, Can., 1961-66; mem. faculty Laval U. Faculty of Law, 1966—, dean, 1973-77, prof. emeritus, 2003—. Commonwealth fellow St. John's Coll., Cambridge U., 1977-78 Mem. Assn. Can. Law Tchrs. (pres. 1972-73, chmn. conf. law deans 1975-76), Que. Bar, Canadian Bar, Royal Soc. Can. Home: 2542 de la Falaise Sillery PQ Canada G1T 1W3 Office: Cite Universitaire Universite Laval Quebec City PQ Canada

VERGER, JOANNE, state representative; Attended, Northwestern State U., La. State U. Cert. speech therapist. State rep., dist. 9 Oreg. House Rep., Salem, 2001—; former mayor City of Coos Bay; co-owner Verger Chrysler. Mem. com. Rules, Restricting, and Pub. Affairs, Transportation. Mem. state bd. Oreg. Easter Seal Soc.; chair campaign United Way; mem. bd. Southwest Oreg. C.C. Found. Named One of Oreg.'s 6 Outstanding Women, 1993. Office: 900 Court St NE H-372 Salem OR 97301

VERGHESE, ABRAHAM CHEERAN, internist, educator, writer; b. Addis Ababa, Ethiopia, May 30, 1955; came to U.S., 1980; s. George and Mary Verghese; children: Steven, Jacob. MD, Madras (India) U., 1979; MFA, U. Iowa, 1991; DSc (hon.), Swarthmore Coll., 2001. Diplomate Am. Bd. Internal Medicine, Am. Bd. Infectious Diseases, Geriatrics., and ulmonary Medicine. Intern Govt. Gen. Hosp., Madrass Med. Coll., 1979-80; resident, chief resident E. Tenn. State U., Johnson City, 1980-83, instr. in medicine, 1982-83, asst. prof. medicine, 1985-88, assoc. prof. medicine, 1988-90; tchg. asst. medicine Boston U., 1983-85; chief infectious diseases VA Med. Ctr., Johnson City, 1986-90, asst. chief medicine, 1988-90; vis. assoc. U. Iowa, Iowa City, 1990-91; prof. medicine Tex. Tech. U., El Paso, Tex., 1991—2002; chief infectious diseases Tex. Tech. Regional Acad. Health Ctr., El Paso, 1991-97; prof. medicine, dir. Ctr. for Med. Humanities and Ethics, U. Tex. Health Scis. Ctr., San Antonio, 2002—. Author: My Own Country: A Doctor's Story of a Town and Its People in the Age of AIDS, 1994, (with others) Infection in the Nursing Home, 1990. Named Tchr. of Yr. Internat. Medicine residents and Alpha Omega Alpha E. Tenn. State U., 1989; recipient James Michener fellowship to Writer's Workshop U. Iowa. Fellow ACP (publs. coms.), Royal Coll. Physicians Can., Infectious Diseases Soc. Am., Coll. Chest Physicians; mem. Am. Geriat. Soc., Am. Fedn. for Clin. Rsch., Am. Soc. Microbiology, Soc. for Exptl. Biology and Medicine. Office: UTHSCSA Mail Code 7730 7703 Floyd Curl Dr San Antonio TX 78229 Home: 9 Inwood Fork San Antonio TX 78248

VERGON, FREDERICK PORTER, JR., lawyer; b. Mesa, Ariz., June 12, 1944; s. Frederick Porter and Adalaide (Boyd) V.; children: Frederick Porter III, Heather Boyd, Sarah McCrea. BA, Denison U., 1966; JD, Case Western Res. U., 1969; postgrad., Cleve. Marshall Coll. Law, 1969-70. Bar: Ohio 1969, U.S. Dist. Ct. Ohio 1970, U.S. Supreme Ct. 1980. Assoc. McNeal & Schick, Cleve., 1969-79; ptnr. McNeal Schick, Archibald & Biro, Cleve., 1979-85; assoc. Cronquist Smith Marshall & Weaver, Cleve., 1985-86; ptnr. Smith Marshall Weaver & Vergon, Cleve., 1986—. Mem. ABA, Ohio State Bar Assn., Cleve. Bar Assn., Def. Rsch. Inst., Ohio Assn. Civil Trial Attys., Internat. Assn. Def. Counsel. Republican. Presbyterian. Office: Smith Marshall Weaver & Vergon 500 National City-E 6 Bldg Cleveland OH 44114 Office Phone: 216-781-4994.

VERHAAREN, HAROLD CARL, lawyer; b. Salt Lake City, Apr. 11, 1938; m. Cynthia Mary Hughes, Nov. 25, 1964; children: Scott Harold, Steven Robert, Jill, Brent Carl, Brian Hughes. JD, U. Utah, 1965. Bar: Utah 1965, US Dist. Ct. Utah 1965, US Ct. Appeals (10th Cir.), 1968, US Supreme Ct. 1978. Law clk. to chief justice Utah Supreme Ct., 1964-65; v.p., bd. dirs. Nielsen & Senior PC, Salt Lake City, 1994—2001. Judge pro tem Small Claims Ct. Salt Lake County, 1978-85; shareholder Nielsen and Sr., 1992-. Chmn. Mt. Olympus Planning Dist., 1971-85; active Boy Scouts Am., 1967-97. Recipient Silver Beaver award Boy Scouts Am. Mem. Utah Bar Assn., Salt Lake County Bar Assn., Am. Arbitration Assn. (panel arbitrators), Delta Theta Phi, Phi Kappa Phi, Phi Eta Sigma. Mem. Lds Ch. Office: 60 E South Temple 11th Fl Salt Lake City UT 84111 E-mail: hcv@ns-law.com.

VERHAGEN, TIMOTHY, utilities executive; married; 3 children. BA, St. Thomas U.; JD cum laude, St. Louis U. Cert. Soc. Human Resources Mgmt. Asst. atty. gen. State of Mo., 1974—76; atty. Shugart Thomson & Kilroy, Kans. City, Mo., 1976—78; sr. atty. The Marley Co., 1978—85, v.p. human resources, 1985—93, United Dominion Industries, Ltd., Charlotte, NC, 1993—98, sr. v.p. human resources, 1998—2001; v.p. human resources Cinergy Corp., Cin., 2001—. Office: Cinergy Corp 139 E 4th St Cincinnati OH 45202

VERHALEN, ROBERT DONALD, consultant; b. Chgo., July 6, 1935; s. William Joseph and Pearl Evelyn (Anderson) V.; m. Phyllis Scandridge, Jan. 11, 1958; children: Elizabeth L., David S. BA, U. Iowa, 1963; MPH, U. N.C., 1965, DrPH, 1972. Expediter Fansteel Metall. Corp., North Chicago, Ill., 1957-58; tech. writer Collins Radio Co., Cedar Rapids, Iowa, 1958-59; rsch. aide Dept. Physics and Astronomy, Iowa City, 1960-63; sanitarian Lake County Health Dept., Waukegan, Ill., 1963-64; cons. safety mgmt. Ga. Dept. Pub. Health, Atlanta, 1965—67; instr. U. N.C., Chapel Hill, 1968-70; chief task force Pres.'s Commn. on Product Safety, Washington, 1969-70; asst. dir. Bur. Product Safety FDA, Washington, 1970-73; assoc. dir. U.S. Consumer Product Safety Commn., Washington, 1973-95; pres. Verhalen & Assocs., McLean, Va., 1995—; gen. ptnr. advotec Investment Ltd. Partnership, McLean, 1997—; chmn. Elmstreet Tech. Group, 1999—. Pres.-elect found. bd. Sch. Pub. Health U. N.C., Chapel Hill, 2000—, guest lectr., 1975—, Walter Reed Army Med. Ctr., Washington, 1982—. Mem. editorial bd. Jour. Safety Rsch.; developer Nat. Electronic Injury Surveillance System; contbr. articles to profl. jours. Sgt. USMC, 1953-57. Mem. Am. Coll. Epidemiology, Soc. Epidemiologic Rsch., Am. Pub. Health Assn., Am. Statis. Assn., Sr. Exec.'s Assn. (charter), Sr. Exec. Svc. Lutheran. Avocation: sailing. Home: 640 Live Oak Dr Mc Lean VA 22101-1563 Office: Verhalen & Assocs 6867 Elm St Ste 300 Mc Lean VA 22101-3871 E-mail: verhalenr@aol.com.

VERHEY, JOSEPH WILLIAM, psychiatrist, educator; b. Oakland, Calif., Sept. 28, 1928; s. Joseph Bernard and Anne (Hanken) V.; BS summa cum laude, Seattle U., 1954; MD, U. Wash., 1958; m. Darlene Helen Seiler, July 21, 1956. Intern, King County Hosp., Seattle, 1958-59; resident Payne Whitney Psychiatric Clinic, N.Y. Hosp., Cornell Med. Center, N.Y.C., 1959-62, U. Wash. Hosp., Seattle, 1962-63; pvt. practice, Seattle, 1963-78; mem. staff U. Providence Hosp., 1963-78, Fairfax Hosp., 1963-78, VA Med. Center, Tacoma, 1978-83, chief inpatient psychiatry sect., 1983—; clin. instr. psychiatry U. Wash. Med. Sch., 1963-68, clin. asst. prof. psychiatry, 1968-82, clin. assoc. prof., 1982—; cons. psychiatry U.S. Dept. Def., Wash. State Bur. Juvenile Rehab.; examiner Am. Bd. Psychiatry and Neurology. Diplomate Am. Bd. Psychiatry and Neurology. Fellow N. Pacific Soc. Psychiatry and Neurology, Am. Psychiat. Assn.; mem. AMA, Am. Fedn. Clin. Rsch., World Fedn. Mental Health, Soc. Mil. Surgeons of U.S., Wash. Athletic Club, Swedish Club (life). Home: 1100 University St Seattle WA 98101-2848 Office: Va Med Ctr Tacoma WA 98493-0001

VERHOEK, SUSAN ELIZABETH, botany educator; b. Columbus, Ohio, 1942; m. S.E. Williams; 1 child. Student, Carleton Coll., 1960-62; BA, Ohio Wesleyan U., 1964; MA, Ind. U., 1966; PhD, Cornell U., 1975. Herbarium supr. Mo. Bot. Garden, St. Louis, 1966-70; asst. prof. Lebanon Valley Coll., Annville, Pa., 1974-82, assoc. prof., 1982-85, prof., 1985—. Vis. researcher Cornell U., Ithaca, N.Y., 1982-83; content cons. Merrill Pub. Co., 1987-89; vis. profl. Chgo. Bot. Garden, 1991. Author: How to Know the Spring Flowers, 1982; contbr. articles to profl. jours., newspapers, and bulls. Trustee Lebanon Valley Coll., Annville, 1979-82, 84-90, 92-98; dir. Lebanon Valley Coll. Arboretum, 1996—. Mem. Soc. for Econ. Botany (pres. 1985-86), Bot. Soc. Am., Am. Assn. Bot. Gardens and Arboreta. Office: Lebanon Valley Coll Dept Biology Annville PA 17003-0501 Office Phone: 717-867-6178. Business E-Mail: verhoek@lvc.edu.

VERHOEVEN, CHARLES K. lawyer; BBA with distinction, U. Iowa, 1985, JD with high distinction, 1988. Assoc. Cravath, Swaine & Moore, N.Y.C., 1988—93; ptnr., head No. Calif. offices Quinn Emanuel et al, Redwood Shores, Calif., 1993—. Mem.: Iowa Law Rev., 1986—87, articles editor:, 1987—88. Named one of Top 20 Lawyers in Calif. Under 40 Yrs. Old, Calif. Law Bus. Mem.: ABA, Assn. Bar City of New York, State Bar N.Y., State Bar Calif. Office: Quinn Emauel et al 555 Twin Dolphin Dr Ste 560 Redwood City CA 94065 Business E-Mail: charlesverhoeven@quinnemanuel.com.

VERHOEVEN, PAUL, film director; b. Amsterdam, Netherlands, July 18, 1938; PhD in Maths., Physics, U. Leiden. Dir. (films) Wat Zien Ik?, 1971, Turkish Delight, 1973, Keetje Tippel, 1975, Spetters, 1981, The Fourth Man, 1983, Robocop, 1987, Total Recall, 1990, Basic Instinct, 1992, Showgirls, 1995, Starship Troopers, 1997, Hollow Man, 2000, (TV) Hitchhiker, Floris, 1969, (documentary with the Royal Netherlands Navy) Het Korps Mariniers, 1965; dir., co-screenwriter Soldier of Orange, 1979, Flesh and Blood, 1985. Office: Care Beth Swofford 9830 Wilshire Blvd Beverly Hills CA 90212-1804

VERING, JOHN ALBERT, lawyer; b. Marysville, Kans., Feb. 6, 1951; s. John Albert and Bernadine E. (Kieffer) V.; m. Ann E. Arman, June 28, 1980; children: Julia Ann, Catherine Ann, Mary Ann. BA summa cum laude, Harvard U., 1973; JD, U. Va., 1976. Bar: Mo. 1976, U.S. Dist. Ct. (we. dist.) Mo. 1976, U.S. Ct. Appeals (10th cir.), 1980, U.S. Ct. Appeals (4th cir.) 1987, Kans. 1990, U.S. Dist. Ct. Kans. 1990; arbitrator, mediator. Assoc. Dietrich, Davis, Dicus, Rowlands, Schmitt & Gorman, Kansas City, Mo., 1976-81, ptnr., 1982—. Editor: U. Va. Law Rev., 1974-76. Bd. dirs. Greater Kansas City YMCA Southwest Dist., 1987. Mem.: Labor and Employment Law Com. (chmn. 2003), Kansas City Metro Bar Assoc., Harvard Club (adv. bd. schs. com. Kansas City 1977—2004, v.p. 1981—82, 1992—93, pres. 1994—96). Roman Catholic. Home: 1210 W 68th Ter Kansas City MO 64113-1904 Office: Armstrong Teasdale LLP 2345 Grand Blvd Ste 2000 Kansas City MO 64108-2617 Office Phone: 816-221-3420. Business E-Mail: jvering@armstrongteasdale.com.

VERINK, ELLIS DANIEL, JR., metallurgical engineering educator, consultant; b. Peking, China, Feb. 9, 1920; s. Ellis Daniel and Phoebe Elizabeth (Smith) V.; m. Martha Eulala Owens, July 4, 1942; children: Barbara Ann, Wendy Susan. BS, Purdue U., 1941; MS, Ohio State U., 1963, PhD, 1965. Registered profl. engr., Fla., Pa., Calif. Mgr. chem. sect., sales devel. divsn. Alcoa, New Kensington, Pa., 1946-59, mgr. chem. and petroleum indsl. sales Pitts., 1959-62; assoc. prof. metall. engring. U. Fla., Gainesville, 1965-68, prof. materials sci. and engring., 1968—, disting. svc. prof., 1984-91, prof. emeritus, 1991—; pres. Materials Cons., Inc., 1970—. Cons. Aluminum Assn., Washington, 1966-84; mem. U.S. nuclear waste tech. rev. bd., 1989-97. Author: Corrosion Testing Made Easy, The Basics, 1993; editor: Methods of Materials Selections, 1968, Material Stability and Environmental Degradation, 1988; contbr. articles to profl. jours. Pres. Gainesville YMCA, 1977. Recipient Sam Tour award ASTM, 1979, Donald E. Marlowe award Am. Soc. Engring. Edn., 1991; recipient Disting. Alumnus award Ohio State U., 1982, Disting. Faculty award Fla. Blue Key, 1983; named Tchr.-Scholar of Year U. Fla., 1979 Fellow Metall. Soc. of AIME (pres. 1984, Educator of Yr. award 1988), Am. Soc. Materials Internat., Nat. Assn. Corrosion Engrs. Internat. (bd. dirs. 1984-87, Willis Rodney Whitney award; mem. Masons, Shriners, Kiwanis, Sigma Xi, Tau Beta Pi. Republican. Presbyterian. Office: U Fla Dept Materials Sci Eng Gainesville FL 32611 Home: Apt M224 7805 NW 28th Pl Gainesville FL 32606-8659

VERLICH, JEAN ELAINE, writer, public relations consultant; b. McKeesport, Pa., July 5, 1950; d. Matthew Louis and Irene (Tomko) V.; m. S(tanley) Wayne Wright, Sept. 29, 1979 (div. June 1988). Student, Bucknell U., 1968-69; BA, U. Pitts., 1971. Pres. sec. Com. to Re-elect Pres., S.W. Pa., 1972; adminstrv. asst. Pa. Rep. James B. Kelly III, 1972-73; reporter Beaver (Pa.) County Times, 1973-74; proofreader Ketchum, MacLeod & Grove, Pitts., 1975-76; cmty. rels. specialist PPG Industries, Pitts., 1976-77; editor PPG News, 1977-79, sr. staff writer, 1979-84, comm. coord., 1984-85; pub. rels. assoc. Glass Group, 1986-87; mgr. pub. rels. Glass Group PPG Industries, 1987-92; account mgr. Maddigan Comm., Pitts., 1992-93; owner JV Comm., Pitts., 1993—. Mem. Internat. Assn. Bus. Communicators (bd. dirs. Pitts. chpt. 1981, v.p. pub. rels. Pitts. chpt. 1982, v.p. programs Pitts. chpt. 1985, pres. Pitts. chpt. 1986), Travelers Aid Soc. Pitts. (bd. dirs. 1992-95, v.p. 1994-95), Phi Beta Kappa, Delta Zeta, Automotive Pub. Rels. Coun. Office: JV Comm PO Box 11114 Pittsburgh PA 15237-0414 Office Phone: 724-933-0242. E-mail: jverlich@jvcommunications.com.

VERMA, ARUN K. mathematician, educator; b. Dibrugarh, India, June 1955; 3 children. MSc, Dibrugarh U., India, 1977; Diploma, PhD, Indian Inst. of Tech., Kharagpur, India, 1980. Lectr. in math. Regional Engring. Coll., Silchar, India, 1984—89; rsch. assoc. Hampton U., Hampton, Va., 1989—89, vis. lectr. in math., 1989—92, asst. prof. of math., 1992—93, assoc. prof. of math., 1993—2001, prof. of math., 2001—03. Reader for AP calculus Ednl. Testing Svcs., Princeton, NJ, 1998—2004; ASEE summer faculty fellow NASA Langley Rsch. Ctr., Hampton, Va., 2000; U.S. EdD project cons. Ala. State U., Montgomery, Ala., 2002—03; Schev project cons. Norfolk State U., Norfolk, Va., 2002—03; faculty summer rsch. participant Oak Ridge Inst. for Sci. and Rsch., Oak Ridge, Tenn., 1993—93. Coord. Yorktown 4th July Committe, Yorktown, Va., 2002—04; elected com. mem. Internat. Baccalaureate Adv. Coun., Yorktown, Va., 2000—04; nominated com. mem. New Horizon Governors Sci. & Tech. Adv. Com., Hampton, Va., 2000—04; v.p. Hindu Temple of Hampton Roads, Chesapeake, Va., 2000—04. Named Leader in Edn., Hewlett-Packard Inc., 2000; recipient William C. Lowry Outstanding Math. Tchr. award, coll. level, Va. Coun. of Teachers of Math., 2001, 2002 QEM (Quality Edn. for Minorities) Excellence in Math. and/or Sci. Tchg. award, 2002. Mem.: Nat. Tech. Assn., Va. Coun. of Teachers of Math., Math. Assn. of Am., Sigma Xi. Office: Hampton U E Queen St Hampton VA 23668 Personal E-mail: akverma@cox.net. E-mail: arun.verma@hamptonu.edu.

VERMA, DEVESH, pharmaceutical executive, researcher; s. Dinesh Chandra and Kiran Verma; m. Reema Prakash, July 8, 2000; 1 child, Saransh. BS, Indian Inst. of Tech., 1993; MS, U. of Minn., 1994, PhD, 2000. Sr. scientist Bios Group, Superior, Colo., 2001; assoc. dir. MarketRx, Inc, Bridgewater, NJ, 2001—. Ops. rsch. developer Delta Air Lines - Delta Tech., Atlanta, 1999—2001. Contbr. articles to profl. jours. Recipient Presdl. Silver medal, Indian Inst. of Tech., Kharagpur, 1993. Achievements include research in a process model to manage multiple- concurrent new product development projects.

VERMA, DINESH, ophthalmologist, researcher; b. New Delhi, Nov. 9, 1957; s. Anand Prakash and Chander Kanta Verma; m. Sumita Kher, May 15, 1989; 1 child, Nitish. MBBS, Maulana Azad Med. Coll., New Delhi, 1974—78; MD in Ophthalmology, All India Inst. Med. Scis., New Delhi, 1980—83. Cert. Gen. Med. Coun., 1983, Calif. Med. Bd., 2002. Cons. ophthalmologist with spl. interest in vitreoretinal surgery Hull Royal Infirmary, Kingston-upon-Hull, England, 1994—2001; hon. sr. clin. lectr. U. Hull, Kingston-upon-Hull, England, 1998—2001; vis. assoc. prof., ophthalmology Wilmer Eye Inst., Johns Hopkins U. Hosps., Balt., 2001—02; assoc. prof., clin. ophthalmology Doheny Eye Inst., L.A., 2002—. Author: (book) Relative Happiness. Sec. Brit. Indian Ophthalmologists Social Club, London, 1997—2001; pres. Maulana Azad Med. Coll. Old Students Alumni, Kingston-upon-Hull, England, 2000—01, Hull & East Yorkshire Hindu Soc., Kingston-upon-Hull, England, 1999—2001; joint sec. Ophthalmic Rsch. Assn., New Delhi, 1981—82, sec., 1982—83. Grantee, PPP Found., London, 2001—02. Fellow: Royal Coll. Ophthalmologists (examiner 1998—2001), Royal Coll. Surgeons Edinburgh (examiner 1997—2001); mem.: Assn. for Rsch. in Vision and Ophthalmology, Am. Telemedicine Assn., Am. Acad. Ophthalmology. Hindu. Achievements include development of the first Virtual Reality Simulator for Eye Surgery; invention of Maculog, a device to measure the posturing time for patients undergoing Macular Hole Surgery; first to do laser scleral buckling using a CO2 laser. Avocations: sketching, painting, writing. Office: Doheny Eye Inst 1490 San Pablo St DEI-3611 Los Angeles CA 90033 Personal E-mail: dverma36@hotmail.com. E-mail: dverma@usc.edu.

VERMA, INDER M. biochemist; b. Sangrur, Punjab, India, Nov. 28, 1947; MSc, Lucknow U., India, 1966; PhD in Biochemistry, Weizmann Inst. Sci., Rehovot, Israel, 1971. From asst. prof. to assoc. prof. Salk Inst., 1974-83; sr. mem. Molecular Biology & Virology Lab, 1983-85; prof. Molecular Biology, 1985-95; prof. Lab. Genetics Salk Inst., 1995—. Fellow Jane Coffin Childs Meml. Fund, 1970-73; Reverend Soloman B. Caulker Meml. fellow, 1967-70; adj. assoc. prof. U. Calif. San Diego, 1979-83, adj. prof. Biology, 1983—; mem. Virology Study Sec., 1981-85, elected mem., Inst. of Medicine, 1999. Recipient medal Outstanding Scientist N. Am. Scientists of Indian Origin, 1985-86; merit award NIH, 1987, outstanding investigator award, 1988; bd. trustees Salk Inst., 1989-91 & 94—; mem. acad. coun., 1989—; vchmn. Fac. and Acad. coun., 1989-90 & 94-95; chmn., 1991-92 & 96-97, prof. Molecular Biology, Am. Cancer Soc., 1990; lectr. Purdue U., 1991, Sch. Med. Vanderbilt U., 1992, TATA Meml. Hosp., Bombay, India, 1992, U. Chgo., 1992, Queenstown, New Zealand, 1993, N.Y.U., 1993, Bar-Ilan U., Ramat Gan, Israel, and others. Mem. Nat. Acad. Sci., Am. Cancer Soc. Office: Salk Inst Biol Studies 10010 N Torrey Pines Rd La Jolla CA 92037-1099

VERMA, SATYA BHUSHAN, optometrist, educator; b. Multan, Punjab, India; s. Hari C. and Satwanti (Girdhar) V.; m. Asha C. Valecha, Dec. 28, 1974; children: Pooja, Kajal. DR OPT, Sch. Optometry GEH, Aligarh, India, 1964; BA, Delhi U., 1968; AO, U. Calif. Berkeley, 1971; OD, Pa. Coll. Optometry, 1975. Diplomate Am. Acad. Optometry, Pub. Health and Environ. Optometry. Refractionist Eye Dept. Willingdon Hosp., New Delhi, India, 1967-70; assoc. Sch. Optometry U. Calif., Berkeley, 1970-71; assoc. Pa. Coll. Optometry, Phila., 1971-75, asst. prof., 1976—. Cons. East Coast Migrant Health, Washington, 1990—. Contbr. chpts. in books and articles to profl. jours. Bd. dirs. Bridgeport-Upper Merion Lions Club, pres. 1987; chair scholarship com. AIP Found., Morrestown, N.J., 1994—; del. White House Conf. on Aging, 1995. Named Optometrist of Yr., Am. Optometric Assn., 1998; recipient Disting. Svc. award Prevent Blindness Am., 1998, Disting. Practitioner in Optometry Nat. Acads. Practice, 2000; primary care health policy fellow DHHS, 2003. Fellow Am. Acad. Optometry (Carl C. Koch Meml. award 2002); mem. APHA (chair vision care sect.), Nat. Coun. Aging (bd. dirs., exec. com., chair health promotion inst.), Nat. Vol. Orgn. for Ind. Living for Aging (chair 1992-94), Pa. Optometric Assn. (pres. 1996, past pres. 1997—, OD of Yr. 1997, 86, George Gottschalk Meml. award 1985), Chester-Delaware County Optometric Soc. (pres. 1982-84, OD of Yr. 1997, 86). Democrat. Hindu. Avocations: golf, tennis. Office: Pa Coll Optometry 8360 Old York Rd Elkins Park PA 19027-1516 E-mail: satya@pco.edu.

VERMA, SURJIT KUMAR, retired school system administrator; b. India, May 17, 1940; arrived in Canada 1966; s. Sohara Lal and Gian Devi V.; m. Raj Verma; 1 child, Sonia. MEd, St. Francis Xavier U., N.S., 1975; postgrad., Dalhousie U., N.S., U. Ottawa, Ont., Can, 1979. Cert. tchr. Nova Scotia. Sci. dept. head Halifax County Bedford Dist. Sch. Bd., N.S., Canada, 1968-88, curriculum supr., 1988-94; ret., 1995. Served on C.T.F. Project Overseas Can. Teams, W.I., Nigeria, 1976, 77; mem. provincial sci. task force, biology rev. com., elem. sci. Nova Scotia Dept. Edn.; mem. Internat. Sci. Symposium, 1979; mem. selection panel PromoSci. Program. Natural Scis. and Engring. Rsch. Coun. of Can.; mem. exec. coun. N.S. Inst. Sci.; worksop presenter numerous sci. workshops. Contbr. to profl. jours. Chmn. First Metro Halifax Dartmouth Reg Sci. Fair, 1975; co-chmn. Canada Wide Sci Fair, 1984. Recipient Sci. Tchg. Achievement Recognition award, U.S. Nat. Sci. Tchrs. Assn. and Am. Gas Assn., 1993, Profl. Devel. award, N.S. Tchrs. Union, Tchg. Excellence in Sci., Tech. and Math. award, Prime Min. Can., 1993, 1994, Sci. on Display award, NASCO, 1993—94, Outstanding Achievement in Sci. Edn. award, Halifax County Sch. Bd., 1993, Surjit Verma award for tchg. excellence created in his honor, Halifax County Bedrod Dist. Sch. Bd., 1994, Michael Smith award, Industry Can., 1996, Maritimer of the Week award, Atlantic TV and Can. TV Network, 2003, Maritimer of Week award, Atlantic T.V. and Can. T.V. Network, 2003; fellow, U. Ottawa, 1979; scholar, N.S. Tchrs. Union, 1979; grad. fellow, Dalhousie U., 1980, Math. Sci. Tech. Edn. fellow, Royal Bank Queen's U., 1994, rsch. devel. grantee, Dalhousie U., 1979, Can./N.S. Tech. Devel. grantee, 1995. Mem. Nova Scotia Inst. Sci. (coun. mem.), Natural Sci. and Engring. Rsch. Coun. (mem. selection panel promosci. project). Avocations: jogging, yoga. Home: 49 Rosewood Ave Timberlea NS Canada B3T 1C6 E-mail: rsverma49@yahoo.com.

VERME, ALBERTO J. investment banker; b. Peru; BA in Econs., Denison U., 1979; MBA, Columbia U., 1984. With The World Bank, 1979—83; joined The First Boston Corp., 1983, co-head emerging markets, 1988—90; dir. and head Credit Suisse First Boston, Spain, 1990—92; pres. MG Global Capital, London, 1992—94; CEO MG Valores, Madrid, Metallgesellschaft AG, 1992—94; chmn. L.Am. Investment Bank Citigroup (formerly Salomon Bros.), 1994—, global head energy, power and chems., 1994—, mng. dir. and global head investment banking global corp. and investment banking group, 1994—. Office: Citigroup Global Corp and Investment Banking Group 390 Greenwich St New York NY 10013*

VERMEER, MAUREEN DOROTHY, sales executive; b. Bronxville, N.Y., Mar. 21, 1945; d. Albert Casey and Helen (Valentine Casey) Vermeer; m. John R. Fassnacht, Feb. 11, 1966 (div. 1975); m. George M. Dallas Peltz IV, Oct. 26, 1985. Grad., NYU Real Estate Inst., 1976. Lic. real estate broker, notary pub., N.Y. With Douglas Elliman, N.Y.C., 1965-74, mgmt. supr., 1974-78, v.p., 1978-83; real estate broker Rachmani Corp., N.Y.C., 1983-84; v.p. sales and mktg. Carol Mgmt. Corp., N.Y.C., 1984-90; v.p. mktg. The Sunshine Group, N.Y.C., 1990; v.p., sec., bd. dirs. H.J. Kalikow & Co., N.Y.C., 1991—. Mem. Real Estate Bd. N.Y. (bd. dirs., residential mgmt. com.), Assn. Real Estate Women (bd. dirs. charitable fund). Republican. Presbyterian. Avocations: skiing, scuba diving. Home: 111 Broadway Norwood NJ 07648-1412 Office: H J Kalikow & Co 101 Park Ave Fl 25 New York NY 10178-0002

VERMEIL, DICK, professional football coach; b. Calistoga, Calif., Oct. 30, 1936; m. Carolyn Drake; 3 children. Head coach UCLA, 1974—75, Phila. Eagles, 1976—82; football coach St. Louis Rams, 1997-2000; pub. spkr. Nationwide Spkrs. Bur., Beverly Hills, Calif., 2000—01; head coach Kansas City Chiefs, 2001—. Tv analyst with CBS, ABC. Named Coach of Yr. on four levels, high sch., jr. coll., NFL Coach of the Yr. 1980, 1999, nat. collegiate Divsn. I, NFL; named first fulltime spl. teams coach in NFL history, L.A. Rams, 1969. Career highlights include: head coach Super Bowl XXXIV champion St. Louis Rams, 2000, becoming the oldest coach in NFL history to win a Super Bowl; only coach in history to win both the Super Bowl and the Rose bowl; only 4th coach in history to lead two different teams to Super Bowl (Phil., St. Louis). Office: Kansas City Chiefs One Arrowhead Drive Kansas City MO 64129*

VERMETTE, RAYMOND EDWARD, clinical laboratories administrator; b. Lewiston, Maine, June 30, 1942; m. Ernestine Pero, Dec. 29, 1963; children: Tamara, Gregory. BS in Bacteriology, U. Maine, 1964; MS in Biochemistry, U. Wis., 1966; MBA, Temple U., 1973; master tchr.'s cert., Cath. Diocese Boston, 1981. Cert. in pers. mgmt., Va. Supr. animal toxicology Hazleton Labs., Vienna, Va., 1967-71; pers. mgr. Damon Clin. Lab., Phila., 1971-73, ops. mgr., 1973-75, gen. mgr. Needham Heights, Mass., 1975-90; v.p. ops. Damon Corp., Needham Heights, 1983-87, corp. v.p., 1987-89, sr. v.p., 1990—93; sr. v.p., gen. mgr. Corning/MetPath, Westwood, Mass., 1994-95; ret., 1995. Vis. lectr. fin. mgmt. and bus. adminstrn. Framingham State Coll., 1978—84; instr. mgmt. Newbury Jr. Coll., Boston, 1976—79; health care mgmt. cons., 2001—. Author: (with B. Kliman and E. Kolowrat) What You Should Know About Medical Lab Tests, 1979. V.p. fin. com., Framingham, Mass., 1982—84; mem. capital budget com. Town of Framingham, 1987;

mem-elect Framingham Town Meeting, 1987—90, Govt. Study Com., 1995—97, mem. fin. com., 1997—2001; chmn. bd. religious edn. Cath. Ch., Framingham, 1981—84, co-chmn. pre-marriage preparation coun., 1981—99, organist, 1979—. Democrat. Home: 11 Willowbrook Dr Framingham MA 01702-5515

VERMEULE, CORNELIUS CLARKSON, III, museum curator; b. Orange, N.J., Aug. 10, 1925; s. Cornelius Clarkson, Jr. and Catherine Sayre (Comstock) V.; m. Emily Dickinson Townsend, Feb. 2, 1957 (dec. Feb. 6, 2001); children: Emily D. Blake, Cornelius Adrian Comstock. Grad., Pomfret Sch., 1943; AB, Harvard, 1949, MA, 1951; PhD, U. London, Eng., 1953; DHL (hon.), Boston Coll., 1995. Instr. fine arts, then asst. prof. U. Mich., 1953-55; asst. prof. classical archaeology Bryn Mawr (Pa.) Coll., 1955-57; curator classical art Mus. Fine Arts, Boston, 1956-96, curator emeritus, 1996—, acting dir., 1972-73, hon. visitor ancient art, 2002—; assoc. curator coins Mass. Hist. Soc., 1965-71, curator, 1971—. Lectr. fine arts Smith Coll., 1960-64, Boston U., Harvard, Wellesley Coll.; vis. prof. Yale, 1969-70, 72-73; Thomas Spencer Jerome lectr. U. Mich., 1975-76; vis. prof. Boston Coll., 1978-97; vis. prof. U. Aberdeen, Scotland, 1993; pres. Internat. Com. to Save Jewish Catacombs of Italy, 1980-84, chmn., 1984-98, dir. 1998-2000; cons. classical art Worcester Art Mus., 1998-2001. Author: (with N. Jacobs) Japanese Coinage, 1948, 2d edit., 1972, Bibliography of Applied Numismatics, 1956, The Goddess Roma, 1959, 2d edit., 1974, Dal Pozzo-Albani Drawings, 1960, European Art and the Classical Past, 1964, Drawings at Windsor Castle, 1966, Roman Imperial Art in Greece and Asia Minor, 1968, Polykleitos, 1969, Numismatic Art in America, 1971, (with M. Comstock) Greek Etruscan and Roman Bronzes, 1972, (with N. Neuerburg) Catalogue of the Ancient Art in the J. Paul Getty Museum, 1973, Greek and Roman Sculpture in Gold and Silver, 1974, Greek and Roman Cyprus, 1976, (with M. Comstock) Sculpture in Stone, 1976, Greek Sculpture and Roman Taste, 1977, Roman Art: Early Republic to Late Empire, 1978, (with A Herrmann) The Ernest Brummer Collections, Vol. II, 1979, Greek Art: Socrates to Sulla, 1980, The Jewish Experience in Roman Art, 1981, Masterpieces of Greek and Roman Sculpture in America, 1982, Greek Art: Prehistoric to Perikles, 1982, Numismatic Studies, 1983, Alexander the Great Conquers Rome, 1985, The Cult Images of Imperial Rome, 1986, Numismatic Art of the Greek Imperial World, 1987, Philatelic Art in America, 1987, (with M. Comstock) Sculpture in Stone and Bronze, 1988, (with A. Brauer) Stone Sculptures, The Greek, Roman and Etruscan Collections of the Harvard University Art Museums, 1990, (with others) Le Sport dans la Grèce Antique, 1992, Du Jeu à la Compétition, 1992, (with others) El Deporte en la Grecia Antigua, La génesis del olimpismo, 1992-93, (with others) Vase-Painting in Italy, 1993, (with others) Eye of the Beholder, Masterpieces from the Isabella Stewart Gardner Museum, 2003, Art and Archaeology of Antiquity, Vols. I-IV, 2001-04; mem. editl. bd. Minerva, 2002—. Trustee Cardinal Spellman Philatelic Mus., 1980-93. Served to 1st lt. AUS, 1943-47. Recipient Bicentennial medal Boston Coll., 1976; Fulbright fellow, 1951-53; Guggenheim fellow, 1968 Fellow AAAS, Am. Numis. Soc. (life), Royal Numis. Soc., Soc. Antiquaries; mem. Coll. Art Assn. (life), Archaeol. Inst. Am. (life) German Archaeol. Inst., Holland Soc. N.Y., Colonial Lords of Manors in Am., Mass. Hist. Soc. (hon.); Tavern Club (medalist 1986, Boston). Home: 47 Coolidge Hill Rd Cambridge MA 02138-5509 Office: Mus Fine Arts 465 Huntington Ave Boston MA 02115-5597 *To teach, collect and record the past, as exemplar for the present, as prologue to the future, can there be any better use of a historian's and archaeologist's professional life?*

VERMILYE, PETER HOAGLAND, banker; b. N.Y.C., Jan. 17, 1920; s. Herbert Noble and Elise Tace (Hillyer) V.; m. Lucy Shaw Mitchell, Oct. 14, 1950; children: Peter H., Dana R., Andrew R., Mary S. AB, Princeton U., 1940. V.p. pension investments J.P. Morgan & Co. and Morgan Guaranty Trust, 1940-64; ptnr. State St. Research & Mgmt., Boston, 1965-69; pres. Alliance Capital Mgmt., N.Y.C., 1970-77; sr. v.p., chief investment officer Citibank, N.Y.C., 1977-84; chmn. Baring Am. Asset Mgmt., Boston, 1984-89; sr. advisor Baring Asset Mgmt., 1990-95, Harbor Capital Mgmt., Boston, 1996—. Chmn. emeritus Huntington Theatre, 1989-96; bd. dirs. Engelhard Hanovia, Breadstreet Holdings Corp. Trustee Boston U., 1970—. Mem.: Brook, Somerset, Myopia. Home: 157 School St Manchester MA 01944-1236 also: 107 Chestnut St Boston MA 02108-1038 Office: Harbor Capital Mgmt 125 High St Fl 26 Boston MA 02110-2704 Address: 75 State St Ste 2700 Boston MA 02109

VERMILYEA, STANLEY GEORGE, prosthodontist, educator; b. Portland, Oreg., Jan. 29, 1946; s. Stanley Edmonds and Hattie Willamina (Bittner) V.; m. Barbara Jean Koester Ternus, June 23, 1967 (div. Dec. 1979); 1 child, Sheryl Eileen; m. Ileana Esther Villamarzo, July 3, 1980; children: Michael Enrique, Josue Jorge. BS, Portland State Coll., 1970; DMD, U. Oreg., Portland, 1971; MS in Dental Materials, U. Mich., 1976; cert. in prosthodontics, Walter Reed Army Med. Ctr., Washington, 1985. Diplomate Am. Bd. Prosthodontics. Commd. 2d lt. U.S. Army, 1971, advanced through grades to col., 1985, dentist, 1971-76; rschr. dental materials U.S. Army Inst. Dental Rsch., Washington, 1976-80, chief dental materials rsch., 1980-83; prosthodontist U.S. Army, various locations, 1983-89, co-dir. residency in prosthodontics Washington, 1989-92, ret., 1992; asst. prof. Coll. Dentistry Ohio State U., Columbus, 1992-95, chmn. primary care, 1996—, assoc. dean clin. affairs, 2001—. Contbr. chpt. to book and articles to profl. jours. Fellow Am. Coll. Prosthodontists, Acad. Gen. Dentistry; mem. Internat. Assn. Dental Rsch. Achievements include research on the corrosion characteristics of dental alloys as well as the compositions and microstructural features of dental materials. Office: Ohio State U Coll Dentistry 305 W 12th Ave Columbus OH 43210-1267 E-mail: vermilyea.1@osu.edu.

VERMYLEN, PAUL ANTHONY, JR., oil company executive; b. N.Y.C., Dec. 5, 1946; s. Paul Anthony and Nancy Primrose (Barr) Vermylen; m. Robin S. Collins, Jan. 24, 1970; children: Robert T.C., Nancy Barr, Sarah Morgan, Paul Anthony III. AB, Georgetown U., 1968; MBA, Columbia U., 1971. V.p. Citibank N.A., N.Y.C., 1971-78; treas. Commonwealth Oil Refining Co., San Antonio, 1978-81, v.p. fin., chief fin. officer, 1981-82; v.p., chief fin. officer, dir. Meenan Oil Co., Inc., Syosset, NY, 1982—91, pres., 1992—2001, Meenan Oil Co., L.P., 1992—2001; chmn. Kestrel Energy Co., Inc., Huntington, NY, 2002—. Bd. dirs. Petroleum Industry Rsch. Found., 1992—2002. Bd. dirs. Huntington Arts Coun., N.Y.C., 1983—89, v.p., 1986—87, pres., 1987—89; bd. dirs. Cold Spring Harbor Whaling Mus., 1995—2000; bd. advisors Cold Spring Harbor Lab. DNA Learning Ctr., 1991—2000; bd. regents Georgetown U., Washington, 1997—2003; trustee Girls Prep. Charter Sch., N.Y.C., 2004—, bd. dirs., 2004—. Mem.: Empire State Petroleum Assn. (bd. dirs. 1994—2001), N.Y. Yacht Club, Cold Spring Harbor Beach Club. Office: 6900 Jericho Tpke Syosset NY 11791-4499

VERNARELLI, MICHAEL JOSEPH, economics educator, consultant; b. Rochester, N.Y., Nov. 24, 1948; s. S. John and Angelica Dolores (Morabito) V.; m. Joan Ann Taylor, Oct. 4, 1975; children: Jacqueline Andrea, Laurel Aileen. BA in Econs., U. Mich., 1970; MA in Econs., SUNY, Binghamton, 1974, PhD in Econs., 1978. Account analyst Travelers Ins. Co., Rochester, 1970-71; rsch. assoc. Ctrl. Adminstrn. SUNY, 1975-76; prof. econs. Rochester Inst. Tech., 1976—, chmn. dept., 1987—. Cons. econs. Rochester Downtown Devel. Corp., 1980; rsch. economist divsn. housing rsch. HUD, Washington, 1980-81, vis. scholar, 1980; pres., forensic economist Rochester Econ. Cons., 1983—; vis. prof. U.S. Bus. Sch. in Prague, 1992-96. Contbg. author: Federal Housing Policy and Desegregation, 1986. Mem. Brighton (N.Y.) Bd. Archtl. Rev., 1990-91, mem. planning bd., 1991-98. Recipient Eisenhart award Rochester Inst. Tech., 1987; grantee SUNY, Binghamton, 1974. Mem. Am. Econ. Assn., Nat. Assn. Forensic Economists, Ea. Econ. Assn., Greater Rochester C. of C. (panel mem. bus. trends com. 1987—), Omicron Delta Epsilon. Roman Catholic. Avocation: golf. Home: 133 Esplanade Dr Rochester NY 14610-3325 Office: Rochester Inst Tech Rochester NY 14623-0887 Office Phone: 585-475-2455. Personal E-mail: mjvern11@aol.com. Business E-Mail: mjvgss@rit.edu.

VERNAVA, ANTHONY MICHAEL, lawyer; b. N.Y.C., May 13, 1937; s. Michel Antonio Vernava and Ana Avellina Guerriero. BS, Georgetown U., 1959; JD, Harvard U., 1962; LLM, NYU, 1965; MA in L.Am. Studies/Internat. Fin., George Washington U., 1999. Bar: N.Y. 1962, U.S. Dist. Ct. (so. and ea. dists.) N.Y. 1963, U.S. Ct. Appeals (2nd cir.) 1963, Mich. 1965, U.S. Dist. Ct. (ea. dist.) Mich. 1966, U.S. Tax Ct. 1966, U.S. Supreme Ct. 1966, Ill. 1973. Atty. Reid & Priest, N.Y.C., 1962-63, IBM Corp., Armonk, N.Y., 1963-65; assoc. prof. Wayne State U., Detroit, 1965-68, prof., 1968-72; pvt. practice law Detroit and Chgo., 1972-75; prof. law So. Meth. U., Dallas, 1975-76; prof. law, consulting atty. U. Detroit Sch. Law, 1976-95; pvt. practice internat. cons. Fairfax, Va., 1995—. Arbitrator Mich. Employment Rels. Commn., Detroit, 1988-95. Contbr. articles to profl. jours. Mem. ABA, N.Y. State Bar. Avocations: international travel, pre-colombian civilizations, boating, hiking. Office: PO Box 99 Oakton VA 22124-0099

VERNAZZA, TRISH BROWN (TRISH EILEEN BROWN), visual artist, art therapist, sculptor; b. Tampa, Fla., Mar. 22, 1958; d. Burrell Joseph and Katharine Stowell (Weekly) B. BFA in Art History, U. South Fla., 1993; MA in Clin. Feminist Psychology, New Coll. Calif., 1997; postgrad., U. Calif., Berkeley, 1997. Lic. marriage and family therapist, art therapist; older adult tchr. Flight attendant Pan Am. World Airways, N.Y.C., 1989-91; art therapist jail psychiat. svcs. Haight Ashbury Free Clinics, Tampa, 1997-99; art instr. to older and disabled adults, 1999—; program mgr. Mental Health Sys., 2002—; pvt. practice psychotherapy Oceanside, 2003—. Judge John's Seafood Festival, Madeira Beach, Fla., program mgr., Mental Health Sys., 2002—04. Artist: worked with HIV Women/AIDS Artreach phase 3, sculpture, 1994; group shows include Centre Gallery, U. So. Fla., 1994, U. Mobile Ala., 1994, Ctr. for Contemporary Art, Tampa, 1994, Fla. State U. Gallery and Mus., Tallahassee, 1994, Valencia C.C., Orlando, Fla., 1993, Tandemn Art Ctr., Venice, Fla., 1993, 4th Ann. Fla. Biennal, Richmond Art Ctr., Calif., 1996, calendar Richmond Art Ctr., 1997, Sonoma Art Festival, 1997, Napa Valley Mustard Festival, 1998, Sebastopol Art Ctr., 1999; author: Women Art & Mental Illness; works included in pvt. collections; contbr. articles to profl. jours.; presenter festivals, confs. and workshops. Vol. art/crafts instr. Substance Abused Mothers Against Drugs, Tampa, 1993; vol. docent Salvador Dali Mus., St. Petersburg, Fla., 1986-88; mem. Women's Caucus for Art; active multicultural workshops arts & crafts for children, Clearwater, Fla., 1995; intersession instrs. arts & crafts for children, Alameda, Calif., 1995-98; vol. art therapist chronic mentally ill adults Berkeley Creative Living Ctr., 1996-97. Recipient Hillsborough County Emerging Artist award; named to Wall of Tolerance So. Poverty Law, Ala.; named Woman of Merit, North County San Diego; grantee Serpent Source Found. women, San Francisco. Mem. Women in Psychology, Calif. Assn. Marriage and Family Therapists, San Diego North County Assn. Marriage Family Therapists, North County African-Am. Women's Assn., Oceanside Mus. Art. Democrat. Avocations: art therapist and visual artist with a feminist, female and feminine voice addressing social, political and gender issues. Office Phone: 760-439-8874. E-mail: info@TrishV.com.

VERNER, JAMES MELTON, lawyer; b. Selma, Ala., Sept. 19, 1915; s. Singleton Foster and Jennie (Harris) V.; m. Gretchen Gores, Aug. 12, 1939; children: Ann Verner Picardo, James Singleton, William Melton. Student, Biltmore Coll., 1932-34; AB, U. N.C., 1936, LL.B., 1938. Bar: N.C. 1938, Tenn. 1947, D.C. 1950, Va., 1986. Assoc. firm Gover & Covington, Charlotte, N.C., 1938; law clk. atty. gen. N.C., 1938-40; atty. CAB, Washington, 1940-43; asst. gen. counsel Chgo. & So. Airlines, Memphis, 1946-47; atty. Air Transport Assn. Am., Washington, 1947-49; hearing examiner CAB, 1949-50, exec. asst. to chmn., 1950, exec. dir., 1950-53; from atty. to ptnr. Turney & Turney, 1953—60; ptnr. firm Verner, Liipfert, Bernhard, McPherson & Hand, Chartered (and predecessor firms), 1960-88; hon. mem. bd. dirs., spl. coun. Piper Rudnick (formerly Verner, Liipfert, Bernhard, McPherson & Hand, Chartered, Washington, 1988—. Assoc. editor: N.C. Law Rev, 1937-38. Former mem., chmn. policy bd. Legal Counsel for Elderly, Washington. Served as lt. (j.g.) USNR, 1943-46; legal officer Naval Air Transport Svc., 1945-46. Mem. ABA, Order of Golden Fleece, Cosmos Club (Washington). Home: 900 N Taylor St # 2104-2106 Arlington VA 22203-1858 Office: Piper Rudnick 1200 Nineteenth St NW Washington DC 20003-6132 *My belief is that if you treat other people fairly and trust them, you will seldom be disappointed and will be the better for it.*

VERNEY, RICHARD GREVILLE, paper company executive; b. Providence, Aug. 24, 1946; s. Gilbert and Virginia Ruth (Piggott) Verney; m. Dorothy Howard, Aug. 26, 1967; children: Virginia F., Elizabeth I., Heather B., Eric B. AB, Brown U., 1968. Mgmt. trainee Monadnock Paper Mills, Bennington, NH, 1969-70, asst. gen. mgr., 1970, exec. v.p., 1970-76, pres., 1977-85, chmn., CEO, 1978—, Monadnock Non-Wovens, LLC, 1998—, Monadnock Specialty Coatings, LLC, 2000—. Mem. exec. com. Crotched Mt. Found., Greenfield, NH, 1974—87, trustee, 1974—, St. George's Sch., Newport, RI, 1978—93, chmn., 1985—89, hon. trustee, 1993—, Monadnock Cmty. Hosp., 1993—2000, v.p., 1997—99; trustee Nantucket Conservation Found., Inc., 1994—, pres., 1998—. Mem.: Bus. Industry Assn. N.H. (bd. dirs. 1991—, mem. exec. com. 1998—2004), Boston Paper Trade Assn., Sales Assn. Paper Industry, Am. Forest and Papers Assn. (chmn. exec. bd. pulp consumers divsn. 1980—82, chmn. splty. packaging and indsl. divsn. 1984—85, chmn. cover and text exec. com. 1989—91, bd. dirs. 1991—98, chmn. printing/writing exec. com. 2002—03), N.Y. Yacht Club (N.Y.C.), Nantucket Yacht Club (Mass.), Algonquin Club (Boston). Republican. Episcopalian. Home: PO Box 145 The Verney Farm Bennington NH 03442-0145 Office: Monadnock Paper Mills Inc 117 Antrim Rd Bennington NH 03442-4205

VERNIERO, PETER G. former state supreme court justice; b. Montclair, NJ, Apr. 30, 1959; married; 2 children. BA summa cum laude, Drew U., 1981; JD, Duke U., 1984. Law clk. to Justice Robert L. Clifford NJ State Supreme Ct., 1984; with Pitney, Hardin, Kipp & Szuch, Morristown, NJ, 1985—87; dir. Herold & Haines P.A., Warren, NJ, 1990—93; chief counsel, chief of staff Gov. Christine Whitman, Trenton, NJ, 1994—95; atty. gen. State of N.J., Trenton, 1996—99; assoc. justice N.J. Supreme Ct., Trenton, 1999—2004. Adj. prof. bus. law County Coll. Morris, 1986. Exec. dir. Rep. State Com., 1989—90.

VERNON, CARL ATLEE, JR., retired wholesale food distributor executive; b. Topeka, Aug. 15, 1926; s. Carl Atlee and Capitola May (Jarboe) V.; m. Marion Leila Colton, May 7, 1950; children— Mary Catherine, Matthew Fowler, Susan Elizabeth. BS, Yale U., 1947. Merchandising mgr. Fleming Cos., Topeka, 1957-61, dir. merchandising, 1961-66, dir. info. services, 1966-72, v.p. info. services, 1972-74, v.p. regional systems, 1974-79, sr. v.p. mktg. services Oklahoma City, 1979-88. Chmn. Shawnee County chpt. ARC, Topeka, Kans., 1957-58. Served to ensign USNR, 1944-46 Republican. Episcopalian. Avocations: golf, gardening, travel.

VERNON, DARRYL MITCHELL, lawyer; b. N.Y.C., May 4, 1956; s. Leonard and Joyce (Davidson) V.; m. Lauren Lynn Bernstein, Aug. 21, 1982. BA in Math., Tufts U., 1978; JD, Yeshiva U., 1981. Bar: N.Y. 1982, U.S. Dist. Ct. (so. and ea. dists.) N.Y. 1982, U.S. Ct. Appeals (2d cir.) 1987. Assoc. Hochberg & Greenberg, N.Y.C., 1981—82; ptnr. Greenberg & Vernon, 1982—83, Law Offices of Darryl M. Vernon, 1983—; pres., ptnr. Vernon & Ginsburg, LLP, 1989—. Spkr. in field. Contbr. articles to profl. jours. Samuel Belkin scholar Yeshiva U., 1979. Mem. Assn. Bar City N.Y. (com. legal issues pertaining to animals). Office: 261 Madison Ave New York NY 10016-2303 Office Phone: 212-949-7300.

VERNON, GARY WAYNE See LEVOX, GARY

VERNON, HEIDI, international business educator; b. Washington, Mar. 3, 1938; d. Raymond and Josephine (Stone) V.; m. Lawrence N. Wortzel, Dec. 23, 1956 (dec. Feb. 1996); children: Joshua C., Jennifer R. Stiller; m. F. Gerard Adams, Oct. 12, 1997. AB, Rutgers U., 1960; AM, Boston U., 1978, PhD, 1980. Owner Heidi Wortzel's Cooking Sch., Newton, Mass., 1970-75; prof. Northeastern U., Boston, 1980—. Sr. prof. Prasetiya Mulya Grad. Sch. Mgmt., Jakarta, Indonesia, 1987—; sr. cons. Global Resources, Corona de Mar, Calif., 1992—. Author: Business and Society, 1990, 6th edit., 1998, Lowell: The Corporations and the City, 1992; co-author: Strategic Management in the Global Environment, 1989, 3rd edit., 1997. Fellow Ea. Acad. Mgmt., 1994. Mem. Eastern Acad. Mgmt. (bd. mem., sec. 1988-91), Acad. Mgmt. (divsn. chair 1992), Acad. Internat. Bus. Democrat. Avocations: cooking, photography, gardening. Home: 39 Stafford Rd Newton MA 02459-1818 Office: Northeastern Univ 313 Hayden Boston MA 02115 Office Phone: 617-373-4756. E-mail: h.vernon@neu.edu.

VERNON, JACK ALLEN, otolaryngology educator, laboratory administrator; b. Kingsport, Tenn., Apr. 6, 1922; s. John Allen and Mary Jane (Peters) Vernon Hefley; m. Betty Jane Dubon, Dec. 12, 1946 (div. 1972); children: Stephen Mark, Victoria Lynn; m. Mary Benson Meikle, Jan. 2, 1973 BA in Psychology, U.Va., 1948, MA in Psychology, 1950, PhD in Psychology, 1952. Instr. psychology Princeton U., N.J., 1952-54, asst. prof., 1954-60, assoc. prof., 1960-64, prof., 1964-66; prof. otolaryngology Oreg. Health Sci. U., Portland, 1966—, also dir. Oreg. Hearing Rsch. Ctr. Author: Inside the Black Room, 1963; editor: Tinnitus, Q&A's, Tinnitus, Treatments and Relief, Mechanisms of Tinnitus; inventor in field. Adv. Office Civil Defense, Washington, 1961-62. Served to 2d lt. USAAF, 1943-44 Recipient Guest of Honor award 1st Internat. Tinnitus Seminar, 1979, Opticon Focus on People award, 2001. Mem. Assn. Rsch. in Otolaryngology (pres. 1973-74), Am. Acad. Ophthalmology and Otolaryngology, Rotary. Democrat. Avocations: woodworking, sailing, skiing, reading. Office: Oreg Hearing Rsch Ctr 3181 SW Sam Jackson Park Rd Portland OR 97201-3011

VERNON, LILLIAN, mail order company executive; b. 1927; d. Herman and Erna Menasche; m. Paolo Martino; children: Fred, David. DCS(hon.), Mercy Coll., Dobbs Ferry, N.Y., 1984, Coll. New Rochelle; DSc in Bus. Adminstrn. (hon.), Bryant Coll.; LLD (hon.), Baruch Coll.; LHD (hon.), Old Dominion U.; DCS (hon.), Mercy Coll.; DCS Coll. New Rochelle (hon.); D. in Bus. Adminstrn. (hon.), Bryant Coll.; LLD (hon.), Baruch Coll. Founding chmn. Lillian Vernon, Rye, NY, 1951—. Lectr. in field. Contbr. articles to profl. jours. Trustee Coll. Human Svcs., Bryant Coll.; mem. adv. bd. Giraffe Project Girl Scout Coun. Tidewater; mem. adv. bd. Women's News; mem. bd. overseers Columbia U. Bus. Sch., NYU; mem. adv. com. Citizens Amb. Program; mem. bus. com. Met. Mus. Art; bd. govs. The Forum; mem. nat. com. The Kennedy Ctr. for Performing Arts, Washington; active The Ellis Island Reopening Com.; Bd. dirs. Westchester County, Ctr. Preventive Psychiatry, Va. Opera, Children's Mus. Arts, Retinitis Pigmentosa Found. Named Va. Press Women Newsmaker of Yr., woman of Yr., Women's Direct Response Group and Westchester County Fedn. Women's Clubs, Hampton Rds. Woman of Yr., So. New Eng. Entrepreneur of Yr.; named to Acad. Women Achievers, YWCA, Direct Mktg. Assn. Hall of Fame, Conn. Women's Hall of Fame; recipient Disting. Achievement award, Lab. Inst. Merchandising, Entrepreneurial award, Women's Bus. Owners of N.Y., 1983, Bravo award, YWCA, Woman of Achievement award, Woman's NEws, Nat. Hero award, Big. Bros./Big Sisters, Legend in Leadership award, Emory U., A Woman Who Has Made a Differene award, Inter. Womens Forum, medal of honor, Ellis Island, Bus. Leadership award, Gannett Newspapers, Outstanding Bus. Leader award, Northwood Inst., Congl. Record Commendation award, Crystal award, Coll. Human Svcs., City of Peace award, Bonds of Israel, Svc. award, Sr. Placement Bur., Excellence award, Westchester Assn. Women Bus. Owners, Commendation in Cong. Record, Magnificent Seven award, Bus. and Profl. Women, Woman of Distinction award, Birmingham So. Coll. Mem.: Nat. Retail Fedn. (bd. dirs.), Women's Forum, Com. of 200, Am. Stock Exch. (listed co. adv. com.), Am. Bus. Conf. (dir.), Lotos Club. Office: Lillian Vernon Corp 1 Theall Rd Rye NY 10580-1450 Office Phone: 916-925-1200.

VERNON, WESTON, III, (WES VERNON), broadcaster, writer, actor; b. N.Y.C., Aug. 23, 1931; s. Weston, Jr. and Adelaide (Neilson) V.; m. Alida Steinvoort, Oct. 5, 1951; children: Rosanne, Weston IV, Diane, John Randall. *Wes Vernon comes from a family of lawyers. His father, Weston Vernon Jr., was a longtime partner in the New York law firm Milbank-Tweed. An uncle George D. Neilson served for 50 years as a Superior Court judge in Washington. Vernon opted instead for a career in broadcasting. His mentor was the late Arch L. Madsen, President, Bonneville International, Inc. Vernon and his wife of over 50 years, the former Alida Steinvoort, have four children and nine grandchildren. Ancestors are Utah pioneers.* Student, Utah State U., 1949-50, Brigham Young U., 1953-54. Early broadcasting career on staff of radio stas., in Utah and Wyo., 1950-54; news and announcer KBMY, Billings, Mont., 1954-63; news dir., polit. specialist KSL Radio-TV, Salt Lake City, Utah, 1963-68; bur. chief Bonneville Internat. Corp., Washington, 1968-72; corr. CBS Radio Stas. News Svc. CBS Radio, Washington, 1972-97; host CBS Crosstalk, 1975-97. *Wes Vernon pioneered and won awards for local radio news and editorial policy at station KBMY Billings, Montana. An editorialist rival said Vernon had "a quick mind" and "an abundant supply of moral courage." In Salt Lake City, Utah, Vernon's work as Political Specialist for KSL Television/Radio attracted the attention of management at the parent firm, Bonneville International, which made him its first Washington Bureau Chief. For 25 years he was correspondent for CBS Radio, Washington, where he was "a winner" who served "with distinction" (according to his last supervisor there). He is currently a writer/broadcaster/actor.* Columnist The High Green, The Timetable, Washington corr. Carstens Publs., Inc.; actor:. Bd. dirs. Winding-Orchard Citizens Assn., Wheaton-Glenmont, Md., 1974-77, 86—, pres., 1975-76. Served with AUS, 1951-52. Recipient Journalism awards Mont. A.P. Press Stas., 1960, Journalism awards Utah Bar Assn., 1965, Journalism awards Utah Broadcasters Assn., 1965-66, Nat. Press Club. Mem. SAG, AFTRA (exec. bd. Balt.-Wash. local 1997—), Am. Legion (comdr. Yellowstone Post 4 1962-63), Chesapeake Rlwy. Assn. (pres. 1992-94, bd. dirs.). Office: 1605 Billman Ln Silver Spring MD 20902-1417 E-mail: baan@comcast.net.

VERON, J. MICHAEL, lawyer, writer; b. Lake Charles, La., Aug. 24, 1950; s. Earl Ernest and Alverdy (Heyd) V.; m. Melinda Anne Guidry, Jan. 2, 1993; children: John Heyd, Katharine Leigh, Dylan Michael Earl. BA, Tulane U., 1972, JD, 1974; LLM, Harvard U., 1976. Bar: La. 1974, U.S. Dist. Ct. (we. dist.) La. 1977, U.S. Dist. Ct. (ea. dist.) La. 1979, U.S. Dist. Ct. (mid. dist.) La., 1983, U.S. Dist. Ct. (ea. dist.) Tex. 1992), U.S. Ct. Appeals (5th cir.) 1981, U.S. Ct. Appeals (fed. cir.) 1996, U.S. Tax Ct. 1988. Law clk. to presiding justice La. Supreme Ct., New Orleans, 1974-75; sole practice Lake Charles, 1976-78; ptnr. Scofield, Gerard, Veron, Singletary & Pohorelsky (formerly Scofield, Gerard, Veron, Hoskins & Soileau), Lake Charles, 1978—. Instr. legal method and rsch. Boston U., 1975-76; lectr. environ. law McNeese State U., 1976-79; faculty Tulane Trial Adv. Inst., 1980; adj. prof. La. State U. Sch. Law, 1993-2000. Author: The Greatest Player Who Never Lived, 2000, The Greatest Course That Never Was, 2001; mem. bd. editors Tulane Law Rev., 1972-73, assoc. editor, 1973-74. Mem. athletic adv. com. Tulane U., 1983-86; pres. Krewe of Barataria, 1980-86. Named to La. State U. Law Ctr. Hall of Fame, 1993. Mem. U.S. Golf Assn. (sectional affairs com.), La. Golf. Assn. (bd. dirs., pres. 1990), Order of Coif, Maritime Law Assn., Lake Charles Country Club (pres. 1986). Roman Catholic. Avocations: golf, gin rummy, athletics. Home: 9 Par Dr Lake Charles LA 70605-5925 Office: Scofield Gerard Veron Singletary & Pohorelsky 1114 Ryan St Lake Charles LA 70601-5252 E-mail: mveron@sgvsp.com.

VERONA, ANDREI, mathematician, educator; b. Bucharest, Romania, Aug. 24, 1943; s. Renato and Maria Verona; m. Maria Elena Cioranu, July 31, 1968; 1 child, Andrei. PhD, U. Bucharest, 1966. Rschr. Math. Inst., Bucharest, 1966—75, INCREST, Bucharest, 1975—81, Max-Planck Inst. Math., Bonn, Germany, 1981—82, Inst. Advanced Study, Princeton, NJ, 1982—83; vis. prof. Ohio State U., Columbus, 1983—84; prof. Calif. State U., L.A., 1984—. Author books; contbr. articles to profl. jours. Office: California State University Dept Mathematics Los Angeles CA 90032 Business E-Mail: averona@calstatela.edu.

VERONIS, GEORGE, geophysics educator; b. New Brunswick, N.J., June 6, 1926; s. Nicholas Emmanuel and Angeliki (Efthimakis) V.; m. Anna Margareta Olsson, Nov. 8, 1963; m. Catherine Elizabeth, Jan. 29, 1949 (div. Nov. 1962); children— Melissa, Benjamin. A.B., Lafayette Coll., 1950; Ph.D., Brown U., 1954; M.A. (hon.), Yale U., 1966; DSc (hon.) Lafayette Coll. 1997. Staff meteorologist Inst. Advanced Study, Princeton, 1953-56; staff mathematician Woods Hole Oceanographic Inst., Mass., 1956-64, mem. staff, dir. geophys. fluid dynamics summer program, 1959—, assoc. prof. MIT, Cambridge, 1961-64, research oceanographer, 1964-66; prof. geophysics and applied sci.

Yale U., New Haven, 1966—, Henry Barnard Davis prof., 1985—, chmn. geology and geophysics, 1976-79, dir. applied math, 1979-93. Editor Jour. Marine Rsch., 1973 ; contbr. articles to profl. jours. Served with USN, 1943-46. Fellow Am. Acad. Arts and Scis., Am. Geophys. Union; mem. NAS, Norwegian Acad. Scis. (Robert L. and Bettie P. Cody award 1989, Henry Stommel Rsch. award 1997). Greek Orthodox. E-mail: george.veronis@yale.edu.

VERPLANCK, WILLIAM SAMUEL, psychologist, educator; b. Plainfield, N.J., Jan. 6, 1916; s. William Samuel and Kathryn (Tracy) V. BS, U. Va., 1937, MA, 1938; PhD, Brown U., 1941. Asst. prof. Ind. U., 1946-50; asst. prof. Harvard, 1950-55, acting asso. prof., 1955-56; research asso. Stanford U., 1956-57; asso. prof. Hunter Coll., 1957-59; prof. U. Md., 1958-62; prof. psychology U. Tenn., 1963-81, head dept., 1963-73; founder, chmn. Resource Assocs., Inc., 1980-88. Bd. dirs. Cambridge Ctr. for Behavioral Sci., 1990-93. Author: (with others) Modern Learning Theory, 1953. Bd. trustees Cambridge Ctr. Behavioral Studies, 1995-2000. Served to lt. USNR, 1943-46. Recipient travel grant Am. Philos. Assn., 1953 Fellow APA, Am. Psychol. Soc., Assn. Study Animal Behavior, AAAS; mem. Ea. Psychol. Assn., Psychonomic Soc. (founder, past sec.-treas., bd. govs.), Sigma Xi, Sigma Alpha Epsilon. Home: 1509 Duncan Rd Knoxville TN 37919-8632 E-mail: wverplan@utk.edu./wverplan.com. *The history of psychology is largely constituted of a succession of fads overlying the continuity given by a few plausible technological methods which have been progressively misapplied, with little critical concern for their social, political or scientific consequences.*

VERPLANK, SCOTT RACHAL, professional golfer; b. Dallas, July 9, 1964; m. Kim Verplank; children: Scottie, Hannah, Emma. BS in Bus., Okla. State U., 1986. Winner Western Open (PGA Tour), 1985, Buick Open (PGA Tour), 1988, World Cup of Golf (individual), 1998. U.S. Amateur champion 1984, NCAA champion 1986. Avocations: reading, kids, sports. Office: c/o PGA Box 109601 100 Ave of Champions Palm Beach Gardens FL 33410

VERRECCHIA, ALFRED JOSEPH, toy company executive; b. Providence, Feb. 19, 1943; s. Alfred Augustus and Elda Lucy (Tortolani) V.; m. Geraldine Macari, June 11, 1964; children: Michael, Michele, Melisa, Lisa. BS, U. R.I., 1967, MBA in Fin., 1971; Doctorate (hon.), Johnson & Wales U., 1991. Joined as jr. accountant Hasbro, Inc., Pawtucket, RI, 1965, v.p. fin., 1980-82, sr. v.p. fin., CFO, 1982-86, exec. v.p. fin., CFO, 1986-89, exec. v.p., 1989, pres. Hasbro mfg. svcs., 1989, co-COO, 1989, COO, domestic toys, exec. v.p. global ops., CFO, 1990—96, exec. v.p., pres., global ops., 1996—99, exec. v.p., pres., global ops and develop., 1999; exec. v.p., global ops., CFO Hasbro Inc., Pawtucket, 1999—2000; pres., COO, CFO Hasbro, Inc., Pawtucket, 2000—01, pres., COO, 2001—03, pres., CEO, 2003—. Bd. dirs. Hasbro Inc., Old Stone Corp., FM Global. Chmn. Bradley Hosp., East Providence, R.I.; pres. R.I. Pub. Expenditure Coun., Providence; bd. mem. Bd. of Govs. for Higher Edn., Providence, U. R.I. Coll. Bus., Kingston, R.I. Mem. Toy Mfrs. Am. (bd. mem.). Office: Hasbro Inc 1027 Newport Ave Pawtucket RI 02862*

VERRETT, SHIRLEY, soprano; b. New Orleans, May 31, 1931; d. Leon Solomon and Elvira Augustine (Harris) V.; m. Louis Frank LoMonaco, Dec. 10, 1963; 1 dau., Francesca. AA, Ventura (Calif.) Coll., 1951; diploma in voice (scholarship 1956-61), Juilliard Sch. Music, 1961; MusD (hon.), Coll. Holy Cross, Mass., 1978. CPA, Cert. real estate broker. Faculty U. Mich. Sch. Music, 1996—, James Earl Jones disting. univ. prof. voice, 1999—. Mem. adv. bd. Opera Ebony. Recital debut Town Hall, N.Y.C., 1958; appeared as Irina in Lost in the Stars, 1958; orchestral debut Phila. Orch., 1960; operatic debut in Carmen, Festival of Two Worlds, Spoleto, Italy, 1962; debuts with Bolshoi Opera, Moscow, 1963, N.Y.C. Opera, 1964, Royal Opera, Covent Garden, 1966, Maggio Fiorentino, Florence, 1967, Met. Opera, 1968, Teatro San Carlos, Naples, 1968, Dallas Civic Opera, 1969, La Scala, 1970, Vienna State Opera, 1970, San Francisco Opera, 1972, Paris Opera, 1973, Opera Co. Boston, 1976, Opera Bastille, Paris, 1990; guest appearances with all major U.S. symphony orchs.; toured Eastern Europe and Greece with La Scala chorus and orch., 1981; TV debut on Ed Sullivan Show, 1963; TV performances include: Great Performances series, live performance of Macbeth at La Scala, Santuzza in Cavalleria Rusticana; film debut Maggio Musicale, 1989, Macbeth, 1986; rec. artist, RCA, Columbia, ABC (Westminster), Angel Everest, Kapp, Philips Records and Deutsche Grammophon. Recipient Marian Anderson award, 1955, Nat. Fedn. Music Clubs award, 1961, Walter Naumberg award, 1958, Blanche Thebom award, 1960; named Chevalier Arts and Letters (France), 1970, Commandeur, 1984; John Hay Whitney fellow, 1959; Ford Found. fellow, 1962-63; Martha Baird Rockefeller Aid to Music Fund fellow, 1959-61; grantee William Matteus Sullivan Fund, 1959; grantee Berkshire Music Opera, 1956; recipient Achievement award Ventura Coll., 1963, Achievement award N.Y. chpt. Albert Einstein Coll. Medicine, 1975; 2 plaques Los Angeles Sentinel Newspaper, 1960; plaque Peninsula Music Festival, 1963; Los Angeles Times Woman of Yr. award, 1969 Mem. Mu Phi Epsilon. Office: U Mich Sch Music 1100 Baits Dr Ann Arbor MI 48109-2085 E-mail: verrett@umich.edu.

VERRILL, CHARLES OWEN, JR., lawyer; b. Biddeford, Maine, Sept. 30, 1937; s. Charles Owen and Elizabeth (Handy) V.; m. Mary Ann Blanchard, Aug. 13, 1960 (dec.); children: Martha Anne, Edward Blanchard, Ethan Christopher, Elizabeth Handy, Matthew Lawton, Peter Goldthwait; m. Diana Baber, Dec. 11, 1993. AB, Tufts U., 1959; LLB, Duke U., 1962. Bar: D.C. 1962. Assoc. Weaver & Glassie, 1962-64, Barco, Cook, Patton & Blow, 1964-66, ptnr., 1967, Patton, Boggs & Blow, 1967-84, Wiley, Rein & Fielding, Washington, 1984—. Adj. prof. internat. trade law/internat. bus. transaction Georgetown U. Law Ctr., Washington, 1978—, Charles Fahy Disting. adj. prof., 1993; vis. sr. lectr. internat. trade law Duke U. Law Sch., 1998—; conf. chmn. The Future of Internat. Steel Industry, Bellagio, Italy, 1984, U.S. Agenda for Uruguay Round, Airlie House, Warrenton, Va., 1986, Polish Joint Venture Law, Cracow, Poland, 1987, Internat. Steel Industry II, Bellagio, 1987, Bulgaria and the GATT, Washington, 1977; chair, spkr. Protection of Intellectual Property from Theft and Piracy Abroad Southwestern Legal Found. Fgn. Investment Symposium, 1995, chair, panel on NAFTA 2 1/2 Years Later, 1996; nat. adv. bd. Natural Resources Coun. of Maine, 2002—; panel mem. CPR Washington, 2003—. Local dir. Tufts U. Ann. Fund, 1965-69; mem. Duke Law Alumni Coun., 1972-75; trustee Internat. Law Inst., 1981—, chmn. bd. trustees, 1983-87; apptd. to roster of dispute settlement panelists World Trade Orgn., 1995, 97; chmn. adv. bd. Inst. for Advancement of Svc., 1997—; adv. com. rules U.S. Ct. Internat. Trade, 1998—; chmn. D.C. Cable Television Adv. Com., 1999—; bd. visitors Duke U. Law Sch., 2000—. Mem. ABA, Internat. Bar Assn., D.C. Bar Assn., Order of Coif, Theta Delta Chi, Phi Delta Phi, Met. Club (Washington), Chevy Chase Club (Md.), Tarratine Club (Dark Harbor, Maine). Home: 3000 Q St NW Washington DC 20007-3080 Office: 1776 K St NW Washington DC 20006-2304 Office Phone: 202-719-7323. E-mail: cverrill@wrf.com.

VERRILL, F. GLENN, advertising executive; b. N.Y.C., Dec. 17, 1923; s. Ralph Francis and Rose (Cuva) V.; m. Jean Demar, Aug. 25, 1946; children: Gary, Joan. AB, Adelphi Coll., 1949; A.M., Harvard U., 1950. With Batten, Barton, Durstine & Osborn, Inc., 1952—98, v.p., 1964; creative dir. Batten, Barton, Durstine & Osborn, Inc. (Burke Dowling Adams div.), Atlanta, 1965-70, exec. v.p., gen. mgr., 1970-71, pres., 1971-88, chmn., 1988—98, also dir. parent co. Author: Advertising Procedure, 1983, rev. edit., 1986, 88. Mem. adv. bd. U. Ga.; vice chmn. bd. overseers Coll. Bus. Adminstrn., Ga. State U.; bd. dirs. Atlanta Humane Soc., pres., 1980-81; chmn. Advanced Advt. Inst. Atlanta, 1981; mem. Peabody award com., 1984—90; bd. dirs. Atlanta Coll. of Art, 1990. With USAAF, 1943-46. Mem. Am. Assn. Advt. Agys. (nat. dir. 1973—), Atlanta Athletic Club, Cherokee Club, Harvard Club (Atlanta). Episcopalian. Home: 1730 Winterthur Close Atlanta GA 30328 Office: BBDO Atlanta Inc Box 720717 Atlanta GA 30358

VERRILL, JOHN HOWARD, museum director; b. Biddeford, Maine, June 17, 1947; s. Charles Owen and Elizabeth Martha (Handy) V.; m. Carol Christine Cory, Sept. 8, 1967; 1 child, Nathan Lawrence. BA, Campbell U., 1969. Tchr. St. Mary's County Schs., Leonardtown, Md., 1969-73; sales mgr. Kable News Co., N.Y.C., 1973-79; contract adminstr. Fischbach and Moore, L.K. Comstock, Lanham, Md., 1979-83; agrl. entrepreneur Jubilee Farm, Hebron, Md., 1983-87; mus. mgr. NASA, Wallops Island, Va., 1985; exec. dir. Purnell Mus., Snow Hill, Md., 1986-93, Ea Shore of Va. Hist. Soc., Onancock, Va., 1993 . Faculty mem. Seminar for Hist. Adminstrn. at Colonial Williamsburg, 1999-2000. Editor: (book) Trustee, Board Member Handbook, 1995. Pres. Wicomico County Fair, Salisbury, Md., 1986, S.E. Shore Travel Coun., Salisbury, 1988, Lions Club, Hebron, Md., 1991; active Hist. Adminstrn. 1999-2000. Recipient Gov.'s citation, Maryland Gov. Schaeffer, 1994. Mem. Am. Assn. Mus., S. Ea. Mus. Conf. (mentor 1994)), Va. Assn. Mus. (mentor 1997), Am. Assn. State and Local History, Small Mus. Assn. (chmn. 1990, bd. dirs. 1997—), Rotary Club Melfa, Va. (pres. 1995), Ea. Shore Barrier Islands Ctr. (bd. dirs. 1995—). Episcopalian (Lay Eucharistic Minister). Avocations: home restoration, gardening, boating, travel. Office: Ea Shore Va Hist Soc PO Box 193 Onancock VA 23417-0193 E-mail: kerr@esva.net.

VERRILLI, CATHERINE JEAN, music educator, soprano; b. Stamford, Conn., Nov. 29, 1965; d. Rudolfo Rinaldo and Carolyn Berger Verrilli; m. Karl Alan Van Beckum, July 15, 1989. MusB in voice, Shenandoah Conservatory, Winchester, Va., 1984—88; MusM in voice, U. Mich., Ann Arbor, 1990—92; D in music, U. Md., Coll. Park, 1993—97. Adj. prof. music St. Mary's Coll. Md., St. Mary's City, 1997—99; assoc. prof. music St. Cloud State U., Minn., 1999—. Presenter, lecture recital Coll. Music Soc. Regional Conf., Sweetbriar, Va., 1998; competition coord. William Kapell Internat. Piano Competition, College Park, Md., 1998; lecture, presenter Minn. Music Educators Assn., Minneapolis, 2003. Singer: (soloist, opera characters) performances at the John F. Kennedy Ctr. for the Performing Arts, Pan Am. Symphony, Chesapeake Chorale, Chesapeake Chamber Orchestra, Trio Lorca, Arts Club of Wash., Renwick Gallery of Nat. Mus. Named Regional Winner, Nat. Assn. of Tchrs. of Singing Artists, 1997; recipient Summa Cum Laude, U. Mich., 1992, U. Md., 1997, Winner, Gov.'s Grant, NATS, 1997, Finalist, Judges' Discretionary prize, Wash. Internat. Competition for Singers, 1997. Fellow: Phi Kappa Phi, Sigma Alpha Iota (hon.; patroness 2002—04); mem.: Nat. Assn. Tchrs. Singing, Nat. Italian Am. Found., Pi Kappa Lamba. Wiccan. Avocations: reading, gardening, yoga. Office: Music Dept St Cloud State U 720 Fourth Ave S Saint Cloud MN 56301 Business E-Mail: cverrilli@stcloudstate.edu.

VERRILLO, RONALD THOMAS, neuroscience educator, researcher; b. Hartford, Conn., July 31, 1927; s. Francesco Paul and Angela (Forte) V.; m. Violet Silverstein, June 3, 1950; children: Erica, Dan, Thomas. BA, Syracuse (N.Y.) U., 1952; PhD, U. Rochester, 1958. Asst. prof. Syracuse U., 1957-62, rsch. assoc., 1959-63, rsch. fellow, 1963-67, assoc. prof., 1967-74, prof., 1974-94, prof. emeritus, 1995—, assoc. dir. Inst. Sensory Rsch., 1980-84, dir., 1984-93, dir. grad. neurosci. program, 1984-93. Advisor com. on hearing, bioacoustics and biomechanics NRC. Author: Adjustment to Visual Disability, 1961 (award 1962); contbr. chpts. to books, articles to profl. jours. With USN, 1945-46. Fellow Am. Found. for Blind, 1956, NATO, 1970; grantee NSF, 1969-72, 84-87, NIH, 1972—; recipient Internat. Sensory Aids award, 1998. Fellow Acoustical Soc. Am. (Silver medal 1999); mem. Soc. for Neurosci., N.Y. Acad. Scis., Sigma Xi (Rsch. award 1982). Home: 312 Berkeley Dr Syracuse NY 13210-3031 Office: Syracuse U Inst Sensory Rsch 621 Skytop Rd Syracuse NY 13244-5290 Office Phone: 315-443-4164. Business E-Mail: ron_verrillo@isr.syr.edu.

VERRONE, PATRIC MILLER, lawyer, writer; b. Glendale, NYC, Sept. 29, 1959; s. Pat and Edna (Miller) V.; m. Margaret Maiya Williams, 1989; children: Patric Carroll Williams, Marianne Emma Williams, Theodore Henry Williams. BA, Harvard U., 1981; JD, Boston Coll., 1984. Bar: Fla. 1984, Calif. 1988, U.S. Dist. Ct. (mid. dist.) Fla. 1984, U.S. Dist. Ct. (ctrl. dist.) Calif. 1995, U.S. Ct. Appeals (9th cir.) 1995. Assoc. Allen, Knudsen, Swartz, DeBoest, Rhoads & Edwards, Ft. Myers, Fla., 1984-86; writer The Tonight Show, Burbank, Calif., 1987-90. Adj. prof. Loyola Law Sch., LA, 1998—2000; lectr. U. Calif., LA, 2002—. Dir., prodr., writer The Civil War-The Lost Episode, 1991; writer: The Larry Sanders Show, 1992—94, The Critic, 1993—95; prodr., writer The Simpsons, 1994—95, 2002—, Muppets Tonight!, 1995—97 (Emmy award Best Children's Program, 1998), Pinky and the Brain, 1998, Futurama, 1998—2002 (Environ. Media award, 2000, 2003, WGA award nominee, 2004, Emmy nominee, 1999, 2001, 2003, 2004, Emmy award for outstanding animated program, 2002, 2002, Writers Guild award nominee, 2004, Annie award nominee, 2004); editor: Harvard Lampoon, 1978—84, Boston Coll. Law Rev., 1983—84, Fla. Bar Jour., 1987—88, L.A. Lawyer, 1994—; issue editor Ann. Entertainment Law Issue, 1995—2003; contbr. articles to profl. jours. including Elysian Fields Quar., Baseball and the American Legal Mind, White's Guide to Collecting Figures, Frank Sinatra: The Man, The Music The Legend, Bongo Comics. Bd. dirs. Calif. Confedn. of Arts, 1994-98, Mus. Contemporary Art, 1994-95. Mem. ABA (vice-chair arts, entertainment and sports law com. 1995-96), Calif. Bar, Calif. Lawyers for Arts, L.A. County Bar Assn. (sec. barristers exec. com., chmn. artists and the law com., steering com. homeless shelter project, intellectual property and entertainment law sect., state appelate jud. evaluation com., legis. activity com.), Fla. Bar Assn., Writers Guild Am. West (exec. com. animation writers caucus, bd. dirs., membership fin. com. 1999-2001, sec., treas., 2001—, chmn. 2001-04 contract negotiating com., chair organizing com. 2001—, vice-chmn. 2004, animation writers caucus, Animation Writing award 2002), Harvard Club Lee County (v.p. 1985-86), Harvard Club So. Calif. Republican. Roman Catholic. Avocations: baseball, history. Home and Office: PO Box 1428 Pacific Palisades CA 90272-1428

VERRONE, RICHARD BURKS, archivist, educator; s. I. Richard and Carol Crumpler Verrone. BA, Hampden-Sydney Coll., Hampden-Sydney, Va., 1989; MA, U. N.C., Wilmington, 1996; PhD, Tex. Tech Univ., 2001. Adj. instr. Honors Coll., Tex. Tech U., Lubbock, 2004—; instr. Dept. of Outreach and Extended Studies, Tex. Tech U., 2002—; adj. instr. Dept. of Humanities, Lubbock Christian U., 2001—. Manuscript editor Enslow Pub. Co. Contbr. articles to encys., revs. to jours. Exec. bd. Tex. Tech U. Lifelong Learning Cmty., 2002—04. Named Most Outstanding Grad. Student, Dept. of History, Tex. Tech U., 1999—2000; scholar J. William Fulbright Fgn. scholar, Inst. of Internat. Edn., 2000—01, Phi Alpha Theta scholar, Dept. of History, Tex. Tech U., 1999, Ernest Wallace-Phi Alpha Theta scholar, 1998, Internat. Edn. Fee scholar, Tex. Tech U. Divsn. of Internat. Edn., 1998. Mem.: Soc. for Mil. History (assoc.), Soc. for the Historians of Am. Fgn. Rels. (assoc.), Am. Hist. Assn. (assoc.), Oral History Assn. (assoc.), Phi Beta Delta (assoc.), Phi Kappa Phi (assoc.), Phi Alpha Theta (assoc.; treas. 1997—98). Office: The Vietnam Archive Texas Tech Univ PO Box 41041 Lubbock TX 79409-1041 Office Phone: 806-742-9010. Office Fax: 806-742-0496. E-mail: richard.verrone@ttu.edu.

VERRY, WILLIAM ROBERT, retired mathematics researcher; b. July 11, 1933; s. William Richard and Maurine Houser (Braden) V.; m. Bette Lee Ronspiess, Nov. 20, 1955 (div. 1981); children: William David, Sandra Kay Verry Motor, Steven Bruce, Kenneth Scott; m. Jean Elizabeth Morrison, Oct. 16, 1982; step-children: Lucinda Jean Hale, Christine Carol Hale Fortner, Martha Jean Johnson, Brian Kenneth Lackey, Robert Morrison Lackey. BA, Reed Coll., 1955; BS, Portland State U., 1957; MA, Fresno State U., 1960; PhD, Ohio State U., Columbus, 1972. Instr. chemistry Reedley (Calif.) Coll., 1957-60; ops. rsch. analyst Naval Weapons Ctr., China Lake, Calif., 1960-63; ordnance engr. Honeywell Ordnance, Hopkins, Minn., 1963-64; sr. scientist Litton Industries, St. Paul, 1964-67; project mgr. Tech. Ops., Inc., Alexandria, Va., 1967-70; rsch. assoc. Ohio State U., Columbus, 1970-72; prin. engr. Computer Sci. Corp., Falls Church, Va., 1972-77; mem. tech. staff MITRE Corp., Albuquerque, 1977-85; C3 program dir., assoc. prof. math. sci. Clemson U., S.C., 1985-87; dep. dir. Riverside Rsch. Inst., Rosslyn, Va., 1987-91; mgr. Hillcrest Gardens, Livermore, Calif., 1992-98, ret., 1998. Founder, minister Christian Love Ctr.; founder, v.p. Interfaith Sharing, Inc., 1994-98. Mem. Inst. for Ops. Rsch. and the Mgmt. Scis. Home: PO Box 765 24 Snowden Cutoff Rd White Salmon WA 98672 E-mail: billverry@gorge.net.

VERSCH, ESTHER MARIE, artist; b. Santa Monica, Calif., May 27, 1927; d. Claro Contreras Santellanes and Juana Hernandez; m. Chester Ray Fraelich, Nov. 14, 1943 (div. Nov. 1964); children: Joe Fraelich, Diane Fraelich Foster Preston; m. Terry Lee Versch, June 21, 1969; stepchildren: Fred, Roman, Joseph, Terry Jr., Michael. Student, East L.A. Coll., Pasadena City Coll. Lic. vocat. nurse. Nurse pvt. dr.'s office, L.A., 1968-69, U. So. Calif. Med. Ctr., L.A., 1963-68; artist Altadena, Calif., 1972—. Artist: (front cover) Library Services L.A., 1983, Christmas card for Western Greeting Inc., (back cover) Moccasin Tracks, 1984-85; one woman shows include Republic Fed. Savings, Altadena, Calif., Pasadena Pub. Libr., Whites Art Store and Gallery, La Canada, Calif., 1979, Windmill Gallery, 1985; group exhibitions: Women Artists of the West Internat. Exhibition and Sale, Cody Western and Wildlife Classyc, 1979, Nat. Cowgirl Hall of Fame, Hereford, Tex., 1978, Beauty for the Beast Benefit, 1980, Ducks Unltd. Invitational Art Show, Taylor, Mich., 1986-87, Lawrence (Kans.) Indian Art Show, Mus. Anthropology, 1989-90, Snake River Showcase, Lewiston, Idaho, 1992, Women Artists of the West, 1992, 98, 99, Death Valley 49's Invitational Art Show, 1994-2000, 2001, George Ohr Cultural Arts and Cultural Ctr., Biloxi, Miss., 1998, Western and Wildlife Invitational Art Show, Estes Park, Colo., 2000, WAOW Art Show Pinedale, Wyo, 2002, Art and Music Festival, Dublin, Ohio, 2002; collections: Johnson Humrick House Mus., Coshocton, Ohio, and other private collections; illustrator back cover Moccasin Tracks, 1984-85. Vol. nurses aide City View Hosp., L.A., 1960-63; vol. Arroyo Rep., Pasadena, Calif., St. Luke Hosp., Pasadena, 1990-94, flu immunization ARC, 1977-78. Recipient Gold medal for watercolor San Gabriel Fine Arts, 1979, Best of Show award for watercolor Am. Indian and Western, 1990, Hon. mention San Gabriel Fine Arts, 1990, 3rd Place Watercolor Women Artists of the West Saddle Back Art Gallery, 1982. Mem. Women Artists of the West (emeritus mem., treas., asst. sec., editor West Wind, membership chmn.), Ohio Art League, Coshocton Art Guild. Republican. Roman Catholic. Avocations: walking, gardening, sewing. E-mail: everschart@newsguy.com.

VERSCHOOR, CURTIS CARL, business educator, consultant; b. Grand Rapids, Mich., June 7, 1931; s. Peter and Leonene (Dahlstrom) V.; m. Marie Emilie Kritschgau, June 18, 1952; children— Katherine Anne, Carolyn Marie, John Peter, Carla Michelle. BBA with distinction, U. Mich., 1951, MBA, 1952; EdD, No. Ill. U., 1977. CPA; cert. mgmt. acctg., cert. fin. planner, cert. fraud examiner, cert. internal auditor; chartered fin. cons. Pub. accountant Touche, Ross, Bailey & Smart (C.P.A.'s), 1955-63; with Singer Co., 1963-68, asst. controller, 1965-68; controller Colgate-Palmolive Co., 1968-69; asst. controller bus. products group Xerox Corp., 1969-72; controller Baxter Internat., 1972-73; CFO, v.p. fin. Altair Corp., Chgo., 1973-74; prof. DePaul U., Chgo., 1974-94, ledger and quill alumni rsch. prof., 1994—; pres. C.C. Verschoor & Assocs., Inc., 1981—. Part-time instr. Wayne State U., 1955-60. Author: Audit Committee Briefing: Understanding the 21st Century Audit Committee Governance Roles, 2000, Audit Committee Briefing: Facilitating New Audit Committee Responsibilites, 2001, Governance Update 2003: Impact of the New Initiatives, 2003; contbg. editor: Jour. Accountancy, 1961-62, Jour. Internal Auditing, 1985—, Strategic Fin., 1999—; editl. adv. bd. Acctg. Today, 1991—. Trustee Hektoen Inst. Med. Rsch., Chgo., 1996—. Served with AUS, 1953-55. Recipient Elijah Watts Sells award Am. Inst. C.P.A.'s, 1953; rsch. scholar Ctr. for Bus. Ethics, Bentley Coll. Mem. AICPA, Fin. Execs. Inst., Am. Acctg. Assn., Inst. Mgmt. Accts., Inst. Internal Auditors, Nat. Assn. Corp. Dirs., Assn. Cert. Fraud Examiners, Internat. Assn. Bus. and Soc., Soc. for Bus. Ethics, Beta Gamma Sigma, Beta Alpha Psi, Delta Pi Epsilon, Phi Kappa Phi, Phi Eta Sigma. Home: 231 Wyngate Dr Barrington IL 60010-4840 Office: DePaul Univ One E Jackson Blvd Chicago IL 60604-2287 E-mail: cverscho@condor.depaul.edu.

VERSFELT, DAVID SCOTT, lawyer; b. Mineola, N.Y., Feb. 17, 1951; s. William H. and Ruth (Gerland) V.; m. Mary Deborah Garber, Aug. 31, 1974; children: Christopher L., William S., Kathryn H. AB, Princeton U., 1973; JD, Columbia U., 1976. Bar: N.Y. 1977, U.S. Dist. Ct. (so. and ea. dists.) N.Y. 1977, U.S. Ct. Appeals (D.C. cir.) 1979, U.S. Ct. Appeals (2d and 7th cirs.) 1980, U.S. Supreme Ct. 1980, U.S. Ct. Appeals (9th cir.) 1981, U.S. Ct. Appeals (3d cir.) 1982, Ct. Internat. Trade 1990, U.S. Ct. Appeals (fed. cir.) 1994, U.S. Ct. Appeals (6th cir.) 1996. Mem. vol. divsn. Legal Aid Soc., N.Y.C., 1985-88, Partnership for a Drug-Free Am., 1989—. Mem. ABA, Fed. Bar Coun., Phi Beta Kappa. Office: Kirkpatrick & Lockhart LLP 599 Lexington Ave New York NY 10022-6030 E-mail: dversfelt@kl.com.

VERSHBOW, ALEXANDER R. ambassador; m. Lisa Vershbow; two children. BA in Russian and East European Studies, Yale Coll., 1974; MS in Internat. Rels., Columbia U., 1976. Various fgn. svc. positions, 1977—; dir. Office of Soviet Union Affairs U.S. Dept. of State, 1988-91; prin. dep. asst. Sec. of State for European and Can. Affairs, 1993-94; spl. asst. to pres. and sr. dir. European Affairs Nat. Security Coun., 1995-97; U.S. amb. NATO and permanent rep. to North Atlantic Coun., 1998—2001; U.S. amb. to Russian Fedn., 2001—. Contbr. articles to profl. jours. Recipient Anatoly Sharansky Freedom award Union of Couns. of Soviet Jews, 1990, 1st ann. Joseph J. Kruzel award, Sec. of Def. William Cohen, 1997, Disting. Honor award Dept. State, 2001. Office: U S Embassy in Moscow Bolshoy Devyatinskiy Pereulok No 8 121099 Moscow Russia

VERSIC, LINDA JOAN, nurse educator, research company executive; b. Aug. 27, 1944; d. Robert and Kathryn I. (Fagird) Davies; m. Ronald James Versic, June 11, 1966; children: Kathryn Clara, Paul Joseph. RN, Johns Hopkins Sch. of Nursing, 1965; BS in Health Edn., Ctrl. State U., 1980; MS in Edn., Nova Southeastern U., 2000. Asst. head nurse Johns Hopkins Hosp., Balt., 1965—67; staff Nurse Registry Miami Valley Hosp., Dayton, Ohio, 1973—90; instr. Miami Jacobs Jr. Coll. Bus., Dayton, 1977—79; pres. Ronald T. Dodge Co., Dayton, 1979—86, chmn. bd., 1987—; chmn. bd. dirs. A-1 Travel, Inc. Instr. Warren County Career Ctr., Ohio, 1980—84, coord. diversified health occupations, 1984—2003, career pathways coord., 2003—. Coord. youth activities, mem. steering com. Queen of Apostles Cmty.; active Miami Valley Mil. Affairs Assn., Glen Helen, Friends of Dayton Ballet, Dayton Art Inst., Cin. Art Mus. Recipient Excellence in Tchg. award, 1992, award for Project Excellence, 1992. Mem.: Am. Vocat. Assn., Ohio Vocat. Assn., Welsh Soc. Cin., South Slavic Club of Greater Dayton, Johns Hopkins Club, Vocat. Indsl. Clubs Am. (chpt. advisor 1982—). Roman Catholic. Home: 1601 Shafor Blvd Dayton OH 45419-3103 Office: Ronald T Dodge Co PO Box 41630 Dayton OH 45441-0630 Office Phone: 937-439-4497. E-mail: LVersic.rt@donet.com.

VERSTANDIG, TONI GRANT, federal agency administrator; b. Pitts., Jan. 15, 1953; d. Louis A. and Ruth M. (O'Block) Grant; m. Lee L. Verstandig, Feb. 20, 1982; 1 stepchild, Scott B.; 1 child, Grant L. BA, Boston U., 1974; AD, Stephens Coll., 1972. Legis. asst. subcom. on agrl. labor House Com. on Edn. and Labor, 1976-77; staff dir. subcom. on accts. House Adminstrn. Com., 1977-78; mem. profl. staff subcom. on internat. security/sci. affairs House Com. on Fgn. Affairs, 1978-86; mem. profl. staff Com. on Fgn. Affairs, 1986-93; dep. asst. sec. of state Near Ea. affairs U.S. Dept. of State, Washington, 1993—. Cons. to com. on fgn. affairs U.S. Ho. of Reps., 1978-93, staff dir. subcom. accts., com. on house adminstrn., prin. legis. asst. to Congressman John N. Dent. Vol. cons. on fgn. policy and nat. security Clinton-Gore Presdl. Campaign, 1992. Recipient Spl. Merit of Honor commendation Mayor Kevin White. Office: Dept of State Near Eastern Affairs 2201 C St NW Rm 6244 Washington DC 20520-0001

VER STEEG, CLARENCE LESTER, historian, educator; b. Orange City, Iowa, Dec. 28, 1922; s. John A. and Annie (Vischer) Ver S.; m. Dorothy Ann De Vries, Dec. 24, 1943; 1 child, John Charles. AB, Morningside Coll., Sioux City, Iowa, 1943; MA, Columbia U., 1946, PhD, 1950; LHD, Morningside Coll., 1988. Lectr., then instr. history Columbia U., N.Y.C., 1946-50; mem. faculty Northwestern U., Evanston, Ill., 1950—, prof. history, 1959—, dean grad. sch., 1975-86. Vis. lectr. Harvard U., 1959-60; mem. council Inst. Early Am. History and Culture, Williamsburg, Va., 1961-64, 68-72, chmn. exec. com., 1970-72; vis. mem. Inst. Advanced Study, Princeton, N.J., 1967-68; chmn. faculty com. to recommend Master Plan Higher Edn. in Ill., 1962-64; mem. Grad. Record Exam. Bd., 1981-86, chmn., 1984-86; bd. dirs. Ctr. for Research Libraries, 1980-85, Council Grad. Schs. in U.S., 1983-87; pres. Assn. Grad. Schs., 1984-85; mem. steering com. Grad. Research Project, Consortium on Financing Higher Edn., 1981-85; mem. working group on talent Nat. Acad. Scis., 1984-87; mem. Higher Edn. Policy Adv. Com. to OCLC, Online Computer Library Ctr., 1984-87. Author: Robert Morris,

Revolutionary Financier, 1954, A True and Historical Narrative of the Colony of Georgia, 1960, The American People: Their History, 1961, The Formative Years, 1607-1763, 1964 (Brit. edit.), 1965, The Story of Our Country, 1965, (with others) Investigating Man's World, 6 vols., 1970, A People and a Nation, 1971, The Origins of a Southern Mosaic: Studies of Early Carolina and Georgia, 1975, World Cultures, 1977, American Spirit, 1982, rev. edit., 1990; sr. author: Heath Social Studies, 7 Vols., 1991, Planning at Northwestern University in the 1960s, 1993; editor: Great Issues in American History, From Settlement to Revolution 1584-1776, 1969; editl. cons.: Papers of Robert Morris, vols. I-IX, 1973-99; contbr. articles to profl. jours. Served with USAAF, 1942-45. Decorated Air medal with 3 oak leaf clusters; 5 Battle Stars; Social Sci. Research Council fellow, 1948-49, George A. and Eliza Gardner Howard Found. fellow, 1954-55, Huntington Library research fellow, 1955, Am. Council Learned Socs. sr. fellow, 1958-59, Guggenheim fellow, 1964-65, NEH sr. fellow, 1973; Northwestern U. Clarence L. Ver Steeg Professorship established in his honor, 1997. Mem. AAUP, Am. Hist. Assn. (nominating com. 1965-68, chmn. 1967-68, Albert J. Beveridge prize 1952, hon. mention 1991 Eugene Asher Disting. Teaching award), Orgn. Am. Historians (editorial bd. Jour. Am. History 1968-72), So. Hist. Assn. (nominating com. 1970-72). Presbyterian. Home: Apt 311 Two Arbor Ln Evanston IL 60201-4216 Office: Northwestern Univ Dept History Evanston IL 60208-0001 Business E-Mail: c-ver@nww.edu.

VER STEEG, DONNA LORRAINE FRANK, nurse, sociologist, educator; b. Minot, N.D., Sept. 23, 1929; d. John Jonas and Pearl H. (Denlinger) Frank; m. Richard W. Ver Steeg, Nov. 22, 1950; children: Juliana, Anne, Richard B. BSN, Stanford, 1951; MSN, U. Calif., San Francisco, 1967; MA in Sociology, UCLA, 1969, PhD in Sociology, 1973. Clin. instr. U. ND Sch. Nursing, 1962-63; USPHS nurse rsch. fellow UCLA, 1969-72; spl. cons., mem. adv. com. on physicians' assts. and nurse practitioner progs. Calif. State Bd. Med. Examiners, 1972-73; asst. prof. UCLA Sch. Nursing, 1973-79, assoc. prof., 1979-94, asst. dean, 1979-81, chmn. primary ambulatory care, 1976-87, assoc. dean, 1983-86, prof. emeritus, chair primary care, 1994-96, prof. emeritus, 1996—. Co-prin. investigator PRIMEX Project Family Nurse Practitioners, UCLA Ext., 1974—76; assoc. cons. Calif. Postsecondary Edn. Commn., 1975—76; spl. cons. Calif. Dept. Consumer Affairs, 1978; accredited visitor Western Assn. Sch. and Coll., 1985; mem. Calif. State Legis. Health Policy Forum, 1980—81; mem. nurse practitioner adv. com. Calif. Bd. RN, 1995—97; mem. Edn. Industry Interface, Info. Devel. Mktg. Sub Com., 1995—99, recruitment, 1999—2001; archivist Calif. Strategic Planning Com. Nursing/Colleagues in Caring Project, 1995—. Contbr. chpts. to profl. books, articles to profl. jours. Recipient Leadership award Calif. Area Health Edn. Ctr. Sys., 1989, Commendation award Calif. State Assembly, 1994; named Outstanding Faculty Mem., UCLA Sch. Nursing, 1982. Fellow Am. Acad. Nursing; mem. AAAS, AAUW, ANA (pres. elect Calif. chpt. 1977-79, pres. 1979-81, interim chair Calif. 1995-96), Nat. League Nursing, Calif. League Nursing, N.Am. Nursing Diagnosis Assn., Am. Assn. History Nursing, Stanford Nurses Club, Sigma Theta Tau (Alpha Eta chpt. Leadership award Gamma Tau chpt. 1994), Sigma Xi. Home: 708 Swarthmore Ave Pacific Palisades CA 90272-4353 Office: UCLA Sch Nursing Box 956917 Los Angeles CA 90095-6917

VERTEFEUILLE, CHRISTINE SIEGRIST, judge; b. New Britain, Conn., Dec. 10, 1950; BA in Polit. Sci., Trinity Coll., 1972; JD, U. Conn., 1975. Pvt. practice, 1975-89; judge Conn. Superior Ct., 1989—99; adminstrv. judge Waterbury Jud. Dist., 1994-99, complex litig. judge, 1999; judge Appellate Ct., 1999-2000; assoc. justice Conn. Supreme Ct., 2000—. Alternate mem. Waterbury and New Haven (Conn.) Grievance Panels, 1985-89; faculty Conn. Judges Inst., 1989-94. Recipient Jud. award Conn. Trial Lawyers Assn., 1995. Mem. Conn. Bar Assn. (mem. exec. com. real property 1988-89). Office: Supreme Ct Bldg 231 Capitol Ave Hartford CT 06106

VERTICCHIO, RICK, lawyer; b. Litchfield, Ill., July 10, 1953; s. Paul C. and Marge (Lacy) V.; children: Gina Maria, Jonathan Barry, Juliana; m. Heidi Fritz, Nov. 24, 2000; children: Margaret, Mia. BA with honors, Ill. Coll., Jacksonville, 1975; JD with honors, So. Ill. U., 1978. Bar: Ill. 1978, U.S. Dist. Ct. (cen. and so. dists.) Ill. 1980, U.S. Ct. Appeals (4th cir.) 1980. Mem. Verticchio & Verticchio, Gillespie, Ill., 1978—. Asst. pub. defender Macoupin County, 1980-86. Editor So. Ill. Law Jour. Recipient William Jennings Bryant award for polit. sci. Ill. Coll., 1975, C.J.S. award for legal scholarship, 1977, Order of Barrister for appellate advocacy, 1978. Democrat. Roman Catholic. Home: 17509 Ridge Dr Carlinville IL 62626 Office: Verticchio & Verticchio 100 E Chestnut St Gillespie IL 62033-1501 Office Phone: 217-839-4411. E-mail: verticchiolaw@dtnspeed.net.

VERTREACE-DOODY, MARTHA MODENA, English educator, poet; b. Washington, Nov. 24, 1945; d. Walter Charles and Modena Kendrick Vertreace; m. Timothy S. Doody. BA, D.C. Tchrs. Coll., 1967; MA, Roosevelt U., 1972, MPH, 1973; MS, Mundelein Coll., 1981; MFA, Vermont Coll., 1996. Tchr. English Roosevelt H.S., Gary, Ind., 1967-72; disting. prof. English Kennedy-King Coll., Chgo., 1976—. Adv. bd. mem. City Mag., Chgo., 1984-86, Seams Mag., 1986-87; poetry fellow Hawthornden Internat. Retreat for Writers, Lasswade, Scotland, 1992, 93, Writers Ctr., Dublin, Ireland, 1993; adj. prof. English Columbia Coll., Chgo., 1993—. Author: Second House from the Corner, 1986, Under a Cat's-Eye Moon, 1991, Kelly in the Mirror, 1993, Oracle Bones, 1994, Cinnabar, 1995, Light Caught Bending, 1995, Maafa: When Night Becomes a Lion, 1996, Second Mourning, 1998, Smokeless Flame, 1998, Dragon Lady: Tsukimi, 1999; editor: Class Act mag., 1988-91. Contest judge White Eagle Coll. Press, Ill., 1994, Triton Coll., 1994; poet-in-residence St. Thomas the Apostle Cath. Ch., Chgo., 1996; mem. Harper Square Adv. Bd., 1997. Mem. MLA, Soc. for the Study Midwestern Lit., Soc. Writers Children's Lit., Ill. Assn. Tchrs. English, Midwest Regional Conf. Tchg. English in Two-Yr. Coll. Democratic Socialist. Roman Catholic. Avocations: travel, poetry, music. Home: 5232 S Greenwood Ave Chicago IL 60615-4316 Office: Kennedy-King Coll 6800 S Wentworth Ave Chicago IL 60621-3728 Office Phone: 773-602-5182. E-mail: mvertreace-doody@ccc.edu.

VERTS, LITA JEANNE, university administrator; b. Jonesboro, Ark., Apr. 13, 1935; d. William Gus and Lolita Josephine (Peeler) Nash; m. B. J. Verts, Aug. 29, 1954 (div. 1975); 1 child, William Trigg. BA, Oreg. State U., 1973; MA in Lingustics, U. Oreg., 1974; postgrad., U. Hawaii, 1977. Librarian Forest Research Lab., Corvallis, Oreg., 1966-69; instr. English Lang. Inst., Corvallis, 1974-80; dir. spl. svcs. Oreg. State U., Corvallis, 1980-96, faculty senator, 1988-96; ret., 1996. Editor ann. book: Trio Achievers, 1986, 87, 88; contbr. articles to profl. jours. Precinct com. Rep. Party, Corvallis, 1977-80; adminstrv. bd. 1st United Meth. Ch., Corvallis, 1987-89, mem. fin. com., 1987-93, tchr. Bible, 1978—; bd. dirs. Westminster Ho., United Campus Ministries, 1994-95; adv. coun. Disabilities Svc., Linn, Benton, Lincoln Counties, 1990-99, vice-chmn., 1992-93, chmn. 1993-94; citizen adv. bd. on Transit, 1998—, intercity steering com., 1999—, Corvallis Downtown Parking Commn., 1999—; Oreg. Longterm Care Ombudsman, 1999—. Mem. N.W. Assn. Spl. Programs (pres. 1985-86), Nat. Coun. Ednl. Opportunities Assn. (bd. dirs. 1984-87), Nat. Gardening Assn., Alpha Phi (mem. corp. bd. Beta Upsilon chpt. 1990-96). Republican. Methodist. Avocations: gardening, photography, golf. Home: 530 SE Mayberry Ave Corvallis OR 97333-1866 E-mail: l.verts@comcast.net.

VERTUN, ALAN STUART, lawyer; b. N.Y.C., Feb. 11, 1951; s. Simon and Dorothy (Weber) V.; m. Marion Vertun, May 20, 1983; children: Laura, Jeffrey, Amy. AB, UCLA, 1973; JD, Southwestern U., 1976. Bar: Calif. 1976. Atty. Potscrubber, Inc., L.A., 1978-81, NIS Corp., L.A., 1981-84; pvt. practice L.A., 1984—. Vol. Am. Cancer Soc., L.A., 1985-95, LIFE, L.A., 1984-87. Mem. Los Angeles County Bar Assn. Office: 4250 Wilshire Blvd # 203 Los Angeles CA 90010-3508 Office Phone: 323-937-1793. E-mail: avertun@hotmail.com.

VERVILLE, ELIZABETH GIAVANI, federal official; b. N.Y.C., July 13, 1940; d. Joseph and Gertrude (Levy) Giavani. BA, Duke U., 1961; LLB, Columbia U., 1964. Bar: Mass. 1965, U.S. Supreme Ct. 1970, D.C. 1980. Assoc. Snow Motley & Holt, successor Gaston Snow & Ely Bartlett, Boston, 1965-67; asst. atty. gen. Commonwealth of Mass., Boston, 1967-69; atty. advisor for African affairs U.S. Dept. State, Washington, 1979-72, asst. legal adviser for East Asian and Pacific affairs, 1972-80, dep. legal adviser, 1980-89; dep. asst. sec. state Bur. Politico-Mil. Affairs Bur. Politico-Mil. Affairs, Washington, 1989-92, sr. coord., 1992-95; dir. for global and multilateral affairs Nat. Security Coun., Washington, 1995-98; dep. dir. Critical Infrastructure Assurance Office, Washington, 1998-2000; spl. rep. Bur. Narcotics and Law Enforcement, Washington, 2000-01; acting dep. asst. sec. Bur. Internat. Narcotics and Law Enforcement, Dept. State, Washington, 2001—02, sr. advisor, 2002—. Recipient presdl. rank of meritorious exec., 1985, 90, 2003, presdl. rank disting. exec., 1988. Mem. Am. Soc. Internat. Law, Coun. on Fgn. Rels. Home: 3012 Dumbarton Ave NW Washington DC 20007-3305 Office: Bur Internat Narcotics & Law Enforcement State Dept Washington DC 20520-0001 Office Phone: 202-647-0456. E-mail: vervilleeg@state.gov.

VERWAAYEN, BEN J.M. communications company executive; M in Law and Internat. Politics, State U. of Utrecht. Mgr. pub. rels. to various mgmt. positions ITT Nederland, 1975-83, exec. v.p., dir. opers., 1983-88; pres. PTT Telecom BV (Royal PTT Nederland NV), 1988-97; exec. v.p., COO Lucent Technologies, Inc., Murray Hill, N.J., 1997-99, vice-chmn., 1999—. Mem. Bankers Trust European Adv. Bd.; adv. coun. ING; chmn. supr. bd. Endemol Entertainment. Office: Lucent Technologies Inc 600 Mountain Ave New Providence NJ 07974-2008

VESCOVO, DIANE KIRKLAND, federal judge; b. 1955; BA in History, U. Va., 1976; JD, Memphis State U., 1980. Bar: Tenn. 1980. Atty. Lloyd C. Kirkland, Jr., Memphis, 1981-87, Internat. Paper Co., Memphis, 1987-92, Wolff, Ardis, P.C., Memphis, 1992-95; magistrate judge U.S. Dist. Ct. (we. dist.), Memphis, 1995—. Mem. Phi Beta Kappa. Office: US Dist Ct 341 Federal Bldg 167 N Main St Memphis TN 38103-1816 Fax: 901-495-1387.

VESELINOVIČ, DRAŠKO, stock exchange executive; b. Ljubljana, Slovenia, Feb. 26, 1959; s. Branko and Breda (Pokorn) V.; children; Eva, Gal. M of Internat. Fin., U. Ljubljana, 1986, DSc in Econs., 1996. Fgn. exch. dealer Ljubljanska Bank, fgn. exch. and internat. treasury mgr.; assoc. prof. Faculty of Econs.; fin. adviser Slovene Govt.; CEO Ljubljana Stock Exch., gen. mgr., 1993—. Founder The Yugoslav Stock Exch., 1989. Author: Foreign Exchange in Developed World & in Yugoslavia, 1988, Foreign Exchange Trading, 1991, Stock Exchange Handbook, 1991, 95, Options and Other Derivative Financial Instruments, 1998, Aphorisms, 1996, 2002, Foreign Exchange Act with a Commentary and By-laws, 1999; contbr.more than 200 articles to profl. jours. Mem.: Tennis Assn. Slovenia (v.p.). Avocations: tennis, music. Office: Ljubljana Stock Exchange Inc Slovenska c 56 1000 Ljubljana Slovenia E-mail: drasko.veselinovic@ljse.si.

VESELL, ELLIOT SAUL, pharmacologist, educator; b. NYC, Dec. 24, 1933; s. Harry and Evelyn (Jaffe) Vesell; m. Kristen Paige Peery, Mar. 24, 1968; children: Liane Clark, Hilary Peery. AB magna cum laude, Harvard U., 1955, MD magna cum laude, 1959; DSc (hon.), Phila. Coll. Pharmacy & Sci., 1988; PhD (hon.), Philipps U., Marburg, Germany, 1991. Intern, children's med. svc. Mass. Gen. Hosp., Boston, 1959-60; rsch. assoc. Rockefeller U., NYC, 1960-62; resident medicine Peter Bent Brigham Hosp., Boston, 1962-63; clin. assoc. Nat. Inst. Arthritis Metabolic Diseases, NIH, Bethesda, Md., 1963-65; head sect. pharmacogenetics Nat. Heart Inst., NIH, Bethesda, 1965-68; Evan Pugh prof. pharmacology Pa. State U., Hershey, 1968—, asst. dean grad. edn., 1973-96, chmn. dept. pharmacology Coll. Medicine, 1968—2000, Bernard B. Brodie prof., 1991—. Pfizer vis. prof.; Burroughs Wellcome vis. prof. Editor: The Life and Works of Thomas Cole, 1964, Progress in Basic and Clin. Pharmacology, 1990, others; contbr. articles to profl. jours. Recipient Von Humboldt award, 1988. Fellow: AAAS, Royal Soc. Medicine (Frohlich vis. prof. 1985); mem.: Am. Soc. Clin. Pharmacology Therapeutics (Oscar B. Hunter Meml. award 1991), Am. Coll. Clin. Pharmacology (pres. 1980—82, Disting. Investigator award 1999), Am. Soc. Pharmacology Exptl. Therapeutics (sec.-treas. 1995—98, Exptl. Therapeutics award 1971, Harry Gold award clin. pharmacology 1985), Am. Soc. Clin. Investigation, Assn. Am. Physicians, Phi Beta Kappa, Alpha Omega Alpha. Office: Pa State U Coll Medicine Dept Pharmacology PO Box 850 Hershey PA 17033-0850 Office Phone: 717-531-8285. Business E-Mail: esol@psu.edu.

VESELY, IVAN, biomedical engineer; BSCE, U. Western Ont., London, Canada, 1983, PhD, 1987. Scientist Robarts Rsch. Inst., London, 1989—94; mem. staff Cleve. Clinic Found., 1994—2004; H. Russell Smith prof. cardiothoracic surgery, dir. cardiothoracic surgery rsch. Saban Rsch. Inst. of Children's Hosp. L.A., Keck Sch. Medicine, U. So. Calif., 2004—. Mem.: Internat. Soc. Applied Cardiovasc. Biology (mem. exec. com. 2003). Achievements include research in mechanisms of failure of artificial heart valves. Office: Saban Rsch Inst Children's Hosp LA Keck Sch Medicine - Univ So Calif 4650 Sunset Blvd Mailstop #137 Los Angeles CA 90027

VESELY, SUZANNE ARAAS, school librarian, educator; d. Frederick Joseph and Edythe Kuzma Araas; m. William Benjamin Vesely, Apr. 28, 1984. BA, Trinity Coll., Washington, 1968; MS, U. Wyo., 1971; PhD, U. Iowa, 1996, MLS and Info. Sci., 1999. Cert. acad. track U. of Iowa Ctr. for the Book, 2000. Rsch. asst. Louis Falco Archives, U. Iowa, Iowa City, 1998—99; libr. asst. Noun-Smith Iowa Women's Archives, Iowa City, 2000—01; copyright/ref. libr. Forsyth Libr., Ft. Hays State U., Kans., 2001—. Adv. coun. virtual coll. Ft. Hays State U., Kans., 2002—04, faculty senate alt., 2002—; head copyright and intellectual property ctr. Forsyth Libr., Ft. Hays State U., Kans., 2002—; copyright and intellectual property cons. Friends U., Wichita, Kans., 2003—03; mem. tenure planning com. Forsyth Libr., 2004. Creator (exhibitions) Martin Luther King: The Rest of the Dream; contbr. articles to profl. jours. Treas., pub. rels. and advt. com. Martin Luther King Day Planning Com., Hays, Kans., 2002—03; spkr., orgn. Coll. and Univ. librs. sect. statewide workshop Spkr.'s Bur., Ft. Hays State U., Kans., 2003—04; mem. Diversity Awareness Com., Hays, Kans., 2002—03; asst., facilitator computer skills for 50+, Ft. Hays State U., Kans., 2003—03. Mem.: ALA (publicity com. 2000—02, new members round table archives com. 2002—04, database preparation subcom. 2002—04, chair self-study and resource allocation com. 2004—, mem. scholarship and rsch. ad hoc com. 2004), Soc. of Am. Archivists, Roundtable on Info. Access and Tech., Libr. and Info. Tech. Round Table, Ref. and User Svcs. Assn., Kans. Libr. Assn. (summer inst. com.), New Members Round Table Archives Com., ALA, New Members Round Table, ALA, Beta Phi Mu (scholarship 1997—98). Avocations: hiking, gardening, jazz and blues events, meditation. Office: Fort Hays State Univ 135 FL 600 Park Ave Hays KS 67601 Business E-Mail: svesely@fhsu.edu.

VESETH, MICHAEL AARON, economics professor; b. Tacoma, Wash., Nov. 4, 1949; s. Einar Melven and Mary Jane (Morgan) Veseth; m. Sue Ann Trbovich, July 24, 1976. BA, U. Puget Sound, 1972; MS, Purdue U., 1974, PhD, 1975. Rsch. assoc. Adv. Commn. on Intergovtl. Relations, Washington, 1974—75; asst. prof. econs. U. Puget Sound, Tacoma, 1975—80, assoc. prof., 1980—87, prof., 1987—2003, prof. internat. polit. economy, 2003—, dir. internat. polit. economy program, 1993—, acad. advisor WGBH Commanding Heights website, 2002. Vis. prof. Bologna Ctr. Johns Hopkins SAIS, 1997. Author: Public Finance, 1984, Introductory Macroeconomics, 1980, 1981, 1984, Introductory Microeconomics, 1981, Introductory Economics, 1981, Coursebook for Economics, 1981, Economics: Cost and Choice, 1987, Mountains of Debt, 1990, Introduction to International Political Economy, 1996, 2001, Selling Globalization, 1998, New York Times: The Rise of the Global Economy, 2002, International Political Economy, UNESCO Encyclopedia, 2002, Globaloney: Unraveling the Myths of Globalization, 2005.

VESPA, NED ANGELO, photographer; b. Streator, Ill., May 31, 1942; s. Ned James and Evelyn Blanche (Flanigan) V.; m. Carol DeMasters, Sept. 11, 1976; 1 child, Nicole Marie; 1 son by previous marriage, James Paul. BS, So. Ill. U., 1965. Photographer Milw. Jour. Co., 1965-95, Milw. Sentinel, 1965-95; ret., 1995; freelance, 1995—. Mem. Nat. Press Photographers Assn., Wis. News Photographers Assn. (past pres.), Milw. Press Photographers. Home: 38309 Genesee Lake Rd Oconomowoc WI 53066-8614

VESPER, CAROLYN F. newspaper publishing executive; Assoc. pub., sr. v.p. advt. USA TODAY, Arlington, Va. Office: 7950 Jones Branch Dr Mc Lean VA 22108-0001

VESPER, HUBERT WALTER, food scientist, researcher; PhD, U. Munich. Rsch. chemsit Ctrs. for Disease Control, Atlanta, 1996—. Office: CDC/NCEH/DLS 4770 Buford Hwy NE MS F25 Atlanta GA 30341 E-mail: hvesper@cdc.gov.

VESPER, ROSE, state legislator; m. Lee Vesper; children: Stephanie, Jennifer, Jessica. BA, Xavier U., 1960; MA, Midwestern U., 1967. Past mem. Ohio Valley Regional Devel. Commn., Ohio Water and Sewer Rotary Commn.; pres. Ohio Clermont County Farm Bur.; rep. Ohio State Ho. Reps. Dist. 72. Mem. Nat. Fedn. Rep. Women; chmn. Clermont County Rep. Party, 1990—, Southwestern Ohio Rep. Leadership; owner, operator beef cattle/crop farm. Named Clermont County Farm Woman of Yr., 1988; recipient Disting. Svc. award Ohio Med. Polit. Action Com., 1988, Coop. Ext. Agts. Assn. award, 1990, Frances Boltom award Ohio League Young Reps., 1990. Mem. Richmond Hist. Soc., Clermont, Brown and Clinton County C. of C., State Med. Assn., Farm Bur., Farmers Union. Home: 1174 Watkins Hill Rd New Richmond OH 45157-9504 Office: Ohio Ho of Reps State House Columbus OH 43215

VESPOLI, LEILA L. energy executive, lawyer; b. 1959; BS, Miami (Ohio) U.; JD, Case Western Reserve U. Bar: Ohio 1984. From atty. to sr. atty. Ohio Edison, Akron, Ohio, 1985—97; assoc. gen. counsel First Energy Corp., Akron, Ohio, 1997—2000, gen. counsel, 2000—, v.p. 2000—01, sr. v.p., 2001—. Bd. dirs. NJ Central Power & Light. Bd. trustees Cleveland Opera, The NEOUCOM Found. Named a Women of Professional Excellence, YWCA. Mem.: Greater Cleveland General Counsel Assn., Ohio C. of C., Energy Assn. of Pa. (bd. dirs., chair exec. electric com.), NJ Utilities Assn. (bd. dirs.). Office: First Energy Corp 76 S Main St Akron OH 44308*

VESSEY, JOHN WILLIAM, JR., army officer; b. Mpls., June 29, 1922; s. John William and Emily (Roche) V.; m. Avis Claire Funk, July 18, 1945; children: John William, David, Sarah. BS, U. Md., 1963; MS, George Washington U., 1967; LLD, Concordia Coll., St. Paul, 1978, U. Md., 1983, Concordia Sem., St. Louis, 1983; DMS (hon.), Norwich U., Northfield, Vt., 1985; grad., Command and Gen. Staff Coll., 1958, Indsl. Coll. Armed Forces, 1966. Commd. 2nd lt. U.S. Army, 1944, advanced through grades to gen., 1976; comdr. U.S. Army Support Command Thailand, 1970-71; chief Mil. Assistance Adv. Group, 1972-73; dir. ops. Dept. Army, 1973-74; comdr. 4th Inf. Div. Ft. Carson, Colo., 1974-75; dep. chief of staff-ops. Dept. Army Washington, 1975-76; comdr.-in-chief UN Command/U.S. Forces in Korea Seoul, 1976-79; comdr.-in-chief Republic of Korea/U.S. Combined Forces Command, 1978-79; vice chief of staff U.S. Army, 1979-82; chmn. Joint Chiefs of Staff, 1982-85; ret. U.S. Army, 1985; presdl. emissary to Hanoi for POW/MIA matters, 1987-93. Bd. dirs. Nat. Flag Day Com.; mem. bd. vistors UMUC; chmn. bd. Ctr. Preventive Action, Def. Sci. Bd. Decorated D.S.C., Def. D.S.M., D.S.M., AF D.S.M., Navy D.S.M., Legion of Merit, Bronze Star, Air medal, Joint Svcs. Commendation medal, Army Commendation medal, Purple Heart (U.S.), Presdl. Medal of Freedom, decorated by govts. of Austria, Belgium, Chile, Colombia, Germany, France, Greece, Honduras, Korea, Luxembourg, Norway, Pakistan, Saudi Arabia, Spain, Thailand, Uruguay; recipient State of Minn. Disting. Svc. medal, Excellence in Diplomacy award Am. Acad. of Diplomacy, Sylvanus Thayer award USMA, Alumni Achievement award and Disting. Pub. Svc. award George Washington U., Disting. Alumnus award U. Md., Golden Plate award Am. Acad. Achievement, Adm. John M. Will award N.Y. Coun. Navy League, hon. award Nat. League Families. Mem. VFW (Eisenhower medal), Assn. U.S. Army (George Marshall medal), Army Aviation Assn., U.S. Armor Assn., Coun. Fgn. Rels. (chair bd. dirs. ctr. for prevention action), Phi Kappa Phi. Lutheran.

VESSOT, ROBERT FREDERICK CHARLES, physicist, researcher; b. Montreal, Que., Can., Apr. 16, 1930; s. Robert Charles Ulysses and Marguerite Yvonne (Giauque) V.; m. Norma Newman Wight, Apr. 18, 1959; children: Judith Norma, Margaret Anne, Nancy Elizabeth. BA, McGill U., 1951, MSc, 1954, PhD, 1956. Mem. research staff MIT, 1956-60; mgr. Maser Research and Devel., Varian Assos., Hewlett Packard, Beverly, Mass., 1960-69; sr. physicist Harvard-Smithsonian Center for Astrophysics, Cambridge, Mass., 1969-2001, rsch. assoc., 2002—. Contbr. articles to profl. jours.; patentee in field. Served with RCAF, 1951-53. Recipient medal for outstanding sci. achievement NASA, 1978, I.I. Rabi award IEEE, 1993. Fellow Am. Phys. Soc.; mem. Eastern Yacht Club. Office: 60 Garden St Cambridge MA 02138-1516 Business E-Mail: rvessot@cfa.harvard.edu.

VEST, CHARLES MARSTILLER, retired academic administrator; b. Morgantown, W.Va., Sept. 9, 1941; s. Marvin Lewis and Winifred Louise (Buzzard) V.; m. Rebecca Ann McCue, June 8, 1963; children: Ann Kemper, John Andrew. BS in Mech. Engring., W.Va. U., 1963; MS in Mech. Engring., U. Mich., 1964, PhD, 1967; degree (hon.), Mich. Tech. U., 1992, W.Va. U., 1994, Ill. Inst. Tech., 1998, U. Notre Dame, 1998, Musashi Inst. Tech., 1999, NC State U., 2002. Asst. prof., then assoc. prof. U. Mich., Ann Arbor, 1968—77, prof. mech. engring., 1977—90, assoc. dean acad. affairs Coll. Engring., 1981—86, dean Coll. Engring., 1986—89, provost, v.p. acad. affairs, 1989—90; pres. MIT, Cambridge, 1990—2004. Bd. dirs. E.I. du Pont de Nemours and Co., IBM, Math. for Am., Ithaka Harbors, Inc., Blanchette Rockefeller Neurosci. Inst.; vis. assoc. prof. Stanford (Calif.) U., 1974-75; mem. Commn. on the Intelligence Capabilities of the U.S. Regarding Weapons of Mass Destruction; mem. Ctr. for Strategic and Internat. Studies Commn. on Sci. Comm. and Nat. Security; mem. Mass. Gov.s Coun. on Econ. Growth and Techn. 1990-99; chmn. Presdl. Adv. Com on Redesign of Space Stat., 1993-94, chmn. U.S. Dept. Energy Task Force on Future of Sci. Programs; vice chmn. Coun. on Competitiveness. Author: Holographic Interferometry, 1979; assoc. editor Jour. Optical Soc. Am., 1982-83; contbr. articles to profl. jours. Trustee Woods Hole Oceanographic Inst., Univ. Corp. for Advanced Internet Devel., WGBH Ednl. Found.; adv. trustee TIAX adv. bd., Environ. Rsch. Inst. Mich. Recipient Excellence in Rsch. award U. Mich., 1980, Disting. Svc. award, 1972, Disting. Visitor award U. La Plata, Argentina, 1979, Centennial medal Am Soc. Engring. Edn., 1993, Arthur M. Bueche award Nat. Acad. Engring., 2000, Nat. Leadership award Phi Kappa Psi, 1999., Pres.' award Accrediation Bd. for Engring. and Tech., 2002. Fellow AAAS, Am. Acad. Arts and Scis., Optical Soc. Am., ASME; mem. NAE, Assn. Women in Sci., Sigma Xi, Tau Beta Pi, Pi Tau Sigma. Presbyterian.

VEST, GAYLE SOUTHWORTH, obstetrician, gynecologist; b. Duluth, Minn., Apr. 7, 1948; d. Russell Eugene and Brandon (Young) Southworth; m. Steven Lee Vest, Nov. 27, 1971; 1 child, Matthew Steven. BS, U. Mich., 1970. Diplomate Am. Bd. Ob-Gyn. Intern in ob-gyn. Milw. County Gen. Hosp., 1974-75, So. Ill. U. Sch. Medicine, 1975-78; pvt. practice Chapel Hill (N.C.) Ob-Gyn., 1978-80; asst. attending physician dept. ob-gyn. U. N.C. Sch. Medicine, Chapel Hill, 1978-80; clin. assoc. dept. ob-gyn. Duke U. Med. Ctr., Durham, N.C., 1978-80; pvt. practice Big Stone Gap (Va.) Clinic, 1980-88, Norwise Ob-Gyn. Assocs., Norton, Va., 1988—. Fellow: ACOG; mem.: Wise County Med. Soc., Med. Soc. Va., Va. Ob-Gyn. Soc., Christian Med. and Dental Assn., Am. Soc. Reproductive Medicine. Avocations: skiing, kayaking, travel. Office: Norwise Ob-Gyn Assocs 102 15th St NW Ste 301 Norton VA 24273-1616 Office Phone: 276-679-1623.

VEST, GEORGE SOUTHALL, retired diplomat; b. Columbia, Va., Dec. 25, 1918; s. George Southall and Nancy Margaret (Robertson) V.; m. Emily Barber Clemons, June 21, 1947; children— Jeannie, George, Henry BA, U. Va., 1941, MA, 1947. Fgn. service duty SHAPE and NATO, Quito, Ottawa, Paris; dir. bur. polit. mil. affairs Dept. State, asst. sec. of state for European affairs, 1977-81; ambassador to European Communities Brussels, 1981-85; dir. gen. Fgn. Svc. Dept. State, Washington, 1985-89, career amb., 1987-89, ret., 1989. Served to capt. U.S. Army, 1941-46, ETO Mem. Phi Beta Kappa Episcopalian. Avocations: bicycling, gardening. Home: 5307 Iroquois Rd Bethesda MD 20816-3104

VEST, HYRUM GRANT, JR., retired horticultural sciences educator; b. Salt Lake City, Sept. 23, 1935; s. Hyrum and Josephine Gwendolyn (Lund) V.; m. Gayle Pixton, Sept. 18, 1958; children: Kelly, Lani, Kari, Kamille, Kyle. BS, Utah State U., 1960, MS, 1964; PhD, U. Minn., 1967. Pathologist, agronomist U.S. Dept. Agr., Beltsville, Md., 1967-70; vegetable breeder Mich. State U., East Lansing, 1970-76; dept. head dept. hort. and landscape architecture Okla. State U., Stillwater, 1976-83; head dept. hort. scis. Tex A & M U., College Station, 1983-89; head dept. plants, soils and biometeorology Utah State U., Logan, 1989-95, assoc. dir. Utah Agrl. Experiment Sta., 1995-2000; mem. Nat. Plant Genetics Resource Bd., Washington, 1982-88; ret., 2000. Served to 1st lt. U.S. Army, 1960-63. Univ. research fellow Utah State U., 1963-64 Fellow Am. Soc. Hort. Sci. Republican. Mem. Lds Ch. Home: 368 Spring Creek Rd Providence UT 84332-9432 E-mail: gvest@cc.usu.edu.

VEST, R. LAMAR, church administrator; b. Belton, SC, July 24, 1940; m. Iris Vest, 1958 (dec. 2001); m. Vickie Underwood, Feb. 16, 2002; 6 children. BS, Lee U.; MA, Church of God Theological Seminary; D, Lee U. Began ministry, 1955; ordained, 1965; dir. Ch. of God Media Ministries, 1994—96, 1st asst., gen. overseer, 1996—99, presiding bishop. Chmn. Nat. Assn. Evangelicals, first-vice-chmn., second vice-chmn., bd. dir.; chmn. bd. trustee Am. Bible Soc., exec. com.; guest spkr. at various conferences, seminars, conventions, and local churches around the world. Author: (book) What a Life, The Church and Its Youth, Spiritual Renewal, The Pain and the Glory, Spiritual Balance-Reclaiming the Promise; co-author (with Steven J. Land): Reclaiming Your Testimony: Your Story and the Christian Story; contbr. articles to profl. jours. State/regional youth and Christian edu. dir. for youth ministry in Okla., Calif. Nev., and Md.-Del.-DC.; exec. leader Dept. Youth and Christian Edu., 1976—84; sec. Pentecostal Charismatic Churches NAm.; presidium Pentecostal World Fellowship; pres. Lee U., Cleve., 1984—86. Mem.: Am. Bible Soc. (trustee 1990—94, exec. com. 1994—). Office: Nat Assn Evangelicals PO Box 1325 Azusa CA 91702-1325*

VESTAL, ALLAN W. dean, law educator; BA, Yale U., 1976, JD, 1979. Tchr. partnership and corp. law, comml. law, and real estate Washington and Lee U. Sch. Law, 1989—2000; dean U. Ky. Coll. Law, Lexington, 2000—. Practiced law for ten yrs., Wis., Iowa. Publ. (treatise with Prof. Hillman and Dean Weidner) The Revised Uniform Partnership Act; contbr. chapters to books, articles to law revs. Mem.: Am. Law Inst. Office: Coll Law U Ky Lexington KY 40506-0048

VESTAL, JOSEPHINE BURNET, lawyer; b. Iowa City, June 13, 1949; d. Allan Delker and Dorothy (Walker) V. Student, Williams Coll., 1970; BA, Mt. Holyoke Coll., 1971; JD, U. Wash., 1974. Bar: Wash. 1974, U.S. Dist. Ct. (we. dist.) Wash. 1974, U.S. Ct. Appeals (9th cir.) 1984, U.S. Ct. Appeals (D.C. cir.) 1984, U.S. Dist. Ct. (ea. dist.) Wash. 1993. Ptnr. Selinker, Vestal, Klockars & Andersen, Seattle, 1974-80; assoc. Williams, Kastner & Gibbs, Seattle, 1981-87; mem. Williams, Kastner & Gibbs, PLLC, Seattle, 1988—. Mem. ABA (labor and employment sect.), Def. Rsch. Inst. (labor and employment sect.), Wash. State Bar Assn., King County Bar Assn. Office: Williams Kastner & Gibbs PLLC 4100 Twp Union Sq PO Box 21926 Seattle WA 98111-3926 Office Phone: 206-233-2894. E-mail: jvestal@wkg.com.

VESTAL, KATHERINE R. language educator; b. Elkin, N.C., Dec. 4, 1961; d. Lowell R. and Faye P. Vestal. BA in Spanish, U. N.C., 1984; MDiv, Southeastern Bapt. Theol. Sem., 1991; MEd in Spanish, U. N.C., 1997. Tchr. Spanish Alleghany High Sch, Sparta, NC, 1984—89, West Rowan High Sch., Mt. Ulla, 1992—99; instr. Spanish Rowan-Cabarrus C.C., Salisbury, 1999—. Mem. group home study task force Social Svcs., Salisbury, NC, 2003. Mem.: Fgn. Lan. Instrs. Cmty. Colls., Fgn. Lan. Assn. N.C. Southern Baptist. Office: RCCC PO Box 1595 Salisbury NC 28145

VESTAL, MARILYN ANITA, writer, researcher, educator; b. Pitts., May 28, 1950; d. Elmo Foucheaux and Mary Alice (Hayes) Vestal; 1 child, Daven Remley. BS in Child and Family Devel., Va. Tech., 1974; MBA in Mgmt., Tex. Tech. U., 1980; PhD in Conflict Mgmt., Nova Southeastern U., 2001. Vol. Peace Corps, Dominican Republic, 1974-76; child devel. tng. specialist Tex. Tech. U., Lubbock, 1977-80; methods analyst supr. Cmty. Progress Coun., York, PA., 1980-81; program adminstr. East Coast Migrant Head Start Project, 1982-84; mgmt./fiscal specialist, data mgmt. project coord. Head Start Resource and Tng. Ctr., U. Md., 1984-87; exec. dir. Child Care Cons., Inc., Pa., 1987-90; mgmt. cons., mediator, 1990—. Assoc. prof. human resources mgmt. Webber Coll., 1993-97; assoc. prof. mgmt. orgn. devel. Ea. Mennonite U., 2000-; adj. prof. conflict resolution Nova Southeastern U., 2001-; cons. S.C. Ednl. TV, 1992-96, U. Md., Head Start Resource and Tng. Ctr., 1988-92, South Fla. C.C., 1995, Region IV Mgmt. Inst., Tuskeegee U., 1995, DHHS/Administration on Children and Families, Washington, 1991—, Wheelock Coll., 1997-98, Aspen Sys.; presenter numerous papers at confs., workshops. Mem. editl. bd.: 4th R, Assn .for Conflict Resolution, 2003—. Facilitator Wellspring Retreat, Family Enrichment Ctr., Archdiocese of Miami, 1998-2000; arbitrator Nat. Assn. Securities Dealers, 1998-; mem. Nat. Peace Corps Assn., Soc. for Human Resources Mgmt., 2001—, Consortium on Peace Rsch., Ed., Devel., 2000-02, Assn. for Conflict Resolutions, 1999-; mem., bd. dirs. Child Care Cons., Inc., York, 1990-91, bd. pres. Mediation Svcs. Conflict Resolution, 2000-02; bd. dirs. Atkins House, York, 1989-90. Recipient Margaret Sangar award Planned Parenthood, 1975, Beyond War award, 1987, Cert. Recognition Dept. Interior, 1976; Head Start Rsch. scholar, 1999-2000. Mem. Broward County Mediators Assn. Roman Catholic. Avocations: tennis, travel, culture. E-mail: vestala@suscom.net.

VESTAL, THEODORE MERRILL, education educator; b. Sherman, Tex., Sept. 11, 1933; s. Merrill Madison Vestal and Grace Truman Moore; m. Patricia Lou Botefuhr, Aug. 25, 1956; children: Charles Merrill, Theodore Edward, Grace Suzanne Thomson. BA in Govt., U. North Tex., 1955; MA in Polit. Sci., Stanford U., Calif., 1958, PhD in Polit. Sci., 1962. Asst. to the asst. sec. for edn. Dept. HEW, Washington, 1966—67; assoc. dir. U.S. Peace Corps, Addis Ababa, Ethiopia, 1964—66; assoc. dean Briarcliff Coll., Briarcliff Manor, NY, 1967—69; resident dir. Ednl. Resources Ctr. USNY, New Delhi, 1969—71; dean of continuing edn. Austin Coll., Sherman, Tex., 1973—78; pres. Calif. Inst. of Integral Studies, San Francisco, 1979—83; sr. vis. fellow U. of Tulsa, 1983—87; prof. Okla. State U., Stillwater and Tulsa, 1988—. Pres. Ted Vestal & Assocs., Tulsa, 1983—. Author: (nonfiction book) International Education: Its History and Promise for Today, 1994, Ethiopia: A Post-Cold War African State, 1999, The Eisenhower Court and Civil Liberties, 2002. Ethiopian Rsch. Coun., Washington, 2003—; cons. Friends of Ethiopia and Eritrea, 1990—94; contbr. and editor of pan-ethiopia forum Ethiopia Policy Inst., Grand Rapids, Mich., 2000—04; cons. on history Ethiopian Am. History and Culture Symposium, Washington, 2002—04. 1st lt. Chem. Corps USAR, 1959. Recipient Outstanding Polit. Scientist, Okla. Polit. Sci. Assn., 2001—02. Mem.: Mortar Bd. (hon.). Unitarian Universalist. Avocation: opera singing. Home: 3030 S Quaker Ave Tulsa OK 74114-5322 Office: Okla State U 534 Math Scis Bldg Stillwater OK 74078-1060 E-mail: vestal@okstate.edu.

VETAL, BRADLEY S. service company executive; Degree in mech. engring. cum laude, U. Mich. Various positions Aeschliman Equipment Co.; v.p. Ea. ops. Matrix Svc. Mid-Continent, Inc., 1991—92; pres. Matrix Svc., Inc., 1992—; v.p. tank divsn. Matrix Svc. Co., 1996—99, pres., CEO, dir., 1999—. Office: 10701 E Ute St Tulsa OK 74116

VETSCHER, TIMOTHY JOHN, reporter, television anchorman; b. St. Paul, Minn., Mar. 4, 1976; s. John T. and Mary J. V. BA, Marquette U., 1998. Writer WDJT-TV, Milw., 1997; reporter KSAX-TV, Alexandria, Minn., 1998; reporter, anchor KLKN-TV, Lincoln, Nebr., 1999; news reporter WHBQ-TV, Fox 13, Memphis, 1999—. Columnist Marquette Tribune, 1996-98; talk show host WMUR Radio. Recipient Best Investigative Story award Nebr. AP, 2000. Mem. Soc. Profl. Journalists, Radio and TV News Dirs. Assn. Democrat. Roman Catholic. Avocations: golf, reading, travel, opera. Office: WHBQ-TV 485 S Highland St Memphis TN 38111-4391 E-mail: timothy376@aol.com.

VETTER, DAVID R. lawyer, data processing executive; b. 1959; BA, Bucknell U., 1981; JD, U. Fla., 1984. Bar: 1984. Sr. v.p., gen. counsel, sec. Tech Data Corp., Clearwater, Fla. Mem. ABA.

VEVERKA, DONALD JOHN, lawyer; b. Chgo., July 20, 1935, s. John Edward and Irene Cecelia (Wasil) V.; m. Mary Almjeld, May 27, 1967 (dec.); children: Tanya, Holly, Marc. BS, Loyola U., Chgo., 1957; JD, DePaul U., 1963. Bar: Ill. 1963, U.S. Dist. Ct. (no. dist.) Ill. 1963, U.S. Ct. Appeals (7th cir.) 1963, U.S. Supreme Ct. 1968. Asst. state's atty. civil appeals sect. Cook County State's Attys. Office, 1963-67; asst. atty. gen. appeals sect. Ill. Atty. Gen. Office, 1967-68; house counsel Kenilworth Ins. Co., 1968-69; ptnr. Bradshaw, Speranza, Veverka & Brumlik, 1969-72; spl. asst. atty. gen., 1970-72; ptnr. Speranza & Veverka, Chgo., 1972-73, 74-90, Veverka Rosen & Haugh, 1990—. Officer Henehan Donovan Isaacson Speranza & Veverka, Ltd., Chgo., 1973-74; bd. dirs., officer DePaul Law Coun., 1972-83; mem. Ill. Supreme Ct. Com. on Pattern Jury Instrns. Assoc., 1973-96, chmn., 1993-96. Author: How To Buy or Sell Your Home Without a Lawyer, 1982; also articles. Bd. dirs. LaGrange Cmty. Meml. Hosp., 1979-89, officer, 1982-85, pres., 1986 87; bd. dirs. Rich Port YMCA, 1981—, chmn., 1997-99; trustee Village of LaGrange Park, Ill., 1981-95; police bd. Village of LaGrange Park, 1979-80, 2000—. 1st lt. U.S. Army, 1967-69; capt. Res. Mem. ABA (faculty mem. Nat. Inst. Appellate Advocacy 1980, Ill. chmn. young lawyers com. on jud. selection 1971-72), Ill. State Bar Assn. (mem. com. on corrections reform 1973, also past mem. spkrs. bur., young mems. conf.), Bar Assn. Seventh Fed. Cir. (Ill. chmn. meetings com. 1976), DePaul Alumni Assn. (governing bd. 1975-82), Chgo. Athletic Assn., Phi Alpha Delta, Blue Key, Rich Port YMCA Men's Club, Oak Brook Park Dist. Racquet Club. Roman Catholic. Home: 709 N Park Rd La Grange Park IL 60526-1428 Office: 180 N Michigan Ave Chicago IL 60601-7401 Office Phone: 312-372-3665. *Notable cases include: Witherspoon vs. Ill., U.S. Supreme Ct. Case involved the qualification of jurors in death penalty cases.*

VEYNA, ADRIENNE MARIE, exercise specialist; b. Denver, Nov. 27, 1979; d. Arlene and Timothy Rightsell(Stepfather), Julian Benny Veyna III. BS, Colo. State U., 2003. Specialist exercise physiology Clinix Health Svcs. Colo., Centennial, 1998—. Intern, student leader health promotions Hartshorm Health Svcs. Colo. State U., Fort Collins, 2002—03. Scholarship for Hispanic Students of Employees, GM, 1998. Achievements include patents for Teaching Educators about Health (T.E.A.C.H.), a 12-week health and wellness program for teachers. Avocations: running, skiing. Personal E-mail: adrienneveyna@yahoo.com.

VEZERIDIS, MICHAEL PANAGIOTIS, surgeon, educator; b. Thessaloniki, Greece, Dec. 16, 1943; came to U.S., 1974; s. Panagiotis and Sofia (Avramidis) V.; m. Therese Mary Statz; children: Peter Statz, Alexander Michael. MD, U. Athens, 1967; MA ad eundem (hon.), Brown U., 1989. Diplomate Am. Bd. Surgery. Fellow surg. rsch. Harvard Med. Sch./Mass. Gen. Hosp., Boston, 1974-77; resident U. Mass., Worcester, 1977-80; fellow in surg. oncology Roswell Park Meml. Inst., Buffalo, 1980-81, attending surgeon, 1981-82; staff surgeon VA Med. Ctr., Providence, 1982-84; asst. prof. surgery Brown U., Providence, 1982-88; chief surg. oncology VA Med. Ctr., Providence, 1984—, assoc. chief surgery, 1986-98, chief surgery, 1998—; cons. in surgery R.I. Hosp., Providence, 1987—; surg. oncologist Roger Williams Med. Ctr., Providence, 1989—; assoc. dir. divsn. surg. oncology Brown U., Providence, 1989—, assoc. prof. surgery, 1988-94, prof., 1994—; prof. surgery Boston U. Sch. Medicine, 1999—. Chmn. profl. edn. com. R.I. divsn. Am. Cancer Soc., Providence, 1987-89, pres.-elect 1989-91, pres. 1991-93, del. dir. to nat. bd. dirs., 1993-96, mem. Nat. Assembly of the Am. Cancer Soc., 1997-2003, mem. internat. activities adv. com., 2003-, bd. dirs. New Eng. divsn., 1997-2001, chief med. officer New Eng. divsn., 1999-2001; chmn. R.I. State Cancer Liaison Program Am. Coll. Sugeons, 1999—, mem. commn. on cancer, 2003-; vis. prof. U. Patras (Greece) Med. Sch., 1988; mem. sci. adv. com. Clin. Rsch. Ctr., Brown U., Providence, 1989-91. Contbr. articles to profl. jours. and chpts. in med. books. Mem. parish coun. Ch. of Annunciation, Cranston, R.I., 1985-91; v.p. Hellenic Cultural Soc. Southeastern New Eng., Providence, 1987-89. Decorated Navy Commendation medal; named Profl. Fed. Employee of Yr., R.I. Fed. Exec. Coun., 1987; recipient St. George medal Am. Cancer Soc.; Merit Rev. Cancer Rsch. grantee VA, 1983-89. Fellow ACS (treas. R.I. chpt. 1996-2000, pres.-elect 2000-2002, pres. 2002-2004); mem. Soc. Surg. Oncology, Assn. for Acad. Surgery, Am. Soc. Clin. Oncology, N.Y. Acad. Scis. (life), Soc. for Surgery Alimentary Tract, Am. Assn. for Cancer Rsch., Collegium Internat. Chirurgiae Digestivae, Assn. Mil. Surgeons U.S., Soc. for Metastasis Rsch., New Eng. Cancer Soc., New Eng. Surg. Soc., Quidnessett Country Club. Greek Orthodox. Avocations: classical music, reading, fencing, tennis, squash, cross country skiing. Home: 50 Limerock Dr East Greenwich RI 02818-1643 Office: Univ Surg Assocs Ste 470 Two Dudley St Providence RI 02905 Office Phone: 401-331-1036.

VEZIROGLU, TURHAN NEJAT, mechanical engineering educator, energy researcher; b. Istanbul, Turkey, Jan. 24, 1924; came to U.S., 1962; s. Abdul Kadir and Ferruh (Bürün) V.; m. Bengi Isikli, Mar. 17, 1961; children: Emre Alp, Oya Sureyya. A.C.G.I., City and Guilds Coll., London, 1946; B.Sc. with honors, U. London, 1947; D.I.C., Imperial Coll., London, 1948; PhD, U. London, 1951. Engring. apprentice Alfred Herbert Ltd., Coventry, U.K., 1945; project engr. Office of Soil Products, Ankara, Turkey, 1953-56; tech. dir. M.K.V. Constrn. Co, Istanbul, 1957-61; assoc. prof. mech. engring. U. Miami, Coral Gables, Fla., 1962-65, prof. Coral Fables, Fla., 1966—, dir. grad. studies mech. engring. Coral Gables, Fla., 1965-71, chmn. dept. mech. engring., 1971-75, assoc. dean research Coll. Engring., 1975-79, dir. Clean Energy Research Inst., 1974—. UNESCO cons., Paris; vis. prof. Middle East Tech. U., Ankara, 1969 Editor-in-chief: Internat. Jour. Hydrogen Energy, 1976—. Pres. Learning Disabilities Found., Miami, 1972-73, advisor, 1974-80. Recipient Turkish Presdl. sci. award Turkish Sci. and Tech. Research Found., 1975; named hon. prof. Xian Jiaotong U., China, 1982 Fellow AAAS, ASME, Instn. Mech. Engrs.; mem. Internat. Assn. Hydrogen Energy (pres. 1975), AIAA, Assn. Energy Engrs., Am. Nuclear Soc., Am. Soc. Engring. Edn., AAUP, Internat. Soc. Solar Energy, Systems Engring. Soc., Sigma Xi Home: 4910 Biltmore Dr Miami FL 33146-1724 Office: U Miami Clean Energy Rsch Inst PO Box 248294 Miami FL 33124-8294 Office Phone: 305-284-4666. Business E-Mail: veziroglu@miami.edu. *Hydrogen energy system will provide the world with clean and abundant energy, while doing away with pollution, acid rains and the greenhouse effect. It is a noble and worthwhile goal to strive for.*

VIAMONTE, MANUEL, surgeon; b. Havana, Cuba, Feb. 3, 1958; came to U.S., 1959; s. Manuel Jr. and Maria Eugenia (Rosado) V.; m. Olga del Carmen Gonzalez, APr. 14, 1966; children: Manuel Aurelio, Michael Alexander. BS, U. Miami, 1986; MD, U. Fla., 1986. Diplomate Am. Bd. Surgery, Am. Bd. Colon and Rectal Surgery, Nat. Bd. Med. Examiners; cert. controlled substances, advance trauma life support. Intern, resident in gen. surgery U. Miami, Jackson Meml. Hosp., Fla., 1986-91; fellow in colon and rectal surgery St. Luke's/Roosevelt Hosp. Ctr., Columbia Coll. Physicians and Surgeons, N.Y.C., 1991-92; clin. asst. prof. surgery sch. medicine U. Miami, 1992—. Presenter in field. Contbr. articles to profl. jours. Fellow ACS (assoc.); mem. AMA, Am. Soc. Colon and Rectal Surgeons, Fla. Med. Assn., Med. Soc. of State of N.Y., Dade County Med. Assn., N.Y. County Med. Soc. Republican. Roman Catholic. Avocations: spearfishing, scuba diving. Office: 9195 Sunset Dr Ste 230 Miami FL 33173-3488

VIANI, JAMES LAURENCE, lawyer; b. Kincaid, Ill., Dec. 24, 1932; s. Frank Jerome and Alfonsina V.; m. Virginia Lee Wilson, Dec. 27, 1958; children: Theresa, Diana, Deborah. BS, Millikin U., 1954; LLB, Wash. U., St. Louis, 1957. Bar: Ill. 1957, Mo. 1957. Assoc. Blackmar, Swanson, Midgley, Jones & Eager, Kansas City, Mo., 1958-59, Stinson, Mag & Fizzell, Kansas City, 1960-62; ptnr. Stinson, Mag & Fizzel, Kansas City, 1962-87, chmn. corp. dept., 1979-87, cons. ptnr., 1988-92. Br. bd. chmn. YMCA, Kansas City, 1979-81. With U.S. Army, 1957-63. Mem. ABA, Phi Kappa Phi, Order of the Coif. Republican. Avocations: hiking, reading, farming. Home: 11106 Belleview Ave Kansas City MO 64114-5115

VIATCHENKO-KARPINSKI, SERGE, biophysicist, researcher; b. Kyiv, Ukraine, May 24, 1961; s. Vsevolod Viatchenko-Karpinski and Nina Alekseeva. MS, Kyiv State U., Phys. Dept., Ukraine, 1984; PhD in Biophysics, Bogomoletz Inst. of Physiology, Ukraine, 1995. Rsch. assoc. Bogomoletz Inst. of Physiology, Kyiv, Ukraine, 1994—95, Inst. of Neuroscience U. of Cologne, Germany, 1995—97; sr. rschr. Bogomoletz Inst. of Physiology, Kyiv, Ukraine, 1997—98; rsch. assoc. Tex. Tech U. HSC Physiology, Lubbock, 1998—2001, instr., 2001—. Mem.: N.Y. Acad. of Scis., Biophysical Soc., German Physiol. Soc., Ukrainian Biophysical Soc., Ukrainian Physiol. Soc. Avocations: fishing, travel. Office: Tex Tech U HSC Physiology 3601 4th St Lubbock TX 79430 Office Phone: 1-806-743-2561. Office Fax: 1-806-743-1512. E-mail: serge.karpinski@ttuhsc.edu.

VIATOR, JOHN A. biomedical physicist, military officer; s. John Dunis and Fujiko Viator. BS, U. Wash., 1985; MS, U. Oreg., 1993, Oreg. Grad. Inst., 1997; PhD, Oreg. Health & Sci. U., 2001. Engr. Conix Rsch., Springfield, Oreg., 1992—95; postdoctoral rschr. Beckman Laser Inst., Irvine, Calif., 2000—03; sr. rsch. assoc. Oreg. Health & Sci. U., Portland, 2003—; sr. scientist Blue Rd. Rsch., Gresham, Oreg., 2003—; vis. rschr. Beckman Laser Inst., Irvine, Calif., 2003—. Author (actor): (stage play) Nightshift with William. Lt. comdr. USN, 1985—2003. Decorated Navy Achievement medal USN; fellow Ruth L. Kirschstein Nat. Rsch. Svc. award, NIH, 2003—; grantee Rsch. grant, Am. Soc. for Laser Medicine and Surgery (ASLMS), 2003. Mem.: SPIE, The Internat. Soc. for Optical Engring., Soc. for Indsl. and Applied Math., Am. Soc. for Laser Medicine and Surgery, Sigma Xi (v.p., uc irvine chpt. 2002—03). Roman Catholic. Achievements include patents pending for Photoacoustic imaging of skin. Home: 1329 NE Hancock St #4 Portland OR 97212 Office: Dept of Dermatology OP06 3181 SW Sam Jackson Pk Rd Portland OR 97239 Office Phone: 503-494-8066. Home Fax: 503-418-4266; Office Fax: 503-418-4266. Personal E-mail: viatorinst@yahoo.com. E-mail: viatorinst@yahoo.com.

VIAULT, RAYMOND G. food company executive; b. N.Y.C., Sept. 19, 1944; m. Lucille Viault; children: Lisa, Deborah, Russell. Bachelor's degree, Brown U.; MBA, Columbia U. Pres., CEO Kraft Jacobs Suchard, Zurich, Switzerland; CEO Jacobs Suchard A.G. (acquired by Kraft Gen. Foods), 1990-93; pres. Maxwell House Coffee Co. Kraft Gen. Foods, v.p., gen. mgr. desserts divsn.; with Gen. Mills, Mpls., 1996—, vice-chmn., 1996—, also bd. dirs.; responsible for meals divsn., baking divsn. Pillsbury U.S. Bakery and Food Svc. Bd. dirs. Cereal Ptnrs. Worldwide, VF Corp. Newell Rubbermaid. Bd. overseers Columbia Grad. Sch. Bus., N.Y.C.; trustee Lawrenceville Sch., N.J.; bd. dirs. United Way Mpls., Minn. Internat. Ctr., Technoserve. Office: PO Box 1113 One General Mills Blvd Minneapolis MN 55440-1113

VICARI, ANDREW, artist; b. Port Talbot, Wales, Apr. 20, 1938; s. Vittorio Vicari and Italia Bertani. Student, Slade Sch. of Art, London, 1951-53. Represented in many permanent and pvt. collections including: Dallas Mus. Fine Arts, Nat. Libr. Wales, Mus. Tel-Aviv, Contemporary Arts Soc. Great Britain, Tate Gallery, Columbus Mus. Fine Arts, Poldi Pezzoli Mus., Milan, Mus. Petit Palais, Modern Art, Geneva, David Lloyd Kreeger Coll., Washington, IBM Coll. Armonk, N.Y., Palais Princier, Monaco; group exibits include: Retrospective Chinese Ministry of Culture, Palais des Beaux Arts, Beijing, 1995, From War to Peace in the Gulf, Vicari Opus of 225 paintings, 1990-2000, Ministry of the Interior, Paris, 2000, many others; commd. paintings include: King of Saudi Arabia, Interpol and CRS France; author: Triumph of the Bedouin, 1984; illustrator: (poems) From the Orient and the Desert, 1984, La Vigonade a Vicari (by Louis Pauwels), 1989, (BBC film) Outrageous Fortune: Life of Andrew Vicari, 1997, the Mystery of Memory, 2002. World patron Beacon Millenium Trust. Decorated chevalier Order of Merit (Monaco); mem. The Guild of Freeman of the City of London, 2002, Liveryman of Wales, 2002; brigadier d'honneur Compagnie Republicaine de Securite (France); recipient European Beaux Arts prize, 1995; recipient Beaux Arts prize European Parliament and Coun. Europe, 1995. Fellow London Zool. Soc.; mem. East India and Pub. Schs. Club (London), Cardiff (Wales) and County Club, Bristol Channel Yacht Club, Lords Cricket Ground London, Marylebone Cricket Club, Rotary Internat. (hon.). Avocations: tennis, squash, gourmet cuisine. Home: The East India Club 16 St James' Square London SW1Y 4LH England Fax: 0044 07092006234. E-mail: executive@andrew.vicari.com.

VICARY, WILLIAM CHARLES, JR., director sales and marketing; b. Dearborn, Mich., Nov. 27, 1956; s. William Charles and Nancy Jane (Ternes) V.; m. Sandra Kay Leach, Mar. 24, 1990. AS in Liberal Arts, Henry Ford C.C., 1977; BS in Packaging Engring., Mich. State U., 1980. Packaging engr. GM, Dayton, Ohio, 1980-83, Sanders Assoc., Nashua, N.H., 1983-84; corp. packaging engr. Mack Trucks, Inc., Allentown, Pa., 1984-86; mktg. coord. Fluor Daniel, Inc., Greenville, S.C., 1986-91; mgr. bus. devel. Simons Engring., Greenville, S.C., 1991-95; venue coord. and cons. ACOG and Planit Sports, Greenville, S.C., 1996-97; dir. food & beverage Sverdrup Facilities Inc., St. Louis, 1997-98; dir. corp. mktg. and sales SSOE Inc., Toledo, 1998—. Venue coord-yatching Atlanta Com. for Olympic Games, Savannah, Ga., 1996; pres. Planit Sports & Events, Greer, S.C., St. Louis, 1995—. Co-chairperson & founder Golf for Greenville, 1990, 91. Mem. KC. Avocations: golf, boating music art. Office: SSOE Inc 1001 Madison Ave Ste A Toledo OH 43624-1585 Home: 406 Arlington Ave E Oldsmar FL 34677-3803 Fax: (419) 255-6101.

VICE, ROY LEE, history educator; b. Lynchburg, Va., Oct. 12, 1950; s. Cline Lowell and Ruth Burchell (Newman) V. BA in History, BS in Physics, Carson-Newman Coll., 1972; MA in History, U. Chgo., 1976, PhD in History, 1984. Lectr. Continuing Edn. program U. Chgo., 1985-86, 87-88, rare books asst. univ. librs., 1986; asst. prof. Pacific Luth. U., Tacoma, 1986-87, Clemson (S.C.) U., 1988-90, Wright State U., Dayton, Ohio, 1990-95, assoc. prof., 1995—. Contbr. articles to profl. jours. Vol. tutor CYCLE Cabrini-Green Projects, Chgo., 1981—86; vol. lectr. LaSalle St. Ch., Chgo., 1989—98, 2000—04. With U.S. Army, 1972—74. Mem. Am. Hist. Assn., 16th Century Studies Conf. Democrat. Baptist. Home: 229 E 2nd St Dayton OH 45402-1719 Office: Wright State U Dept History 3640 Colonel Glenn Hwy Dayton OH 45435-0001 Business E-Mail: roy.vice@wright.edu.

VICHIOLA, CHRISTOPHER MICHAEL, educator, writer; b. Bridgeport, Conn., Apr. 27, 1959; s. Michael Richard and Delores (Distaci) Vichiola; m. Tracey Vichiola, Nov. 12, 1997; children: Michael, Christopher, Anthony. AS, Western Conn. State U., 1981, BA, 1983; grad., Colonel James "Bo" Gritz's Spec. Forces Green Beret On-Field Med. Surg. Sch. Cert. nursing asst. Martial arts tchr. Am. Bujinkan Dojo, Danbury, Conn., 1993—; tchr., distbr. Ctr. for Action, Kamiah, Idaho, 1997—; with Home Depot, 1998—, A&P Foodmart, 1999—2003, Price Chopper Grocery, 2003—. Educator, cons. Primerica Fin. Svcs., Danbury, 1997—; educator Christic Inst. Law Firm, Washington, 1995—. Author: Above the Law - The Real Story's Files, 1995, Above the Law Part II, 1995, The Real Story of Christopher Vichiola and Colonel Gritz, 1997, The Real Story of Christopher Vichiola's and Colonel Gritz's Training, 1997. Educator Rev. Jesse L. Jackson's Rainbow Coalition, Washington, 1992—, Mayor Eugene Eriquez Dem. Party, Danbury, 1987—, Rep. Jack Brooks, 1991—, Gov. Michael Dukakis, 1989—. Black belt in Ninjutsu, 1997; recipient Eagle award Col. James "Bo" Gritz, 1997, Spike Navy Seal Scuba badge Col. James "Bo" Gritz, 1997. Avocations: camping, scuba diving, basketball, football, martial arts.

VICK, COLUMBUS EDWIN, JR., retired civil engineering design firm executive; b. Jacksonville, Fla., Nov. 8, 1934; s. Columbus Edwin Sr. and Lucretia (Dean) V.; m. Laura Anne McGowan, Mar. 28, 1964; children: Jennifer, Carolyn, Elizabeth. BSCE, N.C. State U., 1956, MSCE, 1960. Registered profl. engr., 15 states. Rsch. asst. N.C. State Civil Engring. Dept., Raleigh, 1958-60; transp. planning engr. Harland Bartholomew & Assocs., Memphis, 1960-64, office and project mgr. Raleigh, 1964-67; prin., co-founder Kimley-Horn and Assocs. Inc., Raleigh, 1967-72, pres., 1972-92; chmn., 1992-2000. Bd. dirs. Wachovia Bank, Design Profls. Coalition Am. Cons. Engrs. Coun. Co-author: North Carolina Atlas; contbr. articles to profl. jours. Past pres., bd. dirs. N.C. State U. Engring. Found.; past pres. bd. assocs. Meredith Coll.; past dir. N.C. State U. Alumni Assn.; bd. visitors N.C. State

U.; past 2d v.p. Bapt. State Conv. of N.C.; bd. dirs. Assoc. Bapt. Press, Bibl. Recorder; trustee Kenan Inst. for Engring. Tech. and Sci., Gardner Webb U., Meredith Coll.; mem. bd. advisors Wake Forest U. Sch. Divinity. Named Disting. Engring. alumnus N.C. State U., 1991. Fellow ASCE (Outstanding Young Engr. award ea. br. N.C. sect. 1966), Inst. Transp. Engrs. (Outstanding Individual Activity award so. sect. 1978, Disting. Svc. award so. sect. 1981, Lifetime Svc. award N.C. sect. 1995); mem. NSPE (Disting. Svc. award), Am. Con. Engrs. Coun., Am. Inst. Cert. Planners, Profl. Svcs. Mgmt. Assn. (Coll. of Fellow), N.C. Soc. Engrs. (Outstanding Engring Achievement award 1992). Baptist. Home: 2205 Nancy Ann Dr Raleigh NC 27607-3318 Office: Kimley-Horn and Assocs Inc 3001 Weston Pky Cary NC 27513-2301 E-mail: ed.vick@kimley-horn.com.

VICK, EDWARD HOGE, JR., advertising executive; b. N.Y.C., Feb. 27, 1944; s. Edward Hoge and Margaret Jane (Sprankle) V.; m. Nancy Jane Newcomer; Children: Joshua D., Charlie, Jane. AB, U. N.C., 1966; MS, Northwestern U., 1971. With Benton & Bowles, Inc., N.Y.C., 1971-75, Ogilvy & Mather, Inc., N.Y.C., 1975-83; exec. v.p., dir. account service Ammirati & Puris Inc., N.Y.C., 1983-85, pres., chief operating officer, 1985-90; pres., CEO Levine, Huntley, Vick & Beaver, N.Y.C., 1990-94, Young & Rubicam N.Y., 1994-96, chmn., CEO, 1997—. Author: An Examination of the Creative Process, 1971. Bd. vis. U. N.C. Decorated Bronze Star (2). Mem. Am. Assn. Advt. Agys. (bd. dirs.), Advt. Edn. Found. (bd. dirs.), St. Andrew's Soc. Republican. Presbyterian. Home: 501 Guard Hill Rd Bedford NY 10506 Office: Young & Rubicam 285 Madison Ave New York NY 10017

VICK, JAMES ALBERT, publishing executive, consultant; b. Norwalk, Conn., Feb. 5, 1945; s. James Albert and Madeline (Mayew) V.; m. Deborah M. Ashley, Dec. 23, 1964 (div. Oct. 1974); children: James Ashley, Guy Robert; m. Susan Jane Collins, May 14, 1977; 1 child, Jonathan Scott. BS, Boston U., 1967. Dist. mgr. McGraw Hill Pub. Co., N.Y.C., 1969-75, Cahners Pub. Co., N.Y.C., 1975-79; mgr. advt. ASCE, N.Y.C., 1979-82; v.p. mktg. Bill Communications, N.Y.C., 1982-87; pub. Thomas Pub. Co., N.Y.C., 1987-95; v.p. Web Property Devel. Poppe Tyson, 1995-96; exec. v.p. sales/mktg. Lawyers Weekly Publs., Boston, 1996-98; v.p. publ. Phillips Publ./KIPI, White Plains, N.Y., 1998-2000; pub., staff dir. IEEE Spectrum Mag., N.Y.C., 2000—. Cons. Carvajal, Calle, Columbia, 1984, McLarens, London, 1987; pubs. com. Am. Bus. Media. Capt. USAR, 1967-70, Vietnam. Mem. IEEE (comms. soc., computer soc.), Bus. Mktg. Assn. (cert. bus. communicator), Soc. Plastics Engrs., Princeton Club, Port Royal Golf Club, Elks. Episcopalian. Avocations: golf, sailing, antique restoration. Home: 473 Judd Rd Easton CT 06612 Office: IEEE Spectrum Mag 3 Park Ave Ste 1701 New York NY 10016-5997 Fax: 212-419-7589. Office Phone: 212-419-7767. E-mail: j.vick@ieee.org., javick@att.net.

VICK, JEFFREY HARRISON, music educator, musician; b. Denver, Nov. 5, 1965; s. Donald James and Sharlene Marie (Savage) Vick; m. Jacquelyn Campeau, Nov. 20, 1999; 1 child, Teresa Irene. BS in Music, U. Ariz., 1989; MEd in Music, Mont. State U., 1991. Cert. music tchr. grades K-12 Mont., secondary tchr. grades 7-12, secondary tchr. music, Office of Pub. Instrn., State Mont. Music educator Bozeman (Mont.) Pub. Schs., 1990—91, Willow Creek (Mont.) Sch., 1991—92, Anderson Sch. Dist. #41, Bozeman, 1993—. Pvt. percussion tchr., Bozeman, 1989—; prin. timpanist and percussionist Bozeman Symphony Orch., 1989—, Intermountain Opera Assn., Bozeman, 1990—, Mont. Ballet Co., Bozeman, 1993—; prin. timpanist Mont. Summer Symphony, Helena, 1998—2002; libr., coach Mont. chamber music workshop Mont. State U., Bozeman, 1990—, adj. instr. music, 1992—96, adv. bd. Mont. chamber music workshop, 1998—2003; dist. and state music festival adjudicator, 1994—; clinician Internat. Conf. on Percussion Music, Tucson, 1995; founding dir. PercOrchestra, Bozeman, 2000—; mem. Flutes and Friends, 2000. Composer: (band) Theme and Variations, 1984, (percussion) Escalation and Denouement, 1985, (Gamelan) Permulaan Baru, 2001, Musik Percobaan, 2001, Baru Saja Lahir, 2002, Kreasi Bagi Guru Besar, 2003, Rekan Imbangan, 2004, Asmara Nyanyian, 2003; editor (newsletter): Montana Percussion News, 1998—; musician: (Concerto with Orchestra) MILHAUD: Concerto for Percussion, 1991, SVOBODA: Concerto for Marimba, 1996, (Chamber Recital) Nat. Arts Festival, 1992, (Chamber Recital with Cascade Quartet) KULESHA: Quintet-Sonata, 1998, (Chamber Recital with Mistral Duo) UNG: Spiral, 1999, (Concerto with Percussion Ensemble) MCCARTHY: Concerto for Marimba, Percussion and Synthesizers, 2001. Recipient Individual Artist Fellowship award, Mont. Arts Coun., 1992—93. Mem.: NEA, Mont. Music Educators Assn., Music Educators Nat. Conf., Percussive Arts Soc. (sec. Ariz. chpt. 1986—87, v.p. Ariz. chpt. 1987—88, sec. Mont. chpt. 1998—), Am. Fedn. Musicians (exec. bd. local 709 1996—99, pres. local 709 1999—2002), Phi Delta Kappa (profl. rsch. grant 1999). Avocations: collecting instruments and masks, photography, world music. Home: 529 South Black Ave Bozeman MT 59715-5301 Office: Anderson Sch Dist #41 10040 Cottonwood Rd Bozeman MT 59718 Personal E-mail: jvick@metnet.state.mt.us.

VICK, MICHAEL, professional football player; b. Newport News, Va., June 26, 1980; Attended, Va. Tech. Football player Atlanta Falcons, 2001—. Named to NFC Pro-Bowl, 2002. Office: Atlanta Falcons 4400 Falcon Pkwy Flowery Branch GA 30542*

VICK, NICHOLAS A. neurologist; b. Chgo., Oct. 3, 1939; MD, U. Chgo., 1965. Diplomate Am. Bd. Neurology. Intern U. Chgo. Hosps., 1965, resident in neurology, 1966-68; fellow in neurology NIH, Bethesda, Md., 1968-70; staff Evanston (Ill.) Hosp., 1975—; prof. neurology Northwestern U. Med. Sch., Evanston, Ill., 1978—. Office: Evanston Hosp Dept Neurology 2650 Ridge Ave Evanston IL 60201-1781 Office Phone: 847-570-2570. Business E-Mail: nvick@enh.org.

VICK, PAUL ASHTON, lawyer; b. Rochester, N.Y., Sept. 30, 1945; s. Robert A. and Dorothy Lou (Flanders) V.; Joyce M. Vick, NOv. 28, 1998; children—Jennifer, Christopher, Benjamin. B.A., Kalamazoo Coll., 1967; M.Div., Colgate Rochester Div. Sch., 1971; postgrad. New Eng. Sch. Law, 1972-73; J.D., SUNY-Buffalo, 1975. Bar: N.Y. 1976, U.S. Dist. Ct. (we. dist.) N.Y. 1976. Dir. Southeast Area Coalition Family Counseling, Rochester, 1969-72; assoc. firm Sullivan, Peters, Burns and Holtzberg, Rochester, 1976-79; ptnr. firm Sullivan, Peters, Burns, Holtzberg & Stander, Rochester, 1980-81, firm Phillips, Lytle, Hitchcock, Blaine & Huber, Rochester, 1982— . Trustee Immanuel Bapt. Ch., Rochester, 1984—; bd. dirs. Cameron Community Ministries, Rochester, 1983-88, Alternatives for Battered Women, Rochester, 1981-96. Mem. Monroe County Bar Assn. (exec. council estate and trust sect. 1983—96). Democrat. Lodge: Masons. Office: Phillips Lytle Hitchcock Blaine & Huber 1400 First Federal Plz Rochester NY 14614-1981 Home: 70 Whitestone Ln Rochester NY 14618-4113 E-mail: pvick@phillipslytle.com.

VICK, SUSAN, playwright, educator, director, actress; b. Raleigh, NC, Nov. 4, 1945; d. Thomas B. Jr. and Merle (Hayes) V. MFA, So. Meth. U., 1969; PhD, U. Ill., 1979. Prof. drama/theatre and dir. theatre WPI, 1981—; playwright Excuse Me For Living Prodns., Cambridge, Mass., 1989—, Festival Fringe, Edinburgh, 1989—; dir. WPI New Voices in N.Y. Dreams Abridged, Samuel French Festival, 2004. Playwright Ensemble Studio Theatre, N.Y.C., 1981-83; founder WPI Ann. New Voices Festival of Original Plays, 1982. Editor: (2 vols.) Playwrights Press, Amherst, 1988—; playwright: When I Was Your Age, 1982, Ord-Way Ames-Gay, 1982, Investments, 1985, Half Naked, 1989, Quandary, 1983, Meat Selection, 1984, Give My Love to Everyone But, 1989; appeared in plays including Rip Van Winkle, 1979, Why I Live at The P.O., 1982, The Play Group, 1984-85, Present Stage, 1985, Sister Mary Ignatius Explain It All, 1986, Wipeout, 1988, Bogus Joan, 1992-93; dir. play Give My Love to Everyone But, 1990 (Edinburgh Festival); theatre editor: Sojourner The Women's Forum, 1995-98; dramatist, script cons. Clyde Unity Theatre, Glasgow, Scotland, 1992-93, 1999-2000. Dir., Women's Community Theatre, Amherst, 1981-84, Upstart, Wis., 1994; head Kew Montessori Ctr. Faculty fellow U. Ill., 1976-77, Bd. of Trustees Award for Outstanding Tchg., WPI, 1997. Mem. U.S. Inst. for Theatre Tech., Nat. Assn. Schs. of Theatre, New Eng. Theatre Conf., Inc., Drama League, Dramatists Guild (assoc.), Soc. Stage Dirs. and Choreographers (assoc.), U.S. Inst. Theatre Tech., New England Theatre Conf., Nat. Assn. Schs. Theatre, Alpha Phi Omega (Svc. to Students award 1996). Avocations: puppets, frogs, travel. Office: WPI 100 Instit Rd Worcester MA 01609-2280 Office Phone: 508-831-5682. Business E-Mail: svick@wpi.edu.

VICKERS, GEORGE ROSS, non-profit organization executive, sociology educator; b. Evanston, Ill., Dec. 26, 1943; s. George Warren and Frances Louise (Ross) V.; m. Irene Silverblatt, Oct. 13, 2001. Student, Northwestern U., 1966-68; MA, Washington U., 1970, PhD, 1973. Staff sociologist Russell Sage Found., N.Y.C., 1973-75; prof. Bklyn. Coll. and the Grad. Ctr., CUNY, N.Y.C. and Bklyn., 1975-97; exec. dir. Washington Office of Latin Am., 1993—2001, also bd. dirs.; regional dir. for Latin Am. Open Society Inst., 2002—. Bd. dirs. Inst. for Ctrl. Am. Studies, N.Y.C., Hemisphere Initiatives, Cambridge, Latin Am. Working Group, Washington, DC. Author: The Formation of the New Left, 1975, Prologue to Sociology, 1977. Mem. presdl. del. to observe the elections in El Salvador, Pres. of the U.S., El Salvador, 1994; U.S. Spl. Ambassador to Guatamala, 2000. Mem. Am. Sociol. Assn., L.Am. Studies Assn. (chair com. on acad. freedom and human rights 2002-03). Avocation: running. E-mail: gvickers@osi-dc.org.

VICKERS, LEE LOUISE, minister; b. Suffern, N.Y., Dec. 20, 1954; d. Chester E. and Dorothy Jean (Allen) Vickers; 1 child, Seth. Dipl. summa cum laude, We. Bapt. Coll., 1977; A in Forestry, Flathead Valley C.C., 1979, A, 1980; BA in Liberal Arts, Regents Coll., 1988. Sec.-clk. Glacier Ch., Kalispell, Mont., 1988—91; pastor Indep. Ministry, Mont., 1991—. Clk. Nat. Flood Svcs., Kalispell, 2001—. Poem, E Duo Unum, 1993; author: Earth and Sky, 2002. Firefighter, dept. sec. Marion (Mont.) Vol. Fire Dept., 1996—98. With U.S. Army, 1982—84. Avocations: Bee Gees fan, reading, poetry. Home: PO Box 9155 Kalispell MT 59904

VICKERS, MARCIA, journalist; BA, Meredith Coll., 1983; MA, Columbia U. Grad. Sch. Journalism. Editor-in-chief On Wall St., Securites Data Pub./Thomson; contbr. NY Times Sunday Bus. Section, 1996—98; dept. editor markets and investments Bus. Week, 1999—2000, assoc. editor, prin. markets reporter, 2000—. Adj. prof.; appeared on Moneyline, CNNfn, ABC News' World News Tonight with Peter Jennings, Nat. Pub. Radio, Money Talks, WABC-TV, NY. Recipient Medill/Strong Fin. Writing award, 1999, 2000. Office: Bus Week 1221 Ave of the Americas 43rd Fl New York NY 10020 Office Phone: 212-512-2511.

VICKERS, MARK STEPHEN, business educator, travel industry executive, sculptor, painter; b. Vallego, Calif., Sept. 11, 1957; s. John Frederick and Anna Ruth (Boschell) V. BA in Bus. Adminstrn., Azusa Pacific U., 1979; grad. studies, U. Bourgogne, Dijon, France, 1986-87. Dir. public relations Azusa Pacific div. Bus., 1977-78; copywriter Pennington, Inc., Fullerton, Calif., 1978; dir. communications Glendora (Calif.) C. of C., 1979; asst. mgr., dir. public relations Burbank (Calif.) C. of C., 1979-82, exec. dir., 1982-84; v.p. Astra Tours and Travel, Los Angeles, 1984-86; custom group cons. Marquis Tours, Vallejo, 1987—; bus. instr. St. Patrick's High Sch., Vallejo, 1987—; pres. US Sportsmarque, 1987—. Author: Selling Art on the Internet, 2000, Right-Brained Guide to a Left-Brained Industry, 2002; columnist, poet and contbg. editor Calif. Chamber Execs. Assn. Newsletter and Burbank Bus. Today mag. Coordinator Burbank Trade Fair Festival. Recipient Eagle Scout award Boy Scouts Am., 1971; Bus. award Bank of Am., 1975; Outstanding Young Man of Am. award U.S. Jaycees, 1982; Calif. State Senate Resolution award, 1984. Mem. Am. Chamber Execs. Assn., Calif. Chamber Execs. Assn., Los Angeles Public Interest Radio and TV Ednl. Soc. Clubs: Toastmasters (Burbank); San Fernando Valley Press (pres.). Office Phone: 707-642-2933. E-mail: marques@neteze.com.

VICKERS, NANCY J. academic administrator; BA, Mt. Holyoke Coll., 1967, LHD (hon.), 1999; MA, Yale U., 1971, PhD, 1976. Prof. French and Italian Dartmouth Coll., 1973—87; prof. French, Italian, and comparative literature U. Southern Calif., 1987—97, dean curriculum and instrn. Coll. Letters, Arts and Scis., 1994—97; pres. Bryn Mawr Coll., 1997—. Vis. prof. Harvard U., U. Pa., UCLA; bd. dirs. Bryn Mawr Bank Corp.; bd. govs. Coun. Dante Soc. Am. Recipient Presdl. medal Outstanding Leadership and Achievement, Dartmouth Coll., 1991; fellow vis. fellow, Princeton U. Office: Bryn Mawr Coll 101 N Merion Ave Bryn Mawr PA 19010-2899

VICKERS, SELWYN M. surgeon; BA in Natural Scis., Johns Hopkins U., 1982, MD, 1986. Diplomate Am. Bd. Surgery. Instr. surgery Johns Hopkins Hosp., Balt., 1993—94; asst. prof. surgery U. Ala., Birmingham, 1994—99, assoc. scientist, 1995—2002, co-dir. Pancreaticobiliary Ctr., 1998, assoc. prof. surgery, 1999—2003, prof. surgery, chief sect. gastrointestinal surgery, John H. Blue chair gen. surgery, 2000—. Surg. oncology fellow Johns Hopkins U., 1993—94, surg. rsch. fellow, 1988—90; co-dir. Minority Health & Rsch. Ctr. U. Ala., Birmingham, 2002, sr. scientist Comprehensive Cancer Ctr, 02. Recipient Resident Rsch. award, Balt. Acad. Surgery, 1990, Young Clinician award, Soc. for Surgery Alimentary Tract, 1998—99; Robert Wood Johnson rsch. fellow, 1995—99. Fellow: James IV Assn. Surgeons, Inc.; mem.: Alpha Omega Alpha. Office: U Ala-Birmingham 406 Kracke Bldg 1922 7th Ave S Birmingham AL 35294-0016 Office Phone: 205-934-5147. E-mail: smu@uab.edu.

VICKERS, STANLEY, biochemical pharmacologist; b. Blackpool, Eng., Sept. 27, 1939; arrived in U.S., 1962, naturalized, 1979; s. Norman Stanley and Hannah (Snape) Vickers; m. Florence Margaret Foster, Jan. 6, 1975. BSc, London U., 1962; PhD, SUNY, Buffalo, 1967. Fellow U. Kans., Lawrence, 1966-69; sr. rsch. pharmacologist Merck & Co., West Point, Pa., 1969-71, rsch. fellow, 1971-81, sr. rsch. fellow, 1981-2001; ret., 2001. Assoc. editor: Current Drug Metabolism, 1999—2001; contbr. articles to profl. jours. Mem.: AAAS, Internat. Soc. Study Xenobiotics, N.Y. Acad. Scis., Am. Chem. Soc., Am. Soc. Pharmacology and Exptl. Therapeutics. Achievements include patents in field. Avocations: golf, skiing, health club activities.

VICKERY, BYRDEAN EYVONNE HUGHES (MRS. CHARLES EVERETT VICKERY JR.), retired library services administrator; b. Apr. 18, 1928; d. Roy Franklin and Margaret Cordelia (Wood) Hughes; m. Charles Everett Vickery, Jr., Nov. 5, 1948; 1 child, Camille. Student, Flat River (Mo.) Jr. Coll., 1946-48; BS in Edn., S.E. Mo. State Coll., 1954; MLS, U. Wash., 1964; postgrad., Wash. State U., 1969-70. Tchr. Ironton (Mo.) Pub. Schs., 1948-56; elem. tchr. Pasco (Wash.) Sch. Dist. 1, 1956-61, jr. high sch. libr., 1961-68, coord. librs., 1968-69; asst. libr. Columbia Basin Cmty. Coll., Pasco, 1969-70; head libr., dir. Instructional Resources Ctr., Pasco, 1970-78, dir. libr. svcs., 1979-87, assoc. dean libr. svcs., 1987-90, ret., 1990; owner Vickery Search & Research, Pasco, 1990-99. Chmn. S.E. Wash. Libr. Svc. Area, 1977-78, 88-90; bd. dirs. Pasco-Kennewick Cmty. Concerts, 1977-88, pres., 1980-81, 87-88, Pasco-Kennewick Cmty. Concerts, treas., 1991-99; bd. dirs. Mid-Columbia Symphony Orch., 1983-89; trustee Wash. Commn. Humanities, 1982-85; bd. mem. Arts Coun. Mid-Columbia Region, 1991-93. Author, editor: Library and Research Skills Curriculum Guides for the Pasco School District, 1967; author (with Jean Thompson), also editor Learning Resources Handbook for Teachers, 1969. Recipient Woman of Achievement award Pasco Bus. and Profl. Women's Club, 1976. Mem. ALA, AAUW (2d v.p. 1966-68, corr. sec. 1969), Wash. Dept. Audio-Visual Instrn., Wash. Libr. Assn., Am. Assn. Higher Edn., Wash. Assn. Higher Edn., Wash. State Assn. Sch. Librs. (state conf. chmn. 1971-72), Tri-Cities Librs. Assn., Wash. Libr. Media Assn. (community coll. levels chmn. 1986-87), Am. Assn. Rsch. Libr., Soroptimist Internat. Assn. (rec. sec. Pasco-Kennewick chpt. 1971-72, treas. 1973-74, pres. 1978-80, v.p. 1989-90, treas. 1991, found. & awards chmn. 1995-96), Columbia Basin Coll. Adminstrs. Assn. (sec.-treas. 1973-74), Pacific N.W. Assn. Ch. Libr., Women in communications, Pasco Bus. and Profl. Women's Club, PEO-HJ (corr. sec. 2002-), Farmington Presbyn. Manor (adv. bd. 2003—), Am. Legion Aux. (mem. 2003-) Gen. Fedn. Women's Clubs of Mo., Beta Sigma Phi, Delta Kappa Gamma, Phi Delta Kappa (sec. 1981-82, Outstanding Educator award 1983).

VICKERY, EDWARD DOWNTAIN, lawyer; b. Fort Worth, Tex., May 1, 1922; s. Charles Richard and Margaret May Vickery; children: Anne Vickery Stevenson, E.D. Jr. AS, North Tex. Agrl. Coll., 1941; BA, U. Tex., 1947, JD with honors, 1948. Bar: Tex. 1948, U.S. Dist. Ct. (so. dist.) Tex. 1948, U.S. Ct. Appeals (5th cir.) 1950, Bd. Immagration Appeals 1952, U.S. Supreme Ct. 1953. From assoc. to sr. ptnr. Royston, Rayzor, Vickery & Williams, Houston, 1948-55, sr. ptnr., 1955-98, of counsel, 1999—. Chmn. bd. dirs. First Nat. Bank Bellaire, Katy Bank, Tradition Bank, Houston. Deacon First Presbyn. Ch., Houston, 1958-64, elder 1965-94; mem. Brazos Presbyn. Ch., 1972-77, chmn. 1976-77; bd. trustees Austin (Tex.) Presbyn. Theol. Sem., 1976-85, 86-95, v. chmn. 1978-83, chmn. 1983-85, 89-95; bd. trustees Tex. Presbyn. Found. 1978-85. Fellow Am. Coll. Trial Lawyers, Internat. Acad. Trial Lawyers (Am. chpt.); mem. Internat. Assn. Ins. Counsel, Am. Judicature Soc., Maritime Law Assn. U.S. (exec. com. 1977-80), Hist. Soc. Supreme Ct. U.S., Tex. Assn. Def. Counsel (bd. dirs. 1965-67), Tex. Bar Found. (Houston chpt.), Tulane Admiralty Law Inst. (program, planning com., adv. bd., 1965-92), Propellor Club U.S. (nat. pres. 1965-66, 66-67, nat. first v.p. 1964-65, nat. exec. com. 1961-85, port of Houston pres. 1961-62), U. Tex. Littlefield Soc., Chancellor's Coun., T Assn., Longhorn Found., Law Sch. Found., Houston Club, Lakeside Country Club. Home: 22507 Blue Canyon Dr Katy TX 77450 Office: Royston Rayzor Vickery & Williams LLP 1001 McKinney Ste 1100 Houston TX 77002-6418 E-mail: ed.vickery@roystonlaw.com.

VICKERY, JON LIVINGSTONE, neurologist; b. Freeport, Ill., May 30, 1955; s. Eugene Livingstone and Millie Margaret (Cox) V.; m. Diane Antoinetti; children: Daniel Scott, John Michael. BA, Northwestern U., 1976; MD, U. Ill., Chgo., 1980. Diplomate Nat. Bd. Med. Examiners. Resident in neurology U. Va., Charlottesville, 1980-84; staff neurologist Pinnacle Health Sys., Harrisburg, Pa., 1984—; v.p. Pa. Neurol. Assocs., Lemoyne, Pa., 1984—2004, pres., 2004—; assoc. prof. of medicine Hershey Med. Ctr., Pa. State U., 1984-99; chief of medicine Holy Spirit Hosp., Camp Hill, Pa., 1992-95. Asst. coach Dickinson Coll. Fencing Team. Fellow Am. Acad. Neurology; mem. AMA, Dauphin County Med. soc. (del. 1985-98), U.S. Fencing Coaches Assn., U.S. Fencing Assn. (life), U.S. Fencing Coaches Assn. (cert. moniteur de armes), Am. Orchid Soc. (cert. judge, mem. conservation com, 1989-91), Beaufort Hunt Club (bd. dirs.), Masons, Shriners. Avocations: fencing, photography, raising orchids, theater, breeding Hanoverian horses. Office: Pa Neurol Assocs 110 Lowther St Lemoyne PA 17043-2012

VICKERY, RAYMOND EZEKIEL, JR., international business consultant, lawyer; b. Brookhaven, Miss., Apr. 30, 1942; s. Raymond Ezekiel and Clarene Helen (Dickens) V.; m. Raymond Clair Brown, Dec. 23, 1967 (div. June 1976); m. Ann Morgan, June 25, 1979; children: Raymond Morgan, Philip Dickens. AB, Duke U., 1964; postgrad., U. Sri Lanka, 1964-65; LLB, Harvard U., 1968. Assoc. Hogan & Hartson, Washington, 1968-77, ptnr. McLean, Va., 1985-93, Johnson & Vickery, Vienna, Va., 1977-81, Reed Smith Shaw & McClay, McLean, Va., 1981-85; asst. sec. for trade devel. U.S. Dept. Commerce, Washington, 1993-97; prin. Vickery Internat., 1977—; pvt. practice Washington, 1997—; of counsel Williams Aron & Assocs., Washington, 2002—. Adj. prof. internat. transactions George Mason U., Fairfax, Va., 1997-99. Contbr. articles to profl. jours. Del. Va. Gen. Assembly, Richmond, 1974-80; mem. Dem. Com., Farifax County, Va., 1971-93; Dem. nominee for Congress, Va., 1992; mem. State Ctrl. Com., Va., 1993; mem. Libr. Bd., Fairfax County, 1972-74. Fulbright scholar, 1964. Mem. ABA, Va. Bar Assn., D.C. Bar Assn., City Club, Phi Beta Kappa, Omicron Delta Kappa. Baptist. Avocations: fishing, horseback riding. Home: 2733 Willow Dr Vienna VA 22181-5310 Office: 1101 Pennsylvania Ave NW Washington DC 20004-2514

VICKERY, WILLIAM, arts administrator; B, M, Juilliard Sch.; studies with the late Roger Smith. Dir. music program NEA, Washington, 1987-89; pres., mng. dir. The St. Paul Chamber Orch., 1989—93; exec. dir. Ark. Symphony Orch., Little Rock. Asst. dean Aspen Music Sch.; orch. mgr. Juilliard Sch., guest lectr.; mem. Seaver/NEA Condr.'s Award panel. Performances with the Met. Opera Orch., the Greenwich (Conn.) Philharm., and in N.Y.C. Former exec. v.p. Aspen Music Festival; mem. adv. com. Minn. Chorale. Recipient Yamaha Internat. award. Office: Ark Symphony Orch 2417 N Tyler St Little Rock AR 72207-3740

VICKREY, ROBERT FISCHER, publishing executive, broadcast executive; b. Mendota, Ill., May 21, 1944; s. Gail Sabin and Marie Augusta (Fischer) Vickrey; m. Barbara Ann Harmon, May 30, 1970; 1 child, Robert James. Student, Ill. Valley CC, 1963-64, Dana Coll., 1964. Account exec. Daily News Tribune, La Salle, Ill., 1968-71; v.p. Daily News-Tribune, La Salle, 1985—; account exec. La Salle County Broadcasting Corp., 1971-72, sales mgr., 1972-84, v.p., 1984—, Miller Group Media, 1992—. Founder, v.p. No. Ill. Indsl. Devel. Corp., 1985—86; founder, pres. Ill. Econ. Devel. Coun., 1997—; bd. dirs. Tri-County Fin. Group, 1st State Bank, Mendota, Ill. Pub. relations com. Starved Rock Area coun. Boy Scouts Am., 1972—76; pres. Ill. Econ. Devel. Coun., 2000—; alt. del. Rep. Nat. Conv., 2000, del., 2004—; chmn. LaSalle County Rep. Ctrl. Com., 2000—04; dep. state ctrl. committeeman Ill. Rep. Party; bd. dirs. United Way Ill. Valley, 1973—75, pub. rels. com., 1980—82; bd. dirs. Ill. Gaming Bd., 1992—2000, Canal Corridor Assn., 1996—; chmn. Ill. Gaming Bd., 1999—2000; trustee U. Ill., 2001—, civil svc. merit commn., 2001—03, exec. com., 2002—. Served with U.S. Army, 1966—68. Mem.: AMVETS (life), Nat. Assn. Broadcasters, DAV, Ill. Valley Area C. of C. (past pres.), Gov.'s Club (Ill.), Wilde Waters Yacht Club (Ottawa, Ill.), Elks. Home: 902 16th St Peru IL 61354-1821 Office: 426 2nd St La Salle IL 61301-2334

VICTOR, A. PAUL, lawyer; b. N.Y.C., Nov. 6, 1938; s. Samuel L. and Sophie (Ostrow) V.; m. Ellen Grabois, Aug. 30, 1959; children: Stephanie, Rebecca, Diana. BBA, U. Mich., 1960, JD with distinction, 1963. Bar: N.Y. 1964, D.C. 1964. Atty. antitrust div. U.S. Dept. Justice, Washington, 1963-66; assoc. Kirkland, Ellis & Rowe, Washington, 1966-68, Weil, Gotshal & Manges, N.Y.C., 1968-72, ptnr., 1972—. Adj. prof. law Fordham U., N.Y.C., 1983—; mem. adv. bd. Ctr. for Am. and Internat. Law, Dallas, 1984—; bd. dirs. Toray Industries (Am.) Inc., N.Y.C., 1987—; presenter in field. Contbr. numerous articles to law revs., other legal publs. regarding U.S. internat. antitrust and trade law. Mem. visitors com. U. Mich. Law Sch., 1980—; trustee Mass. Sch. of Law, Andover, 1989—, chmn., 1998—; sec. Japan Soc., N.Y.C., 1999-2000; bd. dirs. N.Y. chpt. Juvenile Diabetes Rsch. Found., 1994-99, 2004—. Mem. ABA (vice-chair sect. antitrust law 1994-95, mem. coun. 1983-86, 91-94, chmn. internat. antitrust com. 1982-85, 87-90), Internat. Bar Assn., N.Y. State Bar Assn., Order of Coif. Jewish. Avocations: golf, travel, swimming. Office: Weil Gotshal & Manges LLP 767 5th Ave Fl Concl New York NY 10153-0119 Office Phone: 212-310-8110. Business E-Mail: paul.victor@weil.com.

VICTOR, ANN MICHELE, musician, educator; d. Tony and Marllys Ruth Victor. MusB, Kent State U., 1977, MusM, 1979. Tchr. cert. Univ. Tex. at Austin, 1989. Instr. cello & double bass Lamar U., Beaumont, Tex., 1980—83; orch. dir. Bowie Jr. High Ector ISD, Odessa, Tex., 1990—92, Baytown Jr. Sch., Baytown, Tex., 1992—95, Alief (Tex.) ISD, 1995—97, Macario Garcia Mid. Sch., Sugar Land, Tex., 1997—2002, Sartartia Mid. Sch., Sugar Land, Tex., 2000—. Tchr., adminstrv. co-coord. U. Tex. String Project, Austin, 1985—87; pvt. cello instr., 1990—; co-condr. strings orch. Houston Youth Symphony, 1999—. Fellow, AAUW, 1997. Mem.: Tex. Music Adjudicators Assn., Tex. Orch. Dirs. Assn., Tex. Classroom Tchrs. Assn., Tex. Music Educators Assn., Am. String Tchrs Assn., Musician's Union Local 111. Baptist. Office: Sartartia Mid Sch Orch 8125 Homeward Way Sugar Land TX 77479 Office Phone: 281-634-6333. Personal E-mail: ann_victor@hotmail.com. E-mail: ann.victor@fortbend.k12.tx.us.

VICTOR, JACK, former health association executive, consultant; b. N.Y.C., Aug. 11, 1935; s. William and Sadye (Eichenbaum) Victor; m. Ellen Lieb, Aug. 14, 1966; children: Nicole, Jason. AA, Boston U., 1955; BA, CCNY, 1957; MA, New Sch., N.Y.C., 1959; PhD, Yeshiva U., N.Y.C., 1968. Project dir. Greenleigh Assocs., N.Y.C., 1973—76; rsch. dir. Columbia U. Sch. Social Work, N.Y.C., 1976—79; dir., rsch. and tng. Human Resources Ctr., Albertson, NY, 1979—85, dir., grants adminstrn., 1985—88; dir., grants and contracts Adelphi U., Garden City, NY, 1988—91; sr. assoc. Metis Assocs., N.Y.C., 1991—92; dir. devel. World Rehab. Fund, N.Y.C., 1992—93, sr. healthcare program planner, 1993—95, project dir., 1996—98, pres., 1998—2001, pres. emeritus, 2001—. Pres. L.I. Ptnrs., Farmingdale, NY, 1992—98; cons. Victor Assocs., N.Y.C., 1995—; dir. Ptnrs. of the Ams., Washington, 1999—, Brain

Injury Soc., N.Y.C., 2002—. Contbr. articles to profl. jours. Recipient Gralnick award, World Assn. Psychosocial Rehab., Spirit of Hope award, World Rehab. Fund, 2001; Mary Switzer fellow, Nat. Rehab. Assn., 1983. Mem.: APA, Ea. Psychol. Assn. Avocations: music, theater, sports. Office: World Rehab Fund 386 Park Ave S New York NY 10016-8804

VICTOR, MICHAEL GARY, lawyer, physician; b. Detroit, Sept. 20, 1945; s. Simon H. and Helen (Litsky) V.; children: Elise Nicole, Sara Lisabeth. Bar: Ill. 1980, U.S. Dist. Ct. (no. dist.) Ill. 1980, U.S. Ct. Appeals (7th cir.) 1981; diplomate Am. Bd. Legal Medicine, Am. Bd. Emergency Medicine, 2003. Pres. Advocate Adv. Assocs., Chgo., 1982-95; asst. prof. medicine Northwestern U. Med. Sch., Chgo., 1982—; pvt. practice law Barrington, Ill., 1982—; lectr. U. Ill., Chgo., 1999—. Dir. emergency medicine Loretto Hosp., Chgo., 1980-85, chief. sect. of emergency medicine St. Josephs Hosp., Chgo., 1985-87; v.p. Med. Emergency Svcs. Assocs., Buffalo Grove, Ill., 1989; v.p. MESA Mgmt. Corp.; of counsel Bollinger, Ruberry & Garvey, Chgo. Author: Informed Consent, 1980; Brain Death, 1980; (with others) Due Process for Physicians, 1984, A Physicians Guide to the Illinois Living Will Act, The Choice is Ours!, 1989. Recipient Svc. awards Am. Coll. Emergency Medicine, 1973-83. Fellow Am. Coll. Legal Medicine (bd. govs. 1996-97, alt. del. to AMA House of Dels. 1996-97), Chgo. Acad. Legal Medicine; mem. Am. Coll. Emergency Physicians (pres. Ill. chpt. 1980, med.-legal-ins. coun. 1980-81, 83-84), ABA, Ill. State Bar Assn., Am. Soc. Law and Medicine, Chgo. Bar Assn. (med.-legal coun. 1981-83), AMA, Ill. State Med. Soc. (med.-legal coun. 1980-86, 88), Chgo. Med. Soc. Jewish. Home and Office: 153 Aberdour Ln Palatine IL 60067-8001 Office Phone: 847-934-8404. E-mail: mgv@northwestern.edu.

VICTOR, ROBERT EUGENE, real estate corporation executive, lawyer; b. N.Y.C., Dec. 17, 1929; s. Louis and Rebecca (Teitelbaum) V.; m. Dorothy Saffir, Oct. 14, 1951; children— Priscilla Saffir Victor Faubel, Pandora Saffir. LL.B., St. John's U., 1953, JD, 1968. Bar: N.Y. bar 1953, Calif. bar 1965. With firm Szold and Brandwen, N.Y.C., 1953-54; atty. Dept. Army, Phila., 1955-56; with Hughes Aircraft Co., Culver City, Calif., 1956-62; v.p., gen. counsel Packard Bell Electronics Corp., Los Angeles, 1962-70; sr. v.p., gen. counsel Cordon Internat. Corp., Los Angeles, 1970-78; also dir.; gen. counsel Am. Harp Soc., 1969-85; pres., bd. dirs. Vanowen Realty Corp., 1978-93; chmn., pres., bd. dirs. Dobere Realty, Inc., 2000—. Mem. Los Angeles County Bar Assn., Masons. Office: 722 Walden Dr Beverly Hills CA 90210-3125

VICTORA, RANDALL HARRY, physicist, researcher; b. Elmhurst, Ill., Dec. 14, 1957; s. Roger R. and Ruth V. Victora; m. Nancy L. Rhodes, Sept. 12, 1987; children: Denise S., Michelle M. BS in Math., BS in Physics, MIT, 1976—80; PhD, U. Calif., Berkeley, 1980—85. Sr. rsch. scientist Eastman Kodak Co., Rochester, NY, 1985—91, rsch. assoc., 1991—98; assoc. prof. U. Minn., Mpls., 1998—2001, prof., 2001—, dir., ctr. for micromagnetics and info. tech. (MINT), 2003—. Program co-chair INTERMAG Conf., 1995, MMM/INTERMAG Conf., 2001; univ. adviser Info. Storage Industry Consortium, San Diego, 2001—03; gen. chair Conf. on Magnetism and Magnetic Materials, 2005. Guest editor: Jour. Applied Physics, 1993—94; editor: Handbook of Magneto-Optical Data Recording, 1997; contbr. more than 60 articles to profl. jours. Recipient Bell Labs. fellowship, 1983, Westinghouse Sci. Talent Search award winner, 1976, Tech. Achievement award, Nat. Storage Industry Consortium, 2001. Fellow: IEEE, Am. Physical Soc., Magnetics Soc. ADCOM. Achievements include first demonstration of quantitative accuracy in micromagnetic predictions for hysteresis; 9 patents issued. Avocation: golf. Office: Univ Minn 200 Union St SE Minneapolis MN 55455-0154 Office Phone: 612-625-1825.

VICTORIA, CHRISTA, composer, director; d. Camille J. Billops and James V. Hatch(Stepfather), Margaret Carlisle and Lynus V. Richards, Stanford Webb; m. Helmut Georg Meier-Staude, June 22, 1995. Student, U. Calif., Berkeley, 1975—78, CUNY, 1992. Composer/musical dir. secound run Klub Ka- The Blues Legend, 2002; composer/musical dir. Klub Ka - A Blues Legend- U. Iowa, 2002—; musical dir. The Good Faith, N.Y.C., 2004—. Performer Europe, Far East, India. Singer (actor): (theatre, film and live performance) CD - Journey Within The Heart. Office Phone: 646-339-6232. Personal E-mail: christvictorious@aol.com.

VICTORIA, DONDYSH L. piano educator; b. Moscow, July 8, 1963; d. Leon M. and Jane N. Dondysh; m. Gary Katz, June 28, 1991; children: Samuel A. Katz, Elizabeth F. Katz. MusM, Manhattan Sch. Of Music, N.Y., 1988. Concert pianist Soesterberg Music Festival, Amsterdam, Netherlands, 2002, WQXR, Radio Sta., N.Y.C., 2002. Pub. performances Long Island Pub. TV Sta., Southempton, NY, 2001. Composer performance of own piano compositions, (publ.) Children's Art, (CD) piano recital featuring works of Shumann, Bach, Chopin, and Rachmaninoff, 2001, Bach - 6 Partitas, 2004. Recipient prize, Young Artist Competition; Full Scholarship, Juilliard Sch. of Music, 1976—79, Mannes Coll. of Music, 1979—81. Mem.: MTNA (assoc.), Piano Tchrs. Congress of N.Y. (assoc.). Home: 141 Oakdene Ave Leonia NJ 07605 Personal E-mail: katzga@yahoo.com.

VICTORSON, MICHAEL BRUCE, lawyer; b. Fairmont, W.Va., July 13, 1954; s. Morton Jerome and Deborah (Jacobson) V.; m. Janet Harris, Mar. 8, 1981; children: David Solomon, Sara Lorraine. BA, W.Va. U., 1976, JD, 1979. Bar: W.Va. 1979, U.S. Dist. Ct. (so. and no. dists.) W.Va. 1979, U.S. Dist. Ct. (ea. dist.) Ky. 1986, U.S. Ct. Appeals (4th cir.) 1980, U.S. Supreme Ct., 1992. Assoc. Love, Wise, Robinson and Woodroe, Charleston, W.Va., 1979-83, Robinson & McElwee LLP, Charleston, 1983-84, ptnr., 1985-99; mem. Jackson Kelly PLLC, Charleston, 1999—. Spkr. in field. Contbr. articles to profl. jours. Chmn. appeal bd. U.S. Selective Svc. System, So. Dist. W.Va., Charleston, 1983—; lawyers' chmn. United Way Kanawha Valley, Charleston, 1988-92, chmn. profl. divsn., 1992-93, admissions com., 1990-92; treas., bd. dirs. Med. Eye Bank W.Va., Charleston, 1989—, treas., 2000—; bd. dirs. Sunrise Collectors Club, 2002—; trustee B'nai Jacob Synagogue, 1992-94, v.p. 1997-2001, pres. 2001-; trustee Federated Jewish Charities of Charleston, Inc., 1998—, vis. com. W.Va. U. Coll. Law, 1996-2000. Mem. ABA, Internat. Assn. Jewish Lawyers and Jurists, Am. Law Firm Assn. (products liability steering com., bd. dirs. 1998-99), W.Va. Bar Assn., W.Va. State Bar Assn., Kanawha County Bar Assn., Def. Rsch. Inst., Def. Trial Counsel W.Va. (charter, bd. govs. 1992-98), Order of Coif, Phi Beta Kappa, Phi Delta Phi, Phi Kappa Phi, Pi Sigma Alpha. Office: Jackson Kelly PLLC PO Box 553 Charleston WV 25322-0553 E-mail: mvictorson@jacksonkelly.com.

VICTORY, JEFFREY PAUL, state supreme court justice; b. Shreveport, La., Jan. 29, 1946; s. Thomas Edward and Esther (Horton) V.; m. Nancy Clark Victory, Jan. 20, 1973; children: Paul Bradford, William Peter, Christopher Thomas, Mary Katherine. BA in History and Govt., Centenary Coll., 1967; JD, Tulane U., 1971. Bar: La. 1971. Ptnr. Tucker, Jeter, Jackson & Victory, Shreveport, 1971-82; dist. ct. judge 1st Jud. Dist. Ct., Shreveport, 1982-90; appellate judge 2d Circuit Ct. of Appeal, Shreveport, 1991-95; assoc. justice Supreme Ct. La., 1995—. Bd. dirs. CODAC Drug Abuse, Shreveport; mem. La. Sentencing Commn. La. NG, 1969-75. Mem. ABA, Shreveport Bar Assn., La. Bar Assn. Republican. Baptist. Avocations: tennis, motorcycles, classic cars. Office: Supreme Ct 301 Loyola Ave New Orleans LA 70112-1814

VICTORY, NANCY, federal agency administrator; BA, Princeton U.; JD, Georgetown U. Ptnr. Wiley, Rein & Fielding, Washington; asst. sec. for comm. and info. Dept. Commerce, Washington, 2001—, adminstr. Nat. Telecom. and Info. Adminstrn., 2001—. Office: Wiley Rein Fielding LLP 1776 K St NW Washington DC 20006

VIDAILLET, HUMBERTO J., JR., physician, researcher; b. Santiago, Cuba, Sept. 24, 1954; arrived in U.S., 1968; s. Humberto J. and Caridad Vidaillet; m. Debbie Vidaillet, June 6, 1981; children: Kelsey, Daniel, Corbin. MD, U. Okla., 1981. Resident in internal medicine Mayo Clinic, Rochester, Minn., 1981-84; tng. in cardiology/electrophysiology Duke U. Med. Ctr., Durham, N.C., 1984-87; dir. cardiac electrophysiology Marshfield (Wis.) Clinic, 1987—; assoc. clin. prof. medicine U. Wis. Sch. Medicine, Madison, 1994-2000, clin. prof. medicine, 2000—. Prof. medicine U. Chile Sch. Medicine, 1994; cons. prof. medicine Inst. Med. Sci., Sch. Medicine, Medellin, Colombia, 1999; med. dir. arrhythmia svcs. St. Joseph Hosp., Marshfield, 1992—; cons. in field. Contbr. articles to profl. jours. Parish coun. Our Lady of Peace Cath. Ch., Marshfield, 1996-2001; bd. dirs. Univ. Found., U. Wis.; exec. com. Marshfield; vice chmn. bd. trustees Marshfield Clinic Rsch. Found., 1990-93, 2000-03, elected clin. physician rep. to bd. trustees, 2000—, vice-chair, 2003—; coord., local prin. investigator clin. trials of med. rsch. Am. Heart Assn. sr. investigator award, 1997, 15th Annual Gwen D. Sebold Rsch. Fellow ACP (chair internat. com. 1989-92, winner clin. paper competition 1984, 86, 87, faculty ann. sci. sessions), Am. Coll. Cardiology (mem. edn. com., faculty sci. ann. sessions sr. investigator award, 2000), Am. Coll. Chest Physicians; mem. N.Am. Soc. Electrophysiology and Pacing (faculty ann. sci. sessions), Heart Rhythm Soc. (faculty ann. sessions), Internat. Soc. of Internal Medicine (sci. program commn.), Inter Am. Congress Cardiology (sci. program com. 2003), Intern Am. Coll. Cardiology (US rep. to sci. com., faculty ann. sci. session), Human Rights Workers Internat., Netsuke Collectors Soc. Office: Marshfield Clinic 1000 N Oak Ave Marshfield WI 54449-5702 Office Phone: 715-387-5477. Business E-Mail: vidaillet.humberto@marshfieldclinic.org.

VIDAL, ALEJANDRO LEGASPI (ANDY VIDAL), architect; b. Kawit, Cavite, The Philippines, May 3, 1934; came to U.S. 1954; s. Antonio and Patrocinia Santonil (Legaspi) V.; m. Fe Del Rosario, Aug. 16, 1962; 1 child, Alex Anthony. BS in Architecture, Mapua Inst. Tech., 1962. Registered arch., The Philippines. Prin. A.L. Vidal Arch., Manila, The Philippines, 1962-63; staff arch. Vinnell Wall & Green, Agana, Guam, 1963-64; project engr. Dillingham Corp. of Nevada, Hawaii and Guam, 1964-74; sr. project mgr., preconstrn. svc. mgr. Fletcher-Pacific Constrn. Co. Ltd., Honolulu, 1974-96; prin. A.L. Vidal Constrn. Cons., Honolulu, 1996-2000, A.L. Vidal Arch., Cavite, The Philippines, 1996-2000. Designer, builder first application of integrated aluminum forming sys. for high rise concrete construction. Active Rep. Presdl. Task Force, Washington, 1980-88, Rep. Senatorial Com., Washington, 1980-88. With USN, 1954-58, Korea. Mem. VFW (life), Am. Mgmt. Assn., Soc. Am. Mil. Engrs., Am. Legion, U. Hawaii Found., Chancellor's Club, Disabled Am. Vets., Comdrs. Club. Roman Catholic. Avocations: golf, swimming, volunteer work. Home: 1051 Kaluanui Rd Honolulu HI 96825-1321 E mail: avidal96825@yahoo.com.

VIDAL, DAVID JONATHAN, insurance company executive, journalist; b. Bayamón, P.R., Oct. 11, 1946; s. Jesus Maria and Ercira Audacia (Mejia) V.; m. Watuza Leal, Jan. 25, 1975; 1 child, Katalyn. AB cum laude, Princeton U., 1968; student, Sch. Advanced Internat. Studies, Washington, 1982-83; MBA, Columbia U., 1991. Reporter The Caracas (Venezuela) Daily Jour., 1969-70; reporter, news editor AP, Caracas, N.Y., Sao Paulo, 1970-73, corr. Brasilia, Brazil, 1973-75; reporter, bur. chief N.Y. Times, N.Y.C. and Rio de Janeiro, 1975-80; spl. asst., White House fellow Dept. State, Washington, 1980-81; cons. U.S. AID, Washington, 1981-82; dept. mgr. task force Pres.'s Pvt. Sector Survey on Cost Control, Washington, 1982-83; exec. dir. Nat. Commn. Secondary Schooling for Hispanics, Washington, 1983-84; dir. pub. affairs N.Y.C. Partnership, 1984-85; asst. v.p. Continental Ins., N.Y.C., 1985-95; v.p. Coun. on Fgn. Rels., N.Y.C., 1995-97; dir. rsch. global corp. citizenship The Conf. Bd., N.Y.C., 1997—; pub. Across the Board, 2001—. Adj. prof. journalism Columbia U. Grad. Sch. Journalism, N.Y.C., 1985-86; bd. dirs. Pub. Affairs Coun., Washington, 1988-95; trustee Found. for Pub. Affairs, Washington, 1989-95; mem. Contbns. Adv. Group, 1988-95, chmn., 1994-95; mem. corp. adv. group Schomburg Ctr. for Rsch. in Black Culture, 1988-95, Ad Hoc Com. on Charter Revision, 1988, Nat. Hispanic Agenda, 1988; mem. adv. group Latino Leadership Fund, 1991-95; vice-chmn. Nat. Civic League, 1999—. Author: (newspaper series) NY Times, 1980; pub. Across the Board, 2001—; contbr. articles and reports in field. Trustee N.Y. Theol. Sem., N.Y.C., 1990—; mem. Coun. Fgn. Rels.; prin. Coun. for Excellence in Govt., Washington, 1992—; dir. Coun. on Internat. Ednl. Exch., N.Y.C., 1997—2003; elder, trustee West End Presbyn. Ch., N.Y.C., 1986—. Recipient Hispanic Achievement award Wall Street chpt. IMAGE, N.Y.C., 1989; Fulbright scholar, Washington and Venezuela, 1968. Fellow Royal Soc. for Encouragement of Arts, Manufacturers and Commerce; mem. N.Y. Regional Assn. Grantmakers (dir., sec. 1988-95), Nat. Inst. Industry Assn. (corp. adv. group 1990-95), Nat. Civic League, Coun. on Fgn. Rels. Democrat. Office: The Conf Bd 845 3rd Ave New York NY 10022-6601 E-mail: david.vidal@conference-board.org.

VIDAL, GORE, writer; b. West Point, N.Y., Oct. 3, 1925; s. Eugene L. and Nina (Gore) V. Grad., Phillips Exeter Acad., 1943; DLitt (hon.), Brown U., 1988. Author, 1946—. Author: (novels) Williwaw, 1946, In a Yellow Wood, 1947, The City and the Pillar, 1948, The Season of Comfort, 1949, A Search for the King, 1950, Dark Green, Bright Red, 1950, The Judgment of Paris, 1952, Messiah, 1954, Julian, 1964, Washington, D.C, 1967, Myra Breckinridge, 1968, Two Sisters, 1970, Burr, 1973, Myron, 1974, 1876, 1976, Kalki, 1978, Creation, 1981 (Prix Deauville 1983), Duluth, 1983, Lincoln, 1984, Empire, 1987, Hollywood, 1990, Live From Golgotha, 1992, The Smithsonian Institution, 1998, The Golden Age, 2000, Perpetual War for Perpetual Peace, 2002, Dreaming War: Blood for Oil and the Cheney-Bush Junta, 2002 (under name Edgar Box) Death in the Fifth Position, 1952, Death Before Bedtime, 1953, Death Likes It Hot, 1954, The Essential Vidal, 1998; (short stories) A Thirsty Evil, 1956; (plays) Visit to a Small Planet, 1957, The Best Man, 1960, (Broadway revived 2000) Romulus, 1962, Weekend, 1968, An Evening with Richard Nixon, 1972, (essays) Rocking the Boat, 1962, Sex, Death, and Money, 1968, Reflections upon a Sinking Ship, 1969, Homage to Daniel Shays, 1973, Matters of Fact and of Fiction, 1977, The Second American Revolution, 1982 (Nat. Book Critics Circle award for criticism 1982), Armageddon?, 1987 (London), United States: Essays 1952-1992, 1993 (Nat. Book award for nonfiction 1993), The Last Empire, 2001; (films) The Catered Affair, 1956, I Accuse, 1958, The Left-Handed Gun, 1958, The Scapegoat, 1959, Suddenly Last Summer, 1959, The Best Man, 1964 (Cannes Critics prize 1964), Is Paris Burning?, 1966, The Last of the Mobile Hotshots, 1970; (teleplays) Barn Burning, 1954, Dark Possession, 1954, Smoke, 1954, Visit to a Small Planet, 1955, Dr. Jekyll and Mr. Hyde, 1955, A Sense of Justice, 1955, Summer Pavilion, 1955, The Turn of the Screw, 1955, Stage Door, 1955, A Farewell to Arms, 1955, The Death of Billy the Kid, 1955, Honor, 1956, The Indestructible Mr. Gore, 1959, Dress Gray, 1986, Billy the Kid, 1989; actor: Fellini Roma, 1978, Bob Roberts, 1992, With Honors, 1994, others, (memoirs) Screening History, 1992, Palimpsest, 1995. Mem. Pres.'s Adv. Com. on Arts, 1961-63; Dem.-Liberal candidate for U.S. Congress, 1960, candidate for Dem. nomination from Calif., 1982; co-chmn. The New Party, 1970-71. Served with AUS, 1943-46. Named hon. citizen Ravello, Italy, 1983, Chevalier de l'Ordre des Arts et des Lettres, France, 1995. Office: Thunders Mouth Press 245 W 17th St 11th Fl New York NY 10011-5300

VIDAL, MAUREEN ERIS, theater educator, actress; b. Bklyn., Mar. 18, 1956; d. Louis and Lillian (Kaplan) Hendelman; m. Juan Vidal, June 25, 1974 (div. Sept. 1981); m. Guillermo Eduardo Uriarte, Dec. 22, 1986. BA, Bklyn. Coll., 1976, MS, 1981. From english tchr. to drama tchr. N.Y.C. Bd. Edn., 1976—2002, chair women's history dept., 1984—, dean, 1997—, drama tchr., 2002—. Mem PETA Humane Soc. Mem.: AFTRA, Gorilla Soc., Nat. Anti-Vivisection Soc. (mem. physicians' com. responsible medicine), Heights Players Theater Co. (arranger theatrical performance for residents of homeless shelters 1986—2003, exec. bd., sec. 1993—, actress), Doris Day Animal League, Delta Psi Omega. Avocations: travel, white-water rafting, scuba diving, skydiving, theater. Home: 3380 Nostrand Ave Brooklyn NY 11229-4056 Office: I S 318 101 Walton St Brooklyn NY 11206-4311 also: Heights Players 26 Willow Pl Brooklyn NY 11201-4513 Office Phone: 718-782-0589. E-mail: MVidal4942@aol.com.

VIDAL, MERCÈ, art historian, education educator; b. Esplugues de Llobregat, Barcelona, Spain, May 5, 1950; d. Lluis Vidal and Rosa Jansà. Art hist., U. of Barcelona, 1969—74, PhD in art history, 1989. Sr. lectr. Sch. of Arch., Barcelona, 1973—78, Faculty of Edn., Barcelona, 1974—90. Adv. bd. Direcció Gen. Patrimoni Artistic Generalitat de Catalunya, Barcelona, 1989—90. Contbr. articles. Mem. of comm. act Congrés de Cultura Catalana, Barcelona, 1975—77. Recipient Prize Nat. Arts Plàstiques 1991, Generalitat of Catalonia, 1992. Mem.: AICA. Office: Dept of Art History UniversitatBCN Baldiri Reixach s/n Barcelona 08028 Spain Office Phone: 93 333 34 66. Office Fax: 93 449 85 10. E-mail: vidal@trivium.gh.ub.es.

VIDAL, RONALD ANTHONY, otolaryngology; b. N.Y.C., 1951; MD, SUNY, 1977. Diplomate Am. Bd. Otolaryngology. Resident in gen. surgery Millard Fillmore Hosp., Buffalo, N.Y., 1977-79; resident in otolaryngology U. Affiliated Hosp., Buffalo, 1979-82; ptnr. Assocs. Clinton, 1983—, mem. mgmt. com., 1996-2000; pres. med. staff Mercy Health Ctr., Clinton, Iowa, 1994-95; chmn. mgmt. com. Assocs. Clinton, 1999-2000; chmn. dept. surgery and chmn. credentials com. Samaritan Health Sys. Mercy Med. Ctr., Clinton, Iowa, 1997. Bd. dirs. Gateway Physician Hosp. Orgn. Mem. ACS, IMS, Am. Acad. Otolaryngology Head and Neck Surgery. Office: Springdale Dr & 13th Ave N Clinton IA 52732 Office Phone: 563-243-2511.

VIDALE, JOHN EMILIO, geologist; b. Phila., Mar. 15, 1959; s. Guido Levi and Rosemary (Jacobson) V.; 1 child, Laura. BS, Yale U., 1981; PhD, Calif. Inst. Tech., 1986. Scientist U. Calif., Santa Cruz, 1987-90, U.S. Geol. Survey, Menlo Park, Calif., 1991-95; assoc. prof. UCLA, 1995-99, prof., 1999—, acting dir. Inst. Geophysics and Planetary Physics, 2002—03, interim dir., 2003—04. Editor Bulletin Seismology Soc. Am., 1988-93; contbr. articles to profl. jours. Gilbert fellow U.S. Geol. survey, 1994-95; co-recipient James B. Macelwane Young Investigator medal Am. Geophys. Union, 1994 Fellow Am. Geophys. Union (Macelwane medal 1994). Home: 10421 Colina Way Los Angeles CA 90077-2041 Office: UCLA Dept Earth & Space Sci PO Box 951567 Los Angeles CA 90095-1567 Business E-Mail: vidale@ucla.edu.

VIDAS, VINCENT GEORGE, engineering executive; b. Phila., May 25, 1931; s. Joseph and Blanche (Misch) V.; m. Judith Weber, Oct. 15 1955; children: Lisa Louise, Jeffrey Vincent, Kristen Judith. BSEE, Drexel U., 1959, MSEE, 1964. Systems engr. RCA, Moorestown, N.J., 1959-65, Sci. Mgmt. Assn., Haddonfield, N.J., 1965-67; CEO SEMCOR, Inc., Mt. Laurel, N.J., 1967-99; also bd. dirs.; chmn., owner, bd. dirs. Edn. Mgmt. Corp., Cherry Hill, N.J., 1991-93; COO, dir. Advanced Comm. Systems, Fairfax, Va., 1999—. Staff Sgt. USAF, 1949-53. Mem. IEEE. Avocations: chess, tennis, photography, music. Office: SEMCOR Inc 815 E Gate Dr Mount Laurel NJ 08054-1240

VIDAVER, ANNE MARIE, plant pathology educator; b. Vienna, Mar. 29, 1938; came to U.S., 1941; d. Franz and Klara (Winter) Kopecky; children: Gordon W.F., Regina M. BA, Russell Sage Coll., 1960; MA, Ind. U., 1962, PhD, 1965. Lectr. U. Nebr., Lincoln, 1965-66, rsch. assoc., 1966-72, asst. prof., 1972-74, assoc. prof., 1974-79, prof. plant pathology, 1979—, interim dir. Ctr. Biotech., 1988-89, 97-00, head dept. plant pathology, 1984-2000, 2003—; chief scientist USDA's NRICGP, 2000—02. Contbr. articles to profl. jours. and books; patentee in field. Recipient Pub. Svc. award Nebr. Agri-Bus., 1977, Sci. award for excellence NAMA, New Orleans, 1991. Fellow AAAS, Am. Phytopath. Soc., Am. Soc. Microbiology; mem. Intersoc. Consortium for Plant Protection, Internat. Soc. Plant Pathology, Alliance for Prudent Use of Antibiotics. Avocations: indoor gardening, reading. Office: U Nebr Dept Plant Pathology Lincoln NE 68583-0722 E-mail: avidaver1@unl.edu.

VIDEBÆK, BENTE A. humanities educator; b. Tveje Merløse, Sjaelland, Denmark, Oct. 13, 1950; d. Jørgen Kristian and Agnete Nellie Jensen; m. Flemming Videbaek, Nov. 28, 1984; children: Christian David Videbaek, Thomas Erik Videbaek. Cand. Mag., U. Copenhagen, 1978; PhD, Northwestern U., Evanston, Ill., 1992. Tenured tchr. Nordvestsjaellands Voksenundervisningscenter, Holbaek, Denmark, 1973—84; lectr. SUNY, Stony Brook, NY, 1997—; adj. asst. prof. Suffolk County C.C., Selden, 1993—. Author: (criticism) The Stage Clown in Shakespeare's Theatre; contbr. MLA's Guide to Teaching Hamlet; editor: (college textbook) Revenge Tragedies. Mem.: MLA. Office: SUNY Nicholls Rd Stony Brook NY 11790 Personal E-mail: bvidebaek@optonline.net.

VIDELL, JARED STEVEN, cardiologist; b. Phila., Apr. 9, 1947; s. Harry and Rose (Malken) V.; m. Cyla Trocki, Dec. 27, 1969; children: Haviv Elana, Mikhael Alon, Samara Pilar. BEd, U. Miami, 1969; DO, Phila. Coll. Osteo. Medicine, 1976. Resident and chief resident in internal medicine Atlantic City (N.J.) Med. Ctr., 1976-79; fellow in cardiovascular diseases Albert Einstein Med. Ctr., Phila., 1979-81; rsch. fellow in nuclear cardiology Deborah Heart and Lung Ctr., Browns Mills, N.J., 1981-82, dir. employee health svcs., 1982-84; asst. dir. cardiology Pritikin Longevity Ctr., Downington, Pa., 1984-87; cardiologist, dir. clin. lab. Physician Care, P.C., Towanda, Pa., 1987-90; from co-chmn. intensive care to dir. cardiac stress lab. Meml. Hosp., Towanda, 1987-90; dir. house staff, intensive/cardiac care Lower Bucks Hosp., Bristol, Pa., 1992-94; dir. house staff ICU-CCU North Phila. Health Systems, 1994-97; med. dir. North Phila. Health Sys. Girard Med. Ctr., 1997—, chmn. clin. medicine, 1997—. Med. dir. Am. Cancer Soc. chpt., 1989-90; state peer rev. KEPRO, 1989-90. Contbr. rsch. articles to profl. jours. Maj. M.C. USAR, Maj. USMC Res. Fellow: Am. Coll. Angiology; mem.: AMA, Nat. Assn. Managed Care Physicians, Alumni Assn. Phila. Coll. Osteo. Medicine, Phila. County Med. Soc., Pa. Med. Soc., Am. Soc. Law, Medicine and Ethics, Internat. Platform Assn., Am. Coll. Physician Execs., Internat. Soc. Endovascular Surgery, Internat. Soc. Internal Medicine, Am. Soc. Internal Medicine, Am. Coll. Chest Physicians. Avocations: squash, bicycling, cross country skiing, travel, fishing. Home: 408 N Exeter Ave Margate City NJ 08402-1868

VIDLER, ANTHONY, architecture educator, dean; BA in Architecture and Fine Arts, diploma in Architecture, Cambridge U., Eng. Mem. faculty Sch. Architecture Princeton U., 1965—93, chair PhD com. and dir. European cultural studies, William R. Kenan Jr. chair architecture, 1990; prof. and chair dept. art history UCLA, 1993, prof. and chair dept. art history and prof. Sch. Architecture, 1997; acting dean Irwin S. Chanin Sch. Architecture The Cooper Union, 2001—02, dean Irwin S. Chanin Sch. Architecture, 2002—. Getty scholar Getty Ctr. History Art and Humanities, 1992—93. Author: The Writing of the Walls: Architectural Theory in the Late Enlightenment, 1987, Claude-Nicolas Ledoux: Architecture and Social Reform at the End of the Ancient Regime, 1990, The Architectural Uncanny: Essays in the Modern Unhomely, 1992, Antoine Grumbach, 1996, Warped Space: Architecture and Anxiety in Modern Culture, 2000. Recipient awards, Guggenheim Found., NEH. Office: The Cooper Union for Advancement of Sci and Art Cooper Sq New York NY 10003-7120

VIDOVICH, MARK A. paper products executive; CEO Day Runner, Inc., Irvine, Calif., 1986-2000, chmn. bd. dirs., 2000—.

VIDRICKSEN, BEN EUGENE, food service executive, state legislator; b. Salina, Kans., June 11, 1927; s. Henry and Ruby Mae Vidricksen; m. Lola Mae Nienke, Jan. 20, 1950 (div.); children: Nancy, Janice, Ben, Penelope, Jeffery. AB, Kans. Wesleyan U., 1951. Field supt. Harding Creamery divsn. Nat. Dairy Products, Kearney, Kans., 1951-52, plant mgr. Kraft divsn. O'Neill, Nebr., 1952-59; owner Vidricksen's Food Svc., Salina, 1959—. Cons. in field; mem. Kans. Senate, 1979—, asst. majority leader; chmn. joint bldg. constrn. com., legis. and congl. apportionment com., legis. post audit, econ. devel., transp. and utilities, pub. health and welfare, fed. and state affairs, govtl. orgn., spl. interim com. on efficiency in state govt., 1983; del. White House Conf. on Tourism and Travel, 1995, 96; mem. Hennessy/USAF Worldwide Food Svc. Evaluation Team, 1978, 79. Mem. Salina Airport Authority, 1972-84, chmn., 1976-77; chmn. Rep. Ctrl. Com., County of Saline, Kans., 1974-79; adv. coun. SBA, 1982—, chmn. adv. coun. small bus. devel. ctr.; mem. adv. bd. Salvation Army; past chmn. Salina Conv. and Tourism Bur.; vice chmn. Kans. Turnpike Authority, 1995—. Served with USN, 1945-46. Recipient Salut au Restaurateur award Fla. State U., 1974, Gov.'s Spl. award Kans. Assn. Broadcasters, Guardian award Nat. Fedn. Indep. Bus., 1989, Promotion of Tourism and Travel award Travel Ind. Assn. Kans., 1989, Support of Kans. Nat. Guard award Kans. Adjutant Gen., 1990, Good Citizenship award Kans. Engring. Soc., 1991, 92, Freedom award NRA, 1994, Kans. Nat. Guard award Excellence, 1997; named Nat. Rep. Legislator of Yr., Nat. Rep. Legislators Assn., 1991, Assoc. of Yr., Am. Womens Bus. Assn., 1992. Mem. USAF Assn., Assn. U.S. Army, Nat. Rep. Legislators Assn., Am. Legis. Exch. Coun.,

Pan Am. Hwy. Assn. (Internat. Achievement award 1992, Road Buiulders award 1995), North Salina Bus. Assn. (past pres.), Internat. Brdige, Tunnel and Tpke. Assn., Kans. Restaurant Assn. (past pres., Restaurateur of Yr. 1973), Kans. Tourism and Travel Commn., Kans. Film Commn., Nat. Restaurant Assn. (dir. 1977—), Travel Industry Assn. Kans. (dir.), VFW (life), Salina C. of C. (past bd. dirs.), Am. Legion, Optimists, North Salina Lions Club, Elks, Moose, Eagles, Masons (knight commdr. Scottish rite 1994), Shriners. Office: State Senate State Capitol Topeka KS 66612

VIE, RICHARD CARL, insurance company executive; b. St. Louis, Sept. 26, 1937; s. George William and Geraldine Vie; m. Joan Kay Wilschetz, June 4, 1960. Student, St. Louis U., U. Mo. With Reliable Life Ins. Co., St. Louis, 1962-79; pres. Commonwealth Life Ins. Co., St. Louis, 1979-82; pres., chmn. bd. dirs. United Ins. Co. Am., Chgo., 1983—; sr. v.p., bd. dirs. Unitrin, Inc., 1990-92, pres., CEO, 1992—. Chmn. Life Insurers Conf., 1994; trustee Life Underwriters Tng. Coun. Bd. dirs. Concordia U. Found., 1985-94, Valparaiso U., 1995—. Lt. USN, 1958-62. Mem. The Racquet Club St. Louis, Execs. Club Chgo. Office: Unitrin Inc 1 E Wacker Dr Chicago IL 60601-1802

VIEGAS, HERMAN HERMOGIO, mechanical engineer; b. Bombay, Dec. 10, 1946; arrived in U.S., 1968; s. Joseph A.B. and Maria F.R.L. Viegas; m. Sharon Ann Krizan, Oct. 20, 1979; children: Joseph, Katrina, Eric. BE, U. Bombay, 1968; MS, N.D. State U., Fargo, 1970; MBA, U. St. Thomas, Mpls., 1995. Prof. engr., Minn. Engr. Lundquist, Wilmar & Assoc., St. Paul, 1971, Setter, Leach & Lindstrom, Mpls., 1972, A. Epstein & Sons, Chgo., 1971—72, Thermo King, Mpls., 1972—82, sr. engr., 1982—95, sect. engr. mgr., 1995—2000, cons. engr., 2000—. Contbr. articles to profl. jours. Fellow: ASME (history and heritage com. 2000—, Thomas Edison award 2000); mem.: Cryogenic Soc. Am. Achievements include patents in field. Avocations: running, volleyball, bridge. Office: Thermo King Corp 314 W 90th St Minneapolis MN 55420

VIEGAS, LOUIS PAUL, real estate salesperson, retired postmaster; b. Bklyn., Aug. 24, 1940; s. Jack and Antoinette (Cappiello) V.; m. Charlotte Sonia Storey, May 28, 1967; children: Cindy, Tracy. AAS. in Bus., N.Y. Inst. Tech., 1978, BS in Bus., 1979; postgrad., St. John's U., Queens, N.Y., 1987. Lic. real estate assoc. Traffic asst. Berkshire Chem. Corp., N.Y.C., 1956-59; engrng. aide Bd. Higher Edn., N.Y.C., 1959-61; letter carrier U.S. Postal Svc., Bklyn., 1961-68, supr., 1968-79, area mgr., 1979-82, mgr., deliveries & collections, 1982-85, dir. city ops., 1985-87, postmaster, 1987-92; ret., 1992; cons. U.S. Postal Svc., N.Y.C., 1995-99; sales assoc. Sung and Assocs. Real Estate Corp., 2000—. Mem. Northeast Region Speakers Bur., N.Y., N.J., New Eng., 1985—. Mem. Assn. for the Help Retarded Children, Nassau County, N.Y., 1974-89, Valley Stream Civilian Patrol, Valley Stream, N.Y., 1984-86, Nassau County Foster Parents Assn., 1982-87. Named Man of Yr. Holy Name Soc. Bklyn., 1986, Christopher Columbus Assn., Bklyn., Staten Island, 1987, Bklyn. Jewish Postal Workers Welfare League, 1989. Mem. Nat. League Postmasters of U.S., Nat. Assn. Postal Suprs., Sons of Italy. Republican. Roman Catholic. Avocation: photography. Office: Sung and Assocs Real Estate Corp 31 W Merrick Rd Valley Stream NY 11580-9998 E-mail: lou@barps.com.

VIEHE, KARL WILLIAM, mathematics educator, lawyer, investment banker; b. Allentown, Pa., Aug. 12, 1943; s. John Sage and Margaret (Higgs) V. BA in Govt. and Econs., Am. U., 1965, MA in Econs., 1968; JD, Howard U., 1981; MLT in Taxation, Georgetown U., 1982. Bar: D.C. 1983, U.S. Tax Ct. 1984, U.S. Ct. Internat. Trade 1988, U.S. Ct. Appeals (4th cir.) 1988, U.S. Ct. Appeals (D.C. cir.) 1985, U.S. Supreme Ct. 1988. Instr. math. and Russian lang. St. Albans Sch., Washington, 1968-69; pres., CEO Investment-Futures Group, Washington, 1968-84; prof. math. and stats. U. D.C., 1971—. Gen. counsel Promstroy Bank Russia, 1996-97; adj. prof. internat. law and fin. Am. U., 1972—; adj. prof. internat. law and bus. George Washington U., 1986—; internat. advt. dir. Washingtonian Mag., 1972-75; mgmt. program chmn. Fla. Inst. Tech., 1983-85; adj. faculty Internat. Law Inst., Washington, 1986—, Internat. Devel. Law Inst., Rome, 1987—; v.p., gen. counsel James A. Tilley Co., Investment Bankers, Washington, Moscow, 1994-95; chmn., CEO Horizons-Northstar Capital Mgmt. Co., Washington, 1995-97; gen. counsel U.S. Congrl. Philharmonic Orch., 1998-99; co-chmn. U.S. IRS Ann. Conf. on Current Issues in Internat. Taxation, 1986-88, Dept. Commerce Ann. Conf. on Current Issues in Internat. Trade, 1994-97; internat. adv. bd. McGeorge Sch. Law, 1987—; presenter in field. Contbr. articles to profl. jours. Vice-chmn. bd. dirs., gen. counsel U.S. Congrl. Philharmonic Soc. Mem. ABA, Am. Econ. Assn., Am. Fin. Assn., Am. Arbitration Assn. (comml. panel, internat. panel), Washington Fgn. Law Soc. (bd. dirs.), D.C. Bar Assn., U.S. Congl. Philharmonic Soc. (vice-chmn. bd. govs.). Avocations: piano, photography, triathlons, marathons, tennis. Home: 2401 H St NW Apt 707 Washington DC 20037-2581 Office: Horizons & Northstar Capital Mgmt Co 1700 Pennsylvania Ave NW Washington DC 20006-4704

VIEHE, RICHARD B. podiatrist; m. Margaret Viehe; children: Anne, Thomas, Andrew. BS, Cornell U.; MD in Podiatric Medicine, Calif. Coll. Podiatric Medicine, 1971. Resident in podiatry Lincoln Cmty. Hosp., Calif.; staff physician Children's Hosp. of Orange County; Coastal Cmtys. Hosp., Santa Ana; Coll. Hosp., Costa Mesa; Fountain Valley Cmty. Hosp.; Hoag Meml. Presbyn. Hosp., Newport Beach; St. Joseph Hosp., Orange County, & Western Med. Ctr., Santa Ana; pvt. practice Newport Ctr. Podiatry Group, Newport Beach, Calif.; dir. surgical residency Western Medical Center, Santa Ana. Bd. trustee Calif. Coll. of Podiatric Medicine, 1987—; diplomat Am. Bd. of Podiatric Surgery & Am. Bd. of Podiatric Examiners. Fellow: Am. Coll. of Foot & Ankle Surgeons; mem.: Nat. Acad. of Practice, Am. Podiatric Med. Assn. (pres. 2001), Orange County Podiatric Med. Assn. (past pres.), Calif. Podiatric Med. Assn. (past pres.), Alpha Gamma Kappa, Pi Delta. Office: Newport Ctr Podiatry Group 1303 Avocado Ave Ste 195 Newport Beach CA 92660*

VIEIRA, MEREDITH, television personality; b. Providence, Dec. 30, 1951; m. Richard Cohen June 14, 1986; children: Benjamin, Gabriel, Lily Max. BA in English (magna cum laude), Tufts U., 1975. News announcer WORC-Radio, Worcester, Mass., 1975; reporter, anchor WJAR-TV, Providence, R.I.; reporter WCBS-TV, N.Y.C., 1979-82; from reporter to news correspondent CBS News, N.Y.C., 1982-93; chief correspondent ABC News, N.Y.C., 1993—; co-host The View, N.Y.C., 1997—; host Lifetime TV's Intimate Portrait, 1999—. Host The Miss America Pageant, 1998; narrator ABC TV special Open Sesame: The Making of Arabian Nights, 2000; host ABC special The Beatles Revelution, 2000, ABC TV Network's Countdown to Oscar, 2000, Who Wants to Be a Millionaire, 2002. Recipient Front Page award Newswoman's Club of N.Y., 1991, Robert F. Kennedy journalism award, 1995, Woman of Yr. award, City of Hope, 2001, six Emmy awards for reporting; honored by Anti-Defamation League; Found. Am. Women Radio and T.V., 1997. Office: ABC 320 W 66th St New York NY 10023-6304

VIELOT, ALAIN J. elementary school educator; arrived in U.S., 1964; s. Kleber and Marie Claire Vielot. BA in Sociology, Howard U., 1977; MA in French Lit., MA in Psychology, Lausanne (Switzerland) U., 1981; BA in Edn., Fla. Internat. U., 1993. Analyst Sociology and Psychology Think-Tank, Washington, 1982—87; tchr. Dade County Pub. Schs., Miami, Fla., 1988—; head songwriter Hilltop Records. Recipient Editor's Choice award, Nat. Libr. Poetry, 1996. Mem.: United Tchrs. Dade County, Am. Soc. Poets, Internat. Soc. Poets (Internat. Poet Merit award 1995). Roman Catholic. Avocations: football, basketball, soccer, dance, music. Home: 4841 SW 152 Ct Miami FL 33185 Office: North Miami Elem Sch 655 NE 145th St Miami FL 33163

VIENER, JOHN D. lawyer; b. Richmond, Va., Oct. 18, 1939; s. Reuben and Thelma (Kurtz) V.; m. Karin Erika Bauer, Apr. 7, 1969; children: John D. Jr., Katherine Bauer Viener Riordan. BA, Yale U., 1961; JD, Harvard U., 1964. Bar: N.Y. State 1965, U.S. Supreme Ct. 1970, U.S. Dist. Ct. (so. dist.) N.Y. 1974, U.S. Tax Ct. 1975. Assoc. Satterlee, Warfield & Stephens, N.Y.C., 1964—69; sole practice N.Y.C., 1969—76; sr. ptnr. Christy & Viener, N.Y.C., 1976—98, Salans, Hertfeld, Heilbronn, Christy & Viener, N.Y.C., 1999—2000; prin., dir. BFD Capital Beteiligungs GmbH, 2001—. Founder, bd. dirs., gen. counsel Foxfire Fund, Inc., 1968—88; gen. counsel, bd. dirs. Landmark Communities, 1970—99, Am. Continental Properties Group, 1978—, NF&M Internat., Inc., 1976—2003, Singer Fund, Inc., 1979—, Immunotherapy, Inc., 1997—99, Tupper Broadcasting Group Cos., 1996—, Viener Found., 1991—; gen. counsel Nat. Cancer Found. Cancer Care, 1982—85, Troster, Singer & Co., 1970—77; bd. dirs. Gen. Financiere Immob. et Commer. S.A., 1985—89; spl. counsel fin. instns., investment banking and securities concerns; real estate and tax advisor. Bd. dirs. York Theatre Co., 1999-2001, The N.Y. Pops, 1999-2002. Mem.: Internat. Polo Club, Palm Beach Polo Club, Washington Club, Manursing Island Club, Fairfield County Hounds, Meeker Brook Sporting Assn. Office: 620 Fifth Ave New York NY 10020-2402

VIERCK, CHARLES JOHN, JR., neuroscience educator, scientist; b. Columbus, Ohio, July 6, 1936; s. Charles John and Esther (Amadon) V.; m. Cheryl Stogner; children: Kenneth Christopher, Karl Frederick. B.Sc., U. Fla., 1959, M.Sc., 1961, PhD, 1963. Postdoctoral fellow U. Pa., Phila., 1963-65; asst. prof. U. Fla., Gainesville, 1965-71, assoc. prof., 1971-77, prof., 1977—. Adj. prof. U. N.C., Chapel Hill, 1977—; dir. Ctr. Neurobiol. Scis. U. Fla., Gainesville Editor: (textbook) Basics of Neuroscience, 1974; contbr. articles to profl. jours., also chpts. to books; mem. editorial bd. Somatosensory Motor Research, Am. Pain Soc. Jour. Grantee NIH, NIMH, NSF, VA, 1966— Mem. Soc. Neurosci., Internat. Assn. Study Pain Democrat. Avocations: jazz, golf. Home: 9331 NW 15th Pl Gainesville FL 32606-5580 Office: U Fla PO Box 100244 Gainesville FL 32610-0244 E-mail: vierck@ufbi.ufl.edu.

VIERECK, PETER, poet, historian, educator; b. N.Y.C., Aug. 5, 1916; s. George S. and Margaret (Hein) V.; m. Anya de (Markov), June 1945 (div. May 1970); children: John, Alexis, Valerie Edwina and John Gibbs; m. Betty Martin (Falkenberg), Aug. 30, 1972. BS summa cum laude(hon.), Harvard U., 1937, MA, 1939; Henry fellow Christ Ch., Oxford U., Eng., 1937—38; PhD, Harvard U., 1942; LHD (hon.), Olivet Coll., 1959. Tchg. asst. Harvard U., 1941—42, instr. German lit., tutor history and lit. dept., 1946—47; instr. history U.S. Army U., Florence, Italy, 1945; asst. prof. history Smith Coll., 1947—48, vis. lectr. Russian history, 1948—49; assoc. prof. Modern European, Russian history Mt. Holyoke Coll., 1948—55, prof., 1955. Vis. lectr. Am. Culture Oxford U., 1953; Whittal lectr. in poetry Libr. of Congress, 1954, 63, 79; Fulbright prof. Am. poetry and civilization U. Florence, Italy, 1954-56; Elliston chair poetry lectr. U. Cin., 1956; vis. lectr. U. Calif., Berkeley, 1957; Disting. William R. Kenan prof. Mt. Holyoke Coll., 1979; charter mem. Council Basic Edn.; vis. poet Russian Am. cultural exchange program Dept. State, USSR, 1961; vis. rsch. scholar 20th Century Fund, USSR, 1962-63; vis. scholar Rockefeller Study Ctr., Bellagio, Italy, 1977; vis. artist and scholar Am. Acad., Rome, 1949-50, 78; dir. poetry workshop N.Y. Writers Conf., 1965-67; rsch. fellow Huntington Library, San Marino, Calif., 1978. Author: Metapolitics: From the Romantics to Hitler, 1941 Swedish edit., 1942, Italian, 1948, rev. edit., 2003, Terror and Decorum, poems, 1948, reprinted, 1972, Who Killed the Universe, novelette included in anthology New Directions Ten, 1948, Conservatism Revisited: The Revolt Against Revolt 1815-1949, (English edit, 1950), Strike Through the Mask, New Lyrical Poems, 1950, reprinted, 1972, The First Morning: New Poems, 1952, reprinted, 1972, Shame and Glory of the Intellectuals, 1953, rev. edit., 1965, reprinted 1978, Dream and Responsibility, The Tension Between Poetry and Society, 1953, The Unadjusted Man; a New Hero for Americans, 1956, reprinted, 1973, revised expanded edit, Conservatism: From John Adams to Churchill, 1956, reprinted, 1978, The Persimmon Tree, poems, 1956, Inner Liberty, The Stubborn Grit in the Machine, 1957, The Tree Witch: A Verse Drama, 1961, reprinted, 1973, Meta-politics, The Roots of the Nazi Mind, 1961, rev. expanded edit. 1965, Conservatism Revisited and The New Conservatives: What Went Wrong; rev. paperback edits., 1962, 65, reprinted hardcover, 1978, New and Selected Poems, 1932-67, 1967, Archer in the Marrow: The Applewood Poetry Cycles of 1967-87, 1987, Tide and Continuities: Last and First Poems, 1995, Meta-politics: From Wagner and the German Romantics to Hitler, 2003, expanded edit.; Unadjusted Man in an Overadjusted Age, 2004, Conservatism Revisited, 2004, expanded edit.; author of selections in symposium books: Strict Wilderness Discoveries in Poetry and History, 2004 Towards a World Cmty., 1950, Mid-century Am. Poets, 1950, Arts in Renewal, 1951, The New American Right, 1955, Edn. in a Free Soc., 1958, The Radical Right, 1962, Soviet Policy Making, 1967, Outside Looking In, 1972, A Question of Quality, 1976, The So. Calif. Anthology, 1987, rev. editions, 1987, 89, Decade: New Letters Anthology of the 80's, 1990; contbg. essays and poems to popular magazines, and profl. journals, monograph on Conservatism in Ency. Brit., 1974. Sgt. U.S. Army, 1943-45, served in Africa and Italy. Decorated 2 battle stars; awarded Tietjens prize for poetry, 1948, Pulitzer prize for poetry, 1949; recipient Most Disting. Alumnus Award Horace Mann School for Boys, 1958, Poetry Translation Award Translation Center, Columbia U., 1978, Sadin poetry prize N.Y. Quar., 1977, Golden Rose Award New Eng. Poetry Club, 1981, Varoujan prize, 1983, New Eng. Poetry Club prize, 1998, Anne Sexton prize Agni mag., 1999; Guggenheim fellow, Rome, 1949-50; Rockefeller Found. rschr. in history Germany, summer 1958; NEH sr. rsch. fellow USSR, 1969; Mass. Artists Found. fellow, 1978. Mem. Am. Hist. Assn., Oxford Soc., Poetry Soc. Am., P.E.N., Phi Beta Kappa. Clubs: Harvard, N.Y.C. and London; Bryce, Oxford, Eng. Home: 12 Silver St South Hadley MA 01075-1616 *After 86 years of books, scars, and sugar plums, my rock bottom thought on life is a line of Vachel Lindsay: "Courage and sleep are the principal things.".*

VIERLING, H. PHILIP, medical device company executive; With Empi, Inc., St. Paul, 1986—, v.p., officer, 1997-99, pres., COO, 1999—. Office: 599 Cardigan Rd PO Box 26500 Saint Paul MN 55126-4099

VIERMETZ, KURT F. banker; b. Augsburg, Bavaria, Germany, Apr. 27, 1939; came to U.S., 1985; s. Alfons and Claire (Bruck) V.; m. Felicitas Kempe, May, 1966; 1 child, Maximilian Grad., Heilig Kreuz Coll., Germany, 1957. With Morgan Guaranty Trust Co. of N.Y., Frankfurt, Fed. Republic Germany, 1966-69, asst. v.p., 1969-71, v.p. Paris, 1971-82, sr. v.p. for Central Europe N.Y.C., 1982-85; vice chmn. Morgan Guaranty Trust Co. N.Y., 1990—; also bd. dirs. Morgan Guaranty Trust Co. of N.Y., N.Y.C.; vice chmn. J.P. Morgan & Co., Inc., 1990—2000; gen. mgr. Saudi Internat. Bank, London, 1975-77; chmn., supervisory bd. HypoVereinsbank, Munich; treas. J. P. Morgan & Co. Inc., NY; chmn. supervisory bd. Bayerishce Hypo und Vereinsbank, AG, Munich, 1999—2003; dep. chmn., supervisory bd. Bayerishce Hypo und Vereinsbank AG, Munich, 2003—. Author books and articles on internat. fin. to profl. publs. Mem. Am. C. of C. in Germany Roman Catholic. Office: HypoVereinsbank Am Tucherpark 16 80538 Munich Germany

VIERTEL, GEORGE JOSEPH, lawyer, arbitrator, mediator, consulting engineer; b. N.Y.C., June 10, 1912; s. William and Marie Dorothy (Reichert) V.; 1 child, Elise V. Robertson. BSCE, NYU, 1934; LLB, LaSalle U., Chgo., 1952; cert., Old Dominion U., 1963; student, Alliance Francaise, Paris, 1971; JD (hon.), Bernadean U., 1973; PhD (hon.), USUA, 1977. Bar: Va. 1954, D.C., 1972, Md., 1981, U.S. Dist. Ct. (ea. dist. Va.) 1954, U.S. Ct. Appeals (4th cir.) 1954, U.S. Tax Ct. 1954, U.S. Supreme Ct. 1957, U.S. Claims Ct. 1961, U.S. Dist. Ct. Hawaii 1962, U.S. Ct. Appeals (9th cir.) 1963, U.S. Dist. Ct. (D.C. dist.) 1972, U.S. Ct. Appeals (7th cir.) 1972, U.S. Ct. Appeals (D.C. cir.) 1973, Ct. Appeals Md. 1981, U.S. Ct. Mil. Appeals 1973, U.S. Dist. Ct. Md. 1981; registered profl. engr. Md., Va., D.C., N.Y., Wis.; cert. expedited dispute settler; cert. arbitrator Superior Ct. D.C.; lic. real estate broker, Md. Freelance constrn. estimator, 1952-57; asst. engr. N.Y.C. Housing Authority, 1934, Bd. Transp. N.Y.C, 1933-34; supr. constrn. M. Shapiro & Son, N.Y.C.; engr. N.Y.C. Bd. Water Supply; asst. resident engr. Langley Field Sta., Va.; civil engr. Nat. Adv. Com. for Aeronautics (now known as NASA), Langley Field, 1940-48; assoc. Williams, Coile, Blanchard, Architects and Engrs., Newport News, Va., 1948-50; ptnr., chief engr. Assoc. Architects and Engrs., Newport News, 1950-61; asst. to dir. Office of Constrn. and Facility Mgmt. U.S. Dept. Energy, Wash., 1977-79; sole practice law Va., 1954—, 1972—, Md., 1981—. Arbitrator, mediator D.C. Superior Ct., Balt. City Cir. Ct., among others. Contbr. articles to profl. jours. Lt. U.S. Army Corps Engrs., 1934-39. Fellow ASCE (life, pres. local chpt. 1965-67); mem. Bar Assn. Montgomery County, Assn. for Conflict Resolution. Home and Office: 4407 Pinetree Rd Rockville MD 20853-1320 Office Phone: 301-589-7060.

VIESSMAN, WARREN, JR., civil engineering educator emeritus, researcher; b. Balt., Nov. 9, 1930; s. Warren and Helen Adair (Berlinckee) V.; m. Gloria Marie Scheiner, May 11, 1953 (div. Apr. 1975); children: Wendy, Stephen, Suzanne, Michael, Thomas, Sandra; m. Elizabeth Gertrude Rothe, Aug. 8, 1980; children: Heather, Joshua. B in Engrng., Johns Hopkins U., 1952, MS in Engrng., 1958, DEng, 1961. Registered profl. engr., Md. Engr. W. H. Primrose & Assocs., Towson, Md., 1955-57; project engr. Johns Hopkins U., Balt., 1957-61; from asst. to assoc. prof. N.Mex. State U., Las Cruces, 1961-66; prof. U. Maine, Orono, 1966-68, U. Nebr., Lincoln, 1968-75; sr. specialist Libr. Congress, Washington, 1975-83; prof., chmn. U. Fla., Gainesville, 1983-90, assoc. dean for rsch. and grad. study, 1990-91, assoc. dean for acad. programs, 1991—. Vis. scientist Am. Geophys. Union, 1970-71; Maurice Kremer lectr. U. Nebr., 1985, 2001; lectr. Harvard U. Water Policy Seminar, 1988; Wayne S. Nichols Meml. Fund lectr. Ohio State U., 1990; mem. steering com. on groundwater and energy U.S. Dept. Energy, 1979-80; mem. task group on fed. water rsch. U.S. Geol. Survey, 1985-87; mem. com. of water sci. and tech. bd. NAS, 1986-90; mem. water resources working group Nat. Coun. on Pub. Works Improvement, 1987; chmn., chief of engrs. Environ. Adv. Bd., Washington, 1991-93; chmn. solid and hazardous waste mgmt. adv. bd. State U. Sys. Fla. Co-author: Water Supply and Pollution Control, 1993, Water Management: Technology and Institutions, 1984, Introduction to Hydrology, 1996; contbr. over 167 articles to profl. jours. Mem. Water Mgmt. Com., Gainesville, 1983-88, Fla. Environ. Efficiency Study Commn., 1986-88. 1st lt. U.S. Army C.E., 1952-54, Korea. Recipient Comdr.'s award for pub. svc. U.S. Dept. Army, 1993. Fellow ASCE (hon. mem., Julian Hinds award 1989), Am. Water Resources Assn. (nat. pres. 1990, Icko Iben award 1983, Henry P. Caulfield Jr. medal 1996), Univs. Coun. on Water Resources (pres. 1987, Warren A. Hall medal 1994), Sigma Xi, Tau Beta Pi. Avocations: scuba diving, woodworking. Office: U Fla Coll Engring PO Box 116450 Gainesville FL 32611-6450 Office Phone: 352-392-2312. Business E-Mail: wvies@eng.ufl.edu.

VIEST, IVAN M(IROSLAV), consulting structural engineer; b. Bratislava, Slovakia, Czechoslovakia, Oct. 10, 1922; came to U.S., 1947, naturalized, 1955; s. Ivan and Maria (Zacharova) V.; m. Barbara K. Stevenson, May 23, 1953. Ing., Slovak Tech. U., Bratislava, 1946; MS, Ga. Inst. Tech., 1948; PhD, U. Ill., 1951; D. honoris cause (hon.), Tech. U. Kosice, 2002. Registered profl. engr., Pa. Research asst. U. Ill., Urbana, 1948-50, research assoc., 1950-51, research asst. prof., 1951-55, research assoc. prof., 1955-57; bridge research engr. Am. Assn. State Hwy. Ofcls., Nat. Acad. Scis., Ottawa, Ill., 1957-61; structural engr. Bethlehem Steel Corp., Pa., 1961-67, sr. structural cons., 1967-70, asst. mgr. sales engrng. div., 1970-82; pvt. cons. structural engr. IMV Cons., 1983—. Cons. in field. Author: Composite Construction, 1958, History of Engineering Foundation, 1991, Composite Construction--Design for Buildings, 1997, Seventy-Five Years of the Lehigh Valley Section, 1997. Recipient Constrn. award Engring. News Record, 1972, Special Achievement award, Am. Inst. Steel Constrn., 2004; named to Hall of Fame, Ga. Inst. of Tech., 1998. Fellow AAAS, Am. Concrete Inst. (Wason Rsch. medal 1956); mem. NAE, ASCE (hon., v.p. 1973-75, Rsch. prize 1958, Ernest E. Howard award 1991), Internat. Assn. Bridge and Structural Engrng., Transp. Rsch. Bd. (emeritus 1999—), Czechoslovak Soc. Arts and Scis. (exec. v.p. 1992-93), Earthquake Engrng. Rsch. Inst., Saucon Valley Country Club (Bethlehem). Achievements include research in steel and concrete structures including bridges and bldgs. Office Phone: 610-865-1041.

VIETH, GIFFORD DUANE, lawyer; b. Omaha, Sept. 20, 1923; s. Walter E. and Irene E. (Horn) V.; m. Jane G. Richardson, Feb. 16, 1952; children: Peter D., Robert R., Jane G. BA, U. Iowa, 1947, JD, 1949. Bar: Iowa 1949, D.C. 1949, U.S. Dist. Ct. Iowa 1953, U.S. Dist. Ct. Md. 1955, U.S. Ct. Claims 1958, U.S. Ct. Appeals (3d cir.) 1960, U.S. Dist. Ct. (ea. dist.) Wis. 1965, U.S. Supreme Ct. 1966, U.S. Ct. Appeals (2d cir.) 1970, U.S. Ct. Appeals (7th cir.) 1971. Ptnr. Arnold & Porter, Washington, 1949—. Mem. D.C. Commn. on Budget and Financial Priorities, 1989-90. Trustee Iowa Law Sch. Found., Iowa City, 1971-88, Fed. City Council, Washington, 1972—. With USAAF, 1942-45, ETO. Mem. ABA, D.C. Bar Assn., Iowa State Bar Assn., Columbia Country Club, Burning Tree Club, Met. Club. Lutheran. Avocation: golf. Home: 4407 Chalfont Pl Bethesda MD 20816-1812 Office: Arnold & Porter 555 12th St NW Ste 1202 Washington DC 20004-1200

VIETOR, HAROLD DUANE, federal judge; b. Parkersburg, Iowa, Dec. 29, 1931; s. Harold Howard and Alma Johanna (Kreimeyer) V.; m. Dalia Artemisa Zamarripa Cadena, Mar. 24, 1973; children: Christine Elizabeth, John Richard, Greta Maria. BA, U. Iowa, 1955, JD, 1958. Bar: Iowa 1958. Law clk. U.S. Ct. Appeals 8th Circuit, 1958-59; ptnr. Bleakley Law Offices, Cedar Rapids, Iowa, 1959-65; judge Iowa Dist. Ct., Cedar Rapids, 1965-79, chief judge, 1970-79; U.S. dist. judge U.S. Dist. Ct. for So. Dist. Iowa, Des Moines, 1979-96, chief judge, 1985-92, sr. U.S. dist. judge, 1997—. Lectr. at law schs., legal seminars U.S. and Japan. Contbr. articles to profl. jours. in U.S. and Japan. Served with USN, 1952-54. Mem. Iowa Bar Assn. (pres. jr. sect. 1966-67), Iowa Judges Assn. (pres. 1975-76), 8th Cir. Dist. Judges Assn. (pres. 1986-88). Office: US Dist Ct 221 US Courthouse 123 E Walnut St Des Moines IA 50309-2035

VIETS, HERMANN, college president, consultant; b. Quedlinburg, Fed. Republic Germany, Jan. 28, 1943; came to U.S., 1949, naturalized, 1961; s. Hans and Herta (Heik) V.; m. Pamela Deane, June 30, 1968; children: Danielle, Deane, Hans, Hillary BS, Polytech. U., 1965, MS, 1966, PhD, 1970. Fellow von Karman Inst., Brussels, 1969-70; group leader Wright-Patterson AFB, Dayton, Ohio, 1970-76; prof. Wright State U., Dayton, Ohio, 1976-81; assoc. dean W.Va. U., Morgantown, 1981-83; dean U. R.I., Kingston, 1983-91; pres. Milw. Sch. Engring., 1991—. Chmn. bd. dirs. Precision Stampings, Inc., Beaumont, Calif., 1977—; bd. dirs. Gehl Co., West Bend, Wis., Astro Med, Inc., West Warwick, R.I., Wenthe-Davidson Engrng. Co., New Berlin, Wis., Max Kade Inst. for German-Am. Studies, Discovery World, Milw. County Rsch. Park Corp.; cons. USAF Aero Propulsion Lab., Dayton, 1976-80, Covington & Burling, Washington, 1976-77; cons. in field. Patentee in aero. field; contbr. numerous articles to profl. jours. Mem. Greater Milw. Com.; dir. Competitive Wis., Gov. Regional H.S. Excellence Co., 1994, Gov.'s Export Strategy Commn., 1994; trustee Pub. Policy Forum. Recipient Tech. Achievement award USAF, 1974, Sci. Achievement award, 1975, Gov.'s Sci. and Tech. award State of R.I., 1987, Goodrich Pub. Svc. award, 1990, Citation R.I. Legislature, 1987, 90, 91, Outstanding Alumnus award aerospace engrng. dept. Poly. U., 1994; Disting. Alumnus Poly. U., 1995, Engr. of Yr. award Engrs. and Scientists of Milw., 1997; named Hon. Citizen Fachhochschule Luebeck, Germany, 1998; postdoctoral fellow NATO, 1969-70, NASA, 1965-69. Fellow AIAA (assoc., acad. affairs com. 1998—, Best Tech. Paper award Allegheny-Pitts. sect. 1982); mem. German Assn. for Luft and Raumfahrt, German-Am. Heritage Soc. (bd. dirs.), Nat. Assn. Independent Coll. and Univ. (bd. dirs.), Am. Soc. Engring. Edn., Japan-Am. Soc. (bd. dirs. 1994), Soc. Mfg. Engrs., Rotary, Sigma Xi, Phi Kappa Phi, Tau Beta Pi, Sigma Gamma Tau. Avocations: antique automobiles, beer steins, notgeld currency. Home: 4216 N Lake Dr Milwaukee WI 53211-1722 Office: Milw Sch Engring 1025 N Broadway Milwaukee WI 53202-3109

VIETZKE, WESLEY MAUNDER, internist, educator; b. Ft. Defiance, Ariz., Jan. 1, 1938; s. Paul Carl Franz and Alice Rose (Maunder) V.; m. Barbara Joan Feroe, Apr. 2, 1966; children: Gay Elizabeth, Robert Paul. BA, DePauw U., 1959; MD, Johns Hopkins U., 1963. Diplomate Am. Bd. Internal Medicine. Intern Grace-New Haven Hosp., 1963-64; resident Yale-New Haven Hosp., 1964-65, 67-68; asst. prof. medicine U. Conn., Farmington, 1969-70, assoc. dean, 1971-75; asst. clin. prof. medicine Yale U., New Haven, 1975—2000. Asst. to dir. health plan Yale U., 1981-84; physician in charge Kaiser Permanente, Stamford, Conn., 1986-90. Contbr. articles to profl. jours. Lt. comdr. USPHS, 1965-67. Fellow ACP; mem. Phi Beta Kappa, Alpha Omega Alpha. Democrat. Avocations: painting, travel. Home and Office: 15 W Haycock Point Rd Branford CT 06405-5307 E-mail: wesvietzke@comcast.net.

VIEZER, TIMOTHY WAYNE, economist, investment company executive; b. Cleve., Jan. 13, 1959; s. Lawrence Stephen and Elaine Pearl (Thompson) V.; m. Jody Claire Russell, Oct. 14, 1988 (div. Aug. 1993); 1 child, Jessica

Marlene; m. Joani Sue Yoakum, Sept. 21, 1996. BBA, BA with honors, Kent State U., 1982, MA in Econs., 1987, MA, 1989; PhD in Agrl. Econs., Ohio State U., 1998. CFA 2002. Adminstrv. asst. Arthur Andersen & Co., Cleve., 1985; corp. economist Centerior Energy Corp., Cleve., 1985-90, grad. tchg. assoc. Ohio State U., Columbus, 1990-91; grad. rsch. assoc. Nat. Regulatory Rsch. Inst., Columbus, 1991-93; asst. economist Huntington Nat. Bank, Columbus, 1991-92; portfolio analyst State Tchrs. Retirement Sys. Ohio, Columbus, 1993-99; sr. equities investment officer Sch. Employees Retirement Sys. Ohio, Columbus, 1999—. Instr. econs. Cuyahoga CC, Parma, Ohio, 1989-90; lectr. Baldwin-Wallace Coll., Berea, Ohio, 1989-90, Ohio Dominican Coll., Columbus, 1991, Capital U., 1991-95, Columbus State CC, 1992-93, Otterbein Coll., 1993-2000, Franklin U., 1994-2000, Ohio State U., 2001-. Co-author: The Soviet Occupation of Afghanistan, 1986; contbr. articles to profl. jours. Named one of Outstanding Young Men of Am. US Jaycees, 1981. Mem. Am. Econ. Assn., Am. Fin. Assn., Nat. Assn. Bus. Economists, Assn. Investment Mgmt. and Rsch., Internat. Assn. Bus. Forecasting (asst. sec. 1986, bd. dirs. 1987), Columbus Assn. Bus. Economists (past pres.), Am. Real Estate Soc., Soc. Quantitative Analysists, Chgo. Quantitative Alliance. Roman Catholic. Home: 231 E Como Ave Columbus OH 43202-1212 Office Phone: 614-222-5925. E-mail: tviezer@ohsers.org.

VIG, VERNON EDWARD, lawyer; b. St. Cloud, Minn., June 19, 1937; s. Edward Enoch and Salley Johanna (Johnson) V.; m. Susan Jane Rosenow, June 10, 1961; 1 child, Elizabeth Karen. BA, Carleton Coll., 1959; LLB, NYU, 1962, LLM, 1963; postdoctoral studies, Univ. Paris, Fac. de Droit, 1964. Bar: N.Y. 1962; avocat, Paris, 1992. Assoc. Cleary, Gottlieb, Steen & Hamilton, Paris, 1964, Donovan, Leisure, Newton & Irvine, N.Y.C. and Paris, 1965-72, ptnr., 1972-86, LeBoeuf, Lamb, Greene & MacRae, LLP, N.Y.C., Brussels, 1986—2001, of counsel, 2002—. Editor: NYU Law Rev. Sr. warden Grace Ch., Bklyn., 1986-2001. George F. Baker scholar, Fulbright scholar, 1963-64, Ford Found. scholar, 1963-64. Mem. ABA (internat. and antitrust sects.), N.Y. State Bar Assn. (chmn. antitrust sect. 1987-88), Assn. of Bar of City of N.Y., Internat. Bar Assn., Union Internat. des Avocats, Heights Casino (bklyn.), Merriewold Club (Forestburgh, N.Y., bd. dirs. 1985-91), Phi Beta Kappa. Episcopalian. Office: LeBoeuf Lamb Greene & MacRae LLP 125 W 55th St New York NY 10019-5369 E-mail: vvig@llgm.com.

VIGDOR, JUSTIN LEONARD, lawyer; b. N.Y.C., July 13, 1929; s. Irving Barton and Ida (Devins) V.; m. Louise Martin, Mar. 8, 1952; children: Robert, Jill Vigdor-Feldman, Lisa Vigdor-Peck, Wendy Vigdor-Hess. LLB magna cum laude, St. John's U., 1951; LLM, N.Y.U., 1952. Bar: N.Y. 1951, U.S. Supreme Ct 1951, Fla. 1975. Counsel Boylan, Brown, Code, Vigdor & Wilson LLP, Rochester, NY, 1958—. Bd. dirs.IEC Electronics Corp.; former mem. faculty Nazareth Coll.; mem. N.Y. Uniform Law Commn., Nat. Conf. Uniform Law Commrs. Contbr. articles to profl. jours. Bd. dirs. AAA Western/Central N.Y., Found. for Jewish Cmty., Ames Amzalak Meml. Trust; pres. AAA N.Y. State, Inc., Al Sigl Ptnrs. Foundn., also past pres.; chmn. N.Y. State IOLA Fund. Served with JAGC, AUS, 1952-54. Recipient Community Svc. award, 1960, award for Svc. to Community and Legal Profession, 1983, Disting. Svc. award N.Y. State Assn. County Clks., 1985. Fellow Am. Bar Found., N.Y. Bar Found. (Nathaniel award for cmty. svc. and profl. accomplishment); mem. Fla. Bar Assn., N.Y. State Bar Assn. (past pres. Ho. of Dels.), Monroe County Bar Assn. (past pres.), Estate Planning Coun., Am. Arbitration Assn. (nat. panel 1962—), N.Y. State C. of C. (Disting. Svc. award 1964), Irondequoit Country Club. Democrat. Jewish. Home: 16 Tobey Woods Pittsford NY 14534-1824 Office: Boylan Brown Code Vigdor & Wilson LLP 2400 Chase Sq Rochester NY 14604 Office Phone: 585-232-5300. Business E-Mail: jvigdor@boylanbrown.com. E-mail: jvigdor@aol.com.

VIGIER, FRANÇOIS CLAUDE DENIS, city planning educator; b. Geneva, Oct. 14, 1931; s. Eugene Henri Rene and Françoise (Dupuy) V. BArch, MIT, 1955; M in City Planning, Harvard U., 1959, PhD, 1967. Architect UN Relief and Works Agy., Jordan, 1955-57; designer Town Planning Cons., Cambridge, Mass., 1957-58; mem. faculty Harvard Grad. Sch. Design, Cambridge, 1960—, prof. city planning and urban design, 1968-85, Charles Dyer Norton prof. regional planning, 1985—, dir. Ctr. Urban Devel. Studies, 1987—, chmn. spl. programs, 1982-86, chmn. dept. urban planning and design, 1992-98. Vis. lectr. art Dartmouth Coll., 1962, 64; vis. critic urban design U. N.C., 1963; cons. Ford Found. Latin Am. program, 1964-65, Ednl. Svcs., Inc., 1966; dir. Harvard Ctr. Environ. Design Studies, 1967-69; pres. Nash-Vigier Inc., Cambridge, 1965-91. Author: Change and Apathy: Liverpool and Manchester During the Industrial Revolution, 1970, Housing in Tunis, 1987; contbr. articles to various periodicals. Decorated Knight, Order of Merit, France, 1995. Mem. Am. Inst. Cert. Planners, Am. Planning Assn. Home: 27 Fayerweather St Cambridge MA 02138-3329 E-mail: FVigier@gsd.harvard.edu.

VIGIL, DAVID CHARLES, lawyer; b. Bklyn., Jan. 29, 1944; s. Charles S. and Kathleen A. (Liebert) V. BA, U. Colo., 1966; JD, U. N.Mex., 1969. Bar: Colo. 1969, U.S. Dist. Ct. Colo. 1969, U.S. Ct. Appeals (10th cir.) 1969, U.S. Supreme Ct. 1974. Pvt. practice, Denver, 1969-80, 96—; ptnr. Vigil & Vigil, Denver, 1980-96; broker Perry & Butler Realty, Denver, 1996-97, Keller Williams Realty, Denver, 1997—. Bd. dirs. Archdiocesan Housing Commn. Inc., 1998—2003, Housing for All, 1999—2003. Grantee Nat. Inst. for Trial Advocacy, 1983. Mem.: NITA Advs. Assn., Cath. Lawyers Guild, Colo. Hispanic Bar Assn. (bd. dirs. 1986—89, treas. 1988), Assn. Trial Lawyers Colo., Am. Arbitration Assn. (comml. arbitrator 1993—95), Denver Bar Assn. (mem. jud. selection and benefits com. 1975—90, chmn. 1988—90), Colo. Bar Assn. (mem. ethics com. 1973—79, legal fee arbitration com. 1980—92), ATLA, ABA, Elks. Personal E-mail: davidcvigil@msn.com.

VIGIL, EUGENE LEON, retired federal agency administrator, cell biologist; b. Chgo., Mar. 14, 1941; s. Marcelo Raymond and Anna (Lewus) V.; m. Suan M. Davis, Jan. 22, 1963 (div. Sept. 1989); children: Michael, Jennifer, Aimee; m. Marcia Janice Holden, Apr. 18, 1993 (div. Aug. 2004). BS, Loyola U., 1963; MS, U. Iowa, 1965, PhD, 1967. NIH postdoc. fellow U. Wis., 1967-69; pub. health trainee U. Chgo., 1969-71, Danforth tutor, 1970; asst. prof. Marquette U., Milw., 1971-79, U. Md., College Park, 1979-81, rsch. assoc., 1981-88; plant physiologist USDA/ARS, Beltsville, Md., 1988-95; program dir. NIH, Bethesda, Md., 1995-98, sci. rev. adminstr., 1998—2001. Program chmn. Histochem. Soc., N.Y.C., 1976-79, councilor 1979-82; study sect. mem. cell biology NSF, Washington, 1983-87; mem. minority affairs com. Am. Soc. Cell Biology, Bethesda, 1991-97; chmn. min. affr com., mem. exec. com. Am. Soc. Plant Physiology, Rockville, Md., 1995-97. Author, editor: Botanical Cytochemistry, 1980. Pres. Milw. Hort. Soc.; precinct chmn. Rep. Party, Chgo. Predoctoral fellow NIH, U. Iowa, Iowa City, 1966, fellow German Acad. Exch., Munich, 1975; grantee NATO, Munich and Heidelberg, Germany, 1976, NSF, 1979. Mem.: Internat. League Antiquarian Booksellers, Antiquarian Booksellers Assn. Am., Rotary (group sec. Beltsville, Md. 1998—99, pres.-elect 1999—, pres. 2000—02). Home: 308 Kwanzan Dr Lynden WA 98264-1703

VIGIL, HENRY P. information technology executive; BA in Philosophy, MBA, Stanford U. From dir. mktg. to corp. v.p. Microsoft, Redmond, Wash., 1990, corp. v.p. consumer strategy & partnerships. Bd. dir. Artist Trust. Founder City Yr. Seattle. Office: One Microsoft Way Redmond WA 98052-6399

VIGIL, JEFFREY L. infant and child products manufacturing executive; b. 1954; BS in Acctg., U. Wyo., 1976. Sr. auditor Arthur Andersen & Co., 1976; internal auditor Guaranty Bank and Trust Co., 1979; v.p., treas., contr. Sunnyside Mines, Inc., 1989-90; v.p. fin. Energy Fuels Corp., 1980; v.p. acquisitions Northwestern Growth Corp., Huron, S.D., 1993; v.p. fin. and adminstrn., treas., sec. Koala Corp., Denver, 1996—. Mem. AICP. Office: Unit D 11600 E 53d Ave Denver CO 80239-2312 E-mail: ir@koalabear.com.

VIGIL-GIRON, REBECCA, state official; b. Taos, N.Mex., Sept. 4, 1954; d. Felix W. and Cecilia (Santistevan) Vigil; 1 child, Andrew R. AA in Elem. Edn., N.Mex. Highlands U., 1978, BA in French, 1991. Sec., project monitor, customer svc. rep. Pub. Svc. Co. N.Mex., 1978-86; sec. of state N.Mex., 1987-90, 98—; exec. dir. N.Mex. Commn. Status of Women, 1991; electoral observer UN, Angola, Africa, 1992, Internat. Found. Electoral Sys., Dominican Republic, 1994, 1996, Washington, 1996. Participant AMPART, Mex., 1991. Dem. nominee U.S. Hr. Reps., 1990. Named among 100 Most Influential Hispanics in Nation, Hispanic Bus. Mag., 1990; recipient Trio Achievers award S.W. Assn. Student Assistance Programs, 1993, Gov.'s award Outstanding N.Mex. Women, 1994. Mem. Albuquerque Hispano C. of C. (membership rep., sr. sales mktg. rep., corp. rels. coord.) Democrat. Office: Office of the New Mexico Secretary of State State Capitol North Annex, Suite 300 Santa Fe NM 87503

VIGNEAULT, ALAIN, professional hockey coach; b. Quebec City, Can., May 14, 1961; m. Josée Doucet; children: Andréanne, Janie. Head coach Can. Nat. Jr. Team, 1989-91; coach Trois-Rivières Draveurs, QMJHL, Beauport Harfangs, QMJHL, 1995-97; asst. coach Ottawa Senators, NHL; head coach Montreal Canadiens, 1997—2000; Coach PEI Rocket (formerly Montreal), Charlottetown, Canada, 2003—. Office: PEI Rocket Charlottetown Civic Center 46 Kensington Rd C1A 5H7 Charlottetown PE Canada

VIGNERI, JOSEPH WILLIAM, lawyer; b. Decatur, Ill., July 28, 1956; s. Joseph Paul and Thelma Lucille (Pettus) V.; children: Craig Ashley, Emily Carmela. BA in Polit. Sci., Millikin U., 1980; JD cum laude, St. Louis U., 1983. Bar: Ill. 1983, U.S. Dist. Ct. (ctrl. dist.) Ill. 1983, U.S. Supreme Ct. 1990. Assoc. Rosenberg, Rosenberg, Bickes, Johnson & Richardson, Decatur, 1983-86; ptnr. Brilley & Vigneri, Decatur, 1986-88; pvt. practice, Decatur, 1988-92; ptnr. Vigneri & Robinson, Decatur, Ill., 1993-95; pvt. practice Decatur, 1995—; asst. pub. defender Macon County, Ill., 1999—. Past mem. job. svc. employer com. Ill. Dept. Employment Security. Past mem. profl. adv. com. Vis. Nurses Assn.; past bd. dirs., treas. Macon County Mental Health Assn. Mem. ABA (sect. real property, probate and trust law, com. spl. needs and tech. com., vice chmn. gen. practice com. 1991-92, family law subcom., editor newsletter), Ill. Bar Assn. (sec. individual rights sect. 1986, mem. bus. advice and fin. planning sect. coun. 1995-97), Decatur Bar Assn. (continuing legal edn. com. 1994-95, tech. com. 1996-97). Republican. Roman Catholic. Office: 136 W Washington St Decatur IL 62522-3102 Office Phone: 217-422-9992. E-mail: jvigneri@earthlink.net.

VIGNERON, ALLEN HENRY, theology studies educator, rector, auxiliary bishop; b. Mt. Clemens, Mich., Oct. 21, 1948; s. Elwin E. and Bernadine K. (Kott) V. AB in Philosophy, Sacred Heart Sem., Detroit, 1970; STL in Fundamental Theology, Pontifical Gregorian U., 1977; PhD in Philosophy, Cath. U. Am., 1987. Ordained deacon Roman Cath. Ch., 1973, ordained priest, 1975, titular bishop, 1996. Assoc. pastor Our Lady Queen of Peace Ch., Harper Woods, Mich., 1975-79; asst. prof. philosophy and theology Sacred Heart Major Sem., Detroit, 1985—; addetto of the secretariat of his Holiness the Pope The Holy See, Vatican City, 1991-94; rector, pres. Sacred Heart Major Sem., Detroit, 1994—; auxiliary bishop Archdiocese of Detroit, 1996—. Adj. prof. theology Pontifical Gregorian U., Rome, 1992-94. Roman Catholic. Office: Sacred Heart Major Sem 2701 W Chicago Detroit MI 48206-1704

VIGNOLA, ANDREW MICHAEL, SR., systems management executive; b. N.Y.C., Sept. 6, 1938; Student in bus. adminstrn., CCNY, 1956-59. Programmer trainee Citibank, N.Y.C., 1959-60; programmer analyst Soc. Savs., Hartford, Conn., 1960-63; mgr. on-line data ctr. NCR Corp., Boston, 1963-67; cons., sr. ptnr. Computer Assistance, Inc., Hartford, 1967-72; v.p. info. sys. svc. divsn. Soc. for Savs., Hartford, 1972-80; pres. Solar Svcs., Inc. subs. Soc. for Savings, 1977-80; sr. v.p., dir. info. svcs. Dime Savs. Bank, N.Y.C., 1980-83; v.p. info. svcs. group Advest, inc., Hartford, 1983-85; pres. Cosine Inc., Meriden, Conn., 1985-90; exec. v.p., COO I.G.I.C., Great Neck, N.Y., 1993-99; mgmt. cons., 1999—. Former mem. faculty Conn. Savs. Sch. Fin. and Mgmt.; lectr. in field. Mem. Data Processing Mgmt. Assn. (pres., chmn. bd. Hartford chpt. 1976-77). Contbr. articles to profl. jours.; inventor banking brokerage interface. Mem. Data Processing Mgmt. Assn. (pres., chmn. bd. Hartford chpt. 1976-77). Address: PO Box 3265 Waterbury CT 06705

VIGORITO, PHILIP MICHAEL, lawyer; b. Niles, Ohio, June 25, 1957; s. Philip Anthony and Annette Lucille (Pezzano) V.; m. Sharon Kay Patrick, July 14, 1995; children: Michael, Philip, Nicholas. BS in Applied Sci., Youngstown (Ohio) State U., 1984; JD cum laude, U. Akron, Ohio, 1989. Bar: Ohio 1989, U.S. Dist. Ct. (no. dist.) Ohio 1989. Assoc. Baker, Meekison & Dublikar, Canton, Ohio, 1987-92, Law Offices of Marty White, Warren, Ohio, 1992-94; pvt. practice Warren, 1994—. Mem. Ohio State Bar Assn., Trumbull County Bar Assn. Roman Catholic. Avocations: hunting, fishing, camping, exercise. Office: 552 N Park Ave Warren OH 44481

VIGTEL, GUDMUND, museum director emeritus; b. July 9, 1925; came to U.S., 1948, naturalized, 1966; s. Arne Jonsen and Elisabeth (Petri) V.; m. Solveig Lund, 1951 (div. 1964); 1 child, Elisabeth; m. Carolyn Gates Smith, July 18, 1964; 1 child, Catherine Higdon. BFA, U. Ga., 1952, MFA, 1953; DFA (hon.), Atlanta Coll. Art, 1991. Adminstrv. asst. Corcoran Gallery Art, Washington, 1954-61, asst. dir., 1961-63; dir. High Mus. Art, Atlanta, 1963-91, dir. emeritus, 1991—. Contbr. articles and essays to profl. publs. With Royal Norwegian Air Force, 1944-45. Decorated Chevalier des Arts et Lettres, Min. of Culture, France, 1985; recipient Order of Merit 1st Class, Fed. Republic Germany, 1989, The James R. Short Lifetime Achievement award, 2003. Home: 2082 Golfview Dr NW Atlanta GA 30309-1210

VIIL, HEINO, retired engineer; b. Riisipere, Estonia, Dec. 18, 1919; arrived in U.S., 1951; s. Johannes Friedrich and Pauline (Jahnsohn) Viil; m. Ella Toomet, Apr. 30, 1941 (div. 1949); m. Mirdza Berzins, July 25, 1953; children: Brunolf, Silvia. PhD, Albert-Ludwigs U., Freiburg, Germany, 1950; BS, Drexel U., Phila., 1962; MS, George Washington U., 1967, SUNY, Buffalo, 1974. Preliminary engr. Proctor & Schwartz, Phila., 1951—62; rsch. engr. Robertshaw, King of Prussia, Pa., 1962—63; ops. analyst Vitro Labs., Silver Spring, Md., 1963—68; devel. engr. Bell Aerospace Co., Buffalo, 1968—74; sr. engr. Singer, Kearfott, Wayne, NJ, 1974—78; sr. mem. tech. staff ITT Def. Comm. Divsn., Nutley, NJ, 1978—94; ret., 1994. Mem.: Alpha Sigma Lambda. Home: 543 Main St Little Falls NJ 07424-2448

VIJAYARAMAN, PUGAZHENDHI, medical educator; m. Vasanthi Pugazhendhi, Dec. 10, 1993; children: Adithya Pugazhendhi, Avani Pugazhendhi. MD, JIPMER, Pondicherry, India, 1990—93. Internal Medicine Am. bd. of internal Medicine, 1997, Cardiovascular Diseases Am. bd. of Internal Medicine, 2000, Cardiac Electrophysiology Am. bd. of Internal Medicine, 2001. Asst. prof. of internal medicine Med. Coll. Va, Va. Commonwealth U., Richmond, Va., 2002—; dir., cardiac electrophysiology divsn. McGuire VA Med. Ctr., Richmond, Va., 2002—. Dir., pacemaker, arrhythmia services McGuire VA Med. Ctr., Richmond, Va., 2002—. Contbr. articles various profl. jours. Recipient Best Outgoing Student, Madurai Med. Coll., 1989, Outstanding Academic Achievement in Cardiovasc. Medicine, Montefiore Med. Ctr., Dept. Cardiology, NY, 2000, Leo Davidoff Socs. Outstanding Achievement Tchg., Albert Einstein Coll. Medicine, Yeshiva U., NY, 1997. Mem.: Am. Heart Assn., Va. Dept. of Health (licentiate), Am. Coll. of Cardiology (assoc.). Office: McGuire Veterans Affairs Med Ctr 1201 Broadrock Blvd 111J3 Richmond VA 23049

VIJAYARATNAM, KANAPATHIPILLAI, civil and environmental engineer, consultant, director, educator; b. Analaitivu, Sri Lanka, May 10, 1948; arrived in Eng., 1979, naturalized, 1990; s. Kathirvelu Kanapathipillai and Parvathy Ponniah; m. Sakuntala Mylwaganam, Oct. 31, 1979. BSc in Engring. with honors, U. Ceylon, Peradeniya, 1971; M Engring., Asian Inst. Tech., Bangkok, 1977; MSc in Pub. Health (Environ.) Engring., Imperial Coll. U. London, 1982; cert. sustainable bus. challenge, World Bus. Coun. Sustainable Devel., 1999; Diploma, Imperial Coll., London, 1982. Chartered engr., U.K. Instr. civil engring. U. Ceylon, Peradeniya, 1972; civil engr. Mahaweli Devel. Bd., Colombo, Sri Lanka, 1972-75, Renardet Engring., Singapore, 1977-80; engr. Chanton Engring. Ltd., Middlesex, 1984-85, S.P. Collins Assocs., Cambridge, U.K., 1985-86; cons. civil engr. Coulsdon, U.K., 1986-88; sr. engr. Neilcot Constrn. Ltd., Kent, U.K., 1988-90; engr. clean water dept. Binnie & Ptnrs., Cons. Engrs., Redhill, U.K., 1990-94; sr. engr. grade 1 SMHBinnie Cons. Engrs., K.L., Malaysia, 1995-96; dep. project mgr., prin. engr. S.S.P. Consulting Engrs., Kuala Lumpur, Malaysia, 1996-97, engring. cons., 1998-99; mng. dir. Rosebury Cons., Ltd., 1999—. Exec. dir. AITA-Net (Europe), Internat. Cons. Consortium, 2001—; orig. contbr. to re-engring. of water ind. orgs., 1996, Broader Edu. of Civil Engs. in 21st Century, 1995, Integrated River Basin Devel., 1977, Cost and Performance Optimization of Water Treatment System (conceptual and mathematical), 1982, overview of criterian decision making, Water Mgmt. Resources, 1994, Assessment of Mathematical Multi-Objective/Gilerion Approaches to Water Resources Mgmt., Eng., 1994, Sustainable Development of Infrastructure in Water and Environ. Engring., 1996, Environmentally Sound Dam and Water Power Devel., 1995, Emergence and Complexity in Urban Environmental Engring Mgmt. in 21st Century, 1999, Environ. Engring. Edn. in 21st Century, 1999, 2003, and Future Dir. Tech. Edn. in Asia, 1999, Project Mgmt. Water Supply and Treatment Projects in Asia, 1995, Future Direction Engring. Edn. for a Sustainable World in the New Millenium, 2000, 2003, Sustainable Water Supply for Asian City, 2001, 2003, Sustainable Waste Management, 2001, leading contbr. Talking Forum of www.bbc.co.uk on engring., sustainable devel. & public policy issues, 2002; contbr. leading numerous BBC -Have your say (Eng.'s pub. policy) forum, 2002; prof. and dean Sch. of Engring. Mgmt., Sustainable Devel. and Pub. Policy Am. U. London, 2003-; presenter in field. Contbr. articles to profl. jours. U.K. Govt. scholar, 1976-77; NATO Advanced Inst. grantee, 1981, UNESCO/Colo. State U. grantee, 1981; named one of 500 Leaders of New Century, 1999, Asians in Millennium, 100 Eminent Tamils of 20th Century. Mem. ASCE, Royal Instn. London, Instn. Civil Engrs. London, Internat. Water Assn., Internat. Assn. Hydraulic Rsch. and Engring., Internat. Assns. Water Resources and Water Power Internat. Ctr. Engring. Edn., Water and Environ. Mgmt. (charter). Avocations: golf, travel, reading, writing, fine arts, tennis. Home: 1 Ashcroft Rise Coulsdon Surrey CR5 2SS England E-mail: vijay@vijayaratnam.com.

VIKESLAND, PETER JOHN, environmental engineering educator, researcher; b. Boulder, Colo., Mar. 30, 1971; s. John Peter and Angela Mae Vikesland; m. Judy Chun, July 29, 1995. BA, Grinnell Coll., Iowa, 1993; PhD, U. of Iowa, 1998. Postdoctoral scholar The Johns Hopkins U., Balt., 1999—2001; asst. prof. Va. Tech, Blacksburg, 2002—. Author: (phd dissertation) Monochloramine Loss in the Presence of Ferrous Iron (AWWA Dissertation award and AEESP Hon. Mention Dissertation award, 1999), (jour. articles) Environ. Sci. and Tech. Fellow Abel Wolman Doctoral Fellowship, Am. Water Works Assn., 1996; grantee U.S. Nat. Sci. Found. Career award, 2004—; Grant, Am. Water Works Assn. Rsch. Found., 2002—04, 2002—. Mem.: Am. Geophys. Union, Assn. of Environ. Engring. and Sci. Profs., Am. Water Works Assn., Am. Chem. Soc. Office: Virginia Tech 415 Durham Hall Blacksburg VA 24061 Office Phone: 540-231-3568. Business E-Mail: petervikesland@vt.edu.

VIKTORA, RICHARD EMIL, lawyer; b. Chgo., July 1, 1943; s. Emil J. and Lillian B. (Smatlak) V.; m. Anne Marie Kus, Feb. 20, 1971. BS, U. Ill., 1965; JD, John Marshall Law Sch., 1969. Bar: Ill. 1969, U.S. Dist. Ct. (no. dist.) Ill. 1969, U.S. Ct. Appeals (7th cir.) 1970, U.S. Supreme Ct. 1975, N.Y. 1981, U.S. Dist. Ct. (so. and ea. dists.) N.Y. 1983. Assoc. Menk, Johnson & Bishop, Chgo., 1969-73; litigation group counsel, regulatory counsel, asst. sec. G.D. Searle & Co., Skokie, Ill., 1973-80; asst. sec., dir. gen. svcs. Revlon, Inc.; asst. sec. Revlon Group, Inc., N.Y.C., 1980-92; gen. counsel Skidmore, Owings & Merrill LLP, N.Y.C., 1992—. Lawyer; b. Chgo., July 1, 1943; s. Emil J. and Lillian B. (Smatlak) V.; m. Anne Marie Kus, Feb. 20, 1971. B.S., U. Ill., 1965; JD, John Marshall Law Sch., 1969. Bar: Ill. 1969, U.S. Dist. Ct. (no. dist.) Ill. 1969, U.S. Ct. Appeals (7th cir.) 1970, U.S. Supreme Ct. 1975, N.Y. 1981, U.S. Dist. Ct. (so. and ea. dists.) N.Y. 1983. Assoc. Menk, Johnson, & Bishop, Chgo., 1969-73; instr. John Marshall Law Sch., Chgo., 1970-73; litigation group counsel, regulatory counsel, asst. sec. G.D. Searle & Co., Skokie, Ill., 1973-80; asst. sec., dir. gen. svcs. Revlon, Inc., also asst. sec. Revlon Group, Inc., N.Y.C., 1980-92; gen. counsel Skidmore Owings & Merrill LLP, N.Y.C., 1992—. Zoning adminstr. Village of Bartlett (Ill.), 1974, chmn. Plan Commn., 1975, trustee, 1975-79. Mem. ABA, Ill. State Bar Assn., Chgo. Bar Assn., Def. Research Inst., Am. Corp. Counsel Assn., Assn. Trial Lawyers Am., Def. Assn. N.Y., Assn. of Bar of City of N.Y., Westchester-Fairfield Corp. Counsel Assn., Order of John Marshall Law Sch., Delta Theta Phi (scholar Key), Anvil Club (East Dundee, Ill.), Masons. Republican. Roman Catholic. Zoning adminstr. Village of Bartlett, Ill., 1974, chmn. Plan Commn., 1975, trustee, 1975-79. Mem. ABA, Ill. State Bar Assn., Chgo. Bar Assn., Def. Rsch. Inst., Am. Corp. Counsel Assn., Assn. Trial Lawyers Am., Def. Assn. N.Y., Assn. of Bar of City of N.Y., Westchester-Fairfield Corp. Counsel Assn., Order of John Marshall Law Sch., Delta Theta Phi (scholar Key), Anvil Club (East Dundee, Ill.), Masons. Republican. Roman Catholic. Home: 11 Saddle Hill Ln Stamford CT 06903-2309 Office: Skidmore Owings & Merrill LLP 14 Wall St New York NY 10005-2101 E-mail: richard.e.viktora@som.com.

VILA, ADIS MARIA, lawyer, business and government executive, academic administrator, educator; b. Cuba, Aug. 1, 1953; d. Calixto Vila and Adis C. Fernandez. BA with distinction, Rollins Coll., 1974; JD with honors, U. Fla., 1978; LLM with high honors, Institut Universitaire de Hautes Estudes Internationales, Geneva, 1981; MBA, U Chgo., 1997. Bar: Fla. 1979, DC 1984. Assoc. Paul & Thomson, 1979-82; White House fellow Office Pub. Liaison, Washington, 1982-83; spl. asst. to sec. state for inter-Am. affairs Dept. State, Washington, 1983-86; dir. Office of Mex. and Caribbean Basin, Dept. Commerce, Washington, 1986-87; sec. Dept. Adminstrn., State of Fla., 1987-89; asst. sec. for adminstrn. USDA, Washington, 1989-91; vis. fellow Nat. Def. U., Washington, 1992-93; v.p. internat. devel. Vigoro Corp., Chgo., 1994-95; v.p. govt. affairs regulatory policy, Carribean & Latin Am. Nortel Networks, 1997-2000; pres., CEO Vila & Assocs., 2001—; prof. Huizenga Grad. Sch. Bus. Nova Southeastern U. Vis. asst. prof. Fla. Internat. U., 1993—94; mem. adv. bd. Ams. Global Asset Mgmt. Fund, 1999—; v.p. external affairs Miami Dade C.C., 2002—03; adj. prof. internat. bus. strategy and internat. law Nova Southeastern U., 2002—04. Trustee So. Ctr. Internat. Studies, 1987—. Named one of 100 Most Influential Hispanics, 1988; Paul Harris fellow, Rotary Internat., 1983, U.S.-Japan Leadership fellow, 1991—92, Eisenhower Exch. fellow, Beca Fiore, Argentina, 1992. Mem.: Women Execs. in State Govt. (bd. dirs. 1987—89), Am. Coun. Young Polit. Leaders (bd. dirs. 1984—), Internat. Women's Forum, Coun. Fgn. Rels. (term mem. 1987—92), Dade County Bar Assn. (bd. dirs. young and lawyers sect. 1979—87). Republican. Roman Catholic. Avocations: tennis, skiing, golf, theater, art.

VILA, ROBERT JOSEPH, television host, designer, real estate developer; b. Miami, Fla., June 20, 1946; s. Roberto and Esperanza (Robles) Vila; m. Diana Barrett, Oct. 3, 1975; children: Christopher, Monica, Susannah. AA in Architecture, Miami Dade Jr. Coll., 1966; BS in Journalism, U. Fla., 1969. Editor English Lang. Cons., Stuttgart, Fed. Republic of Germany, 1971; stagehand Wurttemburg State Theatre, Stuttgart, 1972; project mgr. Barrett Assocs., Boston, 1973-74; pres. R.J. Vila, Inc., Boston, 1975-85; host This Old House Sta. WGBH-TV, Boston, 1978-89; host Bob Vila's Home Again, Cape Cod and Chgo., 1990—. Author: This Old House, 1980, Bob Vila's This Old House, 1982, Guide to Building Materials, 1986, Guide to Buying Your Dream House, 1990, Bob Vila's Tool Box, 1993, Bob Vila's Guide to Historic Homes of New England, 1993, Bob Vila's Guide to Historic Homes of the South, 1993, Bob Vila's Guide to Historic Homes of the Mid-Atlantic, 1993, Bob Vila's Workshop, 1994, Bob Vila's Guide to Historic Homes of the Midwest and Great Plains, 1994, Bob Vila's Guide to Historic Homes of the West, 1994 (A&E Spl.), Bob Vila's Guide to Historic Homes, 1996, Bob Vila's American Home mag., 1996, Bob Vila's Complete Guide to Remodeling Your Home, 2002. Bd. dirs. Nat. Alliance to End Homlessness, Washington, Coll. Summit. Recipient Emmy award, New Eng. Region, 1979, Nat. Region, 1985. Mem.: SAG (Screen Actors Guild), AFTRA (Am. Fedn. TV Radio Artists). Roman Catholic. Avocations: sailing, fishing, bicycling, gardening, woodworking. Office: BVTV Inc 115 Kingston St Boston MA 02111

VILAR, ALBERTO W. investment company executive; b. Cuba, Oct. 4, 1940; BA, Washington and Jefferson Coll., 1962; MBA, Iona Coll., 1969. Co-founder, pres., profile mgr. Amerindo Investment Advisors, San Francisco,

1985—. Active in philanthropic, healthcare, and cultural endeavors; founder Alberto Vilar Global Fellows in the Performing Arts. Roman Catholic. Office: Amerindo Investment Advisors Ste 2300 1 Embarcadero Ctr San Francisco CA 94111

VILARDI, AGNES FRANCINE, real estate broker; b. Monson, Mass., Sept. 29, 1918; m. Frank S. Vilardi, Dec. 2, 1939 (dec.); 2 children. Cert. of Dental assisting, Pasadena Jr. Coll., 1954. Lic. real estate broker; grad. Realtor Inst. Real estate broker, owner Vilardi Realty, Yorba Linda, Calif. Cons. in property mgmt. Mem. Am. Dental Asst. Assn., North Orange County Bd. Realtors (sec./treas. 1972). Home and Office: 18982 Villa Ter Yorba Linda CA 92886-2610

VILAS, FAITH, aerospace scientist; b. Evanston, Ill., Apr. 14, 1952; d. Jack Jr. and Faith McCrea (Lehman) V.; m. Larry Wayne Smith, July 5, 1986. BA, Wellesley (Mass.) Coll., 1973; MS, MIT, 1975; PhD, U. Ariz., 1984. Sr. rsch. asst. Cerro Tololo Inter-Am. Obs., La Serena, Chile, 1975-77; sr. assoc. scientist Lockheed Electronics Co., Houston, 1977-78; vis. rsch. scientist NRC, Johnson Space Ctr., Houston, 1984-85; space scientist NASA, Johnson Space Ctr., Houston, 1985—; discovery program scientist NASA Hdqs., Washington, 2001—02; chief planetary astronomy group Johnson Space Ctr., 2002—. Editor: (with C.R. Chapman and M.S. Matthews) Mercury, 1988; mem. editl. bd. Icarus, 2001—03. Bd. dirs. Vatican Observatory Found., 1996—. Mem. Am. Astron. Soc. (div. planetary scis. nominating com. 1988-91, sec. 1992-95, vice chmn. 1995-96, chmn. 1996-97, prize com. chmn. 1997-98), Johnson Space Ctr. Nat. Mgmt. Assn. (chair Am. enterprise com. 1987-88, Shield Excellence award 1988). Episcopalian. Avocations: travel, flying, emergency medicine. Office: NASA Johnson Space Ctr Code SR Houston TX 77058 Office Phone: 281-483-5056. E-mail: Faith.Vilas-1@nasa.gov.

VILASUSO, FRANCISCO X. anesthesiologist; b. Havana, Cuba, Jan. 24, 1953; MD, U. Miami Sch. Medicine, 1980. Diplomate Am. Bd. Anesthesiology, Am. Bd. Pain Mgmt. Intern Jackson Meml. Hosp., Miami, 1980-81, resident, 1981-83; dir. pain mgmt. svcs. Miami Pain Inst. Clin. asst. prof. U. Miami Sch. Medicine. Fellow Am. Coll. Anesthesiology; mem. AMA, Am. Soc. Anesthesiology, Am. Soc. Regional Anesthesia, Internat. Anesthesia Rsch. Soc. Home: 321 Costanera Rd Miami FL 33143-6565 Office: 6280 Sunset Dr Ste 503 Miami FL 33143-4870

VILCEK, JAN TOMAS, immunologist, medical educator; b. Bratislava, Czechoslovakia, June 17, 1933; came to U.S., 1965, naturalized, 1970. s. Julius and Friderika (Fischer) V.; m. Marica F. Gerhath, July 28, 1962 MD, Comenius U., Bratislava, 1957; CSc (PhD), Czechoslovak Acad. Sci., Bratislava, 1962. Fellow Inst. Virology, Bratislava, 1957-62, head of lab., 1962-64; asst. prof. microbiology NYU Med. Ctr., N.Y.C., 1965-68, assoc. prof., 1968-73, prof., 1973—. Chmn. nomenclature com. WHO, 1981—86; mem. adv. com. Am. Cancer Soc., 1981—87, chmn., 1983; mem. sci. adv. bd. Max Planck Inst., Munich, 1987—95; pres. Vilcek Found., 2003—. Author: Interferon, 1969; editor in chief Archives of Virology, 1975-86, Cytokine and Growth Factor Revs., 1995—; editor: Interferons and the Immune System, 1984, Tumor Necrosis Factor: Structure, Function and Mechanism of Action, 1991, Cytokine Reference, 2000; mem. editl. bd. Virology, 1979-81, Archives of Virology, 1986-92, Infection and Immunity, 1983-85, Antiviral Rsch., 1984-88, Jour. Interferon and Cytokine Rsch., 1988—, Jour. Immunological Methods, 1986—, Natural Immunity and Cell Growth Regulation, 1986-92, Jour. Immunology, 1987-89, Lymphokine Rsch., 1987-94, Jour. Biol. Chemistry, 1988-90, ISI Atlas Sci., Immunology, 1988-89, Jour. Cellular Physiology, 1988—, Cytokine, 1989—, Biologicals, 1989-95, Acta Virologica, 1991—, Internat. Archives of Allergy and Immunology, 1992-98, Folia Biologica, 1993-96, Cellular Immunology, 1993-96, Jour. of Inflammation, 1994-97, Cytokines, Cellular & Molecular Therapy, 1998—; contbr. articles to profl. jours.; co-inventor of anti-inflammatory drug infliximab used in rheumatoid arthritis and Crohn's disease. Mem. rev. panel Israel Cancer Rsch. Fund, 1993-96; mem. fellowship rev. com. Am. Heart Assn., 1992-94. Recipient Rsch. Career Devel. award, USPHS, 1968—73, Recognition award, Japanese Inflammation Soc., 1989, Outstanding Investigator award, Nat. Cancer Inst., NIH, 1991—98, Elliott Osserman award for disting. svc. in support of cancer rsch., 1996, Disting. Alumnus award and medal, Comenius U., Bratislava, 2001; grantee, USPHS, numerous other orgns. Fellow AAAS; mem. Am. Soc. Microbiology, Am. Assn. Immunologists, Internat. Soc. Interferon and Cytokine Rsch. (hon. life), Czech Immunology Soc., Internat. Cytokine Soc. (hon. life, pres. 1997-98), Czechoslovak Soc. Microbiology. Office: NYU Med Ctr 550 1st Ave New York NY 10016-6402 E-mail: jan.vilcek@med.nyu.edu.

VILCHES-O'BOURKE, OCTAVIO AUGUSTO, accounting company executive; b. Havana, Cuba, Aug. 15, 1923; came to the U.S., 1962, naturalized, 1967; s. Bartolome and Isabel Susana (O'Bourke) Vilches; m. Alba Del Valle Junco, July 24, 1954; 1 son, Octavio Roberto. CPA, U. Havana, 1949, JD, 1951, PhD in Econ. Scis., 1953. Owner Octavio Vilches & Assocs., Havana, 1949-61; comptr. United R.R. of Cuba, 1950-53; cons. econ. affairs Cuban Dept. Labor, Havana, 1953; auditor Cuban Dept. Treasury, 1952-59; pres. Roble Furniture, Inc., San Juan, P.R., 1963-65; owner Hato Rey, P.R., 1963—; pres. Mero Constrn. Corp., San Juan, 1973. Mem. Circulo Cubano P.R., Colegio Contadores Publicos en el Exilio, Colegio Abogados en el Exilio, Cuban Nat. Bar Assn., Nat. Soc. Pub. Accts., Am. Club (Miami, Fla.). Republican. Home: Golden Gate 146 Turquesa St San Juan PR 00920 Office: Condominio El Centro II Ste 1402 Hato Rey PR 00920 Address: PO Box 190300 San Juan PR 00919-0300 Office Phone: 787-754-8242.

VILCHEZ, RICARDO S. library supervisor; b. Masaya, Nicaragua, Jan. 20, 1953; s. Adrian Zamora and Maria M. Vilchez; children: Ricardol E., Nidia E. BA, Fordham U., 1990; MBA, CES, Managua, Nicaragua, 1978; diploma, Inst. of Christian Econs., 1982; MLS, Pratt Inst., Bklyn., 1995. With Nat. Police Nicaragua, Managua, 1968-72; presdl. asst. Govt. Nicaragua, 1972-74; libr. asst. Ctrl. Bank Libr., Managua, 1974-75; asst. presdl. office Ctrl. Bank Managua, 1975-79; libr. supervisor Fordham U., N.Y.C., 1989—. Editor (CD) Los Motivos Del Lobo, 2000. V.p. Nicaraguan Children's Found., N.Y.C., 1999—; cultural dir. Nicaraguan Support Group, N.Y.C., 1999—; pres. Comision Hispana Pro Obra Rubén Dario N.Y., 1998—. Mem. Am. Libr. Assn., Am. Soc. Info. Sci., Libr. Congress. Republican. Roman Catholic. Avocations: cultural activities, travel, walking, rare books, community activities. Home: 13 Van Pelt Ave Staten Island NY 10303-2478 Office: Fordham U 113 W 60th St New York NY 10023-7484

VILCHEZ, VICTORIA ANNE, lawyer; b. Tampa, Fla., Aug. 10, 1955; d. Angel and Mary Ida (Guarisco) V.; m. Louis J. Deutsch; children: Matthew Stephen Williams, Michael Paul Williams, Heather Margaret Williams. BA, Fla. State U., 1977; JD, Mercer U., 1980. Bar: Fla. 1980. Trial atty. Office Pub. Defender, Miami, Fla., 1980-83; pvt. practice, 1983—. Rep. Nat. Conf. on Women and Law, Atlanta, 1978; traffic magistrate Palm Beach County Ct., 1991-95. Vol. Cath. Home for Children, Miami, 1983-84; mem. Coun. Cath. Women; class 1994 Leadership Palm Beach County. Recipient cert. of achievement 8th Nat. Conf. Juvenile Justice, 1981, Livingstone Hall award Juvenile Justice ABA, 1998; grantee Mercer U., 1977. Mem. Fla. Bar, Fla. Assn. Women Lawyers (sec., newsletter editor Palm Beach County chpt. 1985-86, mentor chair 2003-03), Palm Beach County Bar Assn., Fla. State U. Alumni Assn., Palm Beach County Hispanic Bar Assn. (pres.-elect 1990-91, pres. 1991-92, bd. dirs. 1990—, treas. 1993-94, 94-97), Legal Aid Soc. Palm Beach (bd. dirs. 1992—, v.p. 1999-2001, pres. 2001-03), West Palm Beach Kiwanis Club, Leadership Palm Beach County (grad. 1994, bd. govs. 1999-2001). Roman Catholic. Office: 900 Osceola Dr Ste 200 West Palm Beach FL 33409 Office Phone: 561-471-0001. E-mail: Vilchezlaw@palmbeachbar.org.

VILES, ANDREW MICHAEL, English language educator; b. Prineville, Oreg., Oct. 22, 1959; s. Melvin Ernest and Mary Service Viles; m. Carla Ann Chadwick, Aug. 8, 1981; children: Nicholas Chadwick, Tyler James, Jerome Mason, Carson Michael, Rayna Grace Pearl. BA, Oreg. State U., 1983; MFA, U. of Mich., 1987; PhD, U. of Oreg., 1997; Associates, Blue Mountain C.C., Pendleton, Oregon, 1977—79. Bar: Confederated Tribes of Siletz Indians of Oreg. 1991. Instr., counselor U. Oreg., Eugene, 1987—89; editor Confederated Tribes of Siletz Indians of Oreg., Siletz, 1989, Siletz Free Press, Inc., Eugene, 1989—93; instr. N.W. Indian Coll., Bellingham, Wash., 1993, U. Oreg., Eugene, 1997—98; assoc. judge Confederated Tribes of Siletz Indians of Oreg., Siletz, 1997—99; instr. Ln. C.C., Eugene, 1999—. Cons. Indian Edn. Program, Portland, Oreg., 1995, Connections Across Cultures, Eugene, 1998—99, Oreg. Diversity Inst., Salem, 2002, Umista/Rites of Passage, Eugene, 2002—. Editor: (periodical) Siletz News II (Best Editl. or Column, Native Am. Journalists Assn., 1992). Mem. parent steering com. Indian Edn. Program, Eugene, 1990—94; mem. Siletz Free Press, Inc., Eugene, 1989—2003. Recipient Hon. Mention, NW Mag., 1988, Best News Story, 3rd Pl. award, Native Am. Journalist Assn., 1992, Grad. scholarship, Am. Indian Grad. Scholarship Commn., 1995—96, Grad. Tchg. fellowship, U. Oreg., 1991—97, Ford scholarship, Consortium on Intercollegiate Cooperation, 1986—87, Grad. award, Confederated Tribes of Siletz Indians of Oreg., 1996—97; grantee, Ochoco Scholarship Commn., 1977—83, Ward Rhoden Scholarship Commn., 1977—81. Mem.: MLA, Sigma Tau Delta, Phi Kappa Phi. Home: 1541 Taft Eugene OR 97402 Office: Lane C C Dept of English 4000 E 30th Ave Eugene OR 97405 Personal E-mail: kaynineteeth@netscape.net. E-mail: vilesa@lanecc.edu.

VILES, HENRY, pathologist; b. Cali, Colombia, Dec. 24, 1938; s. Pedro and Tulia V.; m. Mary Jo Oliver, Oct. 10, 1980; children: Maurice, Andres, Tabatha, Joshua. MD, U. del Valle, Colombia, 1968. Diplomate Am. Bd. Pathology. Rotating intern Hosp. U. del Valle, Cali, 1967-68; resident in pathology Stamford (Conn.) Hosp., 1971-75, chief pathology resident, 1975-76; dir. labs. Mayfield (Ky.) Cmty. Hosp., 1976—, Jackson Purchase Med. Ctr., 1976—. Fellow AAAS, Coll. Am. Pathologists, Am. Soc. Microbiology. Home: 309 Lakeview Dr Mayfield KY 42066-4765 Office: 1099 Medical Center Dr Mayfield KY 42066-1159

VILIM, NANCY CATHERINE, advertising agency executive; b. Quincy, Mass., Jan. 15, 1952; d. John Robert and Rosemary (Malpede) V.; m. Geoffrey S. Horner, Feb. 16, 1992; children: Matthew Edward Cajda, Megan Catherine Cajda, Margaret Horner. Student, Miami U., Oxford, Ohio, 1970-72. Media asst. Draper Daniels, Inc., Chgo., 1972-74; asst. buyer Campbell Mithun, Chgo., 1974-75; buyer Tatham, Laird & Kudner, Chgo., 1975-77; media buyer Adcom, Inc. div. Quaker Oats Corp., Chgo., 1977-79; media supr. G.M. Feldman, Chgo., 1979-81; v.p. media dir. Media Mgmt., 1981-83; v.p. broadcast dir. Bozell, Jacobs, Kenyon & Eckhardt, Chgo., 1983-88; v.p., media mgr. McCann-Erickson, Inc., 1989—2002; broadcast supr. OMD USA, Chgo., 2002—04; sr. media buyer GSD&M, Chgo., 2004—. Judge 27th Internat. Broadcast Awards, Chgo., 1987. Co-pres. Immaculate Conception Religious Edn. Parents Club, 1995-96. Recipient Media All Star awards Sound Mgmt. Mag., N.Y.C., 1987. Mem. Broadcast Advt. Club Chgo., Mus. Broadcast Communications, NAFE. Office: GSD&M 625 N Michigan Ave Chicago IL 60601

VILLA, JOHN KAZAR, lawyer; b. Ypsilanti, Mich., June 9, 1948; s. John Joseph and Susie (Hoogasian) V.; m. Ellen A. Edwards, June 3, 1990. AB, Duke U., 1970; JD, U. Mich., 1973. Bar: D.C. 1973. Trial atty. U.S. Dept. Justice, Washington, 1973-77; assoc. Williams & Connolly, Washington, 1977-81, ptnr., 1981—. Author: legal treatises. Office: Williams & Connolly 725 12th St NW Washington DC 20005-5901

VILLABLANCA, JAIME ROLANDO, medical neuroscientist, educator; b. Chillàn, Chile, Feb. 1929; arrived in U.S., 1971, naturalized, 1985; s. Ernesto and Teresa (Hernàndez) V.; m. Guillermina Nieto, Dec. 3, 1955; children: Amparo C., Jaime G., Pablo J., Francis X., Claudio I. Bachelor in Biology, Nat. Inst. Chile, 1946; licentiate medicine, U. Chile, 1953, MD, 1954. Cert. neurophysiologist. Rockefeller Found. postdoctoral fellow in physiology John Hopkins and Harvard Med. Schs., 1959-61; Fogarty internat. rsch. fellow in anatomy UCLA, 1966-68, assoc. research anatomist and psychiatrist, 1971-72; assoc. prof. psychiatry and biobehavioral scis. UCLA Sch. Medicine, 1972-76; prof. psychiatry and biobehavioral scis. UCLA, 1976—, prof. neurobiology, 1977—. Mem. faculty U. Chile Sch. Medicine, 1954-71, prof. exptl. medicine, 1970-71; vis. prof. neurobiology Cath. U. Chile Sch. Medicine, 1974; cons. in field. Author numerous rsch. papers, book chpts., abstracts; chief regional editor Developmental Brain Dysfunction, 1988-99. Decorated Order Francisco de Miranda (Venezuela), 1987; recipient Premio Reina Sofia, Madrid, 1990, Lifetime Achievement award UCLA Sch. Medicine, 2001; fellow Rockefeller Found., 1959-61, Fogarty Internat. Rsch. fellow NIH, 1966-68; grantee USAF Office Sci. Rsch., 1962-65, Found. Fund Rsch. Psychiatry, 1969-72, USPHS-Nat. Inst. Child Human Devel., 1972-96, USPHS-Nat. Inst. Drug Abuse, 1981-85, USPHS-Nat. Inst. Neurol. Disorders and Stroke, 1988-92, Fgn. Scientist Traveling grant Tokyo Met. Govt., 1995. Mem. AAAS, AAUP, Sleep Rsch. Soc. (Significant Early Contbr. award 2003), Mental Retardation Rsch. Ctr., Brain Rsch. Inst., Internat. Brain Rsch. Orgn., Am. Physiol. Soc., Soc. for Neurosci., Assn. Venezolana Padres de Niños Excepcionales, Soc. Child and Adolescent Psychiatry and Neurology (Chile, hon.), Johns Hopkins Med. and Surg. Assn., Sigma Xi. Home: 200 Surfview Dr Pacific Palisades CA 90272-2911 Office: UCLA Dept Psychiatry & Biobehavioral Scis Los Angeles CA 90024-1759 Office Phone: 310-825-5195. Business E-Mail: jvillablanca@mednet.ucla.edu.

VILLAFRANCA, JOSEPH J. pharmaceutical executive, chemistry educator; b. Silver Creek, N.Y., Mar. 23, 1944; s. Joseph Nicholas and Mildred (Dolce) C.; children: Jennifer, June, Evan. BS, SUNY, Fredonia, 1965; PhD, Purdue U., 1969. From asst. prof. to prof. Pa. State U., University Park, 1971-76, Evan Pugh prof. chemistry, 1986—; v.p. drug discovery Bristol Myers Squibb, Princeton, N.J., 1992—. Cons. Monsanto Corp., St. Louis, 1985-89, Eastman Kodak Co., Rochester, N.Y., 1985-87. Author over 190 sci. publs. Mem. Am. Chem. Soc. (councilor 1986-89), Am. Soc. for Biochemistry and Molecular Biology, Biophys. Soc., Protein Soc. Avocation: skiing. Office: Bristol-Myers Squibb Pharm Res Inst PO Box 4000 Princeton NJ 08543-4000

VILLAIRE, HOLLY HENNEN HOOD, theater producer, director, actress, educator; b. Yonkers, N.Y., Apr. 11, 1944; d. John Wilson and Adele Jelonek (Deer) Hood. *Father was one of "10 Best Trial Attorneys in New York State." Grandfather: Colonel Duncan Hood, President of McKinley's Aid-de-Camp; great grandfather: Civil War General John Bell Hood, CSA (Fort Hood's namesake), descendant of Kentucky pioneer Colonel Richard Callaway. Great-grandfather: Franklin Wilson, Arizona's Attorney General and first U.S. Congressman. She's also descended from Nashville's founder, General James Robertson and Judge Alfred Hennen of New Orleans. Mother's parents: Helen Wyszynski and John Jelonek, emigrated from Poland and Germany, met and married in Wilmington, Delaware. Her sisters: Victoria Hood, Social Security Administration Supervisor, and Donna Hood Pointer (MBA), Certified Senior Iyengar Yoga Instructor.* BA (summa cum laude), U. Detroit, 1964; MA, U. Mich., 1967. Cert. of studies Centre Dramatique Nat. du Sud Est, France, 1965. Assoc. artistic dir. Hamm & Clov Stage Co., Yonkers, NY, 1973—2001, producing artistic dir., 2001—; prodr. Olympic Arts Festival (Ensemble Studio Theatre), 1984; asst. prof. Allentown Coll. (now called De Sales U.), 1991—92, Vassar Coll., 1992. Dir. grad. showcases Am. Musical and Dramatic Acad., 1992—95; screening, finals judge U. Resident Theatre Assn. Auditions, 1993—95; finals judge Region 2 Am. Coll. Theatre Festival, 1993—94; guest spkr. Disting. Artist Forum with James Earl Jones, U. Mich., 1993; guest artist, S.W. Gas Disting. Artist lectr. UNLV, Las Vegas, 1994; forum prodr. Actor's Ctr., 1996; casting cons. Stratford Festival Theatre, Conn., 1998; adj. prof. Mercy Coll., 2000—. Actor: Antony and Cleopatra (Pitts. Press award as Best Actress, 1989), (Off-Broadway play) God Bless You, Mr. Rosewater, Bklyn. Acad. Music Theatre Company (BAM), (Christopher Reeve's benefit with John Lithgow) Coming Around Again: A Concert in Tribute to Christopher Reeve, Princeton, N.J., 1997; (Broadway plays) Habeas Corpus, Scapino; dir.: Car, Berlin Festival, 1973; dir., conceived Anam, 2001, Anam Cara, 2003, Of Pubs and Parishes, 2004; actor: (internat. theatre) On Borrowed Time, Munich, 1965, Our Town, Munich, 1966, Return the Rain, London, 1971, This Property is Condemned, Paris, 1972, Eyes of Chalk, Edinburgh Festival, 1972, Talk to Me Like the Rain and Let Me Listen, Paris, 1972. Arts Alive grantee, Westchester Arts Coun. (NYSCA), 2003, 2004. Mem.: Actor's Equity Assn., AFTRA, SAG. E-mail: info@hammandclov.org.

VILLA-KOMAROFF, LYDIA, molecular biologist, educator, university official; b. Las Vegas, N.Mex., Aug. 7, 1947; d. John Dias and Drucilla (Jaramillo) V.; m. Anthony Leader Komaroff, June 18, 1970. BA, Goucher Coll., 1970; PhD, MIT, 1975; DSc (hon.), St. Thomas U., 1996, Pine Manor Coll., 1997; PhD (hon.), Goucher Coll., 1997. Rsch. fellow Harvard U., Cambridge, 1975-78; asst. prof. dept. microbiology U. Mass. Med. Ctr., Worcester, 1978-81, assoc. prof. dept. molecular genetics micro, 1982-85; assoc. prof. dept. neurology Harvard Med. Sch., Boston, 1986-95; sr. rsch. assoc. neurology Children's Hosp., Boston, 1985-95, assoc. dir. mental retardation rsch. ctr., 1987-94; prof. dept. neurology Northwestern U., Evanston, Ill., 1995—2002, assoc. v.p. rsch., 1995-97, v.p. rsch., 1998—2002; v.p. for rsch., COO, Whitehead Inst. for Biomed. Rsch., Cambridge, Mass., 2003—; sr. lectr. Sloan Sch. Mgmt., MIT, 2003—. Mem. mammalian genetics study sect. NIH, 1982-84, mem. reviewers rsch., 1989, mem. neurol. disorders program project rev. com., 1989-94; mem. adv. bd. Biol. Sci. Directorate, NSF, 1994-99; bd. dirs. Nat. Ctr. Genome Rsch., 1995-2000, TransKaryotic Therapies, 2003—; mem. adv. coun. Nat. Inst. Neurol. Disorders and Stroke, NIH, 2000-04; bd. trustees Pine Manor Coll., 2004—. Contbr. articles and abstracts to profl. jour.; patentee in field. Recipient Hispanic Engr. Nat. Achievement award, 1992, Nat. Achievement award Hispanic Mag., 1996; inducted Hispanic Engr. Nat. Achievement Hall of Fame, 1999;selected 50 most important Hispanics by "business & Tech., Hispanic Engr. & Info. Tech." mag. 2003; Helen Hay Whitney Found. fellow, 1975-78; NIH grantee, 1978-85, 89-96. Mem. AAAS (bd. dirs. 2000—), Am. Soc. Microbiology, Assn. for Women in Sci., Soc. for Neurosci., Am. Soc. Cell Biology, Soc. for Advancement Chicanos and Native Ams. in Sci. (founding, bd. dir. 1987-93, v.p. 1990-93). Office: Whitehead Inst Biomed Rsch 9 Cambridge Ctr Cambridge MA 02142 Office Phone: 617-258-7190. Business E-Mail: lvk@wi.mit.edu.

VILLARI, JACK C. performing arts executive, arts entrepreneur; b. Cleve., Nov. 18, 1938; s. Sam and Grace (Zingale) V.; m. Kathleen R. Sims, Sept. 25, 1965; children: Maria, Brian. BA, Govs. State U., University Park, Ill., 1978. Singer, producer musical revues, supper clubs, broadway musicals, U.S., 1958-70; pres. Am. Dance Ctr., Homewood and Orland Park, Ill., 1971—; artistic dir. Am. Dance Ctr. Regional Ballet Co., 1973—. Dance adminstrv. dir. Prairie State Coll., Chicago Heights, Ill., 1979-98, Govs. State U., University Park, Ill., 1971-76, Chgo. Conservatory Coll., Chgo., 1977-79; prodn. asst. Warner Bros. Hanna-Barbera, Walt Disney Prodns.; mem. performing arts adv. com., Moraine Valley Cmty. Coll., 2001—. Author: Official Guide to Disco Dance Steps, 1978; created original ballet "Hansel and Gretel", 1976; creator dinner/show Holiday Fantasy, 2000-- (award); asst. choreographer USO Tour to the Far East, 1970. Estab. continuing dance classes Cmty. Recreation Depts., Olympia Fields, Crete, Frankfort, Frankfort Sq., Hazel Crest, Park Forest, Oak Forest, Oak Lawn, Mokena, Homewood-Flossmoor, Tinley Park, Palos Park, Palos Hills, Sauk Village; prodn. coord. Urban Gateways, Chgo. With U.S. Army, 1961—67. Grantee Midwest Suburban Pub., 1973—, Ill. Arts Coun., 1982 and 1986, ARCO Corp., 1984, Target, 1995—, City Proclamation, 1996; recipient congrl. cert. Ill., 1984, Internat. Gold Medal Ballet Bolshoi Soloists Ballet and Cultural Exch., 1978; named Outstanding Dance Educator Am., Dance Mag., 1980. Mem. Prairie State Coll. Performing Arts Coun. (mem. adv. com. 1985-92), Morality in Media. Roman Catholic. Avocation: songwriting. Home: 1037 Wingate Rd Olympia Fields IL 60461-1604 Office: Am Dance Ctr 1933 Ridge Rd Homewood IL 60430-1904 also: 10464 W 163d Pl Orland Park IL 60467

VILLAR-PALASI, CARLOS, pharmacology educator; b. Valencia, Spain, Mar. 3, 1928; came to U.S., 1963; s. Vicente Villar Bolinaga and Teresa (Palasi-Pinazo); m. Amparo Gosalvez-Sobrino, Aug. 17, 1957 (dec. July 1978); children: Victor, Carlos, Juan Jose, María Amparo. MS in Chemistry, U. Valencia, Spain, 1951; PhD in Biochemistry, U. Madrid, Spain, 1955; MS in Pharmacy, U. Barcelona, Spain, 1962. Rsch. fellow med. sch. U. Hamburg, Fed. Republic of Germany, 1953-54, Spanish Rsch. Coun., Madrid, 1954-57, Case Western Res. U., Cleve., 1960-63; rsch. assoc. Spanish Rsch. Coun., Madrid, 1960-63, Case Western Res. U., Cleve., 1963-64, U. Minn., Mpls., 1964-65, asst. prof., 1965-69; assoc. prof. U. Va., Charlottesville, 1969-72, prof., 1972—. Invited speaker Fedn. European Biochem. Soc., 1969, 96. March Found. fellow, 1957; recipient Rsch. award Cleve. Diabetes Found., 1960, NIH, 1967-69. Mem. AAAS (Rsch. award 1960-62), Am. Soc. Pharmacology, Am. Soc. Biol. Chemistry. Roman Catholic. Avocations: horse riding, camping. Office: U Va Med Sch Dept Pharmacology 1300 Jefferson Park Ave Charlottesville VA 22903-3363 Home: 406 Carlton RD Charlottesville VA 22902-5930

VILLARREAL, CARLOS CASTAÑEDA, engineering executive; b. Brownsville, Tex., Nov. 9, 1924; s. Jesus Jose and Elisa L. (Castañeda) V.; m. Doris Ann Akers, Sept. 10, 1948 (dec. 1995); children: Timothy Hill, David Akers; m. June Ricchezza McElroy, Oct. 3, 2002. BS, U.S. Naval Acad., 1948; MS, U.S. Navy Postgrad. Sch., 1950; LLD (hon.), St. Mary's U., 1972. Registered profl. engr. Commd. ensign U.S. Navy, 1948, advanced through grades to lt., 1956; comdg. officer U.S.S. Rhea, 1951, U.S.S. Osprey, 1952; comdr. Mine Div. 31, 1953; instr. elec. engring. U.S. Naval Acad., 1954—56; resigned, 1956; mgr. marine and indsl. operation Gen. Electric Co., 1956—66; v.p. mktg. and adminstrn. Marquardt Corp., 1966-69; adminstr. Urban Mass Transit Adminstrn., Dept. Transp., Washington, 1969-73; commr. Postal Rate Commn., 1973-79, vice chmn., 1975-79; v.p. Washington ops. Wilbur Smith and Assocs., 1979-84, sr. v.p., 1984-86, exec. v.p., 1987—, also bd. dirs. Lectr. in field; mem. industry sector adv. com. Dept. Commerce; mem. sect. 13 adv. com. Dept. Transp., 1983-86. Contbr. articles to profl. jours. Devel. com. Wolftrap Farm Park for the Performing Arts, 1973-78; coun. mem. St. Elizabeth Ch., 1982-86, chmn. fin. com.; bd. edn. St. Elizabeth Sch.; bd. dirs. Assoc. Catholic Charities, 1983-86; chmn. fin. com. Cath. Charities, USA; active John Carroll Soc. Decorated knight Sovereign Mil. Hospitaller Order St. John of Jerusalem of Rhodes and Malta, 1981, Knight Equestrian Order of the Holy Sepulchre of Jerusalem, 1995, Knight Commdr., 2003; recipient award outstanding achievement Dept. Transp. Fellow ASCE, Am. Cons. Engrs. Coun. (vice chmn. internat. com.); mem. IEEE, NSPE (pres. D.C. soc. 1986-87, bd. dirs. 1988-91), Am. Pub. Transit Assn., Soc. Naval Architects and Marine Engrs., Soc. Am. Mil. Engrs., Am. Rds. and Transp. Builders Assn. (chmn. pub. transp. adv. coun.), Transp. Rsch. Bd., Washington Soc. Engrs., Internat. Bridge, Tunnel and Turnpike Assn., Inst. World Politics, Inst. Traffic Engrs., Intelligent Transp. Soc. Am. (chmn. fin. com., bd. dirs.), Univ. Club, Army-Navy Club (pres. 1999-2004). Republican. Roman Catholic. Office: Wilbur Smith Assocs 2921 Telestar Ct Falls Church VA 22042-1205 Office Phone: 703-698-9780. Business E-Mail: cvillarreal@wilbursmith.com.

VILLARREAL, JUNE PATRICIA, sales consultant; b. Atlantic City, Sept. 26, 1929; d. Edmund N. and Dorothy R. (McDowell) Ricchezza; m. Ottavio Gelmi, Dec. 16, 1954 (div. 1964); 1 child, Alessandra; m. Robert Joseph McElroy, Oct. 16, 1970 (dec. May 1974); m. Carlos Castañeda Villarreal, Oct. 3, 2002. Student, Temple U., 1947-48, Georgetown U., 1951-53. Staff mem. Am. Consulate Gen., Milan, 1954; legis. asst. U.S. Senate, Washington, 1956; social sec. Amb. of Finland, Washington, 1958; adminstrv. asst., translator Roosevelt and Clark Lobbyists, 1958—59; legis. asst. to congressman Washington, 1960-65; sr. assoc. Gillmore M. Perry Co., Washington, 1965-76; sales exec., cons., 1980-87; ptnr. Mfrs. Representatives Internat., Washington, 1987-97; ret. Pres. Spanish-Portugese Study Group, 1994—95. Mem.: AAUW, Pan Am. Round Table, Equestrian Order Holy Sepulchre of Jerusalem (Lady Comdr. 2003—), Georgetown U. Alumni Assn., John Carroll Soc., Army Navy Club (Washington). Republican. Roman Catholic. Home: 4000 Cathedral Ave NW Apt 208B Washington DC 20016-5254

VILLAVECES, JAMES WALTER, allergist, immunologist; b. San Luis Obispo, Calif., Nov. 4, 1933; s. Robert and Solita (Combariza) V. BA, UCLA, 1955; MD, U. Calif. Med. Sch., 1960. Cert. Am. Bd. Allergy and Immunology, 1974, recertified, 1993. Intern Sawtelle VA Hosp., L.A., 1960-61; preceptorship in adult allergy L.A. County Hosp., L.A., 1964-66; fellow in allergy

White Meml. CCM, L.A., 1966-67; chief allergy divsn. Ventura (Calif.) Med. Ctr., 1969-87; practice medicine specializing in allergy-immunology Ventura, 1984—. Inventor, cons. Sprixx: Alcohol-gel Clip on Dispensers, 2001—; cons. Bio-Dynamics Co., Ventura, 1975-80, Norwich-Eaton and Pharmacia and 3M, Ventura, 1980-85; founder botanical weed allergy walks, 1970; producer Ventura County cities street-tree guide for asthma patients; pharmacy and therapeutics com. Wellpoint (Blue Cross Calif.) Inc., 1995-99, former cons. and lectr. in field. Writer, prodr., editor films; contbr. articles on biology of pollens and molds of Ventura County to profl. jours.; patentee in field. Bd. dirs. Am. Lung Assn., Ventura, 1969-85, pres., 1974, advisor air pollution control com., 1971-74; judge Ventura Sci. Fair, 1970-85. Recipient Commendation, County Bd. Suprs., Ventura, 1974; named one of Am.'s Top Physicians Consumer's Rsch. Coun. of Am., 2003. Fellow Am. Acad. Allergy, Asthma, Immunology, Am. Coll. Allergy Asthma, Immunology; mem. Calif. Soc. Allergy-Immunology, Calif. Med. Assn., Ventura County Med. Assn., Gold Coast Tri-County Allergy Soc. (pres. 1987), CAL Club (hon.), Ventura County Sports Hall of Fame (mem. founding bd.), Mensa. Republican. Achievements include development of infection protection device for hospital and food service establishments. Avocations: writing, photography, lecturing, pistol target shooting, fishing. Home: 928 High Point Dr Ventura CA 93003-1415 Office: Dudley Profl Ctr 4080 Loma Vista Rd Ste M Ventura CA 93003-1811 Office Phone: 805-656-0433. E-mail: lv4080@aol.com.

VILLECCO, ANTHONY CHARLES, tenor, travel company executive, consultant; b. Binghamton, N.Y., May 4, 1956; s. Louis Vito Villecco and Jeanne Maxine Roys. AA with honors, Broome C.C., 1992; BA cum laude, Binghamton U., 1998. Notary pub. State of NY, 1980. NYSSMA Vocal Adjudicator NY State Schools Music Assoc., 1998. Author (professional performer/singer-actor): Silent Stars Speak: Interviews With Twelve Cinema Pioneers; singer: (tenor soloist) Oratorio/Musical Theatre; contbr. writing; performer: Cabaret, Into The Woods, Sweeney Todd, Man of La Mancha, Three Penny Opera, Creation, Handel Messiah, Magnificat. Past pres. Binghamton Classic Films, Binghamton, NY, 1996—2000; mem. Broome County Arts Coun., 1998—2004. Recipient Golden Key Nat. Honor Soc., Binghamton U., 1995—; Lois Tyrell Music scholar, Broome C.C., 1988. Mem.: So. Tier Silents (life; founder, dir. 2003—04), Phi Theta Kappa (Hon. soc Broome c.c. 1989). Liberal. Avocations: singing, writing, travel, movies, humane society. Home: 742 Tunnel Rd Port Crane NY 13833 Office: Binghamton University-Travel: Adm 512 PO Box 6000 Binghamton NY 13902-6000 Office Phone: 607-777-2039. Personal E-mail: tvtenor@aol.com.

VILLELA, DANIEL ANTUNES MACIEL, electrical engineer, researcher; b. Rio de Janeiro, May 30, 1974; arrived in U.S., 1998; s. Tarciso José Pereira and Monica Antunes Maciel Villela; m. Sylvia G. Garcia-Villela, July 6, 2002; 1 child, Adrian J. Garcia-Villela. Degree in electrical engring. cum laude, Fed. U. Rio de Janeiro, 1996, MS, 1998; M in philosophy, Columbia U., 2003. Grad. rsch. asst. Fed. U., Rio de Janeiro, 1997—98, Columbia U., NYC, 1998—; rschr. AT&T Rsch., Florham Park, NJ, 2001; tchg. asst. Columbia U., NYC, 2002—; rschr. IBM Rsch., NY, 2003. Contbr. articles to profl. jours. Vol. Portuguese tchr. lang. exch. program Internat. House, N.Y.C., 2000. Recipient tchg. assistantship, Columbia U., 2002, doctorate scholarship, Dept. of Sci. and Tech. of Brazilian Govt., 1998—2002, grad. study scholarship, Dept. of Edn. of Brazilian Govt., 1997—98, Conf. Travel grant, ACM SIGCOMM, 2002. Mem.: IEEE (tech. reviewer Comms. Soc. 2000, tech. reviewer Network mag.). Roman Catholic. Achievements include research in analysis, definition of algorithms and system design of server sharing collectives for content distribution in computer networking; analysis and design of scalability mechanisms for multicast protocols in computer networking. Avocations: travel, cooking, music, theater, volleyball. Office: Columbia U Rm 1312 500 W 120th St New York NY 10027 E-mail: dvillela@ieee.org.

VILLELA, KHRISTAAN DAVID, art educator; b. Mexico City, Mex., Aug. 11, 1969; s. Rene David Villela and Ann Yellen Villela. BA, Yale U., New Haven, 1990; MA, U. of Tex., 1993, PhD, 2001. Dir. Thaw Art History Ctr., Santa Fe, N.Mex., 1998—. Assoc. prof. art history Coll. Santa Fe, 1998—. Author: (academic works) Contemporary Mexican Design and Architecture; contbr. articles to profl. jours. Pres. Recursos de Santa Fe, 2000—02; v.p. Sci. Inst. Ethnographic Rsch., Albuquerque, 2000—02; dir. Ctr. Arts and Symbolism Ancient Am., San Marcos, Tex., 2002, Intermezzo Santa Fe Opera, 1999—2002. Recipient Yale Club Princeton prize, 1988, Adrian Van Sinderen Book prize, Bienecke Libr., Yale U., 1988; fellow Pre-Doctoral fellow, Ford Found., 1990—93. Mem.: Coll. Art Assn., Assn. Latin Am. Art, Grolier Club NYC, Sigma Chi. Avocations: book collecting, opera. Office: College of Santa Fe Art Dept 1600 St Michael's Dr Santa Fe NM 87505 E-mail: kvillela@csf.edu.

VILLELLA, EDWARD JOSEPH, ballet dancer, educator, choreographer, artistic director, performing arts administrator; b. L.I., N.Y., Oct. 1, 1936; s. Joseph and Mildred (DeGiovanni) Villella; m. Janet Greschler (div.); 1 child, Roddy; m. Linda Carbonetta; children: Christa Francesca, Lauren. BS in Marine Transp., N.Y. State Maritime Coll., 1957; LHD (hon.), Boston Conservatory, 1985, hon. degree, Union Coll., Schenectady, N.Y., 1991; DHL (hon.), St. Thomas U., Miami, Fla., 1994, U. S.C., 1997; DFA (hon.), SUNY Maritime Coll., Bronx, 1998; Doctor (hon.), Fla. Atlantic U., 2000, U. N.C., Asheville, 2002, Coll. Charleston, 2002. Mem. N.Y.C. Ballet, 1957, soloist, 1958-60, prin. soloist, 1960-83; artistic dir. Ballet Okla., Oklahoma City, 1983-86; founding artistic dir., CEO Miami (Fla.) City Ballet, 1985—. Vis. artist U.S. Mil. Acad., West Point, 1981—82; vis. artist Salute to Balanchine residency Harvard U., 1999—2000; vis. prof. dance U. Iowa, 1981; resident Heritage chair arts and cultural criticism George Mason U.; Dorthy F. Schmidt artist-in-residence Coll. of Arts and Letters, 2000—01. Dancer Symphony C., Scotch Symphony, We. Symphony, Donizetti Variations, Swan Lake, La Source, The Nutcracker, Agon, Stars and Stripes, The Prodigal Son, The Figure in the Carpet, 1960, Electronics, 1961, A Midsummer Night's Dream, 1962, Bugaku, 1963, Tarantella, 1964, Harlequinade, 1965, The Brahms-Schoenberg Quartet, 1966, Jewels, 1967, Symphony in Three Movements, 1972, Schéhérazade, 1975, choreographer Narkissas, 1966, Shostakovitch Ballet Suite, 1972, Shenandoah, 1975, Gayane Pas de Deux, 1972, Salute to Cole, 1973, Sea Chanties, 1974, Prelude, Riffs and Fugues, 1980, dancer TV The Ed Sullivan Show, Bell Telephone Hour, Mike Douglas Show, TV spl. Harlequin, 1975 (Emmy award); co-author (autobiography): Prodigal Son, 1991. Mem. Nat. Coun. Arts, 1968—74; chmn. Commn. for Cultural Affairs, N.Y.C., 1978; bd. visitors N.C. Sch. for Arts; mem. adv. panel Nat. Endowment for Arts; trustee Wolf Trap Found. for Arts. Named Miamian of Yr., UNICO Nat., 1993, Miracle Maker, Big Bros. Big Sisters of Greater Miami, 2003; named to Fla. Artists Hall of Fame, 1997, Dance Hall of Fame, 2004; recipient Dance Mag. award, 1964, Lions of Performing Arts award, N.Y. Pub. Libr., 1987, Capezio Dance award, 1989, Gold medal, Nat. Soc. Arts and Letters, 1990, William G. Anderson Merit award, AAHPERD, 1991, Nat. Medal of Arts award, 1997, Kennedy Ctr. Honors, 1997, Cultural Soc. award, Bklyn. Ctr. for Performing Arts at Bklyn. Coll., 1998, Am. Irreplaceable Dance Treasures: The First 100; Robert J.H. Kiphuth fellow, Yale U., 2001, Hon. Theater Arts Br. fellow, U.S. Imperial Soc. Tchrs. Dancing, 2003.

VILLERS, PHILIPPE, mechanical engineer; b. Paris, June 20, 1935; arrived in U.S., 1940, naturalized, 1946; s. Raymond and Garda (Schmidt) Villers; m. Annie Louise Young, July 13, 1957 (div. 1973); children: Jocelyn Anne(dec.), Renata Jane; m. Katherine Stephan, 1973; children: Noel Stephan, Carolyn Grace. AB in Applied Scis. cum laude, Harvard U., 1955; SM in Mech. Engring, MIT, 1960. Mem. mfg. tng. program GE, 1955-58; project engr. Perkin-Elmer Corp., Wilton, Conn., 1959-62; project engr. Apollo Antenna pointings sensor Barnes Engring. Co., Stamford, Conn., 1962-65; project mgr. Advanced Products Ctr., Link Group, Gen. Precision, Inc., Binghamton, NY, 1965-67; mgr. advanced products Concord Control, Inc., Boston, 1967-69; co-founder, sr. v.p., dir. Computervision Corp., Bedford, Mass., 1969-80; founder, pres., dir. Automatix, Inc., Billerica, Mass., 1980-84; chmn. bd. Automatix Inc., Billerica, Mass., 1984-86; founder, pres., dir. Cognition Inc., 1985-88. Bd. dirs. Xyvision, Inc., Wakefield, Mass., chmn., 1992—94; bd. dirs. Grainpro Inc., Concord, Mass., pres., 1996—; bd. dirs. Conflict Mgmt. Group, Cambridge, Mass., Quitnet, Inc., Cambridge Innovations, Voxiva Inc. Del. Dem. Nat. Conv., 1988, 1992; mem. Dem. Town Com., Wilton, 1963, Concord, Mass., 1978—, chmn., 1984—96; mem. Harvard Com. Univ. Resources, 1981—92; mem. various vis. coms. MIT, 1981—91; mem. vis. com. Nat. Bur. Stds., 1981—84; trustee U. Lowell, 1985—91; founder, pres. Families U.S.A. Founds. (formerly Villers Found.), Washington, 1981—, Bay State Retiree Vol. Coun., Concord, 1989—92. Grad. fellow, NSF, 1959—60. Mem.: ACLU (pres. com. 1981—, bd. dirs. Physicians Human Rights 1991—94), ASME, IEEE, Soc. Mfg. Engrs., Unitarian-Universalist Assn. (pres. coun. 1982—86), Amnesty Internat. (bd. dirs. 1990—96, ombudsman 1992—96, mem. exec. com. 1994—96, mem. leadership coun. 1995—, coord. group 15 1998—), Sigma Xi. Achievements include patents for process welding aluminum liners to steel surfaces, horizon sensor for visible wavelength; infrared roughness testing instrument; improved thermopile construction thermal die marker; method for long term storage of a bulk biologically active commodity; pioneer design and feasibility study for solar sail applications for interpanetary probe propulsion and stabilization. Home: 20 Whits End Rd Concord MA 01742-5411 Office: 200 Baker Ave Ste 309 Concord MA 01742-2170 Office Phone: 978-371-7400. Business E-Mail: pvillers@igc.org.

VILLFORTH, JOHN CARL, engineer, health physicist; b. Reading, Pa., Dec. 28, 1930; s. Carl and Grace L. (Fichthorn) Villforth; m. Joanne E. Heine, Sept. 12, 1953; children: Mary Jane Villforth Smith, Elaine, Jennifer Villforth Veazy. BS in San. Engring., Pa. State U., 1952, MS, 1954; MS in Physics, Vanderbilt U., 1958. Cert. Am. Bd. Health Physics. With USPHS, 1961-90; dir. Ctr. Devices and Radiol. Health, 1969-90, asst. surgeon gen., 1972-90, chief engr., 1985-89; pres. Food and Drug Law Inst., Washington, 1990—2001. Bd. dirs. Vasogen Inc., EduNeering Inc. Served to capt. USAF, 1954—61. Decorated Meritorious Svc. medal, D.S.M. (2), Outstanding Svc. medal; recipient Outstanding Engring. Alumnus award, Pa. State U., 1987, Recognition award, HHS, 1987, Disting. Alumni award, FDA, 2000; Univ. Alumni fellow, Pa. State U., 2002. Mem.: USPHS Commd. Officers Assn. (chmn. bd. dirs. 1999—2000), Regulatory Affairs Profl. Soc., Internat. Radiation Protection Assn., Health Physics Soc. (pres. 1976—77, Elda Anderson award 1970), FDA Alumni Assn. (chmn. 2001—). *Understand the problem! Too much energy is wasted and too many relationships are strained because we fail to understand the underlying problem before we embark on a solution.*

VILLIA, MORRIS SABASTIAN, music producer, publishing executive, writer; b. Plaquemine, La., Nov. 21, 1960; s. Morris Villia and Doretha Calloway. Care initiator EMP Internat./FMP Am., New Orleans, 1985; music prod. MSV Record and Prod., New Orleans, 1989—; writer/author MSV Prod. Inc., New Orleans, 1989—; exec. dir. Holographic Enterprises, 1986—; owner Sign and Logo Enterprises, New Orleans, 1997—98, MSV Record and Prod., New Orelans, La., 1990—, music cons. New Orleans, 1990—. Writer/cons. MSV Prod., Inc., New Orleans, 1990—, pub. adv., 1990—; mentor spkr. MSV Productions, Inc., New Orleans, 2000—. Author: (book) God Ghetto, 2000. Recipient hon. mention, World of Poetry, 1990, MSV Inc., 1989. Fellow: The Leukemia and Lymphoma, No. Am. Hunting Club; mem.: ASPCA. Avocations: writing, boxing. Home: PO Box 4273 New Orleans LA 70178 Office: MSV Record & Production Inc PO Box 4273 New Orleans LA 70178

VILLINGER, NITI, management educator; D, U. Cambridge, Eng., 1996. Brand cons. Audi AG, Ingolstadt, Germany, 1996; market rschr. Siemens AG, Munich, 1997—98; asst. prof. mgmt. Hawaii Pacific U., Honolulu, 2000—. Recipient Best Paper at a Conf. award, IBER, 2003; fellow, Sloan Found., 1990; grantee, Rotary Found., 2002, Fulbright Found., 2003; scholar, Rotary Found., 1990—91. Mem.: Acad. Internat. Bus., Acad. Mgmt. (Best Paper nomination 2003), Soroptimists. Office: Hawaii Pacific U 1166 Fort St Mall FS-305 Honolulu HI 96813 Office Phone: 808-544-0227.

VILSACK, THOMAS, governor; b. Pitts., Dec. 31, 1950; adopted s. Bud and Dolly Vilsack; m. Christie Bell, Aug. 1973; children: Jess, Doug. B in History, Hamilton Coll., Clinton, N.Y., 1972; JD, Albany Law Sch., 1975. Pvt. practice, Mt. Pleasant, Iowa, 1975—87; mayor City of Mt. Pleasant, Iowa, 1987—92; senator State of Iowa, 1992-98, gov., 1999—. Chmn. Midwest Gov. Conf., Dem. Gov. Assn.; mem. Nat. Gov. Assn. (exec. com.). Bd. dir. United Way, Mt. Pleasant. Mem. Mt. Pleasant C. of C. (pres.), Rotary (pres.). Democrat. Office: Office of the Governor State Capitol Bldg Des Moines IA 50319-0001

VILTER, RICHARD WILLIAM, internist, educator; b. Cin., Mar. 21, 1911; s. William Frederick and Clara (Bieler) V.; m. Sue Potter, Aug. 17, 1935 (dec. Aug. 19, 2003); 1 son, Richard William, Jr. (dec.). AB, Harvard U., 1933, MD, 1937. Diplomate: Am. Bd. Internal Medicine. Intern, resident internal medicine Cin. Gen. Hosp., 1937-42, founding dir. divsn. hematology/oncology, 1945-56, asst. dir. dept. internal medicine, 1953-56, dir., 1956-78; assoc. prof. medicine U. Cin. Coll. Medicine, 1948-56, Gordon and Helen Hughes Taylor prof., 1956-78, prof. medicine on spl. assignment, 1978-81, prof. medicine emeritus, 1981—, asst. dean, 1945-51. Cons. VA, 1947—; cons. hematology Good Samaritan Hosp., Cin.; cons. physician Christ, Drake hosps., Cin.; mem. sci adv. bd. Nat. Vitamin Found., 1953-56; spl. cons. nutrition and anemias in Egypt WHO, 1954; cons. Pan Am. Sanitary Bur. Anemias of Kashiorkor in Guatemala and Panama, 1955; mem. Am. Cancer Soc. Com. on Investigation and Therapy of Cancer, 1960-64, chmn. 1964; chmn. hematology sect. NIH, 1965-69, nat. adv. com. anemia malnutrition Rsch. Ctr. Chiengmai, Thailand, 1967-75. Assoc. editor Jour. Clin. Investigation, 1951-52; contbr. to profl. publs. Recipient Joseph Goldberger award AMA, 1960, Daniel Drake medal U. Cin., 1985, Golden Apple award U. Cin., 1985, award for excellence U. Cin., 1990, Daniel Drake Humanitarian award Acad. Medicine, Cin., 1991, 1st recipient U. Cin. Coll. Medicine Lifetime Tchg. award, 1995; Richard W. and Sue P. Vilter endowed professorship U. Cin. Coll. Medicine est. and funded 1999. Master ACP (past gov. Ohio bd. regents, sec. gen. 1973-78, pres.-elect 1978-79, pres. 1979-80, pres. emeritus 1984, Laureat award Ohio chpt. 2002); mem. Federated Coun. for Internal Medicine (chmn. 1979-80), Clin. and Climatol. Assn. (v.p. 1982-83), Assn. Am. Physicians, Am. Soc. Clin. Nutrition (pres. 1960-61), Am. Soc. Clin. Investigation, Ctrl. Soc. Clin. Rsch. (coun. mem. 1957-60), Am. Soc. Hematology, Am. Bd. Nutrition, Internat. Soc. Hematology, Cin. Lit. Club (pres. 1990-91), Phi Beta Kappa, Alpha Omega Alpha, Nu Sigma Nu. Home: 5 Annwood Ln Cincinnati OH 45206-1419 Office: U Cin Med Ctr Cincinnati OH 45267-0001 Business E-Mail: vilterr@ucmail.uc.edu.

VIMONT, RICHARD ELGIN, lawyer; b. Lexington, Ky., Aug. 3, 1936; s. Richard Thompson and Christine Frazee (Anderson) V.; m. Louise Marie Salyer, Sept. 20, 1960; children: Richard Thompson II, Margaret Anderson; m. 2d, Martha Jane Murray, Nov. 13, 1982 (div.); m. Mary Ann Farley, May 31, 1997. BS, U. Ky., 1958, JD, 1960. Bar: Ky. 1960, U.S. Dist. Ct. (ea. dist.) Ky. 1964, U.S. Ct. Appeals (2d and 6th cirs.) 1964, U.S. Supreme Ct. 1966, U.S. Ct. Appeals (2d cir.) 1998. Assoc. Brown, Sledd and McCann, 1960-64; ptnr. Core, Vimont and Combs, 1964-68, Breckenridge, Vimont and Amato, 1968-70, Anggelis, Vimont and Bunch, 1970-78, Vimont and Wills PLLC, Lexington, 1978—, mng. mem., 1998—. Asst. commonwealth atty., 1973-75; vis. prof. Transylvania U., 1978-80, Midway Coll., 1992; bd. dirs. Equitania Ins. Co.; mng. dir. Equitania Ins. Co., 1990-93, pres., CEO, 1993-95; gen. counsel Pavenstedt Pauli (U.S.A.), Inc., 1990-92; adj. prof. U. Kent. Coll. of Law, 1998. City commr., Lexington, 1971-72; chmn. Lexington Mounted Police Bd., chair, 1997-2000; bd. dirs. Ky. World Trade Ctr., 1990-97, Lexington Ballet Co., 1989-90; ch. parliamentarian Christian Ch. (Disciples of Christ). Fellow U. Ky., U. Kent. Mem. ABA, Am. Acad. Trial Attys., Ky. Bar Assn., Ky. Acad. Trial Attys., Fayette County Bar Assn., Lexington C. of C., Thoroughbred Club of Am., Lexington Polo Club, Spindletop Hall Club (bd. dirs. 1978-81, 86-90), Rotary (sec. Lexington endowment 1994-97, Paul Harris fellow). Democrat. Office: 155 E Main St Fl 3 Lexington KY 40507-1300

VINATIERI, ADAM MATTHEW, professional football player; b. Yankton, South Dakota, Dec. 28, 1972; s. Paul and Judy; m. Valerie Vinatieri. B.S. in Fitness and Wellness, S. Dakota State. Kicker New England Patriots, 1996—. Named to AFC Pro-Bowl Team, 2003. Achievements include kicked game winning field goal in Super Bowl XXXVI, XXXVIII. Office: c/o New England Patriots 1 Patriot Place Foxboro MA 02035*

VINCE, APRIL RENEE, social worker; b. Findlay, Ohio, Apr. 30, 1974; d. James Dwight and Barbara Louise Elsea; m. Richard Dale Vince Jr. BA, Coll. Wooster, 1996; M Social Sci. Adminstrn., Case Western Res. U., 1998. LCSW Ohio. Social worker, counselor, adminstr. Nursing Care Ctr., Cleve., 1998—99; case mgr. breast and cervical cancer program Cuyahoga County Bd. Health, Cleve., 1999—. Mem. adv. coun. Ohio Dept. Aging, Columbus, 2004—. Mem. Case Wester/Mandel Sch. Alumni Bd., Cleve., 1999—2003. Avocations: reading, writing, exercise, singing.

VINCENSI, AVIS A. sales executive, medical educator; b. Hazardville, Conn., July 10, 1949; d. George P. Vincensi and Hilda G. (Boucher) Vincensi(dec.). AS in Bus., Holyoke (Mass.) CC, 1987. Registered diagnostic med. sonographer, radiologic tech., radiography, mammography. X-ray technologist Baystate Med. Ctr., Springfield, Mass., 1969—73, Cooley Dickinson Hosp., Northampton, Mass., 1971—73, Holyoke Hosp., 1974—87, sonographer, 1973—82, sonographer, supr. Providence Hosp., Holyoke, 1982—87; sonographer Diagnostic Imaging, Springfield, Mass., 1987—90; product specialist/product mktg. sales Corometrics Med. Sys., Wallingford, Conn., 1991—96; diagnostic reagent rep. Sigma Diagnostics, St. Louis, 1996—2002; clin. adj. prof. Springfield Tech. CC, 1999—2002, assoc. prof., 2002—, bd. dirs., 1999—, assoc. prof., dept. chair diagnostic med. sonography, 2002—. Recipient 2 Gold medals and 1 Silver medal Tai Chi competition, 2002. Mem.: Am. Inst. Ultrasonic Medicine, Am. Registry Diagnostic Med. Sonographers. Home: 101 Acushnet Ave Springfield MA 01105-2218 E-mail: avincensi@stcc.edu.

VINCENT, CARL G., JR., real estate portfolio manager; b. Milford, Del., June 30, 1964; s. Carl G. Sr. and Phylis F. (Cash) V.; m. Rhonda L. Ross, May 26, 1990. BS, Oral Roberts U., 1985, MBA, 1988; JD, U. Tulsa, 1991. Bar: Okla. 1991; real property adminstr., facility mgmt. adminstr. BOMI Inst.; cert. facility mgr. Internat. Facilities Mgmt. Assn. Real estate market analyst 1st Am. Realty, Tulsa, 1985-87; real estate fin. analyst Boston Mgmt. Co., Tulsa, 1987-91; real estate tax cons. Burke & Nickel, Tulsa, 1991-94; dir. Tulsa ops. Ruffin Properties, Tulsa, 1994—. Bus. advisor Alzheimers Found., Tulsa, 1991—; adj. prof. mktg., internat. bus. and econs., 1992—. Contbr. articles to profl. publs. Recipient Chair award Order of Curule. Mem. Phi Delta Phi, Phi Alpha Phi. Office: Ruffin Properties 7130 S Lewis Ave Ste 950 Tulsa OK 74136-5427

VINCENT, CHARLES EAGAR, JR., sports columnist; b. Beaumont, Tex., Mar. 24, 1940; s. Charles Eagar and Hazel Ruth (Balston) V.; m. Mary Jacquelyn Bertman, Aug. 8, 1959 (div. Jan. 1969); children: Lisa Marie, Dixie Ann, Charles Joseph, John Patrick; m. Patricia Helene Skinner, Mar. 28, 1970 (div. Apr. 1985); 1 child, Susanna Lee; m. Karen Judith Peterson, Aug. 17, 1985. Student, Victoria Coll., 1958-59. Reporter Victoria (Tex.) Mirror, 1958-59, Taylor (Tex.) Daily Press, 1959-60; sports writer Beaumont (Tex.) Jour., 1960-62; sports editor Galveston (Tex.) Tribune, 1962-63; sports writer San Antonio Express-News, 1963-69, Sandusky (Ohio) Register, 1969-70, Detroit Free Press, 1970-85, sports columnist, 1985-99. Author: Welcome to My World, 1994, Broken Wings, 1998, Men of Courage; Women of Strength, 2004; co-author: (with Richard Bak) The Corner, A Century of Memories at Michigan and Trumbull, 1999. Recipient 4th Pl. award Nat. AP Sports Editors, 1981, 5th Pl., 1989, 92, Sister Mary Leila Meml. award, 1991, Mich. Columnist of Yr. award, 1991, 97; Afro-Am. Night honoree, 1991, Mich. Writer of the Yr. Nat. Sportscasters and Sportswriters, 1998. Mem. Baseball Writers Assn. Am. Avocations: travel, cooking, geneology. Personal E-mail: Vincentcharlie@hotmail.com.

VINCENT, DAVID RIDGELY, management consulting executive; b. Detroit, Aug. 9, 1941; s. Charles Ridgely and Charlotte Jane (McCarroll) V.; m. Margaret Helen Anderson, Aug. 25, 1962 (div. 1973); children: Sandra Lee, Cheryl Ann; m. Judith Ann Gomez, July 2, 1978; 1 child, Amber; stepchildren: Michael Jr., Jesse Joseph Flores (dec.). BS, BA, Calif. State U., Sacramento, 1964; MBA, Calif. State U., Hayward, 1971; PhD, Somerset U., 1991. Cert. profl. cons. to mgmt., 1994. Sr. ops. analyst Aerojet Gen. Corp., Sacramento, 1960-66; contr. Hexcel Corp., Dublin, Calif., 1966-70; mng. dir. Memorex, Vienna, Austria, 1970-74; sales mgr. Ampex World Ops., Friebourg, Switzerland, 1974-76; dir. product mgmt. NCR, Sunnyvale, Calif., 1976-79; v.p. Boole & Babbage Inc., Sunnyvale, 1979-85; gen. mgr. Inst. Info. Mgmt., Sunnyvale Calif., Calif., 1979-85; pres., CEO The Info. Group, Inc., Santa Clara, Calif., 1985—. Author: Perspectives in Information Management, Information Economics, 1983, Handbook of Information Resource Management, 1987, The Information-Based Corporation: stakeholder economics and the technology investment, 1990, Reengineering Fundamentals: Business Processes and the Global Economy, 1994-96; contbr. monographs and papers to profl. jours. U.S. Soccer Fedn. soccer referee emeritus. Mem.: Product Devel. and Mgmt. Assn., Am. Mktg. Assn., Nat. Investor Rels. Inst., Assn. Fin. Profl., World Future Soc., Soc. Competitive Intelligence Profl., Am. Electronics Assn., Nat. Alliance Bus. Econ., Silicon Valley Roundtable, Soc. Info. Mgmt. (treas.). Home and Office: 2821 Kalliam Dr Santa Clara CA 95051-6838 Address: TIG PO Box Q Santa Clara CA 95055-3756 Office Phone: 408-983-1560. E-mail: dvincent@tig-usa.com.

VINCENT, FREDERICK MICHAEL, SR., neurologist, educator; b. Detroit, Nov. 19, 1948; s. George S. and Alyce M. (Borkowski) Vincent; m. Patricia Lucille Cordes, Oct. 7, 1972; children: Frederick Michael Jr., Joshua Peter, Melissa Anne. BS in Biology, Aquinas Coll., 1970; MD, Mich. State U., 1973. Intern St. Luke's Hosp., Duluth, Minn., 1974-75; resident in neurology Dartmouth Med. Sch., Hanover, NH, 1975-77, instr. dept. medicine, chief resident neurology, 1977-78; chief neurology sect. Munson Med. Ctr., Traverse City, Mich., 1978-84; asst. clin. prof. medicine and pathology Mich. State U., East Lansing, 1978-84, chief sect. neurology Coll. Human Medicine, 1984-87, clin. prof. psychiatry and internal medicine, 1989—, clin. prof. medicine, 1990—, clin. prof. neurology and ophthalmology, 2001—; pvt. practice Lansing, Mich., 1987—. Clin. and rsch. fellow neuro-oncology Mass. Gen. Hosp., Boston, 1985; clin. fellow in neurology Harvard Med. Sch., Boston, 1985; cons. med. asst. program Northwestern Mich. Coll., Traverse City, 1983—84; neurology cons. radio call-in show Sta. WKAR, East Lansing, 1984—2000, Sta. WCMU-TV, 1987, 1993—. Author: (book) Neurology: Problems in Primary Care, 1987, 2d edit., 1993; contbr. articles to profl. jours. Fellow, NSF, 1969, Nat. Multiple Sclerosis Soc., 1971. Fellow: ACP, Am. Bd. Legal Medicine, Am. Assn. Electrodiagnostic Medicine (computer electronics com. 1995—98, profl. practice com. 1999—2000, practice rev. panel 2000—03), Am. Acad. Neurology (program accreditation devel. subcom. 1993—2001), Am. Bd. Forensic Examiners, Am. Heart Assn.; mem.: Am. Coll. Legal Medicine, Am. Soc. Neurorehab., Soc. for Neuro-Oncology, Movement Disorders Soc., Am. Clin. Neurophysiology Soc., Am. Soc. Clin. Oncology, Univ. Club, Alpha Omega Alpha. Roman Catholic. Office: 1515 Lake Lansing Rd Ste F1 Lansing MI 48912-3752 Office Phone: 517-374-1055. Business E-Mail: vincen11@msu.edu.

VINCENT, HAL WELLMAN, marine corps officer, investor; b. Pontiac, Mich., Sept. 27, 1927; s. Harold and Glenda (Wellman) V.; m. Virginia Bayler, June 9, 1951; children: David B., Dale W., Deborah K. Vincent Minder. Student, Navy V-5 program Western Mich. Coll./Colgate U., 1945; BS, U.S. Naval Acad., 1950; postgrad., Marine Officers Basic Sch., 1950, Flight Sch., 1952, Test Pilot Sch., 1955, Navy Fleet Air Gunnery Sch., 1958, Air Force Fighter Weapons Sch., 1959, Marine Corps Command and Staff Coll., 1964, Indsl. Coll., 1969, Marine Air Weapons Tng. Unit, 1972. Commd. 2d lt. U.S. Marine Corps, 1950, advanced through grades to maj. gen., 1974; rifle and machinegun platoon comdr. Camp Lejeune, N.C., 1951; fighter pilot El Toro, Calif. and, Korea, 1953-54; test pilot Flight Test Div., Patuxent River, Md., 1955-57; ops. officer, squadron asst. and fighter pilot El Toro, 1958-59; conventional weapons project test pilot Naval Air Weapons Test Ctr., China Lake, Calif., 1960-62; squadron ops. and exec. officer El Toro and Japan, 1962-64; aviation specialist Marine Corps amphibious warfare presentation team and staff officer Quantico, Va., 1965-66; comdg. officer 2d Marine Aircraft Wing fighter-attack squadron, Beaufort, S.C., 1967-68; exec. officer Marine Aircraft Group, Vietnam, 1969; logistics staff officer Fleet Marine Force Pacific, Hawaii, 1970-72; comdg. officer Marine Aircraft Group, Yuma, Ariz., 1972-73; chief of staff 3d Marine Aircraft Wing, El Toro, 1973-76; dep.

chief. of staff plans and policy to Comdr. in Chief Atlantic, Norfolk, Va., 1976-78; comdg. gen. 2d Marine Aircraft Wing, Cherry Point, N.C., 1978-80; dep. comdg. gen. Fleet Marine Force Atlantic, Norfolk, 1980-81; ret., 1981; pvt. investor, 1981—. Flight test pilot; preliminary pilot, evaluator new mil. aircraft. Contbr. numerous articles on tactics and conventional weapons delivery, flight test stability and control to various mil. publs. Decorated Legion of Merit with 2 gold stars, D.F.C., Bronze Star with combat V, Air medal with star and numeral 14, Honor medal 1st class, Cross of Gallantry with gold star (Republic of Vietnam). Mem. SAR, Soc. Exptl. Test Pilots, Early Pioneer Naval Aviators, Marine Corps Aviation Assn., Mach 2 Club, Marbella Country Club. Achievements include invention of triple ejector rack for delivery of conventional bombs, 1961; devel. of fighter tactics in F8 and F4 aircraft, 1958-69; flew 165 models of fgn. and U.S. mil. aircraft; flew 8 models of fixed wing and helicopters on 242 combat missions; first Marine to fly MACH-2; pilot for 59 years. E-mail: hwvincent@webtv.net. *In all 36 years in the service I am convinced that war is bad, and little is accomplished in the long term by warfare. However when National policy dictates a war, then we must not limit what can be done. We must win! My thought "Winning isn't everything, it's the only thing!" When I must go to battle I want to be allowed to "fight to win".*

VINCENT, JAMES LOUIS, biotechnology company executive; b. Johnstown, Pa., Dec. 15, 1939; s. Robert Clyde and Marietta Lucille (Kennedy) V.; m. Elizabeth M. Matthews, Aug. 19, 1961 (div. 1998); children: Aimee Archelle, Christopher James; m. Joyce Anne Fitzgibbons, Dec. 30, 1999 (div. 2002). BSME, Duke U., 1961; MBA in Indsl. Mgmt., U. Pa., 1963; DBA (hon.), U. New Haven, 1998. Mgr. Far East divsn. Tex. Instruments, Inc., Tokyo, 1970—72; pres. Tex. Instrument Asia, Ltd., Tokyo, 1970—72; v.p. diagnostic ops., pres. diagnostics div. Abbott Labs., North Chgo., Ill., 1972—74, group v.p., bd. dirs., 1974—81, exec. v.p., COO, bd. dirs., 1979—81; corp. group v.p., pres. Allied Health and Sci. Products Co. Allied Corp., Morristown, NJ, 1982—85; CEO Biogen, Inc., Cambridge, Mass., 1985—97, 1999—2000, chmn. bd., 1997—2002; ret., 2002. Bd. dirs. Found. for Nat. Tech. Trustee Duke U., Com. for Econ. Devel.; bd. overseers Wharton Grad. Bus. Sch., U. Pa Recipient Young Exec. Achievement Young Execs. Club, Chgo., 1976, Disting. Alumni award Duke U., 1988, Biotech. award Wall St. Transcript, 1997. Mem. Mass. Bus. Roundtable, The Comml. Club Boston, Algonquin Club Boston, The Links (N.Y.C.). Republican. Presbyterian.

VINCENT, JIM, performing company executive; b. N.J. m. France Nguyen; children: Lena, Claire, June. Studied at, Wash. Sch. of Ballet, Harkness House of Ballet, N.C. Sch. of the Arts. Profl. dancer Jim Kylian's Netherlands Dans Theater, Nacho Duato's Compania Nacional de Danza in Spain; asst. artistic dir. Compania Nacional de Danza, 1990—94; concept designer, show dir. Disneyland Paris, 1997; artistic dir. Hubbard St. Dance Chgo., 2000—. Ballet master Nederlands Dans Theater II, Compa a Nacional de Danza, Opera National de Lyon. Office: Hubbard Street Dance Chgo 1147 W Jackson Blvd Chicago IL 60607

VINCENT, JOHN BERTRAM, chemist, educator; b. Cape Girardeau, Mo., July 10, 1962; s. Jack Donald and Patricia Illers Vincent; m. Sharon Ellen Nevels; children: Allisa, Christina. BS, Murray (Ky.) State U., 1984; PhD, Ind. U., 1988. Postdoctoral rsch. assoc. U. Va., Charlottesville, 1988-90, NIH postdoctoral fellow, 1990-91; asst. prof. chemistry U. Ala., Tuscaloosa, 1991-96, assoc. prof., 1996-2001, prof., 2001—, Faculty Tchg. fellow Coll. Arts and Scis., 2002—. Contbr. over 150 articles and abstracts to profl. jours. Recipient Outstanding Commitment to Tchg. award U. Ala. Alumni Assn., 1999, Outstanding Honor Program Faculty award U. Ala. Honors Student Assn., 1998. Mem. Am. Diabetes Assn., Ala. Acad. Sci., Coun. on Undergrad. Rsch., Soc. Biol. Inorganic Chemistry, Am. Chem. Soc. (sec. Ala. sect. 1996-97). Presbyterian. Home: 716 53d Ct E Tuscaloosa AL 35404 Office: U Ala Dept Chemistry Tuscaloosa AL 35487-0336 Fax: (205) 348-9104. E-mail: nevels@dbtech.net., jvincent@bama.ua.edu.

VINCENT, JOHN K. prosecutor; U.S. atty. ea. dist., Calif., 2002; dir. criminal div. U.S. Atty. Office Ea. Dist., Calif., 2003—.

VINCENT, MARK See DIESEL, VIN

VINCENT, NORMAN FULLER, broadcast executive; b. Boston, Oct. 5, 1930; s. Norman Harrison and Marian Bernice (Fuller) V.; m. Karen Ann Walter, June 21, 1969. BA, Denison U., 1953. Sales mgr. Sta. WMBR, Jacksonville, Fla., 1956-62; gen. mgr. Sta. WZOK, Jacksonville, 1962-66; owner, pres. Norm Vincent Sound Recording Studios, Inc., Jacksonville, 1966-75; dir. radio ops. Sta. WJCT, Jacksonville, 1975-91; announcer, narrator radio, TV film and video, talking books, 1991—. Producer, host (radio): Swing Time with Norm Vincent, 1992—. Served with USN, 1953-56; to comdr. USNR, 1958-80. Mem.: Advt. Fed. Am., Jacksonville C. of C. (armed svcs. com.), Navy League, Exch. Club, Sigma Alpha Epsilon. Republican. Episcopalian. Home: 2110 The Woods Dr Jacksonville FL 32246-1016

VINCENT, NORMAN L. retired insurance company executive; b. Milw., July 21, 1933; s. Victor V. Vincent and Hilda I. (Boedecker) Vincent Patlow; m. Arlene Page, Jan. 31, 1953 (div. 1978); children: J. Todd, Meg; m. Donna Jean Doll, Aug. 8, 1980. BS, U. Wis., 1957; MS, Purdue U., 1958, PhD, 1960. Diplomate Am. Bd. Profl. Psychology; registered psychologist., Ill., C.P.C.U., C.L.U. Supr. agy. research State Farm Ins. Cos., Bloomington, Ill., 1960-63, dir. agy. research., 1963-66, asst. v.p. agy., 1966-69, asst. v.p exec., 1969-70, v.p. data processing, 1970-94; systems v.p., 1994-95. Pres. Bloomington Bd. Edn., 1974-77; bd. dirs. YMCA, Bloomington, 1971-85. Served with M.I. U.S. Army, 1953-55. Mem. AAAS Home: W332 N 5861 Meadowlark Ct Nashotah WI 53058-9528

VINCENT, THOMAS JAMES, retired manufacturing company executive; b. Balt., Mar. 17, 1934; s. Thomas Alonzo and Helen Geraldine (Cloman) V.; divorced; children: Wayne S., Robin K. MS, MIT, 1968. Div. gen. mgr. Fairchild Industries, St. Augustine, Fla., 1969-72; pres. T.J. Vincent Properties Ltd., St. Augustine, 1972-75, Pacific Concrete & Rock Co., Honolulu, 1975-77, Ramsey Engring. Co., St. Paul, 1977-80, Kobe Inc., L.A., 1980-84, Milchem Inc., Houston, 1984-85, York (Pa.) Internat. Corp., 1985-88, also bd. dirs., cons.; chmn., CEO Hawaii Seafood Growers, Inc., Kahuku, 1990-92. Author: Fairplan, 1962; publ.: The Boss Upstairs, The Father Raymond Brennan Story, 2004. Founder, pres. Thomas J. Vincent Found. Inc., Kaneohe, Hawaii, 1990—; founder, v.p., treas. Winter Park (Fla.) Family Health Ctr., Inc., 1995—. Named one of Outstanding Young Men in Am., Jaycees, 1965; Alfred P. Sloan fellow MIT, 1967; recipient Rsch. for Progress Achievement award, 1972. Avocations: deep sea fishing, orchid growing. Home and Office: 44-447 Kanoehe Bay Dr Kaneohe HI 96744

VINCENT, THOMAS LANGE, political science professor; b. Sept. 16, 1935; MS, Oreg. State U., 1960; PhD, U. Ariz., 1963. Prof. U. Ariz., Tucson, 1963—2001, prof. emeritus, 2001—. Home: 5225 W Lazy C Dr Tucson AZ 85745-9052 Office Phone: 520-621-2325.

VINCENT, VAL D. state legislator; b. Middlebury, Vt., June 15, 1948; m. John W. Vincent; 4 children. BA, Castleton State Coll., 1975. Tchr.; bus. owner; rep. State of Vt., 1991—. Bd. dirs. Small Bus. Devel. Ctr., Human Resources Investment Bd. Mem. Lund Family Ctr. Bd., Gov.'s Inst. Home: PO Box 131 Waterbury VT 05676-0131

VINCENTI, WALTER GUIDO, aeronautical engineer, emeritus educator; b. Balt., Apr. 20, 1917; s. Guido A. and Agnes (Nicolini) V.; m. Joyce H. Weaver, Sept. 6, 1947; children— Margaret Anna, Marc Guido. AB, Stanford U., 1938, Aero. Engr., 1940. Aero. research scientist NACA, 1940-57; prof. aero. and astronautics and history of tech. Stanford U., 1957-83, prof. emeritus, 1983—. Cons. to industry, 1957—; mem. adv. panel engring. sec. NSF, 1960-63. Author: (with Charles H. Kruger, Jr.) Introduction to Physical Gas Dynamics, 1965, (with Nathan Rosenberg) The Britannia Bridge, 1978, What Engineers Know and How They Know It, 1990; also papers.; co-editor (with Milton Van Dyke) Annual Review of Fluid Mechanics, 1970-76. Served with USN, 1945-46. Recipient Gold medal Pi Tau Sigma, 1948, Engr.-Historian award ASME, 1997; Rockefeller Pub. Service award, 1956; Guggenheim fellow, 1963 Fellow AIAA; mem. Internat. Acad. Astronautics (corr.), Soc. History Tech. (Usher prize 1984, Leonardo da Vinci medal 1998), Nat. Acad. Engring., Phi Beta Kappa, Sigma Xi, Tau Beta Pi. Home: 13200 E Sunset Dr Los Altos CA 94022-3427 Office: Stanford U Stanford CA 94305 Business E-Mail: sts@stanford.edu.

VINCI, JOHN NICHOLAS, architect, educator; b. Chgo., Feb. 6, 1937; s. Nicholas and Nicolina (Camiola) V. B.Arch., Ill. Inst. Tech., 1960. Registered architect, Ill., Mo., Mich., Pa., NCARB. Draftsman Skidmore, Owings, Merrill, Chgo., 1960-61; with City of Chgo., 1961; stencil restorer Crombie Taylor, Chgo., 1961-62; designer Brenner, Danforth, Rockwell, Chgo., 1962-68; architect Vinci, Inc., Chgo., 1977-95; ptnr. Vinci/Hamp, Architects, Inc., Chgo., 1995—; lectr. Roosevelt U., Chgo., 1969-72, Ill. Inst. Tech., Chgo., 1972-90, adj. prof., 1999. Author: (booklet) Trading Room-Art Inst. Chgo., 1977; contr. articles to profl. jours.; exhbn. designer. Bd. dirs. Music of Baroque, Chgo., 1976—87, Mies Van Der Rohe Soc., 2003—; mem. adv. com. Commn. on Chgo. Archtl. and Hist. Landmarks, 1971—83, Millennium Pk., Chgo., 2000—; exec. sec. Richard Nickel Com., Chgo., 1972—; chmn. Howard Van Doren Shaw Soc., 1994—2001; mem. Friends of the Farnsworth Ho., 2001—, Landmark Preservation of Ill. Fellow AIA; mem. Soc. Archtl. Historians, Frank Lloyd Wright Home and Studio Found., Art Inst. Chgo., The Corp. of YADDO, Chgo. Hist. Soc., Arts Club of Chgo. Roman Catholic. Home: 3152 N Cambridge Ave Chicago IL 60657-4613 Office: Vinci/Hamp Architects Inc 1147 W Ohio St Chicago IL 60622-6472

VINCIGUERRA, SALVATORE JOSEPH, scientific instrument company executive; b. Methuen, Mass., Jan. 21, 1938; s. Joseph Frederick and Erminia (Bonnacorsi) V.; m. Grace Stevens, Apr. 20, 1963; children: Elizabeth, Catherine, Joseph, Suzanne. BSE, Princeton U., 1959; MBA, Harvard U., 1968. Systems analyst GE, Phoenix, 1962-63; cons. Arthur D. Little, Inc., Cambridge, Mass., 1964-66; with Instron Corp., 1968—; contr. Canton, Mass., 1968-71; treas., 1971-76; gen. mgr. Asia/Pacific Ops. Toyko, 1976-81; v.p., gen. mgr. Western Hemisphere Ops. Canton, 1981-85; pres., 1985—, Serro Fluidics, Inc., Nashua, N.H., 1995—. Dir. Lytron Inc., Woburn, Mass. Dir. Japan Soc. Boston, 1986—; corp. mem. Children's Mus. Boston, 1984—. Mem. High Tech. Council, Internat. Bus. Ctr. Clubs: Harvard (Boston); Harvard of Japan (Toyko) (treas. 1978-81). Office: 705 Plantation St Worcester MA 01605-2039

VINDERSCHMITT, BERNARD V. data processing executive; MSEE, U. Pa.; MBA, Rider U. Various positions RCA; past v.p., gen. mgr. Zilog; CEO Xilinx, 1984—96, chmn. bd., 1996—. Office: Xilinx Inc 2100 Logic Dr San Jose CA 95124-3400

VINE, NAOMI, museum administrator; b. Seattle; MA and PhD, U. Chgo., 1976; postgrad., Emory U., 1991—. Dir. of edn. Mus. of Contemporary Art, Chgo., 1980-86; chief curator Dayton (Ohio) Art Inst., 1986-88; assoc. dir. High Mus. of Art, Atlanta, 1988; chief exec. ofr., pres. Orange County Mus. of Art, Newport Beach, Calif. Address: Orange Cty Museum of Art 850 San Clemente Dr Newport Beach CA 92660

VINECOUR, ONEIDA AGNES, nurse; b. Port Arthur, Tex., Oct. 15, 1917; d. Ernest Eugene and Gertrude Mary (Wooldridge) Thorn; m. Seymour Vinecour, Jan. 14, 1943 (dec. 1976); children: Seymour Jacob, Rebecca Leah. Diploma, St. Mary's Hosp. Sch. Nursing, Port Arthur, 1939; postgrad., cert. Surg. Tech., Anesthesia, Cook County Hosp., 1939-40; postgrad. U. Chgo., 1939-40, Tex. Coll. Mines, 1943, U. Tex. Health Ctr. R.N., cert. occupational audiometric technician, occupl. spirometric technician. Operating room supr., instr. Schumpert Meml. Hosp., Shreveport, La., 1940-41; anesthetist St. Joseph Hosp., Albuquerque, 1941-42; operating room supr., instr. Lynn City Hosp. (Mass.), 1946-48; staff anesthetist St. Mary's Hosp., Port Arthur, Tex., 1951-53, in service dir., 1971-73; staff nurse Tyler County Hosp., Woodville, Tex., 1964-65; dept. head, supr. Park Pl. Hosp., Port Arthur, 1965-71; operating room supr. Mid-County Hosp., Nederland, Tex., 1973-81; staff nurse Baptist Meml. Hosp., Beaumont, Tex., 1973-81; part time staff Health Care Svcs., Port Arthur, 1983—; indsl. nurse Synpol Inc., 1984-86; staff nurse Texaco Chem. Plant, Port Arthur, 1986-92, Olsten Health Care Svcs., 1992—, staff nurse Huntsman Petro-Chem. Corp., 1996—. Served as officer U.S. Army Nurse Corps, 1942-46. Mem. Am. Nurses Assn., Mass. Nurses Assn., Tex. State Nurses Assn., Assn. Occupational Health Nurses. Republican. Methodist. Home: 2502 Glenwood Dr Port Arthur TX 77642-2639

VINEGRAD, ALAN, prosecutor; Graduate Magna Cum Laude, U. Pa, 1980; JD, NYU, 1984. Staff acct. Price Waterhouse & Co.; clerk Honorable Leonard B. Sand, US Dist. Ct. for the Southern Dist., NY; private practice Meister Leventhal & Slade, 1985—90; chief of general crimes US Atty. Office, Brooklyn, NY, 1990—94, chief of civil rights, 1994—97, chief of the Criminal Div., 1999—; interim US Atty. US Atty. Office, Eastern Dist., New York, 2001. Adj. prof. New York Law Sch., 1996—; guest lectr. Brooklyn Law Sch., Cardoza Sch. Law, Fordham Law Sch., Hofstra Law Sch., New York U. Law Sch., Yale Law Sch., Dept. Justice's Office of Legal Edu. Recipient Atty. Gen. award for Distinguished Service, Stimson Medal for Outstanding Prosecutor, US Atty. Office for Eastern Dist. of NY. Office: US Attorney US Courthouse 147 Pierrepont St Brooklyn NY 11201

VINENT-CANTORAL, AIDA R. mediator; b. Havana, Cuba, Nov. 8, 1948; arrived in U.S., 1959; d. Roberto M. Vinent and Carmen; m. Ennio Cantoral, Dec. 26, 1979 (div. 1981); 1 child, Alfredo Cantoral. BA, Alverno Coll., 1969; MA, Marquette U., 1971, cert. dispute resolution, 1998; cert. negotiating labor agreements, Harvard U., 2000, U. Mich., 2002, Northwestern U.; cert. mediation sys. design, U. Tex.; postgrad., U. So. Tex. Coll. Law, 2004. Fed. Mediation and Conciliation Inst., 2004. Family health asst. Milwaukee County Dept. Human Svcs. & Hosp., 1975—; human svcs. case coord. Milwaukee County Dept. Human Svcs. and Hosp., 1998—; mediator pvt. practice Milw., 1979—; mediator Milwaukee County Family Ct., 1998—, USPS, 1998—, Bus. to Bus., 1998—, CHIPS, 1997, Wis. Spl. Edn. Mediation Sys., 2001—; case mgr. Milw. Co. Disability Svs., 1996—. Cons. in field. Active ACR, 1998—, Wis. Assn. Homicide Investigators, 2000—. Named Human Svcs. Worker of Yr., Wis. Foster Parents, 1980. Mem.: Wis. Coun. Problem Gambling, Wis. Assn. Mediators. Republican. Address: PO Box 462 Greendale WI 53129-0462 Office Phone: 414-550-8772. E-mail: avinent@aol.com.

VINER, PETER, communications executive; 1 child, Christine. Profl. Mgmt., Harvard, 1980. Cert. Can. Advertising Agy. Practitioner, 1970. Pres. Telemedia Comms. Ontario, Inc., 1980-84, CKVU TV, Vancouver, 1980—84; pres., CEO CanWest Broadcasting Ltd., Toronto, 1990—93; CEO CanWest Global Comm. Corp., Toronto, 1997-99, chmn., 1999—; publisher National Post, 2001—03; exec. v.p. CanWest Global Comm. Corp., 2003—. Office: 31 Barber Greene Rd Toronto ON Canada M3C 2A2 E-mail: pviner@canwest.com.

VINES, JAMES, lawyer; b. Dec. 1959; BS, JD, Washington & Lee U. Law clk. to Judge Robert R. Merhige, U.S. Dist. Ct.; law clk. to Chief Justice William H. Rehnquist, U.S. Supreme Ct., 1989—90; assoc. King & Spalding, Atlanta, 1990—93; exec. dir., gen. counsel for environ. affairs Bridgestone/Firestone, Nashville, 1993—2000; ptnr. Baker, Donelson, Bearman & Caldwell, Nashville, 2000—02; U.S. atty. Mid. Dist. Tenn., 2002—. Office: 110 Ninth Ave S Ste A961 Nashville TN 37203

VINET, LUC, physicist; b. Montreal, Apr. 16, 1953; s. Jean and Françoise (Ouellette) V.; m. Letitia Muresan, May 19, 1989; children: Jean-François, Laurent, Stéphane, Sophie Andrée. BSc, U. Montreal, 1973, MSc, 1974, PhD, 1980; D, U. P.& M. Curie, Paris, 1979. Rsch. assoc. MIT, Cambridge, 1980—82; rsch. fellow, asst. prof., assoc. prof. U. Montreal, Canada, 1982—92, prof. physics, 1992—99; vice prin. (acad.) McGill U., Montreal, 1999—2001, provost, vice prin. (acad.), 2001—. Invited prof. U. Cath. de Louvain, 1980-81; vis. scholar MIT, Cambridge, 1987; vis. prof. UCLA, 1989-90; dir. Ctr. Rsch. Math., Montreal, 1993-99. Editor: Particle Physics and Quantum Field Theory, 1995, Symmetries and Integrability of Difference Equations, 1995, Quantum Groups Integrable Models and Statistical Systems, 1993, Group Theoretical Methods in Physics, 1989. Grantee FCAR, 1984—, NSERC, 1982—, rsch. fellow, 1982-92. Mem. APS, AMS, SIAM, CAP, CMS. Achievements include contributions in theoretical physics and mathematics - symmetry studies of difference equations; algebraic interpretation of q-special functions using quantum groups; applications of Berry potentials in the nuclear collective model; identification of Lie superalgebras as dynamical algebras in quantum mechanics; development of dimensional reduction in Yang Mills theories.

VINEY, DONALD WAYNE, philosophy educator; b. Shawnee, Okla., Feb. 13, 1953; s. Wayne and Wynonna Rose Viney; m. Christine Elizabeth Hailey, Sept. 1975 (div. 1984); 1 child, Jennifer Michelle; m. Rebecca Nell Viney, May 25, 1985. BA in Philosophy, Colo. State U., 1977; MA in Philosophy, U. Okla., 1979, PhD in Philosophy, 1982. Part-time faculty English East Ctrl. U., Ada, Okla., 1982-84; adj. lectr. philosophy U. Okla., Norman, 1982-84; asst. prof. philosophy Pittsburg (Kans.) State U., 1984-89, assoc. prof., 1989-96, prof., 1996—. Author: Charles Hartshorne and the Existence of God, 1985, Incidents in the Life and Death of Jules Lequyer, 1999; translator: Translation of Works of Jules Lequyer: The Hornbeam Leaf, The Dialogue of the Predestinate and the Reprobate, and Eugene and Theophilus, 1998; editor: Questions of Value: Beginning Readings for Philosophy, 1998, A Brief Guide to Logic and Critical Thinking for Nonvulcans, 1998; bd. editors U. Press Kans., 1989-92; co-editor (with Marjorie Donovan) The Practice of Social Science and History, 1990-95; editor-in-chief, founder Logos-Sophia, 1988—; editl. bd. Midwest Quar., 1987—, acting editor-in-chief, 1991, acting book rev. editor, 1997; abstractor Process Studies, 1994—; editor Universitas, 1996—; contbr. articles and book revs. to profl. jours. Mem. Am. Philos. Assn., Soc. Christian Philosophers, Ctr. Process Studies, Kans. Philos. Assn., Alpha Mu Gamma, Phi Kappa Phi. Democrat. Methodist. Home: 2003 Countryside Dr Pittsburg KS 66762-3525 Office: Pittsburg State U 1705 N Broadway St Pittsburg KS 66762-3023

VINIAR, DAVID, investment banker; B. in Economics summa cum laude, Union Coll., 1976; MBA, Harvard U., 1980. Joined Goldman Sachs, 1980, ptnr., 1992-96, mng. dir., 1992—94, dep. CFO, 1994—98; CFO Goldman Sachs Group, L.P., 1999, Goldman Sachs, 1999—, exec. v.p., 1999—, head, fin. div. and co-head credit risk mgmt. and advisory and firm wide risk, 2001—02, head, operations, tech. and fin. div., 2002—. Bd. trustees Union Coll. Recipient CFO Excellence Award for Risk Management, CFO mag., 2001. Office: Goldman Sachs 85 Broad St New York NY 10004*

VINING, JOSEPH (GEORGE JOSEPH VINING), law educator; b. Fulton, Mo., Mar. 3, 1938; s. D. Rutledge and Margaret (McClanahan) V.; m. Alice Marshall Williams, Sept. 18, 1965; children: George Joseph IV, Spencer Carter. BA, Yale U., 1959, Cambridge U., 1961, MA, 1970; JD, Harvard U., 1964. Bar: DC 1965. Atty. Office Dep. Atty. Gen., Dept. Justice, Washington, 1965; asst. to exec. dir. Nat. Crime Commn., 1966; assoc. Covington and Burling, Washington, 1966-69; asst. prof. law U. Mich., 1969-72, assoc. prof., 1972-74, prof., 1974-85, Hutchins prof., 1985—. Sir Edward Youde prof., Hong Kong, 2002. Author: Legal Identity, 1978, The Authoritative and the Authoritarian, 1986, From Newton's Sleep, 1995, The Song Sparrow and the Child, 2004. NEH sr. fellow, 1982-83, Bellagio fellow Rockfeller Found., 1997. Fellow Am. Acad. Arts and Scis.; mem. ABA, D.C. Bar Assn. (life), Am. Law Inst. (life), Century Assn. Office: U Mich 964 Lega Rsch Ann Arbor MI 48109-1215

VINING, MARGARET SIMMONS, historian, curator; d. George R. Simmons and Keturah Hill Garner; m. Robert Winfield Vining, July 15, 1960 (dec.); children: Suzanne Simmons Vining Brownlow, Robert Winfield, Edwin Martin. MA, The George Wash. U., 1981. Mus. curator/historian Smithsonian Instn., Washington, 1983—. Curator several maj. mus. exhbns. Author: (dictionary of am. history) Military Uniforms; contbr. articles to profl. jours. Mem.: Smithsonian Instn. Women's Coun. (exec. com. 2001—02), U.S. Commn. of Mil. History (assoc.; trustee and bd. mem. 2000—03, sec.-gen.). Dc Statehood Party. Episcopal. Home: 150 12th Street NE Washington DC 20002 Office: Smithsonian Institution NMAH 4014 Washington DC 20560-0620 E-mail: viningm@si.edu.

VINKEN, PIERRE JACQUES, publishing executive; b. Nov. 25, 1927; MD, U. Utrecht, 1955; postgrad., U. Amsterdam, The Netherlands, 1957-63; D (hon.), U. Paris, 1981. Staff neurosurgeon Univ. Clinic, Amsterdam, 1964-69; pres., chief editor Excerpta Medica Found., Amsterdam and Princeton, NJ, 1962-88; mng. dir. Elsevier Pub. Co., Amsterdam, 1972-78, chmn. bd. dirs., 1979-95, Reed Elsevier, London, 1993-95. Chmn. Netherlands del. Intergovernmental Unisist Conf., Paris, 1970; mem. Netherlands Unisist Commn., 1971—79, Nat. Sci. Policy Coun., The Hague, 1983—90; prof. med. database informatics U. Leyden, 1975—93; chmn. supervising bd. Halder Holdings, The Hague, Netherlands, Blue Horse Prodns., Rotterdam, Netherlands, Medialand, Amsterdam, Optas, Rotterdam, Trust Theater Co.; bd. dirs. Wereldhave Investment Co., Logica, Aalberts Industries, Revisor, Nat. Acad. Arts, Internat. Rights-Collecting and Distbns. Agys. Founder, editor-in-chief: book Handbook of Clinical Neurology, 78 vols.; editor: sci. books; contbr. articles to profl. jours. Pres. Internat. Congress Patient Counselling, 1976—79; chmn. Netherlands Commn. Bibliography and Documentation, 1972—81; dep. chmn. European Pubs. Coun.; chmn. Hiscom, Leyden, 1987—98, The Lancet, London, 1991—95; bd. dirs. Pearson, London, 1988—91, The Economist, London, 1989—92; mem. soc. adv. coun. Tinbergen Inst., Rotterdam, 1996—2000. Recipient award, Royal Netherlands Acad. Sci., 1997. Mem.: European Info. Providers Assn. (pres. 1980—83), Peruvian Soc. Psychiat. Neurology and Neurosurgery (hon.), Amsterdam Neurol. Soc. (hon.), French Neurol. Soc. (hon.), Neurol. Soc. India (hon.), Netherlands Rep. Soc. (founder 1996), Order of Orange Nassau (comdr.), Order of Netherlands' Lion (knight), Order Hipolitó Unanue (comdr.). Home: 142 Bentveldsweg 2111 EE Aerdenhout Netherlands Personal E-mail: vinken@quicknet.nl.

VINROOT, RICHARD ALLEN, lawyer, mayor; b. Charlotte, N.C., Apr. 14, 1941; s. Gustav Edgar and Vera Frances (Pickett) V.; m. Judith Lee Allen, Dec. 29, 1964; children: Richard A., Laura Tabor, Kathryn Pickett. BS in Bus. Adminstrn., U. N.C., 1963, JD, 1966. Bar: N.C. 1966, U.S. Dist. Ct. (ea., mid. and we. dists.) N.C. 1969, U.S. Ct. Appeals (4th cir.) 1969. Ptnr. Robinson, Bradshaw & Hinson, P.A., Charlotte, 1969—. Mayor City of Charlotte, 1991-95; bd. dirs. Martin-Marietta Materials Inc. Tchr. sr. h.s. sunday sch. Myers Park Presbyn. Ch., 1970—, ruling elder, 1970-76, 78-84, 96—, chmn. of session, 1984; mem. Charlotte City Coun., 1983-91. With U.S. Army, 1967-68, Vietnam. Recipient Bronze Star, 1968; named Mcpl. Leader of the Yr. Am. City & County Mag., 1995. Mem. ABA, VFW, N.C. Bar Assn., Mecklenburg County Bar Assn. (sec. 1976, bd. dir. 1970-76), Mecklenburg County Vietnam Vets. Assn., Mecklenburg County Eagle Scouts Assn., Am. Legion, Phalanx Lodge Mason. Republican. Presbyterian. Office: Robinson Bradshaw & Hinson PA 1900 Independence Ctr 101 N Tryon St Ste 1900 Charlotte NC 28246-0103

VINSON, BETH W. systems analyst, web site designer; b. Atlanta, Nov. 3, 1957; d. James W. and Sue P. Waldroop. AAS, Southwestern C.C., Sylva, N.C., 1979; BS in Bus. Adminstrn., Western Carolina U., 1996. Web developer/arch. U.S. Army - MI BN, Tuzla, Bosnia-Herzegovina, 2001—02; sr. systems analyst AMSEC - NETWARCOM, Virginia Beach, Va., 2003—. Prin. info. engr. U.S. Joint Forces Command, Norfolk, Va., 2000—01. Author: (novels) multiple. Recipient Cert. of Appreciation - Commdg. Gen., U.S. Army - Bosnia, 2001—02.

VINSON, KEVIN RAYMOND, music educator; s. Michael Curtis and Karla Rae Vinson; m. Shannon Marie Deitz, June 16, 2001; 1 child, Abigail Marie. BS in Music Edn., Ind. U. of Pa., Indiana, Pa., 1992—96. Music tchr. Titusville Area Sch. Dist., Titusville, Pa., 1997—. Mem.: NEA, Pa. State Edn. Assn., Music Educators Nat. Conf., Pa. Music Educators Assn.

VINSON, LAURENCE DUNCAN, JR., lawyer; b. Gadsden, Ala., Mar. 17, 1947; BS with hons., U. Ala., Tuscaloosa, 1969; JD, U. Ala., 1973. Bar: Ala., U.S. Dist. Ct. (no., mid. and so. dists.) Ala., U.S. Ct. Appeals (11th cir.), U.S. Supreme Ct. Assoc. Bradley Arant Rose & White, LLP, Birmingham, Ala., 1973-79, ptnr., 1979—. Bar: Ala. 1973, U.S. Dist. Ct. (no. dist.) Ala. 1973, U.S. Supreme Ct. 1977, U.S. Ct. Appeals (11th cir.) 1981, U.S. Dist. Ct. (so. dist.) Ala. 1989, U.S. Dist. Ct. (mid. dist.) Ala. 1991. Chmn. Ala. Uniform Comml. Code Revisions Coms., 1991-2004. Mem. ABA, Birmingham Bar Assn., Ala. State Bar, Ala. Law Inst., Order of Coif, Phi Beta Kappa, Omicron Delta Kappa. Office: Bradley Arant Rose & White LLP One Federal Pl 1819 5th Ave N Birmingham AL 35203-2104 Business E-Mail: lvinson@bradleyarant.com.

VINSON, LEILA TERRY WALKER, retired gerontological social worker; b. Lynchburg, Va., July 28, 1928; d. William Terry and Ada Allen (Moore) Walker; m. Hughes Nelson Vinson, Aug. 11, 1951; children: Hughes Nelson, William Terry. Student, Agnes Scott Coll., 1946-48; BA, U. Ala., Tuscaloosa, 1950; postgrad., U. Ala., Birmingham, 1980-81, U. Va., 1950-51. Cert. gerontol. social worker, Ala. Tchr. English and Latin Marion County Bd. Edn., Hamilton, Ala., 1952-59; social worker I Marion County Dept. Pensions and Security, 1963-72, gerontol. social worker II, 1972-85; ret., 1985. Bd. dirs. Marion County Dept. Human Resources, 1985—; bd. mem. Clyc Nix Libr., Bevill Coll. Cmty. Theatre, 1992—; spkr. gen. subjects. Recipient Ala. Woman Committed to Excellence award Tuscaloosa coun. Girl Scouts U.S., 1987; named Mrs. Marion County, PTA, Gwin, Ala., 1969, Woman of Yr. Town of Hamilton, 1980, New Retiree of Yr. Ala. Ret. State Employees Assn., 1988, Woman of Yr. BPW, 1985; Gessener Harrison fellow U. Va., 1950-51. Mem. AAUW, DAR (flag chmn. Bedford chpt. 1988-90), UDC, Bus. and Profl. Women's Club (dist. dir. 1984-86, Outstanding Dir. award 1986), Ala. Fedn. Women's Club. Home: PO Box 1112 Hamilton AL 35570-1112 also: Military Rd Hamilton AL 35570

VINSON, WILLIAM THEODORE, lawyer, diversified corporation executive; BS, USAF Acad., 1965; JD, UCLA, 1969. Bar: Calif. 1970. Judge advocate USAF, 1970-74; trial counsel Phillips Petroleum, San Mateo, Calif., 1974-75; atty. Lockheed Corp., Westlake Village, Calif., 1975-90, v.p. & sec., 1990-92, v.p., gen. couns., 92-95; v.p., chief counsel Lockheed Martin Corp., Westlake Village, 1995-98; cons. Lockheed Corp., Westlake Village, 1998; dir. Siemens Govt. Svcs., Inc., 2001—. Bd. dirs. Westminster Free Clinic, 2001—. Office: 5560 E Napoleon Ave Oak Park CA 91377-4746

VINTZILEOS, ANTHONY MARK, obstetrician-gynecologist; b. Athens, Greece, Dec. 15, 1950; s. Mark and Barbara (Prokopiou) V.; m. Colleen Ann McBride, June 25, 1977 (div.); children: Mark, Matthew, Michael; m. Cathylynn Pike, Dec. 30, 1989; children: Barbara, William. MD, Athens U. Med. Sch. Intern Monmouth Med. Ctr., Long Branch, N.J., 1976-77; resident St. Josephs Hosp. Med. Ctr., Paterson, N.J., 1977-81; dir. maternal fetal medicine & obs., prof. Robert Wood Johnson Med. Sch.; dir. maternal fetal medicine & obs. Maternal fetal medicine fellow U. Conn. Health Ctr., Farmington, N.J., 1981-83. Mem. Am. Coll. Ob gyn. Home: 4 Sky High Ter Bridgewater NJ 08807-1201 Office: 125 Paterson St New Brunswick NJ 08901

VINYARD, WALTER DARNALL, lawyer; b. Roanoke, Va., Feb. 6, 1943; s. W. Darnall and Claiborne (Wood) V.; m. Joanne Nusrala, June 12, 1971; children: Emily Darnall, Abigail Devin, Julia Claiborne. AB cum laude, Coll. William and Mary, 1964; JD, Columbia U., 1967. Bar: Va. 1969, D.C. 1979. Atty. U.S. SEC, Washington, 1968-72; sr. counsel Am. Ins. Assn., Washington, 1972-79; ptnr. Alston & Bird, Washington, 1979-84, Zuckert, Scoutt & Rasenberger, Washington, 1984-92; prin. Vinyard & Assocs., Washington, 1992—. Contbr. articles to profl. jours. Mem. ABA (chair emeritus com. on fin. instns. sect. tort and ins. practice), French-Am. C. of C. (pres. 1995-98). Episcopalian. Avocations: horses, gardening. Office: 555 13th St NW Washington DC 20004-1109

VIOLA, BILL, artist, writer; b. N.Y.C., Jan. 25, 1951; s. William John and Wynne Viola; m. Kira Perov; children: Blake, Andrei. BFA, Syracuse U., 1973, DFA, 1995, Sch. Art Inst. Chgo., 1997, Calif. Coll. Arts & Crafts, Oakland, 1998, Mass. Coll. Art, 1999, Calif. Inst. of the Arts, Valencia, 2000, U. Sunderland, Eng., 2000. Tech. dir. Art/Tapes/22 Video Studio, Florence, Italy, 1974-76; artist-in-residence Sta. WNET, N.Y.C., 1976-83, WXXI-TV, Rochester, NY, 1979, Sony Corp., Atsugi Labs., Japan, 1980-81, San Diego Zoo, 1984; instr. Calif. Inst. of Arts, Valencia, 1983; represented by James Cohan Gallery, N.Y.C. Solo exhbns. include The Kitchen Ctr., N.Y., 1974, Everson Mus. Art, Syracuse, N.Y., 1975, Mus. Modern Art, N.Y.C., 1979, 87, Whitney Mus. Art, N.Y.C., 1982, Musee d'Art Moderne, Paris, 1983, Mus. Contemporary Art, L.A., 1985, Fukui Prefectural Mus. Art, Fukui City, Japan, 1989, Staditsche Kunsthalle Düsseldorf, 1992, Moderna Musee, Stockholm, 1993, Museo Nacional Centro de Arte Reina Sofia, Madrid, 1993, Musee Cantonal des Beaux-Arts, Lausanne, Switzerland, 1993, Whitechapel Art Gallery, London, 1993, Tel Aviv Mus. Art, 1994, Musée d'Art Contemporain, Montreal, 1993, Centro Cultural/Banco de Brazil, Rio de Janeiro, 1994, 46th Venice Biennale, 1995, Festival d'Automne Paris, 1996, Bill Viola: A 25 Year Survey Exhbn., Whitney Mus. Am. Art, N.Y., travels to Whitney Mus. Am. Art, 1997, L.A. County Mus. Am. Art, 1998, Stedelijk Mus., Amsterdam, 1998, Mus. Pur Moderne Kunst and Shirnkunstalle Dominkankloister, Germany, 1999, San Francisco Mus. Modern Art, 1999, Art Inst. Chgo., 1999-2000, 2KM, Karlsruhe, Germany, 2000, James Cohan Gallery, N.Y., 2000, Anthony d'Offay Gallery, London, 2001, Bill Viola: Going Forth By Day, Deutsche Guggenheim Berlin, 2002; group exhbns. include De Saisset Art Gallery and Mus., Santa Clara, Calif., 1972, Whitney Mus. Am. Art, 1975-87, 89, 93, Stedelijk Mus., Amsterdam, 1984, Carnegie Mus. Art, Pitts., 1988, Kölnischer Kunstverein, Cologne, Germany, 1989, Israel Mus., Jerusalem, 1990, Musée Nat. d'Art Moderne, Ctr. Georges Pompidou, Paris, 1990, Martin Gropius Bau, Berlin, 1991, Mus. Moderne Kunst, Frankfurt, Germany, 1991, Royal Acad., London, 1993, Denver Art Mus., Columbus (Ohio) Art Mus., 1994, Anthony d'Offay Gallery, London, 1995, Mus. Modern Art, N.Y.C., 1995, Tate Gallery, London, 1995, Albright-Knox Art Gallery, 1996, Fabric Workshop, Phila., 1997, MOMA, N.Y., 1999, La Beauté, Found Cartier, 2000, Tate Modern, London, 2000, Nat. Gallery, London, 2000, James Cohan Gallery, NY, 2001; spl. screening film: Dèserts, Vienna, Austria, 1994, WhiteCahpel Art Gallery, London, 2001, 49th Venice Biennale, 2001, Perth Festival, Australia, 2001, Commune di Ferrara, Italy, 2001, Musse d'Art Contemporian de Montreal, Canada, 2001; commns. include The Stopping mind, Mus. Moderne Kunst, Frankfurt, 1991, Nantes Triptych, Dèlegation aux Arts Plastiques, Nantes, France, 1992, Slowly Turning Narrative, Isnt. Comtemporary Art, Phila., Va. Mus. Fine Art, Richmond, 1992, Tiny Deaths, Biennale d'Art Contemporain de Lyon, France, 1993, Dèserts, Konzerthause, Vienna, 1994, 3e Biennale d'Art contemporaire de Lyon, Musée d'art contemporain, Lyon, France, 1995, Helaba Main Tower, Frankfurt, Germany, 2000, Gotesborgs Musiken, Sweden, 2001, Deserts, Konzerthaus, Vienna, 2001, Deserts, Carnigie Hall, New York, 2001, Deserts, Royal Festival Hall, London, 2001, Deserts, IRCAM, Centre Pomidou Main Hall, Paris, 2001, others; composer: (album) David Tudor-Rainforest IV, 1981; (video) Chott el-Djerid, Anthem, 1983, Hatsu-Yume, 1981, The Reflecting Pool, 1977-79, The Space Between the Teeth, 1976, Bill Viola: Selected Works, 1986, I Do Not Know What It Is I Am Like, 1986, The Passing, 1991, The City of Man, 1989, Nantes Triptych, 1992, Slowly Turning Narritive, 1992, Tiny Deaths, 1993, The Greetings, 1995, The Crossing, 1996, The Quintet of Remembrance, 2000, The Quintet of the Unseen, 2000, The Quintet of the Astonished, The Quintet of the Silent, 2000, Surrender, 2001, Catherine's Room, 2001, Five Angles for the Millenium, 2001, Going Forth By Day, 2002. Japan/U.S. Creative Arts fellow NEA, 1980, Rockefeller Found. Video Artist fellow, 1982, Visual Artist fellow NEA, 1983-89, Guggenheim Meml. Found. fellow, 1985, Intercultural Film/Video fellow Rockefeller Found., 1991; recipient Jury prize U.S. Film and Video Festival, 1982, Grand prize, 1983, Jury prize Video Culture/Can., 1983, Grand prize for video art, 1984, First prize for video art Athens (Ohio) Film/Video Festival, 1984, Maya Deren award Am. Film Inst., 1987, First prize Festival Internat. d'Art Video et des Nouvelles Images Electroniques de Locarno, 1987, John D. and Catherine T. MacArthur Found. award, 1989, Skowhegan medal, 1993, First prize Festival Internat. de Video, Cidade de Vigo, Spain, 1993, Medienkunstpreis, Siemens Kulturprogramm and Zentrum fur Kunst und Medientechnologie, Germany, 1993; scholar-in-residence The Getty Rsch. Inst. for History of Art and Humanities, L.A., 1998. Office: 282 Granada Ave Long Beach CA 90803 E-mail: info@billviola.com.

VIOLA, MARY JO, art history educator; b. Yonkers, N.Y., July 25, 1941; d. William F. and May (Cleary) O'Connor; m. Jerome Joseph Viola, June 21, 1967 (dec. Feb. 1990). BA in Fine Arts, Coll. of Mt. St. Vincent, 1963; MA in Art History, NYU, 1966; MPhil in Art History, CUNY, 1983, PhD in Art History, 1992. Art history tchr. Georgian Ct. Coll., N.J., 1965-66, Hollins Coll., Roanoke, Va., 1966-67, Marymount Coll., Tarrytown, N.Y., 1967-71, Baruch Coll., CUNY, N.Y.C., 1974-97, Bklyn. Coll., 1990-97, Parsons Sch. of Design, N.Y.C., 1991-93, Rutgers U., 1993-95, Bronx C.C. CUNY, 1997—. Curator exhbns. Baruch Coll. Gallery, N.Y.C., 1987-88. Editor: A World View of Art History, 1985; art exhibited at Tribes Gallery, N.Y.C., 1996; creater ednl. videos. Rschr. for ethnic festivals, N.Y.C., 1993—. Fellow Nat. Trust for Hist. Preservation, 1964, Marymount Coll., 1970, Boston Mus. Fine Arts/CUNY, 1978, Luce Found., 1988. Mem. Coll. Art Assn., Historians of Am. Art, City Lore. Avocations: tai chi, argentine tango, ballroom dance. Home and Office: 37 Roosevelt St Yonkers NY 10701-5823

VIOLENUS, AGNES A. retired school system administrator; b. N.Y.C., May 17, 1931; d. Antonio and Constance Violenus. BA, Hunter Coll., 1952; MA, Columbia U., 1958; EdD, Nova U., 1990. Tchr. N.Y. State Day Care, N.Y.C., 1952-53, N.Y.C. Bd. Edn., 1953-66; asst. prin. N.Y.C. Elem. and Jr. H.S., 1966-91; student tchr. supr. dept. edn., adj. lectr. CCNY, 1997. Adj. instr. computer dept. continuing edn. divsn. York Coll., N.Y.C., 1985-88, Hunter Coll., N.Y.C., 1998—; adj. instr. tchr. mentor program grad. edn divsn. CCNY, 1990-91; reviewer ednl. and instrnl. films; judge news and documentary Emmy awards NATAS, 1995, 97, 2000, 2002. Co-author: LOGO: K-12, 1980; contbr. articles to profl. jours. Mem. mid-Manhattan br. NAACP, mem. com. on Afro-Am. acad., cultural, and tech. olympics; life mem. Girl Scouts U.S., N.Y.C.; bd. visitors Manhattan Psychiat. Ctr., 1995, pres., 2000, chair 1999—; vol. advisor math., sci., computers Workshop Ctr., CCNY, 1995-97; bd. dirs. Hunter Coll. Scholarship and Welfare Fund. Recipient Dedicated Svc. award Coun. Suprs. and Adminstrs., Appreciation award Aerospace Edn. Assn., 1985, Significant Contbn. award Am. Soc. for Aerospace Edn., 1985, Leaders' Day Cert. of Appreciation, Girl Scouts U.S., 1997. Mem. ASCE, AAUW, Am. Ednl. Rsch. Assn., Assn. Advancement of Computing in Edn., Assn. Computers in Math. and Sci. Tchg., Soc. for Info. Tech. and Tchr. Edn., Assn. for Women in Sci., Nat. Tech. Assn., N.Y. Acad. Scis. (scientists in schs. program 1995), Nat. Assn. Negro Bus. and Profl. Women's Clubs (scholarship com. 1989—, family math. com. 1995, rec. sec. 1994-95, profl. award 1997), Nat. Black Child Devel. Inst. (bd. dirs. 1991—, sci. exhibit com. 1995, v.p. 1999, co-chair entering coll. zone program 1999, 2000, pub. policy com. 1991—, Bridge Bldr.'s award 1995), Schomburg Ctr. Rsch. in Black Culture Schomburg Corp. (vols. adv. com. 1992—, bd. trustee, co-chair corp. task force on African-Am. in math., sci. and tech. 1992—, pres. 1995-98, treas. 1999-2000), Doctorate Assn. N.Y. Educators, N.Y. Alliance Black Sch. Educators, Hunter Coll. Alumni Assn. (bd. dirs. 1993—, rec. sec. 1996-99, treas. 1999—2002, named to Hall of Fame 1998), Bank St. Alumni Coun. Greater N.Y. (asst. sect. 1991-93), Wistarians Alumni Hunter Coll. (exec. com. 1990—, pres. 1990-94). Democrat. Roman Catholic. Avocations: music, genealogy.

VIOLET, WOODROW WILSON, JR., retired chiropractor; b. Sept. 19, 1937; s. Woodrow Wilson and Alice Katherine (Woods) V.; m. Judith Jane Thatcher, June 15, 1963; children: Woodina Lonize, Leslie Alice. Grad. with honors, U.S. Army Med. Svc. Sch., 1955; student, Ventura Coll., 1961-62; grad., L.A. Coll. Chiropractic, 1966. Pvt. practice chiropractic medicine, Santa Barbara, Calif., 1966-73, London, 1973-74, Carpinteria, Calif., 1974-84. Past mem. coun. roentgenology Am. Chiropractic Assn. Former mem. Parker Chiropractic Rsch. Found., Ft. Worth. With USAF, 1955-63. Recipient award merit Calif. Chiropractic Colls., Inc., 1975, cert. of appreciation Nat. Chiropractic Antitrust Com., 1977. Mem.: Nat. Geog. Soc., Delta Sigma. Patentee surg. instrument. E-mail: jjv@redrock.net.

VIORST, JUDITH STAHL, writer; b. Newark, Feb. 2, 1931; d. Martin Leonard and Ruth June (Ehrenkranz) Stahl; m. Milton Viorst, Jan. 30, 1960; children: Anthony Jacob, Nicholas Nathan, Alexander Noah. BA, Rutgers U., 1952; grad., Washington Psychoanalytic Inst., 1981. Author: (children's books) Sunday Morning, 1968, I'll Fix Anthony, 1969, Try It Again Sam, 1970, The Tenth Good Thing About Barney, 1971 (Silver Pencil award 1973), Alexander and the Terrible Horrible No Good Very Bad Day, 1972, My Mama Says There Aren't Any Zombies, Ghosts, Vampires, Creatures, Demons, Monsters, Fiends, Goblins or Things, 1973, Rosie and Michael, 1974, Alexander, Who Used to Be Rich Last Sunday, 1978, The Good-Bye Book, 1988, Earrings!, 1990, The Alphabet from Z to A (with Much Confusion on the Way), 1994, Alexander, Who's Not (Do You Hear Me? I Mean It!) Going to Move, 1995, Super-Completely and Totally the Messiest, 2001; (poetry) The Village Square, 1965-66, It's Hard to Be Hip Over Thirty and Other Tragedies of Married Life, 1968, People and Other Aggravations, 1971, How Did I Get to Be Forty and Other Atrocities, 1976, If I Were in Charge of the World and Other Worries, 1981, When Did I Stop Being Twenty and Other Injustices, 1987, Forever Fifty and Other Negotiations, 1989, Sad Underwear and Other Complications, 1995, Suddenly Sixty and Other Shocks of Later Life, 2000; (with Milton Viorst) The Washington Underground Gourmet, 1970, Yes Married, 1972, A Visit From St. Nicholas (To a Liberated Household), 1977, Love and Guilt and the Meaning of Life, Etc., 1979, Necessary Losses, 1986, Murdering Mr. Monti, 1994, Imperfect Control, 1998, You're Officially a Grown-Up, 1999, Grown-up Marriage, 2003; (musical) Love and Shrimp (book and lyrics), 1990; (HBO children's movie) Alexander and the Terrible, Horrible, No Good, Very Bad Day (book and lyrics), 1990, children's stage musical, 1998, (musical) Alexander, Who's Not Not Not Not Not Going to Move (book and lyrics), 2003. Recipient Emmy award for poems used in Anne Bancroft Spl., 1970. Jewish.

VIORST, MILTON, writer; b. Paterson, N.J., Feb. 18, 1930; s. Louis and Betty (LeVine) Viorst; m. Judith Stahl, Jan. 30, 1960; children: Anthony, Nicholas, Alexander. BA summa cum laude, Rutgers U., 1951; student (Fulbright scholar), U. Lyon, France, 1952; MA, Harvard U., 1955; MS, Columbia U., 1956. Reporter Bergen (N.J.) Record, 1955-56, Newark StarLedger, 1956-57, Washington Post, 1957-61; Washington corr. N.Y. Post, 1961-64; syndicated columnist Washington Evening Star, 1971-75; staff writer New Yorker, N.Y.C., 1987-93; Ferris prof. journalism Princeton (N.J.) U., 1995-96. Lectr. in field. Author: (book) Hostile Allies: FDR and deGaulle, 1965, Great Documents of Western Civilization, 1965, Fall from Grace: The Republican Party and the Puritan Ethic, 1968, Hustlers and Heroes, 1971, Fire in the Streets: America in the 1960's, 1980, Making a Difference: The Peace Corps at Twenty-Five, 1986, Sands of Sorrow: Israel's Journey from Independence, 1987, Reaching for the Olive Branch: UNRWA and Peace in the Middle East, 1990, Sandcastles: The Arabs in Search of the Modern World, 1994, In The Shadow of the Prophet: The Struggle for the Soul of Islam, 1998, What Shall I Do With This People? Jews and the Fractious Politics of Judaism, 2002; contbr. articles to profl. jours.; contbg. corr.: Washington Quar. Mem. nat. adv. com. Mid. East Policy Coun.; chmn. Fund Investigative Journalism, 1969—78; bd. dirs. Georgetown Day Sch., 1977—80, Inst. World Affairs. Officer USAF, 1952—54. Recipient Columbia Journalism Alumni award, 1992, Human Rights award, UN Assn. DC, 2002; Woodrow Wilson Sr. fellow, 1973—79, Alicia Patterson fellow, 1979, Sr. scholar, Mid. East Inst. Mem.: Coun. Fgn. Rels., Author's Guild, Soc. Profl. Journalists, PEN, Am. Peace Now, Phi Beta Kappa. E-mail: mviorst@aol.com.

VIRELLI, LOUIS JAMES, JR., lawyer; b. Phila., Nov. 4, 1948; s. Louis James and Elaine Antoinette (Colombo) V.; m. Barbara Ann Rotella, Aug. 22, 1970; children: Louis J. III, Christopher F. BE in Mech. Engring., Villanova U., 1970; JD, U. Tenn., 1972. Bar: Pa. 1973, U.S. Patent and Trademark Office, 1973, U.S. Ct. Customs and Patent Appeals 1974, U.S. Dist. Ct. (we. dist.) Pa. 1976, U.S. Dist. Ct. (ea. dist.) Pa. 1977, U.S. Ct. Appeals (9th cir.) 1980, U.S. Ct. Appeals (D.C. cir.) 1982, U.S. Supreme Ct. 1982. Patent atty. Sperry New Holland Co., New Holland, Pa., 1973-74; assoc. counsel Westinghouse Co., Pitts., 1974-76; assoc. Paul & Paul, Phila., 1976-80, ptnr., 1980-84; patent counsel Nat. Starch and Chem. Co., Bridgewater, N.J., 1984-88, asst. gen. counsel, intellectual property, 1988-92, gen. counsel, intellectual property, 1992-95; asst. gen. counsel Patents Unilever U.S., Inc., Edgewater, NJ, 1988—95; v.p. gen. patent counsel Unilever N.V., P.L.C., Edgewater, NJ, 1995—96, sr. v.p., gen. patent counsel, 1997—, sr. v.p., gen. counsel intellectual property, 2003—. Arbitrator U.S. Dist. Ct. (ea. dist.) Pa., Phila., 1982-84. Mem.: ABA, Assn. Corp. Patent Counsel (treas., v.p., pres.), Phila. Patent Law Assn., NJ Patent Law Assn., Intellectual Property Owners Assn. (bd. dirs.). Office: Unilever US Inc 45 River Rd Edgewater NJ 07020-1017 also: Unilever PLC Unilever House Blackfriars London England E-mail: louis.virelli@unilever.com.

VIRGO, JOHN MICHAEL, economist, researcher, educator; b. Prestbury Village, Eng., Mar. 11, 1943; s. John Joseph and Muriel Agnes (Franks) V.; m. Katherine Sue Ulmrich, Sept. 6, 1980; 1 child, Debra Marie Riekstins. BA, Calif. State U., Fullerton, 1967, MA, 1969, Claremont Grad. U., 1971, PhD, 1972. Instr. econs. Whittier (Calif.) Coll., 1970-71, Calif. State U., Fullerton and Long Beach, 1971-72, Claremont (Calif.) Grad. Sch., 1971-72; asst. prof. econs. Va. Commonwealth U., Richmond, 1972-74; assoc. prof. mgmt. So. Ill. U., Edwardsville, 1975-83, prof., 1984—. Bd. dirs., founder Internat. Health Econ. & Mgmt. Inst., Edwardsville, 1983-87. Author: Legal & Illegal California Farmworkers, 1974; author, editor: Health Care: An International Perspective, 1984, Exploring New Vistas in Health Care, 1985, Restructuring Health Policy, 1986; founder, editor-in-chief Internat. Advances in Econ. Rsch.; contbr. articles to profl. jours. Served with USN, 1965-68. Mem. AMA, Am. Econ. Assn., Am. Soc. Assn. Execs., Internat. Atlantic Econ. Soc. (founder, exec. v.p., mng. editor Atlantic Econ. jour. 1973—), European Econ. Assn., Allied Social Scis. Assn. (chmn. exec. confs. 1982-84), Western Econs. Assn., Western Econ. Assn., So. Econs. Assn., Media Club (St. Louis). Democrat. Roman Catholic. Avocations: tennis, skiing. Home: 5277 Lindell Blvd Saint Louis MO 63108-1223 Office: Internat Atlantic Econ Soc 2nd Fl 4949 W Pine Blvd Saint Louis MO 63108-1431 Office Phone: 314-454-0100. Business E-Mail: iaes@iaes.org.

VIRKHAUS, TAAVO, symphony orchestra conductor; b. Tartu, Estonia, June 29, 1934; came to U.S., 1949; s. Adalbert August and Helene Marie (Sild) V.; m. Nancy Ellen Herman, Mar. 29, 1969. MusB U. Miami, 1955; MusM Eastman Sch. of Music, Rochester, 1957, DMA, 1967. Dir. music U. Rochester (N.Y.), also assoc. prof. Eastman Sch., Rochester, 1967-77; music dir., condr. Duluth (Minn.) Superior Symphony Orch., 1977-94; guest condr. Rochester Philharm., Minn. Orch., Balt. Symphony, Vancouver Symphony and others, 1972—; music dir., condr. Hunstville (Ala.) Symphony Orch., 1989-2003, condr. emertius, 2003—; guest condr. at Tallinn, Estonia, 1978, 88, 90, 92, 93, 94, 99; lectr. U. Minn.-Duluth, U. of Wis.-Superior. With U.S. Army, 1957-58, USAR, 1957-61. Recipient Howard Hanson Composition award, 1966, Am. Heritage award JFK Libr. for Minorities, 1974; Fulbright scholar, Musickhochschule, Cologne, 1963. Mem. Am. Symphony Orch. League, Condrs. Guild, Am. Fedn. of Musicians. Composer: Violin Concerto, 1966, Symphony No. 1, 1976, Symphony No. 2, 1979, Symphony No. 3, 1984, Symphony No. 4, 1989, Symphony No. 5, 1994, Violin Concerto No. 2, 1995. Republican. Lutheran. E-mail: tvirkhaus@knology.net.

VIRKLER, MARK WILLIAM, religious educator; b. Lowville, N.Y., Mar. 25, 1952; s. Clayton Einbeck and Lillian Amelia V.; m. Patricia Claire, Dec. 16, 1972; children: Charity, Joshua. BA, Roberts Wesleyan Coll., 1974; ThM, Miami Christian U., 1985; PhD, Carolina Christian U., 1994. Youth pastor Avon (N.Y.) Wesleyan Ch., 1971-74; asst. pastor Yorkshire (N.Y.) Free Meth. Ch., 1975; assoc. pastor Curriers (N.Y.) Cmty. Ch., 1976; founding pastor Pioneer Christian Fellowship, Arcade, N.Y., 1976-82; asst. pastor Full Gospel Tabernacle, Orchard Park, N.Y., 1982-89; pres. Communion with God Ministries, Elma, N.Y., 1989—. Pres. Christian Leadership U., Elma, 1994—, Covenant Enterprises, Elma, 1994—; dir. Christian Restoration Fellowship Internat., Elma, 1998—. Author: Communion With God, 1983, Dialogue With God, 1985, Counseled By God, 1989, Naturally Supernatural, 1990, Go Natural, 1994. Avocations: reading, writing, researching, family time. Office: Communion with God Ministries 1431 Bullis Rd Elma NY 14059-9656 Office Phone: 716-652-6990. Business E-Mail: mark@cluonline.com.

VIROSTEK, ROBERT JOSEPH, physician; b. Braddock, Pa., July 4, 1938; AB, Dartmouth Coll., 1960; MD, U. Cin., 1963. Intern Harrisburg Gen. Hosp., 1963-64, resident, 1964-67; dept. head Champlain Valley Physicians Hosp. Med. Ctr., Plattsburgh, N.Y., 1990-91, pres. med. staff, 1997-99; assoc. prof. U. Vt. Med. Sch., 1997—; pvt. practice; v.p. med. staff Champlain Valley Physicians Hosp. Med. Ctr., 2001—03, pres. med. staff, 2003. Mem. Upper Hudson Prenatal Svcs. Network, chmn. bd., 2003—. Mem. AAGL, ACOG, AFS, AIUM, AMA. Office: Lake Champlain ObGyn PC 206 Cornelia St Ste 306 Plattsburgh NY 12901-2789

VIRTEL, JAMES JOHN, lawyer; b. Joliet, Ill., May 15, 1944; BA cum laude, Loras Coll., 1966; JD cum laude, St. Louis U., 1969. Bar: Mo. 1969, Ill. 1969. Atty. Armstrong, Teasdale, Schlafly & Davis (now called Armstrong Teasdale LLP), St. Louis, 1976—. Adj. prof. law St. Louis U., 1995-99; regent Loras Coll., Dubuque, Iowa, 1996—. Editor: St. Louis U. Law Jour., 1968-69. Fellow Am. Coll. Trial Lawyers; mem. Ill. State Bar Assn., Mo. State Bar Assn. Office: Armstrong Teasdale LLP 1 Metropolitan Sq Ste 2600 Saint Louis MO 63102-2740 E-mail: jvirtel@armstrongteasdale.com.

VIRTUE, TED, investment company executive; Grad., Middlebury Coll. Sr. v.p. Drexel Burnham Lambert; exec. v.p., head global fin., mem. mgmt. com., bus. coun., client com. Bankers Trust; pres. BT Alex. Brown Inc. (merged with Deutsche Bank), bd dirs.; pres. Deutsche Bank Alex. Brown; mem. exec. com. Deutsche Bank; CEO DB Capital Ptnrs., MidOcean Ptnrs., NYC. Bd. dirs. Noveon, Inc., Celerity Group, Inc., Ctr. Parcs UK. Office: MidOcean Ptnrs 320 Park Ave Ste 1700 New York NY 10022 Office Phone: 212-497-1400.

VISBAL, JONATHAN RALPH, communications executive; b. Lima, Peru, Sept. 17, 1957; arrived in U.S., 1959; s. Ralph Albert and Elizabeth Victoria (Krystyniak) V. BA, U. Colo., 1979; MBA, Stanford U., 1984. Network mgr. AT&T Long Lines, San Francisco, 1980-81, ops. mgr. Gardena, Calif., 1981-82; mgr. market devel. Latin Am. Pacific Telesis Internat., San Francisco, 1984-85; dir. mktg. and sales Pacific Telesis Iberica, Madrid, 1986, mng. dir., 1986-87; internat. product mgr. Octel Communications Corp., Milpitas, Calif., 1987-90; group product mgr. Internat. Octel Comms., Milpitas, Calif., 1990-91; mktg. dir. Octel Comms. Europe, London, 1991-92, sales and mktg. dir., 1993-95; v.p. mktg. Octel Comms. USA, 1995—97; v.p. internat. bus. devel. Lucent Techs., 1997—99; mng. dir. Silicon Valley office Spencer Stuart, San Mateo, Calif., 2000—. Student lectr. Stanford U., 1984; adj. prof. U. San Francisco, 1999—. Tchr. Jr. Achievement, Gardena, 1982. Named Outstanding Young Man of Am. U.S. Jaycees, 1983. Mem. Omicron Delta Upsilon. Roman Catholic. Avocations: windsurfing, skiing, motorcycles, harmonica. Office: Spencer Stuart 2988 Campus Dr 3d Fl San Mateo CA 94403

VISCARDI, PETER G. risk management and environmental affairs executive; b. NYC, Dec. 28, 1947; s. Peter and Louise (Johnson) Viscardi; m. Margaret E. McGowan, Sept. 11, 1971 (dec. 2001); children: Margaret, Peter; m. Linda M. Gawel, Sept. 26, 2003. BA, Hunter Coll., 1970. CPCU. Ins. mgr. Jaffie Contracting Co., Inc., N.Y.C., 1971-73; ins. adminstr. Otis Elevator Co., N.Y.C., 1973, supr. ins. adminstrn., 1974; dir. adminstrn. Finsure divsn. Studebaker-Worthington, Inc., N.Y.C., 1975-78, corp. risk mgr./exec. v.p., chief oper. officer, 1978-80; mgr. corp. ins. Fortune Brands, Inc. (formerly Am. Brands), N.Y.C., 1980-81, mgr. corp. ins. and real estate, 1981-87, dir. corp. ins. Old Greenwich, Conn., 1987-90, dir. risk mgmt. and environ. affairs, 1990-99; cons. Shirley, NY, 2000—03; sr. mgr. Ernst & Young, 2003—. Mem. edit. bd.: Risk and Benefits Mag., 1987—89, 1991—92, instnl. investor adv. bd.:, 1997. Mem. adv. bd. ACE Bermuda, 1999—2003. Mem.: Air and Waste Mgmt. Assn., Nat. Assn. Environ. Mgrs., Nat. Assn. Mfrs. (risk mgmt. and environ. quality coms. 1990—99), Risk and Ins. Mgmt. Soc., Am. Mgmt. Assn. (ins. and risk mgmt. coun.), Soc. CPCUs. Office Phone: 212-773-2358. E-mail: peviscardi@cs.com.

VISCHER, HAROLD HARRY, manufacturing executive; b. Toledo, Oct. 17, 1914; s. Harry Philip and Hazel May (Patterson) V.; m. DeNell Meyers, Feb. 18, 1938; children: Harold Harry, Robert P., Michael L. BBA, U. Toledo, 1937. With Ohio Bell Telephone Co., 1937-38; with Firestone Tire & Rubber Co., Toledo, 1948-61, nat. passenger tire sales mgr., 1953-57, dist. mgr., 1957-61; with Bandag Inc., Muscatine, Iowa, 1961-80; exec. v.p., pres. Bandag Inc. (Rubber and Equipment Sales group), 1975-80; also dir.; pres., gen. mgr. Hardline Internat., Inc., Jackson, Mich., 1980-82; chmn. Tred-X Corp., 1982—. Mem. City Council, Muscatine, 1964-76; chmn., mem. Dist. Export Council Iowa, 1964-81; chmn. Muscatine United Way, 1969-70; mem. adv. bd. Engring. Coll. Iowa State U., 1970-81; mem. Muscatine Light & Water Bd., 1979-80. Elected to Nat. Tire Dealers and Retreaders Assn. Hall of Fame, 1988, to Internat. Tire Retreading and Repairing Hall of Fame, 1990. Mem. Nat. Tire and Retreaders Suppliers Group Assn. (chmn. 1979-80, exec. com. 1977-80), Tire Retread Info. Bur. (exec. com. 1974-81), Am. Retreading Assn. (adv. bd. 1970-72), Retreading Industry Assn., Industry Man of Yr. 1979), Christian Business men's Com., Gideons. Republican. Home: 13500 Vischer Rd Brooklyn MI 49230-9022

VISCLOSKY, PETER JOHN, congressman, lawyer; b. Gary, Ind., Aug. 13, 1949; s. John and Helen (Kauzlaric) V. BS in Acctg., Ind. U.-Indpls., 1970; JD, U. Notre Dame, 1973; LL.M. in Internat. and Comparative Law, Georgetown U., 1983. Bar: Ind., D.C., U.S. Supreme Court. Legal asst. Dist. Atty.'s Office, N.Y.C., 1972; assoc. Benjamin, Greco & Gouveia, Merrillville, Ind., 1973-76, Greco, Gouveia, Miller, Pera & Bishop, Merrillville, Ind., 1982-84; assoc. staff appropriations com. U.S. Ho. of Reps., Washington, 1976-80, assoc. staff budget com., 1980-82; mem. U.S. Congress from 1st dist. Ind., 1985—; mem. appropriations com., subcoms. treasury, postal svc., gen. govt. and military constrn. Democrat. Roman Catholic. Office: US House of Reps 2313 Rayburn Hob Washington DC 20515-1401 also: 701 E 83d Ave Ste 9 Merrillville IN 46410

VISCOLI, DAVID ANTHONY, music educator; s. Sergio Aloysius and Lois Kathryn Viscoli; m. Kimberly Musser, July 21, 2001. MusB, U. Tex., 1987; MusM, U. So. Calif., 1989, D Mus. Arts, 1992. Instr. piano Calif. Bapt. U., Riverside, 1990—95; assoc. prof. music, piano Minn. State U., Mankato, 1999—. Piano performance examiner Internat. Piano Performance Exams. Com., Taiwan, 2004; guest instr. Chung-Ang U., Anseong-Si, Republic of Korea, 2003; guest and master class tchr. Nat. Taiwan U. Arts, Taipei, 2003; soloist, chamber musician Japanese Embassy, Taiwan, Nat. U. Arts, Taiwan, U. Wash., U. Oreg., U. Calif., Santa Barbara, others. Recipient 2d prize piano competition, Carmel Music Soc., 1995, Recognition for Exemplory Dedicated Svc., N.Mex. Sec. of State, 2001, winner Calif. and Golden West piano competition, Nat. Fedn. Music Clubs, 1993—94. Mem.: Minn. Music Tchrs. Assn., Music Tchrs. Nat. Assn. Avocations: travel, backpacking.

VISCOVICH, SIR ANDREW JOHN, educational management consultant; b. Oakland, Calif., Sept. 25, 1925; s. Peter Andrew and Lucy Pauline (Razovich) V.; m. Roen Shirley Mulvana, Apr. 19, 1952 (div. Feb. 1985); children: Randal Peter, Andra Clair; m. Elena Beth Wong, Apr. 28, 1991; 1 child, Alison Wong. BA, U. Calif., Berkeley, 1949; MA, San Francisco State U., 1960; EdD, U. Calif., Berkeley, 1973; cert. labor dispute resolution, Golden Gate U., 1976. Assoc. supt. Oakland Unified Sch. Dist., Calif., 1970-77; supt. Palm Springs (Calif.) Unified Sch. Dist., 1976-79, Garvey Sch. Dist., Rosemead, Calif., 1979-88, Berkeley (Calif.) Unified Sch. Dist., Stockton, Calif., 1988-90; pres. Ctr. for Ednl. Rsch. in Adminstrn., Stockton, Calif., 1990—. Adj. prof. U. Calif., Berkeley, 1965-67, Calif. State U., Hayward, 1970-76, L.A., 1971-8; exec. dir. Marcus Foster Edn. Found., Oakland, 1975-76; cons. Spanish Ministry Edn., 1987—, Republic of China Ministry Edn., Taipei, Taiwan, 1986-89, Croatian Ministry Edn., Zagreb, 1993—, Marriott Sch. Svcs, 1992—, CSHQH, Idaho; pre-sch. dir. Oakland Unified Sch. Dist., 1974-76; asst. dir. Bay Area Bilingual Edn. League, 1971-75; dir. Bay Area Tchr. Ctr., 1974, asst. dir. Far West Ednl. Lab., 1974; adj. assoc. prof. Calif. State U. at L.A.and Hayward, U. South Fla., U. Oreg., Coll. of Holy Names; exec. dir. ANRO Cons., Inc., Calif., 1973-82; state adminstr. Coachella Unified Sch. Dist., Thermal, Calif., 1992; nat. dir. supt. consulting svcs. Sodexho Marriott Corp., 1992-99. Author: Language Programs for the Disadvantaged, 1965, R.E.S. Plus, 1978; contbr. The School Principal, 1978. Chair United Way, Pasadena, Calif., 1985; pres. Croatian Scholarship Found., San Ramon, Calif., 1993-94. Served to ens. USNR, 1959-64. Recipient award for innovations in alternative schools Behavioral Rsch. Lab., San Francisco, 1973; named Knight of Civil Order of Merit King Juan Carlos of Spain, 1990. Mem. Am. Mgmt. Assn., Am. Assn. Sch. Adminstrs., Assn. Calif. Sch. Adminstrs., Calif. City Sch. Supts., Calif. Tchrs. Assn. (John Swett award 1978), Tau Kappa Epsilon. Avocations: golf, reading, travel. ultralite flying. Home: 3754 Fort Donelson Dr Stockton CA 95219-3211

VISEK, WILLARD JAMES, nutritionist, animal scientist, physician, educator; b. Sargent, Nebr., Sept. 19, 1922; s. James and Anna S. (Dworak) V.; m. Priscilla Flagg, Dec. 28, 1949; children: Dianna, Madeleine, Clayton Paul. B.Sc. with honors (Carl R. Gray scholar), U. Nebr., 1947; MSc (Smith fellow in agr.), Cornell U., 1949, PhD, 1951; MD (Peter Yost Fund scholar), U. Chgo., 1957; DSc (hon.), U. Nebr., 1980. Diplomate Nat. Bd. Med. Examiners, 1960. Grad. asst., lab. animal nutrition Cornell U., 1947-51; AEC postdoctoral fellow Oak Ridge, 1951-52; research assoc., 1952-53; research asst. pharmacology U. Chgo., 1953-57, asst. prof., 1957-61, assoc. prof., 1961-64; rotating med. intern U. Chgo. Clinics, 1957-58, 58-59, 59; prof. nutrition and comparative metabolism, dept. animal sci. Cornell U., Ithaca, N.Y., 1964-75; prof. clin. sci. (nutrition and metabolism) Coll. Medicine and dept. food sci. U. Ill. Coll. Agr., Urbana-Champaign, 1975—; prof. dept. internal medicine U. Ill. Coll. Medicine, Urbana-Champaign, 1986-93, prof. emeritus, 1993—. Bd. dirs. Coun. Agriculture, Sci. and Tech., 1994-97; bd. sci. advisors Coun. Sci. and Health, 1994—; Brittingham vis. prof. U. Wis. Madison, 1982-83; Hogan meml. lectr. U. Mo., 1987; mem. subcom. dog nutrition com. animal nutrition NRC-Nat. Acad. Sci., 1965-71; adv. coun. Inst. Lab. Animal Resources, NRC-Nat. Acad. Sci., 1966-69; sub-com. animal care faciltities Survey Inst. Lab. Animal Resources, 1967-70; cons., lectr. in field; mem. sci. adv. com. diet and nutrition cancer program Nat. Cancer Inst., 1976-81; mem. nutrition study sect. NIH, 1980-84; chmn. membership com. Am. Inst. Nutrition-Am. Soc. Clin. Nutrition, 1978-79, 80-83, 85; cons. VA, NSF, indsl. orgns.; Wellcome vis. prof. in basic med. scis. Oreg. State U., 1991-92; bd. sci. counselors USDA, 1989-91. Mem. editl. bd. Jour. Nutrition, 1980-84, editor, 1990-97; mem. editl. bd. Physiol. Rev., 1995-2001; contbr. articles to profl. jours. Bd. dirs. Coun. for Agrl. Sci. and Tech., 1994-97; active local Boy Scouts Am. Served with AUS, 1943-46. Recipient alumni award Nebr. 4-H, 1967, 97, alumni award U. Chgo., 1997, faculty merit award U. Ill. Coll. Medicine, 1988, Alumni Achievement award U. Nebr., 1997, U. Chgo., 1997; Nat. Cancer Inst. spl. fellow MIT, rsch. fellow Mass. Gen. Hosp., 1970-71; sr. scholar U. Ill., 1988. Fellow AAAS, Am. Inst. Nutrition (Osborne and Mendel award 1985), Am. Soc. Animal Sci. (chmn. subcom. antimicrobials, mem. regulatory agency com. 1973-78); mem. Am. Physiol. Soc., Soc. Pharmacology and Exptl. Therapeutics, Am. Inst. Nutrition (council 1980-83, 85-86), Soc. Exptl. Biology and Medicine, Am. Soc. Clin. Nutrition, Am. Therapeutic Soc., Am. Gastroenterol. Assn., Am. Bd. Clin. Nutrition, Innocents Soc., Fedn. Am. Socs. Exptl. Biology (sci. steering group life scis. rsch. office, adv. com. 1986-92), Am. Bd. Nutrition (bd. dirs.), Am. Soc. Nutritional Scis. (Conrad Elvehjem award 1996), Nat. Dairy Coun. (rsch. adv. com. 1987-91, vis. prof. nutrition program 1981-92), Gamma Alpha (pres. 1948-49), Phi Kappa Phi (pres. 1981-82), Alpha Gamma Rho (pres. 1946-47), Gamma Sigma Delta. Presbyterian (elder). Home: 1405 W William St Champaign IL 61821-4406 Office: U Ill 190 Med Sci Bldg 506 S Mathews Ave Urbana IL 61801-3618 Office Phone: 217-244-2797. Business E-Mail: w-visek@uiuc.edu.

VISH, DONALD H. lawyer, pension fund administrator; b. Ft. Benning, Ga., Jan. 18, 1945; s. D. H., Jr. and Dorris (Parrish) Vish; m. Catherine Pence Hamilton, Aug. 20, 1966 (div. 1986); children: Donald Hamilton, Daphne Mershon Sullivan. BA in English, Bellarmine Coll., 1968; JD cum laude, U. Louisville, 1971. Bar: Ky. 1971, Fla. 1972, U.S. Ct. Appeals (6th cir.) 1974, U.S. Ct. Claims 1994. Sec., gen. counsel Gen. Energy Corp., Lexington, Ky., 1978-83; ptnr. Wyatt, Tarrant & Combs, Lexington, 1980-88, Frost Brown Todd, Lexington, 1988-89, 1991-98; gen. counsel Ky. Coal Producers' Self-Ins. Fund, 1992-98; sec., gen. counsel AIK Workers Compensation Fund, 1998—, exec. v.p., 2002—. Apptd. assoc. solicitor U.S. Dept. Interior, 1989—91; assoc. prof. Coll. Law U. Ky., Lexington, 1977—80, adj. assoc. prof. mineral law, 1979—85. Co-author: American Law of Mining, 2d edit., 1984; co-editor, co-author: Coal Law and Regulation, 1983—93, Kentucky Election Law, 1995. Trustee Syre Sch., Lexington, 1980—88, chmn. bd. dirs., 1986—88; mem. Blue Grass coun. Boy Scouts Am., 1988—93; apptd. gov. Ky. Registry Election Fin., 1991—93; bd. dirs. Highlands Cmty. Ministries, 2001—. Fellow: Am. Bar Found. (life); mem.: ABA (chmn. coal com., natural resources sect. 1987), Ky. Bar Assn. (mem. ethics com. 1983—85, chair residency com. 1998—), Fla. Bar, Am. Judicature Soc., Eastern Mineral Law Found. (trustee 1979—91, mem. exec. com. 1979—82, chmn. coal subcom. 1984—85), Am. Law Inst., Louisville Bar Assn. (life), Ky. Bar Found. (life). Office: Parrent and Vish 9700 Park Plz Ave Ste 107 Louisville KY 40241 Home: 5020 Nitta Yuma Dr Harrods Creek KY 40027 Office Phone: 502-327-8800. Personal E-mail: donaldvish@att.net.

VISHNIAC, ETHAN TECUMSEH, astronomy educator; b. New Haven, Sept. 29, 1955; s. Wolf Vladimir and Helen Frances (Simpson) V.; m. Ilene Joy Busch, June 13, 1976; children: Cady Anne, Miriam Rachel. BS and BA summa cum laude, U. Rochester, 1976; MA, PhD, Harvard U., 1980. Rsch. assoc. Princeton (N.J.) U., 1980-82; lectr. U. Tex., Austin, 1982-84, asst. prof., 1984-88, assoc. prof., 1988-93, prof., 1993-98, Johns Hopkins U., Balt., 1998—. Assoc. editor Phys. Rev. Letters, 1995-97; sci. editor Astrophys. Jour., 1997—; contbr. numerous articles to profl. jours. Recipient Presdl. Young Investigator, 1985; Alfred Sloan fellow, 1986. Fellow Am. Phys. Soc.; mem. Am. Astron. Soc. (Helen B. Warner prize 1990), Internat. Astron. Union. Office: Johns Hopkins U Dept Physics and Astronomy 3400 N Charles St Dept And Baltimore MD 21218-2680 Office Phone: 410-516-7269. E-mail: ethan@pha.jhu.edu.

VISKANTA, RAYMOND, mechanical engineering educator; b. Lithuania, July 16, 1931; came to U.S., 1949, naturalized, 1955; s. Vincas and Genovaite (Vinickas) V.; m. Birute Barbara Barpsys, Oct. 13, 1956; children: Renata, Vitas, Tadas. BSME, U. Ill., 1955; MSME, Purdue U., 1956, PhD, 1960; DEng (hon.), Tech. U. Munich, 1994. Registered profl. engr., Ill. Asst. mech. engr. Argonne (Ill.) Nat. Lab., 1956-59, student rsch. assoc., 1959-60, assoc. mech. engr., 1960-62; assoc. prof. mech. engring. Purdue U., West Lafayette, Ind., 1962-66, prof. mech. engring., 1966-86, Goss disting. prof. engring., 1986—. Guest prof. Tech. U. Munich, Germany, 1976-77, U. Karlsruhe, Germany, 1987; vis. prof. Tokyo Inst. Tech., 1983. Contbr. over 500 tech. articles to profl. jours. Recipient Sr. U.S. Scientist award Alexander von Humboldt Found., 1975, Sr. Rsch. award Am. Soc. Engring. Edn., 1984, Nusselt-Reynolds prize, 1991, Thermal Engring. award for Internat. Activity, Japan Soc. Mech. Engrs., 1994, Alumni award for Disting. Svc. U. Ill.-Urbana-Champaign, 2000; Japan Soc. for Promotion of Sci. fellow, 1983. Fellow ASME (Heat Transfer Meml. award 1976, Max Jakob Meml. award 1986, Melville medal 1988), AIAA (Thermophysics award 1979); mem. AAAS, NAE, Acad. Engring. Scis. Russian Fedn. (fgn.), Lithuanian Acad. Scis. (fgn.), Sigma Xi, Pi Tau Sigma, Tau Beta Pi. Home: 3631 Chancellor Way West Lafayette IN 47906-8809 Office: Purdue Univ 585 Purdue Mall West Lafayette IN 47907-2088 Office Phone: 765-494-5632. Personal E-mail: rviskanta@insightbb.com. Business E-Mail: viskanta@ecn.purdue.edu.

VISOCKI, NANCY GAYLE, information services consultant; b. Dumont, N.J., May 13, 1952; d. Thomas and Gloria Visocki. BA in Math., Manhattanville Coll., 1974; MS in Ops. Rsch. and Stats., Rensselaer Poly. Inst., 1977. Rsch. asst. Coll. Physicians and Surgeons Columbia U., N.Y.C., 1974-75; programmer analyst R. Shriver Assocs., Parsippany, N.J., 1977-79; sr. tech. rep. GE Info. Svcs. Co., East Orange, N.J., 1979-81, mgr. project office Morristown, N.J., 1981-83, tech. dir., 1983-87, tech. mgr., 1988-89, area mgr. sys. devel. and consulting Parsippany, 1989-92, area tech. mgr. sys. devel. and cons., Fin. Info. Sys., 1992-93, sr. cons. info. svcs., 1993-98, project mgr. e-commerce sys. integration, 1998-2000; mgr. Major e-commerce Applications Practice, 2000—03. Active Western Hills Christian Ch., Tranquility, N.J., 1986—; vol. Women's Ctr., Hackettstown, N.J., 1989-93; class fundraising and gift chmn. Rensselaer Poly. Inst., Troy, N.Y., 1991-95; vol. Elfun Soc., 1981—. Manhattanville Coll. grantee, Purchase, N.Y., 1970-71; tuition fellow Rensselaer Poly. Inst., 1975-77. Mem. NAFE, Elfun, Women of Accomplishment. Avocations: tai chi, hiking, bicycling, reading, yoga. Personal E-mail: ngv2@verizon.net.

VISOVSKY, NICK JOHN, research scientist; b. N.Y.C., Mar. 16, 1951; s. George and Mary Visovsky; m. Gail Catherine Wilks, Nov. 24, 1979. B in Tech., CCNY, 1976. Sr. scientist Corning (N.Y.) Inc., 1989—. Contbr. articles to profl. jours. Achievements include patents for Replicating a Nanoscale Pattern; research in adhesion and wetting hysteresis of a metal (mercury) on an oxide glass in air and nitrogen; the effect of dry-etching upon AMLCD substrate glasses; fabrication of micrometer and nanometer scale structures in silica sol-gel films using electron beam writing methods; patents for Insertion probe system for continuous measurement of pH level in process lines. Office: Corning Inc Sp Pr 2 Corning NY 14831 E-mail: visovskyn@corning.com.

VISSER, RICHARD EDGAR, minister; b. South Weymouth, Mass., Apr. 28, 1937; s. Edgar and Marjorie (McPhee) V.; m. Carol Naomi Edwards, June 21, 1958; children: Andrew, Thomas, Peter. AB, Gordon Coll., 1958, BS, 1959; BD, Gordon Div. Sch., 1962, MRE, 1965; D Ministry, Asbury Theol. Sem., 1983. Ordained to ministry Am. Bapt. Chs. in U.S.A., 1962. Pastor Acton-Milton Mills Bapt. Ch., Milton Mills, NH, 1962—65; First Bapt. Ch., Derry, N.H., 1966-69; min. edn. Peters Creek Bapt. Ch., Library, Pa., 1969-73; pastor 1st Bapt. Ch., Warren, Pa., 1973-79, min. ch. edn. and music St. Albans, W.Va., 1980-83, sr. pastor Waynesburg, Pa., 1983—2003; co- pastor First Baptist Church, Warren, Pa., 2003—. Pres. Clergymen's Assn. of Derry, 1967-69; founder, chmn. Pitts. Ch. Edn. Conv., 1972-73; clk. Pitts. Bapt. Assn., 1971-73; pres. Ministerial Assn., Warren, 1975-76, St. Albans, 1982-83, Waynesburg, 1988-90, 99-2001; moderator Ten Mile Assn. Waynesburg, 1985-87; pres., Ten Mile Assn. Mins. and Spouses, 2001—03; co-founder, vice chmn. Ten Mile and Monogahela Assns. Lic. Lay Pastor Tng. Program, 1988-90; chairperson Am. Bapt. Ch. Leadership Inst. Western Pa., 1993-2002; pres. Am. Bapt. Chs. of Pa. and Del., 1991-92, chmn. Sunday Sch. team, 1987-90, exec. com., 1987-94, 1997-2002 chrmn. Budget Commn. 2004-2005; mem. gen. bd., bd. ednl. ministries Am. Bapt. Chs. U.S.A., 1997-2002,mem. comms. com., 1999-2002, com. of 100 for Renewal, 1992-98; mem. Ministers and Missionaries Benefit Bd., 1999-2002, mem. comms. com., 1999-2002, chmn. benefits com., 2000-2002. Founder, chmn. Warren (Pa.) Community Chorus, 1974-78; pres. Warren County Health and Welfare Coun., 1975-77; chmn. Forest-Warren Counties Human Svcs. Adv. Commn., 1978-79; co. chmn. Greene County Human Svcs. Adv. Commn., Pa., 1988-96, vice chmn., 2000—02, chmn. mental health com., 2000—02, mem. sr. outreach and referral coalition, 2001-03; chmn. Greene County chpt. ARC, 1989-91; bd. dirs. Greene County Meml. Hosp., 1989—02; bd. dirs. Comty. Found. Greene County, 2000—03, vice chmn. 2001—03; mem. emergency food and shelter bd. Greene County FEMA, 1985-2003. Recipient Apollo award, Alderson-Broaddus Coll., Phillipi, W. Va., 1995, Disting. Cmty. Svc. award, Greater Waynesburg C. of C., 2002. Mem. Am. Bapt. Mins. Coun. (Excellence in Ministry award 2000, v.p. Pa. and Del. chpt. 1978-79), Rotary (v.p. Waynesburg Club 1990-91, pres. 1991-92). Avocations: walking, reading, singing. Office: 1st Bapt Ch 303 W High St Waynesburg PA 15370-1209 Home: 207 N Parker St Warren PA 16365-2952 E-mail: firstbaptist@alltel.net. *I feel that sometimes people avoid leadership roles because they can be demanding. I do not seek leadership roles, but when I see needs and suggest possible solutions, these roles often seem to find me. I have found that an open, ordinary person such as I can make a difference and enjoy some rich rewards.*

VISSER, THOMAS DURANT, social studies educator, writer; s. William Warren and June Frances Visser. BSBA, U. N.H., 1973; MS in Hist. Preservation, U. Vt., 1986. Assoc. prof. U. Vt., Burlington, 1985—. Author: (book) Field Guide to New England Barns and Farm Buildings (Pioneer Am. Soc. Kniffen Award, 1998). Mem. dist. environ. commn. Vt. Environ. Bd., 1991—98. Office: Univ Vt History Dept 133 S Prospect St Burlington VT 05405

VISSER, VALYA ELIZABETH, physician; b. Chgo., Oct. 2, 1947; d. Roy Warren and Tania Eugenia (Morozoff) Nelson; children: Kira Elizabeth Visser, Michael Philip Visser. BS, Iowa State U., 1968; MD, U. Iowa, 1973. Diplomate Am. Bd. Pediatrics, Sub-Bd. Neonatal-Perinatal Medicine. Resident pediatrics U. Iowa Hosps. and Clinics, Iowa City, 1976; fellow neonatology Children's Mercy Hosp., Kansas City, 1978; asst. prof. pediatrics U. Kans. Sch. Medicine, Kansas City, 1978-81; staff pediatrician U.S. Army Med. Corps., Ft. Bragg, N.C., 1981-83; attending neonatologist Carolinas Med. Ctr., Charlotte, 1983—. Chair dept. pediatrics Carolinas Med. Ctr., Charlotte, 1999—; conf. chair Extracorporeal Life Support Orgn., Ann Arbor, Mich., 1993-95. Major Med. Corps., 1981-83. Fellow Am. Acad. Pediatrics. Mem. Unitarian-Universalist Ch. Avocation: music. Office: Carolinas Med Ctr Dept Pediatrics PO Box 32861 Charlotte NC 28232-2861

VISTE, ARLEN ELLARD, chemistry professor; b. Austin, Minn., Aug. 13, 1936; s. Arthur E. and Edith L. (Kehret) V.; m. Elizabeth Ann Lindbeck, June 14, 1959; children: Solveig, David, Mark. BA, St. Olaf Coll., 1958; PhD, U. Chgo., 1962. Asst. prof. chemistry St. Olaf Coll., Northfield, Minn., 1962-63; NSF fellow Columbia U., N.Y.C., 1963-64; asst. prof. Augustana Coll., Sioux Falls, S.D., 1964-68, assoc. prof., 1968-73, prof., 1973—, prof. emeritus, 2002—. Contbr. articles to profl. jours. Mem. Am. Chem. Soc., Royal Soc. Chemistry (London), S.D. Acad. Sci., Midwest Assn. Chemistry Tchrs. in Liberal Arts Colls., Phi Beta Kappa, Sigma Xi. Home: 1500 W 30th St Sioux Falls SD 57105-3622 Office: Augustana Coll Chemistry Dept Sioux Falls SD 57197-0001 Business E-Mail: arlen_viste@augie.edu.

VISWANATH, GUTTALU RAMACHANDRA RAO, mathematics educator, consultant, researcher; b. Mandya, Karnataka State, India, Sept. 24, 1940; s. Guttalu Chandrashekariah Ramachandra Rao (Late) and Guttalu R. Subamma (Late); m. Padma Guttalu Viswanath, Aug. 26, 1970 (dec. Oct. 17, 1980); m. Leelavathi Guttalu Viswanath, Aug. 2, 1981; 1 child, Bramara G. BSc in Physics, Chemistry and Math., U. Mysore, India, 1960; MSc in Math., Karnataka U., Dharwar, India, 1963; MA in Math., U. Md., College Park, 1968; PhD in Math., Cath. U. Am., Washington, 1972. Cert. tchr. Md., 1974. Asst. prof. math. Howard U., Washington, 1968—74; tchr. Balt. Poly., 1974—75; asst. prof. math. St. Pauls Coll., Lawrenceville, Va., 1977—78; prof. math. S.C. State U., Orangeburg, 1978—. Rsch. scholar dept. chem. engring. Indian Inst. Sci., Bangalore, Karnataka State, India, 1963—65; grad. rsch./tchg. asst. U. Md., College Park, 1965—68; ops. rsch. analyst Comm. Command, U.S. Army, Ft. Huachuca, Ariz., 1984, 7Th Signal Command, U.S. Army, Ft. Ritichie, Md., 1986; faculty rsch. fellow Rsch. Directorate, U.S. Army Missile Command, Redstone Arsenal, Huntsville, Ala., 1988; math. statistician U.S. Army - Dugway (Utah) Proving Grounds, 1990; faculty reserach fellow Irdd Rome Labs., USAF, Griffis AFB, NY, 1992; faculty rsch. fellow NFESC USN, Port Hueneme, Calif., 1994. Author: (text book) Complex Analysis An Introductory Course (Faculty Devel. grant, 1999), A First Course In Calculus - With Emphasis On Concepts And Problem Solving, Calculus II - With Emphasis On Concepts And Problem Solving. Recipient Pres. of India prize, Karnataka U., Dharwar, India, 1963; grantee, Howard U., 1971, S.C. State U., 1999; Rsch. scholarship, Indian Inst. Sci., Bangalore, 1963 - 1965, Grad. Rsch./ Tchg. assistantships, U. Md., 1965 - 1968. Mem.: Am. Math. Soc., Kappa Mu Epsilon (hon.). Hindu. Achievements include research and publ. in the area of complex analysis; research in at the Nat. Lab; Established Excellence in Math. Award to recognize the best students in math., SC State U., Orangeburg, 1966; organized and funded resurrection of an ancient Sri Gopala Krishna Temple, Guttalu, Mandya District, India, 1996. Home: 4073 Cedric St Orangeburg SC 29118 Office: Box 7493 Dept Math SC State U 300 College St NE Orangeburg SC 29117 Office Phone: 803-536-8695. E-mail: viswanath@scsu.edu.

VISWANATHAN, GOPALAKRISHNAN, metallurgist, researcher; b. Trichy, India, Dec. 20, 1964; arrived in U.S., 2000; s. Viswanathan Muthuswamy Iyer and Lalitha Viswanathan; m. Sivagamasundari Gopalakrishnan, Jan. 22, 1999; children: Balaji, Siddharth. MS, Bharathidasan U., Tamil Nadu, India, 1987; MS in Engring., Regional Engring. Coll., Madras, India, 1992; PhD in Metallurgy, Indian Inst. Tech., Madras, India, 1999. Lectr. Mookambigai Coll. Engring., Tamil Nadu, India, 1987—92; rschr. Indian Inst. Tech., Madras, India, 1993—99; scientist, dir. Madras, India, 1999—2000; metallurgist Controlled Thermal Tech., Phoenix, 2000—01, Superior Shot Penning Inc., Houston, 2001—. Contbr. articles to profl. jours. Mem.: Thermal Spray Soc., Am. Soc. for Materials. Achievements include establishing a treatment procedure for critical parts of a fast breeder test reactor. Home: 12919 Windfern Rd Houston TX 77064 Office: Superior Shot Penning Inc 13930 Luthe Rd Houston TX 77039

VISWANATHAN, RAMASWAMY, physician, educator; b. Coimbatore, India, Aug. 20, 1949; came to U.S., 1972; s. Thiruvalangadu and Bhavani Krishnamurthy Ramaswamy; m. Kusum Ramakrishna, June 15, 1980; children: Vikram, Vivek, Vidya. MB, BS, U. Madras, 1972; D of Med. Sci., SUNY, 1989. Diplomate Am. Bd. Psychiatry and Neurology, geriatric psychiatry, addiction psychiatry, Am. Bd. Internal Medicine. Med. intern Bklyn.-Cumberland Med. Ctr., 1972-73; resident in internal medicine L.I. Jewish-Hillside Med. Ctr.-Queens Hosp. Ctr. Affiliation, N.Y.C., 1973-74; resident in psychiatry SUNY Health Sci. Ctr., Bklyn., 1974-77, fellow in psychosomatic medicine, 1976-78, fellow in research tng. in psychiatry, 1977-79, mem. staff, 1978—, clin. asst. prof. psychiatry, 1979-87, instr. in medicine, 1979—, clin. assoc. prof., 1987-90, assoc. prof. clin. psychiatry, 1990—, assoc. dir. med.-psychiat. liaison svc., 1981-83, 84-97, acting dir., 1983-84, dir., psychiat. liaison svc., 1998—, med. dir. Anxiety Disorders Clinic, 1982—, mem. com. cancer edn. and preventive oncology, 1983-92, dir. course on life-threatening illness, dying and death, 1984-89, dir. med. interviewing course, 1985-89, dir. doctor-patient relationship course, 1989-90, dir. intro. to clin. medicine-human dimension course, 1990-98, cons. AIDS unit, 1989—, with student evaluation and promotion com., 1989-94, with course dirs.' com., 1989-98; mem. exec. com. Univ. Hosp., 1992-96; internal medicine residency program rev. com. SUNY Health Sci. Ctr., 1994—; cons. Bklyn. VA Med. Ctr., 1986-89; pvt. practice medicine specializing in psychiatry, psychosomatic medicine, behavior therapy, hypnosis and sex therapy Bklyn., 1978—. Mem. task force on doctoring experience curricular reform, 1997—. Contbr. articles to profl. jours. Curriculum coun. Herricks Pub. Sch. Dist., 1992-95. Fellow ACP, Am. Psychiat. Assn. (dep. rep. Asian-Am. caucus 1996-99, RG rep. 1999—, assembly com. on procedures, 1997—, com. on consultation, liaison psychiatry and primary care edn. 1992-98, coun. on internat. affairs 1992-95, 97—, nominating com. 1997-98, assembly com. on planning 1998—, cert. excellence in med. evaluation 1999), Indian Psychiat. Soc. (life), Acad. Psychosomatic Medicine; mem. AMA, Bklyn. Psychiat. Soc. (councillor, pres. elect 1988-90, pres. 1990-92, chmn. com. on AIDS, 1990-92, chmn. com. on consultation-liaison psychiatry 1990-92, chmn. disaster response com. 1991-92, chmn. legis. and pvt. practice com. 1992-96, chmn. legis. com. 1996—, chmn. internat. affairs com. 1992-94), Am. Acad. Psychiatry and the Law (rsch. com. 1998—, internat. rels. com. 1998—, Assn. Advancement Behavior Therapy, Soc. Liaison Psychiatry (bd. dirs. 1986-90, 93-96, sec. 1987-88), Anxiety Disorders Assn. Am., N.Y. State Psychiat. Assn. (com. on govt. health programs 1988-94, task force on practice guidelines, legis. com., chmn. edn. com. 1992-96), Soc. Exploration Psychotherapy Integration, Indo-Am. Psychiat. Assn. (founder, life, exec. com. 1979-85, 92—, sec. 1992-94, pres.-elect 1994-96, pres. 1996-98, Sci. and Svc. award 1990). Office: SUNY Health Sci Ctr 450 Clarkson Ave # 127 Brooklyn NY 11203-2056

VITA, STEVEN, poet; b. Chgo., July 16, 1960; s. John and Rosemarie V. BA in Art and English, Denison U., 1982; MFA in English, CUNY, 1985. Founder, editor Veery, Chgo., 1991—. *"John Bayley of Oxford University analyzes, 'Vita is a poet of great promise as well as performance. He has affinities with a very distinguished kind of poet-one might call them in School of Contingency-whose doyen is of course John Ashbery.'"--KSUI-FM National Public Radio (NPR), Iowa City. "He is, I believe, that increasingly rare bird,*

the true original."--Daniel Weissbort, The University of London, "The Heart of Tents." "Sir Stephen Spender, who first published W.H. Auden and whose own poetry was brought to the literary public by T.S. Eliot, calls Vita's abilities as a poet 'gifted'."--Daily Southtown. Author: The Heart of Tents, 1991. Mem. Am. Philos. Assn.

VITALE, DAVID J. former banker; b. 1946; With First Nat. Bank of Chgo. subs. First Chgo. NBD Corp., 1968—, exec. v.p., 1986—, First Chgo. NBD Corp., 1986—, also bd. dirs., 1992—; vice chmn., pres. First Nat. Bank Chgo., 1995—99; CEO Chgo. Bd. Trade, 2001—02; chief adminstrv. officer Chgo. Public Schools, 2003—.

VITALE, GERALD LEE, financial services executive; b. Chgo., Apr. 3, 1950; s. Le Roy Allen and Gilda Leanora (Rasori) V. BS in Psychology, Loyola U., Chgo., 1972. Fin. mgr. Mellon Fin., Chgo., 1973-76; credit mgr. Kemper Ins. Co., Chgo., 1976-78; pres., CEO Tribune Employees Credit Union, Chgo., 1978-96. Pres. NCR Credit Union User Group, Dayton, Ohio, 1984-91; CEO, Gerald Equity Resources, Inc., 1996—; mem. adv. bd. Ill. Gov.'s Credit Union, 1993-98; dir. fin. Rush Cancer Inst., 2000-2001. Co-host Chicagoland Cable (CLTV) TV Fin. Reports, Tribune Broadcasting, 1993-96. Mem. Habitat for Humanity, 1998—, Nat. Rep. Senatorial Com., 2002; counselor youth motivation Chgo. C. of C. and Industry, 1980—97, mem. adv. bd., 1984—96; counselor Hire the Future, 1988—96; vol. Red Cloud Athletic Assn., 1993—2000, Friends of Providence-St. Mel, 1993—; mem. Chgo. Coun. Fgn. Rels., 1995—98; mem. Coun. of 1000 Nat. Italian-Am. Found., 1995—99, Humane Soc. U.S., 1997—; mem. fin. svcs. com. Exec. Club City of Chgo., 1993—99; mem. Ctr. Study of Presidency, 1993—97, Filene Inst., 1992—96, Ill. Arts Alliance, 1996—98, George Bush Presdl. Libr. Found., 2002—, GOP Action Com., 1992—97; life mem. Rep. Nat. Com., 1977—; mem. Ill. Rep. Party, 2002—. Recipient award, Eisenhower Commn., 2002. Mem.: Fgn. Policy Rsch. Inst., Greater Garfield C. of C. (bd. dirs. 1992—95), The Carter Ctr., Am. Enterprise Inst., Nat. Assn. Investors (corp. mem. 1999—), Nat. Assn. State Chartered Credit Unions (bd. dirs. 1995—97, region V dir.), Midwest Assn. Credit Unions (bd. dirs. 1992—96), Am. Mgmt. Assn., Heritage Found., Sky Line Club, Monroe Club (bd. dirs. 1995—99). Roman Catholic. Avocations: hiking, rowing, long-distance walking. Home: 1636 N Wells St Apt 2410 Chicago IL 60614-6020 Office: GER Inc 1636 N Wells St Apt 2410 Chicago IL 60614-6020 E-mail: gerinc@aol.com.

VITALE, PATTY A. pediatrician, consultant, medical educator; MD, Jefferson Med. Coll., 1998; MPH in Epidemiology, U. Calif., San Diego. Diplomate American Board of Pediatrics. Intern pediat. U. Calif., San Diego, 1998—99, resident pediat., 1999—2001, fellow cmty. pediat.; fellow pub. health San Diego State U., 2001—03; asst. prof. pediat. U. Medicine and Dentistry, NJ; full-time cons. child abuse. Mem.: AMA (Excellence in Medicine Leadership award 2004), Am. Acad. Pediat. Office: U Docs Pavilion #1100 42 E Laurel Rd Stratford NJ 08084

VITE, FRANK ANTHONY, realtor; b. Aurora, Ill., Feb. 9, 1930; s. Frank A. and Rose (Cosentino) V.; grad. Marmion Mil. Acad., 1948, student Sch. Mgmt., U. Notre Dame, 1958; D.B.A. (hon.), Hillsdale Coll., 1972; m. Barbara Ann Decio, Oct. 23, 1954; children: Bradley Scott, Mark Steven, Michael Lee, Leslie Ann, Lisa Ann. Plant engr. Lyon Metal Products, Aurora, 1951-52, purchasing agt., 1953-54; became sales mgr., exec. v.p., owner, dir. Skyline Homes, Inc., Elkhart, Ind., 1954; pres., owner B&F Realty, Inc., No. Ind. Appraisal Co., Golden Falcon Homes, Inc.; real estate broker; dir. 1st Nat. Bank, Elkhart, Ind. Trustee Hillsdale (Mich.) Coll., Holy Cross Coll., South Bend, Ind.; bd. dirs. Ind. Commn. Higher Edn. Served with AUS, 1952-53, Korea. Mem. Elkhart Bd. Realtors, Nat. Sales Execs. Assn., Ind. Real Estate Assn., Nat. Inst. Real Estate Brokers, Holy Name Soc. Republican. Clubs: K.C. (4 deg.), Knight of Malta, Elks. Office: 1300 Cassopolis St Elkhart IN 46514-3248 Home: 9 Colonia Miramonte Paradise Valley AZ 85253

VITEK, RICHARD KENNETH, retired scientific instrument company executive; b. Chgo., Feb. 1, 1935; s. Martin and Mildred (Veverka) V.; m. Marilyn Y. Young, June 23, 1956; children: Christine, Debra, Evelyn. AB, Albion Coll., 1956; MS, U. Mo., 1958, profl. degree in chemistry, 1994. Rsch. chemist Allied Chem. Corp., Morristown, NJ, 1959—64, AEC/Nat. Lead Co., Cin., 1957; sales mgr. Aldrich Chem. Co., Inc., Milw., 1964-66, dir. mktg., 1966-68; pres., chmn. Camag, Inc., 1968-79, Fotodyne Inc. and Variquest Techs., Inc., Hartland, Wis., 1980—; ret. Contbr. articles to profl. jours. and books. Co-founder Chem. Rsch. Found.; Florentine Opera Co.; bd. dirs. various civic and indsl. orgns.; chmn. bd. trustees, pres. U. Mo., Rolla; trustee Opera Am. Recipient Disting. Alumni award Albion Coll., 1994, Disting. Alumni Achievement award U. Mo., 1998. Mem. Am. Chem. Soc., Coun. Ind. Mgrs., Wis. Acad. Scis., Arts and Letters, Ind. Bus. Assn. Wis., Wis. Bus. Assn. Congregationalist. Achievements include 8 patents; discovery of Bismuth Dimethylglyoxime and F3NO. Office: PO Box 704 Brookfield WI 53008

VITEK, VACLAV, materials scientist; b. Olomouc, Czechoslovakia, Sept. 10, 1940; came to U.S., 1978; s. Josef and Ruzena V.; m. Ludovita Stankovicova, Aug. 5, 1972; children: Adrian Joseph, Clementine Mary. BSc in Physics, Charles U., Prague, 1962; PhD in Physics, Czechoslovakian Acad. Scis., Prague, 1966; hon. doctorate, Tech. U. Brno, 1999. Research assoc. dept. metall. materials sci. and research fellow Wolfson Coll., Oxford (Eng.) U., 1967-75; research officer Central Elec. Research Labs., Central Elec. Generating Bd., Leatherhead, Eng., 1975-78; prof. materials sci. and engring. U. Pa., 1978—. Vis. prf. U. Groningen, The Netherlands, 1985-86. Recipient Humboldt award for sr. scientists, Germany, 1992-93, Acta metallurgica Gold medal, 1996, Mach medal Czech Acad. Scis., 1999. Fellow Inst. Physics (London), Am. Soc. Metals Internat., Metals, Minerals Materials Soc.; mem. Am. Phys. Soc., Materials Rsch. Soc. Office: U Pa Dept Materials Sci and Engring 3231 Walnut St Philadelphia PA 19104-6202 E-mail: vitek@lrsm.upenn.edu.

VITETTA, ELLEN S. microbiologist educator, immunologist; BA, Conn. Coll.; MS, NYU, 1966, PhD, MD, 1968. Prof. microbiology Southwestern Med. Sch., U. Tex., Dallas, 1976—; dir. Cancer Immunobiology Ctr., U. Tex., Dallas, 1988—; Sheryle Simmons Patigian Disting. chair in cancer immunobiology Southwestern Med. Sch., U. Tex., Dallas, 1989—. Bd. sci. coun. NCI Cancer Treatment Bd., 1993; sci. adv. bd. Howard Hughes Med. Inst., 1992—; Kettering selection com. GM Cancer Rsch. Foun., 1987-88; task force NIAID in Immunology, 1989-90; mem. sci. bd. Ludwig Inst., 1983—. Mem. editl. bd.: Advances in Host Defense Mechanisms, 1983—, Annual Review of Immunology, 1991—, Bioconjugate Chemistry, 1989-93, Cellular Immunology, 1984-93, Current Opinions in Immunology, 1992—, FASEB Journal, 1987—, Internat. Jour. of Oncology, 1992—, Internat. Soc. Immunopharmacology, 1989—, Jour. of Immunology, 1975-78, Molecular Immunology, 1978-93; assoc. editor Cancer Research, 1986—; Immunochemistry sect. editor: Jour. of Immunology, 1978-82; co-editor in chief: Therapeutic Immunology, 1992—. Recipient Women's Excellence in Sci. award Fedn. Am. Soc. Exptl. Biology, 1991, Taittinger Breast Cancer Rsch. award Komen Found., 1983, Pierce Immunotoxin award, 1988, NIH Merit award, 1987—, U. Tex. Southwestern Med. Sch. Faculty Teaching awards 1989, 91, 92, 93, 94, FASED Excellence in Sci. award, 1991, Abbot Clinical Immunology award Am. Soc. Microbiologists, 1992, Past State Pres. award Tex. Fed. Bus. Profl. Women's Club, 1993, Richard and Hinda Rosenthal Found. award Am. Assn. Cancer Rsch 1995, Charlotte Friend award Am. Assn. Cancer Rsch., 1995, AAAS Mentreny award, 2002. Mem. Am. Assn. Immunologists (pres. 1994), Nat. Acad. Scis., Am. Acad. Microbiology (hon.). Achievements include co-discovery of IL-4, development of immunotoxins and identification of IgD on murine B cells. Office: Univ Texas Cancer Immunobiol Ctr 6000 Harry Hines Blvd Dallas TX 75235-5303 Address: 6914 Pemberton Dr Dallas TX 75230-4260 E-mail: ellen.vitetta@utsouthestern.edu.

VITEZ, MICHAEL, reporter; b. Washington, 1957; m. Maureen Fitzgerald; children: Timmy, Sally, Jonathan. Degree, U. Va., 1979. Past reporter Hartford Courant, Washington Star, Virginian-Pilot, Norfolk; reporter Phila. Inquirer, 1985—. Co-recipient Pulitzer Prize for explanatory journalism, 1997. Office: Phila Inquirer PO Box 8263 Philadelphia PA 19101-8263

VITHARANA, PADMAL M. management educator; BS, Univ. Wis., La-Crosse, 1988, MBA, 1990, PhD, 2000. Asst. prof. Syracuse U., Syracuse, NY, 2000—. Author: (ieee transactions on software engring.) Computer-Mediated Group Support, Anonymity and the Software Inspection Process: An Empirical Investigation; actor: (ieee transactions on software engring.) Knowledge-based Repository Scheme for Storing and Retrieving Business Components: A Theoretical Design and an Empirical Analysis; author: (communications of the acm) Risks and Challenges of Component-based Software Development, Component-based Software Development: Design, Retrieval, and Assembly. Office: Syracuse U Schoolof Mgmt Suite 400 Syracuse NY 13244

VITIELLO, MICHAEL V. gerontologist, educator; s. Americo M. and Ann Carillo Vitiello(Stepmother). AB, Columbia U., 1969—73; PhD, U. of Wash., 1973—80. Asst. prof. of psychiatry and behavioral sciences U. of Wash., Seattle, 1985—87, assoc. prof. of psychiatry and behavioral sciences, 1987—93, prof. of psychiatry and behavioral sciences, 1993—; assoc. dir. Northwest Geriatric Edn. Ctr., 2004—. Editor-in-chief (for the americas) sleep medicine reviews Elsevier Sci. Ltd., Oxford, United Kingdom, 1997—; spl. asst. to the vice provost for rsch. U. of Wash., 1998—2002, asst. vice provost rsch., 2002—03, dir., grant and contract initiative, 1999—2003; head, circadian rhythms sect. Sleep Rsch. Soc., Chgo., 2001—; program com. Associated Profl. Sleep Societies, Chgo., 2001—. New Investigator Rsch. award, Nat. Inst. on Aging, 1983—86, Ind. Scientist Career award, NIMH, 1994—99, 1999—2004, Sleep Medicine Rsch. and Ednl. Found. Grant, Am. Acad. of Sleep Medicine, 2002—03. Fellow: Gerontol. Soc. of Am.; mem.: Internat. Coll. of Geriatric Psychoneuopharmacology, European Sleep Rsch. Soc., Sleep Rsch. Soc. (bd. of dirs. 2001—04). Independent. Avocations: cooking, travel, reading, photography, hiking. Home: 5134 26th Ave NE Seattle WA 98105 Office: U Wash Psychiatry Box 356560 Seattle WA 98195 6560 Office Phone: 206-616-3444. Personal E-mail: vitiello@u.washington.edu. E-mail: vitiello@u.washington.edu.

VITKOWSKY, VINCENT JOSEPH, lawyer; b. Newark, Oct. 3, 1955; s. Boniface and Rosemary (Ofack) Vitkowsky; m. Mary Gunzburg, May 16, 1981 (div. 1997); children: Vincent Jr., Victoria, Pierce; m. Pandora Strasler, Sept. 18, 1999. BA, Northwestern U., 1977; JD, Cornell U., 1980. Bar: NY 1981. Assoc. Hart and Hume, N.Y.C., 1980-84, Kroll & Tract, 1984-87; of counsel Nixon, Hargrave, Devans & Doyle, 1988-89; ptnr. Buchalter, Nemer, Fields & Younger, 1990-95, Edwards & Angell LLP, 1996—. Mem. panel arbitration London Ct. Internat. Arbitration; lectr. in field. Contbr. articles to profl. jours. Mem. ABA (com. chmn.), Am. Arbitration Assn. (internat. panel arbitrators), Internat. Bar Assn. (com. officer), Assn. Bar City of NY, Cornell Club, Federalist Soc. Law and Pub. Policy (mem. exec. com. internat. and nat. security practice group, steering com. N.Y. chpt.), IBA Human Rights Inst. (officer, com. on interventions and trial observations). Home: 422 E 72d St Apt 15E New York NY 10021 Office: Edwards & Angell LLP 750 Lexington Ave Fl 12 New York NY 10022-1253 Office Phone: 212-756-0238. E-mail: vvitkowsky@edwardsangell.com.

VITRAC, JEAN-JACQUES CHARLES, international business consultant; b. Paris, May 31, 1942; came to U.S., 1972; s. Jean Bernard Vitrac and Paulette Aimée (Buisson) Mannerheim; m. Roswitha Kahling, Sept. 11, 1965; children: Emmanuel, François, Catherine. Diploma, Faculty of Law, Aix, France, 1963; post grad. in mktg., Institut National Du Marketing, Paris, 1972; post grad. in econ. scis., Institut Superieur Sciences Economiques, Paris, 1979. Devel. officer Europe-Africa Internat. Jaycees, Geneva, 1968-70; dir. econ. affairs Internat. Jaycees, Coral Gables, Fla., 1970-72; mktg. cons. Bernard Krief Internat., Paris, 1973-79; strategy cons. Euro-PacRim Internat., Walnut Creek, Calif., 1980—. Owner Domaine Becquet Winery, Valley Springs, Calif.; chair task force on multinat. strategies Ctrl. Bank of France, Paris, 1974-78; mktg. cons. Aérospatiale, Paris, 1978; bd. dirs. Capsule Française Inc., Napa, Calif.; asst. prof. mktg. Inst. Français de Gestion, Paris, 1973-79; U.S. chmn. L'Entreprise Demain, Brussels, 1982-98; no. Calif. chmn. World Tech. Execs. Network, 1987-90. Author: Discover Export, 1974; co-author: Doing Business in California, 1989; editor World Tech. Execs. Network Review, 1989-90. Bd. dirs. E. Bay Internat. Trade Coun., 1996-97; chair parish coun. St. Patrick's Ch., 1998, 99; trustee Mark Twain St. Joseph's Hosp. Found., 1999-2004, exec. bd. mem., pub. rels. com. co-chair, 2000-2001; elected to Calaveras County Rep. Ctrl. Com., 2001. Named knight Equestrian Order of Holy Sepulchre of Jerusalem. Mem. KC (dep. grand knight 1998, treas. 1999-2001, Grand Knight 2001-2002, trustee 2002-04), Am. Assn. Polit. Cons., Art Ranaissance Found. (hon., chair Calif. chpt. 1994—), Classical Philharmonic (v.p. 1995-96), Cal-France Coun. (v.p. 1996-97), Kiwanis Internat (gov.'s cabinet, div. com. svc. 1996-97), French War Vets. (No. Calif. chpt. pres. 1996-97), Napa Kiwanis Club (disting. pres. 1993, bd. dirs. Calif.-Nev.-Hawaii Found. 1996-98), Wine Inst., Calaveras Wine Assn., West Calaveras Rotary (founding pres. 2000-2001), Jackson Rotary. Republican. Roman Catholic. Home: Becket's Ranch PO Box 467 Valley Springs CA 95252 Office: Euro PacRim Int Corp 2173 Hwy 12 East PO Box 1418 Valley Springs CA 95252-1418 Office Phone: 209-772-3469. E-mail: californieusa@yahoo.fr.

VITRANO, FRANK, supermarket executive; b. 1955; With Pathmark Stores Inc., Carteret, N.J., 1972—, v.p., treas., exec. v.p., CFO, treas., 1998—. Office: Path Mark Stores Inc 200 Milik St Carteret NJ 07008

VITT, DAVID AARON, medical manufacturing company executive; b. Phila., Aug. 3, 1938; s. Nathan and Flora B.; m. Renee Lee Salkever, Oct. 20, 1963; children: Nadine Lori Einiger, Jeffrey Richard. BS, Temple U., 1961. Sales engr. X-Ray Corp., Phila., 1961-65, Midwest Am., Chgo., 1965-67, product mgr., 1967-68, product mgr. regional sales, 1968-70; dir. mktg. Valtronic & Living Wills, Bronx, NY, 1970-74; v.p., gen. mgr. dental divsn. Siemens Med. Sys. Inc., Iselin, NJ, 1974—86, past corp. v.p., gen. mgr. dental divsn.; CEO, pres. Pelton & Crane, Charlotte, NC, 1986-89; v.p. govt. sales, ret. Siemens Med. Sys., 1994; founder, pres., CEO D.A.V., Inc., 1995—; founder, co-owner RealDental.com. Pres. Denx Am. Inc., 1998; industry rep. to Am. Nat. Stds. Inst.; co. rep. U.S.-USSR Trade and Econ. Coun.; co-founder Enter Am. Group Exec. Consultants. Bd. dirs. Am. Fund for Dental Health; apptd. mem. Charlotte Mecklenburg Cmty. Rels. Com.; mem. bd. visitors U. N.C., Charlotte; officer, mem. exec. com. Jr. Achievement. Served in USAR, 1961-68. Mem. Am. Mgmt. Assn. (bd. dirs. N.J. chpt.), Am. Mktg. Assn., Am. Dental Trade Assn. (bd. dirs.), Dental Mfrs. Am. (past pres.), Am. Acad. Dental Radiology, Charlotte C. of C. (bd. advisors), Acad. Gen. Dentists (bd. mem. found.), Masons (32d deg.), Shriners. Republican.

VITTER, DAVID, congressman; b. May 15, 1961; m. Wendy Baldwin; children: Sophie, Lise and Airey (twins). BA magna cum laude, Harvard U.; MA in History/Econs. with highest honors, Oxford U.; JD with honors, Tulane U. Bus. atty., La.; mem. La. Ho. of Reps., 1971-99, U.S. Congress from 1st. dist. La., 1999—, mem. transp. and judiciary com., govt. reform com., approp. com., 1999—. Adj. prof. law Tulane U., Loyola U., New Orleans. Articles editor Tulane Law Rev. Lecotr. St. Francis Xavier Cath. Ch., Metairie, La. Rhodes scholar. Mem. Phi Beta Kappa. Republican. Office: 414 Cannon House Ofc Bldg Washington DC 20515-0551

VITTETOE, MARIE CLARE, retired clinical laboratory science educator; b. Keota, Iowa, May 19, 1927; d. Edward Daniel and Marcella Matilda Vittetoe. BS, Marycrest Coll., 1950; MS, W.Va. U., 1971, EdD, 1973. Staff technologist St. Joseph Hosp., Ottumwa, Iowa, 1950-70; instr. Ottumwa Hosp. Sch. Med. Tech., 1957-70, St. Joseph Hosp. Sch. Nursing, Ottumwa, 1950-70; asst. prof. U. Ill., Champaign-Urbana, 1973-78; prof. clin. lab. scis. U. Ky., Lexington, 1978-94. Mem. Sisters of Humility of Mary, 1946—; chair Congregation of Humility of Mary; clin. lab. asst. 6 clinics in Haiti. Author: Vittetoe Family Tree and Scrapbook, 2000, Peiffer-Berg Family Tree and Scrapbook, 2000, Lutz/Peiffer Family Tree Update, 2002, Vittetoe Family Tree Update, 2002; contbr. articles to profl. jours. Vol. hosp. labs., Haiti, 1999—. Named Ky. Col., Marie Vittetoe award for excellence in svc. named for her, U. Ky., 1999; recipient Kingston award for Creative Tchg., Recognition award for svc. to edn., Commonwealth of Ky. Coun. on Higher Edn., disting. grad. award, Nat. Cath. Ednl. Assn., 1995, devel. of youth award, Iowa 4-H Found., 1996, award for devel. Best Little Lab. in Haiti, 2002. Mem. Am. Soc. for Med. Tech. (chmn. 1986-89, Profl. Achievement award 1991, Ky. Mem. of Yr. award 1994), Am. Soc. Clin. Lab. Scis., Am. Soc. Clin. Pathologists (assoc.), Alpha Mu Tau, Phi Delta Kappa, Alpha Eta. Avocations: walking, genealogy.

VITTON, JOHN JOSEPH, education educator; b. Trimountain, Mich., Sept. 4, 1930; s. John Joseph and Minne Claire Vitton; m. Mary Lee Sherman, May 29, 1957; children: Michael, James, Elizabeth, Thomas, Charles, Kathleen. BS Metall. Engring., Mich. Tech. Univ., Houghton, Mich., 1951; MBA, Ohio State Univ., Columbus, Ohio, 1956; PhD, Univ. Nebr., Lincoln, Nebr., 1982. Metall. engring. Ladish Co., Milw., 1951—53; regular officer, Lt. Col. USAF, 1953—82, dir., 1970—71; squardon comdr. Offutt AFB, Omaha, 1974—76; asst. prof. econ. USAF Acad., Colo. Springs., Colo., 1965—68; instr. Univ. Nebr. Omaha, Omaha, 1980—82; assoc. prof. NW Mo. State Univ., Maryville, Mo., 1982—86, Univ. N.D., Grand Forks, ND, 1986—2001, chmn. mgmt. dept., 2001—04. Author: (case studies) NACRA Proceedings, 1994—; contbr. articles pub. to profl. jour. Campaign mgr. Henry Doorly Zoo, Omaha, 1979—80; pres., bd. dirs. Columbia Pk. Towers Assoc., Grand Forks, Mich., 2000—03; founder, player Ohio State Univ. Ice Hockey, Columbus, Ohio, 1956; coach, devel. USAF Ice Hockey Team Club, Colo. Springs, Colo., 1966. Lt. col. USAF, 1953—80, USA, Thailand. Mem.: N. Am. Case Rsch. Assn., Acad. Mgmt., Gamma Beta Sigma. Republican. Avocations: ice hockey, photography, swimming, travel, baseball coach. Home: Columbia Pk Towers 2200 S 29th N 21 Grand Forks ND 58201 Office: Mgmt Dept Box 8377 2934 Centennial Dr Grand Forks ND 58202

VITTOR, KENNETH MARK, lawyer; b. L.I. BS, Cornell U., 1971; JD, U. Chgo., 1974. Assoc. Cahill, Gordon & Reindel, N.Y.C., 1974-80; atty. McGraw-Hill Cos., N.Y.C., 1980-95, various positions to exec. v.p., gen. counsel The McGraw-Hill Cos., Inc., N.Y.C., 1995—. Chmn. Libel Def. Resource Ctr., 1999-2000. Mem. Copyright, Patent and Trademark Commn., Freedom to Read Commn., Assn. of Am. Pubs., Mag. Pubs. Am. (chmn. legal affairs com.), Lawyers Commn. (chmn. libel, privacy and first admendment sub-com. 1983-86). Office: The McGraw-Hill Cos Inc 48th Fl 1221 Avenue Of The Americas New York NY 10020-1001

VITTY, RODERIC BEMIS, retired financial planner, publishing executive; b. St. Johnsbury, Vt., July 28, 1933; s. Clarence Lucian and Leota (Cobleigh) V.; m. Virginia Gable, March, 1960 (div. 1983); children: Roderic G., Virginia A., David P., Suzanne L.; m. Patricia Lyster, June 21, 1986. BS, U.S. Mil. Acad., 1955; MS in Fin. Svcs., Am. Coll., Bryn Mawr, Pa., 1977, MS in Mgmt., 1987; postgrad. exec. mgmt. program, Columbia U., 1985. CLU; chartered fin. cons.; cert. fin. planner. With Conn. Gen. Life Ins. Co. (CIGNA-Lincoln Fin. Advisor), 1960, mgr. br. office, 1968—, mgr. Greater Phila. office, 1981—, mktg. gen. mgr., 1983—85, gen. mgr., regional v.p., 1985—94. Pub., owner Vt. Heritage press, Caber Pub. Ltd. Trustee St. Johnsbury Acad., Vt., 1993—, co-chair capital campaign, 1999; mem assembly of overseers Dartmouth-Hitchcock Med. Ctr. Served with inf. U.S. Army, 1955-59, Pa. N.G., 1961-68. Recipient GAMA Master Agy. Builder award, 1982-92, Nat. Mgmt. awards (20), 1972-92, Outstanding Agy. awards (9), CIGNA; named to CIGNA Hall of Fame, 1998. Mem. West Point Soc. Phila. (pres. 1969-71, 89-94, emeritus, 1994), Nat. Assn. Ins. and Fin. Advisors, South Jersey Fin. Planning Coun., Internat. Assn. Fin. Planners, Soc. of Fin. Svc. Profls., So. N.J. Gen. Agts. and Mgrs. Assn. (pres. 1979-80), Nat. GAMA (regional v.p. 1986-89, treas., exec. com. 1991-94), Assn. Grads U.S. Mil. Acad. (trustee 1992—, pres. Class of 1955, 1995-2000), Army Athletic Assn., Sunnybrook Swim Club, Cherry Hill Raquet Club, Riverton Country Club, Quechee Club Vt., St. Johnsbury Country Club, Safari Club Internat., Chevaliers du Tastevin, Union League Phila., St. Andrews Soc. Vt., Masons (32 deg.), Shriners, K.T. Presbyterian. Address: Twildoon Lodge-Angell Trail PO Box 151 Quechee VT 05059-0151

VITVITSKY, JACK, physician assistant; b. White Plains, N.Y., Mar. 8, 1945; s. Alexander Jack and Helen Louise Virginia (Rider) V. BS, U. Rochester, 1968; AAS, Cuyahoga C.C., Cleve., 1978; postgrad., SUNY, Plattsburgh, 1964-66, 73-74, Liberty U., 1994—. Cert. first aid and CPR instr. ARC; cert. EMT instr. N.Y.; cert. ground and flight instr., instrument instr., multi-engine instr., written test examiner FAA. Physician's asst. Planned Parenthood No. N.Y., 1979-84, Dr. David P. Gorman, Malone, N.Y., 1980-81, N.Y. State Dept. Corrections, Dannemora, N.Y., 1981-84, N.Y. State Office Mental Retardation and Devel. Disabilities, Tupper Lake, N.Y., 1984-85, N.Y. State Dept. Corrections, Raybrook, NY, 1985—2002; ret., 2002; owner Adirondack Computer Testing Ctr., 1996—; assoc. sales rep. Primerica Fin. Svcs., Plattsburg, NY, 2002—04; bus driver Franklin County Assn. Sr. Citizens at Saranac Lake Ctr., NY. Contbr. articles to profl. jours. Active Lake Placid Vol. Ambulance Svc., Inc., 1975—, Nat. Ski Patrol System, 1975—; mem. aviation explorer program Boy Scouts Am. With U.S.Army Res., 1981-84, N.Y. Army N.G., 1984—. Mem. Am. Acad. Physician Assts. (cons. minority affairs com. 1999-2001), N.Y. State Soc. Physician Assts., Soc. Army Physician Assts. (del. to Am. Acad. Physician Assts. Ho. of Dels.), Adirondack Soc. Physician Assts. (sec. 1996—), Mid-Hudson Assn. Physician Assts., Fellowship Christian Physician Assts. (sec. 1992-97), Exptl. Aviation Assn., Aircraft Owners and Pilots Assn., U.S. Army Flight Soc. of Flight Surgeons, NRA, Gun Owners Am. Republican. Avocations: snowshoeing, skiing, writing, woodworking, equine activities. Home: 451 Old Military Rd Lake Placid NY 12946-1824 Office: NY Army NG 147 Warren St Glens Falls NY 12801 also: Adirondack Computer Testing Ctr Adirondack Regional Airport Box 209A Saranac Lake NY 12983

VITZ, PAUL CLAYTON, psychologist, educator; b. Toledo, Aug. 27, 1935; m. Evelyn Birge; 6 children. BA high honors in Psychology, U. Mich., 1953; PhD, Stanford U., 1962. Instr. psychology Pomona (Calif.) Coll., 1962-64; asst. prof. NYU, 1965-70, assoc. prof., 1970-85, dir. psychology dept. undergrad. program, 1973-79, prof., 1985—, acting dir. master's program, 1988-89, 90-91, acting dir. grad. program, 1989-90. Adj. prof. John Paul II Inst. on Marriage and Family, Washington, 1990-2003, Internat. Acad. Philosophy, 1994-98, Inst. for Psychol. Scis., 2000—; lectr. in field. Author: Psychology as Religion: The Cult of Self-Worship, 1977, 2d edit., 1994, (with A.B. Glimcher) Modern Art and Modern Science: The Parallel Analysis of Vision, 1984, Censorship: Evidence of Bias in Our Children's Textbooks, 1986, Sigmund Freud's Christian Unconscious, 1988, Faith of the Fatherless: The Psychology of Atheism, 1999; editor: (with S. Krason) Defending the Family: A Sourcebook, 1998; contbr. articles to profl. jours., chpts. to books. Rsch. grantee Nat. Inst. Mental Health, 1963-64, 64-66, 66-67, Nat. Inst. Neurol. Diseases and Blindness grantee, 1970-73, 73-74, Shalom Found. grantee, 1974-78, Nat. Inst. Edn. grantee, 1983, 84-85, Dept. Edn. grantee, 1986-87. Office: NYU Dept Psychology New York NY 10003

VIVIANO, JOSEPH P. food products executive; BBA, Xavier U. With Delmonico Foods, Inc., 1960-66; pres. Delmonico Foods, Inc. (acquired by Hershey Foods Corp. 1966), San Giorgio Macaroni Co. subs. Hershey Foods Corp., San Giorgio-Skinner Co. subs. Hershey Foods Corp.; v.p. ops. Hershey Foode Corp.; sr. v.p., pres. Hershey Chocolate; pres., COO Hershey Foods Corp., vice chmn., 1999—. Office: Hershey Foods Corp 100 Crystal A Dr Unit 8 Hershey PA 17033-9702

VIVIO, FRANK MICHAEL, education educator, researcher; b. Norway, Mich., Apr. 16, 1945; s. Frank Joseph and Ann Marie Vivio; m. Patricia NMN Moulas, Dec. 28, 1969; children: Frank, Nicholas, Christopher. BS, Mich. State Univ., E. Lansing, MI, 1967, MS, 1972, PhD, 1974. HS instr. Benton Harbor HS, Benton Harbor, Mich., 1967—72; asst. dir., spl. program Mich. State Univ., E. Lansing, Mich., 1974—76; planning and evalu. officer E./W. Ctr., Honolulu, 1976—80; asst. dir., ed. program Argonne Nat. Lab., Argonne, Ill., 1980—. Cons. Univ. of Alberta & World Bank, Alberta, Canada, 1980; panel mem. Nat. Acad. of Sci., Wash., DC, 1991—93. Author: (evaluation report) Internat. Atomic Energy Agy., 1984, (evaluation reports) Dept. of Energy Ed., 1986—96. Pres. Naperville Mcpl. Band, Naperville, Ill., 1997. Mem.: Naperville Mcpl. Band (section head 2001—). Avocation: music. Home: 25 W 101 Cape Rd Naperville IL 60540 Office: Argonne Nat Lab 9700 So Cass Ave Argonne IL 60439

VIVONA, DANIEL NICHOLAS, chemist; b. Chgo., Apr. 13, 1924; s. Daniel and Mary Rose (Lomonico) V.; m. Helen Mary Belanger, Sept. 14, 1950; 1 child, Daniel Maurice. Student, Chgo. City Coll., 1941-42; BA, U. Maine, 1951; MS, Pa. State U., 1953; postgrad., Purdue U., 1953-56. Instr. chemistry Purdue U., Lafayette, Ind., 1955-56; with Minn. Mining and Mfg. Co., St. Paul, 1956-86, sr. chemist, 1969-79, info. scientist, 1979-81, quality assurance sr. chemist, 1981-86, cons., 1986—. With USAAF, 1943-45. Decorated Air medal with oak leaf clusters, DFC. Dow Corning fellow, 1952-53. Mem. Am. Chem. Soc., Phi Beta Kappa. Roman Catholic. Home: 3253 Kraft Cir N Lake Elmo MN 55042-9720 Office: Beta of Dan Vivona 3253 Kraft Circle N Lake Elmo MN 55042-0128

VIZARD, MICHAEL, periodical editor; Degree in Journalism, Boston (Mass.) U. Editor PC Week, Computerworld, Digital Review; editor news InfoWorld, 1995—96, exec. news editor, 1996—99, editor-in-chief, 1999—2002; editor-in-chief CRN CMP Media, 2002—. Office: CMP World-wide Media Networks 600 Community Drive Manhasset NY 11030-3150

VIZCAINO, HENRY P. mining engineer, consultant; b. Hurley, N.Mex., Aug. 28, 1918; s. Emilio D. and Petra (Perea) V.; m. Esther B. Lopez, Sept. 16, 1941; children: Maria Elena, Rick, Arthur, Carlos. BS in Engring., Nat. U., Mexico City, 1941; geology student, U. N.Mex., 1951-54. Registered profl. engr. With Financiera Minera S.A., Mexico City, 1942-47; gen. mgr. Minas Mexicanas S.A., Torreon, Mex., 1947-51; exploration engr. Kerr McGee Corp., Okla., 1955-69; cons. Albuquerque, 1969-75, 84—; regional geologist Bendix Field Engring., Austin, Tex., 1976-79, staff geo-scientist Grand Junction, Colo., 1979-81; sr. geologist Hunt Oil Co., Dallas, 1981-84. Contbr. articles to profl. publs. Mem. AIME, Internat. Platform Assn., Aircraft Owners and Pilots Assn., Rotary, Elks. Republican. Congregationalist. Home and Office: 214 Lynn Oaks Ave Thousand Oaks CA 91320-4755

VIZQUEL, OMAR ENRIQUE, professional baseball player; b. Caracus, Venezuela, Apr. 24, 1967; Grad. high sch., Caracus. With Seattle Mariners, 1989-93; shortstop Cleve. Indians, 1994—. Recipient Winner Am. League Golden Glove, 1993-96. Office: Cleve Indians 2401 Ontario St Cleveland OH 44115-4003

VIZY, KALMAN NICHOLAS, research physicist, educator; b. Gyor, Hungary, July 7, 1940; came to U.S., 1954, naturalized, 1962; s. Joseph and Helen Julianna (Meleg) V.; m. Mary Anne Smith, Aug. 31, 1968; children: Anne Katharine, Edward Kalman. B Engring. Sci., Cleve. State U., 1964; MS, John Carroll U., 1967; PhD, Walden U., 1990. Registered profl. engr., N.Y. Apprentice design engr. Warner & Swasey, Cleve., 1959-64; tchr., head dept. scis. Byzantine Ednl. Ctr., Parma, Ohio, 1964-67; rsch. physicist Eastman Kodak Rsch. Labs., Rochester, N.Y., 1967-79, corp. tech. and sci. advisor, 1080-91, worldwide tech. lectr., 1980—. Adj. prof. physics Rochester Inst. Tech., 1968—, Roberts Wesleyan Coll., 1993—, SUNY, Brockport, 2001—; adj. asst. prof. radiology U. Rochester Med. Ctr., 1990—. Mem. Rochester-Rennes Sister Cities Com., 1977—. Recipient Excellence in Tchg. award Rochester Inst. Tech., 1980. Mem. ASME, NSPE, Am. Soc. Photogrammetry (cert. photogrammetrist, cert. remote sensing specialist, autometric award 1975), N.Y. State Soc. Profl. Engrs., Am. Assn. Physics Tchr., Am. Assn. Physicists in Medicine, Optical Soc. Am. (house chmn. 1975), Am. Phys. Soc., Soc. Photog. Scientists and Engrs. (inter-soc. rep. 1975-79), Soc. Info. Displays, Am. Coll. Radiology, Rochester Acad. Scis. (v.p. 1993-98), Health Physics Soc. (pres. 1999-00). Achievements include inventions in field. Home and Office: 16 Clearview Dr Spencerport NY 14559-1118

VLACH, JIRI, electrical engineering educator, researcher; b. Prague, Czechoslovakia, Oct. 5, 1922; emigrated to Can., 1969; s. Frantisek and Bozena (Papouskova) V.; m. Dagmar Gutova, Oct. 22, 1949; 1 son, Martin. Dipl.eng., Tech. U. Prague, 1947, C.Sc., 1957. With Research Inst. for Radio Communications, Prague, 1948-67, head math. dept., until 1967; vis. prof. U. Ill., Urbana, 1967-69; prof. elec. engring. U. Waterloo (Ont., Can.), 1969—. Author: Computerized Approximation and Synthesis of Linear Networks, 1969, (with others) Computer Methods for Circuit Analysis and Design, 1983, 2d edit., 1994, Basic Network Theory with Computer Applications, 1992; assoc. editor IEEE Trans. on Circuits and Systems, 1979-80, 87-88, 98—. Fellow IEEE (life); mem. Eta Kappa Nu Home: 355 Craigleith Dr Waterloo ON Canada N2L 5B5 Office: U Waterloo 200 University Ave West Waterloo ON Canada N2L 3G1

VLACHOS, PETER GEORGE, economics professor; b. Apr. 4, 1944; s. George Peter and Thelma Lucille (Ridenour) Vlachos. BA, U. Cin., 1966, MA, 1967, PhD, 1969. Econ. affairs officer UN, Bangkok, 1975; assoc. prof. econs. and quantitative methods U. Hawaii, Honolulu, 1969—83; prof. Shanghai Inst. Internat. Econ. Mgmt., 1984—; staff planner City and County of Honolulu Dept. Gen. Planning, 1986, Hawaii State Dept. Land and Natural Resources, 1987—88; mgr. customer support Chase Manhattan Bank, NY, 1989—90; ind. economist, 1983—. Cons. in field; vis. prof. Waseda U., Tokyo, 1973, Aoyama Gakuin Daigaku, Tokyo, 1977, Xavier U., Cin., 1973, Cin., 77, Roosevelt U., Honolulu, 1986—89, Wright State U., Dayton, 1989—; coord. U.S. Bur. Census, Dayton and Springfield, Ohio, 2000. Editor: Jour. Readings in Managerial Econs., 1975; contbr. articles to profl. jours. Vol. Atherton br. YMCA, Honolulu, 1971—84; mem. Neighborhood Bd. 8, Neighborhood Commn., Honolulu, 1979—81. Grantee, U. Hawaii, U. Cin., Saudi Arabian Govt. Mem.: NEA, AAUP, Hawaii Edn. Assn., Western Econ. Assn., Am. Econ. Assn. Eastern Orthodox. E-mail: pvlachos45402@yahoo.com.

VLADECK, BRUCE CHARNEY, health services administrator, policy educator; b. N.Y.C., Sept. 13, 1949; s. Stephen Charney and Judith (Pomarlen) V.; m. Fredda Wellin, Aug. 5, 1973; children— Elizabeth Charney, Stephen Isaiah, Abigail Sarah. BA, Harvard U., 1970; MA, U. Mich, 1972, PhD in Polit. Sci., 1973. Assoc. social scientist N.Y.C.-Rand Inst., 1973-74; asst. prof. Columbia U., N.Y.C., 1974-78, assoc. prof., 1978-79; asst. commr. health planning and resources devel. N.J. Dept. Health, Trenton, 1979-82; asst. v.p. Robert Wood Johnson Found., Princeton, N.J., 1982-83; pres. United Hosp. Fund, N.Y.C., 1983-93; adminstr. HCFA, Washington, 1993-97; prof. health policy and geriatrics Mt. Sinai Med. Ctr., N.Y.C., 1997—. Mem. N.Y. State Coun. on Health Care Financing, Albany, 1978-92; mem. com. on nursing home regulation Inst. Medicine, Washington, 1983-85, chmn. com. on health care for homeless people, 1986-88, mem. prospective payment assessment com., 1986-93; mem. Nat. Bipartisan Commn. on Future of Medicare, 1997-98. Author: Unloving Care: The Nursing Home Tragedy, 1981. Contbr. numerous articles to profl. publs. Fellow N.Y. Acad. Medicine; mem. Inst. Medicine, Nat. Acad. Scis., Phi Beta Kappa. Home: 1212 5th Ave New York NY 10029-5210 Office: Mt Sinai Med Ctr Box 1062 1 Gustave Levy Pl New York NY 10029 Office Phone: 212-241-3845. E-mail: bruce.vladeck@mountsinai.org.

VLADECK, JUDITH POMARLEN, lawyer; b. Norfolk, Va., Aug. 1, 1923; BA, Hunter Coll., 1945; JD, Columbia U., 1947. Bar: NY 1947, US Supreme Ct. 1962. Assoc. Conrad & Smith, N.Y.C., 1947-51; sole practice N.Y.C., 1951-57; mem. Vladeck, Elias, Vladeck & Engelhard P.C., N.Y.C., 1957—; sr. ptnr. Vladeck, Waldman, Elias & Englehard, P.C., N.Y.C. Adj. prof. Fordham Law Sch. Mem. adv. bd. Inst. for Edn. and Rsch. on Women and Work, Cornell U.; bd. dirs. N.Y. Civil Liberties Union, 1963-68; bd. dir., counsel Tamiment Inst., Inc.; bd. dirs. lawyers' coordinating com. AFL-CIO; bd. mem. Non-Traditional Employment for Women. Recipient Hunter Coll. Profl. Achievement award, 1992, Edith Spivack award, 1998, Women of Power and Influence award NY NOW, 1998, ORT Jurisprudence award, 1996; elected to Hunter Coll. Hall of Fame, 1988; Non-Traditional Employment for Women named building Judith P. Vladeck Ctr. for Women, 1989; Margaret Brent Award, ABA 2002; Columbia Law Sch. Assoc. Medal for Excellence, 2003; NEW 25th Anniv. Equity Leadership Award, 2003. Fellow Am. Bar Found., Coll. of Labor and Employment Lawyers; mem. ABA (co-chmn. labor law and equal employment coms., N.Y. State Bar Assn. (labor law com.), Assn. of Bar of City of N.Y., N.Y. County Lawyers Assn., Fed. Bar Assn., Women's Bar Assn., Am. Arbitration Assn. (panel of arbitrators), Columbia Law Sch. Alumni Assn. (bd. dir.), Harlem Inst. Fashion (counsel, bd. dir.). Home: 115 Central Park W New York NY 10023-4153 Office: Vladeck Waldman Elias & Engelhard 1501 Broadway Ste 800 New York NY 10036-5560 Office Phone: 212-403-7300. E-mail: jvladeck@vladeck.com.

VLADEM, STEVEN ALLEN, writer, motivational speaker, film producer; b. Chgo., July 24, 1949; s. Arthur and Elaine Edythe (Ascher) Vladem. BA with honors and distinction, U. Ill., Chgo., 1970; MEd in Math., Northeastern Ill. U., Chgo., 1973; MA in Ednl. Adminstrn./Supervision, Roosevelt U., Chgo., 1975; ScD, London Sch. Applied Rsch., 1993. Tchr. math. Chgo. Bd. Edn., 1971-81, statistician and evaluator dept. rsch. and evaluation, 1979; supr. program svcs. Dept. Planning, Chgo. City Hall, 1981; coord. alt. sch. without walls program Chgo. Met. HS, 1982-87, coord. computer assisted instrn., 1987-91; developer ednl. software Chgo., 1987-92; freelance computer cons., 1987-92; writer/lectr., 1994—; prodr. Image Lost Film, 2003—. Lectr. in field; mktg. cons. Enoch Searle Prodns., 2001—, Cosmic Films, 2001—; motivational spkr. Profl. Spkrs. Bur. Internat., 2001—. Author: (poetry) The Jigsaw People, 1997; exhibitions include Gallery Art, Internat. Congress Arts and Commn., Keble Coll., Oxford U., Eng.; prodr.: Image Last Films, 2003—; exec. prodr.: (films) Gein, 2003. Mem. Internat. Parliament Safety and Peace, Palermo, Italy, 1993—95; bd. dirs. Nat. Coalition health Care Reform, 1998—; founder coun. London Diplomatic Acad., Internat. Diplomatic Acad., Albert Schweitzer Inst., Chgo. Coun. Fgn. Rels., Internat. Fellowship Christians and Jews; sec.-gen. United Cultural Conv.; hon. amb. laureates Jr. Achievement and Chgo. Assn. Bus. and Industry, 1990; support group leader, outreach vol. Nat. Keratoconus Found., L.A., 1995—; docent Tour of Old Town Old Town C. of C., Chgo., 1993; patron various arts orgns.; vol. Sight Savers Internat., Karen Or Ctr. Multi-Handicapped Blind Children, State of Ill. Transplant Program, 2003, Am. Transplant Assn., Cinema for Deaf Film Festival, 2003; judge Daniel Webster Acad. Poets Competition, 1998; nominator Col.'s Way Award. Finalist, U.S. Nat. Memory Championship, N.Y.C., 1997; named John W. Rogers Educator of the Yr., Jr. Achievement, Chgo., 1990; named to Wall of Tolerance, Civil Rights Meml. Ctr., 2003; recipient Congress Star of Distinction, Internat. Congress Arts and Comm./St. John's Coll., Cambridge U., 1992, medal of Merit, Republic of Peru, 1992, Alzheimers Rsch. award, Alzheimers Assn. Am., 2000, Internat. Peace prize, 2002, Congl. medal of Excellence, 2002, Am. medal of Honor, 2002. Mem. NATAS, Ill. Prodn. Alliance, Internat. Platform Assn. (bd. govs. internet team, red carpet com., Gold Ribbon Most Popular Artist 1995), United Writers Assn. (life fellow), World Univ. Roundtable, Toastmasters Internat., Internat. Order of Merit (Cambridge, Eng.), Daniel Webster Acad. Poets (Cert. of Merit 1995), Chrysopoets, Order of Templars of Jerusalem (knight), Lofsensic Ursinius Order (knight comdr.), World Order of Sci. Edn. Culture. (knight-cavalier), Am. Order Excellence, Order of San Ciriaco (count), Internat. Diplomatic Acad., Am. Legion (gold medal, sch. leadership award 1967), Rotary Club, Lions Club. Avocations: cinema, musical theatre, backgammon, architecture, world travel. Home and Office: Evanston Pl 1715 Chicago Ave # 218 Evanston IL 60201-6404 Address: Profl Spkrs Bur Internat 1112 5th Ave Ste 101 Worthington OH 43085 E-mail: stevevladem@yahoo.com.

VLADUTIU, ADRIAN O. physician, educator; b. Bucharest, Romania, Aug. 5, 1940; came to U.S., 1969, naturalized 1974; s. Octavian and Veturia (Chirescu) V.; m. Georgirene D. Therrien; children: Christina Lynn, Catherine Joy. MD, Sch. Medicine, Bucharest, 1962; PhD in Immunopathology, Sch. Medicine, Jassy, Romania, 1968. Diplomate Am. Bd. Pathology. Asst. prof. physiopathology Sch. Medicine, Bucharest, 1968-71; assoc. prof. pathology SUNY Sch. Medicine, Buffalo, 1978-81, prof. pathology, 1981—; pathologist Buffalo Gen. Hosp., 1974—, dir. clin. labs., 1982—2001, prof. microbiology, 1982—, prof. medicine, 1985—. Cons. Niagara Falls (N.Y.) Meml. Hosp., 1976—82, Tri-County Hosp., Gowanda, NY, 1991—93; acting head dept. pathology Buffalo Gen. Hosp, 1985—86; dir. lab. Deaconess Hosp. Buffalo, 1982—91, Columbus Meml., Buffalo, 1996—98. Author: Pleural Effusion, 1986; contbr. chapters to books, articles to profl. jours. Med. Rsch. Coun. Can. fellow, 1968, Buswell fellow, 1969; recipient rsch. prize Ministry Edn. Romania, 1965, rsch. award NIH, 1985. Fellow: ACP, Nat. Acad. Clin. Biochemistry, Coll. Am. Pathologists; mem.: Soc. Exptl. Biol. Medicine, Am. Soc. Investigative Pathology, Am. Assn. Immunologists. Achievements include first demonstration of the association of autoimmunity with major histocompability antigens. Home: 80 Oakview Dr Buffalo NY 14221-1420

VLAMIS, SUSAN (SUZANNE) ANNE, editor, photographer; d. Steve Anthony and Anne Lillian Vlamis. BA in English, Long Island U., Bklyn., 1966. Intensive Film Summer Workshop NYU, 1989. Free-lance photographer, N.Y.C., 1967—72; copy asst. to features editor BRIDE'S Mag. Conde Nast, N.Y.C., 1967—68; editl. asst. Victor Riesel-Labor Columnist, N.Y.C., 1969; staff photographer The AP, N.Y.C., 1974—85, news photo editor special projects, 1998—; supervising newsfeatures photo editor AP NewsFeatures, N.Y.C., 1985—98. Sci., health rschr. Dr. Joy C. Zagoren, PhD, N.Y.C., 1999—. Photo editor (biography) John Wayne, prodn. asst. (public access TV) Cable Doctor and Speak Out, photographer (book) Moments In Time - 50 Years of Associated Press News Photos 1985, 1st edit., The Sports 100 - The 100 Greatest Athletes of the 20th Century, 1999, One Day In Our World, Moments In Time- 60 Years of AP News Photos, The Olympics At 100, Am. Photographers, photo editor (biography) Bing Crosby, art reviewer (newspaper) The Jersey City Jour.; one-woman shows include Restoring Lady Liberty, 1986, Jazz Musicians, 1991, Commemorative Photo Exhibition 9/11, Gallery of Graphic Arts and Morning Calm Gallery, 2001, Welfare Island and other Photographs, Long Island U., 1972. V.p. of zoning com. 79th St. Neighborhood Assn., NY, 2002—03; bd. mem., v.p. Sarah Herzog Hosp., Jerusalem, 2002—. Recipient Photographers Sports award, World Press, 1975. Mem.: N.Y. Press Photographers Assn. (1st prize Feature Story for "Centennial Restoration, St. Pat's Cathedral" 1979), Am. Film Inst. (assoc.), Ocean Conservancy, Cousteau Soc., World Wild Life Found., Audobon Soc., George Eastman House N.Y.C. Collecter Club, Sierra Club. Independent. Roman Catholic. Avocations: collect fine arts and illustrated books, yoga, dance, swimming, scuba diving. Home: 405 E 82nd St New York NY 10028 Office: The Associated Press 50 Rockefeller Pl New York NY 10020 Business E-Mail: svlamis@ap.org.

VLAZNY, JOHN GEORGE, bishop; b. Chgo., Feb. 22, 1937; s. John George and Marie Hattie (Brezina) V. BA, St. Mary of the Lake Coll., Mundelein, Ill., 1958; STL, Pontifical Gregorian U., Rome, 1962; MA in Classics, U. Mich., 1967; MEd, Loyola U., 1972; LLD (hon.), U. Portland, 1999. Ordained priest Roman Cath. Ch., 1961, consecrated bishop Roman Cath. Ch., 1983. Assoc. pastor St. Paul of the Cross Ch., Park Ridge, Ill., 1962—63, St. Clement Ch., Chgo., 1963—68, St. Aloysius Ch., Chgo., 1968—72, pastor, 1979—81; assoc. pastor St. Sylvester Ch., Chgo., 1972—74, Precious Blood Ch., Chgo., 1974—79; faculty Quigley Prep., North Chgo., Ill., 1963—79, dean of studies, 1969—79; rector Niles Coll., Chgo., 1981—83; aux. bishop Archdiocese of Chgo., 1983—87; Episcopal vicar Vicariate I, Chgo., 1983—87; bishop Episc. Ch., Winona, Minn., 1987—97; archbishop Diocese of Portland, 1997—. Pres. Presbyteral Senate, Chgo., 1976—77; mem. Diocesan Clergy Personnel Bd., Chgo., 1981—84, chmn., 1983—84. Bd. dirs. NED, Latino Tng. Ctr., Chgo., 1980—81, Sacred Heart Sch. Theology, Hales Corners, Wis., 1986—, St. Mary's Coll., Winona, 1987—. Mem.: Nat. Conf. Cath. Bishops (various coms. 1983—), Nat. Comms. Found. (bd. dirs. 1990—). Roman Catholic. Avocations: music, running.

VLCEK, DONALD JOSEPH, JR., food distribution company executive, consultant, business author, executive coach; b. Chgo., Oct. 30, 1949; s. Donald Joseph and Rosemarie (Krizek) V.; m. Claudia Germain Meyer, July 22, 1978 (div. 1983); 1 child, Suzanne Mae; m. Valeria Olive Russell, Nov. 11, 1989; children: James Donald, Victoria Rose. BBA, U. Mich., 1971. Cert. facilitator Adizes Inst. Gen. mgr. Popps Inc., Hamtramck, Mich., 1969-76; pres. Domino's Pizza Distbn. Corp., Ann Arbor, Mich., 1978-93, chmn., 1993-94, also bd. dirs.; pres. Don Vlcek & Assocs., Ltd., Plymouth, Mich., 1994—; CEO Beaver Buddies, LLC, Plymouth, Mich.; master franchisee Beaver Tails Can., Inc., Mich., Ind., Ill., Ohio, Wis. Profl. speaker, personal coach, seminar leader, bus. cons., workshop facilitator; trustee Domino's Pizza Ptnrs. Found.; bd. dirs. RPM Pizza Inc., Gulfport, Miss., Dimango Corp., South Lyon, Mich.; sr. v.p. distbn. and tech. Domino's Ohio Commissary, Zanesville; pres. Morel Mountain Corp.; judge 1994 Duck Stamp contest U.S. Dept. Interior, Jr. Fed. Duck Stamp Contest, 1995; bd. dirs. Beaver Tails Can. Author: The Domino Effect, 1992 (Best of Bus. award ALA 1992, Soundview's Top 30 Business books of 1993), SuperVision, 1997, Job Planning and Review System Manual, 1997, 2001; (audio cassette tape series Super Vision; contbr. articles to profl. jours. Bd. dirs. Men's Hockey League of Oak Park, Mich., 1973-78; asst. coach Redford Scorpions Jr. Travel Hockey Team. Named Person of Yr. Bd. Franchises, Boston, 1981; recipient Teal award Ducks Unltd., 1992, State Major Gifts Chmn. award, 1992, 93, State Chmn.'s award, 1992, State Major Gifts award, 1994, Russ Bengal award, 2003, Mr. Producer awrad, 1997, 98, 2000, others. Mem. Am. Soc. of Tng. Dirs., Mich. Steelheaders Assn. (life), Ducks Unltd. (life, Domino's Pizza chpt. treas., sponsor, chmn. 1988—, Mich. state bd. dirs., life sponsor, chmn. 1989, 91-92, state trustee 1992-98, hon. trustee 2001—, chmn. exec. com. 1992-94, major gifts chmn. 1993-98, chmn. strategic devel. com. 1994, sponsor in perpetuity Grand Slam Life, Heritage sponsor, recipient Russ Bengal award, 2003), Mich. United Conservation Club (life), Whitetails Unltd. (life), Pheasants Forever (life), Midstates Masters Bowling Assn. (bd. dirs. 1976-85), Barton Hills Country Club (golf com., capt. dist. team), U. Mich. Alumni Assn. (life), Domino's Lodge/Drummond Island Wildlife Habitat Found. (pres., chmn. bd.), Vlcek Family Wildlife Found. (pres., chmn. bd.), Elks (life), Die Hard Cubs Fan Club, Greater Detroit C. of C., Profl. Spkrs. Assn. of Mich. (bd. dirs. 1997-99), Mich. Soc. Assn. Execs., Sm. Bus. Assn. Mich., Nat. Spkrs. Assn., Profl. Spkrs. Ill. (profl.), Internat. Coaching Fedn. (cert. master), Am. Soc. Tng. Dirs. Republican. Roman Catholic. Avocations: hunting, fishing, hockey, collecting wildlife art, coins, and sports cards and memorabilia. Home: 9251 Beck Rd N Plymouth MI 48170-3336 Office: Don Vlcek & Assoc Ltd PO Box 701353 Plymouth MI 48170-0963 Office Phone: 734-459-2285.

VLEISIDES, GREGORY WILLIAM, lawyer; b. Kansas City, Mo., June 17, 1950; s. William Chris and Irene Helen (Karos) V. BA, U. Kans., 1972; JD, U. Mo., Kansas City, 1976. Bar: Mo. 1977, U.S. Dist. Ct. (Mo.) 1977, U.S. Ct. Appeals (8th cir.) 1977, U.S. Ct. Fed. Claims 1990, U.S. Supreme Ct. Law clk. presiding justice Circuit Ct. of Jackson County, Kansas City, 1976-78; assoc. Tierney & Ernst, Kansas City, 1978-86; of counsel Law Office of F. Lee Bailey, Boston, 1982-88; assoc. Turner & Boisseau, Kansas City, 1986-89; mng. ptnr. Vlesides, Donnelly & O'Leary, Kansas City, 1989—. Regional counsel Video Software Dealers Assn., Overland Park, Kans., 1986-89; v.p. legal affairs Nuvidia, LLC. Author: (with others) Challenges to Court Action in Child Abuse and Neglect Cases, 1976, Opening Statements by Julien, 1994, Stein on Closing Arguments, 1994. Mem. ABA, ATLA, Mo. Assn. Trial Lawyers, Kansas City Bar Assn. Republican. Greek Orthodox. Home: 3008 W 84th Pl Leawood KS 66206-1309 Office: Vleisides Donnelly & O Leary LC 4006 Central PO Box 10084 Kansas City MO 64161-0084 Office Phone: 816-931-9500. E-mail: gvleisides@sprintmail.com.

VO, HIEU N. architect; b. Cantho City, Cantho, Vietnam, June 2, 1963; s. Tan T. Vo, Tiet L. Lam; m. Hanh T. none. AA, L.A. Pierce Coll., 1994; BArch (hon.), Calif. State Poly. U., 1998. Project mgr. Underwood Assocs. Architects, Decatur, Ala., 1998—99, L. Hughes Assoc. Architects, Huntsville, Ala., 2000—. Named to The Talent Roster for Disting. Acad. Performance, The Coll. Bd.s Coll. Scholarship Svc., 1993; recipient Concour d'Elegance, Calif. State Poly. U. Coll. of Environ. Design, 1998, Internat. Biog. Centre's 21st award for Achievement. Mem.: AIA (assoc.), Golden Key (life; California State Polytechic University, Pomona, Outstanding Achievement Scholastic and Excellent 1997). Home: 429 Barrington Hills Dr Madison AL 35758 Personal E-mail: HVO24@aol.com.

VO, HUU DINH, pediatrician, educator; b. Hue, Vietnam, Apr. 29, 1950; arrived in U.S., 1975; s. Chanh Dinh and Dong Thi (Pham) Vo; children: Katherine Hao-An, Karyn Bao-An, Hugh Hung. MD, U. Saigon, 1975. Diplomate Am. Bd. Pediat. Adminstr. bilingual vocat. tng. Cmty. Care and Devel. Svc., LA, 1976-77; resident in pediat. Univ. Hosp., Jacksonville, Fla., 1977-80; physician, surgeon, chief med. officer Lanterman Devel. Ctr., Pomona, Calif., 1980-92, chief med. staff, 1984-88, coord. med. ancillary svc., 1984-88, 91—; physician Pomona Valley Cmty. Hosp., 1988-90; asst. clin. prof. Loma Linda (Calif.) Med. Sch., 1985-92; chief med. officer So. Reception Ctr. and Clinic., Norwalk, Calif., 1992-98; physician, surgeon F.C. Nelles Youth Facility, 1998—; med. dir. CTC - HGS Youth Facility, 2004—. Bd. dirs. Pomona Med. Clinic Inc. Radio talk show host, 1997—. Nat. co-chair mem. Vietnamese Am. Cmty. U.S., 1993—95, chmn., bd. comptrs., 1998—; pres. Vietnamese Cmty. Pomona Valley, 1983—85, 1987—95, 1999—, chmn., 1993—95; bd. dirs. YMCA, Pomona, 1988—92, Sch.-Cmty. Partnership, Pomona, 1988—92, ARC, Pomona, 1995—. Mem.: AMA (Physician Recognition award 1989, 1992, 1998), Vietnamese-Am. Physicians Assn. LA and Orange County (founding mem., sec. 1982—84, bd. dirs. 1987—90), LA Pediat. Soc. Republican. Buddhist. Avocations: tennis, soccer, reading, singing, music. Office: Pomona Med Clinic 1182 E Holt Ave Pomona CA 91767 Office Phone: 909-623-8502. Personal E-mail: drhuuvo@hotmail.com.

VO, NGHIA VAN, materials scientist, electrical engineer; b. Saigon, Vietnam, July 18, 1969; arrived in United States, 1997; s. Nga Van Vo and Hoa Thi Do. BSc in Computer Sci. and Applied Math., U. Adelaide, Australia, 1992, BEE, 1993, BSc in Exptl. Physics with honors, 1994; PhD in Materials Engring., U. Wollongong, NSW, Australia, 1997. Cert. sys. engr. Microsoft, 2003. Solid state devices engr. CSIRO, Australia Telescope Nat. Facility, Marsfield, NSW, 1991-92; radio astronomer U. Adelaide, 1993-94; sr. advisor, mentor Wegrona Coll., Wollongong, 1994-96; materials rschr. inst. Materials Tech. and Mfg., Wollongong, 1994-97; rsch. scientist, fellow Los Alamos (N.Mex.) Nat. Lab., 1997-98; materials scientist Intermagnetics Gen. Corp., Schenectady, NY, 1998—2001; lead engr. Gen. Electric Power Sys., Schenectady, 2001—03. Referee Philos. Mag. B, 1997-2003, Jour. Superconductivity, 1997—, Jour. Materials Rsch., 1997—, Superconductor Sci. and Tech., 1997—. Contbr. numerous articles to profl. jours. Referee U.S. Soccer Fedn. Rsch. fellow, Los Alamos Nat. Lab., 1997, NRIM Japan, 1997. Mem. IEEE, AIME, Materials Rsch. Soc. Avocations: classical guitar, swimming, music, reading, martial arts.

VOEGELI, VICTOR JACQUE, history educator, dean; b. Jackson, Tenn., Dec. 21, 1934; s. Victor Jacque Voegeli and Winnie Lassiter; m. Anna Jean King, Oct. 14, 1956; children: Victor Jacque, Charles Lassiter. BS, Murray State Coll., 1956; MA, Tulane U., 1961, PhD, 1965. Instr. history Tulane U., 1963-65, asst. prof., 1965-67; asst. prof. history Vanderbilt U., 1967-69, assoc. prof., 1969-73, prof. history, 1973-98, chmn. history dept., 1973-76, dean Coll. Arts and Sci., 1976-92, acting dean Coll. Arts and Sci., 1996-97, prof. emeritus, dean emeritus, 1998—. Author: Free But Not Equal: The Midwest and the Negro During the Civil War, 1967. Served with U.S. Army, 1956-58. Nat. Endowment Humanities grantee, 1969-70, 72 Mem. So. Hist. Assn. Address: 2110 Golf Club Ln Nashville TN 37215-1224

VOEGTLIN-ANDERSON, MARY MARGARET, secondary school educator, music educator; b. Seattle; d. Joseph Walter and Veronica Margaret (Conroy) Voegtlin; m. Terry Lee Anderson, Mar. 19, 1977 (div. July 20, 1982). BA cum laude, Marylhurst U., 1963; postgrad., U. Wash., 1963—65, Oakland U., 1968, Seattle Pacific U., 1982—84. Cert. std. tchg. grades K-12 Wash. Profl. cellist Oreg. Symphony, Portland, 1962—63; tchr. music and humanities Chinook Mid. Sch., Seattle, 1963—89, gifted edn. specialist, 1983—89; tchr. music, music dept. chair Highline H.S., Seattle, 1989—, tchr. honors English, 1989—. Contralto soloist Mt. Baker Pk. Presbyn. Ch., 1966—68, U. Congl. Ch., Seattle, 1968—73; profl. singer Seattle Opera Co., 1968—70; vocal coach, advisor Highline Jazz Ensemble, Seattle, 1990—2004; pvt. piano, cello and voice tchr., Seattle, 1991—; astronomy club advisor Highline H.S., Seattle, 1998—2004; dir. Highline Dist. Youth Orch., 2003—04, Burien Sr. Choir, 2003; trustee Sunlight Waters Corp., 2002—. Contbr. articles to profl. jours. Officer, sec. 46th Legis. Dist. Dem. Party, Seattle, 1974—78, chairperson Initiative 314 Campaign, 1975; Wash. state conv. del. Dem. Party, Olympia, 1976, Dem. precinct chairperson Seattle, 1976—77. Fulbright Scholarship grantee, Nat. Tchrs. Performance Inst., Oberlin Coll., Ohio, 1970.

Mem.: NEA, Nat. Coun. Tchrs. English, Seattle Astron. Soc., Music Educators' Nat. Conf. Roman Catholic. Avocations: astronomy, reading, bicycling, writing, hiking. Office: Highline HS 225 S 152nd St Seattle WA 98148

VOELL, RICHARD ALLEN, retired private investor; b. Chgo., Dec. 29, 1933; s. John Herman and Esther Frances (Anderson) V.; m. Virginia Charlotte Broderick, Dec. 20, 1958; children: David Broderick, Gregory Jon, Jeffrey Scott. BA, U. Ill., 1956; MBA, U. Hawaii, 1960. With Beatrice Foods Co., Chgo., 1958-79, group mgr. recreational products group, 1971-73, corp. v.p., 1973-75, vice chmn., 1975-79; pres., chief operating officer Penn Central Corp., Greenwich, Conn., 1979-81, chief exec. officer, 1981; pres., chief exec. officer The Rockefeller Group, N.Y.C., 1982-95. Chmn. Harbor Rock Corp.; mem. adv. bds. Fiat and Club Med; mem. bds. SPA Exor and Con Edison; vice chmn. N.Y.C. Partnerships. Chair nominating com. Wildlife Conservation Soc.; chmn. Bus. Coun. for UN, 1982-97; mem. adv. bd. Ctr. for Sustainable Fisheries—Rosentiel Sch. Marine and Atmospheric Sci. 1st lt. AUS, 1956-58. Mem. UN Assn. (vice chmn.), Chief Execs. Orgn., Coun. on Fgn. Rels., Econ. Club N.Y. (past chmn.), Rockefeller Ctr. Club, Greenwich (Conn.) Country Club, Riverside (Conn.) Yacht Club, Chgo. Club, U. Ill. Founders Club. E-mail: pigoose@aol.com.

VOELLER, JOHN GEORGE, engineer; b. Denver, Colo. s. John George and Catherine Eunice V.; m. Sheila Kay Voeller, Oct. 19, 1951. BME, Ga. Tech. U., 1971. Registered profl. engr., Kans., Mich. Field engr. Westinghouse, N.Y.C., 1971-73, start-up engr. Atlanta, 1973-74; nuclear strec engr. Black and Veatch, Kansas City, Mo., 1974-77, dir. engring. info. tech., 1977-88, prin. in charge of info. tech., 1989-94, chief tech. officer, 1994-95, chief knowledge officer, chief tech. officer, 1997—. Bd. dirs. e-Builder, Boca Raton, Fla., Design Build Ptnrs., N.Y.C., CERF; adv. bd. CII, Austin, Tex. Author: (3 vol. set) I.T. User Survival Guide, 1986-94; patentee in field. Recipient Enterprise Value award CIO Mag., 1997, Ed Forrest award AEC Systems Conv., 1999. Mem. AAAI, AAAS, ACM, IEEE Computer Soc. Avocations: astronomy, die cast, music, exotic car history, robotics. Office: Black and Veatch 11401 Lamar Overland Park KS 66211

VOELLGER, GARY A. business consulting executive, retired air force officer; BS in Indsl. Rels. Pers. Mgmt., San Jose State U., 1967; grad., Squadron Officer Sch., 1971; M in Psychology, Peperdine U., 1976; grad., Air Command Staff Coll., Maxwell AFB, 1979, Air War Coll., 1988; cert. in Joint Flag Officer War Fighting, Maxwell AFB, 1997; cert.in sr. mgrs. govt. seminar, Harvard U., 1997. Commd. 2d. lt. USAF, 1967, advanced through grades to maj. gen., 1996; pers. officer 379th Combat Support Grp., Wurtsmith AFB, Mich., 1967-69; undergrad. navigator trng. Mather AFB, Calif., 1969-69; weapons sys. officer 46th Tactical Fighter Squadron, MacDill AFB, Fla., 1970-70; weapons syss. officer 91st Tactical Fighter Squadron, Royal Air Force Bentwaters, Eng., 1970-72; undergrad. pilot tng. Laredo AFB, Tex., 1972; F-111 transition tng. Nellis AFB, Nev., 1973-73; F-111 pilot 428th Tactical Fighter Squadron, Takhli Royal AFB, Thailand, 1973-74; F-111 instr. pilot, flight comdr., standardization and evaluation flight examiner 523rd Tactical Fighter Squadron, 27th Tactical Fighter Wing, Cannon AFB, N.Mex., 1974-79; air ops. staff officer, politico-mil. affairs officer, asst. dep. dir. Joint Nat. Security Coun. Matters Hdqs. USAF, Washington, 1980-84; comdr. 55th Tactical Fighter Squadron, Royal Air Force, Upper Heyford, Eng., 1984-87; asst. dep. comdr. ops. 20th Tactical Fighter Wing, Royal Air Force; dep. comdr. ops. 4450th Tactical Group, Nellis AFB, Nev., 1988-89, vice comdr., 1989-90; comdr. 552nd Air Control Wing, Tinker AFB, Okla., 1990-92, Coll. Aerospace Doctrine, Rsch. and Edn., Air U., Maxwell AFB, Ala., 1992-93, 43rd Air Refueling Wing, Malmstrom AFB, Mont., 1993-94, 92nd Air Refueling Wing, Fairchild AFB, Wash., 1994-95, 437th Airlift Wing, Charleston AFB, S.C., 1995-96; dir. ops. Hdqs. Air Mobility Command, Scott AFB, Ill., 1996-98; NATO force comdr. Hdqs. NATO Airborne Early Warning Force, Mons, Belgium, 1998-2000; ret. USAF; prin. Booz Allen Hamilton, O'Fallon, Ill. Decorated D.D.S.M., Legion of Merit with oak leaf Cluster, Bronze Star medal, Meritorious Svc. medal with two oak leaf clusters, Air medal with oak leaf cluster, Armed Forces Expeditionary medal, Rep. Vietnam Gallantry Cross with Palm. Office: Booz Allen & Hamilton Inc 1728 Corporate Crossing O Fallon IL 62269

VOEVODSKY, VLADIMIR, mathematician; b. Russia, June 4, 1966; BS in Math., Moscow State U., 1989; PhD in Math., Harvard U., 1992. Prof. Inst. for Advanced Study, 2002. Vis. position Inst. for Advanced Study, Harvard U., Max Planck Inst. for Math.; mem. faculty Northwestern U., 1996; Sloan fellow, 1996—98. Co-author: Cycles, Transfers and Motivic Homology Theories, 2000. Recipient Fields medal, 2002, rsch. grants, NSF, Clay Prize fellowship, 1999, 2000. Office: Inst for Advanced Study Sch Math Fuld 116 Einstein Dr Princeton NJ 08540

VOGEL, ANNETTE-BARBARA, violinist, educator; arrived in U.S., 1999; d. Helmuth and Katharina Vogel. Diploma, Sweelinck-Konservatorium, Amsterdam, Netherlands, 1986—91; artist diploma, U. So. Calif., L.A., 1990; student, Folkwang-Hochschule, Essen, Germany, 1993, student, 1997; artist diploma, Coll.-Conservatory, Cin., 1995. Artist-in-residence U. Va., Charlottesville, 1994—95; docent Folkwang-Hochschule, Essen, Germany, 1995—98; concertmaster Folkwang Chamber Orch., Essen, 1995—97, Niederrheinische Sinfoniker, Krefeld, Germany, 1997—98; asst. prof. violin U. Iowa, Iowa City, 1999—2003; asst. prof., violin U. Western Ontario, London, Canada, 2004—. Founder, artistic dir. Magisterra! Internat. Chamber Music Festival. Avocations: literature, art, cooking, travel, sports.

VOGEL, ARTHUR ANTON, clergyman; b. Milw., Feb. 24, 1924; s. Arthur Louis and Gladys Eirene (Larson) V.; m. Katharine Louise Nunn, Dec. 29, 1947; children: John Nunn, Arthur Anton, Katharine Ann. Student, U. of South, 1942-43, Carroll Coll., 1943-44; B.D., Nashotah House Theol. Sem., 1946; MA, U. Chgo., 1948; PhD, Harvard, 1952; S.T.D., Gen. Theol. Sem., 1969; D.C.L., Nashotah House, 1969; D.D., U. of South, 1971. Ordained deacon Episcopal Ch., 1946, priest, 1948; teaching asst. philosophy Harvard, Cambridge, Mass., 1949-50; instr. Trinity Coll., Hartford, Conn., 1950-52; mem. faculty Nashotah House Theol. Sem., Nashotah, Wis., 1952-71, asso. prof., 1954-56, William Adams prof. philosophical and systematic theology, 1956-71, sub-dean Sem., 1964-71; bishop coadjutor Diocese of West Mo., Kansas City, 1971-72, bishop, 1972-89; rector Ch. St. John Chrysostom, Delafield, Wis., 1952-56; dir. Anglican Theol. Rev., Evanston, Ill., 1964-69; mem. Internat. Anglican-Roman Cath. Consultation, 1970-90, Nat. Anglican-Roman Catholic Consultation, 1965-84, Anglican chmn., 1973-84; mem. Standing Commn. on Ecumenical Relations of Episcopal Ch., 1957-79; mem. gen. bd. examining chaplains Episcopal Ch., 1971-72. Del. Episcopal Ch., 4th Assembly World Council Chruches, Uppsala, Sweden, 1968, and others. Author: Reality, Reason and Religion, 1957, The Gift of Grace, 1958, The Christian Person, 1963, The Next Christian Epoch, 1966, Is the Last Supper Finished?, 1968, Body Theology, 1973, The Power of His Resurrection, 1976, Proclamation 2: Easter, 1980, The Jesus Prayer for Today, 1982, I Know God Better Than I Know Myself, 1989, Christ in His Time and Ours, 1982, God, Prayer and Healing, 1995, Radical Christianity and the Flesh of Jesus, 1995; editor: Theology in Anglicanism, 1985; contbr. articles to profl. jours. Vice chmn. bd. dirs. St. Luke's Hosp., Kansas City, Mo., 1971, chmn., 1973-89. Research fellow Harvard, 1950 Mem. Am. Philos. Assn., Metaphys. Soc. Am., Soc. Existential and Phenomenological Philosophy, Catholic Theol. Soc. Am. Episcopalian. Home: 4203 W 94th Terrace Apt 111 Prairie Village KS 66207 E-mail: akvogel@swbell.net.

VOGEL, CARL E. telecommunications industry executive; B in Fin. and Acctg., St. Norber Coll., DePere, Wis. With Jones Intercable, 1983; exec. v.p. EchoStar Comm. Inc., 1994—97; chief exec. Star Choice Comm., 1998; chmn., chief exec. Primestar Inc., 1998—99; exec. v.p., COO AT&T Broadband, 1999; sr. v.p. Liberty Media Corp., 1999—2001; pres., CEO Charter Comm. Inc., 2001—. Bd. dirs. C-SPAN, CableLabs. Mem.: Nat. Cable TV Assn. (bd. dirs.). Office: 12405 Powerscourt Dr Ste 100 Saint Louis MO 63131-3660

VOGEL, CARL-WILHELM ERNST, biomedical scientist, clinical pathologist; b. Hamburg, Germany, Mar. 9, 1951; came to U.S., 1979; s. Erich Hermann Walter and Lisbeth Klara (Barbulla) V.; m. Candice G. McMullan, 1989. MD, U. Hamburg (Germany), 1976; diploma in biology, 1980, PhD in Biochemistry, 1986. Diplomate Am. Bd. Pathology; cert. Bd. Lab. Medicine and Bd. Med. Biochemistry (Germany). Predoctoral rsch. fellow Tropical Inst., Hamburg, 1973-75; intern Univ. Hosps., Hamburg and Kiel, Germany, 1976-78; postdoct. rsch. fellow Rsch. Inst. Scripps Clinic, La Jolla, Calif., 1979-82; asst. prof. biochemistry and medicine Georgetown U., Washington, 1982-87, assoc. prof., 1987-91, adj. prof., 1991-99, resident in medicine, pathology, allergy/immunology, 1984-86, 88-89; prof., chmn. dept. biochemistry and molecular biology U. Hamburg, Germany, 1990-99; prof. pathology U. Hawaii John A. Burns Sch. Medicine, Honolulu, 1999—, dir. Cancer Rsch. Ctr., 1999—. Mem. Vincent T. Lombardi Cancer Rsch. Ctr., Washington, 1982-92; mem. Internat. Ctr. for Interdisciplinary Studies of Immunology, Washington, 1982-94, sci. dir., 1987-91; vis. prof. pathology and lab. medicine Ind. U.-Purdue, Indpls., 1996-97; mem. examiner Bd. Lab. Medicine (Germany), 1991-99, Bd. Med. Biochem. (Germany), 1998-99; cons. to biomed. corps. Mem. edtl. bd. Jour. Devel. and Comparative Immunology, 1984-96. Recipient Nat. Cancer Inst./NIH Rsch. Career Devel. award; overseas rsch. fellow Studienstiftung des Deutschen Volkes, 1978-79, U.S.A. rsch. fellow Deutsche Forschungsgemeinschaft, 1980-82; NIH rsch. grantee, 1983-94, 99—. Fellow Am. Soc. Clin. Pathology, Coll. Am. Pathologists; mem. AMA, AAAS, Am. Chem. Soc., German Soc. Biochemistry and Molecular Biology, Am. Soc. Microbiology, Am. Assn., Immunologists, Am. Soc. Biochemistry and Molecular Biology, Am. Assn. Cancer Rsch., Am. Soc. Clin. Oncology, European Soc. Med. Oncology, Am. Soc. Tropical Medicine and Hygiene, Internat. Soc. Devel. and Comparative Immunology, Am. Fedn. Med. Rsch., Gesellschaft Immunologie, Gesellschaft Deutscher Chemiker, Am. Soc. Clin. Investigation, Am. Soc. Investigative Pathology, German Soc. Cell Biology, German Soc. Lab. Medicine, Japanese Biochem. Soc., Australasian Soc. Immunology, Japanese Cancer Assn., German Cancer Soc., European Assn. Cancer Rsch., Hawaii Med. Assn., Sigma Xi. Office: Cancer Rsch Ctr Hawaii 1236 Lauhala St Honolulu HI 96813-2424 Fax: 808-586-3052. Office Phone: 808-586-3013. E-mail: cvogel@crch.hawaii.edu.

VOGEL, CEDRIC WAKELEE, lawyer; b. Cin., June 4, 1946; s. Cedric and Patricia (Woodruff) V. BA, Yale U., 1968; JD, Harvard U., 1971. Bar: Ohio 1972, Fla. 1973, U.S. Tax Ct. 1972, U.S. Supreme Ct. 1975. Ptnr. Vogel, Heis, Wenstrup & Cameron, Cin., 1972-96; sole practice, 1997—. Bd. dirs. Pro Srs., 1994—. Chmn. mem.'s com. Cin. Art Mus., 1987-88; chmn. auction Cin. Hist. Soc., 1985; local pres. English Speaking Union, 1979-81, nat. bd. dirs., 1981; chmn. Keep Cin. Beautiful, Inc., 1994-96; active Bravo! Cin. Ballet, 1989; chmn. Act II Nutcracker Ball, 1987-88; bd. dirs. Merc Libr., 1991-98; bd. dirs. Cin. Preservation Assn., 1990-93, Cin. Opera Guild, 1997-99; vice chmn. Children's Heart Assn. Reds Rally, 1989; bd. dirs. Cin. Country Day Sch., 1983, pres. Alumni Coun. and Ann. Fund, 1983. Mem.: Fla. Bar Assn., Cin. Bar Assn., Yale Alumni Assn. (del. 1984—87), Harvard Law Sch. Assn. Cin. (pres. 1997—99, 2003—), Heimlich Inst. (trustee 1987—2001), Harvard Club of Cin. (bd. dirs. 1996—98, pres. 1999—2000), The Lawyers Club Cin. (pres. 1995), Cincinnatus, Cin. Yale Club (pres. 1980—81, 1996—97). Republican. Home: 2270 Madison Rd Cincinnati OH 45208-2659 Office: 817 Main St Ste 800 Cincinnati OH 45202-2183 Office Phone: 513-421-4225.

VOGEL, CONRAD DAVID, artist; b. White Plains, N.Y., Apr. 17, 1954; AA, Arts Students League, N.Y.C., 1973; student, N.Y. Studio Sch., 1973—74, New Sch. for Social Rsch., N.Y.C., 1973—74; BA, Sarah Lawrence Coll., 1977. Author and illustrator The Adult Coloring Book of the Civil War, 1996; one-man shows include Red Bar, N.Y.C., 1983, 7th St. Gallery, 1985, Nolo Contendere Gallery, 1985, Nada Gallery, 1986, Jon Gerstad Gallery, 1987, Vitrine Hortense Stahl, Paris, 1990, 1991, 1993, Fraunces Tavern, N.Y.C., 1999—2000, exhibited in group shows at Stamford Mus., Conn., 1987, Henry St. Settlement, N.Y.C., 1989, Foire Internationale d'Art Contemporain, Paris, 1991, World Fin. Ctr., N.Y.C., 1993, Pushkin Mus., Moscow, 1993, Millennium Group, N.Y.C., 2002, Soho, 2002, Fusion Arts Mus., 2003, Angel Orensanz Ctr., 2003, numerous others, Represented in permanent collections Mus. Modern Art, Patterson Mus. Art, N.J.; contbr. art to newspapers and mags. Recipient Award of Merit, N.Y. Soc. Publ. Designers, 1975, exhbn. funding, Artists Space, 1986, N.Y. State Coun. for the Arts, 1986. Avocations: reading, American history, drawing. Office Phone: 212-989-2604.

VOGEL, DAVID SETH, lawyer; b. N.Y.C., July 11, 1955; s. Joshua Selig and Muriel Rita Vogel; m. Patrice Louise Jaxon; children: Claire, Jack. AB, Amherst Coll., 1973—77; JD magna cum laude, Boston U., 1979—82. Law clerk Hon. Frank M. Johnson, Jr., 11th Circuit Ct. of Appeals, Montgomery, Ala., 1982—83; assoc. Perkins Coie Law Firm, Seattle, 1983—84; dep. prosecutor King County Prosecutor's Office, Seattle, 1984—89; assoc. Levinson Friedman Law Firm, Seattle, 1989—92; prin. Law Offices of David S. Vogel, Seattle, 1992—. Editor: Boston U. Law Rev. Pres. Vashon-Maury Island Cmty. Coun., Vashon Island, Wash., 1986—93, bd. mem., 1985—2000, Vashon Household, Vashon Island, Wash., 1996—2003; chair Vashon Town Plan Com., Vashon Island, Wash., 1992—96. Recipient Cmty. Svc. award, Vashon-Maury Island Audubon Soc., 1994, Pilchuck Audubon Soc., 1997. Mem.: ABA, Wash. Assn. Criminal Defense Lawyers, Brain Injury Assn., Wash. State Trial Lawyers Assn., Assn. of Trial Lawyers of Am., Wash. State Bar Assn., Seattle-King County Bar Assn., WSTLA Eagles. Liberal. Jewish. Avocations: fishing, hiking, camping. Office: Law Offices of David Vogel 2025 First Ave Penthouse Ste A Seattle WA 98121 Personal E-mail: dsvogel@earthlink.net.

VOGEL, EZRA F. sociology educator; b. Delaware, Ohio, July 11, 1930; s. Joseph H. and Edith (Nachman) V.; m. Suzanne Hall, July 5, 1953 (div.); children: David, Steven, Eva; m. Charlotte Ikels, Nov. 3, 1979. BA, Ohio Wesleyan U., 1950; MA, Bowling Green State U., 1951; PhD, Harvard U., 1958; LittD (hon.), Kwansai Gakuin, 1980, Wittenberg Coll., 1981, Bowling Green State U., 1982, U. Md., 1983, Albion Coll., 1988, Chinese U., Hong Kong, 1992, Ohio Wesleyan, 1996; LittD (hon.), U. Mass., Lowell, 1996, Yamaguchi U., 1998, Monterrey Inst., 2002. Rsch. fellow Harvard (for work in Japan), 1958-60; asst. prof. Yale U., 1960-61; rsch. assoc., lectr. Harvard U., 1961-67, prof., 1967—, Henry Ford II rsch. prof. social scis., 1990—, assoc. dir. East Asian Rsch. Ctr., 1967-73, dir., 1973-77, chmn. council East Asian studies, 1977-80, dir. program on U.S.-Japan relations, 1980-87, hon. chmn. program on U.S.-Japan rels., 1988—, mem. faculty council, 1981-84; nat. intelligence officer for East Asia Nat. Intelligence Coun., 1993-95, dir. Fairbank Ctr. East Asian Studies, 1995-99; dir. Asia Ctr. Harvard U., 1997-99, rsch. prof., 2000—. Mem. Joint Com. on Contemporary China, 1968-75, Com. on Scholarly Communication with Peoples Republic China, 1973-75, Joint Com. Japanese Studies, 1977-79 Author: Japan's New Middle Class, 1963, Canton Under Communism, 1969, Japan As Number One, 1979, Comeback, 1985, The Impact of Japan on a Changing World, 1987, One Step Ahead in China, 1989, The Four Little Dragons, 1991, Is Japan Still Number One?, 2000; co-editor: (with Norman W. Bell) A Modern Introduction to the Family, 1960, (with George Lodge) Ideology and National Competitiveness, Living With China, 1997, (with Ming Yuan and Akihiko Tanaka) The Golden Age of the U.S.-China Japan Triangle, 2002; editor: Modern Japanese Organization and Decision-Making, 1975. Trustee Ohio Wesleyan U., 1970-75, 80-94. Served with AUS, 1951-53. Recipient Harvard faculty prize for book of year, 1970, Japan Found. prize, 1996, Japan Soc. prize 1998; Guggenheim fellow, 1972 Mem. Assn. Asian Studies (bd. dirs. 1970-72), Am. Acad. Arts and Scis. Home: 14 Sumner Rd Cambridge MA 02138-3018 E-mail: efvogel@fas.harvard.edu.

VOGEL, H. VICTORIA, psychotherapist, trauma, post-traumatic stress disorder and addiction recovery counselor and educator, author; BA, U. Md., 1968; MA, NYU, 1970, 75; MEd, Columbia U., 1982, postgrad., 1982—; cert., Am. Projective Drawing Inst., 1983; CASAC, New Sch. U. for Social Rsch., 2000. Diplomate Am. Acad. Experts in Traumatic Stress; cert. addiction recovery counselor, expert in traumatic stress, alcohol and substance abuse counselor, addictions treatment, addiction counseling alcohol and substance abuse. Art therapist Childville, Bklyn., 1962-64; tchr. Montgomery County (Md.) Jr. H.S., 1968-69; with H.S. divsn. N.Y.C. Bd. Edn., 1970—; guidance counselor, instr., psychotherapist in pvt. practice. Guidance counselor, instr., psychotherapist in pvt. practice; clin. counseling cons. psychoanalysis and devel. studies, art/play therapy The Modern Sch., 1984—; art/play therapist Hosp. Ctr. for Neuromuscular Disease and Devel. Disorders, 1986—; employment counselor-adminstr. N.Y. State Dept. Labor Concentrated Employment Program, 1971-72; intern psychotherapy and psychoanalysis psychiat. divsn. Ctrl. Islip Hosp., 1973-75, Calif. Grad. Inst., L.A.; intern psychol. counseling and rehab. N.J. Coll. Medicine, Newark, 1979. Author: The Never Ending Story of Alcohol, Drugs and Other Substance Abuse, 1992, Variant Sexual Behavior and the Aesthetic Modern Nudes, 1992, Psychological Science of School Behavior Intervention, 1993, Joycean Conceptual Modernism: Relationships and Deviant Sexuality, 1995, Electronic Evil Eyes, 1995 (U.S. Cert. of Recognition, 1996), Psychological Paradigms of Alcohol Violence Suicide Trauma Addiction Variant Pathologies PTSD and Schizophrenia, 1999. Mem. com. for spl. events NYU, 1989; participant clin. and artistic perspectives Am. Acad. Psychoanalysis Conf., 1990, participant clin. postmodernism and psychoanalysis, 1996; aux. police officer N.Y. Police Dept., 1994—; chair bylaws com. Columbia U., 1995—. Mem.: ACA, AAAS, APA, Tchrs. Coll. Adminstrv. Women in Edn., Assn. Humanistic Psychology (exec. sec. 1981), Art/Play Therapy, N.Y. Art Tchrs. Assn., Am. Acad. Experts Traumatic Stress (diplomate in expert traumatic stress), Am. Soc. Group Psychotherapy and Psychodrama (publs. com. 1984—), Am. Orthopsychiat. Assn., Am. Psychol. Soc., Phi Delta Kappa (editor chpt. newsletter 1981—84, exec. sec. Columbia U. chpt. 1984—, chmn. nominating com. for chpt. officers 1986—, rsch. rep. 1986—, pub. rels. exec. bd. dirs. 1991, NYU chpt. v.p. programs 1994—).

VOGEL, HENRY ELLIOTT, retired university dean and physics educator; b. Greenville, S.C., Sept. 16, 1925; s. Henry Lamprecht and Alice (Cousins) V.; m. Barbara Argyle Gladden, Aug. 16, 1953; children: Alisabeth, Henry L. II, Barbara Alice, Susan Marie. BS, Furman U., 1948; MS, U. N.C., 1950, PhD, 1962. Instr. dept. physics Clemson (S.C.) U., 1950-52, asst. prof. physics, 1952-59, assoc. prof., 1959-65, prof., 1965-67, prof., head physics dept., 1967-71; prof., dean Clemson (S.C.) U. Coll. Scis., 1971-87, prof. physics, 1987-90, dean emeritus, prof. emeritus dept. physics and astronomy, 1990—. Mem. S.C. ad hoc com. for NSF exptl. program to stimulate competitive research, 1978-87; mem. tech. adv. bd. S.C. Research Authority, 1984-87. Served with AUS, 1943-45. Decorated Bronze Star, Purple Heart. Mem. Am. Phys. Soc., Am. Assn. Physics Tchrs., Sigma Xi, Sigma Pi, Alpha Epsilon Delta. Address: 222 Wyatt Ave Clemson SC 29631-3003 E-mail: henryvgl@aol.com.

VOGEL, HOWARD STANLEY, lawyer; b. NYC, Jan. 21, 1934; s. Moe and Sylvia (Miller) V.; m. Judith Anne Gelb, June 30, 1962; 1 son, Michael S. BA, Bklyn. Coll., 1954; JD, Columbia U., 1957; LLM in Corp. Law, NYU, 1969. Bar: NY 1957, U.S. Supreme Ct. 1964. Assoc. Whitman & Ransom, NYC, 1961-66; with Texaco Inc., 1966-99, gen. atty., 1970-73, assoc. gen. counsel, 1973-81, gen. counsel Tex. Philanthropic Found. Inc., 1979-82; gen. counsel Jefferson Chem. Co. Texaco Chems. Can. Inc., 1973-82; assoc. gen. tax counsel, gen. mgr. adminstrn. Texaco Inc., White Plains, NY, 1981-99; counsel Allegaert Berger & Vogel LLP, NYC, 1999—. Gen. tax counsel Texaco Found. Inc., 1995-99; pres., dir. 169 E. 69th Corp., 1981—. Served to 1st lt. JAGC, U.S. Army, 1958-60. Mem. ABA, Assn. Bar City of NY, Fed. Bar Coun., Assn. Ex-Mems. of Squadron A., Princeton Club (NYC). Home: 169 E 69th St Apt 9D New York NY 10021-5163 Office: 18th Fl 111 Broadway Fl 18 New York NY 10006-1901 Office Phone: 212-571-0550. E-mail: hvogel@abv.com.

VOGEL, JAMES EDMOND, plastic surgeon; b. NYC, Mar. 11, 1956; BS in Biochemistry, Bowdoin Coll., Maine, 1978; MD, Mount Sinai Sch. Medicine, 1982. Intern New England Med. Ctr., Boston, 1982—83, surgery residency, 1982—84, U. NC, Chapel Hill, NC, 1984—87; fellowship plastic surgery Johns Hopkins Hospital, Balt., 1987—91, assist. chief service plastic surgery, 1989—90, assist. prof. surgery div. of plastic surgery, 1989—. Diplomat Nat. Bd. Med. Examiners, 1983. Fellow: Am. Coll. of Surgeons; mem.: Internat. Soc. of Hair Restoration Surgery (bd. of governors 1993—98, pres. 1996—97, exec. com. 1996—99, chmn. sci. com. 1993—99), Northeastern Soc. of Plastic & Reconstructive Surgeons, Nathan Womack Surgical Soc., Md. Breast Soc., Johns Hopkins Med. Soc., Balt. County Med. Soc., Am. Soc. of Aesthetic Plastic Surgery, Am. Soc. of Plastic Surgeons. Office: Woodholme Med Bldg 1838 Greene Tree Rd Ste 420 Baltimore MD 21208

VOGEL, JEFFREY C. commissioner; m. Kathy Vogel; children: Sam, Chase. BS in Acctg., U. Wy., 1983. Dep. banking commr. Wy. Banking Divsn., commr., divsn. banking, dept. audit, 2002—. Office: 122 W 52nd St Cheyenne WY 82002

VOGEL, MICHAEL N. journalist, writer, historian; b. Buffalo, May 26, 1947; s. Ralph John and Florence Helen (Pohlmann) V.; m. Stasia Zoladz, Aug. 28, 1971; children: Charity Ann, Rebecca Marie, Alex Christian. BA in English, Canisius Coll., 1969; MA in English, So. Ill. U., 1970. Journalist Buffalo News, 1970—, dep. editl. page editor. Assoc. prof. journalism Buffalo State U. Coll., 1979-80. Author: Maritime Buffalo, 1990, Echoes in the Mist, 1991, America's Crossroads, 1993. Pres. Buffalo Lighthouse Assn., Inc., 1985—; co-founder St. Michael's Sch. at Greycliff, Derby, N.Y., 1987; pres. Buffalo Newspaper Guild, 1994-96; bd. dirs. Landmark Soc. Niagara Frontier, 1990-91, Western N.Y. Heritage Inst., 1994-98, Friends of N.Y. State Newspaper Project, 1996—; pres. Am. Lighthouse Coord. Com.; founding trustee Nat. Lighthouse Ctr. and Mus.; adv. bd. Great Lakes Lighthouse Mus. 1st lt. U.S. Army, 1971-73. Recipient numerous awards including One to One Media award, 1978, 79, Newspaper Editorial Workshop award, 1979-80, N.Y. State AP award, 1982-90, Am. Planning Assn. award, 1987. Mem. U.S. Lighthouse Soc., Gt. Lakes Hist. Soc., Buffalo & Erie County Hist. Soc. (Augspurger award 1989, Niederlander award 1990), Buffalo Mus. Sci. Roman Catholic. Avocations: sailing, photography, reading. Home: 6540 Lake Shore Rd Derby NY 14047-9755 Office: Buffalo News PO Box 100 Buffalo NY 14240-0100

VOGEL, NELSON J., JR., lawyer; b. South Bend, Ind., Oct. 13, 1946; s. Nelson J. and Carolyn B. (Drzewiecki) V.; m. Sandra L. Cudney, May 17, 1969; children: Ryan C., Justin M., Nathan J., Lindsey M. BS cum laude, Miami U., Oxford, Ohio, 1968; JD cum laude, U. Notre Dame, 1971. Bar: Ind. 1971, Mich. 1971, U.S. Dist. Ct. (no. dist.) Ind. 1971, U.S. Tax Ct. 1972, U.S. Ct. Appeals (5th cir.) 1975, U.S. Ct. Claims 1980. Acct. Coopers & Lybrand, South Bend, 1969-71; assoc. Barnes & Thornburg, South Bend, 1971-76, ptnr., 1977—. Lectr. U. Notre Dame, South Bend, 1971, 74-80; instr. Ind. U., South Bend, 1971-74; vice-chair Barnes & Thornburg, 2001—, mng. ptnr. South Bend office, 2001—; trustee Project Future, St. Joseph Co., 2002—. Pres. Big Bros./Big Sisters, South Bend, 1978-79; bd. pres. South Bend Regional Mus. Art, 1984-86; mem. ethics com. Meml. Hosp., South Bend, 1986-94; bd. advisors Goshen Coll. Fmaily Bus. program, 1993-99; bd. dirs. Madison Ctr., 2003-. Mem. Nat. Employee Stock Ownership Plan Assn. (sec.-treas. Ind. chpt. 1993-95), Nat. Assn. State Bar Tax Sec. (exec. com. 1982-84), Ind. State Bar Assn. (chmn. taxation sect. 1981-82, Citation of Merit 1979), Ind. Assn. Mediators, Mich. Bar Assn. (tax sect.), Ind. State H.S. Hockey Assn., Inc. (bd. dirs. 1998-2001, treas. 1998-2001), Michiana World Affairs Coun. (bd. dirs. 1992-96), Michiana World Trade club (bd. dirs. 1992-96), Mental Health Assn. St. Joseph County (bd. dirs. 1997-2001). Home: 1146 Dunrobbin Ln South Bend IN 46614-2150 Office: Barnes & Thornburg 600 1st Source Bank 100 N Michigan St Ste 600 South Bend IN 46601-1632 Office Phone: 219-237-1162., 574-237-1162. Business E-Mail: nvogel@btlaw.com.

VOGEL, PAULA ANNE, playwright; b. Washington, Nov. 16, 1951; d. Donald Stephen and Phyllis (Bremerman) Vogel. BA, Cath. U., 1974; doctoral studies, Cornell U., 1974-77. Instr. theatre and women's studies Cornell U., Ithaca, N.Y., 1978-81; prodn. supr. Theatre on Film & Tape, N.Y.C., 1983-85; prof. Creative Writing Program, Brown U., Providence, 1985—. Author: (plays) Meg, 1977 (Nat. Playwright award Am. Coll. Theatre Festival), And Baby Makes Seven, 1984, Desdemona, 1985, The Oldest Profession, 1988, The Baltimore Waltz, 1992 (Obie award for best play, 1992), Hot 'N' Throbbing, 1994, The Mineola Twins, 1996, How I Learned to Drive, 1996 (Pulitzer prize, 1998, Obie award, 1997, N.Y. Drama Critics Drama Desk award for best play, 1997, Lucille Lortel award, 1997, Outer Critics' Circle award, 1997). Recipient Bunting award, Radcliffe-Harvard Colls., 1990, Pew

Charitable Trust Sr. Residency award, 1995, Laura Pels award, 1999; grantee Fund for New Am. Plays, 1994; playwright fellow NEA, 1981, 1990, Guggenheim fellow, 1995. Fellow: McDowell Colony; mem.: New Dramatists. Office: Brown U PO Box 1852 Providence RI 02912-1852

VOGEL, ROBERT LEE, retired college administrator, clergyman; b. Phillipsburg, Kans., Sept. 27, 1934; s. Howard and Marie V.; m. Sally M. Johnson, June 3, 1956; children— Susan, Kirk BA, Wartburg Coll., 1956; B.D., M.Div., Wartburg Theol. Sem., 1960, D.D. (hon.), 1976. Ordained to ministry Am. Lutheran Ch., 1960. Organizing pastor Faith Luth. Ch., Golden, Colo., 1960-65; regional dir. div. youth activity Am. Luth. Ch., Chgo., 1965-67, dir. parish resources, div. youth activity Mpls., 1967-69; sr. pastor Our Savior's Luth. Ch., Denver, 1969-73; exec. asst. to pres. Am. Luth. Ch., Mpls., 1973-80; pres. Wartburg Coll., Waverly, Iowa, 1980-98; interim pres. Grand View Coll., 1999. V.p. Internat. Luther League, Am. Luth. Ch., 1953-58, pres., 1958-60; ofcl. observer Luth. World Fedn. Assembly, 1957; mem. com. on laity Am. Luth. Ch., 1964-67. Mem. nominating com., theol. edn. coord. com. Evang. Luth. Ch. Am., 1996—. Recipient Alumni citation Wartburg Coll., 1978 Mem. Coun. Ind. Colls., Iowa Assn. Ind. Colls. and Univs. (chmn. bd. 1987-88), Luth. Ednl. Conf. N. Am. (pres. 1988-89), Nat. Assn. Ind. Colls. and Univs. (commn. mem.). Home and Office: 900 Saint Paul St Denver CO 80206-3940

VOGEL, SALLY THOMAS, psychologist, social worker, educator; b. Joplin, Mo., July 3, 1925; d. Clyde Albert Thomas and Kathryn (Waite) Thompson; m. F. Lincoln Vogel, Sept. 4, 1946; children: Kathryn Duchin, Linda, Robert L. BA, Beaver Coll., 1947; MEd, North Adams State Coll., 1969; EdS, Seton Hall U., 1995. Case worker Pa. Dept. Welfare, Phila., 1947-48; high sch. tchr. Downington High Sch., Coatesville, Pa., 1969-71; sch. social worker Delaware Valley High Sch., Frenchtown, N.J., 1970-84; study team coord. Holland Twp. Sch., Milford, N.J., 1975-85, sch. social worker, 1975-90, guidance counselor, 1990-94; sch. psychologist Lake Shore Sch. Dist., St. Clair Shores, Mich., 1998—2004. Instr. in Parent Effectiveness and Tchr. Effectiveness, Hunt County Adult Edn., N.J., 1975-84; advanced trainee Edn. Tng. Inst., Calif., 1984-89; presenter in field. Acting exec. dir. Big Bros./Big Sisters (founder), Hunterdon County, N.J., 1976. Recipient Ed Kiley Svc. award Big Bros./Big Sisters, 1978. Mem.: AAUW, NASP, MASP. Office: Lake Shore Sch Dist Admin Bldg Harper St Clair Shores Saint Clair Shores MI 48081

VOGEL, STEVEN MICHAEL, philosopher, educator; b. N.Y.C., Feb. 21, 1954; s. Amos and Marcia V.; m. Jane Ann Henderson, June 18, 1988; children: Anna, Jesse. AB, Yale U., 1975; MA, Boston U., 1977, PhD, 1984. From asst. prof. philosophy Denison U., Granville, Ohio, 1984-90, assoc. prof., 1990-96, prof., 1996—, chair dept. philosophy, 1992—97, 2000—04. Author: Against Nature, 1996. Mem. Am. Philos. Assn., Internat. Soc. Environ. Ethics, Soc. Phenomenology & Existential Philosophy. Office: Dept Philosophy Denison Univ Granville OH 43023 Office Phone: 740-587-6579.

VOGEL, SUSAN CAROL, nursing administrator; b. Hartford, Conn., Oct. 9, 1948; d. Morton B. and Esther (Riback) Worshoufsky. Diploma in nursing, Grace Hosp., New Haven, 1969; B in Healthcare Mgmt., U. La Verne, 1991, M in Health Adminstrn., 1994. RN, Calif.; cert. nephrology nurse, Nephrology Nurse Cert. Bd. Oper. rm. nurse New Britain (Conn.) Gen. Hosp., 1970-72; staff nurse oper. rm. Parkview Cmty. Hosp., Riverside, Calif., 1972-74; staff nurse dialysis, IV team Cedars-Sinai Med. Ctr., L.A., 1974-82; clin. nurse III dialysis UCLA, 1982-88; nurse mgr. inpatient dialysis UCLA Med. Ctr., 1988-93; adminstr. South Valley Regional Dialysis Ctr., Encino, Calif., 1993—; pres. Renal Replacement Therapies, Inc. Bd. dirs. End Stage Renal Disease Network 18, med. rev. bd., 1996—2000, treas. Author: (with others) Review of Hemodialysis for Nurses and Dialysis Personnel, 7th edit., 2002, Vascular Access, Principles & Practices, 4th edit., 2002; editor Nephrology Nursing Jour., 2000-02. Mem. med. rev. bd. End Stage Renal Disease Network 18, 1996-2000; pres. Calif. Dialysis Coun., 2002—. Mem. NAFE, Am. Nephrology Nurses Assn. (pres. L.A. chpt. 1990-92, 96-98, nat. chairperson hemodialysis spl. interest group 1993-95), Nat. Kidney Found. Avocations: travel, skiing. Office: South Valley Regional Dialysis Ctr 17815 Ventura Blvd Ste 100 Encino CA 91316-3600

VOGEL, THOMAS TIMOTHY, surgeon, educator, lay worker; b. Columbus, Ohio, Feb. 1, 1934; s. Thomas A. and Charlotte A. (Hogan) V.; m. M.M. Darina Kelleher, May 29, 1965; children: Thomas T., Catherine D., Mark P., Nicola M. AB, Coll. of Holy Cross, 1955; MS, Ohio State U., 1960, PhD, 1962; MD, Georgetown U., 1965. Pvt. practice surgery, Columbus, 1971-2001; chmn. liturgy com., pres. parish coun. St. Catharine Parish, Columbus, 1971-73; chmn. diocesan adminstrn. com. Diocesan Pastoral Coun., Columbus, 1972-73, chmn., 1973-75; vice prefect Sodality of Holy Cross, 1953-55; mem. Ohio Bishop's Adv. Coun., Columbus, 1976-79. Clin. asst. prof. surgery Ohio State U., Columbus, 1974—; past trustee Peer Rev. Sys., Inc.; assoc. med. dir. United Health Care, Columbus, 1997-2000; cons. Rehabilitation Svcs.; commr., surveillance utilization rev. mem. Medicaid, State of Ohio, 1998-2000; assoc. med. dir. Palmetto GBA, 1999—. Contbr. articles to profl. jours. Bd. dirs. St. Vincent's Children's Ctr., 1975-83, chmn., 1981-82; past chmn. bd. trustees St. Joseph Montessori Sch. Named Knight of the Holy Sepulchre, Equestrian Order of the Holy Sepulchre of Jerusalem, 2001; recipient Layman's award, Columbus Ea. Kiwanis, 1972. Mem. ACS, Am. Physiol. Soc., Assn. for Acad. Surgery, Ohio State Med. Assn. (del. 1993—), Sigma Xi, Delta Epsilon Sigma. Roman Catholic. Home: 247 S Ardmore Rd Columbus OH 43209-1701 Office: 621 S Cassingham Rd Columbus OH 43209-2403 E-mail: vogel.3@osu.edu.

VOGEL, VICTOR GERALD, medical educator, researcher; b. Bethlehem, Pa., Mar. 14, 1952; s. Victor Gerald Jr. and Margaret Moser (Smith) V.; m. Saralyn Sue Schaffner, June 25, 1977; children: Heather Marie, Christiaan Keith. Diplomate Am. Bd. Internal Medicine, Am. Bd. Preventive Medicine, Nat. Bd. Med. Examiners. Resident in internal medicine Balt. City Hosps., 1978-81; fellow in med. oncology Johns Hopkins Oncology Ctr., Balt., 1983-86; Andrew W. Mellon fellow Johns Hopkins Sch. Hygiene Pub. Health, Balt., 1984-86; asst. prof. medicine and epidemiology U. Tex./M.D. Anderson Cancer Ctr., Houston, 1986-93, assoc. prof. clin. cancer prevention, 1993-95; asst. prof. epidemiology U. Tex. Sch. Pub. Health, Houston, 1987-95; prof. medicine and epidemiology U. Pitts. Cancer Inst./Magee-Womens Hosp., 1996—, dir. MAGEE/UPCI breast cancer program, 1996—2002, dir. MAGEE/UPCI breast cancer prevention program, 2003—. Epidemiologist Tex. breast screening project Am. Cancer Soc., 1986-93; mem. data and safety monitoring bd. Women's Health Initiative, NIH, 1994—; bd. dirs. Nat. Surg. Adjuvant Breast and Bowel Project Found., Inc., 1997—, AMC Cancer Ctr., Denver, 1996-99; protocol chmn. Nat. Cancer Inst. Study of Tamoxifen and Raloxifene. Contbr. articles to profl. jours. Founding mem. Nat. Surg. adjuvant Breast and Bowel Project Found., Inc.; founding pres. Internat. Soc. Cancer Risk Assessment and Mgmt., 2003. Served with USPHS, 1981-83. Named Med. Vol. of Yr., Am. Cancer Soc., 1983, award 1987, career devel. award, 1990-93; fellow Susan G. Komen Breast Cancer Found., 1990-93. Fellow Am. Coll. Preventive Medicine, ACP; mem. Am. Soc. Clin. Oncology, Am. Soc. Preventive Oncology, Christian Med. and Dental Assn., Am. Assn. Cancer Rsch. Republican. Presbyterian. Avocation: flying. Office: U Pittsburgh Cancer Inst Magee-Womens Hosp 300 Halket St Rm 3524 Pittsburgh PA 15213-3108 Office Phone: 412-641-6500. Business E-Mail: vvogel@magee.edu.

VOGEL, WERNER PAUL, retired machine company executive; b. Louisville, June 15, 1923; s. Werner George and Emma (Bartman) Vogel; m. Helen Louise Knapp, Oct. 2, 1954. B Mech. Engring., U. Louisville, 1950. With Henry Vogt Machine Co., Louisville, 1942—86, asst. plant supt., 1957—60, plant supt., 1961—73, v.p., 1974—86. Trustee City of Strathmoor, Ky., 1959—61; clk. City of Glenview Manor, Ky., 1967—73, trustee, 1974—75, treas., 1986—89; mem. adv. coun. Lindsey Wilson Coll., 1988—2003; bd. dirs. Louisville Protestant Altenheim, 1979—80, pres., 1985—90, ret. With USAAF, 1944—46. Mem.: ASME, Sigma Tau, Tau Beta Pi. Republican. Methodist. Home: 29 Glenwood Rd Louisville KY 40222-6168

VOGEL, WILLIAM DICKERMAN, financial services executive; b. N.Y.C., Oct. 21, 1961; s. Ralph B. and Mabel (Harris) V.; m. Mary Anne Taylor. AB, Harvard Coll., 1984. CFA. Rsch. asst. George W. Ball, Princeton, N.J., 1986; corp. search cons. Korn/Ferry Internat., Hong Kong, 1987; equity rsch. analyst The Boston Co., Boston, 1988-93; telecom. analyst Nat. West Securities, N.Y.C., 1993-95; sr. v.p., head telecomm. equity rsch. Dillon, Read & Co., N.Y.C., 1996; mng. dir., head telecomm. equity rsch. NationsBanc Montgomery Securities, N.Y.C., 1997-98; sr. v.p. strategic planning Winstar Comm., N.Y.C., 1999-2000; ind. cons., 2000—02; founding ptnr. Context Ptnrs., LLC, 2003—. Author: Strategic Assessment, Regional Bell Telephone Cos., 1994. Trustee St. Paul's Sch., Concord, N.H. Mem. Assn. Investment Mgmt. and Rsch., Boston Security Analysts Soc., N.Y. Soc. Security Analysts, New Eng. Hist. and Geneal. Soc. Avocations: tennis, skiing, mountain biking, geneal. rsch.

VOGELEY, CLYDE EICHER, JR., engineering educator, artist, consultant; b. Pitts., Oct. 19, 1917; s. Clyde Eicher and Eva May (Reynolds) V.; m. Blanche Wormington Peters, Dec. 15, 1947; children: Eva Anne, Susan Elizabeth Steele. BFA in Art Edn., Carnegie Mellon U., 1940; BS in Engring. Physics, U. Pitts., 1944, PhD in Math., 1949. Art supr. Pub. Sch. Sys., Spingdale, Pa., 1940—41; rsch. engr. Westinghouse Rsch. Labs., East Pittsburgh, Pa., 1944—54; adj. prof. math. U. Pitts., 1954—64; sr. scientist Bettis Atomic Power Lab., West Mifflin, Pa., 1956—59, supr. tech. tng., 1959—71; mgr. Bettis Reactor Engring. Sch., West Mifflin, 1971—77, dir., 1977—92; cons. U.S. Dept. Energy, Washington, 1992—95. Cons. Bettis Atomic Power Lab., W. Mifflin, 1954-56; U.S. Navy Nuclear Power Schs., Mare Island, Calif., Bainbridge, Md., 1959-69. Author: (grad. sch. course) Non-linear Differential Equations, 1954; (rev. text) Ordinary Differential Equations, Rev. edit. 5, Shock and Vibration Problems, Rev. Edit. 6, 1991; rsch. report distributed to Brit., Can. and U.S. Govts. for use in design of airborne radar systems, 1944; oil painting represented in permanent Latrobe collection; acrylics, water colors and Christmas card designs in several pvt. collections; oil painting included in Barbara H. Nakle's A Unique Vision of Art, 1997, water color included in collection Superior Ct. of Pa. 1999. Pres., trustee Whitehall (Pa.) Pub. Libr., 1985. Recipient letter of commendation naval reactors br. USN, 1992. Mem. IEEE (life), Am. Phys. Soc., Assoc. Artists Pitts. (hon.), Pitts. Watercolor Soc., Sigma Xi, Sigma Pi Sigma, Sigma Tau. Presbyterian. Achievements include patents for Automatic Continuous Wave Radar Tracking System, Modulating Signals Passing Along Ridged Waveguides, Ridged Waveguide Matching Device, Method for Joining Several Ridged Waveguides, Antenna Feed Modulation Unit, others. Home: c/o Susan Steele 102 Appletree Dr Beaver PA 15009 *My life as an artist, scientist, and teacher has been a wonderful journey - made richer by my family, teachers, friends, colleagues, and students. It has never seemed like work.*

VOGELGESANG, SANDRA LOUISE, business executive, writer, consultant; b. Canton, Ohio, July 27, 1942; d. Glenn Wesley and Louise (Forry) Vogelgesang; m. Geoffrey Ernest Wolfe, July 4, 1982. BA, Cornell U., 1964; MA, Tufts U., 1965, MA in Law and Diplomacy, 1966, PhD, 1971. With Dept. State, Washington, 1975-97, policy planner for sec. state and European Bur., 1975-80, dir. Econ Policy Office, Orgn. Econ. Coop. and Devel., 1981-82, econ. minister U.S. Embassy, Ottawa, Can., 1982-86, dep. asst. sec. Internat. Orgn. Affairs Bur., 1986-89; dep. asst. adminstr. Office Internat. Activities Environ. Protection Agy., Washington, 1989-92; with Dept. State, Washington, 1992; sr. policy advisor Agy. for Internat. Devel., 1993; U.S. amb. to Nepal Dept. State, Washington, 1994-97; pres. Everest Assocs. and Himalaya, 1997—. Bd. dirs. Ctr. for Econ. Devel. and Population Activities; mem. women and conservation com. World Wildlife Fund, 1997—, mem. Nat. Coun., 1999—; bd. advisors Am.'s Soc., N.Y.C., 1986—89; mem. Pres.'s Coun. of Cornell Women Cornell U., 1998—; adv. com. Dept. of Treasury com. on Internat. Child Labor Enforcement, 1999—; writer, cons. internat. devel. issues. Author: Long Dark Night of the Soul, The American Intellectual Left and the Vietnam War, 1974, American Dream-Global Nightmare: The Dilemma of U.S. Human Rights Policy, 1980. Bd. dirs. Crafts Ctr., 1999-2000. Recipient Meritorious Service awards, 1973, 74, 82, 83, 86, Disting. Honor award, 1976 Dept. State, Pres.' Disting. Service award, 1985. Mem. Council on Fgn. Relations. Office: 9009 Charred Oak Dr West Bethesda MD 20817-1923 E-mail: everest.associates@erols.com.

VOGELMAN, JOSEPH HERBERT, scientific engineering company executive; b. N.Y.C., Aug. 18, 1920; s. Jacob and Sabina (Weingarten) V.; m. Norma Schneider, Dec. 8, 1946; children: Jeffrey Allan, Leslie Sue, Linda Leigh. BS, CCNY, 1940; M.E.E., Poly. Inst. Bklyn., 1948, D.Elec. Engring., 1957. Registered profl. engr., N.Y., N.J. Project engr. Signal Corps Engr. Labs., Belmar, N.J., 1943-45; chief devel. br. Watson Labs., Eatontown, N.J., 1945-50; chief scientist Rome Air Devel. Center, Griffiss AFB, N.Y., 1951-52, chief electronic warfare lab., 1953-56, dir. communications, 1956-59; v.p., dir. Capehart Corp., N.Y.C., 1959-64; dir. electronics Chromalloy Am. Corp., N.Y.C., 1964-67, gen. mgr. pocket fone div., 1966-67, v.p., 1967-73; v.p., dir. Cro-Med Bionics Corp., 1968-73; vice chmn. bd., dir. Laser Link Corp., 1968-73; chief scientist, dir. Orentreich Found. for Advancement Sci., 1973—; pres. Vogelman Devel. Corp., 1973—. Chmn. tech. adv. com. Compupix, Inc., 1984-86. Contbr. articles to profl. jours. and encys.; patentee in field. Served with AUS, 1942-43. Recipient Outstanding Performance award USAF, 1957 Fellow AAAS, IEEE; mem. Titulaire, Societe Francaise de Electroniciens et des Radio Electriciens, N.Y. Acad. Scis., Sigma Xi, Eta Kappa Nu. Home: 48 Green Dr Roslyn NY 11576-3221 Office: 910 5th Ave New York NY 10021-4155 E-mail: dr.jhv@juno.com.

VOGEL-SPROTT, MURIEL DORIS, psychology educator, researcher; b. Waterloo, Can., Aug. 20, 1934; d. Henry and Anne Ellen (Stroh) V.; m. David Arthur Sprott, Dec. 16, 1961; children: Anne Ellen, Jane Barry. BA, McMaster U., Can., 1955; MA, U. Toronto, 1957; PhD, 1960. Rsch. assoc. Addiction Rsch. Found., Toronto, 1959-61; asst. prof. psychology U. Waterloo, Canada, 1961-65; assoc. prof., 1965-69; prof., 1969-96; rsch. prof., 1996-97; disting. prof. emerita, 1997—. Author: Alcohol Tolerance and Social Drinking, 1992; contbr. numerous chpts. and rsch. papers in profl. publs. in field. Recipient Rsch. award AA Found. for Traffic Safety, 1988; named Disting. Psychopharacologist, Can. Psychol. Assn., 1988, grantee Govt. and Pvt. agys. in Can. and USA. Fellow APA, Can. Psychol. Assn., Psychonomic Sci. Office: Dept Psychology University of Waterloo Waterloo ON N2L3G1 Canada E-mail: mvogel@watarts.uwaterloo.ca.

VOGELSTEIN, BERT, oncology educator; b. Balt., Md., June 2, 1949; BS in Math., U. Pa., 1970; MD, Johns Hopkins U. Sch. Medicine, 1974. Rsch. assoc. Nat. Cancer Inst., 1976—78; pediatric intern and resident Johns Hopkins U. Sch. Medicine, Balt., 1974—76, asst. prof., 1978—83, assoc. prof., 1983—89, Clayton prof. oncology, 1989—, Howard Hughs Med. Inst. investigator, 1995—, prof. pathology, 1998—. Advisor NIH Sci. Rev. Groups, Nat. Cancer Inst.; bd. reviewing editors Science; assoc. editor Molecular Cell and Cancer Cell; sci. adv. bd. U, Calif., San Francisco, Cancer Ctr., GMP Genetics, Morphotek; sci. review bd. Pediatric Brain Tumor Found., US. Assoc. editor: Genes, Chromosomes and Cancer, mem. bd. reviewing editors: Sci. mag.; contbr. articles to profl. jours., 99 US patents in the field. Recipient William Allan award, Am. Soc. of Human Genetics, Alfred G. Knudson award, Nat. Cancer Inst., Anne & Jason Farber Lecture award, Am. Acad. Neurology, 1991, Internat. award, Gairdner Found., 1992, Medal of Honor, Am. Cancer Soc., 1992, Richard Lounsbery award, NAS, 1993, Baxter Rsch. award, Assn. Am. Med. Coll., 1994, laureates Passano Found., 1994, G.H.A. Clowes Meml. award, Am. Assn. Cancer Rsch., 1995, Charles S. Mott prize, GM Cancer Rsch. Found., 2000. Mem.: NAS, Am. Philosophical Soc., Inst. Medicine, Am. Acad. Arts and Scis. Achievements include revolutionizing our understanding of complex genetic mutations that occur when an normal bowel epithelial cell is transformed into a malignant cell. Office: Johns Hopkins U Sch Med Dept Oncology 424 N Bond St Baltimore MD 21231-1000*

VOGELSTEIN, JOHN L. venture capitalist; b. N.Y.C., Dec. 9, 1934; s. Hans A. and Ruth E. (Krieger) V.; m. Jacqueline C. Wolf, Sept. 5, 1957 (div. Sept. 1983); children: Hans A. II, Andrew W.; m. Lee Gibouleau, Dec. 29, 1983. Grad., The Taft Sch., 1952; student, Harvard U., 1954. Assoc. Lazard Freres & Co., N.Y.C., 1954-64, ptnr., 1964-66; v.p. E.M. Warburg, Pincus & Co., Inc., N.Y.C., 1967-70, exec. v.p., 1970-82, vice chmn., 1982—. Bd. dirs. Mattel, Inc., Hawthorne, Calif., Ingersoll Newspapers, Inc., Princeton, N.J., Community Newspapers, Inc., Princeton, JPT Holdings, Inc., N.Y.C., Adv0-System, Inc., Windsor, Conn., Magma Copper Co., San Manuel, Ariz, NH Acquisition Corp., Princeton; vice-chmn., bd. of overseers, Leonard N. Sch. of Bus., NYU; trustee, NYU, Temple Emanu-El; mem. bd. govs., RAND Grad. Sch. Trustee The Taft Sch., Watertown, Conn., 1982—, Prep for Prep, N.Y.C., 1983—; bd. dirs. N.Y. City Ballet, 1989—. Mem.: Jewish Mus. (pres.). Office: EM Warburg Pincus & Co Inc 466 Lexington Ave Fl 10 New York NY 10017-3147

VOGES, LINDA KAY, mathematics educator, telecommunications engineer; b. Oklahoma City, Oct. 23, 1946; d. James W. and Betty J. (Palmer) Bolt; m. Erich Nolan Voges, Jan. 26, 1991; 1 child: Virginia Lynn Simon. BS in Edn., East Ctrl. U., Ada, Okla., 1968; MS, U. North Tex., 1972; EdD, Baylor U., 1998. Cert. secondary math. tchr., Tex., planning engr. Southwest Bell Tel. Co. Math. tchr. Arlington (Tex.) Ind. Sch. Dist., 1970-71; tel. engr. Bell Tel. Co., Dallas, 1973-81; planning engr. Southwestern Bell Tel. Co., Dallas, 1982-89, mgr., course developer, 1990; dept. chair ctr. for applied learning Tex. State Tech. Coll., Waco, 1991-94; tech.-prep. curriculum coord. McLennan C.C., Waco, 1994-95; workforce edn. coord. Tex. Higher Edn. Coordinating Bd., Austin, 1995-96; asst. prof. Concordia U., Austin, 1996-99; program specialist Tex. Coun. on work Force Econs., Office of the Gov., Austin, 1999-2000; ednl. designer Viviance New Edn., Austin, 2000—; dir. sect. edn. Concordia U., Austin, 2000—02, edn. prof., 2000—; lectr., cohort coord. U. Tex., Austin. Planning and zoning bd. dirs. City of Woodway, Tex., 1992-95; rschr. Tex. Senate Edn. Com. Austin, 1995-98; campaign coord. YMCA-YWCA, Waco, Tex., 1991; vol. Jr. Achievement, Dallas, 1988; pub. sch. vol. Dallas Ind. Sch. Dist., 1987-89. Recipient Key Contrb. awards, Southwestern Bell Tel. Co., Dallas, 1987—89, Project Amigos, 1999—2002; grantee Project Passage, 1994. Mem.: AAUP (campus rep. 1997—98), Assn. Tex. Profl. Educators, Nat. Coun. Tchrs. Math., Kappa Delta Pi (rec. for blind and dyslectic com.). Avocations: writing, research, politics, theater. Home: 118 Royal Oak Ln Lakeway TX 78734-4520 Office: State of Tex 1100 San Jacinto Austin TX 78701 Office Phone: 512-232-4146. E-mail: voges@swbell.net.

VOGL, OTTO, polymer science and engineering educator; b. Traiskirchen, Austria, Nov. 6, 1927; came to U.S., 1953, naturalized, 1959; s. Franz and Leopoldine (Scholz) V.; m. Jane Cunningham, June 10, 1955; children: Eric, Yvonne. PhD, U. Vienna, 1950; Doctorate (hon.), U. Jena, Germany, 1983, Poly. Inst., Iasi, Romania, 1992, Osaka U., Japan, Slovak Acad. Scis., 2001. Instr. U. Vienna, 1948-55; research asso. U. Mich., 1953-55, Princeton U., 1955-56; scientist E.I. Du Pont de Nemours & Co., Wilmington, Del., 1956-70; prof. polymer sci. and engring. U. Mass., 1970-83, prof. emeritus, 1983—; Herman F. Mark prof. polymer sci. Poly. U., Bklyn., 1983-95, prof. emeritus, 1996—. Guest prof. Kyoto U., 1968, 80, Osaka U., 1968, 96, Royal Inst. Stockholm, 1971, 87, U. Freiburg, Germany, 1973, U. Berlin, 1977, Strasbourg U., 1976, Tech. U. Dresden, 1982, Wuhan (China) U.; Monbusho prof. Kyoto Inst. Technology, Japan, 1996; guest Soviet Acad. Sci., 1973, Polish Acad. Sci., 1973, 75, Acad. Sci. Romania, 1974, 76; cons. in field. Chmn. com. on macromolecular chemistry Nat. Acad. Sci. Author: Polyaldehydes, 1967, (with Furukawa) Polymerization of Heterocyclics, 1973, Ionic Polymerization, 1976, (with Simionescu) Radical Co and Graftpolymerization, 1978, (with Donaruma) Polymeric Drugs, 1978, (with Donaruma and Ottenbrite) Polymers in Biology and Medicine, 1980, (with Goldberg and Donaruma) Targeted Drugs, 1983, (with Immergut) Polymer Science in the Next Decade, 1997, (with Kitayama and Hatada) Macromolecular Design of Polymeric Materials; contbr. articles to profl. jours. Sr. fellow Japan Soc. Promotion of Sci., 1980; recipient Fulbright award, 1976, Humboldt prize, 1977, Chemistry Pioneer award, 1985, Gold medal City of Vienna, Austria, 1986, Exner medal, 1987, Mark medal, 1989, Honor Ring, City of Traiskirchen, 1989; golden hon. diploma U. Vienna, 2000, Hon. Cross of Arts and Scis., Rep. of Austria, 2000, Culture prize City of Traiskirchen, 2002, hon. medal SAS Polymer Rsch. Inst, 2003. Fellow AAAS; mem. Am. Chem. Soc. (chmn. div. polymer chemistry 1974, chmn. Conn. Valley sect. 1974, award applied polymer chemistry 1990, Herman F. Mark award 2000), Am. Inst. Chemistry (chmn. Pioneer Award 1985), Austrian Chem. Soc. (hon.), Japanese Soc. Polymer Sci. (award 1991), N.Y. Acad. Sci., Austrian Acad. Sci., Royal Swedish Acad. Sci., Pacific Polymer Fedn. (pres.), Slovak Chem. Soc. (hon.), Croatian Chem. Soc. (hon. mem.), Soc. Polymer Sci. Japan (life), Sigma Xi. Home: 12 Canterbury Ln Amherst MA 01002-3536 Office: U Mass Dept Polymer Sci and Engring Amherst MA 01003-4530 E-mail: vogl@polysci.umass.edu., voglotto@aol.com.

VOGLER, FREDERICK WRIGHT, French language educator; b. Burlington, Vt., May 27, 1931; s. Curtis Linville and Marion (Wright) V.; m. Mary Frances Angle, Aug. 27, 1965; 1 child, Robert BA, U. N.C., 1953, MA, 1955, PhD, 1961; postgrad, U. Strasbourg, France, 1953-54. Instr. U. N.C., Chapel Hill, 1961-62, asst. prof., 1963-66, assoc. prof., 1966-78, prof. French, 1978—, assoc. dean arts and scis., 1976-87, dir. undergrad. studies French and Italian, 1989-95; asst. prof. U. Iowa, Iowa City, 1962-63. Cons. Ednl. Testing Service, Princeton, N.J., 1967-70 Author: Vital d'Audiguier and the Early 17th Century French Novel, 1964; editor: Moliere Mocked: Three Contemporary Hostile Comedies, 1973; contbr. articles on French lit. and cultural history to profl. jours. Served to 1st lt. U.S. Army, 1955-65 Fulbright Commn. scholar, Washington, Paris, 1953; So. Fellowship Bd. fellow, Chapel Hill, 1955 Mem. Am. Assn. Tchrs. French, Swiss Am. Hist. Soc. Episcopalian. Home: 1010 Dawes St Chapel Hill NC 27516-3010 E-mail: fwvogler@email.unc.edu.

VOGT, ALBERT RALPH, forester, educator, program director; BS in Forest Mgmt., U. Mo., 1961, MS in Tree Physiology, 1962, PhD in Tree Physiology, 1966. Instr. in dendrology U. Mo., Columbia, 1965-66; asst. prof. rsch. tree physiology Ohio State U., 1966-69, assoc. prof., assoc. chmn. rsch. and adminstrn. forestry, 1969-76, prof., chmn. dept. adminstrn. and tchg. forestry, 1976-85; prof., dir. sch. natural resources U. Mo., 1985—2003, prof. emeritus, 2003—. Mem. Mo. Forest Heritage Initiative, Gov.'s Task Force Environ. Edn., Mo. Gov.'s Energy Coalition, Mo. Citizens Com. Soil, Water, and State Parks; co-chair steering com. 3d Forestry Edn. Symposium, 1991; co-chair external rev. dept. forestry So. Ill. U., Carbondale, 1993; co-chair external rev. Sch. Forest Resources Pa. State U., 1995; chair external rev.forestry U. Wis., Madison, 1997; chair on-site S.A.F. accreditation rev. dept. forest and natural resources Purdue U., 2003. Office: U Mo Sch Natural Resources 105H Natural Resources Bldg Columbia MO 65211-0001 Office Phone: 573-882-1627. E-mail: vogta@missouri.edu.

VOGT, ERICH WOLFGANG, physicist, academic administrator; b. Steinbach, Man., Can., Nov. 12, 1929; s. Peter Andrew and Susanna (Reimer) V.; m. Barbara Mary Greenfield, Aug. 27, 1952; children: Edith Susan, Elizabeth Mary, David Eric, Jonathan Michael, Robert Jeremy. BS, U. Man., 1951, MS, 1952; PhD, Princeton U., 1955; DSc (hon.), U. Man., 1982, Queen's U., 1984; LLD (hon.), U. Regina, 1986; DSc (hon.), Carleton U., 1988, U. B.C., 1999; LLD (hon.), Simon Fraser U., 1996. Rsch. officer Chalk River (Ont.) Nuclear Labs., 1956-65; prof. physics U. B.C., Vancouver, 1965-95, prof. emeritus, 1995—, assoc. dir. TRIUMF Project, 1968-73, dir. TRIUMF Project, 1981-94, v.p. univ., 1975-81; chmn. Sci. Council B.C., 1978-80. Co-editor: Advances in Nuclear Physics, 1968—; Contbr. articles to profl. jours. Decorated officer Order of Can.; recipient Centennial medal of Can., 1967 Fellow Royal Soc. Can., Am. Phys. Soc.; mem. Can. Assn. Physicists (past pres., gold medal for achievement in physics 1988). Office: Triumf 4004 Wesbrook Mall Vancouver BC Canada V6T 2A3 Office Phone: 604-222-1047.

VOGT, HARTMUT, education educator; b. Berlin, Oct. 18, 1923; s. Alfred and Luise (Thiele) Vogt; m. Helga Hellebrand, July 16, 1952. Cert. in tchg., U. Berlin, 1950, PhD, 1956. State tchr., Berlin, 1950-51; from lectr. to asst. prof. U. Berlin, Tübingen, Marburg, 1951-70; full prof. U. Dortmund, 1970-89, prof. emeritus, 1989—. Author: several books in field; contbr. articles to profl. jours. 1st lt. German Air Force, 1941—45. Mem.: Flying Club. Avocation: flying. Home: Otterbach 80 H 18 D-53902 Bad Muenstereifel Germany Office: Univ Dortmund Emil-Figge-Strasse 50 D-44221 Dortmund 50 Germany

VOGT, KATHLEEN CUNNINGHAM, musician, music educator; b. Ellwood City, Pa., July 3, 1951; d. Joseph Edward and Dorothea Cunningham Vogt. BS summa cum laude in Music Edn., Duquesne U., 1973, M in Music edn., 1975. Cert. Tchr Nat. Bd., 2003. Tchr., band and choral dir. Diocese of Pitts. Schs., 1973—79; tchr., band dir. Carrick HS, 1980—84; band dir., drama tchr. Hanahan (SC) HS, 1984—2004, Sangaree Mid. Sch. Instr. percussion Duquesne U., Pitts., 1975—79; adj. prof. Charleston So. U., SC, 2001—; guest clinician and conductor, 1975—. Musician: Pitts. Symphony Orch., Charleston Symphony Orch., Lowcountry Winds, Charleston (SC) Cmty. Band. Mem. Hanahan Area Arts Coun. Mem.: Nat. Bd. Cert. Tchrs., All Berkeley County Music Educators, Nat. Band Assoc., Nat. Baton Twirling Assn., Nat. Twirling Judges Bur. (Inducted into Baton Twirling Hall of Fame 2002), Am. Sch. Band Dirs. Assn., SC Band Dirs. Assn. (Outstanding Performance award 1985—2004, SC State Marching Band Champions 1986, 1987, 1988, 1991), SC Music Educators Assn., Music Educators Nat. Conf., Pi Lambda Theta, Phi Beta Mu. Home: 504 Greenmeadow Rd Goose Creek SC 29445 Personal E-mail: katyvogt@aol.com.

VOGT, MARTHA DIANE, lawyer; b. Albertville, Ala., Sept. 22, 1952; m. Robert A. Vogt, May 26, 1973. BA, Oakland U., 1974; JD, Wayne Law Sch., 1980. Bar: Mich. 1980, U.S. Ct. Appeals (4th cir.) 1985, Fla. 1988, U.S. Ct. Appeals (6th cir.) 1990, U.S. Ct. Appeals (11th cir.) 1996. Ptnr. Clark, Klein & Beaumont, Detroit, 1980-92, Bavol & Vogt, Tampa, Fla., 1992-95; pvt. practice Law Office of M. Diane Vogt, Tampa, Fla., 1995—. Adj. prof. Wayne Law Sch., Detroit, 1987-92; instr. U. South Fla., 1995. Author: The Silicone Solution, 1999; co-author: Lawyer Retention: Improving Job Satisfaction for Lawyers. Mem. ABA, DRI, State Bar of Mich. Assn., The Fla. Bar Assn. Office: Law Office M Diane Vogt 800 S Dakota Ave Apt 201 Tampa FL 33606-2855

VOGT, PETER K. oncologist; b. Broumov, Czech Republic, Mar. 10, 1932; BS dr. honoris causa, U. Würzburg, Germany, 1955; PhD, U. Tübingen, Germany, 1959; postgrad., Max-Planck Inst., Tübingen, 1955—59, U. Calif., Berkeley, 1959—62. Asst. prof. pathology U. Colo. Sch. Medicine, Denver, 1962—66, assoc. prof. pathology, 1966—67; assoc. prof. microbiology U. Wash., Seattle, 1967—69, prof. microbiology, 1969—71; Hastings prof. microbiology U. So. Calif., L.A., 1971—78, Hastings Disting. prof. microbiology, 1978—80, Hastings Disting. prof. microbiology and chair dept. microbiology, 1980—93; dept. molecular and exptl. medicine, head divsn. oncovirology Scripps Rsch. Inst., LaJolla, Calif., 1993—. Mem. sci. bd. advisors Nat. Cancer Inst., 1996—, German Cancer Ctr., Heidelberg. Mem. editl. bd. Virology, Current Topics in Microbiology and Immunology, Jour. Molecular Medicine, Cancer Rsch., Cell Growth and Differentiation, Archives of Biochemistry and Biophysics, 1994—99, Jour. Virology. Named McGinnis lectr., Duke U., 1999, Princess Takamatsu lectr., 1995, Calif. Scientist of the Yr., 1975; recipient Charles S. Mott prize, GM Cancer Rsch. Found., 1991, Howard Taylor Ricketts award, U. Chgo., 1991, Internat. prize in virology, ICN, 1989, Bristol Myers award, 1989, Paul-Ehrlich and Ludwig-Darmstaedter prize, 1988, Robert J. and Claire Pasarow award, 1987, Waterford Biomed. Sci. award, 1986, Ernst Jung prize for medicine, 1985, Alexander von Humboldt award, Fed. Republic Germany, 1984, Disting. Tchg. award, U. Wash., 1970—71, U. So. Calif., 1974, 1976, 1985, Irene-Vogeler prize, Max-Planck Soc., 1976, Assocs. award for creative scholarship and rsch., U. So. Calif., 1975, Studienstiftung des Deutschen Volkes, 1955. Fellow: Am. Acad. Microbiology; mem.: AAAS, NAS, Am. Philos. Soc., IOM, Deutsche Akademie der Naturforscher Leopoldina, Internat. Soc. Differentiation, Japanese Cancer Assn. (hon.), Am. Chem. Soc., Am. Assn. for Cancer Rsch., Am. Soc. Virology, Am. Soc. Microbiology (councilor 1976—77, chmn. virology divsn. 1975, vice chmn. virology divsn. 1973—74). Office: Scripps Research Inst Dept Molecular/Exptl Medicine 10550 N Torrey Pines Rd La Jolla CA 92037

VOGT, ROCHUS EUGEN, physicist, researcher; b. Neckarelz, Germany, Dec. 21, 1929; came to U.S., 1953; s. Heinrich and Paula (Schaefer) V.; m. Micheline Alice Yvonne Bauduin, Sept. 6, 1958; children: Michele, Nicole. Student, U. Karlsruhe, Germany, 1950-52, U. Heidelberg, 1952-53; SM, U. Chgo., 1957, PhD, 1961. Asst. prof. physics Calif. Inst. Tech., Pasadena, 1962-65, assoc. prof., 1965-70, prof., 1970—2002, R. Stanton Avery disting. svc. prof., 1982—2002, R. Stanton Avery disting. svc. prof. and prof. physics emeritus, 2002—, chmn. faculty, 1975-77, chief scientist Jet Propulsion Lab., 1977-78, chmn. div. physics, math. and astronomy, 1978-83, acting dir. Owens Valley Radio Obs., 1980-81, v.p. and provost, 1983-87. Vis. prof. physics MIT, 1988-94; dir. Caltech/MIT Laser Interferometer Gravitational Wave Observatory Project, 1987-94. Author: Cosmic Rays (in World Book Ency.), 1978, (with R.B. Leighton) Exercises in Introductory Physics, 1969; contbr. articles to profl. jours. Fulbright fellow, 1953-54; recipient Exceptional Sci. Achievement medal NASA, 1981, Profl. Achievement award U. Chgo. Alumni Assn., 1981. Fellow AAAS, A. Phys. Soc. Achievements include research in astrophysics and gravitation. Office: Calif Inst Tech 103-33 1200 E California Blvd Pasadena CA 91125-0001 Office Phone: 626-395-3800. Business E-Mail: vogt@caltech.edu.

VOHS, JAMES ARTHUR, health care program executive; b. Idaho Falls, Idaho, Sept. 26, 1928; s. John Dale and Cliff Lucille (Packer) Vohs; m. Janice Hughes, Sept. 19, 1953 (dec. Oct. 1999); children: Lorraine, Carol, Nancy, Sharla. BA, U. Calif., Berkeley, 1952; postgrad., Harvard Sch. Bus., 1966. Employed by various Kaiser affiliated orgns., 1952—92; chmn., pres., CEO Kaiser Found. Hosps. and Kaiser Found. Health Plan, INc., Oakland, Calif., 1975—92, chmn. emeritus; chmn. bd. dirs. Holy Names Coll., 1981—92; chmn. Marcus Foster Inst., 1981—. Chmn. Fed. Res. Bank San Francisco, 1991—94. Mem. Oakland Bd. Port Commrs., 1993—96; bd. dirs. Oakland-Alameda County Coliseum Complex, 1986—96, Bay Area Coun., 1985—94, chmn., 1991—92. With U.S. Army, 1946—48. Mem.: Inst. Medicine NAS.

VOIGHT, JACK C. state official; b. New London, Wisconsin, Dec. 17, 1945; s. Oscar C. and Thelma J. (Hamm) V.; m. Martha J. (Wolfe), July 14, 1973; children: Carly and Emily. BS, U. Wis., Oshkosh, 1971. Claims adjuster U.S. F and G Ins. Co., Appleton, Wis., 1971-74; ins. agy. owner Voight Ins. Agy., Appleton, Wis., 1974—; state treas. State of Wis., 1995—. Bank organizer Am. Nat. Bank, Appleton, Wis. 1992-94; real estate broker Voight Realty and Ins., Appleton, 1977-92. Pres. Appleton Northside Bus. Assn., 1982; alderman city coun., City of Appleton, 1983-83, pres., 1992-93; Sgt. U.S. Army, 1968-70. Decorated Bronze Star; named Citizen of Yr. Appleton Northside Bus. Assn., 1990. Mem. Nat. Assn. State Treas., Midwest State Treas. Assn. (pres. 1996-97); Appleton Noon Optimist Club (pres. 1980). Republican. Presbyterian. Avocations: gardening, politics. Office: State Treas Wis PO Box 7871 Madison WI 53707-7871 E-mail: jack.voight@ost.state.wi.us.

VOIGHT, JON, actor; b. Yonkers, N.Y., Dec. 29, 1938; s. Elmer and Barbara (Camp) V.; m. Lauri Peters, 1962 (div. 1967); m. Marcheline Bertrand, Dec. 12, 1971 (div.); children: James Haven, Angelina Jolie. BFA, Cath. U., 1960; studied with, Sanford Meisner and Samantha Harper, N.Y.C. Stage appearances include O Oysters Revue, 1961, The Sound of Music, 1961, A View from the Bridge, 1965, Romeo and Juliet, 1966, The Tempest, 1966, Two Gentlemen of Verona, 1966, That Summer-That Fall, 1967 (Theatre World award 1967), A Streetcar Named Desire, 1973, The Hashish Club, 1975, Hamlet, 1976, The Seagull, 1992; TV appearances include Cimarron Strip, Gunsmoke; films include Fearless Frank, 1967, Hour of the Gun, 1967, Out of It, 1969, Midnight Cowboy, 1969 (Acad. award nom. best actor 1969, NY Critics Circle award 1969, L.A. Film Critics award best actor 1969, BAFTA award most promising newcomer 1969, Golden Globe award most promising newcomer 1969), Catch-22, 1970, The Revolutionary, 1970, Deliverance, 1972, The All American Boy, 1973, Conrack, 1974, The Odessa File, 1974, End of the Game, 1976, Coming Home, 1978 (Acad. award best actor 1978, Golden Globe award 1978, Cannes Internat. Film festival award 1978, NY Film Critics best actor award 1978, L.A. Film Critics award best actor 1978), The Champ, 1979 (Golden Globe award 1979), Runaway Train, 1985 (Acad. award nominee best actor 1986, London Film Critics award nominee 1986, Golden Globe best actor 1986), Desert Bloom, 1986, Eternity, 1990, Heat, 1995, Mission Impossible, 1996, Rosewood, 1997, Anaconda, 1997, Most Wanted, 1997, The Rainmaker, 1997, Boys Will Be Boys, 1997, U Turn, 1997, I Once Had a Life, 1998, Enemy of the State, 1998, Varsity Blues, 1999, A Dog of Flanders, 1999, Pearl Harbor, 2001, Lara Croft: Tomb Raider, 2001, Zoolander, 2001, Ali, 2001, Holes, 2003, Karate Dog, 2004, The Manchurian Candidate, 2004, Superbabies: Baby Geniuses 2, 2004; TV films include Chernobyl: The Final Warning, 1991, The Last of His Tribe, 1992; actor, prodr., co-writer film Lookin' To Get Out, 1982, the Fixer, 1998; actor, prodr. film Table for Five, 1983, A Tribute to Dustin Hoffman, 1999, Noah's Ark, 1999, Second String, 2000.*

VOIGT, BARTON R. state supreme court justice; BA and MA in Am. History, law degree, U. Wyo. Atty., Thermopolis, Wyo.; former Hot Springs County atty.; former county ct. judge; former dist. judge Douglas, Wyo.; justice Wyo. Supreme Ct., 2001—. Office: 2301 Capitol Ave Cheyenne WY 82001

VOIGT, CYNTHIA, writer; b. Boston, Feb. 25, 1942; d. Frederick C. and Elise (Keeney) Irving; married, 1964 (div. 1972); m. Walter Voigt, Aug. 30, 1974; children: Jessica, Peter. BA, Smith Coll., 1963. High sch. tchr. English, Glen Burnie, Md., 1965-67; tchr. English Key Sch., Annapolis, Md., 1968-69, dept. chmn., 1971-79, tchr., dept. chmn., 1981-88. Author: Homecoming, 1981, Tell Me If the Lovers Are Losers, 1982, Dicey's Song, 1982 (John Newbery medal 1983), The Callender Papers, 1983 (Edgar award 1984), A Solitary Blue, 1983, Building Blocks, 1984, Jackeroo, 1985, The Runner, 1985 (Silver Pencil award 1988, Deutscher Jugend Literator Preis 1989, ALAN award 1989), Come a Stranger, 1986, Izzy, Willy Nilly, 1986 (Calif. Young Reader's award 1990), Stories About Rosie, 1986, Sons From Afar, 1987, Tree by Leaf, 1988, Seventeen Against the Dealer, 1989, On Fortune's Wheel, 1990, The Vandemark Mummy, 1991, Orfe, 1992, Glass Mountain, 1991, David and Jonathan, 1992, The Wings of a Falcon, 1993, When She Hollers, 1994, Bad Girls, 1996, Bad, Badder, Baddest, 1997, Elske, 1999, It's Not Easy Being Bad, 2000, Bad Girls in Love, 2002.

VOIGT, ELLEN, literature educator; BA, Converse Coll.; MFA, U. Iowa. Prof. poetry MIT; prof. Goddard Coll., Warren Wilson Coll., Asheville, NC, 1981—. Tchr. Bread Loaf Writers' Conf., Aspen Writer's Conf., Ind. Writers' Conf., Napa Writer's Conf., Catskills Writers' Conf., RopeWalk Writers' Conf. Author: (poems) Claiming Kin, 1976, The Forces of Plenty, 1983, The Lotus Flowers., 1987, Two Trees, 1992, Shadows of Heaven, 2002 (Nat. Book award finalist), (sonnet) Kyrie, 1995 (Nat. Book Critics' Circle award finalist, Teasdale Poetry prize); co-editor (with Gregory Orr): Poets Teaching Poets: Self and the World; author: The Flexible Lyric, 2001. Fellow, Acad. Am. Poets, 2002; grantee, Vt. Coun. Arts, NEA, Guggenheim Found. Office: Warren Wilson Coll PO Box 9000 Asheville NC 28815

VOIGT, HEIDI M. music educator; d. Charles John and Anno Montgomery; m. John Voigt, Apr. 5, 1975; children: Heather, Jacob, Luke, Noah, Hannah. Pianist Magnolia Bible Ch., Magnolia, Tex., 2001—; worship leader/pianist Faith Family Fellowship, Magnolia, Tex., 2000—03; piano tchr. Magnolia, Tex., 2001—. Mem.: Conroe Music Teachers Assn., Tex. Music Teachers Assn., Music Teachers Nat. Assn. Republican. E-mail: heidivoigt@sbcglobal.net.

VOIGT, RICHARD, lawyer; b. Oskaloosa, Iowa, Jan. 20, 1946; s. Franz Otto Wilhelm and Minni (Heilbrunn) V.; m. Annemarie H. Riemer, Oct. 2, 1976; children: Samuel, Nicholas. BA, Conn. Wesleyan U., 1968; JD, U. Va., 1974. Bar: Va. 1974, U.S. Dist. Ct. (ea. dist.) Va. 1979, Conn. 1981, U.S. Dist. Ct. Conn. 1982, U.S. Ct. Claims 1982, U.S. Ct. Appeals (4th cir.) 1982. Assoc. counsel regional litigation Solicitor's Office Osha Div., 1978-80; staff atty. U.S. Dept. Labor, Washington, 1974-78; prin. Siegel, O'Connor, Schiff, Zangari & Kainen, P.C., 1981-88, 87-88; ptnr. Cummings & Lockwood, Hartford, 1988—2003, McCarter & English, Hartford, 2003—. Contbg. author: ABA Treatise on Occupational Safety and Health Law, 1988; contbr. articles to profl. jours. Bd. dirs. Urban League Greater Hartford, 1984-88, Isnt. for Non-Profit Tng. and Devel., 1991-95, Hartford Proud and Beautiful, 1995—, Greater Hartford Arts Coun., 2001—. Mem. ABA (labor and employment law sect., OSHA com., litigation sect.), Conn. Bar Assn. (labor employment law sect., employment discrimination com., com. on alternative dispute resolution). Avocations: acrylic design, history, sports. Office: McCarter & English LLP 36th Floor Cityplace I Hartford CT 06103

VOINOVICH, GEORGE V. senator, former governor; b. Cleve., July 15, 1936; m. Janet Voinovich; 3 children. BA, Ohio U., 1958; JD, Ohio State U., 1961; LL.D. (hon.), Ohio U., 1981. Bar: Ohio 1961, U.S. Supreme Ct. 1968. Asst. atty. gen. State of Ohio, 1963-64; mem. Ohio Ho. of Reps., 1967-71; auditor Cuyahoga County, Ohio, 1971-76; commr., 1977-78; lt. gov. State of Ohio, 1979; mayor City of Cleve., 1979-89; gov. State of Ohio, 1991-98; U.S. senator from Ohio, 1999—. Pres. Nat. League Cities, 1984-85; trustee U.S. Conf. Mayors; chmn. Midwestern Govs. Conf., 1991-92, Coun. Gt. Lakes Govs., 1992-94. Recipient cert. of Merit award Ohio U., Humanitarian award NCCJ, 1986; named one of Outstanding Young Men in Ohio Ohio Jaycees, 1970; one of Outstanding Young Men in Greater Cleve. Cleve. Jaycees; Disting. Urban Mayor award Nat. Urban Coalition, 1987; named to All-Pro City Mgmt. team City & State Mag., 1987. Mem. Rep. Govs. Assn. (vice chmn. 1991-92, chmn. 1992-93), Nat. Govs. Assn. (chmn. edn. action team on sch. readiness 1991, chmn. child support enforcement work group 1991-92, mem. strategic planning task force 1991-92, mem. human resources com., co-chmn. task force on edn. 1992-93, mem. exec. com. 1993-98, co-lead gov. on fed. mandates, chmn. 1997-98), Omicron Delta Kappa, Phi Alpha Theta, Phi Delta Phi. Republican. Office: US Senate 317 Hart Bldg Washington DC 20510-0001

VOITLE, ROBERT ALLEN, college dean, physiologist; b. Parkersburg, W.Va., May 12, 1938; s. Ray Christian and Ruby Virginia (Hannaman) V.; m. Linda Ellen Loveday, Dec. 5, 1975; children: Robert Allen, Elizabeth Anne, Christian Blair, Vanessa Virginia. BS, W.Va. U., 1962; MS, W.Va., 1965; PhD, U. Tenn., 1969. Asst. in poultry U. Tenn., Knoxville, 1965-69; asst. prof. physiology U. Fla., Gainesville, 1969-75, assoc. prof., 1975-79; prof., head dept. poultry Calif. Poly. State U., San Luis Obispo, 1979-81; dean Coll. Agr., Auburn U., Ala., 1981—2000, prof. poultry sci., 2000—. Cons. Columbia Bank for Coops., S.C., 1972 Contbr. articles to sci. jours. Pres., other offices Alachua County Fair Assn., Gainesville, 1969-79. Recipient Pub. Service award Alachua County Commn., 1975; recipient Tchr. of Yr. award U. Fla., 1977, Golden Feather award Calif. Poly. Inst., 1982 Mem. Poultry Sci. Assn., So. Poultry Sci. Assn., Gainesville Jaycees (JCI senatorship), Sigma Xi, Gamma Sigma Delta Clubs: Elks. Episcopalian. Home: 2247 Longwood Dr Auburn AL 36830-7105 Office: Auburn U Coll Agr Auburn AL 36849 Office Phone: 334-844-2603. Business E-Mail: rvoitle@ag.auburn.edu.

VOJCANIN, SAVA ALEXANDER, lawyer; b. Oak Lawn, Ill., Oct. 15, 1964; s. Jovan and Lili (Yovanovich) V.; m. Valerie S. Rupich, Oct. 12, 2002; 1 child: John William. Diploma, Culver Mil. Acad., 1981; BA with distinction, DePauw U., 1985; JD, Washington U., 1988. Bar: Ill. 1988, U.S. Dist. Ct. (no. dist.) Ill. 1989, U.S. Dist. Ct. (no. dist.) Tex. 1996. Assoc. Schaffenegger, Watson & Peterson Ltd., Chgo., 1988-91, Clausen Miller P.C., Chgo., 1991-98, ptnr., 1999—, shareholder, 2002—. Editor: Law, Culture and Values, 1989. Mem. Mayor's Adv. Coun. on Immigrant and Refugee Affairs, Chgo., 1992-97; trustee St. Basil Orthodox Ch. of Lake Forest, 1997—, sec. bd. trustees, 1999-2002, nominating com., 2002--. Mem.: Chgo. Bar Assn., Serbian Bar Assn. Am. (treas. 1999—2000, sec. 2000—01, v.p. 2001—02, pres. 2002—03, bd. dirs.). Orthodox. Office: Clausen Miller PC 10 S LaSalle St Chicago IL 60603-1098 Office Phone: 312-855-1010. Business E-Mail: svojcanin@clausen.com.

VOJTA, PAUL ALAN, mathematics professor; b. Mpls., Sept. 30, 1957; s. Francis J. and Margaret L. V. B in Math., U. Minn., 1978; MA, Harvard U., 1980, PhD, 1983. Instr. Yale U., New Haven, 1983-86; fellow Math. Scis. Rsch. Inst., Berkeley, Calif., 1986-87, Miller Inst. for Basic Rsch., Berkeley, 1987-89; assoc. prof. U. Calif., Berkeley, 1989-92, prof., 1992—. Mem. Inst. for Advanced Study, Princeton, 1989-90, 96-97. Author: Diophantine Approximations and Value Distribution Theory, 1987. Recipient perfect score Internat. Math. Olympiad, 1975. Mem. Am. Math. Soc. (Frank Nelson Cole Number Theory prize 1992), Math. Assn. Am., Phi Beta Kappa, Tau Beta Pi. Avocations: computer, skiing. Office: Univ Calif Dept Math 970 Evans Hall # 3840 Berkeley CA 94720-3840

VOKETAITIS, ARNOLD MATTHEW, bass-baritone, educator; b. East Haven, Conn., May 11, 1930; s. Mathew Joseph and Agnes Mary (Pilvelis) V.; m. Marion Lee Dever, June 1959 (div. 1967); children: Arnold Mathew Jr., Paul Stanley; m. Nijole Lipciute, Sept. 6, 1968. BS in Bus. Adminstrn, Quinnipiac Coll., 1954. Dir. opera program De Paul U., Chgo., 1987-89. Lectr. techniques for mus. stage, author singing technique Northwestern U., Evanston, Ill., 1986; mem. adv. panels in music and ethnic affairs Ill. Arts Coun.; mem. panel for opera and mus. theatre NEA; faculty mem. Brevard (N.C.) Summer Music Ctr., 1987, 88; artist-in-residence for opera and voice Auburn U., Ala., 1990-93; artist/mgr. for pianists, formed Keyboard Artists Internat., 1998. Condr. master classes in singing; author on voice technique; operatic debut with N.Y.C. Opera, 1958, European debut at Liceo, Barcelona, Spain, 1968; mem. Met. Opera Nat. Co., appeared with maj. operatic and symphonic orgns. in U.S., Can., Mex., Cen. Am., S.Am., Lyric Opera of Chgo., 1966-84, 89, rec. artist for Desto, Vox, Columbia, RCA; recitalist appearances on Pay-TV; classical soloist U.S. Army Band, Washington. Served as sgt. U.S. Army, 1954-56. Recipient 1st place award, Conn. Opera Assn. auditions, 1957, Rockefeller Found. award, 1964, Lithuanian Man of Yr. award, 1990, Disting. Alumni award, Quinnipiac U., 1991. Mem. AFTRA, Am. Guild Mus. Artists (life), Actors Equity. Avocations: golf, fishing, theater. *I have felt very strongly over the years that opera was written to be enjoyed, not revered, and that it cried out to be acted as well as sung. With television's influence on the viewer, necessity became reality and my hopes are being realized.*

VOKSHOOR, AMIR, neurosurgeon; b. Tehran, Iran, Aug. 17, 1970; s. Mir Hashem Vokhshoor zadeh and Mihan Jamali. BS, Old Dominion U., 1988—92. M.D. Med. Coll. of Va., 1996. Spine surgery resident fellow U. of South Fla., 2001; staff neurosurgeon So. Calif. Permanente Med. Group, Woodland Hills, Calif., 2002—. Neurosurgical resident Ohio State U. Med. Ctr., 1996—2002. Recipient Honors Rsch. in Neuroanatomy, Old Dominion U., 1992; A.D. Williams Rsch. Fellowship award, Med. Coll. of Va., 1994. Mem.: AMA, N.Am. Spine Soc., ARGOS N.Am. (bd. mem. 2003), Am. Assn. of Neurol. Surgeons (assoc.), Alpha Omega Alpha. Avocation: travel. Office: Woodland Hills Med Ctr NEUROSURG 5601 De Soto Avenue Woodland Hills CA 91365 Office Phone: 818-719-3519.

VOLAKIS, JOHN LEONIDAS, engineering educator; b. Chios, Greece, May 13, 1956; came to U.S., 1973; s. Leonidas I. and Maria L. (Makarigakis) V.; m. Maria I. Papouras, 1985; children: Leo, Alexandro. BE summa cum laude, Youngstown State U., 1978; MS, Ohio State U., 1979, PhD, 1982. Mem. tech. staff Rockwell Internat., Columbus, Ohio, Lakewood, Calif., 1982-84; asst. prof. elec. engrng. and computer sci. U. Mich., Ann Arbor, 1984-89, assoc. prof., 1989-94, prof. computer sci., 1994—, prof. elec. engrng., dir. radiation lab, 1998-2000; Chope chmn., prof. engrng., dir. ElectraSci. Labs. Ohio State U., Columbus, 2003—. Gen. chmn. IEEE Antennas and Propagation Internat. Symposium and Radio Sci. Meeting, 1993; mem. tech. coms COMPUMAG Conf., 1994, 95, 98, Advanced Computational Electromagnetics Conf., 1995, 96; mem. Senate Assembly, U. Mich. rsch. policies and acad. affairs coms., 1994-97, elec. engrng. dept. exec. com., 1997-99, grad. divsn. com., 1990—; dir. electrosci. lab., 2003—; co-chair IEEE Antennas and Propagation Internat. Symposium, 2003. Co-author: (books) Approximate Boundary Conditions in Electromagnetics, 1995, Finite Element Methods for Electromagnetics, 1998; contbr. chpts. or articles to 20 other books, more than 210 articles to refereed jours., 240 tech. papers to sci. symposiums or confs.; assoc. editor IEEE Antennas and Propagation Transactions, 1989-93, IEEE Antennas and Propagation Mag., 1992—, Radio Sci., 1994-97, Jour. Electromagnetics Waves and Applications, 1995-2003; co-inventor slot spiral antenna with integrated balun and feed, patent pending. Fellow IEEE (numerous coms. including adminstrv. com. 1996-99, past chmn. antennas symposium), IEEE Antennas and Propagation Soc. (pres.-elect 2002-03); mem. Internat. Union of Radio Sci., Sigma Xi, Phi Kappa Phi, Tau Beta Pi. Office: Ohio State U 1320 Kinnear Rd Columbus OH 43212

VOLBERDING, PAUL ARTHUR, academic physician; b. Rochester, Minn., Sept. 26, 1949; s. Walter A. and Eldora M. (Prescher) V.; m. Juline Christofferson, June 15, 1971 (div. June 1976); m. Mary M. Cooke, June 6, 1980; children: Alexander, Benjamin, Emily. AB, U. Chgo., 1971; MD, U. Minn., 1975. Resident in internal medicine U. Utah, Salt Lake City, 1975-78; fellow in oncology U. Calif., San Francisco, 1978-81; dir. med. oncology San Francisco Gen. Hosp., 1981—, dir. AIDS program, 1983—; dir. Ctr. for AIDS Rsch. U. Calif., San Francisco, 1988—, prof. medicine, 1990—. Bd. dirs. Dignity Ptnrs. Inc., 1996—; elected mem., Inst. of Medicine, 1999. Editor: Medical Management in AIDS, 1986; editor Jour. of AIDS, 1990—. Fellow ACP, AAAS; mem. Internat. AIDS Soc. (founder, chmn. bd.). Office: U Calif San Francisco San Francisco AIDS Program 995 Potrero Ave San Francisco CA 94110-2859

VOLBERG, HERMAN WILLIAM, electronics engineer, consultant; b. Hilo, Hawaii, Apr. 6, 1925; s. Fred Joseph and Kathryn Thelma (Ludloff) V.; m. Louise Ethel Potter, Apr. 26, 1968 (dec.); children: Michael, Lori. BSEE, U. Calif., Berkeley, 1949. Project engr. Naval Electronics Lab., San Diego, 1950-56; head solid state rsch. S.C. div. Gen. Dynamics, San Diego, 1956-60; founder Solidyne Solid State Instruments, La Jolla, Calif., 1958-60; founder, v.p. electronics divsn. Ametek/Straza, El Cajon, Calif., 1960-66; founder, cons. H.V. Cons., San Diego, 1966-69; sr. scientist Naval Ocean Systems Ctr., Oahu, Hawaii, 1970-77; chief scientist Integrated Scis. Corp., Santa Monica, Calif., 1978-80; founder, pres. Acoustic Sys. Inc., Goleta, Calif., 1980-84, Invotron, Inc., Murray, Utah, 1984—; sr. scientist Reson, Inc., Santa Barbara, Calif., 1992—. Cons. Lockheed-Martin, 1985—, U. Utah Ctr. for Engrng. Design, 1991; cons. on autonomous underwater vehicle sonar systems Mitsui/U. Tokyo, 1992; lectr. solid state course UCLA and IBM, 1956-62; instr. Applied Tech. Inst., Columbia, Md., 1988—; contbr. to undersea acoustical rsch. and devel. programs European Union, 1990—. Contbr. articles to IRE Bull., IEEE Ocean Electronics Symposium, IEEE/MTS Oceans, UDT Conf. Procs. Mem. adv. panels for advanced sonar systems and for high resolution sonars, USN, 1970-77. 1st lt. U.S. Army, 1944-47, ETO. Recipient award of merit Dept. Navy, 1973, 94. Mem.: NRA, AAAS, IEEE (life), Math. Assn. Am., N.Y. Acad. Scis., Acoustical Soc. Am., Air Force Assn., U.S. Naval Inst., Mine Warfare Assn., Marine Tech. Soc., Planetary Assn., Libr. Congress Assocs. (charter), Old Crows, Am. Legion, Elks, Masons. Achievements include patents for device for detecting and displaying the response of tissue to stimuli, high rate neutralizer (HIRAN), crane high-voltage sensing system. Home and Office: 41 W 6830 S Murray UT 84107-7124 Personal E-mail: hwv@aros.net.

VOLCKER, PAUL A. economist; b. Cape May, N.J., Sept. 5, 1927; s. Paul A. and Alma Louise (Klippel) V.; m. Barbara Marie Bahnson, Sept. 11, 1954 (dec. June 1998); children: Janice, James. AB summa cum laude, Princeton U., 1949, LLD (hon.), 1982; MA, Harvard U., 1951, LLD (hon.), 1985. Economist Fed. Res. Bank N.Y., 1952-57, pres., 1975-79; economist Chase Manhattan Bank, N.Y.C., 1957-61, v.p., dir. planning, 1965-68; with Dept. Treasury, Washington, 1961-65, 69-74, dep. under sec. monetary affairs, 1963-65, under sec., 1969-74; chmn. bd. govs. Fed. Res. Bd., Washington, 1979-87. Prof. internat. econ. policy Princeton U., 1988-95; chmn. Nat. Commn. on Pub. Svc., 1987-90, Internat. Acctg. Stds. Com., Trilateral Commn., 1990-2001, Internat. House & Fin., Svcs. Vol. Corps. Sr. fellow Woodrow Wilson Sch. Pub. and Internat. Affairs, 1974-75. Mem. Am. Coun. Germany (dir.), Japan Soc. (dir.), Inst. Internat. Econs. (dir.).

VOLDMAN, STEVEN HOWARD, electrical engineer; b. Rochester, NY, Sept. 8, 1957; s. Carl Jerome and Blossom (Passer) V.; m. Annie Curry Brown, July 1986; children: Aaron Samuel, Rachel Pesha. BS, U. Buffalo, 1979; MS, MIT, 1981, EE, 1982; MS in Engrng. Physics, U. Vt., 1986, PhD, 1991; postgrad., IBM, 1988-91. Engrng. asst. R.E. Ginna Nuclear plant Rochester Gas & Electric, N.Y., 1977, 78; rsch. assoc. MIT, Boston, 1979-81, rsch. assoc. high voltage rsch. lab., 1981-82; staff level engr. IBM, Burlington, Vt.,

1982—, 4-Mb DRAM devel. staff, 1985-88, 16-Mb DRAM devel. staff, 1991-93, 0.25 um advanced logic devel., 1993—, 0.15 um development, SOI devel., SIGE devel., SEMATECH esd testors and testing chmn., 1997—, SiGe devel., 2000—, SiGeC devel., 2001—, sr. engr., 2002—. Adv. engr. IBM, 1993—, sr. engr., 2003—; bd. dir. Conf. on Judaism in Rural New Eng., Inc.; tech. program com. Internat. Reliability Physics, Symposium, Taiwan, Electrostatic Discharge Conf.; coord. SEMATECH Electrostatic Discharge tech. benchmarking group, 1996—, Integrated Reliability Workshop, 1999, Internat. Reliability Physics Symposium, 2002, Elec. Overstress/Electrostatic Discharge Symposium, 1998, tech. program chmn., 2000, steering com., 2000—01, vice-chmn., 2001, bd. dir., gen. chmn., 01, tech. roadmap chmn.; tech. com. Internat. Reliability Physics Symposium, chmn. subcom. electrostatic discharge/latchup, 2002—03; liaison SEMATECH/ESDA; chmn. EOS/ESD Device Testing Std. Com. on Transmission Line Pulse, 2001—; steering com. Electrostatic Discharge Symposium, 2002—03, gen. chmn., 2002; tech. program com. Taiwan Electrostatic Discharge Conf., Internat. Conf. on Electromagnetic App, Taipei, Taiwan; bd. gov. Taiwan ESD Symposium, Singapore Internat. Phys. and Failure Analysis. Contbr. articles Sci. Am., Internat. ESD Jour., ESD Threshold, Tech. Program Com. of Taiwan Internat. Conf. on Electromagnetic Applications and Compatibility, 2004., Electron Device Meeting, Conf. on Elec. Insulation and Dielectric Phenomena, Transaction Elec. Devices, Computational Method in Elec. Engring., Numerical Analysis of Sem. Devices and Integrated Crcts., Device Rsch. Conf., Electrochem. Soc., Internat. Conf. on Microelectronic Test Structures, IEEE Transaction on Nuclear Sci., ECS Low Temperature Procs., Jour. Applied Physics, Jour. Electrostats. Discharge and Elec. Overstress, others. Bd. dir. Ohavi Zedek Synagogue, 1986—90, bd. gov., 2001—; bd. dir. U. Vt. Hillel, 1999—. Fellow IEEE; mem. Electrostatic Discharge Assn. (bd. dirs., stds. com. chmn. transmission line pulse device 5.5 2001—, edn. com., bd. dirs., symposium gen. chmn., tech. com.), MIT Club Vt., subcommittee chmn. Internat. Reliability Physics Symposium, 2004-2005, Sigma Xi, Phi Eta Sigma, Tau Beta Pi. Democrat. Achievements include over 130 patents in field. Office Phone: 802-769-8368. E-mail: a108501@us.ibm.com.

VOLENTINE, RICHARD J., JR., lawyer; b. Tampa, Fla., Apr. 2, 1955; s. Richard J. Sr. and Mary Francis (Shaw) V.; m. Susan Ruth Zimmerman, May 16, 1981; children: Rachel Elizabeth, Scott Thomas, Melissa Mary. BS, Spring Hill Coll., 1977; JD, U. Ala., 1980. Bar: Ala. 1980, Mo. 1982, Fla. 1984. Staff atty. Ala. Jud. Coll., Tuscaloosa, 1980-81; staff counsel Citicorp Person-to-Person, Inc., St. Louis, 1982; regional counsel Citicorp Person-to-Person Corp., Tampa, 1982-84; asst. gen. counsel Citicorp Savs. Fla., Miami, 1984-85; assoc. counsel Nationwide Capital Corp., Atlanta, 1985-86; regional atty. FDIC, Atlanta, 1986-88; gen. counsel, v.p. Altus Bank, Mobile, Ala., 1988-90; v.p., assoc. gen. counsel Chase Home Mortgage Corp., Tampa, Fla., 1990-91; sr. v.p., chief legal officer Prudential Bank, Atlanta, 1991—. Mem. ABA, Am. Corp. Counsel Assn., Ala. Jud. Coll. Faculty Assn. (hon.). Republican. Roman Catholic. Avocations: playing golf and other sports, photography, writing. Home: 2688 Tritt Springs Dr Marietta GA 30062-5268 Office: Prudential Bank 1 Ravinia Dr Ste 1000 Atlanta GA 30346-2103

VOLGIN, DENYS V. medical researcher; b. Melitopol, Ukraine, Apr. 19, 1973; s. Victor E. Volgin and Ludmila I. Volgina; m. Valeria Dovbik, June 12, 2003; 1 child, Anastasia; 1 child from previous marriage, Darya D. Volgina. MS biology, chemistry(hon.), Melitopol State Pedagogical U., Ukraine, 1990—95; PhD physiology of human and animals, Bogomolets Inst. Physiology, Kiev, Ukraine, 1996—99. Asst. tchr. physiology Melitopol State Pedagogical U., Ukraine, 1995—96; postgraduate rschr. Bogomolets Inst. Physiology, Kiev, 1996—99; postdoctoral rschr. U. Pa., Phila., 1999—2002, rsch. assoc., 2002—. Recipient Faculty Career Advancement award, Am. Sleep Medicine Found., 2004; fellow Soros Fellowships, Internat. Renaissance Found., 1994, 1996. Mem.: Internat. Soc. Neurochemistry, Am. Acad. Sleep Medicine. Christian. Achievements include research in Pharmacological correction of hypoxic states; Study of the role of nitric oxide in central control of breathing in neonatal animals; Single-cell gene expression profiling of upper airway motoneurons; Study of GABAergic mechanisms in hypothalamic neurons involved in sleep/wake regulation. Avocations: poetry, exercise. Home: 4032 Spruce St Philadelphia PA 19104 Office: Univ Pa 3800 Spruce St 209 E/Vet Philadelphia PA 19104 Office Phone: 215-898-6258. Business E-Mail: dvolgin@vet.upenn.edu. E-mail: dvolgin@vet.upenn.edu.

VOLGY, THOMAS JOHN, political science educator, organization official; b. Budapest, Hungary, Mar. 19, 1946; BA magna cum laude, Oakland U., 1967; MA, U. Minn., 1969, PhD, 1972. Prof. polit. sci. U. Ariz., Tucson; dir. U. Teaching Ctr.; mayor City of Tucson, 1987-91. Exec. dir. Internat. Studies Assn., 1995—; chmn. telecom. com. U. Conf. Mayors, 1988—; Dem. nominee for congress, 1998; cons. H.S. curriculum project Ind. U. Author: Politics in the Trenches, 2001; co-author: The Forgotten Americans, 1992; editor: Exploring Relationships Between Mass Media and Political Culture: The Impact of Television and Music on American Society, 1976; contbr. articles to profl. jours.; producer two TV documentaries for PBS. Mem. Nat. Women's Polit. Caucus Conv., 1983, U.S. Senate Fin. Com., 1985, U.S. Ho. of Reps. Telecomm. Com., 1988—, Polit. Sci. Adminstrn. Com., 1986, Gov.'s Task Force on Women and Poverty, 1986, United Way, 1985-87; bd. dirs. Honors Program, 1981—, U. Teaching Ctr., 1988—, Tucson Urban League, 1981, Ododo Theatre, 1984, So. Ariz. Mental Health Care Ctr., 1987, Nat. Fedn. Local Cable TV Programmers; chmn. Internat. Rels. Caucus, 1981, 86—, Transp. and Telecommunications Com. Nat. League Cities, 1986, 88-91. NDEA scholar, 1964-76; NDEA fellow, 1967-70; recipient Oasis award for oustanding prodn. of local affairs TV programming; named Outstanding Young Am., 1981, Outstanding Naturalized Citizen of Yr., 1980; faculty research grantee U. Ariz., 1972-75, 77-78. Mem. Pima Assn. Govts., Nat. Fedn. Local Cable Programmers. Democrat. Jewish. Office: U Ariz Polit Dept Sci Tucson AZ 85721-0001

VOLK, AUSTIN N. insurance company executive; b. N.Y.C., Dec. 28, 1918; s. Nicholas and Helen Volk; m. Rae Petigrue Volk, Aug. 17, 1979; children: Deborah Saliba, John Glidden, James L.P. Glidden, Gordon G. Glidden. BA in Econ., Brown U., Providence, 1941. V.p. Nicholas Volk & Co. Inc., N.Y.C., 1946—55, pres., 1955—75. Pres. Nat. Naval Res. Surface Policy Bd., Omaha, 1964—66; mem. Nat. Naval Res. Policy Bd., Washington, 1967—69. Pres. Englewood Cemetery Assn., NJ, 1988—; trustee, chmn. Naval War Coll. Found., 1997—99; councilman, coun. pres. City of Englewood, NJ, 1955—59, mayor, 1959—63, 1965—67; assemblyman State of N.J., Trenton, 1968—72. Capt. USNR, 1941—73, PTO, WWII, ATO. Mem.: N.Y. Coun., Navy League (pres. 1982—84, Teddy Roosevelt Leadership award 1982), N.Y. Commandery, Naval Order of U.S. (pres. 1990—92). Avocations: swimming, tennis. Home: 139 Chestnut St Englewood NJ 07631 also: 37 S Beach Rd Southampton NY 11968

VOLK, CECILIA ANN, elementary school educator; b. Greensburg, Ind., Mar. 8, 1956; d. Paul George and Ruth (Martin) Volk. BS, Purdue U., 1978; MA in Edn., Ball State U., 1984. Cert. K-Primary tchr., Ind. Tchr. spl. edn. Greensburg Cmty. Schs., 1978-79; tchr. Decatur County Day Care, Greensburg, 1979-81; tchr. 1st grade St. Louis Sch., Batesville, Ind., 1983-91, kindergarten tchr., 1991—, tchr. kindergarten, 1991—. Mem. ASCD, Am. Assn. Family and Consumer Scis., Nat. Assn. Edn. Young Children, Ind. Assn. Edn. Young Children, Nat. Coun. Tchrs. Math., Ind. Home Econs. Assn., Nat. Cath. Ednl. Assn., Purdue Alumni Assn., Delta Kappa Gamma. Home: 1035 N Broadway St Greensburg IN 47240-1309 Office: St Louis Sch 17 E Saint Louis Pl Batesville IN 47006-1397

VOLK, KENNETH HOHNE, lawyer; b. Hackensack, N.J., Nov. 8, 1922; s. Henry L. and Constance (Brady) V.; m. Joyce Geary, May 11, 1954; children: Christopher H., Cynthia. BS, U.S. Naval Acad., 1946; LLB, Yale U., 1953. Ptnr. Burlingham, Underwood, N.Y.C., 1955-92; of counsel McLane, Graf, Raulerson & Middleton, Portsmouth, N.H., 1992—. Speaker various symposia and confs. on maritime law. Assoc. editor Am. Maritime Cases; contbr. articles to profl. jours. Pres. Maritime Assocs., N.Y.C., 1967-68; chmn. bd. dirs. Seamen's House YMCA, N.Y.C., 1971-76; sec., bd. dirs. Seamen's Ch. Inst., N.Y.C., 1977-92; bd. dirs. Strawbery Banke Mus., Portsmouth, N.H.; mem. adv. bd. Tulane Admiralty Law Inst. Fellow Am. Bar Found., Am. Coll. Trial Lawyers; mem. ABA, Assn. Bar of City of N.Y., Maritime Law Assn. U.S. (exec. com. 1977-80, pres. 1990-92), Comite Maritime Internat. (titulary mem.), Quaker Hill Country Club (pres. 1976-78). Republican. Espicopalian. Avocations: reading, hiking, fishing. Office: McLane Graf Raulerson & Middleton 100 Market St Portsmouth NH 03801 Office Phone: 603-436-2818.

VOLK, KRISTIN, advertising agency executive; b. Phila., Feb. 26, 1953; d. Richard H. and Doris (Colasanti) V. BS in Biology, Tufts U., 1976; MPH, Boston U. Sch. Med., 1981. Rsch. technician Beth Israel Hosp., Boston, 1976; rsch. asst. Dana-Farber Cancer Inst., Boston, 1976-78; sr. rsch. asst. Beth Israel Hosp., Boston, 1978-81; rsch. supr. Schneider Parker Jakuc Advt., Boston, 1981-86; v.p., assoc. rsch. dir. HBM/Creamer, Boston, 1986-88, Della Femina McNamee, Boston, 1988-90; v.p., dir. rsch. Lawner Reingold Britton & Ptnrs., Boston, 1990-93; sr. v.p., dir. consumer insight group Arnold Fortuna Lawner & Cabot, Boston, 1993-95; exec. v.p., dir. consumer insight group Arnold Comm., Inc., Boston, 1995-99; exec. v.p., dir. strategic planning Deutsch Boston, 1999—2001; exec. v.p., chief mktg. officer Arnold Worldwide, N.Y.C., 2001—. Guest lectr. colls. and univs., Boston. Contbr. articles to profl. jours. Mem. Am. Assn. Advt. Agencies (account planning group com., chmn. conf. 1998), Ad Club N.Y. Home: 180 W 20th St Apt 10F New York NY 10011

VOLK, NORMAN HANS, financial executive; b. N.Y.C., Jan. 10, 1935; s. Hans and Mary (Zurl) V.; m. Karlyn Schram, Aug. 17, 1959; children: Kari, Heidi, Jenny. BA, Valparaiso (Ind.) U., 1957; MA, Marquette U., Milw., 1959. Dir. pub. rels. Wagner Coll., N.Y.C., 1961-62; asst. to owner Alan M. Wood, N.Y.C., 1962-72; sr. v.p. Bessemer Trust Co., N.Y.C., 1972-85; pres. Chamberlain & Steward, N.Y.C., 1985—. Trustee John Hartford Found., N.Y.C., 1979—. With U.S. Army, 1959-61. Mem. Univ. Club, Univ. Glee Club of N.Y.C., Doubles Club. Lutheran. Home: 445 Walton Rd Maplewood NJ 07040-1119 Office: 400 Park Ave New York NY 10022-4406

VOLK, PATRICIA GAY, fiction writer, essayist; b. NYC, July 16, 1943; d. Cecil Sussman and Audrey Elaine (Morgen) Volk; m. Andrew Blitzer, Dec. 21, 1969; children— Peter Morgen, Polly Volk BFA cum laude, Syracuse U., 1964; student, Sch. Visual Arts, N.Y.C., 1968, New Sch., 1975, Columbia U., 1977-88. Art dir. Appelbaum & Curtis, N.Y.C., 1964-65, Seventeen Mag., Triangle Publs., N.Y.C., 1966-68; copywriter Doyle, Dane, Bernbach, Inc., N.Y.C., 1969-88, also sr. v.p., creative mgr., 1969-87, sr. v.p.- assoc. creative dir., 1987-88; columnist N.Y. Newsday, 1995-96; fiction instr. Yeshiva Coll. Fiction instr. Playwrights Horizon Theater Sch., Marymount Coll. Author: The Yellow Banana, 1985 (Word Beat Press Fiction Book award 1984), White Light, 1987, All it Takes, 1990, Stuffed: Adventures of a Restaurant Family, 2001; contbr. articles to N.Y. Times mag., Redbook, Allure, Mirabella, Family Circle, The New Yorker, The Atlantic, Playboy, others; contbr. short stories to popular and small press publs. and anthologies. Recipient Stephen E. Kelly award, 1983, Various Andy, Clio, Effie and One Show awards, 1970—88, Yaddo fellow, 1983, 1999, 2001, MacDowell fellow, 1984, 2000. Mem.: PEN, Century Assn., Author's Guild, Juliana Berner's Anglers.

VOLK, STEPHEN RICHARD, diversified financial services company executive, investment banker, lawyer; b. Boston, Apr. 22, 1936; s. Ralph and Miriam (Rose) V.; m. Veronica J. Brown, June 19, 1959 (dec. Feb. 1989); children: Jeffrey A., Andrew M., Michael J.; m. Diane Kemelman, Apr. 22, 1990; 1 child, Anne. Grad. cum laude, Dartmouth Coll., 1957; JD, Harvard U., 1960. Bar: N.Y. 1961. Assoc. Shearman & Sterling, N.Y.C., 1960-68, ptnr., 1968—88, dep. sr. ptnr., 1988-91, sr. ptnr., 1991—2001; vice chmn. Credit Suisse First Boston, N.Y.C., 2001—02, mem. exec. bd. and operative com., chmn., 2002—04; mem. exec. bd. Credit Suisse Group, 2003—04; vice chmn. Citigroup Inc., 2004—. Bd. dirs. Trizec Properties, Inc., ContiGroup Cos. Inc., Consol. Edison, Inc., 1996; trustee Consol Edison Co. N.Y.C., Inc., 1998 Mem. dean's adv. bd. Harvard Law Sch., 1997. Fellow Am. Bar Found.; mem. ABA (com. on securities regulation 1974), Assn. Bar City N.Y., Harvard Law Sch. Assn., N.Y.C., 1999, Coun. on Fgn. Rels., Univ. Club, Phi Beta Kappa. Office: Citigroup Inc 399 Park Ave New York NY 10043*

VOLKEMA, MICHAEL A. office furniture manufacturer; Chmn., CEO Meridian Inc., Spring Lake, Mich.; pres., CEO Coro Inc., Zeeland, Mich., Herman Miller Inc., Zeeland, 1995—, chmn., 2000—. Office: Herman Miller Inc 855 E Main Ave Zeeland MI 49464-0302

VOLKER, DALE MARTIN, state legislator, lawyer; b. Lancaster, NY, Aug. 2, 1940; s. Julius J. and Loretta (O'Neill) Volker; m. Carol A. Suchyna, Nov. 28, 1970; children: Martin Andrew, Mark Dale, Meredith Ann. BA, Canisius Coll., 1966; JD, SUNY, Buffalo, 1966. Bar: NY 1967. Police officer Village of Depew, NY, 1966—72; assemblyman NY State Assembly, Albany, 1972—74; mem. NY State Senate, Albany, 1975—, Fowler and Volker, Lancaster, NY. Mem.: Erie County Bar Assn., Eagles, Moose, Elks. Republican. Roman Catholic. Home: 92 Center Dr Depew NY 14043-1706 Office: Rm 427 State Capitol Albany NY 12247 Address: 5441 Broadway Lancaster NY 14086-2123 Office Phone: 716-685-4805. Business E-Mail: volker@senate.state.ny.us.

VOLKHARDT, JOHN MALCOLM, food company executive; b. Chester, Pa., Apr. 13, 1917; s. George Thomas and Evelyn (Mitchell) V.; m. Linda J. Volkhardt; children: Michael, Jacqueline, Janet, Dana. AB cum laude, Brown U., 1939. Product mgr. Vick Chem. Co., N.Y.C., 1939-48; gen. mgr. Northam Warren Co., Stamford, Conn., 1948-56, Rit div. Best Foods Co., N.Y.C., 1956-58; with Best Foods div. CPC Internat. Inc., Englewood Cliffs, N.J., 1958-78, exec. v.p., 1968-71, pres., 1971-78; pres. North Am. div. CPC Internat. and exec. v.p. CPC Internat., 1978-82, group v.p., 1979; v.p. CPC, 1971-78, dir., 1977-82; pres., chmn. Full Circle Corp., Moss Creek, 1985-91; pres. Water Oak Utility, 1985-91. Dir. Storm Eye Inst., 2002—05. Chmn. bd. Keep Am. Beautiful, Inc., 1979-82, chmn. bd. trustees, 1982. Recipient Herbert Hoover award Nat. Assn. Wholesale Grocers Am.; honoree Nat. Jewish Hosp., 1976. Mem. Phi Beta Kappa.

VOLKMAN, ALVIN, retired physician, research scientist, educator; b. Bklyn., June 10, 1926; s. Henry Phillip and Sarah Lucille (Silverstein) V.; m. Winifred Joan Grinnell, June 12, 1947 (div. Aug. 1967); children: Karl Frederick, Nicholas James, Rebecca Jane Evans, Margaret Rose Werrell, Deborah Ann Falls; m. Carol Ann Fishel, Jan 26, 1973 (dec. Sept. 1992); 1 child, Natalie Fishel; 1 stepchild, Jeffrey C. Moore; m. A. Suzanne Hiss, Oct. 6, 1997. BS, Union Coll., 1947; MD, U. Buffalo, 1951; D in Philosophy, U. Oxford, Eng., 1963. Diplomate Nat. Bd. Med. Examiners, Am. Bd. Pathology. Intern Mt. Sinai Hosp., Cleve., 1951-52; rsch. fellow dept. anatomy Western Res. U. Sch. Medicine, 1952-54; resident, then sr. resident, then asst. in pathology Peter Bent Brigham Hosp., Boston, 1956-60; asst. prof. pathology Columbia U. Coll. Physicians and Surgeons, 1960-66; asst. mem., then assoc. mem. Trudeau Inst., Saranac Lake, N.Y., 1966-67; prof. dept. pathology East Carolina U. Sch. Medicine, Greenville, N.C., 1977—, acting chmn. dept. pathology, 1989-90, assoc. dean for rsch. and grad. studies, 1989-95, prof. emeritus, 1995—, ret., 1999. Mem. NIH study sect. immunological scis., 1975-79, chmn., 1977-79. Contbr. articles to sci. jours. Served to lt. USNR, 1954-56. Am. Cancer Soc. scholar, 1961-63, Arth and Rheumat Found. fellow, 1952-54. Mem. AAAS, Am. Soc. Investigative Pathology, Am. Assn. Immunologists, Am. Soc. Hematology, Reticuloendothelial Soc., Am. Soc. Microbiologists, N.Y. Acad. Scis., Soc., Leukocyte Biology (hon. life). E-mail: alvolk@cox.net.

VOLKMANN, FRANCES COOPER, psychologist, educator; b. Harlingen, Tex., May 4, 1935; d. Edward O. and Elizabeth (Bass) C.; m. John Volkmann, Nov. 1, 1958 (dec.); children: Stephen Edward, Thomas Frederick. AB magna cum laude, Mt. Holyoke Coll., 1957; MA, Brown U., 1959, PhD, 1961; DSc, Mt. Holyoke Coll., 1987. Rsch. assoc. Mt. Holyoke Coll., South Hadley, Mass., 1964-65; lectr. U. Mass., Amherst, 1964-65, Smith Coll., Northampton, Mass., 1966-67, asst. prof., 1967-72, assoc. prof., 1972-78, prof. psychology, 1978—, dean faculty, 1983-88, Harold E. Israel and Elsa M. Siipola prof. psychology, 1988—, acting pres., 1991. Vis. assoc. prof. Brown U., Providence, 1974, vis. prof., 1978-82; vis. scholar U. Wash., Seattle, summer 1977. Contbr. articles to profl. jours. Trustee Chatham Coll., 1987-95; mem. City Coun., Northampton, 1998—. USPHS fellow, 1961-62; NSF grantee, 1974-78; Nat. Eye Inst. grantee, 1978-82 Fellow APA, AAAS, Optical Soc. Am.; mem. Ea. Psychol. Assn., Soc. Neurosci. Psychonomic Soc., Assn. Rsch. in Vision and Ophthalmology, New Eng. Assn. Schs. and Colls. (vice chair commn. instns. higher edn. 1991-93, chair 1993-95).

VOLKMAR, FRED ROBERT, psychiatrist, educator; b. Highland, Ill., Mar. 26, 1950; s. Fred Harwood and Ella Josephine (Smith) Volkmar; m. Elizabeth Anne Wiesner, Sept. 2, 1984; children: Lucy Amelia, Emily Louisa. BS, U. Ill., 1972; MA, MD, Stanford U., 1976. Diplomate Am. Bd. Psychiatry and Neurology. Resident psychiatry Stanford U., Calif., 1976—80; fellow child psychiatry Yale U., New Haven, 1980—82; asst. prof. Child Study Ctr., 1982—88, assoc. prof., 1988—98, prof., 1998—, Irving B. Harris chair, 2003—. Cons. psychiatrist Benhaven Sch., New Haven, 1984—, med. dir., 1982—85; mem. sci. com. Nat. Ctr. for Clin. Infant Programs, Washington, 1985. Recipient Sandoz award, 1980, Ittelson award, Am. Psychiat. Assn., Faculty Scholar award, William T. Grant Found., 1982, Rsch. Career award, NIMH, 1983; James scholar, Laughlin fellow, 1982. Mem.: Am. Acad. Child Psychiatry, Soc. for Rsch. in Child Devel., Phi Beta Kappa. Democrat. Avocations: astronomy, photography, sailing. Office: Yale U Child Study Ctr 230 S Frontage Rd New Haven CT 06519-1124 Office Phone: 203-785-2510. Business E-Mail: fred.volkmar@yale.edu.

VOLKOW, NORA DOLORES, medical research center director; b. Mexico City, Mar. 27, 1956; m. Steven Adler. BA, Modern Am. Sch., Mexico City, 1974; MD, Nat. U. Mex., 1980; postgrad. in Psychiatry, NYU, 1980-84. Diplomate Am. Bd. Psychiatry and Neurology. Rsch. asst. Registro Nacional de Anat. Path., Mexico City, 1975-76, Miles Lab. Exp. Therap., Mexico City, 1977-78; intern St. Anne Psychiat. Hosp., Paris, 1979-80; residency NYU Dept. Psychiatry, 1981—84; asst. prof. U. Tex. Med. Sch., Houston, 1984-87; attending physician psychiat. unit Herman Hosp., Houston, 1985-87; assoc. scientist dept. medicine Brookhaven Nat. Lab., Upton, NY, 1987-89, assoc. chief of staff, Clinical Rsch. Ctr., 1990, dir. Nuclear Medicine, 1994—2003, dir, NIDA/DOE Imaging Ctr., 1997—2003, assoc. dir. life sciences, 1999—2003; assoc. prof. dept. psychiatry SUNY, Stony Brook, 1991—2003, assoc. dean, Sch. Med., 1997—2003; lecturer, Psychiatry Dept. Columbia Univ.; dir. Nat. Inst. on Drug Abuse (NIDA), Washington, 2003—. Mem. Adv. Com. for Minority Tng. in Psychiatry, Washington, 1991—; mem. study sect. in clin. neuroscis. NIH, Washington, 1992—; elected mem., Inst. Medicine, 2000. Co-editor: Positron Emission Tomography in Schizophrenia Research, 1991. Named Innovator of the Yr., U.S. News and World Report, 2000; recipient Premio Robins award, U. Mex., 1978, Premio Gabino Barrera award, 1981, Laughlin fellowship, Am. Coll. Psychiatry, 1984, Scanditronix scholarship, 1985, Paul C. Aebersold award, Soc. of Nuclear Medicine, 2003. Office: Nat Inst on Drug Abuse NIH Rm 5274 6001 Executive Blvd Bethesda MD 20892-9581

VOLL, JOHN OBERT, history professor; b. Hudson, Wis., Apr. 20, 1936; s. Obert Frank and Ruth Olivia (Seaberg) V.; m. Sarah Lynne Potts, June 12, 1965; children: Sarah Layla, Michael Obert. AB summa cum laude, Dartmouth Coll., 1958, PhD (Ford Found. fellow), 1969; AM (Danforth fellow), Harvard U., 1960. Instr. history U. N.H., Durham, 1965-69, asst. prof., 1969-74, assoc. prof., 1974-82, prof., 1982-95, chair dept., 1988-91; prof. Georgetown U., Washington, 1995—, dep. dir. Ctr. for Muslim-Christian Understanding, 1996—2004, dir., 2004—. Mem. history and social scis. adv. com. Coll. Bd. 1983-86, chmn. European history and world cultures achievement test com., 1985-88; tchg. fellow Harvard U., 1969. Harvard Ctr. for Middle Eastern, Studies Vist. Com., 2003-. Author: Historical Dictionary of the Sudan, 1978, 2nd edit., 1992, Islam Continuity and Change in the Modern World, 2nd edit., 1994; (with others) The Sudan: Unity and Diversity, 1985, Eighteenth Century Renewal and Reform in Islam, 1987, Sudan: State and Society in Crisis, 1991, Islam and Democracy, 1996, Makers of Contemporary Islam, 2001; contbr. articles to profl. jours. Mem. bd. Ecumenical Ministry U. N.H., 1974-78, pres., 1975-77; chmn. social action Durham Cmty. Ch., 1974-75, mem. ch. coun., 1977-78, deacon, 1986—. Sheldon traveling fellow, 1960-61, U. N.H. summer fellow, 1969, 89, NEH fellow, 1971-72, Fulbright faculty rsch. abroad fellow, 1978-79, Inst. Advanced Studies fellow Hebrew U., 1984-85; recipient Egyptian Presdl. medal, 1991. Mem. Am. Coun. Learned Socs. (del. 1989-96, del. exec. com. 1989-92, bd. dirs. 1990-92), New England Hist. Assn. (sec. 1975-78, v.p. 1981, pres. 1982), Sudan Studies Assn. (bd. dirs. 1981-82, co-exec. dir. 1990-94), N.H. Coun. on World Affairs (bd. dirs. 1978-95), Am. Hist. Assn. (chmn. program com. 1999), Mid. East Studies Assn. (bd. dirs. 1987-89, pres. 1992-93), Am. Coun. for Study of Islamic Socs. (bd. dirs. 1989—, v.p. 1989-91), N.H. Humanities Coun. (bd. dirs. 1991-95). Mem. United Ch. of Christ. Home: 4000 Cathedral Ave NW Apt 652B Washington DC 20016-5205 Office: Ctr Muslim Christian Understanding Georgetown U Washington DC 20057-0001 Office Phone: 202-687-8375. E-mail: vollj@georgetown.edu.

VOLLA, STEVEN L. food products executive; Sr. v.p. Universal Health Svcs.; CEO Am. Healthcare Mgmt. Co., 1989—94; founder, non-exec. chmn. Primary Health Sys., 1994—2001; non-exec. chmn. Pathmark Stores, Carteret, NJ, 2002—. Mem. audit com. Sun Healthcare Group, Inc.; bd. dir. audit com. Brown Schs. Am., chmn.; bd. dir. Pathmark, Health Risk Mgmt. Named Turnaround Entrepreneur of Yr., Ernst & Young Inc. Mag., 1993, 1994. Office: Pathmark Stores 200 Milik St Carteret NJ 07008

VOLLEN, ROBERT JAY, lawyer; b. Chgo., Jan. 23, 1940; s. Ben N. and Rose (Belonsky) V.; m. Judith Paula Spector, Aug. 12, 1961; children: Steven, Neil, Jennifer. AB, U. Mich., 1961; JD, U. Chgo., 1964. Bar: Ill. 1964, D.C. 1965, U.S. Supreme Ct. 1975. Atty. appellate sect. Civil Div., U.S. Dept. Justice, Washington, 1964-65; asso. firm Schiff Hardin & Waite, Chgo., 1965-70, partner firm, 1971-72; gen. counsel BPI (Bus. and Profl. People for Pub. Interest), Chgo., 1972-83; ptnr. Schwartz & Freeman, Chgo., 1983-87; chmn. Restorion, LLC, 2003—. Mem. vis. com. U. Chgo. Law Sch., 1978-81. Mem. ABA (ho. of dels. 1974-76), Chgo. Coun. Lawyers (gov. 1972-76, 79-81). Home: 2 Kingswood Ct Deerfield IL 60015-1912 Office Phone: 847-945-3711. E-mail: rvollen@ameritech.net., rvollen@restorion.com.

VOLLKOMMER, MICHAEL T. credit reporting company executive; CFO, v.p. Alumax Inc., Atlanta; corp. v.p., contr. Equifax, Inc., Atlanta. Office: Equifax Inc 1550 Peachtree St NW Atlanta GA 30309

VOLLMER, HELEN, public relations executive; B Journalism, M Radio/TV/Film, U. Tex. Copywriter for maj. retail outlet; acct. exec. Ruder & Finn; v.p., mgr. client rels. Bozell & Jacobs Pub. Rels.; CEO Vollmer Pub. Rels. Office: Vollmer Pub Rels 800 Travis, Ste 501 Houston TX 77002-5706

VOLLUM, ROBERT BOONE, management consultant; b. Abington, Pa., Sept. 13, 1933; s. Charles Milton and Marion (Yocum) V.; m. Gayle Lorraine Timmerman, July 8, 1956; children: Robert Boone III, Jeffrey Charles. BS in Engring. and Sci., U.S. Naval Acad., 1955. Sr. cons., group leader Stevenson, Jordan & Harrison, Inc., N.Y.C., 1959—65; asst. to pres., plant supt., sales engr. W.L. Gore & Assocs., Inc., Newark, Del., 1965—69; gen. mgr. Philmont Pressed Steel subs. Gulf & Western Industries, Inc., Bethayres, Pa., 1969—72; gen. mgr. Air Shields divsn. Narco Sci. Industries, Inc., Hatboro, Pa., 1972—75; pres. Advanced Airflow Tech., Inc., Warminster, Pa., 1975—76, R.B. Vollum & Assocs., Huntingdon Valley, Pa., 1986—, RBV Mktg. Inc., Willow Grove, Pa., 1992—; chmn. bd. dirs., CEO SFM Technologies, Willow Grove, 1994—. Prin. mfg. cons. Sperry Corp., Blue Bell, Pa., 1976-84; dir. cons. Creative Output, Inc., Milford, Conn., 1984-86; spkr. in field. Contbr. articles to profl. jours. Bd. dirs. Upper Moreland Little League, 1965-76. Served to lt. USN, 1955-59. Fellow Am. Prodn. and Inventory Control Soc. (chpt. pres. 1984-85); mem. soc. Mfg. Engrs (sr. mem.), Computer and Automated Systems Assn. (sr. mem.). Republican. Episcopalian. Home: 525 Overlook Ave Willow Grove PA 19090-2818 Office: PO Box 206 Huntingdon Valley PA 19006-0206 Office Phone: 215-784-9011. Personal E-mail: rbvollum@rbvollum.com.

VOLMAN, DAVID HERSCHEL, chemistry professor; b. LA, July 10, 1916; s. Carl Herman and Blanche (Taylor) V.; m. Ruth Clare Jackson, Sept. 15, 1944 (dec. Dec. 2001); children: Thomas Peter, Susan Frances, Daniel Henry. BA, UCLA, 1937, MS, 1938; PhD, Stanford U., 1940. Mem. faculty U. Calif.-Davis, 1940—41, 1946—, prof. chemistry, 1956-87, emeritus prof. chemistry, 1987—, chmn. dept., 1974-81, chmn. Acad. Senate, 1971-72; rsch. chemist OSRD, 1941-46; rsch. fellow Harvard U., 1949-50. Vis. prof. U. Wash. 1958. Editor: Advances in Photochemistry, 1983-98; mem. editl. bd. Jour. Photochemistry and Photobiology, 1972-98; contbr. articles to profl. jours. Grantee Rsch. Corp. Am.; grantee NIH; grantee U.S. Army Rsch. Office; grantee NSF;Std. Oil Co. fellow, 1940; Guggenheim fellow, 1949-50. Mem. Am. Chem. Soc., Inter Am. Photochem. Soc., Sigma Xi. Office: U Calif Davis Dept Chemistry 1 Shields Ave Davis CA 95616 Office Phone: 530-752-0960.

VOLPE, ANGELO ANTHONY, former university president, chemistry educator; b. Nov. 8, 1938; s. Bernard Charles and Serafina (Martorana) V.; m. Jennette Murray, May 15, 1965. BS, Bklyn. Coll., 1959; MS, U. Md., 1962, PhD, 1966; M in Engring. (hons.), Stevens Inst. Tech., 1975. Rsch. chemist USN Ordnance Lab., Silver Spring, Md., 1961-66; from asst. prof. to prof. chemistry Stevens Inst. Tech., Hoboken, N.J., 1966-77; chmn. dept. chemistry East Carolina U., Greenville, N.C., 1977-80, dean Coll. Arts and Scis., 1980-83, vice chancellor for acad. affairs, 1983-87; pres. Tenn. Technol. U., Cookeville, 1987-2000, pres. emeritus, 2000—. Adj. prof. textile chem. N.C. State U., Raleigh, 1978-82; guest lect. Plastics Inst. Am., Hoboken, 1967-82. Contbr. articles to profl. jours. Recipient Ednl. Svc. award Plastics Inst. Am., 1973; named Freygang Outstanding Tchr., Stevens Inst. Tech., 1975. Mem. Am. Chem. Soc., Tenn. Acad. Scis., Sigma Xi, Phi Kappa Phi. Democrat. Roman Catholic. Avocations: golf, reading. Home: 734 Loweland Rd Cookeville TN 38501-2888 E-mail: avolpe@tntech.edu.

VOLPE, BRUCE THOMAS, neurologist; b. NYC, 1947; BS, Yale Coll., 1969; MD, Yale U. Sch. Medicine, 1973. Bd. cert. neurology 1980, bd. cert. internal medicine 1976. Intern U. Chgo., 1973—74, resident in internal medicine, 1974—75, Columbia Presbyn. Hosp., 1975—77; resident in neurology Cornell-NY Hosp., 1977; prof. neurology and neuroscience Weill Med. Coll., Cornell U., Burke Med. Rsch. Inst. Contbr. articles in profl. jour. Office: Burke Med Rsch Inst 785 Mamaroneck Ave White Plains NY 10605 also: Cornell U Med Ctr Dept Neurology 525 E 68th St New York NY 10021-4870 Office Phone: 914-597-2835., 914-597-2835. Office Fax: 914-597-2976. Business E-Mail: volpe@rockvax.rockefeller.edu.

VOLPE, EDMOND L(ORIS), college president; b. New Haven, Nov. 16, 1922; s. Joseph D. and Rose (Maisano) V.; m. Rose Conte, May 20, 1950; children: Rosalind, Lisa. AB, U. Mich., 1943; MA, Columbia U., 1947, PhD, 1954. Instr. NYU, 1949-54; mem. faculty CCNY, 1954-74, prof. English, 1968-74, chmn. dept., 1964-70; pres. Richmond Coll., 1974-76, Coll. S.I., NY, 1976-94. Fulbright prof. Am. lit., France, 1960-61. Author: A Reader's Guide to William Faulkner, 1964, The Comprehensive College, 2001, A Reader's Guide to William Faulkner: The Novels Reissued, 2003, A Reader's Guide to William Faulkner: The Short Stories, 2004; also anthologies and coll. text books.; co-editor: Eleven Modern Short Novels. Bd. dirs. S.I. United Way, 1975—, S.I. coun. Boy Scouts Am., 1977-84, S.I. Doctors Hosp., 1977-78, Snug Harbor Cultural Ctr., 1978-83, St. Vincent's Hosp., 1979—; mem. N.Y.C. Mayor's Commn. on Bias, 1986-88. With AUS, 1943-46. Recipient Commendatore Order of Merit, Republic of Italy, Cmty. Svc. award Italian Club S.I., Humanitarian award S.I. Jewish Found. Sch., Mills G. Skinner award S.I. br. N.Y. Urban League, Christopher Columbus award Columbian Assn. Bd. Edn., Disting. Cmty. Svc. award YMCA, Cmty. Svc. award S.I. Women's divsn. Am. Com. on Italian Migration, Outstanding Achievement award Guiseppe Mazzini Lodge of Sons of Italy; named Educator of Yr. Am. Legion Richmond County. Mem. MLA, Am. Studies Assn., Assn. Dept. English (exec. com. 1969-71), Am. Assn. State Colls. and Univs. (task force ednl. opportunites for the aging, rsch. and liason com., com. internat. programs, health affairs com.), Am. Assn. Higher Edn., Am. Assn. Colls. for Tchr. Edn., Am. Assn. Univ. Profs., Am. Coun. Edn., Am. Studies Assn., Assn. Colls. and Univs. N.Y., Assn. Depts. of English (nat. exec. com.), Coll. English Assn. (nat. bd. dirs.), Consortium Internat. Programs, Inst. Internat. Edn., Inc., Mid. States Assn. Colls. and Schs., Andiron Club N.Y. (pres. 1972-75).

VOLPE, ELLEN MARIE, secondary school educator; b. Bronx, N.Y., Aug. 2, 1949; d. George Thomas and Mary (Popadinecz) Soloweyko; m. Ronald Edward Volpe, May 22, 1971; children: Keith, Daniel, Christopher, Stephanie. BBA, Pace U., 1971; MA in Teaching, Sacred Heart U., 1986. Tchr. Conn. Bus. Inst., Stratford, 1979-80, Katherine Gibbs Sch., Norwalk, Conn., 1980-89; adj. instr. So. Cen. Community Coll., New Haven, 1986-87, Salt Lake C. C., Phillips Jr. Coll., Salt Lake City, 1992-93; instr. Bryman Sch., Salt Lake City, 1990-92; tchr. Indian Hills Mid. Sch., Sandy, Utah, 1993-99, vocational dept. chmn.; tchr. MaST Cmty. Charter Sch., Phila., 1999-2001; office mgr. Basilicato & Levesque, CPA, North Andover, Mass., 2004—. Bus. team leader reaccreditation and tech. coms. Indian Hills Mid. Sch., 1996, vocat. dept. chair; mem. curriculum rev. com. Katharine Gibbs Sch., 1989-90. Avocations: ceramics, gardening. Home: 103 Juniper Ln Tewksbury MA 01876-1281 Office: Basilicato & Levesque CPA 33 Walker Rd North Andover MA 01845 E-mail: compteach50@hotmail.com., sprgrndma@aol.com.

VOLPE, ERMINIO PETER, biologist, educator; b. N.Y.C., Apr. 7, 1927; s. Rocco and Rose (Ciano) Volpe; m. Lesley D. Volpe, 1992; children: Laura Elizabeth, Lisa Lawton, John Peter. BS, CCNY, 1948; MA, Columbia U., 1949, PhD (Newberry award 1952), 1952. Asst. zoologist Columbia U., N.Y.C., 1948-51; instr. biology CCNY, N.Y.C., 1951-52; asst. prof. zoology Newcomb Coll., Tulane U., 1952-81, chmn. dept. zoology, 1954-64, 64-66, 69-79, W.R. Irby disting. prof. biology, 1979-81, assoc. dean Grad. Sch., 1967-69; prof. basic med. scis. (genetics) Mercer U. Sch. Medicine, Macon, Ga., 1981—. Cons. Nat. Commn. for Undergrad. Edn. in Biol. Scis., 1964-71; mem. steering com. Biol. Scis Curriculum Study, 1966-70; panelist NRC, 1967-70; mem. U.S. Nat. Commn. for UNESCO, 1968-72; regional lectr. Sigma Xi, 1970-72; lectr. Elderhostel, 1988-98; chmn. Advanced Placement Test in Biology, Ednl. Testing Service, 1975-80. Author: (textbook) Understanding Evolution, 2000, Human Heredity and Birth Defects, 1971, Patterns and Experiments in Developmental Biology, 2001, Man, Nature, and Society, 1975, The Amphibian Embryo in Transplantation Immunity, 1980, Biology and Human Concerns, 1993, Patient in the Womb, 1984, Test-Tube Conception: A Blend of Love and Science, 1987; mem. editl. bd. jour. Copeia, 1962-63; assoc. editor Jour. Exptl. Zoology, 1968-76, 84-85; editor jour. Am. Zoologist, 1975-80; contbr. articles to profl. jours. Served with USNR, 1945-46. Fellow AAAS; mem. Genetics Soc. Am., Am. Soc. Zoologists (pres. 1981), Am. Soc. Naturalists, Soc. Devel. Biology, Soc. Study Evolution, Am. Soc. for Cell Biology, Am. Soc. Human Genetics, Phi Beta Kappa (v.p. Tulane U. chpt. 1962), Sigma Xi (pres. Tulane U. chpt. 1964, faculty award 1972.) Home: 1105 Bond St Macon GA 31201-1602 Office: Mercer Univ Sch Medicine 1550 College St Macon GA 31207-1500

VOLPE, JOSEPH, opera company general manager; b. Brooklyn, NY, July 2, 1940; m. Jean Anderson Volpe. Apprentice carpenter The Met. Opera, N.Y.C., 1964—66, master carpenter, 1966—78, technical dir., 1978—81, assist. mgr., 1981—90, gen. mgr., 1990—. Office: The Met Opera Lincoln Ctr W 64th & Broadway New York NY 10023

VOLPE, JOSEPH, Canadian government official; b. Monteleone, Puglia, Italy, Sept. 21, 1947; married; 4 children. MA in Edn., U. Toronto, Can. Mem. Can. Parliament, 1988—; parliamentary sec. to the min. health Govt. Can., 1996—98, chair standing com. on health, 1998—99, chair standing com. on natural resources and govt. ops., 1999—2000, min. human resources and skills devel., 2003—. Office: House of Commons Ottawa ON Canada K1A 0A6 also: Human Resources Devel Place du Portage Phase IV 14th Fl 140 Pr Gatineau PQ Canada K1A 0J9*

VOLPE, JOSEPH JOHN, pediatric neurologist, educator; b. Salem, Mass., Dec. 17, 1938; s. John Rosario and Anne Eleanor (Femino) V.; m. Sara Lee Solov, June 2, 1980; children from previous marriage: Joanna Marie, Joseph Anthony, John Matthew. BA, Bowdoin Coll., 1960; MD, Harvard U., 1964. Diplomate Am. Bd. Pediatrics, Am. Bd. Neurology and Psychiatry with spl. competence in child neurology. Pediatric intern Mass. Gen. Hosp., Boston, 1964-65, pediatric resident, 1965-66, neurology and pediatric resident, 1968-71; rsch. assoc. Nat. Inst. Child Health and Human Devel., Bethesda, Md., 1966-68; asst. prof. pediatrics and neurology Washington U. Med. Sch., St. Louis, 1971-76, assoc. prof. pediatrics and neurology, 1976-79, prof. pediatrics and neurology, 1979—, prof. biol. chemistry, 1980-90, dir. div. pediatric neurology, 1984-90; Bronson Crothers prof. neurology Harvard Med. Sch., Boston, 1990—; neurologist in chief Children's Hosp., Boston, 1990—. Author: Neurology of the Newborn, 1981, 4th edit., 2000; contbr. over 300 articles to profl. jours. Capt. USPHS, 1966-68. Recipient Weinstein-Goldenson award United Cerebral Palsy Assn., 1985; rsch. grantee NIH, 1973—, March of Dimes Nat. Found., 1985-87. Mem. Nat. Acad. Scis. Inst. Medicine. Office: Children's Hosp 300 Longwood Ave Boston MA 02115-5737

VOLPE, PETER ANTHONY, surgeon; b. Columbus, Ohio, Dec. 17, 1936; s. Peter Anthony and Jeanette Katherine (Volz) V.; m. Suzanne Stephens, Sept. 5, 1959; children: John David, Michael Charles; m. Kathleen Ann Townsend, Mar. 28, 1978; 1 child, Mark Christopher; m. Theresa Ann Morse, Aug. 27, 2000. BA cum laude, Ohio State U., 1958, MD summa cum laude, 1961. Diplomate Am. Bd. Surgery, Am. Bd. Colon and Rectal Surgery (pres. 1988). Pvt. practice, San Francisco, 1969—; sr. ptnr. Volpe, Chui, Abel, Yee, Sternberg, San Francisco, 1987—; clin. prof. surgery U. Calif., San Francisco, 1995—. Asst. clin. prof. surgery U. Calif., San Francisco, 1972-95, clin. prof., 1995—; chmn. dept. surgery St. Mary's Hosp. and Med. Ctr., San Francisco, 1978-90. Contbr. articles to profl. jours. Lt. USN, 1962—64. Fellow ACS (bd. govs. 1988-94), Am. Soc. Colon and Rectal Surgeons (treas. 1985-89, pres. 1990); mem. San Francisco Surg. Soc., San Francisco Med. Soc. Republican. Roman Catholic. Office: Volpe Chiu Abel and Yee Sternberg 3838 California St San Francisco CA 94118-1522 Office Phone: 415-668-0411.

VOLPE, RALPH PASQUALE, retired insurance company executive; b. Souderton, Pa., Sept. 20, 1936; s. Pasquale S. and Katie M. (Hartzell) V.; m. Marie F. Romano, Feb. 6, 1962; children: William, Anthony, Lynda. BA in Polit. Sci., Pa. State U., University Park, 1963. Claim cons. Aetna Life & Casualty Co., King of Prussia, 1964-97; litig. cons. Hartford Ins., King of Prussia, 1998—2003; ret., 2003. Mem. Upper Merion Twp. Bd. Suprs., 1974-79, 82-87, 94—, chmn., 1984, 86-87, 96-97, 2003-04, vice-chmn., 1985, 95; 2d v.p. Montgomery County Assn. Twp. Ofcls., 1995-97, pres., 1997-99; mem. exec. bd. Greater Valley Forge Transp. Mgmt. Assn., 1994-2003; mem. Upper Merion Govt. Study Commn., 1974, Rt. 202 Exec. Com., 1994-2003; chmn. Montgomery County Dem. Campaign, 1975, chmn. Upper Merion Dems., 1980-81; chmn. blue ribbon panel Montgomery County Waste Sys. Authority, 1997-98. With U.S. Army, 1959-61. Recipient Good Govt. award Upper Merion Jaycees, 1977, Excellence in Govt. award King of Prussia C. of C., 1997. Mem.: Southeastern Assn. Twp. Ofcls., Pa. State Assn. Twp. Suprs. (chmn. rules com. 1997—2000, chmn. resolution-legislation com. 2002—04), Valley Forge Hist. Soc., Chapel Four Chaplains, Legion (hon.), Valley Forger Order Sons of Italy in Am. # 1776, Optimists. Republican. Roman Catholic. Home: 240 Strawberry Ln King Of Prussia PA 19406

VOLPE, RICHARD GERARD, insurance accounts executive, consultant; b. Sewickley, Pa., Apr. 10, 1950; s. Ralph Carl and Louise P. (Cosentino) V.; m. Janet Lynn Henne, May 10, 1986; 1 child, John Ralph. BA, Vanderbilt U., 1972. CPCU 1978. Trainee, asst. mgr. Hartford (Conn.) Ins. Group, 1973-74; v.p. sales Roy E. Barker Co., Franklin, Tenn., 1975-80; asst. v.p., product mgr. comml. ins. Nat. Farmers Union Ins., Denver, 1980-82; prin. R.G. Volpe & Assocs, Denver, 1982-85; acct. exec. Millers Mut. Ins., Aurora, Colo., 1985-89; pres, CEO AccuSure, Inc., Arvada, Colo., 1989—; acct. exec. J.R. Misken, Inc., Denver, 1990-92, The Prudential, Colorado Springs, 1992-2001; sr. fin. rep. Principal Fin., Denver, 2001—. Edn. chmn. Insurors Tenn., Nashville, 1978-79; new candidate chmn. Mid-Tenn. chpt. CPCU, Nashville, 1979-80; cons. Bennett Nat. Bank Colo., mktg. mgr., 1989-90; cons. Colo. Plains Ins., Inc., 1987-90. Contbr. articles to profl. jours. Dem. chmn. Williamson County, Tenn., 1979; campaign mgr. legis., Franklin, 1979-98; legis. chmn. Centennial Life Underwriters, 1998, 2000, 02; del. Rep. State Caucus, 1998, 2000; mem. dist. com. Arapaho Dist., Denver Area coun. Boy Scouts Am., 2000. Named Hon. Col. Gov. Tenn., 1979; recipient Hertiage Soc., Boy Scouts of Am., 2004. Fellow Life Underwriters Tng. Coun.; mem. Soc. Property and Casualty Underwriters, Centennial Life Underwriters, Million Dollar Roundtable (qualifying mem.), South Metro Denver C. of C., Order of the Arrow. Roman Catholic. Avocations: skiing, camping, hiking, biking, sailing. Home: 10908 Snow Cloud Trl Littleton CO 80125-9210 Office: Principal Fin 7600 E Eastman Ave Ste 300 Denver CO 80231 also: Prin Fin 7600 E Eastman Ave Ste 300 Denver CO 80231 Office Fax: 303-751-1214. Business E-Mail: volpe.richard@principal.com.

VOLPÉ, ROBERT, endocrinologist, researcher, educator; b. Toronto, Ont., Can., Mar. 6, 1926; s. Aaron G. and Esther (Shulman) V.; m. Ruth Vera Pullan, Sept. 5, 1949 (dec. Jan. 1997); children: Catherine, Elizabeth, Peter, Edward, Rose Ellen. MD, U. Toronto, 1950. Intern U. Toronto, 1950-51, resident in internal medicine, 1951-52, 53-55, fellow in endocrinology, 1952-53, NRC fellow, 1955-57, sr. rsch. fellow dept. medicine, 1957-62, McPhedran fellow, 1957-65, from asst. prof. to prof., 1962—74, prof., 1974—92, prof. emeritus, 1992—, dir. divsn. endocrinology and metabolism, 1987-92, chmn. centennial com., 1987-88; attending staff St. Joseph's Hosp., Toronto, 1957-66; active staff Wellesley Hosp., Toronto, 1966-2000, St. Michael's Hosp., Toronto, 2000—; dir. endocrinology rsch. lab. Wellesley Hosp., 1968-97, physician-in-chief, 1974-87. Trans-Atlantic vis. prof. Caledonia Endocrine Soc., 1985; Hashimoto Meml. lectr. Kyushu U., Fukuoka, Japan, 1992; K.J.R. Wightman vis. prof. Royal Coll. Physicians, Can., 1994; celebratory lectr. commemorating 200th anniversary of birth of Robert Graves, Dublin, Ireland, 1996. Author: Systematic Endocrinology, 1973, 2d edit., 1979, Thyrotoxicosis, 1978, Auto-immunity in the Endocrine System, 1981, Auto-immunity and Endocrine Disease, 1985, Thyroid Function and Disease, 1987, Autoimmune Diseases of the Endocrine System, 1990, The Autoimmune Endocrinopathies, 1999; past editl. bd. mem. Jour. Clin. Endocrinology and Metabolism, Clin. Medicine, Clin. Endocrinology, Annals Internal Medicine, Endocrine Pathology, American Journal of Physiology, Opinions in Endocrinolgy Metabolism, Thyroid; mem. editl. bd. Jour. Royal Soc. Medicine; contbr. over 320 articles to profl. jours. Nat. med. advisor Thyroid Found. Can., 1990—. Served Royal Can. Naval Vol. Res., 1943—45. Decorated officer Order of Can.; recipient Goldie medal for med. rsch. U. Toronto, 1971, Novo-Nordisk prize Irish Endocrine Soc., 1990, Commemorative medal Queen's Golden Jubilee, 2003; Med. Rsch. Coun. Can. grantee, 1960-97. Master ACP (gov. for Ont. 1978-83); fellow Royal Coll. Physicians Can. (coun. 1988-96, chmn. ann. meetings com. 1988-94, sci. program com. 1988-94, chmn. rsch. com. 1994-96, v.p. medicine 1994-96), Royal Coll. Physicians Edinburgh and London, Royal Soc. Medicine (editl. bd.); mem. AAAS, Can. Soc. Endocrinology and Metabolism (past pres., Sandoz prize lectr. 1985, Disting. Svc. award 1990), Toronto Soc. Clin. Rsch. (Baxter prize lectr. 1984), Can. Soc. Clin. Investigation (Disting. Svc. award 1998), Am. Thyroid Assn. (pres. 1980-81, Disting. Scientist award 1991), Assn. Am. Physicians, Endocrine Soc., Am. Fedn. Clin. Rsch., Can. Soc. Nuclear Medicine (Jamieson prize lectr. 1980), Can. Inst. Acad. Medicine, N.Y. Acad. Sci., European Thyroid Assn. (corr.), L.Am. Thyroid Assn. (corr.), Soc. Endocrinology and Metabolism of Chile (hon.), Caledonia Soc. Endocrinology (hon.), Japan Endocrine Soc. (hon., gold medal 1986), Order of Can. (officer), Alpine Ski Club (bd. dirs. 1987-89), U. Toronto Faculty Club. Home: 400 Walmer Rd Apt 1829 Toronto ON Canada M5P 2X7 Office: 600 Sherbourne Ste 211 Toronto ON Canada M4X 1W4 E-mail: robertvolpe@bellnet.ca. *Rigid adherence to high standards and integrity is essential. Do what is worth doing now, not tomorrow.*

VOLPERT, RICHARD SIDNEY, lawyer; b. Cambridge, Mass., Feb. 16, 1935; s. Samuel Abbot and Julia (Fogel) V.; m. Marcia Flaster, June 11, 1958; children: Barry, Sandy, Linda, Nancy. BA, Amherst Coll., 1956; LL.B. (Stone scholar), Columbia U., 1959. Bar: Calif. bar 1960. Atty. firm O'Melveny & Myers, Los Angeles, 1959-86, ptnr. L.A., 1967-86, Skadden, Arps, Slate, Meagher & Flom, L.A., 1986-95, Munger, Tolles & Olson, L.A., 1995—. Pub. Jewish Jour. of Los Angeles, 1985-87 . Editor, chmn.: Los Angeles Bar Jour, 1965, 66, 67, Calif. State Bar Jour, 1972-73. Chmn. cmty. rels. com. Jewish Fedn.-Coun. L.A., 1977-80; bd. dirs. Jewish Fedn.-Coun. Greater L.A., 1976-99, v.p., 1978-81; pres. Los Angeles County Natural History Mus. Found., 1978-84, trustee, 1974—, chair bd. dirs., 1992-97, pres., bd. govs., 1997—; chmn. bd. councilors U. So. Calif. Law Ctr., 1979-85; vice chmn. Nat. Jewish Cmty. Rels. Adv. Coun., 1981-84, mem. exec. com., 1978-85; bd. dirs. U. Judaism, 1973-89, bd. govs., 1973-89; bd. dirs. Valley Beth Shalom, Encino, Calif., 1964-88; mem. capital program major gifts com. Amherst Coll., 1978-86; bd. dirs., mem. exec. com. L.A. Wholesale Produce Market Devel. Corp., 1978-95, v.p., 1981-93, pres. 1993-96; mem. exec. bd. L.A. chpt. Am. Jewish Com., 1967—, pres., 1999-2002, nat bd. dirs., 2000—; vice-chmn. Los Angeles County Econ. Devel. Coun., 1978-81; bd. dirs. Jewish Cmty. Found., 1981—, Brandeis-Bardin Inst., 1995-2000, L.A. Chamber Orch., 2002—; mem. Pacific S.W. regional bd. Anti Defamation League B'nai B'rith, 1964—. Named Man of Year, 1978 Fellow Am. Bar Found.; mem. Los Angeles County Bar Assn. (trustee 1968-70, chmn. real property sect. 1974-75), Los Angeles County Bar Found. (trustee 1977-80, 96-99), Calif. Bar Assn. (com. on adminstrn. justice 1973-76), Am. Coll. Real Estate Lawyers (bd. govs. 1996-99), Anglo-Am. Real Property Inst. (treas. 1995-98), Amherst Club of So. Calif. (dir. 1968-69, pres. 1972-73), City Club (L.A.). Jewish. Home: 16055 Royal Oak Rd Encino CA 91436-3913 Office: Munger Tolles & Olson 355 S Grand Ave 35th Fl Los Angeles CA 90071-1560 Office Phone: 213-683-9101. Business E-Mail: volpertrs@mto.com.

VOLPI, MIKE, computer company executive; BSME, MSME, MBA, Stanford U. Former product devel. engr. and product mktg. mgr. optoelectronics divsn. Hewlett Packard; v.p. bus. devel. Cisco Systems, Inc., San Jose, Calif., 1994—, sr. v.p. bus. devel. and alliances, 1999—2000, chief strategy officer, 2000—02, chief strategy officer, v.p. internet switching and svcs. group, sr. v.p. routing tech. group, 2002—. Bd. dirs. Equinix, Inc., TIBCO Software, Opsware Inc. Office: Cisco Systems Inc 170 W Tasman Dr San Jose CA 95134

VOLTZ, STERLING ERNEST, physical chemist, researcher; b. Phila., Apr. 17, 1921; s. Harry John and Gertrude Irene (Derr) V.; m. Betty Morgan, Nov. 6, 1943; children: Sandra Elizabeth, Karen Lee. BA, Temple U., 1943, MA, 1947, PhD, 1952. Rsch. chemist Houdry Process Corp., Linwood, Pa., 1951-58; group leader Sun Oil Co., Marcus Hook, Pa., 1958-60, supervising engr. GE, Phila., 1960-62, cons. liaison scientist Valley Forge, Pa., 1962-68; rsch. assoc. Mobil Rsch. & Devel. Corp., Paulsboro, N.J., 1968-80, adminstrv., 1980-86; pvt. practice Media, Pa., 1986—. Contbr. articles to Jour. Phys. Chem., Jour. Am. Chem. Soc., Jour. Organic Chemistry, Analytical Chemistry, Jour. Soc. Automotive Engrs., Jour. Chem. and Engring. Data, Jour. Am. Inst. Chem. Engrs. and others. Lt. (j.g.) USN, 1943-46, ETO. Mem. AAAS, Am. Chem. Soc. (Phila. sect.), Catalysis Soc., Catalysis Club. Phila. (sec.-treas., chmn., dir. 1957-60), Am. Legion, Disabled Am. Vets., Sigma Xi. Achievements include 23 patents for Simulation of Catalytic Cracking Process, for Compatible Mixtures of Coal Liquids and Petroleum Based Fuels, for Reactivation of Automotive Exhaust Oxidation Catalyst, for Increasing Antiknock Value of Olefinic Gasoline, for Preparation of Aromatic Hydrocarbons, for Process for Dehydrocyclizing Heterocyclic Organic Compounds, for Alumina Stabilized by Thoria to Resist Alpha Alumina Formation, for Method of Treating Chromium Oxide, others; invention of plastic dry bag; co-development of commercial methanol-to-gasoline process, of fuel cell for space power applications, including first successful operation in space flight; development of catalysts and processes for petroleum and petrochemical conversions, of electronic apparatus to measure dielectric properties during oxidation reactions and establish reaction kinetics; establishment of relationship between catalytic properties, surface chemistry, and semiconductivity properties of metal oxide catalysts; research on catalytic systems for automotive emissions control including kinetic model of oxidation of carbon monoxide and hydrocarbons. Home: 6 E Glen Cir Media PA 19063-4712

VOLZ, CHARLES HARVIE, JR., lawyer; b. Richmond, Va., Sept. 15, 1925; s. Charles Harvie and Mary V. (Mallory) V.; m. Constance A. Lewis, July 30, 1976; children: Charles Harvie III, Judith C. BS, U. Ala., 1950, JD, 1951. Bar: Ala. 1951, U.S. Dist. Ct. Ala., U.S. Ct. Appeals (5th cir.), U.S. Ct. Mil. Appeals, U.S. Ct. Appeals (11th cir.), U.S. Supreme Ct. 1962. Spl. agt. FBI, 1951; claim mgr. Allstate Ins. Co., 1952-54; claims atty. State Farm Ins. Co., 1954-57; ptnr. Roberts, Orme & Volz, 1957-59; sole practice Montgomery, 1961-63; asst. dir. Dept. Indsl. Rels., State of Ala., 1959-63; pntr. Volz, Capouano, Wampold & Prestwood, 1963-84, Volz & Volz, 1984-95, Volz, Prestwood & Hanan, 1995—2001; of counsel Prestwood and Assocs., 2001—. Note editor Ala. Law Rev., 1950-51. Campaign dir. March of Dimes, 1958, Am. Cancer Soc., 1967; exec. sec. Gov.'s Com. on Employment of Physically Handicapped, 1959-62; mem. Pres.'s Com. on Employment of Physically Handicapped, 1959-62; pres., bd. dirs. Montgomery chpt. Am. Cancer Soc. 2nd lt. USAAF, 1943-45. Recipient Outstanding Service award Am. Cancer Soc., 1967 Mem. ATLA (state committeeman 1973-75), Am. Arbitration Assn. (mem. nat. panel), ABA, Ala. Bar Assn., Ala. Trial Lawyers Assn., Farrah Law Soc., Montgomery County Club, Masons, Kiwanis, Phi Alpha Delta. Methodist. Home: 1638 Cobblestone Ct Montgomery AL 36117-1713 Office: 350 Adams Ave Montgomery AL 36104-4204

VOLZ, WILLIAM HARRY, law educator, administrator; b. Sandusky, Mich., Dec. 28, 1946; s. Harry Bender and Belva Geneva (Riehl) V. BA, Mich. State U., 1968; MA, U. Mich., 1972; MBA, Harvard U., 1978; JD, Wayne State U., 1975. Bar: mich. 1975. Atty. pvt. practice, Detroit, 1975-77; mgmt. analyst Office of Gen. Counsel, HEW, Woodlawn, Md., 1977; from asst. prof. to prof. Wayne State U., Detroit, 1978—86, prof., 1986—99, dean, 1997—99; dir. Ctr. for Legal Studies Wayne State U. Law Sch., 1996-97. Cons. Merrill Lynch, Pierce, Fenner & Smith, N.Y.C., 1980-83, City of Detroit Law Dept., 1982, Mich. Supreme Ct., Detroit, 1981; ptnr. Mich. CPA Rev., Southfield, 1983-85; expert witness in product liability, comml. law and bus. ethics; pres. Wedgewood Group. Author: Managing a Trial, 1982; contbr. articles to legal jours.; mem. editl. bds. of bus. and law jours. Internat. adv. bd. Inst. Mgmt., L'viv, Ukraine, Legal counsel Free Legal Aid Clinic, Inc., Detroit 1976-996, Shared Ministries, Detroit, 1981, Sino-Am. Tech. Exch. coun., China, 1982; chair advt. rev. panel BBB, Detroit, 1988-90; pres. Mich. Acad. Sci., Arts and Letters, 1995-96, 98-2000, bd. dirs.; pres. Common Ground, PLAYERS; bd. dirs. Greater Detroit Alliance Bus., Olde Custodian Fund. Mem.: ABA, The Wedgewood Group (pres.), Players, Amateur Medicant Soc. (commissionaire 1981—85), Harvard Bus. Sch. Club Detroit, Econ. Club Detroit, Detroit Athletic Club, Beta Alpha Psi, Alpha Kappa Psi, Golden Key. Home: 3846 Wedgewood Dr Bloomfield Hills MI 48301-3949 Office: Wayne State U Sch Bus Adminstrn Cass Ave Detroit MI 48202 Office Phone: 313-577-4694.

VOM SAAL, WALTER, psychology educator; b. NYC, Nov. 29, 1944; s. W. Rudolf and Jane (Towle) vom S.; children: Daniel, Laura, Jeffrey. BA, Columbia U., 1966; MA, McMaster U., 1967, PhD, 1969. Asst. prof. psychology Princeton (N.J.) U., 1969-74; assoc. prof. Millersville (Pa.) U., 1974-79, prof. psychology, 1979-86, assoc. v.p., 1986-89; provost and v.p. acad. affairs SUNY, Oneonta, 1989-94, acting pres. Plattsburgh, 1993-94, prof. psychology, 1989—. Named Disting. tchg. fellow Commonwealth of Pa., 1979, Disting. Tchg. chair, 1979. Mem. Phi Beta Kappa. Home: 103 Elm St Oneonta NY 13820 Office: SUNY 502 Fitzelle Hall Oneonta NY 13820

VON ARX, DOLPH WILLIAM, food products executive; b. St. Louis, Aug. 30, 1934; s. Adolph William and Margaret Louise (Linderer) von A.; m. Sharon Joy Landolt, Dec. 21, 1957; children: Vanessa von Arx Gilvarg, Eric S., Valerie L. BSBA, Washington U., St. Louis, 1961; LHD, St. Augustine Coll., 1988. Account exec. Compton Advt., N.Y.C., 1961-64; v.p. mktg. Ralston Purina Co., St. Louis, 1964-69; exec. v.p. mktg. Gillette Personal Care Div., Chgo., 1969-72; exec. v.p. gen. mgmt. group T.J. Lipton Inc., Englewood Cliffs, N.J., 1973-87; pres., chief exec. officer R.J. Reynold Tobacco Co., Winston-Salem, N.C., 1987-88; chmn., chief exec. officer Planters LifeSavers Co., Winston-Salem, 1988-91. Bd. dirs. Internat. Multi Food, Mpls., Hosp. Ptnrs. Am., Charlotte, N.C., No. Trust Fla. Corp., Miami, Cree Rsch. Inc., Durham, N.C., Ruby Tuesday Inc., BMC Fund Inc., Hosp. Ptnrs. Am., Charlotte, N.C.; chmn. Morrison's Restaurant Atlanta, 1996-98. Bd. visitors

U. N.C., 1988-92; chmn. bd. trustees Wake Forest U. Grad. Sch. Mgmt., 1988-96; pres. bd. trustees N.C. Dance Theater, Winston-Salem, 1989-90; bd. dirs. Forsyth Meml. Hosp., 1988-92, Naples Conservancy, Naples Philharm. Ctr. for Arts, Fla. Arts Coun., Reynolds Mus. Am. Art, Naples Cmty. Hosp., chmn., 1994-99, bd. dirs. health care sys., chmn., 1995—; mem. chmn.'s cir. Collier County Econ. Devel. Coun., Naples; chmn. Regional Bus. Alliance, Naples, Fla., 2004—. Mem. Belle Haven Club (Greenwich) (bd. dirs. 1983-87), Naples Yacht Club, Univ. Club (N.Y.C.), Linville Ridge Country Club (Linville, N.C.), Royal Poinciana Club (Naples, Fla.), Port Royal Club (Naples). Avocation: tennis. Home: 3663 Rum Row Naples FL 34102

VON BAILLOU, ASTRID, executive search consultant; b. Neutitschein, Czech Republic, Mar. 2, 1944; d. Karl von Baillou and Angela Stillfried; m. Dennis Hallam Bigelow, Oct. 21, 1967 (div. Oct. 1994). BA in English, Sweet Briar Coll., 1965. Creative dir. Freeman Advt., Washington, 1969-72; on-air reporter, prodr. PBS, BBC, London Weekend TV, N.Y.C., 1972-80; v.p. Sci. Program Group TV, Washington, 1980-82; pres. Cullen & Casey, N.Y.C., 1982-86; sr. v.p. Ruder Finn, N.Y.C., 1986-87; pres. Baillou Internat., N.Y.C., 1988-94; prin., mgmt. dir. Kinser & Assocs., N.Y.C., 1994-2000; ptnr. Kinser & Baillou, N.Y.C., 2000—. Home: 1245 Park Ave Apt 19F New York NY 10128-1740 Office Phone: 212-534-2161. E-mail: search@kinserbaillou.com.

VON BARGEN, SALLY, stock image photography company executive; BA in Psychology, U. Calif., Santa Cruz; MEd, Seattle U. Circulation dir. CommTek Comm.; founding v.p. sales and mktg. Netlink; cons. Gen. Instruments, Citicorp, Fingerhut and Viacom; advisor and orgnl. cons. to CEO and pres. Photo Disc, founding mem. mgmt. team, co-pres.; pres. Getty One, Seattle. Mem. Satellite Broadcasting Assn. (nat. bd. dirs.). Office: Getty Images Inc 701 N 34th St Ste 400 Seattle WA 98103-3415

VON BERNUTH, CARL W. lawyer, diversified corporation executive; b. Feb. 2, 1944; BA, Yale U., 1966, LLB, 1969. Bar: N.Y. 1970, Pa. 1990. Corp. atty. White & Case, 1969-80; assoc. gen. counsel Union Pacific Corp., N.Y.C., 1980-83, dep. gen. counsel fin. and adminstrn., 1984-88, v.p., gen. counsel Bethlehem, Pa., 1988-91, sr. v.p., gen. counsel, 1991-97, sr. v.p., gen. counsel and sec. Omaha, 1997—. Mem. U. Pa. Inst. for Law and Econs. Mem. Am. Corp. Counsel Assn., Practicing Law Inst. Office: Union Pacific Corp 1416 Dodge St Rm 1230 Omaha NE 68179-0001

VON BERNUTH, ROBERT DEAN, agricultural engineering educator, consultant; b. Del Norte, Colo., Apr. 14, 1946; s. John Daniel and Bernice H. (Dunlap) von B.; m. Judy M. Wehrman, Dec. 27, 1969; children: Jeanie, Suzie BSE, Colo. State U., 1968; MS, U. Idaho, 1970; MBA, Claremont (Calif.) Grad. Sch., 1980; PhD in Engring., U. Nebr., 1982. Registered profl. engr., Calif., Nebr. Agrl. product mgr. Rain Bird Sprinkler Mfg., Glendora, Calif., 1974-80; instr. agrl. engring. U. Nebr., Lincoln, 1980-82; from assoc. prof. to prof. U. Tenn., Knoxville, 1982-90; prof. Mich. State U., East Lansing, 1990—, chmn., 1992-96. V.p. Von-Sol Cons., Lincoln, 1980-82; prin. Von Bernuth Agrl. cons., Knoxville, East Lansing, 1982—. Patentee in field. With USNR, 1970—98, Vietnam. Decorated DFC (2); recipient Disting. Naval Grad. award USN Flight Program, Pensacola, Fla., 1970. Fellow Am. Soc. Agrl. Engrs.; mem. ASCE, Irrigation Assn. (Person of Yr. 1994), Naval Res. Assn. Avocations: flying, skiing, antique tractors. Office: Mich State U Sch of Constrn Mgmt 213 Farrall Hall East Lansing MI 48824-1323

VON BETZEN, VALERIE, artist; d. Warren Betz Von Betzen and Eleni (Panagakos) Poulos. Student, Pratt Inst., 1966—67. One-woman shows include Katharina Rich Perlow Gallery, N.Y.C., 1997, 2000, 2002, Morpeth Gallery, Hopewell, N.J., 2002, Butler Inst. Am. Art, Youngstown, Ohio, 2003, exhibitions include Allentown Art Mus., 1992, 1998, Cheekwood Mus., Nashville, 1994, San Bernardino County Mus., Redlands, Calif., 1995, Palm Springs (Calif.) Desert Mus., 1997, Albright-Knox Art Gallery, Buffalo, NY, 1998, 1999, Butler Inst. Am. Art, Youngstown, Ohio, 2003. Recipient award, Phillips Mill Ann. Art Exhibit, New Hope, 1987, 1992, 1994, 1996, 1997, 1999, 2003, Hunterdon Mus., Clinton, N.J., 1991, 1995, NYU Small Works Show, 1995; grantee, Elizabeth Greenshields Found., Montreal, Can., 1999, Johnson (Vt.) Studio Ctr., 1997; residency, Millay Colony for the Arts, Austerlitz, N.Y., 1999. Mem.: N.Y. Artists Equity. Independent. Avocation: drawing. Home: PO Box 6986 FDR Sta New York NY 10150 Home (Summer): Box 124 Durham PA 18039 Office Phone: 610-253-3896.

VON BRANDENSTEIN, PATRIZIA, production designer; Prodn. designer The Mirisch Agy., L.A., 1978—. Prodn. designer films including Heartland, 1979, Breaking Away, 1979, Ragtime, 1981 (Academy award nomination best art direction 1981), Silkwood, 1983, Amadeus, 1984 (Academy award best art direction 1984), A Chorus Line, 1985, The Money Pit, 1986, No Mercy, 1987, The Untouchables, 1987 (Academy award nomination best art direction 1987), Working Girl, 1988, The Lemon Sisters, 1990, Postcards From the Edge, 1990, Billy Bathgate, 1992, Sneakers, 1992, Leap of Faith, 1993, Six Degrees of Separation, 1993, The Quick and the Dead, 1995, Just Cause, 1995, The People vs. Larry Flynt, 1996, A Simple Plan, 1998, Man on the Moon, 1999, Shaft, 2000, It Runs in the Family, 2002, The Emperor's Club, 2002; costume designer films including Between the Lines, 1977, Saturday Night Fever, 1977, A Little Sex, 1982.

VON BRAUN, PETER CARL MOORE STEWART, business executive; b. Greenwich, Conn., June 24, 1940; s. Carl Conrad and Martha Irwin (Moore) von B.; m. Elisabeth Esser, July 1, 1967 (div. Dec. 1980); m. Denene Jensen, Sept. 26, 1987; children: Christina Stewart, Alexander Stewart. BA with high honors, Yale U., 1964; PhD summa cum laude, U. Cologne, 1966. Assoc. McKinsey & Co., Inc., N.Y.C., 1966-72, prin., 1972-77; chief internat. program devel. Order of St. John, London, 1977-80; exec. dir. Sight Programme, London and Sultanate of Oman, 1977-84; mng. ptnr. Leyton Assocs., Greenwich, 1980—; chmn., CEO Am. Microtrace Corp., Virginia Beach, Va., 1987-95, RusPetrol (USA), LLC, Greenwich, Conn., 1989-99. Mng. dir. LabelADD, LLC, Greenwich, Conn., 1987—; chmn. Leix LLC, Riverside, Conn., 2000—, Best Candle Co., Riverside, Conn., 2001—. Author: Die Verteidigung Indiens, 1968, How to Save a Life, 1977, How to Save An Eye, 1981; contbr. articles to profl. jours.; producer (film) How to Save a Life, 1977. Chmn. Battle Harbour Found., Greenwich, 1972—; vestryman Trinity Parish, N.Y.C., 1977-84; chmn. Anglican Svc. Tng. & Relief Orgn., London, 1986—; bd. dirs. Presiding Bishop's Fund, N.Y.C., 1977-81; mem. exec. bd. Greenwich Coun. Boy Scouts Am. With USN, 1956-58, U.S. Army, 1958-64. Decorated knight of grace and knight of justice Order of St. John, companion with star Order of Merit (Cyprus), other fgn. and U.S. decorations; Fulbright scholar, 1964-66. Mem.: Cavalry, Guards Polo (London); N.Y. Yacht (N.Y.C.), Yale Club, Indian Harbor Yacht Field Club (Greenwich, Conn.), Battle Harbour Yacht (Newfoundland, Can.), Commodore, Stewart Soc. (Edinburgh). Republican. Episcopalian. Avocations: sailing, military history, cooking. Home: 36 Zaccheus Mead Ln Greenwich CT 06831-3753

VONCANNON, BRIAN EVERETT, writer, scriptwriter, radio personality; s. Mary Jane and Charles Everett Voncannon. AA in applied sci., Ctrl. Piedmont C.C., 1995—98; D in naturology, Am. Inst. of Holistic Theology, 1994—96. General Law Enforcement Cert. NC Tng. and Standards Commn., 1990, Chemical Analyst of Breath NC HHS, 1998, cert. Profl. Trainer Nat. Fedn. of Profl. Trainers, 1995. Police officer Concord City Police Dept., Concord, NC, 1990—95; dep. sheriff/swat officer Cabarrus County Sheriff's Dept., Concord, NC, 1997—2002; author EveningStorm Enterprises, Midland, NC, 1997—; cmty. radio dj/rec. studio owner EveningStorm Radio, Midland, NC, 2002—. Swat officer Cabarrus County Sheriff's Dept., Concord, NC, 1998—2002. Author: (book) Chronic Fatigue Syndrome: Living with the Unknown, Shadows: Diary of a Ninja, Cherokee Blue Eyes: Keeping the Heritage Alive, Living Behind the Shield: A Modern Warrior's Path to Bravehood, Completing the Circle: The Hathcock Indian Blood, (screenplays) The Keepers, Orbit. Sound tech. First Bapt. Ch. of Locust, Locust, NC, 1985—2000. E-6 staff sgt. US Army Reserves, 1991—99, Concord, North Carolina. Decorated Army Achievement medal US Army, Disting. Honor Grad. award US Army Inf. Tng. Ctr., Ft. Benning, Ga., Cert. of Recognition for Cold War Svc. Dept. of Def., Nat. Def. Svc. medal US Army. Democrat-Npl. So. Bapt. Avocations: martial arts, physical fitness activities, outdoor activities, creating native american crafts, travel. Home: 13101 Pine Bluff Rd Midland NC 28107 Office: EveningStorm Enterprises 13101 Pine Bluff Rd Midland NC 28107 E-mail: eveningstorm@earthlink.net.

VON DECK, JOSEPH FRANCIS, secondary school educator, researcher; b. Athol, Mass., Jan. 6, 1931; s. Robert and Imelda May Von Deck; m. Evelyn Strachan, Feb. 24, 1958; children: Scott Andrew, Philip Henry. BA in History, U. Mass., 1961; MEd in History, Fitchburg State Coll., 1971. Cert. secondary tchr. history Mass. Tchr. history Oakmont Regional High Sch., Ashburnham, Mass., 1961—67, chair dept. history, 1967—96, tchr. advanced placement U.S. history, 1996—2002; ret., 2002. Cons. Mass. Hist. Soc., Ashburnham, 1998. Contbr. articles to profl. jours. Moderator Town of Ashburnham, 1971—72; hist. commr. Hist. Commn., 1985—. With USN, 1948—52, with USN, 1955—59. Grantee Horace Mann grantee, Ash-West Regional Sch. Com., So. Ashburnham, Mass., 1985, Nat. Def. Ednl. Adminstrn., 1965, 1967. Mem.: Civil War Round Table (founder, v.p. 1983—85), Ashburnham Hist. Soc., Assn. for Preservation Civil War Sites. Democrat. Avocations: writing, history, travel. Office: Oakmont Regional High Sch Oakmont Dr Ashburnham MA 01430

VONDERBRINK, GERALD WILLIAM, retired academic administrator, property manager; b. Cin. s. Richard Bernard and Marguerite Grady Vonderbrink; widowed; children: David Jerome, Diane Edwards, Philip Gerald, Joseph Paul. BSBA, Xavier U., 1950; MBA, U. Dayton, 1966. Jr. acct. Alexander Grant, Cin., 1950-51; sr. acct. Hathaway & Hathaway, Cin., 1951-54; contr. Aerosonic Instrument Co., Cin., 1954-56; fin. analyst GE, Cin., 1956-57; contr. Coll. Conservatory of Music, Cin., 1958-61; v.p. fin. affairs U. Dayton, Ohio, 1961-92, asst. exec. v.p., 1993-98. Contbr. articles to profl. jours. Pres. Ohio Assn. Coll. and Univ. Bus. Officers, 1967-68; sec./treas. Ctrl. Assn. Coll. and Univ. Bus. Officers, 1968-69; mem. fin. aid com. Nat. Assn. Coll. and Univ. Bus. Officers, Washington, 1978; chmn. bd. dirs. U. Dayton Libr. Advancement Assn., 1999—; treas. bd. dirs. Places, Inc., Dayton, 1999-2001; bd. dirs. Dakota Ctr., Dayton, 1999-2001, Caring Families, Inc., Dayton, 1996-2001. Cpl. U.S. Army Signal Corps, 1946-48, Japan. Democrat. Roman Catholic. Avocations: tennis, bridge.

VONDER HAAR, THOMAS H. meteorology educator; b. Quincy, Ill., Dec. 28, 1942; m. Dee M. Clark, 1980; children: Kim, Kurt, Nicholas, Krista, Matthew. BS, St. Louis U., 1963; MS, U. Wis., 1964, PhD in Meteorology, 1968. Assoc. scientist meteorology Space Sci. & Engring. Ctr. U. Wis., Madison, 1968-70; assoc. prof. meteorology Colo. State U., Ft. Collins, 1970-77, prof. atmospheric sci., 1977—, univ. disting. prof., 1994, head dept. atmospheric sci., 1974-84, acting dean Coll. Engring., 1981-82. Cons. U.S. Army, ITT Aerospace, Sci. and Tech. Corp., World Meteor Orgn. UN, Ball Aerospace Corp., 1969—. Mem. Am. Meteorol. Soc., Sigma Xi. Office: Coop Inst Rsch in Atmosphere Colo State U Fort Collins CO 80523-1375

VON DER HEYDEN, KARL MUELLER, retired manufacturing executive; b. Berlin, July 18, 1936; arrived in U.S., 1957, naturalized, 1967; s. Werner and Erika (Mueller) von der Heyden; m. Mary Ellen Terrell, Aug. 17, 1963; children: Ellen, Eric. Student, Free U., Berlin, 1959-61; BA, Duke, 1962; MBA, U. Pa., 1964. CPA Pa. Mgmt. trainee Berliner Bank, Berlin, 1955-57; sr. staff acct. Coopers & Lybrand, Phila., 1963-66; asst. comptr., corporate comptr. Pitney-Bowes, Inc., Stamford, Conn., 1966-74; v.p., contr. PepsiCo., Inc., Purchase, 1974-77; v.p. fin. Pepsi-Cola Co., 1977-79, v.p. mfg., 1979-80; v.p. fin., treas. H.J. Heinz Co., Pitts., 1980-83, sr. v.p. fin., CFO, also bd. dirs., 1983-89; exec. v.p., CFO RJR Nabisco Inc., N.Y.C., 1989-93, co-chmn., CEO, 1993; pres., CEO Metallgesellschaft Corp., N.Y.C., 1993-94; sr. advisor Clipper Group, 1994-97. Chmn. Fin. Acctg. Stds. Adv. Coun., 1995—96; vice-chmn., ret. PepsiCo, Inc., Purchase, NY, 1996—2001; bd. dirs. Federated Dept. Stores, Inc., Aramark Corp., Exult, Inc. Trustee Duke U., Am. Acad., Berlin, Nat. Humanities Ctr., Univ. Club, N.Y.C. Home: 15 Khakum Wood Rd Greenwich CT 06831-3728 Office: Ste 100 2 Sound View Dr Greenwich CT 06830

VON DER HEYDT, JAMES ARNOLD, federal judge; b. Miles City, Mont., July 15, 1919; s. Harry Karl and Alice S. (Arnold) von der H.; m. Verna E. Johnson, May 21, 1952. BA, Albion (Mich.) Coll., 1942; JD, Northwestern, 1951. Bar: Alaska 1951. Pvt. practice, Nome, 1953-59; judge superior ct. Juneau, Alaska, 1959-66; from judge to sr. judge U.S. Dist. Ct. Alaska, Alaska, 1966—; U.S. commr. Nome, Alaska, 1951—; U.S. atty. div. 2 Dist. Alaska, 1951-53; mem. Alaska Ho. of Reps., 1957-59. Author: Mother Sawtooth's Nome, 1990, Alaska, The Short and Long of It, 2000. Pres. Anchorage Fine Arts Mus. Assn. Recipient Disting. Alumni award Albion Coll., 1995. Mem. Alaska Bar Assn. (mem. bd. govs. 1955-59, pres. 1959-60), Am. Judicature Soc., Masons (32d degree), Shriners, Phi Delta Phi, Sigma Nu. Avocations: researching arctic bird life, creative writing. Office: US Dist Ct 222 W 7th Ave Box 40 Anchorage AK 99513-7564 Office Phone: 907-677-6254.

VON DER SCHMIDT, EDWARD, III, neurosurgeon, veterinarian; b. Jan. 13, 1953; BS in Animal Sci., Rutgers U., 1975; DVM, Cornell U., 1979; MD, U. Medicine and Dentistry N.J., Newark, 1984. Diplomate Nat. Bd. Med. Examiners, Am. Bd. Neurol. Surgery. Veterinarian Secaucus (N.J.) Animal Hosp., 1979-82; pvt. practice vet. medicine NJ, 1980-85; gen. surg. intern Washington Hosp. Ctr., Washington, 1984-85; resident in neurosurgery George Washington U. Med. Ctr., Washington, 1985-90; pvt. practice neurosurgery Princeton (N.J.) Healthcare Ctr., 1990—. Neurosurgeon Robert Wood Johnson U. Hosp., New Brunswick, NJ, St. Peter's Med. Ctr., New Brunswick, Somerset Med. Ctr., Somerville, NJ; chief neurosurgery sect. Med. Ctr. Princeton; mem. search com. for chief divsn. neurosurgery U. Medicine and Dentistry N.J./Robert Wood Johnson Med. Sch. Mem.: AAAS, AMA, N.J. Soc. Med. Specialty (pres. 2000—02), Coun. State Neurosurgical Safety (mem. reform commn. 2001, vice chmn. N.E. quadrant 2003—), Am. Assn. Med. Transcription (bd. dirs. Ctrl. N.J. chpt.), Am. Coll. Physician Execs., Soc. Exec. Physicians, Soc. Critical Care Medicine, N.J. Neurosurgical Soc. (trustee at large 2000—, sec. treas. 1998—2000), N.Y. Acad. Sci., Middlesex Med. Soc. (sec. 2003, del.), Middlesex County Med. Soc., Med. Soc. N.J., Congress Neurol. Surgeons (mem. joint sect. disorders spine and peripheral nerves), Am. Assn. Neurol. Surgeons, Alpha Zeta (Best Freshman award). Home: 140 Hodge Rd Princeton NJ 08540-3014 Office: Princeton Healthcare Ctr 419 N Harrison St Ste 204 Princeton NJ 08540-3521

VONDRACEK, M. JON, communications executive; b. Chgo., Oct. 23, 1938; s. Milo J. and Genevieve H. V.; m. Elisabeth B. Vondracek, May 8, 1965. BA, Lawrence U., 1964. Journalist Washington Post, NY Times, Time Mag., Washington, 1961—66; sec., dir. comm. Georgetown U. Ctr. for Strategic and Internat. Studies, Washington, 1966—86; v.p. corp. pub. affairs Young & Rubicam, NYC, 1986—87; adv. to the pres. Ctr. for Strategic and Internat. Studies, Washington, 1987—89; v.p. The Johnson Found., Racine, Wis., 1989—95, CSIS, 1995—2000, v.p. and advisor to pres., 2000—03. Trustee Lawrence U., 1998-2001; mng. dir. World Affairs Coun. Washington, 2001-2003. Mem. Nat. Press Club, Met. Club of Washington, Union League Club of NY, Univ. Club of Washington, Racine Yacht Club. Office: Export Import Bank of the US 811 Vermont Ave NW #1278 Washington DC 20571 E-mail: mjon.vondraced@exim.gov.

VON DREHLE, RAMON ARNOLD, lawyer; b. St. Louis, Mar. 12, 1930; s. Arnold Henry and Sylvia E. (Ahrens) Von D.; m. Gillian Margaret Turner, Sept. 13, 1980; children by previous marriage: Carin L., Lisa A., Courtney A. BS, Washington U., St. Louis, 1952; JD, U. Tex., Austin, 1957; postgrad, Parker Sch. Internat. Law, Columbia U., 1965. Bar: Tex. 1956, Mich. 1957, U.S. Supreme Ct. 1981. Sr. atty. Ford Motor Co., Dearborn, Mich., 1957-67; assoc., asst. gen. counsel Ford of Europe, Inc., Brentwood, Essex, Eng., 1967-75, v.p., gen. counsel, 1975-79; v.p. legal Ford Motor Credit Co., Dearborn, 1979-87; v.p., gen. counsel Am. Road Ins. Co., Dearborn, 1979-87; exec. dir. legal affairs Ford Fin. Services Group, Dearborn, 1987-91; leader in residence Walsh Coll., Mich., 1992. Panelist large complex case program Am. Arbitration Assn., 1993—; advisor to Czech Republic Ministry of Privatization, Prague, 1993-94; leader Russian Def. Conversion Project, 1995-96; lectr. in Ea. Europe, 1995; pres. Focus Internat. LLC, 1995—. Article editor: Tex. Law Rev, 1956-57. Trustee Birmingham Unitarian Ch., 1966-67. Served to 1st lt. AUS, 1952-54, Korea. Mem. ABA, Mich. Bar Assn., Tex. Bar Assn., Internat. Bar Assn., Am. Fin. Svcs. Assn. (chmn. 1990-91, bd. dirs. 1981-91), Fin. Svcs. Coun. (bd. dirs. 1987-91), Washington U. Alumni Club Detroit (past pres.), Order of Coif, Tower Club (Tysons, Va.), Confrèrie des Chevaliers du Tastevin (France, Washington), Royal Automobile Club (London), Cosmos Club (Washington). Mem. Christ Ch. Home and Office: 519 Princess St Alexandria VA 22314-2332 E-mail: rvond2@aol.com.

VON ESCHEN, LISA A. lawyer; BA, Coll. of William and Mary, 1986; JD, NYU, 1991. Bar: Calif. 1991. Mem. bd. dirs. Western Law Ctr. for Disability Rights. Mem.: Women Lawyers Assn. L.A., Assn. Bus. Trial Lawyers, L.A. County Bar Assn. (vol. Pro Bono Domestic Violence Project, mem. labor and employment sect.). Office: Latham and Watkins LLP 633 W Fifth St Ste 4000 Los Angeles CA 90071

VON ESCHEN, ROBERT LEROY, electrical engineer, consultant; b. Glasgow, Mont., Oct. 3, 1936; s. Leroy and Lillian Victoria (Eliason) Von E.; m. Carolyn Kay Frampton, Dec. 14, 1965 (dec. Feb. 1999); children: Eric Leroy, Marc Alfred. BSEE, Mont. State U., 1961; postgrad., U. Liberia, Lakeland C.C., Glendale C.C. Registered profl. engr., Pa. Hydro constrn. engr. U.S. Army Corps of Engrs., Mont. and S.D., 1961-62; hdqrs. chief engr. Eagle Constrn. Co., Colo., 1962; resident transp./distbn. elec. engr. Stanley Cons., Inc., West Africa, 1962-63, hydro cons., startup engr., 1965-66; with Stanley Cons., 1962-68, Gilbert Assoc./United Energy Svc., 1968-92; performance based assessment program sect. engr., maintenance planning engr., condition assessment survey sec. mgr. Gilbert Assocs., Inc., Tex., 1992—. Bd. dirs. Kidsworld Multimedia; cons. engr. fossil power plant, Ky., Colo., Mo., Korea; site project mgr., Ariz., Aruba; nuclear constrn. startup engr., Pa., Ala., Ohio; safety sys. functional inspector, Calif., Wis., Oreg.; performance based assessment program project mgr., Tex.; tech. cons. World Bank, Liberia; engring. cons. USN, Manila, 1967; founding dr. Madison Comptr. Soc., Ohio, 1983-85; v.p., dr. Boy Scouts Am., 1981-84. Founder, dir. Madison (Ohio) Computer Soc., 1983-85; v.p., bd. dirs. N.E. coun. Boy Scouts Am., Painesville, 1983-85. Recipient Silver Beaver award Boy Scouts Am., 19 other awards. Mem. IEEE, NRA, NPSE, NARP, Soc. Am. Mil. Engrs., Nat. Def. Indsl. Orgn., Profl. Engring. Soc. Ohio, Profl. Engring. Soc. Tex., Masons (life), Shriners. Avocations: target and skeet shooting, construction design, computers, electronics. Office: Mason & Hanger Mason Corp PO Box 30020 Amarillo TX 79120-0020 Home: 1001 S Girl Scout Rd Amarillo TX 79124-2135

VON ESCHENBACH, ANDREW C. director National Cancer Institute, oncologist; b. Phila., Pa., Oct. 30, 1941; MD, Georgetown U., 1967. Diplomate Am. Bd. Urology. Intern U. Pa./Phila. Gen. Hosp., 1967—68; resident gen. surgery Pa. Hosp., Phila., 1971—72, resident urology, 1972—75; fellow urol. oncology U. Tex. MD Anderson Hosp., Houston, 1976—77, prof. urology, 1977—2002, chmn. dept. urology, 1983—96, exec. v.p., chief acad. officer, dir. program ctr. Genitourinary Cancer, 1997—2002, founding dir., Prostate Cancer Research Prog., 1996; dir. Nat. Cancer Inst., NIH, Bethseda, Md., 2002—. Lt. comdr. U.S. Navy Medical Corps. Recipient Julie Rogers award, Achievement award in prostate cancer, Partners in Courage, Medical award, Cancer Counseling, Certificate of Meritorious Service for outstanding contbn. to prostate disease research, Uniformed Services U. of the Health Sci. Mem.: AMA, Soc. Surg. Oncology, Am. Urologists Assn., Am. Cancer Soc. (pres.-elect 2002). Office: Nat Cancer Inst, NIH 31 Center Dr Bldg 31 Rm11A48 Bethesda MD 20892

VON ESSEN, THOMAS, protective services official; b. Bklyn. m. Rita Von Essen; children: Pamela, Erica, Marc, Tom. BA in Econs., St. Francis Coll. Bklyn.; MEd, C.W. Post; grad., N.Y.C. Fire Dept. Sch., 1970. Firefighter Fire Dept. N.Y.C., 1970-85; from del. to pres. N.Y.C. Firefighters, 1985-96; commr. Fire Dept. N.Y.C., 1996—. Office: Fire Dept NY 9 Metrotech Ctr Brooklyn NY 11201-5431 Fax: 718-999-1031.

VON FETTWEIS, YVONNE CACHÉ, archivist, historian; b. L.A., Nov. 28, 1935; d. Boyd Eugene and Georgette Louisa (Tilmann) Adams; m. Maurice Lee Caché, Jan. 8, 1955 (div. 1962); children: Maurice C.B. II, Michele-Yvonne (Mrs. Vernon Young Sr.); m. Rolland Phillip von Fettweis, July 22, 1967. BA, Wagner Coll., 1954; postgrad, Am. U., 1973, Bentley Coll., 1981. Legal sec., asst. Judge, Davis, Stern, Orfinger & Tindall, Daytona Beach, Fla., 1961-66; head rec. sect., bd. dirs. 1st Ch. Christ Scientist, Boston, 1969-71, rsch. assoc., 1971-72, adminstrv. archivist, 1972-78, sr. assoc. archivist, 1979-84, records adminstr., 1984-91, div. mgr. records mgmt./orgnl. archives, 1991-92, divsn. mgr. ch. history, 1992—, divsn. mgr. ch. history and healing ministry, 1995; divsn. mgr. ch. history, 1995-96; ch. historian 1st Ch. Christ Scientist, Boston, 1996—. Cons. Christian Sci. Bd. Dirs., 1999—, pres. of Mother Ch., 2002-; mem. Religious Pub. Rels. Coun. Co-author: Mary Baker Eddy: A Lifetime of Healing, 1996, Mary Baker Eddy: Christian Healer, 1997, The New Woman and the New Church: The Lincoln Women, 2001. Trustee Ch. Hist. Trust, 1995—; exec. sec. Volusia County Goldwater campaign, Daytona Beach, 1964; mem. Christian Sci. Bd. Lectureship, 1998. Mem. Soc. Am. Archivists (editor The Archival Spirit), Automated Records and Techniques Task Force, Am. Mgmt. Assn., Orgn. Am. Historians, Ctr. for Study Presidency, Religious Pub. Rels. Coun., New Eng. Archivists, Assn. Records Mgrs. and Adminstrs. (bd. dirs. 1983—), Assn. Coll. and Rsch. Librs., Bay State Hist. League, Order Ea. Star, Order Rainbow (bd. dirs. 1972-77). Republican. Christian Scientist. Home: 147 Bosarvey Dr Ormond Beach FL 32176-6662 Office: 1st Ch Christ Sci 175 Huntington Ave # A240 Boston MA 02115-3117

VON FRAUNHOFER-KOSINSKI, KATHERINA, bank executive; b. N.Y.C. m. Jerzy Kosinski, Feb. 15, 1987 (dec. May 3, 1991). Student, St. Joseph's Convent, London, Clark's Coll. Various positions Robert W. Orr & Assocs., N.Y.C.; with traffic dept. Compton Advt., Inc., N.Y.C., 1956-63; acct. exec. J. Walter Thompson Co., N.Y.C., 1963-69; product mgr. Natural Wonder line Revlon Co., N.Y., 1969-71; pres. Scientia Factum, Inc., N.Y.C., 1971—, Polish Am. Resources Corp., N.Y.C., 1992—, pres., CEO, 1992—2002. Chmn. Am. Bank in Poland, 1990—2001; bd. dirs. DZ Bank Polska, Warsaw, 1997—. Co-founder Westchester Sports Club. Assoc. fellow Timothy Dwight Coll./Yale U., 1997—. Avocations: skiing, horse/polo, swimming, photography. Home: 60 W 57th St New York NY 10019-3909

VON FURSTENBERG, BETSY, actress, writer; b. Neiheim Heusen, Germany, Aug. 16, 1931; d. Count Franz-Egon and Elizabeth (Johnson) von F.; m. Guy Vincent de la Maisoneuve (div.); 2 children.; m. John J. Reynolds, Mar. 26, 1984. Attended Miss Hewitt's Classes, N.Y. Tutoring Sch.; prepared for stage with Sanford Meisner at Neighborhood Playhouse. Made Broadway stage debut in Second Threshold, N.Y., 1951; appeared in Dear Barbarians, 1952, Oh Men Oh Women, 1954, The Chalk Garden, 1955, Child of Fortune, 1956, Nature's Way, 1957, Much Ado About Nothing, 1959, Mary Mary, 1965, Paisley Convertible, 1967, Avanti, 1968, The Gingerbread Lady, 1970 (toured 1971), Absurd Person Singular, 1976; off Broadway appearances include For Love or Money, 1951; toured in Petrified Forest, Jason and Second Man, 1952; appeared in Josephine, 1953; subsequently toured, 1955; What Every Woman Knows, 1955, The Making of Moo, 1958 (toured 1958), Say Darling, 1959, Wonderful Town, 1959, Season of Choice, 1959, Beyond Desire, 1967, Private Lives, 1968, Does Anyone Here Do the Peabody, 1976; appeared in Along Came a Spider, Theatre in the Park, N.Y.C., 1985; appeared in film Women Without Names, 1950; TV appearances include Robert Montgomery Show, Ed Sullivan Show, Alfred Hitchcock Presents, One Step Beyond, The Mike Wallace Show, Johnny Carson Show, Omnibus, Theatre of the Week, The Secret Storm, As the World Turns, Movie of the Week, Your Money or Your Wife, Another World; writer syndicated column More Than Beauty; contbr. articles to newspapers and mags. including N.Y. Times Sunday Arts and Leisure, Saturday Rev. of Literature, People, Good Housekeeping, Art News, Pan Am Travel; co-author: (novel) Mirror, Mirror, 1988. Avocations: tennis, painting, photography.

VON FURSTENBERG, DIANE SIMONE MICHELLE, fashion designer, writer, entrepreneur; b. Brussels, Dec. 31, 1946; came to U.S., 1969; d. Leon L. and Liliane L. (Nahmias) Halfin; m. Eduard Egon von Furstenberg, July 16, 1969 (div.); children: Alexandre, Tatiana. Student, U. Madrid, 1965 66, U. Geneva, 1966-68. Founder, pres. Diane von Furstenberg Studio, L.P., N.Y.C., 1970—; pres. Diane Von Furstenberg Ltd., N.Y.C.; founder Salvy, Paris, 1985. Pioneer TV shopping with creative and live on-air selling Silk Assets collection, 1992; returns to retail as designer DIANE line of signature dresses, including the wrap, 1997. Author: Diane Von Furstenberg's Book of Beauty; Beds, 1991, The Bath, 1993, The Table, 1996, DIANE: A Signature Life, 1998; contbg. editor Vanity Fair mag., 1993. Recipient Ellis Island Medal of Honor, 1986. *Honesty in all ways: honest products, honest and straight approach to needs.**

VON FURSTENBERG, GEORGE MICHAEL, economics educator, researcher; b. Germany, Dec. 3, 1941; came to U.S., 1961; m. Gabrielle M. Freiin Koblitz von Willmburg, June 9, 1967; 1 child, Philip G. PhD, Princeton U., 1967. Asst. prof. econs. Cornell U., Ithaca, N.Y., 1966-70; assoc. prof. econs. Ind. U., Bloomington, 1970 73, prof., 1976-78, Rudy prof. econs., 1983—; Robert Bendheim prof. econ. and financial policy Fordham U., N.Y.C., 2000—03; sr. staff economist Council Econ. Advisors, Washington, 1973-76; div. chief research dept. IMF, Washington, 1978-83. Project dir. Am. Coun. Life Ins., Washington, 1976-78; sr. advisor Brookings Instn., Washington, 1978-90; vis. sr. economist planning and analysis staff Dept. State, Washington 1989-90; Bissell-Fulbright vis. prof. Can.-Am. rels. U. Toronto, 1994-95. Contbg. author, editor: The Government and Capital Formation, 1980, Capital, Efficiency and Growth, 1980, Acting Under Uncertainty: Multidisciplinary Conceptions, 1990, Regulation and Supervision of Financial Institutions in the NAFTA Countries and Beyond, 1997; editor: International Money and Credit: The Policy Roles, 1983; co-author: Learning from the World's Best Central Bankers, 1998; co-editor: Monetary Unions and Hard Pegs: Effects on Trade, Financial Development, and Stability, 2004; assoc. editor Rev. of Econs. and Stats., 1987-92, Open Econs. Rev., 1997—; contbr. articles to profl. jours. Fulbright grantee to Poland, 1991-92. Mem. N.Am. Econs. and Fin. Assn. (pres. 2000), Am. Econ. Assn. Roman Catholic. Avocation: tennis. Office: Indiana U Dept Economics Wylie Hall Bloomington IN 47405 Office Phone: 812-855-4764. Business E-Mail: vonfurst@indiana.edu.

VONGERICHTEN, JEAN-GEORGES, food service executive; b. Strasbourg, Alsace; arrived in U.S., 1985; Studied with chef Paul Hueberlin, Auberge de l'Ill. Worked with Paul Bocuse L'Oasis Market, Paris; worked with master chef Louis Outhier L'Oasis, France; chef Oriental Hotel, Bangkok; opened Meridian Hotel, Singapore, Mandarin Hotel, Hong Kong, Lafayette, Boston, 1985, exec. chef N.Y.C., 1986; opened Jo Jo, 1991, Vong, N.Y.C., London, 1995, Hong Kong, 1997, Chgo., 1999, Mercer Kitchen, N.Y.C., 1998, The Lipstick Cafe, Prime, Las Vegas, Nev., 1998, Dune, Bahamas, 2000, V Steakhouse, N.Y.C., 2004. Author: Simple Cuisine, Jean-Georges: Cooking at Home with a Four-Star Chef, 1998, Simple to Speculate, 2000; appeared Martha Stewart Show, Live! with Regis and Kathie Lee, Today Show, Good Morning Am., Food Network, (TV series) Julia's Kitchen with Master Chefs with Julia Child, 1995. Named Jo Jo Best New Restaurant of Yr., Esquire Mag., Chef of Yr., Outstanding Chef, James Beard Found., 1998; recipient four stars for Lafayette, N.Y. Times, three stars for Jo Jo, three stars for Vong, four stars for Jean Georges, 1997, Best New Restaurant award for Jean Georges, James Beard Found., 1998. Office: Jean Georges Mgmt LLC 111 Prince St New York NY 10012

VON GIERKE, HENNING EDGAR, biomedical science educator, former government official, researcher; b. Karlsruhe, Germany, May 22, 1917; arrived in U.S., 1947, naturalized, 1977; s. Edgar and Julie (Braun) Von Gierke; married; 2 children. Dipl. Ing., Karlsruhe Tech., 1943, Dr. Engr., 1944. Asst. in acoustics Karlsruhe Tech., 1944—47, lectr., 1946; cons. Aerospace Med. Research Labs, Wright-Patterson AFB, Ohio, 1947—54, chief bioacoustics br., 1954—63, dir. biodynamics and bionics div., 1963—88; assoc. prof. Ohio State U., 1963—88; clin. prof. Wright State U., 1980—. Mem. com. hearing bioacoustics and biomechanics NRC, 1953—93, chmn., 1990—93, bioastronaut com., 1959—61; mem. adv. com., flight medicine and biology NASA, 1960—61. Author numerous tech. publs., book chpts.; patentee in field. Fellow: Am. Inst. Med. and Biol. Engring., Coll. Fellows, Aerospace Med. Assn. (v.p. 1966—67, E. Liljenkrantz award 1966, A.D. Tuttle award 1974, John Paul Stapp award 2004), Inst. Environ. Scis. (hon.), Acoustical Soc. Am. (pres. 1979—80, Silver medal 1981, Gold medal 1999); mem.: Internat. Acad. Astronautics, Mil. Audiology Assn. (hon.), Biomed. Engring. Soc., Inst. Noise Ctrl. Engring., Internat. Acad. Aviation and Space Medicine, NAE. Achievements include research in bioacoustics, acoustics, biomechanics and bioengring. Home: 1325 Meadow Ln Yellow Springs OH 45387-1219

VON GIZYCKI, ALKISTIS ROMANOFF, research scientist, educator, scholar, writer; b. Famagusta, Cyprus; arrived in U.S., 1967; d. Costas and Evangelia Lillian Victoria Kyprianou; m. Nicholas Romanoff, 1977 (dec.); m. Walter Von Gizycki, Sept. 19, 1981 (div. Dec. 1992); children: Bernard, Elsa. BA with honors, RMWC, Lynchburg, Va., 1967-71; MA in Psychology, New Sch. U., 1976-78. Educator, counselor Bilingual Bd. Edn., Nicosia, Cyprus, 1971-86; bus. devel. Bucci Trading Co., Nicosia, Cyprus, 1981-86; rschr., writer freelance, 1986—. Officer ch. bd. Fifth Ave. Presbyn. Ch. 1979—; vol. ch. and civic leader. Fulbright grantee; recipient Gen. Excellence award, valedictorian Am. Acad., Nicosia, Cyprus, 1967, Vol. award J.P. Morgan Chase Found., 1995, Outstanding Performance award J.P. Morgan Chase, 1997. Mem. NOW, AAUW, NY Acad. Sci. (assoc.), Am. Psychol. Assn. Avocations: theater, films, reading, music, ballet. E-mail: alk12345@aol.com.

VON GUNDEN, HEIDI, music educator; b. San Diego, Calif., July 13, 1940; d. C. F. and Evangeline Cecilia Von Gunden. MusB, Mount St. Mary's Coll., 1963; MA, Calif. State U., 1971, U. Calif. San Diego, 1973, PhD, 1975. Asst. prof. So. Ill. U., Carbondale, 1975—79; assoc. prof. U. Ill., Urbana, 1979—. Author: The Music of Vivian Fine, 1998 (Deems Taylor ACAP award, 2000). Office: Univ Illinois Sch Music 1114 Nevada St Urbana IL 61801

VON HAKE, MARGARET JOAN, librarian; b. Santa Monica, Calif., Oct. 27, 1933; d. Carl August and Inez Garnet (Johnson) von Hake. BA, La Sierra U., 1955; MS in Library Sci., U. So. Calif., 1963. Tchr. Newbury Park (Calif.) Acad., 1955-60, librarian, 1957-60; circulation librarian Columbia Union Coll., Takoma Park, Md., 1962-67, library dir., 1967—, assoc. prof., 1990—. Mem. ALA, Md. Libr. Assn., Congress of Acad. Libr. Dirs. of Md. (exec. dir. 1999-00), Md. Ind. Coll.and Univ. Assn. Libr. Dirs. Round Table (chair 1996-98), Assn. Seventh Day Adventist Librs. (newsletter editor 1981-83, pres. 1989-90), Sligo Federated Music Club (pres. 1988-89, yearbook co-editor 2000—). Republican. Office: Columbia Union Coll 7600 Flower Ave Takoma Park MD 20912-7796

VON HILSHEIMER, GEORGE EDWIN, III, neuropsychologist; b. West Palm Beach, Fla., Aug. 15, 1934; s. George E. Jr. and Dorothy Sue (Bridges) Von H.; m. Catherine Jean Munson, Dec. 27, 1968 (div. Oct. 1987); children: Dana Ghermine, George E., Alexandra; m. Jonnie Mae Warner, June 29, 1991. BA, U. Miami, 1955; PhD, Saybrook Inst., 1977. Diplomate Acad. Psychosomatic Medicine, Am. Bd. Behavioral Medicine, Am. Acad. Pain Mgmt., Am. Bd. Cert. Managed Care Providers, Am. Acad. Psychol. Treating Addiction, Nat. Register Neurofeedback. Sr. min. Humanitas, NYC, 1959-64; cons. Pres. Kennedy's Commn. Nat. Vol. Svc., Juvenile Del., Migratory Labor, 1963-64; headmaster Summerlane Sch., North Branch, NY, 1964-69; supt. Green Valley Sch., Orange City, Fla., 1969-74; neuropsychologist Growth Insts., Twyman's Mill, Va., 1974-79, Growth Inst., DeLand, Fla., 1980-82; assoc. health profl. Maitland, Fla., 1982—2004; pvt. practice biofeedback trainer and hypnotist, 1998—. Cons. Sci. Adv. Bd. EPA, Washington, 1974-84; chmn. Certification Bd., Internat. Coll. Environ. Medicine, 1991-94; mem. Bd. Assn. Diagnostic Efficiency and Brief Therapy, dir. curriculum, 1993-94; cons. Ont. Correctional Inst., Toronto, 1970-95. Author: How to Live With Your Special Child, 1970, Understanding Problems of Children, 1975, Allergy, Toxins and the LD Child, 1977, Psychobiology of Delinquents, 1978, Depression Is Not a Disease, 1989, Brief Therapy, 1993, Brief Therapy: Antecedent Scientific Principles, 1994; editor Human Learning, Washington, 1974-94; editor: Jour. of ANT, ANT Trails, 1998—. Mem. spl. bd. Fla. Symphony Orch., 1992-93. With mil. intelligence U.S. Army, 1957-59. Fellow Royal Soc. Health (life), Internat. Coll. Applied Nutrition, Acad. Psychosomatic Medicine; mem. Assn. Neurotrainers (pres. 1998), Toastmasters, Phi Kappa Phi, Omicron Delta Kappa, Alpha Sigma Phi. Mem. Ch. Of Brethren. Achievements include establishment of minor physical anomalies as significant predictor of physical and mental disease; demonstrated that treatment by neurofeedback significantly reduced criminal recidivism and that delinquency is a function of physical disease; demonstrated that ADHD and pain respond to neurofeedback; introduced treatment of schizophrenia by neurofeedback through Electro Dermal Response; introduced treatment of irritable bowel syndrome by neurofeedback; contributor to proof that alcoholism responds to EEG biofeedback. Office: AAT 125 S Swoope Ave Ste 109 Maitland FL 32751-5784 Office Phone: 407-644-6464. E-mail: drvonh@mindspring.com.

VON HIPPEL, ERIC ARTHUR, innovation educator; b. Boston, Aug. 27, 1941; s. Arthur Robert and Dagmar von Hippel; m. Jessie Roberta Janjigian; children: Christiana Dagmar, Eric James. BA, Harvard U., Cambridge, Mass., 1964; MS, MIT, 1966; PhD, Carnegie-Mellon U., Pitts., 1973; D in econ. (hon.), Ludwig Maximilans Univ., 2004. Engring. mgr. Graphic Sciences, Inc, Danbury, Conn., 1966—69; cons. McKinsey and Co., N.Y.C., 1970—72; prof. Sloan School of Management, MIT, Cambridge, 1973—; head Innovation and Entrepreneurship Group. Pres. Lead User Concepts Inc, Cambridge, 1996—. Author: (Book) The Sources of Innovation, 1988; contbr. articles to scholarly jours. Named Sir Walter Scott Disting. Prof., Australian Grad. Sch. Mgmt., 1997—98; fellow, Canadian Inst. for Advanced Rsch., 1995—97; grantee, NSF, Alfred P. Sloan Found., 3M; Nortel Networks; NYNEX; Xerox; Bush,Boake,Allen,Bell-Atlantic. Achievements include patents for facsimile technology. Avocation: industrial archaeology. Office: MIT Rm E52-566 50 Memorial Dr Cambridge MA 02141 Business E-Mail: evhippel@mit.edu.

VON HIPPEL, PETER HANS, chemistry educator, molecular biology researcher; b. Goettingen, Germany, Mar. 13, 1931; came to U.S., 1937, naturalized, 1942; s. Arthur Robert and Dagmar (franck) von H.; m. Josephine Baron Raskind, June 20, 1954; children: David F., James A., Benjamin J. BS, MIT, 1952, MS, 1953, PhD, 1955. Phys. biochemist Naval Med. Research Inst., Bethesda, Md., 1956-59; from asst. prof. to assoc. prof. biochemistry Med. Sch. Dartmouth Coll., 1959-67; prof. chemistry, mem. Inst. Molecular Biology U. Oreg., 1967-79, dir. Inst. Molecular Biology, 1969-80, chmn. dept. chemistry, 1980-87; rsch. prof. chemistry Am. Cancer Soc., 1989—. Chmn. biopolymers Gordon Conf., 1968; mem. trustees vis. com. biology dept. MIT, 1973—76; mem. bd. sci. counsellors Nat. Inst. Arthritis, Metabolic and Digestive Diseases NIH, 1974—78, mem. coun. Nat. Inst. Gen. Med. Scis., 1982—86, mem. dir.'s adv. com., 1987—92; bd. dirs. Fedn. Am. Socs. for Exptl. Biology, 1994—98; mem. NIH-CSR panel on boundaries for sci. rev., 1998—2003, mem. joint steering com. for pub. policy, 1998—. Mem. editl. bd. Jour. Biol. Chemistry, 1967-73, 76-82, Biochem. Biophys. Acta, 1965-70, Physiol. Revs., 1972-77, Biochemistry, 1977-80, Trends in Biochem. Soc., 1987—, Protein Sci., 1990-95; editor Jour. Molecular Biology, 1986-94; contbr. articles to profl. jours., chpts. to books. Lt. M.S.C. USNR, 1956-59. Recipient Merck award Am. Soc. Biochem. and Molecular Biology, 2000; NSF predoctoral fellow, 1953-55; NIH postdoctoral fellow, 1955-56; NIH sr. fellow, 1959-67; Guggenheim fellow, 1973-74 Fellow: Am. Acad. Arts and Scis.; mem.: AAAS, Am. Philosophic Soc., Fedn. Am. Scientists, Nat. Acad. Scis., Biophys. Soc. (coun. 1970—73, pres. 1973—74), Am. Soc. Biochem. and Molecular Biology, Am. Chem. Soc., Sigma Xi. Home: 1900 Crest Dr Eugene OR 97405-1753

VON HOELLE, JOHN JACOB LEWIS, publisher, commercial developer; b. Miami, Fla., Sept. 21, 1940; s. John Charles and Susan Ann (Lewis) von H.; m. Jan Behringer, Oct. 7, 1961; children: Eric, Christopher, Thimothy, Andrew, Ellen. MS, U. Cambridge, Eng., 1966. V.p. MNI Corp., N.Y.C., 1969-79, McCall's Pubs., N.Y.C., 1979-81; pres. Dyne-Am. Publs., Wilmington, 1981-95; dir. publs. Oak Knoll Press, New Castle, Del., 1995—. Bd. dirs. St. Paul's Bibliographies, Winchester, U.K., Agamemnon Corp., Wilmington, Del; cons. Smithsonian Instn., Washington; spkr. internat. antiquarian and pub. convs., 1980—. Author: Collector's Encyclopedia, 1983, 1984, 1986, Sound and Glory, 1990, Godfather of the Brandywine, 1994, Tales of the Eastern Shore, 1995, The Lewis Chronicles, 1996, In Search Of, 1999, The Silence of Them, 2000, The Bibliography of Cold War Intelligence Literature, 2002, Bio-bibliography of Ernesto Che Guevara, 2003, The Song of I'bram, 2003, various other books on history, biography and short stories, Tales from a Forgotten War, 2004, short stories; editor, co-pub.: The British Libr., 1995—, Libr. of Congress, 2000—. Lt. col. USAF, 1958-62, USAFR, 1964-91. Recipient N.Y. award for scholarship and rsch. TCI, 1986, Taylor-Peabody award in Am. lit., 1995. Mem. Assn. Am. Pubs., Nat. Writers Assn., Internat. Assn. Fgn. War Corrs., Assn. Former Intelligence Officers (Washington, D.C.), Royal Cambrian Geneal. Soc. Avocations: writing, Mayan and Mesopotamian archaeology, collecting Cold War espionology books and cuneiform tablets. Office: Oak Knoll Press 310 Delaware St New Castle DE 19720-5037

VON HOFF, DANIEL DOUGLAS, physician, oncologist; b. Oshkosh, Wis., Apr. 29, 1947; MD, Columbia U., 1973. Diplomate Am. Bd. Internal Medicine, Am. Bd. Oncology. Intern Calif.-Moffit Hosp., 1973-74, resident, 1974-75; physician Audie Murphy VA Hosp., Tex., 1975—, St. Luke's Hosp., Tex., 1975—, SW Tex. Meth. Hosp., 1975—; prof. medicine, oncology U. Tex. Health Scis. Ctr., San Antonio, 1975—. Mem. AMA, Am. Assn. Cancer Rsch. (Richard and Hinda Rosenthal Found. award 1997), Am. Coll. Physicians, Am. Soc. Clin. Oncology. Office: U Tex Health Scis Ctr 8122 Datapoint Dr Ste 700 San Antonio TX 78229-3271 also: CTRC/IDD 14960 Omicron Dr San Antonio TX 78245-3215

VON HOFFMAN, NICHOLAS, writer, former journalist; b. N.Y.C., Oct. 16, 1929; s. Carl and Anna (Bruenn) von H.; m. Ann Byrne, 1950 (div.); children: Alexander, Aristodemos, Constantine; m. Patricia Bennett, 1979 (div.). Grad., Fordham Prep. Sch., 1948. Assoc. dir. Indsl. Area Found., Chgo., 1954-63; mem. staff Chgo. Daily News, 1963-66, Washington Post, 1966—76; columnist N.Y. Observer, 1993—; contbg. writer Archtl. Digest, 1996—. Author: Mississippi Notebook, 1964, Multiversity, 1966, We Are The People Our Parents Warned Us Against, 1968, Two, Three, Many More, 1969, Left at The Post, 1970, (with Garry Trudeau) Fireside Watergate, 1973, Tales From the Margaret Mead Taproom, 1976, Make-Believe Presidents: Illusions of Power from McKinley to Carter, 1978, Organized Crimes, 1984, Citizen Cohn, 1988, Capitalist Fools, 1992, Hoax, 2004; also articles.

VON HOLDEN, MARTIN HARVEY, psychologist; b. Bronx, N.Y., May 29, 1942; s. Leon and Gertrude (Fishbein) Von H.; m. Virginia T. Brown, Dec. 17, 1971; 1 child, Mark Walter; children by previous marriage: Sandi Gwen Bitton, David Lawrence; 1 stepchild, Theresa Ann Brilli-Rogers. BA, NYU, 1964; MA, U. Toledo, 1965; D Pub. Adminstrn., NYU, 1981. Sr. psychologist N.Y. State Dept. Mental Hygiene, Rockland State Hosp., Orangeberg, 1966-67, team leader, 1970-71, dir. interdisciplinary tng. team, 1971-73; chief of service Metro Unit Harlem Valley Psychiat. Ctr., Wingdale, N.Y., 1973-74, dep. dir. programs, 1974-75; dep. dir. treatment svcs. Pilgrim Psychiat. Ctr., West Brentwood, N.Y., 1975-76; dir. Matteawan State Hosp., Beacon, N.Y., 1977, Ctrl. N.Y. Psychiat. Ctr., Marcy, N.Y., 1977-82; exec. dir. Rochester (N.Y.) Psychiat. Ctr., 1982-97; privatization project mgr. Fla. Dept. Children & Families, Tallahassee, 1997-98; from svc. team coord. to adminstr. G. Pierce Wood Meml. Hosp., Arcadia, Fla., 1998-2000; adminstr. G. Pierce Wood Meml., Arcadia, Fla., 2000—02; ops. mgmt. cons. mgr. DeSoto Juvenile Correctional Facility, 2002—. Assoc. dir. Inst. Motivation Rsch., Croton-on-Hudson, N.Y., 1965-73; dir. Martin H. Von Holden Assocs., motivation rsch., Fairlawn, N.J., 1970-74; cons. psychologist, group therapist Green Haven Correctional Facility, Stormville, N.Y., 1970-77; cons. psychologist, group therapist Auburn (N.Y.) Correctional Facility, 1977-94, Butler Correctional Facility, 1994-96, Willard Drug Treatment Ctr., 1997; clin. assoc. prof. dept. psychiatry Sch. Medicine, U. Rochester, 1983-97; spkr. nat. and internat. profl. confs. including 2nd World Congress on Prison Health Care, 1983. Contbr. articles to profl. jours. Mem. adv. coun. N.Y. State Commn. Quality Care to Mentally Disabled, 1989-97. Capt. MSC, U.S. Army, 1967-70. Recipient James Gordon Bennett prize NYU, 1964, Outstanding Achievement award United Way of N.Y. State, 1994. Fellow Am. Assn. Mental Health Adminstrs. (cert. mental health adminstr.); mem. Am. Psychol. Assn., Am. Correctional Assn., Am. Assn. Correctional Psychologists, Assn. Facility Dirs. N.Y. State Office Mental Health (pres. 1984-85), Order of Arrow, Psi Chi Jewish. Home: 1250 Peppertree Ln Port Charlotte FL 33952-1357 Office Phone: 863-491-5367 x2254.

VON HONTS, JACQUELINE JAY, artist, educator; b. San Antonio, Nov. 25, 1940; d. Emory Ralph and Helen Marie (Elder) Honts. BA in Painting, Trinity U., 1957; cert. in illustration, layout and design, Parsons Sch. of Design, 1959; MFA, U. Ams., 1964; PhD in Interrelated Studio Arts, N.Y. U., 1987; cert. in illustration, layout and design, Parsons Sch. of Design. Instr. San Antonio Coll., 1967-73, St. Mary's U., San Antonio, 1969-82, State U. N.Y., Buffalo, 1974-76, Niagara C.C., Niagara Falls, 1975, Dallas Independent Sch. Dist., 1981-82, San Antonio Mus. Art, 1994, 95, instr., adminstr., 1989, 91, 93-95, Trinity U., San Antonio, 1996, Northside Sch. Dist., 1997; art dir., owner Love Tex. Gallery SA Internat. Airport, 1982-99. Sr. artist Family Circle Mag., N.Y.C., 1959-62; asst. promotional dir. Better Homes and Gardens, N.Y.C., 1974-75; spkr. in field. Prin. work include sculptures Lake Travis, Austin, Tex., Hemisfair Playground, San Antonio, Colonial Hills Meth. Ch., and several private collections; executed murals Internat. Ptnrs. Ams. Internat. Conf., San Antonio, 1981, Modern Pentathlon Olympic Ctr., L.A., 1984, Am. Women in Radio and TV Nat. Conv., San Antonio, Trade Through the Ages Internat. Conv., San Antonio, Univ. Health Sys. Hosp.; one woman show include Instituto Mexicano-Norteamericaon de Relaciones Culturales, Mexico City, Am. Haus, West Berlin, McNay Mus., San Antonio, MGM Grand Hotel, Las Vegas, Nev., SOHO Gallery, N.Y.C., Art League Gallery, San Antonio, Gallery One, N.Y., Rockport Ctr. for the Arts, Tex., exhibited in group shows at Intstituto Peruano-Norteamericano, Lima, Peru, Bright Shawl, San Antonio, Witte Mus., San Antonio, Ursuline Gallery, San Antonio, Jacob Javits Ctr., N.Y.C.; comml. artist for Bapt. Radio-TV Commn., Ft. Worth, Sta. KXAS-TV, Dallas, Sta. WFAA-TV, Dallas, Dem. Nat. Conv., 1976, TV News Network, Morristown, N.J., Sta. WBEN-TV, Buffalo; ct. rm. artist Watergate Trial N.Y. Times. Cover designer Bapt. Sunday Sch. Bd., Nashville, Tenn. Recipient Benedictine Liqueur award Jules Wile Sons, 1977, 1st prize in sculpture Dallas Art Edn. Assn., 1981; named one of Outstanding Young Women in Tex., 1970; grantee HEB, 1996, U.S. State Dept., 1989; scholar Ford Salute to Edn., 1994, 95, 96, San Antonio Tchrs. Coun., San Antonio Dept. Arts and Cultural Affairs. Mem. Tex. Ptnrs. of the Ams. (dir. cultural 1972-98), San Antonio Art League. Baptist. Home: PO Box 13023 San Antonio TX 78213-0023

VON KAENEL, HOWARD J. army officer; b. Ft. Knox, Ky., Oct. 26, 1946; BS, U.S. Mil. Acad., 1969; Rhodes Scholar, MA in Philosophy, Politics and Econs., Oxford (Eng.) U., 1973. Commd. 2d lt. U.S. Army, 1969, advanced through grades to maj. gen., with field arty., 1969, regimental / DIVARTY comdr., 1989—91; comdg. gen. III Corps Arty., Ft. Sill, Okla., 1992-94; dep. under sec. for policy Office of Sec. of Def., Washington, 1994-96; dep. dir. strategy, plans and policy directorate Office of Dep. Chief Staff for Ops. and Plans, Washington, 1996, dir. strategy, plans and policy directorate, 1996-98; mil. dep. for internat. affairs Office of Dep. Under Sec. of Army, Washington, 1998—, acting dep. under sec. of Army for Internat. affairs, 1999. MIT seminar XXI, 1986; sr. fellow Brookings Instn., 1989. Decorated Def. DSM, Legion of Merit with 2 oak leaf clusters, Bronze Star medal with 3 oak leaf clusters, others.*

VON KALINOWSKI, JULIAN ONESIME, lawyer; b. St. Louis, May 19, 1916; s. Walter E. and Maybelle (Michaud) von K.; m. Penelope Jayne Dyer, June 29, 1980; children by previous marriage: Julian Onesime, Wendy Jean von Kalinowski. BA, Miss. Coll., 1937; JD with honors, U. Va., 1940. Bar: Va. 1940, Calif. 1946. Assoc. Gibson, Dunn and Crutcher, L.A., 1946-52, ptnr., 1953-85, mem. exec. com., 1962-82, adv. ptnr., 1985—; CEO, chmn. Litigation Scis., Inc., Culver City, Calif., 1991-94, chmn. emeritus Torrance, Calif., 1994-96, Dispute Dyamics, Inc., Torrance, Calif., 1996-2000. Instr. Columbia Law Sch., Parker Sch. Fgn. and Comparative Law, 1981; instr. antitrust law So. Meth. Sch. of Law, 1982-84, bd. visitors, 1982-85; bd. dirs. W.M. Keck Found.; faculty Practising Law Inst., 1971, 76, 78-80; instr. in spl. course on antitrust litigation Columbia U. Law Sch., NYC, 1981; lawyers dels. com. to 9th Cir. Jud. Conf., 1953-67; UN expert Mission to People's Republic China, 1982. Contbr. articles to legal jours.; author: Antitrust Laws and Trade Regulation, 1969, desk edit., 1981; gen. editor: World Law of Competition, 1978, Antitrust Counseling and Litigation Techniques, 1984; gen. editor emeritus Antitrust Report. With USN, 1941-46, capt. Res. ret. Fellow Am. Bar Found., Am. Coll. Trial Lawyers (chmn. complex litigation com. 1984-87); mem. ABA (ho. of dels. 1970, chmn. antitrust law sect. 1972-73), State Bar Calif. (Anti-Trust Lawyer of Yr. award 2000), L.A. Bar Assn., U. Va. Law Sch. Alumni Assn. (mem. deans adv. coun.), Calif. Club, L.A. Country Club, La Jolla Beach and Tennis Club, Phi Kappa Psi, Phi Alpha Delta. Republican. Episcopalian. Home: 12320 Ridge Cir Los Angeles CA 90049-1151 Office: 12320 Ridge Cir Los Angeles CA 90049-1151

VON KANEL, DANNY RENARD, minister, writer; b. Macon, Miss., Sept. 10, 1955; s. Louis Simon and Madge Lorraine Von Kanel; m. Beverly Gay Allen, Sept. 10, 1977; children: Daniel Allen, Bradford Ryan. B in Ch. Music, William Carey Coll., Hattiesburg, Miss., 1977; M in Ch. Music, New Orleans Theol. Sem., 1983. Ordained min. Bapt. Ch., 1984; state music specialist Miss. Min. of music/youth First Bapt. Ch., Vandalia, Ill., 1984—87, Florala, Ala., 1987—90, Purvis, Miss., 1990—92, min. of music/edn. Lucedale, Miss., 1993—97; min. of music/sr. adults Liberty (Miss.) Bapt. Ch., 1998—2001; min. of music/edn. First Bapt. Ch., Franklinton, La., 2001—. Ch. growth cons. Framework Ministries, Franklinton, 2001—; publicity chmn. Southea. Area Leadership Tng. Conf., 1991. Author: Built by the Owner's Design (A Positive Approach to Building Your Church God's Way), 2003. V.p. Vandalia Ministerial Alliance, 1986, pres., 1987. Recipient award, Writer's Digest, 1999. Mem.: Miss. Singing Churchmen. Republican. Southern Baptist. Avocations: writing, reading, sports. Home: 826 10th Ave Franklinton LA 70438 Office: First Baptist Ch 950 Self St Franklinton LA 70438 Office Phone: 985-839-3427. E-mail: dannyruk@huntcom.net.

VON KANN, CLIFTON FERDINAND, aviation and space executive, software executive; b. Boston, Oct. 14, 1915; s. Alfred and Lyllian (Kaufman) von K.; m. Sallie Emery Flint, Oct. 6, 1938 (div. May 1965); children: Curtis Emery, Lisa Christine; m. Kathryn Heyne, July 18, 1965. AB cum laude, Harvard U., 1937, MBA, 1948, D in Aero. Sc. (hon.), 1984; grad., Arty. Sch., 1942, Command and Gen. Staff Sch., 1945, Armed Forces Staff Coll., 1954, Nat. War Coll., 1957. Commd. 2d lt., F.A. U.S. Army, 1938, advanced through grades to maj. gen., 1962; various combat assignments, North Africa, Sicily and Italy, 1942-45; mem. War Dept. gen. staff, 1945-46; with Office Comptr., Dept. of Army, 1948-51; with CIA, 1951-53; comdg. officer 7th Inf. Div. Arty., 8th Army, 1954; with Korean Mil. Adv. Group, 1954-55; with Hdqrs. Army Forces Far East and 8th Army, Japan, 1955-56; asst. div. comdr. 82d Airborne Div. Ft. Bragg, N.C., 1957-59; dir. army aviation Dept. Army, 1959-61; J-3 U.S. Strike Command, Tampa, Fla., 1961-62; comdg. gen. 1st cavalry div. Korea, 1962-63; comdg. gen. U.S. Army Aviation Ctr., 1963-65; ret., 1965; v.p. ops. and engring. Air Transport Assn. Am., 1965-70, sr. v.p. ops. and airports, 1970-80; pres. Nat. Aeron. Assn., 1980-89; chmn. bd. Nat. Aeronautic Assn., 1989-90, chmn. emeritus, 1992—. Decorated Silver Star, Legion of Merit; Cross of Mil. Valor (Italy); recipient Charles Edwin Webb Meml. medal Pa. Mil. Coll., 1964, mil. rev. award Command and Gen. Staff Coll., 1964, Clifford W. Henderson award for achievement, 1990, Dept. Transp./FAA award for disting. svc., 1990. Mem. Am. Helicopter Soc. (chmn. bd. 1962-63, pres. 1961-62), World Aerospace Edn. Assn. (bd. dirs. 1987-93, pres. 1990-91, Fedn. Aeronautique Internat. (v.p. 1980-88, pres. 1988-90), Black Tie Club (Washington; pres. 1978-79), Aero Club (Washington; pres. 1969), Harvard Varsity Club (Cambridge), Met. Club (Washington), Nat. Aviation Club (pres. 1974-75). Clubs: Harvard Varsity (Cambridge); Metropolitan, Nat. Aviation (pres. 1974-75). Home and Office: Apt 502 4200 Massachusetts Ave NW Washington DC 20016-4752 E-mail: cvonkann@aol.com.

VON KAPPELHOFF, DORIS See DAY, DORIS

VON KENNEL, GARY PHILLIP, marketing company executive; b. cin, Aug. 17, 1948; s. Harry Phillip and Dorothy (Lanzer) Von K.; m. Jane Louise Endean, June 27, 1970; children: Andrew Phillip, John Benjamin. BA, U. Ky., 1971. Sales trainee Gillette-Personal Care Co., Cin., 1972-74, sales rep., 1972-74, project mgr. graphics Boston, 1975-77; mgr. brand promotions Miller Brewing Co., Milw., 1977-80; v.p. Target Mktg., Chgo., 1980-81; pres. Promotional Services Group, Dallas, 1981-86, Multi-Dimension Mktg., Inc., Dallas, 1986-99; CEO TLP Inc., Dallas, Dallas, 1999—. Presbyterian. Home: 6032 Deloache Ave Dallas TX 75225-2809 Office: TLP Inc Dallas Harwood Ctr 1999 Bryan St Fl 28 Dallas TX 75201-6868

VON KLEMPERER, KLEMENS, historian, educator; b. Berlin, Nov. 2, 1916; came to U.S., 1938; s. Herbert O. and Frieda (Kuffner) Von K.; m. Elizabeth Lee Gallaher, Dec. 19, 1953; children— Catharine Lee, James Alfred Abitur, Französisches Gymnasium, Berlin, 1934; MA, Harvard U., 1940, PhD, 1949; MA, Cambridge U., 1974. Vis. prof. Stanford U., Palo Alto, Calif., 1960; prof. history Bonn U., Fed. Republic Germany, 1963-64; L. Clark Seelye prof. history Smith Coll., Northampton, Mass., 1960-87, prof. emeritus, 1987—. Vis. prof. Amherst (Mass.) Coll., 1989, 91, 96; vis. fellow Trinity Coll., Oxford, Eng., 1982. Author: Germany's New Conservatism, 1957, Mandate for Resistance, 1969, Ignaz Seipel: Christian Statesman, 1972, German Resistance Against Hitler: The Search for Allies Abroad 1938-1945, 1992, The German Incertitudes, 1914-1945, 2000; editor: A Noble Combat. The Letters of Shiela Grant Duff and Adam von Trott, 1988, "Für Deutschland" Die Männer des 20 Juli, 1994; contbr. articles to profl. jours. Served with AUS, 1943-46, ETO Recipient Austrian Cross of Honor for Sci. and Art 1st class, 1997; Guggenheim Found. fellow, 1957-58; Fulbright fellow, 1957-58, 63-64; Overseas fellow Churchill Coll., Cambridge, Eng., 1973-74; Inst. for Advanced Study fellow, Berlin, 1986; Am. Philos. Soc. grantee, 1977-78, Am. Council of Learned Socs. grantee, 1978-79 Mem. Am. Hist. Soc. (chmn. conf. group for central European history 1982-83) Clubs: Century (N.Y.C.). Avocations: playing recorder; mountaineering; hiking. Home: 23 Washington Ave Northampton MA 01060-2822 Office: Smith Coll Northampton MA 01063-0001 Office Phone: 413-585-3705. Business E-Mail: kvonklem@smith.edu.

VON KLITZING, KLAUS, research facility administrator, physicist; b. Schroda, June 28, 1943; s. Bogislav and Anny (Ulbrich) von K.; m. Renate Falkenberg, May 27, 1971; children: Andreas, Christine, Thomas. Diploma, Tech. U. Braunschweig, 1969; PhD, U. Wuerzburg, 1972; Habilitation, 1978. Faculty mem. Tech. U., Munich, 1980-84; dir. Max Planck Inst. FKF, Stuttgart, 1985—. Recipient Nobel prize in physics Royal Swedish Acad. Sci., 1985. Office: Max Planck Inst Feskörperforschung Heisenbergstr 1 D-70569 Stuttgart Germany

VON KNORRING, HENRIK JOHAN, publisher; b. Lisbon, Portugal, Dec. 20, 1943; came to U.S., 1978; s. Helge and Denise (Halla) von K.; m. Robin Ellis Evans, Oct. 1966; children: Katharina Elizabeth, Helena Alexandra. MA, Oxford U., Eng., 1963. Joint mng. dir. Chapman and Hall Ltd., London, 1973-78; group mktg. dir. Associated Book Pub. Ltd., London, 1977-78; pres. Routledge Inc., N.Y.C., 1978—. Office: Routledge 29 W 35th St Fl 10 New York NY 10001-2291

VON KOHORN, BARON RALPH STEVEN, retired investment banker, author; b. Chemnitz, Germany, Dec. 14, 1919; arrived in N.Z., 1963; s. Baron Oscar and Valerie (Wirth) von K.; m. Jillian Annette Bussell, Feb. 25, 1967; children by previous marriage: Karen Janne, Kirk Steven. Student, U. So. Calif., U. Mich. Dep. chmn. various world wide bus. orgns., 1945-62; ret. Settlor von Kohorn Family Trust Controlling Genrock Group of Cos., N.Z. and Australia. Author: Abstract Paintings by Forty New Zealand Artists, 1966; What You Always Wanted to Know about Single Sideband Radio and Never Dared to Ask, 1976, VHF/FM Marine Radio, 1977, Columbia Cruises South, 1977, Columbia Cruises North, 1978, Management of a General Ancillary Licence for Clubs, 1978, Your Guide to Marine Search and Rescue, 1980; co-author, cartographer: A Cruising Man's Guide to the Marlborough Sounds, 1979, A Cruising Guide-Cape Palliser to Marlborough Sounds and Tasman Bay, 1982, The Sounds Crusing Guide, including Cape Palliser to Farewell Spit, 1986, The Cohorn Clan, 1987, The Cohorn Clan 2, 1988, New Zealand Cruising Guide-Central Area, 1989, 2d edit., 1994, 3rd edit., 1999, The Cohorn Clan 3, 1996. Founding sr. v.p., dir. Am. C. of C., 1965-74; bd. dirs. Am. Edn. Found. (Fulbright), 1965-94, Kennedy Meml. Fellowship, 1972-94, East-West Ctr., Honolulu, 1972-78; selector Eisenhower Fellowships, 1966-68, 78, 81, 86; trustee Wellington Visual Arts Trust, 1968-72, Found. for Newborn Child, 1977-96, N.Z. Oral History Archives, 1981-94, Wellington Maritime Mus., 1989-96, founder, pres.; trustee, dir. N.Z. Sports Found., 1977-85, gov., 1986-94, hon. life mem.; nat. treas. N.Z. Water Safety Coun., 1979-87, Small Boat Safety Com., 1977-90; com. chmn. N.Z. Yachting Fedn., hon. life mem. Recipient Graham Hayter trophy, 1973-74, 78-79; Lane Bryant Internat. Vol. award, 1969, Water Safety award Minister of Internal Affairs, 1987, Merit award Minister of Transport, 1987, Outstanding Vol. Svc. award Wellington, N.Z., 1987, Tribute of Appreciation award U.S. Govt., 1987, N.Z. Yacht Cruising award. Fellow Inst. Dirs. (London), N.Z. Inst. Mgmt. (counselor); mem. Royal Yachting Assn. (London, life), Past Commodores Assn. N.Z. (pres.), Internat. Order Past Commodores (internat. v.p. 1982-93, v.p. emeritus 1993—, hon. life mem., patron 1996), N.Z. Am. Assn., Wellington Planetarium Soc. (life, vice-chmn. 1968-73), Inst. Advanced Motorists (life, vice-chmn. 1969-73), Mus. Wellington (life, boardroom named in his honor), Nat. Press Club, Wellesley Club (Wellington), Tattersalls Club (Sydney), U. Club, Royal N.Z. Yacht Club, Royal Port Nicholson Yacht Club (life), Mana Cruising Club (life, past commodore) Home: Herbert Gardens 186 The Terrace Wellington New Zealand Home (Summer): 122 Alexandra Parade Alexandra Headland QLD 4575 Australia

VON KRENNER, WALTHER G. artist, writer, art consultant and appraiser; b. West Germany, June 26, 1940; s. Frederick and Anna-Marie (von Wolfrath) von K.; m. Hana Renate Geue, 1960; children: Michael P., Karen P. Rschr. Buddhist U., Bangkok; curator, v.p. Gallery Lahaina, Maui, Hawaii; pres. Internat. Valuation Honolulu, Hawaii, 1973-80; owner Al Hilal Arabians, Mont.; instr. aikido, 1962—; founder, dir. Sandokan Aikido Schs., 1981. Named to U.S. Martial Arts Hall of Fame. Mem. Am. Soc. Appraisers (sr. mem.; pres., dir.). Avocation: aikido (8th degree black belt). Home: PO Box 1338 Kalispell MT 59903-1338 E-mail: asil@centurytel.net.

VON LINSOWE, MARINA DOROTHY, information systems consultant; b. Indpls., July 21, 1952; d. Carl Victor and Dorothy Mae (Quinn) von Linsowe; m. Clayton Albert Wilson IV, Aug. 11, 1990; children: Kira von Linsowe Parker, Lara Carla von Linsowe-Wilson, Tami Cheri von Linsowe-Wilson. Student Am. River Coll., Portland State U. Cert. Prodn. and Inventory Mgmt. Verbal operator Credit Bur. Metro, San Jose, Calif. and Portland, Oreg., 1970-72; computer clk. Security Pacific Bank, San Jose, 1972-73; proof operator Crocker Bank, Seaside, Calif., 1973-74; proof supr. Great Western Bank, Portland, 1974-75; bookkeeper The Clothes Horse, Portland, 1976-78; computer operator Harsh Investment Co., Portland, 1978-79; data processing mgr. Portland Fish Co., 1979-81; data processing mgr. J & W Sci. Inc., Rancho Cordova, Calif., 1981-83; search and recruit specialist, data processing mgr. Re:Search Exec. Recruiters, Sacramento, Calif., 1983; sr. systems analyst Unisys Corp. (formerly Burroughs), 1983-91; sr. systems cons. FileNet Corp., Portland, Oreg., 1991-92; owner Optimal System Svcs., Portland, Oreg., 1992—; bus sys. analyst, software design and devel., mfg. specialist Portland. First violinist Am. River Orch. Recipient Bank of Am. Music award, 1970. Mem. NAFE, Am. Prodn. and Inventory Control Soc. (cert.), Am. Mgrs. Assn., MENSA, Data Processing Mgmt. Assn. Republican. Lutheran. Address: 3280 SW 170th Ave Apt 1780 Beaverton OR 97006-8612

VON MEHREN, ARTHUR TAYLOR, lawyer, educator; b. Albert Lea, Minn., Aug. 10, 1922; s. Sigurd Anders and Eulalia Marion (Anderson) von M.; m. Joan Elizabeth Moore, Oct. 11, 1947; children: George Moore, Peter Anders, Philip Taylor. S.B., Harvard U., 1942, LL.B., 1945, PhD, 1946; Faculty of Law, U. Zurich, 1946-47; Faculte de Droit, U. Paris, 1948-49; Doctor iuris (h.c.), Katholieke U., Leuven, 1985, U. Pantheon-Assas (Paris II), 2000. Bar: Mass. 1950, U.S. Dist. Ct. Mass. 1980. Law clk. U.S. Ct. Appeals (1st cir.), 1945-46; asst. prof. law Harvard U., 1946-53, prof., 1953-76, Story prof., 1976-93, prof. emeritus, 1993—, dir. East Asian legal studies program, 1981-83; acting chief legislation br., legal div. Occupation Mil. Govt. U.S.,Germany, 1947-48, cons. legal div., 1949. Tchr. Salzburg Seminar in Am. Studies, summers 1953, 54; Fulbright rsch. prof. U. Tokyo, Japan, 1956-57, Rome, Italy, 1968-69; cons. legal studies Ford Found., New Delhi, 1962-63; vis. prof. U. Frankfurt, summer 1967, City Univ. Hong Kong, 1995; Ford vis. prof. Inst. Advanced Legal Studies, U. London, 1976; assoc. prof. U. Paris, 1977; Goodhart prof. legal sci. U. Cambridge, 1983-84, fellow Downing Coll., 1983-84, hon. fellow, 1984—; fellow Wissenschaftskolleg zu Berlin, 1990-91. Author: The Civil Law System: An Introduction to the Comparative Study of Law, 1957, 2d edit. (with J. Gordley), 1977, Law in the United States: A General and Comparative View, 1988, (with D.T. Trautman) The Law of Multistate Problems: Cases and Materials on the Conflict of Laws, 1965, (with S. Symeonides and W. Perdue) Conflict of Laws: American, Comparative, International, 1998, 2d edit., 2003, International Commercial Arbitration, 1999, (with J. Varady, J. Barcelo) 2d edit., 2002, Theory and Practice of Adjudicatory Authority in Private International Law: A Comparative Study of the Doctrine, Policies and Practices of Common- and Civil-Law Systems, 2002 (Canada Prize Internat. Acad. Comparative Law), Hague Academy of International Law, Collected Courses, Vol. 295; mem. editl. bd. Am. Jour. Comparative Law, 1952-86; contbr. articles to profl. jours.; editor: Law in Japan-The Legal Order in a Changing Soc., 1963; mem. editl. com. Internat. Ency. Comparative Law, 1969—. Mem. U.S. Del. Hague Conf. pvt. internat. law, 1966, 68, 76, 80, 85, 93, 96, 2001. Decorated Order of the Rising Sun with golden rays (Japan); Guggenheim fellow, 1968-69; inst. fellow Sackler Inst. Advanced Studies, 1986-87. Mem. ABA (Leonard J. Theberge Award for Pvt. Internat. Law 1997, Sect. of Internat. Law and Practice), Am. Acad. Arts and Scis., Institut de Droit Internat., Japanese Am. Soc. Legal Studies, Am. Soc. Comparative Law (bd. dirs., former pres.), Am. Soc. Polit. and Legal Philosophy, Phi Beta Kappa. Office: Harvard Law Sch/ AR-231 1545 Massachusetts Ave Cambridge MA 02138-2903 Office Phone: 617-495-3193. E-mail: vonmehre@law.harvard.edu.

VON MEHREN, GEORGE M. lawyer; b. Boston, Nov. 2, 1950; s. Arthur Taylor and Joan Elizabeth (Moore) von M.; m. Barbara A. Ruggiero; children: Paige Elizabeth, Reed Carl. AB, Harvard U., 1972, JD, 1977; BA, Cambridge U., Eng., 1974, MA, 1985. Bar: Ohio 1977. Assoc. Squire, Sanders & Dempsey, Cleve., 1977-86, ptnr., 1986—, mem. mgmt. com., 1990-93, co-chmn. internat. litig. practice group, 1998—. Mem. adv. com. U.S. Dist. Ct. (no. dist.) Ohio, 1991-95; del. 59th Conf. of the Sixth Jud. Cir. of the U.S. Co-author: Non-US Firms, How to Enforce Your Foreign Trade Secrets in the US, United States Ligigation Yearbook, 1999; editor: Harvard Law Rev., 1975-77. Trustee Rainbow Children's Mus., 1998—2001, Beck Ctr. for the Arts, 1999—2001. Mem.: Union Club. Office: Squire Sanders & Dempsey 127 Public Sq Ste 4900 Cleveland OH 44114-1304

VON MEHREN, ROBERT BRANDT, retired lawyer; b. Albert Lea, Minn., Aug. 10, 1922; s. Sigurd Anders and Eulalia Marion (Anderson) von M.; m. Mary Katharine Kelly, June 26, 1948 (dec. Mar. 1985); children: Carl S., John M., Katharine, Jane, Margaret; m. Susan Heller Anderson, Apr. 2, 1988. BA summa cum laude with philosophical oration, Yale U., 1943; LLB magna cum laude, Harvard U., 1946. Bar: N.Y. 1946, U.S. Supreme Ct. 1954. Law clk. to Judge Learned Hand U.S. Ct. Appeals (2d cir.), 1946-47; law clk. to Assoc. Justice Stanley Reed U.S. Supreme Ct., 1947-48; assoc. Debevoise & Plimpton, N.Y.C., 1946, 48-57, ptnr., 1957-93, of counsel, 1994-95, ret., 1995. Arbitrator in internat. and other matters; sr. lectr. in law Wharton Sch. U. Pa., Phila., 1985-86; legal counsel Prep. Commn. for Internat. Atomic Energy Agy., N.Y.C., 1956-57; trustee Practising Law Inst., N.Y.C., 1972-96, emeritus, 1996, pres., 1979-86, chmn. bd., 1986-96. Bd. editors Harvard Law Rev., 1944-46, Am. Jour. Internat. Law, 1981-89, hon. editor, 1990-2000; contbr. articles to profl. jours. Trustee Axe Houghton Found., N.Y.C., 1965—; bd. dirs. Legal Aid Soc., N.Y.C., 1966-70; pres. Harvard Law Sch. Assn. N.Y., 1982-83. Mem. Assn. Bar City N.Y., Internat. Law Assn. (vice chmn. 1989—, pres. Am. br. 1978-86, chmn. exec. com. 1986-92), Coll. of Comml. Arbitrators, Coun. on Fgn. Rels., Univ. Club, Century Assn. N.Y.C., The Comml. Bar Assn. (hon. mem.). Home: 925 Park Ave New York NY 10028-0210 Office: 919 3rd Ave 46th Fl New York NY 10022 Office Phone: 212-909-6588. Business E-Mail: rbvonmeh@debevoise.com.

VON MERING, OTTO OSWALD, anthropology educator; b. Berlin, Oct. 21, 1922; came to Switzerland, 1933, to U.S., 1939, naturalized, 1954; s. Otto O. and Henriette (Troeger) von M.; m. Shirley Ruth Brook, Sept. 11, 1954; children: Gretchen, Karin, Gregory, Hilary, Celia. Grad., Belmont Hill Sch., 1940; BA in History, Williams Coll., 1944; PhD in Social Anthropology, Harvard U., 1956. Instr. Belmont Hill Sch., Belmont, Mass., 1945-47, Boston U., 1947-48, Cambridge Jr. Coll., 1948-49; rsch. asst. lab. social rels. Harvard U., 1950-51, Boston Psychopathic Hosp., 1951-53; Russell Sage Found. fellow N.Y.C., 1953-55; asst. prof. social anthropology U. Pitts. Coll. Medicine, 1955-60, assoc. prof., 1960-65, prof. social anthropology, 1965-71; prof. child devel. and child care U. Pitts. Coll. Allied Health Professions, 1969-71; prof. anthropology and family medicine U. Fla., 1971-76, prof. anthropology in ob-gyn, 1979-84, prof. anthropology and gerontology, 1986-96, prof. anthropology and gerontology emeritus, 1998, joint prof. dept. medicine, coll. medicine, 1994-96. Lectr. Sigmund Freud Inst., Frankfurt, Germany, 1962-64, Pitts. Psychoanalytical Inst., 1960--71, Interuniv. Forum, 1967-71; tech. adviser Maurice Falk Med. Fund, 1964-75; Fulbright vis. lectr., 1962-63; Richard-Merton guest prof. Heidelberg U., Germany, 1962-63; vis. prof. Dartmouth, 1970-71; vis. lectr. continuing edn. Med. Coll. Pa., 1990-92, vis. lectr. U. Sheffield, Eng.,1995, U. Liverpool, 1995, U. Augsburg, 1997, U. Heidelberg, 1997; hon. vis. prof. U. Coll. London Med. Sch., 1997; bd. dirs. Tech. Assistance Resource Assocs., U. Fla., 1979-84; supr. grad. study program Ctr. Gerontologic Studies, U. Fla., 1983-85, assoc. dir. 1985-86, dir. 1986-96, prof. emeritus 1998; mem. coordinating com. Geriatric Edn. Ctr., Coll. Medicine, U. Fla., 1986-96; mem. med. selection com. Coll. Medicine U. Fla., 2000—; mem. adv. bd. nursing programs Santa Fe C.C., 2001—; mem. nat. tech. expert panel on long-term care Health Care Financing Adminstrn., Washington; mem. adv. bd. Internat. Exch. Ctr. on Gerontology State U. System of Fla., 1987-92; adv. bd. Second Season Broadcasting Network, Palm Beach, Fla., 1989-92, Fla. Policy Exch. Ctr. on Aging, State U. System Fla., 1991-95, Assoc. Health Industries of Fla., Inc., Nat. Shared Housing Resource Ctr., Balt.; cons. mental hosps. Author: Remotivating the Mental Patient, 1957, A Grammar of Human Values, 1961, (with Mitscherlich and Brocher) Der Kranke in der Modernen Gesellschaft, 1967, (with Kasdan) Anthropology in the Behavioral and Health Sciences, 1970, (with Maria Alvarez) Aging, Demography and Well-Being in Latin America, 1989; (with R. Binstock and L. Cluff) The Future of Long Term Care, 1996; also articles; commentary editor: Human Organization, 1974-76; corr. editor Jour. Geriatric Psychiatry, 1990-98; mem. editl. bd. Med. Anthropology, 1976-84, Ednl. Gerontology, 1990-2002, Australasian Leisure for Pleasure Jour., 1995-2000, Jour. Cross-Cultural Gerontology, 1996-2002. Mem. nat. adv. bd. Nat. Shared Housing Resource Ctr., 1994-95; pres. Dedicated Alt. Resources for the Elderly, 1996-98; mem., bd. dirs. No. Ctrl. Fla. chpt. Alzheimer's Assn., 1996—2002; bd. dirs. Shepherd's Ctrs. Am., Gainesville, 1998-2000; adv. bd. nursing programs, Santa Fe C.C., Gainesville, 2001—. Recipient Fulbright-Hayes Travel award, 1962-63; grantee Wenner-Gren Found., N.Y., 1962-63, Am. Philos. Soc., 1962-63, Maurice Falk Med. Fund, 1970-71, US-DHHS, 1979-83, Walter Reed Army Inst. Rsch., 1987-91. US-ADA/Fla. Dept. of Elder Affairs, 1993-94; spl. fellow NIMH, 1971-72. Fellow AAAS, Am. Anthrop. Assn. (mem. James Mooney award com. 1978-81, vis. lectr. 1961,-62, 71-74, 91-92), Am. Gerontol. Soc., Royal Soc. Health, Acad. Psychosomatic Medicine, Am. Ethnological Soc., Soc. Applied Anthropology, Royal Anthrop. Inst.; mem. Assn. Am. Med. Colls., Assn. Anthrop. Gerontol. (pres.-elect 1991-92, pres. 1992-93), Am. Fedn. Clin. Research, Am. Public Health Assn., Canadian Assn. Gerontology, British Soc. Gerontology, Med. Group Mgmt. Assn., World Fedn. Mental Health, Internat. Assn. Social Psychiatry (regional counselor 1973-81), Internat. Hosp. Fedn., Help Age Internat. (London). Home: 818 NW 21st St Gainesville FL 32603-1027 Office: U Fla Ctr Gerontological Studies Turlington Hall Gainesville FL 32611 Office Phone: 352-376-9512. *Three guides to conduct I value most: always search for the best fit of fact, argument, and experience. Every first remedy must be amended quickly. When the past disturbs the present, more work on the future is needed.*

VONNEGUT, KURT, JR., writer; b. Indpls., Nov. 11, 1922; s. Kurt and Edith Sophia (Lieber) V.; m. Jane Marie Cox, Sept. 1, 1945 (div. 1979); children: Mark, Edith, Nanette; adopted nephews: James, Steven and Kurt Adams; m. Jill Krementz, 1979, 1 child, Lily. Student, Cornell U., 1940-42, U. Chgo., 1945-47, MA in Anthropology, 1971. Reporter Chgo. City News Bur., 1946; pub. relations with Gen. Electric Co., 1947-50; free-lance writer N.Y.C., 1950-65, 74—; lectr. writers workshop U. Iowa, Iowa City, 1965-67; lectr. in English Harvard U., Cambridge, Mass., 1970; disting. prof. CCNY, 1973-74; of counsel Jacob Medinger & Finnegan LLP, N.Y. Author: (novels) Player Piano, 1951, Sirens of Titan, 1959, Mother Night, 1961, Cat's Cradle, 1963, God Bless You, Mr. Rosewater, 1964, Slaughterhouse-Five, 1969, Breakfast of Champions, 1973, Slapstick, or Lonesome No More, 1976, Jailbird, 1979, Deadeye Dick, 1982, Galápagos, 1985, Bluebeard, 1987, Hocus Pocus, 1990, Timequake, 1997, (collected stories) Welcome to the Monkey House, 1968; (play) Happy Birthday, Wanda June, 1970; (TV Script) Between Time and Timbuktu or Prometheus-5, 1972; (essays) Wampeters, Foma and Granfalloons, 1974; (Christmas Story with illustrations by Ivan Chermayeff) Sun Moon Star, 1980; (autobiographical collage) Palm Sunday, 1981, (collection of speeches and essays) Fates Worse Than Death, 1991, Timequake, 1997, (collection of short stories) Bagombo Snuff Box, 1999; also short stories, articles, revs. Served with inf. AUS, 1942-45. Guggenheim fellow, 1967-68. Mem. Nat. Inst. Arts and Letters (recipient Lit. award 1970). Office: c/o Donald C Farber of counsel Jacob Medinger & Finnegan LLP 1270 Avenue of the Americas New York NY 10020 Fax: (212) 332-7235. Office Phone: 212-332-7735. E-mail: dcfarber@jmfnylaw.com.

VON RAFFLER-ENGEL, WALBURGA (WALBURGA ENGEL), linguist, cross-cultural communications specialist, lecturer, writer; b. Munich, Sept. 25, 1920; came to U.S., 1949, naturalized, 1955; d. Friedrich J. and Gertrud E. (Kiefer) von R.; m. A. Ferdinand Engel, June 2, 1957; children: Lea Maxine, Eric Robert von Raffler. DLitt, U. Turin, Italy, 1947; MS, Columbia U., 1951; PhD, Ind. U., 1953. Free-lance journalist, 1949-58; mem. faculty Bennett Coll., Greensboro, NC, 1953-55, U. Charleston (formerly Morris Harvey Coll.), W.Va., 1955-57, Adelphi U., CUNY, 1957-58, NYU, 1958-59, U. Florence, Italy, 1959-60, Istituto Postuniversitario Orgn. Aziendale, Turin, Italy, 1960-61, Bologna Center of Johns Hopkins U., 1964; assoc. prof. linguistics Vanderbilt U., Nashville, 1965-77, prof. linguistics, 1977-85, prof. emerita, sr. rsch. assoc. Inst. Pub. Policy Studies, 1985—2002, dir. linguistics program, 1978—85; chmn. com. on linguistics Nashville U. Ctr., 1978—85; Italian NSF prof. Psychol. Inst. U. Florence, Italy, 1986-87; prof. NATO Advanced Study Inst., Cortona, Italy, 1988; pres. Kinesics Internat., 1988—. Vis. prof. linguistics Shanxi U., Peoples Republic China, 1988-2002; vis. prof. U. Ottawa, Ont., Can., 1971-72, Lang. Scis. Inst., Internat. Christian U., Tokyo, 1976, U. Paris, Sorbonne, 1965-67, 1978-79; grant evaluator NEH, NSF, Can. Coun.; manuscript reader Ind. U. Press, U. Ill. Press, Prentice-Hall; advisor Trinity U., Simon Frazer U.; dir. internat. seminar Cross-Cultural Comm., 1986-87; mem. Ctr. for Global Media Studies, 1999; State Dept. Italy del. to Congress of the Hague; lectr. in field; specialist in non-verbal comm. Author: Il prelinguaggio infantile, 1964, The Perception of Nonverbal Behavior in the Career Interview, 1983, The Perception of the Unborn Across the Cultures of the World, Japanese edit., 1993, English edit., 1994 (transl. into Chinese), A Traveler's Guide to Cross-Cultural Business Communications, 2000; co-author: Language Intervention Programs, 1960-75; editor, co-editor 12 books; author films and videotape; contbr. of 500 articles to profl. jours. in Engish, Itialian, French, German, Chinese, Japanese. Grantee Am. Coun. Learned Socs., NSF, Can. Coun., Ford Found., Kenan Venture Fund, Japanese Ministry Edn., NATO, UNESCO, Finnish Acad., Meharry Med. Coll., Internat. Sociol. Assn., Internat. Coun. Linguists, Tex. A&M U., Vanderbilt U., others. Mem. AAUP, Internat. Linguistic Assn., Linguistic Soc. Am. (chmn. Golden Anniversary film com. 1974, emerita 1985—), Linguistic Assn. Can. and the U.S., Internat. Assn. for Applied Linguistics (com. on discourse analyses, sessions chmn. 1978), Lang. Origins Soc. (exec. com. 1985-97, chmn. internat. congress, 1987), Internat. Sociol. Assn. (rsch. com. for sociolinguistics, session co-chmn. internat. conf. 1983, session chmn. profl. conf. 1983), Internat. Coun. Psychologists, Internat. Assn. for Intercultural Comms. Studies, Internat. Assn. for Study of Child Lang. (v.p. 1975-78, chmn. internat. conf. Tuscan Acad. Scis., Florence, Italy 1972), Inst. for Nonverbal Comm. Rsch. (workshop leader 1981), Southeastern Conf. on Linguistics, 1980— (hon. mem. 1985—), Semiotic Soc. Am. (organizing com. Internat. Semiotics Inst. 1981), Nat. Assn. Scholars, Tenn. Assn. Scholars (bd. dirs. 1998-99), Internat. Assn. for Intercultural Comms. Studies (panel organizer 1999), United Europe Movement (sect. chmn. 1944-45), Internat. Comm. Assn., Internat. Pragmatics Assn. Achievements include being instrumental in forcing Vanderbilt U. to enroll women on an equal basis with men. Home and Office: 2455 Brighton Oaks San Antonio TX 78231 *In the social sciences theories come and theories go. Carefully collected and objectively analyzed data are useful for generations and the cleanest research design in the lab does not equal a moderately neat design in the naturalistic setting.*

VON REYN, C. FORDHAM, infectious disease physician; b. Montour Falls, N.Y., Sept. 24, 1945; m. Janet Elizabeth Goldberger, June 18, 1967; children: Leah Edana, Adam Daniel, Charles Alexander. AB, Dartmouth Coll., 1967, BMS, 1969; MD cum laude, Harvard U., 1971. Diplomate Am. Bd. Internal Medicine, Am. Bd. Infectious Diseases. Intern in medicine Beth Israel Hosp., Boston, 1971-72, jr. resident in medicine, 1972-73, sr. asst. resident in medicine, 1975-76; clin. fellow in infectious disease Beth Israel Hosp., Children's Hosp. Med. Ctr., Dana-Farber Cancer Ctr., Boston, 1976-77; clin. assoc. in medicine U. N.Mex. Sch. Medicine, Albuquerque, 1973-75, clin. assoc. in family & cmty. medicine, 1974-75, outpatient attending dept. medicine, 1976-77, inpatient attending dept. medicine, 1978-79; instr. epidemiology sch. medicine Tufts U., Boston, 1974, 76; adj. asst. prof. clin. medicine Dartmouth Med. Sch., Hanover, N.H., 1978-85, lectr. microbiology, 1978—, adj. assoc. prof. clin. medicine, 1986-87, assoc. prof. clin. medicine, 1988-91, attending physician infectious disease svc. dept. medicine, co-dir. infectious disease block scientific basis of medicine, 1988—, assoc. prof. medicine, 1991-94, prof. medicine, 1994—; dir. microbiology, hosp. epidemiologist infectious disease dept. Concord (N.H.) Hosp., 1977-88; cons. staff Mary Hitchcock Meml. Hosp., Hanover, 1977-88, clin. staff, 1988—; hosp. epidemiologist, chief infectious disease section Dartmouth-Hitchcock Med. Ctr., Hanover, 1988—. Cons. physician infectious diseases Vets. Adminstrn. Hosp., White River Junction, Vt., 1990—; asst. physician Harvard U. Health Svcs., Cambridge, 1975-77; pres. Concord Clinic Inc., 1984-85; section chief internal medicine Concord divsn. Hitchcock Clinic, 1985-88; cons. global program on AIDS World Health Orgn., 1987. Mem. editl. bd. Current Issues in Public Health, 1993—; mem. internat. editl. adv. bd. AIDS and Society, 1989—; contbr. articles to profl. jours. and chpts. in books. Pres. Frontiers of Knowledge Found., Concord, N.H., 1982-83; v.p. Concord Cmty. Music Sch., 1984-85, pres., 1986-88; trustee Am. Red Cross, Concord, 1986-88, N.H. AIDS Found., Manchester, 1989—; chmn. N.Mex. Task Force on Rabies, 1974, U.S. del. Congress of the Internat. Physicians for the Prevention of Nuclear War, Helsinki, 1984; mem. N.H. AIDS Adv. Com., 1985-87; mem. Commr.'s Task Force on HIV/AIDS Divsn. of Pub. Health Svcs., N.H., 1990— and numerous others. Med. officer USPHS, 1973-75. Recipient Gov.'s Spl. award for Pub. Svc., Santa Fe, N.Mex., 1975. Fellow Infectious Disease Soc. Am.; mem. Am. Soc. Microbiology, Internat. Immunocomprised Host Soc., Internat. AIDS Soc., Northern New England Infectious Disease Soc. (v.p. 1990-92, pres. 1992-94), Physicians for Social Responsibility, Soc. for Hosp. Epidemiology Am., Alpha Omega Alpha. Home: 44 Waterman Hill Rd Norwich VT 05055-9686 Office: Dartmouth-Hitchcock Med Ctr Infectious Disease Sect One Medical Ctr Dr Lebanon NH 03756

VON RHEIN, JOHN RICHARD, music critic, editor; b. Pasadena, Calif., Sept. 10, 1945; s. Hans Walter and Elsa Maryon (Brossmann) von R. AA, Pasadena City Coll., 1965; BA in Eng., UCLA, 1967; BA in Music, Calif. State U., Los Angeles, 1970. Music reviewer Hollywood (Calif.) Citizen-News, 1968-70; music editor and critic, dance critic Akron (Ohio) Beacon

Jour., 1971-77; music critic Chgo. Tribune, 1977—; prof. music appreciation Rio Hondo Jr. Coll., Calif., 1970-71. Lectr., TV host, rec. annotator. Author (with Andrew Porter): Bravi; contbr. revs. and articles to World Book Ency., revs. and articles to 1994 Yr. Book, revs. and articles to 1995 Yr. Book, revs. and articles to 1996 Yr. Book, revs. and articles to 1997 Yr. Book, revs. and articles to 1998 Yr. Book, revs. and articles to 1999 Yr. Book, revs. and articles to 2000 Yr. Book, revs. and articles to 2001 Yr. Book, revs. and articles to 2002 Yr. Book, revs. and articles to New Grove Dictionary of Music, revs. and articles to Stagebill, revs. and articles to Opera Now, revs. and articles to High Fidelity/Mus. Am., revs. and articles to Ovation, revs. and articles to L.A. Times, revs. and articles to Boston Globe, revs. and articles to Vanity Fair, revs. and articles to Fanfare, revs. and articles to Am. Record Guide, revs. and articles to others. Music Critics Assn.-Kennedy Center for Performing Arts fellow, 1972, 75; recipient Peter Lisagor award Soc. Profl. Journalists, 1999. Mem. Music Critics Assn. (edn. com., dir. 1988), Ravinia Critics Inst. (dir. 1988). Office: Chgo Tribune Co 435 N Michigan Ave Chicago IL 60611-4066 E-mail: jvonrhein@tribune.com.

VON ROSEN, RUDIGER, stock exchange executive; b. Grucholin, June 21, 1943; Diploma, U. Frankfurt, 1970; PhD, 1973. With Deutsche Bundesbank, 1974-86; exec. vice-chmn. Fedn. German Stock Exchanges, 1986-93; speaker bd. mng. dirs. Frankfurter Wertpapierbörse AG, Frankfurt, 1990-92; mem. bd. mng. dirs. Deutsche Börse AG, Frankfurt, 1993-94, mng. dir., 1995—, Deutsche Aktieninstitut EV, Frankfurt. Hon. prof. Frankfurt U., 1998. Office: Deutsches Aktieninstitut EV Borsenplatz 5 D-60313 Frankfurt am Main Germany Office Phone: +49-69-92915-21. E-mail: rosen@dai.de.

VON RYDINGSVARD, URSULA KAROLISZYN, sculptor; b. Deensen, Germany, July 26, 1942; came to U.S., 1950; d. Ignacy and Konegunda (Sternal) Karoliszyn; m. Paul Greengard. BA, MA, U. Miami, Coral Gables, Fla., 1965; postgrad., U. Calif., Berkeley, 1969-70; MFA, Columbia U., 1975; PhD (hon.), Md. Inst. Art, 1991. Instr. Sch. Visual Arts, N.Y.C., 1981-82; asst. prof. Pratt Inst., Bklyn., 1978-82, Fordham U., Bronx, N.Y., 1980-82; assoc. prof. Yale U., New Haven, 1982-86; prof. grad. divsn. Sch. Visual Arts, N.Y.C., 1986—. One-woman shows include Laumeier Sculpture Gallery, St. Louis, 1988, Capp St. Project San Francisco, 1990, Lorence-Monk Gallery, N.Y.C., 1990-91, Zamek Ujazdowski Contemporary Art Ctr., Warsaw, Poland, 1992, Storm King Art Ctr., Mountainville, N.Y., 1992-94, Galerie Lelong, N.Y.C., 1994, Weatherspoon Art Gallery, Grensboro, N.C., 1994, Univ. Gallery, Amherst, 1995, Mus. Art, Providence, 1996, Mus. Art R.I. Sch. Design, Providence, 1996, Yorkshire Sculpture Pk., Wakefield, England, 1997, Nelson-Atkins Mus., Kansas City, Mo., 1998, Madison (Wis.) Art Ctr., 1998, Chgo. Cultural Ctr., 1998, Indpls. Mus. Art, 1999, The Contemporaty Mus., Honolulu, 1999, Barbara Krakow Gallery, Boston, 1999, Galerie Lelong, Zurich, 2000, N.Y.C., 2000, Doris C. Freedman Plz., Ctrl. Pk., N.Y.C., 2000, Neuberger Mus. Art, SUNY, Purchase, 2002; exhibited in group shows at Contemporary Arts Ctr., Cin., 1987, Damon Brandt Gallery, N.Y.C., 1989, Met. Mus. Art, N.Y.C., 1989-93, Whitney Mus. Contemporary Art, 1990, Cultural Ctr., Chgo., 1991, Ctrl. Bur. Art Exhbns., Warsaw and Krakow, Poland, 1991, The Cultural Space/Exit Art, N.Y.C., 1992, Galerie Lelong, N.Y.C., 1993, Denver Art Mus. and Columbus Art Mus., 1994—, others; outdoor exhbns include Pelham Bay Park, Bronx, N.Y., 1978, Neuberger Mus., Purchase, N.Y., 1979, Artpark, Lewiston, N.Y., 1979, Laumeier Sculpture Park, St. Louis, 1989-94, Walker Art Ctr., Mpls., 1990-93, Oliver Ranch, Geyserville, Calif., Storm King Art Ctr., Mountainville, N.Y., 1992-93; contbr. articles to profl. jours. Fulbright Hays travel grantee, 1975; grantee N.Y. State Coun. Arts, Am. the Beautiful Fund, Nat. Endowment for Arts, Creative Artists Program Svc.; Griswald traveling grantee Yale U., 1985; Guggenheim fellow, 1983-84; Nat. Endowment for Arts individual artists grantee, 1986-87; recipient Acad. award in Art, Am. Acad. Arts and Letters, 1994, Alfred Jurzykowski Found. Fine Arts award, 1996, Joan Mitchell award, N.Y., 1997. Studio: 429 S 5th St Brooklyn NY 11211-7425 E-mail: art@galerielong.com.

VON SAUERS, JOSEPH F. lawyer; b. N.Y.C. s. Joseph F. and Margaret von Sauers; m. June A. von Sauers. BEE, Manhattan Coll., 1980; MBA, Pepperdine U., 1987; JD, Southwestern U., 1991; LLM, Columbia U., 1995; DBA, North Central U., 2001. Bar: Calif. 1992, D.C. 1993, Minn. 1993, Tex. 1993, Colo. 1994, U.S. Patent and Trademark Office. Contracts negotiator Hughes Aircraft Co., El Segundo, Calif., 1985-92; atty. Jones, Day, Reavis & Pogue, Dallas, 1992-94, Loeb & Loeb, LLP, L.A., 1995-97, Gray, Cary, Ware & Freidenrich, Palo Alto, Calif., 1997-98; dep. gen. coun. Roland Corp. U.S., L.A., 1998—. Active Calif. Lawyers for Arts, L.A., 1996; guest spkr. Loyola U., L.A., 1996. Contbr. articles to profl. jours. Capt. USNR. Recipient Kuwait Liberation medal Saudi Arabian/Kuwaiti Govts., 1992, 96, Joint Svcs. Commendation medal, Navy Commendation medal (2), Navy Achievement medal; Wildman scholar Southwestern U., 1987-91. Mem. Naval Res. Assn., L.A. County Bar Assn. Avocations: sailing, golf, tennis.

VON SCHACK, WESLEY W. energy services company executive; b. NY, 1944; married. AB, Fordham U., 1965; MBA, St. John's U., Jamaica, N.Y., 1971; doctorate, Pace U., 1990. Chmn., CEO, pres. DQE, Pitts., 1986-96, ret., 1996; chmn., pres., CEO N.Y. State Electric and Gas Corp., Binghamton, 1996-99, chmn. bd. dirs., 1999—; chmn., pres., CEO Energy East Corp., Albany, N.Y., 1998—. Bd. dirs. Mellon Fin. Corp., Energy East Corp., AEGIS Ins. Svcs., Inc. Trustee Gettysburg Nat. Battlefield Mus. Found. Mem.: Am. Gas Assn. Found. (trustee). Office: Energy East Corp PO Box 12904 Albany NY 12212-2904 E-mail: wwvonschack@energyeast.com.

VON STADE, FREDERICA, mezzo-soprano; b. Somerville, N.J., June 1, 1945; m. Peter Elkus, 1973 (div.); children: Jennie, Lisa; m. Michael G. Gorman, Jan. 1991. Student, Mannes Coll. Music, N.Y.C., Ecole Mozart, Paris; DMus (hon.), Yale U., 1985. Former nanny, salesgirl; sec. Am. Shakespeare Festival. Debut in Le nozec di Figaro with Met. Opera, 1970, later resident mem., Covent Garden debut, 1975; appeared with opera cos. including Paris Opera, San Francisco Opera, Salzburg Festival, London Royal Opera, Spoleto Festival, Boston Opera Co., Santa Fe Opera, Houston Grand Opera, La Scala; recital artist, soloist with symphony orchs.; appeared in operas The Marriage of Figaro, Faust, The Magic Flute, Don Giovanni, Tales of Hoffman, Rigoletto, Der Rosenkavalier, The Seagull, Werther, The Barber of Seville, The Dangerous Liasons, Le Nozze di Figaro; albums Frederica Von Stade Sings Mozart-Rossini Opera Arias, French Opera Arias, Pelleas and Melisande, Idomeneo, La Sonnambula, Simple Gifts with Mormon Tabernacle Choir, Songs of the Cat with Garrison Keillor; created roles of Nina in the Seagull (Pastieri), 1974, Tina in the Aspern Papers (Argento), 1988; starred in Dominick Argento's Casa Guidi, 1985, Carnegie Hall, N.Y.C.; rec. artist EMI. Mem. Am. Guild Mus. Artists Roman Catholic. Avocations: tennis, skiing, dance. Office: Columbia Artists Mgt Inc Arbib/Treuhaft Div 165 W 57th St New York NY 10019-2201

VON STUDNITZ, GILBERT ALFRED, state official; b. Hamburg, Germany, Nov. 24, 1950; came to U.S., 1954. s. Helfrid and Rosemarie Sofie (Kreiten) von S. BA, Calif. State U., L.A., 1972. Adminstrv. hearing officer State of Calif., Montebello, 1987-91, mgr. III driver control policy unit Dept. Motor Vehicles Sacramento, 1991-93; ops. mgr. Driver Safety Review, 1993-95; contract mgr. State Dept. Health Svcs., 1995-97; staff mgr. licensing ops. policy Dept. Motor Vehicles, Sacramento, 1997-2000; Welfare-to-Work regional mgr. State Health and Human Svcs. Agy., Sacramento, 2000; regional mgr. State Labor and Workforce Devel. Agy., 2002—. Author: Aristocracy in America, 1989; editor publs. on German nobility in U.S., 1986—. Active L.A. Conservancy, West Adams Heritage Assn., dir., 1989-91. Fellow: Internat. Soc. for Chivalric Rsch., Entente Cordiale for Chivalric and Heraldic Traditions; mem.: Nat. Assn. Managed Care Regulators, Driver Improvement Assn. Calif. (v.p. 1992—96, dir. media rels. 1996—), Calif. State mgrs. Assn., Orders and Medals Soc. Am., Sierra Club, Assn. German Nobility in N.Am. (pres. 1985—), Benicia Hist. Soc., Intertel, Mensa, Phi Sigma Kappa (v.p. chpt. 1978). Roman Catholic. Avocations: genealogical research, collecting. Home: 1101 W 2nd St Benicia CA 94510-3125

VON TERSCH, LAWRENCE WAYNE, engineering educator, dean; b. Waverly, Iowa, Mar. 17, 1923; s. Alfred and Martha (Emerson) Von T.; m. LaValle Sills, Dec. 17, 1948; 1 son, Richard George. BS, Iowa State U., 1943, MS, 1948, PhD, 1953. From instr. to prof. elec. engring. Iowa State U., 1946-56; dir. computer lab. Mich. State U., 1956-83, prof. elec. engring., chmn. dept., 1958-65, assoc. dean engring., 1965-68, dean, 1968-89, dean emeritus, 1989—. Author (with A. W. Swago) Recurrent Electrical Transients, 1953. Mem. IEEE; mem. Sigma Xi, Tau Beta Pi, Eta Kappa Nu, Phi Kappa Phi, Pi Mu Epsilon Home: 4282 Tacoma Blvd Okemos MI 48864-2734 Office: Michigan State U Coll Engring East Lansing MI 48823 Personal E-mail: vontersc@egr.msu.edu.

VON TUNGELN, GEORGE ROBERT, retired university administrator, economics consultant; b. Golconda, Ill., July 18, 1931; s. Cecil Ernest and Rachel Elizabeth (Wright) von T.; m. Marilyn Ruth Burris, Nov. 6, 1955; children— Stuart, Cheryl, Brenda, Sonya, Eric. BS, So. Ill. U., 1951, MS, 1956; PhD, U. Ga., 1974. Asst. mgr. exptl. farms So. Ill. U., Carbondale, 1951-52; instr., research asst. Pa. State U., 1955-58; asst. prof. to prof. agrl. sci. Clemson (S.C.) U., 1958-85, asst. to dean internat. programs, 1977-85; cons. econs. and internat. econ. devel. El Paso, 1985—. Pres. P.T.O., 1973 Contbr. articles to profl. jours. Served with AUS, 1952-54. Mem. Assn. U.S. Univ. Dirs. Internat. Agrl. Programs, Partners of Americas, West Tex. Football Officials Assn., Phi Kappa Phi, Gamma Sigma Delta. Clubs: S.C. Football Ofcls. Assn, Sertoma (chmn. bd. 1972). Republican. Baptist. Home and Office: 547 Cocula Ave El Paso TX 79932-2731

VON VOLBORTH, ALEXIS, geochemist, geological engineering educator; b. Viipuri, Finland, July 11, 1924; came to U.S. 1955, naturalized; m. Nadia Hasso, 1947; children: Tatyana, Swetlana, Maria, Gregory, Anna, Nicholaus H.W., Elisabeth. *First church records on the Volborth family appear with Herman Volbordt (dec. 1622) in Barby, a Swedish settlement on River Elbe, Saxony. His son Herman (b. 1609) moved to Nordhausen, Harz. His son was Johann Christian Volborth (b. 1738, Nordhausen). His son, Johann Friedrich August von Volborth (b. 1768), emigrated to St. Petersburg, Russia around 1790. He was pastor general in St. Petersburg and vice president, General Consortium, Evangelical Lutheran Church of Russia. He was granted hereditary nobility by Czar Nicholas I in 1824. His son was Alexis von Volborth's great grandfather, Carl Alexander (b. 1800), who was a doctor of medicine, paleontologist, mineralogist, founder of the Mineralogical Society of Russia, state counselor, and chief physician at the Royal Marine Hedaquaters, St. Petersburg. The mineral Volborthite and a fossil Volborthella were named in his honor. Alexis von Volborth's grandfather, Woldemar (b. 1838), served as Chancellor, Royal Chancellory, St. Petersburg. His father, Alexis (b. 1889) has a PhD in Chemistry from Universtiy of Bonn. He was a colonel in the Semyonovsky regiment in WWI, and emigrated to Finland in 1920.* PhC, U. Helsinki, 1950, PhLic and PhD in Geology-Mineralogy, 1954. Mineralogist, rsch. assoc., assoc. prof., prof. U. Nev., Reno, 1956-68; Killam vis. prof. geology, Killam rsch. prof. Dalhhousie U., Can., 1968-72; vis. prof. NASA Lunar Sci. Inst., U. Houston, 1972-73; vis. rsch. chemist U. Calif., Irvine, 1973-76; prof. geology and chemistry N.D. State U., 1975-78; prof. geology, scientist Nucleaar Radiation Ctr., Wash. State U., Pullman, 1978-79; prof. geochemistry and chemistry Mont. Coll. Mineral Sci. and Tech., Butte, 1979-94, prof. geol. engring., 1987-92, dir. accelerator lab., 1983-86, sr. radiation safety officer, 1983-86; prof. emeritus Mont. Tech./U. Mont., Butte, 1995—. Prin. investigator Stoichiometry Study Lunar Rocks, NASA, 1972-73; cons. AEC, 1961-63, NASA, 1965-73, Anaconda Co., 1968, Atomic Energy Orgn. Iran, 1975, King Abdul Aziz U., Jeddah, Saudi Arabia, 1975-76, Johns Manville Corp., Chevron, 1980-83, Pegasus Gold Inc., 1987, Placer Dome Inc., Echo Bay, Inc., 1990; U.S. rep., del. 2d Conf. on Natural Reactors, IAEC, Paris, 1977; U.S. rep. Internat. Geol. Correlation Program, 1990-96; interpreter, Russian translator in Soviet Siberia for U.S. and Can. mining cos., 1990-96. *Granted: Cross of Malta, Knight of Justice, O.S.J., Sovereign Order of St. John of Jerusalem, Knights of Malta, May 27, 1972.* Contbr. articles to profl. jours. Traveling rsch. fellow Outokumpu Found., U. Vienna, U. Heidelberg, 1954-55, Hoover fellow Calif. Inst. Tech., 1955-56, sr. fellow Australian Acad. Sci., 1965, fellow Guggenheim Found., 1965-66; fossil Elkoceras Volborthi named in his honor. Fellow Mineral. Soc. Am., Am. Inst. Chemists; mem. Am. Chem. Soc., Am. Nuclear Soc., Soc. Econ. Geologists, Internat. Precious Metals Inst. Home and Office: PO Box 80 Dayton MT 59914-0080 Office Phone: 406-849-5830. E-mail: aalex000@centurytel.net.

VON ZUBEN, FRED G. corporate executive; CEO, pres. Newark Group, Cranford, N.J. Office: Newark Group 20 Jackson Dr Cranford NJ 07016-3609

VOOGT, JAMES LEONARD, medical educator; b. Grand Rapids, Mich., Feb. 8, 1944; married; 3 children. Student, Calvin Coll., 1962-64; BS in Biological Sci., Mich. Tech. U., 1966; MS in Physiology, Mich. State U., 1968, PhD in Physiology, 1970. Fellow, lectr. dept. physiology U. Calif., San Francisco, 1970-71; asst. prof. dept. physiology and biophysics U. Louisville Sch. Medicine, 1971-77, assoc. prof. dept. physiology and biophysics, 1977; assoc. prof. dept. physiology U. Kans. Sch. Medicine, 1977-82, prof. physiology, 1982—. Assoc. dean rsch. U. Kans. Sch. Medicine, 1982—84, chmn. dept. physiology, 1993—2001; vis. prof. Erasmus U., 1985. Mem. editl. bd. Endocrinology, 1984-86, 89-92, Am. Jour. Physiology, 1984-88, Doody's Jour., 1995-98; ad hoc reviewer Neuroendocrinology, Sci., Biology of Reproduction, Life Scis., Jour. Endocrinology, Molecular Cellular Neuroscis., Procs. Soc. Exptl. Biology and Medicine, biochm. endocrinology study sect. NIH, 1992, reproductive endocrinology study sect., 1994-98; reviewer grants NSF; editor sci. procs. Rsch. Week, 1982-83; contbr. over 120 articles to profl. publs., 4 chpts. to books. Grantee NIH, 1972-85, 88—, NSF, 1985-86, 91-94, Ctr. on Aging, 1988, Nat. Inst. Drug Abuse, 1991-93; fellow Japan Soc. Promotion of Sci., 1993; recipient Outstanding Young Alumni award Mich. Tech. Univ., 1974, Honors in Edn., Med. Student Voice, 1990; inducted Mich. Tech. U. Acad. of Scis. and Arts, 2000. Mem. AAAS, Endocrine Soc., Internat. Soc. Neuroendocrinology (charter mem.), Am. Physiol. Soc. (pub. affairs adv. com. 1983-87) Soc. Neuroscis., Phi Kappa Phi, Sigma Xi. Office: Dept Molecular and Integrative Physiology U Kans Med Ctr 3901 Rainbow Blvd Kansas City KS 66160-0001

VOOK, FREDERICK LUDWIG, physicist, consultant; b. Milw., Jan. 17, 1931; s. Fred Ludwig and Hedwig Anna (Werner) V.; m. Frederica Jean Sandin, Aug. 16, 1958; children: Eric Robert, Dietrich Werner. BA with honors, U. Chgo., 1951, BS, 1952; MS, U. Ill., 1954, PhD in Physics, 1958. With Sandia Labs., Kirtland AFB East, N.Mex., 1958-94; div. supr., 1962-71; mgr. dept. research, 1971-78; dir. research, 1978-94; pvt. cons., 1994—. Editor: Radiation Effects in Semiconductors, 1968; co-editor: Applications of Ion Beams to Metals, 1974. Mem. coll. engring. adv. bd. U. Ill.; mem. policy bd. Nat. Nanofabrication Facility Cornell U.; mem. basic energy sci. adv. com. Panel on Value of Basic Rsch; mem. Okla. State Univ. Ctr. for Laser and Photonics Rsch. adv. bd. U. Chgo. and U. Ill. scholar and fellow. Fellow Am. Phys. Soc.; mem. IEEE (sr. mem.), Böhmische Physikalische Gesellschaft, Phi Beta Kappa, Sigma Xi. Office Phone: 505-884-4754. E-mail: fandfvook@msn.com.

VOORHEES, JAMES DAYTON, JR., lawyer; b. Haverford, Pa., Nov. 14, 1917; s. James Dayton Voorhees and Elsa Denison Jameson; m. Mary Margaret Fuller, Sept. 5, 1942 (dec. Apr. 1991); children: J. Dayton III, Susan F. Voorhees-Maxfield, Jane Voorhees Kiss; m. Rosemarie Stewart, Jan. 7, 2004. BA, Yale U., 1940; JD, Harvard U., 1943. Bar: N.H. 1947, Colo. 1948, U.S. Dist. Ct. Colo. 1948, U.S. Ct. Appeals (10th cir.) 1949, U.S. Ct. Appeals (5th cir.) 1956, U.S. Supreme Ct. 1960. Assoc. Johnson & Robertson, Denver, 1947-50; atty. Conoco Inc., Denver, 1950-56; ptnr. Moran, Reidy & Voorhees, Denver, 1956-78, Kutak, Rock & Huie, Denver, 1978-80; ptnr., counsel Davis, Graham & Stubbs, Denver, 1980—. Mem. Denver Bd. Edn., 1965-71, pres. 1967-69. Lt. comdr. USNR, 1941-46, ATO, PTO. Mem.: ABA, Denver Bar Assn., Colo. Bar Assn., University Club, Denver Country Club.

VOORHEES, JOHN JAMES, dermatologist, department chairman; BS, Bowling Green U., 1959; MD, U. Mich., 1963. Intern U. Mich., 1963-64, resident in dermatology, 1966-69, asso. prof. dermatology, 1972-74, prof., 1974—; chief dermatology service Univ. Hosp., Ann Arbor, 1975; chmn. dept. dermatology U. Mich., 1975—. Contbr. articles to profl. jours., chpts. in books. Recipient Taub Internat. Meml. award for psoriasis research, 1973, 86, Henry Russel award U. Mich., 1973; Herzog fellow Am. Dermatol. Assn., 1968-70 Mem. Am. Soc. Clin. Investigation, Am. Soc. Pharmacology and Exptl. Therapeutics, Am. Assn. Pathologists, Central Soc. Clin. Research, Soc. Investigative Dermatology, Dermatology Found., Skin Pharmacol. Soc., Assn. Profs. Dermatology, Am. Soc. Cell Biology, Am. Acad. Dermatology, Am. Dermatol. Assn., Alpha Omega Alpha. Office: U Mich Med Ctr Dept Dermatology 1910 Taubman Health Care Ctr Ann Arbor MI 48109

VOORHEES, RICHARD LESLEY, federal judge; b. Syracuse, N.Y., June 5, 1941; s. Henry Austin and Catherine Adeline (Fait) V.; m. Barbara Holway Humphries, 1968; children: Martha Northrop, Steven Coerte. BA, Davidson Coll., 1963; JD, U. N.C., Chapel Hill, 1968. Bar: N.C. 1968, U.S. Dist. Ct. (we. dist.) N.C. 1969, U.S. Tax Ct. 1969, U.S. Ct. Appeals (4th cir.) 1978, U.S. Dist. Ct. (mid. dist.) N.C. 1981. Mem., ptnr. Garland, Alala, Bradley & Gray, Gastonia, N.C., 1968-80; pvt. practice Gastonia, N.C., 1980-88; judge U.S. Dist. Ct., Charlotte, N.C., 1988—, chief judge, 1991-98. Mem. N.C. State Rep. Exec. Com., Gaston County Rep. Com., chmn., 1979-83, U.S. Jud. Conf. Com., 1993—, case mgmt. and ct. adminstrn. com., 4th Cir. Ct. Appeals Jud. Coun., 1992-93; chmn. Gaston County Bd. Elections, Gastonia, 1985-86; alt. del. Rep. Nat. Conv., Kansas City, Kans., 1976. 1st lt. U.S. Army, 1963-65, U.S. Army Res., 1963-69. Mem. N.C. Bar Assn., Fed. Judges Assn., Dist. Judges Assn. Avocation: boating. Office: US Dist Ct WDNC 195 Fed Bldg 401 W Trade St Charlotte NC 28202-1619

VOORHEES, STEPHANIE ROBIN FAUGHT, retired art educator; b. Indpls., Dec. 18, 1951; d. Edward Francis and Dorothy Marie (Teague) Faught; m. James Osborn Voorhees, June 19, 1999. BFA, Montclair (N.J.) State U., 1973, postgrad., 1974-76. Substitute tchr. Woodbridge (N.J.) Twp. Bd. of Edn., 1971-73, elem. art tchr., 1973-84, 85-86; middle sch. art tchr Colonia (N.J.) Middle Sch., 1984-85; high sch. art tchr. Woodridge HS, 1986—90; middle sch. art tchr. Avenel (N.J.) Middle Sch., 1990-94; art tchr. John F. Kennedy H.S., Iselin, N.J., 1994-98, ret., 1998. Spkr. Woodbridge River Watch, 1991; pvt. art tchr., 1983-93; yearbook advisor Woodbridge H.S., 1989-90, Avenel Mid. Sch., 1991-94, John F. Kennedy H.S., 1995-98; play set designer, 1989, 94-97. Illustrator: Care of the Lower Back, 1975, Touching All the Bases, 1993; profl. muralist. Campaign vol. Rep. Party, Woodbridge, 1992; sec. to the producer Fgn. Broadcast Svc. Dem./Rep. Nat. Convs., Miami, 1972. Recipient Gov.'s Tchr. Recognition award NJ State Dept. of Edn., 1992, Excellence in Edn. award Woodbridge C. of C., 1992. Mem. AAUW, Woodbridge Twp. Fedn. of Tchrs. (v.p. 1980-83, pres. 1983-95, cert. of merit, 1982), Art Educators of N.J., Met. Mus. of Art, Manatee County Vets. Coun. (sr. v.p.), Ecology Club (advisor 1990-94), Am. Legion Aux. 325 (historian 2000-01, treas. 2001-2003), Am. Legion (sec. 2003-, treas. post 325, sec. post 30), Cabane 880 (historian 2000-01, garde de la port 2001-02, condr. 2003—), VFW Post 10141 Ladies Aux. (sec. 2000, sr. v.p. 2001-03). Baptist. Avocations: singing, playing piano, dance, writing, cruise travel. Home: 29 River Isles Bradenton FL 34208-9003

VOORSANGER, BARTHOLOMEW, architect; b. Detroit, Mar. 23, 1937; s. Jacob H. and Ethel A. (Arnstein) V.; m. Lisa Livingston, 1964; m. Catherine Hoover, Sept. 10, 1983 (dec. Dec. 2001); children: Roxanna Virginia (dec.), Matthew Ansley; m. Peggy Loar, June 5, 2004. AB cum laude, Princeton U., 1960; diplome, Fontainebleau, 1960; MArch, Harvard U., 1964. Assoc. Vincent Ponte, Montreal, Que., Can., 1964-67, I.M. Pei & Ptnrs., 1968-78, dir., 1975-78; co-chmn. Voorsanger & Mills (Architects), NYC, 1978-90; founder, prin. Voorsanger & Assocs., Architects, NYC, 1990—; founder Taylor/Voorsanger Urban Designers, 1991. Lectr. Bennington (Vt.) Coll., U. Pa., Columbia U., Harvard U.; guest critic, lectr. Yale U., Pratt Inst., CUNY, R.I. Sch. Design, U. Cin., Syracuse U., U. Tex., Arlington; mem. adv. bd. Parson Sch. Architecture; mem. archtl. rev. panel Port Authority of NY & NJ; advisor to Samsung Corp., Korea. Exhbns. include: NYU, Archtl. Assn., London, Harvard Grad. Sch. Design, Vacant Lots Housing Study, NY, Deutsches Architeckur Mus., Frankfurt, Mus. Finnish Architecture, Avery Lib. Centennial Exhbn. Columbia Univ., Helsinki, Bklyn. Mus.; major projects include: Le Cygne Restaurant, Neiman houseboat, NYU Midtown Ctr., NYU Bus. Sch. Library, La Grandeur housing, NYU dormitories, Hostos Cmty. Coll., NY; finalist Bklyn. Mus. masterplan internat. competition, expansion and master plan Pierpont Morgan Libr., Wethersfield Carriage Mus., Amenia, NY; Montana and Wyoming Residences; Advanced Tng. Ctr., NYU, New York Apt., NYC, Riverdale (NY) Jewish Ctr.; fellow J. Pierpont Morgan Libr., NY, Asia Soc., NY, Brody Residence, VA, Daniels/Falks Residence, Ariz., Port Authority NY/NJ Air Traffic Control Towers, Univ. Art Mus., U. Va., Asia Soc. and Mus., NYC, Olana Mus., Hudson, NY; winner competition for Nat. World War II Mus., New Orleans. Mem. vis. com. RI Sch. Design, U. Tex., Arlington; mem. Pt. Authority NY/NJ Ground Zero Archive, NY Hist. Soc., also mem. archtl. cir. steering com.; chmn. bd. advisors Temple Hoyne Buell Ctr., Study Am. Architecture, Columbia U., NYC, 1989—; mem. adv. bd. Parsons Sch. Architecture; chair archtl. rev. panel Port Authority NY, NJ; bd. dirs. Worldesign Found.; mem. Regent's Panel NY State U., NY State Regents' Com. on Schs; pres. NY Found. for Architecture 2000-01. 1st lt. US Army, 1960-61. Recipient Cannon prize NAD, awards NYC chpt. AIA, AIA/Better Homes, Bard City Club, Interiors mag., Stone Inst., AIA/Libr., Lumen, Pratt Inst., NYU, NYC Art Commn.; competition winner Nat. WWII Mus., New Orleans. Fellow: AIA (numerous offices, including pres. N.Y.C. chpt. 1987, Nat. Honor award, N.Y. State award); mem.: Alumni Coun. Grad. Sch. Design Harvard (editl. bd. Harvard Design mag.), Wadawanuck Club, Century Assn., Sir John Soane Mus. Found., Archtl. League NYC (bd. dirs.), Ellis Island Yacht Club (commodore 2001—). Office: 246 W 38th St Fl 14 New York NY 10018-5805

VORA, MANU KISHANDAS, chemical engineer, quality consultant; b. Bombay, Oct. 31, 1945; s. Kishandas Narandas and Shantaben K. (Valia) V., m. Nila Narotamdas Kothari, June 16, 1974; children: Ashish, Anand. BSChemE, Banaras (India) Hindu U., 1968; MSChemE, Ill. Inst. Tech., Chgo., 1970, PhD in ChemE, 1975; MBA, Keller Grad. Sch. Mgmt., Chgo., 1985. Grad. asst. Ill. Inst. Tech., 1969-74; rsch. assoc. Inst. Gas Tech., Chgo., 1976-77, chem. engr., 1977-79, engring. supr., 1979-82; mem. tech. staff AT&T Bell Labs. (now Lucent Techs.), Holmdel, N.J., 1983-84, Naperville, Ill., 1984—, mgr. customer satisfaction, 1990-96, voice of the customer mgr., 1997-2000; pres., CEO Bus. Excellence, Inc., 2000—. Adj. faculty mem. Ill. Inst. Tech., Chgo., part-time, 1993—; spkr. in field. Invited editor Internat. Petroleum Encyclopedia, 1980. Chmn. Save the Children Holiday Fund Drive, 1986-99; trustee Avery Coonley Sch., Downers Grove, Ill., 1987-91; pres., dir. Blind Found. for India, Naperville, 1989—. Recipient Non-Supervisory AA award Affirmative Actions Adv. Com., 1987, 92, 97, Outstanding Contbn. award Asian Am. for Affirmative Actions, 1989, Disting. Svc. award Save the Children, 1990, Ann. Merit award Chgo. Assn. Tech. Socs., 1992. Fellow Am. Soc. for Quality (standing rev. bd. 1988—, editl. re. bd. 1989, tech. media com. 1989, mixed media rev. bd. 1994, nat. quality month regional planning com. 1989-94, nat. cert. com. 1989-94, chmn. cert. process improvements subcom. 1990-94, testimonial awards 1995, 96, 2001, 02, exec. bd. Chgo. sect., vice chmn. sect. affairs 1993-94, sect. chmn. 1994-95, nat. dir. at large, 1996-98, nat. dir. 1998-2000, v.p. 2000-2002, vice chmn. investing in quality campaign, spl. award 1991, Century Club award 1992, Founders' award 1993, Joe Lisy Quality award 1994, Grant medal 2001); mem. Ill. Team Excellence award (chief judge 1993-99, steering com. 1993-99, award). Hindu. Avocations: reading, photography, travel, philanthropic activities. Home: 1256 Hamilton Ln Naperville IL 60540-8373 Office: Bus Excellence Inc PO Box 5585 Naperville IL 60567-5585 Office Phone: 630-548-5531. E-mail: manuvora@yahoo.com.

VORCE-TISH, HELENE R. writer; d. Palmer Lemuel Vorce and Adelaide Catherine Miller; m. Charles Ronald VanBuren, Dec. 23, 1950 (div. Aug. 1967); children: Gail Rae, Karen Helene; m. William David Tish, Oct. 20, 1978 (dec.). BA in Psychology, Mich. State U., 1950, tchrs. cert. in English, 1961; M in English, U. N.Mex., 1968. Secondary tchr. English and creative writing Grant Unified Tchrs. Dist., Sacramento. Leader writing workshops Friends of the Libr., Placerville and Cameron Park, Pa., 1998—; literacy spkr. in field, Calif., 2003. Author: (novels) The Wounds of Hate, 2001, Challenging the Forces of Hate, 2002; regular contbr.: Foothill Times; contbr. articles to

jours. Fellow: Am. Soc. Journalists and Authors, Calif. Writers Club (bd. mem. 1999—2000). Avocations: tennis, swimming, jogging. Home: 3473 Santos Cir Cameron Park CA 95682 Office Phone: 530-677-3327.

VORENBERG, MICHAEL, history educator; b. Boston, Mass., July 20, 1964; s. John and Martha Sherwood Vorenberg; m. Katherine Philbrick, Jan. 16, 1963; 1 child, Emma Reynolds. AB, Harvard U., 1986, AM, 1990, PhD, 1995. Asst. SUNY-Buffalo, History Dept., Buffalo, 1996—99; asst. prof. Brown U., History Dept., Providence, 1999—. Author: Final Freedom: The Civil War, the Abolition of Slavery, and the Thirteenth Amendment (ACLS Grant, 2003). Mem.: Orgn. of Am. Historians, Am. Hist. Assn. Office: Brown U Hist Dept Box N 142 Angell St Providence RI 02912 Personal E-mail: michael_vorenberg@brown.edu. E-mail: michael_vorenberg@brown.edu.

VORT, ROBERT A. lawyer; b. Newark, Sept. 24, 1943; s. Saul S. and Ruth J. (Jacobson) Vort; m. Elizabeth Hornstein, June 25, 1968 (div. Nov. 1979); m. Marcelle Greenstein, Nov. 18, 1979 (div. Jan. 1991); children: Joel, Abigail, Rebecca; m. Tina Kruh, Feb. 4, 1996; 1 child, Hannah. BS in Econs., U. Pa., 1965; JD, Columbia U., 1968. Bar: N.J. 1968, N.Y. 1970, U.S. Ct. Appeals (2d and 3d cirs. 1975), U.S. Ct. Appeals (9th cir.) 1980, U.S. Ct. Appeals (5th cir.) 1981, U.S. Ct. Appeals (fed. cir.) 1984, U.S. Dist. Ct. N.J. 1968, U.S. Dist. Ct. (so. and ea. dists.) N.Y. 1984, U.S. Supreme Ct. 1977. Law clk. to Hon. Theodore I. Botter Superior Ct. of N.J., 1968-69; assoc. Davis & Cox, 1969-71, Israel B. Greene, 1971-73; sole practitioner, 1973-82; ptnr. Balk, Goldberger, Seligsohn, O'Connor & Rhatican, 1982-84, Kirsten, Friedman & Cherin, 1986; pvt. practice, 1984-85, 87-88; ptnr. Goldberg, Mufson & Spar, West Orange, N.J., 1988-91; counsel Donald Friedman, West Orange, 1991-92; pvt. practice Tenafly, N.J., 1997—; ptnr. Pearce, Vort & Fleisig LLC, Hackensack, N.J., 2001—. Mem. ABA (litigation sect., family law sect., legal econs. sect.), N.J. State Bar Assn. (appellate practice subcom.), Bergen County Bar Assn. Office: Pearce Vort & Fleisig LLC Court Plaza North 25 Main St Hackensack NJ 07601 Office Phone: 201-342-3400. Business E-Mail: rvort@vortlaw.com.

VOS, JORIS MICHAEL, diplomat; b. Ede, Netherlands, Mar. 17, 1940; s. Willam Vos and Eva Louise Douwes Dekker; m. Yvonne Marguerite Rydemark, Oct. 1, 1966; children: Sebastiaan F.A., Annabelle M.C. JD, U. Utrecht, Netherlands, 1964. 3d sec. of embassy Netherlands Embassy, Prague, 1968-70, 2d sec. of embassy Accra, Ghana, 1970-72; polit. officer for Middle Easat Ministry of Fgn. Affairs, The Hague, 1972-74, prin. pvt. sec. to fgn. min., 1974-77, dir. for Atlantic coop. and security affairs, 1977-80; polit. counsellor Netherlands Embassy, The Hague, 1982-86, ambassador Canberra, Australia, 1986-90, Moscow, 1990-93, Washington, 1997—; under sec. for polit. affairs Ministry Fgn. Affairs, The Hague, 1993-97. Avocations: classical music, fine arts, literature, golf, skiing. Home: 2347 S St NW Washington DC 20008-4015 Office: Netherlands Embassy 4200 Linnean Ave NW Washington DC 20008-3896

VOSBECK, ROBERT RANDALL, architect; b. Mankato, Minn., May 18, 1930; s. William Frederick and Gladys (Anderson) V.; m. Phoebe Macklin, June 21, 1953; children: Gretchen, Randy, Heidi, Macklin. BArch, U. Minn., 1954. Various archtl. positions, 1956-62; ptnr. Vosbeck-Vosbeck & Assocs., Alexandria, Va., 1962-66, VVKR Partnership, Alexandria, 1966-79; exec. v.p. VVKR Inc., 1979-82, pres., 1982-88; prin. Vosbeck/DMJM, Washington and Alexandria, Va., 1989-94; v.p. DMJM Arch. and Engring., 1990-94; pvt. practice archtl. cons., 1994—. Mem. Nat. Capital Planning Commn., 1976-81, U.S./USSR Joint Group on Bldg. Design and Constrn., 1974-79; mem. Nat. Park System Adv. Bd., 1984-88. Archtl. works include Pub. Safety Ctr., Alexandria, Va., 1987, Yorktown (Va.) Visitors Ctr, 1976, Frank Reeves Mcpl. Office Bldg., Washington, 1986, Fed. Bldg., Norfolk, Va., 1979, Jeff Davis Assocs. Office Complex, Arlington, Va., 1991, Westminster Continued Care Retirement Community, Lake Ridge, Va., 1993. Pres. Alexandria Jaycees, 1960-61; v.p. Va. Jaycees, 1962-63; pres. Alexandria Ch. of Com., 1974-75. Engring. officer USMC, 1954-56. Recipient Plaque of Honor, Fedn. Colegios Architects, Republic of Mexico, Alumni Achievement award U. Minn. Coll. Arch., 2001, hon. fellowship Colegios Architects of Spain, Royal Archtl. Inst. Can., Soc. Architects of Mex.; named Outstanding Young Man in Va., 1963, Acadamecian, Internt. Acad. Arch. Fellow AIA (bd. dirs. 1976-78, v.p. 1979-80, pres. 1981), Internat. Union Architects (coun. 1981-87), Nat. Trust Hist. Preservation. Presbyterian. Home and Office: 770 Potato Patch Dr Unit A Vail CO 81657-4462

VOSBECK, WILLIAM FREDERICK, JR., architect; b. Mankato, Minn., May 13, 1924; s. William Frederick and Gladys (Anderson) V.; m. Elizabeth Just, Aug. 2, 1947; children: Lee, William Frederick III, Lynn, James Stephen. Student, U. Notre Dame, 1943, Cornell U., 1945; BArch, U. Minn., 1947. Ptnr. Vosbeck & Ward, Alexandria, Va., 1957-62, Vosbeck Vosbeck & Assos. (changed to Vosbeck Vosbeck Kendrick Redinger, Architects, Engrs., Planners), Alexandria, 1962-68; chmn. bd. dirs. VVKR, Inc., merged with Suter & Suter, Basel, Switzerland. Bd. dirs. Dominion Resources Va. Power, Crestar Fin. Corp. Prin. works include Nat. Automobile Dealers Assn. Hdqs., Am. Trucking Assn. Hdqs., Woodrow Wilson Rehab. Bldgs. and campus planning. Mem. Gov.'s Com. Employment Handicapped, 1973; trustee Va. Found. Ind. Colls., Va. Mus. Fine Arts, Va. C. of C.; vis. design critique, U. Va. Architecture; mem. Alexandra Hosp. Bd., pres., 1970. With USMCR, 1943-50. Recipient Wash. Acad. Sci. Nat. Capital award for achievement in arch., Nat. Rehab. Assn. citation tech. svcs., Gargoyle award, T. David Fitz-Gibbon Archt. Firm awrd, numerous honor and merit awards Va. Soc. AIA, Va. Mus. Fine Arts, Outstanding Achievement award Engring. News Record, 1977. Fellow AIA (pres. Va. chpt. 1971), Sigma Alpha Epsilon Found., Belle Haven Country Club, Cosmos Club, Rotary. Home: 7512 Fort Hunt Rd Alexandria VA 22307-1924 Office: Vosbeck Assocs 211 N Union St Alexandria VA 22314-2643 Fax: 703 683-4707.

VOSBURG, BRUCE DAVID, lawyer; b. Omaha, June 17, 1943; s. Noble Perrin and Dena V. (Ferrari) V.; m. Susan Simpson, May 27, 1972; children: Margaret Amy, Wendy Christine, Bruce David. BA, U. Notre Dame, 1965; BSME, 1966; JD, Harvard U., 1969. Bar: Nebr. 1969, Ill. 1970, U.S. Supreme Ct. 1974. Law clk. U.S. Dist. Ct. Nebr., 1969-70; assoc. Kirkland & Ellis, Chgo., 1970-72; ptnr. Fitzgerald & Schorr, Omaha, 1972—. Author: Financing Small Businesses, 1981, Securities Law Practice, 1987, Securities Law-Going Public, 1989, Trade Secret Protection, 1994, Protecting Intellectual Property, 1998, Intellectual Property Law, 2000. Pres. Children's Crisis Ctr., 1984-85, bd. dirs., 1973-84, Childrens Savinds Inst. 1985-86, bd. dirs. 1984-90; pres. Nebr. Tennis Assn., 1976-77; mem. Leadership Omaha, 1979; chmn. bd. dirs. City of Omaha Parks and Recreation, 1985-92; founding dir. Friends of the Parks, 1988; bd. dirs. Omaha Pub. Libr. Found., 1997—, pres., 1999—; bd. dirs. Western Heritage Mus., 1998—; exec. com. U.S. Tennis Assn., 2004—. Named to, Nebr. Tennis Hall of Fame. Fellow Nebr. Bar Found.; mem. ABA, Nat. Assn. Bond Attys., Nebr. Bar Assn. (chmn. securities com.), Omaha Bar Assn. (exec. coun. 1983-86), Rotary (dir. 1993-98), USTA/Mo. Valley Tennis Assn. (chmn. grievance com. 1978—), Am. Intellectual Property Lawyers Assn., Tau Beta Pi. Republican. Roman Catholic. Office: Ste 400 13220 California St Omaha NE 68154-5228 Office Phone: 402-342-1000.

VOSBURG, KATHY D, tax specialist, consultant; b. Zeeland, Mich., Feb. 24, 1952; d. Donald L and Thelma K Schutte; m. Duane W Vosburg, July 13, 1973; 3 children. AA in acctg., Davenport U., 1973, BBA, 1996. Enrolled agent. Income tax cons. Self-Employed, 1981—; legis. asst. State of Mich., 1998—2000; county commr. Macomb County, Mich., 2003—. Trustee Chesterfield Hist. Soc., Holly, Mich., 2001—; trustee, bd. dirs. Compassion Pregnancy Ctr., Clinton Twp., 2003. Mem.: Nat. Assn. Tax Professionals (mem. bd. dirs.), Rotary Club (Anchor Bay). Home: 47395 Sugar Bush New Baltimore MI 48047 Office: Macomb County Bd Commr 1 So Main Mount Clemens MI 48043

VOSE, KATHRYN KAHLER, marketing and communication executive; b. Denton, Tex., Aug. 18, 1953; d. James and Martha Kahler; m. William O. Vose, June 1, 1996. BA in Sociology, Sophie Newcomb Coll. Tulane U., 1975; MA in Mass Communications, U. Minn., 1977. Corr. newspapers, N.Y.C., Mpls.; nat. corr. Newhouse Newspapers, Washington; comm. dir. U.S. Dept. Edn.; v.p. comm. & mktg. Campaign for Tobacco-Free Kids, Washington. Panelist Washington Week In Review; vis. fellow Woodrow Wilson Nat. Fellowship Found; adviser World Health Orgn.; contbr. Nat. Acad. Scis. Recipient Crystal Medallion award AMA, Clarion award Assn. Women Comm., Silver Inkwell award Internat. Assn. Bus. Communicators, Mercury Grand award MerComm Internat., Thoth (2) awards Pub. Rels. Soc. Am., Assoc. Press Mng. Editors Pub. Svc. award. Mem. Nat. Press Club (pres. 1991, bd. govs.). Home: 3351 Tennyson St NW Washington DC 20015-2442 Office: Nat Ctr Tobacco Free Kids 1707 L St NW Ste 800 Washington DC 20036-4209

VOSEVICH, KATHI ANN, writer, editor, scholar; b. St. Louis, Oct. 12, 1957; d. William and Catherine Mildred (Kalinowski) V.; m. James Hughes Meredith, Sept. 6, 1986. AB with honors, St. Louis U., 1980, MA, 1983; PhD, U. Denver, 1988. Tchg. fellow St. Louis U., 1980-83, acad. advising fellow, 1983-84; tchg. fellow U. Denver, 1985-87; prof. ESL, BNM Talensch., Eden, The Netherlands, 1988-91; instr. English, mentor U. Ga., Athens, 1992-94; vis. asst. prof. Colo. Coll., Colorado Springs, 1994; sr. tech. writer and editor Titan Client/Server Techs., Colorado Springs, 1994-96, head documentation, libr., 1996-97; documentation mgr. Beechwood, Colorado Springs, 1997-98, tech. mgr., 1998-99; tech. writer Microsoft, Redmond, Wash., 1999-2000; documentation and process mgr. Sprint, Denver, 2000; practice and group mgr. e-bus. Sprint Corp., Denver, 2000—02, svc. launch mgr. Mobile Computing Svcs., 2002—03, strategic market mgr., 2003—. Forensic judge USAF Acad., Colo., 1987-88; edn. officer Volkel (The Netherlands) Air Base, 1988-91; instr. English European divsn. U. Md., The Netherlands and Belgium, 1989-91. Author: Customer Care User's Guide, 1996, Interview with Joseph Heller, 1999, Conversations with Joseph Heller in Understanding the Literature of World War II, 1999, Office Update, 1999-2000, Tutoring the Tudors, 2000, Sprint Takes Messaging into the Future, 2003; editor: Subscription Services System Documentation, 1996, Titan Process Documentation, 1994-96; copy editor: Language, Ideas, and American Culture; War, Literature and the Arts; contbr. over 100 electronic texts and articles to profl. jours. Colo. scholar U. Denver, 1985-86, grad. dean scholar, 1988; NEH fellow U. Md., 1994 Mem. MLA, Phi Beta Kappa, Alpha Sigma Nu. Roman Catholic. Avocations: writing, drawing, raising Bernese mountain dogs. Office: Sprint Ste 1400 1099 18th St Denver CO 80202

VOSKA, KATHRYN CAPLES, consultant, facilitator; b. Berkeley, Calif., Dec. 26, 1942; d. Donald Buxton and Ellen Marion (Smith) Caples; m. David Karl Nehrling, Aug. 15, 1964 (div. Nov. 1980); children: Sandra E. Nehrling, Barbara M. Nehrling, Melissa A. Nehrling-Holmgren; m. James Edward Voska, Aug. 31, 1985. BS, Northwestern U., 1964; MS, Nat.-Louis U., 1989. Cert. teacher, Ill.; cert. career mgmt. fellow practitioner Inst. Career Cert. Internat. Tchr. pub. schs., Northbrook and Evanston, Ill., 1964-65; acting phys. dir. YWCA, Evanston, Ill., 1975; quality control technician Baxter Travenol, Morton Grove, Ill., 1978-80; sr. quality assurance analyst Hollister Inc., Libertyville, Ill., 1980-85; info. ctr. trainer, tech. training mgr. Rand McNally, Skokie, Ill., 1985-92; cons., facilitator Capka & Assocs., Skokie and Kansas City, 1992—; dir. edn. Nat. Office Machine Dealers, 1992-94; career and mgmt. cons. Right Mgmt. Cons., Overland Park, Kans., 1994—. Pvt. practice estate conservator. Telephone worker Contact Chgo. Crisis Hotline, 1989-90; CPR instr. trainer Amer. Heart Assn., Chgo., 1977-89; aquatic dir. YMCA, Evanston, Ill., 1969-80; rep. Alumnae Panhellenic Coun., Evanston, 1969-75; grad. Leadership Overland Park, 1996, mem. 15th anniv. special task force. Mem. ASTD (bd. dirs. Kansas City chpt. 1997-99), ASCD, Soc. Human Resource Mgmt., Midwest Soc. Profl. Cons., Assn. for Mgmt. Orgn. Design, Chgo. Orgn. Data Processing Educators, Chgo. Computer Soc., Info. Ctr. Exch. of Chgo., Assn. Quality and Participation, Am. Soc. for Quality (teller N.E. Ill. sect. 1982-84), Internat. Soc. for Performance Improvement, Assn. Career Profls. Internat. (founding pres. Kansas City chpt. 2002-04, nat. bd. dirs. 2000—, nat. bd. v.p., pres.-elect 2002-04, nat. bd. pres. 2004—, chmn. internat. membership drive 2004), Learning Resource Network. Presbyterian. Avocations: scuba diving, swimming, hiking, camping, travel. Home: 1001 E 118th Ter Kansas City MO 64131-3828 Office: Right Mgmt Cons 7300 W 110th St Ste 800 Overland Park KS 66210-2387 Office Phone: 913-323-2309. Personal E-mail: kvoska@kc.rr.com. Business E-Mail: kathy.voska@right.com.

VOSS, JAMES S. astronaut; b. Cordova, Ala., Mar. 3, 1949; m. Suzan Curry; 1 child. BSc in Aerospace Engring., Auburn U., 1972; MSc in Aerospace Engring., U. Colo., 1974, PhD (hon.), 2000. Commd. 2d lt. U.S. Army, advanced through grades to col., various assignments; vehicle integration test engr. NASA, Houston, 1984—87, astronaut, 1988—. Astronaut Space Shuttle Atlantis, 1991, Space Shuttle Discovery, 1992, Space Shuttle Endeavour, 1995, Space Shuttle Atlantis, 2000, Space Shuttle Discovery, lived on Internat. Space Sta., 2001. Decorated Def. Meritorious Svc. medal U.S. Army, Def. Superior Svc. medal, Def. Meritorious Svc. medal. Avocations: woodworking, skiing, softball, racquetball, scuba diving. Office: Astronaut Office CB NASA Johnson Space Center Houston TX 77058

VOSS, JANICE E. astronaut; b. South Bend, Ind., Oct. 8, 1956; d. James R. and Voss. Student, U. Okla., 1973—75; BSc in Engring Sci., Purdue U., 1975; MSc in Elec. Engring., MIT, 1977; student, Rice U., 1977—78; PhD in Aero. & Astronautics, MIT, 1987. Co-op NASA, Houston, 1973—75, crew tnr., 1977—87; with Orbiatl Sci. Corp., 1987—90; astronaut NASA, 1991—. Astronaut space mission on STS-57, 1993, space mission on STS-63, 1995; payload comdr. space mission on STS-83, 1997; astronaut space mission on STS-94, 1997, space mission on STS-99, 2000. Fellow, NSF, 1976, Howard Hughes fellow, 1981, Zonta Amelia Earhart fellow, 1982. Mem.: AIAA. Avocations: reading, dance, volleyball, flying. Office: Astronaut Office CB NASA Johnson Space Center Houston TX 77058

VOSS, JERROLD RICHARD, architecture educator; b. Chgo., Nov. 4, 1932; s. Peter Walter and Annis Lorraine (Hayes) V.; m. Jean Evelyn Peterson, Aug. 21, 1954; children— Cynthia Jean, Tania Hayes. B.Arch., Cornell U., 1955; M. City Planning, Harvard U., 1959; PhD (Bus. History fellow, Univ. fellow, IBM fellow), 1971. Asst. prof. U. Calif., 1960-61; asst. prof., asso. prof. U. Ill., 1961-69; asso. prof. Harvard U., 1969-71; prof. city and regional planning Ohio State U., Columbus, 1971—, chmn. dept. city and regional planning, 1971-79; dir. Ohio State U. (Knowlton Sch. Architecture), 1981-96, prof., 1996-2000, dir., prof. emeritus, 2000—. UN advisor to Govt. Indonesia, 1964-65; social affairs officer UN Secretariat, 1970-71; project mgr. UN Task Force on Human Environment, Thailand, 1975-76; dir. rsch. and devel. UN Ctr. for Human Settlements (Habitat), 1979-81; cons. Ill. Dept. Devel., J.S. Bolles & Assocs., UN Office Tech. Cooperation, UN Devel. Program, AID, Bechtel Nat. Inc., other pvt. and pub. orgns.; mem. external examiners team United Arab U., 1992—. Author: Human Settlements: Problems and Priorities; Contbr. articles to profl. jours. Mem. pub. policy com. Smithsonian Instn., 1970-73; bd. dirs. Champaign County United Community Council, 1965-69, Columbus Theatre Ballet Assn., 1972-75. Served to 1st lt. U.S. Army, 1955-57. Mem. Acad. for Contemporary Problems (asso.), Am. Am. Inst. Planners, Am. Soc. Engring. Edn., Internat. Center for Urban Land Policy (London). Office: 190 W 17th Ave Columbus OH 43210-1320

VOSS, JOAN SARAH, administrative assistant, writer; b. Aberdeen, Md., June 13, 1964; d. Carl Anthony Dugo and MaryAnn Catherine Sullivan. Grad., St. Barbara H.S., Chgo. Sec. Branham Newspaper Sales, Chgo., 1983—90; adminstrv. asst. Lake Forest (Ill.)Hosp., 2003—. Freelance writer, 1996—. Author poetry; contbr. articles to mags. Mem.: Children's Internat., Feed the Children. Roman Catholic. Avocation: art. Home: 1021 Dawes St Libertyville IL 60048

VOSS, K. DIRK, social sciences educator, researcher; b. Scharfoldendorf, Germany, Oct. 18, 1963; s. Dieter and Ingeborg Voss. BA Arbitur, Theodor Huess Gymnasium, Aalen, Germany, 1985; MA, Goettingen U., Germany, 1991, U. Okla., 1994, PhD, 2001. Instr. U. Okla., 1997—2001; vis. asst. prof. Stephen F. Austin State U., Nagagdoches, Tex., 2001—02; asst. prof. St. Louis Cmty. Coll., 2003—. Home: Apt 408 2350 Timberview Rd Saint Louis MO 63122 Office: St Louis Community Coll 11333 Big Bend Saint Louis MO 63122 E-mail: dvoss@stlcc.edu.

VOSS, MELINDA, health care association administrator; MPH, U. Minn, 1999. Staff writer The Des Moines Register; exec. dir. Assn. Health Care Journalists. Coord., health journalism masters program U. Minn., adj. instructor; chair Council Nat. Journalism Organizations. Casey Journalism Fellow, American Press Institute Fellow on Aging, Mini-Fellow, Henry J. Kaiser Family Found., 1997. Mem.: Investigative Reporters and Editors, Journalism and Women Symposium. Office: U Minn Sch Journalism 206 Church St SE Minneapolis MN 55455 Office Phone: 612-624-8877. Office Fax: 612-626-8251. Business E-Mail: melinda@umn.edu.

VOSS, OMER GERALD, truck company executive; b. Downs, Kans., Sept. 14, 1916; s. John and Grace (Bohlen) V.; m. Annabelle Katherine Lutz, June 20, 1940; children— Jerrol Ann, Omer Gerald. AB, Ft. Hays (Kans.) State Coll., 1937; JD, U. Kans., 1939. Bar: Kans. bar 1939. With Internat. Harvester Co., 1936-79, v.p. farm equipment div., 1962-66, exec. v.p., dir., 1966—, vice chmn., 1977-79. Served with USAAF, 1943-46. Mem.: Chicago, Commercial, Westmoreland Country.

VOSS, PETER S. investment company executive; CEO, chmn. of bd., pres. New Eng. Investment Cos. LP, Boston. Office: New Eng Investment Cos LP 399 Boylston St Boston MA 02116-3305

VOSS, REGIS DALE, agronomist, educator; b. Cedar Rapids, Iowa, Jan. 4, 1931; s. Francis Joseph and Mary Valeria (Womichil) V.; m. Margaret Anne Mitchell, Nov. 24, 1956; children: Lori Anne, John Patrick, David James. BS, Iowa State U., 1952, PhD, 1962. cert. profl. agronomist. Agriculturist Tenn. Valley Authority, Muscle Shoals, Ala., 1962-64; prof. Iowa State U., Ames, 1964-99, prof. emeritus, 1999—. Co-contbr. chpt. to: Fertilizer Technology and Use, 1985, Soil Testing and Plant Analysis, 1990; assoc. editor Jour. Prodn. Agr., 1988-92. Pres. FarmHouse Frat. Alumni Assn. Bd., Ames, 1990. 1st lt. USAF, 1952-56, Korea., sec. treas. Iowa State U. Retirees Assn., 2003-2004 Recipient Burlington No. Found. award Iowa State U., 1990, disting. svc. award Iowa State U. Ext., 1996, Iowa Master Farmer Exceptional Svc. award, 1998. Fellow AAAS, Am. Soc. Agronomy (bd. dirs. 1976-78, Agronomic Extension Edn. award 1984, Agronomic Achievement award 1989, Werner L. Nelson award 1992), Soil Sci. Soc. Am. (bd. dirs. 1980-83). Republican. Roman Catholic. Achievements include development of field laboratory for training of crop advisors on diagnosis of crop problems; research on effects of soil amendments on chemical indices and crop yields and economic analysis of crop yield. Office: Iowa State Univ Agronomy Hl Ames IA 50011-0001 E-mail: rvoss@iastate.edu.

VOSS, WILLIAM CHARLES, retired oil company executive; b. Buffalo, Sept. 22, 1937; s. William T. and Dorathea S. (Grotke) V.; m. Marilyn Erickson, Sept. 6, 1958; children: William, John, Douglas. AB with honors, Harvard U., 1959, MBA with honors, 1961. With Northwestern Refining Co., St. Paul Park, 1961-70, v.p. adminstrn., 1969-71; with Ashland Oil Inc., Ky., 1971-89, v.p., 1973-79, adminstrv. v.p., 1979-80, sr. v.p., group operating officer, 1980-89; pres. Ashland-Warren Inc., 1979-83, APAC, Inc., 1980-82, 83-86. Mem. Am. Chem. Soc. Republican. Home: 6756 N Fleur de Lane Stone Lake WI 54876

VOTAW, JOHN FREDERICK, educational foundation executive, educator; b. Richmond, Va., May 9, 1939; s. Frederick Lee and Katherine (B.) V.; m. Joyce Marie Miller, June 8, 1961; children: Laura, Cynthia, Mary, John Jr. BS, U.S. Mil. Acad., 1961; MA in History, U. Calif., Davis, 1969; grad., U.S. Army Colls., 1970, grad., 1985; PhD in History, Temple U., 1991. Commd. 2d lt. U.S. Army, 1961, advanced through grades to lt. col., 1976; comdr. Company C 1st bn. 69th Armor U.S. Army, Hawaii, 1964-65; comdr. Troop A 1st Squadron 11th ACR U.S. Army, South Vietnam, 1966-67, comdr. C&C Squadron 11th ACR, 1975-77; asst. prof. history U.S. Mil. Acad., West Point, N.Y., 1970-73, asst. dean for plans and programs, 1980-81, asst. prof., 1981-82; dep. dir. U.S. Army Mil. History Inst., Carlisle Barracks, Pa., 1983-86; ret. U.S. Army, 1986; dir. First Divsn. Mus., Wheaton, 1986—; exec. dir. Cantigny First Divsn. Found., Wheaton, 1991—. Adj. asst. prof. history Dominican U. (formerly Rosary Coll.), River Forest, Ill., 1991-98, adj. assoc. prof. history, 1998—; dir. Col. Robt. R. McCormick Rsch. Ctr., Wheaton, 1991-2002; series editor Cantigny Mil. History Series. Contbg. author: The D-Day Encyclopedia, 1993, The Encyclopedia of American Wars - The First World War, 1994, The European Powers in the First World War: An Encyclopedia, 1996, Encyclopedia of the Vietnam War, 3 vols., 1998, A Guide to the Study and Use of Military History, 1979, History in Dispute, vol. 5, Encyclopedia of American Military History, 3 vols., 2003; contbr. articles to profl. jours. Mem. adv. com. Ctr. for the Study of Force and Diplomacy, Temple U., 1996—. Decorated Legion of Merit, Bronze Star with "V" device, Purple Heart (3 awards) and others. Mem. Am. Hist. Assn., Orgn. Am. Historians, Soc. for Mil. History (trustee 2001—), Am. Assn. Mus., U.S. Naval Inst. (life), U.S. Army War Coll. Alumni Assn. (life), Ret. Officers Assn. (life), Disabled Am. Vets., Assn. Grads. U.S. Mil. Acad., U. Calif. Davis Alumni Assn. (life), Am. Vets. (life), Am. Legion (life), Kiwanis (Wheaton club 1986—, pres. 1991-92), Phi Alpha Theta, Phi Kappa Phi (life). Avocations: reading, writing, classical music, golf. Office: First Divsn Mus at Cantigny 1 S 151 Winfield Rd Wheaton IL 60187-6097 E-mail: jvotaw@tribune.com.

VOTAW, TY M. golf association commissioner; b. Salem, Ohio; m. Paula Votaw; children: Sam, Caroline. BS in Journalism summa cum laude, Ohio U., 1984; JD cum laude, U. NC, 1987. Atty. Taft, Stettinius & Hollister, Cin.; gen. counsel Ladies Profl. Golf Assn. (LPGA), Daytona Beach, Fla., 1991-92, spl. asst. to commr., 1992-99, v.p. bus. affairs, 1997—99, commr., 1999—. Bd. dir. Ladies Profl. Golf Assn., World Golf Found., Golf 20/20; mem. First Tee Oversight Com. Achievements include playing a key role in the establishment of the World Congress of Women's Golf. Avocations: collector of first edition books, music. Office: c/o LPGA 100 International Golf Dr Daytona Beach FL 32124-1092 Office Phone: 904-274-6200. Office Fax: 386-274-1099.*

VOTH, ALDEN H. political science educator; b. Goessel, Kans., May 4, 1926; s. John F. and Helena (Hildebrandt) V.; m. Norma E. Jost, Aug. 18, 1956; children: Susan, Thomas. BA, Bethel Coll., 1950; MS in Econs., Iowa State U., Ames, 1953; PhD in Internat. Rels., U. Chgo., 1959. Assoc. prof. polit. sci. Upland (Calif.) Coll., 1960-63; prof. polit. sci. San Jose (Calif.) State U., 1963-65, 67-91, prof. emeritus, 1991—. Vis. prof. polit. sci. Am. U. in Cairo, 1965-67. Author: Moscow Abandons Israel, 1980, (with others) The Kissinger Legacy, 1984. Trustee Pomona (Calif.) Valley Am. Assn. UN, 1963; participant China Ednl. Exch., 1996. Am. U. in Cairo Rsch. grantee, 1966; Nat. Coun. on U.S.-Arab Rels. fellow, 1990—. Home: 1385 Kimberly Dr San Jose CA 95118-1426 Office: San Jose State U One Washington Sq San Jose CA 95192 Personal E-mail: ahvoth@aol.com.

VOTH, DOUGLAS W. dean, educator; MD, U. Kans., 1959. Diplomate Am. Bd. Internal Medicine, 1966. Intern U. Kans. Sch. Medicine, Kansas City, 1959—60, resident in internal medicine, 1960—61, 1964—65, assoc. prof. medicine, 1971—73, prof. medicine, chair dept. and dir. residency program, 1974—84, pres. corp., 1978—84; fellow in infectious diseases Upstate Med. Ctr., Syracuse, NY, 1961—64; mem. sect. infectious diseases Kans. U. Med. Ctr., 1965—73; prof. medicine U. Okla. Sch. Medicine, 1973—74; med. dir., chief med. svc. King Fahad Hosp, Al Baha, Saudi Arabia, 1985—86; overseas advisor Royal Coll. Physicians, England, 1987—; prof. medicine U. Okla. Coll. Medicine, Oklahoma City, 1987—, acting chair dept. neurology, 1990—92, exec. dean, 1992—96; dean Faculty of Medicine and Health Scis., United Arab Emirates, 1996—2000; dir. med. edn. Sheikh Zayed Hosp., Abu Dhabi, 2000—01; dir. alumni and devel. U. Okla. Health Scis. Ctr., 2001—02; dean U. Okla. Coll. Pharmacy, Oklahoma City, 2002—. Trustee U. Presbyn.

Neurol. Inst., Oklahoma City, 1994—96. Fellow: ACP, Infectious Diseases Soc. Am. Office: Univ of Okla Coll of Pharmacy PO Box 26901 Oklahoma City OK 73190 Office Phone: 405 271-6485. Business E-Mail: douglas-voth@ouhsc.edu.

VOUDOUKIS, IGNATIOS JOHN, internist, cardiologist; b. Skalohorion, Lesvos, Greece, July 8, 1927; came to U.S., 1955; s. John Ignatios and Christina (Hatzilias) V.; m. Penny Christakos, July 15, 1962; 1 child, Christine Antoinette. MD, Nat. U. Athens, 1954. Intern Meml. Hosp., Albany, N.Y., 1955-56; resident Episcopal Hosp., Phila., 1956-58, Hahnemann Med. Coll. and Hosp., Phila., 1958-59; fellow in cardiology Jackson Meml. Hosp. and U. of Miami, Fla., 1959-61, Jewish Gen. Hosp., Montreal, 1961-63; rsch. assoc. in cardiology Maine Med. Ctr., Portland, 1963-64; assoc. physician Henry Ford Hosp., Detroit, 1964-67; adj. instr. medicine Wayne State U., Detroit, 1969, clin. asst. prof. medicine, 1973, clin. assoc. prof. internal medicine, 1981—; pvt. practice Detroit, 1967—. Active staff Harper Hosp., Detroit, Hutzel Hosp., Detroit. Mem. lab. facilities coun. Dept. Pub. Health, State of Mich., 1968-74; pres. Hypertension Coord. and Planning Coun. of Southeastern Mich., 1974. Recipient St. Paul Medallion, Greek Orthodox Diocese and Archdiocese of N. and S. Am., Detroit, 1986. Fellow ACP, Am. Coll. Angiology; mem. Am. Soc. Nephrology, Am. Soc. Hypertension (charter), Hellenic Univ. Club (pres. 1968-69), Detroit Athletic Club. Greek Orthodox. Office: Hutzel Hosp Profl Bldg 4727 Saint Antoine St Ste 402 Detroit MI 48201-1461

VOWLES, RICHARD BECKMAN, literature educator; b. Fargo, N.D., Oct. 5, 1917; s. Guy Richard and Ella (Beckman) V.; m. Ellen Noah Hudson, Aug. 1, 1942 (div. 1969); children: Elizabeth Ellen, Richard Hudson. BS, Davidson Coll., 1938; postgrad., U. N.C., 1938-39, U. Stockholm, 1939-40; MA, Yale U., 1942, PhD, 1950. Engr. Hercules Powder Co., Wilmington, Chattanooga, 1941-43, chemist Rohm & Haas, Knoxville, Tenn., 1943-44; econ. cons. War Dept., 1944; Am. vice consul Gothenburg, Sweden, 1945-46; asst. prof. English Southwestern U., Memphis, 1948-50, Queens U., N.Y.C., 1950-51; asso. prof. English U. Fla., 1951-60; prof. Scandinavian and comparative lit. U. Wis., Madison, 1960-85, prof. emeritus, 1985—, chmn. comparative lit., 1962-63, 64-67, 71-72, chmn. Scandinavian studies, 1977-80. Am. specialist in Scandinavia Dept. State, summer 1963; vis. prof. N.Y.U., summer 1964, U. Helsinki, Finland, spring 1968, Stockholm, 1969; lectr., Sydney, Australia, 1975, Paris, 1975; master ceremonies Santa Fe Scandinavian Film Festival, 1984 Editor: Eternal Smile, 1954, Dramatic Theory, 1956, Comparatists at Work, 1968; Adv. editor: Nordic Council Series, 1965-70, Herder Ency. of World Lit; contbr. articles to profl. jours. Am.-Scandinavian Found. fellow Stockholm, 1939-40, Lassen fellow Am. Scandinavian Found., 1986; Fulbright fellow Copenhagen, 1955-56; Strindberg fellow Stockholm, 1973; Swedish govt. research award, 1978; Norwegian Govt. fellow, summer 1978 Mem. Modern Lang. Assn., Soc. Advancement Scandinavian Study (mem. exec. com.), Internat. Comparative Lit. Assn., Am. Comparative Lit. Assn. (adv. bd.), Strindberg Soc., Phi Beta Kappa. Home: 1115 Oak Way Madison WI 53705-1420

VOYCHECK, GERALD LOUIS, nursing home administrator, social worker; b. Wilkes-Barre, Pa., Mar. 10, 1944; s. Martin Vojcik and Lottie (Lukashefska) V. BA, Quincy Coll., 1968; MA, Sangamon State U., 1981; postgrad., So. Ill. U., 1981-82. Joined Franciscan Bros. Holy Cross., 1964. Tchr. St. James Trade Sch., Springfield, Ill., 1968-71; evening librarian Springfield Coll., 1968-69; cataloger St. Francis Convent, Springfield, 1971-72; worker child care Lt. Joseph P. Kennedy, Palos Park, Ill., 1972-73; technician mental retardation Good Shepherd Manor, Momence, Ill., 1973-75; asst. adminstr. Bro. James Ct., Springfield, 1975-76, adminstr., 1976-79, 96—, social worker, 1979—; exec. dir. Springfield Devel., 1985-86. Instr. Lincoln Land Community Coll., Springfield, 1981—; interpreter Ill. Dept. Mental Health, Springfield, 1986; sec. Franciscan Bros. Holy Cross, 1973-76, bd. dirs., 1985—. Vol. Acquired Immune Deficiency Disease, sexual assault counseling. Mem. Polish Nat. Alliance. Republican. Roman Catholic. Avocations: food microbiology, horticulture. Home: 2500 Saint James Rd Springfield IL 62707-9736 Office: Brother James Ct Sangamon Avenue Rd Springfield IL 62707-9731

VOYIADJIS, GEORGE ZINO, civil engineer, educator; b. Cairo, Dec. 15, 1946; s. Zino Dimitri and Eleni (Mavridou) V.; m. Christina George Tziortzi, Nov. 4, 1978; children: Helena G., Andrew G. BSc with highest honors, Ain Shams U., Cairo, 1969; MSc, Calif. Inst. Tech., 1970; DSc, Columbia U., 1973. Sr. stress analyst Nuclear Power Svcs., Inc., N.Y.C., 1973-75, EBASCO Svcs., Inc., N.Y.C., 1975; assoc. prof. U. Petroleum and Minerals, Dhahran, Saudi Arabia, 1975-80; Boyd prof. civil engring. La. State U., Baton Rouge, 1980—, acting assoc. dean Grad. Sch., 1992-94, chmn., Bingham C. Stewart Disting. prof. dept. civil and environ. engring., 2001—. Editor: Mechanics of Materials Interfaces, 1986, Advances in the Theory of Plates and Shells, 1990, Microstructural Characterization in Constitutitve Modeling of Metals and Granular Media, 1992, Damage in Composite Materials, 1993, Advances in Damage Mechanics: Metals and Metal Matrix Composites, 1999; mem. editl. bd. Internat. Jour. Plasticity; contbr. over 200 articles on mech. behavior of solids, profl. publs.; editor: Damage Mechanics with Finite Elements: Practical Applications with Computer Tools, 2001. Recipient best paper prize Canadian Soc. Mech. Engring. Transactions, 1984. Fellow ASCE, ASME, Am. Acad. Mechanics; mem. Am. Soc. Engring. Educators, Soc. Engring. Sci., Sigma Xi. Democrat. Achievements include study of bridging of length scales and modeling mechanical behavior of metals and metal matrix composites; refined theory of plates and shells and numerical simulation of elasto-plastic contact problems and damage mechanics; organized conferences and symposia in behavior of materials. Home: 12718 N Oak Hills Pky Baton Rouge LA 70810-3243 Office: La State U Dept Civil & Environ Engring 3508-B CEBA Bldg Baton Rouge LA 70803 Office Phone: 225-578-8668. E-mail: voyiadjis@eng.lsu.edu.

VRABEL, JOSEPH P. lawyer; b. Adams, Mass., Feb. 8, 1948; BA, Lake Forest Coll., Ill., 1970; JD, Boston Coll., 1977; Mediator Cert., Harvard U., 1997. Bar: Mass., N.Y. Shareholder atty. Cope & Wilson, PC, 1979—84; sr. ptnr. Bowditch & Dewey, 1984—2001; v.p., gen. counsel Capital Risk Mgmt., Framingham, Mass., 2001—. Adj. prof. bus. law grad.-MBA program Babson Coll. Founder Crossroads Cmty. Found.; trustee Framingham State Coll.; treas., trustee Longfellow's Wayside Inn; former chmn. United Way MetroWest; trustee MCLE; dir. John J. Tobin Found., Maynard Food Pantry, Inc.; steering com. Equal Justice Coalition; former regional dir. Am. Cancer Soc.; mem. Maynard Town Counsel. Mem.: ABA, Worcester County Bar Assn., South Middlesex County Bar Assn., Boston Bar Assn., N.Y. Bar Assn., New Eng. Bar Assn. (bd. dirs.), Mass. Bar Assn. (chmn. bldg. and ops. com. 1988—, budget and fin. com. 1992—, exec. com. 1995—, governance task force 1996—98, sec. 1998—99, dues restructuring task force 1999—2000, v.p. 1999—2000, treas. 2000—01, by-law com. 2001—02, pres.-elect 2001—02, pres. 2002—03). Office: Capital Risk Mgmt 1661 Worcester Rd Ste 303 Framingham MA 01701

VRABLIK, EDWARD ROBERT, import/export company executive; b. Chgo., June 8, 1932; s. Steven Martin and Meri (Korbel) V.; m. Bernice G. Germer, Jan. 25, 1958; children: Edward Robert, II, Scott S. BS in Chem. Engring, Northwestern U., 1956; MBA, U. Chgo., 1961; postgrad., MIT, 1970. Registered profl. engr., Ill. Dir. indsl. mktg. Eimco Corp., 1956-61; dir. indsl. mktg. and planning Swift & Co., Chgo., 1961-68; v.p., gen. mgr. Swift Chem. Co., Chgo., 1968-73; pres., chief exec. officer Estech Gen. Chems. Corp., Chgo., 1973-86; pres. Kare Internat. Inc., Chgo., 1986—. Pres. Julius and Assocs., Inc., Kare Internat., Inc.; bd dirs. Potash Phosphate Inst., Consol. Fertilizers, Ltd.; mem. mgmt. com. Esmark Inc., Korbel, Inc., Mister Lawn Care, Inc. Author; patentee in field. Bd. dirs., v.p. Northwestern U. Tech. Inst.; trustee Future Farmers Am. Mem. Internat. Superphosphate Mfrs. Assn. (dir.), Am. Inst. Chem. Engrs., Fertilizer Inst. (dir.) Clubs: Butler Nat. (Oak Brook, Ill.). Lutheran. Home: 631 Thompsons Way Palatine IL 60067-4653 Office: 141 W Jackson Blvd Chicago IL 60604-2992 Office Phone: 847-358-4948.

VRALSTED, LEANN CHRISTINE, music educator; b. Billings, Mont., May 19, 1952; d. Ernest and Elenaor Christine Wyttenbach; m. Howard E. Vralsted, Aug. 27, 1978; children: Todd H. Vratsted, Kevin H., Bryan H. BA in Music Performance and German, Rocky Mountain Coll., 1974; MA in Music Performance, U. Wyo., 1976. Instr. piano Casper Coll., Wyo., 1976—78, pvt. practice, Billings, Mont., 1978—, Rocky Mountain Coll., 1996—. Mem.: Billings Tchrs. Assn. (chmn. 1995—). Republican. Lutheran.

VRANCIK, BARBARA A. lawyer; BBA, U. Miami, 1976; JD, DePaul U., 1979. Bar: Ill. 1979, N.Y. 1985. Law clk. to Hon. Robert Eisen, Bankruptcy Ct. for No. Dist. Ill., Chgo., 1979-80; ptnr. Sidley & Austin, N.Y.C. Editor DePaul Law Rev., 1978-79. Office: Sidley & Austin 875 3d Ave New York NY 10022 Fax: 212-906.2021. E-mail: burancik@sidley.com.

VRANICAR, MICHAEL GREGORY, lawyer; b. Hammond, Ind., Mar. 11, 1961; s. Melvin G. and Maryann R. (Szarek) V.; m. Marianna C. Livas, May 28, 1994. BSEE, U. Ill., 1983; JD, U. San Diego, 1987. Bar: Calif. 1987, Ill. 1988. Engr. Gen. Dynamics, San Diego, 1983-88; judge advocate USMC, Okinawa, Japan, 1988-91; assoc. Stellato & Schwartz, Chgo., 1992-94, ptnr. Plesha & Vranicar, Chgo., 1995—2001; atty. Fitch Even Tabin & Flannery, Chgo., 2001—. Arbitrator Cook County Arbitration Bd., Chgo., 1994—; judge regional competition Nat. Moot Ct., Chgo., 1992. Mem. Marine Corps Scholarship Found., Chgo. Ball Com. Lt. Col. USMC Res., 2001-. Mem. Chgo. Bar Assn., Okinawa Bench and Bar Assn., Am. Legion, Intellectual Property Lawyer's Assn., Chgo., Inst. Electrical and Electronics Engrs. Republican. Roman Catholic. Office: Fitch Even Tabin Flannery 120 S LaSalle Ste 1600 Chicago IL 60603

VRANISH, JOHN MICHAEL, electrical engineer, researcher; b. Brainerd, Minn., May 20, 1939; s. John Paul and Louise Ann (Jenkins) V.; m. Dorothy Jean Ward, June 27, 1980; children: John Christopher, Anthony Brian. BS, U.S. Mil. Acad., 1962; MSEE, George Washington U., 1973. Staff engr. robotics rsch. Naval Surface Weapons Ctr., White Oak, Silver Spring, Md., 1971-82, Nat. Bur. Standards, Gaithersburg, Md., 1982-86; staff engr. space mechanisms and space robotics Goddard Space Flight Ctr., Greenbelt, Md., 1986—. Mem. tech. task force Office of Sec. Def., 1981-82, fact finding com., 1981; cons. U.S. Congress, 1983, 87, 96; spkr. in field. Inventor capaciflector, 3-D sprags, carrier-less anti-backlash transmission, robotic deriveter, magnetostrictive direct drive rotary motor, spin bearings, continuously variable planetary transmission, gear bearings, flexure wedges, conformal robot gripper, stepping flexures, 3-D interactive display, screw locking "clickless" wrench; conformal robot gripper; multiple patents in several patentee, licensor in field; contbr. articles to books, jours. and various publs. Capt. U.S. Army, 1962—70. Mem. Robotics Internat. of Soc. Mfg. Engrs. (charter, award 1981). Holder world record for precision non contact robotic assembly in space; holder world record in single stage gear reduction; actuator upgrade designee, F-35 joint strike fighter. Home: 900 Truro Ln Crofton MD 21114-1207 Office: NASA/Goddard Space Flight Ctr Code 544 Greenbelt MD 20771-0001 E-mail: jvranish@mscmail.gsfc.nasa.gov., jmvranish@home.com.

VRANNA, JEFFREY, music educator; b. Dickinson, ND, Aug. 22, 1950; s. Warren Pletan and RoseMary Vranna; m. Dorothy Leone Renner, June 23, 2000. BS in Composite Music, Dickinson State U., 1972; MusM, U. No. Colo., 1987. Tchr. instrumental and vocal music Terry (Mont.) Pub. Schs., 1972—74; grad. asst., asst. condr. univ. band, tchr. asst. U. Mont., Missoula, 1974—75; instrumental music tchr. Cut Bank (Mont.) Pub. Schs., 1975—78; real estate bus. mgr. Dakota, Inc., Dickinson, 1978—80; real estate mgr. GM Homes, Dickinson, 1980—82; music tchr. Belfield (ND) Pub. Schs., 1982—89; dir. bands, music tchr. Dickinson Pub. Schs., 1989—. Mem. Helena (Mont.) Civic Orch., 1974—75, Missoula Civic Symphony, 1974—75, Dickinson Elks Band, 1978—, dir., 1980—; dir., solosit Centennial Ch. Choir, 1989; french horn Prairie Brass Quartet, 1990—91; French horn Bismarck-Mandan Symphony Orch., 1996—; dir. McDonald's Roughrider Band, Dickinson, 1991—94; mem. staff Internat. Peace Gardens Music Camp, 1989; dir., chaperone ND H.S. Centennial Band, 1988—89; cert. music adjudicator ND. Pres. Dist. 7 Music Tchrs., Cut Bank, 1978, Belfield Edn. Assn., v.p., 1986—87; dir. sr. choir St. John Luth. Ch., 1981—93. Mem.: NEA, Nat. Bandmaster's Assn., ND Edn. Assn., ND Music Educators Assn. (pres. 1994—97), ND H.S. Activities Assn. (mem. music adv. coun. 1989—2003, del. leader Am.-Soviet Youth Exch. 1991, 1992, pres.-elect 1993—94, chmn. music adv. coun. 2000—03), Music Educators Nat. Conf. (chmn. ND All-State com. 1992—96). Avocations: gardening, home remodeling. Home: 34 E 9th St Dickinson ND 58601 Office: Dickinson HS North Empore Rd Dickinson ND 58601 Office Phone: 701-456-0030. Fax: 701-456-0019.

VRATIL, JOHN LOGAN, state legislator, lawyer; b. Great Bend, Kans., Oct. 28, 1945; s. Frank and Althea (Shuss) V.; m. Kathy Hoefer, June 21, 1971 (div. Dec. 1985); m. Anne Whitfill, Mar. 7, 1986 (div. Dec. 1992); m. Teresa Hobbs, Mar. 15, 1996; children: Alison, Andy, Ashley. BS in Edn., U. Kans., 1967; postgrad., U. Southampton, Eng., 1967-68; JD, U. Kans., 1971; postgrad., U. Exeter, Eng., 1972. Bar: Kans. 1971, U.S. Dist. Ct. Kans. 1971, U.S. Ct. Appeals (10th and 8th cirs.) 1975. From assoc. to ptnr. Bennett, Lytle, Wetzler & Winn, Prairie Village, Kans., 1972-83; with Lathrop & Gage, Overland Park, Kans., 1983—; mem. Kans. Senate from 11th dist., 1998—, v.p., 2003—. Contbr. articles to profl. jours. Mem. recreation commn. Prairie Village, 1982-83, mem. planning commn., 1983-84; v.p. Usher Mansion Hist. Found., Lawrence, Kans., 1990—. Fellow ABA Found.; mem. ABA, Kans. Bar Assn. (pres. 1995-96, gov. 1988-97), Kans. Bar Found. (trustee 1996-2002), Johnson County Bar Assn. (pres. 1979), Kans. Sch. Attys. Assn. (pres. 1985), Overland Park C. of C. (bd. dirs. 1985-94, pres. 1988). Republican. Avocations: sports, hunting, reading. Office: Lathrop & Gage 10851 Mastin Blvd Ste 1000 Overland Park KS 66210-2007 Address: Kansas Senate State Capitol Rm 522S Topeka KS 66612 Office Phone: 913-451-5100. E-mail: jvratil@lathropgage.com., vratil@senate.state.ks.us.

VRATIL, KATHRYN HOEFER, federal judge; b. Manhattan, Kans., 1949; BA, U. Kans., 1971, JD, 1975; postgrad., Exeter U., 1971-72. Bar: Kans. 1975, Mo. 1978, U.S. Dist. Ct. Kans. 1975, U.S. Dist. Ct. (we. dist.) Mo. 1978, U.S. Dist. Ct. (ea. dist.) Mo. 1985, U.S. Ct. Appeals (8th cir.) 1978, U.S. Ct. Appeals (10th cir.) 1980, U.S. Ct. Appeals (11th dist.) 1983, U.S. Supreme Ct., 1995. Law clk. U.S. Dist. Ct., Kansas City, Kans., 1975-78; assoc. Lathrop Koontz & Norquist, Kansas City, Mo., 1978-83; ptnr. Lathrop & Norquist, Kansas City, 1984-92; judge City of Prairie Village, Kans., 1990-92. Bd. dirs. Kans. Legal Bd. Svcs., 1991-92; mem. adminstrv. com. Jud. Conf. of the U.S., 2000—. Bd. editors Kans. Law Rev., 1974-75, Jour. Kans. Bar Assn., 1992—. Mem. Kansas City Tomorrow (XIV); bd. trustees, shepherd-deacon Village Presbyn. Ch.; nat. adv. bd. U. Kans. Ctr. for Environ. Edn. and Tng., 1993-95; bd. dirs. Kans. Legal Svcs., 1991-92. Fellow Kans. Bar Found., Am. Bar Found.; mem. ABA (editl. bd. Judges Jour. 1996—), Am. Judicature Soc., Nat. Assn. Judges, Fed. Judges Assn., Kans. Bar Assn. (mem. bench bar com., 2000—), Mo. Bar Assn., Kansas City Met. Area Bar Assn., Johnson County Bar Assn., Assn. Women Judges, Lawyers Assn. Kansas City, Supreme Ct. Hist. Soc., Kans. State Hist. Soc., U. Kans. Law Soc. (bd. govs. 1978-81), Kans. U. Alumni Assn. (mem. Kansas City chpt. alumni bd. 1990-92, nat. bd. dirs. 1991-96, bd. govs. Adams Alumni Ctr. 1992-95), Chancellor's Club, Williams Ednl. Fund, Jayhawks for Higher Edn., Homestead Country Club Prairie Village (pres. 1985-86), Native Sons and Daus of Kans. (life), Jr. League Wyandotte and Johnson Counties, Order of Coif, Kans. Inn of Ct. (master 1993—, pres. 1999-2000), Phi Kappa Phi. Republican. Presbyterian. Office: 511 US Courthouse 500 State Ave Kansas City KS 66101-2403

VREDENBURGH, JUDY, youth organization executive; m. Donald Vredenburgh; 1 child. BA, U. Pa., 1970; MBA, U. Buffalo, 1975. Various positions in retail; exec. v.p., gen. mdse. mgr. Sizes Unlimited/Lerner Women; CEO Chess King; sr. v.p. March of Dimes, 1993—99; CEO and pres. Big Brothers Big Sisters of Am., 1999—. Bd. dirs. Generations United, Big Sister; bd. overseers Sch. Arts and Sciences, U. Penn. Office: Big Brothers Big Sisters of Am Nat Office 230 N 13th St Philadelphia PA 19107*

VREDEVOE, DONNA LOU, research immunologist, microbiologist, educator; b. Ann Arbor, Mich., 1938; BA in Bacteriology, UCLA, 1959, PhD in Microbiology, 1963. USPHS postdoctoral fellow Stanford (Calif.) U., 1963—64; instr. bacteriology UCLA, 1963, postgrad. rsch. immunologist dept. surgery Ctr. Health Scis., 1964-65, asst. rsch. immunologist dept. surgery Ctr. Health Scis., 1964-67, asst. prof. Sch. Nursing, Ctr. Health Scis., 1967-70, assoc. prof., 1970-76; prof. Sch. Nursing, Ctr. Health Scis., 1976—, assoc. dean Sch. Nursing, 1976-78, acting assoc. dean Sch. Nursing, 1985-86, asst. dir. space planning Cancer Ctr., 1976-78, dir. space planning, 1978-90, cons. to lab. nuc. medicine and radiation biology, 1967-80, acting dean Sch. Nursing, 1995-96. Chair acad. senate UCLA, 1999—2000, vice chancellor acad. pers., 2001—. Contbr. articles to profl. publs. Postdoctoral fellow USPHS, 1963-64; Mabel Wilson Richards scholar UCLA, 1960-61; rsch. grantee Am. Cancer Soc., Calif. Inst. Cancer Rsch., Calif. divsn. Am. Cancer Soc., USPHS, Am. Nurses Found., Cancer Rsch. Coordinating Com. U. Calif., Dept. Energy, UCLA. Mem Am. Soc. Microbiology, Am. Assn. Immunologists, Am. Assn. Cancer Rsch., Nat. League Nursing (2d v.p. 1979-81), Sigma Xi, Alpha Gamma Sigma, Sigma Theta Tau (nat. hon. mem.). Office: UCLA Chancellor's Office 2147 Murphy Hall PO Box 951405 Los Angeles CA 90095-1405

VREE, ROGER ALLEN, lawyer; b. Chgo., Oct. 2, 1943; s. Louis Gerard and Ruby June (Boersma) V.; m. Lauren Trumbull Gartside, Mar. 29, 1969; children: Jonathan Todd, Matthew David. BA, Wheaton Coll., 1965; MA, Stanford U., 1966, JD, 1969. Bar: Ill. 1969, U.S. Dist. Ct. (no. dist.) Ill. 1969. Assoc. Sidley & Austin, Chgo., 1969—75; ptnr. Sidley Austin Brown & Wood LLP, Chgo., 1975—. Mem.: ABA, Univ. Club (Chgo.). Office: Sidley Austin Brown & Wood LLP Bank One Plz 10 South Dearborn Chicago IL 60603-2000 E-mail: rvree@sidley.com.

VREELAND, ROBERT WILDER, retired electronics engineer; b. Glen Ridge, N.J., Mar. 4, 1923; s. Frederick King and Elizabeth Lenora (Wilder) V.; m. Jean Gay Fullerton, Jan. 21, 1967; 1 son, Robert Wilder. BS, U. Calif., Berkeley, 1947. Electronics engr. Litton Industries, San Carlos, Calif., 1948-55; sr. devel. electronics engr. U. Calif. Med. Ctr., San Francisco, 1955-89; ret. Cons. electrical engring; speaker 8th Internat. Symposium Biotelemetry, Dubrovnik, Yugoslavia, 1984, RF Expo, Anaheim, Calif., 1985, 86, 87. Contbr. articles to profl. jours., also to internat. meetings and symposiums; patentee in field. Recipient Chancellor's award U. Calif., San Francisco, 1979; cert. appreciation for 25 years' service U. Calif., San Francisco, 1980. Mem. IEEE, Am. Radio Relay League (pub. svc. award 1962). Home: 45 Maywood Dr San Francisco CA 94127-2007

VREELAND, RUSSELL GLENN, accountant, consultant; b. Princeton, N.J., Apr. 27, 1960; s. Glenn Earl and Barbara Ann (Jungels) Vreeland; m. Traci Ann Harbold, Dec. 17, 1988; children: Hans Russell, Anna Patricia. BSBA, Bloomsburg (Pa.) U., 1982. CPA Pa., Md. Sr. acct. Louis H. Linowitz & Co., Trenton, N.J., 1982-85; tax supr. Horty & Horty, P.A., Wilmington, Del., 1985-87; tax mgr. Stewart Waddell & Co. P.A., Columbia, Md., 1988-92; assoc. in charge of tax Hillman & Glorioso, P.L.L.C., Vienna, Va., 1993-98; ptnr. Vreeland & Assocs., LLC, 1998—, Vreeland & Co., Ltd., 2001—. Spkr. in field. Author: Foreign Sales Corporations - A Primer, 1992, Exporting - Are You Ready?, 1993; contbr. articles to profl. jours. Mem. Sykesville (Md.) Econ. Devel. Commn., 1998—2001; chair Sykesville Budget Com., 2000—, Sykesville Capital Improvement Com., 2000—; chmn. fin. com. Woodland Village Condominium Assn., 1989—90; mem. Sykesville Town Coun., 2000—, pres., 2002—; mem. Sykesville Hist. Dist. Commn., 2002—; com. chair Sykesville Centennial, 2003—04; co-chair fin. com. Messiah Luth. Ch., 2000—. Mem.: AICPA (adv. group mem. partnership taxation com. 1997—98, apptd. mem.partnership taxation com. 1998—99, tax divsn., mgmt. consulting svcs. divsn., accredited bus. valuations), Inst. Bus. Appraisers, Md. Assn. CPAs (mem. fed. taxation com. 1990—91). Republican. Lutheran. Office: Vreeland & Assocs LLC 7200 Norris Ave Sykesville MD 21784-6642 Personal E-mail: rgv_cpa@msn.com.

VRENTAS, JAMES SPIRO, chemical engineering educator; b. Danville, Ill., Apr. 14, 1936; s. Spiro and Evanthia (Guintonis) V.; m. Christine Mary Jarzebski, June 8, 1975; children: Catherine Eva, Jennifer Marie. BS, U. Ill., 1958; MSChE, U. Del., 1961, PhD, 1963. Rsch. engr. Dow Chem. Co., Midland, Mich., 1963-69, sr. rsch. engr., 1969-72; asst. prof. Ill. Inst. Tech., Chgo., 1972-73, assoc. prof., 1973-76, prof., 1976-80, Pa. State U., University Park, 1980-85, Dow prof., 1985—. Contbr. articles to profl. jours. Recipient William H. Walker Nat. Rsch. award AIChE, 1981, Charles Stein Materials Rsch. award, 1989. Mem. AIChE. Greek Orthodox. Achievements include development of theories for diffusion, rheology, and sorption in polymers. Home: 1705 Princeton Dr State College PA 16803-3260 Office: Pa State U 119 Fenske Lab University Park PA 16802-4400 Business E-Mail: jsv1@psu.edu.

VRIS, THOMAS W. surgeon; b. Elkins, W.Va., Apr. 27, 1951; s. Thomas and Barbara (Johns) V.; children: Tracy, Courtney. BA, Columbia U., 1973; MD with honors, NYU, 1979. Diplomate Am. Bd. Otolaryngology. Resident Harvard Sch. Medicine, Boston, 1979-81, Yale U., New Haven, 1982-85; fellow in plastic surgery, Heiden, Switzerland, 1985; attending surgeon, chief ENT and facial plastic surgery Norwalk (Conn.) Hosp., 1985—; pvt. practice Yale U., New Haven, 1985—; asst. chief of staff Norwalk Hosp., 2001—03. Mem. tchg. staff Sch. Medicine Yale U., New Haven; trustee Fairfield County Med. Soc., 1995-2000, Norwalk Hosp., 2001-03. Mem. Norwalk Med. Soc. (treas. 1991-92, pres. 1994-95), Columbia Club, Am. Acad. Otolaryngology Head and Neck Surgery, Saugatuck Harbor Yacht Club. Republican. Episcopalian. Office: 10 Mott Ave Ste 3-1 Norwalk CT 06850-3348

VRUWINK, AMY SUE, state legislator; b. May 22, 1975; BS, Marion Coll., Fond du Lac, Wis., 1997. Former congl. aide; mem. Wis. State Assembly, Madison, 2002—, sec. Minority Caucus, 2003—. Democrat. Office: State Capitol Rm 412N PO Box 8953 Madison WI 53708 Address: 9425 Flower Ln Milladore WI 54454

VU, JOSEPH DUONG, financial educator; b. Hanoi, Vietnam, Mar. 13, 1952; s. Phuong and Nhan (Trinh) V.; m. Huyen Tran T. Do, July 1, 1978; children: Christine, Daniel. BBA, Ohio U., 1973; MBA, U. Chgo., 1975, PhD in Fin., 1984. Asst. prof. Loyola U., Chgo., 1981-85, U. Ill., Chgo., 1985-88; assoc. prof. fin. DePaul U., Chgo., 1988—. Author: Investment Management, 1993. Mem. Am. Fin. Assn., Vietnamese Assn. Ill. (pres. 1993-98). Avocation: tennis. Office Phone: 312-362-5121. E-mail: jvu@depaul.edu.

VU, QUAT THUONG, electrical engineer; b. Vietnam, Aug. 5, 1944; came to U.S., 1988; s. Mao Quy and Phung Thi Vu; children: Hien T., Duc T. BSEE, U. Ky., 1965; MSEE, Calif. Inst. of Tech., 1967, PhDEE, 1970. Dean MINH-DUC U. Coll. Engring., Saigon, Vietnam, 1971-75; rschr. Hochiminh City, Vietnam, 1977-87, CNRS-CRN, Strasbourg, France, 1987-88, Calif. Inst. of Tech., Pasadena, 1989-90, Intel Corp., Santa Clara, Calif., 1990—. Achievements include over a dozen patents in field. Office: Intel Corp M/S SC1-05 2200 Mission College Blvd Santa Clara CA 95052 E-mail: quat.t.vu@intel.com.

VUCANOVICH, BARBARA FARRELL, retired congressman; b. Fort Dix, N.J., June 22, 1921; d. Thomas F. and Ynez (White) Farrell; m. Ken Dillon, Mar. 8, 1950 (dec. 1964); children: Patty Dillon Cafferata, Mike, Ken, Tom, Susan Dillon Anderson; m. George Vucanovich, June 19, 1965 (dec. Dec. 1998). Student, Manhattanville Coll. of Sacred Heart, 1938-39. Owner, operator Welcome Aboard Travel, Reno, 1968-74; Nev. rep. for Senator Paul Laxalt, 1974-82; mem. 98th-104th Congresses from 2d Nev. dist., 1983-96; chmn. appropriations subcom. on military construction; Rep. natl. committeewoman Nev. Rep. Party, 1996-2000. Pres. Nev. Fedn. Republican Women, Reno, 1955-56; former pres. St. Mary's Hosp. Guild, Lawyer's Wives. Mem.: Hidden Valley Country (Reno). Roman Catholic.

VUKAS, RONALD, publishing executive; Exec. v.p. Inst. Real Estate Mgmt., Chgo., 1990—. Office: Inst Real Estate Mgmt 430 N Michigan Ave Chicago IL 60611-4011

VUKMIR, LEAH, state legislator; b. Apr. 26, 1958; m. George Vukmir; children: Elena, Nicholas. BSN, Marquette U., Milw., 1980; MSN, U. Wis., 1983. Cert. pediat. nurse practitioner, RN Wis. Faculty nursing St. Mary's Med. Ctr., Children's Hosp. of Wis.; mem. Wis. State Assembly, Madison, 2002—, vice chair edn. reform com., mem. children and families com., mem. econ. devel. com., mem. criminal justice com., mem. health com. Lectr. in field; guest panelist Sunday Insight TV show; rsch. fellow Wis. Policy Rsch. Inst.; past pres. Parents Raising Ednl. Stds. in Schs. Contbr. articles to profl. jours. Vol. speedskating referee ASU; mem. stds. and assessment subcom. Gov. Tommy Thompson's Task Force on Edn. and Learning, Wis.; mem. English/lang. arts task force Coun. on Model Acad. Stds.; mem. choir Annunciation Greek Orthodox Ch. Recipient Alumni Achievement award, Brookfield East H.S., 2002, Unsung Hero award, Ctr. for Edn. Reform, Washington, 1998. Mem.: West Allis Speedskating Club. Republican. Greek Orthodox. Office: State Capitol Bldg Rm 307 N PO Box 8953 Madison WI 53708 Address: 2544 N 93d St Wauwatosa WI 53226

VUKSANOVIĆ, MIRO, library director, writer; b. Krnja Jela, Montenegro, May 4, 1944; s. Milutin and Koja (Grdinić) V.; m. Milana Dzuver; children: Danilo, Jelena. Grad., U. Belgrade, Yugoslavia, 1969. Secondary sch. tchr. Tech. Sch., Sombor, Yugoslavia, 1970-75; dir. City Libr. Karlo Bijelicki, Sombor, 1975-88, Biblioteka Matice srpske, Novi Sad, Serbia and Montenegro, 1988—. Author: (novels) Kletva Peka Perkova, 1977, Gradista, 1989, Daleko bilo, 1995, Semolj gora, 2000, Tocilo, 2001, Kucni krug, 2003; (short stories) Gorske oci, 1982, Nemusti jezik, 1984, Vucji tragovi, 1987; (poems) Tamooni, 1992, Moracnik, 1994, other writings. Recipient Miroslavljevo jevandelje, Meml. of Vuk, Politika, Borba, Assn. of Writers of Vojvodina, Oct.'s prize, Prosveta, Vuk's prize, Svetozar Čorović prize. Mem. Assn. of Writers (pres. 1985-86), Fedn. Socs. of Writers Belgrade (pres. 1984-86), Fedn. Socs. of Librs. Yugoslavia (pres. 1985-87), Fedn. Nat. Librs. (pres. 1988-92), Serbian Sci. and Cultural Soc. Matica srpska (collaborator 1988, mem. adminstrv. com. 1988, v.p. 2004). Office: Matice Srpske Libr Matice Srpske 1 21000 Novi Sad Serbia and Montenegro

VUKSTA, MICHAEL JOSEPH, surgeon; b. Pitts., Apr. 25, 1926; s. Michael and Mary Sarah (Hanulya) V.; m. Dorothy Ann Bosak, Sept. 12, 1953; children: Patricia, Michael, Carol, Janet. BA, Youngstown State U., 1949; MD, Ohio State U., 1957. Diplomate Am. Bd. Surgery. Enlisted USN, advanced through grades to capt., 1974; intern St. Elizabeth Hosp., Youngstown, Ohio, resident in gen. surgery, 1958-62; pvt. practice gen. surgery Youngstown, 1962-89; head blue team surgery Oak Knoll U.S. Naval Hosp., Oakland, Calif., 1989-93; assoc. prof. surgery NEOUCOM. Capt. USN retired. Fellow ACS, Am. Coll. Sports Medicine, Southwestern Surg. Congress; mem. Nat. Athletic Trainers Assn. (advisor). Byzantine Catholic. Home: 131 Lovett Pl Pensacola FL 32506-5265

VULEVICH, EDWARD, JR., prosecutor; b. Nov. 5, 1933; s. Edward J. and Minnie R. V.; m. Diane Misko; children: Erin, Jan, John. AB, U. Ala., 1955, JD, 1957. Bar: Ala., U.S. Supreme Ct., U.S. Ct. Appeals (11th cir.) Ala., U.S. Ct. Appeals (5th cir.) Ala. Atty. U.S. Dept. Justice, Mobile, Ala., 1969—, chief civil divsn. Office: US Attys Office 63 S Royal St Ste 1600 Mobile AL 36602-3245

VULGAMORE, ALLISON, performing arts administrator; BMus, Oberlin Coll. Former gen. mgr., artistic adminstr., mgr. ops. Nat. Symphony Orch., Washington; former gen. mgr. N.Y. Philharm. Orch., N.Y.C.; pres. Atlanta Symphony Orch., 1993—. Bd. dirs. Oberlin Coll.; mem. arts challenge panel in music NEH. Bd. dirs. Midtown Alliance; mem. Vision 2000 Econ. Devel. Collaborative; Cultural Olympiad and opening ceremonies coord. Centennial Olympic Games, Atlanta, 1996. Am. Symphony Orch. League fellow, 1980. Mem. Atlanta Rotary. Office: Atlanta Symphony Orchestra Robert W Woodruff Arts Ctr 1293 Peachtree St NE Ste 300 Atlanta GA 30309-3552

VULGAMORE, MELVIN L. retired college president; b. Springfield, Ohio, July 19, 1935; s. Leo Beeman and Della Marie (McCoy) V.; m. Ethelanne Oyer, Feb. 17, 1957; children: Allison Beth, Sarah Fith Vulgamore Evans. BA with honors, Ohio Wesleyan U., 1957; BD, Harvard U., 1960; PhD, Boston U., 1963; LLD, Albion Coll., 1997. Chmn., prof. religion Ohio Wesleyan U., Delaware, 1962-78, assoc. dean faculty, 1972-73, dean acad. affairs, 1973-78; v.p., provost U. Richmond, Va., 1978-83; pres. Albion Coll., Mich., 1983-97, chancellor, 1997—98; pres. emeritus, 1998—. Vis. prof. Am. U. Beirut, 1971-72; vis. scholar Harvard U., 1995. Contbr. articles to profl. jours. Trustee Howe Mil. Sch., Ind., 1984-97; mem. Mich. Coun. for Humanities, 1985-89, 96-97. Mem. Am. Acad. Religion, Tillich Soc. N.Am., Harvard Faculty Club, St. Botolph Club, Nat. Press Club, Phi Beta Kappa, Omicron Delta Kappa, Delta Sigma Rho, Pi Sigma Alpha. Avocations: bicycling, tennis, classical music, antique collecting and refinishing. Home: 175 Pleasant St New London NH 03257-4817

VUMBACCO, JOSEPH V. health services executive; BA, Bowdoin Coll.; JD, Syracuse u. Atty. Mudge, Rose, Guthrie and Alexander; sr. v.p. F&M Schaefer Corp.; exec. v.p. The Turner Corp.; pres., CEO Health Mgmt. Assocs., Inc., Naples, Fla., 1996, pres., 1997, CEO, 2001—. Office: Health Mgmt Assocs Inc Ste 500 5811 Pelican Bay Blvd Naples FL 34108-2710

VUOTO, ANTHONY, corporate financial executive; BA, Princeton U.; MBA, Wharton Sch. Bus., U. Pa. Pres. consumer lending divsn. Bank One Corp., pres., COO First USA Bank; vice chmn., CFO Providian Fin. Corp., San Francisco, 2002—. Office: Providian Fin Corp 201 Mission St San Francisco CA 94105

VURAL, VOLKAN, Turkish representative to UN; b. Istanbul, Turkey, Dec. 29, 1941; married. Grad., Ankara U. With Turkish Ministry Fgn. Affairs, 1964—; internat. officer, polit. dept. NATO Hdqrs., 1976-82; head econ. dept., envoy, dep. dir. gen. bilateral econ. aff. Ministry Fgn. Affairs, 1982-87; Turkish amb. to Tehran, 1987-88, Moscow, 1988-93; dep. under-sec., amb., spokesman Ministry Fgn. Affairs, 1993, chief advisor to prime min., dep. under-sec., 1993-95; Turkish amb. Bonn, Germany, 1995-98; rep. from Turkey to UN, 1998—. Office: Permanent Del of Turkey/UN 821 U N Plz Fl 11 New York NY 10017-3520

VYAS, GIRISH NARMADASHANKAR, virologist, immunohematologist; b. Aglod, India, June 11, 1933; came to U.S., 1965, naturalized, 1973; s. Narmadashankar P. and Rukshmani A. (Joshi) V.; m. Devi Ratilal Trivedi, Apr. 3, 1962; children: Jay, Shrikrishna. B.Sc., U. Bombay, 1954, M.Sc., 1956, PhD, 1964. Postdoctoral fellow Western Res. U., 1965-66; mem. faculty U. Calif., San Francisco, 1967—, chief blood bank, 1969-88, prof. lab. medicine, 1977—; dir. transfusion rsch. program, 1985—. WHO cons., S.E. Asia, 1980; cons. in field; mem. com. viral hepatitis NRC, 1974-76; mem. task force blood processing Nat. Heart and Lung Inst., 1972-73; sci. program com. Am. Assn. Blood Banks, 1971-76; com. immunoglobulin allotypes WHO, 1974-76; mem. U.S. del. immunologists to Romania and Hungary, 1980; mem. FDA com. on blood and blood products, 1987-92; cons. to VA on med. rsch., 1985, UN Devel. Program in India, 1986, others; chmn. Transmed Biotech Inc., South San Francisco, 1989-94, chmn. IABS Blood Com., 2003—. Author: Hepatitis and Blood Transfusion, 1972, Laboratory Diagnosis of Immunological Disorders, 1975, Membrane Structure and Function of Human Blood Cells, 1976, Viral Hepatitis, 1978, Viral Hepatitis and Liver Disease, 1984, Use and Standardization of Chemically Defined Antigens, 1986, Transfusion-associated Infections and Immune Response, 1988, Molecular Approaches to Laboratory Diagnosis, 1996, Advances in Transfusion Safety, 2000; also 225 research papers. Recipient Julliard prize Internat. Soc. Blood Transfusion, 1969; named Outstanding Immigrant in Bay Area Communities by Mayor of Oakland, Calif., 1969; Fulbright scholar France, 1980 Mem. AAAS, Am. Soc. Hematology (chmn. com. on transfusion medicine 1989-90), Am. Assn. Immunologists, Internat. Assn. for Biol. Standardization (coun. 1992-2000, chmn. com. on blood), Internat. Assn. Biologics (coun. and chair com. on blood). Democrat. Hindu. Office: U Calif Lab Med S 561 San Francisco CA 94143-0100 Office Phone: 415-476-4678. E-mail: vyas@itsa.ucsf.edu. *Truth alone wins. Truth in our actions manifests beauty in character. Beauty in character brings harmony into the home. Harmony in the home produces order in our society. Order in our society leads to peace in the nation. And peace in the nation can win for us universal prosperity and happiness for mankind, only if individuals practice truth in their actions.*

VYAZOVKIN, SERGEY, chemist, educator; b. Kazan, Russia, Feb. 20, 1960; came to U.S., 1995; s. Valentin and Irma Vyazovkin; m. Sasha Vyazovkin, Oct. 1, 1983; 1 child, Polina. BS, Belorussian U., Minsk, 1982, PhD in Chemistry, 1989. Rsch. prof. U. Utah, Salt Lake City, 1998—2001; prof. U. Ala., Birmingham, 2001—. Editor: Thermochem. Acta, Thermochim. Acta. Lise Meitner Rsch. fellow Austrian Rsch. Fund, 1992, 93, NATO rsch. fellow, 1994. Mem. NATAS. Office: U Ala Dept Chemistry 901 S 14th St Birmingham AL 35294

VYDARENY, KAY HERZOG, radiologist, medical educator; b. Chgo., Nov. 26, 1942; MD, U. Mich., 1968. Diplomate Am. Bd. Radiology. Intern Blodgett Meml. Med. Ctr., Grand Rapids, Mich., 1968—69; resident in diagnostic radiology Mich. State U., Grand Rapids, 1975—80; prof. radiology Emory U., Atlanta; radiologist Emory U. Hosp., Atlanta. Mem.: Am. Roentgen Ray Soc., Am. Assn. Women in Radiology, Assn. Univ. Radiologists, Am. Coll. Radiology (pres. 2001—02), Radiol. Soc. N.Am.

VYKUKAL, EUGENE LAWRENCE, wholesale drug company executive; b. Caldwell, Tex., June 26, 1929; s. Henry J. and Anna P. (Polansky) V.; m. Judith Anderson, Jan. 1, 1977; children— Anna K., Mark Roman, Laura Roman, Geni. BS in Pharmacy, U. Tex., Austin, 1952. Pharmacist Scarborough's Pharmacy, Baytown, Tex., 1952-53; pharmacist Gene Vykukal's Pharmacy, Clifton, Tex., 1953-57; with Southwestern Drug Corp. (name now Bergen Brunswig Drug Co.), 1957-86; gen. sales mgr. Southwestern Drug Corp., Dallas, 1966-67, v.p., dir. sales, 1967-75, exec. v.p., dir. sales, 1975-81, exec. v.p., 1980-81, pres., chief exec. officer, 1981-86, vice chmn., 1985-86, dir., 1966-86; asst. dean for devel., lectr. Coll. Pharmacy U. Tex., Austin, 1991—, mem. adv. coun. Pharm. Found., chmn., 1978—; sr. v.p. profl. affairs Bergen Brunswig Corp., Bergen Brunswig Drug Co., 1986—. Mem. centennial endowment com. U. Tex., 1980—; bd. dirs. Baylor U. Med. Center Found., Dallas; mem. indsl. adv. coun. Coll. Pharmacy, U. Ky., 1990—. Recipient Disting. Alumni award U. Tex. Coll. Pharmacy, 1979, William J. Sheffield Disting. Alumni award U. Tex. at Austin Coll. Pharmacy, 1987, Legend of Pharmacy award U. Tex. Coll. Pharmacy Alumni Assn., 1997. Mem. Nat. Wholesale Druggists Assn. (chmn. sales mgmt. com. 1972-73, dir. 1980—, chmn. bd. 1985-86, 1st vice chmn. 1983—, chmn. exec. com. 1987—, Timothy Barry award 1990), Am. Pharm. Assn., Tex. Pharm. Assn. (long range planning com. 1983—), Wholesale Druggist Assn. Tex. (pres. 1978-79), Drug Travelers Assn. Tex. (pres. 1977-78), Sales and Mktg. Execs. Dallas (dir. 1971-72). Roman Catholic. Office: U Tex Coll Pharmacy Pharmacy Bldg Austin TX 78712-1074 *The quality of life in our great country has been enhanced by the tremendous strides made in our health care delivery system over the past three decades. To have served in the pharmaceutical segment has been very rewarding.*

WAAGE, MERVIN BERNARD, lawyer; b. Spirit Lake, Iowa, May 12, 1944; s. Bernard and Pearl Peterson W.; children: Love Lee, Mark Warren. BA, Northwestern Coll., Roseville, Minn., 1966; MDiv, Southwestern Sem., 1969; JD, So. Methodist U., 1974. Bar: Tex. 1974, U.S. Dist Ct. (no. dist.) Tex. 1974, U.S. Dist. Ct. (ea. dist.) Tex. 1976, U.S. Supreme Ct. 1977, U.S. Tax Ct. 1978, U.S. Ct. Claims, 1978, U.S. Dist. Ct. (we. dist) Tex. 1988, U.S. Ct. Appeals (5th cir.) 1989. Asst. dist. atty. Denton County (Tex.) Atty.'s Office, 1974-76; pvt. practice law Denton, Tex., 1977—. Bankrupcy trustee, 1980-87. Mem. Tex. Bar Assn., Tex. State Bar (v.p. bankruptcy com., 2002-), Tex. Bd. Legal Specialization (cert. in consumer bankruptcy 1986, cert. in bus. bankruptcy 1988). Republican. Baptist. Avocation: singing. Office: Waage & Waage LLP 8350 S Stemmons St Denton TX 76210-2424

WAAGE, SISSEL, environmental services administrator; PhD, U. of Calif., Berkeley. Cert. environ. sci., policy, and mgmt. V.p. R&D program The Natural Step; program officer World Wildlife Fund. Author: (book) Ants, Galileo, and Gandhi: Designing the Future of Business through Nature, Genius, and Compassion. Achievements include research in integration of environmental and social issues into core business strategy and operations.

WAALAND, IRVING THEODORE, retired aerospace design executive; b. Bklyn., July 2, 1927; s. Trygve and Marie Waaland; m. Helen Rita Katz, Apr. 7, 1961; children: Theodore, Neil, Elizabeth, Scott, Diane. B of Aero. Engring. magna cum laude, NYU, 1953. Project engr. Grumman Corp., Bethpage, NY, 1953—74; v.p., B-2 Chief Designer Northrop Corp., Pico Rivera, Calif., 1974—93. Patentee in field. With USAF, 1946-48. Fellow AIAA (Aircraft Design award 1989, Aircraft Design cert. merit 1989, Wright Bros. lectr. in Aeronautics 1991); mem. NAE, Am. Def. Preparedness Assn. (Leslie E Simon award 1990), SAE (Aerospace Engring. Leadership award 1993). Home: 3161 Alta Vista # D Laguna Woods CA 92637

WAAS, ANDREA SUE, nonprofit foundation administrator; b. Kansas City, Mo., Mar. 5, 1958; d. Willis Albert Waas. BS in Journalism, U. Kans., 1980; MBA, Cardinal Stritch Coll., 1990. Founder Wings of Light, Inc., Phoenix, 1995—. Contbr. Wings newsletter. Mem. Am. Soc. Assn. Execs. Avocation: flying. Office: Wings of Light Inc PMB 448 16845 N 29th Ave # 1 Phoenix AZ 85053 E-mail: awaaswings@aol.com.

WABER, HARRY EDWARD, insurance agency executive; b. Phila., May 2, 1911; s. Max and Hattie (Sonnenfeld) W.; m. Raechal Kravitz, Oct. 8, 1935 (dec.); children: Beth Rebecca Love, Michael David. BS in Econs., U. Pa., 1933. With Montgomery Scott & Co., Phila., 1933-35, Waber & Co., 1935-56, Waber-Odell, 1956-75, Trio Mgmt., 1963-75; founder, chmn. Main Line Agy., Inc., Wynnewood, Pa., 1960—. Founder Montgomery Gen. Agy., Inc., Wynnewood, 1962; underwriting mem. Lloyds, 1977—. Trustee Fedn. Jewish Agys.; vice chmn. Allied Jewish Appeal; bd. dirs. Akiba Acad., Torah Acad., Phila. Jewish Archives Ctr., Beth Jacobs Schs.; bd. govs. Greenhill condominium Assn.; treas. Lower Merion Cmty. Watch. With U.S. Army, 1943-46. Decorated Army Commendation medal; recipient cert. of merit Big Bros., 1961; C.P.C.U. Mem. Soc. Chartered Property and Casualty Underwriters, Locust Club, White Manor Country Club (past pres.), Bryn Mawr Kennel Club (past gov.), B'nai Brith, Bala Golf Club. Home: 1001 City Ave Apt Wa-704 Wynnewood PA 19096-3938

WACHENFELD, TIMOTHY H. aeronautical engineering executive; Gen. mgr. Gen. Electric Aircraft Engines, Cin. Recipient Leadership in Quality Mgmt. award AIAA, 1994. Office: GE Aircraft Engines 1 Neumann Way Cincinnati OH 45215-1915

WACHMAN, MARVIN, retired academic administrator; b. Milw., Mar. 24, 1917; s. Alex and Ida (Epstein) W.; m. Adeline Lillian Schpok, Apr. 12, 1942; children: Kathleen M., Lynn A. BS, Northwestern U., 1939, MA, 1940; PhD, U. Ill., 1942; LLD (hon.), U. Pa., 1964, Lincoln (Pa.) U., 1970, Del. Valley Coll. Sci. and Agr., 1973, Med. Coll. Pa., 1982, Bloomfield Coll., 1987, Albright Coll., 1991; DHL (hon.), Gratz Coll., 1973; LittD (hon.), Jewish Theol. Sem. Am., 1973, Drexel U., 1980; LHD (hon.), Colgate U., 1975, Widener U., 1976; DSc (hon.), Thomas Jefferson U., 1980; LHD, U. New Eng., 1997; DHL, Phila. Coll. Textiles and Sci., 1999. Asst. in history U. Ill., 1940-42; instr. Biarritz Am. U., Biarritz, France, 1945-46; vis. asst. prof. San Diego State Coll., summer 1948, U. Minn., 1950; assoc. prof. history U. Md. in Europe, 1952-53; from instr. to prof. Colgate U., 1946-61, dir. upper class core program, 1956-61; pres. Lincoln (Pa.) U., 1961-70; v.p. acad. affairs Temple U., 1970-73, pres., 1973-82, chancellor, 1982-2000, Dir. Salzburg Seminar in Am. Studies, 1958-60, pres. Fgn. Policy Rsch. Inst., 1983-89; acting exec. dir. Pa. Higher Edn. Assistance Agy., 1989; acting pres. Phila. Coll. Textiles and Sci., 1991; pres. Albright Coll., 1991-92. Past chmn. Nat. Ctr. for Higher Edn. Mgmt. Sys.; specialist in Africa for State Dept., 1965, 68; mem. adv. coun. World Learning, Inc.; mem. Colgate Nat. Coun.; chmn. emeritus Collegis, Inc. Author: History of Social-Democratic Party of Milwaukee, 1897-1910, 1945; contbr. articles to profl. jours. and newspapers, also chpts. in books. Mem. adv. coun. Greater Phila. Urban Affairs Coalition, World Affairs Coun.; vice chair Fgn. Policy Rsch. Inst.; hon. dir. Phila. Contributionship; trustee emeritus Balch Inst. Ethnic Studies; mem. bd. overseers Coll. V.I.; hon. trustee Albright Coll.; hon. life trustee Temple U. With U.S. Army, 1942—46. Mem. NAACP, Am. Studies Assn. (past mem. exec. com.), AAUP (past pres. Colgate U. chpt.), Am. Hist. Assn., ACLU, Pa. Assn. Colls. and Univs. (past chmn., pres. 1993), Phi Beta Kappa. Office: Temple U Philadelphia PA 19122-6096 Office Phone: 215-204-6275. E-mail: marvin.wachman@temple.edu.

WACHOB, TOM WEBB, JR., retired obstetrician-gynecologist; b. El Paso, Ill., July 16, 1923; s. Tom Webb and Esther Della (Cooper) W.; m. Patricia Klemm, June 20, 1944 (div. 1952); children: William K., Robert T.; m. Susan Ann Niederwimer, Nov. 15, 1952 (dec. May 1992); children: Carol Ann, Thomas S., James C.; m. Dorothy Boyd Gray Riggin, June 12, 1996. BS, Ill. Wesleyan U., 1944; MD, U. Ill., 1946. Diplomate Am. Bd. Ob-Gyn. Rotating intern St. Elizabeth Hosp., Lafayette, Ind., 1946-47; resident in ob-gyn. St. Louis City Hosp., 1949-50, St. Elizabeth Hosp., Lafayette, 1950-52; with So. Clin., Ark. and Tex., 1952—54, Howard Cmty. Hosp., Kokomo, Ind., 1954—85. Mem. ACOG, AMA, Cen. Assn. Obstetricians and Gynecologists, Ind. Ob-Gyn. Soc. (pres. 1968), Kokomo Rotary Club (pres. 1965), Belleair Country Club, Kokomo Country Club. Republican.

WACHOWSKI, ANDY, film director; b. Chgo., Dec. 29, 1967; Motion picture dir., writer, prodr. (With brother Larry) exec. prodr., writer, dir. films Bound, 1996 (Internat. Fantasy Film award 1997, nominee spl. grand prize Deauville Film Festival, hon. mention Stockholm Film Festival), The Matrix, 1999 (Saturn award for best dir., Saturn award nominee for best writer, Sierra award nominee 2000, Las Vegas Film Critics Soc. Best Original Screenplay, nominee best fgn. film Norwegian Internat. Film Festival 2000), Assassins, 1995 (story, hon. mention Stockholm Film Festival), The Matrix Reloaded, 2003. Office: EON Entertainment 400 Warner Blvd Bldg 81 Burbank CA 91522-0001

WACHOWSKI, LARRY, film director; b. Chgo., June 21, 1965; m. Thea Bloom, Oct. 30, 1993 (div. Dec. 2002). Motion picture dir., writer, prodr. (With brother Andy) exec. prodr., writer, dir. films Bound, 1996 (Internat. Fantasy Film award 1997, nominee spl. grand prize Deauville Film Festival, hon. mention Stockholm Film Festival), The Matrix, 1999 (Saturn award for best dir., Saturn award nominee for best writer, Sierra award nominee 2000, Las Vegas Film Critics Soc. Best Original Screenplay, nominee best fgn. film Norwegian Internat. Film Festival 2000), Assassins, 1995 (story, hon. mention Stockholm Film Festival), The Matrix Reloaded, 2003, The Matrix Revolutions, 2003. Office: EON Entertainment 4000 Warner Blvd # 81 Burbank CA 91522-0001 Address: William Morris Agy care Dave Wirtschafter 151 El Camino Dr Beverly Hills CA 90212

WACHS, ALAN L, quality assurance engineer; b. Kalamazoo, Mich., Oct. 25, 1959; s. Melvin W and Eulene S Wachs. AB, Cornell U., Ithaca, NY, 1977—81; MS, U. of Ill., Urbana, 1981—82, PhD, 1982—86. Postdoctoral rsch. assoc. Lawrence Livermore Nat. Lab., Livermore, Calif., 1986—89; mem. of tech. staff Oak Ridge Nat. Lab., 1989—91, quality assurance specialist, 1991—96; process engr. and quality engr. Ion Bond, West Chicago, Ill., 1997—2000; sr. quality engr. Shure Inc., Evanston, Ill., 2000—03; verification engr. Vapor Bus. Internat., Buffalo Grove, Ill., 2004—. Author / co-author (26 scientific publications). Mem.: AAAS, Am. Soc. for Quality. Achievements include Recognition for developing award-winning products and implementing quality management systems. Avocations: hiking, camping, folkdancing. Home: 1640 Maple #1403 Evanston IL 60201

WACHS, DAVID V. retired apparel executive; b. Phila. Attended, U Penn Wharton, 1948. With Charming Shoppes Inc., Bensalem, 1950-95, CEO, 1988-95; ret., 1995. Cons. David Wachs Exec. Offices, King of Prussia, 1995—. Office: David Wachs Exec Offices 215 W Church Rd Ste 108 King Of Prussia PA 19406-3209

WACHS, MARTIN, urban planning educator, author, consultant; b. NYC, June 8, 1941; s. Robert and Doris (Margolis) W.; m. Helen Pollner, Aug. 18, 1963; children: Faye Linda, Steven Brett. BCE, CUNY, 1963; MS, Northwestern U., 1965, PhD, 1967. Asst. prof. U. Ill., Chgo., 1967-69, Northwestern U., Evanston, Ill., 1969-71; assoc. prof. urban planning UCLA, 1971-76, prof., 1976-96; dir. U. Calif. Transp. Ctr., 1996-99; prof. civil and environ. engring. and city/regional planning U. Calif., Berkeley, 1996—, dir. Inst. Transp. Studies, 1999—. Vis. disting. prof. Rutgers U., New Brunswick, N.J., 1983-84; mem. exec. com. Transp. Rsch. Bd., 1995—2004, chmn., 2000; vis fellow Oxford (Eng.) U., 1976-77. Author: Transportation for the Elderly: Changing Lifestyles, Changing Needs, 1979, Transportation Planning on Trial, 1996, also numerous articles; editor: Ethics in Planning, 1984, The Car and the City, 1992. Mem. steering com. L.A. Parking Mgmt. Study, 1976-78; bd. dirs. L.A. Commuter computer, 1978-94, mem. Calif. Commn. on Transp. Investment, 1995. Served to capt. Ordnance Corps, U.S. Army, 1967-69. Recipient Pike Johnson award Transp. Rsch. Bd., 1976, Disting. Tchg. award UCLA Alumni Assn., 1986, Disting. Planning Educator award Calif. Planners Found., 1986, W.N. Carey Disting. Svc. award Transp. Rsch. Bd., 2002, Disting. Educator award Coun. U. Transp. Ctrs., 2003; Guggenheim fellow, 1977, Humanities fellow Rockefeller Found., 1980; Rsch. lectr Soc. Sigma Xi, 2004—. Fellow: Am. Inst. Cert. Planners, Am. Coun. Edn.; mem.: ASCE, Inst. Transp. Engrs., Cosmos Club (Washington). Jewish. Home: 1106 Grizzly Peak Blvd Berkeley CA 94708-1704 Office: U Calif Berkeley Inst Transp Studies 109 Mclaughlin Hall Berkeley CA 94720-1720 Office Phone: 510-642-3585. Business E-Mail: mwachs@berkeley.edu.

WACHS, SAUL PHILIP, Jewish education educator; b. Phila., Dec. 24, 1931; s. Abraham and Annette (Schaller) W.; m. Barbara Ruth Eidelman, Jan. 27, 1957 (dec. 1997); children: Sharona Rachel, Hillel Eliezer, Devorah Leah, Aviva Marcia (dec.); m. Diane Ruth Cover, Feb. 6, 2000. Hebrew tchr. diploma, Gratz Coll., 1951; BS in Edn., Temple U., 1953; BRE, Jewish Theol. Sem., 1956, B in Sacred Music, 1959, D Pedagogy (hon.), 1989; MA, Ohio State U., 1966, PhD, 1970. Dir. edn. Congregation Tifereth Israel, Columbus, Ohio, 1960-70, Park Ave Synagogue, N.Y.C., 1970-72; asst. prof., dir. Jewish edn. program Brandeis U., Waltham, Mass., 1972-75; dean Gratz Coll., Phila., 1975-80, Rosaline B. Feinstein prof. of Jewish edn., chair dept., 1980—. Bd. dris. Jewish Edn. Assembly, N.Y.C., 1965-70, Akiba, Merion, Pa., 1975—, Beth Hillel-Beth El, Wynnewood, Pa., 1984-88, Coun. for Jewish Edn., N.Y.C., 1970-74; vis. lectr. Hebrew U., 1986-89, tutor, 1988-89, vis. rschr., 1985; vis. professorial lectr. Am. U.-George Washington U.; vis. prof. Jewish Theol. Sem. Am.; vis. instr. Coll. of Jewish Studies, Cleve., 1965-69; cons. United Synagogue Dept. Edn., 1980—, Herzlia United Schs., Cape Town, 1989—; mem. ethical adv. com. Jewish Family and Children's Svc., Phila.; vis. prof. Balt. Hebrew U., 1998-2000, U. Judaism, 1998-, Jewish Theol. Sem., 1998,. Co-author texts: Judaism, 1979, Jewish Education, 1991, also curriculum materials; contbr. articles to religious publs. Mem. Soviet Jewry com. Phila Jewish Community Rels. Coun.; bd. dirs. Akiba Hebrew Acad., 1992—. Recipient Aaron Zacks award Am. Assn. for Jewish Edn., 1959, Behrman House award for lifetime achievement Jewish Educators Assembly, 1995, Ateret Kavod award United Synagogue. Mem. ASCD, Coalition for Jewish Edn., Assn. for Jewish Studies, Assn. Instns. of Higher Learning in Jewish (past pres.), Phi Delta Kappa. Home: 346 E Lancaster Ave Apt 102 Wynnewood PA 19096-2221 E-mail: wachscover@home.com., swachs@gratz.edu. *"Happiness consists of the fulfillment of the need to be needed." (Abraham Joshua Heschel). Teaching can make a person happy because a teacher is needed.*

WACHSMAN, HARVEY FREDERICK, lawyer, neurosurgeon; b. Bklyn., June 13, 1936; s. Ben and Mollie (Kugel) W.; m. Kathryn M. D'Agostino, Jan. 31, 1976; children: Dara Nicole, David Winston, Jacqueline Victoria, Lauren Elizabeth, Derek Charles, Ashley Max, Marea Lane, Melissa Roseanne. BA, Tulane U., 1958; MD, Chgo. Med. Sch., 1962; JD, Bklyn. Law Sch., 1976. Bar: Conn. 1976, N.Y. 1977, Fla. 1977, D.C. 1978, U.S. Supreme Ct. 1980, Pa. 1984, Md. 1986, Tex. 1987, cert.: Am. Bd. Legal Medicine, Am. Bd. Profl.

Liabiloty Attys.; diplomate Nat. Bd. Med. Examiners. Intern surgery Kings County Hosp Ctr, Bklyn., 1962-63; resident in surgery Kingsbrook Med. Ctr., Bklyn., 1964-65; resident in neurol. surgery Emory U. Hosp., Atlanta, 1965-69; practice medicine specializing in neurosurgery Bridgeport, Conn., 1972-74; sr. ptnr. Law Offices of Harvey F. Wachsman, MD, JD, LLP, Great Neck, NY, 2001—; of counsel firm Queller, Fisher, Dienst, Serrins, Washor & Kool, LLP, N.Y.C., of counsel. Trustee SUNY, chmn. health sci. and hosp. com.; pres., CEO Found. Excellence & Ethics in Medicine. Author: American Law of Medical Malpractice, Vol. I, 1980, 2d edit., 1992, American Law of Medical Malpractice, Vol. II, 1981, 2d edit., 1993, American Law of Medical Malpractice, Vol. III, 1982, 2d edit., 1994, Cumulative Supplement to American Law of Medical Malpractice, 1981, 82, 83, 84, 85, American Law of Medical Malpractice, 2d edit., Vols. I, II and II, Lethal Medicine, 1993; mem. editl. bd. Legal Aspects of Med. Practice, 1978-82. Trustee SUNY, chmn. health sci. and hosp. com. Fellow: Assn. Trial Lawyers Am., Royal Soc. Medicine (London), Royal Soc. Arts (London), Am. Coll. Legal Medicine (mem. bd. govs. 1986, chmn. edn. com. 1983—, chmn. 1985, chmn. nat. meeting New Orleans 1988, nat. meeting, bd. dirs. ACLM Found.), Royal Soc. Medicine; mem.: ABA, Nassau-Suffolk Trial Lawyers Assn., Fairfield County Med. Soc., Nassau County Bar Assn., Pa. Trial Lawyers Assn., Tex. Trial Lawyers Assn., Md. Trial Lawyers Assn., Fla. Acad. Trial Lawyers, Conn. Trial Lawyers Assn., N.Y. Trial Lawyers Assn., N.Y. Acad. Scis., D.C. Bar Assn., Fla. Bar Assn., Conn. Bar Assn., N.Y. Bar Assn., Congress Neurol. Surgeons, Cosmos (Washington), Cosmos Club (Washington). also: 233 Broadway New York NY 10000 E-mail: hwachsman@quellerfisher.com. *In my pursuit of knowledge and excellence in the fields of neurosurgery and the law, I have found that arming oneself with the power of knowledge is truly the key to helping others. Let one's goal in life be to help others, and he shall always find fulfillment, challenge and hope.*

WACHTEL, ALBERT, writer, educator; b. N.Y.C., Dec. 20, 1939; s. Jacob and Sarah Rose (Kaplansky) W.; m. Sydelle Farber, Mar. 9, 1958; children: Sally Rose, Seth Laurence, Stephanie Allyson, Synthia Laura, Jonathan Benjamin, Jessica Eden, Jacob Ethan. BA, CUNY, 1960; PhD, SUNY, Buffalo, 1968. Instr. SUNY, Buffalo, 1963-66, asst. to dean, 1966-68; asst. prof. U. Calif., Santa Barbara, 1968-74; prof. English, creative writing Pitzer Coll., The Claremont (Calif.) Colls., 1974—. Playwright: Paying the Piper, 1968, Prince Hal, 1995; co-editor Modernism: Challenges and Perspectives, 1986; author: The Cracked Looking Glass: James Joyce and the Nightmare of History, 1992; contbr. stories, creative essays to lit. jours., newspapers, and mags. NDEA fellow, 1960-63, fellow Creative Arts Inst., U. Calif., Berkeley, 1970, NEH Summer Inst., Dartmouth Coll., 1987; Danforth Found. assoc., 1970, NEH Seminar, Cornell U., 1998. Jewish. Office: Pitzer Coll Claremont Colls Claremont CA 91711-6101 Office Phone: 909-607-3641. E-mail: awachtel@pitzer.edu.

WACHTEL, HOWARD K. mathematician, educator; BA, Washington U., St. Louis, 1979; MA, U. Wis., 1981; ArtsD, U. Ill., Chgo., 1994. Asst. prof. math. York Coll. CUNY, Jamaica, 1998—2001, Del. Valley Coll., Doylestown, Pa., 2001—03; assoc. prof. math. Goldey-Beacon Coll., Wilmington, Del., 2003—. Contbr. articles to profl. jours., chpts. to books. Judge Bucks County Sci. Fair, 2002, L.I. Math. Fair, 2000. Grantee Rsch. grantee, Rsch. Found. of PSC-CUNY, 2001; scholar Chancellor's Hon. scholar, Washington U., 1975, Nat. Merit scholar, Nat. Merit Scholarship Found., 1975. Mem.: Nat. Coun. of Tchrs. of Math., Math. Assn. of Am., Am. Math. Soc., Am. Mensa, Phi Beta Kappa. Avocations: chess, shogi, folk dancing, classical music. Office: Goldey-Beacon Coll 4701 Limestone Rd Wilmington DE 19808 Home: 10 Colony Blvd Apt 509 Wilmington DE 19802-1457 Personal E-mail: quadratic@juno.com.

WACHTEL, JOHN STEVEN, obstetrician, gynecologist; b. Chgo., Oct. 18, 1950; s. Hans and Lillian (Kriloff) W.; m. Mary Louise Lee, June 24, 1973; children: Hanna, Josh, Leah, Noah. BS, Stanford (Calif.) U., 1972; MD, U. Calif., San Diego, 1976. Diplomate Am. Bd. Ob-Gyn. Intern U. Calif. San Diego, La Jolla, 1976-77; resident in ob-gyn. Stanford U., 1977-80, clin. prof.; obstetrician Stanford U. Hosp., 1980—. Mem. AMA, Am. Coll. Ob-Gyn., Calif. Med. Assn., San Mateo County Med. Soc., Santa Clara County Med. Soc. Office: Menlo Med Clinic 1300 Crane St Menlo Park CA 94025-4283

WACHTEL, NORMAN JAY, lawyer; b. N.Y.C., June 1, 1941; s. A. Allen and Lillian (Rolnik) W.; m. C. Robin Fixler, June 12, 1969; children: Jonathan, Charles. AB, U. Pa., 1963, LLB, 1966; LLM, Boston U., 1967. Bar: N.Y. 1967. Assoc. Demov, Morris & Hammerling, N.Y.C., 1968-78, ptnr., 1978-87, Rogers & Wells, N.Y.C., 1987-96, of counsel, 1996—2003, Clifford Chance US LLP, N.Y.C., 2003—. Bd. advisors 1st Am. Title Ins. Co. N.Y., 1982—. Author: (chpt.) Real Estate Titles, 1984. Office: Clifford Chance US LLP 200 Park Ave Ste 5200 New York NY 10166-0005 Personal E-mail: dex1125@aol.com. Business E-Mail: norman.wachtel@cliffordchance.com.

WACHTELL, ESTHER, non-profit management executive, consultant; b. June 30; m. Thomas Wachtell, Jan. 27; children: Roger Bruce, Wendy Anne, Peter James. BA in Phil., Conn. Coll.; MA in Literature, Cornell U. Pres. Music Ctr. of Los Angeles County; founder, pres. The Wachtell Group, TWG, Inc. Lectr. UCLA Grad. Sch. of Mgmt. Bd. visitors George L. Graziadio Sch. of Bus. Pepperdine U.; bd. dirs. The Ventura County Mus. of History and Art; chair U. So. Calif Ctr. Philanthropy and Pub. Policy; bd. dirs. Children's Hosp. L.A. Mem.: Regency Club (bd. dirs.). Fax: 805-649-3303.

WACHTLER, SOL, law educator, retired judge, arbitration corporation executive, writer; b. N.Y.C., Apr. 29, 1930; s. Philip Henry and Fay (Sobel) W.; m. Joan Wolosoff, Feb. 23, 1952; children: Lauren Jane, Marjorie Dru, Alison Toni, Philip Henry. BA, Washington and Lee U., 1951, LLB, 1952, postgrad., 1980, LLD (hon.), 1981, New Eng. Sch. Law, 1978, Bklyn. Law Sch., 1978, Hofstra U., 1980, SUNY, 1981, Syracuse U., Dowling Coll., 1990, Thomas M. Cooley Law Sch., 1990, New. Eng. Law Sch.; LHD (hon.), LIU, Coll. of St. Rose. Bar: N.Y. 1956. Justice N.Y. State Supreme Ct., 1968-72; judge N.Y. State Ct. Appeals, Albany, 1972-84; chief judge State of N.Y., Albany, 1985-93; prof. law Touro Law Sch., 1997—. Guest lectr. Bklyn. Law Sch., Hofstra Law Sch., Yale U. Sch. Law, Albany Law Sch., St. John's Law Sch., 1968-77, USIA, Munich, Germany, 1973, Stuttgart, Germany, 1977, U. Leyden, Amsterdam, Stockholm, 1988, Madrid, 1989; chmn. NY State Fair Trial/Free Press Conf., NY State Commn. on Bicentennial of US Constitution.; bd. dirs. Confs. Chief Justices; trustee Nat Jud. Coll. Author: After the Madness, 1997, Blood Brothers, 2003; critic-at-large New Yorker mag., 1996; contbr. articles to legal jours. Councilman Town of North Hempstead, N.Y., 1963-65, chief exec., 1965-67; mem. Nassau County Bd. Suprs., 1965-67, chmn. com. pub. safety, 1965-67; trustee L.I. Jewish-Hillside Med. Ctr., 1970-98, L.I. U.; exec. com. North Shore L.I. Jewish Health Sys., 1998—; bd. overseers Nelson A. Rockefeller Inst. Govt.; dist. chmn. Boy Scouts Am., 1968-69; trustee Cerebral Palsy Assn., Assn. for Help of Retarded Children, 1966-67. Mem. Am. Law Inst., Assn. N.Y. State Supreme Ct. Justices, ABA, N.Y. State Bar Assn., Nassau County Bar Assn., Order of Coif, Phi Delta Phi. Jewish. Home: 10 Stonehill Dr N Manhasset NY 11030-4438 E-mail: SWCADRE@aol.com. *As a people, we are fond of the observation that ours is a nation of laws and not of men. It too, like the words of our great laws, seems to lend security, a sense of certainty, and a predictability to the paths we travel. In the law particularly, the thought that past generations have separated right from wrong and good from evil can be comforting. Yet, here again, if we will just scratch the surface, we will find that the greatest responsibility for our national welfare does not rest with statutes carved in stone but with the principles, conscience, and morality of the individuals who constitute this generation.*

WACHTMANN, LYNN R. state legislator; m. Trudy Blue; children: Cory, Aaron. Grad., Four County Joint Vocat. Sch. Owner, pres. Maumee Valley Bottlers, Inc., Napoleon, Ohio; ptnr. Culligan Water Conditioning; former councilman City of Napoleon; mem. Ho. of Reps., Ohio, 1985—98, Ohio Senate from 1st dist., Columbus, 1999—, chmn. health, human svcs. and aging com., mem. energy, natural resources, environment, highways and transp., ins., commerce and labor coms. Vol. fundraiser Crisis Pregnancy Ctrs. of N.W. Ohio, Bryan; vol. Orphan Grain Train; mem. Rep. Ctrl. Com.; Sunday sch. tchr., usher St. Paul Luth. Ch.; bd. dirs. Ohio Water Quality Assn. Named Nat. Legislator of Yr., Am. Legis. Exch. Coun., 1994, State Legislator of Yr., Nat. Retail Fedn., 1996, Legislator of Yr., Am. Legion; recipient Bobcat Legis. award, 1993, Watchdog of the Treasury award, United Conservatives of Ohio, Oustanding Freshman Legislator of Yr. award, 2000, Grad. Wall of Fame award, Four County Joint Vocat. Sch., 1997, Legislator of Yr. Defender of Life award, Ohio Right to Life, 1997, Conservation Legis. award, League of Ohio Sportsmen Nat. Wildlife Fedn., 1997, Guardian of Small Bus. award, Nat. Fedn. Ind. Bus., 1998. Mem.: NRA, Ohio Twp. Assn., Nat. Assn. Sportsman Legislators, Am. Legis. Exch. Coun. (state chmn.), Ohio Right to Life Soc., Gideon's Internat., Ohio Farm Bur., Pheasants Forever, Ducks Unlimited. Republican. Office: Rm # 040 Senate Bldg Columbus OH 43215

WACHTMEISTER, COUNT WILHELM H. F. diplomat; b. Vanas, Sweden, Apr. 29, 1923; s. Gustaf and Margaretha (Trolle) W.; m. Ulla Leuhusen, 1947; children: Anna, Erik. LLD, U. Stockholm, Sweden, 1946. Attache Swedish Ministry for Fgn. Affairs, 1946-47; attache Swedish Embassy, Vienna, Madrid and Lisbon, 1947-50; 2d sec. Swedish Ministry Fgn. Affairs, Stockholm, Sweden, 1950-55; 1st sec. Swedish Embassy, Moscow, 1955-58; personal asst. to UN Sec. Gen., 1958-61; head UN sect. Fgn. Ministry, Stockholm, 1962-65, dep. under-sec. polit. affairs, 1965-66; ambassador to Algeria Swedish Embassy, 1966-67; under-sec. for polit. affairs Swedish Ministry Fgn. Affairs, Stockholm, 1968-74; Swedish ambassador to U.S. Swedish Embassy, Washington, 1974-89; dean diplomatic corps in Washington, 1986-89. Sr. advisor to chmn. AB Volvo, 1989-94. Mem. Soc. Cin. (France), Nya Sällskapet, Swedish-Am. C. of C. (chmn. 1993-95), Met. Club of Washington, Fed. City Club, Washington, Sällskapet, Stockholm. Avocation: tennis. Address: Karlavagen 59A SE 11449 Stockholm Sweden Fax: 46854569733.

WACKER, SUSAN REGINA, creative design director; b. Red Bank, NJ, Apr. 29, 1954; d. Durward Richard and Margaret Rose (Williams) W., m. Edward W. Donle. BFA, Pratt Inst., 1978, cert. computer graphics/electronic pub., 2001. Asst. art dir. Lesley-Hille Inc., NYC, 1975-79; art dir. Kasica, Lefton, Brown, Inc., NYC, 1979-80, Marinelli & Hnath Assoc., Inc., NYC, 1980-82; sr. design dir. Elizabeth Arden Co., NYC, 1982-99; art dir. L'Oreal Retail Divsn., NYC, 2000—02; design cons. SRW Design, Pittsfield, Vt., 2002—. Exhibited at The Nature of Diamonds, Mus. Natural History, NYC, 1997-98; patentee in field. Recipient (4) DESI awards, 1980, ANDY award, 1980, Fragrance Found. award, 1988, 91, 92, Silver award NJ Packaging Execs. Club, 1990, ADDY Excellence citation, 1991, Edison Best New Products Gold Medal award, 1991, (2) Gold awards Nat. Paperbox & Packaging Assn., 1992, (2) Gold awards, 1994, Silver award Paperboard Packaging Coun., 1993, Excellence award, 1993, Silver Excellence award Nat. Paperbox & Packaging Assn., 1993, (10) Silver Excellence awards, 1994, Mobius 1st Place Statuette award, 1995, Gold award Nat. Paperboard Coun., 1995, Prix Francois 1st de L'Emballage de Luxe, 1995, OMA Gold award, 1995, Oscar de L'Emballage Prestige à Lyon, 1995, Mobius award First Place Statuette for Elizabeth Taylor's Black Pearls perfume product line/package design, 1996, OMA Gold award for Elizabeth Arden's 5th Avenue tester display, 1996, OMA Bronze award for Elizabeth Taylor's Black Pearls tester display, 1996, Lagerfeld, Jako Mdsg., 1998, CPC "Package of the Month" (October), Elizabeth Arden's 5th Avenue fragrance line, 1996, Natl. Paperboard Packaging Conc. award, 1996, OMA Bronze award Lagerfeld JAKO Mdsg. Program, 1998. Mem. Internat. Perfume Bottle Assn., Cosmetic Exec. Women Found., Fashion Group Internat.(publ. com.), Annette Green Mus. at Fragrance Found. Avocations: skiing, tennis, horseback riding, photography. Office: SRW Design 19 Schoolhouse Dr PO Box 567 Pittsfield VT 05762 E-mail: srwacker@aol.com., srwdesign@comcast.net.

WACKER, WARREN ERNEST CLYDE, physician, educator; b. Bklyn., Feb. 29, 1924; s. John Frederick and Kitty Dora (Morrissey) W.; m. Ann Romeyn MacMillan, May 22, 1948; children: Margaret Morrissey, John Frederick. Student, Georgetown U., 1946—47; MD, George Washington U., 1951; MA (hon.), Harvard U., 1968. Intern George Washington U. Hosp., 1951-52, resident in internal medicine, 1952-53; resident Peter Bent Brigham Hosp., Boston, 1953-55; Nat. Found. Infantile Paralysis fellow, 1955-57; investigator Howard Hughes Med. Inst., Boston, 1957-68; from faculty to prof. hygiene Harvard U., Cambridge, Mass., 1955-71, assoc. prof. medicine, 1968—71, 1971—89, Henry K. Oliver prof. hygiene emeritus, 1995, acting master Mather House, 1974-75, acting master Kirkland House, 1975-76, master Cabot House, 1978-84; sr. med. cons. Risk Mgmt. Found., Cambridge, 1992—. Dir. health svcs. Harvard U., Cambridge, 1971-89; vis. scholar St. Mary's Hosp. Med. Sch., 1964; vis. prof. U. Tel Aviv, 1987; chmn. bd. Applied Mgmt. Sys., Burlington, Mass., 1982-97, Millipore Corp., Bedford, Mass., 1971-94. Author: Magnesium and Man, 1981; sec., editl. adv. bd. Biochemistry, 1962-76; assoc. editor Magnesium; mem. editl. bd. Toxiogical and Environ. Chemistry, 1989-; contbr. articles to med. and sci. jours. Vestryman St. Paul's Episc. Ch., Brookline, Mass., 1965-68, 76-79, 91-94; bd. dirs. Harvard Cmty. Health Plan, Boston, 1973-84, mem. fin. com., 1984-86, mem. corp., 1986-96; bd. dirs. Bishop Rhinelander Found., Cambridge, 1973-76, 78-84, Controlled Risk Ins. Co., 1976-78; pres. bd. overseers Peter Bent Brigham Hosp., Boston, 1979-84; trustee Brigham and Women's Hosp., Boston, 1984-89, Risk Mgmt. Found., 1979-92; mem. mgmt. bd. MIT, 1985-95; mem. corp. Mt. Auburn Hosp., Cambridge, 1986—; mem. adv. bd. hospitality program Episc. Diocese Mass., 1989-95. 1st lt. USAAF, 1942-45. Decorated Air medal, D.F.C., Liberation medal, Greece; named Disting. Alumnus, George Washington U., 1963; recipient Cert. of Merit, Soc. Magnesium Rsch., 1985. Mem. AMA, Am. Chem. Soc., Am. Soc. Biol. Chemistry, Am. Soc. Clin. Investigation, Mass. Med. Soc., ACP, Am. Coll. Health Assn. (pres. 1981, Boynton award 1986), Biochemistry Soc. (London), Am. Coll. Nutrition, Harvard Club (Boston), Sigma Xi, Alpha Omega Alpha. Home: 91 Glen Rd Brookline MA 02445-7764 Office: Risk Mgmt Found 101 Main St Cambridge MA 02142-1519 Office Phone: 617-679-1216. Business E-Mail: wwacker@rmf.harvard.edu.

WACKERBAUER, RENATE ANNA, physicist; b. Geisenhausen, Bavaria, Germany, Sept. 23, 1963; came to U.S., 1998; d. Rudolf and Anna Wackerbauer. Diploma in physics, Tech. U. Munich, 1990, vordiploma in physics, 1985; PhD in Physics (Nonlinear Dynamics), Ludwig-Maximilian U., Munich, 1995. Rsch. scientist Max-Planck-Inst. Extraterrestrial Physics, Munich, 1990-96, Max-Planck Inst. Complex Systems, Dresden, Germany, 1996-98, W.Va. U., Morgantown, 1998-2001; asst. prof. physics U. Alaska, Fairbanks, 2001—. Presenter 5th United European Gastroenterology Week, Paris, 1996; poster presenter internat. confs.; session chair Chaos Conf., Munich, 1993; conf. organizer Physics Session, Nat. Summer Sch. on Complex Systems, Tutzing, Germany, 1995; invited spkr. numerous instns., 1988—. Contbr. articles to profl. jours., including Chaos, Phys. Rev. Letters, Phys. Rev. E, Gastroenterology, Gut, others; contbr. chpts. to books. Fellow Max-Planck Soc., 1994. Mem. Am. Phys. Soc. (divsn. biol. physics, group statis. and nonlinear physics), German Phys. Soc. (divsn. condensed matter physics). Achievements include research in modeling of biological systems: neuron models, plasmodium; spatiotemporal complexity in reaction-diffusion systems, population dynamics; stochastic dynamical systems with few/many degrees of freedom: stabilization and synchronization phenomena, noisy neuronal assemblies, small-world topology; nonlinear time-series/image analysis; applications to natural systems. Office: U Alaska Dept Physics PO Box 755920 Fairbanks AK 99775-5920

WACKER-BRAWLEY, MARGARET, communications executive; b. Dec. 12, 1951; d. Warren Ernest Clyde and Ann Romeyn (MacMillan) W.; m. Richard Warren Brawley, Feb. 26, 1994. BA, Carnegie Mellon U., 1974. Promotion specialist Millipore Corp., Billerica, Mass., 1974-77, dir. comm. Lab. Products divsn., 1981-82, corp. comm. mgr., 1982-88, human resources project mgr., 1989-93, sr. acct. mgr. biosci. divsn., 1993-94, mgr. tech. pubs. and life sci. promotion, lab. & health care products divsn., 1994-95, mgr. mktg. comm., analytical products divsn., 1995—; dir. advt. IVAC divsn. Eli Lilly Co., San Diego, 1977-79, dist. sales mgr. L.A., 1979-80; bus. unit mgr. Sage divsn. Orion Rsch., Cambridge, Mass., 1980-81. Counselor to handicapped individuals in bus. Democrat. Episcopalian. Avocations: computer aided illustration, graphic design and desktop publishing, collage. Home: The Brook House 77 Pond Ave Apt 701C Brookline MA 02445-7114 Office: Millipore Corp 80 Ashby Rd Billerica MA 01821-3405 Business E-Mail: rwbmwb@rcn.com.

WACKERMANN, WILLIAM, publishing executive; married; 3 children. Grad., Villanova U., 1989. Mktg. mgr. Bus. Week; various positions Vanity Fair, corp. mgr., 1995—96; N.Y. advt. mgr. Conde Nast Traveler, 1996—97, advt. mgr., 1997—98, assoc. pub., 1999—2000, House & Garden, 1998—99; v.p. and pub. Details mag., 2000—04, Glamour mag., 2004—. Named Mag. Pub. of Yr., Delaney Report, 2002; recipient Media Mavens award, Advt. Age, 2003. Office: Glamour Mag Conde Nast Bldg 4 Times Sq New York NY 10036-6522*

WACKYM, PHILLIP ASHLEY, surgeon, researcher, otolaryngologist; b. Balt., Dec. 25, 1957; s. Phillip Adeeb and Elsie Jean Wackym; m. Jeremy JoAlice Miller, June 25, 1983; 1 child, Ashton Rhys. BA in Chemistry, Calif. State U., Fullerton, 1980; MD, Vanderbilt U., 1985. Diplomate Am. Bd. Otolaryngology, 1992. Resident in surgery UCLA Med. Ctr., L.A., 1985—86, resident in neurosurgery, 1986—87, resident in head and neck surgery, 1987—91; asst. prof. surgery UCLA Sch. Medicine, L.A., 1991—95; fellow otology, neuro-otology and skull base surgery U. Iowa, Iowa City, 1991—92, vis. asst. prof. otolaryngology, 1991—92; assoc. prof. Mt. Sinai Sch. Medicine, N.Y.C., 1995—98; prof./chmn. dept. otolaryngology and communication scis. Med. Coll. Wisc., Milw., 1998—, chief divsn. otology and neuro-otologic skull base surgery, 1998—. Guest examiner Am. Bd. Otolaryngology, 1994—96, 2002; chief ear svc. Mt. Sinai Med. Ctr., N.Y.C., 1995—98, dir. molecular biology lab., 1995—98, bd. dirs. Assn. Attending Staff, 1995—98; mem. hearing study sect. Ctr. for Sci. Revs., NIH, Bethesda, Md., 1996—2000. Author: (thesis) Laryngoscope, 1996 (Fowler award, 1997); mem. editl. bd. Laryngoscope, 1996—. Recipient Clin. Investigator award, Nat. Inst. Deafness and Other Comm. Disorders/NIH, L.A., 1991—95, First Ind. Rsch. and Transition award, 1995—2000, Baron Rsch. award, Triological Soc., Western Sect., 1990, 1993, Torok award, Am. Neurotolgy Soc., 1993. Fellow: ACS, N.Y. Acad. Sci., Am. Laryngol., Rhinol. & Otologic Soc. (sec. & treas. Middle sect. 2002—); mem.: Am. Acad. Otolaryngology Head and Neck Surgery Found. (chmn. grants and prizes com. 1997—2000, coord. for rsch. 2002—, Honor award 1998), Am. Otologic Soc. Episcopalian. Achievements include: 125 jour. publs., 33 textbook chpts., 1 textbook, 1 videotape, 78 invited presentations, 45 submitted presentations. Office: Dept Otolaryngology Med Coll Wisc 9200 W Wisconsin Ave Milwaukee WI 53226-3522 E-mail: wackym@mcw.edu.

WACZIARG, ROMAIN THOMAS, social sciences educator; b. Geneva, Jan. 6, 1970; s. Francis Marie and Annick Marie (Jeanne) Wacziarg; m. Magali Aline Delmas, July 6, 2001; 1 child, Claire Audrey. BA in econ., pub. policy, Inst. D'Etudes Politiques, France, 1989; MA in econ., U. De Paris-Dauphine, France, 1992, Harvard U., 1996, PhD in econ., 1998. Asst. prof., econ. Stanford U., Calif., 1998—2002; nat. fellow Hoover Inst., Stanford, 2002—03; assoc. prof., econ. Stanford U., 2002—; faculty rsch. fellow Nat. Bur. of Econ. Rsch., Cambridge, Mass., 2002—. Cons. The World Bk., Wash., 1996—97. Contbr. articles various profl. jours., chapters to books various profl. text. Edward Teller Nat. fellow, Hoover Inst., 2002—03. Mem.: Am. Econ. Assn., Econometric Soc. Achievements include invited spkr. to numerous presentations and conf. Avocations: classical music, mountain climbing. Home: 105 Peter Coutts Cir Stanford CA 94305 Office: Stanford Grad Sch of Bus 518 Meml Way Stanford CA 94305 Office Fax: 650-725-7979. E-mail: wacziarg@gsb.stanford.edu.

WADDELL, DOUGLAS HOWARD, family physician; b. Bluff City, TN, May 6, 1943; s. Cecil Howard and France Daisy (Boling) W.; m. Luz Isabel Garza, Jan 2, 1971; children: Amy, Christopher, Brandon. BS in Biology, Chemistry, Carson-Newman Coll., Jefferson City, Tenn., 1965; MD, U. Tenn., 1969. Diplomate Am. Bd. Family Practice. Intern Baylor U. Med. Ctr., Dallas, 1970; physician, owner Launey Med. Clinic, Dallas, 1971-82, Beltline North Med. Clinic, Dallas, 1983-85, Atrium Med. Clinic, Dallas, 1985—. Fellow Am. Acad. Family Physicians; mem. Tex. Med. Assn., Dallas County Med. Soc., Tex. Acad. Family Physicians (bd. dirs. state assn., past sec., treas., v.p., pres. Dallas chpt.), Am. Coll. Occupational and Environ. Medicine. Republican. Baptist. Avocations: gardening, boating, cooking. Home: 10473 Epping Ln Dallas TX 75229-6310 Office: Atrium Med Clinic 14465 Webb Chapel Rd Ste 111 Dallas TX 75234-3600 Office Phone: 972-247-6900.

WADDELL, JOHN COMER, electronics distribution company executive; b. Bridgeport, Conn., Sept. 10, 1937; s. John and Dorothy Margot (Comer) W. BA, Yale U., 1959; MBA, Harvard U., 1965. Assoc. R.W. Pressprich & Co., N.Y.C., 1965-68; ptnr. Glenn, Green & Waddell, N.Y.C., 1968-80; exec. v.p. Arrow Electronics, Inc., Melville, N.Y., 1969-80, chmn. bd., 1980—. Served with U.S. Navy, 1960-63. Office: Arrow Electronics Inc 25 Hub Dr Melville NY 11747-3509

WADDELL, M. KEITH, human resources specialist; From v.p. to vice chmn., CFO, treas. Robert Half Internat. Inc., Menlo Pk., Calif., 1986—93, vice chmn., 1999—, CFO, 1999—, treas., 1999—. Office: Robert Half International Inc 2884 SandHill Rd Menlo Park CA 94025*

WADDELL, WALTER HARVEY, chemist; b. Chgo., Sept. 26, 1947; BS in Chemistry, U. Ill., 1969; PhD in Chemistry, U. Houston, 1973. Rsch. assoc. Columbia U., N.Y., 1973—75; asst. prof. Carnegie-Mellon U., Pitts., 1975—79, assoc. prof., 1979—83; sr. rsch. chemist Goodyear Tire and Rubber, Akron, Ohio, 1983—85, sect. head, 1985—90; sr. scientist PPG Industries, Pitts., 1990—96; mgr. Exxon Mobil Chem., Houston, 1996—. Spkr. in field. Contbr. articles to profl. jours. Mem.: ACS (Sparks-Thomas award 1994, Melvin Mooney award 2003), Am. Soc. Patent Holders. Achievements include patents in field. Office: Exxon Mobil Chemical 5200 Bayway Dr Baytown TX 77520

WADDELL, WILLIAM JOSEPH, pharmacologist, toxicologist; b. Commerce, Ga., Mar. 16, 1929; s. John Daniel and Lillian Marie (Vollrath) W.; m. Grace Carolyn Marlowe, Oct. 19, 1974; children: William Joseph, James Glenn, Martin Christie, Amy Alison. AB in Chemistry, U. N.C., 1951, MD, 1955. Postdoctoral research fellow U. N.C. Sch. Medicine, 1955-58, asst. prof. pharmacology, 1958-62, asso. prof., 1962-72; asso. prof. oral biology U. N.C. Sch. Medicine (Dental Research Center), 1967-69, prof., 1969-72, asso. dir., 1968-72; prof. pharmacology U. Ky. Coll. Medicine, Lexington, 1972-77; prof., chmn. dept. pharmacology and toxicology U. Louisville, 1977-97, emeritus chmn., 1997—, prof. emeritus, 1998—. Centennial Alumni Disting. vis. prof. U. N.C. Sch. Medicine, 1979 Contbr. articles to profl. jours. Fellow Acad. Toxicological Scis.; mem. Am. Soc. for Pharmacology and Exptl. Therapeutics, Am. Physiol. Soc., Am. Teratology Soc., Internat. Soc. for Study Xenobiotics, Soc. for Exptl. Biology and Medicine, Soc. Toxicology, Sigma Xi. Home: 14300 Rose Wycombe Rd Prospect KY 40059-9024 Office: U Louisville Dept Pharmacology Louisville KY 40292-0001 Business E-Mail: bwaddell@louisville.edu.

WADDEN, RICHARD ALBERT, environmental engineer, educator, science administrator, consultant; b. Sioux City, Iowa, Oct. 3, 1936; s. Sylvester Francis and Hermina Lillian (Costello) Wadden; m. Angela Louise Trabert, Aug. 9, 1975; children: Angela Terese, Noah Albert, Nuiko Clare. Student, St. John's U., Collegeville, Minn., 1954-56; BSChemE, Iowa State U., 1959; MSChemE, N.C. State U., 1962; PhD in Chem. and Environ. Engring., Northwestern U., 1972. Registered profl. engr., Ill., cert. indsl. hygienist. Engr. Linde Co., Tonnawanda, NY, 1959-60, Humble Oil Co., Houston, 1962-65; instr. engring. Pahlavi U. Peace Corps, Shiraz, Iran, 1965-67; tech. adviser Ill. Pollution Control Bd., Chgo., 1971-72; asst. dir. Environ. Health Resource Ctr. Ill., Chgo., 1972-74; from asst. prof. to assoc. prof. environ. and occupational health scis. Sch. Pub. Health U. Ill., Chgo., 1972—79, prof., 1979—2003, dir., 1984-86, 88-92, dir. Office Tech. Transfer Ctr. Solid Waste Mgmt. and Rsch., 1987-92, dir. indsl. hygiene and hazardous waste tng. programs Occupl. Safety and Health Ctr., 1987—2002, prof. emeritus, 2003—. Vis. scientist Nat. Inst.

Environ. Studies, Japan, 1978—79, invited scientist, Japan, 1983, Japan, 84, Japan, 88; cons. air pollution control, health implications energy devel., indoor air pollution. Author: (book) Energy Utilization and Environmental Health, 1978; author: (with P. A. Scheff) Indoor Air Pollution, 1983; author: Engineering Design for Control of Workplace Hazards, 1987; contbr. articles to profl. publs. Vis. scholar, Northwestern U., Evanston, Ill., 1997; Sr. Internat. fellow, Fogarty Internat. Ctr.-NIH, 1978—79, 1983, WHO fellow, 1984. Mem.: AIChE, Am. Conf. Govtl. Indsl. Hygienists, Am. Indsl. Hygiene Assn., Air and Waste Mgmt. Assn., Am. Acad. Indsl. Hygiene (diplomate), Am. Acad. Environ. Engrs. (diplomate), Am. Chem. Soc. Address: 816 16th St Wilmette IL 60091

WADDEN, THOMAS ANTHONY, psychologist, educator; b. Richmond, Va., Sept. 3, 1952; s. Thomas Antony Jr. and Mary Lloyd (Cradock) W.; m. Jan Robin Linowitz, Nov. 11, 1984; children: David Joseph, Michael James, Steven Zachary. AB magna cum laude, Brown U., 1975; PhD, U. N.C., 1981; MA (hon.), U. Pa., 1994. Psychology intern Boston VA Med. Ctr., 1980-81; instr. in psychology U. Pa. Sch. Medicine, Phila., 1981-82, asst. prof. psychology, 1982-87, assoc. prof. psychology, 1987-91, prof. psychology, 1994—; prof. psychology, dir. clin. tng. Syracuse (N.Y.) U., 1992-93. Clin. dir. Obesity Rsch. Group, U. Pa., Phila., 1983-91, dir. Weight and Eating Disorders Program, 1994—; dir. Ctr. for Health and Behavior, Syracuse U., 1992-93. Author (with K.D. Brownell): LEARN PRogram for Weight Control, 1998; assoc. editor: Annals of Behavioral Medicine, 1990—93, mem. editl. bd.: Internat. Jour. Eating Disorders, Jour. Cons. and Clin. Psychology, Obesity Rsch.; editor (with T.B. VanItallie): Treatment of the Seriously Obese Patient, 1992; editor: (with A.J. Stunkard) Obesity: Theory and Therapy, 1993, Handbook of Obesity Treatment, 2002; contbr. chapters to books; writer: numerous sci. papers. Recipient Nat. Rsch. Svc. award NIMH, 1983-85, Rsch. Scientist Devel. award, 1987-91, 94-2000, Midcareer Investigator award in patient oriented rsch., 2003—. Mem. APA, Soc. Behavioral Medicine (bd. dir. 1987-90), Assn. for Advancement of Behavior Therapy (New Rschr. award 1986), Acad. Behavioral Medicine, No. Am. Assn. for the Study of Obesity (v.p. 2003-04), Germantown Cricket Club, Cosmos Club, Phi Beta Kappa, Sigma Xi. Democrat. Avocations: tennis, squash, symphonic music, guitar. Home: 433 Bolsover Rd Wynnewood PA 19096-1301 Office: U Pa Ste 3029 3535 Market St Philadelphia PA 19104-2641 Business E-Mail: wadden@mail.med.upenn.edu.

WADDINGTON, RAYMOND BRUCE, JR., English language educator; b. Santa Barbara, Calif., Sept. 27, 1935; s. Raymond Bruce and Marjorie Gladys (Waddell) W.; m. Linda Gayle Jones, Sept. 7, 1957 (div.); children: Raymond Bruce, Edward Jackson; m. Kathleen Martha Ward, Oct. 11, 1985. BA, Stanford U., 1957; PhD, Rice U., 1963; postdoctoral (Univ. fellow in Humanities), Johns Hopkins U., 1965-66. Instr. English U. Houston, 1961-62; instr. U. Kans., 1962-63, asst. prof., 1963-65; asst. prof. English lit. U. Wis., Madison, 1966-68, assoc. prof., 1968-74, prof., 1974-82; prof. English lit. U. Calif., Davis, 1982—. Author: The Mind's Empire, 1974, Aretino's Satyr, 2004; co-editor: The Rhetoric of Renaissance Poetry, 1974, The Age of Milton, 1980, The Expulsion of the Jews, 1994; mem. editl. bd. The Medal, 1991, Renaissance Quar., 2000; sr. editor: Sixteenth Century Jour.; editor: Praeger Series on the Early Modern World. Huntington Library fellow, 1967, 75; Inst. Research in Humanities fellow, 1971-72; Guggenheim fellow, 1972-73; NEH fellow, 1977, 83; Newberry Library fellow, 1978; Am. Philos. Soc. grantee, 1965. Mem. Renaissance Soc. Am., Milton Soc. Am., Am. Numismatic Soc., 16th Century Studies Conf. (pres. 1985), Brit. Art Medal Soc., Logos Club. Home: 39 Pershing Ave Woodland CA 95695-2845 Office: U Calif Dept English Davis CA 95616 E-mail: rbwaddington@ucdavis.edu.

WADDLE, JOHN FREDERICK, former retail chain executive; b. Somerset, Ky., July 1, 1927; s. Lewis Everett and Anna Hail (Prather) W.; m. Catherine Joan Osborn, June 3, 1977; children: Lewis Victor, Joan Catherine, John Frederick. BS, U. Ky., 1949; MS, NYU, 1952. With Sears, Roebuck and Co., Chgo., 1949-85, nat. mgr. toys, 1969-72, asst. to sr. exec. v.p. merchandising, 1972-76, group nat. merchandising mgr., 1977-78, v.p. children's apparel, 1978-82; mng. dir., exec. v.p. Sears World Trade, Inc., Chgo., 1982-85. Served with USN, 1945-46. Republican. Presbyterian. E-mail: cathwaddle@aol.com.

WADDOCK, SANDRA, finance educator; d. John Joseph and Rita Voisin Waddock; 1 child, Benjamin Waddock Wiegner. BA, Northeastern U., Boston, 1969; MA, Boston Coll., Chestnut Hill, 1973; MBA, Boston U., 1979—79, DBA, 1985. Prof. mgmt. Boston Coll., Chestnut Hill, 1986—. Editor: Jour. of Corp. Citizenship. Fellow: Ctr. for Corp. Citizenship at Boston Coll. Avocation: folk music. Office: Boston Coll Carroll School of Mgmt Chestnut Hill MA 02467 E-mail: waddock@bc.edu.

WADDY, CALISTA ANNE, music educator, musician; b. Warner Robins, Ga., Nov. 14, 1975; d. Richard Craig and Annelle Still Moser; m. Ben Lee Waddy, Nov. 4, 2000. B Music Therapy, Fla. State U., 1999. Music therapist Under Mus. Constrn., Alphonetta, Ga., 1999—2001; self-employed harpist, therapist Atlanta Harpist, Covington, Ga., 2001—03, Macon (Ga.) Harpist, 2003—; prof. harp Mercer U., Macon, 2003—. Mem. nat. songbook com. Alpha Chi Omega, 1996; music therapist Focus, Atlanta, 2000—03. Named Mrs. Covington Internat., 2003. Mem.: Nat. String Tchrs. Assn., Am. Harp Soc., Nat. Music Tchrs. Assn. Republican. Baptist. Avocations: computers, piano. Home: 113 Lotus Point Dr Macon GA 31220 Office: Macon Harpist 113 Lotus Point Dr Macon GA 31220 E-mail: Maconharpist@yahoo.com.

WADDY, LAWRENCE HEBER, religious writer; b. Sydney, Australia, Oct. 5, 1914; came to U.S., 1963; s. Percival Stacy and Etheldred (Spittal) W.; m. Laurie Hancock, July 10, 1972. BA, Oxford (Eng.) U., 1937, MA, 1945. Asst. master Winchester Coll. Eng., 1938-42; headmaster Tonbridge Sch., Eng., 1949-62; edn. officer BBC, Eng., 1962-63; chaplain The Bishop's Sch., La Jolla, Calif., 1963-67; lectr. in Greek and Latin lit. U. Calif., San Diego, 1969-80; vicar Ch. of Good Samaritan, University City, Calif., 1970-74; hon. asst. St. James By The Sea Episcopal Ch., La Jolla, 1975—. Author: Pax Romana & World Peace, 1950, The Bible as Drama, 1975, Drama in Worship, 1978, Symphony, 1976, A Parish By the Sea, 1988, Shakespeare Remembers, 1994, First Bible Stories, 1994, Florence Nightingale, 1996. Chaplain, British Navy, 1942-46. Recipient Drama 1st prize BBC, 1964. Republican. Episcopalian. Home: 5910 Camino De La Costa La Jolla CA 92037-6550 E-mail: lawrencewaddy@yahoo.com.

WADDY, PATRICIA A. architectural history educator; b. Cannelton, Ind., July 29, 1941; d. Luther and Gertrude Viola (Brandyberry) W. BA, Rice U., 1963; MA, Tulane U., 1965; PhD, NYU, 1973. Vis. lectr. Carnegie-Mellon U., Pitts., 1970-71; asst. prof., 1971-77; assoc. prof. archtl. history Syracuse U., NY, 1977-91, prof., 1991—2002, Disting. prof. architecture, 2002—. Vis. lectr. Cornell U., Ithaca, N.Y., 1977, vis. assoc. prof., 1980. Author: Seventeenth-Century Roman Palaces: Use and The Art of the Plan, 1990 (Alice Davis Hitchcock award 1992); co-author: (with D. DiCastro and A.M. Pedrocchi) Il Palazzo Pallavicini Rospigliosi e la Galleria Pallavicini, 2000; editor Nicodemus Tessin the Younger, Traicté dela decoration interieure (1717), 2002. Fulbright grantee, Rome, 1968-69; fellow Am. Acad. in Rome, 1970, Nat. Humanities Ctr., 1984-85, Samuel H. Kress sr. fellow Nat. Gallery Art, 1994-95, NEH fellow, 1998-99, Guggenheim fellow, 1999-00, Am. Coun. Learned Soc. fellow, 1978. Mem. Soc. Archtl. Historians (book rev. editor Jour. 1985-88, editor 1990-93, 2d v.p. 1993-94, 1st v.p. 1994-96, pres. 1996-98), Coll. Art Assn., Renaissance Soc. Am. Office: Syracuse U Sch Architecture Syracuse NY 13244-1250 E-mail: pwaddy@syr.edu.

WADE, BEN FRANK, college administrator; b. Roanoke, Va., July 20, 1935; s. Frank Hart and Clyde Temple (Weaver) W.; m. Janice Marie Wine, June 14, 1958; children— Andrea Marie, Laurel Faye BA, Bridgewater Coll., 1957; MDiv cum laude, United Theol. Sem., 1960; STM, Boston U., 1961; MS, Columbia U., 1966; PhD, Hartford Sem. Found., 1966. Prof. Shenandoah Coll., Winchester, Va., 1963-65, United Theol. Sem., Dayton, Ohio, 1965-69, James Madison U., Harrisonburg, Va., 1969-71; acad. dean Brevard Coll., N.C., 1971-73, Fla. So. Coll., Lakeland, Fla., 1973-77; pres. Westmar Coll., LeMars, Iowa, 1977-79; provost Bridgewater Coll., Va., 1979-85; v.p., acad. dean Fla. So. Coll., Lakeland, Fla., 1985-96, v.p., dean emeritus, 1996—. Mem., chmn. accreditation visit teams So. Assn. Colls. and Schs., State Council Higher Edn. Va.; vis. lectr., cons. Divsn. chmn. YMCA Capital Funds Campaign, Lakeland, Fla., 1975; ret. mem. Fla. Annual Conf., United Meth. Ch. Named Disting. Alumnus, Bridgewater Coll., 1994, Hon. Alumnus, Fla. So. Coll., 1996; Hartzler fellow Hartford Sem. Found., 1961-62, 62-63. Mem. Theta Chi Beta, Phi Eta Sigma, Omicron Delta Kappa. Avocations: breadmaking, saddle horses, music. Home: 3733 Highland Fairways Blvd Lakeland FL 33810-5765 Home (Summer): 387 Mt Crawford Ave Bridgewater VA 22812

WADE, BILL, airport executive; Gen. mgr. Met. Oakland (Calif.) Internat. Airport, 1994—. Office: Met Oakland Intl Airport 1 Airport Dr Box 45 Oakland CA 94621-1430

WADE, DANIEL M. recreational facility executive, hotel executive; With Circus Circus, Las Vegas, Nev., Holiday Casino, Las Vegas, The Maxim, Las Vegas, Aladdin Hotel, Las Vegas; v.p. ops. Harrah's, Las Vegas; pres., gen. mgr. MGM Marina Hotel, Las Vegas; from various sr. level positions to vice chmn. MGM Mirage MGM Grand Hotel, Inc., Las Vegas, 1990—2001, vice chmn. MGM Mirage, 2001—. Office: MGM Mirage 3600 Las Vegas Blvd South Las Vegas NV 89109

WADE, DAVID STUART, surgeon; b. Guthrie, Okla., July 21, 1955; MD, Uniformed Svcs. U. Health Sci., 1981. Diplomate Am. Bd. Surgery. Intern Naval Hosp., Bethesda, Md., 1981, resident in gen. surgery Portsmouth, 1982-86; fellow in surg. oncology Roswell Park Meml. Inst., Buffalo, 1987-89; from head dept. surgery to dir. surg. svc. Naval Hosp., Oakland, Calif., 1992-95; head dept. surgery Nat. Naval Med. Ctr., Bethesda, 1996, chief clin. staff, 1997-99, dep. comdr., 1999-2000; dep. for edn., tng. and pers. Bur. of Medicine, 2000-01; comdg. officer Naval Sch. Health Scis., Bethesda, 2001—02; fleet surgeon Cmdr. U.S. Naval Forces, Europe, 2002—. E-mail: davidswade2002@yahoo.com.

WADE, DWYANE, professional basketball player; b. Chicago, Jan. 17, 1982; m. Siohvaughn Wade; 1 child. Student, Marquette U. Player Miami Heat, 2003—. Mem. U.S. Olympic Basketball Team, Athens, 2004. Named to NBA All-Rookie First team, 2004. Office: c/o Miami Heat American Airlines Arena 601 Biscayne Blvd Miami FL 33132*

WADE, ED, professional sports team executive; From pub. rels. intern to v.p., gen. mgr. Phila. (Pa.) Phillies, 1977—98, v.p., 1998—, gen. mgr., 1998—; pub. rels. asst. Houston (Tex.) Astros, 1977—79, pub. rels. dir., 1979—81, Pitts. (Pa.) Pirates, 1981—86. Mailing: 3501 S Broad St Philadelphia PA 19148*

WADE, EDWIN LEE, author, lawyer; b. Yonkers, N.Y., Jan. 26, 1932; s. James and Helen Pierce (Kinne) W.; m. Nancy Lou Sells, Mar. 23, 1957; children: James Lee, Jeffrey K. BS, Columbia U., 1954; MA, U. Chgo., 1956; JD, Georgetown U., 1965. Bar: Ill. 1965. Fgn. svc. officer U.S. Dept. State, 1956-57; mktg. analyst Chrysler Internat., S.A., Switzerland, 1957-61; intelligence officer CIA, 1961-63; industry analyst U.S. Internat. Trade Commn., 1963-65; gen. atty. Universal Oil Products Co., Des Plaines, Ill., 1965-72; atty. Amsted Industries, Inc., Chgo., 1972-73; chief counsel dept. gen. svcs. State of Ill., Springfield, 1973-75; sr. atty. U.S. Gypsum Co., Chgo., 1975-84; gen. atty. USG Corp., 1985, corp. counsel, 1986, asst. gen. counsel, 1987, corp. sec., 1987-90, corp. sec., asst. gen. counsel, 1990-93; prin. Edwin L. Wade, 1993-95; instr. Roosevelt U., Chgo., 1995-96. Author: (books) Constitution 2000: A Federalist Proposal for the New Century, 2000, Talking Sense at Century's End: A Barbarous Time...Now What?, 2000; editor: Let's Talk Sense, A Pub. Affairs Newsletter, 1994-98. Fellow Chgo. Bar Assn. (life); mem. ABA, Ill. Bar Assn., Am. Philatelic Soc., Royal Philatelic Soc. Can. Home: 434 Mary Ln Crystal Lake IL 60014-7257 Office: Let's Talk Sense Publishing Co PO Box 6716 Chicago IL 60680-6716

WADE, GLEN, electrical engineer, educator; b. Ogden, Utah, Mar. 19, 1921; s. Lester Andrew and Nellie (Vanderwerff) W.; m. LaRee Bailey, Mar. 20, 1945; children: Kathleen Ann, RaLee, Lisa Jean, Mary Sue. BS in Elec. Engring, U. Utah, 1948, MS, 1949; PhD, Stanford U., 1954. Research group leader, asso. prof. elec. engring. Stanford U., 1955-60; asso. dir. engring., microwave and power tube div. Raytheon Co., 1960-61, asst gen. mgr. research div., 1961-63; dir. Sch. Elec. Engring., Cornell U., 1963-66, J.P. Levis prof. engring., 1963-66; prof. elec. engring. U. Calif. at Santa Barbara, 1966—. Indsl. advisor U. R.I., 1961-63; vis. lectr. Harvard, 1963; cons. to industry, 1956—; vis. prof. Tokyo U., 1971; Fulbright-Hays lectr., Spain, 1972-73; cons. mem. Dept. Def. Adv. Group Electron Devices, 1966-73; Spl. Chair prof. Nat. Taiwan U., 1980-81, internationally renowned fgn. scholar lectureship, 1988; UN vis. prof. Nanjing Inst. Tech., 1986; UN vis. prof. S.E. U. People's Republic of China, 1989, Nat. Com. Sci. and Tech. vis. prof. U. Guanajuato, Mex., 1994—; elected mem. The Electromagnetics Acad., 1990. Editor: Transactions on Electron Devices, 1961-71, IEEE Jour. Quantum Electronics, 1965-68; series editor: Harcourt Brace Jovanovich, 1964—; contbr. articles to profl. jours. U.S. del. Tech. Cooperation Program internat. meeting, 1970. Served with USNR, 1944-46. Recipient ann. award Nat. Electronics Conf., 1959, Outstanding Teaching award Acad. Senate, U. Calif., Santa Barbara, 1977, Prof. of Yr. award U. Calif. at Santa Barbara Mortar Bd. Sr. Honor Soc., 1988, Hon. Chairmanship award Twentieth Acoustical Imaging, 1992, Disting. Alumnus award Engring. Coll. U. Utah, 1998. Fellow IEEE (life; mem. adminstrv. com. profl. group election devices 1960-71, mem. publs. bd., chmn. info. processing com., mem. exec. com. 1971-72, dir. 1971-72, chmn. ednl. activities bd. 1971-72, editor proc. 1977-80, Centennial award 1984, Millennium medal 2000); mem. Am. Phys. Soc., Phi Kappa Phi, Tau Beta Pi, Sigma Xi, Eta Kappa Nu (Outstanding Young Elec. Engr. award 1955) Home: 1098 Golf Rd Santa Barbara CA 93108-2411 Office Phone: 805-893-2508. E-mail: wade@ece.ucsb.edu.

WADE, JAMES O'SHEA, editor, writer; b. Atlanta, June 17, 1940; s. Richard J. and Mary Clare (O'Shea) W.; m. Linda Norman, June 19, 1971; 1 child, Christopher Scott. AB magna cum laude, Harvard U., 1962. Editor Blaisdell Pub. Co., N.Y.C., 1963-65; asst. to pres., sr. editor Macmillan Co., 1966-69; editor-in-chief World Pub. Co., 1969-71; v.p., editorial dir. David McKay Co., 1971-74; founder, pres. Wade Pub. Co., Inc., N.Y.C., 1975-78; exec. v.p. Rawson, Wade Pubs., Inc., N.Y.C., 1978-82; sr. editor Crown Pubs., Inc., N.Y.C., 1982-85, exec. editor, 1985-95, v.p., 1988-95; with Ind. Editors Group, 1996—. Mem. Century Club (N.Y.C.), Iroquois/D.U. Club (Harvard), Hasty-Pudding Inst. 1770 (Harvard U.). Democrat. Home and Office: 1565 Baptist Church Rd Yorktown Heights NY 10598-5812 Personal E-mail: jedit@westnet.com.

WADE, JIMMIE L. automotive executive; CFO, pres., sec. Advance Stores, Roanoke, Va. Office: Advance Stores 5673 Airport Rd Roanoke VA 24012

WADE, JUNE BOOTH, secondary school educator; b. St. Petersburg, Fla., Dec. 24, 1934; d. Monroe Phillippi and Julia Lenoir (Burdett) Booth; m. Charles Wade, Feb. 18, 1956; children: Susan Wade Infanzon, John Eric. BSJM, U. Fla., 1956. Tchr. English and journalism Hillsborough County Schs., Tampa, Fla. Mem. Nat. Coun. Tchrs. English, Fla. Coun. Tchrs. English, Hillsborough Coun. Tchrs. English, Delta Kappa Gamma. West Hillsboraigh Chapter, Ret. Educators of FL.

WADE, KAREN, federal agency administrator; b. Cortez, Colo. m. John W. Wade (div.). Student, U. Colo., 1960-62; B.Bus., Ft. Lewis Coll., 1962-64; postgrad., U. No. Ariz., 1973, U. Tenn., Knoxville, 1977. So. region trail coord. Appalachian Trail Project Nat. Park Svc., 1978-83; mgmt. asst. Shenandoah Nat. Park, Va., 1983-85; supt. Ft. McHenry Nat. Monument and Historic Shrine Hampton Nat. Hist. Park, Balt., 1985-87; supt. Guadalupe Mountains Nat. Park, Tex., 1987-90, Wrangell-St. Elias Nat. Park and Preserve, Alaska, 1990-94, Great Smoky Mountains Nat. Park, Gatlinburg, Tenn., 1994—, dir., 1999—. Office: Dir Intermountain Reg Nat Park Svc PO Box 25287 Denver CO 80225-0287 also: 12795 Alameda Pky Denver CO 80228 E-mail: karen_wade@nps.gov.

WADE, MAGGIE, newscaster; b. Crystal Springs, Miss. married; 2 children. Student, Jackson State U., Miss. Coll. Reporter WHJT-FM; radio announcer, mktg. rschr., weekend news anchor WJDX-MISS 103; anchor WLBT, Jackson, Miss.; adj. prof. Belhaven Coll., Jackson, Miss. Miss. rep. Presdl. Summit, 1997; mem. adv. bd. So. Christian Svcs. for Children and Youth; bd. dirs. Friends of Children's Hosp., U. Med. Ctr., Miss. Pub. Edn. Forum, Coun. on Reform and Excellence, Jackson Pub. Schs., United Way Ctrl. Miss.; Olympic Torchbearer; spkr. in field. Actor: (films) A Time to Kill, Ghosts of Mississippi. Active United Negro Coll. Fund, Easter Seals, Santa's Toy Chest; mem. Word of Faith Christian Ctr.; bd. dirs. Salvation Army, River Oaks Hosp., Diabetes Found. Miss. Named Outstanding Young Mississippian, Miss. Jr. C. of C., Woman of Yr., Alcorn State U., Outstanding Career Woman, Jackso9n Sales and Mktg. Execs., Woman of Yr., State Martin Luther King, Jr. Com.; named one of Outstanding Young Women in Am.; named to Hall of Fame, Miss. Families for Kids; recipient over 150 awards, Angel in Adoption award, Congl. Coalition on Adoption, Top 40 under 40 Bus. award, Miss. Bus. Journ., Svc. to Mankind award, Miss., Meritorious Leadership award, Tougaloo Coll., Vernon Dahmer award for svc. to children, State NAACP, Svc. to Edn. award, Jackson State U. Office: WLBT 715 S Jefferson St Jackson MS 39201

WADE, MICHAEL ROBERT ALEXANDER, marketing specialist; b. N.Y.C., June 29, 1945; s. Burton Jean and Celia (Handleman) W.; m. Carole Kay West, Aug. 25, 1974. AB, U. Chgo., 1967; postgrad. in pub. adminstrn., Am. U., 1967-71; MBA in Fin., NYU, 1975. Program analyst, mgmt. intern HUD, 1967-71; dep. dir. Mgmt. Comm. and Briefing Ctr. U.S. Price Commn., 1972; asst. exec. sec. policy coordination U.S. Cost of Living Coun., 1973-74; assoc. dir. U.S. Indochina Refugee Program, 1975-76; pres. China Trade Devel. Corp. Chgo., 1977—. Participant with W.R. Grace & Co. in Alaska oil and gas prodn. Recipient Meritorious Svc. award Exec. Office of Pres., 1972, Disting. Svc. award U.S. Cost of Living Coun., 1974. Mem. Soc. Contemporary Art, Internat. Bus. Coun. MidAm. (bd. dirs.). Office: China Trade Devel Corp 2049 Century Park E Ste 480 Los Angeles CA 90067-3117 Office Phone: 310-556-8091. E-mail: CHINA-TRADE@worldnet.att.net.

WADE, NIGEL, former editor in chief; b. New Zealand; Editor in chief Chgo. Times, 1996—2000. Recipient Ethics in Jour. award, 1999; grantee Nieman Fell., Harvard U. Office: Chgo Sun Times 401 N Wabash Ave Chicago IL 60611-5642

WADE, REBA, music teacher, pianist; b. Dresden, Tenn., Apr. 30, 1938; d. John Buford and Willie Ruth (Todd) Tilley; m. Ronald Lee Wade, July 22, 1956; children: Tony Lee, Randy Neal. Student, U. Tenn., Martin, 1976-80. Tchr. pvt. studio, Martin, 1962-70, 76—, Sharon (Tenn.) Sch., 1968, Westview H.S., Martin, 1976--79, Greenfield (Tenn.) Sch., 1984-86; mgr., dir. Wade Bros., Martin, 1965-71, High Variety Show Mems., Martin, 1994—. Tchr., accompanist for students, shows, groups, auditions and on radio and TV; profl. pianist; vice consul Internat. Biog. Ctr., 2002, 03, 04, advisor to dir.-gen., 2002. Prodr. Wade Bros. Rec., 1969, student recs., 1988-90, 97-2003; author lyrics, music original compositions including Little Cowboy, 1963, I Love My Jesus, 1963, Christmas Time, 1964, Happy Happy Day, 1964, Love, 1964, Oh How I Love You, 1965, Dear Mis-Fortune, 1965, Red Lace, 1965, Crazy Little Feeling, 1967, All Because of Christmas Day, 1968, Mean Mean Mama, 1968, God is Like This, 1979, Little Dreams, 1992, also tnr., prodr., 1988-90, 97-2001; performer Christmas music The White House, 1997-98, Pentagon Party, 1998; performer World Wide Air Show RAF, Fairford, Eng., London, 1999; recorded 3CDs (total 32 songs and pieces on piano), Nasville, Tenn., 2000, 2001, Christmas CD (9 songs), 2003; recorded 18 songs and pieces on piano, Hilltop Recording Studio, Nashville, Tenn., 2000, 12 others, 2001, 10 more songs, 2003; prodr. five reco. sessions Hilltop Recording Studio, Nashville, tenn., 2000; tnr. students Cerebral Palsy Telethon WBBJ TV, Jackson, Tenn., 1995-2002. Active in civic affairs, 1947-; judge music festival U. Tenn., Martin, 2000-01, 2002, fall performance, 2000-01, 2002-03, Kiwanis Club Talent Show, 2000-01; active Martin Elem. Chorus, 2001; fundraiser Big Cypress Tree State Park, 2000-01, Dickson (Tenn.) Police Dept., 2000, Relay for Life, 1992-; planner, tnr. fund raiser program local fire dept. to buy new fire truck, 2000, entertainment fund raiser local town to install new lights in town, 2000; vice consul Internat. Biog. Ctr., 2002-, advisor to dir. gen., 2002-. Recipient Vol. Svc. award State of Tenn. Recreation and Parks Assn., 2001; selected for the crowning of ABI World Laureate; nominated for Am. medal of Honor, 2002; recipient Companion of Honor award, 2002, Universal Award of Accomplishment, ABI, 2002; named Internat. Woman of the Yr., 2001 Fellow Internat. Biog. Assn. (life); mem. SAI (life, social chmn. 1979), Songwriters Guild Am., Music Tchrs. Nat. Assn., Philharm. Music Club (v.p. 1983-84, pres. 1985), Am. Coll. Musicians, Dem. Women. Baptist. Avocations: music writing, interior decorating and designing, travel, church and charity work, political and military entertaining. Home: 208 Melody Dr Martin TN 38237-5535

WADE, ROBERT GLENN, engineering executive; b. Sturgeon, Mo., Nov. 21, 1933; s. Robert Clifford and Mildred Guinn (Bartee) W.; m. Geraldine Harris, Dec. 27, 1959; 1 child, Carolyn Ruth. BSCE, U. Mo., 1955. Registered profl. engr., Mo., Kans. Structural engr. Carter-Waters Corp., Kansas City, Mo., 1958-62; project mgr. Pfuhl & Stevson, Kansas City, 1962-76; prin. Stevson-Hall & Wade, Inc., Kansas City, 1976-82; pres. Structural Engring. Assocs., Inc., Kansas City, 1982-85, chmn., CEO, 1985-98. Mem. Mo. Bd. Architects, Engrs. and Land Surveyors, 1992-2000; mem. Midwest Concrete Industry Bd., pres., 1975-76. Co-author: Quality Assurance for Consulting Engineers, 1986. Com. mem. Downtown Coun., Kansas City, 1990. lst lt. USAF, 1956-58. Recipient lst Merit award Midwest Concrete Industry Bd., 1976, award of excellence Am. Inst. Steel Constrn., 1982, Excellence in Design award Prestressed Concrete Inst., 1988, Disting. Svc. award Nat. Coun. of Examiners for Engring. and Surveying, 2001. Fellow ASCE (pres. Kansas City sect. 1986-87, Leadership award 1987); mem. Am. Cons. Engrs. Coun. (firm rep., bd. dirs. 1987-88), Cons. Engrs. Coun. Mo. (firm rep., pres. 1986-87, Svc. award 1987). Avocation: golf. Office: Structural Engring Assocs 101 W 11th St Kansas City MO 64105-1803 Personal E-mail: rwade4@kc.rr.com.

WADE, THOMAS EDWARD, electrical engineering educator, university research administrator; b. Jacksonville, Fla., Sept. 14, 1943; s. Wilton Fred and Alice Lucyle (Hedge) W.; m. Ann Elizabeth Chitty, Aug. 6, 1966; children: Amy Renee, Nathan Thomas, Laura Ann. BSEE, U. Fla., Gainesville, 1966, MSEE, 1968, PhD, 1974. Cert. rsch. adminstr., 1992. Interim asst. prof. U. Fla., Gainesville, 1974-76; prof. elec. engring. Miss. State U., Starkville, 1976-85; state-wide dir. microelectronics rsch. lab. Miss., 1978-85; assoc. dean, prof. elec. engring. U. South Fla., Tampa, 1985—. Dir. Engring. Indsl. Experiment Sta., 1986-93, exec. dir. Ctrs. for Engring. R&D, 1985-90, mem. presdl. faculty adv. com. for rsch. and tech. devel., 1986-88, mem. fed. demonstration project com. for contracts and grants, 1986-88; mem. adv. bd. USF Exec. Fellows Program, 1987-91; chmn. evaluation task force applied rsch. grants program High Tech. and Industry Coun. State of Fla., 1988-90, vice chmn. microelectronics and materials subcoms. 1987-93, mem. telecom. subcom., 1988-89, chmn. legis. report com. FHTIC, 1989-90, chmn. U. sabbatical com., 1997-98; vice chmn. subcom. on microelectronics and materials Enterprise Fla. Innovation Partnership, 1993-94, chmn. univ. sabbatical com., 1997-98; mem. Tampa Bay Internat. Super Task Force, 1986-92, vice chmn. edn. com. 1988; dir. Fla. Ctr. for Microelectronics Design and Test, 1986-88; bd. dirs. NASA Ctr. Comml. Devel. of Space Comm. Ctr., Fla., 1990-93; bd. trustees Trinity Coll. Fla., 1997—, exec. com. 1998—, chmn. strategic planning com., 2001-; bd. trustees Toccoa Falls Coll., 2002; bd. dirs. New Tampa YMCA; rev. panel govt.-univ.-industry rsch. round table for fed. demonstration project NAS, 1988; solid state circuit specialist Applied Micro-circuits Corp., San Diego, 1981-82; sr. scientist NASA Marshall Space Flight Ctr., Huntsville, Ala., 1983; scientist Trilogy Semiconductor Corp., Santa Clara, Calif., 1984; organizer, chmn. Very Large Scale Integrated/Ultra

Large Scale Integrated Multilevel Interconnection Conf., Seminar and Exhbn., editor procs., 1991—; organizer, gen. chmn. Dielectrics for Ultra Large Scale Integrated Multilevel Interconnection Conf., 1995—, Chem.-Mech.-Polish Planarization for Ultra Large Scale Integration, 1996—, Conductors for Ultra Large Scale Integrated Multilevel Interconnection Conf., 2000—; cons. in field. Author: Polyimides for Very Large Scale Integrated Applications, 1984, (U.S. Army handbook) Modern Very Large Scale Integrated Circuit Fabrication Processes, 1984, Photosensitive Polyimides for Very Large Scale Integrated Applications, 1986, Very Large Scale Multilevel Interconnection Advanced Metals Tutorial, 1996—, Very Large Scale Multilevel Interconnection Tutorial, 1987—; contbr. chpts. on electronics to World Book encys., 1997; contbr. over 125 articles to profl. jours. Active First Bapt. Ch., Temple Terrace, Fla., vice-chmn. bd. deacons 1989-90, chmn. bd. deacons, 1990-91, 93-94, chmn. pastor search com., 1990-91, vice-chmn. long range planning com., 1989-91, vice-chmn. pastor search com., 1994-95, dir. adult coed III Sunday sch. dept., 1993-94, ch. coun., 1994-95, ch. trustee, 1999—, mem. constn. and bylaws com., 1997-99, trustee, 1999—; treas. Tampa Palms Owners Assn., 1994-95, chmn. home decorating com., 1997; vol., United Fund, Miss. State U., 1983-85. Recipient Outstanding Engring. Tchg. award Coll. Engring. U. Fla., 1976, Outstanding Tchg. Incentive program award State of Fla., 1998, Cert. of Recognition NASA (5 times), 1981-88, Outstanding Rsch. award Sigma Xi, 1984, Outstanding Contbn. to Sci. and Tech. award Fla. Gov., 1989, 90, Outstanding Undergrad. Tchg. award U. South Fla., 1999. Mem. AAAS, NSPE, IEEE (sr. mem., guest editor periodical 1982, gen. chmn. Internat. Very Large Scale Integrated Multilevel Interconnection Conf. annually 1984-90, editor conf. procs., 1984-90, chmn. acad. affairs com. CHMT Soc., 1984-86, gen. chmn. univ./govt./industry microelectronics symposium, 1981, tech. program commn., 1991, bd. dirs. workshop on tungsten and other refractory metals 1987-90), Am. Soc. Engring. Edn. (gen. chmn. engring. rsch. coun. ann. meeting 1987, chmn. engring. rsch. coun. adminstrv. com. 1987-90, chmn. coun., 1990-92, session chmn. ann. meeting 1990, 92, bd. dirs. 1990-92, mem. nominations com. 1992-94, mem. long range planning com. 1992-95, Centennial Cert. 1992, 2d Century Cert. 1993), World Future Soc. Internat. Soc. Hybrid Microelectronics, Assn. U.S. Army (bd. dir. Suncoast chpt. 1991-93), Soc. Photo Optical Instrumentation Engring., Univ. Faculty Senate Assn. of Miss. (organizer 1985), Am. Vacuum Soc., Am. Phs. Soc., Am. Electronics Assn., Am. Inst. Physics, Nat. Coun. Univ. Rsch. Adminstrn., Soc. Rsch. Adminstrs (external rels. com. for SRA 1988-91), Fla. Engring. Soc. (v.p. edn. com. 1987-92, pres. 1989-90, bd. dirs. 1989-90, Fla. engring. found. trustee 1989-90, ann. meeting steering com. 1989-90, Outstanding Svc. to the Profession award 1992), Soc. Am. Mil. Engring., Order of Engrs., 1991, Sigma Xi (v.p. 1985), Tau Beta Pi (Fla. Alpha chpt. pres. 1969, 71, faculty advisor Miss. Alpha chpt. 1977-85, faculty advisor Fla. Gamma chpt. 1986—, Outstanding hon. soc. advisor award 1994), Eta Kappa Nu (pres. U. Fla. chpt. 1968, Org. Charter Chpt. U. South Fla. 1998, faculty adv. Kappa Xi chpt. 1998—, Outstanding Honor Soc. Adv. award 1998-99), Sigma Tau, Omicron Delta Kappa, Soc. Am. Inventors, Fla. Blue Key (v.p. 1972, sec. 1971), Epsilon Lambda Chi (founder 1970, pres. 1971). Club: Downtown Tampa Rotary (Paul Harris fellow 1987,94, 2000, perfect attendance award 1986—, chmn. com. on environ. issues 1990), Rotary Club New Tampa (organizer, charter mem., pres. 1995-96, v.p. 1996-97, mem. exec. com. 1996—, dir. internat. svc. 1997-98, sr. dir. 1998-99, 99-2001). Avocations: collecting antique furniture, carpentry, restoring antique sports cars, basketball. Home: 5316 Witham Ct E Tampa FL 33647-1026

WADE, TYRA V. manufacturing executive; b. Cheyenne, Wyo., Jan. 8, 1957; d. Larry Emil Schieck and Wanda Frances Reimer. Student, South Mountain Coll., 1991-97. Cert. trainer/instr. Mgr. Holiday Inn, Homestead, Fla., 1977-80, Legion Club, Alliance, Nebr., 1980-87; supr. Motorola, Phoenix, 1987-2000; mgr. S.W. Traffic Systems, 2001—. Baptist. Avocations: art, computers, cooking. Home: 14910 S 43rd Ave Laveen AZ 85339-3262

WADHAMS, TIMOTHY, consumer products company executive; CPA Coopers & Lybrand, 1972; joined Masco Corp., Taylor, Mich., 1976, various positions MascoTech, 1984—2000, v.p. fin., CFO, 2001—04, sr. v.p., CFO, 2004—. Office: Masco Corp 21001 Van Born Rd Taylor MI 48180

WADKINS, LANNY LANSTON, professional golfer; b. Richmond, Va., Dec. 5, 1949; s. Jerry Lanston and Francis Ann (Burnett) W.; m. Rachel Irene Strong, Jan. 2, 1971; 1 child, Jessica. Student, Wake Forest U. Profl. golfer PGA, 1971—. Mem. numerous nat. teams including Walker Cup (2), 1969, 71, World Amateur Cup, 1970, Ryder Cup (8), 1977, 79, 83, 85, 87, 89, 91, 93, Ryder Cup Capt., 1995, World Cup (3), 1977, 84, 85, U.S. vs. Japan (2), 1982, 83, Nissan Cup, 1985, Dunhill Cup, 1986, Kirin Cup, 1987, Asahi Glass Four Tours, 1991; golf analyst, CBS Sports, 2003-. Winner 1968, 70 So. Amateur champion, Sahara Invitational, 1972, PGA, 1977, World Series of Golf, 1978, Can. PGA, 1978, Tournament Players' Championship, 1979, 82, 83, (4) 1978 Victoria PGA Championship (Australia), Can. PGA Championship, 1979 Bridgestone Open (Japan), L.A. Open, 1979, Phoenix Open, 1982, Greater Greensboro, 1983, Bob Hope Desert Classic, 1985, Doral Ryder, 1987, 1984 World Nissan Championship (Japan), Hawaiian Open, 1988, 91, Colonial Open, 1988, Anheuser Busch Classic, 1990, 1990 Fred Meyer Challenge, PGA of AmericaPlayer of Yr., 1985, Greater Hartford Open, 1992, 2000 ACE Group Classic, among others. Address: PGA America/Senior Tour 100 Ave of the Champions PO Box 109601 Palm Bch Gdns FL 33410-9601

WADLEIGH, KEVIN RICHARD, mathematician; b. Joplin, Mo., Aug. 23, 1959; s. George Richard and Johnie Kathalyn Wadleigh; m. Laurie Susan Smetzer, May 7, 1983; children: Leslie Anne, John Richard. BS in Math., Oral Roberts U., 1980; MS in Applied Math., U. of Tulsa, 1982; EdD in Math., Okla. State U., 1986. Rsch. cons. Amoco Prodn. Co., Tulsa, 1981—86; software engr. E-Systems, Garland, Tex., 1986—88; tech. mktg. specialist Convex Computer Corp., Richardson, Tex., 1989—94; software engring. specialist Raytheon, Garland, Tex., 1995—95; software engring. master Hewlett-Packard Co., Richardson, 1996—. Author: (text) Software Optimization for High Performance Computing; contbr. tech. articles to profl. jours. Mem.: Soc. of Indsl. and Applied Math. Presbyterian. Achievements include patents for Cache Bank Conflict Avoidance and Cache Collison Avoidance; Mechanism for Calculation of One-Dimensional Fast Fourier Transform. Avocations: piano playing, genealogy.

WADLEY, FREDIA STOVALL, state commissioner; b. Winchester, Tenn. BS, Tenn Tech U., 1967; MD, U. Tenn., 1969; MSHPA, U. Cin., 1978. Diplomate Am. Bd. Pediats. Pediat. intern City of Memphis Hosp., 1970, pediat. resident, 1971-72; clin. instr. pediats. dept. pediats. U. Tenn. Ctr. for Health Scis., Memphis, 1973-74; pvt. practice Winchester, Tenn., 1974-75; instr. phys. assessment course dept. nursing U. Tenn., Chattanooga, 1975-76; dir. med. svcs. Dept. Health and Environ. Southeast Region, Chattanooga, 1975-80, regional dir., 1981-83; chief med. officer Dept. Health and Environ. Commr.'s Office, Nashville, 1984-87; dir. Met. Health Dept., Nashville, 1987-95; commr. Dept. Health, Nashville, 1995-97; state med. dir. Tenn. Health Srvcs. Bureau, 1997—; clin. asst. prof. dept. pediats. Meharry Med. Coll., 1985—; mem. faculty staff preventive medicine divsn. Quillen Dischner Med. Coll., 1985-87; now commr. Dept. Health, Nashville. Vol. faculty mem. dept. nursing U. Tenn. Ctr. for Health Scis., Memphis, 1977-83, U. Tenn., Knoxville, 1977-83; mem. preventive medicine resident adv. com. Meharry Family Medicine Dept., 1988—; adj. assoc. prof. nursing dept. family and cmty. health Vanderbilt U., 1988—; presenter in field. Contbr. articles to profl. jours. Mem. HSA III Task Force on Ambulatory Health Care Problems, 1977, HSA III Bd., 1981-82; mem. southeast Tenn. regional placement com. Tenn. Med. Loan Scholarship Program, 1978-79; bd. dirs. Southeast Tenn. Chpt. Kidney Found., 1981, Vol. Healthcare Sys., Inc., 1988-90, Vanderbilt AIDS Project, 1990, United Way Mid. Tenn., 1992-95, ARC, 1992; mem. Tenn. Sch. health Coalition, 1985—, Cmty. Coalition for Minority Health, 1988, Mayor's Substance Abuse Action Team, 1990; active Brentwood United Meth., Sunday Sch. tchr. 6th grade, 1984-87; chmn. Tenn. AIDS Adv. Com., 1987-88, Davidson County Child Fatality Rev. Team, 1994-95, others. Mem. AMA, APHA (Charles G. Jordan award for outstanding accomplishments in field of pub. health so. br. 1981), Southern Health Assn. (chmn. awards com. and governing coun. 1981-83, pres. 1989-90, spl. meritorious award for outstanding contbns. to orgn. and pub. health 1992), Tenn. Pub. Health Assn. (pres. 1990-91, spl. meritorious award 1993), Tenn. Health Officers, Tenn. Pediat. Soc., Tenn. Med. Assn., Nashville/Davidson County Acad. Medicine, Davidson County Pediat. Soc. Office: Health Svcs Bureau 425 5th Ave N Fl 3D Nashville TN 37247-0001*

WADLEY, M. RICHARD, consumer products executive; b. Lehi, Utah; s. Merlyn R. and Verla Ann (Ball) W.; m. Nancy Zwiers; children: Lisa Kathleen, Staci Lin, Eric Richard, Nicole Marie. BS, Brigham Young U., 1967; MBA, Northwestern U., 1968. Brand asst. packaged soap and detergent divsn. Procter & Gamble Co., Cin., 1968-69, asst. brand mgr. packaged soap and detergent divsn., 1970-71, brand mgr. Dawn detergent, 1972-73, copy supr. packaged soap and detergent divsn., 1974-75, brand mgr. Tide detergent, 1975-77, assoc. advt. mgr. packaged soap and detergent divsn., 1977-81; corp. product dir. Hallmark Cards, Inc., Kansas City, Mo., 1982-83, Ambassador Cards divsn. Hallmark Cards, Inc., 1983-85; v.p., gen. mgr. feminine protection divsn. Tambrands Inc., Lake Success, NY, 1986-88; sr. v.p. Bongrain, Inc., N.Y.C., 1988-89, pres., CEO AltaDena Inc. divsn. City of Industry, Calif., 1989-91, pres. The Summit Group, 1991-93; chmn., CEO, bd. dirs. T-Chem Products Inc., Santa Fe Springs, Calif., 1993-99; CEO The Bayshore Group, 1999—. Bd. dirs. Legacy Interactive, Life Point, Inc., Funosophy, Inc.; adj. prof. MBA program Pepperdine U., 1998—99. Bd. dirs. Long Beach Opera, 1991-95, L.I. Friends of the Arts, 1986-88; mem. adv. bd. Bus. Sch. Calif. State U., Long Beach, 1991-93. Avocations: civil war history, tennis, travel. E-mail: rwbayshore@aol.com.

WADLINGTON, WALTER JAMES, law educator; b. Biloxi, Miss., Jan. 17, 1931; s. Walter and Bernice (Taylor) Wadlington; m. Ruth Miller Hardie, Aug. 20, 1955; children: Claire, Charlotte, Ian(dec.), Susan, Derek Alan. AB, Duke U., 1951; LLB, Tulane U., 1954. Bar: La. 1954, Va. 1965. Pvt. practice, New Orleans, 1954—55, 1958—59; asst. prof. Tulane U., 1960—62; mem. faculty U. Va., 1962—, prof law, 1964—, James Madison prof., 1970—2002, James Madison prof. emeritus, 2002—, prof. legal medicine Med. Sch., 1979—2002, Harrison Found. rsch. prof., 1990—92. Tutor civil law U. Edinburgh, Scotland, 1959—60; vis. Tazewell Taylor prof. law Coll. William and Mary, 1986; med. malpractice program dir. Robert Wood Johnson, 1985—91, mem. adv. com. clin. scholars program, 1989—97; chmn. nat. adv. bd. Improving Malpractice Prevention and Compensation Sys., 1994—98; Disting. Health Law Tchr. Am. Soc. Law, Medicine and Ethics; trustee-at-large Edn. Commn. Fgn. Med. Grads., 1995—2003. Author (with O. Brien): Cases and Materials on Domestic Relations, 1970, 5th edit., 2002, Family Law in Perspective, 2001; author: (with Waltz and Dworkin) Cases and Materials on Law and Medicine, 1980; editor-in-chief: Tulane U. Law Rev., 1953—54; author (Davis, Scott, and Whitebread): Children in the Legal System, 2d edit., 1997, Children in the Legal System, 3rd edit., 2004. Fulbright scholar, U. Edinburgh, 1959—60. Mem.: Am. Law Inst., Inst. of Medicine of NAS, Found. Advancement Internat. Med. Edn. and Rsch. (bd. dirs., sec. 2001—03). Home: 1620 Keith Valley Rd Charlottesville VA 22901-3018 Office: U Va Sch Law 580 Massie Rd Charlottesville VA 22903-1738 Office Phone: 434-924-3471. E-mail: wwadlington@earthlink.net.

WADLINGTON, WARWICK PAUL, English language educator; BS, U.S. Mil. Acad., 1961; MA, Tulane U., 1966, PhD, 1967. Asst. prof. English U. Tex., Austin, 1967-72, assoc. prof., 1972-78, prof., 1978—, Joan Negley Kelleher Centennial prof., 1987—2001, emeritus, 2002—. Author: The Confidence Game in American Literature, 1975, Reading Faulknerian Tragedy, 1987, As I Lay Dying: Stories Out of Stories, 1992; contbr. articles to profl. jours. With U.S. Army, 1961-64. Decorated Air medal. Office: U Tex Dept English Austin TX 78712

WADLOW, JOAN KRUEGER, retired academic administrator, construction executive; b. LeMars, Iowa, Aug. 21, 1932; d. R. John and Norma I. (IhLe) Krueger; m. Richard R. Wadlow, July 27, 1958; children: Dawn, Kit. BA, U. Nebr., 1953, PhD, 1963; MA, Fletcher Sch. Law and Diplomacy, 1956; cert., Grad. Inst. Internat. Studies, Geneva, 1957. Mem. faculty U. Nebr., Lincoln, 1966-79, prof. polit. scis., 1964-79, assoc. dean Coll. Arts and Scis., 1972-79; prof. polit. scis., dean Coll. Arts and Scis., U. Wyo., Laramie, 1979-84, v.p. acad. affairs, 1984-86; prof. polit. sci., provost U. Okla., Norman, 1986-91; chancellor U. Alaska, Fairbanks, 1991-99. Cons. on fed. grants; bd. dirs. Alaska Sea Life Ctr., Key Bank Alaska; mem. Commn. Colls. N.W. Assn.; pres. Lan Constrn., Inc., 1999—. Author articles in field. Bd. dirs. Nat. Merit Scholarship Corp., 1988-97, Lincoln United Way, 1976-77, Bryan Hosp., Lincoln, 1978-79, Washington Ctr., 1986-99, Key Bank of Alaska, Alaska SeaLife Ctr.; v.p., exec. commr. North Ctrl. Assn., pres., 1991; pres. adv. bd. Lincoln YWCA, 1970-71; mem. def. adv. com. Women in the Svcs., 1987-89; mem. cmty. adv. bd. Alaska Airlines; mem. Univ. Pres.'s Mission to Israel, 1998; mem. bd. dirs. Netarts Oceanside Sanitary Dist., 2002-04. Recipient Mortar Board Tchg. award, 1976, Alumni Scholar Achievement award Rotary Internat., 1998, Alumni Achievement award U. Nebr., 2003; Seacrest Journalism fellow 1953-54, Rotary fellow, 1956-57, fellow Conf. Coop. Man, Lund, Sweden, 1956. Mem. NCAA (divsn. II pres. coun. 1997-99), Internat. Studies Assn. (co-editor Internat. Studies Notes 1978-91), Nat. Assn. State Univs. and Land-Grant Colls. (exec. com. coun. acad. affairs 1989-91, chair internat. affairs counsel 1996-97), Western Assn. Africanists (pres. 1980-82), Assn. Western Univs. (pres. 1993), Coun. Colls. Arts and Scis. (pres. 1983-84), Greater Fairbanks C. of C., Gamma Phi Beta. Republican. Congregationalist. Address: Chancellor Emerita PO Box 246 Oceanside OR 97134-0246 E-mail: wadlow@oregonvos.net.

WADMAN, WILLIAM WOOD, III, educational director, technical research executive, consulting company executive; b. Oakland, Calif., Nov. 13, 1936; s. William Wood, Jr., and Lula Fay (Raisner) W.; children: Roxanne Alyce Wadman Hubbling, Raymond Alan (dec.), Theresa Hope Wadman Boudreaux; m. Barbara Jean Wadman; stepchildren: Denise Ellen Varine Skrypkar, Brian Ronald Varine. M.A., U. Calif., Irvine, 1978. Cert. program mgr. tng. Radiation safety specialist, accelerator health physicist U. Calif. Lawrence Berkeley Lab., 1957-68; campus radiation safety officer U. Calif., Irvine, 1968-79; dir. ops., radiation safety officer Radiation Sterilizers, Inc., Tustin, Calif., 1979-80; prin., pres. Wm. Wadman & Assocs. Inc., 1980—; mem. operational review team Princeton U. Rsch. Campus TOKOMAK Fusion Test Facility, 1993-94; technical project mgr. for upgrades projects Los Alamos Nat. Lab. 1994-96, tech. project mgr. for 3 projects, 1995—; mem. team No. 1, health physics appraisal program NRC, 1980—, operational readiness review team to Princeton U. Rsch. Campus TOKOMAK Fusion Test Facility, 1993-94; cons. health physicist to industry; lectr. sch. social ecology, 1974-79, dept. community and environ. medicine U. Calif., Irvine, 1979-80, instr. in environ. health and safety, 1968-79, Orange Coast Coll., in radiation exposure reduction design engring. Iowa Electric Light & Power; trainer Mason & Hanger-Silas Mason Co., Los Alamos Nat. Lab.; instr. in medium energy cyclotron radiation safety UCLBL, lectr. in accelerator health physics, 1966, 67; curriculum developer in field; subject matter expert Los Alamos Nat. Lab., Earth and Environ. Scis., Tech. Support Office. Active Cub Scouts; chief umpire Mission Viejo Little League, 1973. Served with USNR, 1955-63. Recipient award for profl. achievement U. Calif. Alumni Assn., 1972, Outstanding Performance award U. Calif., Irvine, 1973. Mem. Health Physics Soc. (treas. 1979-81, editor proc. 11th symposium, pres. So. Calif. chpt. 1977, Professionalism award 1975), Internat. Radiation Protection Assn. (U.S. del. 4th Congress 1977, 8th Congress 1992), Am. Nuclear Soc., Am. Public Health Assn. (chmn. program 1978, chmn. radiol. health sect. 1979-80), Campus Radiation Safety Officers (chmn. 1975, editor proc. 5th conf. 1975), ASTM, Project Mgmt. Inst. Club: UCI Univ. (dir. 1976, sec. 1977, treas. 1978). Contbr. articles to tech. jours. Achievements include research in radiation protection and environmental sciences; Avocations: sailing, Tae Kwon Do, wood working, numesmantics. Home: 3687 Red Cedar Way Lake Oswego OR 97035-3525 Office: 675 Fairview Dr Ste 246 Carson City NV 89701-5428 *Personal philosophy: The continuous practice of patience, openmindedness, and open communication provide the essential ingredients for a full, satisfying personal and professional life. The timing of major decisions is not a matter of heart, but the culmination of the effective use of the practices above.*

WADSWORTH, DYER SEYMOUR, retired lawyer; b. N.Y.C., June 16, 1936; s. Seymour and Phoebe Armistead (Helmer) W.; m. Beverley Allen Dunn Barringer, Feb. 2, 1963; children: Sophia, Jennifer. BA, Yale U., 1959; JD, Harvard U., 1962. Bar: N.Y. 1963, Pa. 1979. Assoc. Humes, Andrews & Botzow, N.Y.C., 1962-64; with Inco Ltd. and subs., 1964-96; asst. gen. counsel Inco Ltd., N.Y.C., 1982-96; pres. Inco U.S., Inc., N.Y.C., 1993-96. Chmn., bd. dirs. Barringer Crater Co., Flagstaff, Ariz., 1996—; chmn., CEO, treas., dir. Cass County Iron Co., Linden, Tex., 1992—. Gen. counsel Baseline Fin. Svcs., Inc., N.Y.C., 1997-2000, The Sailors Snug Harbor, Sea Level, N.C., 1987-2000; chmn., bd. dirs. Amsterdam Nursing Home Corp., N.Y.C., 1986-2000; trustee Isaac Tuttle Fund for the Aged, N.Y.C., 1968-96; bd. dirs. Frenchman Bay Conservancy, Hancock, Maine, 1997—. Named Trustee of Yr. N.Y. Assn. Homes and Svcs. for the Aging, 1995. Mem. Meteoritical Soc., Univ. Club, Ivy League Club, Union Club, (N.Y.C.), Pilgrims Soc. (N.Y.C.), Yale Club Suncoast (dir. 2001—, pres. 2002-04). Home: 8466 Lockwood Ridge Rd PMB 304 Sarasota FL 34243-2951

WADSWORTH, FRANK WHITTEMORE, foundation executive, literature educator; b. N.Y.C., June 14, 1919; s. Prescott Kingsley and Elizabeth (Whittemore) W.; m. Roxalene Harriet Nevin, Oct. 22, 1943 (dec. 1979); Susan, Roxalene; m. Deborah Yohalem, Dec. 22, 1980. AB, Princeton U., 1946, PhD, 1951. Instr. English Princeton (N.J.) U., 1949-50; instr. to assoc. prof. English UCLA, 1950-61; prof. English, dean div. humanities U. Pitts., 1962-67; acad. v.p. SUNY-Purchase, 1967-78, prof. lit., 1967-89, emeritus, 1989—; nat. rep. Woodrow Wilson Nat. Fellowship Found., 1958-61, trustee, 1973—2003; vice-chmn. bd. trustees, 1992—2003; trustee Wenner-Gren Found., N.Y.C., 1970—, chmn. bd. trustees, 1977-87, vice-chmn. bd. trustees, 1992—. Author: The Poacher from Stratford, 1958, contbr. articles to publs. Served to lt. (j.g.) USNR, 1942-45. Woodrow Wilson fellow, 1946-47; Scribner fellow, 1948-49; Folger Shakespeare Library fellow, 1961; Guggenheim fellow, 1961-62 Mem. MLA, Am. Soc. Theatre Research, Malone Soc., Phi Beta Kappa Clubs: Princeton. Home: 430 Sterling Rd Harrison NY 10528-1316

WADSWORTH, JACQUELINE DORÈT, private investor; b. San Diego, June 15, 1928; d. Benjamin H. Dilley and Georgia E. (Elliott) Dilley Waters; m. Charles Desmond Wadsworth Jr., June 16, 1954 (dec. 1963); 1 child, Georgia Duncan Wadsworth Barber. BS, U. Oreg., 1950; MA, San Diego State U., 1952. Cert. tchr. Calif., Oreg. Dir. Jr. Red Cross, San Diego County chpt. ARC, 1952-59, asst. dir. leadership ctrs. for 8 western states, 1954-59; pvt. investor, comml. real estate and property devel., 1974—. Interior designer J. Wadsworth Interiors, La Jolla, Calif., 1990—2002. Vol. chair nat. conv. ARC, San Diego, 1966; vol., fundraiser San Diego Symphony Orch. Orgn., 1974-83; mem. Gold Ribbon Patron com. San Diego Symphony, 1995-99; friends mem., vol. San Diego Mus. Art, 1958—, Asian Arts Coun., 1996—; mem. Scripps Found. for Medicine and Sci., 1990—; life mem., fund raiser, bd. dirs., chmn. Scripps, Mercy Hosp. Aux., 1965—; life mem., chair, bd. dirs. Social Svc. Aux., 1968—. Recipient Svc. award Mercy Hosp. Aux., 1967-70. Mem. Japanese Garden Soc. of San Diego, Globe Gilders Theatre Aux. (activity chairperson 1966-85), San Diego Zool. Soc. (curator 1976—), Mingei Internat., Palladian Soc. (San Diego County chpt.), Mus. Contemporary Art San Diego, San Diego Natural History Mus. Republican.

WADSWORTH, OLIVER, actor, playwright; b. Beverly, Mass., May 7, 1962; s. Oliver F. and Ellen (Glessner) Wadsworth. BA, Hampshire Coll., Amherst, Mass., 1986; MFA, NYU, N.Y.C., 1988. Resident Yaddo, 1995, McDowell, 1992, Millay, 1993. Author: (plays) Struggles in Daddy's Dress, —, The Family Tree, —; actor: (plays) Enemy of the People, 1998, Peter Pan, 1998, Bread and Roses, 1998, Usual Suspect, 1998—, Wally's Ghost, 1999, Endpapers, 2002, Angels in America (part 1 and 2), 2002 (Arizoni award (Best Principal Actor in Play), 2002), Fully Committed, 2002, Orestes, 2003—, Misalliance, 2003—, Stones in His Pockets, 2003—. Vol. crisis intervention GMHC, N.Y.C., 1989—93. Recipient Best Performance award, Metroland Newsweekly, Albany, N.Y., 2002, Best Play for Wally's Ghost, Obie Award, N.Y.C.; grantee Fox Found. Fellowship grantee, Diverse Forms Artists grantee, N.Y. State Coun. for the Arts, Franklin Furnace Emerging Artist grantee. Mem.: AFTRA, Actor's Equity Assn. Home: 510 E 13th St #3 New York NY 10009

WADSWORTH, ROBERT DAVID, advertising agency executive; b. Prestbury, Cheshire, Eng., May 20, 1942; came to U.S., 1978; s. Eric and Irene (Thorpe) W.; m. Kathleen O'Meara, Dec. 13, 1968; children: Tracey, Charles Robert. BA, U. Natal, S. Africa, 1963. With Lever Bros. S. Africa, 1960-66, sr. brand mgr., 1964-66, Gen. Foods S. Africa, 1967; account exec. London Press Exch., S. Africa, 1968, Grant Advt., S. Africa, 1969; dir., then mng. dir. Cen. Advt., Johannesburg, S. Africa, 1970-73; dir. new bus. coord. McCann-Erickson, South Africa, 1973-78; sr. v.p., mng. rep., new bus. coord. McCann-Erickson, Inc., N.Y.C., 1978-82; client dir., exec. v.p. Lintas, N.Y.C., 1983-90; dir. corp. strategy, regional dir. So. Africa Lintas Worldwide, N.Y.C., 1991-97; cons. Midlothian, Va., 1998—. Home and Office: 14018 Bayport Landing Ter Midlothian VA 23112-2038

WADSWORTH, STEVE, recreational facility executive; BS in Engring., U. Va.; MBA, UCLA. Prin. Windsor Pk. Group, L.A., Calif.; sr. v.p., CFO Walt Disney Co., North Hollywood, Calif., 1993—95, with Disney Online, 1995—99; pres. Walt Disney Internet Group, Walt Disney Co., North Hollywood, Calif., 1999—. Spkr. in field. Office: Walt Disney Co 5161 Lankershim Blvd North Hollywood CA 91601

WADZINSKI, MARY BETH, administrative assistant; b. Wausau, Wis., Apr. 26, 1953; d. Erwin Fredrick Hackbart and Selma Ruth Margaret Krueger; m. William R. Wadzinski, June 20, 1987 (div. June 1997); children: Bethany Dawn, Andrew William. AS, Northcentral Tech. Coll., 1973. Typist Wausau (Wis.) Abstract and Title Co., 1973-76; adminstrv. asst. Marathon County Dept. Social Svcs., Wausau, 1977—. Author poems, songs. Recipient Poet Merit award, Am. Poetry Assn., 1989, Editors Choice awards, Nat. Libr. Poetry, 1996—98, 2001, Honorable Mention award, Iliad Press, 1996—98. Mem.: Famous Poets Soc. (Shakespeare Trophy of Excellence 2002, Poet of Yr. medallion 2002, Diamond Homer trophy 1996, Recognition award 1998, Poet of Yr. medallion 1999, Diamond Homer trophy 1999, Recognition award 2001), Internat. Poetry Hall of Fame, Internat. Soc. Poets. Democrat. Lutheran. Avocations: shopping, garage sales, writing, singing. Home: 1113 N 6th Ave Wausau WI 54401-2747

WAECKERLE, JOSEPH, emergency physician, educator; b. Kansas City, Mo., June 20, 1946; MD, U. Mo., 1972. Bd. cert. emergency medicine, bd. cert. sports medicine. Intern Akron Hosp., 1973; resident Truman Med. Ctr., Kansas City, Mo., 1973—75; clin. prof. U. Mo. Sch. Medicine, Kansas City, Mo., 1996—; chmn. dept. emergency medicine Bapt. Med. Ctr., Kansas City, Mo.; med. officer Kansas City divsn. FBI, Leawood, Kans.; chmn. dept. emergency care Menorah Med. Ctr., Overland Park, Kans.; chmn. dept. emergency medicine Rsch. Med. Ctr., Kansas City, Mo. Former club physician Kansas City Chiefs; former pres. U. Assn. for Emergency Medicine (now Soc. for Acad. Emergency Medicine); pres. Emergency Physicians Found. Kansas City, 1995—99. Author (with others): Emergency Medicine Clinics of North America-Bioterrorism, 2002; editor: Annals Emergency Medicine, 1989—2002; editor emeritus:, 2002—. Fellow: Am. Coll. Emergency Physicians (bd. mem. 1981—84, chmn. nuc., biol., and chem. task force); mem.: Emergency Medicine Residents' Assn. (founder). Office: Bapt Luth Med Ctr Emergency Medicine 6601 Rockhil Rd Kansas City MO 64131

WAELSCH, SALOME GLUECKSOHN, geneticist, educator; b. Danzig, Germany, Oct. 6, 1907; arrived in U.S., 1933, naturalized, 1938; d. Ilya and Nadia Gluecksohn; m. Heinrich B. Gluecksohn, Jan. 8, 1943; children: Naomi Barbara, Peter Benedict. Student, U. Konigsberg, Germany, U. Berlin, 1927—28; PhD, U. Freiburg, Germany, 1932; DSc (hon.), Columbia U., 1995. Rsch. assoc. in genetics Columbia U., 1936—55; assoc. prof. anatomy Albert Einstein Coll. Medicine, 1955—58, prof., 1958—63, prof. molecular genetics, 1963—, chmn. dept. genetics, 1963—76. Mem. study sects. NIH. Author: contbr. numerous articles on devel. genetics. Recipient Nat Medal of Sci.,

Pres. Clinton, 1993, Thomas Hunt Morgan medal, Genetics Society of America, 1999. Fellow: Am. Acad. Arts & Scis., AAAS; mem.: The Royal Soc., Am. Soc. Human Genetics, Am. Soc. Naturalists, Soc. Devel. Biology, N.Y. Acad. Scis. (hon.), Genetics Soc., Am. Assn. Anatomists, Am. Soc. Zoologists, NAS, Sigma Xi. Office: Albert Einstein Coll Med 1300 Morris Park Ave Bronx NY 10461-1926 E-mail: gradus@aecom.yu.edu.

WAETZMAN, LARRY SAMUEL, planning company executive; b. Reading, Pa., Dec. 11, 1945; s. Joseph and Lilyan B. (Berliner) W.; m. Bonnie Lynn Samuels, July 27, 1969; children: Ross, Evan, Melissa. BA, Franklin & Marshall Coll., 1967; MA, U. Wis., 1968; postgrad., Nova U., Temple U., Harvard U. Lic. profl. planner, N.J. Dir. of planning Borough of Norristown, Pa., 1972-74; dir. cmty. devel. Twp. of Haverford, Havertown, Pa., 1974-80; sr. planning cons. Govt. Studies & Systems, Phila., 1980-81; ptnr. Tredinnick/Waetzman Assocs., Havertown, 1981-87; prin. The Waetzman Planning Group, Ardmore, Pa., 1987-2001; pres. Waetleman Planning Group Inc., 2001—. Pres. Congregation Ner Tamid, Springfield, Pa., 1989-91. Served to 1st lt. U.S. Army, 1969-72. Mem. Am. Soc. Consulting Planners (pres. 1998-2000), Am. Planning Assn. (pres. eastern Pa. chpt. 1981-85), AICP, Pa. Planning Assn. (bd. dirs. 1981-85), N.J. Assn. Cons. Planners. Avocation: skiing. Home: 2725 Pine Valley Ln Ardmore PA 19003-1718 E-mail: lsw@waetzmanplanning.com.

WAFER, DOUGLAS DREW, environmental engineer; b. Monroe, La., June 18, 1964; s. Tom Drew and Ruth (Knotts) W. BS in Indsl. Engring., La. State U., 1991. Registered profl. engr., La. Motorcycle technician Am. Honda Motors Corp., Baton Rouge, 1983-84; pvt. practice computer sys. engr. Baton Rouge, 1987-92; environ. quality specialist State of La. Dept. Environ. Quality, Kenner, 1992-93, engr.-in-tng., 1993—. Engr. air quality divsn.-analysis La. Dept. Environ. Quality, 1992—. Programmer software in field; designer machine vise design. T.H. Harris scholar, 1982. Mem. NSPE, NSPE Engrs. in Govt., La. Engring. Soc., Air Force Assn. Democrat. Baptist. Avocations: computer programming, Karate, running. Home: 1834 Wimpole St Baton Rouge LA 70815-4947 Office: Bldg 4 Ste 420 201 Evans Rd New Orleans LA 70123-5230

WAFER, THOMAS J., JR., newspaper publisher; Pub. The Daily Breeze, Torrance, Calif., 1993—. Office: 5215 Torrance Blvd Torrance CA 90503-4009

WAGAR, (WALTER) WARREN (WALTER WAGAR), historian, educator; b. Balt., June 5, 1932; s. Walter (Warren) and Laura Stoner Wagar; m. Dorothy Bowers, Dec. 19, 1953; children: John, Bruce, Steven, Jennifer. AB, Franklin & Marshall Coll., 1953; MA, Ind. U., 1954; PhD, Yale U., 1959; DHL (hon.), U. Maine, 1996. From instr. to assoc. prof. Wellesley (Mass.) Coll., 1958-66; assoc. prof., then prof. U. N.Mex., Albuquerque, 1966-71; prof., disting. tchg. prof. SUNY, Binghamton, 1971—2002, prof. emeritus, 2002—. Author: H.G. Wells and the World State, 1961, The City of Man, 1963, Building the City of Man, 1971, Good Tidings: The Belief in Progress from Darwin to Marcuse, 1972, Books in World History, 1973, World Views: A Study in Comparative History, 1977, Terminal visions: The Literature of Last Things, 1982, A Short History of the Future, 1989, 3d rev. edit., 1999, The Next Three Futures, 1991, Memoirs of the Future, 2001; editor: H.G. Wells: Journalism and Prophecy, 1964, European Intellectual History Since Darwin and Marx, 1967, Science, Faith, an Man: European Thought Since 1914, 1968, The Idea of Progress Since the Renaissance, 1969, History and the Idea of Mankind, 1971, The Open Conspiracy: H.G. Wells on World Revolution, 2002; mem. editl. bd. Futures Rsch. Quar. Fulbright scholar, London, 1957-58; fellow Am. Coun. Learned Socs., London, 1963-64, NEH, 1974-75. Mem. World Future Soc., N.Y. State Assn. European Historians (pres. 1977-78), H.G. Wells Soc. (v.p. 1988—), Soc. for Utopian Studies. Home: 724 Pickwick Dr Vestal NY 13850 E-mail: wwagar@stny.rr.com.

WAGENER, HOBART D. retired architect; b. Sioux Falls, S.D., May 10, 1921; s. Frank Samuel and Beatrice (Hobart) W.; m. Violet LaVaughn, Dec. 16, 1944; children: Diane Kay Wagener, Jeffrey Scott, Shaw Bradley. BArch, U. Mich., 1944. Registered architect, Colo. Draftsman Eggers & Higgins, Architects, N.Y.C., 1946-47, Pietro Belluschi, Architect, Portland, Oreg., 1947-50; designer James Hunter, Architect, Boulder, Colo., 1950-53; prin. Hobart D. Wagener Assocs., Boulder, 1953-77; prin. ptnr. Wagener Vander-Vorste, Architects, Boulder, 1977-86; ret., 1986. Mem. selection com. Colo. Supreme Ct., Denver, 1968-72. Co-author: The School Library, 1962; work pub. in Archtl. Record, Sunset mag., N.Y. Times, House Beautiful, 25 Years of Record Houses. Chmn. Boulder Planning Commn., 1966; pres. Boulder C. of C., 1971. Lt. (j.g.) USN, 1944-46, PTO. Named Outstanding Designer for past 50 yrs. Hist. Boulder, 1983; also numerous nat. and regional design awards. Fellow AIA (pres. Colo. 1973, Colo. Architect of Yr. award 1985, pres. award N.Mex. chpt. 1998), Lions (pres. Boulder 1965). Avocations: travel, golf. Address: 1730 Avenida Del Mundo Coronado CA 92118-3021 E-mail: arclib@msn.com.

WAGER, MICHAEL, manufacturing executive; Pres. Robert H. Wager Co. Address: Robert H Wager Co 570 Montroyal Rd Rural Hall NC 27045-9550

WAGES, ROBERT COLEMAN, equity investor; b. Casablanca, Morocco, Aug. 28, 1963; came to U.S., 1963; s. Dan Sims and Sara Mae (Miller) W.; m. Tara Shamattee Sarwan, July 18, 1992; children: John Coleman, Thomas Sims; 1 stepchild, Jason Anthony Squillace. AB in Chemistry with honors, Princeton U., 1985. Cons. Oliver, Wyman & Co., N.Y.C., 1985—87; from assoc. to mng. dir. Castle Harlan, Inc., N.Y.C., 1987—2001, mng. dir., 2001—. Bd. dirs. Dearborn Risk Mgmt., Inc., N.J., Gravograph New Hermes LLC, Atlanta, Stackteck Sys., Inc., Toronto, Ont., Can., Carret Holdings, Inc., N.Y.C. Sponsor Student/Sponsor Partnership, N.Y.C., 1987-91, All Saints Episcopal Ch., vestry 1994-95, treas. 1995. Republican. Episcopalian. Avocations: sailing, travel, photography, scuba diving. Office: Castle Harlan Inc 150 E 58th St New York NY 10155-0002 Business E-Mail: rwages@castleharlan.com.

WAGGENER, RONALD EDGAR, radiologist; b. Green River, Wyo., Oct. 6, 1926; s. Edgar Fleetwood and Mary Harlene (Hutton) W.; m. Everina Ann Stalker, Aug. 1, 1948; children: Marta, Nancy, Paul, Daphne. Student, Colo. A&M U., 1944; student, Oreg. State U., 1945; BS, U. Nebr., 1949, MS, 1952, PhD, 1957, MD cum laude, 1954, postgrad., 1955-58, St. Bartholomew's, London, 1956-57. Diplomate Am. Bd. Radiology. Intern U. Nebr. Hosp., 1954-55, resident, 1955-56, 57-58; radiation therapist Nebr. Meth. Hosp., Omaha, 1965-70, chmn. cancer com., 1964-89, dir. cancer and radiation therapy, 1964-89, dir. dept. radiology, 1970-89, dir. cancer fellowship program, 1977-89; instr. radiology U. Nebr., Omaha, 1958, asst. prof., 1959-61, radiation therapist, 1959-65, assoc. prof., 1962-80, clin. assoc. prof., 1981—. Pres. Highland Assocs. Ltd., Omaha, 1977-89; mem. cancer com. Children's Meml. Hosp., Omaha, 1970-89. Contbr. articles to profl. jours. With C.E., U.S. Army, 1944-46. Fellow AEC, 1952-53, Am. Cancer Soc., 1956-57. Fellow Am. Coll. Radiologists; mem. Nebr. Radiology Soc. (pres. 1963-64), Sigma Xi, Alpha Omega Alpha, Phi Nu. Home: PO Box 666 Pinedale WY 82941-0666 Office: 13304 W Center Rd Omaha NE 68144-3453

WAGGENER, THERYN LEE, retired law enforcement professional; b. Cedar Rapids, Iowa, Sept. 7, 1941; s. Walter and Hollis Angisa (Fowler) W.; m. Zoetta Jean Hamilton, May 30, 1967; 1 child, Drugh Kincade. BBA, Nat. U., 1977, MBA. 1979; JD, Tex. So. U., 1980. Traffic officer Calif. Hwy. Patrol, San Diego, 1966-72; owner, operator Am. Nat. Chem., San Diego, 1972-82; chief investigator N.Mex. Real Estate Commn., Albuquerque, 1983-86, Nev. Real Estate Divsn., Carson City, 1986—89; lt., shift comdr. Nev. Dept. Prisons, Ely, 1989-2000. Prof., Sierra Nev. Coll., Incline Village, 1988-89, Western Nev. Community Coll., Carson City, 1987-89. Mem. Washoe County (Nev.) Rep. Cen. Com., 1989. With USN, 1960-65. Mem. Nat. Assn. Real Estate Lic. Law Ofcls. (enforcement and investigative com. 1987-89), Toastmasters, Rotary, Lions, Masons, Shriners, Nu Beta Epsilon. Avocations: skiing, golf, horses, flying. E-mail: theryn@sbcglobal.net.

WAGGONER, JAMES CLYDE, lawyer; b. Nashville, May 7, 1946; s. Charles Franklin and Alpha (Noah) W.; m. Diane Dusenbery, Aug. 17, 1968; children: Benjamin, Elizabeth. BA, Reed Coll., 1968; JD, U. Oreg., 1974. Bar: Oreg. 1974, U.S. Dist. Ct. Oreg. 1975, U.S. Ct. Appeals (9th cir.) 1980, U.S. Tax Ct. 1979, U.S. Supreme Ct. 1979. Clk. to presiding justice Oreg. Supreme Ct., Salem, 1974-75; assoc. Martin, Bischoff & Templeton, Portland, Oreg., 1975-78, ptnr., 1978-82, Waggoner, Farleigh, Wada, Georgeff & Witt, Portland, 1982-89, Davis Wright Tremaine, Portland, 1990—. Contbr. articles to profl. jours. Fulbright scholar U. London, 1968-69. Mem. ABA, Oreg. Bar Assn., Multnomah Bar Assn., Reed Coll. Alumni Assn. (v.p. 1988, pres. 1989, bd. mgmt.) Alzheimers Assn. of Columbia-Willamette (v.p. 1992, pres. 1993), Order of Coif, Phi Beta Kappa. Democrat. Avocations: wood turning, calligraphy. Office: Davis Wright Tremaine 1300 SW 5th Ave Ste 2300 Portland OR 97201-5682 Office Phone: 503-778-5326. Business E-Mail: jimwaggoner@dwt.com.

WAGGONER, JAMES VIRGIL, chemicals company executive; b. Judsonia, Ark., Oct. 29, 1927; s. Loren Dye and Vera (Meacham) W.; m. M.E. June Howell; children: Liz Waggoner Quisenberry, Jay. BS in Chemistry and Math., Ouachita Bapt. U., 1948, DSc (hon.), 1990; MS in Organic Chemistry and Math., U. Tex., 1950. Successively rsch. chemist, sales asst., asst. sales mgr., sales mgr. Monsanto, Texas City, Tex., 1950-57, dir. sales Springfield, Mass., 1957-59, product adminstr. St. Louis, 1959-61, dir. sales, 1961-63, dir. mktg., 1963-67, bus. dir., 1967-68, gen. mgr. petrochems. div., 1972-76, gen. mgr. cycle-safe div., 1976, corp. v.p., mng. dir. Plastics & Resins Co., 1977, group v.p., 1978-80; pres. petrochem. and plastics unit El Paso Co., Odessa, Tex., 1980-83; cons. to petrochem. industry Houston, 1984-85; pres., CEO Sterling Chems., Inc., Houston, 1986-96; pres., owner, CEO JVW Investment Ltd., Houston, 1996—. Mem. adv. bd. 1st Comml. Bank, N.A., Little Rock; bd. dirs. Kirby Corp., Houston, Mail-Well Holdings, Inc., Englewood, Colo. Chmn. adv. coun. Coll. Natural Scis., U. Tex., Austin; mem. devel. coun. Ouachita Bapt. U.; bd. dirs. Tex. Rsch. League; bd. dirs., chmn. Good Samaritan Found., 1993-94; supporter, patron Star of Hope Mission; corp. leader, contbr. United Way, Texas City, LaMarque Area, Houston; mem. chmn.'s adv. bd. Rep. Nat. Conv. Mem. Nat. Petroleum Refiners Assn. (v.p., bd. dirs., exec. com.), Tex. Assn. Taxpayers (bd. dirs.). Avocations: golf, art collecting. Home: 11 Shadder Way Houston TX 77019-1415 Office: 1111 Bagby St Ste 2420 Houston TX 77002-2554 *In my opinion, the greatest single character trait that separates those who excel and achieve from those who don't is their constant committment to excellence and to strive for continuing improvement.*

WAGGONER, LAWRENCE WILLIAM, law educator; b. Sidney, Ohio, July 2, 1937; s. William J. and Gladys L. Waggoner; m. Lynne S. Applebaum, Aug. 27, 1963; children: Ellen, Diane. BBA, U. Cin., 1960; JD, U. Mich., 1963; PhD, Oxford (Eng.) U., 1966. Assoc. Cravath, Swaine & Moore, N.Y.C., 1963; prof. law U. Ill., Champaign, 1968-72, U. Va., Charlottesville, 1972—74, U. Mich., Ann Arbor, 1974-84, Lewis M. Simes prof. law, 1987—. Dir. rsch., chief reporter joint editorial bd. for Uniform Trust and Estate Acts, 1986-94, dir. rsch., 1994—, joint editl. bd. uniform trust and estate acts; reporter restatement (3d) of property, 1990—; adviser restatement (3d) of trusts, 1993—. Author: Family Property Law: Wills, Trusts, and Future Interests, 3d edit., 2002, Uniform Trust and Estate, 2004—, California and Uniform Trust and Estate Statutes, 2004—. Served to capt., U.S. Army, 1966-68. Fulbright scholar Oxford U., 1963-65. Mem. Am. Law Inst., Am. Coll. Trust and Estates Counsel, Internat. Acad. Estate and Trust Law. Office: U Mich Law Sch 625 S State St Ann Arbor MI 48109-1215 Office Phone: 734-763-2586.

WAGGONER, PAUL EDWARD, agricultural scientist; b. Appanoose County, Iowa, Mar. 29, 1923; s. Walter Loyal and Kathryn (Maring) W.; m. Barbara Ann Lockerbie, Nov. 3, 1945; children— Von Lockerbie, Daniel Maring S.B., U. Chgo., 1946; MS, Iowa State Coll., 1949, PhD, 1951. From asst. to chief scientist Conn. Agrl. Expt. Sta., New Haven, 1951-71, vice dir., 1969-71, dir., 1972-87, disting. scientist, 1987—. Mem. panels on policy implications of global warming NAS, 1989-91; chmn. sci. adv. bd. Giant Sequoia Nat. Monument, 2001-02. Contbr. articles to profl. jours. Served to capt. USAAF, 1943-46 Guggenheim fellow, 1963 Fellow AAAS (chmn. climate changes and water resources com. 1986-89), Am. Phytopath. Soc.; mem. NAS, Am. Meteorol. Soc. (Outstanding Achievement in Biometerology award 1967), Conn. Acad. Sci. and Engring., Recipient of the Anton-de- Bary Medal, 1996, Grads Club. Achievements include rsch. in mathematical simulation of plant disease epidemics, hydrologic role of foliar pores, climate change on agriculture and water resources, how much ten billion can spare for nature. Home: 314 Vineyard Point Rd Guilford CT 06437-3255 Office: Conn Agrl Expt Sta PO Box 1106 New Haven CT 06504-1106 E-mail: paul.waggoner@po.state.ct.us.

WAGGONER, ROBERT, chef; Studied with Michael Roberts, Trumps, 1981—83; studied with Jacques Lameloise, Charles Barrier, Pierre Gagnaire, Gerard Boyer, Mark Meneau, France; studied with Jean Paul Coupal, Caracas, Venezuela. Owner restaurant Le Monte Cristo, France; chef with Jean Pierre Silva Le Vieux Moulin, Beaune, 1991; chef Turnberry Isle, Fla., 1993, The Wild Boar, Nashville, Charleston Grill, 2002—. Guest appearances fine dining establishments James Beard Ho., N.Y.C. Appeared (TV series) Gourmet Getaways with Robin Leach, Great Chefs of the South, Nashville's Talk of the Town, Ralph Emery Show, The Food Network's In Food Today, appearances with food reporter Burt Wolf (TV series) The Travel Channel, CNN, PBS Stas. nationwide, host Salute to Southern Chefs. Supporter nat. relief hunger charity Share our Strength. Office: Charleston Grill Charleston Pl Hotel 244 King St Charleston SC 29401

WAGLE, SUSAN, state legislator, small business owner; b. Allentown, Pa., Sept. 27, 1953; m. John Thomas Wagle, Apr. 3, 1980; children: Julia Marie, Andrea Elizabeth, John Timothy, Paul Thomas. BA in Elem. Edn. cum laude, Wichita State U., 1979, post grad., 1979-82. Tchr. Chisholm Trail Elem., Kans., 1979-80; tchr. emotionally disturbed, special edn. Price Elem., Kans., 1980-82; real estate investor Kans., 1980—; prin. Wichita Bus. Inc., Kans., 1983—; mem. Kans. Ho. Reps. from 99th dist., Topeka, 1990, 92, 94-2000; speaker pro tem Kans. Ho. Reps., Topeka, 1994-2000; mem. Kans. Senate from 30th dist., Topeka, 2001—. Mem. Am. Legis. Exchange Coun. (state chmn., nat. bd. dirs., Outstanding Legis. of Yr. award 1994), Farm Bur., Nat. Fedn. Ind. Bus., Nat. Restaurant Assn., Wichita Ind. Bus. Assn. Home: 14 N Sandalwood St Wichita KS 67230-6612

WAGLE, UDAYA, educator; s. Kaladhar and Madhu M. Wagle; m. Karuna Khanal, June 30, 1999; 1 child, Ava S. MS in Nonprofit Mgmt., Ea.U., St. Davids, Pa., 1997; Ph.D. (candidate), U.Mass., Boston, 2004. Program officer Inst. for Integrated Devel. Studies, Kathmandu, Nepal, 1991—95; rsch. assoc. U. Mass., Boston, 1998—, lectr., 2001—. Rsch. cons. USC, LA, 2001—02. Contbr. articles to profl. jours. Grantee Dissertation Rsch. Grant, U. Mass. Boston, 2002, Craig R. Bollinger Meml. Rsch. Grant, 2002. Mem.: Ea. Econ. Assn. (assoc.), Am. Polit. Sci. Assn. (assoc.). Achievements include research in urban poverty issues in Kathmandu. Office: U Mass 100 Morrissey Blvd Boston MA 02125

WAGMAN, GERALD HOWARD, retired biochemist; b. Mar. 4, 1926; s. David and Sophie (Milinsky) W.; m. Rhoda Kirschner, Dec. 9, 1948; children: Jan Donald, Neil Mark. BS, Lehigh U., 1946; MS, Va. Poly. Inst. and State U., 1947. Tech. rsch. asst. Squibb Inst. for Med. Rsch., New Brunswick, N.J., 1947-49, 54-57; mgr. Yankee Radio Corp., N.Y.C., 1950-54; assoc. biochemist Schering Corp. (now Schering-Plough Rsch. Inst.), Kenilworth, N.J., 1957-58, biochemist, 1958-68, sect. leader, 1969-70, from mgr. antibiotics dept. to prin. scientist, 1970-89, mgr. libr. info. ctr., 1989-93; ret., 1993. Freelance tech. writer, editor, cons., 1993—; adv. bd. Nat. Cert. Commn. in Chemistry and Chem. Engring., 1985-88. Author: Chromatography of Antibiotics, 1973, rev. edit., 1984, The Handy HamBook, 1994; mem. editl. bd. Antimicrobial Agents and Chemotherapy, 1971-74; co-editor: Isolation, Separation and Purification of Antibiotics, 1978, Natural Products Isolation, 1989; contbr. chpts. in books and articles to profl. jours.; patentee in field. Coun. mem. Troop 23 Boy Scouts Am., 1964-66; comm. officer East Brunswick Civil Def. and Disaster Control, 1966-71; mem. sci. adv. com. East Brunswick Bd. Edn., 1960-68; bd. dirs. Tamarack N. Homeowners Assn., pres., 1989-93, treas., 1994—. Recipient Pub. Svc. award, Am. Radio Relay League, 1965. Chartered chemist, Gt. Britain; fellow Am. Inst. Chemists; mem. AAAS, ALA, Spl. Libra. Assn., Am. Chem. Soc., Am. Soc. Microbiology, Am. Inst. Biol. Scis., Soc. Indsl. Microbiology, Soc. Applied Microbiology (Gt. Britain), Royal Soc. Chemistry, Sigma Xi, Tau Delta Phi. Home and Office: 17 Crommelin Ct East Brunswick NJ 08816-2406

WAGMAN, ROBERT JOHN, journalist, writer; b. Chgo., Nov. 11, 1942; s. Albert Alan and Rosamond (Horner) Wagman; m. Carol Ann Mueller, Jan. 30, 1965; children: Jennifer, Patricia, Marilyn. AB, St. Louis U., 1966, MA, 1968, JD, 1971. Analyst Dun & Bradstreet, 1965-67; with CBS News, 1967-71, 74-77; asst. to dean St. Louis U. Sch. Law, 1971-74; Washington bur. chief N.Am. Newspaper Alliance, 1977-80, Ind. News Alliance, 1980-82; columnist Newspaper Enterprise Assn., 1980-95. Sr. corr. Soccertimes, VP, Washington, SMA Global. Author, co-author Hubert Humphrey, The Man and His Dream, 1978, Citizens Guide to the Tax Revolt, 1979, Asbestos: The Silent Killer, 1982, Lord's Justice, 1985, Instant Millionaires, 1986, The Nazi Hunters, 1988, The First Amendment Book, 1991, 2d edit., 1996, World Almanac Guide to the Supreme Court, 1993, Blood Oath, 1994, Hong Kong, 1997, And Beyond, 1997; editor: World Almanac of U.S. Politics, 1994—2000. Recipient Thomas Stokes award in Journalism.

WAGNER, ALAN CYRIL, television and film producer, consultant, performing arts educator; b. N.Y.C., Oct. 1, 1931; s. Joseph and Isabelle (Chanson) W.; m. Martha Celia Dreyfus, Mar. 11, 1956; children: David Mark, Susan Jill, Elizabeth Celia. BA, Columbia U., 1951, MA in English, 1952. Mgr. network programs Benton & Bowles, Inc., N.Y.C., 1957-61; dir. program devel. CBS, N.Y.C., 1961-68, v.p. program devel. Hollywood, Calif., 1968-73, v.p. program planning and devel. N.Y.C., 1973-75, v.p. nighttime programs, 1975-78, v.p. programs, 1978-82; pres., chief exec. officer The Disney Channel, N.Y.C., 1982-83; pres., CEO Alan Wagner Prodns., Inc., N.Y.C., 1983—; exec. v.p. feature and TV devel. and prodn. Grosso-Jacobson Entertainment Corp., N.Y.C., 1985-90; pres. Boardwalk Entertainment, N.Y.C., 1990-97, chmn., 1997—. Sr. program cons. Todays Cath. Cable Network, 1999-; adj. assoc. prof. visual arts NYU, 1993-98; lectr. Met. Opera Guild, CUNY, Wagner Soc. Prodr., dir., host program Living Opera, Stas. WNYC-WNYC-FM, N.Y.C., 1958-68; host radio broadcasts N.Y.C. Opera Co., 1978-80; panelist, commentator Met. Opera broadcasts, 1996—; contbr., Opera News, 2001—, Playbill, 2004—; exec. prodr. film Reunion at Fairborough, 1985; prodr. TV pilot We're Puttin' on the Ritz, 1986; author: Prima Donnas and other Wild Beasts, 1961; exec. con. The Gunfighters, Diamonds; supervising prodr. Cop Talk: Behind the Shield, 1988, 89, True Blue, TV movie and series, 1989, A Family for Joe, TV movie and series, 1989-90, TV series Counterstrike, 1990-93, Top Cops, 1989-94; exec. prodr. TV movies Spenser: Ceremony, Spenser: Pale Kings and Princes, 1993, Spenser: The Judas Goat, Spenser: A Savage Place, 1994, Wounded Heart, 1995, Hearts Adrift, Reasons of the Heart, 1996, TV series The Marriage Counselor, 1994. Lt. (j.g.) USNR, 1953-57. Recipient Evelyn Burkey Meml. award Writers Guild Am., 1983, Silver Circle award NATAS, 1999. Mem. NATAS, Brit. Acad. Film and TV Arts, Wagner Soc. N.Y., Columbia U. Alumni Assn. Avocations: opera, other music, sound reproduction, baseball, other sports. Office: Boardwalk Entertainment 210 E 39th St New York NY 10016-2754 E-mail: aw.boardwalk@infohouse.com. *A decent and abiding respect for the opinions and talents of the creative community on one hand, and the consuming community on the other, has always served as the necessary framework for any decision making in both my professional and personal life. The doers and the thinkers are crucially important, but no more so than those for whom they do and think. If I can serve as an effective middle man, a good part of my life's objective is realizable.*

WAGNER, ALEXANDER JOHANNES, physicist, educator; m. Heather Jean Ummel-Wagner, Oct. 10, 2000. Diploma in Math., Diploma in Physics, U. Bielefeld, Germany, 1990; MS in Physics, U. Bielefeld, 1994; PhD in Theoretical Physics, Oxford (Eng.) U., 1997. Postdoctoral rsch. asst. MIT, Cambridge, Mass., 1998—99, U. Edinburgh, Scotland, 2000—02; asst. prof. N.D. State U., Fargo, 2002—. Presenter in field. Achievements include research in lattice boltzmann; spinodal decomposition; viscoelasticity. Office: ND State Univ Dept Physics Administration Dr Box 5566 Fargo ND 58105-5566 E-mail: alexander.wagner@ndsu.nodak.edu.

WAGNER, ALYSON KAY (ALY WAGNER), professional soccer player; b. San Jose, Calif., Aug. 10, 1980; Majored in combined scis., Santa Clara U., Calif., 1999—2002. Soccer player, midfielder U.S. Women's Nat. Team, 1998—; team mem. San Diego Spirit, 2003—. No. 1 draft pick San Diego Spirit, WUSA, 2003. Finalist Hermann trophy, 2001, Mo. Athletic Club award, 2001; named second team All-Am, NSCAA, 2000, first team All-Am, 2001, first team All-Am., 2002, Offensive MVP, NCAA Final Four, 2001, Female Player of Yr., Soccer Am., 2001; recipient Top VII award, NCAA, 2002, Mo. Athletic Club Hermann trophy, 2002. Office: US Soccer Fedn 1801 S Prairie Ave Chicago IL 60616

WAGNER, ANN, political organization executive; m. Ray Wagner; children: Raymond III, Stephen, Mary Ruth. BSBA, U. Mo., 1984. Mem. com. Lafayette Twp.; chmn. com. St. Louis County Republican Ctrl. Com.; mem. Mo. Fedn. Republican Women; dir. ho. and senate redistricting commn. Mo. Republican Party, 1991, chmn., 1999—; Mo. state exec. dir. Bush/Quayle Campaign, 1992; advisor Ashcroft for Senate Campaign, 1994; 2nd congl. dist. chair Dole for Pres. Campaign, 1996; co-chmn. Republican Nat. Com., Wash., 2001—. Chair Mo. Rep. Party. Mem.: Republican Nat. Conv. Mid-western State Chmn.'s Assn. (com. on arrangements 2000, del. 2000, del. chmn. 2000). Office: Mo Rep Party 204 East Dunklin Jefferson City MO 65101

WAGNER, ANNICE MCBRYDE, judge; BA, law degree, Wayne State U. With Houston and Gardner; gen. counsel Nat. Capital Housing Authority; people's counsel D.C.; assoc. judge Superior Court D.C., 1977-90, D.C. Ct. Appeals, 1990—, now chief judge. Mem. teaching team, trial advocacy workshop Harvard U. Office: Dist of Columbia Court of Appeals 500 Indiana Ave NW Ste 6000 Washington DC 20001-2131

WAGNER, ARTHUR WARD, JR., lawyer; b. Birmingham, Ala., Aug. 13, 1930; s. Arthur Ward and Lucille (Lockheart) W.; m. Ruth Shingler, May 11, 1957; children: Celia Wagner Minter, Julia Wagner Dolce, Helen Wagner McAfee. BSBA, U. Fla., 1954, JD, 1957. Bar: Fla. 1957, U.S. Dist. Ct. (so. dist.) Fla. 1957, U.S. Dist. Ct. (mid. dist.) Fla. 1975. Ptnr. Wagner & McAfee, P.A., West Palm Beach, Fla., 1959-2000; ret., 2000—. Lectr. in field. Author: Art of Advocacy: Jury Selection, 1981; co-author: Anatomy of Personal Injury Lawsuit I & II, 1968 and 1981. Mem. 15th Jud. Nominating Com., Palm Beach City, 1979—82, 4th Dist. Nominating Commn., Palm Beach City, 1982—86; mem. pres.'s coun. U. Fla.; vestry Holy Trinity Parish, v.p., 2002—; bd. dirs., pres.-elect U. Fla. Found., 1996—. Fellow Internat. Acad. Trial Lawyers, Am. Coll. Trial Lawyers, Internat. Soc. Barristers, Am. Bd. Trial Advs.; mem. Assn. Trial Lawyers Am. (pres. 1975-76, hon. life trustee Roscoe Pound Found.), So. Trial Lawyers Assn. (pres. 1991), U. Fla. Law Coll. Alumni (mem. bd. govs.). Democrat. Episcopalian.

WAGNER, BARRY J. lawyer; Grad., Hamilton Coll., 1963, Harvard U., 1966. Sec., gen. counsel Omnicom Group, 2003—. Office: Imnocom Group Inc 437 Madison Ave New York NY 10022

WAGNER, BILLY, professional baseball player; b. Tannersville, Va., July 25, 1971; Student, Ferrum Coll. Baseball player Houston Astros, 1995—. Named 1st Houston pitcher to win Rolaids Relief Man award. Achievements include holds the single-season NCAA record for most strikeouts per nine innings (19.1 in 1992); Division III mark for most career K's (327 in 182.1 innings); fewest hits allowed per game (1.58 in 1992). Office: Houston Astros Po Box 288 Houston TX 77001-0288

WAGNER, BRUCE STANLEY, marketing professional; b. San Diego, Aug. 1, 1943; s. Robert Sheldon and Janet (Lowther) Wagner; m. Elizabeth Pearsall Winslow, Oct. 4, 1975; children: Sage Elizabeth, Alexander Winslow. BA, Dartmouth Coll., 1965; MBA, U. Pa., 1984. Sr. v.p. Grey Advt., Inc., N.Y.C., 1967-81; exec. v.p., chief oper. officer Campaign '76 Media Comm., Inc., Washington, 1975-76; exec. v.p., bd. dirs. Ross Roy, Inc., Bloomfield Hills, Mich., 1981-91, Ross Roy Group, Inc., Bloomfield Hills, Mich., 1991-94; v.p. mktg. and comms. ITT Automotive Inc., Auburn Hills, Mich., 1995-99; pres. Wagner & Co., Ltd., Birmingham, Mich., 1999—2000; v.p. mktg. and corp. comms. MSX Internat. Inc., Southfield, 2001—03; pres. Wagner & Co., Ltd., Birmingham, 2004—. Mem. parents bd. Bucknell U., pres. parents bd., 1999—2000, mem. bus. adv. bd., chmn., 2003—. Mem.: Am. Assn. Advt. Agys. (chmn., bd. govs. Mich. coun. 1985—86, bd. govs. ctrl. region 1988—94), Wharton Alumni Assn. (chmn. 1983—85), Birmingham Athletic Club, Orchard Lake Country Club, Detroit Athletic Club, Wharton Club Mich. (bd. dirs. 1985—90). Home and Office: Wagner & Co Ltd 975 Arlington Rd Birmingham MI 48009-1684

WAGNER, CHARLENE BROOK, publishing consultant, elementary school educator; b. L.A. d. Edward J. and Eva (Anderson) Brook; children: Gordon, Brook, John. BS, Tex. Christian U., 1952; MEd, Sam Houston U., 1973; postgrad., U. Tex., Austin, 1975, Tex. A&M U., 1977. Sci. educator Spring Branch Ind. Sch. Dist., Houston, 1970-98; ret., 2000; dir. CompuKidZ, Houston, 1998—2000; cons. Scott Foresman, Addison Wesley, Ginn, Houston. Cons. Scott Foresman Pub. Co., Houston, 2000-01; owner Sci. Instrnl. Sys. Co., 1988—; dir. Compukidz. Mem. Houston Symphony League, 1992, Mus. Fine Arts, Mus. of Art of Am. West, Houston, 1989, Mus. Natural Scis., Women's Christian Home, Houston, 1991; mem. Houston Grand Opera Guild, mem. exec. bd. 1999-2000, rec./corr. sec.; social chmn. Encore, 1988; mem. Magic Circle Rep. Women's Club. Mem.: AAUW, NAFE, NEA, Internat. Platform Assn., Spring Branch Edn. Assn., Tex. State Tchrs. Assn., Heather and Thistle Soc., Wellington Soc. for Arts (Houston chpt.), Clan Anderson Soc., Art League Houston, Shepherd Soc., Watercolor Arts Soc. (Houston), Houston Highland Games Assn., Space City Ski Club. Episcopalian. Avocations: painting, watercolor media. Home: 2670 Marilee Ln Apt B54 Houston TX 77057-4264 E-mail: wagner2670@aol.com.

WAGNER, CHERI J. business owner; b. Mar. 9, 1963; Owner, mgr. Wagner Constrn., Lake Arrowhead, Calif., 1980-94, Blind Ambitions, Skyforest, Calif., 1994—. Mem. C. of C., Soroptomists, Nat. Fedn. Ind. Bus., Humane Soc., Arrowhead Bldg. Contractors Assn., Mountain Women's Assn. Office: 22788 Via Santana Nuevo CA 92567-9636 Office Phone: 951-928-5517. E-mail: poker4me247@msn.com.

WAGNER, CHRISTIAN NIKOLAUS JOHANN, materials engineering educator; b. Saarbrucken-Dudweiler, Germany, Mar. 6, 1927; arrived in U.S., 1959, naturalized, 1969; s. Christian Jakob and Regina (Bungert) W.; m. Rosemarie Anna Mayer, Apr. 5, 1952; children— Thomas Martin, Karla Regine, Petra Susanne. Student, U. Poitiers, France, 1948-49; Licence es Sci., U. Saar, Ger., 1951, Diplom-Ingenieur, 1954, Dr.rer.nat., 1957 Research asst. Inst. fur Metallforschung, Saarbrucken, 1953-54; vis. fellow M.I.T., 1955-56; research asso. Inst. fur Metallforschung, 1957-58; teaching, research asst. U. Saarbrucken, 1959; asst. prof. Yale U., New Haven, Conn., 1959-62, assoc. prof., 1962-70; prof. dept. materials engring. UCLA, 1970-91, prof. emeritus, 1991—, chmn. dept., 1974-79, asst. dean undergrad. studies Sch. Engring. and Applied Sci., 1982-85, acting chmn., 1990-91. Vis. prof. Tech. U., Berlin, 1969, U. Saarbrücken, 1979-80 Contbr. articles to profl. jours. Recipient U.S. Sci. Humboldt award, U. Saarbrucken, 1989—90, 1992. Fellow Am. Soc. Metals Internat.; mem. Am. Crystallographic Assn., Minerals, Metals and Materials Soc. Home: 37621 Golden Pebble Ave Palm Desert CA 92211-1430 Office: UCLA 6532 Boelter Hl Los Angeles CA 90095-0001 E-mail: cwagner@dc.rr.com.

WAGNER, CURTIS LEE, JR., judge; b. Nov. 8, 1928; m. Jeanne E. Allen (dec.); children: Curtis L. III, Rex A. Student, Tenn. Poly. Inst., 1947-49; LLB, U. Tenn., 1951. Bar: Tenn. 1952. Assoc. Kramer, Dye, McNabb and Greenwood, Knoxville, Tenn., 1951-54; atty.-adv. gen. crimes and fraud sect. Criminal Divsn. Dept. Justice, Washington, 1954-56; trial atty. Dept. Justice, Washington, 1954-60; assigned to Ct. of Claims sect. Civil Divsn., Washington, 1956-60; spl. asst. comms., transp. and utilities JAG Dept. Army, Washington, 1960-64; chief Regulatory Law Divsn., Washington, 1964-74; adminstrv. law judge FERC, Washington, 1974-79, chief adminstrv. law judge, 1979—. Mem. civilian lawyer career com., 1960-74; chmn. JAG incentive awards com. 1960-74; mem. Army Staff Awards Bd., 1964-74, Army Environ. Policy Council, 1972-74. Dist. commr. Nat. Capital Area coun. Boy Scouts Am., 1967-69; mem. Bd. Govts. Watergate of Alexandria Condo, 1996—; commr. Alexandria Redevel. and Pub. Housing Commn., 1996-2000. Decorated Meritorious Civilian Svc. award, Exceptional Civilian Svc. award; recipient citation for outstanding performance Dept. Army, 1961-74, Scouter's Tng. award Boy Scouts Am., 1965, Scoutmaster's Key, 1966, Commr.'s Key, 1968, Commr.'s Arrowhead Honor, 1966, Silver Beaver award 1969. Mem. Order of Arrow, Annapolis Yacht (parliamentarian) Club. Methodist. Office: Fed Energy Regulatory Comm 888 1st St NE Washington DC 20426-0002 Office Phone: 202-502-8500. E-mail: curtis.wagner@ferc.gov.

WAGNER, CYNTHIA GAIL, editor, writer; b. Bethesda, Md., Oct. 3, 1956; d. Robert Cheney and Marjory Jane (Kletzing) W. BA in English, Grinnell Coll., 1978; MA in Comms., Syracuse U., 1981. Editl. asst. The Futurist/World Future Soc., Bethesda, Md., 1981—82, staff editor, 1982-85, asst. editor, 1985-91, sr. editor, 1991-92, mng. editor, 1992—. Editor: (newsletter) Futurist Update, 2000—; columnist: 3-2-1 Contact, 1994; contbr. Encyclopedia of the Future, 1995, The 21st Century, 1999. Mem. Theatre Comm. Group, Washington Shakespeare Reading Group. Avocation: theater. Office: The Futurist World Future Soc 7910 Woodmont Ave Ste 450 Bethesda MD 20814-3066 Business E-Mail: cwagner@wfs.org.

WAGNER, DARRYL WILLIAM, lawyer; b. Dixon, Ill., Jan. 14, 1943; s. Earl L. and Lois Mae W.; m. Susan A. Aldrich; children: Peter Alan, Nicholas William. BA, Northwestern U., 1965, JD, 1968. Bar: Ill. 1968, U.S. Dist. Ct. (no. dist.) Ill. 1969, U.S. Ct. Appeals (7th cir.) 1971, Calif. 1982. Sr. counsel Sidley Austin Brown & Wood, Chgo., 1969—. Dir. Housing Options for People to Excell, Inc., 1992-94, 96—. Co-author: Illinois Municipal Law: Subdivisions and Subdivisions in Controls, 1978, 81. Mem. ABA, Internat. Assn. Attys. and Execs. in Corp. Real Estate, Ill. State Bar Assn., Chgo. Bar Assn. Presbyterian. Home: 526 A San Ysdiro Rd Santa Barbara CA 93108 Office: Sidley Austin Brown & Wood 555 W 5th St Ste 4000 Los Angeles CA 90013-3000 E-mail: dwagner@sidley.com., wwagneresq@springmail.com.

WAGNER, DONALD BERT, healthcare consultant; b. York, Pa., July 27, 1930; s. Bert Daniel and Mary Elizabeth (Roelke) W.; m. Janet Louise Bankert, July 12, 1952; children: Kimberly, Susan, David, John. Student, Franklin & Marshall, 1948-50; BS in Phys. Therapy, Columbia U., 1952; MHA, Baylor U., 1960. Commd. 2d lt. USAF, 1952, advanced through grades to brig. gen., 1982; physical therapist Randolph AFB, San Antonio, 1952-55; asst. adminstr. USAF/RAF S. Ruislip, London; adminstr. USAF/RAF Bentwaters, Ipswich, Eng., 1955-58; various adminstrv. roles USAF Hosps. and Commands, Europe and U.S., 1958-73; dep. comdr. USAF Sch. Health Care Sci., Wichita Falls, Tex., 1973-75; adminstr. Wilford Hall Med. Ctr., San Antonio, 1975-79; chief med. svc. corps Office Surgeon Gen. USAF, San Antonio, 1979-82; dep. surgeon gen. USAF Med. Svc. Ctr., San Antonio, 1981-82, ret., 1982; adminstr., assoc. v.p. M. D. Anderson/U. Tex. Cancer Ctr., Houston, 1982-85; chief exec. officer Meml. Southwest Hosp., Houston, 1985-91; v.p. Meml. Hosp. System, Houston, 1985-91, interim hosp. chief, 1991—; mem. adv. bd. Grad. Program in Healthcare Adminstrn. Texas Women's U., Houston. Adj. prof. Baylor and Trinity U., San Antonio, 1975-82; assoc. prof. U. Houston, St. Louis U., 1982-88; exec. officer Woodlands Hosp., Angleton-Danbury Hosp., Prevention and Recovery Ctr., Bellville Hosp., MHHS Long Term Acute Care Hosp.; cons., El Salvador, Nicaragua, China, Saudi Arabia, Japan, Korea, 1991-2002. Bd. dirs. Hospice at the Med. Ctr., 1982-2001, Child Advocates, Houston, 1985-89, Kidney Found., Houston, 1985-88, Westland YMCA, Houston, 1985-88, 90-94, Greater Houston Hosp. Coun., 1983-87, Sam Houston area Alzheimer's Assn. 1990-94; mem.n. external adv. bd. Sch. Allied Health, U. Tex. Med. Br.; mem. adv. bd. gradrogram healthcare adminstrn. Tex. Women's U., Houston. Named Disting. Alumnus Baylor U. Program in Healthcare Adminstrn, 1993. Fellow Am. Coll. Healthcare Execs. (edn. com., ethics com., comm. com.), Royal Soc. Health; mem. Am. Hosp. Assn. (bd. dirs. hosp. rsch. and edn. found. 1990—), Tex. Hosp. Assn., Assn. Mil. Surgeons U.S. (Ray E. Brown award 1982, Outstanding Sr. Level Healthcare Exec. Ache Regents award 1991), Am. Mgmt. Soc. Republican. Methodist. Avocation: music. Home: 1746 Carriage Way Sugar Land TX 77478-4201 Office: Meml Healthcare System 9401 Southwest Fwy Houston TX 77074-1807 Office Phone: 713-448-6982. Business E-Mail: don_wagner@mhhs.org.

WAGNER, DOROTHY MARIE, retired senior creative designer, artist; b. Chgo., Jan. 12, 1926; d. William Christopher and Margaret Frances (Rowell) W. Student, Kalamazoo Coll., 1943-45; BS, Western Mich. U., 1947; BFA, Art Ctr. Coll. Design, L.A., 1962. Dir. electroencephalography lab. Bronson Hosp., Kalamazoo, 1945-51; dir. EEG lab. Terr. Hosp., Kaneohe, Hawaii, 1951-55, UCLA Med. Ctr., 1955-60; sr. creative designer GM Tech. Ctr. Styling, Warren, Mich., 1962-82. Cons. in EEG, Army Hosp., Honolulu, 1950-55; dir. sales and rental gallery Pt. Huron (Mich.) Mus., 1989-93, art and painting instr., 1992-96. Recipient Best of Show award Ea. Mich. Internat. Art Show, 1992, 1st pl. award, 1988, 89, 94. Mem. Blue Water Art Assn. (pres. 1990-96), Orion Art Ctr. Episcopalian. Avocations: horseback riding, showing in dressage, breeding and raising racing greyhounds, water color and acrylic painting, stained glass design and fabrication. Home: 14841 Pine Knoll Rd Capac MI 48014-1913 E mail: dot@glis.net.

WAGNER, EDWARD KURT, publishing company executive; b. N.Y.C., Sept. 29, 1936; s. Kurt Henry and Julia Marie (Selesky) W.; m. Ann Marie Philbin, Jan. 31, 1959; children: Denise, Steven, Kenneth, Jeanne. BBA, St. Francis Coll., 1961. With Pitman Pub. Corp., N.Y.C., 1952-75, v.p., treas., 1968-71, exec. v.p., 1971-75; financial mgr. Dun-Donnelley Pub. Corp., N.Y.C., 1975-76, contr. gen. book div., 1976-77; sr. mgr. contr.'s dept. Dun & Bradstreet, Inc., N.Y.C., 1977-78, asst. contr., 1978-83, contr., 1983-88, v.p., contr., 1989-96; ret., 1996—. Home: 55 Shoal Rd Jackson NJ 08527

WAGNER, ERIC ARMIN, sociology educator; b. Cleve., May 31, 1941; s. Armin Erich and Florence (Edwards) W. AB, Ohio State U., 1964; MA, U. Fla., 1968, PhD, 1973. Instr. sociology Ohio U., Athens, 1968-73, asst. prof., 1973-75, assoc. prof., 1975-83, prof., 1983-97, chmn. sociology and anthropology, 1974—78, 1986—91, 1994—97, vice chmn. faculty senate, 1982—84, prof. emeritus, 1997. Contbr. articles on internat. sports and soc. to books and profl. jours. Dir. Planned Parenthood of Southeast Ohio, 1990-96, pres. 1992-94. Mem. Internat. Sociol. Assn., Midwest Assn. Latin Am. Studies (pres. 1979-80), U.S. Orienteering Fedn. (dir. 1976-82, sec.-treas. 1976-79, v.p. 1979-80, sec. 1980-82), Delta Sigma Phi. Presbyterian. Home: 2615 NW 82d St Gainesville FL 32606-8638

WAGNER, FLORENCE ZELEZNIK, telecommunications executive; b. McKeesport, Pa., Sept. 23, 1926; d. George and Sophia (Petros) Zeleznik; m. Francis Xavier Wagner, June, 18, 1946; children: Deborah Elaine Wagner Franke, Rebecca Susan Wagner Schroettinger, Melissa Catherine Wagner Good, Francis Xavier, Robert Francis. BA magna cum laude, U. Pitts., 1977, MPA, 1981. Sec. to pres. Tube City Iron & Metal Co., Glassport, Pa., 1944-50; cons. Raw Materials, Inc., Pitts., 1955; gen. mgr. Carson Compressed Steel Products, Pitts., 1967-69; ptnr. Universal Steel Products, Pitts., 1970-71; gen. mgr. Josh Steel Co., Braddock, Pa., 1971-78; owner Wagner's Candy Box, Mt. Lebanon, Pa., 1979-80; borough sec./treas. Borough of Pennsbury Village, Allegheny County, Pa., 1980-88; ptnr. Tele-Communications of Am., Burgettstown, Pa., 1984-86; trustee Profit-Sharing Trust, Pension Trust Josh Steel Co., Burgettstown, 1986-88, Consol, Inc., Upper St. Clair, 1989—. Mem. Foster Parents; sec. Sch. Bd. St. Bernard Cath. Elem. Sch., Mt. Lebanon, Pa., 1995—98; vol. Pitts.-Carlow GED Literacy program, 1997—98, Upper St. Clair Libr.; Mem. Jefferson Twp. Planning Commn.; mem. Washington County, Pa. Mem. AAUW, Pitts. Symphony Soc., Pitts. Ballet Theater Guild, Soc. Pub. Adminstrn. (founder U. Pitts. br.), Acad. Polit. Sci., U.S. Strategic Inst., Southwestern Pa. Sec. Assn., Alpha Sigma Lambda (past treas., sec., pres.). Republican. Home: 1611 Upper Saint Clair Dr Pittsburgh PA 15241-2648 E-mail: fwagner@libcom.com.

WAGNER, FREDERICK REESE, retired language educator; b. Phila., Apr. 15, 1928; m. Barbara Alexander Brady, May 9, 1959 (div. 1968); 1 child, Christopher A. BA summa cum laude, Duke U., 1948, MA, 1949, PhD, 1971. Advt mgr Prentice-Hall, Inc., N.Y.C., 1955-57; promotion mgr. Harper & Row, N.Y.C., 1957-65; instr. English Duke U., Durham, N.C., 1967-69; asst. prof. Hamilton Coll, Clinton, N.Y., 1969-73, assoc. prof., 1973-78, prof. English, chmn. dept., 1978-90, prof. English, 1990-95, ret., 1995. Author: Famous Underwater Adventurers, 1962; Submarine Fighter of the American Revolution, 1963; Patriot's Choice: The Story of John Hancock, 1964; Robert Morris, Audacious Patriot, 1976. Mem. Thoreau Soc. (pres. 1984-86), Hawthorne Soc., Phi Beta Kappa. Home: 2160 Bleecker St Apt A-215 Utica NY 13501

WAGNER, FREDERICK WILLIAM (BILL WAGNER), lawyer; b. Daytona Beach, Fla., Apr. 13, 1933; s. Adam A. and Nella (Schroeder) W.; m. Ruth Whetstone; children: Alan Frederick, Darryl William, Thomas Adam. BA, U. Fla., 1955, LLB with honors, 1960. Bar: Fla. 1960, U.S. Supreme Ct. 1967, D.C. 1989; cert. civil trial lawyer, Fla. Bar; cert. aviation lawyer, Fla. Bar. Pvt. practice law, Miami, Fla., 1960-63, Orlando, Fla., 1963-65, Tampa, Fla., 1965—; ptnr. Nichols, Gaither, Beckham, Colson, Spence & Hicks, Tampa, 1965-67; ptnr., shareholder Wagner, Vaughan & McLaughlin (P.A. and predecessor names), 1967—. Mem. Gov.'s Jud. Nominations Commn., 1971-72, Constnl. Jud. Nominations Commn., 1972-75; mem. Fla. Bd. Bar Examiners, 1974-77, emeritus mem., 1995—; chmn. Civil Procedure Rules Com. Fla. Bar, 1977-78; bd. govs. Fla. Bar, 1978-83; trustee Roscoe Pound Inst., 1984-92; mem. civil jury instrn. com. Fla. Supreme Ct., 1985-2003. Contbr. articles to profl. jours. 1st lt. USAF, 1955-57. Fellow Am. Bar Found., Am. Coll. Trial Lawyers, Internat. Acad. Trial Lawyers, Am. Bd. Trial Advs.; mem. ATLA (bd. govs. 1973-80, 84-89, chmn. pub. affairs dept. 1984-89, treas. 1982-84, v.p. 1986-87, pres.-elect 1987-88, pres. 1988-89), Am. Inns of Ct. Found. (trustee 1996-2000), Acad. Fla. Trial Lawyers (bd. dirs. 1965-84, pres. 1972-73), Bay Area Trial Lawyers Assn. (v.p. 1966-68), Am. Law Inst. (coun. 1993—), Lawyer-Pilots Bar Assn., Fla. Bar Found., U. Fla. Alumni Assn., Nat. Bd. Trial Advocacy (cert. civil), Assn. Personal Injury Lawyers, Australian Plaintiff Laywers Assn., Pan European Orgn. Personal Injury Lawyers, So. Trial Lawyers Assn., Nat. Transp. Safety Bd. Bar Assn., Tampa Bay Trial Lawyers Assn. Democrat. Methodist. Home: 901 Mariner Way Tampa FL 33602-5759 Office: Wagner Vaughan & McLaughlin 601 Bayshore Blvd Ste 910 Tampa FL 33606-2786 Office Phone: 813-225-4000. Business E-Mail: Bill@WagnerLaw.com.

WAGNER, GARY WAYNE, educational administrator; b. Washington, Iowa, Sept. 5, 1946; s. Wayne Earl and Beulah (Lowry) W.; children: Michael, Jeff, Aaron, Nathan, Caleb. BA, Sioux Falls Coll., 1968; MDiv, Colgate Rochester Divinity Sch, 1972; postgrad., Fuller Theol. Sem., 1987—. Admissions counselor Sioux Falls (S.D.) Coll., 1968-69; pastor First Bapt. Ch., Sac City, Iowa, 1972-75; chaplain Bacone Coll., Muskogee, Okla., 1975-76, dir. devel., 1976-79, Green Lake (Wis.) Conf. Ctr., 1979-84, Alderson Broaddus Coll., Phillipi, W.Va., 1984-88; v.p. univ. rels. Phillips U., Enid, Okla., 1988-93; dir. devel. & mktg. Omniplex Sci. Mus., Oklahoma City, 1993-96; pres., CEO Rainbow Acres, Camp Verde, Ariz., 1996—. Adv. bd., Kakwang Prof. Acad., Shantou, China, 1986—; bd. dirs. Am. Baptist Homes and Hosp. Assn. Author devotional works, articles. Mem. CASE, Bapt. World Alliance (chmn. devel. co. 1986-88), Am. Bapt. Pub. Rels. Assn. (pres. 1982-83), Nat. Soc. Fund Raising Execs., Am. Assn. Mental Retardation. Avocations: photography, travel. Office: Rainbow Acres PO Box 1326 2120 W Reservation Loop Rd Camp Verde AZ 86322 Office Phone: 928-567-5231. Business E-Mail: president@rainbowacres.com.

WAGNER, GERALDINE MARIE, nursing educator, consultant; b. Renton, Wash., Apr. 12, 1948; d. Ernest F. and Vera P. (Temiraeff) W. AA, Pasadena City Coll., 1970; BA cum laude, Calif. State U., Northridge, 1977; BSN, Calif. State U., L.A., 1982; MEd summa cum laude, Azusa Pacific U., 1993. Cert. pub. health nurse, Calif. Dept. Health Svcs. In utilization mgmt. Blue Cross, Woodland Hills, Calif., 1987-88, Healthmarc, Pasadena, Calif., 1988-90; nursing educator, asst. dir. vocat. nursing program Casa Loma Coll., L.A., 1991-92, dir. program planning and devel., and coord. continuing edn. Lake View Terrace, 1992-93; dir. vocal. nursing program Glendale (Calif.) Career Coll., 1994-95; with patient care rev. svcs. U. So. Calif. U. Hosp., L.A., 1996—; med.-legal nurse cons., 2000—. Capt. Nurse Corp, U.S. Army, 1979-84. Mem.: VFW, Fellowship of Cath. Scholars, Nat. Assn. Cath. Nurses, Computer Using Educators, Nat. Coun. Tchrs. of Math., Am. Math. Soc., Civil War Soc., Assn. of Hebrew Catholics, Inst. of Religious Life, Res. Officers Assn. of U.S., Army Nurse Corps. Assn., AMVETS, Cath. War Vets, Assn. U.S. Army, U.S. Naval Inst., Mil. Officer Assn. Am., Order of Preachers, Nat. Maritime Hist. Soc., Soc. Cath. Social Scientists, Am. Legion, Sigma Theta Tau, Pi Lambda Theta. Roman Catholic. Home: 924 Rock Rose Ln Lompoc CA 93436 Office Phone: 805-735-3575. E-mail: srgmwagnerop@earthlink.net.

WAGNER, HAROLD A. industrial gas and chemical company executive; b. Oakland, Calif., Nov. 12, 1935; s. Harold A. and Lurline Frances (Madsen) Wagner; m. Marcia Kenaston, July 17, 1956; children: Sandra Wagner Boyce, Kristi Wagner Schwiering, Tracey, Eric. BS in Mech. Engring., Stanford U., 1958, SEP, 1982; MBA, Harvard U., 1963. Regional sales mgr. ind. gases U.S. Air Products & Chems., Allentown, Pa., 1963—70; mgr. GM ind. gases U.K.Air Products & Chems., 1970—76; regional sales mgr. GM Ind. Gases Continental Europe, 1976—80, GM Ind. Gases U.S., 1980—81; v.p. sales ind. gases div. FM, 1981—82; v.p. corp. planning Air Products & Chems., 1982—87, v.p. bus. div. chems., 1987—88; pres. AP Europe, 1988—90, exec. v.p., 1990—91, pres., COO, 1991—92, past chmn. pres., CEO; chmn., pres., CEO, dir. Air Products and Chems., 1992—2001, chmn., CEO, dir. 1st lt. USAF, 1958—61. Avocations: squash, photography. Home: 1306 Prospect Ave Bethlehem PA 18018-4917 Office: Air Prods & Chems Inc 7201 Hamilton Blvd Allentown PA 18195-1501

WAGNER, HARVEY ARTHUR, nuclear engineer, consultant; b. Ann Arbor, Mich., Jan. 2, 1905; s. Emanuel M. and Emma (Kiebler) W.; m. Eleanor Mary Bond, July 6, 1929. BS in Mech. Engring., U. Mich., 1927; D.Eng., Lawrence Inst. Tech., 1969. With Proctor & Gamble Co., 1927-28; with Detroit Edison Co., 1928-70, exec. v.p., 1969-70; cons. engr., 1970-96; chmn., dir. Overseas Adv. Assocs., Inc., 1974-96. Mem. Detroit Bd. Water Commrs., 1952-60; Trustee Nat. Sanitation Found., 1965-82 Author papers in field. Recipient Disting. Alumnus award U. Mich. Coll. Engring., 1953, Outstanding Alumni Achievement award, 1989; Sesquincentennial award as outstanding exec. and nuclear power cons. U. Mich., 1967; cert. pub. service Fed. Power Commn., 1964 Fellow ASME, Am. Nuclear Soc. (Cisler Award, 1994), Engring. Soc. Detroit (pres. 1968-69); mem. Nat. Acad. Engring., Tau Beta Pi, Phi Kappa Phi. Home: 15191 Ford Rd Apt 205 Dearborn MI 48126-4654

WAGNER, HENRY NICHOLAS, JR., physician; b. Balt., May 12, 1927; s. Henry N. and Gertrude Loane Wagner; m. Anne Barrett Wagner, Feb. 1951; children: Henry N., Mary Randall, John Mark, Anne Elizabeth. AB, Johns Hopkins U., 1948, MD, 1952; DSc (hon.), Washington Coll., Chestertown, Md., 1972, Free U., Brussels, 1985; MD (hon.), U. Gottingen, 1988. Chief med. resident Osler Med. Svc., Johns Hopkins Hosp., Balt., 1958—59; asst. prof. medicine, radiology Johns Hopkins Med. Instns., 1959—64, assoc. prof., 1964—65, prof. environ health scis., dir. divn. nuclear medicine and radiation health scis., 1965—, dir. divsn. radiation health scis. Contbr. articles to profl. jours. With USPHS, 1955—57. Recipient Georg von Hevesey medal, 1976. Fellow: ACP; mem.: AMA (coun. sci. affairs, Sci. Achievement award 1991), Balt. City Med. Soc. (past pres.), Am. Soc. Clin. Investigation, Assn. Am. Physicians, Rsch. Socs. Council (past pres.), Am. Fedn. Clin. Rsch. (past pres.), Soc. Nuclear Medicine (past pres.), Am. Bd. Nuclear Medicine (founding mem.), World Fedn. Nuclear Medicine and Biology (past pres.), Inst. Medicine, Phi Beta Kappa. Office: John's Hopkins Med Instns 600 N Wolfe St Baltimore MD 21287-0005

WAGNER, JAMES MILLER, funeral director; b. Louisville, Ky., June 3, 1965; s. William Henry and Jane (Miller) Wagner. Funeral dir., Hanover Coll., 1988. Apprentice, funeral dir., embalmer Highlands Funeral Home Inc., Louisville, 1989—; funeral dir. Bosse Funeral Home, Inc., Louisville, 1995—. Sec. bd. dirs. Louisville Hist. League, 1989—99. Mem.: Falls Cities Funeral Dirs. Assn., Rotary Club Louisville. Roman Catholic. Avocation: history. Home: 3501 Illinois Ave #A16 Louisville KY 40213 Office: Bosse Funeral Home Inc 1355 Ellison Ave Louisville KY 40204 Office Phone: 502-451-8440.

WAGNER, JAMES WARREN, academic administrator, engineering educator; b. Washington, July 12, 1953; s. Robert Earl and Bernice (Bittner) W.; m. Debbie Kelley, July 31, 1976; children: Kimberly Renee, Christine Kelley. BSEE, U. Del., 1975; MS, Johns Hopkins U., 1978, PhD, 1984. Electronics engr. U.S. FDA, Washington, 1975-84; asst. prof. Johns Hopkins U., Balt., 1984-88, assoc. prof., 1988-93, prof., 1993-97, chmn. dept. materials scis. and engring., 1993-97; prof. materials sci. and engring., dean Case Sch. Engring. Case Western Res. U., Cleve., 1998—2000, provost, 2000-01, interim pres., 2001—02; pres. Emory U., Atlanta, 2003—. Contbr. articles to profl. jours. Regional v.p. Chesapeake Bay Yacht Racing Assn., Annapolis, Md., 1982; elder Presbyterian Ch. U.S.A. Mem. IEEE, Optical Soc. Am., Laser & Electro-Optics Soc., Biomed. Engring., Soc. Exptl. Mechanics (Peterson award 1988). Presbyterian. Achievements include contributions to the field of optical metrology applied to materials characterization, especially advanced holographic and laser-based ultrasonic methods. Office: Emory Univ Office of the Pres Atlanta GA 30322

WAGNER, JODY M. treasurer; b. Canton, Ohio; m. Alan L. Wagner; children: Rachael, Jason, Elizabeth, Maxwell. Undergrad. degree in Econs., Northwestern U., Evanston, Ill., 1977; grad. degree in law, Vanderbilt U., Nashville, 1980. Bar: Tenn. 1980, Va. 1984. With Kaufman and Canoles PC, Norfolk, Va., 1981—2002; state treas. Va., 2002—. Office: Commonwealth of Va Dept of Treasury 101 N 14th St Richmond VA 23218

WAGNER, JOHN LEO, lawyer, former magistrate judge; b. Ithaca, N.Y., Mar. 12, 1954; s. Paul Francis and Doris Elizabeth (Hoffschneider) W.; m. Marilyn Modin, June 18, 1987. Student, U. Nebr., 1973-74; BA, U. Okla., 1976, JD, 1979. Bar: Okla. 1980, Calif. 1999, U.S. Dist. Ct. (we. dist.) Okla. 1980, U.S. Dist. Ct. (no. and ea. dists.) Okla. 1981, U.S. Dist. Ct. (ctrl. dist.) Calif. 2000, U.S. Ct. Appeals (10th cir.) 1982. Assoc. Franklin, Harmon & Satterfield Inc., Oklahoma City, 1980-82; ptnr. Franklin, Harmon & Satterfield, Inc., Oklahoma City, 1982; assoc. Kornfeld, Franklin & Phillips, Oklahoma City, 1982-85, ptnr., 1985; magistrate judge U.S. Dist. Ct. No. Dist. Okla., Tulsa, 1985-97; dir. Irell & Manella LLP Alt. Dispute Resolution Ctr., Newport Beach, Calif., 1997—. Pres. U. Okla. Coll. Law Assn., 1991-92. Fellow Am. Coll. Civil Trial Mediators, Internat. Acad. Mediators, Fed. Magistrate Judge's Assn. (dir. 10th cir. 1987-89); mem. ABA, 10th Cir. Edn. Com., Okla. Bar Assn., Council Oak Am. Inn of Cts. (pres. 1992-93), Jud. Conf. U.S. (com. ct. adminstrn. and case mgmt. 1992-97), CPR-Georgetown Commn. Ethics and Standards in ADR. Republican. Office: Irell & Manella LLP Alt Dispute Resolution Ctr 840 Newport Center Dr Ste 400 Newport Beach CA 92660-6321 Office Phone: 949-760-5288. E-mail: jwagner@irell.com., usmag1@cox.net.

WAGNER, JOHN RUSSELL, mechanical engineering educator, researcher; BS, U. Buffalo, 1983, MS in mech. engring., 1985; PhD in mech. engring., Purdue U., 1989. Cert. Profl. Engineer, Ind., 1996. Millard Filmore Coll. instr. U. of Buffalo, Buffalo, 1984; rsch. asst. mech. engring. Purdue U., West Lafayette, Ind., 1985—89; sr. project engr. & tech. leader Delphi Delco Electronics Systems, 1989—98; instr. mech. engring. tech. Purdue U., Kokomo, Ind., 1995—97; assoc. prof. mech. engring. Clemson U., SC,

1998—. Author: (book) Mechatronics System Design - Laboratory Manual. Grantee Honda Initiation Grant, Honda Motor Co., 2003; scholar Gustav & Greta Zimmer Scholarship, U. of Buffalo, 1981, 1982. Mem.: Soc. Automotive Engineers (Clemson U. Faculty Advisor 1998—, Ralph R. Teetor Ednl. Award 2003), Inst. Elec. and Electronic Engineers, ASME (chair, automotive & transp. systems com. 2002—03, panel 2004—), Am. Soc. Engring. Educators, Pi Tau Sigma, Tau Beta Pi Engring., Sigma Chi Sci. Office: Clemson U 212 Fluor Daniel Engring Building Clemson SC 29634-0921 E-mail: jwagner@clemson.edu.

WAGNER, JOHN WALDORF, music educator, researcher; b. Oak Park, Ill., Feb. 11, 1937; s. Albert Benjamin and Ethel Margaret Wagner; m. Bobbie Baker Wagner, Nov. 23, 1960; children: Benjamin Baker, Daniel Andrew. MusB, DePauw U., 1959; MusM, Fla. State U., 1961; DPhil, Ind. U., 1965. From asst. prof. to prof. music Newberg Coll., SC, 1965—2002, chair music depot., 1988—2000; ret. Author: The New Grove Dictionary of Music and Musicians, 2d edit., 2000; editor: The Music of James HEwitt, 1980. Mem.: Am. Musicological Soc. (chpt. treas.), Soc. Am. Music, Internat. Clarinet Soc. Home: 905 Amelia St Newberry SC 29108

WAGNER, JUDITH BUCK, investment firm executive; b. Altoona, Pa., Sept. 25, 1943; d. Harry Bud and Mary Elizabeth (Rhodes) B.; m. Joseph E. Wagner, Mar. 15, 1980; 1 child, Elizabeth. BA in History, U. Wash., 1965; grad., N.Y. Inst. Fin., 1968. Registered Am. Stock Exch., N.Y. Stock Exch., investment advisor. Security analyst Morgan, olmstead, Kennedy & Gardner, L.A., 1968-71, Boettcher & Co., Denver, 1972-75; pres. Wagner Investment Mgmt., Denver, 1975—. Chmn. The Women's Bank, N.A., Denver, 1977-94, organizational group pres., 1975-77; chmn. Equitable Bankshares Colo., Inc., Denver, 1980-94; pres. Equitable Bank of Littleton, Colo., 1985; lectr. Denver U., Metro State, 1975-80. Author: Woman and Money series Colo. Woman Mag., 1976, moderator "Catch 2' Sta. KWGN-TV, 1978-79. Pres. Bit Sisters Colo., Denver, 1977-82, bd. dirs., 1972-83; bd. fellows U. Denver, 1985-90; bd. dirs. Red Cross, 1980, Assn. Children's Hosp., 1985, Colo. Health Facilities Authority, 1978-84, Jr. League Cmty. ADv. Com., 1979-82, Bros. Redevel., Inc., 1979-80; mem. agy. rels. com. Mile High United Way, 1978-81, chmn. United Way Venture Way, 1978-81, chmn. United Way Venture Grant com., 1980-81; bd. dirs. Downtown Dener, Inc., 1988-95; bd. dirs., v.p., treas. The Women's Found. Colo., 1987-91; treas., trustee, v.p., Graland Country Day Sch., 1990-97, pres., 1994-97; trustee Denver Rotary Found., 1990-95, Hunt Alternatives Fund, 1992-97; trustee The Colo. Trust, 1998—, chmn., 2003—. Recipient Making It award Cosmopolitan Mag., 1977, Women on the Go award, Savvy Mag., 1983, Minouri Yasoui award, 1986, Salute Spl. Honoree award, Big Sisters, 1987; named one of the Outstanding Young Women Am., 1979; recipient Woman Who Makes A Difference award Internat. Women's Forum, 1987, Maverick Thinker award Urban Park, 2003. Fellow Assn. Investment Mgmt. & Rsch.; mem. Women's Forum Colo. (pres. 1979), Women's Found. Colo., Inc. (bd. dirs. 1986-91), Denver Soc. Security Analysts (bd. dirs. 1976-83, v.p. 1980-81, pres. 1981-82), Colo. Investment Advisors assn., Rotary (treas. Denver chpt. found., pres. 1993-94), Leadership Denver (Outstanding Alumna award 1987), Pi Beta Phi (pres. U. Wash. chpt. 1964-65). Office: Wagner Investment Mgmt Inc Ste 240 3200 Cherry Creek South Dr Denver CO 80209-3245

WAGNER, JULIA A(NNE), retired editor; b. Alexandria, Va., Feb. 15, 1924; d. Luigi and Domenica (Di Giammarino) Coppa; widowed. BA, George Washington U., 1948, MA, 1950. With U.S. Govt., Washington, 1941-55, publs. editor, 1951-55; editl. asst. Dell Pub. Co., N.Y.C., 1956-59, mng. editor, 1959-72, editor-in-chief, 1973-87; ret., 1987.

WAGNER, LAWRENCE M. diversified financial services company executive; Exec. v.p., COO The Hillman Co., Pitts., pres., CEO. Bd. mem. Black Rock Inc. Vice chair, v.p. Pa. Economy League; bd. mem. Allegheny County United Way. Office: The Hillman Company 1900 Grant Bldg Pittsburgh PA 15219*

WAGNER, LESLIE, lawyer; b. Houston, July 18, 1953; d. Jacob and Geraldine (Harris) W. BA cum laude, U. Tex., 1975; JD, U. Houston, 1980. Bar: Tex. 1980, U.S. Dist. Ct. (so. dist.) Tex. 1981. Trial atty. civil rights EEOC, Houston, 1981-84; pvt. practice Houston, 1984—85, 1987—88, 2004—; dir. law placement U. Houston Law Ctr., 1985-87; employee rels. atty, sr. employee rels. analyst The Meth. Hosp. System, Houston, 1988—97; employee rels. cons. Prudential Fin., Houston, 1997—2003; equal employment affirmative action cons., 2004—. Cons. EEOC, Houston, 1984—; v.p., treas. Houston Soc. Healthcare Human Resources Adminstrns., 1995-97; dir., gen. counsel Hematology/Oncology Assistance Resource Coalition, 1995-2002. Editor: U. Houston Law Rev., 1979, assoc. editor, 1980. Mem. health and edn. com. Jewish Cmty. Ctr., Houston, 1983-85; polit. cons. Houston, 1984-85. Named Honors Day Honoree U. Tex., 1971; Arts and Scis. scholar U. Tex., 1971-74. Mem. ABA (com. employee and labor rels. 1983-85, employment rights com. gen. practice sect. 1986), ATLA, Houston Bar Assn., Tex. Young Lawyers Assn. (job fair com.), Tex. Hosp. Assn., Soc. of Human Resources Mgmt., Nat. Assn. Law Placement (careers com. 1986-87, minority placement com. 1987), Am. Studies Assn., Houston Festival Dancers (treas. 1976-77), Eta Phi Sigma. Democrat. Avocations: creative writing, dance, reading. Home: 5407 Wigton Dr Houston TX 77096-4005 E-mail: leslie.wagner@earthlink.net.

WAGNER, LYNN EDWARD, lawyer; b. Mt. Holly, N.J., Feb. 10, 1941; m. Maureen Elizabeth Bach, May 25, 1973; children: Daniel Preston, Matthew Evan. BS, Drexel U., 1965; JD, Duke U., 1968. Bar: Mass. 1968, US Dist. Ct. Mass. 1968, Fla. 1972, US Ct. Appeals (5th cir.) 1972, US Supreme Ct. 1972, US Dist. Ct. (mid. dist.) Fla. 1974, US Dist. Ct. (we. dist.) Pa. 1975, US Ct. Appeals (4th cir.) 1977, US Ct. Appeals (11th cir.) 1978, US Ct. Appeals (DC cir.) 1980, US Ct. Appeals (3d cir.) 1985, US Dist. Ct. (so. dist.) Fla. 1991, US Dist. Ct. (no. dist.) Fla. 1992; cert. arbitrator and mediator, Fla. 1995. Assoc. Foley, Hoag & Elliot, Boston, 1968-70; asst. prof. law U. Fla., Gainesville, 1971-73; sr. trial atty. US EEOC, Washington, 1973-74; ptnr. Berkman, Ruslander, Pohl, Lieber & Engel, Pitts., 1975-84, Kirkpatrick & Lockhart, Pitts., 1985-86, Rumberger, Kirk, Caldwell, Cabaniss, Burke & Wechsler, Orlando, 1986—94, Baker & Hostetler, Orlando, 1995-97, Wagner & Solomon PA, Winter Park, Fla., 1997—; pres. Litig. Alternatives, Inc., Winter Park, 2000—. Bd. dirs. Fla. Legal Svcs., Inc.; mem. arbitration and mediation panels Fla. Cts. Fed. Mediation and Conciliation Svc., Nat. Mediation bd., World Intellectual Poperty Orgn., Nat. Futures Found., Am. Health Attys. Assn., Fla. Dispute Resolution Consortium, Nat. Assn. Securities Dealers, Nat. Arbitration Forum, Am. Arbitration Assn.; adj. prof. Barry U., 2002, U. Fla. Coll. Law, 2004—. Mem. Pa. Dept. Labor, United Mine Workers and Bitumineous Coal Operators Assn., NY Stock Exchange; With USAR, 1960-66. Mem.: ABA (litig. sect., employment law sect., dispute resolution sect., labor and employment law sect.), Pa. Coun. Mediators, Million Dollar Advocates Forum (pres. Fla. chpt., workplace, arbitration coms.), Assn. for Conflict Resolution, Leading Am. Attys. (employment, comml. and constrn. litig. and dispute resolution coms.), Fla. Acad. Profl. Mediators, Fla. Bar Assn. (labor sect., dispute resolution sect.), Pa. Bar Assn. (labor sect., dispute resolution sect.). Avocations: fishing, hiking, travel. Home: 526 Alokee Ct Lake Mary FL 32746-2218 Office: 2180 N Park Ave Ste 318 Winter Park FL 32789 Office Phone: 407-875-0922. E-mail: lwagner@taflaw.com.

WAGNER, MARILYN FAITH, retired elementary school educator; b. Salinas, Calif. d. Clay Chester and Gladys Edna (Wiley) W. AA, Hartnell Coll., Salinas, 1956; BA, San Jose (Calif.) State U., 1958; MA in Computer Edn., U.S. Internat. U., San Diego, 1987; diploma, Inst. Children's Lit., Redding Ridge, Conn., 1981. Cert. elem. tchr., cross-cultural lang. acad. devel., tech. in edn., Calif. Tchr. Hollister (Calif.) Elem. Sch., 1958—60, Greenfield (Calif.) Schs., 1958—2000, Alum Roc, Union Sch. Dist., San Jose, 1960—2000; ret., 2000; substitute and contract tchr. Alum Roc Union Sch. Dist., San Jose, Calif., 2001—. Mem. Calif. Ret. Tchrs. Assn., Spartan Found., Monterey Bay Aquarium.

WAGNER, MARY ANN, human resources executive; b. St. Louis, May 24, 1947; d. John Gerard and Carmela Lucy (Cozza) Blethroad; 1 child, John Patrick. BA, Webster U., St. Louis, 1979, MA, 1982. Tchr. Our Lady of Fatima, St. Louis, Wetterau, St. Louis; personnel mgr. Venture, St. Louis, 1979-81, customer svc. coord. O'Fallon, Mo., 1981-84, personnel mgr., 1984-86; regional personnel mgr., 1986-88; dir. tng. and devel., 1988-92; divsn. v.p. dir. of assoc. rels. May Merchandising, St. Louis, 1995-98; sr. v.p. human resources Meier & Frank, Portland, Oreg., 1998-2001; sr. v.p. May Mdse. Co., St. Louis, 2001—. Adj. prof. Webster U., 1990-95. Bd. of Dir., Daniel Webster Soc.; v.p. State Bd. of Dir., Interval Svc. Orgn. for Young Women; bd. of Dir., Urban League Mem. AAIM Mgmt. Assn., Am. Soc. Tng. and Devel., Am. Mgmt. Assn. Roman Catholic. Avocations: antiques, music, sports. Home: 325 Perceval Dr Saint Charles MO 63304-5708

WAGNER, MARY KATHRYN, sociology educator, former state legislator; b. Madison, S.D., June 19, 1932; d. Irving Macaulay and Mary Browning (Wines) Mumford; m. Robert Todd Wagner, June 23, 1954; children: Christopher John, Andrea Browning. BA, U. S.D., 1954; MEd, S.D. State U., 1974, PhD, 1978. Sec. R.A. Burleigh & Assocs., Evanston, Ill., 1954-57; dir. resource ctr. Watertown (S.D.) Sr. High Sch., 1969-71, Brookings (S.D.) High Sch., 1971-74; asst. dir. S.D. Com. on the Humanities, Brookings, 1976-90; asst. prof. rural sociology S.D. State U., 1990-96; mem. S.D. Ho. of Reps., 1981-88, S.D. Senate, 1988—92. Mem., pres. Brookings Sch. Bd., 1975-81; chair fund dr. Brookings United Way, 1985; bd. dirs. Brookings Chamber music Soc., 1981-98, Advance and Career Learning Ctr. Named Woman of Yr., Bus. and Profl. Women, 1981, Legislator Conservationist of Yr., Nat. and S.D. Wildlife Fedn., 1988. Mem. Population Assn. Am., Midwest Sociol. Soc., Rural Sociol. Soc., Brookings C. of C. (mem. indsl. devel. com. 1988-98), PEO, Rotary. Republican. Episcopalian. Avocations: reading, gardening, music, golf, bridge. Home: 24497 N Playhouse Rd Keystone SD 57751-6653 E-mail: drswagnerrtmk@aol.com.

WAGNER, MARY MARGARET, library and information science educator; b. Mpls., Feb. 4, 1946; d. Harvey F.J. and Yvonne M. (Brettner) W.; m. William Moore, June 16, 1978; children: Lebohang Y.C., Nora M. BA, Coll. St. Catherine, St. Paul, 1969; MLS, U. Wash., 1973; PhD, U. Minn., 2003. Asst. libr. St. Margarets Acad., Mpls., 1969-70; libr. Derham Hall High Sch., St. Paul, 1970-71; youth worker The Bridge for Runaways, Mpls., 1971-72; libr. Guthrie Theater Reference and Rsch. Libr., Mpls., 1973-75; asst. br. libr. St. Paul Pub. Libr., 1975; assoc. prof. dept. info. mgmt. Coll. St. Catherine, St. Paul, 1975—. Del. Minn. Gov.'s Pre-White House Conf. on Librs. and Info. Svcs., 1990; mem. Minn. Pre-White House Program Com., 1989-90, Continuing Libr. Info. and Media Edn. Com. Minn. Dept. Edn., Libr. Devel. and Svcs., 1980-83, 87-2002; mem. cmty. faculty Met. State U., St. Paul, 1980—; mem. core revision com. Coll. St. Catherine, 1992-93, faculty budget adv. com., 1992-95, faculty pers. com., 1989-92, 2001—, acad. computing com. 1991-96, ednl. policies com., 1998-01; chair curriculum subcom. Minn. Vol. Cert. Com., 1993—. Contbr. articles to profl. jours. Bd. dirs. Christian Sharing Fund, 1976-80, chair, 1977-78. Grantee U.S. Embassy, Maseru, Lesotho, Africa, Brit. Consulate, Maseru, Fed. Inst. for Mus. and Libr. Scis., various founds.; Upper Midwest Assn. for Intercultural Edn. travel grantee Assoc. Colls. Twin Cities. Fellow: Higher Edn Consortia for Urban Affairs (bd. dirs. 1998—); mem.: ALISE (chair internat. rels. com. 2001—03), ALA (libr. book fellows program 1990—91), Minn. Ednl. Media Orgn., Minn. Libr. Assn. (pres. 1981—82, chair continuing edn. com. 1987—90, steering com. Readers Adv. Roundtable 1989—91), Spl. Libr. Assn., Am. Soc. Indexers, Am. Soc. Info. Sci. Office: Coll St Catherine Dept Info Mgmt 2004 Randolph Ave Saint Paul MN 55105-1750 E-mail: mmwagner@stkate.edu.

WAGNER, MARY SATTERWHITE, education educator; b. Brownsville, Tex., Dec. 11, 1948; d. Fred Guy and Helen Bellinghausen Satterwhite; m. Charles Raymond Wagner, Aug. 22, 1970; children: Charles Raymond Jr., Helen Pearl. BS, Tex. A & I U., 1970, MS, 1973. Cert. Tchr. Tex., 1970. Grad. asst. Tex. A & I U., Kingsville, 1971—72; secondary classroom tchr. Brownsville (Tex.) Ind. Sch. Dist., 1973—85; asst. prof. U. of Tex. Brownsville & Tex. Southmost Coll., 1985—. Home: 515 Honeydale Rd Brownsville TX 78520 Office: Univ of Tex Brownsville 80 Fort Brown Brownsville TX 78520 Office Phone: 956-574-6611. Office Fax: 956-574-6637. E-mail: mwagner@utb.edu.

WAGNER, MELINDA, musician, composer; b. Phila., 1957; m. James Saporito; children: Benjamin, Olivia. Grad., U. Chgo., U. Pa. Studied with Richard Wernick, George Crumb, Shulamit Ran, Jay Reise. Instr. U. Pa., Swarthmore Coll., Syracuse U., Hunter Coll. Works performed by: Chgo. Symphony, Am. Composers Orchestra, Chamber Music Soc. of Lincoln Ctr., Ill. Chamber Orchestra, Oakland East Bay Symphony; commissioned works: Barlow Found., Fromm Found. Harvard U., Mary Flagler Carey Charitable Trust, Chgo. Symphony Orchestra, N.Y. New Music Ensemble, Am. Brass Quintet; composer Falling Angels, commissioned by Chgo. Symphony Orchestra, premiered in 1993, performed by Am. Composers Orchestra, 1995, Chgo. Symphony, 1996, Concerto for Flute, Strings, and Percussion (Pulitzer prize in Music 1999), commissioned and premiered by Paul Lustig Dunkel and Westchester Philharmonic, 1998, Extremity of Sky, premiered by Emanuel Ax, Chicago Symphony Orch., 2003. Fellow Guggenheim Meml. Found., Howard Found., 1996; resident fellow MacDowell Colony, Yaddo; grantee Ill. Arts Coun., N.Y. State Coun. on Arts; recipient three ASCAP Found. Young Composer awards. Mem. ASCAP (panelist ASCAP Deems Taylor Competition, ASCAP Found. Morton Gould Grants to Young Composers Program; recipient numerous ASCAP Standard Special awards).

WAGNER, MICHAEL GRAFTON, investor, management consultant; b. Greenville, Ohio, May 31, 1935; BA, Vanderbilt U., 1957. With Henny Penny Corp., Eaton, Ohio, 1957-76, sales rep., 1957-60, dir. advt., 1960-63, dir. mktg., 1963-68, pres., CEO, 1968-76, Henny Penny Ltd., Toronto, Ont., Can.; pvt. investor, 1976—. Pres. Schaefer Corp., Madison, Ala., 1979—81; cons., pvt. investor Rair Sys., Inc., Nashville, 1985—87; nat. accounts mgr. spl. products and projects Vulcan Hart Corp. divsn. Premark Corp., 1987—89, Wagner Investments, 1989—2003; dir. sales and mktg. Chef Specialties. Area chmn. Vanderbilt U. Endowment Fund, Nashville, 1961-66, 70-74; fin. chmn. Tenn. Rep. Com., 1977-78. Mem. Nat. Commadore Club, Alpha Tau Omega. Episcopalian (sec.-treas., warden 1969-71). Home: 1602 Hillmeade Dr Nashville TN 37221-5210 E-mail: sixdad6@comcast.net.

WAGNER, NANCY HUGHES, secondary school educator, state legislator; b. Raleigh, N.C., Sept. 27, 1943; d. Eugene Anderson and Miriam St. Clair (Morgan) Hughes; m. Clarence Cobaugh Wagner II, Sept. 12, 1970; children: Morgan Anderson, Cobaugh Wagner III. BA, Salem Coll., Winston-Salem, N.C., 1965; MS, Wilmington (Del.) Coll., 1989. Tchr. Milford (Del.) Sch. Dist., 1965-66, Capital Sch. Dist., Dover, Del., 1966-70, 89—; job specialist Jobs for Del. Grads., Dover, 1987-89; rep. Del. Ho. of Reps., Dover, 1992—, former chair small bus., chair judiciary com., sch. to work coord., 1998—. Mem. parents bd. U. Del., Newark, 1991-93; bd. visitors Del. State U., Dover, 1995—; bd. dirs. Modern Maturity Ctr., Dover, 1995—, 801 House Aid in Dover, 1995—, Because We Care, Dover, 1995—; mem. Kent County Parks and Recreation Commn., Dover, 1990-92; pres. South Run Crossing Civic Assn., Springfield, Va., 1982-85, PTA Dover H.S., 1987-89; mem. Rep. State Com., Kent County Rep. Women's Club; bd. dirs. Murphy Sch., 1991—. Mem. AAUW, C. of C., Nat. Coun. State Legislators, Coun. of State Govts., Capital Edn. Assn., Del. Edn. Assn., Capital City Rotary Club, Delta Kappa Gamma Soc. Internat. Republican. Presbyterian. Avocations: reading, politics, travel. Home: 283 Troon Rd Dover DE 19904-2370 Office: House of Reps Legis Hall Rm 117 PO Box 1401 Dover DE 19903-1401

WAGNER, NORMAN ERNEST, corporate education executive; b. Edenwold, Sask., Can., Mar. 29, 1935; s. Robert Eric and Gertrude Margaret (Brandt) W.; m. Catherine Hack, May 16, 1957; children: Marjorie Dianne, Richard Roger, Janet Marie. BA, MDiv, U. Sask., 1958; MA, U. Toronto, 1960, PhD in Near Eastern Studies, 1965; LLD, Wilfrid Laurier U., 1984. Asst. prof. Near Eastern studies Wilfrid Laurier U., Waterloo, Ont., 1962-65, assoc. prof., 1965-69, prof., 1970-78, dean grad. studies and rsch., 1974-78; pres. U. Calgary, Alta., Can., 1978-88; chmn. bd. Alta. Natural Gas Co., Ltd., 1988—93; pres. emeritus U. Calgary, Can., 1988-95; chmn. Knowledge at Work Ltd., 1995—; chmn., CEO Auxano Philatelic Svcs., Inc., 2002—. Bd. dirs., chmn. Terry Fox Humanitarian Award Program; pres. The Corp. Higher Edn. Forum, 1996-2000. Author: From Chaos to Wisdom: A Framework for Understanding, 1998, Emerging Saskatchewan: The Postal History of Assiniboia, 2002, (with others) The Moyer Site: A Prehistoric Village in Waterloo County, 1974. Mem. Adv. Coun. on Adjustment, OCO '88, Alta. Heritage Found. for Med. Rsch., Nat. Adv. Bd. Sci. and Tech., Internat. Trade Adv. Com. Decorated officer Order of Can. Mem. Can. Soc. Bibl. Studies. Lutheran. Home: 1320 720 13th Ave SW Calgary AB Canada T2R 1M5 Office: Auxand Philatelic Svcs Inc 207 525 11th Ave SW Calgary AB Canada T2P 0C9 E-mail: newal1@aol.com.

WAGNER, PATRICIA HAMM, lawyer; b. Gastonia, N.C., Feb. 1, 1936; d. Luther Boyd and Mildred Ruth (Wheeler) Hamm; married; children: David Marion, Michael Marion, Laura Marion. AB summa cum laude, Wittenberg U., 1958; JD with distinction, Duke U., 1974. Bar: N.C. 1974, Wash. 1984. Asst. univ. counsel Duke U., Durham, N.C., 1974-75, assoc. univ. counsel health affairs, 1977-80; atty. N.C. Meml. Hosp., 1975-77; assoc. N.C. Atty. Gen. Office, 1975-77, Powe, Porter & Alphin, Durham, 1980-81, prin., 1981-83; assoc. Williams, Kastner & Gibbs, 1984-86, Wickwire, Goldmark & Schorr, 1986-88; spl. counsel Heller, Ehrman, White & McAuliffe, 1988-90, ptnr., 1990—. Arbitrator Am. Arbitration Assn., 1978—; arbitrator, pro tem judge King County Superior Ct., 1986—; tchr. in field. Mem. bd. vis. Law Sch. Duke U., 1992-98; bd. dirs. Seattle Edn. Ctr., 1990-91, Metroctr. YMCA, 1991-94, Cmty. Psychiat. Clinic, Seattle, 1984-86; bd. dirs., sec.-treas. N.C. Found. Alternative Health Programs, Inc., 1982-84; bd. dirs., sec.-treas. N.C. Ctr. Pub. Policy Rsch., 1976-83, vice-chmn., 1977-80; mem. task force on commitment law N.C. Dept. Human Resources, 1978; active Def. Rsch. Inst. 1982-84; bd. dirs. Law Fund, 1992—, v.p., 1993-97, pres., 2000-01; mem. ADR Roundtable, 1996-2001. Fellow Am. Bar Found.; mem. ABA (mem. ho. dels. Seattle-King County Bar Assn. 1991-94, mem. litigation sect.), Am. Soc. Hosp. Attys., Am. Law Inst., Wash. State Bar Assn. (mem. domestic rels. task force 1991-93), Seattle-King Bar Assn. (mem. bd. trustees 1990-93, sec. bd. 1989-90, chair judiciary and cts. com. 1987-89, mem. King County Superior Ct. delay reduction task force 1987-89, mem. gender bias com. 1990-94, chair 1990-91), Wash. Def. Trial Lawyers (chmn. ct. rules and procedures com. 1987, co-editor newsletter 1985-86), Wash. State Soc. Hosp. Attys., Wash. Women Lawyers (treas. 1986, 87). Office: Heller Ehrman White & McAuliffe Ste 6100 701 5th Ave Seattle WA 98104-7098 E-mail: pwagner@hewm.com.

WAGNER, PAUL ANTHONY, JR., education educator; b. Pitts., Aug. 28, 1947; s. Paul A. and Mary K. Wagner; children: Nicole S., Eric P., Jason G., Emily Ryanne. BS, N.E. Mo. State U., 1969; MEd, U. Mo., 1972; MA in Philosophy, 1976, PhD in Philosophy of Edn., 1978. Internal expeditor electromotive div. GM, La Grange, Ill., 1970-71; instr. Moberly (Mo.) Jr. Coll., 1972-73, U. Mo., Columbia, 1973-78, acting dir. instl. rsch. and planning, 1990-92, dir. univ. self study, 1991-92; instr. Mo. Mil. Acad., 1978-79; prof. edn. and philosophy U. Houston-Clear Lake, Atrium Cir. Disting. Rsch. Prof., 1980, Chancellor's Disting. Svc. Prof., 1985, dir. Inst. Logical and Cognitive Studies, 1980—, dir. Project in Profl. Ethics, 1989—, chmn. Dept. Edn. Found., 1989-92, 2003—; adj. prof. bus. mgmt. U. Houston-Victoria, chmn. edn. dept., 2003—. Judge Sears Intercollegiate Ethics Bowl, Dallas, 1998; pres. Wagner & Assoc. Ednl. Consulting, 1988-93; dir. Tex. Ctr. for Study Profl. Ethics in Tchg., 1988-95; rsch. assoc. Ctr. for Moral Devel., Harvard U., 1985-86; vis. scholar Stanford U., Palo Alto, Calif., 1981; cons. total quality mgmt. Golden Gate U., 1992-93, M.D. Anderson Cancer Ctr. and Hosp., 1992-93, U. Houston-Victoria, 1993; cons. strategic planning Houston Chronicle Newspaper, 1997; chair So. Accreditation of Coll. and Sch. steering com. U. Houston, Clear Lake, 1990-93, pres. faculty senate, 1999-2001; chair planning and budgeting com., 1996-98, chair, Univ. Life com., 2003-2007, Houston Tenneco Marathon, 1992-94; steering com. Trilateral Conf. and Supershow Greater Houston Partnership, 1994-95; cons., ethics trainer Am. Leadership Forum, 1995-98; chair Tchr. Cert. Coun. 2000-; planning com. Tex. Ethics in Govt. Ann. Conf., 1995-98;; adj. prof. ethical theory U. Houston, 2000—; faculty exec. com. U. Houston Sys., 1999-2001, chair univ. life com., 2003— faculty senate exec. comm., 1999— dept. chair Ednl. Found., 2003—; cons. in field. Author: (with F. Kierstead) The Ethical Legal and Multicultural Founds. of Teaching, 1992, Understanding Professional Ethics, 1996, Wagner-Kierstead Moral Self-Assessment Protocol, 2d edit., 2002; contbr. articles to profl. jours. on sci. edn., mgmt. theory and philosophy of edn.; Mem. editl. bd. Jour. of Thought, 19815, Focus on Learning, 1982-85; editorial cons. Instrnl. Scis., 1981-83; editorial assoc. Brain and Behavioral Scis., 1985. Vice-chmn. Human Rights Com., Columbia, Mo., 1978-79; Sunday sch. tchr. Mary Queen Cath. Ch., Friendswood, Tex., 1979-85; founding bd. dir. Bay Area Symphony Soc., 1983-85; capital campaign com. Soc. Prevention Cruelty to Animals, 1989-91; publicity com. Am. Cancer Soc., Houston chpt., 1989-92; cons. in strategic planning M.D. Anderson Cancer Ctr. vol. divsn., 1992-93; steering com. City of Houston Emerging Bus. Conf., 1994-95, Trilateral Conf., Greater Houston Partnership, 1994-95; active Houston Bus. Promise; chair strategic planning com. Leadership Houston, 1996-98; bd. dirs. Houston Vol. Ctr., Leanna Spraianno Dance Co., 1999-2002, Baker Inst., 1998-2001, chair, 1999-2001; bd. dirs. Hope Village Friendswood, Tex.; ann. leadership briefing com. Rice U., 2001-03; mem. Linda Lorelle Scholarship Com., 1995—, Project Grad Coordinating Coun., 1994-96, pres., 1995-96; emcee, expert commentator for pub. TV, Channel 8, Houston, 1989-2002. Sgt. Mo. N.G., 1970-76; mem. choir Queen of Angels Cath. Ch., Dickinson, Tex., 2003—. Recipient Cert. of Appreciation, City of Columbia, 1978; K.E. Graessle scholar, 1968, Mo. Peace Studies Inst. grantee, 1971. Mem. AAUP, Assn. Applied and Profl. Ethics, Am. Assn. Pub. Adminstrs. (ethics com.), Am. Philos. Assn., Assn. Philosophers in Edn. (exec. bd., v.p.), Philosophy of Edn. Soc. (exec. sec.-treas., hospitality chair 1995-96), Am. Ednl. Studies Assn., Philosophy Sci. Assn., S.W. Philosophy Edn. Soc., Tex. Network for Tchr. Tng. in Philosophy for Children (bd. dirs. 1983-90), Tex. Ctr. for Ethics in Edn. (bd. dirs. 1990-98), Tex. Ednl. Found. Soc. (pres. 1995-98), Tex. Assn. Coll. Tchrs., So. Assn. Colls. Coord., Houston Bar Assn. (steering com. NAFTA Conf. 1993-94), Informal Logic Assn., Leadership Houston, Friends Hermann Pk., Clearlake Cir. (chair 1979-85), Phi Delta Kappa, Kappa Delta Pi. Roman Catholic. Avocations: running, reading, opera, ballet. Home: RR 4 Box 217 Navasota TX 77868-9413 Office: U Houston 2700 Bay Area Blvd Rm 338 Houston TX 77058-1002 Office Phone: 281-283-3571. Business E-Mail: Wagnov@cc.uth.edn.

WAGNER, RICHARD, athletics consultant, former baseball team executive; b. Central City, Nebr., Oct. 19, 1927; s. John Howard and Esther Marie (Wolken) W.; m. Gloria Jean Larsen, May 10, 1950; children— Randolph G., Cynthia Kaye. Student, pub. schs., Central City. Gen. mgr. Lincoln (Nebr.) Baseball Club, 1955-58; mgr. Pershing Mcpl. Auditorium, Lincoln, 1958-61; exec. staff Ice Capades, Inc., Hollywood, Calif., 1961-63; gen. mgr. Sta. KSAL, Salina, Kans., 1963-65; dir. promotion and sales St. Louis Nat. Baseball Club, 1965-66; gen. mgr. Forum, Inglewood, Calif., 1966-67; asst. to exec. v.p. Cin. Reds, 1967-70, asst. to pres., 1970-74, v.p. adminstrn., 1975, exec. v.p., 1975-78, gen. mgr., 1977-83, pres., 1978-83, Houston Astros Baseball Club, 1985-87; spl. asst. Office of Baseball Commr., 1988-93; asst. to chmn. Major League Exec. Coun., 1993-94. Pres. RGW Enterprises, Inc., Phoenix, 1978-87. Served with USNR, 1945-47, 50-52. Named Exec. of Yr., Minor League Baseball, Sporting News, 1958. Republican. Methodist.

WAGNER, RICHARD E. economist, educator; b. Jamestown, ND, Apr. 28, 1941; s. Herbert and Dorothy Mae King; m. Barbara Helen (Westgate) W., June 9, 1962; children: Stephanie Wagner Tice, Valerie Wagner Smith. AA, Fullerton (Calif.) Jr. Coll., 1961; BS, U. So. Calif., 1963; PhD, U. Va., 1966. Asst. prof. econs. U. Calif., Irvine, 1966-68, Tulane U., New Orleans, 1968-73; prof. econs. Va. Poly. Inst. and State U., Blacksburg, 1973-79, Auburn (Ala.) U., 1979-81, Fla. State U., Talahassee, 1981-88; Holbert L. Harris prof. econs. George Mason U., Fairfax, Va., 1988—. Sr. fellow, chmn. acad. adv. bd. Pub. Interest Inst., Mt. Pleasant, Iowa, 1995—. Author: Democracy in Deficit, 1977, To Promote the General Welfare, 1989, The Economics of Smoking, 1991, Trade Protection in the United States, 1995; editor: Public Choice and Constitutional Economics, 1988, Charging for Government, 1991, Limiting Leviathan, 1999, Federalist Government in

Principle and Practice, 2001, Politics, Taxation, and The Rule of Law, 2002. Mem. Am. Econ. Assn., So. Econ. Assn. (exec. com. 1987-88), Internat. Inst. Pub. Fin., Internat. Soc. New Instl. Econs., Pub. Choice Soc. Home: 11845 Clara Way Fairfax Station VA 22039 Office: George Mason U Dept Econs Fairfax VA 22030 Office Phone: 703-993-1132. E-mail: rwagner@gmu.edu.

WAGNER, ROBERT EARL, retired agronomist; b. Garden City, Kans., Mar. 6, 1921; s. Fay Arthur and Margaret (Longbottom) W.; m. Bernice Bittner, Aug. 7, 1948; children— Robert Earl, James Warren, Douglas Alan. BS, Kans. State Coll., 1942; MS, U. Wis., 1943, PhD, 1950. Forage crops specialist Ft. Hays Expt. Sta., Hays, Kans., 1943-45; asso. agronomist Plant Industry Sta., U.S. Dept. Agr., Beltsville, Md., 1945-48, research agronomist, asst. project leader pasture and range project, 1951-54, research agronomist, project leader western pasture and range project, 1954-56; prof., head dept. agronomy U. Md., 1956-59; regional dir. American Potash Inst., 1959-66, also Found. for Internat. Potash Research, v.p. both orgns., 1966-67; dir. Coop. Extension Service, U. Md., 1967-75; pres., bd. dirs. Potash Inst., 1975-77, Potash and Phosphate Inst., 1977-88, pres. emeritus, 1988—, chmn., bd. dirs. Potash & Phosphate Inst. Can., 1975-88; pres., bd. dirs. Found. for Agronomic Rsch., 1980-87; owner Wagner Performance Cattle, Stone Mountain, Ga., 1985—. Bd. dirs., mem. exec. com. Internat. Fertilizer Devel. Ctr., 1975-98; chmn. Nat. Ext. Com. on Orgn. and Policy; mem. U.S. del. 7th Internat. Grassland Congress, New Zealand. Author tech., popular publs.; Editor: Proc. Sixth Internat. Grassland Congress. Recipient Medallion award Am. Forage and Grassland Coun., Disting. Grasslander award, 1994; award Md. Farm Bur.; Disting. Svc. award in agr. Kansas State U., 1985, Disting. Alumnus award, 1990; Cert. of Disting. Citizenship, State of Md.; Robert E. Wagner Efficient Agr. award established in his honor; Disting. Grasslander award Am. Forage and Grassland Coun., 1994; named to Am.'s Registry of Outstanding Profls., 2003. Fellow AAAS, Am. Soc. Agronomy (chmn. grassland com., mem. exec. com., bd. dirs., pres. N.E. br.), Crops Sci. Soc. Am., Soil Sci. Soc. Am.; mem. Grassland Coun. (pres.), Am. Soc. Range Mgmt., Cosmos Club (Washington), Atlanta Athletic Club, Sigma Xi, Alpha Zeta, Gamma Sigma Delta, Phi Kappa Phi. Presbyterian. Home: 1495 Parkview Blvd Stone Mountain GA 30087-1016 Office: 655 Engineering Dr Norcross GA 30092-2822

WAGNER, ROBERT WALTER, photography, cinema and communications educator, media producer, consultant; b. Newport News, Va., Nov. 16, 1918; s. Walter George and Barbara Anne Wagner; m. Betty Jane Wiles, Nov. 21, 1948; children: Jonathan R., Jeffrey A., Jennifer J. BSc, Ohio State U., 1940, MA, 1941, PhD, 1953. Motion picture writer-dir. Office War Info., N.Y.C. and Washington, 1942-43; writer-dir. Office Coord. Interam. Affairs for South and Ctrl. Am., 1943-44; chief info. Divsn. Mental Hygiene, Ohio Dept. Pub. Welfare, 1944-46; dir. divsn. motion pictures Ohio State U., Columbus, 1946-58, prof. comms., photography and cinema, 1960—, chmn. dept. photo-cinema, 1966-74. Pres. Univ. Film Found., 1979-85; writer, dir. James Thurber's Columbus Town, 1990, Images of the Depression, 1990; writer, prodr. TV series The Last of the Silents, 1975; internat. cons. comms.; bd. dirs. Am. Film Inst., 1974-81; mem. faculty U. So. Calif., 1958 59, U. P.R., 1961, 66, 68, San Jose State U., 1967, Ariz. State U., 1971, Concordia U., Montreal, 1980, 81, Danish Nat. Film Sch., 1983, 94, Emerson Coll., Boston, 1987. Author film series: Series of Motion Picture Documents on Communication Theory and New Educational Media, 1966; co-author: The American Tintype, 1999; editor: Education of Film Maker, 1975; co-producer: Cognizant Media, Studio City, Calif., 1997, The View from Malabar, 2000; curator: Pioneers of The American Tintype, Columbus Mus. of Art, 2003. Recipient Disting. Svc. award Columbus Cmty. Film Coun., 1986, Disting. Svc. award Ohio State U., 1988, Ohiana Pegasus award, 1985; Ency. Brit. fellow, 1953; Sr. Fulbright fellow, Peru, 1976. Fellow Soc. Motion Picture and TV Engrs. (Eastman Gold Medal award 1981); mem. Acad. TV Arts and Scis. (Disting. Svc. award 1966), Univ. Film/Video Assn. (bd. editors jour. 1975-85, editor jour. 1956-75), Internat. Congress Schs. Cinema and TV (v.p. 1964-82), Assn Ednl. Comm. and Tech. (bd. editors jour. 1976—), Torch Club (Columbus, pres. 1996), curator, The Art of Humane Propaganda, Columbus Mus. of Art, 2001, Photography in The Midwest, Encl. of The Midwest, 2004. Home: 1353 Zollinger Rd Columbus OH 43221-2939

WAGNER, ROD, library director; b. Oakland, Nebr., Sept. 14, 1948; s. Francis Lynn and Doris Jean (Egbers) W.; m. M. Diane Kennedy, June 14, 1969; children: Jennifer, Brian, James. BA Social Sci. Edn., Wayne (Nebr.) State Coll., 1970; MA Polit. Sci., U. Nebr. Lincoln, 1971; MA Libr. Sci., U. Mo., 1981. Rsch. coord. Nebr. Libr. Commn., Lincoln, 1972, planning, evaluation, rsch. coord., 1972-73, adminstrv. asst., 1973-74, dep. dir., 1974-87, dir., 1988—. Bd. dirs. Nebr. Ctr. for the Book, Nebr. Devel. Network; mem. Nebr. Universal Svcs. Adv. Bd., 1998—. Mem. state govt. coun. Nebr. Info. Tech. Commn., 1999—. With U.S. Army N.G., 1970-77. Mem. ALA (contbr. yearbook 1981-84), Assn. Specialized and Cooperative Libr. Agys. (bd. dirs. 1998-2000), Nebr. Libr. Assn. (pres.-elect 1993-94, pres. 1994-95), Chief Officers State Libr. Agys., Western Coun. State Librs. (pres. 1992-93). Presbyterian. Home: 3205 W Pershing Rd Lincoln NE 68502-4844 Office: NE Libr Commn 1200 N St Ste 120 Lincoln NE 68508-2023 E-mail: rwagner@nlc.state.ne.us.

WAGNER, ROY, anthropology educator, researcher; b. Cleve., Oct. 2, 1938; s. Richard Robert and Florence Helen (Mueller) W.; m. Brenda Sue Geilhausen, June 14, 1968 (div. Dec. 1994); children: Erika Susan, Jonathan Richard. AB, Harvard U., 1961; AM, U. Chgo., 1962, PhD, 1966. Asst. prof. anthropology So. Ill. U., Carbondale, 1966-68; assoc. prof. Northwestern U., Evanston, Ill., 1969-74; prof. U. Va., Charlottesville, 1974—, chmn. dept., 1974-79. Mem. cultural anthropology panel NSF, Washington, 1981-82. Author: (novels) Habu, 1972, The Invention fo Culture, 1975, Lethal Speech, 1978, Symbols That Stand for Themselves, 1986, An Anthropology of the Subject, 2000. Social Sci. Research Council faculty research grantee, 1968; NSF postdoctoral research grantee, 1979. Fellow Am. Anthropol. Assn. Avocation: student hot-air balloon pilot. Home: 726 Cargil Ln Charlottesville VA 22902-4302 Office: U Va Dept Anthropology University Station Charlottesville VA 22906

WAGNER, SAMUEL ALBIN MAR, records management executive, educator; b. Brighton, Colo., Feb. 23, 1942; s. Jacob Doer and Leota Garnet (Wilson) W.; m. Donna Dee Person, Mar. 20, 1987; children: Kurt, Andrea, Autumn, Jan, Arthur. BA in History, U. Colo., 1964, MA in History, 1965; STB (MTS) in History of World Religions, Harvard U., 1968; cert. in archival adminstrn., U. Denver, 1978. cert. records mgr. 1983; cert. archivist 1994. Archival asst. Harvard U. & Harvard Bus. Sch., 1965-68; asst. curator we. hist. collections U. Colo., 1968-70; sr. asst. archivist Cornell U., Ithaca, NY, 1971-73; editor Brighton Blade, Ft. Lupton Press, Colo., 1973-77; city archivist City of Providence, 1978-80; state records analyst Wyo. State Archives, Cheyenne, 1979-83; pres. Records Mgmt. Cons. Internat., 1983—; records mgr. Ft. Collins (Colo.) Police Dept., 1984-87; pub. records adminstr. State RI, Providence, 1987-90; asst. prof. master archival studies program U. BC, Vancouver, Canada, 1990-93; editor Mo. State Archives, Jefferson City, 1994-96; prodr. community access Sta. JCTV, Jefferson City, 1994-96; chief NJ Bur. Records Mgmt., Trenton, 1996—; pres. Historic Rsch. Svcs., Jefferson City, Trenton, 1994—. Instr. Chapman, U., 1981-87, Colo. State U., 1985-87, Lincoln U., 1995-96, U. BC, 1990-93; speaker in field. Author: Brighton Reflections, 1976, Adams County: Crossroads of the West, 1977, Directory of Automated Records Management Systems, 1985-91, Crossroads of the West: A History of Brighton and the Platte Valley, 1977; editor The Fort Lupton Story, 1977, Adams County Colorado: A Centennial History, 2002, Moving Archives, 2002; contbr. articles to profl. jours. Officer, bd. dirs. Adams County Hist. Soc., 1973-77; county historian Adams County, Brighton, 1976-77; mem. Brighton Human Rels. Commn., 1977-78; bd. dirs. Brighton Bicentennial Com., 1975-76, Ft. Lupton Bicentennial Com., 1975-76, RI RSVP, 1978-80, mem. RI Pub. Records Adv. Coun., 1987-90, RI Hist. Records Adv. Bd., 1987-90; chmn. info. profls. legis. task force Freedom of Info. and Privacy Assn., 1991-93; chmn. oral history project Cole County Hist. Soc., 1996. Recipient Hist. Preservation award Adams County Hist. Soc., 1978, award Freedom of Info. and Privacy Assn., 1993; grantee Ethnic Heritage Project Colo. Humanities Coun., 1977, Humanities and Social Scis. U. BC, 1993, Nat. Historic Pub. & Records Commn., 1988-92; Ford Found. fellow, 1964-65. Mem. Assn. Records Mgrs. and Adminstrs. (pres. No. Colo. chpt. 1984-85, v.p. Ocean State chpt. 1987-90, bd. dirs., editor Vancouver chpt. 1991, bd. dirs. Ctrl. NJ chpt. 2000—, pres. 2002—), records mgmt. standards and glossary task forces, Mem. Yr. 1985, microcomputer/PC industry action com., chmn. 1984-86, editor Software Dir. 1985-91, co-chmn. tech. applications com. 1989-90, chmn. Archives ISG 1997-99, ISG mid-year seminar program com. 1998-2002, mgr. edn. sector 1999-2002), Inst. Cert. Records Mgrs. (regional coord., exam proctor, grader 1982—, cert. records mgr. 1983), Soc. Am. Archivists (com. automated records and techniques 1990-94, select com. task force on automated records and techniques 1994—1998, chmn. MicroMARC users group 1994-96, rep. joint SAA-ARMA Com. 1995-97), Nat. Assn. Govt. Archivists an Records Adminstrs., Archives Assn. B.C. (freedom of info. and privacy legis. com. 1990-93), Assn. Can. Archivists (electronic records select com. 1991-93, Acad. Cert. Archivists (outreach com. 1996-98, mem. commn. on future of archival enterprise 1999—2000), Pub. Sector Mgrs. Assn., Am. Civil Liberties Union, Nature Conservancy, Am. Hist. Soc. of Germans from Russia (charter), Mid-Atlantic Regional Archives Conf. (program com. 1999-2000, 2002—). Democrat. Unitarian Universalist. Avocations: local history, art, photography, film and tv production. Home: 387 N 6th Ave Brighton CO 80601 Office Phone: 609-530-3204. Business E-Mail: albin.wagner@sos.state.nj.us.

WAGNER, TERRANCE CARL, automotive executive; b. Cin., Sept. 15, 1960; s. Thomas Anthony and Laverne Stella Wagner; m. Mary Louise Baghdoian, June 25, 1988; 1 child, Collin Caimin. BS, U. Dayton, 1981; MS, Purdue U., 1983; PhD, U. Mich., 1993. Cert. Six Sigma Black Belt 2002. Mgr. Ford Motor Co., Dearborn, Mich., 2002 . Engr. Ford Motor Co., 1983—93, engine devel. supr., 1993—95, engine design supr., 1995—99. Contbr. articles various profl. jours. Scholar Presdl. scholarship, U. Dayton, 1977-1981. Master: Am. Sail Inst.; mem.: ASME, Soc. of Automotive Engrs. Achievements include research in developing a simple efficient algorithm for decoupling large optimization problems. Formulation was basis for numerous additional developments @UM Design Laboratory; developing measurement technique to extract 3-D flow field information by rotating a single hot-wire anemometer; incorporated non-linear programming techniques into thermo-fluid models of engine performance. One of early developers of these techniques. Office: Ford Motor Co 21500 Oakwood Blvd Dearborn MI 48121 E-mail: twagner3@ford.com.

WAGNER, THOMAS JOSEPH, lawyer, insurance company executive; b. Jackson, Mich., June 29, 1939; s. O. Walter and Dorothy Ann (Hollinger) Wagner; m. Judith Louise Bogardus, Jan. 15, 1961; children: Ann Louise, Mark Robert, Rachel Miriam. BA, Earlham Coll., 1957; JD, U. Chgo., 1965. Bar: Ill. 1968, U.S. Supreme Ct. 1975. Asst. to gov. State of Ill., Springfield, 1966—67, legal counsel, adminstrv. asst. to treas., 1967—70; adminstrv. asst. U.S. Senator Adlai E. Stevenson Washington, 1970—77; sr. v.p. govt. affairs divsn. Am. Ins. Assn., Washington, 1977—80; staff v.p. Ina Corp., Washington; v.p., chief counsel Property Casualty Group, CIGNA Corp., Phila., 1986—88, sr. v.p., corp. sec., 1988—91, exec. v.p., gen. counsel, 1992—2001; ret., 2001. Former trustee Eisenhower Exch. Fellowships, Inc.; past chmn. Phila. Crime Commn.; former bd. dirs. Inst. Law and Econs., U. Pa. Pub. Svc. fellow, Syracuse U., 1965—66. Mem.: ABA (bus. law com.), U.S.-Pacific Econ. Cooperation Coun., Am. Corp. Counsel Assn.

WAGNER, WILLIAM GERARD, university dean, physicist, consultant, information scientist, investment manager; b. St. Cloud, Minn., Aug. 22, 1936; s. Gerard C. and Mary V. (Cloone) W.; m. Janet Agatha Rowe, Jan. 30, 1968 (div. 1978); children: Mary, Robert, David, Anne; m. Christiane LeGuen, Feb. 21, 1985 (div. 1989); m. Yvonne Naomi Moussette, Dec. 4, 1995. BS, Calif. Inst. Tech., 1958, PhD (NSF fellow, Howard Hughes fellow), 1962. Cons. Rand Corp., Santa Monica, Calif., 1960-65; sr. staff physicist Hughes Research Lab., Malibu, Calif., 1960-69; lectr. physics Calif. Inst. Tech., Pasadena, 1963-65; asst. prof. physics U. Calif. at Irvine, 1965-66; assoc. prof. physics and elec. engring. U. So. Calif., L.A., 1966-69, prof. depts. physics and elec. engring., 1969—, dean div. natural scis. and math. Coll. Letters, Arts and Scis., 1973-87, dean interdisciplinary studies and developmental activities, 1987-89, spl. asst. automated record services, 1975-81; founder program in neural, informational & behavioral scis., 1982—. Chmn. bd. Malibu Securities Corp., L.A., 1971—; cons. Janus Mgmt. Corp., L.A., 1970-71, Croesus Capital Corp., L.A., 1971-74, Fin. Horizons Inc., Beverly Hills, Calif., 1971—; allied mem. Pacific Stock Exch., 1974-82; fin. and computer cons. Hollywood Reporter, 1979-81; mem. adv. coun. for emerging engring. techs. NSF, 1987-89; cons. Wagner Tech. Solutions, L.A., 2001—. Contbr. articles on physics to sci. publs. Richard Chase Tolman postdoctoral fellow, 1962-65 Mem. Am. Phys. Soc., Nat. Assn. Security Dealers, Sigma Xi. Home: 2828 Patricia Ave Los Angeles CA 90064-4425 Office: U So Calif Hedco Neurosci Bldg Los Angeles CA 90089-0001 Office Phone: 213-740-7839.

WAGONER, ANNA MILLS, prosecutor; BA, Agnes Scott Coll.; JD, Wake Forest U. Assoc. Woddson, Linn, Sayers, Lawther, Short and Wagoner, 1985—87, ptnr., 1987—90; judge Rowan County Dist. Ct., 1990—2001; U.S. atty. mid. dist. U.S. Dept. Justice, NC, 2001—. Office: PO Box 1858 Greensboro NC 27402

WAGONER, DAVID EVERETT, lawyer, arbitrator; b. Pottstown, Pa., May 16, 1928; s. Claude Brower and Mary Kathryn (Groff) W.; children: Paul R., Colin H., Elon D., Peter B., Dana F.; m. Jean Morton Saunders; children: Constance A., Jennifer L., Melissa J. BA, Yale U., 1950; LLB, U. Pa., 1953. Bar: D.C. 1953, Pa. 1953, Wash. 1953. Law clk. U.S. Ct. Appeals (3d cir.), Pa., 1955-56; law clk. U.S. Supreme Ct., Washington, 1956-57; ptnr. Perkins & Coie, Seattle, 1957-96. Panel mem. of arbitration forum worldwide including People's Republic of China, B.C. Internat. Comml. Arbitration Ctr., Hong Kong Internat. Arbitration Centre, London Ct. Internat. Arbitration, AAA's Internat. Ctr. Dispute Resolution, CPR Inst. Dispute Resolution. Mem. sch. com. Mcpl. League Seattle and King County, 1958—, chmn., 1962-65; mem. Seattle schs. citizens coms. on equal ednl. opportunity and adult vocat. edn., 1963-64; mem. Nat. Com. Support Pub. Schs.; mem. adv. com. on community colls., to 1965, legislature interim com. on edn., 1964-65; mem. community coll. adv. com. to state supt. pub. instrn., 1965; chmn. edn. com. Forward Thrust, 1968; mem. Univ. Congl. Ch. Council Seattle, 1968-70; bd. dirs. Met. YMCA Seattle, 1968; bd. dirs. Seattle Pub. Schs., 1965-73, v.p., 1966-67, 72-73, pres., 1968, 73; trustee Evergreen State Coll. Found., chmn. 1986-87, capitol campaign planning chmn.; trustee Pacific NW Ballet, v.p. 1986. Served to 1st lt. M.C., AUS, 1953-55 Fellow Coll. Comml. Arbitrators, Am. Coll. Trial Lawyers (mem. ethics com., legal ethics com.), Chartered Inst. Arbitrators, Singapore Inst. Arbitrators; mem. ABA (chmn. standing com. fed. jud. improvement, chmn. appellate advocacy com., mem. commn. on separation of powers and jud. independence), Wash. State Bar Assn., Seattle-King County Bar Assn., Acad. Experts, Swiss Arbitration Assn., Nat. Sch. Bds. Assn. (bd. dirs., chmn. coun. Big City bds. edn. 1971-72), English-Speaking Union (v.p. Seattle chpt. 1961-62), Chi Phi. Office: Internat Arbitration Chambers US BankCtr 1420 5th Ave Fl 22 Seattle WA 98101-4087 Home: 3916 E Pine St Seattle WA 98122-3517 Office Phone: 206-224-2872. E-mail: email@davidwagoner.com.

WAGONER, DAVID RUSSELL, writer, educator; b. Massillon, Ohio, June 5, 1926; s. Walter Siffert and Ruth (Banyard) W.; m. Patricia Lee Parrott, July 8, 1961 (div. June 1982); m. Robin Heather Seyfried, July 24, 1982; children: Alexandra Dawn, Adrienne Campbell. BA in English, Pa. State U., 1947; MA in English, Ind. U., 1949. Instr. English DePauw U., 1949-50; instr. Pa. State U., 1950-53; asst. prof. U. Wash., 1954-57, assoc. prof., 1958-66, prof., 1966-2000, prof. emeritus, 2000—. Elliston lectr. U. Cin., 1968; editor Poetry NW, 1966-02; poetry editor Princeton U. Press, 1977-81, Mo. Press, 1983—. Author: (poetry books) Dry Sun, Dry Wind, 1953, A Place to Stand, 1958, The Nesting Ground, 1963, Staying Alive, 1966, New and Selected Poems, 1969, Working Against Time, 1970, Riverbed, 1972, Sleeping in the Woods, 1974, Collected Poems, 1976, Who Shall Be the Sun?, 1978, In Broken Country, 1979, Landfall, 1981, First Light, 1983, Through the Forest, 1987, Walt Whitman Bathing, 1996, Traveling Light: Collected and New Poems, 1999, The House of Song, 2002; (novels) The Man in the Middle, 1954, Money, Money, Money, 1955, Rock, 1958, The Escape Artist (also film 1982), 1965, Baby, Come on Inside, 1968, Where is My Wandering Boy Tonight?, 1970, The Road to Many a Wonder, 1974, Tracker, 1975, Whole Hog, 1976, The Hanging Garden, 1980; editor: Straw for the Fire: From the Notebooks of Theodore Roethke, 1943-63, 1972. Recipient Morton Dauwen Zabel prize Poetry mag., 1967, Blumenthal-Leviton-Blonder prize, 1974, 2 Fels prizes Coordinating Coun. Lit. Mags., 1975, Tietjens prize, 1977, English-Speaking Union prize, 1980, Sherwood Anderson award, 1980, Ruth Lilly Poetry prize, 1991, Levinson prize, 1994; Union League Prize, 1987, Pacific N.W. Booksellers award, 2000; Guggenheim fellow, 1956, Ford fellow, 1964, Nat. Inst. Arts and Letters grantee, 1967, Nat. Endowment for Arts grantee, 1969 Mem. Acad. Am. Poets (chancellor 1978—2000), Soc. Am. Magicians, Nat. Assn. Blackfeet Indians (asso.) Home: 5416 154th Pl SW Edmonds WA 98026-4348 Office: U Wash PO Box 354330 Seattle WA 98195-4330 E-mail: renogawd@aol.com.

WAGONER, G. RICHARD, JR., automotive company executive; b. Wilmington, Del., Feb. 9, 1953; BS in Econs., Duke U., 1975; MBA, Harvard U., 1977. Analyst in treas.'s office, mgr. Latin Am. financing, dir. Can. and overseas borrowing, dir. capital analysis and investment GM, N.Y., 1977-81, treas. Sao Paulo, Brazil, 1981-84, exec. dir. fin., 1984-87, v.p., fin. mgr., 1987-88, group dir. strategic bus. planning, 1988-89, v.p. fin., 1989-91, pres., 1992-93, head Worldwide Purchasing Group, 1993-94, exec. v.p., pres. North Am. ops., 1994-98, pres., COO, 1998—2000, pres., CEO, 2000—03, chmn., CEO, 2003—, also bd. dirs. Chmn. bd. visitors Fuqua Sch. Bus. Duke U.; trustee Detroit County Day Sch. Mem. Soc. Automotive Engrs. (mem. VISION 2000 exec. com.). Office: GM Corp 300 Renaissance Ctr Detroit MI 48265-0001

WAGONER, GERALDINE VANDER POL, music educator; b. Kankakee, Ill., Sept. 16, 1931; d. Ralph and Josie (Mieras) VanderPol; children: Joel Timothy, Stephanie Anne. BA, Central U. Of Iowa, 1954; MA, Montclair State Coll., 1968; postgrad., Juilliard Sch. Music, 1955-56, 66-67, NYU, Royal Conservatory, Toronto, 1971, Mozarteum, Salzburg, Austria, 1972. Music specialist Bd. Edn., Edison, NJ, 1954—74, Ridgewood, 1975-95; dir. Musical Spheres Co., 1995—. Mem. Amb. to Amb. program Russian Conservatories, 1998. Composer: tonal rhythmic curriculum for assessing children. Trustee, Hudson Symphony Orch., 1965-71; mem. Met. Mus. of Art, Teaching fellow NYU, 1990-91; adj. prof. music William Paterson Coll., Wayne, N.J. Mem. Profl. Music Tchrs. Guild (cert. for highest goals and achievements 1966), Nat. Music Tchrs. Nat. Assn., N.J. Music Tchrs. Assn., Am. Orff Schulwerk Assn., NEA, Music Educators Nat. Conf., Nat. Guild Piano Tchrs. (judge 2003—), Met. Opera Guild, Netherland-Am. Found., Collegiate Chorale N.Y.C. 1995—, Lyceum Soc. of N.Y. Acad. Scis., Netherland Club, Coll. Club. Office Phone: 201-825-9045. E-mail: wagonerg@optonline.net.

WAGONER, RALPH HOWARD, academic administrator; b. Pitts., May 30, 1938; s. Richard Henry and Charlotte (Stevenson) W.; m. Wilma Jo Staup, Dec. 21, 1961; children: Amanda Jane, Joseph Ryan. AB in Biology, Gettysburg Coll., 1960; MS in Ednl. Adminstrn., Westminster Coll., 1963; PhD, Kent State U., 1967; postgrad., MIT, 1973, Dartmouth Coll., 1979. Prin., tchr., coach Williamsfield (Ohio) Elem. and Jr. High Sch., 1960-62; dir. elem. edn. Pymatuning Valley (Ohio) Local Schs., 1962-64, asst. supt. instrn., 1964-65; acad. counselor, asst. to dean coll. edn. Kent (Ohio) State U., 1965-66, instr. edn., 1966-67; asst. prof. Drake U., Des Moines, 1967-70, assoc. prof., 1970-71, chmn. dept. elem. edn., 1968-70, chmn. dept. tchr. edn., 1970-71, acad. adminstrn. intern Am. Council Edn., Office of Pres., 1971-72, asst. to pres., 1972-77, dir. devel., 1975-77; v.p. pub. affairs and devel., prof. Western Ill. U., Macomb, 1977-87, pres., 1987-93, Augustana Coll., Sioux Falls, SD, 1993—2000, Lutheran Ednl. Conf. of N.Am. Adj. prof. San Francisco Theol. Sem., 1971; mem. senate Drake U., 1968-77; sponsor interhall council Western Ill. U., 197893, mem. BOG/UPI task force on incentives for faculty excellence, co-chmn., faculty mentor, 1985-93; cons. in field. Co-author: (with L. Wayne Bryan) Societal Crises and Educational Response: A Book of Readings, 1969, (with Robert L. Evans) The Emerging Teacher, 1970, (with William R. Abell) The Instructional Module Package System, 1971, Writing Behavioral Objectives or How Do I Know When He Knows, 1971; contbr. articles to profl. jours. Chmn. Mid-Ill. Computer Consortium, 1980, 85, Western Ill. Corridor of Opportunity, 1987-93; mem. Pres.' Regional Adv. Coun., 1977-87; mem. investments com. McDonough County YMCA; mem. exec. com. Macomb Area Indsl. Corp.; trustee Robert Morris Coll., 1983-88, Chgo. and Carthage, Ill., 1983-88; bd. dirs. Ill. Coun. Econ. Edn., 1987-93, McDonough County United Way Dr., 1980-82; bd. trustees The Cornerstone Found. LSS of Ill., 1990-96; mem. Sioux Falls Tomorrow Task Force, 1993-94; bd. dirs. S.D. Symphony, 1993—, Edn. Telecomms. State of S.D., 1993—, Sioux Falls Devel. Found., 1993—, Children's Inn, 1993—, Sioux Valley Physicians Alliance, 1995—, LECNA, 1996—; life trustee Lutheran Social Svcs., 1996—. Recipient Man of Yr. award Andover Rotary Club, 1964, Quax Honor award, 1969-70, Disting. Alumni award Gettysburg (Pa.) Coll., 1991; named McDonough County Citizen of Yr., Elks, 1982. Fellow Am. Coun. Edn. (cons. fund raising 1984-87); mem. Am. Assn. State Colls. and Univs. (com. econ. devel. 1988, com. on athletics 1987), Ednl. Computing Network (chmn. policy bd. 1985-87), Assn. Midcontinent Univs. (coun. dels. 1987-93), Gateway Conf. (coun. dels. 1987-93), Coun. for Advancement and Support of Edn. (discussion leader, speaker, 1975, 77, 80, 84, 86, 91, 92, 93, 94, Citation award 1981, 83, Grand award 1982, Bronze award 1985, Silver award 1986), Macomb C. of C. (exec. com., bd. dirs.), Ill. Chamber Econ. Devel. Policy Task Force, Blue Key (hon.), Omicron Delta Kappa, Phi Eta Sigma (hon.), Phi Mu Alpha. Lodges: Rotary. Lutheran. Home: 2505 S Poplar Dr Sioux Falls SD 57105-4946 Office: Augustana Coll 2001 S Summit Ave Sioux Falls SD 57197-0001

WAGONER, ROBERT VERNON, astrophysicist, educator; b. Teaneck, N.J., Aug. 6, 1938; s. Robert Vernon and Marie Theresa (Clifford) W.; m. Lynne Ray Moses, Sept. 2, 1963 (div. Feb. 1986); children: Alexa Frances, Shannon Stephanie; m. Stephanie Brewster, June 27, 1987. BME, Cornell U., 1961; MS, Stanford U., 1962, PhD, 1965. Rsch. fellow in physics Calif. Inst. Tech., 1965-68, Sherman Fairchild Disting. scholar, 1976; asst. prof. astronomy Cornell U., 1968-71; assoc. prof., 1971-73; assoc. prof. physics Stanford U., 1973-77, prof., 1977—. George Ellery Hale disting. vis. prof. U. Chgo., 1978; mem. Com. on Space Astronomy and Astrophysics, 1979-82, theory study panel Space Sci. Bd., 1980-82, physics survey com. NRC, 1983-84; grant selection com. NSERC (Can.), 1990-93; active Laser Interferometer Gravitational-Wave Obs. Sci. Collaboration. Contbr. articles on theoretical astrophysics and gravitation to profl. jours., mags.; co-author Cosmic Horizons, 1982; patentee in field. Sloan Found. rsch. fellow, 1969-71; Guggenheim Meml. fellow, 1979; grantee NSF, 1973-90, 2000-03, NASA, 1982-99. Fellow Am. Phys. Soc.; mem. Am. Astron. Soc., Internat. Astron. Union, Tau Beta Pi, Phi Kappa Phi Office: Stanford U Dept Physics Stanford CA 94305-4060 Office Phone: 650-723-4561. Business E-Mail: wagoner@stanford.edu.

WAGONER, RUSSELL A. music educator; b. Indpls., July 21, 1971; s. Gordon L. and Martha J. Wagoner. BA in Music Edn., Ball State U., 1993; MusM in Choral Conducting, U. Cin., 2000. Cert. tchr. Ind., N.Y. Dir. choral activities LaPorte (Ind.) H.S., 1993—98; tchg. asst. U. Cin. Coll. Conservatory Music, 1998—99; mgr., asst. mgr. Vocal Arts Ensemble Cin., 1998—2000; dir. choral activities Tappan Zee H.S., Orangeburg, NY, 2000—; dir. music, organist Franklin Lakes(N.J.) United Meth. Ch., 2000—. Adjudicator Fedn. Music Clubs, LaPorte, 1996—98; music dir., pianist Front Row Ctr., Pearl River, NY, 1997—; coach accompanist Opera Theatre Lucca, Italy, 1998; clinician Ind. Choral Dirs. Assn., Indpls., 1998; asst. dir., accompanist Mini-Singers, Cin., 1999—2000. Pianist, composer: albums Once Upon a Midnight, 1998, pianist: albums On the Wings of Song, 2000; composer: (musical) One Forever Kiss, 2004. Recipient Alumni citation, Ball State U., 1998. Mem.: N.Y. State Sch. Music Assn., Am. Choral Dirs. Assn. (state chmn. on women's choirs 1990—). Office: Tappan Zee HS 15 Dutch Hill Rd Orangeburg NY 10962

WAGONER, RUTH R, education coach; b. Louisville, Ky., Feb. 25, 1950; d. Joseph Edward and Patricia Jane Richardson; m. James Reagan Wagoner, Aug. 18, 1973; 1 child, Amanda Lee. PhD, Univ. of KY, Lexington, KY, 1994; MA, Western KY Univ., Bowling Green, KY, 1973; BA, Bellarmine Univ., Louisville, KY, 1971. Prof. Bellarmine Univ., Louisville, 1973—. Ed. coach Bellarmine Mock Trial, Louisville, 1985—. Recipient Reynoldson Award, Am. Mock Trial Assoc./ Des Moines, Iowa, 1987, 1991, Neal Smith Award, 1993, Reynoldson Award, 1994, 1998—99. Mem.: Am. Mock Trial Assoc. (exec. comm.- sec. 2002—04). Home: 3115 Brownsboro Rd Louisville KY 40206 Office Phone: 502-452-8417. E-mail: rwagoner@bellarmine.edu.

WAGONER, WALTER DRAY, JR., lawyer; b. New Haven, Dec. 25, 1942; s. Walter D. and Mariana (Parcells) Wagoner; m. Rosa Nilda Morales, Jan. 22, 1980; children: David, William Carlos, Brenda, Lisa. BA, Yale U., 1965, LLB, 1970. Bar: Conn. 71, U.S. Dist. Ct. Conn. 71. Staff atty. New Haven Legal Assistance Assn., 1970—74, mng. atty., 1974—76, dir. legal edn., 1976—78; sole practice New Haven, 1978—. Chmn. New Haven City Commn. Cultural Affairs, 1977—79; trustee Conn. Pub. TV, 1977—83, U.S. Bankruptcy Ct. for Dist. Conn., 1983—87. Mem.: Conn. Bar Assn., Loizenos Club (hon.). Democrat. Office: 840 Elm St New Haven CT 06511-4010 Office Phone: 203-624-7759. E-mail: wdwagoner@yahoo.com.

WAGONFELD, JAMES B. gastroenterologist; b. Bronx, N.Y., Jan. 30, 1946; m. Judith Wagonfeld; children: Temira Lital, Ariella Lirit. BA, NYU, 1966; MD, U. Health Scis., Chgo., 1970. Diplomate Nat. Bd. Med. Examiners, in internal medicine and gastroenterology Am. Bd. Internal Medicine. Med. intern Duke U. Med. Ctr., Durham, N.C., 1970-71; jr. asst. resident in medicine U. Chgo. Hosps. and Clinics, 1971-72, sr. asst. resident in medicine, 1972-73, NIH fellow in gastroenterology, 1973-75, instr. medicine, 1975-76; asst. prof. medicine U. Oreg. Health Scis. Ctr., Portland, 1976-78; attending physician Portland VA Hosp., 1976-78; pvt. practice Digestive Health Specialists, Tacoma, 1979—93; dir. gastrointestinal study unit Tacoma Gen. Hosp., 1987—; co-dir. gastrointestinal diagnostic nit St. Joseph Hosp. and Health Care Ctr., 1988-90. Cons. FDA panel on rev. of vitamins, minerals, and hematinic drug products, 1974-75. Contbr. articles to profl. jours. Physician Benita Juarez Clinic, Chgo., 1971-73, Cardiac Rehab. Program Tacoma-Pierce County Family YMCA, 1980-84; advisor Portlan dAssn. for Childbirth Edn., 1976-78, RESOLVE, An Advocacy Orgn. for Infertile Couples, 1976-78, Colon Cancer Screening in Sr. Citizens, Multinomah County Pub. Health Dept. and Southwest Wash. Health Dist., 1977-78; scientific advisor Shaw Meml. Lecture series, Oreg. Med. Assn., 1977-78; bd. med. advisors Pacific Northwest Soc. of Gastrointestinal Assts., 1982; trustee Charles Wright Acad., 1984-87, chmn. devel. com., 1985-87, chmn. edn. fund, 1985-86. Recipient NIH rsch. award, 1975-76. Fellow ACP, Am. Coll. Gastroenterology; mem. AMA, Am. Gastroenterologic Assn., Am. Soc. for Gastrointestinal Endoscopy, Pacific Northwest Endoscopy Soc., The Wilderness Med. Soc., Wash. State Med. Assn., Med. Soc. Pierce County, Alpha Omega Alpha. Office: Digestive Disease Cons 1901 S Union Ave Ste B-4006 Tacoma WA 98405-1898 Office Phone: 206-272-5127.

WAGSTAFF, GRAYSON, musicologist, educator; s. George and Olive (Clay) Wagstaff; m. Deborah K. Boyd, Dec. 1, 2000. MusB, James Madison U., 1986; PhD in Musicology, U. Tex., 1995. Vis. prof. Va. Commonwealth U., Richmond, 1995—; asst. prof. U. Ala., Tuscaloosa, 1997—; assoc. prof. Rome Sch. Music, Cath. U. Am., Washington, 2000—; dir. L.Am. Ctr., Grad. Study Music, 2002. Contbr. articles to profl. jours.; editor: Encomium Musicae, 2002. Grantee, Cushwa Found., Ctr. Mexican Studies. Mem.: Am. Musicol. Soc. Avocations: travel, dogs, art, antiques, reading. Office: Cath U Am Rome Sch Music Washington DC 20064

WAHBA, MARCELLE M. ambassador; b. Calif., Dec. 1948; m. Derek M. Farwagi; 1 child, Morwenna O. Farwagi. BA in Polit. Sci., Western Coll. for Women. Dep. policy officer Near East Office U.S. Info. Agy., 1987—88; press attaché, embassy spokesperson Dept. State, Cairo, 1988—91, pub. affairs officer Am. Embassy Cyprus Nicosia, 1991—95, counselor for press and cultural affairs Amman, Jordan, 1995—99, Cairo, 1999—2001, U.S. amb. to United Arab Emirates Washington, 2001—. Office: DOS Amb 6010 Abu Dhabi Pl Washington DC 20521

WAHINGTON, ANTHONY WILLIAM, volunteer coordinator; b. Balt., Md., July 20, 1976; s. Chester and Joyce Ann Washington. BS, Frostburg State U., 1999. Program mgr. Frostburg State U., Frostburg, Md., 2000—01; asst. dir. Frostburg State U., Ctr. for Volunteerism and Nat. Svc., 2001—02; stage crew Ctr. Stage Theatre, Balt., 2002; vol. coord. Md. Sci. Ctr., Balt., 2003—. Adv. bd. mem. Allen HallSTARS!, Frostburg State U., 2000—02; com. mem. Frostburg State U. Leadership Com., 2000—02; bd. mem. Frostburg State U. Pres. Bd on Affirmative Action and Equal Employment Opportunities, 2001—02. Com. mem. Spl. Olympics of Alleghany County, Cumberland, Md., 1999—2002, Am. Cancer Soc., Relay for Life, Frostburg, 2001—02. Recipient Pres. Student Svcs. award, Corp. for Nat. Comm. Svc., 2000, CEO award, 2001, Govs. Cert. for Volunteerism, Govs. Office on Svc. and Volunteerisms, 2000—02, Daily Point of Light award, Points of Light Found., 2004, Govs. citation, State of Md., 2004. Independent. Achievements include development of Thanksgiving sponsor a family program at Frostburg State U; the roots African Am. Theatre Org., Frostburg State U. Avocations: writing and performing poetry, volunteering, trumpet, bass, sports. Office: Md Sci Ctr 601 Light St Baltimore MD 21230 E-mail: twashington@mdsci.org.

WAHL, ARTHUR CHARLES, retired chemistry educator; b. Des Moines, Sept. 8, 1917; s. Arthur C. and Mabel (Mussetter) W.; m. Mary Elizabeth McCauley, Dec. 1, 1943; 1 child, Nancy Wahl Miegel. BS, Iowa State Coll., 1939; PhD, U. Calif., Berkeley, 1942. Group leader Los Alamos (N.Mex.) Nat. Lab., 1943-46; assoc. prof. chemistry Washington U., St. Louis, 1946-53, Farr prof. of radiochemistry, 1953-83, prof. emeritus, 1983—. Cons. Los Alamos Nat. Lab., 1950—. Author, editor: Radioactivity Applied to Chemistry, 1951; contbr. articles to profl. jours. NSF fellow, 1967; recipient Sr. Vis. Scientist Humboldt award Humboldt Found., 1977. Mem. Am. Chem. Soc. Office: Los Alamos Nat Lab Ms # 514 Los Alamos NM 87545-0001 E-mail: awahl@lanl.gov.

WAHL, BERNT RAINER, mathematician, writer, application developer; b. Santa Monica, Calif., June 24, 1960; s. Bruno W. and Ursula (Nunn) Wahl. BA in Math., U. Calif., Santa Cruz, 1984, BS in Physics, 1986; MBA, U. Calif., Davis, 1999; cert. in mgmt. tech., U. Calif., Berkeley, 2000; MA in Multimedia, Calif. State U., Hayward, 2001; Knowledge Revolution cert., Stanford U., 2000. Founding mem. Berkeley Macintosh User Group, 1984—; CEO Dynamic Software, Berkeley, 1986—; mem. Bootstrap Inst., Fremont, Calif., 1996—; chief creative officer Yellow Giant, Oakland, Calif.; CEO Datahunt, Inc., 2001, Infoseek Corp., 2000—01. Tech. advisor Reliacom, Reston, Va., Quantal, Berkeley, Jhane Barnes, Inc., NY, Walt Disney Corp., Sunnyvale, Calif., 1995—, Internat. Justice Mission, Washington, UN Devel. Program, MAVCAP Venture Fund, Malaysia; lectr. U. Calif., Berkeley, Davis, Santa Cruz, 1995—99; adj. prof. bus. Golden Gate U., San Francisco; prof. bus./multimedia Calif. State U., Hayward; vis. prof. Multimedia U., Malaysia, 2002—; multimedia super corridor advisor Cyberjaya, Malaysia. Author: (book) Chaos, 1988, Exploring Fractals, 1995; co-author: Virtual Playhouse, 1994; host (video series) Fractals, 1995, Information Technology, 1996; dir., prodr.: (films) Swing City, 1999. Fulbright fellow, 2002. Mem.: AAAS, Internat. Radio Engrs. and Elec. Engrs., IEEE Computer Soc., Urban Land Inst., Assn. Computing Machinery, Nat. Ednl. Film and Video Festival (jury chair). Avocations: olympic photography, America Cup Heart of Am. also: Quantal 1936 University Ave Ste 355 Berkeley CA 94704-1071 Home: 1463 Kimball Ct Concord CA 94518-1230 E-mail: berntww@wahl.org.

WAHL, FLOYD MICHAEL, geologist; b. Hebron, Ind., July 7, 1931; s. Floyd Milford and Anne Pearl (DeCook) W.; m. Dorothy W. Daniel, July 4, 1953; children: Timothy, David, Jeffrey, Kathryn. AB, DePauw U., 1953; MS, U. Ill., 1957, PhD, 1958. Cert. profl. geologist. Prof. geology U. Fla., Gainesville, 1969-82, assoc. dean Grad. Sch., 1974-80, acting dean, 1980-81; exec. dir. Geol Soc Am., Boulder, Colo., 1982-94; ret., 1994. Contbr. articles to profl. jours. Served to cpl. U.S. Army, 1953-55. Recipient Outstanding Tchr. award U. Ill., 1967 Fellow Geol. Soc. Am. (Outstanding Svc. award 1994); mem. Am. Inst. Profl. Geologists (chpt. pres.), Sigma Xi

WAHL, HOWARD WAYNE, retired construction company executive, engineer; b. Hitterdal, Minn, Jan. 17, 1935; s. Milo Ormenzo and Esther Marie (Sorensen) W.; m. Carroll May Pollock, Aug. 16, 1958; children: Jeffrey David, Michael Edward, Nancy Elizabeth. BCE, U. Washington, 1957. Registered engr., Calif., NY, Mich., Ohio, Md. Structural engr. Bechtel Corp., San Francisco, 1956-69, project engr. Gaithersburg, Md., 1969-72; chief civil engr. Bechter Power Corp., San Francisco, 1972-74, mgr. engring. and constrn., 1975-78; v.p., mgr. Ann Arbor Power Div.-Bechtel, Mich., 1978-84; dir. Bechtel Group, Inc., 1982-91; pres. Bechtel Ea. Power Corp., Gaithersburg, 1984-88; mng. dir. Bechtel Power Corp., San Francisco, 1988-89; pres. European region Bechtel Corp., Paris, 1989-91; ret., 1991; pres. Pacific Voice Track, Las Vegas, 1996—2002. Dir. Ann Arbor Bank-1st Am., 1978-84. Contbr. articles to profl. jour. Campaign chmn. Washtenaw County United Way, Ann Arbor, 1982; chmn. Turkish-US Bus. Coun., Washington, 1988-90; mem. exec. coun. Boy Scouts Am., Ann Arbor, 1978-84; mem. devel. coun. U Wash. Coll. Engring.; trustee emeritus Desert Rsch. Inst. U. Nev., Reno. Mem. ASCE (life), Am. Concrete Inst., U. Mich. Pres. Club and Victors Club, U. Washington Pres. Club. Republican. Presbyterian. Avocations: woodworking, gardening, cooking, antique cars, hiking. Home: 170 Canyon Dr Napa CA 94558-1255

WAHL, RICHARD LEO, radiologist, educator, nuclear medicine researcher; b. Iowa, July 13, 1952; s. Max Henry and Josephine Elizabeth (Hogan) Wahl; m. Sandra K. Moeller, June 28, 1975; children: Daniel, Matthew, Peter, Katherine. BA in Chemistry, Wartburg Coll., 1974; MD, Washington U., St. Louis, 1978. Diplomate Am. Bd. Nuc. Medicine (pres. 1998-), Am. Bd. Radiology. Intern U. Calif., San Diego, 1978—79; resident in radiology Mallinckrodt Inst. Washington U., 1979—82, fellow in nuc. medicine and immunology, 1982—83; asst. prof. U. Mich. Med. Ctr., Ann Arbor, 1983—87, assoc. prof., 1987—90, prof., 1990—2000; dir. gen. nuc. imaging, dir. radiopharm. program U. Mich. Cancer Ctr., 1999—; prof., dir. nuc. medicine, vice chair tech. and new bus. devel. Johns Hopkins U., Balt., 2002—. Mem. exptl. immunology study sect. NIH, Bethesda, Md., 1990—94; sec. Am. Bd. Nuc. Medicine, 1997, chmn., 98. Editor: 2 textbooks; contbr. more than 240 articles to profl. jours., chapters to books. Named Eugene Prendegreer New Horizon lectr., RSNA, 1999; recipient Disting. Scientist award, Acad. Molecular Imaging, 2001, Jerome W. Conn rsch. award, U. Mich., 1989; grantee ACS, Dept. of Army; rsch. grantee, NIH. Fellow: Am. Coll. Radiology, Am. Coll. Nuc. Physicians; mem.: AMA, Inst. for Clin. Positron Emission Tomography (bd. dirs., pres. 1996), Am. Assn. for Cancer Rsch., Am. Soc. for Clin. Investigation, Radiol. Soc. N.Am., Soc. Nuc. Medicine (Marc Tetalman award 1986, Berson and Yalow rsch. award 1992, Hounsfield rsch. award 1992). Achievements include 10 patents in field. Avocations: reading, sports. Office: Johns Hopkins Outpatient Ctr Divsn Nuclear Medicine 601 N Caroline St Rm 3223 Baltimore MD 21287

WAHL, WILLIAM BRYAN, marketing professional, real estate officer; b. Aurora, Colo., Dec. 17, 1963; s. Harold Edward Wahl and Dianne (Fowler) Armstrong. BBA in Mgmt., St. Edward's U., 1987; MBA in Gen. Bus., Kent Coll., 1991; PhD in Bus., U. San Moritz, 1999. Asst. store mgr. Handy Dan, Austin, Tex., 1981-88; real estate broker Powell/Armstrong Realty, Austin, 1985—88, S&W Realty, Austin, 1988—; nat. mktg. dir. Am. Home Products, Austin, 1988—; pres. Wahl Success Systems, Austin, 1989—, project mgr. applied materials, 1995—98; procurement mgr. Dell Computer Corp., 2000—; pres. O.H.S. Prodns., 2000—, Brigadier Group LLC, 2003—. Bd. dirs. Pahl Enterprises, Austin, 1988—. Named Outstanding Citizen, Berkeley Davis, Inc., Berkeley, Calif., 1988. Mem. Austin Assn. Life Underwriters, Austin Bd. Realtors, Tex. Assn. Realtors, Nat. Assn. Realtors, Nat. Assn. Life Underwriters, Mktg. and Distributive Edn. Roman Catholic. Avocations: black belt in taekwondoe, golf, weightlifting. Home: 1206 Greenlawn Blvd Round Rock TX 78664-6918

WAHL, WILLIAM JOSEPH, JR., information systems specialist; b. Pottsville, Pa., Jan. 19, 1947; s. William Joseph and Edith (Adams) W.; m. Mary Ellen Trautman, Oct. 17, 1964; children: Patricia Marie, William Joseph III, Monica Marie, Michael Anthony. MS in Bus. Policy, Columbia U., 1983. Dir. info. sys. IBM Corp., White Plains, N.Y., 1979-84, group dir. mgmt. control sys., 1985-87, group dir. info. sys. and telecom., 1988-92; chief info. officer IBM Personal Sys. Group, Somers, N.Y., 1992-94; dir. worldwide fullfillment sys.ecommunications IBM, Somers, N.Y., 1995-98; v.p., mem. svc. tech. Am. OnLine, Inc., Dulles, Va., 1999, exec. v.p. internal computing, 2000—. Rsch. affiliate NYU Stern Sch. Bus., N.Y.C., 1991—; ops. mgmt. advisor Columbia Grad. Sch. Bus., N.Y.C., 1988—. Mem. Beta Gamma Sigma. Avocations: fishing, stamp collecting/philately, music. Home: 43426 Turnberry Isle Ct Leesburg VA 20176 Office: Am OnLine Inc 22260 Pacific Blvd Dulles VA 20166

WAHLBERG, MARK, actor; b. Dorchester, Mass., June 5, 1971; Appeared in films The Substitute, 1993, Renaissance Man, 1994, The Basketball Diaries, 1995, No Fear, 1995, Boogie Nights, 1997, Traveller, 1997, The Big Hit, 1998, Three Kings, 1999, The Corruptor, 1999, The Yards, 1999, The Perfect Storm, 2000, The Planet of the Apes, 2001, Rock Star, 2001, The Truth About Charlie, 2002, The Italian Job, 2003. Office: Provident Financial Mgmt Wennberg 10345 W Olympic Blvd Los Angeles CA 90064

WAHLBERG, PHILIP LAWRENCE, former bishop; b. Houston, Jan. 18, 1924; s. Philip Lawrence and Ella Alieda (Swenson) W.; m. Rachel Conrad, June 1, 1946; children: David, Christopher, Pauli, Sharon. AA, Tex. Luth. Coll., 1942, DD (hon.), 1963; BA, Lenoir Rhyne Coll., Hickory, N.C., 1944; MDiv, Luth. Theol. Sem., Columbia, S.C., 1946. Ordained to ministry United Luth. Ch. in Am., 1946. Pastor St. Luke Luth. Ch., Thunderbolt, Ga., 1946-50, Redeemer Luth. Ch., Wilmington Island, Ga., 1946-50, St. Mark Luth. Ch., Corpus Christi, Tex., 1950-59; pres. Tex.-La. Synod, United Luth. Ch. Am., Austin, Tex., 1959-62; bishop Tex.-La. Synod, Luth. Ch. Am., Austin, Tex., 1963-87; acting dir. devel. Luth. Outdoor and Retreat Ministries Southwest, 1987-88; legis. liaison Tex. Impact, Austin, 1989-91; interim coord. Regional Ctr. for Mission Evang. Luth. Ch. in Am., Dallas, 1991-92; mem. devel. staff Luth. Sem. Program of Southwest, 1992—; mem. com. on appeals, also chmn. Evang. Luth. Ch. in Am., 1988-95, hearing officer, 1995-98. Also mem. exec. coun. Luth. Ch. in Am., N.Y.C., 1980-87, chmn. com. on legal matters, 1984-87; mem. mgmt. com. Divsn. for Mission in N.Am., N.Y.C., 1972-80, chmn., 1972-76; bd. dirs. Bd. Am. Missions, N.Y.C., 1963-72, chmn., 1968-72; bd. dirs. Luth. Sch. Theology, Chgo., 1967-87. Author articles in religious jours., sermons; author theol. cassette, 1973. Named Disting. churchman Tex. Luth. Coll., 1978; Disting. Alumnus, Lenoir Rhyne Coll., 1962; named Man of Year, Thunderbolt, Ga. C. of C., 1950. Democrat. Avocations: winemaking, golf, choral singing. Office: 5804 Cary Dr Austin TX 78757-3108

WAHLE, ELLIOTT, retail executive; BS in Commerce, Rider U. Asst. dir. minor league ops. N.Y. Yankees, N.Y.C.; dir. player personnel Toronto (Can.) Blue Jays; founding pres., gen. mgr. Toys "R" Us Can., 1983—95; pres., CEO Dylex Ltd., Canada; from v.p. and gen. mgr. Times Sq. Store to pres. Babies "R" Us Toys "R" Us, Inc., Wayne, NJ, 2000—02, pres. Babies "R" Us, 2002—, pres. Kids "R" Us, 2003—. Mem. exec. com. Toys "R" Us, Inc.; mem. adv. bd. Sch. Retail Ryerson U., Toronto; chmn. Retail Coun. Can. Dir. Canadian Spl. Olympic Found.; mem. major gifts campaign United Way. Office: Toys R Us Inc 1 Geoffrey Way Wayne NJ 07470-2030

WAHLEN, EDWIN ALFRED, lawyer; b. Gary, Ind., Mar. 12, 1919; s. Alfred and Ethel (Pearson) W.; m. Alice Elizabeth Condit, Apr. 24, 1943 (div. 1983); children: Edwin Alfred, Virginia Elizabeth, Martha Anne; m. Elizabeth L. Corey, Nov. 23, 1984. Student, U. Ala., 1936-38; AB, U. Chgo., 1942, JD, 1948. Bar: Ill. 1948. Practiced in, Chgo., 1948—; mem. firm Haight, Goldstein & Haight, 1948-55; ptnr. Goldstein & Wahlen, 1956-59, Arvey, Hodes, Costello & Burman (and predecessor), 1959-91, Wildman, Harrold, Allen & Dixon, 1992—. Author: Soldiers and Sailors Wills: A Proposal For Federal Legislation, 1948. Served to 2d lt. AUS, 1942-46. Decorated Silver Star medal, Bronze Star medal. Mem. ABA, Ill. Bar Assn., Chgo. Bar Assn., Order of Coif, Phi Beta Kappa, Phi Alpha Delta. Home: 1250 Breckenridge Ct Lake Forest IL 60045-3875 Office: 225 W Wacker Dr Chicago IL 60606-1224

WAHLKE, JOHN CHARLES, political science educator; b. Cin., Oct. 29, 1917; s. Albert B.C. and Clara J. (Ernst) W.; m. Virginia Joan Higgins, Dec. 1, 1943; children: Janet Parmely, Dale. AB, Harvard U., 1939, MA, 1947, PhD, 1952. Instr., asst. prof. polit. sci. Amherst (Mass.) Coll., 1949-53; assoc. prof. polit. sci. Vanderbilt U., Nashville, 1953-63; prof. polit. sci. SUNY, Buffalo, 1963-66, U. Iowa, 1966-71, SUNY, Stony Brook, 1971-72, U. Iowa, Iowa City, 1972-79, U. Ariz., Tucson, 1979-87, prof. emeritus, 1988—, ret. Author: (with others) The Legislative System, 1962, Government and Politics, 1966, The Politics of Representation, 1978; co-author: Introduction to Political Science—Reason, Reflection, and Analysis, 1997. Served to capt., F.A. AUS, 1943-46. Decorated Air medal with 2 oak leaf clusters, ETO Ribbon, 6 Battle Stars. Mem. AAAS, Am. Polit. Sci. Assn. (past pres.), Internat. Polit. Sci. Assn., So. Polit. Sci. Assn., Midwest Polit. Sci. Assn. (past pres.), Western Polit. Sci. Assn., Southwestern Polit. Sci. Assn., Assn. Politics and the Life Scis. (Founders award 1997), Internat. Soc. of Polit. Psychology. Home: 5462 N Entrada Catorce Tucson AZ 85718-4851

WAHLS, HARVEY EDWARD, civil engineer, educator; b. Evanston, Ill., Aug. 8, 1931; s. Albert C. and Lydia E. (Kutz) W.; m. Margaret B. Waggoner, Sept. 3, 1960; children: Richard A., Nancy K. BSCE, Northwestern U., Evanston, Ill., 1954, MS, 1955, PhD, 1961. Registered profl. engr., N.C. Instr. civil engring. Worcester (Mass.) Poly. Inst., 1955-57, asst. prof., 1957-60; instr. Northwestern U., 1957-59; asst. prof. N.C. State U., Raleigh, 1960-63, assoc. prof., 1963-69, prof. civil engring., 1969-97, assoc. dept. head, 1983-97, prof. emeritus, 1997—. Cons. in field. Fellow ASCE (chair geotech. divsn. 1982-83); mem. ASFE, Am. Soc. Engring. Edn., Internat. Soc. Soil Mechanics and Geotech. Engring., U.S. Nat. Soc. for Soil Mechanics and Found. Engring. (sec. 1985-2001). Office: NC State U PO Box 7908 Raleigh NC 27695-7908

WAHOSKE, MICHAEL JAMES, lawyer; b. Ripon, Wis., June 4, 1953; children: Jennifer, John. BA with highest honors, U. Notre Dame, 1975, JD summa cum laude, 1978. Bar: Minn. 1978, U.S. Dist. Ct. Minn. 1979, U.S. Ct. Appeals (7th cir.) 1979, U.S. Ct. Appeals (8th and 9th cirs.) 1980, U.S. Ct. Appeals (10th cir.) 1982, U.S. Supreme Ct. 1982, U.S. Ct. Appeals (6th cir.) 1988, U.S. Ct. Appeals (fed. cir.) 1989, U.S. Ct. Appeals (D.C. cir.) 1992, U.S. Ct. Appeals (4th cir.) 1994, U.S. Ct. Appeals (11th cir.) 1996, Supreme Ct. of Winnebago Tribe of Nebr., 1996. Law clk. to judge Luther M. Swygert U.S. Ct. Appeals (7th cir.), Chgo., 1978-79; law clk. to chief justice Warren E. Burger U.S. Supreme Ct., Washington, 1979-80; assoc. Dorsey & Whitney, Mpls., 1980-85, ptnr., 1986—. Adj. prof. law U. Minn., Mpls., 1981-83. Exec. editor U. Notre Dame Law Rev., 1977-78; co-editor: Freedom & Education: Pierce v. Society of Sisters Reconsidered, 1978. Recipient Vol. Recognition award Nat. Assn. Attys. Gen., 1993, Spl. Recognition award, 2003; Supreme Ct. Reception honors State and Local Legal Ctr., 1991, 92, 93, 95. Fellow: Am. Acad. Appellate Lawyers; mem.: FBA, ABA (standing com. on Amicus Briefs 1997—2002), Hennepin County Bar Assn., Minn. Bar Assn., U.S. Ct. Appeals (8th cir.) Bar Assn., Phi Beta Kappa. Office: Dorsey & Whitney LLP Ste 1500 50 S Sixth St Minneapolis MN 55402-1498

WAHWEAH, LINDA MCNEIL, insurance agent, writer; b. Albuquerque, New Mex., Apr. 2, 1955; d. Ernest Neil and Elizabeth Ann (Murane) Lemke; m. Eugene Gerald Wahweah, Feb. 14, 1979 (div. June 2001). Bus., Cannon's Internat. Bus. Coll., 1976. Legal sec. Manpower Gen. Dynamic, San Bernardino, Calif., 1980—82; ins. c.s.r. p.l. and comml. Ctrl. City Ins. Agy., San Bernardino, 1982—84; ins. office mgr. Bankers Life Ins., Riverside, Calif., 1984—85; ind. ins. agt. Am. Family Life Ins., Redlands, Calif., 1985—88; civil rights adv. Walker River Palute Tribe, Schurz, Nev., 1989—95; freelance writer Native Am. Civil Rights, San Clemente, Calif., 1996—2003; chronical specialist Native Am. Civil Union, San Bernardino and West Cajon, 2000—03. Promotor specialist Karaoke of Inland Empire, San Bernardino, 2000—03; council mem. Native Am. Civil Rights Union, 1992—95, fellow founder, 1993. Author: Poetry's "Guardian" Best Poems and Poets of 2003. Lobbyist Walker River Piaute Tribe, Schurz, Nev., 1993—95, civil rights adv. San Clemente, 1995—96. Recipient World Champion Amateur Poet, Internat. Soc. Poets, 2002, No. Am. Poet of Merit, Internat. Libr. Poetry, 2002, New Country Female Vocalist, CCMA of Inland Empire, 1999. Mem.: San Bernardino County Bar Assn., Am. Poetry Assn., Am. Lit. Guild. Democrat. Ch. Of Christ. Avocations: writing, karoake, cooking, sewing.

WAIDELICH, DONALD LONG, electrical engineer, consultant; b. Allentown, Pa., May 3, 1915; s. John A. Sr. and Maisie Hamilton (Long) W.; m. Florence Emma Bennethum, June 6, 1939; 1 child, Ann Louise. BEE, Lehigh U., 1936, MS, 1938; PhD, Iowa State U., 1946. Registered profl. engr., Mo. Instr., asst. prof. electrical engring. U. Mo., Columbia, 1938-44, assoc. prof., prof., 1946-85, prof. emeritus, 1985—, assoc. head engring. experiment sta., 1955-60, chair dept., 1960-61; electrical engr. Naval Ordnance Lab., Silver Spring, Md., 1944-46. Cons. Naval Electronics Lab., San Diego, 1948-50, Argonne (Ill.) Nat. Lab., 1950-60, Nat. Aeronautics & Space, Green Belt, Md., 1961-70, Hughes Aircraft Co., Santa Monica and El Segundo, Calif., 1970-88; Fulbright prof. Cairo U., 1950-52, U. New South Wales, Sydney, Australia, 1960-62. Author: (with G. Lago) Transients in Electrical Circuits, 1958. Com. mem. Civic and U. Retirees, Columbia, Mo., 1985-95. Recipient Rsch. award Sigma Xi, 1977, Missouri Honor award, Distinguished Service, 1986. Fellow IEEE (life, Excellence award 1985), AIEE, Inst. Radio Engrs., 1961; mem. Am. Assn. Univ. Profs. (life), Am. Soc. Engring. Edn. (life), Nat. Soc. Profl. Engrs. (life). Episcopal. Achievements include research on rectifiers, electromagnetic testing of materials, steady-state transforms, microwave antennas, electrostatics, and electromagnetic fields; worked on magnetic and electric fields in space; involved with design of international communication satellites. Home: 104 E Ridgeley Rd Columbia MO 65203-3530 Office: U Mo Dept Elec & Comp Engring 7 W Engineering Bldg Columbia MO 65211

WAILAND, GEORGE, lawyer; b. Munich, Mar. 14, 1947; came to U.S., 1951; s. Max and Bella (Grylak) W.; m. Adele M. Rosen, Aug. 20, 1972; children: J. Zachary, William J. BS, NYU, 1969, JD, 1972. Bar: N.Y. 1973, U.S. Supreme Ct. 1976, U.S. Dist. Ct. (so., ea. dists.) N.Y. 1973, U.S. Dist. Ct. (no. dist.) N.Y. 1981, U.S. Claims Ct. 1979, U.S. Tax Ct., 1979, U.S. Ct. Appeals (2d cir.) 1973, U.S. Ct. Appeals (fed. cir.) 1982, U.S. Ct. Appeals (4th cir. and 9th cir.) 1986, U.S. Ct. Appeals (7th cir.) 1987. Assoc. Cahill Gordon & Reindel LLP, N.Y.C., 1972-80, ptnr., 1980—. John Norton Pomeroy scholar NYU, 1970. Home: 1050 Park Ave New York NY 10028-1031 Office: Cahill Gordon & Reindel LLP 80 Pine St Fl 17 New York NY 10005-1790 Office Phone: 212-701-3212.

WAIN, CHRISTOPHER HENRY FAIRFAX MORESBY, retired actuary, insurance and investment consultant; b. Toronto, Ont., Can., Nov. 21, 1918; came to U.S., 1923; s. Andrew Martin and Eve Margaret (Fairbain) W.; m. Jeane Crawford Thomas, June 26, 1948; children: Christopher H. Jr., Margot Crawford. BA, UCLA, 1940. CLU. Actuarial student Occidental Life of Calif., L.A., 1946-48; various positions including v.p., actuary Prudential Ins. Co. Am., Newark and L.A., 1948-83; ins. and investment cons. L.A., 1984—2003. Mem. various coms. Am. Coun. Life Ins., Washington, 1965-83. Capt. U.S. Army, 1941-45. Regents scholar UCLA, 1938-39. Fellow Soc. Actuaries; mem. Am. Acad. Actuaries.

WAINSCOTT, JAMES LAWRENCE, accountant; b. LaPorte, Ind., Mar. 31, 1957; s. James J. and Frances J. (Cunningham) W. BS magna cum laude, Ball State U., 1979; MBA U. Notre Dame, 1987. CPA, Ind.; cert. mgmt. acct.; cert. internal auditor; cert. info. systems auditor; chartered fin. analyst. Sr. auditor Geo. S. Olive & Co., CPAs, Indpls. and Valparaiso, Ind., 1979-82; fin. mgr. Midwest div. Nat. Steel Corp., Portage, Ind., 1982-88, mgr. pension investments, Pitts., 1988-90, asst. treas., asst. sec., Pitts., 1991-92; treas., asst. sec., Mishawaka. Ind., 1993-95, v.p. & treas., AK Steel Holding Corp., Middletown, OH, 1995—, CFO, AK Steel Holding Corp., 1998—, sr. v.p., CFO,

1999—; cons. Edward J. Wainscott, CPA, LaPorte, Ind., 1982—; instr. acctg. Purdue U.-Westville, 1980-82, Valparaiso U., 1980-84. Advisor Jr. Achievement, 1984; vol. Am. Cancer Soc., Valparaiso Income Tax Assistance Program, Valparaiso Community/Univ. Campaign; pres., treas. Midwest Steel Employees Fed. Credit Union; pres. Midwest Steel Employees Assn.; mem. Ball State U. Cardinal Connection; mem. N.W. Ind. Open Housing Council; chmn. dean's adv. council Valparaiso U.; bd. dirs. Youth Svc. Bur. St. Joseph County; chmn. fin. com. Good Shepherd Parish, Cin., 1999-2001. Mem. Ind. CPA Soc. (chmn. chpt. activities com. 1985-86, chpt. bd. dirs. 1983-86, chpt. pres. 1984-85, chmn. chpt. task force, Pres. award 1994, state bd. dirs. 1987-90), Nat. Assn. Accts. (chpt. bd. dirs. 1982-86, chpt. pres. 1983-84; Past Pres. award 1984), Am. Inst. CPA's, Inst. Mgmt. Acctg., Inst. Internal Auditors, Inst. Chartered Fin. Analysts, Assn. for Investment Mgmt. and Rsch., Chgo. Soc. Fin. Analysts, U. Notre Dame Exec. MBA Alumni Assn., Mensa, Blue Key, Golden Key, Intertel, Delta Sigma Pi. Roman Catholic. Avocations: music, chess, coin collecting, sports, travel. Home: 11990 Millstone Ct Loveland OH 45140-6220 Office: AK Steel Holding Corp 703 Curtis St Middletown OH 45043

WAINTROOB, ANDREA RUTH, lawyer; b. Chgo., Dec. 23, 1952; d. David Samuel and Lees (Carson) W. AB, Brown U., 1975; JD, U. Chgo., 1978. Bar: Ill. 1978, U.S. Dist. Ct. (no. dist.) Ill. 1978, U.S. Dist. Ct. (cen. dist.) Ill. 1996, U.S. Ct. Appeals (7th cir.) 1982, U.S. Supreme Ct. 1989. Assoc. Vedder, Price, Kaufman and Kammholz, Chgo., 1978-84; ptnr. Vedder, Price, Kaufman, Chgo., 1984-94, Franczek Sullivan, P.C., Chgo., 1994—. Mem. Chgo. Bar Assn., Nat. Coun. Sch. Attys. Home: 5428 S Harper Ave Chicago IL 60615-5506 Office: Franczek Sullivan 300 S Wacker Dr Ste 3400 Chicago IL 60606-6708

WAINWRIGHT, CARROLL LIVINGSTON, JR., lawyer; b. N.Y.C., Dec. 28, 1925; s. Carroll Livingston and Edith Katherine (Gould) W.; m. Nina Walker, July 2, 1948; children: Delos Walker, Mark Livingston. AB, Yale U., 1949; LL.B., Harvard U., 1952. Bar: N.Y. 1953. With Milbank, Tweed, Hadley & McCloy (and predecessor), N.Y.C., 1952-58, 60-62, ptnr., 1963—. Asst. counsel Gov. N.Y., 1959-60; mem. State Commn. Jud. Conduct, 1974-83; hon. dir. U.S. Trust Corp.; hon. trustee U.S. Trust Co. N.Y.; adj. prof. law Washington and Lee U. Sch. Law, 1991-97; mem. governing bd. N.Y. Community Trust, 1991—. Hon. trustee Am. Mus. Natural History; trustee Edward John Noble Found.; trustee Boys' Club N.Y., 1966—, pres., 1986-94, hon. trustee, 1999; vice-chmn. Cooper Union Advancement Sci. and Art, 1988-95, hon. trustee; trustee Ch. Pension Fund and Affiliates, 1974-91, treas. 1974-78; mem. univ. coun. Yale U., 1978-81; mem. vestry Trinity Ch., N.Y.C., 1983-90; dir. Greater Yellowstone Coalition, 1992-98, 99—. Served with USMCR, 1943-46. Mem. ABA, N.Y. State Bar Assn., Assn. Bar City N.Y. (treas. 1970-73, v.p. 1975-76), Union Club, Down Town Assn. (pres. 1985-92), Maidstone Club (pres. 1970-73). Home: 57 Dunemere Ln East Hampton NY 11937-2705 Office: Milbank Tweed Hadley & McCloy 1 Chase Manhattan Plz Fl 46 New York NY 10005-1401 Office Phone: 212-530-5332.

WAINWRIGHT, DALE V. judge; b. Tenn. B, Howard U., 1983; JD, U. Chgo., 1988. With Andrews & Kurth, Houston, Haynes & Boone, Houston; dist. judge. Harris County, 1999—2002; justice Tex. Supreme Ct., 2002—. Fellow: Houston Bar Found., Tex. Bar Found.; mem.: ABA, Houston Bar Assn., State Bar Tex. Office: Tex State Supreme Ct PO Box 12248 Austin TX 78711

WAINWRIGHT, DAVID STANLEY, intellectual property professional; b. New Haven, May 23, 1955; s. Stanley Dunstan and Lillian (Karelitz) W.;m. Catherine Demetra Kefalas, Aug. 11, 1984; children: Maxwell Stanley Hector, Eric George Alexander. BSc in Physics with 1st class honors, Dalhousie U., Halifax, N.S., 1976; MSc in Physics, U. B.C., Vancouver, 1979. Registered patent agt., U.S., Can. Model plant supr., scientist, technician Moli Energy Ltd., Maple Ridge, Canada, 1978-84, project leader cell devel., 1984-88, cell devel. mgr., 1988-90, Moli Energy (1990) Ltd., Maple Ridge, 1990-92, mgr. intellectual property, 1992-98; patent agt. Ballard Power Sys., Burnaby, 1998—. Contbr. articles to profl. jours. Mem. Patent and Trademark Inst. Can. Home: 2585 W 1st Ave Vancouver BC Canada V6K 1G8 Office: Ballard Power Sys Inc 9000 Glenlyon Pky Burnaby BC Canada V5J 5J9 Office Phone: 604-412-8602. Business E-Mail: david.wainwright@ballard.com.

WAINWRIGHT, GEORGE, judge; b. Wilson County, N.C., Dec. 10, 1943; s. George Sr. and Susan Wainwright; m. Carol McChesney; children: Kennon, Ashton. Undergrad. degree, U. N.C., 1966; JD, Wake Forest U., 1984. Agribus. and real estate positions, Wilson, 1966-81; with Wheatly, Wheatly, Nobles & Weeks, Beaufort, N.C., 1986-90; apptd. judge Dist. Ct., 1991; resident Superior Ct. judge for N.C. Jud. Dist. 3B, 1994; justice Supreme Ct. N.C., 1999—. With USCGR, 1966-72 Morehead scholar, 1966. Mem. N.C. Bar Assn., Lookout Rotary Club. Presbyterian. Office: Supreme Ct NC Justice Bldg PO Box 1841 Raleigh NC 27602-1841

WAINWRIGHT, PAUL EDWARD BLECH, construction company executive; b. Annapolis, Md., Jan. 28, 1917; s. Richard and Alice Sorrel (Blech) W.; m. Helen Mae Rogers, July 10, 1941; children— Richard, Paul Edward Blech, John. BS in Civil Engring, Va. Mil. Inst., 1938. Cost engr. Turner Constrn. Co., N.Y.C., 1938-40, cost engr., asst. supt., 1945-46; cost. engr. for contractors Pacific Naval Air Bases, Honolulu, 1940-42; with Dillingham Corp., Honolulu, 1946-82, asst. v.p., then v.p., 1961-69, group v.p. constrn., 1969-82; cons. constrn. Honolulu, 1982—. Bd. dirs. Hawaii Visitors Bur., 1967, Goodwill Industries Hawaii, 1965-70; pres. Citizens Adminstrn. of Justice Found., 1968, Hawaii Epilepsy Soc., 1975. Served with AUS, 1942-45. Decorated Legion of Merit, Bronze Star, Air medal. Mem. Am. Soc. Mil. Engrs., Beavers, Gen. Contractors Assn. Hawaii (pres. 1966), Hawaii C. of C. (dir. 1964-65), Waikiki Yacht Club, Outrigger Canoe Club. Republican. Episcopalian. Home: 4301 Providence Point Pl SE Issaquah WA 98029-6270

WAINWRIGHT HENBEST, MARGARET A. state representative; b. L.A., Aug. 13, 1953; m. Michael Henbest; children: Ryan, Daniel, Kevin. BS in Health Scis., Oreg. U., 1976; MS, Calif. State U., Long Beach, 1984. Pediatric nurse practitioner, pvt. practice, 1984—86; pediatric nurse practitioner, Child Abuse Clinic St. Luke's Regional Med. Ctr., 1991—; asst. prof. nursing Boise State U., 1988—91; state rep. dist. 16A Idaho Ho. of Reps., Boise, 1996—, mem. revenue and taxation com.; mem. CHIPS task force, 1998; chmn. joint legis. oversight com., 2000—; mem. mental health interim com., 1996. Small benefit plan com. Idaho Dept. Commerce, 1994—95. Mem.: ASPAC, ANA, St. Joseph's Home & Sch. Assn. (pres.), Nat. Assn. Pediatric Nurse Practitioners and Assocs., Idaho Nurses Assn. (legis. com. chair nurse practitioner group 1990—), Child Abuse Law Mentors, Mountain States Group (bd. dirs., pres.), Kids Count (bd. dirs.), Discovery Ctr. Idaho (past bd.), Rotary. Democrat. Office: State Capitol PO Box 83720 Boise ID 83720-0038

WAISANEN, CHRISTINE M. lawyer, writer; b. Hancock, Mich., May 27, 1949; d. Frederick B. and Helen M. (Hill) W.; m. Apr. 21, 1979; children: Jeffrey Hunt, Erick Hill. BA with honors, U. Mich., 1971; JD, U. Denver, 1975. Bar: Colo. 1975, D.C. 1978. Labor rels. atty. U.S. C. of C., Washington, 1976-79; govt. rels. specialist ICI Americas, Inc., Wilmington, Del., 1979-87; dir. cultural affairs City of Wilmington, 1987; founder, chief writer Hill, Katzenstein & Waisanen, 1988—. Chmn. Delaware State Coastal Zone Indsl. Control Bd., 1993—. Mem. Fed. Bar Assn., Jr. League of Wilmington (v.p. 1985-86), Women's Rep. Club of Wilmington (bd. dirs. 1988-93), U. Mich. Club of Del. (pres. 1999—). Republican. Presbyterian. Home: 1609 Mt Salem Ln Wilmington DE 19806-1134

WAIT, CHARLES VALENTINE, banker; b. Albany, NY, May 28, 1951; s. Newman Edward Jr. and Jane Caroline (Adams) W.; m. Candace Ellin Hollar, May 27, 1978; children: Charles Valentine Jr., Christopher David, Alexandra Dallas Wait. BA, Cornell U., 1973; cert. in banking, Rutgers U., 1981; LHD (hon.), SUNY Empire State Coll., 2001. Asst. v.p. The Adirondack Trust Co., Saratoga Springs, N.Y., 1974, treas., 1978-81, sec., treas., 1981-84, pres., 1984—. Trustee NY Bus. Devel., 1997-2003; mem. Saratoga County Indsl. Devel. Agency, 1998—; mem. Yaddo Corp., Saratoga Springs, 1996—, sec., asst. treas., 1997—, asst. treas., 1998—; class A dir. Fed. Res. Bank NY, 2003— Trustee Skidmore Coll., Saratoga Springs, 1984-2002, Nat. Mus. Dance, Saratoga Springs, 1987-2002, Charles R. Wood Found., 1991-98, NY Racing Assn., Saratoga Hosp., 2003—; trustee Nat. Mus. Racing, 1988-91, v.p., 1989-91; treas. Saratoga Performing Arts Ctr., 1987, chmn., 1989-97, Saratoga Care, Inc., 2002—; chmn. Saratoga Springs City Ctr. Authority, 1983-89, Saratoga Care, Inc., Face of the Future Capital Campaign. Named Outstanding New Yorker, NY State Jaycees, 1984, Disting. Citizen, Saratoga Springs Sr. Citizens, 2002; recipient Pvt. Sector Initiative award, Pres. Ronald Reagan, Commitment to Cmty. award, NY State Bus. Coun., 1983, Liberty Bell award, Saratoga County Bar Assn. for cmty. svc., Good Scout award, Twin Rivers Coun., 1997, Exec. of Yr. award, Capital Dist. Bus. Rev., 1999, Denis Kemball-Cook award, 2003, Lucy Skidmore Scribner award, Skidmore Coll., Saratoga Springs, 2003, Sam Walton Bus. Leader award, 1997; Paul Harris fellow Dist. 7190, 1997. Mem. Ind. Bankers Assn. of N.Y. State (bd. dirs., sec. 1986-87), N.Y. Bankers Assn. (bd. dirs. 1987, treas. 1995—, chmn. 1997-99), N.Y. State Bankers Retirement System (trustee 1987-95, vice chmn., chmn. 1992-94), Am. Inst. Banking (Counsel of Yr. 1976), Greater Saratoga C. of C., Pillar Soc. Republican. Home: 658 N Broadway Saratoga Springs NY 12866-1624 Office: The Adirondack Trust Co 473 Broadway Saratoga Springs NY 12866-2262

WAIT, GEORGE WILLIAM, sales executive; b. Balt., Oct. 23, 1958; s. Frank H., Jr. and Betty (Cartwright) Wait; m. Susan Erwin, Oct. 16, 1982; children: J. Stokes, Hannah S., C. Sam, Addy M. BSBA, Western Carolina U., 1982. From sales rep. to regional sales asst. Gen. Mills Inc., Kinston, N.C., 1982-85, dist. sales mgr. Charlotte, N.C., 1985-87, product sales mgr. Mpls., 1987-89, mgr. promotions and merchandising Raleigh, N.C., 1989-90, regional merchandising mgr., 1990—, regional tri healthway dir., 1992—, mgr. bus. devel., 1993—, corp. ops. mgr. Cary, N.C., 1995—. Author: The Job Plan, 1991, How to Approach Meaningful Reclaim Reduction, 2002; guest columnist: Cary News, 2001. Head coach '84 Explorers Soccer Team, 1990—; pres. A. V. Baucom-Elem. Sch. PTO, Apex, NC, 1991—93; mem. Indian Guides YMCA, 1991—, mem. youth com., 1995—; asst. scout master Boy Scouts Am., 1996—; mem. adv. com. Wake County Bd. Edn., 1996—, chmn. adv. coun., 1997—99; chmn. Dist. 8 adv. coun. Wake County Sch. Bd., 2003—; pres. Davis Dr. Mid. Sch., 1997—98, 1998—99, pres. PTA, 1997 99; chmn. Wake County Fun Festival, Apex Adv. Coun. Bd. Edn., 1997—99; area v.p. Wake County PTA Coun., 1998—99; mem. Wake County Health Schs. Task Force, 2003—. Named to Order of Arrow, Boy Scouts Am., 1999. Mem.: Grocery Mfrs. Retail Assn., KC (3d degree), Lambda Chi Alpha. Republican. Roman Catholic. Avocations: golf, weightlifting, reading, swimming. Office: Gen Mills Inc PO Box 4349 Cary NC 27519-4349

WAIT, LEA, writer, small business owner; b. Boston, Mass., May 26, 1946; d. George W Wait and Sally Eleanor Smart; m. Robert Joseph Thomas, Oct. 28, 2003; children: Caroline Yoon Kyung Childs, Alicia Yupin Gutschenritter, Rebecca Siu Kuen Wynne, Elizabeth Purnima. BA, Chatham Coll., Pitts., 1968; MA, NYU, N.Y.C., 1974; DWD, NYU, 1978. Author: (historical fiction) Stopping To Home, (mystery novel) Shadows At The Fair: An Antique Print Mystery (nominated for Agatha for best first mystery, 2003), (historical novel) Seaward Born, (mystery novel) Shadows On The Coast Of Maine: An Antique Print Mystery, (historical novel) Wintering Well, (mystery novel) Shadows On The Ivy: An Antique Print Mystery. Mem.: Maine Antique Dealers Assn., Mystery Writers Am., Sisters in Crime, Maine Alliance Writers and Pubs. (sec. 2002—), Nat. Coun. for Single Adoptive Parents. Home: PO Box 225 Edgecomb ME 04556 Personal E-mail: leawait@clinic.net.

WAIT, SAMUEL CHARLES, JR., academic administrator, educator; b. Albany, N.Y., Jan. 26, 1932; s. Samuel C. and Isabel M. (Cassedy) W.; m. Carol D. Petrie, June 6, 1957; children: Robert J., Alison R. BS in Chemistry, Rensselaer Polytechnic Inst., 1953, MS in Physical Chemistry, 1955, PhD in Physical Chemistry, 1956. Postdoc. teaching fellow U. Minn., 1958-59; visiting asst. prof. Carnegie Inst. Tech., 1959-60; rsch. sci. Nat. Bur. Standards, 1960-61; from asst. prof. to prof. of chemistry Rensselaer Poly. Inst., Troy, N.Y., 1961—, from asst. dean of sci. to assoc. dean of sci., 1974—, acting dean of sci., 1978-80, 88-89. Dir. Cooperative Coll. Sci. Improvement Program, Troy, 1972-73, Rsch. Participation for High Sch. Tchrs., Troy, 1962-67; asst. dir., prof. M of Sci. in Natural Scis. Program, Troy, 1962-74. Author: Scattering of Laser Radiation, 1971; contbr. articles to profl. jours. Pres. dist. 2 Niskayuna (N.Y.) Fire Co., 1970-72, mem. 1966-; mem. Niskayuna Bd. Fire Commrs., 1978-83; trustee Dudley Obs., 1978—, v.p., 1980-91, pres., 1991-2001; mem. math., sci. and tech. adv. com. Schenectady County C.C., 1976—, chmn., 1977-78; vice chmn. Schenectady County Fire Adv. Bd., 1978-79; mem. Schenectady County Hazardous Materials Team, 1991-2002. Recipient Disting Faculty award Rensselaer Alumni Assn., 1988, Alumni Key award, 1994, Rensselaer Alumni Admission award of excellence, 1993, Rensselaer Alumni Assn. Albert Fox Demers medal, 1997, Rensselaer Alumni Fellow award, 2003; named fellow Rsch. Corp., 1954-55, Eastman Kodak Co., 1955-56; Fulbright scholar, 1956-58. Mem. Am. Chem. Soc., Rensselaer Premed. Soc., Sigma Xi, Alpha Epsilon Delta, Phi Theta Kappa. Office: Rensselaer Poly Inst 1C 05 Sci Ctr 110 8th St Troy NY 12180-3522 Business E-Mail: waitsc@rpi.edu.

WAITE, CHARLES MORRISON, food company executive; b. Chgo., Oct. 1, 1932; s. Norman and Lavinia M. (Fyke) W.; m. Barbara Chowning Wham, Aug. 21, 1954; children: Susan R., Charles M., John B., David T. BA, Yale, 1954; MBA, Harvard, 1958. Mgr. planning and analysis Standard Fruit & Steamship Co., New Orleans, 1958-62, v.p., exec. v.p., 1969-72, dir., 1972-76; div. mgr. Standard Fruit Co., La Ceiba, Honduras, 1962-69; dir. Standard Fruit Tropical Charities, Inc., 1970-76; sr. v.p. Castle & Cooke, Inc., Honolulu, 1972-76; exec. v.p. Castle & Cooke Foods, San Francisco, 1974-76; pres. United Fruit Co., Boston, 1976-77; sr. v.p. United Brands Co., Boston, 1976-77; pres. Genoa Packing Co., Boston, 1977-78, Catelli Foods, Inc., 1979-90, Howard Foods Inc., Danvers, Mass., 1990—, also bd. dirs. Bd. dirs. Rock of Ages Corp., Barre, Vt., Swenson Granite Co., Concord, N.H. Served to 1st lt. USAF, 1955-57. Mem. Zeta Psi. Clubs: Harvard (Boston). Republican. Episcopalian. Home: 520 Cherry Valley Rd Gilford NH 03249-7841 Office: Howard Foods Inc 5 Ray St Danvers MA 01923-3531

WAITE, CHARLES PRESCOTT, entrepreneur; b. Manchester, Conn., Mar. 30, 1930; s. Earl M. and Virginia (Clark) W.; m. Catherine Corbett, Apr. 21, 1951 (div. Feb. 1985); children: Charles P. Jr., David C., Catherine C., Patricia C.; m. Angela Peterson, Feb. 16, 1985. BS, U. Conn., 1957; MBA, Harvard U., 1959. V.p. Am. Research & Devel. Corp., Boston, 1960-66; ptnr., pres. Greylock Mgmt. Corp., Boston, 1966—. Bd. dirs. Stellar Computer Corp., Newton, Mass., Floating Point Systems, Beaverton, Oreg., Micom Sytems, Simi Valley, Calif., Data Input Output Corp., Kirkland, Wash., Lumber Mutual Ins. Co., Framingham, Mass. Trustee Kenyon Coll., Gambier, Ohio, 1985—, Dana Hall Sch., Wellesley, Mass., 1974-84. Served to lt. col. U.S. Army, USAR, 1951-73. Republican. Congegationalist. Clubs: Algonquin (Boston), Harvard (Boston and N.Y.C.). Avocation: european traveling. Home: 85 E India Row Boston MA 02110-3320 Office: Brett Levy 40 Court St Boston MA 02108-2202

WAITE, DAVID ALLEN, software development executive; b. Canton, N.Y., June 7, 1947; s. Kelsey Arden and Helen Gladys (Pollock) W.; m. Dorretta Carlyle Richardson, Aug. 28, 1971; 1 child, Rebecca. BA, SUNY, Potsdam, 1969; MBA, Columbia U., 1992. Assoc. programmer IBM Corp., Poughkeepsie, N.Y., 1969-73, Burlington, Mass., 1973-76, staff programmer, 1976—79, Essex Junction, Vt., 1976—79, devel. programmer, mgr. Lexington, Ky., 1979-84, Poughkeepsie, 1985-92; from total quality mgr. to v.p. product devel. coord. ILX Systems, NYC, 1992—2002; sr. v.p. product mgmt. Thompson Fin., NYC, 2003—, sr. v.p. retail mktg. data, 2004—. Contbr. articles to profl. jours. Mem.: Am. Soc. for Quality, Assn. for Computing Machinery, Columbia U. Bus. Sch. Alumni Club of N.Y. (sec. 1996—98, pres. 1998—2000), Columbia U. Bus. Sch. EMBA Alumni Assn. (pres. 1994—96). Avocations: sailing, cooking, golf, gardening. Home: 6 Candlewood Dr New Providence NJ 07974-1615 Office: Thomson Fin 111 Fulton St New York NY 10038-2776 E-mail: dwaite92@alumni.gsb.columbia.edu.

WAITE, DENNIS VERNON, investor relations consultant; b. Chgo., Aug. 26, 1938; s. Vernon George and Marie G. Waite; m. Christine Rene Hibbs; 1 child, Kip Anthony. BA, U. Ill., 1968; MS in Journalism, Northwestern U., 1969. Fin. reporter, columnist Chgo. Sun-Times, Chgo., 1969-76; asst. prof. Northwestern U., Evanston, Ill., 1978-79; assoc. prof. Mich. State U., East Lansing, 1979-82; ptnr. Fin. Rels. Bd., Inc., Chgo., 1982-90, sr. ptnr., 1991-97, sr. counselor, 1997—. Reporter, producer econ. affairs Sta. WTTW-TV, Sta. WBBM-TV, Chgo., 1973-76; adj. faculty English, Coll. of DuPage, 1998—. Mem. editorial adv. bd. alumni relations U. Ill., Chgo., 1980-84, 90-94. With USAF, 1956-60, PTO. Rutgers U. fellow, 1972. Mem. Medill Alumni Assn. (bd. dirs. 1989-92). Avocations: reading, writing, study of ancient history. Office: Financial Relations Bd John Hancock Ctr 875 N Michigan Ave Ste 2250 Chicago IL 60611-1805

WAITE, DONALD EUGENE, medical educator, consultant; b. Columbus, Ohio, Aug. 25, 1925; s. Sidney B. and Louise Alice (Lipsey) W.; children: David L., Larry R., James A., Steve C., Debra J., Julie A., Craig D., Tracy E., Christopher R. DO in Osteo. Medicine, U. Osteo. Medicine and Health Scis., 1953, MPH, U. Calif., Berkeley, 1979. Intern Doctors Hosp., Columbus, Ohio, 1955-56; pvt. practice Columbus, 1956-72; prof. family medicine Mich. State U., East Lansing, 1972-90, prof. emeritus, 1990—. Cons. Environ. Health Conss., Columbus, East Lansing, 1990—; mem. occupl. health del. to Poland, Hungary and Czechoslovakia, 1992; mem. Aerospace Med. Assn. del. to People's Republic of China, 1993. Author: Your Environment, Your Health and You, 1991, Environmental Health Hazards, 1994, 2d edit., 2002. Med. examiner FAA, East Lansing, 1964-90; asst. scoutmaster Boy Scouts Am., East Lansing, 1980-83. With USN, 1943-45. Mem. Am. Osteo. Assn., Am. Coll. Occupl. Medicine, Aerospace Med. Assn., Ohio Osteo. Assn., Mich. Assn. Osteo. Physicians. Avocations: skiing, fishing, hunting. Home: 117 Agate Way Williamston MI 48895-9434 Office: Mich State U Dept Family Medicine East Lansing MI 48824 Office Phone: 517-353-4730. Personal E-mail: waited@msu.edu.

WAITE, LAWRENCE WESLEY, osteopathic physician, educator; b. Chgo., June 27, 1951; s. Paul J. and Margaret E. (Cresson) W.; m. Courtnay M. Snyder, Nov. 1, 1974; children: Colleen Alexis, Rebecca Maureen, Alexander Quin. BA, Drake U., 1972; DO, Coll. Osteo Medicine and Surgery, Des Moines, 1975; MPH, U. Mich., 1981. Diplomate Nat. Bd. Osteo. Med. Examiners; bd. cert. family practice, neuromusculoskeletal medicine, OMM and holistic medicine. Intern Garden City Osteo Hosp., Mich., 1975-76; practice gen. osteo. medicine Garden City, 1979-82, Battle Creek, 1982-96, La Crosse, Wis., 1996—; sect. head Onalaska Family Practice, 1999—2002, coord. rsch., chmn. dept., 1996—99, chmn. integrative medicine edn./rsch. com., 2002—04, vice chair, dept. integrative medicine, 2004—. Cons. Nat. Bd. Examiners Osteo. Physicians and Surgeons, 1981—88, 1998—; chief med. examiner Calhoun County, 1991—93; preceptor U. Wis. Med. Sch., 1997—2000, assoc. clin. prof., 2000—, Mich. State U. Coll. Osteo. Medicine, East Lansing, 1979—97, Lakeview Gen. Osteo. Hosp., Battle Creek, Mich., 1983—87, Des Moines U. Osteo. Med. Ctr., 2001—; mem. profl. adv. coun. Good Samaritan Hosp., Battle Creek, 1982—83; exec. bd. Primary Care Network, 1994—96; assoc. clin. prof. Des Moines U. Coll. Osteo. Medicine, 2002—. Writer TV program Cross Currents Ecology, 1971; editor radio series Friendship Hour, 1971-72 Bd. dirs. La Crosse YMCA, 2000-03, Internat. Log Rolling Assn., 2000-; bd. dirs., instr. Hospice Support Services, Inc., Westland, Mich., 1981-86; exec. bd. officer Battle Creek Area Urban League, 1987-91; bd. dirs., mem. exec. com. Clearwater Farm Found., Inc., 1999—; vestryman St. Thomas Episcopal Ch., 1990-93; bd. mem. Eagle Bluff Environ. Learning Ctr., Lanesboro, 2003-; leader Boy Scouts Am. Served to lt. comdr. USN, 1976-79. U. Wis. fellow, Madison, 2004—; State of Iowa scholar, 1969. Mem. AMA, Population Inst. (population action coun. 1984-99, Am. Pub. Health Assn., Population Inst., Aerospace Med. Assn., Natl. Eagle Scounts Assn. (life), Am. Osteo. Assn., S. Cen. Osteo. Assn. (officer, state del. 1983-96), Am. Acad. Osteopathy, Bermuda Hist. Soc. (life), Wis. Ctr., Academically Talented Youth, Brotherhood St. Andrews (life). Avocations: geography. medieval history, genealogy. Home: 2110 Evenson Dr Onalaska WI 54650-8772 Office: Gundersen Lutheran 3100 S Kinney Coulee Rd Onalaska WI 54650-8512 Business E-Mail: lwwaite@gundluth.org.

WAITE, STEPHEN HOLDEN, lawyer; b. Rochester, N.Y., Dec. 5, 1936; s. Richard Holden and Judith H. (Lapp) Waite; m. Sarah T. Caswell, Aug. 20, 1960 (dec. Mar. 1996); m. Martha Gay Stewart, Jan. 4, 1997; children: Sarah T., Richard H. BA, Amherst Coll., 1958; JD, Yale U., 1961. Bar: N.Y. 1961. Mem. firm Nixon, Hargrave, Devans & Doyle, Rochester, NY, 1961-69; v.p., counsel Lincoln First Banks Inc., Rochester, 1969-73, sr. v.p., 1973-77, exec. v.p., 1978-81, CFO, 1973-81; sr. v.p. Schlegel Corp., 1981-82; mem. firm Harris, Beach, Wilcox, Rubin & Levey, Rochester, 1982-88, Underberg & Kessler, Rochester, 1988—. Past chmn. Rochester Area Hosp. Assn.; mem. strategic planning commn. Monroe Cmty. Hosp.; past bd. dirs., treas. Hosp. Trustees N.Y. State; past bd. dirs., past chmn. Ctr. Govtl. Rsch.; treas. Planned Parenthood Rochester/Syracuse Region; bd. dirs. Planned Parenthood Rochester/Syracuse region; past bd. dirs. Mercy Flight Ctrl., Inc., Highland Hosp., Monroe County Long Term Care, Inc., Rochester Regional Rsch. Libr. Coun., Hosp. Assn. N.Y. State, Health Futures for Rochester, Harley Sch., Hearing and Speech Ctr. Rochester. With U.S. Army, 1962. Mem.: Monroe County Bar Assn., N.Y. State Bar Assn., Country Club Rochester. Home: 7 Woodcliff Ter Fairport NY 14450-4209 Office: 1800 Chase Sq Rochester NY 14604-1910 Office Phone: 585-258-2826.

WAITE, VERNER STUART, retired surgeon; b. Lindsay, Calif., Aug. 16, 1928; s. Albert Crew Waite and Helen Fowle; m. Elizabeth Souchick, Nov. 5, 1955; children: Peter Stuart, Elizabeth Ruth, Eva Ann, Amelia Catherine, Susan Marie, Alexander Crew. AA, Compton Jr. Coll., 1948; BA, U. Calif., Berkeley, 1950; MD, U. Chgo., 1954. Intern L.A. VA Hosp., 1954-55; resident in surgery St. Louis City Hosp., 1958-61; fellow in surgery Ellis Fischel Cancer Ctr., Colulmbia, Mo., 1961-63; pvt. practice surgery Lynwood and Downey, Calif., 1963-97. Bd. dirs. Downey Hosp., 1994; active Lynwood Sch. Bd., 1967-75; med. exec. com. St. Francis Hosp.; pres. Family Support Ctr. of Downey, 1999-2000. Fellow ACS; mem. Semmelweis Soc. (founder, pres. 1986-97), Lynwood Exch. Club, Downey Exch. Club. Republican. Avocation: stamp collecting/philately. Home: 5243 Vista Del Sol Cypress CA 90630

WAITE-FRANZEN, ELLEN JANE, academic administrator; b. Oshkosh, Wis., Feb. 17, 1951; d. Earl Vincent and Margaret (Luft) W.; m. Thomas H. Dollar, Aug. 19, 1977 (div. July 1984); m. Kent Hendrickson, Mar. 26, 1994 (div. Dec. 1995); m. Scott Franzen, Apr. 4, 1998. BA, U. Wis., Oshkosh, 1973; MLS, U. Wis., Milw., 1977. Head of cataloging Marquette U., Milw., 1977-82; head catalog libr. U. Ariz., Tucson, 1983-85; assoc. dir. libr. Loyola U., Chgo., 1985-86, acting dir. libr., 1986-87, dir. libr., 1987-94, v.p. acad. svcs., 1994-97; assoc. provost for info. svcs. U. Richmond, 1997-99, v.p. for info. svcs., 1999—2002; v.p. for computing and info. svcs. Brown U., Providence, 2002—. Cons. Loyola U., Chgo., 1984, Boston Coll., 1986, U. San Francisco, 1989; bd. trustees Online Computer Lib. Ctr., Dublin, Ohio, 1994-2000. Contbg. author: Research Libraries and Their Implementation of AACR2, 1985; author: (with others) Women in LC's Terms: A Thesaurus of Subject Headings Related to Women, 1988. Mem. ALA. Avocation: photography. Office: Brown U Computing and Info Svcs Box 1885 Providence RI 02912-1885 E-mail: ewaite@brown.edu.

WAITES, ROBERT GUINN, utilities executive; b. Laurel, Miss., July 12, 1950; s. Robert Leland Waites and Ida Doris (Gordon) Robinson; m. Lynda Gay Tubertini, Nov. 25, 1972; children: Julie G. Burran, Andrea G. BS, U. So. Miss., 1972; JD, Miss. Coll., 1976. Commd. 2d lt. U.S. Army, 1972, advanced through grades to capt., 1980, res., 1980; legal counsel Miss. House Reps., Jackson, 1976-89, Legis. Environ. Protection Coun., Jackson, 1989-90; dep. dir. Miss. Pub. Utilities Staff, Jackson, 1990-96, exec. dir., 1996—. Mem. ABA, Miss. State Bar Assn., Miss. Rep. Party, Kappa Sigma (Outstanding Mem. award 1972). Methodist. Avocations: golf, biking. Home: 179 Apple Blossom Dr Brandon MS 39047-7686 Office: Miss Pub Utilities Staff 550 High St Jackson MS 39201-1113

WAITES, WILLIAM ERNEST, advertising executive; b. Detroit, Dec. 14, 1934; s. William Ernest and Jean (Bryant) W.; m. Susanne Pinkett, Jan. 5, 1957; children: Bryant Andrew, Randel Schumann. BA, Mich. State U., 1956. Sr. v.p., creative dir. Young & Rubicam, Detroit, 1973-77, mng. dir. Adelaide, Australia, 1977-79, sr. v.p., dir. creative svcs. Chgo., 1979-81; vice chmn., chief creative officer Stone & Adler, Chgo., 1981-83; sr. v.p., group creative dir. Ogilvy & Mather, Chgo., 1983-89; pres. Huryup & Waites Creative Cons., Ft. Myers, Fla., 1989-94. Chmn. The Spiro Group, Inc., 1994-2001, Double W. Ltd., Taos, N.Mex., The Waites Group; co-owner Aboriginals: Art of the First Person, Sanibel, Fla. Bd. trustees Calusa Nature Ctr. and Planetarium; bd. dirs. Lee County Alliance of Arts. Capt. USAF, 1957-60. Mem. Advt. Fedn. S.W. Fla. (past pres.), Fla. Direct Mktg. Assn., Southwest Fla. Attractions Assn., Lee County Hotel Motel Assn., Cape Coral C. of C., S.W. Fla. C. of C., Greater Fort. Myers C. of C., Sanibel-Captiva Islands C. of C., Ft. Myers Mus. Found., Lambda Chi Alpha. Office: 6296 Corporate Ct Ste B202 Fort Myers FL 33919-3535 E-mail: sanibelart@earthlink.net.

WAITS, JOHN A. lawyer; b. Greenville, Miss., June 6, 1947; BA summa cum laude, U. Miss., 1969; MA with honors, U. Va., 1973; JD, NYU, 1977. Bar: N.Y. 1978, U.S. Dist. Ct. (ea. and so. dists.) N.Y. 1978, D.C. 1988. Counsel to Ho. Agrl. Subcom. U.S. Ho. of Reps., Washington, 1979-80, adminstrv. asst. to Congressman David R. Bowen, 1980-82; ptnr. Winston & Strawn, Washington, 1992. Fulbright scholar. Mem. Assn. Bar City N.Y. Office: Winston & Strawn 1400 L St NW Ste 800 Washington DC 20005-3508

WAITS, THOMAS ALAN, composer, actor, singer; b. Pomona, Calif., Dec. 7, 1949; s. Frank W. and Alma (Johnson) McMurray; m. Kathleen Patricia Brennan, Aug. 10, 1980; children: Kellesimone Wylder, Casey Xavier, Sullivan Blake. Composer 18 albums including Closing Time, 1973, The Heart of Saturday Nite, 1974, Nighthawks at the Diner, 1975, Small Change, 1976, Foreign Affairs, 1978, Blue Valentine, 1979, Heart Attack and Vine, 1980, One From the Heart, 1981, Swordfishtrombones, 1983, Rain Dogs, 1985, Anthology, 1985, Frank's Wild Years, 1987, Big Time, 1988, Bone Machine, 1992, Night on Earth, 1992, The Black Rider, 1993, Beautiful Maladies, 1998, Mule Variations, 1999 (Grammy Award, 1999), Alice, 2002, Blood Money, 2002; composer (film scores) One from the Heart, 1983, Streetwise, 1985, Night on Earth, 1991; co-author music and songs (with Kathleen Brennan) for Night on Earth, 1991, End of Violence, 1997, Bunny, 1999, Liberty Heights, 2000, Big Bad Love, 2002, Pollock, 2002, Dead Man Walking, film American Heart; composer songs and music for The Black Rider opera, Hamburg, Germany, 1990; composer songs and music, writer (with Kathleen Brennan) Alice Avant Garde opera, Hamburg, 1992, opera Woyzeck (recipient Italian Dramt Critics award for Best Musical, 2003), Copenhagen, 2000; actor (musical) Frank's Wild Years, 1986, (stage play) Demon Wine, 1989; appeared in films Paradise Alley, 1978, The Outsiders, 1983, Rumble Fish, 1983, The Cotton Club, 1984, Down by Law, 1986, Ironweed, 1987, Candy Mountain, 1987, Big Time, 1988, Cold Feet, 1989, The Bearskin, 1991, Queen's Logic, 1991, At Play in the Fields of the Lord, 1991, Bram Stoker's Dracula, 1992, Short Cuts, 1993, Mystery Men, 1999, Coffee & Cigarettes, 2003. Recipient Acad. Award nomination Best Song Score for One from the Heart, 1983; Grammy award for best alternative album Bone Machine, 1992, Grammy award for Mule Variations as best contemporary folk music, 2000, Dramalogue award for actor Demon Wine, Danish Theater award for Woyzeck as best musical, 2001. Mem. ASCAP (Founders award for career achievement in songwriting 2001), Musicians Union Local 47, SAG, AFTRA, Motion Picture Acad. Office: care Howard Grossman 10960 Wilshire Blvd Ste 2150 Los Angeles CA 90024-3807

WAITT, ROBERT KENNETH, lawyer; b. Seattle, Apr. 25, 1931; s. Charles Kenneth and Willa E. (Ryan) W.; m. Jane Dallam, Dec. 7, 1933; children: Mark Robert, Julie Lynn Reid. Student, Wash. State Coll., 1949-50, 52-53; LLB, Gonzaga U., 1957, JD, 1967. Bar: Wash. 1957, U.S. Supreme Ct., 1990. Assoc. Morrissey, Hedrick & Dunham, Seattle, 1957-59; ptnr. Benson & Waitt, Seattle, 1959-60; assoc. Walsh & Margolis, Seattle, 1960-62; ptnr. Murray, Dunham & Waitt, Seattle, 1962-81, Waitt, Johnson & Martens, Seattle, 1981-90, of counsel, 1990—99; retired, 1999. Judge King County Dist. Ct., Issaquah Dist., 1965-81, City of Issaquah Mcpl. Ct., 1961-81; chmn. City Issaquah Civil Service Commn., 1963-69; chmn. Gonzaga Law Council, Gonzaga U. Sch. Law, Spokane, Wash., 1983-85; regent Gonzaga U., 1982-88. With USMC, 1950-52. Mem. Wash. Bar Assn., Tradition Golf Club. Home: 3815 E Lake Sammamish Shorelane SE Sammamish WA 98075

WAITT, THEODORE W. computer company executive; b. Sioux City, Iowa, Jan. 18, 1963; m. Joan Waitt; 4 children. Attended, U. Iowa. Founder, chmn. Gateway Inc., Poway, 1985—, CEO, 1985—2004. Established Waitt Family Found., 1993. Office: 14303 Gateway Pl Poway CA 92064*

WAITTS, JAMES ROBERT, marketing professional; b. Glen Ridge, N.J., Nov. 16, 1964; s. Robert Rocco and Joan Lee Waitts; m. Annette Waitts, Oct. 17, 1992; children: Carla Rose, Julia Marie. BA, Hartwick Coll., 1987. Telemarketer Crown Roll Leaf Inc., Paterson, NJ, 1987-88, 1989-92, mgr. telesales, 1993-95, new product devel. staff, 1996-99, COO/mktg., 2000—. Mem. Tag and Label Mfrs. Inst., Document Mgmt. Industries Assn., Internat. Sign Assn. Republican. Avocations: guitar, music. Office: Crown Roll Leaf Inc 91 Robert Waitts Ave Paterson NJ 07503

WAITZKIN, HOWARD BRUCE, internist, sociologist, educator; b. Akron, Ohio, Sept. 6, 1945; s. Edward and Dorothy (Lederman) W.; m. Stephany Borges, Mar. 13, 1983 (div.); 1 stepchild, Daren; 1 child, Sofia. BA summa cum laude, Harvard U., 1966, MA, 1969, MD, PhD, 1972. Diplomate Am. Bd. Internal Medicine, Am. Bd. Geriatric Medicine. Resident in medicine Stanford U. Med. Ctr., Calif., 1972-75, Robert Wood Johnson clin. scholar depts. sociology-medicine, 1973-75; sr. resident in medicine Mass. Gen. Hosp., Boston, 1977-78; assoc. prof. sociology, clin. asst. prof. medicine U. Vt., Burlington, Vt., 1975-77; vis. assoc. prof. health and med. scis. U. Calif., Berkeley, 1978-82, clin. asst. prof. medicine San Francisco, 1978-82; internist La Clínica de la Raza, Oakland, Calif., 1978-82; prof. medicine and social scis. U. Calif., Irvine, 1982-96, chief div. gen. internal medicine and primary care, 1982-90; med. dir. U. Calif.-Irvine-North Orange County Community Clinic, Anaheim, 1982-90; prof. family and cmty. medicine, internal medicine, sociology, and Latin Am. studies U. N.Mex., Albuquerque, 1997—. Regional rep., nat. sec. bd. dir. Physicians for Nat. Health Program, Cambridge, Mass., 1989-91; cons. documentary Health Care Across the Border, Nat. Pub. TV, NYC, 1989-90, documentary on US health care system Nat. TV Austria, 1991; cons. BBC, 1992, Pew Health Professions Commn., 1992-94, Assn. Am. Med. Colls., 1992-93, Robert Wood Johnson Found., 1992, Rsch. and Tng. Group in Social Medicine, Santiago, Chile, 1990—, Eisenhower Rural Health Ctr., Idyllwild, Calif., 1995-96, office of pres. breast cancer rsch. initiative U. Calif, 2001; lectr. med. sociology U. Amsterdam, The Netherlands, 1977; vis. prof. Northwestern U., 1994, U. Ill., Chgo., 1994, U. Wash., 1996, U. N.Mex., 1996, U. Ky., 1996, U. Guadalajara, 1997, 2002, 03, Simon Fraser U., 1997, U. Campinas, Brazil, 1999, Cornell Med. Coll., 1999, U. Utah, 2002, Nat. Inst. Pub. Health, Cuernavaca, Mex., 2003-04, Robert Wood Johnson Sch. Medicine and Dentistry, NJ, 2003-04; expert panel on comm. with elderly patients Nat. Inst. Aging, 1997; prin. investigator US Agy. for Healthcare Rsch. and Quality, NIMH, 2003-04, Robert Wood Johnson Found., 2003-04. Co-author: The Exploitation of Illness in Capitalist Society, 1974; author: The Second Sickness: Contradictions of Capitalist Health Care, 1983, paperback edit., 1986, revised edit., 2000, The Politics of Medical Encounters: How Patients and Doctors Deal with Social Problems, 1991, paperback edit., 1993, At the Front Lines of Medicine: How the Health Care System Alienates Doctors and Mistreats Patients...and What We Can Do About It, 2001; mem. editl. bd. Internat. Jour. Health Svc., Social Problems, Western Jour. Medicine, Cambio y Salud (Chile), Investigacion en Salud (Mex.). Cons. on health policy Jesse Jackson Presdl. Campaign, 1988; bd. dir., mem. com. on litigation Orange County Pub. Law Ctr., 1990-96. Fellow in ind. study & rsch. NEH, 1984-85, Fulbright fellow, 1983, 88-90, 93-94, sr. fellow NIA, 1989-91, Fogarty Internat. Ctr., NIH, 1994-98, Fulbright New Century Scholar, 2001-02, Guide to Am. Top Physicians, 2002-, John Simon Guggenheim Meml. Found. fellow, 2002-, Jonathan Mann Award for Lifetime Commitment to Pub. Health and Social Justice Issues, N.Mex. Pub. Health Assn., 2003. Fellow ACP, Am. Acad. Physician and Patient, Soc. for Applied Anthropology; mem. APHA, Am. Sociol. Assn. (nat. coun.-at-large med. sociology sect. 1989-92, coord. resolution process concerning nat. health program 1990-91, Leo G. Reeder award for disting. career in medicine and social sci., 1997), Soc. Gen. Internal Medicine, Phi Beta Kappa. Avocations: music, athletics, gardening, mountain hiking. Office: U NMex Dept Family and Cmty Med MSC 09 5060 2400 Tucker NE Rm 173 Albuquerque NM 87131-0001 E-mail: waitzkin@unm.edu.

WAIXEL, VIVIAN, journalist; b. Norfolk, Va., July 22, 1946; d. Julius and Julia (Heimann) W.; m. Steven E. Scharbach, Aug. 24, 1969. BS in Communication, Simmons Coll., 1967; MA in Communication, U. Wis., 1971; PhD in Journalism (hon.), Simmons U., 2002. Teaching asst. U. Wis., Madison, 1967-69; reporter Wis. State Jour., Madison, 1969-72, The Record, Hackensack, N.J., 1972-74, bus. editor, 1974-76, assignment editor, 1976-86, sports editor, 1986-88, chief news editor, 1988-92, mng. editor, 1992-97, editor, 1997-2000, v.p., exec. editor, 2000—, Herald News, West Paterson, N.J., 2000—. Recipient Tribute to Women and Industry award, YWCA, 1976. Avocations: snorkeling, fitness walking, music, reading. Office: The Record 150 River St Hackensack NJ 07601-7155

WAJENBERG, ARNOLD SHERMAN, retired librarian, educator; b. Indpls., Apr. 11, 1929; s. Henry and Hazel L. (Johnson) W.; m. Joyce E. Dunham, Sept. 6, 1952; 1 child, Earl S. BA, Butler U., Indpls., 1951, MA, 1953, U. Chgo., 1955. Cataloger U. Chgo. Library, 1953-69; catalog librarian U. Ill., Chgo., 1969-74, asst. catalog librarian Champaign-Urbana, 1974-78, prin. cataloguer, 1979-94; retired, 1994; prof. library adminstrn. U. Ill., Champaign-Urbana. Prin. educator, Ill. Tng. Program for Implementation of Anglo-Am. Cataloguing Rules, 2d edit., 1979-80; mem. editorial policy com. Dewey Decimal, 1981-92; Ill. rep. cataloging adv. com., Online Computer Libr. Ctr. 1979-82, cataloging and database svcs. adv. com., 1989-92. Author: FLC FEDLINK AACR 2 Cataloging Manual for Federal Libraries, 1981; contbr. articles to profl. jours. Mem. ALA (com. on cataloging: description and access 1981-86, mem.-at-large exec. com. cataloging and classification sect. 1982-86) Avocations: walking, science fiction. Home: 240 Donald Dr Goffstown NH 03045-6214

WAJER, RONALD EDWARD, management consultant; b. Chgo., Aug. 31, 1943; s. Edward Joseph and Gertrude Catherine (Rytelny) W.; m. Mary Earlene Hagan, July 5, 1969; children: Catherine, Michael. BSIE, Northwestern U., 1966; MBA, Loyola U., Chgo., 1970. Cert. mgmt. cons. Inst. Mgmt. Cons. Project engring. mgr. Procter & Gamble, Chgo., 1966-67; indsl. engring. mgr. Johnson & Johnson, Bedford Park, Ill., 1967-71; project mgr. Jewel Cos., Franklin Park, Ill., 1971-73; divsn. engring. mgr. Abbott Labs., North Chicago, Ill., 1973-79; pres. bus. engring. divsn. R.E. Wajer & Assocs., Northbrook, Ill., 1979—. Contbr. articles to profl. jours. Sec. Downtown Redevel. Commn., Mt. Prospect, Ill., 1977-78; fundraising vol. Maryville Acad., Des Plaines, 1985—; bd. dirs. Lattof YMCA, Des Plaines, 1994-96; profl. advisor Sch. for New Learning, DePaul U., 1994—; mem. indsl. sector com. Lincoln Found. for Bus. Excellence, 1997-99. Recipient Cmty. Svc. award Chgo. Lighthouse for the Blind, 1989, Cert. of Merit, Village of Mt. Prospect, 1978. Mem. Inst. Indsl. Engrs. (cmty. svc. chmn. 1984), Inst. Mgmt. Cons. (exec. v.p., bd. dirs. 1987-94), Assn. Mgmt. Cons. (ctrl. regional v.p. 1985-87), Midwest Soc. Profl. Cons., Northwestern Club Chgo. Roman Catholic. Office: Bus Engring 5 Revere Dr Ste 200 Northbrook IL 60062-8000 Office Phone: 847-824-0809. Business E-Mail: rewajer@busnengg.com.

WAJSGRAS, DAVID C. manufacturing executive; m. Teena Wajsgras; 3 children. BS in Acctg., U. Md.; MBA in Fin., Am. U. CPA. CFO Maserati Automobile, Balt.; sr. auditor Coopers & Lybrand; contr. Contellation Investments, C.G.I.; from contr. to v.p. fin. UNC Inc., Annapolis, Md.; various sr. fin. positions AlliedSignal, Inc., Morristown, NJ, 1992—97; corp. contr. Engelhard Corp., Iselin, NJ, 1997—99; v.p., contr. Lear Corp., Southfield, Mich., 1999—2002, sr. v.p., CFO, 2002—. Mem.: Fin. Execs. Inst. Office: Lear Corp 21557 Telegraph Rd Southfield MI 48076-5008

WAKASHIGE, BENJAMIN TAKA, librarian; b. Paia, Hawaii, Sept. 3, 1947; s. Akio and Asayo (Tagawa) W.; m. Diane Marie, Dec. 29, 1969; children: David B.A., Kristen J.A. B.A. with honors, Western N.Mex. U., 1969; M. in Librarianship, Emporia State U., 1970. Reference librarian Birmingham-So. Coll., Ala., 1972-74; regional librarian for blind and physically handicapped Maine State Library, 1974-75, N.Mex. State Library, Santa Fe., 1975-77; project dir. Am. Indian Library Cultural Ctr. Project, U. N.Mex., Albuquerque, 1979-80; dist. library media coordinator Zuni Pub. Schs., N.Mex., 1980-82; library dir. U. Albuquerque, 1982-85; library dir. Albuquerque Acad., from 1985; state librarian N.Mex. State Libr., 1998-. Editor: (with others) Haiku and Haiga, 1970. Served with U.S. Army, 1970-72. Emporia State U. HEA Title II fellow, 1970. Mem. N.Mex. Library Assn. (pres. 1982-83), ALA, N.Mex. Book League, Greater Albuquerque Library Assn., N.Mex. Adv. Council Libraries. Democrat. United Ch. Christ. Office: State Library 1209 Camino Carlos Rey Santa Fe NM 87505

WAKATSUKI, LYNN Y. commissioner; Commr. fin. instns. divsn. fin. instns. Dept. Commerce and Consumer Affairs, Honolulu, 1995—. Office: Dept Commerce Consumer Affairs Divsn Fin Instns PO Box 2054 Honolulu HI 96805

WAKE, DAVID BURTON, biology professor; b. Webster, S.D., June 8, 1936; s. Thomas B. and Ina H. (Solem) W.; m. Marvalee Hendricks, June 23, 1962; 1 child, Thomas Andrew BA, Pacific Luth. U., 1958; MS, U. So. Calif., 1960, PhD, 1964. Instr. anatomy and biology U. Chgo., 1964-66, asst. prof. anatomy and biology, 1966-69; assoc. prof. zoology U. Calif., Berkeley, 1969-72, prof., 1972-89, John and Margaret Gompertz prof., 1991-97, prof. integrative biology, 1989—2003, prof. emeritus integrative biology, 2003—, faculty rsch. lectr., 2004. Dir. Mus. Vertebrate Zoology U. Calif., Berkeley, 1971-98; curator Herpetology Mus. Vertebrate Zoology, U. Calif., 1969-2003; vis. Alexander Agassiz prof. Mus. Comparative Zoology, Harvard U., 2002. Author: Biology, 1979; co-editor: Functional Vertebrate Morphology, 1985, Complex Organismal Functions: Integration and Evolution in the Vertebrates, 1989. Recipient Quantrell Teaching award U. Chgo., 1967, Outstanding Alumnus award Pacific Luth. U., 1979, Joseph Grinnell medal Mus. Vertebrate Zoology, 1998, Henry S. Fitch award Am. Soc. Ichthyologists and Herpetologists, 1999; grantee NSF, 1965—; Guggenheim fellow, 1982. Fellow AAAS, Am. Acad. Arts and Scis.; mem. NAS, NRC (bd. biology 1986-92), Am. Philos. Soc., Internat. Union for Conservation of Nature and Natural Resources (chair task force on declining amphibian populations 1990-92), Am. Soc. Zoologists (pres. 1992), Am. Soc. Naturalists (pres. 1989), Am. Soc. Ichthyologists and Herpetologists (bd. govs.), Soc. Study Evolution (pres. 1983, editor 1979-81), Soc. Systematic Biology (coun. 1980-84), Herpetologist's League (Disting. Herpetologist 1984). Home: 999 Middlefield Rd Berkeley CA 94708-1509 Business E-Mail: wakelab@uclink.berkeley.edu.

WAKE, MARVALEE HENDRICKS, biology professor; b. Orange, Calif., July 31, 1939; d. Marvin Carlton and Velvalee (Borter) H.; m. David B. Wake, June 23, 1962; 1 child, Thomas A. BA, U. So. Calif., 1961, MS, 1964, PhD, 1968. Tchg. asst., instr. U. Ill., Chgo., 1964, asst. prof., 1968—69; lectr. U. Calif., Berkeley, 1969—73, asst. prof., 1973—76, assoc. prof., 1976—80, prof. zoology, 1980—89, chmn. dept. zoology, 1985—89, chmn. dept. integrative biology, 1989—91, 1999—2002, assoc. dean Coll. Letters and Sci., 1975—78, prof. integrative biology, 1989—2003, Chancellor's prof., 1997—2000, prof. of the Grad. Sch., 2004—. Mem. NAS/NRC Bd. on Sustainable Devel., 1995-99, NSF Bio Adv. Commn., 1997-2002; Smithsonian Sci. Commn., 2001-02. Editor, co-editor: Hyman's Comparative Vertebrate Anatomy, 1979, The Origin and Evolution of Larval Forms, 1999; co-author: Biology, 1978; contbr. articles to profl. jours. NSF grantee, 1978—; Guggenheim fellow, 1988-89. Fellow: AAAS (chair Biology Sect. G 1998), Calif. Acad. Sci. (trustee 1992—98, hon. trustee 1998—), Am. Acad. Arts and Scis.; mem.: Am. Inst. Biol. Sci. (pres.-elect 2004), World Congress of Herpetology (sec. gen. 1994—97), Internat. Union Biol. Scis. (U.S. nat. com. 1986—, chair 1992—95, sec. gen. 1994—2000, pres. 2000—04), Soc. Integrative Comparative Biology (pres. 2001—03), Am. Soc. Ichthyologists and Herpetologists (bd. govs. 1978-84, 1986-91, pres. 1984). Office: U Calif Dept Integrative Biology 3060 VLSB Berkeley CA 94720-3140

WAKE, RICHARD W. food products executive; b. 1953; BS, U of Illinois. With Aurora (Ill.) Eby-Brown Co., Inc., 1975—, co-pres., 1983—. Office: 280 Shuman Blvd Ste 280 PO Box 3067 Naperville IL 60566-7067

WAKE, THOMAS G. food products executive; Co-pres. Eby-Brown Co., Naperville, Ill., now co-chief exec., 1983—. Office: Eby Brown Co 280 Shuman Blvd Ste 280 Naperville IL 60563-2578

WAKEFIELD, STEPHEN ALAN, lawyer; b. Olney, Ill., Oct. 18, 1940; s. George William and Blanche Lucille (Sheesley) W.; children from previous marriage: Melissa Hawley, Tracy Wakefield, Stephen Alan Jr.; m. Patricia Ann McGuire, Nov. 29, 1980; 1 child, Mark. LLB, U. Tex., Austin, 1965. Bar: Tex. 1965. Assoc. Baker & Botts, Houston, 1965-70, ptnr., 1974-84, sr. ptnr., chmn. energy dept., 1986-89; atty. Federal Power Commn., Washington, 1970-72; dep. asst. sec. energy programs Dept. Interior, Washington, 1972-73, asst. sec. energy and minerals, 1973-74; asst. adminstr. Fed. Energy Office, Washington, 1973-74; vice chmn., gen. counsel United Energy Resources, Inc., Houston, 1985-86; pres. United Gas Pipe Line Co., Houston, 1985-86; exec. v.p. MidCon Corp., 1985-86; gen. coun. Dept. Energy, Washington, 1989-91; ptnr. Akin, Gump, Strauss, Hauer & Feld, L.L.P., 1991-97; sr. v.p., gen. coun. Southern Co., 1997-2001; sr. counsel Southern Co., 2001—. Bd. visitors M.D. Anderson Cancer Ctr.; bd. govs. Robert Packard Ctr. ALS Rsch. Johns Hopkins U. Mem. Tex. Bar Assn., Capital City Club (Atlanta). Home: 201 Blackland Dr NW Atlanta GA 30342-4405 Office: Southern Company Ste 1400 270 Peachtree St NW Atlanta GA 30303-1263 E-mail: sawakefield@mindspring.com., sawakefi@southernco.com.

WAKEMAN, FREDERIC EVANS, JR., historian, educator; b. Kansas City, Kans., Dec. 12, 1937; s. Frederic Evans and Margaret Ruth (Keyes) W.; married He Lea Liang; children: Frederic Evans III, Matthew Clark, Sarah Elizabeth. BA, Harvard Coll., 1959; postgrad., Institut d'Etudes Politiques, U. Paris, 1959-60; MA, U. Calif., Berkeley, 1962, PhD, 1965. Asst. prof. history U. Calif., Berkeley, 1965-67, assoc. prof., 1968-70, prof., 1970-89, Haas prof. Asian Studies, 1989—, dir. Ctr. Chinese Studies, 1972-79; humanities research prof., vis. scholar Corpus Christi Coll., U. Cambridge, Eng., 1976-77, Beijing U., 1980-81, 85. Acad. adviser U.S. Ednl. Del. for Study in China; chmn. Joint Com. Chinese Studies Am. Coun. Learned Socs./Social Sci. Rsch. Coun.; sr. adviser Beijing office NAS; pres. Social Sci. Rsch. Coun., 1986-89, chmn. com. on scholarly comm. with China, 1995-2000; dir. Inst. East Asian Studies, Berkeley, 1990-2001; vis. prof. U. Heidelberg, Germany, 2000; hon. prof. China People's U. Author: Strangers at the Gate, 1966, History and Will, 1973, The Fall of Imperial China, 1975, Conflict and Control in Late Imperial China, 1976, Ming and Qing Historical Studies in the People's Republic of China, 1981, The Great Enterprise, 1986, Shanghai Sojourners, 1992, Policing Shanghai, 1995, Shanghai Badlands, 1996, China's Quest for Modernization, 1997, Reappraising Republican China, 2000, Spymaster, 2003. Harvard Nat. scholar, 1955-59; Tower fellow, 1959-60; Fgn. Area fellow, 1963-65; Am. Coun. Learned Socs. fellow, 1967-68; Guggenheim fellow, 1973-74; NRC fellow, 1985. Mem. Am. Acad. Arts and Scis., Am. Hist. Assn. (pres.), Am. Philos. Soc., Shanghai Acad. Social Scis. (fgn.). Home: 501 Delancey St Apt 409 San Francisco CA 94107-1432 Office: U Calif Inst East Asian Studies Berkeley CA 94720-0001 Office Phone: 510-643-9496. Business E-Mail: jingcha@socrates.berkeley.edu.

WAKOSKI, DIANE, poet, educator; b. Whittier, Calif., Aug. 3, 1937; d. John Joseph and Marie Elvira (Mengel) W. BA in English, U. Calif., Berkeley, 1960. Writer-in-residence Mich. State U., East Lansing, 1976—, Univ. disting. prof., 1990—. Vis. writer Calif. Inst. Tech., 1972, U. Va., 1972-73, Wilamette U., 1973, Lake Forest Coll., 1974, Colo. Coll., 1974, U. Calif., Irvine, 1974, Macalester Coll., 1975, U. Wis., 1975, Hollins Coll., 1974, U. Wash., 1977, Whitman Coll., 1976, Emory U., 1980-81, U. Hawaii, 1978. Author: books Coins and Coffins, 1962, Discrepancies and Apparitions, 1966, Inside The Blood Factory, 1968, The George Washington Poems, 1967, The Magellanic Clouds, 1969, The Motorcycle Betrayal Poems, 1971, Smudging, 1972, Dancing On The Grave of A Son Of A Bitch, 1973, Trilogy, 1974, Virtuoso Literature For Two and Four Hands, 1976, Waiting For the King of Spain, 1977, The Man Who Shook Hands, 1978, Cap of Darkness, 1980, The Magician's Feastletters, 1982, The Collected Greed: Parts I-XIII, 1984, The Rings of Saturn, 1986, Emerald Ice: Selected Poems 1962-87, 1988 (William Carlos Williams prize 1989), Medea The Sorceress, 1991, Jason the Sailor, 1993, The Emerald City of Las Vegas, 1995, Argonaut Rose, 1998, The Butcher's Apron: New & Selected Poems, 2000. Named Univ. Disting. Prof., Mich. State U., 1990, Author of Yr., Mich. Libr. Assn., 2003; recipient award, Mich. Arts Found., 1989, Disting. Faculty award, Mich. State U., 1989; grantee Cassandra Found., 1970, N.Y. State Cultural Coun., 1971—72, Guggenheim Found., 1972—73, Fullbright, 1984, Mich. Arts Coun., 1988. Office: Mich State U 207 Morrill Hall East Lansing MI 48824-1036 E-mail: dwakoski@aol.com., wakoski@pilot.msu.edu.

WAKS, JAY WARREN, lawyer; b. Newark, Dec. 6, 1946; m. Harriet, July 27, 1969; children: Jonathan Warren, Allison Lindsay. BS, Cornell U., 1968, JD, 1971. Bar: N.Y. 1972, U.S. Ct. Appeals (2d cir.) 1972, U.S. Dist. Ct. (no. dist.) N.Y. 1972, U.S. Dist. Ct. (so. & ea. dists.) N.Y. 1973, U.S. Ct. Appeals (3d cir.) 1983, U.S. Dist. Ct. D.C. 1985, U.S. Supreme Ct. 1991. Law clk. to Hon. Inzer B. Wyatt U.S. Dist. Ct. So. Dist. N.Y., 1971-72; assoc. Kaye, Scholer, Fierman, Hays & Handler, N.Y.C., 1972-80; ptnr. Kaye Scholer LLP, N.Y.C., 1981—, chmn. employment and labor law practice/litigation, chmn. ADR practice group, mem. e-commerce practice group and internat. practice group; Kevin Becraft Lectr. Cornell U., ILR Sch., Inst. for Workplace Studies. Bd. dirs., gen. counsel Legal Momentum; advisor restatement of the law third-employment law Am. Law Inst., 2004—. Bus. Watch columnist Nat. Law Jour., 1990—; contbg. author numerous articles to profl. jours. Chair Work in Am. Inst., 2002—04; mem. employment disputes com. CPR Inst. Dispute Resolution, 1988—, chair, 1991—, mem. exec. com.; mem. coun. Cornell U., 2000—, admin. com. coun., chair admissions com., 2002—, nat. chmn. Cornell Law Sch. ann. fund, 2001—, chmn. 20th, 25th and 30th reunion campaigns Cornell Law Sch., former nat. co-chair Cornell Law Sch. dean's spl. leadership commn. Class of '68, major gifts com., co-chair, 2002, chmn. law sch. adv. coun., devel. exec. com. Cornell Law Sch., 2004—. Named among #1 employment def. lawyers in N.Y., Chambers USA Guide, among nation's best litigators in employment law, The Nat. Law Jour., 1992, among best lawyers in N.Y. and among 7 best corp. side labor/employment lawyers, N.Y. Mag., 1995, Top of the Docket column for success in high-profile public sector case, Am. Lawyer, 2002; recipient recognition for svc. to diversity efforts, Cornell Black Alumni Assn.; profiled in Cornell Law Forum, 2004. Mem. ABA (spkr. ann. meetings sect. labor and employment), State Bar Calif. (assoc.), N.Y. State Bar Assn. (co-chair employment alternative dispute resolution com., labor and employment law sect., exec. com. 1995-99), Assn. Bar of City of N.Y. (chmn. labor and employment law com. 1990-93), Fed. Bar. Coun. (sustaining). Avocations: swimming, tennis, skiing, bicycling. Office: Kaye Scholer LLP 425 Park Ave New York NY 10022-3506 Office Phone: 212-836-8558. E-mail: jwaks@kayescholer.com.

WAKSBERG, JOSEPH, statistical company executive, researcher; b. Kielce, Poland, Sept. 20, 1915; s. Harry and Anna (Kalichstein) W.; m. Roslyn Karr, Dec. 25, 1941; children: Arlene, Mark. BS, CCNY, 1936; postgrad., NYU, 1936-37, Am. U., 1941-43. Project dir. WPA, Phila., 1938-40; assoc. dir. stats. U.S. Bur. Census, Washington, 1940-73; chmn. bd. dirs. Westat, Inc., Rockville, Md., 1973—. Tchr. U. Mich., Ann Arbor, 1968-75; statis. cons. CBS, N.Y.C., 1967-90, UN, 1975-81, Voter News Svc., N.Y.C., 1992-96. Editor: Telephone Survey Methodology, 1988; assoc. editor Survey Methodology, 1992—; contbr. articles to profl. jours. Mem. tech. adv. com. United Jewish Communities, N.Y.C., 1978—. Recipient Gold medal U.S. Dept.

Commerce, 1965. Fellow Am. Statis. Assn. (bd. dirs., chair several sects.); mem. Internat. Statis. Inst., Internat. Assn. Survey Statisticians (mem. coun. 1975-77). Office: Westat Inc 1650 Research Blvd Rockville MD 20850-3195 E-mail: wakshej1@westat.com.

WAKSLER, FRANCES CHAPUT, sociologist, educator; b. Cambridge, Mass., Jan. 8, 1942; d. Hervé Chaput and Helen Egan; m. Norman H. Waksler, May 25, 1962. BA cum laude, Boston Univ. Coll. of Libral Arts, 1966; MA, Boston Univ. Graduate Sch., 1968; PhD, Boston Univ., 1973. Instr. Wheelock Coll., Boston, 1972—73, asst. prof., 1973—80, assoc. prof., 1980—2002, prof. sociology, 2002—. Author (with Jack D. Douglas): The Sociology of Deviance: An Introduction; author: The Little Trials of Childhood and Children's Strategies for Dealing with Them; editor: Studying the Social Worlds of Children; editor Erving Goffman's Sociology: Human Studies Spl. Issue, Intersubjectivity as a Practical Matter: Human Studies Spl. Issue, Human Studies 25th Anniversary Issue, assoc. editor Human Studies, 1998—. Mem.: Soc. Phenomenology and Existential Philosophy, Ea. Sociol. Soc., Soc. Phenomenology and the Human Scis. (exec. bd. 2001—04, featured scholar 2001). Achievements include pioneering work in the sociological studies of childhood and theoretical contributions to the sociological study of face-to-face interaction, intersubjectivity, and medicine; from phenomenological, ethnomethodological, and symbolic interactionist perspectives. Avocations: dog training, gardening. Office: Wheelock College 200 The Riverway Boston MA 02215 Personal E-mail: fwaksler@comcast.net.

WAKSMAN, BYRON HALSTED, neuroimmunologist, experimental pathologist, educator, medical association administrator; b. N.Y.C., Sept. 15, 1919; s. Selman A. and Bertha (Mitnik) W.; m. Joyce Ann Robertroy, Aug. 11, 1944; children: Nan, Peter. BS, Swarthmore Coll., 1940; MD, U. Pa., 1943. Intern Michael Reese Hosp., Chgo., 1944; fellow Mayo Found., 1946-48; NIH fellow Columbia U. Med. Sch., 1948-49; assoc., then asst. prof. bacteriology and immunology Harvard Med. Sch., 1949-63; rsch. fellow, then assoc. bacteriologist (neurology) Mass. Gen. Hosp., 1949-63; prof. microbiology Yale U., 1963-74, prof. pathology, 1974-78, chmn. dept., 1964-70, 72-74, prof. pathology and biology, 1979-89; v.p. rsch. programs Nat. Multiple Sclerosis Soc., N.Y.C., 1979-87, v.p. rsch. and med. programs, 1987-89; adj. prof. pathology NYU, 1979—, rsch. prof. biomedicine and sci. edn., 2002—, dir. (ad interim) programs for prep. edn. sci. and medicine, 2002—03, sr. advisor collaborative edn. programs, 2003—; vis. scientist in neurology Harvard U., 1990—. Mem. expert panel immunology WHO, 1963—83; microbiology fellowships panel and study sect. mem. NIH, 1961—69; bd. trustees Found. for Microbiology, 1968—, pres., 1970—2000, chmn. bd. trustes, 2001—; bd. trustees Biosis, 1988—91; dir. sci. writing fellowships program Marine Biol. Lab., Woods Hole, Mass., 1990—95; Humboldt prof. Max Planck Inst., Martinsried, 1991—92; dir. European Initiative for Communicators Sci., 1992—95; chmn. bd. Sci. Counsellors Nat. Inst. Aging, 1977—79. Contbr. articles to profl. jours.; editor: Progress in Allergy/Chemical Immunology, 1962—; mem. editl. adv. bd.: Cellular Immunology, 1970—95, Immunol. Comms., 1970—95, Inflammation, 1975—90, assoc. editor: Bacteriol. Revs., 1963—67, Jour. Immunology, 1962—66, Internat. Archives Allergy and Applied Immunology, 1962—95. Served as psychiatrist AUS, 1944-46. Fellow Am. Acad Arts and Scis.; mem. Am. Assn. Immunologists (councillor 1965-70, pres. 1970-71), Brit. Soc. Immunology, Am. Soc. Microbiology (councillor 1967-71), Am. Acad. Microbiology, Am. Acad. Neurology, Am. Neurol. Assn. Home: 300 E 54th St New York NY 10022-5018 Office: NYU Sch Medicine Dept Pathology 550 1st Ave New York NY 10016-6402 Office Phone: 212-263-0042. Business E-Mail: bhw1@nyu.edu.

WAKUMOTO, YOSHIHIKO, electronics company executive, grants executive; b. Bunkyo-Ku, Tokyo, June 4, 1931; s. Yoshitaro and Fumie (Oka) W.; m. Reiko Tanaka, Mar. 28, 1959; children: Yoshiaki, Yoshiyuki. BA, Tokyo U., 1955; postgrad., Columbia U., 1960-61. Dep. mgr. license negotiation Toshiba Corp., Tokyo, 1964-67, mgr. overseas mfg. ops., 1967-72, mgr. fin. divsn., 1972-74, gen. mgr. internat. fin. divsn., 1974-81, gen. mgr. internat. affairs divsn., 1981-88, v.p., dep. group exec.-internat. staff group, 1988-91, exec. v.p. for corp. planning, info. sys. and group cos., 1991-95, exec. v.p. for internat. rels., 1995-96, advisor, 1996—2001; exec. dir. Japan Found. Ctr. for Global Partnership, Tokyo, 1996—2002; spl. asst. to the pres. The Japan Found., 2002—. Mem., Japan Nat. Com. United World Colls., 1996—2002; dir. The Am. Studies Found., 1997—; chairperson CARE Japan, 2003—; pres. Japan Assn. for Cultural Exchange, 2004—. Co-author: Foreign Exchange Risk and International Financial Strategy, 1973, The Run-up of 21st Century, 1991; translator: Management By Exception, 1968. Mem. Internat. House of Japan, Japan Inst. Internat. Affairs, Japanese Assn. for Cultural Exchange (pres. 2004—), Fgn. Corr. Club Japan (assoc.). Home: 3-43-18 Hongo Bunkyo-ku Tokyo 113-0033 Japan Office: Japan Found Ctr Global Ptnr 1-12-32 Akasaka Mori Bldg Minato-ku Tokyo 107-6021 Japan Office Phone: 81-3-5562-3542. E-mail: waksan@tcn-catv.ne.jp.

WALBAUM, ROBERT C. lawyer; b. Springfield, Ill., Nov. 13, 1933; s. George Crum and Mary Emma (Taylor) W.; m. Anita P. Walbaum, Aug. 6, 1960; children: John Taylor, Charles Robert. Student, Bradley U., Peoria, Ill., 1951-53; BS in Commerce, U. Ill., Urbana, 1955; JD, Washington, St. Louis, 1960. Bar: Ill. 1961, U.S. Dist. Ct. (so. dist.) Ill. 1964, U.S. Ct. Appeals (7th cir.) 1973, U.S. Supreme Ct. 1989. With Chgo. Title and Trust Co., 1960-61; asst. states atty. County of Sangamon, Springfield, Ill., 1961-63; pvt. practice Springfield, 1963—. Atty. City Springfield, 1964-69, Village Pleasant Plains, Ill., 1970-93; tech. advisor Ill. Dept. Law Enforcement, 1969-73; counsel Springfield Park Dist., 1984—; dir. Pleasant Plains State Bank, 1982-95. Mem. Sangamon County Bd. Suprs., 1962-75, chmn., 1974; bd. dirs. Washington St. Mission, Springfield, 1966-90, pres. 1983-86. Served with U.S. Army, 1955-57. Mem. ABA, Ill. State Bar Assn., Sangamon County Bar Assn., Illini Country Club, Sangamo Club. Republican. Episcopalian. Episcopalian. Address: 1049 W Woodland Ave Springfield IL 62704-2863 E-mail: walbaumlaw@sbcglobal.net.

WALBERG, HERBERT JOHN, psychologist, educator, consultant; b. Chgo., Dec. 27, 1937; s. Herbert J. and Helen (Bauer) W.; m. Madoka Bessho, Aug. 20, 1965; 1 child, Herbert J. III. BE in Edn. and Psychology, Chgo. State U., 1959; ME in Counseling, U. Ill., 1960; PhD in Ednl. Psychology, U. Chgo., 1964. Instr. psychology Chgo. State U., 1962-63, asst. prof., 1964-65; lectr. edn. Rutgers U., New Brunswick, N.J., 1965-66; asst. prof. edn. Harvard U., Cambridge, Mass., 1966-69; assoc. prof. edn. U. Ill., Chgo., 1970-71, prof., 1971-84, rsch. prof., 1984—, external examiner, 1981. External examiner, 1981; ednl. cons. numerous orgns.; external examiner Monash U., 1974, 76, Australian Nat. U., 1977; speaker in field; former coord. worldwide radio broadcasts on Am. Edn. Voice of Am., USIA, Office Pres. U.S., cons. Ctr. for Disease Control U.S. Pub. Health Svcs., 1985-90. Author, editor 49 books; chmn. editl. bd. Internat. Jour. Ednl. Rsch., 1985—; contbr. over 350 articles to profl. jours., chpts. to books. Mem. Chgo. United Edn. Com., also other civic groups, 1971-86; bd. dirs. Family Study Inst., 1987; chmn. bd. dirs. Heartland Inst., 1995. Nat. Inst. Edn. rsch. grantee, 1973, NSF rsch. grantee, 1974, March of Dimes rsch. grantee, 1976, numerous others. Fellow AAAS, Am. Psychol. Assn., Royal Statis. Soc.; mem. Internat. Acad. Edn. (founding), Am. Ednl. Rsch. Assn., Assn. for Supervision and Curriculum Devel., Brit. Ednl. Rsch. Assn., Nat. Soc. for Study Edn., Evaluation Rsch. Soc., Internat. Acad. Scis., Phi Delta Kappa (Disting. Rsch. award U. Chgo. chpt. 1971, cert. of recognition 1985), Phi Kappa Phi (hon.). Lutheran. Avocation: travel. Home: 180 E Pearson St Apt 3607 Chicago IL 60611-2135 Office: U Ill 1040 W Harrison St Chicago IL 60607-7129

WALBESSER, HENRY HERMAN, computer science educator; b. Buffalo, May 9, 1935; s. Henry Herman and Florence (Schoenl) W.; m. Diane L. Walker, Aug. 16, 1958; children: Henry, Kathleen, James. BS, SUNY, Buffalo, 1958; MA, U. Md., 1960, PhD, 1965; DSc, U. of the Republic, Uruguay, 1976. Asst. prof. U. Tex., Austin, 1961-63; assoc. dir. AAAS, Washington, 1963-68; assoc. prof. U. Md., College Park, 1968-76, assoc. dean/assoc. provost, 1971-76, prof., chair Catonsville, 1976-92, prof. emeritus, 1992—; prof. Baylor U., Waco, Tex., 1992—, dean, 1992-96. Author: Evaluation Model, 1965, Integrity and Higher Education, 2001, A Brief Primer on Teaching: For New University Personnel, 2002, Imagination, 2003; co-author: Descriptive Data Analysis, 1991, Inferential Data Analysis, 1994; contbr. articles to profl. jours.; author: An Introduction to Data Analysis for Computer Scientists and Engineers, 2003. Active adv. bd. Gov.'s Econ. Devel. Office, Annapolis, Md., 1988-91, Strecker Mus., Waco, 1992—, Lyric Opera of Waco, 1997—; worker Habitat for Humanity, Waco, 1996—. Fulbright-Hays fellow, 1967, 68, SEAMEO fellow, 1981, 82, OECD fellow, 1988. Fellow: AAAS; mem.: Nat. Hist. Soc. Democrat. Baptist. Avocations: bioinformatics, history of university presidents, gardening. Home: 400 Show Mt Waco TX 76712 Office: Baylor U PO Box 97356 Waco TX 76798-7356 Office Phone: 254-710-6846. Business E-Mail: henry_walbesser@baylor.edu.

WALBRIDGE, JOHN, foreign language educator; b. Lake Forest, Ill., Apr. 28, 1950; s. John T. Jr. and Mary Lou (Sailor) W.; m. Linda Strickland, May 27, 1972 (dec. 2002); children: John, Nathaniel, m. Frances Trix, June 26, 2004. BA, Yale U., 1973; PhD in Near Eastern Langs., Harvard U., 1983. V.p. No. Land and Lumber Co., Escanaba, Mich., 1980-87; gen. editor Bahai Ency. Project, Wilmette, Ill., 1987-91; asst. editor Ctr. for Iranian Studies, Columbia U., N.Y.C., 1991-93; prof. Near Eastern langs. Ind. U., Bloomington, 1993—. Author: The Science of Mystic Lights, 1992; translator: The Storm (Kahlil Gibran), 1993, The Beloved (Kahlil Gibran), 1994; mem. editl. bd. Bibliotheca Persian, 1993-96. Baha'I. Avocation: model railroading. Home: 3125 S Snoddy Rd Bloomington IN 47401-9615

WALBRIDGE, WILLARD EUGENE, broadcasting executive; b. Republic, Pa., Mar. 11, 1913; s. Peter D. and Anna (Higbee) W.; m. Marietta H. Arner, Nov. 15, 1941; 1 child, Peter F. AB, U. Mich., 1936. Salesman, Sta. WWJ, Detroit, 1939-43; mgr. Sta. WWJ-TV, Detroit, 1946-53; exec. v.p., gen. mgr. Sta. WJIM AM-TV, Lansing, Mich., 1953 54, Sta. KTRK-TV, Houston, 1954-70; sr. v.p. corp. affairs Capital Cities Communications, Inc., 1970-78, cons., 1978-81; sr. cons. Hill & Knowlton, Inc., Houston, 1987—. Dir. Houston Lighting & Power Co., Houston Industries, Inc., 1975-83, Internat. Systems & Controls, Inc., Tex. Commerce Med. Bank. Pres., Greater Houston Community Found.; bd. dirs. Salvation Army, Houston Area council Boy Scouts Am., Houston Grand Opera Assn.; mem. nat. bd. govs. ARC, 1974-80, also bd. dirs. Houston chpt., 1965-83, chmn. Houston chpt., 1972-75; chmn. bd. TV Info. Office, N.Y.C., 1965-70; trustee Mus. Broadcasting, 1978-82. Served from ensign to lt. USNR, 1943-46. Decorated Silver Star. Mem. Maximum Service Telecasters (dir. 1971-81), Houston Assn. Community TV (dir. 1972-82), Internat. Radio and TV Fedn. (dir. 1969-76), Nat. Assn. Broadcasters (dir. 1965-70, chmn. bd. 1970-71), U.S. C. of C. (dir. 1975-81), Houston C. of C. (dir. 1971-83, chmn. bd. 1975-76), Houston Council Fgn. Relations (chmn. 1977-78) Home and Office: Apt 207 2828 Bammel Ln Houston TX 77098-1129 Office: Hill & Knowlton Inc Niels Esperson Bldg 808 Travis St Fl 21 Houston TX 77002-5706

WALBURN, JOHN CLIFFORD, mental health services professional; b. Marion, Ind., Apr. 6, 1945; s. Rex Raymond and Norma Jane (Clifford) W.; m. Linda Sue Spall, Sept. 21, 1968 (div. Dec. 1987); 1 child, Geoffrey Jacob; m. Mitzi Lynn Johnson, June 20, 1992; 1 child, Abigail Rae. BS, Ball State U., 1969, MA, 1975; JD, I.U., Indpls., 1991. Bar: Ind. 1992. Planner Metro. Planning Commn., Muncie, Ind., 1970-72; dir. adult svcs. Del. County Assn. for Retarded, Muncie, Ind., 1972-76; exec. dir. Fayette-Union Assn. for Retarded, Connersville, Ind., 1976-83; cons. Ind. Protection and Advocacy, Indpls., 1984-86; case mgr. Ind. Dept. Mental Health, Indpls., 1986-87; exec. dir. Cardinal Svc. Mgmt., New Castle, Ind., 1987-2000; founding ptnr. Creative Human Resource Solutions, New Castle, Ind., 1998—; exec. dir. Cmty. Alternative, Southeast Divsn. of Rescare, Jeffersonville, Ind., 2000—. Ofcl. Ind. Spl. Olympics, 1973—; chmn. Ind. Residential Mgmt. Com., 1991—; cons. DLG Cons. and Mktg. Svc., Ind., 1992; treas. Cmty. Action, So. Ind. Co-author: Feldman/Walburn Habilitation System, 1988; photo, drawing artist, 1978—. Treas. cmty. action, So. Ind., Madison Area C. of C. With USN, 1965-67. Named Ky. Col., Commonwealth of Ky., 1978. Mem. Am. Assn. Mental Retardation (bd. dirs. 1991-98), Ind. Assn. Rehab. Facilities (bd. dirs. 1996—, Pres.'s award 1998), Madison Area C. of C. Avocations: sports, playing/listening to music, movies, art, reading fiction. Home: 2559 So College Hill Dr Hanover IN 47243-9177 Office: RES-CARE Twenty-Five-O-One Pl 6200 E Hwy 62 Ste 675 Jeffersonville IN 47130

WALCH, PETER SANBORN, museum director, publisher; b. Portland, Maine, Oct. 10, 1940; s. J. Weston and Ruth Dyer (Sanborn) W.; m. Margaret S. Segal, June 29, 1962 (div. 1983); children: Maximilian F.S., Abigail M.; m. Linda P. Tyler, Aug. 3, 1990. BA, Swarthmore Coll., 1962; MFA, Princeton U., 1964, PhD, 1968. Asst. prof. fine arts Pomona Coll., Claremont, Calif., 1966-68, Vassar Coll., Poughkeepsie, N.Y., 1968-69, Yale U., New Haven, 1969-71; assoc. prof. U. N.Mex., Albuquerque, 1971-85, dir. Art Mus., 1985—. Chmn., bd. dirs. J. Weston Walch, Pub., Portland, 1990—. Author: (exhbn. catalog) French Eighteenth-Century Oil Sketches, 1980, French Oil Sketches and the Academic Tradition, 1994; editor N.Mex. Studies in the Fine Arts jour., 1978-86. Mem. Contemporary Art Soc., Cogawesco Club. Home: 1520 Columbia Dr NE Albuquerque NM 87106-2635 Office: Univ NMex Art Mus Fine Arts Ctr Albuquerque NM 87131-0001

WALCH, TIMOTHY GEORGE, library administrator; b. Detroit, Dec. 6, 1947; s. George Louis Walch and Margaret Mary (Shields) DeSchryver; m. Victoria Irons, June 24, 1978; children: Thomas Emmet, Brian Edward. BA, U. Notre Dame, 1970; PhD, Northwestern U., 1975. Assoc. dir. Soc. Am. Archivists, Chgo., 1975-79; grants analyst Nat. Hist. Publ. Commn., Washington, 1979-81; budget analyst Nat. Archives, Washington, 1981-82, editor Prologue, 1982-88; asst. dir. Hoover Presdl. Libr., West Branch, Iowa, 1988-93, dir., 1993—. Author: Catholicism in America, 1989, Pope John Paul II, 1989, Parish School, 1996, reprinted, 2003, others; editor: Herbert Hoover & Harry S Truman, 1992, Immigrant America, 1994, At the President's Side, 1997, Herbert Hoover & Franklin D. Roosevelt, 1998, Uncommon Americans, 2003, and others; assoc. editor: U.S. Cath. Historian, 1983—; guest columnist Cedar Rapids Gazette, 1996—; contbr. History News Svc., 2002—. Recipient Journalism award U.S. Cath. Press Assn., 1986, 1st place publ. award Nat. Assn. Govt. Communicators, 1988, U.S. Archivist's award Nat. Archives, 1993, Iowa Gov.'s Vol. award, 1995, 97, Dominican Veritas Forum award, 1996, Rogus Lecture, U. Dayton, 1999, Williams Lecture, La. State U., Shreveport, 2000, Hatfield Lecture, Oreg. Hist. Soc., 2003. Mem. Orgn. Am. Historians, U.S. Cath. Hist. Soc., Rotary Internat. Home: 65 N Westminster St Iowa City IA 52245-3833 Office: Hoover Presdl Libr PO Box 488 West Branch IA 52358-0488 Office Phone: 319-643-6029. Personal E-mail: Twalch47@aol.com. Business E-Mail: timothy.walch@nara.gov.

WALCHER, ALAN ERNEST, lawyer; b. Chgo., Oct. 2, 1949; s. Chester R. and Dorothy E. (Kullgren) W.; children: Dustin Alan, Michael Alan, Christopher Ray. BS, U. Utah, 1971, cert. in internat. rels., 1971, JD, 1974. Bar: Utah 1974, U.S. Dist. Ct. Utah 1974, U.S. Ct. Appeals (10th cir.) 1977, Calif. 1979, U.S. Dist. Ct. (cen. dist.) Calif. 1979, U.S. Ct. Appeals (9th cir.) 1983, U.S. Dist. Ct. (ea., no., and so. dists.) Calif. 1994. Sole practice, Salt Lake City, 1974-79; ptnr. Costello & Walcher, L.A., 1979-85, Walcher & Scheuer, 1985-88, Ford & Harrison, 1988-91, Epstein Becker & Green, 1991—; judge pro tem Los Angeles Mcpl. Ct., 1986-91; dir. Citronia, Inc., Los Angeles, 1979-81. Trial counsel Utah chpt. Common Cause, Salt Lake City, 1978-79. Robert Mukai scholar U. Utah, 1971. Mem. Soc. Bar and Gavel (v.p. 1975-77), ABA, Fed. Bar Assn., Los Angeles County Bar Assn., Century City Bar Assn., Assn. Bus. Trial Lawyers, Phi Delta Phi, Owl and Key. Home: 17933 Sunburst St Northridge CA 91325-2848 E-mail: awalcher@ebglaw.com., alan1002@earthlink.net.

WALCHER, KATHLEEN, state official; b. Sept. 20, 1948; Clk. of ct. of Common Pleas, Huron County; civil sheriff deputy; deputy clk.; state rep. State of Ohio, 58th Dist., 2002—. Mem.: Juvenile and Family Law (vice-chair), Econ. Devel. and Tech., County and Twp. Govt., Agr. and Natural Resources. Republican. Office: 77 South High St 12th Fl Columbus OH 43215-6111

WALCOTT, CHARLES, neurobiology and behavior educator; b. Boston, July 19, 1934; s. Charles Folsom and Susan (Cabot) W.; m. Jane Clayton Taylor, Aug. 14, 1976; children: Thomas Stewart, Samuel Cabot. AB, Harvard U., 1956; PhD, Cornell U., 1959. Asst. prof. div. engring. and applied physics Harvard U., Cambridge, Mass., 1961-65; asst. prof. biology Tufts U., Medford, Mass., 1965-67; assoc. prof. dept. biology SUNY, Stony Brook, 1967-74, prof. dept. biology, 1974-81; prof., exec. dir. Cornell Lab. of Ornithology, Ithaca, N.Y., 1981-93, Louis Agassiz Fuertes dir., 1992-95; prof. neurobiology and behavior Cornell U., 1981—, dir. divsn. biol. scis., 1998-99, assoc. dean of the univ. faculty, 2000—03, dean of univ. faculty, 2003—. Cons., dir. Elem. Sci. Study, Watertown, Mass., 1961-67; dir. 3-2-1- Contact, Children's TV Workshop, N.Y.C., 1978—80; dir. L.A. Fuertes. Contbr. many rsch. papers to sci. jours. Dir. sci. TV, Mass. Audubon, Lincoln, 1959-61. Avocations: gardening, sailing, photography. Home: 84 Besemer Hill Rd Ithaca NY 14850-9636 Office: Cornell U Dept Neurobiology Behavior W255 Seeley Mudd Hall Ithaca NY 14853 Office Phone: 607 254 4382. Business E-Mail: cw38@cornell.edu.

WALCOTT, DEREK ALTON, poet, playwright; b. Castries, St. Lucia, Jan. 23, 1930; s. Warwick and Alix W.; m. Fay Moston, 1954 (div. 1959); 1 son; m. Margaret Ruth Maillard, 1962 (div.); 2 daus.; m. Norline Metivier (div.). BA, U. West Indies, Kingston, Jamaica, 1953, DLitt, 1972. Former tchr., St. Lucia, Grenada, Jamaica; poet-in-residence Hollins Coll., Roanoke, VA, 1980; prof. English Boston U. Founding dir. Trinidad Theatre Workshop, 1959—; lectr. Rutgers U., Yale U.; vis. prof. Columbia U., 1981, Harvard U., 1982, Boston U., 1985. Author: (poetry) Twenty-Five Poems, 1948, Epitath for the Young: A Poem in XII Cantos, 1949, Poems, 1953, In A Green Night: Poems, 1948-1960, 1962, Selected Poems, 1964, The Castaway and Other Poems, 1965 (Heinemann award Royal Soc. Lit. 1966), The Gulf and Other Poems, 1969 (Cholmondeley award 1969), Another Life, 1973 (Jock Campbell/New Statesman prize 1974), Sea Grapes, 1976, Selected Verse, 1976, The Star-Apple Kingdom, 1979, The Fortunate Traveller, 1981 (Heinemann award Royal Soc. Lit. 1983), Selected Poetry, 1981, Midsummer, 1984, Collected Poems, 1948-1984, 1986 (L.A. Times Book Rev. prize 1986), The Arkansas Testament, 1987, Omeros, 1990 (W.H. Smith Literary award 1991), Selected Poetry, 1993, Antiles: Fragments of Epic Memory, 1993, The Bounty, 1997; (plays) Henry Christophe: A Chronicle in Seven Scenes, 1950, Henry Dernier, 1951, Wine of the Country, 1953, The Sea at Dauphin: A Play in One Act, 1953, Ione: A Play with Music, 1957, Drums and Colours: An Epic Drama, 1958 (Jamaica Drama Festival prize 1958), Ti-Jean and His Brothers, 1958, Malcochon; or, Six in the Rain, 1959, Dream on Monkey Mountain, 1967 (Obie award 1971), In a Fine Castle, 1970, The Joker of Seville, 1974, The Charlatan, 1974, O Babylon!, 1976, Remembrance, 1977, Pantomime, 1978, The Isle Is Full of Noises, 1982, The Last Carnival, 1986, Beef, No Chicken, 1986, A Branch of the Blue Nile, 1986, The Odyssey, 1992. Recipient Guinness award, 1961, Nat. Writer's Coun. prize Welsh Arts Coun., 1979, Queen Elizabeth II Gold Medal for poetry, 1988, Nobel Prize for Lit., 1992; Rockefeller Found. fellow, 1957, 58; Eugene O'Neill Found.-Wesleyan U. fellow, 1969; MacArthur Found. grantee, 1981; decorated Order of the Hummingbird, Trinidad and Tobago, 1969. Achievements include being the founder of Trinidad Theater workshop. Home: 71 Saint Marys St Boston MA 02215 Office: 165 Duke of Edinburgh Ave Diego Martin Trinidad and Tobago also: care Farrar Straus & Giroux 19 Union Sq W New York NY 10003-3304

WALCOTT, JOHN L. communications executive; b. Paterson, NJ, Aug. 29, 1949; s. Henry Richards Jr. and Katharine McCauley (Fearing) W.; m. Nancy Bittles, Aug. 11, 1973; children: Jennifer James, Allison Tierney, Elizabeth Bittles. BA, Williams Coll., 1971. With Ridgewood (NJ) News, 1972, The Record, Hackensack, NJ, 1972—77; econ. corr., nat. polit. corr., chief diplomatic corr. Newsweek, 1977—86; nat. security corr. Wall St. Jour., 1986—89; fgn. editor, nat. editor US News & World Report, 1989—96; fgn. editor, news editor Knight Ridder, Inc., 1997—2002, bur. chief, 2002—. U.S. Rep. U.N. Conf. on Media, Igls, Austria, 1983; mem. Georgetown U. Sch. Fgn. Svc. Leadership Seminar, Washington, 1985. Co-author: (with David C. Martin) Best Laid Plans: The Inside Story of America's War Against Terrorism, 1988. Named Disting. Friend, Georgetown U. Sch. Fgn. Svc., 1985—; recipient Edward Weintal prize Georgetown U., 1988, Edwin M. Hood award Nat. Press Club, 1983, Freedom of the Press award, 1995, Overseas Press Club award, 1983, 84, Newspaper Guild of N.Y. award, 1985. Mem. Overseas Writers Club (pres. 1986-88), White House Correspondents Assn., Sigma Delta Chi. Presbyterian. Office: Knight Ridder Newspapers One Metro Ctr Ste 1000 700 12th St NW Washington DC 20005-3994

WALCOTT, ROBERT, health facility administrator, priest; b. Boston, July 31, 1942; s. Robert and Rosamond (Pratt) W.; m. Diane Palmer, Sept. 3, 1966; 1 child, Sara. BA, Coll. of Wooster, 1964; MDiv, Ch. Div. Sch., Berkeley, Calif., 1967; M Healthcare Adminstrn., Ohio State U., 1972. Ordained Episc. priest, 1968. Planning specialist Health Planning and Devel. Coun., Wooster, Ohio, 1972—73, asst. dir., 1974—75, St. Joseph Hosp., Lorain, Ohio, 1975—78, assoc. dir., 1978—81; CEO Lakeside Meml. Hosp., Brockport, NY, 1981—85; adminstr. Dent Neurologic Inst., Buffalo, 1986—87, Oak Hills Nursing Ctr., Lorain, 1994; pastor Ch. of Transfiguration, Buffalo, 1988—91, St. Michael and All Angels Ch., Uniontown, Ohio, 1991—93; adminstr.-in-tng. Chapel Hill Cmty., Canal Fulton, Ohio, 1993; interim adminstr. Regina Health Ctr., Richfield, Ohio, 1994—95; adminstr. Ohio Pythian Sisters Home, Sophia Huntington Parker Home, Medina, 1995—2001, Homestead I and II Nursing Homes, Painesville, Ohio, 2002—02; longterm care ombudsman Luth. Met. Ministries, Cleve., 2002—. Housing com. Tremont Devel. Corp., Cleve., 1994—, bd. dirs., 1997-2002; steering com. Habitat for Humanity, Cleve., 1994-97; chair trustees Tremont West Devel. Corp., 2000-2002. Fellow Am. Coll. Healthcare Execs. Democrat. Avocations: travel, reading. Home: 2173 W 7th St Cleveland OH 44113-3621 Office: Luth Met Ministries 2800 Euclid Ave Ste 200 Cleveland OH 44115 E-mail: bobwal31@aol.com.

WALD, ARNOLD, gastroenterologist; b. N.Y.C., June 10, 1942; s. Jack and Ruth (Fox) W.; m. Ellen Faith Rashkow, June 26, 1966; children: Elissa Karen, Eric Lawrence. BA, Colgate U., 1964; MD, SUNY, N.Y.C., 1968. Diplomate Am. Bd. Internal Medicine, Am. Bd. Gastroenterology; lic. physician, Pa. Intern Kings County Hosp., Bklyn., 1968-69, resident, chief resident, 1969-71; fellow in medicine Johns Hopkins Hosp., Balt., 1973-75; asst. prof. medicine U. Pitts. Sch. Medicine, 1978-83, assoc. prof., 1983-91, prof., 1991—; chief gastroenterology divsn. Montefiore U. Hosp., Pitts., 1991-95; assoc. chief divsn. gastroenterology and hepatology U. Pitts. Med. Ctr., 1993—2000, dir. fellowship tng. and edn. divsn. gastroenterology, hepatology and nutrition, 1999—. Head gastroenterology unit Montefiore Hosp., Pitts., 1985-91; mem. adv. bd. Internat. Found. Bowel Dysfunction, 1992—; bd. dirs. Pitts. chpt. Nat. Found. Ileitis and Colitis, Inc., 1980-84. Contbr. articles to profl. jours and books. Maj. U.S. Army, 1971-73. Master Am. Coll. Gastroenterology (bd. trustees 1991-98, gov. western Pa. 1988-90, chmn. internat. rels. com. 1993); fellow ACP; mem. Am. Gastroent. Assn., Ctrl. Soc. Clin. Rsch. (councillor 1985-90, chmn. gastroent. sect. 1989-90), Am. Motility Soc., Internat. Found. for Functional Gastrointestinal Disorders, Gastroenterology Rsch. Group, Pa. Soc. Gastroenterology. Democrat. Jewish. Avocations: tennis, reading, hiking. Home: 1143 Shady Ave Pittsburgh PA 15232-2809 Office: U Pitts Med Ctr 200 Lothrop St Pittsburgh PA 15213-2546 Office Phone: 412-648-9241.

WALD, BERNARD JOSEPH, lawyer; b. Bklyn., Sept. 14, 1932; s. Max and Ruth (Mencher) W.; m. Francine Joy Weintraub, Feb. 2, 1964; children—David Evan, Kevin Mitchell. B.B.A. magna cum laude, CCNY; J.D. cum laude, NYU, 1955. Bar: N.Y. 1955, U.S. Dist. Ct. (so. dist.) N.Y. 1960, U.S. Dist. Ct. (ea. dist.) N.Y. 1960, U.S. Ct. Appeals (2d cir.) 1960, U.S. Supreme Ct. 1971. Mem. Herzfeld & Rubin, P.C. and predecessor firms, N.Y.C., 1955—. Mem. ABA, N.Y. State Bar Assn., Assn. Bar City N.Y., N.Y. County Lawyers Assn. Office: Herzfeld & Rubin PC 40 Wall St Ste 5400 New York NY 10005-2301 E-mail: bwald@herzfeld-rubin.com.

WALD, FRANCINE JOY WEINTRAUB (MRS. BERNARD J. WALD), physicist, academic administrator; b. Bklyn., Jan. 13, 1938; d. Irving and Minnie (Reisig) Weintraub; m. Bernard J. Wald, FEb. 2, 1964; children: David Evan, Kevin Mitchell. Student, Bklyn. Coll., 1955-57; BEE, CCNY, 1960; MS, Poly. Inst. Bklyn., 1962, PhD, 1969. Engr. Remington Rand Univac

divsn. Sperry Rand Corp., Phila., 1960; instr. Poly. Inst. Bklyn., 1962-64, adj. rsch. assoc., 1969-70; lectr. N.Y. C.C., Bklyn., 1969, 70; instr. sci. Friends Sem., N.Y.C., 1975-76, chmn. dept. sci., 1976-94; instr. sci., chmn. dept. sci. Nightingale-Bamford Sch., N.Y.C., 1994-99. Adj. asst. prof. NYU. NDEA fellow, 1962-64. Mem. AAAS, Am. Phys. Soc., Am. Assn. Physics Tchrs., Assn. Tchrs. in Ind. Schs., N.Y. Acad. Scis., Nat. Sci. Tchrs. Assn.; Sigma Xi, Tau Beta Pi, Eta Kappa Nu.

WALD, FRANCIS JOHN, state legislator; b. N.D., Apr. 8, 1935; s. Anton S. and Magdelena (Bosch) W.; m. Sharon Kay Mischel, 1961; children: Kirk James, Mark Allen, Jo Lynn, Laura, Cara, Maria, Michael, Joe. BSBA, U. N.D., 1959. Pres., ins. broker Wald Agy. Inc., Dickinson, N.D., 1973—; mem. from dist. 37 N.D. State Ho. of Reps., Bismarck, 1979-83, 85—, chmn. appropriations, edn. and environ. coms., speaker of the ho. Commr. Midwestern Higher Education Commission, 2001—. Mem. exec. com. Conf. of Ins. Legislators. Recipient Korean Occupation award. Mem. Dickenson C. of C. (past pres.), N.D. Profl. Ins. Agts., Am. Legion, Rotary, KC, Elks, Alpha Tau Omega. Address: 433 7th St E Dickinson ND 58601-4525

WALD, MICHAEL LEONARD, economist; b. Balt., Jan. 5, 1951; s. Leonard Marvin and Frances (Kosinski) Wald; m. Marlena Malmstedt, June 10, 1972. BA, Am. U., 1972. Mgr. Woodward and Lothrop Dept. Store, Washington, 1972-75, Hecht Co., Washington, 1975-76; store mgr. W.J. Sloane & Co., Washington, 1976-77; economist U.S. Bur. Labor Stats., Balt., 1977-85, Washington, 1985-86, Atlanta, 1986-96, S.E. regional economist, 1996—. Lectr. fed. compensation issues. Mem. editl. bd. HR Atlanta, 1993—95; contbr. articles to profl. jours.; reviewer Monthly Labor Rev., 1992—, peer reviewer ACA Jour., 1995—99. Bd. dirs. Athens (Ga.) Habitat for Humanity, 1990—93; venue mktg. liaison mgr. 1996 Centennial Olympic Games. Recipient Commr.'s award for Outstanding Mgmt. Performance, 2000, Sec.'s Exceptional Achievement award, 2001. Mem.: Atlanta Econ. Club (officer 2003—04), Indsl. Rels. Rsch. Assn., Nat. Assn. Bus. Econ., Atlanta Compensation Assn. (v.p. 1992—94, pres. 1996), World at Work, Alpha Tau Omega. Avocations: reading, home improvement, travel, labor history, economic development. Home: 5015 Fawn Valley Dr Loganville GA 30052-3879 Office: US Bur Labor Stats 61 Forsyth St SW Ste 7t50 Atlanta GA 30303-8817 Office Phone: 404-331-3415. Business E-Mail: wald_m@bls.gov.

WALD, NIEL, public health educator; b. N.Y.C., Oct. 1, 1925; s. Albert and Rose (Fischel) W.; m. Lucienne Hill, May 24, 1953; children: David, Phillip. AB, Columbia U., 1945; MD, NYU, 1948. Sr. hematologist Atomic Bomb Casualty Commn., Hiroshima, Japan, 1954-57; head biologist health physics divsn. Oak Ridge Nat. Lab., 1957-58; med. rsch. and tchg. specializing in radiation medicine and cytogenetics Pitts., 1958—; mem. faculty U. Pitts. Grad. Sch. Pub. Health and Med. Sch., 1958—2004, prof. radiation health, 1962-91, prof. environ. and occupl. health, 1991—2004, prof. radiology, 1965—2004; prof. human genetics U. Pitts., 1991—2004, prof. emeritus, 2004; chmn. dept. radiation health U. Pitts. Grad. Sch. Pub. Health and Med. Sch., 1969-76, 77-89, chmn. dept. occupl. health, 1975-76, chmn. dept. indsl. environ. health scis., 1976-77. Dir. radiation medicine dept. Presbyn.-Univ. Hosp., 1966—; med. dir. Clin. Cytogenetics Lab., U. Pitts., 1982-99, radiation cytogenetics cons., 1999—; dir. U.S. Dept. Energy postdoctoral fellowship program in radiation scis., 1997-2004; cons. U.S. NRC Office of Nuc. Materials Safety and Safeguards, mem. adv. panel for decontamination of Three Mile Island Nuc. Power Sta. Unit 2, 1981-93, cons. adv. com. on reactor safeguards, 1989-94; mem. U.S. working group on health effects, U.S.-USSR Joint Coordinating Com. for Civilian Nuc. Reactor Safety, 1989-92; cons. USN, nuc. industries and utilities; chmn. radiol. health study sect. USPHS, 1967-71; mem. Nat. Coun. Radiation Protection and Measurements, 1969-81, consociate mem., 1981—; mem. Gov. Pa. Adv. Com. Atomic Energy Devel. and Radiation Control, 1966-84, chmn., 1974-76; mem. Pa. Dept. Environ. Protection adv. com. on low level radioactive waste disposal, 1985—; mem. U.S. nuc. tech. adv. group Internat. Stds. Orgn., 2003--. Contbr. numerous articles to sci. and med. publs. Served to capt. M.C. USAF, 1952-54. Recipient Health Physics Faculty Rsch. award U.S. Dept. Energy, 1992-95. Mem. Health Physics Soc. (pres. 1973-74), Am. Pub. Health Assn. (governing coun. 1971-73, program devel. bd. 1973-74), Radiation Rsch. Soc. (assoc. editor jour. 1965-68), Soc. Nuc. Medicine (assoc. editor jour. 1959-69), Am. Soc. Human Genetics, Am. Coll. Occupl. & Environ. Medicine, AAAS, AMA, Internat. Soc. Hematology. Achievements include research in the diagnosis and treatment of accidental human radiation injury, in human radiation dosimetry by automatic image analysis of radiation-induced chromosome aberrations, in the cytogenetics of murine radiation-induced leukemia and in health studies of irradiated human populations in U.S., Japan and Russia. Office: U Pitts Grad Sch Pub Health A-744 Crabtree Hl Pittsburgh PA 15261-0001 E-mail: wald@pitt.edu.

WALD, PATRICIA MCGOWAN, retired federal judge; b. Torrington, Conn., Sept. 16, 1928; d. Joseph F. and Margaret (O'Keefe) McGowan; m. Robert L. Wald, June 22, 1952; children: Sarah, Douglas, Johanna, Frederica, Thomas. BA, Conn. Coll., 1948; LLB, Yale U., 1951; HHD (hon.), Mt. Vernon Jr. Coll., 1980; LLD, LLD, Hofstra U., 1991, New Eng. Coll., 1991, Vermont Law Sch., 1995, Yale U., 2001. Bar: D.C. 1952. Clk. to Hon. Jerome Frank U.S. Ct. Appeals, 1951—52; assoc. Arnold, Fortas & Porter, Washington, 1952—53; mem. D.C. Crime Commn., 1964—65; atty. Office of Criminal Justice, 1967—68, Neighborhood Legal Svc., Washington, 1968—70; co-dir. Ford Found. Project on Drug Abuse, 1970, Ctr. for Law and Social Policy, 1971—72, Mental Health Law Project, 1972—77; asst. atty. gen. for legis. affairs U.S. Dept. Justice, Washington, 1977—79; judge U.S. Ct. Appeals (D.C. cir.), 1979—99, chief judge, 1986—91; judge Internat. Criminal Tribunal for Former Yugoslavia, The Hague, Netherlands, 1999—2001. Author: Law and Poverty, 1965; co-author: Bail in the United States, 1964, Dealing with Drug Abuse, 1973; bd. editors: ABA Jour., 1978—86; contbr. articles to profl. jours. Trustee Ford Found., 1972—77, Phillips Exeter Acad., 1975—77, Agnes Meyer Found., 1976—77, Conn. Coll., 1976—77; active Carnegie Coun. on Children, 1972—77. Mem.: ABA-Ctrl. and Ea. European Law Inst. (exec. bd. 1994—99), Inst. Justice Initiative, Am. Acad. Arts and Scis., Am. Law Inst. (coun. mem. 1979—, exec. com. 1985—99, 2d v.p. 1988—93, 1st v.p. 1993—98), Open Soc. Inst. (chair justice initiative 2002—, chair), Phi Beta Kappa. Office: 2101 Connecticut Ave NW Washington DC 20008

WALD, RICHARD CHARLES, broadcasting executive; b. N.Y.C. s. Joseph S. and Lily (Forstate) W.; m. Edith May Leslie; children: Matthew Leslie, Elizabeth Tole, Jonathan Simon. BA, MA, Columbia U.; AB, Clare Coll., Cambridge. From reporter to mng. editor N.Y. Herald Tribune, 1955-66; asst. mng. editor Washington Post, 1967; exec. v.p. Whitney Communications Corp., N.Y.C., 1968; pres. NBC News, 1968-77; sr. v.p. ABC News, 1978; prof. Columbia U., 1999. Chmn. bd. Columbia Daily Spectator. Annotator: (with James Bellows) The World of Jimmy Breslin, 1967. Office: ABC News 47 W 66th St New York NY 10023-6290 E-mail: richard.c.wald@abc.com.

WALD, SYLVIA, artist; b. Phila., Oct. 30, 1915; Ed., Moore Inst. Art, Sci. and Industry. One-woman shows include U. Louisville, 1945, 49, Kent State Coll., 1945, Nat. Serigraph Soc., 1946, Grand Central Moderns, N.Y.C., 1957, Devorah Sherman Gallery, Chgo., 1960, New Sch., 1967, Book Gallery, White Plains, N.Y., 1968, Benson Gallery, Bridgehampton, L.I., 1977, Knoll Internat., Munich, 1979, Amerika Havs, Munich, 1979, Aaron Berman Gallery, N.Y.C., 1981, Hirschltadler Gallery, 1994, New Britain (Conn.) Mus., 1994, Dongah Art Gallery, Seoul, Korea, 1995, Hanlim Art Gallery, Daejun, 1995-96, Kwanju City Art Mus, Pusanm Korea, Dong Shin U., Kwangju, 1996, Chosun U. Mus., Kwanju City, 2001, Chosun Univ. Mus. Art, Kwangsu, Korea, 2002, Tenri Gallery, N.Y.C., 2004; exhibited in group shows at Nat. Sculpture Soc., 1940, Sculpture Internat., Phila., 1940, Chgo. Art Inst., 1941, Bklyn. Mus., 1975, Library of Congress, 1943, 52, 58, Smithsonian Instn., 1954, Internat. Print Exhbn., Salzburg and Vienna, 1952, 2d Sao Paulo Biennial, 1953, N.Y. Cultural Center, 1973, Mus. Modern Art, N.Y.C., 1975, Benson Gallery, Bridgehampton, L.I., 1982, Dumon-Landis Gallery, New Brunswick, N.J., 1982-83, Suzuki Gallery, N.Y.C., 1982, Sid Deutch Gallery, N.Y.C., 1983, Aaron Berman Gallery, N.Y.C., 1983, Full House Gallery, Kingston, N.J., 1984, Nabi Gallery, Sag Harbor, N.Y., 1989, Worcester Mus., 1991, Boston Mus. Fine Arts, 1991, Hirschl & Adler Gallery, N.Y.C., 1993, Parrish Mus., Southampton, 2002, others; represented in permanent collections Aetna Oil Co., AAUW, Ball State Tchrs. Coll., Bibliotheque Nat., Paris, Bklyn. Mus., Howard U., State U. Iowa, Library of Congress, U. Louisville, Nat. Gallery, Mus. Modern Art, Phila. Mus., N.C. Mus., Rose Mus. Art at Brandeis U., Whitney Mus., N.Y.C., Finch Coll. Mus., N.Y.C., U. Nebr., Ohio U., U. Okla., Princeton, Victoria and Albert Mus., Walker Gallery, Worcester (Mass.) Art Mus., Guggenheim Mus., N.Y.C., Grunewald Mus., UCLA, Rutgers Mus., N.J., Aschenbach Collection Mus., San Francisco, Grunewald Coll. Mus. UCLA, Wellesley Coll.; acquisitions Yale U. Art Gallery, 1998, Cleve. Mus., 1998; contbr. articles to profl. jours. Address: 417 Lafayette St New York NY 10003-7005

WALDBAUM, JANE COHN, art history educator; b. Jan. 28, 1940; d. Max Arthur and Sarah (Waldstein) Cohn. BA, Brandeis U., 1962; MA, Harvard U., 1964, PhD, 1968. Rsch. fellow in classical archaeology Harvard U., Cambridge, Mass., 1968-70, 72-73; from asst. prof. to assoc. prof. U. Wis., Milw., 1973-84, prof. art history, 1984—2002, chmn. dept., 1982-85, 86-89, 91-92, adj. prof. anthropology, 2002—. Dorot rsch. prof. W.F. Albright Inst. Archaeol. Rsch., Jerusalem, 1990-91; vis. scholar Hebrew U. Jerusalem, 1989-91. Author: From Bronze to Iron, 1978, Metalwork from Sardis, 1983; author (with others), co-editor: Sardis Report I, 1975; mem. editl. bd. Bull. Am. Schs. Oriental Rsch., 1994-98, Near Eastern Archaeology, 2000-2002; contbr. numerous articles to profl. jours. Woodrow Wilson Found. fellow, dissertation fellow, 1962-63, 65-66, NEH postdoctoral rsch., Jerusalem, 1989-90; grantee Am. Philos. Soc., 1972, NEH, summer 1975, U. Wis.-Milw. Found., 1983. Mem. Am. Schs. Oriental Rsch. (bd. trustees 2003—), Soc. for Archaeol. Sci., Israel Exploration Soc., Archaeol. Inst. Am. (exec. com. 1975-77, chmn. com. on membership programs 1977-81, nominating com. 1984, chmn. com. on lecture program 1985-87, acad. trustee 1993-98, 1st v.p. 1999—2002, pres. 2003-, com. profl. responsibilities 1993—, fellowships com. 1993-99, gold medal com. 1993-99, chair 1996-97, Near East Archaeology interest group 1993—, chair ann. meeting com. 1999—2002, chair regional meetings com. 1999—2002, pers. com., governance com., devel. com., fin. com.), W.F. Albright Inst. Archaeol. Rsch. (trustee 1996—, mem. governance com. 1996—), Wis. Soc. Jewish Learning (trustee 1993-99), Milw. Soc. Archaeol. Inst. (bd. dirs., pres. 1983-85, 91-95, 97-99), Phi Beta Kappa. Office: U Wis Dept Anthropology PO Box 413 Milwaukee WI 53201-0413 E-mail: JCW@uwm.edu.

WALDECK, JOHN WALTER, JR., lawyer; b. Cleve., May 3, 1949; s. John Walter Sr. and Marjorie Ruth (Palenschat) W.; m. Cheryl Gene Cutter, Sept. 10, 1977; children: John III, Matthew, Rebecca. BS, John Carroll U., 1973; JD, Cleve. State U., 1977. Bar: Ohio 1977. Product applications chemist Synthetic Products Co., Cleve., 1969-76; assoc. Arter & Hadden, Cleve., 1977-85, ptnr., 1986-88, Porter, Wright, Morris and Arthur, Cleve., 1988-90, ptnr. in charge, 1990-96; ptnr. Walter & Haverfield LLP, Cleve., 1996—, mem. exec. com., 2003—. Bd. advisors Litigation Mgmt., Inc., 2000—. Chmn. Bainbridge Twp. Bd. Zoning Appeals, Chagrin Falls, Ohio, 1984-94; trustee Greater Cleve. chpt. Lupus Found. Am., 1978-91, sec., 1979-86; trustee LeBlond Housing Corp., Cleve., 1990-96, sec., 1996, Univ. Circle, Inc., 1993-97, Fairmount Ctr. for Performing and Fine Arts, Novelty, Ohio, 1993-96, sect., 1994-95; bd. dirs. Geauga County Mental Health Recovery Svc. Bd., Chardon, Ohio, 1988-97, treas., 1991-93, vice-chmn., 1993-95, chmn., 1995-97; mem. bd. advisors Palliative Care Svcs., Cleve. Clinic Cancer Ctr., 1989-91. Mem. Ohio State Bar Assn. (real property sect. bd. govs. 1992), Greater Cleve. Bar Assn. (real property, corp. banking sect, co-chair real estate law inst. 1990, 95, 96). Roman Catholic. Avocations: beekeeping, gardening, jogging. Home: 18814 Rivers Edge Dr W Chagrin Falls OH 44023-4968 Office: Walter & Haverfield LLP suite 3500 1301 E Ninth St Cleveland OH 44114 Office Phone: 216-781-1212. Business E-Mail: jwaldeck@walterhav.com.

WALDEGRAVE, LORD (LORD WALDEGRAVE OF NORTH HILL), financial services company executive; b. Aug. 15, 1946; s. Earl Waldegrave; m. Caroline Burrows, 1977; 4 children. Grad., Corpus Christi Coll., U. Oxford, Eng. Fellow All Souls Coll., U. Oxford, Eng., 1971-86; mem. ctrl. policy rev. staff Cabinet Office, 1971-73; mem. polit. staff Office of Prime Min., London, 1973-74; head Office Leader of Opposition, London, 1974-75; justice of peace Inner London Juvenile Ct., 1975-79; M.P. for Bristol West Ho. of Commons, London, 1979-97; parliamentary under sec. state Brit. Dept. Edn. and Sci., 1981-83, Brit. Dept. Environ., 1983-85, min. state for environ. and countryside, 1985-87, min. state for planning, 1986-88, min. state for housing, 1987-88; min. state Fgn. and Commonwealth Office, 1988-90; sec. state for health, 1990-92; chancellor Duchy of Lancaster, 1992-94; min. agr., fisheries and food London, 1994-95; chief sec. to treasury, 1995-97; exec. dir. Dresdner Kleinwort Benson, London, 1998—. Dir. Bank of Ireland Fin. Svcs. (U.K.), plc, FLIT plc, Waldegrave Farms Ltd., Henry Sotheran Ltd.; chmn. Rhodes Trust, 2002—, Nat. Mus. Sci. and Industry, 2002—. Author: The Binding of Leviathan, 1977. Kennedy Fellow Harvard U., U.S.A., Disting. Fellow Au Souls Coll., Oxford, Eng. Mem. Beefsteak Club, Pratt's Club, Clifton Club (Bristol). Office: Dresdner Kleinwort Wasserstein 20 Fenchurch St London EC3 P3DB England

WALDEK, DAVID P. pharmaceutical executive; BS in Econs., MBA in Fin., U. Rochester. Sr. acct. Ernst & Young; from asst. contr. to contr. NAMIC; v.p. fin. Boston Sci./NAMIC; CFO, treas. Albany (N.Y.) Molecular Rsch., Inc. Office: Albany Molecular Rsch Inc 21 Corporate Cir Albany NY 12212-5098

WALDEN, DANA, broadcast executive; BA in Comm., U. So. Calif. Formerly with Bender, Goldman & Helper; former v.p. mktg. Arsenio Hall Comm., Paramount; former sr. v.p. media and corp. rels. 20th Century Fox TV, v.p. current programming, 1994—96, former v.p. drama, former sr. v.p. drama, former exec. v.p. drama devel., co-pres., 1999—. Named to Women in Entertainment Power List, Hollywood Reporter, 1999—2003. Mem.: Hollywood Radio and TV Soc. (v.p. 2003—). Office: 20th Century Fox TV 10201 W Pico Blvd Bldg 88 Rm 29 Los Angeles CA 90035

WALDEN, GREG, congressman; b. The Dalles, Oreg., Jan. 10, 1957; m. Mylene Walden; 1 child. BS in Journalism, U. Oreg., 1981. Owner Columbia Gorge Broadcasters, Inc., The Dalles, 1986—; mem. Oreg. Ho. of Reps., 1989-95, house majority leader, 1991-93; mem. Oreg. Senate, 1995-97, asst. majority leader, 1995-97; press sec., chief of staff Congressman Denny Smith, Washington, 1981-86; mem. U.S. Congress from 2d Oreg. dist., Washington, 1999—, mem. com. on energy and commerce, com. on resources. Dir. Columbia Bancorp. Bd. dirs., exec. com. Assoc. Oreg. Industires; bd. dirs. Oreg. Health Scis. Found.; former dir. Hood River Meml. Hosp. Named Outstanding Young Oregonian, Oreg. Jaycees, 1991, Legislator of the Yr., Nat. Rep. Legislators Assn., 1993. Mem. Hood River C. of C., Nat. Fedn. Ind. Bus., Elks, Rotary. Republican. Office: US Ho Reps 1404 Longworth HOB Washington DC 20515 also: 843 E Main St Ste 400 Medford OR 97504-7137 E-mail: greg.walden@mail.house.gov.

WALDEN, JAMES WILLIAM, accountant, educator; b. Jellico, Tenn., Mar. 5, 1936; s. William Evert and Bertha L. (Faulkner) Walden; m. Eva June Selvia, Jan. 16, 1957 (dec. Aug. 1988); 1 child, James William; m. Hattie Nan Lamb, Jan. 6, 1990 (div. June 1992); m. Janet Faulkner, Aug. 12, 1993 (div. May 2001); m. Louise Davis, Apr. 28, 2004. BS, Miami U., Oxford, Ohio, 1963; MBA, Xavier U., Cin., 1966. CPA, Ohio. Tchr. math. Middletown (Ohio) City Sch. Dist., 1963-67, Fairfield (Ohio) High Sch., 1967-69; instr. accounting Sinclair Community Coll., Dayton, Ohio, 1969-72, asst. prof., 1972-75, assoc. prof., 1975-78, prof., 1978-89, prof. emeritus, 1991—. Cons., public acct.; mem. adj. faculty in acctg. Capital U., 1980—. Group comdr., fin. officer, chief staff Ohio Wing, CAP. Served with USAF, 1954-59. Mem.: Ohio Soc. CPAs, Greater Hamilton Estate Planning Coun., Nat. Soc. Pub. Accts., Pub. Accts. Soc. Ohio (pres. S.W. chpt. 1985—86), Springboro C. of C. (bd. dirs., treas.), Kiwanis (pres. Springboro chpt.), Butler County Torch Club, Lions, Rotary, Am. Legion (life), Beta Alpha Psi. Home: PO Box 469 Springboro OH 45066-0469 Office: Sinclair C C 265 N Main St Springboro OH 45066-9255 Office Phone: 937-748-3736.

WALDEN, JANET C. lawyer; AB, Brown U., 1976; JD, NYU, 1979. Bar: N.Y. 1979. Assoc. Rubin Baum Levin Constant & Friedman, N.Y.C., 1979-86, Schulte, Roth & Zabel LLP, N.Y.C., from 1986, ptnr. Mem. ABA, Assn. Bar City N.Y. Office: Schulte Roth & Zabel LLP 900 #d Ave New York NY 10022 E-mail: janet.walden@srz.com.

WALDEN, JOHN, retail executive; married; 5 children. B, U. Ill.; JD, Ill. Inst. Tech.; M, Northwestern U. Former exec. Storage Tech. Corp., Ameritech Corp.; former pres., COO Peapod, Inc., Skokie, Ill.; pres., Best Buy.com subs. Best Buy Co., Inc., 1999—2002, exec. v.p. human capital and leadership, 2002—. Office: Best Buy Co Inc 110 SE 6th St Fort Lauderdale FL 33301

WALDEN, JOSEPH LAWRENCE, career officer; b. Paducah, Ky., Oct. 2, 1956; s. Thomas Lorenzo and Betty Jo (Miller) W.; m. Julia Kay Johnson, Oct. 9, 1982; children: Amber Marie, Bobbi Michelle. BS in Rural Sociology, N.C. State U., 1978; MBA, Fla. Inst. Tech., Melbourne, 1988; MS in Sys. Mgmt., Fla. Inst. Tech., 1989; grad., USAF Command and Staff Coll., 1990, U.S. Army/Command Gen. Staff, 1992, U.S. Air War Coll., 1997; MS in Strategic Planning, U.S. Army Command/Gen. Staff Coll., 2001. Commd. U.S. Army, 1978, advanced through grades col., to date, supply platoon leader 25th Inf. divsn., 1979-81, supply control officer, 1981-82, installation supply officer Signal Sch., 1983, brigade logistics officer 2d Signal Brigade, 1983-84; co. comdr. Co. B, 3rd Batallion, 2d Signal Brigade, Ft. Gordon, 1984-86; logistics plans officer Combat Devel., Quartermaster Sch., Ft. Lee, Va., 1988-89; chief gen. support U.S. Army Quartermaster Sch., Ft. Lee, 1989-91; assigned to U.S. Army Command and Gen. Staff Coll., Ft. Leavenworth, Kans., 1991-92; exec. officer 19th Corps Materiel Mgmt. Ctr., Wiesbaden, Germany, 1992-94; chief supply mgmt. 3D Corps Support Command, Wiesbaden, 1994-95; comdr. Materiel Mgmt. Ctr., Ft. Irwin, Calif., 1995-97; program mgr. Logistics Reengring., Ft. Lee, Va., 1997-99; sr. fellow adv. operational art Ft. Leavenworth, Kans., 1999-2000; mem. faculty U.S. Army Sch. Advanced Mil. Studies, 2000-2001; comdr. nat. tng. Ctr. Theater Support Command, Ft. Irwin, Calif., 2001—03; dir. Sch. of Command Preparation, Ft. Leavenworth, Kans., 2003—04, Supply Chain Rsch. Inst., 2004—. Mem. adj. faculty St. Leo Coll., Ft. Lee, 1988-91; mem. faculty City Coll. of Chgo., 1994-95, Webster Univ., 2004—; pres. Walden Fitness Systems, Ft. Leavenworth, 1984-92. Author: The Forklifts Have Nothing To Do!, 2003; contbr. articles to profl. jour. Mem. Bldg. Code Appeals Bd., City of Hopewell, 1988-91; vol. staff Negro Leagues Baseball Mus., Kansas City, Mo., 2001. Armed Forces Powerlifting Champion, 1983, Va. State Powerlifting Champion, 1990, Kans. State Powerlifting Champion, 1992, Nat. Powerlifting Champion, 1992, European Armed Forces Powerlifting Champion, 1993, 94; Supply Chain Practitioner of Yr., 2004. Mem. APICS (cert. fellow in prodn. and inventory mgmt.), Internat. Soc. of Logistics, Warehousing Edn. and Rsch. Coun. (mem. edn. com.), Material Handling Mgmt. Soc., Va. Assn. of U.S. Powerlifting Fedn. (pres. 1989-91), U.S. Golf Assn., Am. Sunbathing Assn., Fellowship Christian Athletes, Fla. Sheriffs Assn., San Diego Zool. Soc., Assn. Quartermasters, Mus. Tolerance, Save the Manatee Club. Republican. Methodist. Avocations: powerlifting (1992 Nat. Champion), naturist, golfing, top 20 logistics exec. for 2002-2003. E-mail: joewalden@aol.com.

WALDEN, MARY L, nurse, educator; b. Mishawaka, Ind., May 19, 1954; d. Bob and Wanda Butler; m. Jerry L Walden, May 11, 1974; 1 child, Amy Catherine. ADN, NE Miss. C.C., 1973—75; BSN, Univ. of North Ala., 1996—97; MSN, Alcorn State U., 2002—04. Registered RN, Miss. Bd. of Nursing, Miss., 1975, cert. Wound, Ostomy, and Continence Nurse, Wound, Ostomy, and Continence Nursing Bd., 1997. RN Gilmore Meml. Hosp., Amory, Miss., 1975—87, Miss. Pub. Health, Amory, Miss., 1987—91; home health care North Miss. Med. Ctr., Tupelo, Miss., 1991—2002; wound care mgr. Gilmore Meml. Hosp., Amory, Miss., 2002—. V.p. U. of North Ala. Nursing Honor Soc., Florence, Ala., 2004—. Pres. Wound, Ostomy, Continence Nursing Certification Bd., Milw., 2002—. Recipient Wound, Ostomy, Continence Nurse of the Yr., Miss. Nurses Assn., 2001, J.T. GIlbert award for Clin. Excellence, Miss. Home Care Assn., 1993. Mem.: WOCN Soc., Miss. Nurses Assn., Sigma Theta Tau. Presbyn. Home: 30047 Lake Monroe Aberdeen MS 03973 Office: Gilmore Meml Hosp 1105 Earl Frye Blvd Amory MS 38821 E-mail: mwalden@direcway.com.

WALDEN, PHILIP MICHAEL, recording company executive, publishing company executive; b. Greenville, S.C., Jan. 11, 1940; s. Clemiel Barton and Carolyn Hayes (McClendon) W.; m. Peggy Hackett, Sept. 13, 1969; children: Philip Michael, Amantha Starr. AB in Econs., Mercer U., 1962. Pres. Phil Walden & Assocs., 1961, Capricorn Records, Inc., 1969—. Campaign chmn. Macon Muscular Dystrophy Assn., 1975; chmn. Macon Heritage Found.; mem. In-Town Macon Neighborhood Assn.; Mem. nat. finance com. Jimmy Carter for Pres.; mem. Com. for Preservation of the White House; mem. nat. adv. bd. NORML; bd. dirs. Brandywine Conservancy; mem. Presdl. Inaugural Com., 1977; trustee Ga. Trust for Historic Preservation., Mercer Univ. Press, Otis Redding Meml. Found.; founder Otis Redding Scholarship Fund, Mercer U., Phil Walden scholarship; bd. dirs. Atlanta Preservation Ctr., Otis Redding Found. Served to 1st lt. Adj. Gen. Corps AUS, 1963-65. Recipient Gold and Platinum Record awards, pub. awards; Big Bear award Mercer U., 1975; Martin Luther King, Jr. Humanitarian award, 1977; Human Relations award Am. Jewish Com., 1978 Mem. Common Cause, Middle Ga. Hist. Soc., Nat. Assn. Rec. Arts and Scis., Rec. Industry Assn. Am. (dir.), Nat. Assn. Rec. Merchandisers, Phi Delta Theta Alumni Assn., Atlanta Coll. of Art, Camp Sunshine, Ga. Trust for Historic Preservation, Capitol City Club.

WALDEN, SHELTON HARRISON, radio personality, educator; s. Herman B. Walden and Sarah Louise Harrison. BA in Polit. Sci., Fordham U., 1984. Radio broadcaster WBAI Radio, N.Y.C., 1986—. Prodr., radio host, jounalist Walden's Pond. Home: 10 River Rd #10E New York NY 10044 Office: Walden's Pond Prodns 10 River Rd #10E New York NY 10044 E-mail: shelton@waldenspond.com.

WALDER, DEBBY JEAN, program director, quality manager, nursing service administrator, nurse, educator; b. Watertown, S.D., Nov. 25, 1947; d. James Russell and Gladys Elizabeth (Owen) W. BSN with honors, S.D. State U., 1970; MSN, U. Minn., 1977. Staff nurse VAMC, Mpls., 1970-71, instr., 1971-75, coord., 1976-77, trainee-assoc. chief nursing svc. for edn., 1977, assoc. chief nursing svc. for edn. Wilmington, Del., 1977-80, Richmond, Va., 1980-83, chief nurse svc. Huntington, W.Va., 1983-85, Cin., 1985-87; quality mgmt. coord. VA Hosp., Madison, Wis., 1987-91; clin. program mgr., dir. risk mgmt. VA Hdqrs., Washington, 1991-96, dir. risk mgmt., program dir. ext. peer rev. program, 1995—. Adj. faculty Med. Coll. Va., Richmond, 1980-82; basic cardiac life support instr.-trainer Am. Heart Assn., Richmond, 1980-83; clin. prof. Marshall U. Sch. Nursing, Huntington, 1983-85. Mem. task force Richmond Area chpt. Am. Heart Assn. Recipient Outstanding Cardiopulmonary Resuscitation Instr. award Richmond Area chpt. Am. Heart Assn., 1982, Achievement award VAMC, Richmond, 1983, Recognition award for excellence in mgmt., VAMC, Huntington, 1983, Spl. Contbn. award, 1992-95, 98, 99, Unsung Heroes award, 1994; Bush Found. fellow, 1975-76. Mem. Nat. Assn. Quality Assurance Profls., Phi Kappa Phi, Sigma Theta Tau (Phi chpt. scholar 1969-70), Nat. Assn. Quality Assurance Profls., Pi Lambda Theta. Roman Catholic. Office: VA Cen Office Office Quality Mgmt 810 Vermont Ave NW Washington DC 20420-0001

WALDERA, WAYNE EUGENE, crisis management specialist; b. Cayuga, N.D., Mar. 23, 1930; s. Bernard Cyril and Eleanor Nee (Kugler) W.; m. Eva Jenzene Personius, Jan. 13, 1958; children: Anthony, Lori, Mia, Shauna. BSBA, N.D. State U., 1952. With Gamble-Skogmo, 1954-88; pres. Gamble div. Gamble-Skogmo, Mpls., 1972-88; pres., CEO Retail Resource Co., Mpls., 1988-89, Amdura Corp., Denver, 1989-92, also bd. dirs.; chmn. Sullivan Waldera, Inc., Mpls., 1992-93; prin., CEO Waldera & Co. Inc., Mpls., 1993—. 1st lt. USAF, 1952-54. Home: 12125 62nd St Waconia MN 55387-9411 Office: Waldera & Co Inc 15500 Wayzata Blvd Ste 604-208 Wayzata MN 55391-1435 E-mail: wwaldera@uswest.net.

WALDHAUSEN, JOHN ANTON, retired surgeon, educator, editor; b. N.Y.C., May 22, 1929; s. Max. H. and Agnes H. (Stettner) W.; m. Marian Trescher, June 4, 1957; children: John H., Robert Rodney, Anthony Gordon Scarlett. BS magna cum laude, Coll. Great Falls, 1950; MD, St. Louis U., 1954. Diplomate Am. Bd. Surgery (bd. dirs. 1985-88), Am. Bd. Thoracic Surgery (bd. dirs. 1989-95). Intern Johns Hopkins Hosp., 1954-55, resident, 1955-57; clin. asst. Nat. Heart and Lung Inst., NIH, 1957-59; resident Hosp. U. Pa., 1959, Ind. U. Med. Ctr., 1960-62; practice medicine specializing in cardiothoracic surgery Indpls., 1962-66, Phila., 1966-70; mem. staff Milton S. Hershey Med. Ctr., Hershey, Pa., 1969-96. From instr. to asst. prof. Ind. U. Med. Ctr., 1962—66; assoc. prof. surgery U. Pa., Phila., 1966—70; prof. surgery Pa. State U. Coll. Medicine/Milton S. Hershey Med. Ctr, 1966—83, chmn. dept. surgery, 1969—94, sr. mem. grad. faculty, 1970—94, interim provost, dean, 1972—73, assoc. dean health care, 1973—75, assoc. dean and dir. Univ. Physicians, 1993—96, prof. surgery, 1994—99, J.W. Oswald prof., 1983—94, J.W. Oswald prof. emeritus, 1999—; trustee U. Great Falls, Mont., 2001—04. Mem. editl. bd. Jour. Cardiovasc. Surgery, 1985-93, Jour. Pediatric Surgery, 1972-78, Jour. Thoracic and Cardiovasc. Surgery, 1982, editor, 1994-2000; cons. editor Archives of Surgery, 1972-74; contbr. chpts. to books and articles to med. jours. Served with USPHS, 1957-59. Recipient Career Devel. award USPHS, 1964. Fellow AAAS; mem. AMA, ACS (chpt. pres. 1974-75, gov. 1979-85, chmn. adv. coun. cardiothoracic surgery 1992-97), Am. Acad. Pediat., Am. Assn. Surgery of Trauma, Am. Coll. Cardiology (sec. 1981-82, trustee 1984-89, mem. editl. bd. jour. 1983, assoc. editor 1986-89), Am. Fedn. Clin. Rsch., Am. Heart Assn., Am. Physiol. Soc., Am. Soc. Artificial Internal Organs, Am. Assn. Thoracic Surgery (1st v.p. 1990-91, pres. 1991-92), Am. Surg. Assn. (1st v.p. 1984-85), Ctrl. Surg. Assn., Internat. Cardiovasc. Soc. (chpt. recorder 1969-74), Pa. Assn. Thoracic Surgery (pres. 1977-78), Thoracic Surgery Dirs. Assn. (pres. 1977-79), Societe International de Chirurgie (membership chmn. 1987-92, treas. 1992-94), Soc. Clin. Surgery (treas. 1971-80, v.p. 1981-82, Pres. 1982-83), Soc. Surg. Chairmen, Soc. Thoracic Surgeons, Soc. Univ. Surgeons, Soc. Vascular Surgery, So. Surg. Assn., Sigma Xi, Alpha Omega Alpha. Home: 515 Bridgeview Dr Lemoyne PA 17043 Office: Pa State U Coll Med MS Hershey Med Ctr PO Box 850 Hershey PA 17033-0850 Office Phone: 717-531-8330. Personal E-mail: jwaldhausen@aol.com.

WALDHAUSEN, JOHN HENRY TRESCHER, pediatric surgeon, educator; b. Washington, D.C., Sept. 19, 1958; s. John Anton and Marian Trescher Waldhausen; m. Donna Hosterman, Dec. 18, 1983 (div. Nov. 2002); children: Tessa Marie, Elizabeth Trescher. BA, Haverford Coll., 1980; MD, Pa. State Coll., 1986. Resident U. Va., Charlottesville, 1986—92; fellow in pediat. surgery Children's Hosp., U. Wash., Seattle, 1992—94; attending surgeon Children's Hosp. and Regional Med. Ctr., Seattle, 1994—, dir. surg. edn., 1996—, program dir. pediatric surgery fellowship, 2004. Asst. prof. surgery U. Wash. Sch. Medicine, Seattle, 1994—2000, assoc. prof. surgery, 2000—, assoc. dir. 4th yr. med. student surg. clerkship, 2001—. Contbr. chapters to books, articles to profl. jours.; author: (manual) Pediatric General & Thoracic Surgery Residents Manual, 2003. Named one of Best Drs. in Seattle, Seattle Mag., 2001—02, Best Drs. in Am., Consumers Rsch. Coun. of Am., 2004; recipient Lange Med. Pub. award, 1986, Acad. Excellence, UpJohn Pharm., 1990. Fellow: Am. Acad. Pediat., Am. Coll. Surgeons; mem.: Am. Pediat. Surg. Assn. Episcopalian. Avocations: hiking, reading, sailing. Office: Children's Hosp and Regional Med Ctr 4800 Sand Point Way NE Seattle WA 98105 Office Phone: 206-987-2039. Business E-Mail: john.waldhausen@seattlechildrens.org.

WALDHORN, ARTHUR, literature educator, researcher, scriptwriter; b. N.Y.C., Sept. 30, 1918; s. David Mark Waldhorn and Carolyn Barnett; m. Hilda Kurland, Dec. 24, 1942 (dec. 1999); children: Valerie M. Auerbach, Stephen Edward. B.A. with honors in English, NYU, 1938, PhD in English and Am. Lit., 1950. Instr. English CCNY, N.Y.C., 1945—53, asst. prof. English, 1953—57, prof. English, 1967—78; vis. adj. prof. English NYU, 1978—81. Dir. Davis Ctr. for Performing Arts CCNY, 1972—73; Fulbright prof., Italy, 1958, England, 65, Japan, 73. Author: (television documentary) The Stations of Bach; editor: Ernest Hemingway, Good Reading; author: Reader's Guide to Ernest Hemingway. Recipient 125th Anniversary Svc. award medal, CCNY, 1973. Mem.: MLA (life). Democrat. Home: 7 Stuyvesant Oval New York NY 10009 Office: The City College of New York 135 Street Convent Ave New York NY 10031 Personal E-mail: hawk22@nyc.rr.com.

WALDKOETTER, RAYMOND OLIVER, psychologist, consultant; b. Indpls., Oct. 25, 1928; s. Raymond Oliver Waldkoetter, Sr. and Viola Simmons Waldkoetter; m. Mary Frances McBane, Sept. 25, 1953; children: Lisa K. Keenan, Greta A. Banner, Eric R., William H., Janet M. Turko, Olivia E. BS in Edn., Ind. U., 1951, MS in Edn., 1955, EdD in Psychol. Studies, 1963. Cert. psychologist Ind. Health Professiosn Bur. Dir. student activities U. Toledo, 1957—59; expatriate tutor Techiman Tng. Coll., Abetifi, Ghana, 1959—60; counselor Testing Bur. Depauw U., Greencastle, Ind., 1960—61; rsch. psychologist Enlisted Evaluation Ctr., Ft. Harrison, Ind., 1961—63, tech. advisor, 1965—73; dean of students Shepherd Coll., Shepardstown, W.Va., 1963—64; sr. rsch. psychologist Army Rsch. Inst., Alexandria, Va., 1974—82; consulting psychologist U.S. Army Soldier Support Ctr., Ft. Harrison, 1982—93; pvt. practice consulting psychologist Greenwood, Ind., 1993—. Mem. bd. advisors The Monroe Inst., Faber, Va., 1986—. Capt. USMC, 1951—59. Recipient Harry Greer award, Internat. Mil. Testing Assn., USN, 1983, Comdrs. award for Civil Svc., Dept. of the Army, 1993. Mem.: APA, Masons, Phi Delta Kappa, Theta Xi. Methodist. Achievements include personnel rating form design; sound-wave acoustic therapy; occupational analysis for performance enhancement. Avocations: reading, parapsychology, travel. Home: 906 S Haven Rd Greenwood IN 46143-2623

WALDMAN, ANNE LESLEY, poet, performer, editor, publisher, educational administrator; b. Millville, N.J., Apr. 2, 1945; d. John Marvin and Frances (Le Fevre) W.; m. Reed Eye Bye; 1 son, Ambrose. BA, Bennington Coll., 1966. Dir. The Poetry Project, St. Marks Ch. In-the-Bowery, N.Y.C., 1968-78; dir. Jack Kerouac Sch. of Disembodied Poetics at Naropa Inst., Boulder, Colo., 1974—. Adj. faculty Inst. Am. Indian Arts, Santa Fe; bd. dirs. Com. for Internat. Poetry, Eye and Ear Theatre, N.Y.C.; poet-in-residence with Bob Dylan's Rolling Thunder Rev.; dir. Naropa Study Abroad in Bali, Indonesia, 1998; guest dir. Schule fur Dichtung, Vienna, 1999. Author: (poetry) On the Wing, 1968, O My Life, 1969, Baby Breakdown, 1970, Giant Night, 1970, No Hassles, 1971, Life Notes, 1973, Fast Speaking Woman, 1975, Journals and Dreams, 1976, Shaman, 1977, Countries, 1980, Cabin, 1981, First Baby Poems, 1982, Makeup on Empty Space, 1983, Invention, 1986, Skin Meat Bones, 1986, The Romance Thing, 1987, Blue Mosque, 1988, Helping the Dreamer: New and Selected Poems, 1989, Not a Male Pseudonym, 1990, Lokapala, 1991, Troubairitz, 1993, Iovis: All is Full of Jove, 1993, Kill or Cure, 1994, Iovis II, 1997; editor: Nice To See You: Homage to Ted Berrigan, 1991, The Beat Book, 1996, (anthologies) The World Anthology, 1969, Another World, 1972, Talking Poetics From Naropa Institute vol. 1, 1978, vol. 2, 1979, Out of This World, 1991, (with Andrew Schelling) Disembodied Poetics: Annals of the Jack Kerovac School, 1994, (with Anselm Hollo and Jack Collom) Polemics; translator (with Andrew Schelling) Sons & Daughters of the Buddha, 1996; publisher: anthologies Angel Hair Books, N.Y.C., Full Ct. Press, N.Y.C.; recordings: The Dial-a-Poem Poets Disconnected, Anne Waldman/John Giorno, Fast Speaking Woman, The Nova Convention, Big Ego, Uh-oh Plutonium!, 1982, Crack in My World, 1986, Assorted Singles, 1990; performance videos include Eyes in All Heads, 1990, Live at Naropa, 1991, Battle of the Bards, 1991; featured on nat. pub. radio show All Things Considered, also featured in the poetry documentary Poetry In Motion. Dir. summer writing program Naropa; organizer Surrealist, Objectivist, Feminist, Pan Am. Ecology, Performance Confs., and The Robert Creeley Symposium. Recipient Dylan Thomas Meml. award New Sch., N.Y.C., 1967, Blue Ribbon Am. Film Festival, Nat. Literary Anthology award, 1970; named Heavyweight Champion Poet, 1989, 90; Cultural Artists Program grantee, 1976-77; NEA grantee, 1979-80; recipient Shelley Meml. award, 1996. Mem. PEN Club, Amnesty Internat. Office: c/o Naropa Inst 2130 Arapahoe Ave Boulder CO 80302-6602

WALDMAN, BEN, information technology executive; AB summa cum laude in Computer Sci., Harvard U., 1989. From devel. mgr. to corp. v.p. Microsoft, Redmond, Wash., 1989—2000, corp. v.p. mobile devices divsn., 2000—. Mem.: Phi Beta Kappa. Office: One Microsoft Way Redmond WA 98052 6399

WALDMAN, DANIEL M. lawyer; b. 1945; BA, Franklin & Marshall Coll.; JD, Georgetown U., 1971. Bar: NJ. Ptnr. Waldman & Moriarty, Red Bank, NJ. Mem.: Assn. County Bar Pres., Monmouth Bar Assn. (former pres.), NJ Bar Assn. (pres. 2001—02). Office: 212 Maple Ave Red Bank NJ 07701

WALDMAN, MICHAEL, economist, educator; b. Paterson, N.J., May 12, 1955; s. Henry and Nettie Waldman; m. Karen Voris, July 9, 1982 (div. Jan. 1992); m. Lisa Berki, July 18, 1999; children: David Henry, Emma Nicole. BS in Econs., MIT, 1977; PhD in Econs., U. Pa., 1982. From asst. prof. to prof econs. UCLA, 1983-93; prof. econs. Cornell U., Ithaca, N.Y., 1991-97, Charles H. Dyson prof. in mgmt., 1997—. Vis. prof. econs. Yale U. Sch. Orgn. and Mgmt., New Haven, 1989—90, U. Chgo. Grad. Sch. Bus., 1997—99. Co-editor: Jour. Econ. Perspectives, 2000—; assoc. editor: Quar. Jour. Econs., 2000—; contbr. articles to profl. jours. Mem.: Western Econ. Assn., Soc. Labor Economists, Royal Econ. Soc., Econometric Soc., Am. Econ. Assn. (program com. 2004). Office: Cornell U Johnson Grad Sch Mgmt Sage Hall Ithaca NY 14853 Business E-Mail: mw46@cornell.edu.

WALDMAN, SCOTT ARTHUR, medical educator, medical association administrator; b. Bklyn., Oct. 22, 1953; MD, Stanford U., 1987. Diplomate Am. Bd. Internal Medicine. Assoc. prof. medicine, pharmacy Thomas Jefferson U., Phila. Fellow, ACCP; mem.: AMA, AFCR, ACP, Endoscopi Soc., Am. Soc. Clin. Pharmacology (pres.). Office: Thomas Jefferson U Divsn Clin Pharm Dept 1100 Walnut St Philadelphia PA 19107-5563

WALDMAN, SEYMOUR MORTON, lawyer; b. N.Y.C., Aug. 6, 1926; s. Louis and Bella B. Waldman; m. Lois Citrin, Aug. 5, 1951; children: David, Daniel, Michael, Ellen. BA, Columbia U., 1948, LLB, 1950. Bar: N.Y. 1950, U.S. Ct. Appeals (1st, 2d, 3d, 4th, 5th, 6th and D.C. cirs.), U.S. Dist. Ct. (so. dist.) N.Y., U.S. Dist. Ct. (ea. dist.) N.Y., U.S. Supreme Ct. 1956. From assoc. to ptnr. Waldman & Waldman, N.Y.C., 1950-82; ptnr., of counsel Vladeck, Waldman, Elias & Engelhard, P.C., N.Y.C., 1982—; atty. Village of Croton-Hudson, N.Y., 1972—, chair zoning bd. appeals, 1963-72, trustee hosp. for Joint Diseases Orthopaedic Inst., 1968-93. With USN, 1944-46. Mem. ABA, N.Y. State Bar Assn., Phi Beta Kappa. Avocation: tennis. Office: Vladeck Waldman Elias & Engelhard PC 1501 Broadway Ste 800 New York NY 10036-5560

WALDMANN, THOMAS ALEXANDER, medical researcher, physician; b. N.Y.C., Sept. 21, 1930; s. Charles Elizabeth (Sipos) Waldmann; m. Katharine Emory Spreng, Mar. 29, 1958; children: Richard Allen, Robert James, Carol Ann. AB, U. Chgo., 1951; MD, Harvard U., 1955; PhD (hon.), U. Med. Sch., Debrecin, Hungary, 1991. Diplomate Am. Bd. Allergy and Immunology. Intern Mass. Gen. Hosp., Boston, 1955—56; clin. assoc. Nat. Cancer Inst. NIH, Bethesda, Md., 1956—58, sr. investigator, 1958—68, head immunophysiology sect., 1968—73, chief metabolism br., 1971—. Cons. WHO, 1975, 78; bd. dirs., v.p. Found. for Advanced Edn. in Scis., Bethesda, 1980—2002, treas., 1988—90, v.p., 1990—92; William Dameshek vis. prof. U. Calif., Irvine, 1984; mem. med. adv. bd. Howard Hughes Med. Inst., 1987—93; vis. com. mem. Harvard Med. Sch., Boston, 1988—94; mem. sci. adv. com., chmn. Mass. Gen. Hosp., 1992—96; chmn. sci. adv. bd. HealthCare Investment Corp., Princeton, NJ, 1986—. Author: Plasma Protein Metabolism, 1970; contbr. articles to profl. jours. With USPHS, 1956—58, 1959—63, 1975—94. Named Man of Yr., Am. Leukemia Soc., 1980; recipient Henry M. Stratton medal, Am. Hematology Soc., 1977, G. Burroughs Mider award, NIH, 1980, Disting. Svc. medal, Dept. Health and Human Svcs., 1983. Fellow: Am. Acad. Allergy (Bela Schick award 1974, John M. Shelton award 1984, Lila Gruber prize 1986, Simon Shubitz prize 1987, CIBA-GEIGY Drew award 1987, Milken Family Med. Found. Disting. Basic Scientist prize 1991, Artois Latour Internat. Rsch. prize 1991, Bristol-Myers Cancer prize 1992, Paul Ehrlich medal 1997); mem.: NAS (chmn. 1985—), Clin. Immunology Soc. (pres. 1988), Am. Soc. Clin. Investigation (mem. editl. bd. 1978—80, 1983—88), Assn. Am. Physicians, Hungarian Acad. Scis. (hon.), Inst. Medicine, Am. Acad. Arts and Scis. Achievements include the defining of structure of multisubunit IL-2 receptor; identifying novel cytokine IL-15; introduction of different forms of IL-2R-directed therapy using alpha and beta-emitting radionuclide chelate versions of humanized monoclonal antibodies (Zenapax) for treatment of cancer; introduction of analysis of immunoglobulin gene rearrangements to define clonality and classifying human lymphoid neoplasia; discovered intestinal lymphangectiasia and allergic gastroenteropathy. Office: Nat Inst Health 10 Center Dr Bethesda MD 20892-1374 Office Phone: 301-496-6656. Business E-Mail: tawald@helix.nih.gov.

WALDMEIR, PETER NIELSEN, journalist; b. Detroit, Jan. 16, 1931; s. Joseph John and Helen Sarah (Nielsen) W.; m. Marilyn C. Choma; children—Peter William, Patti Ann, Lindsey Marilyn, Christopher Norman. Student, Wayne State U., 1949-58. From mem. staff to gen. columnist Detroit News, 1949—72, gen. columnist, 1972—2004. Pres. Old Newsboys Goodfellow Fund, Detroit, 1988. With USMC, 1951-53. Recipient Headliners award Nat. Headliners Club, 1971, SDX Lifetime Achievement award, 2000; named Mich. Sports Writer of Yr., Nat. Sportscasters and Sportswriters, 1967, 69, 71; Heart award Variety Club Internat., 1985; inducted Mich. Journalism Hall of Fame, 2000. Mem. Sigma Delta Chi. Roman Catholic. Personal E-mail: pwaldmeir@aol.com.

WALDO, JAMES CHANDLER, lawyer; b. Seattle, Oct. 23, 1948; s. Burton Chandler and Margaret (Hoar) W.; m. Sharon B. Waldo; children: Sara K., William K., John J. Grad., Whitman Coll., 1970; JD, Willamette U., 1974. Bar: Wash. 1974, U.S. Ct. Appeals (9th cir.) 1976. Exec. asst. Dept. of Labor, Washington, 1974-76; asst. U.S. atty. Justice Dept., Seattle, 1976-79; of counsel ESTEP & LI, Seattle, 1979-80; ptnr. Gordon, Thomas, Honeywell, Malanca, Peterson & Daheim LLP, Seattle, 1981—. Chmn. N.W. Renewable Resources Ctr., Seattle, 1984-97, Wash. State Energy Strategy Com., 1991-93; spl. counsel on Water for Gov., 2001—. Trustee Western Wash. U., 1981-93. Recipient Outstanding Alumnus of Yr. Whitman Coll., 1994, Dir.'s award Wash. Dept. Fisheries, 1986, Pres.'s award Assn. Wash. Bus., 1988, Outstanding Citizen award Western Assn. Fish & Wildlife Agys., 1987. Republican. Office: Gordon Thomas Honeywell Malanca Peterson & Daheim LLP PO Box 1157 Tacoma WA 98401-1157

WALDO, ROBERT LELAND, retired insurance company executive; b. Pittsville, Wis., Sept. 1, 1923; s. Elmer Harley and Edith Viola (Senter) W.; m. Elaine Anne Jossie, June 4, 1947; children: Daniel Robert, Thomas Parker, Susan Jeanne. BA, U. Wis., 1949, JD, 1951. Assoc. atty. Foley & Lardner, Milw., 1951-59; asst. sec., asst. gen. counsel Wis. Gas Co., Milw., 1959-69; v.p., gen. counsel Verex Corp. and Subss., Madison, Wis., 1969-72; exec. v.p., sec. Verex Corp. and subs., Madison, Wis., 1972-78, pres., chief operating officer, 1978-82, pres., chief exec. officer, 1982-85, chmn., chief exec. officer, 1985-86. Served as sgt. U.S. Army, 1943-46, ETO. Mem. Wis. Bar Assn., Dane County Bar Assn., Mortgage Ins. Co.'s Am. (pres. 1980-82), Maple Bluff Country Club. Republican. Methodist. Avocations: travel, golf. Home: 818 Charing Cross Rd Madison WI 53704-6010

WALDOCK, WILLIAM DAVID, aeronautical science and aviation safety educator; b. Ft. Worth, Tex., Aug. 4, 1952; s. Wallace Gordon and Annabelle (Wolfe) W.; m. Barbara A. Wisler, Sept. 14, 1974; children: Andrew, Kathleen. BA in History, U. Fla., 1975; student, Miami-Dade Coll., Miami, Fla., 1977-78; M of Aero. Sci. with honors, Embry-Riddle Aero. U., 1982; postgrad., Kennedy-Western U. Prof. aero. sci. Embry-Riddle Aero. U., Prescott, Ariz., 1982—, chief investigator aircraft accidents, 1991—, assoc. dir. Ctr. Aerospace Safety Edn., 1986—, dir. Robertson Aviation Safety Ctr., 1995—. Pres., chief cons. Sys. Safety, Inc., Prescott, 1990—; cons. Am. West Airlines, Phoenix, 1996-99; presenter numerous safety confs. Contbr. articles to profl. publs.; guest various T.V. shows. Lt. comdr. USCG, 1975-96, ret. Mem. SAFE Assn. (Gen. Spruance award for Outstanding Contbns. to Safety Through Edn. 1990), Aircraft Owners and Pilots Assn., Aircraft Rescue and Firefighting Working Group, Am. Soc. Safety Engrs., World Safety Orgn. (cert.), Internat. Soc. Air Safety Investigators (pres. Ariz. chpt. 1987—). Achievements include over 150 field investigations; research in accident history. Office: Embry-Riddle Aero U Bldg 21 3700 Willow Creek Rd Prescott AZ 86301-3721 E-mail: wwaldock@msn.com.

WALDON, ALTON RONALD, JR., judge; b. Lakeland, Fla., Dec. 21, 1936; s. Alton Ronald and Rupert Juanita (Wallace) W.; m. Barbara De Costa, June 3, 1961; children: Alton III, Dana Olive, Ian Patrick. BS, John Jay Coll., 1968; JD, N.Y. Law Sch., 1973. Capt. N.Y.C. Housing Authority Police Dept., 1962-75; dep. commr. N.Y. State Divsn. Human Rights, 1975-82; assemblyman N.Y. State Assembly, 1983-86; congressman U.S. Ho. Reps., Washington, 1986-87; commr. N.Y. State Commn. Investigation, 1987-90; senator N.Y. State, 1991-00; judge Ct. of Claims State of N.Y., 2000—. Bd. dirs. USO Met. N.Y. Recipient Thurgood Marshall fellow, N.Y. State Trial Lawyers Assn., 1970-73. Mem. Met. Black Bar Assn., Macon B. Allen Bar Assn., Comus Club N.Y., Alumni Assn. N.Y. Law Sch., Alumni Assn. John Jay Coll., Masons (33 deg.), Sigma Pi Phi. Democrat. Roman Catholic. Avocation: sports. Office Phone: 212-361-8140. E-mail: awaldon@courts.state.ny.us., awaldon@nyc.rr.com.

WALDRON, JANET E. state commissioner; Sr. legis. analyst Legis. Office of Fiscal and Program Rev.; dir. legis. affairs Ctrl. Maine Power Co.; dir. adminstrn. Dept. Conservation; asst. sec. of state State of Maine, commr. dept. adminstrv. and fin. svcs., 1994—. Mem. Intergovernmental Task Force; co-chair Info. Tech. Task Force; chair Telecom. and Info. Tech. Planning Project. Office: Adminstrv & Fin Svcs Dept 78 State House Sta Augusta ME 04333-0078

WALDRON, KAREN, development, construction, and management company executive; m. Shawn Ricci. Chairperson/sr. v.p. F&W Mgmt.; pres. Bent Tree Farm Ltd., The Ctr. at Walnut Grove; chairperson, CEO Fralin and Waldron, Inc., Roanoke, Va. Mem. bd. visitors Radford U.; mem. exec. bd. Roanoke Valley Horse Show; pub. bd. dirs., chair Va. Horse Ctr. Avocations: horse industry, Pilates instruction, yoga, dance. Office: Fralin and Waldron Inc Ste 200 PO Box 24018 3130 Chaparral Dr Roanoke VA 24018

WALDROP, ROBERT L. utilities executive; B in Mktg., Lamar U.; JD, South Tex. Coll. Law. Bar: Tex. Power cons. mktg. dept. Houston Lighting & Power Co., 1972, v.p. pub. affairs, 1988—93, group v.p. external affairs, 1993—96, exec. v.p., gen. mgr. energy svcs., 1996—97; sr. v.p. corp. comm. Reliant Energy, Inc., 1997, Reliant Resources, Inc., Houston, 1997—. Mem. adv. bd. Houston Hispanic C. of C., Houston Zool. Soc.; bd. dirs. Houston 2012 Found. Mem.: Pub. Rels. Soc. Am., Am. Leadership Forum, State Bar Tex. Office: Reliant Energy Exec Offices PO Box 2286 Houston TX 77252-2286

WALDSTEIN, DANIEL ERIC, science educator; b. Aberdeen, South Dakota, Feb. 20, 1974; s. Sammy James and Linda Ruth Waldstein; m. Jessica Anne Bradshaw, May 15, 2004. BS, Minn. State U., Mankato, 1992—96; PhD, Cornell U., Ithaca, NY, 1996—2000. Rsch. assoc. Mich. State U., East Lansing, 2000—02; asst. rsch. prof. S.W. Mo. State U., Mountain Grove, 2002—. Author: (novels) The War That Never Was, (jour. publications) Jour. of Econ. Entomology, (jour. publ.) The Can. Entomologist. Sunday sch. tchr. First Bapt. Ch., Mountain Grove, Mo., 2003—. Grantee, Mich. Dept. of Environ. Quality, 2001—03. Mem.: Entomol. Soc. of Am. Home: 3890 Kemper Rd Mountain Grove MO 65711 Office: SW Mo State U 9740 Red Spring Rd Mountain Grove MO 65711 Personal E-mail: waldregenbook@yahoo.com. Business E-Mail: dew898f@smsu.edu.

WALDSTEIN, GAIL P. pediatric pathologist, writer; b. Bklyn., Apr. 9, 1942; d. Milton Herman Waldstein and Dorothea Schlegel; m. Mark Levine, June 1965 (div. Jan. 1976); children: Sarah Levine, Samantha Levine, Saul Levine; m. Bruce Hansen, Apr. 1990 (div. Sept. 1992). BA, Douglass Coll., 1964; MD, Temple U., 1968. Pediatric intern Univ. Colo. Hlth. Sci. Ctr., 1968—69, residency in path., 1971—72; residency in pediatric path. The Children's Hosp., Denver, 1969—72, assoc. pediat. pathologist, 1973—92; pediat. pathologist Toledo Hosp., 1993—95, Childrens Hosp. Mich., Detroit, 1995—97; part-time pediat. pathologist Presbyn. Med. Ctr., Denver, 1997—2001. Asst./assoc. prof. U. Colo. Sch. Medicine, Denver, 1973—92; assoc. pathologist Wayne State Med. Sch., Detroit, 1995—97; chair credentials com. Children's Hosp., Denver, 1982—90. Author poems, essays, short stories, novels. Fellow, Rocky Mountain Women's Inst., 1997—98, Colo. Coun. Arts, 2001, Helene Wurlitzer Found., 2002. Mem.: Colo. Author's League. Home: 180 Cook St #308 Denver CO 80206

WALE, KEVIN E. automotive executive; b. Melbourne, Australia, 1954; B Commerce (hon.), U. Melbourne. Fin. mgr. Holden, 1975—83; mem. fin. staff GM, New York, 1983—85; dir. fin. Holden, 1985—93, dir. sales, mktg., 1993—98; exec.-in-charge ops. GM Asia Pacific Ltd., Singapore, 1998—2001; v.p. Gen. Motors Europe, 2001—; mng. dir. Vauxhall Motors, 2001, chmn., mng. dir., 2002—. Office: GM Corp PO Box 300 300 Renaissance Ctr Detroit MI 48265-3000

WALEN, HARRY LEONARD, historian, lecturer, author; b. Winchester, Mass, June 26, 1915; s. Harry Leonard and Alice (Garland) W.; m. Elizabeth Rowe Benson, June 26, 1939; children: Harry Benson, Kimball Frederick, Robert Leonard. AB cum laude, Harvard U., 1937, AM, 1942. Tchr. Los Alamos Ranch Sch., N.Mex., 1937-42, head English dept., 1939-42; tchr. English Groton Sch., Mass., 1942-46; instr. English, faculty marshal Newton Jr. Coll., 1946-51; tchr. English and journalism Newton HS, Newtonville, Mass., 1946-51, adminstr., 1951-55; directing editor secondary sch. English textbooks Ginn and Co., Boston, 1955-61; prin. Needham HS, Mass., 1961-72, career and post secondary guidance counselor, 1972-79. Mem. Regional Interviewing Com. for Overseas Grants and Fellowships, 1961-84; mem. planning com. Task Force on High Sch. Graduation Requirements, Mass Dept. Edn., 1976-80. Author: (books) The Family Travel-Camper, 1955, (with E. Gordon and others) Types of Literature, American Literature, English Literature, 1964, The Memory Book of the New England Association of Teachers of English, 1981, The Sons of the American Revolution 1962-82: An Historical Anthology, 1984; (monographs) English Learning Environments, 1972, History of the Order of Founders and Patriots of America, 1982, Centennial History, 1996; co-author Alluring Rockport, rev. edit. 1986, The Little Old Meeting House and How It Grew; (poetry) Images and Perceptions, 1996; editor The English Leaflet, 1947-54; cons. editor on career edn. New Voices Series, 1978; poet laureate, Rockport, 1998, 99; contbr. chpts., articles, poems to books, profl. jour. and periodicals. Alderman City of Newton, Mass., 1961-72; corp. mem. USS Mass. Meml. Com., Inc., 1972—, bd. dir., 1984-91, honorary dir., 1995—; chmn. edn. com. N.E. Conf. NCCJ, 1972-82, mem. study mission to Israel, 1974; vice chmn. New Eng. Conf. on Quality of Life, Boston, 1973; mem. Newton Regional Adv. Manpower Planning Bd., 1973-77; pres. counseling svc. YMCA, Greater Boston, 1976-7; chmn. Newton Highlands Bd. Christian Edn., 1974-75; pres. bd. trustees weekday ch. sch.; 1st Congl. Ch., Rockport, Mass., ch. historian, 1982-2002; del. Mass. Conf. United Ch. Christ, 1989-96. John Hay fellow, 1965; Mass. Dept. Edn. Commonwealth fellow, 1971; recipient citation U.S. Commr. Edn., 1971, citation New Eng. Assn. Schs. and Colls., 1984, cert. of Appreciation, City of Newton, 1971, Service award, YMCA, 1978. Mem. Nat. Council Tchr. English (assoc. chmn. nat. conv. 1965, chmn., co-founder Emeritus Assembly 1979-83, various other coms. and offices, Citation 1969), Nat. Assn. Secondary Sch. Prin., Headmasters Assn. (life), New Eng. Assn. Tchr. English (life, past pres., chmn. ann. C. S. Thomas award com. 1975-96, historian 1978—, Thomas award 1978), Mass. Secondary Sch. Prins. Assn. (diploma standards com. 1973-78, Bronze plaque 1974), Mass. Council Tchr. English (co-founder), Mass. Schoolmasters Club (past pres., hon. life), MENSA, Friends of Jackson Homestead, Newton Hist. Soc. (life, past pres.), Los Alamos (N.Mex.) Hist. Soc. (life), Sandy Bay Hist. Soc. (pres. 1983-86), Greater Boston Guidance Club (hon.), Nat. Gavel Soc., New Eng. Hist. and Geneal. Soc., SAR (pres. state 1979-81, nat. trustee 1981-83, historian gen. 1983-86, sec. Mus. Bd.

1982-88, Minuteman award 1985), Gen. Soc. Mayflower Descs. (mem. nat. exec. com. 1990-93), Mass. Soc. Mayflower Descs. (gov. 1985-88, dep. gov. gen. 1988-93), Pilgrim John Howland Soc. (pres. 1987-99, pres. emeritus 1999—, led pilgrimage to Eng., 1989), Mass. Huguenot Soc. (pres. 1990-92, nat. del. 1983-92), Descs. Colonial Clergy, Soc. Colonial Wars, Navy League US (life), Sons and Daus. of 1st Settlers of Newbury (pres. 1982-84), Piscataqua Pioneers (pres. 1990-91), Order of Crown of Charlemagne, Order Founders and Patriots (nat. treas. 1978-81, dep. gov. gen. 1981-84, exec. com. 1992-2000, councillor gen. Mass. 1984—, NH, 1987-90, 93—, gov. 1992-95, councillor gen. 1993—, Nat. Disting. Svc. award 1996), Boston Athenaeum, Harvard Club, Boston Authors Club (pres. 1995-96), English Lunch Club (pres. 1975-82), Friday Evening Club (most venerable 1979-86), Sandy Bay Yacht Club, Masons (32d degree, 50-Yr. award). Home: 15 Penzance Rd Rockport MA 01966

WALENDOWSKI, GEORGE JERRY, accounting and business educator; b. Han-Minden, Germany, Mar. 25, 1947; came to US, 1949; s. Stefan (dec.) and Eugenia (Lewandowska) W. AA, LA City Coll., 1968; BS, Calif. State U., LA, 1970, MBA, 1972; cert. completion, Inst. Mgmt. Accts., 2000—. Cert. community coll. instr. acctg. and mgmt., Calif. Acct. Unocal (formerly Union Oil Co. Calif.), LA, 1972-76, data control supr., 1976-78, acctg. analyst, 1978-79; sr. fin. analyst Hughes Aircraft Co., El Segundo, Calif., 1979-83, fin. planning specialist, 1983-84, program controls specialist, 1984-86, bus. mgmt. specialist, 1986-92, bus. analyst, 1993-95. Adj. instr. bus. math. L.A. City Coll., 1976-80, acctg., 1980-97, 99—, mem. acctg. adv. com., 1984, 87, 89, 99, acctg. and bus. Pasadena City Coll., 1996-2001, 03; reviewer conf. papers. Contbr. articles to profl. jours. Mem. commn. Rep. Pres. Task Force, 1986. Recipient Medal of Merit, Rep. Presdl. Task Force, 1984, cert. of merit, named registered life mem. commn., 1986, named Honor Roll life mem., 1989; recipient Vice-Presdl. Cert. of Commendation, Rep. Nat. Hall of Honor, 1992, Rep. Congl. cert. of Appreciation, 1993, Rep. Congl. Order of Freedom award Nat. Rep. Congl. Com., 1995, Recognition award LA chpt. Strategic Leadership Forum, 1983. Mem.: Midwest Fin. Assn. (program rev. com. 2002), Ea. Fin. Assn. (program rev. com. 2000), Soc. Advancement Mgmt. (editl. rev. bd. Advanced Mgmt. Jour. 1999—, selection com. mem. Internat. Conf. 2000), Nat. Bus. Edn. Assn., Am. Acctg. Assn. (competitive manuscript com. 1997—98, reviewer tchg. curr. sect. 1998, tchg. and curriculum sect. two-yr. coll. issues com. 1998—99), Inst. Mgmt. Accts. (author's cir. L.A. chpt. 1980, mem. editl. adv. bd. Strategic Fin. and Mgmt. Acctg. Quarterly 2002—, Robert Half author's trophy 1980, cert. of appreciation 1980, 1983), Acad. Mgmt. (reviewer social issues in mgmt. divsn. 1991, mgmt. edn. and devel. disvsn. program rev. com. 1998, 1999, reviewer bus. policy and strategy divsn. 2002—04, reviewer for acad. of mngmt. learning & ed. Jour. 2003), U.S. Chess Fedn., Delta Pi Epsilon, Beta Gamma Sigma. Republican. Roman Catholic. Home: 426 N Citrus Ave Los Angeles CA 90036-2632 Office: LA City Coll 855 N Vermont Ave Los Angeles CA 90029 Personal E-mail: geowalen@msn.com.

WALES, GWYNNE HUNTINGTON, retired lawyer; b. Evanston, Ill., Apr. 18, 1933; s. Robert Willett and Solace (Huntington) W.; m. Janet McCobb, Feb. 8, 1957; children— Thomas Gwynne, Catherine Anne, Louise Carrie. AB, Princeton U., 1954; JD, Harvard U., 1961. Bar: N.Y. 1962. Assoc. White & Case, N.Y.C., 1961-69, ptnr., 1969-2000, resident ptnr. Brussels, 1969-75, Ankara, Turkey, 1998-2000. Served with USN, 1954-58. Mem.: Am. Law Inst. (life), Round Hill (Greenwich, Conn.), Mountain Lake Colony House (Lake Wales, Fla.). Home: 25 Mountain Lake Lake Wales FL 33898

WALES, PATRICE, school system administrator; b. Washington, Sept. 9, 1935; d. Robert Corning and Bernadette Mary (Dyer) W. BA, Dunbarton Coll. of Holy Cross, 1957; MTS, Cath. U. Am., 1978; PhD, U. Md., 1993. Cert. tchr., supt., Md. Tchr. mid. sch. St. Marys, Laurel, Md., 1960-61; tchr. high sch. St. Vincent Pallotti High Sch., Laurel, Md., 1962-65; instr. nursing sch. St. Mary's Sch. Nursing, Huntington, W.Va., 1965-66; tchr. St. Vincent Pallotti High Sch., Laurel, Md., 1967-76, adminstr., 1976—2004, chair sci. dept., 1962-80, dean students, 1976-87; sponsorship dir. St. Vincent Pallotti HS, Laurel, Md., 1988—2004. Bd. dirs. St. Vincent Pallotti HS, Laurel; trustee St. Joseph's Hosp., Buckhannon, W.Va., 1990-2004, v.p. 2003; dir. German Exch. Program, Laurel, Ahlen, Germany, 1976-96, Maesawa H.S. Exch., Japan, 1997; exec. sec. US Nat. Coord. Coun. Senator Sisters Senate Archdiocese of Washington, 1993-2003, pres., 1998-2001. NSF grantee, 1967, 69, 71; recipient Youth Ministry award Archdiocese of Washington, 2004. Mem. ASCD, Nat. Cath. Edn. Assn., Nat. Soc. Daughters of Am. Revolution (chaplain Toaping Castle chpt.), Am. Governance and Leadership Group (gen. councilor to superior gen. Pallottine missionary sisters, 2004—). Roman Catholic. Avocations: walking, bicycling, choir, travel. Home: Casa Generalizia Viale delle Mura Aurelie 7/B I-00165 Rome 20707-4032 Italy Office Phone: (011 39) 06 39 36 35 1.

WALES, ROSS ELLIOT, lawyer; b. Youngstown, Ohio, Oct. 17, 1947; s. Craig C. and Beverly (Bromley) W.; m. Juliana Fraser, Sept. 16, 1972; children: Dod E., J. Craig. AB, Princeton U., 1969; JD, U. Va., 1974. Bar: Ohio 1974, U.S. Dist. Ct. (so. dist.) Ohio 1974, U.S. Ct. Appeals (5th cir.) 1979. Assoc. Taft, Stettinius & Hollister, Cin., 1974-81, ptnr., 1981—. Pres. U.S. Swimming, Inc., Colorado Springs, 1979-84, U.S. Aquatic Sports, Inc., Colorado Springs, 1984-88, 94-98; dir. Child Welfare League Am., 2003-. Pres. Cin. Active to Support Edn., 1987-88; chmn. sch. tax levy campaign, Cin., 1987; trustee The Childrens Home Cin., 1987—, v.p., 1995-98, pres., 1998-2002; trustee Cin. State Tech. and C.C., 1994—, sec. bd., 1995-98, vice-chmn., 1998-2000, chair 2000-02; pres. Cin. Arts Sch., Inc., 2000-01; sec. Greater Cin. Arts and Edn. Ctr., 1996—; mem. Anti-Doping Rev. Bd., U.S. Anti-Doping Agy., Colo. Springs. Mem. ABA, Ohio Bar Assn., Cin. Bar Assn., Internat. Swimming Fedn. of Lausanne, Switzerland (sec. 1988-92, v.p. 1992-2000). Presbyterian. Office: 425 Walnut St Ste 1800 Cincinnati OH 45202-3923 Office Phone: 513-357-9351. Business E-Mail: wales@taftlaw.com.

WALES, WALTER D. physicist, researcher; b. Oneonta, N.Y., Aug. 2, 1933; s. Walter D. and Anna Laura (Brockway) W.; m. Margaret Irene Keiter, June 19, 1955; children: Stephen Dirk, Carolyn Sue. BA, Carleton Coll., 1954; MS, Calif. Inst. Tech., 1955, PhD, 1960. Instr. physics U. Pa., Phila., 1959-62, asst. prof., 1962-64, assoc. prof., 1964-72, prof., 1972—, chmn. dept. physics, 1973-82, assoc. dean, 1982-87, acting dean, 1987-88, assoc. dean, 1988-92, dep. provost, 1992-95, interim dean, 1996-98, ombudsman, 1999-2001, interim assoc. provost, 2002—04; assoc. dir. Princeton (N.J.)-Pa. Accelerator, 1968-71; staff physicist AEC, 1972-73. Fellow Am. Phys. Soc.; mem. Am. Assn. Physics Tchrs. Achievements include research in exptl. particle physics. Home: 404 Drew Ave Swarthmore PA 19081-2406 Office: 209 S 33rd St Philadelphia PA 19104-6317 Business E-Mail: wales@physics.upenn.edu.

WALHOUT, JUSTINE SIMON, chemistry professor; b. Aberdeen, S.D., Dec. 11, 1930; d. Otto August and Mabel Ida (Tews) S.; m. Donald Walhout, Feb. 1, 1958; children: Mark, Timothy, Lynne, Peter. BS, Wheaton Coll., 1952; PhD, Northwestern U., 1956. Instr. Wright City Community Coll., Chgo., 1955-56; asst. prof. Rockford (Ill.) Coll., 1956-59, assoc. prof., 1959-66, 81-89, prof., 1989-96, prof. emeritus, 1996—, dept. chmn., 1987-95; cons. Pierce Chem. Co., Rockford, 1968-69; trustee Rockford (Ill.) Coll., 1987-91. Contbr. articles to profl. jours. Mem. Ill. Bd. Edn., 1974-81. Mem. AAUW (Ill. bd. dirs. 1985-87), Am. Chem. Soc. (councilor 1993-99), Rockford LWV (bd. dirs. 1983-85, 2002-04), Sigma Xi. Presbyterian. Home: 320 N Rockford Ave Rockford IL 61107-4547 Office: Rockford Coll 5050 E State St Rockford IL 61108-2311

WALI, MOHAN KISHEN, environmental science and natural resources educator; b. Kashmir, India, Mar. 1, 1937; came to U.S., 1969, naturalized, 1975; s. Jagan Nath and Somavati (Wattal) W.; m. Sarla Safaya, Sept. 25, 1960; children: Pamela, Promod. BS, U. Jammu and Kashmir, 1957; MS, U. Allahabad, India, 1960; PhD, U. B.C., Can., 1970. Lectr. S.P. Coll., Srinagar, Kashmir, 1963-65; rsch. fellow U. Copenhagen, 1965-66; grad. fellow U. B.C., 1967-69; asst. prof. biology U. N.D., Grand Forks, 1969-73, assoc. prof., 1973-79, prof., 1979-83, Hill rsch. prof., 1973; dir. Forest River Biology Area Field Sta., 1970-79, Project Reclamation, 1975-83; spl. asst. to univ. pres., 1977-82; staff ecologist Grand Forks Energy Rsch. Lab. U.S. Dept. Interior, 1974-75; prof. Coll. Environ. Sci. and Forestry SUNY, Syracuse, 1983-89, dir. grad. program environ. sci., 1983-85, prof. Sch. Natural Resources, 1990—, dir. Sch. Natural Resources, assoc. dean Coll. Agr., 1990-93; dir. Environ. Sci. Grad. program Ohio State U., Columbus, 2001—. Vice chmn. N.D. Air Pollution Adv. Coun., 1981-83; co-chair IV Internat. Congress on Ecology, 1986. Editor: Some Environmental Aspects of Strip-Mining in North Dakota, 1973, Prairie: A Multiple View, 1975, Practices and Problems of Land Reclamation in Western North America, 1975, Ecology and Coal Resource Development, 1979, Ecosystem Rehabilitation-Preamble to Sustainable Development, 1992; co-editor Agriculture and the Environment, 1993; sr. editor Reclamation Rev., 1976-80, chief editor, 1980-81; chief editor Reclamation and Revegetation Rsch., 1982-87; contbr. articles to profl. jours. Recipient B.C. Gamble Disting. Tchg. and Svc. award, 1977. Fellow AAAS, Nat. Acad. Scis. India; mem. Ecol. Soc. Am. (chmn. sect. internat. activities 1980-84), Bot. Ecol. Soc., Can. Bot. Assn. (dir. ecology sect. 1976-79, v.p. 1982-83), Am. Soc. Agronomy, Am. Inst. Biol. Sci. (gen. chmn. 34th ann. meeting), Internat. Assn. Ecolog (co-chmn. IV Internat. Congress Ecology), Internat. Soc. Soil Sci., N.D. Acad. Sci. (chmn. editl. com. 1979-81), Sigma Xi (nat. lectr. 1983-85, pres. Ohio State chpt. 1993-94, pres. Syracuse chpt. 1984-85, Outstanding Rsch. award U. N.D. chpt. 1975). Office: Ohio State U Sch Natural Resources 2021 Coffey Rd Columbus OH 43210-1044

WALI, SIMA, foundation administrator; b. Kandahar, Afghanistan, Apr. 7, 1951; came to U.S., 1978; d. Mohammad and Shafiqa (Sharifi) W. BA, Kabul U., Afghanistan, 1970; MA, Am. U., 1984, Smith Coll., 2002, PhD honoris causa, 2003, Shenandoah U., 2003. Asst. to consular officer Am. Embassy, Kabul, 1970-71; asst. to program tech. rep. U.S. Peace Corps, Kabul, 1971-78; communications officer New Trans Century Found., Washington, 1978-82; asst. to dir. Refugee Women in Devel., Project of OEF Internat., Washington, 1982-83, dir., 1983-86; exec. dir. Refugee Women in Devel. Inc., Washington, 1986-96, pres., 1996—; del. His Majesty the Former King of Afghanistan UN Peace Talks, Bonn, 2001; chief organizer Afghan Women's Summit Democracy, Brussels, 2001. Mem. adv. bd. Global Fund for Women, 1992—. Contbr. articles to profl. publs., chpt. to book. Bd. dirs. Refugee Trauma Ctr., Harvard U., 1987-89; bd. dirs. Mem. expert's com. Women's Commn. for Refugee Women and Children, 1990-94; mem. adv. com. Refugee Policy Group; rep. refugee women and devel., human rights of uprooted people at nat. and internat. confs.; bd. dirs., chair Fund for the Future of Our Children, 1995-99; dir. gender, human rights, forced migration Creative Assocs. Internat., Inc., 1996; pres. Rufugee Women in Devel., Inc., 1996; advisor Women for Women Internat., 1997—; mem. Sisterhood Is Global Inst., 1986—, v.p. 1985-2003, treas. 2004; found. mem. Ppolicy Coun. on Afghan Women, 2003—. Recipient N.Y. Assn. New Ams. Outstanding Contbn. award, 1988, Gloria Steinem: Women of Vision award, 1989, Women in Leadership award Women's Commn. for Refugee Women and Children, 1992, Resourceful Women award, 1995, Amnesty Internat. Ginetta Sagan Human Rights award, 1999; named finalist Ortho 21st Centruy Woman, NOW and Ortho Pharm. Co., Women of Distinction George Washington U., 1992. Office: Refugee Women in Devel Inc R Strauss Bldg 1333 New Hampshire Ave NW Washington DC 20036-1564 Office Phone: 703-931-6442. Business E-Mail: refwid@erols.com.

WALKE, DAVID MICHAEL, business advisory, consulting and research executive; b. Mt. Vernon, N.Y., Dec. 30, 1954; s. Charles Philip and Elinor Mae (Denner) W.; m. Linda Susan Berkover, Nov. 26, 1978; children: Evan Matthew, Hilary Rose. BS in Acctg., Syracuse U., 1976. Account exec. Ecom Cons., Inc., N.Y.C., 1976-79, Anametrics, Inc., N.Y.C., 1979-81, Ruder, Finn & Rotman, Inc., N.Y.C., 1981-82; prin. Morgen-Walke Assocs., Inc., N.Y.C., 1982—2000, mng. ptnr.; CEO, dir. FINDS/SVP consulting, 2001—. Mem. Nat. Investor Rels. Inst., Gilda's Club Westchester (bd. dirs.). Office: Morgen-Walke Assocs Inc 50th Fl 380 Lexington Ave Fl 50 New York NY 10168-0002*

WALKEN, CHRISTOPHER, actor; b. Astoria, N.Y., Mar. 31, 1943; s. Paul Walken; m. Georgianne Thon, 1969. attended Hofstra U., studied with Wynn Handman, Actors Studio. Stage appearances include Broadway, off-Broadway and regional theatres throughout U.S. and Can.; Broadway debut in J.B. 1959; other stage appearances include Best Foot Forward, West Side Story, Macbeth, The Lion in Winter (Clarence Derwent award 1966), Hamlet, The Rose Tatoo (Theatre World's Most Promising Personality 1966-67), Romeo and Juliet, The Seagull, The Night Thoreau Spent in Jail (Joseph Jefferson award 1970-71), Kid Champion (Obie award 1975), Miss Julie, Sweet Bird of Youth, Hurlyburly, 1984, Cinders, 1984, A Bill of Divorcement, 1985, Coriolanus, 1988, Othello, 1992, (also playwright) Him, 1995; films include The Anderson Tapes, 1971, Next Stop Greenwich Village, The Sentinel, 1977, Roseland, 1977, Annie Hall, 1977, The Deer Hunter, 1978 (N.Y. Film Critics Best Supporting Actor award 1978, Acad. award Best Supporting Actor 1979), Last Embrace, 1979, Dogs of War, 1981, Heavens Gate, 1980, Pennies From Heaven, 1981, The Happiness Cage, 1982, The Dead Zone, 1983, Brainstorm, 1983, A View to a Kill, 1984, At Close Range, 1986, Deadline, 1987, Puss in Boots, 1988, The Milagro Beanfield War, 1988, Biloxi Blues, 1988, Communion, 1989, King of New York, 1990, Homeboy, 1991, The Comfort of Strangers, 1991, McBain, 1991, All American Murder, 1992, Batman Returns, 1992, True Romance, 1993, A Business Affair, 1994, Wayne's World II, 1994, Pulp Fiction, 1994, Search and Destroy, 1995, Nick of Time, 1995, The Addiction, 1995, The Prophecy, 19954, The Funeral, 1996, Basquiat, 1996, The Wild Side, 1996, Things To Do in Denver When You're Dead, 1995, Last Man Standing, 1996, Touch, 1997, Mousehunt, 1997, Excess Baggage, 1997, Suicide Kings, 1997, Sleepy Hollow, 1999, Blast From the Past, 1999, Kiss Toledo Goodbye, 1999, Vendetta, 1999, Antz (voice), 1998, Illuminata, 1998, New Rose Hotel, 1998, The Prophecy II, 1998, Trance, 1998, Scotland PA, 2001, Joe Dirt, 2001, America's Sweethearts, 2001, Chelsea Walls, 2001, The Affair of the Necklace, 2001, Jungle Juice, 2001, Poolhall Junkies, 2002, The Country Bears, 2002, Plots with a View, 2002, Catch Me If You Can, 2002 (Best Actor in Supporting Role, British Acad. Film Award (BAFTA)2003), Kangaroo Jack, 2003, Gigli, 2003, The Rundown, 2003, Man on Fire, 2004, Envy, 2004, The Stepford Wives, 2004; TV films include Sarah, Plain and Tall, 1991 (Emmy nominee), Skylark, 1993, Scam, 1993; The Opportunists, 1999, The Prophecy III: The Ascent, 1999, Sarah, Plain and Tall: 3, 1999; (TV series) Saturday Night Live (Am. Comedy award 2001), Naked City, 1958, Hawaii Five-O, 1968, Kojak, 1973; (TV mini-series) Julius Caesar, 2002.*

WALKER, ALAN C. anthropologist, educator; b. Leicester, Eng., Aug. 23, 1938; arrived in U.S., 1973; s. Cyril and Edith Walker; m. Patty L. Shipman, Apr. 20, 1976; 1 child, Simon B. BA with honors, U. Cambridge, Eng., 1962; PhD, U. London, 1967; DSc (hon.), U. Chgo., 2000. Lectr. Makerere U. Coll., Kampala, Uganda, 1965—69; sr. lectr. Nairobi U., Kenya, 1969—73; assoc. prof. Harvard U., Cambridge, Mass., 1973—78; prof. Johns Hopkins U., Balt., 1978—95; prof. anthropology Pa. State U., University Park, 1995—96, Disting. prof., 1996—2002, Evan Pugh prof., 2002—. Author: over 170 articles to profl. jours.; editor: several books. With Royal Air Force, 1957—59. Recipient Internat.Fyssen prize, Paris, Rhone Poulenc prize, London; fellow, Guggenheim Found., MacArthur Found. Fellow: Royal Soc., NAS (assoc.); mem.: Am. Acad. Arts and Scis. Achievements include discovery of and analysis of fossil primates and humans in East Africa. Avocations: goldsmithing, jewelry. Office: Pennsylvania State Univ Dept Anthropology 409 Carpenter Bldg University Park PA 16802

WALKER, ALICE, writer; b. Eatonton, Ga., Feb. 9, 1944; d. Willie Lee and Minnie (Grant) W.; m. Melvyn R. Leventhal, Mar. 17, 1967 (div. 1976); 1 dau., Rebecca Walker Leventhal. BA, Sarah Lawrence Coll., 1966; PhD (hon.), Russell Sage U., 1972; DHL (hon.), U. Mass., 1983. Co-founder, pub. Wild Trees Pr., Navarro, Calif., 1984-88. Writer in residence, tchr. black studies Jackson State Coll., 1968-69, Tougaloo Coll., 1970-71; lectr. literature Wellesley Coll., 1972-73, U. Mass., Boston, 1972-73; disting. writer Afro-American studies dept. U. Calif., Berkeley, 1982; Fannie Hurst Prof. of Literature Brandeis U., Waltham, Mass., 1982; cons. Friends of the Children of Miss., 1967. Author: Once, 1968, The Third Life of Grange Copeland, 1970, Five Poems, 1972, Revolutionary Petunias and Other Poems, 1973 (Nat. Book award nomination 1973, Lillian Smith award So. Regional Coun. 1973), In Love and Trouble, 1973 (Richard and Hinda Rosenthal Found. award Am. Acad. and Inst. of Arts and Letters 1974) Langston Hughes: American Poet, 1973, Meridian, 1976, Goodnight, Willie Lee, I'll See You in the Morning, 1979, You Can't Keep a Good Woman Down, 1981, The Color Purple, 1982 (Nat. Book Critics Circle award nomination 1982, Pulitzer Prize for fiction 1983, Am. Book award 1983), In Search of Our Mothers' Gardens, 1983, Horses Make a Landscape Look More Beautiful, 1984, To Hell With Dying, 1988, Living By the Word: Selected Writings, 1973-1987, 1988, The Temple of My Familiar, 1989, Her Blue Body Everything We Know: Earthling Poems, 1965-1990, 1991, Finding the Green Stone, 1991, Possessing the Secret of Joy, 1992, (with Pratibha Parmar) Warrior Marks, 1993, (with others) Double Stitch: Black Women Write About Mothers & Daughters, 1993, Everyday Use, 1994, Alice Walker Banned: The Banned Works, 1996, Everything We Love Can Be Saved: A Writer's Activism: Essays, Speeches, Statements and Letters, 1997, The Same River Twice, 1997; editor: I Love Myself When I'm Laughing... And Then Again When I'm Looking Mean and Impressive, 1979, By The Light of My Father's Smile, 1998, The Way Forward is With a Broken Heart, 2000, Absolute Trust in the Goddness of the Earth: New Poems, 2003. Recipient first prize Am. Scholar essay contest, 1967, O. Henry award for Kindred Spirits, 1986, Nora Astorga Leadership award, 1989, Fred Cody award for lifetime achievement Bay Area Book Reviewers Assn., 1990, Freedom to Write award PEN Ctr. USA West, 1990; Bread Loaf Writer's Conf. scholar, 1966; Merrill writing fellowship, 1967; McDowell Colony fellowship, 1967, 77-78; National Endowment for the Arts grantee, 1969, 77; Radcliffe Inst. fellowship, 1971-73; Guggenheim fellow, 1977-78. Address: Random House Inc 1745 Broadway #B1 New York NY 10019-4305

WALKER, ALLEN LYON, engineer; b. Wellsboro, Pa., Jan. 30, 1943; s. Joseph Dewitt and Louise (Thompson) W.; m. Jean Barbara Hickson, Aug. 11, 1979 (div. Jan. 1985); 1 child, Iain Lyon Walker; m. Mary Ann Knowlton Walker, Jan. 30, 1987. A in Engring. Mech., Williamsport (Pa.) Tech. Inst., 1963; Grad., U.S. Army Aviation Sch., 1970, U.S. Army Test Pilots Sch., 1970, U.S. Army Comd./Gen. Staff, Coll., Ft. Leavensworth, Kans., 1991. Lic. comml. pilot, FAA. Exptl. lab. tech. Ille Electric Corp., Williamsport, 1963-65; commd. 2nd lt. U.S. Army, 1965, advanced through grades to maj., 1966, ret., 1995; tool engr. Ingersoli Rand Corp., Painted Post, N.Y., 1965-66; aviator, test pilot U.S. Army, Vietnam, 1966-68, aircraft maintenance officer, 1969-72, co. comdr., 1969-72; maintenance engr. Ingersoll Rand Corp., Painted Post, N.Y., 1972-75; logistics mgr. Bell Helicopter Internat., Kermanshah, Iran, 1975—77; base supply mgr. Gen. Devices/Grumman, Kermanshah, Iran, 1977—79; field engr. Northrop Grumman Corp., Phila., 1980—. Adv. Army of the Rep. of Vietnam, Anh-Khe, 1967, English instr., 1967. Author treatise, 1990. Founding warden Internat. Order of St. Vincent, Holy Nativity, Rockledge, Pa., 1992-98, life mem.; dist. commr. Cradle of Liberty coun. Boy Scouts Am., Phila., 1994-99, coun. commr., 1999-2004, adv. coun., 2004—. Maj. U.S. Army, 1966-72, Vietnam, Europe. Decorated Bronze Star, Air medal, Meritorious Svc. medal; recipient Silver Beaver award, Boy Scouts Am., award of merit, Cradle of Liberty coun. Boy Scouts Am., Disting. Commr. award, Daniel C. Beard Masonic Scouter's award, Boy Scouts Am.; James E. West Found. fellow. Mem.: SAR, Soc. Logistics Engrs. (vice-chmn. 1982—85), Mil. Order of Loyal Legion of U.S., Lyons Family Assn. (v.p. 1972—75), Brit. Officers Club of Phila. (sec. 1990—93), Royal Order Scotland, Nat. Sojourners, Knights Templar, Shriners (comdr. Legion of Honor 2000), Masons (32d degree, past master 2001—03). Republican. Episcopalian. Avocations: genealogy, scouting, astronomy. Home: 419 Huntingdon Pike Rockledge PA 19046-4449 Office: Naval Inventory Control Pnt 700 Robbins Ave Philadelphia PA 19111-5008

WALKER, ANTOINE DEVON, professional basketball player; b. Chgo., Aug. 12, 1976; 1 child, Crystal. Student, U. Ky., 1996. Forward Boston Celtics, 1996—. Named to 1996-97 NBA All Rookie First Team. Avocations: dance, bowling, video games. Office: c/o Boston Celtics 151 Merrimac St Ste 5 Boston MA 02114-4714

WALKER, BARABARA J. interior designer, writer; b. Maryville, Tenn., June 23, 1940; d. Clarence K. and Virgina Grace Walker; m. G. Richard Geldbaugh (div.); children: Mark Richard Geldbaugh, Susan Michele Geldbaugh. Lic. Fla. State Bd. Arch. and Interior Design, 1958. Owner Park Pl. A Good Design Shop, Manchester Ctr., Vt., 1974—78; prin. designer, pres. Interior Design Concepts, LTD, Manchester, Vt., 1974—89; owner Bellwether Gallery, Manchester Ctr., Vt., 1980—88; pres., prin. buyer Beli Internat., Manchester, Vt., 1988—96; product design and develop. S.R. Guggenheim Mus., Biltmore Antique Stores, Source Internat., Paracelso Boutiques, 1993—95; interior designer Walker Designs, Ft. Lauderdale, Fla., 1994—. Author: Bali Style, 1995. Appt. mem. of hist. preservation adv. bd. City of Ft. Lauderdale, 2004—; bd. dirs. Vt. Folklife Mus., Middlebury, Vt., 1989—92. Mem.: Nat. League of Am. Penn Women. Avocations: photography, tennis, boating, nature studies. Home: 69 Marsh Lane Dorset VT 05251 Office: Walker Designs 401 Riveria Isle Dr Fort Lauderdale FL 33301 Office Phone: 954-629-8143.

WALKER, BARBARA DODSON, cultural organization administrator, consultant, lecturer, researcher; b. Washington, Jan. 18, 1930; d. Joseph Norman Dodson and Naomi Althea Neal; m. James Dent Walker; children: James Dent, Barbara Ann Brissett, Althea Elizabeth Davi, Susan Victoria. BS, Miner Tchrs. Coll., Washington, 1951; EdM, Fed. City Coll., Washington, 1972. Cert. tchr. Tchr. DC Pub. Sch., Washington, 1951—83; rec. sec. Afro-Am. Hist. and Geneal. Soc., Washington, 1989—92, nat. pres., 1993—. Dir. Fedn. of Geneal. Socs., 1997—; coun. mem. Assn. Study of African-Am. Life and History, 2002—; mem. DC Hist. Records Adv. Bd., 2003—. Contbr. book and periodical indexes, articles to profl. jours., chapters to books. Recipient Dist. Svc. award, Afro-Am. Hist. and Geneal. Soc., 1989, DC Geneal. Soc., 2001. Mem.: Nat. Geneal. Soc., Hist. Soc. of Washington. Avocations: reading, collecting books, music boxes, angels. Home: 1320 Sheperd St NW Washington DC 20011 Office: Afro-Am Hist & Geneal Soc PO Box 73067 Washington DC 20056-7306

WALKER, BEATRIZ ALEM, language educator; b. Montevideo, Uruguay, 1958;, permanent resident, 2002; d. Miguel Ronald and Nela Flor de Liz Alem; m. Jack C Walker, 1979; children: Ana Maria Parker, Amanda, Ashley Trevino, J.C. BAS, Abilene Christian U., 1996; MEd, Abilene Christian U, 1999; MA in romance languages, Tex. Tech. U., 2002, student. Tchg. cert. Abilene Christian U., 1997, cert. of proficiency in english U. Mich., 1979, Alianza Cultural Uruguay, 1979, bi-lingual sec. cert. 1977. Spanish instr. Abilene Ind. Sch. Dist., Abilene, Tex., 1997—99, Abilene Christian U., 1999—; grad. asst. to cert. officer Abilene Christian U., Dept. Edn., 1996; asst. with spanish lags Abilene Christian U., Dept. Fgn. Languages, 1996; translator for channel 5 Montevideo, Uruguay, 1991—92; bilingual sec. to Dr. Dan C. Coker Abilene Christian U., Dept. Missions, 1982—83; bilingual sec. La Iglesia de Cristo, 1977—79. Cons. culture and lang. Bridges to the World, Abilene; state textbook rev. panel me. Tex. Edn. Agy., Austin, 2000. Recipient Nat. Honor Soc., Phi Eta Sigma, ACU Chpt., 1995, Sigma Delta Pi, Tex. Tech. Chpt., 2000. Mem.: Am. Assn. teachers of Spanish and Portugese, Am. Coun. Tchg. of Fgn. Languages, Phi Delta Kappa. Avocations: travel, writing, photography. Office: Abilene Christian U Dept Fgn Languages Box 28275 Abilene TX 79699

WALKER, BETSY ELLEN, consulting and systems integration company executive; b. Atlanta, Sept. 14, 1953; d. John Franklin and Betty Louise (Brown) W.; children: William Franklin, Samuel Elliott. BA summa cum laude, Duke U., 1974; MBA, Harvard U., 1978. Mgmt. trainee First Atlanta, 1974, officer, 1975-76; analyst Coca Cola, Atlanta, 1977; bus. analyst Am. Mgmt. Systems Inc., N.Y.C., 1978-80, prin., 1981, v.p., 1982-99, dir. fin. svcs. group, 1982-90, IBM Svcs. sector group, 1990-92, fin. strategic initiatives group, 1993; dir. fin. industry Strategic Alliance Group, 1994-96, area dep. dir. fin. industry groups, 1996-97; COO, bd. dirs. Security First Network Bank, Atlanta, 1999. Mem. mgmt. policy com. Am. Mgmt. Systems, 1988-99, mem. corp. operating group; pres. B.E. Walker Assoc., Inc., 1999-2003. J. Spencer Love fellow Harvard U., 1976-78. Mem. Alexandria North Ridge Citizens

Assn. (exec. bd. 1994-96), Harvard Bus. Sch. Club (bd. mgrs. Madison Green 1990-91, treas.), Phi Beta Kappa, Pi Mu Epsilon. Office: Security First Network PO Box 1220 Rocky Mount NC 27802-1220 Personal E-mail: bewalker@mindspring.com.

WALKER, BETTE, automotive executive; BS in Bus. Mgmt., U. NH; student, Bosotn U. Tech. dir. Latin Am. Digital Equip. Corp.; IT exec. auto. sector safety restraint sys. AlliedSignal, Inc.; v.p., CIO Delphi Corp., Troy, Mich., 1997—. Office: World Hdqrs 5725 Delphi Dr Troy MI 48098-2815

WALKER, BRIGITTE MARIA, translator, linguistic consultant; b. Stolp, Germany, Sept. 20, 1934; came to U.S., 1957; d. Joseph Karl and Ursula Maria Margot Ehrler; m. John V. Kelley (div.); 1 child, John V. Jr.; m. Edward D. Walker, July 3, 1977. Grad., Erlangen Translator's Sch., Germany, 1956; grad. fgn. corres., Berlitz Sch., Germany, 1956. Bilingual sec., translator Spencer Patent Law Office, Washington, 1959-62; office mgr., translator I. William Millen, Millen and White, Patent Law, Washington, 1962-67; prin. Tech. Translating Bur., Washington, 1967-68, St. Petersburg Beach, Fla., 1968—. Cons. for patent law offices, Washington, 1962—; ofcl. expert for ct. Paul M. Craig, Patent Atty., Rockford, Ill., 1981; cons. to sci. editor Merriam-Webster, Inc., Springfield, Mass., 1987—. Author: German-English/English-German Last-Resort Dictionary for Technical Translators, 1991, (poetry) The Other Side of the Mirror, 1992 (Poetry award Nat. League Am. Pen Women 1994); co-translator: The Many Faces of Research, 1980; holder of trademark in field. Evaluator fgn. textbooks Pinellas County Sch. Bd., St. Petersburg, 1987, German judge, 1988. Recipient Recogninition award Pinellas County Sch. Bd., 1988, Meritorious Pub. Svc. award City of St. Petersburg Beach, 1987, poetry award Nat. League Am. Pen Women, 1994, 99, 2000, essay award, 1996, short story award, 1997, Grand prize for poem DDDD Publs., 1998. Mem. Mensa (Winner Nat. award Best Fiction 1996). Democrat. Lutheran. Avocations: swimming, aerobics, piano, painting. Home: Pasadena Apts #428 1885 Shore Dr S Saint Petersburg FL 33707-4746

WALKER, BRUCE EDWARD, anatomy educator; b. Montreal, Que., Can., June 17, 1926; s. Robinson Clarence and Dorothea Winston (Brown) W.; m. Lois Catherine McCuaig, June 26, 1948; children: Brian Ross, Dianne Heather, Donald Robert, Susan Lois. BS, McGill U., 1947, MS, 1952, PhD, 1954; MD, U. Tex. at Galveston, 1966. Instr. anatomy McGill U., 1955-57; asst. prof. anatomy U. Tex. Med. Br., 1957-61, assoc. prof. anatomy, 1961-67; prof. Mich. State U., East Lansing, 1967—, chmn. dept., 1967-75. Contbr. articles to profl. jours. Mem. Am. Assn. Anatomists, Teratology Soc., Am. Assn. for Cancer Rsch. Office: Mich State U Dept Radiology and Anatomy East Lansing MI 48824-1316

WALKER, CARLENE MARTIN, state senator; BS, Brigham Young U., 1969. Supr. coding & data entry the Wirthlin Group, 1982-86; cons. D.K. Shifflet & Assocs., 1987-88; ptnr., mgr. Covecrest Properties, 1978-99; dir. adminstrn. Energy Lock, Inc., 1992-99; tech. recruiter Manpower Tech., 1999-2000; mem. Utah State Senate, Salt Lake City, 2001—. Cons. Wash. Times Newspaper, 1987-88. Bd., chair fundraising com. Granite Edn. Found., 1989-90; chmn., founder of the bd. Repub. Womens Political Action Com. Office: 4085 E Prospector Dr Salt Lake City UT 84121

WALKER, CAROLYN PEYTON, English language educator; b. Charlottesville, Va., Sept. 15, 1942; d. Clay M. and Ruth Peyton. BA with distinction in Am. History/Lit., Sweet Briar Coll., 1965; cert. in French, Alliance Francaise, Paris, 1966; EdM, Tufts U., 1970; MA in English and Am. Lit, Stanford U., 1974, PhD in English Edn., 1977. Tchr. elem. and jr. h.s., Switzerland, 1967-69; tchr. elem. grades Boston Sch. System, 1966-67, 69-70, Newark (Calif) Unified Sch. System, 1970-72; instr. divsn. Humanities Canada Coll., Redwood City, Calif., 1973, 76-78; instr. Sch. Bus. U. San Francisco, 1973-74; evaluation cons. Inst. Profl. Devel., San Jose, Calif., 1975-76; asst. dir. Stanford U. Learning Assistance Ctr., Calif., 1972—77, dir., 1977—84, supr. counselors, tutors and tchrs., 1972-84; lectr., dept. English Stanford U., 1977-84; lectr. Stanford U. Sch. Edn., 1975-84; pvt. practice corp. tng., 1983—; prof. dept. English San Jose State U., 1984-93, dir. The Writing Ctr. dept. English, 1986—93, dir. Steinbeck Rsch. Ctr., 1986—87; mem. faculty U. Calif., Santa Cruz, Berkeley, 1995—. Condr. reading and writing workshops, 1972-1994; reviewer Random House Books, 1978-95, Rsch. in the Teaching of English, 1983-95, Course Tech., Inc.; bd. dirs. The Tech Mus. of Innovation, San Jose, 1983-84; head cons. to pres. to evaluate college's writing program, San Jose City Coll., 1985-87, cons. U. Texas, Dallas, 1984; numerous testing programs; Ednl. Testing Svc., 1985-88; English dept. Writing Ctr., 1986-93; spkr. in field.; cons. in field. Author: Handbook for Teaching Assistants at Stanford University, 1977, Learning Center Courses for Faculty and Staff: Reading, Writing, and Time Management, 1981, How to Succeed as a New Teacher: A Handbook for Teaching Assistants, 1978, ESL Courses for Faculty & Staff: An Additional Opportunity to Serve the Campus Community, 1983, (with Karen Wilson) Tutor Handbook for the Writing Center at San Jose State University, 1989, (with others) Academic Tutoring at the Learning Assistance Center, 1980, Writing Conference Talk: Factors Associated with HIgh and Low Rated Writing Conferences, 1987, Lifeline Mac: A Handbok for Instructors in the Macintosh Computer Classrooms, 1989, Communications with the Faculty: Vital Links for the Success of Writing Centers, 1991, Coming to America, 1993, Teacher Dominance in the Writing Conference, 1992, Instant Curriculum: Just Add Tutors and Students, 1993; editor newsletter Environ. Vols. Inc., Palo Alto, Calif., 1999-2003; contbr. chpts. to Black American Literature Forum, 1991; contbr. articles to profl. jours. Founding mem. Tech. Mus. of Innovation, San Jose, Calif., 1995; vol. fundraiser Peninsula Ctr. for the Blind, Palo Alto, Calif., 1982—2001, The Resource Ctr. for Women, Palo Alto, 1975—76, Pathways Hospice, 2002—; vol. Gamble Garden Ctr., 1989—. Recipient Award for Outstanding Contbns., U.S. HEW, 1979, award ASPIRE (federally funded program), 1985, two awards Student Affirmative Action, 1986, award Western Coll. Reading & Leanring Assn., 1984; numerous other awards and grants. Mem.: Tech. Mus. Innovation. Home: 2350 Waverley St Palo Alto CA 94301-4143 Office Phone: 650-321-6466.

WALKER, CHARLES B. chemicals company executive; b. 1939; Attended, Univ. of Richmond, Richmond, VA, 1961. With Southern States Co-Op, Inc., 1961-64, Albemarle Paper Mfg. Co., 1965-68; pres. Spotless Stores, Richmond, Va., 1969-74; with State Comp. State of Va., 1974-81, sec. adminstrn. and fin., 1978; v.p. Ethyl Corp., Richmond, 1981 ; now CFO, vice chmn., tng. dir. Ethyl Corp, Richmond. Office: Albemarle Corp PO Box 1335 Richmond VA 23218

WALKER, CHARLES D. astronaut; b. Bedford, Ind., Aug. 29, 1948; s. Donna Lake Walker; m. Susan Y. Flowers; 1 child. BS in Aero. and Astronautical Engring., Purdue U., 1971; DSc (hon.), St. Louis Coll. Pharmacy, 1985. Civil engring. technician, land acquisition specialist, forest firefighter U.S. Forest Svc.; design engr. Bendix Aerospace Co.; project engr. Naval Sea Systems Command; test engr., Aft Propulsion Subsys. for Space Shuttle orbiters McDonnell Douglas Corp., 1977, original mem. Space Mfg. Team (laster Electrophoresis Ops. in Space, EOS), chief test engr., payload specialist, EOS commercialization project, 1979—86, spl. asst. to pres. Space Systems Co., 1986; sr. mgr., space programs bus. devel. and mktg. Boeing Co. Ops., Washington. Industry mem. numerous NASA task forces; mem. NRC Space Applications Bd.; faculty course advisor, lectr. Internat. Space U., 1988; nat. panel mem. NASA/Industry Manned Flight Awareness Program, NASA/Industry Edn. Initiative; bd. dirs. Challenger Ctr. Space Sci. Edn.; trainer various NASA astronaut crews; astronaut Space Shuttle missions 41-D, 51-D and 61-B; chmn. organizing com. World Space Congress, 1992. Contbr. articles to profl. jours. and mags., chapters to books. Bd. mem. Astronauts Meml. Found.; vol. chmn., bd. dirs. Spacecause. Named Ky. Col., Commonwealth of Ky., 1990; recipient Space Flight medals, NASA, 1984—85, Aerospace Laurels award, Aviation Week and Space Tech. Mag., 1985, Engring. Astronaut Alumnus award, Purdue U. Schs. Engring., Lindbergh award, AIAA, St. Louis sect., 1986. Mem.: Assn. Space Explorers (bd. dirs.), Nat. Space Soc. (bd. dirs., past pres.). Achievements include patents for electrophoresis apparatus with flow control. Office: Astronaut Office/CB NASA Johnson Space Ctr Houston TX 77058*

WALKER, CHARLES DODSLEY, conductor, organist; b. N.Y.C., Mar. 16, 1920; s. Marshall Starr and Maude Graham (Marriott) Walker; m. Janet Elizabeth Hayes, May 30, 1949 (dec. Feb. 1997); children: Peter Hayes, Susan Starr; m. Elizabeth Ann Phillips, Jan. 14, 2001. BS, Trinity Coll., 1940; AM, Harvard U., 1947. Organist, choirmaster Am. Cathedral, Paris, 1948-50, Ch. of the Heavenly Rest, N.Y.C., 1951-88; music dir. Blue Hill Troupe, Ltd., N.Y.C., 1955-90, Chapin Sch., N.Y.C., 1961-85; mem. organ faculty Union Theol. Sem., N.Y.C., 1962-73, NYU, N.Y.C., 1968-80; dean, music dir. Berkshire Choral Inst., Sheffield, Mass., 1982-91; organist, choirmaster Trinity Episcopal Ch., Southport, Conn., 1988—. Contbr. articles to profl. jours. Lt. comdr. USNR, 1942—46. Recipient Disting. Alumnus award, Cathedral Choir Sch., 1988. Fellow: Am. Guild Organists (nat. pres. 1971—75); mem.: Canterbury Choral Soc. (founder, condr. 1952—), Am. Fedn. Musicians, St. Wilfrid Club, Bohemians. Avocations: travel, photography. Home: 160 W 96th St Apt 15N New York NY 10025-9212 Office: Trinity Episcopal Ch 651 Pequot Ave Southport CT 06890-1416 Office Phone: 203-255-0454 x307. Personal E-mail: dodsley@aol.com.

WALKER, CHARLES URMSTON, retired university president; b. Bolivar, Pa., June 20, 1931; s. Charles William and Frances May (Urmston) W.; m. Cherie Hall Duckworth, Aug. 7, 1959; children: Douglas Leland, Christy Lynn. BA, U. Pitts., 1953; MA, Columbia U., 1958; PhD, Stanford U., 1964; LLD (hon.), Kanto Gakuin U., 1979; LHD (hon.), Linfield Coll., 1992. Asst. prof. English Rockford (Ill.) Coll., 1958-61; dept. head, residence dir. Menlo Coll., Menlo Park, Calif., 1961-64; v.p., dean Hamline U., St. Paul, 1964-70; pres. Russell Sage Coll., Troy, N.Y., 1970-75, Linfield Coll., McMinnville, Oreg., 1975-92, pres. emeritus, 1992—; ednl. cons., 1992—; dir. managed programs Ford Family Found., Roseburg, Oreg., 1993-98. Bd. dirs. 1st Fed. Savs. & Loan, McMinnville, Wespro Ins. Co., Oreg. Mut. Ins. Co.; mem. Univ. Pres. Initiative, IIE/USIA/NATO, Brussels, 1991. Bd. dirs. South Tillamook County Libr., 1994; pres. Neskowin (Oreg.) Chamber Music; co-chair bldg. com. First Bapt. Ch., McMinnville; bd. dirs., mem. exec. com., dir. Oreg. Coun. Humanities; trustee, vice chair Ford Family Found.; chair Oreg. Cultural Trust, pres. Found. Better Oregon. Warg scholar U. Pitts., 1949-51; Univ. fellow Stanford U., 1963-64; Hill Found. grantee, St. Paul, 1970; Paul Harris fellow Rotary Internat., 1987; recipient Community Svc. award Troy, N.Y. Troy C. of C., 1975, First Citizen award McMinnville, Oreg., 1989; named Man of Yr., Troy C. of C., 1975. Mem. Univ. Club (Portland), Rotary (past pres. McMinnville). Home: 1324 SW Gilorr St Mcminnville OR 97128-6617 E-mail: cwalkc@oregoncoast.com.

WALKER, CHARLS EDWARD, economist, consultant; b. Graham, Tex., Dec. 24, 1923; s. Pinkney Clay and Sammye D. (McCombs) W.; m. Harmolyn Hart, June 24, 1949; children: Carolyn, Charls Edward. BBA, U. Tex., 1947, MBA, 1948; PhD in Econs., U. Pa., 1955. Instr. fin. U. Tex., 1947-48, asst. prof., then assoc. prof., 1950-54; instr. fin. U. Pa. Wharton Sch., 1948-50; fin. economist Fed. Res. Bank Phila., 1953; with Fed. Res. Bank Dallas, 1954-61, v.p., econ. adviser, 1958-61; economist Republic Nat. Bank Dallas, 1955-56; asst. to sec. treasury, 1959-61; exec. v.p. Am. Bankers Assn., N.Y.C., 1961-69; under sec. treasury, 1969-72; dep. sec., 1972-73. Adj. prof. U. Tex., Austin, 1986—, Tex. A&M U., 2000-2003; bd. dirs. Washington Campus, Nat. Coun. Econ. Edn.; chmn., CEO Charls E. Walker Assocs., Inc., 1973-96; disting. vis. prof. Emory U., 2000-02. Co-editor: The Bankers Handbook, New Directions in Federal Tax Policy, The Consumption Tax: A Better Alternative, 1987, Intellectual Property Rights and Capital Formation, 1988, The U.S. Savings Challenge, 1990; contbr. articles to profl. jours. and newspapers, chpts. to books. Founder, chmn. emeritus Am. Coun. for Capital Formation; co-founder Com. on the Present Danger, 1976, chmn. Pres.'s adv. coun. on minority enterprise, 1973-75; co-chmn. Presdl. Debates, 1976; founder, chmn. Bretton Woods Com.; chmn. Ronald Reagan's Task Force on Tax Policy, 1980; sr. advisor Ctr. for Deliberative Polling, U. Tex., 1996-, Stanford U., 2003-. Recipient Alexander Hamilton award U.S. Dept. Treasury, Urban League award, Baker award for Exemplary Svc. to Econ. Edn., 1991, Disting. Svc. award, 2002, Pro Bono Meritas award Coll. Liberal Arts U. Tex., 2003; named Disting. Alumnus, U. Tex., 1994. Mem.: Coun. Fgn. Rels., Sea Island (Ga.) Club, Congl. Club (Bethesda, Md.), Burning Tree Club. Home: 10120 Chapel Rd Potomac MD 20854-4143 Home (Winter): 105 Biltmore Saint Simons GA 31522 *What's good for the public interest ultimately is good for every person, business, or other group in the nation. This, combined with modern application of the Golden Rule, about sums it up.*

WALKER, CLARENCE EUGENE, psychology educator; b. Monongahela, Pa., Jan. 8, 1939; s. Lewis G. Walker and Olga T. Brioli; div.; children: Chad Eugene, Kyle Lewis, Cass Emanuel. BS in Psychology summa cum laude, Geneva Coll., 1960; MS in Clin. Psychology, Purdue U., 1963, PhD in Clin. Psychology, 1965. Lic. psychologist, Okla. Psychology trainee West 10th St. VA Hosp., Indpls., 1962—63; intern in clin. psychology Riley Children's Hosp., West 10th St. VA Hosp., Indpls., 1963—64; asst. prof. Westmont Coll., 1964—68; pvt. practice clin. psychology Santa Barbara, Calif., 1965—68; from asst. prof. to assoc. prof. Baylor U., 1968—74; pvt. practice clin. psychology Waco, Tex., 1970—74; assoc. prof. med. sch. U. Okla., Oklahoma City, 1974—80, prof. med. sch., dir. pediatric psychology tng. program, 1980—95, prof. emeritus, 1995; chief pediatric psychology svc. Okla. Children's Meml. Hosp., 1974—80, dir. out-patient pediatric psychology clinic, 1974—80; assoc. chief mental health svcs. Children's Hosp. Okla., 1980—95; pres. Psychol. Cons., Inc., 1998—. Cons. Head Start Program, Waco, 1968-70, VA Hosp, Waco, 1969-74, VA Ctr., Temple, Tex., 1969-74, Region XII Ednl. Svc. Ctr., Waco, 1971-74, Rusk (Tex.) State Hosp., 1972-74, Bapt. Children's Home, Oklahoma City, 1975-79; rsch. cons. Los Alamos (N.Mex.) Pub. Schs., 1975-79; chmn. divsn. edn. and psychology Westmont Coll., 1966-68; consulting psychologist, 1995—. Author: Learn to Relax, 1975, 3d edit., 2001, (with P. Clement, A. Hedberg and L. Wright) Clinical Procedures for Behavior Therapy, 1981, (with B.L. Bonner and K. Kaufman) The Physically and Sexually Abused Child, 1988, others; editor: The History of Clinical Psychology in Autobiography, vol. I, 1992, vol. II, 1993, (with M.C. Roberts) Handbook of Clinical Child Psychology, 1983, 3d edit., 2001; contbr. articles to profl. jours. Fellow APA; mem. AAAS, Southwestern Psychol. Assn. (pres. 1977), Okla. Psychol. Assn. (pres. 1983), Soc. Pediatric Psychology (pres. 1986), Ctrl. Tex. Psychol. Assn. (pres. 1973), Sigma Xi. Avocations: reading, wine tasting, travel. Office Phone: 405-341-7399. Business E-Mail: genewalker@iname.com.

WALKER, CLARENCE WESLEY, lawyer; b. Durham, N.C., July 19, 1931; s. Ernie Franklin and Mollie Elizabeth (Cole) W.; m. Ann-Heath Harris, June 5, 1954; children: Clare Ann, Wesley Gregg. AB, Duke U., 1953, LL.B., 1955. Bar: N.C. 1955. Assoc. Mudge Stern Baldwin & Todd, 1955-59; ptnr. Kennedy, Covington, Loddell & Hickman, Charlotte, N.C., 1961—. Bd. dirs. Lawyers Mut. Liability Ins. Co., Legal Services Corp. N.C., Oakwood Homes Corp. Glendale Group, Ltd.; lectr. N.C. Bar Found. Continuing Legal Edn. Insts., N.C. Jud. Planning Com., 1978-79; pres. Pvt. Adjudication Found. Chmn. bd. mgrs. Charlotte Meml. Hosp. and Med. Ctr., 1981-87; trustee N.C. Ctrl. U., 1979-83; vice-chmn. Charlotte-Mecklenburg Hosp. Authority, 1988-99; adv. bd. Ctrl. Piedmont Paralegal Sch.; trustee Carolinas Healthcare Found., Charlotte Country Day Sch., 1977-81; state chmn. Nat. Found. March of Dimes, 1968-70; chmn. Charlotte Park and Recreation Commn., 1970-73; bd. dirs. Charlotte Symphony, 1965-71, Bethlehem Ctr., 1975-77, N.C. Recreators Found., 1973-75; adv. bd. Charlotte Children's Theatre, 1972; bd. dirs. Charlotte C. of C., 1970-72; bd. visitors Duke U. Law Sch.; dir., gen. campaign chmn. United Way Ctrl. Carolinas, 1985. Fellow Am. Bar Found.; mem. N.C. Bar Assn. (pres. 1978-79, gov. 1971-75), ABA (state del. 1980-89, assembly del. 1989-97, bd. govs. 1997-2000, chair audit com. 2000—) 26th Jud. Dist. Bar Assn., Mecklenburg Bar Found. (trustee), Am. Law Inst., Order of Coif, Phi Eta Sigma, Phi Beta Kappa. Democrat. Methodist. Home: 1047 Ardsley Rd Charlotte NC 28207-1815 Office: Kennedy Covington Lobdell & Hickman Hearst Tower 47th Fl 214 N Tryon St Charlotte NC 28202

WALKER, COREAN JONES, evangelist; b. Marion, Ind., Mar. 27, 1952; d. Arthur Lee and Millie Mae Jones; 1 child, Jennifer Nicole. Diploma, Marion HS, Marion, Ind., 1970; diploma word processing, Ind. Bus. Coll., Marion, Ind., 1987—89. Evangelist. Dist. coord. Ind. One Ch. One Child, Marion, Ind., 1991—92; dir., fin. coord. Caring Hands Ministry, Marion, Ind., 1997—2003; editor-light centennial New Light Bapt. Ch., Marion, Ind., 2001—02. Editor: (newsletter) Light Centennial, 2001; author: (book) Walk With Me Lord, 2002, Inspirations of Love, 2003. Exec. sec. B for City Coun., Marion, Ind., 2003; founder Arthur Lee Jones- Millie Mae Jones Ministries; group leader Purpose Driven Women; founder His Women Outreach Ministry; bd. mem. Faith Tabernacle Outreach Ministries. Recipient Corean Walker Day Proclamation, City of Muncie, James P. Carey-Mayor, 1991, Ind. One Ch. One Child, Elaine Walters/So. Bend Ind., 1991, Cert. of Recognition, Famous Poets-Mark Schramm/ Talent, Oreg., 2001, Editor's Choice award, Internat. Libr. Poetry, 2004. Baptist. Starting "Caring Hands" a ministry that has helped 1,100 children have a nice Christmas- also in helping 250 children with Easter baskets. Assisting in adoptions for special needs children; intercessor for Kids Hope; assistance directory of Crowned With His Glory Ministries. Home: 2125 So Florence St Marion IN 46953 Personal E-mail: evancjn@yahoo.com.

WALKER, CRAIG M. cardiologist, medical association administrator; b. Boug, La. Grad., Nicholls State U., La. State U. Diplomate Am. Bd. Cardiology, Am. Bd. Internal Medicine, bd. cert. in interventional cardiology. Intern, resident Ochsner Found. Hosp.; rsch. and tchg. fellow Harvard U. Med. Sch., Boston; founder, med. dir. Cardiovasc. Inst. of the South, Houma, La.; med. dir. Cardiac Catheterization Lab., Terrebonne Gen. Med. Ctr., Houma, La. Lectr. in field. Contbr. articles to profl. jours. Named one of Ten Outstanding Young Americans, U.S. Jr. C. of C., 1992. Fellow: ACP, ACC, Am. Heart Assn. Coun. on Clin. Cardiology, Am. Soc. Laser Medicine and Surgery, Am. Coll. Chest Physicians, Soc. Cardiac Angiography and Interventions, Internat. Coll. Angiology, Am. Soc. Cardiovasc. Interventionists. Office: Cardiovasc Inst South 225 Dunn Street Houma LA 70360

WALKER, CRAIG MICHAEL, lawyer; b. Vermont, 1947; m. Patricia A. Magruder; two children. BA, Williams Coll., 1969; JD, Cornell U., 1972. Bar: N.Y., 1973, U.S. Dist. Ct. (so. dist.) N.Y., 1975, U.S. Ct. Appeals (2d cir) 1975, U.S. Supreme Ct., 1976. Assoc. Alexander and Green, N.Y.C., 1972—80, ptnr., 1980—86, chmn. litigation dept., 1985—86; ptnr. Walter, Conston, Alexander, and Green P.C., N.Y.C., 1987—89, Rogers and Wells, LLP, N.Y.C., 1990—99, Clifford, Chance, Rogers, and Wells, LLP, NYC, 2000—02; spl. trial counsel Clifford Chance US, LLP, NYC, 2002—03; ptnr., spl. trial counsel Walker Law, LLP, Pound Ridge, NY, 2004—. Contbr. author: New York Forms of Jury Instruction, 1992; contbr. articles to profl. journals. Fellow Am. Bar Found.; mem. ABA, N.Y. State Bar Assn., Def. Rsch. Inst., Fed. Bar Coun. Democrat.

WALKER, DALE MAXWELL, city official; b. Big Rapids, Mich., Dec. 18, 1947; s. Lewis M. and Hilma I. (Windquist) W.; m. Joanne Kay Richmond, June 22, 1968; children: Christina Elizabeth, Heather Marie. BS, Ferris State U., 1970; MBA, Ctrl. Mich. U., 1981. Cert. govt. fin. mgr. Dir. fin. City of Owosso, Mich., 1970-74; internal auditor John Wesley Coll., 1974—76; corp. treas. Mich. Bapt. Homes, Detroit, 1976-77; dir. fin. City of Cadillac, Mich., 1977—. Pres. Gospel Bookstore, Inc., Cadillac, 1983-98; bd. dirs. Workplace Ministry, 2001—. Bd. dirs. Wexford County United Way, 1980-82, Shiawassee County United Way, 1971-72; sec.-treas. Cadillac Police and Fire Retirement System, 1977-87, bd. dirs. 1987—; chmn. Mcpl. Employees Retirement System, Mich., 1997—. Fellow Govtl. Fin. Officers Assn. U.S. and Can. (Profl. Achievement award 1984-2004); mem. Mich. Mcpl. Fin. Officers Assn. (bd. dirs. 1983-85), Internat. City Mgrs. Assn., Mich. Mcpl. Treas. Assn., Mcpl. Treas. Assn. U.S. and Can. (bd. dirs. 1982-84), McGuires Golf Club. Republican. Baptist. Avocations: golf, swimming, reading. Home: 901 Lincoln St Cadillac MI 49601-2035 Office: 200 N Lake St Cadillac MI 49601-1829 Office Phone: 231-775-0181. E-mail: finance@cadillac-mi.net.

WALKER, DAN, mayor, business consultant; Mem. Torrance City Coun., 1978—92, 1994—2002; mayor City of Torrance, Calif., 2002—. Del. South Bay Cities Coun. Govts., L.A. County Sanitation Dist., South Bay Econ. Devel. Partnership; mem. Planning Commn., 1975—77. Mem. L.A. Regional Quality Control Bd.; bd. dirs. Friends of Child Advs. Office: 3031 Torrance Blvd Torrance CA 90503 E-mail: dwalker@tornet.com.

WALKER, DAVID A(LAN), finance educator; b. York, Pa., Jan. 5, 1941; s. Arthur Benjamin and Alva (Strasbougher) Walker; m. Audrey Thayer, Aug. 21, 1982; children: Matthew Billett, Elizabeth Penniman Bilhartz. BA, Pa. State U., 1962; MS, Iowa State U., 1964, PhD, 1968. Asst. prof. Pa. State U., 1968-70; economist FDIC, 1970-76, 78-80; vis. assoc. prof. Northwestern U., 1976-77; dir. rsch. Office Comptroller Currency, 1977-78; assoc. prof. fin. Georgetown U., 1980-82, prof., 1982-92, assoc. dean, 1985-87, John A. Largay prof., 1992—. Chair governing bd. Credit Rsch. Ctr., 1997—; dir. Capital Mkts. Rsch. Ctr., 1989—; hon. com. mem. Wall St. Inst., 2002-; advisor US Dept. Treas., US SBA; cons. field. Co-author textbooks; editor Jour. Fin. Rsch., 1981-87; co-editor Jour. Small Bus. Fin., 1992-95; mem. editl. bd. Jour. Fin. Rsch., Fin. Mgmt., J.F.Q.A., Fin. Rev., Quar. Rev. Econ. and Fin., Jour. Small Bus. Fin.; contbr. articles to profl. jours. NDEA fellow, 1962-64. Mem. Am. Econ. Assn., So. Fin. Assn. (bd. dirs.), Ea. Fin. Assn. (bd. dirs.), Fin. Mgmt. Assn. (v.p. 1990-91, pres. 1994-95, trustee 1995—, chair bd. trustees 1999—), Beta Gamma Sigma. Republican. Home: 4416 Que St NW Washington DC 20007 Office: Georgetown U Sch Bus Washington DC 20057-0001 Office Phone: 202-687-4582. E-mail: walkerd@georgetown.edu.

WALKER, DAVID ELLIS, JR., educator, minister, consultant; b. Richmond, Va., Oct. 5, 1938; s. David Ellis and Laura Eloise (Vaughan) W.; m. Sandra Suzanne Barnes, Feb. 3, 1964; children: David Ellis III, Virginia Suzanne Walker Frizzell, Cindy Poole Key, Michelle Poole Clark. BA, David Lipscomb U., 1960; MA, U. Fla., 1961, PhD, 1969. Ordained to ministry Ch. Christ, 1954. Instr. Jacksonville (Fla.) U., 1963-65; min. Ch. of Christ, 1954—; prof. Middle Tenn. State U., Murfreesboro, 1965—. Acting chmn. dept. speech Middle Tenn. State U., 1984, 1990, dir. debate, 1965-70, pres. faculty senate, 1983-84; coord. comm. studies,1969-81, 97-99; cons. in field. Editor Jour. of NonTraditional Education, 1992-96; contbr. articles to profl. jours. Grad. fellow U. Fla., 1961-63; grantee Mid. Tenn. State U., 1967, 72, 77-78, 88-90, 92-94, David Walker scholar Mid. Tenn. State U., 1993—. Mem. NEA, Tenn. Comm. Assn. (v.p. 1973-74, pres. 1974-75, 2003-04, editor jour. 1977-85, Educator of Yr. 2002-03.), Tenn. Intercollegiate Forensic Assn. (pres. 1966-67, exec. sec. 1967-68), So. States Comm. Assn., Tenn. Edn. Assn., Pi Kappa Delta (gov. province of S.E. 1966-68), Phi Kappa Phi (chpt. treas. 1989-90). Avocations: reading, walking. Home: Ste 202 910 Murfreesboro Rd Franklin TN 37064 Office: Mid Tenn State U Dept Of Speech And Theatre Murfreesboro TN 37132-0001 Office Phone: 615-898-2270. Business E-Mail: dwalker@mtsu.edu.

WALKER, DAVID MICHAEL, US government officer; b. Birmingham, Ala., Oct. 2, 1951; s. David Sellers and Dorothy Ann (West) W.; m. Mary Carmel Etheredge, June 12, 1971; children: Carol Marie, James Andrew. BS in Acctg., Jacksonville U., 1973; Sr. Exec. Govt. Cert., Harvard U., 1986; PhD in Bus. Adminstrn. (hon.), Bryant Coll., 2002; PhD in Pub. Svc. (hon.), Lincoln Meml. U., 2004. CPA, Fla., Tex. Sr. auditor Price Waterhouse & Co. and Coopers & Lybrand, Jacksonville, Fla., 1973-76; dir. personnel Coopers & Lybrand, Atlanta and Houston, 1976-79; Ea. regional mgr. Source Svcs. Corp., Washington, 1979-83; acting exec. dir. and dep. exec. dir. Pension Benefit Guaranty Corp., Washington, 1983-85; dep. asst. sec. U.S. Dept. of Labor, Washington, 1985-87, asst. sec., 1987-89; ptnr., global mng. dir. human capital svcs. practice Arthur Andersen LLP, Atlanta, 1989-98; U.S. comptroller gen. U.S. Gen. Acctg. Office, Washington, 1998—. Author: Retirement Security-Understanding and Planning Your Financial Future, 1996; co-author: Delivering on the Promise: How to Attract, Manage and Retain Human Capital, 1998; contbr. articles, editl. adv. bd. several profl. jours. Gov. bd. Internat. Orgn. Supreme Audit Instns. chmn. strategic planning, acctg., reporting, and numerous other not-for-profit bds. and adv. coms., mem.; mem. fin. acctg. stds. adv. com.; chmn. U.S. Intergovtl. Audit Forum; chmn. U.S. Joint Fin. Mgmt. Improvement Program, Ctr. Continuous Auditing. Recipient numerous pub. svc., profl. and industry awards for outstanding svc. and contbns. Mem. AICPA Group of 100 (past chmn. employee benefit plans com.), Nat. Acad. Pub. Adminstrn., Nat. Acad. Social Ins., Coun. for Excellence in Govt., Concord Coalition, Sons of Am. Revolution, Cosmos Club. Roman Catholic.

Home: 9061 Tower House Pl Alexandria VA 22308-2758 Office: US Gen Acctg Office 441 G St NW Ste 700 Washington DC 20548-0001 Office Phone: 202-512-5500. E-mail: walkerd@gao.gov.

WALKER, DEWARD EDGAR, JR., anthropologist, educator; b. Johnson City, Tenn., Aug. 3, 1935; s. Deward Edgar and Matilda Jane (Clark) W.; m. Candace J. Arroyo; children: Alice, Deward Edgar III, Mary Jane, Sarah, Daniel, Joseph Benjamin. Student, Ea. Oreg. Coll., 1953-54, 56-58, Univ. of the Americas, 1958-59; BA in Anthropology with honors, U. Oreg., 1960-61, PhD in Anthropology, 1964; postgrad., Wash. State U., 1962. Asst. prof. anthropology George Washington U., Washington, 1964-65, Wash. State U., Pullman, 1965-67, research collaborator, 1967-69; assoc. prof., chmn. dept. Sociology/Anthropology, lab. dir. U. Idaho, Moscow, 1967-69; prof. U. Colo., Boulder, 1969—, research assoc. in population processes program of inst. behavioral sci., 1969-73, assoc. dean Grad. Sch., 1973-76. Founder, v.p. Walker Rsch. Group, Ltd., Boulder, Colo., 1995. Founder, co-editor Northwest Anthropol. Rsch. Notes, 1966—; editor, Plateau Vol.: Handbook of North American Indians, 1971-98; author, co-author 150 books, reports, articles and papers. Mem. tech. steering panel Hanford Environ. Dose Reconstrn. Project, 1988-95, Basalt Waste Isolation Project, Hanford, 1986-88; advisor on Native Am. affairs. With U.S. Army, 1954-62. Fellow NSF, 1961, NDEA, 1961-64. Fellow Am. Anthropol. Assn. (assoc. editor Am. Anthropologist 1973-74), Soc. Applied Anthropology (hon. life, exec. com. 1970-79, treas. 1976-79, chmn. 1960-2000, cons., expert witness western tribes, editor Human Orgn. 1970-76, rschr. over 65 projects with 150 monographs, articles, reports, and papers, editor High Plains Applied Anthropologist); mem. AAAS, Am. Acad. Polit. and Social Scis., N.W. Anthropol. Conf. Avocations: geology, mining, ranching. Home: PO Box 4147 Boulder CO 80306-4147 Office: U Colo PO Box 233 Boulder CO 80309-0233 E-mail: walkerde@spot.colorado.edu. *I have been both lucky and happy to have had the opportunities to do so many wonderful things in my life as an anthropologist.*

WALKER, DONALD ANTHONY, economist, educator; b. Mar. 6, 1934; s. Timothy Anthony and Helen (Walker) W.; m. Patricia Ann McKeage, Feb. 14, 1961; 1 dau., Valerie Alana. AB, Tex. State U., 1952; MA, U. Tex., 1956; PhD, Harvard U., 1961. Asst. prof. econs. Miami U., Oxford, Ohio, 1961-67, assoc. prof. econs., 1967-69; prof. econs. Indiana U. Pa., 1969-88, chmn. dept., 1969-98, Univ. prof., 1988-98, Univ. prof., prof. econs. emeritus, 1999—. Author: Walras's Market Models, 1996, Advances in General Equilibrium Theory, 1997; editor: William Jaffé's Essays on Walras, 1983, Money and Markets: Essays by Robert W. Clower, 1984, Perspectives on the History of Economic Thought, 1989, Welfare Economics and the Theory of Economic Policy, 1995, Jour. of the History of Econ. Thought, 1989—98, Economics, Welfare Policy and the History of Economic Thought, 1999, Equilibrium, 2000, The Legacy of Léon Walras, 2001; co-editor (with J.P. Potier): La correspondance entre Aline Walras et William Jaffé, 2004; contbr. articles to profl. jours. Recipient Commonwealth of Pa. Distinguished Acad. Service award, 1974, Ind. U.-Pa. Disting. Research Award, 1984; Harvard fellow, 1956-57, 57-58; Henry Lee Meml. fellow, 1957-58 Mem. History of Econs. Soc. (pres. 1987-88), Walras Soc. (pres. 1997-2000). Home: 48 Shady Dr Indiana PA 15701-3245

WALKER, DONALD EZZELL, retired academic administrator; b. Springfield, Mo., July 13, 1921; s. Edward Everett and Cecilia (Ezzell) W.; m. Ann Lathrop, Dec. 17, 1943; 1 son, Craig Lathrop. AB, U. So. Calif., 1943, M.Th., 1947; PhD, Stanford U., 1954; L.H.D. (hon.), Southeastern Mass. U., 1973. Recreational dir. club work All Nations Found., Los Angeles, 1941-42, Wilshire Meth. Ch., Los Angeles, 1942-43; asst. minister Vincent Meth. Ch., Los Angeles, 1943-44; minister Encinitas Meth. Ch., 1945-47; teaching asst. Stanford U., 1947-49; instr. sociology San Diego State Coll., 1949-51, asst. prof. sociology, 1951-54, assoc. dean students, counseling, 1954-56, dean counseling, 1956-58, v.p. acad. affairs, 1968-71, acting pres., 1971-72; dean of students San Fernando Valley State Coll., Northridge, Calif., 1958-60; pres. Idaho State U., 1960-64; dean of students Sonoma State Coll., Rohnert Park, Calif., 1964-66; vice chancellor student affairs U. Calif., Irvine, 1966-68, sr. lectr. Grad. Sch. Administrn., 1967-68, fellow Univ. Coll., 1967-68; pres. Southeastern Mass. State U., N. Dartmouth, 1972-83; chancellor Grossmont-Cuyamaca Community Coll. Dist., El Cajon, Calif., 1983-92; ret., 1992. Author: (with others) Readings in American Public Opinion; The Effective Administrator: A Practical Approach to Problem-Solving, Decision-Making, and Campus Leadership, 1979; Never Try to Teach a Pig to Sing: Wit and Wisdom for Leaders, 1996; contbr. (with others) articles to profl. jours. Home: 8661 Lake Murray Blvd Apt 19 San Diego CA 92119-2842

WALKER, DONALD J. automotive systems company executive; b. London, Ont., Can., Aug. 29, 1956; s. Cyril Reginald and Margaret Marilyn (Wallace) W. BSc, U. Waterloo, Ont., 1987. Sr. engr., supt. GM; asst. to chair Magna Internat. Inc., 1987—89, v.p. product devel., 1989-90, exec. v.p., COO, 1990-92, pres., CEO, 1992-2001, Intier Automotive Inc., Newmarket, Canada, 2001—. Bd. dirs. Covisint, Yves Landry Found. Co-chmn. Can. Auto Partnership Coun., 2002—. Mem.: Automotive Parts Mfrs. Assn. (bd. dirs. 1993—2000), Assn. Profl. Engrs. Ont. (Gold medal 1999). Office: Intier Automotive Inc 521 Newpark Blvd Newmarket ON Canada L3Y 4X7 E-mail: don_walker@intier.com.

WALKER, DONALD MURRAY, minister; b. Lansing, Mich., Oct. 10, 1938; s. Paul H. and Margaret V. (Holloway) W.; m. Jacquelyn Touchstone, June 7, 1958; children: Donalyn Renee Scoggins, S. Denise Walker. BS, Lee U., 1977; MA, Ashland U., 1978; MDiv, Ch. of God Theol. Sem., 1980; EdD, Southeastern Nova U., 1983. Ordained to ministry Ch. of God, 1968. Evangelist Ch. of God, Minot, N.D., 1958-60, state dir. youth and Christian edn. Indpls., 1960-64, pastor, 1964-70, state dir. youth and Christian edn., 1970-74, 1974-78, 1978-82; pres. Northwest Bible Coll., Minot, 1982-86; state overseer Ch. of God, N.D., S.D., 1984-86, asst. dir. gen. edn. dept., 1986-88, state overseer, 1988-93, 1993-98, mem. exec. coun., 1994-98; pres. Ch. of God Theol. Sem., Cleveland, Tenn., 1998—. Chmn. Ch. of God Chaplains Commn., Cleveland, 1990-94. Bd. dirs., chmn. bldg. com. Lee U., 1994-98. Home: 1845 Partridge Rd NW Cleveland TN 37312-2128 Office: 900 Walker St NE Cleveland TN 37311-5234 *While there are many issues and crises in life that we often do not understand our attitude toward our faith in God and His mercy can never be dictated by our circumstances.*

WALKER, DORIS ISAAK, writer, historian, educator; b. Cleve. d. Alphonse Charles and Rose Emma (Gibbons) Isaak; children: Brent Evan Walker, Blair Dana Walker; m. Jack Pierson Smith, 2001. AB, Case Western Reserve U.; postgrad., Northwestern U., U. Calif., Irvine. Publs. editor Brunswick Corp., Chgo.; pub. rels. mgr. Dana Point (Calif.) Harbor, 1970-84; field rsch. writer Kessler Exch., L.A., Calif., 1984-89. Instr. Calif. history South Orange County Coll. Dist.; lectr. in field. Author: A Guide Book of Philatelic-Numismatic Covers, 1970, Dana Point Harbor/Capistrano Bay: Home Port for Romance, 1981, The Whales of Capistrano Bay, 1982, Sections of Orange, 1989, Orange County Adventures with Children, 1997, The Heritage of San Clemente, 2000, Coastal Reflections, 2001, Mission Viejo: The Ageless Land, 2004; contbr., editor, photographer newspapers, mags. Commr. Orange County Hist. Commn., 1994—; founder, coord. Dana Point Festival of Whales, 1975-84. Recipient over 100 awards including Am. History award DAR, Clarion award, Unique Coverage award Women in Comm., Woman of Distinction award Capistrano Bay Area, Soroptimist Internat., Crisis Comm. Award Internat. Coun. Indsl. Editors, cert. of recognition Calif. State Senate; named Orange County Woman of Achievement in Comm., YWCA. Mem. AAUW (pres. San Clemente-Capistrano Bay br.), Nat. Fedn. Press Women (Nat. first place history book award), Calif. Media Profls., Calif. Press Women (pres. Orange County dist., state sec.), Dana Point Hist. Soc. (hon. life, co-founder, dir.), San Juan Capistrano Hist. Soc. (dir.), Orange County Hist. Soc. (dir.), Dana Point Lighthouse Soc. (hon. life), Friends of Libr. (hon. life). Avocations: travel, photography. Office: PO Box 546 Dana Point CA 92629-0546 Office Phone: 949-496-6677. Personal E-mail: homeports@aol.com. E-mail: homeports@aol.com.

WALKER, DOUGLAS, computer developement company executive; Graduate, Vanderbilt U., 1976. With Western Data Corp., Seattle, 1976-80, Walker, Richer & Quinn, Inc., Seattle, 1980—, now pres., 1989—, CEO. Office: Walker Richer & Quinn Inc 1500 Dexter Ave N Seattle WA 98109-3032

WALKER, DOUGLAS C. banker; b. Betheleham, Pa. BA, Princeton U., 1970; MBA, Harvard U., 1978. Asst. v.p. J.P. Morgan, 1970-76; gen. ptnr. Brown Bros. Harriman & Co., N.Y.C. Bd. dirs. Asten Group, Inc., Magee Reiter Automotive, Inc., Nat. Lands Trust. Bd. dirs. U. Pa. Mus., Acad. Natural Scis. Office: Brown Bros Harriman & Co 1531 Walnut St Philadelphia PA 19102-3098

WALKER, DUARD LEE, medical educator; b. Bishop, Calif., June 2, 1921; s. Fred H. and Anna Lee (Shumate) Walker; m. Dorothea Virginia McHenry, Aug. 11, 1945; children: Douglas Keith, Donna Judith, David Cameron, Diane Susan. AB, U. Calif. - Berkeley, 1943, MA, 1947; MD, U. Calif. - San Francisco, 1945. Diplomate Am. Bd. Microbiology. Intern, U.S. Naval Hosp., Shoemaker, Calif., 1945—46; asst. resident internal medicine Stanford U. Service San Francisco Hosp., 1950—52; asso. prof. med. microbiology and preventive medicine U. Wis., Madison, 1952—59, prof. med. microbiology, 1959—88, prof., chmn. med. microbiology, 1970—76, Paul F. Clark prof. med. microbiology, 1977—88, prof. emeritus, 1988—, prof., chmn. med. microbiology, 1981—88. Cons. Naval Med. Rsch. Unit, Gt. Lakes, Ill., 1958—74; mem. microbiology tng. com. Nat. Inst. Gen. Med. Scis., 1966—70; mem. nat. adv. Allergy and Infectious Diseases Coun., 1970—74; mem. adv. com. on blood program rsch. ARC, 1978—79; mem. study group on papovaviridae Internat. Com. on Taxonomy of Viruses, 1976—90; mem. vaccines and related biol. products adv. com. FDA, 1985—89; mem. rev. panel postdoct. rsch. fellowships for physicians Howard Hughes Med Inst., 1990—93. Served to lt. (j.g.) USNR, 1943—46, served to capt. USNR, 1953—55. Fellow NRC postdoctoral virology, Rockefeller Inst. Med. Rsch., N.Y.C., 1947—49, USPHS immunology, George Williams Hooper Found., U. Calif., San Francisco, 1949—50. Fellow: Infectious Diseases Soc. Am., Am. Acad. Microbiology, Am. Pub. Health Assn.; mem.: Arts and Letters, Wis. Acad. Scis., Am. Soc. Virology, AAUP, Reticulendothelial Soc., Soc. Exptl. Biology and Medicine, AAAS, Am. Soc. Microbiology, Am. Assn. Immunologists, NAS. Home: 618 Odell St Madison WI 53711-1435 Office: U Wis Med Sch 1300 University Ave Madison WI 53706-1510 Office Phone: 608-233-9279. Personal E-mail: dlwalke1@facstaff.wisc.edu.

WALKER, EARL, food service executive; CFO, controller, treas. Jitney-Jungle Stores of Am., Inc., Jackson, Miss. also: Jitney-Jungle Stores of Am Inc 1770 Ellis Ave Ste 200 Jackson MS 39204-3613 Office: Jitney-Jungle Stores of Am Inc Ste D20 1855 Lakeland Dr Jackson MS 39216-4947 Fax: (601) 346-2169.

WALKER, EDWARD KEITH, JR., retired management consultant, retired military officer; b. Annapolis, Md., Jan. 23, 1933; s. Edward Keith and Miriam (Whitmore) W.; m. Carol Ann Turner, June 12, 1954 (dec. June 14, 2002); children: Lynn Walker Streett, Wendy Louise. BS, U.S. Naval Acad., 1954; postgrad., Armed Forces Staff Coll., 1966; MBA in Fin. Mgmt., George Washington U., 1970. Commd. ensign U.S. Navy, 1954, advanced through grades to rear admiral, 1981; force supply officer COMSUBLANT Norfolk, Va., 1975-78; exec. officer SPCC Mechanicsburg, Pa., 1978-80; comdr. Naval Supply Ctr., Puget Sound, Bremerton, Wash., 1980-81; Atlantic Fleet supply officer CINCLANTFLT Norfolk, 1981-83; asst. comptroller Navy Dept., Washington, 1983-84; comdr. Naval Supply Systems Command and 35th chief supply corps Washington, 1984-88; v.p. adminstrn. and corp. strategy Resource Cons. Inc., Vienna, Va., 1989-2000, v.p. emeritus, 2000—. Bd. dirs. Herley Industries. Decorated D.S.M., Legion of Merit (3 awards); recipient Def. Superior Service medal, 1983 Mem. Vinson Hall Corp. (bd. dirs., chmn. 2003), Naval Acad. Found. (trustee), U.S. Navy Meml. Found. (bd. dirs., treas.), Supply Corps Found. (past pres.), Supply Corps Assn. (past pres.), U.S. Naval Inst., Am. Soc. Naval Engrs., Naval Submarine League, Naval Order U.S. (life), Surface Navy Assn. (life), Navy League U.S. (life), Naval Acad. Alumni Assn. (life), Mil. Officers Assn. (life), N.Y. Yacht Club, Chesapeake Yacht Club. Republican. Episcopalian. Home: 3520 Saylor Pl Alexandria VA 22304-1831 Office: Resource Cons Inc 2650 Park Tower Dr Ste 800 Vienna VA 22180-3862 Office Phone: 571-226-3008. *There is no greater satisfaction than to see your people succeed, and then to insure they get the credit.*

WALKER, EDWARD S., JR., diplomat; b. Abington, Pa., June 13, 1940; s. Edward Stanley and Rosabel Dunlop (Gould) W.; m. Wendy Jane Griffiths, Apr. 7, 1973; Kathryn Erica, Christopher James. BA, Hamilton Coll., 1963; MA, Boston U., 1965. Joined Fgn. Svc., Dept. State, Washington, 1967; polit. officer Am. Embassy, Tel Aviv, 1969-73; staff asst. Nr. Ea. affairs Fgn. Svc., Dept. State, Washington, 1974-75; Arabic lang. trainee Fgn. Svc. Inst., Lebanon, Tunis, Egypt, 1975-77; polit. officer Am. Embassy, Damascus, Syria, 1977-79; spl. asst. Pres.'s personal rep., Washington, 1980-82; exec. dir. Office of Dep. Sec. State, Washington, 1982-84; mem. Royal Coll. Def. Studies, London, 1984-85; dep. chief of mission Am. Embassy, Riyadh, Saudi Arabia, 1985-88; dep. asst. sec. Dept. State, 1988-89; U.S. amb. to United Arab Emirates Abu Dhabi, 1989-92; dept. permanent rep. to UN, N.Y.C., 1993-94; U.S. amb. to Egypt Cairo, 1994-97; U.S. amb. to Israel Tel Aviv, 1997-00; asst. sec. Dept. State, 2000—. With U.S. Army, 1962-65. Decorated Order of Independence (Abu Dhabi); recipient Superior Honor award Dept. State, 1975, Meritorious Honor award, 1976, Disting. Civilian Svc. award Dept. Def., 1997. Episcopalian. Office: NEA Rm 6242 Dept Of State Washington DC 20520-0001

WALKER, FRANCIS JOSEPH, lawyer; b. Aug. 5, 1922; s. John McSweeney and Sarah Veronica (Meechan) W.; m. Julia Corinne O'Brien, Jan. 27, 1951; children: Vincent Paul, Monica Irene Hylton, Jill Marie Nudell, John Michael, Michael Joseph, Thomas More. BA, St. Martin's Coll., 1947; JD, U. Wash., 1950. Bar: Wash. Asst. atty. gen. State of Wash., 1950-51; pvt. practice Olympia, Wash., 1951—. Gen. counsel Wash. Cath. Conf., 1967-76. Lt. (j.g.) USNR, 1943-46; PTO. Home and Office: 2723 Hillside Dr SE Olympia WA 98501-3460 E-mail: fjwalker@comcast.net.

WALKER, FRANK DILLING, market research executive; b. Indpls., Dec. 31, 1934; s. Frank D. and Dorothy Mae (Cole) W.; m. Jane Tatman, Aug. 25, 1979; children— Steven F., Leah R. BA, DePauw U., 1957. Chmn., CEO Walker Group, Indpls., 1960-95, Walker Clin. Evaluations, Inc., Indpls., 1986-95; chmn. Walker Info., 1995—. Bd. dirs. Am. United Life Ins. Co., NBD Ind. Nat. Bank, State Life Ins. Co.; frequent speaker on market rsch. to various groups. Contbr. articles trade publs. Past mem. Indpls. Hist. Preservation Commn.; bd. dirs. Ind. Repertory Theatre, Meth. Hosp., United Way of Greater Indpls.; adv. council Indpls. Mus. Art, Buchanan Counseling Center; former chmn. Central Ind. Better Bus. Bur.; former chmn. Indpls. Econ. Devel. Corp.; trustee Children's Mus. Indpls., Univ. Indpls.; former bd. dirs. Jr. Achievement Central Ind., mem. adv. council; trustee The Children's Mus., YMCA Found.; bd. dirs. Citizens Gas and Coke Utility. With USAF, 1958-60. Mem. Council Am. Survey Research Orgns. (past chmn. bd.), Am. Mktg. Assn. (past pres. Ind. chpt.), Indpls. Sales and Mktg. Execs. Assn. (past pres.), Indpls. C. of C. (past chmn.), Mktg. Rsch. Assn. (hon. life), Sigma Chi. Republican. Methodist. Office: Walker Info Ste 100 3939 Priority Way South Dr Indianapolis IN 46240-3833

WALKER, FRED ELMER, broadcast executive; b. Trenton, N.J., May 31, 1931; s. Elmer and Adele F. (Decker) W.; m. Catharine Middleton Sullivan, Nov. 26, 1952; children: Catharine Walker Bergstrom, Elizabeth Walker Phillips, Frederick Christopher. Student, Trenton State Coll., 1952, NYU, 1953. Dir. pub. relations Sta. WPTZ-TV, Phila., 1953; v.p., gen. mgr. Sta. WTTM-AM, Trenton, 1956-59; gen. sales mgr. Sta. KYW-AM, Cleve., 1959-62; v.p., gen. mgr. Sta. KDKA-AM, Pitts., 1962-65, Sta. KYW-TV, Phila., 1965-67, Sta. KPIX-TV, San Francisco, 1967-69, Sta. WLWT-TV, Cin., 1969-71; pres. Broad St. Communications Corp., New Haven, 1971-85; v.p. radio group Westinghouse Broadcasting, N.Y.C., 1985-88; exec. v.p. Broad St. Ventures, N.Y.C., 1988—. Pres. Broad St. TV Corp., 1988-96, Broad St. Mgmt. Corp., 1988-96; bd. dirs. Broadcast Music, Inc., 1984-87, Call for Action, Washington, 1993-2000. Bd. dirs. Long Wharf Theatre, New Haven, WXEL-TV, 1998—; chmn. Long Wharf Theatre Future Fund campaign, 1983-85, chmn. devel., 1986-90, chmn. and pres., 1990-97; mem. Pres.'s Coun. Albertus Magnus Coll.; trustee Hamden Hall Country Day Sch., chmn. devel. com.; chmn. 250th fund dr. United Ch. Christ, 1987-89; chmn. Call For Action, Washington, 1994-2000; trustee Fla. Stage. Recipient Alfred P. Sloan award, 1954, Ohio State Ednl. award, 1953; fellow Berkeley Coll. Yale U., 1976. Mem. Radio Advt. Bur. (dir.), TV Bur. Advt., Nat. Assn. Broadcasters, New Haven Lawn Club. Democrat. E-mail: fredewalk1@aol.com.

WALKER, GEORGE EDWARD, academic administrator, physicist; b. Chillicothe, Ohio, Nov. 5, 1940; s. Cecil Edward Walker and Delia Jesse Auxier; m. Erika Ilse Bopp, June 6, 1964; children: Elizabeth, Patricia, Christopher. BA, Wesleyan U., 1962; MS, Case Western Res. U., 1964, PhD, 1966. Postdoctoral rsch. assoc. Los Alamos (N.Mex.) Nat. Lab., 1966—68, Stanford U., Palo Alto, Calif., 1968—70; prof. physics Ind. U., Bloomington, 1970—2004, assoc. dean Coll. Arts and Scis., 1976—79, chair dept. physics, 1986—89, assoc. v.p. for rsch., dean Grad. Sch., 1989—91, v.p. for rsch., dean Grad. Sch., 1991—2003; sr. scholar Carnegie Found. for Advancement of Tchg., Stanford, Calif., 2001—. Vis. scientist Brookhaven Nat. Lab., 1977; cons. Lawrence Livermore (Calif.) Nat. Lab., 1984—95; mem. program adv. com. Los Alamos Nat. Lab., 1989—92, chair program adv. com., 1990—91; mem. com. on outreach and tech. transfer Nat. Assn. State Univs. and Land-Grant Colls., Washington, 1990—95, mem. exec. com. coun. on rsch. policy and grad. edn., 1995—99, chair coun. on rsch. policy and grad. edn., 1997—98, bd. dirs., 1999—2001, Coun. Grad. Schs., Washington, 1992—97, chair, 1995; mem. exec. com. Midwest Assn. Grad. Schs., 1994—98, chair, 1996; mem. adv. bd. Peterson's Grad. Guide, 1994—95, Pew Charitable Trusts, 1999, Woodrow Wilson Found., 2000—; mem. grad. record examinations bd. Ednl. Testing Svc., Princeton, NJ, 1997—2001, mem. policy coun. test of English as a Fgn. Lang., 1997—2001, chair policy coun., 1997—2001, mem. exec. and policy com., 1997—2002, mem. fin. com., 1997—2002; chair Livermore Physics N-Divsn. Tech. Rev. Com., 1997—; mem. Physics and Advanced Techs. Directorate Rev. Com., 1997—; cons., evaluator North Ctrl. Assn., 1998—. Team capt. United Way Monroe County, Bloomington, 1989—2003; bd. dirs. Brown County Playhouse, Bloomington, 1992—. Grantee, NSF, 1970—96. Fellow: Am. Phys. Soc.; mem.: Com. on Instnl. Cooperation (mem. grad. deans group 1991—2003, mem. sr. rsch. officers group 1991—2003), Assn. Am. Univs. (mem. steering com. project on doctoral rsch. 1993—95, mem. exec. com. 1993—98, mem. coun. on fed. rels. 1995—2002, bd. pres. assn. grad. schs. 1997), Am. Assn. Physics Tchrs. Achievements include research in basic theories and interpretation of experiments in intermediate nuclear physics. Office: Carnegie Found for Advancement of Tchg 51 Vista Ln Stanford CA 94305

WALKER, GEORGE HERBERT, III, ambassador, former investment banking company executive; b. St. Louis, Mar. 16, 1931; s. George H. and Mary (Carter) W.; m. Sandra E. Canning, Dec. 23, 1955 (div. Oct. 1962); children: Mary Elizabeth, Wendy, Isabelle; m. Kimberly Gedge, July 27, 1968 (div. Jan. 1977); children: George H. IV, Carter; m. Carol Banta, Feb. 21, 1987. BA, Yale U., 1953; LL.B., Harvard U., 1956. Bar: Conn. 1956. Gen. ptnr. G.H. Walker & Co. (later G.H. Walker, Laird Inc.), 1961-74; sr. v.p., also bd. dirs. White, Weld & Co. Inc., 1974-75; chmn. bd. dirs. G.H. Walker & Co., 1973-74; exec. v.p. Stifel Nicolaus & Co., 1976-78, pres., CEO, 1978-92, chmn., 1982—2001, chmn. emeritus, 2001—, also bd. dirs.; US amb. to Hungary US Dept. State, Budapest, 2003—. Civilian aide to sec. U.S. Army for Ea. Mo., 1973-80; bd. dirs. Laidlaw Corp., Laclede Steel Co., Eck-Adams Corp.; bd. govs. Midwest Stock Exch., 1982-88. Bd. dirs. Downtown St. Louis Inc., 1975-90, chmn., 1984-86; bd. dirs. Webster U., chmn. bd., 1987-92; trustee Mo. Hist. Soc., St. Louis Children's Hosp., 1972-92, Jefferson Nat. Expansion Meml. Assn., 1992; vestryman St. Ann's Ch., Kennebunkport, Maine; mem. Mo. Rep. Ctrl. Com., 1983—; adv. bd. St. Louis Area coun. Boy Scouts Am., 1989—; trustee investment trust Episcopal Diocese of Mo.; hon. bd. dirs. Anti-Drug Abuse Edn. Fund, Inc., 1990—; bd. dirs. St. Louis Zoo, 1992. With USAF, 1956-58. Mem. Rotary (St. Louis club). E-mail: walkergh@stifel.com.*

WALKER, GEORGE KONTZ, law educator; b. Tuscaloosa, Ala., July 8, 1938; s. Joseph Henry and Catherine Louise (Indorf) W.; m. Phyllis Ann Sherman, July 30, 1966; children: Charles Edward, Mary Neel. BA, U. Ala., 1959; LLB, Vanderbilt U., 1966; AM, Duke U., 1968; LLM, U. Va., 1972; postgrad. (Sterling fellow), Law Sch. Yale U., 1975-76. Bar: Va. 1967, N.C. 1976. Law clk. U.S. Dist. Ct., Richmond, Va., 1966-67; assoc. Hunton, Williams, Gay, Powell & Gibson, Richmond, 1967-70; pvt. practice Charlottesville, Va., 1970-71; asst. prof. Law Sch. Wake Forest U., Winston-Salem, N.C., 1972-73, assoc. prof. Law Sch., 1974-77, prof. Law Sch., 1977—, mem. bd. advisors Divinity Sch., 1991-94; Charles H. Stockton prof. internat. law U.S. Naval War Coll., 1992-93. Vis. prof. Marshall-Wythe Sch. Law, Coll. William and Mary, Williamsburg, Va., 1979-80, U. Ala. Law Sch., 1985; cons. Naval War Coll., 1976—, Nat. Def. Exec. Res., 1991—, Naval War Coll., Internat. Law Dept. Adv. Bd., 1993—. Author: The Tanker War, 1980-88, 2000; contbr. articles to profl. jours. With USN, 1959-62, capt. USNR, ret. Woodrow Wilson fellow, 1962-63; decorated Order of the long Leaf Pine; recipient Joseph Branch Alumni Svc. award, Wake Forest, 1988, Meritorious Unit Commendation, USN, 1992-93; named Hon. Atty. Gen. N.C., 1986. Mem.: ABA, Internat. Inst. Humanitarian Law, Maritime Law Assn., Am. Law Inst., Am. Judicature Soc., Internat. Law Assn. (exec. com. Am. br. 2001—), Am. Soc. Internat. Law (exec. coun. 1988—91), N.C. Bar Assn. (v.p. 1997—98), Va. Bar Assn., Order of Barristers (hon.), Piedmont Club, Phi Delta Phi, Sigma Alpha Epsilon, Phi Beta Kappa, Order of the Coif (hon.). Democrat. Episcopalian. Home: 3321 Pennington Ln Winston Salem NC 27106-5439 Office: Wake Forest U Sch Law PO Box 7206 Winston Salem NC 27109-7206

WALKER, GEORGE THEOPHILUS, JR., composer, pianist, music educator; b. Washington, June 27, 1922; s. George Theophilus Sr. and Rosa (King) W.; children: Gregory, Ian. MusB, Oberlin Coll., 1941; student of, Rudolf Serkin, Rosario Scalero; Artist Diploma, Curtis Inst. music, 1945; D of Mus. Arts, U. Rochester, 1957; DFA (hon.), Lafayette Coll., 1982; MusD (hon.), Oberlin Coll., 1983; student of, Nadia Boulanger; MusD (hon.), Curtis Inst. Music, 1997; DHL (hon.), Montclair State U., 1997; MusD (hon.), Bloomfield Coll., 1997; DFA (hon.), Spelman Coll., 2001. Instr. Dillard U., New Orleans, 1953-54; instr. Dalcroze Sch. Music, N.Y.C., 1960-61, New Sch. Social Research, N.Y.C., 1961; instr. to assoc. prof. Smith Coll., Northampton, Mass., 1961-68; assoc. prof. U. Colo., Boulder, 1968-69; disting. prof. Rutgers U., Newark, 1976-92, prof. emeritus, 1992. Concert pianist Nat. Concert Artists, N.Y.C., 1950-53, Columbia Artists, N.Y.C., 1959-60; adj. prof. Peabody Inst. Johns Hopkins U., Balt., 1975-78; disting. prof. U. Del., Newark, 1975-76. Composer: Sonata for 2 Pianos (Harvey Gaul prize 1963), numerous sonatas, cantatas and concertos, Concerto for Cello and Orch., 1982, Sinfonias for Orch. Bd. dirs. Am. Bach Found., 1988; mem. Mary Flagler Cary Trust Commn., 1998. Recipient award Am. Acad. and Inst. Arts and Letter, 1982, Koussevitsky award, 1988, Pulitzer prize, 1996, L.J. Govs. award 1997, Koussevitsky award 1998, Mary Flagler Cary Charitable Trust award, 1998, Dorothy Maynor Arts Citizens award, 2000, A.I. duPont award Del. Symphony, 2001, Classical Roots award Detroit Symphony, 2001; grantee Smith Coll., U. Colo., Rutger U. Rsch. Coun., NEA, N.J. State Coun. for Arts; Fulbright fellow, 1957, John Hay Whitney fellow, 1958, Guggenheim fellow, 1969, 88, Rockefeller fellow, 1971, 74; Disting. scholar U. Rochester, 1996; commd. N.Y. Philharm., Kennedy Ctr., Cleve. Orch., Boston Symphony, N.J. Symphony, Am. Guild of Organists; inducted Am. Classical Music Hall of Fame, 2000. Mem. ASCAP, Am. Acad. Arts and Letters (mem.-elect), Am. Bach Found. (bd. dirs. 1988), Am. Symphony League. Democrat. Avocations: tennis, photography, audio. Home: 323 Grove St Montclair NJ 07042-4223

WALKER, GLORIA LEE, training services executive; b. Oklahoma City, Dec. 31, 1942; d. Russell Holland and Ethel Wanita (Kierig) Walker; m. Thomas William Rupprath, June 3, 1966 (div. Feb. 1995); children: Robert Rupprath, John Rupprath. BA in Sociology, U. S.C., 1965; MS in Elem. Edn., U. Nebr., 1971; EdD in Adminstrn., Fla. Atlantic U., 1986. Ops. rsch. analyst U.S. Bur. Mines, Washington, 1988-90; employment devel. specialist IRS,

Dallas, 1991-92; pres. AMERITRAIN, Dallas/Lubbock, Tex., 1992—. Author: Training a Diversified Workforce, 1993, Developing Training Materials, 1995, Instructing Diversified Employee, 1995, Seminars in Training, 1995.

WALKER, GORDON BEVERLEY MOORE, JR., business educator; b. N.Y.C., Oct. 10, 1944; s. Gordon Beverley Moore and Nancy Holton Walker; m. Jane Edwards, June 15, 1977 (div. Sept. 1983); 1 child, Emma; m. Nancy Niebuhr, Mar. 22, 1984; children: Hugh Curran, Ian Moore. BA, Yale U., 1966; MBA, U. Pa., 1976, PhD, 1982. Assoc. prof. Sloan Sch. Mgmt., MIT, Cambridge, Mass., 1981-86, Wharton Sch., U. Pa., Phila., 1986-91, Sch. of Orgn. and Mgmt., Yale U., New Haven, 1991-93; prof., chair Cox Sch. of Bus., So. Meth. U., Dallas, 1993—. Cons. numerous orgns., 1990—. Contbr. book Modern Competitive Strategy, 2003, articles to profl. jours. 1st lt. USMC, 1967-70. Decorated Bronze star; recipient numerous grants including NSF, 1987-89, 95-97. Mem.: Am. Sociol. Assn., Acad. Mgmt., Yale Club of Dallas (pres. 2001—02, 2003—). Home: 331 Ridgebriar Dr Richardson TX 75080-1920 Office: Cox Sch Bus So Meth U Dallas TX 75275-0333 Office Phone: 214-768-2191. E-mail: gwalker@mail.cox.smu.edu.

WALKER, GORDON DAVIES, former government official, writer, lecturer, consultant; b. Logan, Utah, July 10, 1944; s. Rudger Harper and Fawn Lucile (Davies) W.; m. Carlene Martin, June 5, 1968; children— Kimberly Anne, Kelly Anne, Gordon Davies Jr., Bradford Martin AB, Brigham Young U., 1968; MBA, Harvard U., 1971. Project dir. Becker Research Co., Boston, 1969-71; dir. mktg. Am. Nat. Enterprises, Salt Lake City, 1971-72; v.p., dir. Sweetwater Properties, Salt Lake City, 1972-76; gen. ptnr. Covecrest Properties, Salt Lake City, 1976—; spl. asst. to sec. HUD, Washington, 1981-82, dep. under sec., 1983-86; cons. real estate, fin. Commerce Cons., Washington, 1986-87; pres., chief exec. officer Deseret Fed. Savs. and Loan, Salt Lake City, 1987-88; pres. U.S. Resources, Inc., Phoenix, 1988-92, also bd. dirs.; pres. Energy Lock Inc., Salt Lake City, 1992—2002; exec. dir. Utah chpt. Alzheimer's Assn., 2002—; dir. housing cmty. devel. State of Utah, 2003—. Author: Finance Your Own Way to Success, 1980; Develop Your Way to Success, 1981; Hottest New Ideas of the 1980's, 1982. Rep. state del., Salt Lake City, 1974; del. Rep. Nat. Conv., 1988 Mem. Nat. Assn. Realtors Mem. Lds Ch.

WALKER, HENRY GILBERT, health care executive, consultant; b. Gowanda, N.Y., Feb. 16, 1947; s. Henry George and Grace Dayton (Moore) W.; m. Elaine Ruth Darbee, July 18, 1970 (div. Dec. 1979); 1 child, Matthew Case; m. Patricia Ann Andrade, May 14, 1983; children: Michael David, Christopher John. BS in Indsl. Engring., Cornell U., 1969; MBA, U. Chgo., 1975. Evening adminstr. Rush-Presbyn. St.-Luke's Med. Ctr., Chgo., 1973-75; mgmt. cons. Booz, Allen & Hamilton, Chgo., 1975-79; regional adminstr., v.p. S.W. Community Health Service, Albuquerque, 1979-83, adminstr., v.p., 1983-86; exec. v.p. Presbyn. Healthcare Services, Albuquerque, 1986-92; pres., CEO Tucson Med. Ctr., 1992—95, Health Ptnrs. of Ariz., 1995—97, Providence Health System, Seattle, 1997—2004; ptnr. Andrade Walker Consulting, LLC, Bellevue, Wash., 2004—. Bd. dirs. Park Dist., Elmhurst, Ill., 1978, 1979; mem. Dist. III Cmty. Action Com., Albuquerque, 1985; divsn. chmn. United Way of Albuquerque, 1985, 1988. Recipient Hosp. Survey award U. Chgo., 1975, Bachmeyer award U. Chgo., 1975, Outstanding Midshipman award Cornell U., 1969; named one of Emerging Healthcare Leaders, Healthcare Forum, 1985, 86, Healthcares Up and Comers, Modern Healthcare Mag., 1987. Mem.: Healthcare Forum (bd. dirs., chmn.), N.Mex. Hosp. Assn. (chmn. bd. dirs. 1983—85, treas.). Democrat. Presbyterian. Avocations: reading, hiking, skiing.

WALKER, HOWARD ERNEST, lawyer; b. Mobile, Ala., Mar. 3, 1944; s. Ernest W. and Denise (Kearney) W.; m. Michelle Ann Pinsonneault, June 20, 1992. BA, U. Ill., 1966; JD, Boston U., 1974. Bar: R.I. 1974. Assoc. Hinckley, Allen & Snyder, Providence, 1974-80, ptnr., 1980—2004. Trustee Providence Pub. Libr., 1978-2000, pres., 2002—; vice chmn. programs; trustee R.I. Wild Plant Soc., 1995-97—; trustee R.I. Civic Chorale & Orchestra, 1988-95; dir. South Shore Mental Health Ctr., 1997—, v.p. 2000—; trustee and sec. Hopkinton Land Trust, 2000—; mem. Hopkinton Planning Bd., 2002—, sec., 2003—. Lt. USNR, 1967-71. Mem. ABA, R.I. Bar Assn. (chmn. superior ct. bench/bar com. 1990-93, 94-95, Dorothy Lohmann Cmty. Svc. award 2003), Maritime Law Assn. of U.S., Nat. Assn. R.R. Trial Counsel, Phi Kappa Phi, Phi Beta Kappa. Avocations: Western Americana, natural history. Home: 39A Berrie Ln PO Box 118 Rockville RI 02873-0118 Office: PO Box 299 Hope Valley RI 02832 Office Phone: 401-539-6767. E-mail: hewlaw@direcway.com.

WALKER, HUGH DYSON, educator, deacon; b. Plymouth, N.H., Feb. 21, 1934; s. Hubert and Lena May (Bosence) W.; m. Sandra Ann Peary, Dec. 21, 1957; children: Christopher, Sarah, Andrew, Gregory, Anne. BA, U. N.H., 1956; MA, U. Calif., L.A., 1960, PhD, 1971. Lectr. U. Md., Tokyo, 1962-65; from asst. prof. history to prof. U. Wis., Stevens Point, Wis., 1965-73, prof., 1973—. Contbr. articles to profl. jours. With USNR, 1956-58. Mem. Assn. Asian Studies (Korean studies com.), Mongolian Soc., Midwest Japan Seminar. Avocation: golf. Office: Univ Wis History Dept Stevens Point WI 54481

WALKER, IRVING EDWARD, lawyer; b. Balt., Jan. 31, 1952; s. Bertram and Mildred (Shapiro) W.; children: Brandon Harris, Aaron Seth, Emily Celeste. BA, Duke U., 1973; JD, U. Md., 1978. Bar: Md. 1978, U.S. Dist. Ct. Md. 1978, U.S. Ct. Appeals (4th cir.) 1980, U.S. Supreme Ct. 1995, U.S. Ct. Appeals (3d cir.) 2001. Assoc. Frank, Bernstein, Conaway & Goldman, Balt., 1978-85, ptnr., 1986-91; ptnr. Miles & Stockbridge, Balt., 1991-2001; ptnr. Saul Ewing LLP, Balt., 2001—. Chair Bankruptcy & Creditors Rights Group, 1991-2000. Contbg. author: Bankruptcy Deskbook, 1986. Bd. dirs. Jewish Cmty. Ctr. Greater Balt., 1986-88, Temple Emanuel of Balt., Inc., 1996-2002. Mem. ABA, Md. Bar Assn., Bar Assn. Balt. City (chmn. bankruptcy and bus. law com. 1989-90), Am. Bankruptcy Inst., Bankruptcy Assn. Dist. Md. (pres. 1992-93, chmn. Balt. chpt. 1989-91), Order of Coif. Avocations: soccer, weightlifting. Office: Saul Ewing LLP 100 S Charles St 15th Fl Baltimore MD 21201 Office Phone: 410-332-8672. E-mail: iwalker@saul.com.

WALKER, JAMES E. academic administrator, educator; b. Phenix City, Ala. s. Curtis and Mamie (Milner) W.; m. Gwendolyn Pompey, Dec. 22, 1968; children: Jamell E., Jabrina E. BS, Ala. State U., 1963; MA, Atlanta U., 1967; EdD, Pa. State U., 1972; LhD, Mt. St. Mary's Coll., 1991. Chmn., tchr. Parks Jr. High Sch., Atlanta, 1967-69; instr. Western Mich. U., Kalamazoo, 1971; asst. prof. spl. edn. So. Ill. U., Edwardsville, 1972-74; exec. asst. to supt. Bryce Hosp., Tuscaloosa, Ala., 1975-77; chmn. spl. edn. Ill. State U., Normal, 1977-80; dean edn. Calif. State U., Hayward, 1980-87; v.p. provost U. No. Colo., Greeley, 1987-91; pres. Mid. Tenn. State U., Murfreesboro, 1991—2000, So. Ill. U., 2000—. Adj. prof. U. Ala., Tuscaloosa, 1975-77; presenter in field. Author: Behavior Management: A Practical Approach for Educators, 1987, 5th edit., 1992. Commr. Boy Scouts Am., Nashville, 1992—; mem. Black Health Care Task Force, Nashville, 1992—. USDE/BEH fellow Pa. State U., 1969-72, State of Ga. Dept. Edn. fellow, 1966-67; recipient Outstanding Alumni award Ala. State U., 1986, Coll. Edn. Alumni award Pa. State U., 1988. Mem. AAUW, Am. Assn. Higher Edn., Rotary. Democrat. Roman Catholic. Avocations: reading, travel, golf. Office: Mid Tenn State U Office of Pres 110 Cope Adminstrn Bldg Murfreesboro TN 37132-0001

WALKER, JAMES HARPER, retired security firm executive, writer; b. Cleve., Ohio, Jan. 29, 1936; s. Roy Hubert and Susie May Walker; m. Barbara Jean Woods, Feb. 15, 1962; children: James Randolph, Mark Lawrence, John Ireland. BA, Lake Erie Coll., 1968. Charter life underwriter Ohio, 1971. Agt., staff mgr., sales mgr. Monumental Ins. Co, Cleve., 1962—72; police officer, detective Waite Hill (Ohio) Police Dept., 1974—81; asst. chief police Huron Rd., East Cleve., 1981—84; area mgr. The Wackenhut Corp., Louisville, 1985—94; ret. Author: (novel) Man In Blue (Libr. of Congress award), Inside Your Local Police, (children short story) Bushytail the Squirrel. Dir. save a sight fund Lions Club, Willoughby, Ohio, 1976—78; mem. police fellowcraft team Masonic Lodge, Willoughby 302, Ohio, 1976—81. Staff sgt. U.S. Army, 1953—56. Recipient Hon. Cert., Internat. Soc. Poets, 1994. Mem.: Masons. Independent-Republican. Avocations: writing, golf, travel. Home: 44 Pfrimmers Chapel Rd Corydon IN 47112 Personal E-mail: jwalk010@aol.com.

WALKER, JAMES STEVEN, osteopath, emergency physician; b. Hobart, Okla., Feb. 4, 1951; BS in Zoology, Okla. State U., 1973, MS in Zoology, 1975, DO, 1978. Diplomate Am. Bd. Emergency Medicine. Intern Osteo. Hosp., South Bend, Ind., 1978-79; resident in emergency medicine Darnall Army Cmty. Hosp., Ft. Hood, Tex., 1983-85; mem. staff Univ. Hosp., Oklahoma City, 1985-88; prof. emergency medicine U. Okla. Health Scis. Ctr., 1988-2001, clin. prof. surgery, 2001—; emergency physician Okla. Heart Hosp., 2001—. Mem. AMA, Am. Osteo. Assn., Am. Acad. Emergency Medicine, Am. Coll. Emergency Physicians, Am. Coll. Osteo. Emergency Physicians, Soc. of Acad. Emergency Medicine, Wilderness Med. Soc.

WALKER, JEFFREY CLEMENS, venture capitalist; b. Knoxville, Tenn., Sept. 22, 1955; s. William Clemens and Joyce Hazel (Harkins) W.; m. Suzanne Marie Connelly, Apr. 27, 1984; children: Courtney, Ryan, Morgan, Hunter. BS, U. Va., 1977; MBA, Harvard U., 1981. CPA, Tex.; cert. mgmt. acct., Tex. Sr. auditor, cons. Arthur Young & Co., Houston, 1977-79; assoc. Chem. Bank, NYC, 1981-82, v.p., 1982-83; ptnr. Chase Capital Ptnrs., NYC, 1984-87, mng. ptnr., 1988—95; co-founder, gen. ptnr. JP Morgan Ptnrs. at JP Morgan Chase & Co., 1984—, vice-chmn., mng. ptnr., 1988—, dir., 1995—. Bd. dirs. Timothys, Inc., Toronto, Monet Corp., NYC, Guitar Ctr., LA, Metroplex Corp., NJ, Doaneroducts, Mo., Metakote, Lima, Ohio, Chase Asia Fund, NYC, Chase Equity Ptnrs, NYC, Thomas Jefferson Found. (Monticello), JP Morgan Chase Found.; dir. Domain, 1-800-Flowers, Metroplex, Doane Pet Care, House of Blues, Metokote, Axis Ins. and Guitar Center; chmn., NPower NY, Finance Com., U. Va.; serves on adv. bd., Solera Capital; mem.Investment Com., JPMorgan Partners Asia, JP Morgan Private Equity Partners Select, and JPM organ Horizon Funds Mem. Young Pres. Orgn.; chmn. Bd. Edn., Wilton, Conn.; bd. dirs. WPA Theatre, NYC; pres. of bd. of trustees, McIntire Sch., U. Va. Endowment, chmn., Finance Com.; dir., NYC Investment Fund, Lincoln Center Film Soc., The Big Apple Circus, The Internat. Center of Photography, Wilton Y; bd. trustees, Morgan Library and St. Luke's School Mem. AICPA, Nat. Venture Capital Assn., Nat. Assn. Small Bus. Investment Cos. (bd. govs., vice chmn.), Silver Spring Country Club, Golf Club of Purchase, Pawling Mountain Hunt Club, wilton Riding Club, Beta Gamma Sigma. Republican. Unitarian Universalist. Home: 360 New Canaan Rd Wilton CT 06897-3331 Office: JP Morgan Ptnrs 1221 Ave of the Americas New York NY 10020 Office Phone: 212-899-3400. Office Fax: 212-899-3401.

WALKER, JENNIE LOUISE, not-for-profit fundraiser, consultant; b. Ft. Hood, Tex., Nov. 27, 1962; d. Homer Lee and Jennie Louise (Smith) Walker; m. Philip Jerome King, Apr. 23, 1994 (div. Mar. 1999). BA in Speech Comm., Columbus State U., 1984, postgrad., 1985, Mercer U., 1987-90. Intern Senator Mack Mattingly, Washington, 1984, Congressman Richard Ray, Washington, 1984; rsch. asst. Robinson Humphrey Co., Inc., Atlanta, 1985-89; mktg. asst. Norrell Corp., Atlanta, 1989 90; dir. rsch. Carter Ctr., Inc., Atlanta, 1990-94, Boys & Girls Clubs Am., Atlanta, 1994-2000; dir. philanthropic initiatives WEBMD Found., Inc., Atlanta, 2000; assoc. dir. Global Philanthropists Cir. Synergos Inst., NYC, 2000—02; pres., CEO Jennie Walker Co., Inc., NYC, 2001—. Mem. adv. bd. The Found Ctr., Atlanta, 1997—2000, Found. Ctr., Atlanta, 1997—2000. Vol. Atlanta Project, 1992, Sta. WPBA-TV, Channel 30, Musicians on Call N.Y., 2001—, Lyric Chamber Music Soc. N.Y., 2000—; mem. adv. bd. Ga. Addiction Pregnancy and Parenting Family Enrichment Ctr, 1994—96; mem. Music Mgrs. Forum U.S., 2003—; vol. Richard Ray for Congress Campaign Com., 1984. Mem.: DAR, NARAS (assoc.), Nashville Songwriters Assoc. Internat., Women in Music (mem. 2002—), Assn. Ind. Music Pubs., Assn. Ind. Music Publ., Nat. Acad. Popular Music, Spl. Libr. Assn., Soc. Competitive Intelligence Profls., Am. Prospect Rsch. Assn. (pres. Ga. chpt. 1993—94, 1996—97), Nat. Acad. Songwriters, Broadcast Music, Inc., Ga. Music Industry Assn. (bd. dirs. 1991—93, publicity chair 1991—93, v.p. 1992—93, 1995—98, bd. dirs. 1995—2000, fundraising chair 1995—2000, pres. 1998—2000, pres. emeritus, advisor 2000—, Pres. award for vol. svc. 1997), Nat. Soc. Fundraising Exec., Columbus State U. Alumni Assn. Methodist. Avocations: songwriting, singing. Office: 435 W 57th St #15-S New York NY 10019 Office Phone: 212-541-7456. Business E-Mail: jennie@jenniewalker.com.

WALKER, JEWETT LYNIUS, clergyman, church official; b. Beaumont, Tex., Apr. 7, 1930; s. Elijah Harvey and Ella Jane (Wilson) W.; m. Dorothy Mae Croom, Apr. 11, 1965; children: Cassandra Lynn, Jewett L., Kevin, Michelle, Ella, Betty Renne, Kent, Elijah H. BA, Calif. Western U., 1957; MA, Kingdom Bible Inst., 1960; B Religious Edn., St. Stephens Coll., 1966, DD, 1968; LLD, Union Bapt. Sem., 1971; postgrad., St. Paul Sch. Theology, 1979, Southwestern Bapt. Theol. Sem., 1985-86; grad., Nat. Planned Giving Inst., 1981, Philanthropy Tax Inst., 1982; DD, Clinton Jr. Coll., 1992. Ordained to ministry African Methodist Episcopal Zion Ch., 1957. Pastor Shiloh A.M.E. Zion Ch., Monrovia, Calif., 1961-64, Martin Temple A.M.E. Zion Ch., L.A., 1964-65, 1st A.M.E. Zion Ch., Compton, Calif., 1965-66, Met. A.M.E. Zion Ch., L.A., 1966-73, Logan Temple A.M.E. Zion Ch., San Diego, 1973-74, Rock Hill A.M.E. Zion Ch., Indian Trail, NC, 1974-79, Bennettsville A.M.E. Zion Ch., Norwood, NC, 1979-86, Price Meml. A.M.E. Zion Ch., Concord, NC, 1986-89, Mt. Zion A.M.E. Zion Ch., Hickory Grove, SC, 1989-91, Lancaster, SC, 1993—2001, Mt. Moriah A.M.E. Zion Ch., Richburg, SC, 2001—03, New Hope A.M.E. Zion Ch., Richburg, 2003—. Sec.-treas. dept. home missions, brotherhood pensions and relief African Methodist Episcopal Zion Ch., Charlotte, N.C., 1974-92; mem. exec. bd. Prophetic Justice Unit Com. Nat. Coun. Chs., co-chairperson pers. com.; mem. World Meth. Coun., del. 14th World Conf. Author: Is There a Man in the House, 1975, Lets Get Serious about Missions, 1991, Issues Facing the Ministry, 1991, The Denominational Dollar, 1992, also articles. Chmn. Minority Affairs Adv. Com., Mecklenburg County; trustee Clinton Coll., dir. planned giving, 1992; trustee Rock Hill, Lomax-Hannon Coll., Greenville, Ala., Union Bapt. Theol. Sem., Birmingham, Ala.; bd. mgrs. McCrorey br. YMCA; pres. Am. Ch. Fin. Svc. Corp., Carolina Home Health Svc. Inc., Meth. Life Ins. Soc. Inc., bd. trustees State N.C. Coll. Found., Inc., 1987, del. Presbyn. Ptnrs. in Ecumenism Nat. Coun. Chs. Christ, 1986, pres., 1988—; pres. Walker Funeral Home Inc. (formerly The House of Irma Funeral Home), Concord, Am. Ch. Econ. Devel. Corp.; del. Presbyn. Ch. U.S. Gen. Assembly, 1985; mem. citizens parole accountability com. Mecklenburg County, Charlotte, 1993; mem. planned giving adv. bd. Livingston Coll., Salisbury, N.C.; pres. Jewett L. Walker & Assocs.; chmn. minority affairs adv. com. Mecklenburg County; com. mem. Charlotte Mecklenburg Citizen Parole Accountability Com., 1994, vice chmn., 1998; pres. Pardue St. Apts. Inc., Lancaster, S.C., 1997—, Am. Ch. Econ. Devel. Corp., 1999; elected to jud. coun. African Meth. Episcopal Zion Ch., 2000; mem. adv. bd. mechanics Charlotte, 2001--, Farmers Bank, 2001--. Fellow Nat. Assn. Ch. Bus. Adminstrs., Ch. Bus. Adminstrn., Presbyn. Ch. Bus. Adminstrn. Assn.; mem. NAACP (life), Nat. Soc. Fund Raising Execs., Am. Bible Soc. (state dir. vols., N.C. and S.C. dir. vol.), Nat. Spkrs. Bur., Christian Ministries Mgmt. Assn., Am. Soc. Assn. Execs., Funeral and Cremation Soc. South, Inc. (founding mem. 1998), Shriners, Masons (33 deg.), Prince Hall Affiliation. Republican. Home: 910 Bridlepath Ln Charlotte NC 28211-2022 Office: 4501 Walker Rd Charlotte NC 28211-2047

WALKER, JOAN H. marketing and communications executive; m. George Walker. BA, Rutgers U., New Brunswick, 1968, MA in Sociology, 1973. Sr. exec. mktg. and govt. N.J. State Govt., 1973-83; pres. Richmann & Ptnrs., 1983-88; exec. v.p. Saatchi & Saatchi, 1988-90; mng. dir. mktg. comm. NYNEX Corp., 1990-93; pres., CEO Bozell Pub. Rels., N.Y.C., 1993-96; ptnr. Bozell Sawyer Miller Group, 1996; sr. v.p. corp. comm. Ameritech, Chgo., 1996-99; sr. v.p. global pub. affairs Monsanto (merged with Pharmacia & UpJohn, now Pharmacia), Skolie, Ill., 1999—2002; exec. v.p. corp. mktg. and comm. Qwest Comm. Internat., 2002—. Dir. Qwest Found.; mem. bd. trustees Colo. Symphony Orch. Office: Qwest Comm Internat 1801 California St Denver CO 80202 E-mail: Joan.H.Walker@am.pnu.com.

WALKER, JOHN H. textile manufacturing company executive; Fin. contr. U.K. divsn. Heuga Holding BV, 1972-88; various positions Interface, Inc. (formerly Heuga Holding BV), 1988-95, v.p. sales and mktg. Europe; pres. Interface Europe, 1995-96, sr. v.p., pres., CEO, 1996—. Bd. dirs. Interface, Inc. Office: Interface Inc 2859 Paces Ferry Rd SE Ste 2000 Atlanta GA 30339-6216

WALKER, JOHN LEONARD, lawyer; b. Wash., Oct. 5, 1947; BS in Econs., U. Pa., 1969; JD, NYU, 1972. Bar: Miss. 1972, U.S. Ct. Appeals (5th cir.) 1973, U.S. Supreme Ct. 1975. Staff atty. Cmty. Legal Svc. of Miss., Jackson, 1972—73; ptnr. Johnson and Walker, Jackson, Miss., 1973—76; pvt. practice Jackson, Miss., 1976—78; ptnr. Walker, Brookings & Walker, Jackson, Miss., 1978—82, Walker and Walker, Jackson, Miss., 1982—. City atty., Bolton, Miss., 1973—94; bd. dirs. Ctrl. Miss. Legal Svcs., 1976—92. Mem.: Miss. Trial Lawyers Assn. (bd. dirs., exec. com. 1983—87), Assn. Trial Lawyers Am., Nat. Bar. Assn., Nat. Conf. Black Lawyers (past chmn., Miss. chpt.). Home: 450 Fairfield Dr Jackson MS 39206 Office: 1410 Livingston Ln Ste A Jackson MS 39213

WALKER, JOHN MERCER, JR., federal judge; b. N.Y.C., Dec. 26, 1940; s. John Mercer and Louise (Mead) W.; m. Cristy West, June 20, 1980 (div. Apr. 1983); m. Katharine Kirkland, Feb. 14, 1987. BA, Yale U., 1962; JD, U. Mich., 1966. Bar: NY 1969, U.S. Dist. Ct. (so. dist.) NY 1971, US Ct. Appeals (2d cir.) 1972, US Supreme Ct. 1977, US Ct. Appeals (D.C. cir.) 1982. Maxwell Sch. Pub. Adminstrn. fellow, state counsel Republic of Botswana, Africa, 1966-68; assoc. Davis, Polk and Warwell, NYC, 1969-70; asst. U.S. atty. U.S. Dist. Ct. (so. dist.) NY, NYC, 1971-75; assoc. to ptnr. Carter, Ledyard and Milburn, NYC, 1975-81; asst. sec. enforcement ops. Dept. Treasury, Washington, 1981-85; judge U.S. Dist. Ct. (so. dist.) N.Y., 1985-89, US Ct. Appeals (2nd cir.), Conn., 1989—, chief judge, 2000. Adj. prof. NYU Law Sch., 1995—; gen. counsel Nat. Coun. on Crime and Deliquency, N.Y.C., 1977-81; chmn. Fed. Law Enforcement Tng. Ctr., Washington, 1981-85; spl. counsel Adminstrv. Conf. U.S., Washington, 1986-92; mem. budget com. jud. conf. Inst. Jud. Adminstrn., 1992—, dir., 1992—. Del. Rep. Nat. Conv., Detroit, 1980. With USMCR, 1963-67. Recipient Alexander Hamilton award Sec. of Treas., Washington, 1985, Secret Service Honor award, 1985. Mem. ABA, D.C. Bar Assn., Assn. Bar City of NY, Fed. Judges Assn. (pres. 1993-95). Republican. Episcopalian. Office: US Cir Ct 157 Church St New Haven CT 06510-2100

WALKER, JOHN P. pharmaceutical executive; Pres., CEO Arris Pharm. Corp., South San Francisco; chmn. & CEO Axys Pharms Inc., San Francisco. Office: Axys Pharm Inc 180 Kimball Way South San Francisco CA 94080-6218

WALKER, JOYCE MARIE, secondary school educator; b. Kansas City, Kans., Jan. 24, 1948; d. Frank Cornelius and Inez (Pennington) W.; divorced; 1 child, Kevin Cornelius. BS, U. Ark., Pine Bluff, 1972. Cert. ch. adminstr. Bus. tchr. U.S. Trade Sch., Kansas City, 1972-74; exec. sec. Kansas City Mo. Sch. Dist., 1974-77; tchr. vocat. bus. Aurora (Colo.) Pub. Sch., 1977—. Vocat. bus. tchr. Pioneer C.C., 1975 77; amb. Aurora Pub. Schs., 1999—. Mem. Aurora Human Rels. Martin Luther King Jr. Com., 1986—; sec., supt. Sunday sch. Macedonia Bapt. Ch., 1985—, evangelism counselor, 1992—; 2d v.p. E.L. Witchfield Missionary Soc., 1989; chmn. We. States Fgn. Mission, 1990. Mem. Nat. Coun. Negro Women, Nat. Assn. Bus. Educators, NAACP (Aurora br. 1990—), Delta Sigma Theta (v.p. Denver chpt. 1998-2002, pres. 2002—). Avocations: tennis, bowling, sewing. Home: 12948 E 48th Ave Denver CO 80239-4408 Office: Aurora Pub Schs 11700 E 11th Ave Aurora CO 80010-3758

WALKER, JUANITA MOFFETT, retired elementary school educator; b. Edwards, Miss., Jan. 31, 1939; d. Fred Douglas and Matlean Allen Moffett; m. Tommy Lewis, June 11, 1962; children: Tommy Jr., Edward, Roland. AA, Utica (Miss.) Jr. Coll., 1959; BA, Jackson State U., 1961; MA, Purdue U., 1995; postgrad., Black Hills State U., Spearfish, S.D., Ind. U. Cert. tchr. Miss., S.D., counselor Ind. Tchr. Burgland H.S., McComb, Miss., 1961, Oglala Cmty. H.S., Pine Ridge, SD, 1962—69, Wirt H.S., Gary, Ind., 1969—71, West Side H.S., Gary, Ind., 1971—78; counselor Pulaski Mid. Sch., Gary, Ind., 1978—82, Bailly Mid. Sch., Gary, Ind., 1982—91, Edison Mid. Sch., Gary, Ind., 1991—2001. Testing coord. Bailly and Edison Mid. Schs., 1982—95; dept. chmn. Edison Mid. Sch., 1991—2001; chmn. guidance career day Bailly Mid. Sch., 1982—90. Author: Church Folk, 2001; co-host cable TV show. Historian Gary Civic Chorale, 1980—; founder, pres. Gary Writers Workshop, 2001—; mem. Friends of Libr., Gary, 2000—. Mem.: Lake County Ret. Tchrs. Assn., Alpha Kappa Alpha. Avocations: singing, playing keyboards, travel, public speaking, reading.

WALKER, KARA, artist; b. Stockton, Calif., Nov. 26, 1969; BA in Painting/Printmaking, Atlanta Coll. Art, 1991; MFA in Painting/Printmaking, R.I. Sch. Design, 1994. One-woman shows include Ctr. Curaltorial Studies, Bard Coll., Annandale-on-Hudson, N.Y., 1995, Nexus Contemporary Arts Ctr., Atlanta, 1995, Wooster Gardens/Brent Sikkema, N.Y.C., 1995, 1998, Bernard Toale Gallery, Boston, 1996, Huntington Beach (Calif.) Arts Ctr., 1997, U. Chgo., 1997, Contemporary Arts Ctr., Cin., 1997, Henry Art Gallery, U. Wash., Seattle, 1997, The Carpenter Ctr., Harvard U., Cambridge, Mass., 1997, San Francisco Mus. Modern Art, 1997, The Forum, St. Louis, 1998, Vienna State Opera House, Austria, 1998, The Print Ctr., Phila., 1998, Galleri Index, Stockholm, 1998, Contemporary Arts Mus., Houston, 1999, Calif. Coll. Arts and Crafts, Oliver Art Ctr., Oakland, 1998, Brent Sikkema, N.Y., 1998, Gallery 100, Atlanta, 1991, McKinney Ave. Contemporary, Dallas, 1999, exhibited in group shows at New Visions Gallery, Atlanta, 1991, exhibited in group shows, Atlanta, 1991, exhibited in group shows, MU Gallery, Boston, 1993, exhibited in group shows, Providence, 1994, exhibited in group shows, Paul Morris Gallery, N.Y.C., 1995, Mills Gallery, Boston, Inst. Contemporary Art, 1996, Greg Kucera Gallery, Seattle, 1997, Stephen Friedman Gallery, London, 1998, Elaine L. Jacob Gallery, Wayne State U., Detroit, 1999, numerous others; author: Freedom, A Fable, A Curious Interpretation of the Wit of a Negress in Troubled Times; contbr. articles to profl. jours. Recipient John D. and Catherine T. MacArthur Found.; fellow Individual Artist's fellow, Art Matters, Inc.; scholar Presdl. scholar, Atlanta Coll. Art, Ida Blank Ocko scholar. Office: care Brent Sikkema 530 West 22d St New York NY 10011

WALKER, KATHRYN A. telecommunications industry executive; B in Civil Engring., SD State U.; MS, degree in Engring., U. Mo. Asst. v.p. human resources Sprint Tech. Svcs., 1995—97; v.p. product mgmt. Sprint Bus., 1997—2002; sr. v.p. network svcs. global Markets group Sprint Corp., 2002—03, exec. v.p. network svcs., 2003—. Office: 6200 Sprint Pkwy Overland Park KS 66251

WALKER, KENNETH ADLEY, aluminum fabricating company executive; b. Hartford, Conn., May 16, 1949; s. George Gould and Elizabeth Mae (Parcher) W.; m. Ruth Ann Danowski; children: Kenneth, Gregory, Daniel. BSME with honors, Cornell U., 1971; M in Adminstrv. Sci., Johns Hopkins U., 1978; M in Fin., Loyola Coll., Balt., 1981; postgrad., U. Md., 1990—. Test engr. Koppers Co. Inc., Balt., 1971-72, project engr., 1973; mgr. accessory equipment Environ. Elements Corp., Balt., 1974-76, mgr. scrubber/ filter products, 1976-82, gen. mgr. water treatment systems, 1983-88; v.p. ops. Washington Aluminum Co., Balt., 1988-94, pres., 1994—, also bd. dirs.; pres. TriFab, Inc., 1994—. Bd. dirs. Md. Healthcorp, Inc., 1992-94, Dovco Indsl. Fabricators, Inc., TriFab, Inc.; pvt. industry rep. Gov.'s Com. Study Anticipated Sewage Treatment Needs, State of Md., 1986-88. Patentee method and system cleansing a filter bed; patent issued for Modular Bd. dirs. Greater Balt. Med. Ctr., 1986-94, sec. 1992-94, mem. fin. and bldg. coms., 1986-94, mem. credentials com., 1998—; bd. dirs. Towson (Md.) Presbyn. Kindergarten, 1986-89, v.p. 1987-89; asst. scoutmaster, scoutmaster Boy Scouts Am., 1990—. Mem. Am. Welding Soc., Cornell Soc. Engrs., Quill and Dagger Soc., Autocrossers, Inc., UMBC Coll. of Engrg. (indsl. adv. bd.), 1999—, Adirondack Mountain Club, Porsche Club Am., Adirondack 46ers, U.S. Orienteering Fedn., Appalachian Mtn. Club, Quantico Orienteering Club, Aluminum Assn. (mem. engring. task force 1993—), Am. Alpine Club, Tau Beta Pi, Delta Chi.

Republican. Avocations: skiing, golf, winter mountaineering, autocrossing, orienteering. Office: Washington Aluminum Co Knecht Ave Baltimore MD 21229 Home: PO Box 1068 Chester VT 05143-1068

WALKER, KENNETH DALE, automotive service company executive; b. Ft. Worth, Feb. 25, 1948; s. Billy Glenn and Jo Ann (Prestridge) W.; m. Cheri Lee Propp, Feb. 28, 1969 (div. Aug. 1980); children: Joel Glenn, Corbett Dale; m. Vickie Lynn Franklin, Sept. 27, 1980; children: Kristi Lynn, Carolyn Christine. BBA, U. Tex., 1970. CPA, Tex. Mgr. Arthur Young & Co., Ft. Worth, 1970-76; controller, v.p. fin. Big 4 Automotive, Ft. Worth, 1976-80, v.p. ops West Tex., 1980-82, v.p. retail, 1982-84; chief fin. officer southwest region AI Automotive Corp., Ft. Worth, 1984-86, v.p. ops., chief operating officer southwest region, 1986-88; owner Kenneth D. Walker Consulting Turn Around Mgmt. Projects, 1988; pres., CEO Cardis Corp., Buena Park, Calif., 1989-92, Parts Industry Corp., Memphis, 1992-96, Meineke Discount Muffler Shops, Inc., 1996—. Instr. project bus. Jr. Achievement, Ft. Worth, 1981; bd. dirs. All Pro Program, Inc., Andolusia, Ala., 1978-84. Bumper to Bumper Program, Ft. Worth, 1987-88. Recipient Automotive Replacement Edn. award Northwood Inst., 1987. Mem. Inst. Internal Auditors (v.p. 1975-76, pres. 1976), Automotive Warehouse Distbr. Assn. (chmn. fin. stats. com. 1984-87, chmn. univ. faculty 1986-87, bd. govs. 1986—, chmn. bd. dirs. 1995, Pursuit of Excellence award 1986), TPC-Southwind Club. Methodist. Avocations: golf, skiing. Office: Meineke Discount Muffler 128 S Tryon St Ste 900 Charlotte NC 28202-5000

WALKER, LARRY KENNETH ROBERT, professional baseball player; b. Maple Ridge, B.C., Dec. 1, 1966; Grad. high sch., B.C., Can. With Montreal Expos, 1989-94; outfielder Colo. Rockies, 1995—. Named "The Sporting News" Nat. League All-Star Team, 1992, "The Sporting News" NAt. League Silver Slugger Team, 1992; recipient Gold Glove as outfielder, 1992-93. Office: Colo Rockies Coors Field 2001 Blake St Denver CO 80205-2008

WALKER, LAURIE SHANNON, psychologist, counselor; b. Harrisburg, Pa., Apr. 29, 1958; d. Don Lockwood Lucas and Muriel Mae Schmidt; m. James Robert Walker, Aug. 29, 1982; children: Adrienne, Alexis, Alyssa. BA, Dickenson Coll., Carlisle, Pa., 1980; MS, Millersville U., Pa., 1993; doctoral student, Union Inst. and U., Cin., 2001—. Lic. psychologist 1997, profl. counselor. Counselor Craig & Associates, York, Pa., 1992—95; psychologist Tressler Luth. Svcs., Mechanicsburg, Pa., 1995—98, Mazzihi & Sullivan, 1995—98, Guidance Associates of Pa., Camp Hill, 1998—99; pvt. practice Laurie S. Walker, M.S., L.P.C., Loveland, Colo., 1999—. Contbr. articles to profl. jours. and periodicals. Group facilitator R25 Sch. Dist., Loveland, Colo., 2002—. Mem.: APA. Democrat. Avocations: reading, writing, film and theatre reviewing. Home: 1020 Arapahoe Ave Berthoud CO 80513 Office: Laurie S Walker MS LPC Ste B 2114 Lincoln Ave Loveland CO 80538

WALKER, LAWRENCE HOWARD, JR., music educator, department chairman; b. Phila., Feb. 26, 1955; s. Lawrence Walker Sr. and Daisy Walker; m. Sheila Patricia Roberts, July 18, 1981; children: Lauren, Iris. BS, Va. State U., 1978, MEd, 1981. Cert. tchr. Va. Tchr. Chesterfield Sch., Va., 1978, Fairfax Co. (Va.) Pub. Sch., 1978—. Dept. chair Fairfax (Va.) Pub. Sch., camp dir. Home: 13314 Lockgate Pl Herndon VA 20171-4028

WALKER, LELAND JASPER, civil engineer; b. Fallon, Nev., Apr. 18, 1923; s. Albert Willard and Grayce (Wilkinson) W.; m. Margaret Frances Noble, Jan. 21, 1946; children: Thomas, Margaret, Timothy. BS in Civil Engring, Iowa State U., 1944; D. Eng. (hon.), Mont. State U., 1983. Engr. with various govtl. depts., 1946-51, 53-55; v.p. Wenzel & Co. (cons. engrs.), Great Falls, Mont., 1955-58; pres., chmn. bd. No. Engring. and Testing, Inc., Great Falls, 1958-88. Pres. Ind. Labs. Assurance Co., 1977-79; bd. dirs. Mont. Power Co., Entech Inc., 1982-92, Lewis and Clark Biologicals, Inc., 1989-92, Applied Tech., Inc. Pres., trustee Endowment and Rsch. Found. Mont. State U., 1969-82, Mont. Deaconess Hosp., Great Falls, 1959-67. McLaughlin Rsch. Inst. Biol. Scis., 1989-92, Mont. Sch. Deaf and Blind Found., 1984—; trustee Rocky Mountain Coll., 1977-80, Dufresne Found., 1979-87; chmn., bd. dirs. Mont. Tech. Svcs. Adv. Coun. adv. coun. Engring. Coll. Mont. State U.; bd. dirs. Mont. State Fair, Engring. Socs. Commn. on Energy, 1977-79, Mont. Bd. Sci. and Tech., 1983-88, Great Falls Chamber Found., 1989-91, trustee Great Falls Public Libr. Found., 1995-2001. Named to Mont. Engrs. Hall Fame, 2003. Fellow ASCE (pres. 1976-77), AAAS, Cons. Engrs. Coun. (pres. Mont. 1971), Accrediting Bd. Engring. and Tech. (v.p. 1978-79, pres. 1980-83); mem. Nat. Acad. Engring., Am. Coun. Ind. Labs. (hon., sec. 1973-76), Meadowlark Country Club, Pachyderm Club (bd. dirs., v.p. 1992-94), Chi Epsilon (nat. hon.), Tau Beta Pi (hon.). Republican. Methodist. Home: 1200 32nd St S Apt 9 Great Falls MT 59405-5333

WALKER, LEROY TASHREAU, university chancellor, coach; b. Atlanta, June 14, 1918; s. Willie and Mary Elizabeth (Thomas) W.; m. Katherine McDowell, Dec. 31, 1938 (dec.); children— LeRoy, Carolyn BS, Benedict Coll., 1940, PhD (hon.); MA, Columbia U., 1941; PhD, NYU, 1957; PhD (hon.), Defiance Coll.; D of Sports Sci., U.S. Sports Acad.; LLD (hon.), Ea. Ky. U. and N.C. Cen. U., Wake Forest U., 1993, Morehouse U., 1993; DHL (hon.), Tuskegee U., 1993, Duke U., 1995; LHD (hon.), U. N.C., 1995, Queens Coll., 1995; Dr.Humanities, Princeton U., 1996. Chmn. dept. phys. edn., coach basketball, football, track and field Benedict Coll., Columbia, S.C., 1941-42; chmn. dept. phys. edn., coach basketball, football, track and field Bishop Coll., Marshall, Tex., 1942-43, Prairie View State U., 1943-45; chmn. dept. phys. edn. and recreation, coach basketball, football, track and field N.C. Cen. U., Durham, 1945-73, vice-chancellor for univ. relations, 1974-83, chancellor, 1983-86, chancellor emeritus, 1986—. Ednl. specialist Cultural Exchange Program, Dept. State, 1959, 60, 62,; dir. program, planning and tng. Peace Corps, Africa, 1966-68; coach Ethiopian and Israeli teams Olympic Games, Rome, 1960; adviser track and field teams throughout world; mem. U.S. Collegiate Sports Coun., 1971; chmn. Coll. Commrs. Assn., 1971-74; chmn. track and field com. Athletic Union U.S.A., 1973-75; head coach U.S. track and field team Olympic Games, Montreal, 1976; chmn. bd. U.S. Olympic Festival, 1987—; mem. exec. bd., treas. U.S. Olympic Com., pres., 1992—; chef de mission for 1992 Barcelona Olympic Games, 1991—; sr. v.p. sports Atlanta Com. for the Olympic Games 1996, 1991—. Author: Manual of Adapted Physical Education, 1960; Physical Education for the Exceptional Student, 1965; Championship Techniques in Track and Field, 1969, Track and Field for Boys and Girls, 1983; also articles Bd. dirs. U.S.A.-China Rels. Com.; bd. trustees U.S. Olympic Com.; pres. Athletic Congress, U.S. Olympic Com., 1992—; pres. Spl. Olympics World championship Bd. Recipient James E. Shepard Outstanding Tchr. award Hamilton Watch Co., 1964, U. N.C. Systems Bd. Govs. award, 1989; Achievement award Cen. Intercollegiate Athletic Assn., 1967; Disting. Alumnus award Benedict Coll., 1968, Disting. Service award Kiwanis Internat., 1971, City of Durham, 1971, Durham C. of C., 1973, Gov.'s Ambassador of Goodwill award, 1974; O. Max Gardner award, 1976; N.C. Disting. Citizen award, 1977; Achievement in Life award Ency. Brit., 1977, Achievement award Sertoma; Heritage award YMCA, 1988, Robert Giegengack award The Athletics Congress, 1990, Amb. award Pres.' Coun. on Phys. Fitness and Sports, 1991, Disting. Alumni award NYU, 1993, Jim Corbett award Nat. Assn. Coll. Athletic Dirs., 1993; named to N.C. Hall of Fame, 1975, S.C. Hall of Fame, 1977, Nat. Assn. Sport and Phys. Edn. Hall of Fame, 1977, N.C. Cen. U. Hall of Fame, 1984, U.S. Olympic Hall of Fame, 1987, Ga. Hall of Fame, 1988, Benedict Coll. Hall of Fame, N.C. Soc. award The Olympic Order by Internat. Olympic Com., 1995, Toastmasters Golden Camel award, 1996, 100 Blackmen Disting. Leadership award, 1996. Mem. Am. Alliance Health, Phys. Edn., Recreation, and Dance (nat. pres.; Honor award 1972, Gulick award), NEA, U.S. Track Coaches Assn. (Nat. Track Coach of Yr. 1972), N.C. Assn. Health, Phys. Edn., Recreation and Dance (Honor award 1971; v.p. div., dir.), Internat. Assn. Athletic Fedns. (U.S. rep. 1976—), Sigma Delta Psi, Alpha Phi Omega, Omega Psi Phi Episcopalian.

WALKER, LORENE, retired elementary school educator; b. Clovis, N.Mex., July 27, 1911; d. Jessie H. and Tille Eula (Harlan) Black; m. Carl Westley Walker, June 9, 1934; children: Wesley, Charles. BS, N.Mex. State U., 1933; M of Family Life, Ctrl. Wash. U., 1959, postgrad., 1956—74. Tchr. home econs. Floyd Sch., near Portales, N.Mex., 1933-34, Navajo Meth. Mission, Farmington, N.Mex., 1947-48; home agt. ext. svc. Wash. State Coop. Ext. Svc., Yakima, 1948-56; family life, counseling tchr. West Valley Sch., Yakima, 1956-71, spl. elem. reading tchr., 1971-75; tour organizer, leader Mission Tour, Yakima, 1966-98; trainer missioners United Meth. Ch., Yakima, 1998—. Coord. 4-H camps, fairs and programs Wash. Coop. Ext. Svc., Yakima, 1950-56. Chairperson Experiment for Internat. Living, Yakima Valley Rep. Women's Club, 1960-67; docent, tour leader Yakima Valley Mus., 1976—; trustee Found. Pacific Northwest United Meth. Ch., 1984—; pres. Columbia River dist. United Meth. Ch., 1987-88, chairperson global missions, 1993-94; chair Tour With a Mission, 1966-2003; del. World Meth. Conf., Brighton, Eng., 2001. Mem. AAUW (treas. 1962-66, bd. dirs., chair internat. rels. 1962-89; spl. honor award 1989), United Meth. Women (pres. 1987-89, active local, dist. confs. Pacific N.W. Conf., spl. recognition 1989), Wesleyan Svc. Guild Meth. Women. (officer 1964-68), Yakima Woman's Century Club (active local orgns.), Ret. Tchrs. Yakima County Assn. (active local orgns.), Alpha Delta Kappa (pres. 1967-69). Avocations: gardening, travel, needle-crafts, international political and cultural news. Home: 101 N 48th Ave Apt 25A Yakima WA 98908-3179

WALKER, LORENZO GILES, surgeon, educator; b. Phila., June 29, 1957; s. Manuel Lorenzo and Romaine Yvonne (Smith) W.; m. Yvonne Ruiz; children: Zachary Giles, Benjamin Lee, Cassidy Leigh. BA cum laude, U. Pa., 1978; MD, Harvard U., 1982. Diplomate Am. Bd. Orthopaedic Surgery, Nat. Bd. Med. Examiners; lic. surgeon, Mass., Calif.; cert. added qualification hand surgery, 1993; recertified orthopedic surgery and hand surgery, 2003. Intern in surgery New Eng. Deaconess-Harvard Surg. Svc., Boston, 1982-83, asst. resident in surgery, 1983-84; resident in orthop. surgery Harvard U., Boston, 1985-88; fellow in hand surgery UCLA Med. Sch., 1988-89, asst. clin. prof. orthop. surgery, 1988—, attending physician dept. orthop. Hand Clinic, 1996-98; ptnr. Ventura Orthop. Hand and Sports Med. Group, Calif., 1994-98; solo practice hand surgery, 1998—. Staff physician St. John's Plasant Valley Hosp., Camarillo, Calif., St. John's Regional Med. Ctr., Oxnard, Calif., Cmty. Meml. Hosp., Ventura, Calif.; attending physician, cons. Sepulveda, Calif. VA Hosp.; presenter in field. Cons. reviewer Clin. Orthopaedics and related Rsch., 1990-92; contbr. numerous articles to profl. jours. Vol. Spl. Olympics, Ventura, 1994-96, Direct Relief Internat., Santa Barbara, Calif., 1994-96, Ventura County Rescue Mission, 1994-98. Recipient Cert. of Appreciation, Am. Heart Assn., 1994; UCLA faculty fellow, 1988-89. Mem. Am. Soc. for Surgery of the Hand, Am. Assn. for Hand Surgery, AMA, Calif. Med. Assn., Calif. Orthopaedic Assn., Calif. Ringside Physician, Ventura County Med. Soc., Internat. Soc. Aquatic Medicine, Western Orthopaedic Assn., Orthopaedic Overseas, UCLA Hand Club, Arthroscopy Assn. N.Am., Alpha Epsilon Delta, Onyx Honor Soc., Philomathean Soc. Avocations: photography, scuba diving, sports memorabilia, fishing, travel. Home: 3041 Shadow Mesa Cir Thousand Oaks CA 91360-1061 Office Phone: 805-485-7764.

WALKER, LUCY DORIS, secondary school educator, writer; b. Ridgeway, NC, May 6, 1953; d. Edgerton Verl and Mary Ellen (Williams) Plummer; m. William A. Walker Jr., June 21, 1969 (div. Aug. 1974); 1 child, Lucretia Marie. BA in English Edn., Fairleigh Dickinson U., 1975; MA in Theater Arts, Montclair State U., 1977. Cert. English and theater arts tchr., N.J. Tchr., dir., actor, writer Ctr. Modern Dance Edn., Hackensack, NJ, 1978; writer, dir. Am. Theater Actors, NYC, 1978-79; tchr. multicultural hub Ctr. Internat. Studies, Cultural Events, Teaneck HS, Teaneck, NJ, 1979—; coord. Teaneck Arts Acad. at Teaneck HS, Teaneck, NJ, 2002—. Artistic dir. Teaneck H.S. dance ensemble, 1989—; program coord. African and African-Am. Studies Resource Ctr., 1990—; instructional leader for fine and performing arts, coord. Teaneck Arts Acad. Writer and choreographer various plays, 1979-95. Recipient Acad. Achievement award Fairleigh Dickinson U. Opportunities Program, 1974, Black Heritage award Nat. Assn. Negro Bus. & Profl. Women's Clubs, 1991. Mem. NEA, NJ Edn. Assn. Democrat. Baptist. Avocations: sewing, gardening, hiking, painting, music. Home: 363 Washington Pl Englewood NJ 07631-3232 Office: Teaneck HS 100 Elizabeth Ave Teaneck NJ 07666-4713 E-mail: walkplum@aol.com.

WALKER, LULA NORIEGA, secondary administrator; b. Alexandria, Va., Nov. 20, 1944; d. Eugene and Ruth Elizabeth (Lowe) Noriega; m. James J. Walker Sr., Sept. 29, 1979; children: Lynn, James, Melvin, Sean, Ronald; m. Jim Patterson. BS in Agrl. and Tech., U. N.C., 1966; MLS, SUNY, Stony Brook, 1976; PD, L.I. U., 1982. Cert. sch. adminstr., N.Y.; cert. English tchr. N.Y. Tchr. High Point (N.C.) Pub. Schs.; chairperson, English tchr. Westbury (N.Y.) Pub. Schs.; asst. prin. N. Babylon (N.Y.) Pub. Schs. Mem. SANYS, ASCD. Home: 139 Craig Ave Freeport NY 11520-1532

WALKER, MARGARET SMITH, real estate company executive; b. Lancashire, Eng., Oct. 14, 1943; came to U.S., 1964; d. Arthur Edward and Doris Audrey (Dawson) Smith; m. James E. Walker, Feb. 6, 1992. Lic. real estate agt., Hawaii. Broker Lawson-Worrall Inc. (now Mary Worrall/Sotheby), Honolulu, 1974-81; pres. Maggie Parkes & Assocs., Inc., Honolulu, 1981—. Bd. dirs. Aloha State Dressage Soc., Honolulu, 2001, Hawaii Opera Theatre, 2002—, com. chmn., chmn. Opera Ball, 1997. Mem. Am. Horse Shows Assn., Hawaii Horse Shows Assn., Outrigger Canoe Club. Episcopalian. Avocations: dressage riding, horse show management. Office: PO Box 25083 Honolulu HI 96825-0083

WALKER, MARK A. lawyer; b. N.Y.C., June 24, 1941; s. Joseph and Eleanor (Junger) W.; m. Tania Khodjamirian; children: Marie, Andrew. BA, Stanford U., 1963; LLB, Yale U., 1966. Bar: N.Y. 1967, U.S. Dist. Ct. (so. dist.) N.Y. 1977. Assoc. Cleary, Gottlieb, Steen & Hamilton, Paris, Brussels and N.Y., 1966-75, ptnr. N.Y.C., 1975—. Mem. Assn. Bar City N.Y. E-mail: mwalker@cgsh.com.

WALKER, MARTHA YEAGER, state senator, businesswoman; b. May 15, 1940; m. H. Jarrett Walker; children: Meredyth, Brent, Melissa. BS, W.Va. U. Mem. W.Va. Ho. of Reps., Charleston, 1990-92, W.Va. Senate, Charleston, 1993—. Mem. fin. com., govt. orgn. com., health and human resources com., pensions com., rules com., enrolled bills com.; with Byrd Inst. Studies, U. Charleston. Mem. W.Va. Dem. Exec. Com., Charleston Zoing Appeals Bd., Ctr. for Econ. Options, Byrd Inst. Govt. Studies, U. Charleston; former mem. Cabin Creek Health Ctr.; former treas. Kanawha County Pvt. Industry Coun.; active Literacy Vols. W.Va.; bd. dirs. Poison Control Ctr., Cabin Creek Health Ctr., Multiple Sclerosis Soc. W.Va., W.Va. Children's Health Policy Bd., Gov.'s Cabinet on Children and Families, Regional Contracting Assistance Ctr., Charleston Capitol Market, Literacy Vols. of Am.; sustaining mem. Jr. League Charleston; treas. PIC Kanawha County. Mem. Charleston C. of C., W.Va. U. Alumni Assn., Rotary. Democrat. Presbyterian. Office: WVa Senate 1900 Kanawha Blvd E Rm 439M Charleston WV 25305-0009 also: 11 Quail Cove Rd Charleston WV 25314-1634

WALKER, MARY L. federal agency administrator, lawyer; b. Dayton, Ohio, Dec. 1, 1948; d. William Willard and Lady D. Walker; 1 child, Winston Samuel. Student, U. Calif., Irvine, 1966-68; BA in Biology/Ecology, U. Calif., Berkeley, 1970; postgrad., UCLA, 1972-73; JD, Boston U., 1973. Bar: Calif. 1973, U.S. Supreme Ct. 1979. Atty. So. Pacific Co., San Francisco, 1973-76; assoc. Richards, Watson & Gershon, L.A., 1976-78, ptnr., 1979-82; dep. asst. atty. gen. lands div. U.S. Dept. Justice, Washington, 1982-84; dep. solicitor U.S. Dept. Interior, Washington, 1984-85; asst. sec. for environment, safety and health U.S. Dept. Energy, Washington, 1985-88; spl. cons. to chmn. bd. Law Engring., Atlanta, 1988-89; v.p., West Coast and the Pacific Law Environ., Inc., San Francisco, 1989; ptnr., head environ. law dept. Richards, Watson & Gershon, San Francisco, 1989-91; ptnr. Luce, Forward, Hamilton & Scripps, San Diego, 1991-94; ptnr. and head San Diego Environ. Practice Group Brobeck, Phleger & Harrison, LLP, San Diego, 1994—2001; gen. counsel air force U.S. Dept. Defense, Washington, 2001—. U.S. commr. InterAm. Tropical Tuna Commn., 1989—95; mem. adv. bd. Floresta, Inc. Bd. dirs. Endowment for Cmty. Leadership, 1987—2000, Global Involvement Through Edn., 1998—2001. Mem. Calif. Bar Assn., San Diego Bar Assn., BIOCOM (bd. dirs. 1991-2001, pres. 1994), Profl. Women's Fellowship-San Diego (co-founder, bd. dirs. 1996-2001, pres. 1996-97), World Affairs Coun., Renaissance Women. Republican. Office: US Dept Defense Gen Counsel 1740 Air Force Pentagon Washington DC 20330-1740

WALKER, MICHAEL ANGUS, economist, director; b. Corner Brook, New Foundland, Sept. 11, 1945; m. Janet Walker; children: Margot, Joel. BA, St. Francis Xavier U., 1966; MA, U. We. Ontario, 1967, PhD, 1969. Instr. U. We. Ontario, Canada, 1968—69; with Bank of Can., 1969—72; instr. Carleton U., Canada, 1971; with Fed. Dept. Fin., Canada, 1973—74; exec. dir. The Fraser Inst., Vancouver, Canada, 1974—. Bd. dir. Mancal Corp., The Milton and Rose D. Friedman Found. Office: The Fraser Inst 4th Floor 1770 Burrard St Vancouver BC Canada V6J 3G7

WALKER, MICHAEL CHARLES, SR., retirement services executive; b. Rochester, N.Y., Mar. 4, 1940; s. Charles Boyle and Evelyn Esther (Young) W.; m. Patricia Ann Camelio, Feb. 2, 1963; children: Michael Charles Jr., Lyn, Lea, Matthew. BA, U. Colo., 1962; MBA, Columbia Pacific U., 1982, DBA, 1984. Adminstrv. trainee Lincoln Rochester (N.Y.) Trust Co., 1962-64, mktg. officer, 1964-68; asst. v.p. Lincoln First Bank of Rochester, 1968-72, v.p., 1972-77; pres. M.C. Walker Co., Inc., Spencerport, N.Y., 1977-80; exec. dir. The Valley Manor, Rochester, 1980-85; pres., CEO Presbyn. Homes & Svcs. Genesee Valley, Inc., Rochester, 1999—. Lectr. SUNY, Brockport, 1982—89; v.p., dir. Kilian and Caroline Schmitt Found., Rochester, 1985—; mem. adv. bd. Chase Manhattan 1st Bank, Rochester, 1989—92; trustee Rochester Hearing and Speech Ctr., 1989—95, chmn., 1993—94; bd. dirs. Genesee Region HOme Care Assn., Rochester, 1990—2000; trustee Greater Rochester C. of C., 1981—89. Author: Introduction to Bank Marketing Research, 1969, rev. edit., 1972, Practical Handbook of Marketing Definitions, 1970; contbr. articles to profl. jours. Leader task force Spencerport Ctrl. Schs. Bd. Edn., 1977, 80-81, 85; chmn. Monroe County Svs. Bond Com., Rochester, 1972-97; mem. United Way Evaluation Team, 1990-94; bus. adv. bd. SUNY, Brockport, 1993—; mem. N.Y. State Bd. Profl. Med. Conduct, 1993—; profl. adv. com. Self Help for Hard of Hearing, 1994-96. Recipient Pres.'s Geneseekers award, Rochester Area C. of C., 1979, Innovation of Yr. award, NYAHSA, 1989, Cmty. Svc. award, Self Help for Hard of Hearing, 1997, Patriotic Svc. award, U.S. Treasury, 1997. Mem. Am. Assn. Homes for Aging (various coms.), Am. Mktg. Assn. (pres. Rochester chpt. 1969-70), N.Y. State Bankers Assn. (pres. residential mortgage com. 1975-76), N.Y. Assn. Homes and Svcs. for Aging (various coms.), Ridgemont Country Club, Rochester Rotary, Am. Legion. Episcopalian. Avocations: golf, reading, travel, physical fitness. Office: Homes & Svcs Genesee Valley Inc 1570 East Ave Rochester NY 14610-1610

WALKER, MORT, cartoonist; b. El Dorado, Kans., Sept. 3, 1923; s. Robin A. and Carolyn (Richards) W.; m. Catherine Prentice, Aug. 24, 1985; children: Greg, Brian, Polly, Morgan, Marjorie, Neal, Roger, Whitney, Cathy, Jr., Priscilla Student, Kansas City Jr. Coll., 1941-42, Washington U., St. Louis, 1943-44; BA, U. Mo., 1948; LL.D., William Penn Coll., 1981. Designer Hallmark Greeting Cards, 1941; editor Dell Pub. Co., 1948-49; free lance cartoonist Saturday Evening Post, other popular mags., 1948-50. Scholar in residence Mo. U., 1992. Comic strip artist King Features, 1950—; creator Beetle Bailey, 1950, Hi and Lois, 1954, Sam's Strip, 1961, Boner's Ark, 1968, Sam and Silo, 1977, The Evermores, 1982, Betty Boop and Felix, 1984, (for United Features) Gamin and Patches, 1987; author: Most, 1971, Land of Lost Things, 1973, Backstage at the Strips, 1975, The Lexicon of Comicana, 1981, The Best of Beetle Bailey, 1984, The Coconut Crew, 1997, (autobiography) Mort Walker's Private Scrapbook, 2001; contbr. to numerous anthologies and textbooks. Mem. Pres.'s Com. to Hire Handicapped, People to People Com. Exhbn. touring group show Met. Mus. Art, N.Y.C., 1951; chmn. Internat. Mus. Cartoon Art. Served to 1st lt. AUS, 1943-46, ETO. Decorated chevalier Order Arts and Letters (France), 2000; recipient Outstanding Cartoonist award The Banshees, 1955, Il Secolo XIX award (Italy), 1972, Adamson award (Sweden), 1975, 88, Segar award, 1977, 4th Estate award Am. Legion, The Jester, 1979, Power of Printing, 1977, NCS Golden T-Square award, 1999, Disting. Civilian Svc. award U.S. Army; named Man of Yr. NCCJ, 1988. Mem. Nat. Cartoonists Soc. (pres. 1959-60, Reuben award 1953, award for best humor strip of 1966, 69, Mus. Cartoon Art Hall of Fame 1989), Artists and Writers, Newspaper Features Coun. Authors Guild, Soc. Illustrators, Nat. Press Club, Silvermine Club (Norwalk, Conn.), Greenwich Country Club, Quechee Club (Vt.), Kappa Sigma (Man of Yr. 1988). Office: care King Features Syndicate 888 7th Ave New York NY 10019 *If I enjoy my own life that's one life enjoyed. But if I can help others enjoy their lives more, many lives are made more enjoyable.*

WALKER, NATHAN C. foundation administrator, minister, educator; b. Munich, Dec. 31, 1975; s. Steve K. and Mary C. Walker. BFA, Emerson Coll., 1998; MA, postgrad., Columbia U., 2002—, Union Theol. Sem., N.Y.C., 2002—. Cert. tchr. comm. and performing arts pre-K-12 Mass. Instr. Western Nev. C.C., Carson City, 1995—99; founder The da Vinci Coll. Found., Minden, Nev., 1998—; advisor NYU, 1999—2000; instr. Lake Tahoe C.C., South Lake Tahoe, Calif., 1999; program coord. dept. medicine, divsn. infectiuos diseases Columbia U., N.Y.C., 2000—02; interim dir. religious edn. Fourth Universalist Soc., N.Y.C., 2002—04. Min. pvt. weddings and funerals, 2002—; curriculum writer Union Theol. Sem., 2003; guest preacher Unitarian Universalist Cmty. Ch., Glen Allen, Va., 2003; artist in residence Nev. Arts Coun., 2000—04; grant writer Soc. for Jewish Edn., Columbia U. Tchrs. Coll. Author: (children's book) Peace in the Dark; playwright Of Age (1st pl. Boston Playwrights Theater, 1998), A Kite's Tale. Mem. Columbia U. Senate, 2002—. Recipient Univ. Pres. and Coll. Pres. Diversity awards, Columbia U., 2003; scholar, Am. Conservatory Theater, 1993. Mem.: Unitarian Universalist Min. Assn., Religious Edn. Assn., Kappa Delta Pi. Unitarian Universalist. E-mail: nw163@columbia.edu.

WALKER, OLENE S. governor; b. Ogden, Utah, Nov. 15, 1930; d. Thomas Ole and Nina Hadley (Smith) W.; m. J. Myron Walker, 1957; children: Stephen Brett, David Walden, Bryan Jesse, Lori, Mylene, Nina, Thomas Myron. BA, Brigham Young U., 1954; MA, Stanford U., 1954; PhD, U. Utah, 1986; HHD (hon.), Weber State U., 1997. V.p. Country Crisp Foods, 1969-92; mem. Utah Ho. of Reps. Dist. 24; lt. gov. State of Utah, 1993—2003, gov., 2003—. Mem. Salt Lake Edn. Found. bd. dirs. 1983-90; dir. community econ. devel.; mem. Ballet West, Sch. Vol., United Way, Commn. on Youth, Girls Village, Salt Lake Conv. and Tourism Bd.; mem. adv. coun. Weber State U. Mem. Nat. Assn. Secs. of State (Western chmn., nat. lt. gov.'s conf., pres. 1997-98). Mem. Lds Ch. Office: Off of Gov E Off Bldg Ste E220 PO Box 14220 Salt Lake City UT 84114-2220

WALKER, PAUL HOWARD, retired lawyer; b. Baldwyn, Miss., Feb. 10, 1923; s. Howard Earl and Frances Caroline (McElroy) W.; m. Gwendolyn Yvonne Loomis, June 17, 1950; children: Michael D., Melinda K. Student, E. Miss. Jr. Coll., 1940-41, La. State U., 1941-43, U. Mo., 1943-44; JD with honors, George Washington U., 1948; BA, George Washington U, 2000; LL.M., George Washington U., 1949; postgrad., Harvard U., 1975-82. Bar: D.C. 1948, Md. 1959, Mass. 1969. Atty.-editor U.S. Tax Ct., Washington, 1950-53; asst. gen. counsel Life Ins. Assn. Am. (now Am. Coun. of Life Ins.), Washington, 1953-68; tax counsel New Eng. Mut. Life Ins. Co., Boston, 1968-86, ret., 1986—. Mem. tax policy adv. bd. Taxation with Representation Fund, Washington, 1975; adv. coun. Hartford Inst. on Ins. Taxation, Conn., 1981-83. Contbr. articles to profl. jours.; mem. adv. bd. Estate Planning Mag., 1973-86, Compensation Planning Jour., 1973-86. Trustee New Eng. Coll., Henniker, N.H., 1978-90, trustee emeritus, 1990—; chancellor New Eng. Diocese Anglican Ch. in Am., 1981-2002; sr. warden St. Columba Anglican Ch., Dudley, Mass., 2002—. Served with AUS, 1943-45; to capt. USAFR, 1951-63. Decorated Silver Star, Bronze Star, Combat Infantry Man's Badge, EAME Ribbon with 2 battle stars. Mem.: SAR (pres. Mass. Soc. 1981—83, nat. trustee 1983—85, chancellor gen. 1986—88, pres. gen. 1992—93), ABA, The Am. Legion, Sons of Confederate Vets., Soc. of the War of 1812 in Mass. (state pres. 1996—97), Hon. Order of Ky. Cols., Masons, Knights Templar (comdr. Boston Commandery No. 2 1997—98, named Knight Comdr. of Temple of Grand Encampment 1997, Knight York Cross of Honor 2001). Republican. Home and Office: 85A Seminary Ave Apt 347 Newton MA 02466-2648 E-mail: pwalker@lasell.edu.

WALKER, PEGGY JEAN, retired social work agency administrator; b. Carbondale, Ill., Aug. 9, 1940; d. George William and Lola Almeda (Black) Robinson; children: Edith Nell, Keith Alan. BA, So. Ill. U., 1962, PhD, 1986; MSW, Washington U., St. Louis, 1967. Lic. clin. social worker. Caseworker,

casework supr. Ill. Dept. Pub. Aid, 1964-71; child welfare adminstr. Ill. Dept. Children and Family Svc., 1971-75; mem. faculty social work program So. Ill. U., 1975-79; exec. dir. Western divsn. Children's Home Soc. Fla., Pensacola, 1979-2000; ret., 2000; program and acreditation cons., 2000—. Apptd. to Fla. State Coord. Coun. for Early Childhood Devel., 1994-99, corp. programs and accreditation coord., 1999-2000; adj. adv. bd. dept. social work U. West Fla., 1982—; appt. by Fla. Dept. Edn. to task force Edn. for Children of the Homeless, 1989-99, Dept. Children and Families, Dist. Task Force on Family Preservation and Support Svcs., 1985-99, chmn. 1988, 89; mem. steering com. Fla. Healthy Mothers/Healthy Babies, 1990-99; peer reviewer, team leader Coun. on Accreditatin of Svcs. for Families and Children, 1990—; program and accreditation cons. 2000. Co-chair chief judge Children's Coun., 1984-99; mem. Juvenile Justice Coun., 1994-99, chmn., 1996. Recipient Disting. Cmty. Svc. award United Way Escambia County, 1993, Peer of Yr. award Coun. on Accreditation, 2003. Home: 613 Silverthorn Rd Gulf Breeze FL 32561-4625 E-mail: pwalker080940@cs.com.

WALKER, PETER, landscape architect; BS in Landscape Arch., U. Calif., Berkeley, 1955; postgrad., U. Ill., 1956; M in Landscape Arch., Harvard U., 1957. Resident Am. Acad. in Rome, 1991; co-founer Sasaki, Walker Assocs., Inc., 1957—75; prin., consulting prin., chmn. The S.W.A. Group, 1975—83; founder, prin. Peter Walker & Ptnrs. Landscape Arch. Inc., Berkeley, Calif., 1983—. Instr. landscape arch. Harvard U. Grad. Sch. Design, 1958—59, adj. prof., 1976—91, acting dir. Urban Design Program, 1977—78, chmn. dept. landscape arch., 1978—81, Charles Eliot chair, 1992; vis. critic MIT, 1959; dir. The S.W.A. Group Summer Sch., 1973—83; chmn. dept. landscape arch. U. Calif., Berkeley, 1997—99; guest lectr. and spkr. in field. Co-author: Invisible Gardens: The Search for Modernism in the American Landscape; mem. editl. bd.: Landscape Arch., 1988—91. Named co-winner, World Trade Ctr. Site Meml. Competition, 2003; named to Inst. Honor, AIA, 1992. Fellow: Inst. for Urban Design, Am. Soc. Landscape Archs. Office: Peter Walker and Ptnrs 739 Allston Way Berkeley CA 94710*

WALKER, PHILIP CHAMBERLAIN, II, health care executive; b. Big Spring, Tex., July 7, 1944; s. Philip Chamberlain and Mary Catherine (St. John) W.; m. Linda Jane Holsclaw, Jan. 21, 1978; children: Shannon M., Meghan M. BA, Cen. Wash. State Coll., 1970; MS, U. Idaho, 1971. Exec. dir. Multnomah Found. for Med. Care, Portland, Oreg., 1972-81; chief exec. officer Peer Rev. Orgn. for Wash. State, Seattle, 1981-84; dir. Preferred Provider Orgn. devel. Provident Life and Accident, Chattanooga, 1984-88; v.p. Maxicare Health Plans, LA, 1988-91; v.p., gen. mgr. Maxicare Health Plans Midwest, Chgo., 1991-92; pres. Health Plus, Peoria, Ill., 1992—; CEO, chmn. bd. HCH Adminstrn., Peoria, Ill., 1992-98; sr. v.p. Health Care Horizons, Albuquerque, 1992-98; exec. v.p. Proctor Health Sys., 1998—. Bd. dir. RMR Group, HCH Adminstrn., Health Care Horizons; cons. to numerous orgns. Contbr. articles to profl. jour. Mem. bd. dirs. Boys and Girls Club Peoria, 2003—, v.p., 2004—; bd. dirs. Hult Health Edn. Ctr.; bd. dir. Cancer Ctr. for Health Living, 2001—03; bd. dirs. Ctrl. Ill. United Way; bd. mem. Central Ill. Regional Adv. Bd. Multiple Sclorsis Assn., 2002—; chmn. Hult Health Edn. Ctr., 1999—2003. With USAF, 1961—66, Vietnam. Mem.: Creve Coeur Club (bd. govs., pres.). Office: 5409 N Knoxville Ave Peoria IL 61614 Office Phone: 309-689-8600. Business E-Mail: phil.walker@proctor.org.

WALKER, PHYLLIS LEVONNE, elementary school educator; b. Waxahachie, Tex., Aug. 25, 1967; d. Vernon Randall Brown and Carolyn Sue Crabtree; m. James Kenneth Walker, Dec. 28, 1985; children: Sky, Kenyon, Felicity. B Christian Edn., Bethany Bible Coll., 2003. Tchr. New Life Christian Sch., Athens, Tex., 1986—87, Columbia Christian Sch., West Columbia, Tex., 1993—; Christian educator First Assembly of God, Athens, Tex., 1988—93. Dir. Christian edn. Ministerio Hispano-Centro Cristiano, West Columbia, 1993—97; coach Bible Quiz, West Columbia, 1998—. Author: (short stories) Dr. Luke's Real Characters, 2001, (play) Christmas Spirit, 2002. Campaign dir. Walker for City Coun., West Columbia, 2003. Recipient Educators High Merit Poet award, Creative Comm., 2002. Avocations: reading, poetry, music, theater, travel. Office: Columbia Christian Sch 725 W Brazos West Columbia TX 77486 E-mail: ccs@thechristiancenter.org.

WALKER, R. TRACY, retired personnel director; b. North Wilkesboro, N.C., July 27, 1937; m. Nena Watkins; children: Randy, Kirk. Student, Wilkes C.C., Wake Forest U. With CMI Industries Inc., Elkin, N.C., 1967-99, plant human resource mgr.; ret., 1999; mem. N.C. Ho. of Reps., 1999—. Commr. Wilkes County, 1978-96, past mem. region "D" coun. govts., regional econ. devel. coun., indsl. park com., chmn. regional transp. com., mem. regional adv. com. to WNCREDC, liaison Advantage West and region "D" coun. govts.; past chmn. region"D" coun. govts. Wilkes County, northwestern housing authority, past mem. bd. edn., 1972-76, airport authority; past vice-chmn., chmn. Wilkes County Commrs.; past bd. dirs. Blue Ridge Water Assn.; pres. Northwestern Devel. Assn.; trustee Health Ins. N.C. Assn. County Commrs.; mem. N.C. Regional Econ. Devel. Comm.; apptd. mem. N.C. Adv. Coun. Vocat. and Technical Edn., 1972-76, N.C. Dept. Correction, 1984-92; Rep. candidate for N.C. Commr. of Labor, 1996; candidate N.C. House, 1998, 2000. With USAF, 1955-59. Recipient Leadership award Western N.C., 1996. Office Phone: 919-733-5935.

WALKER, RADFORD, computer system architect; b. Pueblo, Colo., Apr. 12, 1957; s. Frank M. and Marian F. Walker; m. Sharon L. Stevens, Dec. 27, 1980; children: Rader Steele, Tova Sidnee Ann, Nyssa Radell Turney, Tacita Wynn Tansey. BS, Wichita State U., 1979; MS, U. Colo., 1992, MEWSE, 2001. Lab. asst. Dr. Paul Tasch, Wichita, Kans., 1978; asst. staff mgr. Southwestern Bell, St. Louis, 1979-82; sys. analyst Mountain Bell, Denver, 1983-87; mem. tech. staff U S WEST, Denver, 1988-92, sr. mem. tech. staff, 1994-97; mem. tech. staff U S WEST Advanced Tech., Boulder, Colo., 1993; sr. info. tech. architect Qwest, Thornton, Colo., 1998—. Editor newspaper Above The Line, 1989-96; exec. editor newspaper The Walker Squaker, 1994—; contbr. articles to profl. jours. Bd. dirs. Metro Wastewater Reclamation Dist., Denver, 1997—; commr. Thornton Devel. Authority, 1997—; mem. city coun. City of Thornton, 1997—; fair dir. Denver Metro Region Sci. Fair, Eastlake, Colo., 1997-2000; bd. dirs. Thornton Arts Scis. Hist. Cultural Orgn., 1997—; mem. North Front Range Trnasp. Alternatives Feasibility Study, Denver, 1999—; bd. dirs., judge Colo. Sci. and Engring. Fair, 1985—. NSF grantee, 1978; recipient Outstanding Young Man of Am. award V.I.P. Awards Ltd., 1985. Mem. IEEE Computer Soc., Am. Assn. Artificial Intelligence, Assn. Computing Machinery (chair Denver chpt. 1990-92), Platte Valley Model R.R. Club (pres. 1984—, past sec., Logo Design award 1989). Avocations: model railroading, lapidary, paleontology, nascar auto racing. Office: Qwest 1005 17th St Rm 1300 Denver CO 80202 E-mail: radford@qwest.net.

WALKER, RANDALL H. air transportation executive; b. Boulder City, Nev. m. Terry Walker; 6 children. BS in Acctg. magna cum laude, Brigham Young U. Budget analyst Clark County (Nev.) Mgr.'s Office; bus. mgr. Las Vegas Met. Police Dept.; dep. city mgr. City of Las Vegas; Las Vegas rep. to Nev. State Legislature; asst. county mgr. Clark County, dir. dept. fin.; dep. dir. Clark County Dept. Aviation, now dir. Office: c/o McCarran Internat Airport PO Box 11005 Las Vegas NV 89111-1005

WALKER, RANDOLPH MEADE, minister; b. Heathsville, Va., Mar. 24, 1950; s. Levi Robeson and Elsie Tolson Walker; m. Deloris Adair Walker; children: Jennifer Michelle, John Randolph. BA, Hampton U., 1972; MA, U. Memphis, 1976, PhD, 1990; LLD, LeMoyne-Owen Coll., 2002. Pastor Pilgrim Rest Bapt. Ch., Henning, Tenn., 1976—82; sales exec. AC-DELCO Divsn. GM Corp., Memphis, 1972—86; pastor New Phila. Bapt. Ch., Memphis, 1982—96; assoc. prof. LeMoyne-Owen Coll., Memphis, 1987—2002; pastor Castalia Bapt. Ch., Memphis, 1998—. Bd. mem. Shelby County Hist. Com., Memphis, 2002—. Mem. NAACP, Memphis, 1976—, Urban League, Inc., Memphis, 1982—, Kiwana's Inst., Memphis, 2002—. Recipient Svc. award, Memphis Theol. Sem., 2003. Mem.: So. Conf. of African Am. Studies, Memphis Bapt. Ministerial Assn., West Tenn. Hist. Soc. Democrat. Baptist. Avocations: baseball, football, basketball, reading, writing. Office: Castalia Bapt Ch 1540 Castalia St Memphis TN 38114 E-mail: rmwalker@midsouth.rr.com.

WALKER, RAYMOND JOHN, physicist; b. L.A., Oct. 26, 1942; s. Raymond Osmund and Marie Dorothy (Peterman) W. BS, San Diego State U., 1964; MS, UCLA, 1969, PhD, 1973. Rsch. assoc. U. Minn., Mpls., 1973-77; rsch. geophysicist Inst. Geophysics and Planetary Physics UCLA, 1977—, prof. in residence Inst. Geophysics and Planetary Physics and Dept. Earth and Space Sci., 1999—. Mgr. planetary plasma interactions node, 1990-, and project scientist, 1992-96, NASA Planetary Data System; mem. numerous coms. on space physics and the mgmt. of space physics data NRC and NASA. Contbr. articles to profl. jours. Mem. AAAS, Am. Geophys. Union (chair info. tech. com. 1990-92, Edward A. Flinn III award 1996), Am. Astron. Soc. (div. Planetary Sci.). Achievements include research in magnetospheric physics, in planetary magnetospheres, in global magnetohydrodynamic simulation of solar wind-magnetosphere interaction, in data management, in magnetic field modeling. Home: 11053 Tennessee Ave Los Angeles CA 90064-1936 Office: UCLA IGPP 405 Hilgard Ave Los Angeles CA 90095-1567 Office Phone: 310-825-7685. E-mail: rwalker@igpp.ucla.edu.

WALKER, RICHARD BRIAN, chemistry professor; b. Quincy, Mass., May 14, 1948; s. George Edgar and Eva Mary (Taylor) W. BS in Biochemistry, U. So. Calif., 1970; PhD in Pharm. Chemistry, U. Calif., San Francisco, 1975. Rsch. assoc. Oreg. State U., Corvallis, 1975-76, U. Wash., Seattle, 1976-78; lectr. U.S. Internat. U., San Diego, 1978-81, Hamdard Sch. Pharmacy, New Delhi, India, 1981-82; rsch. scientist Biophysica Found., San Diego, 1982-83; assoc. prof. chemistry U. Ozarks, Clarksville, Ark., 1983-84; asst. to assoc. prof. chemistry U. Ark., Pine Bluff, 1984-96, prof. chemistry, 1996—. Prin. investigator minority biomed. rsch. support program NIH, Bethesda, Md., 1986—; project dir. Ark. Systemic Sci. Initiative; rev. in field. Contbr. articles to profl. jours. Coord. home Bible fellowship The Way Internat., Pine Bluff, 1984-99; judge Ctrl. Ark. Sci. Fair, Little Rock, 1986—. NIH rsch. grantee, 1986, 89, 93. Mem. Am. Chem. Soc., Ark. Acad. Scis., Am. Assn. Pharm. Scientists, Sigma Xi. Avocations: fishing, golf, skiing. Office: 1200 University Dr Pine Bluff AR 71601-2799 E-mail: walker_r@vx4500.uapb.edu.

WALKER, RICHARD DAVID, civil engineer, educator; b. Washington, Feb. 19, 1931; s. Stanton and Amelia (Ramseyer) W.; m. Alice Patricia Davis, June 6, 1953; children: Patricia Vawn, Jean Brianne, Sharyl Elise. B.C.E., U. Md., 1953; M.C.E., Purdue U., 1955, PhD, 1961. Instr., Purdue U., 1957-61; asst. prof. Va. Poly. Inst., 1961-62, assoc. prof., 1962-68, prof., 1968-96, head dept. civil engring., 1970-83; prof. emeritus, 1996. Author: (with R.D. Krebs) Highway Materials, 1971. Mem. Montgomery County Rep. Com. Lt. USAF, 1955—57. Fellow ASCE; mem. ASTM (sec. com. C-9 on concrete and concrete aggregates 1970-76), Transp. Research Bd., Am. Soc. for Engring. Edn., Sigma Xi, Chi Epsilon. Presbyterian (elder 1973—). Home: 701 Broce Dr Blacksburg VA 24060-2803 *Have respect for others, their opinions and beliefs. At the same time, stand firm for what you believe. Remember, even a firmly rooted tree stands because it is flexible and can bend with the wind. Concerning goals, avoid rigidity; include service to others, then set goals sufficiently general to embrace the total purpose God has for you in this life.*

WALKER, RICHARD HAROLD, pathologist, educator; b. Cleve., Dec. 2, 1928; s. Harold Deford and Bernice Margaret (Wright) W.; m. Carolyn Franklin, Sept. 28, 1954; children: Bruce, Lynn, Cara, Leah. BS, Emory U., 1950, MD, 1953. Intern City of Memphis Hosps., 1953-54; resident in pathology Coll. Medicine U. Tenn., Memphis, 1954-55, 57-59, prof. pathology, 1966-70; Am. Cancer Soc. clin. fellow U. Tenn. Coll. Medicine, 1957-59; med. dir. blood bank and transfusion svc. City of Memphis Hosps., Memphis, 1961-70; chief of blood bank and transfusion service William Beaumont Hosp., Royal Oak, Mich., 1970-95, med. dir. Sch. Med. Tech., 1970-91. Clin. prof. pathology Sch. Medicine Wayne State U., Detroit, 1982-95. Contbr. articles on blood transfusion, blood group genetics and transfusion medicine to med. jours. Capt. USNR ret. Recipient Murray Thelin Humanitarian award Memphis chpt. Nat. Hemophilia Found., 1968 Mem. AMA, Coll. Am. Pathologists, Am. Soc. Clin. Pathologists (Disting. Svc. award 1977, Ward Burdick award 1992), Am. Assn. Blood Banks (pres. 1976-77, John Elliott Meml. award 1986), Tenn. Assn. Blood Banks (L.W. Diggs award 1986), Internat. Soc. Blood Transfusion, Am. Soc. for Histocompatibility and Immunogenetics. Republican. Presbyterian. Home: 4204 Fleet Landing Blvd Atlantic Beach FL 32233-4590

WALKER, RICHARD HENRY, lawyer; b. Wilmington, Del., Dec. 29, 1950; s. Henry H. and Mary L. (Meister) W. BA, Trinity Coll., 1972; JD, Temple U., 1975. Bar: Pa. 1976, U.S. Supreme Ct. 1977, N.Y. 1978, D.C. 1981. Law clk. to Hon. Collins J. Seitz U.S. Ct. Appeals (3rd cir.), Wilmington, Del., 1975-76; assoc., ptnr. Cadwalader, Wickersham & Taft, N.Y.C., 1976-91; regional dir. N.E. office U.S. SEC, N.Y.C., 1991-95, gen. counsel Washington, 1996-98, dir. enforcement, 1998—2001; gen. counsel Corp. Investment Bank, Deutsche Bank, 2001—. Fellow Am. Bar Found.

WALKER, RICHARD HUGH, orthopaedic surgeon; b. Elgin, Ill., Jan. 29, 1951; m. Wendy Allen; children: Ashley Elizabeth, Blake Allen, Emily Paige. AB cum laude, Occidental Coll., 1973; MD, U. Chgo., 1977. Diplomate Nat. Bd. Med. Examiners, Am. Bd. Orthopaedic Surgery. Jr. resident in surgery UCLA, 1977-79; jr. resident in orthopaedic surgery Stanford (Calif.) U., 1979-81, sr. resident, 1981-82, chief resident, 1982-83; clin. mem. divsn. orthop. surgery, sect. lower extremity reconstructive surgery Scripps Clinic, La Jolla, Calif., 1983—, co-dir. lower extremity reconstructive surgery fellowship, divsn. orthopaedic surgery, 1989—, assoc. head. divsn. orthopaedic surgery, 1990-97, chmn. dept. surgery, 1998—, v.p. surg. svcs., 2001—. Staff physician dept. surgery Green Hosp. of Scripps Clinic, La Jolla, 1983—, mem. exec. com., 1994—2001, chief of staff, 1995—97; Team physician San Diego Padres, 1983—86, team physician, 1995—99; Clin. instr. dept. orthopaedics and rehab. U. Calif., San Diego, 1983—92, asst. clin. prof., 1992—; Mem. bd. dir. Scripps Clinic Med. Group, La Jolla, 1992—, mem. exec. com., 1998—, med. dir. surg. specialties, 1998—2001, mem. joint exec. bd., 1992— 93. Cons. reviewer Clin. Orthopaedics and Related Rsch., 1989—, Jour. Bone and Joint Surgery, 1994—; contbr. articles to profl. jours. Mem. AMA, ACS, Am. Acad. Orthopaedic Surgeons, We. Orthopaedic Assn. (program chmn. San Diego chpt. 1994-95, treas. 1995-96, v.p. 1996-97, pres. 1997-98, Resident Paper award 1983), Calif. Orthopaedic Assn., Assn. Arthritic Hip and Knee Surgery (charter mem. 1991), Am. Assn. Hip and Knee Surgeons, Assn. Bone and Joint Surgeons (Nicholas Andry Rsch. award 1997). Office: Scripps Clinic Divsn Orthop Surgery 10666 N Torrey Pines Rd La Jolla CA 92037-1092 Office Phone: 858-554-9882. Business E-Mail: rwalker@scrippsclinic.com.

WALKER, RICHARD K. lawyer; b. Knoxville, Tenn., Oct. 21, 1948; BA with honors, U. Kans., 1970, JD, 1975; student, U. Bonn, Germany; grad. student, U Tübingen, Germany. Bar: Ariz. 1975, D.C. 1977, U.S. Supreme Ct. 1977. Asst. prof. law U. S.C., 1977-81, assoc. prof. law, 1981-82; ptnr. Bishop, Cook, Purcell & Reynolds, Washington, 1981-90, Winston & Strawn, Washington, 1990-93; dir. Streich Lang, Phoenix, 1993-2000; ptnr. Quarles & Brady Streich Lang, Phoenix, 2000—. Bd. trustees Ariz. Theatre Co., 1995-2001; bd. dirs. Phoenix Cmty. Alliance, 2001—. Fulbright Direct Exchange scholar. Mem. ABA, Labor and Employment Law Sec. (mem. equal employment opportunity law com. and devel. of the law under the NLRA com., 1979—), Litigation Sec. (mem. class actions and derivitive suits com. and trial pratice com., 1998—, mem. employment rels. and labor law com., 1979—), Ariz. Assn. Def. Counsel (bd. dirs. 1997-2000). Office: Quarles & Brady Streich Lang LLP Renaissance One 2 N Central Ave Phoenix AZ 85004-2345 E-mail: rwalker@quarles.com.

WALKER, ROBERT DIXON, III, retired surgeon, urologist, educator; b. Rochester, N.Y., July 22, 1936; s. Robert Dixon, Jr. and Virginia (Weir) W.; m. Joyce Ann Copeland, June 23, 1961; children— Sherri Lynn, Lisa Marie, Jeffrey Alan. BA, BS, Carson-Newman Coll., 1959; MD, U. Miami, Fla., 1963. Intern Wake Forest U., 1964; resident in surgery U. Fla., 1968, asst. prof., 1970-74, assoc. prof., 1974-76, prof. surgery, 1976—, dir. admissions Coll. Medicine, 1976-79; instr. U. Tenn., 1969-70, chief divsn. urology, 1998-2000; chief of staff Shands Teaching Hosp., 1976; ret. Assoc. editor: Jour. Urology. Served to comdr. USNR, 1968-70. Fellow ACS (gov.); mem. Assn. Univ. Urologists, Am. Urol. Assn. (editorial bd. Update Series), Am. Assn. Genitourinary Surgeons, Soc. Pediatric Rsch., Soc. Pediatric Urology (exec. com., sec., pres.), Am. Acad. Pediatrics (sec., chmn. urology sect.), Fla. Urologic Soc. (sec., pres.). Home: 5184 Atlantic Vw Saint Augustine FL 32080-7142

WALKER, ROBERT HARRIS, historian, writer, editor; b. Cin., Mar. 15, 1924; m. Grace Burtt; children: Amy, Rachel, Matthew. BS, Northwestern U., 1945; MA, Columbia U., 1950; PhD, U. Pa., 1955. Edn. specialist U.S. Mil. Govt., Japan, 1946-47; instr. Carnegie Inst. Tech., 1950-51, U. Pa., 1953-54; asst. prof., dir. Am. studies U. Wyo., 1955-59; asso. prof. George Washington U., 1959-63, prof. Am. civilization, 1963-94, dir. Am. studies program, 1959-66, 68-70. First dir. edn. and pub. programs NEH, 1966-68; fellow Woodrow Wilson Internat. Ctr., 1972-73, Rockefeller Rsch. Ctr., 1979, Hoover Instn., Huntington Libr., 1980; specialist grants to Japan, Germany, Thailand, Iran, Greece, Israel, Brazil, China, People's Republic of Korea, Hong Kong, 1964-91; Fulbright lectr., Australia, New Zealand, Philippines, 1971, Sweden, France, West Germany, Norway, all 1987; Am. Coun. Learned Socs. alt. del. UNESCO Gen. Info. Program, 1978—; co-founder Algonquin Books, 1982. Author: Poet and Gilded Age, 1963, Life in the Age of Enterprise, 1967, American Society, 1981, 2d edit., 1995, Reform in America (nominated for Pulitzer prize in history), 1985, (with R.H. Gabriel) Course of American Democratic Thought, 3d edit., 1986, Cincinnati and the Big Red Machine, 1988, Everyday Life in Victorian America, 1994; editor, compiler: American Studies in the U.S., 1958, American Studies Abroad, 1975, Reform Spirit in America, 1976, 85, American Studies: Topics and Sources, 1976, Frieds of Raoul Wallenberg, 1987-1997, 1998; editor: Am. Quar., 1953-54; sr. editor: Am. Studies Internat., 1970-80, Am. studies series for Greenwood Press, 1972—, over 100 vols. Founding mem. Japan-U.S. Friendship Commn., 1977-80; founding pres. Friends of Raoul Wallenberg Found., 1987-99. With USNR, 1943-46, 50. Mem. Am. Studies Assn. (nat. pres. 1970-71), Cosmos Club, Phi Beta Kappa. Office: 200 Riverside Blvd #4J New York NY 10069-0907

WALKER, ROBERT MARTIN, writer, minister; b. Fairbanks, Alaska, Aug. 18, 1954; s. Robert Lee and Helen Eileen (Palmer) W.; m. Donna Lee Henry, May 20, 1977; children: Robert Brandon, Matthew Lee. BA, So. Meth. U., 1975, MTh, 1978; MBA, 1979; STM, Yale Y., 1985. Ordained to ministry United Meth. Ch., 1977. Assoc. pastor Oak Lawn United Meth. Ch., Dallas, 1978-79; editor United Meth. Reporter North Tex. Ann. Conf., Dallas, 1979-81; sr. pastor Richland United Meth. Ch., Richardson, Tex., 1982-84, Darien (Conn.) United Meth. Ch., 1985-93, 1st Ch. of Round Hill, Greenwich, Conn., 1999—. Chair pastoral adv. com. Stamford (Conn.) Hosp., 1989-91. Author: The Jesus I Knew, 1996, Politically Correct Parables, 1996, Politically Correct Old Testament Stories, 1997, You Might Be a United Methodist If, 1998, Encounters with the Living God, 2000; co-author: 365 Meditations for Families, 2001. Pres. Darien Clergy Assn., 1991-93; v.p. Interfaith Hospitality Network, Darien, 1992-94; mem. adv. bd. Kids in Crisis, Greenwich, Conn., 1995-97. Avocations: rowing, tennis, squash. Home: 9 McCrea Ln Darien CT 06820-5902 Office: 464 Round Hill Rd Greenwich CT 06831

WALKER, ROBERT ROSS, social worker; b. Haverhill, Mass., May 26, 1954; s. Bertram Ross and Ann Elizabeth (Glass) W.; m. Jean Marie Webster, June 16, 1979; children: Jennifer Elizabeth, Heather Jean. BS in Human Devel., U. Mass., Amherst, 1976; MEd, Tufts U., 1980. Diplomate Nat. Assn. Forensic Counselors; lic. social worker, Mass.; cert. domestic violence counselor. Field instr. Salem State Coll., Fitchburg State Coll., Haverhill, 1976; continuing edn. instr. No. Essex C.C., Haverhill, Mass., 1976; res. police officer City of Haverhill, 1978—; counselor Hampstead (N.H.) Hosp., Haverhill, 1979-81; social worker Mass. Dept. Social Svcs., Haverhill, 1980-91, supr. Lawrence, 1991—. Spl. edn. cons. to area office, rep. Haverhill/Newburyport area interdeptl. human svc. team; spkr. burs., acct. exec. Merrimack Valley United Fund, Dept. Social Svcs., Merrimack Valley Sexual Assault Com. Bd. dirs. ARC, Haverhill, 1976-91, water safety, first aid and CPR instr., sec., 1984-89, co-chmn. Youth Red. Cross and Disaster Com., chmn. Haverhill chpt., 1989-91, Merrimac Valley chpt., 1991—, vice-chmn., 1991-93, sec. 1993-96; fire responder; steering com. Haverhill/Newburyport Human Svcs. Coalition; bd. dirs. Haverhill Youth Commn., 1971-72; vestry mem. Trinity Episcopal Ch. Recipient Boy Scouts Am. award, ARC award, Clara Barton award ARC, Vol. award Merrimack Valley United Fund, Commonwealth Mass. Pride in Performance Recognition award, Pub. Safety award Elks, Jewish Am. War Vets. award. Mem. Am. Personnel and Guidance Assn., Svc. Employees Internat. Union, Am. Fedn. Musicians, Nat. Honor Soc., Nat. Eagle Scout Assn., Alpha Phi Omega, Kappa Kappa Psi. Home: 1 Twelve Rod Way Haverhill MA 01830-1840 Office: Dept Social Svcs 1 Twelve Rod Way Haverhill MA 01830 Office Phone: 978-557-2567.

WALKER, ROBERT S. government agency administrator; BS in Edn., Millersville U., Pa.; MA in Polit. Sci., U. Del.; LLD (hon.), Franklin and Marshall Coll. Tchr. H.S.; Rep. congressman 16th dist. Pa. Ho. of Reps., Washington; chmn., CEO Wexler & Walker Pub. Policy Assocs. Chief dep. whip, chmn. leadership, spkr. pro tempore, chmn. sci. com., vice chmn. budget com. Ho. of Reps. Recipient Disting. Svc. medal, NASA, 1996. Republican. Office: Aerospace Commn Ste 940 Crystal Gateway One 1235 Jefferson Davis Hwy Arlington VA 22202-3283

WALKER, ROBERT SMITH, former congressman; b. Bradford, Pa., Dec. 23, 1942; s. Joseph Erdman and Rachael Viola (Smith) W.; m. Sue Ellen Albertson, Apr. 13, 1968. BS, Millersville (Pa.) U., 1964; MA in Polit. Sci, U. Del., 1968; LLD (hon.), Franklin & Marshall Coll., 1998. Tchr. Penn Manor High Sch., Lancaster, Pa., 1964-67; legis. asst. to Congressman Edwin D. Eshleman, 1967-74, adminstrv. asst., 1974-76; mem. 95th-104th Congresses from 16th Pa. dist., Washington, D.C., 1977-96, chmn. House Com. Sci.; vice chmn. house budget com., chmn. house Rep. leadership, 1995-97; chief dep. minority whip, 1989-95; spkr. pro tempore, 1996; chmn. Wexler & Walker Pub. Policy Assocs., Washington, 1997—. Adv. bd. Innerlink, 2001; chmn. Commn. on the Future of the U.S. Aerospace Industry, 2001—02; mem. Nat. Academies Aeronautics and Space Engring. Bd., 2004, Pres.'s Commn. on the U.S. Postal Svc., 2003, Pres.'s Commn. on Space Exploration, 2004. Co-author: Congress-The Pennsylvania Dutch Representatives, 1774-1974, Can You Afford This House, 1978, House of Ill Repute, 1987, Space: The Free Market Frontier, 2003, Crossroads: The Future of American Politics, 2003; columnist: UPI, 2001, Space: The Free Market Frontier, 2003; contbr. articles to profl. jours. Trustee Aerospace Corp., 1997—, Vice Chmn., 2004-, Space Found., 1997—, Susquehana Valley Ctr. Pub. Policy, 1998—. With Pa. NG, 1967-73, bd. dirs., Space Devel., 2001-. Recipient NASA Disting. Svc. medal, 1996; fellow Millersville U., 1996-2001, Franklin & Marshall Coll., 1997-2001. Mem. Am. League of Lobbyists (bd. dirs. 2000—). Republican. Presbyterian. Office: Wexler & Walker Pub Policy Assocs 1317 F St NW Ste 600 Washington DC 20004-1157 Office Phone: 202-638-2121. E-mail: walker@wexlerwalker.com. *The revolution sweeping politics, economics, culture and technology will produce new opportunities but at the same time will demand a new way of thinking about our economy and our society. The wealth of information available to each individual means that government and business must think in terms of individualized approaches.*

WALKER, ROGER GEOFFREY, geology educator, consultant; b. London, Mar. 26, 1939; s. Reginald Noel and Edith Annie (Wells) W.; m. Gay Parsons, Sept. 18, 1965; children: David John, Susan Elizabeth. BA, Oxford (Eng.) U., 1961, DPhil in Geology, 1964. NATO postdoctoral fellow in geology Johns Hopkins U., Balt., 1964-66; from asst. to assoc. prof. McMaster U., Hamilton, Canada, 1966-73, prof. geology, 1973-98, prof. emeritus, 1998—. Tchr. 80 profl. short courses on various aspects of oil exploration in clastic reservoirs, Can., U.S., Brazil, Australia, Japan, Italy, Venezuela, Norway; mem. grant selection com. earth scis. sect. Nat. Scis. and Engring. Rsch. Coun. Can., 1981-84; Judd A. & Cynthia S. Oualline Centennial lectr. U. Tex., Austin, 1986; vis. scientist Denver Rsch. Ctr., Marathon Oil Co., Littleton, Colo., 1973-74, Amoco Can. Petrol Co., Calgary, Alta., 1982; vis. fellow Australian Nat. U., Canberra, 1981; vis. prof. Fed. U. Ouro Preto, Brazil, 1987, 89, 90, 91, Fed. U. Rio Grande do Sul, Brazil, 1992; adj. prof. U. Regina, 1997—; pres. Roger Walker Cons., Inc., 1997—. Editor: Facies Models, 1979, 3d edit., 1992; contbr. over 140 articles to profl. jours. Recipient oper. and strategic

grants Nat. Scis. and Engring. Rsch. Coun. Can., 1966—. Fellow: Royal Soc. Can.; mem.: Internat. Assn. Sedimentologists (spl. lectr., Korea, Japan 2003, Henry Clifton Sorby medal 2002), Can. Assn. Univ. Tchrs., Soc. Sedimentary Geology (Francis J. Pettijohn medal 1997), Soc. Econ. Paleontologists and Mineralogists (hon.; assoc. editor 1970—78, pres. eastern sect. 1975—76, coun. for mineralogy 1979—80), Am. Assn. Petroleum Geologists (Disting. lectr. 1979—80, Disting. Educator award 1999), Can. Soc. Petroleum Geologists (Link award 1983, R.J.W. Douglas Meml. medal 1990), Geol. Assn. Can. (assoc. editor 1977—80, Past Pres.'s medal 1975, Disting. Svc. award 1994, Logan medal 1999). Achievements include research in sedimentary facies analysis, sedimentology of turbidites, quantitative basin analysis, sedimentology of Western Canadian Cretaceous clastic wedge. Home and Office: Roger Walker Cons 83 Scimitar View NW Calgary AB Canada T3L 2B4 E-mail: walkerrg@telus.net.

WALKER, RONALD EDWARD, psychologist, educator; b. East St. Louis, Ill., Jan. 23, 1935; s. George Edward and Marnella (Altmeyer) W.; m. Aldona M. Mogenis, Oct. 4, 1958; children: Regina, Mark, Paula, Alexis. BS, St. Louis U., 1957; MA, Northwestern U., 1959, PhD, 1961. Lectr. psychology Northwestern U., 1959-61; faculty dept. psychology Loyola U., Chgo., 1961—, asst., then assoc. prof., 1961-68, prof., chmn. dept., 1965—73, prof. emeritus, 1999—, acting dean Coll. Arts and Scis., 1973-74; dean Loyola U. (Coll. Arts and Scis.), 1974-80, academic v.p., 1980-81, sr. v.p., dean faculties, 1981-89, exec. v.p., 1989-99. Cons. VA, Chgo., 1965-74; Am. Psychol. Assn.-NIMH; vis. cons., 1969; vis. scientist Am. Psychol. Assn. NSF, 1968; Cook County (Ill.) rep. from Ill. Psychol. Assn., 1969-72; cons.-evaluator North Cen. Assn., 1986-99. Contbr. articles to profl. jours. Bd. trustees St. Francis Hosp., Evanston, Ill., 1986—92, Chgo. Archdiocesan Sems., 1985—97, Loyola Acad., Wilmette, Ill., 1987—93, St. Louis U., 1988—97; bd. dirs. Holy Family Villa Nursing Home, Lemont, Ill., 2002—. Recipient Disting. Psychologist of Yr. award Ill. Psychol. Assn., 1986. Home: Unit 5I 1630 Sheridan Rd Wilmette IL 60091-1835

WALKER, RONALD HUGH, retired management consultant; b. Bryan, Tex., July 25, 1937; s. Walter Hugh and Maxine (Tarver) W.; m. Anne Lucille Collins, Aug. 8, 1959; children: Lisa, Marjorie, Lynne. BA, U. Ariz., 1960. With Allstate Ins. Co., Pasadena, Calif., 1964-67, Hudson Co., 1967-69; asst. to sec. interior, 1969-70; founder, 1st dir., staff asst. to Pres. U.S. White House Advance Office, 1970-72; spl. asst. to Pres., 1972-73; dir. Nat. Park Service, Washington, 1973-75; cons. Saudi Arabia, 1975; assoc. dir. World Championship Tennis, 1975-77; pres. Ron Walker & Assocs., Inc., Dallas, 1977-79; sr. ptnr., mng. dir. Korn/Ferry Internat., Washington, 1979-2000; ret., 2000. Bd. dirs., chmn. Guest Svcs. Inc., Mullin Cons., Inc., Vinson & Co.; chmn. NOVAVAX. Bd. dirs. U.S.S. Arizona Found. and Memorial; founder, chmn. emeritus Order of Raft, 1972; spl. presdl. del. to Prime Min. Indira Gandhi's funeral New Delhi, 1984; spl. presdl. del. to Games of XXIV Olympiad Seoul, 1988; trustee Nat. Outdoor Leadership Sch., Nat. Fitness Found., Pres.'s Coun. on Phys. Fitness and Sports, 1981—85; bd. dirs., exec. com. NCAA Found.; bd. dirs. Meridian Internat.; mem. Ctr. for Study of Presidency, 1988—95; chmn. Freedom Found. at Valley Forge, 1989—2000; trustee Ford's Theater, Washington; men's chair Project Hope Ann. Ball, 1989, 1990, 1991; chmn. ann. dinner Boys and Girls Clubs Am., 1993; chmn. 50th Presdl. Inauguration, Dedication Richard Nixon Libr., Birthplace, 1990, bd. dirs., 1990; nat. chair Celebrities and Sports for Bush-Quayle; mem. over-site com. U.S. Rowing, 1993; mem. com. Preservation of White House, 1973—75; mem. Nat. Pk. Adv. Bd., 1973—75, Nat. Pk. Found., 1973—75, John F. Kennedy Ctr. for Performing Arts, 1973—75, Friends of Nancy Hanks Ctr.; bd. trustees Mridian House Internat., 1992—; mem. USA Gymnasium Found., 1993—99; trustee U. Ariz. Found.; chair Nat. Pk. Found. Alumni Assn.; bd. dirs Saquaro Nat. Park; vol. Nixon/Agnew Campaign, 1968, transition and inauguration team, 1969; vice chmn., mem. Pres.'s Commn. on Bicentennial U.S. Constn., 1985—88; mem. Coun. for Excellence in Govt., 1988—; mgr., CEO Rep. Nat. Conv., 1984, sr. advisor, 1988, 1992, 1996, 2000, 2004, Bush/Quayle Presdl. Campaign, 1988, Bush/Cheney Presdl. Campaign, 2000, 2004, 2004, Bush/Cheney Inauguration; hon. chmn. Cheney Inaugural Activities; mem. leadership adv. bd. NCAA; bd. dirs. Grand Teton Nat. Pk. Found., Saquaro Nat. Pk. Found. Capt. U.S. Army, 1961—64. Recipient Disting. Citizen award U. Ariz., 1973, Outstanding Svc. award Dept. Interior, 1975, Centennial Medallion award U. Ariz., 1989, Ellis Island Congl. medal of honor, 1992, Lincoln medal Ford's Theater, 2002. Mem. NCAA (bd. dirs. 1992-2003, exec. com. 1992-2003), Econs. Club of Washington, Met. Club of Washington, Congl. Country Club, Georgetown Club, City Club of Washington, Univ. Club. of N.Y., Burning Tree Club, Phi Delta Theta (named to Hall of Fame, 1991). Republican. Methodist. Home (Winter): 13535 Placita Montanas de Oro Tucson AZ 85737 E-mail: roadrunnerrhw@aol.com.

WALKER, RONALD R. writer, editor, educator; b. Newport News, Va., Sept. 2, 1934; s. William R. and Jean Marie (King) W.; m. O. Diane Mawson, Apr. 16, 1961; children: Mark Jonathan, Steven Christopher. BS, Pa. State U., 1956; postgrad., Harvard U., 1970-71. Reporter, news editor, sr. editor, editorial page editor, mng. editor San Juan Star (P.R.), 1962-73, Washington columnist, 1982-84, city editor, 1984-87; instr. journalism Pa. State U., State College, 1973-74; asst. prof. Columbia U. Grad. Sch. Journalism, N.Y.C., 1974-76; editor The Daily News, V.I., 1976-77; press sec. Gov. V.I., 1978-79; spl. asst., chief of staff Rep. James H. Scheuer, U.S. Congress, 1980-82, Resident Commr. Jaime B. Fuster, U.S. Congress, 1987-92; spl. asst., press sec. Resident Commr. Antonio J. Colorado, 1992-93; ind. profl. writer, weekly columnist editl. page San Juan Star, 1993—; regular columnist St. John Times, 1997—. Contbr. articles to nat. mags. and jours. including The Nation, The N.Y. Times, The Washington Post, and others. Served with U.S. Army, 1957-59. Nieman fellow in journalism Harvard U., 1970-71. Mem. Soc. Nieman Fellows, Leica Hist. Soc. Am. Address: PO Box 1358 St John VI 00831-1358 E-mail: ronwalker@viaccess.net.

WALKER, ROSLYN ADELE, retired museum director; b. Memphis, Tenn., July 26, 1944; Student Gen. Studies, U. Poitiers, France, 1965; BS in Art Edn. with high honors, Hampton U., 1966; MA in History of Art, Indiana U., 1969, PhD in History of Art, 1991. Registrar Mus. African Art, Washington, 1968-69; coord. Univ. Art Gallery U. Mass., Amherst, 1969-70; temporary registrar Fed. Dept Antiquities Nat. Mus., Lagos, Nigeria, 1970; curator of collections Inst. African Studies U. Idaban, Nigeria, 1973-75; curator ethnographic art collection Univ. Mus. Ill. State U., Normal, 1975-81, interim adminstr., 1975, adminstr., 1975-77, dir., 1977-81; curator Nat. Mus. African Art Smithsonian Instn., Washington, 1981-93, sr. curator, 1993-97, dir., 1997—2002; sr. curator The Arts of Africa, the Pacific and the Americas Dallas Mus. Art, Margaret McDermott curator African art. Rsch. asst. Mus. Modern Art, N.Y.C., 1971-72, guest curator African Women/African Art, The African-Am. Inst., N.Y.C., 1976, Lakeview Mus. Arts and Scis., Peoria, Ill., 1981; instr. in primitive art U. Mass., Amherst, 1969-70, in African decorative art USDA Grad. Sch., Washington, 1984. in Art in Africa, Dept. Art History, U. Md., College Park, 1990; vis. lectr. Afro-Am. Art, Ind. U., Bloomington, 1970-71, lectr. 1971-72, summer program, U. Idaban, Nigeria, 1974; asst. prof. Art Dept., Ill. State U., Normal, 1975-81. Author: (with Roy Sieber) African Art in the Cycle of Life, 1987, Olowe of Ise: A Yoruba Sculptor to Kings, 1998; contbr. catalogs for exhibitions of African Art to Royal Acad. of Arts, London, 1995, Guggenheim Mus. N.Y. and Afro-Am. Hist. and Cultural Mus., Phila., 1996; contbr., reviews, essays and articles to profl. jours. and mags. Mem. visual arts and crafts adv. panel Washington Commn. on the Arts. Recipient Ford Found. Fgn. Study grant, 1965, Faculty Rsch. grant, U. Mass., 1970, Fgn. Lang. fellowship Ind. U., Bloomington, 1971, Grant in Aid, Ind. U., 1972, Rsch. Fund grant (collections-based), Smithsonian Instn., Washington, 1994; named Twenty Yr. Student, Hampton U., 1986. Mem. Arts Coun. African Studies Assn. (past bd. dirs.), ArTable, Assn. Art Mus. Dirs.

WALKER, SALLY BARBARA, retired glass company executive; b. Bellerose, N.Y., Nov. 21, 1921; d. Lambert Roger and Edith Demerest (Parkhouse) W. Diploma, Cathedral Sch. St. Mary, 1939; AA, Finch Jr. Coll., 1941. Tchr. interior design Finch Coll., 1941-42; draftsman AT&T, 1942-43; with Steuben Glass Co., N.Y.C., 1943—, exec. v.p., 1959-62, exec. v.p. ops., 1962-78, exec. v.p. ops. and sales, 1978-83, exec. v.p., 1983-88, ret., 1988. Pres. 116 E. 66th St. Corp. Mem. Fifth Ave. Assn., Rockaway Hunting Club, Lawrence Beach Club, Colony Club, English-Speaking Union, Garden Club of Lawrence, City Garden Club of N.Y.C. Republican. Episcopalian. Home: 116 E 66th St New York NY 10021-6547

WALKER, SAVANNAH T. retired executive assistant, legislative assistant; b. Lubbock, Tex., Nov. 23, 1930; d. John Hansford and Lenore Belle (Muecke) Tunnell; m. Julius Waring Walker, Jr., July 29, 1956; children: Savannah Waring, Lucile Lenore, George Julius Stewart. BA, Tex. Tech. U., 1951; student, Radcliffe Coll., 1951. Cert. secondary sch. tchr., Tex. Tchr., English and journalism Phillips (Tex.) Ind. Sch. Dist., 1951-52; asst. to congressman Mahon U.S. Congress, Washington, 1952-54, admisntrv., exec. asst., 1954-58, 63-66; legis. asst. to chmn. House Appropriations U.S. Ho. of Reps., Washington, 1973-78; exec. asst. to v.p. Nat. Assn. Mfrs., Washington, 1985-89; exec. asst. to pres. Ogilvy Pub. Rels. Worldwide, Washington, 1990-99; sr. mgr. Pres. of the Americas, Ogilvy Pub. Rels. Worldwide, 2000—01. Vol., fundraiser for charitable orgns., Chad and Eng., 1966-73; pres. Am. Women in London, 1971-72, Am. Women in Liberia, Monrovia, 1979-80. Mem. AAUW, PEO, Am. Women in the Arts Mus., DAR, Internat. Women's Club (founder pres.) (Ouagadougou, Burkina Faso), Delta Delta Delta. Avocations: church work, bridge, reading, needlecrafts, writing. Home: 3801 Jenifer St NW Washington DC 20015-1917 Personal E-mail: julwalk@aol.com.

WALKER, SCOT WILLIAM P. writer, real estate investor; b. Washington, July 10, 1944; s. William Francis and Patricia Vittum Walker; life ptnr. Tri P. Pham, Aug. 14, 1989. BA, Kings Coll., Briarcliff Manor, N.Y., 1966; MEd, U. Md., 1971. Tchr. Calvert County Bd. Edn., Prince Fredrick, Md., 1971—74; salesman Parklawn Cemetery, Rockville, Md., 1971—74; pres. Patrick Michaels Enterprise, Washington, 1974—89; writer Washington, 1989—. Author: These Forty Years Have Flown So Fast, 2002, (short stories) Winston Churchills American Cousin, 2001, (plays) November 22, Eternal Bliss, numerous poems. Officer bd. mem. Grenway Downs Ctr. Assn., 1998—; mem. Anacostia River Commn., Washington, 1985—95. Recipient Martha Epostio Award, Home Health Assembly of N.J., 2001. Mem.: Md. State Tchr. Assn., Acad. Am. Poets. Republican. Avocations: gardening, travel, mentoring. Home: 2805 Bolling Rd Falls Church VA 22042 Personal E-mail: scotwalker2004@yahoo.com.

WALKER, SUZANNAH WOLF, language educator; b. Akron, Ohio, May 3, 1954; d. Robert Patton and Katherine Jane (Guglielmi) Wolf Jr.; m. Timothy Gordon Walker, Dec. 23, 1988 (div. Dec. 21, 1992). BA in Secondary Edn., U. Akron, 1976; MA in Pub. Rels., Kent State U., 1987. Tchr. English, Spanish Cuyahoga Falls (Ohio) City Sch., 1977—96; tchr. English DOD Dependents Sch., Wurzburg, Germany, 1981—82; tchr. English, Spanish Canton (Ohio) City Schs., 1999—. Mem. supt. adv. com. Cuyahoga Falls City Sch., 1995, bldg. rep., 1992—95, Canton City Schs., 2000—03. Pub. rels. intern Ronald McDonald House, Cleve., 1985. Mem.: NEA, Canton Profl. Educators Assn. (mem. exec. com. 2003—), N.E. Ohio Fgn. Lang. Assn., Ohio Fgn. Lang. Assn., Cuyahoga Falls Edn. Assn., Ohio Edn. Assn. Home: 3430 E Prescott Cir Cuyahoga Falls OH 44223 Office Phone: 330-454-7717.

WALKER, THOMAS MICHAEL, school psychologist; b. Waycross, Ga., May 5, 1945; s. Hazel Mae (Thomas) W.; divorced; children: Ettoria Elizabeth, Tom. BSEd, MEd, U. Ga., Athens, 1982, EdS, 1985. Cert. sch. psychologist, Ga. Farmer, Blackshear, Ga., 1966—; land developer, 1969—; postal worker U.S. Postal Svc., Blackshear, 1967-73; sch. psychologist Hart County Bd. Edn., Hartwell, Ga., 1985-98, Pierce County Bd. Edn., Blackshear, Ga., 1998—. Mem. APA, Nat. Assn. Sch. Psychologists, Ga. Assn. Sch. Psychologists. Home: 5339 Trudie Rd Blackshear GA 31516-8211

WALKER, THOMAS RAY, city aviation commissioner; AB in Art, Dartmouth Coll., 1970; BArch, Ill. Inst. Tech., 1977. Project mgr. Lohan Assocs., 1977-86; v.p. design and constrn. The Chgo. Dock and Canal Trust, 1986-91; exec. dir. Pub. Bldg. Commn. of Chgo., 1991-95; commr. dept. transp. City of Chgo., 1995-99; commr. Chgo. Dept. of Aviation, City of Chgo., 2000—. Prin. works include Soldier Field World Cup renovation, Chgo., Wright Coll. Addition, Chgo. Pub. Schs. capital improvement program, Cityfront Ctr., Chgo., MarketTower Officer Bldg., Indpls., Episcopal Sch. of Dallas Libr./Fine Arts addition, Frito-Lay Nat. Hdqs., Plano, Tex. Vice chmn. Chgo. Area Transp. Study; commr. State St. Commn.; mem. com. Newhouse arch. fellowship program Chgo. Arch. Found.; mem. Chgo. Planning Commn.; mem. selection com. cmty. svc. fellowship Chgo. Cmty. Trust; mem. TRB steering com. Conf. Transp. Issue in Large U.S. Cities; mem. Conf. Minority Transp. Officials; trustee Chgo. Music and Dance Theater; chmn. leadership coun. Met. Open Cmtys.; co-chmn. adv. bd./housing com. Met. Planning Coun. 1st lt. USAF, 1970-72. Mem. Intelligent Transp. Soc. of Am. (bd. dirs.), Nat. Assn. City Transp. Ofcls. (chmn.), Nat. Orgn. Minority Architects, Urban Land Inst., Lambda Alpha Internat. Office: O'Hare Internat Airport Dept of Aviation PO Box 66142 Chicago IL 60666-0142

WALKER, TIMOTHY BLAKE, lawyer, educator; b. Utica, N.Y., May 21, 1940; s. Harold Blake and Mary Alice (Corder) W.; m. Sandra Blake; children: Kimberlee Corder, Tyler Blake, Kelley Loren. AB magna cum laude, Princeton U., 1962; JD magna cum laude, U. Denver, 1967, MA in Sociology, 1969. Bar: Colo. 1968, Calif. 1969, Ind. 1971. Asst. prof. law U. Pacific, 1968-69; vis. assoc. prof. U. Toledo, 1969-70; assoc. prof. Indpls. Law Sch., Ind. U., 1970-71, U. Denver, 1971-75, prof., 1975-99; prof. emeritus, 1999—; dir. adminstrn. of justice program U. Denver, 1971-78; pvt. practice Denver, 1972-79; of counsel Robert T. Hinds, Jr. & Assocs. PC, Littleton, Colo., 1980-85; ptnr., of counsel Cox, Mustain-Wood, Walker & Schumacher, Littleton, 1985—. Cons., lectr. in field; rsch. on lay representation in adminstrv. agys., Colo., 1975-76. Contbr. articles to profl. jours.; editor: Denver Law Jour., 1966-67; editor-in-chief: Family Law Quar., 1983-92. Mem. Ind. Child Support Commn., 1970-71; pres. Shawnee (Colo.) Water Consumers Assn., 1975-84, 93-95; del. Colo. Rep. Conv., 1978. Colo. Bar Assn. grant, 1975-76. Fellow: Am. Bar Found., Internat. Acad. Matrimonial Lawyers, Am. Sociol. Assn., Am. Acad. Matrimonial Lawyers; mem.: ABA (vice chmn. child custody subcom., sec. Family Law sect. 1992—93, vice chmn., sec. 1993—94, chmn. elect family law sect. 1994—95, chmn. 1995—96, chmn. child custody task force 2000—, alimony, maintenance and support com. 2000—, family sect. del. ho. of dels. 2000—), Colo Trial Lawyers Assn., Ind. Bar Assn., Colo. Bar Assn., Calif. Bar Assn. Presbyterian. Home: 13138 Whisper Canyon Rd Castle Rock CO 80108-9281 Office: 1900 Olive St Denver CO 80220-1857 also: 6601 S University Blvd Littleton CO 80121-2913 *Law and justice require the combination of intellectual self-discipline and an awareness of human dignity. The path of the law is often twisted and circuitous, and my goal has been to leave the trail better than I found it.*

WALKER, TIMOTHY CRAIG, transportation executive; b. Huntington, W.Va., Jan. 16, 1945; s. John Paul and Marjorie Frances (Withers) W. BA, Northwestern U., 1967; B of Fgn. Trade, Am. Grad. Sch. Internat. Mgmt., 1968. Mgmt. trainee to dir. OIM/internat. mktg. ops. NCR Corp., Dayton, Ohio, 1968—79; v.p. mktg. Do-Ray Lamp Co., Inc., Colorado City, Colo., 1979—87; v.p. sales and mktg. Truck-Lite Co., Inc., Jamestown, NY, 1984—; pres., COO Truck-Lite Internat., Inc., 1990—, also bd. dirs. Recruiter Am. Grad. Sch. Internat. Mgmt., 1971—. Bd. dirs. Valley Human Resources, United Way Agy., 1980-84, Goodwill Industries of Pueblo, Colo., 1983-84; mem. Working Group for U.S. Dept. Commerce MOSS Talks. Recipient Pres.'s award 1st alumnus Am. Grad. Sch. Internat. Mgmt., 1976, award for excellence in internat. advt., 1968; named to Automotive Hall of Fame. Mem. Transp. Safety Equipment Inst. N.Am. (chmn. mktg. and statis. com. 1980-82), European Transport Maintenance Coun. (bd. dirs. 1991-93), Heavy Duty Bus. Forum (bd. dirs.), Heavy Duty Mfrs. Assn. (bd. govs. 1987-95, sec. 1990-91, 95-96, vice chmn. 1997, chmn. 1998), Overseas Automotive Coun. (bd. dirs.), Pueblo Area C. of C. (transp. com. 1981-84), Coun. Fleet Specialists (mfrs. liaison com. 1989-91), 500 Automotive Execs. Club. Republican. Presbyterian. Home: PO Box 1263 Jamestown NY 14702-1263 Office: Truck-Lite Co PO Box 387 Jamestown NY 14702-0387 E-mail: tcwbhx@aol.com., twalker@truck-lite.com.

WALKER, VALAIDA SMITH, university administrator; b. Phila., Dec. 22, 1932; d. Samuel and Rosa (Lee) Smith. BS in Math. and Phys. Edn., Howard U., Washington, 1954; MEd in Spl. Edn., Temple U., 1970, EdD in Spl. Edn., 1973. Jr. H.S. math. tchr., Balt., 1955-58, Albuquerque, 1964-65; tchr. emotionaly disturbed and socially maladjusted children Phila., 1965-66; demonstration tchr., 1968-70; tchg. assoc., coord./supr. resource rm. tchr. tng. program Temple U., Phila., 1970-72; commr. mental retardation Southeastern region Dept. Pub. Welfare, Commonwealth Pa., 1973-74; program dir. Woodhaven Ctr. Mentally Retarded Temple U., Phila., 1974-76, chairperson dept. spl. edn., 1980-83, assoc. dean Coll. Edn., 1983-84, assoc. vice provost undergrad. programs, 1984-90, interim vice provost adminstrn., 1987-90, acting v.p. student affairs, 1990-92, prof. dept. spl. edn., 1974—, v.p. student affairs, 1992—. Past mem. steering com., chairperson cmty. svcs. task force subcom. Pres. Com. on Mental Retardation; exec. advisor Caribbean Assn. Mental Retardation, 1982-89; mem. adv. panel on spl. edn. Commonwealth Pa., 1985-93; hearing office Pa. Dept. Edn., 1978-91; gov.'s apointee Profl. Stds. and Practices Commn., 1980-83; field reader U.S. Office Edn., Bur. Handicapped, 1980-93; expert witness Pennhurst State Instn. Ct. Case, 1973-74. Bd. dirs. Elwyn Insts., 1983—, chairperson edn. and tng. com., 1984-86; chair curriculum and nominations com. William Penn Adult Cmty. Sch. Adv. Bd., 1976; bd. mem. Rebecca Gratz Assn., Phila. Recipient svc. award Chapel of Four Chaplains, cert. of honor Alumni Assn. Temple U., Phila., 1990, Svc. award Kappa Alpha Phi, Phila., 1995; named Spl. Educator Yr., Sigma Pi Epsilon Delta, 1983, Tchr. of Yr. Sigma Pi Epsilon Delta, Phila., 1995. Fellow Am. Assn. Mental Retardation (pres.-elect, program chair 1986-87, pres. 1987-88). Baptist. Office: Temple U 1801 N Broad St Philadelphia PA 19122-6003

WALKER, VAUGHN R. federal judge; b. Watseka, Ill., Feb. 27, 1944; s. Vaughn Rosenworth and Catharine (Miles) W. AB, U. Mich., 1966; JD, Stanford U., 1970. Intern economist SEC, Washington, 1966, 68; law clk. to the Hon. Robert J. Kelleher U.S. Dist. Ct. Calif., L.A., 1971-72; assoc. atty. Pillsbury Madison & Sutro, San Francisco, 1972-77, ptnr., 1978-90; judge U.S. Dist. Ct. (no. dist.) Calif., San Francisco, 1990—. Mem. Calif. Law Revision Commn., Palo Alto, 1986-89; bd. advisors Law and Econs. Ctr., George Mason U., 1999—. Dir. Jr. Achievement of Bay Area, San Francisco, 1979-83, St. Francis Found., San Francisco, 1991-97, 98—. Woodrow Wilson fellow U. Calif., Berkeley, 1966-67. Fellow Am. Bar Found.; mem. ABA (jud. rep., antitrust sect. 1991-95), Lawyers' Club of San Francisco (pres. 1985-86), Assn. Bus. Trial Lawyers (dir. 1996-98), Am. Law Inst., Am. Saddlebred Horse Assn., San Francisco Mus. Modern Art, Bohemian Club, Olympic Club, Pacific-Union Club. Office: US Dist Ct 450 Golden Gate Ave San Francisco CA 94102-3482

WALKER, VICKI L. state senator; m. Steven Walker; children: Adam, Sara. Ct. reporting program, Lane C.C., 1980—83; BS in Polit. Sci., U. Oreg., 1978. State sen. Oreg. State Senate, Salem, 1999—; ct. reporter Salem, 1983—. Mem.: Oreg. Ct. Reporters Assn., Am. Found. for Suicide Prevention-NW. Democrat. Office: 900 Court St NE S-210 Salem OR 97301

WALKER, VIOLA, writer, educator; b. Chgo. d. Ernest and Marie Walker. AA, Olive Harvey Coll., Chgo.; BE, Chgo. State U., MEd, 1991. Tchr. Chgo. Housing, 1980—86, Chgo. Pub. Sch., 1986—2001. Author: (children's book) Marie's Dad, 2002, (teen book) Ted, 2003, (book) The Selling Out of the Church, 2004. Achievements include invention of removable vehicle trunk organizer. Avocations: fishing, writing, drawing, painting, rollerskating. Home: 722 W 82d St Chicago IL 60620

WALKER, W. JACK, retired small business owner; b. Sept. 30, 1919; s. John Wesley Walker, Mattie Alma (Gilbert) Walker; m. Loraine Walker; 1 child, Gayle Walker Threet. BBA, U. Tenn., 1940; DHL (hon.), Knoxville Coll., 1988. Owner W.Jack Walker Rolling Store, 1946—51, Walker Market, Knoxville, Tenn., 1954—78; cons. Ernest Youngblood Assocs., Knoxville, 1978—. Bd. govs. Club LeConte, 1977—; bd. dirs. St. Mary's Health Sys., Inc., Cmty. Found. East Tenn., Wellness Cmty. Knoxville, Child & Family Svcs., Salvation Army, Presbyn. Homes of Tenn., Inc., Tenn. Valley Agrl. & Indsl. Fair, v.p. exec. com., 1984—; chmn. investment com. Monday Found., 1990—; bd. dirs. Sr. Citizens Home Assistance Svcs., Pellissippi State C.C. Found., Union Planters Bank, 1990—, Blount Hearing and Speech Found.; deacon Ctrl. Bapt. Ch. Bearden; chmn. bd. First Tenn. Bank, Knoxville, Tenn., 1977—86. With U.S. Coast Guard. Named Retailer of Yr., Tenn. Retail Merchants Assn., 1977, Salesman of Yr., 1978; recipient Outstanding Leadership award, ARC, 1968, Outstanding Svc. award, Castle Heights Mil. Acad., 1980, Pres.'s award, Knoxville Area Urban League, 1987, Disting. Svc. award, Arthritis Found., 1988, Book of Golden Deeds award, Knoxville Exch. Club, 1985, Brotherhood-Sisterhood award, Nat. Conf. Christians and Jews, 1987. Mem.: Masons (32d degree), YMCA Knoxville (Red Triangle award, Man of Yr. 1968), U. Tenn. Pres.'s Club, Rotary Club Knoxville. Home: 719 Clubhouse Way Knoxville TN 37909 Office: Ernest Youngblood Assocs 1810 Ailor Ave Ste E Knoxville TN 37921

WALKER, W. LAWRENCE, JR., newspaper publishing executive; Exec. v.p. & bus. mgr. Newspaper Agency, 1987—90; pres., CEO, San Antonio Express-News, 1990—. Office: San Antonio Express-News PO Box 2171 San Antonio TX 78297-2171 also: San Antonio Express News Ave E and Third Street San Antonio TX 78205

WALKER, WALDO SYLVESTER, biologist, educator, academic administrator; b. Fayette, Iowa, June 12, 1931; s. Waldo S. and Mildred (Littelle) W.; m. Marie J. Olsen, July 27, 1952 (div.); children: Martha Lynn, Gayle Ann; m. Rita K. White, June 16, 1984. BS cum laude, Upper Iowa U., Fayette, 1953; MS, U. Iowa, 1957, PhD, 1959; D of Sci. (hon.), Upper Iowa U., 2004. Mem. faculty Grinnell (Iowa) Coll., 1958, assoc. dean coll., 1963-65, chmn. div. Natural Scis., 1968-69, dean of adminstrn., 1969-73, exec. v.p., 1973-77, dean coll., 1973-80, provost, 1977-80, exec. v.p., 1980-90, exec. v.p. and treas., 1988-90, v.p. for coll. svcs., 1990-95, prof. biology, 1968-2001, prof. emeritus, 2001—. Research assoc. U. B.C. Dept. of Botany, 1966-67. Author articles on plant physiology, ultrastructural cytology. Served with U.S. Army, 1953-55. Fellow NSF Sci. Faculty, 1966-67; recipient NSF research grants, 1960-63, 68. Mem. Am. Assn. Colls., Am. Conf. Acad. Deans (nat. chmn. 1977-78), Am. Assn. Higher Edn., Sigma Xi. Home: 1920 Country Club Dr Grinnell IA 50112-1130 Address: Grinnell Coll PO Box H2 Grinnell IA 50112-0805 E-mail: walkerws@iowatelecom.net.

WALKER, WALTER FREDERICK, professional basketball team executive; b. Bradford, Pa., July 18, 1954; m. Linda Walker. Diploma, U. Va.; MBA, Stanford U., 1987; BA, U. Va., 1976. Chartered Fin. Analyst. Player Portland (Oreg.) Trail Blazers, 1976-77, Seattle SuperSonics, 1977-82, pres., CEO, 1994—; player Houston Rockets, 1982-84; with Goldman Sachs and Co., San Francisco, 1987-94; prin. Walker Capital, Inc., San Francisco, 1994. Mem. USA gold medal World Univ. Games basketball team, 1973; broadcaster basketball Raycom Network, 1989-94; cons. Seattle SuperSonics, 1994. Bd. dirs. Advanced Digital Info. Corp., Drexler Tech. Corp. Named 1st team Acad. All-Am. U. Va.; named to Pa. State Sports Hall of Fame. Nat. trustee Boys and Girls Clubs of Am. Office: Seattle SuperSonics 351 Elliott Ave W Seattle WA 98119-4101 E-mail: wwalker@sonics-storm.com.

WALKER, WILLIAM BOND, painter, retired librarian; b. Brownsville, Tenn., Apr. 15, 1930; s. Marshall Francis and Mary Louise (Taylor) W. BA, State U. Iowa, 1953; M.L.S., Rutgers U., 1958. Librarian-trainee Donnell br. N.Y. Public Library, N.Y.C., 1955-57; reference librarian/cataloger Met. Mus. Art, N.Y.C., 1957-59; chief librarian Bklyn. Mus., 1959-64; supervisory librarian Library of Nat. Collection Fine Arts and Nat. Portrait Gallery, Smithsonian Instn., Washington, 1964-80; Arthur K. Watson chief librarian Thomas J. Watson Library, Met. Mus. Art, N.Y.C., 1980-94; ret., 1994. Adj. lectr. Columbia U. Sch. Library Service, 1987-88. Author: annotated bibliography American Sculpture, 18th-20th Century, 1979; retrospective exhbn. paintings, 1954-96, Pittsfield, Mass., 1996-97; solo and group exhbns. Columbia County, N.Y., Berkshire County, Mass., 1997-2003. Mem. ALA, Art

Libns. Soc. N.Am (pres. 1975, Disting. Svc. award, 1992), Geneal. and Biog. Soc. (corr.), Phi Beta Kappa. Home: 54 Queechy Lake Dr PO Box 237 Canaan NY 12029-0237 E mail: lakequeechy@taconic.net.

WALKER, WILLIAM D. physicist, educator, researcher; b. Nov. 23, 1923; s. William D. and Mildred Ramsey Walker; m. Suzanne Porter, Dec. 23, 1946 (div. Oct. 1975); m. Constance Kalbach, Oct. 16, 1975; children: Nancy Walker Davis, Elizabeth Walker Schenkel, Samuel. BA, Rice U., 1944; PhD in Physics, Cornell U., 1949. Asst. prof. Rice U., Houston, 1949-51; lectr. U. Calif., Berkeley, 1951-52; asst. prof. U. Rochester, NY, 1952-54; from asst. prof. to prof. U. Wis., Madison, 1954-71; prof. physics Duke U., Durham, NC, 1971-98; chmn. dept. physics U. Wis., Madison, 1964-66, Max Mason disting. prof., 1969-71, Disting. faculty fellow, 2002; J.B. Duke disting. prof. Duke U., Durham, NC, 1990-94, chmn. dept. physics, 1975-81, prof. emeritus, 1994—. Chmn. users com. Argonne Nat. Lab., Lemont, Ill., 1960-63; mem. users com. Fermi Nat. Accelerator Lab., Aurora, Ill., 1971-74, chmn., 1973; mem. physics adv. bd. NSF, Washington, 1962-65; bd. dirs. Oak Ridge Assn. U., 1975-81. Contbr. 200 articles to profl. jour.; discovered several elementary particles. Deacon Episc. Ch., 1964-71; elder Presbyn. Ch., 1993—. Fellow Am. Phys. Soc. Avocation: tennis. Home: 907 Green St Durham NC 27701-1507 Office: Duke U Physics Dept Box 90305 Durham NC 27708 E-mail: walker@phy.duke.edu. *My life was renewed and rebuilt at age 35 by Jesus Christ. Any success I may have had is due to him.*

WALKER, WILLIAM EASTON, surgeon, educator, lawyer; b. Glasgow, Scotland, Aug. 7, 1945; came to U.S., 1969; s. William Telfer and Josephine Blair (Easton) W.; m. Mary Fraley Cooley, June 23, 1973; children— Sarah Cooley, Blair Easton, Denton Arthur Cooley, William Easton, II MD, Glasgow U., Scotland, 1968; PhD, Johns Hopkins U., 1975; JD, South Tex. Coll Law, 1993. Diplomate Am. Bd. Surgery, Am. Bd. Thoracic Surgery, Am. Bd. Vascular Surgery. Intern, resident Johns Hopkins U., Balt., 1969-75; resident Vanderbilt U., Nashville, 1975-79; assoc. prof., dir. div. thoracic and cardio-vascular surgery U. Tex. Med. Sch., Houston, 1979-94. Cons. M.D. Anderson Hosp., Houston, 1979—. Recipient Harwell Wilson award Vanderbilt U., Nashville, 1979 Fellow ACS, So. Surg. Assn., Royal Coll. Surgeons, Am. Coll. Cardiology; mem. Am. Assn. Thoracic Surgery, Coun. Fgn. Rels., Houston Country Club, Belle Meade Country Club, Cosmos Club (Washington), Krewe of Endymion (New Orleans), Phi Beta Kappa, Sigma Xi. Republican. Presbyterian. Avocations: law, bridge, Wagner, WWI, cooking. Home and Office: 2831 Sackett St Houston TX 77098-1125 Office Phone: 713-520-0021. Personal E-mail: wew2001@swbell.net.

WALKER, WILLIAM HAMILTON, civil engineer, educator; b. Brookline, Mass., Dec. 28, 1934; s. William A. and Ingeborg (Thorkilsen) W.; m. Shirley Ann Ackerman, Nov. 3, 1962; children: William Franklin, John Hamilton. BS, U. Mass., 1956; MS, U. Ill., 1958, PhD, 1963. Rsch. asst. U. Ill., Urbana, 1956-61, instr. civil engring., 1961-63, asst. prof., 1963-68, assoc. prof., 1968-90, prof., 1990—99, assoc. head dept., 1985—, prof. emeritus, 1999—. Cons. to various govt. agys. and industry, 1965—. Contbr. articles to profl. jours. Trustee Windsor Park Fire Protection Dist., Champaign, Ill., 1972—. Mem. ASCE (pres. cen. Ill. sect. 1984); mem. Am. Soc. for Engring. Edn., Sigma Xi, Tau Beta Pi, Phi Kappa Phi. Presbyterian. Avocations: photography, videography, travel, bird watching. Home: 2402 Melrose Dr Champaign IL 61820-7607 Office: U Ill 205 N Mathews Ave Urbana IL 61801-2350 Office Phone: 217-333-6948. Business E-Mail: whwalker@uiuc.edu.

WALKER, WILLIAM TIDD, JR., investment banker; b. Detroit, Sept. 5, 1931; s. William Tidd and Irene (Rhode) W.; m. Patricia Louise Frazier, Sept. 10, 1953; children: Donna Louise, Carol Ann, Sally Lynn, Alyssa Jane. Student, Stanford, 1950. Stockbroker William R. Staats & Co., Los Angeles, 1952-57, sales mgr., 1957-58, syndicate partner, 1958-65; sr. v.p. Glore Forgan, William R. Staats Inc., N.Y.C., 1965-68; partner, exec. com. Lester, Ryons & Co., Los Angeles, 1968; exec. v.p. Bateman Eichler, Hill Richards Inc., Los Angeles, 1969-85. Pres., CEO, WTW Inc.; chmn., CEO Walker Assocs.; bd. dirs. Digid, Inc., Health Scis. Group, Inc., King-Thomason Group, Inc., Supralife Internat., Stone Mountain Data Ctrs. Inc., Desert Health Products Inc., Viastar Media Corp.; adv. mem. Am. Stock Exch., 1981—. With USAF, 1949-52. Mem. Securities Industry Assn. (dir. nat. syndicate com., chmn. Calif. Dist. 10), Pacific Coast Stock Exch. (bd. govs. 1971-72), Investment Bankers Assn. (nat. pub. rels. com. 1966—), Bond Club L.A. (pres. 1973), Calif. Yacht Club. Office: Walker Assocs PO Box 10684 Beverly Hills CA 90213-3684

WALKER, WOODROW WILSON, retired lawyer, timber farmer, real estate investor; b. Greenville, Mich., Feb. 19, 1919; s. Craig Walker and Mildred Chase; m. Janet K. Keiter, Oct. 7, 1950; children: Jonathan Woodrow, William Craig, Elaine Virginia. BA, U. Mich., 1943; LLB, Cath. U., 1950. Bar: D.C. 1950, U.S. Supreme Ct. 1958, Va. 1959. Operator family farm, 1937-39; dir. Libr. of Congress Fed. Credit Union, 1957-60; atty. Am. law div. legis. reference Libr. Congress, Washington, 1951-60; pvt. practice, Arlington, Va., 1960-2000. Counsel, bd. dirs. Calvary Found., Arlington, 1970-85, first pres., 1972; judge moot ct. George Mason Law Sch., 1986; owner-operator Walker Farm Front Royal, Va., 1972—. Co-author rsch. publs. for U.S. Govt.; featured in Washington Post. V.p. Jefferson Civic Assn., Arlington, 1955-61; pres. Nellie Custis PTA, Arlington, 1960-61; sec. Arlington County Bd. Equalization Real Estate Assessment, 1962, chmn. 1963; com. chmn. Arlington Troop 108 Boy Scouts Am., 1964-69; mem. Arlington County Pub. Utilities Commn., 1964-66, vice chmn., 1965-66; pres. Betschler Class Adult Sunday Sch., Calvary United Meth. Ch., Arlington, 1965. Served with U.S. Army, 1943-45, PTO. Cited for notable deed in conduct of his legal duties Washington Post, 1996. Mem. ABA, Arlington County Bar Assn., Va. Farm Bur., Va. Cattleman's Assn. Methodist. Democrat. Home and Office: 2822 Ft Scott Dr Arlington VA 22202-2307

WALKER-WILLIAMS, HOPE DENISE, administrator, business consultant; b. Chgo., Dec. 24, 1952; d. Welmon and Mary Ann (Brefford) Walker; children: Albert Lee, Ebony Emani Denise. Student, Ill. State U., 1971-72; BA in Psychology, St. Ambrose Coll., 1985, postgrad., 1985-87, Harvard U. Grad. Sch. Design, summer 1981, Nat. Assn. Collegiate Women Athletic Adminstrs./Higher Edn. Resources Inst., 1995, No. Ill. U., 1998—2000. Social svc. dir. Friendly House, Davenport, Iowa, 1977-78; data collector, cons., 1978; supr. summer youth employment program Cmty. Employment Tng. Act, Davenport, 1978; lead organizer Central and Western Neighborhood Devel. Corp., Davenport, 1978-79; exec. dir. Inner City Devel. Corp., Davenport, 1980-83; owner Midwestern Internat. Mktg. Assocs., San Francisco, 1983; ops. mgr. Dramatic Mktg. Assn., San Francisco, 1983-85; adminstrv. asst. Parker Ross Assocs., 1984-85; crisis intervention counselor Cath. Social Svcs., 1985-86; adminstrv. intern Scott County Iowa, 1985-86; from counselor to dir. advising Marycrest Coll., Davenport, 1986-90; dir. spl. svcs. Augustana Coll., Rock Island, Ill., 1990-97, asst. dean of student svcs., 1991-97. Cons. Dramatic Mktg. Assocs., San Francisco, 1997—; coord. student athlete support svcs. No. Ill. U., Dekalb, 1999—2001; asst. dir. athletics student svcs., athletic dept. U. Iowa, Iowa City, 2001—; bus. cons., incorporator, sec. bd. dirs. United Neighbors Inc., 1980; bd. dirs. Cmty. Health Care, 1978—80; v.p., treas. Athletes Say More Edn., 1980; treas., exec. com. F&A Cmty. Warehouse, 1982—; bd. dirs. HELP Legal Aid, v.p., 1990, pres., 91; allocations panel United Way, 1987—89. Author narrative and final report for oral history project, 1979. Bkacl belt, 1st Dan Choe's TKD, Iowa City, 2002. Recipient Cert. of Appreciation, Palmer Jr. Coll. Davenport, 1979, Personal Dedication plaque, Jr. Achievement, 1988—90, cert. of merit, Ch. of Women United, 1983, Cert. of Appreication, Choe's TKD, 2002; Presdl. grant, Palmer Jr. Coll., 1979, grantee, NEH, 1979. Mem. NAFE, Assn. Black Women Higher Edn., Nat. Assn. Women Edn. (nat. treas. 1993, Dorothy Truex award for Emerging Profls. 1994), Nat. Assn. Acad. Advisors for Athletics (membership com. 2000—, minority concerns com., liaison to legis. affairs com. Region III 2001-02), Quad Cities Career Womens Network (treas., exec. com.), Assn. Acad. Affairs Adminstrs. (bd. dirs. 1989-96, award for new profls. 1989, treas. 1992-96), Nat. Assn. for Blacks at Predominately White Instns. (v.p. fin.), Nat. Acad. Advisors Assn., Nat. Assn. Acad. Advisors (bd. dirs. 1988), Quad Cities Assn. Black Sch. Educators (founding, charter, treas. 1993), Quad City Negro Heritage Soc., Assn. Black Profls. (chair), Nat. Assn. Black MBAs, Alpha Kappa Alpha (chair connection com. Xi Eta Omega chpt. 1989, 2001, internat. stds. com. 1994-98), Tau Psi Omega (pres. 2004), Quad Cities Strivers Inc. (bd. dirs.). Office Phone: 319-335-8867.

WALKOWIAK, VINCENT STEVEN, lawyer; b. Apr. 22, 1946; s. Vincent Albert and Elizabeth (Modla) W.; m. Linda Kae Schweigert, Aug., 1968; children: Jenifer, Steven. BA, U. Ill., 1968, JD, 1971. Bar: Ill. 1971, Minn. 1971, Tex. 1981, U.S. Ct. Appeals (8th cir.) 1971, (5th cir.) 1982, U.S. Dist. Ct. (ea., we., so., and no. dists.) Tex. 1982. Assoc. Dorsey, Marquart, Windhorst, West & Halladay, Mpls., 1971-74; ptnr. Fulbright & Jaworski LLP, Houston, 1982—. Prof. Fla. State U., Tallahassee, 1974-76, So. Meth. U., Dallas, 1976-84. Editor: Uniform Product Liability Act, 1980, Trial of a Product Liability Case, vol. 1, 1981, vol. 2, 1982, Preparation and Presentation of Product Liability, 1983, Attorney Client Privilege in Civil Litigation, 1997. Office: Fulbright & Jaworski LLP 2200 Ross Ave Ste 2800 Dallas TX 75201-2784 Office Phone: 214-855-8037. E-mail: vwalkowiak@fulbright.com.

WALKOWITZ, DANIEL JAY, historian, filmmaker, educator; b. Paterson, N.J., Nov. 25, 1942; s. Sol and Selda (Margel) W.; m. Judith Rosenberg, Dec. 26, 1965; 1 child, Rebecca Lara. AB, U. Rochester, 1964, PhD, 1972; postgrad., U. Grenoble, France, 1965. Lectr. in history U. Rochester, N.Y., 1967-69; instr. history Renssalaer Poly. Inst., Troy, N.Y., 1969-71; asst. prof. history Rutgers U., New Brunswick, N.J., 1971-78, NYU, N.Y.C., 1978-81, assoc. prof., 1981-88, co-dir. pub. history program, 1981-89, prof., 1988—, dir. met. studies, 1989—, dir. coll. honors, 2004—. Ptnr., film producer PastTimes Prodns., N.Y.C., 1982-97; vis. prof. U. Calif. Irvine, 1982, Johns Hopkins U., 1991-92, Stanford U., 2002; editorial sec. Radical History Rev., N.Y.C., 1985-89; bd. dirs. N.Y. Marxist Sch., 1987-90. Author: Worker City, Company Town, 1978, Working With Class, 1999; co-author: Workers of the Donbass Speak, 1995; film project dir. The Molders of Troy, 1980; co-editor: Workers in the Industrial Revolution, 1974, Working-Class America, 1984, Memory and the Impact of Political Transformation in Public Space, 2004, Social History of the United States in the 20th Century, 2004—; video dir., co-prodr., dir., writer: Perestroika From Below, 1990; co-prodr., writer Public History Today. Grantee, Nat. Endowment Humanities, 1976, 78, 82; Affiliate fellow Stanford Humanities Ctr., 2001 02. Mem. Nat. Coun. Pub. History (bd. dirs. 1986-89), Am. Hist. Assn., Orgn. Am. Historians, Oral History Assn. Avocation: international folk dance. Office: NYU Dept Met Study Porgram New York NY 10003 E-mail: daniel.walkowitz@nyu.edu.

WALKUP, CHARLOTTE LLOYD, lawyer; b. N.Y.C., Apr. 28, 1910; d. Charles Henry and Helene Louise (Wheeler) Tuttle; m. David D. Lloyd, Oct. 19, 1940 (dec. Dec. 1962); children: Andrew M. Lloyd, Louisa Lloyd Hurley; m. Homer Allen Walkup, Feb. 4, 1967. AB, Vassar Coll., 1931; LLB, Columbia U., 1934. Bar: N.Y. 1935, U.S. Supreme Ct. 1939, U.S. Dist. Ct. D.C. 1953, Va. 1954. Asst. solicitor Dept. Interior, Washington, 1934-45; asst. gen. counsel UNRRA, Washington and London, 1945-48; assoc. and cons. firms Washington, 1953, 55, 60; atty., spl. asst. Office Treasury, Washington, 1961-65, asst. gen. counsel, 1965-73. Cons. Rogers & Wells, Washington, 1975-86. Editor Columbia Law Rev., 1933-34, Life Stories of a Celebrated Lawyer: Memoirs of Charles H. Tuttle, Esq., 2002. Pres. Alexandria Cmty. Welfare Coun., 1950-52; bd. dirs. Alexandria Coun. Human Rels., 1958-60, New Hope Found., 1977. Recipient Meritorious Svc. award Dept. Treasury, 1970, Exceptional Svc. award, 1973, Career Svc. award Nat. Civil Svc. League, 1973; named Hon. fellow Harry S. Truman Libr. Inst. Mem. Columbia U. Alumni Assn., Phi Beta Kappa. Democrat. Episcopalian. Home: 4800 Fillmore Ave Apt 1251 Alexandria VA 22311-5077 E-mail: walkup@comcast.net.

WALKUP, HOMER ALLEN, lawyer, writer; b. Dunloup, W.Va., Jan. 28, 1917; s. Homer Allen and Lillie Belle (Harris) W.; m. Edna Mae Tucker, Nov. 19, 1941 (dec. 1966); m. Charlotte M. Tuttle Lloyd, Feb. 4, 1967; children: Homer Allen, Randolph Michael, Pamela Susan. AB, W.Va. U., 1935, LLB, 1938; LLM, Georgetown U., 1947. Bar: W.Va. 1938, U.S. Supreme Ct. 1946, U.S. Ct. Fed. Claims 1978, U.S. Ct. Appeals (fed. cir.) 1982, U.S. Ct. Claims 1982, U.S. Ct. Appeals Armed Forces 1984. Sole practice, W.Va., 1938-42; complaint atty. W.Va. Office OPA, Charleston, 1942; commd. ensign USNR, 1942, advanced through grades to capt., 1963; appellate judge Navy Ct. Mil. Rev., 1966-68; dep. asst., JAG of Navy, 1968-73; ret., 1973; sole practice, Summersville, W.Va., 1974-90. Mem. governing bd. Alexandria (Va.) Mental Health Ctr., 1988-92; bd. dirs. United Way Nat. Capital Area, 1990—. Mem. ABA, ATLA, Fed. Bar Assn., W.Va. State Bar, W.Va. Bar Assn., Bar Assn. D.C., Fed. Cir. Bar Assn., Judge Advs. Assn., Navy-MarCorps Retired Judge Advs. Assn., Am. Judicature Soc., Mil. Order World Wars, Res. Officers Assn., Ret. Officers Assn., Order of Coif. Democrat. Presbyterian. Club: Mil. Dist. Washington Officers. Contbr. in field. Office: Ste 1251 4800 Fillmore Ave Alexandria VA 22311-5077

WALKUP, JOHN KNOX, lawyer; m. Betsy Walkup; children: Alice, Margaret. BA magna cum laude, Centre Coll. Ky.; JD, Harvard U. Law clk. to Chief Justice Tenn. Supreme Ct., 1972—73; formerly in pvt. practice Burson & Walkup, Memphis; chief counsel, staff dir. subcom. govtl. affairs U.S. Senate; chief dep. atty. gen. State of Tenn., 1985—89, solicitor gen., 1989—93, atty. gen., 1997—99; former ptnr. Gullett, Sanford, Robinson & Martin, Nashville; with Wyatt, Tarrant & Combs, Nashville, 1999—. Former part-time asst. county atty. Shelby County, Tenn.; lectr. Law Sch. Vanderbilt U., 1993—95. Mem.: ABA, Nashville Bar Assn., Tenn. Bar Assn. Office: Wyatt Tarrant & Combs 2525 W End Ave # 1500 Nashville TN 37203-1423

WALKUP, MARY ROE, state legislator; b. Kennedyville, Md., May 4, 1924; d. William Benjamin and Catharine Cooper (Roe) Groves; m. Harry Ernst Walkup, 1945; children: Mary Anne, Harry Ernst Jr., Margaret Louise, Robert Douglas. BSN, U. Md., 1945. RN, Md. Nurse U. Md. Hosp., Balt., 1945-46; mem. Md. Ho. of Dels., Annapolis, 1995—. Editor Kent Conservation News, 1972-78. Women's vice chmn. Md. 1st Congl. Dist. Rep. Com., 1970-74; legis. chmn. Md. Fedn. Rep. Women, 1970-72; spl. asst. to census chmn. Kent County, Md., 1970, census chmn., 1970, commr., 1978-86; pres. Rep. Women's Club Kent and Queen Anne's County, Md., 1973-77; sec. Md. Rep. Ctrl. Com., 1974-78; mem. citizens adv. com. Chesapeake Bay Program, 1988—, chmn., 1989-91; mem. Md. Water Quality Adv. Com., 1988—; charter mem., bd. dirs. Kent Conservation Inc., 1989—, sec., 1969-72, pres., 1972-74, 91-93; v.p. Nat. Wildlife Fedn., 1972-78, alt. del., 1977. Named Conservationist of Yr., Md. Wildlife Fedn., 1977, Outstanding Md. Rep. Woman of Yr. and Thomas Sone award Md. Rep. Ctrl. Com., 1977.

WALKUP, ROBERT E. mayor; b. Ames, Iowa, Nov. 14, 1936; m. Beth Walkup; 3 children; 2 stepchildren. BS in Indsl. Engring., Iowa State U. Exec. Rockwell Internat., Fairchild Republic; sr. exec. Hughes Aircraft Co.; mayor Tucson, Ariz., 1999—. Chmn. Greater Tucson Econ. Coun.; founder, first chmn. Ariz. Space Commn.; vol. Tucson Cmty. Food Bank; co-founder Pima-Santa Cruz County Sch.-to-Work Program; co-founder El Centro Cultural de las Americas. Capt. U.S. Army. Republican. Avocations: playing guitar, sketching, studying astronomy, restoring antique cars and motorcycles. Office: City Hall 255 W Alameda St Tucson AZ 85701-1362 Fax: 520-791-4213. Business E-Mail: email_mayor@mail.ci.tucson.az.us.

WALL, BARBARA WARTELLE, lawyer; b. New Orleans, Sept. 30, 1954; d. Richard Cole and Ruth Druhan (Power) Wartelle; m. Christopher Read Wall, June 21, 1980; 2 children. BA, U. Va., 1976, JD, 1979. Bar: N.Y. 1980, U.S. Dist. Ct. (so. and ea. dists.) N.Y. 1980. Assoc. Satterlee & Stephens, N.Y.C., 1979-85; asst. gen. counsel Gannett Co., Inc., Arlington, Va., 1985-90, sr. legal counsel, 1990-93, v.p., sr. legal counsel, 1993—. Mem. ABA (past chair forum on comm. law), N.Y. State Bar Assn., Assn. of Bar of City of N.Y. Republican. Home: 5026 Tilden St NW Washington DC 20016-2334 Office: Gannett Co Inc 7950 Jones Branch Dr Mc Lean VA 22102-0320

WALL, BETTY JANE, real estate consultant; b. Wichita Falls, Tex., Mar. 23, 1936; d. Albert Willis and Winnie Belle (Goodloe) Beard; m. Richard Lee Wall, Feb. 21, 1959; 1 child, Cynthia Lynn. BS, Vocat.Home Econs. Edn, U. Okla., 1958; MEd, Midwestern U., 1959. Lic. real estate salesperson, Tex. Tchr. San Diego County Schs., 1959-60, Long Beach (Calif.) City Schs., 1960-61, Norman (Okla.) Kindergarten Assn., 1961-65; real estate salesperson WestMark Realtors, Lubbock, Tex., 1983-85; now ind. real estate salesperson Lubbock, 1985—. Coll. adviser Nat. Panhellenic Conf., Tex., 1979-91; judge talent and beauty pageants, Tex. N.Mex., Okla., 1984—. Treas. Lubbock Symphony Guild, 1985-87, v.p. ways and means com., 1987-88, chmn. ball, 1990, pres. elect, 1993-94, pres., 1994-95; bd. dirs. Tex. Assn. of Symphony Orchs., 1994-95, Ballet Lubbock, 1996-98, 2000—; bd. dirs. Miss Lubbock Pageant, 1992—; co-chmn. Performance Lubbock' 96, 1996; mem. Lubbock Arts Festival Com., 1997-98. Recipient Tex. Tech. U. Outstanding Greek Alumni award, 1994, Tex. Tech. Chancellor's Coun. Mem. Tex. Real Estate Assn., Jr. League Lubbock (treas. 1976-78, sustaining advisor fin. com. 1979-83, hdqrs. commn. advisor 1989-94), Mus. Tex. Tech. Univ. (chmn. planetarium com. 1996, trustee 1997—, bd. dirs., mus. league 1992-2002, pres. 2002, v.p. 2002-2003), Lubbock C. of C., Lubbock Women's Club (bd. dirs. 1996-2000, pres. 1999-2000, pres. hist. found. 1999-2000), Tex. Tech. U. Faculty Women's Club (v.p. and pres. 1967-69, Lubbock chpt. Achievement Rewards for Coll. Sci. bd. 1995-96), Alpha Chi Omega (nat. coun., nat. panhellenic del. 1978-83, 88-90, nat. v.p. membership 1985-88, nat. v.p. collegians 1990-92), Mus. Tex. Tech U. Assn. (v.p. mus. league 2002-2003), Lubbock Alumnae Panhellenic (pres. 2003-04). Avocations: needlepoint, travel, music. Home and Office: 3610 63rd Dr Lubbock TX 79413-5308

WALL, CAROLYN RAIMONDI, communications executive; b. Springfield, Mass., July 2, 1942; d. Amedio G. and Celestina F. (Penna) Raimondi; m. Peter M. Wall, Oct. 24, 1964 (div. 1972); children: Christina, Suzanne; m. Warren J. Keegan, June 17, 1984 (div. 1989). AB, Trinity Coll., Washington. Advt dir. Beldoch Industries, N.Y.C., 1972-74; promotion dir. Fairchild Pubs., N.Y.C., 1974-76; v.p., pub. Adweek, N.Y.C., 1976-83; assoc. pub. N.Y. Mag., N.Y.C., 1983-84, pub., 1984-85; exec. v.p. consumer div. Murdoch Mags., 1985-87; v.p., gen. mgr. Sta. WNYW, N.Y.C., 1987—92; dir. News America Holdings; exec. v.p. corp. devel. and sales News America, 1992—95; pres. Cowles Bus. Media, 1995-96, WBIS-TV, 1996-98; pub. Newsweek, 1998—2001, dir. mktg. and comms., 2001; ptnr. Quintacom, 2002—. Mem. bus. adv. bd. Lubin Schs. Bus., Pace U., 1982-88; bd. dirs. N.Y. Urban League, Found. for Minority Interests in Media, MacDuffie Sch., Internat. Radio and TV Found. Mem. Internat. Radio and TV Soc., N.Y. TV Acad. Arts and Scis., Advt. Women N.Y. (bd. dirs., pres. 1981-83). Mem. Advt. Women of N.Y. (bd. dirs., pres. 1981-83) Democrat. Roman Catholic.

WALL, CHARLES R. lawyer; BA hist., Grinnell Coll., Iowa, 1967; JD, Univ. of Mo. Law Sch., Mo., 1970. Assoc. and ptnr. Shook, Hardy & Bacon, Kans. City, Mo., 1970—90; v.p. and assoc. gen. coun. Philip Morris Co. Inc., New York, NY, 1990—94, sr. v.p., litig., 1994—95, dep. gen. coun., 1995—2000; gen. coun. and sr. v.p. Altria Group, Inc. (formerly Philip Morris Co. Inc.), New York, NY, 2000—. Mem.: bd. dirs. NY City Opera, Neurosciences Inst., La Jolla, Calif. Office: Altria Group Inc 120 Park Ave New York NY 10017 Office Phone: 917-663-5000.

WALL, CLARENCE VINSON, state legislator; b. Athens, Ga., Oct. 17, 1947; s. Clarence Jacob and Fannie Lucile (Clark) W.; m. Linda Gail Mason, Dec. 6, 1969 (div. 1980); 1 child, Jeffrey Vinson. Grad. high sch., Lawrenceville, Ga., 1965. Rep. Ga. Ho. of Reps., Lawrenceville, 1973-82, 85-96. Staff sgt. Ga. Air N.G., 1967-73. Republican. Baptist. Home: 458 Springlake Rd Lawrenceville GA 30045-5090

WALL, DONALD ARTHUR, lawyer; b. Lafayette, Ind., Mar. 17, 1946; s. Dwight Arthur and Myra Virginia (Peavey) W.; m. Cheryn Lynn Heinen, Aug. 29, 1970; children: Sarah Lynn, Michael Donald. BA, Butler U., 1968; JD, Northwestern U., 1971. Bar: Ohio 1971, U.S. Dist. Ct. (no. dist.) Ohio 1973, U.S. Supreme Ct. 1980, Ariz. 1982, U.S. Dist. Ct. (no. dist.) W.Va. 1982, U.S. Ct. Appeals (6th cir.) 1982, U.S. Dist. Ct. Ariz. 1983, U.S. Ct. Appeals (9th and 10th cirs.) 1984, U.S. Ct. Appeals (5th cir.) 1988. Assoc. Squire, Sanders & Dempsey, Cleve., 1971-80, ptnr., 1980-82, Phoenix, 1983—. Spkr. at profl. meetings; program moderator. Contbr. articles to profl. jours. Trustee Ch. of the Saviour Day Ctr., Cleveland Heights, 1979-82; mem. adminstrv. bd. Ch. of Saviour, Cleveland Heights, 1980-83; fin. com. Paradise Valley (Ariz.) United Meth. Ch., 1986-87; bd. dirs., divsn. commr. North Scottsdale (Ariz.) Little League, 1983-92; bd. dirs. Epilepsy Found. N.E. Ohio, 1976-82, pres., 1981-82; bd. dirs. N.E. Cmty. Basketball Assn., 1993-99; bd. visitors U. Ariz. Law Sch., 1996—; bd. mgrs. Scottsdale-Paradise Valley YMCA, 1999—. Mem. ABA (torts and ins. practice and litigation sect., past chmn. r.r. law com., litigation sect.), Def. Rsch. Inst., Ariz. Bar Assn. (labor and trial practice sects.), Maricopa County Bar Assn., Ariz. Assn. Def. Counsel. Methodist. Office: Squire Sanders & Dempsey LLP 40 N Central Ave Ste 2700 Phoenix AZ 85004-4498 E-mail: dwall@ssd.com.

WALL, DUANE, lawyer; b. Amadarko, Okla., Jan. 10, 1940; BA, So. Nazarene U., 1962; JD, U. Okla., 1965; LLM, NYU, 1966. Bar: (N.Y.) 1969. Resident White & Case LLP, London, 1972—76, 1980—81, mng. ptnr. N.Y.C., 2000—. Mem.: ABA, Internat. Law Assn. (Am. br.), Assn. of Bar of City of N.Y., N.Y. State Bar Assn. Office: White & Case 1155 Ave of the Ams New York NY 10036

WALL, FREDERICK THEODORE, retired chemistry educator; b. Chisholm, Minn., Dec. 14, 1912; s. Peter and Fanny Maria (Rauhala) W.; m. Clara Elizabeth Vivian, June 5, 1940; children: Elizabeth Wall Ralston, Jane Vivian Wall. B.Chemistry, U. Minn., 1933, PhD, 1937. Mem. faculty chemistry dept. U. Ill., 1937-64, dean grad. coll., 1955-63; prof., chmn. dept. chemistry U. Calif., Santa Barbara, 1964-66, vice chancellor rsch., 1965-66; vice chancellor grad. studies and research, prof. chemistry U. Calif. at San Diego, 1966-69; exec. dir. Am. Chem. Soc., Washington, 1969-72; prof. chemistry Rice U., Houston, 1972-78. Pres. Assn. Grad. Schs., 1961; trustee Inst. Def. Analyses, 1962-64; mem. governing bd. Nat. Acad. Scis.-NRC, 1963- 67. Author: Chemical Thermodynamics, 1958; editor Jour. Phys. Chemistry, 1965-69. Mem. Am. Chem. Soc. (Pure Chemistry award 1945, dir. 1962-64), Finnish Chem. Soc. (corr.), Am. Acad. Arts and Scis., Nat. Acad. Scis. Achievements include early work on Monte Carlo computer simulation of macromolecular configurations and of basic reaction probabilities.

WALL, GERARD W. physiologist, researcher; b. NYC, Dec. 19, 1956; s. Marion Calbot-Wall. BSc, SUNY, Stony Brook, 1976—79; MSc, Kans. State U., 1980—82, PhD in Sci., 1982—86. Plant physiologist USDA, Phoenix, 1986—. Achievements include research in Global Change. Office: USDA 4331 E Broadway Rd Phoenix AZ 85040 Business E-Mail: gwall@uswcl.ars.ag.gov.

WALL, JANET G. state legislator; b. Portsmouth, N.H., Nov. 21, 1949; two children. BS, U. N.H., 1971. Rep. dist. 9 N.H. Ho. Reps. Water commr. Madbury, N.H., chmn. bd. dirs.; commr. Straf County exec. commn., 1989—, Straf County Coop. Extension Svc., 1992—; jud. com. N.H. Ho. Reps. Chmn. Heritage Collections Com., 1990—; govt. adv. commn. Peace Redevel.; dir. Madbury Hist. Preservation Project; project coord. Madbury Forum. Mem. Durham Hist.Soc. (past pres., bd. dirs., com. chair), Durham-Green Bay Rotary (dir. RADAR), Lee Hist. Soc., Durham Hist. Assn. Home: 4 Pudding Hill Rd Madbury NH 03820-7001 Office: NH State Senate State Capital Concord NH 03301

WALL, JEFF F. urban planner; b. Baton Rouge, July 26, 1950; s. Charles W. and Lula E. Wall; m. Mary Florea Wall; children: Lauren E., Jeff Troy, Mary Rebecca, Amanda K. Cantu. BSBA, La. State U., 1972; MBA, U. Dallas, 1980. CPA 1979; cert. pub. mgr. 2001, fraud examiner 1992. Mgmt. trainee Am. Bank & Trust, Baton Rouge, 1972—73; asst. cashier North Dallas Bank and Trust, Dallas, 1973—76; sr. credit analyst Mercantile Nat. Bank, 1976—77; loan officer Ford Motor Credit Co., 1977—80; v.p. InterFirst Bank, 1980—83; sr. v.p. 1st Bank Las Colinas, 1983—89; ops. specialist FDIC/RTC,

1990—95; cons. fin. industry pvt. practice, 1995—96; sr. v.p. Extraco Bank, Waco, 1996—99; v.p. Sunbelt Savings, Dallas, 1998—99; dir. housing and cmty. devel. svcs. City of Waco, Waco, 1999—. Adj. prof. Le Tourneau U., 1993; bd. dirs. Bus. Resource Ctr., Downtown Waco, Inc. Founding mem. Faith Covemant Svcs., Inc. Avocations: soccer, sports.

WALL, KENNETH E., JR., lawyer; b. Beaumont, Tex., Apr. 6, 1944; s. Kenneth E. and W. Geraldine (Peoples) W.; m. Marjorie Lee Hughes, Dec. 21, 1968; children— Barbara, Elizabeth, Kenneth. Grad. Lamar U., 1966, U. Tex.-Austin, 1969. Bar: Tex. 1969, U.S. Supreme Ct. 1979. Asst. city atty., Beaumont, 1969-73, city atty., 1973-84; with firm Olson & Olson, Houston, 1984—; dir. Tex. Mcpl. League Ins. Trust, 1979-84, vice chmn., 1983-84; counsel S.E. Tex. Regional Planning Commn., 1974, 76. Active Boy Scouts Am., Girl Scouts U.S.A. Mem. Nat. Inst. Mcpl. Law Officers (chmn. com. on local govt. pers. 1979-81, 82-84), State Bar Tex., Tex. City Attys. Assn. (pres. 1982-83), Jefferson County Bar Assn. (dir. 1975-77), Houston Bar Assn., Phi Delta Phi. Methodist. Office: 2727 Allen Pkwy Houston TX 77019 Office Phone: 713-533-3800. Business E-Mail: kwall@olsonolson.com.

WALL, LARRY, computer scientist, web programmer; m. Gloria Biggar, 1979; children: Heidi, Geneva, Lewis, Aron. Grad., Seattle Pacific U., 1976. With Seagate, NetLabs; programmer NASA Jet Propulsion Lab., Pasadena, Calif., Unisys; rschr., developer O'Reilly & Assocs., Sebastopol, Calif. Recipient award, Free Software Found., 1998. Achievements include creating PERL (Practical Extraction and Report Language) Script. Office: OReilly and Assocs 1005 Gravenstein Hwy North Sebastopol CA 95472*

WALL, M. DANNY, financial services company executive; BArch, N.D. State U., 1963. Exec. dir. Urban Renewal Agy., Fargo, N.D., 1964-71, Salt Lake City Redevel. Agy., 1971-75; dir. legis. Office U.S. Senator Jake Garn, Washington, 1975-78; minority staff dir. Senate Com. for Banking, Housing and Urban Affairs, Washington, 1979-80, staff dir., 1980-86, Rep. staff dir., 1987; chmn. Fed. Home Loan Bank Bd./Fed. Home Loan Mortgage Corp., Washington, 1987-89; dir. Office Thrift Supervision (formerly Fed. Home Loan Bank Bd.), 1989-90; fin. svcs. cons., 1990—2003; sr. v.p. Dougherty Funding LLC, 1997—2003; pres. GMAC Comml. Mortgage Bank. Office Phone: 801-567-2686. E-mail: dan_wall@gmaccm.com.

WALL, MARK EMANUEL, banker, engineer, consultant; b. N.Y.C., Mar. 12, 1937; s. Jacob Bernard and Eva (Goldstein) W.; m. Diane Nachbar, Dec. 5, 1962; children: Michael Edward, Stephen Philip. BEE cum laude, CCNY, 1957; M in Engring., Moore Sch., 1962; postgrad., N.Y.U., 1962-68. Registered profl. engr., N.J., N.Y. With tech. staff RCA Labs., Astro Elec. Div., Princeton, N.J., 1957-62; dir. R&D Computer Scis. Corp., Paramus, N.J., 1962-75; pres. Tech. Fin. Svcs., Fair Lawn, N.J., 1975-80; dir. digital sys. Western Union Telegraph co., Upper Saddle River, N.J., 1977-81; v.p. Chase Manhattan Bank N.a., N.Y.C., 1981-87, NYNEX Corp., White Plains, N.Y., 1987-94; v.p. engring. NYNEX Allink Co.; v.p., chief tech. The Data Group; dir. network mgmt. engring. Info. Sys. Group; prin. ALLMARK Internat., Ltd., 1994—. Vis. assoc. prof. Stevens Inst. Tech., Hoboken, N.J., 1979-81; adv. bd. Bramson ORT Inst., N.Y.C., 1980-84. Trustee Radburn Assn., Fair Lawn, 1981-85, pres. bd. trustees, 1985. Mem. IEEE, Eta Kappa Nu. Office Phone: 201-791-9535. E-mail: allmarkint@hotmail.com.

WALL, MATTHEW J., JR., surgeon, research scientist; b. June 22, 1958; s. Matthew J. and Anne V. W.; m. Barbara M. Wall; children: Christopher Matthew, Patrick Joseph. BS, Rice U., Houston, 1980; MD, Baylor Coll. Medicine, Houston, 1984. Diplomate Am. Bd. Surgery, Am. Bd. Thoracic Surgeons, Am. Bd. Surg. Critical Care. Resident gen. surgery Baylor Affiliated Hosp., Houston, 1984-89, resident cardiothoracic surgery, 1989-91; asst. prof. surgery Baylor Coll. Medicine, Houston, 1991-95, assoc. prof. surgery, 1995—, prof. Michael E. DeBayey dept. surgery, 2004—, dep. program dir. thoracic surgery residency, 1999—, program dir. surg. critical care residency, 1999—; dir. trauma and critical care svcs. Ben Taub Gen. Hosp., Houston, 1993-99, dep. chief surgery, 1993—, exec. dir. trauma and critical care, 2000—, chief thoracic surgery, 2000—. Contbr. chpts. to books, articles to jours. Fellow ACS (chair south Tex. 1994-2001), Am. Assn. Surgery Trauma, Soc. Thoracic Surgeons; mem. AAAS, Assn. Advancement Med. Instrumentation, Assn. Academic Surgeons, Tex. Surg. Soc., Harris County Med. Soc. Office: Baylor Coll Medicine One Baylor Plz Houston TX 77030

WALL, ROBERT J. author, researcher; b. N.Y.C., June 1, 1936; s. Joseph L. and Kathleen W. BA, CCNY, 1978; diploma, N.Y. Sch. Interior Design, 1995. Archtl. renderer ann. announcement circulars N.Y. Soc. Archs., 1960s. With U.S. Army, 1955-57, ret. Mem. Disable Am. Vets. (life), Am. Legion (life). Roman Catholic. Avocations: reading, writing, collecting books, collecting art work. Home: 12401 Davis Blvd Fort Myers FL 33905-1701

WALL, SONJA ELOISE, nursing administrator; b. Santa Cruz, Calif., Mar. 28, 1938; d. Ray Theothornton and Reva Mattie (Wingo) W.; m. Edward Gleason Holmes, Aug. 1959 (div. Jan. 1968); children: Deborah Lynn, Lance Edward; m. John Aspesi, Sept. 1969 (div. 1977); children: Sabrina Jean, Daniel John; m. Kenneth Talbot LaBoube, Nov. 1, 1978 (div. 1989); 1 child, Tiffany Amber; m. Charles Borsic, July 2002. BA, San Jose Jr. Coll., 1959; BS, Madonna Coll., 1967; postgrad., Wayne State U., 1967—68; student, U. Mich., 1968—70. RN, Calif., Mich., Colo. Staff nurse Santa Clara Valley Med. Ctr., San Jose, Calif., 1959-67, U. Mich. Hosp., Ann Arbor, 1967-73, Porter and Swedish Med. Hosp., Denver, 1973-77, Laurel Grove Hosp., Castro Valley, Calif., 1977-79, Advent Hosp., Ukiah, Calif., 1984-86; motel owner LaBoube Enterprises, Fairfield, Point Arena, Willits, Calif., 1979—; staff nurse Northridge Hosp., L.A., 1986-87, Folsom State Prison, Calif., 1987; co-owner, mgr. nursing registry Around the Clock Nursing Svc., Ukiah, 1985—; critical care staff nurse Kaiser Permanente Hosp., Sacramento, 1986-89; nurse Snowline Hospice, Placerville, Calif., 1989-92; carepoint home care and travel nurse Hosp. Staffing Svcs. Inc., Placerville, 1992-94, interim home health nurse, 1994-95; nurse Finders Home Health Care, 1996; owner Sunshine Manor Residential Care Home, Placerville, 1995—, Rainbow Manor Residential Care Home, 2000—02; psychol. and trauma RN Folsom State Prison, 2002—04, Calif. Dept. Mental Health, Calif., 2004—. Owner Royal Plantation Petites Miniature Horse Farm. Contbr. articles to profl. jours. Leader Coloma 4-H, 1987-91; mem. mounted divsn. El Dorado County Search and Rescue, 1991-93; docent Calif. Marshall Gold Discovery State Hist. Park, Coloma, Calif. Mem. AACN, NAFE, Oncology Nurses Assn., Soc. Critical Care Medicine, Am. Heart Assn. (CPR trainer, recipient awards), Calif. Bd. RNs, Calif. Nursing Rev., Calif. Critical Care Nurses, Soc. Critical Care Nurses, Alzheimers Aid Soc. No. Calif., Am. Motel Assn. (beautification and remodeling award 1985), Nat. Hospice Nurses Assn., Cmty. Residential Care Assn. Calif., Soroptimist Internat. Calif., Am. Miniature Horse Assn. (winner nat. grand championship 1981-83, 85, 89), DAR (Jobs Daus. hon. mem.), C. of C. of El Dorado County, Kiwanis, Cameron Park Country Club. Republican. Episcopalian. Avocations: pinto, paint and miniature horses, real estate development, swimming. Home and Office: Sunshine Manor Residental Care Home Care and Around Clock Nursing Svc 3112 Washington St Placerville CA 95667-5825 Fax: 530-622-2233. Office Phone: 530-622-3940. E-mail: sunshinemanor@directcon.net.

WALLA, CATHERINE ANNE, nursing administrator, educator; b. Chgo., Oct. 18, 1948; d. Louis Bernard and Mary Louise W.; m. Robert Joseph Murphy, July 2, 1972 (div. Oct. 1979); 1 child, Meghan Anne. BS, Loyola U., 1971, BSN, MA, 1978; M of Nursing, UCLA, 1988. RN Calif. Staff nurse Wadsworth VA Hosp., L.A., 1978-79; charge, staff nurse UCLA Med. Ctr., L.A., 1979-81; clin. rsch. nurse specialist L.A. County & U. So. Calif. Med. Ctr., L.A., 1981-84; asst. prof. Bethune-Cookman Coll., Daytona Beach, Fla., 1984-86; dir. perinatal rsch. L.A. County & U. Soc. Calif., 1986-90; coord. ob-gyn. rsch. Cedars-Sinai Med. Ctr., L.A., 1990—; asst. clin. prof. UCLA Sch. Nursing, 1990—. Cons. in field. Co-author: (chpts.) Maternity Nursing, 1991, 97, Diagnostic Medical Sonography, 1992, 97, Protocols for High Risk Pregnancy, 1996, Genetic Disorders and Pregnancy Outcome, 1997; Fetal Therapy, 1999; contbr. articles to profl. jours. Rsch. grantee Bethune Cookman Coll., 1985. Mem. APHA, Am. Inst. Ultrasound Medicine, Monterey Bay Aquarium, Long Beach Aquarium. Avocations: herptology, salt water aquariums, hiking, fictional writing, multi-cultural cooking. Home: 29044 Lake Dr Agoura Hills CA 91301-2947 Office: Cedars-Sinai Med Ctr Dept Ob-Gyn 8700 Beverly Blvd Los Angeles CA 90048-1865

WALLACE, ANDERSON, JR., lawyer, educator; b. Cleve., Sept. 24, 1939; s. Anderson and Agatha Lee (Culpepper) Wallace; m. Kristine Lee Gough; children: Anderson III, Whitney, Nicole Belcher. BA, George Washington U., 1962, JD, 1964, LLM, 1966. Bar: Tex. 68, U.S. Dist. Ct. (no. dist.) Tex. 68, U.S. Ct. Claims 68, U.S. Tax Ct. 68, U.S. Ct. Appeals (5th cir.) 68, U.S. Supreme Ct. 71, U.S. Ct. Appeals (11th cir.) 81. Program mgmt. asst. NASA, Washington, 1962—64; atty. U.S. Dept. Treasury, Washington, 1964—66; tax atty. Price Waterhouse & Co., Atlanta, 1966—67; tax ptnr. Jackson, Walker, Winstead, Cantwell & Miller, Dallas, 1967—84; dir. in charge tax dept. Baker, Mills & Glast, P.C., Dallas, 1984—93; pres. Anderson Wallace, Jr., P.C., Attys., Dallas, 1993—. Instr. Sch. Law So. Meth. U. Trustee S.W. Mus. Sci. and Tech., Dallas, 1974—, Girls Found. Dallas Inc.; chmn. Inst. on Employee Benefits, Southwestern Found., 1976. Mem.: ABA. Office: 3328 Purdue Ave Ste 100 Dallas TX 75225-7635 Office Phone: 214-739-1714. E-mail: awallacejr@sbcglobal.net.

WALLACE, ANDREW GROVER, physician, educator, medical school dean; b. Columbus, Ohio, Mar. 22, 1935; s. Richard Homes and Eleanor Bradley (Grover) W.; m. Kathleen Barrick Altvater, June 22, 1957; children: Stephen Andrew, Michael Bradley, Kathleen Claude. BS, Duke U., 1958, MD, 1959. Diplomate Am. Bd. Internal Medicine. Intern medicine Duke U. Hosp., Durham, N.C., 1959-60, asst. resident, 1960-61; fellow NIH, Bethesda, Md., 1961-63; chief resident medicine Duke U., Durham, 1963-64, asst. prof., 1965-67, assoc. prof., 1967-71, chief, divsn. cardiology, 1970-81, prof. medicine, 1971—, Walter Kempner prof. medicine, 1973; vice chancellor health affairs, chief exec. officer Duke U. Hosp., Durham, 1981-87; v.p. health affairs Duke U., 1987-90; dean Dartmouth Med. Sch., Hanover, N.H., 1990-98. V.p. for health affairs Dartmouth Coll., 1990-98; cons. program project com., cardiology adv. com. and pharmacology study sect. Nat. Heart and Lung Inst., cardiovascular merit rev. bd. VA. Co-author: (with R.S. Williams) Biological Effects of Physical Activity, 1989; mem. editl. bd. Am. Jour. of Physiology, 1965-70, Jour. of Pharmacology and Exptl. Therapeutics, 1966-71, Jour. of Molecular and Cellular Cardiology, 1970-75, Jour. of Clin. Investigation, 1973-78. Pres. Durham YMCA Swim Assn., 1975-77; bd. dirs. Durham C. of C.; co-chmn. Nat. Jr. Olympics, 1976. Markle scholar, 1965-70 Mem. AAAS, AAMC, NAS, Inst. of Medicine, Am. Fedn. for Clin. Rsch. (coun.), Am. Soc. Internal Medicine, Am. Soc. Clin. Investigation, Am. Heart Assn. (coun. on clin. cardiology), Am. Physiol. Soc., Biomed. Engring. Soc., Soc. Med. Adminstrs., Assn. Am. Med. Colls. (adv. com. electronic residency 1992-94, generalist initiative 1993-95, mission and orgn. 1994-2000, exec. coun. 1996-98), N.H. Med. Soc., So. Soc. Clin. Investigation. Home: 2112 Faucette Mill Rd Hillsborough NC 27278-7553

WALLACE, ANTHONY FRANCIS CLARKE, anthropologist, educator; b. Toronto, Ont., Can., Apr. 15, 1923; s. Paul A.W. and Dorothy Eleanor (Clarke) W.; m. Betty Louise Shillott, Dec. 1, 1942; children: Anthony, Daniel, Sun Ai, Samuel, Cheryl, Joseph. BA, U. Pa., 1948, MA, 1949, PhD, 1950; L.H.D. (hon.), U. Chgo., 1983. Instr. anthropology Bryn Mawr Coll., 1948-50; asst. instr. anthropology U. Pa., research sec. Behavioral Research Council, 1951-55; research asst. prof. U. Pa., 1952-55, vis. assoc. prof., 1955-61, prof., 1961—, chmn. dept., 1961-71, Geraldine R. Segal prof. Am. social thought, 1980-83, Univ. prof. anthropology, 1983-88, prof. emeritus, 1988—. Sr. research assoc. anthropology Eastern Pa. Psychiat. Inst., 1955-60, dir. clin. research, 1960-61, med. research scientist, III, 1961-80; mem. tech. adv. com. N.J. Psychiat. Inst., 1958; cons. disaster studies NRC, 1956-57; cons. Phila. Housing Authority, 1952; mem. research adv. com. Commonwealth Mental Health Research Found., 1960-61, U.S. Office Edn., 1965-68; mem. behavioral scis. study sect. NIMH, 1964-68; mem. NRC, 1963-66; mem. various adv. coms. NIMH, 1962—; mem. social sci. adv. council NSF, 1969-72 Author: King of the Delawares: Teedyuscung, 1700-1763, 1949, Culture and Personality, 1961, rev. edit., 1970, Religion: An Anthropological View, 1966, Death and Rebirth of the Seneca, 1970, Rockdale: The Growth of an American Village in the Early Industrial Revolution, 1978, Social Context of Innovation, 1983, new ed., 2003. St. Clair, 1987, The Long, Bitter Trail, 1993, Jefferson and the Indians, 1999, Revitalizations and Mazeways, 2003. Bd. mgrs. Founds. Fund for Research in Psychiatry, 1969-71. Served AUS, 1942-45. Recipient Bancroft prize in Am. History, 1979, Dexter prize in History of Technology, 1989, Caroline Bancroft prize in history, 2000; Guggenheim fellow, 1978-79 Fellow Am. Anthrop. Assn. (pres. 1971-72),; mem. Nat. Acad. Scis., Am. Philos. Soc., Am. Acad. Arts and Scis. Home: 614 Convent Rd Aston PA 19014-1208 Office: Univ PA Dept Anthropology 33rd and Spruce Sts Philadelphia PA 19104

WALLACE, ARTHUR, JR., retired college dean; b. Muskogee, Okla., June 12, 1939; s. Arthur and Edna (Collins) W.; m. Claudina Young, Oct. 4, 1969; children: Dwayne, Jon, Charles. BS, Langston U., 1960; MS, Okla. State U., Stillwater, 1962, PhD, 1964. Dir. commodity rsch. Gen. Foods Corp., White Plains, N.Y., 1964-67; v.p., sr. economist Merrill Lynch & Lionel D. Edie & Co., N.Y.C., 1968-71; econ. cons. Wall St. fin. instns. Group IV Econs., N.Y.C., 1972-76; mgr. U.S. and Can. econs. Internat. Paper Co., N.Y.C., 1976-78, chief economist, 1978-82, dir. corp. affairs and policy analysis, 1982-83, corp. sec. Purchase, N.Y., 1983-87, v.p., corp. sec., 1987-93; pres. Internat. Paper Co. Found., 1983-93; dean coll. bus. San Francisco State U., 1993-98; ret.

WALLACE, BARBARA BROOKS, writer; b. Soochow, China, Dec. 3, 1922; came to U.S., 1938; d. Otis Frank and Nicia Brooks; m. James Wallace Jr., Feb. 27, 1954; 1 child, James V. BA, UCLA, 1945. Script sec. Foote, Cone & Belding, Hollywood, Calif., 1946-49; tchr. Wright MacMahon Secretarial Sch., Beverly Hills, Calif., 1949-50; head fund drive Commerce and Industry Divsn. ARC, San Francisco, 1950-52. Author: Claudia, 1969 (Nat. League of Am. Pen Women Juvenile Book award 1970), Andrew the Big Deal, 1970, The Trouble with Miss Switch, 1971, Victoria, 1973, Can Do, Missy Charlie, 1974, The Secret Summer of L.E.B. (Nat. League of Am. Pen Women Juvenile Book award 1974), Julia and the Third Bad Thing, 1975, Palmer Patch, 1976, Hawkins, 1977, Peppermints in the Parlor, 1980 (William Allen White award 1983), The Contest Kid Strikes Again, 1980, Hawkins and the Soccer Solution, 1981, Miss Switch to the Rescue, 1981, Hello, Claudia, 1982, Claudia and Duffy, 1982, The Barrel in the Basement, 1985, Argyle, 1987, 92, Perfect Acres, Inc., 1988, The Twin in the Tavern, 1993 (Edgar award Mystery Writers Am. 1994), Cousins in the Castle, 1996, Sparrows in the Scullery, 1997 (Edgar award 1998), Ghosts in the Gallery, 2000, Secret in St. Something, 2001, Miss Switch Online, 2002, The Perils of Peppermints, 2003. Mem. Children's Book Guild of Washington, Alpha Phi. Episcopalian. Home and Office: 104 Stewart Ave #2 Alexandria VA 22301-1173 E-mail: jimbob4@comcast.net.

WALLACE, BECKY WHITLEY, protective services official; BA in Criminal Justice, Montgomery C.C. Police officer City of Troy (N.C.), 1974-75; deputy sheriff Montgomery County (N.C), 1975-78, 82-94; alcohol law enforcement agt. N.C. Dept. Crime Control & Pub. Safety, Greensboro, 1978-82; U.S. marshal N.C., 1994—. Recipeint Leadership N.C. Stanley Frank award, Breaking the Glass Ceiling award Nat. Ctr. Women in Policing; named Disting. Woman of N.c., Coun. Women. Mem. Fed. Law Enforcement Officers' Assn., N.C. Women's Law Enforcement Assn., Nat. Sheriffs Assn., N.C. Sheriff's Assn., Montgomery County Law Enforcement Assn., Profl. Women's Assn. Office: US Post Office 324 W Market St Greensboro NC 27401-2544

WALLACE, BEN, professional basketball player; b. White Hall, Ala., Sept. 10, 1974; m. Chanda Wallace. Student, Va. Union, 1996. Basketball player Wash. Bullets, 1996—99, Orlando Magic, 1999—2000; forward-ctr. Det. Pistons, 2000—. Mem. USA Team. Named NBA Defensive Player of Yr., 2002, 2003; named to NBA All-Defensive Team, 2002, 2003, 2004. Achievements include mem. of NBA Championship Team, 2004. Office: Palace of Auburn Hills 2 Championship Dr Auburn Hills MI 48326

WALLACE, CAROL, editor at large; b. Chgo. BS in Comm., U. Ill., 1971. With Phila. Daily News, Rochester Times-Union, Tribune Pub. Co., N.Y. Daily News, N.Y.C., 1979—82; sr. writer People Mag., N.Y.C., 1982—85, sr. editor, 1985—88, 1990—92, asst. mng. editor, 1991—94, dep. mng. editor, 1994—97, mng. editor, 1997—2002; editor at large Time Inc., N.Y.C., 2003—. Writer, host The Wallace Report for Daytime, Heart/ABC Women's Network, 1982—84; editor Us Mag., 1988—90. Co-author: The Portable Best Friend, 1996. Recipient Front Page award, Newswomen's Club N.Y., 1982. Office: Time Inc Rockefeller Ctr New York NY 10020-1393

WALLACE, DANIEL, writer; Author: Big Fish, 1998, Ray in Reverse, 2000, Watermelon King, 2003, Crossroads, 2004; contbr. stories to mags. Office: Penguin Publicity 375 Hudson St New York NY 10014*

WALLACE, DON, JR., law educator; b. Vienna, Apr. 23, 1932; s. Don and Julie (Baer) Wallace; m. Daphne Mary Wickham, 1963; children: Alexandra Creed, Sarah Anne, Benjamin James. BA with high honors, Yale U., 1953; LL.B. cum laude, Harvard U., 1957. Bar: N.Y. 1957, D.C. 1978. Assoc. Fleischmann, Jaeckle, Stokes and Hitchcock, N.Y.C., 1959-60, Paul, Weiss, Rifkind, Wharton and Garrison, N.Y.C., 1957-58, 60-62; rsch. asst. to faculty mem. Harvard Law Sch., Cambridge, Mass., 1958-59; regional legal adv. Middle East AID, Dept. State, 1963-65, dep. asst. gen. counsel, 1965-66; assoc. prof. law Georgetown U. Law Ctr., Washington, 1966-71, prof., 1971—2002; chmn. Internat. Law Inst., Washington, 1969—; adj./emeritus prof. Georgetown U. Law Ctr., Washington, 2002—. Cons. AID, 1966-70, UN Centre on Transnat. Corps., 1977-78; counsel Wald, Harkrader & Ross, Washington, 1978-86, Arnold & Porter, 1986-89, Shearman & Sterling, 1989-98, Morgan, Lewis & Bockius, 1998—; legal advisor State of Qatar, 1979-82; chmn. adv. com. on tech. and world trade Office of Tech. Assessment, U.S. Congress, 1976-79; mem. Sec. of State's Adv. Com. on Pvt. Internat. Law, 1979—; mem. U.S. del. UN Conf. on State Succession in Respect of Treaties, Vienna, 1978; mem. U.S. del. new internat. econ. order working group UN Commn. Internat. Trade Law, Vienna, 1981—; vis. com. Harvard Law Sch., 1996-97; mem. panel of judges World Trade Orgn., 1996-2000. Co-author: Internat. Business and Economics: Law and Policy; author: International Regulation of Multinational Corporations, 1976, Dear Mr. President: The Needed Turnaround in America's International Economic Affairs, 1984; editor: A Lawyer's Guide to International Business Transactions, 1977-87; contbr. numerous articles on internat. trade and law to profl. jours., books revs. on law and bus. to profl. jours. Coord. Anne Arundel County (Md.) Dem. Nat. Com., 1972-79; sec. Chesapeake Found., 1972-73; nat. chmn. Law Profs. for Bush and Quayle, 1988, 92, for Dole and Kemp, 1996; v.p., bd. govs. UNIDROIT Found., Rome, 1997—. Fulbright fellow, 1967, Eisenhower Exch. fellow, 1976. Mem. ABA (chmn. sect. internat. law 1978-79, ho of dels. 1982-84, mem. adv. bd. Ctrl. European and Eurasian Law Initiative), Am. Law Inst., Internat. Law Assn., Shaybani Soc. of Internat. Law (v.p.), Cosmos Club, Met. Club, Coun. Postgraduate Sch. Internat. Bus. and European Law, European Ctr. Peace and Devel. Home: 2800 35th St NW Washington DC 20007-1411 Office: Georgetown U Law Ctr 600 New Jersey Ave NW Washington DC 20001-2022 Office Phone: 202-247-6006. E-mail: wallace@ili.org.

WALLACE, DONALD JOHN, III, rancher; b. Houston, May 17, 1941; s. D. J., Jr. and Doris Jill (Gano) Wallace; m. Patricia Anne McShane, Sept. 3, 1964 (div. 1984); children: Donald John IV, Megan; m. Nena Jo Isenhower, June 1, 1985 (div. 1989); 1 child, Andrew; m. Kay Fulkerson, May 31, 1997. BBA in Mktg., Texas A&M U., 1963. Regional sales dir. Orkin Exterminating Co., Inc., Dallas, 1977-79, br. mgr., 1979-80, dist. mgr., 1980-83, comml. region mgr., 1983-85, regional sales dir., 1985-86; owner Omega Telex, Dallas, 1986-88; rancher Valley View, Tex., 1988—. Mem. Tex. Structural Pest Control Bd., Austin, 1983—84; leader Big Mineral Trail Riders Club Boy Scouts Am.; bd. dirs. Frank Buck Zoo, Gainesville, Tex., 1997—98; pres. Frank Buck Zool. Soc.; bd. dirs. North Tex. Med. Found. Mem.: Dalla Pest Control Assn., Tex. Pest Control Assn., Nat. Pest Control Assn. Republican. Roman Catholic. Avocations: hiking, fishing, hunting, skiing, horseback riding. Home: 1034 Trails End Valley View TX 76272-6114 Personal E-mail: donandkay@cooke.net.

WALLACE, EDNA MARIE, paralegal; b. Indpls., July 22, 1945; d. William T. and Agnes L. (Pierce) Branson; m. James Michael Wallace; children: Penny Sue Wallace-Steele, Brandi Michael Wallace-Coffin. Paralegal Cert., Am. Inst. Paralegal Studies, Oak Brook Terrace, Ill., 1988. Paralegal, office adminstr. Baldwin & Baldwin, Danville, Ind., 1985—90; paralegal Tucker, Surface, Fehribach, Indpls., 1990—92; paralegal, office adminstr. Hebenstreit & Moberly, 1992—96; paralegal Kroger, Gardis & Regas, 1996—2002, Whitham, Hebenstreit & Zubek, LLP, 2002—. Presenter in field. Paralegal adv. bd. St. Mary of the Woods Coll., 1999—. Mem. ABA (assoc.), Nat. Fedn. Paralegal Assns. (registered paralegal), Indpls. Bar Assn. (chair paralegal exec. com. 1998-2000, 2002-03, Legal Awareness com., Placement com., CLE comm., Paralegal of Yr. 1999), Ind. State Bar Assn. (paralegal com.), Ind. Paralegal Assn. (bd. dirs. legis. sect. chair 1999-2003, chair ethics sect. 2000-03, Lifetime Achievement award 2002), Bus./Profl. Women, Order Eastern Star, Job's Daus. (adult leader 1986-2000, bd. dirs. ednl. found. 1997-2000), Epsilon Sigma Alpha (pres. chpt. 1988-90). Republican. Baptist. Office: Whitham Hebenstreit & Zubek LLP 151 N Delaware St # 2000 Indianapolis IN 46204 E-mail: emw@whzlaw.com.

WALLACE, EDWARD L. biomedical researcher, consultant; b. Orange, N.J., Feb. 27, 1921; s. Thomas Leo and Mary Frances Wallace; m. Mary Ann Ostrowski, Feb. 3, 1980; children: Thomas Edward, Patricia Vargas. PhD, U. Chgo., 1957. Asst. prof. Harvard U., Cambridge, Mass., 1954—55; prof. U. Chgo., 1957—58, SUNY, Amherst, 1959—90; pres. Ctr. for Mgmt. Systems, Naples, Fla., 1983—. Rsch. cons., Williamsville, NY, 1960—82, Ctr. for Mgmt. Systems, Naples, Fla., 1983—; sci. advisor Charlotte Geyer Found., Sarasota, Fla., 1995—; ptnr. Talisman Ltd., Vienna, 1998—. Author: Securing a Safer Blood Supply. Mem. strategic planning com. ARC, Washington, 1992—94; project leader: health care task force Aspen Inst., Aspen, Colo., 1995—96; vice chmn. biomed. svcs. com. ARC, Washington, 1986—89; chmn., bd. dirs. Nat. Blood Data Resource Ctr., Bethesda, Md., 1997—2002. 1st lt. USAAF, 1942—45, ETO. Fellow: AAAS; mem.: Nat. Blood Data Resource Ctr. (chmn. bd. dirs. 1997—2002), Am. Assn. Blood Banks (Disting. Svc. award 1997), Beta Gamma Sigma. Avocations: tennis, photography. Home: 485 Spinnaker Ct Naples FL 34102 Office: Ctr for Mgmt Systems 485 Spinnaker Ct Naples FL 34102 Personal E-mail: tw@naples.net.

WALLACE, EDWIN RUTHVEN, IV, psychiatrist, neuropsychiatrist psychotherapist; b. Portsmouth, Va., Mar. 10, 1950; s. Edwin Ruthven III and Laura Essie (Catron) W.; m. Laura Martin Elmore, May 13, 1972; children: Laura Martin, Edwin Ruthven V. BS cum laude, U. S.C., 1970, BA magna cum laude, 1976; MD, Med. U. S.C., 1973; MA summa cum laude, Johns Hopkins U., 1978. Diplomate Am. Bd. Psychiatry and Neurology. Intern in neurology Richland Meml. Hosp., Columbia, S.C.; resident in psychiatry and neurology William S. Hall Psychiat. Inst., Columbia, S.C., 1973-75, chief resident, 1975-76; postdoctoral fellow in neuropsychiatry and hosp. psychiatry Yale U. Sch. Medicine, New Haven, 1977; postdoctoral fellow in history of science and medicine Sch. Medicine Johns Hopkins U., Balt., 1978; asst. prof. neuropsychiatry Sch. Medicine U. S.C., Columbia, 1978-80; asst. prof. psychiatry Yale U. Sch. Medicine, New Haven, 1980-82; assoc. prof., vice chmn. dept. psychiatry & health behavior Med. Coll. Ga., Augusta, 1982-87, prof. psychiatry and health behavior, 1987-95, acting chmn. Dept. Psychiatry, 1987-90; prof. social work U. Ga. Grad. Sch., Athens, 1988—; clin. prof. psychiatry and health behavior Med. Coll. Ga., 1995—; rsch. prof. bioethics and med. humanities U. S.C., 1995—, adj. prof. history, philosophy & religious studies, 1996—. Instr. in neuropsychiatry U. S.C. Sch. Medicine, 1975-76; cons. Army Health Svc. Command, U.S. Army Med. Corps, 1986-94, VA Hosps. Augusta, 1988-94; mem. history and libr. com., Am. Psychiat. Assn., Washington, 1986-89; vis. scholar Com. on Conceptual Foundations of Sci., U. Chgo., 1990. Author: Dynamic Psychiatry in Theory and Practice, 1983, Spanish edit., 1991, Freud and Anthropology: a History and Reappraisal, 1983 Japanese edit., 1993, Historiography and Causation in Psychoanalysis, 1985, Italian edit., 1991, 140 articles and chpts. in scholarly

and profl. jours. and edited books and encyclopedias; sr. editor: Essays in the History of Psychiatry, 1980; mem. editl. bd. Bull. of History of Medicine, Balt., 1980-88, Second Opinion: Jour. Health, Faith and Ethics, Chgo., 1987-95, Rev. of Psychoanalytic Books, 1995-97; sr. edit. bd. Philosophy, Psychiatry and Psychology, 1993—. Trustee J.B. White Nat. Charitable Found., Augusta, 1988-98; co-capt. Inner City Soup Kitchens, Augusta, 1984-87. Recipient NEH fellowship, 1990. Mem. AAAS, AMA, Am. Hist. Assn., Am. Assn. for the History of Medicine, Am. Coll. Psychiatrists, Assn. for Advancement of Philospy and Psychiatry (co-founder, exec. com.), Group for the Advancement of Psychiatry, Phi Beta Kappa, Alpha Epsilon Delta. Episcopalian. Fax: 803-777-4575.

WALLACE, EMILY MITCHELL, writer, editor, educator; d. George Lafayette and Prewitt Carlisle (Evans) Mitchell; m. Gregory Merrill Harvey, June 14, 1969; m. Robert Arthur Wallace, June 8, 1954 (div. 1964). BA, Southwest Mo. State, 1958; MA, Bryn Mawr Coll., Pa., 1959, PhD, 1965. Tutor, history and lit. Curtis Inst. of Music, Phila., 1957—58, chair English dept., 1976—78, 1979—83; lit. tchr. The Shipley Sch., Bryn Mawr, Pa., 1959—60; instr. to asst. prof. U. Pa., 1962—67; vis. asst. prof. Swarthmore Coll., Pa., 1967—68, 1969—70; interdisciplinary seminar leader Yale U., 1979; rsch. assoc. Ctr. Visual Culture Bryn Mawr Coll., 2003—. Mem. sponsoring com. Marianne Moore Fund for Poetry, Bryn Mawr Coll., 1975—; mem. adv. com. Rosenbach Mus. and Libr., Phila., 1980—; curriculum cons. Cooper Union of Art, Sci. and Tech., NY, 1984—85; interdisciplinary rsch. scholar in poetry and visual arts; writer photographic essays and multimedia lectrs. scholarly and acad. audiences, double-screen lectrs. confs. and symposia univs. and mus. Author: (book) A Bibliography of William Carlos Williams, 1969; guest editor (periodical) W.C. Williams Review, Centennial Issue, 1983, PAIDEUMA (Spcl. James Laughlin Vol.), 2002; author: (photo essay) Youthful Days and Costly Hours: The Education of Ol' Ez and Billy Williams at Penn, U. Pa. Conf. Papers, 1983, Athena's Owls: The Education of Marianne Moore and Hilda Doolittle, Bryn Mawr '09' in Poesis, 1985, Some Friends of Ezra Pound, 1986, Saffron Honey: A Love Song by William Carlos Williams, 2001, Why Not Spirits?-The Universe is Alive in Ezra Pound and China, 2003. Mem. bd. dirs. Am. Found., Bok Tower, Fla., 1976—86; shareholder The Libr. Co., Phila., 1981—; lifetime mem. Friends of the Bryn Mawr Coll. Libr., Pa., 1996—; mem. Yale Libr. Assocs., Franklin Inn., Phila. Grantee Workman Traveling fellowship, Bryn Mawr Coll., Eng., France, Italy, 1961—62, AAUW fellowship, Am. Assocs. of Univ. Women, 1968—69, Inaugural Beinecke fellow, Yale U., 1987, Everett Helm Vis. fellow, Lilly Libr., Ind. U., 2003. Mem.: Modern Lang. Assn., Harvard Humanities Ctr. Faculty Arts and Scis., Conn. Acad. Arts and Sci., Assn. Lit. Scholars and Critics, Emily Dickinson Soc., H.D. Soc., Ezra Pound Soc., William Carlos Williams Soc. (first pres.), Marianne Moore Soc., Wallace Stevens Soc., Henry James Soc., Ernest Hemingway Soc., Merion Cricket Club. Democrat. Avocations: chess, music, travel, gardening, tennis. Home: 1939 Panama St Philadelphia PA 19103-6609 Office Phone: 610-718-0503. E-mail: emwallace@aol.com.

WALLACE, F. BLAKE, aerospace executive, mechanical engineer; b. Phoenix, Jan. 10, 1933; BMechE, Calif. Inst. Tech., 1955; MS in Engring., Ariz. State U., 1963, PhD in Engring., 1967. Preliminary design engr. Pratt & Whitney, East Hartford, Conn., 1955-59; chief engr. advanced tech. Garrett Corp., Phoenix, 1959-80; mgr. advanced plans and programs Aircraft Engine Group GE, Evendale, Ohio, 1981-83; gen. mgr. Allison div. GM, Indpls., 1983-93, v.p., 1987-93; chmn. & CEO Allison Engine Co., Indpls., 1993-95; retired, 1995. Author numerous tech. papers. Fellow AIAA (chmn. air breathing propulsion tech. com. 1977-78, Air Breathing Propulsion award 1991), U.S. Advanced Ceramic Assn. (chmn. 1987-89).

WALLACE, FRANKLIN SHERWOOD, lawyer, director; b. Bklyn., Nov. 24, 1927; s. Abraham Charles and Jennie (Etkin) Wolowitz; m. Eleanor Ruth Pope, Aug. 23, 1953; children: Julia Diane, Charles Andrew. Student, U. Wis., 1943-45; BS cum laude, U.S. Mcht. Marine Acad., 1950; LLB, JD, U. Mich., 1953. Bar: Ill. 1954. Practice law, Rock Island, Ill.; ptnr. Winstein, Kavensky & Wallace. Asst. state's atty. Rock Island County, 1967-68; local counsel UAW at John Deere-J.I. Case Plants. Former bd. dirs. Tri City Jewish Ctr.; former trustee United Jewish Charities of Quad Cities; former bd. dirs. Blackhawk Coll. Found. Mem. ABA, Ill. Bar Assn. (chmn. jud. adv. polls com. 1979-84), Rock Island County Bar Assn., Am. Trial Lawyers Assn., Ill. Trial Lawyers Assn., Nat. Assn. Criminal Def. Lawyers, Ill. Appellate Lawyers Assn., Am. Judicature Soc., Blackhawk Coll. Found. Democrat. Jewish. Home: 3405 20th Street Ct Rock Island IL 61201-6201 Office: Rock Island Bank Bldg Rock Island IL 61201 Home: 36571 Tallowood Dr Palm Desert CA 92211 Office Phone: 309-794-1515. E-mail: fnewallace@aol.com.

WALLACE, GERI LYNN, special education educator, landscape architect; b. Mt. Vernon, Ohio, Aug. 27, 1951; d. Richard William and Patricia Ann (Bunn) W. BS in Edn., Ashland (Ohio) Coll., 1973. Cert. tchr. health and phys. edn. Facility locator, foreman, budget analyst United Telephone Co., Mansfield, Ohio; tchr. Mt. Vernon Developmental Ctr. Named Boss of Yr., Jaycees, 1978. Mem. NEA, Devel. Edn. Assn. Address: 109 Park Rd Mount Vernon OH 43050-3825

WALLACE, GLADYS BALDWIN, librarian; b. Macon, Ga., June 5, 1923; d. Carter Shepherd and Dorothy (Richard) Baldwin; m. Hugh Loring Wallace Jr., Oct. 14, 1941 (div. Sept. 1968); children: Dorothy, Hugh Loring III. BS in Edn., Oglethorpe U., 1961; MLS, Emory U., 1966; EdS, Ga. State U., 1980. Libr. pub. elem. schs., Atlanta, 1956-66; libr. Northside HS, 1966-87. Episc. Cathedral St. Philip. Author: The Time of My Life, 1994, Glorious Grass, 2003. Mem. High Mus. Art, Madison-Morgan Cultural Ctr. Recipient Poet of Merit award, 1999; Ga. Dept. Edn. grantee, 1950, NDEA grantee, 1963, 65. Mem.: Am. Assn. Univ. Women, Atlanta Hist. Soc., Am. Assn. Ret. Persons, Atlanta Bot. Garden, Ga. Women of Achievement. Home: NC 6 136 Peachtree Memorial Dr NW Atlanta GA 30309-1096

WALLACE, GUY WILLIAM, management consultant; b. Harvey, Ill., Aug. 22, 1952; s. Willis James and Orpah Linda (Rademacher) W.; m. Karen Margaret Bakke Kennedy, Feb. 20, 1981 (div. July 1996); m. Margaret Ann Johnson, Feb. 8, 1997 B Radio/TV/Film, U. Kans., 1979. Inside salesperson Wickes Lumber, Lawrence, Kans., 1976-79, program devel. Saginaw, Mich., 1979-81; tng. project supr. Motorola, Schamburg, Ill., 1981-82; ptnr. Svenson & Wallace, Inc., Naperville, Ill., 1982-97; ptnr., pres. Curriculum Architecture Design & Devel. Inst., Inc., Naperville, 1998—. Dir. Internat. Soc. for Performance Improvement, Washington, 1999-2000. Author: T&D Systems View, Lean-ISD, 2000; co-author: Quality Roadmap, 1994; developer (tng. program) Product Management Process Training, 1987 (finalist Best Instrnl. Product 1989). With USN, 1972-75. Mem.: ASTD, Internat. Soc. for Performance Improvement (bd. dirs. 1999—2001, pres.-elect 2002—). E-mail: guy.wallace@caddi.com.

WALLACE, HARRY LELAND, lawyer; b. San Francisco, June 26, 1927; s. Leon Harry and Anna Ruth (Haworth) W.; 1 child, Mary Ann Wallace Frantz. AB in Govt.; BS in Bus, Ind. U., 1949; JD, Harvard U., 1952. Bar: Wis. 1953. Law clk. U.S. Supreme Ct. Justice Sherman Minton, Washington, 1952-53; assoc. firm Foley & Lardner, Milw., 1953-61, partner, 1961-96. retired, 1996; officer and/or dir. various corps. Treas. Mequon-Thiensville Sch. Bds., 1966-67, 71-73, pres., 1965-66, 67-71, 73-75; bd. dirs. Milw. County Assn. for Mental Health, 1970-76, Milw. Mental Health Found., 1983-94; chmn. financing policies com. Gov.'s Commn. on Edn., 1969-70; mem. Gov.'s Task Force on Sch. Financing and Property Tax Reform, 1972-73; chmn. Gov.'s Commn. on State-Local Rels. and Fin. Policies, 1975-76; trustee Pub. Policy Forum, 1976-92, sec., 1984-86, pres., 1986-88. With USN, 1945-46. Mem. Wis. Bar Assn., Am. Law Inst., Phi Beta Kappa, Beta Gamma Sigma, Delta Tau Delta. Clubs: Milwaukee. Methodist. Home: 1913 Somerset Ln Northbrook IL 60062-6067

WALLACE, HENRY JARED, JR., lawyer; b. Pitts., Oct. 26, 1943; s. Henry Jared and Jane (Bowman) Wallace. BA, Harvard U., 1965, JD, 1968. Bar: Pa. 1969, U.S. Supreme Ct. 1973. With Reed Smith, Pitts., 1968—94; pvt. practice Pitts., 1995—. Served with U.S. Army, 1968-70. Mem. Duquesne Club, Fox Chapel Golf Club, Harvard-Yale-Princeton Club (Pitts.). Home and Office: 149 Ridgeview Dr New Kensington PA 15068-9389

WALLACE, J. CLIFFORD, federal judge; b. San Diego, Dec. 11, 1928; s. John Franklin and Lillie Isabel (Overing) Wallace; m. Virginia Lee Schlosser, 1957 (dec.); m. Elaine J. Barnes, Apr. 8, 1996 (dec.); m. Dixie Jenee Robison Zenger, Apr. 2, 2001. BA, San Diego State U., 1952; LLB, U. Calif., Berkeley, 1955. Bar: Calif. 1955. With Gray, Cary, Ames & Frye, San Diego, 1955—70; judge U.S. Dist. Ct. (so. dist.), Calif., 1970—72, U.S. Ct. Appeals (9th cir.), San Diego, 1972—96, chief judge, 1991—96, sr. judge, 1996—. Contbr. articles to profl. jours. Stake pres. San Diego East LDS Ch., 1962—67, regional rep., 1967—74, 1977—79. With USN, 1946—49. Mem.: Inst. Jud. Adminstrn., Am. Bd. Trial Advocates. Mem. Lds Ch. Office: US Ct Appeals 9th Cir 940 Front St Ste 4192 San Diego CA 92101-8918 *My principles, ideals and goals and my standard of conduct are embodied in the Gospel of Jesus Christ. They come to fruition in family life, service, industry and integrity and in an attempt, in some small way, to make my community a better place within which to live.*

WALLACE, JAMES WENDELL, lawyer; b. Clinton, Tenn., July 13, 1930; s. John Nelson and Rose Ella (Carden) W.; m. Jeanne Mary Ellen Newlin; children: Karen Wallace Young, Michael James. Student, Syracuse U., 1952-53; BS, U. Tenn., Knoxville, 1959; JD, U. Tenn., 1958. Bar: Calif. 1959, U.S. Dist. Ct. (ctrl. dist.) Calif. 1959, U.S. Ct. Appeals (9th cir.) 1977, U.S. Supreme Ct. 1964. Sec., legal counsel Guidance Tech., Inc., Santa Monica, Calif., 1958-65; sr. atty., asst. sec. Varian Assocs., Palo Alto, Calif., 1965-67; gen. counsel, asst. sec. Electronic Splty. Co., Pasadena, Calif., 1967-69, asst. gen. counsel, asst. sec. The Times Mirror Co., L.A., 1969-75, assoc. gen. counsel, asst. sec., 1976-85, assoc. gen. counsel, sec., 1985-89; dir., v.p., sec. Flintridge Asset Mgmt. Co., San Marino, Calif., 1990—. Mem. editl. bd. Tenn. Law Rev., 1956-58. Served with USAF, 1951-55. Mem. Jonathan Club, Phi Delta Phi, Phi Kappa Phi. Home: 5822 Briartree Dr La Canada Flintridge CA 91011-1825

WALLACE, JANE HOUSE, retired geologist; b. Ft. Worth, Aug. 12, 1926; d. Fred Leroy and Helen Gould (Kixmiller) Wallace. AB, Smith Coll., 1947, MA, 1949; postgrad., Bryn Mawr Coll., 1949-52. Geologist U.S. Geol. Survey, 1952-97; chief Pub. Inquiries Offices, Washington, 1964-72, spl. asst. to dir., 1974-97, dep. bur. ethics counselor, 1975-97, Washington liaison Office of Dir., 1978-97; ret., 1997. Recipient Meritorious Service award Dept. Interior, 1971, Disting. Svc. award, 1976, Sec.'s Commendation, 1988, Smith Coll. medal, 1992. Fellow Geol. Socs. Am., Washington (treas. 1963-67); mem. Sigma Xi (assoc.)

WALLACE, JEANNETTE OWENS, state legislator; b. Scottsdale, Ariz., Jan. 16, 1934; d. Albert and Velma (Whinery) Owens; m. Terry Charles Wallace Sr., May 21, 1955; children: Terry C. Jr., Randall J., Timothy A., Sheryl L., Janice M. BS, Ariz. State U., 1955. Mem. Los Alamos (N.Mex.) County Coun., 1981-82; cons. County of Los Alamos, 1983-84; chmn., vice chmn. Los Alamos County Coun., 1985-88; cons. County of Los Alamos, Los Alamos Schs., 1989-90; rep. N.Mex. State Legislature, 1991—. Mem. appropriations and fin. govt. and urban affairs, N.Mex., 1991—, legis. fin. com., Indian affairs, radioactive and hazardous materials, co-chmn. Los Alamos County's dept. energy negotiating com., 1987-88; mem. legis. policy com. Mcpl. League, N.Mex., 1986-88; mem. legis. fin. com. Info. Tech. and Energy Coun., radioactive & hazardous materials com., medicaid oversight com., legis. coun., info. tech., LANL oversight com., energy coun. Bd. dirs. Tri-Area Econ. Devel., 1988-94, 96—, Crime Stoppers, Los Alamos, 1988-92, Los Alamos Citizens Against Substance Abuse, 1989-94; mem. N.Mex. First, Albuquerque, 1989-2003; legis. chmn. LWV, 1990; mem. Los Alamos Rep. Women, pres., 1989-90; bd. dirs. Los Alamos Commerce and Devel., 1990—. Mem. Los Alamos Bus. & Profl. Women (legis. chmn. 1990), Los Alamos C. of C., Mana del Norte, Kiwamis. Methodist. Avocations: tennis, needlecrafts, reading. Home: 1913 Spruce Los Alamos NM 87544-3041 E-mail: wallace@losalamos.com.

WALLACE, JESSE WYATT, pharmaceutical scientist; b. Canton, Ga., Jan. 24, 1925; s. Jesse Wyatt and Lula (Wyatt) W.; m. Myra Brown, Jan. 2, 1949; children: Karin, Kimberly, Stephen, David. BBA magna cum laude, U. Ga., 1954; MS, Ga. Inst. Tech., 1960. Chmn. svc. groups Ga. Tech, Atlanta, 1953-57; adminstrv. mgr. Am. Viscose Corp., Marcus Hook, Pa., 1957-61; various exec. positions FMC Corp., Phila., 1961-85; pres., dir. Wallco Internat. Corp., Wilmington, Del., 1985-89, 96—; v.p., sec. Pharm. Svc. and Tech., Inc., Woodbury, N.J., 1989-95. Adv. bd. Pharm. Tech. Conf., 1986—. Editor: Controlled Release Systems, 1988; contbr. Encyclopedia, 1989; contbr. articles to profl. jours; author (manual) Problem Solver, 1980. Vice chmn. Ch. Deacons, Wilmington; v.p., pres. Wilmington Gideons, 1969-71; v.p., bd. dirs. ACA Acad., 1971-73; vice chmn. Del. Family Found., 1990—. Lt. USN, 1943-46, 50-53. Recipient Publ. award Pharm. Technology, 1989. Fellow Acad. Pharm. Scis., Am. Asnsn. of Pharm. Scientists; mem. Internat. Platform Assn., La. Fedn. Internat. Pharm., Am. Assn. Pharm. Scientists, Mensa, Delta Sigma Pi (life), Delta Mu Delta. Republican. Baptist. Avocations: family, reading, golf, racquet ball, travel. Office: Wallco Internat Corp 1106 Grinnell Rd Wilmington DE 19803-5126 E-mail: jessewallace@comcast.net.

WALLACE, JOHN E. judge; m. Barbara Wallace. Degree in Polit. Sci., U. Del., 1964; JD, Harvard U. Atty. Montgomery, McCracken, Walker & Rhoads, Phila.; mem. appellate div. N.J. Superior Ct., 1992; judge State Supreme Ct. N.J., 2003—. Coach Washington Twp. H.S. With U.S. Army, Vietnam. Democrat. Office: Richard J Hughes Justice Complex 25 Market St PO Box 970 Trenton NJ 08625

WALLACE, JOHN LOYS, aviation services executive; b. Decatur, Tex., July 31, 1941; s. John K. and Flora Viola (Lundsen) Montgomery W.; m. Linda M. Jackson, May 18, 1962; children— John, Amy Lynn, Katherine Lea, Elizabeth D'Ann Student, U. Tex.-Arlington, 1961-65, North Tex. State U., Denton, 1960-61. V.p. acctg. svcs. Cooper Airmotive, Dallas, 1975-77, v.p. fin., 1977-80, exec. v.p., gen. mgr. Gen. Aviation div., 1980-82; exec. v.p. fin., adminstrn. Aviall, Dallas, 1982-85; exec. v.p., chief oper. officer Aviall, Inc., Dallas, 1985-89, pres. Gen. Aviation Svcs. div., 1989-93; ret., 1993. Mem. Fin. Execs. Inst., North. Dallas C. of C., U.S./Mex. C. of C. (bd. dirs.), Chif Exec.'s Round Table, Cotton Creek Club, Delta Sigma Phi. Republican. Presbyterian. Avocations: gardening, fishing, golf. Home: 3651 Pinehurst Cir Gulf Shores AL 36542-9052

WALLACE, JOHN MITCHELL MAVER See DUFFY-KING, JAN

WALLACE, JOYCE IRENE MALAKOFF, internist; b. Phila., Nov. 25, 1940; d. Samuel Leonard and Henrietta (Hameroff) Malakoff; m. Lance Arthur Wallace, Aug. 30, 1964 (div. 1974); 1 dau. Julia Ruth; m. Arthur H. Kahn, Oct. 7, 1979 (div. 1986); 1 son, Aryeh N. Kahn. AB, Queens Coll., CUNY, 1961; postgrad., Columbia U., 1962-64; MD, SUNY, 1968. Diplomate Am. Bd. Internal Medicine. Intern St. Vincent's Hosp. Med. Ctr., N.Y.C., 1968-70; practice medicine N.Y.C., 1970-71; resident Manhattan VA Hosp., N.Y.C., 1972, Nassau County Med. Ctr., East Meadow, N.Y., 1972-73; practice medicine North Conway, NH, 1973—74; practice medicine specializing in internal medicine N.Y.C., 1976—; med. dir. FROST'D Primary Care, 1999—2003. Mem. attending staff Nassau County Med. Ctr., 1974, St. Vincent's Hosp. and Med. Ctr., N.Y.C., 1977—; asst. prof. medicine Mt. Sinai Med. Sch., N.Y.C.; pres. Found. for Rsch. on Sexually Transmitted Diseases, Inc., 1986-89, exec. and med. dir., 1989-2003. Fellow ACP, N.Y. Acad. Medicine; mem. Am. Med. Women's Assn., N.Y. County, N.Y. State Med. Socs. Office: 32 W 18th St New York NY 10011

WALLACE, JULIA DIANE, newspaper editor; b. Davenport, Iowa, Dec. 3, 1956; d. Franklin Sherwood and Eleanor Ruth (Pope) W.; m. Doniver Dean Campbell, Aug. 23, 1986; children: Emmaline Livingston Campbell, Eden Jennifer Campbell. BS in Journalism, Northwestern U., 1978. Reporter Norfolk (Va.) Ledger-Star, 1978-80, Dallas Times Herald, 1980-82; reporter, editor News sect. USA Today, Arlington, Va., 1982-89, mng. editor spl. projects, 1989-92; mng. editor Chgo. Sun-Times, 1992-1996; exec. editor Statesman Jour., 1996—98; mng. editor Arizona Republic, Phoenix, 1998—2000, Atlanta Journal and Constitution, Atlanta, 2001—02, editor, 2002—. Mem. Am. Soc. Newspaper Editors. Mailing: The Atlanta Journal Constitution P O Box 4689 Atlanta GA 30302 Office: Atlanta Journal Constitution 72 Marietta St NW Atlanta GA 30303

WALLACE, JULIAN CRAIG, psychology educator, researcher; s. James L. and Julia C. Wallace; m. Larissa Jerae Klein, Apr. 14, 1999. BS in Psychology, U. of Tenn., Chattanooga, 1998; MA in Indsl./Orgnl. Psychology, U. of West Fla., Pensacola, 2001; PhD in Indsl./Orgnl. Psychology, Ga. Inst. of Tech., 2004. Instr. psychology Ga. Inst. of Tech., Atlanta, 2001—04; asst. prof. indsl./orgnl. psychology Tulane U., New Orleans, 2004—. Cons. Vodanovich & Assocs., Pensacola, 1999—2002. Contbr. articles to profl. jours. Campaign supporter; active mem. and supporter of faith values. Recipient Merit Grad. scholarship, U. of West Fla., 2000—01, small rsch. grant, Ga. Tech, 2004. Mem.: APA (assoc.), Acad. of Mgmt. (assoc.), Am. Psychol. Soc. (assoc.), Soc. for Indsl./Orgnl. Psychology (assoc.). Achievements include research in personal and situational characteristics of workers to improve workplace safety. Office: Tulane Univ 2007 Percival Stern Hall New Orleans LA 70118 Personal E-mail: craigwallace@comcast.net or parputt5@aol.com.

WALLACE, KARL KENNETH, JR., physician, radiologist; b. Farmville, Va., June 12, 1932; s. Karl Kenneth and Frances Virginia (Newman) W.; m. Patricia Laughbaum, June 19, 1954; children: Karl Kenneth III, Elizabeth, John, Patricia. BA, Hampden-Sydney Coll., 1954; MD, Med. Coll. Va., 1958. Diplomate Am. Bd. Radiology, Am. Bd. Nuc. Medicine. Rotating intern Med. Coll. Va. Hosps., 1958-59; radiology resident Duke U., 1959-62; chmn. dept. radiology Virginia Beach (Va.) Gen. Hosp., 1963-91; prof. radiology U. Va., Charlottesville, 1992—99, prof. radiology emeritus, 1999—. Bd. dirs. Va. divsn. Am. Cancer Soc., Richmond, 1973-84. Fellow Am. Coll. Radiology (pres. 1994-95, chmn. bd. chancellors 1992-94); mem. Radiol. Soc. N.Am., Coun. Med. Splty. Socs., Am. Roentgen Ray Soc., Soc. for Nuclear Medicine, Am. Inst. Ultrasound in Medicine, Med. Soc. Va. (speaker ho. of dels. 1976-80), Soc. Thoracic Radiology. Office: U Va Dept Radiology PO Box 170 Charlottesville VA 22902-0170

WALLACE, KEN, magazine publisher; BBA, St. John's U. With Reader's Digest mag., 1967-1983; v.p. advt. Sylvia Porter's Personal Finance mag., 1983-87; v.p., advt. dir. Parade mag., 1987-93; v.p., pub. Prevention mag., Emmaus, Pa., 1993-98, v.p. mag. divsn., 1998—. Office: Prevention 733 3rd Ave Fl 15 New York NY 10017-3204 also: Prevention Rodale Press Inc 33 E Minor St Emmaus PA 18098-0001

WALLACE, MARK ALLEN, hospital executive; b. Oklahoma City, Apr. 24, 1953; s. William Howell and Mollie Marie (Godsy) W.; children: Emily, Benjamin. BS, Okla. Bapt. U., 1975; MS, Washington U., St. Louis, 1978. Adminstrv. asst. Bapt. Med. Ctr., Oklahoma City, 1975-77; adminstrv. resident Meth. Hosp., Houston, 1977-78; asst. v.p. Tex. Meth. Hosp., Houston, 1978-80, v.p., 1980-83, sr. v.p., 1983-89; pres., CEO Tex. Children's Hosp., Houston, 1989—. Adj. instr. Washington U., 1984—; adj. asst. prof. Tex. Womans U., Houston, 1983—; bd. dirs., chmn. fin. com., treas. Greater Houston Hosp. Svc. Corp., 1986-90; bd. trustees, Nat. Assn of Children's Hospitals and Related Institutions Contbr. articles to profl. jours. Chmn. campaign drives United Way, Houston, 1984, 86, corporate walk for Juvenile Diabetes Found. Walk to Cure Diabetes, 2000; class chmn. alumni vision for excellence and growth for future campaigns Okla. Bapt. U., 1982; bd. dirs. Tex. Gulf Coast chpt. March of Dimes Birth Defects Found., 1985-91, Zoological Society of Houston, Sam Houston Area Coun. of the Boy Scouts, World Health & Golf Assn., Greater Houston Partnership (vice-chair Flood Control Task Force), Greater Houston Community Found.; bd. governors, Houston Forum; active mem. Second Baptist Ch., Houston, Young Presidents' Orgn., and Houston Country Club Recipient Emerging Leaders in Health Care award Healthcare Forum Mag. and Korn/Ferry Internat., 1987. Fellow Am. Coll. Healthcare Execs. (com. on membership, subcom. on recruitment 1990—, Robert S. Hudgens Meml. award, 1992, Young Healthcare Exec. of Yr., 1992); mem. Am. Heart Assn. (med. adv. com. 1990-91), Healthcare Forum (pres. emerging leaders alumni group 1988-91), Am. Hosp. Assn., Tex. Hosp. Assn. (bd. dirs., bd. dirs. polit. action com. 1988—, chmn. bd. trustees, 1998-1999), Greater Houston Hosp. Coun. (bd. dirs. 1991—, chmn. 1993-1994), Houston Area Health Care Coalition, Childrens Hosp. Assn. Tex. (pres. 1992—, chmn. 2002-2003), Tex. Gulf Coast Arthritis Found. (bd. dirs. 1990-91). Republican. Baptist. Office: Tex Children's Hosp PO Box 300630 Houston TX 77230-0630 Address: Tex Children's Hosp 6621 Fannin St Houston TX 77030*

WALLACE, MARY ELAINE, opera director, author; m. Robert House. BFA cum laude, U. Nebr., Kearney, 1940; MusM, U. Ill., 1954; postgrad., Music Acad. West, Santa Barbara, Calif., 1955, Eastman Sch. Music, 1960, Fla. State U., 1962. Prof. voice, dir. opera La. Tech. U., Ruston, 1954-62, SUNY-Fredonia, 1962-69, So. Ill. U.-Carbondale, 1969-79; dir. Marjorie Lawrence Opera Theatre, Opera on Wheels; adminstrv. adviser Summer Playhouse, Carbondale; stage mgr. Chautauqua Opera Co., N.Y., 1963; asst. mus. dir., condr. Asolo Festival, Sarasota, Fla., 1961; music editor, critic The Chautauquan Daily; adjudicator Met. Opera auditions; exec. sec. Nat. Opera Assn., 1981-91. Co-author: Opera Scenes for Class and Stage, 1979, (with Robert Wallace) More Operas Scenes for Class and Stage, 1990, Upstage Downstage, 1992. Founding mem. bd. dirs. Rockwall Alliance for the Arts, 2001; founding bd. dirs. Rockwall Musicfest, Rockwall, 2002. Recipient Lifetime Achievement award Nat. Opera Assn., 1998, Alumni award U. Nebr., 1998, Disting. Alumna Kearney Pub. Schs., 2004. Mem. Nat. Opera Assn. (pres. 1974, 75), Music Tchrs. Nat. Assn., Nat. Assn. Tchrs. Singing, AAUP, AAUW, Met. Opera Guild, Mortar Bd., Sigma Tau Delta, Pi Kappa Lambda, Phi Beta, Alpha Psi Omega, Delta Kappa Gamma Address: 3106 Lakeside Dr Rockwall TX 75087-5319 E-mail: mehouse@flash.net.

WALLACE, MATTHEW EDWARD, actor; b. St. Louis, Nov. 23, 1973; s. Jerry Lee and Joanne Wallace; m. Tina Jo Hagens, Mar. 27, 2004. BFA in regional theatre, Webster U. Conservatory of Theatre Arts, 1992—96. Actor Horse Cave Theatre, Horse Cave, Ky., 1996—96; artistic dir. Dolphinback Theatre Co., Chgo., 1999—2001; actor/booking mgr. HealthWorks Theatre, Chgo., 1998—2001; actor Greasy Joan and Co., Chgo., 1999—2000, Ky. Shakespeare Festival, Louisville, 2001—, Derby Dinner Playhouse, Clarksville, Ind., 2003—. Artistic assoc. Ky. Shakespeare Festival, 2001—; artistic dir. Double JJ Resort, Rothbury, Mich., 2000; tchr. Children's Theatre of Charlotte, NC, 2001; judge and respondant Am. Coll. Theatre Festival, Milw., 2001; actor/booking mgr. HealthWorks Theatre, Chgo., 1998—2001; tchr. Childrens Theatre of Charlotte, Charlotte, NC, 2001; actor Greasy Joan and Co., Chgo., 1999—2000, Pub. Theatre of Ky., Bowling Green, Ky., 2003, Horse Cave Theatre, Horse Cave, Ky., 1996. Actor: St. Croix Festival Theatre, 2002, Ky. Shakespeare Festival, 2001; (films) Forrest Gump, 1993, LaSposa, 2004, Beauty of The Southland, 1996. Roman Catholic. Personal E-mail: mrmattwall@aol.com.

WALLACE, MATTHEW WALKER, retired entrepreneur; b. Salt Lake City, Jan. 7, 1924; s. John McChrystal and Glenn (Walker) W.; m. Constance Cone, June 22, 1954 (dec. May 1980); children: Matthew, Anne; m. Susan Struggles, July 11, 1981. BA, Stanford U., 1947; MCP, MIT, 1950. Prin. planner Boston City Planning Bd., 1950-53; v.p. Nat. Planning and Rsch., Inc., Boston, 1953-55; pres. Wallace-McConaughy Corp., Salt Lake City, 1955-69, Ariz. Ranch & Metals Co., Scottsdale, 1969-84, Idaho TV Corp., Channel 6, ABC Boise, 1976-78; chmn. Wallace Assocs., Inc., Salt Lake City, 1969-98. Dir. 1st Interstate Bank, Salt Lake City, 1956—90, Wells Fargo Bank Cmty. Bd., 2000, Arnold Machinery Co., 1988—, Roosevelt Hot Springs Corp., 1978—; mem. adv. bd. Mountain Bell Tel. Co., Salt Lake City, 1975—85. Pres. Downtown Planning Assn., Salt Lake City, 1970; chmn. Utah State Arts Coun., Salt Lake City, 1977; chmn. hon. bd. Planned Parenthood; humanities and scis. coun. Stanford U., athletics bd., alumni assn. exec. bd., bd. vis. sch. law; nat. adv. bd. U. Utah Coll. Bus.; lifetime dir. Utah Symphony Orch.; chmn. arts, adv. coun. and Capital Campaign Westminster Coll. Lt. (j.g.) USN, 1944-46, PTO.

Recipient Contbn. award Downtown Planning Assn., 1977, Gov.'s award in the Arts, 1991, Utah Nat. Guard Minuteman award, 1994. Mem. Am. Inst. Cert. Planners (charter), Am. Arts Alliance (bd. dirs. 1991), Alta Club (dir.), Cottonwood Club (pres. 1959-63), Salt Lake Country Club (dir.), Desert Island Golf and Country Club (Rancho Mirage, Calif.), Flat Rock Club (Island Park., Idaho pres. 1994-98), Phi Kappa Phi (hon., life). Home: 2230 E Parleys Terr Salt Lake City UT 84109-1530

WALLACE, MICHELE, writer, educator; b. N.Y.C., Jan. 4, 1952; d. Robert Earl Wallace and Faith Ringgold; m. Eugene Nesmith, Dec. 22, 1989 (div. Nov. 2002). BA, CCNY, 1974, MA in English, 1990; PhD in Cinema Studies, NYU, 1998. Asst. prof. English CUNY, 1989—91; assoc. prof. English, women's studies and film CUNY and CUNY Grad. Ctr., 1991—97, prof., 1998. Pres. Art Without Walls, 1974. Author: Black Macho and the Myth of the Superwoman, 1979, Invisibility Blues: Pop to Theory, 1990, Black Popular Culture, 1992, Dark Designs and Visual Culture, 2004, Invisibility Blues: From Pop to Theory and Back Again, 2004; columnist: The Village Voice, 1996; contbr. to newspapers and popular mags. including Ms., The Village Voice, The Nation, The N.Y. Times, Art Forum, Art In America; editor: Women in Art, 1971; mem. editl. bd.: Social Identities, Women and Therapy. Founding mem. Nat. Black Feminist Orgn., 1974; pres. Women Students and Artists for Black Art Liberation, 1970—76. Mem.: PEN, MLA, Oscar Micheaux Soc., Soc. Cinema Studies, Am. Studies Assn., Phi Beta Kappa.

WALLACE, MICHELE, media company executive; Assignment editor Sta. WVUE-TV, ABC, New Orleans, News 12, all-news cable channel, L.I., N.Y.; with Medialink Inc., N.Y.C., 1989—; now v.p. global ops. Office: Medialink Inc 708 3rd Ave Fl Dave9 New York NY 10017-4201 E-mail: mwallace@medialink.com.

WALLACE, MIKE, television interviewer and reporter; b. Brookline, Mass., May 9, 1918; s. Frank and Zina (Sharfman) Wallace; m. Lorraine Perigord (dec.); children: Peter(dec.), Christopher, Pauline; m. Mary Yates, June 28, 1986. AB, U. Mich., 1935—39, hon. degree, 1987, U. Mass., 1978, U. Pa., 1989. Associated with radio, 1939—; TV, 1946—; commentator CBS-TV, 1951—54, TV interviewer, reporter, 1951—; CBS news corr., 1963—; co-editor 60 Minutes, CBS, 1968—. Author: Mike Wallace Asks, 1958; author: (with Gary Paul Gates) Close Encounter, 1984. Recipient Robert Sherwood award, 19 ATVAS Emmy awards, George Foster Peabody awards, 1963—71, 1998, DuPont Columbia Journalism award, 1972, 1983, Carr Van Anda award, 1977, Thomas Hart Benton award, 1978. Mem.: Century Assocs., Sigma Delta Chi. Office: CBS News 60 Minutes 524 W 57th St New York NY 10019-2924

WALLACE, MIKE, race car driver; Race car driver Biagi Brothers. Recipient Champion, Winston Racing Series Mid-Am. Region, 1990, Busch Series/Indpls. Raceway Park, 1994. Office: Mike Wallace Fan Club PO Box 4450 Mooresville NC 28117

WALLACE, NORA ANN, lawyer; b. Phila., May 24, 1951; AB, Vassar Coll., 1973; JD cum laude, Harvard U., 1976. Bar: N.Y. 1977. Mem. Willkie Farr & Gallagher, N.Y.C. Trustee Vassar Coll., Bklyn. Acad. Music, Bklyn. Acad. Music Endowment Trust; pres. Harvard Law Sch. Assn. of N.Y.C.; bd. dirs. Joseph Collins Found. Office: Willkie Farr & Gallagher 787 7th Ave New York NY 10019-6099

WALLACE, PAULA S. academic administrator; 3 children. BA, Furman U.; MEd, EdS, Ga. State U. Co-founder Savannah Coll. Art and Design, 1979, pres., 2000—. Author of children's books. Mem. Skidaway Island United Meth. Ch., Savannah, Ga. Film and Videotape Commn., Ga. C. of C.; bd. dirs. B. B. & T. Bank, Nat. Mus. Women in the Arts. Recipient Oglethorpe Bus. and Profl. Women award, James T. Deason Human Rels. award; named Outstanding Young Woman of Am., Ky. Col.; named to Savannah Bus. Hall of Fame. Office: Savannah Coll Art and Design PO Box 3146 622 Drayton St Savannah GA 31402-3146

WALLACE, RASHEED, professional basketball player, marketing professional; b. Sept. 17, 1974; s. Jackie Wallace; m. Fatima Sanders, July 18; 3 children. Attended, U. N.C. Prof. basketball player Washington Wizards, 1995—96, Portland Trailblazers, 1996—2004, Atlanta Hawks, 2004, Detroit Pistons, 2004—; CEO Dir. Hit Studios, Phila., 2002—. Founder Rasheed A. Wallace Found., Phila., 1997. Named to NBA All-Star Team, 2000, 2001. Achievements include mem. NBA Championship Team, 2004. Office: c/o Detroit Pistons 2 Championship Dr Auburn Hills MI 48326*

WALLACE, RICHARD, editor, writer; b. Bronxville, N.Y., May 25, 1947; m. Elisabeth Beeftink, May 24, 1969; 1 child, Eric B. BA, Columbia U., 1974. Reporter, editor, contbr. varius industry and bus. pubs., Electronic News, EE Times, 1976-92; editor-in-chief Electronic Engring. Times, Manhasset, NY, 1992—98; editor, dir. EE Times, 1998—. Office: CMP Media LLC Electronic Engring Times 600 Community Dr Ste 1 Manhasset NY 11030-3875

WALLACE, RICHARD LEE, chancellor; BS in Journalism, Northwestern U., 1958; PhD in Econs., Vanderbilt U., 1965. From instr. to asst. prof. Fla. State U., 1961-66; from asst. prof. to prof. U. Mo., Columbia, 1967-77, interim dean Grad. Sch., 1978-79, assoc. dean, 1979-82, interim dean Coll. Arts Scis., 1982-83; assoc. provost Mo. U., Columbia, 1983-85, from assoc. v.p. to v.p., 1985-89, v.p. acad. affairs, 1989-96, chancellor, 1996—. Recipient Faculty Svc. award Nat. Continuing Edn. Assn., 1990, J. Rhoads Foster award, 1995, award Northwestern Medill Sch. Journalism, 1998. Mem. Nat. Forum Sys. Chief Acad. Officers, Nat. Assn. State Univs. Land-Grant Colls. (chmn. coun. acad. affairs, com. econ. higher edn.). Office: Univ Missouri Columbia Office of the Chancellor 105 Jesse Hall Columbia MO 65211-1050 E-mail: WallaceR@missouri.edu.

WALLACE, RICK, marketing professional; Dir. mktg. and procurement Alliant Foodsvc., Deerfield, Ill., to 1996, v.p. category mgmt., 1996—. Office: Alliant Food Service 9933 Woods DR Skokie IL 60077-1057

WALLACE, ROANNE, hosiery company executive; b. Greenwood, Miss., Dec. 18, 1949; d. Robert Carter and Lois Anne (Vick) Wallace. BM, U. Tenn., 1971; MA, U. NC, 1976; MBA, Wake Forest U., 1982. Exec. dir. Am. Bd. Clin. Chemistry, Winston, Salem, NC, 1977-78; adminstrv. officer Forsyth County Office Emergency Mgmt., 1978-79, sr. asst. dir., 1979-82; with Sara Lee, 1982—; mktg. dir. Hanes Her Way Intimates, Sara Lee Hosiery, Just My Size, 1988—; product mgr. L'eggs Products, Inc., 1986-88. Mem. adv. coun. Forsyth County Office Piedmont Emergency Mgmt., Winston-Salem, NC; bd. dirs. Piedmont Opera Theatre, Inc. Recipient Miss University of Tenn., Tenn., 1970. Home: 803 Devon Ct Winston Salem NC 27104-1263 Office: Sara Lee Intimates and Hosiery 5650 University Pkwy Winston Salem NC 27105-1312 Office Phone: 336-519-3534. Business E-Mail: roanne.wallace@saralee.com.

WALLACE, ROBERT B. medical educator; BSM Medicine, Northwestern U., 1964, MD, 1967; MSc Epidemiology, SUNY, 1972. Intern internal medicine Cornell U., N.Y., 1967—68, resident internal medicine, 1968—69; instr. dept. medicine Emory U. Medicine, 1969—70; instr. dept. social and preventive medicine SUNY, Buffalo, 1970—72; asst. prof. preventive medicine and internal medicine Coll. Medicine U. Iowa, 1972—75; assoc. prof. preventive medicine and internal medicine Coll. Medicine U. Iowa, 1975—79, head epidemiology sect. dept. preventive medicine Coll. Medicine, 1976—85, prof. preventive medicine and internal medicine Coll. Medicine, 1979—99, head dept. preventive medicine Col. Medicine, 1986—94, dir. cancer ctr., 1994—98, prof. epidemiology Coll. Pub. Health, 1999—. Mem.: Nat. Acad. Scis., Inst. Medicine (bd. health promotion and disease prevention 1994—), Nat. Inst. Aging (nat. adv. coun. 1994—98), U.S. Preventive Svs. Task Force (sec. office assistance DHHS 1990—95), Alpha Omega Alpha. Office: U Iowa Coll Pub Health 5190 Westlawn Iowa City IA 52242

WALLACE, ROBERT BRUCE, retired surgeon; b. Washington, Apr. 12, 1931; s. William B. and Anne E. W.; m. Betty Jean Newel, Aug. 28, 1955; children: Robert B., Anne E., Barbara N. BA, Columbia U., 1953, MD, 1957. Diplomate: Am. Bd. Surgery, Am. Bd. Thoracic Surgery. Chmn., prof. dept. surgery Mayo Clinic and Mayo Med. Sch., Rochester, Minn.; bd. govs. Mayo Clinic, 1968-79; prof. dept. surgery Georgetown U. Sch. Medicine, 1980—, chmn. dept. surgery, 1980-95, surgeon and chief univ. hosp., 1980-95; retired, 1995. Trustee Mayo Found., 1970—78; chmn. sci. adv. com. LeDucq Found., 2000—. Mem. ACS (bd. govs. 1975-79), Am. Surg. Assn., Soc. Clin. Surgery, Am. Assn. Thoracic Surgery (pres. 1994-95), Internat. Cardiovascular Soc., Soc. Vascular Surgery, Thoracic Surgery Found. Rsch. & Edn. (bd. dirs. 1993-2001, pres. 1998-2001). Home: 1322 Darnall Dr Mc Lean VA 22101-3009 E-mail: rbwallace@cox.net.

WALLACE, ROBERT EARL, geologist; b. NYC, July 16, 1916; s. Clarence Earl and Harriet (Wheeler) W.; m. Gertrude Kivela, Mar. 19, 1945; 1 child: Alan R. BS, Northwestern U., 1938; MS, Calif. Inst. Tech., 1940, PhD, 1946. Geologist U.S. Geol. Survey, various locations, 1942-98, regional geologist Menlo Park, Calif., 1970-74, chief scientist Office of Earthquakes, Volcanoes and Engring., 1974-87, emeritus, 1987-98; asst. and assoc. prof. Wash. State Coll., Pullman, 1946-51; prof. emeritus U. Nev., Reno, 1998—2003. Adv. panel Nat. Earthquake Prediction Evaluation Coun., 1980-90; adv. com. Stanford U. Sch. Earth Sci., 1972-82; engring. criteria rev. bd. San Francisco Bay Conservation and Devel. Commn., chmn. 1981-92. Contbr. articles to profl. jours. Recipient Alfred E. Alquist award Calif. Earthquake Safety Found., 1995. Fellow AAAS, Geol. Soc. Am. (chmn. cordillidan sect. 1967-68, Career Contbn. award Structural Geology and Tectonics, 2002), Earthquake Engring. Rsch. Inst. (hon. 1999), Calif. Acad. Scis. (hon.); mem. Seismol. Soc. Am. (medalist 1989) Avocations: birding, amateur radio, water color painting.

WALLACE, RUSTY, race car driver; b. St. Louis, Aug. 14, 1956; m. Patti Wallace; children: Greg, Katie, Stephen. Stock race car driver, 1980—; mem. Miller Genuine Draft team. Named winner, NASCAR Winston Cup, 1989, Miller High Life, 1989, Champion Spark Plug 400, 1989, Bud at the Glen, 1989, Valleydale Meats 500, 1989, 1991, Goodwrench 500, 1989, 1993, 1994, Pontiac Excitement 400, 1989, 1997, Coca-Cola 600, 1990, Banquet Frozen Foods 300, 1990, Miller Genuine Draft 500, 1991, Miller Genuine Draft 400, 1992, 1993, 1st Union 400, 1993, Slick 50 300, 1993, Tyson/Holly Farms 400, 1993, AC Delco 500, 1993, Hooters 500, 1993, Split Fire 500, 1993, 1994, Hanes 500, 1993, 1994, 1995, Food City 500, 1993, 1999, 2000, UAW-GM 500, 1994, Bud 500, 1994, Miller 400, 1994, 1995, 1996, Goody's 500, Martinsville, 1994, 1996, Goody's 500, Bristol, 1994, 1996, Save Mark 300, 1996, Miller 500, 1996, Dura Lube/KMart 500, 1998. Office: NASCAR PO Box 2875 Daytona Beach FL 32120-2875

WALLACE, SAMUEL TAYLOR, health system administrator; b. Blytheville, Ark., Sept. 2, 1943; m. Sara Billow, Apr. 30, 1992. BS, U. Mo., 1965; M.H.A., Washington U., St. Louis, 1970. Asst. adminstr. Hillcrest Med. Ctr., Tulsa, 1969-75; adminstr. St. Luke's Meth. Hosp., Cedar Rapids, Iowa, 1975-81, pres., 1981-95, Iowa Health Sys., Des Moines, 1995—. Bd. dirs. Vol. Hosp. Am., Dallas, 1982-94, Iowa Golf Charities, 2001-; chmn. bd. dirs. Vol. Hosp. Iowa, Cedar Rapids, 1983-87; bd. dirs. Greater Des Moines Partnershp, 1996—, Physician Mgmt. Resources, 1996—2000, Health Enterprise of Iowa, 1995-2000; mem. Cedar Rapids coun. Boy Scouts Am., 1983, Mid-Iowa coun., 1995—. Served to capt. M.S.C. U.S. Army, 1965-68, Vietnam. Recipient Silver Beaver award Boy Scouts Am., 1980, Silver Antelope award, 1992; James E. West fellow, 1994, Dist. Eagle Scout, 2002. Fellow Am. Coll. Healthcare Execs. (Iowa bd. regents 1982-84, 88-95, interim gov. Dist. 5 1999-2000); mem. Iowa Hosp. Assn. (dir. 1982-85). Lodges: Rotary (Cedar Rapids pres. 1986-87). Republican. Methodist. Office: Iowa Health Sys 1200 Pleasant St Des Moines IA 50309-1406

WALLACE, SIDNEY, radiologist; b. Phila., Feb. 26, 1929; s. Carl and Sylvia Wallace; m. Marsha Joan Baker, Nov. 26, 1959; children: Stewart, Andrea, Michael J. BA, Temple U., 1949, MD, 1954. Asst. prof. radiology Jefferson Med. Coll., Phila., 1965-66; assoc. prof. M.D. Anderson Cancer Ctr., Houston, 1966-69, prof., 1969—, head sect. clin. radiology, 1969-84, dep. chmn. dept. radiology, 1984-89, chmn. dept., 1989-92, dep./acting head divsn. diagnostic imaging, 1992-93, dep. head rsch. divsn. diagnostic imaging, 1993—. Prof. Med. Sch. U. Tex., Houston, 1972—; mem. sci. adv. bd. Angiogenesis Techs., Inc., Vancouver, B.C., Can., 1993-95; cons. Hermann Hosp., Houston, 1971—, St. Lukes Episc. Hosp., Houston, 1975—. Editor: Interventional Radiology, 1991; contbr. chpts. to: Leukemia-Lymphoma, 1970, Radiologic Contributions to Pediatric Radiology, 1977. With U.S. Army, 1956-58. Fulbright lectr. Fulbright Commn., Brazil, 1994, 5th Ann. Leeds lectr., U. Leeds, Eng., 1983; rsch. grantee. Fellow Am. Coll. Radiology, Soc. Cardio-vasc. and Interventional Radiology (chmn. fellowship com. 1988). Achievements include research in high affinity Tamoxifen derivatives and uses thereof, in efficient microcapsule preparation and method of use, in self-expanding filter of percutaneous insertion, in closure prosthesis for transcatherter placement. Office: MD Anderson Cancer Ctr 1515 Holcombe Blvd Houston TX 77030-4009

WALLACE, STEVEN R. college president; m. Amelia Wallace; children: Devon, Michael. AA, Chaffey C.C., 1972; BS in Psychology, MS in Psychology, Calif. State U., San Bernardino; D in Higher Edn. Adminstrn., Claremont Grad. U., 1989. Vp. adminstrv. svcs. Lakeland C.C., Ohio, 1981-90; pres. Austin C.C., Minn., 1990-92, Inver Hills C.C., Minn., 1992-97, Fla. C.C., 1997—. Adj. faculty Chaffey C.C., faculty Innovative Learning Ctr., dist. dir. learning disabilities, dir. mktg. and legis. affairs. Bd. dirs. Communities in Schs. and Enterprise North Florida. Mem. C. of C. (bd. dirs.), Jacksonville Symphony Assn. (bd. dirs.). Office: Fla Cmty Coll 501 W State St Jacksonville FL 32202-4086

WALLACE, STEWART S. career military officer; b. Nov. 15, 1944; Commd. 2d lt. U.S. Army, advanced through grades to maj. gen. comdg. gen., 1996—.

WALLACE, TERRY CHARLES, SR., retired technical administrator, researcher; b. Phoenix, May 18, 1933; s. Terry Milton Wallace and Fair June (Hartman) Wallace Timberlake; m. Yvonne Jeannette Owens, May 21, 1955; children: Terry Charles, Randall James, Timothy Alan, Sheryl Lynn, Janice Marie. BS, Ariz. State U., 1955; PhD, Iowa State U., 1958. Staff Los Alamos Nat. Lab., 1958-71, dep. group leader, 1971-80, group leader, 1980-83, assoc. divsn. leader, 1983-89, tech. program coord., 1989-91, ret., 1991. Sr. tech. adv. SAIC, Inc., 1994-95; ptnr. Stonewall Enterprises, Los Alamos, 1966-71. Contbr. chpts., articles to profl. jours.; patentee in field. Fundraiser Los Alamos County Republican Party, N.Mex., 1983-84. Served to 1st lt. Chem. Corps, U.S. Army, 1959-61. Mem. Am. Chem. Soc., AAAS, Lab. Retiree Group, Inc. (Los Alamos, treas., bd. dirs. 1995-98), Los Alamos Ret. and Sr. Orgn. (pres., bd. dirs. 1999-2002), Mil. Order World Wars (MG Franklin E. Miles chpt. adj. 1997-99, 2003, treas. 2000-02). Methodist. Home and Office: 1913 Spruce St Los Alamos NM 87544-3041

WALLACE, THOMAS C(HRISTOPHER), editor, literary agent; b. Vienna, Dec. 13, 1933; came to U.S., 1938; s. Don and Julia (Baer) W.; m. Lois Kahn, July 19, 1962 (div. May 2000); 1 son, George Baer; m. Barbara Shortt, Nov. 12, 2000. Grad., Peddie Sch., 1951; BA, Yale U., 1955, MA in History, 1957. Editor G.P. Putnam Sons, N.Y.C., 1959-63; with Holt, Rinehart & Winston, N.Y.C., 1963-81, editor-in-chief gen. books divsn., 1968-81; v.p., sr. editor Simon and Schuster, N.Y.C., 1981; editor W.W. Norton, N.Y.C., 1982-87; v.p. Wallace Lit. Agy., N.Y.C., 1987-98; pres. T. C. Wallace, Ltd., N.Y.C., 1998—. Bd. dirs. Roger Klein Found. Mem. PEN, Yale Club, Century Assn. (N.Y.C.). Office: Ste 2005 215 Park Ave S New York NY 10003 E-mail: tcwallace2@aol.com.

WALLACE, VICTOR LEW, computer science educator; b. Bklyn., Mar. 20, 1933; s. Frank Hobart and Victoria (Schwerthoffer) W.; m. Mary E. Jamieson, June 23, 1962; children: Robert Joseph, Andrew Gilbert. BEE, Poly. Inst. N.Y., 1955, MEE, 1957; PhD in Elec. Engring., Computer Sci., U. Mich., 1967. Mem. tech. staff Bell Telephone Labs., N.Y.C., 1954-55; mathematician-programmer IBM Corp., N.Y.C., 1955-57; instr. elec. engring. U. Mich., Ann Arbor, 1957-61, research scientist, 1959-69; assoc. prof. computer sci. U. N.C., Chapel Hill, 1969-76; prof. computer sci. U. Kans., Lawrence, 1976—2001, chmn. dept. computer sci., 1976-84, prof. emeritus, 2001—. Acad. vis. U. London, Eng., 1970; cons. Los Alamos (N.Mex.) Nat. Lab., 1975-78, Honeywell Corp., Phoenix, 1982-87; cons. in field., 1962—. Co-author: To Compute Numerically--Concepts and Strategies, 1983; contbr. articles to profl. jours. Mem. IEEE (sr., life), AAUP, Assn. Computing Machinery, Inst. Ops. Rsch. & Mgmt. Scis., Sigma Xi. Democrat. Congregationalist. Home: 1509 Massachusetts St Lawrence KS 66044-4253 Office: U Kans Nichols Hall (ITTC) 2335 Irving Hill Rd Lawrence KS 66045-7612 Business E-Mail: wallace@ku.edu.

WALLACE, WALTER C. lawyer, government official; b. N.Y.C., Mar. 25, 1924; m. Frances Helm, Apr. 5, 1963; 1 dau., Laura. BA magna cum laude, St. John's U., Hillsdale, N.Y., 1948; LLB with distinction, Cornell U., 1951. Bar: N.Y. 1952, Calif. 1954, D.C. 1975, U.S. Dist. Ct. (no. dist.) Calif. 1954, U.S. Ct. Appeals (9th cir.) 1954, D.C. 1975, U.S. Dist. Ct. D.C. 1975, U.S. Ct. Appeals (D.C. cir.) 1975. Assoc. Cahill, Gordan & Reindel, N.Y.C., 1951-54; exec. asst. Sec. of Labor, Washington, 1955-60, asst. sec. of labor for manpower and employment, 1960-61; gen. counsel Presdl. R.R. Commn., Washington, 1961; v.p. labor rels. Hudson Pulp & Paper Corp., N.Y.C., 1963-73; pres. Bituminous Coal Operators Assoc., Washington, 1974-75; ptnr. Ables & Wallace, Washington, 1977-80; prin. Law Offices Walter C. Wallace, N.Y.C., 1981-82; mem. Nat. Mediation Bd., Washington, 1982—, chmn., 1983, 85, 88. U.S. del. Internat. Labor Orgn. Conf. on Labor Rels. in Timber Industry, Geneva, 1958; asst. to cabinet com. on oil imports chaired by John Foster Dulles, 1958. Mem. bd. editors Cornell Law Quar., 1950-51. Bd. dirs. Nat. Safety Coun., Washington, 1974-75; asst. to chmn. United Givers Fund, Washington, 1956, mem. admission and allocations com., 1957-58. Staff sgt. U.S. Army, 1943-45, ETO. Decorated Bronze Star; recipient Presdl. commendation Pres. Eisenhower, Washington, 1961, Disting. Svc. award United Givers Fund, 1956, Disting. Svc. award Nat. Mediation Bd., 1990. Mem. Calif. Bar Assn., N.Y. State Bar Assn., D.C. Bar Assn., Order of Coif. Republican. Roman Catholic. Home: 55 Central Park W New York NY 10023-6003

WALLACE, WILLIAM, III, engineering executive; b. Bklyn., June 7, 1926; s. William and Ruth (Fitch) W.; m. Dorothy Ann Reimann, Aug. 2, 1969 (dec.); 1 child, Andrew William. B.E.E., Union Coll., 1947. Registered prof. engr., 22 states. Test engr. Gen. Electric Co., Schenectady, 1947; engr. Ebasco Services Inc., N.Y.C., 1948-67, chief elec. engr., 1967-70, mgr. projects, 1970-73, v.p. Atlanta office Norcross, Ga., 1973-76, exec. v.p. N.Y.C., 1976-80, dir., pres., chief exec. officer, 1980-82, chmn., chief exec. officer, 1982-86, also bd. dirs.; cons., 1986—. Bd. dirs. McNab Corp. Chmn. bd. advisors Sch. engring., N.C. State U., 1986-89; mem. adv. bd. trustees Union Coll., 1997-2000; trustee Poly. Prep. Country Day Sch., 1990-2002; trustee Saddle River Day Sch.; deacon West Side Presbyn. Ch., Ridgewood, N.J., 1988-90, 96-2000, elder, 1990-93, trustee, 2000-2003. Mem. IEEE (sr.), NSPE, N.J. State Soc. Profl. Engrs., World Rehab. Fund (bd. dirs. 1986-96), N.Y.C. C. of C. and Industry (bd. dirs. 1980-88), Delta Upsilon (vice chmn. Ednl. Found. 1986-95). Republican. Home and Office: 84 Buckhaven Hl Upper Saddle River NJ 07458

WALLACE, WILLIAM BRIAN, sales executive; b. Memphis, June 28, 1978; s. William Lee and Melissa Lee Wallace. BBA in Acctg. summa cum laude, BBA in Fin. summa cum laude, U. Memphis, 2002. V.p. sales and mem. rels. First South Credit Union, Bartlett, Tenn., 2001—02, sr. sales mgr., 2002—. V.p. membership Memphis Jaycees, 2001—02, bd. dirs., 2001—02, webmaster, 2001—02; vol. Nat. Kidney Found., Memphis, 2002, St. Jude Children's Rsch. Hosp., Memphis, 2000—03. Named one of Memphis's Top 40 Under 40, Memphis Bus. Jour., 2003; recipient award, Tenn. Soc. CPAs, 2002. Mem.: Golden Key, Phi Kappa Phi, Beta Gamma Sigma, Beta Alpha Psi. Republican. Roman Catholic. Avocations: travel, reading, gardening, sketching, writing. Office: First South Credit Union 6445 Stage Rd Bartlett TN 38134 Office Phone: 901-380-7552. E-mail: bwallace@firstsouth.com.

WALLACE, WILLIAM HALL, economic and financial consultant; b. Senatobia, Miss., Aug. 8, 1933; s. Woodard Harvey and Cellie (Carter) W.; m. Margaret Jaeger, Mar. 7, 1964 (dec. 1978); children: Amy Margaret, William Douglas, John Richard Bruce; m. Virginia Wilson, Aug. 25, 1979. BBA, U. Miss., 1955, MBA, 1956; PhD, U. Ill., 1962. Asst. prof. econs. Duke U., Durham, NC, 1962-67; v.p. Fed. Res. Bank Richmond, Va., 1967-73; prof. econs. N.C. State U., Raleigh, 1973-74; staff dir. Fed. Res. Bd., Washington, 1974-80; 1st v.p., COO Fed. Res. Bank Dallas, 1981-91; prof. fin., dean Coll. Bus. and Pub. Adminstrn. Old Dominion U., Norfolk, Va., 1991-94; ret., 1994; pres. Wallace Cons., Inc., 1994—. Co-dir. Eurasia Found. Program in Banking & Fin. Markets for Russia and CIS, 1994-95; tchr. Israel Coll., Tel Aviv, 1998-2000; adj. prof. econs. U. North Tex., Denton, Tex., 2001—. Trustee Dallas Hist. Soc.; mem. Dallas Com. Fgn. Rels. Served to 1st lt. U.S. Army, 1956-58. Mem. Am. Econs. Assn., Am. Statis. Assn., Ctrl. Dallas Assn. (exec. com.), Greater Dallas C. of C. (edn. com. 1984-88, chmn. edn. com. 1989-90), Rotary. Methodist. Office: U North Tex Dept Econs Wooten Hall 353 Denton TX 76203 Home: 7777 Glen America Dr Apt 114 Dallas TX 75225-1834 Office Phone: 940-369-7984. E-mail: whw2511@aol.com.

WALLACE DE CORNWALL, CLINTON H. media consultant; b. Montego Bay, Jamaica; s. E. Herbert Wallace and Elbemire Violette Forbes; m. Marina Olga-Yvonne Wallace De Cornwall, Dec. 1995. BS in Comm., NYU, 1995; MA in Media, Canterbury U., U.K., 2002. Notary pub. Calif., cert. French Lit. U. De Paris. Media rels. asst. Warlock Records, N.Y.C., 1992—93; news rm. asst. NBC News, 1993—94; media cons. Antoine Breton and Assocs., Paris, 1994—; co-founder Photoglobo, Strausbourg, France, 1999—2003; staff photographer Globe Photos, Inc., N.Y.C., 1999—2003; corr. Euroimagen, Madrid, 2002—03; media cons. D'ouzio and Assocs., Beverly Hills, Calif., 2000—03, Fusion Publicity, West Hollywood, 2001—, Verbana and Assocs., Burbank, 2002—, Amplified Pub. Relats., 2003—04. Founder Photmundo Internat., Granada, Spain, 1993. Editor: Talawah Jours., 1999, Brazil Explore, 2002; photographer Latin Style, 2001. Fellow: Hon. Order Ky. Cols.; mem.: Am. Fedn. Televisoin and Radio Artists, Mus. of Making Music. Avocations: photography, travel, archaeology, French literature, writing. Home: 270 N Canon Dr #1712 Beverly Hills CA 90210 Office Phone: 310-585-4637.

WALLACE DOUGLAS, JEAN, conservationist; b. Des Moines, Iowa, June 30, 1920; d. Henry A. and Ilo Wallace; m. Wallace Leslie Douglas, Oct. 12, 1946; children: David, Joan, Ann. BA, Connecticut Coll., 1943. Pres. Wallace Genetic Found., Washington, D.C., 1965—. Past bd. dirs. America The Beautiful, Am. Bird Conservancy, Cornell Lab. of Ornithology, The Land Inst., Wallace House Birthplace, The Accokeek Found., Am. Farmland Trust, Concern, Henry A. Wallace Inst. for Alternative Agr. Office: Wallace Genetic Found Ste 220 4900 Massachusetts Ave NW Washington DC 20016-4358

WALLACH, ALAN, art historian, educator; b. Bklyn., June 8, 1942; s. Israel and Vivian (Esner) W.; m. Phyllis Rosenzweig, Jan. 3, 1988. BA, Columbia U., 1963, MA, 1965, PhD, 1973. Assoc. prof. Kean Coll., Union, N.J., 1974-89; Ralph H. Wark prof. art and art history, prof. Am. studies Coll. William and Mary, Williamsburg, Va., 1989—. Vis. prof. UCLA, 1982-83, Stanford (Calif.) U., 1987, CUNY, 1988, U. Mich., 1989; co-curator Nat. Mus. Am. Art, Washington, 1991-94. Author: (with William Truettner) Thomas Cole: Landscape into History, 1994; Exhibiting Contradiction: Essays on the Art Museum in the United States, 1998; mem. editl. bd. Am. Quar., 2000-03; contbr. articles to profl. jours. Sr. Postdoctorate Rsch. award Smithsonian Inst., 1985-86. Mem. Am. Studies Assn., Coll. Art Assn. (bd. dirs. 1996-2000), Assn. Art Historians. Home: 2009 Belmont Rd NW Washington DC 20009-5449 Office: Coll William and Mary Dept Art and Art History Williamsburg VA 23187-8795 Office Phone: 757-221-2530. E-mail: axwall@wm.edu.

WALLACH, ANNE JACKSON See JACKSON, ANNE

WALLACH, DAN, lumber company executive; CFO 84 Lumber Co., Eighty Four, Pa. Office: 84 Lumber Co 1019 Rte 519 Eighty Four PA 15330-2813

WALLACH, ELI, actor; b. Bklyn., Dec. 7, 1915; s. Abraham and Bertha (Schorr) W.; m. Anne Jackson, Mar. 5, 1948; children: Peter Douglas, Roberta Lee, Katherine Beatrice. AB, U. Tex., 1936; MS in Edn, CCNY, 1938; student, Neighborhood Playhouse Sch. of Theatre, 1940; hon. doctorate, Emerson Coll., Boston, Sch. for Visual Arts, 1991. Corp. mem., dir. Neighborhood Playhouse Sch. Theatre. Actor, 1945—; Broadway plays include Antony and Cleopatra, 1948, Mr. Roberts, 1949-50, Rose Tatoo, 1950-52, Camino Real, 1953, Mademoiselle Colombe, 1953, Teahouse of the August Moon, 1954-55, London prodn., 1954, Major Barbara, 1956, Rhinoceros, 1961, Luv, 1964, Promenade All, 1972, Twice Around the Park, 1983, Opera Comique, Kennedy Ctr. Performing Arts, 1987, The Flowering Peach, Fla., 1987, Broadway, 1994, Cafe Crown, 1989; appeared off-Broadway prodn. Typists and the Tiger, 1962-63, London prodn., 1964, Saturday, Sunday, Monday, 1974, (with wife and 2 daus.) Diary of Anne Frank, 1977-78, Visiting Mr. Green, 1997; off-Broadway in Tennessee Williams Remembered, 1999; on tour Down the Garden Paths, 1998-99; appeared in: nat. tour co. Waltz of the Toreadors, 1973-74; appeared in TV film Executioner's Song, 1982, Murder By Reason of Insanity, 1985, Monday Night Mayhem, 2000, TV series Batman, 1966, Kojak, 1973, Highway to Heaven, 1984, Our Family Honor, 1985, L.A. Law, 1986, Law & Order, 1990, The Education of Max Bickford, 2001-02, TV miniseries Christopher Columbus, 1985, The Education of Max Bickford, 2002; motion pictures include Baby Doll, 1955, The Misfits, 1960, The Victors, 1962, Lord Jim, 1964, How To Steal a Million, The Good, the Bad and the Ugly, The Tiger Makes Out, Band of Gold, Zig-Zag, Cinderella Liberty, 1973, Crazy Joe, 1973, Movie, Movie, 1976, Sam's Son, 1985, Tough Guys, 1986, Rocket to the Moon,1986, Nuts, 1987, The Impossible Spy, 1987, Godfather III, 1990, The Two Jakes, 1990, Article 99, Mistress, 1991, Night and the City, 1991, Honey, Sweet Love, 1993, Two Much, 1995, The Associate, 1996, Keeping the Faith, 2000, (TV movie) Monday Night Mayhem, 2002. Served to capt. Med. Adminstrn. Corps AUS, World War II. Recipient Donaldson, Theatre World, Variety, Antoinette Perry, Drama League awards, Brit. Film Acad. award, 1956, Disting. Alumnus award U. Tex., 1989. Original mem. Actors Studio. Office: Paradigm 200 W 57 St Ste 900 New York NY 10019

WALLACH, ERIC JEAN, lawyer; b. NYC, June 11, 1947; s. Milton Harold and Jacqueline (Goldschmidt) W.; m. Miriam Grunberger, Mar. 21, 1976; children: Katherine, Emily, Peter. BA, Harvard U., 1968, JD, 1972. Bar: N.Y. 1973, U.S. Dist. Ct. (so. and ea. dists.) N.Y. 1973, U.S. Dist. Ct. (no. dist.) N.Y. 1989, U.S. Ct. Appeals (2nd cir.) 1973, (3d cir.) 1996, U.S. Tax Ct. 1976. Assoc. Webster & Sheffield, N.Y.C., 1972-77, Rosenman & Colin, N.Y.C., 1977-80, ptnr., 1981-96, mem. mgmt. com., 1993-96, chmn. employment practice group, 1985-96; ptnr., chmn. employment practice group Kasowitz, Benson, Torres & Friedman LLP, N.Y.C., 1996—. Presenter, chmn. CLE programs, Practising Law Inst., Cambridge Inst., others. Mem. editl. bd. You and the Law, 1992-96; contbr. articles to profl. jours. Sec.-treas. Art Dealers Assn. Am., Inc., N.Y.C., 1985-96; trustee C.G. Jung Found. for Analytical Psychology; trustee Am. Jewish World Svc., Inc., N.Y.C., 1989-97, chmn., 1995-97; dir. N.Y. Jr. Tennis League. Mem. Harvard Club N.Y.C. (admissions com. 1992-94), Sunningdale Country Club, Poughkeepsie Tennis Club. Democrat. Avocations: sports, travel, reading. Home: 940 Park Ave New York NY 10028 also: 16 Buttonwood Ln Rhinebeck NY 12572-3510 Office: Kasowitz Benson Torres & Friedman LLP 1633 Broadway New York NY 10019 Office Phone: 212-506-1750. Business E-Mail: ewallach@kasowitz.com.

WALLACH, HOWARD FREDERIC, psychiatrist; b. Chgo., Sept. 4, 1923; s. Leo and Mildred (Ebert) W.; m. Laurie Rochelle Gettleman, Sept. 15, 1945 (div. July 1968); children: Joan, John, Richard; m. Gloria Bunny Jackman, July 14, 1968; children: Rand, Steve, Beth. MD, U. Ill., Chgo., 1946; M.Social Psychiatry, UCLA, 1969. Diplomate Am. Bd. Psychiatry and Neurology. Intern Cook County Hosp., Chgo., 1946—47, resident internal medicine, 1947—49; pres. Mount Sinai Hosp. Med. Rsch. Found., 1952—64; asst. clin. prof. psychiatry UCLA, 1968—80, assoc. clin. prof., 1980—; chief allied mental health Brentwood VA Hosp., L.A., 1970—72; chief psychiatry Sepulveda VA Hosp., L.A., 1972—74; pvt. practice L.A. Bd. govs. Cedars-Sinai Med. Ctr., L.A., 1985—, mem. exec. com., 2000—; cons. VA Med. Ctr., L.A., 1982-90; developer maj. high rise apts., Chgo., 1951-64. Contbr. articles to profl. jours. Sec. Am. Psychiat. Found., Washington, 1990-99; bd. dirs. Nat. Mus. Health and Medicine, Washington, 1989-99; v.p. Jewish Family Svc. of L.A., 1997-98; bd. dirs., pres. Young Men's Jewish Charities, Chgo., 1951-62; mem. Cook County Blue Ribbon Commn., 1959-63. 1st lt. U.S. Army, 1943-46. Recipient Bronze award Boys Clubs of Am., 1962, Pres.'s Spl. Achievement award So. Calif. Psychiat. Soc., 1991. Fellow Am. Coll. Psychoanalysts, Am. Psychiat. Assn. (exec. com. 1982-88), Am. Acad. Psychoanalysis; mem. Calif. Psychiat. Assn. (pres. 1986-88), So. Calif. Psychiat. Soc. (pres. 1979-80, mem. coun. 1975-83), Alpha Omega Alpha. Avocations: photography, computers, golf, walking, presidential manuscript collecting. Office: 2080 Century Park E Los Angeles CA 90067-2001 E-mail: hfwallach@yahoo.com.

WALLACH, IRA DAVID, lawyer, business executive; b. N.Y.C., June 3, 1909; s. Joseph and Della (Kahn) W.; m. Miriam Gottesman, Dec. 25, 1938. BA, Columbia U., 1929, JD, 1931, LLD (hon.), 1983, U. Maine, 1983. Bar: N.Y. 1932. Practiced in, N.Y.C., 1932-45; exec. v.p. Gottesman & Co., Inc. (name changed to Central Nat.-Gottesman Inc. 1984), N.Y.C., 1952-56, pres., CEO, 1956-74, chmn., CEO, 1974-79, chmn., 1979-2001, sr. vice chmn., 2001—, also bd. dirs. Exec. v.p. Ctrl. Nat. Corp., N.Y.C., 1952-56, pres., CEO, 1956-74, chmn., CEO, 1974-79, chmn., 1979—; exec. v.p. Eastern Corp., Bangor, Maine, 1951-52; dir., pres. Sejak Corp., N.Y.C., dir., exec. v.p. Cenro Corp., N.Y.C. Pres. D.S. and R.H. Gottesman Found., 1956—, bd. dirs., 1941—; chmn., dir. Miriam and Ira D. Wallach Found., 1956—; co-founder, chmn. emeritus East West Inst., 1981—; bd. dirs. Internat. Peace Acad., People for the Am. Way Found. Lt. USNR, 1943-46. Mem. Am. Bar Assn., Assn. of Bar of City of N.Y., N.Y. Co. Lawyers Assn. Home: 5 Sherbrooke Rd Scarsdale NY 10583-4429 Office: 3 Manhattanville Rd Purchase NY 10577-2116

WALLACH, LESLIE ROTHAUS, architect; b. Pitts., Feb. 4, 1944; s. Albert and Sara F. (Rothaus) W.; m. Susan Rose Berger, June 15, 1969; 1 child, Aaron. BS in Mining Engring., U. Ariz., 1967, BArch, 1974. Registered architect, Ariz.; registered contractor, Ariz. Prin. Line and Space LLC, Tucson, 1978—. Mem. awards jury Sunset mag., 1997, Ariz. Homes of Yr., 1997, L.A. AIA; keynote spkr. various confs. Representative projects include Ariz. Sonora Desert Mus. Restaurant Complex, Tucson, Elgin Elem. Sch., Ariz., Hillel Student Ctr. U. Ariz., Tucson, Boyce Thompson Southwestern Arboreteum Vis. Ctr., Superior, Ariz., San Pedro Riparian Ctr., Sierra Vista, Ariz., Nat. Hist. Trails Ctr., Casper, Wyo., 2002, Vis. Ctr. and Arborteum, Flagstaff, Ariz., 2001, Regional Libr., Phoenix, 2002, Poetry Ctr. for U. Ariz., 2003, City of Phoenix Regional Libr., U. Ariz.; contbr. Sunset Mag., Architecture Mag. and Fine Homebuilding; pub.: Space and Society (Italy), Hinge (Hong Kong), Wallpaper (London); exhibited at U. Ariz., AIA Nat. Conv., Washington, The Dutch Jour., Objekt, 2003 . Bd. dirs Tucson Regional Plan, Inc.; pres. Civitas Sonoran (The Environ. Design Coun. of the U. of Ariz. Coll. of Arch.). Recipient Roy P. Drachman Design award, 1982, 85, 93, 2001, Electric League Ariz. Design award, 1987, 88, Gov. Solar Energy award, 1989, Desert Living awards citation, 1991, Ariz. Architect's medal, 1989, Disting. Alumni award U. Ariz., 1998, also 35 additional design awards, including 4 received in 1995, winner $25,000 prize, nat. Endowment of the Arts, 2002, Coll. of Architecture Alumni of Yr., U. Az., 2001. Fellow AIA (Ariz. Honor award 1989, 92, 96, AIA/ACSA Nat. Design award 1991, Western Mountain region Design award 1992, 96, CA AIA/Phoenix Homes and Gardens Home of the Yr. Honor award 1992, 96, Western Region Silver medal 1996); mem. SAC AIA (past pres., Design award 1985, 88, 90), Western Mountain Region AIA (named Firm of Yr. 1999). Office: Line and Space 627 E Speedway Blvd Tucson AZ 85705-7433 E-mail: studio627@lineandspace.com.

WALLACH, MAGDALENA FALKENBERG (CARLA WALLACH), writer; b. Brussels; d. Carl Albert and Renee Antoinette (Meunier) Falkenberg; m. Philip Charles Wallach, Mar. 5, 1950. Student, Columbia U., Hunter Coll., New Sch. for Social Rsch. Pub. Williams Falkenberg Advt. Assocs., Inc., N.Y.C., 1951-55. Author: Reluctant Weekend Gardener, 1971, Interior Decorating with Plants, 1976, Gardening in the City, 1976, Garden in a Teacup, 1978; contbr. articles to N.Y. Times, Glamour, Working Woman, Greenwich Time, Stamford Adv, others. Former bd. dirs. ARC, N.Y.C.; active Bruce Mus., 1987-2001, chmn. spl. events 75th anniversary gala, chmn. Renaissance Ball, bd. dirs., also other fundraising activities; former bd. dirs., v.p. Greenwich Adult Day Ctr. Mem. Nat. League Am. PEN Women (pres. Greenwich br. 1987-92, Owl award 1996), Authors Guild, Garden Writers Assn., English-Speaking Union (past bd. dirs. Greenwich br.), Alliance Francaise, Nat. Inst. Social Scis. Roman Catholic. Avocations: gardening, reading, travel, music, theater. Home: 126 W Lyon Farm Dr Greenwich CT 06831-4352

WALLACH, MARK IRWIN, lawyer; b. May 19, 1949; s. Ivan A. and Janice (Grossman) W.; m. Karla L. Wallach, 1996; children: Kerry Melissa, Philip Alexander; stepchildren: Daniel Kanter, Rachel Kanter, Adam Kanter. BA magna cum laude, Wesleyan U., 1971; JD cum laude, Harvard U., 1974. Bar: Ohio 1974, U.S. Dist. Ct. (no. dist.) Ohio, 1974, U.S. Ct. Appeals (6th cir.) 1985, U.S. Supreme Ct. 1985. Law clk. U.S. Dist. Ct., Cleve., 1974-75; assoc. Baker & Hostetler, Cleve., 1975-79; chief trial counsel City of Cleve., 1979-81; assoc. Calfee, Halter & Griswold, Cleve., 1981-82, ptnr., 1982—, co-chmn. litigation dept., 2004—. Mem. fed. ct. adv. com. U.S. Dist. Ct. (no. dist.) Ohio, 1991-95; chmn. bd. trustees Ohio Group Against Smoking Pollution, 1986 90; trustee Cleve. chpt. Am. Jewish Com., 1986—, sec. 1989-91, v.p., 1991-95, pres., 1995-97; bd. trustees Citizens League of Greater Cleve., 1978-79, 87-92. Author: Christopher Morley, 1976. Pres. Wesleyan Alumni Club, Cleve., 1983-87, 92—; trustee Lyric Opera, Cleve., 1995—, pres., 1996-98, Ratner Schs., 1994-96; pres. Performing Arts Together, 1997-2001; trustee The Sculpture Ctr. 2001—, pres., 2001—; trustee Bellefaire Jewish Children's Bur., 2001—. Mem. ABA, Ohio Bar Assn., Fed. Bar Assn., Cuyahoga County Law Dirs. Assn., The Cleve. Racquet Club, Greater Cleve. Bar Assn., The Club at Soc. Ctr. Avocations: reading, bicycling, space exploration, politics. Home: 2758 Claythorne Rd Shaker Heights OH 44122-1938 Office: Calfee Halter & Griswold 1400 McDonald Investment Ctr 800 Superior Ave E Ste 1800 Cleveland OH 44114-2688 Office Phone: 216-622-8344. E-mail: mwallach@calfee.com.

WALLACH, MORTON L. scientist; s. Herman and Helen Wallach; m. Harriet Myers, Dec. 10, 1959 (div. Oct. 15, 1969); children: Bonalynn, Richard, Hillary. BS in Chemistry, Wayne State U., 1951—55, PhD in Phys. Chemistry, 1955—59. Sci. advisor & tech. operation mgr. Polysar, Inc., Leominster, Mass., 1987—90; pres./ceo PEL Associates, Groton, Conn., 1975—. Expert Teltech Network of Experts, Mpls., 1990—; v.p. Ocean Tech. Found., 2000—; indsl. affiliate U. of Conn., Groton, Conn., United States, 2001—. Author (25 pubs. & five books): (science & technology) PEL Ann. Update: Recent Progress in Polymer/Plastics Tech. Fellow Fulbright, State Dept., USA, 1960. Mem.: Licensing Executives Soc., Conn. Tech. Coun., Soc. of Plastics Engineers, Am. Chem. Soc. Achievements include invention of novel sensors, coatings, plastics, polymer films; first to Polymer Films, Polymer Blends, Plastics Nucleating Agents; patents pending for Novel Sensors; New Marine Coatings; development of of light scattering theory and applications to polymers and colloids. Avocations: swimming, travel. Home: 23 Wildwood Rd Groton CT 06340 Office: PEL Associates 1084 Shennecossett Rd Groton CT 06340 E-mail: mlwallach@pelassociates.com.

WALLACH, PATRICIA, councilwoman, retired mayor; b. Chgo. m. Ed Wallach; 3 children. Grad., Pasadena City Coll. Mem. city coun. City of El Monte, Calif., 1990-92, mayor, 1992-99, elected mem. of city coun., 2003—. Ret. tchr.'s aide Mountain View Sch. Dist. Past trustee El Monte Union High Sch. Dist., L.A. County High Sch. for the Arts; amb. of goodwill Zamora, Michoacan, Mex., Marcq-en-Baroeul, France, Yung Kang, Hsiang, Republic of China, Minhang, Peoples Republic of China; bd. dirs. Cmty. Redevel. Agy., El Monte Cmty. Access TV Corp.; mem. PTA, Little League Assns.; v.p. exec. bd., treas. Foothill Transit. Mem. League of Calif. Cities, San Gabriel Valley Coun. of Govts., Independent Cities Assn., U.S./Mex. Sister Cities Assn., Sister Cities Internat., Women of the Moose, El Monte Women's Club. Office Phone: 626-580-2001.

WALLACH, ROBERT CHARLES, obstetrician, gynecologist, educator; b. Bklyn., Jan. 2, 1935; s. Irving T. and Saralta W.; m. Judith Leffert, Apr. 1, 1968; 1 son, Theodore Hugh Kendall. BA with honors (N.Y. State Regents scholar), Swarthmore Coll., 1956; MD, Yale U., 1960. Intern Beth Israel Hosp., N.Y.C., 1960-61, resident in Ob-Gyn, 1961-65; sr. clin. trainee divsn. chronic diseases USPHS, 1965-66; fellow in gynecol. oncology SUNY, Bklyn., 1965-66; practice medicine specializing in ob-gyn N.Y.C., 1966—; chief ob-gyn Gouverneur Hosp., N.Y.C., 1966-76; dir. ob-gyn Beth Israel Med. Ctr., N.Y.C., 1977-89, dir. emeritus, cons., 1989—; prof. ob-gyn., dir. emeritus divsn. gynecol. oncology NYU Sch. Medicine, 1990—. Asst. vis. obstetrician-gynecologist Kings County Hosp. Ctr., 1965-71, clin. prof. Mt. Sinai Sch. Medicine, N.Y.C., 1977—1990; clin. prof. 1990-1992, profl.lectr. 1992-, attending obstetrician-gynecologist Mt. Sinai Hosp., 1970-94, Orthopaedic Inst., Hosp. for Joint Diseases, N.Y.C., 1979—, Tisch U. Hosp., N.Y.C.; lectr. SUNY, Bklyn., 1967—, Yale U. Sch. Nursing, 1971-73; dir. gynecol. oncology Bellevue Hosp., N.Y.C., 1990-2000; cons. in ob-gyn St. Agnes Hosp., White Plains, N.Y., 1971-92; gynecologist Doctors Hosp. Beth Israel Med. Ctr. Singer Divsn., N.Y.C., Lenox Hill Hosp., N.Y.C., N.Y. Hosp. Queens Divsn. Author: New Choices, New Chances, 1982, A Primer of Gynecologic Oncology, 1995; contbr. articles to profl. jours. Regents' scholar, N.Y., 1952, 1956. Fellow ACS, Am. Coll. Obstetricians and Gynecologists, N.Y. Obstet. Soc.; Soc. Gynecol. Oncologists,N.Y. Acad. Medicine (sec. sect. on ob.-gyn. 1975-76, chmn. 1976-77, com. on pub. health, subcom. on maternity and family planning 1982—), N.Y. Acad. Sci., N.Y. Cancer Soc., N.Y. Obstet. Soc., Assn. Profs. Ob-Gyn., Internat. Soc. Gynecol. Pathologists, European Soc. Gynecol. Oncology. Office: 700 Park Ave New York NY 10021-4930

WALLACH, STEPHEN JOSEPH, cardiologist; b. Bklyn., Dec. 16, 1942; s. Frank and Sylivia B. (Meisel) W.; m. Vicki Wallach, June 30, 1968; children: Jonathan, Rachel. BS in Pharmacy, L.I. U., 1965; MD, U. Okla., 1969. Intern Emory Affiliated, Atlanta, 1960-70, med. resident, 1970-71; gen. med. officer USN, 1971-74; med. resident USN Naval Res. Med. Ctr., Phila., 1974-75, fellow cardiology, 1975-76, mem. staff intermal medicine, 1976-77; asst. prof. John Burns Sch. Medicine, Honolulu, 1977-78; pvt. practice cardiology Queens Med. Ctr., Honolulu, 1978—, chief dept. medicine, 1993-2000, dir. utilization mgmt., dir. inhospital svcs., 1998. Clin. assoc. prof. medicine John A. Burns Sch. Medicine, 1998. Bd. dirs. Am. Heart Assn., Honolulu, 1980-86, pres. Honolulu chpg., 1994-95. Ltd. comdr. USNR, 1971. Fellow Am. Coll. Cardiology; mem. Honolulu County Med. Assn. (pres. 1990-91), Hawaii Med. Assn. (pres. 1991-92), Hawaii Soc. Internal Medicine (pres. 1996—). Jewish. Avocations: movies, hiking, music. Office: Queens Med Ctr 1301 Punchbowl St Ste 206 Honolulu HI 96813-2413

WALLACH, STEVEN ERNST, lawyer, pilot; b. N.Y.C., Mar. 21, 1944; s. Eduard Herbert Wallach and Karin (Wassermann) Grunebaum; m. Stefany Gay Rosehill (div. Oct. 1990); children: Shelby Karin, Shawna Beth; m. Geri Joan Grieco, Nov. 21, 1992. BS, USAF Acad., 1965; MS summa cum laude, U. So. Calif., 1971; JD magna cum laude, Nova U., 1986. Bar: Fla. 1986, D.C. 1988, U.S. Dist. Ct. (so. dist.) Fla. 1987, U.S. Dist. Ct. (mid. dist.) Fla. 1989, U.S. Dist. Ct. Ariz. 1989; cert. airline transport pilot, 1969; bd. cert. aviation law, 1998. Systems analyst Hughes Aircraft Co., L.A., 1971-72; airline capt. Eastern Air Lines, Miami, 1972-91; atty. Barwick, Dillian & Lambert P.A., Miami Shores, Fla., 1987-96; atty., ptnr. Thornton Davis & Murray, P.A., Miami, 1996-98. Aviation mgmt. cons. PRC Speas, Lake Success, N.Y., 1977-83, TRAMCO, Cambridge, Mass., 1972-77, A.V. lawyer, 1997, Steven Wallach Assoc., 1998—. Trustee Karin Grunebaum Cancer Found., Cambridge, 1979—. Capt. USAF, 1965-70. Decorated DFC, 5 air medals. Avocation: flying. Home: 2600 S Ocean Blvd Apt 21-E Boca Raton FL 33432

WALLACK, STANLEY S. healthcare administrator; b. Sept. 6, 1941; BA, Antioch Coll., 1964; PhD in Econs., Washington U., St. Louis, 1969. Mem. faculty U. Ill., Champaign; dep. asst. dir. Congl. Budget Office for Health Income Assistance, Washington, 1971-75; dir. divsn. health resources U.S. Office Asst. Sec. for Planning and Evaluation, HEW, 1971-75; mem. faculty, exec. dir. Schneider Inst. for Health Policy, Brandeis U., Waltham, Mass.; chmn. bd. dirs., CEO LifePlans, Inc., 1993-97. Developer Social Health Maintenca Orgn.; prin. investigator Health Policy Rsch. Consritium/HCFA; dir. Pew Doctoral Program; co-dir. Kaiser Found. Ctr. for State Svcs.; co-prin. investigator NIDA Ctr. for Drug Abuse Svcs. Rsch. Contbr. articles to profl. publs. Office: PO Box 549110 415 South St # MS035 Waltham MA 02454-9110 E-mail: wallack@brandeis.edu.

WALLANCE, GREGORY J. lawyer; b. Washington, Oct. 24, 1948; s. Donald Aaron Wallance and Shula Cohen; m. Elizabeth Van Veen, Jan. 4, 1981; children: Daniel, Carina, Lisanne. BA, Grinnell Coll., 1970; JD, Bklyn. Law Sch., 1976. Bar: N.Y. 1977, U.S. Dist. Ct. (ea. dist.) N.Y. 1977, U.S. Dist. Ct. (so. dist.) N.Y. 1978, U.S. Ct. Appeals (2d cir.) 1980, U.S. Dist. Ct. (no. dist.) 1989, Clk. to Hon. Jacob Mishler, N.Y.C., 1976-77; assoc. Paul, Weiss, Rifkind, Wharton & Garrison, N.Y.C., 1977-79, asst. U.S. atty., U.S. Atty's. Office, N.Y.C., 1979-85; assoc. Kaye Scholer Fierman Hays & Handler, N.Y.C., 1985-88; ptnr. Kaye, Scholer, Fierman, Hays & Handler, 1988—; chief litigation counsel Kidder Peabody & Co., Inc., 1995—. Author: Papa's Game, 1981; assoc. prodr. (HBO) Sakharov, 1981; co-host The Law Show, (BBC), 1998; columnist Nat. Law Jour., 1993-98; contbr. articles to profl. jours. Vol. VISTA, N.Y.C., 1970-72. Mem. ABA, Assn. for Bar of City of N.Y. Office: Kaye Scholer Fierman Hays & Handler 425 Park Ave New York NY 10022-3506

WALLAU, ALEX, broadcast executive; b. Ft. McPherson, Ga. BA, Williams Coll. Head on-air promotion ABC Sports, 1976—86, boxing analyst, 1986—93; v.p. ABC TV Network, Walt Disney Co., Burbank, Calif., 1993—96; exec. v.p. ABC TV Netowrk Ops. and Adminstrn., Walt Disney Co., Burbank, Calif., 1996—98, pres., 1998—2000, ABC TV Network, Walt Disney Co., Burbank, Calif., 2000—. Office: ABC Inc 500 S Buena Vista St Burbank CA 91521-4551

WALLEM, PAUL SIGURD, financial planner; b. Ottawa, Ill., Mar. 14, 1934; s. Sigurd and Bertha Elene W.; m. Joan B. Wallem, Aug. 12, 1956; children: Jeffery, Linda, Stephen. BS, U. Ill., 1956. CFP. Terr. and sales mgr. Internat. Harvester Co., Chgo., 1958-66, export mgr., 1966-68; pres. Wallem Internat., Belvidere, Ill., 1969-86; owner Wallem Assocs., Rockford, Ill., 1986—. Chmn., bd. trustees Highland Hosp., Belvidere, 1977-79; founding dir. Vintage Wings and Wheels Mus., Poplar Grove, Ill., 1996—. 1st lt. U.S. Army, 1956-58. Republican. Methodist. Avocation: aviation. Office: Wallem Assocs 6068 Palo Verde Dr Rockford IL 61114

WALLEN, CARL JOSEPH, JR., education educator; b. Glendale, Calif., Dec. 12, 1931; s. Carl Joseph and Winifred (Batten) W.; m. LaDonna Leigh Stanley, Nov. 29, 1959; children: Erik Stanley, Todd Alan, Michael Carl. BA, U. Calif., Santa Barbara, 1956; MA, San Francisco State U., 1960; EdD, Stanford U., 1962. Tchr. 5th grade Mt. Eden Sch. Dist., Hayward, Calif., 1956-58; tchr. 3d and 6th grades Pacifica (Calif.) Sch. Dist., 1958-60; grad. asst. Stanford U., Palo Alto, Calif., 1960-62; asst. prof. Oreg. State U., Corvallis, 1962-65; assoc. prof. tchg. rsch. Oreg. Sys. Higher Edn., Monmouth, 1965-67; assoc. prof. U. Oreg., Eugene, 1967-73, dir. of U.S. Office of Edn. fellowship program, 1972-73; prof., chmn. dept. elem. edn. Ariz. State U., Tempe, 1973-78, prof., 1978-97, prof. emeritus, 1997—. Cons. to schs., dists. and state depts. edn. in Oreg. and Ariz., 1962—. Author: Competency in Teaching Reading, 1973, 82, Cognition and Effective Instruction, 1993, 94, 95, 96; co-author: Effective Classroom Management, 1978, Fraud Recognition: Claims Adjustors, 1993; also monographs and jour. articles. Mem. com. Am. Friends Svc. Com., Oreg. and Ariz., 1963—; co-founder, pres. Ariz. Ctr. to Reverse Arms Race, Phoenix, 1978-82; rep. Ariz. Ecumenical Coun., 1978—, pres., 1990-93, prison visitation and support, 1997—. With U.S. Army, 1952-54. U.S. OfficeEdn. fellow, 1972-73. Mem. Am. Ednl. Rsch. Assn., Phi Delta Kappa. Democrat. Mem. Soc. Of Friends. Avocations: woodworking, stained glass making, gardening. Home: 525 E Alameda Dr Tempe AZ 85282-3822 E-mail: clwallen@aol.com.

WALLENDER, MICHAEL TODD, lawyer; b. Schenectady, N.Y., Apr. 8, 1950; s. Kenneth Clark and Martha Lee (Getty) W.; m. Joyce Ann Mushaw, June 3, 1978; children: Kristina Lee, Michael David. BA, Colgate U., 1972; JD, Harvard U., 1975. Law asst. N.Y. State Supreme Ct. Appellate Div., Albany, 1975-76; assoc. DeGraff, Foy, Conway, Holt-Harris & Mealey, Albany, 1976-80, ptnr., 1981-90. Counsel N.Y. State Assn. Realtors, Albany, 1981—, Albany County Bd. Realtors, 1985-92, Capital Regional Multiple Listing Svc., Albany, 1986—, Greater Capitol Assn. Realtors, 1992—. Author: Realtors and the Law of Agency, 1988. Mem. ATLA, ABA, Lawyers for Justice in Ireland, N.Y. State Bar Assn., Albany County Bar Assn., Ft. Orange Club, Mohawk Golf Club, Colgate Club (capital dist. chpt., Albany), Saratoga Reading Rm. Avocation: thoroughbred horse racing. Home: 209 Agostino Ave Niskayuna NY 12309-1331 Office: 90 State St Ste 1501 Albany NY 12207-1714

WALLENMEYER, WILLIAM ANTON, retired physicist; b. Evansville, Ind, Feb. 3, 1926; s. William Anton and Mindie (Madden) W.; m. Diane Mae Hankins, June 1, 1952; children: Wendy, Jon, Ann, Timothy. BS, Purdue U., 1950, MS, 1954, PhD, 1957, PhD (hon.), 1989. Jr. rsch. assoc. Brookhaven Nat. Lab., LI, NY, 1954—55; asst. prof. physics Wabash Coll., Crawfordsville, Ind., 1955-56; dir. accelerator divsn. Midwestern U. Rsch. Assn., Madison, Wis., 1957-62; dir. divsn. high energy physics U.S. Dept. Energy, Germantown, Md., 1962-87; pres. Southeastern Univ. Rsch. Assn., Washington, 1987-92; spl. asst. to pres. Univ. Rsch. Assn., Washington, 1993-94. With Air Corps U.S. Army, 1944—46. Fellow AAAS, Am. Phys. Soc. Home: 1204 Azalea Dr Rockville MD 20850-2024

WALLER, EDWARD MARTIN, JR., lawyer; b. Memphis, July 2, 1942; s. Edward Martin and Freda (Lazarov) W.; m. Laura Jayne Rhodes, June 18, 1982; children: Lauren, Jonathan, Melissa. BA, Columbia U., 1964; JD, U. Chgo., 1967. Bar: Fla. 1967. Assoc. Fowler, White, Boggs, Banker, P.A., Tampa, Fla., 1967-72, ptnr., 1972—. Mem.: ABA (standing com. professionalism chmn. 1995—97, banking and fin. transactions com., litig. sect. 1978—82, co-chmn. 1983—87, coun. 1990—92, budget officer 1996—2000, litig. sect.), Bay Area Legal Svcs. (bd. dirs. 2003—), Hillsborough County Bar Assn., Fla. Bar Assn., Fla. Supreme Ct. Commn. on Professionalism. Democrat. Jewish. Office: Fowler White Boggs Banker PO Box 1438 Tampa FL 33601-1438

WALLER, EPHRAIM EVERETT, retired association executive; b. Sioux City, Iowa, Aug. 10, 1928; s. Everett and Ruth Emma (Little) W.; m. Virginia Louise Harper, Oct. 3, 1959. BA, U. Iowa, 1951, MA, 1959; grad., Strategic Intelligence Sch., 1955, Army Security Agy. Sch., 1962, Nat. Cryptologic Sch., 1966, Comd. and Gen. Staff Coll., 1966; grad. with honors, State Dept. Fgn. Svc. Inst., 1967, Turkish Lang. Sch., 1968; grad., Indsl. Coll. Armed Forces, 1972; EdD with honors, U. S.D., 1981. Cert. fgn. area specialist, cryptologist. Commd. 2d lt. U.S. Army, 1951, advanced through grades to lt. col., 1967, retired, 1979; exec. dir. Midwest Agrl. Chems. Assn., Sioux City, Iowa, 1981-95; cons., 1996—; ret. mem. sci. and regulatory oversight coun. Am. Crop Protection Assn., Washington, 1990-95; mem. interregional coord. coun. Joint Body U.S. Regional Agrl. Assns., Dawson, Ga., 1991-95. Contbr. articles to profl. jours. Mem. coms. 1st Congrl. Ch., Sioux City, 1937—. Decorated Bronze Star, Cross of Gallantry with Silver Star, Legion of Merit with oak leaf cluster, Chinese and Vietnamese Honor medals, Meritorious Svc. medal with oak leaf cluster, Joint Svc. Commendation medal with oak leaf cluster, Army Commendation medal with oak leaf cluster, Army Gen. Staff badge, Vietnamese Combat Merit medal; Asia Found. scholar U. Iowa; recipient Outstanding Leadership in the Industry award Am. Crop Protection Assn., 1995, Leadership in Cmty. and Pub. Edn. award Chem. Prodrs. and Distbrs. Assn., 1993-94, Dedication and Svc. to Agrl. Industry award Ill.

Fertilizer and Chems. Assn., 1987, Dean Roy Exceptional Svc. award Midwest Agrl. Chems. Assn., 1985, Industry Vision award Mid Am. Crop Protection Assn., 1995, Significant Svc. to Agr. and Agrl. Chems. Industry award So. Crop Protection Assn., 1981-95, Outstanding Leadership in the Industry award Am. Crop Protection Assn., 1995, Don Kenna Excellence in Coalition Bldg. and Pub. Rels. award Fertilizer and Ag-Chem. Affiliated Assns., 1994. Mem. Ret. Officers Assn., Siouxland C. of C. (com. mem. 1981-95), Interprofl. Inst., Scottish Rite, Masons, Eastern Star, Phi Delta Kappa, Delta Sigma Rho. Avocations: swimming, hiking, travel, stamp collecting/philately, writing. Home: 2847 Valley Dr Sioux City IA 51104-4071

WALLER, HAROLD MYRON, political science educator; b. Detroit, Oct. 12, 1940; s. Allan L. and Lillian R. (LeVine) W.; m. Diane Carol Goodman, June 28, 1966; children: Sharon, Dahvi, Jeffrey. SB, MIT, 1962; MS, Northwestern U., 1966; PhD, Georgetown U., 1968. Asst. prof. McGill U., Montreal, 1967-71, assoc. prof., 1971-93, prof., 1993—, chmn. polit. sci. dept., 1969-74, 89-90, acting chmn., 1980-81, 86-87, assoc. dean (acad.) faculty arts, 1991-94, acting dean faculty arts, 1994-95, chair N.Am. studies program, 2003—04. Pres. McGill Assn. Univ. Tchrs., Montreal, 1978-79; fellow Jerusalem Ctr. Pub. Affairs, 1980—; dir. Can. Ctr. Jewish Community Studies, Montreal, 1980—. Co-author: Maintaining Consensus: The Canadian Jewish Polity in the Postwar World, 1990; co-editor: Canadian Federalism: From Crisis to Constitution; contbg. editor: Middle East Focus; mem. editorial bd. Jewish Political Studies; chmn. editorial bd. Viewpoints; contbr. numerous articles to profl. jours. and books in field. Com. chmn. Can. Jewish Congress, Montreal, 1971-74; chair, nat. exec. Can. Profs. for Peace in Middle East, Toronto, 1975-85; pres. Akiva Sch., Montreal, 1984-85; com. chmn. Jewish Edn. Council, Montreal, 1986-88. Recipient Nat. Jewish Book award Jewish Book Coun., N.Y.C., 1991; Grad. fellow NSF, Washington, 1965-66, Leave fellow Social Sci. Humanities Rsch. Coun., Ottawa, 1981-82. Mem. Am. Polit. Sci. Assn., Can. Polit. Sci. Assn., Assn. Jewish Studies, Assn. Sociol. Study of Jewry, Assn. Israel Studies, Faculty Club, Sigma Xi, Pi Sigma Alpha. Jewish. Avocations: travel, athletics, reading, politics. Office: McGill U Dept Polit Sci 855 Sherbrooke St W Montreal QC Canada H3A 2T7 Office Phone: 514-398-4806. Business E-Mail: harold.waller@mcgill.ca.

WALLER, JIM D. former holding company executive; Pres. Ithaca Holdings, Wilkesboro, NC, 1985—91, CEO, pres., chmn., 1991—2000.

WALLER, JOHN HENRY, author; b. Paw Paw, Mich., May 8, 1923; s. George and Marguerite (Rowland) W.; m. Barbara Steuart Hans, Sept. 2, 1947; children: Stephanie Robinson, Gregory, Maria. BA, U. Mich., 1946. Vice consul U.S. Fgn. Svc., Iran, 1947-53, 2d sec., 1960-62, spl. asst. to ambassador New Delhi, India, 1955-57, 68-71; polit. analyst State Dept., Washington, 1962-68; insp. gen. CIA, Washington, 1976-80; free-lance author Washington, 1968—. Bd. dirs. internat. affairs dept. Va. Mil. Inst. Author: (pen name John Rowland) Hostile Co-existance, history of Sino-Indian Relations, 1988, Gordon of Khartoum: The Saga of a Victorian Hero, (pen name John McGregor) Tibet, A Chronicle of Exploration, 1970, Beyond the Khyber Pass, 1990, The Unseen War in Europe, 1996, The Devil's Doctor, 2002; contbr. articles to popular history to profl. jours. Recipient Career Svcs. award Nat. Civil Svc. League, 1979, 80, Disting. Intelligence medal CIA, 1980. Mem. Washington Inst. Fgn. Affairs (bd. dirs.), Cosmos Club (Washington), Office of Strategic Svcs. Soc. (chmn. bd. dirs.). Home: 800 Ridge Dr Mc Lean VA 22101-1624

WALLER, JOHN HENRY, JR., state supreme court justice; b. Mullins, S.C., Oct. 31, 1937; s. John Henry and Elnita (Rabon) Waller; m. Jane McLaurin Cooper, Nov. 16, 1963 (div.); children: John Henry III, Melissa McLaurin; m. Debra Ann Meares, May 9, 1981; children: Ryan Meares, Rand Ellis. AB in Psychology, Wofford Coll., 1959; LLB, JD, U. S.C., 1963. Mem. S.C. Ho. of Reps., 1967—77, S.C. Senate, 1977—80; judge S.C. Cir. Ct., 1980—94; assoc. justice S.C. Supreme Ct., 1994—. Capt. U.S. Army, 1959—60. Mem.: Millins Rotary Club (1st pres.), Shriners, Masons. Avocations: woodworking, golf, water sports, skiing. Office: SC Supreme Ct 103 Main St PO Box 1059 Marion SC 29571-1059 also: SC Supreme Ct Supreme Court PO Box 11330 Columbia SC 29211-1330

WALLER, JOHN LOUIS, anesthesiology educator; b. Loma Linda, Calif., Dec. 1, 1944; s. Louis Clinton and Sue (Bruce) W.; m. Jo Lynn Marie Haas, Aug. 4, 1968; children: Kristina, Karla, David. BA, So. Coll., Collegedale, Tenn., 1967; MD, Loma Linda U., 1971. Diplomate Am. Bd. Anesthesiology. Intern Hartford (Conn.) Hosp., 1971—72; resident in anesthesiology Harvard U. Med. Sch.-Mass. Gen. Hosp., Boston, 1972—74, fellow, 1974—75; asst. prof. anesthesiology Emory U. Sch. Medicine, Atlanta, 1977—80, assoc. prof., 1980—86, prof., 1986—2001; chmn. dept. anesthesiology Emory U. Sch. Med., Atlanta, 1986—2000; chief anesthesiology Emory U. Hosp., Atlanta, 1986-94, med. dir., 1993-95; assoc. v.p. info. svcs. Woodruff Health Scis. Ctr., 1995-97; chief info. officer Emory U. System Healthcare, Atlanta, 1995-97; prof. anesthesiology Med. U. S.C., Charleston, 2002—, chmn. dept. anesthesia and perioperative medicine, 2002—. Cons. Arrow Internat., Inc., Reading, Pa., 1988—; mem. adv. com. on anesthetic and life support drugs FDA, Washington, 1986—92; numerous vis. professorships and lectures. Contbr. articles to med. jours. Maj. M.C., USAF, 1975-77. Recipient cert. of appreciation Office Sec. Def., 1983. Fellow: Am. Coll. Chest Physicians, Am. Coll. Anesthesiologists; mem.: AMA, Assn. Cardiac Anesthesiologists, Soc. Acad. Anesthesia Chmn. (councillor 1989—), Assn. Univ. Anesthesiologists, Internat. Anesthesia Rsch. Soc. (trustee 1984—2002, sec. 1996—98, chair 1998—2000), Soc. Cardiovascular Anesthesiologists (pres. 1991—93), Am. Soc. Anesthesiologists. Avocations: fishing, sailing, swimming. Office: Med U SC Dept Anes and Perioperative Medicine 165 Ashley Ave Ste 525 Charleston SC 29425

WALLER, MARY BELLIS, psychotherapist, education educator, consultant; b. Milw., May 18, 1940; d. Ernest Anthony and Hazel Mary (Addie) Bellis; m. Michael I. Waller, May 9, 1987 (dec. Nov. 1996); children: Eric B. Griswold, Andrew D. Griswold, Megan E. Griswold Simone BS, U. Wis., Milw., 1969, MS, 1971, PhD, 1992. Coord. Wis. Coalition for Ednl. Reform, Milw., 1971-74; instr. U. Wis., Milw., 1974-77; exec. dir. Worker Rights Inst., Milw., 1977-87; adj. prof. Nat. Coll. Edn., Evanston, Ill., 1981-96; preceptor, clin. program coord. U. Wis.-Parkside, Kenosha, 1987-96; Wis. lead cons. Emprise Designs, 1993-97; psychotherapist, dir. outreach programs Achievement Assocs., Ltd., 1998—; clin. assoc. prof. U. Wis., Milw., 2002—. Cons. on drug-affected children; ctr. scientist Ctr. for Addiction and Behavioral Health Rsch., 1996—; pres. Program Devel. and Evaluation, 1993—, Priority Group, Inc., 1998—. Author: Crack-Affected Children: A Teacher's Guide, 1993, Lady of the Manor: Medieval Cooking with Herbs, 1994; author numerous articles on drug-affected children. Mem. ASCD, NAEYC, Am. Ednl. Rsch. Assn., Assn. Tchr. Educators, Phi Delta Kappa (Disting. Svc. award 1992). Home: 8316 N Regent Rd Milwaukee WI 53217-2736 E-mail: mwaller@execpc.com.

WALLER, MICHAEL E. publishing executive; Grad, Milliken U., Decatur, Illinois, 1963. Editor Hartford (Conn.) Courant, 1990-94, pub., CEO, 1994-97, Baltimore Sun, Md., 1997—. Office: Baltimore Sun 501 N Calvert St Baltimore MD 21278-0001

WALLER, PATRICIA FOSSUM, transportation executive, researcher, psychologist; b. Winnipeg, Man., Can., Oct. 12, 1932; d. Magnus Samuel and Diana Isabel (Briggs) Fossum; m. Marcus Bishop Waller, Dec. 27, 1957; children: Anna Estelle, Justin Magnus, Martha Wilkinson, Benjamin Earl. AB in Psychology cum laude, U. Miami, Coral Gables, 1953, MS in Psychology, 1955; PhD in Psychology, U. N.C., 1959. Psychology intern VA Hosp., Salem, Va., 1956; psychology instr. Med. Sch. U. N.C., Chapel Hill, 1957; USPHS postdoctoral fellow R.B. Jackson Lab., Bar Harbor, Maine, 1958-60; psychologist VA Hosp., Brockton, Mass., 1961-62; psychology lectr. U. N.C., Chapel Hill, Greensboro, 1962-67, assoc. dir. driver studies Hwy. Safety Rsch. Ctr. Chapel Hill, 1967-89, founding dir. Injury Prevention Rsch. Ctr., 1987-89; dir. Transp. Rsch. Inst. U. Mich., Ann Arbor, 1989-99, sr. rsch. scientist emerita, prof. emerita, 1999—; sr. rsch. scientist Ctr. for Transp. Safety, Tex. Transp. Inst. Tex. A&M U., 2002—. Bd. dirs. Intelligent Transp. Soc. Am., Washington, 1991—99, Traffic Safety Assn. Mich., Lansing, 1991—99; bd. advisors Eno Transp. Found., Inc., Lndnsdowne, Va., 1994—97; chair group 5 coun. Transp. Rsch. Bd. of NRC, Washington, 1992—95; chmn. Task Force Operation Regulations, 1974—76, mem. study com. devel. ranking rail safety R&D projects, 1980—82, chmn. group 3 coun. operation, safety and maintenance transp. facilities, 1980—83, mem. IVHS-IDEA tech. rev. panel, 1993—2000, chair workshop human factors rsch. in hwy. safety, 1992, chair ad hoc com. environ. activies, 92, mem. task force on elderly drivers, 1990—93, mem. com. vehicle user characteristics, 1983—86, mem. com. planning and adminstrn. of transp. safety, 1986—92, mem. com. alcohol, other drugs and transp., 1986—98, numerous other coms., mem. spl. coms. including Inst. Medicine Dana Award com., 1986—90, com. of 55MPH nat. maximum speed limit, 1983—84; mem. motor vehicle safety rsch. adv. com. Dept. Transp., Washington, 1991—94; reviewer JAMA, Jour. Studies on Alcohol, Jour. of Gerontology, Am. Jour. Pub. Health; apptd. Pres. Coun. Spinal Cord Injury, 1981; apptd. advisor Nat. Hwy. Safety Adv. Com. to Sec. U.S. Dept. Transp., 1979—80, 1980—83, chair nat. motor carrier adv. com., 1997—98; author numerous reports on transp. to govtl. coms. and univs. Author: (with Paul G. Shinkman) Instructor's Manual for Mogan and King: Introduction to Psychology, 1971; author: (with others) Psychological Concepts in the Classroom, 1974, Drinking: Alcohol in American Society—Issues and Current Research, 1978, The American Handbook of Alcoholism, 1982, The Role of the Civil Engineer in Highway Safety, 1983, Aging and Public Health, 1985, Young Driver Accidents: In Search of Solutions, 1985, Alcohol, Accidents and Injuries, 1986, Transportation in an Aging Society: Improving the Mobility and Safety for Older Persons, 1988, Young Drivers Impaired by Alcohol and Drugs, 1988; mem. editorial bd. Jour. Safety Rsch., 1979—; assoc. guest editor Health Edn. Quar., 1989; assoc. editor Accident, Analysis, and Prevention, 1978-84, mem. editorial bd., 1976-87; contbr. articles to profl. jours. Grantee HHS, 1982, 92-97, NIH; named Widmark laureate Internat. Coun. Alcohol, Drugs and Traffic Safety, 1995; Dist. Alumnus Awd., Dept. Psych., UNC Chapel Hill, 1997; recipient James J. Howard Trailblazer award Nat. Assn. of Govs. Hwy. Safety Reps., 1998, Svc. Awd., Intelligent Transportation Soc. of Amer., 1999; World Traffic Soc. Awd., 1999, World Safety Symposium, 1999; Lifetime Acheivement Awd., Mich. Traffic Safety Summit, 1999. Mem. AAAS, APA (Harold M. Hildreth award 1993), APHA (injury control and emergency health svcs. sect., Disting. Career award 1994, transp. rsch. bd., Roy W. Crum award for rsch. contbns. 1995), Assn. for the Advancement of Automotive Medicine (chmn. human factors sect. 1978-80, bd. dirs. 1979-82, pres. 1981-82), Coun. Univ. Transp. Ctrs. (exec. com. 1991-93), Transp. Rsch. Bd., Ea. Psychol. Assn., Sigma Xi. Democrat. Avocations: gardening, reading. Office: 1779 Crawford Dairy Rd Chapel Hill NC 27516 E-mail: pwaller@umich.edu.

WALLER, PETER WILLIAM, public relations executive; b. Kewanee, Ill., Oct. 1, 1926; s. Ellis Julian and Barodel (Gould) Waller; m. Anne-Marie Appelius van Hoboken, Nov. 10, 1950; children: Catherine, Hans. BA with honors, Princeton U., 1949; MA with honors, San Jose State U., 1978. Bur. chief Fairchild Publs., San Francisco, 1953-55; freelance writer Mountain View, Calif., 1956-57; pub. rels. coord. Lockheed Missiles and Space, Sunnyvale, Calif., 1957-64; info. mgr. 1st missions to Jupiter, Saturn, Venus NASA Ames Rsch. Ctr., Mountain View, 1964-83, mgr. pub. info., 1983-95; cons. NASA-Ames Galileo, Lunar Prospector, 1996-97; prodr. space films PacPAW Assoc., 1998—. Speechwriter to pres. Lockheed Missles and Space, 1960—64. Prodr.: (documentaries) Jupiter Odyssey, 1974 (Golden Eagle, 1974); prodr., writer NASA Aero. program, 1984; contbr. articles to profl. jours., encyclopedias. Cons. preservation Lake Tahoe Calif. Resources Agy., Sacramento, 1984. Mem.: No. Calif. Sci. Writers Assn., Sierra Club. Democrat. Congregationalist. Avocations: skiing, travel, architecture, construction, hiking. Home: 3655 La Calle Ct Palo Alto CA 94306-2619 Personal E-mail: pwaller@sbcglobal.net.

WALLER, ROBERT JAMES, writer; b. Aug. 1, 1939; s. Robert Sr. and Ruth W.; m. Georgia Ann Wiedemeier (div. 1997); 1 child, Rachael. Student, U. Iowa, 1957-58, U. No. Iowa, 1958; PhD, Ind. U., 1968. Prof. mgmt. U. No. Iowa, Cedar Falls, 1968-91, dean bus. sch., 1979-85. Author: Just Beyond the Firelight: Stories & Essays, 1988, One Good Road is Enough: Essays, 1990, The Bridges of Madison County, 1992, Slow Waltz in Cedar Bend, 1993, Old Songs in a New Cafe: Selected Essays, 1994, Border Music, 1995, A Thousand Country Roads: An Epilogue to the Bridges of Madison County, 2002; recorded album The Ballads of Madison County, 1993, Puerto Vallarta Squeeze, 1996. Recipient Literary Lion award New York Public Library, 1993. Office: care Aaron Priest Literary Agy 708 3rd Ave Fl 23 New York NY 10017-4201

WALLER, ROBERT REX, ophthalmologist, educator, foundation executive; b. N.Y.C., Feb. 19, 1937; s. Madison Rex and Sally Elizabeth (Pearce) W.; m. Sarah Elizabeth Pickens, Dec. 27, 1963; children: Elizabeth, Katherine, Robert Jr. BA, Duke U., 1958; MD, U. Tenn., 1963. Diplomate Am. Bd. Ophthalmology (dir. 1982—, vice chmn. 1988-89, chmn. 1989—). Intern City of Memphis Hosps., 1963-64; resident in internal medicine Mayo Grad. Sch. Medicine, Rochester, Minn., 1966-67, resident in ophthalmology, 1967-70, faculty, 1970—; assoc. prof. ophthalmology Mayo Clinic, Rochester, Minn., 1974-78, prof., 1978—; chmn. dept. ophthalmology Mayo Med. Sch., Rochester, Minn., 1974-84, cons., 1970—, bd. govs., 1978-93, chmn., 1988-93; trustee Mayo Found., Rochester, 1978—, pres., CEO, 1988-98, pres. emeritus, 1999—. Chmn. bd. trustees Healthcare Leadership Coun., Washington, 1999-2001. Contbr. chpts. to books, articles to profl. jours. Elder 1st Presbyn. Ch., Rochester, 1975-78; mem. Rochester Task Force on Pub. Assembly Facilities, 1983-84. Oculplastic Surgery fellow U. Calif. San Francisco, 1973. Mem. AMA, Minn. State Med. Assn., Zumbro Valley Med. Assn., Am. Acad. Ophthalmology, Am. Ophthalmol. Soc., Orbital Soc., Am. Soc. Ophthalmic Plastic and Reconstructive Surgery, Minn. Acad. Ophthalmology and Otolaryngology, Memphis Country Club, Old Baldy Golf Club, Augusta Nat. Golf Club, Alpha Omega Alpha, Delta Tau Delta. Presbyterian. Avocations: golf, travel, photography, dogs. Home: 199 Greenbriar Dr Memphis TN 38117-3238 E-mail: RWaller@mayo.edu.

WALLER, STEPHEN, air transportation executive; b. 1949; Student, New Zealand U., 1970-74. Courier, country mgr., european mktg. mgr. DHL Airways, Inc., London, 1975-80, Tehran, Iran, 1975-80, v.p. field svcs. Redwood City, Calif., 1980-93, sr. v.p. Network Trans. divsn., 1994—. Office: DHL Worldwide Express 50 California St Ste 500 San Francisco CA 94111-4608

WALLER, WILLIAM LOWE, JR., state supreme court justice; b. Miss., Feb. 9, 1952; s. Bill Sr. and Carroll (Overton) W.; m. Charlotte Brawner, Aug. 4, 1979; children: William, Jeannie, Clayton. BA in Bus., Miss. State U., 1974; JD, U. Miss., 1977; grad., U.S. Army War Coll. Bar: Miss. 1977. Ptnr. Waller and Waller, 1977-97; judge City of Jackson, Miss., 1995-96; justice Miss. Supreme Ct., Jackson, 1998, presiding justice, 2004—. Chmn. lawyer referral svc. Miss. State Bar, 1987-89; chmn. Miss. Pub. Defenders Task Force, 2000; mem. Study Commn. on the Miss. Jud. Sys.; panelist Miss. Pro Bon Svc. Tchr. Sunday sch. First Bapt. Ch., Jackson, Miss.; past gen. counsel Ctrl. Miss. chpt. Lupus Found. Am.; bd. dirs., chmn. Jackson Coun. Neighborhoods B.G. With USAR, 2004. Mem. ABA, Miss. Bar Assn., Christian Legal Soc., Am. Legion, Miss. Nat. Guard Assn. (sec., chmn. legis. com., bd. dirs., nat. guard Miss. Army 1975-2004). Office: PO Box 117 Jackson MS 39205-0117

WALLER, WILMA RUTH, retired secondary school educator and librarian; b. Jacksonville, Tex., Nov. 15, 1921; d. William Wesley and Myrtle (Nesbitt) W. BA with honors, Tex. Woman's U., 1954, MA with honors, 1963, MLS with honors, 1976. Tchr. English Dell (Ark.) High Sch., 1953-54, Jefferson (Tex.) Ind. Schs., 1954-56, Tyler (Tex.) Ind. Schs., 1956-68; librarian Wise County Schs., Decatur, Tex., 1969-71, Thomas K. Gorman High Sch., Tyler, 1971-74, Sweetwater (Tex.) Ind. Sch. Dist., 1974-86; ret. Lectr., book reviewer for various clubs. Active in past as vol. for ARC, U. Tex. Health Ctr. Ford Found. fellow, 1959; recipient Delta Kappa Gamma Achievement award, 1992. Mem. UDC, Smith County Ret. Sch. Pers., Bible Study Group, Delta Kappa Gamma. Republican. Baptist. Avocations: reading, gourmet cooking, piano, writing letters. Home: 1117 N Azalea Dr Tyler TX 75701-5206 Office Phone: 903-593-6039.

WALLERSTEIN, JUDITH SARETSKY, psychologist, researcher; b. N.Y.C., Dec. 27, 1921; d. Samuel Saretsky and Augusta (Tucker) Weinberger; m. Robert S. Wallerstein, Jan. 26, 1947; children: Michael, Nina, Amy. BA, CUNY, 1943; MS, Columbia U., 1946; PhD in Psychology, Lund (Sweden) U., 1978. Sr. lectr. U. Calif., Berkeley, 1966—91, sr. lectr. emeritus, 1991—; dir. Calif. Children of Divorce Project, Marin County, 1971—. Founder, former exec. dir. Judith Wallerstein Ctr. Family in Transition, Corte Madera, Calif., 1980—93. Author: (book) Surviving the Breakup, 1980, Second Chances, 1989, The Good Marriage, 1995, The Unexpected Legacy of Divorce, 2000, What About the Kids, 2003; contbr. articles to profl. jours. Mem. adv. com. on family law Calif. Senate Subcom. Adminstrn. of Justice, 1977—79; mem. task force family equity Calif. State Senate, 1986. Recipient Koshland award in social welfare, San Francisco Found., 1975, René Spitz award, Denver Psychoanalytic Soc., 1991, Geri Taylor Meml. award, No. Calif. Psychiat. Soc., 1993, Presdl. citation, APA Divsn. Family Psychology, 1995, Dale Richmond award, Am. Acad. Pediat., 1996, award, ABA Section on Family Law, 2001, Presdl. citation, APA, 2001; fellow, Ctr. Advanced Study in the Behavioral Scis., Stanford, Calif., 1979—80, Rockefeller Found. Study Ctr., Bellagio, Italy, 1992. Mem.: NASW, Internat. Psychoanalytical Assn., Assn. Family Conciliation Cts., Assn. Child Psychoanalysis (mem. exec. coun. 1977—80), Am. Orthopsychiat. Assn., San Francisco Psychoanalytic Soc. (interdisciplinary mem.), N.Y. Freudian Soc. (hon.), Am. Psychoanalytic Assn. (hon.), Phi Beta Kappa. Achievements include principal investigator follow-up study effects of divorce on children and their parents; principal investigator study of good marriages. Office Phone: 415-435-3417.

WALLERSTEIN, RALPH OLIVER, physician; b. Dusseldorf, Germany, Mar. 7, 1922; arrived in U.S., 1938, naturalized, 1944; s. Otto R. and Ilse (Hollander) Wallerstein; m. Betty Ane Christensen, June 21, 1952; children: Ralph Oliver, Richard, Ann. AB, U. Calif., Berkeley, 1943; MD, U. Calif., San Francisco, 1945. Diplomate Am. Bd. Internal Medicine. Intern San Francisco Hosp., 1945—46, resident, 1948—49, U. Calif. Hosp., San Francisco, 1949—50; research fellow Thorndike Meml. Lab., Boston City Hosp., 1950—52; chief clin. hematology San Francisco Gen. Hosp., 1953—87; mem. faculty U. Calif., San Francisco, 1952—, clin. prof. medicine, 1969—, prof. emeritus of medicine. Bd. govs. Am. Bd. Internal Medicine, 1975—83, chmn., 1982—83. Capt. M.C. U.S. Army, 1946—48. Mem.: ACP (gov. 1977—87, chmn. bd. govs. 1980—81, regent 1981—87, pres. 1988—89), AMA, Western Assn. Physicians, Western Soc. Clin. Rsch., Internat. Soc. Hematology, Calif. Acad. Medicine, Inst. Medicine, Am. Assn. Blood Banks, Am. Soc. Internal Medicine, Am. Fedn. Clin. Rsch., Am. Clin. and Climatol. Assn., San Francisco Med. Soc., Am. Soc. Hematology (pres. 1978), Gold Headed Cane Soc. Republican. Home: 3447 Clay St San Francisco CA 94118-2008 E-mail: rowmdsf@aol.com.

WALLERSTEIN, ROBERT SOLOMON, psychiatrist; b. Berlin, Jan. 28, 1921; s. Lazar and Sarah (Guensberg) W.; m. Judith Hannah Saretsky, Jan. 26, 1947; children: Michael Jonathan, Nina Beth, Amy Lisa. BA, Columbia U., 1941, MD, 1944; postgrad., Topeka Inst. Psychoanalysis, 1951-58. Assoc. dir., then dir. rsch. Menninger Found., Topeka, 1954-66; chief psychiatry Mt. Zion Hosp., San Francisco, 1966-78; tng. and supervising analyst San Francisco Psychoanalytic Inst., 1966—; clin. prof. U. Calif. Sch. Medicine, Langley-Porter Neuropsychiat. Inst., 1967-75, prof., chmn. dept. psychiatry, also dir. inst., 1975-85, prof. dept. psychiatry, 1985-91, prof. emeritus, 1991—. Vis. prof. psychiatry La. State U. Sch. Medicine, also New Orleans Psychoanalytic Inst., 1972-73, Pahlavi U., Shiraz, Iran, 1977, Fed. U. Rio Grande do Sul, Porto Alegre, Brasil, 1980; mem., chmn. rsch. scientist career devel. com. NIMH, 1966-70; fellow Ctr. Advanced Study Behavioral Scis., Stanford, Calif., 1964-65, 81-82, Rockefeller Found. Study Ctr., Bellagio, Italy, 1992. Author: 20 books; mem. editl. bd.: numerous profl. jours.; contbr. articles pub. over 335 to profl. jours. With AUS, 1946-48. Recipient Heinz Hartmann award N.Y. Psychoanalytic Inst., 1968, Disting. Alumnus award Menninger Sch. Psychiatry, 1972, J. Elliott Royer award U. Calif., San Francisco, 1973, Outstanding Achievement award No. Calif. Psychiat. Soc., 1987, Mt. Airy gold medal, 1990, Mary Singleton Sigourney award, 1991, Outstanding Contbn. to Psychoanalytic Edn. award Internat. Fedn. Psychoanalytic Edn., 1999. Fellow ACP, Am. Coll. Psychoanalysts, Am. Psychiat. Assn., Am. Orthopsychiat. Assn.; mem. Am. Psychoanalytic Assn. (pres. 1971-72), Internat. Psychoanalytic Assn. (v.p. 1977-85, pres. 1985-89, hon. v.p. 1999—), Group for Advancement Psychiatry, Mexican Psychoanalytic Assn. (hon.), Brit. Psycho-Analytical Soc. (hon.), Phi Beta Kappa, Alpha Omega Alpha. Home: 290 Beach Rd Belvedere CA 94920-2472 Office Phone: 415-435-3417.

WALLEY, BYRON See CARD, ORSON SCOTT

WALLEY, JAMES MARVIN, JR., engineering executive, management consultant, real estate company executive; b. Orange, Calif., Oct. 25, 1947; s. James Marvin Sr. and Edna Amelia (Rohr) W.; m. Marynelle Lorimer Walley, Apr. 28, 1990; children: Charlotte, Elizabeth, Edward, Joseph. BSCE, Tulane U., 1970; MSCE, George Washington U., 1974; MBA in Fin., U. So. Miss., 1980. Registered profl. engr., Tex., Va.; cert. property mgr., lic. broker. Commd. ensign USN, 1970, advanced through grades to lt. comdr. Civil Engr. Corps, served in, 1970-71, resigned, 1981; exec. v.p. SPW, Inc., Dallas, 1981-84; chief ops. officer, ptnr. Montgomery Cos., Inc., Dallas, 1984-87; sr. v.p. Law Engring., Inc., Dallas, 1988-94; pres., COO Cura, Inc., Dallas, 1995. Pres., CEO Geo. Marine, Inc., 1996; v.p. Archon Group, 1997—. Vice chmn., chmn. ARC, 1985, sec.; councilman University Park City, 1998-2002. Rear Admiral Civil Engr. Corps, USN Res. Fellow: ASCE; mem.: Soc. Am. Mil. Engrs., Seabee Meml. Scholarship Assn. (pres. 2001—03), Leadership Dallas Alumni (pres. 1986), Tulane Alumni Coun. Assn. (pres. 1989), Salesmanship Club Dallas, Masons (32d Degree, KCCH). Republican. Roman Catholic. Avocations: golf, skiing. Address: RADM CEC USNR 600 E Las Colinas Blvd Ste 400 Irving TX 75039

WALLFESH, HENRY MAURICE, business communications company executive, editor, writer; b. N.Y.C., June 15, 1937; s. David Shibe and Rose (Silk) W.; m. Suzanne Krakowitch, Dec. 26, 1960; children: Saundra Kay, Gerald Bruce. Grad. indsl. and labor rels., Cornell U., 1958. Editor, co-pub. Indsl. Rels. News, N.Y.C. and Stamford, Conn., 1960-67; pres., chief exec. officer RAI div. Hearst Bus. Communications, N.Y.C., 1968-91, sr. v.p., editor at large, 1991; pres. Whale Communications, Inc., Stamford, Conn., 1992—. Pres. Indsl. Rels. Inst., Stamford, 1964-67; founder, bd. dirs. Internat. Soc. Pre-Retirement Planners, 1975-88; bd. dirs. VSOP Mktg., Boston. Author: Implications of the Age Discrimination in Employment, 1977, When a CEO Retires, 1978. Bd. dirs. Aging in Am., N.Y.C., 1985-90, N.Y.C. Anti-Defamation League, 1987-89; mem. alumni bd. dirs. Cornell Inst. Labor Rels., 1995—. Capt. inf. USAR, 19658-67. Recipient Corp. Achievement award Nat. Assn. for Sr. Living Industries, 1990; inducted into Internat. Soc. Pre-Retirement Planners Hall of Fame, 1988. Mem. Roxbury Swim and Tennis Club (bd. dirs. 1975-78), Cornell Club. Jewish. Avocations: tennis, theater, writing. Home and Office: 341 Biltmore Ln Somerset NJ 08873-6004

WALLHAUSEN, MILDRED CAROLYN, publisher; b. N.Y.C., Apr. 3, 1914; d. James Meroe and Frances (Bronson) Savell; m. Arthur Louis Wallhausen Sr., Sept. 25, 1936 (dec. Nov. 1969); children: Art L. Jr., Elizabeth Gail. Grad., Brown Bus. Coll., 1932. Proofreader Daily Am. Rep., Poplar Bluff, 1933-36; co-owner Enterprise-Courier, Charleston, 1936-69, pub., 1969—, East Prairie (Mo.) Eagle, 1969—. Illustrator: (children's book) Bobby Butterfly, 1986; watercolor artist. Mem. Mo. Gov.'s Adv. Coun., Comprehensive Health Planning Coun., 1969-73; mem. Bootheel CHP Coun., 1971-72, Charleston Park and Recreation Bd., 1972-77, Sr. Citizens Housing Project, 1973, Miss. County TB Assn., 1945-53, S.E. Mo. Regional Coun. Alcoholism and Drug Abuse, 1976-78, Miss. County Child Welfare Coun., 1974-77; bd. dirs. Miss. County Child Devel. Ctr., 1974-77; pres. Eugene Field Elem. Sch. PTA, 1948, Charleston H.S. PTA, 1935; chpt. mother FHA, 1955, 62; mem. Miss. County Cmty. Chs.; commr. East Prairie Housing Authority, 1992—;

SEMO State U. Copper Dome Soc.(pres. coun.), mem. citizens adv. bd. S.E. U., Cape Girardeau KRCU-Public Radio, 1996-1999. Inducted Mo. Press Assn. Hall of Fame, 2000. Mem. NAACP, S.E. Mo. Press Assn (pres. 1981, historian 1982-), Miss. County Sheltered Workshops (bd. mem. 1985-), Am. Legion Aux, Citizens' Adv. Bd. 1997-99. Republican. Episcopalian. Office: Enterprise-Courier 206 S Main Charleston MO 63834

WALLIN, JAMES PETER, lawyer; b. Huntington, N.Y., May 9, 1958; s. Jerome Peter and Margaret Mary (Gilvarry) W.; m. Julia Katherine Springen, Aug. 11, 1984; children: James Peter Jr., Thomas George, Katherine Grace, Sarah Elizabeth. BA in Econs., SUNY, Stony Brook, 1980; JD, N.Y. Law Sch., 1983. Bar: N.Y. 1984. Counsel Alliance Capital Mgmt., N.Y.C., 1982-86; assoc. Cole & Dietz (now Winston & Strawn), N.Y.C., 1986-87; counsel The Dreyfus Corp., N.Y.C., 1987-88; gen. counsel Yamaichi Capital Mgmt. Inc., N.Y.C., 1988-92, Yamaichi Internat. (Am.) Inc., N.Y.C., 1992-94, Evergreen Asset Mgmt. Corp., 1994-97; dir. Covenance Group Morgan Stanley Investment Mgmt., N.Y.C., 1997—. Faculty Practicing Law Inst., N.Y.C., 1992—. Author: (seminar materials) Broker Dealer Regulation, 1992. Avocations: aviation, skiing, sailing. Home: PO Box 90 Cold Spring Harbor NY 11724-0090

WALLIN, JEAN R. state legislator; b. Hibbing, Minn., Jan. 13, 1934; Student, U. Minn. Mem. N.H. Ho. of Reps., Concord, 1967-69, 75, N.H. Ho. of Reps. (dist. 15), Concord, 77-79, 96—; mem. local and regulated revenues com. N.H. Ho. of Reps., Concord, 1996—. Mediator. Chmn. N.H. Liquor Commn.; mem. Dem. Nat. Com.; pres. Nashua Bd. Edn., 1974-75. Mem. N.H. Mediators Assn. Unitarian Universalist. Office: NH Legis State House Concord NH 03301

WALLIN, LELAND DEAN, artist, educator; b. Sioux Falls, SD, Oct. 14, 1942; s. Clarence Forrest and Leona Mae (McInnis) W.; m. Meredith Maria Hawkins, Mar. 26, 1977; 1 child, Jessica Hawkins. Student, Columbus Coll. Art and Design, 1961-62; BFA in Painting, Kans. City Art Inst., Mo., 1965; MFA in Painting, U. Cin. with Cin. Art Acad., 1967. Prof. drawing, painting, sculpture St. Cloud State U., Minn., 1967-86; prof. Queens Coll., CUNY, Flushing, NY, 1983-84; prof., coord. MFA painting Marywood U., Scranton, Pa., 1985-90; prof. painting and drawing East Carolina U., Greenville, NC, 1992—; advisor Painting Guild, 1993—94. Lectr. Carnegie-Mellon U., Pitts., 1988; curator Philip Pearlstein Retrospective Exhibit, Scranton, 1988; juror Belin Arts Grant Com., Waverly, Pa., 1989; vis. prof. painting East Carolina U., Greenville, 1992-93; judge, juror No. Nat. Art Competition, 1993. One-man shows include Mpls. Coll. Art and Design, 1978, Harold Reed Gallery, 1983, Gallery Henoch, NYC, 1991, exhibited in group shows at Bklyn. Mus., 1983, Greenville County Mus. Art, SC, 1983, Mus. Modern Art, Fla., 1993, Huntsville Mus. Art, 1994, San Bernardino County Mus. Internat., Calif., 1995, Contemporary Realism, 1996, Downey (Calif.) Mus. Art, 1998, Palm Springs Desert Mus., 1999, Fine Arts Ctr., Sacramento, 1999, Internat. Ctr. Arts, Loredo, Tex., 2000, Bellevue Art Mus., Wash., 2001, Morris Mus. Art, Ga., 2001, Huntsville Mus. Art, Ala., 2002, Miss. Mus. Art, 2002, Represented in permanent collections represented in various collections; contbr. articles to profl. jours. Named Outstanding Tchr., East Carolina U., 1994, 95; recipient numerous rsch. awards East Carolina U., 1994—. Mem. Coll. Art Assn. Am., Pa. Soc. Watercolor Painters. Home: 218 York Rd Greenville NC 27858-5601

WALLING, ARTHUR KNIGHT, orthopedist; b. Oskaloosa, Iowa, Apr. 25, 1950; m. Rebecca Lynn; children: Christopher Albert, Eleanor Eckhoff. BS, Iowa State U., 1972; MD, Creighton U., 1976. Diplomate Nat. Bd. Med. Examiners, Am. Bd. Orthopedic Surgeons. Resident in surgery Creighton Univ. Affiliated Hosps., Omaha, 1976-77; resident in orthopedic surgery U. South Fla. Affiliated Hosps., Tampa, 1977-80; fellow in musculoskeletal pathology U. Fla., 1980-81, clin. instr., 1981-82; acting chief orthopedic surgery James A. Haley VA Hosp., Tampa, 1982-85; chief orthopedic surgery H. Lee Moffitt Cancer Ctr., Tampa, 1985-89, 96—; clin. prof. U. South Fla., Tampa, 1989—. Vis. asst. prof. U. So. Fla., 1982-85; dir. Tampa Orthopedic Program, 1991—; bd. dirs. Fla. Orthopedic Inst., 1989—; chief orthopedics H. Lee Moffitt Cancer Ctr., 1996—. Fellow Am. Acad. Orthopedic Surgeons; mem. AMA, Am. Orthopedic Assn., Am. Bone and Joint Surgeons, Am. Orthopedic Foot and Ankle Soc., Internat. Soc. Limb Salvage, So. Med. Assn., Southeast Oncology Group, So. Orthopedic Group, Assn. Bone & Joint Surgeons, Pediat. Oncology Group, Fla. Orthopedic Soc., Bay Area Orthopedic Soc., Pediat. Oncology Group, Hillsborough County Med. Soc., U. Fla. Orthopedic Assn., U. South Fla. Orthopedic Alumni Assn. Office: Fla Orthopedic Inst 4175 E Fowler Ave Tampa FL 33617-2011

WALLING, CHEVES THOMSON, chemistry professor; b. Evanston, Ill., Feb. 28, 1916; s. Willoughby George and Frederika Christina (Haskell) W.; m. Jane Ann Wilson, Sept. 17, 1940; children— Hazel, Rosalind, Cheves, Janie, Barbara AB, Harvard, 1937; PhD, U. Chgo., 1939. Rsch. chemist E.I. duPont de Nemours, 1939-43, U.S. Rubber Co., 1943-49; tech. aide Office Sci. Research, Washington, 1945; sr. rsch. assoc. Lever Bros. Co., 1949-52; prof. chemistry Columbia U., N.Y.C., 1952-69; Disting. prof. chemistry U. Utah, Salt Lake City, 1970-91, prof. chemistry emeritus, 1991—. Author: Free Radicals in Solution, 1957, Fifty Years of Free Radicals, 1995; also numerous articles. Fellow AAAS; mem. Nat. Acad. Scis., Am. Acad. Arts and Scis., Am. Chem. Soc. (editor jour. 1975-81, James Flack Norris award 1970, Lubrizol award 1984) Home: PO Box 537 Jaffrey NH 03452-0537 Office Phone: 603-532-6557.

WALLING, DONOVAN ROBERT, educational book editor; b. Kansas City, Mo., Jan. 9, 1948; s. Donovan Ernest and Dorothy Jane (Goyette) W.; m. Diana Lynn Eveland, Oct. 19, 1968 (dec. 1991); children: Katherine Anne, Donovan David, Alexander James. BS in Edn., Kans. State Tchrs. Coll., 1970; MS, U. Wis., Milw., 1975. Cert. tchr., adminstr., Wis., Ind. Tchr. Sheboygan (Wis.) Area Sch. Dist., 1970-81, 83-86, coord. lang. arts and reading, 1986-91; tchr. Dept. Def. Dependents Schs., Zweibruecken, Germany, 1981-83; dir. instrnl. svcs. Carmel (Ind.)-Clay Schs., 1991-93; dir. publs. and rsch. Phi Delta Kappa Internat., Bloomington, Ind., 1993—. Mem. adj. faculty U. Wis., Oshkosh, 1986-91, Silver Lake Coll., Manitowoc, Wis., 1987-91. Author: Complete Book of School Public Relations, 1982, How To Build Staff Involvement in School Management, 1984, Teachers as Leaders, 1994, Rethinking How Art Is Taught, 2000; also numerous articles. Mem. ASCD, Nat. Coun. Tchrs. English, Internat. Reading Assn., Phi Delta Kappa (v.p. Cen. Ind. chpt. 1992-93). Avocations: writing, painting. Office: Phi Delta Kappa Internat PO Box 789 Bloomington IN 47402-0789 Office Phone: 800-766-1156. Business E-Mail: dwalling@pdkintl.org.

WALLINGER, M(ELVIN) BRUCE, lawyer; b. Richmond, Va., Dec. 27, 1945; s. Melvin W. and Ellen Scott (Barnard) W.; m. Rosemary Moore Hynes, Aug. 8, 1970; children: Mary Moore, Ann Harrison, Carrie. BA, U. Va., 1968, JD, 1972. Bar: Va. 1972, U.S. Dist. Ct. (we. dist.) Va. 1972, U.S. Ct. Appeals (4th cir.) 1976, U.S. Supreme Ct. 1978, U.S. Dist. Ct. (ea. dist.) Va. 1986; mediator and arbitrator for Am. Arbitration Assn. (Comml., Employment and Large, Complex Case panels). Assoc. Wharton, Aldhizer & Weaver, Harrisonburg, Va., 1972—76, ptnr., 1976—2004, Hoover Penrod, Harrisonburg, Va., 2004—. Pres., Shenandoah County Libr. Foun., Edinburg, Va. Fellow ABA, Am. Coll. Trial Lawyers, Va. Law Found.; mem. Va. Bar Assn. (exec. com. 1996-99), Harrisonburg Bar Assn. (pres. 1984), Va. State Bar (pres. young lawyers conf. 1981-82, chmn. 6th dist. disciplinary com. 1988-89), Va. Assn. Def. Attys. (pres. 1989-90). Avocations: bicycling, scuba diving. Office: Hoover Penrod 342 South Main Street Harrisonburg VA 22801 Office Phone: 540-433-2444.

WALLINGFORD, ANNE, writer, editor, project developer; b. Chgo., June 29, 1949; d. Lester Arlyn and Roseanne (Jones) W. BS in Edn., Chgo. State U., 1975. Cert. elem. and mid. sch. tchr., Ill. Profl. dressmaker Annie's Original's, Chgo., 1968-72; instr., asst. prin., St. Bonaventure Sch., Chgo., 1972-81; instr., chair sci. dept. Our Lady of Lourdes Sch., Chgo., 1981-87; product designer, catalog mgr. FSC Ednl., Inc., Mansfield, Ohio, 1988-91; interim dir. pub. rels. Shelby Meml. Hosp., 1991-92; founder, dir. Anne Wallingford WordSmith, Chgo., 1992—. Instr. English lit. and bus. writing North Ctrl. Tech. Coll., 1991-92; catalog cons. Lab-Aids, Inc., 2002. Editor/writer: Steck-Vaughn, ZCI Edn., Gale Rsch., WCTS/McGraw-Hill, Quarasan Group, Proof Positive/Farrowlyne, McGraw Hill Higher Edn., 2000—, Lucas Mfg., Kemtec, Sci. First, Ctrl. Sci., Fisher Sci., 1992—94, catalog/product developer: ETA, 1992—95, Sargent-Welch, 1993—; catalog cons. WGBH of Boston, 2001—02; catalog cons.: Lab.-Aids, 2002, Basic Sci., 2003; contbr. articles to profl. jours. Active The Vol. Ctr., Mansfield, 1992-93, steering com. Wright Community Ctr., 1991; treas. Wolfram St. Block Club, Chgo., 1975-78. Recipient Gold award Adler Planetarium, Chgo., 1985. Mem. Nat. Writerss Union, Chgo., Women in Pub. (Individual Excellence in Prodn., 1994, 95), Soc. Tech. Communicators, Profl. Freelance Assn. (founder, pres., 1991-92), Editl. Freelancers Assn., Mensa. Avocations: telecommunications, reading, theater, museums. Office: 6155 N Moody Ave Chicago IL 60646-3806

WALLINGTON, PATRICIA MCDEVITT, computer company executive; b. Phila., July 29, 1940; d. James J. and Mary (Eschbach) McDevitt; m. William R. Wallington; 1 child, Colleen Xydis. BBA, U. Pa., 1975; MBA, Drexel U., 1978; postgrad. mgmt. devel., Harvard U., 1981. Project mgr. Fidelity Mut., Phila., 1965-72, Penn Mut. Ins. Co., Phila., 1972-77; mgr. info. systems Sun Info. Svcs., Phila., 1977-81; dir. info. systems Sun Exploration & Prodn. Co., Dallas, 1981-87; sr. v.p., chief info. officer Mass. Mut. Life Ins. Co., Springfield, 1987-89; corp. v.p., chief info. officer Xerox Corp., Rochester, NY, 1989—99; pres. CIO Assocs., Sarasota, Fla., 2000—. Mem. MBA adv. bd. Baylor U., Waco, Tex., 1986-88; bd. dirs. FINA, Inc., Middlesex Mut. P&C Co. Mem. adv. bd. Handicap Ctr.-HUP, Phila., 1978-80; v.p. fin. Girls Club Dallas, 1986-87. Named one of Top 100 Women in Tech., 1994, Hall of Fame, 1997, CIO mag., 1997. Mem. Soc. for Info. Mgmt.*

WALLIS, BEN ALTON, JR., lawyer; b. Llano County, Tex., Apr. 27, 1936; s. Ben A. and Jessie Ella (Longbotham) W.; children from previous marriage: Ben a. III, M. Jessica; m. Joan Mery, 1987. BBA, U. Tex., 1961, JD, 1971; postgrad., Law Sch. So. Meth. U. Bar: Tex. 1966, U.S. Dist. Ct. (no. dist.) Tex. 1971, U.S. Ct. Appeals D.C. 1974, U.S. Dist. Ct. D.C. 1975, U.S. Dist. Ct. (we. dist.) Tex. 1975, U.S. Dist. Ct. (no. dist.) Calif. 1983, U.S. Ct. Appeals (5th cir.) 1975, U.S. Ct. Appeals (8th cir.) 1980, U.S. Ct. Appeals (11th cir.) 1981, U.S. Dist. Ct. (ea. dist.) Wis. 1983, U.S. Supreme Ct. 1974. Pvt. practice, Llano, 1966-67, Dallas, 1971-73; investigator, prosecutor State Securities Bd. Tex., 1967-71; v.p. of devel. Club Corp. Am., Dallas, 1973; assoc. counsel impeachment task force U.S. Ho. of Reps. Com. on Judiciary, Washington, 1974; prin. Law Offices of Ben Wallis, P.C., San Antonio, 1974—. Chmn. Nat. Land Use Conf., 1979-81; mem. Gov.'s Areawide Planning Adv. Com., 1975-78; pres. Inst. Human Rights Rsch., 1979-2000. Mem. ATLA, FBA, Coll. of State Bar of Tex., State Bar Tex. (former chmn. agr. tax com.), D.C. Bar Assn., San Antonio Bar Assn., Delta Theta Phi, Delta Sigma Pi. Republican. Baptist. Office: GPM South Tower 800 NW Loop 410 Ste 350 San Antonio TX 78216-5619 Office Phone: 210-525-1500. E-mail: wallis@stic.net.

WALLIS, CARLTON LAMAR, librarian; b. Blue Springs, Miss., Oct. 15, 1915; s. William Ralph and Tellie (Jones) W.; m. Mary Elizabeth Cooper, Feb. 22, 1944; 1 child, Carlton Lamar. BA with spl. distinction, Miss. Coll., 1936; MA, Tulane U., 1946; B.L.S., U. Chgo., 1947; L.H.D., Rhodes Coll., Memphis, 1980. English tchr., coach Miss. Pub. Schs., 1936-41; teaching fellow Miss. Coll. and Tulane U., 1941-42; chief librarian Rosenberg Library, Galveston, Tex., 1947-55; city librarian Richmond, Va., 1955-58; dir. Memphis Pub. Library, 1958-80, ret., 1980. Author: Libraries in the Golden Triangle, 1966; contbr. articles to library jours. Trustee Belhaven Coll., 1978-82, Nat. Ornamental Metal Mus., 1989—. Served as chief warrant officer AUS, 1942-46. Decorated Bronze Star. Mem. ALA (chmn. library mgmt. sect. 1969-71), Pub. Library Assn. (dir. 1973-77), Tex. Library Assn. (pres. 1952-53), Va. Library Assn., Southwestern Library Assn. (exec. bd. 1950-55), Southeastern Library Assn. (chmn. pub. library sect. 1960-62), Tenn. Library Assn. (pres. 1969-70, Distinguished Service award 1979, Intellectual Freedom award 1998). Presbyterian (elder). Club: Egyptian (pres. 1973-74). Home: 365 Kenilworth Pl Memphis TN 38112-5405

WALLIS, DEBORAH, curator; b. Salina, Kans., Mar. 17, 1971; BS, Kans. State U., Manhattan, 1993; MA in Mus. Studies, U. Nebr., Lincoln, 1994. Registrar Richrd Nixon Libr. and Birthplace, Yorba Linda, Calif., 1995—98; dir., curator Nat. Mus. of Roller Skating, Lincoln, Nebr., 2000—. Mem.: Nebr. Mus. Assn. (bd. mem. 2002—). Office: Nat Mus Roller Skating 4730 South St Ste 2 Lincoln NE 68506

WALLIS, DIANA LYNN, artistic director; b. Windsor, Eng., Dec. 11, 1946; d. Dennis Blackwell and Joan Williamson (Gatcombe) W. Grad., Royal Ballet Sch., Eng., 1962-65. Dancer Royal Ballet Touring Co., London, 1965-68; ballet mistress Royal Ballet Sch., London, 1969-81, dep. ballet prin., 1981-84; artistic coord. Nat. Ballet of Can., Toronto, 1984-86, assoc. artistic dir., 1986-87, co-artistic dir., 1987-89; free-lance prod., tchr. London; dep. artistic dir. English Nat. Ballet, London, 1990-94; artistic dir. Royal Acad. Dance, 1994—. Fellow Imperial Soc. Tchrs. Dancing. E-mail: lwallis@rad.org.uk.

WALLIS, DONALD WILLS, lawyer; b. Wilkes-Barre, Pa., Aug. 22, 1950; s. Donald and Hazel (Jansen) W.; m. Kathryn Macon Waggoner, Aug. 28, 1971; children: Neill Jansen, Kathryn Spencer. AB, Duke U., 1971, JD, 1974. Bar: Fla. 1974, U.S. Tax Ct. 1975, U.S. Dist. Ct. (mid. dist.) Fla. 1977, U.S. Ct. Appeals (5th cir.) 1978, U.S. Claims Ct. 1978, U.S. Supreme Ct. 1979. Assoc. Mahoney, Hadlow, Chambers & Adams, Jacksonville, Fla., 1974-78; mem. firm Fisher, Tousey & Wallis, P.A., Jacksonville, Fla., 1978-89; ptnr. Holland & Knight LLP, Jacksonville, Fla., 1989—2003; gen. coun., treas. Holland & Knight Consulting LLC, Jacksonville, Fla., 2001—02; mem. firm Rogers Towers, P.A., Jacksonville, 2003—. Co-author: Bank Holding Companies: A Practical Guide to Bank Acquisitions and Mergers, 1978; tax notes editor: The Florida Probate System, 1977; contbg. editor Jour. Partnership Taxation, 1989-95. Chmn. Duke U. Alumni Admissions Adv. Com., Jacksonville, 1986-2000; pres. Beaches Fine Arts Series, Inc., Jacksonville Beach, Fla., 1990-2000. Recipient Charles A. Dukes award Outstanding Vol. Svc., 2000, Vol. of the Yr. award Vol. Jacksonville, Inc., 2000. Mem. ABA (taxation sect.), Fla. Bar (tax sect., bd. cert. tax atty.), Jacksonville Bar Assn. (tax sect.), Duke U. alumni assn. (admissions com. 1974—), Selva Marina Country Club, Inc. (bd. govs. 1987-89), Duke Club Greater Jacksonville (bd. dirs. 1993—, pres. 2004—). Avocations: sailing, scuba diving, backpacking, bicycling. Office: Rogers Towers PA 1301 River Place Blvd Ste 1500 Jacksonville FL 32207-5776 also: 1 Cedar Hollow Dr Stirling NJ 07980-1214 Office Phone: 904-346-5776. Business E-Mail: dwallis@rtlaw.com.

WALLIS, JOHN JAMES (JIMMY WALLIS), comedian, impressionist, ventriloquist, comedy writer, Internet site designer; b. Searcy, Ark., Mar. 21, 1939; s. Prentiss Bascom and Maxine (James) W.; children: Lori Diana Wallis Bledsoe, Shauna Kathleen. Grad., Okla. U., 1960. Advisor Am. Acad. for Entertainment at U.S. Vets. Hosps., N.Y.C., 1988-97. Nat. TV debut Art Linkletter's Hollywood Talent Scouts, 1966; entertained troops in S.E. Asia, 1967-70; performed with Ann Murray, Lou Rawls, Lola Falana, Ben Vereen, Al Hirt, Debbie Reynolds, Rip Taylor, Suzanne Somers, others; performed in numerous clubs including Tropicana, Las Vegas, The Sahara, Las Vegas, The Flamingo, Las Vegas, Chauteau Champlain, Montreal, The Cave, Vancouver, The Paradise Island Casino, The Bahamas, The Superstar Theater, Atlantic City, Riviera, Las Vegas, Harrah's, Reno, The Reno Hilton, Las Vegas Hilton, Flamingo Hilton, Disneyland, L.A.; featured in Royal Caribbean Cruise Lines, Premier's Disney Theme Cruises, Norwegian Cruise Lines, Holland Am. and Celebrity Cruise Lines, Night of the Stars, Las Vegas; featured in Distinguished Oklahomans (Victoria Lee). Named Okla.'s Top Comedian, Okla. Ho. of Reps.; recipient Am. Legion medal. Avocations: photography, scuba diving, computers, tennis, target shooting.

WALLIS, OLNEY GRAY, lawyer; b. Llano, Tex., July 27, 1940; s. Ben Alton and Jessie Ella (Longbotham) W.; m. Linda Lee Johnson, June 29, 1963; children: Anne, Brett. BA, U. Tex., 1962, JD, 1965. Bar: Tex. 1965, U.S. Dist. Ct. (so. dist.) Tex. 1966, U.S. Ct. Mil. Appeals 1968, U.S. Surpeme Ct. 1970, U.S. dist. Ct. (we. dist.) Tex. 1976, U.S. Ct. Appeals (5th cir.) 1977, U.S. Tax Ct. 1980, U.S. Ct. Appeals (10th cir.) 1981, U.S. Ct. Appeals (11th cir.) 1983, U.S. Dist. Ct. (no. dist.) Tex. 1985, U.S. Dist. Ct. (ea. and we. dists.) Ark. 1985, U.S. Ct. Appeals (8th cir.) 1985. Assoc. Brown & Cecil, Houston, 1965-66, asst. U.S. atty. Dept. Justice, Houston, 1971-74; mem. Jefferson, Wallis & Sherman, Houston, 1975-81, Wallis & Pruitt, Houston, 1981-87, Wallis and Short, Houston, 1987—. Instr. U. Md., Keflauik, Iceland, 1968-69; mem. faculty continuing legal edn. U. Houston, 1981-84. Capt. USAF, 1969-70. Decorated Air Force Commendation medal. Mem. Assn. Trial Lawyers Am., Am. Judicature Soc., Tex. Trial Lawyers Assn., Houston Bar Found., Phi Delta Phi, Phi Kappa Tau. Office: Wallis & Short 4300 Scotland St Houston TX 77007-7328 Office Phone: 713-956-1300. E-mail: ogwlawyer@earthlink.net.

WALLIS, RICHARD FISHER, physicist, researcher; b. Washington, May 14, 1924; s. William F. and Alberta (Sigelen) W.; m. Mary Camilla Williams, Aug. 20, 1955; children: Maria Fisher, Sylvia Camilla. BS, George Washington U., 1945, MS, 1948; PhD, Cath. U. Am., 1952. Postdoctoral fellow (U. Md.), College Park, 1951-53; chemist Applied Physics Lab. Johns Hopkins U., Silver Spring, Md., 1953-56, physicist Naval Rsch. Lab., Washington, 1956-66, 67-69, head semiconductors br., 1958-66, 67-69; prof. physics U. Calif., Irvine, 1966-67, 69—; prof. emeritus, 1993—; chmn. dept. physics U. Calif., Irvine, 1972-75, 80-83. Vis. prof. U. Paris, 1975-76, 79, 85. Author: (with Maradudin and Dobrzynski) Handbook of Surfaces and Interfaces, 1980, (with Balkanski) Many-Body Aspects of Solid State Spectroscopy, 1986, (with Balkanski) Semiconductor Physics and Applications, 2000; editor: Lattice Dynamics, 1965, Localized Excitations in Solids, 1968 (with Stegeman) Electromagnetic Surface Excitations, 1986, (with Birman and Sebenne) Elementary Excitations in Solids, 1992; contbr. articles to profl. jours. Served with U.S. Army, 1945-46. Recipient Pure Sci. award Naval Rsch. Lab., 1964, Disting. Alumni Achievement award George Washington U., 1991. Fellow Am. Phys. Soc., AAAS; mem. Philos. Soc. Washington, Phi Beta Kappa, Sigma Xi Home: 2635 Alta Vista Dr Newport Beach CA 92660-4102 Office: U Calif Dept Physics Irvine CA 92697-0001

WALLIS, ROBERT RAY, psychologist; b. Hardwood, Okla., Sept. 1, 1927; s. Walter William and Osie Oma (Luckett) W.; m. Joan Elaine Martino, Sept. 10, 1955; children: Rosalie, Glenn, Damon, Gina, Darren. Student, Southwestern Inst. Tech., 1945; BA, U. Okla., 1951, Ed.M., 1960, PhD, 1963. Lic. psychologist, Pa., N.J. From psychology intern to dir. div. psychology Greater Kansas City Mental Health Found., 1962-71; from fellow to chief psychologist Western Mo. Mental Health Center, Kansas City, 1965-71; from program dir. to exec. dir. Horizon House Inc., Phila., 1971-79; chief exec. officer Ancora Psychiat. Hosp., Hammonton, N.J., 1979-81; individual practice clin. and cons. psychology, Medford, N.J., 1981-97; propr. Wallis Printing Ctr., Phila., 1985-91; clin. supr. Alcoholism and Psychotherapy Assocs., Medford, N.J., 1985-98, Middlesex Counseling Assocs., Cranbury, N.J., 1985-89. From asst. prof. to chmn. div. psychology dept. psychiatry, U. Mo., Kansas City Sch. Medicine, 1965-71. Contbr. articles to profl. jours. Served with USNR, 1945-46. Mem. Am. Psychol. Assn. Home and Office: 3225 Park Cir Manhattan KS 66503-2429

WALLISON, FRIEDA K. lawyer; b. N.Y.C., Jan. 15, 1943; d. Ruvin H. and Edith (Landes) Koslow; m. Peter J. Wallison, Nov. 24, 1966; children: Ethan S., Jeremy L., Rebecca K. AB, Smith Coll., 1963; LLB, Harvard U., 1966. Bar: N.Y. 1967, D.C. 1982. Assoc. Carter, Ledyard & Milburn, N.Y.C., 1966-75; spl. counsel divsn. market regulation SEC, Washington, 1975; exec. dir., gen. counsel Mcpl. Securities Rulemaking Bd., Washington, 1975-78; ptnr. Rogers & Wells, N.Y.C. and Washington, 1978-83, Jones, Day, Reavis & Pogue, N.Y.C. and Washington, 1983-98; mem. Govtl. Acctg. Standards Coun., Washington, 1984-90, Nat. Coun. on Pub. Works Improvement, Washington, 1985-88; vice chair environ. fin. adv. bd. EPA, 1988-92. Contbr. articles to profl. jours. Fellow Am. Bar Found.; mem. N.Y.C. Bar Assn.

WALLMAN, RICHARD F. electronics company executive; b. 1951; BSEE, Vanderbilt U., 1972; MBA, U. Chgo., 1974. Asst. contr. sales and mktg., asst. corp. contr. Chrysler Corp.; gen. asst. contr. IBM, 1993-94, v.p., contr., 1994-95; sr. v.p., CFO AlliedSignal, 1995-99, Honeywell, 1999—.

WALLMANN, JEFFREY MINER, author; b. Seattle, Dec. 5, 1941; s. George Rudolph and Elizabeth (Biggs) W. BS, Portland State U., 1962; PhD, U. Nev., 1998. Pvt. investigator Dale Sys., N.Y.C., 1962-63; asst. buyer, mgr., pub. money bidder Dohrmann Co., San Francisco, 1966-69; dir. pub. rels. London Films, Cinelux-Universal, Trans-European Publs., 1970-75; editor-in-chief Riviera Life mag., 1975-77; instr. U. Nev., Reno, 1990—, Regis U., 2003—. Instr. U. Nev., Las Vegas, 1998—, U. Phoenix, 2001—, Regis U., 2003—. Author: The Spiral Web, 1969, Judas Cross, 1974, Clean Sweep, 1976, Jamaica, 1977, Deathtrek, 1980, Blood and Passion, 1980, Brand of the Damned, 1981, The Manipulator, 1982, Return to Conta Lupe, 1983, The Celluloid Kid, 1984, Business Basic for Bunglers, 1984, Guide to Applications Basic, 1984, The Western: Parables of the American Dream, 1999, (under pseudonym Leon DaSilva) Green Hell, 1976, Breakout in Angola, 1977, (under pseudonym Nick Carger) Hour of the Wolf, 1973, Ice Trap Terror, 1974, (under pseudonym Margaret Maitland) The Trial, 1974, Come Slowly, Eden, 1974, How Deep My Cup, 1975, (under pseudonym Amanda Hart Douglass) First Rapture, 1972, Jamaica!, 1978, (under pseudonym Grant Roberts) The Reluctant Couple, 1969, Wayward Wives, 1970, (under pseudonym Gregory St. Germain) Resistance # 1: Night and Fog, 1982, Resistance #2: Magyar Massacre, 1983, (under pseudonym Wesley Ellis) Lonestar on the Treachery Trail, 1982, numerous others, (under pseudonym Tabor Evans) Longarm and the Lonestar Showdown, 1986, (under pseudonym Jon Sharpe) Trailsman 58: Slaughter Express, 1986, numerous others in Trailsman series, also others under pseudonyms; co-author: (under pseudonym William Jeffrey) Duel at Gold Buttes, 1980, Border Fever, 1982, Day of the Moon, 1983, The Western: Parables of the American Dream, 1999; contbr. articles and short stories to Argosy, Ellery Queen's Mystery Mag., Alfred Hitchcock's Mystery Mag., Zane Grey Western, Venture, Oui, TV Guide. Mem. Mystery Writers Am., Sci. Fiction Writers Am., We. Writers Am., Nat. Coun. Tchrs. English, Crime Writers Am., Nev. state Coun. Tchrs. English, Esperanto League N.Am., We. Lit. Assn., Internacia Soc. Amikeco Kaj Bonvolo, Sci. Fiction Rsch. Assn., Internat. Assn. Fantastic in the Arts, We. Lit. Assn. Office: care of Barry Malzberg PO Box 61 Teaneck NJ 07666-0061

WALLNER, MARY JANE, state legislator, director child care organization; b. St. Louis, Oct. 25, 1946; d. Arthur M. and Frances (Fulkerson) Bills; m. Nicholas Anthony Wallner, Mar. 10, 1967; children: Jenny, Jessy. BS in Child and Family, U. N.H., 1971; postgrad. Wheelock Coll., 1974-76. Child care worker Newmarket (N.H.) Day Care, 1967-69, dir., 1971-72; tchr. Exeter (N.J.) Head Start, 1969-70; dir. Merrimack Valley Day Care, Concord, N.H., 1973—; mem. N.H. Ho. of Reps. (dist. 24), Concord, 1980—. VISTA vol. Jane Adams Hull House, Chgo., 1966; bd. dirs. N.H. Womens Lobby, Concord, 1991—, Meritorious Svc. award, 1988; bd. dirs. N.H. Task Force for the Prevention Child Abuse, Concord, 1985-91; trustee Trust Fund for the Prevention Child Abuse, Concord, 1987-91. Recipient Friend of Children award N.H. Group Home Assn., 1988, Commitment to Young Children award N.H. Assn. for the Edn. Young Children, 1989, Voice for Children award Child and Family Svcs., 1990. Mem. Zonta (sec. 1980—). Democrat. Office: Merrimack Valley Day Care Svcs 19 N Fruit St Concord NH 03301-2989

WALLOCK, TERRENCE J. lawyer; JD, UCLA, 1970. Bar: Calif. 1971. V.p., gen. counsel Denny's Inc.; sr. v.p., sec., gen. counsel Vons Cos., Arcadia, Calif., 1990—; now sr. v.p., sec., gen. counsel Ralphs Grocery Co., L.A., 1990-98, ret., 1998. Office: Ralphs Grocery Co PO Box 54143 Los Angeles CA 90054-0143

WALLOT, JEAN-PIERRE, archivist, historian; b. Valleyfield, Que., Can., May 22, 1935; s. Albert and Adrienne (Thibodeau) W.; m. Denyse Caron; children: Normand, Robert, Sylvie. BA, Coll. Valleyfield, 1954; lic. es lettres, MA in History, U. Montreal, 1957, PhD in History, 1965; D (hon.), U. Rennes, France, 1987, U. Ottawa, Can., 1996. Reporter Le Progres de Valleyfield,

1954-61; from lectr. to prof. dept. history U. Montreal, 1961-85, dept. chmn., 1973-75, vice-dean studies faculty arts and scis., 1975-78, vice-dean rsch. Faculty Arts and Scis., 1979-82, academic v.p., 1982-85. Nat. archivist, Can., 1985-97; historian Nat. Mus. Man, Ottawa, Ont., 1966-69, assoc. prof. U. Toronto, 1969-71; prof. Concordia U., Montreal, Que., 1971-73; vis. prof. U. Ottawa, 1997—, dir. Ctr. de Rsch. en Civilisation Canadienne-Francaise, 2000—; dir. Etude Assn. Ecole Pratique des Hautes Etudes en Scis. Sociales, Paris, 1975, 79, 81, 83, 85, 87, 89, 94. Author: Intrigues françaises et americaines au Canada, 1965; author: (with John Hare) Les Imprimés dans le Bas-Canada, 1967; author: Confrontations, 1971; author: (with G. Paquet) Patronage et Pouvoir dans le Bas-Canada, 1973; author: Un Quebec qui bougeait, 1973; editor (with R. Girard): Memoires de J.E. McComber, bourgeois de Montréal, 1981; editor: (with J. Goy) Evolution et eclatement du monde rural, 1986; editor: Constructions identitaires et pratiques sociales, 2002, Le débat qui n'a pas eu lieu: la Commission Pepin-Robarts, 2003. Pres. internat. adv. com. on Memory of the World UNESCO, 1993—98. Decorated officer Order Arts et Lettres, France; officer Order of Can., 1991; recipient Marie Tremaine medal, 1973, Tyrrell medal, 1982, Royal Soc. Centenary medal, 1994, Jacques Ducharme prize, 1997, Queen's Jubilee medal, 2002; Faculty of Arts and Scis. U. de Montreal Merit medal, 2004. Fellow Royal Soc. Can. (sect. pres. 1985-87, pres. 1997-99); mem. Am. Antiquarian Soc., Acad. des Lettres du Quebec, Inst. d'Histoire l'Amerique Francaise (pres. 1973-77), Can. Hist. Assn. (pres. 1982), Assn. Can.-Francaise l'Avancement Scis. (pres. 1981-83, emeritus mem.), Assn. Archivists Que., Assn. Can. Archivists, Internat. Coun. on Archives (v.p. 1988-92, pres. 1992-96, pres. emeritus). Roman Catholic. Office: U Ottawa CDtr Rsch PO Box 450 Sta A Ottawa ON Canada K1N 6N5 Office Phone: 613-562-5710. E-mail: jpwallot@uottawa.ca.

WALLS, CARL EDWARD, JR., food service executive; b. Sept. 9, 1948; s. Carl E. and Melba Rene W.; m. Doris Duhart, Aug. 1, 1970; children: Carl Edward, Forrest Allen. Student, San Antonio Coll., 1966-68. Divsn. mgr. Sears Roebuck & Co., San Antonio, 1967-73, area sales mgr., 1973-78; svc. cons. Southwestern Bell, 1978-79, acct. exec., 1979-82; acct. exec., industry cons. AT&T Info. Sys., 1983-88, acct. mgr., 1988-89; gen. mgr. Tex. State Govt., 1989-95, group sales mgr., 1998-99; solutions gen. mgr. AT&T, 1999—2001; v.p. Louie LeDeaux Restaurant, 2001—. Mem. citizens adv. com. Tex. Senate, 1975-81; legis. aide Tex. Ho. of Reps., 1981-85; commr. Alamo Area cou. boy Scouts Am., 1970-79, Capitol Area coun., 1980—, nat. jamboree staff, 1973, 77, 81, 85, 89, 93; mem. Rep. Nat. Com., 1980—, Rep. Presdl. Task Force, 1980—, Rep. Senatorial Club, 1981—. Recipient Patriotic Svc. award U.S. Treasury Dept., 1975-76, Scouters Key and Commrs. award Boy Scouts Am., Disting. Merit award Boy Scouts Am., 1978. Mem. Scouting Collectors Assn. (pres. South Ctrl. region 1979-80, v.p. region 1980-81, sec. 1983-86), U. Ark. Alumni Assn. (life), Am. Legion. Home: 11712 D K Ranch Rd Austin TX 78759-3770

WALLS, CARMAGE LEE, JR., newspaper publisher/executive, consultant; b. Cleveland, Tenn., May 4, 1962; s. Carmage Lee Walls Sr. and Sarah (Smith) Bailey; m. Jeanne Marie Waller, June 4, 1989. BA in Journalism and English, U. Ala., Birmingham, 1988. Writer Birmingham News, 1987; exec. v.p. Cleveland Newspapers Inc., Birmingham, 1989—; pres., creative dir. Walls New Media, Inc., 1997—. Bd. trustees Magic City Art Connection, Birmingham, 2001—. Republican. United Methodist.

WALLS, JAMES DOUGLAS, minister; b. Washington, Aug. 1, 1931; s. George Washington and Emma (Benson) W.; m. Donna Marie Payne, June 16, 1962; children: Quentin Douglas, Janice Marie. Student, Washington Bible Inst., 1957-61; DD, Faith Evangelistic Christian Coll., Detroit, 1990, So. Calif. Sch. Ministry, Inglewood, 1991; HHD (hon.), Faith Evang. Christian Schs., Detroit, 1991. Ordained to ministry Ch. of God, 1960. Pastor Ch. of God, Xenia, Ohio, 1968—; mem. program and planning com., nominating com. Nat. Assn. Ch. of God, West Middlesex, Pa., 1983-89, coord. nat. preachers clinic, 1986—2000, mem. mass comm. bd., 1988-92, mem. ch. rels. bd., 1989-93, chief ops. officer, 2000—. Chair. bd. dirs. Women's Abuse of Substance Intervention Tactics, 1990-94 Editor Words of Truth, 1972-84, Xenia Herald, 1988-2000. Mem. Cumberland Ridge Civic Assn., Columbus, Ohio, 1971—. With U.S. Army, 1952-54. Mem. Urban Christian Leadership Assn., Xenia Area Assn. Chs., African Am. Ministerial Alliance, Ohio State Ch. of God Missionary Bd. Home: 3032 Pine Valley Rd Columbus OH 43219-1643

WALLS, MARTHA ANN WILLIAMS (MRS. B. CARMAGE WALLS), publishing executive; b. Gadsden, Ala., Apr. 21, 1927; d. Aubrey Joseph and Inez (Cooper) Williams; m. B. Carmage Walls, Jan. 2, 1954; children: Byrd Cooper, Lissa Walls Vahldiek. Student pub. schs., Gadsden. Pres., dir. Walls Newspapers, Inc., 1969-70; sec., treas., dir. Summer Camps, Inc., Guntersville, Ala., 1954-69; CEO, pres., dir. So. Newspapers, Inc., Houston, 1970—; pres., dir. So. Newspapers of Ala., Inc., Scottsboro. V.p., dir. Ft. Payne (Ala.) Newspapers, Inc. Bay City (Tex.) Newspapers, Inc., Galveston Newspapers, Inc.; dir. Monroe (Ga.) Newspapers, Inc.; bd. dirs. Jefferson Pilot Corp., Greensboro, N.C., 1990-98, Jefferson-Pilot Life Ins. Co., 1990-98, Jefferson Pilot Comm., 1990-98. Bd. dirs. Montgomery Acad., 1970-74. Mem.: Soc. Profl. Journalists. Episcopalian. Office: So Newspapers Inc 1050 Wilcrest Dr Houston TX 77042-1608

WALLS, ROBERT HAMILTON, JR., lawyer; b. Austin, Tex., May 19, 1960; s. Robert Hamilton Sr. and Anita L. (Hoffman) W.; m. Nancy R. Ghormley, Aug. 11, 1984. BBA in Petroleum, U. Tex., 1983, JD, 1985. Bar: Tex. 1985. Assoc. Vinson & Elkins, Houston, 1985—; dep. gen. coun. Enron Corp., Houston, 1992—2002, exec. v.p. & gen. coun., 2002. Mem. ABA, Tex. Bar Assn., Houston Bar Assn. Office: Office of Gen Coun Enron Corp 1400 Smith St PO Box 1188 Houston TX 77251-1188

WALLS, WESLEY (CHARLES WESLEY WALLS), professional football player; b. Pontotoc, Miss. m. Christy; children: Alexandria Bailey, Wesley Colton. Student, U. Miss. Tight end, long snapper, backup holder on punts San Francisco 49ers, 1989-93; winner Super Bowl XXIV, 1989; tight end New Orleans Saints, 1994-96, Carolina Panthers, 1996—. Named to Pro Bowl, 1996, 97, 98, 99; named second-team All-Pro, AP, Coll. and Pro Football Newsweekly, 1996, 99, second-team All-Pro, Football Digest, first-team All-NFC, Football News, United Press Internat., 1996, All-NFC selection Pro Football Weekly, Football News, 1999; recipient first-team All-NFC honors Football News, United Press Internat., 1997. Office: Carolina Panthers 800 S Mint St Ste 2 Charlotte NC 28202-1502

WALLS, WILLIAM WALTON, JR., management consultant; b. Phila., Oct. 3, 1932; s. William Walton and Mary Crown (Elliott) W.; m. Nina Catherine deAngeli, July 1, 1961; 1 child, Deborah. BSME, Swarthmore Coll., 1959. With Boeing Helicopters, Phila., 1959-96, v.p. light helicopter joint venture, 1988-91, v.p. devel. programs, 1991-92, v.p. rsch. and engring., 1992-96; small high-tech. bus. cons. Ridley Park, Pa., 1996—. Cons. in field. Chmn. aerospace adv. coun. Pa. State Coll., 1974-79; mem. NATO Indsl. Advisors Group, 1988-93; mem. bd. advisors Rotocraft Ctr. Excellence, Rensselaer Polytech. Inst., 1982-84 Mem. Am. Helicopter Soc. (pres. 1988-89, chmn. 1989-90). Republican. Avocations: personal computer applications, classical music, travel, aerobic exercise. Home: 502 Harrison St Ridley Park PA 19078-3208

WALLSKOG, JOYCE MARIE, nursing educator, psychologist; b. Melrose Park, Ill., Apr. 20, 1942; BSN, Alverno Coll., 1977; MSN, U. Wis., Milw., 1982; PhD, Marquette U., 1992. RN, Wis.; lic. psychologist; diplomate Am. Coll. Forensic Examiners. Staff nurse St. Mary's Hill Hosp., Milw., 1977-78, Waukesha (Wis.) Meml. Hosp., 1978-80, clin. nurse specialist, 1980-87; asst. prof. nursing Marquette U., Milw., 1986—; psychotherapist Psychiat. Assocs. Comprehensive Services, Ltd., Milw., 1982-85; nurse psychotherapist Counseling and Wellness Ctr., Waukesha, 1982—; adv. practice nurse prescriber, 1995—. Cons. Alverno Coll., Milw., 1983-84, Health Care Cons., Sussex, Wis., 1985—; coord. Waukesha Premenstrual Syndrome Program, 1980—; nurse psychotherapist Stress Mgmt. and Mental Health Svcs., Waukesha, 1991-94; co-founder Turning Point Mental Health and Cons. Svcs., Waukesha, 1994—; advanced practice nurse prescriber, 1995—. Contbr. articles to profl. jours. Bd. dirs. Waukesha County Mental Health Assn., 1982; mem. Waukesha County Unified Svcs., 1984; adv. bd. Northwest Rehab. Ctr., 1992-94; advisor Resolve Through Sharing, 1986-2001, Women's Health Svcs., 1987-2001; advisor Parish Nurse Program. Mem. ANA (coun. psychiat. and mental health nursing), Wis. Nurses Assn. (rep. Wis. Coalition on Sexual Misconduct by Psychotherapists and Counselors 1988-93), Delta Upsilon Sigma, Phi Lambda Delta. Office: Ctr for Behavioral Health 721 American Ave Ste 501 Waukesha WI 53188-5071 E-mail: wallskogj@aol.com.

WALLSTROM, TIMOTHY C. physicist; b. Resht, Iran, 1958; s. Ira C. and Doris E. Wallstrom; m. Leslie Hornung, Oct. 17, 1992. BA in History, MS in Physics, Stanford U., 1979; PhD in Physics, Princeton U., 1988. Postdoctoral fellow Los Alamos Nat. Lab., N.Mex., 1992—95, tech. staff mem., 1995—. Mem.: Am. Math. Soc., Phi Beta Kappa, Stanford Chpt. Office: Los Alamos Nat Lab Theoretical Division MS B213 Los Alamos NM 87545

WALLYN, JOAN M. social worker, writer; d. Richard Joseph and Helen Marie Wallyn. BBA, Valparaiso U., 1981, BSW, 1982; MSW, La. State U., 1983. LCSW. Social worker State of La., Baton Rouge, 1984—. Contbr. chapters to books, articles to profl. jours. Drug task force East Baton Rouge Parish Club; bd. dirs. Pennington YMCA, Baton Rouge, 2001—03; bd. dirs., sec. St. Nicholas Cmty. Found., Baton Rouge, 2000—03. Mem.: Svc. Corp. Ret. Execs., Romance Writers Am. (treas. Baton Rouge chpt. 1999—2000, newsletter editor 2000). Avocations: writing, horseback riding, painting. Home: PO Box 83933 Baton Rouge LA 70884

WALMER, EDWIN FITCH, lawyer; b. Chgo., Mar. 24, 1930; s. Hillard Wentz and Anna C. (Fitch) W.; m. Florence Poling, June 17, 1952; children: Linda Diane Walmer Dennis, Fred Fitch. BS with distinction, Ind. U., 1952, JD with high distinction, 1957. Bar: Wis. 1957, U.S. Dist. Ct. (ea. dist.) Wis. 1957. Assoc. Foley & Lardner, Milw., 1957-65, ptnr., 1965-90, ret., 1990. Served to 1st lt. U.S. Army, 1952-54. Recipient Cal. C. Chambers award Culver (Ind.) Mil. Acad., 1948. Fellow Am. Coll. Trust and Estate Counsel; mem. Order of Coif, Dairymen's Country Club (Boulder Junction, Wis.), Vineyards Country Club (Naples, Fla.), Phi Eta Sigma, Beta Gamma Sigma. Republican. Congregationalist. Avocations: golf, fishing. Office: Foley & Lardner 777 E Wisconsin Ave Ste 3800 Milwaukee WI 53202-5367

WALMSLEY, JAMES NAYLOR, hydroponic farming executive; b. Rockford, Ill., Sept. 6, 1929; s. James A. and Louella H. (Gage) W.; m. Ann Walmsley (divorced); children: Dana, Lauren, Michael, Daryl Lynn; m. Helga Walmsley (div.); children: Kristen V., Tanya J. Student, George Washington, 1950-52, Loyola U., 1953-55, Northwestern U., 1955. Investment banker Hornblower & Weeks, Chgo., 1955-61; pres. Manin Internat. Inc., Chgo., 1961-72, Jinga Hydroponic Farms Ltd., Chgo., 1972—, Bahedeshar Ltd., tech. R & D, Clarksburg, W.Va., 1995—; mng. dir. Manin Internat., Inc., Las Vegas, Nev., 2000—. Active Points of Light Found., Children Def. Fund; rep. W.Va. Rep. Presdl. Roundtable, 2001; hon. chmn. grassroots campaign Rep. Hdqrs., 2002. With USN, 1949-53. Recipient Internat. Am. award, 1987. Mem. Royal Horticulture Soc., Am. Horticulture Soc., N.Y. Acad. Scis., The Heritage Found. Republican. Avocations: travel, art, reading. Office: Bahedeshar Ltd 728 Milford St Clarksburg WV 26301 Office Phone: 304-623-4670. Office Fax: 304-623-4745.

WALNER, ROBERT JOEL, lawyer; b. Chgo., Dec. 22, 1946; s. Wallace and Elsie W.; m. Charlene Walner; children: Marci, Lisa. BA, U. Ill., 1968; JD, De Paul U., 1972; MBA with distinction, Northwestern U., 1991. Bar: Ill. 1972, Fla. 1973, U.S. Dist. Ct. (no. dist.) Ill. 1972, U.S. Ct. Appeals (7th cir.) 1972; counselor of real estate; cert. mediator. Atty. SEC, Chgo., 1972-73; pvt. practice Chgo., 1973—; adminstrv. law judge Ill. Commerce Commn., Chgo., 1973-76; atty. Allied Van Lines, Inc., Broadview, Ill., 1976-79; sr. v.p., gen. counsel, corp. sec. The Balcor Co., Skokie, Ill., 1979-92; prin. fin. ops. Balcor Securities divsn. The Balcor Co., Skokie, 1984-92, pres., 1989-92; of counsel Lawrence, Walner & Assocs., Ltd., Chgo., 1992-93; sr. v.p., gen. counsel, corp. sec. Grubb & Ellis Co., Northbrook, Ill., 1994—2001, exec. v.p., chief adminstrv. and legal officer, corp. sec., 2001—03; of counsel Pircher, Nichols & Meeks, Chgo., 2003—; nat. chmn. tax, regulatory and legis. com. Counselors of Real Estate, 2003—. Mem. securities adv. com. to Ill. Sec. of State, 1984-94; mem. editl. bd. Real Estate Securities Jour., Real Estate Securities and Capital Markets; program chmn. Regulators and You seminar. Contbr. chpts. to books, articles on real estate and securities law to profl. jours.; assoc. editor De Paul U. Law Rev. Mem. Kellogg Career Devel. Com., 1992-94, Kellogg Bus. Adv. Com., 1992-2001; mem. enterprise forum MIT, 1992—, mem. exec. com., 1993-94. With USAR, 1968-73. Mem. ABA, Ill. Bar Assn., Chgo. Bar Assn., Fla. Bar Assn., Am. Real Estate Com. (pres. com. 1985-90), Real Estate Syndication Com. (chmn. 1982-85), Ill. Inst. Continuing Legal Edn., N.Am. Securities Adminstrs. Assn. Inc. (industry adv. com. to real estate com., 1987-89), Real Estate Securities and Syndication Inst. of Nat. Assn. Realtors (chmn. regulatory and legis. com., 1984, 87, group v.p. 1987, exec. com. 1987-90, specialist, real estate investment), Nat. Real Estate Investment Forum (chmn. 1985, 88), Real Estate Investment Assn. (founder, exec. com. 1990-92, bd. dirs. 2004—), Kellogg Alumni Club (bd. dirs., event chmn. 1996-98, v.p., exec. com. 1998-99), Beta Gamma Sigma.

WALPIN, GERALD, lawyer; b. N.Y.C., Sept. 1, 1931; s. Michael and Mary (Gordon) W.; m. Sheila Kainer, Apr. 13, 1957; children: Amanda Eve, Edward Andrew, Jennifer Hope. BA, CCNY, 1952; LLB cum laude, Yale Law Sch., 1955. Bar: N.Y. 1955, U.S. Supreme Ct. 1965, U.S. Ct. Appeals (2d cir.) 1960, (6th cir.) 1969, (3d cir.) 1976, (8th cir.) 1982, (9th cir.) 1983, (llth cir.) 1983, (7th cir.) 1984, U.S. Ct. Claims 1984. Law clk. to Hon. E.J. Dimock U.S. Dist. Ct. (so. dist.) N.Y., N.Y.C.; law clk. to Hon. F.P. Bryan U.S. Dist. Judge (so. dist.) N.Y., N.Y.C., 1955-57; asst. U.S. atty., chief spl. prosecutions U.S. Atty. Office, N.Y.C., 1960-65; sr. ptnr. Katten Muchin Zavis Rosenman predecessor firms, N.Y.C., 1965—2002, chmn. litigation dept., 1985-96, counsel, 2002—. Adv. com. Fed. Ct. So. Dist. N.Y., 1991-98; co-chmn. lawyers divsn. Anti-Defamation League, N.Y., 1994-97; bd. dirs. Ctr. for Individual Rights, 1997—; pres. Fed. Bar Coun., 2002—. Editor Yale Law Jour., 1953-54, mng. editor, 1954-55; contbr. articles to profl. jours. Pres. Parker Jewish Inst. for Health Care and Rehab., New Hyde Park, N.Y., 1987-90, trustee, 1979—; bd. dirs. Fund for Modern Cts., N.Y.C., 1985-91; mem. law com. Am. Jewish Com., 1980—; mem. Com. for Free World, N.Y.C., 1983-91; trustee, mem. exec. com. United Jewish Appeal-Fedn. Jewish Philanthropies, N.Y.C., 1984-96; mem. Nassau County Crime Commn., 1970; pres. Kensington Civic Orgn., Gt. Neck, N.Y., 1972-73. Recipient Quality of Life award United Jewish Appeal Fedn., 1978, Human Rels. award Am. Jewish Com., 1982, Gift of Life award Jewish Inst. Geriatric Care, 1987, Learned Hand award Am. Jewish Com., 1990, Human Rels. award Anti-Defamation League, 1998. Mem. ABA, Fed. Bar Coun. (chmn. modern cts. com. 1989, v.p. 1991-95, chmn. bench and bar liaison com. 1994-95, vice chmn. 1995-97, chmn. bd. dirs. 1997-99, pres. 2002—), Federalist Soc. (chmn. litigation sect. 1996-99, mem. bd. visitors 1999—), Univ. Club. Republican. Jewish. Home: 875 Park Ave New York NY 10021-0341 Office: KMZ Rosenman 575 Madison Ave Fl 20 New York NY 10022-2511 Office Phone: 212-940-7100. E-mail: gerald.walpin@kmzr.com. *My life should be an appropriate response to God and this country for providing me with the opportunities I have had: Contribution to our society and strengthening of our country's steadfast opposition to discrimination for or against anyone based on race, religion or sex.*

WALRATH, HARRY RIENZI, retired minister; b. Alameda, Calif., Mar. 7, 1926; s. Frank Rienzi and Cathren (Michlar) W.; m. Dorothy M. Baxter, June 24, 1961; 1 son, Gregory Rienzi. AA, City Coll., San Francisco, 1950; BA, U. Calif., Berkeley, 1952; MDiv, Ch. Div. Sch. of Pacific, 1959. Ordained deacon Epsicopal Ch., 1959, priest, 1960. Dist. exec. San Mateo area Boy Scouts Am., 1952-55; curate All Souls Parish, Berkeley, Calif., 1959-61; vicar St. Luke's, Atascadero, Calif., 1961-63, St. Andrew's, Garberville, Calif., 1963-64; assoc. rector St. Luke's Ch., Los Gatos, 1964-65, Holy Spirit Parish, Missoula, Mont., 1965-67; vicar St. Peter's Ch., Litchfield Park, Ariz., 1967-69; also headmaster St. Peter's Schs., Litchfield Park, Ariz., 1967-69; chaplain U. Mont., 1965-67; asst. rector Trinity Parish, Reno, 1969-72; coord. counciling svcs. Washoe County Coun. Alcholism, Reno, 1972-74; adminstr. Cons. Assistance Svcs., Inc., Reno, 1974-76; pastoral counselor, contract chaplain Nev. Mental Health Inst., 1976-78; contract mental health chaplain VA Hosp., Reno, 1976-78; mental health chaplain VA Med. Ctr., Reno, 1978-83, staff chaplain, 1983-85, chief chaplain svc., 1985-91, triage coord. mental health, ret., 1991. Per diem chaplain Washoe Med. Ctr., Reno, 1993; assoc. priest Trinity Epsicopal Ch., Reno, 1995; assoc. Mountain Ministries, Susanville, Calif., 1995—. Author: God Rides the Rails-Chapel Cars on American Railroads at the Turn of the Century, 1994. Dir. youth Paso Robles Presbytery; chmn. Diocesan Commn. on Alcoholism; cons. teen-age problems Berkeley Presbytery; mem. clergy team Epsicopal Marriage Encounter; chaplain Make A Wish Found., 1998-2000; mem. at-large Washoe dist. Nev. area coun. Boy Scouts Am., scoutmaster troop 73, 1976, troop 585, 1979-82, asst. scoutmaster troop 35, 1982-92, assoc. adviser area 3 Western region, 1987-89, regional com. Western Region, 1989-90; lodge adviser Tannu Lodge 346, Order of Arrow, 1982-87; docent coun. Nev. Hist. Sch., 1992; South Humboldt County chmn. Am. Cancer Soc.; trustee Cmty. Youth Ctr., Reno. With USNR, 1944-46. Decorated Pacific Theatre medal with star, Am. Theatre medal, Victory medal, Fleet Unit Commendation medal; recipient dist. award of merit Boy Scouts Am., St. George award Episc. Ch.-Boy Scouts Am., Silver Beaver award Boy Scouts Am., 1986, Founders' award Order of the Arrow, Boy Scouts Am., 1995; performance awards VA-VA Med. Ctr., 1983, 84; named Arrowman of Yr., Order of Arrow, Boy Scouts Am. Cert. substance abuse counselor, Nev. Mem. Ch. Hist. Soc., U. Calif. Alumni Assn., Nat. Model R.R. Assn. (life), Sierra Club Calif., Missoula Coun. Chs. (pres.), Rotary, Alpha Phi Omega. Democrat. Home: 4822 Ramcreek Trl Reno NV 89509-8029

WALRATH, PATRICIA A. state legislator; b. Brainerd, Minn., Aug. 11, 1941; d. Joseph James and Pansy Patricia (Drake) McCarvill; m. Robert Eugene Walrath, Sept. 1, 1961; children: Karen, Susan, David, Julie. BS, Bemidji State U., 1962; MS, SUNY, Oswego, 1975. Cert. secondary math. tchr., N.Y., Mass. Programmer analyst Control Data Corp., Mpls., 1962-65; crewleader dept. commerce U.S. Census, Middlesex County, Mass., 1979-80; selectman Town of Stow, Mass., 1980-85; tchr. math. Hale Jr. High Sch., Stow, 1981-82; instr. math. Johnson & Wale Coll. Hanscom AFB, Bedford, Mass., 1983-84, test examiner, 1983-84; state rep. 3d Middlesex dist. State of Mass., Boston, 1985—. Mem. ways and means com. Mass. Ho. of Reps., 1987—92, 1996, mem. joint coms. on local affairs, 1993—95, mem. pub. svc. com., 1993—96, mem. election law com., 1985—86, 1995—96, mem. sci. and tech. com., 1995—96, mem. commerce and labor com., 1996, mem. govt. regulations com., 96, chmn. com. long term debt and capital expenditures, 1997—2001, asst. whip, floor chair, 2001—. Chmn. Mass. Indoor Air Pollution Commn., Boston, 1987-88; mem. Stow Dem. Com., 1988—. Recipient Disting. Svc. award Auburn N.Y. Jaycees, 1976. Mem. LWV (pres. 1973-76, dir. fin. 1977-78), Mass. Legislators' Assn., Mass. Dem. Leadership Coun. (v.p. 1991-92, co-chmn. 1993-94, treas. 1995-99), Mass. Women's Legis. Caucus (chair 1986). Roman Catholic. Avocations: gardening, stamp collecting/philately, travel. Home: 20 Middlemost Way Stow MA 01775-1363 Office: State Capital RM481 Boston MA 02133 E-mail: Rep.PatriciaWalrath@hou.state.ma.us.

WALSER, SANDRA TERESA JOHNSON, rehabilitation nurse, preceptor; b. Lexington, N.C., Dec. 9, 1951; d. Thomas Victory and Mary Johnson; m. Ellis Kent Walser, Nov. 14, 1970; children: Andrea Elise, Joshua Kent, Jonathan Patrick. ADN, Forsyth Tech. Community Coll., Winston-Salem, N.C., 1989. RN, N.C. Nurse physical neuro brain injury rehab. unit Forsyth Meml. Hosp., Winston-Salem, 1989—. Mem. Assn. Rehab. Nurses (cert. rehab. RN), Christian Nurses Fellowship. Home: 497 Baileys Chapel Rd Advance NC 27006-7141

WALSH, ANNMARIE HAUCK, research firm executive; b. N.Y.C., May 5, 1938; d. James Smith and Ann-Marie (Kennedy) Hauck; m. John F. Walsh, Jr., Aug. 20, 1960; children: Peter Hauck, John David. BA, Barnard Coll., 1961; MA, Columbia U., 1969, PhD, 1971. Sr. staff mem. Inst. Pub. Adminstrn., N.Y.C., 1961-72, pres., 1982-89, trustee, Gulick scholar, 1989—, dir. programs in Ctrl. Europe and NIS, 1991—; dir. Ctr. for Urban and Policy Studies, CUNY Grad. Ctr., N.Y.C., 1972-79, Govs.' Task Force on Regional Planning, N.Y., Conn., N.J., 1979-81. Disting. vis. prof. Bklyn. Coll., CUNY, 1991-93; adj. prof. Robert Wagner Sch. Pub. Svc., NYU, 1998—; cons. pub. enterprise, civil svc., urban and regional mgmt., tng., pub. fin. adminstrn. reform UN, China, Indonesia, Bangladesh, Czech Republic and Slovakia, Poland, Macedonia, Uzbekistan, Kazakstan, state and local govts., U.S. Postal Svc., U.S. Dept. Transp., Senate com. govt. ops. Author: Urban Government for Zagreb, Yugoslavia, 1968, Urban Government for Lagos, Nigeria, 1968, Urban Government for the Paris Region, 1968, The Urban Challenge to Government: An International Comparisons of Thirteen Cities, 1969, The Public's Business: Politics and Practices of Government Corporations, 1978, 2d edit., 1980, Designing and Managing the Procurement Process, 1989, Privatization-Implications for Public Management, 1996; editor: Agenda for a City, 1970. Project dir. 20th Century Fund, Pub. Enterprise, 1972-76, pub.-pvt. partnerships, 1989-93; bd. dirs. Ralph Bunche Inst., UN, 1978-82, Regional Plan Assn., 1987-91. Herbert Lehmann fellow, 1966-69 Fellow, Nat. Acad. Pub. Adminstrn. (bd. dirs. 1996—); mem. Phi Beta Kappa. Office: Inst Pub Admistrn 411 Lafayette St Ste 303 New York NY 10003-7032

WALSH, CHARLES RICHARD, retired banker; b. Bklyn., Jan. 30, 1939; s. Charles John and Anna Ellen Walsh; m. Marie Anne Goulden, June 24, 1961; children: Kevin C., Brian R., Gregory M. BS, Fordham U., 1960; MBA, St. John's U., 1966, D of Comml. Scis. (hon.), 1985. V.p. Mfrs. Hanover Trust Co., Hicksville, N.Y., 1974-80, sr. v.p., 1980-86, exec. v.p., 1986-90, group exec., mem. mgmt. com., 1990-92; exec. v.p., group exec. Chem. Banking Corp., Hicksville, N.Y., 1992-95, The Chase Manhattan Corp., 1995-97; ret., 1997. Bd. dirs. Mastercard Internat.; bd. dirs., former chmn. Eastern States Monetary Svcs., Lake Success, N.Y., 1978-88; former pres., CEO, bd. dirs. The Bankcard Assn., Hicksville, 1988-91. Sustaining mem. Rep. Nat. Com., 1978—; vice chmn. adv. bd. St. John's U., 1982—. With USAR, 1960, 61-62. Mem. N.Y. State Bankers Assn. (former bd. dirs., mem. gov. coun., chmn. consumer banking divsn.), Am. Bankers Assn. (mem. govt. rels. coun., chmn. bank card divsn., mem. exec. com., former mem. comms. coun. and chmn. edn. com.), Am. Mgmt. Assn., N.Y. Credit and Fin. Mgmt. Assn., Soc. Cert. Consumer Credit Execs. (cert.), Beta Gamma Sigma, Omicron Delta Epsilon, North Hempstead Country Club, Gov.'s Club Kiawah Island (S.C.), Kiawah Island Club. Republican. Home: 9 Blueberry Ln Oyster Bay NY 11771-3901 also: 107 Goldeneye Dr Kiawah Island SC 29455-5773

WALSH, CHRISTINE ANN, cardiologist; b. Bklyn., Dec. 31, 1947; d. Martin and Loretta (Lesniewski) Kull; m. Sean Michael Walsh, June 10, 1978; children: Kathleen, Sean, Stephen. BS, Fordham U., 1969; MD, Yale U., 1973. Diplomate Am. Bd. Pediatrics, Am. Bd. Critical Care Medicine, Am. Bd. Pediatric Cardiology. Intern, then resident Babies Hosp., N.Y., Columbia-Presbyn. Med. Ctr., N.Y.; fellow in pediatric cardiology Columbia U., N.Y., asst. prof. Coll. Physicians and Surgeons, 1980-84; asst. prof. Albert Einstein Coll. of Medicine, N.Y.C., 1984-91; asst. attending physician N.C. Bronx Hosp., 1984—; asst. attending pediatrician Jacobi Med. Ctr., Bronx, 1984—; dir. Pediat. Dysrhythmia Ctr. Montefiore Med. Ctr., Bronx, 1984—, from asst. to assoc. attending pediatrician, 1984-98, attending pediatrician, 1998—, chief sect. pediat. cardiology, 2002—; assoc. prof. pediat. Albert Einstein Coll. of Medicine, Bronx, 1991-98, prof., 1998—, co-chair admissions com., 1998—. Cons. Adult Arrhythmia Svc., Montefiore Med. Ctr., Pacemaker Ctr., epilepsy unit, Cranio-facial Ctr.; postdoctorate in cardiac electrophysiology and phramcology Columbia U. Coll. Physicians and Surgeons, N.Y.C., 1978—80. Editor: Adolescent Medicine, State of Art Revs., Adolescent Cardiology; contbr. articles to profl. jours. Bd. dirs. Velo-Cardio-Facial Syndrome Ednl. Found., N.Y.C., 1995—. Grantee, Albert Einstein Interdivisional, 1995, 1999. Fellow: Am. Acad. Pediat., Am. Coll. Cardiology; mem.: N.Y. Soc. Pediatric Critical Care Assn., Am. Heart Assn., Pediat. Electrophysiology Soc., Pediatric Cardiology Soc. (treas. 1987—88, sec. 1988—89, v.p. 1989—90, pres. 1990—91), N.Am. Soc. Pacing and Electrophysiology, Assn. Yale Alumni

Medicine (sec.), Phi Beta Kappa. Avocations: gardening, skiing, scuba diving, piano, camping. Home: PO Box 238 Flushing NY 11363-0238 Office: Montefiore Med Ctr 111 E 210th St Bronx NY 10467-2401 Office Phone: 718-741-2310.

WALSH, CHRISTOPHER THOMAS, biochemist, department chairman; b. Boston, Feb. 16, 1944; married; 1 child. BA, Harvard U., 1965; PhD in Life Sci., Rockefeller U., 1970. Helen Hay Whitney Found. fellow Brandeis U., 1970-72; from asst. prof. to prof. chemistry and biology MIT, 1972-87, assoc. dir. Whitaker Coll. Mgmt., 1979-82, Uncas and Helen Whitaker prof., 1980-85, Karl Taylor Compton prof., 1985-87, chmn. chemistry dept., 1982-87; David Wesley Gaiser prof. Harvard U., 1987-91, chmn. dept. biol. chemistry and molecular pharmacology Med. Sch., 1987—, Hamilton Kuhn prof., 1991—; pres. Dana-Farber Cancer Inst., Boston, 1992-95. Cons. Merck, Sharp & Dohme Rsch. Labs., 1975-81, Monsanto Corp. Res. Labs., 1980-81, Johnson & Johnson, 1982-83, Hoffman LaRoche, 1982—, Genzyme & Bioinfo Assocs., 1983—, Firmenich, S A, 1986-90, Enzymatics, 1988—, Biotage, 1989—; mem. panel rsch. grants study NSF, 1977-79, panel study sect. biochemistry NIH, 1978-82, gen. med. coun., NIH, 1983-85, Chemal Rsch. Group, WHO, 1984-86; co-chmn. Gordon Rsch. Conf. Enzymes, Coenzymes & Molecular Biology, 1978, Conf. Methanogenesis, 1984; chmn. study sect. biochemistry NIH, 1982—; lectr. in field. Alfred P. Sloan Found. fellow, 1975-77, Camille and Henry Dreyfus Tchr.-Scholar grantee, 1976-80; recipient Eli Lilly award, 1979. Mem. NAS, Inst. Medicine-NAS, Am. Acad. Arts & Sci., Am. Soc. Biol. Chemists, Am. Chem. Soc., Am. Soc. Microbiology Achievements include research in enzymatic reation mechanisms, phosphoryl and pyrophosphoryl transfers, flavin-dependent enzymes, membrane biochemistry and mechanism of active transport. Office: Harvard Med Sch Dept Bio Chem/Mol Pharm 240 Longwood Ave Boston MA 02115-5701

WALSH, DANIEL FRANCIS, bishop; b. San Francisco, Oct. 2, 1937; Grad., St. Joseph Sem., St. Patrick Sem., Catholic U. Am. Ordained priest, Roman Catholic Ch., 1963. Ordained titular bishop of Tigia, 1981; aux. bishop of San Francisco, 1981-87; bishop of Reno-Las Vegas, 1987—2002; bishop of Santa Rosa, 2002—. Roman Catholic. Address: Bishop of Santa Rosa PO Box 1297 Santa Rosa CA 95402

WALSH, DAVID ALLAN, theater director; b. Toronto, Can., Sept. 12, 1947; s. Francis Larimer and Margaret Allan Walsh; children: Vanessa, Siobhan. BA with honors, U. Windsor, Ont., 1969; grad. cert. in theatre sci., U. Toronto, 1972. Stage mgr. Can. Opera Co., Toronto, 1972—74; asst. dir. English Nat. Opera, London, 1976—80, Frankfurt Opera, Germany, 1980—84; asst. artistic dir. Vancouver Opera, Canada, 1984—87; head, prodn. Scottish Opera, Glasgow, 1987—91; dir., opera studio Victoria Conservatory, Canada, 1993—95, Vancouver Acad., Canada, 1995—98; asst. dir. Dusseldorf Opera, Germany, 1998—2002; dir., opera U. Minn., Mpls., 2002—. Avocations: running, tennis, hiking, theater. Home: 1049 5th St SE Minneapolis MN 55412 Office: Univ Minn Sch Music 2106 Fourth St South Minneapolis MN 55455 Business E-Mail: walsh057@umn.edu.

WALSH, DAVID GRAVES, lawyer; b. Madison, Wis., Jan. 7, 1943; s. John J. and Audrey B. Walsh; married; children: Michael, Katherine, Molly, John. BBA, U. Wis., 1965; JD, Harvard U., 1970. Bar: Wis. Law clk. Wis. Supreme Ct., Madison, 1970-71; ptnr. Walsh, Walsh, Sweeney & Whitney, Madison, 1971-86; ptnr.-in-charge Foley & Lardner, Madison, 1986—95. Bd. regents U. Wis., 2003-; bd. dirs. Nat. Guardian Life, Madison, 1981—; lectr. U. Wis., Madison, 1974-75, 77-78, v.p. Regents U. of Wis. Chmn. State of Wis. Elections Bd., Madison, 1978. Lt. USN, 1965-67, Vietnam. Recipient Disting. Bus. Alumnus award U. Wis. Sch. Bus., 1997. Maple Bluff Country Club (Madison) (pres. 1987). Roman Catholic. Avocations: tennis, golf, fishing. Home: 41 Fuller Dr Madison WI 53704-5962 Office: Foley & Lardner PO Box 1497 Madison WI 53701-1497

WALSH, DAVID JAMES, lawyer; b. Dubuque, Iowa, Aug. 10, 1949; s. James and Helen Walsh; m. Alice Chebba; children: Elizabeth, James. BA, Loras Coll., 1971; JD, U. Wis., 1974; MBA, Alaska Pacific U., 1990; postgrad. in Internat. Bus., City U. London, 1991. Bar: Wis. 1974, Alaska 1975. Asst. dist. atty. State of Alaska, Anchorage, 1975-78; pvt. practice Anchorage, 1974-75, 78-90; co-founder, chmn. exec. com. Internat. Assn. Ins. Suprs., 1992-95; dir. ins. State of Alaska, 1990-95; gen. counsel Domestic Brokerage Group Am. Internat. Group, N.Y.C., 1995-98; pres. Nat. Assn. Ins. Commrs., 1994; exec. v.p., corp. counsel Swiss Re Life & Health, Stamford, CT. Mem. Gov.'s Transition Team, 1982-83; mem. U.S./Alaska R.R. Transfer Team, 1982-84; vice chmn. State Rolyalty Oil and Gas Adv. Bd., 1985-87; bd. dirs. IFNY; adj. prof. law Pace U. Chmn. Anchorage Mcpl. Assembly, 1976-86; bd. dirs. Alaska Mcpl. League, 1976-86, pres., 1980; mem. exec. bd. Greater N.Y. coun. Boy Scouts Am., 1997—. Mem. Assn. Internationale de Droit des Assurances (presdl. coun. 1995—). Office: Swiss Re Life & Health 969 High Ridge Rd Stamford CT 06905-1608

WALSH, DENNIS P. government agency administrator; m. Barbara A. O'Neill; children: Steven, Rose. BA summa cum laude in govt., Hamilton Coll., 1976; JD cum laude, Cornell Law Sch., 1983. Mem. Nat. Labor Rels. Bd., 2000—01; mem. Nat. Labor Relations Bd., 2002—; chief counsel to Margaret A Browning, 1994—97, and to Wilma B. Liebman, 1997—2000; atty. Nat. Labor Rels. Bd., 1984—89; assoc. Spear, Wilderman, Borish, Endy, Browning & Spear, Phila., 1989—94. Office: Franklin Court Bldg 1099 14th St NW Washington DC 20570-0001

WALSH, DENNY JAY, reporter; b. Omaha, Nov. 23, 1935; s. Gerald Jerome and Muriel (Morton) W.; m. Peggy Marie Moore, Feb. 12, 1966; children by previous marriage— Catherine Camille, Colleen Cecile; 1 son, Sean Joseph. B.J., U. Mo., 1962. Staff writer St. Louis Globe-Democrat, 1961-68; asst. editor Life mag., N.Y.C., 1968-70, assoc. editor, 1970-73; reporter N.Y. Times, 1973-74, Sacramento Bee, 1974—. Served with USMC, 1954-58. Recipient Con Lee Kelliher award St. Louis chpt. Sigma Delta Chi, 1962; award Am. Polit. Sci. Assn., 1963; award Sigma Delta Chi, 1968; Pulitzer prize spl. local reporting, 1969; 1st prize San Francisco Press Club, 1977 Office: Sacramento Bee 21st & Q Sts Sacramento CA 95816 Office Phone: 916-321-1189. Business E-Mail: dwalsh@sacbee.com.

WALSH, DIANA CHAPMAN, academic administrator, sociologist, educator; b. Phila., July 30, 1944; d. Robert Francis and Gwen (Jenkins) Chapman; m. Christopher Thomas Walsh, June 18, 1966; 1 child, Allison Chapman. BA in English, Wellesley Coll., 1966; MS in Journalism, Boston U. Sch. of Pub. Comm., 1971; PhD in Health Policy, Boston U., 1983; LHD (hon.), Boston U, 1994, Amer. Coll. of Greece, Athens, 1995, U. Mass., Amherst, 1999, Northeastern U., 2003. Dir. info., edn. Planned Parenthood League, Newton, Mass., 1971—74; sr. program assoc. Dept Pub. Health, Boston, 1974—76; assoc. dir. Boston U. Health Policy Inst., 1985—90; prof. Sch. Pub. Health, Sch. Medicine, Boston U., 1987—90, adj. prof. pub. health, 1990—; Florence Sprague Norman and Laura Smart Norman prof., chair dept. health and social behavior Harvard Sch. Pub. Health, 1990—93, adj. prof., 1993—; pres. Wellesley Coll., 1993—. Author: (book) Corporate Physicians, 1987; editor: Women, Work and Health: Challenges to Corporate Policy, 1980, (book series) Industry and Health Care, 1977—80; co-author: Payer, Provider, Consumer, 1977; contbr. articles to profl. jours. Bd. dirs. Planned Parenthood League of Mass., 1974—79, 1981—85, bd. overseers, 1993—94; trustee Occupl. Physicians Scholarship Fund, 1987—94, WGBH Ednl. Found., 1993—2000. Recipient Book of the Yr. award, Am. Jour. Nursing, 1980; fellow, Kellogg Nat. fellow, 1987—90. Mem.: AHA, AASA, Consortium on Financing Higher Edn., State Street Corp., Mass. Pub. Health Assn., Soc. for the Study of Social Problems, Am. Sociol. Assn. Avocations: gender and health, social policy, writing, skiing. Office: Wellesley Coll Office of the Pres 106 Central St Wellesley MA 02481-8268

WALSH, DIANE, pianist; b. Washington, Aug. 16, 1950; d. William Donald and Estelle Louise (Stokes) W.; m. Henry Forbes, 1969 (div. 1979); m. Richard Pollak, 1982. MusB, Juilliard Sch. Music, 1971; MusM, Mannes Coll., 1982. N.Y.C. debut Young Concert Artists Series, 1974; founding mem. Mannes Trio, 1983-94; solo appearances include: Kennedy Ctr. for Performing Arts, Washington, 1976, Met. Mus., N.Y.C., 1976, Wigmore Hall, London, 1980, Merkin Concert Hall, 1989, Miller Theatre, 1994, 96; with Mannes Trio: Lincoln Ctr.'s Alice Tully Hall, Libr. of Congress, 1987; appeared with maj. orchs. worldwide, including St. Louis Symphony, Indpls. Symphony, San Francisco Symphony, Am. Symphony, Austin (Tex.) Symphony, Bavarian Radio Symphony of Munich, Berlin Radio Symphony, Radio Symphony Frankfurt, Radio Symphony Stuttgart; has toured Europe, N.Am., S.Am., C.Am., Russia; Marlboro Festival, 1982, Bard Festival, 1990-99, Santa Fe (N.Mex.) Festival, 1995; recs. for Nonesuch Records, 1980, 82, Book-of-Month Records, 1985, Music and Arts, 1990, CRI, 1991, Koch, 1995, Biddulph Records, 1998, Stereophile, 1998, Newport Classic, 1998, Sony, 2000, Arabesque, 2004, Bridge, 2004; artistic dir. Skaneateles Festival, 1999-2004; mem. piano and chamber music faculty Mannes Coll. Music, 1982—. Recipient 3d prize Busoni Internat. Piano Competition, Italy, 1974, 2nd prize Mozart Internat. Piano Competition, Salzburg, Austria, 1975, 1st prize Munich Internat. Piano Competition, 1975, Naumburg Chamber Music award, 1986; NEA grantee, 1981.

WALSH, DOLORES ANN GONCZO (LORRY WALSH), special education educator; b. Detroit, Sept. 3, 1933; d. Joseph John and Dolores (Carey) Gonczo; m. Bernard Waldrup, Aug. 23, 1958 (div. 1980, dec. 2000); children: Elizabeth, Carey, Leslie, Bernard III; m. Deleon Walsh, Sept. 3, 1982 (dec. 1990). Student, Barat Coll., 1951-52; PhB, U. Detroit, 1955; MPS, Manhattanville Coll., 1978. Tchr. 2d grade East Detroit (Mich.) Pub. Schs., 1955-58; tchr. 4th grade Birmingham (Ala.) Schs., 1958-59, St. Francis Xavier Sch., Birmingham, 1959-62; homebound tchr. Greenburg Ctrl. 7, Hartsdale, NY, 1969-73, tchr. spl. edn., 1973-91, mid. states h.s. evaluation team, 1982—90; ret., 1991. Tchr. English, China, summer 1998; mem. Middle States Evaluating Team of High Schs., 1082-90. Dist. leader Dem. Party Greenburgh, 1981-91; sec. Greenburgh Health Cen. Bd., Greenburgh, N.Y., 1986-91; leader Girl Scouts U.S., 1968-69; CCD tchr. Convent of Sacred Heart, Greenwich, Conn.; vol. West Valley Art Mus., 1992-2001, Cath. Ctr., 1998—. Mem. Ariz. Alumnae of Sacred Heart (pres. 2001-03), Delta Zeta. E-mail: lorry2@quik.com.

WALSH, DON, marine consultant, executive; b. Berkeley, Calif., Nov. 2, 1931; s. J. Don and Marguerite Grace (Van Auker) W.; m. Joan A. Betzmer, Aug. 18, 1962; children— Kelly Drennan, Elizabeth McDonough BS, U.S. Naval Acad., 1954; MS, Tex. A&M U., 1967, PhD, 1968; MA, San Diego State U., 1968. Commd. ensign USN, 1954, advanced through grades to capt., 1974, officer-in-charge Bathyscaph Trieste, 1959-62, comdr. in USS Bashaw, 1968-69; dir. Inst. Marine and Coastal Studies, prof. ocean engring. U. So. Calif., L.A., 1975-83; pres., CEO Internat. Maritime, Inc., L.A., 1976—; mng. dir. Deep Ocean Engring., Inc., 1990—2000, also bd. dirs. Dir. Ctr. for Marine Transp. Studies, U. So. Calif., 1980-83, Coastal Resources Ctr., 1990-94; trustee USN Mus. Found., 1989—; mem. Nat. Adv. Com. on Oceans and Atmosphere, 1979-85; bd. govs. Calif. Maritime Acad., 1985-95; pres. Parker Diving, 1989-94. Editor, contbr.: Law of the Sea: Issues in Ocean Resource Management, 1977, Energy and Resources Development of Continental Margins, 1980, Energy and Sea Power: Challenge for the Decade, 1981, Waste Disposal in the Oceans: Minimizing Impact, Maximizing Benefits, 1983; editor Jour. Marine Tech. Soc., 1975-80; mem. editorial bd. U.S. Naval Inst., 1974-75. Bd. dirs. Charles and Anne Lindbergh Found., 1996—. Decorated Legion of Merit (2); Woodrow Wilson Internat. Ctr. for Scholars fellow, 1973-74. Fellow Marine Tech. Soc., Acad. Underwater Arts and Scis., Explorers Club (hon. life, bd. dirs. 1994-2000, Explorers Medal, 2001); mem. AAAS, Soc. Naval Archs. and Marine Engrs., Am. Soc. Naval Engrs., Navy League, Navy Inst., Adventurers Club (hon. life), Am. Geog. Soc. (hon. life), Nat. Acad. Engring. Home and Office: Internat Maritime Inc 14758 Sitkum Ln Myrtle Point OR 97458-9726 E-mail: imiwalsh@worldnet.att.net.

WALSH, DONNA M. state legislator; b. Trenton, N.J., Jan. 28, 1943; m. Henry Walsh, Jr.; one child, Henry III. BA, U. R.I., 1971, MA, 1976. Tchr. Hope Valley Sch., R.I., 1971-88, Chariho Mid. Sch., R.I., 1998—; mem. R.I. Senate, Dist. 25, Providence, 1996—. Mem. judiciary com. R.I. State Senate, health com., edn. and welfare com. Mem. R.I. Bd. Regents for Elem. and Secondary Edn.; pres. bd. trustees Cross Mills Libr.; mem. Cross Mills Ladies Fire Co. Aux.; mem. Chariho Bus. and Profl. Women, Charlestown and Hopkinton Hist. Socs.; me. Charlestown Charter Commn., 1980; mem. Charlestown Town Coun., 1982-84; chair Charlestown Dem. Town Com., 1991-93. Mem. Nat. Sci. Tchrs. Assn., Charlestown C. of C. Democrat. Office: RI State Senate PO Box 1380 Charlestown RI 02813-0905 Address: RI State Senate State House Providence RI 02903 E-mail: sen-walsh@rilin.state.ri.us.

WALSH, EDWARD JOSEPH, toiletries and food company executive; b. Mt. Vernon, N.Y., Mar. 18, 1932; s. Edward Aloysius and Charlotte Cecilia (Borup) W.; m. Patricia Ann Farrell, Sept. 16, 1961; children: Edward Joseph, Megan Simpson, John, Robert. BBA, Iona Coll., 1953; MBA, NYU, 1958. Sales rep. M & R Dietetic Labs., Columbus, Ohio, 1955-60; with Armour & Co., 1961-71, Greyhound Corp., 1971-87; v.p. toiletries div. Armour Dial Co., Phoenix, 1973-74, exec. v.p., 1975-77; pres., CEO Armour Internat. Co., Phoenix, 1978-84; pres. The Dial Corp. (formerly Armour-Dial Co.), Phoenix, 1984-87, chief exec. officer, 1984-87; pres., chief exec. officer Purex Corp., 1985; chmn., chief exec. officer The Sparta Group Ltd., Scottsdale, Ariz., 1988—. Bd. dirs. Guest Supply Inc., New Brunswick, NJ, 1988—2001, WD-40 Co., San Diego, Nortrust Holding Corp., Phoenix, No. Trust Bank of Ariz., N.A., Inc., Matrixx Initiatives, Inc., Phoenix; mem. bd. advisors Universal Tech. Inst., Phoenix, Brother to Brother Internat., 1988—2001; dir. Exec. Svc. Corp. Ariz., 1996—2000. Trustee Scottsdale Meml. Health Found., 1995-98; pres. Mt. Vernon Fire Dept. Mems. Assn., 1960-61. Served with U.S. Army, 1953-55, Germany. Recipient Loftus Lifetime Achievement award, Iona Coll., 2004. Mem. Am. Mgmt. Assn., Nat. Meat Canner Assn. (pres. 1971-72), Cosmetic, Toiletries and Fragrance Assn. (bd. dirs. 1985—87), Nat. Food Processors Assn. (bd. dirs.). Republican. Roman Catholic. Office: The Sparta Group Ltd 6623 N Scottsdale Rd Scottsdale AZ 85250-4421

WALSH, ELIZABETH JAMESON, musician; b. Panhandle, Tex., Oct. 23, 1913; d. Edwin Reece and Lela (Blackshear) Jameson; m. Thomas Norris Walsh, Nov. 1, 1951 (dec. May 5, 1990); children: Thomas Edwin, Richard Malcolm, Lela Elizabeth. MusB, U. North Tex., 1941, MusM, 1942. Cert. tchr. music. Piano tchr. U. North Tex., Denton, 1940-42; music tchr. Perryton HS, Tex., 1942-43, Plainview HS, Tex., 1943-45; choir dir. Presbyn. and Disciples Ch., Plainview, 1943-45; music tchr. Dallas Pub. Sch., 1945-53; organist, choir dir. Midway Hills Ch., Dallas, 1954-60; piano tchr. Hockaday Pvt. Sch., Dallas, 1960-70; music tchr. Dallas Pub. Sch., 1970-82; organist, choir dir. Greenville Ave. Christian Ch., Dallas, 1975-82, Grace Meth. Ch., Dallas, 1982-91, St. Andrews Episcopal Ch., Farmers Branch, Tex., 1991—, Christ United Meth. Ch., 2001—. Composer (operetta) Day in Mexico, 1971, various titles for choir, 1996—; author: The Echo Tower, 1987, The House on the Hill, 1989, Uncle Willie (biography); appeared as Cleopatra as Caesar and Cleopatra, Dallas Little Theatre, 1933, Jane in Jane Eyre, Amarillo Little Theatre, 1935, Anna in Anna and the King of Siam, Northway Ch. Players, 1971, Uncle Willie (biolgraphy), 2004. Mem. Dallas Civic Chorus, 1960-65, Dallas Symphony Chorus, 1970-75, Farmer's Br. Women's Club, 1995—; v.p. Mus. Arts, 2003—. Recipient 2nd prize in Nat. Recording Contest, Nat. Piano Guild, 1973. Mem. Dallas Music Tchr. Assn., Dallas chpt. Am. Guild Organists, Musical Arts Club (sec. 2001-03, 1st v.p. 2003—), Daus. of Republic of Tex. (chaplain 1993-95, pres. James Butler Bonham chpt. 1997—, sec. 2003—, Mamie Wynne Cox award 1995, sec. 1995-97, 2003, chmn. yearbook), Pro Musica (pres. 1976-77, 85-86, 2001—, sec. 2003-2005, asst. sec. 2003—, treas. 1980-81, 96-97), Pi Beta Phi, Mu Phi Epsilon. Avocations: reading, travel. Home: 14339 Tanglewood Dr Farmers Branch TX 75234-3855

WALSH, FRANCIS RICHARD, law educator, lawyer, arbitrator; b. Newark, Jan. 1, 1924; s. Francis R. Sr. and Loretta Anne (Norton) W.; m. Ethel Anne Walsh, Mar. 12, 1944; 1 child, Jeffrey R. BSBA, Seton Hall U., 1943; JD, Georgetown U., 1948. Prof. Law Sch. Georgetown U., Washington, 1949-51; law clk. to presiding justice U.S. Ct. Appeals (9th cir.), San Francisco, 1948-49; chief broadcast bur. FCC, Washington, 1970-71; pvt. practice San Francisco, 1954-70; prof. law U. San Francisco, 1951-54, 71-74, dean, prof. law, 1957-70; prof. law Hastings Coll. of Law, U. Calif., San Francisco, 1974—. Lt. USNR, 1943-46, PTO. Roman Catholic. Avocations: golf, travel. Home: 28 Spring Rd Kentfield CA 94904 Office: Hastings Coll Law 200 Mcallister St San Francisco CA 94102 Office Phone: 415-565-4600.

WALSH, GEORGE WILLIAM, publishing company executive, editor, author; b. N.Y.C., Jan. 16, 1931; s. William Francis and Madeline (Maass) W.; m. Joan Mary Dunn, May 20, 1961; children— Grail, Simon. BS, Fordham U., 1952; MS, Columbia U. Sch. Journalism, 1953. Copy editor, reporter Cape Cod Standard-Times, Hyannis, Mass., 1955; communications specialist IBM, N.Y.C., 1955-58; editorial trainee Time, Inc., 1958-59; writer-reporter Sports Illus., N.Y.C., 1959-62; book editor Cosmopolitan, N.Y.C., 1962-65, mng. editor, 1965-74; editor-in-chief, v.p. Ballantine Books div. Random House, N.Y.C., 1974-79, Macmillan Pub. Co., N.Y.C., 1979-85; pub. cons., 1985—. Author: Gentleman Jimmy Walker, 1974, Public Enemies, 1980, Damage Them All You Can--Robert E. Lee's Army of Northern Virginia, 2002, Whip the Rebellion--Ulysses S. Grant's Rise to Command, 2004. Served with AUS, 1953-55. Mem. Assn. Am. Pubs. Clubs: Univ. (N.Y.C.); Pamet Harbor Yacht and Tennis (Truro, Mass.). Roman Catholic. Home: 35 Prospect Park W Brooklyn NY 11215-2370 Office Phone: 718-622-7431. E-mail: edchief@aol.com.

WALSH, GERALDINE FRANCES, nursing administrator; b. Phila., July 3, 1946; d. Raymond S. and Marie Ruth (Lipsett) Lore; m. Harry G. Walsh, Jan. 29, 1966; children: Michael, Gregory. AA, No. Va. Community Coll., 1979; BS, St. Joseph's Coll., Windham, Maine, 1987, postgrad. Cert. in nursing adminstrn.; cert. dir. nursing adminstrn. long term care; lic. nursing home adminstr. Charge nurse, asst. head nurse Parkview Hosp., Phila., 1968-73; staff nurse JFK Med. Ctr., Edison, 1973-76; clin. nursing supr., charge nurse med.-surg. Loudoun Hosp. Ctr., Leesburg, Va., 1976-88; asst. dir. nursing Loudoun Long Term Care Ctr., Leesburg, 1988-95; dir. nursing Inova Cameron Glen Care Ctr., Reston, Va., 1995-99, Integrated Health Svcs. No. Va., 1999—. Recipient Nursing Achievement award. Fellow Nat. Assn. Dirs. Nursing; mem. ANA, NAFE, Nat. League Nursing, Va. League Nursing, Va. Nurses Assn., Am. Coll. Healthcare Execs. (student assoc. mem.), Assn. Healthcare Adminstrs. of Nat. Capitol Area, Va. Orgn. Nurse Execs. Address: 208 Birdie Rd Locust Grove VA 22508-5116 E-mail: walshge@attglobal.net.

WALSH, GERRY O'MALLEY, lawyer; b. Houston, Dec. 22, 1936; d. Frederick Harold and Blanche (O'Malley) W. BS, U. Houston, 1959; JD, South Tex. Coll. Law, 1966. Bar: Tex. 1966, U.S. Dist. Ct. (so. dist.) Tex. 1967, U.S. Dist. Ct. (we. dist.) Tex. 1976; cert. elem. tchr., Tex. Elem. tchr., Houston, 1959-65; instr. bus. law U. Houston, 1966-67; pvt. practice Houston, 1966—. Lectr. legal, jud. and civic orgns. Adviser, den mother Sam Houston coun. Boy Scouts Am.; mem. Mus. Fine Arts. Recipient den mother award Sam Houston coun. Boy Scouts Am. Mem. ABA, Houston Zool. Assn., Houston Archeol. Soc., Bus. and Profl. Women's Assn. (Woman of Yr. 1973), Am. Judicature Soc., Tex. Criminal Lawyers Assn., Harris County Criminal Lawyers Assn., Tex. Trial Lawyers Assn., State Bar Tex., Houston Bar Assn., U. Houston Alumni Assn., So. Tex. Coll. Law Alumni Assn., Nat. Criminal Def. Lawyers Assn., Zeta Tau Alpha (best mem. and rec. sec. 1958), Sigma Chi (award 1958). Office Phone: 713-864-4898.

WALSH, JAMES, retail supermarket executive; CFO Meijer, Grand Rapids, Mich. Office: Meijer 29129 Walker St NW Grand Rapids MI 49544 Office Fax: (616) 453-6067.

WALSH, JAMES JOSEPH, lawyer; b. New Orleans, June 21, 1948; s. Francis Michael and Violet (Young) W.; m. Priscilla Robson Ferris, Oct. 12, 1972; children: Caitlin Marian, Alison Robson. BA, La. State U., 1970, JD, 1975. Bar: La. 1975, Mich. 1977, U.S. Ct. Appeals (6th cir.) 1981, U.S. Supreme Ct. 1991. Law clk. Mich. Ct. Appeals, Detroit, 1975-77; assoc. Bodman LLP, Detroit, 1977-84, ptnr., 1984—. Counsel Outdoor Advt. Assn. Mich. Editor: La. Law Rev., 1975. Named to Hall of Fame, La. State U. Law Sch., 1988. Mem. ABA, State Bar Mich., Washtenaw County Bar Assn., Ann Arbor Club, Detroit Athletic Club, Mich. C. of C., Jefferson City Buzzards. Avocations: fishing, gardening, carpentry. Home: 8025 Mast Rd Dexter MI 48130-9301 Office: Bodman Longley & Dahling 110 Miller Ave Ste 300 Ann Arbor MI 48104-1339 Office Phone: 734-930-0237. Business E-Mail: jwalsh@bodmanllp.com.

WALSH, JAMES PATON, composer; b. Spring Valley, NY, Sept. 4, 1957; s. James Jerome and Carol Jean Walsh; m. Janna Karen Saslaw, May 19, 1956. BA, Columbia Coll., 1981; MA, Columbia U., 1984, D of Musical Arts, 1992. Adj. prof. Columbia U., N.Y.C., 1992—93, U. North Tex., Denton, 1994—95, Loyola U., New Orleans, 1996—. Guitarist, pianist, composer The Other Planets, New Orleans, 2003—; bassist, composer Anacrusis, Suffern, NY, 1971—94; condr. Naked Orch., New Orleans, 1999—; bassist, music dir. Michael Ray and the Cosmic Krewe, 1997—; bassist, creative dir. The Improvisational Arts Coun., 2000—; bassist, songwriter The Bureaucrats, N.Y.C., 1984—2001; lead guitarist Wampum, 1984—94; bassist, composer Malibu Dolfins, 1979—82, The Blue Universe, New Orleans, 2001—; music dir., composer Sorceror Jones. Composer (electronic music): Digital Study #1 (Columbia U. Electronic Music Prize, 1989), Zen Tryptich (performed at Merce Cunningham Dance Studio, 1992); composer: (saxophone and tape) Zoomability (selected for performance at inaugural concert of the Brandeis Electro-acoustic Music Studio, broadcast on WGBH radio Boston, 1992); composer: (piano) Fantasia for Solo Piano (Performed on North-South Consonance Concert Series, 1980), The Relativity Cycle; composer: (big band) The Heart of Diego Rivera, Sunny's Late Night Hammer (performed by Dartmouth Coll. Jazz Band, 2000); composer: (chamber orchestra) Caprice for Ten Instruments (performed at Composer's Conf., 1992); producer, conductor, arranger, composer: compact disk Brief Repairs on the Gradually Unravelling Spool in the Sense Continuum, composer, musician, producer: compact disk Gardens, Improvisational Arts Council, composer, producer: single Big Time, musician, songwriter: compact disk Blue Moon, Sherman Ewing, co-producer: compact disk Funk If I Know, Michael Ray and the Cosmic Krewe; musician: Sharin The Groove - Celebrating the Music of Phish; composer: Memories of Illegal Music; composer: (symphony) Leviathan, Ashes; composer: (violin) Songs of Courtship; composer: (clarinet and viola) Dancing Like Children; composer: Crossing The Bar, (films) Stalker (Gold Medal Short Film, Houston Film Festival, 1997); contbr. articles to profl. jours.; performer: The New Orleans Jazz and Heritage Festival, The Ann Arbor Jazz Festival, The Aspen Jazz Festival, The Umbria Jazz Festival, The Mellon Jazz Festival, Street Scene. Exec. dir. Guild Of Composers, N.Y.C., 1992—2001; artistic dir. The Improvisational Arts Coun., New Orleans, 2000—03; co-producer The Zeitgeist Creative Music Festival, 2001—02; curator Zeitgeist Thursday Night Concert Series, New Orleans, 2000—01. Recipient Big Easy awards, Best Funk Band, Michael Ray and the Cosmic Krewe, Gambit Weekly, 1999, Best of the Beat, Offbeat Mag., 2001; fellow, Wellesley Coll., 1992; William J. Mitchell fellow, Columbia U., 1982. Democrat. Home: 1532 Lowerline Street New Orleans LA 70118 Office: Loyola University New Orleans 6363 St Charles Avenue New Orleans LA 70118 Personal E-mail: mx3@bellsouth.net.

WALSH, JAMES THOMAS, congressman; b. Syracuse, N.Y., June 19, 1947; m. DeDe Ryan; 3 children. BA, St. Bonaventure U., 1970. Agrl. extension agt. Peace Corps, 1970-72; mktg. exec. telecommunications co., 1974-88; exec.-in-residence telecommunications inst. Coll. Tech. SUNY, Utica, Rome, N.Y., 1986-87; common councilor City of Syracuse, 1977-85, pres. common coun., 1986-88; mem. U.S. Congress from 25th N.Y. dist., Washington, 1989—; mem. appropriations com., military constrn. subcom., chmn. VA, HUD and Ind. Agys. subcom. Republican. Office: US House of Reps 2369 Rayburn Hob Washington DC 20515-3225 also: PO Box 7306 Syracuse NY 13261-7306 also: 1180 Canandaigua Rd Palmyra NY 14522-3831

WALSH, JANICE MAUREEN, counselor, educator; b. Monroe, Ga., June 17, 1948; d. Herschel Thomas and Joan (Williford) Scott; m. Dennis Warner Anderson, June 24, 1967 (div. Sept. 1988); children: Jeffrey, Timothy; m. Francis Raymond Walsh, July 6, 1993 (dec. Sept. 1998). AA, Windward C.C.,

1988; BA, U. Hawaii, 1990; MBA, Chaminade U., Honolulu, 1991, advanced profl. cert., 1992. Cert. clin. hypnotherapist Hawaii, 1998. Instr. Windward C.C., Kaneohe, Hawaii, 1991-92; prof. Chaminade U., Honolulu, 1993; instr., counselor Kapiolani C.C., Honolulu, 1993-99, asst. prof., 1999—. Cons. Changing Me, Kailua, Hawaii, 1993-99. Mem. disaster action team Hawaii Red Cross. Mem. ACA, Hawaii Counseling Assn. (treas., pres., past pres. 1990-97), Nat. Career Devel. Assn., Guild of Hypnotists, Hawaii Career Devel. Assn. (treas. 1995-97), Soroptomist Internat. of Windward Oahu. Avocations: bridge, movies, crossword puzzles. Office: Kapiolani C C 4303 Diamond Head Rd Honolulu HI 96816-4421

WALSH, JOHN, museum director; b. Mason City, Wash., Dec. 9, 1937; s. John J. and Eleanor (Wilson) W.; m. Virginia Alys Galston, Feb. 17, 1962; children: Peter Wilson, Anne Galston, Frederick Matthiessen. BA, Yale U., 1961; postgrad., U. Leyden, Netherlands, 1965-66; MA, Columbia U., 1965, PhD, 1971; LHD (hon.), Wheaton Coll., 2000. Lectr., rsch. asst. Frick Collection, N.Y.C., 1966-68; assoc. higher edn. Met. Mus. Art, N.Y.C., 1968-71, assoc. curator European paintings, 1970-72, curator dept. European paintings, 1972-74, vice-chmn., 1974-75; adj. asso. prof. art history Columbia U., N.Y.C., 1969-72, adj. prof., 1972-75; prof. art history Barnard Coll., Columbia U., N.Y.C., 1975-77; Mrs. Russell W. Baker curator paintings Mus. Fine Arts, Boston, 1977-83; dir. J. Paul Getty Mus., Malibu, Calif., 1983-2000, dir. emeritus, 2000—. Vis. prof. fine arts Harvard U., 1979; mem. governing bd. Yale U. Art Gallery, 1975—, Smithsonian Coun., 1990-2000; mem. Inst. for Advanced Study, Princeton, 2000; trustee Burlington Mag. Found., 1999-; adj. prof. history of art Yale U., 2003. Author: Things In Place: Landscapes and Still Lifes by Sheridan Lord, 1995, Jan Steen, The Drawing Lesson, 1996, The J. Paul Getty Museum and Its Collections: A Museum for the New Century, 1997, Bill Viola: The Passions, 2002; contbr. articles to profl. jours. Mem. Dem. County Com., N.Y.C., 1968-71; mem. vis. com. Fogg Mus., Harvard U., 1982-87; bd. fellows Claremont U. Ctr. and Grad. Sch., 1988-2000. With USNR, 1957-63. Fulbright grad. fellow The Netherlands, 1965-66 Mem. Am. Acad. Arts and Scis., Coll. Art Assn., Am. Assn. Mus., Archaeol. Inst. Am., Am. Antiquarian Soc., Assn. Art Mus. Dirs. (trustee 1986-90, pres. 1989-90), Century Assn. N.Y.C. Office: J Paul Getty Mus 1200 Getty Center Dr Ste 1000 Los Angeles CA 90049-1687

WALSH, JOHN, television show host; b. Dec. 26, 1945; m. Reve Walsh; three children. Founder Adam Walsh Child Resource Ctr., Straight Shooter; bd. dirs Nat. Ctr. for Missing and Exploited Children. Exec. prod., actor TV movie If Looks Could Kill; prodr. Street Smart Kids (Emmy nomination); creator The New America's Most Wanted: America Fights Back. Named one of the fifty most beautiful people, People Mag., 1996, named one of the hundred Ams. who changed history, CBS Portraits; recipient three times U.S. Marshals Man of the Year, Spl. Recognition award U.S. Atty. Gen.; honored in the Rose Garden four times by three U.S. Pres. Office: Americas Most Wanted PO Box Crime TV Washington DC 20016-9126

WALSH, JOHN ALFRED, retired social worker; b. N.Y.C., N.Y., June 4, 1927; s. Joseph Thomas and May Catherine (Moran) Walsh; m. Gwendolyn Ann Stockton, Apr. 13, 1952; children: Ralph, Carl, Nils. BA cum laude, St. Mary's U., Balt., 1949; M in Social Svc., Fordham U., 1954. Lic. clin. social worker, nursing home adminstr., marriage/family therapist. Social worker Cath. Charities, Bklyn., 1949—56; supr. after care clinics Ancora (N.J.) Psychiat. Hosp., 1956—57; dir. social svc. Trenton (N.J.) Psychiat. Hosp., 1958—68; asst. supt. Hunterdon Devel. Ctr., Clinton, NJ, 1968—91; ret. Author: (pamphlet) Fabulous Rosts, 1982. V.p. Warren County Hist. Soc., Belvidere, NJ, 1990—, Assn. Hunterdon Devel. Ctr., Clinton, 1991—; mem. bd. edn. Belvidere Sch. Dist., 1991—2001. Capt. U.S. Army, 1953—66. Avocation: collecting stamps and post cards. Home: 703 Oxford St Belvidere NJ 07823

WALSH, JOHN CHARLES, metallurgical company executive; b. Indpls., Sept. 8, 1924; s. John Charles; children: Michael S., Carolyn Ann, Anne D. BS, Notre Dame U., 1949. Auditor Herdrich Boggs & Co., Indpls., 1949—78; with P.R. Mallory & Co., Inc., 1978—; pres. Walgang Co. Inc., Indpls., 1970—. V.p., treas. P.R. Mallory & Co., 1971. Served with USMCR, 1943-45. Mem. Fin. Execs. Inst., Indpls. C. of C., Ind. Hist. Soc., Econ. Club, Notre Dame Club, Rotary. Home: 4974 Shadow Rock Cir Carmel IN 46033-9500 Office: Ste B2 598 W Carmel Dr Carmel IN 46032-2667

WALSH, JOHN E., JR., business educator, consultant; b. St. Louis, Apr. 28, 1927; s. John E. and Ann M. (Narkewicz) W. BS, U.S. Naval Acad., 1950; MBA, Washington U., St. Louis, 1957; DBA, Harvard U., 1960. Asst. prof. Washington U., St. Louis, 1959-60, assoc. prof., 1960-68, prof., 1968-2001, prof. emeritus, 2001—; vis. assoc. prof. Stanford U., 1964-65; vis. prof. INSEAD, Fontainebleau, France, 1970. Mem. exec. com. Econ. Strategy Inst. Author: Preparing Feasibility Studies in Asia, 1971, Guidelines for Management Consultants in Asia, 1973, Planning New Ventures in International Business, 1976, (with others) Strategies in Business, 1978, Management Tactics, 1980, International Business Case Studies: For the Multicultural Market Place, 1994, Joint Authoring: Managing Cultural Differences, 1994. Mem. State of Mo. leadership initiative to former Soviet Union, Poland, Hungary, 1990; mem. coun. Kearny Found., Internat. Ho., Washington U. 1st lt. USAF, 1950-54. Zurn Found. fellow, 1958; Presdl. fellow Am. Grad. Sch. Internat. Mgmt. Mem. Harvard Club N.Y.C. E-mail: walshjejr@aol.com.

WALSH, JOHN F. government agency administrator; m. Ann Groark; 2 children. B in bus. admin., Auinnipiac U. Gov. to vice chmn. US Postal Svc. Bd of Gov., 1999—2006; retired pres. Ninth Sq. Assn., Inc., New Haven, 1992—98; chmn. New Haven Parking Authority, 1992—98; purchasing agent City New Haven, 1978—90; dir. support svcs. New Haven Police Dept. With U.S. Army. Office: Bd of Gov, US Postal Svc 475 L'Enfant Plaza SW Washington DC 20260-0001

WALSH, JOSEPH MICHAEL, magazine distribution executive; b. N.Y.C., Jan. 19, 1943; s. John Redmond and Bridget Judith (Donovan) W.; m. Theresa Rose Vericker, Oct. 3, 1964; children— Joseph, Matthew, Teresa Ann, John, James BBA in Acctg., Iona Coll., 1964. With Peat, Marwick, Mitchell & Co., C.P.A.s, N.Y.C., 1964-70, audit supr., until 1970; asst. to chmn. bd. and pres. Cadence Industries Corp., West Caldwell, N.J., 1970-71, v.p., 1971-74, exec. v.p., 1974-87; pres. subs. Curtis Circulation Co., 1972-74, chmn., chief exec. officer, 1982—; pres. Data Services for Health, 1976-77, U.S. Pencil and Stationery Co., 1977-79, Perfect Subscription Co. (merger Perfect Sch. Plans, Perfect Telephone Plan, Moore Cottrell and Keystone Readers Service), 1980-83. Mem. AICPA, N.Y. State Soc. CPAs, K.C. Office: Curtis Circulation Co 730 River Rd New Milford NJ 07646-3048

WALSH, JOSEPH RICHARD, lawyer, bank executive; b. Atlanta, May 10, 1951; s. Joseph Radamaker and Meta Lucille (Cole) Walsh; m. Elisabeth Clare Kane, July 27, 1980; children: Lindsay Carolyn, Dana Elisabeth, Cameron Marisa. B in Indsl. Engring., Ga. Inst. Tech., 1973; JD, U. Ga., 1976; ML in Taxation, Georgetown U., 1984. Bar: Ga. 1976, U.S. Dist. Ct. (no. dist.) Ga. 1976, U.S. Ct. Appeals (5th cir.) 1976, Va. 1978, U.S. Ct. Appeals (4th cir.) 1978, DC 1979, U.S. Ct. Appeals (11th cir.) 1982, U.S. Claims Ct. 1983, U.S. Tax Ct. 1983, Calif. 1984, U.S. Dist. Ct. (no. dist.) Calif. 1984, U.S. Ct. Appeals (9th cir.) 1984. Indsl. engr. So. Rlwy. Sys., Atlanta, 1973—74; atty. ICC, Washington, 1977—78, atty., asst. rail merger coord., 1979—84; assoc. Fulbright & Jaworski, Washington, 1978—79; counsel Bank Am. Nat. Assn., San Francisco, 1984—85, sr. counsel, 1985—98, asst. gen. counsel, 1998—. Counselor Athens (Ga.) Legal Aid and Defender Soc., 1976; instr. comml. law San Francisco Law Sch., 1987—92. Co-author: (book) Federal Regulatory Process: Practice and Procedure, 1981. Campaign vol. Jimmy Carter Presdl. Campaign, NH, 1976. Named Outstanding Young Men Am., U.S. Jaycees, 1982; Nat. Merit scholar, Ga. Inst. Tech., 1969, NSF grantee, 1972. Mem.: ABA, Am. Inst. Indsl. Engrs., San Francisco Leasing Lawyers Forum, San Francisco Bar Assn., Calif. Bar Assn., Va. Bar Assn., Fed. Bar Assn., Ga. Bar Assn., DC Bar Assn., Calif. Nature Conservancy, Sierra Club, Commonwealth Club Calif., Lawyers Club (San Francisco), Alpha Pi Mu, Tau Beta Pi, Phi Kappa Phi. Office: Bank of Am N A CA5-705-04-01 555 California St 4th Fl San Francisco CA 94137-0001 E-mail: joseph.r.walsh@bankofamerica.com.

WALSH, JUANITA, theater educator, actress; b. Milw., May 03; d. Melvin John and Evelyn Dorothy (Heinrich) W.; m. Mark Jeffrey Rowen, Sept. 14, 1980. BFA, Stephens Coll., 1972; cert. speech, U. Wis., Milw., 1981. Mem. faculty NYU, 1985-89, Marymount Manhattan Coll., 1989-92, Temple U., Phila., 1991, Rutgers U., New Brunswick, N.J., 1992-93, HB Studio, N.Y.C., 1985-2000; prof. NYU, 1997-2000. Founder, artistic dir. Actors Alliance Inc,. N.Y.C., 1986-90. Off-Broadway performances include Grandma Sylvia's Funeral, 1997-98, Tribute to Uta Hagen, 1995; regional performance in Glass Menagerie, 2001, Baker's Wife, 2002; co-star TV show Ed, 2002, TV miniseries War of China's Fate, 1999; starred in films The Two Henrys, Fresh Cut Grass, Crutch, 2003, The Color of Truth, 2004. Mem. Actors Equity Assn., SAG, AFTRA. Avocation: gardening. E-mail: jwract@yahoo.com.

WALSH, KENNETH ANDREW, biochemist; b. Sherbrooke, Que., Can., Aug. 7, 1931; s. George Stanley and Dorothy Maud (Sangster) W.; m. Deirdre Anne Clarke, Aug. 22, 1953; children: Andrew, Michael, Erin. BSc in Agr., McGill U., 1951; MS, Purdue U., 1953; PhD, U. Toronto, 1959. Postdoctoral fellow U. Wash., Seattle, 1959-62, from asst. prof. to assoc. prof. Biochemistry, 1962-69, prof. Biochemistry, 1969—, chair, 1990-2000. Author (book) Methods in Protein Sequence Analysis, 1986. Mem. The Protein Soc. (sec.-treas. 1987-90), Am. So. Biochemistry/Molecular Biology. Office: U Wash PO Box 357350 Seattle WA 98195-7350

WALSH, KERRI LEE, Olympic athlete; b. Aug. 15, 1978; d. Tim and Margie. BA in Am. Studies, Stanford U., 1999. Player BVA Tour, 2001, FIVG Internat. Tour, 2001—, AVP Tour, 2003—; beach volleyball player Team USA, Sydney Olympic Games, 2000, Team USA, Athens Olympic Games, 2004. Named First Team All-Am., 1995—99, Pro Beach Volleyball Rookie of the Yr., 2001, AVP Best Offensive Player, 2003, AVP Most Valuable Player, 2003, AVP Team of the Yr. (With Misty May), 2003. Achievements include only second person in history to be named First Team All-Am. four years in a row, Stanford U., 1995-1999; FIVB World Champions with partner Misty May, 2002, 2003; Gold medal (with Misty May), Beach Volleyball, Athens Olympic games, 2004. Office: c/o USOC One Olympic Plz Colorado Springs CO 80909*

WALSH, KEVIN, newspaper editor; Bur. chief AP, Miami, Fla., 1996—. Address: 9100 NW 36th St Ste 104 Miami FL 33178-2432

WALSH, LAWRENCE EDWARD, lawyer; b. Port Maitland, N.S., Can., Jan. 8, 1912; came to U.S., 1914, naturalized, 1922; s. Cornelius Edward and Lila May (Sanders) W.; m. Mary Alma Porter; children: Barbara Marie, Janet Maxine (Mrs. Alan Larson), Sara Porter, Dale Edward, Elizabeth Porter (Mrs. Joseph Wells). AB, Columbia, 1932, LL.B., 1935; LL.D., Union U., 1959, St. John's U., 1975, Suffolk U., 1975, Waynesburg Coll., 1976, Vt. Law Sch., 1976. Bar: N.Y. 1936, D.C. 1981, Okla. 1981, U.S. Supreme Ct. 1951. Spl. asst. atty. gen. Drukman Investigation, 1936-38; dep. asst. dist. atty. N.Y. County, 1938-41; assoc. Davis Polk Wardwell Sunderland & Kiendl, 1941-43; asst. counsel to gov. N.Y., 1943-49; counsel to gov., 1950-51; counsel Pub. Service Commn., 1951-53; gen. counsel, exec. dir. Waterfront Commn. of N.Y. Harbor, 1953-54; U.S. judge So. Dist. N.Y., 1954-57; U.S. dep. atty. gen., 1957-60; partner firm Davis, Polk & Wardwell, 1961-81; counsel firm Crowe & Dunlevy, Oklahoma City, 1981—. Ind. counsel Iran/Contra investigation, 1986-93; chmn. N.Y. State Moreland Commn. Alcoholic Beverage Control Law, 1963-64; pres. Columbia Alumni Fedn., 1968-69; dep. head with rank of amb. U.S. del. meetings on Vietnam, Paris, 1969; counsel to N.Y. State Ct. on Judiciary, 1971-72; 2d cir. mem. U.S. Cir. Judge Nominating Commn., 1978-80. Author: (Book) Firewall The Iran-Contra Conspiracy and Cover-Up, 1997, The Gift of Insecurity, 2003. Trustee emeritus Columbia U., Mut. Life Ins. Co., N.Y. Recipient medal for excellence Columbia U., 1959, Law Sch., Columbia U., 1980, John Jay award Columbia Coll., 1989. Fellow Am. Bar Found., Am. Coll. Trial Lawyers; mem. Am. Law Inst., ABA (pres. 1975-76), N.Y. State Bar Assn. (pres. 1966-67), Oklahoma County Bar Assn., Okla. State Bar Assn., Internat. Bar Assn., Assn. of Bar of City of New York, N.Y. County Lawyers Assn., Fed. Bar Coun., Law Soc. Eng. and Wales (hon.), Can. Bar Assn. (hon.), Mexican Bar Assn. (hon.), The Century Assn., Oklahoma City Golf and Country Club, Beta Theta Pi. Presbyterian. Home: 1902 Bedford Dr Oklahoma City OK 73116-5306 Office: 1800 Mid Am Towers Oklahoma City OK 73102

WALSH, M. EMMET, actor; b. Ogdensburg, N.Y., Mar. 22, 1935; BBA, Clarkson Coll., 1958; student, Am. Acad. Dramatic Arts, 1959-61. Appeared in films, including Raising Arizona, Ordinary People, The Milagro Beanfield War, Romeo and Juliet, Winterdance, My Best Friend's Wedding, Twilight, A Time To Kill, Albino Alligator, Free Willy II, Snow Dogs, Music of Chance, White Sands, Narrow Margin, The Mighty Quinn, Clean and Sober, Harry and The Hendersons, Fletch, Missing in Action, Back to School, Blood Simple, Blade Runner, Silkwood, Sundown, Brubaker, Raise the Titanic, Fast Walking, Reds, The Jerk, Straight Time, At Long Last Long, Serpico, What's Up Doc?, They Might Be Giants, Midnight Cowboy, End of the Road, Cannery Row, Straight Time, Slap Shot, Cold Turkey, The Traveling Exceuctioner, Alice's Restaurant, Airport '77, Wild Wild West; TV shows include Frasier, Sandy Duncan Show, Bonanza, Mind of the Married Man, The Rockford Files, All in the Family, Bob Newhart Show, The Waltons, Little House on the Prairie, Early Edition, Tales from the Crypt, Home Improvement, The Outer Limits, X Files, The Abduction of Kari Swenson, Resting Place, The Woman Who Willed a Miracle, The Guardian, Tracy Lilman's Traiter Tales, Charlies Laurencio, HBO series The Mind of the Married Man; Broadway shows include That Championship Season, Does the Tiger Wear a Necktie?, The Beauty Part; Off-Broadway shows include Death of a Well-Loved Boy, 1967, Shepherds of the Shelf, 1961, Are You Now Or Have You Ever Been?; also appeared in regional theatre and summer stock; voices include Scooby Doo.

WALSH, MARIAN C. state legislator; BA, Newton Coll. Sacred Heart, 1976; MTh, Harvard U., 1982; JD, Suffolk U., 1986. Chief adminstrv. officer, dir. fin., devel. and planning Suffolk County Dist. Atty. Office, Boston, 1979-85; asst. dir., govt. rels. legis. agt. Mass. Med. Soc., Waltham, 1985-86; practice law, Milton, 1987—; mem. Mass. Ho. of Reps., Boston, 1989-92, mem. judiciary, ethics, banks and banking coms.; mem. Mass. Senate, Boston, 1993—. Adj. prof. law Newbury Coll., 1987-88; adj. prof. ethics Fisher Coll., 1990—. Mem., bd. dirs. YMCA; active West Roxbury Hist. Soc., Neighborhood Assn., Friend of Shattuck Shelter. Home: 651 W Roxbury Pkwy Chestnut Hill MA 02467-3225 Office: Mass Ho of Reps State House Rm 405 Boston MA 02133

WALSH, MARIE LECLERC, nurse; b. Providence, Sept. 11, 1928; d. Walter Normand and Anna Mary (Ryan) Leclerc; m. John Breffni Walsh, June 18, 1955; children: George Breffni, John Leclerc, Darina Louise. Grad., Waterbury Hosp. Sch. Nursing, Conn., 1951; BS, Columbia U., 1954, MA, 1955. Team leader Hartford (Conn.) Hosp., 1951-53; pvt. duty nurse St. Luke's Hosp., N.Y.C., 1953-57; sch. nurse tchr. Agnes Russel Ctr., Tchrs. Coll. Columbia U., N.Y.C., 1955-56; clin. nursing instr. St. Luke's Hosp., N.Y.C., 1957-58; chmn. disaster nursing ARC Fairfax County, Va., 1975; course coord. occupational health nursing U. Va. Sch. Continuing Edn., Falls Church, 1975-77; mem. disaster steering com. No. Va. C.C., Annandale, 1976; adj. faculty U. Va. Sch. Continuing Edn., Falls Church, 1981; disaster svcs. nurse ARC, Wichita, Kans., 1985-90, disaster svcs. nurse Seattle-King County chpt. Seattle, 1990-96; ret. Rsch. and statis. analyst U. Va. Sch. Continuing Edn. Nursing, Falls Church, 1975; rsch. libr. Olive Garvey Ctr. for Improvement Human Functioning, Inc., Wichita, 1985. Sec. Dem. party, Cresskill, N.J., 1964-66; county committeewoman, Bergen County, N.J., 1965-66; pres., v.p., Internat. Staff Wives, NATO, Brussels, Belgium, 1978-80; election officer, supr. Election Bd., Wichita, 1987, 88; v.p. McLean Newcomers, 1997-99, pres., 1999-2000. Mem. AAAS, AAUW, N.Y. Acad. Sci., Pi Lambda Theta, Sigma Theta Tau. Avocations: travel, gardening. Home: 8800 Prestwould Pl Mc Lean VA 22102-2231

WALSH, MATHEW M. M. construction executive; Grad., St. Ignatius Coll. Prep. Sch., U. Notre Dame. CEO, pres. Walsh Group, Inc., Chgo. Mem.: Union League Club. Office: Walsh Group Inc 929 W Adams St Chicago IL 60607-3021

WALSH, MICHAEL J. lawyer; b. Portland, Oreg., Sept. 4, 1932; s. Frank M.J. and Elisemary (Derbes) W.; m. June Griffin, Nov. 28, 1959; children: Molly, Erin, Kathryn (dec.), Anne. BA, U. Portland, 1954; JD, Georgetown U., 1959. Bar: D.C. 1959, Oreg. 1959, U.S. Ct. Appeals (fed. and 9th cirs.) 1959, U.S. Tax Ct. 1959, U.S. Supreme Ct. 1968. Law ck. to presiding justice Oreg. Supreme Ct., Salem, 1959-60; mng. ptnr. Rankin, Walsh, Ragen and Roberts, Portland, 1960-75; pvt. practice Portland, 1976—81; ptnr. Walsh and Conolly, Portland, 1982-83; of counsel McEwen, Hanna, Gisvold and Rankin, Portland, 1983-85, Bullivant, Houser, Bailey, Pendergrass, & Hoffman, Washington, 1985—. Chmn. Employees Compensation Appeals Bd. US Dept. Labor, Washington, 1985—2003, sr. counsel Adminstrv. Appeals Bd., 2003—; legal counsel Reagan-Bush '84, Nat. Hdqs., Washington, 1983—84. Chmn. legal dev. March of Dimes, 1967; chmn. admissions Georgetown U., Oreg., 1972-83; trustee Christie Sch., 1974-78; trustee Cath. Charities Oreg., 1966-72, pres. 1971; trustee Parry Ctr. for Children, 1967-73, v.p. 1970-71; trustee Portland Tennis Ctr. Assn., 1972-83, pres. 1976-82; bd. dirs. Portland Traffic Safety Commn., 1981-83. Served with JAGC, USAF, capt. res. Mem. Am. Judicature Soc., Am. Trial Lawyers Assn., Nat. Assn. Coll. and Uiv. Attys., Am. Arbitration Assn., D.C. Bar Assn., Oreg. Bar Assn. (mem. various coms.), Multnomah County Bar Assn., Portland C. of C. (bd. dirs. 1975-78, chmn. legis. coun. 1975), John Carroll Soc., Thomas More Soc. Clubs: Georgetown Univ. (Oreg.) (pres. 1966). Home: 3273 Sutton Pl NW # B Washington DC 20016-3537 Office Phone: 202-693-5039.

WALSH, NAN, artist, painter, sculptor, consultant; b. N.Y.C., Nov. 4, 1932; d. Joseph Edward and Mary Ellen (White) Heinl; m. Albert Anthony Walsh, July 10, 1954 (dec. Oct. 9, 2002); children: Maryellen, Nanette, Mark, Gregg (dec.). BS in Elem. Edn., Fordham U., 1954; postgrad., Nat. Acad. Sch. Fine Arts, Art Life Studio Inc., White Plains and Portchester, N.Y., 1984-94, V.K. Jonynas, L.I., N.Y., 1968-88, Art Ctr. No. N.J., 1996—2002. Fashion model Martha Clyde, N.Y.C., 1951-54; tchr. Yonkers (N.Y.) Pub. Schs., 1953-55; gallery dir. Mamaroneck Artists Guild, Larchmont, N.Y., 1988-95; fine artist, art juror, cons., 1995—. Membership juror Mamaroneck Artists Guild, Larchmont, 1982-84, membership juror chair, 1996-98, mem. adv. bd., 1996-98; mem. Ctr. for Contemporary Printmaking, 1998—. One-woman shows and juried exhbns. Westchester and N.Y.C., 1976—; works represented in corp. and pvt. collecitons. Hostess chairperson Citizens for John Lindsay, Gracie Mansion, N.Y., 1970; mem. Studio Twelve, pres., show chair, 1972-80; mem. Katonah Mus. Art. Recipient numerous 1st place awards for art. Mem. Nat. League Am. Penwomen, Nat. Mus. Women in the Arts, N.Y. Soc. Women Artists, Guild Creative Art, N.Y. Artists Equity, Mamaroneck Artists Guild (v.p. 1982, 83, membership chair 1992-95 Fordham U. Art Club (show chair 1965-80). Avocations: gardening, bridge, tennis, swimming, travel.

WALSH, NICOLAS EUGENE, rehabilitation medicine physician, educator; b. Mpls., July 1, 1947; s. Leonard Cyril and June Alice Walsh; m. Wendy Sarah Allnutt, June 1, 1973; children: Meghan, Rorey, Katlin, Alaine. BS, USAF Acad., 1969; MS, Marquette U., 1974; MD, U. Colo., 1979. Asst. prof. naval sci. Marquette U., Milw., 1972—74; from asst. prof. to assoc. prof. rehab. medicine U. Tex. Health Sci. Ctr., San Antonio, 1982—89, prof., chmn. rehab. medicine, 1989—, exec. assoc. dean Sch. Medicine, 1999—2000, disting. prof., 2001—. Dir. Am. Bd. Phys. Medicine and Rehab., Rochester, Minn., 1994—, sec., 1996—98, chmn., 1998—; pres., CEO Univ. Physician Group, 1998—2001. Author book chpts.; editor: Rehabilitation of Chronic Pain, 1991; editor-in-chief Archives of Phys. Medicine and Rehab., Chgo., 1994—2000. Named Health Care Profl. of Yr., Gov.'s Com. for Disabled Persons, 1989; recipient Excellence in Rsch. award, Am. Jour. Phys. Medicine and Rehab., 1991. Fellow: Am. Acad. Phys. Medicine and Rehab. (Richard and Hinda Rosenthal Found. award 1991, Zieter lectr. 2003), Am. Bd. Pain Medicine (v.p. 1993—94, sec. 1994—96); mem.: Phys. Medicine and Rehab. Edn. and Rsch. Found. (pres. 1993—2000, Excellence in Rsch. award 1991), Assn. Acad. Physiatrists (v.p. 1993—95, pres. 1996—98). Office: U Tex Health Sci Ctr Mail Code 7872 7703 Floyd Curl Dr San Antonio TX 78229-3900 Office Phone: 210-567-5350. Business E-Mail: walshn@uthscsa.edu.

WALSH, PATRICIA MAACK, special education educator; b. Yokohama, Japan, Sept. 10, 1950; d. Johan Gustof and Dorothy Maack; m. Frederic Peterson Walsh, Sept. 10, 1971; children: Audra Louise Walsh Lexin, Frederic Maack. AA in Art, Weber State U., 1972, BS in Child Devel., 1973; BS in Elem. Edn., Peru State Coll., 1988; MS in Psychology, U. La Verne, 1991; MS in Spl. Edn., Calif. State U., Northridge, 1996. Clear credential in spl. edn., Calif. Tchr. spl. edn. Papillion (Nebr.)-LaVista Sch. Dist., 1988-89, Eastside Union Sch. Dist., Lancaster, Calif., 1989-96, Antelope Valley Union H.S. Dist., Lancaster. Advisor H.S. Stds. Com., Lancaster, 1997—. Exit pole worker Rep. Women's Club, Palmdale, Calif., 1996. Mem. Coun. for Exceptional Children, Calif. Assn. Resource Specialists (cert.), Assistance League, Delta Kappa Gamma. Methodist. Avocations: art, travel, ministry with children. Office: Lancaster H S 44701 32nd St W Lancaster CA 93536-7023

WALSH, PATRICK CRAIG, urologist; b. Akron, Ohio, Feb. 13, 1938; s. Raymond Michael and Catherine N. (Rodden) W.; m. Margaret Campbell, May 23, 1964; children— Christopher, Jonathan, Alexander. AB, Case Western Res. U., 1960, MD, 1964. Intern in surgery Peter Bent Brigham Hosp., Boston, 1964-65, asst. resident in surgery, 1965-66; asst. resident in pediatric surgery Children's Hosp. Med. Center, Boston, 1966-67; resident in urology U. Calif.-Los Angeles Med. Center, 1967-71; dir. Brady Urol. Inst., urologist-in-chief Johns Hopkins Hosp., Balt., 1974—; prof., dir. dept. urology Johns Hopkins U. Sch. Medicine, 1974—. Contbr. articles to med. jours. Served to comdr. M.C. USN, 1971-73. Recipient Charles F. Kettering medal GM Cancer Rsch. Found., 1996. Mem. Soc. Univ. Surgeons, Am. Assn. Genitourinary Surgeons, Clin. Soc. Genitourinary Surgeons, Am. Urol. Assn., Endocrine Soc., Am. Surg. Assn. Inst. Medicine of NAS, Alpha Omega Alpha. Roman Catholic. Office: Johns Hopkins Med Inst 600 N Wolfe St Baltimore MD 21287-0005

WALSH, PAUL S. food products executive; Chmn., pres., CEO Pillsbury Co., Mpls. Office: Pillsbury Co 200 S 6th St Ste 200 Minneapolis MN 55402-6005

WALSH, PETER JOSEPH, physics educator; b. N.Y.C., Aug. 21, 1929; s. Peter and Mary Ellen (Kelly) W.; m. Rosemarie Imundo, May 13, 1952; children: Kathleen, Mary Ellen, Susan, Carole, Karen. BS, Fordham U., 1951; MS, N.Y.U., 1953, PhD, 1960. Research physicist Westinghouse Elec. Co., Bloomfield, N.J., 1951-60; supervisory physicist Am. Standard, Piscattaway, N.J., 1960-62; prof. Fairleigh Dickinson U., 1962-93; prof. emeritus, 1993—. Vis. rsch. scientist MIT, 1977; vis. prof. electronics and elec. engring. U. Sheffield, 1978-79; NASA fellow U. Santa Clara, 1980; Am. Soc. Engring. Edn. Navy fellow Naval Rsch. Labs., 1981, 82, 86, NASA Langley, 1987, Air Force fellow Hanscom AFB, 1988, Kirtland AFB, 1990; vis. prof. U. Genoa, 1984; vis. scholar Stanford U., 1984-85, cons. physics to 20 labs., 1963—; chmn. bd. trustees EMS Ednl. Corp., 1982—. Author: Dark Side of Knowledge, articles in field; patentee in field. Mem. Am. Phys. Soc., AAAS, N.J. Acad. Sci., Sigma Xi (sec. 1969) Home: 40 Saint Josephs Dr Stirling NJ 07980-1224 E-mail: peterj@gowebway.com.

WALSH, PETER JOSEPH, marketing professional; b. Newport, RI, Jan. 22, 1948; s. Alexander Ronald and Mary (O'Connell) W.; m. Virginia Diana Santore, May 11, 1978 (div. May 1992); children: Bridget, Peter, Lara, Elizabeth, Vanessa. BA, Santa Clara U., 1970; MA, Johns Hopkins U., 1978. V.p. Noblemet Internat., N.Y.C., 1978-80; mktg. dir. Multi-Arc Scientific Coatings, St. Paul, Minn., 1980-88; sr. v.p. Projects Devel., Inc., N.Y.C., 1988-91; pres. Kiser Rsch., Inc., Washington, 1990-93; v.p. Sonalysts, Inc., Waterford, Conn., 1993—. Bd. dirs. Conn. Tech. Coun., 2002—. Bd. dirs.

Portsmouth Abbey Sch. Alumni, Portsmouth, RI, 1996—2000, Mystic Coast and Country, 2002—. Roman Catholic. Avocations: tennis, golf, running. Home: 9 Mt Vernon St Newport RI 02840 Office: Sonalysts Inc 215 Parkway N Waterford CT 06385-1209

WALSH, PETER L. arts administrator, writer, consultant, researcher, art critic; b. N.Y.C., Jan. 14, 1951; s. Dwight Rolfe and Jane Rae Walsh. AB, Oberlin Coll., 1973; M in Liberal Arts, Harvard U., 1985. Asst. dir. pub. programs Mus. Cmparative Zoology, Harvard U., Cambridge, Mass., 1974-78, dir. publs. and info. art museums, 1979-92; dir. campaign and devel. comms. Mus. Fine Arts, Boston, 1992-94, cons., writer, 1994—; dir. info. and instnl. rels. Davis Mus. and Cultural Ctr., Wellesley (Mass.) Coll., 1994-99; chmn. Mass. Art Commn., Boston, 1996—. Cons., writer Met. Mus. Art, N.Y.C., 1999—2001; founding organizer Art Mus. Image Consortium, Pitts., 1996—99, cons., 2000—01; cons., rschr. writer Jemison Inst. Dartmouth Coll., Hanover, NH, 2000—01, cons. writer pub. affairs, 2002—, cons. writer Com. on Race in the Acad., 2002—03; art critic WBUR-NPR, Boston, 2001—; cons. Jan Krukowski & Co., N.Y.C., 2002—. Contbg. author: A Cloud on Sand, 1990, The Great Image Debate, 1996, Computing and Visual Culture, 1999, Democracy and New Media, 2003; author: (exhbn. guide) van Gogh, 1998, Gauguin, 2002, Egypt Exhbn., 2002, (report) Report on the Race Matter, Conf. at Dartmouth Coll., 2003; contbr. articles to profl. jours. including Jour. Am. Assn. Info. Sci., Archives and Mus. Informatics. Mem.: Coll. Art Assn. (chmn. com. on intellectual property 2001—02). Office: Mass Art Commn State House Rm 61-G Boston MA 02133 Fax: 617-727-5400. E-mail: plwalsh@mindspring.com

WALSH, PHILIP CORNELIUS, retired mining executive; b. Harrison, N.J., May 23, 1921; s. Philip Cornelius and Frances (Prendergast) Walsh; m. Alexandra Somerville Tuck, May 19, 1945 (dec. Sept. 1993); children: Eugenie Philbin Flaherty, Philip C.C., Frances Cummings, Alexander Tuck, Nicholas Holladay, Elizabeth Lovering; m. Peggy Flanigan McDonnell, Oct. 13, 1996. BA, Yale U., 1943; member of the Class of 1944. With W.R. Grace & Co., Lima, Peru and N.Y.C., 1946-71; v.p. parent co., chief operating officer Latin Am. group, 1961-71, group exec. corp. adminstrv. group, 1970-71; v.p. Cerro Corp., 1972-74, Newmont Mining Corp., 1974-80; chmn. bd. Foote Mineral Co., Exton, Pa., 1979-80; dir. Cyprus Minerals Co., 1980—85; vice chmn. St. Joe Minerals Corp., 1980-85; chmn. bd. Chilean Lithium Co. Ltd., 1980-94; dir. T. Rowe Price Assocs., Inc., 1986—2000; ret., 2000. Past dir. Peabody Coal Co., Piedmont Mining Co.; bd. advisors Fond Elec.; mem. Nat. Strategic Minerals and Metals Program Adv. Commn. Mem. Harding Twp. Bd. Edn., NJ, 1960—66, Harding Twp. Com., 1966—72, police commr., 1966—72; trustee Morristown Meml. Hosp., 1969—79; vis. com. Colo. Sch. Mines, Global Sys. and Cultures. 1st lt. U.S. Army. Decorated Silver Star, Purple Heart. Mem.: AIME (Saunders gold medal 1992, Disting. Mem. award 1993), Am. Soc. (hon. dir.), Pan Am. Soc. U.S. (past vice chmn.), Am. Assn. Order of Malta (past chancellor), Fed. Assn. Order of Malta, Edgartown Golf Club, Essex Hunt Club, Edgartown Yacht Club (commodore 1993—95), Racquet and Tennis Club, Somerset Hills Country Club, Sigma Xi, Phi Beta Kappa. Republican. Roman Catholic. Home: Pleasant Valley Peapack NJ 07977

WALSH, RAYMOND JOHN, medical educator; b. Dec. 13, 1947; married; 2 children. BS in Zoology, U. Mass., 1969; PhD in Anatomy, Tufts U., 1976. Rsch. asst. dept. comparative pathology New Eng. Regional Primate Rsch. Ctr., 1969-72; postdoctoral rsch. fellow dept. ob-gyn. Royal Victoria Hosp., McGill U., Montreal, 1976-78; asst. prof. anatomy George Washington U., Washington, 1978-82, assoc. prof., 1982-91, interim chmn. anatomy, 1990-95, prof. and chmn. anatomy, 1995—. Participant numerous ednl. confs.; lectr. in field; sponsor Ednl. Commn. for Fgn. Med. Grads., Quaid-i-Azam Med. Coll. Bahawalpur, Pakistan, 1992-93; external examiner dept. anatomy Kuwait U., 1993, 94. Contbr. numerous articles and abstracts to profl. jours. Chmn. anatomical bd. Dept. Human Svcs., D.C. Govt., 1992—. Grantee Biomed. Rsch. Support, 1978-79, 85-86, 90-91, NINCDS, 1979-83, 83-85, NSF, 1986-90, Souers Fund, 1994-95. Mem. Am. Assn. Anatomists (local organizing com. ann. meeting 1987), Soc. Neurosci., Internat. Brain Rsch. Orgn., Soc. for Applied Learning Tech., Am. Assn. Neurol. Surgeons (local organizer workshop 1994), Washington Soc. for Electron Microscopy (chmn. sponsor site orgn. com. 1980). Office: George Washington Univ Dept Anatomy & Cell Biology 2300 I St NW Washington DC 20037-2336

WALSH, ROBERT JOSEPH, psychotherapist; b. Chgo., Sept. 16, 1948; s. Robert Paul Walsh and Louise Tirado; children: Brigid, Justin, Clare. BA, Loyola U., 1970; MA, Governors State U., 1974. Cert. counselor. Family svc. facilitator LaGrange (Ill.) Area Spl. Edn., 1996-98; social worker Sch. Dist. 107, Burr Ridge, Ill., 1998—; therapist R.J. Walsh and Assocs., Western Springs, Ill., 1979—. Author: The Complete Guide to Private Practice, 2000. Parent edn. vol. YMCA, LaGrange, 1996-99; advisor Lyons Twp. Youth Com. Bd., LaGrange, 1979-80. Named Vol. of Yr. Young Mens Christian Assn., 1997, Counselor of Yr. Am. Mental Health Counselors, 1999. Mem.: ACA (pub. policy and legis. com. 2001—, chair 2002—), Ill. Mental Health Counselors Assn. (chair managed care task force 1993—, bd. dirs. 1994—), Jackson Park Yacht Club (sec. exec. bd. 1999—). Democrat. Roman Catholic. Avocations: sailing, scuba diving. Home: 234 S Madison La Grange IL 60525 Office: RJ Walsh & Assocs 822 W Hillgrove Western Springs IL 60558 E-mail: Walshgasp@aol.com.

WALSH, ROBERT K. dean; AB, Providence Coll., 1964; JD, Harvard U., 1967. Bar: Calif. 1967, Ark. 1979. Assoc. McCatchen, Black, Verleger & Shea, L.A., 1967-70; asst. prof. Villanova (Pa.) U., 1970-71, assoc. prof., 1971-73, prof., 1973-76; ptnr. Friday, Eldredge & Clark, Little Rock, 1981-89; dean, prof. Wake Forest Sch. Law, Winston-Salem, N.C., 1989—. Mem. ABA (chair accreditation com. 1984-86, chair standards rev. com. sect. legal edn. 1991—), N.C. Bar Assn. (chair bar bench and law schs. com. 1990-92, v.p., bd. govs. 1994-95). Office: Wake Forest Sch Law Dean's Office PO Box 7206 Winston Salem NC 27109-7206

WALSH, ROGER N. psychiatry, philosophy, anthropology and religious studies educator; b. Brisbane, Australia, July 3, 1946; arrived in U.S., 1972; s. Nugent William and Patricia Walsh; m. Frances Elizabeth Vaughan, June 30, 1985. B in Med. Sci., U. Queensland, Australia, 1968; diploma in psychology, U. Queensland, 1969, MD, 1970, PhD, 1972. Diplomate Am. Bd. Psychiatry and Neurology, lic. physician Calif. Rsch. fellow U. Queensland, Brisbane, 1969; intern Repatriation Hosp., Brisbane, 1971; resident in psychiatry Stanford (Calif.) U., 1972—75, Foundations Fund fellow, 1975—77; prof. psychiatry U. Calif., Irvine, 1978—, prof. philosophy, 1986—, prof. anthropology, 1991—, prof. religious studies, 2003—. Mem. internat. adv. com. Internat. Sch. Psychotherapy, St. Petersburg, 1996—, The Peace U., Berlin, 1996—; mem. internat. sci. adv. com. European Transpersonal Assn., Rome, 1996—. Author: Essential Spirituality, 1999, The Spirit of Shamerism, 2004, Higher Wisdom, 2004; editor: Meditation, 1984 (Outstanding Acad. Book of Yr., 1985), Beyond Ego, 1993; sr. editor: Revision Jour., 1980—85. Mem. adv. bd. Dzogchen Found., Cambridge, 1996—. Scholar, Fulbright scholar, 1972. Mem.: Internat. Transpersonal Assn. (bd. dirs. 1992—95), Physicians for Human Rights. Achievements include discovery of plasticity of geriatric brain; seven common practices in the world religions; enhanced perceptual sensitivity induced by meditation.

WALSH, THOMAS CHARLES, lawyer; b. Mpls., July 6, 1940; s. William G. and Kathryne M. Walsh; m. Joyce Williams, Sept. 7, 1968; children: Brian Christopher, Timothy Daniel, Laura Elizabeth Smith. BS in Commerce magna cum laude, St. Louis U., 1962, LLB cum laude, 1964. Bar: Mo. 1964, U.S. Dist. Ct. (ea. dist.) Mo. 1964, U.S. Ct. Appeals (8th cir.) 1968, U.S. Supreme Ct. 1971, U.S. Ct. Appeals (6th cir.) 1972, U.S. Ct. Appeals (5th cir.) 1974, U.S. Ct. Appeals (D.C. cir.) 1980, U.S. Ct. Appeals (7th cir.) 1982, U.S. Ct. Appeals (9th cir.) 1987, U.S. Ct. Appeals (4th cir.) 1989, U.S. Ct. Appeals (11th and fed. cirs.) 1992, U.S. Ct. Appeals (2d and 10th cirs.) 1993. Jr. ptnr. Bryan, Cave, McPheeters & McRoberts, St. Louis, 1964-73; ptnr. Bryan Cave LLP, St. Louis, 1974—; mem. exec. com. Bryan Cave LLP, St. Louis, 1980-96. Mem. 8th Cir. Adv. Com., 1983-86. Bd. dirs. St. Louis Symphony Soc., 1983-95. With U.S. Army, 1965-66; lt. USNR, 1966-71. Fellow Am. Coll. Trial Lawyers, Am. Acad. Appellate Lawyers; mem. Mo. Bar Assn., St. Louis Bar Assn., Am. Law Inst., Mo. Athletic Club, Bellerive Country Club. Roman Catholic. Office: Bryan Cave LLP 1 Metropolitan Sq 211 N Broadway Saint Louis MO 63102-2733 Office Phone: 314-259-2284. Business E-Mail: tcwalsh@bryancave.com.

WALSH, THOMAS FRANCIS, JR., producer, writer, director; b. N.Y.C., Aug. 15, 1956; s. Thomas Francis and Catherine Alice (May) W.; m. Adriana Mia Stastny, Oct. 19, 1996; children: Barron, Arielle, Thomas III. BFA, NYU, 1977. Pres. Tom Walsh Prodns. Inc., N.Y.C. and Del., 1977-89; chmn., CEO I.D.L. Inc., N.Y.C. and Calif., 1989-91, Wonderland Dream Factory Inc., Calif. and Del., 1991-93, Enteraktion Inc. and Enteraktion Studios, Inc., Miramar, Fla., 1993—, also prodr., dir. 8 new entertainment web series, prodr., dir. Kidsline (TV), 2002—. Prodr.: (feature film) Denial, 1991; (CD-ROM) The Arrival, 1996; exec. prodr.: (TV) We Dare You!, 1982, House to House, 1982, Mismatch, 1979; prodr., dir.: The Whole Truth, 1977, (TV) Global Trade with Toms Travis, 2002; prodr., dir., writer (TV) 14 Stories, 2002, Newsoes, 2003; created and developed more than 175 creatures and characters for TV, movies and animation. Scholar Helena Rubenstein Co., N.Y.C., 1976-77; recipient 1st prize for best TV show Conn. Assn. Profl. Communicators, 1974, Bronze and Silver awards Nat. Forensic League, 1977, Kate Garland award NYU/Columbia Pictures, 1976. Mem. Psi Upsilon (Delta chpt.), Alpha Epsilon Rho. Avocations: boating, diving, trains. Office: Enteraktion Inc/NBC Studios 15000 Peacock Plz Miramar FL 33027 E-mail: tomwalsh@enteraktion.com.

WALSH, THOMAS JAMES, environmental engineer, consultant; b. Phila., Nov. 20, 1957; s. Thomas Michael and Rita Elizabeth Walsh; m. Karen Aileen Rohler, Apr. 5, 1986; children: Laura, Christina, Kimberly. BS, Pa. State U., 1979, M in Environ. Pollution Control, 1984; MS, U. Cin., 2001. Cert. Inst. Profl. Environ. Practice 1995. Environ. scientist GPU Nuc., Middletown, Pa., 1979—86; project engr. Ill. Power Co., Clinton, 1986—87; environ. compliance mgr. Westinghouse, Cin., 1987—92; sr. tech. mgr. Fluor Fernald, Cin., 1992—2004; gen. mgr. Environ. Analysis & Solutions, LLC, Fairfield, Ohio, 2002—. Ind. safety rev. com. Fluor Fernald, 1999—2001; spkr.'s bur. Westinghouse, 1987—92; emergency response team GPU Nuc., Westinghouse, Fluor, Ill. Power Co., 1979—2004. Coach, meet dir. Sacred Heart Boosters Assn., Fairfield, 1997; team leader United Way, Fernald, 1999; science-by-mail scientist McKinley, Canton, Ohio, 1993—95. Mem.: AAAS, Air and Waste Mgmt. Assn., Am. Meteorol. Soc. Roman Catholic. Avocations: weather forecasting, running, reading, coaching. Office: Environ Analysis and Solutions LLC 4513 Rita Mae Dr Fairfield OH 45014 Office Phone: 513-305-0538. E-mail: tomwalsh75@aol.com.

WALSH, THOMAS JOHN, infectious disease physician, oncologist, researcher, educator; BA in Biology/Chemistry, Assumption Coll., Worcester, Mass., 1974; MD, The Johns Hopkins U., 1978. Diplomate in internal medicine, infectious diseases, med. oncology Am. Bd. Internal Medicine. Resident in medicine Michael Reese Hosp., U. Chgo., 1978-82; fellow pathology Johns Hopkins Hosp. and Univ., Balt., 1979-80; fellow infectious diseases U. Md., Balt., 1982-85, fellow med. oncology, 1985-86, Nat. Cancer Inst., Bethesda, Md., 1986-87, sr. staff fellow, 1987-88, med. officer, 1988-93, sr. investigator, 1993—, head mycology unit, 1993—, chief immunocompromised host sect., 1996—; assoc. prof. U. Md. Sch. Medicine, Balt., 1992-98, prof., 1998—. Lectr. The Johns Hopkins U. Sch. Medicine, Balt., 1985—. Contbr. chpts. to Management of Infections in Patients with Cancer, 1985, Critical Problems in Trauma Care, Vol. II Medical Management, Current Therapy in Hematology/Oncology, 1987, Diagnosis and Therapy of Systemic Mycoses, 1989, Respiratory Diseases in the Immunosuppressed Host, 1990, Hematology: Basic Principles and Practice, 3d edit., 1999, Medical Microbiology, 3d edit., 1991, Pediatric AIDS, 1990, Current Therapy in Critical Care Medicine, 1990, Emerging Targets in Antibacterial and Antifungal Chemotherapy, 1991, The Principles and Practice of Medical Intensive Care, 1993, Aspergillus: The Biology and Industrial Applications, 1991, New Strategies in Fungal Disease, 1992, Oral Fungal Infections in Immunocompromised Patients, 1991, Current Therapy in Pediatric Infectious Diseases, 3d edit., 1993, Hematopoietic Growth Factors and Mononuclear Phagocytes, 1993, Fungal Diseases of the Lung, 2d edit., 1993, Manual of Clinical Microbiology, 7th edit., 1994, Infectious Diseases, 1994, Infectious Complications of Cancer, 1995, Principles and Practice of Pediatric Oncology, 2d edit., 1996, Current Therapy in Adult Medicine, 4th edit., 1997, Cutaneous Infection and Therapy, 1997, Manual of Bone Marrow Transplantation, 1997, Adrenomedullin, 1998, Transplant Infections, 1998, Hunter's Tropical Medicine, 1999, Cancer: Principles and Practice of Oncology, 2001, others; editor: Medical Mycology. Infectious Diseases Clinics of North America, Vols. I an II, 2002-03; contbr. more than 400 articles to profl. jours. and 300 rsch. abstracts. Capt. USPHS, 1998—, NIH. Recipient Med. Mycology Fellow award Nat. Found. for Infectious Diseases, 1984, Young Investigator award ICAAC and Am. Soc. Microbiology, USPHS Commendation medal, 1993, 01, Outstanding Svc. medal, USPHS, 1996. Fellow ACP, Am. Acad. Microbiology, Infectious Diseases Soc. Am., Am. Coll. Chest Physicians. Achievements include development of exptl. and clin. found. for new approaches to diagnosis, treatment and prevention of invasive candidiasis and aspergillosis in immunocompromised patients; devel. of new understanding of pathogenesis, diagnosis, and treatment of emerging mycoses; devel. new approaches to augmentation of host defenses in neutropenic hosts against invasive mycoses. Office: NIH 9000 Rockville Pike Bethesda MD 20892-0003 Office Phone: 301-496-7103.

WALSH, THOMAS JOSEPH, neuro-ophthalmologist; b. NYC, Sept. 18, 1931; s. Thomas Joseph and Virginia (Hughes) W.; m. Sally Ann Maust, June 21, 1958; children: Thomas Raymond, Sara Ann, Mary Kelly, Kathleen Meghan. BA, Coll. Fordham, 1954; MD, Bowman Gray Med. Sch., 1958; degree in Mgmt., Yale U., 1998. Intern St. Vincent's Hosp., N.Y.C., 1958-59; resident ophthalmology Bowman Gray Med. Sch., Winston-Salem, N.C., 1961-64; fellow neuro-ophthalmology Bascom Palmer Eye Inst., Miami, Fla., 1964-65; practice medicine specializing in neuro-ophthalmology Stamford, Conn., 1965—; dir. neuro-ophthalmology service, asst. prof. ophthalmology and neurology Yale Sch. Medicine, New Haven, 1965-74, assoc. prof., 1974-79, prof., 1979—, also bd. permanent officers; dir. ophthalmology Stamford Hosp., 1978-83; mem. staff St. Joseph Hosp., Yale New Haven Hosp. Cons. to surgeon gen. army in neuro-ophthalmology Walter Reed Hosp., Washington, 1966—, VA Hosp., West Haven, 1965—, Silver Hill Found., New Canaan, Conn., 1974—; adj. prof. Dartmouth Med. Sch.; telemedicine bd. ORBIS Internat.; cons. mem. of bd. Obis Internat.; lectr. in field. Contbr. articles to various publs. Adv. bd. Stamford Salvation Army, 1972-92; med. bd. Darien Nurses Assn., Conn., 1972—; surgeon Darien Fire Dept., 1969—. With AUS, 1959-61. Decorated Knight of Malta; Centennial fellow Johns Hopkins, 1976; named one of Top Opthalmologists, Best Doctors.com, 2004 Mem. AMA, Conn., Fairfield County med. socs., Acad. Ophthalmology, Oxford Ophthal. Congress, Acad. Neurology, Am. Assn. Neurol. Surgeons, Internat. Neuro-Ophthalmology Soc., Soc. Med. Cons. to Armed Forces, Cosmos Club (Washington), Darien County Club, Yale Club (N.Y.C.), Lions, Army-Navy Club, Orbis Internat. (cybermedicine bd. mem.). Office: 1250 Summer St Ste 205 Stamford CT 06905-5318 Office Phone: 203-785-2020. Personal E-mail: twalsh13@optonline.net.

WALSH, W. TERENCE, lawyer; b. Toledo, Ohio, Nov. 18, 1943; s. Walter James and Ann (Gifford) W.; m. Patricia Jane Walker, Dec. 17, 1966; children: Christopher O'Brien, Ryan Kerrick, Ann Elisabeth. AB, Brown U., 1965; JD, Emory U., 1970. Bar: Ga., 1971, U.S. Dist. Ct. (no. dist.) Ga., 1971, U.S. Ct. Appeals (11th cir.), 1971, U.S. Supreme Ct., 2003. Assoc. Alston, Miller & Gaines, Atlanta, 1970-76, ptnr., 1976-83, Alston & Bird, Atlanta, 1983—. Lectr. various seminars on bus. litig., appellate procedure, juvenile law, ethics, and professionalism. Contbr. articles to profl. jours. Co-founder Truancy Intervention Project, 1991—; chmn. Kids In Need of Dreams, Inc., 1993-; bd. dirs. Family Connection Partnership, 2002-, Georgians for Children, 1993-2002, The Bridge, 1994-99, Ga. Justice Project, 1987-97, Juvenile Justice Fund, 2000—, Ga. Acad., 1999-2002, Family Connection Partnership, 2001—; bd. dirs. Atlanta Legal Aid Soc., Inc., 1976-98, pres., 1987; chmn. Capital Area Mosaic, 1994-96; chmn. sch. bd. Christ the King Sch., 1982-84; alumni trustee Brown U., 1994-2001; chmn. State Bar Com. on Children and the Cts., 1996—; bd. dirs. Child Placement Project Adv. Bd. Supreme Ct. Ga., 2000—. Recipient cmty. svc. award Martin Luther King, Jr. Ctr. for Nonviolent Social Change, 1995. Fellow: Ga. Bar Found.; mem.: ABA (juvenile justice sect., Livingston Hall Juvenile Justice award 1999), Gate City Bar Assn., Atlanta Bar Assn. (bd. dirs. 1987—93, pres. 1991—92, Charles E. Watkins award 1994, S. Phillip Heiner award 1994, David Pollard award 1995), State Bar Ga. (bd. govs. 1979—99, pres. young lawyers sect. 1980—81, H. Sol Clark award 1987, Chief Justice's award for cmty. svc. 1998), Emory Law Alumni Assn. (exec. com. 1990—98, Disting. Law Alumnus award 2000). Avocations: sports, gardening, reading. Office: Alston & Bird 1201 W Peachtree St NW Ste 4200 Atlanta GA 30309-3449 Office Phone: 404-881-7161. E-mail: twalsh@alston.com.

WALSH, WILLIAM ALBERT, management consultant, former naval officer; b. Gilman, Ill., Aug. 15, 1933; s. Lawrence Eugene and Myrtle R. (Mulder) W.; m. Joan Elizabeth Kennedy, Dec. 28, 1957; children: Kathryn, Michael, Julie. BS in Commerce, U. Notre Dame, 1955; MS in Mgmt. with distinction, U.S. Naval Postgrad. Sch., Monterey, Calif., 1962; MS in Internat. Affairs with honors, George Washington U., 1972. Commd. ensign U.S. Navy, 1955, advanced through grades to rear adm., 1981; exec. asst. to dep. chief naval ops. (Surface Warfare), Washington, 1974-76; comdg. officer USS Juneau, San Diego, 1976-78; comdr. Amphibious Squadron Three, San Diego, 1978-79; head plans and policy div., comdr. rapid deployment naval forces Comdr. in Chief U.S. Pacific Fleet, Honolulu, 1979-81; comdr. Amphibious Group Eastern Pacific, San Diego, 1981-82; dir. surface warfare div. Office Chief Naval Ops., Pentagon, Washington, 1983-85; ret., 1985; pres. Air/Space Am., San Diego, 1986-89, W.A. Walsh Enterprises, 1990—. Decorated Legion of Merit with 2 gold stars, Bronze Star, Navy Commendation medal U.S.; Disting. Service Order 2d Class Vietnam

WALSH, WILLIAM ARTHUR, JR., lawyer; b. Washington, Mar. 17, 1949; children: Jesse Creighton, Patrick McKay. BS in Econs. and Fin., U. Md., 1972; JD, U. Richmond, 1977. Bar: Va. Ptnr. Hunton & Williams LLP, Richmond, Va., 1977—. Adv. bd. for law rev. U. Richmond. Trustee, bd. dirs. Va. Commonwealth U. Real Estate Found.; mem. Va. Commonwealth U. Real Estate Circle of Excellence. Mem. Va. Bar Assn., Am. Coll. Real Estate Lawyers. Home: 4705 Leonard Pky Richmond VA 23226-1337 Office: Hunton & Williams LLP Riverfront Plz East Tower 951 E Byrd St Richmond VA 23219-4074 Office Phone: 804-788-8378. Business E-Mail: wwalsh@hunton.com.

WALSH, WILLIAM DESMOND, investor; b. N.Y.C., Aug. 4, 1930; s. William J. and Catherine Grace (Desmond) W.; m. Mary Jane Gordon, Apr. 5, 1951; children: Deborah, Caroline, Michael, Suzanne, Tara Jane, Peter. BA, Fordham U., 1951; JD, Harvard U., 1955. Bar: N.Y. 1955. Asst. U.S. atty. So. dist. N.Y., N.Y.C., 1955-58; counsel N.Y. Commn. Investigation, N.Y.C., 1958-61; mgmt. cons. McKinsey & Co., N.Y.C., 1961-67; sr. v.p. Arcata Corp., Menlo Park, Calif., 1967-82; chmn. Sequoia Assocs. LLC, 1982—; pres., CEO Atacra Liquidating Trust, 1982-88. Chmn. bd. dirs. Consol. Freightways Corp., Vancouver, Wash., Neuroscis. Inst./Scripps, Ameriscape, Inc., Cornelius, Oreg., Creativity Inc., Van Nuys; bd. dirs. URS Corp., San Francisco, UNOVA, Evertt, Wash., Am. Ireland Fund, Digital Safety Techs., Inc., Lebanon, Tenn. Bd. overseers Hoover Inst. Mem. N.Y. State Bar Assn., Harvard Club (N.Y.C. and San Francisco), Fordham Club No. Calif., Knights of Malta (amb. to Bolivia). Home: 279 Park Ln Atherton CA 94027-5448 Office: 1550 El Camino Real Ste 220 Menlo Park CA 94025 Office Phone: 650-321-9400. E-mail: bill@sequoiaassociates.com.

WALSH, WILLIAM EGAN, JR., electronics executive; b. Springfield, Mass., Dec. 2, 1948; s. William Egan and Veronica (Maroney) W.; m. Terese Anne Sullivan, Oct. 25, 1952; children: Brian, Kathleen, John, Kevin. BA in Physics, Holy Cross, 1970; MS in Physical Oceanography, U.S. Naval Sch., Monterey, Calif., 1971; MBA, U. North Fla., 1975. Oceanographer Sippican, Inc., Marion, Mass., 1975-77, mktg. mgr., 1977-80, from v.p. to sr. v.p., 1980-90, pres., CEO, 1990—, also bd. dirs., 1990—. Bd. dirs. Phys. Scis., Inc., Andover, Mass. Lt. USN, 1970-75, lt. comdr. USNR, 1976-80. Mem. Marine Tech. Soc. Roman Catholic. Avocations: boating, jogging, racquetball, photography. Office: Sippican Inc 7 Barnabas Rd Marion MA 02738-1421

WALSHAW, L. SCOTT, commissioner; BA in Art History, BA in Econ., Calif. State U.; MBA, U. Nev. Sr. examiner Nev. Fin. Instns., Carson City, Nev.; asst. nat. bank examiner Office the Comptr. the Currency, Carson City, Nev.; commr. Fin. Instns., Carson City, Nev., 1983—. Past chmn. Am. Coun. State Savs. Supr.; past chmn., trustee Inst. Supr. Edn.; past mem. state liaison com. Fed. Fin. Instns. Examination Coun. Office: State Nev Fin Instns Divsn 406 E 2nd St Ste 3 Carson City NV 89701-4758

WALSHOK, MARY LINDENSTEIN, academic administrator, sociology educator; b. Sept. 10, 1942; BA, Pomona Coll., 1964; MA in Sociology, Ind. U., 1966, PhD in Sociology, 1969. Asst. prof. sociology Calif. State U., Fullerton, 1972-75; dir. women's programs, assoc. dean U. Ext. U. Calif., San Diego, 1975-80, dean, 1981-87; assoc. prof. sociology U. Calif., San Diego, 1981-87, assoc. vice-chancellor pub. programs, adj. prof. sociology, 1990—. Adj. prof. Stockholm Sch. Econ.; bd. dirs. Calif. Coun. Humanities, San Diego Cmty. Found., Girard Found., Eureka Communities. Author: Blue Collar Women, 1982, Knowledge Without Boundaries, 1995; contbr. over 50 articles to profl. jours. Address: 150 12th St Del Mar CA 92014-2315 E-mail: mwalshok@ucsd.edu.

WALSKE, M(AX) CARL, JR., physicist; b. Seattle, June 2, 1922; s. Max Carl and Margaret Ella (Fowler) W.; m. Elsa Marjorie Nelson, Dec. 28, 1946; children: C. Susan, Steven C., Carol A. BS in Math. cum laude, U. Wash., 1944; PhD in Theoretical Physics, Cornell U., 1951. Staff, asst. theoretical divsn. leader Los Alamos Sci. Lab., 1951-56; dep. rsch. dir. Atomics Internat., Canoga Park, Calif., 1956-59; sci. rep. AEC in U.K., London, 1961-62; theoretical physicist RAND Corp., 1962-63; sci. attache U.S. missions to NATO and OECD, Paris, 1963-65; staff mem. Los Alamos Sci. Lab., 1965-66; asst. to sec. def. atomic energy commn. Dept. Def., 1966-73, chmn. military liaison com. atomic energy commn.; pres., COO Atomic Indsl. Forum, Inc., Washington, 1973-87. Chmn. Upper Hood Canal Watershed Mgmt. Com., 1994-2000; budget steering com. Kitsap County, 1996, budget com., 1997-99, participant strategic planning, 1997, planning commn., 1998-2000. Lt. (j.g.) USNR, 1943-51. Recipient Disting. Civilian Svc. medal Dept. Def. Fellow Explorers Club, Am. Phys. Soc.; mem. Am. Nuc. Soc., Poulsbo Yacht Club (trustee 1996-98), Phi Beta Kappa, Sigma Xi. Home: PO Box 370 Silverdale WA 98383-0370 E-mail: cwalske@wavecable.com. *To seek out positions which appeared the most challenging and personally satisfying; to gain my reward through self-respect rather than public recognition; to expend extra effort as an offset to my limitations.*

WALSS, RODOLFO J. obstetrician-gynecologist, artist; b. Monclova, Coahuila, Mex., June 13, 1945; came to U.S., 1992; s. Rodolfo and Maria Consuelo W.; m. Maria Eugenia Aurioles, Dec. 17, 1967; children: Eugenia, Consuelo, Rodolfo, Patricia, Leonardo. MD, U. Coahuila (Mex.), Torreón, 1970. Diplomate Am. Bd. Ob-Gyn. Intern Ohio Valley Med. Ctr., Wheeling, W.Va., 1973-74; resident U. W.Va. Ohio Valley Med. Ctr., Wheeling, W.Va., 1974-77; prof. obstetrics faculty of medicine U. Coahuila (Mex.), Torrón, 1978-92, prof. gynecology faculty of medicine, 1982-92; chief ob-gyn svc. Mexican Social Security Inst., Torrón, 1986-90, chief divsn. ob-gyn., 1990-92; ob-gyn. Women Healthcare Group, Brownsville, Tex., 1992—2003; chief ob-gyn. Columbia Valley Regional Med. Ctr., Brownsville, 1994-97, mem. edn. com., 1997—; pvt. practice Brownsville, 1997—; vice chief of state, 2003; chief of staff Valley Regional Med. Ctr., 2004. Contbr. 22 articles to profl. jours. Fellow Am. Coll. Ob-Gyn., ACS; mem. Am. Soc. Reproductive Medicine, AMA, Tex. Med. Assn. Avocation: painting. Home: 24 Summit Dr Brownsville TX 78521-3610 Office: Alton Bloor Blvd Ste 260 Brownsville TX 78523

WALSTON, LOLA INGE, dietitian; b. Chgo., Jan. 26, 1943; d. Willy and Ingeborg (Smith) Neumann; m. Steven Ward Walston, Aug. 5, 1967; children: Bradley, Scott. BS, No. Ill. U., 1965; MS, U. Iowa, 1967. Registered, lic. dietitian. Asst. dietary dir. Alaska Hosp. Med. Ctr., Anchorage, 1973-76; cons. dietitian Mercer County Hosp., Coldwater, Ohio, 1979; profl. svc. cons. Health Care and Retirement Corp. Am., Lima, Ohio, 1981-84; dietary dir. Estes Health Care Ctr., Montgomery, Ala., 1979-80, Mercy Meml. Hosp., Urbana, Ohio, 1984-86, Dairy & Nutrition Coun. Mid East, Dayton, Ohio, 1987-89. Cons. Sharonview Nursing Home, South Vienna, Ohio, 1987-1997, Columbia House, Springfield, Ohio, 1987—; Miami Health Care Ctr., Troy, Ohio, SCOPE Nutrition Program for the elderly, Fairborn, Ohio, CLS Nutrition Program, Bellefontaine, Ohio, 1987-90, Westview Acres Care Ctr., Eaton, Ohio, 1988-97, St. John's Nursing Home, Springfield, 1989-95, Oakwood Village, Springfield, 1989-97, Villa Springfield, Springfield, Ohio, 1988-04, Covington (Ohio) Care Ctr., 1990-91, Champaign Nursing Home, 1993-97, Covenant House, 1993, Toward Independence, Inc., 1995—, Hospitality Homes, 1999-2003. Mem. com. Tecumseh coun. Boy Scouts Am., 1984—. Mem.: AAUW, Dayton Dietetic Assn. (treas. 1995—96, nominating com. chair 1997—98, mktg. com. chair 1998—2000, mem. com. 2000—02, nominating com. chair 2002—03), Ohio Cons. Dietitians Health Care Facilities (chmn. 1982—84, treas.-elect 1996—97, treas. 1997—98, chmn. elect 2001—02, chmn. 2002—03, past chmn. adv. 2003—), Ohio Dietetic Assn., Am. Dietetic Assn., Hilltoppers Club (pres. 1982—83, Fairborn, Ohio). Avocations: camping, sewing, knitting, crocheting, cooking.

WALSTON, RODERICK EUGENE, federal official; b. Gooding, Idaho, Dec. 15, 1935; s. Loren R. and Iva M. (Boyer) W.; m. Margaret D. Grandey; children: Gregory Scott W., Valerie Lynne W. AA, Boise Jr. Coll., 1956; BA cum laude, Columbia Coll., 1958; LL.B. scholar, Stanford U., 1961. Bar: Calif. 1961, U.S. Supreme Ct. 1973. Law clk to judge U.S. Ct. Appeals 9th Cir., 1961-62; dep. atty. gen State of Calif., San Francisco, 1963-91, head natural resources sect, 1969-91, chief asst. atty. gen. pub. rights div., 1991-99; spl. dep counsel Kings County, Calif., 1975-76; gen. counsel Metropolitan Water Dist. So. Calif., 2000—02; dep. solicitor U.S. Dept. Interior, 2002—. Mem. environ. and natural resources adv. coun. Stanford (Calif.) Law Sch. Contbr. articles to profl. jours.; bd. editors: Stanford Law Rev., 1959-61, Western Natural Resources Litigation Digest, Calif. Water Law and Policy Reporter; spl. editor Jour. of the West. Co-chmn. Idaho campaign against Right-to-Work initiative, 1958; Calif. rep. Western States Water Coun., 1986—; environ. and natural resources adv. coun., Stanford Law Sch. Nat. Essay Contest winner Nat. Assn. Internat. Rels. Clubs, 1956, Stanford Law Rev. prize, 1961; recipient Best Brief award Nat. Assn. Attys. Gen., 1997; Astor Found. scholar, 1956-58. Mem. ABA (chmn. water resources com. 1988-90, vice chmn. and conf. chmn. 1985-88, 90—), Contra Costa County Bar Assn., U.S. Supreme Ct., Hist. Soc., Federalist Soc., World Affairs Coun. No. Calif. Office: Office of the Solicitor U S Dept of the Interior 1849 C St N W Washington DC 20240

WALT, MARTIN, physicist, consulting educator; b. West Plains, Mo., June 1, 1926; s. Martin and Dorothy (Mantz) W.; m. Mary Estelle Thompson, Aug. 16, 1950; children: Susan Mary, Stephen Martin, Anne Elizabeth, Patricia Ruth. BS, Calif. Inst. Tech., 1950; MS, U. Wis., 1951, PhD, 1953. Staff mem. Los Alamos Sci. Lab., 1953-56; research scientist, mgr. physics Lockheed Missiles and Space Co., Palo Alto (Calif.) Rsch. Lab., 1956-71, dir. phys. scis., 1971-86, dir. research, 1986-93; cons. prof. Stanford U., 1986—. Mem. adv. com. NRC, NASA, Dept. Def., U. Calif. Lawrence Berkeley Lab. Author 2 books; contbr. articles to sci. jours. Served with USNR, 1944-46. Wis. Research Found. fellow, 1950-51; AEC fellow, 1951-53 Fellow Am. Geophys. Union, Am. Phys. Soc.; mem. Am. Inst. Physics (bd. govs.), Fremont Hills Country Club. Home: 12650 Viscaino Ct Los Altos Hills CA 94022-2517 Office: Stanford U Starlab Packard 352 Stanford CA 94305

WALTER, CHARLES SEBASTIAN, Roman Catholic priest; b. Grafton, W.Va., Aug. 19, 1940; s. Sebastian Julius Walter and Mary Elizabeth Macdonald. BA, U. San Diego, 1962; B in Sacred Theology, Pontifical Urban U., Rome, 1964, Licentiate in Sacred Theology, 1966; DMin, Cath. Theol. Union, 1999. Ordained priest Roman Cath. Ch., 1966. Prin. Sacred Heart Seminary, Cin., 1966-68; missionary Diocese of Witbank, South Africa, 1968-74; asst. gen. Comboni Missionaries, Rome, 1975-79, provincial superior Cin., 1980-86; missionary Archdiocese of Lima, Peru, 1987-90; prof. theology Faculty of Theology, Lima, 1991-95; assoc. dir., adj. prof. Cath. Theol. Union, Chgo., 1999—. Bd. dirs. Peru Peace Network, Jefferson City, Mo. Trustee Cath. Theol. Union, Chgo., 1995-99. Mem. Am. Soc. Missiology (editl. bd. 1997), Assn. Profs. of Mission. Home and Office: Chgo Ctr Global Ministries 5401 S Cornell Ave Chicago IL 60615-5664

WALTER, GEORGE ANTHONY, elementary school educator; b. Cin., July 16, 1948; s. George Winton and Yvonne Iola (Rivard) W. AA, Brevard C.C., 1968; BA in Edn., U. Fla., 1970; MEd, Stetson U., 1978. Tchr. Brevard County Sch. Sys., Vierra, Fla., 1971—. V.p. Rockledge Little League, 1991—; v.p. bd. dirs. Fla. Miss Softball, 1988; pres. bd. dirs. Rockledge Miss Softball, 1988-89; mem. Rep. Nat. Party. With U.S. Army, 1970-76, USAR. Recipient Newspapers in Edn. cert. Fla. Today, 1997. Mem. Brevard Fedn. Tchrs., Am. Legion. Republican. Avocations: photography, softball. Home: 155 Becora Ave Merritt Island FL 32953-3141

WALTER, HAROLD M. lawyer; b. Balt., 1957; BA, Franklin Marshall Coll., 1979; JD, U. Md., 1982. Bar: Md. 1983, N.Y. 1997, U.S. Dist. Ct. Md. 1990, U.S. Dist. Ct. (so. and ea. dists.) N.Y. 1997, U.S. Ct. Appeals (4th cir.) 1992, U.S. Ct. Appeals (3d cir.) 1997, U.S. Supreme Ct. 1995. Law clk. Ct. Spl. Appeals, Md., 1982—83; ptnr. Tydings & Rosenberg LLP, Balt., 1983—. Steering com. industrywide litig. Def. Rsch. Inst. Named one of Top Ten Most Winning Attys., The Nat. Law Jour., 2002. Mem.: ABA (forum com. comms. law, forum com. entertainment and sports industries), N.Y. State Bar Assn., Md. State Bar Assn., Balt. (Md.) County C. of C. Office: Tydings & Rosenberg LLP 100 East Pratt St Baltimore MD 21202*

WALTER, INGO, economics professor; b. Kiel, Fed. Republic of Germany, Apr. 11, 1940; s. Hellmuth and Ingeborg (Moeller) W.; m. Jutta Ragnhild Dobernecker, June 28, 1963; children: Carsten Erik, Inga Maria. AB summa cum laude, Lehigh U., 1962, MS, 1963; PhD, NYU, 1966. Asst. prof. econs. U. Mo., St. Louis, 1965-67, assoc. prof., chmn. dept., 1967-70; prof. econs. and fin. Stern Sch. Bus. Adminstrn. NYU, N.Y.C., 1970—, assoc. dean academic affairs, 1970-79, chmn. internat. bus. and fin. depts., 1980-85, Dean Abraham L. Gitlow chair, 1987-90; Charles Simon chair, dir. NYU Ctr., 1990—2003; Seymour Milstein chair fin., corp. governance and ethics, dir. NYU Global Bus. Inst., 2003—. Prof. internat. mgmt. (joint appointment) INSEAD, Fontainebleau, France, 1985—; cons. in field. Author. editor 28 books including Secret Money, 1985, 2d edit., 1990, Global Banking, 3d edit., 2003, Universal Banking in the United States, 1994, Street Smarts, 1997. High Finance in the Euro-Zone, 2000, Mergers and Acquisitions in Financial Services, 2004; contbr. articles to profl. jours. Recipient Bernhard Harms medal, 1992; Ford Found. fellow, 1974-76, Rockefeller Found. fellow, 1977-78. Mem. Am. Econ. Assn., Am. Fin. Assn., Acad. Internat. Bus., Royal Econ. Soc., So. Econ. Assn., Phi Beta Kappa, Beta Gamma Sigma, Omicron Delta Epsilon. Home: 77 Club Rd Montclair NJ 07043-2528 Office: NYU Stern Sch Bus 44 W 4th St New York NY 10012-1106 E-mail: iwalter@stern.nyu.edu.

WALTER, J. JACKSON, consultant; b. Abington, Pa., Nov. 6, 1940; s. Joseph Horace and Edith Wilson (Jackson) W.; m. Susan Draude, Feb. 3, 1978; 1 child, Allison K. Vann. AB, Amherst Coll., Mass., 1962; LLB, Yale U., New Haven, 1966. Sec. Fla. Dept. Bus. Regulation, Tallahassee, 1976-79; dir. U.S. Office Govt. Ethics, Washington, 1979-82; pres. Nat. Acad. Pub. Adminstrn., Washington, 1982-84, Nat. Trust Historic Preservation, Washington, 1984-92; exec. dir. Waterford (Va.) Found., 1996-98. Chmn. Amendment I, Inc. Co-author: America's Unelected Government, 1983. Contbr. articles to profl. jours. Mem. Nat. Acad. Pub. Adminstrn., Met. (Washington) Club.

WALTER, JOHN, newspaper editor; Mng. editor Atlanta Jour. and Constn. Office: Atlanta Journal-Constitution PO Box 4689 72 Marietta St NW Atlanta GA 30303-2899

WALTER, JOHN FREDERICK, historical researcher, genealogist; b. Bklyn., Sept. 27, 1939; s. William O. and Madeline (Dittrich) W.; m. Margaret Killeen, Feb. 9, 1963; children: Mark, Michael, Robin, Brian. Student, St. John's U., 1955-61. Records mgr. Ladenburg Thalmann & Co., N.Y.C., 1961-76, W.R. Family Assocs., N.Y.C., 1976-94; dir., owner Inst. for Civil War Rsch., Middle Village, N.Y., 1994—. Author: The Confederate Dead in Brooklyn. Merit badge counselor Boy Scouts Am., Middle Village, 1990—. Sgt. U.S. Army Res., 1961-65. Mem. Nat. Geneal. Soc., Co. Mil. Historians, Assn. Profl. Genealogists, Cartophilic Soc. Great Britain. Roman Catholic. Avocations: walking, volleyball, racquetball, cigarette card collecting. Home and Office: 79-13 67 Dr Middle Village NY 11379 E-mail: icwrjohn@aol.com.

WALTER, KENNETH GAINES, library director; b. Atlanta, Mar. 14, 1932; s. Gaines Winningham and Freddie Lou (Thigpen) W.; m. Eva Lou McClelland, June 10, 1965; children: Regina Eileen, Kevin Michael. BA, Emory U., 1954, MS, 1958; postgrad., U. Vienna, Austria, 1962; MSLS, U. N.C., Chapel Hill, 1966; EdD, U. Ga., 1995. Asst. cataloging libr. Ohio U., Athens, 1961-65, head cataloging libr., 1965-68, faculty rep. Baptist Student Union New Haven, 1965-68; asst. dir. librs. U. S.C., Columbia, 1968-75; dir. librs. Ga. So. U., Statesboro, 1975-84; dir. libr. svcs. So. Conn. State U., New Haven, 1985-97, dir. libr. svcs. emeritus, 1997—. Cons. libr. strategic planning, budgeting, evaluation of book collections; faculty advisor Delta Tau Delta, Statesboro, 1976-83; book reviewer Libr. Jour., 1970-78. Contbr. articles to profl. jours. Mem. Conn. State U. Sys. Lib. Autom. RFP com., 1991-93, lib. dirs. com., 1985-97, Conn. Coun. Acad. Lib. Dirs., 1989-97 (emeritus mem. 1997—), Interagy. Libr. Planning Com., Hartford, Conn., 1986-89; mem. com. in-state svc. Conn. Acad. Libr. Dirs., 1985-89; mem. cataloging bd. New Haven Colony Hist. Soc., 1987-89; mem. Statesboro-Ga. So. Community Chorus, 1980-84; chmn. bd. suprs. CORE Credit Union, Statesboro, 1978-81. Staff sgt. U.S. Army, 1956-57. Recipient scholarship Emory U., 1950-53; Fulbright scholar, 1961-62; grantee Austrian Govt., 1961-62. Mem. ALA (life), Ga. Acad. Libr. Dirs., Ga. regents com. 1975-83 (sub com. coop. purchasing, 1978-1980, autom., 1980-1983, a/v 1975-1978), Assn. Coll. and Rsch. Librs., Libr. Adminstrn. and Mgmt. Assn., Reference and User Svcs. Assn., Southeastern Libr. Assn., Ga. Libr. Assn., Conn. Libr. Assn., Cen. Ga. Assoc. Librs. (pres. 1980-82), East. Ga. Libr. Triangle (pres. 1976-83), Ga. Acad. Sci., Ga. Assn. Coll. and Rsch. Librs. (pres. 1983), Rotary (New Haven), Sigma Gamma Epsilon, Beta Phi Mu, Phi Delta Kappa, Delta Tau Delta. Baptist. Avocations: camping, rock collecting, stamp collecting/philately, woodworking. Home: 512 Wallingford Rd Cheshire CT 06410-2844

WALTER, LYNN M. geologist, educator; PhD in Geology, U. Miami, 1983. Prof. geol. scis. U. Mich., Ann Arbor. Recipient Disting. Svc. award Geol. Soc. Am., 1999. Achievements include research on aqueous and solid phase geochemistry of sedimentary systems. Office: U Mich 2534 CC Little Bldg 425 E University Ave Ann Arbor MI 48109-1063 Fax: 734-763-4690. E-mail: lmwalter@umich.edu.

WALTER, MICHAEL D. food products executive; BS in Mgmt. and Mktg., Ea. Ill. U. Pres. ConAgra Splty. Grain Products, 1989—96, sr. v.p. trade and procurement, 1996—2000; sr. v.p. commodity procurement and econ. strategy ConAgra Foods, Omaha, 2000—. Mem., dir. Chgo. Bd. Trade. Mem.: Mpls. Grain Exch. Office: ConAgra Foods Inc 1 ConAgra Dr Omaha NE 68102-5001

WALTER, PAUL HERMANN LAWRENCE, chemistry professor; b. Jersey City, N.Y., Sept. 22, 1934; s. Helmuth Justus and Adelaide C. J. (Twardy) W.; m. Grace Louise Carpenter, Aug. 25, 1956; children: Katherine Elizabeth Walter Bousquet, Marjorie Allison Walter Moran. BS, MIT, 1956; PhD, U. Kans., 1960. Rsch. scientist DuPont Cen. Rsch. Dept., Wilmington, Del., 1960-67; prof. chemistry Skidmore Coll., Saratoga Springs, N.Y., 1967-96, chair chemistry and physics, 1975-85, prof. emeritus, 1996—. Translator: (book) Foundations of Crystal Chemistry, 1968; contbr. articles to profl. jours. Fellow Chem. Inst. Can.; mem. AAAS, AAUP (pres. 1984-86), Am. Chem. Soc. (bd. dirs. 1991-99, chmn. 1993-95, pres.-elect 1997, pres. 1998, Radding award 2002), Soc. Quimica de Mexico (hon.). Presbyterian. Achievements include patents in field. Home: 3 Benedictine Retreat Savannah GA 31411-1624 E-mail: phlw@alum.mit.edu.

WALTER, RICHARD LAWRENCE, physicist, researcher; b. Chgo., Nov. 1, 1933; s. Lawrence Barnabas and Marie Ann (Boehmer) Walter; m. Carol Elizabeth Goethals, Dec. 27, 1958; children: Timothy, Susan, Matthew. BS, St. Procopius Coll., 1955; PhD, Notre Dame U., 1960. Teaching asst., research asst. Notre Dame U., 1955-59; research asso. dept. physics U. Wis., 1960-61, instr., 1961-62; asst. prof. physics Duke U., Durham, N.C., 1962-67, asso. prof., 1967-74, prof., 1974—. Vis. staff mem. Los Alamos Sci Lab., 1964, 70, 75; vis. prof. Max Planck Inst fur Kernphysik, Heidelberg, Germany, 1970—71, Fudan Univ, Shanghai and Tsinghua Univ., Beijing, 1985, Fudan Univ., Shanghai and Tsinghua Uni., Beijing, 1991, Fudan Univ., Shanghai and Tsinghua Univ., Beijing, 1994—96, Fudan Univ., Shanghai and Tsinghua Univ., Beijing, 1998; staff Triangle Univs Nuclear Lab, 1970—, assoc. dir., 1998—2001; vis. scientist China Inst. Atomic Energy, Beijing, 1985, Beijing, 91, Beijing, 1994—96, Beijing, 1998. Contbr. articles to profl jours. Scholar Fulbright, 1970—71. Mem.: Environ Metals Group (coun 1973—76), Am Physical Soc, Sigma Pi Sigma (nat coun 1964—68), Sigma Xi. Home: 2818 Mc Dowell Rd Durham NC 27705-5621 Office: Duke Univ Dept Physics PO Box 90305 Durham NC 27708-0305 Business E-Mail: walter@tunl.duke.edu.

WALTER, ROBERT D. wholesale pharmaceutical distribution executive; b. 1945; m. Peggy Walter; children: Matthew, Blane, Peter. BMechE, Ohio U., 1967; MBA, Harvard U., 1970. Founder Cardinal Foods Inc. (acquired by Roundy's Inc. 1988), Dublin, Ohio, 1971-88; CEO, chmn. bd., dir. Cardinal Health, Inc., Dublin, 1971—. Bd. dirs. Bank One Corp., Viacom Inc., Am. Express; bd. trustees Battelle Meml. Inst., Ohio U. Trustee Battelle Meml. Inst., Ohio U. Avocations: golf, running, skiing. Office: Cardinal Health Inc 7000 Cardinal Pl Dublin OH 43017-1092

WALTER, ROBERT IRVING, chemistry professor; b. Johnstown, Pa., Mar. 12, 1920; s. Charles Weller and Frances (Riethmiller) W.; m. Farideh Asghari, Oct. 17, 1973. AB, Swarthmore Coll., 1941; MA, Johns Hopkins U., 1942; PhD, U. Chgo., 1949. Instr. U. Colo., 1949-51, U. Conn., 1953-55; rsch. assoc. Rutgers U., 1951-53; assoc. physicist Brookhaven Nat. Lab., 1955-56; mem. faculty Haverford Coll., 1956-68, prof. chemistry, 1963-68; prof. U. Ill., Chgo., 1968—, prof. emeritus, 1990—. Vis. lectr. Stanford (Calif.) U., winter 1967; acad. guest U. Zurich, 1976; U.S. NAS exch. visitor to Romania, 1982, 88. Mem. Adv. Council Coll. Chemistry, 1966-70. Served with USNR, 1944-46. Grantee U.S. Army Signal Research and Devel. Lab., NIH, NSF, Dept. Energy; NSF fellow, 1960-61 Fellow AAAS; mem. Am. Chem. Soc. (vis. scientist div. chem. edn. 1964-73), Sigma Xi. Achievements include special research preparation, proof of structure, chemical and physical properties of stable aromatic free radicals, C1 reactions and mechanisms in heterogeneous catalysis, reactions of porphyrin bases. Home: 2951 Central St Unit 308 Evanston IL 60201-1284 E-mail: mhry@aol.com.

WALTER, SCOTT, school librarian; b. Van Nuys, Calif., Mar. 11, 1967; s. Meryl Ann Rorer and Peter Vincent Walter; m. Kirsten Elaine Pauli, Oct. 13, 1991; 1 child, Hope Gwendolyn. MS in history and philosophy of edn., MLS, Ind. U.; MA in edn., The Am. U.; MA in Russian area studies, BS in Russian and linguistics, Georgetown U. Asst. dir. for pub. services & outreach Wash. State U. Libraries, Pullman, Wash., 2002—; head, george b. brain edn. libr. Wash. State U., Pullman, Wash., 2001—02. Collection mgr. for edn. Ohio State U. Libraries, 1999—2001; vis. asst. prof. of libr. & info. sci. U. of Ill. at Urbana-Champaign, 2003; vis. asst. prof. of edn. Wash. State U., Pullman, Wash., 2001—03. Editor: (collection of essays) Information Literacy Instruction for Educators: Professional Knowledge for an Information Age. Mem.: Am. Ednl. Rsch. Assn. (chair, communication of rsch. sig 2002—03), Assn. of Coll. & Rsch. Libraries (chair, edn. & behavioral sciences 2003—04). Office: Washington State University 1C Holland/New Library Box 645610 Pullman WA 99164-5610 E-mail: swalter@wsu.edu.

WALTER, SHERYL LYNN, lawyer; b. Morris, Ill., July 18, 1956; d. C. Frank and Margaret (Juhl) W. BA in History cum laude, Grinnell (Iowa) Coll., 1978; JD cum laude, U. Minn., 1984; MPA John F. Kennedy Sch. of Govt., Harvard U., 2003. Bar: Minn. 1984, U.S. Dist. Ct. Minn. 1987, U.S. Ct. Appeals (8th cir.) 1987, D.C. 1989, U.S. Dist. Ct. D.C. 1989, U.S. Ct. Appeals (D.C. cir.) 1989. Law clk. to presiding judge 3d Jud. Dist. of Minn., Rochester, 1984-85; law clk. to Chief Judge Donald P. Lay U.S. Ct. Appeals (8th cir.), St. Paul, 1985-87; assoc. Mayer, Brown & Platt, Washington, 1987-89; gen. counsel Nat. Security Archive, Washington, 1989-94, Assn. Records Review Bd., Washington, 1994-95, Commn. Protecting and Reducing Govt. Secrecy, Washington, 1995-97, dep. spl. counsel U.S. Senate Vets. Affairs com., 1997-98; minority staff dir., chief counsel U.S. Senate Jud. Com., Youth Violence Subcom., 1998-2000; with Office of Legis. Affairs U.S. Dept. of Justice, 2000—03, acting asst. atty. gen., 2001, chief of staff Office of Intelligence & Policy Rev., 2003—. Cons. Amnesty Internat., Washington, 1988-89. Mem. ABA (vice chmn. adminstrv. law sect. govt. info. subcom. 1990-96), D.C. Bar Assn. (steering com., adminstrv. law sect. 1990-97), Am. Soc. Access Profls. (bd. dirs. 1990-98, pres. 1996-97), Brit.-Am. Security Info. Coun. (bd. dirs. 1994-2000), Lawyers Alliance for World Security (bd. dirs. 1994-2000). Office: US Dept Justice 9th and Pennsylvania Ave NW Washington DC 20530

WALTER, VIRGINIA LEE, psychologist, educator; b. Temple, Tex., Oct. 30, 1937; d. Luther Patterson and Virginia Lafayette (Wilkins) W.; m. Glen Ellis, 1958 (div.); children: Glen Edward, David Walter; m. Robert Reinehr, 1963 (div.); 1 son, Charles Allen; m. Robert Bruininks, 1975 (div.). BS, U. Tex.-Austin, 1959, M.Edn., 1967; postgrad. internship program in spl. Edn. Adminstrn., 1970; Ed.D., U. Houston, 1973. Prof. ednl. psychology dept. ednl. psychology U. Minn., Mpls., 1973-85; pres. Sch. Resource Ctr., Austin, Tex., 1985-90; tchr. Llano Pub. Schs., 1988-97; dir. Walter Resources, 1998—. Chmn. State Adv. Coun. for Inservice Tng. Regular Classroom Tchrs., 1977-79; cons. spl. ednl. various sch. dists., state depts. and agys. Editl. cons.: Jour. Ednl. Psychology, 1979, Reading Rsch. Quar., 1982; assoc. editor: Exceptional Children, 1979-84; assoc. editor Teaching Exceptional Children, 1985-89; contbr. articles to profl. jours., papers to profl. confs. Named Minn. Spl. Educator of Yr., 1978; recipient Svc. award Internat. Coun. Exceptional Children, 1978; HEW Office of Human Devel. Svcs. grantee, 1976-80; Dept. Edn. contractee, 1980-83 Mem. Coun. for Exceptional Children, Nat. Assn. Children with Learning Disabilities (dir. Minn. chpt. 1978-80), Nat. Assn. Retarded Citizens, AAUP, Assn. Supervision and Curriculum Devel. Home and Office: 7108 Running Rope Austin TX 78731-2128

WALTER, W. EDWARD, hotel executive, corporate financial executive; Ptnr. Trammell Crow Residential Co.; pres. Bailey Capital Corp.; from sr. v.p. acquisitions to exec. v.p., CFO Host Marriott Corp., Bethesda, Md., 1996 2003, exec. v.p., 2003—, CFO, 2003—. Office: Host Marriott Corp 6903 Rockledge Drive Ste 1500 Bethesda MD 20817

WALTERMIRE, THOMAS ALLEN, financial executive; b. Balt., Oct. 30, 1949; s. William Everett and Emma (Barack) W.; m. Shirley Jean Flinn, June 16, 1972; children: Todd Andrew Barack Waltermire, Kevin Adam Davis Waltermire, Heidi Alexis Nicole Waltermire. BS, Ohio State U., 1971; MBA, Harvard U., 1974. With B.F. Goodrich Co., Akron, Ohio, 1974-89, mgr. corp. fin., 1975-76; asst. treas., 1977-78; asst. contr., 1978-80; dir. planning, analysis chem. group B.F. Goodrich Co., Cleve, 1980, dir. purchasing div., 1981-84, v.p. comml. svcs., 1984, pres. elastomers and latex div. Cleve., 1985-89, v.p. investor rels., 1989-97; COO Geon Co., 1997-99, pres., CEO, 1999-2000; pres. & CEO PolyOne (Geon and M.A. Hanna merger), Cleveland, 2000—. Mem. pres.'s adv. bd. Baldwin Wallace Coll., Cleve., 1983-86; bd. dirs. Community Hall Found., Akron, 1978-82, 1988—. Mem. Internat. Inst. Synthetic Rubber Producers (pres., bd. dirs. N.Am. sect. 1986-89, pres. 1989), Inda Assn. of Nonwovens Industry (vice chmn. 1988-89), Fairlawn County Club. Republican. Methodist. Address: Poly One Ste 36-5000 200 Public Sq Cleveland OH 44114-2304

WALTERS, ALAN WAYNE, judge; b. Georgetown, S.C., Feb. 8, 1963; s. Burl T. and Emily W. Walters; m. Susan Welch, May 13, 1989; children: Robert Alan, Jason Scott. AS in Criminal Justice, Horry-Georgetown Tech. Coll., Conway, S.C., 1996; BS in Edn., So. Ill. U., Carbondale, 1999. Mem. investigations divsn. Georgetown County Sheriff's Dept., 1985-93; law enforcement ofcl. Andrews (S.C.) Police Dept., 1993-94; mem. investigations/crime prevention divsn. Georgetown Police Dept., 1994—2002; summary ct. judge Georgetown County Summary Ct., 2002—. Chmn. Georgetown County Rep. Com., 1997-99, Black River Dist. coun. Boy Scouts Am., 2000—; vice chmn. Georgetown County Easter Seals, 1997—; elder Georgetown Presbyn. Ch., 1998-00; bd. dirs. Horry-Georgetown Tech. Alumni Assn., 1998-2001, Coastal Carolina coun. Boy Scouts Am., 2000—. Named State Dep. Sheriff of Yr., S.C. Sheriff's Assn., 1992. Mem. S.C. Law Enforcement Officers Assn. (State Law Enforcement Officer of Yr. 1996), Rotary (pres. Georgetown chpt. 1999-00, asst. dir. gov. 2002-, Pub. Safety Officer of Yr. award 1992). Home: 306 Kaufman St Georgetown SC 29440-3814 E-mail: alnwltrs@aol.com.

WALTERS, BARBARA ANN, television journalist; b. Boston, Mass., Sept. 25, 1931; d. Lou and Dena (Selett) Walters; m. Lee Gruber, 1963 (div. 1976); m. Merv Adelson, 1986 (div. 1992); 1 child, Jacqueline. BA in English, Sarah Lawrence Coll., 1953; LHD (hon.), Ohio State U., Marymount Coll., 1975, Wheaton Coll., 1983, Temple U., Hofstra U., Ben-Gurion U. Former producer WNBC-TV; former writer CBS News; then with Stas. WPIX and CBS-TV; writer, reporter-at-large Today Show, 1961—63, regular panel mem., 1964—74, co-host, 1974—76; moderator syndicated program Not For Women Only, 1972—76; newscaster ABC Evening News (now ABC World News Tonight), 1976—78; host The Barbara Walters Spls., 1976—; co-host ABC TV news show 20/20, 1984—99, anchor, 1999—; co-exec. prodr., co-owner, co-host The View, ABC, N.Y.C., 1997—; exec. prodr. The Iyanla Show, 2001. Contbr. NBC Radio Network. Contbr. ABC programs Issues and Answers; author: (book) How to Talk With Practically Anybody About Practically Anything, 1970; contbr. to Reader's Digest, Good Housekeeping, Family Weekly; appeared in (films) At Long Last Love, 1975, Crazy Mama, 1975, Goin' South, 1978, Rock 'n' Roll High School, 1979, In God We Trust, 1980. Named Woman Yr. Comm., 1974, Broadcaster Yr., Internat. Radio and TV Soc., 1975, Woman Yr., Theta Sigma Phi; named one of Am.'s 75 Most Important Women, Ladies' Home Jour., 1970, 200 Leaders Future, Time Mag., 1974, 10 Women Decade, Ladies' Home Jour., 1979, Most Important Women 1979, Roper Report, 1979, Women Most Admired Am. People, Gallup Poll, 1982, Am.'s 100 Most Important Women, Ladies' Home Jour., 1983, Women Most Admired Am. People, Gallup Poll, 1984; named to 100 Women of Accomplishment, Harper's Bazaar, 1967, 1971, Hall Fame, Acad. TV Arts and Scis., 1990; recipient Award Yr., Nat. Assn. TV Program Execs., 1975, Emmy award, Nat. Acad. TV Arts and Scis., 1975, 1980, 1982, 1983, Mass Media award, Am. Jewish Com. Inst. Human Relations, 1975, Barbara Walters' Coll. Scholarship in Broadcast Journalism established in her honor, Ill. Broadcasters Assn., 1975, Matrix award, N.Y. Women in Comm., 1977, Hubert H. Humphrey Freedom prize, Anti Defamation League B'nai B'rith, 1978, Pres.'s award, Overseas Press Club, 1988, Lowell Thomas award, Marist Coll., 1990, Lifetime Achievement award, Internat. Women's Media Found., 1991, saluted, Am. Mus. Moving Image, 1992, Lifetime Achievement award, Women's Project and Prodn., 1993, honored for contbn. to broadcast journalism, Mus. TV and Radio, 1996, George Foster Peabody award for her interview with actor Christopher Reeve, 1996, Muse award, NY Women in Film and TV, 1997, Lifetime Achievement award, Daytime Emmy Awards, 2000, Nat. Acad. TV Arts and Scis., 2000, Silver Satellite award, Am. Women Radio and TV. Office: 20/20 147 Columbus Ave Fl 10 New York NY 10023-5900 also: The View 320 W 66th St New York NY 10023-6304*

WALTERS, BETTE JEAN, lawyer; b. Norristown, Pa., Sept. 5, 1946; BA, U. Pitts., 1967; JD, Temple U., 1970, LLM in Taxation, 1974. Bar: Pa. 1970, U.S. Dist. Ct. (ea. dist.) Pa. 1971. Law clk., assoc. William R. Cooper, Lansdale, Pa., 1969-72; spl. asst. to pub. defender Montgomery County (Pa.), 1973; pvt. practice North Wales, Pa., 1972-73; assoc. counsel Alco Standard Corp., Valley Forge, Pa., 1973-79, group counsel mfg., 1979-83; v.p., gen. counsel, sec. Alco Industries, Inc., Valley Forge, 1983—2003. Mem. corp. sponsors com. Zool. Soc. of Phila.; adv. environ. studies program U. Pitts.; bd. visitors Beasley Sch. Law Temple U. Mem. ABA, DAR, Pa. Bar Assn., Montgomery County Bar Assn. Republican. Personal E-mail: b.j.walters@verizon.net.

WALTERS, BILL, former state senator, lawyer; b. Paris, Ark., Apr. 17, 1943; s. Peter Louis and Elizabeth Cecelia (Wilhelm) W.; m. Joyce Leslie Garrett Moore, Jan. 9, 1964 (div. 1970); children: Jamie, Sherry Ann; m. Shirley Ann Dixon, Aug. 20, 1971; 1 child, Sandra. BS, U. Ark., 1966, JD, 1971. Bar: Ark. 1971, U.S. Dist. Ct. Ark. 1971. Asst. prosecuting atty. 12th Jud. Dist. Ark., Ft. Smith, 1971-74; pvt. practice Greenwood, Ark., 1975—; mem. Ark. Senate, Little Rock, 1982-2000. Bd. dirs., sec.-treas. Mineral Owners Collective Assn. Inc., Greenwood; v.p., bd. dirs. Sebastian County Abstract & Title Ins. Co., Greenwood and Ft. Smith, Ark.; mem. Ark. Real Estate Commn., Ark. Abstract and Title Commn. Committeeman Rep. Ctrl. Com. Ark., Ft. Smith, 1980; search pilot CAP, Ft. Smith. Decorated Silver Medal of Valor; recipient Cert. of Honor Justice for Crime's Victims, 1983. Mem. Ark. Bar Assn., South Sebastian County Bar Assn. (pres. 1991-94), Profl. Landmen's Assn. Roman Catholic. Home: PO Box 280 Greenwood AR 72936-0280 Office: 1405 W Center Greenwood AR 72936-3200 Office Phone: 479-996-2122. E-mail: bwalters@waltlaw.net.

WALTERS, DAVID MCLEAN, lawyer; b. Cleve., Apr. 4, 1917; s. William L. and Marguerite (McLean) W.; m. Betty J. Latimer, Mar. 25, 1939 (dec. 1983); 1 child, Susan Patricia (Mrs. James Edward Smith); m. Rebecca Brewer, Feb. 14, 1991. BA, Baldwin-Wallace Coll., 1938, LHD (hon.); LLB, Cleve. Sch. Law, 1943; JD, U. Miami, 1950; LHD (hon.), St. Thomas of Villanova U. Bar: DC 1950, Fla. 1950, Fed. 1950. Judge adminstrv. practices US Dept. Justice, Washington, 1940-50; sr. law ptnr. firm Walters & Costanzo, Miami, Fla., 1950-80; of counsel firm Walters, Costanzo, Russell, Zyne, 1980-85. Amb. to Vatican, 1976-78; fellow internat. medicine, bd. advisors Med. Sch., Boston U., 1985. Chmn. Fla. Harbor Pilot Commn., 1952-54, City of Miami Seaport Commn., 1953-54, Nat. Leukemia Soc., 1965-66, Archbishops Charities Dr., 1975-76; spl. bond counsel Dade County, 1957-58; gen. counsel Dade County Port Authority, 1957-58; vice-chmn. Nat. Dem. Fin. Coun., 1960-77; mem. Gov.'s Adv. Bd. on Health and Rehabilitative Svc., 1976-77; sec.-treas. Inter-Am. Ctr. Authority, 1960-74; bd. advisor St. Thomas Law Sch., 1985-88; personal rep. Pres. Reagan F.D.R. Meml. Commn., 1985; bd. dir. Barry U.; chmn. bd. trustees Variety Children's Hosp.; pres. Miami Children's Hosp. Found., 1980—; founder, pres. emeritus Miami Children's Hosp. Found., 1980-2002; life trustee Gregorian Inst. Found., Rome. Served with Counter Intelligence Corps., US Army, 1943-46. Decorated Bronze Star medal., Knight of the Grandcross, Order St. Gregory the Great; recipient Silver medallion NCCJ, Resolution of Commendation award for civic contbn. Fla. Legislature, 1988. Mem. Am., Fla., Fed., DC, Interam. bar assns., Am. Assn. Knights of Malta (v.p.), Serra Club, Sovereign Mil. Order Malta (master knight 1975—, exec. com. papal visit to US 1987), Omicron Delta Kappa, Lambda Chi Alpha. Democrat. Roman Catholic. Home: 9202 SW 78th Pl Miami FL 33156-7590 also: 5 St Helens Marine Parade Sandycove Dublin Ireland Office: 3000 SW 62nd Ave Miami FL 33155-3065

WALTERS, GEORGE JOHN, oral and maxillofacial surgeon; b. Balt., June 16, 1956; s. George John Sr. and Henrietta Jean (Parker) W.; m. Melanie Ann Goodreau, June 23, 1989. BS, Loyola Coll., 1978; DDS, U. Md., 1983; postgrad., John Hopkins, 1991, U. Pa., 1992, postgrad., 1993. Cert. argon laser. Rsch. asst. dept. otolaryngology The Johns Hopkins Sch. Medicine, Balt., 1978-79; ind. learning ctr. technician Balt. Coll. Dental Surgery, Dental Sch., U. Md., 1980-81; audio-visual technician U. Md. Law Sch., Balt., 1981-82, res. material circulation asst., 1982-83; resident gen. practice residency York (Pa.) Hosp., 1983-84; resident dept. anesthesia The Med. Coll. of Pa. and Hosp., Phila., 1984-85; resident dept. dentistry div. oral and maxillofacial surgery U. Md. Med. System, Balt., 1985-89, chief adminstrv. resident dept. dentistry, 1988-89; assoc. in oral and maxillofacial surgery Miller Oral Surgery and Pa. Jaw Treatment Ctr., Harrisburg, Pa., 1989-91; ptnr. Oral and Maxillofacial Surgery, Panama City, Fla., 1991-95; individual practice oral and maxillofacial surgery Panama City, Fla., 1995—. Explorer advisor for health career explorer post Balt. Coll. Dental Surgery, Dental Sch., U. Md., 1981, dental rsch. student com., 1982, vol. for recruitment of minority students, 1983; testifier Sen. House Com. on Medicaid Funding, State House, Annapolis, Md., 1987-88; lectr. Gulf Coast C.C., 1991—. Copntbr. to profl. jours. Health vol. overseas Nepal Mission for Cleft Lip and Palate, 1989; vol. Guatemala Med. Mission Cleft Lip and Palate, 1994; bd. dirs. Am. Cancer Soc. Bay County, 1996-97; chmn. Cath. sharing appeal St. Bernadette's Ch., Panama City, 1996-98, eucharistic min.; lectr. St. Romalotto's Parish. John Hopkins fellow 1989. Mem. ADA, Am. Assn. Oral and Maxillofacial Surgery, Mid. Atlantic Soc. Oral and Maxillofacial Surgery, Bay County Dental Soc. (sec./treas. 1997-98, v.p. 1998-99), Fla. Dental Soc., N.W. Dental Soc. Fla., Fla. Soc. Oral and Maxillofacial Surgery, Gorgas Odontological Soc., Rotary, Bay County Civil War Roundtable, Gamma Pi Delta. Roman Catholic. Avocations: golf, boating, baseball, travel, reading. Office: 2202 State Ave Ste 200 Panama City FL 32405-4582 Home: 1906 Dewitt St Panama City FL 32401-4049

WALTERS, GLEN ROBERT, banker; b. Mpls., Sept. 11, 1943; s. Sterling Thomas and Mildred Eunice (Parkinson) W.; m. Gail Elvira Engelsen, June 11, 1966; children — Nicole Marie, Brent Aaron, Hillary Renee. BA, U. Minn., Mpls., 1965, postgrad., 1965-67; banking degree, Stonier Grad. Sch. Banking, Rutgers U., New Brunswick, N.J., 1982. Comml. banker 1st Nat. Bank, Mpls., 1967-83, sr. v.p. human resources, 1983-90; sr. v.p. Firstar Bank Minn., Mpls., 1990-2001, US Bank, Mpls., 2001—. Served to sgt. USNG, 1967-73 Republican. Presbyterian. Office: US Bank 9633 Lyndale Ave S Minneapolis MN 55420

WALTERS, ISAAC CLAYTON, theater educator, director; b. Provo, Utah, Nov. 10, 1971; s. Lawrence Clayton Walters and Carol Jeane Thovy; m. Shannyn Sue Thompson, Aug. 16, 1994; children: Christopher Clayton, Michael Paul. BA, Brigham Young U., 1997; MFA, Columbia U., 2001. Adj. prof. Utah Valley State Coll., Orem, Utah, 2000—01; asst. prof. Ind. U., South Bend, Ind., 2001—. Dir.: (plays) Barrabbag, 2000, Images of the Soul, 2001, Hayfever, 2002. Campaign mgr. Larry Walters for Utah Legis., Provo, Utah, 2000. Mem.: Soc. Stage Dirs. and Choreographers, Network Ensemble Theaters. Mem. LDS Ch. Home: 1067 Woodward Ave South Bend IN 46616 Office: Indiana Univ South Bend 1700 Mishawaka Ave South Bend IN 46634-7111

WALTERS, JANE, state agency administrator; MusB, BA in Music History, Rhodes Coll.; MA in Counseling, U. Memphis; PhD in Sch. Adminstrn., Duke U. Tchr., counselor Messick H.S., Memphis, asst. prin.; asst. dir. computer svcs. Memphis City Schs.; prin. Craigmont Jr. H.S., 1974-79, Craigmont Jr. and Sr. H.S., 1979-95; 21st commr. edn. State Dept. Edn., Nashville, 1995—99; exec. dir. Ptnrs. in Pub. Edn., 1999—; prin. Grizzlies Acad., Memphis, 2003—. Adv. com. edn. depts. Rhodes Coll, Christian Brothers Com., Tenn. Arts Acad.; cons. College Bd. advanced placement program. Grant reader NEA; mem. Goals for Memphis Edn. Com.; bd. dirs. World Affairs Coun, Nat. Coun. Christians and Jews, Memphis Coun. Internat. Visitors, Memphis Youth Symphony, Am. Cancer Soc., Memphis chpt. Office: 204 North Second St Memphis TN 38103

WALTERS, JEFFERSON BROOKS, musician, retired real estate broker; b. Dayton, Ohio, Jan. 20, 1922; s. Jefferson Brooks and Mildred Frances (Smith) W.; m. Mary Elizabeth Espey, Apr. 6, 1963 (dec. July 22, 1983); children: Dinah Christine Basson, Jefferson Brooks; m. Carol Elaine Clayton Gillette, Feb. 19, 1984. Student, U. Dayton, 1947. Composer, cornetist, Dayton, 1934—; real estate broker, 1948-88; ret., 1988. Condr., composer choral, solo voice settings of psalms and poetry Alfred Lord Tennyson; composer Crossing the Bar (meml. performances U.S. Navy band), 1961; composer The Yorktown Grand March (Good Citizenship medal SAR, 1988). Founder Am. Psalm Choir, 1965; apptd. deferred giving officer Kettering (Ohio) Med. Ctr., 1982-85. Served with USCGR, 1942-45, PTO, ETO. Mem.: SAR (life), Masons (32d degree). Brethren Ch. Home: 4113 Roman Dr Dayton OH 45415-2423

WALTERS, JESSE RAYMOND, JR., state supreme court justice; b. Rexburg, Idaho, Dec. 26, 1938; s. Jesse Raymond and Thelma Rachael (Hodgson) W.; m. Harriet Payne, May 11, 1959; children: Craig T., Robyn, J. Scott. Student, Ricks Coll., 1957-58; BA in Polit. Sci., U. Idaho, 1961, JD, 1963; postgrad., U. Washington, 1962; LLM, U. Va., 1990. Bar: Idaho 1963; U.S. Dist. Ct. Idaho 1964, U.S. Ct. Appeals (9th cir.) 1970. Law clk. to chief justice Idaho Supreme Ct., 1963-64; solo practice Boise, Idaho, 1964-77; atty. Idaho senate, Boise, 1965; dist. judge 4th Jud. Dist., Idaho, 1977-82, adminstrv. dist. judge, 1981-82; chief judge Idaho Ct. Appeals, Boise, 1982-97. Chmn. magistrate's commn. 4th jud. dist.; chmn. Supreme Ct. mem. services; chmn. Criminal Pattern Jury Instrn. Com.; mem. Civil Pattern Jury Instrn. Com. Republican committeeman Boise, 1975-77; mem. Ada County Rep. Ctrl. Com., 1975-77. Mem. Idaho Bar Assn. (bankruptcy com.), Idaho Adminstrv. Judges Assn., ABA, Am. Judicature Soc. (dir.), Assn. Trial Lawyers Am., Idaho Trial Layers Assn., Coun. Chief Judges Ct. Appeals (pres. 1994-95), Boise Estate Planning Coun., Jaycees (nat. dir. 1969-70, pres. Boise chpt. 1966-67), Lions, Elks, Eagles. Mem. Lds Ch. Office: Supreme Ct Idaho PO Box 83720 Boise ID 83720-3720

WALTERS, JOHN P. federal official; BA, Mich. State U.; MA, U. Toronto. Acting asst. dir. and program officer div. edn. programs NEH, 1982—85; asst. to sec. U.S. Dept. Edn., 1985—88; dep. dir. supply reduction Office Nat. Drug Control Policy, Washington, 1991—93; pres. Philanthropy Roundtable, 1996—2001; dir. Office Nat. Drug Control Policy, Washington, 2001—. Vis. fellow Hudson Inst., 1993; instr. polit. sci. Mich. State U., Boston Coll. Co-author: (book) Body Count: Moral Poverty and How to Win America's War Against Crime and Drugs. Pres. New Citizenship Program. Office: Exec Office of Pres Office Nat Drug Control Policy 750 17th St NW Washington DC 20503

WALTERS, JOHN SHERWOOD, retired newspaperman; b. Junction City, Ark., May 15, 1917; s. John Thomas and Cora (McBride) W.; m. Claire Dailey, June 1, 1941; children: Elizabeth Claire, Mary Dailey (dec.). BA, La. Tech. Inst., 1939; MA, La. State U., 1941. Editor Ruston (La.) Daily Leader, 1940; reporter Baton Rouge Morning Adv., 1941; rating examiner Jacksonville Naval Air Sta., 1941-42; reporter Fla. Times-Union, Jacksonville, 1943, 44-53, city editor, 1953-60; exec. editor Times-Union and Jacksonville Jour., 1960-78, asso. pub., 1978-82, ret., 1982. Asst. prof. journalism La. Tech. Inst., 1943-44; mem. jud. Nominating Commn., 1st Dist. Ct. Appeals of Fla. Bd. dirs. Duval County chpt. A.R.C., chmn., 1966-67; charter trustee U. North Fla. Found., Inc., pres., 1973-75; chmn. council advisers U. North Fla., 1975; bd. dirs. Health Planning Council, N.E. Fla. Cancer Program, Jacksonville Blood Bank. Mem. Am. Soc. Newspaper Editors, Fla. Soc. Newspaper Editors (pres. 1971-72), Alpha Lambda Tau, Sigma Delta Chi. Clubs: Rotarian (Jacksonville) (sec. 1970-71, pres. 1971-72); Timuquana Country. Democrat. Methodist. Home: Apt 19 2950 Saint Johns Ave Jacksonville FL 32205-8719

WALTERS, JOHNNIE MCKEIVER, lawyer; b. Hartsville, S.C., Dec. 20, 1919; s. Tommie Ellis and Lizzie Lee (Grantham) W.; m. Donna Lucile Hall, Sept. 1, 1947; children: Donna Dianne Walters Gent, Lizbeth Kathern Walters Kukorowski, Hilton Horace, John Roy. AB, Furman U., 1942, LLD, 1973; LLB, U. Mich., 1948. Bar: Mich. 1948, N.Y. 1955, S.C. 1961, D.C. 1973. Atty. office chief counsel IRS, Washington, 1949-53; asst. mgr. tax div. law dept. Texaco, Inc., N.Y.C., 1953-61; ptnr. firm Geer, Walters & Demo, Greenville, SC, 1961-69; asst. atty. gen. tax div. Dept. Justice, Washington, 1969-71; commr. IRS, 1971-73; ptnr. firm Hunton & Williams, Washington, 1973-79, Leatherwood Walker Todd & Mann, P.C., Greenville, 1979-95; exec. v.p., gen. counsel Colonial Trust Co., 1996—. Bd. dirs. Textile Hall Corp., Greenville, Colonial Trust Co. Mem. S.C. Coun. on Competitiveness, 1987-91. With USAF, 1942—45. Fellow Am. Coll. Tax Counsel (founding regent), Am. Coll. Trust and Estate Counsel, Am. Bar Found., S.C. Bar Found. (bd. dirs. 1988-92); mem. ABA (taxation sect.), S.C. Bar (chmn. taxation sect. 1983-84), Rotary (pres. local club 1968-69). Republican. Baptist. Office: Colonial Trust Co PO Box 2817 Greenville SC 29602-2817 Home: 125 Hummingbird Ridge Greenville SC 29605-5305 Office Phone: 864-370-0737.

WALTERS, JUDITH RICHMOND, neuropharmacologist; b. Concord, N.H., June 20, 1944; d. Samuel Smith and Hazel Albertina (Stewart) Richmond; m. James Wilson Walters, Aug. 23, 1969 (div. 1992); children: James Richmond, Gregory Stewart, Douglas Powers. BA, Mt. Holyoke Coll., 1966; PhD, Yale U., 1972. Postdoctoral fellow dept. psychiatry Yale U. Med. Sch., New Haven, rsch. assoc. dept. pharmacology, asst. prof. dept. psychiatry; unit chief neurophysiol. pharmacology sect. exptl. therapeutics br. Nat. Inst. Neurol. Disease and Stroke, Bethesda, Md., 1976-81, sect. chief physiol. neuropharmacology sect., 1981—. Mem. sci. adv. bd. Hereditary Disease Found., L.A., 1977-80, 82-86, Tourette Syndrome Assn., 1992—; mem. bd. sci. counselors Nat. Inst. on Alcohol Abuse and Alcoholism, 1992-95; mem. Inst. of Medicine Com. to Raise the Profile of Rsch. on Substance Abuse, 1995-96. Sect. editor Neuroscience.net, 1996—; contbr. more than 100 articles on neuropharmacology and neurophysiology to profl. jours. Recipient NIH Dir.'s award, 1994. Mem. Am. Soc. Pharmacology and Exptl. Therapeutics, Soc. for Neurosci. (mem. com. 1995-98). Home: 3615 Littledale Rd Kensington MD 20895-3435 Office: NIH Bldg 10 Rm 5C106 Bethesda MD 20892

WALTERS, KATHY, elementary school educator; b. Follansbee, W.Va., Nov. 4, 1945; d. Albert and Mary Ezzi; m. Tom Walters; children: Matt Paul, Erin Elizabeth. Tchr. Kyren Del Cealo Sch., Tempe, Ariz., 1994—. Republican. Roman Catholic. Avocations: swimming, dog walking. Home: 1930 E Calle De Arcos Tempe AZ 85284

WALTERS, LAWRENCE CHARLES, advertising executive; b. Cin., Apr. 1, 1948; s. Lawrence Simpson and Mary Josephine (Koerner) W.; m. Ann Morley Reifenrath, Jan. 15, 1983. Assoc. in Advt., U. Cin., 1969. Art dir. J. Walter Thompson, Chgo., 1972-78; sr. art dir. Needham Harper and Steers, Chgo., 1978-81; advt. creative dir. ACOM, Quaker, Chgo., 1981-83; co. group creative dir. Tatham, Laird, Kudner, Chgo., 1983-99; exec. creative dir. Euro R.S.C.G. Tatham, Chgo., 1996—. With the USMC, 1966-69. Democrat. Roman Catholic. Avocations: music writing, white water canoe racing, tennis, water color painting. Office: Euro RSCG Tatham 36 E Grand Ave Chicago IL 60611-3506

WALTERS, MARK DOUGLAS, obstetrician, gynecologist; b. Toledo, July 21, 1954; s. Donald Walters; m. Virginia Walters; children: Samantha, Maxwell, Zoe. BS in biology, U. Cincinnati, 1976, MD, Ohio State U., 1980. Cert. Am. Bd. Ob-Gyn. Intern Tufts U. Sch. Medicine, Boston, 1980—81, resident in ob-gyn., 1981—84; asst. prof. dept. ob-gyn. U. Tex. Health Sci. Ctr., San Antonio, 1984—90; assoc. prof. dept. reproductive biology and ob-gyn. Case Western Reserve U. Sch. Medicine, Cleve., 1990—93; med. dir. Women's Health Ctr. U. Hospitals of Cleve., 1990—93; chief gynecology sect. VA Med. Ctr., Cleveland, 1992—93; vice-chmn. dept. ob-gyn., head sect. gen. gynecology, dir. urogynecology The Cleve. Clinic Found., 1993—, dir. fellowship program in urogynecology/reconstructive pelvic surgery, 1997—. Author: (book) Clinical Urogynecology, 1993, Urogynecology and Reconstructive Pelvic Surgery, 2d edit., 1999. Recipient Ann. Resident Tchg. award, MetroHealth Med. Ctr., 1996, 1999, 2000, 2002. Fellow: Am. Coll. of Obstetricians and Gynecologists; mem.: Cleve. Soc. of Ob-gyn., Soc. of Gynecologic Surgeons, Am. Urogynecology Soc., Jour. of Gynecologic Surgery (editl. bd.), Internat. Urogynecology Jour. (editl. bd.). Office: Cleve Clinic Found Dept Ob-gyn 9500 Euclid Ave Desk A81 Cleveland OH 44195 Office Phone: 216-445-6586. E-mail: walterm@ccf.org.

WALTERS, MATTHEW PAUL, recreational facility executive, consultant; b. Columbus, Ohio, Aug. 3, 1977; s. Thomas Edward and Kathy Ann Walters. BA, Ottawa U., 2002; MBA in concentration mktg., U. La Verne. Mktg., and pub. rels. Artist Direct, Encino, Calif., 1998—2000; owner Adventure Ventures, Tempe, Ariz., 1998—. Vol. plan creator Good Samaritan Hosp., Phoenix, 2001. Mem.: IndUS Entrepreneur. R-Liberal. Roman Catholic. Avocations: running, basketball. Personal E-mail: matt.walters@ptk.org.

WALTERS, MILTON JAMES, investment banker; b. Hornell, N.Y., May 21, 1942; s. James Henry and Frances Eleanor (Simmons) W.; m. Caroline Houck, May 24, 1963; children: Melissa Ann, Gregory Thomas, Timothy Allen. BA, Hamilton Coll., 1964. Trainee Mfrs. Hanover, 1964-65; with A.G. Becker Paribas Inc., N.Y.C., 1965-84; mng. dir. Smith Barney, N.Y.C., 1978—84, Prudential Securities, N.Y.C., 1997-99; pres. Tri-River Capital, 1988—. Bd. dirs. Quest Products, Decision One, Fredericks of Hollywood, Sun Healthcare Group. Trustee Hamilton Coll., Clinton, N.Y., 1983-88, Friends Acad., Locust Valley, N.Y., 1981-91; pres. 16 Sutton Pl. Apt. Corp. Mem. Econ. Club N.Y., Mill River Club. Republican. Office: Tri-River Capital PO Box 128 New York NY 10150-0128 Office Phone: 212-581-5777. E-mail: mjw@tririv.com.

WALTERS, PHILIP RAYMOND, foundation executive; b. Frankfort, Ind., Jan. 26, 1938; s. Raymond and Ruth Edna (Grimes) W.; m. Sharon Pearl Wilfong, May 31, 1958 (div. Nov. 1992); children: Raymond (dec.), Robert, Sharon Ruth; m. Candace Gina Oden, Jan. 29, 1994. BSBA, Olivet Nazarene Coll., 1959; JD, Ind. U., Indpls., 1969; postgrad., NYU, 1969-70. Bar: Ind. 1969, U.S. Dist. Ct. (so. dist.) Ind. 1969. Co-corp. counsel Ind. Farm Bur. Ins., Indpls., 1975-79; dir. gift and estate planning Orlando (Fla.) Regional Healthcare Found., 1991-96; assoc. v.p. planned giving Arthritis Found., Atlanta, 1996—. Dep. atty. gen. State of Ind., Indpls.; planned giving officer Wheaton (Ill.) Coll.; campaign dir. Ketchum, Inc., Pitts.; dir. planned giving Presbyn. Sch. Christian Edn., Richmond, Va.; presenter in field. Contbr. articles to profl. jours. Mem.: Assn. Fundraising Profls., Nat. Com. on Planned Giving. Republican. Presbyterian. Avocations: golf, auto racing, reading. Home: 897 Cutler Rd Longwood FL 32779-3525

WALTERS, RITA, councilwoman; b. Chgo., Aug. 14, 1930; children: David, Susan, Philip. BA, Shaw U., Raleigh, N.C., 1975; MBA, UCLA, 1984. Tchr. adult divsn. L.A. Sch. Dist., 1975-79; instr. Ednl. Founds. Dept. Calif. State U., L.A., 1981; pres. L.A. Bd. Edn., 1985-88; city councilwoman L.A., 1991—. Chair Arts Health and Humanities Com., Public Works, Budget & Fin. Office: City Hall Rm 508 200 N Main St Los Angeles CA 90012-4110

WALTERS, ROBERT ANCIL, physicist, mathematician; b. Russell Springs, Ky., Mar. 12, 1915; s. Robert Edmund Lee and Talitha Margaret (Wilson) W.; m. Etha Jane McKinley, Feb. 2, 1943; 1 child, Robert Ancil II; m. Sandra Faye Roy, June 29, 1969; 1 child, Forrest Wayne. BS, Western Ky. U., 1941; postgrad., George Washington U., 1943-45, Agrl. Grad. Sch., 1947-48, Am. U., 1951-52. H.S. asst. prin. Russell County Bd. Edn., 1941-42; physicist, head exterior ballistics U.S. Naval Weapons Lab., Dahlgren, Va., 1942-59; pres. Walters Ins. and Investment Counselor, Dahlgren, 1948-80; engr., head systems planning U.S. Naval Space Surveillance, Dahlgren, Va., 1959-69; R&D specialist, physicist interdisplinary math. cons. U.S. Naval Warfare Lab., Dahlgren, 1969-75. Pres. Navel Weapons Lab. Fed. Credit Union, Dahlgren, 1968-74; bd. examiners Potomac River Naval Com., Washington, 1953-56; biology lab. instr. Western Ky. U., Bowling Green, 1935-36. Chmn. Old Dominion Eye Bank, Richmond, Va., 1975-76; co-chair Dem. Party, Ky., 1937-42; pres. Nat. Fedn. Fed. Employees, Washington, 1963-69. Recipient Nat. Quality award Nat. Assn. Life Underwriters, 1976; named Ky. Col., gov. of Ky., 1976, Outstanding Citizen of Yr., VFW, 1981, Guest of Honor King George County Fall Festival, 1994. Mem.: Lions Internat. (dep. dist. gov. 1976—77, Disting. Svc. award 1975, Melvin Jones fellow 2001). Baptist. Home: 5460 Potomac Dr PO Box 877 Dahlgren VA 22448-0877 Office Phone: 540-663-3300. Personal E-mail: bobwalterssr@aol.com.

WALTERS, ROBERT F. diversified financial services company executive; Sr. v.p., chief info. officer John Hancock Life Ins. Co., Boston, 1995—2001, exec. v.p., 2001—; exec. v.p. and chief info. officer John Hancock Fin. Svcs., Inc., Boston, 2001—. Bd. dirs. Essex Corp., John Hancock Subs. LLC. Office: John Hancock Fin Svcs Inc John Hancock Pl PO Box 111 Boston MA 02117

WALTERS, RONALD OGDEN, mortgage banker; b. Holcombe, Wis., July 13, 1939; s. Ogden Eugene and Josephine Ann (Hennekens) W.; m. Margaret Ellen Weisheipl, July 14, 1962; children— Laurie, Cheryl, Michael, Patrick Student, U. Wis., 1959-62. Mgr. Thorp Fin., LaCrosse, Wis., 1962-65, regional mgr. Milw., 1965-69, ITT Consumer Fin. Corp., Milw., 1969-74, sr. v.p. Brookfield, Wis., 1974-90, exec. v.p. adminstrn., 1990-92; CEO Ideal Fin. Corp., Brookfield, 1993—, USA Funding Corp., Brookfield, Wis., 1993—. Mem. Wis. Fin. Services Assn. (pres. 1980) Republican. Roman Catholic. Avocations: boating, fishing, hunting. Home: 812 Back Bay Delafield WI 53018-1528 also: 17035 W Wisconsin Ave Brookfield WI 53005-5734 E-mail: rowmew@earthlink.net.

WALTERS, ROSS A. federal judge; Magistrate judge U.S. Dist. Ct. (so. dist.) Iowa, 1994—. Office: US Courthouse Rm 440 123 E Walnut St Des Moines IA 50309-2035

WALTERS, SHERWOOD GEORGE, management consultant, educator; b. Detroit, May 9, 1926; s. George Henry and Helen (Parker) Walters; m. Alexandra Sielcken, Sept. 4, 1952; children: Margaret Taylor Clifford, Karen Chapin, George Alexander II, Virginia Sherwood McFee. BA cum laude, W. Md. Coll., 1949; MS, Columbia U., 1950; MBA with distinction, Columbia U. Grad. Sch. Bus., 1953; PhD honors scholar, cert. specialist in Latin Am. affairs, NYU, 1960. Assoc. prof. econ. sociology Coll. Bus. Econ., Lehigh U., Bethlehem, Pa., 1950-60; exec. v.p., dir. ctrs., retail planning mgr. Mobil Oil, NYC, 1960-65; exec. officer, mktg. dir. Gen. Tire & Rubber Internat. Plastics Co., Chem. Plastics Divsn., Akron, Ohio, 1965-70; prof. Rutgers U. Bus. Sch., Newark, 1970—93, prof. emeritus mgmt. studies, 1993—; founding dir. interfunctional mgmt. program Rutgers U., Newark, 1970-88, founding dir. PhD mgmt. program. Former rsch. dir. U.S. Small Bus. Devel. Coun.; former co-dir. E.I. DuPont de Nemours Interdisciplinary Rsch. Team; dir. mgmt., fin., sci. various internat. programs in Romania, PR, Sweden, No. Ireland, France, 1971—2004; evaluator, emissary Industry-Univ. Coop. Rsch. Ctrs. Program NSF, 1980—2004; evaluator, emissary Industry Univ. Coop. Rsch. Ctrs. Program, 1980—2004; cons. in field. Co-author: 7 books, including Marketing Management Veiwpoints, 2d edit., 1970, Mandatory Housing Finance Programs, 1975, Managing the Industry University Cooperative Research Centers: a Guide for Directors and Other Stakeholders, 1998; contbr. articles to profl. publs. and reports, 7 books, 3 seminars; prodr., dir., participant (radio program) Breakfast with the Walters, WEST/NBC, Easton, Pa., 1953—60. Adv. nat. rep. congl. com. on tax reform, 2001; chmn. NJ Gov. Pub. Utility Commn. Task Force, 1973—75, U./Indsl. Partnerships, John Von Neumann Ctr., Princeton U., 1986; hon. chmn. bus. adv. coun. Nat. Rep. Congl. Com., 2003—04; elder, trustee, co-dir. Christian Edn. Com. Topsail Presbyn. Ch., Hampstead, NC; co-dir. Christian Edn. Com.; bd. trustees Alumni Award, McDaniel Coll. 1st lt. Inf./Quatermaster Corps U.S. Army, 1944—47, ETO. Recipient Rep. Presdl. Legion of Merit, Excellence award, NSF, 2004, Bd. Trustees Alumni award, McDaniel Coll.; Spl. Studies scholar, Ford Found., Harvard U. Bus. Sch., Cambridge, Mass. Fellow: Am. Acad. Polit. Sci.; mem.: Newcomen Soc., Beta Gamma Sigma. Avocation: deep sea fishing. Home: 110 Topsail Watch Ln Hampstead NC 28443-2728 Office Phone: 910-329-0663. E-mail: s.george.walters@worldnet.att.net.

WALTERS, SUE FOX, business executive, accountant; b. Louisville, June 9, 1941; d. Thomas Burke and Reva Crick Fox; m. Hugh Alexander Walters (dec. 2001); children: Thomas Wade Walters, Alexandra Walters Ebling. Student, N.C. State U., Ky. Wesleyan Coll. Acct., paralegal for fin. instns. and firms; ct. adminstr. 45th Jud. Cir. Ct., Ky.; v.p., treas. Alexander and Assocs., CATV cons. firm, Greenville, Ky.; corp. adminstr., pub. corp. Bellevue, Wash.; sr. acctg. specialist Japanese/Am. automotive mfg. co., Bowling Green, Ky.; land

developer. Pres., Jr. Woman's Club Greenville, 1964-65, Woman's Club of Greenville, 1976-78; vice gov. 2nd dist. Ky. Fedn. Women's Clubs, 1980. Avocations: historical preservation, design, antiques, dogs, flying. Home: 151 N Main St Greenville KY 42345-1503

WALTERS, WILLIAM BEN, chemistry professor; b. Highland, Kans., Apr. 26, 1938; s. Ben Guthrie and Dolly Varden (Shaw) W.; m. Barbara Lulu Sternaman, Aug. 5, 1962; children: Katharine, David. AS, Highland Coll., 1957; BS, Kans. State U., 1960; PhD, U. Ill., 1964. Asst. prof. MIT, Cambridge, 1965-70; assoc. prof. chemistry U. Md., College Park, 1970-77, prof., 1977—, assoc. chmn. dept., 1982-86. Vis. prof. U. Louvain, Belgium, 1978; chair U. Senate, 1999-00; mem. physics adv. com. GANIL, 2003-2006. Recipient Nuclear Chemistry award Am. Chemical Soc., 2001; Guggenheim fellow Oxford U., 1986-87, Von Humboldt fellow Univ. Mainz, 2001-02. Mem. Am. Phys. Soc., European Phys. Soc., Am. Chem. Soc. (chmn. div. nuclear chemistry 1986), Rotary (bd. dirs. College Park 1990-91, 2000—). Office: U Md Dept Chemistry College Park MD 20742-0001 E-mail: wwalters@umd.edu.

WALTERS-LUCY, JEAN MARIE, personal growth educator, consultant; b. St. Louis, Feb. 7, 1941; d. James Blaine Davenport and Helen Elizabeth (Vosbrink) Davenport; m. John E. Walters, Sept. 26, 1959 (div. Oct. 1975); m. Marvin Lucy, Aug. 13, 1988; children: Steven John, Debra Jean, Jeffrey Scott, Cynthia Leigh. D of Metaphys., Coll. of Metaphys., 1977; cert. reality therapist, Inst. Reality Therapy, 1982; DDiv, Ch. of Metaphys., 1977, Universal Life Ch., 1980. Personal growth cons., St. Louis, 1978—; tchr. personal growth Maryville U., St. Louis, 1988—, St. Louis C.C., 1992—. Co-host McKenna-Walters Psychotherapy radio show, Sta. KXOK, 1985; pres., sr. cons. Psi Bus. Cons., St. Louis, 1980-85; founder, pres. Mind Dynamics, St. Louis, 1980-83; cons. Ctr. for Aging Studies, U. Mo., Kansas City, 1979-80; founder, v.p. Found. for Transformation, Spiritual Transformation Found. Author: (novels) Game of Life, Dreams & Symbology of Life, Look, Ma, I'm Flying, Choosing Health, Set Yourself Free, Evolution: The Master Plan; columnist: St. Louis Globe Dem., 1983—84, St. Louis Home Mag., 1985, St. Louis Fax Daily; prodr.: Transformation Radio; host: Transformation Radio, www.success-talk.com; prodr.: www.success-talk.com; columnist: Yes You Can, 1999—, host syndicated radio show: Positive Moments, 2000—01. Avocations: travel, writing, decorating, creative activities. E-mail: Jean@Spiritualtransformation.com.

WALTHER, DALE JAY, lawyer; b. Elko, Nev., Oct. 15, 1948; s. Harold V. and Beryl H. (Brand) W.; m. Kazue Mori, Sept. 25, 1975; children— Kent, Brian, Nolan, Lisa, Curtis, Katie. B.A., Northwestern U., 1972; postgrad., Notre Dame U. summer law program, Japan, 1974; J.D., Calif. Western Sch. Law, 1975. Bar: Alaska 1975. Assoc. Law Offices Murphy Clark, Anchorage, 1975-80; ptnr. Clark, Walther & Flanigan, Anchorage, 1980-93, ptnr. Walther & Flanigan, Anchorage, 1993— . Mem. Anchorage Bar Assn., Alaska Bar Assn., ABA, Order of Barristers, Am. Arbitration Assn., Phi Alpha Delta. Lodge: Elks. Home: PO Box 100428 Anchorage AK 99510-0428 Office: Walther & Flanigan 1029 W 3rd Ave Ste 250 Anchorage AK 99501

WALTHER, JOSEPH EDWARD, health facility administrator, retired physician; b. Indpls., Nov. 24, 1912; s. Joseph Edward and Winona (McCampbell) W.; m. Mary Margaret Ruddell, July 11, 1945 (dec. July 1983); children: Mary Ann Margolis, Karl, Joanne Landman, Suzanne Conran, Diane Paczesny, Kurt. BS, MD, Ind. U., 1936; postgrad., U. Chgo., Harvard U., U. Minn., 1945-47; DSc (hon.), Ind. U., 1997, Purdue U., 1998. Diplomate Nat. Bd. Med. Examiners, Am. Bd. Internal Medicine, Am. Bd. Gastroenterology. Intern Meth. Hosp. and St. Vincent Hosp. of Indpls., 1936-37; physician, surgeon U.S. Engrs./Pan Am. Airways, Midway Island, 1937-38; chief resident, med. dir. Wilcox Meml. Hosp., Lihue, Kauai, 1938-39; internist, gastroenterologist Meml. Clinic Indpls., 1947-83, med. dir., pres., chief exec. officer, 1947—; founder, pres. Doctors' Offices Inc., Indpls., 1947—; founder, pres., chief exec. officer Winona Meml. Found. and Hosp. (now Walther Cancer Inst.), Indpls., 1956—. Clinical asst. prof. medicine Ind. U. Sch. Medicine, Indpls., 1948-93, clin. asst. prof. emeritus, 1993—. Author: (with others) Current Therapy, 1965; mem. edit. rsch. bd. Postgrad. Medicine, 1982-83; contbr. articles to profl. jours. Bd. dirs. March of Dimes, Marion County div., 1962-66, Am. Cancer Soc., Ind. div., 1983-92. Col. USAAF, 1941-47, PTO. Decorated Bronze Star, Silver Star, Air medal; named to Pres.'s Cir., Ind. U., 1999; recipient Disting. Alumni Svc. award, 2001, Sing the Heroes award, Ind. U. Sch. Medicine, 2001, Healthcare Heroes Award for Corp. Achievement in healthcare, 2002, Living Legend award, Ind. Hist. Soc., 2003. Mem.: AMA (del. 1970—76), Hoosier Hundred, Marion County Med. Assn., Ind. Med. Assn., Soc. Cons. to Armed Forces, Am. Coll. Gastroenterology (pres. 1970—71, master and charter, Weiss award 1988), Ind. U. Alumni Assn. (life), 702 Club, Indpls. Athletic Club, Waikoloa Golf and Country Club (Hawaii), Highland Golf and Country Club (hon.). Republican. Home: 3266 N Meridian St Ste 104 Indianapolis IN 46208-5846 Office: Walther Cancer Inst 3202 N Meridian St Indianapolis IN 46208-4646

WALTHER, STEVEN T. lawyer; b. Reno, Nev., July 18, 1943; BA in Russian, U. Notre Dame, 1965; JD, U. Calif., Berkeley, 1968. Bar: Nev. 1968, (U.S. Dist. Ct. Nev.) 1969, Calif. 1986, (U.S. Ct. Appeals (9th cir.)) 1991, (U.S. Supreme Ct.). Guest lectr. Nat. Jud. Coll., chair exec. bd., 2001—; pres. legal adv. bd. Martindale-Hubbell LexisNexis, 2001—; panelist U.S. Magistrate Panelist, U.S. Magistrate Selection Panel, 1990; chair internat. bus. task force Coll. Bus. Adminstrn., U. Nev., Reno. Author: The Globalization of the Rule of Law and Human Rights; contbr. articles to profl. jours. Master: Am. Law Inst. (mem. consultative group transnat. civil procedure, mem. consultative group internat. jurisdiction and judgments); mem.: ATLA, ABA (bd. govs. 1995—97, fin. com. 1995—97, spl. adv. com. on internat. activities 1997—98, exec. adv. bd. 1998—2000, mem. UN coord. com. 1998—, subcom. on internat. jud. rels., mem. sect. on bus. and internat. law), Internat. Assn. Gaming Attys., Nev. Trial Lawyers Assn. Gaming Attys., Am. Inns of Ct. (Bruce R. Thompson chpt.), Nat. Conf. Bar Pres., Inc. (mem. sponsorship com. 1994—95), Washoe County Bar Assn., Calif. Bar Assn., Nev. Bar Assn. (gov., bd. govs. 1978—91, pres. 1990—91), Phi Delta Phi (trustee 2002—, bd. trustees 1990—94). Mailing: PO Box 30000 Reno NV 89520 Office: Walther Key Maupin Oats Cox & LeGoy Lakeside Profl Plz 3500 Lakeside Ct Reno NV 89509

WALTHIE, T. H. chemicals executive; Degree in chem. engring. summa cum laude, Tech U. Delft, Netherlands. Mem. spl. assignments program Dow Europe, 1970—72, prodn. engr. chlorinated solvents plant, 1972—74, various purchasing positions Rotterdam, Netherlands, 1974—78; bus. mgr. Dow Chem. Iberica, 1978—82; mgr. hydrocarbon feedstock supplies Dow Europe, Horgen, Switzerland, 1982—86, bus. v.p. hydrocarbons, 1986—89, v.p. polyurethanes, 1989—91, mgr. thermosets bus. group, 1991—92, mgr. automotive group, 1992—95, global v.p. hydrocarbons and energy, 1995—2000; bus. group pres. Dow Chem. Corp., 2000—. Mem.: Assn. Petro-Chem. Producers Europe (pres. 1998, mem. steering com. 1997, pres. 1998), Internat. Isocyanate Inst. (pres.), European Isocyanate Producers Assn. (v.p.). Office: Dow Chem Co 47 Building Midland MI 48067

WALTNER, BEVERLY RULAND, artist; b. Kansas City, Mo.; d. Harry George and Ruth Anna (Laitner) Waltner, Jr. Student Columbia U., 1950-51, Yale U., 1951-53; B.A., U. Miami, Fla., 1955; M.F.A., No. Ill. U., 1968; postgrad. Kent State U., summer 1968. Tchr. art pub. schs. N.Y., Fla., Mo., Ill., 1960-65; instr. art Barry Coll., Miami Shores, Fla., 1969-70; artist-designer, Coral Gables, Fla., 1972—; One-woman shows: Art Gallery, No. Ill. U., DeKalb, 1968, Lyons Meml. Library, Point Lookout, Mo., 1968, Jewish Community Ctr. Gallery, Kansas City, Mo., 1969; juried exhbns. include: New Horizons in Painting, North Shore Art League, 1966, 68, Chautauqua Exhbn. Am. Art, 1968-73, 78, 10th Midwestern Bienniel, Joslyn Mus., 1968, Mid-Am. I, Nelson Gallery and St. Louis Mus., 1968, Nat. Soc. Painters in Casein and Acrylic, 1969, 70, 72, 73, Ark. Nat., Ark. State U., 1970, 35th Ann. Mid-Yr. Show, Butler Inst. Am. Art, 1970, Ann. Exhbn. Am. Painting, Soc. Four Arts, 1971, 74, IV and V Ann. Pan. Am. Exhbns., 1972, 73; represented in permanent collections: No. Ill. U., Arlen Realty Mgmt., Inc., Alexander Muss and Sons, Equitable Life Assurance Soc. U.S., Gen. Devel. Corp., Zuckerman-Vernon Corp., also numerous pvt. collections. Recipient 1st place award Ann. Chautauqua Exhbn. of Am. Art, 1968, Louis E. Selden award, 1972; top award New Horizons in Painting Show, 1966, honorable mention, 1968. Mem. Artists Equity Assn., Cultural Execs. Council Profl. Artists Guild (treas. 1977-78, v.p. 1978-79, editorial staff newsletter 1977—), Chautauqua Art Assn., Coral Gables C. of C. (cultural affairs com. 1979—).

WALTON, ALAN GEORGE, venture capitalist; b. Birmingham, Eng., Apr. 3, 1936; s. Thomas George and Hilda (Glover) W.; m. Jasmin Yvonne Christensen, Sept. 1, 1958 (dec. Nov. 1970); children: Kimm A., Keir D.A.; m. Elenor Jean McElliott, Aug. 6, 1977; children: Kristin M., Sherri L. PhD, U. Nottingham, Eng., 1960, DSc, 1973. Rsch. assoc. Ind. U., Bloomington, 1960-62; asst. prof. chemistry Case Western Res. U., Cleve., 1962-66, assoc. prof., 1966-69, assoc. prof. macromolecular sci., 1969-71, prof., 1971-81, dir. lab. for biol. macromolecules, 1972-81; pres., CEO Univ. Genetics Co., 1981-86, chmn., 1986-87; sr. ptnr. Oxford Biosci Ptnrs., Westport, Conn., 1987—; chmn. Oxford Biosci. Corp., 1992—. Vis. lectr. biol. chemistry Harvard Med. Sch., 1971; mem. Pres. Carter's Task Force on Sci. and Tech.; U.S. project officer Rudjer Boskovic Inst., Zagreb, Yugoslavia, 1967—75; bd. dirs. Acadia Pharma, Targacept Inc., Alexandria R.E.I.T., Rsch. Am.; chmn. Psychiat. Genomics Inc., Asterand Inc., Avalon Therapeutics. Author: Formation and Properties of Precipitates, 1967, Biopolymers, 1973, Structure and Properties of Amorphous Polymers, 1980, Polypeptide and Protein Structure, 1981, Recombinant DNA, 1981, Yearbook of Genetic Engineering and Biotechnology, 1983, 85, 88, (biography) Beneath This Gruff Exterior There Beats a Heart of Plastic, 2000. Bd. dirs. Friends of Nottingham U. Recipient Israel State medal, 1972, Case Inst. Centennial Scholar medal, 1981. Mem. Nat. Venture Capital Assn., Sigma Xi (Research award 1973), Pi Kappa Alpha. Home: 11 Beachside Common Westport CT 06880 Office: Oxford Biosci Corp 315 Post Rd W Westport CT 06880-4739 Personal E-mail: awalton@onbio.com.

WALTON, ALICE L. bank executive; b. Newport, Ark., Oct. 7, 1949; d. Sam and Helen (Robson) W. BBA, Trinity U., 1971; D. of Bus. Adminstrn. (hon.), S.W. Bapt. U., 1988. Investment analyst First Commerce Corp., New Orleans, 1972-75; dir., v.p. investments Walton Enterprises, Bentonville, Ark., 1975—; retail & investment broker E.F. Hutton Co., New Orleans, 1975-79; vice chair, investment dir. Walton Bank Group, Bentonville, Ark., 1982-88; former pres., chair, CEO Llama Co./Llama Asset Mgmt. Co., Fayetteville, Ark. Dean's adv. coun. U. Ark. Coll. Bus. Adminstrn., Fayetteville, 1989-90; internat. judge Students in Free Enterprise, Springfield, Mo., 1990; bd. trustees The Asia Soc., N.Y.C., 1991. Chairperson N.W. Ark. Coun., Fayetteville, 1990—; bd. dirs. Pillar's Club-United Way, Easter Seals Soc.-Arkansan of Yr., Walton Arts Ctr. Coun., Fayetteville, Ark. Named Disting. Bus. Lectr. Cen. State U., Edmond, Okla., 1989.

WALTON, ANTHONY JOHN (TONY WALTON), theater and film designer, book illustrator; b. Walton on Thames, Eng., Oct. 24, 1934; s. Lancelot Henry Frederick and Hilda Betty (Drew) W.; m. Julie Andrews, May 10, 1959 (div. 1968); 1 child, Emma Kate; m. Genevieve LeRoy, Sept. 12, 1991; 1 stepchild, Bridget. Student, Oxford Sch. Tech. Art and Commerce, 1949-52, Slade Sch. Fine Art, London, 1954-55. Designer settings, costumes for theater prodns., London, off-Broadway, 1957-60, Broadway, 1961—; Broadway prodns. include Pippin, 1972 (Tony award 1972-73, Drama Desk award 1972-73), Shelter, 1973 (Drama Desk award 1972-73), Chicago, 1975, Sophisticated Ladies, 1981, The Real Thing, 1984, Hurlyburly, 1984, I'm Not Rappaport, 1985, House of Blue Leaves, 1986 (Tony award 1985-86), Drama Desk award 1985-86), Front Page, 1986, Social Security, 1986 (Drama Desk award 1985-86), Anything Goes, 1987, Grand Hotel, 1989, Six Degrees of Separation, 1990, The Will Rogers Follies, 1991, Death and the Maiden, 1992, Conversations with My Father, 1992, Four Baboons Adoring the Sun, 1992, Guys and Dolls, 1992 (Tony award 1991-92, Drama Desk award 1991-92), Tommy Tune Tonight, 1992, She Loves Me, 1993, A Grand Night for Singing, 1993, Laughter on the 23rd Floor, 1993, Picnic, 1994, A Christmas Carol, N.Y.C., 1994, Company, 1995, Moonlight, 1995, A Fair Country, 1996, A Funny Thing Happened on the Way to the Forum, 1996, The Shawl, 1996, Make Someone Happy, Bay St. Theater Festival, 1997, Not Waving, 1997, Steel Pier, 1997, King David, 1997, 1776, 1997; The Cripple of Inishmaan, 1998; Noel & Gertie, 1998; House, 1998; Ashes to Ashes, 1999; Annie Get Your Gun, 1999; On Raftery's Hill, 2000 (Dublin and London); If Love Were All, 1999; Taller Than a Dwarf, 2000, Uncle Vanya, 2000, The Man Who Came To Dinner, 2000, Our Town, 2002, Blithe Spirit, 2002, I'm Not Rappaport, 2002, Nobody don't Like Yogi, 2003, The Boy Friend, 2003; dir., designer The Importance of Being Earnest, 1996, Major Barbara, 1997, Where's Charley?, 2004; dir. Noel Coward in Two Keys Bay St. Theatre Festival, 1996; dir. Missing Footage, 1999; dir., co-writer, costume designer Oops! The Big Apple Circus Stage Show, 1999; ballets, principally San Francisco Ballet Co., Am. Ballet Theatre, Peter and the Wolf, Dance Theatre of Harlem "St. Louis Woman", 2003, Lincoln Ctr., N.Y.C.; films include Mary Poppins, A Funny Thing Happened on the Way to the Forum, Murder on the Orient Express, The Wiz, All That Jazz (Acad. award with Philip Rosenberg 1980), Prince of the City, Star 80, The Glass Menagerie, 1987, Regarding Henry, 1991, Our Town, 2003; operas in London, 1963-68, Spoleto, Italy, 1965, Santa Fe, 1975, San Francisco, 1992, Chgo., 1993; author: Adelie Penguin in Wonders, 1981; illustrator (books) Wonders, 1981, The Importance of Being Earnest, 1973, Lady Windemere's Fan, 1973, Popcorn, 1972, God Is a Good friend, 1969, Witches Holiday, 1971, Dumpy the Dump Truck, 2000, Dumpy at School, 2000, others. Served with RAF, 1952-54. Recipient Emmy award Death of a Salesman, 1986; named to Theatre Hall of Fame, 1991; elected to Interior Design Hall of Fame, 1993. Mem.: Acad. Motion Picture Arts and Scis., Costume Designers Guild Calif., United Scenic Artists. Office: care Martino ICM 40 W 57th St New York NY 10019-4001

WALTON, BILL (WILLIAM THEODORE WALTON III), sportscaster, former professional basketball player; b. La Mesa, Calif., Nov. 5, 1952; s. Theodore and Gloria W.; m. Lori Walton; children: Adam, Nathan, Luke, Christopher. Grad., UCLA, 1974. Team center Portland Trail Blazers, 1974-79, capt., 1976-77; with Los Angeles Clippers (formerly San Diego Clippers), 1979-85, Boston Celtics, 1985-87; sportscaster NBC Sports, 1993—. Mem. NCAA Divisional Championship Team, 1972-73, NBA Championship Teams, 1977, 86. Recipient James E. Sullivan Meml. award, 1974, James Naismith award, 1972, 73, 74, Adolph Rupp trophy, 1972, 73, 74, NBA Sixth Man award, 1986; named NBA Most Valuable Player, 1978. Home: 1010 Myrtle Way San Diego CA 92103-5123

WALTON, BILL R. retail executive; CFO Belk Stores Svcs. Inc., Charlotte, N.C., sr. v.p. Office: Belk Stores Svcs Inc 2801 W Tyvola Rd Charlotte NC 28217-4525

WALTON, CARMELITA NOREEN, retired nursing administrator; b. Chgo., Nov. 15, 1926; d. Elmo Augusta and Evelyn Mae (Terry) Desobrey; 1 child by previous marriage: Michael Jerome. Student, St. Marys Coll., U. Notre Dame, 1943-45; grad., Cook County Sch. Nursing, Chgo., 1949; BA in Behavioral Social Sci., DePaul U., 1993. Cert. nursing adminstr. ANCC; cert. correctional health profl. Head nurse, supr., nurse clinician Cook County Hosp., Chgo., 1951-71; supr. U. Chgo. Hosps. and Clinics, 1963-68; DON, Woodlawn Child Health Ctr., Chgo., 1968-69; DON prison health care Cermak Health Svcs., Cook County Jail, Chgo., 1973-93; ret., 1993. Nurse cons. Quality Mgmt., In-Svc. Edn.; med.-surg. staff nurse; cons., surveyor Nat. Commn. on Correctional Health Care, speaker 13th ann. conv., 1989, apptd. to bd. certification correctional health, 1991—. Contbr. articles to profl. jours. Recipient Superior Pub. Svc. award City of Chgo., 1984. Mem. APHA, ANA (coun. nursing adminstrn.), Ill. Nurses Assn., Nat. League Nursing, Am. Assn. Diabetes Educators. Democrat. Roman Catholic. Home: 5050 S Lake Shore Dr Chicago IL 60615-3200

WALTON, CAROLE LORRAINE, clinical social worker; b. Harrison, Ark., Oct. 20, 1949; d. Leo Woodrow Walton and Arlette Alegra (Cohen) Armstrong. BA, Lambuth Coll., Jackson, Tenn., 1971; MA, U. Chgo., 1974. Diplomate Clin. Social Work, Acad. Cert. Social Workers; bd. cert. diplomate; lic. clin. social worker. Social worker Community Mental Health, Flint, Mich., 1971-72, clin. social worker Westchester, Ill., 1974-76; dir. self-travel program Chgo. Assn. Retarded Citizens, 1973; coord. family svcs. Inner Harbors Psych. Hosp., Douglasville, Ga., 1976-83; sr. mental health clinician Northside Mental Health Ctr., Atlanta, 1983—; pvt. practice clin. social work Atlanta, 1997—2001. Mem.: NASW, Ga. Soc. for Clin. Work (pres. 1981—82, 1993—95, ethics co-chair 2003—). Avocation: tennis. Office: Northside Mental Health Ctr 1140 Hammond Dr Ste J-1075 Atlanta GA 30328-7145 Office Phone: 770-842-3761.

WALTON, CHARLES MICHAEL, civil engineering educator; b. Hickory, N.C., July 28, 1941; s. Charles O. and Virginia Ruth (Hart) W.; m. Betty Grey Hughes; children: Susan, Camila, Michael, Gantt. BS, Va. Mil. Inst., 1963; MCE, N.C. State U., 1969, PhD, 1971. Research asst. N.C. State U., Raleigh, 1967-71; transp. planning engr. N.C. Hwy. Commn., Raleigh, 1970-71; asst. prof. civil engring. U. Tex., Austin, 1971-76, assoc. prof., 1976-83, prof., 1983—, Bess Harris Jones Centennial prof. natural resource policy studies, 1987-91, Paul D. and Betty Robertson Meek Centennial prof. engring., 1991-93, Ernest H. Cockrell Centennial chair engring., 1993—, chmn. dept. civil engring., 1988-96. Transp. cons., 1970—; assoc. dir. Ctr. for Transp. Rsch. U. Tex., 1980-88; chmn., exec. com. Transp. Rsch. Bd., NRC, 1991, Disting. Lectr., 1994. Contbr. articles to profl. jours. Past chmn. Urban Transp. Commn., Austin. Recipient Disting. Engring. award N.C. State U., 1995, Joe J. King Profl. Engring. Achievement award U. Tex. at Austin, 1995-96, W.N. Carey Jr. Disting. Svc. award Transp. Rsch. Bd., 1998, George S. Bartlett award AASHTO, Transp. Rsch. Bd., ARTBA, 2000 Fellow ASCE (Harland Bartholomew urban planning award 1987, Frank M. Masters transp. engring. award 1987, James Laurie prize 1992, Francis C. Turner lectr. 1999), Inst. Transp. Engrs.; mem. NSPE, NAE, Intelligent Transp. Soc. Am. (tech. coord. coun., past chair bd. dirs., past chair tech. coord. coun.), Am. Rd. and Transp. Assn. (western v.p., past pres. edn. divsn.), Soc. Automotive Engrs., Urban Land Inst., Inst. for Ops. Rsch. and Mgmt. Scis., Soc. Am. Mil. Engrs., Internat. Rd. Fedn. (bd. dirs.), Internat. Rd. Ednl. Found. (bd. dirs.), Austin C. of C. (Leadership Austin program). Democrat. Methodist. Home: 3404 River Rd Austin TX 78703-1031 Office: U Tex Dept Civil Engring Dept Civil Engring ECJ Hall Ste 6 3 Austin TX 78712 Office Phone: 512-471-1414. Business E-Mail: cmwalton@mail.utexas.edu.

WALTON, CONRAD GORDON, SR., retired architect; b. Houston, June 18, 1928; s. John Edward and Evelyn Lucile (Gordon) W.; m. Rilda Ellen Akin, Dec. 10, 1954; children: Conrad Gordon Jr., Evelyn Coleman, Roberta Agnes. BS (Walsh scholar), Rice U., 1951; postgrad., U. Houston, 1955. Registered architect, Tex., NCARB, ret. Past pres. DCW Architects, Inc. Mem.: AIA (emeritus). Home: 9014 Springview Ln Houston TX 77080-1755

WALTON, DAN GIBSON, lawyer; b. Houston, Mar. 26, 1950; s. Dan Edward and Lucy Frances (Gibson) W.; m. Martha Sandlin, June 24, 1972; children: Cole Gibson, Emily Wyatt. BA with honors, U. Va., 1972; JD with honors, U. Tex., 1975. Bar: Tex. 1975, U.S. Dist. Ct. (so. dist.) Tex. 1977, U.S. Ct. Appeals (D.C. cir.) 1975, U.S. Ct. Appeals (5th cir.) 1981, U.S. Supreme Ct. 2001; bd. cert. in civil trial law. Law clk. to hon. Malcolm R. Wilkey D.C. Ct. Appeals (D.C. cir.), 1975-76; assoc. Vinson & Elkins, Houston, 1976-82, ptnr., 1982—. Bd. dirs. The Meth. Hosp., Houston. Bd. dirs. Tex. Equal Access to Justice Found., 2000—, State Bar of Tex., 1999-2002, South Tex. Coll. Law, Houston, 1994—, Briarwood Sch./Brookwood Cmty., Houston, 1991—, Alley Theatre, 2003—; trustee St. John's Sch., Houston, 1997—, Good Samaritan Found., 1998—, Cullen Trust for Health Care, 2002—; co-chancellor Tex. Ann. Conf., United Meth. Ch., 1996—; admission commn. U.S. Dist. Cts. for So. Dist. Tex.; chiar U.S. Magistrate Judge Merit Selection Com. Fellow Am. Bar Found., Tex. Bar Found., Houston Bar Found. (chair 1994), Houston Bar Assn. (pres. 1998-99), Garland Walker Am. Inn of Ct. (master), Am. Bd. Trial Advocates (assoc.), Internat. Soc. Barristers, Internat. Assn. Def. Counsel, Tex. Assn. Def. Counsel. Avocations: golf, skiing. Office: Vinson & Elkins LLP 2300 First City Tower 1001 Fannin St Ste 3201 Houston TX 77002-6706 Office Phone: 713-758-2026.

WALTON, DEWITT TALMAGE, JR., dentist; b. Macon, Ga., May 25, 1937; s. DeWitt T. Sr. and Jimmie (Braswell) W.; m. Joan Robinson, June 11, 1960; children: Jimmie Walton Paschall, Gwen N., Gayle N., Joy A. BS, Howard U., 1960, DDS, 1961. Pvt. practice, Macon, 1963—. Chmn. dental adv. com. Ga. Dept. Med. Assistance; dental svcs. adv. com. Dept. Physical Health, Ga. Dept. Human Resources; adv. bd. dirs. Wachovia Bank, Macon-Warner Robins area; bd. dirs. The Ga. Dept. Cmty. Affairs. Fin. chmn. Boy Scouts Am., Piedmont/Creek Dist., 1978-80, exec. bd., 1978-82, v.p. exec. com., 1983-84; apptd. Bibb County Bd. Edn., 1969-73; vice chmn. Macon-Bibb County Transit Authority, 1981-87; dir. exec. com. Devel. Corp. Mid. Ga., 1984-91; sec.-treas. Urban Devel. Authority, Macon-Bibb County, 1984-87; trustee Macon Heritage Found., 1983-87; bd. dirs. Ctrl. Ga. Speech and Hearing Ctr., 1984-87, Boys' Club Macon, Inc., 1986, 87, 88, The Grand Opera House, 1988, 89, 90, Booker T. Washington Ctr., 1993, Pub. Edn. Found., 1995—, Douglass Theater, 1995—; mem. oversight com. Minority Bus. Assistance Program, 1984-91; active Bibb County Commn. on Excellence in Edn., 1984; trustee United Way Macon-Bibb County, 1985, 86, 87; deacon, elder, treas. Washington Ave. Presbyn. Ch.; active Downtown Coun., Coalition for Polit. Awareness, So. Poverty Law Ctr., NAACP; mem. "Cmty. Hero"-torchbearer Olympic Torch Relay for 1996 Olympic games, Atlanta; advisory bd. Wachovia Bank, Macon, Warner-Robins, 1999—; apptd. bd. dirs. Ga. Dept. Cmty. Affairs, 1999—, Cmty. Found. Ctrl. Ga., 2001—. With U.S. Army, 1961-63. Recipient Cert. of Appreciation State Bar of Ga., Citizenship award Bibb County Voter's Registration League, Inc., 1977, Cmty. Svc. award NAACP, 1982, Cmty. Svc. award Alpha Kappa Alpha Sorority, 1982, Meritorious Svc. award United Negro Coll. Fund, 1983, Comml. Bldg. of Yr. award Macon Heritage Found., 1983, Faithful Svc. award Bibb County Dept. Family and Children's Svcs., 1983-90, Lifetime Achievement award for cmty. svc., Boys' and Girls' Clubs, 2002, citation Macon-Bibb County Beautification Clean Cmty. Commn., 1983-84, Cert. appreciation Macon-Bibb County Econ. Opportunity Coun., 1984, Outstanding Svc. award So. Poverty Law Ctr., 1984, Proclamation Mayor George Israel Svc. on Macon-Bibb County Transit Authority, 1984, Outstanding Alumni award Coll. Dentistry Howard U., 1985, award for Outstanding Svc. Macon-Bibb County Urban Devel. Authority, 1987, award for Outstanding Svc. Macon-Bibb County Transit Authority, 1987, cert. Appreciation Close-Up Found., 1988, cert. Appreciation Ga. Dental Edn. Found., 1988, Cmty. Svc. award United Way Macon-Bibb County, 1988, cert. Disting. Svc. Devel. Corp. Middle Ga., 1990, Continuous Corp. Support award Entrepreneurship and Black Youth Program U. Ga., 1990, cert. Recognition Outstanding Svc. So. Poverty Law Ctr., 1990, cert. Appreciation Keep Macon-Bibb Beautiful Commn. and Cherry Blossom Festival, 1990, James E. Carter award Ga. Dental Soc., 1993; named Olympic Torchbearer, 1996. Fellow Acad. Gen. Dentistry (Membership award 1983-85), Acad. Dentistry Internat., Am. Coll. Dentists, Ga. Dental Assn. (hon.), Internat. Coll. Dentists, Pierre Fauchard Acad.; mem. AAAS, ADA (alt. del. Ga. 1986-91, life mem.), Am. Analgesic Soc., Am. Endodontic Soc., Am. Fund Dental Health, Am. Sch. Health Assn., Am. Soc. Dentistry for Children, Nat. Dental Assn. (life), Nat. Rehab. Assn., Ga. Dental Soc. (pres., 1978, Citizenship award 1979-80, Humanitarian award 1981-82, James E. Carter Jr. award 1993), North Ga. Dental Soc. (pres. 1978-79), Cen. Dist. Dental Soc. (peer rev. com., legis. com., alt. del. to Ga. Dental Assn. 1982, 83, 84, del. 1984, 85, 86, 87), Bibb County Dental Soc. (charter), Acad. Continuing Edn., Fed. Dentaire Internat. (life), Pres'. Club Howard U. (life), Am. Running and Fitness Assn. (life), Greater Macon C. of C. (bd. dirs. 1995-97), Macon Tracks, Sigma Pi Phi, Omega Psi Phi (life). Presbyterian. Avocations: walking, jogging, aerobics, coin collecting/numismatics, real estate. Home: 2988 Malibu Dr Macon GA 31211-2609 Office: DeWitt T Walton Jr DDS 591 DT Walton Sr Way Macon GA 31201-7504

WALTON, EDMUND LEWIS, JR., lawyer; b. Salisbury, Maryland, Sept. 4, 1936; s. Edmund Lewis and Iris Tull (White) W.; m. Barbara (Post), Sept. 18, 1965; children: Southy E. and Kristen P. BA, Coll. William and Mary, 1961, JD (Godwin scholar), 1963. Bar: Va., 1963, U.S. Dist. Ct. (ea. dist.) Va., 1964, U.S. Supreme Ct., 1971, U.S. Dist Ct. (we. dist.) Va., 1972, U.S. Ct. Appeals (4th cir.), 1980. Grad. asst. Coll. William and Mary, 1961-62; assoc. Simmonds, Coleburn, Towner & Carman, Arlington, Fairfax, Va., 1963-68,

ptnr., 1968-74, Putbrese and Walton, McLean, Va., 1975; pvt. practice, 1976-82; sr. ptnr. Walton and Adams P.C., 1983—2003, Reston, Va., 2003—. Judge pro tem Fairfax County Cir. Ct., 1977—; commr. in chancery, 1990-97, legis. com. Va. State Bar, 1974-76; bus. law sect. exec. com., 1983-88, (sec. 1984-85, vice chmn. 1985-86, chmn. 1986-87). Editor: William and Mary Law Sch. Rev. 1961-63. Bd. dir. Home Run Acres Civic Assn. 1968-70, v.p. 1969-70; bd. dir. McLean Citizens Assn., 1976-79, 1st v.p. 1977-78; bd. dir., pres. Rocky Run Citizens Assn., 1973-74; bd. dir. Langley Sch. Inc., 1975-77, treas. 1976-77; mem. Fairfax County Rep. Com., 1966-82, chmn. 1970-72; del. Rep. Nat. Conv. 1972; mem Va. Rep. Ctrl. Com. 1974-77, exec. com. 1976-77; chmn. Providence Dist. Rep. Com., 1968-70; mem. 10th Congl. Dist. Rep. Com. 1970-77, vice chmn. 1974-76, chmn. 1976-77, mem. 8th Congl. Dist. Rep. Com. 1967-70; v.p. Arlington County Young Reps., 1965-66, counsel Arlington County Rep. Com. 1965-66; bd. dir. McLean Planning Com. 1975-79, chmn. 1976-77; bd. dir. McLean Office Sq. Condominium Assn., 1979-83, pres. 1979-82; chmn. Tysons Corner Citizens Task Force 1977-78; mem. Fairfax County Coun. on Arts; bd. dir. Fairfax YMCA 1974-75; bd. dir. Friends of Turkey Run Farm, 1981—, counsel 1981—, mem. exec. com. 1981-83. Served in U.S. Army 1956-59. Named Bus. Citizen of Yr., McLean, Va., 1996. Fellow ABA Found. (life), Va. Law Found. (dir. 1991-97, mem. com. on continuing legal edn. 1990-93, chmn. 1992-93); mem. ABA, Am. Law Inst., Va. Bar Assn. (spl. com. to study rules of ethics 1981-84, membership com. 1981-84, exec. com. 1982-88, chmn. 1984-85, pres. elect 1985-86, pres. 1986-87), Va. Continuing Legal Edn. Bd. (chmn. 1995-98), Arlington County Bar Assn., Fairfax County Bar Assn. (ct. com. 1975-77, dir. 1976-77), McLean Bar Assn. (dir. 1978-79, 80-83, sec. 1978-79, pres. 1980-82), Va. Trial Lawyers Assn., Am. Judicature Soc., William and Mary Law Sch. Assn. (dir. 1970-76), Fairfax County C. of C. (dir. ex officio 1981-83), McLean C. of C. (bd. dir. 1995-96), McLean Bus. and Profl. Assn. (dir. 1976-85, 89-90, pres. 1981-83), Washington Golf and Country Club, Daufuskie Island Club, Lowes Island Club, Phi Alpha Delta. Episcopalian. Home: 2032 Mayfair Mclean Ct Falls Church VA 22043-1760 Office: 1925 Isaac Newton Sq Ste 250 Reston VA 20190 Office Phone: 703-790-8000. Business E-Mail: ewalton@walton-adams.com.

WALTON, G. CLIFFORD, family practice physician; b. Richmond, Va., Jan. 5, 1968; s. Eugene Marion and Mary Ann (McNabb) W.; m. Tami Marie Daniel, June 26, 1998. BS summa cum laude, Hampden-Sydney Coll., 1990; MD, Med. Coll. Va., 1994. Intern Med. Coll. Va., Richmond, 1994-95; resident Blackstone (Va.) Family Practice, 1995-97; pvt. practice, Kenbridge, Va., 1997-99, Richmond, 1996—. Med. examiner Va. Dept. Health, Powhatan, 1996—; mem. housestaff coun. Med. Coll. Va., 1995-97. Sci. fair judge Southside Va. H.S., Farmville, 1988-97. Mem. AMA, Am. Acad. Family Physicians, Med. Soc. Va., Phi Beta Kappa, Sigma Xi, Omicron Delta Kappa. Avocations: baseball card collecting, gardening, photography. Home: 1640 Jeter Rd Powhatan VA 23139-6907 Office: Patient First 8110 Midlothian Tpke Richmond VA 23235-5100 Office Phone: 804-320-8160.

WALTON, HAROLD VINCENT, former agricultural engineering educator, academic administrator; b. Christiana, Pa., June 17, 1921; s. Howard King and Alice Lauretta (Kirk) W.; m. Velma Purvis Braun, June 24, 1946; children: H. Richard, Marilyn J. Walton Friedersdorf, Carol A. BS in Agrl. Engring., Pa. State U., 1942, MS in Agrl. Engring., 1950; PhD in Agrl. Engring., Purdue U., 1961. Test engr. Gen. Electric Co., Schenectady, 1943-45; instr. Pa. State U., 1947-50, asst. prof. agrl. engring., 1950-52, assoc. prof., 1952-61, prof., 1961, 76-85, head dept. agrl. engring., 1976-85, ret., 1985; prof., chmn. dept. agrl. engring. U. Mo.-Columbia, 1962-69, chief of party, 1969-71, prof., 1971-76. Cons. OAS, Trinidad and Tobago, 1980, Ptnrs. of Ams., Brazil, 1984. Served with U.S. Army, 1945-46. Fulbright scholar, Cyprus, 1989-90 Fellow Am. Soc. Agrl. Engrs. (bd. dirs. 1967-69, 85-87). Republican. Personal E-mail: hwalton3002@adelphia.net.

WALTON, JAMES MELLON, investment company executive; b. Pitts., Dec. 18, 1930; m. Ellen Carroll; 4 children. BA, Yale U.; MBA, Harvard U. With Gulf Oil Corp., Phila., Houston, Pitts., Tokyo, Rome, 1958-67; pres. Carnegie Inst., Pitts., 1968-84, Carnegie Mus. Natural History and Mus. of Art, Pitts., 1968-84, Carnegie Library, Pitts., 1968-84; life trustee, pres. emeritus Carnegie Inst. and Carnegie Library, Pitts., 1984—. Vice chmn. bd. dirs. MMC Group Inc.; bd. dirs. New Ireland Fund, Inc. Mem. sponsoring com. Penn's Southwest Assn.; trustee emeritus Carnegie-Mellon U.; treas. Carnegie Hero Fund Commn.; dir. World Affairs Coun. of Pitts., One Hundred Friends of Pitts. Art; trustee Sarah Scaife Found. Inc., Extra Mile Found.; chmn. Vira I. Heinz Endowment; mem. Cultural Dist. Devel. Com. Lt. U.S. Army, 1954-56. Office: 525 William Penn Way Ste 3902 Pittsburgh PA 15219-1710 E-mail: jmwa@earthlink.net.

WALTON, JERRY W. trucking executive; b. Ft. Worth, 1946; Degree, U. Tex., 1968. With Peat Marwick, 1968—91, ptnr., 1976—91, mng. ptnr. Little Rock office, 1982—91; exec. v.p. fin. and adminstrn., CFO J. B. Hunt Transport Svcs., Inc., Lowell, Ark., 1991—; also bd. dirs. Office: JB Hunt Transport Svc 615 JB Hunt Corp Dr Lowell AR 72745*

WALTON, JON DAVID, lawyer; b. Clairton, Pa., Sept. 18, 1942; s. Thomas Edward and Matilda Lucy (Sunday) W.; m. Carol Jeanne Rowland, Sept. 15, 1964; children: David Edward, Diane Elizabeth. BS, Purdue U., 1964; JD, Valparaiso U., 1969. Bar: Pa. 1969. Atty. U.S. Steel Corp. (now USX Corp.), Pitts., 1969-73; asst. gen. counsel Harbison-Walker Refractories, Pitts., 1973-75, gen. counsel, 1975-81, v.p., gen. counsel, 1981-83; regional gen. counsel Dresser Industries, Inc., Pitts., 1983-86; gen. counsel, sec. Allegheny Ludlum Corp., Pitts., 1986-90, v.p., gen. counsel, sec., 1990-96, Allegheny Techs. Inc., Pitts., 1996—, sr. v.p., gen. counsel, sec., 1997—. Trustee Westminster Coll., 1997—; pres., bd. dirs. Music for Mt. Lebanon, 1996—; bd. dirs. Pitts. Youth Golf Found., 1991--; clk. of session Southminster Presbyn. Ch., 1998-2001. Mem. ABA, Pa. Bar Assn., Allegheny County Bar Assn., Am. Soc. Corp. Secs. (former pres. regional group), Am. Corp. Counsel Assn., Am. Arbitration Assn. (panel arbitrators), Duquesne Club, Valley Brook Country Club, Rolling Rock Club. Home: 137 Hoodridge Dr Pittsburgh PA 15228-1803 Office: Allegheny Technologies Inc 1000 Six PPG Pl Pittsburgh PA 15222-5479 E-mail: jwalton@alleghenytechnologies.com.

WALTON, JOSEPH CARROLL, investor; b. Frankfurt, Fed. Republic Germany, Nov. 23, 1955; (parents Am. citizens); s. James Mellon and Ellen Marie (Carroll) W.; m. Molly Erwin, Mar. 23, 1985; 3 children. BA in Eng. Lit., Williams Coll., 1979; MBA, U. Tex., 1983. Pvt. investor, Pitts. Dir. Amy's Ice Creams Inc., Austin, Tex., Physicians Data Corp., Atlanta; trustee Scaife Family Found., Pitts. Trustee Children's Hosp. Pitts. Recipient Outstanding Advisor award Jr. Achievement, 1984. Mem.: Rolling Rock (Ligonier, Pa.); Beaumaris Yacht (bd. dirs., Ont., Can.). Office: 525 William Penn Way Ste 3902 Pittsburgh PA 15219-1707

WALTON, MADALYN CAROL, music educator; b. Alexandria, La., Nov. 5, 1949; d. Willie James Walters and Dona Maxine Self; m. Thomas L. Walton, June 14, 1969; children: Suanne Marie, Alicia René. B in Sacred Music, Gulf-Coast Bible Coll., Houston, 1972; MEd, U. Mo., 1988. Cert. Nat. Bd. Cert. Tchr., 2003. Choral tchr. Rolla (Mo.) HS, 1983—84, St. James (Mo.) HS, 1984—88; elem. music tchr. Davenport (Fla.) Elem., 1988—90, Hillcrest Elem., Lake Wales, Fla., 1990—. Contbr. editor (book) Polk County Curriculum Guide Grades K-5, 1999. Min. of music First United Meth. Ch., 1998—2001. Mem.: Fla. Music Edn. Assn., Music Educators Nat. Conf. Republican. Mem. Ch. Of God. Avocations: scrapbooks, church music, travel, theater. Home: 736 Hunt Dr Lake Wales FL 33853 Office: Hillcrest Elem 1051 State Rd 60E Lake Wales FL 33853 Office Phone: 863-678-4055. E-mail: madalyn_walton@allvantage.com.

WALTON, MARK T. water transportation company executive; Pres., chmn. Travis Boats & Motor Inc., Austin, 1979—. Office: Travis Boats & Motors 12116 Jekel Cir #102 Austin TX 78727-6111

WALTON, MAURINE ISABEL, social worker; b. Denver, June 22; d. Roman and Julia Fass Engle; m. Earl Anderson, Nov. 5, 1943 (dec. Jan. 7, 1974); children: Rene Anderson, Erlin Anderson, Jim Anderson; m. Harris George Walton, June 15, 1985. BS, Met. State U., 1984; MSW, Denver University, 1985. Social worker Introduced independant living program for foster childern while working at Aspira, 1992. Pres. Newcomers Club, Santa Maria, Calif., 1988. Nominee Women of the Yr., S.M. Womans Network, 1991. Mem.: AAUW (treas. 1999—2000), Leota Club (pres. 1973—74), Ea. Star. Democrat. Achievements include development of indep. living program for foster children, 1992. Avocation: golf. Home: 985 Foxenwood Dr Santa Maria CA 93455

WALTON, MORGAN LAUCK, III, lawyer; b. Woodstock, Va., July 30, 1932; s. Morgan Lauck Jr. and Frances (Allen) W.; m. Jeannette Freeman Minor, Mar. 4, 1961; children: Morgan Lauck IV, Charles Lancelot Minor, Christopher Allen, Laura Cathlyn Hirschfeld. BA, Randolph-Macon Coll., 1953; LLB, U. Va., 1959. Bar: Va. 1959, N.Y. 1959, U.S. Ct. Appeals (2d cir.) 1959, U.S. Dist. Ct. (ea. and so. dists.) N.Y. 1960, U.S. Dist. Ct. (we. dist.) Va. 1988. Assoc. Donovan Leisure Newton & Irvine, N.Y.C., 1959-68, ptnr., 1968-84; counsel FDIC, Washington, 1989-90, asst. gen. counsel, 1990-97; mem. editl. adv. bd. Free Advice, San Francisco, 1997—. Contbr. articles to profl. jours. Trustee Randolph-Macon Acad., Front Royal, Va., 1987-92, trustee emeritus, 2002—; trustee Unitarian Ch. Shenandoah Valley, Stephens City, Va., 1987—; mem. coun. Law Sch. U. Va., 1989-92; treas. Shenandoah Valley Music Festival, Woodstock, 1986-87; chmn. bd. All Souls Ch., N.Y.C., 1974-76; active Shenandoah County Dem. Com., 1999—; assoc. dir. Lord Fairfax Soil & Water Bd., 2004-. With U.S. Army, 1953-56. Mem. Univ. Club (N.Y.C.), Collectors Club, Order of Coif, Phi Beta Kappa. Democrat. Home: 908 Kern Springs Rd Woodstock VA 22664-3216

WALTON, R. KEITH, academic administrator, lawyer; BA, Yale U., 1986; JD, Harvard U., 1990. Bar: Ga. Assoc. King & Spaulding, Atlanta, 1991-93; law clk. for Judge. U.W. Clemon U.S. Dist. Ct. (no. dist.) Ala., Birmingham, 1990-91; chief of staff Office Enforcement Dept. Treas., Washington, 1993-96; sec. of univ. Columbia U., N.Y.C., 1996—, polit. sci. lectr., 1997. Del. Young Leaders Conf., 1998. Del. Interpol, Rome, 1994, Beijing, 1995; treas. Yale Coll. Class of 1986, 1985-96, dep. dir. White House Security Rev., Washington, 1994-95; sr. advisor Good Ol' Boy Round Up Rev., Washington, 1995-96; U.S. Del., UN Crime Commn., Vienna, 1996; mem. adv. bd. Human Rights Watch, 1997—; bd. dirs. Sanctuary for Families, Apollo Theatre Found., Orch. St. Luke's. Mem. Am. Law Inst., Coun. for U.S. and Italy, Coun. Fgn. Rels. (adv. bd. 1997—), Enterprise Found. (N.Y. adv. bd. 1997—), Century Assn. Office: Columbia U Office of Sec 211 Low Meml Libr 535 W 116th St New York NY 10027-7030

WALTON, RALPH GERALD, psychiatrist, educator; b. Darlington, Eng., Aug. 18, 1942; came to U.S., 1950; s. Kenneth and Paula (Weissman) W.; m. Ellen Paula Liebling, Feb. 15, 1970 (div. 1980); children: Deborah, Rachel; m. Mary Elaine Hultburg, Sept. 27, 1981; children: Lisa, Jonathan. AB, U. Rochester (NY), 1963; MD, SUNY, Syracuse, 1967. Diplomate Am. Bd. Psychiatry and Neurology. Intern Strong Meml. Hosp., Rochester, 1967-68, resident in psychiatry, 1968-71; asst. prof. psychiatry Sch. Medicine U. Rochester, 1973-76; chief psychiatry Jamestown (NY) Gen. Hosp., 1976-88; commr. mental health Chautauqua County, Jamestown, 1985-88; chmn. dept. psychiatry Western Res. Care Sys., Youngstown, Ohio, 1988-98; prof., chmn. dept. psychiatry N.E. Ohio Univs. Coll. of Medicine, Rootstown, 1998—. Med. dir. Profl. Recovery Plus Alcoholic Clinic, Youngstown, 1992—. Contbr. chpts. to books, articles to profl. jours. Maj. U.S. Army, 1971-73, Panama. Fellow Am. Psychiat. Assn. Jewish. Office: PO Box 240 Youngstown OH 44501-0240 Office Phone: 330-884-3621. E-mail: rwalton193@aol.com.

WALTON, REGGIE BARNETT, judge; b. Feb. 8, 1949; m. Debra Walton; 1 child, Danon. BA, W.Va. State Coll., 1971; JD, Am. U., 1974. Staff atty. Defender Assn. Phila., 1974-76; asst. U.S. atty. Office of U.S. Atty., Washington, 1976-80, chief career criminal unit, 1979-80; assoc. judge Superior Ct. D.C., 1981—89, 1991—2001; exec. asst. U.S. atty. Office of U.S. Atty., Washington, 1980-81; dep. presiding judge criminal divsn. Superior Ct. D.C., 1986-89; assoc. dir. Office Nat. Drug Control Policy, Exec. Office of Pres., Washington, 1989-91; sr. White House advisor for crime, 1991; U.S. dist. judge U.S. Dist. Ct. for D.C., Wasington, 2001—. Mem. U.S. Dept. Justice and ABA Ctrl. and East European Law Initiative Reform Project, Irkutsk, Russia, 1996; instr. SEAK, Inc., 1993, 97, Criminal Practice Inst., Washington, 1996, 97, Ctrl. and East European Law Inst., ABA, 1996, Harvard U., 1994—; mem. faculty Nat. Jud. Coll., Reno, Nev., 1999—, George Washington U. Law Ctr., 1992—; instr. Nat. Inst. Trial Advocacy, Georgetown U. Law Sch., Washington, 1983—, U.S. Dept. Justice, 1993, ABA Traffic Ct. Sem., Washington, 1984, 87; disting. guest lectr. Lincoln U., Jefferson City, Mo., 1991, Albany (Ga.) State Coll., 1991; lectr. U.S. Atty.'s Office, Washington, 1979-81, D.C. Bar Assn., 1980, Graterford (Pa.) State Prison, 1974-76. Contbr. article to profl. jours. Active Big Brothers; mem. task force on interscholastic programs D.C. Pub. Schs., 1987; hon. mem. Capital Ballet Guild, Inc., 1989; mem. D.C. Cares, Inc., 1990; mem. Nat. Ctr. for Missing and Exploited Children, bd dirs., 1990-91; bd. dirs. Robert A. Shuker Scholarship Fund., Inc., 1993—, Hillcrest Children's Ctr., 1994-96; co-chmn. pub. safety com. D.C. Agenda Project, Fed. City Coun., 1995—. Recipient Dean's award Washington Coll. Law, 1989, Disting. Svc. award Young Lawyers sect. Bar Assn. D.C., 1989, H. Carl Moultrie award D.C. br. NAACP, 1989, Sec.'s award Dept. Vets. Affairs, 1990, James R. Waddy Meritorious Svc. award W.Va. State Coll. Nat. Alumni Assn., 1990, County Spotlight award Nat. Assn. Counties, 1990, William H. Hastie award Jud. coun. Nat. Bar Assn., 1993, Honorable Robert A. Shuker Meml. award Asst. U.S. Attys. Assn., 1997, Friendship award Best Friends Found., 1998, Disting. Alumni award Am. U., 1999, Angel award Bridging the Gap Tri-County Inc., Mt. Sinai Bapt. Ch., 2000, North Star award Washington Coll. of Law, Am. U., 2000, among others. Mem. ABA (lawyer competency com. 1984-87, del. nat. conf. state trial judges 1986), D.C. Bar Assn. (criminal instrns. com. 1984-86), Washington Bar Assn., Nat. Inst. Trial Advocacy Advocates Assn., Am. Inns of Ct. Republican. Office: US Dist Ct for DC 333 Constitution Ave NW Washington DC 20001-2131 E-mail: waltonrb@dcsc.gov.

WALTON, ROBERT LEE, JR., plastic surgeon; b. Lawrence, Kans., May 30, 1946; s. Robert L. and Thelma B. (Morgan) W.; m. Elisabeth K. Beahm, Oct. 7, 2000; children: Marc, Morgan, Lindsey. BA, U. Kans., 1968; MD, U. Kans., Kansas City, 1972. Diplomate Am. Bd. Surgery, Am. Bd. Plastic Surgery. Resident in surgery Johns Hopkins Hosp., Balt., 1972-74, Yale-New Haven (Conn.) Hosp., 1974-78; chief of plastic surgery San Francisco Gen. Hosp., 1979-83; prof. and chmn. dept. plastic surgery U. Mass. Med. Ctr., Worcester, 1983-94; prof., chmn dept. plastic surgery U. of Chicago, 1994—. Contbr. articles to profl. jours. Founder Projecto Mira Found. for Handicapped Children, Santurce, P.R., 1990. Mem. ACS, Am. Assn. Plastic Surgeons, Am. Soc. Plastic and Reconstructive Surgery, Am. Soc. Reconstructive Microsurgery, Alpha Omega Alpha. Office: U Chgo Sect Plastic Surgery MC6035 5841 S Maryland Ave Chicago IL 60637-1463 Office Phone: 773-702-4111. E-mail: rwalton@surgery.bsd.uchicago.edu., notlaw72@sbcglobal.net.

WALTON, RODNEY EARL, lawyer; b. Corvallis, Oreg., Apr. 28, 1947; s. Ray Daniel Jr. and Carolyn Jane (Smith) W. BA, Coll. of Wooster, 1969; JD, Cornell U., 1976; MA in History, Fla. Internat. U., Miami, 2001. Bar: Fla. 1976, U.S. Dist. Ct. (so. dist.) Fla. 1976, U.S. Dist. Ct. (mid. dist.) Fla. 1977, U.S. Supreme Ct. 1980, U.S. Ct. Appeals (11th cir.) 1981. Assoc. to jr. ptnr. Smathers & Thompson, Miami, Fla., 1976-87; ptnr. Kelley, Drye and Warren, Miami, 1987-93; atty. Heinrich Gordon Hargrove Weihe & James, P.A., Ft. Lauderdale, 1994-97. Adj. instr. U.S. mil. history Fla. Internat. U., 2001, adj. instr. modern U.S. history, 2003—04. Sec. bd. dirs. Kings Creek Condominium Assn., Miami, 1984-89, treas., 1984, pres., 1990-91. 1st lt. U.S. Army, 1969-73, Vietnam. Decorated Bronze Star. Mem. ABA, Fla. Bar. Republican. Methodist. Avocations: travel, reading, tennis, history. Home: 7985 SW 86th St Apt 430 Miami FL 33143-7014 Personal E-mail: rodneyearlwalton@aol.com.

WALTON, ROGER ALAN, public relations executive, mediator, writer; b. Denver, June 25, 1941; s. Lyle R. and Velda V. (Nicholson) W.; m. Helen Anderson. Attended, U. Colo., 1960-63. Govt. rep. Continental Airlines, Denver, 1964-72; dir. pub. affairs Regional Transp. Dist., Denver, 1972-77; pub. affairs cons. Denver, 1977—; res pub. info. officer Fed. Emergency Mgmt. Agy., 1995-96; pres. Colo. Times Pub. Co., 1999-2000; internet mediator for Square Trade, 2000—. Pres. Colo. Times Pub. Co. Author: Colorado-A Practical Guide to its Government and Politics, 1973-92, 6th rev. edit., 1990, Colorado Gambling - A Guide, 1991; columnist The Denver Post newspaper, 1983—, The Rocky Mountain Jour., 1977-81. Mem. U.S. Presdl. Electoral Coll., Washington, 1968; commr. U.S. Bicentennial Revolution Commn., Colo., 1972-76, U.S. Commn. on Bicentennial of U.S. Constn., Denver, 1985-90, pres.; trustee Arapahoe County (Colo.) Libr. Bd., 1982-86; chmn. lobbyist ethics com. Colo. Gen. Assembly, 1990-91. Republican. Avocations: reading, fishing, photography. Home and Office: 12550 W 2d Dr Lakewood CO 80228-5012

WALTON, S. ROBSON, discount department store chain executive; b. 1945; s. Sam Moore W.; married. BA, U. of Arkansas, 1966; grad., Columbia U., 1969. Formerly with Conner, Winters, Ballaine, Barry & McGowen; with Wal-Mart Stores Inc., Bentonville, Ark., 1969—, sr. v.p., 1978-82, also bd. dirs., vice chmn. bd., 1982-92, chmn., 1992—. Office: Wal-Mart Stores Inc 702 SW 8th St Bentonville AR 72716-6299

WALTON, STANLEY ANTHONY, III, lawyer; b. Chgo., Dec. 10, 1939; s. Stanley Anthony and Emily Ann (Pouzar) W.; m. Karen Kayser, Aug. 10, 1963; children: Katherine, Anne, Alex. BA, Washington and Lee U., 1962, LLB, 1965. Bar: Ill. 1965, U.S. Dist. Ct. (no. dist.) Ill. 1966, U.S. Ct. Appeals (7th cir.) 1966. Ptnr. Winston & Strawn, Chgo., 1965-89, Sayfarth Shaw Fairweather, Chgo., 1989-96. Trustee Village of Hinsdale (Ill.), 1985-89; bd. dirs. Washington and Lee Law Sch., Lexington, Va., 1975-78, bd. dirs. univ. alumni, 1983-87, pres., 1986-87; bd. dirs. UNICEF, Chgo., 1983; pres. Hinsdale Hist. Soc., 1979-81, 2001—, St. Isaac Jogues PTA, 1980; sec. Hinsdale Cmty. Svc., 2000—; bd. dirs. Hinsdale Ctrl. Found., 2000—. Mem. Ill. State Bar Assn., Phi Alpha Delta, Hinsdale Golf Club. Republican. Roman Catholic. Home and Office: 6679 Snug Harbor Dr Willowbrook IL 60527 Office Phone: 630-887-9216.

WALTON, TRACY MATTHEW, JR., radiologist; b. Columbia, SC, Nov. 12, 1930; MD, Howard U., 1961. Diplomate Am. Bd. Radiology. Intern Freedmans Hosp., Washington, 1961-62, resident in radiology, 1962-66; pvt. practice Washington. Mem. AMA, Am. Coll. Radiology, Nat. Med. Assn. (pres. 1994-95). Address: 7506 Ninth St NW Washington DC 20012-1602 Office Phone: 202-396-8600.

WALTRIP, DARRELL LEE, race car driver; b. Owensboro, Ky., Feb. 5, 1947; s. Leroy and Margaret Jean (Evans) Waltrip; m. STephanie Hamilton Rader, Aug. 15, 1969; children: Jessica Leigh, Sarah. Student, Ky. Wesleyan Coll. Driver for Junior Johnson & Assocs., Rick Hendrick Motor Sports; owner Darrell Waltrip Honda Volvo, 1994—. Named Driver of Yr., Nat. Motorsports Press Assn., 1977, Olsonite Driver of Yr., 1979, winner, Winston Cup, 1982, Nat. Assn. Stock Car Auto Racing Championship, 1985, Winston Cup Championship, 1981, 1982, 1985, Coca Cola 600, 1985, 1988, 1989, Wrangler 500, 1985, Bisch 500, 1986, Budweiser 400, 1986, Holly Farms 400, 1986, Goody's 500, 1987, 1988, 1989, Motorcraft 500, 1989, Daytona 500, 1989, Champion Spark Plug 500, 1991. Mem.: Nat. Assn. Stock Car Auto Racing. Republican. Presbyterian. Achievements include top motor sport money winner worldwide with more than 7.5 million dollars.

WALTRIP, MICHAEL, professional race car driver; b. Owensboro, Ky., Apr. 30, 1963; m. Elizabeth Waltrip; children: Caitlin Marie, Margaret Carol. Stock car racer, 1981—. Recipient Most Popular Driver awards, NASCAR Dash Series, 1983, 1984. Achievements include Mini-Modified divsn. track championship Ky. Motor Speedway, 1981; NASCAR Touring Goody's Dash Series, 1982-84, including series title 1983; NASCAR Winston Cup Series, 1985—, including 2d-place in Rookie of Yr. race, 1986; 2d-place 1988 Miller 500 at Pocono; NASCAR Busch Series Grand Nat. divsn. career includes 7 victories, 11 poles. Avocations: golf, tennis. Office: 222 Raceway Dr Mooresville NC 28117-6510

WALTRIP, ROBERT L. environmentalist; b. Austin, Tex., 1931; BBA in Mgmt., U. Houston, 1954. With Heights Funeral Home, 1954—62; founder, chmn. bd. dirs., chief exec. officer Service Corp. Internat., Houston, 1962—; founder, chmn. bd. dirs. Waltrip Enterprises Inc., Houston, 1982—; with Tanknology Corp. Internat., Houston, 1988—, Tanknology Environ. Inc., Houston, 1989—. Office: Service Corp International 1929 Allen Pky Houston TX 77019-2507 also: Tanknology Environ Inc 5225 Hollister St Houston TX 77040-6205

WALTS, ANN E. pathologist; b. N.Y.C., Oct. 4, 1944; d. Abraham and Lillian Schleifer; m. Leonard F. Walts, June 12, 1973; 1 child, Avram D. BS, Bklyn. Coll., 1965; MD, U. Pa., 1971. Intern Hebrew U. Hadassah Med. Ctr., Jerusalem, 1972—73; resident Cedars Sinai Med. Ctr., L.A., 1973—77, pathologist, 1977—. Contbr. articles to profl. jours. Mem.: Am. Soc. Clin. Pathology, Internat. Acad. Pathology, Am. Soc. Cytopathology. Jewish. Avocations: reading, travel, hiking, photography. Office: Cedars-Sinai Med Ctr 8700 Beverly Blvd Los Angeles CA 90048

WALTUCK, DAVID, chef, restaurant owner; m. Karen Waltuck. Student, CCNY, Culinary Inst. Am. Lunch chef La Petite Ferme; chef, co-owner (SoHo, Grand St) Chanterelle, N.Y.C., 1979—89, chef, co-owner (TriBeCa, Harrison St.), 1989—. Recipient James Beard Found. award, 2004. Office: Chanterelle 2 Harrison St New York NY 10013-2810

WALTZ, ALAN KENT, clergyman, denominational executive; b. Normal, Ill., Oct. 10, 1931; s. James Edwin Sr. and Ethel Leona (Hawkins) W.; m. Mary Joyce Horton, June 5, 1966; children: Sharon Kay, Reid Alan. BA, Ill. Wesleyan U., 1953; MDiv, Garrett Theol. Sem., Evanston, Ill., 1957; MA, Northwestern U., 1958, PhD, 1961. Ordained to ministry United Methodist Ch., 1957. Pastor Braceville Meth. Ch., Ill., 1954-56; denominational exec. United Meth. Ch., 1960-98; asst. dir. Bd. Missions, Phila., 1960-64; asst. gen. sec. Coun. on Fin., Evanston, 1964-68; assoc. gen. sec. Gen. Coun. on Ministries, Dayton, Ohio, 1969-84, Gen. Bd. Discipleship, Nashville, 1984-98. Author: Images of the Future, 1980, To Proclaim the Faith, 1983, Facts and Possibilities, 1987, A Dictionary for United Methodists, 1991; editor book series Into Our Third Century, 1981-84. Trustee Ill. Wesleyan U., Bloomington, 1984-93.

WALTZ, JAMES RICHARD, physician; b. Massillon, Ohio, June 30, 1935; AB, Ohio U., 1957; MD, Ohio State U., 1962. Intern Milw. County Hosp., 1962-63; resident U. Ill. Rsch. Edn. Hosps., 1963-67; gen. surgeon Liberty Hosp. Mem. ACS. Office: 15724 Oakmont Dr Kearney MO 64060-9251

WALTZ, JOSEPH MCKENDREE, neurosurgeon, educator; b. Detroit, July 23, 1931; s. Ralph McKinley and Bertha (Seelye) W.; m. Janet Maureen Journey, June 26, 1954; children: Jeffrey McKinley, Mary Elaine, David Seelye, Stephen McKendree; m. Marilyn Liska, June 5, 1967; 1 child, Tristana McKendree. Student, U. Mich., 1950; BS, U. Oreg., 1954, MD, 1956. Diplomate Am. Bd. Neurol. Surgery. Surg. intern U. Mich. Hosp., 1956-57, gen. surg. resident, 1957-58, clin. instr. neurosurgery, 1960-63; neurosurg. assoc. St. Barnabas Hosp., N.Y.C., 1963—; assoc. dir. Inst. Neurosci., 1974—, dir. dept. neurol. surgery, 1977—2002; attending Neurosci. Inst. Our Lady of Mercy, 1998—. Assoc. cons. in neurosurgery Englewood (N.J.) Hosp., 1964—; assoc. prof. neurosurgery NYU Med. Str., 1974—; asst. prof. dept. surgery (neurosurgery) N.Y. Coll. Osteo. Medicine, 1989—; mem. alumni bd. U. Mich. Med. Ctr., 1995; dir. Med. Ct. Graphics. Author: (chpt.) Cryogenic Surgery, Neurology, 1982, Advances in Neurology, 1983, Textbook of Stereotactic and Functional Neurosurgery, 1997; contbr. articles to profl. jours. Mem. sci. adv. bd. Dystonia Med. Research Found., 1980—; trustee St. Barnabas Hosp., 1980—. Served to capt. M.C. AUS, 1958-60. Recipient

Bronze award Am. Congress Rehab. Medicine, 1967, World Cmty. Svc. award Rotary, Disting. Trustee award United Hosp. Fund, 1995. Mem. AMA, Am. Paralysis Assn., World Soc. Stereotactic and Functional Neurosurgery, Congress Neurol. Surgeons, Math. Assn. Am., Internat. Neural Network Soc., Soc. for Cryobiology, N.Y. State Med. Soc., Bronx County Med. Soc., N.Y. State Neurosurg Soc., Nat. Ski Patrol, Phi Beta Pi. Achievements include spl. rsch. on neurophysiology and treatment of epilepsy, basal ganglia disorders, abnormal movement disorders, cerebral palsy, also neurosurg. application stereotactic thalamic surgery and spinal cord stimulation. Home: Four B Island South 720 Milton Rd Rye NY 10580-3258 Office: 150 Purchase St Ste 7 Rye NY 10580

WALTZ, KATHLEEN M. publishing executive; b. Mar. 6, 1954; m. Bill Raffel, 1990; stepchildren: Jamie, Jenny. BA, DePaul U.; postgrad., Northwestern U. Telemarketer Chgo. Tribune, 1973, mgr. recruitment advt., 1987, dir. customer satisfaction, 1989—90, dir. classified advt., 1990—95, v.p./dir. of developing bus., 1995—97; v.p., gen. mgr. Sun-Sentinel Co., Fla., 1997—98; CEO, pres., pub. Daily Press, Newport News, Va., 1998—2000, Orlando Sentinel Comm., 2000—. Bd. dirs. United Way. of Va. Peninsula, Peninsula Allice for Econ. Devel. WHRO Found. and Greater Peninsula Now; bd. dirs., exec. com. Hampton Roads Partnership; ABC/NAA liaison com., sr. exec. resource corps. Coll. of William and Mary. Mem. So. Newspapers Pub. Assn. (diversity com.). Avocations: travel, golf, gardening. Office: Orlando Sentinel 1000 N Garland Ave Orlando FL 32801*

WALTZ, KATHY, publishing executive; m. Bill Raffel; stepchildren: Jamie, Jenny. BA in Liberal Arts, DePaul U.; postgrad., Northwestern U., 1991. Dir. classified advt., dir. customer satisfaction Chgo. Tribune, 1973—97, v.p., dir. developing businesses, 1995—97; v.p., gen. mgr. Sun-Sentinel Co., Ft. Lauderdale, Fla., 1997—98; pres., pub., CEO Daily Press, Hampton Roads, Va., 1998—2000, Orlando (Fla.) Sentinel, 2000—. Avocations: gardening, golf, history, travel. Office: Orlando Sentinel Comms 633 N Orange Ave Orlando FL 32801

WALTZ, MARCUS ERNEST, retired prosthodontist; b. Brownsville, Oreg., July 29, 1921; s. Roswell Starr and Eva Ione (Cherrington) W.; m. Constance Jean Elwood, May 31, 1952 (div. Nov. 1973); children: Melody Ann, Martha Louise, Kathryn Jean, Holly Jay, Joy Evalyn, Ross Elwood; m. Shelby Annette Schwab, June 10, 1975. AB, Willamette U., 1942; DMD, U. Oreg., 1945. Cert. Nev. State Bd. Dental Examiners. Practice dentistry, Forest Grove, Oreg., 1946-52; practice dentistry specializing in prosthodontics Reno, 1954-95; ret., 1995. Councillor Pacific Coast Dental Conf., bd. dirs., 1979-84; pres. Pacific Coast Soc. of Prosthodontics, 1983; mem. Nev. State Bd. Dental Examiners, 1960-66, pres., 1964. Contbr. essays to dentistry jours. Mem. State of Nev. Selective Svc. Appeals Bd., 1970-76, pres., 1974-76. Lt. USN, 1945-46, 52-54, Korea. Decorated Combat Medics award, Battle Stars (oak leaf cluster). Fellow Internat. Coll. Dentistry, Acad. Dentistry Internat.; mem. ADA, Northern Nev. Dental Soc. (pres. 1959), Nev. Dental Assn., Nev. Acad. Gen. Dentistry (pres. 1974), Sigma Chi, Omicron Kappa Upsilon. Reno Exec. Club (dir. 1960-66, pres. 1964-65), Sigma Tau (pres. 1941-42), Masons (32 degree), Shriners, Jesters. Democrat. Methodist. Avocations: outdoor activities, arranging choral music. Home: 715 Manor Dr Reno NV 89509-1944

WALTZ, SUSAN, international relations educator; Former chmn. Amnesty Internat., London, England, 1993-98; prof. internat. pub. policy Gerald Ford Sch. Pub. Policy U. Mich., Ann Arbor, 2001—. Bd. dirs. Am. Friends Svc. Com., 2000—. Office: Ford Sch Public Policy Michigan U 611 Tappan St Ann Arbor MI 48109 Office Phone: 734-615-8683. Business E-Mail: swaltz@umich.edu.

WALUK, STANLEY PETER, corporate engineering official; b. Palmer, Mass., July 29, 1943; s. Stanley John and Bertha Rose (Mozden) W.; A.S. in E.E., Northeast Inst., 1963; B.S. in Indsl. Engring., Western New Eng. Coll., 1973; postgrad. in forensic engring. and patent law Brown U., 1983; postgrad. in product liability law Providence Coll., 1981; m. Mary Ann Mechonski, June 6, 1964; 1 dau., Angela Kim. Quality control mgr., chief engr. Gavitt Wire and Cable Co., Brookfield, Mass., 1963-71; spl. project engr. TRW-Holyoke Wire and Cable Co., South Hadley, Mass., 1971-74; plant mgr. Standard Wire and Cable Co., Attleboro, Mass., 1974-75; v.p., gen. mgr. Lyall Electric, Kendallville, Ind., 1975; tech. dir. Miller Electric Co. (Carol Cable Co.), Woonsocket, R.I., 1976-83; engring. mgr. Judd Wire Inc. div. High Voltage Engring., 1983-90; corp. mgr. quality and standards Judd Wire, Inc., 1990-92; cons. wire and cable engring., 1975—; owner, mgr., W Ma Assocs., Deerfield, Mass., 1992—; dir. engring. and quality Am. Electric Cable Co., Holyoke, Mass., 1994-98; engring. and purchasing mgr. Coleman Cable Co., Longmeadow, Mass., 1998—. mem. tech. adv. panel Underwriters Lab., also rep. Industry Adv. Conf. Aux. staff officer USCG; mfg. insp. rep. FAA, 1985—. Mem. ASTM, Nat. Fire Protection Assn., Stat. Process Control Soc., Internat. Electrotech. Comm. (mem. com.), Am. Inst. Indsl. Engrs., Wire Assn., Am. Soc. Quality Control, Soc. Automotive Engrs., Am. Mgmt. Soc. (affiliate), Providence Engring. Soc. (affiliate), U.S. Coast Guard Aux. (staff officer), U.S. Yacht Racing Union. Expert in elec. engring. and consumer elec. products. Home and Office: 3 Oak Knoll Dr South Deerfield MA 01373-9672 Personal E-mail: wmaassoc@aol.com.

WALWORTH, ARTHUR, author; b. Newton, Mass., July 9, 1903; s. Arthur Clarence and Ruth Richardson (Lippincott) W. Grad., Phillips Andover Acad., 1921; BA, Yale U., 1925. Ednl. dept. Houghton Mifflin Co., 1927-43; staff OWI, 1943; Staff Medomak Camp, Washington, Maine, summers 1943-63. Author: School Histories at War, 1938, Black Ships Off Japan, 1946, Cape Breton, 1948, The Medomak Way, 1953, Woodrow Wilson, 2 vols, 1958, 1 vol., 1967, 78, America's Moment: 1918, 1977, Wilson and His Peacemakers, 1986 Recipient Pulitzer prize in biography, 1958 Mem.: Cosmos Club. Home: North Hill 865 Central Ave Apt D506 Needham MA 02492-1338

WALZ, CARL E. astronaut; b. Cleve., Sept. 6, 1955; m. Pamela J. Glady; 2 children. BS in Physics, Kent State U., 1977; MS in Solid State Physics, John Carroll U., 1979. Commd. 2d lt. USAF, 1977, advanced through grades to col.; with Atomic Energy Detection Sys. 1155th Tech. Ops. Squadron, McClellan AFB, Calif., 1979—82; flight test engr. USAF Test Pilot Sch., Edwards AFB, Calif., 1983—84, F-16 Combined Test Force, Edwards AFB, Calif., 1984—87; flight test mgr. Detachment 3 Air Force Flight Test Ctr., 1987—90; astronaut NASA, Houston, 1990—; mission specialist STS-108 Endeavour, Internat. Space Sta., 2001—02. Named to, Ohio Vets. Hall of Fame; recipient Disting. Alumnus award, Kent State U., 1997. Mem.: Kent State U. Alumni Assn., Am. Legion. Achievements include logged over 231 days in space; mission specialist STS-51 Discovery (1993); Orbiter flight engr. STS-65 Columbia (1994); U.S. record for 196 days in space; mission specialist STS-79 Atlantis (1996). Avocations: piano, vocal music, sports, lead singer MAX-Q (rock-n-roll band). Office: Astronaut Office/CB NASA Johnson Space Ctr Houston TX 77058

WALZ, KENT, publishing executive; Degree in Econs., We. N.Mex. U., 1972; JD, U. N.Mex., 1976. Editor Silver City Daily Press; supr. burs. The AP, 1972—84; asst. editor Albuquerque (N.Mex.) Jour., 1985—95, editor, 1995—. Office: Albuquerque Jour Albuquerque Jour Newsroom 7777 Jefferson St NE Albuquerque NM 87109-4360

WALZER, JUDITH BORODOVKO, academic administrator, educator; b. N.Y.C., May 27, 1935; d. Isidore and Ida (Gins) Borodovko; m. Michael L. Walzer, June 17, 1956; children— Sarah, Rebecca BA, Brandeis U., 1958, MA, 1960, PhD, 1967. Dir. office women's edn. Radcliffe Coll., Cambridge, Mass., 1974-77, assoc. dean., 1976-77; Allston Burr sr. tutor, asst. dean for co-edn. Harvard Coll., Cambridge, Mass., 1977-80; asst. to the pres. Princeton U., N.J., 1980-85; provost New Sch. U., N.Y.C., 1985-98, prof. lit., 1998—. Mem. adv. com. Overseas Sch., Hebrew U. in Jerusalem, 1989—. Democrat. Jewish. Office: New Sch U 65 W 11th St New York NY 10011 E-mail: walzer@newschool.edu.

WALZER, NORMAN CHARLES, economics professor; b. Mendota, Ill., Mar. 17, 1943; s. Elmer J. and Anna L. Walzer; m. Dona Lee Maurer, Aug. 22, 1970; children: Steven, Mark. BS, Ill. State U., Normal, 1966; MA, U. Ill., 1969, PhD, 1970. Rsch. dir. Cities and Villages Mcpl. Problems Com., Springfield, Ill., 1974-84; vis. prof. U. Ill., Urbana, 1977-78; prof. econs. Western Ill. U., Macomb, 1978—, chmn. dept. econs., 1980-89, dir. Ill. Inst. Rural Affairs, 1988—, interim dean coll. bus. and tech., 1993-95. Author: Cities, Suburbs and Property Tax, 1981, Government Structure and Public Finance, 1984; editor: Financing State and Local Governments, 1981, Rural Community Economic Development, 1991; co-editor: Financing Local Infrastructure in Non Metro Areas, 1986, Financing Economic Development in The 1980s, 1986, Financing Rural Health Care, 1988, Rural Health Care, 1992, Rural Community Economic Development, 1992, Local Economic Development: International Trends and Issues, 1995, Community Visioning Programs: Practice and Principles, 1996, Public-Private Partnerships for Local Economic Development, 1998, Cooperative Approach to Community Economic Development, 2000, Local Government Innovations, 2000, American Midwest: Managing Change in Rural Transition, 2003, Cooperatives and Development: Applications for the 21st Century, 2003. Mem. Am. Econs. Assn., Ill. Econs. Assn. (pres. 1979-80), Mid-Continent Regional Sci. Assn. (pres. 1985-86). Office: Western Ill U Ill Inst Rural Affairs 518 Stipes Hall Macomb IL 61455

WAMBACH, ABBY (MARY ABIGAIL WAMBACH), Olympic athlete; b. June 2, 1980; Grad., Univ. of Florida. Mem. U.S. Nat. Soccer Team, 2001—; professional soccer player Washington Freedom, 2002—03; mem. U.S. Women's Olympic Soccer Team, Athens, 2004. Named WUSA All-Star game MVP, 2002, WUSA Rookie of the Year, 2002, WUSA First Team All-Star, 2003, MVP Founders Cup Champions match, 2003; named to WUSA All-Star Team, 2002—03. Achievements include mem. U.S. Women's Gold medal Soccer Team, Athens Olympic games, 2004; scored overtime game winning goal in olympic gold medal game, Athens Olympic games, 2004; mem. Founders Cup Championship Team, Washington Freedom, 2003. Office: c/o US Soccer Federation 1801 S Prairie Ave Chicago IL 60616*

WAMBAUGH, JOSEPH A., JR., author; b. Pitts., Jan. 22, 1937; s. Joseph Aloysius and Anne (Malloy) W.; m. Dee Allsup, Nov. 26, 1955; children: Mark (dec.), David, Jeannette. BA, Calif. State Coll., L.A., 1960; MA, Calif. State Coll., Los Angeles, 1968. Police officer, L.A., 1960-74. Author: The New Centurions, 1971, The Blue Knight, 1972, The Onion Field, 1973 (Edgar Allan Poe award Mystery Writers Am. 1974), The Choirboys, 1975, The Black Marble, 1978, The Glitter Dome, 1981, The Delta Star, 1983, Lines and Shadows, 1984 (Rodolfo Walsh prize Internat. Assn. Crime Writers 1989), The Secrets of Harry Bright, 1985, Echoes in the Darkness, 1987, The Blooding, 1989, The Golden Orange, 1990, Fugitive Nights, 1992, Finnegan's Week, 1993, Floaters, 1996, The Fire Lover, 2003. Served with USMC, 1954-57.

WAMBOLD, RICHARD LAWRENCE, manufacturing executive; b. Wilbraham, Mass., Jan. 19, 1952; s. Richard A. and Virginia M. (Reid) W.; m. Patricia Bentley, Aug. 24, 1974; children: Lauren, Carolyn, Robin. BA, U. Tex., 1974, MBA, 1977. From systems cons. to strategic planning mgr. Tenneco, Inc., Houston, 1977-81, asst. to chmn. and chief exec. officer, 1981-84, pres. Tenneco Ventures Inc., 1984-88, v.p. corp. planning and devel., 1988—; exec. v.p., gen. mgr. Internat. Bus. Group, J.I. Case Co., Racine, Wis., 1988—. Mem. Nat. Venture Capital Assn. Avocation: sailing. Office: J I Case 700 State St Racine WI 53404-3392 also: Headquaters 1900 West Field Court Lake Forest IL 60045

WAMP, ZACH, congressman; b. Ft. Benning, Ga., Oct. 28, 1957; m. Kim Wamp; 2 children. Student, U. N.C., U. Tenn. Chmn. Hamilton County Rep. Party, 1987; regional dir. Tenn. Rep. Party, 1989; v.p. Charter Real Estate Corp., 1989-92; comml. and indsl. real estate broker Fletcher Bright Co., 1992-94; mem. U.S. Congress from 3d Tenn. dist., 1995—, mem. sci. com., transp. and infrastructure com., approp. com., budget com., former mem. small bus. com., vice chmn. water resources and environment subcom. Republican. Office: US House Reps 2447 Rayburn Ho Office Bldg Washington DC 20515-4203

WAMPLER, LLOYD CHARLES, retired lawyer; b. Spencer, Ind., Nov. 4, 1920; s. Charles and Vivian (Hawkins) W.; m. Joyce Ann Hoppenrath, Sept. 28, 1950 (dec. 1954); 1 child, Natalie Gay (dec.); m. Mary E. Shumaker, Sept. 16, 1982 AB, Ind. U., 1942, JD, 1947. Bar: Ind. 1947, U.S. Supreme Ct. 1971. Instr. bus. law U. Kans., 1947-49; dep. atty. gen. Ind., 1949-50; mem. legal com. Interstate Oil Compact Commn., 1950; asst. pub. counselor Ind., 1950-53; mem. Stevens, Wampler, Travis & Fortin, Plymouth, 1953-83; claim counsel Am. Family Ins. Group, Indpls., 1983-88; ret., 1988. Mem. Ind. Rehab. Services Bd., 1978-86; Dem. nominee for judge Ind. Supreme Ct., 1956. With USNR, 1942-46 Mem. ABA, Am. Judicature Soc., Ind. Bar Assn. (bd. mgrs. 1975-77), Indpls. Bar Assn., Ind. Acad. Sci., Ind. Def. Lawyers Assn. (bd. dirs. 1967-72, v.p. 1970, pres. 1971-72), Ind. Hist. Soc., Marshall County Hist. Soc. (bd. dirs. 1969-75), Sagamore of the Wabash, Am. Legion, Phi Delta Phi. Home: 4000 N Meridian St Indianapolis IN 46208-4034

WAMUTOMBO, DIKEMBE MUTOMBO MPOLONDO MUKAMBA JEAN JACQUE See MUTOMBO, DIKEMBE

WAN, FREDERIC YUI-MING, mathematician, educator; b. Shanghai, Jan. 7, 1936; arrived in U.S., 1947; s. Wai-Nam and Olga Pearl (Jung) W.; m. Julia Y.S. Chang, Sept. 10, 1960. SB, MIT, 1959, SM, 1963, PhD, 1965. Mem. staff MIT Lincoln Lab., Lexington, 1959-65; instr. math. MIT, Cambridge, 1965-67, asst. prof., 1967-69, assoc. prof., 1969-74; prof. math., dir. Inst. Applied Math. and Stats. U. B.C., Vancouver, 1974-83; prof. applied math. and math. U. Wash., Seattle, 1983-95, chmn. Dept. Applied Math., 1984-88, div. dean scis. coll. arts and scis., 1988-92; prof. math., prof. mech. and aero. engring. U. Calif., Irvine, 1995—, vice chancellor rsch., dean grad. studies, 1995-2000, faculty athletics rep., 2000—04. Program dir. Divsn. Math. Sci. NSF, 1986-87, divsn. dir., 1993-94; cons. indsl. firms and govt. agys.; mem. MIT Ednl. Coun. for B.C. Area of Can., 1974-83. Assoc. editor Jour. Applied Mechanics, 1991-95, Can. Applied Math. Quar., Studies in Applied Math., Jour. Dyn. Discrete, Continuous and Impulsive Sys., 1994-97, Natural Resource Modeling 1985-88, Internat. Jour. Solids & Structures; contbr. articles to profl. jours. Sloan Found. award, 1973, Killam sr. fellow, 1979. Fellow AAAS, ASME, trustee, NSF Inst. Pure & Applied Mathematics, UCLA (chmn. 1999-2001, past chmn. 2001-03) fgn. mem. Russian Acad. Natural Scis., mem. Am. Acad. Mechanics (sec. fellows 1984-90, pres.-elect 1992-93, pres. 1993-94), Soc. Indsl. and Applied Math., Can. Applied Math. Soc. (coun. 1980-83, pres. 1983-85, Arthur Beaumont Disting. Svc. award 1991), Am. Math. Soc., Math. Assn. Am., Sigma Xi. Home: 22 Urey Ct Irvine CA 92612-4077 Office: U Calif Irvine Dept Math Rm 267 MST Bldg Irvine CA 92697-3175 Office Phone: 949-824-5529. E-mail: fwan@uci.edu.

WAN, JULIA CHANG, retired science educator; b. Hong Kong, Oct. 13, 1937; d. Charles S.Y. and Lucy (Wong) Chang; m. Frederic Y.M. Wan, Sept 10, 1960. BA, Wellesley Coll., 1960, MA, 1970; EdD, Boston Coll., 1978. Mem. staff Bio Rsch. Inst., Cambridge, Mass., 1960-64; physics tchr. Watertown (Mass.) H.S., 1970-73; sci. dir. Watertown Pub. Schs., 1973-79; curriculum dir. Fed. Way Sch. Dist., Fed. Way, Wash., 1979-83; asst. supt. Bainbridge Island (Wash.) Sch. Dist., 1983-93; program dir. NSF, Washington, 1993-95; dir. Ctr. for Excellence in Sci. and Math. Edn. Calif. State U., Fullerton, 1995-2000. Mem. accreditation com. N.W. Assn. Schs. and Colls., Boise, Idaho, 1981-95; mem. edn. opportunity coun. AAAS, Washington, 1995-99; bd. dirs. Challenger Ctr., Alexandria, Va., 1997-2000. Author: Designing School Health Education Curricula, 1992, 2d edit. 1995; contbr. articles and revs. to sci. mags. Bd. dirs. NOW, 1985-88; mem. Commn. on Asian-Am. Affairs, Olympia, Wash., 1990-93; bd. trustees Girls, Inc., Orange County, Calif., 1995-2000. Recipient award profl. excellence We. Wash. U., Bellingham, 1988, exemplary program award Met. Life Found., N.Y.C., 1989; grantee: NSF (numerous), Arlington, Va., 1989-2000, Beckman Found., Irvine, Calif., 1998-2000. Mem. ASCD, Am. Ednl. Rsch. Assn., Nat. Sci. Tchrs. Assn. Office: Calif State U Fullerton PO Box 6850 Fullerton CA 92834-4565 E-mail: Jwan@fullerton.edu.

WAND, PATRICIA ANN, librarian; b. Portland, Oreg., Mar. 28, 1942; d. Ignatius Bernard and Alice Ruth (Suhr) W.; m. Francis Dean Silvernail, Dec. 20, 1966 (div. Jan. 19, 1986); children: Marjorie Lynn Silvernail, Kirk Dean Silvernail. BA, Seattle U., 1963; MAT, Antioch Grad. Sch., 1967; AMLS, U. Mich., 1972. Vol. Peace Corps, Colombia, S.Am., 1963-65; secondary tchr. Langley Jr. High Sch., Washington, 1965-66; asst. libr. Wittenberg U. Libr., Springfield, Ohio, 1967-69; secondary tchr. Caro (Mich.) High Sch., 1969-70; assoc. libr. Coll. of S.I. (N.Y.) Libr., 1972-77; head, access svcs. Columbia U. Librs., N.Y.C., 1977-82; asst. univ. libr. U. Oreg., Eugene, 1982-89; univ. libr. The Am. U., Washington, 1989—. Cons. Bloomsburg (Pa.) U. Libr., 1990, Banco Ctrl., Ecuador, 1998, Am. U. Sharjah, UAE, 1999; bd. dirs. CAPCON, ERIC Clearinghouse on Higher Edn. Adminstrn. Contbr. articles to profl. jours. Pres. West Cascade Returned Peace Corps Vols., Eugene, 1985-88; v.p. Friends of Colombia, Washington, 1990—; speaker on Peace Corps, 1965—, libr. and info. svcs., 1979—. Honors Program scholarship Seattle U., 1960-62, Peace Corps scholarship Antioch U., 1965-66; recipient Beyond War award, 1987, Fulbright Sr. Lectr. award Fulbright, 1989, Disting. Alumnus award Sch. of Info. and Libr. Studies, U. Mich., 1992. Mem. ALA (chmn. com. on legislation 1997-98), Assn. Coll. and Rsch. Librs. (chair budget and fin. bd. dirs. 1987-89, chair WHCLIS task force 1989-92, chair govt. rels. com. 1993-94, chair internat. rels. com. 1996-98), On-line Computer Librs. Ctr. (adv. com. on coll. and univ. librs. 1991-96), D.C. Libr. Assn. (bd. dirs. 1993-98, pres. 1996-97). Home: 4854 Bayard Blvd Bethesda MD 20816-1785 Office: Am Univ Libr 4400 Massachusetts Ave NW Washington DC 20016-8046

WANDELL, BRIAN A. neuroscientist, educator; BS in Math. and Psychology, U. Mich., 1973; PhD in Social Sci., U. Calif., Irvine, 1977. Postdoctoral fellow U. Pa.; from asst. to assoc. prof. Stanford U., Calif., 1979—88, prof., 1988—. Isaac and Madeline Stein family prof., 2002—. Author: Foundations of Vision; assoc. editor: Jour. Vision, Jour. Neuroscience and Neural Networks; contbr. articles to profl. jours. Named McKnight Sr. Investigator, 1997; recipient Edridge-Green Medal in Ophthalmology for work in visual neurosciences, 1997, Macbeth prize, Inter-Soc. Color Coun., 2000. Fellow: Optical Soc. Am.; mem.: NAS (Troland Rsch. award 1986). Office: Jordan Hall Stanford Univ Stanford CA 94305

WANDER, HERBERT STANTON, lawyer; b. Cin, Ohio, Mar. 17, 1935; s. Louis Marvin and Pauline (Schuster) W.; m. Ruth Cele Fell, Aug. 7, 1960; children: Daniel Jerome, Susan Gail, Lois Marlene. AB, U. Mich., 1957; LLB, Yale U., 1960. Bar: Ohio 1960, Ill. 1960. Law clk. to judge US Dist. Ct. (no. dist.) Ill., 1960—61; ptnr. Pope Ballard Shepard & Fowle, Chgo., 1961—78, Katten Muchin Zavis Rosenman, Chgo., 1978—. Trustee Michael Reese Found., 1991-; bd. dir. Tel. & Data Systems, Chgo., 1968-, Advance Ross Corp., 1991-96; mem. legal adv. com. to the bd. gov. NY Stock Exch., 1989-92; mem. legal adv. bd. Nat. Assn. Securities Dealers, Inc., 1996-99. Editor: (jour.) Bus. Law Today, 1992-93; editor-in-chief: (jour.) The Bus. Lawyer, 1993-94; contbr. numerous articles to profl. jour. Bd. dir. Jewish Fedn. Met. Chgo., 1972—, pres., 1981-83; bd. dir. Jewish United Fund, 1972—, pres., 1981-83, chmn. pub. affairs com., 1984-87, gen. campaign chmn., 1993; former regional chmn. nat. young leadership cabinet United Jewish Appeal; vice-chmn. large city budgeting conf. Coun. Jewish Fedns., 1979-82, bd. dir., 1980—, exec. com., 1983-84. Mem. ABA (sec. bus. law sect. 1992-93, vice-chair 1993-94, chair-elect 1994-95, chair 1995-96, apptd. to commn. on multidisciplinary practice 1998), Ill. State Bar Assn., Chgo. Bar Assn., Yale Law Sch. Assn. (exec. com. 1982-86), Std. Club, Econ. Club, Northmoor Country Club, Phi Beta Kappa. Home: 70 Prospect Ave Highland Park IL 60035-3329 Office: Katten Muchin Zavis Rosenman 525 W Monroe St Ste 1600 Chicago IL 60661-3693 E-mail: hwander@kmzr.com.

WANDERMAN, SUSAN MAE, lawyer; b. Mar. 12, 1947; d. Leo and Muriel D. Wanderman. AB, Wheaton Coll., Norton, Mass., 1967; JD, St. John's U., 1970; LLM, NYU, 1976. Bar: N.Y. 1971, U.S. Dist. Ct. (ea. and so. dists.) N.Y. 1972, U.S. Ct. Appeals (2d cir.) 1973, U.S. Supreme Ct. 1974. Asst. legal officer, legal dept. Chem. Bank, N.Y.C., 1972—75; 2d v.p. legal dept. Chase Manhattan Bank N.A., N.Y.C., 1975—82; asst. gen. counsel Citicorp Svcs., Inc., N.Y.C., 1982—84; v.p. Citibank, N.A., N.Y.C., 1984—. Instr. bus. law and law for the layman LaGuardia C.C., 1976—77; law day spkr. Queens County Supreme Ct., 1979—83; mem. Cmty. Bd. 6, Queens County, N.Y.C., 1987—. Contbr. articles to legal publs. Past vol. N.Y. State Bar Assn. Lawyers in the Classroom. Mem.: ABA, Queens County Bar Assn., N.Y. State Bar Assn. Office: Citibank NA One Court Sq Long Island City NY 11120

WANDERS, HANS WALTER, banker; b. Aachen, Germany, Apr. 3, 1925; came to U.S., 1929, naturalized, 1943; s. Herbert and Anna Maria (Kusters) W.; m. Elizabeth Knox Kimball, Apr. 2, 1949; children: Crayton Kimball, David Gillette. BS, Yale U., 1947; postgrad. Grad. Sch. Banking, Rutgers U., 1961-64. With GE, 1947-48, Libbey-Owens-Ford Glass Co., 1948-53, Allied Chem. Co., 1953-55, McKinsey & Co., Inc., 1955-57; from asst. cashier to v.p. No. Trust Co., Chgo., 1957-65; v.p. Nat. Blvd. Bank, Chgo., 1965-66, pres., 1966-70; exec. v.p. Wachovia Bank & Trust Co., N.A., Winston-Salem, N.C., 1970-74, chmn., 1977-85, vice chmn., 1985-88, also bd. dirs.; pres. Wachovia Corp., Winston-Salem, 1974-76, 85-87, chmn., 1977-85, vice chmn., 1987-88, also bd. dirs.; pres., chief exec. officer 1st Wachovia Corp. Services, Inc., Winston-Salem, 1986-88, ret., 1988; dir. Exxon Supply Co., 1989-94, Goody's Mfg. Corp., 1989-94, Gulf Resources, Inc., 1989-92, Turnpike Properties, Inc., 2001—. Chmn. Winston-Salem Found. Com., 1981-82; bd. dirs. N.C. Textile Found., N.C. Engring. Found., Inc., 1971-88; trustee, mem. exec. com. Salem Coll. and Acad., 1986-91, Tax Found., 1982—, vice chmn., 1984-86, chmn., 1986-88, chmn. exec. com., 1989; mem. bd. visitors Fuqua Sch. Bus., Duke U., 1978-89, N.C. Japan Ctr., 1982—; mem. nat. corps. com. United Negro Coll. Fund; mem., chmn. N.C. Bd. Econ. Devel., 1989-93; corporator Belmont Hill Sch., 1996—. Lt. USNR, 1943-46, 51-53. Mem. Am. Bankers Assn. (chmn. mktg. divsn. 1979-80, dir. 1971-73), Assn. Res. City Bankers, Conf. Bd. (So. regional adv. coun.), Assn. Bank Holding Cos. (bd. dirs., exec. com. 1981-83), Chgo. Club, Commonwealth Club Chgo., Twin City Club Winston Salem, Old Town Club Winston-Salem, Roaring Gap Club N.C. Home: 10 Graylyn Pl Winston Salem NC 27106 Office: Wachovia Corp 420 W 4th St Ste 202-A Winston Salem NC 27101-2837 Office Phone: 336-732-5923.

WANDYCZ, PIOTR STEFAN, history educator; b. Krakow, Poland, Sept. 20, 1923; s. Damian Stanislaw and Stefania (Dunikowska) W.; m. Maria Teresa Chrzaszcz, Aug. 13, 1963; children: Anna, Joanna, Antoni. BA, Cambridge U., 1948, MA, 1952; PhD, London U., 1951; MA (hon.), Yale U., 1968; PhD (hon.), Wroclaw U., Poland, 1993; DHC, Sorbonne U., Paris, 1997, Jagiellonian U., 2000. Instr. to assoc. prof. history Ind. U., 1954-66; fellow Harvard's Russian Rsch. Ctr., 1963-65; assoc. prof. history Yale U., 1966-68, prof., 1968-89, chmn. Russian and East European coun., 1974-76, 81-83, Bradford Durfee prof., 1989-97, prof. emeritus, 1997—. Vis. prof. history Columbia U., 1967, 69, 74 Author: Czechoslovak-Polish Confederation and Great Powers, 1956, France and Her Eastern Allies, 1962, Soviet-Polish Relations, 1969, The Lands of Partitioned Poland, 1974, United States and Poland, 1980, August Zaleski, 1980, Polska i Zagranica, 1986, The Twilight of French Eastern Alliances, 1988, Z Dziejow dyplomacji, 1988, Polish Diplomacy 1914-1945, 1988, The Price of Freedom, 1992, 2nd edit., 2001, Die Freiheit und ihr Preis, 1993, Pod zaborami, 1994, Cena wolnosci, 1995, 2d edit., 2003, Laisves Kaina, 1997, Stredni Evropa v Dejinach, 1998, Tsenata na svobodata, 1999, Z Pilsudskim i Sikorskim, 1999, Il prezzo della liberta, 2001, O Federalizmie i emigracji, 2003, Pax Europaea, 2003; co-author: Historia Europy Srodkowo-Wschodniej, 2000; contbr. articles to profl. jours.; mem. editl. bd. Slavic Rev., Internat. History Rev., Polish Rev., Polin., East European Politics and Soc. Served as 2d lt. Polish Army, 1942-45. Decorated Comdr.'s Cross of Polonia Restituta; recipient Alfred Jurzykowski Found. award in history, 1977; fellow Guggenheim Found., Ford Found., Rockefeller Found., Am. Philos. Soc., Am. Coun. Learned Socs., Social Sci. Rsch. Coun., Internat. Rsch. and Exchs. Bd. Mem. AAAS (Wayne Vucinich prize 1989), Am. Hist. Assn. (George Louis Beer prize 1962, 89), Polish Hist. Assn. (hon.), Polish Acad. Arts and Scis., Polish Acad. Scis., Polish Inst. Arts and Scis. (pres. 1999—), Polish Soc. Abroad (A. Lenkszewicz prize 1991, Oscar

Halecki History award 1997), Czechoslovak Acad. of Scis. (Hlavka medal 1992), Czechoslovak Soc. Arts and Scis. Home: 27 Spring Garden St Hamden CT 06517-1913 Office: Yale U Dept History New Haven CT 06520-8324

WANEK, TODD, retail executive; CEO Ashley Furniture Industries, Arcadia, Wis., 2002—. Office: Ashley Furniture Industries One Ashley Way Arcadia WI 54612

WANEK, WILLIAM CHARLES, public relations executive; b. Ridgewood, N.Y., Oct. 21, 1932; s. William John and Anna (Benes) W.; m. Robbie Gene Fairbanks, Feb. 14, 1974; children: William Robert, Jennifer Leigh. BA in English, CCNY, 1954; MA in Psychology, The New Sch. Social Rsch., N.Y.C., 1982. Asst. editor Soap Chem. Spltys. Mag., N.Y.C., 1956-58; editor in chief Maintenance Supplies Mag., N.Y.C., 1958-60; acct. exec. O.S. Tyson & Co. Inc., N.Y.C., 1960-62; dir. advt. and pub. rels. Pa. Glass Sand Corp., N.Y.C., 1962-64; sr. acct. exec. McCann Erickson Inc., N.Y.C., 1964-66; acct. supr. Burson-Marsteller Assocs., N.Y.C., 1966-71; exec. v.p. Gibbs & Soell Inc., N.Y.C., 1971—. With U.S. Army, 1954-56. Mem. Am. Agrl. Editors Assn., Nat. Agri-Mktg. Assn. (bd. dirs. ea. chpt. 1974-76), Nat. Assn. Farm Broadcasters. Presbyterian. Avocations: horticulture, classical music, theater, reading, swimming. Office: Gibbs & Soell Inc 600 3rd Ave Fl 6 New York NY 10016-1903

WANG, ALBERT HUAI-EN, lawyer; b. Tainan, Taiwan, Feb. 21, 1967; s. Tien-Yu Wang and Shiu-Yin Chen. BA magna cum laude, MA magna cum laude, UCLA, 1990; JD, Cornell U., 1994. Bar: N.Y. 1995. Tax specialist KPMG Peat Marwick, L.A., 1990-91; tchr. asst. Cornell Law Sch., 1993; assoc. Willkie Farr & Gallagher, N.Y.C., 1994-99, Schulte Roth & Zabel LLP, N.Y.C., 1999—2001. Legal counsel, adv. coun. Asian Am. Bus. Devel. ctr., N.Y.C., 1999—2002; dir. Baldor Specialty Foods, Inc., 2001—. U. Calif. regent scholar, 1986-90, Alumni scholar UCLA, 1986, Departmental scholar, 1989. Mem.: ABA, Asian Fin. Soc. (adv. coun. mem. 2002—), Orgn. Chinese Ams. (N.Y. chpt.), U.S.-China Lawyers Soc. (bd. dirs. 2002—), Chinese Fin. Soc. (dir., legal counsel 2000—02), N.Y. State Bar Assn., Chinese Am. Voters Assn. of Queens (dir. N.Y. chpt. 1999—2001), Asia Soc., China Inst., Phi Beta Kappa, Omicron Delta Epsilon, Phi Delta Phi. Democrat. Home: 138-10 Franklin Ave Apt 5N Flushing NY 11355-3305 Office: Phillips Nizer LLP 666 Fifth Ave New York NY 10103-0084 Office Phone: 212-977-9700. Business E-Mail: awang@phillipsnizer.com.

WANG, ALBERT JAMES, violinist, educator; b. Ann Arbor, Mich., Nov. 19, 1958; s. James and Lydia (Ebenhoch) Wang; m. Bridget Renee Becker, June 30, 1987 (div. 2000); children: Ona Lenore, Kevin Lewis. MusB, Ind. U., 1979; MusM, U. Mich., 1981; DMA, Am. Conservatory, 1993. Prin. second violin Baton Rouge Symphony Orch., 1981-82; first violin Valcour String Quartet, Baton Rouge, 1981-82, Loyola String Quartet, 1982-83; mem. Lyric Opera Chgo. Orch., 1982—; mem. Orch. Ill., Chgo., 1982-88; prin. 2d violin Internat. Symphony Orch., Port Huron, Mich., 1984; 1st violin Internat. String Quartet, Port Huron, 1984; concertmaster, soloist Chgo. Chamber Orch., 1985-88, Chgo. Philharm., 1985—; mem. Grant Park Symphony Orch., Chgo., 1986-87; concertmaster, soloist Birch Creek Music Festival, Wis., Woodstock (Ill.) Mozart Festival Orch., 1988-90; concertmaster Rockford (Ill.) Symphony Orch., 1990-91, Northwestern Music Festival Orch., 1990—; soloist, concertmaster Pro Musica Orch. of Mauritius, 1992-93; soloist, concertmaster China tour Classical Symphony Orch., 1994, 95; soloist, concertmaster Midwest Symphony Orch., 1995-96; music dir. Baroque Masterplayers, 1994—; soloist, concertmaster Met. Arts Orch., 1995-98. Artist-in-residence St. Clair Coll., Port Huron, 1984, Elgin C.C., 1994—97; lectr. Am. Conservatory Music, Chgo., 1989—92; Fulbright lectr. Francois Mitterand Conservatory of Music, Quatre Bornes, Mauritius, 1992—93; asst. prof. violin Roosevelt U., 1993—2002; adj. prof. violin Wheaton (Ill.) Coll., 1997—2000; adj. asst. prof. violin Moody Bible Inst., Chgo., 1997—2000; v.p. sales and mktg. Music Edn. Publs., Inc., Coral Springs, Fla., 1997—98. Numerous solo, recital and chamber music appearances and master classes throughout U.S., Can., France, Mauritius and China; recs. and broadcasts by Mauritian Nat. Radio and WFMT Chgo. Fine Arts Sta., PBS, Nat. Pub. Radio, and Chinese Nat. Radio and TV; numerous world premieres; recs. on New World Records and with Slavic Projection Ensemble; N.Y. recital debut at Carnegie Hall, 1998; adjudicator for state and nat. music competitions; contbr. articles and revs. to profl. jours. Vol. ARC, Literacy Vols. Am., Chgo. Pub. Librs., United Way; bd. advisors Prism Music Festival, 1984—, Am. Chamber Symphony, 1985, Symphony II, 1993-94. Fulbright grantee, 1992-93; recipient 1st prize Ann Arbor (Mich.) Symphony Competition, 1976, Soc. Am. Musicians Competition, Chgo., 1984, Internat. Concerts Atlantique Competition, N.Y.C., 1989, Chgo. Park Dist. Competition, 1991, 2nd prize Biennial Adult Artist Competition, 1992, Helmuth Fuchs Performance award 1998; selected to Arts Am. Touring Artist Roster, 1993; finalist Lilly Fellows Program in Humanities and the Arts, Valparaiso U., 1994, Harry and Sarah Zelzer Fellowship and prize; recipient Leo Sowerby medal, 1994; Christian Performing Artists' fellow. Mem. ASCAP, Am. Fedn. Musicians, Am. String Tchrs. Assn., Coll. Music Soc., Chamber Music Am., Am. Music Ctr., Music Tchrs. Nat. Assn., Christian Performing Artists' Fellowship. Avocations: powerlifting, fishing, travel, woodworking. Home: 6110 N Glenwood Ave Chicago IL 60660-1804 Office: Lyric Opera Chgo 20 N Wacker Dr Chicago IL 60606-2806

WANG, ALLAN XU HUI, physician; b. Xindeng, Zhejiang, China, May 14, 1955; s. Helen Hui Fu Wang and Ruo Nan Shi; m. Hui Huang, May 31, 1985; 1 child, Susan Shubai. CMD, Shanghai U. Chinese Medicine, 1977, Post CMD, 1985. Physician Shanghai Yueyang Hosp./Coll. TCM, China, 1977-84; prof. Shanghai U. Chinese Medicine, 1985-93; pres. Inst. Traumatology and Orthopedics/Shanghai Acad. TCM, China, 1985-93; v.p. Internat. Med. Rsch., China, 1993-99, Internat. Med. Rsch. (Botanic Lab), Brea, Calif., 1999-2001; chmn., pres. NeoMedicine, Tustin, Calif., 2000—; prof. Internat. Hygienic Med. Acad., 2000—, All China Uni-Sci. Rsch. Ctr., 2000—. Commr. Task Force on Cancer Pain of IASP, 1993—. Patentee in field; contbr. articles to profl. jours. Spl. subsidy expert China State Coun., 1992—, China scientist and inventist, 1995; recipient cert. for world-famous med. experts and qualified personnel World Pharm. Rsch. Ctr., 1997. Mem. All China Soc. Rheumatism (commr. 1988-2000), All China Com. Preventing and Treating Rheumatism (vice-chmn. 1994—). Avocations: art, music, sports, reading. E-mail: NeoMedicine@CS.com.

WANG, ARTHUR WOODS, retired publisher; b. Port Chester, N.Y., Oct. 7, 1918; s. Israel and Madolin (Woods) W.; m. Mary-Ellen Mackay, Aug. 13, 1955; 1 son, Michael Anthony. BS, Bowdoin Coll., 1940; postgrad., Columbia U., 1949—52. Advt. rsch. McCann-Erickson, Inc., 1940-41; editor Doubleday & Co., 1942-43, Alfred A. Knopf, Inc., 1943, T.Y. Crowell (Pub.), 1943-47; with E.M. Hale & Co., Eau Claire, Wis., 1947-52; editor A.A. Wyn, Inc., 1952-55; co-founder, pres., editor-in-chief Hill & Wang, Inc., 1956-71; pub., editor-in-chief Hill & Wang divsn. Farrar, Straus & Giroux, Inc., N.Y.C., 1971-87; sr. editor Hill and Wang divsn. Farrar, Straus & Giroux, Inc., N.Y.C., 1988-98, ret., 1998. Exhibitions include Beinecke Rare Book and Manuscript Libr., Yale U., 2002. Home: 100 Newbury Ct Apt 205 Concord MA 01742-4155

WANG, BAOLIANG (BOB WANG), applications scientist, researcher; b. Xinji, Hebei, China, Jan. 9, 1963; came to U.S., 1988; s. Yuzhuang and Shuyin (Yang) W.; m. Haiying Li, May 15, 1987; children: George, May. BS, Nankai U., Tianjin, China, 1978-82; PhD, U. Ill., Chgo., 1993. Lectr. Hebei Tchrs. U., 1985-88; postdoctoral rschr. U. Ill., Chgo., 1993-94; sr. applications scientist, applications rsch. mgr. Hinds Instrument, Inc., Hillsboro, Oreg., 1995—. Recipient 2 R&D 100 awards. Achievements include research in polarization modulation instrumentation; investigation of vibrational Zeeman effect using magnetic vibrational circular dichroism; Fourier transform infrared-vibrational circular dichroism spectroscopy; invention of a highly sensitive birefringence measurement system known as EXICOR; measurement of optical rotation. Home: 16254 NW Joscelyn St Beaverton OR 97006-7258 E-mail: bwang@hindspem.com.

WANG, BUQIAN, materials research scientist; b. Nantong, China, Sept. 8, 1938; came to U.S., 1984, citizen, 1999; s. Jizhou Wang and Shujun Zhu; m. Zheng-Rong Shui, July 1, 1962; children: Xiao-Dan, Jue. BS, Xian Jiaotong U., China, 1961, PhD, 1979. Teaching asst., lectr., assoc. prof. Xian Hwy. U., China, 1961-84, prof., dir. Tribology Rsch. Inst., 1987-88; sr. rsch. scientist, cons. Metalspray Internat., Inc., Richmond, Va., 1992—. Vis. scientist, staff scientist Lawrence Berkeley Lab., U. Calif., 1985-87, 88-92; cons. in field. Author: Corrosion and Particle Erosion, 1989; contbr. over 100 articles to profl. jours. V.p. Chinese Student & Vis. Scholar Assn., Berkeley, 1986-87. Recipient Sci. & Tech. award, Xian Hwy. U., 1976, Xian City, 1978, Heat Treatment award, Chinese Sci. & Tech. Assn., 1980; vis. scholar SUNY, Mat. Sci. & Engring. Dept., Stony Brook, 1984-85. Mem. Nat. Assn. Corrosions Engrs., Am. Soc. Materials Internat. Avocations: photography, folk songs, stamp collecting/philately, hiking. Home: 408 Whitaker Rd Richmond VA 23235-4056 Office: FBE Tech Ctr Metalspray United 2713 Oak Lake Blvd Midlothian VA 23112 E-mail: BQ.Wang@metalspray.com.

WANG, CHAO CHENG, mathematician, engineer; b. Peoples Republic of China, July 20, 1938; came to U.S., 1961; s. N.S. and V.T. Wang; m. Sophia C.L. Wang; children: Ferdinand, Edward. BS, Nat. Taiwan U., 1959; PhD, Johns Hopkins U., 1965. Registered profl. engr., Tex. Asst. prof. Johns Hopkins U., Balt., 1966-68, assoc. prof., 1968-69; prof. Rice U., Houston, 1968-79, Noah Harding prof., 1979—, chmn. math. sci. dept., 1983-89, chmn. mech. engring. and materials sci., 1991-94. Author numerous books in field; contbr. articles to profl. jours. Named Disting. Young Scientist Md. Acad. Sci., 1968. Mem. ASME, Soc. Natural Philosophy (treas. 1985-86), Am. Acad. Mechs. Office: Rice Univ Dept Mech Engring Materials Sci Houston TX 77251

WANG, CHARLES B. professional sports team executive; b. Shanghai, Rep. China, Aug. 19, 1944; arrived in U.S., 1952; BS in Math., Queens Coll., 1967. Programming trainee Columbia U. Riverside Rsch. Inst., Islandia, NY; v.p. sales Std. Data Corp.; CEO Computer Assocs., Islandia, 1976—2000, chmn., 1980—2002, chmn. emeritus; owner, CEO N.Y. Islanders, Uniondale, 1999—; co-owner N.Y. Dragons (arena football). Author: Techno Vision, 1994, Techno Vision II: Every Executive's Guide to Understanding and Mastering Technology and the Internet, 1997. Founder The Smile Train; active Nat. Ctr. for Missing and Exploited Children, Make-A-Wish Found. Avocations: cooking, basketball. Address: NY Islanders Nassau Veterans Meml Coliseum Uniondale NY 11553

WANG, CHARLES PING, engineering executive; b. Shanghai, Republic of China, Apr. 25, 1937; came to U.S., 1962; s. Kuan-Ying and Ping-Lu (Ming) W.; m. Lily L. Lee, June 29, 1963. BS, Taiwan U., Republic of China, 1959; MS, Tsinghua U., Singchu, Republic of China, 1961; PhD, Calif. Inst. Tech., 1967. Mem. tech. staff Bellcomm, Washington, 1967-69; research engr. U. San Diego, 1969-74; sr. scientist Aerspace Corp., Los Angeles, 1976-86; pres. Optodyne, Inc., Compton, Calif., 1986—. Adj. prof. U. Calif., San Diego, 1979-90; pres. Chinese-Am. Engr. and Scientists Assn. So. Calif., Los Angeles, 1979 81; program chmn. Internation Conf. of Lasers, Shanghai, 1979-80; organizer and session chmn. Lasers Conf., Los Angeles, 1981-84, program chmn., Las Vegas, 1985. Editor in chief Series in Laser Tech., 1983-91; contbr. articles to profl. jours.; inventor discharge excimer laser. Calif. Inst. Tech. scholar, 1965. Fellow Am. Optical Soc., AIAA (assoc., jour. editor 1981-83). Office: Optodyne Inc 1180 W Mahalo Pl Compton CA 90220-5443 Office Phone: 310-635-7481. Personal E-mail: optodyne@aol.com.

WANG, CHEN CHI, electronics company, real estate, finance company, investment services, and international trade executive; b. Taipei, Taiwan, Aug. 10, 1932; came to U.S., 1959, naturalized, 1970; s. Chin-Ting and Chen-Kim Wang; m. Victoria Rebisoff, Mar. 5, 1965; children: Katherine Kim, Gregory Chen, John Christopher, Michael Edward. BA in Econs., Nat. Taiwan U., 1955; BSEE, San Jose State U., 1965; MBA, U. Calif., Berkeley, 1961. With IBM Corp., San Jose, Calif., 1965-72; founder, CEO Electronics Internat. Co., Santa Clara, Calif., 1968-72, owner, gen. mgr., 1972-81; reorganized as EIC Group, 1981-2000; chmn. bd., CEO EIC Investment Corp., 1982—; dir. Systek Electronics Corp., Santa Clara, 1970-73; founder, sr. ptnr. Wang Enterprises (name changed to Chen Kim Enterprises 1982), Santa Clara, 1974-75, Hanson & Wang Devel. Co., Woodside, Calif., 1977-85; chmn. bd. Golden Alpha Enterprises, San Mateo, Calif., 1979-99; mng. ptnr. Woodside Acres-Las Pulgas Estate, Woodside, 1980-85; founder, sr. ptnr. DeVine & Wang, Oakland, Calif., 1977-83, Van Heal & Wang, West Village, Calif., 1981-82; founder, chmn. bd. EIC Fin. Corp. (now EIC Investment Corp.), Redwood City, Calif., 1985-90; chmn. bd. Maritek Corp., Corpus Christi, Tex., 1988-89; chmn. EIC Internat. Trade Corp., Lancaster, Calif., 1989-90, EIC Capital Corp., Redwood City, 1990-91. Mng. mem. Sixtieth West, LLC, 1997—2004, Land Investment Co. Calif., LLC, 1998—, Aceh Capital, LLC, 1998—. Author: Monetary and Banking System of Taiwan, 1955, The Small Car Market in the U.S., 1961. Served to 2d lt., Nationalist Chinese Army, 1955-56. Mem. Internat. Platform Assn., Tau Beta Pi. Mem. Christian Ch. Home: 195 Brookwood Rd Woodside CA 94062-2302 Office: ACE Group Head Office Bldg 2055-2075 Woodside Rd Redwood City CA 94061-3355 Business E-Mail: chenwang@acecapgroup.com.

WANG, CHEN-KU, retired library director; b. Peiping, China, July 18, 1924; s. Bing-fong Wang and Fong-gen Hsia; m. Shuo-fen Wang, Aug. 15, 1946; children: Pei-chi, Sheng-shiang, Sheng-Wen. MA, Peabody Coll. Tchrs., 1959; LLD (hon.), Ohio U., 1988. Prof. Nat. Taiwan Normal U., Teipei, 1960-94; dir. Nat. Ctrl. Libr., China, 1977-89, ret., 1994. Dir. Ctr. for Chinese Studies, 1977-89. Author: Selection and Acquisition of Library Materials, 1978; hon. editor Jour. Libr. and Info. Sci., 1975—. Decorated knight comdr. Silvestri, Vatican; recipient Disting. Svc. award Chinese-Am. Libr. Assn.and Libr. Assn. China, 1986, 87. Mem. Libr. Assn. China (pres. 1992-97).

WANG, CHI HUA, chemist, education educator; b. Beijing, Apr. 18, 1921; arrived in U.S., 1948; s. Wen Ru and Liu Shih Wang; m. Nancy Yang Wang; 1 child, Fong. BS, St. John's U., Shanghai, 1945; MS, Fu-Jen U., Peking, 1947; PhD, St. Louis U., 1951. Instr. in chemistry Brandeis U., 1953—55, asst. prof., 1955—60, assoc. prof. of chemistry, 1960—62; sr. scientist Arthur D. Little Inc., Cambridge, 1962—64; assoc. prof. in chemistry Wellesley Coll., 1964—68, dir. molecular biology program, 1966—68; assoc. prof. of chemistry U. of Mass., Boston, 1968—70, prof. of chemistry, 1971—99, prof. of chemistry emeritus, 1999—. Cons. Arthur D. Little Inc., Mass., 1964—80; vis. prof. of chemistry The Chinese Acad. of Sci., Taiwan U., Tsing-hua U., Taipei, 1966, The PhotoChemistry Inst., The Chinese Acad. of Sci., Beijing, 1980, Jilin U., 1980, Chinese Acad. of Sci., Beijing, 1983, The Chinese Acad. of Sci., Organic Chemistry Inst., Chengdu, 1985, The Grad. Sch., The Chinese Acad. of Sci., Beijing, 1987, 91, 94. Contbr. numerous articles to various jours., 1953—90; author: (book) An Intro. to the Fundamentals of Phys. Organic Chemistry, 1990. Grantee, Brandeis U., 1951—53. Avocation: oriental art. Home: 106 Pleasant St Lexington MA 02421

WANG, CHIA PING, physicist, researcher; b. The Philippines; came to U.S., 1963, naturalized; (parents Chinese citizens). s. Guan Can and Tah (Lin) W. *Born in the Philippines, Chinese by birth. Grandparents and parents were business proprietors. Received basic training in nuclear electron physics and theoretical physics from Professor Sir Norman Alexander, student of Lord Rutherford, and Professor Otto Frisch, University of Cambridge, and closely associated with Otto Frisch for more than 20 years; and also with Professor Sir Denys Wilkinson. Built a modified Wilkinson discriminator for double beta decay and comic-ray experiments in China, and one in Hong Kong.* BS, U. London, 1950; MS, Brit. U. Malaya in Singapore (now U. Singapore), 1951; PhD in Physics, Brit. U. Malaya (now U. Singapore) and U. Cambridge, 1953; DSc in Physics (hon.), U. Singapore, 1972. Asst. lectr. U. Malaya, Singapore, 1951—53; mem. faculty Nankai U., Tientsin, China, 1954—58, prof. physics, 1956—58, head electron physics divsn., 1955—58; head electron physics Lanchow (China) Atomic Project, 1958; faculty Hong Kong U., Chinese U., Hong Kong, 1958, prof. physics, 1959—63, acting head physics, math. depts., 1959; rsch. assoc. lab. nuc. studies Cornell U., Ithaca, NY, 1963—64; assoc. prof. space sci. and applied physics Cath. U. Am., Washington, 1964—68; assoc. prof. physics Case Inst. Tech., Case Western Res. U., Cleve., 1966—70; vis. scientist, vis. prof. Cavendish Lab., U. Cambridge (Eng.), Inst. Theoretical Physics, U. Louvain (Belgium), Cosmic Ray Lab., U.S. Naval Rsch. Labs. (concurrently U. Md.) MIT, 1970—75; rsch. physicist radiation lab. U.S. Army Natick (Mass.) R & D Command, 1975— Steering com. sci. and tech. directorate U.S. Army Natick R & D Command, 1993—; steering com. nuc. physics divsn. Nankai U., Tientsin, 1956-58; vis. scientist, vis. prof. U. Cambridge (Eng.), U. Leuven, Belgium, U.S. Naval Rsch. Labs., U. Md., MIT, 1970-75. *Initiated extensive air shower project in China; first to convert in 1963 picosecond pulses to pulse-heights; discovered in 1965-1968 from more than 50 experiments the many-subunit (parton) structure of the nucleon and other hadrons, opening up the field of multiparticle production in high-energy physics; and the 3-quark-qq-bar (called Ylon, later, Valence quarks- sea quarks) structure of the nucleon from electron-, neutrino-, meson, and nucleon-nucleon high-energy scattering experiments at the Cavendish Laboratory in 1970-72; performed one of the first experiments at the Fermi National Laboratory's (then) 200 GeV accelerator in 1972; and work on laser interferometry (with Otto Frisch), thermal Physics, microwaves, Laser, quantum fields, and Cosmology.* Co-author: Atomic Structure and Interactions of Ionizing Radiations with Matter in Preservation of Food by Ionizing Radiation, 1982; contbr. over 80 articles to profl. jours. Recipient Outstanding Performance award Dept. Army, 1980, Quality Increase award, 1980, Sustained Superior Performance awards, 1990, 96. Mem. AAAS, Am. Nuc. Soc., Am. Phys. Soc., Inst. Physics London (chartered physicist), N.Y. Acad. Scis., Sigma Xi. Achievements include pioneering research in nucleon sub-structure (now often referred to as parton), established quantum fluctuating 3-quark-many-qq-bar (called Ylon, later known as Valence Quarks, Sea Quarks) nuclear sub unit structure from MIT/SLAC/CERN deep inelastic electron-neutrino-nucleon scattering experiments; multiparticle production, cosmic radiation, picosecond time to pulse-height conversion, thermal physics, power law of laser steel melting, microwaves absorption and scattering, initiating cosmic-ray extensive air shower research in China; visualizing with Otto Frisch the sinusoidal interference laser light waves in Frisch's laser interferometer. Office: US Army Natick Lab/MIT 28 Hallett Hill Rd Weston MA 02493-1753 Office Phone: 781-899-6751. Personal E-mail: chiapingwang@yahoo.com.

WANG, CHUAN-BAO, chemist, research scientist; b. Huaining, Peoples Republic China, Jan. 1, 1964; s. Guojia and Nan (He) Wang; m. Xiaojing Zhang, Sept. 24, 1988; children: Derek S., Janet Z. BS, Anyhui Normal U., Wuhu, China, 1985; MS, U. Sci. and Tech., Hefei, China, 1988; PhD, Peking U., Beijing, 1991. Asst. prof. Peking U., Beijing, 1991—94; rsch. scientist Lehigh U., Bethlehem, Pa., 1994—98; sr. chemist, project mgr. Indsl. Sci. Corp., Oakdale, Pa., 1998—. Contbr. articles to profl. jours.; patentee formaldehyde production. Fellow, Japan Soc. for Promotion of Sci., 1994. Mem.: Am. Assn. for Advanced Soc., N.Am. Catalysis Soc., Am. Chem. Soc., Pitts.-Cleve. Catalysis Soc. (treas. 1999—2003). Avocations: jogging, reading, music. Home: 505 Jonathan Ct Oakdale PA 15071 Office: Indsl Sci Corp 1001 Oakdale Rd Oakdale PA 15071 E-mail: cbwang8@yahoo.com.

WANG, CHUNG SHAN, physicist; b. Fukien, China, Dec. 16, 1937; came to U.S., 1964; s. Pey-jen and I-jen (Liu) W.; m. Kaiwen K. Mao, June 2, 1969 (div. Sept. 1988); children: Alicia K., Jason K. BS, Nat. Cheng Kung U., 1962; MS, U. Idaho, 1966, PhD, 1969. Asst. prof. SUNY, Albany, 1969-77; staff scientist Systems and Applied Sci. Corp., College Park, Md., 1977-78; rsch. staff Tech. Svc. Corp., Silver Spring, Md., 1978-79; tech. staff Tex. Instruments, Inc., Suitland, Md., 1979-81; sr. physicist Vitro Corp., Rockville, Md., 1981-99, BAE Sys., Rockville, Md., 2000—. Contbr. articles to profl. jours. Mem. Am. Geophys. Union. Avocation: ballroom dancing. Home: 12 Sebastiani Blvd Gaithersburg MD 20878-4120 Office: BAE Systems 1601 Research Blvd Rockville MD 20850-3173 E-mail: chung.wang@baesystems.com.

WANG, CHUNG-HSIAO, industrial engineer; b. Taipei, Taiwan, Dec. 30, 1968; arrived in U.S., 1994; s. Chih-Chun Wang and Hsiu-Yueh Wang Lin; m. Li-Ming Liu, Jan. 31, 2002. BS, Tunghai U., Taichung, Taiwan, 1991; MS, Iowa State U., 1997, PhD, 2001. Rsch. asst. Electric Power Rsch. Ctr., Iowa State U., Ames, 1995—99; instr. indsl. engring. Iowa State U., 2000; prin. rsch. asst. EPRI, 1999—2001; fin. engr., model analyst LG&E Energy LLC, Louisville, 2001—. Contbr. articles to profl. jours. 2d lt. Taiwan Army, 1991—93. Recipient Grad. Rsch. Excellence award, Iowa State U., 2001. Mem.: Inst. of Ops. Rsch. and the Mgmt. Scis., Inst. Indsl. Engrs., Phi Kappa Phi. Avocations: astronomy, reading. Home: 2400 Mellwood Ave #406 Louisville KY 40206 Office: LG&E 220 W Main St Louisville KY 40202 Office Phone: 502-627-3825. Business E-Mail: chung-hsiao.wang@lgeenergy.com.

WANG, DELIANG, computer scientist, educator; b. He County, China, Jan. 27, 1963; came to U.S., 1988; s. Shiwu Wang and Xianzheng Song; m. Ping Bai, Jan. 19, 1991. BS, Peking U., Beijing, 1983, MS, 1986; PhD, U. So. Calif., 1991. Asst. rsch. fellow Inst. Computing Tech. Academia Sinica, Beijing, 1986-87; rsch. asst. U. So. Calif., L.A., 1988-90; asst. prof. Ohio State U., Columbus, 1991-96, assoc. prof., 1997—2001, prof., 2001—. Vis. scientist Harvard U., Cambridge, 1998-99. Assoc. editor (jour.) Neurocomputing, 1995—, Neural Computing and Applications, 1996—, IEEE Transactions Neural Networks, 1998—; contbr. articles to profl. jours. NSF rsch. initiation award, 1992, Office of Naval Rsch. young investigator awardee, 1996. Mem. IEEE (sr.), I Neural Networks Soc., IEEE Signal Processing Soc., Internat. Neural Network Soc. Achievements include contributions to temporal sequence learning/processing, revealing learning mechanisms in anuran visual perception and oscillatory associative memory; co-discovered mechanism of selective gating and co-ingrained LEGION networks; applying LEGION networks to visual and auditory scene analysis. Office: Ohio State U Dept Computer & Infor Sci 2015 Neil Ave Columbus OH 43210-1210 E-mail: dwang@cis.ohio-state.edu.

WANG, DONNA HUI, investigative medicine director; b. Guangdong, China, Aug. 20, 1961; d. Xuanwu and Huijuan Wang; m. Eugene J. Yu; 1 child, Eunice Yu. MD, Sun Yat-Sen Med. U., Guangzhou, China, 1984; postdoc. fellow, Eastern Va. Med. Sch., Norfolk, 1990. Resident Sun Yat-Sen Ophthalmic Ctr., Sun Yat-Sen Med. U., Guangzhou, China, 1984-85; vis. scholar dept. surgery and physiology Bowman Gray Sch. Medicine, Winston-Salem, N.C., 1985-87; rsch. assoc. dept. physiology Eastern Va. Med. Sch., Norfolk, 1987-90, asst. prof. dept. physiology, 1990-93; asst. prof. dept. internal medicine U. Tex. Med. Branch, Galveston, Tex., 1993-97, assoc. prof. dept. internal medicine, 1997-99; scientist, dir. histochemical core Sealy Ctr. for Molecular Cardiology, U. Tex. Med. Sch., Galveston, 1994-99; prof. dept. medicine Michigan State U., East Lansing, 1999—. Dir. Investigative medicine, Dept. Medicine, Mich. State U., East Lansing, 1999—; mem. Pub. Com. Am. Heart Assn. Coun. for High Blood Pressure, Dallas, 1999-02. Editor: Angiotensin Protocol, Methods in Molecular Medicine, 2000; contbr. articles to profl. jours. Chair The Session of Physiology and Genetics of Angiotensin I and II Receptors, The 68th Scientific Sessions of Am. Heart Assn., Anaham, Calif., 1995, The Session of Hypertension, Am. Physiol. Soc., San Francisco, 1998; peer reviewer Am. Heart Assn-Western State Affiliates Peer Review, San Francisco, 1998-99; mem. prof. com. The Microcirculatory Soc. Inc., San Diego, 1997-01. Recipient First Ind. Rsch. Support Transition award, Nat. Inst. Health, 1993, 98, 1997 Outstanding Young Investigator Travel award, The Microcirculatory Soc., Inc., Hoechst Marion Roussel 1998 Young Scholar award, The Am. Soc. Hypertension, 1998, Established Investigator award Am. Heart Assn., 1999-03. Fellow Am. Heart Assn. Coun. for High Blood Pressure Rsxh. Pub. com. mem., 1995—, Cardiovascular sect., Am. Physiol. Soc. Woman in Physiology com. mem., 1999—; mem. The Microcirculatory Soc. Inc. Office: Dept Medicine B316 Clinical Ctr East Lansing MI 48824 Fax: 517-432-1326. E-mail: donna.wang@ht.msu.edu.

WANG, FAHUI, geographer; arrived in U.S., 1991; PhD, Ohio State U., 1995. Assoc. prof. No. Ill. U., DeKalb, 2002—. Office: No Ill U 118 Davis Hall Dekalb IL 60115-2854 E-mail: fwang@niu.edu.

WANG, FREDERICK MARK, pediatric ophthalmologist, medical educator; b. N.Y.C., Feb. 17, 1948; Student, Northwestern U., 1968; MD, Yeshiva U., 1972. Diplomate Am. Bd. Ophthalmology, Am. Bd. Pediats., Nat. Bd. Med. Examiners. Intern in pediats. H.C. Moffitt-U. Calif. San Francisco Hosps., 1972-73; resident in pediats. Bronx Mcpl. Hosp. Ctr.-Albert Einstein Coll. Medicine, 1973-74, resident in ophthalmology, 1976-79; Heed fellow in ophthalmology and strabismus Children's Hosp. Nat. Med. Ctr., Washington, 1979-80; asst. prof. ophthalmology Albert Einstein Coll. Medicine, Bronx, 1980-82, asst. clin. prof., 1982-85, assoc. clin. prof., 1985-95, clin. prof., 1995—, asst. prof. pediats., 1980-82, asst. clin. prof. pediats., 1982-92; dir. pediat. ophthalmology and strabismus svc. Montefiore Med. Ctr., Bronx, 1980-90. Cons. ophthalmologist Children's Evaluation & Rehab. Ctr., Rose Kennedy Ctr. for Rsch. in Mental Retardation and Human Devel., Bronx, 1980—, Craniofacial Ctr., Montefiore Med. Ctr., Bronx, 1980—; attending physician in ophthalmology Bronx Mcpl. Hosp./Montefiore Med. Ctr., 1980—; asst. attending physician in ophthalmology North Ctrl. Bronx Hosp., 1980-98; attending physician Strabismus Svc., N.Y. Eye & Ear Infirmary, N.Y.C., 1982-99, attending surgeon, 1999—; mem. dept. ophthalmology Lenox Hill Hosp., N.Y.C., 1988—; sci. reviewer Jour. Am. Acad. Ophthalmology, 1980-86; mem. profl. adv. bd. Found. for Children with Learning Disabilities, N.Y.C., 1983-89; mem. sci. adv. bd. The Glaucoma Found., N.Y.C., 1986-92; mem. profl. adv. bd. Nat. Assn. for Visually Handicapped, N.Y.C., 1988—; coord. pediat. sect. Greater N.Y. Ophthalmology Clin. Lectr. Series, 1990-93; mem. Velo-Cardio-Facial Syndrome Ednl. Found., 1994—, nominating com., 1995—. Mem. editl. bd. Jour. Pediat. Ophthalmology and Strabismus, 1998—; contbr. articles to profl. jours., chpts. to books. Referee, U.S. Soccer Fedn. Maj. med. officer USAF, 1974-76. Mem. Am. Acad. Pediats., Am. Acad. Ophthalmology, Am. Assn. for Pediat. Ophthalmology and Strabismus, N.Y. Soc. for Pediat. Ophthalmology and Strabismus (program chmn. 1987-89, pres. 1990-92), N.Y. Soc. for Clin. Ophthalmology (corr. sec. 1988-90, membership chmn. 1990-91, program chmn. 1991-92, pres. 1992-93), N.Y. Acad. Medicine (sec. sect. on ophthalmology 1993-94, sect. chmn. 1995-96), Alpha Omega Alpha. Avocations: fishing, chess, swimming, soccer refereeing. Office: Pediat Ophthalmology NY 30 E 40th St New York NY 10016-1201 Office Phone: 212-684-3980.

WANG, GAOFENG, engineer, educator; b. China, Dec. 1965; m. Xiaoqing Fang; 1 child, Wavelet. BS in Physics, Hubei U., Wuhan, China, 1983; MS in Radio and Space Physics, Wuhan U., Hubei, China, 1988; PhD in Elec. Engring., U. Wis., Milw., 1993; PhD in Sci. Computing, Stanford U., Calif., 2001. Scientist Tanner Rsch., Inc., Pasadena, Calif., 1993—96; prin. engr. Synopsys, Inc., Mountain View, Calif., 1996—2000. Chief tech. officer Intpax, Inc., San Jose, Calif., 2000—. Contbr. over 70 articles to profl. jours. Grantee SBIR Co-Principal Investigator Phase II Award, $600K, U.S. Army Rsch. Office, 1996, SBIR Co-Principal Investigator Phase I Award, $70K, 1995. Mem.: IEEE. Achievements include patents for 3; patents pending for 4.

WANG, GEORGE K.F. international lawyer; b. Nanking, China, Jan. 2, 1927; m. Lei Lei, Jan. 10, 2000. LLB, Soochow U., Taipei, Taiwan, 1957; LLM, Golden State U., 1982, PhD, 1984. Internat. lawyer, Taiwan, U.S., 1976—; prof. law Nat. Taiwan U., 1977-80, Golden State U., L.A., 1984-86. Advisor, Yunnan Province, China, 1997—, legal advisor, Wego Chiang, Comr. in Chief Taiwan, 1992-94; def. atty., USAF, 327 Divsn., Taiwan, 1978-80; legal advisor ex-premier Taiwan, 1978-80. Author: Domestic Relation, 1961, Jade Warrior, 2000. Chmn. Dr. Sun Yat-Sen Internat. Found., L.A., 1990; sr. Rep., U.S. Reps. Abroad, Taiwan, 1980. Mem. Internat. Bar Ass.n, Am. Immigration Lawyer Assn., Taiwan Bar Assn., Chinese Am. Assn. (chmn.). Avocations: writing, reading, travel. Home: 15585 Facilidad St Hacienda Heights CA 91745-5204 E-mail: georgekf28@hotmail.com.

WANG, GREG G. education educator, consultant; s. Zheng Aihua and Xiansu Wang; m. Zhengxia Dou, Aug. 20, 1982; 1 child, Alice David Wang Dou. BA in Edn., Yan'an U., China, 1982; MS in Agrl. Econs., Chinese Acad. of Agrl. Scis., Beijing, 1987; MA in Mgmt., Pa. State U., 1995, PhD in Human Resource Devel., 1998. Pres. PerformTek, LLC, West Chester, Pa., 2001—; asst. prof. James Madison U., Harrisonburg, Va., 2002—. Program mgr. instrnl. design Motorola, Schaumburg, Ill., 1997—98; lead instrnl. designer Gen. Electric, Shelton, Conn., 1998—99; tng. assoc. Pa. Power and Light Co., Berwick. Author: (rsch.) Human Resource Devel. Quar., Human Resource Devel. Rev., Edn. Tech., Performance Improvement Quar., Performance Improvement Jour., 2002 Tng. & Performance Yearbook, Am. Soc. of Tng. and Devel. Grantee Analysis of Nat. Reporting Sys. on Va. Adult Learning Programs, Adult Edn., Va. Dept. of Edn., 2002—03, Rsch. on E-learning Abandonment, The Industry E-learning Consortium, 2003, Rsch. on cross culture comparison of E-learning in the U.S., China and Russia, Internat. Rsch. and Exch. Bd., 2003—04. Mem.: Human Resource Devel. Accreditation Assn. (founding bd. mem.), Va. Adult and Continuing Edn. Assn. (corr.), Am. Evaluation Assn. (corr.), Soc. for Human Resource Mgmt. (corr.), Internat. Soc. for Performance Improvement (corr.), Acad. of Human Resource Devel. (corr.). Achievements include research in Developed tng. and consulting on learning evaluation and return on investment (ROI) methods for bus. and industries, internat. speaker on human capital and ROI measurement. Home: 1233 Wordsworth Ct Harrisonburg VA 22802 Office: James Madison Univ 800 S Main St MSC 1908 Harrisonburg VA 22807

WANG, GUANGMIAO, business executive, consultant; b. Ninghai, China, Jan. 19, 1947; came to U.S., 1992; s. Yuegnan and Hehua (Zhou) W.; m. Guiyan Xu, May 1, 1973; children: Haixiang, Haijia. BA, Hangzhou Coll. Fgn. Lang., China, 1969; grad., Shanghai Jiaotong U., China, 1985, U. N.D., 1993; postgrad., Heriot-Watt U., Edinburgh, U.K., 1997—. Supr. Heiman Ship Co., China, 1971-74; lectr. Zhejiang U. Tech., Hangzhou, 1974-91; exec. Kin Lin Corp., Kansas City, Mo., 1997—, Jia Xiang Inc., Springfield, Mo., 1997—. Cons. Heimen Bus. Assn., 1972-74. Contbr. articles to profl. jours. U. N.D. grantee, 1992. Mem. Zhejiang Lang. Assn. (advisor 1980-91), N.Am. Chinese Restaurant Assn. (dir. 1997—), Phi Beta Delta. Avocations: golf, boating, photography, collecting stamps and coins. Office: PO Box 12489 Pittsburgh PA 15231-0489

WANG, GWO JAW, orthopaedic surgery educator; Lillian T. Pratt prof. and chmn. orthopedic surgery U. Va. Sch. Medicine, Charlottesville; pres. Kaohsiung (Taiwan) Med. U., 2000—. Recipient U. Va. Pres.'s Report award, 1992, Otto Aufranc award, Hip Soc. and Am. Acad. Orthop. Surgeons, 1992, 1997, Stinchfield award, 1986, Nicholas Andry award, 1998. Office: Kaohsiung Med Univ 100 Shih Chuan 1st Rd Kaohsiung Taiwan Office Fax: 886-7-3212062. E-mail: gwojaw@cc.kmu.edu.tw.

WANG, HONG, engineer, researcher; b. Qianjiang, Hubei, China, June 27, 1963; s. Chuanzhong Wang, Qiande Liu; m. Lili Yu; 1 child, Yu. B Engring., Wuhan U. of Hydraulic and Elec. Engring., Hubei, China, 1983; M Engring., Wuhan U. of Hydraulic and Elec. Engring., Hubai, China, 1986; D Engring., Wuhan U. of Hydraulic and Elec. Engring., Hubei, China, 1991; PhD, Mich. Tech. U., 2001. Lectr. Wuhan U. of Hydraulic and Elec. Engring., China, 1986—92, assoc. prof., 1992—95; vis. scholar dept. mining and geol. engring. U. Ariz., Tucson, 1995—96; rsch. asst. dept. mech. engring.-engring. mechanics/mining engring. Mich. Tech. U., Houghton, 1996—2001; postdoctoral rschr. dept. mech. engring. Johns Hopkins U., Balt., 2001—04; postdoctoral rschr. Oak Ridge Nat. Lab., Oak Ridge, Tenn., 2004—. Visiting Engineer Geo-Eng Australia PTY LTD, Morwell, Victoria, Australia, 1994—94; Field Engineer The 9th Hydroelectric Constructional Bureau, Qinzheng, Guizhou, China, 1990—90. Author: (journal) Acta Materialia, 2004, Wear, 2002, Journal of the Mechanics and Physics of Solids, 2002, Wear, 2001, (Ph.D. Dissertation) Mechanics of Material Removal during the Formation of Single-Grit Rotating Scratch with a Conical Tool, 2001, (journal) International Journal of Rock Mechanics and Mining Science, 1997, (book) Properties of Fissured Rock Mass and Constructional Mechanics of Tunnel System, 1993 (The First Class Award of Science and Technology Progress, Wuhan Univ. of Hydr. and Elec. Eng., 1995), Mechanics of Jointed and Fractured Rock, 1992 (The First Class Award of Science and Technology Progress, Wuhan Univ. of Hydr. and Elec. Eng., 1994), (journal) Journal of Wuhan University of Hydr. and Elec. Eng., 1994, Chinese Journal of Hydraulic Engineering, 1993, (D.E. Dissertation) Statistical Fracture Mechanical Analysis and Joint Network Simulation Technique of Rocks, 1991, (journal) Sichuan Water Power, 1991 (The Third Class Award of Science and Technology Progress, The Ministry of Electric Industry, China, 1992), Site Investigation Science and Technique, 1990, Journal of Yangtze Institute of Science Research, 1990 (The Third Class Award of Science and Technology Award, The Ministry of Water Conservancy, China, 1994), Journal of Wuhan Univerity of Hydr. and Elec. Eng., 1989, Chinese Journal of Rock Mechanics, 1988, Fracture and Strength of Rock and Concrete, 1986. Mem.: ASME, Soc. Exptl. Mech., Sigma Xi. Home: 244 N Purdue #101 Oak Ridge TN 37830 Office: Oak Ridge Nat Lab Metals and Cermaics Divsn PO Box 2008 Oak Ridge TN 37831 Office Phone: 865-574-4501. Office Fax: 865-574-6098. Business E-Mail: wangh@ornl.gov.

WANG, JAMES CHUO, biochemistry and molecular biology educator; b. Kiangsu, China, Nov. 18, 1936; came to U.S., 1960; s. Chin and H.-L. (Shih) W.; m. Sophia Shu-lan Hwang, Dec. 23, 1961; children: Janice S., Jessica A. BS, Nat. Taiwan U., 1959; MA, U. S.D., 1961; PhD, U. Mo. Coll. Arts and Sci., 1964. Asst. instr. Nat. Taiwan U., Taipei, 1959-60; rsch. fellow in chemistry Calif. Inst. Tech., Pasadena, 1964-66; asst. prof. chemistry U. Calif. at Berkeley, 1966-69, assoc. prof., 1969-74, prof., 1974-77; prof. biochemistry and molecular biology Harvard U., Cambridge, Mass., 1977-88, Mallinckrodt prof. biochemistry and molecular biology, 1988—; Chiron lectr. U. Calif., Berkeley, 1994. Chancellor's Disting. lectr. U. Calif., Berkeley, 1984; mem. molecular biology study sect. NIH, 1988-91, chair, 1990-91; disting. faculty lectr. U. Tex., M.D. Anderson Cancer Ctr., 1989. Mem. editl. bd. Quar. Rev. Biophysics, 1988-94. Guggenheim fellow Guggenheim Found., 1986-87; recipient Disting. Alumnus award U. Mo. Coll. Arts and Scis., 1991. Fellow Am. Acad. Arts and Scis.; mem. NAS (molecular biology award 1983), Third World Acad. Scis., Academia Sinica (Taipei). Office: Harvard University Dept Molecular/Cellular Biology 7 Divinity Ave Cambridge MA 02138-2019

WANG, JAW-KAI, bioengineering educator; b. Nanjing, Jiangsu, China, Mar. 4, 1932; arrived in U.S., 1955; s. Shuling and Hsi-Ying (Lo) W.; m. Kwang Mei Chow, Sept. 7, 1957 (div. Oct. 1989); children: Angela C.C., Dora C.C., Lawrence C.Y.; m. Bichuan Li, Sept. 25, 1999. BS, Nat. Taiwan U., 1953; MS in Agrl. Engring., Mich. State U., 1956, PhD, 1958. Registered profl. engr., Hawaii. Faculty agrl. engring. dept. U. Hawaii, Honolulu, 1959-93, assoc. prof., chmn. dept. agrl. engring., 1964-68, prof., chmn. dept. agrl. engring., 1968-75, prof. biosys. engring., 1994—2000, prof. molecular bioscis. dept., 2000—02; prof. emeritus U. Hawaii-Manoa, Honolulu, 2004—, dir. Aquaculture Program, 1990-96; spl. asst., Internat. Rsch. Dept., Office of Internat. Cooperation and Devel. U.S. Dept. Agr., 1988; pres. Aquaculture Tech., Inc., 1990—. Co-dir. internat. sci. and edn. coun. USDA; vis. assoc. dir. internat. programs and studies office Nat. Assn. State Univs. and Land-Grant Colls., 1979; vis. prof. Nat. Taiwan U., 1964-65, 2000-01, U. Calif., Davis, 1980; hon. prof. coll. pharmacology Tianjing U., China, 2003; cons. U.S. Army Civilian Adminstrn., Ryukus, Okinawa, 1965, Internat. Rice Rsch. Inst., Philippines, 1971, Pacific Concrete and Rock Co. Ltd., 1974, AID, 1974, Universe Tankships, Del., 1980-81, World Bank, 1981, 82, ABA Internat., 1981-85, Internat. Found. for Agrl. Devel./World Bank, 1981, Rockefeller Found., 1980, Orizaba, Inc., 1983, Agrisys./FAO, 1983, Info. Processing Assocs., 1984, County of Maui, 1984, 85, Dept. of State, 1985, Alexander and Baldwin, 1986; mem. expert panel on agrl. mechanization FAO/UN, 1984-90; sr. fellow East-West Ctr. Food Inst., 1973-74; dir. Info. Sys. and Svcs. Internat., Inc., 1986-90; mem. bd. on agr. and natural resources The Nat. Acads., 2004—; panel mem. Vietnam Edn. Found., 2004. Author: Irrigated Rice Production Systems, 1980; editor: Taro-A Review of Colocasia Esculenta and its Potentials, 1983; mem. editl. bd. Aquacultural Engring., 1982—. Recipient Exemplary State Employee award State of Hawaii, 1986, State of Hawaii Disting. Svc. award Office of Gov., 1990. Fellow Am. Soc. Agrl. Engrs. (chmn. Hawaii sect. 1962-63, chmn. grad. instrn. com. 1971-73, various coms., Engr. of Yr. 1976, Tech. Paper award 1978, Kishida Internat. award 1991), Am. Inst. Med. and Biol. Engring.; mem. NAE, Aquaculture Engring. Soc. (pres. 1993-95), Sigma Xi, Gamma Sigma Delta (pres. Hawaii chpt. 1974-75), Pi Mu Epsilon. Office: U Hawaii MBBE Dept 1955 East West Rd Honolulu HI 96822 *To be allowed a continuing search for truth even when you are doubting its existence, is to be blessed.*

WANG, JIA, educator; b. Wenzhou, Zhejiang, China, Dec. 25, 1968; came to the U.S., 1990; p. KeQiang Wang and DanPing Cai. BA, Wenzhou Tchrs.' U., 1988; MS, Ft. Valley State U., 1992; PhD, UCLA, 1996. Sr. statistician Applied Mgmt. and Planning Group, L.A., 1995-97; asst. dir., sr. rsch. assoc. Ctr. for Pacific Rim Studies UCLA, 1997—2002, sr. rsch. and project dir. Ctr. for Study of Evaluation, 2003—. Cons. The World Bank, Washington, 1997--, WHO, Geneva, Switzerland, 1999-2002. 1st author: (book) Measuring Country Performance on Health: Selected Indicators for 115 Countries, 1999; contbr. articles to profl. jours. Univ. fellow UCLA, 1992-96. Mem. AAAS, Am. Ednl. Rsch. Assn., Comparative and Internat. Edn. Soc. Avocations: reading, hiking, travel. Office: UCLA-CRESST 10945 LeConte Ave, Ste 1400E Los Angeles CA 90095 E-mail: jiawang@ucla.edu.

WANG, JIAN, physical chemist, researcher; b. Weiyuan, Sichuan, China, Mar. 3, 1971; s. Fengyan Wang and Shufen Deng; m. Lingyun Zhu, Apr. 16, 1974. BS, Peking U., Beijing, China, 1992, PhD, 1998. Postdoctoral fellow U. Tex., Austin, 1999—2001; rsch. assoc. Boston U., 2001—. Contbr. articles to profl jours. including: Japanese Jour. Applied Physics, 1996, Japanese Journal of Applied Physics, 1996 (DuPont Prize, 1997), Chemical Physics Letters, 1997 (Star of Photoelectronics, 1997). Co-founder and v.p. Austin Peking U. Alumni Assn., 2000—01. Mem.: AAAS, N.Y. Acad. Scis., Am. Chem. Soc. Avocations: photography, reading, travel, sports. Office: 590 Commonwealth Ave Boston MA 02215 Home: 141 Spruce St #3 Watertown MA 02472-1921 Business E-Mail: jianwang@chem.bu.edu.

WANG, JIN, research scientist; s. Lianru Wang and Yuliang Zhang; m. Xiaoyan Guo; 1 child, Jerry. Ph D, U. So. Calif., L.A., Calif., 1995. Scientist Ctr. for Monitoring Rsch., Arlington, Va., 1995—2000; network solution specialist Hewlett Packard Co., Reston, Va., 2000—. Contbr. articles to profl. jour. Fellow, Keck Found., 1997. Mem.: Am. Geophys. Union, IEEE. Achievements include research in artificial intelligence application in seismic network; optimum array signal processing. Home: 4297 Country Squire Ln Fairfax VA 22032 Office: Hewlett & Packard Co 10700 Parkridge Blvd Reston VA 20191

WANG, JOHN, not-for-profit company executive; b. Taipei, Taiwan, July 29, 1947; s. Stephen and Marcelle Wang; m. Lilly Ying, Jan. 9, 1989; children: Christina, Scott. BA, Queens Coll., N.Y.C., 1972. Urban planner Dept. City Planning, N.Y.C., 1972—80; freelance writer/cons., 1980—85; exec. dir. Chinese Am. Local Devel. Corp., N.Y.C., 1985—90; pres. John Wang Assocs., N.Y.C., 1990—94, Asian Am. Bus. Devel. Ctr., N.Y.C., 1994—. Mem. N.Y. State Small Bus. Adv. Bd., 1990—93, 1995—98; del. White House Conf. on Small Bus., 1995; mem. adv. coun. Lower Manhattan Devel. Corp., N.Y.C., 2002—. Organizer Empire State Bldg. Lighting in Honor of Lunar New Year, 2000—03. Staff sgt. USAF, 1966—69. Named an Everyday Hero, Newsday, 2002; journalism fellow, Columbia U., 1980—81. Avocations: photography, fishing. Office: Asian Am Bus Devel Ctr 150 Lafayette St New York NY 10013

WANG, JOHN CHENG HWAI, communications engineer, researcher; b. Beijing, Feb. 12, 1934; s. Hwa Lung and Shu Shiang (Shia) W.; m. Rosa Jenny Chu, Sept. 9, 1967; children: Sophia, Maria, Nina, Amy. BS, U. Md., 1959; MS, U. Pitts., 1968. Engr. Chesapeake Instrument Corp., Shadyside, Md., 1959-64; rsch. scientist Rsch. Ctr. U.S. Steel Corp., Monroeville, Pa., 1964-67; asst. prof. Pa. State U., New Kensington, 1967-69; rsch. engr. FCC, Washington, 1969—. Cmn. working party ionospheric propogation, Internat. Telecom. Union (ITU), Geneva, 1983-. Contbr. articles to profl. jours. Fellow IEEE. Avocations: astronomy, bridge, chinese history. Office: FCC 445 12 St SW Washington DC 20554-0001

WANG, JOHN XIAOWU, computer company executive; b. Hefei, Anhui, China, July 6, 1958; arrived in U.S., 1982; s. Zhi Dao Wang and Xian Zhen Fang; m. Lin Hu, Aug. 24, 1985; children: Fanny, Kathy, Bill. B in Physics, U. Sci. and Tech. China, Hefei, 1982; MS, NYU, 1984, PhD in Physics, 1990. Sr. engr. Micromath, Salt Lake City, 1990-92; chmn., chief engr. Poly Software Internat. Ltd., Salt Lake City, 1992-95, pres., CEO, 1995—, software engr. Pearl River, NY, 2000—. Contbr. articles to profl. jours. James Arthur fellow, NYU, 1990. Home: 7 Kerry Ct Pearl River NY 10965-3034 Business E-Mail: wang@polysoftware.com.

WANG, JOSEPHINE JUNG-SHAN, language educator, translator; d. Hsiian Chang and Yen-Yi Lan; children: Charlotte C., Kenneth C. BA, Queens Coll., CUNY, Flushing, 1966; MA, George Washington U., 1969. Lang. instr. Montgomery Coll., Rockville, Md., 1975—2002; spl. asst. U.S. Dept. Edn., Washington, 1988—89; mem., Pres.'s Intergovtl. and Adv. Coun. of Edn., 1989—92; instr., Mandarin Montgomery City Pub. Schs., Md., 1990—. Mem., sr. coun. City of Gaithersburg, Md., 2003—; mem. St. Raphael's Cath. Ch. Taft sr. fellow, Catholic U. Mem.: NEA, Montgomery Retired Tchrs. Assn., West Deer Park Homeowners Assn., Queens Coll. Alumni Assn., George Washington U. Alumni Assn., Mid-Montgomery Rep. Club. Republican. Roman Catholic. Home: 382 W Deer Park Rd Gaithersburg MD 20877

WANG, JUI HSIN, biochemistry educator; b. Beijing, Mar. 16, 1921; arrived in U.S., 1946; s. Lieh and Sun Li (Sun) W.; m. Yen Chan Yang, Apr. 2, 1949 (dec. 1993); children: Jane, Nancy. BS, Nat. S.W. Assoc. U., Kunming, China, 1945; PhD, Washington U., St. Louis, 1949; MA (hon.), Yale U., 1960. Postdoctoral fellow radiochemistry Washington U., 1949-51; mem. faculty Yale U., New Haven, 1951-72, prof. chemistry, 1960-62, Eugene Higgins prof. chemistry, 1962-65, Eugene Higgins prof. chemistry and molecular biophysics, 1965-72; Einstein prof. sci. SUNY, Buffalo, 1972—. Rschr. molecular structure and biochem. activity, superconductivity. Contbr. articles to profl. jours., chapters in books. Guggenheim fellow Cambridge U., 1960-61. Fellow AAAS, Am. Acad. Arts and Scis.; mem. Am. Chem. Soc., Am. Soc. Microbiology, Yale Chemists Assn., Am. Soc. for Biochemistry and Molecular Biology, Am. Phys. Soc., Biophys. Soc., Am. Assn. Cancer Rsch., Academia Sinica, Materials Rsch. Soc., Am. Assn. Cancer Rsch., Sigma Xi. Home: 755 Renaissance Dr Apt 206 Williamsville NY 14221-8046 Office: SUNY Dept Chemistry Buffalo NY 14260-0001 Personal E-mail: juiwang@acsu.buffalo.edu. Business E-Mail: kac@acsu.buffalo.edu.

WANG, KIM, real estate broker, librarian; m. Harry Wang; children: Elaine, Steve, Leslie. B in History, U. Colo.; MLS, U. Calif., Berkeley. Former libr. U. So. Calif., Hughes Aircraft; property mgr. and real estate broker. Mem. Nat. Mus. and Libr. Svcs. Bd., Washington, 2004—. V.p. La Terrazza Homeowners Assn.; former parks and recreation commr., planning commn. mem. City of Rancho Palos Verdes; bd. mem. Libr. Calif. Bd.; mem. Cultural Arts Commn., Torrance, Calif.; trustee Marymount Coll., Palos Verdes, Calif.; former bd. mem. Am. Heart Assn., Torrance. Mem.: AARP, AAUW (Torrance br.), LWV (Torrance br.), Am. Contract Bridge League, Torrance Sister City Assn., Torrance Hist. Soc., Torrance Hist. Assn., Torrance Chamber Toastmasters, Torrance Area C. of C. Office: Inst Mus and Libr Svcs 1100 Pennsylvania Ave NW Washington DC 20506*

WANG, KUNG-LEE, economics consultant; b. Pei Tai-Ho, Hopei, China, Aug. 12, 1925; came to U.S., 1947; s. Cheng-Fu Wang and Funghin Liu; m. Christine Wen, Aug. 15, 1959 (div.); 1 child, Christopher Ching-Yu. BA, Yenching U., 1947; MA, Brown U., 1950; MBA, Columbia U., 1958; MPA, Harvard U., 1965. Acct. in charge fiscal mgmt. Bushwick Hosp., Bklyn., 1952-55; economist, civilian and mil. ops. analyst, internat affairs C-E-I-R., Inc., Washington, 1955-60; cons., 1960-61; chief qualitative econs. analysis, Bur. Mines U.S. Dept. Interior, Washington, 1960-82; pres. KLW Internat., Inc., 1982—, Chi Am Metals & Energy, Inc., 1983-86. Vice chmn. Chinatown Devel. Corp., 1983—96, chmn., 1996—99; pres. The Truth Coun. for Second World War in Asia, 2000—; vice chmn. MLS Inc., 1986—87, AmerAsia Inc., 1988—89, pres., 1989; dir. Internat. Data Applications Inc., 1969—71, Yenching Grad. Inst., 1994—; L.P. mng. dir. North Gallery Place Assoc., L.P., 1995—99; econ. ops. advisor to ministry econ. affairs Republic of China, 1969—71; cons. ops. rsch. office Johns Hopkins, Bethesda, Md., 1960—61; trustee OCA Endowment Fund, 1988—, chmn. bd. trustees, 2002—05; pres. U.S.-China Coun. Internat. Exch. Inc., 1988—; founding chmn. Chinese Heritage Ctr., Inc., 1991—94; ethnic advisor U.S. OEO, 1972—75; dir. Com. of 100, 1990—, exec. dir., 1993—95; pres. Civic League of Brookmont, 1963—64; coord. Chinese-Am. Leadership Coun., 1971—73; pres. Rho Psi Found., Inc., 1967—97; nat. v.p. Asian-Pacific Am. C. of C., 1983—84; co-founder, dir. Asian Pacific Am. Heritage Coun., Inc., 1979—97, pres., 1982—83; co-founder, nat. dir. Asian Am. Voters Coalition, 1985—91; co-founder, bd. dirs. Nat. Chinese Am. Voters League, 1984—91; founder, nat. pres. Orgn. Chinese Ams. Inc., 1973—77, nat. treas., v.p. fin., 1979—81, hon. mem., 1982; chmn. U.S.-China Capital Cities Friendship Coun., 1984—94; dir. Md. Civil Rights Coalition, 1990—92; v.p.-U.S. ea. states The Global Alliance for Preserving the History of World War II in Asia, Inc., 2001—; v.p. Yenching Ednl. Found., 2003—. Contbr. articles to encys. and profl. jours. Recipient Engr. of Yr. award Am. Inst. Mining, Metall. and Petroleum Engrs., 1976, Mineral Economist of Yr. award, 1984, award Asian and Pacific Am. Civil Rights Alliance, 1983, Ellis Island medal Honor Nat. Ethnic Coalition Found., 1993; Nat. Inst. Pub. Affairs fellow, 1965. Mem. Am. Soc. Pub. Adminstrn., Kennedy Sch. Govt. Alumni Assn. of Harvard U. (bd. dirs. 1978-82), Asian-Am. Bus. Roundtable (pres. 1989-95), Am. Econs. Assn., Rho Psi. Mem. Chinese Christian Ch. Home: 1940 Dundee Rd Rockville MD 20850-3137 Office: 1940 Dundee Rd Rockville MD 20850-3137 E-mail: uscc@uschinacouncil.org.

WANG, LEON RU-LIANG, civil engineer, educator; b. Canton, China, June 15, 1932; came to US, 1959; s. Huai-Kao and Yuen-Chin (Ho) W.; m. Joyce Chieh-Chun Tien, July 22, 1961; children: Frank Yu-Heng, Mark Yu-Da, Cindy Chi-Wen. BSC.E., Cheng-Kung U., Tainan, Republic of China, 1957; MSC.E., U. Ill., 1961; ScD, MIT, 1965. Asst. prof. civil engring. Rensselaer Poly. Inst., Troy, NY, 1965-69, assoc. prof. civil engring., 1969-80; prof. civil engring. U. Okla., Norman, 1980-84, Old Dominion U., Norfolk, Va., 1984-95, chair civil engring. dept., 1984-90, prof. emeritus civil engring. dept., 1995—. Adj. prof. civil and structural engring. dept. Hong Kong U. Sci. and Tech., 1993-95; tech. cons. Watervliet (NY) Arsenal, 1966-80. Editor: Rsch. for Multiple Hazard Mitigations, 1983, Seismic Evaluation of Lifeline Systems-Case Studies, 1986. Founding mem. Chinese Cmty. Ctr., Albany, 1973. Recipient rsch. awards NSF, 1976—. Fellow ASCE (br. pres. 1987-88), Hong Kong Inst. of Engr.; mem. Earthquake Engr. Rsch. Inst., Am. Soc. Engring. Edn., Chinese-Am. Assn. Nat. Hazard Mitigation Rsch. (founding mem.).

WANG, LIN, physicist, computer science educator, computer software consultant; b. Dandong, China, June 11, 1929; came to U.S., 1961, naturalized, 1972; s. Lu-Ting and Shou-Jean (Sun) W.; m. Ingrid Ling-Fen Tsow, July 8 1961; children: W. Larry, Ben. BS in Physics, Taiwan U., 1956; MS in Physics, Okla. State U., 1965, PhD in Physics, 1972. Mem. physics faculty Cheng Kung U., Tainan, China, 1957-61; asst. prof. physics Southwestern Okla. State U., Weatherford, 1965-72; prof., chmn. physics dept. N.E. Coll. Arts and Sci., Maiduguri, Nigeria, 1973-75; mem. tech. staff Pacific Engring. Corp., Bellevue, Wash., 1976-78; sr. software engr., Far East cons. Electro-Sci. Industries, Inc., Portland, Oreg., 1979-82; mem. sr. computer sci. faculty South Seattle C.C., 1983—. Mem. Assn. for Computing Machinery, Am. Phys. Soc., AAUP. Avocations: classical music, world travel. Home: 9214 181st Ave E Bonney Lake WA 98390-7187

WANG, LU-HAI, medical educator, scientist, researcher; b. Tonan Jien, Yuin Lin Shien, Taiwan, Sept. 2, 1947; s. Bun-Chin Wang and Tsoo Huang; m. Mei-Hui Teng, Mar. 14, 1944; children: Sophia F., Sandra T. PhD, U. Calif., Berkeley, 1976. Postdoctoral fellow Univ. Calif., Berkeley, 1976—77, Rockefeller U., N.Y.C., 1977—79. asst. prof., 1979—85, assoc. prof., 1985—88; assoc. prof. with tenure The Mt. Sinai Sch. of Medicine, N.Y.C., 1988—92, prof., 1992—2001. Study sect. mem. NIH, Bethesda, Md., 1988—98; sci. cons. Nat. Health Rsch. Inst., Taipei, Taiwan, 1996; hon. prof. Peking Union Med. Coll., China, 1998; rschr. in field. Recipient Jr. Faculty award, Am. Cancer Soc., 1979, Career Rsch. Devel. award, NIH; scholar Am. Leukemia

Soc. Mem.: Soc. Chinese Biochemists in Am., Am. Soc. Advancement Scis., N.Y. Acad. Sci., Am. Soc. Microbiology. Office: Mount Sinai Sch Medicine Dept Microbiology 1 Gustave Levy Pl New York NY 10029 Office Phone: 212-241-3795.

WANG, MING DE, engineer; b. Yibin, Sichuan, Peoples Republic of China, July 04; came to U.S., 1994; d. Xisheng and Shoumai (Wu) W.; m. Guoxian Zhang, Oct. 4, 1970; 1 child, Ying. BSc in Chemistry, Nankai U., Tianjin, China, 1978, MSc in Organic Chemistry, 1981; PhD in Chemistry, U. Ottawa, Ont., Can., 1993. Rsch. asst. Nankai U., Tianjin, 1978-81, lectr., 1981-87; rsch. asst. in chemistry U. Ottawa, Can., 1987-89, rsch. asst., 1989-93; postdoctoral fellow in chemistry SUNY, Albany, 1994-95, U. Ottawa, 1995-96; process engr. Hadco Santa Clara, Calif., 1996-98, Carolina Circuits, C-MAC of Am., Inc., Greenville, S.C., 1998—. Co-author 3 chpts. to books; contbr. 16 articles to profl. jours. Cert. instr. CPR, ARC, SUNY, Albany, 1994—. Recipient scholarship Ont. Min. Edn. and Tng., 1992, Sci. and Tech. award Nat. Edn. Com. Peoples Republic of China, 1990. Mem. Am. Chem. Soc., Chem. Inst. Can., China Chem. Soc. Avocations: gospel music, classic movies, travel. Home: 107 Raleigh Ct Simpsonville SC 29681-1981 Office: Carolina Circuits C-MAC of Am Inc 200 Fairforest Way Greenville SC 29607-4609 E-mail: mwang@carolina.cmac.com., Inchrist-1@excite.com.

WANG, NANCY, pathologist, educator; b. An-Wei, China, Sept. 2, 1944; m. Tingchung Wang; children: Jessie, Melissa. BS, Nat. Taiwan U., 1966; MS, U. Minn., 1968, PhD, 1978. Diplomate Am. Bd. Med. Genetics. Instr. Dept. Pathology & Lab. Med. U. Minn., Mpls., 1978-79, asst. prof., 1980-82, Dept. Pathology, Tulane Med. Sch., 1982-83, assoc. prof., 1984-86, U. Rochester, N.Y., 1986-93, prof., 1993—. Mem.: Am. Assn. Human Gennetics. Business E-Mail: nancywang@urmc.rochester.edu.

WANG, PETER ZHENMING, physicist; b. Quanzhou, Fujian, People's Republic of China, Nov. 30, 1940; came to U.S., 1983; s. Guohua and Shunhua (Chen) W.; m. Grace Ruhui Xu, Mar. 14, 1967; children: Yili, Yile. MS, Qinghua U., Peking, People's Republic of China, 1964; postgrad., U. Tex., Dallas, 1983-84. Sr. engr. Particle Accelerator Inst., Shanghai, 1964-83; electronic engr. Benchmark Media Systems, Inc., Syracuse, N.Y., 1984-87; project engr. McGaw Inc., Carrollton, Tex., 1988—. Physicist High Energy Physics Inst., Peking, 1978-79. Co-author: (book) Vacuum World, 1984. Tchr. Bible study, Plano, Tex., 1990. Baptist. Achievements include research and design of a variety of proton and electron accelerators for low energy nuclear physics experiments, industries and hospitals; design of 50 GEV proton synchrotron, design of audio distribution amplifiers and consoles for BBC, ABC, and other TV and radio stations; development and design of air bubble detector, pressure transducer and noise reduction solution for the microprocessor based infusion therapy instrument used in hospitals. Home: 1510 Chesterfield Dr Carrollton TX 75007-2847 Office: McGaw Inc 1601 Wallace Dr Carrollton TX 75006-6666

WANG, PINGHUA, education educator; arrived in US, 1991; d. Wenhui and Maifang (Zhang) Wang; m. Weimin Zheng, Jan. 1, 1989; children: Claus Congcui Zheng, William Haocui Zheng. BS, Suzhou U., China, 1984; MS, Nanjing Normal U., China, 1990; PhD, U. SC, 1996. Asst. prof. Nanjing Normal U., 1984—91, Floyd Coll., Rome, Ga., 1996—2000, assoc. prof., 2000—. Home: 13 Limerick Ct Cartersville GA 30120 Office Phone: 706-295-6306. Business E-Mail: pwang@floyd.edu.

WANG, Q. EDWARD, history professor; s. Xiaocang and Shifen Wang; m. Ni Gao, July 21, 1987. B.A., East China Normal U., Shanghai, 1982, M.A., 1984; Ph.D., Syracuse U., 1992. Lectr. East China Normal U., Shanghai, 1984—87, U. RI, Kingston, 1991—92; asst. prof. dept. history Rowan U., Glassboro, NJ, 1992—97, assoc. prof., 1997—2001, chair dept. history, 1998—, prof., 2001—. Pres. Chinese Historians in U.S., N.Y.C., 1992—93. Author: The Idea of History in the West, 1998, Postmodernism and Historiography: A Chinese-Western Comparison, 2000, Inventing China through History: The May 4th Approach to Historiography, 2001; editor: Turning Points in Historiography: A Cross-Cultural Perspective, 2002. Fellow, DAAD, 1995, Ctr. for Chinese Studies, Ctrl. Libr., Taiwan, 1999; Rsch. fellow, Chiang Ching-kuo Found., 2002—. Mem.: Internat. Soc. for Intellectual History, Assn. for Asian Studies, Am. Hist. Assn. Liberal. Avocations: swimming, travel. Office: History Dept Rowan U 201 Mullica Hill Rd Glassboro NJ 08028 Office Phone: 856-256-4819.

WANG, QIGUI, materials engineer, researcher; b. Funing, Jiangsu, China, Nov. 23, 1960; arrived in U.S., 1997, permanent resident, 1998; s. Chengchao and Yun (Guo) Wang; m. Jiaping Zhang, Mar. 3, 1961; 1 child, Weike. Bachelor in Sci. and Engring., Nanjing Inst. of Tech., Nanjing, Jiangsu, China, 1982; MSc in Sci. and Engring., SE U., Nanjing, Jiangsu, China, 1987; PhD, U. Queensland, Brisbane, Australia, 1997. Lectr. Nanjing (Jiangsu) Inst. of Tech., China, 1982—87; asst. prof. SE U., Nanjing, China, 1988—92; vis. rsch. scientist Fed. U. of Rio Grande do Sol(UFRGS), Porto Alegre, Brazil, 1992—94; rsch. scholar Australian Government's Coop. Rsch. Ctr. (CAST), Brisbane, Australia, 1994—97; postdoctoral rsch. scientist Worcester (Mass.) Poly. Inst., 1997—99; sr. rsch. engr. Aerotek, Saginaw, Mich., 1999—2000; sr. materials engr. Gen. Motors Corp, Saginaw, Mich., 2000—. Consulting engr. Metall. Machinery Plant of Jiangsu Province, Nanjing, China, 1982—87; sr. consulting engr. Nanjing (Jiangsu) Non-Ferrous Metals Corp, China, 1987—89, Nanjing Motors Corp., Nanjing, Jiangsu, China, 1989—92. Contbr. articles to profl. jours., 1997. Named for The Best Rsch. Work, The Sci. and Tech. Com. of Jiangsu Province, China, 1991; recipient OPRS Scholarship, Australian Edn. Dept., 1994-1997, CAST Rsch. Scholarship, The U. of Queensland, Australia, 1994-1997, Rsch. Fellowship, Brazilian Rsch. Coun. (CNPq), 1992-1994, Rsch. Found. of Rio Grande do Sul (FAPERGS), Brazil, 1992-1994, The Best Undergraduate Thesis award, The State Edn. Com. of China, 1982. Mem.: Am. Foundrymen's Soc., Am. Soc. Materials Internat. (chpt. sec. 2001, vice chair 2002), The Minerals, Metals & Materials Soc. Achievements include Chinese patent. Avocations: coin collecting/numismatics, stamp collecting/philately, travel.

WANG, QIN, computer engineer, researcher; b. Lishui, Zhejiang, China, Jan. 15, 1973; d. Jixu Wang and Xuewen Chen; m. Ying Hu. PhD, Iowa State U., 1998—2001. Rsch. asst. Iowa State U., Ames, Iowa, 1998—2001; sr. hardware engr. EMC, Hopkinton, Mass., 2001—. Contbr. articles to profl. jours. (Best Thesis Award, 1998). Recipient PACE, Iowa State U., 1998, ABD, 2001, Best Grad. award, Zhejiang Province, 1995, 1998, Best Thesis award, 1995, 1998, Siemens prize, Siemens Inc., 1996, Nari award, Chinese State Power, 1997, Outstanding Student award, Zhejiang Univ., 1991—94; scholar Grad. Coll. scholar, Iowa State U., 1998—2001, First Level Outstanding Student Scholarship, Zhejiang Univ., 1991—94. Mem.: IEEE, Soc. Women Engrs., Nat. Scholars Honor Soc., Delta Epsilon Iota, Tau Beta Pi, Sigma Xi. Personal E-mail: qwanghz@yahoo.com.

WANG, QIN, medical educator; d. Dayou Wang and Yanying Yan. MD, Wannan Med. Coll., China, 1982; MS, Shanghai Second Med. U., C, 1990. Attending physician Shanghai Ruijin Hosp., 1990—94; rsch. fellow U. So. Calif., Palm Springs, 1994—95; postdoctoral fellow N.J. Med. Sch., U. Md.-N.J., Newark, 1995—2000, faculty N.J. Med. Sch., 2000—. Contbr. articles to profl. jours. Recipient Trainee Investigator award, 1995, N.J. Cancer Rsch. award for sci. excellence, 1997, Gallo award for outstanding cancer rsch., 1999; Breast Cancer Rsch. fellowship, 1997, Breast Cancer fellowship, Found. of U. Md.-N.J., 1997. Mem.: AAUP, Am. Found. for Clin. Rsch.

WANG, RICHARD Y. emergency physician, osteopath; b. Taiwan, 1961; DO, N.Y. Coll., 1986. Diplomate Am. Bd. Emergency Medicine, Am. Coll. Med. Toxicology. Intern Metro Hosp., Phila., 1986-87; resident in emergency medicine Sparrow Hosp./Ingham Med. Ctr., East Lansing, Mich., 1987-90; fellow in clin. toxicology N.Y.C. Poison Control/Bellev, 1990-92; mem. staff R.I. Hosp., Providence; assoc. prof. Brown Univ., Providence, 1992—2001; mem. staff Grady Health Sys., Atlanta, 2001—. Mem. Am. Coll. Emergency Physicians, Am. Acad. Clin. Toxicology, Am. Coll. Med. Toxicology, European Assn. Poison Ctrs. and Clin. Toxicologists. Office: Nat Ctr Environ Health Ctrs Disease Control and Prevention 4770 Buford Hwy MS F-17 Atlanta GA 30341

WANG, SAM SHU-YI, mechanical engineer, educator; b. Chungking, Szechuan, China, Sept. 21, 1936; arrived in U.S., 1963; s. San-Chuan and Mayhsun (Chen) Wang; m. Jine Yang, Aug. 27, 1966. BSME, Nat. Cheng Kung U., Tainan, Taiwan, 1959; MS in Mech. and Aerospace Sci., U. Rochester, 1965, PhD in Computational Hydrodynamics, 1968. Registered profl. engr., Miss. Asst. design engr. Yue Loong Motors Corp., Taipei, Taiwan, 1960-61; rsch. asst. Nat. Chengking U., Tainan, 1961-63; tchg. and rsch. asst. U. Rochester, NY, 1963-67; from asst. prof. to assoc. prof. mech. engring. U. Miss., University, 1967—81, prof., 1981—, Barnard disting. prof., 1988—, acting chmn. dept., 1982-83, dir. Nat. Ctr. Computational Hydrosci. and Engring., 1983—. Gen. chmn. Internat. Conf. Finite Elements Water Resources, 1980, Internat. Symposium Sediment Transport Modeling, 1989, Internat. Conf. Hydro-Sci. and Engring., 1993; pres., prin. rsch. engr. Computational Engring. Rsch. Inst., Inc., Oxford, Miss., 1983—; UN expert UN Devel. Program, 1987. Prin. editor: Finite Element in Water Resources, 1980, River Sedimentation, 1986, Developments in Theoretical and Applied Mechanics, 1988; editor: Sediment Transport Modeling, 1989, Advances in Hydro-Science and Engineering, Vol. I, parts A and B, 1993. Recipient Ralph R. Teetor award, Soc. Automotive Engrs., 1975, Outstanding Faculty award, Miss. Legislature, 1989; Sr. Faculty Rsch. grantee, U. Miss., 2002. Fellow: ASCE (Hydraulic Engring. Achievement award 1988, Hans Albert Einstein award for Sedimentation Rsch. 2003), AIAA (assoc. Spl. award 1979, Space Shuttle Falg plaque 1984); mem.: Chinese Soc. Theoretical and Applied Mechanics (hon.). Avocations: travel, chess, stamp and coin collecting. Office: U Miss NaCtr Computational Hydrosci and Engring University MS 38677 Office Phone: 662-915-7788. Business E-Mail: wang@ncche.olemiss.edu.

WANG, SAMUEL JAMES, physician; s. John S and Betty S Wang; m. Andrea Beth Hawkins; children: Kira Emily children: William Joseph. PhD, Stanford U., 1992, MD, 1996. Informatics rschr. Partners HealthCare Sys., Boston, 1999—2002; resident in internal med. Newton Wellesley Hosp., 2003—04; resident in radiation oncology U. Tex. Health Sci. Ctr., San Antonio, 2004—. Fellow in med. informatics, Harvard/MIT, 1999. Home: 11146 Vance Jackson #4401 San Antonio TX 78230 Personal E-mail: samuel@stanfordalumni.org.

WANG, SHIH-HO, electrical engineer, educator; b. Kiangsu, China, June 29, 1944; came to U.S., 1968; BEE, Nat. Taiwan U., Taipei, 1967; MEE, U. Calif., Berkeley, 1970, PhD in Elec. Engring., 1971. Asst. prof. elec. engring. U. Colo., Colo. Springs, 1973-76, Boulder, 1976-77; asst. prof. electrical engring. U. Md., College Park, 1977-78, assoc. prof., 1978-84; prof. U. Calif., Davis, 1984—. Cons. Lawrence Livermore (Calif.) Nat. Lab., 1986-88; scientific officer Office Naval Research, Arlington, Va., 1983-84. Assoc. editor Internat. Jour. Robotics and Automation, 1986-90. Served to 2d lt. China Air Force, Taiwan, 1967-68. Mem. IEEE (hon. mention award control systems soc. 1975). Office: Univ Calif Dept Elec Computer Engring Davis CA 95616 Business E-Mail: shwang@ucdavis.edu.

WANG, SHUNZHU, humanities educator, researcher, translator; b. Yaancheng, China, June 21, 1957; arrived in U.S., 1992; s. Decai Wang and Jinbao Xu; m. Aiping Chen, Feb. 13, 1980; 1 child, Ying. BA in English Lang. and Lit., Suzhou U., China, 1980; MA in English Edn., Wayne State U., 1994; PhD in Comparative Lit., Purdue U., 2001. Tchr. Yancheng (China) H.S., 1980—84; lectr., program coord. Yancheng Inst. Edn., 1984—89; assoc. dir. English dept. Nanjing (China) Coll. Comm., 1989—92; tchg. asst. Bennington (Vt.) Coll., 1999—. Referee Mosaic (acad. jours.), 2000—. Author: Contemporary Western Rhetoric, 2 vols. (in Chinese), 1998; contbr. articles to profl. jours. Mem.: MLA, Am. Coun. Tchg. Fgn. Langs., Am. Comparative Lit. Assn. Office: Bennington Coll Rte 67A Bennington VT 05201 E-mail: shunzhu@bennington.edu.

WANG, SHUZHOU, mathematician, educator, research scientist; arrived in U.S., 1987; m. Yuxue Gao, Feb. 4, 1986; children: Albert Mian, Moses Muyi. BS, Wuhan Inst. of Hydraulic and Electric Engring., 1983; PhD, U. Calif., Berkeley, 1993. Asst. prof. U. of Ga., Athens, 1999—2003, assoc. prof., 2003—. Adj. asst. prof., NSF postdoctoral fellow U. Calif., Berkeley, 1996—99. Grantee, NSF, 2000—03. Mem.: Am. Math. Soc. Achievements include first to several families of compact qauntum groups that lead to a new direction of research in the field. Office: U Ga Dept Math Athens GA 30602

WANG, SUSAN S. manufacturing executive; BA in Acctg., U. Tex.; MBA, U. Conn. CPA, Calif. With Price Waterhouse & Co., N.Y.C.; various fin. and acctg. mgmt. positions Xerox Corp., Westvaco Corp.; dir. fin. Solectron Corp., Milpitas, Calif., 1984, v.p. fin., CFO, 1986, sr. v.p., 1990—, also bd. dirs. Mem. adv. bd. YWCA, Santa Clara County; chairperson Fin. Exec. Rsch. Found. Recipient Top Women in Industry award YWCA; named one of San Francisco Bay Area's most powerful corp. women. Mem. AICPA, N.Y. State Soc. CPA, Fin. Execs. Inst. Office: Solectron Corp 777 Gibraltar Dr Milpitas CA 95035-6328

WANG, SUWEN, physicist, researcher; b. Yangzhou, China, May 14, 1959; came to U.S., 1982; s. Changrong Wang and Yun Zhang; m. Xiao Shuang Fu, Apr. 3, 1994; children: Oliver Shizi Wang, Alice Fuzi Wang. BS, Nanjing (China) U., 1982; MS, La. State U., 1983; PhD, Duke U., 1988. Postdoctoral fellow Duke U., Durham, N.C., 1988-89; postdoctoral rsch. assoc. Manchester (Eng.) U., 1989-90; rsch. assoc. U. Mass., Amherst, 1990-92; sr. rsch. scientist Stanford (Calif.) U., 1992—. Cons. Cadence Sys., Inc., San Jose, Calif., 1996—. Contbr. articles to sci. jours.; inventor in field. Mem. Am. Phys. Soc., Sigma Xi. Achievements include being one of the first to discover non wetting of superfluid helium on cesium substrate with the third sound technique; contributions to the field of crit. phenomena by studying properties of liquid helium; contributions to studying of gravitational physics and relativity. Office: Stanford Univ GP-B HEPL Stanford CA 94305

WANG, TIANSHU, music educator, musician; b. Shenyang, China, Feb. 12, 1969; arrived in US, 1993; d. Guan Wang and Jue Yu; m. Jian Xu, Aug. 8, 1993; children: Kevin Yilun children: David Yakun. MusB, Shanghai (China) Conservatory Music, 1991; MusM, U. Ariz., 1995, D in Musical Art, 1999. Lectr. Shanghai Conservatory Music, 1991—93; vis. asst. prof. Sweet Briar (Va.) Coll., 1999—2002; asst. prof. Capital U., Columbus, Ohio; prof. of piano Shenyang (China) Conservatory of Music. Recipient Best Performance award, The Tcherepnin Soc. NY, 1989, First prize, Green Valley Piano Competition, 1993, Nat. Young Artist Piano Competition, 1995. Mem.: Coll. Music Soc., Music Tchrs. Nat. Assn., Phi Beta Delta. Home: 958 Gray Dr Pickerington OH 43147 Office: Capital Univ 1 College and Main Columbus OH 43209 Office Phone: 614-236-6410. Business E-Mail: twang@capital.edu.

WANG, TING, mechanical engineering educator; BSME, Tatung Inst. Tech., Taipei, Taiwan, 1977; MSME, SUNY, Buffalo, 1981; PhD in Mech. Engring., U. Minn., 1984. Dir. Energy Conversion and Conservation Ctr., U. New Orleans, prof. dept. mech. engring.; dir. gas turbine lab. Clemson (S.C.) U. Contbr. articles to profl. publs. Endowed chair Jack and Reba Matthy Energy Rsch. Fellow ASME (mem. gas turbine com., heat transfer com., biomass and alternative fuels com., George Westinghouse Silver medal 1998). Achievements include research in gas turbine application, integrated gasification combined cycle, mist/steam cooling for advanced turbine systems, heat transfer enhancement and drag reduction on micro-structured surfaces, impingement cooling on a moving surface, turbulent and transitional flows, energy conservation in residential housing. Office: Energy Conversion & Conservation Ctr Univ New Orleans New Orleans LA 70148-2200 E-mail: twang@uno.edu.

WANG, TSUEY TANG, science educator, venture capitalist; b. Tainan, Taiwan, Nov. 12, 1932; came to U.S., 1958; s. Shih-Neng and Tsun (Chen) W.; m. Margaret Mei-Tieh Lin, June 12, 1965; children: David, Marjorie, Vanessa. BS, Cheng Kung U., Tainan, 1955; PhD, Brown U., 1965. Asst. prof. Poly. U. N.Y., Bklyn., 1965-67; disting. mem. tech. staff AT&T Bell Labs., Murray Hill, N.J., 1967-88; vis. prof. Rutgers U., New Brunswick, N.J., 1988—; pres., chmn. bd. dirs. Transpac Capital Corp., Springfield, NJ, 1988—. Vis. prof. Tokyo U. Agr. and Tech., 1984, mem. indsl. adv. bd. Nat. Ctr. Composite Materials, U. Del., 1986-89; bd. dirs. Internat. Power Devices, Inc., Boston, 1989-99; spl. invited vis. prof. Japan Ministry Edn., Tokyo, 1992; bd. dirs. Nat. Assn. Investment Cos., Washington, 1990-94. Author: (chpt.) Polymer Blends, 1978, (chpt.) Optical Telecommunications, 1979; editor: The Applications of Ferroelectric Polymers, 1988; patentee in field. Recipient Borden Corina Keen fellow Brown U., 1961. Fellow Am. Phys. Soc.; mem. ASME, Soc. Advancement Material and Process Engring., Materials Rsch. Soc., N.Y. Acad. Scis. Achievements include research in spinodal decomposition in polymer blends; melting point depression in compatible polymer blends. Office: Rutgers Univ Chem and Biochem Engring Piscataway NJ 08854 E-mail: tsuey@rci.rutgers.edu.

WANG, VERA, fashion designer; b. Manhattan, N.Y., 1949; d. Cheng Ching Wang; m. Arthur Becker, June 22, 1989; children: Cecilia, Josephine. Grad., Sarah Lawrence Coll., New York. Sr. fashion editor Vogue, N.Y.C.; design dir. Ralph Lauren Women's Wear, N.Y.C., 1987-89; prin. Vera Wang Bridal House Ltd., N.Y.C., 1990—; expanded to ready-to-wear, fragrance, eyewear, footwear, fine jewelry, and a home collection. Designer for Olympic figure skaters including Nancy Kerrigan's silver medal performance at the 1994 Olympics. Author: Vera Wang on Weddings, 2001. Achievements include first to successfully fuse high style and fashion with the tradition and symbolism of the bridal industry; designing wedding and red carpet gowns for Hollywood's elite. Office: Vera Wang Bridal House 225 W 39th St Fl 10 New York NY 10018-3103*

WANG, WEI, chemist, researcher; b. Dongtai, Jiangsu, China, Oct. 27, 1966; s. Changgui Wang and Yulin Fu; m. Hjijuan Zhang, Sept. 12, 1994. BS in Sci., Nanjing (China) Normal U., 1988; MS, Shanghai Inst. Material Medica, 1993; PhD in Sci., N.C. State U., 2000. Tchr. chemistry Sizao H.S., Dongtai, 1988-90; rsch. scientist East China U. Sci. and Tech., Shanghai, 1993-94; rsch. assoc. U. Okla. Health Scis. Ctr., Oklahoma City, 1994-96; rsch. scientist dept. chemistry U. Ariz., Tucson, 2000—. Contbg. author: Methods in Molecular Medicine, 1998, Peptide and Protein Drug Delivery, 1998; contbr. articles to sci. jours., including Current Medicinal Chemistry, Chem. Comm., Jour. Peptide Rsch. Univ. scholar Nanjing Normal U., 1985-87; Glaxo fellow N.C. State U., 1998-99. Mem. AAAS, Am. Chem. Soc., Am. Peptide Soc., Phi Lambda Upsilon. Office: U Ariz Dept Chemistry 1306 E University Blvd Tucson AZ 85721

WANG, WILLIAM KAI-SHENG, law educator; b. NYC, Feb. 28, 1946; s. Yuan-Chao and Julia Ying-Ru (Li) W.; m. Kwan Kwan Tan, July 29, 1972; 1 child, Karen You-Chuan. BA, Amherst Coll., 1967; JD, Yale U., 1971. Bar: Calif. 1972. Asst. to mng. partner Gruss & Co., N.Y.C., 1971-72; asst. prof. law U. San Diego, 1972-74, asso. prof., 1974-77, prof., 1977-81, Hastings Coll. Law, U. Calif., San Francisco, 1981—. Vis. prof. law U. Calif., Davis, 1975—76, Hastings Coll. Law, U. Calif., 1980, UCLA, 1990, Villanova U., 1999, Bklyn. Law Sch., 2000, Leiden (Netherlands) U., 2004; cons. White Ho. Domestic Policy Staff, Washington, 1979; mem. investment policy oversight group Law Sch. Admissions Coun.; mem. steering com. Legal Svcs. for Entrepreneurs; mem. nat. adjudicatory coun. NASD. Co-author: Insider Trading, 1996, supplements; contbr. articles to newspapers, mags., scholarly jours.; editor; mem. editl. bd.: Internat. and Comparative Corp. Law Jour. Mem. State Bar Calif., Am. Law Inst., Assn. of Am. Law Schs. (mem., then chair com. on audit and assn. investment policy 1995-98). Home: 455 39th Ave San Francisco CA 94121-1507 Office: U Calif Hastings Coll Law 200 McAllister St San Francisco CA 94102-4978 Office Phone: 415-565-4666. Business E-Mail: wangw@uchastings.edu.

WANG, WILLIAM WEIQI, physician; b. Shanghai, June 3, 1962; s. Junmin Wang and Shanlai Gan; m. Yujia Tang Wang, Nov. 1999. MD, Shanghai Med. U., 1985; PhD, U Medicine and Dentistry N.J., Newark, 1995. Fellow NIMH, Bethesda, Md., 1995-96; rsch. assoc. Baylor Coll. Medicine, Houston, 1997-98; resident in psychiatry Washington U., St. Louis, 1998—2002; attending psychiatrist SSM Healthcare, St. Louis, 2002—. Author: Psychiatry Pearls of Wisdom, 1999, Psychiatry for the Boards, 2002; contbr. articles to profl. jours. Recipient Clin. Rec. awrad Shanghai Bur. Pub. Health, 1988. Mem. AMA, Am. Psychiat. Assn., Am. Acad. Neurology, Am. Soc. for Biochemistry and Molecular Biology, So. Med. Assn. Avocations: fine arts, poetry, history. Office: 330 First Capital Dr Ste 410 Saint Charles MO 63301 E-mail: wwwang@rocketmail.com.

WANG, X. T. (XIAOTIAN WANG), psychologist, educator; b. Beijing, Oct. 10, 1957; arrived in U.S., 1987; s. Zhong Wang, Nancy Zilin Tian; m. Ying Shi, May 19, 1957; 1 child, Geng. M in Patho-physiology, Jinan U., China, 1985; MA in Physiol. Psychology, Beijing Med. U., 1991; PhD, N.Mex. State U., 1993. Lectr. Jinan U. Med. Sch., Guangzhou, China, 1986—87; grad. ass. N.Mex. State U., 1987—93; asst. prof. U. SD, Vermillion, 1993—98, assoc. prof., 1998—2003, prof., 2003—. Vis. scientist Max Planck Inst., Berlin, 1998—99; vis. prof. Hong Kong U. Sci. and Tech. Sch. Bus. and Mgmt., Hong Kong, 2000—01, Peking U., Beijing, 2004. Mem. editl. bd.: Jour. Behavioral Decision Making, 2002—, guest editor: Jour. Bioeconomics, 2001—02; contbr. chapters to books, articles to profl. jours. Grantee, NSF, 1999—2003, James McDonnell Found., 2000; scholar Nat. Grad. scholar, Dept. Edn. China, 1982. Mem.: Human Behavior and Evolution Soc. (Young Investigator award 1992), Soc. for Judgement and Decision Making, Psychonomic Soc., Acad. Mgmt., Behavioral and Brain Scis. (assoc.). Home: 849 Valley View Dr Vermillion SD 57069 Office: Univ SD 414 East Clark St Vermillion SD 57069 Office Phone: 605-677-5183. Personal E-mail: xtwang@usd.edu. Business E-Mail: xtwang@usd.edu.

WANG, XI CHENG (DAVID WANG), mechanical engineer; b. Shanghai, Aug. 25, 1939; came to U.S., 1985; B Mech. Engring., Jiao Tong U., 1961; M Mech. Engring., CUNY, 1987. Engr. Guang-Yao Lighting Equipment Mfg. Corp., 1969-79; dir. tchg. and rsch. divsn. machine mfg. Shanghai U., 1979-85; engr. ACE Envelope Corp., 1988-92; corp. engr. Nat. Envelope Corp., 1992-97, asst. v.p., 1997-99, v.p. R & D, 1999—. Contbr. many articles to profl. publs. Persecuted by Communist Party, 1957-79, honor reinstated 1979. Recipient Nat. Sci. award Govt. of China, 1978, Outstanding Sci. and Tech. Achievement award Municipality of Shanghai, 1978. Mem. ASME. Achievements include research in accuracy analysis of machine tools; theory of metal cutting; optimal design of mechanical systems; design of machine tools and metal cutting tools. E-mail: xc.wang@earthlink.net.

WANG, XIAODONG, biomedical researcher, educator; BS in Biology, Beijing Normal U., 1984; PhD in Biochemistry, U. Tex., Dallas, 1991. Fellow Damon Runyon-Walter Winchell Cancer Rsch. Fund, 1991; George L. MacGregor disting. chair, prof. biomed. sci. U. Tex. S.W. Med. Ctr., Dallas, 1991—. Recipient Eli Lilly award, Am. Chem. Soc., 2000, Paul Marks prize, Meml. Sloan-Kettering Cancer Ctr., 2001, Hackerman award, The Welch Found., 2002, Molecular Biology by a Young Scientist award, NAS, 2004. Mem.: Soc. Chinese Biomed. Scientists in Am. (Young Investigator award 1999), Ray Wu Soc., Am. Soc. Cell Biology, Am. Soc. Biochemistry and Molecular Biology (Schering-Plough award 2000), Am. Assn. Cancer Rsch. Office: Univ Tex Southwestern Med Ctr Dallas/Biomed Sci 5323 Harry Hines Blvd Dallas TX 75390 also: Howard Hughes Med Inst 4000 Jones Bridge Rd Chevy Chase MD 20815-6789

WANG, XING, power systems engineer; b. Haerbin, Heilongjiang, China, June 25, 1970; arrived in U.S., 2001; s. Shaohu Wang and Jianshan Mao; m. Ying Xiao. PhD, Brunel U., London, 2001. Power systems engr., rschr. Electric Power Rsch. Inst., Beijing, 1991—96, team leader energy mgmt. sys., 1997—98; power systems engr. Alstom Esca Corp., Bellevue, 2001—. Recipient China Nat. award sci. and tech., 1997. Mem.: IEEE Power Engring.

Soc. (sr.). Office: Alstom Esca Corp 11120 NE 33rd Pl Bellevue WA 98004 Home: 17305 NE 18th Pl Bellevue WA 98008-3140 Personal E-mail: xingwang@yahoo.com. Business E-Mail: xing.wang@tde.alstom.com.

WANG, XINGWU, physics educator; b. Hangzhou, China, Feb. 19, 1953; came to U.S., 1982; s. Jinguang and Xiuying (Lin) W. BS, Harbin N. Eng. Inst., 1978; MS, Hangzhou U., 1981; PhD, SUNY, Buffalo, 1987. Tchr., technician Hangzhou N. Sch., China, 1978-81; tchr. physics Hangzhou U., 1981-84; rsch. asst. SUNY, Buffalo, 1984-87, rsch. assoc., 1987-88; asst. prof. elec. engring. Alfred U., 1988-93, assoc. prof., 1993-97, prof., 1997—. Physics educator; b. Hangzhou, China, Feb. 19, 1953; came to U.S., 1982; s. Jinguang and Xiuying (Lin) W. BS, Harbin N. Eng. Inst., 1978; MS, Hangzhou U., 1981; PhD SUNY, Buffalo, 1987. Tchr., technician Hangzhou N. Sch., China, 1978-81; tchr. physics Hangzhou U., 1981-84; rsch. asst. SUNY, Buffalo, 1984-87, rsch. assoc., 1987-88; asst. prof. elec. engring. Alfred U., 1988-93, assoc. prof., 1993-97, prof., 1997—. Mem. Am. Phys. Soc. Mem. Am. Phys. Soc. Home: PO Box 1133 Alfred NY 14802-0133 Office: Alfred U Dept Elec Engring Alfred NY 14802 E-mail: fwangx@alfred.edu.

WANG, XUEMING, application developer, educator; m. Di Cao. PhD, W.Va. U., 1998. Sun Java 2 Cert. Architect Sun Microsystems, 2003. Cons. Pitts. Bus. Consulting, Denver, 1998—99; sr. software engr. NDCHealth, Pitts., 1999—. Asst. prof. China U. of Mining & Tech, Beijing, 1987—94. Achievements include design of Temporal flow Simulator for Belt Capacity Optimum Design. Office: NDCHealth Corp - Pharmacy Divsn 530 Lindbergh Dr Coraopolis PA 15108 Home: 1618 Lilac Ln Crescent PA 15046-3812 Office Phone: 1(412)474-1025. Personal E-mail: wangx@comcast.net. E-mail: xueming.wang@ndchealth.com.

WANG, YA-HUI, conductor; b. Taiwan; arrived in U.S., 1986; Degree in Piano Performance and Conducting, Curtis Inst. Music, Peabody Conservatory. Apprentice condr. Chgo. (Ill.) Symphony Orch., 1995—96; music dir. Fort Smith (Ark.) Symphony, 1996—97; asst. condr. Detroit (Mich.) Symphony Orch., 1997—99; music dir. Akron (Ohio) Symphony Orch., 1999—2003; vice music dir. Evergreen Symphony Orch., Taipei, Taiwan, 2004—. Music dir. Omaha Nebr. Youth Orchs.; prin. condr. Chgo. (Ill.) Encore Chamber Orch.; guest condr. in field. Recipient Tokyo (Japan) Competition prize, 1994, Dimitri Mitropoulos Competition prize, Athens, Greece, 1996, Nicolai Malko Competition prize, Copenhagen, Denmark, 1998. Office: Akron Symphony Orchestra 17 N Broadway Akron OH 44308

WANG, YANG, cardiologist, educator, medical researcher; b. Tangshan, China, May 12, 1923; s. Yu-Shen and Jun-Rong (Bo) Wang; m. Helen S. Huang; children: Dale, Cynthia, Jennifer, Heather. MB, Nat. Shanghai Med. Coll., 1948; MD, Harvard U., 1952. Diplomate Am. Bd. Internal Medicine, cert. cardiovasc. diseases. Intern, then resident Mass. Gen. Hosp., Boston, 1952-57, fellow in cardiology, 1957-58; fellow in cardiovascular physiology Mayo Found., Rochester, Minn., 1958-59; dir. cardiac catherization lab. U. Minn. Hosp., 1959—86; from instr. to prof. of medicine (cardiology) U. Minn. Med. Sch., Mpls., 1959—93, prof. emeritus, 1993—. Contbr. chapters to books, articles to profl. jours. Bd. dirs. Minn. Mus. Art, St. Paul, 1984—90, MacPhail Ctr. Music; session elder Presbyn. Ch., St. Paul. Capt. M.C. USAF, 1954—56. Fellow: AAAS, ACP, Am. Heart Assn. (cons., mem. internat. program com., mem. Gt. Plains com., pres., bd. dirs. Mpls. chpt. 1973—74), Am. Coll. Cardiology; mem.: Minn. Acad. Medicine (pres. 1997—98), Ctrl. Soc. Clin. Rsch., Assn. Univ. Cardiologists, Alpha Omega Alpha. Achievements include development of rate-pressure product as an index of cardiac work and coronary blood flow; research in cardiovascular response to exercise in normal subjects and in heart disease; in vivo assessment of cardiac valve protheses; treatment of adult congenital heart disease and of coronary disease in diabetes mellitus. Office: FUMC MMC 508 420 Delaware St SE Minneapolis MN 55455-0374 Office Phone: 612-625-5949.

WANG, YANXIN, research scientist; b. Dandong, Liaoning, China, June 19, 1962; arrived in United States, 1995; d. Dianlu Wang and Guiying Chen; m. Wanmin Xin, July 2, 1988; 1 child, Xin. BS, Shenyang (China) Agr. U., 1985, MS, 1988; MS, PhD, Rutgers U., 1999. Sr. lectr. Shenyang Agr. U., 1988-94; postdoc. assoc. U. Tenn., Knoxville, 1999-2000; rsch. assoc. Rutgers U., New Brunswick, N.J., 2000—. Grad. asst. Rutgers U., New Brunswick, 1995-99. Author: Nutrient Gene Interactions in Health & Disease, 2001; contbr. articles to profl. jours. Recipient Rsch. award Agr. Dept. Liaoning, 1992. Mem. AAAS, Am. Soc. Animal Sci., Soc. Exptl. Medicine Biology, N.Am. Assn. Study Obesity. Home: 615 Benner St Highland Park NJ 08904 Office: Rutgers U 96 Lipman Dr New Brunswick NJ 08901 E-mail: wyx@rci.rutgers.edu.

WANG, YEN, nuclear medicine physician, radiologist; b. 1928; MD, Nat. Taiwan U., 1953. Diplomate Am. Bd. Nuclear Medicine, Am. Bd. Radiology. Intern Holy Cross Hosp., Salt Lake City, 1953-54; resident Mercy Hosp., Pitts., 1955-58; with Thomas Jefferson U. Hosp., Phila. Prof. radiology Thomas Jefferson U. Mem. AMA, NMS, Am. Coll. Radiology, Am. Roentgen Ray Soc., Radiol. Soc. N.Am. Office: Thomas Jefferson U Hosp Philadelphia PA 19107-5084 also: VA Med Ctr Philadelphia PA 19104

WANG, YUNZENG, finance educator; arrived in U.S., 1993; m. Si Hu, Sept. 16, 1964; 1 child, Diana. PhD, U. Pa., Phila., 1993—97. Assoc. prof. Case Western Res. U., Cleve., 1999—. Cons. Teradyne Inc., Boston, 1994—97. Author: (research and industry applications) Svc. Parts Logistics Models (George B. Dantzig award, 1998), over 20 jour. articles and book chapters. Named a Jour. Editl. Bd. Mem., Jour. IIE Trans., since 2001, Jour. Mfg. and Svc. Ops. Mgmt., since 2002; scholar Wharton Scholarship PhD Study, Wharton Sch., U. Pa., 1993-1997. Mem.: Inst. Ops. Rsch. and Mgmt. Sci. (hon.). Achievements include research in Creative rsch. in Supply Chain Mgmt. has generated significant impact both to academia and industry. Office: Case Western Res U 10900 Euclid Ave Cleveland OH 44106

WANG, ZHISHUN, biomedical engineer, consultant; s. Xinming Wang and Xianglan Liu; m. Qiong Liu, May 17, 1990; 1 child, Yujun. BS, Beijing U., 1987; MS, Nanjing (China) U., 1991; PhD, SE U., Nanjing, 1997; postgrad., U. Tex., Galveston, 1999—2001. Cert. sr. info. network engr. Jiangsu Computer Info. Ctr., 1995. Dept. chief Nat. Satellite Comm. Sta. Shiyan (China) Br., 1981—88; sr. engr., project mgr. Jiangsu Computer Info. Ctr., Nanjing, 1991—94; rsch. assoc. Lynn Health Sci. Inst., Oklahoma City, 1997—99; prin. bioinformatics scientist U. Tex. Med. Br., Galveston, 2000—. Sr. consulting scientist Video Compression Sci., Inc., San Jose, Calif., 2000—01; vis. prof. Huazhong U. Sci. and Tech., Wuhan, Hubei, China, 2001—. Contbr. chapters to books, articles to profl. jours. Recipient Outstanding Contbn. award, Hubei Adminstrn. Com. Telecom., 1984, 1986, Travel award, Am. Motility Soc., 2000, Young Investigator award, 2002. Mem.: IEEE (reviewer, Young Investigator award 1999, 2001), Functional Brain-gut Rsch. Group, Internat. Electrogastrography Soc., Biomedical Engring. Soc. (assoc.), Am. Gastroenterology Assn. (assoc.). Achievements include development of Deinterlacing of Interlaced Video; invention of High-ratio Still Image Compression Using Minimum Neural Network; Spatio-temporal filtering of video images; Coupling Analysis of Gastric Myoelectrical Activity; Minimum Fuel Neural Network; Chaos-driven Gastric Pacing for the Treatment of Obesity; Robust Time Delay Estimation Using Least Absolute Deviation Neural Network and Its Application to Radar; Super-resolution Time Frequency Analysis of Nonstationary Signals Using Overcomplete Time-frequency Representation; discovery of Chaos in the gut; Fractals and Strange Attractors in Gastric Migrating Myoelectrical Complex Phases. Avocations: swimming, travel, music, computers. Office Phone: 212-543-6153. E-mail: zhwang@utmb.edu.

WANGER, OLIVER WINSTON, federal judge; b. L.A., Nov. 27, 1940; m. Lorrie A. Reinhart; children: Guy A., Christopher L., Andrew G., W. Derek, Oliver Winston II. Student, Colo. Sch. Mines, 1958-60; BS, U. So. Calif., 1963; LLB, U. Calif., Berkeley, 1966. Bar: Calif. 1967, U.S. Dist. Ct. (ea. dist.) Calif. 1969, U.S. Tax Ct. 1969, U.S. Dist. Ct. (cen. dist.) Calif. 1975, U.S. Dist. Ct. (so. dist.) Calif. 1977, U.S. Dist. Ct. (no. dist.) Calif. 1989, U.S. Ct. Appeals (9th cir.) 1989. Dep. dist. atty. Fresno (Calif.) County Dist. Atty., 1967-69; ptnr. Gallagher, Baker & Manock, Fresno, 1969-74; sr. ptnr. McCormick, Barstow, Sheppard, Wayte & Carruth, Fresno, 1974-91; judge U.S. Dist. Ct. (ea. dist.) Calif., Fresno, 1991—. Adj. prof. Humphreys Coll. Law, Fresno, Calif., 1968—70, San Joaquim Coll. Law, Fresno, 1970—94, dean, 1980—83, chair bd. trustees, pres., 1984—94. Fellow Am. Coll. Trial Lawyers, Internat. Acad. Trial Lawyers; mem. Am. Bd. Trial Advs. (pres. San Joaquin Valley chpt. 1987-89, nat. bd. dirs. 1989-91), Am. Bd. Profl. Liability Attys. (founder, diplomate), Calif. State Bar (mem. exec. com. litigation sect. 1989-92, mem. com. on fed. cts. 1989-90), San Joaquin Valley Am. Inn of Ct. (pres. 1992-93), Beta Gamma Sigma. Office: US Dist Ct 5104 US Courthouse 1130 O St Fresno CA 93721-2201

WANGLER, WILLIAM CLARENCE, retired insurance company executive; b. Buffalo, Dec. 7, 1929; s. Emil A. and Viola M. (Roesser) W.; m. Carol B. Sullivan, Aug. 17, 1957; children: Jeffrey W., Eric J. BS, SUNY, Cortland, 1951. Claims adjuster Liberty Mut. Ins. Co., Buffalo, 1954-60, claims supr. Miami, Fla., 1960-65, home office examiner Boston, 1965-68, asst. claims mgr. Cleve., 1968-69, claims mgr. Cleve, 1969-73, div. claims service mgr. Pitts., 1973-79, div. claims mgr., 1979-86, v.p. asst. gen. claims mgr. adminstrn. Boston, 1986-94, ret., 1994. Pres. Claims Mgrs. Counsel, Cleve., 1970; chmn. Nationwide Intercompany Arbitration, Cleve., 1969-70. Loaned exec. Mass. Bay United Way, Boston, 1964; account exec. Pitts. United Way, 1985-86. Served to capt. USMC, 1951-54. Republican. Roman Catholic. Home: 64 Trout Farm Ln Duxbury MA 02332-4609 Personal E-mail: vcwangler@webtv.net.

WANGSNESS, GENNA STEAD, hotel executive, innkeeper; b. Detroit, Feb. 2, 1942; d. William Allen Stead and Genevieve Josephine Schreiber; m. Roger Carroll Wangsness, Dec. 1, 1967; children: Alison Lee Clement, Bijali Anne, Brian William. BA in Liberal Studies, Georgetown U., 1995. Vol. Peace Corps, Tehran, Iran, 1965—67; sec. Office of Pres. Georgetown U., Washington, 1984—86, coord. adminstrv. svcs. Office of Pres., 1986—89, adminstrv. officer dept. surgery, 1989—92, adminstrv. office Sch. Summer and Continuing Edn., 1992—95; exec. asst. to exec. v.p. Am. Soc. Clin. Oncology, Alexandria, Va., 1995—96; pres., innkeeper The Inn at Folkston, Ga., 1997—. Author: Folkston Then and Now 1881-2003, A Self-Guided Walking Tour of Historic Downtown, Folkston, Georgia, 2003. Mem.: Alpha Sigma Lambda. Achievements include establishment of womens studies section at Charlton Public Library. Office: The Inn at Folkston 509 W Main St Folkston GA 31537 Office Phone: 912-496-6256.

WANI, MANSUKHLAL CHHAGANLAL, chemist; b. Nandurbar, Maharastra, India, Feb. 20, 1925; came to U.S., 1958, naturalized, 1977; s. Chhagnalal Kikabhai and Maniben Chhanganlal (Shah) W.; m. Ramila Mansukhlal Dalal, Dec. 4, 1954; 1 child, Bankim M. BS with honors, St. Xavier's Coll., Bombay U., 1947, MS, 1950; PhD, Ind. U., 1962. Lectr. chemistry Bhavan's Coll., Bombay, 1951-58; rsch. asst. Ind. U., Bloomington, 1958-61; rsch. assoc. U. Wis., Madison, 1961-62; prin. scientist Rsch. Triangle Inst., Rsch. Triangle Park, N.C., 1962—. Inventor anticancer drugs. Recipient B.F. Cain Meml. award Am. Assn. Cancer Rsch., 1994, City of Medicine award Durham, N.C., 1994, Award of Recognition Nat. Cancer Inst., 1996, Charles E. Kettering prize GM Cancer Rsch. Found., 2000, Ranbaxy Rsch. award. Mem. AAAS, Am. Chem. Soc., Am. Soc. Pharmacognosy, N.Y. Acad. Scis., India Assn. (pres. 1970-72), Hindu Soc. (dir. 1976-81), Assn. Indians in Am., Indo-Am. Forum, Sigma Xi, Phi Lambda Upsilon. Democrat. Avocations: reading, travel, sports. Home: 2801 Legion Ave Durham NC 27707-1921 Office: Rsch Triangle Inst 3040 W Cornwallis Rd Research Triangle Park NC 27709-2194 Office Phone: 919-541-6685. Business E-Mail: MCW@rti.org.

WANIEK, MARILYN NELSON See NELSON, MARILYN

WANJOHI, ELSIE WAIRIMU, communications educator; b. Nyeri, Kenya, Nov. 17, 1949; came to U.S., 1990; d. David Kinyua and Martha Nyawira Githiru; 1 child, Anne W. BS in Comm., Okla. State U., 1992, MS in Mass Comm., 1994, D in Comm., 1996. Dir. Wambugu, Embu, Thika Inc., Kenya, 1973-87; info. officer Kabete Info. Ctr., Nairobi, Kenya, 1988-90; publs. editor Okla. State U., Stillwater, 1992-96, tchg. asst., 1995-96; asst. prof. Bethune-Cookman Coll., Daytona Beach, Fla., 1996—. Internat. fellow AAUW, 1993-94. Mem. Fla. Pub. Rels. Assn., Phi Kappa Phi. Avocations: tennis, jogging, reading, tv documentaries. Home: 3537 Forest Branch Dr Apt A Port Orange FL 32129-8952 Office: Bethune-Cookman Coll 640 Mary McLeod Bethune Blvd Daytona Beach FL 32114 E-mail: wanjohie@cookman.edu.

WANK, GERALD SIDNEY, periodontist, educator; b. Bklyn., Jan. 20, 1925; s. Joseph and Sadie (Ikowitz) W.; m. Gloria Baum, June 4, 1949; children: David, Stephen, Daniel. BA, NYU, 1945, DDS, 1949; cert. in orthodontia, Columbia U., 1951, cert. in periodontia, 1956. Intern Bellevue Hosp., 1949-50; pvt. practice N.Y.C., Great Neck, N.Y., 1949—; instr. dept. periodontia, oral medicine NYU Dental Sch., 1956-63, asst. clin. prof. dept. periodontia, 1963-67, asst. prof. periodontia, oral medicine, former postgrad. dir. periodontal-prosthesis dept. fixed partial prosthesis, 1970—, clin. assoc. prof. periodontia and oral medicine, 1970-77, clin. prof., 1977—, postgrad. dir. periodontia, 1968-71, Disting. prof. periodontics, 2002; lectr. periodontology Harvard U. Sch. Dental Medicine, 1971—74; vis. lectr. N.Y.C. C.C. Sch. Dental Hygiene, 1960-65, Albert Einstein Coll. Medicine, 1967-96; sr. asst. attending staff North Shore U. Hosp., 1974-77, sr. asst. attending divsn. surgery, 1977—. Cons. orthodontic panel N.Y. State, N.Y.C. depts. health, 1953-80; cons. periodontal prosthesis, Goldwater Meml. Hosp., N.Y.C.; former postgrad. instr. 1st Dist. Dental Soc. Postgrad. Sch., dist. claims com.; lectr. in field; mem. com. admissions N.Y. U. Coll. Dentistry, 1975-86, chmn. fund raising, 1976-77; cons. N.Y. VA Hosp., 1996—. Contbr. to: Practice of Periodontia, 1960, Dental Clinics of North America, 1972, 81, Manual of Clinical Periodontics, 1973; contbr. articles to profl. jours. Capt. USAF, 1953-55. Recipient Alumni Meritorious Service award NYU, 1981, Coll. Dentistry Alumni Achievement award NYU, 1983, Disting. Prof. Periodontics award NYU Coll. Dentistry, 2002. Fellow Acad. Gen. Dentistry, N.Y. Acad. Dentistry (life), Internat. Coll. Dentists (life), Am. Coll. Dentistry (life), Am. Acad. Oral Medicine (pres. N.Y. sect. 1971-72), Am. Pub. Health Assn.; mem. N.Y. Coll. Dentists (dir.), ADA, Dental Soc. N.Y.C. (dir. 1st dist., chmn. ethics com. 1985-86), Fedn. Dentaire Internat., Am. Assn. Dental Schs., N.Y. State Pub. Health Assn., AAUP, Pan Am. Med. Assn. (life), AAAS, ADA, Am. Acad. Periodontology, Sci. Rsch. Soc. Am., Northeastern Soc. Periodontia (life), Am. Acad. Dental Medicine, Acad. Gen. Dentistry, Internat. Acad. Orthodontia, Am. Assn. Endodontists (life), Am. Acad. Periodontia (life), Am. Acad. Oral Medicine (life), NYU Coll. Dentistry Alumni Assn. (dir., sec. 1973-74, v.p. 1974-75, pres. 1976-77), Am. Assn. Endodontists, NYU Coll. Dentistry Dental Assocs. (charter), Acad. Oral Rehab. (hon.), First Dist. Dental Soc. (program chmn. 1984, chmn. continuing edn. 1983, sec., 1985, v.p. Eastern Dental Soc. br. 1986, pres.-elect 1987, pres. br. 1988, bd. dirs. 1989—, Meritorious Svc. award 1997), Am. Acad. Osseointegration (life), NYU Gallatin Assocs., Alumni Fedn. NYU (dir. 1976-81), N.Y. County Dental Soc. (Dist. Claims Com.), Soc. of the Torch, Masons, Century Club, NYU Club, Fresh Meadow Country Club, Omicron Kappa Upsilon (life), Alpha Omega. Jewish. Home and Office: 40 Bayview Ave Great Neck NY 11021-2819 Office: 30 E 40th St New York NY 10016-1201 Office Phone: 516-487-7877.

WANK, MARTIN, writer; b. Bklyn., Feb. 1, 1932; s. Joseph and Fannie Wank; children: Sharon, Linda. BA, Long Is. U.; MA in english lit., Queens Coll., 1968. Author: (book) Freud's Answer, 1998, Sex, Freud and Folly, 2000, Hitler and the Holocaust, 2002. Democrat. Judaism. Avocations: piano, reading, musical composition, samurai sword, japanese history. Home: 41 Garden St Oneonta NY 13820

WANKAT, PHILLIP CHARLES, chemical engineering educator; b. Oak Park, Ill., July 11, 1944; s. Charles and Grace Wankat; m. Dorothy Nel Richardson, Dec. 13, 1980; children: Charles, Jennifer. BS in Chem. Engring., Purdue U., 1966, MS in Edn., 1982; PhD, Princeton U., 1970. From asst. prof. to C.L. Lovell disting. prof. chem. engring Purdue U., West Lafayette, Ind., 1970—, head freshman engring., 1987-95, interim dir. continuing engring. edn., 1996, head interdisciplinary engring., 2000—04. Cons. pharm. firm, 1985-94. Author: Large Scale Ads and Chromatog, 1986, Equil Staged Separations, 1988, Rate Controlled Separations, 1990, Teaching Engineering, 1993, The Effective, Efficient Professor, 2002; patentee in field. With AUS, 1962-64. Recipient award in Separations Sci. and Tech., Am. Chem. Soc., 1994. Mem. AIChE, Am. Soc. Engring. Edn. (Union Carbide Lectr. award 1997), Am. Chem. Soc. Avocations: fishing, canoeing, camping. Office: Purdue U Dept Engring 480 Stadium Mall Dr West Lafayette IN 47907-2100 E-mail: wankat@ecn.purdue.edu.

WANKE, RONALD LEE, lawyer; b. Chgo., June 22, 1941; s. William F. and Lucille (Kleinwachter) W.; m. Rose Klonowski, Oct. 23, 1987. BSEE, Northwestern U., 1964; JD, DePaul U., 1968. Bar: Ill. 1968. Assoc. Wood, Dalton, Phillips, Mason & Rowe, Chgo., 1968-71, ptnr., 1971-84, Jenner & Block, Chgo., 1984--. Lectr. John Marshall Law Sch., Chgo., 1985-94; mem. adv. com. intellectual property program, U. Fla. Coll. Law, 2001-03. Contbr. chpt. to book, articles to Software Law Jour., 1987, Internat. Legal Strategy, 1995. Mem.: ABA, Intellectual Property Law Assn. Chgo. (chmn. inventor svcs. com. 1976, chmn. fed. rules com. 1981). Home: 1806 N Sedgwick St Chicago IL 60614-5306 Office: Jenner & Block 1 E Ibm Plz Fl 4000 Chicago IL 60611-7603 Office Phone: 312-222-9350.

WANN, LAYMOND DOYLE, retired petroleum research scientist; b. Magazine, Ark., Apr. 25, 1924; s. Vernon Cecil and Emma (McCrary) W.; m. Betty Lou Brown, Nov. 6, 1948; children: Jacqueline, Lyndall Doyle. BS in Physics (Phi Eta Sigma scholar), Okla. State U., 1949, MS, 1950. With Conoco Inc., Ponca City, Okla., 1951-84, sr. rsch. scientist, 1957-60, rsch. group leader, 1960-81, assoc. rsch. dir., 1981-84, staff scientist, 1984-85, ret., 1985. Cons. in disciplines of phys. Contbr. articles on elec. and radioactive well-logging, elec. design to profl. jours. Patentee in field. Mem. Mcpl. Airport Bd., Ponca City. Served with AUS, 1942-46; ETO. Decorated Bronze Star. Mem. Am. Petroleum Inst. (chmn. well logging subcom.), IEEE, Aircraft Owners and Pilots Assn., Seaplane Pilots Assn., VFW, Am. Legion, Phi Kappa Phi, Pi Mu Epsilon, Sigma Pi Sigma. Republican. Episcopalian (vestryman). Home: 1501 Monument Rd Ponca City OK 74604-3522 Office: 1000 S Pine St Ponca City OK 74601-7509

WANN, MICHAEL STEPHEN, music educator; b. Baltimore, Md., July 5, 1950; s. William Richard and Mildred Naomi Wann; 1 child, Michael Joseph. BS in Music Edn., Towson (Md.) State U., 1976; MEd, Loyola Coll., 1991; MusM in Edn., Peabody Conservatory @ Johns Hopkins U., 1995. Cert. tchr. Md., 1991. Band dir. Instrumental Program of Md., Lanham, Md., 1976—79, Archbishop Curley High, Baltimore, Md., 1979—80; instrumental music tchr. Balt. County Pub. Schs., Towson, Md., 1981—97, Howard County Pub. Schs., Ellicott City, Md. Curriculum com. mem. Howard County Pub. Schs., 1998—2001; chmn. of the bd. Cmty. Music Ctr. of Md., Inc, Columbia, Md., 1999—. Musician: (TV series) Marriage in the Family. Mem.: Percussive Arts Soc., Am. Fedn. of Musicians, Md. Band Dirs. Assn, Music Educators Nat. Conf. Avocations: golf, tennis, reading, painting. Home: 8332 Ridgely Oak Rd Baltimore MD 21234 Office: Northfield Elementary School 9125 Northfield Rd Ellicott City MD 21042 Personal E-mail: mwann@mail.howard.k12.md.us. E-mail: mwann@mail.howard.k12.md.us.

WANNAMAKER, MARY RUTH, music educator; b. Ft. Collins, Colo., July 29, 1922; d. Jerry Albert and Daisy B. (Burington) Lyman; m. William H. Anderson, June 14, 1944 (dec. 1944); m. John S. Wannamaker, Sept. 7, 1946; children: Lois Wannamaker, Daisy Wannamaker Van Valkenburg. MusB, Colo. State U., 1944; M in Musicology, U. Minn., 1949, M in Ednl. Psychology, 1969. Piano tchr. U. Minn., Mpls., 1945-46; piano tchr. Drake U., Des Moines, 1945-47; prof. piano Kletzing Coll., University Park, Iowa, 1948-49; ednl. cons. Des Moines, 1975-85. Pvt. piano tchr. Des Moines, 1950—. Composer Easter ch. svc., 1965. Vol. Iowa State Hist. Libr., Des Moines, 1990—; pres. Delta Omicron Alumnae, Des Moines, 1946-50, Profl. Women's League, Des Moines, 1974-75, Iowa Pers. & Guidance Assn., Des Moines, 1978-79; violist Des Moines Symphony Orch., 1946-65; mem. Altrusa, 1970-75. Mem. Music Techs. Nat. Assn., PEO, Phi Kappa Phi (scholarship 1944). Avocations: reading, travel, concerts. Home: 200 Buffalo Hills Ln E # 107 Brainerd MN 56401-4555

WANNER, ADAM, medical association administrator, pulmonologist; MD, U. Basel, 1966. Diplomate Am. Bd. Internal Medicine. Intern Phila. Gen. Hosp.; resident Kantonsspital Aarau, fellow, Mt. Sinai Med. Ctr., Miami Beach, Fla.; dir. pulmonary and critical care medicine divsn., endowed chair U. Miami, Fla., vice chmn. rsch. Mem.: Am. Thoracic Soc. (pres.). Office: U Miami Sch Medicine R-47 1600 NW 10th Ave RMSB 7052 Miami FL 33136

WANNER, ADRIAN J. literature educator; b. Bern, Switzerland, Jan. 26, 1960; s. Oscar and Rosette Wanner; m. Catherine Elizabeth Cowhey, July 16, 1989; children: Elizabeth Duffy, Nicholas James, Katrina Maureen. M.A., Zurich U., Switzerland, 1986; Ph.D., Columbia U., 1992. Dept. head German and Slavic Pa. State U., University Park, 2001—. Author: (books) Russian Minimalism, Baudelaire in Russia; translator: (poetry volume) Die Schwarze Silhouette, Alexander Blok: Gedichte. Avocations: piano, choral singing. Home: 241 Waring Ave State College PA 16801 Office: Pa State U 313 Burrowes Bldg University Park PA 16802 Office Phone: 814-865-5481. E-mail: ajw3@psu.edu.

WANNER, ERIC, foundation executive; b. Wilmington, Del., Mar. 14, 1942; s. Edwin and Isabel Smith (Speakman) W.; m. Patricia Attix, June 13, 1964 (div. 1976); children: Noel Edwin, Erin Cole; m. Carla Francesca Seal, June 18, 1983; children: Lindzay Elizabeth. BA, Amherst Coll., 1963; PhD, Harvard U., 1969. Asst. to assoc. prof. Harvard U., Cambridge, Mass., 1968-76; behavioral sci. editor Harvard U. Press, Cambridge, Mass., 1976-82; program officer Alfred P. Sloan Found., N.Y.C., 1982-84, v.p., 1984-86; pres. Russell Sage Found, N.Y.C., 1986—. Trustee Ctr. for Advanced Study in Behavioral Scis., 1993-99; bd. dirs. Dogan Found., Paris, Am. Acad. Polit. Social Sci. Author: Remembering, Forgetting and Understanding Sentences, 1974; editor: Language Acquisition: the State of the Art, 1982; contbr. articles to profl. jours. Fulbright fellow Sussex U., Brighton, Eng., 1979, N.Y. Inst. for Humanities fellow, NYU, 1985-93, Am. Acad. Arts and Scis. fellow, 1994—. Mem. APA, Nat. Acad. Scis. (adv. bd. divsn. behavioral, social scis. and edn.), Cognitive Sci. Soc., Century Assn., Sigma Xi. Office: Russell Sage Found 112 E 64th St New York NY 10021-7383 E-mail: ew@rsage.org.

WANNSTEDT, DAVID RAYMOND, professional football coach; b. Pitts., May 21, 1952; m. Jan Wannstedt; children: Keri, Jami. Student, U. Pitts. Player Green Bay Packers, 1974; asst. coach U. Pitts., 1975-79, Okla. State U., 1979-82, U. So. Calif., 1983-85; def. coord. U. Miami, 1986-89, Dallas Cowboys, 1989-93; head coach Chgo. Bears, 1993-98; asst. head coach Miami Dolphins, 1999-2000, head coach, 2000—. Named to NCAA 2nd team All-East; inducted into Western Pa. Hall of Fame, 1990. Office: Miami Dolphins Halas Hall 7500 SW 30th St Davie FL 33314-1020

WANTLAND, WILLIAM CHARLES, retired bishop, lawyer; b. Edmond, Okla., Apr. 14, 1934; s. William Lindsay and Edna Louise (Yost) W. BA, U. Hawaii, 1957; JD, Okla. City U., 1967; D in Religion, Geneva Theol. Coll., Knoxville, Tenn., 1976; DD (hon.), Nashotah House, Wis., 1983, Seabury-Western Sem., Evanston, Ill., 1983. With FBI, various locations, 1954-59, Ins. Co. of N.Am., Oklahoma City, 1960-62; law clk.-atty. Bishop & Wantland, Seminole, Okla., 1962-77; vicar St. Mark's Ch., Seminole, 1963-77, St. Paul's Ch., Holdenville, Okla., 1974-77; presiding judge Seminole Mcpl. Ct., 1970-77; atty. gen. Seminole Nation of Okla., 1969-72, 75-77; exec. dir. Okla. Indian Rights Assn., Norman, 1972-73; rector St. John's Ch., Oklahoma City, 1977-80; bishop Episcopal Diocese of Eau Claire, Wis., 1980-99; interim bishop of Navajoland, 1993-94; ret., 1999. Adj. prof. Law Sch. U. Okla., Norman, 1970-78; instr. canon law Nashotah House, 1983-97, 2004—; mem. nat. coun. Evang. and Cath. Mission, Chgo., 1977-90; mem. Episcopal Commn. on Racism, 1990-92, Episcopal Coun. Indian Ministries, 1990-95, Standing Commn. on Constn. and Canons, 1992-95; assisting bishop Diocese of Dallas, 2002—, of Ft. Worth, 2000—. Author: Foundations of the Faith,

1982, Canon Law of the Episcopal Church, 1984, The Prayer Book and the Catholic Faith, 1994; The Catholic Faith, The Episcopal Church and the Ordination of Women, 1997; co-author: Oklahoma Probate Forms, 1971; contbr. articles to profl. jours. Pres. Okla. Conf. Mcpl. Judges, 1973; v.p. South African Ch. Union, 1985-95; trustee Nashotah House, Wis., 1981-2000, chmn., 1992-98; bd. dirs. SPEAK, Eureka Springs, Ark., 1983-89; Wis. adv. com. US Civil Rights Commn., 1990-91; support com. Native Am. Rights Fund, 1990—; mem. City Coun. of the City of Seminole, Okla., 2002—, vice mayor, 2003-04; co-chmn. Luth.-Anglican-Roman Cath. Commn. of Wis., 1989-95; pres. Wis. Episc. Conf., 1995-97, Wis. Coun. Chs., 1985-86; mem. Living Ch. Found., 1981-2002; bd. dirs. Seminole Nation Hist. Soc., 1999—; mem. adv. bd. Seminole Hist. Soc., 2003—. Recipient Most Outstanding Contbn. to Law and Order award Okla. Supreme Ct., 1975, Outstanding Alumnus award Okla. City U., 1980, Wis. Equal Rights Coun. award, 1986, Manitou Ikwe award Indian Alcoholism Coun., 1988, Episcopal Synod Pres.'s award, 1995, 2004. Mem. Okla. Bar Assn., Okla. Indian Bar Assn., Oklahoma City Law Sch. Alumni Assn. (pres. 1968) Democrat. Episcopalian. Avocations: canoeing, skin-diving, cross country skiing. E-mail: puca382@mbo.net. *If we truly believe that God reigns, we will so order our lives that such a belief is clearly reflected in all that we do and say; further, such a belief will shape our relations, not only with all other people, but all of God's created order.*

WAPIENNIK, CARL FRANCIS, manufacturing firm executive, planetarium and science institute executive; b. Donora, Pa., Oct. 10, 1926; s. Karl and Rose (Kidzinski) W.; m. Elva Louise Bartron, Nov. 27, 1953; children: Carl Eric, Ellen Louise. BS, U. Pitts., 1953. Prodn. supr. RCA, Canonsburg, Pa., 1953—54; staff physicist Buhl Planetarium and Inst. Popular Sci., Pitts., 1954—64, exec. dir., 1964—82; owner, operator Work-O-Art Miniatures (small mfg. firm), 1983—2003. Patentee means for controlling liquid flow. Mem. Rostraver Twp. Planning Commn., 1965-67; mem. adv. bd. Allegheny C. of C. (formerly North Side Pitts. C. of C.), 1966-67, dir., 1968-73, pres., 1970; mem. adv. coun. Salvation Army, 1978-82; bd. dirs. Bapt. Homes, Pitts., 1982-94; chmn. Rostraver Twp. Mcpl. Water Authority, 1990-94. With USNR, 1945-46. Recipient Man of Yr. award in sci. Pitts. Jaycees, 1969. Mem. Service Core Ret. Execs., Pitts. Bapt. Assn. (bd. dirs. 1976-82), Phi Beta Kappa, Sigma Pi Sigma. Home: 602 Salem Church Rd Belle Vernon PA 15012-2906

WAPNIR, IRENE LEONOR, medical educator; b. Buenos Aires, May 11, 1954; came to U.S., 1963; d. Raul Alberto and Elsa (Michalewicz) W.; m. Ralph Steven Greco; children: Justin Michael, Eric Matthew, Ilana Rose. BA, Goucher Coll., Balt., 1975; MD, U. Autonoma Metropolitana, Mexico City, 1980. Diplomate Am. Bd. Surgery. Intern, resident N.Y. Med. Coll., Bronx, 1980-85; attending physician and asst. prof. surgery Lincoln Hosp.-N.Y. Med. Coll., 1985-87; asst. prof. surgery UMDNJ-Robert Wood Johnson Med. Sch., New Brunswick, 1988-95, chief divsn. comprehensive breast svcs., 1991-93, assoc. prof. clin. surgery, 1995—2000; assoc. prof. surgery Sch. Medicine Stanford (Calif.) U., 2001—. Contbr. articles to profl. jours. Komen Breast Cancer Rsch. grant, fellow UMDNJ-Robert Wood Johnson Med. Sch., 1987-88. Office: Stanford Univ Sch Medicine 300 Pasteur Drive Stanford CA 94305

WARA, DIANE, dean; BS in Biology, Standord U., 1964; MD, U. Calif., Irvine, 1969. Intern in peds. Harbor Gen. Hosp., Torrance, Calif., 1969-70; resident in peds. U. Calif., San Francisco, 1970-72; fellow immunology divsn. dept. peds. USPHS, 1974-75; asst. prof. peds. U. Calif., San Francisco, 1975-79, assoc. prof. peds., 1979-84, prof. peds., 1984—, chief divsn. ped. immunology/rheumatology, program dir. ped., 1985—, assoc. dean for minority and women's affairs sch. med., 1991—. Mem. NIH study sect. on immunological scis., 1985-87, chair, 1987-89; vice chair universitywide task force on AIDS, 1989-92; vice chair ped. core com. AIDS Clinical Trials Group, 1991-92, chair ped. core com., 1992-94; mem. AIDS rsch. adv. com. NIH, 1990-95; mem. AIDS program adv. com. NIAID, 1990-94; mem. GCRC study sect., 1993-97, chair study sect., 1996-97. Contbr. articles to profl. jours. Recipient Eleanor Roosevelt award Am. Cancer Soc., 1983, Rsch. Career Devel. award Nat. Inst. of Child Health and Human Devel., 1978-83. Mem. NAS (elected to Inst. Medicine 1998), Am. Ped. Soc., Am. Rheumatism Assn., Am. Assn. Immunology, Am. Soc. for Clin. Investigation, Soc. for Ped. Rsch., Western Soc. for Ped. Rsch. (sec.-treas. 1979-83, pres. 1990-91). Office: U Calif Childrens Med Ctr 505 Parnassus Ave # M-601 San Francisco CA 94122-2722

WARACH, MARIE, artist; b. N.Y.C., Feb. 19, 1922; d. Jacob and Diena (Friedlander) Sieff; m. Sam Norkin, Feb. 19, 1941 (div. June 1968); children: Richard Norkin, Laura De Sena; m. Bernard Warach, May 30, 1976; stepchildren: Joshua, Jonathan, Beth. Postgrad., Art Students League, 1956—60; BS in Studio Art, Hunter Coll., CUNY, 1980; cert. in art therapy, New Sch., 1982. Registered art therapist, Am. Art Therapy Assn. Sr. photographer Internat. Paper Co., N.Y.C., 1964-72; freelance photographer Jewish Assn. Svcs. for Aged, N.Y.C., 1974-82; art therapist Fedn. Employment and Guidance, N.Y.C., 1982-86; artist East Hampton, N.Y. Exhibited in solo and group shows, L.I. Mem. Artists Alliance of East Hampton (pres. 1996—). Avocations: family, reading, museums, classical music, film. Office Phone: 631-324-7556.

WARAKOMSKI, ALPHONSE WALTER JOSEPH, JR., sales executive, marketing professional; b. NYC, Apr. 1, 1943; s. Alphonse Walter and Mary (Dupnock) Warakomski. BS in Chemistry, St. Bonaventure, 1968; MBA in Mktg., Keller Grad. Sch., 1981. Chemist, lab. mgr. Purification Sci., Geneva, NY, 1968-73; applications engr. Pollution Control Industries, Stamford, Conn., 1973; sales mgr. Kopper's Environ. Elements, Balt., 1974; mktg. specialist, regional mgr. Union Carbide Linde, Chgo., 1975-79; sales engr. Dorr Oliver, Chgo., 1980-81; dir. mktg. and sales Linde AG Lotepro, Valhalla, NY, 1981—2000; ptnr. Mixing and Mass Transfer Techs., Inc., 2000—. Contbr. articles to profl. jours. Mem.: AIChE, Am. Chem. Soc., Water Environment Fedn., Internat. Ozone Assn., Am. Water Works Assn. Home: 8833 N Congress Apt 818 Kansas City MO 64153 Office Phone: 816-584-1969.

WARBECK, STEPHEN, composer; Motion picture and T.V. composer. Composer films Skallagrigg, 1994, O Mary This London, 1994, Nervous Energy, 1995, Element of Doubt, 1996, Brothers in Trouble, 1996, Shakespeare in Love, 1998 (Oscar award 1999, nominee British Acad. award 1999, Anthony Asquith award for film music 1999), My Son the Fanatic, 1998, others; T.V. films include Prime Suspect, 1990, Devil's Advocate, 1995, Truth or Dare, 1996, The Student Prince, 1997, Bright Hair, 1997, Billy Elliot, 2001, Charlotte Gray, 2001, Birthday Girl, 2001, Captain Corelli's Mandolin, 2001, others. Office: Royal Shakespeare Co Waterside Stratford-upon-Avon Warwickshire CV37 6BB England

WARBERG, WILLETTA, concert pianist, writer, piano educator; b. Twin Falls, Idaho, June 2, 1932; d. George William Warberg and Ethel Margaret (Sargent) Warberg-Chandler; m. David Jacob Bar-Illan, Sept. 3, 1954 (div.); children: Daniela, Jeremy Oscar. Student, Colo. Women's Coll., 1950-51, Aspen Music Camp, 1951; studied with, Rudolph Firkusny, 1951-53; BS, Mannes Coll. Music, N.Y.C., 1954. Assoc. food editor Look mag., N.Y.C., 1956-61; food editor Status mag., N.Y.C., 1961-62, Ladie's Home Jour., N.Y.C., 1964-66; photog. stylist Gourmet mag., N.Y.C., 1961-64, freelance writer, photog. stylist, 1965-75; pres., owner Willetta Enterprises, advt. agy., Twin Falls, 1976-84; food columnist, music and arts critic Times News, 1978-87; duo-piano ptnr. with Robert Starer, N.Y.C., Woodstock, 1991—2000; pvt. piano tchr., Saugerties, N.Y., 1991—. Made feasibility study of restaurant situation in Israel, U.S. Dept. State ICA Point 4 Program, Washington and Israel, 1960; artist-in-residence Holy Cross Concert Series, Kingston, N.Y., 1994—. Concert pianist, Idaho, Oreg., Utah, Wash., Colo., N.Y.C., N.Y. State, 1940—; author: Cooking from Scratch, 1976, Space Age Cookery, 1977; syndicated food columnist Willetta Says, 1978-87; contbr. food and sci. articles to Cosmopolitan, Modern Maturity, Esquire, Sun Valley, Sci. Diegest, also other mags. Bd. dirs. N.W. Opera Assn., 1984-87; pres. bd. dirs. Woodstock Lyric Theatre, 1994—; v.p. bd. dirs. Woodstock Chamber Orch., 1993—; chmn. Friends of the Maverick Concerts Inc., Woodstock, N.Y., 1999—. Winner Rocky Mountain talent search contest Salt Lake Tribune and Salt Lake Telegram, 1949. Mem. Nat. Fedn. Music Clubs, Music Tchrs. Nat. Assn. (cert.), Kingston Music Soc. Avocations: designing and sewing clothes, painting still lifes, swimming, developing recipes, writing science fiction book.

WARBURTON, RALPH JOSEPH, architect, engineer, planner, educator; b. Kansas City, Mo., Sept. 5, 1935; s. Ralph Gray and Emma Frieda (Niemann) W.; m. Carol Ruth Hychka, June 14, 1958; children: John Geoffrey, Joy Frances W. Tracey. BArch, MIT, 1958; MArch, Yale U., 1959, M.C.P., 1960. Registered arch., Colo., Conn., Fla., Ill., La., Md., NJ, NY, Tex., Va., DC; registered profl. engr., Conn., Fla., NJ, NY; registered cmty. planner, Mich., NJ; lic. interior designer, Fla. With various archtl. planning and engrng. firms, Kansas City, Mo., 1952-55, Boston, 1956-58, NYC, 1959-62, Chgo., 1962-64; chief planning Skidmore, Owings & Merrill, Chgo., 1964-66; spl. asst. for urban design HUD, Washington, 1966-72, cons., 1972-77; prof. architecture, archtl. engrng. and planning U. Miami, Coral Gables, Fla., 1972-2000, chmn. dept. architecture, archtl. engrng. and planning, 1972-75, assoc. dean engrng. and environ. design, 1973-74, dir. grad. urban and regional planning program, 1973-75, 81, 87-93, prof. emeritus, 2000—. Advisor govt. Iran, 1970, govt. France, 1973, govt. Ecuador, 1974, govt. Saudi Arabia, 1985; cons. in field, 1972—, lectr., critic design juror in field, 1965—; mem./chmn. Coral Gables Bd. Archs., 1980-82. Assoc. author: Man-Made America: Chaos or Control, 1963; editor: New Concepts in Urban Transportation, 1968, Housing Systems Proposals for Operation Breakthrough, 1970, Focus on Furniture, 1971, National Community Art Competition, 1971, Defining Critical Environmental Areas, 1974; contbg. editor: Progressive Architecture, 1974-84; editl. adv. bd.: Jour. Am. Planning Assn., 1983-88, Planning for Higher Edn., 1986-94, Urban Design and Preservation Quar., 1987-94; contbr. over 130 articles to profl. jour.; mem. adv. panel Industrialization Forum Quar., 1969-79, archtl. portfolio jury Am. Sch. and Univ., 1993. Mem. Met. Housing and Planning Coun., Chgo., 1965-67; mem. exec. com. Yale U. Arts Assn., 1965-70; pres. Yale U. Planning Alumni Assn., 1983-89—; mem. ednl. adv. com. Fla. Bd. Architecture, 1975; mem. grievance com. The Fla. Bar, 1996-99; mem code commn.'s Nat. Fire Protection Assn., 1998-. Recipient W.E. Parsons medal Yale U., 1960; recipient Spl. Achievement award HUD, 1972, commendation Fla. Bd. Architecture, 1974, Fla. Trust Hist. Preservation award, 1983, Group Achievement award NASA, 1976; Skidmore, Owings & Merrill traveling fellow MIT, 1958; vis. fellow Inst. Architecture and Urban Studies, NYC, 1972-74; NSF grantee, 1980-82. Fellow AIA (nat. housing com. 1968-72, nat. regional devel. and natural resources com. 1974-75, nat. sys. devel. com. 1972-73, nat. urban design com. 1968-73, bd. dirs. Fla. S. chpt. 1974-75, Edn. Leadership award Miami chpt. 2000, Test of Time Design award Fla. Assn. 2002),, NSPE, ASCE (archtl. engrng. and structural engrng. insts.), Fla. Engrng. Soc. (bd. dirs. 1984-85, Miami chpt. bd. dirs. 1982-83, 84-85), Nat. Acad. Forensic Engrs.; mem. Am. Inst. Cert. Planners (exec. com. dept. environ. planning 1973-74), Am. Soc. Engrng. Edn. (chmn. archtl. engrng. divsn. 1975-76), Dade Heritage Trust (Cmty. Svc. award 2002), Nat. Sculpture Soc. (allied profl.), Nat. Soc. Archtl. Engrs. (founding), Nat. Trust Hist. Preservation (principles and guidelines com. 1967), Am. Soc. Landscape Archs. (hon., chmn. design awards jury 1971, 72), Am. Planning Assn. (Fla. chpt. award excellence 1983), Am. Soc. Interior Designers (hon.), Omicron Delta Kappa, Sigma Xi, Tau Beta Pi. Home and Office: 2825 Cascade Dr Plano TX 75025 4106 Office Phone: 214-495-9892. E-mail: ProfRJWarc@aol.com. *My contribution to society is made through comprehensive determination, design and development activity leading to habitats most suited to the optimum continuing progress of mankind.*

WARCH, RICHARD, former academic administrator; b. Hackensack, N.J., Aug. 4, 1939; s. George William and Helen Anna (Hansen) W.; m. Margot Lynn Moses, Sept. 8, 1962; children: Stephen Knud, David Preston, Karin Joy. BA, Williams Coll., 1961; B.D., Yale Div. Sch., 1964; PhD, Yale U., 1969; postgrad., U. Edinburgh, 1962-63; H.H.D., Ripon Coll., 1980. Asst. prof. history and Am. studies Yale U., 1968-73, asso. prof., 1973-77; asso. dean Yale Coll.; dir. summer plans Yale U., 1976-77; asso. dir. Nat. Humanities Inst., New Haven, 1975-76; v.p. acad. affairs Lawrence U., Appleton, Wis., 1977-79, pres., 1979—2004. Cons. Nat. Humanities Faculty; ordained to ministry United Presbyn. Ch. in U.S.A., 1968; dir. Bank One of Appleton. Author: School of the Prophets, Yale College, 1701-1740, 1973; editor: John Brown, 1973. Rockefeller Bros. Theol. fellow, 1961-62 Mem. Am. Studies Assn., Soc. for Values in Higher Edn., Winnebago Presbytery. Clubs: Rotary.

WARD, ALBERT EUGENE, archaeologist, ethnohistorian, research center executive; b. Carlinville, Ill., Aug. 20, 1940; s. Albert Alan and Eileen (Boston) Ward; m. Gladys Anena Lea, Apr. 26, 1961 (div. Apr. 1974); children: Scott Bradley, Brian Todd; m. Stefanie Helen Tschaikowsky, Apr. 24, 1982. AA, Bethany Luth. Jr. Coll., Mankato, Minn., 1961; BS, No. Ariz. U., 1968; MA, U. Ariz., 1972. Lab. asst., asst., archaeologist Mus. No. Ariz., Flagstaff, 1965-67; rsch. archaeologist Desert Rsch. Inst. U. Nev., Las Vegas, 1968; rsch. archaeologist Archaeol. Survey Prescott Coll., Ariz., 1969-71, rsch. assoc., 1971-73; rsch. archaeologist Ariz. Archaeol. Ctr. Nat. Park Svc., Tucson, 1972-73; rsch. collaborator Chaco Ctr., Albuquerque, 1975; founder, dir. archaeol., rsch. program Mus. Albuquerque, 1975-76; founder, dir., 1976-79; pres. bd. dirs. Ctr. Anthrop. Studies, Albuquerque, 1976—. Lectr. U. N.Mex. C.C., 1974-77, others; contract archaeol. salvage and rsch. projects in N.Mex. and Ariz. Mem. editl. adv. bd. Hist. Archeology, 1978-80; editor: publs. Ctr. Anthrop. Studies, 1978—; contbr. articles to scholarly jours. Grantee Mus. No. Ariz., 1972, S.W. Monuments Assn., 1973, CETA, 1975-79, Nat. Park Svc., 1978-79. Mem.: Preservation of Archaeol. Collections (Am. com.), Am. Com. For Preservation of Archaeological Collections, N.Mex. Archaeol. Coun., Southwestern Anthrop. Assn., Soc. Archaeol. Scis., S.W. Mission Rsch. Ctr., Albuquerque Archaeol. Soc., Archaeol. Soc. N.Mex., Ariz. Archaeol. and Hist. Soc., No. Ariz. Soc. Sci. and Art, Soc. Hist. Archaeology, Soc. Am. Archaeology, Am. Anthrop. Assn., Am. Soc. Conservation. Republican. Lutheran.

WARD, ANGIE, radio personality; Grad., Auburn U. Sportscaster Auburn U.; radio personality WTQR 104, Greensboro, NC. Named Personality of Yr., Country Music Assn., 2000, Country Radio Broadcast, 2001. Office: WTQR 104 2B PAI Pk Greensboro NC 27409

WARD, BUTCH, newspaper editor; Metro editor Phila. Inquirer, mng. editor, 1998—. Office: Phila Inquirer 400 N Broad St Philadelphia PA 19130-4099

WARD, CHARLES RAYMOND, systems engineer; b. Lansing, Mich., Oct. 23, 1949; s. George Merrill and Dorothy Irene (Hupp) W.; m. Sarah Hopkins Eddy, June 23, 1979; children: Katherine Emily, Rachel Elizabeth. BS in Math., Purdue U., 1971; MSEE, Naval Postgrad. Sch., 1977. Commd. ensign USN, 1971, advanced through grades to lt. commdr., served on USS Barbel, 1972-75, served on USS James Madison, 1978-81, served on USS Alabama, 1983-85; strategic navigation project mgr. Strategic Systems Programs, Arlington, Va., 1985-91; surveillance towed array sensor sys., mgr. sys. engrng. Govt. Info. Sys. divsn. TRW, McLean, Va., 1991-95; integrated undersea surveillance sys., mgr. internat. programs TRW, San Diego, 1995-2000; integrated undersea surveillance, mgr. fixed surveillance Command, Control and Intelligence divsn. TRW, 2000—02; asst. program mgr. sys. integration Def.Mission Sys. divsn. Northrop Grumman Mission Sys., 2002—. Editor: Trident Navigation Standard Operating Procedures, 1991, Acoustic Warfare Operating Doctrine, 1992, Surveillance Towed Array Sensor Passive User's Guide, 1994. Chmn. grounds com. Burke (Va.) United Meth. Ch., 1989-97, chmn. worship com., 1993-94; chmn. Camp Va. site adv. com., 2001—; chmn. Julian Retreat Ctr. Task Force, 2002—. Mem. IEEE, Eta Kappa Nu, Sigma Xi. Republican. Achievements include research in automatic depth and pitch control for a near surface submarine. Office: Northrop Grumman Mission Systems 1843 Hotel Circle S San Diego CA 92108-3320 E-mail: chuck.ward@ngc.com.

WARD, CHESTER LAWRENCE, physician, consultant; b. Woodland, Yolo, Calif., June 8, 1932; s. Benjamin Briggs and Nora Elizabeth Ward; m. Sally Diane Ward, Dec. 10, 1960; children: Katharine, Lynda. BA, U. Calif., Santa Barbara, 1955; MPH, U. Calif., Berkeley, 1966; MD, U. So. Calif., 1962; grad., Indsl. Coll. Armed Forces, 1978. Commd. 2d lt., inf. U.S. Army, 1954, advanced through grades to brig. gen., 1980; surgeon 5th Spl. Forces, Ft. Bragg, NC, Vietnam, 1963-64; chief aviation medicine, preventive medicine and aeromed. consultation service Ft. Rucker, Ala., 1967-68; surgeon Aviation Brigade and USA Vietnam Aviation Medicine Cons., 1968-69; flight surgeon Office of U.S. Army Surgeon Gen., 1970-71; physician The White House, Washington, 1971-75, 76; dir. environ. quality rsch. U.S. Army Med. Rsch. and Devel. Commd., 1975-76; comdr. Womack Cmty. Hosp., 1978—80; surgeon XVIII Airborne Corps, Ft. Bragg, 1978-80; comdr. William Beaumont Army Med. Ctr., El Paso, Tex., 1980-82; med. dir. Union Oil Co., Schaumburg, Ill., 1982-83, dir. domestic medicine L.A., 1983-84; exec. dir. continuing med. edn. and clin. prof. emergency medicine U. So. Calif. Sch. Medicine, L.A., 1984-85; dir., health officer Dept. Pub. Health, Butte County, Calif., 1985-95; cons., contractor, pvt. practice medicine, 1996—; med. dir. NorCal EMS, 2001—. Trustee, pres. Oroville Union HS Dist., 1998—2002; chmn. Citizen's Bond Oversight Com., 2003—; apptd. by Gov. Wilson Calif. Commn. Emergency Med. Svcs., past commr. Decorated DSM, Legion of Merit (2), Bronze Star, Air medal (5). Fellow: Aerospace Med. Assn., Am. Coll. Preventive Medicine (past regent); mem.: No. Calif. Emergency Med. Svcs. Inc. (dir., governing bd.), Calif. Med. Assn. (past del.), Butte-Glenn County Med. Soc. (past pres.), Ret. Officers Assn. (past chpt. pres.). Home: 4 Lemon Hill Ct Oroville CA 95966-3700 Office: Enloe Outpatient Ctr 888 Lakeside Vlg Commons Chico CA 95928-3979

WARD (BAILEY), DAISY DALE, writer; b. Dayton, Ohio, June 12, 1931; d. Ennis and Cora Dale (Greene) Ward; m. James Arrelaus Bailey, June 26, 1965 (dec. Dec. 27, 1999); m. Charles Morris Gilham, Dec. 25, 1949 (dec. Feb. 11, 1961); children: James Craige Bailey, Angelia Dale Wood, Linda Yvette Gilham, Lisa Yvonne Matthews. *She documented her family history in her book, The Perfect Law of Liberty. Great-great grandparents Samuel and Lucy Ward and their children were freed from slavery in 1827 by the will of John Ward Sr. All emancipated slaves at least 15 years old were bequeathed $20. Samuel and three other emancipated slaves were bequeathed 294 acres of land. Virginia laws forced Samuel, Lucy, and family to leave money, land, and Pittsylvania County, Virginia. Samuel did not sell his land. The reunions began in the 19th century in Ohio and have continued for over 100 years.* BA, Goddard Coll.; JD, The Am. Sch. of Law. Counselor Camp Fire Girls, Atlanta, 1968—69, cmty. bd., 1969—70; mem. Aux. to the Med. Assn. of Ga., Atlanta, 1970—91, AMA Aux., Inc, Atlanta, 1970—91; rec. sec. Emory U. Woman's Club, Atlanta, 1972—73, Aux. to the Nat. Med. Assn., Inc, Washington, 1986—87; pres.-elect Aux. to the Atlanta Med. Assn., Atlanta, 1974—75, Aux. to the Nat. Med. Assn., Inc, Washington, 1987—88; pres. Aux. to the Atlanta Med. Assn., Atlanta, 1975—76, Aux. to the Nat. Med. Assn., Inc, Washington, 1988—89, region iii v.p., 1975—76; treas. Aux. to the Nat. Med. Assn., Inc., Washington, 1981—84; hon. chair SW Cmty. Hosp. Charity Ball, Atlanta, 1982; vice chair Emory U. Woman's Investment Club, Atlanta, 1983—84, chair, 1984—85; 2nd v.p. Aux. to the Nat. Med. Assn., Inc., Washington, 1985—86; bd. of dirs. Aux. to the Nat. Med. Assn., Inc, Washington, 1981—, NAACP Atlanta Chpt., Atlanta, 1986—90, Habitat for Humanity, Atlanta, 1989—91; mem. of the bd. Nat. Cancer Inst., Washington, 1988—89; chair bd. of dirs. Aux. to Nat. Med. Assn., Inc, Washington, 1989—90; bd. mem. Black Elected County Ofcls. Main Project, Atlanta, 1989—90; parliamentarian Aux. to the Nat. Med. Assn., Inc, Washington, 1990—91; bd. of trustees Sr. Citizen Svcs., Atlanta, 1985—87; mem. Atlanta chpt. CARATS, Inc., 1980—, pres. Atlanta chpt., 1986. Chair-advisory coun. Aux. to the Atlanta Med. Assn., Atlanta, 1976—77; mem Aux. to the Atlanta Med. Assn., Inc, 1968—; chair pres.' coun. Aux. to the Nat. Med. Assn., Inc, Washington, 1995—96. Author: (book) The Perfect Law Of Liberty. Mem. Youth Svc. Guild, Columbus, Ohio, 1963—68; pres. Juliett Federated Club, Newark, Ohio, 1962—64; apptd. to bi-racial panel Gov. of Ga., Atlanta, 1987; bd. of trustees Trinity AME Ch., Atlanta, 1992—; v.p. Atlanta Phys. Medicine & Rehab. Svcs., Inc, 1982—90. Recipient Proclamation, Atlanta City Coun., 1988, Appreciation, Habitat for Humanity-Atlanta, 1991, Trustee of the Yr., Trinity AME Ch., 2002, Pillar of Strength award, Aux. to the Atlanta Med. Assn., Inc, 2002, Appreciation, Aux. to the Nat. Med. Assn., Inc, 1989, Achievement, Region III Aux. to the Nat. Med. Assn., Inc, 1989, Proclamation, Gov. of Ga., 1988, Exceptional Cmty. Leadership Local-State-National, Group Of Concerned Women, 1988, Key To The City of Orlando, Mayor of Orlando, Fla., 1989, Appreciation award, Nat. Mar. of Dimes, 1989, Svc. award, Aux. to the Nat. Med. Assn., Inc, 1989, Ga. State Med. Assn., 1989, Region V Aux. to the Nat. Med. Assn., Inc, 1989, NAACP, 1990, Nefertiti Outstanding Achievement award, Soc. Docta, Inc., 2002, Atlanta (Ga.) Appreciation award, 2002. Mem.: Ohio State U. Presidents Club, Ohio State U. Faculty Club, Alpha Kappa Alpha Sorority. Avocations: writing, travel, reading.

WARD, DAVID, academic administrator, educator; b. Manchester, Eng., July 8, 1938; arrived in U.S., 1960; s. Horace and Alice (Harwood) Ward; m. Judith B. Freifeld, June 11, 1964; children: Michael J.H., Peter F.B. BA, U. Leeds, Eng., 1959, MA, 1961; MS, U. Wis., 1961, PhD, 1963; LittD, U. Leeds, 1992. Lectr. Carleton U., Ottawa, 1963—64; asst. prof. Univ. B.C., Vancouver, 1964—66, U. Wis., Madison, 1966—67, assoc. prof., 1967—70, prof., 1970—, chmn. geography dept., 1974—77, assoc. dean Grad. Sch., 1980—88, provost and vice chancellor acad. affairs, Andrew Clark prof. geography, 1989—94, chancellor, 1994—2000; pres. Am. Coun. on Edn., Washington, 2000—. Mem. exec. com. Argonne Nat. Lab., Ill., 1990—93; dir.-at-large Social Sci. Rsch. Coun., 1991—93; mem. Kellogg Commn. on Future of Land Grant Univs.; chair Internet 2, Consortium Advances Network Devel. Author: Cities and Immigrants, 1970, Geographic Perspectives on Americas Past, 1978, Poverty Ethnicity and the American City, 1989, Landscape of Modernity, 1992; contbr. articles to profl. jours. Fellow Guggenheim fellow, 1970, Einstein fellow, Hebrew U., 1980, Fulbright fellow, Australian Nat. U., 1979. Fellow: Am. Acad. Arts and Scis.; mem.: Assn. Am. Geographers (pres. 1989). Office: One Dupont Circle NW Washington DC 20036-1193 E-mail: president@ace.nche.edu.

WARD, DAVID A. corporate lawyer; Sr. v.p. Owens Ill., Inc., Toledo, gen. counsel, sec. Office: Owens-Ill Inc 1 Seagate Toledo OH 43604-1558

WARD, DAVID ALLEN, sociology educator; b. Dedham, Mass., June 21, 1933; s. Theodore Allen and Jessie Miller (Ketchum) W.; m. Carol Jane Barton, June 10, 1957 (div. 1964); children: Douglas Allen, Andrew Barton; m. Reneé Ellen Light, Mar. 10, 1967. BA, Colby Coll., 1955; PhD, U. Ill., 1960. Asst. prof. Wash. State U., Pullman, 1960-61; asst. research sociologist UCLA, 1961-64; assoc. prof. U. Minn., Mpls., 1965-68, prof., 1968—2002, chmn. dept. sociology, 1984-88, 92-95. Chmn. Salzburg (Austria) Seminar in Am. Studies, 1977; cons. jud. com. U.S. Ho. Reps., Washington, 1984. Co-author: Women's Prison, 1965, Prison Treatment, 1971; co-editor: Delinquency, Crime and Social Process, 1969, Confinement in Maximum Custody, 1981; editorial cons. Jour. Criminal Law and Criminology, 1968-97. Mem. Mpls. Civilan Police Rev. Bd., 1991-94. Liberal Arts fellow Harvard U. Law Sch., 1968-69; Fulbright research fellow, 1971-72; research fellow Norwegian Fgn. Office, Oslo, 1976. Mem.: Am. Soc. Criminology, Am. Sociol. Assn. (chmn. sect. criminology 1976—77). Office: Univ of Minn Dept of Sociology 909 Social Sci Bldg Minneapolis MN 55455

WARD, DAVID HENRY (DAVE WARD), television news reporter, anchorman; b. Dallas, May 6, 1939; s. H.M. and Mary Ward; m. Glenda Lois Odom, Nov. 10, 1959 (div.); children: Linda Ann, David H.; m. Debra Rene Holland, Apr. 25, 1976 (div.); children: Jonathan H., Christopher H. Student, Tyler Jr. Coll., Tex., 1957—59. Announcer Sta. KGKB, Tyler, 1958—60; program dir. Sta. WACO (Tex.), 1960—62; news dir. Sta. KNUZ, Houston, 1962—66; news reporter, photographer, writer, prodr. Sta. KTRK-TV, 1966—. Freelance writer, prodr., cons. Chmn. pub. affairs adv. bd. Houston Bus. Coun.; pub. info. com. Am. Cancer Soc.; pres. bd. dirs. Easter Seal Soc., Harris, Ft. Bend counties; committeeman Houston Livestock Show and Rodeo, 1997—98. Named Man of Yr., Houston Sertoma Club, 1973, TV Personality of Yr., Am. Women in Radio and TV, 1983, Best TV Anchor, Houston Press, 1995, 1996, 2001; recipient Best TV Newscast award, Tex. UPI, 1968, 1972, 1973—80, TV Svc. award, Houston Jaycees, 1982. Mem.: Houston Press Club, Sigma Delta Chi. Baptist. Office: Channel 13 PO Box 13 3310 Bissonnet St Houston TX 77005-2195

WARD, DAVID SCHAD, screenwriter, film director; b. Providence, Oct. 24, 1947; s. Robert McCollum and Miriam (Schad) W.; children: Joaquin Atwood, Sylvana Soto. BA, Pomona Coll., 1967; M.F.A., UCLA, 1970. Scriptwriter: films include Steelyard Blues, 1971, The Sting, 1973 (Acad. award best original screenplay 1973), The Milagro Beanfield War, 1988, (with Nora Ephron and Jeff Arch) Sleepless in Seattle, 1993 (Academy award nominee Best Original Screenplay 1993), (with John Eskow, Ted Elliott and Terry Rossio) The Mask of Zorro; writer, dir. films include Cannery Row, 1981, Major League, 1989, King Ralph, 1991, The Program, 1993, Major League II, 1995, Down Periscope, 1996. Mem.: Acad. Motion Picture Arts and Scis., Dirs. Guild Am. Office: c/o Ben Smith 8942 Wilshire Blvd Beverly Hills CA 90211

WARD, DENITTA DAWN, lawyer; b. Gardner, Kans., Apr. 29, 1963; d. Gerald Dee Ascue and Patricia Diane (Henderson) Ray; m. Kent Alan Ward, July 6, 1991; children: Alexander Patrick, Olivia Caitlyn. BA, U. Kans., 1985; JD magna cum laude, Georgetown U., 1989. Bar: Md. 1989, U.S. Ct. Appeals (fed. cir.) 1990, D.C. 1991, U.S. Ct. Internat. Trade 1991. Rsch. asst. Georgetown U., Washington, 1988-89; jud. clk. U.S. Ct. Appeals for Fed. Cir., Washington, 1989-90; assoc. Donovan Leisure Rogovin Huge & Schiller, Washington, 1990-94; atty. Fed. Election Commn., Washington, 1994-96, Marriott Internat., Inc., 1996-98; sr. v.p., gen. counsel Boulderbiz, Inc., 1999—. Mng. editor Law and Policy in Internat. Bus., 1988-89. Mem. ABA, Ct. of Appeals for Fed. Cir. Bar Assn., Ct. of Appeals of Fed. Cir. Former Jud. Clks. Assn., Order of Coif, Omicron Delta Kappa, Pi Sigma Alpha. Avocations: travel, gardening. Home: 6999 Firerock Ct Boulder CO 80301-3814

WARD, DORIS M. county official; BA in Govt., MS in Edn., Ind. U.; MA in Counseling, San Francisco State U.; PhD in Edn., U. Calif., Berkeley. Tchr. Indpls. Pub. Schs., 1959-67, team leader, supr. tchg. interns, 1967-68; adviser, counselor San Francisco STEP program, 1969-70; coord. curriculum San Mateo County Office of Edn., Redwood City, Calif., 1968-89; mem. bd. govs. San Francisco C.C., 1973-79; mem. bd. suprs. City and County San Francisco, 1980-92, pres. bd. suprs., 1991-92, assessor, recorder, 1992—, elected assessor-recorder, 1996. Adj. assoc. prof. Sch. Edn. Calif. State U., 1969-70, 72-73; advisor to External Masters Degree Program, U. San Francisco, 1972-76; chief cons. Calif. Assembly on regional govt., 1989-92. Contbr. articles to ednl. and polit. jours. Bd. dirs. Nat. Dem. County Officials 1987—, pres. 1994—; mem. Dem. Nat. Com., 1992—, del. 1984, 88, 92, 96 convs. Named Woman of Yr., Zeta Phi Beta, 1984; recipient Disting. Alumni award San Francisco State U., 1993, Disting. Comty. award, U. San Francisco, 1994, Spl. Merit award Sun Reporter Newspaper and numerous other awards for comty. svc. by activist orgns; grantee: NDEA, 1967, 68, Ind. State U., Terre Haute, Ind., Lilly Found., 1967, Rockefeller Found., U. Calif., Berkeley, 1974. Mem. Bay Area Assessors Assn. (sec. 1994, v.p. 95, pres. 96), Calif. Assessors' Assn. (mem. legis. com. 1993, exec. com. 95), Nat. Assn. Counties (bd. dirs. 1989-91, chair human svcs. and edn., 1991-92), Nat. Assn. Black County Officials (bd. dirs. 1987—, regional dir. 1987—), Nat. League of Cities (bd. dirs. 1991-92, vice chair and steering com. Fed. Adminstrn. Intergovtl. Rels. 1990-91), Nat. Black Caucus of Local Elected Officials (bd. dirs. 1987-95), Pi Sigma Alpha, Pi Lambda Theta. Office: City County San Francisco Assessor Recorder Office Rm 190 1 Dr Carlton B Goodlett Pl San Francisco CA 94102-4603

WARD, EDWARD ANTHONY, economist, educator; b. Mattoon, Ill., May 28, 1953; s. Roy and Eleanor Ward; m. Denese Elaine Parker, Aug. 11, 1979; children: Amy Faye, Mark Edward. PhD, U. Nebr. Prof. U. of Mich., Flint, 1987—90, St. Cloud State U., St. Cloud, Minn., 1990—. Contbr. articles to profl. jours. Recipient Student Choice award for Faculty of the Yr., Coll. of Bus. Exec. Coun., 2000, Disting. Prof.award, U. of Mich.-Flint, 1990, Disting. Paper award, Small Bus. Inst. Dirs. Assn., 1989, Econ. Impact Manuscript award, 1990. Mem.: Mensa. Protestant. Avocations: bicycling, weightlifting, travel, backpacking. Home: 2610 Island View Dr Saint Cloud MN 56301 Office: St Cloud State University BB 156 720 Fourth Ave S Saint Cloud MN 56301 Personal E-mail: edward@stcloudstate.edu.

WARD, ERIC R. agricultural products executive; b. Buffalo, N.Y., Dec. 15, 1960; BS magna cum laude, Duke U., 1982; PhD, Washington U., 1988. Tchg. asst. introductory biology Duke U., Durham, NC, 1981, tchg. asst. biol. oceanography Marine Lab., 1982; tchg. asst. lab. methods in molecular biology Washington U., St. Louis, 1983, tchg. asst. gen. genetics, 1983; postdoctoral assoc. agrl. biotech. rsch. unit Ciba-Geigy Corp., Research Triangle Park, NC, 1988—89; scientist II molecular genetics Ciba Agr. Biotech., Research Triangle Park, 1989—90, sr. scientist molecular genetics, 1990—91, 1992—93, project leader biotech.-weed control, 1994—96; interim head Biotech. and Genomics Ctr. Novartis Crop Protection, Inc., Greensboro, NC, 1997, rsch. dir. herbicides, 1997, v.p. U.S. rsch., 1997—98; co-pres. Novartis Agribusiness Biotech. Rsch., Inc., Research Triangle Park, 1999—2000; CEO Cropsolution, Inc., Research Triangle Park, 2001—. Tech. ptnr. Catalysta Ptnrs., Durham, NC; adj. asst. prof. crop sci. dept. N.C. State U., Raleigh; instr. plant physiology IV: gene expression in plant cells U. Porto, Portugal, 1991; project leader biotech.-weed control, internat. field devel. Ciba Crop Protein, Basel, Switzerland, 1994—95. Ad hoc reviewer: Pesticide Sci., Phytopathology, NSF, others. Recipient grad. fellowship, NSF, 1983—86, James Mountain Meml. scholarship, Marine Biol. Lab., 1983, Nat. Merit scholarship, 1978—82. Mem.: N.C. Bioscis. Assn. (bd. dirs.). Office: Cropsolution Inc PO Box 14069 Research Triangle Park NC 27709-4069

WARD, GEOFFREY CHAMPION, author, editor; b. Newark, Ohio, Nov. 30, 1940; s. Frederick Champion and Rachel Duira (Baldinger) W.; m. Diane Raines; children: Nathan, Kelly; 1 stepchild, Garrett. BA, Oberlin Coll., 1962, DHL (hon.), 2004, Wilkes U., 1995. Sr. picture editor Ency. Britannica, Chgo., 1964-68; co-founder, editor Audience mag., Boston, 1969-73; mng. editor Am. Heritage Mag., N.Y.C., 1976-78, editor, 1978-82. Author: Lincoln's Thought and the Present, 1978, Treasures of the Maharajas, 1983, Before the Trumpet: Young Franklin Roosevelt, 1882-1905, 1985, A First-Class Temperament: The Emergence of Franklin Roosevelt, 1989 (Book Critics Cir. award, Francis Parkman prize Soc. Am. Historians, L.A. Times biography prize, Ohioana award), The Civil War: An Illustrated History, 1990, American Originals: The Private Worlds of Some Singular Men and Women, 1991; (with Diane Raines Ward) Tiger Wallahs, Encounters with the Men Who Tried to Save the Greatest of the Great Cats, 1993, Baseball: An Illustrated History, 1994, Closest Companion: The Unknown Story of the Intimate Friendship between Franklin Roosevelt and Margaret Suckley, 1995, The West: An Illustrated History, 1996, (with Michael Nichols) The Year of the Tiger, 1998, Not for Ourselves Alone: Elizabeth Cady Stanton and Susan B. Anthony, 1999, Jazz: A History of America's Music, 2000, (with Dayton Duncan) Mark Twain, 2001, Unforgivable Blackness: The Rise and Fall of Jack Johnson, 2004; editor: The Best American Essays of 1996; (TV documentaries) Huey Long, 1985, Thomas Hart Benton, 1989, Lindbergh, 1990, Nixon, 1990 (Writer's Guild Am. award), The Civil War, 1990 (Emmy award), Reminiscing in Tempo, 1991, Empire of the Air, 1992, The Kennedys, 1992 (Emmy award), George Marshall and the American Century, 1993, Baseball, 1994 (Emmy award), Daley: The Last Boss, 1995, The West, 1996, Theodore Roosevelt, 1996 (Emmy award), Thomas Jefferson, 1997, Frank Lloyd Wright, 1998, Not for Ourselves Alone, 1999, Jazz, 2000, (with Dayton Duncan) Mark Twain, 2001; contbr. articles to mags., jours. Bd. dirs. Save the Tiger Fund. Recipient Christopher awards for The Statue of Liberty, Theodore Roosevelt, Not For Ourselves Alone, Mark Twain, The Christophers, The Civil War, New Eng. Booksellers Assn. award, Am. Booksellers award, Lila Acheson Wallace Readers Digest writers award. Mem. Soc. Am. Historians, Orgn. Am. HIstorians, Serengeti Club, Writers Guild Am., East Inc., Century Assn. Home: 17 C 290 W End Ave New York NY 10023-8106 Office: Brandt &Hochman care Carl Brandt 1501 Broadway Ste 2310 New York NY 10036-5689

WARD, GEORGE FRANK, JR., ambassador; b. Jamaica, NY, Apr. 9, 1945; s. George Frank and Hildegard Louisa (Evans) W.; m. Peggy Elizabeth Coote, June 12, 1965; 1 child, Pamela Ward Priester. BA, U. Rochester, 1965; MPA, Harvard U., 1980. U.S. vice consul Am. Consulate, Hamburg, Germany, 1970-72; ops. officer Office Sec. State, Washington, 1972-74; U.S. consul Am. Consulate Gen., Genoa, Italy, 1974-76; polit. officer Am. Embassy, Rome, 1976-77, exec. asst., 1977-79; polit.-mil. officer U.S. Dept. State, Washington, 1980-84, 1985—88; polit. officer Am. Embassy, Bonn, Germany, 1984—85, dep. chief mission, 1989—92; prin. dep. asst. sec. Bur. Internat. Orgn. U.S. Dept. State, Washington, 1992-96, U.S. amb. to Namibia, 1996-99; dir. prof. tng. program U.S. Inst. Peace, Washington, 1999—; U.S. coord. for humanitarian assistance to Iraq U.S. Dept. State, 2003. Capt. USMC, 1965-69, maj. USMCR, 1969-78. Decorated Vietnamese Cross Gallantry, Naval Commendation medal with combat V; recipient Presdl. Meritorious Svc. award, 1992, 1994, Disting. Honor award, U.S. State Dept., 1992. Fellow: Phi Beta Kappa; mem.: Am. Fgn. Svc. Assn., Fairfax County Aux. Police, Washington Inst. Fgn. Affairs. Anglican. Home: 3404 Walnut Hill Ct Falls Church VA 22042-3546 Office Phone: 202-429-3872. E-mail: gward@usip.org.

WARD, GEORGE TRUMAN, architect; b. Washington, July 24, 1927; s. Truman and Gladys Anna (Nutt) W.; m. Margaret Ann Hall, Sept. 10, 1949; children: Carol Ann Ward Dickson, Donna Lynne Ward Solomon, George Truman, Robert Stephen. BS, Va. Poly. Inst., 1951, MS, 1952; postgrad., George Washington U., 1966. Registered profl. arch., Va., Md., D.C., W.Va., Ohio, N.J., Del., N.C. Archtl. draftsman Charles A. Pearson, Radford, Va., 1950; head archtl. sect. Hayes, Seay, Mattern & Mattern, Radford and Roanoke, 1951-52; with Joseph Saunders & Assocs., Alexandria, Va., 1952-57, assoc. arch., 1955-57; ptnr. Vosbeck-Ward & Assocs., Alexandria, 1957-64, Ward/Hall Assocs., Fairfax, 1964—. Dir. Crestar Bank/Greater Washington Region, 1967-99. Pres. PTA Burke (Va.) Sch., 1970-71; mem. bd. mgrs. Fairfax (Va.) County YMCA, 1964-76; chmn. adv. com. Coll. Arch., Va. Poly. Inst., 1984-90; bd. dirs., mem. investment com. Va. Tech. Found., Inc., 1986-91, 93-98; pres. Springfield Rotary Found,. 1978-79; chmn. county adv. bd. Salvation Army, 1978-79, 89-95, co-chmn. Fairfax County Salvation Army Capital Campaign, 1991-95; mem. Gen. Bd. Va. Bapts., deacon, moderator; mem. bd. vis. Va. Poly. Inst. & State U., 1984-87; trustee Fairfax County Pub. Schs. Edn. Found., Inc. With AUS, 1946-47. Paul Harris fellow; recipient Disting. Svc. award Va. Tech. Alumni Assn., 1988; recipient William H. Ruffner medal Va. Tech., 1996, VSAIA William C. Noland award, 1998, Va. Tech. Coll. Arch. and Urban Studies Lifetime Contbn. award, 1998. Fellow Coll. AIA; mem. AIA (corp., charter Octagon Soc.), No. Va. Soc. AIA (chmn. polit. action com. 1991-93, Disting. Svc. award 1990, treas. Va. soc. 1994-98, Outstanding Achievement award 1996), Rowe Fellowship (charter mem. 1988), Alumni Assn. Va. Poly. Inst. & State U. (bd. dirs., v.p. 1992, pres. 1994), Interfaith Forum on Religion, Art and Arch., Va. Found. for Arch. (trustee), Va. Assn. Professions, Va. C. of C., No. Va. Angus Assn. (pres. 1987-88), Va. Tech. Alumni Assn. (hon., life, bd. dirs. Disting. Svc. award 1988), Masons, Shriners, KT, Rotary (charter mem., pres. Springfield 1973-74, Disting. Svc. award dist. 7610 1995), Tau Sigma Delta, Omicron Delta Kappa, Phi Kappa Phi, Pi Delta Epsilon, Ut Prosim. Baptist. Office: Ward Hall Assoc AIA Ste 300 12011 Lee Jackson Memorial Hwy Fairfax VA 22033-3310 E-mail: gtward@wardhall.com.

WARD, HARRY MERRILL, history professor; b. West Lafayette, Ind., July 30, 1929; s. Hiley L. and Agnes Ward. Student, U. Ill., 1947-49; BA, William Jewell Coll., 1951; MA, Columbia U., 1954, PhD, 1960. Social investigator N.Y.C. Dept. Welfare, 1958-59; asst. prof. Georgetown (Ky.) Coll., 1959-61; from asst. to assoc. prof. Morehead (Ky.) State U., 1961-65; vis. assoc. prof. So. Ill. U., 1967-68; assoc. prof. history U. Richmond, Va., 1965-77, prof. history, 1977—, William Binford Vest prof. history, 1993-99, William Binford Vest prof. history emeritus, 1999—. Cons. in field. Author: The United Colonies of New England, 1643-1690, 1961, Department of War, 1781-1795, 1962, 1981, Unite or Die: Intercolony Relations, 1690-1763, 1971, Statism in Plymouth Colony, 1973, Duty, Honor or Country: General George Weedon and the American Revolution, 1979, Richmond: An Illustrated History, 1985, 1988, Charles Scott and the Spirit of '76, 1988, Major General Adam Stephen and the Cause of American Liberty, 1989, Colonial America, 1607-1763, 1990, American Revolution: Nationhood Achieved, 1763-1788, 1994, General William Maxwell and the New Jersey Continentals, 1997, The War for Independence and the Transformation of American Society, 1999, Between the Lines: Banditti of the American Revolution, 2002; co-author: Richmond During the Revolution, 1775-1783, 1977; contbr. articles to profl. jours. With USMC, 1951—53. Recipient Fraunces Tavern Mus. Book award, 1990, Scholar award in history, Va. Social Sci. Assn., 1992, History prize for disting. achievement, Soc. of the Cin. in the State of N.J., 2004. Fellow: Pilgrim Soc.; mem.: So. Hist. Assn., Orgn. Am. Historians. Office: U Richmond Dept History Richmond VA 23173-0180 Office Phone: 804-289-8345.

WARD, HARRY PFEFFER, hematologist, retired academic administrator; b. Pueblo, Colo., June 6, 1933; s. Lester L. and Alysmai (Pfeffer) W.; m. Betty Jo Stewart, Aug. 20, 1955; children— Stewart, Leslie, Elizabeth, Mary Alice, Amy. AB, Princeton U., 1955; MD, U. Colo., 1959; MS, U. Minn., 1963. Intern Bellevue Hosp., N.Y.C., 1959; resident Mayo Clinic, Rochester, Minn., 1960-63; practice medicine specializing in hematology; chief medicine Denver VA hosp., 1968-72; dean, asso. v.p. U. Colo. Sch. Medicine, 1972-78, prof. medicine, 1972; chancellor U. Ark. Med. Sci., Little Rock, 1979-2000, chancellor emeritus, 2000—. Clin. investigator VA, 1964-67 Chmn. Assn. Acad. Health Ctr., 1993-94. Mem. ACP, AMA, Am. Fedn. Clin. Research, Central Soc. Clin. Investigation, Am. Soc. Hematology, Internat. Soc. Hematology, Western Soc. Clin. Research. Home: 369 Valley Club Cir Little Rock AR 72212-2900 Office: U Ark Med Scis 4301 W Markham St Little Rock AR 72205-7101 E-mail: hpward1@msn.com.

WARD, HILEY HENRY, journalist, educator; b. Lafayette, Ind., July 30, 1929; s. Hiley Lemen and Agnes (Fuller) W.; m. Charlotte Burns, May 28, 1951 (div. 1971); children: Dianne, Carolee, Marceline, Laurel; m. Joan Bastel, Aug. 20, 1977. BA, William Jewell Coll., 1951; MA, Berkeley Bapt. Div. Sch., 1953; MDiv, McCormick Theol. Sem., Chgo., 1955; student, Northwestern U., 1948, 54, 56-57; PhD, U. Minn., 1977. News asst. Christian Advocate, 1953-55; editor jr. publs. David C. Cook Pub. Co., 1956-59; editor Record, Buchanan, Mich., 1960; religion editor Detroit Free Press, 1960-73; asst. prof. journalism Mankato (Minn.) State U., 1974-76; assoc. prof. journalism Wichita (Kans.) State U., 1976; prof. journalism Temple U., Phila., 1977-96, prof. emeritus, 1997—, dir. news-editorial sequence, journalism dept., 1977-80, chmn. dept., 1978-80. Instr. journalism Oakland U., Rochester, Mich., evenings 1963-66. Author: Creative Giving, 1958, Space-age Sunday, 1960, Documents of Dialogue, 1966, God and Marx Today, 1968, Ecumania, 1968, Rock 2000, 1969, Prophet of the Black Nation, 1969, The Far-out Saints of the Jesus Communes, 1972, Religion 2101 A.D., 1975, Feeling Good About Myself, 1983, Professional Newswriting, 1985, My Friend's Beliefs: A Young Reader's Guide to World Religions, 1988, Reporting in Depth, 1991, Magazine and Feature Writing, 1993, Mainstreams of American Media History, 1997; editor: Media History Digest, 1979-94; exec. editor: Kidbits, 1981-82; book editor: Editor and Publisher, 1989-98; contbr. articles to profl. jours., feature articles to newspapers and mags.; also short stories and poems. Religious Pub. Rels. Coun. fellow, 1970; recipient citation Religious Heritage Am., 1962, Leidt award Epsic. Ch., 1969, citation U.S. Am. Revolution Bicentennial Adminstrn., 1976, Text and Acad. Authors citation, 1997. Mem. Religion Newswriters Assn. (pres. 1970-72), Am. Soc. Journalists and Authors, Am. Journalism Historians Assn. (bd. dirs. 1994-96, Kobre lifetime achievement award 1999), Overseas Press Club. Home: PO Box 399 1263 Folly Rd Warrington PA 18976-1422 E-mail: bastel@voicenet.com.

WARD, HINES, JR., professional football player; b. Forest Park, GA, Mar. 8, 1976; B.A. in consumer economics, Univ. of GA, 1997. Wide receiver Pittsburgh Steelers, 1998—. Named to NFL Pro-Bowl, 2001—03. Office: c/o Pittsburgh Steelers 3400 S Water St Pittsburgh PA 15203*

WARD, HORACE TALIAFERRO, federal judge; b. LaGrange, Ga., July 29, 1927; m. Ruth LeFlore (dec.); 1 son (dec.). AB, Morehouse Coll., 1949; MA, Atlanta U., 1950; JD, Northwestern U., 1959. Bar: Ga. 1960. Instr. polit. sci. Ark. A.M. and N. Coll., 1950-51, Ala. State Coll., 1951-53, 55-56; claims authorizer U.S. Social Security Adminstrn., 1959-60; assoc. firm Hollowell Ward Moore & Alexander (and successors), Atlanta, 1960-69; individual practice law Atlanta, 1971-74; judge Civil Ct. of Fulton County, 1974-77, Fulton Superior Ct., 1977-79; U.S. Dist. Ct. judge No. Dist. Ga., Atlanta, 1979-93; sr. judge U.S. Dist. Ct. No. Dist. Ga., Atlanta, 1993—. Lectr. bus. and sch. law Atlanta U., 1965-70; dep. city atty., Atlanta, 1969-70, asst. county atty., Fulton County, 1971-74 Former Trustee Friendship Baptist Ch., Atlanta; mem. Ga. adv. com. U.S. Civil Rights Commn., 1963-65; assisting lawyer NAACP Legal Def. and Edn. Fund, Inc., 1960-70; mem. Jud. Selection Commn., Atlanta, 1972-74, Charter Commn., 1971-72; mem. Ga. Senate, 1964-74, jud. com., rules com., county and urban affairs com.; mem. State Democratic Exec. com., 1966-74; former bd. dirs. Atlanta Legal Aid Soc.; bd. dirs. Atlanta Urban League, Fed. Defender Program, No. Dist. Ga.; trustee Met. Atlanta Commn. on Crime and Delinquency, Atlanta U., Fledgling Found. Mem. Am. Bar Assn., Nat. Bar Assn. (chmn. jud. council 1978-79), State Bar Ga., Atlanta Bar Assn., Gate City Bar Assn. (pres. 1972-74), Atlanta Lawyers Club, Phi Beta Kappa, Alpha Phi Alpha, Phi Alpha Delta, Sigma Pi Phi. Office: US Dist Court 1252 US Courthouse 75 Spring St SW Atlanta GA 30303-3309 Office Phone: 404-215-1330.

WARD, JACKIE M. computer company executive; Student, Ga. State U., Ariz. State U.; completed internat. bus. fellows program, Ga. State U., The London Bus. Sch. With data processing dept. J.P. Stevens Co.; with UNIVAC div. Sperry Rand Corp.; founder, chief exec. officer Computer Generation, Inc., Atlanta, v.p., then pres., 1970. Vice chmn.-elect bd. regents Univ. System Ga., 1987—; commr. Edn. Commn. of States; pres., bd. dirs. Internat. Claim Services Ltd.; mem. Com. of 200. Office: Computer Generation Inc 5775 Peachtree Dunwoody Rd NE Atlanta GA 30342-1556

WARD, JACQUELINE ANN BEAS, nurse, healthcare administrator; b. Somerset, Pa., Oct. 23, 1945; d. Donald C. and Thelma R. (Wable) Beas; divorced; children: Charles L. Jr., Shawn M. BSN, U. Pitts., 1966; MA in Counseling and Guidance, W.Va. Coll. Grad. Studies, 1976; MBA, Columbus Coll., 1983; AS in Health Svcs. Mgmt./Nursing Home Adminstrn., St. Petersburg Jr. Coll., 1997. Cert. advanced nursing adminstrn.; adult living facility adminstr., nursing home adminstr. preceptor. Staff nurse W.Va. U. Hosp., Morgantown, 1966-67; staff nurse, head nurse Meml. Hosp, Charleston, W.Va., 1967-69; staff nurse Santa Rosa Hosp., San Antonio, 1969; staff nurse, supr. Bexar County Hosp., San Antonio, 1970; charge and staff nurse Rocky Mountain Osteo. Hosp., Denver, 1971; from staff nurse to asst. DON Charleston Area Med. Ctr., 1971—82; DON H.D. Cobb Meml. Hosp., Phenix City, Ala., 1982—84; v.p. nursing Venice (Fla.) Hosp., 1984—90, v.p. ops., 1990—94; exec. dir., v.p. Life Counseling Ctr., Osprey, Fla., 1994—95; dir. skilled unit and spl. projects Bon Secours/Venice Hosp., 1995—97; adj. clin. nursing faculty Manatee C.C., Venice, Fla., 1998—99; interim adminstr. DON contracting, Venice, 1999—2000; adminstr. Ctrs. for Long Term Care Venice Beach, Venice, 2000—01, Lake Towers/Sun Terrace Health Care Ctr., Sun City Center, Fla., 2002—. Clin. instr. Chattahoochie Valley C.C., Phenix City, 1982—84; support svcs. cons. Bon Secours Healthcare, Venice, 1996—97, Long Term Care, 1997—98. Office: Sun Terrace Health Care Ctr 105 Trinity Lakes Dr Sun City Center FL 33573 Office Phone: 813-634-3324.

WARD, JACQUELINE SELMA SKLAR, mathematician, educator; b. Boston, Aug. 27, 1966; d. Richard Lewis Sklar and Byrene Laura Paula Freid, Sheila Greenspan (Stepmother); m. William Thomas Ward, Aug. 31, 2001; children: Aeron, Nigel, Emily. BS in Astrophysics, UCLA, 1996; MA in Math., Calif. State U., Fullerton, 1998; PhD in Math. Edn., Fla. State U., 2002. Contbr. articles to profl. jours. Founder, past chmn./pres. UCLA Undergrad. Astrophysics Soc. Mem.: Assn. Women in Math., Nat. Coun. Tchrs. Math., Am. Math. Soc., Math. Assn. Am., Psychology Math. Edn.

WARD, JANET LYNN, magazine editor, sports wire reporter; b. Albany, Ga., Feb. 20, 1955; d. Andrew Johnson and Dorothy Iris (Pepera) W.; m. William Thomas Hankins III, Apr. 25, 1981 (div. Feb. 1990); m. Jack Wilkinson, May 22, 1993. AB in Journalism, U. Ga., 1977; JD, Woodrow Wilson Coll. Law, 1984. Sports editor Marietta (Ga.) Daily Jour., 1977-79, North Fulton extra-Atlanta Jour. Constitution, 1979-80; asst. editor In town extra-Atlanta Jour. Constitution, 1980-84; lawyer Atlanta, 1984-89; editor Am. City & County Mag., Atlanta, 1989—. Democrat. Roman Catholic. Avocations: sports, reading. Home: 372 Oakdale Rd NE Atlanta GA 30307-2070 Office: Am City & County 6151 Powers Ferry Rd NW Atlanta GA 30339-2959 E-mail: jward@intertec.com.

WARD, JEANNETTE POOLE, retired psychologist, educator; b. Honolulu, June 19, 1932; d. Russell Masterton and Bessie Naomi (Hammett) Poole; children: John Russell Ward, Lisa Joy Ward. BA, Birmingham (Ala.) So. Coll., 1963; PhD in Psychology, Vanderbilt U., 1969. NSF summer rsch. asst. U. Iowa, Iowa City, 1962, Vanderbilt U., Nashville, 1963, NASA fellow, 1963-66, NIH postdoctoral fellow, 1966-67; spl. rsch. fellow Duke U., Durham, NC, 1970-71; asst. prof. psychology U. Memphis, 1967-72, assoc. prof., 1972-77, prof., 1977-2000, ret., 2001. Editor: Current Research in Primate Laterality, 1990, Primate Laterality, 1992; mem. editl. bd. Jour. Comparative Psychology, 1988-95, Internat. Jour. of Comparative Psychology, 1995—; contbr. chpts. to books and articles to profl. jours. Fellow APA; mem. Psychonomic Soc., Animal Behavior Soc., Am. Primatology Soc., Southeastern Psychol. Assn., Soc. for Neuroscis., Internat. Soc. for Comparative Psychology (treas. 1989-90, pres.-elect 1996-98, pres. 1998-2000), Sigma Xi (pres. Memphis State U. chpt. 1989-90, rsch. award 1985). Democrat. Avocations: dogs, reading, art, music. E-mail: jeannetteward@cs.com.

WARD, JERRY, state legislator, real estate executive; b. Anchorage, July 19, 1948; m. Margaret Ward; children: Katheleen Bloodgood, Kirsten Deacon, Jeri Ann. Real estate businessman; mem. Alaska Ho. of Reps., 1982-96, Alaska Senate, Dist. E, Juneau, 1996—; chair state affairs com., chair transp. com. Alaska Senate, mem. cmty. and regional affairs com. Past mem. Mcpl. Health Commn.; commr. Mcpl. Transp., Mcpl. Vet. Affairs; rural affairs coord. Dept. Corrections; legis. aide. Decorated Vietnam Svc. medal. Mem. VFW, Am. Legion. Republican. Avocations: fishing, hunting, boating. Office: State Capitol 120 4th St Rm 423 Juneau AK 99801-1142 Fax: 907-465-3766. E-mail: senatorjerryward@legis.state.ak.us.

WARD, JIM, state representative; b. Omaha, Dec. 5, 1957; m. Jeanne Ward. BA, Creighton U., 1981; JD, Washburn Sch. Law, 1985. City prosecutor, 1985—86; asst. dist. atty., 1986—90; guardian Juvenile Ct., 1990—96; mem. Kans. Senate, 1991—92, Kans. Ho. of Reps., 2002—. Mem. Citizens Participation Orgn., 1986—88, Wichita City Coun., 1991, Project Freedom, Wichita Youth Ct. Project. Mem.: Wichita Bar Assn. Democrat. Office: State Capitol Rm 284 W Topeka KS 66612

WARD, JOANN BOETTNER, convention and tourist bureau administrator; BS, U. Wis. Publicity and spl. events dir. Carson, Pirie, Scott & Co., Chgo., 1958-69; mktg. cons. to bd. trustees Masonic Med. Ctr., Chgo., 1969-76; exec. dir. Fond du Lac (Wis.) Conv. and Visitor's Bur., 1976-99; ret., 1999. Mktg. cons. Am. Invesco Shopping Ctrs, Chances R. Systems, Rand McNally, Carson, Pirie, Scott and Co.; Wis. rep. Great Lake Delegation to Tokyo; appointed Sesquicentennial Commn. by Gov. Thompson, 1996-98. Bd. dirs. United Fund; pres., bd. dirs., pres. East Wis. Waters Region, Service League (pres.); trustee 1st Presbyn Ch.; developer Walleye Weekend Festival, developer, 1st breakfast with Santa for 5000, Chgo., Lakeside Winter Celebration, Fond du Lac Fall Flyway; mem. adv. bd. Fond du Lac Jazz Festival, Windhover Ctr. for the Arts; host Internat. Aerobatic Competition, Fond du Lac, 1979-99. Named Woman of Yr. Fond du Lac Bus. and Profl. Women's Club, 1981; recipient award for outstanding contbns. Wis. Tourism Fedn., Pres.' award Internat. Aerobatic Club, 1981, corp. award Chgo. Publicity Club, gold award Nat. Retail Merchants Assn., best spl. event., U.S., Lifetime Achievement award Upper Midwest Conf. and Visitors Bur., 1999, Comm. and Leadership award Toastmasters Internat., 1999, Wisconsin Trailblazer award for lifetime achievement, 1999, JoAnn award Wis. Festival and Events Assn., 2002; inducted into Internat. Festival and Events Assn. Hall of Fame, 1997; honored in Congl. Record, 1999. Mem. Internat. Festivl and Events Assn. (bd. dirs), Wis. Festival and Events Assn. (founder), Wis. Conv. and Visitors Bur. (founding mem., pres., bd. dirs.), Rotary (Paul Harris fellow), Sigma Beta Delta. E-mail: JBWard712@aol.com.

WARD, JOE HENRY, JR., retired lawyer; b. Childress, Tex., Apr. 18, 1930; s. Joe Henry and Helen Ida (Chastain) W.; m. Carlotta Agnes Abreu, Feb. 7, 1959; children: James, Robert, William, John. BS in Acctg., Tex. Christian U., 1952; JD, So. Meth. U., 1964. Bar: Tex. 1964, Va. 1972, D.C. 1974; CPA, Tex. Mgr. Alexander Grant & Co. CPA's, Dallas, 1956-64; atty. U.S. Treasury, 1965-68; tax counsel U.S. Senate Fin. Com., 1968-72; pvt. practice Washington, 1972-83; asst. gen. counsel, tax mgr. Epic Holdings, Ltd. and Crysopt Corp., 1983-87; pvt. practice Washington and Va., 1987-95; ret., 1995. Lt. USNR, 1952-56. Mem. AICPA, Univ. Club. Home: 2639 Mann Ct Falls Church VA 22046-2721

WARD, JOHN ROBERT, internist, educator; b. Salt Lake City, Nov. 23, 1923; s. John I. and Clara (Elzi) W.; m. Norma Harris, Nov. 5, 1948; children: John Harris, Pamela Lyn, Robert Scott, James Alan. BS, U. Utah, 1944, MD, 1946; MPH, U. Calif., Berkeley, 1967; Masters, Am. Coll. of Rheumatology, 1990. Diplomate Am. Bd. Internal Medicine. Intern Salt Lake County Gen. Hosp., 1947-48, asst. resident, 1949-50, resident physician internal medicine, 1950-51, asst. physician, 1957-58, assoc. physician, 1958-69; clin. fellow medicine Harvard U., Boston, 1955-57; instr. medicine Med. Sch. U. Utah, Salt Lake City, 1954-58, asst. prof. Med. Sch., 1958-63, assoc. prof. Med. Sch., 1963, prof. Med. Sch., 1966-93, chmn. dept. preventive medicine Med. Sch., 1966-70, emeritus prof. internal medicine Med. Sch., 1993—, chief div. rheumatology Med. Sch., 1957-88, prof. internal medicine emeritus Med. Sch., 1994—, Nora Eccles Harrison prof. medicine Med. Sch.; attending physician internal medicine Salt Lake City VA Hosp., 1957-70. Nora Eccles Harrison prof. medicine U. Utah Sch. Medicine, Salt Lake City. Served as capt. M.C. AUS, 1951-53. Master Am. Coll. Rheumatology; fellow ACP; mem. Am. Coll. Rheumatology (Disting. rheumatologist award 1994), Utah State Med. Assn. (hon. pres. 1994-95), U. Utah Sch. Medicine Alumni Assn. (Disting. Alumnus 1996). Home: 1249 E 3770 S Salt Lake City UT 84106-2446 Office: U Utah Health Scis Ctr 50 N Medical Dr Salt Lake City UT 84132-0001

WARD, JOHN WESLEY, retired pharmacologist; b. Martin, Tenn., Apr. 8, 1925; s. Charles Wesley and Sara Elizabeth (Little) W.; m. Martha Isabelle Hendley, Dec. 7, 1947; children: Judith Carol, Charles Wesley, Richard Little. AA, George Washington U., 1948, BS, 1950, MS, 1955; PhD, Georgetown U., 1959. Research assoc. in pharmacology Hazleton Labs., Falls Church, Va., 1950-55, head dept. pharmacology, 1955-58, chief depts. biochemistry and pharmacology, 1958-59; with A. H. Robins Co., Richmond, Va., 1959-90, dir. biol. research, 1978-80, dir. research, 1980-82, v.p. research, 1982-89, v.p., gen. mgr. R & D div., 1989-90; ret., 1990. Lectr. in pharmacology Med. Coll. Va., 1960-64, adj. assoc. prof. pharmacology, 1982-90; guest lectr. Seminar on Good Lab. Practices, FDA, Washington, 1979, Chgo., 1979, San Francisco, 1979; apptd. expert pharmacologue toxicologue, France, 1986. Contbr. articles on pharmacology, toxicology and medicinal chemistry to profl. publs. Served with USMC, 1943; Served with USN, 1944-46; Served with U.S. Army, 1944. Mem. AAAS, N.Y. Acad. Sci., Va. Acad. Sci., Am. Chem. Soc., Soc. Toxicology (charter), Am. Soc. Pharmacology and Exptl. Therapeutics, Internat. Soc. Regulatory Toxicology and Pharmacology (charter), Pharm. Mfrs. Assn. (chmn. animal care and use com. 1971-88), Am. Assn. for Accreditation Lab. Animal Care (chmn. bd. trustees 1976-80), Sigma Xi. Clubs: Willow Oaks (Richmond); Cosmos (Washington), Masons (Washington). Achievements include patents in field. Home: 10275 Cherokee Rd Richmond VA 23235-1107 *An appreciation of the responsibility we have to society has set the standards by which I live. These responsibilities are as important as the rights to be gained from society. Those who are unwilling to assume responsibility should have no rights.*

WARD, JONATHAN P. service company executive; BSChemE, U. N.H., 1976; grad. advanced mgmt. program, Harvard Bus. Sch. With R.R. Donnelley, 1977—2001, pres. Merchandise Media and Fin. Svcs. bus. units, mgr. comml. printing operation, v.p., dir. Spartanburg, S.C., mfg. divsn., pres., COO, 1997—2001; pres., CEO ServiceMaster, Downers Grove, Ill., 2001—02, chmn., CEO, 2002—. Dir. Metromail Corp., Siegwerk, Inc. USA, Direct Mktg. Assn., Nat. Assn. Mfrs. Trustee Goodman Theatre, Chgo.; dir. Chgo. Youth Ctrs. Office: The ServiceMaster Co 3250 Lacey Rd Ste 600 Downers Grove IL 60515-1649

WARD, LARRY THOMAS, social program administrator; b. Abington, Va., Sept. 10, 1951; s. Manuel Thomas and Virginia June (Meade) W.; m. Jacqueline June Moore, Aug. 7, 1982 (div. June 1995); 1 child, Nicholas Lawrence; m. Kathleen Denise McCaslin, July 14, 1998. BSW cum laude, U. Md., 1983, MSW, 1984; PhD in Counseling Psychology, Columbia State U., 1997. Lic. social worker. Legis. lobbyist Citizen Action Coalition, Balt., 1982-83; mgmt. cons. United Way Md., Balt., 1983-84; program adminstr. Adams County Office Aging, Gettysburg, Pa., 1985-86; dir. social work Margaret E. Moul Home, York, Pa., 1986-87; coord. employee assistance program, family svc. supr. Family and Children's Svcs., Harrisburg, Pa., 1987-92, cons. drug & alcohol Gettysburg, 1984-86; pres., CEO Impact Sems., Guffey, Colo., 1988-97; pub. Guffey Co., 1992-97; pres., CEO Family Adv., Guffey, 1997—2001; CEO Internat. Child Advocacy Resource Enterprise, Inc., Guffey, 2002—. Author: Meditatinos on Descartes, 1979, A Philosophical Perspective, 1979, Heracles Reborn, 1983, Protective Services for the Elerly, 1984, Why A Psychiatrist, 1985, The blue ridge Summit Project, 1986, The Effects of Office Design on the Delivery of Therapeutic Social Work Services, 1987, Emotional Disorders of the Chronically Disabled Adolscent, 1987, Resistance to School-based EAPs, 1989, 2d edit., 1993, What Healthy Couples Seem to Know, 1990, Good Relationships Have Certain Traits, 1991, Truth, Justice, and the American Way: The Life and Times of Noel Neill, 2003, Noel Neill: Lois Lane Goes West, 2003, Noel Neill: The Original Lois Lane, 2003; exec. prodr. film on courtroom survival techniques, 1996. Ex-officio bd. dirs. Grass Roots, Inc., Columbia, Md., 1984; del. Gov.'s Youth Adv. Coun., Annapolis, Md., 1970-72; mem. consumer adv. coun. Met. Edison Co., Harrisburg, 1986-87. Recipient Original Art award Md. Pub. Broadcasting, 1969. Democrat. Avocations: baseball. Home: 365 Eagles Nest Trl Guffey CO 80820-9624 Office: PO Box 324 Guffey CO 80820-0324

WARD, LESLIE ALLYSON, journalist, editor; b. L.A., June 3, 1946; d. Harold Gordon and Marilyn Lucille (Dahlstead) W.; m. Robert L. Biggs, 1971 (div. 1977); m. Colman Robert Andrews, May 26, 1979 (div. 1988). AA, Coll. San Mateo, 1966; BA, UCLA, 1968, MJ, 1971. Reporter, researcher L.A. Bur. Life mag., 1971-72; reporter, news asst. L.A. bur. N.Y. Times, 1973-76; sr. editor New West mag., L.A., 1976-78, 79-80; L.A. bur. chief US mag., 1978-79; Sunday style editor L.A. Herald Examiner, 1981-82, editor-in-chief Sunday mags., 1982-83, Olympics editor, 1984, sports editor, 1985-86, sr. writer, 1986; sr. editor L.A. Times Mag., 1988-90; travel editor L.A. Times, 1990—. Democrat. Office: LA Times Times Mirror Sq Los Angeles CA 90053

WARD, LESTER LOWE, JR., arts executive, lawyer; b. Pueblo, Colo., Dec. 21, 1930; s. Lester Lowe and Alysmai (Pfeffer) W.; m. Rosalind H. Felps, Apr. 18, 1964; children: Ann Marie, Alison, Lester Lowe. AB cum laude, Harvard U., 1952, LLB, 1955. Bar: Colo. 1955. Pvt. practice, Pueblo, 1957-89; ptnr. Predovich, Ward & Banner, Pueblo, 1974-89; pres., COO Denver Ctr. for Performing Arts, 1989—. Trustee, Thatcher Found., Frank I. Lamb Found., Helen G. Bonfils Found.; pres. bd. trustees Pueblo Pub. Library, 1960-66; trustee St. Mary-Corwin Hosp., 1972-80, pres., 1979-80. With U.S. Army, 1955-57 Named Outstanding Young Man of Yr., Pueblo Jaycees, 1964 Fellow Am. Coll. Trust and Estate Counsel; mem. ABA (ho. of dels. 1986-88), Colo. Bar Assn. (bd. govs. 1977-79, 82-88, pres. 1983-84), Pueblo County Bar Assn. (Outstanding Young Lawyer award 1965, 67, pres. 1976-77), Denver Metro C. of C. (bd. dirs.), Denver Civic Ventures, Harvard Law Sch. Assn. Colo. (pres. 1972), Kiwanis (pres. 1969). Democrat. Roman Catholic. Home: 1551 Larimer St Apt 2601 Denver CO 80202-1638 Office: Denver Ctr Performing Arts 1050 13th St Denver CO 80204-2157 E-mail: lward@dcpa.org.

WARD, LLEWELLYN ORCUTT, III, oil company executive; b. Oklahoma City, July 24, 1930; s. Llewellyn Orcutt II and Addie (Reisdorph) W.; m. Myra Beth Gungoll, Oct. 29, 1955; children: Casidy Ann, William Carlton. Student, Okla. Mil. Acad. Jr. Coll., 1948-50; BS, Okla. U., 1953; postgrad., Harvard U., 1986. Registered profl. engr., Okla. Dist. engr. Delhi-Taylor Oil Corp., Tulsa, 1955-56; ptnr. Ward-Gungoll Oil Investments, Enid, Okla., 1956—; owner L.O. Ward Oil Ops., Enid, 1963—; chmn., CEO Ward Petroleum Corp. Mem. Okla. Gov.'s Adv. Coun. on Energy; rep. to Interstate Oil Compact Commn.; dir. Hydril Corp; chmn., CEO Ward Petroleum Corp. Chmn. Indsl. Devel. Commn., Enid, 1968—; active YMCA; mem. bd. visitors Coll. Engring., U. Okla.; mem. adv. coun. Sch. Bus., trustee Phillips U., Enid, Univ. Bd., Pepperdine, Calif.; Okla. chmn. U.S. Olympic Com., 1986—; Rep. nat. committeeman from Okla., 1982-88; mem. Pres.'s adv. com. on arts Kennedy Ctr. Served with C.E., U.S. Army, 1953-55. Named Chief Roughneck of Yr., Lone Star Steel, 1999. Mem. Ind. Petroleum Assn. Am. (chmn. 1996-98), Okla. Ind. Petroleum Assn. Am. (pres., bd. dirs.), Nat. Petroleum Coun., Enid C. of C., U. Okla. Coll. Engring. Disting. Grads. Soc., Am. Bus. Club (pres. 1964), Masons, Shriners, Rotary (pres. Enid 1990-91), Alpha Tau Omega. Methodist. Home: 900 Brookside Dr Enid OK 73703-6941 Office: 502 S Fillmore St Enid OK 73703-5703 Office Phone: 580-234-3229.

WARD, LLOYD D. appliance company executive; m. Lita; 2 sons. BS Engring, Mich. State U., 1970; MBA, Xavier U. Design engr., group leader engring., product devel., operations, advertising Procter & Gamble Co., 1970-88, gen. mgr. dish care products, 1988; v.p. ops. Pepsi Cola East, 1988-91; pres. Frito-Lay West PepsiCo, 1991-92, pres. Frito-Lay central divsn., 1992-96; exec. v.p., pres. Maytag Appliances, Newton, Iowa, 1996-98, COO, corp. pres., 1998—, CEO, 1999—. Special assignment PepsiCo restaurant internat. bus. Recipient Exec. Yr. award Black Enterprise mag. 1995. Office: 403 W 4th St N Newton IA 50208-3026

WARD, LOUIS EMMERSON, retired physician; b. Mt. Vernon, Ill., Jan. 19, 1918; s. Henry Ben (Pope) and Aline (Emmerson) Ward; m. Nan Talbot, June 5, 1942; children: Nancy, Louis, Robert, Mark; m. Marian Mansfield, Jan. 27, 1979. AB, U. Ill., 1939; MD, Harvard, 1943; MS in Medicine, U. Minn., 1949. Intern Ill. Research and Ednl. Hosp., Chgo., 1943; fellow medicine Mayo Found., 1946—49; cons. medicine, rheumatology Mayo Clinic, 1950—83, chmn. bd. govs., 1964—75. Contbr. articles to profl. jours. Vice chmn. bd. trustees Mayo Found., 1964—76; past bd. dirs. Fund for Republic, Ctr. for Study Dem. Instns., Arthritis Found.; mem. Nat. Coun. Health Planning and Devel., 1976—83. With M.C. U.S. Army, 1944—46. Recipient Achievement award, U. Ill., 1968, Disting. Alumnus award, Mayo Found., 1983. Master: Am. Coll. Rheumatology; mem.: So. Minn. Med. Assn., Zumbro Valley Med. Soc., Minn. Med. Soc., Ctrl. Soc. Clin. Rsch., Nat. Soc. Clin. Rheumatologists, AAAS, AMA, Phi Delta Theta, Alpha Omega Alpha, Sigma Xi, Phi Beta Kappa. Home: Apt 916 211 2nd St NW Rochester MN 55901-2820

WARD, MICHAEL J. rail transportation executive; b. Balt., Sept. 2, 1950; BS, U. Md., 1972; MBA, Harvard U., 1976. Rsch. analyst Chessie Sys., Balt., 1977—80, mgr., coord. analysis-fin., 1980—81, mgr. bus. rsch. Cleve., 1981—82, dir. nat. accts., 1982—84, asst. v.p. coal mktg., 1984—85, Balt., 1984—86; v.p. coal mktg. CSX Distbn. Svcs., Balt., 1986—88; v.p. coal CSX Transp., Jacksonville, 1988—94, gen. mgr. C&O Bus. Unit, v.p. coal Huntington, W.Va., 1994—95, sr. v.p. fin. Jacksonville, 1995—96, CFO, 1995—98, exec. v.p. fin., 1996—98, exec. v.p. coal and merger planning, 1998—99, exec. v.p. coal svc. group, 1999—2000, exec. v.p. ops., 2000, pres., 2000—03, CEO, 2002—03; pres. CSX Corp., Jacksonville, 2002—, chmn., pres., 2003—. Bd. dirs. Ky. Coal Coun., Ashland, Inc., CSX Corp. Bd. dirs. Ctr. Energy Econ. Devel., Take Stock in Children. Mem.: Fla. Coun. 100, Assn. Am. Railroads (bd. dirs.), Phi Kappa Phi, Beta Gamma Sigma. Office: CSX Corp 500 Water St C 900 Jacksonville FL 32202

WARD, MICHAEL W. lawyer; b. Chgo., Aug. 16, 1950; s. John Francis and Mary Frances (Brophy) W.; m. Amy Louise Alsopiedy, June 29, 1974; children: Daniel Joseph, James Patrick. BA, U. Notre Dame, 1972; JD, Ill. Inst. Tech., 1976. Bar: Ill. 1976, U.S. Dist. Ct. (no. dist.) Ill. 1976, U.S. Ct. Appeals (7th cir.) 1976, U.S. Supreme Ct. 1980, U.S. Dist. Ct. (no. dist.) Ill. 1982, U.S. Ct. Appeals (6th cir.) 1985. Asst. state's atty. Cook County, Chgo., 1976-80; assoc. O'Keefe, Ashenden, Lyons & Ward, Chgo., 1980-85, ptnr., 1986—99; pres. Michael W Ward P.C., 1999—. V.p. Northshore Fellowship League, Evanston, Ill., 1982-84; mem. St. Nicholas Sch. Bd., Evanston, 1984-86; bd. dirs. New Horizons Youth Group, Evanston, 1979-85; mem. adv. bd. Cath. Charities, 1989—; mem. fin. coun. St. Nicholas Ch., Evanston, 1988-97. Mem. Ill. State Bar Assn. (pub. utilities section council 1988-90, Chgo. Bar Assn., Fed. Comm. Bar Assn. (charter mem. midwest coordinating com.). Roman Catholic. Home: 1012 Mulford St Evanston IL 60202-3317 Office: Michael W Ward PC 1608 Barclay Blvd Buffalo Grove IL 60089-4523

WARD, MILTON HAWKINS, former mining company executive; b. Bessemer, Ala., Aug. 1, 1932; s. William Howard and Mae Ivy (Smith) W.; m. Sylvia Adele Randle, June 30, 1951; children: Jeffrey Randle, Lisa Adele. BS in Mining Engring., U. Ala., 1955, MS in Engring., 1981; MBA, U. N.Mex., 1974; DEng (hon.), Colo. Sch. of Mines, 1994; PhD, U. London, 1995. Registered profl. engr., Tex., Ala. Supr., engr. San Manuel (Ariz.) Copper Corp., 1955-60; gen. supt. of mines Kerr-McGee Corp., Oklahoma City, N.Mex., 1960-66; gen. mgr. Homestake Mining Co., Grants, 1966-70; v.p. ops. Ranchers Exploration & Devel. Corp., Albuquerque, 1970-74; pres., COO Freeport-McMoRan, Inc., New Orleans, 1974-92, also bd. dirs.; chmn., pres. CEO Cyprus Amax Minerals Co., Englewood, Colo., 1992-99; dir. Kinross Gold (formerly Amax Gold Inc.), 1993-99. Bd. dirs. Mineral Info. Inst., Inc., Internat. Copper Assn.; mem. Geoscience and Environment Ctr's. adv. bd. Sandia Nat. Labs., 1990—. Bd. trustees Western Regional Coun.; bd. dirs. Smithsonian Nat. Mus. Natural History, Nat. Mining Hall of Fame and Mus.; disting. engring. fellow U. Ala., mem. Pres.'s cabinet. Recipient Daniel C. Jackling award and Saunders gold medal Soc. Mining, Metallurgy and Exploration, 1992; inductee Am. Mining Hall of Fame, State of Ala. Engring. Hall of Fame, 1996; Honoree of Yr. Achievement Rewards Coll. Scientists, 1998-99. Fellow Inst. Mining and Metallurgy (London); mem. NAE, AIME (former sect. chmn., Disting. Mem. award), Am. Mining Congress, Nat. Mining Assn. (dir.), Am. Australian Assn., Mining and Metall. Soc. Am. (pres., exec. com.), Can. Inst. Mining and Metall., Nat. Rsch. Coun. (com. on earth and scis.), NAM (natural resources com.), Internat. Copper Assn. (bd. dirs.), Copper Club, Met. Club (Washington), Met. Club (Englewood), Las Campanas Country Club (Santa Fe, N.M.), Ventana Canyon Country Club (Tucson, Ariz.). Republican. Presbyterian. Office: Cyprus Amax Minerals Co Kinross Gold Corp 40 King St W 57th Fl Toronto ON Canada M5H 3Y2

WARD, NARI, sculptor; Artist-in-residence Studio Mus., N.Y.C., 1992—93. One-man shows include Harlem Firehouse Space, N.Y.C., 1993, 1995, New Mus., 1993, Nat. Ctr. Contemporary Art, Grenoble, France, 1994, Deitch Projects, N.Y.C., 1996, exhibited in group shows at numerous shows including Venice, Italy, 1993—, Rijksmuseum and Kroller-Müller Mus., Amsterdam, 1994—, UN Orgn., Geneva, 1995—, Whitney Mus. Am. Art, N.Y.C., 1995—, Lincoln Ctr., 1995—, Sabbath Day Lake Shaker Cmty., New Gloucester, Maine, 1996—, Studio Mus., N.Y.C., 1996—, Masion des Arts, Créteil, France, 1996—, Athens Sch. Fine Arts, 1996—, Harlem Firehouse Space, 1996—, Sch. Art Inst. Chgo., 1997, —, Maine Sch. Art, Portland, 1997—, Centro Atlantico Arte Moderno, Tenerife, Canary Islands, Spain, 1997—, WHO, Geneva, 1998—, Sjohistoriska Mus., Stockholm, 1998—, Am. Acad. Arts and Letters, N.Y.C., 1998—, represented in newspapers and mags., —. Recipient Wilard L. Metcalf award, 1998; Enrice Donati Found. grantee, 1990, Nat. Endowment for Arts grantee, 1994, Pollack Krasner Found. grantee, 1996, Penny McCall Found. grantee, 1997, Wheeler Found. grantee, 1994, Guggenheim Found. fellow, 1992.

WARD, NINA GILLSON, jewelry store executive; b. Boston, Dec. 19, 1950; d. Rev. John Robert and Patricia (Gillson) Baker; m. Jorge Alberto Lievanos, June 6, 1981 (div.); children: Jeremy John Baker, Wendy Mara Baker, Raoul Salvador Baker-Lievanos; m. David Ward, July 24, 1998; stepchildren: Johnna Ward, Tavi Sterling. Student, Mills Coll., 1969-70; grad. course in diamond grading, Gemology Inst. Am., 1983; student in diamondtology designation, Diamond Coun. Am., 1986—. Cert. store mgr., Jewelers Cert. Coun., Jewelers Am. Artist, tchr., Claremont, Calif., 1973-78; escrow officer Bank of Am., Claremont, 1978-81; retail salesman William Pitt Jewelers, Puente Hills, Montclair, Calif., 1981-83, asst. mgr., 1983, mgr. Santa Maria, Calif., 1983-91, corp. sales trainer, 1988-89; sales and design specialist Merksamer Jewelers, Santa Maria, 1991, mgr. San Luis Obispo, Calif., 1991-92, Santa Maria, Calif., 1992-94, diamond specialist cons., 1994-96; pres., ops. mgr. Dancer House Designs, Santa Maria, Calif., 1996; pres. primary jewelry designer Dancer House Design Fine Jewelry, Inc., Kennebunk, Maine, 1997—. Artist tapestry hanging Laguna Beach Mus. Art, 1974; exhibited in Nat. Jeweler's Design Competition, 1999. Mem. Cen. Coast Pla. Adv. Bd., 1992; mem. Rep. Bus. Majority Coun. Recipient Cert. Merit Art Bank Am., 1968, 1st pl. Best of show award for jewelry design Maine Jeweler's Assn., 1998, design award, 2000, Rep. of Yr. Award Maine, 2000, 1st place award crystal divsn. nat. design competition Mfg. Jewelers and Suppliers of Am., 2001. Mem. NAFE, Internat. Platform Assn., Maine Jewelers Assn. (bd. dirs. 1999—), Speaker's Bur., Santa Maria C. of C., Compassion Internat. Republican. Avocations: tapestry weaving, creative writing. Office: PO Box 475 Kennebunk ME 04043-0475

WARD, PETER ALLAN, pathologist, educator; b. Winsted, Conn., Nov. 1, 1934; s. Parker J. and Mary Alice (McEvoy) Ward. BS, U. Mich., Ann Arbor, 1958, MD, 1960. Diplomate Am. Bd. Anat. Pathology, Am. Bd. Immunopathology. Intern Bellevue Hosp., 1960—61; resident U. Mich. Hosp., Ann Arbor, 1961—63; postdoctoral fellow Scripps Clinic, La Jolla, Calif., 1963—65; chief immunobiology br. Armed Forces Inst. Pathology, Washington, 1965—71; prof. dept. pathology, chmn. dept. U. Conn. Health Center, Farmington, 1971—80; prof., chmn. dept. pathology U. Mich., Ann Arbor, 1980—; interim dean U. Mich. Med. Sch., 1982—85, 1st Godfrey D. Stobbe prof. pathology, 1987; Disting. faculty lectr. U. Mich. Biomed. Rsch. Coun., 1989. Cons. VA Hosp., 1980—; mem. rsch. rev. com. NHLBI, NIH, Bethesda, Md., 1978—82, Inst. Medicine/NAS, 1990—; trustee Am. Bd. Pathology, 1988—97, life trustee, 1998—, pres., 1996; bd. dirs. Univs. Assoc. for Rsch. and Edn. in Pathology, Inc., 1978—, pres. bd. dirs., 1988—90; chmn., mem. sch. adv. bd. Armed Forces Inst. Pathology, Washington, 1981—83; mem. pathology A study sect. NIH, 1972—76, chmn., 1976—78; pres.-elect U.S./Can. Acad. Pathology, 1991—92, pres., 1992—93; bd. dirs. Inst. Lab. Resources, NRC. Capt. M.C. U.S. Army, 1965—67. Named Amberson lectr., Am. Thoracic Soc., 2003; recipient Borden Rsch. award, U. Mich. Med. Sch., Ann Arbor, 1960, R&D and Devel. award, U.S. Army, 1969, Meritorious Civilian Svc. award, Dept. Army, 1970, Parke-Davis award, Am. Soc. Exptl. Pathology, 1971, Rous-Whipple award, Am. Soc. Investigative Pathology, 1996, Gold Headed Cane award, 2000. Fellow: Am. Heart Assn., AAAS; mem.: Nat. Acads. Sci. (lifetime nat. assoc.), Mich. Soc. Pathologists, Assn. Am. Physicians, Assn. Pathology Chmn., U.S. and Can. Acad. Pathologists (pres. 1993—94), Am. Assn. Immunologists, Am. Soc. Clin. Investigation, Am. Assn. Pathologists (pres. 1978—79). Office: 1301 Catherine St Rm M5240 PO Box 602 Ann Arbor MI 48106-0602

WARD, RICHARD HURLEY, dean, writer; b. N.Y.C., Sept. 2, 1939; s. Hurley and Anna C. (Mittasch) W.; children from a previous marriage: Jeanne M., Jonathan B.; m. Michelle Pierczynski, June 15, 1987; 1 child: Michelle Sophia. BS, John Jay Coll., CUNY, 1968; M in Criminology, U. Calif., Berkeley, 1969, D in Criminology, 1971. Detective N.Y.C. Police Dept., 1962-70; coord. student activities John Jay Coll., N.Y.C., 1970-71, dean students, 1971-75, v.p., 1975-77, vice chancelor, 1977-93; assoc. chancellor and prof. internat. criminology U. Ill., Chgo., 1993-98; exec. dir. Office Internat. Criminal Justice, 1985-99, exec. v.p. MBF Fdn. Group, Malaysia, 1996-97; dean Coll. Criminal Justice, Sam Houston State U., Huntsville, Tex., 1999—. Vis. prof. Zagazig U., Egypt, Egyptian Police Acad., 1986, East China Inst. Politics and Law, Shanghai, 1990-91; lectr., various confs. in China, Egypt, Russia, Italy, Eng., Peru, Germany, Saudi Arabia, Finland, Taiwan, Vietnam and U.S., 1983—. Author: (with others) Police Robbery Control Manual, 1975; Introduction to Criminal Investigation, 1975, An Anti-Corruption Manual for Administrators in Law Enforcement; (with Robert McCormack) Quest for Quality, 1984; gen. editor Foundations of Criminal Justice, 46 vols., 1972-75; editor: (with Austin Fowler) Police and Law Enforcement, Vol. I, 1972; Police and Law Enforcement, Vol. II, 1975; (with Harold Smith) International Terrorism: The Domestic Response, 1982, International Terrorism: Operational Issues, 1988; co-author: (with James Osterburg) Criminal Investigation: A Method for Reconstructing the Past, 1992, 3d edit., 1999. Mem. Mayor of Chgo.'s Blue Ribbon Pannel on Police Promotion; varsity baseball coach U. Ill., Chgo., 1980-82, John Jay Coll. Criminal Justice, N.U.C., 1971-72; chief investigator Mayor's Commn. Police Integrity, 1998. Cpl. USMC, 1957-61. Recipient Leonard Reisman award John Jay Coll. Criminal Justice, 1968, Alumni Achievement award, 1978, Richard McGee award U. Calif., Berkeley Sch. Criminology, 1971, Friendship medal Peoples Republic of China, 1994, Hans Mattick award Ill. Acad. Criminology, 1999; Justice Dept. fellow U. Calif., Berkeley, 1971. Mem. ASPA, Acad. Criminal Justice Scis. (pres. 1977-78, Founder's award 1985), Internat. Assn. Chiefs of Police (chmn. edn. and tng. sect. 1974-75), Sigma Delta Chi. Office: Sam Houston State U Coll Criminal Justice Huntsville TX 77341 E-mail: on2ward@aol.com.

WARD, RICHARD JOSEPH, university dean, educator, author; b. Beverly, Mass., Nov. 7, 1921; s. Ralph Woodbury and Margaret (Lyons) W.; m. Cecilia Butler, Sept. 1, 1951; children: Timothy, Mary, Richard, Christopher. BS, Harvard U., 1945; MA, U. Mich., 1948, PhD, 1958. Dir. planning AID Mission to Jordan, 1961-63; chmn. econ. dept. C.W. Post Coll., L.I. U., 1960-61, 63-65; chief planning Bur. for Near East and South Asia, AID, 1965-69; mgr. internat. cons. Peat, Marwick, Mitchell & Co., Washington, 1969-75; dean U. Mass. Coll. Bus., Dartmouth, 1975-87, dean, dir. rsch., prof., 1990-96, Chancellor prof. emeritus, 1996; dir. U.S. Internat. U. Sch. Bus., London, 1988-89; cons. in field. Author: Principles of Economics, 1967, Development Problems, 1973, The Palestine State, 1978, Development Horizon '80, 1980; editor: The Challenge of Development, 1967, Grampas Are For All Seasons, 2003; contbr. articles to profl. jours. Bd. dirs. Indsl. Found., 1976-82; bd. dirs. Jr. Achievement, 1977-99, also past pres.; mem. exec. com. World Congress on Violence and Human Co-existence. Lt. USN, 1943-46. Recipient Svc. award AID, Jordan Mission, 1963, Univ. Svc. award U. Mass. Alumni Assn., 1983, Gov.'s Citation for Svc., 1987; Harvard fellow Ford Found., 1957. Mem. Assn. Social Econs. (pres. 1970-71), Ea. Econ. Assn. (exec. com.), Am. Econ. Assn., Harvard Club (pres. 1984-87, regional bd. dirs.S.E. Mass. and R.I. 1989-92), U.S. Signatory/Found. for Human Co-Existence. Home: 20 Pleasant St South Dartmouth MA 02748-3813 Office Phone: 508-992-5554. E-mail: wardjrichard@comcast.net.

WARD, RICHARD VANCE, JR., management executive; b. Montreal, Quebec, Canada, June 19, 1929; s. Richard Vance Ward and Isobel Eugene Mosley; m. Elizabeth Anne Gareau, Aug. 15, 1953; children: Carolyn, Jennifer, Philip, Karen, Katherine. BSc, McGill U., Montreal, 1951; diploma in bus. adminstrn., U. Western Ont., London, Can., 1952. Indsl. engr. CIL Inc., Montreal, Canada, 1952-63, prodn. mgr., 1963-65; prodn. dir. ICI Am. Inc., Stamford, 1965-73, CIL Inc., Montreal, Canada, 1973-76, v.p., 1976-84; pres. CIL Corp. of Am., Stamford, Conn., 1984-89, Ward Assoc. Mgmt. Cons., 1989—. Chmn., pres., dir. Friends of McGill, Inc., NYC; bd. dirs. Chlorine Inst. Washington, mem. exec. com., 1984—86; bd. dir. Cornwall Chem. Inc., CIL Corp. Am., Cansco Chems. Inc., Canada. Mem. Chem. Mfrs. Assn., Sr. Men's Club (dir., pres.), SCORE (chmn.), Exchange Club (dir.). Avocations: sailing, hiking, curling, skiing. Home: 45 Brushy Ridge Rd New Canaan CT 06840-4207 E-mail: wardllc@aol.com.

WARD, ROBERT, composer, conductor, educator; b. Cleve., Sept. 13, 1917; s. Albert E. and Carrie (Mollenkopf) W.; m. Mary Raymond Benedict, June 19, 1944; children: Melinda, Johanna, Jonathon, Mark, Timothy. B.Mus., Eastman Sch. Music, 1939; cert., Juilliard Grad. Sch. Music, 1946; student composition with, Bernard Rogers, Howard Hanson, Frederick Jacobi, Aaron Copland; conducting with, Albert Stoessel, Edgar Schenkman; D.F.A., Duke, 1972; Mus.D., Peabody Inst., 1975; D.F.A., U. N.C., Greensboro, 1992. Tchr. Juilliard Sch. Music, 1946-56; mng. editor, exec. v.p. Galaxy Music Corp., until 1967, dir., 1967—; exec. v.p. Highgate Press, 1967; pres. N.C. Sch. Arts, Winston-Salem, 1967-74, tchr. composition, 1974-79; prof. composition Duke U., Durham, N.C., 1978-87, Mary Duke Biddle prof. music, 1978-87; composer Mus. Natural Sci., N.C., 1999—. Chmn. bd. Triangle Music Theater Assocs. Composer: 1st Symphony, 1942, Hush'd Be the Camps Today, 1943, Second Symphony, 1947, Third Symphony, 1951, Fourth Symphony, 1958, Divertimento for Orchestra, 1961, Earth Shall Be Fair, 1960, He Who Gets

Slapped (Pantaloon) (opera in 3 acts); opera in 4 acts The Crucible, 1962 (Pulitzer Prize in music); Hymn and Celebration (for orch.), 1962; for orch. Invocation and Toccata, 1963; opera in 2 acts The Lady From Colorado, 1964; Let the Word Go Forth, 1965; cantata Sweet Freedom's Song, 1965, Hymn To The Night, 1966; First String Quartet, 1966, Concerto for Piano and Orchestra, 1968; opera Claudia Legare, 1974; Fifth Symphony-Canticles for America, 1976, Sonic Structure (for orch.), 1980; opera Abelard and Heloise, 1981, Minutes Till Midnight, 1982, Dialogues for Violin, Cello and Orchestra, 1983, Concerto for Saxophone and Orchestra, 1984, Raleigh Divertimento for Wind Quintet, 1986, Festival Triptych, 1987, Sixth Symphony, 1988, First Symphonic Set for the New South, 1988, Fanfare, 1988, Second Symphonic Set, 1988, Appalachian Ditties and Dances, 1988, 5x5, 1989, Images of God, 1989, Ballet Music on The Scarlet Letter, 1990, Second Sonata for Violin and Piano, 1990, Bath County Rhapsody, 1991, Serenade for Mallarmé, 1991, By The Way of Memories for Orchestra, 1997, one act opera Roman Fever, 1993, Love's Seasons, 1994, song cycle Sacred Canticles, 1994, The Hill Song, 1996, Brass Ablaze for British Brass Band, 1996, Night Under the Big Sky for Wind Quintet and Piano, 1997, Echoes of America, Trio for Clarinet, Cello and Piano, 1997, Cherish Your Land-Chorus, 2000, Bayou Rhapsody, 2001, Dialogues: A Triple Concerto for Violin, Cello and Piano and Orch., 2002, Seventh Symphony, 2003, Nonet arrangement of Raligh Divertimento, 2003. Bd. dirs. Martha Baird Rockefeller Fund for Music, 1971-82, Am. Symphony Orch. League, 1977-89, Nat. Inst. Music Theatre, 1977-85; mem. music com. Henry St. Settlement; bd. dirs. Durham Arts Coun. Served with AUS, 1942-46. Decorated Bronze Star; MacDowell Colony fellow, 1938; recipient Juilliard Pub. award, 1942, Fine Arts award State of N.C., 1975, Gold Baton award Am. Symphony Orch. League, 1991, Disting. Faculty Alumnus award U. N.C., 1992, A.I. DuPont award of Del. Symphony, 1995; Alice M. Ditson fellow Columbia U., 1944, Guggenheim fellow, 1950, 52, 66-67; Am. Acad. Arts and Letters grantee, 1946. Mem. Nat. Acad. Arts and Letters. Home: The Forest at Duke 2701 Pickett Rd # 4022 Durham NC 27705-5688

WARD, ROBERT ALLEN, JR., advertising executive; b. Summit, N.J., Sept. 25, 1937; s. Robert Allen and Edith Allen (Edith) Seiberling; m. Nancy Prescott, Oct. 3, 1964; children: Victoria, Jennifer, Robert. BA, Yale U., 1959. Electronics analyst and account exec. U.S. Trust Co., N.Y.C., 1959-62; v.p., dir. Progressive Mktg. Svcs., N.Y.C., 1962-63, Coin Depot Corp., Elizabeth, N.J., 1963-68; pres. J.S. Riley Co., Wayne, N.J., 1964-70; pres., dir. C.G.W. Enterprises, Butler, N.J., Carelli, Glynn & Ward Advt. Co., 1969-95, All Hours Answering Svc., Pompton Lakes, N.J., 1969-93; v.p., dir. N.J. Exch., 1969-93; v.p. direct Anserve Inc., 1993—. Pres., dir. B.E.K., Inc., real estate mgmt. co., Wayne, N.J., Litho Four Printers, 1970-88, Healthserve, 1996—; dir. Devon Pubs., Butler, N.J., 1977-78; owner 1250 Rt # 23 LLC, 817 Ringwood Ave. LLC. Pres. Kinnelon PTA, N.J., 1972-73; councilman Kinnelon Borough Coun., 1978-83; police commr., Kinnelon, 1978-83; mem. Kinnelon Drug Adv. Coun., 1978-83; vestry St. David Episc. Ch., Kinnelon, 1969-72, 78-87, 90-93, sr. warden, 1978-87; bd. dirs. Morris Area Coun. Girl Scouts U.S.A., 1977-80, Morris Land Conservancy, 2002—, Inner City Ensemble, 1983-90; bd. dirs. Willing Hands, 1989—, chmn., 2000—; mem. sports awards dinner com. North Jersey March of Dimes, 1986-90; chmn. Yale Alumni Schs. Commn., 1984—; dir. Morris Land Conservancy, 2002—; mem. Christmas Cove Improvement Assn. With USMC, 1959-60, served to capt. USAR and NYNG, 1960-72. Mem. No. N.J. Advt. Club (bd. dirs. 1970-72), Commerce and Industry Assn. of N.J. (Penpac bd. dirs. 1982-90), N.J. Home Builder Assoc. (bd. dirs. 1967-70), Bank Mktg. Assn., Hugueuot Soc., S.A.R., Inner City Ensemble/N.J. Dance Troupe (bd. dirs. 1983-89), Yale Club (trustee, v.p. 1981—, pres. 1993-96, Montclair), Smoke Rise Club (Kinnelon), Smoke Rise Paddle Tennis Club (pres. 1988—). Republican. Home: 393 Ski Trl Kinnelon NJ 07405-2247 Office: Anserve 1250 State Rt 23 Butler NJ 07405-2002 E-mail: medserve@intac.com.

WARD, ROBERT EDWARD, retired political science educator and university administrator; b. San Francisco, Jan. 29, 1916; s. Edward Butler and Claire Catherine (Unger) W.; m. Constance Regina Barnett, Oct. 31, 1942; children: Erica Anne, Katherine Elizabeth. BA, Stanford U., 1936; MA, U. Calif.-Berkeley, 1938, PhD, 1948. Instr. in polit. sci. U. Mich., 1948-50, asst. prof. polit. sci., 1950-54, assoc. prof., 1954-58, prof., 1958-73, Stanford U., 1973-87, dir. Center for Research in Internat. Studies, 1973-87. Cons. in field; advisor Center for Strategic and Internat. Studies, Washington, 1968-87 Author: Modern Political Systems: Asia, 1963, Political Modernization in Japan and Turkey, 1964. Mem. nat. council Nat. Endowment for Humanities, Washington, 1968-73; mem. Pres.'s Commn. on Fgn. Lang.-Internat. Studies, 1978-79; chmn. Japan-U.S. Friendship Commn., 1980-83; mem. Dept. Def. Univ. Forum, 1982-87. Served to lt. (j.g.) USN, 1942-45. Decorated Legion of MErit, 1945; recipient Japan Found. award Tokyo, 1976, Order of Sacred Treasure (Japan), 1983 Fellow Am. Acad. Arts and Scis.; mem. Am. Polit. Sci. Assn. (pres. 1972-73), Assn. Asian Studies (pres. 1972-73), Social Sci. Research Council (chmn. 1969-71), Am. Philos. Soc. Home: Box 8129 501 Portola Rd Portola Valley CA 94028

WARD, RODMAN, JR., lawyer, director; b. Wilmington, Del., Apr. 8, 1934; s. Rodman and Dorcas (Andrews) W.; m. Susan Speakman Hill, Oct. 10, 1959; children: Margery Ward Garnett, Emily Ward Neilson, Rodman III, Jennifer Ward Oppenheimer. BA, Williams Coll., 1956; LLB, Harvard U., 1959. Bar: Del. 1959, D.C. 1959. Partner Prickett, Ward, Burt & Sanders, Wilmington, 1967-79, Skadden, Arps, Slate, Meagher & Flom, Wilmington, 1979—2002, of counsel, 2002—. Bd. dirs. WMB Holdings, Inc. Author: (with Folk and Welch) Folk on the Delaware General Corporation Law, 1987; contbr. articles to profl. jours. Trustee Winterthur Mus. Gardens and Libr., chmn. acad. affairs com.; bd. dirs. The Del. Art Mus. Capt. USAF, 1960—63. Fellow: Am. Coll. Trial Lawyers; mem.: ABA, Am. Judicature Soc., Assn. of Bar of City of N.Y., D.C. Bar Assn., Am. Bar Found. (life), Del. State Bar Assn. (pres. 1989—90), Am. Law Inst., Vicmead Hunt Club, Wilmington Country Club, Wilmington Club. Home: 52 Selborne Dr Wilmington DE 19807-1216 Office: PO Box 636 Wilmington DE 19899-0636 Office Phone: 302-651-3000. Business E-Mail: rward@skadden.com.

WARD, ROGER ALLEN, music educator, musician; b. Rushville, Ill., Aug. 23, 1954; s. Albert Merle and Mary Ellen Ward; m. Jane Marie Merrey, Aug. 22, 1992; 1 child, Samuel Douglas. BFA cum laude, Western Ill. U., 1988, MFA, 1999. Instr. Spoon River Coll., Macomb branch, Canton, Ill., 1996—, Carl Sandburg Coll., Carthage branch, Galesburg, Ill., 1997—. Composer: (violin/cello invention) Musicae Diabolus, 1994, (string quartet) Quatros, 1995, (orchestral work) Sound Patterns, 1996. Democrat. Meth. Office: Carl Sandburg Coll 305 Sandburg Dr Carthage IL 62321-1183 Business E-Mail: rward@sandburg.edu. E-mail: rward@spoonrivercollege.edu., bassclef@frontiernet.net.

WARD, ROGER COURSEN, lawyer; b. Newark, June 19, 1922; s. Waldron Merry and Aline Toppin (Coursen) W.; m. Katharine More Stevens, Oct. 22, 1949; children: James Olney, Alexander More. Grad., Phillips Exeter Acad., 1940; AB, Princeton U., 1943; LL.B., Columbia U., 1949. Bar: N.J. 1949. Law clk. to justice N.J. Supreme Ct., 1951; since practiced in Newark, Morristown, Montclair, N.J.; ptnr. Pitney, Hardin, Kipp & Szuch, 1959-91, counsel, 1991-92, Schwartz, Tobia, Stanziale, Sedita & Campisano, LLP, 1993—. Bd. advisors Am. Inst. Law Tng. Within Office, Phila. 1986-88, Law Hiring and Tng. Report, Chgo., 1983-88. Bd. dirs. United Hosps. Newark, 1965-78, pres., 1973; trustee, v.p. Newark Mus. Assn., 1969-92; bd. dirs. Better Bus. Bur. Greater Newark, 1970-84; mem. Summit Zoning Bd. Adjustment, 1966-70; trustee Eye Inst. N.J., 1973, Pingry Sch., 1966-68, Summit YMCA, 1960-62, Newark Council Social Agys., 1956-60; vice chmn. Newark Mayor's Commn. on Youth, 1958-60. Served to lt. (j.g.) USNR, 1943-46, PTO, ETO. Harlan Fiske Stone scholar Columbia U., 1949. Mem. Essex County Bar Assn., Princeton Club N.Y., Short Hills (N.J.) Club, Phi Beta Kappa. Office: Schwartz Tobia Stanziale Sedita & Campisano LLP 22 Crestmont Rd Montclair NJ 07042 E-mail: wardr@kipslaw.com.

WARD, ROSCOE FREDRICK, engineering educator; b. Boise, Idaho, Dec. 5, 1930; s. Roscoe C. W. and Alice E. (Ward); m. Julia Duffy, June 8, 1963; children: Eric R., David C. Student, U. Oreg., 1949-50; BA, Coll. of Idaho, 1953; postgrad., U. Wash., 1955-57; BS, Oreg. State U., 1959; MS, Wash. State U., 1961; Sc.D., Washington U., St. Louis, 1964. Registered profl. engr., Ohio. Asst. prof. civil engring. U. Mo., Columbia, 1963-65, Robert Coll., Istanbul, Turkey, 1965-67; assoc. prof. civil engring. Asian Inst. Tech., Bangkok, Thailand, 1967-68; assoc. prof. civil engring., assoc. dean Sch. Engring. U. Mass., Amherst, 1968-75; prof. Bogazici U., Istanbul, 1974-75; br. chief biomass energy Dept. Energy, Washington, 1975-79; interregional advisor UN/World Bank, N.Y.C., 1979-83; dean Sch. Applied Scis. Miami U., Oxford, Ohio, 1983-88; prof. paper sci. and engring. Sch. Engring. and Applied Scis. Miami U., Oxford, 1983—. Vis. scientist Csir, Republic of South Africa, 1990-91. Contbr. chpts. to books, articles to profl. jours. Fellow ASCE Home: 4818 Bonham Rd Oxford OH 45056-1423 E-mail: wardrf@muohio.edu.

WARD, SARAH M. lawyer; b. Elizabeth, N.J., 1957; AB, Princeton U., 1981; JD, Fordham U., 1986. Bar: N.Y. 1987. Ptnr. Skadden, Arps, Slate, Meagher & Flom, N.Y.C. Office: Skadden Arps Slate Meagher & Flom 4 Times Sq Fl 24 New York NY 10036-6595

WARD, SELA, actress; b. Meridian, Miss. d. Granberry Holland and Annie Kate Ward. BA, U. Ala. Appearances include: (TV series) Emerald Point, N.A.S., 1983-84, Sisters, 1991— (Emmy award for Lead Actress in Drama Series 1994), Once and Again, 1999-2002 (winner lead actress in a drama series, Emmy award 2000, winner lead actress in a drama series, Golden Globe award 2001), The Rescuers: Two Women, 1997, (TV movies) Rainbow Drive, 1990, Double Jeopardy, 1993, Almost Golden: The Jessica Savitch Story, 1995 (winner lead actress in drama movie Cableace award 1996), Catch a Falling Star, 2000, The Badge, 2002; (films) Rustler's Rhapsody, 1985, Nothing in Common, 1986, Hello Again, 1987, The Fugitive, 1993, My Fellow Americans, 1996, The Reef, 1997, 54, 1998, Rescuers: Stories of Courage, Two Women, 1997, 54, 1998, Dirty Dancing: Havana Nights, 2003, The Day After Tomorrow, 2004; lead actress (TV series) Once and Again, 1999-00; prodr. (Lifetime cable network) documentary Changing Face of Beauty, 2000, Lifetime "Intimate Portrait", 2001. Office: 289 S Robertson Blvd Ste 469 Beverly Hills CA 90211-2834*

WARD, SPRING TINA, history and political science educator; b. Hagerstown, Md., Nov. 28, 1956; d. Raymond Leon and Opal Dorothy (Spade) Ward; m. Robin L. Brna, Dec. 16, 1989. MA, U. Keele, Eng. Mus. dir. City of Hagerstown, Md., 1981—86; dir. pub. rels. YMCA Greater Balt., Balt., 1986—91; asst. prof. history and polit. sci. Hagerstown C.C., 1991—. Clk. session Covenant Ch., 2002—; bd. trustees Hagerstown C.C. Found., 2002—, Leadership Hagerstown, 1999—, Hagerstown Commn. for Women, 1998—2001. Mem.: Washington County Higher Edn. Assn. (co-pres. 1998—2002), LWV (bd. trustees 1993—2002, dir. pub. rels. 1994—). Office: Hagerstown Cmty Coll 11400 Robinwood Dr Hagerstown MD 21742

WARD, STEPHEN M., JR., computer company executive; BSME, Calif. Polytech. U. Joined IBM Corp., Tucson, 1978; v.p. info. tech., gen. mgr. IBM ThinkPad; gen. mgr. IBM's Global Indsl. Sector; chief info. officer, v.p. bus. transformation IBM Corp., sr. v.p., gen. mgr. regional systems group, 2003—. Office: IBM Corp 1 New Orchard Rd Armonk NY 10504

WARD, THOMAS, food products executive; b. June 9, 1958; Co-CEO, pres. Russell Stover Candies, Kansas City, Mo. Fax: 816-842-5593.

WARD, VERNON GRAVES, internist; b. Palisade, Nebr., Mar. 5, 1928; s. Charles Bennett and Mildred Belle (Graves) W.; m. Eleanore Mae Farstveet, Aug. 28, 1952; children: Margo, Alison, Barry. BA, Nebr. Wesleyan U., 1948; MD cum laude, U. Nebr., Omaha, 1954. Diplomate Am. Bd. Internal Medicine. Instr. in anatomy Columbia U., N.Y.C., 1948—50; intern U. Wis., Madison, 1954—55, resident internal medicine, 1955—58, chief resident, physician, 1957—58; fellow in neurophysiology and psychosomatic medicine U. Okla., Oklahoma City, 1960—61; asst. clin. prof. medicine U. Wis., Madison, 1961—62; pvt. practice internal medicine Kearney, Nebr., 1962—67; asst. prof. U. Nebr. Coll. Medicine, Omaha, 1967—69; assoc. clin. prof. medicine U. Nebr., Omaha, 1969—; pvt. practice internal medicine Omaha, 1969—. Chmn. dept. internal medicine Clarkson Hosp., Omaha, 1976-78, 96-98. Contbr. articles to profl. jours. including JAMA, Nebr. State Med. Jour., Wis. State Med. Jour., Am. Heart Jour., Postgrad. Medicine. Pres. Nebr. chpt. Arthritis Found., 1969-71. Lt. Commdr. USNR, 1958-60. Recipient Cmty. Based Tchg. award ACP-ASIM, 2000; named Hutton Traveling Scholar Coll. of Physicians, 1965. Fellow ACP, Am. Coll. Rheumatology; mem. AMA, Nebr. State Med. Soc., Omaha Med. Soc., Am. Soc. Internal Medicine (Cmty.-Based Tchg. award 2000), Am. Psychosomatic Soc., Nebr. Soc. Internal Medicine (pres. 1980-82, Disting. Internist award 1990), Phi Kappa Phi, Alpha Omega Alpha (pres. Nebr. chpt. 1984-85), Phi Chi (grand sec.-treas. 1986—, co-chmn. nat. conv. Omaha 1953), Phi Kappa Tau. Republican. Lutheran. Home: 302 N 54th St Omaha NE 68132-2813 Office: 650 N Doctors Bldg 4242 Farnam St Omaha NE 68131 Office Phone: 402-561-3040.

WARD, WILLIAM E. mayor; b. Lunenburg County, VA, 1933; BA, Virginia State Coll., Petersburg, Va., 1957, MA, 1960; PhD, Clark Univ., Worchester, Mass., 1972; studied, Hampton, African History Inst., 1963, Norfolk State Coll., Am. History Inst., 1967, Carnegie-Mellon Univ., Afro-Am. History Inst., 1969, Am. Forum Internat. Study, Ghana, West Africa, 1972, Univ. West Indies, Kingston, Jamaica, 1977. Mayor City of Chesapeake, Chesapeake, VA., 1990—; tchr. I.C. Norcom H.S., Portsmouth, Va., 1958—62, P.S. 181, Baltimore, Md., 1962—63; asst. prof. Norfolk State Coll., 1968—70; TTT fellow Clark Univ.; assoc. prof. Norfolk State Coll., 1973—79; prof. Norfolk State Univ., 1980—98, chair, history dept., 1997—2000; ret., 2000; part-time tchr., 2000—. Course instr. Clark Univ., 1972; co-dir. In-Svc. Workshop, 1971; cons. Norfolk State Coll., 1971—72, Norfolk Com., 1970—78; participated Econ. Trade Cultural Missions to Japan, Brazil, Taiwan, Israel, Europe, Japan, 1990—99; former host PRIDE, WAVY-TV; chmn., insurance com. Norfolk State Univ., chmn., faculty senate Va. benefits com., chmn., senate grievance com., chmn., black history com., mem., coll. wide coun. tchr. ed., coll. exe. coun., 1971—82, pres. faculty senate, 1975—77. Bd. dir. Norfolk Chesapeake Va. Beach United Way, Tidewater Va. Urban League; mem. Chesapeake City Coun., 1978—, mayor, 1990—; mem. U.S. Conf. Mayors, Chesapeake Forward Civic Orgn.; past pres. Chesapeake Men Progress Civic Orgn., Fernwood Farms Civic League; mem. Hampton Rds. Military Diplomats; chmn. Fourth Congl. Voters League; mem. Va. State Dem. Ctr. Com., WAVY-TV Minority Adv. Bd.; delegate Nat. Dem. Conv., N.Y.C., 1976, San Francisco, 1984; chmn. Hampton Rds. Mayors Chair Caucus, 1995—96; elected to joint subcom. study use of incentives for joint activities by localities appointed by Va. Senate Com. Privileges, 1996; appointed Va. Municipal League Legislative Com., 1997; exe. bd. Tidewater Coun. Boy Scouts Am., 1997—2000; delegate 17th Ann. Jerusalm Conf. Mayors, 1997; 2nd vice chmn. Hampton Rds. Partnership, 1997; bd. dirs. Hampton Rds. Econ. Alliance, 1997; appointed Internat. Task Force, Nat. League Cities, 1998, U.S. Conf. Mayors Task Force Electronic Commerce Internet Tech., 1999. Recipient cmty. svc. award, Kappa Alpha Psi Fraternity, 1970, three yr. acad. fellowship award, Clark Univ., brotherhood award, Christians and Jews, outstanding alumni award, Va. State Univ., 1993, chamber of commerce commendation award, 1994, various cmty. awards, Martin Luther King, Jr. memorial award, Old Dominion Univ., 1995; grantee study in Africa, Clark Univ., 1972. Mem.: Va. Soc. Sci. Assn., Am. Historical Assn., Southern Historical Assn., Assn. Study Negro Life History, Va. Soc. History Tchrs., Nat. Fatherhood Initiative (co-chair mayor 2001—02), Great Bridge Battlefield Waterways History Found. (pres.), Tidewater Regional Health Coun., Va. World Tech. Fair Commn., Internat. Torch Club, Kappa Alpha Psi. Democrat. Office: Office of Mayor 306 Cedar Rd Chesapeake VA 23322 E-mail: wward@council.chesapeakeva.net.

WARD, WILLIAM FRANCIS, JR., real estate investment banker; b. Everett, Mass., Aug. 23, 1928; s. William Francis and Helen (Schriber) W.; m. Elaine L. Wilson, June 11, 1950 (dec. Oct. 1993); children: Jeffrey W., Gary T., Michelle A., Gregory W., Suzanne M.; m. Marie-Louise Buchheit, Nov. 5, 1994. BS, U.S. Mil. Acad., 1950; MBA, Harvard U., 1956; LLB, La Salle U., 1966; LLD (hon.), So. Vermont U., 1996; HHD (hon.), N.Y. Coll. of Podiatric Medicine, 2003. Commd. 2d lt. U.S. Army, 1950; resigned, 1956; econ. analyst E.I. duPont de Nemours & Co., Inc., Wilmington, Del., 1956-58; sec. N.Y. State Bridge Authority, Poughkeepsie, 1958-60; div. contr., dir. mktg. svcs. GAF Corp., N.Y.C., 1960-63; asst. to pres. Grosset & Dunlap, Inc., 1963-65, v.p., 1965-67; contr. Dun & Bradstreet, 1967-71, v.p., 1968-71; chmn. bd., pres. Dun-Donnelley Pub. Corp., 1971-77; from v.p., treas. to pres. Gestam, Inc., 1981-86; chief Army Res., 1986-91, comdr. U.S. Army Res. Command, 1990—91; chmn., pres. Realicam, 1985—. Bd. dirs. Quotron Electronics, Inc., Empire Nat. Bank, Eastern Savs. Bank, Apple Bank for Savs., Corinthian Broadcasting, Greater N.Y. Bank for Savs.; trustee All-City Funds; mem. adv. bd. Astoria Fin. Bank, Podia Ins. Co.; mem. faculty Dutchess C.C., 1958-60, NYU Sch. Commerce, 1960-64. Pres. Ramapo Central Sch. Dist., 1966-72, 1982-87; mem. facilities and planning bd. Good Samaritan Hosp., 1980-85; chmn. United Way, Rockland County, 1992-94; county chmn. Citizen for Kennedy and Johnson, 1960; Dem. candidate for Ho. of Reps., 1962; chmn. Young Citizens for Johnson and Humphrey, 55 counties N.Y., 1964; exec. v.p. Am. Cancer Soc., 1976-81; bd. dirs. N.Y.C. div. Aerospace Edn. Found., U.S. Army War Coll. Found., West Point Fund, 1979, Franciscan Sisters of the Poor Found., 1980-92; trustee N.Y. Mil. Acad., 1982-86, 91-96, trustee emeritus, 1996—; trustee Assn. Grads. U.S. Mil. Acad., 1993-2003, trustee emeritus, 2003—, exec. com., 1996-2003, chmn. audit com., 1996—; trustee Hist. Soc. Rockland County, 1993-95, N.Y. Coll. Podiatric Medicine, 2000. Served to capt. AUS, 1950-54; to maj. gen. USAR 1978-91. Decorated D.S.M. with 1 oak leaf cluster, Legion of Merit, Meritorious Svc. medal with oak leaf cluster, Air medal with 3 oak leaf clusters, Army Commendation medal with oak leaf cluster, Purple Heart, Army Achievement medal. Mem. West Point Soc. (Washington chpt., Space Coast chpt., N.Y. chpt., pres. 1974-76), Antrim Players, Soc. Harvard Engrs. and Scientists, Fin. Execs. Inst., Newcomen Soc., Res. Officers Assn., Am. Friends of Viet Nam (nat. chmn.), VFW, Am. Legion, Knight of Holy Sepluchre, Disabled Am. Vets., Pilgrim Soc., Army and Navy Club, Squadron "A" Club, Univ. Club (N.Y.), Harvard Club (Washington), Nat. Press Club. Roman Catholic. Home: Summit View Farm 341 17A PO Box 150 Goshen NY 10924-0150 also: 1271 Continental Ave Melbourne FL 32940 E-mail: wward@hvc.rr.com.

WARD-BROWN, DENISE, sculptor, educator; BFA cum laude, Temple U., 1975; MFA summa cum laude, Howard U., 1984. Assoc. prof. U. Washington, St. Louis, 1991—. One-woman shows Cinque Gallery, N.Y.C., 1984, Washington Project for the Arts, Washington, 1984, Bozeman, Mont., 1986, O St. Gallery, Washington, 1989, Montgomery Coll., Tacoma Park, Md., 1989, Fitzpatrick Gallery, Washington, 1989, U. Md., Princess Anne, Md., 1991, Pierce-Arrow Gallery, St. Louis, 1993, St. Louis Art Mus., 1995, Margaret Harwell Art Mus., Poplar Bluff, Mo., 1998; group exhbns. include Corcoran Mus. Art, Washington, 1987, George Washington U., 1987, U. Richmond, Va., 1987, Shippee Gallery, N.y.C., 1987, Strathmore Arts Ctr., Rockville, md., 1988, Rockville Arts Ctr., 1989, Notre Dame Coll., Balt., 1989, No. Va. C.C., Arlington, 1989, The Kunstrum, Washington, 1990, Montgomery Coll., Tacoma Park, Md., 1990, Smithsonian-Anacostia Mus., Washington, 1990, Art St. Louis, 1992, Lindenwood Coll., St. Louis, 1993, Murray State U. Eagle Gallery, 1993, Portfolio Gallery, St. Louis, 1994, U. Wis., Eau Claire, 1994, U. Md., College Park, 1994, St. Louis Design Ctr., 1996, Gene Pool & Assocs., N.Y.C., 1996, Smithsonian Instn., 1996, numerous others. Study grantee Penland (N.C.) Sch. Crafts, 1973, Haystack Mt. Sch. Crafts, Deer Isle, Maine, 1973, 74, Howard U./Ford Found., 1982, 83, Vt. Studio Sch., Johnson, 1986, Geog. Devel. grantee Washington D.C. Commn. on the Arts and Humanities, 1984, 85; Individual Artist grantee Washington D.C. Commn. on the Arts and Humanities, 1986, 87, 89, 91, Mbari, Ritual and Rememory, Regiona Artists' Projects grantee, 1994; Fulbright scholar African Rsch. Program, Ghana, others. Office: Dept Sculpture Sch Art Washington U Camp Box 1031 1 Brookings Dr Saint Louis MO 63130-4862 Fax: 314-935-8412. E-mail: ddwardbr@art.wustl.edu.*

WARDELL, JOHN WATSON, lawyer; b. Mt. Erie, Ill., Oct. 25, 1929; s. Charles R. and Rada (Travers) Wardell; m. Carl J. Gross, Aug. 6, 1955 (div. 1984); children: Michael, Amy, Laurie, Douglas. BA, U. Ill., 1950, JD, 1956. Bar: Ill. 1956, U.S. Dist. Ct. (no. dist.) Ill. 1967. Counsel dept. law Standard Oil Co. (Ind.), 1956—61, Motorola, Inc., Franklin Park, Ill., 1961—68; pvt. practice, 1968—69, 1971—75, 1996—; ptnr. Franz, Franz, Wardell & Lindberg, 1969—70, Wardell & Unvarsky, 1970—71, Wardell & Meinhardt, 1973—74, Wardell & Johnson Ltd. and predecessor, Crystal Lake, Ill., 1976—88, Palmer & Wardell, Schaumburg, Ill., 1987—96; gen. counsel, dir. Matsuo Electronics Am., Inc. Dir. other corps. Contbr. articles to profl. jours. Mem. Gov.'s Adv. Coun., Ill., 1969—73, Lake County Taxpayers Com., 1970—73; bd. dirs. North Barrington (Ill.) Area Assn., 1970—84. With M.C. U.S. Army, 1951—53. Mem.: ABA, U. Ill. Scholarship Soc., N.W. Suburban Bar Assn., Chgo. Bar Assn. (internat. and fgn. law com. 1970—83), Ill. Bar Assn. (chmn. youner mems. conf. 1965—66, coun. en. practice sect. 1971—75, task force on profl. publicity 1976—78, coun. internat. law sect. 1982—86), Turnberry Country Club, Order of the Coif, Phi Kappa Phi, Phi Delta Phi, Phi Beta Kappa. Republican. Office: 675 N North Ct Ste 490 Palatine IL 60067-8173 Office Phone: 847-705-9990.

WARDELL, LINDY CONSTANCE, nonprofit organization administrator; b. Potsdam, N.Y., Apr. 28, 1928; d. Stewart A. and Mabel A. Henderson; m. David F. Constance, Sept. 6, 1947 (dec. Apr. 1984); children: John, Kathryn, Marie, Thomas, Richard; m. Frank M. Wardell, 1989. Student, Powellson Jr. Coll., Syracuse, N.Y., 1946-47, Ctrl. City Bus. Inst., Syracuse, 1946-47. Lic. realtor. V.p. Bicentennial Bus Co., Phila., 1974-77; assoc. cons. Constance & Wallace, Phila., 1976-84; v.p. Trade Devel. Corp., Phila., 1977-84; realtor assoc. Louis Gaev Realtors, Haverford, Pa., 1985-87; pres., chmn. bd. dirs. Darby (Pa.) Cmty. Forum, 1997—; pres., chmn. bd. Darby Borough Hist. Soc., Darby, 1998—. Chmn. Friends of Darby Meth. Meeting Cemetery, 1996—; mem. adv. bd. Delaware County Daily Times, Primos, Pa., 1998-99; bd. dirs. Darby Cmty. Project, 1991—. Author: Images of America, 2003; contbr. articles to newspapers. Pres., Coun. Rep. Women, Newtown Square, Pa., 1977-85; trustee Phila. Fairmount Pk. Hist. Sites com., 2002— Recipient Outstanding Individual Achievement award Delaware County Heritage Commn., 1999; Golden Rule Found. grantee, 1997. Mem Darby Hist. Soc. (founding mem. 1998), Delaware County Hist. Soc. (Coun. of Pres., Lee C. Brown award 2003). Republican. Avocations: genealogical research, arts and crafts, historical research. Home: 16 Winthrop Rd Darby PA 19023-1116

WARDEN, GAIL LEE, health care executive; b. Clarinda, Iowa, May 11, 1938; s. Lee Roy and Juanita (Haley) W.; m. Lois Jean Johnson, Oct. 9, 1965; children: Jay Christopher, Janna Lynn, Jena Marie. BA, Dartmouth Coll., 1960; MHA, U. Mich., 1962. Adminstrv. asst. Blodgett Meml. Hosp., Grand Rapids, Mich., 1962; adj. Dewitt Hosp., Ft. Belvoir, Va., 1963-65; adminstrv. asst. Presbyn.-St. Luke's Hosp., Chgo., 1965-68, asst. to pres., 1968, v.p. adminstrn., 1968-69; exec. v.p. Rush-Presbyn.-St. Luke's Med. Center, Chgo., 1970-76, Am. Hosp. Assn., Chgo., 1976-81; pres., CEO Group Health Coop. Puget Sound, Seattle, 1981-88, Henry Ford Health System, Detroit, 1988—. Past chmn. Am. Hosp. Assn.; bd. dirs. Comerica Bank; mem. governing coun. Inst. Medicine of NAS. Contbr. articles to profl. jours. Bd. dirs. Robert Wood Johnson Found. Served to capt. AUS, 1965. Named one of Ten Outstanding Young Men in Chgo., Jr. Assn. Commerce and Industry, 1968, Nat. Health Care award B'nai B'rith Internat., 1992, CEO award Am. Hosp. Assn.'s Soc. for Healthcare Planning and Mktg., 1993. Mem. NAS, Am. Coll. Hosp. Adminstrs. (named Young Adminstr. of Yr. 1972), Am. Pub. Health Assn., Am. Healthcare Systems, Alpha Chi Rho. Office: Henry Ford Health System 1 Ford Pl Detroit MI 48202-3450

WARDEN, JOHN L. lawyer; b. Evansville, Ind., Sept. 22, 1941; s. Walter Wilson and Juanita (Veatch) W.; m. Phillis Ann Rodgers, Oct. 27, 1960; children: Anne W. Clark, John L., W. Carson. AB, Harvard U., 1962; LLB, U. Va., 1965. Bar: N.Y. 1966, U.S. Ct. Appeals (2d cir.) 1966, U.S. Dist. Ct. (so. and ea. dists.) N.Y. 1967, U.S. Ct. Appeals (10th cir.) 1971, U.S. Supreme Ct. 1972, U.S. Ct. Appeals (D.C. cir.) 1980. Assoc. Sullivan & Cromwell, N.Y.C., 1965-73, ptnr., 1973—. Hon. trustee U. Va. Law Sch. Found.; trustee Am. Ballet Theatre. Editor-in-chief: Va. Law Rev., 1964-65. Fellow Am. Coll. Trial

Lawyers; mem. ABA, Am. Law Inst., N.Y. State Bar Assn., Assn. Bar City N.Y., N.Y. County Lawyers Assn., Knickerbocker Club, Down Town Assn. Club, Doubles Club, Bedford Golf and Tennis Club, Lyford Cay Club. Republican. Episcopalian. Office: Sullivan & Cromwell 125 Broad St Fl 28 New York NY 10004-2489 E-mail: wardenj@sullcrom.com.

WARDEN, RICHARD DANA, government labor union official; b. Great Falls, Mont., Dec. 10, 1931; s. Robert Dickinson and Helen (Leach) W.; m. Barbara Freeman; children from previous marriage: Denise, Michael, Joseph, Jerome. BA, Mont. State U., 1957, MA, 1958. Reporter, then state editor Gt. Falls (Mont.) Tribune, 1959-61; legis. asst. to U.S. Senator Lee Metcalf of Mont., 1962-63; adminstrv. asst. to U.S. Congressman James G. O'Hara of Mich., 1963-67; dep. dir. Office Civil Rights, HEW, 1967-68; legis. rep. AFL-CIO, 1969-70; dir. Washington Research Project Action Council, 1970-72; legis. rep. UAW, 1972-75, legis. dir., 1975-77, 79-91, ret., 1991. Asst. sec. legis. HEW, 1977-79 Served with USN, 1951-54. Congressional fellow, 1961-62; recipient Pub. Affairs Reporting award Am. Polit. Sci. Assn., 1960 Home: 211 Marina Dr Lewes DE 19958

WARDEN, WILLIAM C. lawyer; Exec. v.p., gen. counsel, sec., chief adminstrv. officer Lowe's Cos., Inc., North Wilkesboro, N.C. Office: Lowe's Cos Inc PO Box 1111 North Wilkesboro NC 28659-1111

WARDER, MICHAEL YOUNG, non-profit executive; b. Buffalo, June 29, 1946; s. Thomas Grayston and Norma A. (Young) W.; m. Cheryl Lynn Gilkerson, Feb. 8, 1975; children: Maureen, Amy, Michael Jr. BA, Stanford U., 1968. Tchr. Drew Sch., San Francisco, 1968—69; pres. Internat. Re-edn. Found., San Francisco, 1970—73; sec.-gen. Internat. Conf. on the Unity of Scis., N.Y.C., 1974—79; pres., pub. Newsworld Comm., N.Y.C., 1976—79; dir. adminstrn. Heritage Found., Washington, 1980—83; exec. v.p. Ethics and Pub. Policy Ctr., Washington, 1983—84, The Rockford (Ill.) Inst., 1985—95; v.p. devel. The Claremont (Calif.) Inst., 1995—2001; exec. dir. So. Calif. Children's Scholarship Fund, 2001—. Radio commentator (bi-weekly) Sta. WNIJ-FM NPR Affiliate, DeKalb, Ill., 1991—95; del. leader People to People, USSR, 1991, Rockford Inst., Lithuania, Latvia, Estonia, 1994; del. leader to London Claremont Inst., 1996, del. leader to Hong Kong, 97, del. leader to Israel, 98, del leader to Rome, 2000; guest TV programs Politically Incorrect/ABC, Fox News Channel, MSNBC, others; spkr. in field; polit. analyst in field. Op-ed columnist The Wall Street Jour., USA Today, L.A. Times, The Chgo. Tribune, Chgo. Sun Times, San Francisco Chronicle, San Diego Union Tribune, St. Louis Post Dispatch, Indpls. Star, 1985—; host/prodr. (TV weekly public affairs show) Stateline Newsmakers, 1990-92; columnist (weekly) Rockford Register Star, 1991-92. Recipient Silver Dome award Ill. Broadcasters Assn., 1993, 95, 96; grantee Earhart Found., 1988. Mem.: So. Calif. Grant Makers, L.A. World Affairs Coun., Phila. Soc., Town Hall L.A. Republican. Avocations: travel abroad, history, geography. Office: So Calif Children's Scholarship Fund 626 Wilshire Blvd #515 Los Angeles CA 90017 Business E-Mail: mwarder@sccsf.org.

WARDER, RICHARD CURREY, JR., dean, mechanical aerospace engineering educator; b. Nitro, W.Va., Sept. 30, 1936; s. Richard Currey and Edith Irene (Moser) W.; m. Carolyn Strickler, Mar. 7, 1964 (div. Dec. 1978); children: Jennifer, Jeffrey W.; m. Marjorie Dianne Forney, Jan. 10, 1981. BS, S.D. Sch. Mines, 1958; MS, Northwestern U., 1959, PhD, 1963. Registered profl. engr., Mo., Tenn. Asst. prof. Northwestern U., Evanston, Ill., 1963-65; mgr. energy processes research Litton Industries, Beverly Hills, Calif., 1965-68; assoc. prof. mech. and aerospace engring. U. Mo., Columbia, 1968-72, prof., 1972-94, James C. Dowell prof., 1989-94, chmn. mech. aerospace engring., 1988-94; dean U. Memphis Herff Coll. Engring., 1994—. Program mgr., head resources sect. NSF, Washington, 1974-76; mem. Engring. Accreditation Commn., 2003—; cons. to industry U.S. govt. Bd. dirs. Columbia Montessori Sch., 1971-73; bd. dirs. Columbia Soccer Club, 1976-80, pres., 1978-80; referee Maj. Indoor Soccer League, 1979-83. Fellow: ASME, AIAA (assoc.); mem.: AAAS, Am. Assn. Aerosol Rsch., Am. Soc. Engring. Edn., Am. Phys. Soc. Methodist.

WARDINSKI, BRUCE DAVID, hotel chain executive; b. Ft. Benning, Ga., Apr. 14, 1960; s. Michael Leon and Nancy Kathleen (Long) W. BS in Commerce, U. Va., 1982; MBA, U. Pa., 1987. Various positions Marriott Corp., 1987—93; v.p.- project fin. Host Marriott Corp., 1993—95, sr. v.p.- internat. develop., 1995—96, sr. v.p. and treas., 1996—98; pres., CEO, chmn. Crestline Capital Corp., 1999—2002; pres., CEO Barceló Crestline Corp., 2002—. Bd. dirs. Riverside Civic Assn., Mt. Vernon, Va., 1976-78. Rockwell Internat. Found. fellow, 1985-87. Mem. Am. Inst. CPA's. Roman Catholic. Avocations: running, basketball, carpentry. Office: Crestline Capital Corp 6600 Rockledge Dr Bethesda MD 20817-1806

WARDLAW, KIM A.M. federal judge; b. San Francisco, July 2, 1954; m. William M. Wardlaw Sr., Sept. 8, 1984. Student, Santa Clara U., 1972—73, Foothill C.C., Los Altos Hills, Calif., 1973—74; AB in Comm. summa cum laude, UCLA, 1976, JD with honors, 1979. Bar: Calif., U.S. Dist. Ct. (ctrl. dist.) Calif. 1979, U.S. Dist. Ct. (so. dist.) Calif. 1982, U.S. Dist. Ct. Nev. 1985, U.S. Dist. Ct. (no. dist.) Calif. 1992, U.S. Dist. Ct. Mont. 1993, U.S. Dist. Ct. Minn. 1994, U.S. Dist. Ct. (no. dist.) Ala. 1994, U.S. Dist. Ct. (so. dist.) Miss. 1995, U.S. Supreme Ct. Law clk. U.S. Dist. Ct. Ctrl. Dist. Calif., 1979—80; assoc. O'Melveny and Myers, 1980—87, ptnr., 1987—95; cir. judge U.S. Dist. Ct. Calif., LA, 1995—98, U.S. Ct. Appeals (9th cir.), 1998—. Presdl. transition team Dept. Justice, Washington, 1993; mayoral transition team City of LA, 1995—; bd. govs. UCLA Ctr. for Comm. Policy, 1994—, vice-chair, 1994—; cons. in field. Co-author: The Encyclopedia of the American Constitution, 1986; contbr. articles to profl. jours. Pres. Women Lawyers Pub. Action Grant Found., 1986—87; founding mem. LA Chamber Orch., 1992—; active Legal Def. and Edn. Fund Calif. Leadership Coun., 1993—; active Blue Ribbon of LA Music Ctr., 1993—; del. Dem. Nat. Conv., 1992. Named one of Most Prominent Bus. Attys. in LA County, LA Bus. Jour., 1995; recipient Buddy award, NOW, 1995. Mem.: NOW, ABA, Orgn. Women Execs., Assn. Bus. Trial Lawyers (gov. 1988—), LA County Bar Assn. (trustee 1993—94), Women Lawyers Assn. LA, Calif. Women Lawyers, Mex.-Am. Bar Assn. LA County, Hollywood Womens Polit. Com., Downtown Women Ptnrs., City Club Bunker Hill, Breakfast Club, Chancery Club, Phi Beta Kappa. Mailing: US Court of Appeals 9th Circuit PO Box 193939 San Francisco CA 94119-3939 Office: US Court of Appeals 9th Circuit 95 Seventh St San Francisco CA 94119

WARDLOW, BILL, record industry consultant, entertainer; b. Columbus, Ohio, Jan. 2, 1921; s. Clayton Jesse and Angeline Naomi (Peckham) W. BBA, Ohio State U., 1942; cert., Am. Mgmt. Assn., N.Y.C., 1964. Vice pres. Capitol Records, Los Angeles, 1947-56; gen. mgr. Columbia Record Club, N.Y.C., 1957-61; exec. v.p. Hammond Industries, N.Y.C., 1961-64; assoc. pub. Billboard Mag., N.Y.C., 1964-83; pres. Bill Wardlow & Assocs., Los Angeles, 1983—; ptnr. Dealmakers Connection, Inc., Los Angeles, 1983—; cons. to disco industry, worldwide, 1974-83. Author: (preface) This Business of Disco, 1976, (biography) Against All Odds, 1999; TV appearances include 60 Minutes, Merv Griffin Show, Mike Douglas Show, Ted Turner Network, Good Morning America. Named Father of Disco, Rec. Industry Am., 1976; recipient numerous Gold and Platinum records, 1974-83 Mem. Regines Club (N.Y.C. and Paris). Episcopalian. Home and Office: 2212 Laurel Canyon Blvd Los Angeles CA 90046-1503 *Always be interested in the careers of those around you; i.e., recording artists. Discover them, help in every way possible for them to achieve stardom. And by helping others reach their goals, you have automatically reached yours.*

WARDROP, RICHARD M., JR., former steel holding company executive; b. McKeesport, Pa. BS In Metall. Engring., Pa. State U.; postgrad., U. Pitts. Various positions U.S. Steel Corp., 1968—92, sr. buyer raw materials, 1980—81, supt. flat-rolled products group Gary, Ind., 1981—84, divsn. mgr. for steel prodn., casting and primary rolling, 1984—86, plant mgr. for primary ops., 1986—88, gen. mgr. Mongehela Valley Works, 1988; corp. v.p. engring. and purchasing Washington (Pa.) Steel Corp; v.p. mfg. AK Steel Holding Corp., Middletown, Ohio, 1992—95, CEO, 1995—2003, chmn., 1997—2003. Named Platinum 400 List, Forbes Mag., 1999. Mem.: Am. Iron and Steel Engrs., Am. Soc. Metals Internat. (David Ford McFarland award for achievement in metallurgy 1995), AIME.

WARDROPPER, IAN BRUCE, museum curator, educator; b. Balt., May 11, 1951; s. Bruce Wear and Joyce (Vaz) W.; stepmother: Nancy Hélène (Palmer) W.; m. Laurel Ellen Bradley, May 22, 1982 (div. 1996); 1 child, Chloe Bradley; m. Sarah Anne McNear, June 21, 1997. BA, Brown U., 1973; MA, NYU, 1976, PhD, 1985. Asst. curator European sculpture Art Inst. Chgo., 1982-85, assoc. curator European decorative arts and sculpture, 1985-89, Eloise W. Martin curator European decorative arts and sculpture, and classical art, 1989-2001; Iris and B. Gerald Cantor curator in charge dept. European sculpture and decorative arts Met. Mus. Art, N.Y.C., 2001—. Adj. instr. Drew U., NJ, 1982; vis. asst. prof. Northwestern U., Evanston, Ill., 1986, Sch. of Art Inst. Chgo., 1988; guest scholar J. Paul Getty Mus., Malibu, Calif., 1995; Rhoades lectr. U. Chgo., 1997; exhbns. panelist NEA, 1993, creation and presentation panelist, 98, indemnity panelist, 1998—2001. Co-author: European Decorative Arts in the Art Institute of Chicago, 1991, Austrian Architecture and Design beyond Tradition in the 1990s, 1991, News from a Radiant Future: Soviet Porcelain from the Collection of Craig H. and Kay A. Tuber, 1992, Chiseled with a Brush: Italian Sculpture, 1860-1925, from The Gilgore Collections, 1994, From the Sculptor's Hand: Italian Baroque Terracottas from the State Hermitage Museum, 1998; contbr. articles to profl. jours. NEA fellow, 1976-77, Chester Dale fellow Met. Mus. Art, 1978-79; Kress Found. rsch. grantee, Paris, 1979-81, Am. Philos. Soc. grantee, 1991; named Chicagoan of the Yr. in Arts Chicago Tribune, 1994. Mem. Phi Beta Kappa. Office: Met Mus Art 1000 Fifth Ave New York NY 10028-0198 Office Phone: 212-879-5500 x4980. Business E-Mail: Ian.wardropper@Metmuseum.org.

WARD-STEINMAN, DAVID, composer, music educator, pianist; b. Alexandria, La., Nov. 6, 1936; s. Irving Steinman and Daisy Leila (Ward) W.-S.; m. Susan Diana Lucas, Dec. 28, 1956 (div. 1993); children: Jenna, Matthew; m. Patrice Dawn Madura, May 28, 2001. MusB cum laude, Fla. State U., 1957; MusM, U. Ill., 1958, DMA, 1961; studies with Nadia Boulanger, Paris, 1958-59; postdoctoral vis. fellow, Princeton U., 1970. Grad. instr. U. Ill., 1957-58; mem. faculty San Diego State U., 1961—2003, prof. music, 1968—, disting. prof. music, emeritus prof., 2004, dir. comprehensive musicianship program, 1972—2003, composer in residence, 1961—, univ. research lectr., 1986-87. Faculty Eastman Sch. Music Workshop, 1969, Coll. Music Soc. Nat. Inst. for Music in Gen. Studies, U. Colo., 1983-84, Calif. State Summer Sch. for the Arts, Loyola Marymount U., 1988; Ford Found. composer in residence Tampa Bay (Fla.) Area, 1970-72, Brevard Music Ctr., N.C., 1986; acad. cons. U. North Sumatra (Indonesia), 1982; concert and lecture tour U.S. Info. Agy., Indonesia, 1982; master tchr. in residence Atlantic Ctr. for the Arts, New Smyrna Beach, Fla., 1996; vis. artist in residence Victorian Ctr. for the Arts, Melbourne, Australia, 1997, faculty Coll. Mus. Soc. Nat. Insts., San Diego, 1999, 2001, 2003, Ind., 2003; adj. prof. music Ind. U., 2004. Composer: Symphony, 1959, Prelude & Toccata for orch., 1962, Concerto No. 2 for chamber orch., 1962, ballet Western Orpheus, 1964, Cello Concerto, 1966, These Three ballet, 1966, The Tale of Issoumbochi chamber opera, 1968, Rituals for Dancers and Musicians, 1971, Antares, 1971, Arcturus, 1972, The Tracker, 1976, Brancusi's Brass Beds, 1977; oratorio Song of Moses, 1964; Jazz Tangents, 1967, Childs Play, 1968; 3-act opera Tamar, 1977; Golden Apples, 1981; choral suite Of Wind and Water, 1982; Christmas cantata And In These Times, 1982; Moiré for piano and chamber ensemble, 1983, And Waken Green, song cycle on poems by Douglas Worth, 1983, Olympics Overture for orchestra, 1984, Children's Corner Revisited, song cycle, 1984, Summer Suite for oboe and piano, 1984, Quintessence for double quintet and percussion, 1985, Chroma concerto for multiple keyboards, percussion and chamber orch., 1985, Winging It for chamber orchestra, 1986, Elegy for Astronauts for orchestra, 1986, What's Left for piano, 1987, Gemini for 2 guitars, 1988, Intersections II: Borobudur, Under Capricorn, 1989, Voices from the Gallery, 1990, Cinnabar for viola and piano, 1991, Seasons Fantastic for chorus and harp, 1992, Cinnabar Concerto for Viola and Chamber Orchestra, 1993, Night Winds Quintet # 2 for woodwinds, 1993, Double Concerto for Two Violins and Orchestra, 1995, Prisms and Reflections (3rd Piano Sonata), 1996, Millennium Fanfare for symph. orch., 2000, Millennium Dances for symph. orch., 2001, FIESTA! for symphony orch., 2002, FLIGHT! for 2 Pianos, 2002; recs. include Fragments from Sappho, 1969; Duo for cello and piano, 1974, Childs Play for bassoon and piano, 1974, The Tracker, 1989, Brancusi's Brass Beds, 1984, concert suite from Western Orpheus, 1987, Sonata for Piano Fortified, 1987, Moiré, 1987, 3 Songs for Clarinet and Piano, 1987, Concerto #2 for Chamber Orchestra, 1990, Prisms and Reflections, 1999, Cinnabar, 1999, Sonata for Piano Fortified, 1999, Night Winds, 1999, Borobudur, 1999, Cello Concerto, 2000, Cinnabar Concerto, 2000, Chroma Concerto, 2000, I Am the Wind for voice and chamber ensemble, 2002; commd. by Chgo. Symphony, Joffrey Ballet, San Diego Ballet, San Diego Symphony, numerous others; author: (with Susan L. Ward-Steinman) Comparative Anthology of Musical Forms, 2 vols, 1976, Toward a Comparative Structural Theory of the Arts, 1989. Recipient Joseph H. Bearns prize in Music Columbia U., 1961, SAI Am. Music award, 1962, Dohnanyi award Fla. State U., 1965, ann. BMI awards, 1970—, Broadcast Music prize, 1954, 55, 60, 61; named Outstanding Prof., Calif. State Univs. and Colls., 1968, Outstanding Alumnus of Yr., Fla. State U., 1976; Fulbright sr. scholar La Trobe U. and Victorian Coll. Arts, Victorian Arts Ctr., Melbourne, Australia, 1989-90. Mem. Coll. Music Soc. (nat. bd. for composition 1991-93), Broadcast Music, Inc., Soc. of Composers, inc., Nat. Assn. of Composers U.S.A., Golden State Flying Club. Presbyterian. Office: San Diego State U Dept Music San Diego CA 92182 Business E-Mail: dwardste@mail.sdsu.edu.

WARD-STEINMAN, PATRICE MADURA, music educator; b. Hammond, Ind., May 19, 1952; d. Michael John and Henrietta Pearl (Kaminski) Madura; m. David Ward-Steinman, May 28, 2001. BS in Music Edn., Ind. State U., 1974; MA in Music, San Diego State U., 1981; Dr.Music Edn., Ind. U., 1992. Cert. tchr. Calif. Music tchr. Elliott-Pope Prep Sch., Idyllwild, Calif., 1984—86, Ft. Bragg Pub. Schs., Calif., 1986—88; assoc. instr. Ind. U., Bloomington, 1988—91; asst. prof. Ind. U.-Purdue U., Ft. Wayne, 1991—94, Oberlin Coll. Conservatory of Music, Ohio, 1994—95; assoc. prof., chair dept. music edn. U. So. Calif., L.A., 1995—2003; assoc. prof., chair dept. music Ind. U. Sch. Music, Bloomington, 2003—. Vocal jazz clinician Ctrl. Conn. State U., New Britain, 2000, 02, Music Educators Nat. Conf., Reston, Va., 1998—2003; mem. coun. of reps. Calif. Music Edn. Assn., Portola, 1997—2000. Author: Getting Started with Vocal Improvisation, 1999; contbr. articles to profl. jours. Grantee Outreach in Music grantee, U. So. Calif., 2003. Mem.: Am. Choral Dirs. Assn., Internat. Assn. Jazz Edn., Music Educators Nat. Conf. Avocations: travel, swimming, flying. Office: Indiana Univ Sch of Music 1201 E Third St Bloomington IN 47405 Home: 1159 E Winners Cir Bloomington IN 47401 Office Phone: 812-855-7738.

WARDY, JOE, mayor; b. El Paso, Tex., 1953; s. Joe and Mary Rodriguez Wardy; m. Delores Prouse Wardy; children: Kaleb, David. B in fin., U. of Tex. at El Paso, 1976. With Herman/Miles Trucking, Inc., 1985, ptnr., pres.; COO Miles Group, Inc., 2000; mayor City of El Paso, Tex., 2003—. Mem. Frank Manning Little League Bd.; pres. Franklin Football Booster Club; mem. Tex. Assn. of Football Ofcls.; exec. com. Greater El Paso C. of C.; chmn. El Paso Leadership and Rsch. Coun.; adv. bd. Liberty Mutual Ins. Southwest; bd. dir. North Am. Transp. Alliance, Candlelighters of El Paso; exec. com. Tex. Motor Transp. Assn.; mktg. and mgmt. adv. bd. U. of Tex. at El Paso; v.p. at large Am. Trucking Assn. Office: Joe Wardy, Mayor of El Paso 2 Civic Ctr Plaza, 10th Fl El Paso TX 79901

WARE, ALBERTA, minister, educator; b. Chgo., Mar. 23, 1943; d. Lucille and Lamar, Jr. Coleman(Stepfather); 1 child, Paula Marie West. BS, San Diego State, 1966. Prin. Cabrini-Green Alternative H.S., Chicago, Ill., 1973—77; min., tchr., outreach min., dir. of youth dept. (full & part-time) Christ Universal Temple, Chicago, Ill., 1982—93; program coord., instr. & student affairs asst. City Colleges of Chgo. - Olive/Harvey Coll., Chicago, Ill., 1988—98; asst. pastor South Side Unity Ctr. of Christianity, Chicago, Ill., 1995—97, pastor, 1997—2001; dir. ch. & cmty. moblzn./tng. The Balm In Gilead, N.Y., NY, 1999—. Program dir./ctr. assoc. Nat. Coll. Edn. Ctr. Prog. Devel. in Equal Edn. Opportunity, Evanston, Ill., 1978—81. Mem.: The Coun. Religious AIDS Networks, Nat. HIV Vaccine Comm. Steering Group. Avocations: travel, reading, dance, art, sewing. Office: The Balm In Gilead 130 West 42nd Street New York NY 10036 Personal E-mail: alware@balmingilead.org.

WARE, BENNIE, university administrator; b. Ponca City, Okla., Sept. 21, 1946; s. Clyde Elmer and Lois Aliene (Smith) W.; m. Sheridan Lee Welch, May 28, 1967 (div. 1976); 1 child, Winston Arthur; m. Claudia Borman, Dec. 21, 1979 (div. 1998); children: Jeffrey Bright, Amelia Marie; m. Eleanor Gallagher, Mar. 7, 1998. BS in Chemistry, Okla. State U., 1968; PhD in Biophys. Chemistry, U. Ill., 1972. Asst. prof. chemistry Harvard U., Cambridge, Mass., 1972-75, assoc. prof., 1975-79; prof., chmn. dept. chemistry Syracuse U., 1979-84, Kenan prof. sci., 1984-91, v.p. rsch., 1989-92, v.p. rsch., computing, 1992—. Contbr. articles to profl. jours. Grantee NSF, 1972, 74, 77, 80, 83, 86, 89, NIH, 1972, 74, 76, 77, 79, 81, 84, 86; Alfred P. Sloan fellow, 1976-80. Fellow AAAS; mem. Phi Beta Kappa, Phi Kappa Phi. Achievements include invention of electrophoretic light scattering; first to combine laser light scattering and fluorescence photobleaching recovery to distinguish mutual and tracer diffusion; first to apply laser Doppler velocimetry to protoplasmic streaming. Home: 333 Berkeley Dr Syracuse NY 13210-3041 Office: Syracuse Univ 3-014D Ctr Sci And Tech Syracuse NY 13244-0001 Office Phone: 315-443-2492. Business E-Mail: brware@syr.edu.

WARE, BRENDAN JOHN, retired electrical engineer and utility executive; b. Dublin, Aug. 27, 1932; arrived in U.S., 1959, naturalized, 1967; m. Jane Mills Orth, Oct. 7, 1961; children: Michael, Henry, Frieda. B.E. with honors, Nat. U. Ireland, Dublin, 1954; MSE.E., Newark Coll. Engring., 1967. Various engring. positions Am. Elec. Power Service Corp., N.Y.C., 1960-76, mgr. elec. research and tech. svcs. Columbus, Ohio, 1976-96. Contbr. articles to profl. jours. Fellow: IEEE. Roman Catholic. Home: 2478 Bryden Rd Columbus OH 43209-2132 E-mail: bware@columbus.rr.com.

WARE, CARL, bottling company executive; b. Newnan, Ga., Sept. 30, 1943; s. U.B. and Lois (Wimberly) W.; m. Mary Clark, Jan. 1 1966; 1 son, Timothy Alexander. BA, Clark Coll., 1965; M.P.A., U. Pitts., 1968; postgrad., Carnegie Mellon U., 1965-66. Dir. Atlanta Housing Authority, 1970-73; pres. city council City of Atlanta, 1974-79; v.p. The Coca-Cola Co., Atlanta, 1974-86, sr. v.p., 1986-2000, exec. v.p., 2000—. Dir. Ga. Power Co. Mem. adv. council U.S. Civil Rights Commn., 1983; bd. dirs. Nat. Council Black Agencies, 1983—, United Way of Met. Atlanta, 1983—; trustee Clark Coll. Mem. Gammon Theol. Sem. (trustee), Ga. State U. Found. (trustee), Sigma Pi Phi Democrat. Methodist. Office: The Coca-Cola Co PO Box 1734 Atlanta GA 30301-1734

WARE, CARL, immunologist; s. Utah and Elizabeth Ware; m. Kim Ware, Oct. 28, 1981; children: Austin, Brian. PhD, Univ. Calif., Irvine, 1979. NIH postdoctoral fellow Dana Farber Cancer Inst., Boston, 1981—82; prof. immunology U. Calif., Riverside, Calif., 1982—96; scientist and head Divsn. of Molecular Immunology, La Jolla Inst. for Allergy and Immunology, San Diego, 1996—; prof., dept. biology U. Calif., San Diego, 1997—. Chair, allergy and immunology study sect. NIH, Bethesda, Md., 2002—. Editor: (research journal) The TNF Superfamily; scientist (research) Lymphotoxin ? and LIGHT Cytokine Systems (Nat. Merit Award, Pub. Health Svc., NIAID, 2003). Grantee Anti-herpesvirus Signaling by LT? LIGHT Cytokines, Nat. Inst. for Allergy and Infectious Diseases, 2001-2006. Mem.: Internat. Congress for TNF-Related Cytokines (pres. 2002), Internat. Cytokine Soc. (sec. 1997—2001), Am. Soc. for Biochemistry and Molecular Biology, Am. Assn. of Immunologists (program com. 2003—). Achievements include patents for Lymphotoxin-ab Complexes, Pharmaceutical Preparation and Therapeutic Uses There of. US Patent No. 5, 670, 149. Office: La Jolla Inst for Allergy and Immun 10355 Sci Ctr Dr San Diego CA 92075 Business E-Mail: cware@liai.org.

WARE, DAVID JOSEPH, financial consultant; b. Oberlin, Ohio, Dec. 1, 1928; s. Elmer Edwin and Jessie VanStone (Potter) W.; m. Diane Sue Adams, Sept. 12, 1958 (dec. July 1980); m. Mary Ann Spadafora, Aug. 15, 1981; children: Stacey Whitman, Joel Potter. BA, DePauw U., 1950; postgrad., Miami U., 1950—51, postgrad., 1954—55. CFP. Grain trader Glidden Co., Chgo., 1955-57; dept. mgr. Merrill Lynch, San Francisco, 1958-59; br. and regional mgmt. Dean Witter Reynolds, San Francisco, 1969-92; prin. Experts Co., Mill Valley, Calif., 1992—. Panelist, guest lectr. U. Calif., Berkeley, 1970-71; instr. Golden Gate U., San Francisco, 1987-89; adj. prof. Coll. Fin. Planning, Denver, 1986-87. Counselor Jr. Achievement, San Francisco, 1963; bd. dirs. Jr. C. of C., Mill Valley, 1964, Joint Powers Authority, Marin County, Calif., 1992-96, Marin County Local Agy. Formation Commn., 1995-2000, chmn., 1998-99; com. chmn. San Francisco C. of C., 1975-78; v.p. Marin County Spl. Dists. Assn., 1995; bd. chmn. Strawberry Dist., Marin County, 1996; mem. exec. bd. Calif. Local Agy. Formation Commn., 1998—2000. Recipient Achievement award Chgo. Bd. of Trade, 1956. Mem. Nat. Assn. SEC Dealers (panelist), Assn. Cert. Fin. Planners, Nat. Futures Assn. (panelist), N.Y. Stock Exch. (panelist, disciplinary com. 1975-92), Olympic Club (chmn. house com. 1987), Soc. for Preservation and Encouraging of Barbershop Quartet Singing, Phi Beta Kappa, Alpha Delta Sigma. Republican. Avocations: tennis, handball, sailing, bridge, reading. Home and Office: PO Box 622 Mill Valley CA 94942

WARE, GEORGE HENRY, botanist; b. Avery, Okla., Apr. 27, 1924; s. Charles and Mildred (Eshelman) W.; m. June Marie Gleason, Dec. 21, 1955; children: David, Daniel, Patrick, John. BS, U. Okla., 1945, MS, 1948; PhD, U. Wis., 1955. Asst. prof. Northwestern State U. of La., Natchitoches, 1948-56, assoc. prof., 1956-62, prof., 1962-67; dir. Conservation Sect., No. La. Supplementary Edn. Ctr., Natchitoches, 1967-68; dendrologist Morton Arboretum, Lisle, Ill., 1968-92; adminstr. Urban Vegetation Lab., 1986-92, rsch. fellow in dendrology, 1992-94, dendrologist emeritus, rsch. assoc., 1995—. Vis. prof. U. Okla., Norman, summers, 1957, 61, 63, 64; adj. prof. Western Ill. U., 1972-85; mem. extension faculty George Williams Coll., Downers Grove, Ill., 1969-76, Nat. Coll. Edn., Evanston, Ill., 1972-76, adj. prof. Aurora U., 2003—. Trustee nomination caucus Coll. of DuPage, Glen Ellyn, Ill., 1974-78; bd. dirs. Kane-DuPage Soil and Water Conservation Dist., 1969-81, DuPage Environ. Commn., 1992—, Openlands Project, 1996—; pres. La. Acad. Scis., 1966-67; dir. La. State Sci. Fair, 1966. With USN, 1942-46. Recipient Gold Seal award, Nat. Coun. State Garden Clubs, 1991, Am. Forests Urban Forestry Rsch. medal, 1994, Lifetime Svc. award, Nat. Urban and Cmty. Forestry Adv. Coun., 1995, Hutchinson medal, Chgo. Botanic Garden, 1997, Norman J. Colman award, Am. Nursery and Landscape Assn., 1998, award of merit, Am. Assn. Botanic Gardens and Arboreta, 2000, Liberty Hyde Bailey award, Am. Horticultural Soc., 2002. Mem.: Am. Forests, Nature Conservancy, Ill. Arborist Assn. (pres. 1987—88), Am. Assn. Bot. Gardens and Arboreta, Internat. Soc. Arboriculture (Pres. Commendation award 2000), Southwestern Assn. Naturalists (treas. 1963—69). Office: Morton Arboretum Lisle IL 60532-1293 Office Phone: 630-968-0074. Business E-Mail: gware@mortonarb.org.

WARE, J(OE) ANTHONY, cardiologist; b. Topeka, Dec. 12, 1952; s. Joe F. and Jane C. (Casper) Ware; children: Gabriel, Rachel, Emily. BS summa cum laude, Washburn U., 1974; MD, Kans. U., 1977. Diplomate Am. Bd. Internal Medicine, Am. Bd. Cardiovasc. Disease. Intern, resident Baylor Coll. Medicine, Houston, 1977-81, chief resident, 1981, clin. fellow in cardiovasc. disease, 1981-84; rsch. fellow Beth Israel Hosp., Med. Sch. Harvard U., Boston, 1984-86, assoc. prof. medicine, 1986-97; Sidney L. & Miriam K. Olson prof. cardiology Albert Einstein Coll. Medicine and Montefiore Med. Ctr., N.Y.C., 1997-2001, chief cardiovasc. divsn., 1997-2001; v.p. cardiovasc. rsch. and clin. investigation Eli Lilly and Co., Indpls., 2001—. Dir. CCU Beth Israel Hosp., Med. Sch. Harvard U., 1992—93, dir. vascular biol. unit, 1992—97. Author, editor: book Angiogenesis in Cardiovascular Disease, 1999; contbr. articles to profl. jours. Fellow: Am. Coll. Cardiology; mem.: Molecular Medicine Soc., Assn. Profs. Cardiology, Assn. Univ. Cardiologists, Am. Soc. Clin. Investigation, Am. Heart Assn., Am. Soc. Cell Biology, Am. Soc. Hematology, Assn. Am. Physicians, Interurban Clin. Club. Office: Eli Lilly Corp Ctr DC 0520 Indianapolis IN 46285 E-mail: jaware@lilly.com.

WARE, JUDITH BOYD, education educator; b. NYC, Jan. 20, 1948; d. James Boyd and Emma Coulter Ware; children: Justin, Margaret. B, Lake Erie Coll., 1970; M, U. Colo. at Boulder, 1973. Editor Mountain Guides, Aspen, Colo., 1977; staff Ctr. for Econ. Edn., St. Louis, 1987—88; social studies tchr. Mary Inst., St. Louis, 1981—88, Crossroads Sch., 1988—2001; prof. U. Mo., St. Louis, 1999—2001; adj. prof. Fontbonne U., 2000—; program dir. Mo. Geog. Alliance, St. Louis, 1998—. Bd. mem. Fed. Res. Bank Tchr. Adv. Bd., St. Louis, 1986—. Author (also editor): (book) Hiking Guide to Aspen, 1979; contbr. articles. Bd. mem. The Wolf Sanctuary, St. Louis, 1973—82. Mem.: Mo. Geog. Alliance, Nat. Coun. for Geog. Edn. Com. Curriculum and Instrn. Home: 105 Linden Ave Saint Louis MO 63105 Office: Fontbonne U 6800 Wydown Blvd Saint Louis MO 63105

WARE, RICHARD ANDERSON, foundation executive; b. N.Y.C., Nov. 7, 1919; s. John Sayers and Mabelle (Anderson) W.; m. Lucille Henney, Mar. 20, 1942 (div. 1972); children: Alexander W., Janet M., Bradley J., Patricia E.; m. Beverly G. Mytinger, Dec. 22, 1972. BA, Lehigh U., 1941; M in Pub. Adminstrn., Wayne State U., 1943; D in Social Sci. (honoris causa), Francisco Marroquin U., Guatemala, 1988. Research asst. Detroit Bur. Govt. Research, 1941-42; personnel technician Lend-Lease Adminstrn., Washington, 1942-43; research asso. to asst. dir. Citizens Research Council, Detroit, 1946-56; sec. Earhart and Relm Founds., Ann Arbor, Mich., 1951-70, trustee, pres., 1970-84, trustee, pres. emeritus, 1985—; ret., 1984. Prin. dep. asst. sec. def. for internat. security affairs, Washington, 1969-70; cons. Office Asst. Sec. Def., 1970-73; dir. Citizens Trust Co., 1970-87. Vice pres. Ann Arbor United Fund and Cmty. Svcs., 1968, pres., 1969; asst. dir. Mich. Joint Legis. Com. on State Reorgn., 1950-52; sec. Gov.'s Com. to Study Prisons, 1952-53; com. to chmn. Ann Arbor City Planning Commn., 1958-67; mem. Detroit Com. on Fgn. Rels., 1971-87; mem. coun. Woodrow Wilson Internat. Center for Scholars, 1977-85; vis. com. divsn. social scis. U. Chgo., 1977-85; mem. adv. com. The Citadel, 1977-85; mem. adv. coun. internat. studies program Fletcher Sch., Tufts U., 1979-85; trustee Greenhills Sch., 1973-80, Ann Arbor Area Found., 1977-83, Inst. Fgn. Policy Analysis, 1985-2003, Inst. Polit. Economy, 1985—, Ctr. for Study Social and Polit. Change Smith Coll., 1988—, Pequawket Found., 1989—, Intercollegiate Studies Inst., 1996—; polit. analyst Rep. Nat. Com., Washington, 1964; bd. dirs. The Liberty Fund, Inc., Indpls., 1980—, Bd. Fgn. Scholarships, 1984-90, chmn., 1987-89. With USAAF, 1943-46. Recipient Civilian Meritorious Service medal Dept. Def., 1970; Paul Harris fellow Rotary, 1997. Fellow Mont Pelerin Soc.; mem. Govtl. Research Assoc. (trustee, v.p. 1955-56), Am. Polit. Sci. Assn., Ann Arbor Club, North Conway Country Club, Cosmos Club (Washington), Phi Beta Kappa, Phi Alpha Theta Congregationalist. Home: PO Box 310 Intervale NH 03845-0310 Office: 2200 Green Rd Ste H Ann Arbor MI 48105-1569

WARE, ROBERT K. Internet company executive, researcher, web programmer; b. Dallas, Dec. 6, 1930; s. Clinton L. and Margie Ware; m. Virginia L. Greene, June 8, 1954; children: James K., Janette K. Stalemo, Joan K. BS, U. Tex., Austin, 1958; PhD, Ohio State U., 1961. Rsch. engr. Owens-Ill., Toledo, 1961—67, sect. mgr., 1967—73; rsch. mgr. Johns-Manville, Waterville, Ohio, 1973—76, sr. rsch. assoc. Littleton, 1976—82; UNIX sys. adminstr. U. Denver, 1982—84, Colo. Sch. Mines, Golden, 1984—96; pres. Study Techs., Centennial, Colo., 1996—. Internet search engine programmer Onelook.com. Author: (internet search engine) Onelook.com. Regional chmn., senate election Libertarians, Toledo, 1974. With U.S. Army, 1951—53, Korea. Mem.: Am. Ceramic Soc. Libertarian. Scientologist. Achievements include development of improved way to fully get the meaning of a word, myword.info.

WARE, RUTH WINCHESTER, social worker; b. Asheville, N.C., June 4, 1939; d. William Ernest and Blanche Chandler Winchester; m. Philip Wayne Ware, Jan. 11, 1964; 1 child, Judith Ware Dasseux. BA, Wake Forest U., 1961; MA, Trinity U., 1968; MSW, U. Tenn., 1981, PhD, 1993. LCSW N.C. Clin. social worker Overlook Mental Health Ctr., Knoxville, 1976—91, Child & Family, Inc., 1991—2002; clin. care mgr. ValueOptions, Durham, NC, 2002—. Author: Journey to Root Beer, 2003. Democrat. Unitarian. Home: 6 Chartwell Ct Durham NC 27703

WARE, SUSAN W. historian; b. Wash., DC, Aug. 22, 1950; d. Charles Kline and Charlotte McConnell Wolfe; m. Donald R. Ware, June 10, 1972. BA, Wellesley Coll., 1968—72; MA, Harvard U., 1973, PhD, 1978. Asst. to assoc. prof. NYU, 1986—95; hon. vis. scholar Radcliffe Coll., 1996—97; editor, Notable Am. Women Radcliffe Inst. for Advanced Study, Harvard U., 1997—; vis. lectr., history Harvard U., 2002—. Adv. bd. Schlesinger Libr., Cambridge, Mass., 1988—97, Franklin and Eleanor Roosevelt Inst., Hyde Park, NY, 1986—; assoc. Clio, Inc., Charlotte, Vt., 1996—; exec. bd. Soc. of Am. Historians, N.Y.C., 1990—. Author: (books) Beyond Suffrage: Women in the New Deal, Letter to the World: Seven Women Who Shaped the Am. Century; editor: Forgotten Heroes: Inspiring Am. Portraits from our Leading Historians; author: Holding Their Own: Am. Women in the 1930s, Ptnr. and I: Molly Dewson, Feminism, and New Deal Politics, Still Missing: Amelia Earhart and the Search for Modern Feminism. Home: 16 Hilliard St Cambridge MA 02138 Office: Radcliffe Inst for Advanced Study 10 Garden St Cambridge MA 02138 Personal E-mail: sdware@aol.com. E-mail: ware@radcliffe.edu.

WARE, THADDEUS VAN, government official; b. High Point, N.C., Mar. 31, 1935; s. Elsec and Irene (Myers) W.; m. Doretha Ardella Lee, June 18, 1960; children— Kimberly Melissa, Chrystal Lynn. BA cum laude, Va. Union U., 1957; JD, Howard U., 1960. Bar: Va. bar 1961, D.C. bar 1970, U.S. Supreme Ct. bar 1970. Gen. atty. Office of Solicitor, Dept. Labor, 1961—66; trial counsel Chief Counsel's Office, Fed. Hwy. Adminstrn., 1966—69; staff asst. to Pres. Richard M. Nixon, 1969—70; chief adminstrv. judge, chmn. Bd. Contract Appeals, Dept. Transp., 1987—2003; ret., 2003. Served with AUS, 1960-61. Mem. Va., D.C., U.S. Supreme Ct., Fed. Bar Assns., Urban League, NAACP, Bd. Contract Appeals Judges Assn. (pres. 1988-89), Alpha Phi Alpha, Sigma Delta Tau, Alpha Kappa Mu (Disting. Career Svc. award). Home: 2213 Parallel Ln Silver Spring MD 20904-5446

WARE, WILLIAM BRETTEL, education educator; b. Glen Ridge, N.J., June 17, 1942; s. Howard Brettel and Helen Burd (Dickson) W.; m. Andrea Lou Gartley, June 24, 1967 (div. May 1989); children: Emily Dickson, Matthew Brettel, Erin Johanna Ware; m. Barbara Ann McClave Reynolds, Dec. 26, 1991; adopted children: Dianne Catherine, Kristin Elise. AB, Dartmouth Coll., 1964; MA in Tchg., Northwestern U., 1965, PhD, 1968. Classroom tchr. Chgo. Pub. Schs., 1964-65; asst. prof. U. Fla., Gainesville, 1968-73, assoc. prof., 1973-76, prof., 1976-78, U. NC, Chapel Hill, 1978—, prof. social work, 2004—. Contbr. chpts. to books and articles to profl. jours. Mgr. youth soccer team Ctrl. Carolina Youth Soccer Assn., Chapel Hill, 1980-86. Recipient J. Minor Gwynn professorship Sch. Edn., U. N.C., 1994-95, Chancellor's Award for Disting. Tchg., 1995. Mem. Am. Ednl. Rsch. Assn., Nat. Coun. on Measurement in Edn., N.C. Assn. for Rsch. in Edn. (bd. dirs., pres. 1996-97, treas. 1998—). Home: 907 Bayberry Dr Chapel Hill NC 27517-8378 Office: Sch Edn Univ North Carolina Cb # 3500 Chapel Hill NC 27599-3500

WARE, WILLIAM LEVI, physical education educator, researcher; b. Greenwood, Miss., May 15, 1934; s. Leslie and Catherine (Bowden) W.; m. Lottie Herger, Apr. 26, 1958; children: Felicia Rogene, Trevor Lesleo, Melvinia Simone. BS, Mississippi Valley State U., 1957; MA, Calif. State U., L.A., 1969; PhD, U. So. Calif., 1978. Tchr., coach Greenwood Pub. Schs., 1957-63, Bellflower (Calif.) Unified Sch. Dist., 1963-72; teaching asst. U. So. Calif., L.A., 1972-73; asst. prof. Calif. State U., Northridge, 1973-79; assoc. prof. Miss. State U., Starkville, 1979-90; prof. phys. edn., chmn. dept. Mississippi Valley State U., Itta Bena, 1990—, asst. to pres., 1995-98, cmty. outreach specialist, exec. dir. svc. learning, 1998—. Presenter in field; chmn. Delta Algebra Project Planning & Coordinating Group, 1991-93. Advisor Affirmative Action Adv. Coun., Whittier, Calif., 1977-78; bd. dirs. United Way, Starkville, 1983-86. Recipient Outstanding Svc. award Kiwanis Internat., 1985, Outstanding Educator award Greenwood Cultural Club, 1986, Presdl. citation Nat. Assn. for Equal Opportunity in Higher Edn., 1989; Inducted into Southwestern Athletic Conf. Hall of Fame, 1993; Faculty fellow Found. for Mid-South, 1994. Mem. Phi Delta Kappa (svc. award 1989), Greenwood/Leflore C. of C. (chmn. Leadership Tomorrow 1992-93). Avocations: racquetball, jogging. Office: Miss Valley State U PO Box 620 Itta Bena MS 38941-0620

WARE, WILLIS HOWARD, computer scientist; b. Atlantic City, Aug. 31, 1920; s. Willis and Ethel (Rosswork) W.; m. Floy Hoffer, Oct. 10, 1943; children— Deborah Susanne Ware Pinson, David Willis, Alison Floy Ware Manoli. BSEE, U. Pa., 1941; MSEE, MIT, 1942; PhD in Elec. Engring, Princeton U., 1951. Research engr. Hazeltine Electronics Corp., Little Neck, N.Y., 1942-46; mem. research staff Inst. Advanced Study, Princeton, N.J., 1946-51, North Am. Aviation, Downey, Calif., 1951-52; mem. corp. research staff, research engr. Rand Corp., Santa Monica, Calif., 1952—. Adj. prof. UCLA Extension Service, 1955-68; first chmn. Am. Fedn. Info. Processing Socs., 1961, 62; chmn. HEW sec.'s Adv. Com. on Automated Personal Data Systems, 1971-73; mem. Privacy Protection Study Commn., 1975-77, vice chmn., 1975-77; mem. numerous other adv. groups, spl. coms. for fed. govt., 1959— Author: Digital Computer Technology and Design, vols. I and II, 1963. Recipient Computers Scis. Man of Yr. award Data Processing Mgmt. Assn., 1975, Exceptional Civilian Svc. medal USAF, 1979, Disting. Svc. award Am. Fedn. Info. Processing Socs., 1986, Nat. Computer Sys. Security award Nat. Computer Sys. Lab./Nat. Computer Security Ctr., 1989, Computer Pioneer award IEEE Computer Soc., 1993, Pioneer award Electronic Frontier Found., 1995, Kristain Beckman award Internat. Fedn. Info. Processing, 1999; named one of Fed. 100 of 1994, Fed. Computer Week. Fellow IEEE (Centennial medal 1984), AAAS, Assn. for Computing Machinery; mem. NAE, AIAA, Sigma Xi, Eta Kappa Nu, Pi Mu Epsilon, Tau Beta Pi. Office: 1700 Main St Santa Monica CA 90401-3208 E-mail: willis@rand.org.

WAREHAM, ELLSWORTH EDWIN, cardiothoracic surgeon, educator; b. Avinger, Tex., Oct. 3, 1914; s. Dayton and Goldie Leah Wareham; m. Barbara Nell Nix, May 7, 1950; children: Martin, Robert, Julie, John, Scott. At, Can. Jr. Coll., Coll. Heights, Alta., 1931—33, at, 1935—36, Can. Union Coll., Lacombe, Alta., 1936; MD, Loma Linda U., Calif., 1942; LLD (hon.), Andrews U., Berrien Springs, Mich., 1971. Cert. Am. Bd. of Surgery, 1954, Am. Bd. of Thoracic Surgery, 1955. Intern Seattle Gen. Hosp., 1942; indsl. surgeon Good News Bay Mining Co., Platinum, Alaska, 1942—45; resident fellow in surgery Loma Linda U. Med. Ctr., Calif., 1947—50; resident surgery Bellevue Hosp. Columbia U., NYC, 1950—52; resident thoracic and cardiovasc. surgery Queens Med. Ctr., NYC, 1952—53; resident cardiovasc. surgery svcs. St. Francis Hosp. Cardiac Children, Roslyn, NY, 1954—55; prof. surgery Loma Linda U., 1964—; chief cardiothoracic surgery Loma Linda U. Med. Ctr., 1964—86; acting chmn. dept. of surgery Loma Linda U., 1973—75; staff Loma Linda U. Med. Ctr., 1964—86, Riverside Gen. Hosp., Calif., 1973—75; prof. cardiac surgery King Saud U., Riyadh, Saudi Arabia, 1986—88; admin. dir. Hong Kong Heart Ctr., 1988—. Surgeon and dir., Loma Linda U. mission to Pakistan, India, Thailand and Formosa U.S. Dept. of State, 1963; surgery team Govt. of Greece, Athens, 1967—73; organizer heart surgery affiliation Evangelismos Hosp. and Loma Linda U. Sch. Medicine, 1970—76; surgeon, heart team Loma Linda U., China, 1981. Performer: (films) Atrial Septal Defect, 1964 (Golden Eagle Cine award, Venice Film Festival, 1964); contbr. articles to profl. jours. Lt.(j.g.) USN, 1945—47, PTO. Recipient Outstanding Educator of Am., 1970, award for svc. to people of Pakistan, City of Karachi, 1963, Medallion award for svc. to Greek People, Evangelismos Hosp., Athens, 1967, Golden Medal of Health, Republic of Vietnam, 1974, Outstanding Alumnus, Loma Linda U. Sch. of Med., 1974, Outstanding Contbn. to Medicine, San Bernardino County Med. Soc., 1986, Outstanding Achievement award in medicine, Ministry of Def. and Aviation, Saudi Arabia, 1986, Pres. Commendation, US, 1984, Alumnus of the Yr., Loma Linda U., 1994, Outstanding Contbn., Pasadena divsn., Am. Heart Assn., 1999. Fellow: Am. Coll. of Cardiology, Am. Coll. Surgeons; mem.: AMA, Western Assn. of Thoracic Surgery, Pacific Coast Surg. Assn., Am. Assn. for Thoracic Surgery, San Bernardino County Med. Soc., Calif. Med. Assn., Soc. of Thoracic Surgeons, Alpha Omega Alpha. Republican. Adventist. Achievements include development of heart surgery programs in Saudi Arabia, Hong Kong, developing countries. Mailing: Box 1068 Loma Linda CA 92354

WAREHAM, JOHN L. electronics executive; B in Pharmacy, Creighton U.; MBA, U. Wash. With SmithKline Beecham Corp., Phila., 1968-84, pres. Norden Labs., 1979-84; v.p. diagnostics sys. group Beckman Coulter Inc., Fullerton, Calif., 1984—, pres., COO, 1993-98, pres., CEO, chmn. bd., 1998—. Office: 4300 N Harbor Blvd Fullerton CA 92835-1091

WAREHAM, JOHN P. medical products executive; MS in Pharmacy, Creighton U.; MBA, Washington U. Various positions SmithKline, 1968—79, pres., Norden Labs., 1979—84; v.p., diagnostics sys. group Beckman Coulter, Fullerton, Calif., 1984—93, pres., COO, 1993—98, CEO, 1998—. Mem., adv. coun. Keck Grad. Inst. of Applied Life Scis.; mem., chief exec. roundtable U. Calif., Irvine; mem. Ctr. for Corp. Innovation; mem., bd. trustees Mfrs. Alliance/MAPI; dir., past chmn. AdvaMed; bd. dirs. Steris Corp., 2000—, Beckman Coulter, Fullerton, Calif., 1993—, chmn., bd. dirs., 1999—. Office: Beckman Coulter 4300 N Harbor Blvd Fullerton CA 92834*

WAREHAM, RAYMOND NOBLE, investment professional; b. Rochester, NY, Nov. 20, 1948; s. Simon Harold and Barbara (Snell) W.; m. Cornelia Lee Clifford, June 28, 1975; children: Ellinor Park, Laura Stewart, Cornelia Ashley. BS in Indsl. Engring., Northwestern U., 1970; MBA, Harvard U., 1975. With J.P. Morgan & Co., NY, 1975-80, mgr. dir., head banking industry group, 1988-92, head-corp. fin., 1980-85; exec. dir. J.P. Morgan Securities Ltd., London, 1986-87; mng. dir. corp. fin. dept. J.P. Morgan Securities, NYC, 1992-98; sr. portfolio mgr., mng. dir. Sanford C. Bernstein Alliance Capital, NYC, 1999—. Trustee Am. Sch., Tokyo, 1982-85; elder Brick Presbyn. Ch., NYC, 1989-92; bd. dir. Brick Ch. Day Sch., 1989-92, Juvenile Diabetes Found., 1997-98; pres. bd. trustees Spence Sch., NYC, 1995-2001; Life trustee, 2002-; Lt. Supply Corps, USN, 1970-73. Mem. DERU (Northwestern hon.), Naval War Coll. Found., Union Club (NY), Duxbury (Mass.) Yacht Club, Century Club (Harvard Bus. hon.). Republican. Avocations: athletics, japanese antique furniture, secondary school education. Home: 1148 5th Ave New York NY 10128-0807 Office: Alliance Capital/Sanford C Bernstein 17th Fl 1345 Ave of Americas New York NY 10105-0096

WAREN, ALLAN DAVID, computer information scientist, educator; b. Toronto, Ontario, Can., Nov. 23, 1935; s. David and Sirkka Siiri (Kahara) W.; m. Marion Veronica Halligan, Jan. 25, 1962; children: David, Melissa, Melanie, Jessica. BASc, U. Toronto, 1960; MSEE, Case Inst. Tech., Cleve., 1962, PhD, 1964. Profl. engr., Ontario. Staff engr. Clevite Electronics Research Divsn., Cleve., 1963-66; assoc. prof. Cleve. State U., 1966-69, prof., 1971-93, prof. emeritus, 1993—, interim dean Coll. Bus. Adminstrn., 1990-91, interim assoc. dean, 1997-98, interim dean, 1998-2000; chair of info. tech. Kaplan Coll., 2002. Pres. Com-Share Ltd., Toronto, 1969-71; cons. Gould, Cleve., 1974-84, Texaco, Houston, 1987-88, PPG Industries, Cleve., 1988-92, LTV Steel, 1993-96, Transat Corp., Cleve., 1996-99; v.p. Optimal Methods, Austin, Tex., 1993-2004; expert witness Rose Law Firm, 1993-95, Calfee, Halter & Griswold, 1999-2000. Co-author: Modeling and Optimization with Gino, 1986, Optimization with the IBM Optimization Subroutine Library, 1994, Handbook for IBM OSL, 1994; co-developer computer software GRG2, 1973, What-If-Solver, 1988, Excel Solver, 1991, Borland Quattro Pro Solver, 1991, Lotus1-2-3 Solver, 1997; co-author case study, 1985 (runner-up best case 1985); contbr. articles to profl. jours., chpts. to many books. Recipient Disting. Faculty Rsch. award, Cleve. State U., 1979, First Annual Faculty Rsch. award, Nance Coll. of Bus. Adminstrn., 1993, grant in Ohio Rsch. Challenge Program, State of Ohio, 1988, various other rsch. grants, 1973-84. Mem. IEEE (life), Assn. Computing Machinery, Ops. Rsch. Soc. Am., Math. Programming Soc. Avocations: oriental objects of art, stamp collecting/philately. Home: 9155 Woods Way Dr Willoughby OH 44094-9370 Office: Cleve State U E 24th and Euclid Ave Cleveland OH 44115

WAREN, STANLEY ARNOLD, university administrator, theatre and arts center administrator, director; b. N.Y.C., Mar. 22, 1919; s. Maurice and Minnie (Rosen) W.; m. Florence Rigal, Nov. 21, 1949; 1 child, Mark BSS., CCNY, 1938; MA, Columbia U., 1939, PhD, 1953. Exec. producer, dir. theatre, U.S. and abroad, 1953-70; prof., chmn. dept. speech and theatre CCNY, 1967-72; prof., exec. officer Ph.D. program theatre CUNY, 1972-81, v.p., provost, dep. pres. Grad. Sch., 1981-84; dir. Ctr. for Advanced Study in Theatre Arts, N.Y.C., 1979-82, 84-86. Reviewer NEH, 1978—91; advisor humanities com. Bklyn. Acad. Music, N.Y.C., 1980—81; spl. edn. cons. Dougle Image Theatre, N.Y.C., 1982—90; mem. adv. coun. Roundabout Theatre, N.Y.C., 1985—93; Fulbright-Hayes vis. prof. Nat. Taiwan U., 1986—87; vis. prof. Shanghai Drama Inst., 1988; USIS grant, lectr., Hong Kong, 88, Ctr. for Living and Learning, Marymount Manhattan, 1998—2004, New Sch. U., 2000—03. Dir. musical The Chess King (Taiwan) 1987, Old B Hanging on the Wall (Shanghai), 1988, Judas, Mexico (N.Y.), 1989, Seasoned Citizens Theare Co., 2003-04. Bd. dirs. Women's Inter. Art Ctr., N.Y.C., 1978-82; mem. grants panel N.Y.C. Dept. Cultural Affairs, 1979; bd. dirs. Frank Silvera Workshops for Writers, N.Y.C., 1979-81. Served to capt. USAF, 1942-46 Grantee Herman Goldman Found., 1980-82, NEH, 1980-81, N.Y. Coun. Humanities, USIA/Arts Am., Singapore, 1990. Mem. AAUP, Assn. for Theatre in Higher Edn., Soc. Stage Dirs. and Choreographers, Profl. Staff Congress CUNY, The Drama League (mem. awards nominating com. 1997—). Clubs: The Century Assn. (resident 1984—). Democrat. Avocations: art, tennis, swimming. Home: 465 W End Ave #110 New York NY 10024-4926 Office: Theatre PhD Program Grad Sch 365 5th Ave New York NY 10016-4309

WARFEL, SUSAN LEIGH, editor; b. L.A., Aug. 5, 1959; Ba in Journalism, Sociology, U. So. Calif., L.A., 1981. Bus. reporter L.A. Herald Examiner, 1981-83, Investor's Bus. Daily, L.A., 1983-88, sr. editor, 1988-96, mng. editor, 1996—. Office: Investor's Bus Daily 12655 Beatrice St Los Angeles CA 90066-7303

WARFIELD, GERALD ALEXANDER, composer, writer; b. Ft. Worth, Feb. 23, 1940; s. George Alexander and Geraldine (Spencer) W. Student, Tex. Christian U., 1958-61; BA, North Tex. State U., 1963, M.Mus., 1965; M.F.A., Princeton U., 1967; postgrad., Tanglewood, summers 1963-64. Instr. Princeton, 1968-71; asso. dir. Index of New Mus. Notation, N.Y.C., 1971-75. Lectr. contemporary music notation. Mem. conf. com. Internat. Conf. on New Mus. Notation, Belgium, 1974; chmn. program com. 2d Nat. Conf. Music Theory, 1977 Author: A Beginner's Manual of Music 4B, 1967, Layer Analysis: a Primer of Elementary Tonal Structures, 1976, Writings on Contemporary Music Notations, 1977, How to Write Music Manuscript, 1977, (with others) Layer Dictation, 1978, The Investor's Guide to Stock Quotations, 1982, How To Buy Foreign Stocks and Bonds, 1984, How to Read the Financial News, 1986; (with others) Export-Import Financing, 1986; No Nonsense Guides to the Stock Market, Mutual Funds, Tax-Free Bonds, 1991, Managing Your Stock Portfolio, Money Market Funds, 1993, (with others) Feng Shui Revealed, 1997; composer: Variations and Metamorphoses, 1973 (1st prize Ariz. Cello Soc.); filmstrip Introduction to Musical Notation, 1976; Fantasy Quintet, 1978 (2d prize New Music for Young Ensembles); contbr.: Grove's Dictionary of Music and Musicians, 1976; editor: Longman Music Series, 1976-85; contbr. articles to profl. jours. Mem. Soc. Composers, Inc. (chmn. exec. com. 1972-74, conf. chmn. 9th Ann. Conf., 1974, founding editor Jour. of Music Scores, gen. mgr. 1977-2000, 2002—), Am. Composers Alliance (treas. 1979-96), Coll. Music Soc. (coun., conf. chmn. 1981), Broadcast Music Inc. Home: 410 SW 4th Ave # 4 Mineral Wells TX 76067-5840

WARFIELD, JOHN NELSON, retired engineering educator, consultant; b. Sullivan, Mo., Nov. 21, 1925; s. John Daniel and Flora Alice (Land) W.; m. Rosamond Arline Howe, Feb. 2, 1948; children: Daniel, Nancy, Thomas. BA, BSEE, U. Mo., 1948, MSEE, 1949; PhD, Purdue U., 1952. Assoc. prof. Pa. State U., University Park, 1949-55, U. Ill.-Urbana, 1955-57, Purdue U., West Lafayette, Ind., 1957-58; prof. elec. engring U. Kans., Lawrence, 1958-66; sr. research leader Battelle Meml. Inst., Columbus, Ohio, 1966-74; prof. elec. engring U. Va., Charlottesville, 1974-83; sr. mgr. Burroughs Corp., 1983-84; dir. Inst. for Info. Tech. George Mason U., Fairfax, Va., 1984-87, dir. Inst. for Advanced Study in Integrative Scis., 1987-98; prof. emeritus, 2000—. Cons. IBM, Armonk, N.Y., 1979-82, Saudi Arabian Nat. Ctr. Sci. and Tech., Riyadh, 1978-82, Ghana Coun. for Sci. and Indsl. Rsch., Accra, 1989—, Niagara-Mohawk Power Co., 89, Ford Motor Co., 1990—, Defense Systems Mgmt. Coll., 1990—. Author: Societal Systems, 1976, A Science of Generic Design, 1990, A Handbook of Interactive Management, 1994, Understanding Complexity: Thought and Behavior, 2002, The Mathematics of Structure, 2003; inventor interpretive structural modeling, 1973; editor: IEEE Transactions on Systems, Man, and Cybernetics, 1968-73, Systems Research, 1981-90. Recipient Excellence in Instrn. award Western Electric Co., 1966, Peace Pipe award Ams. for Indian Opportunity, 1987, Best Paper award European Conf. Cybernetics and Systems, 1988, Mayour's cert. City of Austin, 1993, Plaque of Recognition, Mex. Ministry of Social Devel., 1994, Spl. Recognition award Internat. Soc. Design and Process Sci., 1995, Laureate award George Mason U., 2002. Fellow IEEE (life, outstanding contbn. award 1977, Centennial medal 1984, Third Millennium medal 2000), Soc. for Design and Process Sci. (fellow award, 1996); mem. Internat. Soc. Panetics, Assn. for Integrative Studies. Home: 2673 Westcott Cir Palm Harbor FL 34684-1746 E-mail: jnwarfield@aol.com.

WARGO, ANDREA ANN, retired public health official, commissioned officer; b. Pottsville, Pa., Dec. 27, 1941; d. John Andrew and Anna Mary (Blischok) W.; m. Roger Fredrick Sies, Mar. 31, 1981. BS in Biology, Chestnut Hill Coll., 1972; PhD in Biology, Georgetown U., 1978. Educator, adminstr. Cath. Archdiocese Phila., 1961-74; tchg. asst. Georgetown U., Washington, 1974-78, postdoctoral fellow, 1978-80; acting br. chief FDA, Silver Spring, Md., 1980-86, acting chief gen. hosp. and personal use devices, 1986-88; assoc. adminstr. Agy. for Toxic Substances and Disease Registry, Washington, 1988-2001; ret., 2001. Mem. Surgeon Gen.'s Policy Adv. Coun., 1996-2001. Contbr. articles to sci. publs. Grantee NSF, 1972, 73, Kidney Found., 19790-80. Mem. Assn. Women in Sci. (treas. Washington-Balt. chpt. 1979-80), Commd. Officers Assn., Georgetown U. Alumni Assn., Toastmistress Club (pres. Bethesda chpt. 1978-79), Pub. Health Svc. (scientist profl. adv. com., exec. sec. 1984-86, vice chmn. 1986-87), Sigma Xi. Avocations: languages, computers, financial planning, handwriting analysis. Home: 17604 N Stone Haven Dr Surprise AZ 85374

WARGO, LOVETTA LYNN, medical educator, occupational therapist, writer; d. Lewis and Patsy Elaine Hickman; m. George Peter Wargo, July 24, 1998; 1 child, Davey Henry Addams. AAS, J. Sargent Reynolds, 1998. Respiratory Therapy Advance Practice Commonwealth of VA State Bd. for CC, 1998, PALS Provider Am. Heart Assocation, 2002, BLS Instructor Am. Heart Assocation, 2002, Heartsaver First Aid Instructor Am. Heart Assocation, 2004, Registered Respiratory Therapist Nat. Bd. for Respiratory Care, 1999, Respiratory Therapy Commonwealth of Va., 1998, Respiratory Therapy Technology J. Sargeant Reynolds CC/ Va., 1997, Respiratory Therapy Assisting J. Sargeant Reynolds CC/ Va., 1997, Certified Respiratory Therapy Technician Nat. Bd. for Respiratory Care, 1998, ACLS Instructor Am. Heart Assn., 2002, ACLS Provider Am. Heart Assn., 2002, PALS Instructor Am. Heart Assocation, 2002. Educator Riverside Regional Med. Hosp., Newport News, Va., 1998—; item writer Nat. Bd. Respiratory Care, Lenexa, Kans., 2002—, Am. Assn. Cirtical-Care Nurses, Aliso Viejo, Calif., 2003. Mem.: Seaford Women's Club (assoc.), Phi Theta Kappa (assoc.). Achievements include invention of medical education tool. Office: Riverside Regional Medical Hospital 500 J Clyde Morris Blvd Newport News VA 23601

WARHEIT, PETER S. anesthesiologist; b. N.Y.C., Feb. 19, 1952; MD, U. Autonoma, Guadalajara, 1979. Diplomate Am. Bd. Anesthesiology. Intern SUNY, Stony Brook, 1980-81, resident in surgery, 1981-82; resident in anesthesia Mt. Sinai Med. Ctr., N.Y.C., 1982-84, mem. staff, 1984-88, Delray Med. Ctr., Delray Beach, Fla., 1989—2002, West Boca Med. Ctr., Boca Raton, Fla., 1989—2002, chief of staff, 1999—2002, chief of anesthesiology, 1996—2002; mem. staff Wellington (Fla.) Regional Med. ctr., 2003—04, Delray Outpatient Surgery and Laser Ctr., 2004—. Mem. Am. Soc. Anesthesia, Internat. Anesthesia Rsch. Assn., Fla. Soc. Anesthesia. Fax: 561-995-8096. Office Phone: 561-381-2300. E-mail: docpsw@aol.com.

WARICHA, JOAN, publishing executive; BA, Boston U., 1967; MBA, Columbia U., 1980. V.p., editor-in-chief, assoc. pub. Scholastic, Inc., 1968-83; pres. Parachute Press, 1983-96; chmn., CEO Parachute Properties, 1996—; pres. Parachute Pub., 1996—, Parachute Entertainment, 1996—, Parachute Consumer Products, 1996—. Office: Parachute Properties 156 5th Ave New York NY 10010-7002 Office Phone: 212-691-1421. E-mail: jwaricha@parachuteproperties.com.

WARICK, LAWRENCE HERBERT, psychiatrist; b. Warsaw, May 2, 1936; came to U.S., 1949, naturalized, 1954; s. Joseph and Marsha (Beck) W.; m. Elaine Ruth Christensen, Feb. 24, 1963; children: Catherine Ann, David Mark. BS, CCNY, 1956; MD, Albert Einstein Coll. Medicine, 1960; PhD, So. Calif. Psychoanalytic Inst, 1980. Diplomate Am. Bd. Psychiatry and Neurology. Rotating intern L.A. County Gen. Hosp., 1960-61; resident neurology U. So. Calif. Sch. Medicine, L.A. County Gen. Hosp., 1961-62, resident psychiatry, 1962-65; clin. assoc. So. Calif. Psychoanalytic Inst., L.A., 1973-80, instr., 1981—; pvt. practice L.A., 1980—; asst. clin. prof. psychiatry UCLA Sch. Medicine, 1967-97, assoc. clin. prof. psychiatry, 1997—; instr. faculty Psychoanalytic Inst. So. Calif., L.A., 1980—, 1980—. Contbr. chpts. to books and articles to profl. jours. Capt. USAF, 1962-68. Mem. Am. Psychiat. Assn., Am. Acad. Psychiatry and Law, So. Calif. Psychiatry Soc., So. Calif. Psychoanalytic Soc., Phi Beta Kappa. Avocations: swimming, music, hiking, tennis, racketball, reading. Office: 2444 Wilshire Blvd Ste 418 Santa Monica CA 90403-5811

WARINER, JEREMY, Olympic track and field athlete; b. Irving, TX, Jan. 31, 1984; Student, Baylor Univ. Mem. U.S. Olympic Track Team, Athens, 2004. Named Mondo Outdoor Track Athlete of the Yr., USA Track Coaches Assoc., 2004. Achievements include Gold medal, 400m, Athens Olympic games, 2004; NCAA Champion, Indoor 400m, Indoor 4x400m relays, Outdoor 400m, Outdoor 4x400m relay, 2004. Office: c/o USOC 1 Olympic Plaza Colorado Springs CO 80909*

WARING, WALTER WEYLER, English language educator; b. Sterling, Kans., May 13, 1917; s. Walter Wray and Bonnie Laura (Weyler) W.; m. Mary Esther Griffith, Feb. 8, 1946; children: Mary Laura, Helen Ruth, Elizabeth Anne, Claire Joyce. BA, Kans. Wesleyan U., 1939; MA, U. Colo., 1946; PhD, Cornell U., 1949. Tchr., English and chemistry Belleville (Kan.) High Sch., 1939-41; instr. U. Colo., Boulder, 1941-42, 46-47; mem. faculty Kalamazoo Coll., 1949—, prof. English, 1955-85, prof. emeritus, 1985—, chmn. dept., 1953-78, dir. humanities, 1978-83. Ednl. TV lectr.; vis. prof. Kenyon Coll., 1984-86, 90-91. Painter watercolors.; author: Thomas Carlyle, 1978, also articles. Served to 1st lt. AUS, World War II, PTO. Decorated Legion of Merit. Mem. Phi Beta Kappa. Home: 8794 Keller Rd Delton MI 49046-8728

WARING, WILLIAM WINBURN, pediatric pulmonologist, educator; b. Savannah, Ga., July 20, 1923; s. Antonio Johnston and Sue Cole (Winburn) W.; m. Nell Pape Williams, July 19, 1952; children: William Winburn, Benjamin Joseph, Antonio Johnston, Peter Ayraud, Patrick Houstoun Grad., Hotchkiss Sch., Lakeville, Conn., 1942; student, Yale U., 1942-43; MD, Harvard U., 1947. Diplomate Am. Bd. Pediatrics (subbd. of pediatric pulmonology 1985-89). Intern Children's Hosp., Boston, 1947-48; intern, then resident Johns Hopkins Hosp., Balt., 1948-52; practice medicine specializing in pediatrics Jacksonville, Fla., 1955-57; instr. dept. pediatrics Sch. Medicine, Tulane U., New Orleans, 1957-58, asst. prof., 1958-61, assoc. prof., 1961-66, prof. emeritus, 1966—, Jane B. Aron Prof. Pediatrics, 1987-96. Dir. Pediat. Pulmonary Ctr., New Orleans, 1969-88, Cystic Fibrosis Ctr., Tulane U., New Orleans, 1963-88; chmn. profl. tng. com. Cystic Fibrosis Found., 1978-86; cons. La. State Handicapped Children's Assn., 1963-88; mem. pulmonary diseases adv. com. NIH, 1978-80. Co-author: Pro Parvulis: On Behalf of the Little Ones. A History of the Department of Pediatrics, Tulane Medical School, 1834-2003, 2003; co-author, editor: Practical Manual of Pediatrics, 1975, 2d edit., 1982; editor: Harriet Lane Handbook: A Manual for Pediatric House Officers, 1952, Hospital Pediatric Manual, 1958; contbg. author books on pediatric pulmonary disease, also articles in field; assoc. editor Am. Jour. Diseases of Children, 1989-91; mem. editl. bd. Pediatric Pulmonology, 1985-94. Served to capt. M.C., U.S. Army, 1952-54. Recipient Rsch. Career Devel. award, NIH, 1970—72, Edwin L. Kendig, Jr. award for outstanding achievement in pediatric pulmonology, 2004. Fellow Am. Acad. Pediatrics (exec. com. 1966-71), Am. Coll. Chest Physicians; mem. Am. Pediatric Soc., Am. Thoracic Soc. (v.p. 1977). Clubs: Boston, So. Yacht, Wyvern (New Orleans). Republican. Roman Catholic. Avocations: fly fishing; running; computing. Home: 123 Walnut St Apt 905 New Orleans LA 70118-4846 Office: Tulane U Sch of Medicine Dept of Pediatrics 1430 Tulane Ave New Orleans LA 70112-2699

WARITZ, RICHARD STEFAN, toxicologist, researcher; b. Portland, Oreg., Apr. 1, 1929; s. Anton John and Theresa (Stegelmaier) W.; m. Ruth Evelyn White, June 7, 1950; children: Joyce E., Gary S., Sharon J., Carol L. BA, Reed Coll., 1951; PhD, Stanford U., 1957. Diplomate Am. Bd. Toxicology, Acad. Toxicological Scis. Sr. rsch. scientist E.I. DuPont de Nemours & Co., Wilmington, Del., 1957-64, mgr. inhalation toxicology, 1964-72, mgr. bio-scis., 1972-75; sr. toxicologist Hercules Inc., Wilmington, 1975-80, mgr. toxicology, 1980-92; pres. BioSante Internat., Inc., 1992—. Grad. toxicology edn. adv. bd. Rutgers U., Piscataway, N.J., 1980—; life scis. adv. bd. U.S. Army, Aberdeen, Md., 1982-92; toxicology peer rev. bd. U.S. Army Ctr. for Health Promotion and Preventive Medicine, 1992—; vis. prof. toxicology Rutgers U., 1993—. Contbr. articles to profl. jours. Mem.: Am. Chem. Soc., Am. Conf. Govtl. Indsl. Hygienists, Am. Indsl. Hygiene Assn., Internat. Union Toxicol. Socs. (councillor 1983—88), Soc. Toxicology (treas. 1981-85, pres. Mid-Atlantic chpt. 1989). Roman Catholic. Avocations: golf, surf fishing, bowling. Home and Office: 2613 Turnstone Dr Wilmington DE 19808-1638 Office Phone: 302-994-2235. E-mail: waritz.bio@att.net.

WARM, ELLIOT L. lawyer; b. Bronx, Oct. 22, 1947; s. Sally Warm; m. Helene Warm, Oct. 19, 1974; children: Stephanie L, Jessica S. BA summa cum laude, Rutgers Coll., New Brunswick, N.J., 1969; JD, Rutgers U., Newark, 1973. Bar: N.J. 1973. Ptnr. Gutkin, Miller, Selesner & Shapiro, Millburn, NJ, 1976—91; gen. counsel Fidelity Land Devel. Co., Chatham, NJ, 1991—. Adj. instr. of law Rutgers Sch. of Law, Newark, 1991—92. With Army N.G., 1970—76, West Orange, N.J. Mem.: Phi Beta Kappa. Office: Fidelity Land Devel Co 641 Shunpike Rd Chatham NJ 07928 E-mail: ewarm@fidelityland.com.

WARMBROD, CATHARINE PHELPS, educational researcher, consultant; b. Lost Nation, Iowa, July 2, 1929; d. Paul Edward and Ruth Dorthea Phelps; m. J. Robert Warmbrod, Jan. 30, 1965. BA, U. Iowa, 1952; MS, U. Ill., 1965, advanced cert. in edn., 1967. Head supr. student tchrs. in bus. edn. U. Ill., Urbana, 1966-67; chmn. office adminstrn. Columbus (Ohio) State Community Coll., 1970-77; rsch. specialist NCRVE Ohio State U., Columbus, 1977-88, rsch. specialist emeritus, 1988—; prin. Warmbrod Ednl. Svcs., Columbus, 1988-2001. Bd. dirs. Nat. Assn. Industry/Edn. Cooperation, Buffalo, 1980-88. Author: Retraining and Upgrading Workers, 1983; contbr. to profl. pubs.; editor: VocEd Insider for Tech. Edn., 1981. Bd. dirs. Ohio Women, Inc., Columbus, 1986-92, Friendship Village, Dublin, Columbus, 1990—. Mem. Am. Vocat. Assn. (policy com. 1980-83), Assn. Faculty and Profl. Women Ohio State U. (pres. 1984-85), Am. Assn. Cmty. Colls., Am. Tech. Edn. Assn., Delta Pi Epsilon. United Methodist. Office: Warmbrod Ednl Svcs 3853 Surrey Hill Pl Columbus OH 43220-4778

WARMER, RICHARD CRAIG, lawyer; b. Los Angeles, Aug. 12, 1936; s. George A. and Marian L. (Paine) W.; children: Craig McEchron, Alexander Richard. AB, Occidental Coll., 1958; MA, Tufts U., 1959; LLB, NYU, 1962. Bar: Calif. 1963, D.C. 1976. Assoc. O'Melveny & Myers, LLP, Los Angeles, 1962-69, ptnr., 1970-75, mng. ptnr. Washington, 1976-92, mem. mgmt. com., 1986-92, with San Francisco, 1994—. Speaker in field. Contbr. articles to profl. jours. Trustee Law Ctr. Found. NYU, 1981-94; dir. Headland Ctr. for Arts, San Francisco Jazz Orgn. Mem. ABA, D.C. Bar, State Bar Calif., Order of Coif, Phi Beta Kappa, Cosmos Club. Office: O'Melveny & Myers LLP Embarcadero Ctr W 275 Battery St San Francisco CA 94111-3305 E-mail: rwarmer@omm.com.

WARNATH, MAXINE AMMER, organizational psychologist, mediator; b. N.Y.C., Dec. 3, 1928; d. Philip and Jeanette Ammer; m. Charles Frederick Warnath, Aug. 20, 1952; children: Stephen Charles, Cindy Ruth. BA, Bklyn. Coll., 1949; MA, Columbia U., 1951, EdD, 1982. Lic. psychologist Oreg. Various profl. positions Hunter Coll., U. Minn., U. Nebr., U. Oreg., 1951-62; asst. prof. psychology Oreg. Coll. Edn., Monmouth, 1962-77; assoc. prof. psychology, chmn. dept. psychology & spl. edn. Western Oreg. U., Monmouth, 1978-83, prof., 1983-96, prof. emeritus, 1996—. Dir. organizational psychology program, 1983—96; pres. Profl. Perspective Internat., Salem, Oreg., 1987—; cons., dir. Orgn. R&D, Salem, Oreg., 1983—87; seminar leader Endeavors for Excellence program. Author: Power Dynamism, 1987. Mem.: APA (com. pre-coll. psychology 1970—74), Western Psychol. Assn., Oreg. Psychol. Assn. (pres. 1980—81, pres.-elect 1979—80, legis. liaison 1977—78), Oreg. Acad. Sci., N.Y. Acad. Scis., Am. Psychol. Soc. Office: Profl Perspectives Internat PO Box 2265 Salem OR 97308-2265 Office Phone: 503-371-6451. Personal E-mail: mwarnath@comcast.net. Business E-Mail: warnatm@wou.edu.

WARNE, ALAN M. adult education educator, consultant; b. Pierre, SD, Aug. 24, 1945; s. Maynard L. and Ione P. Warne; m. Joan Caulfield, Sept. 7, 1996; children: Alan, Jr. M., Andrea W. White, Amy N. BA in Polit. Sci., Ariz. State U., 1963—67; MA in Ednl. Psychology, Ea. Ky. U., 1969—70; EdD in Continuing Edn., Temple U., 1972—78. Fgn. student advisor Ariz. State U., Tempe, 1966—68; dir., internat. student services U. of Ky., 1968—71; dir., office of internat. services Temple U., 1971—77; exec. dir. Phila. Coun. for Internat. Visitors, 1977—81, Nat. Coun. for Internat. Visitors, Washington, 1981—85; chief exec. officer/vice pres. for programs People to People Internat., Kans. City, Mo., 1986—99; pres. & ceo Entrepreneurial Edn. Found., Kans. City, Mo., 2000—01; sr. program mgr. U. of Kans. Med. Ctr., Kans. City, Kans., 2002—03. Mng. dir. The Brain Inc., Kans. City, Mo., 2000—03; planning cons. Kauffman Ctr. for Entrepreneurial Leadership, Kans. City, Mo., 2000; academic program cons. Rockhurst U., Kans. City, Mo., 2000; mem. U. of Med. Ctr. Continuing Med. Ctr. Statewide Adv. Bd & Governing Com., Kans. City, Kans., 2002—03, Continuing Med. Edn. Adv. Com., U. of Kans., 2002—03. Contbr. curriculum guide Expo 92 (Kans. City-Seville), nat. profl. newsletter Mgmt./Program Planning Articles, admissions guide - internat. student A Model for the Edn. of Fgn. Students. Bd. mem./arts com. Mayor's UN Day Com., Kans. Citry, Mo., 1990—96; site planning com. Kans. City Sch. Dist., Kans. City, Mo., 1990—91; bd. mem./vice chair Nat. Coun. for Internat. Visitors, Washington, 1978—81; founding bd. mem. Consortium for Internat. Citizen Exch., Washington, 1981—85, Caruthers' Arts Alliance, Kans. City, Mo.; scholarship committees rep. U. of Mo.-Kans. City, Kans. City, Mo., 1986—2003; pres./vice pres. Pk. U. Bd. of Visitors, Parkville, Mo., 1995—2001. Recipient Del. Leader - Baltic Nations, Ambassadors, Inc., 1999, Thematic Specialist -Citizen Initiatives (6-US Cities), Inst. of Internat. Edn., 1981; grantee Ednl. Travel Grant, Republic of China Ministry of Edn., 1975. Fellow: Rotary Club Internat. (ednl./scholarship/planning committees 1999—2003); mem.: Assn. of Internat. Educators (regional chair, coord. of nat. job registry, exec. com. 1967—2000), Kans. City Club (membership com. 1993—2003). Avocations: volunteerism, travel, cinema, theater, organizational development. Home: 431 West 70th St Kansas City MO 64113 Office: U of Kans Med Ctr 3901 Rainbow Blvd Kansas City KS 66160-7108 Office Phone: 913-588-4487. Personal E-mail: awarne@aol.com. E-mail: awarne@kumc.edu.

WARNE, WILLIAM ROBERT, economist; b. Washington, Nov. 30, 1937; BA, Princeton U., 1960; MA, Johns Hopkins U., 1974. Provincial advisor U.S. Mission, Vinh Binh, Vinh Long, Vietnam, 1962-64; officer in charge trade, devel. and fin. policy U.S. Mission to European Communities, Brussels, 1974-77; dep. dir. East Asian Econ. Policy, 1977-79; dir. Caribbean affairs U.S. Dept. State, Kingston, Jamaica, 1979-81, charge d'affaires, dep. chief mission, 1981-84, dir. Latin Am. Econ. Policy Washington, 1984-86; counselor for trade, energy, social affairs and agr. U.S. Delegation OECD, Paris, 1986-88; v.p. Midwest Ctr. Exec. Coun. on Fgn. Diplomats, Indpls., 1988-89; pres. Korea Econ. Inst. Am., Washington, 1990-99; instr. Fgn. Svc. Inst., U.S. Dept. State, Washington, 2000—; prof. internat. studies Ewha Woman's U., Seoul, Korea, 2000-2001; instr. Fgn. Svc. Inst. U.S. Dept. State, Washington, 2001—03; prof. internat. studies Korea U., Seoul, 2003. Prof. internat. studies Korea U., Seoul, Republic of Korea, 2003; instr. fgn. svc. Inst. U.S. Dept. State, Wash., 2004—. With U.S. Army, 1960-62.

WARNER, BARRY GREGORY, ecologist, educator; b. Cambridge, Ont., Can., July 20, 1955; s. Gregory O. and Alma (Jansen) W. B in Environ. Studies, U. Waterloo, 1978, MS, 1980; PhD, Simon Fraser U., Burnaby, Can., 1984. Rsch. asst. prof. U. Waterloo, Ont., Ont., 1985-89, rsch. assoc. prof., 1989-91, assoc. prof. geography, 1991-96, prof. biology, earth sci. and geography, 1996—; dir. Wetlands Rsch. Inst., 1991—; U. Neuchatel. Vis. prof. U. Neuchatel, 1993, U. Franche-Comte, Bescon, France, 2002; chair Can. Nat. Wetlands Working Group, 1993—; bd. dirs. Internat. Mire Conservation Group. Editor: Methods in Quaternary Ecology, 1990; co-editor: Wetlands: Envigradients, Boundaries and Buffers, 1996; contbr. articles to profl. jours. Postdoctoral fellow Natural Scis. and Engring. Rsch. Coun. of Can., 1984-85, rsch. fellow, 1985-90; fellow Suisse Nat. Res. Fond, 1993. Fellow Geol. Assn. Can., Soc. Wetland Scientists (pres., v.p. 2000-2003). Office: U of Waterloo Wetlands Rsch Ctr Waterloo ON Canada N2L 3G1 E-mail: bwarner@uwaterloo.ca.

WARNER, BRADFORD H. finance company executive; m. Pamela Warner; 2 children. BA, Brown U.; MBA with distinction, U. Pa. Exec. v.p. BankBoston, 1996—98, vice chmn., 1998—99; vice chmn., investment svcs. Fleet Fin. Corp., 1999—2000, vice chmn., consumer bus. group, 2000—02; exec. v.p., personal fin. svcs. FleetBoston, Boston, 2002—, vice chmn., consumer small bus. svcs., 2002—. Bd. dirs. Consumer Bankers Assn. Bd. dirs. Mass. Mentoring Partnership; chair Fleet Diversity Leadership Coun. Office: FleetBoston Fin Corp 100 Federal St Boston MA 02110

WARNER, CHARLES COLLINS, lawyer; b. Cambridge, Mass., June 19, 1942; s. Hoyt Landon and Charlotte (Collins) W.; m. Elizabeth Denny, Aug. 24, 1964; children: Peter, Andrew, Elizabeth. BA, Yale U., 1964; JD cum laude, Ohio State U., 1970. Bar: Ohio 1970. Assoc. Porter, Wright, Morris & Arthur and predecessor, Columbus, 1970-76, ptnr., 1976—, also mgr. labor and employment law dept., 1988-92. Pres. Peace Corps Svc. Coun., Columbus, 1974—76, Old Worthington (Ohio) Assn., 1976—78, Worthington Ednl. Found., 1994—96, Opera Columbus, 1999—2001; chmn. lawyers sect. United Way, Columbus, 1983—84; mem. alumni adv. coun. Ohio State U., 1998—2004; pres. Alliance for Quality Edn., Worthington, 1987—89. Fellow Am. Bar Found., Ohio Bar Found., Columbus Bar Found., Coll. Labor and Employment Lawyers; mem. ABA (co-chair EEO com. 2000-02, exec. com. Met. Bar Caucus 1992-94, chmn. state and local bar ADR com. 1995-98), Ohio State Bar Assn. (coun. of dels. 1993—, chmn. fed. cts. com. 1992-94), Ohio Met. Bar Assn. (pres. 1991-92), Columbus Bar Assn. (pres. 1991-92, bd. govs. 1982-87, 88-93), Ohio Mgmt. Lawyers Assn. (chair 2004—), FBA, Ohio Assn. Civil Trial Attys. (exec. bd. 1988-97), Ohio State U. Law Alumni Assn. (pres. 1996-97), Nat. Coun. Ohio State U. Coll. Law (pres. 2002—), Capital Club, Yale Club (pres. 1979-81). Avocations: clarinet, singing, tennis. Home: 145 E South St Columbus OH 43085-4129 Office: Porter Wright Morris & Arthur 41 S High St Ste 2800 Columbus OH 43215-6194 Office Phone: 614-227-2013. E-mail: cwarner@porterwright.com.

WARNER, CHARLES DAVID, III, academic administrator; b. Hagerstown, Md., Feb. 2, 1957; s. Charles David Jr. and Ivy Ella Warner; m. Debra Jean Teter, May 25, 1985; children: Betsy, Molly, Charles. B in Music Edn., Shepherd Coll., 1980; M in Music Edn., Towson U., 1985; EdD, Va. Poly. Inst. and State U., 1999. Prof. music Hagerstown C.C., Md., 1989—2001, chair humanities divsn., 2000—03, dir. instrn., 2003—04; exec. dir. Univ. System Md., 2004—. Author: Opinions of Administrators, Faculty, and Students Regarding Academic Freedom and Student Artistic Expression, 2001. Mem. NEA, Phi Kappa Phi. Republican. Lutheran. Avocations: sailing, reading. Home: 17729 Bluebell Dr Hagerstown MD 21740 Office: Univ Sys Md Hagerstown Edn Ctr 20 Public Sq Hagerstown MD 21740 Fax: 301-393-3680. Office Phone: 301-791-4579. E-mail: dwarner@frostburg.edu.

WARNER, DAVID COOK, public affairs educator; b. Boston, Apr. 22, 1940; s. Roger Lewis and Dorothy Flora (Cook) W.; m. Phyllis Gail Erman, July 9, 1967; children: Ann Fitch, Michael Beers. BA, Princeton U., 1963; MPA, Syracuse U., 1965, PhD in Econs., 1969. Rsch. assoc. Ctr. Urban Studies Wayne State U., Detroit, 1969, asst. prof. econs., 1969-71; dep. dir. program analysis and budget N.Y.C. Health and Hosp. Corp., 1971-72; postdoctoral fellow Yale U., New Haven, 1972-73, lectr., 1973-75; assoc. prof. L.B.J. Sch. Pub. Affairs U. Tex., Austin, 1975-81, prof. pub. affairs, 1981—, Wilbur Cohen prof. pub. affairs, 1989—, Vis. prof. pub. health, 1983—; bd. dirs. Brackenridge Hosp., Austin, 1976—83; mem. Tex. Diabetes Coun., 1983—88, chmn., 1985—88; mem. adv. bd. Hogg Found. for Mental Health, 1990—93; vice chair quality methods tech. adv. com. Health Care Info. Coun., 1999—. Author: Health of Mexican Americans in South Texas, 1979, Developing Programs to Prevent and Control Diabetes, 1982, Maternal and Child Health on the U.S.-Mexico Border, 1987, Health Care Across the Border, 1993, NAFTA and Trade in Health Services, 1997, Cost of Diabetes in Texas in 1992, 1996, Getting What You Paid For: Extending Medicare Coverage to Retirees in Mexico, 1999; co-author: Cost of Cancer in Texas, 2001, Investing in Texas: Financing Health Coverage Expansions, 2003; editor: Toward New Human Rights, 1977, Public Affairs Comment, 1978-90; mem. editl. bd. Jour. Health, Politics, Policy and Law, 1975-93; contbr. articles to profl. jours. Mem. U.S.-Mex. Border Health Assn. (chmn. rsch., edn., tng. com. 1982-84), Am. Pub. Health Assn., Tex. Philosophical Soc. Democrat. Congregationalist. Home: 5701 Trailridge Dr Austin TX 78731-4226 Office: U Tex LBJ Sch Pub Affairs Austin TX 78713 Office Phone: 512-471-6277. E-mail: david.warner@mail.utexas.edu.

WARNER, DAVID SAMUEL, anesthesiologist, educator; b. Evanston, Ill., July 20, 1953; s. James Daniel and Marcella Anne Warner; m. Rosanne T. Warner, June 14, 1980; children: Lindsay, Seth. BA, U. Wis., 1976, MD, 1980. Diplomate Am. Bd. Anesthesiology. Resident U. Iowa, Iowa City, 1980-84; rsch. assoc. U. Lund, Sweden, 1984-85; asst. prof. U. Iowa, Iowa City, 1985-89, assoc. prof., 1989-94; prof. anesthesiology Duke U., Durham, N.C., 1994—. Mem. editl. bd. Jour. Neurosurg. Anesthesia, 1989—, Anesthesia and Analgesia, 1995—; contbr. over 170 articles to profl. jours. Grantee, NIH, 1987—. Mem. Soc. for Neurosurg. Anesthesia and Critical Care (pres. 1994-95), Soc. for Neurosci., Am. Soc. Anesthesiologists, Internat. Anesthesia Rsch. Soc. Episcopalian. Home: 1006 Camden Ln Chapel Hill NC 27516-7756 Office: Duke Univ Med Ctr Dept Anesthesiology PO Box 3094 Durham NC 27710-0001 E-mail: warne002@mc.duke.edu.

WARNER, DENNIS ALLAN, psychology educator; b. Idaho Falls, Idaho, Apr. 27, 1940; s. Perry and Marcia E. (Finlayson) W.; m. Charyl Ann DeHart, Dec. 12, 1962; children: Lisa Rae, Sara Michelle, David Perry, Matthew Arie. BS, Brigham Young U., 1964; MS with honors, U. Oreg., 1966, PhD, 1968. Asst. prof. edn. Wash. State U., Pullman, 1968-72, assoc. prof. edn., 1972-78, prof. edn., 1978-85, dir. tchr. edn., 1983-85, prof., chmn. ednl. counseling psychology, 1985-93, interim dir. Partnership Ctr., 1993-94, prof. edn. leadership and counseling psychology, 1994—, assoc. dean Coll. Edn., 1999—, dir. H.S. equivalency program, 2004—. Vis. asst. prof. psychology U. Idaho, Moscow, 1971. Author: Interpreting and Improving Student Test Performance, 1982; contbr. articles to profl. jours. Postdoctoral research assoc. U. Kans., 1976-77. Fellow APA; mem. Delta Kappa. Mem. Lds Ch. Home: 645 SW Mies St Pullman WA 99163-2057 Office: Wash State Univ Coll Edn Cleveland Hl Rm 160B Pullman WA 99164-2114 Office Phone: 509-335-1738. E-mail: dawarner@wsu.edu.

WARNER, DON LEE, dean emeritus; b. Norfolk, N.B., Jan. 4, 1934; s. Donald A. and Cleo V. (Slagel) W.; m. Patricia Ann Walker, Feb. 24, 1957; children: Mark J., Scott Lee. BS in Geol. Engring., Colo. Sch. Mines, 1956, MSc in Geol. Engring., 1961; PhD in Engring. Sci., U. Calif., Berkeley, 1964. Registered profl. engr., Mo., geologist, Mo., Miss., Tex. Geol. engr. Gulf Oil Corp., Casper, Wyo., 1956, Calif. Exploration Co., Guatemala, 1957-58; civil engr. U.S. Forest Svc., Gunnison, Colo., 1958-59; teaching asst. Colo. Sch. Mines, Golden, 1959-61; rsch. asst. U. Calif., Berkeley, 1962-64; rsch. geologist and engr. U.S. Pub. Health Svc., Cin., 1964-67; chief, earth scis. Ohio Basin Region Fed. Water Pollution Control Adminstrn., 1967-69; prof. geol. engring. U. Mo., Rolla, 1969-92, prof. emeritus geol. engring., 1992—, dean emeritus Sch. Mines and Metallurgy, 1992—, chmn., geol. engring., 1980-81, dean Sch. Mines and Metallurgy, 1981-93. Bd. dirs. Underground Injection Practices Coun., 1985-89; mem. adv. com. to Sec. of Interior for Mineral Resources Rsch., 1985-92. Author: Subsurface Wastewater Injection, 1977. Special award scholarship Colo. Sch. Mines, 1951-56, grad. fellowship Colo. Sch. Mines, 1959-51, rsch. fellowship U. Calif., 1962-64; recipient Best Paper award Am. Water Works Assn., 1971. Fellow Geol. Soc. Am.; mem. Am. Inst. Profl. Geologists (cert.), Am. Assn. Petroleum Geologists, Geol. Soc. Am., Nat. Ground Water Assn. (sci. award 1984, disting. lectr. 1986), Ground Water Protection Coun., Blue Key, Soc. Petroleum Engrs., Scabbard and Blade, Theta Tau, Tau Beta Pi. Avocations: fishing, boating, tennis, golf. Office: U Mo-Rolla Sch Mines and Metallurgy 1870 Miner Cir Rolla MO 65409-0001 E-mail: dlw@fidmail.com.

WARNER, DOUGLAS ALEXANDER, III, banker; b. Cin., June 9, 1946; s. Douglas Alexander Jr. and Eleanor (Wright) W.; m. Patricia Grant, May 13, 1977; children: Alexander, Katherine, Michael. BA, Yale U., 1968. Officer's asst. J.P. Morgan & Co., Inc., N.Y.C., 1968-70; asst. treas. J.P. Morgan & Co., Inc., N.Y.C., 1970-72, asst. v.p., 1972-75; v.p. Morgan Guaranty Trust Co., N.Y.C., 1975-85; sr. v.p. J.P. Morgan & Co. Inc., N.Y.C., 1983-87, exec. v.p., 1987-89; mng. dir. Morgan Guaranty Trust Co., N.Y.C., 1989-90, pres., 1990-95, chmn., pres., CEO, 1995—, also bd. dirs. Bd. counselors Bechtel Group, Inc.; bd. dirs. GE Co., Anheuser-Busch Cos., Ind.; chmn. bd. of overseers and mgrs. Meml. Sloan-Kettering Cancer Ctr.; mem. The Bus. Coun. Trustee Pierpont Morgan Libr. Mem. Links Club, River Club, Meadowbrook Club (L.I.). Avocations: golf, skiing, shooting. Home: PO Box 914 New York NY 10268-0914 Office: J P Morgan & Co Inc 60 Wall St New York NY 10005-2888

WARNER, ELEANORE JOYCE, nurse, educator; b. Danville, Ill., July 27, 1940; d. Ralph Harold and Ruby Edgington Dodson; m. John Henry Warner, Oct. 5, 1975. Student, Ft. Wayne Bible Coll., Ind., 1958—59, Moody Bible Inst., Chicago, Ill., 1963—65; diploma, Lake View Meml. Hosp. Sch. of Nursing, Danville, Ill., 1962; State Cert. Midwife, Leeds Hosp.and Queen Elizabeth II Hosp., Leeds and Welwyn Garden City, Eng., 1966. RN, cert. midwife, Coll. of Midwives, Eng., 1966. Asst. head nurse recovery rm. Cook County Hosp., Chgo., 1962—65; asst. head nurse ICU, Ind. Univ. Hosp., Indpls., 1967—75; staff nurse Pike County Meml. Hosp., Louisiana, Mo., 1977—; nurse's aide instr. Maple Grove Lodge, Louisiana, Mo., 2001—. Chair and vice-chair Pike County Rep. Ctrl. Com., Bowling Green, Mo., 1980—2003; vice-chair Ninth Congl. Rep. Com., N.E. Mo., 1988—98; mem. exec. bd. Mo. Bapt. Conv., Jefferson City, 2001—. Republican. Southern Baptist. Home: 307 E Champ Clark Dr Bowling Green MO 63334 Office: Pike County Meml Hosp 2305 W Georgia St Louisiana MO 63353 Personal E-mail: warnerbgmo@webtv.net.

WARNER, EMILY HANRAHAN HOWELL, retired pilot, writer; b. Oct. 30, 1939; m. Julius "Jay" Warner. BA in English, Souther U., Baton Rouge, LA. Kindergarten and elem. sch. tchr.; flight instr. Clinton Aviation Co., 1961—67, rose to positions of chief pilot and flight sch. mgr., 1967—73; pilot Frontier Airlines, 1973—86, Continental Airlines, 1986—88, United Parcel Svc., 1988—90; aviation safety inspector FAA, 1990—2002, aircrew program mgr., 1992—2002. Bd. dirs. Internat. Air Mus., Dayton, Ohio. Author: (children's books) Lily of Watts- A Birthday Discovery, 1969, Lily Takes A Giant Step, (biography) Weaving the Winds, 2003. Co-founder Northeast Women's Ctr., Denver; active with Congress of Racial Equality, ACLU, NAACP. Named to Colo. Aviation Hall Fame, 1983, Nat. Women's Hall Fame, Seneca Falls, NY,

2001; recipient Amelia Earheart award as the Outstanding Woman in US Aviation, 1973. Mem.: Colo. Aviation Hist. Soc., Internat. Soc. Women Airline Pilots (founder), Ninety-Nines: Internat. Orgn. Women Pilots. Achievements include uniform installed in Smithsonian Inst. Air and Space Mus., 1976; first woman hired as pilot by major US airline, 1973.

WARNER, HAROLD CLAY, JR., banker, investment management executive, brokerage house executive; b. Knoxville, Tenn., Feb. 24, 1939; s. Harold Clay and Mary Frances (Waters) W.; m. Patricia Alice Rethorst, Sept. 1, 1961; children: Martha Lee, Carol Frances. BS in Econs, U. Tenn., 1961, PhD, 1965. Asst. to pres. First Fed. Savs., Savannah, Ga., 1965-67; v.p. and economist No. Trust Co., Chgo., 1967-73; sr. v.p. and chief economist Crocker Nat. Bank, San Francisco, 1974-79, sr. v.p. liability mgmt., 1979-82; exec. v.p., dir. fixed income mgmt. BA Investment Mgmt. Corp., 1982-84, dir., pres., COO, 1984-86; dir., pres. Montgomery St. Income Securities, Inc., 1984-86; sr. v.p. Bank of Am., San Francisco, 1982-86; chmn. BA Investment Mgmt. Internat., Ltd., 1985-86; pres. Arthur D. Gimbel, Inc., San Mateo, Calif., 1986-87; exec. v.p., chief investment officer Riggs Nat. Bank Washington, 1987-88; chmn. Riggs Investment Mgmt. Corp., 1988-89; sr. v.p., chief economist Bank of Calif., San Francisco, 1989-93; pres., chief investment officer MERUS Capital Mgmt., San Francisco, 1989-93; pres. Govett Asset Mgmt. Co., 1993-95, Govett Fin. Svcs. Ltd., 1993-95; pres., COO Fisher Investments, Inc., Woodside, Calif., 1996; pres. Warner Fiduciary Counsel, LLC, San Francisco, 1997; 1st v.p., sr. dir. portfolio mgmt. Mellon Pvt. Asset Mgmt., San Francisco, 1998—. Lectr. dept. econs. U. Tenn., 1962-63, Grad. Sch. Bus., Loyola U., Chgo., 1969-73; lectr. Pacific Coast Banking Sch., U. Wash., 1978-79. Chmn. bd. trustees Children's Hosp. and Rsch Ctr. at Oakland. NDEA fellow, 1961-64 Mem. Burlingame Country Club, Pacific-Union Club, Phi Gamma Delta, Phi Eta Sigma, Beta Gamma Sigma, Omicron Delta Kappa, Phi Kappa Phi. Home: PO Box 2449 Yountville CA 94599-2449 Office: 525 Market St 35th Flr San Francisco CA 94105-2743 Office Phone: 415-951-4102. Personal E-mail: warnerfc@msn.com. Business E-Mail: warner.hc@mellon.com.

WARNER, JEAN LOLLICH, poet; b. Clinton, Iowa, June 22, 1916; d. Jens George Christenson and Dibga (Allen) L.; m. Charles Howard Warner, Mar. 26, 1959 (dec.); stepchildren: Judith, Leonard. BA in Elem. Edn., Cornell Coll., Mt. Vernon, Iowa, 1938; MA in Early Childhood Edn., Columbia U., 1945. Tchr. grades 4-6 Mt. Vernon Pub. Sch., 1938-39; tchr. kindergarten-1st grade Lyons Pub. Schs., Clinton, 1939-44; tchr. kindergarten Clinton Pub. Schs., 1945-59. Iowa state rep. Early Childhood Edn. Conf., Washington, 1958, Study Conf. of Childhood in Edn., St. Louis, 1959. Contbr. poetry to American Poetry Anthology, 1984, I Have Need of the Poets, 1984, Hearts on Fire, 1985, Impressions, 1986, Best New Poets of 1989, 1989, Best Poems of the 90's, 1990, Expressions, 1991 (award of merit), Awaken to a Dream, 1991, Poetic Voices of America, 1991, Windows of the World, 1991, Down Peaceful Paths, 1991, Language of the Soul, 1992, Best Poems of 1995, 1995 (Editor's Choice award); contbr. poetry to mags. Sponsor Foster Parents Plan, Warwick, R.I., 1986-92, Children Internat., 1987-92. Summer sch. scholar Rockefeller Found., Duke U., Durham, N.C., 1955. Mem. AAUW (charter), NEA (life), PEO (internat. chpt. sisterhood), Internat. Soc. Poets, Delta Kappa Gamma (charter). Presbyterian. Avocations: reading, china painting, playing organ, knitting, travel. Home: Sarah Harding Retirement Home 308 S Bluff Blvd Room 502 Clinton IA 52732

WARNER, JEAN ROCKWELL, education educator; b. Towanda, Pa., Nov. 9, 1938; d. Henry Tracy and Genevieve Ann (Bryant) Rockwell. AA, Rider U., 1959, BS, 1962, MA, 1964; PhD, NYU, 1970. Instr., dir. student activities evening sch. Rider U., Lawrenceville, N.J., 1962-70, asst. dean evening sch., 1975-76, assoc. prof. undergrad. edn., 1976—; instr. bus. edn. NYU, N.Y.C., 1970-71; asst. prof. bus. edn. Hunter Coll., N.Y.C., 1971-75. Advisor Collegiate Secs. Internat., 1976-90; coord. Ptnrs. in Learning, 1988-94; undergrad. coord. NCATE, 2003—. Author: Informatio Processing For Colleges, 1986, RMT Information Processing Simulation, 1992; contbr. articles to profl. jours. Named Outstanding Young Women of Am., 1968. Mem. N.J. Bus. Educators Assn., Nat. Bus. Educators Assn., Delta Pi Epsilon. Republican. Presbyterian. Avocations: skiing, gardening. Office: Rider U 2083 Lawrenceville Rd Lawrenceville NJ 08648-3099

WARNER, JOHN D. aerospace company executive; b. Glendale, Calif., Jan. 4, 1940; Student, Drury Coll.; bachelor's, master's, PhD in Aero. Engring., U. Mich. Engr. supersonic transport program The Boeing Co., 1968—, engr. Boeing Comml. Airplanes Group, mgr. NASA terminal configured flight-test activity, 1974, chief tech. Boeing Comml. Airplanes Group, dir. devel. new digital auto pilot and navigation sys., 1980-82, mgr. airplane sys. design B-2 program, 1982-85, chief engr., 1985-87, advanced program mgr., 1987, v.p. engring. Boeing Comml. Airplanes Group, 1989-91, v.p. computing, 1991, pres. Boeing computer svcs., 1993-95, pres. Boeing info. and support svcs., 1995-97, sr. v.p., chief adminstrv. officer, 1997—; Boeing Sloan fellow Grad. Sch. Bus. Stanford U., 1976. Active various cmty. orgns.; bd. dirs. Pacific Sci. Ctr., Seattle Alliance Edn., Seattle Found., United Way Endowement Bd., Partnership for Learning, Corp. Coun. Arts, Washington Transp. Alliance. Fellow AIA, Royal Aero. Soc.; mem. NAE. Office: The Boeing Co 7755 E Marginal Way S Seattle WA 98108

WARNER, JOHN EDWARD, advertising executive; b. Troy, N.Y., Mar. 26, 1936; s. George Edward and Ann Frances (Teson) W.; m. Anne Elizabeth Hibbard, Sept. 19, 1959; children: Matthew J., Barbara A., Peter J., Christopher J. BS in Chemistry and Philosophy, Coll. Holy Cross, 1957. Promotion mgr. Union Carbide Corp., N.Y.C., 1957-62; acct. exec. McCann-Erickson, Inc., N.Y.C., 1962-64; pres. Warner, Bicking & Fenwick, Inc., N.Y.C., 1964-84; chmn. Warner, Bicking, Morris & Ptnrs. Inc., 1984-97; pres. Transworld Advt. Agy. network, 1987-97, Quatrefoil, Inc., 1998—. Bd. dirs. Thomas Pub. Co., N.Y.C. Author (non-fiction): Decorating Time Savers by Jack Warner, 2001. Home: 706 Hillcrest Rd Ridgewood NJ 07450-1110 E-mail: jawarner@optonline.net.

WARNER, JOHN HILLIARD, JR., technical services, military and commercial systems and software company executive; b. Santa Monica, Calif., Mar. 2, 1941; s. John Hilliard and Irene Anne (Oliva) W.; m. Helga Magdalena Farrington, Sept. 4, 1961; children: Tania Renee, James Michael. BS in Engring. with honors, UCLA, 1963, MS in Engring., 1965, PhD in Engring., 1967. Mem. staff Marquardt Corp., Van Nuys, Calif., 1963; mem. faculty West Coast U., L.A., 1969-72; mem. staff TRW Systems Group, Redondo Beach, Calif., 1967-70, sect. mgr., 1970-73; mem. staff Sci. Applications Internat. Corp., San Diego, 1973-75, asst. v.p., 1975-77, v.p., 1977-80, corp. v.p., 1980-81, sr. v.p., 1981-87, sector v.p., 1987-89; exec. v.p. Sci. Applications Internat Corp., San Diego, 1989-96, bd. dirs., 1988—; corp. exec. v.p. Sci. Applications Internat. Corp., San Diego, 1996—, chief adminstrv. officer, 2003—. Cons. Rand Corp., Santa Monica, 1964-66; bd. dirs. AMSEC LLC. Contbr. articles to profl. jours. Trustee Scripps Health, 2001—; bd. dirs. Corp. Dirs. Forum, 2001—. AEC fellow, 1963, 66, NSF fellow, 1964, 65. Mem. AIAA, Healthcare Info. and Mgmt. Sys. Soc., Assn. U.S. Army, Air Force Assn., NDIA, Armed Forces Comm. and Electronics Assn., Navy League U.S., La Jolla Chamber Music Soc. (bd. dirs. 1990-97, adv. bd. 1998-2001), San Diego C. of C. (bd. dirs. 2000—), Calif. C. of C. (bd. dirs. 2000—), Calif. Bus. Roundtable, Sigma Nu, Tau Beta Pi. Methodist. Avocations: bicycling, golf, fishing, music. Office: SAIC 10260 Campus Point Dr San Diego CA 92121-1522

WARNER, JOHN MERRITT, legislative staff member; b. Minot, ND, June 28, 1952; s. Glen Roy Warner and Joyce Ione Sherven; m. Janice Jeanne Kundy, June 12, 1982; children: Lisa, Krista, Mallory, Lindsey. BS in bacteriology, ND State U., 1974; BS in history, Minot State U., 1983. Legislator ND Legis., Bismarck, 1996—2004, mem. Janice Joanne legislative coun., budget sect., appropriations. Bd. mem. Minot Symphony Orchestra, 2000—. Democrat. Luth. Home: 33200 331 Ave SW Ryder ND 58779 Office: Legis Rsch Coun 600 E Blvd Bismarck ND 58505 Business E-Mail: jwarner@state.nd.us.

WARNER, JOHN WILLIAM, senator; b. Washington, Feb. 18, 1927; s. John William and Martha Stuart (Budd) W.;wife: Jeanne, children: Mary Conover, Virginia Stuart, John William IV. BS Engring., Washington and Lee U., 1949; LL.B., U. Va., 1953. Law clk. to U.S. judge, 1953-54; spl. asst. to U.S. atty., 1956-57; asst. U.S. atty. Dept. Justice, 1957-60; ptnr. Hogan & Hartson, 1960-68; owner, operator Atoka Cattle Farm, 1961—94; undersec. of navy, 1969-72; sec. of navy, 1972-74; adminstr. Am. Revolution Bicentennial Adminstrn., 1974-76; U.S. senator from Va., 1979—. Mem. environment and pub. works com., rules and adminstrn. com., nat. Rep. senatorial com. Served with USNR, 1944-46; to capt. USMCR, 1949-52. Mem. Bar Assn. D.C. Clubs: Metropolitan. Republican. Episcopalian. Office: US Senate 225 Russell Senate Bldg Washington DC 20510-0001

WARNER, KARL K. prosecutor; BS, U.S. Mil. Acad.; JD, W.Va. U. Gen. counsel to 10th Mountain Div. U.S. Army, 1994—96; legal counsel to Multi-Nat. Force Joint Chiefs of Staff, Haiti, 1994—95, legal counsel to two chmn., joint chiefs staff, 1996—98; gen. counsel U.S. Spl. Ops. Command, 1998—2001; U.S. atty. so. dist. W.Va. U.S. Dept. Justice, 2001—. Office: PO Box 1713 Charleston WV 25326

WARNER, KENNETH E. public health educator, consultant; b. Washington, Jan. 25, 1947; s. Edgar W. Jr. and Betty (Strasburger) W.; m. Patricia A. Hilty, Oct. 1, 1977; children— Peter, Andrew AB, Dartmouth Coll., 1968; MPhil, Yale U., 1970, PhD, 1974. Lectr. dept. health mgmt. and policy Sch. Pub. Health, U. Mich., Ann Arbor, 1972—74, asst. prof., 1974—77, assoc. prof., 1977—83, prof., 1983—, chmn., 1982—88, 1992—95, Richard D. Remington Collegiate prof. pub. health, 1995—2001, dir. Tobacco Rsch. Network, Avedis Donabedian Disting. Univ. prof. pub. health, 2001—. Cons., Washington, 1976—95, Office on Smoking and Health, USPHS, Rockville, Md., 1978—, Inst. Medicine, Nat. Acad. Scis., Washington, 1984—, numerous additional pub. and pvt. orgns.; mem. bd. sci. counselors divsn. cancer prevention and control Nat. Cancer Inst., Bethesda, Md., 1985—89. Author: (with Bryan Luce) Cost-Benefit & Cost Effectiveness Analysis in Health Care, 1982; contbr. articles to profl. jours. Trustee Am. Lung Assn., Mich., Lansing, 1982; mem. subcom. on smoking Am. Heart Assn., Dallas, 1983-87; mem. com. on tobacco and cancer Am. Cancer Soc., N.Y.C., 1984-92; bd. dirs. Am. Legacy Found., 1999-2003. Hon. Woodrow Wilson fellow, 1968; W.K. Kellog Found. fellow, 1980-83; vis. scholar Nat. Bur. Econ. Research, Stanford, Calif., 1975-76; recipient Surgeon Gen.'s medallion Dr. C. Everett Koop, 1989. Fellow Assn. Health Svcs. Rsch.; mem. APHA (leadership award 1990), Am. Econ. Assn., Inst. Medicine, Nat. Assn. Pub. Health Policy, Phi Beta Kappa. Office: U Michigan Dept Health Sch Pub Health Mgmt Policy 109 Observatory St Ann Arbor MI 48109-2029 E-mail: kwarner@umich.edu.

WARNER, KENNETH WILSON, JR., editor, association and publications executive; b. Chgo., Dec. 22, 1928; s. Kenneth Wilson and Ann S. (Knapp) W.; m. Deborah Ann Bollo, Dec. 28, 1982 (div. Apr. 1995); 1 child, Joseph; children by previous marriages: Sara, Seth, Katharin. BS Ed., No. Ill. State Teachers Coll., 1950. Staff editor Bldg. Supply News, Chgo., 1953-56; staff editor Elec. Merchandising, 1956-60; free-lance writer Sarasota, Fla., 1960-66; editor Gunsport Mag., Alexandria and Falls Church, Va., 1966-67, Gunfacts Mag., Arlington, Va., 1968-70, pub., 1968-70; exec. editor Am. Rifleman, Nat. Rifle Assn., Washington, 1971-78, asst. dir. publs. div., 1972-78; editor Am. Hunter, 1973-78, Am. Rifleman, 1976-78; dir. publs. NRA, Washington, 1977-78; editor in chief Gun Digest, Knives Annual-Krause Publs., Inc., Greenville, W.Va., 1979-99; editor, pub. Knives Digest Two Knife Guys Pub., Inc., Chattanooga, 2000—01; pres. Knifeware, Inc., Greenville, W.Va. Cons. firearms and cutlery cos.; co-founder Am. Knife and Tool Inst., 1997. Author: The Practical Book of Knives. 1976; The Practical Book of Guns, 1978. Editor: The Bolt Action, 1976. Contbr. articles to profl. jours. Cpl. U.S. Army. 1951-53. Recipient Cutlery Hall of Fame; inducted into Am. Bladesmith Soc. Hall of Fame, 1999. Mem.: NRA (life), Knifemaker's Guild Am. (assoc.). Office: Prin Office PO Box 52 Greenville WV 24945-0052 Personal E-mail: knifeware@earthlink.net.

WARNER, KRIS, political organization administrator; V.chmn Rep. Party W.Va., 1998—2002, chmn., 2002—. Republican. Achievements include raising more than $100,000 for the Republican party; getting 94 Republican candidates to file to run for the House of Delegates and the State Senate. Office: 5019 MacCorkle Ave, SW South Charleston WV 25303

WARNER, KURT (KURTIS WARNER), professional football player; b. Burlington, Iowa, June 22, 1971; m. Brenda Warner; 4 children. BA in Comm., No. Ill. U. Quarterback Iowa Barnstormers (Arena Football League), 1995—97, Amsterdam Admirals (NFL Europe), 1998, St. Louis Rams (NFL), 1998—2004, N.Y. Giants, East Rutherford, NJ, 2004—. Founder First Things First Found., 1999—. Named NFL MVP, 1999, 2001, Super Bowl XXXIV MVP, 2000; named to, NFL Pro-Bowl, 1999—2001. Achievements include led NFL in passing touchdowns, 1999, 2001, passing yards, completions, 2001; quarterback Super Bowl Championship Team, Super Bowl XXXIV, 2000; tied the NFL record with six consecutive 300-yard passing games during 2000-01 season; set record for highest rated passer in NFL history, 2002; holds Super Bowl record with 414 passing yards; only player in NFL history to record perfect passer rating of 158.3 twice in his career. Office: c/o NY Football Giants Giants Stadium East Rutherford NJ 07073*

WARNER, LAVERNE, education educator; b. Huntsville, Tex., Aug. 14, 1941; d. Clifton Partney and Velma Oneta (Steely) W. BS, Sam Houston State U., 1962, MEd, 1969; PhD, East Tex. State U., 1977. Cert. elem. sch. tchr., Tex. First grade tchr. Port Arthur (Tex.) Ind. Sch. Dist., 1962-64; kindergarten tchr. Burlington (Vt.) Cmty. Schs., 1964-66; first grade tchr. Aldine Sch. Dist., Houston, 1967-68; music tchr. Crawfordsville (Ind.) Cmty. Schs., 1968-71; prof. early childhood edn. Sam Houston State U., Huntsville, 1975—, chmn. faculty senate, 1988-89. Chair faculty senate Sam Houston State U., 1990-91, chair-elect, 1989-90; educator preparation Improvement Initiative, 1996-97. Author: (with P. Berry) Tunes for Tots, 1982; (with K. Craycraft) Fun with Familiar Tunes, 1987, Language in Centers: Kids Communicating, 1991, Theme Escapades, 1992, What If...Themes, 1993; (with Sharon Lynch) Preschool Classroom Solutions, 2004; contbg. editor Good Apple, Inc., 1986-88, 91-93; contbr. over 90 articles to profl. jours. Mem. Huntsville Leadership Inst., 1986-88, chmn. adv. bd. 1987-88, chmn. 1987-88; Community Child Care Assn., Huntsville, 1988-90. Recipient Sam Houston State U. Excellence in Teaching award, 1992, Tchr. Educator of Yr. award Tex. Assn. for Edn. Young Children, 1992, Sammy award Divsn. of Student Life, 1996, Millennium Counselor's award Kappa Delta Pi; grantee Am. Assn. Higher Edn., Tex. Mem. Nat. Assn. Edn. Young Children (life, co-editor Young Children), So. Early Childhood Assn. (chair publs. adv. bd. 1998-2000, bd. dirs. 2002-), Tex. Assn. Coll. Tchrs. (life, past pres.), Tex. Elementary-Kindergarten Nursery Educators (state pres. 1982-84), Tex. Assn. for Edn. Young Children (v.p. 1988-89, newsletter editor, 1991-93, Tchr. Educator of Yr. 1992, pres.-elect 1993-95, pres. 1995-97, so. early childhood rep. 2002-04), Huntsville Leadership Inst. Alumni Assn. (pres. 1988-89), Phi Delta Kappa (area 3H coord. 1986-92, Svc. Key 1987), Sam Houston Assn. for Edn. Young Children (charter, pres-elect, 1991-92, pres. 1992-93, v.p. for membership, advisor 1997—), Sam Houston Univ. Women (pres. 1985-86), Huntsville High Sch. Ex-Students Assn. (charter, pres. 1989-91), Sam Houston Alumni Assn. (bd. dirs. 1996-99, Laverne Warner Early Childhood scholar 2003). Mem. Ch. of Christ. Avocations: music, reading, shopping. Office: Sam Houston State U Coll Edn and Applied Sci Huntsville TX 77341 E-mail: edu_lxw@shsu.edu.

WARNER, MARK R. governor; b. Indpls., Ind., Dec. 15, 1954; m. Lisa Collis; children: Madison, Gillian, Eliza. Bachelors, George Washington U., 1977; JD, Harvard U., 1980. Founding ptnr. Columbia Capital Corp., Alexandria, Va.; gov. State of Va., 2001—. Mem. Nat. Gov. Assn. (chmn.). Founding chmn. Va. Health Care Found.; creator SeniorNavigator.com; founder TechRiders, Va. High-Tech Partnership; co-chmn. Va. Cmtys. in Schs. Found.; mem. Old Presbyn. Meeting House; past bd. dirs. Va. Union U., George Washington U., Appalachian Sch. Law, Va. Found. for Ind. Colls., Va. Math and Sci. Coalition. Office: Office of Gov State Capitol 3d Fl Richmond VA 23219

WARNER, MINER HILL, investment banker; b. N.Y.C., Aug. 13, 1942; s. Bradford Arnold and Nancy (Hill) W.; m. Ellen C. Murphy, Mar. 18, 1972; children— Alix Mallet-Prevost, Lily Wolcott. AB, Harvard U., 1964; C.E.P., Institut d'Etudes Politiques, Paris, 1963; M.Sc. in Econs., London Sch. Econs., 1965; LL.B., U. Pa., 1968; postgrad., NYU. Grad. Sch. Bus. Adminstrn., 1971-73. Bar: N.Y. 1969. Assoc. Shearman & Sterling. N.Y.C., 1968-71; assoc. Salomon Bros. Inc., N.Y.C., 1971-73; v.p. Salomon Bros. Internat. Ltd., London, 1974-78; v.p., mgr. Salomon Bros. Inc., N.Y.C., 1979-87; dir. Merrill Lynch & Co., N.Y.C., 1988-92; pres. Pub. Resources Internat., N.Y.C., 1992-95, chmn., 1996—. Adv. dir. Coun. of the Americas, 1991-93. Mem. Pres.'s Pvt. Sector Survey on Cost Control, Washington, 1982-83; mem. coun. Grad. Theol. Union, Berkeley, Calif., 1998-; vestryman St. John's Ch., Fishers Island, N.Y., 1980-99, sr. warden, 1994-99; regent Cathedral of St. John the Divine, N.Y., 1995-97, trustee, 1997—;English-Speaking Union U.S. (bd. dirs., mem. exec. com. 2002-, mem. task force Gen. Theol. Sem., N.Y., 2000-02; mem. exec. com. Pilgrims, N.Y.C.; trustee N.Y. Hist. Soc. 1985—, chmn. 1994-99, chmn. emeritus, 1999—, Econ. Club, N.Y. Decorated Order of St. John of Jerusalem. Mem. Pub. Securities Assn. (guaranteed loan com. 1980-86), Mayflower Soc. (gov.), Brook Club (sec.), River Club, Met. Club (Washington), Fishers Island Club, Hay Harbor Club (Fishers Island) (former dir.), Links Club. Republican. Episcopalian. Home: 148 E End Ave New York NY 10028-7503 Office: Pub Resources Internat 780 3d Ave Ste 2805 New York NY 10017-2024

WARNER, NEARI FRANCOIS, university president; b. New Orleans, July 20, 1945; d. Cornelius and Enell (Brimmer) Francois; m. Jimmie Duel Warner Sr., June 6, 1970 (div. Sept. 1983); 1 child, Jimmie Duel Jr. BS, Grambling (La.) State U., 1967; MA, Atlanta U., 1968; PhD, La. State U., 1992. Dir. Upward Bound So. U., New Orleans, 1976-89, dean jr. divsn., 1989-94; asst. v.p. acad. affairs Grambling State U., 1994-96, v.p. student affairs, 1996-97, v.p. devel., 1997-99, acting v.p. acad. affairs, 1999, provost, v.p. acad. affairs, 1999—. Sec. Conf. La. Colls./Univs., 1999—; mem. State Funding Task Force, State of La., 1998-99; bd. dirs. La. Endowment for Humanities, 1998—; pres. La. Assn. Student Asst. Program, 1986-88. Preface writer: Interdisciplinary Approach, 1998. Mem. adv. bd. Pupil Progression Commn., New Orleans, 1989-93; mem. task force Gov.'s Tech. Prep., Baton Rouge, 1991-93, Mayor's Task Force for Edn., New Orleans, 1992, Monroe (La.) City Sch., 1995. Named Role model YWCA, New Orleans, 1992, Disting. Alumnae Nat. Assn. Equal Opportunity, Washington, 1996. Mem. AAUW, NAACP, The Links, Inc. (treas. 1999—, Unsung Hero 1993), Alpha Kappa Alpha, Kappa Delta Pi, Pi Gamma Mu Democrat. Baptist. Avocations: reading, bowling. Home: PO Box 989 Grambling LA 71245-0989 Office: Grambling State U PO Box 1170 Grambling LA 71245-1170 E-mail: nfwarner@martin.gram.edu.

WARNER, NELSON ALFRED, dermatologist; b. Detroit, July 31, 1940; s. Stanley Lester and Dorothy Blanch (Nelson) W.; m. Sheryl Lee Pearson, Feb., 1966 (div. Oct. 1976); children: Christine Berea, Jennifer Lee, Pamela Suzanne; m. Kathleen Ann Dailey, Nov. 23, 1976 (div. Oct. 1986); 1 child, Andrew James; m. Jacqueline Patricia Hanks, Sept. 21, 1992 (div. Jan. 1999). AB, Albion Coll., 1962; MD, U. Mich., 1966. Diplomate Am. Bd. Dermatology. Flight surgeon USAF, San Antonio and Nakhon Phanom, Thailand, 1967-69; resident in dermatology Meml. Hosp., U. N.C., Chapel Hill, 1970-73; dermatologist Winter Haven, Fla., 1973—. Author: (with others) Manual for Nurse Practitioners, 1975. Pres. Rotary Club of Cypress Gardens, Winter Haven, Fla., 1981-82; bd. dirs. Theatre of Winter Haven, 1985-87. Capt. USAF, 1967-69. Recipient Alfred P. Sloan scholarship, 1958, U. Mich. Regents Alumni scholarship, 1962, Commendation medal USAF, 1969. Fellow Am. Acad. Dermatology; mem. AMA, Fla. Med. Assn., Fla. Soc. Dermatology, Polk County Med. Assn., Air Force Assn. Avocations: antique and custom automobiles, cooking, guitar playing, motorcycles, garden railroading. Home: 1245 Lake Elbert Dr NE Winter Haven FL 33881-4380 Office: 429 2nd St NW Winter Haven FL 33881-4168

WARNER, PATRICIA ANN, secondary school educator; b. Wooster, Ohio, Dec. 21, 1949; d. Kent Branson and Irene Mae (Graves) W. BA in English, Coll. of Wooster, 1972, MAT in English, 1973. Cert. tchr., Ohio; nat. bd. cert. tchr. adolescence and young adulthood English lang. arts. Instr. in English Orrville (Ohio) H.S., 1974—, Wayne Col., Orrville, Ohio, 1988-91. Named Orrville (Ohio) City Schs. Tchr. of Yr., 1987-88, Jennings Scholar Jennings Found., 1994-95. Mem. NEA, NCTE, Ohio Council of Tchrs. of English and Language Arts. Office: Orrville HS 841 N Ella St Orrville OH 44667-1154

WARNER, PAUL M. prosecutor; BA, Brigham Young U., 1973, JD, 1976, MPA, 1984. With Utah Atty. Gen.'s Office, 1991-98; asst. U.S. atty. U.S. Dept. Justice, Utah, 1998—2001, U.S. atty., 2001—. Office: 185 S State St Ste 400 Salt Lake City UT 84103-4139

WARNER, PETER DAVID, publishing executive; b. Phila., Aug. 15, 1942; s. Robert and Myra (Spector) W.; m. Ruth Bluestein (div. 1982); m. Jill Sansone, 1983; children: Emily, Cynthia, Nicholas. BA, NYU, 1964. Asst. dir. membership and devel. Mus. Modern Art, N.Y.C., 1973-76; editor, promotion dir. Book-of-the-Month Club, N.Y.C., 1976-79; pres. Thames and Hudson, N.Y.C., 1979—. Author: Loose Ends, 1972, Lifestyle, 1986. Mem. The Writers Room (bd. dirs.), The Century Assn. Office: Thames & Hudson Inc 500 5th Ave New York NY 10110-0002

WARNER, RAWLEIGH, JR., oil company executive; b. Chgo., Feb. 13, 1921; s. Rawleigh and Dorothy (Haskins) W.; m. Mary Ann deClairmont, Nov. 2, 1946; children: Alison W. Pyne, Suzanne W. Parsons. Grad., Lawrenceville (N.J.) Sch., 1940; AB cum laude, Princeton U., 1943. Sec., treas. Warner Bard Co., Chgo., 1946-48; with Continental Oil Co., 1948-53, asst. treas., 1952-53; treas. Socony-Vacuum Overseas Supply Co., 1953-55; asst. treas. Mobil Overseas Oil Co., 1955-56; mgr. econs. dept., then mgr. Middle East dept. Socony Mobil Oil Co. Inc., 1956-59; regional v.p. Mobil Internat. Oil Co., 1959-60, exec. v.p., 1960-63, pres., 1963-64; exec. v.p., dir. Mobil Oil Corp. (formerly Socony Mobil Oil Co., Inc.), 1964, pres., 1965-69, chmn. bd., chief exec. officer, 1969-86; chmn. Mobil Corp., 1976-86. Served to capt. F.A., AUS, 1943-45. Decorated Purple Heart, Bronze Star, Silver Star. Mem. Am. Petroleum Inst. Clubs: Augusta (Ga.) Nat. Golf; Links (N.Y.C.); New Canaan Country; Blind Brook (Rye Brook, N.Y.); Jupiter Island (Hobe Sound, Fla.); Seminole (North Palm Beach, Fla.). Republican. Presbyterian. Office: Mobil Corp 375 Park Ave Ste 2901 New York NY 10152-2999

WARNER, ROBERT EDSON, physics educator; b. Gallipolis, Ohio, Apr. 11, 1931; s. Robert and Ada Florence (Roush) W.; m. Mary Lou Clark, June 26, 1954 (div. May 1977); children: Ruth Berlow, Margaret Bushee, Deborah Blackburn, Elizabeth Seth; m. Mary Ann Stepka, Jan. 4, 1986. BS, Antioch Coll., 1954; PhD, U. Rochester, 1959. Asst. prof. physics U. Rochester, 1959-61, Antioch Coll., Yellow Springs, Ohio, 1961-63; asst. to assoc. prof. physics U. Manitoba, Winnipeg, 1963-65; assoc. to full prof. physics Oberlin (Ohio) Coll., 1965—2002, physics dept. chair, 1990-93, Longman prof. natural sci., 1995—2002. Vis. prof. of physics, master tchr. U. Mich., Ann Arbor, 1993-94; users exec. com. Nat. Superconducting Cyclotron Lab., East Lansing, Mich., 1995-98; reviewer NSF; vis. fellowship Japan Soc. for Promotion of Sci., 1995. Contbr. numerous articles to profl. jours.; referee Am. Jour. of Physics and Phys. Rev. Mem. Cleve. Orch. Chorus. Rsch. grantee NSF, 1965-99; postdoctoral fellowship NSF, 1971-72, predoctoral fellowship, 1957-59. Mem. AAUP, Am. Phys. Soc. (faculty mem. for rsch. in undergrad. inst. prize 1999), Audubon Soc. Democrat. Baptist. Avocations: singing, hiking, cross country skiing, reading, conservation activities. Office: Oberlin Coll Physics Dept Oberlin OH 44074 E-mail: robert.warner@oberlin.edu.

WARNER, ROBERT MARK, university dean, archivist, historian; b. Montrose, Colo., June 28, 1927; s. Mark Thomas and Bertha Margaret (Rich) W.; m. Eleanor Jane Bullock, Aug. 21, 1954; children: Mark Steven, Jennifer Jane. Student, U. Denver, 1945; BA, Muskingum Coll., 1949, LL.D. (hon.), 1981; MA, U. Mich., 1953, PhD, 1958; H.H.D. (hon.), Westminster (Pa.) Coll., 1981; L.H.D. (hon.), DePaul U., 1983. Tchr. high sch., Montrose, Colo., 1949-50; lectr. dept. history U. Mich., 1958-66, assoc. prof., 1966-71, prof., 1971-97, prof. emeritus, 1997—, prof. Sch. Info., 1974-97, emeritus, 1997—,

dean Sch. Info. and Library Studies, 1985-92, univ. historian, 1992—, interim dir. Univ. Libraries, 1988-90; asst. in rsch. Bentley Hist. Libr., 1953-57, asst. curator, 1957-61, asst. dir., 1961-66, dir., 1966-80; archivist of U.S., 1980 85. Mem. exec. com. Bentley Hist. Libr., 1988—; bd. visitors Sch. Libr. Sci., Case Western Res. U., 1976-80, chmn., 1980-84, Maxwell Sch. Govt., Syracuse U., 1982-87; chmn. Gerald R. Ford Presdl. Libr. Bldg. Com., 1977-79; bd. dirs., sec. Gerald R. Ford Found., 1987—; trustee Woodrow Wilson Internat. Ctr. for Scholars, 1980-85, chmn. fellowship com., 1983-85; chmn. Nat. Hist. Publs. and Records Commn., 1980-85; mem. exec. com. Internat. Coun. on Archives, 1984-88; pres. 2d European Conf. on Archives, 1989; comptroller gen. U.S. Rsch. and Edn. Adv. Com., 1988-2000; rsch. adv. com. Online Computer Libr. Ctr., 1990-93; bd. govs. Clements Libr., 1988-90, 93—2004, Clark Hist. Libr. Ctrl. Mich. U., 1987—; vis. prof. UCLA, 1993. Author: Chase S. Osborn, 1860-1949, 1960, Profile of a Profession, 1964, (with R. Bordin) The Modern Manuscript Library, 1966, (with C.W. Vanderhill) A Michigan Reader: 1865 to the Present, 1974, (with F. Blouin) Sources for the Study of Migration and Ethnicity, 1979, Diary of a Dream: A History of the National Archives Independence Movement, 1980-1985, 1995. Served with U.S. Army, 1950-52. Recipient Disting. Svc. award Muskingum Coll., 1990, Disting. Svc. award Nat. Hist. Pub. and Records Commn., 1992. Fellow Soc. Am. Archivists; mem. Am. Hist. Assn. (council 1981-85), Orgn. Am. Historians, ALA (council 1986-91), Assn. for Library and Info. Sci. Edn., Presbyn. Hist. Soc. (bd. dirs. 1987-91), Am. Assn. State and Local History, Hist. Soc. Mich. (trustee 1960-66, v.p. 1972-73, pres. 1973-74), Soc. Am. Archivists (mem. council 1967-71, sec., exec. dir. 1971-73, v.p. 1974-75, pres. 1976 77), Am. Antiquarian Soc., Phi Alpha Theta, Beta Phi Mu. Clubs: U. Mich. Research. Lodges: Rotary. Presbyterian. Home: 1821 Coronada St Ann Arbor MI 48103-5066 Office: U Mich Sch Info 550 E University Ave Ann Arbor MI 48109-1092 E-mail: archlib@umich.edu.

WARNER, ROBERTA ARLENE, retired accountant, financial services executive; b. Binghamton, N.Y., Dec. 31, 1938; d. Murrilan Earl and Ethel Margaret (Bell) W. BA, SUNY, Binghamton, 1960; MBA, Ind. U., 1962, MHA with highest distinction, 1973. CPA, N.Y.; lic. nursing home adminstr., N.Y. Sr. acct. Arthur Young & Co., CPA, Buffalo, 1962—66; acctg. supr. Children's Hosp., Buffalo, 1966—68; contr. King Manor Nursing Homes-Ave. Bldg. Corp., Buffalo, 1968—71; asst. dir. health fin. Hosp. Assn. N.Y. State, Albany, 1973—80, dir. health fin., 1980—93, Healthcare Assn. N.Y. State, Albany, 1994—97, dir. data analysis and stds., 1997—98; pres. Roberta A. Warner Co., 1999—2003, ret., 2003. Author articles in field. Trustee Ednl. Found. of Am. Women's Soc. CPA, Am. Soc. Women Accts., 1985-87. Fellow Healthcare Fin. Mgmt. Assn.; mem. AICPA, Am. Acctg. Assn., Am. Soc. Women Accts. (pres. Buffalo chpt. 1967-68), Am. Women's Soc. CPA, N.Y. State Soc. CPA, Ind. U. Alumni Assn. (life), SUNY Binghamton Alumni Assn. (life), Grange. Methodist. Home: 569 NY Rte 79 Windsor NY 13865-2714

WARNER, ROLLIN MILES, JR., economics educator, real estate broker; b. Evanston, Ill., Dec. 25, 1930; s. Rollin Miles Warner Sr. and Julia Herndon (Polk) Clarkson. BA, Yale U., 1953; cert. in law, Harvard U., 1956; MBA, Stanford U., 1960; cert. in edn. adminstrn., U. San Francisco, 1974. Lic. real estate broker Real Estate Cert. Inst., Calif. Asst. to v.p. fin. Stanford U., 1960-63; instr. history Town Sch., San Francisco, 1963-70, instr. econs. and history, dean, 1975—; prin. Mt. Tamalpais, Ross, Calif., 1972-74; dir. devel. Katharine Branson Sch., Ross, 1974-75, instr. econs., history, math. and outdoor edn. Author: America, 1986, Europe, 1986, Africa, Asia, Russia, 1986, Greece, Rome, 1981, Free Enterprise at Work, 1986. From scoutmaster to summer camp commr. Boy Scouts Am., San Francisco, 1956—. Served to lt. USNR, 1953—55, Korea, Pacific, Vietnam. Recipient Silver Beaver award Boy Scouts Am., 1986, Town Sch. medal Town Sch. for Boys Alumni Coun., 1995. Mem.: U.S. Naval Inst., Marines Meml. Assn., South End Rowing Club (San Francisco), Univ. Club (San Francisco), San Francisco Yacht Club (Belvedere, Calif.), Grolier Club NY. Office: Town Sch 2750 Jackson St San Francisco CA 94115-1195 E-mail: warnerrollinm1960@alumni-gsb.stanford.edu.

WARNER, SCOTT DENNIS, investment banker; b. York, Pa., July 13, 1963; s. Earl Dennis and Sandra Glee (Barnhart) W. SB in Elec. Engring., SB in Computer Sci. and Engring., SM in Elec. Engring. and Computer Sci., MIT, 1986; MBA in Fin., U. Chgo., 1990. Intern IBM Corp., Yorktown Heights, N.Y., 1983-86; fin. analyst Merrill Lynch & Co., N.Y.C., 1986-88, assoc., 1990-94, v.p., 1994-95; summer assoc. Goldman, Sachs & Co., N.Y.C., 1989; v.p. Lipper & Co., L.P., N.Y.C., 1995-98, Gerard Klauer Mattison & Co., Inc., N.Y.C., 1998—2002; pres. Warner Capital, S.e.c.s., Luxembourg, 2003—. Nat. Merit scholar, 1981, ROTC scholar, 1981, teaching asst. scholar MIT, 1985, 86; Leon C. Marshall scholar U. Chgo., 1988. Mem. Nat. Eagle Scout Assn., Delta Upsilon Frat. Republican. Presbyterian. Office: Warner Capital Secs 6 Montee Du Grund L-1645 Luxembourg Luxembourg E-mail: scottdwarner@yahoo.com.

WARNER, STEVEN S. dean; s. Eugene Burris, Sr. and Beate U. Warner; m. Tresa Marie Turvin, Oct. 10, 1971; children: Alexandra Lexi Beate, Carson Scott. BSBA, Webber Internat. U., Fla., 1995, MBA, 2002—. Profl. devel. program: NAFSA, Assn. of Profl. Educators 2002, NAFS, Assn. of Internat. Educators 2003, Ednl. Law; U. Vt. 2003; Nat. Coaching Lic. U.S. Soccer Fedn., 1998. Mgr. bookstore Webber Internat. U., Babson Park, Fla., 1992—2002, head men's soccer coach, 1992—2002, dean of men, 1996—98, head women's soccer coach, 1997—2002, dean student devel., 2002—. Mem. Nat. Urea Cycle Disorders Found., La Canada, Calif., 1998. Mem.: NAFSA, Assn. of Internat. Educators, Nat. Soccer Coaches Assn., U.S. Soccer Fedn. (life). Independent. Roman Catholic. Avocations: hunting, fishing, soccer, travel. Office: Webber Internat Univ 1201 N Scenic Hwy Babson Park FL 33827 Office Phone: 863-638-2914. Office Fax: 863-638-2823. E-mail: warnersteve@hotmail.com.

WARNER, SUSAN, federal agency administrator; b. Rochester, N.Y., July 20, 1956; d. Harold J. and Jeannette (Nichols) Warner; divorced; children: Jennifer Lynn, Kathryn Alice. BA, Miami U., Oxford, Ohio, 1978; postgrad., Xavier U. Loan specialist HUD, Columbus, Ohio, 1978-79, Cin., 1979-83; fin. planner IDS Fin. Services, Inc., Cin., 1983-86, Manufacturer's Hanover Mortgage Corp., 1986, Shawmut Mortgage Corp., 1986-87, U.S. Dept. HUD, St. Louis, 1987—. Housing cons., Cin., 1985—. Author: Community Land Coop. Residents' Handbook, 1986. Adv. Cin. Tech. Coll., 1984 ; mem. fin. com. Community Land Coop., Cin., 1985—; exhibits chair Conf. Cin. Women, 1985, corp. patrons chair, 1986, conf. coordinator, 1987—; vol. Am. Cancer soc., 1981-84, March of Dimes, 1996-2003; leader Girl Scouts. Recipient Mercury awards IDS, Cin., 1984, award for superior performance U.S. Inspector Gen. HUD, 1990, Profl. Team 2003 Excellence in Govt. award The Greater St. Louis Fed. Exec. Bd., 2003. Republican. Roman Catholic. Avocations: reading, costume designing, making teddy bears, softball, theater. Home: 771 Seven Hills Ln Saint Charles MO 63304-1436 Office: US Dept HUD 1222 Spruce St Saint Louis MO 63103-2818

WARNER, THEODORE KUGLER, JR., lawyer; b. Phila., Sept. 13, 1909; s. Theodore Kugler and Anna (Allen) W.; m. Dorothy Wark Hoehler, Nov. 23, 1935 (dec. 1985); children: Betsy Ann, Peter Joyce; m. Lynn Howell, May 20, 1995. AB, U. Pa., 1931, LL.B. cum laude, 1934. Bar: Pa. 1934. With Pa. R.R., Phila., 1934-70, chief tax counsel, 1952-58, dir. taxation, 1958-68; v.p. taxes Penn Central, 1968, v.p. accounting and taxes, 1968-69, v.p. corp. adminstrn., 1969-70; pres. Can. So. Ry., 1968-70; v.p. Pitts. & Lake Erie R.R., 1968-70; officer, dir. other Penn Central cos., 1968-70; counsel Duane, Morris & Heckscher, Phila., 1970-71, Harper & Driver, 1975—. Lectr. on consol. returns various tax forums. Bd. suprs. Easttown Twp., Pa., 1962-70, chmn., 1966-70; bd. dirs. Independence Found., 1991—, sec. 1993, pres., 1993-95, sec.-treas., 1996— Mem. ABA, Nat. Tax Assn. (pres. 1965-66), Am. Law Inst. (life mem.), Pa. Bar Assn., Order of Coif, Union League, Masons (33 deg., com. on masonic homes 1970-84, chmn. 1975-77, 81-83, Franklin medal 1983, bd. dirs., treas. Masonic libr. and mus. 1991-99), Tau Kappa Epsilon. Republican. Presbyn. Home: 702 The Touraine 1520 Spruce St Philadelphia PA 19102 Office: 200 S Broad St Ste 1101 Philadelphia PA 19102 Office Phone: 215-985-4009.

WARNER, TOKESHA L, health facility administrator; d. Johnny W. and Mary M. (Wilson) Warner; 1 child, Stefan Wright. BA, Earlham Coll., 1996; postgrad., Walden U., 2002—. Event coord., Nashville, 1996—98; program coord. Vanderbilt Children's Hosp., Nashville, 1999—. Co chmn., diversity workgroup Assn. of U. Ctrs. on Disabilities, Silver Spring, Md., 2003—; chmn. football program Tenn. Police Athletic League, Nashville, 2002—03. Independent. Avocations: creative writing & poetry, nature photography, archaeology of colonial america. Office: Vanderbilt Children's Hosp 2100 Pierce Ave Ste 426 Nashville TN 37212-3573 E-mail: tokesha.warner@vanderbilt.edu.

WARNER, WALTER D. corporate executive, director; m. Susan Dee Hafferkamp, Nov. 15, 1975 (div. 1982); 1 child, Natalie. BS, Drake U., 1975. Ops. officer Iowa-Des Moines Nat. Bank, 1975 78; from v.p. ops. to v.p. mktg. and pub. rels. Cen. Savs. and Loan Assn., San Diego, Calif., 1978-84; pres. The Lomas Santa Fe Cos., Solana Beach, Calif., 1985-91; pres., co-founder Ebert Composites Corp., San Diego, 1991—, also bd. dirs.; pres., CEO Strongwell Ebert LLC, San Diego, 1998-01, also bd. dirs.; CEO Pacific Environ. Sys. LLC, 2001—. Bd. dirs. Torrey Pines Bank, Solana Beach, Lomas Group Inc., Del Mar, Calif., Madison Valley Properties, Inc., La Jolla, Calif., Nature Preserved of Am. Inc., San Clemente, Calif.; pres., bd. dirs. Regents Park Comml. Assn., La Jolla, Strongwell Ebert. Bd. dirs. Inst. of the Ams., La Jolla, 1986-90, mem. internat. coun., 1986-90; chmn. bd. dirs., pres. San Diego chpt. Arthritis Found., 1985-87; dir., pres. Gildred Found., Solana Beach, 1986-90; founding dir., treas. Golden Triangle Arts Found. Mem. Calif. League of Savs. and Loans (mktg. and ops. com. 1982-84), Internat. Forum for Corp. Dirs., Iowa Club San Diego (founding dir. 1984-85). Republican. Protestant. Avocations: tennis, piano.

WARNER, WILLIAM HAMER, applied mathematician; b. Pitts., Oct. 6, 1929; s. John Christian and Louise (Hamer) W.; m. Janet Louise West, June 29, 1957; 1 dau., Katherine Patricia. Student, Haverford Coll., 1946-48; BS, Carnegie Inst. Tech., 1950, MS, 1951, PhD, 1953. Research asso. grad. div. applied math. Brown U., Providence, 1953-55; asst. prof. dept. aerospace engring. and mechanics U. Minn., Mpls., 1955-58, asso. prof., 1958-68, prof., 1968 95, prof. emeritus, 1995—. Author: (with L.E. Goodman) Statics, 1963, Dynamics, 1964; contbr. articles to profl. jours. Mem.: Soc. Natural Philosophy, Math. Assn. Am., Soc. Indsl. and Applied Math., Am. Math. Soc. Office: Univ Minn 107 Akerman Hall 110 Union St SE Minneapolis MN 55455-0153 E-mail: warner@aem.umn.edu.

WARNER-MILLS, SUSAN, organizational and community development consultant; b. Columbus, Ohio, Jan. 1, 1958; d. Robert Lawrence and Elise (Ackley) Mills; m. Thomas Everett Warner, Sept. 14, 1980; 1 child, Robert. BA, Bucknell U., 1979; MPA, Pa. State U., 1991. Office mgr. Tech. Edn. Resource Ctrs., Cambridge, Mass., 1980-81; editl. asst. Daedalus Jour., Cambridge, 1981-82; mng. ptnr. The Lewisburg (Pa.) Inn, 1982—; project dir., Cmty. Connection Project LWV of Pa. Citizen Edn. Fund, Harrisburg, 1995-98; program devel. specialist Cmty. Connection of Pa., 1999—; ptnr. Groupworks Cons., 1998—. Contbr. articles to profl. jours. Pres. LWV Lewisburg Area, 1991-94; citizens jury rev. com., LWV of Pa., 1993, budget com. mem., 1992, bd. dirs. 1997-99; founder Indsl. Roundtable Environ. Mgmt. Ctrl. Pa., 1994; bd. dirs. Merrill Linn Land and Waterways Conservancy, 1993-96; Slifer House Mus., 1992-97; sec., Union County appointee Mid-State Resource Conservation and Devel. Coun., 1992-97; elected mem. Union County Dem. Com., 1984-86; co-founder, dir. Citizens for Social Responsibility, 1982-84. Avocations: swimming, skiing, music, running. Office: 202 S 3rd St Lewisburg PA 17837-1912 E-mail: swm@groupworksconsulting.com.

WARNICK, WALTER LEE, mechanical engineer; b. Balt., May 31, 1947; s. Marvin Paul and Freda (Wilt) W.; m. Metta Ann Nichter, May 2, 1970; children: Ashlie Colleen, Leah Brooke. BS in Engring., Johns Hopkins U., 1969; PhD, U. Md., 1977. Registered profl. engr., Md. Engr. Westinghouse Electric Co., Linthicum, Md., 1969-71, U.S. Naval Rsch. Lab., Washington, 1971-77, U.S. Dept. Energy, Washington, 1977-85, sr. exec., 1985—. Dept. Energy rep. Nat. Acid Precipitation Assessment Program, Washington, 1981-96, dir. Office of Sci. Tech. Info., Washington, 1997—; mem. depository libr. coun. Govt. Printing Office, 2004—. Author: Warnick Families of Western Maryland, 1988, 95, Wilt Families of Western Maryland, 1991, Fazenbaker Family of Western Maryland, 1999. Pres. citizen's adv. com. to Howard County Bd. of Edn., Ellicott City, Md., 1980-82. Mem. ASME, Sigma Xi (pres. DOE/NRC chpt. 1997-98, DOE-wide IT exec. leadership award, 2001, govt.-wide IRMCO award 2001). Office: Us Dept Energy Washington DC 20585-0001 E-mail: walter.warnick@science.doe.gov.

WARNKE, AMY NICHOLLE, state legislator; BA, U. N.D. Rep. Dist. 42 N.D. Ho. of Reps., mem. appropriations com., com. on corrections, chmn. budget sect. on human svcs. Devel. dir. N.D. Cmty. Found.; bd. dirs. Protection and Advocacy Project. Mem.: Kappa Alpha Theta (pres., adv. bd. chmn.). Home: PO Box 12982 Grand Forks ND 58208

WARNOCK, DAVID GENE, nephrologist; b. Parker, Ariz., Mar. 5, 1945; MD, U. Calif., San Francisco, 1970. Diplomate Am. Bd. Internal Medicine, Am. Bd. Nephrology. Intern U. Calif., San Francisco, 1970-71, resident, 1971-73; fellow nephrology NIH, Bethesda, Md., 1973-75; prof. medicine and pharmacology U. Calif., San Francisco, 1983; prof. U. Ala., Birmingham, 1988—; chief nephrology sect. VA Med. Ctr., Birmingham, 1983-88; prof., dir. divsn. nephrology U. Ala., Birmingham, 1988—, prof. medicine & physiology, 1988—. Mem. AAAS, Am. Physiol. Soc., Am. Soc. Clin. Investigation, Am. Soc. Nephrology. Office: U Ala Nephrology Rsch & Tng Ctr Uab Sta Birmingham AL 35294-0001

WARNOCK, JOHN EDWARD, computer company executive; b. Salt Lake City, Oct. 6, 1940; BS in Math. and Philosophy, U. Utah, 1961, MS in Math., 1964, PhD in Elec. Engring. and Computer Sci., 1969. With Evans & Sutherland Computer Corp., Computer Scis. Corp., IBM; prin. scientist Xerox Palo Alto Rsch. Ctr., Calif., 1978-81; co-founder, chmn. Adobe Sys., Inc., San Jose, Calif., 1982—, CEO, 1982—2000. Bd. dirs. Netscape Comm. Corp., Red Brick Sys., Evans & Sutherland Computer Corp. Patentee in field; contbr. articles to profl. jours. and industry mags.; spkr. in field. Chmn. Tech Mus. Innovation; mem. entrepreneurial bd. adv. com. Am. Film Inst. Recipient Computer Achievement award Assn. for Computing Machinery SIGGRAPH, 1989, Tech. Excellence award Nat. Graphics Assn., 1989, ACM Software Sys. award, 1989, Lifetime Achievement award for tech. excellence, PC Mag., 1989, J. Anderson Disting. Achievement award, 1991, Disting. Alumnus award U. Utah, 1995, Cary award Rochester Inst. Tech., 1995; named Entrepreneur of Yr. Ernst & Young, Merril Lynch, Inc., 1991. Mem. NAE. Office: Adobe Sys Inc 345 Park Ave San Jose CA 95110-2704

WARNOCK, WILLIAM REID, lawyer; b. Detroit, July 25, 1939; s. William G. and Margery E. (Ford) W.; m. Sandra L. Klarich, Dec. 27, 1961; children: Cheryl Lynn, Laura Ellen. BBA, U. Mich., 1961, JD with distinction, 1964. Bar: Ill. 1964, U.S. Dist. Ct. (no. dist.) Ill. 1965, U.S. Supreme Ct. 1972, Mich. 1995. With Ross & Hardies, Chgo., 1964-70; regional counsel U.S. Dept. HUD, Chgo., 1970-73; ptnr. Roan & Grossman, Chgo., 1973-82; sole practice Chgo., 1982-85; ptnr. Siegel & Warnock, Chgo., 1985-91; of counsel Donovan & Olsen, Chgo., 1991; pres. William R. Warnock P.C., LaGrange, Ill., 1992—2002, Three Rivers, Mich., 2002—03. Cons. Ill. Dept. Bus. and Econ. Devel., Chgo., 1977-78, Ill. Housing Devel. Authority, Chgo., 1973-78, Council State Housing Financing Agys., Washington, 1975-78; past pres., chmn. Atty.'s Title Guaranty Fund, Inc., Chgo., 1986-88, also bd. dirs., 1976—2003. Author: (legal references) Land Use and Zoning, 1974-88, Ward on Title Examination, 1975, Illinois Real Property Service: Real Estate Exchanges, 1988, Environmental Law and the Real Estate Lawyer, 1989-90. Mem. Ill. State Bar Assn., Am. Coll. Real Estate Lawyers. Republican. Methodist. Avocations: boating, woodworking. Home: 13556 Pleasant View Rd Three Rivers MI 49093-8406 Personal E-mail: warnockwr@aol.com.

WARPINSKI, TERRI L. academic administrator, artist; b. Green Bay, Wis., June 2, 1955; d. Robert J. and Lucille J. (Kehoe) W.; m. Garry B. Fritz, 2001. BA, U. Wis., 1979; MA, U. Iowa, 1982, MFA, 1983. Vis. instr. Sch. Art, U. Fla., Gainesville, 1983-84; prof. dept. arts U. Oreg., Eugene, 1984—, dir. Malheur Photography Workshop, 1984—, assoc. dean Sch. Architecture and Allied Arts, 1997—2004, vice provost for acad. affairs, 2003—. Mem. vis. faculty Arrowmont Sch. Arts and Crafts, Gatlinburg, Tenn., 1990-2000. Pub. art commns., Port of Portland, Oreg. State U., Ctrl. Oreg. C.C., Knight Sch. of Law, U. Oreg. Artist residence Ucross Found., Wyo., 2000; Fulbright fellow rsch. Arava Inst. Environ. Studies, Israel, 2000, 01; Rsch. grantee Ctr. for the Study of Women in Soc., 1996. Mem. Internat. Coun. Fine Arts Deans, Coll. Art Assn., Soc. Photographic Edn. (regional dir. 1987-92, nat. bd. dirs. 2001—, chair nat. bd. 2003—). Office: U Oreg Acad Affairs 206 Johnson Hall Eugene OR 97403 Fax: 541-346-2023. E-mail: tlw@uoregon.edu.

WARPOOL, CHRISTOPHER PAUL, elementary school educator, freelance/self-employed musician; b. Madison, Tenn., Apr. 26, 1973; s. Paul Eugene Warpool and Vicke Diane Barksdale. BS in Music Edn., Austin Perry State U., Clarksville, Tenn., 1998. Tchr./band dir. White House Mid. Sch., Tenn., 1998—. Mem.: Music Educators Nat. Conf., Tenn. Music Educators Assn., Kappa Sigma. Home: 213 Robert Avenue White House TN 37188 Office: White House Middle School 111 Meadows Road White House TN 37188

WARR, ERIC MARK, sociologist, educator; b. Ft. Eustis, Va., June 23, 1952; s. Calvin Eugene Warr; m. Judith Ann Jewell, June 22, 1974; children: Derek Nathaniel, Troy Dashiell. BA in Sociology and Psychology, Pacific Luth. U., 1974; PhD, U. Ariz., 1979. Postdoctoral fellow Washington State U., 1979—81, U. Wash., 1980; asst. prof. Pa. State U., Coll. Sta., Pa., 1981—86; prof. sociology U. Tex., Austin, 1986—. Cons. Nat. Inst. Justice, Washington, 1991—2003; commd. author NAS, Washington, 1994—95; panel mem. nat. consortium for violence rsch. NSF, Washington, 1995. Author: (book) Companions in Crime: The Social Aspects of Criminal Conduct, 2002; mem. editl. bd.: Criminology, 1992—2001, Am. Sociol. Rev., 1998—2000, consulting editor: Am. Jour. Sociology, 2000—02; contbr. articles to profl. jours. Named to U. Tex. Faculty Hall of Fame, UtMost Mag., 1992. Mem.: Am. Statis. Assn. (com. on law and justice stats. 1998—2003), Am. Soc. Criminology, Am. Sociol. Assn. Avocation: piano. Office: Univ Tex Dept Sociology 1 University Station Austin TX 78712 E-mail: mwarr@mail.utexas.edu.

WARREN, ALBERT, publishing executive; b. Warren, Ohio, May 18, 1920; s. David and Clara W.; m. Margaret Yeomans, Jan. 9, 1947; children: Ellen, Paul, Claire, Daniel, Thomas, Joan. BA in Journalism, Ohio State U., 1942. Assoc. editor TV Digest, Washington, 1945-50, sr. editor, 1950-58, chief Washington Bur., 1958-61; chmn., editor, pub. Warren Comm. News, Inc., Washington, 1961—. Lectr. Columbia Grad Sch Journalism, N.Y.C., 1962—75; mem. alumni adv. coun. Ohio State U., Columbus, 1982—88, mem. adv. coun. Sch. Journalism, 1872—; pub. 10 comm. periodicals. Contbr. articles to profl jours. With USNR, 1942—45, PTO. Mem.: Soc. Profl. Journalists (Hall of Fame 1991), US Congress Periodical Gallery, Internat. Radio and TV Soc. Pubs., Cable TV Pioneers, Broadcast Pioneers (Annual Recognition Award 1982, Hall of Fame 1995), Newsletter Pub. Assn. (Hall of Fame 1985), Ind. Newsletter Assn. (co-founder 1963, pres 1965—66), Cosmos Club. Office: Warren Comm News Inc 2115 Ward Ct NW Washington DC 20037-1209

WARREN, ALICE LOUISE, artist; b. Springfield, Mass., May 7, 1927; d. Roland D. and Ella May (McGrath) Eaton Von Der Lancken; m. John Homer Warren, June 5, 1948 (dec. Jan. 1988); children: John David (dec.), Daniel Wayne. Student, N.Y. Sch. Writing, 1952-55, Mansion House Art Sch., 1969, 70, 71; grad., Nat. Landscape Inst., 1960, Famous Writers Sch., 1965; Cert., United UMA Sch., 1967. Home nursing cert.; cert. home health aide paramedical. Nurses aide ARC, Springfield, 1942-45; vol. nurses aid, 1943—44; hot-line councilor Check Line, West Springfield, Mass., 1945-46; freelance columnist New England Homestead, Springfield, 1960-63; freelance columnist, editor Garden Page Woman's Circle, Horticulture mags. Author, photographer: (booklet) Evergreen Shrubs, 1964. solo art exhbns. Mercy Hosp., Arts Unltd. Gallery, 1997, Bay State Med., Springfield, Mass., 1999; featured artist Barnes and Noble Bookstore, Oct. 1999, Westfield Antheneum, 2000; on-line exhbns. MindsIsland.com, 2002, ArtRepsart.com, 2002—, Art-Exchange.com, 2003—. Recipient Bill Curtin award for watercolor, 1983. Mem. Amherst Writers & Artists Inst., Springfield Art League, Scriptures Writers, Mass. Writers Guild (treas. 1963), Tobacco Valley Artists Assn. Avocations: painting, travel, photography, reading.

WARREN, ALVIN CLIFFORD, JR., lawyer, educator; b. Daytona Beach, Fla., May 14, 1944; s. Alvin Clifford and Barbara (Barnes) W.; m. Judith Blatt, Aug. 20, 1966; children— Allison, Matthew. B.A., Yale U., 1966; J.D., U. Chgo., 1969. Bar: Conn. 1970, Pa. 1975. Prof. law U. Conn.-West Hartford, 1969-73, Duke U., Durham, N.C., 1973-74, U. Pa., Phila., 1974-79, Harvard U. Law Sch., Cambridge, Mass., 1979— . Mem. ABA (tax sect.). Contbr. articles to law jours. Office: Law Sch Harvard U Cambridge MA 02138

WARREN, CHARLES DAVID, library administrator; b. Martin, Tenn., June 12, 1944; s. Charles Alton and Evelyn (Bell) W.; children: Aaron David, Meredith Hild, Julia Myers. BS, U. Tenn., 1967; MS, U. Ill., Urbana, 1969. cert. pub. library adminstr. Dir. Shiloh Regional Library, Jackson, Tenn., 1969-72, Cumberland County Pub. Library, Fayetteville, N.C., 1973-79; exec. dir. Richland County Pub. Library, Columbia, S.C., 1979—; v.p. LHW Creations, Inc., 1979—. Bd. dirs. Civic Music Assn., Fayetteville, N.C., 1973-79, Fayetteville Symphony, 1973-78, Fayetteville Arts Commn., 1975; v.p. Friends of Librs. U.S.A., 1994—; mem. Columbia Coord. Coun., 1987-88; chmn. Richland County History Commn., 1987-93; mem. John Cotton Dana Awards Commn., 1994-99. Recipient Lucy Hampton Bostick award, 1993, S.C. Pub. Adminstr. Yr. award, 1993; named Young Man of Yr., Fayetteville Jaycees, 1977, S.C. Libr. of Yr., 1991, Internat. Fedn. Librs., 1997-2001, Order of Silver Crescent, 1999. Mem. ALA (pres. Jr. Member Roundtable 1977, chmn. awards com. 1984), Southeastern Libr. Assn. (pres. pub. libr. sect. 1978), S.C. Libr. Assn. (bd. dirs. 1980), Spring Valley Country Club, Rotary, Kiwanis, Beta Phi Mu. Democrat. Episcopalian. Home: 619 King St #806 Columbia SC 29205 Office: Richland County Pub Libr 1431 Assembly St Columbia SC 29201-3101

WARREN, CLAY, communications educator; b. Lexington Park, Md., Aug. 11, 1946; s. Cassius Clay and Dorothy Dean Warren; m. Gitte Bonde Kolind, May 1, 1985; children: Laura Kolind, Daniel Clay Kolind. BS, U.S. Naval Acad., 1968; MA, U. Colo., 1973, PhD, 1976. Instr. U. Colo., Boulder, 1973-76; asst. prof. semester-at-sea program Inst. Shipbd. Edn., Laguna Hills, Calif., 1977; vis. asst. prof. U. Coll. Cape Breton, Sydney, N.S., Can., 1978, assoc. prof., 1984-90; asst. prof. Shepherd Coll., Shepherdstown, W.Va., 1978-79, U. Hawaii at Manoa, Honolulu, 1979-82; sr. lectr. Internat. People's Coll., Elsinore, Denmark, 1982-84; assoc. prof. George Washington U., Washington, 1990-91, Chauncey M. Depew prof., 1991—. Assoc. cons. M J Solutions, Westport, Conn., 1986—; dir. comm. program George Washington U., Washington, 1990-2002, Warren Consulting, Washington, 1990—. Author: Coming Around, 1986; editor: Inner Visions, Outer Voices, 1988, Democracy Is Born in Conversations, 1998; contbr. articles to scholarly jours. Mem. site team Mil. Installation Vol. Edn. Rev. Project Office of Asst. Sec. of Def., 1992—; nat. coord. CREDIT, Am. Coun. Edn., 1996—. Lt. USN, 1968-71. Latin Am. Teaching fellow Tufts U., 1977, Tompkins Inst. Rsch. fellow, 1987-89; Rudolf Dreikurs Meml. scholar Internat. Com. for Adlerian Summer Schs. and Inst., 1988; named Princeton Seminarian Acad. Consciousness Studies, Princeton U., 1994. Mem. AAUP (v.p. George Washington U. chpt. 1994-98), Nat. Comm. Assn., N.Am. Soc. Adlerian Psychology, Folk Edn. Assn. Am. (exec. coun. 1992-96). Avocations: certified scuba diver, sport parachutist, pvt. pilot, pianist, creative writer. Office: George Washington U 2130 H St NW Ste 707 Washington DC 20052-0001 Office Phone: 202-994-6354. E-mail: claywar@gwn.edu.

WARREN, DANIEL CHURCHMAN, health facility administrator; b. Washington, Sept. 23, 1939; s. Walter Thomas and Laura Katherine W.; m. C. Frederica Lescure, June 5, 1958; 1 child, Christopher C. BS, Roanoke Coll., 1960; MD, Med. Coll. Va., 1964; MPH, U. N.C., 1971; MMAS, U.S. Army Command & Gen. Coll., 1974. Diplomate Nat. Bd. Med. Examiners, Am. Bd. Preventive Medicine, lic. physician VA; ordained Anglican Cath. priest 2002. Intern Georgetown U. Hosp., 1964-65; resident in surgery Med. Coll. Va., 1967-68, William Beaumont Gen. Hosp., 1968-69; resident in preventive medicine Walter Reed Army Inst. Rsch., 1971-73; commd. 2d lt. U.S. Army, 1965, advanced through grades to col., 1986; asst. med. dir. HealthAm. Va., 1986; pvt. practice travel, 1987-89; dir. Peninsula Health Dist., Newport News, Va., 1990—2001; warden Holyrood Sem., 2001—; rector St. Matthews Anglican Cath. Ch., 2002—; warden Scott Sch. Theology, 2003—. Clin. asst. prof. family and cmty. medicine Ea. Va. Med. Sch., Norfolk; cons. Riverside Regional Med Ctr., Newport News. Active Gloucester County Rep. Com., 1987-96, chmn. 1992-95, Gloucester County Redistricting Adv. Com., 1991, 2001; hon. chmn. Combined Va. Campaign United Way the Va. Peninsula, 1992. Fellow Am. Coll. Preventive Medicine, Royal Soc. Medicine; mem. Med. Soc. Va., Mid-Tidewater Med. Soc., Ret. Officers Assn., Cremona Fiddlers. Republican. Anglican. Avocation: English and Virginia history. Office: 215 Main St Newport News VA 23601 E-mail: dwarrenmd@cox.net.

WARREN, DAVID HARDY, psychology educator; b. Chelsea, Mass., July 28, 1943; s. Roland Leslie and Margaret (Hodges) W.; m. Katherine V. Warren; children: Michael Jonathan Warren, Gabriel Kristopher Coy. AB in Psychology, Yale U., 1965; PhD in Child Devel, U. Minn., 1969. Prof. psychology U. Calif., Riverside, 1969—, dean Coll. Humanities and Social Scis., 1977-85, dir. Univ. honors program, 1989-92, chair dept. psychology, 1992-94, exec. vice chancellor, 1994—. Author: Blindness and Early Childhood Development, 1977, 84, Blindness and Children: An Individual Differences Approach, 1994; contbr. articles to profl. jours. Mem. Psychonomic Soc., AAAS. Office: U Calif Office Exec Vice Chancellor Riverside CA 92521-0001

WARREN, DAVID LILES, educational association executive; b. Goldsboro, N.C., Sept. 15, 1943; s. James Hubert and Katherine (Liles) W.; m. Ellen Elizabeth LeGendre, Mar. 1, 1969; children— Jamison, Mackenzie, Katrin BA in English, Wash. State U., 1965; M. Urban Studies, M.Div., Yale U., 1970; PhD, U. Mich., 1976; LittD, Elmhurst Coll., 1994, Moravian Coll., 1994; LLD, Rider U., 1996, Mt. Union Coll., 1997, Centre Coll., 1997, Mercer U., 1998, Franklin and Marshall Coll., 1999; Doctor of Public Service, Rocky Mountain Coll., 1999; LLD, Ky. Wesleyan Coll., 2000; LHD, U. of New Haven, 2001; LittD, Middlebury Coll., 2001. Gen. sec. Dwight Hall, Yale U., New Haven, 1969-76, bd. dirs., 1976—; assoc. dir. community relations Yale U., New Haven, 1976-78; sr. v.p., provost Antioch U., N.Y.C. and Yellow Springs, Ohio, 1978-82; chief adminstrv. officer City of New Haven, 1982-84; pres. Ohio Wesleyan U., Delaware, 1984-93, Nat. Assn. Indep. Colls. and Univs., Washington, 1993—; with Franklin and Marshall Coll., 1999. Cons. to hosps., sch. systems, colls., univs.; bd. dirs. Delaware County Bank; chmn. NCAA Pres. Commn., Div. III, 1990-92. Contbr. chpts. to books, articles to Yale Alumni Mag. Mem. NEw Haven Bd. Alderman, 1973-75; vice chmn. New Haven Commn. on Poverty, 1981-82; pres. North Coast Athletic Conf., 1988-90; justice of peace New Haven Dem. Party, 1974-76; state chmn. People to People, 1987; chmn. Gov.'s Task Force on Dep. Registrar, 1987; chmn. Ohio Five Coll. Commn., 1985-95, Campus Compact Nat. Exec. Com., 1987-88; bd. dirs. U.S. Health Corp., Coun. Ethics and Econs.; exec. com. Great Lakes Colls. Assn., Ctrl. Ohio Symphony Orch.; chmn. Ohio Ethics commn. Fulbright scholar Wash. State U., 1965-66; Rockefeller fellow Yale U., 1966; disting. Centennial Alumnus Wash. State U. Mem. Am. Assn. Higher Edn., Assn. Ind. Colls. Univs. (sec. 1987-88), Univ. Club (Columbus, Ohio), Grad. Club (New Haven), Cosmos Club (Washington), Phi Beta Kappa. Democrat. Presbyterian. Avocations: jogging; writing; tennis. Office: Nat Assn Ind Colls & Univs 1025 Connecticut Ave NW Ste 700 Washington DC 20036-5409

WARREN, DAVID P. stock exchange executive; BA, Wesleyan U.; MBA, Yale Sch. Mgmt. Investment banker CS First Boston, 1987—95; dep. treas. State of Conn., 1995—98; CFO Long Island Power Authority (LIPA), 1998—2000; chief adminstrv. office NASDAQ Stock Exchange, Inc., NYC, 2001, CFO, 2001—. Office: NASDAQ Stock Market Inc 1 Liberty Plz New York NY 10006 Office Phone: 212-401-8742. Office Fax: 212-401-1024.

WARREN, DEAN STUART, artist; b. Mpls., June 30, 1949; s. Jefferson Trowbridge and Dorothy Ann (Edin) Warren; m. Betty Sharon Poe, Aug. 14, 1971; children: Jeremy, Adam. BFA, Fla. Atlantic U., 1973; MA, Northwestern State U., 1975; MFA, Stephen F. Austin State U., 1980. Instr. art Cisco (Tex.) Jr. Coll., 1976-78; staff craftsworker Walt E. Disney Show Prodn. Walt Disney World, Lake Buena Vista, Fla., 1981-83, staff craftsworker staff shop, 1983, property craftsworker, 1983-87, artist preparator animation dept., 1987—; lead prodn. artist Marvac, Inc., Seminole County, Fla., 1983. Founder Dean S. Warren Studio, 1991—; cons. children's edn. program Mt. Dora (Fla.) Ctr. Arts; instr. Bok Tower Gardens Edn. Ctr. Workshop, Lake Wales, Fla., 1996. Author: Runemaster, 1991; Youth Art Symposium, U. Ctrl. Fla., 1993, Children's Art program Atlantic Ctr. Arts, 1995, Edn. Ctr., 1996, one-man shows include Ormond Beach (Fla.) Meml. Art Gallery and Gardens, 1987, U. Ctrl. Fla. Art Gallery, Orlando, 1991, Harris House Atlantic Ctr. Arts, New Smyrna Beach, Fla., 1993, D'Arts Studio Gallery, Milan, 2000, exhibited in group shows at U. Miami, Fla., 1982, Valencia CC Fine Arts Gallery, Orlando, 1989, Polk CC Fine Arts Gallery, Winter Haven, Fla., 1990, U. Ga., Athens, 1990, U. Tampa (Fla.) Scarfone Gallery, 1991, World Cup Soccer, Valencia CC, 1994, Mt. Dora Ctr. Arts, 1996, Crealdé Sch. Art Sculpture Garden, Winter Park, 1997, 2000, 2003, 621 Gallery, Tallahassee, 1998, Barbara Gillman Gallery, Miami Beach, Fla., 1999, D'Arts Studio Gallery, Milan, 1999—2002, Warehouse Gallery, Orlando, 1999—2000, Leonardo DaVinci Mus. Sci. and Tech., Milan, 1999, Walt Disney World, 2000, Alice and William Jenkins Gallery, Crealdé Sch. Art, 2001, Banca Popalare di Milano, Bergamo, Italy, 2001, Postart Gallery, Milan, 2002, Galleria Blanchaert, 2002, Orlando Mus. Art, 1985, Church St. Gallery Contemporary Art, Orlando, 2003, Deland (Fla.) Mus. Art, 2004. Recipient award, U. Ga. Bot. Gardens, Athens, 1980, Valencia CC, 1983, Arts on The Park, Lakeland, Fla., 1995; Artsits in Schs. grantee, Tex. Commn. Arts, 1980. Home: 8069 Wellsmere Cir Orlando FL 32835-5361

WARREN, DIANE, song writer; Owner Real Songs, L.A. Author over 75 top ten pop songs including How Do I Live, I Don't Want to Miss a Thing, If You Asked Me To, Don't Turn Around, Set The Night To Music, I'll Still Love You More, Because You Loved Me, Rhythm of the Night, many others. Office: Realsongs 6363 W Sunset Blvd Fl 8 Hollywood CA 90028-7330

WARREN, DONALD JOHN, retired surgeon, educator; b. New Haven, NY, Jan. 23, 1924; s. John Walls and Jane Margaret (Pendorf) W.; m. Muriel Celia Beach, June 24, 1944 (div. 1980); children: Douglas, Mark, Barbara; m. Betty V. Jones, Apr. 3, 1982. BA, SUNY, Syracuse, 1945, MD, 1947. Cert. surgery. Intern Syracuse U. Hosp., 1947-48; resident in surgery Millard Fillmore Hosp., Buffalo, 1952-56; gen. surgeon USAF, 1956-66, 80-84, ret., 1984; pvt. practice, 1966-75, 1985-88; ret., 1988. Gen. surgeon VA, 1975-80; asst. prof. surgery U. Calif., Davis, 1973-75; asst. clin. prof. surgery, U.S.D., 1977-80. Fellow ACS. Home: 1616 79th Pl Lubbock TX 79423-2402 Personal E-mail: wbettyvan@aol.com.

WARREN, DONALD WILLIAM, physiology educator, dentistry educator; b. Bklyn., Mar. 22, 1935; s. Sol B. and Frances (Plotkin) W.; m. Priscilla Girardi, June 10, 1956; children: Donald W. Jr., Michael C. BS, U. N.C., 1956, DDS, 1959; MS, U. Pa., 1961, PhD, 1963; D in Odontology (hon.), U. Kuopio, Finland, 1991. Asst. prof. dentistry U. N.C., Chapel Hill, 1963-65, dir. Craniofacial Ctr., 1963-2000, assoc. prof., 1965-69, prof., 1969-80, chmn. dept. dental ecology, 1970-85, Kenan prof., 1980—, rsch. prof. otolaryngology, 1985—. Cons. NIH, Bethesda, Md., 1967—, R. J. Reynolds-Nabisco, Winston-Salem, N.C., 1986-99. Contbr. articles to profl. jours. Recipient Honor award Am. Cleft Palate Assn./Craniofacial Assn., 1992, O. Max Garner award U. N.C. Bd. Govs., 1993, honors award Angle Orthodontic Soc., 1998. Fellow AAAS, Internat. Coll. Dentists, Am. Speech and Hearing Lang. Assn. (Editors award 1998, Honors award 2003), Internat. Assn. Dental Rsch., Acoustical Soc. Am., Am. Cleft Palate Assn. (pres. 1981-82, Disting. Svc. award 1984), Am. Cleft Palate Edn. Found. (pres. 1976-77). Avocations: horse related activities, running, farming. Home: PO Box 1356 Southern Pines NC 28388-1356 Office: U NC Sch Dentistry Cb 7450 Chapel Hill NC 27599-0001 E-mail: don_warren@dentistry.unc.edu.

WARREN, ELIZABETH, law educator; BS, U. Houston, 1970; JD, Rutgers U., 1976. Robert Braucher vis. prof. law Harvard U., Cambridge, Mass., 1992-93, Leo Gottlieb prof. law, 1995—. Mem. Nat. Bankruptcy Rev. Commn. Contbr. articles to profl. jours. Named one of 50 Top Women Lawyers Nat. Law Jour., 1998. Mem. Am. Law Inst. (v.p.). Office: Harvard U Law Sch Hauser 200 Cambridge MA 02138

WARREN, ELIZABETH CURRAN, retired political science educator; b. St. Louis, Mo., Aug. 23, 1927; d. Maurice Donovan and Florence Schulte Curran; m. Geoffrey Spencer Warren, June 26, 1949; children: Kathryn Lloyd, Patricia, Michele, Deborah Perry. BA, Bryn Mawr Coll., 1949; MA, U. Kans., 1965; PhD, U. Nebr., 1970. Adj. prof. polit. sci. Loyola U. Chgo., 1977—80, asst. prof. polit. sci., 1980—87, ret., 1987. Cons. Dept. Housing, City of Chgo., 1981; cons. on subsidized housing City of Crystal Lake, Ill., 1982. Author: Legacy of Judicial Policy-Making, 1988, God, Caesar and the Freedom of Religion, 2003; co-author: Impact of Subsidized Housing on Property Values, 1983. Village pres. Village of Glencoe, Ill., 1985—93, trustee, 1974—83; organizer, sec.-treas. Sr. Housing Aid, Glencoe, 1982—2001; mem. Glencoe Garden Club, 1989—, pres., 1997—99. Mem.: Skokie Country Club. Avocations: gardening, skiing, music, swimming, writing. Home: 900 Valley Rd Glencoe IL 60022

WARREN, GLENN JAMES, environmental scientist; b. Milw., Dec. 31, 1951; s. Norbert S. Warren and Lois M. Benski; m. Laurie A. Polacek; children: Benjamin J.P., Christopher J.P., Andrew J.P. PhD, U. Wis., Milw., 1981. Rsch. assoc. U. Mich., Ann Arbor, 1983—88; aquatic biologist U.S. EPA, Chgo., 1988—. Environ. monitoring team leader U.S. EPA, Chgo., 1997—; lead scientist Lake Mich. Mass Balance Study. Officer KAMWI, Kenosha, Wis., 1989—99. Recipient Bronze Medal, U.S. EPA, 2003, 2003. Mem.: Internat. Assn. Gt. Lakes Rsch. Achievements include rsch. on Gt. Lakes. Home: 5623 53rd Ave Kenosha WI 53144 Office: US EPA 77 West Jackson Blvd Chicago IL 60604 E-mail: warren.glenn@epa.gov.

WARREN, JACK HAMILTON, former diplomat and trade policy adviser; b. Apr. 10, 1921; m. Hilary J. Titterington; children: Hilary Warren Nicolson, Martin, Jennifer Warren Part, Ian. Student, Queens U., Kingston, Ont., Can., 1938-41. Joined Dept. External Affairs, Ghana, 1945; assigned London, 1948-51; fin. counsellor Washington, 1952—54, NATO, Paris, 1954—57; asst. dep. minister trade and commerce Ottawa, 1958-64; dep. minister, trade and commerce, 1964-68; dep minister industry, trade & commerce, 1968-71; high commr. to U.K., 1971-75; ambassador to U.S., 1975-77; Can. coord. Gatt multilateral trade negotiations, 1977-79; vice-chmn. Bank of Montreal, 1979-86; prin. trade policy advisor Govt. Que., 1986-94. Served with Royal Canadian Navy, 1941-45; officer Order of Can., 1982. Recipient Pub. Svc. Outstanding Achievement award, 1976. Home: 37 Chemin Larrimac Chelsea QC Canada J9B 2C4

WARREN, JAMES RONALD, retired museum director, writer, columnist; b. Goldendale, Wash., May 25, 1925; stepson H.S. W.; m. Gwen Davis, June 25, 1949; children: Gail, Jeffrey. BA, Wash. State U., 1949; MA, U. Wash., 1953, PhD, 1963. Adminstrv. v.p. Seattle Community Coll., 1965-69; pres. Edmonds Community Coll., Lynnwood, Wash., 1969-79; dir. Mus. of History and Industry, Seattle, 1979-89. Lectr. in field. Author history books; columnist Seattle Post Intelligencer, 1979-92, Seattle Times, 1992-96. Served with U.S. Army, 1943-45, ETO, prisoner-of-war, Germany. Mem. VFW, Am. Ex-POW Assn., 42d (Rainbow) Div. Vets., Rotary, also others. Home and Office: 3235 99th Ave NE Bellevue WA 98004-1803 E-mail: jrgwarren@msn.com.

WARREN, JANE, state representative; b. Torrington, N.Y., Sept. 8, 1950; children: Jeremy, Justin. BA, U. Wyo., 1974, MA, 1980, PhD, 1876. Supr. Youth Crisis Ctr., 1984; dir., therapist, medicator Cmty. Health Ctr., 1984—; child family therapist, 1985—90; adj. prof. U. Wyo., 2000—; state rep. dist. 13 Wyo. Ho. of Reps., Cheyenne, 2000—, mem. labor, health and social svcs., and mgmt. audit coms. Creator adolescent substance abuse prevention programs; adv. com. Albany County Detention Ctr.; founder Sexual Assault/Family Violence Edn. Ctr.; chair Cmty. Svcs. Block Grant Bd., 2000—. Mem.: United Way, Rotary. Democrat. Buddhist. Office: State Capitol Cheyenne WY 82002

WARREN, JENNIFER ELIZABETH, family nurse practitioner; b. Clovis, N.Mex., Nov. 13, 1964; d. Ronald Dwayne and Lillian Ann (Reed) Carter; m. Johnny Lynn Warren Jr., May 18, 1991. BSN, West Tex. State U., 1988; MSN-FNP, West Tex. A&M U., 1998. RN, Tex.; cert. family nurse practitioner. Clin. asst. Northwest Tex. Hosp., Amarillo, 1987-88; neonatal ICU nurse Meth. Children's Hosp., Lubbock, Tex., 1988-98, Covenant Med. Ctr., Lubbock, 1999-2000; family nurse practitioner Covenant Family Health Care Ctr., 2000—03, Garza County Health Clinic, Post, Tex., 2003—. Mem. Am. Acad. Nurse Practitioners, Tex. Nursing Assn., Endometriosis Assn. (organizer/contact, Lubbock leader 1993—), South Plains Nurse Practitioners Assn. Democrat. Methodist. Avocations: gardening, cross-stitch, latch hook, swimming. Home: 1002 W 10th St Post TX 79356-2450 Office: Garza County Health Clinic 608 W 6th St Post TX 79356 Fax: (806) 495-3576.

WARREN, JOHN COOLIDGE, private school administrator, history educator; b. Boston, May 16, 1956; s. William Bradford and Mary-Elizabeth (Coolidge) W.; m. Laura Parker Appell, June 18, 1983; children: Ethan Reynolds Appell, Amanda Pfaltzgraff Appell. BA, Stanford U., 1978, MA, 1980; MEd, Harvard U., 1991, EdD, 1994. Tchr. history Robert Louis Stevenson Sch., Pebble Beach, Calif., 1979-81, Milton (Mass.) Acad., 1981—, chmn. dept. history, 1992-95, acad. dean, 1995—2001, spl. asst. head sch., 2001—. Faculty cons. Ednl. Testing Svc., Princeton, 1990—, William Joiner Ctr., Boston, 1992—; editl. cons. Longman Inc., White Plains, NY, 1991—. Editor: America's Intervention in Vietnam, l987. NEH fellow, 1985, advanced doctoral fellow, Harvard U., 1993. Mem. Am. Hist. Assn., Orgn. Am. Historians, Assn. Asian Studies, World History Assn., Boston Athaneum, Colonial Soc. Mass., Mass. Hist. Soc., Phi Beta Kappa. Avocations: canoeing, fishing. Home and Office: Milton Acad 170 Centre St Milton MA 02186-3338 Office Phone: 617-898-1798.

WARREN, JOHN SHELDON, lawyer, educator; b. Mpls., Apr. 29, 1922; s. Victor Lawrence and Sytske (Korthof) Warren; m. Katrin Einarsdottir, Apr. 11, 1962; 1 child, John Erik; 1 child, Victoria Kristen. BS, U. Minn., 1943; student, U. Notre Dame, 1943; LLB, Hastings Coll. of Law, 1950. Bar: Calif. 1951, US Dist. Ct. (no. dist.)/Calif., US Ct. Appeals (9th cir.). Tax counsel Franchise Tax Bd., Sacramento, 1951—57; ptnr. Loeb and Loeb, Los Angeles, 1957—; now prof. law Layola Law Sch., Los Angeles; cons. GAO, Washington, 1980—82. Contbr. articles law revs. Mem.: ABA (chmn. com. on state and local taxes 1981—83), UCLA Med. Ctr. (bd. advisors 1980—), UCLA Found. (trustee 1976—80), Jonathan. Republican. Episc. Office: Loeb and Loeb One Wilshire Bldg Los Angeles CA 90017

WARREN, JOHN WILLIAM, professional society administrator; b. Clarksville, Ark., June 27, 1927; s. Frederick H. and Fannie Emiline (Casey) W.; m. Marguerette Christine Cohoon, Oct. 9, 1948 (dec. Dec. 1987); children: Catherine Gail, Carolyn Anne, Eve Colette; m. Anna Jane Taylor, Feb. 10, 1990. BA, Abilene Christian U., 1949; MA, U. Ark., 1951; PhD, U. Tenn., 1961. Instr. U. Tenn., Knoxville, 1954—61; assoc. prof. David Lipscomb Coll., Nashville, 1961—62; prof., chmn. English Tenn. Tech. U., Cookeville, 1962—88; assoc. exec. dir. Phi Kappa Phi, Baton Rouge, 1988—92, exec. dir., 1992—99, exec. dir. emeritus, 1999—; v.p. Assn. Coll. Honor Socs., 1999—2001, pres., 2001—03. Author Ofcl. Lit. Map of Tenn., 1976; author: Tennessee Belles-Lettres-Guide to Tennessee Literature, 1976. Mem. Rotary (Cookeville pres. 1972-73), Phi Kappa Phi (Tenn. Tech. U. chpt. pres. 1980, SE region v.p. 1982-88, nat. bd. dirs. 1982-88). Republican. Mem. Ch. of Christ. Avocations: gardening, travel. Personal E-mail: pkpjwarren@aol.com.

WARREN, JOSEPH ADDISON, III, law and history educator; b. Ft. Pierce, Fla., July 23, 1944; s. Joseph Addison and Donna Belle (Fenstermacher) W. BA, Mich. State U., 1966, MA, 1967, PhD, 1976; JD, Thomas M. Cooley Law Sch., 1980. Bar: Mich., 1981, U.S. Supreme Ct. 1985. Prof. history and humanities Lansing (Mich.) C.C., 1969—; pvt. practice law Lansing, 1981—; owner Center Point Press, Lansing, 1998—. Lectr. continuing edn. Mich. State U., East Lansing, 1995—; pub., editor Faculty Advocate Mag., Lansing, 1981-98; dir. Ctr. for Inner Awareness, Inc., Lansing, 1992—; rschr. Ralph Nader's Task Force on Congress, Lansing, 1971-74; forensic photographer Forensic Photographic Svcs., Lansing, 1977—; mem. Gov.'s Adv. Com. on Mich. Meat Stds., Lansing, 1974; co-counsel Wygant V. Jackson vs. Bd. of Edn., 1985; mem. com. on legal edn. State Bar of Mich., Lansing, 1987-89, U.S. Supreme Ct. Author: The Origins of the American Presidency, 1976; contbr. numerous articles to profl. publs. Mem. Mich. Fed. Bar Assn., Mich. State Bar Assn., Am. Acad. of Religion Studies, World Assn. Vedic Studies, Ctr. for Study of the Presidency, Internat. Vedanta Scholars in Indian Civilization, Am. Legal Studies Assn. Avocations: mentoring students and beginning professionals, international travel. Home: 1012 N Washington Ave Lansing MI 48906-4839 Office: 1016 N Washington Lansing MI 48906-4839

WARREN, KATHERINE VIRGINIA, art gallery director; b. Balt., Aug. 10, 1948; d. Joseph Melvin and Hilda Virginia (Thiele) Heim; m. David Hardy Warren; 1 child, Gabriel Kristopher Coy; 1 stepchild, Michael Jonathan Warren. BA, U. Calif., Riverside, 1976, MA, 1980. Asst. curator Calif. Mus. Photography, Riverside, 1979-80, acting dir., 1980-81, asst. dir., curator of edn., 1981-84; dir. univ. art gallery U. Calif., Riverside, 1980—. Bd. dirs. Riverside Arts Found., 1980-89, chmn. bd., 1986-88. Marius De Brabant fellow U. Calif., 1977-79. Mem. Am. Assn. Mus., Western Mus. Conf. Office: Sweeney Art Gallery U Calif Riv Side Riverside CA 92521-0001

WARREN, MARK EDWARD, cruise line executive, lawyer; b. Rochester, Minn., Nov. 26, 1951; s. Edward Joseph and Eunice (Golberg) W.; m. Jasmine Margaret Syracuse, Feb. 18, 1984; children: Natalie, Stephanie. Cert., Instituto de Estudios Europeos, Madrid, 1972; BA, Gustavus Adolphus Coll., St. Peter, Minn., 1974; JD, U. Minn., 1977. Bar: Calif. 1977, U.S. Dist. Ct. (no. and cen. dists.) Calif. 1978, U.S. Ct. Appeals (9th cir.) 1985, U.S. Dist. Ct. (ea. dist.) Calif. 1986, U.S. Dist. Ct. (so. dist.) Calif. 1987, D.C. 1989, U.S. Supreme Ct. 1989, U.S. Ct. Appeals (D.C. cir.) 1989, U.S. Dist. Ct. (D.C. dist.) 1989, U.S. Dist. Ct. Md. 1991, Va. 1992. Assoc. Gibson, Dunn & Crutcher, L.A., 1977-78; spl. asst. to V.P. Walter Mondale Washington, 1979-80; assoc. Gibson, Dunn & Crutcher, L.A., 1980-84, ptnr. L.A. and Washington, 1985-93; sr. v.p., gen. counsel Princess Cruises, L.A., 1993-96; pres. The Gt. Am. Sta. Found., Washington, 1997-99; sr. vp., gen. counsel Norwegian Cruise Line, Miami, Fla., 2003—. Mem. U. Minn. Law Alumni Assn. (bd. dirs. 1990-98). Office: 7665 Corporate Center Dr Miami FL 33126

WARREN, PETER, advertising executive; b. Iran, Sept. 9, 1943; s. Paul and Heda (Adler) W.; m. Carla Ringler, Aug. 26, 1967; children: Jill, Paul. BS, NYU, 1965; MBA, Pace U., 1968. Promotion rsch. analyst Look Mag., N.Y.C., 1965; from media planner to account supr. Ogilvy & Mather, N.Y.C., 1966-72; exec. v.p. Tromson Monroe, N.Y.C., 1972-74; founder, pres. Warren/Kremer Advt., Inc., N.Y.C., 1974—. Mem. Marlboro (N.J.) Twp. Zoning Bd. Adjustment; pres. bd. edn. Freehold Regional H.S.; advisor United Jewish Appeal, Marlboro Bd. Edn., Monmouth County Dem. and Rep. Coms., Marlboro Econ. Devel. Bd.; chmn. Gateway Am. Courtesy and Tng. Com.; exec. com., chair Hospitality Sales and Mktg. Assn. Internat.; exec. bd. mem. NYU Sch. Hospitality, Travel and Tourism. Recipient Effie award Am. Mktg. Assn., 1978. Mem. Hospitality Sales and Mktg. Assn. (co-chmn. mktg. adv. com, numerous platinum, gold, silver and bronze awards 1976-92), Travel and Tourism Rsch. Assn., Caribbean Tourism Orgn. (treas. N.Y.C. chpt., 3 Best of Show awards internat. competition 1982, 83, 85), Advt. Club N.Y. (Addy awards 1982, 83), Alpha Delta Sigma (pres. NYU). Jewish. Avocations: reading, golf, softball, travel, coin collecting/numismatics. Office: Warren/Kremer/Paino Advt Inc 2 Park Ave Rm 1400 New York NY 10016-5701

WARREN, RICHARD JORDAN, newspaper publisher; b. Bangor, Maine, May 28, 1945; s. Richard Kearney Warren and Joanne (Jordan) Van Namee; m. Barbara Burrowes Hall, Mar. 9, 1968 (div.); m. Elizabeth Carter, June 21, 1978; children: Courtney, George, Anne. BA, Trinity Coll., Hartford, Conn., 1968; postgrad. smaller cos. mgmt. program Harvard Bus. Sch., 1977-80. Reporter, The Courant, Hartford, Conn., 1968-71; asst. pub. The Bangor Daily News 1971-84, v.p., 1974—, editor, 1980—, pub., 1984—, also owner; pres., bd. dirs. N.E. Pub. Co., Presque Isle, Maine; dir. Bangor Pub. Co., New Eng. Newspaper Assn., Action Com. Fifty, Quebec-Labrador Found., Atlantic Salmon Found.; mem. Am. Soc. Newspaper Editors, Maine Daily Newspaper Assn., Bangor Mechanic Assn., Land for Maine's Future Bd., Kent Moot Ct., Columbia U. Law Sch., N.Y.C.; adv. bd., past trustee Unity Coll.; apptd. by Pres. Bush U.S. Commr. on The Roosevelt Campobello Island Commn., 2001. Served to 1st lt., Air N.G. Mem. Alexander Graham Bell Assn. Deaf Centennial Bd. (steering com.), Nat. Press Club, Univ. Club, Anglers Club, Penobscot Salmon Club. Office: Bangor Daily News 491 Main St Bangor ME 04401-6862

WARREN, RICHARD KEARNEY, newspaper publisher; b. N.Y.C., Apr. 13, 1920; s. George Earle and Anna (Kearney) W.; m. Joanne Jordan, Sept. 18, 1943 (div. Oct. 1969); children: Richard J., Carolyn; m. Susan Atwood Thibodeau, Oct. 1, 1970. BS, Yale U., 1942; LittD, Ricker Coll., 1971. Shift supt. W.Va ordnance works Gen. Chem. Co., Point Pleasant, 1942-43; dir. Bangor Pub. Co., Maine, chmn. exec. com.; pres. Rockland Courier-Gazette, Inc., also bd. dirs. Bd. dirs. N.E. Pub. Co. Past bd. dirs. William A. Farnsworth Libr. and Art Mus., Bangor YMCA; past trustee Ricker Coll. Lt. (j.g.) USNR, 1943-46. Mem. Maine Daily Newspaper Assn. (pres. 1953-54, 73-74), N.E. Daily Newspaper Assn. (pres. 1959-60), Newspaper Assn. Am., New Eng. Soc. N.Y., N.E. Harbor Fleet (Maine), Penobscot Valley Country Club, Yale Club (N.Y.C.), N.E. Harbor Tennis Club. Home: 28 W Broadway Bangor ME 04401-4541 Office: 96 Harlow St Ste F Bangor ME 04401-4925 also: 3 Huntington Pl Northeast Harbor ME 04662-0663

WARREN, RICHARD M. experimental psychologist, educator; b. N.Y.C., Apr. 8, 1925; s. Morris and Rae (Greenberg) W.; m. Roslyn Pauker, Mar. 31, 1950. BS in Chemistry, CCNY, 1946; PhD in Organic Chemistry, NYU, 1951. Flavor chemist Gen. Foods Co., Hoboken, N.J., 1951-53; rsch. assoc. psychology Brown U., Providence, 1954-56; Carnegie sr. rsch. fellow NYU Coll. Medicine, 1956-57, Cambridge (Eng.) U., 1957-58, rsch. psychologist applied psychology rsch. unit, 1958-59; rsch. psychologist NIMH, Bethesda, Md., 1959-61; chmn. psychology Shimer Coll., Mt. Carroll, Ill., 1961-64; assoc. prof. psychology U. Wis., Milw., 1964-66, prof., 1966-73, rsch. prof., 1973-75, disting. prof., 1975-95, adj. disting. prof., 1995—. Vis. scientist Inst. Exptl. Psychology, Oxford (Eng.) U., 1969-70, 77-78. Author: (with Roslyn Warren) Helmholtz on Perception: Its Physiology and Development, 1968, Auditory Perception: A New Analysis and Synthesis, 1999; contbr. articles to profl. jours. Fellow APA, Am. Psychol. Soc., Acoustical Soc. Am.; mem. AAAS, Am. Chem. Soc., Am. Speech and Hearing Assn., Sigma Xi. Office: U Wis Dept Psychology Milwaukee WI 53201 Office Phone: 414-229-5328.

WARREN, RICHARD WAYNE, obstetrician, gynecologist; b. Puxico, Mo., Nov. 26, 1935; s. Martin R. and Sarah E. (Crump) W.; m. Rosalie J. Franzoia, Aug. 16, 1959; children: Lani Marie, Richard W., Paul D. BA, U. Calif., Berkeley, 1957; MD, Stanford (Calif.) U., 1961. Diplomate Am. Bd. Ob-Gyn. Intern Oakland (Calif.) Naval Hosp., 1961-62; resident on ob-gyn. Stanford Med. Ctr., 1964-67; pvt. practice specializing in ob-gyn. Mountain View, Calif., 1967—. Mem. staff Stanford Hosp., El Camino Hosp.; pres. Warren Medical Corp.; assoc. clin. prof. ob-gyn. Stanford Sch. Medicine. Contbr. articles to profl. jours. With USN, 1961-64. Fellow Am. Coll. Ob-Gyn.; mem. AMA, Am. Fertility Soc., Am. Assn. Gynecologic Laparoscopists, Calif. Med.

Assn., San Francisco Gynecol. Soc., Peninsula Gynecol. Soc., Assn. Profs. Gynecology and Obstetrics, Royal Soc. Medicine, Shufelt Gynecol. Soc. Santa Clara Valley. Home: 102 Atherton Ave Menlo Park CA 94027-4021 Office: 2500 Hospital Dr Mountain View CA 94040-4106

WARREN, RICK DUANE, minister, writer; b. San Jose, Calif., Jan. 28, 1954; s. James Russell and Dorothy Nell (Armstrong) W.; m. Elizabeth Kay Lewis, June 21, 1975; children: Amy Rebecca, Joshua James, Matthew David. BA, Calif. Bapt. Coll., 1977; Master of Divinity, Southwestern Bapt. Theol. Sem., 1979; Doctor of Ministry, Fuller Theol. Sem., 1989. Youth evangelist Calif. So. Bapt. Convention, Fresno, 1970-74; assoc. pastor First Bapt. Ch., Norwalk, Calif., 1974-76; asst. to pres. Internat. Evangelism Assn., Fort Worth, 1977-79; founding pastor Saddleback Valley Community Ch., Mission Viejo, Calif., 1980—; founder Pastors.com. Lectr. Saddleback Ch. Growth Seminars. Author: The Purpose-Driven Church, 1995, Personal Bible Study Methods, 1997, The Power to Change Your Life, 1998, Answers to Life's Difficult Questions, 1999, Planned for God's Pleasure, 2002, The Purpose-Driven Life, 2002 (Gold Medallion award, ECPA Book of the Yr, 2003), The Emerging Church, 2003, Daily Inspiration for the Purpose-Driven Life, 2004. Named Outstanding Preacher of 1977, McGregor Found. Mem. No. Am. Soc. for Ch. Growth. Baptist. Office: Saddleback Valley Comm Ch 24194 Alicia Pky Ste M San Juan Capistrano CA 92691-3927 also: Pastors.com 20 Empire Dr Lake Forest CA 92630-2244*

WARREN, RITA SIMPSON, manufacturing executive; b. Borger, Tex., Jan. 17, 1949; d. William D. and Bobbie J. (Hindman) S.; m. Harry E. Warren, jr., June 10, 1978. BA in Sociology, U. Tex., 1977; MBA, North Tex. State U., 1982. V.p. comms. Tetra Pak, Inc., Dallas, 1977-85; v.p. mktg. Devex, Inc., Dallas, 1986-87; v.p. Neotech Industries, Inc., Irving, Tex., 1987-88; sales mgr. worldwide Optek Tech., Inc., 1989-2001; key account mgr. Alcatel Optronics Inc., 2001—02, Sanmina-SCI, 2003—. Bd. dirs. Dallas Women's Found., 1999-2003; mem. women's resource ctr. adv. com. YWCA of Dallas, 1993-2001. Recipient various awards Dairy and Food Industries Supply Assn., 1979-84, Soc. Visual Comm., 1979, Dallas Ad League TOPS, 1984. Mem. Sportscar Vintage Racing Assn., Hist. Sportscat Racing Assn., Pub. Rels. Soc., Jaguar Owner's Assn. S.W. (co-pres. 1979 83), The Women's Ctr. of Dallas (bd. dirs. WISER 1991-92, Women in Leadership 1993, pres.-elect 1994, pres. 1995, past pres. 1996), Imagine Dallas (pres. 1997-98, bd. dirs. 1995-98). Avocations: classic european automobiles, driving vintage race car, golden retrievers, sailing. Office: 105 W Bethany Dr Allen TX 75013

WARREN, ROBERT LEE, dentist, educator; b. Boone, NC, July 20, 1943; s. John Floyd and Maude Elizabeth (Roark) Warren; m. Deborah Andrews; children: Blaire, Robert, Debin. BS in Biology, Appalachian State U., 1965; postgrad., Duke U., 1967; DDS, U. NC, 1972. Instr. biology and chemistry West H.S., North Wilkesboro, NC, 1965—68; gen. practice dentistry Boone, 1972—. Adj. asst. prof. dept. operative dentistry U. NC Sch. Dentistry, Chapel Hill, 1972—79, adj. asst. prof. dept. fixed prostodontics, 1982—84, adj. asst. prof. operative dentistry, 1987—97. Mem. Watauga County Bd. Edn. Nat. Sci. fellow, Duke U. Master: Acad. Gen. Dentistry (bd. dirs.); mem.: ADA, First Dist. Dental Soc., NC Dental Soc., Boone C. of C., U. NC Dental Alumni Assn. (bd. dirs.), Tar Heel Dental Study Club (pres.), Delta Sigma Delta. Republican. Baptist. Avocations: tar heel sports, show horses, sports cars. Home: 127 Alan Dr Boone NC 28607 Office: R Lee Warren 142 Doctors Dr Boone NC 28607-5018

WARREN, ROSANNA, poet; b. Fairfield, Conn., July 27, 1953; d. Robert Penn Warren and Eleanor Clark; m. Stephen Scully, 1981; children: Katherine, Chiara; stepson, Benjamin. BA summa cum laude, Yale U., 1976; MA, Johns Hopkins U., 1980. Pvt. art tchr., 1977-78; clerical worker St. Martin's Parish, N.Y.C., 1977-78; asst. prof. English Vanderbilt U., Nashville, 1981-82; vis. asst. prof. Boston U., 1982-88, asst. prof. English and modern fgn. langs., 1989-95, assoc. prof. English, 1995—, Emma Mactachlan Metcalf prof. Humanities, 2000—. Poetry cons., contbg. editor Partisan Rev., 1985-98; poet-in-residence Robert Frost Farm, 1990. Author: The Joey Story, 1963, Snow Day, 1981, Each Leaf Shines Separate, 1984, Stained Glass, 1993, Departure, 2003; editor, contbr.: The Art of Translation: Voices from the Field, 1989; editor: Eugenio Montale's Cuttlefish Bones, 1993, Satura, 1998; translator (with Stephen Scully) Euripides' Suppliant Women, 1995, poetry anthologies include In Time, 1995, From This Distance, 1996, Springshine, 1998; contbr. to periodicals including Agni Rev., Am. Poetry Rev., Antioch Rev., Atlantic Monthly, Chelsea, Chgo. Rev., Georgia Rev., Nation, New Republic, New Yorker, N.Y. Times, Paris Rev., Threepenny Rev., Partisan Rev., Ploughshares, Southern Rev., Washington Post. Recipient McLaughlin English prize Yale U., 1973, Charles E. Clark award Yale U., 1976, Nat. Discovery award in poetry 92nd St. YMHA-YWCA, 1980, Newton Arts Coun. award, 1983, Lavan Younger Poets prize Acad. Am. Poets, 1992, Lamont Poetry prize Acad. Am. Poets, 1993, Lila Wallace Writers' Fund award, 1994, Witter Bynner prize in poetry Acad. Arts and Letters, 1994, May Sarton award New Eng. Poetry Club, 1995, Pushcart prize, 2003; named Scholar of House Yale U., 1975-76; Yaddo fellow, 1980; Ingram Merrill grantee, 1983, 93; Guggenheim fellow, 1985-86; Am. Coun. Learned Societies grantee, 1989-90. Fellow: Am. Acad. of Arts and Sci.; mem.: PEN, ALTA, MLA, Am. Acad. Poets (chancellor 2000), Assn. Literary Scholars and Critics (v.p. 2004). Home: 28 Tappan St Roslindale MA 02131-1621 Office: Univ Professors Program Boston Univ 745 Commonwealth Ave Boston MA 02215-1401

WARREN, RUSSELL GLEN, academic administrator; b. Balt., Apr. 29, 1942; s. Clarence N. and Kathryn (Butler) W. BBA, U. Richmond, 1964; PhD, Tulane U., 1968. From asst. prof. to assoc. prof. U. Richmond, Va., 1971—74, dean of Richmond Coll., 1974—76, from asst. to v.p. to asst. to pres., 1976—78; v.p. for acad. affairs U. Montevallo, Ala., 1978-84, James Madison U., Harrisonburg, Va., 1984-90, v.p. acad. affairs, acting pres., 1986—87; pres. N.E. Mo. State U., Kirksville, 1990—94; Disting. prof. econs. and mgmt. Hardin-Simmons U., Abilene, Tex., 1995-97, dir. Ctr. for Rsch. on Teaching and Learning, 1995-97; exec. v.p., provost Mercer U., Macon, Ga., 1997—2002; sr. fellow Nat Assn. Ind. Colls. and Univs., Kiawah Island, SC, 2001—03; prof. econs. So. Wesleyan U., 2003—. Chmn., adv. bd. Coll. Humanities and Social Sci. Coll. Charleston, SC, 1994—. Author: Antitrust in Theory and Practice, 1976, Carpe Diem, 1995. Bd. Dirs. Va. Rural Devel. Corp., Richmond, 1988-90. Capt. U.S. Army, 1969-71. Named One of Outstanding Young Men of Va., Va. Jaycees, 1976. Mem.: Am. Coun. on Edn. (coun. of fellows), Am. Assn. Colls. and Univs. (bd. dirs. 1994—95). Methodist. Avocations: golf, collecting cars. Home and Office: 175 Marsh Island Dr Kiawah Island SC 29455 E-mail: kiawahwarren@cs.com.

WARREN, RUSSELL JAMES, investment banker, consultant; b. Cleve., July 28, 1938; s. Harold Fulton and Agnes Elmenah (Hawkswell) Warren; m. Doris Helen Kenyeres, June 6, 1964. BS, Case Western Res. U., 1960; MBA, Harvard U., 1962. CPA Ohio. With Ernst & Whinney, Cleve., 1962-87, ptnr. in charge merger and acquisition svcs., 1976—87, pres. TransAction Group, 1987—. Bd. dirs. Seneca Capital Mgmt., Inc. Co-author: (book) Implementing Mergers and Acquisitions in the Financial Services Industry, 1985; assoc. editor: Jour. Corp. Growth, 1986—87, mem. editl. bd.:, 1988; contbg. editor: Jour. Buyouts and Acquisitions, 1984—86; contbg. author: venture capital financing study conducted in five countries for Asian Devel. Bank, Malaysia, Indonesia, Pakistan, Sri Lanka, Thailand, 1986. Trustee Case Western Res. U., 1980—, chmn. audit com., 1991—; trustee Cleve. Bot. Garden, 1995—2002, Western Res. Hist. Soc., 1996—2002, chmn. investments com., 1999—2002; trustee Cmty. Improvement Corp. Summit, Medina and Portage Counties, 1992—2000, Cascade CDC, 1992—2000, Brit.-Am. C. of C., Great Lakes Region, 2001—; dir. Univ. Tech., Inc., 1986—88; adv. bd. Shaker Investments, 1992—; v.p. M&A Internat. Inc., 1990—91, pres., 1992; bd. zoning appeals City of Lyndhurst, 1978—, chmn., 1980—82, 1991—93, 2000—01; mem. vis. com. Case Sch. Engring., Weatherhead Sch. Mgmt., 1998—; trustee Fairmont Presbyn. Ch., 1987—93, elder, 1991—93. Mem.: AICPA, Cleve. World Trade Assn., Cleve. Com. Fgn. Rels., Assn. Corp. Growth, Ohio Soc. CPAs, Harvard Club NYC, Catawba Island Club, Mayfield Country Club, Union Club, Jesters. Office: The TransAction Group 500 Hanna Bldg Cleveland OH 44115 Office Phone: 216-348-1666.

WARREN, STEPHEN THEODORE, human geneticist, educator; b. Grosse Point, Mich., Nov. 30, 1953; s. Theodore Stephen and Frances (Fedo) W.; m. Karen Lee Pierce, Aug. 27, 1978; 1 child, Thomas. BS, Mich. State U., 1976, PhD, 1981. Diplomate Am. Bd. Med. Genetics. Grad. asst. Mich. State Univ., East Lansing, 1976-81; rsch. assoc. Univ. Ill., Chgo., 1981-83, instr., 1983-85; asst. prof. Emory U. Sch. of Medicine, Atlanta, 1985-91, assoc. prof., 1991-93, W.P. Timmie prof. human genetics, 1993—, chmn. dept. human genetics, 2001—; investigator Howard Hughes Med. Inst., 1992—2002. Vis. scientist European Molecular Biol. Lab., Heidelberg, Germany, 1984.; cons. Ctrs. for Disease Control, Atlanta, 1988-89, NIH, Bethesda, Md., 1989—; collaborator Ctr. D'Etude du Polymorphysme Humain, Paris, 1989—. Editor-in-chief Am. Jour. Human Genetics, 2000—; mem. editl. bd. Human Molecular Genetics, Am. Jour. Human Genetics, Cytogenetics, Cell Genetics, Mammalian Genome, others; contbr. chpts. to books and more than 200 articles to profl. jorus. Recipient Sigma Xi prize Mich. State Sigma Xi, East Lansing, 1981, NIH fellowship NIH, Bethesda, 1982, Basil O'Connor award March of Dimes, N.Y.C., 1986, Albert E. Levy award Emory Univ., Atlanta, 1987, William Rosen Rsch. award Nat. Fragile X Found., 1996. Mem. Am. Soc. Human Genetics (nominating com. 1991, awards com. 1992— , bd. dirs. 1997—, William Allan award 1999), Am. Soc. Biochemistry and Molecular Biology, Am. Soc. Microbiology, Genetics Soc. Am. Achievements include research on molecular genetic studies of the fragile X syndrome and other human genetic diseases. Home: 2305 Kimbrough Ct Atlanta GA 30350-5635 Office: Emory Univ Sch Medicine 301 Whitehead Bldg 615 Michael St Atlanta GA 30322-4218

WARREN, STEVE, lawyer; Ptnr. Hansen, Jacobsen, Teller, Hoberman, Newman, Warren, Hertz & Goldring LLC, Beverly Hills, Calif. Office: Hansen Jacobsen Teller et al Fl 8 450 N Roxbury Dr Beverly Hills CA 90210-4222

WARREN, STEVEN F. psychologist, educator; PhD of Chiland Devel. Psychology, U. Kans, 1977. Faculty mem. Dept. Spl. Edn. and Psychology Peabody Coll. Vanderbilt U., Nashville, 1982—99; dir. Kans. Mental Retardation and Devel. Disabilities Rsch. Ctr. U. Kans., 2000—01, prof. Human Devel. and Family Life, 2000—, dir. Schiefelbusch Inst. for Life Span Studies, 2001—. Contbr. articles to profl. jours.; editor: Jour. Early Intervention. Recipient Theodore D. Tjossem Nat. Rsch. award, Nat. Down Syndrome Congress, 1999. Mem.: Am. Assn. Mental Retardation (pres. 2002—). Office: Am assn Mental Retardation 444 N Capitol St NW Ste 846 Washington DC 20001-1512

WARREN, SUSAN CAROL, legal assistant, clerk, writer; b. Grand Junction, Colo., Oct. 18, 1948; d. Donald Max and Ruth Alice Nelson; m. William Henry Warren, Jan. 2, 1971; children: Shannon Teresa McCleave, Vanessa Marie Iverson, Rebecca Ann Merritt, Elizabeth Mary Duclos. AD in Legal Assisting suma cum laude, Parks Coll. North, 1999. Customer support rep. Clientlogic, Inc., Las Vegas, 2003—04; recep. United Realty Invest., Las Vegas, 2004—. Author: Who Killed Amy Tyler?, 2002. Independent. Roman Catholic. Avocations: writing, reading, computers. Home: 7319 Clearwater Circle Las Vegas NV 89147 Office Phone: 702-633-4597. Personal E-mail: susanwarren1@cox.net.

WARREN, W. K., JR., oil industry executive; b. 1911; Vice chmn. The William K. Warren Found., Tulsa; also with Warren Am. Oil Co., Tulsa, 1938—, now pres. and chmn. bd. Office: The Warren Office 6585 S Yale Ave Tulsa OK 74136-8384

WARREN, WILLIAM BRADFORD, lawyer; b. Boston, July 25, 1934; s. Minton Machado and Sarah Ripley (Robbins) W.; children: John Coolidge, Sarah; m. Arete B. Swartz, Sept. 20, 1985. AB magna cum laude, Harvard U., 1956, LLB cum laude, 1959. Bar: N.Y. 1960. Assoc. Dewey Ballantine, N.Y.C., 1959-68; ptnr. Dewey Ballantine, LLP, 1968—. Lectr. Inst. Fed. Taxation, NYU, So. Fed. Tax Inst., Practicing Law Inst. Pres. Cintas Found., N.Y.C.; bd. dirs. St. John's Coll., Annapolis and Santa Fe; bd. dirs. emeritus John Carter Brown Libr., Providence, R.I.; adv. bd. dirs. Met. Opera Assn., N.Y.C.; mem. coun. fellows Morgan Libr., N.Y.C. Mem. Am. Law Inst., Am. Coll. Trust and Estate Counsel (former regent), Acad. Am. Poets (bd. dirs., vice chair), Internat. Acad. Estate and Trust Law (former exec. com.), N.Y. State Bar Assn. (chmn. com. taxation of trust and estates sect. 1980-83), Assn. Bar City N.Y., Soc. Mayflower Descs., Harvard Club, Knickerbocker Club, Century Club, Grolier Club (past pres.). Home: 520 E 86th St New York NY 10028-7534 Office: Dewey Ballantine LLP 1301 Avenue Of The Americas New York NY 10019-6022 Office Phone: 212-259-8700. E-mail: wwarren@dbllp.com.

WARREN, WILLIAM KERMIT, retired media company executive; b. Harlem, Ga., May 27, 1941; s. William Kermit and Willie Garnell (Thaxton) Warren; m. Nancy Carolyn Andrews, Sept. 5, 1964; children: Wendy Karen, William Kermit. BA in Journalism, U. Ga., 1964. Reporter Augusta Ga. Chronicle, Ga., 1964-65; reporter Chattanooga Times, Tenn., 1965-66, reporter, city editor, 1971-80; mng. editor Roanoke (Va.) Times & World News, 1980-95; electronic pub. cons., 1995-98; prin. New City Media, Blacksburg, Va., 1998-99. Served to capt USAF, 1966—70. Recipient Best Feature Story Award, Ga AP, 1964. Mem.: AP Managing Eds Asn, Sigma Delta Chi. Episcopalian. Avocation: reading. Home: 3355 Dawn Cir Roanoke VA 24018-3837 E-mail: bwarren33@cox.net.

WARREN, WILLIAM MICHAEL, JR., utilities company executive; b. Bryan, Tex., June 8, 1947; s. William Michael and Rebecca Carolyn (Glass) W.; m. Anne Candler McLeod, June 5, 1968; children: William Powers, Laura Anne, Amy Lynn. BA, Auburn U., 1968; JD, Duke U., 1971. Bar: Ala. 1971. Assoc. Bradley, Arant, Rose & White, Birmingham, Ala., 1971-77, ptnr., 1977-83; v.p., gen. counsel Ala. Gas Corp., Birmingham, 1983-84, pres., chief operating officer, 1984—; pres, chief oper. officer Energen Corp., Birmingham, 1987-91, pres., chief ops. officer, 1991—. Bd. dirs. AmSouth Bank Birmingham N.A., Energen Corp., Ala. Gas Corp., So. Gas Assn., Inst. Gas Tech. Contbr. articles to periodicals. Bd. dirs. Ala. Symphony Assn., 1988-90, pres., 1990—, chmn., 1991-92; chmn. Met. Devel. Bd., 1989-90; trustee Ala. Inst. for Deaf and Blind, 1988—, Children's Hosp. Birmingham, 1988—. 1st lt. USAF, 1971-72. Mem. ABA, Am. Gas Assn. (edn. 2000 com. 1991—), So. Gas Assn. (bd. dirs. 1989—), Inst. Gas Tech. (bd. trustees 1989—), Birmingham Area C. of C. (bd. dirs. 1986—, v.p. 1989), Summit Club (bd. dirs. 1989). Lodges: Rotary. Democrat. Methodist. Home: 3533 Mill Springs Rd Birmingham AL 35223-1637 Office: Energen Corp 605 21st St N Birmingham AL 35203-2707

WARRICK, BROOKE, marketing executive; MS in Psychology, San Francisco State U. Past mktg. dir. VALS program Stanford Rsch. Inst.; pres. Am. Lives, San Francisco, 1989—. Internat. spkr. in field; condr. tng. sessions. various orgns. Author: The Builder's Guide to Moveup Buyers; prodr. (video) An American Portrait. Office: Am Lives Inc 6114 Lasalle Ave Ste 590 Oakland CA 94611-1825

WARRICK, PETER, professional football player; b. Bradenton, Fla., June 19, 1977; Postgrad in political sci., Fla. State Univ. Wide receiver Cin. Bengals, 2001—. Achievements include club record for rushing yards in a season by a wide receiver. Office: Cin Bengals 1 Paul Brown Stadium Cincinnati OH 45202

WARRICK, RUTH, actress; b. St. Joseph, Mo., June 29, 1916; d. Frederick R. Jr. and Annie L. (Scott) W.; m. Erik Rolf (div.); m. Carl Neubert (div.); m. Robert McNamara, (div.); m. L. Jarvis Cushing Jr. (div.). Student, U. Mo.; studies with Antoinette Perry, Brock Pemberton. Cons. High Sch. Drop-out Program, U.S. Dept. Labor, 1962, Job Tng. Corps., 1964-66. Actress: (stage prodns.) Bury the Dead, 1937, Dial M for Murder, 1955, The Thorntons, 1956, Miss Lonelyhearts, 1957, Anna in The King & I, 1957-58, Single Man at a Party, 1959, Take Me Along, 1960, Who's Afraid of Virginia Woolf?, 1965, Long Day's Journey into Night, 1966, The Secret Life of Walter Mitty, 1966, Any Resemblance to Persons Living or Dead, 1971, Misalliance, 1972, Conditions of Agreement, 1972, Irene, 1973-74, Roberta, 1976, Legends, 1987 Butterflies Are Free, 1988, (broadway) Irene, 1971-72, Roberta, 1980, The King and I, 1958-59; (feature films) 34 films including The Corsican Brothers, 1941, Citizen Kane, 1941, Journey into Fear, 1942, The Iron Major, 1943, Forever and a Day, 1943, The Iron Major, 1943, Guest in the House, 1944, Mr. Winkle Goes to War, 1944, China Sky, 1945, Song of the South, 1946, Daisy Kenyon, 1947, Perilous Holiday, 1946, Let's Dance, 1950, The Great Dan Patch, 1949, Three Husbands, 1950, Ride Beyond Vengeance, 1966, How to Steal the World, 1968, The Great Bank Robbery, 1969, (TV series) Father of the Bride, 1961-62, Peyton Place, 1964-67, As The World Turns, All My Children (2 Emmy award nominations); rec. artist Phoebe Tyler Regrets; author: (autobiography) The Confessions of Phoebe Tyler, 1980. Del. Global Forum for Human Survival, Moscow, 1990; bd. dirs. Bus. and Industry for Arts in Edn.; sponsor Learning to Read Through the Arts; co-founder Operation Bootstrap Watts, Calif., 1949-52, 64; regent of Cathedral St. John the Divine, N.Y.C. Recipient Humanitarian award Midland Empire Arthritis Found. given each year in her name, 1976, Arts in Edn. award given each year in her name, 1983, Arts in Edn. award Bus. and Industry for Arts in Edn., 1983, Medal N.Y. Arts Assn., 1996; Emmy Silver Circle, 1997; named Tchr. Cities in Schs., N.Y.C. Schs., 1976, TV-Hall of Fame, 1998. Mem. Bus. and Industry for Arts in Edn. (bd. dirs.), English Speaking Union (bd. dirs.), Juvenille Diabetes Assn. (chair). Avocations: swimming, walking, music, metaphysics. Office: c/o Anthony & Assocs 250 W 57th St Ste 1928 New York NY 10107-0001 also: ABC Press Rels 77 W 66th St Fl 5 New York NY 10023-6201

WARRICK, SHERIDAN, magazine editor; Former editor Pacific Discovery/Calif. Acad. Scis., San Francisco; exec. editor food and nutrition Time Inc.'s Health, San Francisco, 1987 . Author: (book) The Natural History of the UC Santa Cruz Campus, 1983. Office: Time Incs Health 2 Embarcadero Ctr Ste 600 San Francisco CA 94111-3827

WARRING, JEROME THOMAS, management consultant; b. Bloomington, Ind., Feb. 2, 1941; s. Thomas Edward Warring and Ellen Chase Hanna Murphy; 1 child, Frank Anthony. AB in Polit. Sci., Ind. U., 1962, MBA in Fin., 1972. Sr. cons. KMPG/Peat Marwick & Co., LA, 1969-70; v.p. and original equity ptnr. Korn/Ferry Internat., LA, 1971-78; pres. Warring & Assocs., Anaheim Hills, Calif., 1978—, Warring Internat. Ins. Adv. Svcs., Ltd., Anaheim Hills, 1987—. Retained sr. advisor Asia-Pacific bus. devel. strategy, negotiation, and fgn. regulatory affairs Citicorp Global Consumer Ins. Ops., NYC, 1989-93; internat. spkr. in field. Founder, pres. nonprofit Sonshine Youth Svcs. Inc., Bell Gardens, Cudahy, Commerce, Calif., 1976—; pres. Rio Hondo Boys & Girls Club, Bell Gardens, 1978-80; mem. nat. task force com. Boys & Girls Clubs Am., Inc., NYC, 1980-82. Named Man of Yr., Federated Vol. Orgns., Downey, Calif., 1981, Bd. Vol. of Yr., United Way Greater LA, 1995. Mem. Newport-Irvine Rotary, Alexis de Tocqueville Soc. Republican. Reformed Ch. of Am. Avocations: volunteer public service, mountain biking, running, boating, global Christian missions. Office: Warring Internat Adv Svcs Ltd 5673 Stetson Ct Anaheim Hills CA 92807

WARRINGTON, GEORGE D. rail transportation executive; b. Sept. 19, 1952; BA cum laude, Syracuse U., 1974, MPA, 1975. Asst. to dir. divsn. commuter svcs. N.J. Dept. Transp., 1975-77, spl. asst. to commr., 1977-80; dep. exec. dir./chief of staff N.J. Transit Corp. Ops., 1980-88; v.p., gen. mgr. N.J. Transit Rail Ops., 1988-90; dep. commr. N.J. Dept. Transp., 1990-92; exec. dir., pres. Del. River Port Authority and Port Authority Transit Corp., 1992-94; pres. N.E. Corridor Strategic Bus. Unit, Nat. R.R. Passenger Corp. (Amtrak), 1994-98, pres., CEO, 1998—. Bd. dirs. Phila. Belt Line R.R. Office: Nat RR Passenger Corp 60 Massachusetts Ave NE Washington DC 20002-4285 Fax: 202-906-2850.

WARRINGTON, WILLARD GLADE, former university official; b. Macomb, Ill., Oct. 24, 1920; s. Henry K. and Farie V. (Prather) W.; m. Irene Windser, Aug. 9, 1945 (dec. 1969); m. Janette Moffatt Cooper, Apr. 26, 1972; children: David, Steven, Douglas, Jane Ann, Stephen Cooper. B.Ed., Western Ill. State Tchrs. Coll., 1941; MS, U. Ill., 1949, MS, 1950, Ed.D., 1952. Tchr. public high schs., Ill., 1941-42, 45-48; mem. faculty Mich. State U., 1952-58, dir. office evaluation services, 1958-74, asso. dean Univ. Coll., 1974-78, acting dean Univ. Coll., 1978-80, dir. undergrad. univ. div., 1980-85, dir., prof. emeritus, 1986—. Cons. edn.; Ford Found. cons. U. Philippines. Contbr. articles on ednl. measurement to profl. publs.; editorial bd.: Ednl. and Psychol. Measurement, 1968-85. Active Boy Scouts Am., 1957-68. Served to lt. col. USAAF, 1942-45. Mem. Nat. Council on Measurement in Edn. (pres. 1973-74), Am. Ednl. Research Assn., Assn. for Gen. and Liberal Studies (sec.-treas. 1973-79) Methodist. Home: 1211 Ascot Pl Haslett MI 48840

WARRIOR, PADMASREE, communications executive; BSChemE, Indian Inst. Tech.; MSChemE, CornellU. From rschr. to sr. v.p. Motorola, Inc., Schaumburg, Ill., 1984—2003, sr. v.p., 2003—, chief tech. officer, 2003—. Gen. mgr. Thoughtbeam, Inc.; mem. coun. digital economy Tex. Gov.; mem. rev. panel Tex. Higher Edn. Bd.; dir. Ferro Corp. Recipient Women Elevating Sci. and Tech. award, Working Woman Mag., 2001. Office: Motorola Inc 1303 E Algonquin Rd Schaumburg IL 60196

WARSHAUER, IRENE C. lawyer; b. N.Y.C., May 4, 1942; m. Alan M. Warshauer, Nov. 27, 1966; 1 child, Susan. BA with distinction, U. Mich., 1963; LLB cum laude, Columbia U., 1966. Bar: N.Y. 1966, U.S. Dsit. Ct. (so. and ea. dist.) N.Y. 1969, U.S. Ct. Appeals (2d cir.) 1969, U.S. Dist. Ct. (no. dist.) N.Y. 1980, U.S. Supreme Ct. 1972. With 1st Jud. Dept., N.Y. State Mental Health Info. Svc., 1966-68; assoc. Chadbourne Parke Whiteside & Wolff, 1968-75; mem. Anderson Kill & Olick, P.C., N.Y.C., 1975-99, Fried & Epstein, N.Y.C., 2000—. Mediator U.S. Dist. Ct. (so. dist.) N.Y., N.Y. State Supreme Ct.; lectr. Columbia Law Sch., Def. Rsch. Inst., Aspen Inst. Humanistic Studies, ABA, Rocky Mountain Mineral Law Found., CPR Inst. Dispute Resolution; arbitrator NASD EEOC, NYSE, Am. Arbitration Assn. Contbr. chpts. to books, articles to profl. jours. Mem. County Dem. Com., 1968—. Named to Hon. Order Ky. Cols. Mem.: ABA, N.Y. State Bar Assn. (chmn. subcom. mentally disabled and cmty. 1978—82), Assn. Bar City N.Y. (judiciary com. 1982—84, mem. alternative dispute resolution com. 2000—). Avocations: gardening, cooking, birding, theater. Office: Fried & Epstein 1350 Broadway New York NY 10018-7702

WARSHAW, ALLEN CHARLES, lawyer; b. Harrisburg, Pa., Aug. 27, 1948; s. Julius and Miriam (Nepove) W.; m. Shirley Anne Nes, Aug. 23, 1970; children: Christopher James, Andrew Charles, William Robert. BA, U. Pa., 1970; JD, Villanova U., 1973. Bar: Pa. 1973, U.S. Dist. Ct. (ea. and mid. dists.) Pa. 1974, U.S. Ct. Appeals (3d cir.) 1975, U.S. Supreme Ct. 1977, Calif. 1978. Staff atty. Office Atty. Gen., State of Pa., Harrisburg, 1973-79, chief civil litig., 1979-85, dir. civil law, 1985-86; ptnr. Duane, Morris & Heckscher, Harrisburg, 1986—2002; shareholder Klett, Rooney, Lieber & Schorling, Harrisburg, 2002—. Past pres. Mechanicsburg Soccer Assn.; Dem. committeeperson Cumberland County; past bd. dirs. Mechanicsburg Area Sch. Dist.; bd. dirs. Planned Parenthood Susquehanna Valley. Fellow Am. Bar Found.; mem. ABA, ABA Coun. Appellate Lawyers, Fed. Bar Assn., Am. Bankruptcy Inst., Pa. Bar Assn., Dauphin County Bar Assn. Home: 1035 Mccormick Rd Mechanicsburg PA 17055-5970 Office: Klett Rooney Lieber & Schorling 240 N 3d St Harrisburg PA 17101 Office Phone: 717-231-7718. E-mail: acwarshaw@KlettRooney.com.

WARSHAW, ANDREW LOUIS, surgeon, researcher; b. N.Y.C., Feb. 18, 1939; s. David and Florence (Rand) W.; m. Brenda Rose Flavin, Jan. 4, 1986; children: Jordan, Abigail, Daniel; stepchildren: Heather, Gretchen, Brenda. AB, Harvard U., 1959, MD, 1963. Diplomate Am. Bd. Surgery. Intern in surgery Mass. Gen. Hosp., Boston, 1963-64, resident in surgery, 1964-65, 67-70, rsch. fellow in medicine, 1970, chief resident in surgery, 1971; clin. assoc. in gastroenterology NIH, Bethesda, Md., 1965-67; from instr. surgery to prof. surgery Harvard Med. Sch., Boston, 1972-90, Harold & Ellen Danser prof. surgery, 1990-97, W. Gerald Austen prof. surgery, 1997—; assoc. chief surg. svcs. Mass. Gen. Hosp., Boston, 1990-97, chief gen. surgery, 1992-97, chmn. dept. surgery, surgeon-in-chief, 1997—. Editor: Pancreatitis, 1989, Current Practice of Surgery, 1993, The Pancreas, 1998; contbr. more than 400

articles to med. jours., revs.; contbr. to 8 med. ednl. films, videos; editor-in-chief Surgery, 1997—. Trustee Mass. Gen. Hop., Boston, 1999—. Lt. comdr. USPHS, 1965-67. Mem. ACS (pres. Mass. chpt. 1991-92, gov. 1997-2003, health policy steering com. 2001-, 1st v.p. 2004-), Am. Bd. Surgery (chmn. 1992-93, dir. 1985-93), New Eng. Surg. Soc. (pres. 1993-94), Soc. for Surgery of Alimentary Tract (pres. 1997-98), Internat. Assn. Pancreatology (pres. 1998-), Boston Surg. Soc. (pres. 1999-2000), Halsted Soc. (pres. 2002-03). Avocations: photography, fly fishing. Office: Mass Gen Hosp White 506 Boston MA 02114 Business E-Mail: awarshaw@partners.org.

WARSHAW, CAROLE KLEIN, education educator, consultant; d. Irving and Frieda Patlis Klein; m. Gerald Jay Warshaw, June 9, 1956; children: Ms. Jodie Sharon Arrington, Howard Gary, Dr. Joel David. BA, Hunter Coll., N.Y.C., 1957; MS in Spl. Edn., Hofstra U., 1976; Profl. Diploma- Adminstrn., St. John's U., Queens, N.Y., 1987, EdD, 1993. Cert. elem. sch. tchr. N.Y.C. Bd. Edn., 1957, asst. prin. N.Y.C. Bd. Edn., 1989, adminstrn./supr. N.Y. State Dept. Edn., 1987, clin. edn. trainer Fla. Dept. Edn., 2000. Tchr. N.Y.C. Bd. Edn., Queens, 1957—84, tchr. trainer, 1984—89, dir. testing, 1989—90; assoc. prof. Lynn U., Boca Raton, Fla., 1994—, coord. master's program, 1994—, coord. evening edn. programs, 1994—. Liaison to dept. of edn. Lynn U., Boca Raton, 1995—; cons. Florence Fuller Child Devel. Ctrs., Boca Raton, 1999—, Toussaint L'Ouverture H.S., Delray Beach, Fla., 2001—; clin. supervision trainer Fla. Dept. Edn., Boca Raton, 1999—. Contbr. articles to profl. jours. V.p. Coalition of Boynton Beach (Fla.) Residents, 1992—94, Temple Beth Emeth, Bklyn., 1964—65; pres. Palm Shores Homeowners Assn., Boynton Beach, 1993—94. Impact II grantee, N.Y.C. Bd. Edn., 1981. Mem.: Coun. Adminstrs. and Suprs., Coun. for Exceptional Children, Phi Delta Kappa, Kappa Delta Pi (counselor 1997—). Independent. Hebrew. Avocations: bridge, travel, music. Office: Lynn U 3601 N Military Trl Boca Raton FL 33431 Personal E-mail: jecawa@adelphia.net. E-mail: cwarshaw@lynn.edu.

WARSHAW, MARVIN D. conductor, educator, musician; s. Norman Maurice Warshaw and Heartha Joyce Levinson; m. Carol A. Pendleton, May 25, 1986. M in Musical Arts, Yale U., 1980. Pers. mgr., libr., prin. violist, soloist New Haven Symphony Orch., 1977—; pvt. lessons tchr. Wesleyan U., Middletown, Conn., 1997—; faculty instr. Ednl. Ctr. for the Arts, New Haven, 1997—; strings tchr. Coop. H.S. for the Arts and Humanities, New Haven, 1999—; condr. Greater New Haven Concert Orch., 2001—; founding mem., mgr. Wall St. Chamber Players, 1980—; orch. personal mgr., libr. violist Bellingham Festival, 2004—. Head orch. libr. Aspen (Colo.) Music Festival, 1981—98. Office: New Haven Symphony Orch 70 Audubon St New Haven CT 06510

WARSHAW, MICHAEL THOMAS, lawyer; b. Jersey City, June 29, 1950; s. Thomas T. and June C. (Lancaster) W.; m. Mary Jane Egidio, July 12, 1986. BA in Sociology, Coll. of the Holy Cross, 1972; JD, Bklyn. Law Sch., 1975. Bar: N.J. 1976, U.S. Dist. Ct. N.J. 1976, U.S. Ct. Appeals (3d cir.) 1982, N.Y. Ct. of Appeals 1987, U.S. Supreme Ct. 1982. Law sec. to judge N.J. Superior Ct., 1975-76; assoc. Drazin & Warshaw PC, Red Bank, N.J., 1976-88, Magee & Graham, Wall, N.J., 1988-90; pres. Michael T. Warshaw, PC, Red Bank, 1990-95, 2001—; shareholder Warshaw & Barnes, PC, Red Bank, 1995-2001; adj. prof. bus. law Brookdale C.C., Lincroft. Speaker Mock Trial Sem., Young Lawyers div. N.J. Bar Assn., 1984, Discovery Sem., 1986; mem. com. on mcpl. cts. N.J. Supreme Ct., 1984-88; master Hadyn Proctor Inns of Ct., 1999—. Chmn. Red Bank Cath. H.S. Devel. Adv. Coun., 1994—, elder law seminar Trenton Diocese, 1996; trustee Brookdale C.C. Found., 1995—. Mem. ABA, N.J. Bar Assn. (young lawyers divsn., exec. com. 1983-86), N.J. Bar Found. (spkrs. bur.), Monmouth County Bar Assn. (civil practice com. 1985—, chair alternative dispute resolution com.), Christian Bros. Acad. Alumni Assn. (pres. 1993-95), Phi Delta Phi. Roman Catholic. Avocation: golf. Home: 18 Quaker Rd Middletown NJ 07748-3193 Office: 10 W Bergen Pl Ste 202 Red Bank NJ 07701-1500 E-mail: mtwarshaw2000@yahoo.com.

WARSHAW, ROBERTA SUE, lawyer; b. Chgo., July 10, 1934; d. Charles and Frieda (Feldman) Weiner; m. Lawrence Warshaw, July 5, 1959 (div. June 1978); children: Nan R., Adam; m. Paul A. Heise, Apr. 2, 1994. Student, U. Ill., 1952-55; BFA, U. So. Calif., 1956; JD, Northwestern U., 1980. Bar: Ill. 1980. Atty., fin. specialist Housing Svcs. Ctr., Chgo., 1980-84, Chgo. Rehab. Network, 1985-91, 92-95; dir. housing State Treas., State of Ill., Chgo., 1991; sole practitioner, 1995—. Legal worker Sch. of Law, Northwestern U. Legal Clinic, Chgo., 1977-80; real estate developer, mgr., marketer, Chgo., 1961-77; bd. dirs. Single Room Housing Assistance Corp., Lebanon County Mediation Svcs., mediator, sec., 2001; asst. dir. Lebanon Valley Coll. Program, Hania, Crete, 1998. Co-author: (manual) The Cook County Scavenger Sale Program and The City of Chicago Reactivation Program, 1991, (booklet) Fix the Worst First, 1989; co-editor: The Caring Contract, Voices of American Leaders, 1996. Alderman 9th ward City of Evanston, Ill., 1985-93, mem. planning and devel., rules com., unified budget com., chair flood and pollution control com.; pres. Sister Cities Found.; mem. cmty. and econ. devel. policy Nat. League Cities, 1990-93; active Dem. Nat. Com.; bd. dirs. Dem. Ctrl. Com. Evanston, 1973—; elected committeeman Evanston Twp. Dem. Com., 1994-98, dem. committeeman Mt. Gretna Borough, 2000—; del. Dem. Nat. Conv., 1996; Dem. committeeman Mt. Gretna Borough, 2000—; vol. tax preparer; tax counseling for elderly, 2000—; bd. dirs., mediator Lebanon County Mediation Svcs., 2000—, sec., 2001-03, pres., 2003—. Mem. ABA (affordable housing com.), Ill. State Bar Assn., Chgo. Bar Assn. (real estate coms.), Decalogue Soc. Lawyers, Chgo. Coun. Lawyers (housing com.), IRS Tax Counseling for the Elderly (vol. tax preparer). Avocations: politics, travel, hiking, camping, athletic activities. Home: 104 Brown Ave PO Box 537 Mount Gretna PA 17064-0537 E-mail: femdem1@narl.com.

WARSHAW, STANLEY IRVING, federal official, consultant; b. Boston, Nov. 5, 1931; s. Alec and Sarah (Laserson) W.; m. Wanda Faye Capino, Feb., 12, 1992; 1 child from previous marriage, Karen Beth. BS in Ceramic Engring, Ga. Tech. Inst., 1957; Sc.D. in Ceramics, M.I.T., 1961; grad., Advanced Mgmt. Program, Harvard Bus. Sch., 1978. Sr. scientist research div. Raytheon Co., Waltham, Mass., 1961-64; with Am. Standard, Inc., New Brunswick, N.J., 1964-75, gen. mgr. engring. and devel., 1972-75; dir. Ctr. for Consumer Product Tech., Nat. Inst. Stds. and Tech. (formerly Nat. Bur. Stds.), Washington, 1975-80, dir. Office Product Standards Policy, 1981-86, assoc. dir., 1987-89, dir. Office Standards Svcs. Gaithersburg, Md., 1989-93; sr. policy advisor for stds. and tech. U.S. Dept. Commerce, Gaithersburg, 1994-99. Served to capt. U.S. Army, 1951-53. Fellow N.Y. Acad. Scis., Washington Acad. Scis. Home: 555 SE 6th Ave Apt 5B Delray Beach FL 33483-5253 E-mail: swarshaw@adelphia.net.

WARSHAWSKY, ISIDORE, physicist, consultant; b. N.Y.C., May 27, 1911; s. Morris and Esther (Sherman) W. BS cum laude, CCNY, 1930. Physicist Nat. Adv. Com. Aeronautics, Langley Field, Va., 1930-42, chief instrumentation sect. Cleve., 1942-50; chief instrument rsch. br. Nat. Adv. Com. Aeronautics/NASA, Cleve., 1950-72; instrumentation cons. NASA, Cleve., 1972-90, ret., 1990, disting. rsch. cons. (unsalaried), 1990-95. *Some historically more notable inventions are: for studies of an airplane's acrobatic flight, the first mechanical gauge that could record the time history of structural stress in the wing (1935), the first panel plane-acceleration-indicator for the pilot (1937) and the first electrical-signal-recorder that was rugged enough to withstand the plane's vibration (1939); novel circuits that permitted flight use of the new electric strain gauges (1940); precise calibration system for meters used to measure the flow of liquid hydrogen to rocket engines (1961); precise calibration system for determining true pressure indicated by vacuum gauges used in space and in nuclear particle accelerators (1972).* Author: (textbook) Foundations of Measurement and Instrumentation, 1990; author 10 NACA/NASA tech. reports; contbr. 20 articles to sci. jours. and books. Fellow Instrument Soc. Am.; mem. Am. Phys. Soc., Am. Vacuum Soc, Phi Beta Kappa.

WARSHAWSKY, MARK JOEL, federal agency administrator, economist; b. Chgo., Mar. 26, 1958; s. Arthur and Dorothy (Chislof) W.; m. Laura Beth Margolis, June 28, 1987; children: David, Hannah, Avi, Sarah. BA, Northwestern U., 1979; PhD, Harvard U., 1984. Actuary Combined Ins., Chgo., 1979-80; rsch. asst. Nat. Bur. Econ. Rsch., Cambridge, Mass., 1981-82; tutor Harvard U., Cambridge, 1983-84; economist Fed. Res. Bd., Washington, 1984-88, sr. economist, 1989—92; sr. economist Employee Plans IRS, 1992—95; dir., strategic rsch. Teachers Ins. & Annuity Assoc. Coll. Retirement Equity Fund Inst., N.Y.C., 1995—98, dir. rsch., 1998—2001; dep. asst. sec., econ. policy, microeconomic analysis U.S. Dept. Treasury, Washington, 2002—04, asst. sec., econ. policy, 2004—. Contbr. articles to profl. jours. Trustee Actuarial Found., 2000—02. Sloan scholar Harvard U., 1983-84. Mem. Am. Econ. Assn., Am. Risk and Ins. Assn., Fin. Mgmt. Assn., Nat. Assn. Bus. Economists. Republican. Jewish. Office: US Dept Treasury 1500 Pennsylvania Ave NW Rm 3454 Washington DC 20220 Office Phone: 202-622-2200.

WARSHAWSKY, STANFORD SEYMOUR, investment banker; b. Asbury Park, N.J., Oct. 14, 1937; s. Harry and Eva (Holland) W.; m. Sandra Faith Weinstein, Aug. 14, 1960; children: Susan Abrams, Deborah Farfel, Cynthia Mark. BBA, U. Mich., 1959; JD, U. Va., 1962. Lawyer Shearman & Sterling, N.Y.C., 1962-71; from v.p. to co-pres., co-CEO Arnhold and S. Bleichroeder Holdings, Inc., N.Y.C., 1972—94, co-pres., co-CEO, 1994—2003, also bd. dirs., 1977—2003. Bd. dirs. Enzo Biochem, Inc., N.Y., 2002-04; chmn. Arnhold and S. Bleichroeder U.K. Ltd., London, 1998—, First Eagle Funds, N.Y.C., 1994-2003; mem. N.Y. area firms adv. com. N.Y. Stock Exch., N.Y.C., 1998—2003, mem. nominating com., 1998-2000, 2002-2003, chmn., 1999-2000; exch. ofcl. Am. Stock Exch., N.Y.C., 1994-97; co-pres., dir. Arnold and S. Bleichroeder Advisors, LLC., 1997-2003, chmn. Bismarck Capital, LLC, 2004-. Bd. dirs. Gen. Ceramics, Inc., N.Y., 1975-89, Leybold Inficon, Inc., N.Y., 1976-89, Mt. Sinai Ctr. Aux., N.Y.C., 1986-96; vice chmn., The Arthur F. burns Fellowship, 2002—. Mem. N.Y. State Bar Assn., Va. State Bar Assn., Hebrew Free Loan Soc. of N.Y. (bd. dirs. 1985—), German-Am. C. of C. (bd. dirs. 1980—), Met. Club, Harmonie Club, Doubles, India House. Office: Bismark Capital LLC 888 7th Ave New York NY 10019-0302 Office Phone: 212-994-9880.

WARTELL, MICHAEL ALAN, academic administrator; b. Albuquerque, Nov. 4, 1946; s. Richard H. and Betty D. (Davis) Wartell; m. Ruth E. Beachy, Dec. 3, 1977; children: Justin Davis, Richard Harrison. BS, U. N.Mex., 1967; MS, Yale U., 1968, PhD, 1971. Asst. prof. chemistry Met. State Coll., 1971—75, assoc. prof., chmn. dept., 1975—78; dean sch. natural scis., prof. chemistry James Madison U., 1979—84; provost, v.p. acad. affairs Humboldt State U., Arcata, Calif., 1984—89, prof. chemistry, 1984—94; chancellor Ind U. - Purdue U., Ft. Wayne, 1994—. Mem. U.S. Army Sci. Bd., 1981—87; participant various study groups on chem. warfare, decontaminatin, biodefense; cons. U.S. Army, IRT Corp., Sandia Nat. Labs., SRI Internat., JAYCOR, HERO, Boeing Elecs., Battelle; mem. Def. Intelligence Agy. Sci. Adv. Com., 1984—; chmn. bd. visitors Def. Systems Mgmt. Coll., Ft. Belvoir, Va., 1984—, chair, 1985—. Co-author: Engineering Education and A Lifetime of Learning, 1975, Introduction to Chemistry, 1975, Fundamentals of Chemistry, 1980; contbr. articles to profl. jours. Bd. dirs. Humboldt State U. Found., 1984—. Fellow: Am. Acad. Forensic Scis.; mem.: Kappa Nu Epsilon, Am. Assn. Univ. Adminstrs. (evaluation task force 1978—79, stds. and rev. com. 1983—84), Am. Phys. Soc., Am. Chem. Soc., Phi Kappa Phi, Phi Beta Kappa, Sigma Xi. Jewish. Office: Ind U Purdue U 2101 E Coliseum Blvd Fort Wayne IN 46805-1445 E-mail: wartell@ipfw.edu.

WARTH, JAMES ARTHUR, physician, researcher; b. New York City, Apr. 30, 1942; s. Peter and Anne Warth; m. Maria Archer Russell, May 3, 1969; children: David M., Andrew A. BS, Tufts U., 1963, MD, 1967. Diplomate Am. Bd. Internal Medicine, Am. Bd. Hematology, Am. Bd. Oncology. Hematologist Harvard Health Svc. Harvard U., Cambridge, Mass., 1976—77, officer, 1976—77; attending hematologist Harper Grace Hosp., Detroit, 1977—84; asst. prof. medicine Wayne State U., Detroit, 1977—84; rsch. scientist New Eng. Med. Ctr., Boston, 1984—86; attending hematologist, oncologist Faulkner Hosp., Boston, 1986; asst. prof. medicine Tufts U. Sch. Medicine, Boston, 1986, course dir. phys. diagnosis Faulkner Hosp., 1992, assoc. course dir. phys. diagnosis, 1996; dir. dept. medicine, physician asst. program Faulkner Hosp., Boston, 1996—97, course dir., 2001—; lectr. medicine Harvard Med. Sch., Boston, 2000—, patient Dr. II, 2001—, sect. leader hematologic pathophysiology, 2004. Guest appearance NBC affiliate NBC News, Detroit, 1980; cons. in hematology NIH, Bethesda, Md., 1980—83; invited lectr. Columbia U., 1982, Harvard Univ., 1984; vis. prof. Yale Univ., New Haven, 1986; rsch. lectr. NIH, Tarrytown, NY, 1986, cons. in hematology, Md., 87; med. grand rounds spkr. Faulkner Hosp., Boston, 1986, 88, 92, 96, 2004; invited lectr. State Univ. of N.Y., Syracuse, 1991; mem. pharmacy and therapeutics com. Faulkner Hosp., Boston, 1991—; faculty advisor Tufts Univ. Sch. Medicine, 1991—; cons. in hematology Mass. Profl. Rev. Orgn., Waltham, 1991—93; invited lectr. New Eng. Med. Ctr., Tufts Univ., 1992; cons. in hematology Medfield State Hosp., Mass., 1993—99; mem. case devel. com., problem based learning Tufts Univ. Sch. Medicine, 1994—95; chmn. sub com. on anticoagulation of pharmacy and therapeutics Faulkner Hosp., Boston, 1994—; med. grand rounds spkr. Shattuck Hosp., Boston, 1999; invited spkr. Dana Farber Cancer Inst., 1999; Max Millman meml. lectr. in medicine Bay State Med. Ctr., Tufts U., Springfield, Mass., 2000; invited spkr. Dana Farber Cancer Inst., 2003; bd. dir. Faulkner Physicians Assn., Inc., Boston, 1994—; mem. melanoma adv. bd. N.E. region Schering Plough Co., Kenilworth, NJ, 1995; med. grand rounds spkr. Shattuck Hosp., 2003. Author (contbg. author): (textbook) Hematologic Disorders in Maternal-Fetal Medicine, 1990; reviewer: Am. Jour. Hematology, 1986, Jour. Andrology, 1990—92; contbr. articles to profl. jours. Preceptor Nat. Youth Forum, 1996—98. Maj. U.S. Army, 1969—71. Recipient Mark Aisner M.D. Award for Excellence in Tchg. Physical Diagnosis, Tufts Univ. Sch. Medicine, 2001; Spl. Fellow, NIH, 1974—76, rsch. grantee, 1980—83, 1983—86. Fellow: ACP; mem.: Bio-Membranes Sickle Cell Rsch. Group, Am. Fedn. Med. Rsch., Am. Soc. Hematology. Achievements include discovery of new human red blood cell, sequestrocyte accepted into Am. Soc. Hematology slide bank, 1995. Avocations: art, music, architecture, tennis. Office: Faulkner Hosp 1153 Centre St Rm 5950 Boston MA 02130-3446

WARTH, ROBERT DOUGLAS, history educator; b. Houston, Dec. 16, 1921; s. Robert Douglas and Virginia (Adams) W.; m. Lillian Eleanor Terry, Sept. 18, 1945. BS, U. Ky., 1943; MA, U. Chgo., 1945, PhD, 1949. Instr. history U. Tenn., Knoxville, 1950-51; instr. Rutgers U., Newark, 1951-54, asst. prof., 1954-58; vis. prof. Paine Coll., Augusta, Ga., 1960; asso. editor Grolier, Inc., N.Y.C., 1960-62, 63-64; lectr. Hunter Coll., N.Y.C., part time, 1962-63; asso. prof. S.I. C.C., 1964-68; prof. history U. Ky., Lexington, 1968-92, prof. emeritus history, 1992—. Pres. So. Conf. Slavic Studies, 1982-83 Author: The Allies and the Russian Revolution, 1954, Soviet Russia in World Politics, 1963, Joseph Stalin, 1969, Lenin, 1973, Leon Trotsky, 1977, Nicholas II: The Life and Reign of Russia's Last Monarch, 1997. Served with AUS, 1943-44. Sr. scholar award So. Conf. Slavic Studies, 1992. Mem. Am. Hist. Assn., Am. Assn. Advancement Slavic Studies, AAUP Home: 640 Cooper Dr Lexington KY 40502-2277 Office: U Ky Dept History Lexington KY 40506-0001

WARTHEN, HARRY JUSTICE, III, lawyer; b. Richmond, Va., July 8, 1939; s. Harry Justice Jr. and Martha Winston (Alsop) W.; m. Sally Berkeley Trapnell, Sept. 7, 1968; children: Martha Alsop, William Trapnell. BA, U. Va., 1961, LLB, 1967. Bar: Va. 1967, U.S. Ct. Appeals (4th cir.) 1967, U.S. Dist. Ct. (ea. dist.) Va. 1969. Law clk. to judge U.S. Ct. Appeals (4th cir.), Richmond, Va., 1967-68; assoc. Hunton & Williams, Richmond, 1968—. Lectr. in field U. Va. Law Sch., Charlottesville, 1975—77. Trustee exec. com. Hist. Richmond Found., 1986-95, 96-2004, pres., 2000-02; trustee Woodrow Wilson Birthplace and Mus., 1997-2003; dir. exec. com. Preservation Alliance of Va., 1991-97, pres., 1994-96; vice-pres. bd. advisors The Nat. Trust for Historic Preservation, 2003—; elder, trustee endowment fund Grace Covenant Presbyn. Ch.; moderator Hanover Presbytery, Presbyn. Ch. (USA), 1988. Lt. U.S. Army, 1962-64. Fellow Am. Coll. Trust and Estate Counsel, Va. Law Found.; mem. ABA, Richmond Bar Assn., Va. Bar Assn. (chmn. sect. on wills, trusts and estates 1981-89), Antiquarian Soc. Richmond (pres. 1977-78, 98-99), Country Club Va., Deep Run Hunt Club. Republican. Home: 1319 Shallow Well Rd Manakin Sabot VA 23103-2305 Office: Hunton & Williams Riverfront Plz E Tower 951 E Byrd St Richmond VA 23219 Office Phone: 804-788-8414. E-mail: hwarthen@hunton.com.

WARTLUFT, DAVID JONATHAN, retired librarian, minister; b. Stouchsburg, Pa., Sept. 22, 1938; s. Cleaver Milvard and Dorothy (Stump) W.; m. Joyce Claudia Dittmer, June 15, 1963 (dic. Sept. 1988); children: Elizabeth Marie, Deborah Joy, Rebecca Janet, Andrew Jonathan. AB (Trexler scholar), Muhlenberg Coll., 1960; MDiv (Danforth scholar), Luth. Theol. Sem., Phila., 1964; MA (scholar), U. Pa., 1964; MS (Lilly Found. scholar), Drexel U., 1968; DD, Luth. Theol. Sem., Phila., 2003. Asst. chaplain, instr. religion Springfield Coll., Mass., 1962-63; ordained minister Luth. Ch., 1964; pastor Jerusalem Luth. Ch., Allentown, Pa., 1964-66; cataloger, reference libr. Luth. Sem. Phila., 1966-68, asst. libr., 1968-77, dir. libr., 1977—2002, chaplain, 1978-79, dir. 1st yr. field edn., 1979-81, 82-83, faculty sec., 1985—2002; interim pastor New Jerusalem (Pa.) Luth. Ch., 2003—. Mem. comms. com. Northeastern Pa. Synod, 1967—78; archivist Northeastern Pa. Synod, Luth. Ch. Am., 1970—87; conv. com. Northeastern Pa. Synod, 1976; v.p. Luth. Archives Ctr., Phila., 1979—85, bd. dirs.; archivist Northeastern Pa. Synod, Evang. Luth. Ch. Am., 1988—91; libr. cons. Gurkul Luth. Ch., Madras, India, 1989, Huria Kristen Batak Protestant Sem., Pematang Siantar, Sumatra, Indonesia, 1989, Luther Sem., Adelaide, Australia, 1996; chair archives adv. bd. Evang. Luth. Ch. Am., 2000—03. Editor: Tenwork, 1970—84, The Periodical, 1979—84, Luth. Hist. Soc. Eastern Pa.; author: (book indexes) Luther in Mid Career (H. Bronkamm), 1983, Theodicy in the Old Testament (J. Crenshaw), 1983, The Roots of Anti-Semitism (H. Obermann), 1984, The Book of Revelation: Justice and Judgment (E.S. Fiorenza), 1985, Rediscovering Paul (N.R. Peterson), 1985, The Opponents of Paul in Second Corinthians (D. Georgi), 1986, Psychological Aspects of Pauline Theology (G. Theissen), 1986, Ethics of the New Testament (W. Schragg), 1987, Israel's Praise (W. Brueggemann), 1987, Commitment to Unity (W.K. Gilbert), 1988, Paul and His Letters (L. Keck), 1988, Finally Comes the Poet (W. Bruggemann), 1989, Community and Commitment (G. Rupp), 1989, Protest and Praise (J.M. Spenser), 1990, After the Absolute (L. Swidler), 1990, Greeks, Romans and Christians (L. Swidler), 1990, The New Era in Religious Education (P. Babin), 1991, A Commentary on the Book of Amos (S. M. Paul), 1992, The Book of Revelation (J. Roloff), 1993, What is Scripture? (W.C. Smith), 1993, Jesus in the Gospels (R. Schnackenburg), 1995, Amos (Jeremias), 1998, World Religions in America (J. Neusner), 1999, Revolution and Renewal (Campolo), 2000, Nicholas Lyra: The Senses of Scripture (Krey and Smith), 2000, Beleaguered Ruler (W. May), 2001, Practical Theology for Black Churches (D.P. Andrews), 2003, Approaches to Auschwitz (Roth and Rubenstein), 2003; contbr. articles to profl. jours. Active Boy Scouts Am., 1964—66. Mem.: Drexel U. Grad. Sch. Libr. and Info. Sci. Alulmni Assn. (bd. dirs. 1978—80), Mid. States Assn. (accreditation visitor), Assn. Uniting Religion and Art (chmn. membership com., treas. 1995—2002), Paradise Falls Luth. Assn. (chmn. religious activities 1985—86, bd. dirs. 1985—87), Assn. Theol. Schs. in US and Can. (selection panel for libr. grants), Luth. Hist. Conf. (com. on scholarly rsch. and pub. 1981—, constl. revision com. 1984—86, bd. dirs., treas. 1988—94, membership chair 1994—96, editor essays and reports 1996—2000, bd. dirs., treas. 1996—2002), Coun. on Study Religion (liaison com. 1974—77, nominating com. 1978—80, liaison com. 1981—82), Coun. Nat. Libr. and Info. Assn. (counselor 1978—81), Southeastern Pa. Theol. Librs. Assn. (sec. 1970—73, chair planning com. 1986—89), Am. Theol. Libr. Assn. (exec. sec., editor procs. 1971—81, bd. dirs. 1991—94, recording sec. 1995—97, devel. officer 1998—99), Luth. Hist. Soc. Ea. Pa. (life; bd. dirs. 1991—94, v.p. 1994—96), Bea Phi Mu, Phi Sigma Tau, Eta Sigma Phi. Democrat. Personal E-mail: dwartluft@aol.com. *By God's grace I am freed to live a life of joyful service in gratitude.*

WARTMAN, STEVEN, dean, educator; Grad., Cornell U., 1966; MD, Johns Hopkins U., 1970, PhD Sociology, 1979. Diplomate Am. Bd. Internal Medicine. Chief med. svs., chmn. medicine Mount Sinai Med. Ctr., Miami Beach; prof. medicine U. Miami; sr. residency in internal medicine Baltimore City Hosp.; intern in internal medicine Stanford U. Med. Ctr.; resident in internal medicine Yale-New Haven Hosp.; prof. medicine Albert Einstein Coll. Medicine; physician-in-chief L.I. Jewish Med. Ctr.; with Edward Meilman Disting. Chair Medicine; dir. Ctr. Quality Rsch. North Shore-L.I. Jewish Health Sys.; dean U. Tex. Med. Sch. San Antonio, 2000—. Contbr. more than 120 peer-reviewed jour. articles, abstracts, chapters to books. Recipient Leadership and Achievement award, Soc. Gen. Internal Medicine, 1997, Excellence award, U.S. Health Resources and Svcs. Adminstrn., 1999; fellow Internat. in Health Care, Yugoslavia, 1969, Primary Care Policy, USPHS, 1991; scholar Henry Luce, Indonesia, 1975—76, Robert Wood Johnson Clin., Johns Hopkins U., 1976—78. Fellow: ACP; mem.: Alpha Omega Alpha, Phi Beta Kappa. Office: 7703 Floyd Curl Dr San Antonio TX 78229

WARWICK, DIONNE, singer; b. East Orange, N.J., Dec. 12, 1940; m. Bill Elliott (div. 1975); children: David, Damon. Ed., Hartt Coll. Music, Hartford, Conn. As teen-ager formed Gospelaires and Drinkard Singers, then sang background for rec. studio, 1966; debut, Philharmonic Hall, N.Y. Lincoln Center, 1966; appearances include London Palladium, Olympia, Paris, Lincoln Ctr. Performing Arts, N.Y.C.; records include Don't Make Me Over, 1962, Walk On By, Do You Know The Way to San José, What The World Needs Now, Message To Michael, I'll Never Fall In Love Again, I'll Never Love This Way Again, Deja Vu, Heartbreaker, That's What Friends are For; albums include Valley of the Dolls and Others, 1968, Promises, Promises, 1975, Dionne, 1979, Then Came You, Friends, 1986, Reservations for Two, 1987, Greatest Hits, 1990, Dionne Warwick Sings Cole Porter, 1990, Hidden Gems; The Best of Dionne Warwick, Vol. 2, 1992, (with Whitney Houston) Friends Can Be Lovers, 1993, Dionne Warwick and Placido Domingo, 1994, Aquarela Do Brasil, 1994, From the Vaults, 1995, Sings the Bacharach and David Songbook, 1995, Dionne Sings Dionne, 1998, I Say a Little Prayer for You, 2000; TV appearance in Sisters in the Name of Love, HBO, 1986; screen debut Slaves, 1969, No Night, So Long, also, Hot! Live and Otherwise; co-host: TV show Solid Gold; host: TV show A Gift of Music, 1981; star: TV show Dionne Warwick Spl. Founder Dionne Warwick Scholarship Fund, 1968, charity group BRAVO (Blood Revolves Around Victorious Optimism), Warwick Found. to Help Fight AIDS; spokeswoman Am. Sudden Infant Death Syndrome; participant U.S.A for Africa; Am. Amb. of Health, 1987. Recipient Grammy awards, 1969, 70, 80; NAACP Key of Life award, 1990. Address: Arista Records Inc 6 W 57th St New York NY 10019-3901

WASAN, DARSH TILAKCHAND, university official, chemical engineer educator; b. Sarai, Salah, West Pakistan, July 15, 1938; came to U.S., 1957, naturalized, 1974; s. Tilakchand Gokalchand and Ishari Devi (Obhan) W.; m. Usha Kapur, Aug. 21, 1966; children: Ajay, Kern. BSChemE, U. Ill., 1960; PhD, U. Calif., Berkeley, 1965. Asst. prof. chem. engring. Ill. Inst. Tech., Chgo., 1964-67, assoc. prof., 1967-70, prof., 1970—, chmn. dept., 1971-77, 78-87, acting dean, 1977-78, 87-88, v.p. rsch. and tech., 1988-91, provost, 1991—, provost and sr. v.p., 1995-96, v.p., internat. and Motorola chair, 1996—. Cons. Inst. Gas Tech., 1965-70, Chgo. Bridge & Iron Co., 1967-71, Ill. EPA, 1971-72, NSF, 1971, 78-79, 87-89, Nelson Industries, 1976—, B.F. Goodrich Chem. Co., 1976-78, Exxon Rsch. & Engring. Co., 1977-89, Stauffer Chem. Co., 1980-88, ICI Ams., 1988-92, Westinghouse Savannah River Co., 1995-2004, Monsanto, 1999-2004; Procter & Gamble lectr. U. Cin. Editor-in-chief Jour. colloid and Interface sci.; mem. publs. bd. Chem. Engring. Edn. Jour.; mem. adv. bd. Jour. Separations Tech., Current Opinion in Colloid and Interface Sci., Jour. of Dispersion Sci. and Tech.; contbr. articles to profl. jours. Recipient Donald Gage Stevens Disting. Lectureship award Syracuse U., 1991, Jakob J. Bikerman Lectureship award Case Western U., 1994, Robert Gilpin Lectr. award Clarkson U., 1995, MacMoran Disting. Lectureship award Tulane U., 1996, Sidney Ross lectr. award, 1996, Bonnet Dodge Disting. Lectureship award Yale U., 1998, Spl. citation U.S. FDA, 2000. Fellow AIChE (Ernest Thiele award 1989, Thmas Baron award in fluid-particle systems 2002); mem. AAAS, U.S. Nat. Acad. Engring., Am. Chem. Soc. (award in colloid chemistry 2000), Soc. Rheology, Am. Soc. Engring. Edn. (Western Electric award 1972, 3M Lectureship award chem.

engring. divsn. 1991), Am. Physics Inst., Fine Particles Soc. (pres. 1976-77, Hausner award 1982), Sigma Xi. Home: 8705 Royal Swan Ln Darien IL 60561-8433 Office: Ill Inst Tech 3300 S Federal St Chicago IL 60616-3793 E-mail: wasan@iit.edu.

WASCH, WILLIAM KARL, gerontologist, consultant; b. Mt. Vernon, N.Y., May 11, 1931; s. Karl F. and Lina M. (Krauth) W.; m. Susan Beck Wasch, Aug. 23, 1958; children: Christina, William K. Jr., Heidi, Frederick. BA with honors, Wesleyan U., 1952; MS in Bus., Columbia U., 1953. Fin. analyst Std. Oil of N.J., N.Y.C., 1956-59; mktg. rep. Esso Std., N.Y.C., 1959-61; mktg. economist Sinclair Refining Co., N.Y.C., 1961-64; dir. devel. and alumni rels. Wesleyan U., Middletown, Conn., 1965-84; pres. William K. Wasch Assocs., Middletown, 1985—. Builder accessible housing. Author: Home Planning for Your Later Years, 1996. Trustee Wesleyan U., Middletown, 1997-2000, Nat. Coun. on the Aging, Inc., Washington, 1994-96, 98—, Seabury Retirement Cmty., Bloomfield, Conn., 1984-2002; chair Middletown Sr. Affairs Commn., 1996-2002. Lt. j.g. USNR, 1953-56. Mem. Hartford Club, Adelphic Ednl. Fund (sec., treas.), Am. Assn. for Support of Ecological Initiatives (sec., treas.), Phi Beta Kappa. Episcopalian. Avocation: squash. Home and Office: 150 Coleman Rd Middletown CT 06457-5065 Office Phone: 860-346-2967.

WASCOE, THOMAS M. pharmaceutical executive; b. Oct. 10, 1946; B in Polit. Sci., U. Wis., Milw.; MBA, U. Wis., Whitewater. Mgr. employee rels. GE Med. Systems, Milw.; human resource specialist diagnostics divsn. Abbott Labs., Dallas, 1983, numerous mgmt. positions in diagnostics and internat. divsns. Abbott Park, Ill., divisional v.p. human resources diagnostics divsn., sr. v.p. human resources, 1999—. Home: Abbott Labs 100 Abbott Park Rd Abbott Park IL 60064-6400

WASDEN, LAWRENCE, state attorney general; m. Tracey Wasden; children: Sean, Ashley, Cassidy, Blake. B.A., BYU, 1982; JD, U. Idaho, 1985. Bar: Idaho 1985. Dep. pros. atty. Canyon County, Idaho; dep. atty. gen. Idaho State Tax Commn.; dep. chief of staff State of Idaho, Boise, chief of staff to atty. gen., atty. gen., 2003—. Mem.: Idaho State Bar (founding mem., immediate past chmn. govt. and pub. lawyers sect.). Republican. Office: Office Atty Gen PO Box 83720 700 W Jefferson St Boise ID 83720

WASEM, BRUCE WILLIAM, football coach, educator; b. Oberlin, Ohio, Sept. 3, 1946; s. Willis Ira and Marjorie K. Wasem. BA, Bluffton Coll., 1968; MA, Ohio State U., 1976. Tchr., coach Chardon City Sch., Chardon, Ohio, 1968—72, Firelands Local Sch., Oberlin, 1972—74; instr., coach Wilmington Coll., Ohio, 1974—79, asst. prof., coach, 1979—91; instr., asst. coach U. Va. Coll. at Wise (Clinch Valley), 1991—2002, instr., head football coach, 2002—. Org. dist. phone network Common Cause, Ohio, 1972—74. Mem.: Nat. Strength and Conditioning Assn., Am. Alliance Health, Phys. Edn., Rec. and Dance, Am. Football Coaches Assn. (chair, NAIA asst. coach com. 1994—97, mem. rules com. 2002—). Home: 10135 White Oak Rd PO Box 129 Wise VA 24293 Office: U VA Coll at Wise 1 Coll Ave Wise VA 24293 Business E-Mail: bww2e@uvawise.edu.

WASFI, SADIQ HASSAN, chemistry professor; b. Basrah, Iraq, July 1, 1936; established residency in the U.S., 1978; s. Hassan Mohammed and Seniye (Omar) W.; m. Ellen Olivia Schwarz, Nov. 15, 1968; children: Yasmine, Dahlia, Ammar. BS in Chemistry Edn., Baghdad (Iraq) U., 1961; MS in Analytical Chemistry, Georgetown U., 1966, PhD in Inorganic Chemistry, 1971. Lectr. chemistry Basrah U., 1971-77; rsch. assoc. U. Hawaii, Honolulu, 1975-76, Georgetown U., Washington, 1977-78; assoc. prof. Montgomery Coll., Takoma Park, Md., 1978-79; prof. chemistry Del. State U., Dover, 1979—. Vis. assoc. prof. Georgetown U., 1980, 81. Contbr. articles to profl. jours; patent in antimony oxometalate complexes having anti-viral activity, 1991. Mem. Am.-Arab Anti-Discrimination Com. Mem. Am. Chem. Soc., Sigma Xi. Moslem. Home: 286 Pine Valley Rd Dover DE 19904-7111 Office: Del State Univ Dept Chemistry 1200 N Dupont Hwy Dover DE 19901-2202 E-mail: swasfi@dsc.edu.

WASHBURN, BARBARA POLK, cartographer, researcher, explorer; b. Boston, Nov. 10, 1914; m. Bradford Washburn, Apr. 27, 1940; children: Dorothy, Edward, Elizabeth. Grad., Smith Coll., 1935; DSc (hon.), U. Alaska, 1995, Boston U., 1996, Simmons Coll., 2001. Sec. Harvard Biol. Labs., 1936-38; exec. sec. Mus. of Sci., 1939-40; remedial reading tchr. Shady Hill Sch., Cambridge, Mass.; asst. to Henry Bradford Washburn Jr. First ascent of Mt. Bertha, Alaska, 1940, Mt. Hayes, Alaska, 1941; first woman to climb Mt. McKinley, Alaska, 1947; worked with husband on numerous sci. expdns., including Mt. McKinley, the Grand Canyon, Bangkok, London, Nepal, China, Alaska, Zurich, Milan, 1945—; participated in remapping the Grand Canyon for Nat. Geographic/Mus. of Sci., 1971-76; cons. to Govt. of Alaska State Parks Recreational Area in Tokositna Valley, 1980. Editor new chart of Squam Lake, 1977, new map of Presdl. Range, Squam Lake, N.H., 1989; contbr. articles to Anchorage Daily News, 1987. Bd. dirs. Boston Children's Svc. Assn.; overseer Brigham & Women's Hosp., Boston; mem. corp. Fernald Sch., 1976; mem. Cambridge LWV, 1945-50, Mt. Auburn Hosp. Aux., Cambridge, 1945-60; pres. Women's Travel Club of Boston, 1949-51; pres. Cambridge Smith Coll. Club, 1952-54; bd. svc. league Mus. of Sci., 1959-62, sec., 1961-62; chmn. personal interview program for Smith, Alumnae Fund in Boston, 1964-65. Recipient Achievement award 100th Ann. Dinner of the Girl's Latin Sch. Alumni Assn., 1978; honored by Mus. of Sci. with plaque for yrs. of work, 1974, gold medal Royal Scottish Geog. Soc. for Outstanding Contbns. to Cartographic Rsch., 1979, Smith medal for Lifetime Exploration and Mapmaking, 1980, 1st Alexander Graham Bell award of Nat. Geog. Soc., 1980, Centennial award, 1988, award of Yukon Ter. Commr., 1997. Home: 1010 Waltham St Lexington MA 02421-8044

WASHBURN, BRADFORD (HENRY B. WASHBURN JR.), museum administrator, cartographer, photographer; b. Cambridge, Mass., June 7, 1910; s. Henry Bradford and Edith (Hall) W.; m. Barbara Teel Polk, Apr. 27, 1940; children: Dorothy Polk, Edward Hall, Elizabeth Bradford. Grad., Groton Sch., 1929; AB, Harvard U., 1933, A.M., 1960, D.H.L. (hon.), 1975; postgrad., Inst. Geog. Exploration, 1934-35; postgrad. hon. degrees; PhD, U. Alaska, 1951; DSc, Tufts U., 1957, Colby Coll., 1957, Northeastern U., 1958; D.Sc., U. Mass., 1972; DSc, Curry Coll., 1982; DFA, Suffolk U., 1965; DHL, Boston Coll., 1974; LLD, Babson Coll., 1980. Instr. Inst. Geog. Exploration, Harvard U., 1935-42; dir. Mus. Sci., Boston, 1939-80, chmn. of the corp., 1980-85, hon. dir., 1985—. Dir. Mountaineer in Alps, 1926-31; explorer Alaska Coast Range, 1930-40; served as leader numerous mountain, subarctic area explorations; cons. various govtl. agys. on Alaska and cold climate equipment; leader in spl. expdns. investigating high altitude cosmic rays, Alaska, 1947; rep. Nat. Geog. Soc., 17th Internat. Geog. Congress, 1952; leader Nat. Geog. mapping expdns. to Grand Canyon, 1971-75; chmn. Mass. Com. Rhodes Scholars, 1959-64; chmn. arts and scis. com. UNESCO conf., Boston, 1961; mem. adv. com. John F. Kennedy Library, 1977; mem. vis. com. Internat. Mus. Photography, 1978; mem. U.S. Nat. Commn. for UNESCO, 1978; lectr. work of Yukon Expdn., Royal Geog. Soc., London, 1936-37, on mapping Grand Canyon, 1976; lectr. Mus. Imaging Tech., Bangkok, 1989, Royal Geog. Soc., London, on mapping Mt. Everest, 1990; lectr. Antarctica, 1994. Contbr. articles, photographs on Alaska, Alps, glaciers, and mountains to mags., books.; editor, pub. 1st large-scale map Mt. McKinley, Am. Acad. Arts and Scis.-Swiss Found. Alpine Rsch., Bern, 1960; mapped Mt. Kennedy for Nat. Geog. Soc., 1965, Grand Canyon, 1971-74, Muldrow Glacier (Mt. McKinley), 1977; editor new chart, Squam Lake, N.H., 1968, new Grand Canyon map for Nat. Geog. Soc., 1978, Bright Angel Trail map, 1981; photo-mapped Mt. Everest for Nat. Geog. Soc., 1984; dir., pub. large-scale map of Mt. Everest for Nat. Geog. Soc., 1984-88; project chief new 1:50,000 map of Mt. Everest for Nat. Geog. Soc. and Boston Sci. Mus., 1988; pub. Tourist Guide to Mt. McKinley, 1971, new map of Presdl. Range, N.H, 1989; completed new large-scale relief model Mt. Everest, 1990; one-man photographic shows Whyte Art Mus., Banff, Can., Internat. Mus. Photography, N.Y.C., Rochester, N.Y. Bd. overseers Harvard, 1955-61; trustee Smith Coll., 1962-68, Richard E. Byrd Found., 1979-84, Mt. Washington Obs., 1979—; mem. Task Force on Future Financing of Arts in Mass., 1978; hon. bd. dirs. Swiss Found. Alpine Research, 1984—. Recipient Royal Geog. Soc. Cuthbert Peek award for Alaska Exploration and Glacier Studies, 1938, Burr prize Nat. Geog. Soc., 1940, 65, Stratton prize Friends of Switzerland, 1970, Lantern award Rotary Club, Boston, 1978, New Englander of Yr. award New Eng. Coun., 1974, Gold Research medal Royal Scottish Geog. Soc. (with wife), 1979, Alexander Graham Bell award Nat. Geog. Soc., 1980, Disting. Grotonian award Groton Sch., 1979, Explorers medal Explorers Club, 1984, award for lifelong contbns. to cartography and surveying Engring. Socs. New Eng., 1985, King Albert medal of merit, 1994, Commonwealth award State of Mass., 1999; named Bus. Statesman of Yr. Harvard Bus. Sch. Assn., Boston, 1970; named to Acad. Disting. Bostonians Boston C. of C., 1983; one of nine Photographic Masters, Boston U., prize for outstanding contbn. to pub. understanding of geology Am. Geol. inst., 1996, Discovery Lifetime award Royal Geog. Soc., 2000. Fellow Royal Geog. Soc. London (hon., Commonwealth award State of Mass. 1999), Harvard Travelers Club (Gold medal 1959), Nat. Geog. Soc. (with wife, Centennial award 1988), AAAS, Am. Acad. Arts and Scis., Am. Geog. Soc. (hon., major photographic exhibit for ann. conv. 1993—), Commercial Club, Harvard Varsity Club, St. Botolph Club (hon. life), Aero Club of New Eng. Club (hon.), Harvard Mountaineering Club (Cambridge, hon., past pres.), Am. Alpine Club (N.Y.C., hon.), Alpine Club (London, hon.), Sierra Club of San Francisco (hon.), Mountaineers Club (Seattle, hon.), Mountaineering of Alaska Club (hon.); hon. mem. several clubs. Achievements include leading 1st ascent Mt. Crillon, Alaska, 1934, Nat. Geog. Soc. Yukon Expdn., 1935; leading 1st aerial photog. exploration Mt. McKinley, 1936, ascending its summit, 1942, 47, 51; leading 1st aerial exploration St. Elias range, 1938; 1st ascents Mount Sanford and Mount Marcus Baker in Alaska, 1938, Mt. Lucania, Yukon, 1937, Mt. Bertha, Alaska, 1940, Mt. Hayes, Alaska, 1941; 1st ascent West side Mt. McKinley 1951; leader Nat. Geog. Soc. Mt. Everest mapping project, 1981-88; expdn. to S.E. Asia, guest Chinese Acad. Scis., met with King of Nepal, 1988; leader expdn. to Nepal, 1992; 1st laser-distance observation to summit of Mt. Everest, 1992; 50th trip to Alaska to open exhibit of own photos Anchorage Art Mus., 1993; 57th Alaska-Yukon trip on occasion of 60th anniversary of Lucania ascent, 1997. Home: 1010 Waltham St Lexington MA 02421-8044 Office: Science Park Boston MA 02114

WASHBURN, DAVID THACHER, lawyer; b. Claremont, NH, May 2, 1930; s. Walter Henry and Josephine Emmeline (Dana) W.; m. Joycemarie Springer, June 10, 1957 (div. Dec. 1975); children: Margaret Dana, David Thacher Jr., Robert Springer, John Putnam. BA, U. Vt., 1952; JD, NYU, 1955. Bar: N.Y. 1956, D.C. 1970, U.S. Supreme Ct 1970. From assoc. to ptnr. Paul, Weiss, Rifkind, Wharton & Garrison, N.Y.C., 1955—95, of counsel, 1996—. Adj. prof. CUNY Law Sch., 1997-98. Trustee Rye Neck Bd. Edn., Mamaroneck, N.Y., 1971-73, Cambridge (Mass.) Coll., 1980-88, The Yard, N.Y.C., 1986-95, ARIA Found., Inc., Williston, Vt., 1991—; trustee, mem. exec. com. Rare Ctr. for Tropical Conservation, Phila., 1979-80; dir. Sanctuary for Families, Inc., N.Y.C., 1994-2003, mem. exec. com., treas. 1995-2000. Mem. ABA, N.Y. State Bar Assn., Assn. of Bar of City of N.Y., The Coffee House, Doubles, Westchester Country Club. Home: 10 W 66th St New York NY 10023-6206 Office: Paul Weiss Rifkind Wharton & Garrison Fl 2 1285 Ave of the Americas New York NY 10019-6064 E-mail: dwashburn@paulweiss.com.

WASHBURN, DONALD ARTHUR, transportation executive, investor; b. Mankato, Minn., Sept. 24, 1944; s. Donald and Geraldine Helen (Pint) W.; m. Christine Carvell, Aug. 24, 1968; children: Timothy, Abigail. BBA with high honors, Loyola U., Chgo., 1971; MBA, Northwestern U., 1973, JD cum laude, 1978. Bar: Ill. 1978. With prodn. mgmt. dept. J.T. Ryerson/Inland Steel, Chgo., 1963-68; asst. to the pres. G.B. Frank, Inc., 1969-70; cons. Intec, Inc., 1970-72; mktg. mgmt., atty. Quaker Oats, Co., 1972-79; sr. cons. Booz, Allen & Hamilton, 1979-80; from corp. v.p. to exec. v.p. Marriott Corp., Washington, 1980-90; sr. v.p. N.W. Airlines, Mpls., 1990-94, exec. v.p., 1994-98; pres. chmn. N.W. Cargo, 1997—98; chmn. N.W. Aerospace Tng. Corp., 1996—98. Bd. dirs. LaSalle Hotel Properties, Princess House, Inc., Key Tech., Inc., Amedisys, Inc., LAGA, Inc., Victor Plastics, Inc.; law bd. Northwestern U., alumni adv. bd. Kellogg Grad. Sch.; adv. bd. Spell Capital Ptnrs. Fund II, LP, Laborsage, Inc. Contbr. articles to profl. jours. Bd. dirs. Portland Citizens Crime Commn., Hearing and Speech Inst., Citizens Commn. on Homeless, Oreg. Bus. Assn., Stand for Children (nat. bd.). Mem. ABA, Ill. Bar Assn., Friends of the Children (nat. bd. dirs.), Alpha Sigma Nu, Beta Gamma Sigma. Unitarian Universalist.

WASHBURN, JERRY MARTIN, accountant, corporate executive; b. Powell, Wyo., Dec. 31, 1943; s. Roland and Lavon (Martin) W.; divorced; children: Garth, Gavin, Kristina; m. Mary Scatterday. BS in Acctg., Brigham Young U., 1969. CPA, Wash., Idaho, Oreg. Staff acct. Arthur Andersen & Co., Seattle, 1969-70, from sr. auditor to audit mgr. Boise, Idaho, 1971—79; v.p. contr. Washburn Musicland, Inc., Phoenix, 1980-82; mgr., ptnr. Washburn Enterprises, Phoenix, 1977-90; pres. Total Info. Systems, Inc., Phoenix, 1984-90; v.p. KJ Mktg., Inc., Phoenix, 1990-91; dir. mktg. IPRO, Inc., Phoenix, 1991-94; assoc. Perfect Strategies, Inc., Phoenix, 1994—95; v.p., CFO Global Indsl. Products, Inc., Scottsdale, Ariz., 1995—96. Pres./CEO OneSource Techs., Inc., Scottsdale, 1996-2002, dir., chmn. 1999; ptnr. Tatum Ptnrs. LLP, 2002—; mng. mem. Ptnrs. Resource Mgmt., LLC, 2003—; founding dir. Internat. and Commerce Bank, Phoenix, 1985-86; bd. dirs., chmn. audit com. 1source Techs., 2003, AmeriFirst Found., 2004. Mem. AICPA, Inst. Internat. Auditors (pres. Boise chpt. 1974, bd. dirs. Boise and Portland chpts. 1975-77), Am. Mgmt. Soc., Wash. Soc. CPAs, Idaho Soc. CPAs. Republican. Office: OneSource 4800 N Scottsdale Rd Scottsdale AZ 85260-2470 Personal E-mail: washburn3@cox.net. Business E-Mail: jerry.washburn@tatumpartners.com.

WASHBURN, JOAN THOMAS, business owner, art gallery director; b. N.Y.C., Dec. 26, 1929; d. Frank B. and Josephine (Hartman) Thomas; m. Alan Lindsay Washburn, Sept. 26, 1953; children: Brian, Susan. BA, Middlebury (Vt.) Coll., 1951. Asst. Kraushaar Gallery, N.Y.C., 1951-53; dir. pub. rels. Wadsworth Atheneum, Hartford, Conn., 1953-55; dir. contemporary art Graham Gallery, N.Y.C., 1955-67; asst. Cordier-Ekstrom Gallery, N.Y.C., 1967-69; dir. Am. painting dept. Sotheby Parke-Bernet, N.Y.C., 1973-75; pres., dir. Washburn Gallery, N.Y.C., 1971—. Mem. Art Dealers Assn. (bd. dirs. 1989—, v.p. 1991—). Gallery: 20 W 57th St New York NY 10019-3917 Office Phone: 212-397-6780.

WASHBURN, JOHN ROSSER, entrepreneur; b. Hopewell, Va., July 24, 1943; s. Winthrop Doane and Mary Virginia (Overstreet) W.; m. Rebecca m. Wells, Sept. 1991; 1 child, Amanda Ashley Washburn; stepchildren: Eric Joseph Harrison, Leo M. Cicone, Suzann R. Weldon. Student, Louisburg Jr. Coll., 1963-64, U. Richmond Ext., 1967-69, Williams Coll., 1985, Stanford U., 1986-87. Asst. mgr. Liberty Loan Corp., Richmond, Va., 1965-67; loan interviewer Ctrl. Fidelity Bank, Richmond, Va., 1967-69; regional credit/sales supr. Moores Bldg Supplies, Inc., Roanoke, Va., 1969-74; corp. credit mgt. Owens & Minor, Inc., Richmond, 1974-88; fin., investment cons. JA-GO Enterprises, Richmond, 1982-98; prin. agt., owner Washburn Ins. and Fin. Svcs. Group, Richmond, 1996—. Instr., lectr. investment fin., credit mgmt. Washburn Enterprises, 1970—; sec.-treas. Multi-Enterprises, Inc., Richmond, 1988-98; ind. agt. N.Y. Life Ins. Co., Richmond, 1994-98; dir., v.p. Forbes Clin. Rsch. Group, Richmond, 1995—; sr. v.p. E-Com Cons., Inc., Richmond, 1998—; charter mem., ptnr. Nations Bus. Cons. Group, Tysons Corner, Va., 1998—2003; pres., CEO Washburn & Assocs., 2003—. Active Nat. Rep. Congl. Com., 1980—, YMCA, 1979—, Am. Mus. Nat. history, 1982—, U.S. Def. Com., 1981—; mem. Credit Rsch. Found. Mem. Internat. Platform Assn., Nat. Assn. Credit Mgmt. (Appreciation cert. for outstanding svc. 1980-81, pres. ctrl. Va. sect. 1979-80, chmn. legis. com. 1977-79, dir. 1983—), Am. Mgmt. Assn., Nat. Wildlife Fedn., Nat. Assn. Life underwriters (Nat. Quality award 1996, 97), Va. Assn. Life Underwriters, Congressional Club, Hopewell Yacht Club. Episcopalian. Office: Washburn Enterprises PO Box 6826 Richmond VA 23230 Office Phone: 804-262-4797. E-mail: jrwashburn@comcast.net.

WASHBURN, KATHRYN HAZEL, government agency executive; b. L.A., May 22, 1944; d. S. Edward and Hazel Irene Lafler; m. Wilcomb Edward Washburn, Jan. 2, 1985 (Feb. 1997); m. William A. Niskanen, Apr. 23, 2000. BA, UCLA, 1966; MA, George Washington U., 1974. Planner Orange County, Santa Ana, Calif., 1966-70; urban planner So. Calif. Assn. Govt., L.A., 1970-71; planner U.S. Dept. Transp., Washington, 1971, U.S. EPA, Washington, 1972, Hwy. Users Fedn., Washington, 1972-73; regional mgr. North Atlantic NOAA, U.S. Dept. Commerce, Washington, 1974-89; dir. internat. affairs U.S. Dept. Interior, Washington, 1989—. Bd. dirs. Am. Inst. Cert. Planners, Washington, 1977-79, Preservation Md., Balt., 1997—, Salisbury U. Found., 1997—; bd. dirs. Rsch. Ctr. Delmarva History and Culture, Salisbury (Md.) U., 1996—; mem. Chesapeake Day Found. Mem. Nat. Audubon Soc., African Wildlife Found., Nature Conservancy, Sierra Club. Home: 638 A St SE Washington DC 20003 Office: US Dept Interior Dir Internat Affairs 1849 C St NW # Ms4426 Washington DC 20240-0001 E-mail: kwashburn@ios.doi.gov.

WASHBURN, LAWRENCE ROBERT, manufacturing executive; b. Jackson, Mich., Aug. 5, 1941; s. Lawrence Merton and Elvina Marie W.; m. Kay Frances Wieczerzak, Nov. 21, 1970; children: Lawrence Robert II, Alexa Kay. BA in History, Govt., So. Calif. Coll., 1974. Supr., engr. Tool Rsch. & Engring., Inc., Santa Ana, Calif., 1968-77; ops. mgr. Knudsen Systems, Inc., Anaheim, Calif., 1977-86; plant mgr. Flourcarbon, Anaheim, Calif., 1986-88; dir. engring. Ricoh Electronics, Inc., Tustin, Calif., 1988-92; chmn., CEO TEQCOM Industries, Santa Ana, 1992—. Dist. commr. Boy Scouts Am., Orange County, Calif., 1982-90; exec. dir. Immanuel Luth. Ch. & Sch., 1987-92; bd. dirs. Luth. High Sch. Orange County, 1990-96. With USN, 1966-68. Decorated Navy Achievement medal; recipient Scouter medal Boy Scouts Am., 1986, Award of Merit, 1988. Mem. ASME, Soc. Mfg. Engrs., Air Traffic Control Assn., Balboa Bay Club, Ctr. Club. Republican. Avocations: golf, body surfing, backpacking. Office: TEQCOM Industries 1712 Newport Cir Ste O Santa Ana CA 92705-5118 E-mail: teqcom@pacbell.net.

WASHBURN, NAN, conductor; BM in Performance with highest honors, U. Calif., Santa Barbara, 1976; MM in Performance, New England Conservatory of Music, 1979. Mem. faculty New England Conservatory, Boston, 1979-80; artistic dir. Women's Philharmonic, San Francisco, 1980-90, assoc. condr., 1988-90; mem. faculty, condr. classical ensembles Cazadero Music & Arts Ctr., 1982-87; resident condr. Am. Jazz Theater, Oakland, Calif., 1987-97; music dir., condr. Camellia Symphony Orchestra, Sacramento, 1990-96, Orchestra Sonoma (formerly the Rohnert Park Chamber Orch.), 1995—; condr. San Francisco State U. Symphony, 1996-97, Acalenes Chamber Orch., Lafayette, Calif., 1997-98, Channel Islands Symphony Orch., Thousand Oaks, Calif., 1997—. Mem. commissioning program panel Minn. Composer's Forum, 1988, music presenter's panel Calif. Arts Coun., 1992, 93, artist fellowship panel, 1995; guest condr. Antelope Valley Symphony Orch., Lancaster, Calif., 1987, Napa Valley (Calif.) Symphony Orch., 1990, Rudolf Steiner Coll., Sacramento, 1991, Sacramento Symphony Orch., 1989, 91, Women's Philharmonic, San Francisco, Oakland, 1991, Oreg. Mozart Players, Eugene, 1993, Eugene Symphony Orch., 1993, 94, Calif. All-State Honor Orch., Santa Clara, 1994, Columbus (Ohio) Women's Symphony, 1992, 94, Cumberland Valley Chamber Players, Chambersburg, Pa., 1994, Honor Festival Orch., Sacramento, 1993, 95, Berkeley (Calif.) Symphony Orch., 1995, 96, Richmond (Va.) Symphony Orch., 1996, Colo. Symphony Orch., Denver, 1997; lectr. Internat. Congress Women in Music, Atlanta, 1986, Festival New Am. Music, Sacramento, 1987, 90, Condrs. Inst., Columbia, S.C., 1988, conf. Calif. Music Educators Assn., Santa Clara, 1994. Recipient N.Y. Women Composers award, 1992, Role Model award Girl Scouts, 1996, Indy award Sonoma County Independent, 1998, 13 ASCAP awards Am. Symphony Orch. League, 1983, 85-90, 92-97. Mem. Am. Symphony Orch. League, Assn. Calif. Symphony Orchs., Condr.'s Guild, Musicians Union Local 6 (San Francisco), Pi Kappa Lambda. Office: Channel Islands Symphony Orch PO Box 7231 Thousand Oaks CA 91359-7231

WASHBURN, STEWART PUTNAM, management consultant; b. Claremont, N.H., Apr. 6, 1929; s. Walter Henry and Josephine (Dana) W.; m. Josephine F. Foster, Aug. 20, 1960 (dec. 1980); children: Patricia, Alice. BS in Commerce and Econs., U. Vt., 1951; MBA, Harvard U., 1953. Cert. comml. lender. V.p. Worcester County Nat. Bank, Worcester, Mass., 1955-74; v.p., sr. loan officer First Nat. Bank, New Bedford, Mass., 1974-77; sr. v.p., sr. loan officer Durfee Attleboro Bank, Fall River, Mass., 1977-90; mgmt. cons. in comml. lending Fall River, Mass., 1990—. Dir. Bristol Workforce Investment Bd., Fall River, 1982—, chmn., 1987-99; dir. Southeastern Econ. Devel. Corp., Taunton, Mass., 1983—, treas., v.p., pres., 1995-98; dir. Jobs for Fall River 1981—, chair loan com. 1997—; mem. coun., mem. loan com. New Bedford Econ. Devel. Coun.; mem. town mtg., mem. fin. com. Dartmouth, Mass. With U.S. Army, 1953-55. Mem. Inst. Mgmt. Cons. (treas. New Eng. chpt. 1997-2001), Risk Mgmt. Assn. (life, bd. govs. N.E. chpt. 1973-75, chmn. credit policy roundtable 1989, Spl. Svc. award 1989). Avocations: bowling, gardening, fishing. Home: 5 Middle St Dartmouth MA 02748-3427 Office: PO Box 643 Fall River MA 02722-0643 Office Phone: 508-679-5119. E-mail: spwashburn@aol.com.

WASHINGTON, A. EUGENE, medical educator; b. Houston, 1950; MD, U. Calif., San Francisco, 1976. Diplomate Am. Bd. Ob-Gyn., Am. Bd. Gen. Preventive Medicine. Intern USPHS, Staten Island, N.Y., 1976-77; resident Preventive Medicine Harvard U., 1977-79; resident Ob-Gyn. Stanford U., 1986-89; fellow Health Policy Inst. Health PS/U. Calif., San Francisco, 1983-86; prof. Ob-Gyn., Preventive Medicine U. Calif., San Francisco, prof. chair., obstetrics, gynecology, 1989—. Mem. AAAS, APHA, Soc. for Epidemiol. Rsch. Office: U Calif San Francisco PO Box 0132 San Francisco CA 94143-0001

WASHINGTON, ALICE HESTER, human services professional; b. Durham, N.C., Oct. 28, 1960; d. Melvin and Martha Elizabeth (Bridges) Hester; m. Melvin Preston Washington Sr., Aug. 13, 1988; 1 child, Melvin Preston Washington II. BS in Home Econs., N.C. Agrl. and Tech. State U., 1983; grad. cert. in gerontology, Fla. Internat. U., 1995, MSW, 1999. Dietetic technician N.C. divsn. mental health Mental Retardation and Substance Abuse Svcs., Butner, 1984-85; dietary supr. Svcs. Systems, Marriott Corp., Boca Raton, Fla., 1985; dietetic technician HBA Mgmt. Corp., Ft. Lauderdale, Fla., 1986-87; registered dietetic technician Boca Raton (Fla.) Community Hosp., 1987-89; pub. assistance specialist II Fla. Dept. of Children and Families, Lauderhill, 1989-91, human svcs. counselor III, 1993—; case worker Fla. Fin. Assistance Specialists, Inc., Ft. Lauderdale, 1991-93. Mem. Mount Bethel Bapt. Ch. Social Svc. Ministry, Ft. Lauderdale, 1993, Presch. Ministry, 1993—; pres. Saint Luke Primitive Bapt. Ch. Young Matrons Aux., Hollywood, Fla., 1989. Mem. NASW, Phi Alpha Nat. Social Work Honor Soc. Baptist. Avocations: reading, badminton, travel. Office: Fla Dept Children and Families 1400 W Commercial Blvd Ste 115 Fort Lauderdale FL 33309-3782

WASHINGTON, ANTHONY NATHANIEL, mechanical engineer; b. L.A., Jan. 19, 1969; s. Ralph Anthony and Naomi (Jemison) W. BSME, A&M U. Prairie View, 1992; postgrad., U. Phoenix, 1999—. Engr. Detroit Edison Co., 1992-95, GMC, Dayton, Ohio, 1995-96; area supr. Chrysler Corp., Detroit, 1997-99; product engr. Daimler Chrysler Corp., Detroit, 1999—. Mem. Nat. Black MBA Assn., Nat. Soc. Black Engrs., Metro Detroit Optimist Club, Kappa Alpha Psi Fraternity Inc., Pi Tau Sigma. Avocations: sports, music, travel, reading.

WASHINGTON, CHARLES HENDERSON, laser systems designer, consultant; b. Little Rock, Ark., Apr. 8, 1953; s. John David and Antoinette LaVerne (Henderson) W. BA in Comm., U. Ill., 1979; PhD in Comm., Columbia State U. Lineman apprentice IBEW, Springfield, Ill., 1976-80; data comms. specialist State of Ill., Springfield, Ill., 1980-85; v.p. engring. NATAC, Springfield, Ill., 1983—. Cons. North Am. Tec-Hec, Springfield, Ill., 1991-93. Author: Datacom Systems Operation Manual, 1984, Datacom Systems Configuration Manual, 1985. Mem. A. Philip Randolph Inst., Springfield, 1994. With U.S. Navy, 1970-75. Named to Outstanding Young Men of Am., 1984. Mem. AAAS, Internat. Soc. Photo-Optical Engrs., N.Y. Acad. Sci., Omega Psi Phi, Phi Theta Kappa. Methodist.

WASHINGTON, CHRISTOPHER L. education educator; s. William M. Washington and Diana Rochan; m. Shannon Washington; children: Jacques, Faith, Victoria. BA, Western Ill. Univ., Macomb, Ill., 1987, MS, 1990; PhD, Ohio State Univ., Columbus, Ohio, 2002. Adj. faculty Capital Univ., Columbus, Ohio, 1997—99; internal cons. Ohio State Univ., Columbus, Ohio,

1994—99; prof. Franklin Univ., Columbus, Ohio, 1999—2002, program chair, MBA, 2002—03, assoc. dean bus., 2003—. Bd. mem. Columbus Urban League, Ohio, 2003—. Recipient Excellence in Edn., Ohio Mag., 2003, Forty under 40, Bus. First, 2002. Mem.: Acad. of Mgmt., Alpha Phi Alpha (chptr. pres. 1993—). Office: Franklin Univ 201 S Grant Ave Columbus OH 43215 Office Fax: 614-228-8478. Business E-Mail: washingc@franklin.edu.

WASHINGTON, CLARENCE EDWARD, JR., insurance company executive; b. New Orleans, Nov. 20, 1953; s. Clarence Edward and Alice Mildred (Jones) W.; m. Denise Sandra Agard, June 29, 1985. BS cum laude, Xavier U., 1983. Mgr. Time Saver, Inc., New Orleans, 1972-79; budget, fin. analyst Equitable Life Assurance, N.Y.C., 1983-84; actuarial asst. Prudential Life Assurance, Newark, 1984-87; pension mgr. Am. Internat. Life, N.Y.C., 1987—. Mem. Am. Mus. Natural History (assoc.). Democrat. Roman Catholic. Office: Am Internat Life 80 Pine St Fl 13 New York NY 10005-1702

WASHINGTON, DENNIS R. contracting company executive; Equipment operator Guy F. Atkinson Co., Alaska; with King & McLaughlin Construction Co.; founder Washington Construction Co., Missoula, Mont., 1964; chmn., pres., CEO Morrison-Knudsen, 1999; chmn. Washington Group Internat., Inc. (formerly Morrison-Knudsen), Boise, Idaho. Recipient Entrepreneurial award, Montana Ambassadors. Mem.: Horatio Alger Assn., Am. Acad. Of Achievement. Office: Washington Group Internat Inc 720 Park Blvd Boise ID 83729 Office Phone: 208-386-5000. Office Fax: 208-386-7186.*

WASHINGTON, DENZEL, actor; b. Mt. Vernon, N.Y., Dec. 28, 1954; m. Pauletta Pearson; children: John David, Katia, Malcolm and Olivia (twins). BA in Journalism, Fordham U.; student, Am. Conservatory Theatre, San Francisco. With N.Y. Shakespeare Festival, Manhattan Theatre Club, New Fed. Theatre. Actor: (stage prodns.) Coriolanus, 1979, Spell No. 7, The Mighty Gents, Richard III, One Tiger to a Hill, Ceremonies in Old Dark Men, When the Chicken Comes Home to Roost (Audelco award), A Soldier's Play (Obie award 1981), Checkmates, 1988, Split Second, (feature films) Carbon Copy, 1981, A Soldier's Story, 1981, Power, 1986, Cry Freedom, 1987, For Queen and Country, 1988, The Mighty Quinn, 1989, Glory, 1989 (Golden Globe award 1989, Acad. award 1990, NAACP Image award 1990), Heart Condition, 1990, Mo' Better Blues, 1990, Ricochet, 1991, Mississippi Masala, 1992, Malcolm X, 1992, Much Ado About Nothing, 1993, Philadelphia, 1993, The Pelican Brief, 1993, Crimson Tide, 1995, Virtuosity, 1995, Devil in a Blue Dress, 1995, Courage Under Fire, 1996 (NAACP Image award 1997), The Preacher's Wife, 1996, Fallen, 1998, He Got Game, 1998, The Siege, 1998, The Bone Collector, 1999, The Hurricane, 2000 (nominee Best Actor Acad. award 2000, Best Performance by Actor in Motion Picture Drama Golden Globe 2000), Remember the Titans, 2000, Training, Day, 2001 (Best Actor Acad. award 2002, nominee Best Performance by Actor in Motion Picture Drama Golden Globe 2002), John Q, 2002, Out Of Time, 2003, Man on Fire, 2004, The Manchurian Candidate, 2004; actor, dir. prodr. The Antwone Fisher Story, 2002; (TV Movies) Wilma, 1977, License to Kill, 1984, The George McKenna Story, 1986, (TV miniseries) Flesh and Blood, 1979; regular (TV series) St. Elsewhere, 1982-88. Recipient Harvard Found. award, 1996; Am. Conservatory Theater scholar. Avocations: basketball, reading, cooking.

WASHINGTON, DONALD W. prosecutor; BS, U.S. Mil. Acad.; JD, S. Tex. Coll. Law. Capt. U.S. Army, 1977—82; with Conoco Inc., 1982—96, div. counsel, gen. litigation atty., 1991—96; ptnr. Jeansonne and Redmondet, Lafayette, La., 1996—2001; U.S. atty. we. dist. U.S. Dept. Justice, La., 2001—. Capt. USAR, 1982—90. Office: 300 Fannin St Ste 3201 Shreveport LA 71101

WASHINGTON, DONNA JANEL, engineer; b. Chgo., Ill., July 22, 1970; d. Isaac and Delores Jean Washington. Assoc. Degree, Olive Harvey Coll., Chgo., 1989—90; B, Grambling State U., 1991—94; M, Chgo. State U., 2000—02. Tech. support engr. Sq. D Co., Lombard, Ill., 1998—99, Simpson Electric, Elgin, Ill., 1999—2000; applications engr. Littelfuse Inc., Des Plaines, Ill., 2000—03; fed. agt. US Postal Inspection Svc., Pasadena, Calif., 2003—. Author: (screenplays) Pathway's Of Life (Script Mag. Semi Finalist, 2001), Crossing Over, (books of poetry) PASSAGE-Passing Poetry Through A New Millenium (Libr. Of Congress Recognition for poems, 2000). Mem. Ea. Star, Chgo., 1988—2003. Recipient YMCA Mentor award, YMCA, 1998. Mem.: Nat. Honors Soc. Of Criminal Justice, Alpha Kappa Alpha Sorority Inc. Pentecostal.

WASHINGTON, EDDIE, state representative; b. St. Louis, June 8, 1953; m. Flor Washington; children: Tikisha, Malik, Kitanda, Albert, Elias, Asian, Racquel. Student, So. Ill. U. Democrat. Office: 280-S Stratton Office Bldg Springfield IL 62706 Address: 2835 Belvidfere Ste 213 Waukegan IL 60085

WASHINGTON, ERIC T. state supreme court justice; Assoc. Fulbright and Jaworski, Houston and Washington; legis. dir., counsel Rep. Michael Andrews; spl. corp. counsel, prin. dep. corp. counsel; ptnr. Hogan & Hartson, Washington, 1990-95; apptd. Superior Ct., 1995; judge D.C. Ct. Appeals, 1999—. Office: DC Ct Appeals 6th Fl 500 Indiana Ave NW Fl 6 Washington DC 20001-2138

WASHINGTON, GLORIA DUNN, secondary school educator; d. Percy and Eleanor McCoy Dunn; m. Leroy Roosevelt Washington; children: Cheryl Lynn Ford, Gloria Candacy, Daphne Dena Reddick. BA, Baber-Scotia Coll., 1966; MA, U. S. Fla., 1978, Edn. Specialist, 1981. Tchr. Newfane Ctrl. Sch., NY, 1966—67, Auburndale H.S., Fla., 1976—97, North Ctrl. Adult Sch., Auburndale, Fla., 1980—88, Lakeland Sr. H.S., 1998—. Youth dir. St. Mark, Lakeland, Fla., 1985—; founder/sponsor Unified Culture Club, Lakeland, 1991—. Editor: (poems) Polk County Poetry Contest Booklet; co-author: (curriculum) English Curriculum for North Central Adult School, 1984-1985. Chairperson adminstrv. coun. St. Mark United Meth. Ch., Lakeland, 1996—2004. Named English Tchr. Yr., Polk County Coun. Tchrs. English, 1995—96, 1999—2000; recipient, 2003—04. Mem.: Delta Kappa Gamma (pres. 1998—2000, Plague-Outstanding Pres. 2000), Phi Delta Kappa (publicity 2003—). St. Mark United Meth. Achievements include est. Peace and Unity Walk, 1999-. Avocations: reading, writing, playing the piano, collecting clocks. Office: Lakeland High School 726 Hollingsworth Rd Lakeland, FL Office Fax: 863-499-2917. Personal E-mail: gjwash1@acninc.net. E-mail: gloria.washington@polk-fl.net.

WASHINGTON, JAMES WINSTON, JR., artist, sculptor; b. Gloster, Miss., Nov. 10, 1909; s. James and Lizie (Howard) W.; m. Janie R. Miller, Mar. 29, 1943. Student, Nat. Landscape Inst., 1944-47; D.F.A., Center Urban-Black Studies, 1975. Tchr. summer class N.W. Theol. Union Seattle U., 1988. One man shows U.S.O. Gallery, Little Rock, 1943, Foster-White Gallery, Seattle, 1974, 78, 80, 83, 89 (also at Bellevue Art Mus., 89), Charles and Emma Frye Art Mus., Seattle, 1980, 95, Mus. History and Industry, Seattle, 1981; exhibited in group shows Willard Gallery, N.Y.C., 1960-64, Feingarten Galleries, San Francisco, 1958-59, Grosvenor Gallery, London, Eng., 1964, Lee Nordness Gallery, N.Y.C, 1962 Woodside Gallery, Seattle, 1962-65, Foster-White Gallery, Seattle, 1974, 76, 89, 92, Smithsonian Instn., 1974, San Diego, 1977, others; retrospective exhbn. Bellevue Art Mus., Washington, 1989; represented in permanent collections Seattle, San Francisco, Oakland art museums, Seattle First Nat. Bank, Seattle Pub. Libr. YWCA, Seattle, Meany Jr. H.S., Seattle World's Fair, Expo 70 Osaka, Japan, Whitney Mus. Am. Art, N.Y.C.; commd. sculpture: Bird With Covey, Wash. State Capitol Mus., Olympia, 1983, Obelisk with Phoenix and Esoteric Symbols of Nature in granite, Sheraton Hotel Seattle, 1982, Life Surrounding the Astral Alter, In Matrix, owner T.M. Rosenblume, Charles Z. Smith & Assocs., Seattle, 1986, The Oracle of Truth (6 1/2 ton sculpture) Mt. Zion Bapt. Ch., Seattle, 1987, commd. sculptures King County Arts Commn., 1989, Bailey Gatzent Elem. Sch., Seattle, 1991, Twin Eaglets of the Cosmic Cycle (Quincy Jones), 1993, Fountain of Triumph (Bangasser Assocs. Inc.), 1992-93, Seattle, 1993-94, 94-95, Child in Matrix, 1995, Blunt Tail Owl, 1996, Bunny Rabbit and Robbin, 1996; author book of poetry Poems of Life, 1997 (Internat. Hall of Fame Nat. Soc. Poets). Passover leader Mt. Zion Baptist Ch., Seattle, 1974-87; founder James W. Washington, Jr. and Mrs. Janie Rogella Washington Found. Recipient Spl. Commendation award for many contbns. to artistic heritage of state Gov., 1973, plaque City of Seattle, 1973, plaque Benefit Guild, Inc., 1973, arts service award King County Arts Commn., 1984, cert. of recognition Gov. of Wash., 1984, Editor's Choice award Outstanding Achievement in Poetry Nat. Libr. Poetry, 1993; named to Wash. State Centennial Hall of Honor, Wash. State Hist. Soc., 1984; home and studio designated historic landmark (city and state), 1991; Dr. James W. Washington Jr. and Mrs. Janie Rosella Washington Found. established, 1997. Mem. Internat. Platform Assn., Internat. Soc. Poets (life, awards 1993), Profl. Artists Phila., Masons (33d degree). Home: 1816 26th Ave Seattle WA 98122-3110

WASHINGTON, LA TRICE M. social studies educator; d. Shirley Jean Washington Jordan and Howard Eugene Jordan, Sr.(Stepfather). BA Polit. Sci. Summa Cum Laude, St. Augustine's Coll., Raleigh, N.C., 1991; MA Am. Govt. and State and Local Govt., U. Va., Charlottesville, Va., 1994; PhD, Howard U., Washington, 2002. Staff asst. U.S. Rep. Corrine Brown, Washington, 1994—96; legislative asst./corr. U. S. Rep. Corrine Brown, Washington, 1996—97; pub. svc. intern/program analyst NASA Goddard Space Flight Ctr., Greenbelt, Md., 1998—98; classroom tchr. DC Pub. Schs., Washington, 1997—99; classroom tchr. grade 5 Village Learning Ctr. Pub. Charter Sch., Washington, 1999—2000; asst. prof. Otterbein Coll., Westerville, Ohio, 2000—. Author: The Veteran's Millennium Health Care Act of 1999: A Case Study of Role Orientations of the President, Legislators and Interest Groups; contbr. encyclopedia on affirmative action, the encyclopedia on affirmative action. Keynote spkr. Capital U. Black Student Alliance, Columbus, Ohio, 2002—03, NAACP State Youth Coun. Conf. 2004, Dayton, Ohio, 2003—03; youth advisor NAACP Youth Coun., Columbus, Ohio, 2003—04; guest spkr. St. Mark AME Ch., Columbus, Ohio; discussant Nat. Midwest Polit. Sci. Assn. 2004 Conf., Chgo., 2004—04. Recipient Ralph Bunche Scholar Program, Am. Polit. Sci. Assn., 1990, NASA Pub. Svc. Intern/Program Analyst, NASA Goddard Space Flight Sta. Greenbelt MD, 1998; fellow Grad. Fellowship, Va. Higher Edn. Fellowship Com., 1992-1994, Am. Polit. Sci. Assn., 1991-2002; grantee Summer Rsch. Grant, 1990; scholar All Am. Scholar, 1990, 1991; Grad. Fellowship, Va. Governor's Fellowship Com., 1991-1992. Mem.: Midwest Polit. Sci. Assn. (assoc.), Alpha Kappa Mu, Alpha Chi. Office: Otterbein Coll 1 Otterbein Coll Westerville OH 43081 Business E-Mail: lwashington@otterbein.edu.

WASHINGTON, LANTZ H. small business owner; b. Port Huron, Mich., Dec. 13, 1961; s. Felix and Jacqueline Washington; m. Sharline Dobson, Jan. 3, 1991 (div.); 1 child, Lantz Tarvon. Student, Redford H.S., Detroit, 1977-79. CEO Washington Bros. Carpet and Upholstery Cleaning, Detroit. Home: 14901 Mark Twain St Detroit MI 48227-2986

WASHINGTON, LAWRENCE J., JR., chemicals executive; BSChemE, MSChemE, U. Detroit. Mgr. environ. svcs. Dow Chem. Co., Midland, Mich., 1980—87, gen. mgr. western divsn. Pittsburgh, Calif., 1987—90, v.p. Dow North Am. Midland, Mich., 1990—94, corp. v.p. human resources rep., 1994—, corp. v.p. environ., health & safety, and pub. affairs, 1997—. Served for four years USAF. Mem.: Univ. Detroit Mercy (advisory bd. mem.), Mich. Tech. Univ. (advisory bd. mem.), Chem. Bank & Trust Co. (bd. dirs.), Dorinco Reinsurance Co. (bd. dirs.), Liana Ltd. (bd. dirs.). Office: The Dow Chem Co 47 Building Midland MI 48067*

WASHINGTON, MARIAN, women's college basketball coach; b. West Chester, Pa. 1 child, Josie. B.Phys. Edn. and Health, West Chester State Coll., 1970. Tchr. phys. edn. Martin Luther King Jr. H.S., Kansas City, Mo.; grad. asst. health, phys. edn. and recreation U. Kans., Lawrence, 1972, women's athletics dir., 1974-79, head basketball coach, 1974—. Asst. coach 1996 Olympics, Atlanta; coach U.S. Select Team, 1983; mem. Kodak All-Am. selection com.; regional chair for Wade trophy. Commr. Kans. AIAW. Named 1997 Big 12 Coach of the Yr., 1996 Big Eight and Black Coaches Assn. Coach of the Yr., Black Coaches Assn. Women's Coach of the Yr., 1992, Big Eight Conf. Coach of the Yr., 1992, Kans. Basketball Coaches Assn. Women's Coach of the Yr., 1992, Outstanding Black Woman in Sports, Ebony Mag.; recipient William I, Koch Outstanding Woman of the Yr. award, Giant Steps award Ctr. for Study of Sport in Soc. at Northeastern U. and Nat. Consortium for Acads. and Sports, 1995; inductee West Chester State Women's Athletic Hall of Fame. Mem. Black Coaches Assn. (pres. 1993-94), Women's Basketball Coaches Assn. (bd. dirs.). Office: Univ of Kansas/Allen Fieldhouse Women's Athletics Dept 280 Parrott Lawrence KS 66045-0001

WASHINGTON, REGINALD LOUIS, pediatric cardiologist; b. Colorado Springs, Colo., Dec. 31, 1949; s. Lucius Louis and Brenette Y. (Wheeler) W.; m. Billye Faye Ned, Aug. 18, 1973; children: Danielle Larae, Reginald Quinn. BS in Zoology, Colo. State U., 1971; MD, U. Colo., 1975. Diplomate Nat. Bd. Med. Examiners, Am. Bd. Pediat., Pediatric Cardiology. Intern in pediat. U. Colo. Med. Ctr., Denver, 1975-76, resident in pediat., 1976-78, chief resident, instr., 1978-79, fellow in pediatric cardiology, 1979-81, asst. prof. pediat., 1982-1988, assoc. prof. pediat., 1988-90, assoc. clin. prof. pediat., 1990—; staff cardiologist Children's Hosp., Denver, 1981-90; v.p. We. Cardiology Assocs., Divsn. for Fetal, Pediatric and Adult Congential Heart Disease, Denver, 1990—2004; med. dir. Rocky Mountain Pediatrix Cardiology, Denver, 2004—; chief of staff Presbyn./St. Lukes Med. Ctr., 1999-2001. Admissions com. U. Colo. Sch. Medicine, Denver, 1985-89; chmn., bd. dirs. Coop. Health Care Agreements, 1994-98; chmn. dept. pediatrics Presbyn./St. Lukes Med. Ctr, Denver, 1996-99, 2003—, pres.-elect med. staff, 1997-99, chmn. ethics com., 2003—; adv. coun. Nat. Heart Lung Blood Inst., NIH, 1996-98. Cons. editor Your Patient and Fitness, 1989-92; mem. editl. bd. Jour. Pediats., 2004—. Chmn. Coop. Health Care Agreements Bd., State of Colo., 1994-98; adv. bd. dirs. Equitable Bank of Littleton, Colo., 1984-86; bd. dirs. Rocky Mountain Heart Fund for Children, 1984-89, Rainbo Ironkids, 1989-95, Ctrl. City Opera, 1989-95, Cleo Parker Robinson Dance Co., 1992-94, Nat. Coun. Patient Info. and Edn., 1992-98, Children's Heart Alliance, 1993-94, Colo. State U. Devel. Coun., 1994-2003, Caring for Colo. Found., 1999-2001; nat. bd. dirs. Am. Heart Assn., 1992-96; trustee Denver Ctr. Performing Arts, 1994—. Regis U., 1994-99; mem. Gov.'s Coun. Phys. Fitness, 1990-91; bd. govs. Colo. State U., 1996-2004, pres., 2001-03; trustee Colo. Trust, 2002-; trustee Helen Bonfils Found., 2003—. Recipient William E. Morgan Alumnus Achievement award Colo. State U., 2004; named Salute Vol. of Yr. Big Sisters of Colo., 1990; honoree NCCJ, 1994, Physician of Yr., Nat. Am. Heart Assn., 1995. Fellow Am. Acad. Pediat. (cardiology subsect., chmn. sports medicine and fitness com. 2000-2004, chmn. task force on obesity 2003—), Am. Coll. Cardiology, Am. Heart Assn. (coun. on cardiovasc. disease in the young, exec. com. 1988-91, nat. devel. program com. 1990-94, vol. of yr. 1989, pres. Colo. chpt. 1989-90, Torch of Hope 1987, Gold Heart award Colo. chpt. 1990, bd. dirs. Colo. chpt., exec. com. Colo. chpt. 1987-2000, grantee Colo. chpt. 1983-84, mem. editl. bd. Pediat. Exercise Scis. 1988-2002), Soc. Critical Care Medicine; mem. Am. Acad. Pediat. Perinatology, Am. Acad. Pediat./Pediat. Cardiology (exec. com. 1996-2004), N.Am. Soc. Pediat. Exercise Medicine (pres. 1986-87), Colo. Med. Soc. (chmn. sports medicine coun. 1993-94), Leadership Denver 1990, Glenmoor Golf Club. Democrat. Roman Catholic. Avocations: golf, fishing. Office: Rocky Mountain Pediat Cardiology 10103 Ridgegate Pkwy Ste 107 Lone Tree CO 80124 Office Phone: 303-860-9933. E-mail: rlwash@aol.com.

WASHINGTON, STROTHER LEE, JR., mechanical engineer, design engineer; b. Charlottesville, Va., Feb. 9, 1952; s. Strother Lee and Peachie Frances Washington; m. Lillian Juanita Young, May 20, 1978; 1 child, Keyana Latrice. BSME, U. Va., 1974; MS, Johns Hopkins U., 1979. From prin. engr. to assoc. design mgr. Northrop Grumman, Annapolis, Md., 1990—98, mech. engring. mgr., 1998—. Mentor Worthy, Balt., 1998—; coach Amatuer Athletic Union, Balt., 1990—; asst. track coach Bowie (Md.) State U., 1998—2000. Recipient Outstanding Svc. award, United Way, 1995. Mem.: ASME, Am. Design Drafting Assn., Nat. Soc. Black Engrs., Alpha Phi Alpha. Democrat. Baptist. Achievements include invention of modular bouyant fairing panel, translating desktop assembly, connector saver for anphenol connector. Avocations: photography, Antique tools, sports, music, auto restoration. Home: 2085 Ingleside Ct Crofton MD 21114 Office: Northrop Grumman Aviation Blvd Gate 1 Baltimore MD 21203

WASHINGTON, TANYA MONIQUE, law educator; d. Clifton Cedrick and Cynthia Gardner Williams; 1 child, Andre Washington Thomas. BA, James Madison U., Harrisonburg, Va., 1992; JD, U. Md., Balt., 1995; LLM, Harvard U., Cambridge, Mass., 2001. Jud. law clerk Ct. Appeals Md., Balt., 1995—96; corp. def. attorney Piper & Marbury, Balt., 1996—98; Albert M. Sachs fellow Harvard U., Cambridge, Mass., 1998—99, A. Leon Higginbotham fellow, 1999—2000; vis. asst. prof. law U. Md., Balt., 2001—02; asst. prof. law Ga. State U., Atlanta, 2003—. Contbr. articles to profl. jours. Office: Ga State Univ Coll Law PO Box 4037 Atlanta GA 30302-4037

WASHINGTON, WARREN MORTON, meteorologist; b. Portland, Oreg., Aug. 28, 1936; s. Edwin and Dorothy Grace (Morton) W.; m. LaRae Herring, July 30, 1959 (div. Aug. 1975); children: Teri, Kim, Marc (dec.), Tracy; m. Jona Ann, July 3, 1978 (dec. Jan. 1987); m. Mary Elizabeth Washington, Apr., 1995. BS in Physics, Ore. State U., 1958, MS in Meteorology, 1960; PhD in Meteorology, Pa. State U., 1964. Dir. of climate and global dynamics div. Nat. Center Atmospheric Research, Boulder, Colo., 1978-95; affiliate prof. meteorology oceanography U. Mich. at Ann Arbor, 1968-71; mem. Nat. Adv. Com. for Oceans and Atmospheres, 1978-84. Mem. sec. of energy adv. bd. U.S. Dept. Energy, 1990-93. Contbr. articles to meteorol. jours. Mem. Boulder Human Relations Commn., 1969-71; mem. Gov.'s Sci. Adv. Com., 1975-78. Recipient Disting. Alumni award Oreg. State U., 1991, E.B. Lemon Disting. Alumni award Pa. State U., 1991, Le Verrier medal Soc. Meteorol. France, 1995, Bonfils-Stanton Found. award, 2000; inductee NAS portrait collection African Am. in Sci., Engring., and Medicine, 1997; named Sigma Xi Disting. lectr., 1998-99. Fellow AAAS (bd. dirs.), Am. Meteorol. Soc. (pres. 1994, Anderson award 2000); mem. NAE, Am. Philosophy Soc., Am. Geog. Union, Nat. Sci. Bd. (chair 2002—). Home: 725 Pinehurst Ct Louisville CO 80027-3285 Office: PO Box 3000 Boulder CO 80307-3000

WASHINGTON, WILLIAM THOMAS, technical manager, educator; b. N.Y.C., N.Y., Jan. 23, 1952; s. Clifton and Bessie (Campbell) Washington; 1 child, Kara Alyssa. BA, Queens Coll., 1976, MA, 1980; MBA, Dowling Coll., 2001. Prof. U. V.I., St. Thomas, 1980—81, N.Y. U., 1990—2001, Touro Coll., N.Y.C., 1994. Scholar Study Abroad Program UK, CUNY, 1974. Avocations: nature, cinematography. Home: PO Box 300483 Jamaica NY 11430 Personal E-mail: wtwashing@msn.com.

WASHKEWICZ, DONALD E. manufacturing executive; V.p. ops. fluid connectors group Parker Hannifin Corp., Cleve., 1994-97, v.p., pres. hydraulics group, 1997-2000, pres., COO, 2000—01, CEO, 2001—. Office: Parker Hannifin Corp 6035 Parkland Blvd Cleveland OH 44124-4141

WASIK, BARBARA HANNA, psychologist, educator; b. Douglas, Ga., May 29, 1942; d. Frank Joseph and Josephine (Nahoom) Hanna; m. John L. Wasik, June 24, 1966; children— John Gregory, Mark Timothy, Jeffrey Joseph AB, U. Ga., 1963; MA, Fla. State U., 1965, PhD, 1967. Lic. psychologist, N.C. Postdoctoral research fellow Duke U., Durham, N.C., 1967-68; dir. research Ford Found. grant, Durham, N.C., 1968-69; from asst. prof. to assoc. prof. U. N.C., Chapel Hill, 1969-77, prof., 1977—, William R. Kenan Jr. disting. prof., 2003—, assoc. dean Grad. Sch., 1972-75, chmn. div. human devel. and psychol. services, 1975-77, assoc. dean Sch. Edn., 1977-83, 1988—92, sr. investigator Child Devel. Ctr., 1972—. Mem. commn. NAS, 1998—2000; co-facilitator Nat. Forum Home Visiting, 1999—. Assoc. editor Jour. Applied Behavior Analysis, 1972; mem. editorial bd. Behavioral Assessment, 1984-85; contbr. chpts. to books and articles to profl. jours. Mem. N.C. Psychological Assn. (sec. 1982-85, pres. 1988-89), Am. Psychol. Assn. (divsn. 25 sec-treas. 1983-86, coun. rep. 1994-99, bd. edn. affairs 1999-2001, chair bd edn. affairs 2001), Soc. Research in Child Development, Southeastern Psychol. Assn., Assn. Advancement Behavior Therapy. Democrat. Roman Catholic. Home: 609 Brookview Dr Chapel Hill NC 27514-1402

WASIK, JOHN FRANCIS, editor, writer, publisher; b. Chgo., July 2, 1957; s. Arthur Stanley and Virginia Frances (Gray) W.; m. Kathleen Rose. BA in Psychology, U. Ill., Chgo., 1978, MA in Communication, 1988. Sr. editor Consumers Digest Inc., Chgo., 1986—; editor, pub. Conscious Consumer and Co. Newsletters, 1986—. Author: Electronic Business Information Sourcebook, 1987, Green Company Resource Guide, 1992, The Green Supermarket Shopping Guide, 1993, The Investment Club Book, 1995. Mem. Soc. Profl. Journalists, Soc. Environ. Journalists. Office: Consumers Digest Inc 8001 Lincoln Ave # 6 Skokie IL 60077-3695

WASIOLEK, EDWARD, literary critic, language and literature educator; b. Camden, N.J., Apr. 27, 1924; s. Ignac and Mary (Szczesniewska) W.; m. Emma Jones Thomson, 1948; children: Mark Allan, Karen Lee, Eric Wade. BA, Rutgers U., 1949; MA, Harvard, 1950, PhD, 1955; postgrad., U. Bordeaux, France, 1950-51. Teaching fellow Harvard U., Cambridge, Mass., 1953-54, research fellow Russian Research Ctr., 1952-54; instr. English Ohio Wesleyan U., 1954-55; asst. prof. U. Chgo., 1955-60, assoc. prof. English and Russian, 1960-64, prof. Russian and comparative lit., 1964-69, Avalon prof. comparative lit. and Russian, 1969-76, Disting. Services prof. of English, comparative lit., and Slavic studies, 1976—, chmn. comparative lit. program, 1965-83, chmn. dept. Slavic langs. and lit., 1971-77. Vis. prof. Slavic and comparative lit. Harvard, 1966-67 Author: (with R. Bauer) Nine Soviet Portraits, 1955, Crime and Punishment and the Critics, 1961, Dostoevsky: The Major Fiction, 1964, The Notebooks for Crime and Punishment, 1967, The Brothers Karamazov and the Critics, 1967, The Notebooks for the Idiot, 1968, The Notebooks for the Possessed, 1968, The Notebooks for A Raw Youth, 1969, The Notebooks for the Brothers Karamazov, 1970, The Gambler, with Paulina Suslova's Diary, 1972, Tolstoy's Major Fiction, 1978, Critical Essays on Tolstoy, 1986, Fathers and Sons: Russia at the Crossroads, 1993. Addressed UN on Tolstoy, 1988. With USNR, 1943-46. Recipient Quantrell teaching prize U. Chgo., 1961; Laing Press prize, 1972; Research fellow USSR, 1963; Guggenheim fellow, 1983-84 Mem. Modern Lang. Assn., Phi Beta Kappa, Lambda Chi Alpha. Home: 1832 Butterfield Ln Flossmoor IL 60422-2107 Office: Univ Chicago Dept English Chicago IL 60637 E-mail: e-wasiolek@uchicago.edu. *I believe in the life of the mind and I believe with Albert Camus that man's dignity lies in his lucidity: in seeing his fate clearly and in having the courage to accept it. Man is capable of sensitivity, courage, love, and compassion, and all of these are more human because he can think. He is also capable of cruelty, hatred, and destruction, and these are more tolerable because he can reason. Man is not man without reason.*

WASKO, STEVEN E. lawyer; b. Chgo., May 10, 1954; s. Theodore J. and Beverly W.; m. Elaine L. Enger, Oct. 3, 1981 (div. Aug. 1996); 1 child, Christine; m. Deborah Wasko; stepchildren: Tara, Raef, Brooke and Christopher. B in Spl. Studies cum laude, Cornell Coll., 1976; JD cum laude, Kent U., 1979. Bar: Ill. 1979, U.S. Dist. Ct. (no. dist.) Ill. 1979. Assoc. atty. Blanshan & Summerfield, Park Ridge, Ill., 1979-81; ptnr. Summerfield & Wasko, Park Ridge, 1981-86; sole practitioner Steven Wasko and Assocs., Park Ridge, 1986-90, mng. ptnr., 1992-95; ptnr. Wasko & Michaels, Park Ridge, 1990-91, Steponate & Wasko Ltd., Park Ridge and Chgo., 1995—. Dir. Kolan Corp., Park Ridge, 1988—. Great Books leader Field Sch. Dist., Park Ridge, 1997—. Avocations: weight training, watercolors, fine art. Office: 1580 N Northwest Hwy Park Ridge IL 60068-1444

WASKO-FLOOD, SANDRA JEAN, artist, educator; b. N.Y.C., Mar. 12, 1943; d. Peter Edmund and Margaret Dalores (Kubek) Wasko; m. Michael Timothy Flood, June 28, 1969. BA, UCLA, 1965, postgrad., 1968-69, Calif. State U., Northridge, summer 1968; student, Otis Art Inst., L.A., 1969, Marie Kaufman, Rio de Janeiro, 1970-72, Museo de Arte Moderno, 1970-73, Foothill Coll., Los Altos, Calif., 1973-74, Claremont (Calif.) Coll., 1975, U. Wis., Janesville, 1977, Beloit (Wis.) Coll., 1977-78, U. Wis., 1977-78; grad. etching student, Warrington Colescott. Instr. printmaking Washington Women's Arts Ctr., 1983; artist-in-residence U. Md., College Park, 1985; instr. printmaking Arlington (Va.) Arts Ctr., 1984-85; prof. St. Mary's (Md.) Coll., 1985; instr. printmaking Arlington County Lee Arts Ctr., 1989-97; workshop coord. cultural affairs div. Arlington County Cultural Affairs, 1989-97; printmaking instr. Home Studio, Alexandria, Va., 1987—. Condr. workshops Washington Performing Arts Soc., 2002—04. One woman shows include

Wisconsin Women in the Arts Gallery, Madison, 1977, Mbari Art, Washington, 1981, Miya Gallery, Washington, 1981, Slavin Gallery, Washington, 1982, Stuart Mott House, Washington, 1983, Washington Printmakers Gallery, 1986, 88, 91, St. Peter's Ch., N.Y.C., 1989, Montana Gallery, Alexandria, Va., 1991, Montpelier Cultural Arts Ctr., Laurel, Md., 1992, Gallery 10, Washington, 1994, 96, Sch. 33, Balt., 1996; mus. and internat. shows include Boston Printmakers: The 39th North Am. Print Exhbn., Framingham, Mass., Jan.-Mar., 1986, Internat. Graphic Arts Found. and Silvermine Guild Arts Ctr., New Canaan, Conn., Feb., 1988, prints: Washington, The Phillips Collection, Washington, Sept.-Oct., 1988, Contemporary Am. Graphics, Book Chamber Internat., Moscow, 1990, Gallery 10 Artists of Washington D.C. Vartai Gallery, Lithuania, 1994, Peninsula Fine Arts Ctr., Newport News, Va., 1995-96, Riva Sinistra Arte, Florence, Italy, 1997, Contemporary Art Ctr. Va., Virginia Beach, 2000, Charles Sumner Sch. Mus., Washington, D.C., 2001, numerous others; juried shows include Washington Women's Arts Ctr.: Printmakers VII show, 1985, Washington Women's Arts Ctr., 1981, 82, Seventh Ann. Faber Birren Color Show Nat. Juried Open Exhibit, Stamford, Conn., 1987, Acad. of the Arts 25th Ann. Juried Exhbn., 1989, Fla. Printmakers Nat., 1994, S.W. Tex. State U., 1995, Peninsula Fivie Arts Ctr., Newport News, Va., 1998, Washington Women Artists, Womens Caucus for Art, 2001, Rockville Art Place, Md., 2002, Internat. Photography, 2003, and numerous others; invitational shows include Office of the Mayor, Mini Art Gallery, Washington, "Glimpses: Women Printmakers", 1981, Pyramid Paperworks, Balt., 1984, Gallery 10 "Nightmare Show": Washington, D.C., 1987, The Intaglio Process, The Benedicta Art Ctr. Gallery, St. Joseph, Minn., 1988, Women's Caucus for Art, Washington Artists in Perspective, Westbeth Gallery, N.Y.C., 1990, 91, Wesley Theol. Sem., 1992, Balt. City Hall, N.Am. Print Alliance, 1993, The Five Elements Women's Caucus For Art, 1994, WPA/Corcoran Auction, 1999, Washington Theological Union, Washington, 1999, Cannon Rotunda, U.S. House of Reps., Washington, 2000, Charles Sumner Sch. Mus., Washington, 2001, Washington Women Artists Marching into the Millennium, Women's Caucus for Art, 2001 and numerous others; galleries: Slavin Gallery, Washington, D.C., 1981-83, Washington Printmakers Gallery, Washington, 1985-96, White Light Collaborative, Inc., N.Y.C., 1988-89, Montana Gallery, Alexandria, Va., 1989-91, Gallery 10, Washington, 1992-97, Charlevoix Gallery, Albuquerque, NM, 1999, and numerous others; collections include Nat. Mus. of Women in the Arts, Washington, Corcoran Gallery of Art, Washington, Museo de Arte Moderno, Buenos Aires, Cultural Found., USSR, Coll. Notre Dame, Balt., Potomac Hosp., Woodbridge, Md.; dir. Labyrinths for Peace 2000, U.S. Capitol, 2002; featured artist Kali Guide: A Directory of Resources for Women, 2d reprint, 2002. Pres. Washington Area Printmakers, Washington, D.C., 1985-86; pub. rels. dir. Washington Women's Arts Ctr., 1980; bd. dirs. Washington Women's Arts Ctr., 1981-82; program chair D.C. chpt. Women's Caucus for Art, 1998—; founding mem. the Labyrinth Soc., 1999-2000; special projects dir. Labryinth Soc., 2000; cons. Labyrinth Making and Products. Recipient Award of Honorable Mention Nat. Gallery of Art, 1989, Best of Show, Artists Equity Exhibit, Gallery 901, Washington, 1997; grantee Friends of the Torpedo Factory Art Ctr., Alexandria, Va., 1989, D.C. Commn. on the Arts and Humanities Summer Edn. and Sports Program, 2000, 01; individual artists fellow Va. Commn. for Arts, 1994. Mem.: Arts/Sci. Collaborative, Inc. (N.Y.C.), Artists Using Sci. and Tech. (San Francisco), YLEM, The Labyrinth Soc., Washington Sculpture Group, Am. Print Alliance, Md. Printmakers, Women's Caucus for Art, So. Graphics Coun., Pyramic Atlantic, Nat. Print Orgn., Corcoran Gallery/Washington Project for the Arts. Avocations: classical music, hiking, reading. Home: 8106 Norwood Dr Alexandria VA 22309-1331 Studio: 57 N St NW Washington DC 20001-1254 E-mail: sandra@waskoart.com.

WASMUTH, CARL ERWIN, physician, lawyer; b. Pitts., Feb. 16, 1916; s. Edwin Hugo and Mary Blanche (Love) W.; m. Martha Conn., Aug. 25, 1939; children: Carl Erwin; m. Gertrude White Ruth, June 19, 1984; m. Wilhelmina Waterman Devine, May 12, 1990. BS, U. Pitts., 1935, MD, 1939; LLB, Cleve.-Marshall Law Sch., 1959. Diplomate Am. Bd. Anesthesiology. Bar: Ohio 1959. Intern Western Pa. Hosp., Pitts., 1939-40; fellow anesthesiology Cleve. Clinic Found., 1949-51, mem. emeritus staff, 1976—; pvt. practice medicine Dry Run, Pa., 1942-45, Scottdale, Pa., 1945-49; mem. dep. anesthesia Cleve. Clinic, 1951—, head dept., 1967-69; asso. prof. law Cleve.-Marshall Law Sch., 1959-66; adj. prof. Cleve. Marshall Law Sch., 1966-73. Author: Anesthesia and the Law, 1961, Law for the Physician, 1966, Law and the Surgical Team, 1968; Editor: Legal Problems in the Practice of Anesthesiology, 1973; contbg. editor: Hale's Anesthesiology; editorial bd.: Med. World News; Contbr. articles to profl. jours. Trustee Cleve.- Marshall Law Sch., chmn., 1969-71; bd. dirs. Scottdale Hosp. Found; chmn. bd. govs. Cleve. Clinic, 1969-77; trustee Cleve. Clinic Found., 1969-76, v.p., 1973-76; trustee Cleve. Clinic Ednl. Found., 1969-76, v.p., 1973-76; chmn. bd. trustees, pres. Cleve. Marshall Ednl. Found., 1972-81; bd. overseers Coll. Law, Cleve. State U., 1972-76; vis. com. Coll. Law, Case-Western Res. U., 1973-76; trustee United Torch Svcs.; hon. trustee Tucson Symphony Soc., 1983-84, 88; trustee Santa Cruz Med. Found., 1977, pres., 1978; bd. govs. Ohio World Trade Center; trustee Cancer Center Cleve., Ohio Coll. Podiatric Medicine, 1976, Am. Coll. Legal Medicine Research Found., 1984—; mem. U. Ariz. Found., 1978, World Congress Med. Law, 1967—, Keynoter 3d World Congress, 1971; sec. Commn. Med. Malpractice, HEW, 1972-73; vestryman St. Francis-in-the-Valley Episcopal Ch., Green Valley, 1990-93. Named Distinguished Eagle Scout Nat. Council Boy Scouts Am., 1977; named Outstanding Citizen Eagle Cuyahoga council, 1976; Citizen of Year Cleve. Area Bd. Realtors, 1976 Fellow: ACP, Law Sci. Acad., Am. Coll. Chest Physicians, Am. Coll. Legal Medicine (pres. bd. govs. 1966—69), Am. Coll. Anesthesiologists; mem.: ABA, AAAS, AMA, NRC, Cleve. Bar Assn., Cuyahoga County Bar Assn., Ohio Bar Assn., Transplantation Soc. (charter), Cleve. Acad. Medicine, Com. Cadaver Utilization, Nat. Acad. Sci., N.Y. Acad. Scis., Ohio Med. Assn., Acad. Anesthesiology (chmn. program com. 1967), World Fedn. Anesthesiologists (vice chmn. Am. del. 1967), Internat. Anesthesia Rsch. Soc., Cleve. Soc. Anesthesiologists (pres. 1963), Ohio Soc. Anesthesiologists (dir. 1960—69), Am. Soc. Anesthesiologists (dir., pres. 1968, spkr. ho. of dels.), Ariz. Sr. Acad., Gainey Ranch Golf Club (Scottsdale), Old Pueblo Club, The Lakes Club, Mt. Kenya Safari Club (Nanyuki, Kenya), Pleasant Valley Country Club, Tucson Club, Country Club of Green Valley, Lions (past pres. local clubs), Masons, Delta Theta Phi, Phi Rho Sigma. E-mail: cwasmuth@cox.net.

WASOW, OMAR, reporter; BA in Race and Ethnic Rels., Stanford U., Calif., 1992. Coord. voter registration Freedom Summer '92, 1992; asst. dir. Strictly Bus., 1992—93; founder, owner New York Online, 1993—; internet analyst NewsChannel4, N.Y.C., 1995—. Exec. dir. BlackPlanet.com Cmty. Connect, Inc., N.Y.C., 1995—. Co-chair Coalition for Ind. Pub. Charter Schs.; bd. dirs. N.Y. Software Indusry Assn., WorldStudio, The Refugee Project. Fellow Next Generation Leadership program, Rockefeller Found. Office: NBC 30 Rockefeller Plz New York NY 10112

WASS, HANNELORE LINA, educational psychology educator; b. Heidelberg, Germany, Sept. 12, 1926; came to U.S., 1957, naturalized, 1963; d. Hermann and Mina (Lasch) Kraft; m. Irvin R. Wass, Nov. 24, 1959 (dec.); 1 child, Brian C.; m. Harry H. Sisler, Apr. 13, 1978. BA, Tchrs. Coll., Heidelberg, 1951; MA, U. Mich., 1960, PhD, 1968. Tchr. W. Ger. Univ. Lab. Schs., 1958-60; mem. faculty U. Mich., Ann Arbor, 1958-60, U. Chgo. Lab. Sch., 1960-61, U. Mich., 1963-64, Eastern Mich. U., 1965-69; prof. ednl. psychology U. Fla., Gainesville, 1969-92, prof. emeritus, 1992—, faculty assoc. Ctr. for Gerontol. Studies. Cons., lectr. in thanatology. Author: The Professional Education of Teachers, 1974, Dying-Facing the Facts, 1979, 2d edit., 1988, 3d edit., 1995, Death Education: An Annotated Resource Guide, 1980, vol. 2, 1985, Helping Children Cope With Death, 1982, 2d edit., 1984, Childhood and Death, 1984; founding editor (jour.) Death Studies, 1977-92; cons. editor: Ednl. Gerontology, 1977-92, (book series) Death Education, Aging and Health Care, 1980-96; contbr. approximately 200 articles to profl. jours. and chpts. in books. Mem. Am. Psychol. Assn., Gerontol. Soc., Internat. Work Group Dying, Death and Bereavement (bd. dirs.), Assn. Death Edn. and Counseling. Home: 6014 NW 54th Way Gainesville FL 32653-3265 Office: U Fla 346 Norman Hall Gainesville FL 32611-2053 E-mail: wass@nersp.nerdc.ufl.edu .

WASSELL, STEPHEN ROBERT, mathematics educator, researcher; b. Santa Monica, Calif., Jan. 17, 1963; s. Desmond Anthony and Catherine Ann (Stephens) W. BS in arch., U. Va., 1984, MS in math, 1987, PhD in math., 1990, M in computer sci., 1999. Programmer, analyst UNISYS, McLean, Va., 1984-85, graphics artist, 1986; tutor summer transition program U. Va., Charlottesville, 1987-88, tchg. asst., 1986-90; asst. prof. math. Sweet Briar (Va.) Coll., 1990-96, assoc. prof. math., 1996—2002, prof. math., 2002—, dept. chmn., 1996—97, 1999—2002, 2004—05. Prof. of record Ctr. for the Liberal Arts, U. Va., 1991; vis. asst. prof. math., U. Va., Charlottesville, 1992, vis. assoc. prof. computer sci., 1998-99; doctoral cons., Charlottesville, 1989-90. Author: (with Kim Williams) On Ratio and Proportion, 2002; editor: The Golden Section, 2003. Recipient Grad. assistantship award U. Va., 1986-90; Gordon T. Whyburn fellow, 1985-86. Mem. AAUP (Sweet Briar chpt. sec.-treas. 1993-99), Am. Math. Soc., Math. Assn. Am., Am. Solar Energy Soc., Sigma Nu (Beta chpt. treas. 1985-86). Achievements include patents for solar powered lawnmover, for solar shed, for ear muffs. Home: 4500 Monacan Trail Rd North Garden VA 22959-2215 Office: Sweet Briar Coll Dept Math Scis Sweet Briar VA 24595 Office Phone: 434-381-6214. E-mail: wassell@sbc.edu.

WASSENICH, LINDA PILCHER, retired health policy analyst, fund raiser; b. Washington, Aug. 27, 1943; d. Mason Johnson and Vera Bell (Stephenson) Pilcher; m. Mark Wassenich, May 14, 1965; children: Paul Mason, David Mark. BA magna cum laude, Tex. Christian U., 1965; MSW, U. N.C., 1970. Licensed advanced practitioner, cert. social worker, Tex. Counselor family ct. Dallas County Juvenile Dept., Dallas, 1970-73, 75-76; dir. govt. rels. Vis. Nurse Assn., Dallas, 1980-84, exec. officer of hospice, 1984-85; exec. dir. Incest Recovery Assn., Dallas, 1985-86; assoc. exec. dir. Lone Star Coun. Camp Fire, Dallas, 1986-89; exec. v.p. Vis. Nurse Assn. Found., Dallas, 1989-91; dir. policy & resource devel. Vis. Nurse Assn. Tex., Dallas, 1992-99; ret. Field instr. U. Tex. Arlington Sch. Social Work, 1993-99. Contbr. articles to profl. publs. Mem. Leadership Dallas, 1988—89; bd. dirs. Women's Coun. Dallas County, 1986—95, 1999—2001, pres., 1992—93; mem. adv. bd. Maternal Health and Family Planning Dallas, 1990—94; chmn. Dallas County Welfare Adv. Bd., 1991—95; bd. dirs. United Way of Met. Dallas, 1992—94, Youth Impact Ctrs., Dallas, 1993—94, Cmty. Coun. Greater Dallas, 2004—; trustee Simmons Family Found., Dallas, 2000—; active Human Rights Initiative of North Tex., Dallas, 2004—. Recipient Heart award Lone Star Coun. Camp Fire USA, 1990, Laurel award AAUW, Dallas, 1995, Valuable Alumna award Tex. Christian U. Alumni Assn., 2003; named Field Inst. of Yr., U. Tex. Arlington Sch. Social Work, 1999, Golden Rule award finalist JC Penney, 2000. Mem.: LWV (bd. dirs. Dallas 1974—80, pres. 1995—99, bd. dirs. Tex. 1999—, Tex. v.p. pub. rels. 2001—, Myrtle Bales Bulkley award 2000), NASW (co-chmn. Dallas unit 1981—82, chair Tex. nominating com. 1990—92, Tex. bd. dirs., Social Worker of Yr. award 1988, Lifetime Achievement in Social Work award 2002), Assn. Fundraising Profls. (bd. dirs. Dallas chpt. 1994—97, v.p. governance 1995—96, cert., Outstanding Fund Raising Exec. of Yr. 1999), Acad. Cert. Social Workers. Home: 5221 Pebblebrook Dallas TX 75229-5504

WASSER, HENRY, retired American literature and sociology educator; b. Pitts., Apr. 15, 1919; s. Nathan and Mollie (Mendelson) W.; m. Solidelle Felicité Fortier, Aug. 20, 1942; children: Michael Frederick (dec.), Eric Anthony (dec.), Frederick Anthony, Felicity Louise. BA, MA, Ohio State U., 1940; PhD, Columbia U., 1951. Teaching fellow George Washington U., 1940-42; analyst USAAF intelligence, 1941-43; chemist Goodyear Synthetic Rubber Co., 1943-45; from tutor to assoc. prof. City Coll., CUNY, 1946-66; prof. English, dean faculties Richmond Coll., CUNY, 1966-73; v.p. for acad. affairs Calif. State U., Sacramento, 1973-74; prof. English Coll. S.I., CUNY, 1974-89; dir. Center for European Studies, Grad. Sch. CUNY, 1979-93, prof. emeritus of sociology and English, 1989—. Fulbright prof. U. Salonika, Greece, 1955-56; Higher Edn. Seminar assoc. Columbia U., 1961—, co-chair, 1982-87, chair, 1987-89; mem. Colloquium on Higher Edn., Yale U., 1974-75; Fulbright prof. Am. Lit. U. Oslo, 1962-64, dir., prof. Am. Inst., 1963-64; vis. prof. U. Sussex, Eng., 1972, U. Salonika, 1955-56; lectr. in field, Sweden, Norway, Eng., Germany, Poland, Yugoslavia, Italy, Turkey, Greece, Bulgaria; Fulbright prof. Am. Lit. and Civilization U. Bergen, Norway, 1989-90, U. Aveiro, Portugal, 1993; steering com. Internat. Conf. Higher Edn., 1989-2004, exec. dir., 2004—; rsch. scholar comparative higher edn. CUNY, 1989—. Author: The Scientific Thought of Henry Adams, 1956, (with others) Higher Education in Western Europe and North America: A Selected and Annotated Bibliography, 1979, American Literature and Language: A Selected and Annotated Bibliography, 1980; editor: (with Sigmund Skard) Americana Norvegica; Norwegian Contributions to American Studies, 1968, (with others) The Compleat University, 1983, Problems of the Urban University: A Comparative Perspective, 1984, Impact of Changing Labor Force on Higher Education, 1987; editor (with Ulrich Teichler) German and American Universities: Mutual Influences, 1992, Diversification in Higher Education: A Comparative View, 1999; mem. bd. editors History of European Ideas, 1986—, guest editor, summer, 1987; guest editor Higher Edn. Policy, spring, 1994, contbr. articles to newspapers and profl. jours. Faculty trustee CUNY, 1981-86, trustee emeritus, 1986—; bd. dirs. Scandinavian Seminar, 1978-86, sec., 1980-83, vice chmn., 1983-86. Recipient Am. Scandinavian Found. award, 1969, 71, German Acad. Exch. Svc. award, 1973, 80, Swedish Info. Svc. award, 1979, Norwegian Ministry of Culture award, 1983, NEH award, 1984, Foscolo medal U. Pavia, Italy, 1986, German Marshall Fund award, 1985, 87, Atheneum medal U. Pavia, Italy, 1988, Disting. Senator award CUNY Faculty Senate, 1994. Mem. Am. Studies Assn. (pres. Met. N.Y. chpt. 1961-62, mem. nat. exec. coun. 1968-74), Melville Soc. Am. (historian 1969-74), MLA, Am. Scandinavian Found. (fellow 1971), Internat. Assn. Univ. Profs. English, Assn. Upper Level Colls. and Univs. (2d v.p. 1971-72), Assn. for World Edn. (internat. coun.), Phi Beta Kappa (sec. City Coll. chpt. 1957-62, 64-67, pres. CUNY Acad. for Humanities and Scis. 1991—), Henry Adams Soc. (exec. coun. 1994—, pres. 1996-2003), Mass. Hist. Soc. (fellow 2001). Home: 333 E 34th St Apt 16C New York NY 10016-4950 also: 5517 Fieldston Rd Bronx NY 10471-2503 Office: CUNY Academy Grad Sch 365 Fifth Ave New York NY 10016-4309 E-mail: hwasser@gccuny.edu.

WASSERBURG, GERALD JOSEPH, geology and geophysics educator; b. New Brunswick, N.J., Mar. 25, 1927; s. Charles and Sarah (Levine) W.; m. Naomi Z. Orlick, Dec. 21, 1951; children: Charles David, Daniel Morris. Student, Rutgers U.; BS in Physics, U. Chgo., 1951, MSc in Geology, 1952, PhD, 1954, DSc (hon.), 1992; Dr. Hon. Causa, Brussels U., 1985, U. Paris, 1986; DSc (hon.), Ariz. State U., 1987; Dr. (hon.), U. Rennes, 1998; DSc (hon.), U. Turin (Italy), 2000. Rsch. assoc. Inst. Nuc. Studies U. Chgo., 1954-55; asst. prof. Calif. Inst. Tech., Pasadena, 1955-59, assoc. prof., 1959-62, prof. geology and geophysics, 1962-82, John D. MacArthur prof. geology and geophysics, 1982—2001, prof. emeritus, 2001—. Served on Juneau Ice Field Rsch. Project, 1950; cons. Argonne Nat. Lab., Lamont, Ill., 1952-55; former mem. U.S. Nat. Com. for Geochem., com. for Planetary Exploration Study, NRC, adv. coun. Petroleum Rsch. Fund, Am. Chem. Soc.; me. lunar sample analysis planning team (LSAPT) manned Spacecraft Ctr., NASA, Houston, 1968-71, chmn., 1970; lunar sample rev. bd., 1970-72; mem. Facilities Working Group LSAPT, Johnson Space Ctr., 1972-82; mem. sci. working panel for Apollo missions, Johnson Space Ctr., 1971-73; advisor NASA, 1968-88, phys. scis. com., 1971-75, mem. lunar base steering com., 1984; chmn. com. for planetary and lunar exploration, mem. space sci. bd. NAS, 1975-78; chmn. divsn. Geol. and Planetary Scis., Calif. Inst. Tech., 1987-89; vis. prof. U. Kiel, Fed. Republic of Germany, 1960, Harvard U., 1962, U. Bern, Switzerland, 1966, Swiss Fed. Tech. Inst., 1967, Max Planck Inst., Mainz and Heidelberg, Fed. Republic of Germany, 1985, others; invited lectr., Vinton Hayes Sr. fellow Harvard U., 1980, Jaeger-Hales lectr. Australian Nat. U., 1980, Harold Jeffreys lectr. Royal Astron. Soc., 1981, Ernst Cloos lectr. Johns Hopkins U., 1984, H.L. Welsh Disting. lectr. U. Toronto, 1986, Danz lectr. U. Wash., 1989, Goldschmidt Centennial lectr. Norwegian Acad. Sci. and Letters, 1989, Lindsay lectr. Goddard Space Flight Ctr., 1996, other lectureships; plenary spkr. 125th Anniversary Geol. Soc. Sweden, 1996; 60th Anniversary Symposium spkr. Hebrew U., Jerusalem, 1985, 75th Anniversary Symposium spkr., 2000; Lezione Magistrale, Umbria Libri, Perugia, 2003. Served with U.S. Army, 1944-46. Decorated Combat Inf. badge. Recipient Group Achievement award NASA, 1969, Exceptional Sci. Achievement award NASA, 1970, Disting. Pub. Svc. medal NASA, 1973, J.F. Kemp medal Columbia U., 1973, Profl. Achievement award U. Chgo. Alumni Assn., 1978, Goldschmidt medal Geochem. Soc., 1978, Disting. Pub. Svc. medal with cluster NASA, 1978, Wollaston medal Geol. Soc. London, 1985, Sr. Scientist award Alexander von Humboldt-Stiftung, 1985, Crafoord prize Royal Swedish Acad. Scis., 1986, Holmes medal, 1987, Regents fellow Smithsonian Inst., Gold medal Royal Astron. Soc., 1991; named Hon. Fgn. fellow European Union Geoscis., 1983. Fellow Am. Acad. Arts and Scis., Geol. Soc. London (hon.), Am. Geophys. Union (planetology sect., Harry H. Hess medal 1985), Geol. Soc. Am. (life, Arthur L. Day medal 1970), Meteoritical Soc. (pres. 1987-88, Leonard medal 1975), Geochemical Society and the European Assn. for Geochemistry, 1996; mem. Nat. Acad. Scis. (Arthur L. Day prize and lectureship 1981, J. Lawrence Smith medal 1985), Norwegian Acad. Sci. and Letters, Am. Phil. Soc. Achievements include research in geochemistry and geophysics and the application of the methods of chemical physics to problems in the earth scis. Major researches have been the determination of the time scales of nucleosynthesis, connections between the interstellar medium and solar material, the time of the formation of the solar system, the chronology and evolution of the earth, moon and meteorites, the establishment of dating methods using long-lived natural radio-activities, the study of geologic and cosmic processes using nuclear and isotopic effects as a tracer in nature, the origin of natural gases, and the application of thermodynamic methods to geologic systems. Office: Calif Inst Tech Divsn Geol & Planetary Scis Pasadena CA 91125-2500 Office Phone: 626-395-6139. E-mail: isotopes@gps.caltech.edu.

WASSERHEIT, JUDITH N. social services administrator; b. N.Y.C., 1954; m. Jeffrey Harris, 1981; one child. BA cum laude, Princeton U., 1974; MD, Harvard U., 1978; MPH, Johns Hopkins U., 1989. Co-dir., co-developer Harborview Med. Ctr., U. Wash., 1982-84; infectious disease physician Internat. Ctr. for Diarrheal Disease Rsch., 1984-86; asst. chief Sexually Transmitted Disease Clin. Svcs. Balt. City Health Dept., 1986-89; chief Sexually Transmitted Disease Br. Nat. Inst. Allergy and Infectious Diseases, NIH, 1989-92; dir. Sexually Transmitted Disease Prevention Disease Ctr. for Disease Control & Prevention, HHS, 1992—. Editor: Reproductive Tract Infections: Global Impact and Priorities for Women's Health, 1992; contbr. articles to profl. jours. Recipient Spl. Recognition award Pub. Health Svc., 1990, 91, Young Profl. award Maternal-Child Health, APHA, 1991, Presdl. Meritorious Rank award, 1996; Pub. Health Leadership Inst. Scholar, 1993. Mem. Phi Beta Kappa, Sigma Xi.

WASSERMAN, ALBERT, film producer, writer, director; b. N.Y.C., Feb. 9, 1921; s. Martin S. and Beatrice (Schaffer) W.; m. Della Newmark, Aug. 5, 1943 (div. Mar. 1965); children— Paul, Vicki; m. Barbara Alson, June 19, 1968. BS, CCNY, 1941. Pres. Wasserman Prodns., Inc., N.Y.C., 1968-75. Writer documentary, ednl. and indsl. films, 1946-53; freelance writer, dir. TV documentary films, 1953-55; staff writer, dir., prodr., CBS-TV, 1955-60; prodr., dir., writer: NBC News, 1960-67; prodr.: 60 Minutes, 1976-86; writer, prodr., dir.: Out of Darkness; writer film: First Steps; writer, dir. films for: CBS Pub. Affairs Series The Search; prodr., writer dir.: NBC White Paper programs, films for CBS News series The Twentieth Century and CBS Reports; prodr., dir.: TV Spl. The Making of the President, 1972; still photographer and collagist, N.Y.C., 1987—; solo exhbn. at Atlantic Gallery, N.Y.C., 2003; exhibited works at Cortland Jessup Gallery, Provincetown, Mass., 1990-97, Provincetown Art Assn. and Mus., Atlantic Gallery, N.Y.C., 1995-98, 2003, Cast Iron Gallery, N.Y.C., 1995, Cortland Jessup Gallery, N.Y.C., 1997, eyeonart.com, N.Y.C., 2000. Recipient Sylvania TV award, Robert Flaherty film award, Acad. award, 1947, Peabody award for CBS pub. affairs series, Lasker med. journalism awards (2); Edinburgh Film Festival silver medal, 1948, George Polk award, 1960, Journalism award Ohio State U., 1961. Mem. Writers Guild Am. East (treas. 1965-66), Dirs. Guild Am. (eastern regional council 1965-66, 69-70) Home: 259 W 11th St New York NY 10014-2412

WASSERMAN, BARRY L(EE), architect; b. Cambridge, Mass., May 25, 1935; s. Theodore and Adelaide (Levin) W.; m. Wilma Louise Greenfield, June 21, 1957 (div. 1971); children: Tim Andrew, Andrew Glenn; m. Judith Ella Michalowski, Apr. 22, 1979. BA, Harvard U., 1957, M. Arch., 1960. Registered architect, Calif. Assoc. John S. Bolles Assocs., San Francisco, 1960-69; prin. Wasserman-Herman Assocs., San Francisco, 1969-72; prin., dir. Office Lawrence Halprin U Assocs., San Francisco, 1972-76; dep. state architect State of Calif., Sacramento, 1976-78, state architect, 1978-83; prof. dept. architecture, dir. Inst. Environ. Design, Sch. Environ. Design Calif. State Poly. U., Pomona, 1983-87, chair dept. architecture, Coll. Environ. Design, 1988-96, prof. emeritus, 1997—. Program advisor Fla. A&M U., Tallahassee, 1981—83; adv. com. Interior Design Program Calif. State U., Sacramento, 2004—; bd. dirs. Environ. Coun. Sacramento; mem. City of Sacramento Plng. Commn., 2004—; cons. in field. Architect Wasserman House, San Rafael, Calif., 1963 (AIA-Sunset Mag. award of Merit 1965-66), Anna Waden Library, San Francisco, 1969 (AIA award of Merit 1970), Capitol Area Plan, Sacramento, 1977 (Central Valley chpt. AIA Honor award 1979), co-author: Ethics and the Practice of Architecture, 2000. Recipient Awards citation Progressive Architecture 26th awards Program, 1979, Octavius Morgan award Calif. Architects Bd., 2000. Fellow AIA (chmn. architecture in govt. com., 1979, bd.dir. environ. coun. Sacramento, 2004—) Democrat. Jewish. Home: 6456 Fordham Way Sacramento CA 95831-2218 E-mail: blw2@mindspring.com.

WASSERMAN, DAVID H. medical educator, researcher; b. New Orleans, Aug. 24, 1957; m. Doris S. Wasserman; children: Micah Joseph, Mira Rose. BSc in Kinesiology, UCLA, 1979, MSc in Kinesiology, 1981; PhD in Physiology, U. Toronto, 1985. Rsch. asst. dept. respiratory physiology and medicine UCLA, 1979—81, tchg. asst. gen. physiology dept. kinesiology, 1980—81; tchg. asst. gen. physiology dept. physiology U. Toronto, 1982—84; rsch. assoc. dept. molecular physiology and biophysics Vanderbilt U. Sch. Medicine, Nashville, 1985—87, lab. instr. med. sch. physiology dept. molecular physiology and biophysics, 1986—88, course coord., lectr. exercise physiology dept. molecular physiology and biophysics, 1986—, rsch. instr. dept. molecular physiology and biophysics, 1987—88, asst. prof. dept. molecular physiology and biophysics, 1988—92, lectr. tutorials in physiology dept. molecular physiology and biophysics, 1989—90, lectr. metabolic regulation in vivo dept. molecular physiology and biophysics, 1989—, lectr. history physiology dept. molecular physiology and biophysics, 1991—92, assoc. prof. dept. molecular physiology and biophysics, lectr. med. sch. physiology dept. molecular physiology and biophysics, 1992—98, lectr. interdisciplinary grad. program physiology dept. molecular physiology and biophysics, 1992—94, course coord. interaction cell sys. sect. interdisciplinary grad. program, 1994—97, course coord., instr. tutorials in profl. physiology dept. molecular physiology and biophysics, 1995—. Lectr. in field. Mem. editl. bd.: Am. Jour. Physiology: Endocrinology and Metabolism, 1992—, Jour. Applied Physiology, 1996—, assoc. editor: Metabolism, 1996—; contbr. articles to profl. jours. Mem.: European Assn. for Studies in Diabetes, Juvenile Diabetes Found. Internat. (bd. dirs. Tenn. chpt. 1995—, chmn. govt. rels. com. Tenn. chpt. 1996—), Am. Physiol. Soc. (mem. program adv. com. 1988—92, head org. com. interactions endo. and cardiovasc. sys. health/disease 1989—91, sec./treas. endocrinology and metabolism sect. 1992—95, mem. organizing com. integrated biology of exercise 1993—), Am. Coll. Sports Medicine, Am. Diabetes Assn. (mem. rsch. coun. on exercise 1988—, co-advisor tech. report on diabetes and exercise 1993—94, mem. grant rev. panel 1993—96). Office: Vanderbilt U Med Sch Dept Molec Physio & Biophys Light Hl Rm 702 Nashville TN 37232-0001

WASSERMAN, EDWARD ARNOLD, psychology educator; b. L.A., Apr. 2, 1946; s. Albert Leonard and May (Sabin) W. BA, UCLA, 1968; PhD, Ind. U., 1972. Postdoctoral fellow U. Sussex, Brighton, Eng., 1972; from asst. prof. to prof. psychology U. Iowa, Iowa City, 1972-83, prof., 1983—, Stuit prof. exptl. psychology, 1997—. Pres. faculty senate U. Iowa, 1997-98; vis. scientist CNRS, Marseille, France, 1999. Contbr. articles to profl. jours., chpts. to books; assoc. editor several jours. Bd. dirs. Big Bros., Big Sisters, Johnson County, Iowa, 1982-85 Ind. U. fellow, 1968, U. Iowa fellow, 1975, 82, NAS

fellow, former USSR, 1976, James Van Allen Natural Scis. fellow, 1994-95. Fellow APA, Am. Psychol. Soc.; mem. Psychonomic Soc. (governing bd.), Midwestern Psychol. Assn., Phi Beta Kappa. Office: U Iowa Dept Psychology Iowa City IA 52242

WASSERMAN, GERALD STEWARD, psychobiology educator; b. Bklyn., Nov. 22, 1937; s. Julius and Bessie (Weissman) W.; m. Louise Janet Mund, June 17, 1962; children: Mark Daniel, Rachel Lynn. BA, NYU, 1961; PhD, MIT, 1965. Rsch. asst. NYU-Bellevue Med. Ctr., N.Y.C., 1959-61; grad. asst. MIT, Cambridge, Mass., 1961-63, grad. fellow, 1963-65; postdoctoral fellow NIH, Bethesda, Md., 1965-67; asst. prof. U. Wis., Madison, 1967-70, assoc. prof., 1970—75; prof. psychobiology and neurosci. Purdue U., West Lafayette, Ind., 1975—. Author: Color Vision, 1978; mem. editorial bd. Color Rsch. and Application, 1977-80; adv. editor Contemporary Psychology, 1981-87; mem. editorial bd. Biol. Signals and Receptors, 1990-2001; contbr. over 75 articles to profl. jours. Pres. Temple Israel, West Lafayette, Ind., 1984-85. Recipient First Prize Midwest region Johns Hopkins Nat. Search for Computing to Assist the Disabled, Chgo., 1991. Fellow Am. Psychol. Soc., Optical Soc. Am.; mem. Internat. Soc. Psychophysics, Internat. Brain Rsch. Orgn., Acoustical Soc. Am., Soc. Neurosci. Libertarian. Jewish. Achievements include patent for sensory prosthesis; discovered task dependence of sensory coding; development of temporal summation index of mental timing; design of artificial receptor for use in nerve deafness; brain control of photoreceptor timing. Business E-Mail: codelab@purdue.edu.

WASSERMAN, HARRY HERSHAL, chemistry professor; b. Boston, Mass., Dec. 1, 1920; s. Maurice Leonard and Rebecca (Franks) W.; m. Elga Ruth Steinherz, June 1, 1947; children: Daniel M., Diana R., Steven A. BS, MIT, 1941; MA, Harvard U., 1942, PhD, 1949; MA (hon.), Yale U., 1962. Rsch. asst. O.S.R.D. Penicillin Project, 1945; instr., asst. prof. dept. chemistry Yale U., New Haven, Conn., 1948-57, assoc. prof. dept. chemistry, 1957-62, prof. dept. chemistry, 1962-82, Eugene Higgins prof. chemistry, 1982-91; Eugene Higgins prof. chemistry emeritus, 1991—. Cons. Union Carbide Corp., 1956-66, Sandoz Corp., 1966-74, SmithKline Beckman Corp., 1974-80, Ortho Pharms., 1980-94; bd. dirs. Camille and Henry Dreyfus Found. Author numerous articles on organic chemistry in sci. jours. Capt. USAF, 1942-45. Recipient William Devane Tchr.-Scholar award Phi Beta Kappa, 1977, Catalyst Teaching award Chem. Mfrs. Assn., 1985, Oustanding Tchr. award Yale U., 1985, Aldrich Synthetic Chemistry award, Am. Chem. Soc., 1987, Arthur Cope scholar award, 1990. Mem. NAS, Am. Acad. Scis., Conn. Acad. Scis. Avocation: watercolor painting. Office: Yale U Dept Chemistry PO Box 208107 New Haven CT 06520-8107

WASSERMAN, HELENE WALTMAN, art dealer, artist; b. Phila., Jan. 29, 1929; d. William T. and Bertha (Brener) Waltman; m. Richard M. Wasserman, June 23, 1950 (div. 1972); children: Ann Zelver, Ellen Rubinfeld, Stephen; m. Mark C. Cooper, Jan. 22, 1988. BFA, U. Pa., 1951. Pvt. practice art dealer, 1972—. Apptd. appraiser Supreme Ct., State of N.Y., 1978. One-woman shows at Philmont Gallery, Phila., 1964, Roko Gallery, N.Y., 1965; exhibited in group shows at Phila. Mus. Art, Pa. Acad. Fine Arts, Philbrook Mus., Tulsa, Woodmere Gallery, Roko Gallery, 1953-68. Active Nassau County Art Commn., 1968-72; trustee, Sculpture Ctr., N.Y.C., bd. dirs., 1991. Mem. Pvt. Art Dealers Assn., Cosmopolitan Club, Nature Conservancy. Avocations: painting, sculpting, garden design.

WASSERMAN, KATHRYN, photographer; b. Washington, N.C., Apr. 6, 1952; d. Grover C. and Oleta Odum Wood; m. Louis Leslie Wasserman; children: Emily Wasserman Sutton, Bevan Elizabeth. BS magna cum laude, Old Dominion U., 1974. Prin. Rare Light Images, Virginia Beach, Va., 2001—. Exhibited in group shows at Princess Anne Park Arts and Crafts Festival, 2002 (award of merit), The Artists Gallery Marine Art Exhibit, 2002 (hon. mention), Seawall Art Show, 2002 (People's Choice award), 2003 (award of merit), Rawls Mus., 2003 (hon. mention), Lynchburg (Va.) Art Festival, 2003 (Pheasant's Eye award), Va. Highlands Festival, 2003 (hon. mention), Va. Beach Boardwalk Art Show, 2003 (selected for judging, 2003), 2004 (selected for judging, 2004), exhibitions include d'Art Ctrs. Mid-Atlantic Art Exhibit, 2004 (award of merit), Cristallo Gallery Juried Photography Exhbn., 2004 (2d pl. award). Named one of Contemporary Art Center of Va. New Waves, 2004. Avocations: hiking, reading. Home: 2576 Piney Bark Dr Virginia Beach VA 23456 Office Phone: 757-430-7897. Personal E-mail: kwasserman@rarelightimages.com.

WASSERMAN, MARLIE P(ARKER), publisher; b. Chgo., Feb. 14, 1947; d. Theodore E. and Faye (Beller) Parker; m. Mark Wasserman, Nov. 24, 1968; children— Aaron David, Danielle Elizabeth. B.A., Duke U., 1969; M.A., Old Dominion U., 1970. Editor, U. Chgo. Press, 1970-78; sr. editor Rutgers U. Press, New Brunswick, N.J., 1978-83, asst. dir. and editor-in-chief, 1983-87, assoc. dir., editor-in-chief, 1987-94; exec. editor social sciences Routledge, N.Y.C., 1994-95; dir. Rutgers U. Press, New Brunswick, 1995—. Office: Rutgers U Press 100 Joyce Kilmer Ave Piscataway NJ 08854-8045

WASSERMAN, PAUL, library and information science educator; b. Newark, Jan. 8, 1924; s. Joseph and Sadie (Ringelescu) W.; m. Krystyna Ostrowska, 1973; children: Jacqueline R., Steven R. BBA, Coll. City N.Y., 1948; MS in L.S., Columbia, 1949, MS, 1950; PhD, U. Mich., 1960; postgrad., Western Res. U., 1963-64. Advt. mgr. Zuckerberg Co., N.Y.C., 1946-48; asst. to bus. libr. Bklyn. Pub. Library, 1949-51, chief sci. and industry div., 1951-53; librarian, asst. prof. Grad. Sch. Bus. and Pub. Adminstrn., Cornell U., 1953-56, libr., assoc. prof., 1956-62, librarian, prof., 1962-65; dean U. Md. Coll. Library and Info. Scis., 1965-70, prof., 1970-97, prof. emeritus, 1997—. Vis. prof. U. Mich., summers 1960, 63, 64, Asian Inst. Tech., U. Hawaii, U. Hong Kong, summer 1988, Chulalongkorn U., Bangkok, 1990, U. Wash., summer 1991, U. Wis., summer 1991, U. Wis., summer 1992, C.W. Post Coll., L.I. U., 1993, Inst. Sci. and Tech. China, Beijing, 1996; Isabel Nichol lectr. Denver U. Libr. Sch., 1968; market rsch. cons. Laux Advt., Inc., 1955-59, Gale Rsch. Co., Detroit, 1959-60, 63-64; rsch. planning cons. Ind. U. Sch. Bus., 1961-62; cons. to USPHS as mem. manpower tng. rev. com. Nat. Libr. Medicine, 1966-69, Ohio Bd. Regents, 1969, Omngraphics Inc., 1988-91, VITA, summer 1987; dir. Documentation Abstracts, Inc., 1970-73, v.p., 1971-73; Fulbright prof. Warsaw U., 1993-94; rsch. project dir. Kellogg Study, 1996-98. Author: Information for Adminstrators, 1956, (with Fred Silander) Decision Making, 1958, Measurement and Evaluation of Organization Performance, 1959, Sources of Commodity Prices, 1960, 2d edit., 1974, Sources for Hospital Administrators, 1961, Decision Making: An Annotated Bibliography, supplement, 1958-63, 1964, Librarian and the Machine, 1965; Book rev. editor: Adminstrv. Sci. Quar, 1956-61; editor: Service to Business, 1952-53, Directory of University Research Bureaus and Institutes, 1960, Health Organizations of the U.S. and Canada, 1961, and 2d to 4th edit., 1977, Statistics Sources, 1962 and 4th to 8th edits., 1984, (with Bundy) Reader in Library Adminstration, 1968, Reader in Research Methods in Librarianship, 1969; mng. editor: Mgmt. Information Guide Series, 1963-83, Consultants and Consulting Organizations, 1966, 4th edit., 1979, 5th edit., 1982, Who's Who in Consulting, 1968, 2d edit., 1974, Awards, Honors and Prizes: A Sourcebook and Directory, 1969, 2d edit., 1972, 4th edit. Vol. 1, 1978, International and Foreign Awards, 1975, New Consultants, 1973-74, 76-77, 78-79, Readers in Librarianship and Information Science, 1968-78, Ency. Bus. Information Sources, 1971, 3d edit., 1976, 4th edit., 1980, 5th edit., 1983, Library and Information Services Today, 1971-75, Consumer Sourcebook, 1974, 2d edit., 1978, 3d edit., 1980, 4th edit., 1983; series editor: Contributions in Librarianship and Information Science, 1969-99; coordinating mgmt. editor: Information Guide Library, 1971-83, The New Librarianship-A Challenge for Change, 1972; mng. editor: Museum Media, 1973, Library Bibliographies and Indexes, 1975, Ethnic Groups in the United States, 1976, 2d edit., 1982, Training and Development Organizations, 1978, 2d edit., 1983, Speakers and Lecturers: How to Find Them, 1979, 2d edit., 1982, Learning Independently, 1979, 2d edit., 1983, Recreation and Outdoor Life Directory, 1979, Law and Legal Information Directory, 1980, 2d edit., 1982, Ency. Health Info. Sources, 1986, Ency. Sr. Citizen Info. Sources, 1987, Ency. Pub. Affairs Info. Sources, 1987, Ency. Legal Info. Sources, 1987; mem. editorial bd. Social Scis. Citation Index, Inst. Scientific Info., 1972-95, Jour. Library Adminstrn., 1979-89, Social Sci. Info. Studies, 1979—, 1991 Education for Info.: The Internat. Rev. of Education and Tng. in Library and Info. Sci., 1983-88, The Best of Times: A Personal and Occupational Odyssey, 2000, New York from A to Z, 2002, Washington DC from A to Z, 2003. Active U.S. Com. on Edn. and Tng. for Internat. Fedn. for Info. and Documentation, 1993-94. Served with U.S. Army, 1943-46. Decorated Purple Heart, Bronze Star; recipient ALA Ref. Svcs. Divsn./Gale Rsch. Bus. Libr. award, 1997; Fulbright scholar, Sri Lanka, 1986-87. Mem. AAUP, ALA, Am. Soc. Info. Sci., Spl. Librs. Assn. (editor, chmn. publ. project., Disting. Mem. award bus. divsn. 1996—). Home: 4940 Sentinel Dr Apt 203 Bethesda MD 20816-3552 Office: U Md Coll Info Studies College Park MD 20742-0001 E-mail: pw11@umail.umd.edu.

WASSERMAN, RICHARD LAWRENCE, pediatrician, educator; b. Bklyn., Oct. 28, 1948; s. Isidore and Gladys (Glazer) W.; m. Tina D. Rice; children: Jonathan A., Leslie R. BS in Chemistry, Hobart Coll., 1970; PhD, CUNY, 1975; MD, U. Tex. Southwest, Dallas, 1977. Diplomate Am. Bd. Pediatrics, Am. Bd. Allergy and Immunology. Intern Children's Hosp. Phila., 1977-78, resident in pediatrics, 1978-79, fellow in immunology, 1979-80; rsch. assoc. in immunology Rockefeller U., N.Y.C., 1980-82; asst. prof. pediatrics and microbiology U. Tex. S.W. Med. Ctr., Dallas, 1982-88, asst. clin. prof. pediatrics, 1988-99, assoc. clin. prof. pediatrics, 1999—; asst. chief pediatrics Baylor U. Med. Ctr., Dallas, 1989; dir. Immunology Clinic Children's Med. Ctr., Dallas, 1983—2003. Adj. attending physician Mt. Sinai Hosp., N.Y.C., 1981-82; cons. Am. Assn. Blood Banks, Arlington, Va., 1983-95; test devel. com. Nat. Bd. Med. Examiners, 1992—; med. dir. pediatric allergy and immunology North Tex. Children's Hosp., Dallas, 1994—; chmn. Am. Lung Assn. Tex., Dallas, 1999-2000; overseer Jewish Inst. Religion Hebrew Union Coll. Pres. Hobart Coll. Alumnae Coun., 2000-01; overseer Jewish Inst. Religion, Hebrew Union Coll., Cin., 2000— Fellow Am. Bd. Allergy, Asthma and Immunology); mem. Am. Assn. Immunologists, Clin. Immunology Soc., Am. Acad. Allergy Asthma and Immunology (chmn. pub. edn. 1999-2001), So. Soc. for Pediatric Rsch. (coun. 1986-87, Founder's award 1988), Greater Dallas Pediat. Soc. (pres. 1999), Phi Beta Kappa Zeta. Home: 7153 Lavendale Ave Dallas TX 75230-3650

WASSERMAN, RICHARD LEO, lawyer; b. Balt., Aug. 6, 1948; s. Jack B. and Claire (Gutman) W.; m. Manuele Delbourgo, May 13, 1973; children: Alexander E., Lauren E. AB, Princeton U., 1970; JD, Columbia U., 1973. Bar: N.Y. 1975, Md. 1978, U.S. Dist. Ct. (so. and ea. dists.) N.Y. 1975, U.S. Dist. Ct. Md. 1978, U.S. Ct. Appeals (2d cir.) 1975, U.S. Ct. Appeals (4th cir.) 1979, U.S. Supreme Ct. 1982. Law clk. to hon. Roszel C. Thomsen U.S. Dist. Ct. Md., Balt., 1973-74; assoc. Proskauer Rose Goetz & Mendelsohn, N.Y.C., 1974-78, Venable LLP, Balt., 1978-81, ptnr., 1982—, also bd. dirs. Fellow Am. Coll. Bankruptcy, Md. Bar Found.; mem. ABA (bus. bankruptcy com.), Md. Bar Assn. (sec. coun. bus. law sect. 1989-92), Bar Assn. Balt. City (chmn. banking, bankruptcy and bus. law com. 1987-88), Bankruptcy Bar Assn. Dist. Md. (bd. dirs. 1988—, pres. 1990-91), Assn. Bar City N.Y., Am. Bankruptcy Inst., Princeton U. Alumni Assn. Md. (bd. dirs. 1980-98, pres. 1985-87), Suburban Club Baltimore County (bd. govs. 1982-89, 94-98, 2d v.p. 1986-87, sec. 1987-88, pres.-elect 1994-95, pres. 1995-97). Democrat. Jewish. Avocations: tennis, golf, bridge. Office: Venable LLP 1800 Mercantile Bank Bldg Baltimore MD 21201 Office Phone: 410-244-7505. Personal E-mail: rlwasserman@venable.com.

WASSERMAN, ROBERT HAROLD, biology professor; b. Schenectady, Feb. 11, 1926; s. Joseph and Sylvia (Rosenberg) W.; m. Marilyn Mintz, June 11, 1950; children: Diane Jean, Arlene Lee, Judith Rose. BS, Cornell U., 1949, PhD, 1953; MS, Mich. State U., 1951. Research assoc. AEC project U. Tenn., Oak Ridge, 1953-55; sr. scientist med. div. Oak Ridge Inst. Nuclear Studies, 1955-57; assoc. prof. dept. phys. biology N.Y. State Vet. Coll., Cornell U., 1957-63, prof., 1963—, James Law prof. physiology, 1989-97, James Law prof. emeritus, 1998—, acting head phys. biology dept., 1963-64, 71, 75-76, chmn. dept. /sect. physiology, 1983-87, mem. exec. com. div. biol. sci., 1983-87. Vis. fellow Inst. Biol. Chemistry, Copenhagen, 1964-65; chmn. Conf. on Calcium Transport, 1962; co-chmn. Conf. on Cell Mechanisms for Calcium Transfer and Homeostasis, 1970; mem. adv. bd. Vitamin D Symposia, 1976—; mem. adv. bd. Symposia Calcium-Binding Proteins, 1977-2001, chmn., 1977; mem. food and nutrition bd. NRC; cons. NIH, Oak Ridge Inst. Nuclear Studies; mem. pub. affairs com. Fedn. Am. Socs. Exptl. Biology, 1974-77; chmn. com. MPI, NRC; mem. Howard Hughes pre-doctoral fellowship panel, 1999, 2000, 03. Bd. editors: Calcified Tissue Research, 1977-80, Procs. Soc. Exptl. Biol. Medicine, 1970-76, Cornell Veterinarian, Jour. Nutrition; contbr.: articles to profl. jours. Served with U.S. Army, 1944-45. Recipient Mead Johnson award, 1969, Andre Lichtwitz prize INSERM, 1982, W.F. Neuman award Am. Soc. Bone and Mineral Rsch., 1990, merit award NIH, 1993-96; Guggenheim fellow, 1964-65, 72, fellow NSF-OECD, 1964-65. Fellow Am. Inst. Nutrition, mem. Am. Physiol. Soc., Soc. Exptl. Biology and Medicine, AAAS, Nat. Acad. Scis., Sigma Xi, Phi Kappa Phi, Phi Zeta Home: 207 Texas Ln Ithaca NY 14850-1758 Business E-Mail: rhw2@cornell.edu.

WASSERMAN, STANLEY, statistician, educator; b. Louisville, Aug. 29, 1951; s. Irvin Levitch and Jeanne (Plattus) W.; m. Sarah Wilson, Feb. 3, 1974; children: Andrew Joseph, Eliot Miles. BS in Econs., U. Pa., 1973; PhD in Stats., Harvard U., 1977. Asst. prof. U. Minn., Mpls., 1977-82; assoc. prof. U. Ill., Urbana, 1982-88, prof. psychology, stats., sociology, 1988—; prof. Beckman Inst., 1993—. Vis. rschr. Columbia Univ., N.Y.C., 1978; cons., expert witness EEOC, Cleve., 1979-81; cons. V.A. Med. Ctr., Mpls., 1980-82, AT&T Communications, Basking Ridge, N.J., 1988-90. Author: Social Network Analysis, 1994; assoc. editor: Sociological Methodology, 1978-81, Jour. Am. Statis. Assn., 1987—, Psychometrika, 1988-, Am. Statistician, 1993-96, Structural Analysis, 1997-2000; guest editor: Sociol. Methods and Rsch., 1992; book review editor: Chance, 1993—; consulting editor Am. Jour. Sociology, 2000—. Treas. Montessori Sch. of Champaign-Urbana, Savoy, Ill., 1990-92, bd. dirs. WEFT-FM, 2001-03. Grantee NSF, Washington, 1979-81, 84-89, 93-2003, NIH, 1995-98, 2000-, ONR, 2002--; postdoctoral fellow Social Sci. Rsch. Coun., N.Y.C., 1978. Fellow AAAS, Am. Statis. Assn.; mem. Psychometric Soc., Royal Statis. Soc., Classification Soc. N.Am. (sec., treas. 1993-95, bd. dirs. 1996-98. 99-2000, pres. 2002-03), Internat. Network for Social Network Analysis (bd. dirs. 1997--). Achievements include reseach in applied statistics, categorical data analysis, social network analysis. Home: 2066 County Road 125 E Mahomet IL 61853-8907 Office: U Ill 603 E Daniel St Champaign IL 61820-6232 E-mail: stanwass@uiuc.edu.

WASSERMAN, STEPHEN IRA, allergist, immunologist, educator; b. Los Angeles, Dec. 17, 1942; m. Linda Morgan; children: Matthew, Zachary. BA, Stanford U., 1964; MD, UCLA, 1968. Diplomate Am. Bd. Internal Medicine, Am. Bd. Allergy and Immunology. Intern, resident Peter B. Brigham Hosp., Boston, 1968-70; fellow in allergy, immunology Robert B. Brigham Hosp., Boston, 1972-75; asst. prof. medicine Harvard U., Boston, 1975-79, assoc. prof., 1979, U. Calif.-San Diego, La Jolla, 1979-85, prof., 1985—, chief allergy tng. program Sch. Medicine, 1979-85, chief allergy div. Sch. Medicine, 1985-93, acting chmn. dept. medicine, 1986-88, chmn. dept. medicine, 1988-2000, Helen M. Ranney prof., 1992—2001, chief allergy tng.program Sch. Medicine, 2001—. Co-dir. allergy sect. Robert B. and Peter B. Brigham Hosps., 1977-79; dir. Am. Bd. Allergy and Immunology; dir. Am. Bd. Internal Medicine., chair, 1999-2000. Contbr. articles to profl. jours. Served to lt. comdr. USPHS, 1970-72, San Francisco. Fellow Am. Acad. Allergy and Immunology (pres. 1997-98); mem. Am. Soc. Clin. Investigation, Assn. Am. Physicians, Am. Assn. Immunologists, Collegium Internationale Allergologicum, Phi Beta Kappa, Alpha Omega Alpha. Office: U Calif San Diego Stein Clin Rsch Bldg Rm 244 9500 Gilman Dr MC 0637 San Diego CA 92093-0637

WASSERMAN, SUSAN VALESKY, accountant, artist, yoga instructor; b. St. Petersburg, Fla., June 5, 1956; d. Charles B. Valesky and Jeanne I. (Schulz) Morgan; m. Fred Wasserman, III, May 19, 1990; 1 child, Sara Elisabeth. BS in Merchandising, Fla. State U., 1978; BA in Acctg., U. South Fla., 1983. CPA Fla.; ChFC, cert. yoga tchr. Fla. Inst. for Integrated Yoga Studies, 2002, yoga therapist Integrated Yoga Therapy, 2004. Mgmt. trainee Burdines Dept. Stores, Miami, Fla., 1978-79; store mgr. Levi Straus Inc., San Francisco, 1979; pvt. practice acct. St. Petersburg, 1980—; acct., tax and fin. planning specialist Barber, Stowe & Co., St. Petersburg, 1997-98; owner White Egret Yoga Studio, South Pasadena, Fla., 2002—. Exhibitions include Longboat Key (Fla.) Art Ctr., 1993, Fla. Suncoast Water Color Soc., Sarasota, 1994, South Pasadena Artspring, 1998—2000 (Judges award, 1998). Mem.: Internat. Assn. Yoga Therapists, Suncoast Yoga Tchrs. Assn. (dir.), Yoga Alliance. Home and Studio: 7015 Grevilla Ave S Saint Petersburg FL 33707-2050 Office: 5800 4th St N Saint Petersburg FL 33703-1402 Office Phone: 727-347-7354. E-mail: yogisue@tampabay.rr.com.

WASSERMAN-SCHULTZ, DEBBIE, state legislator; b. Forest Hills, N.Y., Sept. 27, 1955; BA in Polit. Sci., U. Fla., 1988, MA, 1990. Mem. Fla. Ho. of Reps., 1992—. Mem. Gov.'s Commn. on Edn., 1996—; mem. legis. adv. coun. So. Regional Edn. Bd., 1995—; bd. dirs. Fla. Distance Learning Network, 1994; mem. Classrooms First Task Force, 1993. Recipient award for outstanding family advocacy Dade County Psychol. Assn., 1993, Giraffe award Women's Advocacy Majority Minority, 1993, Legis. Svc. award Fla. Assn. Women Lawyers, 1993, Quality Floridian award Fla. League of Cities, 1994, AMIT Woman of Yr. award, 1994, Outstanding Legislator of Yr. award Fla. Fedn. Bus. and Profl. Women, 1994, Rosemary Barkett award Acad. Fla. Trial Lawyers, 1995, Woman of Vision award Weizmann Inst. Sci., others; named one of Six Most Unstoppable Women, South Fla. Mag., 1994. Mem. Omicron Delta Kappa. Democrat. Jewish. Avocations: bowling, golf, politics, old houses. Office: 402 S Monroe St Tallahassee FL 32399-6526 also: 2500 Weston Rd Ste 101 Weston FL 33331-3616

WASSERSTEIN, BERNARD MANO JULIUS, historian; b. London, Jan. 22, 1948; came to U.S., 1980; s. Abraham and Margaret (Ecker) W.; m. Janet Barbara Sherrard, Nov. 29, 1981; 1 child, Charlotte Sophia. BA, Oxford U., 1969, MA, 1972, D.Phil., 1974. Rsch. fellow in politics Nuffield Coll. Oxford (Eng.) U., 1973-75, jr. lectr. politics Magdalen Coll., 1973, lectr. politics and internat. rels. Corpus Christi Coll., 1974-76; lectr. modern history U. Sheffield, Eng., 1976-80; assoc. prof. history Brandeis U., Waltham, Mass., 1980-82, prof. history, 1982-96; pres. Oxford Centre for Hebrew and Jewish Studies, Waltham, Mass., 1996—; chmn. dept. Brandeis U., Waltham, Mass., 1986-90, dean grad. sch., 1990-92. Vis. lectr. Hebrew U. of Jerusalem, 1979-80 Author: The British in Palestine, 1978, Britain and the Jews of Europe, 1939-45, 1979, The Secret Lives of Trebitsch Lincoln, 1988 (Golden Dagger award 1988), Herbert Samuel: A Political Life, 1992, Vanishing Diaspora, 1996. Inst. for Advanced Studies fellow Hebrew U. of Jerusalem, 1984-85. Fellow Royal Hist. Soc., Royal Asiatic Soc.; mem. United Oxford Club, Cambridge Univs. Club, Athanaeum (London).

WASSERSTEIN, BRUCE, investment banker; b. N.Y.C., Dec. 25, 1947; s. Morris and Lola Wasserstein; children: Pamela, Ben, Alex. BA with honors, U. Mich., 1967; MBA with high distinction, JD cum laude, Harvard U., 1971; diploma in law, Cambridge U., 1972. Assoc. Cravath, Swaine & Moore, N.Y.C., 1972-77; mng. dir. The First Boston Corp., N.Y.C., 1977-88; pres. Wasserstein, Perella and Co., NYC, 1988—2000; exec. chmn. Dresdner Kleinwort Wasserstein, NYC, 2000—01; CEO Lazard LLC, Paris, 2001—; owner American Lawyer Media, 1997—, The Daily Deal, 1999—, New York Magazine, 2003—. Author: Corporate Finance Law Trustee Dalton Sch. Mem. Council on Fgn. Relations Democrat. Office: Lazard LLC 30 Rockefeller Plaza New York NY 10020

WASSERSTEIN, WENDY, playwright; b. Bklyn., Oct. 18, 1950; d. Morris and Lola Wasserstein. BA, Mt. Holyoke Coll., 1971; MA, CCNY, 1973; MFA, Yale Drama Sch., 1976. Author: (plays) Any Woman Can't, 1973, Happy Birthday, Montpelier Pizz-zazz, 1974, (with Christopher Durang) When Dinah Shore Ruled the Earth, 1975, Uncommon Women and Others, 1975, Isn't It Romantic, 1981, Tender Offer, 1983, The Man in a Case, Miami, 1986, The Heidi Chronicles, 1988 (Pulitzer prize for drama, 1989, Outer Critics Cir. award for best play, 1989, N.Y. Drama Critics Cir. award, 1989, Susan Smith Blackburn prize, 1989), The Sisters Rosensweig, 1991 (Outer Critics Cir. award, 1993), An American Daughter, 1997, Old Money, 2000, (screenplays) Uncommon Women and Others, 1978, The Sorrows of Gin, 1979, (with Durang) House of Husbands, Isn't It Romantic, The Heidi Chronicles, (children's book) Pamela's First Musical, 1995; actress (plays) An American Daughter, Life with Mikey; author: (essays) Bachelor Girls, 1990, Shiksa Goddess, 2003. Recipient Hale Matthews Found. award; grantee Am. Playwrights Project, 1988, Commissioning Program Phoenix Theater; Guggenheim fellow, 1983. Mem.: bd. Channel Thirteen, McDowell Colony, WNET, British Am. Arts Assoc., Dramatists Guild for Young Playwrights, artistic bd. Playwrights Horizons, Coun. Dramatists Guild. Address: c/o Phyllis Wender / Rosenstone Wender 10th Fl 38 E 29th St New York NY 10021

WASSHAUSEN, DIETER CARL, systematic botanist; b. Jena, Germany, Apr. 15, 1938; came to U.S., 1950, naturalized, 1957; s. Heinz P. and Elizabeth A. (Mueller) W.; m. Merrilee M. Locklin, Dec. 23, 1961; children— Lisa A., David B. BS, George Washington U., 1962, MS, 1965, PhD, 1972. Assoc. curator dept. botany Smithsonian Instn., Washington, 1969-76; chmn., curator dept. botany Nat. Mus. Natural History, Washington, 1976—. Recipient Smithsonian Research Found. awards, 1974, 75, Willdenow medal, 1979 Mem. Am. Soc. Plant Taxonomists, Internat. Assn. Plant Taxonomy, Neotropical Field Botanists Assn., Am. Inst. Biol. Scis., AAAS, Assn. Tropical Biology, Sigma Xi. Presbyterian. Achievements include research on systematics of neotropical Acanthaceae, floristic studies in Graminea of Brazil, floristic studies in Begoniaceae, revision of Nat. List Sci. Plant Names. Home: St James Plantation 2931 Legends Dr Southport NC 28461 Office: Nat Mus Natural History 10th St And Constitution Ave N Washington DC 20560-0001 Office Phone: 202-357-2536. E-mail: dmwasshausen@aol.com.

WASSNER, STEVEN JOEL, pediatric nephrologist, educator; b. N.Y.C., Dec. 16, 1946; s. Abraham and Clara (Weitzner) W.; m. Enid K. Kling, June 11, 1972; children: Adam Jacob, Nancy Shane. BS, CCNY, 1968; MD, NYU, 1972. Diplomate Am. Bd. Pediatrics, Am. Bd. Pediatrics Nephrology. Intern, resident Children's Hosp. L.A., 1972-74, fellow in pediatric nephrology, 1974-75; rsch. fellow in pediatric nephrology UCLA, 1975-77; asst. prof. pediat. Pa. State U. M.S. Hershey Med. Ctr., Hershey, 1978-83, assoc. prof., 1983-91, prof., 1991—, vice chmn. dept., 1989-99, chief divsn. pediat. nephrology and hypertension, 1978—, chief divsn. pediatric nephrology and diabetes, 1991-99, vice-chmn. edn., 2000—. Vis. prof. human biochemistry Hebrew U., Hadassah Hosp., 1985-86; dir. Pediatric Diabetes Svc., 1998-99. Contbr. articles to med. jours. Mem. adv. bd. Kidney Found. South Ctrl. Pa., Harrisburg, 1980-90, sci. adv. coun. for pediatric nephrology/urology Nat. Kidney Found., 1986-92, Harrisburg com. for Hebrew U.; bd. dirs. Jewish Family Svc., Harrisburg, 1979-85, pres., 1983-85; bd. dirs. United Jewish Fedn., 1983-85, 94-97, Yeshiva Acad., 1987-90. Recipient Rsch. Career Devel. award NIH, 1983; Musclar Dystrophy Assn. grantee, 1979-81; Sr. Internat. fellow Fogarty Internat. Ctr. NIH, 1985. Fellow Am. Acad. Pediatrics (exec. com. sect. on nephrology, chair program subcom. 1998-2002, chmn. exec. com. sect. on nephrology 2002—), Am. Bd. Pediatrics; mem. Am. Pediatrics Soc., Am. Soc. Nephrology, Internat. Soc. Nephrology, Am. Soc. Pediatrics, Nephrology, Internat. Soc. Pediatric Nephrology, Internat. Pediatric Nephrology Assn. (counsellor 1989-95). Office: MS Hershey Med Ctr PO Box 850 Hershey PA 17033-0850 Office Phone: 717-531-5707. Business E-Mail: swassner@psu.edu.

WASSON, BARBARA HICKAM, music educator; b. Spencer, Ind., Feb. 12, 1918; Student, DePauw U., 1937-38; BA, Vassar Coll., 1939; MusM, Chgo. Mus. Coll., 1944; postgrad., Ind. U., 1962-63. Founder, co-dir. Wasson Piano Studios, Dayton, 1946—; instr. Cedarville (Ohio) Coll., Dayton, 1970-72; adj. prof. Wright State U., Dayton, 1973-78; asst. prof. U. Cin., 1982-87. Named Cert. Tchr. of Yr., Western Dist. of Ohio, 1998, 2001, Family of Yr., Ohio Fedn. Music Clubs, 2002; recipient Family of Yr. award Ohio Fedn. Music Clubs, 2002; MTNA Found. fellow, 2004. Fellow Music Tchr.'s Nat. Assn.; mem. Ohio Music Tchrs. Assn. (pres. 1980-82, chmn. western dist. 1976-78), Dayton Music Club (pres. 1989-91), Mu Phi Epsilon (pres. Dayton alumnae chpt. 1986-88), Dayton Piano Tchrs. Study Club (v.p. 2004-2006). Home: 9620 Belfry Ct Dayton OH 45458-4157 E-mail: WassonPno@aol.com.

WASSON, JAMES WALTER, aircraft electronics manufacturing company executive; b. Pitts., Dec. 9, 1951; s. George Frederick and Dolores Helen (Wuerl) W.; m. Evelyn Fay Gonzales, Dec. 28, 1974; children: Robert, Brian. AST, Pitts. Inst. Aeronautics, 1972; BSET, Northrop U., Inglewood, Calif., 1981; MBA, U. Phoenix, Mesa, 1988, govt. contracts mgmt. cert., 1989. Avionics technician various cos., 1972-74; electronics prodn. mgr. Ostgaard Industries, Gardena, Calif., 1974-75; sr. avionics design engr. Allied Signal Garrett Airesearch Aviation Co., L.A., 1975-81; v.p. engring., co-founder Avionics Engring. Svcs., Inc., Tucson, 1980-81; sr. tech. specialist Northrop Aircraft Div., Hawthorne, Calif., 1981-84; prog. mgr. McDonnell Douglas Helicopter Co., Mesa, Ariz., 1984-93; exec. v.p., co-founder Leading Edge Technologies, Inc., Mesa, 1991-95; mgr. bus. devel. McDonnell Douglas Helicopter Sys., Mesa, 1993-95; dir. advanced tech. devel. Smiths Aerospace, Inc., Grand Rapids, Mich., 1995—2004; chief tech. officer BAE Sys., Johnson City, NY, 2004—. Adj. prof. ops. mgmt., contract mgmt., program mgmt., proposal devel., strategic mgmt., mktg., tech. mgmt., rsch. projects U. Phoenix Online Campus, 1990—, chair Grad. Bus. and Mgmt. Coll., U. Phoenix, W. Mich. Campus, 2000-2004, acad. cabinet, 2001-2003; cons. in field. Author: Avionics Systems Operation and Maintenance, 1993, Business Opportunities in Artificial Intelligence, 1988; contbr. articles to profl. jours. Inventor in field. Com. chmn. industry adv. bd. Northrop U., 1981; chmn. bd. dirs., pres. Alta Mesa Community Assn., 1989; organizer Boy Scouts Am., Mesa, 1988. Named Engr. of Yr., Northrop U., 1980; recipient Disting. Alumnus award Pitts. Inst. Aeronautics, 1981, U. Phoenix, 1996; named to Hall of Fame, Career Colls. Assn., 1991. Mem. AIAA, IEEE, NSPE, Soc. Automotive Engrs., Army Aviation Assn. (chpt. sr. v.p. 1988-91, treas. 1993-95), Nat. Def. Indsl. Assn., Assn. U.S. Army, Am. Helicopter Soc. (chmn. avionics com. 1990), Assn. Avionics Educators, Rotorcraft Industry Tech. Assn. (bd. dirs. 1998-99), Crystal Springs Country Club (fin. com. 2000-01). Republican. Roman Catholic. Avocations: flying, scuba diving, hiking, golf, camping. E-mail: james.wasson@baesystems.com.

WASSON, JEFFREY, music educator; b. Evanston, Ill., Aug. 24, 1948; s. Newton Oliver and Hilda Crowell Wasson. MusB, Northwestern U., 1970, MusM, 1973, PhD, 1987. Instr. music Northwestern U., Evanston, Ill., 1980-85; asst. prof. music Barat Coll., Lake Forest, Ill., 1986-92; dir. music St. Mary of the Angels, Chgo., 1992-97, Barat Coll., Lake Forest, Ill., 1987—, assoc. prof. music, 1992-99, prof. music, 1999-2001, Barat Coll. DePaul U., 2001—02; prof. musicianship DePaul U., Chgo., 2002—. Vis. prof. music, Northwestern U., 1990, 93; bd. mem. New Music Chgo., 1987, 92-94, v.p., 1987-88, pres., 1988-92; Mozart Sinfonia, bd. mem., v.p. Ars Musica Chicago; NEH summer seminar participant, Brandeis U., 1995, Boston U., 2000; lectr. Yale U., U. Leuven, Belgium, U. Mich., Ann Arbor, U. Minn., U. Pitts., Mich. State U., Loyola U. of Chgo., U. Nebr. Editor: A Compendium of American Musicology, 2000; contbr. articles to profl. jours., chpts. to books. Summer seminar grantee NEH, U. Rochester (declined). Mem. NARAS, Am. Musicol. Soc., Am. Guild Organists, Internat. Musicol. Soc., Coll. Music Soc., Club Internationale, Phi Kappa Lambda. Episcopalian. Avocations: fine art collecting, Lionel trains. Office: DePaul Univ School Music 804 W Belden Ave Chicago IL 60614-3296

WASSON, LILA ELIZABETH, educational consultant; b. Bradenton, Fla., Jan. 6, 1924; d. Lawyer and Margaret Jane (Moore) Jenkins; m. Robert Paul Wasson, June 14, 1951; children: Robert Paul, Sandra Wasson Brown, Kathy Elizabeth. BS, Fla. A&M U., 1945, MS, 1968. Tchr. sci. Union Acad., Bartow, Fla., 1946; tchr. phys. edn. Rosenwald High Sch., Panama City, Fla., 1946-51; subs. tchr. Sunflower and Wilson Village Schs., Anchorage, 1960-63; elem. tchr. Hanscom Primary Sch., Hanscom AFB, Mass., 1965-87; ednl. cons. J.B. Enterprises, Bedford, Mass., 1990-91. Master tchr. MA in Teaching program Harvard U., Cambridge, Mass., 1968-71 Author: The Classroom Teacher's Guide: For the Beginning Years and Beyond, 1998. Mem. AAUW (rec. sec. 1990-91), LWV, Mass. Ret. Tchrs. Assn. Democrat. Baptist. Avocations: travel, reading, teaching and promoting children's literature. Home: 26 Gould Rd Bedford MA 01730-1248

WASSON, STEVEN, music educator, piano technician; b. Dayton, Ohio, June 17, 1946; s. Audley Jackson and Barbara Hickam Wasson; m. Emmagene Phyllis Goss, Nov. 27, 1971. MusB, Eastman Sch. Music, Rochester, New York, 1969; MusM, Eastman Sch. Music, 1971; D of Musical Arts, Coll. Conservatory of Music, Cin., 2000. Pvt. music tchr. Wasson Music Studio, Rochester, 1970—72, Milw., 1972—73, Dayton, Ohio, 1974—, piano technician, 1985—. Lectr. in field. Musician: Commemorative Dedications, Op. 40, Smoke And Steel, Op. 15 (Louis Lane prize Eastman Sch. Music, 1968), Paraphrases, Op. 39. Ch. coun. sec. Resurrection Evang. Luth. Ch., Centerville, Ohio, 1989—90. Mem.: BMI (assoc.), Am. Music Ctr., Assn. Wels And Els Composers (assoc.), Am. Composers Forum (assoc.), Am. Coll. Musicians (assoc.), Music Tchrs. Nat. Assn. (assoc.; Ohio state composition chmn. 1983—84). Republican. Avocations: reformation theological studies, linguistics, gardening, bowling. Home and Office: Wasson Music Studio 415 Corona Ave Dayton OH 45419-2606 E-mail: drswssnmuscstd@aol.com.

WASSON-SHAW, CAROL R. music teacher; b. Dayton, Ohio, Feb. 8, 1951; d. Audley Jackson and Barbara (Hickam) Wasson; m. Stephen D. Shaw, Feb. 21, 1981 (div. Apr. 1998); children: Tiffany Elise, Tia Nicole. BMusic in Piano Performance, Wright State U., Fairborn, Ohio, 1978. Pvt. tchr. piano, 1965—; pvt. tchr. violin and viola, 1980—; owner, mentor to music tchrs. Shaw's Music Ctr., Centerville, Ohio, 1993—. Lectr., tcht. piano to preschoolers. Chmn. jr. philharm. Dayton Philharm. Women's Assn., 1979-80; chmn. fundraiser South Dayton Montessori, Kettering, Ohio, 1987-88. Mem. Nat. Guild Piano Tchrs. (chmn. Dayton-Wasson Audition Ctr. 1998—), Music Tchrs. Nat. Assn., Dayton Music Club (chmn. judges Dist. IIIB Jr. Festival 1994—, co-chmn. 1999-2002, chmn. 2001—), Mu Phi Epsilon, Centerville Noon Optimists. Office: Shaw's Music Ctr 35 Marco Ln Centerville OH 45458-3818

WASTAWY, SOHAIR F. library dean, consultant; b. Cairo, Nov. 7, 1954; came to U.S., 1981; s. Fahmy Elsayed Wastawy and Alia Ahmed Shaffie; children: Kareim. BA, Cairo U., 1975, MA, 1978; MLS, Cath. U., 1983; PhD, Simmons Coll., 1987. Micrographics specialist Cairo U., 1975-83; asst. prof. Inst. Pub. Administrn., Riyadh, Saudi Arabia, 1984-85; info. specialist, mktg. dir. Data Processing Services, Cairo, 1983-87; info. researcher Ill. Inst. Tech., Chgo., 1988-91, dir. libr., 1991—. Cons. UN, 1989—. Mem. Egyptian Soc. Info. Sci., Ill. Libr. Assn. Republican. Office: Illinois Inst of Tech Paul V Galvin Libr 35 W 33rd St Chicago IL 60616-3739

WASTBERG, OLLE M. diplomat; b. Stockholm, May 6, 1945; s. Erik and Greta (Hirsch) W.; m. Inger Claesson, Feb. 21, 1968; children: David, Elias. BA, U. Stockholm, 1972. Tchr. polit. sci. U. Stockholm, 1967-68; journalist polit. dept. Expressen, 1968-71; editor-in-chief, 1994-95; rsch. fellow Bus. and Soc. Rsch. Ctr., 1971-76; pres. Aktiefranjandet, 1976-82; mem. Parliament, 1976-82; pres. Swedish Newspaper Promotion Assn., 1983-91; undersec. of state for fin. affairs Ministry of Fin., Stockholm, 1991-93; pres. bd. Nordic Investment Bank, 1992-94, Swedish Broadcasting Corp., 1996-99; consul gen. for Sweden in NY, 1999—. Dir. Stockholm Stock Exchange, 1977-82, 88-92;group of 10 deputies IMF, 1991-93; Swedish del. meeting of ministries of fin., 1992; mem. govt. com. on S. Africa consumer politics and stock market; pres. Bertil Ohlin Inst., 1996-2000. Author books on African problems, immigration politics and econ. topics; contbr. articles to profl. jour. Polit. sec. Liberal Youth Sweden, 1966, v.p., 1996-71; bd. Liberal Party, 1972-93, 97-2000, pres. exec. com., 1982-83; bd. dir. Friends of Hebrew U. of Jerusalem. Recipient Gold medal Swedish Mktg. Group, 1982; Swedish Man of the Yr., NY, 2003. Home: 600 Park Ave New York NY 10021-7010 Office: Consulate Gen of Sweden One Dag Hammarskjold Plz 885 2d Ave 45th Fl New York NY 10017-2201 Office Phone: 212-583-2550. E-mail: olle@wastberg.nu.

WASTERLAIN, CLAUDE GUY, neurologist; b. Courcelles, Belgium, Apr. 15, 1935; s. Desire and Simone (De Taeye) W.; m. Anne Marguerite Thomsin, Feb. 28, 1967; 1 child, Jean Michel. Cand. Sci., U. Liege, 1957, MD, 1961; LS in Molecular Biology, U. Brussels, 1969. Resident Cornell U. Med. Coll., NYC, 1964-67, instr. neurology, 1969-70, asst. prof., 1970-75, assoc. prof., 1975-76, UCLA Sch. Medicine, 1976-79, prof., 1979—, vice chair dept. neurology, 1976—; chief neurology svc. VA Med. Ctr., Sepulveda, Calif., 1976—. Attending neurologist UCLA Ctr. Health Scis., 1976—; chair neurology Greater LA VA Health Care Sys., 1998—. Author, editor: Status Epilepticus, 1984, Neonatal Seizures, 1990, Molecular Neurobiology and Epilepsy, 1992, Progressive Nature of Epileptogenesis, 1996; contbr. articles to med. jours. William Evans fellow, U. Auckland, New Zealand, 1984; recipient N.Y. Neurol. Soc. Young Investigator award, 1965, Rsch. Career Devel. award NIH, 1973-76, Worldwide AES award for rsch. in epilepsy, 1992, Golden Hammer Tchg. award, 1996, Amb. for Epilepsy, Internat. League Against Epilepsy, 2003. Fellow Am. Acad. Neurology; mem. Am. Neurol. Assn., Am. Soc. Neurochemistry (coun. mem. 1991-97), Internat. Soc. Neurochemistry, Am. Epilepsy Soc., Royal Soc. Medicine. Avocations: tennis, skiing, jazz, theater. Office: West LA VA Med Ctr 11301 Wilshire Blvd Los Angeles CA 90073 Office Phone: 310-268-3595. Business E-Mail: wasterla@ucla.edu.

WATABE, NORIMITSU, biology and marine science educator; b. Kure, Hiroshima, Japan, Nov. 29, 1922; came to U.S., 1957; s. Isamu and Matsuko (Takamatsu) W.; m. Sakuko Kobayashi, Dec. 12, 1952; children: Shoichi, Sachiko. BS, 1st Nat. High Sch., Tokyo, 1945; MS, Tohoku U., Sendai, Japan, 1948, DSc, 1960. Rsch. investigator Fuji Pearl Co., Mie-ken, Japan, 1948-52; instr. Prefect U. Mie, Tsu, Mie-ken, 1952-55, asst. prof., 1955-59; rsch. assoc. Duke U., Durham, N.C., 1957-70; assoc. prof. U. S.C., Columbia, 1970-72, prof. biology and marine sci., 1972-93, disting. prof., 1993-94, disting. prof. emeritus, 1994—. Cons, Ford Found., 1968; vis. prof. U. Bonn, Germany, 1976-77; dir. Electron Microscopy Ctr., 19770-95; cons. in field. Author: Studies on Pearls, 1959; editor: Mechanisms of Mineralization, 1976, Mechanisms of Biomineralization, 1980, Hard Tissue Mineralization and Demineralization, 1991; assoc. editor, Jour. Morphology, 1999—; contbr. numerous sci. articles to profl. jours. Recipient Pearl Rsch. award Elmer W. Ellsworth, 1952, alexander Von Humboldt award Govt. of Germany, Russel award U. S.C., 1981; grantee NIH, 1971-76, NSF, 1973-95. Fellow AAAS; mem. Am. Micros. Soc. (life). Avocations: music, piano playing. Home: 3510 Greenway Dr Columbia SC 29206-3416 Office: Dept Biol Sci Univ S Carolina Columbia SC 29208-0001

WATANABE, AUGUST MASARU, physician, medical educator; b. Portland, Oreg., Aug. 17, 1941; s. Frank H. and Mary Y. W.; m. Margaret Whildin Reese, Mar. 14, 1964; children: Nan Reiko, Todd Franklin, Scott Masaru. BS, Wheaton (Ill.) Coll., 1963; MD, Ind. U., 1967. Diplomate Am. Bd. Internal Medicine. Intern Ind. U. Med. Center, Indpls., 1967-68, resident, 1968-69, 71-72, fellow in cardiology, 1972-74; clin. assoc. NIH, 1969-71; clin. instr. medicine Georgetown U. Med. Sch., Washington, 1970-71; mem. faculty Ind. U. Sch. Medicine, Indpls., 1972—2003, prof. medicine and pharmacology, 1978—2003, chmn. dept. medicine, 1983-90; dir. Regenstrief Inst. for Health Care Ind. U. Sch. of Medicine, Indpls., 1984-90; from v.p. to group v.p. rsch. labs. Eli Lilly & Co., Indpls., 1990-94, v.p., pres. labs, 1994-95; exec. v.p. sci. and tech. Eli Lilly and Co., Indpls., 1996—2003; chmn. bd. BioCrossroads, 2003—. Mem. pharmacology study sect. NIH, 1979-81, chmn., 1981-83; mem. cardiovasc.-renal adv. com. FDA, 1982-85, mem. com. A, Nat. Heart, Lung and Blood Inst., 1984-88, chmn., 1986-88; bd. dirs. Guidant Corp.; cons. to fed. govt. and industry. Contbr. articles to profl. jours.; editorial bds. sci. jours. Bd. dirs. Ind. U. Found., 1989—, Indpls. Symphony Orch., 1994—, Regenstrief Found., 1995—, Riley Children's Fund. NIH grantee, 1972-92. Fellow ACP, Am. Coll. Cardiology, Am. Heart Assn. (councils on clin. cardiology and circulation, research rev. com. Ind. affiliate 1978-82, research and adv. com. North Central region 1978-82, adv. com. cardiovascular drugs 1976-79, chmn. com. 1979-81, chmn. program com. council on basic sci. 1982-84, chmn. com. on sci. sessions programs 1985-88, bd. dirs. 1985-88), Am. Coll. Cardiology (govt. relations com. 1979-81, trustee 1982-87); mem. Am. Fedn. Clin. Research (councilor Midwest sect. 1976-77, chmn.-elect Midwest sect. 1977-78, chmn. sect. 1978-79, chmn. sect. nominating com. 1979-80), Am. Soc. Clin. Investigation, Am. Soc. Clin. Pharmacology and Therapeutics, Am. Soc. Pharmacology and Exptl. Therapeutics (exec. com. div. clin. pharmacology 1978-81), Cardiac Muscle Soc., Central Soc. Clin. Research (councillor 1983-86, pres.-elect 1989, pres. 1990), Internat. Soc. Heart Research, Assn. Am. Physicians, Assn. Profs. of Medicine, Sigma Xi. Office: BioCrossroads Baker and Daniels Bldg 300 N Meridian St Ste 950 Indianapolis IN 46204

WATANABE, CORINNE KAORU AMEMIYA, judge, state official, lawyer; b. Wahiawa, Hawaii, Aug. 1, 1950; d. Keiji and Setsuko Amemiya; m. Edwin Tsugio Watanabe, Mar. 8, 1975; children: Traciann Keiko, Brad Natsuo, Lance Yoneo. BA, U. Hawaii, 1971; JD, Baylor U., 1974. Bar: Hawaii 1974. Dep. atty. gen. State of Hawaii, Honolulu, 1974-84, 1st dep. atty. gen., 1984-85, 87-92, atty. gen., 1985-87; assoc. judge Hawaii Intermediate Ct. Appeals, Honolulu, 1992—. Mem. ABA, Hawaii Bar Assn. Office: Hawaii Intermediate Ct Appeals 426 Queen St 2d Fl Honolulu HI 96813

WATANABE, KEN, actor; b. Koide, Niigata, Japan, Oct. 21, 1959; 2 children. Actor: (films) Setouchi shonen yakyu dan, 1984, Kekkon annai mystery, 1985, Tampopo, 1985, Umi to dokuyaku, 1986, Bakumatsu jyunjyoden, 1991, Rajio no jikan, 1997, Kizuna, 1998, Supêsutoraberâzu, 2000, Oboreru sakana, 2001, Sennen no koi-Hikaru Genji monogatari, 2001, Hi wa mata noboru, 2002, T.R.Y., 2003, The Last Samurai, 2003 (Acad. Award nomination for best supporting actor, 2004); (TV series) Kimitachi ga ite boku ga iru, 1992, Ikebukuro West Gate Park, 2000, Hojo Tokumune, 2001. Mailing: c/o Roar 2400 Broadway Santa Monica CA 90404

WATANABE, KYOICHI A(LOYSIUS), chemist, researcher, pharmacology educator; b. Amagasaki, Hyogo, Japan, Feb. 28, 1935; s. Yujiro Paul and Yoshiko Francisca (Hashimoto) W.; m. Krystyna Lesiak; children: Kanna, Kay, Kenneth, Kim, Kelly, Katherine. BA, Hokkaido U., 1958, PhD, 1963. Lectr. Sophia U., Tokyo, 1963; rsch. assoc. Sloan-Kettering Inst., N.Y.C., 1963—66, assoc., 1968—72, 1972—81, prof., 1981—95; rsch. fellow U. Alta., Edmonton, Canada, 1966—68; assoc. prof. Cornell U. Med. Coll., N.Y.C., 1972—81, prof. pharmacology, 1981—98; dir. organic chemistry Codon Pharm., Inc., Gaithersburg, Md., 1996—98; v.p. R&D Pharmasset Inc., Tucker, Ga., 1998—; vis. prof. chem. dept. Emory U., 2003—. Study sect. NIH, Washington, 1981-84. Recipient Szalecki medal, Wojzkowa Akademia Medyczna, 1989, Marie Sklodowska Curie medal, Polish Chem. Soc., 1993, František Šorm Meml. award, Czech Acad. Scis., 2002. Mem. Polish Chem. Soc. (hon.), Russian Acad. Sci. (bd. sci. cons. Engelhardt Inst. Molecular Biology 1994-97). Achievements include rsch. in total synthesis of nucleoside antibiotics, novel heterocycle ring transformation, C-nucleoside chemistry, antiviral and anticancer nucleosides, intercalating agents, modified oligonucleotides, triplex DNA for gene repair.

WATANABE, MAMORU, former university dean, physician, researcher; b. Vancouver, B.C., Can., Mar. 15, 1933; s. Takazo and Nao (Suginobu) W.; m. Marie Katie Bryndzak, June 1, 1974; 1 child, David. MD, McGill U., 1957, PhD, 1963. Intern Royal Victoria Hosp., Montreal, 1957—58, resident in medicine, 1958—63; prof. medicine U. Alta., Edmonton, 1967—74, U. Calgary, 1974—97, head internal medicine, 1974—76, assoc. dean edn., 1976—80, assoc. dean research, 1980—81, acting dean medicine, 1981—82, dean faculty medicine, 1982—92, prof. emeritus, 1997—. Fellow Royal Coll. Physicians and Surgeons (Can.). Home: 162 Pumpridge Place SW Calgary AB Canada T2V 5E6 Office: U Calgary 3330 Hospital Dr NW Calgary AB Canada T2N 1N4 E-mail: watanabe@ucalgary.ca.

WATANABE, PAUL YASHIHIKO, political scientist, educator; b. Murray, Utah, Mar. 14, 1951; s. Hikomune and Ida (Hiraga) W.; m. Gloria Gustafson, Aug. 25, 1975; children: Benjamin Gustafson, Joanna Stahr. BS, U. Utah, 1972; MA, Harvard U., 1975, PhD, 1980. Asst. prof. dept. polit. sci. U. Mass., Boston, 1980-85, assoc. prof., 1985—, chair dept. polit. sci., 1985-90, dir. hons. program, 1990-93, co-dir. inst. Asian Am. studies, 1993—, co-dir., acting dir. pub. policiy PhD program, 1995-96. Author: Ethnic Groups, Congress and American Foreign Policy, 1984. Mem. South Shore area bd. Dept. Social Svc. Com. Mass., Quincy, 1983-89; bd. Overseers Harvard Cmty. Health Plan, Brookline, Mass., 1985-91; mem. acad. adv. com. John. F. Kennedy Libr., Boston, 1991—; bd. dirs. Mass. Immigrant Refugee Advocacy Coalition, Boston, 1992—, Asian Pacific Am. Agenda Coalition, Boston, 1995—; mem. nat. acad. bd. Asian Am. Policy Rev., Cambridge, 1994—. Mem. Phi Beta Kappa. Home: 65 Torrey St South Weymouth MA 02190-2533 Office: Inst Asian Am Studies U Mass 100 Morrissey Blvd Boston MA 02125-3300 E-mail: paul.watanabe@umb.edu.

WATANABE, ROY NOBORU, lawyer; b. Honolulu, July 23, 1947; s. Tadao I. and Clara Y. W. AB, Columbia Coll., 1969; JD, Columbia U., 1973. Bar: N.Y. 1974, U.S. Dist. Ct. (so. and ea. dists.) N.Y. 1976, U.S. Ct. Appeals (2d cir.) 1976. Honors program atty. Office of Labor Rels., Office of Mayor, N.Y.C., 1973-76; assoc. Frankle & Greenwald, N.Y.C., 1976, Cohn, Glickstein, Lurie, Ostrin, Lubell & Lubell, N.Y.C., 1976-79; ptnr. Cohn, Glickstein & Lurie (formerly Cohn, Glickstein, Lurie, Ostrin, Lubell & Lubell, N.Y.C., 1979-88, Spivak, Lipton, Watanabe, Spivak & Moss, 1989—. Guest lectr. labor law Boston Coll., 1982, Union U., 1983, 85, Mercer U., 1997—2001, NYU Law Sch., 1998; mem. faculty Practicing Law Inst., N.Y.C., 1987; panelist, lectr. regional conf. NY State Bar Assn. and NLRB, N.Y.C., 1986; mem. adv. bd. Ctr. for Labor and Employment Law, NYU Sch. Law, 2000—; author, commentator 50th ann. labor conf. NYU, 1997 Contbg. author: NLRA Law and Practice, 1991. Cooperating atty. Asian Am. Legal Def. & Edn. Fund., N.Y.C., 1982—; mem. bd. dirs. lawyers coordinating com. AFL-CIO, 2000—. Nat. Def. Fgn. Language fellow, Columbia U., 1967. Mem. Assn. of Bar of City of N.Y. (labor and employment law com. 1980-83, 86-89, legal and edn. and admission to bar com. 1984-85), N.Y. State Bar Assn. (exec. com., co-chair practice before N.Y. State Labor Rels. Bd. and Nat. Labor Rels. Bd. com. 1989-93, labor arbitration com. 1983—, entertainment, arts and sports law sect. 1989—) Office: Spivak Lipton Et Al 1700 Broadway Fl 21 New York NY 10019-5905 Office Phone: 212-765 2100 Business E-Mail: rwatanabe@spivak-lipton.com.

WATARU, WESTON YASUO, civil engineer; b. Honolulu, Mar. 30, 1957; s. Ralph Mitsuo and Anna Setsuko (Ogami) W.; m. Celine Jacqueline Teasdale, Nov. 1, 1986; children: Maile, Hope, Amber, Adam. BS, U. Hawaii, 1980. Registered profl. engr., Hawaii. Asst. engr. Dames and Moore, Honolulu, 1980-82; civil engr. I City and County of Honolulu Dept. Pub. Works, 1982-84, civil engr. IV, 1985-87, civil engr. V, 1987-89, svc. engr., civil engr. VI, 1989-98, civil engr. VI City and County of Honolulu Dept. Planning and Permitting, 1998—. Mem. utilities coord. com. City and County of Honolulu, 1989—, mem. permit streamlining task force, 1995—. Mem. ASCE, NSPE, Am. Pub. Works Assn., Hawaii Govt. Employees Assn. Avocations: family, sporting events, basketball, reading. Office: City and County of Honolulu Dept Planning and Permitting 650 S King St Dept And Honolulu HI 96813-3078

WATCHMAKER, KENNETH, retail executive; CFO, exec. v.p. Reebok Internat. Ltd., Stoughton, Mass. Office: Reebok Internat Ltd 1895 J W Foster Blvd Canton MA 02021-1099

WATCHORN, WILLIAM ERNEST, venture capitalist; b. Toronto, Ont., Can., Aug. 8, 1943; s. Roy Elgin and Josephine (Swyrida) W.; m. Maureen Emmett, Dec. 28, 1967; 1 child, Meghan. Chartered Acct., Toronto, 1967. Mgr. fin. planning Found. Group of Cos., Toronto, 1968-70; cons. Regional Master Planning Study, Malaysia, 1970-72; controller Selkirk Holdings, Ltd., Toronto, 1972-75; corp. contr. Torstar Corp., Toronto, 1975-78; v.p. fin. Canwest Capital Corp., Winnipeg, Man., 1978-82; exec. v.p. Kaiser Resources Ltd., Vancouver, B.C., 1982; sr. v.p., CFO, Fed. Industries Ltd., Winnipeg, 1982-88; pres., CEO, Fed. Industries Indsl. Group, Winnipeg, 1989-91; CEO, Ensis Corp., Inc., Winnipeg, 1991-97; founder, pres., CEO, Ensis Growth Fund Inc., Ensis Mgmt. Inc., Winnipeg, 1997—; pres., CEO Altura Growth Fund (EVCC) Inc., Altura Mgmt., Inc., Vancouver, Canada, 2002—. Bd. dirs. Ensis Growth Fund Inc., Winnipeg Airports Authority Inc., Altura Growth Fund (EVCC) Inc.; mem. Manitoba Bus. Coun. Bd. dirs. C.D. Howe Inst., Toronto, Can. Stds. Assn. Fellow Man. Inst. Chartered Accts.; mem. Can. Inst. Chartered Accts., Winter Club, St. Charles Country Club. Avocations: squash, golf, tennis. Home: 6453 Southboine Dr Winnipeg MB Canada R3R 0B7 Office: Ensis Growth Fund Inc 200 Graham Ave Ste 1120 Winnipeg MB Canada R3C 4L5

WATERBURY, ELIZABETH FLORIA, conductor; b. Verona, Italy, Sept. 27, 1956; d. John Francis and Floria Maria Leet; m. Robert Franklyn Waterbury, Dec. 20, 1981; 1 child, Dashiell. BA, San Jose State U.; M in piano, Conservatory of Music, 1982; DMA in conducting, UCSB, 1991. Interim Artistic Dir. San Francisco boys choir, 1988—90; asst. condr. Santa Barbara Grand Opera, 1991—92; founder/dir. Santa Barbara Children's Chorus, 1990—98; choral activities Shasta Coll., 1999—. Mem.: Nat. Assn. Tchrs. Singing, Am. Choral Directors Assn. Office: Shasta Coll 11555 Old Oregon Trail Redding CA 96049

WATERBURY, JACKSON DEWITT, retired marketing executive; b. Evanston, Ill., Feb. 4, 1937; s. Jackson D. and Eleanor (Barrows) W.; m. Suzanne Butler, Aug. 27, 1958 (div. Jan. 1970); children: JAckson D. III, Arthur Barrows; m. Lynn Hardin, Mar. 17, 1971 (div. July 1984); 1 child, Timothy Bradford; m. Carolyn Jenkins, Sept. 20, 1986; children: Kathryn Britt, Daniel Jenkins. AB, Brown U., 1959. Acct. exec. D'Arcy Advt. Co., St. Louis, 1958-63, Batz-Hodgson-Neuwohner, Inc., St. Louis, 1963-66; exec. v.p., sec. Lynch, Philips & Waterbury, Inc., St. Louis, 1966-68; pres. Jackson Waterbury & Co., St. Louis, 1968-73; v.p., ptnr. Vinyard & Lee & Ptnrs., St. Louis, 1973-74; pres. Waterbury, Inc., St. Louis, 1975-80, Bright Ideas, Inc., St. Louis, 1977-80; v.p., group supr. Batz-Hodgson-Neuwoehner, St. Louis, 1980-81; sr. v.p. Fawcett McDermott Cavanagh, Honolulu, 1981-82; prin. Waterbury Cons., Honolulu, 1982-88; sr. v.p. planning & rsch. Kenrick Advt., Inc., St. Louis, 1984-86; chmn. Pocket Guide Publs., Inc., Denver, 1986-97, Mountain Sports Sales, Inc., Denver, 1986-89; v.p., group supr. Kerlick Switzer & Johnson, Inc., St. Louis, 1987-88; chmn., CEO Keystone Group, St. Louis, 1988-92; v.p. mktg. Cambridge Engring., Chesterfield, Mo., 1997-2000; ret., 2000. Chmn. publicity U.S. Golf assn. Open Championship, 1964. Bd. dirs. Alice Blake Realtors, 1971-79, Children's Christmas Found., 1966-79; football coach Mo. High Sch. All-Stars, 1966-67, St. Louis U., 1968-70; vice chmn. bd. dirs. Hawaii Soccer Assn., 1981-83. Mem. Ducks Unltd., St. Louis Advt. Producers Assn. (steering com., neogtiating com. 1977-80), Beta Theta Pi. Episcopalian. Home: 118 N Bemiston Ave Saint Louis MO 63105-3811

WATERER, BONNIE CLAUSING, retired secondary school educator; b. Toledo, Sept. 25, 1940; d. Kermit Henry and Helen Ethel (Waggoner) Clausing; m. Louis P. Waterer, June 17, 1961; children: Ryan, Reid. BS in Home Econs. Edn., Ohio State U., 1962; MA in Home Econs. Edn., San Jose State U., 1966. Tchr. James Lick H.S., San Jose, 1963-67, 1973-76; adult edn. instr. Met. Adult Edn. Program, San Jose, 1968-75; home econs. instr. Independence H.S., San Jose, 1976-99, home econs. dept. chair, 1976-80; home econs. coord. East Side Union H.S. Dist., San Jose, 1980-99, coord. coll. and career resource ctrs., 1995-99, ret., 1999—. Child care occupations instr. Ctrl. County Occupl. Ctr., San Jose, 1989-99; child devel. instr. Evergreen Valley Coll., San Jose, 1995 Bd. dirs. NAMI Yavapai County, Ariz. Mem.: AAUW (v.p. Prescott br. 2004—), Home Econs. Tchrs. Assn. Calif. (pres. 1989—91, Outstanding Tchr. award 1987), Calif. Assn. Family and Consumer Sci. (Tchr. of Yr. award 1994), Am. Assn. Family and Consumer Sci., Phi Upsilon Omicron, Delta Kappa Gamma (sec. Prescott br. 2002—), Omicron Nu. Democrat. Methodist. Avocations: travel, computing, cooking, sewing. Home: 1052 Vantage Pt Cir Prescott AZ 86301 E-mail: bh2oer@aol.com.

WATERHOUSE, STEPHEN LEE, management consultant; b. Sanford, Maine, Mar. 31, 1943; s. James William and Evelyn Anita Waterhouse; m. Linda S. Lenge, July 3, 1967; children: Melinda Harwood, James Stephen. AB in Chemistry, Dartmouth Coll., 1965, MBA in Mktg., 1967. Mfg. exec. Procter and Gamble, Boston, Chgo., N.Y.C., 1967-73; cons. to pres. Avon Products, N.Y.C., 1973-75; head European ops. London, 1976-77; sr. exec. officer jewelry div. N.Y.C., 1978-80; v.p. European ops. Revlon, Paris, 1981-82; v.p. U.S. div. Thomas Tilling Ltd., N.Y.C. and London, 1983; chmn., sr. ptnr. Hanover Ptnrs. Ltd., N.Y.C., London, Zurich and Lugano, Switzerland,

1983—; ptnr. Occom Ptnrs. LLC, Boston, 1995—. Alumni coun. mem. Dartmouth Coll., Hanover, N.H., 1979-82, pres. class 1975-80; pres. Dartmouth Coll. Treas. Assn., 1993-95; trustee Hartwick Coll., Oneonta, N.Y., 1995—; bd. dirs. Internat. Festival Statue of Liberty Celebration, N.Y.C., 1986-87. With USAR, 1967-73. Recipient Dartmouth Alumni award, 1992. Mem. Global Exec. Search Profl. Assn., U.K. Inst. Dirs., Friends of Templeton Coll., Oxford U., London Sch. Econs. Club., Yale Club, London Capital Club. Avocations: skiing, travel. Office: 50 E 42nd St Ste 507 New York NY 10017-5405

WATERHOUSE, TRENTON DEAN, marketing director; b. Phoenix, Ariz., Oct. 28, 1968; s. Larry D. and Judith A. (Timmer) W. BSBA, Georgetown U., 1990. Mktg. asst. NYNEX, Washington, 1987-90, syst. engr., 1990-92, Cabletron Sys., Washington, 1992-93; program mktg. mgr. Cabletron Systems Federal, Rochester, N.H., 1993-97, program mktg. dir., 1997-2000; dir. mktg. Aprisma, Portsmouth, NH, 2000—. Contbr. articles to profl. jours. Avocations: reading, fine arts, plays, Broadway shows, dining. Office: Aprisma 273 Corporate Dr Portsmouth NH 03801 E-mail: trent@aprisma.com.

WATERHOUSE, WILLIAM CHARLES, mathematics professor; b. Galveston, Tex., Dec. 31, 1941; s. William Taylor and Grace Louise (Drum) W.; m. Betty Ann Senk, Oct. 11, 1980. AB summa cum laude, Harvard U., 1963, AM, 1964, PhD, 1968. Rsch. fellow NRC/ONR, Cornell U., Ithaca, N.Y., 1968-69; asst. prof. Cornell U., 1969-75; assoc. prof. Pa. State U., University Park, Pa., 1975-80, prof. math., 1980—. Author: Introduction to Affine Group Schemes, 1979; author papers in math. and history of math. Mem. Math. Assn. Am. (Ford awards 1984, 95), Am. Math. Soc. Home: 1335 Harris St State College PA 16803-3022 Office: Pa State U 431 Mcallister Bldg University Park PA 16802-6404

WATERMAN, CHARLES ALBERT, actor, director, retired sales executive; b. New Rochelle, NY, June 15, 1935; s. Burleigh R. and Mabel O. (Thompson) W. BS in Comm., Northwestern U., 1957. Sales rep. The Wall St. Jour., N.Y.C., 1964-66, McCalls Mag., N.Y.C., 1966-67, Holiday Mag., N.Y.C., 1967-69, Time Mag., N.Y.C., 1969-71, Travel & Leisure Mag., N.Y.C., 1971-73; sales mgr. Gambler's World Mag., N.Y.C., 1973-74; travel mgr. Bon Apetit Mag., N.Y.C., 1974-76; founder River Co. Author: The Snappy Poems, 1996, Watermarks, 2003. Dir. Gallery Theatre Round Top Ctr. for the Arts, Damariscotta, Maine, 1991-94; dir. Lincoln County Cmty. Theatre and Orch., Damariscotta, 1997—. Capt. USMCR, 1957-60. Mem. Am. Fedn. Radio and TV Artists, SAG (N.Y.C., L.A.). mem. Actors Equity Assn., 1956-1996. Home: 22 River Rd Apt A Newcastle ME 04553

WATERMAN, CHRISTOPHER, dean; MusB in Composition and Electric Bass, Berklee Coll. Music; PhD in Anthropology, U. Ill. Assoc. prof. music U. Wash., head ethnomusicology program, chair African studies com.; prof. dept. world arts and cultures UCLA, 1996—, chair dept., 1997, acting dean, 2002—04, dean Sch. Arts and Arch., 2004—. Author: Juju: A Social History and Ethnography of an African Popular Music, 1990; co-author: American Popular Music: From Minstrelsy to MTV, 2002. Recipient Ethel Curry Disting. Lectureship in Musicology, U. Mich. Achievements include cited by Rolling Stone magazine for his innovative course on world popular music, 1992. Office: UCLA Sch Arts and Arch Box 951427 303 E Melnitz Los Angeles CA 90095-1427*

WATERMAN, DANIEL, mathematician, educator; b. Bklyn., Oct. 24, 1927; s. Samuel and Anna (Robson) W.; m. Mudite Upesleja, Nov. 4, 1960; children: Erica, Susan, Scott. BA, Bklyn. Coll., 1947; MA, Johns Hopkins U., 1948; PhD, U. Chgo., 1954. Research assoc. Cowles Commn. Research in Econs., Chgo., 1951-52; instr. Purdue U., West Lafayette, Ind., 1953-55, asst. prof., 1955-59, U. Wis.-Milw., 1959-61; prof. Wayne State U., Detroit, 1961-69, Syracuse (N.Y.) U., 1969-96, prof. emeritus, 1996—, chmn. math dept., 1988-94. Cons. Martin-Marietta, Denver, 1960-61; rschr. in real and Fourier analysis, rsch. prof. Fla. Atlantic U., 1997—. Author: Homeomorphisms in Analysis, 1997; editor: Classical Real Analysis, 1985; contbr. articles to profl. jours. Fulbright fellow U. Vienna, 1952-53 Mem. Math. Assn. Am., Am. Math. Soc. (coun. mem.-at-large 1975-78), JMAA (assoc. editor 1997—), Radovi Matematicki (editl. advisor 1986—), Sigma Xi. Home: 7739 Majestic Palm Dr Boynton Beach FL 33437-5413

WATERMAN, MICHAEL SPENCER, mathematics educator, biology educator; b. Coquille, Oreg., 1942; s. Ray S. and Bessie E. Waterman; m. Vicki Lynn Buss, 1962 (div. 1977); 1 child, Tracey Lynn BS, Oreg. State U., 1964, MS, 1966; MA, Mich. State U., 1968, PhD, 1969. Assoc. prof. Idaho State U., Pocatello, 1969-75; mem. staff Los Alamos Nat. Lab., 1975-82, cons., 1982—; prof. math. and biology U. So. Calif., L.A., 1982—, U. So. Calif. Assocs. Endowed Chair, 1991—. Vis. prof. math. U. Hawaii, Honolulu, 1979-80; vis. prof. structural biology U. Calif.-San Francisco, 1982; vis. prof. Mt. Sinai Med. Sch., N.Y.C., 1988; 150th anniversary vis. prof. Chalmers U., 2000; Aisenstadt chair U. Montreal, 2001. Author: Introduction to Computational Biology, 1995; editor: Mathematical Methods for DNA Sequences, Calculating the Secrets of Life, 1995, Genetic Mapping and DNA Sequencing, 1996, Mathematical Support for Molecular Biology, 1999; Annals of Combinatories, Methodology and Computing in Applied Probability, Genomics, Computational Methods in Science and Technology, Acta Biochimica et Biophysica Sinca; editor-in-chief: Jour. Computational Biology; contbr. numerous articles on math. stats., biology to profl. jours. Recipient Internat. award, Gardner Found., 2002; fellow, Guggenheim Found., 1995; grantee, NSF, 1971, 1972, 1975, 1988—, Los Alamos Nat. Lab., 1976, 1981, Sys. Devel. Found., 1982—87, NIH, 1986—99, Sloan Found., 1990—91. Fellow AAAS, Am. Acad. Arts and Scis., Celera Genomics, Inst. Math. Stats.; mem. NAS, Am. Statis. Assn., Soc. Math. Biology, Soc. Indsl. and Applied Math. Office: U So Calif Dept Biol Sci Los Angeles CA 90089-1340

WATERMAN, MIGNON REDFIELD, public relations executive, state legislator; b. Billings, Mont., Oct. 13, 1944; d. Zell Ashley and Mable Erma (Young) Redfield; m. Ronald Fredrick Waterman, Sept. 11, 1965; children: Briar, Kyle. Student, U. Mont., 1963-66. Lobbyist Mont. Assn. Chs., Helena, 1986-90; mem. Mont. Senate, Dist. 26, Helena, 1990—; with pub. rels. dept. Mont. Coun. Tchrs. Math., Helena, 1991-96. Mem. edn., pub. welfare and instns. sub-com. fin. and claims commn. Mont. Senate, rev. oversight com., 1995—, post-secondary policy & budget com., 1995—. Sch. trustee Helena (Mont.) Sch. Dist. 1, 1978-90; bd. dirs. Mont. Hunger Coalition, 1985—; pres. Mont. Sch. Bds. Assn., 1989-90; active Mont. Alliance for Mentally Ill (Mon Ami award 1991). Recipient Marvin Heintz award Mont. Sch. Bds. Assn., 1987, Friends of Edn. award Mont. Assn. Elem. and Middle Sch. Prins., 1989, Child Advocacy award Mont. PTA, 1991, award Mont. Alliance for Mentally Ill, 1991, Outstanding Adv. award Nat. Easter Seals Soc., 1997, Pres.'s award Mont. Assn. Rehab., 1997. Mem. Mont. Sch. Bds. Assn. (Marvin Heintz award 1988, pres.1989-90), Mont. Elem. Sch. Prins., Mont. Parent, Teacher, Student Assn. (child advocacy award 1991). Democrat. Methodist. Home and Office: 530 Hazelgreen Ct Helena MT 59601-5410 Office: Mt State Senate State Capitol Helena MT 59620

WATERMAN, ROBERT A. lawyer; b. L.A., Jan. 4, 1954; m. Leslie Waterman; 2 children. BA summa cum laude, Calif. State U., Long Beach, 1976; JD, U. Calif., Berkeley, 1979. Bar: Calif. 1979. Mem. McCutchen, Doyle, Brown & Enersen, San Francisco; ptnr. Latham & Watkins; sr. v.p., gen. counsel HCA, 1997—. Assoc. editor Calif. Law Rev., 1977-78, note and comment editor, 1978-79. Mem. State Bar Calif. Office: HCA Inc 1 Park Plaza Nashville TN 37203

WATERS, ALICE, executive chef, restaurant owner, writer; b. Chatham, N.J., Apr. 28, 1944; 1 child. Grad. in French Cultural Studies, U. Calif., Berkeley, 1967; postgrad., Montessori Sch., London; degree (hon.), Mills Coll., Oakland, Calif., 1994. Exec. chef, owner Chez Panisse, Berkeley, Calif., 1971—, Chez Panisse Cafe, Berkeley, Calif., 1980—, Cafe Fanny, Berkeley, Calif., 1984—. Mem. adv. bd. U. Calif., Berkeley; active The Garden Project, San Francisco; spkr. in field of food safety and health. Author: Chez Panisse Menu Cookbook, Chez Panisse Vegetables, (storybook and cookbook for children) Fanny at Chez Panisse. Developer Martin Luther King Jr. Mid. Sch. Edible Schoolyard, Berkeley. Named Best Chef in Am., James Beard Found., 1992, Best Restaurant in Am., 1992, Humanitarian of Yr., 1997, Mother of Am. Cooking, N.Y. Times; named one of 10 Best Chefs in the World, Cuisine et Vins du France, 1986; recipient Spl. Achievement award, James Beard Found., 1985, Restaurant and Bus. Leadership award, Restaurants and Instns. Mag., 1987, Barbar Boxer Top Ten Women award, 1991, Le Tour du Monde en 80 Toques, Metziner & Varaut, 1991, Nat. Edn. Diplomate award, 1996. Office: Chez Panisse 1517 Shattuck Ave Berkeley CA 94709-1598

WATERS, BETTY LOU, newspaper reporter, writer; b. Texarkana, Tex., June 13, 1943; d. Chester Hinton and Una Erby (Walls) W. AA, Texarkana Jr. Coll., 1963; BA, East Tex. State U., 1965. Gen. assignment reporter Galveston County Pub. Co., Galveston and Texas City, 1965-68; news and feature writer Ind. and Daily Mail, Anderson, S.C., 1968-69; reporter Citizen-Times newspaper, Asheville, N.C., 1969-74; edn. and med. reporter News Star World Pub. Co., Monroe, La., 1974-79; reporter, writer Delta Democrat Times, Greenville, Miss., 1980-89; staff writer Tyler (Tex.) Morning Telegraph, 1990—. Named Citizen of Yr., Sigma Sigma chpt. Omega Psi Phi, 2001; recipient 1st place award for articles, La. Press Women's Contest, 1978, 1st place for interview, 1979, news media award, N.C. Easter Seal Soc., 1973, 3d place award for feature writing, Miss. Press Assn., 1984, for gen. news, 1983, for investigative reporting, 1988, 1st place for best series of articles, 1990, award for outstanding edn. series, Tex. State Tchrs. Assn., 1998, Sch. Bell award for outstanding series, 1997, Tex. Coll. Women Changing the World award, 2000, hon. mentions, Tex. AP, 1966. Mem. Sigma Delta Chi.

WATERS, CHARLES R., JR., executive editor; married; 3 children. BA in Liberal Arts, U. Ariz. Editor-pub. Mohave Valley News, Bullhead City, Ariz., 1969-73; editor, pub. The Courier, Prescott, Ariz., 1973-84; profl.-in-residence (vis. asst. prof.) U. Kans., 1984-85; asst. city editor, then night/weekend editor metro-state St. Petersburg (Fla.) Times, 1985-86; asst. mng. editor Reno Gazette-Jour., 1986-87, mng. editor, 1987-89, exec. editor, 1989-90; asst. features editor L.A. Times, 1990-97; exec. editor L.A Times Mag., 1997-98, Fresno Bee, 1998—. Keynote spkr. Nat. Writers Workshop nat. conf., Salt Lake City, 1994; writing and editing cons. Dayton (Ohio) Daily News, 1992; law and media seminar panelist Ford Found., 1980. Trustee William Allen White Found., U. Kans., 1991—; dir. Salvation Army, 1974-84, pres. Prescott adv. bd., 1982, bd. dirs. Reno adv. bd., 1988-90, dir. Fresno adv. bd., 1998—. Nev. State Press Assn. (dir., v.p. 1989-90), Ariz. Press Club (dir., v.p. 1982-84). Office: Fresno Bee 1626 E St Fresno CA 93786-0002

WATERS, CRYSTAL, vocalist, songwriter; b. Camden, NJ; BA, Howard U., 1985. With Parole Bd., Washington; represented by Mercury Records, 1989—. Songwriter, Basement Boys, 1987; albums include Surprise, 1991, Storyteller, 1994, Crystal Waters, 1997, The Best of Crystal Waters, 1998. Office: Mercury Records 825 8th Ave New York NY 10019-7416 also: AM PM Entertainment Concepts Inc Vito Bruno 270 Lafayette St Ste 602 New York NY 10012-3327

WATERS, DONALD JOSEPH, information services administrator; b. Balt., Sept. 16, 1952; s. Richard Hunter and Annette Catharine (Hannan) W.; m. Beverly Ann Brent, Apr. 5, 1974; children: Laura Elizabeth, Sarah Elizabeth. BA, U. Md., 1973; M Phil, Yale U., 1976, PhD, 1982. Resource specialist Yale Computer Ctr., New Haven, 1982-84; dir. computer services Yale Sch. Mgmt., New Haven, 1984-87; head, systems office Yale U. Library, New Haven, 1987-92, dir., libr. and adminstrv. systems, 1992-93, assoc. univ. librarian, 1993-97; dir. Digital Libr. Fedn., Coun. Libr. & Info. Resources, New Haven, 1997-99; program officer Andrew W. Mellon Found., N.Y., 1999—. Author: Strange Ways and Sweet Dreams: Afro-American Folklore From the Hampton Institute, 1983. Fellow AAAS; mem. Am. Soc. Info. Sci. Roman Catholic. Avocations: jazz, rowing, cabinet making. Home: 40 Overbrook Rd Madison CT 06443-1834 Office: 140 E 62nd St New York NY 10021-8124 Office Phone: 212-838-8400.

WATERS, GEORGE BAUSCH, newspaper publisher; b. Syracuse, N.Y., July 4, 1920; s. Louis Addison and Mildred Elaine (Bausch) W.; m. Shirley Kessinger Barnard, Sept. 23, 1943; children: Peter, Stephen, Nancy, Kristin, Dean. BA, Syracuse U., 1943. With Rome (N.Y.) Sentinel Co. Pub., 1947—, asst. gen. mgr., 1954-60, gen. mgr., 1960-66, pub., 1966-93, pres., 1993—. Bd. dirs. N.Y. State Photonics Devel. Corp. Chmn. Rome Art and Community Ctr., 1967-85; trustee Stevens Kingsley Found., N.Y.C., 1966—, Kirkland Coll., Clinton, N.Y., 1973-79, Utica Coll. Syracuse U., Utica, 1963-78; past mem. Rome Bd. Edn., Rome Hosp.; bd. dirs. Cen. Assn. Blind. Capt. inf. U.S. Army, 1943-47, ETO. Mem. Am. Newspaper Pubs. Assn., N.Y. State Newspaper Pubs. Assn., N.Y. State Associated Dailies (pres. 1974), Am. Soc. Newspaper Editors, Jervis Libr. Assn. (pres. 1959-65), Soc. Profl. Journalists, Rotary, Ft. Schuyler Club, Yale Club, Washington Press Club, Delta Kappa Epsilon. Republican. Presbyterian. Office: Rome Sentinel Co 333 W Dominick St Rome NY 13440-5791 E-mail: sentinel@rny.com.

WATERS, H. FRANKLIN, federal judge; b. Hackett, Ark., July 20, 1932; s. William A. and Wilma W.; m. Janie C. Waters, May 31, 1958; children—Carolyn Denise, Melanie Jane, Melissa Ann BS, U. Ark., 1955; LL.B., St. Louis U., 1964. Engr., atty. Ralston-Purina Co., St. Louis, 1958-66; ptnr. Crouch, Blair, Cypert & Waters, 1967-81; judge U.S. Dist. Ct. (we. dist.) Ark., from 1981, chief judge, sr. judge, 1997—. Former bd. dirs. Springdale Schs.; former bd. govs. Washington Regional Med. Ctr. Mem. ABA, Ark. Bar Assn., Springdale C. of C. (past bd. dirs.) Office: US Dist Ct PO Box 1908 Fayetteville AR 72702-1908

WATERS, JENNIFER NASH, lawyer; b. Bridgeport, Conn., Dec. 21, 1951; d. Lewis William and Patricia (Cousins) W.; m. Todd David Peterson, Sept. 19, 1981; children: Elizabeth, Andrew. BA, Radcliffe, 1972; JD, Harvard, 1976. Bar: D.C. 1977, U.S. Supreme Ct. 1980. Clk. U.S. Ct. Appeals (D.C. cir.), Washington, 1976-77; assoc. Jones, Day, Reavis & Poque, Washington, 1977-79, Crowell & Moring, Washington, 1979-83, ptnr., 1983—. Mem. ABA (ho. of dels. 1997-99), Fed. Energy Bar Assn. (bd. dirs. 1988-99, v.p. 1994-95, pres. 1996-97). Office: Crowell & Moring LLP 1001 Pennsylvania Ave NW Fl 10 Washington DC 20004-2505

WATERS, JOHN, film director, writer, actor; b. Balt., Apr. 22, 1946; s. John Samuel and Patricia Ann (Whitaker) W. Student, NYU, 1966. Speaker various colls., comedy clubs, U.S., Europe, Australia, 1968—. Writer, dir. films Roman Candles, 1966, Eat Your Makeup, 1968, Mondo Trasho, 1969, Multiple Maniacs, 1970, Pink Flamingos, 1972, Female Trouble, 1974, Desperate Living, 1977, Polyester, 1981, Cry-Baby, 1990, Serial Mom, 1994, Pecker, 1998, Cecil B. DeMented, 2000; writer, dir., actor film Hairspray, 1987; actor Something Wild, 1988, Homer and Eddie, 1990, Sweet and Lowdown, 1999, 21 Jump Street, 1990, Divine Trash, In Bad Taste, 1999, Blood Feast 2: All U Can Eat, 2002, Each Time I Kill, 2002,; author: Shock Value, 1981, Crackpot, 1986, Trash Trio, 1988, Director's Cut, 1997; contbr. articles to N.Y. Times, Am. Film, other mags. Fund raiser AIDS Action Balt.; spokesperson Anti-Violence Campaign, N.Y.C., 1991. John Waters Day named in his honor State of Md., 1985; John Waters Week named in his honor City of Balt., 1988. Mem. AFTRA, SAG, Dirs. Guild Am., Writers Guild Am., Acad. Motion Picture Arts and Scis. Avocation: study of extreme catholic behavior before the reformation. Address: care CAA 9830 Wilshire Blvd Beverly Hills CA 90210*

WATERS, JOHN B. lawyer; b. Sevierville, Tenn., July 15, 1929; s. J. B. and Myrtle (Paine) W.; m. Patsy Temple, Apr. 8, 1953; children: John B., Cynthia Beth. BS, U. Tenn., 1952, JD, 1961; D in Environ. Sci. (hon.), Milligan Coll., 1993. Bar: Tenn. 1961, U.S. Dist. Ct. (ea. dist.) Tenn. 1961, U.S. Supreme Ct. 1969, U.S. Dist. Ct. D.C. 1970. Of counsel Long, Ragsdale & Waters, P.C., Knoxville, Tenn. Mem. hearing com. Bd. Profl. Responsibility Supreme Ct., 1974—80, 1995—2001, Fed. co-chmn. Appalachian Regional Commn., 1968—71; chmn. Sevier County Indsl. Bd., Sevierville Libr. Found.; mem. Gov.'s Com. Econ. Devel.; Tenn. rep. to So. Growth Policies Bd., 1970—74; appointed dir. by Pres. Reagan TVA, Knoxville, 1984, appointed chmn. bd. dirs. by Pres. Bush, 92; bd. dirs. Inst. Nuc. Power Ops., 1985—93; trustee East Tenn. Bapt. Hosp., Knoxville; mem. Tenn.-Tombigbee Waterway Authority, 1993—2000; bd. dirs. East Tenn. Found.; chmn. Leadership Sevier, 1996—2001. Author: Downbound, The Memoirs of John B. Waters, Jr., 2004. Dir. Friends of Great Smoky Mountain Nat. Pk. Lt. USN, 1952—55. Fellow Am. Bar Found. Mem. Tenn. Bar Assn. (pres. 1983-84), Sevier County Bar Assn. (past pres.). Republican. Baptist. Home: Waters Edge 405 Burridge Dr Sevierville TN 37862-3202 also: 119 Commerce St Sevierville TN 37862-3524 Office Phone: 865-453-1051. Business E-Mail: waters@esper.com.

WATERS, JOHN W. minister, educator; b. Atlanta, Feb. 5, 1936; s. Henry and Mary Annie (Randall) W. Cert., U. Geneva, Switzerland, 1962; BA, Fisk U., 1957; STB, Boston U., 1967, PhD, 1970. Ordained to ministry Bapt. Ch., 1967. Min. religious edn. Ebenezer Bapt. Ch., Boston, 1965-67, assoc. min., 1967-69; min. Myrtle Bapt. Ch., West Newton, Mass., 1969, Greater Solid Rock Bapt. Ch., Atlanta, 1980—. Prof. Interdenominational Theol. Ctr., Atlanta, 1976-86, trustee, 1980-83; bd. dirs. Habitat for Humanities, Atlanta, 1984-90; chmn. South Atlanta Joint Urban Ministries, 1983-93; chairperson Coun. Overseers New Era Bapt. Conv. Ctr., 1996-2001; pres. Clayton County Ministers Conf., 2000. Contbr. articles to profl. jours. Mem. Va. Highlands Neighborhood Assn., Atlanta, 1977-87, Butler St. YMCA, 1980-86, South Atlanta Civic League, 1983, others; treas. Prison Ministries with Women, Inc.; v.p. South Met. Ministries Fellowahip, Atlanta, 1990-94. Fund for Theol. Edn. fellow, 1965-67, Nat. Fellowship Fund fellow, 1968-70, Rockefeller doctoral fellow, 1969. Mem. AAUP (chpt. pres. 1971-72), Am. Acad. Religion, Soc. Bibl. Lit., Blacks in Bibl. Studies, New Era Missionary Bapt. Conf. Ga., So. Bapt. Conv. Home: 1516 Niskey Lake Trl SW Atlanta GA 30331-6318 Office: The Greater Solid Rock Bapt Ch 6280 Camp Rd Riverdale GA 30296-2803 Personal E-mail: jwwatersphd@yahoo.com. *In life, each of us faces a variety of choices. The choices made determine our destiny, fate. When more of us assume responsibility and accountability for the choices made, the world in which we live will be decisively better.*

WATERS, LOU, anchorman, correspondent; b. Mpls., July 7, 1938; s. Louis Joseph and Anne Marie Riegert; m. Martha Lee Morin, Feb. 15, 1975; children: Scott, Christopher, Alexander. Student, U. Minn. Reporter Sta. KDWB, Mpls., 1959, Sta. WWTC, Mpls., Sta. KFWB, L.A., Sta. WLBS-FM, N.Y.C., Sta. KNEW, San Francisco; reporter, anchor Sta. KVOA-TV, Tucson, news dir., Sta. KCST-TV, San Diego; asst. sta. mgr., evening anchor Sta. KOLD-TV, CBS, Tucson; co-anchor CNN Today CNN, Atlanta, 1980—89, co-anchor Earlyprime, 1991—. Avocations: golf, photography, music. Office: 1 CNN Ctr NW Atlanta GA 30303-2762

WATERS, MARY BRICE KIRTLEY, federal agency administrator; B, U. Ill.; JD, George Mason U. Bar: D.C. Sr. dir., legis. counsel ConAgra Foods, 1986—2001; asst. sec. congl. rels. USDA, Washington, 2001—; legis. asst. Rep. Larry Hopkins, Ky., 1982—86; dir. agrl. task force Rep. Rsch. Com., 1981—82. Past chair Washington Agrl. Roundtable; mem. Trade Policy Forum. Office: USDA Congl Rels 1400 Independence Ave SW Washington DC 20250

WATERS, MAXINE, congresswoman; b. St. Louis, Aug. 15, 1938; d. Remus and Velma (Moore) Carr; m. Sidney Williams, July 23, 1977; children: Edward, Karen. Grad. in sociology, Calif. State U., L.A.; hon. doctorates, Spelman Coll., N.C. Agrl. &, Tech. State U., Morgan State U. Former tchr. Head Start. Mem. Calif. Assembly from dist. 48, 1976-91, Dem. caucus chair, 1984; mem. U.S.Congress from 35th Calif. dist., 1991—; mem. Banking, Fin., Urban Affairs com., Ho. subcom. on banking, capitol subcom. on banking, employment and tng. subcom. on vets., veterans affairs com., banking and fin. svcs. com., ranking house subcom. on gen. oversight and investigations; chair Congl. Black Caucus. Mem. Dem. Nat. Com., Dem. Congrl. Campaign com.; del. Dem. Nat. Conv., 1972, 76, 80, 84, 88, 92, mem. rules com. 1984; mem. Nat. Adv. Com. for Women, 1978—; bd. dirs. TransAfrica Found., Nat. Women's Polit. Caucus, Ctr. Nat. Policy, Clara Elizabeth Jackson Carter Found. Spellman Coll., Nat. Minority AIDS Project, Women for a Meaningful Summit, Nat. Coun. Negro Women, Black Women's Agenda; founder Black Women's Forum; dep. City Councilman David Cunningham, 1973-76, chief dep. Minority Whip; mem. Congl. Children's Working Group, Congl. Progressive Caucus, Dem. Nat. Com.; chair Dem. Caucus Spl. Com. election Reform; vice chair Steering Com. Mem. Calif. Peer Counseling Assn., Nat. Com. Econ. Conversion and Disarmament; mem. bd. Ctr. Study Sport in Soc., L.A. Women's Found. Democrat. Office: US Ho Reps 2344 Rayburn HOB Washington DC 20515-0001*

WATERS, MICHAEL COOPER, medical center and development corporation executive; b. Cisco, Tex., Oct. 29, 1942; m. Kathy Street, Apr. 17, 1976; children: Tiffany, Allison. Student, Baylor U., 1961-63; BS, Lamar U., 1965; MS, U. Pitts., 1967. Adminstrv. resident U. Tex. Med. Branch Hosp., Galveston, 1966-67; v.p. Meml. Hosp. System, Houston, 1969-78; exec. dir. Bapt. Meml. Hosp., Kansas City, Mo., 1978-80; pres. Hendrick Med. Ctr., Hendrick Med. Devel. Corp., Abilene, Tex., 1980—; dir. First Nat. Bank of Abilene. Bd. dirs. United Healthcare Systems, Kansas City; bd. dirs. Hospice of Abilene, 1981—, Hosp. Receivables, Carrollton, Tex., 1983—, United Way, Abilene, Pastoral Care and Counseling Ctr., 1981— . Served to lt. USPHS, 1967-69. Recipient W.F. Yates medallion William Jewell Coll., Liberty Mo., 1980 Mem. Am. Hosp. Assn., Am. Protestant Hosp. Assn. (bd. dirs. 1983—), Tex. Hosp. Assn. (chmn. Forts and Pecos div. 1983-84), Tex. Asn. Hosp. Auxs. (chmn. 1982-83), Abilene C. of C. (pres. 1986-87), Tex. Hosp. Assn. Bd. (treas. 1985-86, vice chmn. bd. dirs. 1986-87), Bapt. Hosp. Assn. (pres. 1985-87). Republican. Am. Baptist. Club: Abilene Kiwanis. Home: 2713 Southwest Dr Apt 208 Abilene TX 79605-6517 Office: Hendrick Health Systems 1242 N 19th St Abilene TX 79601-2316

WATERS, RICHARD, retired publishing company executive; b. Sterling, Mass., May 13, 1926; s. Sherman Hoar and Viola (Arnold) W.; m. June Hollweg Dorer, Aug. 27, 1949; children: Karl (dec.), Kurt, Kris. BA, Hobart Coll., 1950, LLD hon., 1970; MBA, Harvard U., 1951. Assoc. acct. Hunter & Weldon, N.Y.C., 1953-55; exec. v.p., CFO Reader's Digest Assn., Pleasantville, N.Y., 1955-77; assoc. dean Harvard U. Bus. Sch., Boston, 1977-81; pres., CEO Sporting News, St. Louis, 1981-90, ret., 1990. Bd. dirs. Republic Nat. Bank, N.Y.C., Spectrum Pet Care, Inc. Trustee Hobart Coll., 1971-91, William Smith Coll., 1971-91; regional v.p. Associated Industries N.Y. State, Albany, 1965-79; chmn. bd. Westchester Heart Assn., Port Chester, N.Y., 1975-76; bd. dirs., vice-chmn. Gateway chpt. Nat. Multiple Sclerosis Soc., 1991-95, chmn., 1996-98, chair emeritus 1999—; mem. St. Louis Sports Commn., 1985—; hon. trustee Hobart and William Smith Colls., 1992—; bd. dirs. Buddy Fund, St. Louis, Mo., 2001—; dir. Spectrum Pet Care Inc., 2004-. With USN, 1944-46, PTO; 1st lt. USAF, 1951-53. Mem. Baseball Writers Assn. Am. Clubs: Old Warson Country, St. Louis Club. Republican. Home: 20 Somerset Downs Saint Louis MO 63124-1007 E-mail: somersetdw@aol.com.

WATERS, ROGER ALLEN, music educator; b. Atlanta, Ga., June 12, 1949; s. John Clarence Waters, Virginia Elizabeth Waters; m. Sandra Lynn Smith, Aug. 12, 1978; children: Michael Allen, Melody Elizabeth. BMus, Ga. State U., 1973, MMus, 1981. Lic. min. Salem Bapt. Ch. Dir. choral activities Southwest DeKalb H.S., Decatur, Ga., 1976—82; min. music High Point Bapt. Ch., Covington, Ga., 1982—89, Salem Bapt. Ch., McDonough, Ga., 1989—. Instr. voice Ga. Perimeter Coll., Clarkston, Ga., 1998—; music dir., condr. Covington/Conyers Choral Guild, Covington, Ga., 1985—. Bd. dirs. Covington/Conyers Choral Guild, Covington; deputized sheriff DeKalb County Sheriff's Dept., Decatur, 1970—. Staff sgt. USAF, 1967—73. Mem.: Ga. Music Educators Assn., Am. Choral Dirs. Assn. (state pres. 1991—93), Music Educators Nat. Conf., Nat. Assn. Tchrs. Singing. Republican. Avocations: golf, tennis, mint collectibles, scale trains. Home: 1996 Gibraltar Way Conyers GA 30012

WATERS, ROLLIE O. management consultant; b. Charleston, S.C., Oct. 14, 1942; s. Rollie Robert and Mary Olivia (Brown) W.; m. Stacy Layton Waters, Dec. 31, 1998; children: Wendie Kay, Lauren Olivia. AA, Spartanburg Coll., 1968; BS, U. S.C., 1969; MBA, Pepperdine U., 1980. Cert. mgmt. cons. Supr. comms. and spl. activities Owens-Corning Fiberglas, Aiken, SC, 1970-71,

asst. pers. dir. Fairburn, Ga., 1971-72; pers. dir. Meisel Photochrome Corp., Atlanta, 1972-73, dir. corp. pers. Dallas, 1973-76, asst. v.p., dir. human resources, after 1976; co-founder, sr. ptnr., CEO Waters, Trego & Davis, Dallas, 1976-98; pres., CEO The Waters Cons. Group Inc. Publicity dir., program dir. 35th and 36th North Tex. Pers. Confs.; guest lectr. Lorch Found., London, Calif. Inst. Tech., U. Md., Am. Mgmt. Assn. So. Meth. U.; spkr. in field. Author: (tng. sys.) The Manager, Skill-based Pay for Cities, others; contbr. articles to profl. jours. With USAF, 1962-66. Mem. ASTD, Internat. Pers. Mgmt. Assn., Inst. Mgmt. Cons. (bd. dirs. Texoma chpt.), Soc. Human Resource Mgmt. (nat. compensation and benefits com.), Dallas Pers. Assn. (v.p. membership 1977-78), Am. Compensation Assn., Mensa, Psi Chi, Phi Theta Kappa, Omicron Delta Kappa, Beta Phi Gamma. Office: 2695 Villa Creek Dr Ste 104 Dallas TX 75234-7310 E-mail: rwaters@watersconsulting.com.

WATERS, RONALD V., III, candy company executive; Controller, chief fin. officer Gillette Co., 1993—99; sr. v.p., chief fin. officer William Wrigley Jr., Inc., Chgo., 1999—2003, chief oper. officer, 2004—. Office: William Wrigley Jr Co 410 N Michigan Ave Chicago IL 60611

WATERS, RONALD W. theology studies educator, church executive, pastor; b. Kokomo, Ind., July 23, 1951; s. Ronald Lee and Carolyn Elizabeth (Myers) W.; m. Norma Lee Grumbling Waters, June 16, 1973; 1 child, Melinda Ronee Waters. BA magna cum laude, Ashland (Ohio) Coll., 1973; MA in Comms. with high honors, Wheaton (Ill.) Coll., 1975; MDiv with high honors, Ashland (Ohio) Theol. Seminary, 1985; postgrad., Asbury Theol. Seminary, 1993—2002. Ordained elder Brethren Ch., 1986; lic. minister, 1985-86. Asst. to dir. Bd. of Christian Edn. The Brethren Ch., Ashland, Ohio, 1971-74; mng. editor of publs. Brethren Pub. Co., Ashland, Ohio, 1975-78, asst. to dir. and gen. mgr., 1978-80, exec. dir., 1980-82; dir. of Denom. Bus. The Brethren Ch. Nat. Office, Ashland, Ohio, 1982-84; cons. in mgmt. and computer applications, 1984-85; pastor Mt. Olive Brethren Ch., McGaheysville, Va., 1985-89; dir. Brethren Ch. Ministries The Brethren Ch. Nat. Office, Ashland, Ohio, 1989-95; asst. prof. evangelism Ashland Theol. Sem., 1996-2001; cons. for evangelism and ch. growth The Brethren Ch. Nat. Office, Ashland, 1996—2001; pastor Hammond Ave. Brethren Ch., Waterloo, Iowa, 2002—. Bd. dirs. corp. sec. Brethern Printing Co., Ashland, 1989-96; mem. mission bd. Brethren Ch. Southeastern Dist., 1987-89; mem., sec. exec. bd. Ctrl. Dist., The Brethren Ch., 2002—; mem. statement of faith task force Gen. Conf. Brethern Ch., 1981-84, polity com. 1986-91, 2004-; bd. ref. congl. adv. The Andrew Ctr., Elgin, Ill., 1994-97; founder, tchr. Young Adult Sunday Sch. class Park St Brethern Ch., Ashland, 1990-93; adv. com. Ashland Theol. Sem., 1990-95; mem. evangelism mgmt. team New Life Ministries, Mt. Joy, Pa., 1992-2001; adj. prof. Bethany Theological Seminary, 2002-; spkr. in field. Author: Promise for the Future, 1993, Leader's Manual for Inviting and Welcoming New People, 1995; editor: The Brethren Evangelist mag., 1975-78, New Beginnings mag., 1995-97; contbg. editor LIFE process, 1998-99; contbr. numerous articles to religious jours.; webmaster, www.newlifeministries-nlm.org, 2000—. Mem. adv. coun. World Relief Corp., Wheaton, Ill., 1990-92; dir. vol. ministries Park St. Brethren Ch., 1998-99; sec.-treas. Ohio dist. Mission Bd., 1996-2001. Mem. Am. Soc. Ch. Growth, Nat. Assn. Brethern Ch. Elders. Mem. Brethren Ch. Office: Hammond Ave Brethren Ch 1604 Hammond Ave Waterloo IA 50702

WATERS, SYLVIA, dance company artistic director; BS in Dance, The Juilliard School; studied with, Antony Tudor and Martha Graham; PhD (hon.), State U. N.Y., Oswego, 1997. Prin. dance Alvin Ailey Am. Dance Theater, N.Y.C., 1968—74; artistic dir. Alvin Ailey Repertory Ensemble, N.Y.C., 1974—. Panelist Nat. Endowment for the Arts, N.Y. State Council on the Arts. Office: Alvin Ailey Repertory Ensemble 211 W 61st St Fl 3 New York NY 10023-7832

WATERS, WILLIAM CARTER, III, retired internist, educator; b. Atlanta, Dec. 12, 1929; s. William Carter and Nannie Ellen (Stark) W.; m. Sarah Ann Bankston; children: William Carter IV, Sarah Walker Waters McEntire. AB, Emory U., 1950, MD, 1958. Diplomate in internal medicine and nephrology Am. Bd. Internal Medicine. Resident in internal medicine Grady Meml. Hosp./Emory U., Atlanta, 1958-60, 61-62; fellow in nephrology New Eng. Med. Ctr., 1960-61; practice medicine specializing in internal medicine and nephrology, Atlanta, 1962—2002; from instr. to assoc. prof. Emory U. Sch. Medicine, 1962-70, clin. assoc. prof., 1970-85, clin. prof., 1985—. Chief staff internal medicine Piedmont Hosp., Atlanta, chmn. bd., 1991-94; 1st chmn. bd Promina Health Sys., Atlanta, 1994-96. Contbr. articles to med. jours. Chmn. Piedmont Hosp. Found., 2002—. Served with USAF, 1951—52. Fellow ACP (master: gov. for Ga.); mem. AMA, Med. Assn. Ga., Med. Assn. Met. Atlanta, Am. Soc. Nephrology, S.E. Clin. Club, Atlanta Country Club, Piedmont Driving Club, Big Canoe Club. Methodist. Personal E-mail: drwaters@mindspring.com.

WATERSTON, ROBERT HUGH, medical educator, researcher, medical geneticist, department chairman; b. Detroit, Mich., Sept. 17, 1943; BSE, Princeton U., N.J., 1965; PhD, U.Chgo., 1972; MD, Chgo., 1972. Postdoctoral fellow divsn. cell biology MRC Lab Molecular Biology, Cambridge, England, 1972—74; intern in pediatric medicine Children's Hosp. Med. Ctr., Boston, 1974—75; postdoctoral fellow divsn. cell biology MRC Lab Molecular Biology, Cambridge, England, 1975—76; asst. prof. dept. anatomy and neurobiology Washington U., St. Louis, 1976—89; asst. prof. genetics Washington U. Sch. Medicine, St. Louis, 1980—81, assoc. prof. genetics, 1981—87, prof. genetics, 1987—91, prof. and acting head dept. genetics, 1991—93, James S. McDonnell prof. and chmn. dept. genetics, 1993—; founder Genome Sequncing Center, St. Louis, Minn. Ad hoc mem. Molecular Cytology Study Sect., 1977, 83; regular mem. Molecular Cytology Study Sect., NIH, 1987—88, chmn., 1989—91; mem. NIH, 1985—86; mem. fellowship rev. subcom. Molecular Dystrophy Assn., 1982—87, mem task force on genetics, 1983; mem. organizing com. Fourth Internat. C. elegans Meeting, Cold Spring Habor, NY, 1985; mem. nat. adv. coun. for human genome rsch. NIH, 1998—2002. Contbr. articles (over 80)to profl. jours, 1970; mem. editl. bd. Jour. Cell Biology, 1988—91. Named NIH predoctoral trainee, 1968—71, Am. Heart Assn. Established Investigator, 1980—85; recipient Peter H. Raven Lifetime award, 2000, Gairdner award, 2002, Alfred P. Sloan, Jr. prize, GM Cancer Rsch. Found., 2003; fellow Am. Cancer Soc. (postdoctoral), 1972—74, Muscular Dystrophy Assn. (postdoctoral), 1975—76, John Simon Guggenheim, 1985—86; grantee, NIH, 1997—99, 1998—2001, Merck & Co., 1994—99. Mem.: Am. Soc. Cell Biology: STS, Genetics Soc., Alpha Omega Alpha, Sigma Xi. Office: Washington U Sch Medicine Dept Genetics Box 8232 4566 Scott Ave Saint Louis MO 63110 Address: Genome Sequencing Ctr Box 8501 4444 Forest Park Blvd Saint Louis MO 63108 Office Phone: 314-286-1803. Office Fax: 314-286-1810.

WATERSTON, SAMUEL ATKINSON, actor; b. Cambridge, Mass., Nov. 15, 1940; s. George Chychele and Alice Tucker (Atkinson) W.; m. Lynn Louisa Woodruff, Jan. 26, 1976; children: Graham C., Elisabeth P., Katherine B.; child by previous marriage: James S. BA, Yale U., 1962; student, Sorbonne, Paris, 1960-61. Theatrical appearances include: Indians, Oh Dad Poor Dad, Halfway Up the Tree, Lunch Hour, Hamlet, The Tempest, Measure for Measure, Much Ado About Nothing (Obie, Drama Desk awards), Benefactors, 1986, A Walk in the Woods, 1988, Abe Lincoln in Illinois, 1993-94 (Drama League award 1994), Shakespeare & Szekspir, 1994; film appearances include: The Great Gatsby, 1975, Rancho Deluxe, 1976, Capricorn One, 1978, Interiors, 1978, Sweet William, 1978, Heaven's Gate, 1979, Eagle's Wing, 1983, The Killing Fields, 1984 (Acad. nomination best leading actor), Warning Sign, 1985, Savages, Hopscotch, 1980, Hannah and Her Sisters, 1986, Just Between Friends, 1986, The Devil's Paradise, September, 1987, Welcome Home, 1989, Crimes and Misdemeanors, 1990, Captive in the Land, 1990, Crimes and Misdemeanors, The Man in the Moon, 1991, Mindwalk, 1991, Serial Mom, 1994, Nixon, 1995, The Proprietor, 1996, Shadow Conspiracy, 1997, Le Divorce, 2003; TV films include: Much Ado About Nothing, 1974, The Glass Menagerie, 1975, Diabolique, 1975, Friendly Fire, 1978, Oppenheimer, 1982, Exiled, 1998, A House Divided, 2000, The Matthew Shepard Story, 2002; TV series Q.E.D., 1982, Terrorist on Trial: The United States vs. Salim Ajami; TV miniseries appearance: Oppenheimer, 1980, 82, Gore Vidal's Lincoln, 1988, Nightmare Years, 1989, Lost Civilizations, 1995 (Emmy award for best documentary 1996), Thomas Jefferson, 1997; regular TV series Q.E.D., 1979, I'll Fly Away, NBC-TV, 1991-93 (Emmy award nomination, Lead actor, Drama, 1993), I'll Fly Away: Then and Now, PBS, 1993 (Emmy nomination, Lead Actor - Special, 1994), Law and Order, 1994—, Miracle at Midnight, 1998. Law and Order: Special Victims Unit, 1999, (documentary) Unfinished Journey, 1999. Mem. Actors Equity Assn., Screen Actors Guild, AFTRA Address: care Addis/Wechsler & Assocs 955 Carrillo Dr Fl 3 Los Angeles CA 90048-5400

WATHEN, DANIEL EVERETT, former state supreme court chief justice; b. Easton, Maine, Nov. 4, 1939; s. Joseph Jackson and Wilda Persis (Dow) W.; m. Judith Carol Foren, July 14, 1960; children: Julanne Carol, Daniel Arthur. AB, Ricker Coll., 1962, JD, U. Maine, 1965; LLM (hon.), U. Va. Law Sch., 1988. Bar: Maine 1965. Atty. Wathen & Wathen, Augusta, Maine, 1965-77; trial judge Superior Ct. Maine, Augusta, 1977-81; appellate judge Supreme Jud. Ct. Maine, Augusta, 1981-92, state chief justice, 1992—2001; of counsel Pierce Atwood, 2002—. Office: Pierce Atwood One Monument Sq Portland ME 04101

WATJEN, THOMAS ROS, insurance company executive; With investment and corp. fin. depts. Aetna Life and Casualty, 1981-84; ptnr. Conning and Co., ins. cons. firm, 1984-87; mng. dir. responsible for ins. practice group Morgan Stanley & Co., 1987-94; exec. v.p., CFO Provident Cos., Inc., Chattanooga, 1994—97, vice chmn., dir., 1997—99; exec. v.p., fin. UnumProvident Corp., Chattanooga, 1999—2002, vice chmn., COO, 2002—03, pres., CEO, 2003—. Office: Unum Provident Corp One Fountain Sq Chattanooga TN 37402 E-mail: twatjen@unumprovident.com.

WATKIN, VIRGINIA RUTH, financial professional; b. Pomona, Calif., Sept. 25, 1955; d. Charles Robertson Williams and Ruth (Jones) Kettmann; m. Thomas Peter Watkin, Sept. 10, 1977; children: Shannon Ruth, Dana Erin. AA, Mt. San Antonio Coll., 1975; postgrad., Calif. State U., Fullerton, U. Guadalajara, Riverside (Calif.) City Coll. Mgmt. trainee Local Loan Co., La Puente, Calif., 1977, Morris Plan of Calif., Corona, 1977-78; cons. loan processor Glendale Fed., Riverside, 1978-81, cons. loan officer Riverside and Downey, Calif., 1981-84, sr. cons. loan officer Glendale, 1984-86; asst. v.p., consumer loan mgr. Hemet (Calif.) Fed. Savs. and Loan, 1986-91; underwriter Wells Fargo Bank, Santa Ana, Calif., 1992-93; sr. underwriter 1st Interstate Bank, Pasadena, Calif., 1993-96; reimbursements officer Dept. Veterans Affairs State of Calif., Barstow, 1996—2003; sr. fin. aid counselor Calif. Bapt. U., Riverside, 2003—. Instr. Inst. Fin. Edn. Hemet/San Jacinto (Calif.) chpt. Consumer Fin. Rep. Calif. Community and Jr. Coll. Assn., Walnut, 1975. Mem. Nat. Assn. Female Execs., Calif. Savs. and Loan League (consumer loan com.), Hemet C. of C. Republican. Avocations: reading, water-skiing, fishing, camping, gourmet cooking. Home: 17754 Siskiyou Rd Apple Valley CA 92307-1224

WATKINS, ANGELA MARIE, museum administrator, writer; b. Lexington, Va., Aug. 26, 1962; d. William Woodrow and Dorothy Teaford Watkins. MA in Liberal Studies, Hollins Coll., 1987. Mgr. night reference and circulation Fishburn Libr., Hollins Coll., Roanoke, Va., 1988—89; reference libr. Rockbridge Regional Libr., Lexington, Va., 1994—2001, head reference, 2001—01; mgr. The Toy Mus., Natural Bridge, 2002—. V.p. Soc. Preservation om. Childhood Effects, Natural Bridge, 2003—. Editor: (newsletter and college bulletin) The Hollins Master of Arts in Liberal Studies Class Letter, Newsletter of the Society for the Preservation of American Childhood Artifacts; contbr. articles and revs. to profl. jours. and newspapers. Augusta Marcus scholar, Hollins Coll., 1982, Kent James Brown fellow, U. N.C., Chapel Hill, 1988, 1989. Mem.: SE Tourism Soc., Shenandoah Valley Travel Assn., Roanoke Valley Conventions and Visitors Bur., Blue Ridge Pky. Assn., Am. Toy Mus. Assn., Phi Beta Kappa. Avocations: book collecting, beethoven sonatas, modern architecture, visiting libraries. Home: 290 Ore Bank Lane Natural Bridge Station VA 24579 Office: The Toy Museum at Natural Bridge 6477 South Lee Highway Natural Bridge VA 24578 Personal E-mail: awatkins@hollins.edu. E-mail: info@awesometoymuseum.com.

WATKINS, ANN ESTHER, mathematics professor; b. L.A., Jan. 10, 1949; d. Rex Devere and Burnice Gordine (Duckworth) Hamilton; m. William Earl Watkins, Oct. 5, 1973; children: Mary Ann, Barbara Lee. BA, Calif. State U., Northridge, 1970, MS, 1972; PhD, UCLA, 1977. Instr. math. Los Angeles Pierce Coll., Woodland Hills, Calif., 1975-90; prof. math. Calif. State U., Northridge, 1990—. Editor: (with Albers, Rodi) New Directions in Two Year College Mathematics, 1985; co-author: (with Landwehr) Exploring Data, 1986, 2d edit., 1994, (with Landwehr, Swift) Exploring Surveys, 1987, (with Albers, Loftsgaarden, Rung) Statistical Abstract of Undergraduate Programs in the Mathematical Sciences and Computer Science, 1992 (with Scheaffer, Gnanadesikan, Witmer) Activity-Based Statistics, 1996, 2d edit., (with Scheaffer, Cobb) Statistics in Action, 2004; assoc. editor: American Mathematical Monthly, 1996-2000; editor Coll. Math. Jour., 1989-94; co-editor: (with Apostol, Mugler, Scott and Sterrett) A Century of Calculus, Part II, 1992; mem. editl. bd. Jour. Statis. Edn., 1992-95; mem. adv. bd. Math. Horizons mag., 1992-2001. Grantee NSF, 1987-90, 92—. Mem. Math. Assn. Am. (2d v.p. 1987-88, pres. 2001-03, chair So. Calif. sect. 1988-89, gov. So. Calif. sect. 1995—), Am. Statis. Assn., Nat. Coun. Tchrs. Math. Office Phone: 818-677-2781. Business E-Mail: ann.watkins@csun.edu.

WATKINS, BIRGE SWIFT, investment banker; b. Grand Rapids, Mich., May 2, 1949; s. Robert Goodell and Betty Jane (Swift) W.; m. Elizabeth Beverly Price, Nov. 28, 1985; children: Elizabeth Porter, Benjamin Thorne Swift, Robert William MacIntosh. BA, Alma Coll., 1971; MBA, London Bus. Sch., 1981; MPA, Harvard U., 1989. Staff asst. to Pres. of U.S., Washington, 1974-77; congl. press sec. U.S. Ho. of Reps., Washington, 1977; v.p. Arbor Internat. Inc., McLean, Va., 1980-81; asst. office dir. AID, Washington, 1982-88; asst. dir. Pres.'s Task Force on Internal Pvt. Enterprise, Washington, 1983-85; dep. asst. sec. USDA, Washington, 1989-90; dir. investor outreach Resolution Trust Corp., Washington, 1991-94; ptnr. Benton Resources, Washington, 1994-95; mng. dir. Thornfalcon Internat., 1996-99; sr. v.p. Lifecare Mgmt. Ptnrs., 1999—2002, Friedman, Billings, Ramsey Group, Inc., 2002—03; v.p. Landmark Cmtys., 2003—. Cons. Washington Campus Inc., 1977. Va. Med. Assocs. Inc., Springfield, 1988, U.S. C. of C. Mem. campaign staff Reagan-Bush campaign, Washington, 1980, Bush for President, 1988; mem. transition team office of Pres.-elect Bush, 1988; chmn. bd. trustees Partnership Warrenton Found.; bd. dirs., founder John Singleton Mosby Found. and Mus., Land Trust of Va.; coun. mem. Town of Warrenton, Va., 2002—. Avocations: skiing, running, contemporary art. Home: 832 Blackwell Rd Warrenton VA 20186-2216 Office: Arlington VA Office Phone: 703-658-5200.

WATKINS, CAROL A. special education educator; b. Norfolk, Va., Dec. 7, 1954; d. Bernard Melvin and Jean Everton Dixon; m. William Stanley Watkins, Jr., July 23, 1954; children: William Stanley Watkins III, Bryce Reid. MEd, Va. Commonwealth U., 1986. Postgrad. prof. lic. Commonwealth of Va., 2003. Tchr./ spl. edn. New Kent County Pub. Schools, New Kent, 1984—95; dept. chair Hanover County Pub. Schools, Mechanicsville, Va., 1995—2002, 2003—. Fellow Grad. student tuition, Va. Commonwealth U., 1983-1984; grantee Project Unite Grant, Commonwealth of Va., 1994-1995. Avocations: volunteer- lewis ginter botanical gardens, consultant with the pampered chef*, old church community center member, ptsa faculty representative. Home: 8099 Candleberry Drive Mechanicsville VA 23111 Office: Lee-Davis HS 7052 Mechanicsville Turnpike Mechanicsville VA 23111 E-mail: cwatkins@hanover.k12.va.us.

WATKINS, CAROLE S. human resources specialist, health facility administrator; b. 1960; BA, Franklin U., Columbus, Ohio. Staff The Limited, Columbus, Ohio, 1989—96; v. p. human resources Cardinal Distribution, Columbus, Ohio, 1996—2000; sr. v.p. pharm distbn. and provider svcs. Cardinal Health, Columbus, 2000; exec. v.p. human resources Cardinal Health, Inc., Columbus, 2000—. Office: Cardinal Health 7000 Cardinal Pl Dublin OH 43017

WATKINS, CHARLES BOOKER, JR., mechanical engineering educator; b. Petersburg, Va., Nov. 20, 1942; s. Charles Booker and Haseltine Lucy (Thurston) W. BS in Mech. Engring. cum laude, Howard U., 1964; MS, U. N.Mex., 1966, PhD, 1970. Registered profl. engr., D.C. Mem. tech. staff Sandia Nat. Labs., Albuquerque, 1964-71; asst. prof. dept. mech. engring. Howard U., Washington, 1971-73, prof., chmn. dept. mech. engring., 1973-86; Herbert G. Keyser prof. mech. engring. CCNY, 1986—99, dean Sch. Engring. Cons. U.S. Army, U.S. Navy, NSF, pvt. industries, 1984-85. Rsch. grantee NSF, USN, Nuclear Regulatory Commn., Dept. Energy, NASA; Sandia Labs. doctoral fellow; NDEA fellow. Fellow ASME, AIAA (assoc.); mem. AAAS, Soc. Automotive Engrs. (Ralph R. Teetor award 1980), Am. Soc. Engring. Edn., Am. Soc. Safety Engrs., Sigma Xi, Omega Psi Phi, Tau Beta Pi. Home: 171 Sherman Ave Teaneck NJ 07666-4121 Office: CCNY Sch Engring Convent Ave New York NY 10031

WATKINS, CURTIS WINTHROP, artist; b. Pontiac, Mich., Apr. 9, 1946; s. Robert James and Arvella Marquitta (Chenoweth) W.; m. Gayle Lynn Blom, Dec. 19, 1975; 1 dau., Darcy Ann. Student, Ann Arbor Art Ctr., 1964-66, Kendall Sch. Design, 1966-68, Kraus Hypnosis Ctr., 1966, 70, Arons Ethical Hypnosis Tng. Ctr., 1977. Illustrator, instr. Ann Arbor Art Ctr., 1969-71; owner, dir. Hypno-Art Rsch. Ctr. and Studio, Howell, Mich., 1971—. Research on visualization process of subconscious by doing art work under hypnosis; lectr. hypnosis convs. and schs. One-man shows include LeVern's Gallery, 1969, Rackham Gallery, 1973, Hartland Gallery, 1974, Platt Gallery, 1975, Detroit Artists Guild Gallery, 1975, Golden Gallery, 1977, Cromaine Gallery, 1982, Driggett Gallery, 1982, Mill Gallery, 1983, Walnut Street Gallerya, 1983, Merrill Gallery, 1986, Corbino Gallery, 1986, VanAntwerp, 1991; group shows include Mich. All-State Show, 1980, Mich. State Fine Arts Exhibit, 1980, Washington Internat., 1981, Lansing (Mich.) Art Gallery, 1981, Capitol City Arts Show, 1981, Mich. Ann., 1981, Mich. Ann., 1982-83; illustrator: Handbook of Hypnotic Techniques, 1988. Bd. dirs. 9th Ann. Hartland Art Show, 1975, Livingston Arts and Crafts Assn., 1977-79, Hartland Art Coun., 1974-78. Recipient Dr. Garland H. Fross award, 1989, numerous awards of excellence in art. Mem. Internat. Soc. Artists, Assn. Advance Ethical Hypnosis, Am. Assn. Profl. Hypnologists, Internat. Soc. Profl. Hypnosis, Internat. Platform Assn. Presbyterian. Home: 1749 Pinckney Rd Howell MI 48843-7874 Office Phone: 517-546-6648.

WATKINS, DEAN ALLEN, electronics executive, educator; b. Omaha, Oct. 23, 1922; s. Ernest E. and Pauline (Simpson) W.; m. Bessie Ena Hansen, June 28, 1944; children— Clark Lynn, Alan Scott, Eric Ross. BS, Iowa State Coll., 1944; MS, Calif. Inst. Tech., 1947; PhD, Stanford, 1951. Engr. Collins Radio Co., 1947-48; mem. staff Los Alamos Lab., 1948-49; tech. staff Hughes Research Labs., 1951-53; asso. prof. elec. engring. Stanford, 1953-56; prof., dir. Electron Devices Lab., 1956-64, lectr. elec. engring., 1964-70; co-founder, pres., chief exec. officer, dir. Watkins Johnson Co., Palo Alto, Calif., 1957-67, chmn., chief exec. officer, dir., 1967-80, chmn., dir., 1980-2000. Cons. Dept. Def., 1956-66; mem. White House Sci. Coun., 1988-89. Patentee in field; contbr. articles to profl. jours. Legis. chmn., dir San Meteo County Sch. Bds. Assn., 1959-69; gov. San Francisco Bay Area Coun., 1966-75; Rep. precinct capt. Portola Valley, 1964; vice chmn. San Mateo County Fin. Com., 1967-69; mem. Calif. Rep. Ctrl. Com., 1964-68; trustee Stanford, 1966-69; regent U. Calif., 1969-96, chmn., 1972-74; mem. governing bd. Sequoia Union H.S. Dist., 1964-68, chmn., 1967-68; mem. governing bd. Portola Valley Sch. Dist., 1958-66; mem. bd. overseers Hoover Instn. on War, Revolution and Peace, Stanford, 1969—, chmn., 1971-73, 85-86; adv. policy commn. Santa Clara County Jr. Achievement; trustee Nat. Security Indsl. Assn., 1965-78. Served from pvt. to 1st lt. C.E., O.R.C. AUS, 1943-46. Fellow IEEE (7th region Achievement award 1957, Frederik Philips award 1981), AAAS; mem. Am. Phys. Soc., Am. Mgmt. Assn., Western Electronic Mfrs. Assn. (chmn. San Francisco coun. 1967, v.p., dir.), Calif. C. of C. (dir. 1965-92, treas. 1978, pres. 1981), Nat. Acad. Engring., Mounted Patrol San Mateo County (spl. dep. sheriff 1960-70), San Mateo County Horseman's Assn., San Benito County Farm Bur., Calif. Cattlemen's Assn., Delta Upsilon. Clubs: Palo Alto (Palo Alto), University (Palo Alto); Shack Riders (San Mateo County); Commonwealth (San Francisco); Rancheros Visitadores.

WATKINS, ESTHER SHERROD, secondary school educator, school librarian; b. Port Gipson, Miss., June 4, 1939; d. Raphael Sherrod and Carrie Powell Sherrod Peterson; m. John H. Watkins (dec.); children: Glenna Watkins Tolbert, MD, John Timothy. BA, Tougaloo Coll., Miss., 1960—64; Calif. tchng. credential, Calif. State U. Los Angeles, 1966—72; MA, U. of San Francisco, 1978—79. Sch. reading coord. Samuel Gompers Mid. Sch., Los Angeles, 1968—69, English/reading tchr., 1963—69; English tchr. Robert Frost Mid. Sch., Granada Hills, 1969—79, Sun Valley Mid. Sch., 1979—84; sch. writing coord. Verdugo HS, Tugunga, 1984—95; English tchr. Verdugo Hills HS, 1984—95, libr., 1995—2001. Del. NEA, 2000—01; active union mem. UTLA, 1995—2001. Author: (book) Using Novels to Help High School Students to Cope, 1979. Elder Pasadena Christian Ch., 1969—; nat. bd. Delta Sigma Theta. Mem.: YWCA, Delta Sigma Theta. Achievements include serving as interim counselor co-dept. chair, reading compter coord. and training tchr. supr.

WATKINS, EUGENE LEONARD, surgeon, educator; b. Worcester, Mass., Jan. 4, 1918; s. George Joseph and Marcella Katherine (Akels) W.; A.B. with honors in biology, Clark U., 1940; M.D. (Hood scholar), Harvard U., 1943; m. Victoria Peake, Sept. 23, 1944; children: Roswell Peake, Priscilla Avery. Intern, Roosevelt Hosp., N.Y.C., 1944; resident in surgery, 1944-46, 49-50, asst. resident in surgery, 1948-49; fellow in surgery, clin. rsch. fellow Mass. Gen. Hosp., Boston, 1947-48; practice medicine specializing in surgery, N.Y.C., 1950-56, Morristown, N.J., 1950-90, Denville, N.J., 1956-85, Boonton, N.J., 1961-85; mem. staff Morristown Meml. Hosp., 1950, vice chmn. dept. surgery, 1974-77, chmn., 1959-61, mem. corp.; cons. surgeon St. Clare's Hosp., Denville, N.J., Riverside Hosp., Boonton, N.J., Community Med. Center, Morristown; courtesy surg. staff St. Luke's-Roosevelt Hosp. Center, N.Y.C.; asst. clin. prof. surgery Rutgers U. Coll. Medicine and Dentistry, New Brunswick, N.J., 1972-85; asst. clin. prof. surgery Columbia U. Coll. Phys. and Surg., 1985-90; v.p. chmn. fin. com. Morristown Bd. Health, 1954-56. Served to 1st lt., AUS, 1946. Diplomate Am. Bd. Surgery. Fellow ACS (chmn. N.J. Adv. Com. 1965-77, chmn. N.J. State com. Trauma, 1960); mem. N.J., Morris County med. socs., AMA, Soc. Surgeons N.J. (1st v.p. 1982, pres. 1983), Am. Thoracic Soc., AAAS, Harvard Med. Soc. N.Y. (pres. 1960-61), West Side Med. Soc., Roosevelt Hosp. Alumni Assn. Republican. Presbyterian. Clubs: Harvard (N.Y.C.), Morristown, Morristown Field. Achievements include development of spring-loop surgical suture holder. Home: Unit 419 7501 E Thompson Peak Pkwy Scottsdale AZ 85255-4537

WATKINS, FELIX SCOTT, printing company executive; b. Sutton, W.Va., Nov. 27, 1946; s. Felix Sutton and Helena Sara (Cogar) W.; m. Vivian L. Watkins, June 20, 1970; children: Jeffrey Scott, Jamie Leigh. Student, W. Va. Inst. Tech. Salesman Kingsport (Tenn.) Press, 1971-73; sales mgr. George Banta Co., N.Y.C., 1973-74; prodn. mgr. Fuller Typesetting, Phila., 1974—75; acct. exec. Rocappi, Pennsauken, NJ, 1975—78; pres. Photo Data, Inc., Washington, 1978—91, Signature Printing, Inc., Chantilly, Va., 1991—. Founding mem. Print Polit. Action Com. Mem. Washington Club Printing House Craftsmen, Washington Printing Guild (dir. masters printers divsn.), Printing Industries Met. Washington (chmn. govt. affairs com.), Printing Industries Am. (Chmn.'s Club). Home: 9521 Orion Ct Burke VA 22015-3241 Office: Signature Printing Inc 14310 Sullyfield Cir Ste 200 Chantilly VA 20151-1629

WATKINS, HAROLD ROBERT, minister; b. Wauseon, Ohio, July 30, 1928; s. Orra Lynn and Florence Margaret (Bruner) W.; m. Evelyn Norma Earlywine, June 18, 1950; children: Mark Edwin, Nancy Jo Watkins. AB, Bethany Coll., 1950; MDiv, Lexington Theol. Sem., 1997; DD, Phillips U., 1985, Christian Theol. Sem., Indpls., 1995; BD, Coll. of Bible, 1953. Ordained minister Disciples of Christ, 1950. Min. Park Ave. Christian Ch., Tucson, 1953-56, First Christian Ch., Tuscaloosa, Ala., 1956-57; gen. ch. adminstr. Bd. Ch. Extension of Disciples of Christ, Indpls., 1958-95, pres., 1980-95, pres. emeritus, 2004; mem. faculty Lexington Theol. Sem., 1996-97, 98-99, interim pres., 2001. Chmn. bd. dirs. Discipledata, Inc., Indpls., 1980—94; bd. dirs.

United Church Ins. Co. Trustee Bethany (W.Va.) Coll., 1976—, Nat. City Christian Ch. Corp., Washington, 1981—; bd. dirs. Ecumenical Ch. Loan Fund, Geneva; pres. World Conv. Chs. of Christ, Nashville, 1988-92; bd. dirs. United Ch. of Christ Ins. Bd., 1997—. Recipient Outstanding Alumnus award Bethany Coll., 1975. Mem. Interfaith Forum on Religion, Art and Arch. (dir. officer 1979-95, pres. 1981-82, Elbert M. Conover award 1989). Mem. Christian Ch. Home: 7402 Somerset Bay Apt 118 Indianapolis IN 46240-3495 E-mail: hwatkins@aol.com.

WATKINS, HAYS THOMAS, retired railroad executive; b. Fern Creek, Ky., Jan. 26, 1926; s. Hays Thomas Sr. and Minnie Catherine (Whiteley) W.; m. Betty Jean Wright, Apr. 15, 1950; 1 son, Hays Thomas III. BS in Acctg., Western Ky. U., 1947; MBA, Northwestern U., 1948; LLD (hon.), Baldwin Wallace Coll., 1975, Alderson Broaddus Coll., 1980, Coll. of William and Mary, 1982, Va. Union U., 1987. CPA, Ill., Ohio. With C. & O. Ry. Cleve., 1949-80, v.p. fin., 1964-67, v.p. adminstrv. group, 1967-71, pres., CEO, 1971—73, chmn. bd., CEO, 1973—80; with B. & O. R.R., 1964-80, v.p. finance, 1964-71, pres., CEO, 1971—73, vice chmn. bd., CEO, 1973—80; chmn., CEO Chessie System, Inc., 1973—80; pres. and co-CEO CSX Corp. (merger of Chessie System, Inc. and Seaboard Coast Line Industries, Inc.), Richmond, Va., 1980—82, chmn. bd., CEO, 1982—89, chmn. bd., 1989-91; chmn. emeritus, 1991—. Vice rector bd. visitors Coll. William and mary, 1984-87, rector, 1987-93. With AUS, 1945-47. Named Man of Yr., Modern R.R. mag., 1984; recipient Excellence in Mgmt. award Industry Week mag., 1982. Mem. Nat. Assn. Accts., Am. Inst. C.P.A.'s. Clubs: Commonwealth (Richmond, Va.); Country of Va. (Richmond). Home: 22 Lower Tuckahoe Rd W Richmond VA 23238-6108 Office: CSX Corp 901 E Cary St Ste 1605 Richmond VA 23219

WATKINS, JAMES DAVID, federal official, military officer; b. Alhambra, Calif., Mar. 7, 1927; s. Edward Francis and Louise Whipple (Ward) Watkins; m. Sheila Jo McKinney, Aug. 19, 1950 (dec. Sept. 1996); m. Janet L. McDonough, June 17, 2000; children: Katherine Marie, Laura Jo, Charles Lancaster, Susan Elizabeth, James David, Edward Francis. BS, U.S. Naval Acad., 1949; MSME, Navy Postgrad. Sch., 1958; LHD (hon.), Marymount Coll., 1982, N.Y. Med. Coll., 1988; DSc (hon.), Dowling Coll., 1983, U. Ala., 1991; LLD (hon.), Cath. U. Am., 1985, Mt. Sinai Sch. Medicine, 1993, Calif. U. Pa., 1994; DS (hon.), Coll. William and Mary, 1999. Commd. ensign USN, 1949, advanced through grades to adm., 1979, comdg. officer U.S.S. Snook, 1964-66, exec. officer U.S.S. Long Beach, 1967-69; head submarine/nuclear power distbn. control br. Bur. Naval Pers., Dept. Navy, Washington, 1969-71, dir. enlisted pers. div., 1971-72, asst. chief naval pers. for enlisted pers. control, 1972-73; comdr. Cruiser-Destroyer Group 1 USN, 1973-75; dep. chief naval ops. manpower Dept. Navy, Washington, 1975-78, chief of naval pers., 1975-78, chief Bur. Naval Pers., 1975-78; comdr. U.S. Sixth Fleet USN, 1978-79; vice chief naval ops. Dept. Navy, Washington, 1979-81, comdr.-in-chief U.S. Pacific Fleet, 1981-82, chief naval ops., 1982-86; ret. USN, 1986; chmn. Presdl. Commn. Human Immunodeficiency Virus Epidemic, 1987-88; sec. Dept. Energy, Washington, 1989-93; pres. Joint Oceanographic Instn., 1993-2000, Consortium Oceanographic Rsch. and Edn., 1993-2001. Chmn. Presidentially Apptd. Commn. Ocean Policy, 2001—04. Decorated DSM with 1 gold star, Legion of Merit with 2 gold stars, Bronze Star medal with combat v; recipient Disting. Alumni award, Naval Postgrad. Sch., 1958, Chmn.'s award, Am. Assn. Engring. Socs., 1991, Disting. Grad. award, U.S. Naval Acad., 2001. Mem.: U.S. Naval Acad. Found., Knights of Malta. Roman Catholic.

WATKINS, JERRY WEST, retired oil company executive, lawyer; b. Vernon, Tex., Dec. 10, 1931; s. Terrell Clark and Daisy (West) W.; m. Elizabeth Jill Cole, Sept. 3, 1955. Student, Hendrix Coll., 1949-50, La. Poly. Inst., 1950-51; JD, U. Ark., 1954. Bar: Ark. 1954. Law clk. Supreme Ct. Ark., Little Rock, 1954-55; with Murphy Oil Corp., El Dorado, Ark., 1955-89, sec., gen. atty., 1966-71, sec., gen. counsel, 1971-88, v.p., dir., 1975-88, exec. v.p., 1991-92, also bd. dirs., 1975-89. CEO, bd. dirs. Ocean Drilling and Exploration Co., New Orleans, 1989-91; mem. Ark. Bd. Law Examiners, 1969-74; bd. dirs. Simmons First Bank of El Dorado, N.A., Simmons First Nat. Corp. Mem. Barton Libr. Bd., El Dorado, 1966—89; trustee Ark. State U., 1982—87; bd. dirs. South Ark. Arts Ctr., El Dorado, 1979—82, 1985—88, Warner Brown Hosp., El Dorado, 1984—87, South Ark. Med. Sys., 1987—89, Presbyn. Found. Ark., 1998—, Union County Cmty. Found., 2001—. Mem. ABA, Ark. Bar Assn., Union County Bar Assn. Home: 111 Watkins Dr El Dorado AR 71730-2752

WATKINS, JOAN FRANCES, retired elementary school educator; b. Linwood, N.J., Mar. 8, 1940; d. Francis Joseph and Alberta Catherine (Seabold) W. BS, St. Bonaventure U., 1967. Cert. elem. tchr., N.J. Tchr. various parochial schs., 1961-71, Atlantic City (N.J.) Pub. Schs., 1971—2003; ret., 2003. Mem. Atlantic City Edn. Assn., N.J. Edn. Assn. Roman Catholic. Avocation: working with children. Home: PO Box 714 Northfield NJ 08225-0714

WATKINS, JOAN MARIE, osteopath, occupational medicine physician; b. Anderson, Ind., Mar. 9, 1943; d. Curtis David and Dorothy Ruth (Beckett) W.; m. Stanley G. Nodvik, Dec. 25, 1969 (div. Apr. 1974). BS, West Liberty State Coll., 1965; Cert. of Grad. Phys. Therapy, Ohio State U., 1966; DO, Phila. Coll. Osteo., 1972; M of Health Professions Edn., U. Ill., Chgo., 1986; MPH, U. Ill., 1989. Diplomate Osteo. Nat. Bds., Am. Bd. Preventive Medicine, Am. Bd. Occupl. and Environ. Medicine, Am. Bd. Emergency Medicine. Resident in phys. medicine and rehab. U. Pa., 1973—74; emergency osteo. physician Cooper Med. Ctr., Camden, 1974-79, Shore Meml. Hosp., Somers Point, N.J., 1979-81, St. Francis Hosp., Blue Island, Ill., 1981-82, Mercy Hosp. and Med. Ctr., Chgo., 1982-90, dir. emergency ctr., 1984-88; resident in occupl. and preventive medicine U. Ill., 1988-90; corp. med. dir. occupl. health svc. Univ. Cmty. Hosp., Tampa, 1992—. Fellow Am. Coll. Occupl. and Environ. Medicine, Am. Soc. Preventive Medicine, Fla. Assn. Occupl. and Environ. Medicine (pres. 1999-2001). Avocations: sailing, needlecrafts, swimming. Home: 4306 Harbor House Dr Tampa FL 33615-5408 Office: U Community Hosp Occupational Health Svcs 3100 E Fletcher Ave Tampa FL 33613-4613 Office Phone: 813-615-7755. Office Fax: (813) 615-7711. Business E-Mail: JWatkins@uch.org.

WATKINS, JOHN FRANCIS, management consultant; b. Alhambra, Calif., May 21, 1925; s. Edward F. and Louise (Ward) W.; divorced; children—Stephen, Katherine, John Francis, William. BSCE, U. Tex., Austin, 1947. With Earle M. Jorgensen Co., Lynwood, Calif., 1947-90, sr. v.p. adminstrn., 1978-90, ret.; owner John F. Watkins Assocs., Pasadena, Calif., 1990—. Pres. bd. Poly. Sch., Pasadena, 1978—80, Holy Family Sch., 1994—2002; adv. bd. mem. Serra H.S., Verbum Dei H.S., Dolores Mission Sch., 1996—; mem. Coll. Sci. and Engring. Coun. Loyola Marymount U.; adv. bd. Bishop Mora Salesian H.S., 1994—; mem. Cath. Edn. Found. Archdiocese L.A., 1995—; St. Gabriel pastoral region bd. dirs. Cath. Charities, 1994—; bd. dirs. Boys Republic, Chino Hills, Calif., 1970—, pres., 1977—80; bd. dirs. St. Luke Hosp., Pasadena, 1979—86, chmn. bd., 1982—86; bd. dirs. Econ. Literacy Coun. Calif., 1980—87, Pasadena Mus. of History, 1990—99. Mem. U.S. Navy League (nat. bd. dirs. 1989—, pres. Pasadena coun. 1992-93), Calif. Club, Annandale Golf Club, Serra Club (pres. 1995-97), Valley Club (San Marino, Calif.), Twilight Club (pres. 2002-03). Republican. Roman Catholic. Home and Office: 410 California Ter Pasadena CA 91105-2419 E-mail: jwatkins@pacificnet.net.

WATKINS, JOHN GOODRICH, psychologist, educator; b. Salmon, Idaho, Mar. 17, 1913; s. John Thomas and Ethel (Goodrich) W.; m. Evelyn Elizabeth Browne, Aug. 21, 1932; m. Doris Wade Tomlinson, June 8, 1946; m. Helen Verner Huth, Dec. 28, 1971; children: John Dean, Jonette Alison, Richard Douglas, Gregory Keith, Rodney Philip, Karen Stroobants, Marvin R. Huth. Student, Coll. Idaho, 1929-30, 31-32; BS, U. Idaho, 1933, MS, 1936; PhD, Columbia U., 1941. Instr. high sch., Idaho, 1933-39; faculty Ithaca Coll., 1940-41, Auburn U., 1941-43; assoc. prof. Wash. State U., 1946-49; chief clin. psychologist U.S. Army Welch Hosp., 1945-46; clin. psychologist VA Hosp., American Lake, Wash., 1949-50; chief clin. psychologist VA Mental Hygiene Clinic, Chgo., 1950-53, VA Hosp., Portland, Oreg., 1953-64; prof. psychology U. Mont., Missoula, 1964-84, prof. emeritus, 1984—, dir. clin. tng., 1964-80. Lectr. numerous univs.; clin. asso. U. Oreg. Med. Sch., 1957; pres. Am. Bd. Examiners in Psychol. Hypnosis, 1960-62 Author: Objective Measurement of Instrumental Performance, 1942, Hypnotherapy of War Neuroses, 1949, General Psychotherapy, 1960, The Therapeutic Self, 1978, (with others) We, The Divided Self, 1982, Hypnotherapeutic Techniques, 1987, Hypnoanalytic Techniques, 1992, Ego States: Theory and Therapy, 1997, Adventures in Human Understanding, 2001; contbr. articles to profl. jours. Mem. Internat. Soc. Clin. and Exptl. Hypnosis (co-founder, pres. 1965-67, recipient awards 1960-65), Soc. Clin. and Exptl. Hypnosis (pres. 1969-71, Morton Prince award), Am. Psychol. Assn. (pres. divsn. 30 1975-76, recipient award 1993), Phi Delta Kappa. Home and Office: 413 Evans Ave Missoula MT 59801-5827 *For a complete life one needs a job, a home, a love, a friend, and an enemy. My "enemies" are injustice, war, poverty, illness, and suffering, not people. Make your existence as meaningful as possible. Enjoy life fully, and when it comes time to leave, have no fear or regrets. Seek to leave this world a little better off because you lived. These are my values. Would that I were mature enough always to live up to them.*

WATKINS, LISA M. financial analyst; b. Baytown, Tex., Aug. 14, 1964; d. Bob R. and Ruth (Reeder) Allen; m. Don A. Watkins, Oct. 14, 2000; children: Valerie Ann, Joe Chambers. AA in Bus. Adminstrn., Lee Coll., 1985; BBA in Gen. Bus., U. Houston, Clear Lake, 1987, BS in Finance, 1994, MS in Fin., 1998. Accounts receivable supr. D.E. Harvey Builders, Inc., Houston, 1988-89; document contr. Halliburton, Houston, 1989-90, cost engr., 1990-94, internal auditor, 1994-95, acct., 1995-96, scheduler, 1996-2000; earned value analyst Lockheed Martin Corp., Houston, 2000—04, fin. analyst, 2004—. Methodist. Avocation: cross stitch. Office: Lockheed Martin Corp 2625 Bay Area Blvd Mail Code A8C Houston TX 77058 E-mail: bugsbunny@ev1.net.

WATKINS, SARA, musician; b. June 8, 1981; Mem. bank Nickel Creek; with Sugar Hill Records, 1998—. Musician: (recordings) Nickel Creek, 2000 (Cert. Gold, 2002, 2 Grammy nominations, 2001), This Side, 2002 (Cert. Gold, 2003, Grammy award for Contemporary Folk Album, 2003), (CD) Ten From Little Worlds, Not All Who Wander Are Lost, G.I.gantic, Faraway Land, Let it Fall, 26 Miles, More Than Words, Pickin' on ZZ Top, Philadelphia Folk Festival: 40th Anniversary, Telluride Bluegrass Festival: Reflection, Vol. 1, This is Americana, Vol 1: A View From Sugar Hill, Pickin' on the Rolling Stones, Prancer Returns, Further Down the Old Plank Road. Named Southwest Regional champions, Pizza Hut Internat. Bluegrass Music Showdown, 1994, Ariz. State Fiddle Champion, 1996, Emerging Artist of Yr., IBMA, 2000, Instrumental Group of YR., 2001; named one of Five Music Innovators for the Millennium, Time mag., 2000. Office: Q-Prime 131 S 11th St Nashville TN 37206

WATKINS, SHERRY LYNNE, elementary school educator; b. Bloomington, Ind., Oct. 13, 1944; d. Quentin Odell and Velma Ruth W. BSEd, Ind. U., 1966, MSEd, 1968. Tchr. 4th grade North Grove Elem. Sch., Ctr. Grove Sch. Dist., Greenwood, Ind., 1966-68; tchr. 4th and 6th grades John Strange Sch., Met. Dist. of Wash. Twp., Indpls., 1968-91; tchr. 4th grade Allisonville Sch. Met. Sch. Dist. of Wash. Twp., Indpls., 1991—. Bd. dirs. ISTA Ins. Trust and Fin. Svcs. Mem. People for Ethical Treatment of Animals. Mem.: AAUW, ACLU, NEA (nat. del. 1978—), World Confedn. Orgn. of Tchg. Profls. (del. Costa Rica 1990), Washington Twp. Edn. Assn. (pres. 1986—89), Ind. Tchrs. Assn. (state del. 1966—), Alpha Omicron Pi, Delta Kappa Gamma (chpt. pres. 1992—94, chmn. coordinating coun. Indpls. area 1994—96, state legislature chair 1997—99, state profl. affairs chair 2001—03). Avocations: travel, cultural activities. Office: Allisonville Sch 4920 E 79th St Indianapolis IN 46250-1615 Office Phone: 317-845-9441.

WATKINS, SHIRLEY ROBINSON, agriculture department administrator; BS in Home Econs., U. Ark., Pine Bluff; MEd in Supervision, U. Memphis. Various positions with U. Ark. Ext. Svc.; dir. nutrition svcs. Memphis City Schs.; dep. under sec. Food, Nutrition and Consumer Svcs., USDA, Washington, 1993-95, dep. asst. sec. for mktg. and regulatory programs, 1995-97, under sec. agr., 1997—. Office: Food Nutrition and Consumer Svcs Dept Agr 1400 Independence Ave SW Washington DC 20250-0002

WATKINS, STEPHEN EDWARD, accountant, newspaper executive; b. Oklahoma City, Sept. 1, 1922; s. Ralph Bushnell and Jane (Howell) W.; m. Suzanne Fowler, Aug. 16, 1976; children— Elizabeth Ann Watkins Racicot, Stephen Edward, Jr. BBA, U. N.Mex., 1944. C.P.A., N.Mex. With Peat, Marwick, Mitchell & Co., 1944-67; pres. The New Mexican daily newspaper, Santa Fe, 1967-78, 90—; pvt. practice pub. acctg. Santa Fe, 1978—. Vestryman Ch. of Holy Faith; trustee St. Vincent Hosp., 1979-85, Orchestra Santa Fe, 1976-82, Hist. Santa Fe Found. (pres. 1990). Mem. AICPA, Sons of Am. Revolution, Rotary. Home: 1325 Don Gaspar Ave Santa Fe NM 87505-4627 Office: 223 E Palace Ave Santa Fe NM 87501-1947

WATKINS, SYDNEY LYNN, sales executive; b. Hartford, Conn., Sept. 12, 1964; s. Robert Lee and Joan (Hardy) W. BS, Howard U., 1986, MS, 1989. Cert. U.S. Olympic Acad., Sport Adminstrn. Facility Mgmt. Inst. Water safety instr. Howard U. Satellite Youth Program, Washington, 1986, D.C. Dept. Recreation, Washington, 1986-87, phys. therapeutic recreation specialist, 1987-88; account rep. AT&T, Silver Spring, Md., 1988-90; program assoc. Amateur Athletic Found., L.A., 1991-95; program mgr. L.A. Team Mentoring, 1995-96; ind. cons., 1996—; pharm. sales cons. Wyeth-Ayerst Labs., 1997-99; dist. sales mgr. Takeda Pharms. Am., 1999—. Spl. asst. to pres. Dr. LeRoy T. Walker Found., Durham, N.C., 1993. African Am. Summit fellow NAACP, L.A., 1994; Patricia Roberts Harris grantee Howard U., 1989. Mem. AAHPERD, Alpha Kappa Alpha. Home: #102-355 931 Monroe Dr NE Atlanta GA 30308-1793 E-mail: Rokwest@aol.com.

WATKINS, TED ROSS, social work educator; b. Terrell, Tex., Dec. 2, 1938; s. Daniel Webster and Iva Lucy (Lowrie) W.; m. Betty Diane Dobbs, May 30, 1959; children: Evan Scott, Brett Dobbs, James David. BA in Psychology, U. North Tex., 1961; MSW, La. State U., 1963; D of Social Work, U. Pa., 1976. Staff social worker Mercer County Mental Health Ctr., Sharon, Pa., 1963-65; chief social worker, assoc. exec. Talbot Hall Treatment Ctr., Jonestown, Pa., 1965-70; chief social worker Harrisburg (Pa.) Mental Health Ctr., 1970-71; asst. prof. social work U. Tex., Arlington, 1971-76; dir. counseling svcs. Family Svcs., Inc., Ft. Worth, 1976-79; assoc. prof. social work U. Tex., 1979-85, dir. criminal justice, 1985-87, chair dept. sociology, 1987-91, assoc. prof., grad. advisor social work, 1991-99; assoc. prof., dir. Bachelor of Social Work program S.W. Tex. State U., San Marcos, 1999—2002, prof., 2002—. Cons. in field. Author (with James Callicutt): Mental Health Policy and Practice Today, 1997; author: (with A. Lewellen and M. Barrett) Dual Diagnosis: An Integrated Approach to Treatment, 2001. Tex. del. to Pres.'s Commn. in Mental Health, Austin, 1978. Recipient Golladay Teaching award Coll. Liberal Arts, Arlington, 1990; named Outstanding Profl. Human Svcs., 1972. Mem. NASW (state bd. dirs. 1976-78, 80-82, unit chair, vol. lobbyist 1982), Acad. Cert. Social Workers (lic. master social worker, advanced clin. practitioner), World Assn. for Psychosocial Rehab., Alliance for the Mentally Ill, Nat. Assn. for Rural Mental Health, Nat. Social Sci. Assn. Democrat. Methodist. Avocations: music, painting, camping. Office: Tex State U-San Marcos Sch Social Work 601 University Dr San Marcos TX 78666-4685 E-mail: tw11@swt.edu.

WATKINS, WESLEY WADE, retired congressman; b. DeQueen, Ark., Dec. 15, 1938; s. L. V. and Mary J. W.; m. Elizabeth Lou Rogers, June 9, 1963; children: Sally, Martha, Wade. BS, Okla. State U., 1960, MS, 1961. With USDA, Washington, 1961; asst. dir. admissions Okla. State U., 1963-66; exec. dir. Kiamichi Econ. Devel. Dist. of Okla., 1966-68; founder, owner constrn. and land devel. bus., 1968-76; mem. Okla. Senate, 1975-76, U.S. Congress from 3d Okla. Dist., 1977—91, 1997—2002; mem. ways and means com., human resources suncom., budget com.; pres. World Export Services, Stillwater, Okla., 1991—96. Pres. Higher Edn. Alumni Council of Okla.; Okla. chmn. Nat. Future Farmers Am. Found.; mem. Okla. Health Planning Council.; Pres. Ada (Okla). Growth and Devel. Assn. Served with Air N.G., 1960-66. Recipient Nat. Security Leadership award U.S. Air N.G., 1967, Okla. 4-H Alumni Recognition award, 1978, Disting. Alumnus award Okla. State U. Alumni Assn., 1978, others; named Policymaker of the Yr. Am. Vocational Assn., One of 3 Outstanding Young Men in Okla., Okla. Jaycees, 1968; named to Okla. State U. Hall of Fame, 1989. Mem. C. of C. Clubs: Masons, Lions. Republican. Presbyterian.

WATKINS, WILLIAM, JR., electric power industry executive; b. Jersey City, Aug. 12, 1932; s. William James and Willie Ree (Blount) W.; m. Sylvia I. Mulzac, Oct. 16, 1955; children: Cheryl, Rene, Linda. BBA, Pace U., 1954; MBA, NYU, 1962; postgrad. advanced mgmt. program, U. Mich., 1979; postgrad. exec. program, Edison Electric Inst., 1988. Staff asst. Consol. Edison Co. N.Y., N.Y.C., 1957-64; sys. mgr. Volkswagen Am., Englewood Cliffs, N.J., 1964-71; v.p., dir. adminstrn. New Eng. Power Svc. Co., Westboro, Mass., 1972-82, v.p., dir. human resources, 1986-92; v.p., dist. mgr. Narragansett Electric Co., Providence, 1982-86, exec. v.p., 1992-97; retired. Bd. dirs. Peerless Precision Corp., Lincoln, R.I., 1982-91; mem. bd. advisors Sarasota Pvt. Bank, Fleet Fin. Group, 2001. Chmn. R.I. Urban Project, Providence, 1984, R.I. Coun. for Econ. Edn., Providence, 1984; mem. Gov.'s Commn. on Health Care Reform, 1993-94; trustee R.I. Hosp., 1995-96, Lifespan, 1996-99, Roger Williams U., Bristol, R.I., 1991-94; bd. dirs. R.I. Hosp. Fin. Corp., Providence, 1987-91, Inroads, 1993-97, Leadership R.I., 1993-95, NCCJ, 1993-97; mem. resource and devel. commn. Episcopal Diocese Mass., 1988-92; chmn. bd. trustees RISD, 1998-2000. Recipient Cmty. Svc. award Urban League R.I., 1986, Paris V. Sterett award John Hope Settlement House, 1987, Small Bus. Adminstrn. Adv. of the Yr. award, 1994; named Developer of Yr., Am. Econ. Devel. Coun., 1996. Mem. N.E. Econ. Developers Assn. (bd. dirs. 1993-97), R.I. Urban Bankers Assn., Kappa Alpha Psi, Sigma Pi Phi. Avocations: swimming, biking, hiking, travel, golf. Home: 5114 87th Ct E Bradenton FL 34211-3743

WATKINSON, PATRICIA GRIEVE, museum director; b. Merton, Surrey, Eng., Mar. 28, 1946; came to U.S., 1972; d. Thomas Wardle and Kathleen (Bredl) Grieve. BA in Art History and Langs. with honors, Bristol U., Eng., 1968. Sec. Mayfair Fine Arts and The Mayfair Gallery, London, 1969-71; adminstr. Bernard Jacobson, Print Pub., London, 1971-73; freelance exhbn. work, writer Kilkenny Design Ctr., Davis Gallery, Irish Arts Council in Dublin, Ireland, 1975-76; curator of art Mus. Art, Wash. State U., Pullman, 1978-83, dir., 1984-98; exec. dir. Ft. Wayne (Ind.) Mus. Art, 1998—. Asst. prof. art history Wash. State U., Pullman, 1978; mem. adv. bd. Exhibits USA, 1999—. Co-author, co-editor: Gaylen Hansen: The Paintings of a Decade, 1985. Mem. Assn. Am. Colls. and Univ. Mus. and Galleries (western regional rep. 1987-89), Art Mus. Assn. Am. (Wash. state rep. 1986-87), Internat. Coun. Mus. (modern art com. 1986-89), Wash. Mus. Assn. (bd. dirs. 1984-87), Am. Fedn. Arts (western region rep. 1987-89), Wash. Art Consortium (pres. 1993-95), Western Mus. Assn. (bd. dirs. 1996-98), ARTTABLE. Office: Ft Wayne Mus Art 311 E Main St Fort Wayne IN 46802-1997

WATLEY, NATASHA, Olympic athlete; b. Canoga Pk., Calif., Nov. 27, 1981; d. Edwin and Carolyn. Grad., UCLA, 2003. Mem. U.S. Nat. Team, 2002—, U.S. Women's Softball Team, Athens Olympic Games, 2004. Named NFCA First Team All-Am., 2000, 2001, 2002, 2003, MVP of ISF World Championships, 2002, Pac-10 Player of the Yr., 2003; recipient Honda award for Top College Female Athlete, 2003. Achievements include invention of mem. Gold medal U.S. Nat. Team, ISF World Championships, 2002, Pan Am. Games, 2003, Athens Olympic Games, 2004; mem. NCAA Champion UCLA Bruins, Women's Coll. World Series, 2003. Office: USA Softball Complex 4845 S Shields Blvd Oklahoma City OK 73129*

WATNE, DARLENE CLAIRE, state legislator; b. Minot, N.D., Feb. 11, 1935; d. Charles A. and Anna Marie Widdel (Fjeld) W.; m. Clair A. Watne, Mar. 27, 1954; children: Carmen, Steven, Nancy, Matthew. Court reporting diploma, Minot (N.D.) Bus. Coll., 1975; grad., Real Estate Inst., 1991. Cert. residential real estate specialist, N.D. Exec. sec. Grand Exalted Ruler Elks, Minot, N.D., 1964-75; pres. Bus. Coll., Minot, 1974-76; ct. reporter N.W. Judicial Dist., Minot, 1976-90; real estate broker Watne Realtors Better Homes & Gardens, Minot, 1990-99; mem. N.D. Senate from 5th dist., Bismark, 1994—. Active Joint Civil Svcs. to the Poor, 1995—. Bd. dirs. ARC, Salvation Army, Red Cross; numerous state polit. interim senate coms. Named Minot Woman of Distinction in Bus. and Industry, 1993, Liberty award ND Bar Assn., 2000, named Citizen of Yr. ND Builders Assn., 2001. Republican. Avocations: reading, laking. Home: 520 28th Ave SW Minot ND 58701-7065

WATNE, DONALD ARTHUR, accountant, educator, retired; b. Gt. Falls, Mont., Jan. 18, 1939; BA with high honors, U. Mont., 1960, MA, 1961; PhD, U. Calif., Berkeley, 1977. CPA, Oreg. Acct. Piquet & Minihan, Eugene, Oreg., 1961-65; mgr. capital investment analysis Weyerhaeuser Co., Tacoma, 1965-68; mktg. rep. IBM Corp., Portland, Oreg., 1968-70; dir. EDP Ctr. in Concejo Mcpl., Barquisimeto, Venezuela, 1971-72; prof. acctg. Portland State U., 1976-2001, prof. emeritus, 2001—. Vis. prof. Xiamen (Fujian, People's Rep. China), 1985-86, U. Otago, Dunedin, New Zealand, 1985-86, U. Newcastle, Australia, 1985-86; cons. in field; acctg. qualifications com. Oregon State Bd. Acctg., 1989-98, CPE com., 1998-2001. Author: (with Peter B.B. Turney) Auditing EDP Systems, 2d edit. 1990; contbr. chpts. to books, articles to profl. jours. Del. to Soviet Union citizen amb. program People to People Internat., 1990; active Tng. the Trainers Program, Vilnius, Lithuania, 1993; trustee, treas. First Unitarian Ch. of Portland, 2002-; mem. bd. stewards First Unitarian Ch. of Portland Found., 2002-. Mem.: AICPA, Oreg. Soc. CPAs, Mensa, Mazamas Mountain Climbing Club. Home: 2826 NE 26th Ave Portland OR 97212-3503 Personal E-mail: dawatne@msn.com.

WATRING, WATSON GLENN, retired gynecologic oncologist, educator; b. St. Albans, W.Va., June 2, 1936; m. Roberta Tawell. BS, Washington & Lee U., 1958; MD, W.Va. U., 1962. Diplomate Am. Bd. Ob-Gyn, Am. Bd. Gynecol. Oncology. Intern The Toledo Hosp., 1963; resident in ob-gyn Ind. U., Indpls., 1964-66, Tripler Gen. Hosp., Honolulu, 1968-70; resident in gen. and oncologic surgery City of Hope Nat. Med. Ctr., Duarte, Calif., 1970-71, assoc. dir. gynecol. oncology, sr. surgeon, 1973-77; fellow in gynecol. oncology City of Hope Nat. Med. Ctr. and UCLA Med. Ctr., 1972-74; asst. prof. ob-gyn UCLA Med. Ctr., 1972-77; assoc. prof., sr. gynecologist, sr. surgeon Tufts New Eng. Med. Ctr. Hosp., Boston, 1977-80, asst. prof. radiation therapy, 1978-80; practice medicine specializing in ob-gyn Boston, 1980-82; assoc. prof. ob-gyn U. Mass., Worcester, 1982; regional dir. gynecol. oncology So. Calif. Permanente Med. Group, L.A., 1982-99, asst. dir. residency tng., 1985-99, ret., 1999. Dir. gynecol. oncology St. Margarets Hosp. for Women, Dorchester, Mass., 1977—80; clin. prof. ob-gyn U. Calif., Irvine, 1982—99. Contbr. Mem. ch. coun. Luth. Ch. of the Foothills, 1973—75. Lt. col. M.C. U.S. Army, 1965—71. Fellow: L.A. Obstet. and Gynecol. Soc., Am. Coll. Ob-Gyn; mem.: ACS (Calif. and Mass. chpts.), AAAS, AMA, Obstet. Soc. Boston, Boston Surg. Soc., Mass. Suffolk Dist. Med. Soc., Mass. Med. Soc., New Eng. Cancer Soc., New Eng. Obstet. and Gynecol. Soc., New Eng. Assn. Gynecol. Oncologists (chmn. charter com.), We. Assn. Gynecol. Oncologists (sec.-treas. 1976—81, program chmn. 1984, pres. 1985—), We. Soc. Gynecologists and Obstetricians, Internat. Gynecol. Cancer Soc., Soc. Study Breast Disease, Am. Radium Soc., Soc. Gynecol. Oncologists, Am. Soc. Clin. Oncology, Internat. Soc. Gynecol. Pathologists, Daniel Morton Soc., Sigma Xi. Democrat. Avocation: Avocations: golf, skiing, horticulture.

WATROUS, ROBERT THOMAS, academic director; b. Cleveland, Apr. 20, 1952; s. Frank Thomas and Marie Anne (Kmeicik) W.; m. Robin Joyce (Braun), Mar. 14, 1981 (div. 1993); 1 child, Michael Francis; m. Susan J. (Rupp), Mar. 8, 2003. BS, U. Dayton, Ohio, 1974, MS, 1977. Dir. student ctr. for off campus cmty. rels. U. Dayton, Ohio, 1974—76, resident dir., 1976—78; dir. of housing St. Bonaventure U., Olean, NY, 1978—81; asst. dean of student life housing U. Pa., Kutztown, 1981—86, dir. commuter and jud. affairs, 1986—2004, dean, student svcs. and campus life, 2004—. Faculty senate Kutztown U. Pa. 1986-89, 92-95; mem. Pa. Task Force on Intergroup Behavior in Higher Edn., 1991-94; trainer Pa. Interagy. Task Force on Civil Tension, Harrisburg, Pa., 1989-2001; exec. coun. Adult Learners Consortium, Bloomsburg, Pa., 1990-91; mem. Lehigh Valley Svc. Learning Consortium, 1994—. Bd. mgr. Tri Valley YMCA, Fleetwood, Pa., 1983-94; adv. bd. Crossroads, Kutztown, 1989-94; bd. dir. Jr. Achievement of Berks County, Reading, Pa.,

1990, Reading, Pa., 1990, Reading and Berks Coun. YMCA, 1992-96; mem. Leadership Berks, Reading, 1990, bd. dir. Leadership Berks, 1995—, sec. 1998-99, pres., 2000-04; co-founder Leading Sch. Bd., 1994—; mem. Leadership Alliance Berks, 2004-, YMCA cultural diversity and internat. awareness com., 1994—; mem. Berks County Conflict Resolution Task Force, 1996-2004; v.p. Fleetwood Activities Booster Club, 1998-2002, pres., 1999-2001. Mem. Nat. Assn. Student Pers. Adminstr. (profl. affiliate), Hawk Mt. Coun. Boy Scouts Am. (sustaining mem.), Berks County C. of C. (sch. bd. governance com. 1993-2000), Fleetwood Youth Soccer Club (v.p., pres. 1999), Fleetwood Youth Basketball Assn. (coach 1995-96), Leadership Alliance of Berks, 2003-, Greater Reading Leadrership Alliance, 2004-. Avocations: golf, sports, gardening. Office: Kutztown Univ PO Box 37 Kutztown PA 19530-0037

WATSON, ALEXANDER FLETCHER, organization executive, former ambassador; b. Boston, Aug. 8, 1939; s. Fletcher G. and Alice Victoria (Hodson) W.; m. Judith Dawson Tuttle, June 23, 1962; children: David F., Caitlin H. BA, Harvard U., 1961; MA, U. Wis., 1969. Consular officer Am. Embassy, Santo Domingo, Dominican Republic, 1962-64, Madrid, 1964-66; internat. relations officer Dept. State, Washington, 1966-68, 73-75; polit. officer Am. Embassy, Brasilia, Brazil, 1969-70; prin. officer Am. Consulate, Salvador, Brazil, 1970-73; spl. asst. Dept. State, Washington, Brazil, 1975-77, dir. Office of Devel Fin., 1978-79; dep. chief of mission Am. Embassy, La Paz, Bolivia, 1979-81, Bogota, Colombia, 1981-84, Brasilia, Brazil, 1984-86; U.S. ambassador to Lima, Peru, 1986-89; dep. U.S. permanent rep. to UN, 1989-93; asst. sec. of state for inter-Am. affairs Dept. of State, Washington, 1993 96; v.p., exec. dir. L.Am. and Caribbean region The Nature Conservancy, Arlington, Va., 1996-98; v.p., exec. dir. Internat. Conservation, The Nature Conservancy, Arlington, Va., 1998—. Pres., bd. dirs. Pan Am. Devel. Found., Caribbean/Latin Am. Action; bd. visitors Dept. Def. Ctrs. for Regional Security. Decorated Order of San Carlos (Colombia), Order of Condor (Bolivia), Labor Justice Order of Merit (Brazil), Order of Sun (Peru), Order of Rio Branco (Brazil). Mem. Am. Fgn. Svc. Assn., Coun. on Fgn. Rels., InterAm. Dialogue, Pacific Coun. Internat. Policy, Washington Inst. Fgn. Affairs., Am. Acad. Diplomacy. Office: The Nature Conservancy Internat Hdqs 4245 Fairfax Dr Ste 100 Arlington VA 22203-1650

WATSON, ANTHONY L. health facility executive; b. 1942; Supervising pub. health advisor dept.health edn. and welfare Ctr. for Disease Control, Pub. Health Svc., 1966-70; dep. dir. Comprehensive Health Planning Agy., N.Y.C., 1970-76, Health Planning, N.Y.C., 1976—85; exec. v.p., COO HIP Health Plan of N.Y., 1985—91, chmn., CEO, 1991—. Mem. Community Council of Greater N.Y.; pres, CEO The N.Y. Urban Coalition. Mem. Am. Health Planning Assn., Am. Hosp. Assn. Office: HIP Health Plan of NY 7 W 34th St New York NY 10001-8100

WATSON, ARTHUR DENNIS, federal official; b. Brownsville, Pa., May 11, 1950; s. John Leslie Watson and Margaret Teresa Mastile; m. Kathleen Frances Zaccardo, July 16, 1983; 1 child, Fiona Kathleen; 1 stepchild, John Leslie. BSBA, U. Richmond, 1972; MS in Bus.-Govt. Rels., Am. U., 1977, MA in Lit., 1979; PhD in English Lang. and Lit., Cath. U., 1987. Statis. asst. U.S. Postal Svc. Hdqrs., Washington, 1972—73, economist assoc., 1973—74, staff economist, 1974—77, mktg. analyst, 1977; rate analyst U.S. Postal Rate Commn., Washington, 1977—79, dir. pub. affairs, 1979—82; pub. affairs officer ICC, Washington, 1982—89, dep. dir. pub. affairs, 1989—93, assoc. dir. congl. and pub. affairs, 1993—95; dir. media affairs surface transp. bd. Dept. Transp., Washington, 1996—. Reader Washington Ear Sta. WETA-FM, 1977; pres. Arthur D. Watson and Co., Clifton, Va., 1983—; Washington corr. Linn's Stamp News, Sidney, Ohio, 1983—84; pubs. rels. columnist Arundel Comm., Reston, Va., 1991—92. Contbr. articles to profl. jours. With USCG, 1972—78. Recipient Meritorious Svc. medal, U.S.C.G. Res., 1989, Pub. Svc. award, ICC, 1989, Spl. Achievement award, Surface Transp. Bd., 1999, Merger Response Team Performance award, 2000, Performance award for media and pub. affairs, 2000, Internat. award, Plastic Modelers Soc., 2000, Merger Response Team Performance award, Surface Transp. Bd., 2001, Agy. Performance award Merger team, 2001, Performance award for website enhancements, 2002, Performance award for media and pub. affairs, 2002. Mem.: Assn. Transp. Law, Logistics and Policy, USS Natoma Bay Assn., E. Clairborne Robins Sch. Bus. Alumni Assn. Roman Catholic. Avocations: classical music, reading, writing, model building, travel. Home: 6521 Rockland Dr Clifton VA 20124-2415 Office: Surface Transp Bd 1925 K St NW Ste 845 Washington DC 20423-0001

WATSON, BERNARD CHARLES, educator, foundation administrator; m. Lois Lathan, July 1, 1961; children: Barbra, Bernard Jr. BS, Ind. U., 1951; MEd, U. Ill., 1955; PhD, U. Chgo., 1967; postdoctoral work, Harvard U., 1968; LHD (hon.), Allen U., 1981, LaSalle U., 1987, Spring Garden Coll., Elizabethtown Coll, Beaver Coll., 1988, Harris-Stowe State Coll., Morris Brown Coll., 1989, Millersville U., 1991, N.C. Ctrl. U., 1999; LLD (hon.), Lincoln U., 1974, Fla. Meml. Coll., 1984, Temple U., 1986, Med. Coll. Pa., 1986, Tuskegee U., 1991, Lincoln U., 1992, Morgan State U., 1992, Phila. Coll. Pharmacy and Sci., 1994, Bethune-Cookman Coll., 1995; HHD (hon.), Wilberforce U., 1979; DFA, Univ. of the Arts, 1992; D of Pedagogy, Drexel U., 1992. Tchr., prin. Roosevelt Jr. and Sr. H.S., Gary, Ind., 1955-65; staff assoc. Midwest Adminstrn. Ctr. U. Chgo., 1965-67; assoc. supt. innovative programs Sch. Dist. Phila., 1967-68, dep. supt. for planning, 1968-70; prof., chmn. dept. urban edn. Temple U., Phila., 1970-75, also prof. social foundations Coll. Edn. and prof. urban studies Coll. Liberal Arts, 1970-75, v.p. acad. adminstrn., 1976-81, presdl. scholar, 1994—; pres., CEO William Penn Found, Phila., 1982 93; chmn. HMA Found., Phila., 1994-97. Bd. dirs. Comcast Corp., First Union Bancorp North, First Union Bank, Keystone AAA Club, Keystone Ins. Co., Phila. Contributionship; assoc. edn. Grad. Sch. Edn. Harvard U., 1970-72, mem. vis. com., 1981-87; mem. vis. com. dept. Afro-Am. studies Harvard Coll., 1974-78. Author: In Spite of the System: The Individual and Educational Reform, 1974; editor in chief Cross Reference: A Jour. Pub. Policy and Multi-Cultural Edn., 1976-79, Testing Its Origin, Use and Misuse, 1997, Colored, Negro, Black: Chasing the American Dream, 1997; contbr. numerous articles to profl. jours., chpts. to books. Mem. steering com., mem. exec. com. Nat. Urban Coalition, 1973-89; vice chmn. Nat. Adv. Coun. Edn. Professions Devel., 1967 70, Pa. Coun. on Arts, 1986-93; mem. Nat. Coun. Ednl. Rsch., 1980-82, William T. Grant Found. Commn. Work, Family and Citizenship, 1987-88; sr. vice chmn. bd. trustees Nat. Urban League, 1983-96; vice chmn. bd. dirs. Pa. Conv. Ctr. Authority, 1986—; trustee Thomas Jefferson U., 1993-95; sec. bd. N.J. State Aquarium, 1988-93; chmn. Ave. the Arts Inc., 1992—; mem. fed. judiciary nominating com. Pa., 1981-89; bd. dirs. Friends of the Nelson Mandela Children's Fund, 1996—, Marian Anderson Hist. Soc., 1998—; mem. adv. com. Frederick D. Patterson Rsch. Inst., 1998—; chmn. bd. dirs. Barnes Found., 1999—. Recipient numerous honors and awards for leadership in edn., the arts, and civil rights. Mem. Am. Philosophical Soc., Am. Acad. Polit. and Social Sci., Phi Delta Kappa, Kappa Delta Pi. Office: TUCC 1616 Walnut St Philadelphia PA 19103-5313

WATSON, BRENDA BENNETT, insurance company executive; b. Decatur, Ga., Aug. 26, 1940; d. Robert Joseph and Clarissa Mae (Weekes) Bennett; m. James H. Pair Jr., Apr. 4, 1969 (div. Aug. 1993); children: Richard S. Pair, Randall J. Pair, Ronald G. Pair; m. James Leigh Watson, Sept. 9, 1995. Student, DeKalb Coll., 1971. Lic. property and casualty agt., Fla., Ga., Okla., Tenn., Tex. Underwriter W. K. Stringer Co., Atlanta, 1961-65, Tharpe & Assocs., Atlanta, 1965-68; sr. v.p. Alexander - Howden, Atlanta, 1968-82; exec. v.p., ptnr. Pair Underwriting Mgrs. Inc., Atlanta, 1982-86; pres. Walkingstick-LaGere-Pair Underwriting Mgrs., Inc., Chandler, Okla., 1986-88; exec. v.p., dir. LaGere-Walkingstick Ins. Agy., Chandler, Okla., 1988—. Exec. v.p. Nat. Am. Ins. Co., Chandler, Okla., 1987—, Austin, Tex., 1999—; exec. v.p., bd. dirs. Chandler Ins. Ltd., Cayman Islands, 1985—. Dir., past pres. Gateway to Prevention and Recovery, 1994-98. Mem. Nat. Assn. Ins. Women (pres. Atlanta chpt. 1978-79, Woman of Yr. 1979-80). Republican. Episcopalian. Office: Wells Fargo Bank Bldg 2028 E Ben White Blvd Ste 200 Austin TX 78741 E-mail: bwatson@naico.com.

WATSON, CATHERINE ELAINE, journalist; b. Mpls., Feb. 9, 1944; d. Richard Edward and LaVonne (Slater) W.; m. Al Sicherman (div.); children: Joseph Sicherman, David Sicherman. BA in Journalism, U. Minn., 1967; MA in Teaching, Coll. of St. Thomas, 1971. Reporter Mpls. Star Tribune, 1966-72; editor Picture mag., 1972-78, Travel sect., 1978—2001; editor in chief Galena (Ill.) Gazette, 1990-91. Instr. split rock arts program U. Minn., 1996-2003; sr. travel editor Star Tribune, 2001-. Author: Travel Basics, 1984. Contbr. articles to newspapers and travel mags. and books. Recipient Newspaper Mag. Picture Editor's award Pictures of Yr. Competition, 1974, 75, awards for writing and photography Soc. Am. Travel Writers, 1983-2003, Photographer of Yr. award, 1990, Alumna of Notable Achievement award U. Minn. Coll. Liberal Arts, 1994; rsch. grant Jerome Found./Gen. Mills Found., 2004; named Lowell Thomas Travel Journalist of Yr., 1990. Mem. Am. Newspaper Guild, Soc. Am. Travel Writers, Phi Beta Kappa, Alpha Omicron Pi. Office: 425 Portland Ave Minneapolis MN 55488-1511

WATSON, DAVID COLQUITT, electrical engineer, educator; b. Linden, Tex., Feb. 9, 1936; s. Colvin Colquitt and Nelena Gertrude (Kaesler) W.; m. Flora Janet Thayn, Nov. 10, 1959; children: Flora Janeen, Melanie Beth, Morrie Gaylene, Cheralyn Gail, Nathan David, Amy Melissa, Brian Colvin. BSEE, U. Utah, 1964, PhD in Elec. Engring., 1968. Elec. tech. Hercules Pwoder Co., Magna, Utah, 1961-62; rsch. asst. microwave devices and phys. elecs. lab. U. Utah, 1964-68; sr. mem. tech. staff ESL, Inc., Sunnyvale, Calif., 1968-78, head dept. comm., 1969-70; sr. engring. specialist Probe Systems, Inc., Sunnyvale, Calif., 1978-79; sr. mem. tech. staff ARGO Systems, Inc., Sunnyvale, Calif., 1979-90, GTE Govt. Systems Corp., Mountain View, Calif., 1990-91, sr. cons. Watson Cons. Svcs., 1991 92, 94-97; sr. staff engr. ESL, Inc., 1992-94. Mem. faculty U. Santa Clara, 1978-81, 1992-94, San Jose State U., 1981-92, Coll. Notre Dame, 1992, Chapman U., 1993; sr. engring. specialist Space Sys. Loral, 1997—. Contbr. articles to IEEE Transactions, 1965-79; co-inventor cyclotron-wave rectifier; inventor gradient descrambler. With USAF, 1956-60. NASA fellow, 1968. Mem. IEEE, Phi Kappa Phi, Tau Beta Pi, Eta Kappa Nu. Mem. Lds Ch. Office: Space Sys Loral 3825 Fabian Way Palo Alto CA 94303-4604 E-mail: watson.david@ssd.loral.com. *Personal philosophy: I believe in hard work and strict honesty, in giving full value for consideration received, to God and fellow man or woman.*

WATSON, DENNIS WALLACE, microbiology educator, scientist; b. Morpeth, Ont., Can., Apr. 29, 1914; came to U.S., 1938, naturalized, 1946; s. William and Sarah (Verity) W.; m. Alicemay Whittier, June 15, 1941; children: Catherine W., William V. BSA, U. Toronto, 1934; MS, Dalhousie U., 1937; PhD, U. Wis., 1941, DSc (hon.), 1981. Rsch. assoc. U. Wis., 1942, asst. prof., 1946-49; vis. investigator Rockefeller Inst., 1942; investigator Connaught Lab. Med. Rsch. U. Toronto, 1942-44; assoc. prof. U. Minn., Mpls., 1949-52, prof., 1953-63, head dept. microbiology, 1964-84, Regents prof. microbiology, 1980-84, Regents prof. emeritus, 1984—. Vis. prof. Med. Sch. U. Wash., 1950; mem. Commn. Immunization Armed Forces Epidemiology Bd., 1946-59; mem. bd. sci. counselors, div. biol. standards NIH, 1957-59, mem. allergy and immunology study sect., 1954-58; chmn. tgn. grant com. Inst. Allergy and Infectious Diseases, 1964, mem. adv. coun., 1967-71; mem. microbiology panel Office Naval Rsch., 1963-66; vice chmn. Am. Soc. Microbiology Found., 1973; bd. dirs. Nat. Found. Infectious Diseases, 1976-81 Editorial bd. Infection and Immunity, 1971-72; editorial cons. Medcom Faculty Medicine, 1973—. With AUS, 1944-46. Recipient USPHS Research Career award, 1962-64; Spl. research fellow USPHS, 1960-61 Mem. AAAS, Am. Assn. Immunologists, Am. Chem. Soc., Am. Acad. Microbiology (vice chmn. bd. govs. 1967), Am. Soc. Microbiology (pres. 1969, v.p. Found. 1972-73), Internat. Endotoxin Soc. (hon., life), Soc. Exptl. Biology and Medicine (coun. 1977-79, pres. 1976-77), Lancefield Soc., Sigma Xi, Phi Zeta. Home: 2106 Hendon Ave Saint Paul MN 55108-1419 Office: U Minn Med Sch Dept Microbiology PO Box 196 Minneapolis MN 55440-0196 Office Phone: 651-645-3573. Business E-Mail: watso006@tc.umn.edu.

WATSON, DIANE EDITH, congresswoman; b. L.A., Nov. 12, 1933; d. William Allen Louis and Dorothy Elizabeth (O'Neal) Watson. AA, L.A. City Coll., 1954; BA, UCLA, 1956; MS, Calif. State U., L.A.; PhD, Claremont Grad. Sch., 1987. Tchr., sch. psychologist L.A. Unified Sch. Dist., 1960-69, 73-74; assoc. prof. Calif. State U., L.A., 1969-71; health occupations specialist Bur. Indsl. Edn., Calif. Dept. Edn., 1971-73; mem. L.A. Unified Sch. Bd., 1975-78, Calif. Senate from dist. 26, 1978-98, chairperson health and human svcs. com.; U.S. amb. to Micronesia Dept. of State, 1999-2001; mem. U.S. Congress from 33d Calif. dist., 2001—, mem. govt. reform com. and internat. rels. com. Mem. Legis. Black Caucus, edn. com., budget and fiscal rev. com., criminal procedure com., housing and land use com. Calif State Sen.; del. Dem. Nat. Conv., 1972—; mem. Dem. Nat. Com.; mem. exec. com. Nat. Conf. State Legislators Author: Health Occupations Instructional Units-Secondary Schools, 1975, Planning Guide for Health Occupations, 1975; co-author: Introduction to Health Care, 1976. Recipient Mary Church Terrell award, 1976, Brotherhood Crusade award, 1981, Black Woman of Achievement award NAACP Legal Def. Fund, 1988; named Alumnus of Yr., UCLA, 1980, 82. Mem. Calif. Assn. Sch. Psychologists, L.A. Urban League, Calif. Tchrs. Assn., Calif. Commn. on Status Women. Democrat. Roman Catholic. Office: US Ho Reps 125 Cannon HOB Washington DC 20515-0533

WATSON, DOC (ARTHEL LANE WATSON), vocalist, guitarist, banjoist, recording artist; b. Deep Gap, N.C., Mar. 2, 1923; s. General Dixon and Annie (Greer) Waston; m. Rosa Lee Carlton; children: Eddy Merle(dec.), Nancy Ellen. Ind. rec. artist, touring performer. First appearance Boone (N.C.) Fiddler's Conf., rec. artist Folkways in 1960's, signed with Vanguard Records, 1964, recorded for United Artists, Columbia, Poppy, Sugar Hill, Verve and Flying Fish labels; performer: Newport Folk Festival, 1963, Smithsonian Inst., White House, 1980, Carnegie Hall, 1985; toured in Africa for Dept. State, 1970, also Europe and Japan, albums (many with Merle Watson) Southbound, Red Rocking Chair, The Guitar Album, Riding the Midnight Train (Grammy award for Best Traditional Folk album, 1986), Portrait, Songs for Little Pickers, On Praying Ground (Grammay award for best traditional folk album, 1990); performer (music): (films) Places in the Heart. Recipient Grammy award, 1973, 1974, 1979, 1986, 1990, N.C. award, State of N.C., 1985, Carolina prize N.Y. Times Corp., 1985, Grammy award for Best Traditional Folk Rec., 1990, Nat. Medal of Arts, Pres. of U.S. with NEA, 1997, Nat. Heritage award, NEH, 1988. Office: care Folklore Prodns 1671 Appian Way Santa Monica CA 90401-3258 Fax: 310-458-6005. E-mail: info@folkloreproductions.com.

WATSON, DONALD CHARLES, cardiothoracic surgeon, educator; b. Fairfield, Ohio, Mar. 15, 1945; s. Donald Charles and Pricilla H. Watson; m. Susan Robertson Prince, June 23, 1973; children: Kea Huntington, Katherine Anne, Kirsten Prince. BA in Applied Sci., BSME, Lehigh U., 1968; MSME, Stanford U., 1969; MD, Duke U., 1972. Diplomate Am. Bd. Thoracic Surgery, Am. Bd. Surgery. Intern Stanford U. Med. Ctr., Calif., 1972-73, resident in cardiovasc. surgery, 1973-74, resident in surgery, 1976-78, chief resident in heart transplant, 1978-79, chief resident in cardiovasc. and gen. surgery, 1978-80; clin. assoc. surgery br. Nat. Heart and Lung Inst., 1974-76, acting sr. surgeon, 1976; assoc. cardiovasc. surgeon dept. child health and devel. George Washington U., Washington, 1980-84, asst. prof. surgery, asst. prof. child health and devel., 1980-84, attending cardiovasc. surgeon dept. child health and devel., 1984-89, assoc. prof. surgery, 1984-89; assoc. prof. pediats. U. Tenn.-Memphis, 1984-90, prof. surgery, 1990—, prof. pediats., 1990—, chmn. cardiothoracic surgery, 1984-99, assoc. chief med. officer, 1999—2001. Mem. staff Le Bonheur Children's Med. Ctr., Memphis, 1984—, chmn. cardiothoracic surgery, 1984-99; cons. in field; instr. advanced trauma life support; profl. cons., program reviewer HHS. Contbr. chpts., numerous articles, revs. to profl. publs. Bd. dirs. Internat. Children's Heart Found., Child Health Alliance of the Mid-South. Served to lt. comdr. USPHS, 1974-76. Smith Kline & French fellow Lehigh U., 1967; NSF fellow Lehigh U., 1968; univ. interdepartmental scholar and univ. scholar Lehigh U., 1968. Fellow Am. Coll. Cardiology, Am. Coll. Chest Physicians (forum cardiovasc. surgery, coun. critical care), Southeastern Surg. Congress, Am. Acad. Pediats. (surgery sect.), ACS; mem. Assn. Surg. Edn., Am. Assn. Thoracic Surgery, Soc. Thoracic Surgeons, So. Thoracic Surg. Assn., Am. Thoracic Soc., Assn. Acad. Surgery, Internat. Soc. Heart Transplantation, Am. Fedn. Clin. Rsch., Found. Advanced Edn. in Scis., Andrew G. Morrow Soc., Norman E. Shumway Soc. (multiple bd. dirs.), Coun. on Cardiovasc. Surgery Am. Heart Assn., Soc. Internat. di Chirig., AAAS, N.Y. Acad. Sci., AMA, NIH Alumni Assn., Stanford U. Med. Alumni Assn., Stanford U. Alumni Assn., Lehigh U. Alumni Assn., Smithsonian Assocs., Sierra Club, U. Tenn. Pres.'s Club, LeBonheur Pres's Club, U.S. Yacht Racing Assn., Pilots Internat. Assn., Nat. Assn. Flight Instrs., Aircraft Owners and Pilots Assn., Order Ky. Cols., Crescent Club, Phi Beta Kappa, Tau Beta Pi, Pi Tau Sigma, Phi Gamma Delta. Republican. Presbyterian. Avocations: golf, sailing, racquet sports, flying, computers. Business E-Mail: dwatson@utmem.edu.

WATSON, DONALD RALPH, architect, artist, educator, author; b. Providence, Sept. 27, 1937; s. Ralph Giles W. and Ethel (Fletcher) Pastene; m. Marja Palmqvist, Sept. 8, 1966 (div. Jan. 1984); children: Petrik, Elise; m. Judith Criste, Jan. 3, 1986 (dec. Oct. 8, 2000). AB, Yale U., 1959, BArch, 1962, MEd, 1969. Lic. architect Nat. Council Archtl. Registration Bds. Architect Peace Corps, Tunisia, 1962-64; archtl. cons. Govt. of Tunisia, 1964-65; pvt. practice, Trumbull, Conn., 1969—; dean Sch. Architecture, Rensselaer Poly. Inst., Troy, N.Y., 1990-95, prof., 1990—2001. Frederick C. Baker vis. prof. U. Oreg., 1995; chmn. environ. design program, Yale U., 1979-90; vis. prof. Yale U., 1995-2000. Author: Designing and Building a Solar House, 1977, Energy Conservation Through Building Design, 1979, Climatic Design, 1983, Energy Design Handbook, 1993; editor-in-chief Time Saver Standards: Architectural Design Data, 1997, Time-Saver Standards: Urban Design, 2003. Bd. dirs. Save the Children Fedn., 1979-82. Recipient Honor Design award Conn. Soc. Architects, 1974, Honor Design award region AIA, 1978, 84, 1st award Owens Corning Energy Conservation Bldg. Design Program, 1983, Excellence in housing award Energy Efficient Bldg. Assn., 1988, Lifetime Achievement award Passive and Low Energy Architecture, 1990, Best in Show Watercolors, Soc. Creative Artists, 1999, Green Bldg. Design award NESEA, 2002, Disting. Prof. award ACSA, 2002; Assn. of Collegiate Schs. of Architecture/Am. Metals Climax rsch. fellow, 1967-69; rsch. fellow Rockefeller Found., 1978. Fellow: AIA. Home and Office: 54 Larkspur Dr Trumbull CT 06611-4652

WATSON, DOUG, information technology executive; Asst. v.p. info. tech. Bacardi-Martini; v.p., dir. IT Ams. Bacardi USA Inc., Miami, Fla. Named one of Premier 100 IT Leaders, ComputerWorld, 2003. Office: Bacardi USA Inc 2100 Biscayne Blvd Miami FL 33137-5028*

WATSON, ELIZABETH MARION, protective services official; b. Phila., Aug. 25, 1949; d John Julian and Elizabeth Gertrude (Judge) Herrmann; m. Robert LLoyd Watson, June 18, 1976; children: Susan, Mark, David. BA in Psychology with honors, Tex. Tech. U., 1971. With Houston Police Dept., 1972-92, detective homicide, burglary and theft, 1976-81, lt. records div. northeast patrol div., 1981-84, capt. inspections div., auto theft div., 1984-87, dep. chief west patrol bur., 1987-90, police chief, 1990-92; with Austin, Tex. Police Dept., 1992—, police chief, 1992—. Mem. adv. bd. S.W. Law Enforcement Inst., Richardson,Tex., 1990—. Mem. editorial bd. Am. Jour. Police, 1991—. Mem. Internat. Assn. Chiefs of Police (mem. major cities chiefs, mem. civil rights com.), Police Exec. Rsch. Form, Tex. Police Chiefs Assn. Roman Catholic. Home: 2118 Wychwood Dr Austin TX 78746-7864

WATSON, EMILY, actress; b. London, Jan. 14, 1967; m. Jack Waters, 1995. Motion picture and stage actress. Films include Breaking the Waves, 1996 (nominee Best Actress Oscar 1997, nominee Golden Globe award 1997, Robert award 1997, N.Y. Film Critics Circle award 1996, Nat. Soc. Film Critics award 1996, L.A. Film Critics Assn. New Generation award 1996, European Film award 1996, others), The Mill on the Floss, 1997, Metroland, 1997, The Boxer, 1997, Hilary and Jackie (nominee Best Actress Oscar 1999, nominee Golden Globe award 1999), The Cradle Will Rock, 1999, Angela's Ashes, 1999, Trixie, 2000, Gosford Park, 2001 (SAG award outstanding performance by the cast, 2002), In Search of the Assasin, 2001, Equilibrium, 2002, Punch-Drunk Love, 2002, Red Dragon, 2002. Office: c/o SAG 5757 Wilshire Blvd Los Angeles CA 90036-3635

WATSON, ERIC N. corporate executive; b. Charlotte, N.C., Feb. 26, 1956; s. Climmie Newell and Lula Jane Watson; m. Susan Adele Watson; children: Jarrod, Alexandria. BA, Livingston Coll., 1978. Cert. Inst. Auditors Tools and Techniques; cert. trainer, quality facilitator, claim law assoc. Tchr. English Enderly Pk. Elem. Sch., Charlotte, 1978; claims op. rep. St. Paul Cos., Inc., 1979-82, supr., 1983-89, lead auditor/mgr., 1990-93, claim quality cons., 1994, asst. v.p. global diversity, 1995-98, v.p. global diversity, 1999-2000; exec. dir. diversity Williams, Tulsa, Okla., 2000—. Diversity cons. Guident CPI, St. Paul, Thermo King, St. Paul, Carlson Co., St. Paul, Cargill, Inc., St. Paul, Nat. United Way of Am., Minn., State of Minn., St. Paul, United Negro Coll. Fund, St. Paul, Fed. Res. Bank, St. Paul, Minn. Affirmative Action Coun., St. Paul, State Dept. Internal Revenue, St. Paul, Minn. Cultural Diversity Ctr., St. Paul; corp. rep. TC Diversity Roundtable, Mpls.-St. Paul, Mpls. NAACP, 1999-2000; mem. Def. Rsch. Inst. for Profl. Edn. of Def. Bar, Princeton, N.J., 1991-94. Mem. Multicultural Forum, St. Paul, 1992—, Gov.'s Scholar Program, St. Paul, 1995—, Workforce Diversity Coun., N.Y.C., 1996—. Black Achievers Bd., St. Paul, 1998—, Bus. Social Responsibility, Ca lif., 1998—, Minn. Urban Coalition, 1999—; mentor Minn. 100 Mentoring, St. Paul, 1994—. Mem. Kappa Alpha Psi. Avocations: reading, creative writing, coaching youth sports, mentoring and counseling. Home: 3700 N Narcissus Ave Broken Arrow OK 74012-1706 Office: Williams 1 Williams Ctr PO Box 2400 Tulsa OK 74102-2400

WATSON, EVELYN EGNER, radiation scientist; b. Corbin, Ky., Dec. 15, 1928; d. Edgar Mattison and Bertha Mae (Mayfield) Egner; m. Earl Greene Watson, Nov. 10, 1953; children: Nancy Eileen, Philip Allen. AA, Cumberland Coll., 1946; student, Lincoln Meml. U., 1947-48; BA, U. Ky., 1949; postgrad., U. Tenn., 1968. Math. and sci. tchr. Lynch (Ky.) High Sch., 1949-50; office mgr. Whitley County Sch. System, Williamsburg, Ky., 1950-53; sr. lab. tech. Radiation Internal Dose Ctr. Oak Ridge (Tenn.) Assoc. Univs., 1961-71, scientist, 1971-79, program mgr., 1979-89, program dir., 1989-94; cons. internal dosimetry Tenn., 1994—. Lectr. in field; cons. USFDA, Rockville, Md., 1983-88. Assoc. editor Jour. Nuclear Medicine, 1981-86; editor newsletter Soc. Nuclear Medicine S.E. chpt., 1988-99; co-author: MIRD Primer, 1988; contbr. articles to profl., chpts. to books. Bd. dirs. Youth Haven, Oak Ridge, Tenn., 1970-74, Clinch River Home Health, Clinton, Tenn., 1988-94. Recipient Excellence in Tech. Transfer award Fed. Lab. Consortium, 1985, Lifetime Scientific Achievement award Assn. Women in Sci., 1993. Mem. Soc. Nuclear Medicine (med. internal radiation dose com. 1980—, chmn. 1994—, Marshall Brucer award for Disting. Svc. to S.E. chpt. 1999), Health Physics Soc. (Disting. Svc. award 1981, treas. 1976-77, Lifetime Achievement award 1994), European Assn. Nuclear Medicine, Nat. Coun. on Radiation Protection and Measurements (sci. com. 1986-98), Sigma Xi. Mem. Ch. of Christ. Avocations: reading, word puzzles, handicrafts. Home: 104 New Bedford Ln Oak Ridge TN 37830-8289 E-mail: eew72@comcast.net.

WATSON, GAIL H. retired librarian; b. Hattiesburg, Miss., May 12, 1941; d. Robert Elkin and Virginia Lucille (Swann) Hill; m. Tommy Gene Watson, June 4, 1963; children: James Todd, Thomas Gregory. BA, U. So. Miss., 1963; M in Librarianship, U. S.C., 1975; MEd, Tenn. State U., Nashville, 1983. Tchr. Hawkins Jr. H.S., Hattiesburg, 1963-64, Seminary (Miss.) H.S., 1965-66; libr. Bush River Elem. Sch., Newberry, S.C., 1973-74, Prosperity (S.C.) Elem. Sch., 1974-76; tchr. Franklin County H.S., Winchester, Tenn., 1977-83; libr. South/J.D. Jackson Jr. H.S., Cowan, Tenn., 1983—2003; ret., 2003. Mem. SACS rev. teams, Tenn., 1985—. Tenn. Dept. Edn. grantee, 1995. Mem. ALA, Soc. for Promotion of Christian Knowledge, Franklin County Librs. (chair 1998-2003), Delta Kappa Gamma, Kappa Delta. Democrat. Episcopalian. Avocations: reading, travel. Home: 143 S Carolina Ave Sewanee TN 37375-2405

WATSON, GEORGE HENRY, JR., broadcaster, journalist; b. Birmingham, Ala., July 27, 1936; s. George Henry and Grace Elizabeth (Carr) W.; m. Ellen Havican Bradley, July 13, 1979; children: George H., III, Ellen Havican BA, Harvard U., 1959; MS, Columbia U., 1960. Reporter Washington Post,

1960-61; corr. ABC News, 1962-75, Moscow bur. chief, 1966-69, London bur. chief, 1969-75, v.p., Washington bur. chief, 1976-80; v.p., mng. editor Cable News Network, 1980; v.p. news ABC News, N.Y.C., 1981-85, exec. in charge ABC News Viewpoint, 1981-85, v.p., Washington bur. chief, 1985-93, sr. contbg. editor, 1993-2001; freelance broadcast journalist. Served with U.S. Army, 1958. Recipient Peabody award, 1982, DuPont Columbia award, 1983, nat. news Emmy award, 1984. Mem. Radio Television News Dirs. Assn., Soc. Profl. Journalists, Nat. Press Club, Overseas Press Club (award for best television documentary 1971, citation for excellence 1974), Nat. Press Club, Com. to Protect Journalists, Fgn. Policy Assn., Cosmos Club. E-mail: ebw327@aol.com.

WATSON, GEORGE W. energy executive; BSEE, MBA in Fin. Mktg., Queen's U., Kingston, Can.; grad. advanced mgmt. program, Harvard U., 1988. With Can. Imperial Bank Commerce, Toronto; asst. gen. mgr. world-wide, oil and gas divsn. Calgary, 1981; dir. fin. Dome Petroleum, v.p. fin.; v.p., treas. Amoco Can.; pres., CEO Intensity Resources, 1988-90; CFO TransCanada, 1990-93, pres., 1993-99, CEO, 1994-99; ptnr. Northridge Can. Inc., 1999—2002. CEO WNS Emergent Inc.; chmn. bd. dirs. Badger Daylighting Inc.; bd. dirs. Ranchgate Energy Ltd., Esprit Exploration, Ltd.; chmn. Spirit Energy, Inc., Signal Energy Inc., Blizzard Energy Inc., CODA. Bd. dirs. Queen's U., TGS N. Am. REIT. Office Phone: 403-705-7510. Business E-Mail: george.watson@criticalcontrol.com.

WATSON, GEORGIANNA, librarian; b. Lock Haven, Pa., Feb. 18, 1949; d. George and Anna (Eisenhower) Rhine; children: Sharga Nicolle, George Winfield-Martin. BS in Edn., Lock Haven State U., 1971; MLS, Brigham Young U., 1978; M in Pub. Adminstrn., John Jay Coll. Criminal Justice, N.Y.C., 1986. Tchr. Mifflin County Sch. Dist., Lewistown, Pa., 1971—72; libr. Shiprock Boarding Sch. Bur. Indian Affairs, N.Mex., 1972—79, libr. Ft. Sill Indian Sch. Lawton, Okla., 1979—80; libr. U.S. Mil. Acad., West Point, 1980—83, head pub. services, libr., 1983—. Owner The Paint Pony, Walden, NY. Mem. Southeastern N.Y. Libr. Resource Coun. (continuing edn. com., govt. documents interest group), Southeastern N.Y. Reference Libr. Interest Group, Am. Quarter Horse Assn., Internat. Arabian Horse Assn., Am. Paint Horse Assn., N.Y. State Horse Coun. (Mid-Hudson dir.), Pi Alpha Alpha. Republican. Home: 8 St Michaels Ln Walden NY 12586-2466 Office: US Mil Acad Dept Army West Point NY 10996-1799 E-mail: gwatso@hvc.rr.com.

WATSON, GLENN ROBERT, lawyer; b. Okla., May 2, 1917; s. Albert Thomas and Ethel Amelia W.; m. Dorothy Ann, Feb. 25, 1945; 1 dau., Carol Ann. Student, East Cen. State U., Okla., 1933-36; LL.B., Okla. U., 1939. Bar: Okla. 1939, Calif. 1946. Pvt. practice law, Okla., 1939-41; founding ptnr. Richards, Watson & Gershon, Los Angeles, 1946—2002; ret., 2002; city atty., 1958-65, 78-83, Commerce, Calif., 1960-61, Cerritos, Calif., 1956-64, Victorville, Calif., 1962-63, Carson, Calif., 1968-2000, Rosemead, Calif., 1960-76, Seal Beach, Calif., 1972-78, South El Monte, Calif., 1976-78, Avalon, Calif., 1976-80, Artesia, Calif., 1976-97. Served with USNR, 1942-46. Mem. ABA, Los Angeles County Bar Assn., Am. Judicature Soc., Lawyers Club of Los Angeles (past pres.), Los Angeles World Affairs Council, Internat. Cir., La Canada C. of C. (past pres.), Order of Coif, Phi Delta Phi, Delta Chi. Home: 522 Paulette Pl La Canada CA 91011 Office: Richards Watson & Gershon 355 S Grand Ave 40th Flr Los Angeles CA 90071-3101 E-mail: gwatson@rwglaw.com.

WATSON, H. MITCHELL, JR., business software company executive; Various positions including v.p. mktg. and svcs. IBM; pres., CEO Rolm Co.; pres. Sigma Group, Westport, Conn., 1993-97; chmn. bd. dirs. Mapics Inc., Alpharetta, Ga., 1997—.

WATSON, HARLAN L(EROY), federal official, physicist, economist; b. Macomb, Ill., Dec. 17, 1944; s. Joseph Carroll and Helen Louise (Sanders) Watson; m. Sharon Ann Rinkus Diguette, Apr. 22, 1977. BA in Physics, Western Ill. U., 1967; PhD in Physics, Iowa State U., 1973; MA in Econs., Georgetown U., 1981. Postdoctoral fellow Argonne (Ill.) Nat. Lab., 1973-75; project scientist, then sr. scientist B-K Dynamics, Inc., Rockville, Md., 1975-78; tech. staff TRW Energy Systems Planning Group, Mc Lean, Va., 1978-80; profl. staff mem. subcom. on energy nuclear proliferation and govt. processes Com. on Govtl. Affairs, U.S. Senate, Washington, 1980-81; tech. and sci. cons. Com. on Sci. and Tech., U.S. Ho. of Reps., 1981-86; rep. energy and environ., coord. Com. on Sci., Space and Tech., U.S. Ho. of Reps., 1986-89; sci. adviser to sec. Dept. Interior, Washington, 1989-93, dep. asst. sec. for sci.-water and sci., 1989-90, prin. dep. asst. to sec. for water and sci., 1990-93; rep. spl. asst. subcom. energy, com. sci., space, tech. U.S. Ho. of Reps., Washington, 1993-95, staff dir. subcom. energy and environment, com. sci., 1995—2001; sr climate negotiator, spec rep US Dept State, Washington, 2001—. Contbr. articles to profl. jours. Home: 6719 Tomlinson Ter Cabin John MD 20818-1328 Office: 2201 C St NW Rm 4330 Washington DC 20520-0001 E-mail: WatsonHL@state.gov.

WATSON, HELEN RICHTER, educator, ceramic artist; b. Laredo, Tex., May 10, 1926; d. Horace Edward and Helen Mary (Richter) Watson. B.A., Scripps Coll., 1947; M.F.A., Claremont Grad. Sch. and U. Ctr., 1949; postgrad. Alfred U., 1966; Swedish Govt. fellow Konstfackskolan, Stockholm, 1952-53. Mem. faculty Chaffey Coll., Ontario, Calif., 1950-52; founder ceramic mus., Laredo, Tex., 2003; chmn. ceramics Mt. San Antonio Coll., Walnut, Calif., 1955-57; prof., chmn. ceramics dept. Otis Art Inst., Los Angeles, 1958-81; mem. faculty Otis-Parsons Sch. Design, 1983-88, ret. 1988; studio ceramic artist, Claremont, Calif. and Laredo, Tex., 1949—; design cons. Interpace, Glendale, Calif., 1963-64; artist-in-residence Claremont Men's Coll., 1977. Claremont Grad. Sch. fellow, 1948-49; Swedish Govt. grantee, 1952-53; recipient First Ann. Scripps Coll. Disting. Alumna award, Claremont, 1978. Address: 1906 Houston St Laredo TX 78040-7709

WATSON, JACK CROZIER, retired state supreme court justice; b. Jonesville, La., Sept. 17, 1928; s. Jesse Crozier and Gladys Lucille (Talbot) W.; m. Henrietta Sue Carter, Dec. 26, 1958; children: Carter Crozier (dec.), Wells Talbot. BA, U. Southwestern La., 1949; JD, La. State U., 1956; completed with honor, Appellate Judges Seminar, N.Y. U., 1974, Sr. Appellate Judges Seminar, 1980. Bar: La. 1956. Atty. King, Anderson & Swift, Lake Charles, La., 1956-58; prosecutor City of Lake Charles, 1960; asst. dist. atty. Calcasieu Parish, La., 1961-64; ptnr. Watson & Watson, Lake Charles, 1961-64; judge 14th Jud. Dist., La., 1964-72; judge ad hoc Ct. Appeals, 1st Circuit, Baton Rouge, 1972-73; judge Ct. Appeals, 3rd Circuit, Lake Charles, 1973-79; assoc. justice La. Supreme Ct., New Orleans, 1979-96, ret., 1996; of counsel Bagget, McCall, Burgess, Watson & Gaughan, Lake Charles, 2004—. Faculty advisor Nat. Coll. State Judiciary, Reno, 1970, 73; adj. prof. law summer sch. program in Greece, Tulane U., 1988-2000; adj. prof. law So. U., Baton Rouge, 1998-99; del. NEH Seminar, 1976; La. del to Internat. Conf. Appellate Magistrates, The Philippines, 1977; mem. La. Jud. Coun., 1986-92. 1st lt. USAF, 1950-54. Mem. ABA, La. Bar Assn., S.W. La. Bar Assn. (pres. 1973), Law Inst. State of La., La. Coun. Juvenile Ct. Judges (pres. 1969-70), Am. Judicature Soc., S.W. La. Camellia Soc. (pres. 1973-74), Am. Legion (post comdr. 1963), Lake Charles Yacht Club (commodore 1974), Blue Key, Sigma Alpha Epsilon, Phi Delta Phi, Pi Kappa Delta. Democrat. Baptist. Home (Summer): Grand West Village Leadville CO 80461 Office Phone: 337-478-8888.

WATSON, JAMES DEWEY, molecular biologist, educator; b. Chgo., Apr. 6, 1928; s. James Dewey and Jean (Mitchell) W.; m. Elizabeth Lewis, 1968; children: Rufus Robert, Duncan James. BS, U. Chgo., 1947; PhD in Zoology, Ind. U., 1950; DSc (hon.), U. Chgo., 1961, Ind. U., 1963; LLD (hon.), U. Notre Dame, 1965; DSc (hon.), L.I. U., 1970, Adelphi U., 1972, Brandeis U., 1973, Albert Einstein Coll. Medicine, 1979, Hofstra U., 1976, Harvard U., 1978, Rockefeller U., 1980, Clarkson Coll., 1981, SUNY, 1983; MD (hon.), U. Buenos Aires, Argentina, 1986; DSc (hon.), Rutgers U., 1988, Bard Coll., 1991, U. Cambridge, 1993, Fairfield U., 1993, U. Stellenbosch, 1993, U. Oxford; MD, Charles Univ., Prague, 1998; DSc (hon.), Washington Coll., 1999, U. Judaism, 1999, U. Coll. London, 2000, Ill. Wesleyan U., 2000, Widener U., 2001, Dartmouth, 2001, Trinity Coll., Dublin, 2001. Rsch. fellow NRC, U. Copenhagen, 1950-51; Nat. Found. Infantile Paralysis fellow Cavendish Lab., Cambridge U., 1951-52, 55-56; sr. rsch. fellow biology Calif. Inst. Tech., 1953-55; asst. prof. biology Harvard U., 1955-58, assoc. prof., 1958-61, prof., 1961-76; dir. Cold Spring Harbor Lab., N.Y., 1968-93, pres., 1994—2003, chancellor, 2003—; assoc. dir. Nat. Ctr. for Human Genome Rsch., NIH, 1988-89, dir. Nat. Ctr. for Human Genome Rsch., 1989-92. Newton-Abraham vis. prof. Oxford U., 1994. Author: Molecular Biology of the Gene, 1965, 4th edit., 1986, The Double Helix, 1968, (with John Tooze) The DNA Story, 1981, (with others) The Molecular Biology of the Cell, 1983, 2d edit., 1989, 3d edit. 1994, (with John Tooze and David Kurtz) Recombinant DNA, A Short Course, 1983, 2d edit., 1992, A Passion for DNA, 2000, Genes, Girls and Gamow, 2001, DNA: The Secret of Life, 2003. Named Hon. fellow Clare Coll., Cambridge U., hon. knight of Brit. Empire, 2002; recipient (with F.H.C. Crick) John Collins Warren prize Mass. Gen. Hosp., 1959, Eli Lilly award in biochemistry Am. Chem. Soc., 1959, Albert Lasker prize Am. Pub. Health Assn., 1960, (with F.H.C. Crick) Rsch. Corp. prize, 1962, (with F.H.C. Crick and M.H.F. Wilkins) Nobel prize in medicine, 1962, Presdl. Medal of Freedom, 1977, Kaul Found. award for excellence, 1993, Nat. Biotech. Venture award, 1993, Copley Medal, 1993, Charles A. Dana award, 1994, Lomonosov medal Russian Acad. Sci., 1995, Nat. medal of Sci., 1997, Liberty medal City of Phila., 2000, Benjamin Franklin medal for disting. achievement in scis. Am. Philos. Soc., 2001, Gairdner award, 2002, Lotos Club Medal of Merit, 2004. Mem. NAS (Carty medal 1971), Am. Philos. Soc., Am. Assn. Cancer Rsch., Am. Acad. Arts and Scis., Am. Soc. Biol. Chemistry, Royal Soc. (London), Acad. Scis. Russia, Danish Acad. Arts and Scis. Achievements include co-discovery of Double-Helix DNA. Office: Cold Spring Harbor Lab PO Box 100 Cold Spring Harbor NY 11724-0100

WATSON, JAMES RAYMOND, education educator; b. Blue Isl., Ill., July 29, 1938; s. William James Henry Watson and Edna Mae Stucker; m. Suzette Marie Gehant, July 8, 1969. AB, Marquette Univ., Milw., 1966; MA, Univ. Wisc., Milw., 1969; PhD, So. Ill. Univ., Carbondale, Ill., 1973. Data analyst Clark Oil & Refining, Blue Island, Ill., 1958—59; photographic asst. Waltershoffer's Studio of Photography, Milw., 1961—62; photography instr. Layton Sch. of Art, Milw., 1961—62; asst. prof. Loyola Univ., New Orleans, 1973—77, assoc. prof., 1977—94, prof., 1994—. Pres. SPSGH, 1996—; rsch. assoc. Pic. Univ. of Binghamton, NY, 2002—; assoc. editor Routledge Contintential Phila. Series, N.Y., 2001—. Author: Between Auschwitz and Tradition, 1994, Continental Philosophers in America, 1999, Contemporary Portrayals of Auschwitz, 2000. Exec. com. ACLU Miss., Jackson, Miss., 2002—; bd. dirs. Picayune on Stage, Picayune, Miss., 2001—. Pvt.1st. class U.S. Army, 1962—64. Vis. scholar Max-Planck-Gesellschaft, Berlin, Germany, 1994. Mem.: Soc. for Philos. Study of Genccide & the Holocaust (pres.), Am. Philos. Soc. Avocations: photography, theater, painting. Home: 103 Edgewood Cir Carriere MS 39426 Office: Loyola Univ 6363 St Charles Ave New Orleans LA 70118 Office Phone: 504-865-3940.

WATSON, JEROME ROLAND, marketing professional, researcher; b. Annapolis, Md., Dec. 12, 1944; s. Edward Roland and Louise Elizabeth Watson; m. Patricia Ann Bristow, Dec. 18, 1976; children: Kevin Ryan, Dawn Kimberly. BA in History, Morgan State Coll., 1969; MS in History and Social Sci., Morgan State U., 1977; MBA in Mktg., U. Balt., 1986. Loan rep. Aetna Fin. Svcs., Balt., 1971—72; R&D coord. Blue Cross-Blue Shield Md., Towson, 1972—86; life ins. rep. Met. Life, Pikesville, Md., 1986—88; ind. ins. agt. Timonium, Md., 1988—89; sr. analyst market rsch. Prudential Healthcare Plan, Balt., 1989—97, Kaiser Permanente, Rockville, Md., 1998—. Author: The Churches of Turner Station, 2002, Remembering Our Schools, 2004. Den leader Boy Scouts Am., Balt., 1989—90, asst. scout master, 1990—91. 1st lt. U.S. Army, 1969—70, Vietnam. Recipient Cert. Appreciation, Balt. City Coun., 1991. Mem.: Black Writers Guild Md., Inc., Turner Sta. Heritage Found. (historian 2001—), 15th Art. Assn. Avocations: walking, jazz, attending military air shows, track and field. Home: 1522 King William Dr Catonsville MD 21228 Office: Kaiser Permanente 2101 E Jefferson St Rockville MD 20852

WATSON, JERRY CARROLL, advertising executive; b. Greenville, Ala., Aug. 22, 1943; s. William J. and Georgia Katherine (Mixon) W.; m. Judith Zeigler Brooks, Sept. 16, 1988; 2 child, Theodore William, Hunter Brooks. BS, U. Ala., Tuscaloosa, 1967; MS, U. Va., 1995. Staff writer Phillips, Eindhoven, The Netherlands, 1967-68; mgr. mktg. Fuller & Dees Mktg., Montgomery, Ala., 1968-70; v.p. Univ. Programs, Washington, 1970-73; pres. Coll. & Univ. Press, Washington, 1973-80; ptnr. Direct Response Consulting Svcs., McLean, Va., 1981-96. Bd. dirs. Foxhall Corp., The Art Co., Mustique Co. Founding mem. Am. Inst. Cancer Rsch. Mem. Direct Mktg. Assn., Non-Profit Mailer Fedn., Promotional Mktg. Assn., Nature Conservancy, Sierra Club, Falls Church (Va.) C. of C. (bd. dirs.). Avocations: gardening, astronomy. Home: Apt 402 850 Dolley Madison Blvd Mc Lean VA 22101-1821 Office: Direct Response Cons Svcs 6849 Old Dominion Dr Ste 300 Mc Lean VA 22101-3791 E-mail: watson@drcs.com., watson@mouselink.net.

WATSON, JESSICA LEWIS, writer; b. Urbana, Ill., June 16, 1964; d. Jane Eileen Lewis; m. Bruce S. Watson, Aug. 9, 1986 (div. Apr. 2003). BA in English, U. Ill., 1987; Diploma in Am. Lit., U. Liege, 1988; MA in English, Baylor U., 1994. Social worker Roundhouse, Champaign, Ill., 1988-89; cmty. liaison Krannert Ctr. for the Performing Arts, Urbana, Ill., 1989-90; freelance, writer and author Waco, also Champaign, Ill., 1990—; lectr. in English Baylor U., Waco, Tex., 1996-98; English instr. U. Ill., Urbana, 1988. Author: (books) Bastardy as a Gifted Status in Chaucer and Malory, 1996, Illegitimacy Empowered, 1994.; contbr. articles to nat. jours. Singer Austin Civic Chorus, Tex., 1996-2000. Recipient Literary Touring Program award Tex. Commn. on the Arts, Temple, Longview, Ft. Hood, 1994-97, Helen Chambers Poetry award Baylor U., Waco, 1994; grantee Aspen Writers Found., Colo., 1992. Avocations: modern dance, swimming, playing and singing classical music. Home: 302 S State St # 2 Champaign IL 61820

WATSON, JOANN FORD, theology studies educator; b. Ashland, Ohio, Apr. 11, 1956; d. Laurence Wesley and Edna Lucille (Garber) Ford; m. Duane Frederick Watson, June 2, 1984; 1 child, Christina Lucille. BA, DePauw U., 1978; MDiv, Princeton Theol. Sem., 1981; PhD, Northwestern U., 1984. Ordained to ministry Presbyn. Ch. Asst. prof. hist. theology Ashland (Ohio) Theol. Sem., 1984-86, assoc. prof. theology, 1989-95, chair dept. ch. history and theology, 1989—95, 2003—, H.R. Gill prof. theology, 1996—; chaplain Grady Meml. Hosp., Atlanta, 1986-87; co-pastor Tri-Ch. Parish United Meth. Chs. Northwestern, NY, 1987-89; pastor Camroden Presbyn. Ch., Rome, NY, 1987-89. Clergy commr. del. Gen. Assembly Presbyn. Ch., 1995. Author: Manna for Sisters in Christ, 1989, Mutuality in Christ, 1991, Meditations in Suffering, 1993, Study of Karl Barth's Doctrine of Man and Woman, 1995, Sister to Sister, 1998, Selected Spiritual Writings of Anne Dutton Vol. 1: Letters, 2003. Mem. Hospice Ashland County chpt., 1989—93; assoc. mem. Women's Symphony League, Ashland Symphony Orch., 1989—94; missionary vol. Mother Teresa's Missionaries of Charity, Calcutta, 1988. Recipient Outstanding Faculty Mentor of the Yr. award, Ashland U., 2004; Doctoral fellow, Northwestern U., 1982—84. Mem.: Am. Acad. Religion, Soc. Bibl. Lit., Nat. Assn. Presbyn. Clergywomen, Presbyn. Women in Leadership, Internat. Assn. Women Mins. (mem. exec. bd., trustee 1990—95), Phi Beta Kappa (Outstanding Faculty Mentor award 2001, 2002, Women's Achievement award, Ashland County, Ohio 2003, Outstanding Faculty Mentor award 2004), Alpha Lambda Delta. Republican. Avocations: travel, music, water sports. Office: Ashland Theolog Sem 910 Center St Ashland OH 44805-4007 Office Phone: 419-289-5182.

WATSON, JOHN ALLEN, lawyer; b. Ft. Worth, Sept. 18, 1946; s. John and Mary (Barlow) W.; m. Patricia L. Clardy, Oct. 24, 1946; 1 child, Virginia E. BA, Rice U., 1968; JD, U. Tex., Austin, 1971. Bar: Tex. 1971. Assoc. Fulbright & Jaworski, Houston, 1971-78, ptnr., 1978—. Mem. ABA. Office: Fulbright & Jaworski LLP 1301 McKinney St Ste 5100 Houston TX 77010-3031 E-mail: jwatson@fulbright.com.

WATSON, JOHN LAWRENCE, III, former trade association executive; b. Rome, Ga., Jan. 14, 1932; s. John Lawrence and Mary (Cowen) W.; m. Dorothy Palmer McLanahan, Aug. 9, 1958; children: Mary Palmer Watson Gard, Valerie Catherine Watson Bilbrough, John Lawrence IV. BS, Auburn U., 1954. Trader-over the counter J.C. Bradford & Co., Atlanta, 1957-58; with Robinson Humphrey & Co., Atlanta, 1958-64, dept. head-over the counter, 1964-74, dir. equity trading, 1974-83, dir. capital markets, 1983-85; pres. Security Traders Assn., N.Y.C., 1985-96. Past mem. bd. visitors Babcock Sch. Mgmt. Wake Forest U.; past chmn. Parent's Coun. Wofford Coll.; life trustee Pace Acad.; trustee Securities Industry Found. for Econ. Edn. Named Man of Yr., Equities mag. Mem. Nat. Assn. Securities Dealers (dist. chmn. 1982, bd. govs. 1983-85), Am. Mus. Fin. History (trustee), Capital City Club, Piedmont Driving Club (Atlanta), Ponte Vedra Club, Sawgrass Country Club (Ponte Vedra), Univ. Club (N.Y.C.). Home: 505 Ponte Vedra Blvd Ponte Vedra Beach FL 32082-2317

WATSON, JOHN S. oil company executive; b. Oct. 1956; BA, U. of Calif., Davis, 1978; MBA, U. of Chicago, 1980. Mgr. credit card, products, investor relations Chevron, 1993—95; pres. Chevron Canada, Ltd., 1996—98; dir. Caltex Corp.; v.p. strategic planning Chevron Corp., 1998—2001, v.p. fin., CFO, 2001—. Office: Chevron Corp 6001 Bollinger Canyon Rd San Ramon CA 94583-2324

WATSON, JULIAN See BLAKE, BUD

WATSON, KATHARINE M. state representative; b. Danville, Pa., Nov. 6, 1945; m. James Watson. BS in English, U. Pa., 1967. Formerly owner Coleraine Cons. Pub. Rels.; formerly h.s. English tchr.; former dep adminstr. County of Bucks; mem. Pa. Ho. of Reps., 2001—. Mem. Ctrl. Bucks Sch. Bd., 1985—89, Warrington Twp. Bd. Suprs., 1994—2000, vice chair, 1999—2000. Republican. Office: 159A E Wing Harrisburg PA 17120-2020 also: 1410 West Street Rd Warminster PA 18974 Office Phone: 215-674-0500. E-mail: kwatson@pahousegop.com.

WATSON, KATHY, political organization administrator; b. Skowhegan, Maine; Owner Kathy Watson Co.; mem. Pittsfield Rep. Com., 1982—, Somerset County Rep. Com., 1982—; vice chmn. Maine Rep. Party, 1986-88, 94-98, chmn., 1998—. Co-chmn. Maine women for Reagan/Bush, 1984; county chair Reagan for Pres., 1988, McKernan for Gov., 1990, Snowe for Congress, 1990, 92, Cohen for U.S. Senate, 1990, Snowe for Senate, 1994; mem. Bush adv. com., 1992; del. Rep. Nat. Conv., 1988, 92, 96; mem. rules com. Rep. Nat. Com., 1992, 96. Bd. dirs. Sr. Connections/Bridges. Mem. Assoc. Gen. Contractors Am.

WATSON, KENNETH MARSHALL, physics educator; b. Des Moines, Sept. 7, 1921; s. Louis Erwin and Irene Nellie (Marshall) W.; m. Elaine Carol Miller, Mar. 30, 1946; children: Ronald M., Mark Louis. *Son Mark L. Watson is an author of 14 published books on Java, artificial intelligence, and Common Lisp programming. He lives in Sedona, Ariz., with wife Carol. Web www.markwatson.com.* BS, Iowa State U., 1943; PhD, U. Iowa, 1948; ScD (hon.), U. Ind., 1976. Rsch. engr. Naval Rsch. Lab., Washington, 1943-46; staff Inst. Advanced Study Princeton (N.J.) U., 1948-49; rsch. fellow Lawrence Berkeley (Calif.) Lab., 1949-52, staff, 1957-81; asst. prof. physics U. Ind., Bloomington, 1952-54; assoc. prof. physics U. Wis., Madison, 1954-57; prof. physics U. Calif., Berkeley, 1957-81, prof. oceanography, dir. marine physics lab. San Diego, 1981-93. Cons. Sci. Application Corp.; mem. U.S. Pres.'s Sci. Adv. Com. Panels, 1962-71; adviser Nat. Security Coun., 1972-75; mem. JASON Adv. Panel, 1959-2001; sci. adv. bd. George C. Marshall Inst., 1989—. Author: (with M.L. Goldberger) Collision Theory, 1964; (with J. Welch and J. Bond) Atomic Theory of Gas Dynamics, 1966; (with J. Nutall) Topics in Several Particle Dynamics, 1970; (with Flatté, Munk, Dashen) Sound Transmission Through a Fluctuating Ocean, 1979. Mem. Nat. Acad. Scis. Home: Unit 2008 8515 Costa Verde Blvd San Diego CA 92122-1150 Office: U Calif Marine Physics Lab La Jolla CA 92093-0213 Office Phone: 858-534-6620. Business E-Mail: kmw@mpl.ucsd.edu.

WATSON, MARK S. music educator; BS in Music Edn. magna cum laude, Lebanon Valley Coll., 1980; MusM in Edn., West Chester U., 1988. Cert. tchr. Pa. Dir. bands J.P. McCaskey H.S. Sch. Dist. of Lancaster, Pa., 2001—, tchr. mid. sch. instrumental and gen. music Wheatland Mid. Sch., 1985—2001, tchr. elem. instrumental music, 1981—85. Asst. dir. J. P. McCaskey H.S. Marching Band, Lancaster, 1988—92; dir. Ninth Grade Marching Band Sch. Dist. of Lancaster, 1982—91. Recipient Teen Weekend Favorite Tchr. Award, Lancaster New Era, 1994, Outstanding Young Educator, Lancaster Jaycees. Mem.: NEA, Music Educators Nat. Conf., Lancaster Edn. Assn., Pa. State Edn. Assn., Phi Alpha Epsilon. Office: JP McCaskey High School 445 N Reservoir St Lancaster PA 17602 E-mail: mwatson@lancaster.k.12.pa.ua.

WATSON, MARLAN, reporter; b. Haiti; Student, Spellman Coll.; BS in Music, A.M. and N. Coll. Reporter Sta. WNYW-TV, N.Y.C., 1968—. Actor: (films) Cotton Comes to Harlem, 1969; (Broadway plays) Hello Dolly, 1969; exec. prodr.: (TV series) Brown Sugar. Office: WNYW 205 E 67th St New York NY 10021

WATSON, MAX P., JR., computer software company executive; b. 1946; Grad., La. Tech. U., grad., 1968. With IBM Corp., Houston, 1967-83, Wang Labs., Houston, 1985-90, BMC Software, Inc., Houston, 1985—, pres., CEO, chmn. Office: BMC Software Inc 2101 Citywest Blvd Houston TX 77042-2828

WATSON, NOEL G. construction executive; b. 1936; BSChemE, U. N.D., 1958; postgrad., Colo. Sch. Mines, 1958-60. With Jacobs Engring., 1960-62, AMAX Inc., 1962-65; pres., COO Jacobs Engring. Group Inc., Pasadena, Calif., 1965-92, pres., CEO, 1992—. Office: Jacobs Engring Group 1111 S Arroyo Pkwy Pasadena CA 91105

WATSON, OLIVER LEE, III, aerospace engineering manager; b. Lubbock, Tex., Sept. 18, 1938; m. Judith Valeria Horvath, June 13, 1964; 1 child, Clarke Stanford. BSEE, U. Tex., 1961; MSEE, Stanford U., 1963; MBA, Calif. State U., Fullerton, 1972; cert., U. So. Calif., 1980; cert. comm. & networks, U. Calif., Irvine, 1999. Cert. comm. & networks U. Calif., Irvine, 1999. Mgr. ballistic analysis Rockwell Internat. Autonetics Divsn., Anaheim, Calif., 1973-78, mgr. minuteman systems, 1978-83, mgr. preliminary engring., 1983-84; mgr. analysis group autonetics divsn. Rockwell Internat., Anaheim, Calif., 1984-85, mgr. aircraft sys. autonetics dept., 1985-93, dep. dir. integrated product devel. N.Am. aircraft modification divsn., 1993-94, dep. dir. engring. N.Am. aircraft modification divsn., 1994-96; dep. dir. engring. comm. and combat sys. divsn. Boeing N.Am., Anaheim, 1996-98; skills, process and metrics mgr. Comm. and Battle Mgmt., Anaheim, 1998-99; process, metrics and tools dir. Anaheim Site Engring., Integrated Def. Sys., Anaheim, Calif., 1999—, 2001—. Lectr. engring. Calif. State U., Fullerton, 1981—90, mem. indsl. adv. bd., 1994—, vice-chmn., 1995—97; spkr. welcome address Engring. & Computer Sci. Commencement, 1997; adv. com. Accreditation Bd. for Engring. and Tech., 2000; sec. Elec. Engring. Indsl. Adv. Bd., 2001—; Boeing Ex. Focal CSUF, 2003—; exec. advisor for fin. Anaheim chpt. Boeing Nat. Mgmt. Assn., 2002—03. Co-author Digital Computing Using Fortran IV, 1982; Fortran 77, A Complete Primer, 1986; contbg. author: The World's Best Shortest Stories, 2001. Bd. dirs. Olive Little League, Orange, 1980; vol. Stanford U. Engring. Fund, Orange County, Calif., 1983, regional chmn. 1984-86, So. Calif. chmn. 1986-91; mem. Stanford Assocs., 1988—. Recipient Stanford Assocs. Centennial Medallion award, 1991; fellow N.Am. Aviation Sci.-Engring., L.A., 1962-63, Inst. Advancement Engring., L.A., 1976. Mem. IEEE (sr., sec. v.p. 1974-75, sect. chmn. 1975-76), Nat. Mgmt. Assn. (exec. advisor for fin. Boeing Anaheim chpt. 2002), Jaycees (v.p. Orange chpt. 1973-74), Rockwell-Calif. State Univ. Alumni Club (v.p. 1993, pres. 1993-94), Lido Sailing Club. Republican. Avocations: sailing, swimming, humor writing, scriptwriting, reading. Office: Boeing NAm 031-CA92 3370 E Miraloma Ave Anaheim CA 92806-1911

WATSON, PATRICIA L. library director; b. Jan. 15, 1939; m. Jack Samuel Watson, 1960; children: Bradley, Amanda. BA, Univ. Tenn., 1961, MS in Libr. and Info. Sci., 1975. Cataloging asst. tech. svcs. dept. Knoxville Pub. Libr., 1961-65; adminstrv. asst. Knoxville-Knox County Pub. Libr., 1975-78, head West Knoxville br. libr., 1978-85; dir. Knox County Pub. Libr. System,

1985—. Bd. dirs. Tanasi Girl Scout Coun., 1981-86, KORRNET (Knoxville-Oak Ridge Area Cmty. Network), 1998—; treas. Univ. Tenn. Grad. Sch. Libr and Info. Sci. Alumni Orgn., 1983-84; elder Farragut Presbyn. Ch. Mem. ALA, Tenn. Libr. Assn. (pres. 1992-93), East Tenn. Libr. Assn. (pres. 1988-89), Rotary Internat. Office: Knox County Pub Libr System 500 W Church Ave Knoxville TN 37902-2505

WATSON, PATTY JO, anthropology educator; b. Superior, Nebr., Apr. 26, 1932; d. Ralph Clifton and Elaine Elizabeth (Lance) Andersen; m. Richard Allan Watson, July 30, 1955; 1 child, Anna Melissa MA, U. Chgo., 1956, PhD In Anthropology, 1959, Archaeologist-ethnographer Oriental Inst.-U. Chgo., 1959-60, research assoc., archaeologist, 1964-70, instr. anthropology U. So. Calif., Los Angeles, 1961, UCLA, 1961, L.A. State U., 1961; asst. prof. anthropology Washington U., St. Louis, 1969-70, assoc. prof., 1970-73, prof., 1973—, Edward Mallinckrodt disting. univ. prof., 1993—. Mem. rev. panel NSF, Washington, 1974-76; fellow Ctr. Advanced Study in Behavioral Scis., Stanford, Calif., 1981-82, 91-92. Author: The Prehistory of Salts Cave, Kentucky, 1969, Archaeological Ethnography in Western Iran, 1979; author: (with others) Man and Nature, 1969, Explanation in Archeology, 1971, Archeological Explanation, 1984, Girikihaciyan, A Halafian Site in Southeastern Turkey; author: (editor) Archeology of the Mammoth Cave Area, 1974, Prehistoric Archeology Along the Zagros Flanks, 1983; co-editor: The Origins of Agriculture, 1992, Of Caves and Shell Mounds, 1996. Recipient Arthur Holly Compton Faculty Achievement award Washington U., St. Louis, 2000, Peter H. Raven award for lifetime achievement Acad. Sci. St. Louis, 2002; grantee NSF, 1959-60, 68, 70, 72-74, 78-79, NEH, 1977-78, Nat. Geog. Soc., 1969-75. Fellow Am. Anthropol. Assn. (editor for archaeology 1973-77, Disting. Lectr. award 1994, Disting. Svc. award 1996), AAAS (chair sect. H 1991-92); mem. NAS, Cave Rsch. Found., Am. Acad. Arts and Scis., Am. Philos. Soc., Soc. Am. Archaeology (exec. com. 1974-76, 82-84, editor Am. Antiquity 1984-87, Fryxell medal 1990), Assn. Paleorient (sci. bd.), Nat. Speleological Soc. (hon. life, editorial bd. bull. 1979—, sci. award), Archaeol. Inst. Am. (Gold Medal for Disting. Archaeol. Achievement 1999). Office: Dept Anthropology CB #1114 Washington U Saint Louis MO 63130-4899 E-mail: pjwatson@artsci.wustl.edu.

WATSON, PAUL, photojournalist, correspondent; Photographer The Toronto Star, 1986—, Africa bur. chief, 1992—94, Asian bur. chief, 1994—98; staff writer L.A. Times, 1998—, South Asia bur. chief, 2001—. Recipient Robert Capa gold medal for photography, 1993, Nat. Newspaper award for spot news photography, 1994, Pulitzer Prize for spot news photography, 1994, Nat. Newspaper award for internat. reporting, 1996, George Polk award for internat. reporting, 1999, 2000, Freedom of Press award, Nat. Press Club, 2000. Home: Apt 4 Block 2-C Parkwood Est Rao Tula Ram Marg New Delhi 110022 India Office: D 7/10 Vasant Vihar New Delhi India Fax: 91-11-2617-7-709 E-mail: paulrwatson@yahoo.com.

WATSON, PAULA D. library administrator; b. N.Y.C., Mar. 6, 1945; d. Joseph Francis and Anna Julia (Miksza) De Simone; m. William Douglas Watson, Aug. 23, 1969; children— Lucia, Elizabeth AB, Barnard Coll., 1965; MA, Columbia U., 1966; MSL.S., Syracuse U., 1972. Reference librarian U. Ill., Urbana, 1972-77, city planning and landscape architecture librarian, 1977-79, head documents library, 1979-81; asst. dir. gen. services U. Ill. Library, Urbana, 1981-88, acting dir. gen. svcs., 1988-93, dir. ctrl. pub. svcs., 1989-93, asst. univ. libr., 1993-95, dir. electronic info. svcs., 1995—. Author: Electronic Journals: Acquisition and Management, 2003; contbr. articles to profl. jours. N.Y. State Regents fellow Columbia U., N.Y.C., 1965-66; Council on Library Resources profl. edn. and tng. for librarianship grantee, 1983 Mem. ALA (sec. univ. librs. sect. ALA-Assn. Coll. and Rsch. Librs. 1989-91, com. on instnl. coop., chair pub. svcs. dirs. group, 1997-99, mem. com. inst. coop./OCLC virtual electronic libr. steering com.), Ill. Library Assn. Avocation: gardening. Home: 715 W Delaware Ave Urbana IL 61801-4806 Office: U Ill 246 A Library 1408 W Gregory Dr Urbana IL 61801-3607

WATSON, PETER S. federal agency administrator; married. LLB, Auckland U.; LLM, McGill U.; MIBA, West Coast U. Pvt. practice internat. and bus. law, L.A., Washington, 1976, 78-88; spl. advisor to Pres. Overseas Pvt. Investment Corp.; dir. Asian affairs Nat. Security Coun., 1989-91; commr. U.S. Internat. Trade Commn., 1991—, vice chmn., 1992-94, chmn., 1994-96; pres. and C.E.O. overseas private investment corp. Off. of the Pres., Washington, 2001—. Adj. prof. internat. trade and investment law and internat. bus. law. Contbr. articles to profl. jours. Republican. Office: Overseas Private Investment Corp Off of the Pres 1100 New York Ave NW Washington DC 20527

WATSON, RALPH EDWARD, physician, educator; b. Cin., Apr. 4, 1948; s. John Sherman and Evelyn (Moore) W.; m. Demetria Rencher, Sept. 9, 1972; children: Ralph Edward, Monifa. BS, Xavier U., 1970; MD, Mich. State U., 1976. Diplomate Am. Bd. Internal Medicine; cert. clin. hypertension specialist. Intern U. Cin. Med. Ctr., 1976-77, resident in internal medicine, 1977-79, asst. clin. prof. internal medicine, 1980-88; asst. prof. internal medicine Mich. State U., East Lansing, 1988-94, assoc. prof., 1994—. Attending physician in hypertension clinic Mich. State U., 1988-91, assoc. dir. hypertension clinic, 1991-94, dir. hypertension clinic, 1995—, program dir. transitional yr. residency, 1990-96, assoc. program dir. internal medicine residency, 1996-2003; mem. U.S. HHS Office Minority Health Resource Person Network. Fellow ACP, Internat. Soc. Hypertension in Blacks, Am Assn. Black Cardiologists; mem. Nat. Med. Assn., Am. Soc. Internal Medicine, Lansing Area Am. Heart Assn. (bd. dirs.), Am. Black Cardiologists (chair rsch. com.), Am. Soc. Hypertension, Xavier U. Alumni Assn., Alpha Omega Alpha. Home: 4199 Shoals Dr Okemos MI 48864-3434 Office: Mich State U 338B Clinical Ctr East Lansing MI 48824-1313

WATSON, RAYMOND COKE, JR., engineering executive, academic administrator; b. Anniston, Ala., Aug. 31, 1926; BS, Jacksonville State U.; MSE, U. Ala.; MS, U. Fla.; MBA and PhD in Engring. Sci., Calif. Coast U. Chief engr. Dixie Svc. Co., 1948-54; head dept. physics and engring. Jacksonville State U., 1954-60; v.p. engring. and rsch. Teledyne Brown Engring., 1960-70, chief engr., chief scientist, 1990—2001; dir. continuing edn., engring. and math. U. Ala., Huntsville, 1970-76; pres., prof. engring. and math. Southeastern Inst. Tech., Huntsville, 1976—; owner RC Watson & Assocs., 1980—; pres., CEO Vision Techs. Kinetics, 2000—. Adj. assoc. prof. U. Ala., Huntsville, 1961-70. Contbr. more than 400 articles and reports to profl. jours. Chmn. elec. engring. adv. bd. Ala. A&M U. Recipient NASA Pub. Svc. award; NSF Sci. Faculty Fellow. Mem. IEEE, AIAA, Optical Soc. Am., Ops. Rsch. Soc. Am., Inst. Mgmt. Sci., Internat. Soc. Optical Engrs., Inst. Indsl. Engrs. Achievements include research in defense systems, space systems and electro-optics. Home: 1801 Inspiration Ln SE Huntsville AL 35801-1150 Office: RC Watson & Assocs PO Box 1485 Huntsville AL 35807 E-mail: rxxwatson@aol.com., ray.watson@tbe.com.

WATSON, REBECCA WUNDER, federal agency administrator, lawyer; b. Chgo., Feb. 17, 1952; d. David Hart and Shirley May (Dahlin) Wunder; m. Keith C. Thomson, Oct. 6, 1979 (div. Dec. 1989); m. Gregory B. Watson, Jan. 20, 1996. BA, U. Denver, 1974, MA in LS, 1975, JD, 1978. Bar: Bar: Wyo. 1978, Colo. 1989, D.C. 1995, Mont. 1995. Law clk. U.S. Dist. Ct. for Dist. Wyo., Cheyenne, 1978-80; assoc., then ptnr. Burgess & Davis, Sheridan, Wyo., 1980-88; pvt. practice, Denver, 1988-90; asst. gen. counsel for energy policy Dept. Energy, Washington, 1990-93; of counsel Crowell & Moring, Washington, 1993-95; ptnr. Gough Shanahan Johnson & Waterman, Helena, Mont., 1995—2002; asst. secy. land mgt. U.S. Dept Interior, Washington, 2002—. Contbr. author: ABA Natural Resource Law Handbook, 1993; contbr. articles to law jours. Mem. ABA (chmn. natural resource com. sect. adminstrv. law 1994-97, chmn. pub. lands com. sect. natural resources, energy and environ. law 1997-99), Wyo. Bar Assn., Mont. Bar Assn., Phi Beta Kappa. Republican. Avocations: cooking, reading, travel, hunting. Home: 460 Farmington Rd W Accokeek MD 20607-9412 Office: US Dept Interior Land and Materials Mgt 1849 C St NW Washington DC 20240 Office Phone: 202-208-6734. E-mail: Rebecca_Watson@ios.doi.gov.

WATSON, RICHARD ALLEN, lawyer; b. Oceanside, N.Y., Aug. 11, 1946; s. William Edgar and Grace (Brooks) W.; m. Mary Lee Brown, June 24, 1972; children: Rebecca, Sarah. BA, Hamilton Coll., 1967; JD, Columbia U., 1972. Bar: N.Y. 1973, U.S. Tax Ct. 1974, N.J. 1976. From assoc. to ptnr. Chamberlain, Willi, Ouchterloney & Watson, N.Y.C., 1972—. Mem. Morris Twp. Zoning Bd., N.J., 1981-88; mem. Morris Twp. Coun., 1988—; chmn. Morris Twp. Reps., 1985-89; mayor of Morris Twp., 1991-92, 98-2000; trustee Mark Twain Found., 1994—, The Morris Mus., 1998—. Served with U.S. Army, 1969-71, Vietnam. Mem. ABA, N.J. Bar Assn. Republican. Presbyterian. Home: 5 Quaker Ridge Rd Morristown NJ 07960-6502 Office: Chamberlain Willi Ouchterloney & Watson 15 Maiden Ln Ste 705 New York NY 10038-4029

WATSON, RICHARD THOMAS, lawyer; b. Lakewood, Ohio, Aug. 21, 1933; s. Thomas Earl Watson and Sara Lucille (Whapham) Hadfield; m. Judith C. Briggs, Aug. 6, 1960; children: David, Andrew, Susan (dec.). AB, Harvard U., 1954, JD, 1960. Bar: Ohio 1960. Assoc. Spieth, Bell, McCurdy & Newell, Cleve., 1960, ptnr., 1965, mng. ptnr., 1987 . Bd. dirs. numerous corps. Chancellor Episcopal Diocese of Ohio, Cleve., 1986—; mem. Harvard U. com. on univ. resources, 1992—; bd. trustees Cleve. Mus. Art, 1991—; trustee Case Western Res. U., 1993—. Mem. Union Club Cleve. Office: Spieth Bell McCurdy & Newell 925 Euclid Ave Ste 2000 Cleveland OH 44115-1408 Office Phone: 216-696-4700. E-mail: richardtwatson@worldnet.att.net.

WATSON, ROBERT FRANCIS, lawyer; b. Houston, Jan. 9, 1936; s. Louis Leon and Lora Elizabeth (Hodges) W.; m. Marietta Kiser, Nov. 24, 1961; children: Julia, Melissa, Rebecca. BA, Vanderbilt U., 1957; JD, U. Denver, 1959. Bar: Colo. 1959, U.S. Dist. Ct. (no. dist.) Tex. 1967, U.S. Supreme Ct. 1968, Tex. 1973, U.S. Ct. Appeals (5th cir.) 1973, U.S. Dist. Ct. (so. dist.) Tex. 1980, U.S. Ct. Appeals (11th cir.) 1981. Law clk. U.S. Dist. Ct. Colo., 1960-61; trial atty. SEC, Denver, 1961-67, asst. regional adminstr. Ft. Worth, 1967-72, regional adminstr., 1972-75; ptnr. Law, Snakard & Gambill, P.C., Ft. Worth, 1975-98, of counsel, 1998—; exec. v.p., gen. counsel First Command Fin. Svcs., Inc., Ft. Worth, 1998—. Counsel City of Ft. Worth Police Investigation Commn., 1975; spl. counsel Office Atty. Gen. State Ariz., 1977-78. Contbr. articles to profl. jours. Mem. Ft. Worth Crime Commn., 1987-93. Honoree 27th Ann. Rocky Mountain State-Fed.-Provincial Securities Conf. Fellow: Coll. of State Bar Tex., U. Denver Law Sch. Alumni Coun., Tex. Bar Found. (life), Colo. Bar Assn. (life), Tarrant County Bar Assn., Ft. Worth Club; mem.: ABA, Tarrant County Bar Found., Tex. Bus. Law Found. (bd.dirs. 1988—93), State Bar Tex., Fed. Bar Assn., Shady Oaks Country Club (Ft. Worth), Phi Delta Phi. Republican. Presbyterian. Office: First Command 4100 S Hulen St Fort Worth TX 76109 also: Law Snakard & Gambill PC 1600 W 7th St Ste 500 Fort Worth TX 76102-3819 E-mail: rfwatson@firstcommand.com.

WATSON, ROBERT JOE, health facility administrator, retired career officer; b. Wellington, Kans., Nov. 12, 1934; s. Charles Bruce and Marguerite B. (Scholes) W.; m. Ursula Eschenroeder, Dec. 26, 1983; children: Stephanie, Stacy Watson Bruce, Susannah Watson Gold; stepchildren: Jurgen Wanke, Claudia Beeck. MS in Edn., Kans. State Tchrs. Coll., 1963; MBA, U. Hawaii, 1969; MHA, George Washington U., 1973, EdD, 1976; student, Command-Gen. Staff Coll., 1973, U.S. Army War Coll., 1986. Commd. 2nd lt. U.S. Army, 1963, advanced through grades to col., 1989; stationed at Tripler Army Med. Ctr., Honolulu, 1967-69, USARV Surgeons Office, Long Binh, Vietnam, 1969-70, Surgeon Gen.'s Office, Washington, 1970-74, Walter Reed Med. Ctr., Washington, 1974-76, Acad. Health Svcs., Ft. Sam Houston, Tex., 1976-80, 87-89, 68th Med. Group, Ziegenberg, Germany, 1980-82, U.S. Army Hosp., Ft. Riley, Kans., 1982-84, 34th Gen. Hosp., Augsburg, Germany, 1984-87; ret., 1989; assoc. dir. Student Health Ctr. U. Fla., Gainesville, 1989—. Fellow Am. Coll. Healthcare Execs. (adv., regent 1982-84). Episcopalian. Avocations: tennis, golf, gardening. Office: U Fla Student Health Ctr Gainesville FL 32611 Office Phone: 352-392-1161.

WATSON, ROBERT WINTHROP, poet; b. Passaic, N.J., Dec. 26, 1925; s. Winthrop and Laura Berdan (Trimble) W.; m. Elizabeth Ann Rean, Jan. 12, 1952; children: Winthrop, Caroline. BA, Williams Coll., 1946; postgrad., U. Zurich, 1947; MA, Johns Hopkins, 1950, PhD in English, 1955. Instr. English Williams Coll., 1946, 47-48, 52-53, Johns Hopkins, 1950-52; mem. faculty U. N.C., Greensboro, 1953—, prof. English, 1963-90. Vis. poet, prof. English Calif. State U., Northridge, 1968-69 Author: (poetry) A Paper Horse, 1962, Advantages of Dark, 1966, Christmas in Las Vegas, 1971, Selected Poems, 1974, Island of Bones, 1977, Night Blooming Cactus, 1980, The Pendulum: New and Selected Poems, 1995; (novels) Three Sides of the Mirror, 1966, Lily Lang, 1977, (art book) Betty Watson Paintings, 1999; co-founder The Greensboro Rev., 1966. Swiss-Am. exch. fellow, 1947; grantee Nat. Endowment for Arts, 1973; recipient Am. Scholar Poetry prize, 1959, Lit. award Am. Acad. Inst. Arts Letters, 1977. Home: 4321 Galax Trail Greensboro NC 27410

WATSON, ROYCE ANDREW, retired federal official; b. N.Y.C., Mar. 8, 1932; s. Robert Dealing and Kirsten Marie (Johansen) W.; m. Edith Christine Luik, Aug . 29, 1964; children: Paul Andrew, Gayle Ellen, Jeanne Marie. BS in Chemistry, U. Miami, Coral Gables, Fla., 1954, MS in Microbiology, BBA, 1967, MBA, 1968; PhD, Fla. State U., 1971. Lic. lab. dir., Fla.; cert. med. technologist; ordained deacon Luth. Ch., 1985. Dir. clin. anatomical and blood bank Dept. of Hosps., Miami, Fla., 1957-68; dir. health svcs. planning and state programs Gov.'s Office, Tallahassee, 1968-72; dir. health planning, project officer Nat. Ctr. Health Svcs. Rsch., Washington, 1972-78, 1978-81; br. chief exptl. health delivery sys. HEW/HHS, Washington, 1981—82; chief advisor Office Asst. Sec. for Health and Surgeon Gen. HHS, Washington, Md., 1982—87; pres. Watson & Assocs., Gaithersburg, Md., 1987—2002. Instr. U. Miami Sch. Tech., 1962—99; worldwide health cons.; U.S. del. Internat. Assn. Med. Lab. Tech., 1964—95, WHO, 1968—2001, Pan Am. Health Orgn., 1972—97; instr. pathology U. Miami Med. Sch., 1964—68. Author: Foundations in Relation to Their Partial Involvment in the Financing of the Health Field, 1971; co-author: Medical Education in Florida: Examination of the Issues, 1964, and others; contbr. articles to profl. jours. Deacon Good Shepherd Luth. Ch., Gaithersburg, 1985-2001; bd. dirs. Nat. Pokamonic Orch., Washington, 1986-2002, Nat. Philharm. Orch. and Choir, 2003—. 1st lt. USMCR, 1952-58. Decorated Cross of Colors Internat. Order Rainbow Girls, Royal Order of Scotland, Order of Purple Cross; recipient Outstanding Svc. award, Asst. Sec. for Health/Surgeon Gen., 1982, DeMolay Cross Honor, 1995, DeMolay Legion of Honor, 1999, Red Cross of Constantine, 2001, Svc. award, Soc. Dept. Def., 2001, inducted Hall of Fame, Ft. Hamilton H.S. Fellow: Royal Soc. Health; mem.: VFW, Am. Soc. Clin. Lab. Scis., Md. Soc. Med. Technologists (pres. 1981, 1986, nat. Mem. of Yr. award 1986), Am. Soc. Med. Technologists (pres. Fla. divsn. 1970—72, numerous local, state, nat. and internat. leadership positions, Mem. of Yr. award 1972, 1976), Boy Scouts Am. (Lamb award 1983), Marine Corps League (life), Montgomery County Agrl. Fair (life), Heroes of '76 (comdr. 1994), Nat. Sojourners (pres. Bethesda chpt. 1991—92), Fla. End. Found. (life), Legion of Honor (comdr. 1995—97), Knights of Mecca (regional pres. N.E. Conf. 1998), York Rite (Order of the Purple Cross 1999, Grand High Priest 2002—03, officer York Rite Coll., assoc. regent, Knight of York Cross of Honor 1999), Masons (p.m. 1984, right worshipful past master 1990, pres. Knight Masons of Md. 2000—01, sovereign master 2002—03, Grotto active youth orgns., Top Nat. award Order DeMolay, Md. Master Mason of Yr. 1984), Shriners (Almas, Divan 2000—, chief Rabbou), Scottish Rite (Knight Comdr. Cross of Honor 2000), Am. Legion, Alpha Mu Tau, Alpha Kappa Psi. Republican. Lutheran. Avocations: scuba diving, gardening, skiing, philataly. Home: 16728 Shea Ln Gaithersburg MD 20877-1230

WATSON, RUBIE, museum director; BS in archaeology and anthropology, U. Calif., Berkeley; MS in Anthropology, Rice U.; PhD in Social Anthropology, London Sch. Econs. Assoc. prof. anthropology, acting dir. Asian Studies program U. Pitts.; assoc. curator Peabody Mus. Archeology & Ethnology, sr. lectr. dept. anthropology Harvard U., Cambridge, Mass., 1992-95, assoc. dir., then Howells dir. Peabody Mus., 1995—. Author several books including Inequality Among Brothers: Class and Kinship in South China, 1985; editor: Memory, History, and Opposition under State Socialism, 1994; co-editor: Marriage and Inequality in Chinese Society, 1990, Harmony and Counterpoint: Ritual Music in Chinese Context, 1996. Office: Peabody Mus Archeology Harvard U 11 Divinity Ave Cambridge MA 02138-2019

WATSON, S. MICHELE, school nurse; b. Selma, Ala., Apr. 21, 1965; d. Kenneth and Linda (Bishop) Wilds; m. H. Alan Watson, May 30, 1987. AAS, Cleveland State Community Coll, Tenn., 1987, AS, 1985. RN, Tenn. ICU staff Meml. Hosp., 1987-88; emergency rm. staff Cleveland (Tenn.) Cmty. Hosp., 1988; team leader Bradley Meml. Home Health, Cleveland, 1988-2001; sch. nurse Cleveland City Schs., 2001—. 3635 Georgetown Rd Cleveland TN 37312 Home: 3015 Princeton Hill Dr NW Cleveland TN 37312-1773 E-mail: mwatson@clevelandschools.org.

WATSON, SHARON GITIN, psychologist; b. N.Y.C., Oct. 21, 1943; d. Louis Leonard and Miriam (Myers) Gitin; m. Eric Watson, Oct. 31, 1969; 1 child, Carrie Dunbar. BA cum laude, Cornell U., 1965, MA, U. Ill., 1968, PhD, 1971. Psychologist City N.Y. Prison Mental Health, Riker's Island, 1973-74, Youth Services Ctr., Los Angeles County Dept. Pub. Social Services, L.A., 1975-77, dir. clin. services, 1978, dir. Youth Services Ctr., 1978-80; exec. dir. Crittenton Ctr. for Young Women and Infants, L.A., 1980-89, Assn. Children's Svcs. Agys. of So. Calif., L.A., 1989-92, L.A. County Children's Planning Coun., 1992-99; cons. L.A. County Chief Adminstrv. Office, 2001—; mem. L.A. City Commn. for Children, Youth and Their Families, 2000—, L.A. County Children's Planning Coun., 2001—. Mem. L.A. delegation Pres.'s Summit for Am.'s Future, 1997. Mem. Commn. for Children's Svcs. Family Preservation and Family Support Policy Com., 1989—99, Interagy. Coun. Child Abuse and Neglect Policy Com., 1993—99, Mayor's Com. on Children, Youth and Families, 1993—95; bd. dirs. Adolescent Pregnancy Childwatch, 1985—89, L.A. Ednl. Partnership, 1999—2003, LISC Health Sector, 1996—99, L.A. Roundtable for Children, 1988—94; trustee L.A. Ednl. Alliance for Restructuring Now, 1992—99. Mem.: APA, Assn. Children's Svcs. Agys. So. Calif. (sec. 1981—83, pres. elect 1983—84, pres. 1984—85), Calif. Assn. Svcs. for Children (sec.-treas. 1983—84, pres. elect 1985—86, pres. 1986—87), U.S. Figure Skating Assn. (chmn. sanctions and eligibility 1993—96, membership com. 1996—99, strategic planning com. 2000—02, regional vice chmn. competitions com. 2000—02, sec. 2002—, bd. dirs. 1992—, mem. exec. com. 2002—, nat. competition judge), U.S. Olympics Com. (Jr. Olympics com. 1998—2000), Pasadena Figure Skating Club (pres. 1985—87, 1989—90), So. Calif. Inter-Club Assn. of Figure Skating Clubs (vice chair 1989—91, chair 1991—93). Home and Office: 4056 Camino Real Los Angeles CA 90065-3928 E-mail: sharonla12@aol.com.

WATSON, SOLOMON BROWN, IV, lawyer, business executive; b. Salem, N.J., Apr. 14, 1944; s. Solomon Brown and Denise Amelia W.; m. Bernadette Aldrich, Mar. 18, 1967 (div.); children: Katitti Madrid, Kira Pallis (twins); m. Brenda J. Wilson, Apr. 28, 1984. BA in English, Howard U., 1966; JD, Harvard U., 1971. Bar: Mass. 1972, N.Y. 1977. Assoc. Bingham, Dana & Gould, Boston, 1971-74; corp. sec., asst. gen. counsel N.Y. Times Co., N.Y.C., 1979-89, gen. counsel, 1989-90, v.p., gen. counsel, 1990-96, sr. v.p., gen. counsel, sec., 1996—. Active Vols. Legal Svc., Jobs for Youth Inc., until 1989; v.p. N.Y. Vietnam Vets. Leadership Program, Inc., until 1992, Agent Orange Assistance Fund, Vets. Adv. Bd. 1st lt. U.S. Army, 1966-68. Decorated Bronze Star with oak leaf cluster, Army Commendation medal with oak leaf cluster and V; recipient Nat. Equal Justice award Legal Def. Fund, 2002. Mem. ABA (com. on corp. law depts., mem. task force on corp. responsibility 2002—), Nat. Bar Assn., Assn. Bar City N.Y., Mass. Bar Assn., Newspaper Assn. Am. (mem. legal affairs com.), N.Y. Stock Exch. Home: 341 W 87th St New York NY 10024-2635 Office: NY Times Co 229 W 43rd St New York NY 10036-3959 Business E-Mail: watsons@nytimes.com.

WATSON, STEWART CHARLES, construction company executive; b. Brock, Sask., Can., Sept. 17, 1922; s. Samuel Henry and Elva Jane (St. John) W.; m. Irene Lillian Ahrens, Aug. 4, 1943; children: Judith Gail (Mrs. David Stafford), Wendy Carolyn (Mrs. Rocco Amuso), Ronald James, Candyce Louise. Student, U. Buffalo. With Acme Steel & Malleable Iron Works, Buffalo, 1940—42, Acme Hwy. Products, Buffalo, 1946—55, internat. mktg. mgr., 1955—69; pres. Watson-Bowman Assocs. Inc., Buffalo, 1970—, Kinematics, 1984—. Chmn. bd. Air Stewart Inc.; Internat. lectr. on kinetics of civil engring. structures; mem. U.S. Transp. Rsch. Bd.; bd. dirs. Internat. Bridge of Peace for Bering Strait Crossing. With AUS, 1943-45, ETO. Fellow Am. concrete Inst. (dir. 1984—, Delmar Bloehm award 1984, Charles S. Whitney medal 1987, hon. mem.); mem. ASTM, NAS, Internat. Jts. and Bearings Rsch. Coun. (chmn. 1988—), Internat. Activities Commn., Masons (32 degree), Shriners. Home: 3 Chicory Ln East Amherst NY 14051

WATSON, THOMAS C. lawyer; b. Poplar Bluff, Mo., Feb. 26, 1945; s. William C. and Dorothy E. (Whitson) W.; children: Thomas II, Nathan, Edward, Clay, Luke. BS, U. Memphis, 1967, MEd, 1968; JD, Washington U., St. Louis, 1972. Bar: Mo. 1972, D.C. 1973. Assoc. Morgan, Lewis & Bockius, Washington, 1973-78, ptnr., 1978-79, Crowell & Moring, Washington, 1979-95, Watson & Renner, 1996—. Avocations: hiking, biking, computers, hunting wild fowl. Office: Watson & Renner 1900 M St NW Ste 850 Washington DC 20036

WATSON, THOMAS ROGER, lawyer; b. Concord, N.H., May 14, 1951; s. Roger Edward and Mary (Hannigan) W. BA in Polit. Sci. cum laude, U. N.H., 1973; JD, Franklin Pierce Law Ctr., 1978. Bar: N.H. 1978, U.S. Dist. Ct. N.H. 1978, U.S. Ct. Appeals (1st cir.) 1978, Maine 1982, U.S. Dist. Ct. Maine 1982, U.S. Supreme Ct. 1986. Ptnr. Tybursky & Watson, Portsmouth, N.H., 1979-86, Tybursky, Watson & Harman, Portsmouth, 1987-88, Taylor, Keane, Blanchard, Lyons & Watson, P.A., Portsmouth, 1988-94, Watson, Lyons, & Bosen, P.A., Portsmouth, 1994-99, Watson & Bosen, P.A., Portsmouth, 2000—01, Watson, Bosen, Harman, Venci & Lemire, P.A., Portsmouth, 2001—04, Watson & Lemire, P.A., Portsmouth, 2004—. Del. N.H. Constl. Conv., Concord, 1974. Mem. Maritime Heritage Commn., 1986-95, City of Portsmouth Hist. Dist. Commn., 1992, City of Portsmouth Planning Bd., 1992-94; bd. dirs. N.H. Small Bus. Devel. Ctr., 1993-95, N.H. Main St. Ctr., 1998-2002, sec., 2001-02; mem. adv. bd. Ballet New England, 1997—; bd. advisors N.H. Small Bus. Devel. Ctr., 1992-95; bd. trustees Strawberry Banke Mus., 2000—, sec., 2001-02, chmn., 2002—. Named Portsmouth Citizen of Yr., 1995. Mem. ABA, ATLA (state del. 1996—, chair-elect 1997-98, chair 1998-99, exec. com. 1998-99, co-chair coordinating com. on state rels. 1999-2000, mem. pub. affairs com. 1999-2003, mem. key person com., 2003—, Outstanding State Del. 1997, Wiedeman-Wysocki citation of excellence, 1999, 2000, 2002), N.H. Bar Assn. (bd. govs. 1985-90), N.H. Trial Lawyers Assn. (bd. govs. 1989—, sec. 1982-92, treas. 1993-94, pres. elect 1994-95, pres. 1995-96, chair legis. com. 1992-95, 96-2000, exec. com. 1992--, recipient Pres.'s award 1993, 97, Spl. Recognition award 2000), Rockingham County Bar Assn. (Profl. award 2001), Franklin Pierce Law Ctr. Alumni Assn. (pres. 1985-86), N.H. Bar Found. (bd. govs. 1987-90), Greater Portmouth C. of C. (bd. dirs. 1988-92, chmn. 1990-92), Portsmouth Hist. Soc. (trustee 1994—, pres. 1995-97), Portsmouth Atheneum (propr. 1991—). Office: Watson & Lemire PA PO Box 469 Portsmouth NH 03802-0469 Office Phone: 603-436-7667.

WATSON, THOMAS STURGES, professional golfer; b. Kansas City, Mo., Sept. 4, 1949; s. Raymond Etheridge and Sarah Elizabeth (Ridge) W.; m. Linda Tova Rubin, July 8, 1973 (div.); children: Margaret Elizabeth, Michael Barrett. BS, Stanford U., 1971. Profl. golfer, 1971—. Winner Western Open, 1974, 1977, 1984; winner Byron Nelson Tournament, 1975, 78, 79, 80; winner Brit. Open, 1975, 77, 80, 82, 83; winner, U.S. Open, 1982; winner World Series, 1975, 80; winner Andy Williams San Diego Open, 1977, 80; winner El Prat, 1977; winner Masters, 1977, 81; winner Bing Crosby Nat. Pro-Am Golf Tournament, 1977, 78; winner Tucson Open, 1978, 84; winner Colgate Hall of Fame Classic, 1978, 79; winner Anheuser Busch Golf Classic, 1978; winner Meml. Tournament, 1979; winner Heritage Classic, 1979, 83; winner Tournament of Champions, 1979, 80, 84; Los Angeles Open, 1980, 82; Greater New Orleans Open, 1980, 81; Dunlop Phoenix, 1980, Atlantic Classic, 1981; Nabisco Championship, 1987, Hong Kong Open, 1992; Recipient Vardon Trophy, 1977, 78, 79, Byron Nelson award, 1977-78, 79-80; named to Ryder Cup Team, 1977, 81, 83, 89 (elected capt. 1992—); named Player of Year Profl. Golf Assn., 1977, 78, 79, 80, 82, 84; elected to PGA World Golf Hall of

Fame, 1988, Kans. Golf Hall of Fame, 1991, William H. Richardson award 1990. Mem. U.S. Golf Assn., Profl. Golfers Assn., Golf Course Supts. Assn. of Am. (Old Tom Morris award 1992), Butler Nat. Golf Club, Shadow Glen Club, Preston Trails Golf Club, Oakwood Country Club, Par Club, Blue Hills Country Club, Kansas City Country Club, Royal and Ancient Golf Club St. Andrews. Achievements include being the leading money winner PGA, 1977-80, 84. Address: PGA PO Box 109601 100 Ave of Champions Palm Beach Gardens FL 33418-3665 Office: Tom Watson Designs 1901 W 47th Pl Mission KS 66205

WATSON, WILLIAM HUGHES, news service publisher, network executive; b. York, S.C., Nov. 21, 1950; s. Archie China and LaVerne (Hughes) W.; m. Virginia Thompson, Oct. 14, 1988. Student, U. S.C., 1970-76. Reporter Onion (S.C.) Daily Times, 1980-84; regional editor Soundings, Essex, Conn., 1984-85; mng. editor The Hour, Norwalk, Conn., 1985-87, Record Jour., Meriden, Conn., 1987-91; cons. editor The Hartford (Conn.) Courant, 1991-92; mng. editor Thomson Newspapers Inc., Stamford, Conn., 1992-93; publ., v.p. News USA, Inc., Falls Church, Va., 1994—; CEO, exec. prodr. Washington News Network, Washington, 2001—. Staff sgt. USAFR, 1970-76. Named Ky. Col. Gov. of Ky., 1981, Hon. Citizen Mayor of New Orleans, 1982. Mem.: AP, Soc. Profl. Journalists, Pub. Rels. Soc. Am., Radio-TV News Dirs. Assn., U. S.C. Alumni Assn., Am. Legion, Rotary, Nat. Press Club. Roman Catholic. Avocations: scuba diving, boating, sailing. Office: Washington News Network Inc 400 N Capitol St NW Ste G-50 Washington DC 20001

WATSON-BOONE, REBECCA A. library and information studies researcher, educator; b. Springfield, Ohio, Mar. 7, 1946; d. Roger S. and Elizabeth Boone; m. Dennis David Ash, 1967 (div. 1975); m. Frederick Kellogg, 1979 (div. 1988); m. Peter G. Watson-Boone, May 26, 1989. Student, Earlham Coll., 1964-67; BA, Case Western Res. U., 1968; MLS, U. N.C., 1971; PhD, U. Wis., 1995. Asst. reference libr. Princeton (N.J) U., 1970-76; head cen. reference dept. U. Ariz., Tucson, 1976-83, assoc. dean Coll. Arts and Scis., 1984-89. Loaned exec. Ariz. Bd. Regents, 1988-89; pres. Ctr. for Study of Info. Profls., 1995—2002. Author: Constancy and Change in the Worklife of Research University Librarians, 1998; contbr. articles to profl. jours. Mem. ALA (div. pres. 1985-86, councilor 1988-92), Assn. for Libr. and Info. Sci. Edn., NAFE. Mem. Soc. Of Friends. Office: 7728 County Rd Y Oconto WI 54153 E-mail: rebeccawb@centurytel.net.

WATT, DOUGLAS (BENJAMIN WATT), writer, critic; b. N.Y.C., Jan. 20, 1914; s. Benjamin Douglas and Agnes Rita (Neimann) W.; m. Ray Mantel, Nov. 5, 1937 (div.); children— Richard David, James Douglas; m. Ethel Madsen, Aug. 13, 1951; children— Patricia, Katherine. AB, Cornell U., 1934. Copy boy N.Y. News, 1936-37, radio columnist, 1937-40, drama reporter, 1940-71, sr. drama critic, 1971-87, critic-at-large, 1987-93; staff writer New Yorker mag., 1946-95; profl. song writer; columnist Small World, 1955-70. Pres. Hampton Animal Shelter, 1965-79. Served with USAAF, World War II. Mem. ASCAP, N.Y. Drama Critics Circle (pres. 1975-77) Clubs: Dutch Treat (N.Y.C.) (bd. govs.). Home: 27 W 86th St New York NY 10024-3615 *To say one has achieved success, except perhaps in isolated instances, is an exercise in vanity and contrary to man's experience. At best, some satisfaction can be gained in one's career, and then almost always because of intense effort.*

WATT, DWIGHT, JR., (ARTHUR DWIGHT WATT JR.), computer programming and microcomputer specialist; b. Washington, Jan. 25, 1955; s. Arthur Dwight and Myrtle Lorraine (Putnam) W.; m. Shari Elizabeth Gambrell, July 30, 1988. BA, Winthrop U., 1977, MBA, 1979; EdD, U. Ga., 1989. Cert. computer and internet profl. Inst. Cert. Computer Profls., Microsoft; cert. home fire arms safety, NRA; cert. A+ personal computer technician, CompTIA; cert. sys. engr., sys. adminstr., office user specialist instr.; i-net plus cert. Comptia; Network + cert.; cert. network adminstr. and acad. instr., Cisco; Server + cert. CompTIA. Data processing instr. York Tech. Coll., Rock Hill, S.C., 1977-78; computer ctr. asst. Winthrop U., Rock Hill, 1976-79; data processing instr. Brunswick (Ga.) Coll., 1979-80; system operator, asst. programmer Sea Island (Ga.) Co., The Cloister, 1981; pvt. practice data processing cons. Swainsboro, Ga., 1981—; computer programming/microcomputer specialist instr. Swainsboro Tech. Inst., 1981-96; sr. programmer/analyst Policy Mgmt. Sys. Corp., Columbia, S.C., 1996-97; microcomputer specialist instr. Athens Tech. Coll.-Elbert County Campus, Elberton, Ga., 1997-2001; chair IT dept. Heart of Ga. Tech. Coll., Dublin, 2001—; CIO Ga. Healthcare Sys., Atlanta, 2001. Cons., spkr. in field; chmn. exec. bd. computer curricula Ga. Dept. Tech. and Adult Edn., 1990-92, 2002-, exec. bd. computer curricula, 1994-96, vice chair, 2000-02; chmn. East Ctrl. Ga. Consortium for Computer Occupations, 1990-96; co-facilitator CIS curriculum rev. and update Ga. Tech. Colls., 2001. Author: District Revenue Potential and Teachers Salaries in Georgia, 1989, Structured COBOL for Technical Students, 1998; co-author: District Property Wealth and Teachers Salaries in Georgia, 1990, Factors Influencing Teachers Salaries: An Examination of Alternative Models, 1991, Local Wealth and Teachers Salaries in Pennsylvania, 1992, School District Wealth and Teachers' Salaries in South Carolina, 1993, Test Yourself A+ Certification Practice Exams, 1998. Chmn. Emanuel County chpt. ARC, Swainsboro, 1989-90, 92-93, bd. dirs., 1989-96; pres. United Meth. Men. Swainsboro, 1984-86; trustee Greater Swainsboro Tech. Inst. Found., Inc., 1995-96; bd. dirs. Emanuel Arts Coun. Recipient Nat. Tech. Tchr. of Yr. finalist award Am. Tech. Edn. Assn., 1994; Olympic Cmty. Hero Torchbearer, 1996. Mem. Inst. Cert. Computing Profls., Ga. Bus. Edn. Assn. (dir. dist. 1 1986, 96, dist. sec.-treas. 1993-95, dist. 1 dir.-elect 1995-96, Dist. 1 Postsecondary Tchr. Yr. 1985, State Postsecondary Tchr. Yr. 1995), Profl. Assn. Ga. Educators, Swainsboro Jaycees (Outstanding Young Citizen 1985, treas. 1984-89, pres. 1987-88, pres. S.E. Ga. Jaycee Fair 1995, treas. S.E. Ga. Jaycee Fair 1993-94), Ga. Jaycees (v.p. area C 1988-89, chaplain 1989-90, dir. region 6 1990-91, chmn. state shooting edn. 1991-92, chair Internat. BB Gun Match Championship 1999, co-chair match 2000, treas. match 2002), U.S. Jr. C. of C. (nat. rep. shooting edn. program 1992-95, Shooting Edn. State Program Mgr. Yr. 1992, webmaster Internat. BB Gun Championship match 1999—), Swainsboro-Emanuel County C. of C. (webmaster 2002—), Kiwanis (tech. chair, webmaster 2002—), Emanuel Artist Guild (v.p. 2003—). Methodist. Home: PO Box 1637 206 Hereford Rd Swainsboro GA 30401 Office: 560 Pinehill Rd Dublin GA 31021-1253 Office Phone: 478-274-7775. Personal E-mail: dwight-watt@att.net.

WATT, JOHNATHAN MARK, religious studies educator; b. Sydney, NSW, Australia, May 16, 1957; arrived in U.S., 1967; s. Trevor Lyle and June (Rees) Watt; m. June Marie Hamel, Oct. 15, 1977; children: Nathaniel, Johanna, Benjamin, Zacharias. BS Mag. Journalism, Syrcuse U., 1978; MDiv, Reformed Presbyn. Theol. Sem., Pitts., 1982; MA Linguistics, U. Pitts, 1987, PhD Linguistics, 1995. Ordained minister Reformed Presbyn. Ch. N. Am., 1982. Adj. prof. biblical studies Reformed Presbyn, Theol. Sem., Pitts., 1995—; asst. prof. biblical studies Geneva Coll., Beaver Falls, Pa., 2000—. Author: (Book) Code Switching in Luke and Acts, 1997; contbr. articles to profl jours on bibliosociolinguistics. Mem.: Evangelical Theological Soc., Soc. Biblical Literature. Presbyterian. Office: Geneva Coll 3200 College Ave Beaver Falls PA 15010 E-mail: jwall@geneva.edu.

WATT, JOSEPH MICHAEL, state supreme court chief justice; b. Austin, Tex., Mar. 8, 1947; BA in History, Tex. Tech U., 1969; JD, U. Tex., 1972. Bar: Tex. 1972, Okla. 1974. Pvt. practice, Altus, Okla., 1972-85; judge Dist. Trial Ct., 1985-91; gen. counsel to gov. State of Okla., Oklahoma City, 1991-92; justice Okla. Supreme Ct., Okahoma City, 1992—2003, chief justice, 2003—. Office: Okla State Supreme Ct State Capitol Rm 245 Oklahoma City OK 73105 Fax: 405-521-6982.

WATT, KATHERINE ANN, administrative assistant; b. Wichita, Kans., Jan. 28, 1951; d. Henry Eugene Young, Sr. and Betty Alice Elaine (Myers) Young; m. Willis Martin Watt, Feb. 14, 1970; 1 child, Derek Lee. Student, Manhattan Christian Coll., Kans., 1969—71, Ft. Hays State U., 1986—87; banking diploma, Kans.-Nebr. Schs. Banking, 1993. Cert. Am. Banking Assn., 1991, Svc. Plus Beyond Customer Expectations and Supporting Svc. Excellence Facilitator, 1992. Asst. mgr. Peter Pan Ice Cream Store, Manhattan, Kans., 1970—71; sales assoc. J.C. Penney, Salinas, Kans., 1971—72, Huntsville, Ala., 1972—73, Manhattan, Kans., 1975—76; teller 1st Nat. Bank, 1976—80; teller, sec. Union Story Bank, Ames, Iowa, 1980—83; sales sec. Migro Seed, Inc., Ames, 1983—84; receptionist, sec. Piper-Jaffray Hopwood Inc., Ames, 1984; bank mgr. Emprise Bank, Hays, Kans., 1984—97; receptionist, dir. mktg. Pottroff Accountancy Corp., Manhattan, 1997—2000; adminstrv. asst. to v.p. bus. affairs Meth. Coll., Fayetteville, NC, 2000—. Svc. Plus facilitator Emprise Bank, Hays, Kans., 1992—2000. Mem., actor: Kryiou Drama Group, 1969—71, 1997—2000; mem., actor Chi Rho Players, Ames, Iowa, 1980—84. Site coun. mem. Hays H.S., Kans., 1990—91; choir dir. Hays Christian Ch., 1986—2000; mem., tchr., choir dir. Fayetteville Christian Ch., NC, 2000—. Recipient Leadership cert., Leadership Hays, 1994. Avocations: music, crossword puzzles, reading. Home: 5624 Watersplash Ln Fayetteville NC 28311-0221 Office: Methodist College 5400 Ramsey St Fayetteville NC 28311-1498

WATT, KENNETH EDMUND FERGUSON, zoology educator; b. Toronto, July 13, 1929; s. William Black Ferguson Watt and Irene Eleanor (Hubbard) Dodd; m. Genevieve Bernice Bendig, Oct. 28, 1955; children: Tanis Jocelyn, Tara Alexis. BA with honor, U. Toronto, 1951; PhD in Zoology, U. Chgo., 1954; LLD, Simon Fraser U., 1970. Biometrician Rsch. div. Dept. Lands and Forests, Ont., Canada, 1954-57; sr. biometrician Can. Dept. Agr., Ottawa, Ont., 1957-60; head, statis. rsch. and svcs. Canadian Dept. Forestry, Ottawa, 1960-63; from assoc. prof. to prof. Dept. Zoology, U. Calif., Davis, 1963-93. Author: Ecology and Resource Management, 1968, Principles of Environmental Sciences, 1973, Understanding the Environment, 1982, Taming the Future, 1991. Recipient Gold medal Entomol. Soc., 1969. Achievements include development of new approach to forecasting future based on exhaustive statistic testing of nonlinear math. equations to long runs of historical data; discovery that change through time in real world systems violates Markov principles. Home: 2916 Quail St Davis CA 95616-5711 Office: U Calif Dept Evolution & Ecology Davis CA 95616 *The actual causes of present events are much further back in time than most people suspect. Failure to understand this is why forecasting is such a disaster area.*

WATT, LINDA E. ambassador; married; 2 children. BA, Vanderbilt U., 1973; MA, U. N.Mex., 1975. With Dept. of State, 1976—, London, San Jose, Quito, Moscow; polit. advisor U.S. So. Command, Santo Domingo; U.S. amb. to Panama U.S. Dept. State, 2002—. Office: US Embassy Panama Apo AA 34002 Office Phone: 507-207-7238.

WATT, MELVIN L. congressman, lawyer; b. Mecklenburg County, N.C., Aug. 26, 1945; m. Eulada Paysour; children: Brian, Jason. BS in Bus. Adminstrn., U. N.C., 1967; JD, Yale U., 1970. Atty. Ferguson, Stein, Watt, Wallis, Adkins, & Grensham, 1971-92; state senator N.C., 1985-86; co-owner East Towne Manor, 1989—; mem. U.S. Congress from 12th N.C. dist., Washington, 1993—; mem. fin. svcs. com.; mem. judiciary com., ranking mem. comml. and adminstrv. law subcom. Pres. Mecklenburg County Bar. Active Ctrl. Piedmont C.C. Found., Legal Aid of Southern Piedmont, N.C. NB Community Devel. Corp., Auditorium-Coliseum-Civic Ctr. Authority, United Way, Mint Mus., Family Housing Svcs., Pub. Edn. Forum, Dilworth Community Devel. Assn., Cities in Schs., Housing Authority Scholarship Bd., Morehead Scholarship Selection Com.; bd. visitors Johnson C. Smith Univ. Mem. NAACP (life), N.C. Assn. Black Lawyers, N.C. Acad. Trial Lawyers, Charlotte C. of C. (sports action coun.), West Charlotte Bus. Incubator, Inroads Inc., Phi Beta Kappa. Democrat. Presbyterian. Office: US Ho of Reps 2236 Rayburn House Off Bldg Washington DC 20515-3312

WATT, ROBERT LEE, music educator; b. Neptune, N.J., Jan. 15, 1948; s. Edward Augustus and Eleanora Watt. BA, Calif. Inst. Arts, 1978. Cert. airplane pilot 1975. French horn Boston Ballet, 1968—69, Boston Opera, 1968—69; French horn soloist Boston Pops, 1968—69, Boston Symphony, 1968—69; asst. prin. French horn LA Philharm., 1970—. Faculty Santa Monica (Calif.) Coll., 1985; instr. Calif. State Dominguez Hills, Carson, 1990—, LA City Coll., 2003—. Author: (color and activity book) Story of the Moor's Coloring Book, 1995. Panelist Nat. Endowment for the Arts, Washington, 1989—90. Avocations: fencing, kickboxing, flying, horseback riding. Home: 121 S Hope St #515 Los Angeles CA 90012 Office: LA Philharm 151 S Grand Ave Los Angeles CA 90012 E-mail: bobwatt@pacbell.net.

WATT, WILLIS MARTIN, academic administrator, communications, adult education, leadership educator; b. Ottawa, Kans., Dec. 20, 1950; s. Gerald Omri and Shirley Arlene (Tush) W.; m. Katherine Ann Young, Feb. 14, 1970; 1 child, Derek Lee. BS in Christian Edn., Manhattan Christian Coll., 1976; BS in Secondary Edn.-Speech/Drama, Kans. State U., 1976, MA in Speech/Drama, 1978, PhD in Curriculum/Instrn./Speech, 1980; postdoctoral, Flint Hills Leadership Program, 1999; continuing edn. unit tng., Franklin/Covey, 2000, continuing edn. unit tng., 2002. Ordained to ministry Christian Ch., 1976. Pastor Colony (Kans.) Christian Ch., 1969-71, Barnes (Kans.) Christian Ch., 1974-75, 1975-76; assoc. pastor Burlington (Kans.) Christian Ch., summers 1970-71; pastor Ogden (Kans.) Union Ch., 1979-80; elder, evangelist Hays (Kans.) Christian Ch., 1984-97; grad. tchg. asst. dept. speech, theatre and dance Kans. State U., Manhattan, 1976-78, instr., 1978-80; teaching intern speech/drama Manhattan (Kans.) Christian Coll., 1979; asst. prof. dept. speech comm. Iowa State U., Ames, 1980-84; dir. forensics dept. comm. Ft. Hays (Kans.) State U., 1984-91, chair, 1991-97; v.p. acad. affairs Manhattan (Kans.) Christian Coll., 1997-2000, dept. head adult edn., 1999-2000. Interim min. South Hutchinson (Kans.) Christian Ch., 1999-2000; adj. assoc. prof. dept. speech comm., theater and dance Kans. State U., 1999-2000; divsn. dir. profl. studies Meth. Coll., 2003-04, dean Sch. Info. and Tech., 2004—; dir. orgnl. comm. and leadership, prof. speech Meth. Coll., Fayetteville, N.C., 2000—; dir. Talking Tiger Rsch. Inst., Hays, 1985-91; mem. Comm. Tng. Consulting Svcs., Fayetteville, N.C., 1986—; exec. dir. Chi Rho Players Religious Drama Troupe, Ames, Iowa, 1981-84; adjudicator Am. Coll. Theatre Festival, Region V, 1982-2000; mem. adv. coun. for acad. affairs Ctr. for Policy in Higher Edn., 1999; artistic dir. Kyriou Drama Troupe, Manhattan, 1998-2000. Author: Fundamentals of Speech, 1988, Theory and Application for Effective Bus. and Profl. Presentations, 1994, Fundamentals of Oral Communication: Theory and Practice, 1995, Fundamentals of Oral Communication, 1997, Speech Communication: Theories & Practices, 2001; editor Kans. Speech Jour., 1994-2000; assoc. editor Nat. Forensic Jour., 1987-97; rev. editor The Forensic, 1989-95, Jour. Leadership Edn., 2003—; mem. editl. adv. bd. Privacy on Campus, 1999. Edn. divsn. leader United Way of Ellis County, Hays, 1989, mem. allocations com. Riley County (Kans.) United Way, 1999-2002; Ft. Hays State U. comm. leader, 1992; baseball coach Little League, Ames, Iowa and Hays, 1982-86; bd. dirs. ACTORS Cmty. Theatre, Ames, 1982-84; elder Fayetteville (N.C.) Christian Ch., 2002—. With U.S. Army, 1971-74; mem. facilitator adv. bd. Franklin Corey, Inc., 2004—. Recipient Bronze award Ellis County United Way, 1996, Outstanding Coll. Tchr. award Kans. Speech Comm. Assn., 1996, Editor's Choice awards for numerous poems including Ode to Lost Love and Friends, Green Eyes, Silver and Bronze awards for Poet of Merit Internat. Soc. Poets, 2002; inductee Mid-Am. Edn. Hall of Fame, J. Paul Jewell Ctr., Kansas City, 1998. Mem. Theta Alpha Phi (hon. drama), Pi Kappa Delta (gov. plains province 1986-88, 90-91, Exemplary Svc. award 1987, 91, Svc. award 1993, Order of Highest Distinction 1995), Pi Delta Kappa, Alpha Psi Omega. Avocations: racketball, chess, reading, writing, travel. Home: 5624 Watersplash Ln Fayetteville NC 28311-0221 Office: Meth Coll 5400 Ramsey St Fayetteville NC 28311 Business E-Mail: wmwatt@methodist.edu.

WATTEL, HAROLD LOUIS, economics professor; b. Bklyn., Sept. 30, 1921; s. David Max and Carolyn (Abrams) W.; m. Sara Gordon, Sept. 1, 1946; children: Karen, Jill. BA, Queens Coll., 1942; MA, Columbia U., 1947; PhD magna cum laude, New Sch. Social Research, 1954. Jr. economist WPB, 1942; economist Dept. Agr., 1946; econ. cons. Boni, Watkins & Mounteer, 1952; economist Bur. Bus. and Community Research, Hofstra U., 1954, 57, dir., 1957-58; prof. econs. Bur. Bus. and Community Rsch., Hofstra U., 1957-86, prof. emeritus, 1986—, chmn. dept. econs., 1957-61, chmn. div. bus., 1961—, dean Sch. Bus., 1965-73. Econ. cons. to consumer counsel Staff Gov. N.Y., 1956—58; cons. N.Y. State Moreland Commn. on Alcoholic Beverage Control Law, 1963—64, Legislative Reference Bur. U. Hawaii, 1966, Schenley Industries, 1967—, Ralston Purina Co., 1967—, Am. Can Co., 1965—; econ. cons. Nat. Millinery Planning Bd., 1959—70; ednl. cons. U.S. Merchant Marine Acad., Kings Point, 1972; cons. Bulova Watch Co., 1975—82. Author ann. publ.: The Millinery Industry; Editor: Planning in Higher Education, 1975, Chief Executive Officer Compensation, 1978, The Gross Personal Income Tax, 1981; Contbr. chpts. to books, encys., dictionaries, also reports.; Editor, contbr.: L.I. Bus, 1954-59. Mem. Comprehensive Health Planning Coun., 1970-75; bd. dirs., v. p., N.Y. State unit Am. Lung Assn.; pres. Nassau-Suffolk unit; bd. dirs. Comprehensive Health Planning Coun., Nassau-Suffolk, N.Y., N.Y. State Citizen Coun., Regional Med. Program Nassau-Suffolk, consumer rep., bd. dirs. Island Peer Rev. Orgn., 1990; treas. Parodneck Found.; chair Pronet Citizens Advocacy Ctr., 1997—. Lt. USNR, 1942-46. Edn. fellow, 1949; Hazen Found. fellow, 1952; Ford Found. regional fellow, 1960 Mem. AAUP (chpt. pres. 1953), Middle Atlantic Assn. Colls. Bus. Adminstrn. (pres. 1970-71), Am., Met. econs. assns., N.Y. State Environ. Health Assn. (v.p.), Island Peer Rev. Orgn. (consumer/AARP rep. 1990—), Pi Gamma Mu, Omicron Chi Epsilon, Beta Gamma Sigma (hon. assoc.). Home: 181 Shepherd Ln Roslyn Heights NY 11577-2525 Office: Hofstra U Dept Econ Hempstead NY 11550 Personal E-mail: phdhlw@juno.com.

WATTENBERG, ALBERT, physicist, researcher; b. N.Y.C., Apr. 13, 1917; s. Louis and Bella (Wolff) W.; m. Alice von Neumann, May 23, 1992; children from a previous marriage: Beth, Jill, Nina Diane. BS, Coll. City N.Y., 1938; MA, Columbia, 1939; PhD, U. Chgo., 1947. Spectroscopist Schenley Distilleries, N.Y.C., 1939-42; physicist Manhattan Project, Metall. Lab., Chgo., 1942-46; group leader Argonne Nat. Lab., Chgo., 1946-50; asst. prof. U. Ill., Urbana, 1950-51, prof. physics, 1958—. Research physicist Mass. Inst. Tech., 1951-58 Recipient award for 1st nuclear reactor Am. Nuclear Soc., 1962; Nuclear Pioneer award Soc. Nuclear Medicine, 1977; NSF fellow U. Rome, 1962-63 Achievements include pioneering controlled nuclear reactor.

WATTENMAKER, RICHARD JOEL, archive director, art scholar; b. Phila., Feb. 22, 1941; s. Nathan H. and Frances (Rynes) W.; m. Eva Augusta Oscarsson, June 25, 1968; children: Adrian Ezra, Barnaby Leo. BA, U. Pa., 1963; MA, NYU Inst. Fine Arts, 1965, PhD, 1972; student, The Barnes Found., 1959-66. Dir. Rutgers U. Art Gallery, New Brunswick, N.J., 1966-69; chief curator Art Gallery Ont., Toronto, Can., 1972-78; dir. Chrysler Mus., Norfolk, Va., 1979-80, Flint (Mich.) Inst. Arts, 1980-88, Archives of Am. Art, Smithsonian Instn., Washington, 1990—. Lectr. Barnes Found., 1991-92. Author: The Art of Charles Prendergast, 1968, The Art of Jean Hugo, 1973, Puvis de Chavannes and the Modern Tradition, 1975, William Glackens' Beach Scenes at Bellport, 1988, Dr. Albert C. Barnes and The Barnes Foundation, 1993, Maurice Prendergast, 1994. Trustee Intermus. Conservation Lab., Oberlin, Ohio, 1982-88. Recipient Founders Day award NYU, 1972 Office: Smithsonian Instn Archives of Am Art Victor Bldg Ste 2200 MRC937 PO Box 37012 Washington DC 20013-7012 Office Phone: 202-275-1874. Business E-Mail: wattenmakerr@si.edu.

WATTERS, RICHARD JAMES, professional football player; b. Harrisburg, Pa., Apr. 7, 1969; Degree in design, U. Notre Dame. With San Francisco 49'ers, 1991-94; running back Phila. Eagles, 1995-98, Seattle Seahawks, 1998—2001; currently free agt. Selected to Pro Bowl, 1992-94. Achievements include member San Francisco 49'ers Super Bowl XXIX Champions, 1994, holds NFL postseason single game for most points (30), most touchdowns (5), Jan. 15, 1994 vs N.Y. Giants. Office: Seattle Seahawks 11220 NE 53d St Kirkland WA 98033

WATTERS, SUSAN J. communications executive; b. Lafayette, Ind. m. David J. Steel; children: Colin, Andrew. BA, Bryn Mawr Coll.; MA, Tufts U.; postgrad., Fletcher Sch. Law. Staff writer Christian Sci. Monitor, Boston, Congl. Quar., Washington; bur. chief Fairchild Publs., Washington, 1979-98, Fairchild News Svc., Washington, 1998—. Adj. prof. Am. U., Washington, 1993-94. Office: 68 Observatory Cir NW Washington DC 20008-3611 Office Phone: 202-338-0863.

WATTERSON, SCOTT, home fitness equipment manufacturer; Chmn., CEO ICON Health & Fitness, Inc., Logan, Utah. Office: ICON Health & Fitness Inc 1500 S 1000 W Logan UT 84321-8206

WATTLETON, FAYE (ALYCE FAYE WATTLETON), research and education institute administrator, advocate; b. St. Louis, July 8, 1943; d. George and Ozie (Garrett) Wattleton; m. Franklin Gordon (div.); 1 child, Felicia. BS in Nursing, Ohio State U., 1964; MS in Maternal and Infant Health Care, Columbia U., 1967; LHD (hon.), St. Paul's Coll., 1985, Spelman Coll., 1986; LLD (hon.), Northeastern Univ. Law Sch., 1990; LHD (hon.), Long Island Univ., 1990, Univ. of Pa., 1990, Bard Coll., 1991; HHD (hon.), Oberlin Coll., 1991; LLD (hon.), Wesleyan Univ., 1991; LHD (hon.), Hofstra U., 1992, Haverford Coll., 1992; LHD (hon.), Meadville-Lombar Sem./U. Chicago, 1992; D in Pub. Svc. (hon.), Simmons Coll., 1993. Tchr. Miami Valley Hosp. Sch. Nursing, Dayton, Ohio, 1964-66; asst. dir. Montgomery County Combined Pub. Health Dist., Dayton, 1967-70; exec. dir. Planned Parenthood, Dayton, 1970-78; pres. Planned Parenthood Fedn. Am., Inc., NYC, 1978-92, Ctr. for Advancement of Women, NYC, 1995—. Author: How to Talk to Your Child About Sexuality, 1986, Life on the Line, 1996. Bd. dirs. Inst. for Internat. Edn., Quidel Corp., Savient Pharm., Jazz at Lincoln Ctr., Well Choice Inc.; trustee Columbia U. Recipient Am. Humanist award, 1986, John Gardner award, 1987, APHA award of excellence, 1989, Humanitarian award Congrl. Black Caucus Found., 1989, Claude Pepper Humanitarian award Internat. Platform Assn., 1990, Pioneer of Civil Rights and Human Rights award Nat. Conf. of Black Lawyers, 1990, Florina Lasker award N.Y. Civil Liberties Union Found., 1990, Whitney M. Young Jr. Service award Boy Scouts of Am., 1990, Ministry of Women award Unitarian Universalist Women's Fed., 1990, Spirit of Achievement award Albert Einstein Coll. Medicine of Yeshiva U., 1991, 20th Anniversary Advocacy award Nat. Family Planning and Reproductive Health Assn., 1991, Women of Achievement award Women's Projects and Prodn., 1991, Margaret Sanger award, 1992, Jefferson Pub. Svc. award, 1992, Dean's Disting. Svc. award Columbia Sch. Pub. Health, 1992, Fries prize for improving health,m 2004; named one of Best Mgrs. of Non-Profit Orgns. in Am., Bus. Week, Outstanding Mother Nat. Mother's Day Com., 1997; inducted to Nat. Women's Hall of Fame, 1993. Office: Ctr for Advancement of Women 25 W 43rd St Ste # 1120 New York NY 10036

WATTLEWORTH, ROBERTA ANN, physician, medical educator; b. Sioux City, Iowa, Dec. 26, 1955; d. Roland Joseph and Elizabeth Ann (Ahart) Eickholt; m. John Wade Wattleworth, Nov. 7, 1984; children: Adam, Ashley. BS, Morningside Coll., Sioux City, 1978; D of Osteopathy, Coll. Osteo. Medicine/Surgery, Des Moines, 1981; M.Healthcare Adminstrn., U. Osteo. Med. and Health Scis., Des Moines, 1999; MPH, Des Moines U., 2004. Intern Richmond Heights (Ohio) Gen. Hosp., 1981-82, resident in anesthesiology, 1982-84; anesthesiologist Doctor's Gen. Hosp., Plantation, Fla., 1984-85; resident in family practice J.F. Kennedy Hosp., Stratford, N.J., 1985-87; educator family practice U. Osteo. Medicine and Health Scis., Des Moines, 1987-89; family practitioner McFarland Clinic, P.C., Jewell, Iowa, 1989-94; lectr. family practice Osteopath. Med. Ctr., Des Moines U., 1999—, assoc. prof., chair dept. family medicine, 2003—. Med. dir. nursing home Bethany Manor, Story City, Iowa, 1990-99, Jewell Vol. Fire and Rescue Squad, 1990-99. Bd. dirs. Heartland Sr. Svcs., 1995—99, Iowa Rural Health Assn. Named Nat. Outstanding Osteo. Educator of Yr., Nat. Student Osteo. Med. Assn., 2001—02. Fellow Am. Coll. of Osteo. Family Physicians; mem. Am. Osteo. Assn., Am. Med. Dirs. Assn. (sec.-treas. Iowa chpt. 1997-99), Am. Geriatric Assn., Am. Coll. Osteo. Family Physicians (pres. Iowa chpt. 1995-96), Iowa Osteo. Med. Assn. (trustee 1995-99, v.p. 1999—, pres.-elect, 2000-01, pres. 2001-2002). Lutheran. Avocations: gardening, cooking, painting. Office: 3200 Grand Ave Des Moines IA 50312-4104 Office Phone: 515-271-7816. E-mail: Roberta.Wattleworth@dmu.edu.

WATTS, ANDRÉ, concert pianist; b. Nüremberg, Germany, June 20, 1946; s. Herman and Maria Alexandra (Gusmits) W. Student, Phila. Mus. Acad.; grad., Peabody Conservatory, Balt.; hon. doctorate, Yale U., 1973; HHD, Albright Coll., 1975; MusD (hon.), U. Pa., 1984. First pub. appearance at age 10, Phila. Orch. Children's Concerts, 1955, performed with Phila. Orch., 1956, with Leonard Bernstein and the N.Y. Philharm., 1963, European debut, London

Symphony Orch., 1966, made world concert tour to 16 Asian and Western European cities for U.S. State Dept., 1967, including an appearance at the Berlin Festival, Soviet Union tour with San Francisco Symphony, 1972, appearances as soloist with all major U.S. and European orchs., solo tours, Europe, U.S., Japan, Israel; TV appearances include Live from Lincoln Ctr., Great Performers series Lincoln Ctr., NET TV Spl. with Zubin Mehta and L.A. Philharm., Eugene Ormandy and the Phila. Orch., Casals Festival in P.R. on Arts and Entertainment Network (Emmy award nomination for Outstanding Individual Achievement in Cultural Programming); rec. artist with Angel/EMI and Telarc labels. Decorated Order of Zaire Congo; recipient Grammy award Nat. Acad. Rec. Arts and Scis., 1963; Lincoln Center medallion, 1974, Avery Fisher prize, 1988. Address: Cramer/Marder Artists 127 W 96th St Apt 13B New York NY 10025-6430

WATTS, ANTHONY LEE, bank executive; b. Griffin, Ga., Jan. 24, 1947; s. Edgar Lee and Eula Mae (Benton) W.; m. Barbara Malinda Harp, Oct. 11, 1969; children: Natalie Paige, Barbara Leigh, Melanie Marie. AA, Gordon Mil. Coll., 1967; ABJ, U. Ga., 1969. Conventional loan rep. Fed. Nat. Mortgage Assn., Atlanta, from 1971, asst. regional appraiser, quality control and property mgr., to 1976; v.p., dir. ins. svcs. Ticor Mortgage Ins. Co., Atlanta, 1976-82; v.p., regional sales and exec. v.p. Ticor Indemnity Co., 1982-85; sr. v.p., regional mgr. Ticor Mortgage Ins. Co., Atlanta, 1984, sr. v.p., ea. divsn. mgr., 1984-85; pres. Mt. Vernon Fed. Savs. Bank, Dunwoody, Ga., 1985-95, Mt Vernon Fin. Corp., 1993-95; prin., dir. Banc Mortgage Fin. Corp., 1996-99, vice chmn., co-CEO, 1999—2002, co-pres., 2003—. Lectr. to trade assns. With U.S. Army, 1969-71. Decorated Bronze Star; Paul Harris fellow, 1987. Mem. Ga. Mortgage Bankers Assn., Rotary (past pres. Dunwoody club), Cherokee Town and Country Club (pres. 2002-03), Gridiron Club of U. Ga. Office: 990 Hammond Dr NE Ste 1020 Atlanta GA 30328-5519 Business E-Mail: twatts@bancmortgage.com.

WATTS, BARBARA GAYLE, law academic administrator; b. Covington, Ky., Oct. 18, 1946; d. William Samuel and LaVerne Barbara (Ziegler) W. BA, Purdue U., 1968; MEd, U. Cin., 1969, JD, 1978. Bar: Ohio 1978, U.S. Dist. Ct. (so. dist.) Ohio 1978. Residence dir. Ohio State U., Columbus, 1969-71, asst. dean students, 1971-75; assoc. Frost & Jacobs, Cin., 1978-81; asst. dean U. Cin. Coll. Law, 1981-84, assoc. dean, 1984—. Chair Supreme Ct. of Ohio Commn. on Professionalism, 2003—04. Trustee Summerfair Inc., Cin., 1982-85; bd. dir. Pro-Sr., 1995-2002, sec., 1998-2000; trustee ProKids, 1999—, pres.-elect, 2002-03, pres., 2003-2004. Recipient Disting. Alumni award Purdue U. Sch. Liberal Arts, 2001, U. Cin. Coll. Law, 2002; Schleman fellow Purdue U., 1968, Castleberry fellow AAUW, 1977. Mem. ABA, Ohio State Bar Assn. (Nettie Cronise Lutes award Sect. on Women in the Profession 2000), Cin. Bar Assn. (trustee 1992-98, sec. 1993-94), Nat. Assn. Women in Edn., Order of Coif, Chi Omega. Democrat. Office: U Cin Coll Law Clifton & Calhoun Sts Cincinnati OH 45221-0040

WATTS, BEVERLY L. civil rights executive; b. Nashville, Feb. 4, 1948; d. Willliam E. and Evelyn L. (Bender) Lindsley; 1 child, Lauren. BS in Sociology, Tenn. State U., 1969; MS in Cmty. Devel., So. Ill. U., 1973. Mgr., exec. sec. State of Ill. Minority and Female Bus. Enterprise Program, Chgo.; equal opportunity specialist U.S. Dept. of Health, Edn., and Welfare, Chgo.; reginal dir., civil rights/equal employment opportunity USDA, Chgo.; dir. mgmt. and adv. svcs. Ralph G. Moore and Assocs., Chgo.; exec. dir. Ky. Commn. Human Rights, 1992—. Grad. Harvard U. John F. Kennedy Sch. Govt. State and Local Execs. Program, Leadership Louisville, 1994, Leadership Ky., 1995, Duke U. Strategic Leadership for State Execs., John F. Kennedy Sch. exec. program, Harvard U., 1998; pres. Internat. Assn. Ofcl. Human Rights Agys.; mem. long term planning commn. Ky. Health Policy Bd.; mem. Ohio Valley March of Dimes; mem. equal opportunity com. Ky. Coun. on Postsecondary Edn., Louisville Met. Housing Coalition; mem. Ky. housing adv. com. Leadership Louisville Found. Bd., Bus. & Profl. Women Rover City Bd.; bd. dirs. Metro United Way. Recipient Chgo. Forum Gavel award, BEEP Gold Seal award, NAHRW Individual Human Rights award, So. Women in Pub. Svc. Pacesetter award, River City Woman of Achievement award Bus. and Profl. Women, Ky. Charles W. Anderson Laureate award. Mem. Nat. Urban Affairs Coun., Nat. Coun. Negro Women, Ky. Women's Leadership Network, Chgo. Forum, Affirmative Action Assn., Chgo. Urban Affairs Coun. (pres.), Coalition 100 Black Women, Nat. Coun. Negro Women. Office: Ky Commn on Human Rights 322 W Broadway Fl 7 Louisville KY 40202-2106

WATTS, CLAUDIUS ELMER, III, retired military officer; b. Bennettsville, SC, Sept. 22, 1936; s. Claudius Elmer and Blanche Robey (Wannamaker) Watts; m. Patricia Jane Sims, July 23, 1960; children: Claudius Elmer IV, Patricia Watts Heck. AB in Polit. Sci., The Citadel, 1958; postgrad. (Fulbright scholar), London Sch. Econs. and Polit. Sci., 1958-59; MBA, Stanford U., 1967. Commd. officer USAF, 1958, advanced through grades to lt. gen., 1986, comdr. 438th Mil. Airlift Group, 1979-80, comdr. 63d Mil. Airlift Wing Norton AFB, Calif., 1980-82, asst. dep. chief staff plans Mil. Airlift Command Scott AFB, Ill., 1982-83, dep. chief staff plans Mil. Airlift Command, 1983-84; dir. budget Hdqrs. U.S. Air Force, Washington, 1984-85; sr. mil. asst. to dep. sec. def. U.S. Dept. Def., Washington, 1985-86; compt. USAF, Washington, 1986-89; pres. Citadel, Charleston, SC, 1989-96; ret., 2000. Former adv. coun. grad. sch. bus. Stanford U.; former bd. visitors Air U.; chmn. peer rev. teams NCAA Coun.; former trustee Aerospace Edn. Found.; bd. dirs., chair audit com. Cmty. First Bank S.C.; bd. dirs. Crescent Mortgage Co., Carolina Fin. Corp. Past trustee Palmetto Partnership; past chmn. Marion Sq. Commn.; former bd. dirs., mem. fin. com. Air Force Aid Soc.; mem. bd. advisors Am. Leadership Found. Decorated Def. Disting. Svc. medal, USAF Disting. Svc. medal, Legion of Merit with oak leaf cluster, DFC with two oak leaf clusters, Air medal with 10 oak leaf clusters, Gallantry Cross with Palm, Vietnamese Svc. medal with 2 svc. stars Vietnam. Mem.: VFW, Am. Soc. Mil. Comptrs., Airlift Assn., Air Force Sgts. Assn., Air Force Assn., Am. Legion, Order of Daedalians, Mil. Order World Wars. Methodist. Avocations: golf, reading. Office: 229 Country Club Ln Charleston SC 29412-2208 Business E-Mail: wattsc@a.tadel.edu.

WATTS, DAVID EIDE, lawyer; b. Fairfield, Iowa, June 13, 1921; BA, U. Iowa, 1941, JD, 1942; postgrad., Columbia Law Sch., 1946-47. Bar: Iowa 1942, Mass. 1950, N.Y. 1954. Instr. U. Iowa, Iowa City, 1947-48; asst. prof. U. Pa., 1948-49, Harvard Law Sch., 1949-52; ptnr. Dewey Ballantine, N.Y.C., 1958-90, of counsel, 1990—. Adj. assoc. prof. NYU, 1952-55; vis. lectr. Columbia U., 1954. Contbr. articles to legal jours. Mem. ABA, N.Y. State Bar Assn., Assn. Bar City N.Y., Am. Law Inst., Am. Coll. Tax Counsel, Am. Inst. Tax Policy. Home: 33 W 74th St New York NY 10023-2402 Office: Dewey Ballantine LLP 1301 Ave Of The Americas New York NY 10019-6092

WATTS, DENNIS LESTER, retired military officer; b. Rockford, Ill., Sept. 26, 1947; s. Lester George and Marjorie Doris (Kindell) W.; m. Betty Ann Homb, Oct. 9, 1970; 1 child, Kimberly. BS in Radiol. Tech., Midwestern State U., 1975; MS in Radiol., U. Colo., 1986; postgrad., Nova Southeastern U., 1996—. Lic. med. physicist, Tex. X-ray technician USAF, Wichita Falls, Tex., 1971-76, nuclear medicine technician, 1976-79; commd. capt. U.S. Army, San Antonio, 1979—. Med. physics chief Brooke Army Med. Ctr., Ft. Sam Houston, Tex.; radiation protection officer Reynolds Army Hosp., Ft. Sill, Okla.; med. physicist Berkshire Med. Ctr., Pittsfield, Mass., chmn. radiation safety com.; creator, course dir. Northeastern Conf. on Radiol. Scis.; mem. faculty Breast and Cervical Cancer Tng. Inst. Sch. Medicine Boston U.; adj. instr. Incarnate World Coll., San Antonio; mem. organizing com. World Congress on Med. Physics and Biomed. Engring, San Antonio. Author: (with others) Medical Physics, 1987; mem. editl. bd. Berkshire Med. Jour; rev. Med. Physics; contbr. articles to profl. jours. Mem. Am. Assn. Physicists in Medicine, Health Physics Soc. Mem. Am. Coll. Radiology, Am. Assn. Physicist in Medicine, Health Physics Soc. Avocations: scuba diving, tennis, photography, golf. Home: 8642 Fredericksburg Rd Apt 203 San Antonio TX 78240-1274 Office: Berkshire Med Ctr 725 North St Pittsfield MA 01201-4132 E-mail: dlwatts@vgernet.net.

WATTS, EMILY STIPES, English language educator; b. Urbana, Ill., Mar. 16, 1936; d. Royal Arthur and Virginia Louise (Schenck) Stipes; m. Robert Allan Watts, Aug. 30, 1958; children: Benjamin, Edward, Thomas. Student, Smith Coll., 1954-56; AB, U. Ill., 1958, MA (Woodrow Wilson Nat. fellow), 1959, PhD, 1963. Instr. English U. Ill., Urbana, 1963-67, asst. prof., 1967-73, assoc. prof., 1973-77, prof., dir. grad. studies dept. English, 1977—; bd. dirs. U. Ill. Athletic Assn., chmn., 1981-83; mem. faculty adv. com. Ill. Bd. Higher Edn., 1984—, vice chmn., 1986-87, chmn., 1987-88. Author: Ernest Hemingway and The Arts, 1971, The Poetry of American Women from 1632 to 1945, 1977, The Businessman in American Literature, 1982; contbg. editor: English Women Writers from the Middle Ages to the Present, 1990; contbr. articles on Jonathan Edwards, Anne Bradstreet to lit. jours. John Simon Guggenheim Meml. Found. fellow, 1973-74 Mem. AAUP, Midwest MLA, Am. Inst. Archaeology, Assn. Lit. Scholars Critics, Authors Guild, Ill. Hist. Soc., The Phila. Soc., Phi Beta Kappa, Phi Kappa Phi. Presbyterian. Home: 1009 W University Ave Champaign IL 61821-3317 Office: U Ill 208 English Bldg 608 S Wright St Urbana IL 61801

WATTS, GINNY (VIRGINIA C. WATTS), artist; b. Chester, Pa., Jan. 24, 1931; d. Edwin Swoope Craig and Ruth Irene Tonge; m. Lynch S. Watts, Jr., July 21, 1951 (wid.); children: L. Kenneth, Karen Elizabeth Watts Dick, Monica Faye Watts Malandruccolo, Dawn Ellen Watts Eller; m. Alfred E. Meeds, May 5, 1948 (div. Nov. 1950); children: Brenda Joyce Meeds Parker, Edwin Lewis, Michael Alfred. Student, Del. Tech. and C.C., Georgetown, 1998-99. County coord. Easter Seals, Wilmington, Del., 1985-86; resident advisor Dept. Mental Retardation Kencrest Svcs., Dover, 1986-87, program mgr., 1987-90; fine arts instr. Del. Tech. and C.C., Georgetown, 1998—, 2002—. Instr. workshops Millsboro Art League, Del., 1998—. One person shows include Millsboro Art Gallery, 2000; exhibited in group shows at Del. Art Ctr., 1942—, Del. Tech. and C.C., 1997—, Millsboro Art League and Gallery, Del., 1997—, Fine Arts Event, Rehoboth Beach, Del., 2000, Geyers Art Gallery, Milford, Del., 2000, 01, 2002, others; artist oil, graphite and watercolor paintings, 1942—; group mural: wall of Art Gallery/Del. Tech. C.C., 1998; mural for lobby of Presentations, 2000; fine art work exhibited in offices of U.S. Sen. from Del.; contbr. articles to area newspapers. Vice-pres. Adult Art League, Del. Tech. C.C., 1997—; bd. dirs. Millsboro Art League, 1998—, pres., 2001—; mem. Sussex County Arts Coun., 1997—, Nat. Mus. Women in the Arts; bd. advisors Del. Tech. adult plus program Del. Tech. and C.C.; pres. Adult PLUS Art League, 1998—; pres. Millsboro Art League, 2001-. Recipient Excellence of Artistic Achievement award DAPA and Del. Tech. C.C. Avocations: fitness swimming, hiking, biking, camping, gardening.

WATTS, GLENN ELLIS, union official; b. Stony Point, N.C., June 4, 1920; s. George Dewey and Nellie Viola (Ellis) W.; m. Bernice Elizabeth Willett, Nov. 8, 1941; children: Glenn Ellis II (dec.), Sharon Elizabeth Ann Perlmutter, Marianne Elizabeth Watts Erickson. With Chesapeake & Potomac Telephone Co., Washington, 1941-48, Communications Workers Am., Washington, 1942-85, pres. div. 36, 1948-51, dir. dist. 2, 1951-56, asst. to pres., 1956-65, v.p., 1965-69, sec.-treas. union, 1969-74, pres., 1974-85, pres. emeritus, 1985—. V.p. exec. council AFL-CIO, 1974-85, v.p. emeritus, 1985—; v.p. indsl. union dept., 1968-85, mem. exec. bd. maritime trades dept., 1974-85; mem. Nat. Labor Com. for U.S. Savs. Bonds, 1975; nat. adv. bd. Labor Council for Latin Am. Advancement, 1975-85; mem. labor policy adv. com. for trade negotiations Dept. Labor, 1975-79; mem. industry-labor council White House Conf. on Handicapped Individuals, 1976; chmn. labor subcom. Pres.'s Com. on Employment of Handicapped, 1977; mem. sec.'s adv. council Dept. Commerce, 1976-77; mem. Pres.'s Commn. on Mental Health, 1977-78. Mem. Pres.'s Commn. on the Holocaust, 1978-79; mem. U.S. Holocaust Meml. Coun., 1979-93; past mem. D.C. Appeals and Rev. Bd., D.C. Wage and Hour Rev. Panel, Home Rule for D.C. Com.; mem. nat. advisory com. Nat. Congress Community Econ. Devel., 1974; past chmn. community chest relations com. Nat. Capital Area council Boy Scouts Am., past chmn. James E. West Dist., 1969-71; pres. Health and Welfare Council of Nat. Capital Area, 1967-69; mem. Inter-Am. adv. com. Postal Tel. and Tel. Internat., 1968-74, mem. exec. com., 1977-85, v.p., 1978-81, pres., 1981-85; gen. chmn. United Giver's Fund, 1968, pres., 1971-75; sec. United Way of Am., 1971-76; bd. dirs., treas. United Way Internat., 1974-78; mem.-at-large Dem. Nat. Com., 1974-85, mem. incomes policy study group of domestic affairs task group, 1974-76; trustee, sec.-treas. Am. Inst. Free Labor Devel., 1974-85; mem. U.S. Assn. for Club of Rome, 1978-80; trustee AFL-CIO Human Resources Devel. Inst., 1974-85, George Meany Ctr. for Labor Studies, 1976-85; trustee Ford Found., 1976-88; trustee Aspen Inst. for Humanistic Studies, 1974-89, trustee emeritus, 1989—; trustee Nat. Planning Assn., 1974-80; governing bd. Common Cause, 1974-77; sec.-treas. Ctr. for Mgmt. Services, 1974; hon. vice chmn. Am. Trade Union Council for Histadrut, 1974; mem. nat. adv. council Ariz. Heart Inst., 1974-80; bd. dirs. Am. Arbitration Assn., 1975-79, Am. Productivity Ctr., 1978-82, New Directions, 1977-80, Alliance to Save Energy, 1977-80; mem. nat. com. on coping with interdependence Aspen Program of Humanistic Studies, 1975-77; bd. dirs. Council on Fgn. Rels., 1987-90, Initiative Com. for Nat. Econ. Planning, 1975-76, Overseas Devel. Council, 1987-91; trustee, mem. exec. com. Joint Council Econ. Edn., 1976-79, Collective Bargaining Forum, 1983-92, co-chmn. 1983-87, adv. bd. Collective Bargaining Inst. George Washington U., 1987-92; mem. Commn. on a Nat. Inst. Justice, 1976-79, Trilateral Commn., 1977—, Helsinki Watch, 1978-90, commn. Future U.S.-Mex. Relations, 1987-89, exec. com. Am. Agenda, 1988. Recipient Urban Trade Unionist award Nat. Urban Coalition, 1978, Silver Beaver award, 1965 Unitarian Universalist. Home: 2801 New Mexico Ave NW Apt 804 Washington DC 20007-3910

WATTS, HAROLD WESLEY, economist, educator; b. Salem, Oreg., Sept. 30, 1932; s. Elton and Claire W.; m. Doris A. Roth, Sept. 28, 1951 (div. 1973); children— Michael Lee, Suzanne, Jane Marie, Kristin BA, U. Oreg., 1954; MA, Yale U., 1956, PhD, 1957. From instr. to assoc. prof. Yale U., New Haven, 1957-63; from assoc. prof. to prof. econs. U. Wis., Madison, 1963-76, dir. Inst. Research on Poverty, 1966-71; prof. econs. and pub. policy Columbia U., N.Y.C., 1976-98, prof. econs. and pub. policy emeritus, 1998—, dir. Pub. Policy Rsch. Ctr., 1988-93; sr. fellow Mathematica Policy Research Princeton, N.J., 1979-92; sr. rsch. assoc. Urban Inst., 1994-95. Recipient Paul Lazarsfeld award, 1980; Guggenheim fellow, 1975 Fellow Assn. Pub. Policy Analysis and Mgmt., Econometric Soc.; mem. Am. Econ. Assn., L.I. Wine Coun. (pres. 2000-02). Democrat. Home: 144 Bay Ave Greenport NY 11944-1404 Office: Ternhaven Cellars PO Box 758 Greenport NY 11944 Office Phone: 631-477-8737. Business E-Mail: harold@ternhaven.com.

WATTS, HELENA ROSELLE, military analyst; b. East Lynne, Mo., May 29, 1921; d. Elmer Wayne and Nellie Irene (Barrington) Long; m. Henry Millard Watts, June 14, 1940; children: Helena Roselle Watts Scott, Patricia Marie Watts Foble. BA, Johns Hopkins U., 1952, postgrad., 1952—53. Assoc. engr. Westinghouse Corp., Balt., 1965-67; sr. analyst Merck, Sharp & Dohme, Westpoint, Pa., 1967-69; sr. engr. Bendix Radio divsn. Bendix Corp., Balt., 1970-72; sr. scientist Sci. Applications Internat. Corp., McLean, Va., 1975-84; mem. tech. staff The MITRE Corp., McLean, 1985-94; ret., 1994. Adj. prof. Def. Intelligence Coll., Washington, 1984-85. Contbr. articles to profl. jours. Mem. IEEE, AAAS, AIAA, Nat. Mil. Intelligence Assn., U.S. Naval Inst., Navy League U.S., Air Force Assn., Assn. Former Intelligence Officers, Assn. Old Crows, Mensa, N.Y. Acad. Sci. Republican. Roman Catholic. Avocations: photography, reading. Home: 6541 Franconia Rd # 108 Springfield VA 22150

WATTS, J. C., JR., former congressman, retired professional football player; b. Eufaula, Okla., Nov. 8, 1957; m. Frankie Watts; 5 children. BA in Journalism, U. Okla., 1981. Profl. football player Ottawa and Toronto Teams Can. Football League, 1981-86; youth min. Sunnylane So. Bapt. Ch., Del City, 1987-94; mem. Okla. Corp. Commn., 1990—95, chmn., 1992—95; mem. U.S. Congress from 4th Okla. dist., 1995—2003; mem. armed svcs. com.; mem. special oversight panel on terrorism; chmn. GoPac. Mem. Nat. Drinking Water Adv. Coun.; mem. electricity com. Nat. Assn. Regulatory Utility Commrs; hon. co-chmn. Rep. Nat. Conv., 2000. Bd. of rep. Fellowship of Christian Athletes, Okla. Republican.

WATTS, JESSICA MILAN, director; d. Virginia Maria Quinones, M.D.; BS in biol. sci., La. State U., Shreveport, 1998; MA in gen. coun. and guidance, La. Tech. U., Ruston, 2001. Coun. intern The Ctr. for Families, Shreveport, La., 2000—01, Ctrl. Pk. Elem., Bossier City, La., 2001; program mgr. Alliance for Edn., Shreveport, La., 2001—02, dir. of devel., 2002—03; exec. dir Gingerbread House, Children's Adv. Ctr., Shreveport, La., 2003—. Vol., steering com. mem. Alliance for Edn., Shreveport, La., 2000—01, vol., 2003—. Recipient Phi Eta Sigma Honor Soc., La. State U., Shreveport, 1995—98, Omicron Delta Kappa Leadership Soc., 1997—, Phi Kappa Phi Honor Soc., La.Tech. U., 2001—. Mem.: Am. Coun. Assn., Assn. of Fundraising Prof., Alumni Phi Mu. Avocations: interior decorating, physical fitness, reading, photography. Office: Gingerbread House Bossier/Caddo Children's Advocacy Ctr 513 Jordan St Shreveport LA 71101-4533 Office Phone: 318-674-2900.

WATTS, JOHN, JR., insurance company executive; BA in English, UCLA. Various mgmt. positions Health Net, Northwestern Nat. Life Ins. Co.; regional dir. L.A. sales office Blue Cross of Calif., 1995—97, gen. mgr. large group svcs., 1997; acting sr. v.p., UNICARE comml. accounts large group div. WellPoint Health Networks, Inc.; sr. v.p. large group div. Blue Cross and Blue Shield of Ga. (div. WellPoint Health Networks, Inc.), 2001—03, pres., CEO, 2003—. Office: Blue Cross and Blue Shield of Georgia 3350 Peachtree Rd NE Atlanta GA 30326

WATTS, JOHN RANSFORD, university administrator; b. Boston, Feb. 9, 1930; s. Henry Fowler Ransford and Mary Marion (Macdonald) Watts; m. Joyce Lannom, Dec. 20, 1975; 1 child, David Allister. AB, Boston Coll., 1950, MEd, 1965; MFA, Yale U., 1953; PhD, Union Grad. Sch., 1978. Prof., asst. dean Boston U., 1958-74; prof., dean fine arts Calif. State U., Long Beach, 1974-79; dean and artistic dir. The Theatre Sch./Goodman Sch. Drama, DePaul U., Chgo., 1979-99, prof. and dean emeritus, 1999—. Mng. dir. DePaul U. Merle Reskin Theatre, 1988-99; gen. mgr. Boston Arts Festivals, 1955-64; adminstr. Arts Programs at Tanglewood, 1966-69; producing dir. Theatre Co. of Boston, 1973-75. Chmn. Mass. Coun. on Arts and Humanities, 1968-72; bd. dirs., v.p. Long Beach Pub. Cofp. for the Arts, 1975-79; mem. theatre panel Ill. Arts Coun., 1981-90. With U.S. Army, 1953-55. Recipient Lifetime Achievement award Joseph Jefferson Com., Chgo., 2000. Mem. Mass. Ednl. Comms. Commn., Am. Theatre Assn., Nat. Coun. on Arts in Edn., Met. Cultural Alliance, U.S. Inst. Theatre Tech., League Chgo. Theatres, Chgo. Internat. Theatre Festival, St. Botolph Club (Boston), Univ. Club (Chgo.), Phi Beta Kappa, Phi Kappa Phi.

WATTS, KAREN SOUTHALL, management consultant; d. Martha Ann and John Roderick Southall; m. James David Watts, July 11, 1987; children: Roderick David, Galen Francis. BA, La. State U., 1985. Cert. facilitator REAL Enterprises, 2000. Adj. faculty Alamance C.C., Graham, NC, 1999—2002; cons., life coach Watts Consulting, Hillsborough, NC, 2000—. Author: (poetry collection) Pagan Housewife, 1995, Housewife Caged, 2001, To Go Away and Heal, 2001, Going into Business Without Going Crazy, 2002, So, Now You're the Boss-Management Skills for Entrepreneurs, 2003; actor: (live theater) Kismet (Best Actress, 1983); contbr. articles to profl. jours. Mem.: Coachville, Internat. Assn. of Cert. Coaches, Am. Assn. of Women in Cmty. Colleges. Achievements include development of Mgmt. Soft Skills Tng. Program. Avocations: gardening, singing, yoga, reading. Personal E-mail: wattsconsulting@aol.com.

WATTS, LINDA SUSAN, humanities educator; BA, U. Del., 1981, MA in History, 1983; MA in Am. Studies, Yale U., 1986, PhD in Am. Studies, 1989. Instr. history and Am. studies U. Del., Newark, 1981—83; instr. English and Am. studies Yale U., New Haven, 1984—86, coord. sr. essays and projects in Am. studies, 1987—89; vis. asst. prof. English, Am. studies, and Afro-Am. studies Wesleyan U., Middletown, Conn., 1989—90; asst. prof. Drake U., Des Moines, 1990—95, asst. prof., assoc. dir. women's studies program, 1992—93, assoc. prof. English, 1995—96, assoc. prof. English, assoc. dean Coll. of Arts and Scis., 1996—99; prof. Am. studies, dir. interdisciplinary arts and scis. program U. Wash., Bothell, 1999—2001, prof. Am. studies, interdisciplinary arts and scis. program, 2001—. Author: (book) Rapture Untold: Gender, Mysticism, and 'The Moment of Recognition' in the Writings of Gertrude Stein, 1996, Gertrude Stein: A Study of the Short Fiction, 1999; contbr. book The World Is Our Home: Society and Culture in Contemporary Southern Writing, articles to profl. jours. HIV/AIDS cmty. edn. instr. ARC, Des Moines, 1992—99, HIV/AIDS instr. trainer, 1996—99; vol. literacy tutor Adult Literacy Ctr., Des Moines, 1998—99; vol. mus. visitor svcs. Experience Music Project, Seattle, 2000—01; vol. AIDS Greater Des Moines, 1992—93, SELFHELP Crafts of the World, Des Moines, 1992—94; vol. curriculum cons. and co-instr. Operation Peer Helper, ARC Youth Program, Des Moines, 1993—93; vol. edn. com. mem. AIDS Project of Greater Des Moines, 1993—95; chair HIV/AIDS edn. program com. ARC, Des Moines, 1994—95, vol. mem. HIV/AIDS edn. program com., 1995—99; vol. planning com. mem. World AIDS Day Observance, State of Iowa, Des Moines, 1997—98. Finalist Woodrow Wilson Dissertation Grant in Women's Studies, Woodrow Wilson Found., 1988, Ill.-Nat. Women's Studies Assn. Manuscript award, 1990; nominee Poet of the Yr., Internat. Soc. Poets, 2001; named Semi-Finalist N.Am. Open Poetry Contest, Internat. Libr. of Poetry, 2000, Internat. Libr. Poetry, 2001; recipient Editor's Choice Award for Outstanding Achievement in Poetry, poetry.com, 2000, Internat. Poet of Merit award. Internat. Soc. Poets, 2002, Open Poetry Competition award, King County Pub. Art Program, State of Wash., 2000; Grad. fellow, U. Del., 1981—83, Grad. Sch., Yale U., 1983—87, Marcia Brady Tucker fellow, 1984—85, Sterling fellow, Yale U., 1983—84. Mem.: Phi Beta Kappa, Phi Alpha Theta, Phi Kappa Phi. Office: Univ Wash Bothell Box 358511 11136 NE 180th St Bothell WA 98011-8246 E-mail: lswatts@u.washington.edu.

WATTS, MALCOLM S(TUART) M(CNEAL), retired internist, medical educator; b. N.Y.C., Apr. 30, 1915; s. Malcolm S.M. and Elizabeth (Forbes) W.; m. Genevieve Moffitt, July 12, 1947; children: Pauline, Elizabeth, Malcolm, James. AB, Harvard U., 1937; MD, 1941. Diplomate: Pan Am. Med. Assn. Group practice internal medicine, San Francisco, 1948-76; clin. prof. medicine U. Calif. Sch. Medicine, 1972-89, assoc. dean, 1966-89, clin. prof. medicine emeritus, 1989—, dir. Extended Programs in Med. Edn., 1973-82; dir. Calif. Statewide Area Health Edn. System, 1979-89. Chmn. bd. trustees San Francisco Consortium, 1968-74, trustee, 1974-80, exec. dir., 1981-94; dir. Soc. Med. Coll. Dirs. Continuing Med. Edn., 1975-82, pres., 1980-81; trustee Hospice of San Francisco, v.p., 1979-85; pres. Alliance Continuing Med. Edn., 1979-81. Editor Western Jour. Medicine, 1968-90, Jour. Continuing Edn. in the Health Professions, 1988-91. Served to capt. M.C. AUS, 1942-46. Recipient Outstanding Community Funds and Councils Am., 1964, U. Calif. San Francisco medal, 1983, Disting. Svc. award Alliance for Continuing Med. Edn., 1990, Disting. Svc. award soc. Med. Coll. Dirs. of Continuing Med. Edn., 1991. Master ACP; fellow Am. Coll. Health Care Execs. (hon.); mem. AMA, AAAS, Calif. Acad. Scis., Calif. Acad. Medicine, Am. Med. Writers Assn. (John T. McGovern award 1986), San Francisco Med. Soc. (pres. 1961), Am. Soc. Internal Medicine (pres. 1964-65), Calif. Med. Assn. (bd. dirs. 1962-90), Nat. Inst. Medicine, Soc. Med. Friends Wine, Acad. Mexicana Ciencias Mexicano de Cultura (corr.). Home: 1661 Pine St Apt 1146 San Francisco CA 94109-0426

WATTS, MARY ANN, retired elementary education educator; b. Harrisburg, Pa., Sept. 13, 1927; d. Major Allan and Ellana Susan (Robinson) Brown; m. Spencer R. Watts, June 23, 1951; children: Shelley Lynn, Allison Dee, Howard Allan. BS, Cheyney U., 1949; postgrad., Temple U., 1965—67, Pa. State U., 1969—72, postgrad., 2003—. Tchr. Harrisburg Sch. Dist., 1949-51, 59-69, Balt. Sch. Dist., 1951-57, Reading (Pa.) Sch. Dist., 1969-89. Mem. sch. dist. dress and discipline code com., 1977-79. Corr. Hamburg Item, West Berks Crier. Bd. dirs. Pa. State Assn. Boroughs, mem. resolutions and policy com.; mem. Bernville Borough Coun., 1976-2003, v.p., 1988-93, 96-98; sec., treas. Berks County Borough Assn., 1977-2003; Reach to Recovery vol. Am. Cancer Soc. Recipient Disting. Alumna award for achievement in govt. and politics Cheyney U., 1999. Mem. Women's Polit. Network Pa., Pa. State Edn. Assn.

(life), Pa. Assn. Sch. Retirees, Bernville Woman's Club (pres. 1978-80, 86-88, Woman of Yr. 1985, Grange Cmty. Svc. award 1988), GNO Harrisburg. Democrat. Mem. United Ch. of Christ.

WATTS, NAOMI, actress; b. Shoreham, Kent, Eng., Sept. 28, 1968; d. Peter Watts. Actor: (films) For Love Alone, 1986, Flirting, 1991, Matinee, 1993, Wide Sargasso Sea, 1993, Gross Misconduct, 1993, The Custodian, 1993, Tank Girl, 1995, Children of the Corn IV: The Gathering, 1996, Persons Unknown, 1996, Under the Lighthouse Dreaming, 1997, Dangerous Beauty, 1998, A House Divided, 1998, Strange Planet, 2001, Ellie Parker, 2001, Down, 2001, Mulholland Dr., 2001, The Ring, 2002, Plots with a View, 2002, Rabbits, 2002, Ned Kelly, 2003, Le Divorce, 2003, 21 Grams, 2003 (Acad. Award nomination for best actress, 2004, Screen Actors Guild Award nomination for best actress, 2004); (TV films) Bermuda Triangle, 1996, Timepiece, 1996, The Christmas Wish, 1998, The Hunt for the Unicorn Killer, 1999, The Wyvern Mystery, 2000, The Outsider, 2002; (TV miniseries) Brides of Christ, 1991; (TV series) Home and Away, 1991, Sleepwalkers, 1997. Mailing: Creative Artists Agy 9830 Wilshire Blvd Beverly Hills CA 90212-1825*

WATTS, OLIVER EDWARD, engineering consultancy company executive; b. Hayden, Colo., Sept. 22, 1939; s. Oliver Easton and Vera Irene (Hockett) W.; m. Charla Ann French, Aug. 12, 1962; children: Erik Sean, Oliver Eron, Sherilyn. BS, Colo. State U., 1962. Registered profl. engr., Colo., Calif.; profl. hand surveyor, Colo. Crew chief Colo. State U. Rsch. Found., Ft. Collins, 1962; with Calif. Dept. Water Resources, Gustine and Castaic, 1964-70; land and water engr. CF&I Steel Corp., Pueblo, Colo., 1970-71; engring. dir. United Western Engrs., Colorado Springs., Colo., 1971-76; ptnr. United Planning and Engring Co., Colorado Springs, 1976-79; owner Oliver E. Watts, Cons. Engr., Colorado Springs, 1979—. Dir. edn. local Ch. of Christ, 1969-71, deacon, 1977-87, elder, 1987-96. 1st lt. C.E., AUS, 1962-64. Recipient Individual Achievement award Colo. State U. Coll. Engring., 1981 Fellow ASCE (life; v.p. Colorado Springs br. 1975, pres. 1978); mem. NSPE (pres. Pike's Peak chpt. 1975, sec. Colo. sect. 1976, v.p. 1977, pres. 1978-79, Young Engr. award 1976, Pres.'s award 1979), Cons. Engrs. Coun. Colo. (bd. dirs. 1981-83), Am. Cons. Engrs. Coun., Profl. Land Surveyors Colo., Colo. Engrs. Coun. (del. 1980—), Colo. State U. Alumni Assn. (v.p., dir. Pike's Peak chpt. 1972-76), Lancers, Lambda Chi Alpha. Home: 7195 Dark Horse Pl Colorado Springs CO 80919-1442 Office: 614 Elkton Dr Colorado Springs CO 80907-3514 E-mail: owatts8167@aol.com., OllieWatts@aol.com.

WATTS, ROBERT ALLAN, publisher, lawyer; b. July 4, 1936; s. Richard P. and Florence (Hooker) W.; m. Emily Stipes, Aug. 30, 1958; children: Benjamin H., Edward S., Thomas J. Student, DePauw U., 1954-55; BA, U. Ill., 1959, JD, 1961. Bar: Ill. 1961. Assoc. Stipes Pub. Co., Champaign, Ill., 1962-67, ptnr., editor, 1967—. Treas. Planned Parenthood, 1976-80; mem. Pres.'s Coun., U. Ill.; pres. Friends of Libr., U. Ill., 1980-82; treas. Campaign Rep. Party, 1976-80;; bd. dirs. local United Way, 1972-81, City of Champaign Libr. Found., 1993-. Mem. Ill. Bar Assn., U. Ill. Found., Nat. Acad. Arts (bd. dirs. 1983-89), Champaign Country Club, Saugatuck Yacht Club (commodore), Lake Shore Bath & Tennis Club (pres. 1983-85). Home: 1009 W University Ave Champaign IL 61821-3317 Office: Stipes Publishing Co 204 W University Ave Champaign IL 61820-3912

WATTS, ROBERT GLENN, retired pharmaceutical executive; b. Norton, Va., Apr. 28, 1933; s. Clifford Amburgey and Stella Lee (Cornette) Watts; m. Doris Juanita Slaughter, Aug. 29, 1953 (dec. 1980); children: Cynthia L. Watts Waller, Robert Glenn, Kelly L.; m. Sara Lowry Childrey, Aug. 20, 1982; 1 child, Matthew R. Alexander 1 stepchild, J. Eric Alexander. BA, U. Richmond, 1959. Dir. ops. A.H. Robins Co., Inc., Richmond, Va., 1967-71, asst. v.p., 1971-73, v.p., 1973-75, sr. v.p., 1975-79, exec. v.p., 1979-92; ret., 1992. Bd. dirs. Little Oil Co., BB&T Bank, Fidelity Group. Mem. Pvt. Industry Coun., Richmond, 1983—; sec. YMCA, Richmond, 1984—; bd. dirs. United Way, Richmond, 1982—. With USN, 1952—56. Mem.: Met. Richmond C. of C. (chmn. 1985—86). Episcopalian. Home: 2409 Islandview Dr Richmond VA 23233-2525 E-mail: RGW433@aol.com.

WATTS, RONALD LESTER, retired military officer; b. Seneca, Mo., June 27, 1934; s. Lester N. and Naomi (Montgomery) W.; m. Anita Abelquist, Sept. 26, 1981; 1 child, Christina; children by previous marriage— Elizabeth Ann, Ronald Allen BS in Edn., Pitts. State U., 1956; MS in Polit. Sci., Auburn U., 1976. Commd. officer U.S. Army, 1956, advanced through grades to lt. gen., 1987; asst. div. comdr. 1st Inf. Div., Ft. Riley, Kans., 1981-83; comdg. gen. U.S. Army Readiness, Fort Meade, Md., 1983; dep. comdg. gen. 1st U.S. Army, Fort Meade, Md., 1983-84; comdg. gen. 1st Inf. Div., Ft. Riley, Kans., 1984-86; chief staff Hdqrs. Forces Command, Ft. McPherson, Ga., 1986-87; commdg. gen. VII Corps, 1987-89, ret., 1989; pres. Watts Leadership Devel. Svcs., Greensboro, Ga., 1990—. Decorated D.S.M. with oak leaf cluster, Legion of Merit with 2 oak leaf clusters, Bronze Star, Air medal with 10 oak leaf clusters, Combat Inf. badge, Def. Superior Svc. medal with cluster. Home: 1531 Lighthouse Cir Greensboro GA 30642-3489 Office Phone: 706-453-9367.

WATTS, ROSS LESLIE, accounting educator, consultant; b. Hamilton, Australia, Nov. 10, 1942; came to U.S., 1966; s. Leslie R. and Elsie B. (Horadam) W. m. Helen Clare Firkin, Jan. 15, 1966; children: Andrew David, James Michael. B. Commerce with honors (Commonwealth Govt. scholar 1960-65), U. Newcastle (Australia), 1966; MBA (Ford Found. fellow 1967-68), U. Chgo., 1968, PhD, 1971. Audit clk. Forsythe & Co., Newcastle, Australia, 1960-64, acct., 1964-66; instr. Grad. Sch. Bus., U. Chgo., 1969-70; asst. prof. Simon Sch. Mgmt., U. Rochester (N.Y.), 1971-78, assoc. prof., 1978-84, prof., 1984-86; endowed chair Rochester Telephone Corp., 1986-98; William H. Meckling prof. U. Rochester (N.Y.), 1998—. Prof. commerce U. Newcastle, 1974-76; hon. prof. City U. Hong Kong, 1996—, Xiamen U., China, 1999—; disting. lectr. Hong Kong U. Sci. and Tech., 1994; vis. prof. MIT, 2002; cons. in field. Contbr. articles on acctg. rsch. to profl. jours.; assoc. editor Jour. Acctg. Rsch., 1972-78, Jour. Fin. Econs., 1974-89, Australian Jour. Mgmt., 1976-81; co-editor Jour. Acctg. and Econs., 1979—; editor Jour. Acctg. Abstracts, 1995-97; dir., editor Acctg. Rsch. Network, 1997—; mem. adv. bd. Midland Corp. Fin. Jour., 1983-88, Continental Bank Jour. of Applied Corp. Fin., 1988-94, Bank Am. Jour. Applied Corp. Fin., 1994—; mem. editorial bd. Contemporary Acctg. Rsch., 1983-85; cons. editor Asia Pacific Jour. Acctg. Econs., 1998—. Recipient Notable Contbn. award AICPA, 1979, 80, award Alpha Kappa Psi Found., 1985. Mem. Am. Acctg. Assn. (Outstanding Educator award 2000, Seminal Rsch. award 2004), Am. Fin. Assn., Inst. Chartered Accts. in Australia. Home: 17 Burncoat Way Pittsford NY 14534-2215 Office: U Rochester Simon Sch Mgmt Wilson Blvd Rochester NY 14627-2241 E-mail: Watts@simon.rochester.edu.

WATTS, WILLIAM DAVID, corporate executive, business owner; b. Birmingham, Dec. 2, 1938; s. Edgar Reid and Ruth (Appling) W.; m. Lynda Louise Moseley, Aug. 1964 (div. Aug. 2, 1974); children: William David, Jr., Mark Chadwick; m. Lynn Saccone, June 28, 1975; children: Trudy, Paul William. BS in Indsl. Arts, Auburn U., 1963; student, Dale Carnegie, Birmingham, Ala., 1969, Ed Winner, Hagerstown, Md., 1971-72. Field erector engr. Pangborn Corp., Hagerstown, Md., 1963-64, sales svc. engr., 1964-68, dist. sales engr., 1968-71, acct. exec., 1971-76; owner, pres. Watts Equipment & Supply Co., Atlanta, 1976-89, Blastec, Inc., Alpharetta, Ga., 1989—. Holder 14 U.S. blast machine patents. Ticket chmn. Am. Foundry Soc., Birmingham, 1964-66, arrangements chmn., 1966-68, dir., 1968-69, treas., 1969-72. With USAR, 1957-63. Mem. Atlanta Athletic, Lake Arrowhead Yacht & Country, Masonic Lodge. Avocations: boating, swimming, motorcycling. Office: Blastec Inc 4965 Highway 9 N Alpharetta GA 30004-2922

WATZ, MARTIN CHARLES, brewery consultant; b. St. Louis, Oct. 31, 1938; s. George Michael and Caroline Theresa (Doggendorf) W.; m. Deborah Perkowski; children: Pamela, Kathlene, Karen. BS in Chemistry and Microbiology, SE Mo. State U., 1961; MBA, Washington U., 1966-67. Safety engr. McDonnell-Douglas, 1962-64; sr. brewing chemist Anheuser-Busch, Inc., St. Louis, 1965-68, asst. brewmaster Columbus, Ohio, 1968-79, sr. asst. brewmaster St. Louis, 1979-82, resident brewmaster Baldwinsville, N.Y., 1982-84, Williamsburg, Va., 1984-87; v.p. bakers yeast divsn. Anheuser-Busch Indsl. Products Corp., St. Louis, 1987-88, dir. brewing ops., 1988-89; sr. brewmaster Anheuser-Busch, Ft. Collins, Colo., 1989-99; brewing cons., 1999—. Patentee in field. With USAF, 1962-65. Mem. Master Brewers Assn. Am. (pres., nat. bd. govs.), Am. Soc. Brewing Chemists, Internat. Food Tech. Assocs., Aircraft Owners and Pilots Assn., U.S. Pilots Assn., Profl. Assn. Diving Instrs. Avocations: flying, collectible cars. Home and Office: 1417 N County Rd # 3 Fort Collins CO 80524-9312

WAUD, ROGER NEIL, economist, educator; b. Detroit, Mar. 26, 1938; s. Othneil Stockwell and Mary Josephine (Gough) Waud; children: Heather, Neil. BA, Harvard U., 1960; MA, U. Calif., Berkeley, 1962; PhD (Ford Found. fellow), U. Calif., Berekley, 1965. Asst. prof. bus. econs. Grad. Sch. Bus. U. Chgo., 1964-69; assoc. prof. econs. U. N.C., Chapel Hill, 1969-72, prof., 1972-97, prof. emeritus, 1997—; sr. economist, bd. govs. Fed. Res. Sys., Washington, 1973-75; prof., dir. grad. econs. program Va. Tech., 1997—2002. Cons. Dept. Labor; mem. adv. bd. Taxpayers Ednl. Coalition, 1981; rsch. assoc. Nat. Bur. Econ. Rsch., 1982—92; mem. N.C. Energy Policy Coun., 1986—92; vis. prof. Duke U., 1992—94. Author: Macroeconomics, 5th edit., 1992; mem. editl. bd. So. Econ. Jour., 1970—73, Studies Econs. and Fin., 1995—97; contbr. articles to profl. jours. Mem.: So. Econ. Assn. (exec. com. 1977—79), Am. Econ. Assn.

WAUFORD, J. BEN. architect; b. Lebanon, Tenn. Joined Cooper Carry Inc., 1988, assoc., 1988—92, sr. assoc., 1992—94, assoc. dir., 1994—2000, prin., 2000—. Van Alen fellow. Office: Cooper Carry Inc 6th Fl 38 W 21st St New York NY 10010*

WAUGAMAN, RICHARD MERLE, psychiatrist, psychoanalyst, educator; b. Easton, Pa., Apr. 27, 1949; s. Charles Hoffmeier and Ruth Alviene (Melee) W.; m. Elisabeth Leone Pearson, June 20, 1970; children: Adele Marie, Garrett Dennis. AB, Princeton U., 1970; MD, Duke U., 1973. Cert. psychiatry, 1978, psychoanalysis, 1984. Resident in psychiatry Sheppard-Pratt Hosp., Towson, Md., 1973-76; mem. faculty Washington Sch. Psychiatry, 1983-96; grad. Washington Psychoanalytic Inst., 1984, tng. and supervising analyst, 1989-2001, tng. and supervising analyst emeritus, 2001—; from clin. instr. to clin. assoc. prof. Georgetown U. Sch. Medicine, Washington, 1978-92, clin. prof. psychiatry, 1992—; staff psychiatrist Chestnut Lodge, Rockville, Md., 1986-99. Cons. psychiat. residency program Nat. Naval Med. Ctr., Bethesda, Md., 1994—96; adj. prof. psychiatry Uniformed Svcs. U. of Health Scis., 1999—. Contbr. articles to profl. jours. Mem. Washington Psychoanalytic Soc., Am. Psychoanalytic Assn. (exec. coun. 1993-97, com. on certification 1998-2002), Internat. Psychoanalytic Assn., Am. Psychiat. Assn., Cosmos Club. Methodist. Home: 8109 Horseshoe Ln Potomac MD 20854-3834 Office Phone: 301-654-9771.

WAUGAMAN, RICHARD WILLIAM, sales executive; b. Freedom, Pa., Aug. 29, 1958; s. Harry and Bonita (Reed) Waugaman. Student, Robert Morris Coll., 1984. Cert. travel agt. Purchasing coord. Integrated Supply Network, Lakeland, 1993—98; contract sales rep. The Ledger (A N.Y. Times Co.), Lakeland, Fla., 1998—. Avocations: travel, collecting. Home: #176 202 East Griffin Rd Lakeland FL 33805 Office: The Ledger (A N Y Times Co) 300 West Lime St Lakeland FL 33802 Personal E-mail: PandaBear1958@att.net.

WAUGH, JOHN DOUGLAS, engineer, researcher; b. Buffalo, Jan. 8, 1937; s. John Thomas and Helen Marie Waugh. BSME, U. Buffalo, 1960. Human factors engr. U.S. Army, Watervliet, NY, 1962—65, U.S. Army Rsch. Lab., Aberdeen Proving Ground, Md., 1965—. Asst. dir. tech. Army Rsch. Lab.-Human Rsch. & Engring., Aberdeen Proving Ground, 1993—96; chief systems simulation br. Army Rsch. Lab.-Human Rsch. & Engring. Directorate, Aberdeen Proving Ground, 1999—. Col.-dir. ops. and tng. Md. Def. Force (State Guard), Pikesville, 1995—2004. Served with U.S. Army, 1960—62. Mem.: Watervliet Arsenal Soc. Engrs. (pres. 1964), Human Factors and Ergonomics Soc. (bd. dirs., flight instr.), Harford Flying Club, Inc. Roman Catholic. Achievements include patents for method of acquiring a moving target. Home: 503 Freys Rd Edgewood MD 21040 Office: US Army Rsch Lab Aberdeen Proving Ground MD 21005-5425 Personal E-mail: johnwaugh4@aol.com.

WAUGH, JOHN STEWART, chemist, educator; b. Willimantic, Conn., Apr. 25, 1929; s. Albert E. and Edith (Stewart) W.; married 1983; children: Alice Collier, Frederick Pierce. AB, Dartmouth Coll., 1949; PhD, Calif. Inst. Tech., 1953; ScD (hon.), Dartmouth Coll., 1989. Rsch. fellow in physics Calif. Inst. Tech., 1952-53; mem. faculty MIT, Cambridge, 1953—, prof. chemistry, 1962—, Albert Amos Noyes prof. chemistry, 1973-88, inst. prof., 1989—, emeritus, 1996—. Vis. prof. U. Calif.-Berkeley, 1963-64; lectr. Robert Welch Found., 1968; Falk-Plaut lectr. Columbia U., 1973; DuPont lectr. U. S.C., 1974; Lucy Pickett lectr. Mt. Holyoke Coll., 1978; Reilly lectr. U. Notre Dame, 1978; Spedding lectr. Iowa State U., 1979; McElvain lectr. U. Wis., 1981; Vaughan lectr. Rocky Mountain Conf., 1981; G.N. Lewis meml. lectr. U. Calif., 1982; Dreyfus lectr. Dartmouth Coll., 1984; G.B. Kistiakowsky lectr. Harvard U., 1984; O.K. Rice lectr. U. N.C., Chapel Hill, 1986, Baker lectr. Cornell U., 1990; Smith lectr. Duke U., 1992; sr. fellow Alexander von Humboldt-Stiftung; also vis. prof. Max Planck Inst., Heidelberg, 1972; vis. scientist Harvard U., 1976; mem. chemistry adv. panel NSF, 1966-69, vice chmn., 1968-69; mem. rev. com. Argonne Nat. Lab., 1970-74; mem. sci. and edn. adv. com. Lawrence Berkeley Lab., 1980-86; exchange visitor USSR Acad. Scis., 1962, 75; mem. vis. com. Tufts U., 1966-69, Princeton, 1973-78; mem. fellowship com. Alfred P. Sloan Found., 1977-82; Joliot-Curie prof. École Supérieure de Physique et Chemie, Paris, 1985, 96. Author: New NMR Methods in Solid State Physics, 1978; editor: Advances in Magnetic Resonance, 1965-87; assoc. editor: Jour. Chem. Physics, 1965-67, Spectrochimica Acta, 1964-78; mem. editorial bd. Chem. Revs., 1978-82, Jour. Magnetic Resonance, 1989—, Applied Magnetic Resonance, 1989—. Recipient Irving Langmuir award, 1976, Gold Pick Axe award, 1976, Pitts. award Spectroscopic Soc. Pitts., 1979, Wolf prize, 1984, Pauling medal, 1985, Calif. Inst. Tech. disting. alumnus award, 1987, Killian award, 1988, ISMAR prize, 1989, Richards medal, 1992, Evans award, 1994, Ea. Analytical Symposium award 1996; Sloan fellow, 1958-62, Guggenheim fellow, 1963-64, 72; Sherman Fairchild scholar Calif. Inst. Tech., 1989. Fellow: AAAS, Am. Phys. Soc. (chmn. divsn. chemistry and physics 1983—84); mem.: NAS, Slovenian Acad. Sci. and Arts (fgn. corr.), Internat. Soc. Magnetic Resonance (mem. coun. 1989—95, mem. exec. com. 1996—, v.p. 1997—, pres. 1999—2002), Phi Beta Kappa, Sigma Xi. Office: MIT 6-231 77 Massachusetts Ave Cambridge MA 02139-4307 Office Phone: 617-253-1901. Business E-Mail: jswaugh@mit.edu.

WAUGH, RICHARD B., JR., aircraft company executive, lawyer; b. Cleve., Sept. 1, 1943; s. Richard B. Waugh. BS, Ohio State U., 1965, JD, 1968. Bar: Ohio, Calif. CPA. Asst. prof. econs. and bus. adminstrn. Waynesburg (Ohio) Coll.; sr. tax acct. Price Waterhouse & Co.; sr. tax counsel western region Rockwell Internat. Corp.; corp. dir. tax adminstrn. Northrop Grumman Corp., L.A., from 1978, corp. v.p. taxes, risk mgmt. and bus. analysis, until 1993, corp. v.p., CFO, 1993—. Mem. ABA, AICPA, Calif. Bar Assn., Ohio Bar Assn., Tax Execs. Inst., Fin. Execs. Inst., Leading Chief Fin. Officers. Office: Northrop Grumman Corp 1840 Century Park E Los Angeles CA 90067-2101

WAUGH, RICHARD EARL, banker; b. Winnipeg, Manitoba, Can., Dec. 23, 1947; B Commerce with honors, U. Manitoba, Can., 1970; MBA, York U., York, Can., 1974. Corp. rsch. analyst The Bank of Nova Scotia, Winnipeg, 1970-72, ass.t gen. mgr. Can. corp. banking, 1977-79, asst. gen. mgr., mgr. Toronto br., 1979-81, asst. gen. mgr. corp. banking, 1981-83, gen. mgr. N. Am. corp. banking, 1983—85, sr. v.p. N.Am. corp. banking, Toronto, 1985—91, exec. v.p., 1991—93, sr. exec. v.p., global corp., banking, 1993—95, vice chmn., corp. banking, 1995—98, vice chmn., internat. banking & wealth mgmt., 1998—2003, pres., CEO, 2003—. Bd. dirs. Bank Nova Scotia. Mem. Nat. Club (Toronto), Granite Club (Toronto), Toronto Club. Office: The Bank of Nova Scotia Scotia Plz 44 King St W Toronto ON Canada M5H 1H1

WAUGH, THEODORE ROGERS, orthopedic surgeon; b. Montreal, Sept. 21, 1926; s. Theodore Rogers and Anne Maude (Lawlor) W.; children: Susanne Rogers, Margaret Stewart, Theodore Rogers. BA, Yale U., 1949; MD, CM, McGill U., 1953; DMS, U. Goteborg, Sweden, 1968. Diplomate Am. Bd. Orthop. Surgery. Intern Royal Victoria Hosp., Montreal, 1953-54; asst. resident in pathology McGill U., 1954-55; asst. resident in surgery NYU Bellevue Med. Ctr., 1955-56; asst. resident, resident, fellow N.Y. Orthop. Hosp., Columbia U., 1958-62, instr., clin. asst. prof. orthop. surgery, 1962-68; asst. attending Presbyn. Hosp., N.Y.C., NY, 1962-68; prof., chief divsn. orthop. surgery U. Calif., Irvine, 1968-78; prof., chmn. dept. orthop. surgery NYU Med. Ctr., 1978-96, emeritus prof., 1997—. Adj. prof. surgery, Dartmouth U. Sch. Medicine, 1998-2003, adj. prof. orthopaedics, 2003—. Contbr. numerous articles to profl. jours. Capt., M.C. USAF, 1956-58. Fellow ACS, Royal Coll. Surgeons (Can.), Am. Acad. Orthop. Surgeons, Scoliosis Rsch. Soc., Assn. Bone and Joint Surgeons, Am. Orthop. Assn., Am. Orthop. Soc. for Sports Medicine.; mem. Soc. Colonial Wars, 20th Century Orthopedic Club, Alpha Omega Alpha. Presbyterian. Achievements include developing designer surgical devices used in orthopaedic surgery. Office: Dartmouth-Hitchcock Med Ctr One Medical Center Dr Lebanon NH 03756 E-mail: trwmd@cyberportal.net.

WAVLE, JAMES EDWARD, JR., pharmaceutical company executive, lawyer; b. N.Y.C., July 19, 1942; s. James Edward and Florence Marie (Kehoe) W.; children from previous marriage: James Edward, William Patrick, Robert Thomas, Stephanie Elizabeth; m. Elizabeth Edith Symons Tallett; 1 child, Christopher Andrew; stepchildren: James E. Tallett, Alexander M. Tallett. BA, Adelphi U., 1964; JD, Georgetown U., 1967; LLM, NYU, 1968. Bar: N.Y. bar 1967. With Warner-Lambert Co., Morris Plains, N.J., 1968-87, internat. counsel, 1971-74, assoc. gen. counsel, 1974-77, v.p., gen. counsel, 1977-80, sr. v.p., gen. counsel, 1980-81; corp. sr. v.p. and pres. Parke-Davis Group, 1982-87; pres., CEO Centocor Inc., Malvern, Pa., 1987-92; chmn. Dioscor Inc., Stockton, N.J., 1993-97; chmn., pres., CEO Therics, Inc., Princeton, NJ, 1997—2003. Mem. ABA, Lookaway Golf Club, Stamford Yacht Club.

WAWREJKO COCHRAN, DIANE, performing arts association administrator; BA in Classical Ballet, Mercyhurst Coll., 1978; MFA in Performance & Choreography, Ariz. State U.; student in Dance, U. Surrey. Resident, workshop artist Urban Gateways, Chgo.; prof., dance program dir. U. Tex.-Pan Am.; exec. dir. Nat. Dance Assn. Dancer Ctrl. Ballet of China, first U.S. tour, Laurie Eisenhower and Dances, Repertory Dance Theatre, PBS; contbr. articles to profl. jours. Office: NDA c/o AAHPERD 1900 Association Drive Reston VA 20191-1598

WAWRYTKO, SANDRA ANN, humanities educator; b. Chgo., Ill., Oct. 18, 1951; d. Stanley Andrew Wawrytko and Alyce Valerie Cioch-Wawrytko; m. Charles Wei-hsun Fu, Sept. 29, 1994 (dec. Oct. 15, 1996). BA in Philosophy, Knox Coll., 1972; MA in Philosophy, Washington U., 1975, PhD in Philosophy, 1976. Instr. Washington U., St. Louis, 1973—77; prof. San Diego State U., 1980—. Vis. prof. Chinese Culture U., Yangmingshan, Taiwan, 1984, Fo Guang Buddhist Coll., Kaohsiung, Taiwan, 1990—2004; prin. investigator San Diego State U. Lang. Acquisition Rsch. Ctr., San Diego, 1994—2003; vis. prof. U. San Diego, San Diego, 1978—81; founder, exec. dir. Internat. Soc. for Philosophy and Psychotherapy; founder, pres. Charles Wei-hsun Fu Found. Author: (book) The Undercurrent of Feminine Philosophy in Eastern and Western Thought, 1981, CRYSTAL: Spectrums of Chinese Culture Through Poetry, 1995; editor: (book series) Asian Thought and Culture, (book) North American Institute of Zen Buddhist Studies, (book series) Philosophy and Psychotherapy; contbr. book The Problem of Evil: An Intercultural Exploration, 2000; co-author: (book) The Buddhist Religion, 1996; editor: Rethinking the Curriculum: Toward an Integrated Interdisciplinary Education, 1990, The Problem of Evil, 2000; narrator: interactive CD-ROM Crystals of Chinese Culture, 2000; author (and editor): Saving the Elephant: Asian Encounters with Imperialism, Orientalism, and Gloablization, 2004. Edn. rep. San Diego Sister City Program, Yantai, China, 1985; bd. dirs. San Diego Chinese Hist. Soc. and Mus., 2002—; pres. Charles Wei-hsun Fu Found., San Diego, 1997—. Recipient univ. fellowship, Washington. U., 1974—75, Humanities Advancement Poetry Contest award, Humanities Advancement Com., 1983. Mem.: World Congress of Logotherapy (sec.-gen. 1982—85), Internat. Soc. for Chinese Philosophy (sec., exec. bd. mem. 1990—2003), Phi Beta Delta (governing bd. 2002—03), Phi Beta Kappa (Faculty Lectr. Nu chpt. 2002—03). Avocations: poetry, translating classical Chinese poetry, collecting Asian art and books, creating culinary adventures. Office: San Diego State U Gateway Center San Diego CA 92182 Office Phone: 619-594-5455. Personal E-mail: swawryt1@san.rr.com. E-mail: wawrytko@charlesweihsunfufoundation.org.

WAX, ARNOLD, physician; b. Bklyn., Mar. 11, 1949; s. Emanuel and Eleanor (Greenfield) W.; m. Francine Wax; children: Erin, Rachael, Adam, Benjamin. BS in Pharm. Scis., Columbia U., 1971; MD, SUNY, Buffalo, 1976. Diplomate Nat. Bd. Med. Examiners, Am. Bd. Internal Medicine, Am. Bd. Quality Assurance and Utilization Rev. Physicians, Am. Acad. Pain Mgmt.; lic. physician, Fla., Calif., N.D., Minn., N.Y., Nev., Ariz. Intern, resident Millard Fillmore Hosp., Buffalo, 1976-79; clin. asst. instr. SUNY, 1977-79; instr. medicine U. Rochester, N.Y., 1979-81; dir. internal medicine U. N.D., Grand Forks, 1982-83, clin. asst. prof., 1982-85; pvt. practice Las Vegas, Nev., 1987—. Mem. staff Sunrise Hosp., Las Vegas, Desert Springs Hosp., Las Vegas, Nathan Adelson Hospice, Las Vegas. Contbr. articles to profl. jours. Grantee So. Nev. Cancer Rsch. Found., Ea. Coop. Oncology Group, Gynecol. Oncology Group, North Ctrl. Cancer Treatment Group, S.W. Oncology Group. Fellow Am. Coll. Physicians; mem. AMA, Am. Cancer Soc. (fellow 1979), Am. Soc. Clin. Oncology, Am. Coll. Physicians (gov. State of Nev.), Nev. Oncology So. (v.p.), Nev. Med. Soc., Clark County Med. Soc. (trustee, peer rev. com., treas.), Nev. Peer Rev. Orgn., U. Nev. Las Vegas Found., Nev. Dance Theater, Nev. Opera Theater, Las Vegas Symphony, Nev. Inst. Contemporary Art, Lied Mus., Allied Arts Coun., James Platt White Soc., U. Buffalo Found., Rho Chi (Bronze medal 1971). Home: 2224 Chatsworth Ct Henderson NV 89074-5309 Office: 928 W Sunset Las Vegas NV 89148 Office Phone: 702-952-1251. Business E-Mail: arnold.wax@usoncology.com.

WAX, BENJAMIN, physical education educator, consultant; b. Amory, Miss., June 29, 1968; s. Benjamin and Mae Francis Wax; m. Cynthia Wax, July 30, 1993; 1 child, Dominique. AS, Itawamba CC, Fulton, Miss., 1988; BS, Miss. State U., Starkville, 1991, MS, 1993; PhD, U. Miss., Oxford, 1999. Instr. Miss. State U., Starkville, 1991—92, Lafayette County Sch., Miss., 1992—93, strength coach, 1992—93; instr. U. Miss., Oxford, 1993—98; owner Curves for Women, Greenville, 1996—99, Columbus, 1996—99, Oxford, 1996—99; asst. prof. Miss. Valley State U., Itta Bena, 1999—2002, assoc. prof., 2003—, dir. Health and Fitness Ctr., 2003—; co-founder & pres. LadiesRx Internat. inc., 2004. Fitness cons. Sweat Fitness Club, Oxford, 2000—03; phys. edn. activities coord. sci. program Miss. Valley State U., 2001—, fitness cons., 2002—; dir. Ladies Rx Internat., 2004. Presenter (at profl. meetings). Recipient Minority Nat. Academic Achievement award, 1997, Minority Assoc. Academic award, 1989—91, academic excellence, Alliance for Graduate Education in Mississippi, 2003. Mem.: Nat. Strength and Conditioning Assn., Am. Physiol. Soc., Am. Coll. of Sports Medicine. Office: MS Valley State University box 7270 14000 Hwy 82W Itta Bena MS 38941 E-mail: bjwax_2000@yahoo.com.

WAX, DAVID LOUIS, corporate financial executive; b. Jan. 1953; AB, Brown U. Mng. dir. corp. fin. Rothschild Inc., 1990; various positions Bankers Trust; mng. dir. WL Ross & Co. LLC, N.Y., 2000—. Office: WL Ross & Co LLC Manhattan Tower 19th Fl 101 East 52nd St New York NY 10022

WAX, GEORGE LOUIS, lawyer; b. New Orleans, Dec. 6, 1928; s. John Edward and Theresa (Schaff) W.; LL.B., Loyola U. of South, 1952, B.C.S., 1960; m. Patricia Ann Delaney, Feb. 20, 1965; children: Louis Jude, Joann Olga, Therese Marie. Admitted to La. bar, 1952, practiced in New Orleans, 1954—. Served with USNR, 1952-54. Mem. La. Bar Assn., New Orleans Bar

Assn., Am. Legion, Kiwanis, New Orleans Athletic Club, Suburban Gun and Rod Club, Southern Yacht Club. Roman Catholic. Home: 6001 Charlotte Dr New Orleans LA 70122-2731 Office: 210 Baronne St Ste 1222 New Orleans LA 70112-1714

WAX, NADINE VIRGINIA, retired bank executive; b. Van Horne, Iowa, Dec. 7, 1927; d. Laurel Lloyd and Viola Henrietta (Schrader) Bobzien; divorced; 1 child, Sharlyn K. Wax Munns. Student, U. Iowa, 1970-71; grad. Nat. Sch. Real Estate and Fin., Ohio State U., 1980-81. Jr. acct. McGladrey, Hansen, Dunn (now McGladrey-Pullen Co., CPAs), Cedar Rapids, Iowa, 1944-47; office mgr. Iowa Securities Co. (now Wells Fargo Mortgage Co.), Cedar Rapids, 1954-55; asst. cashier Mchts. Nat. Bank (now U.S. Bancorp.), Cedar Rapids, 1956-75; asst. v.p. Mchts. Nat. Bank (now U.S. Bancorp), Cedar Rapids, 1976-78, v.p., 1979-90; ret., 1990. Vol. St. Luke's Hosp. Aux., Cedar Rapids, 1981—85, SCORE, 1999—2004; bd. dirs., v.p. Kirkwood C.C. Facilities Found., 1970—2004; bd. dirs., treas. Kirkwood C.C., 1984—91; trustee Indian Creek Nature Ctr., Cedar Rapids, 1974—2004, pres., 1980—81; mem. Linn County Regional Planning Commn., 1982—92, Cedar Rapids-Marion Fine Arts Coun., 1994—97; bd. suprs. Compensation Commn. for Condemnation, 1987—92; bd. dirs. Am. Heart Assn., Cedar Rapids, 1983—94; mem. Iowa Employment and Tng. Coun., Des Moines, 1982—83. Recipient Outstanding Woman award, Cedar Rapids Tribute to Women and Industry, 1984. Mem. Fin. Women Internat. (state edn. chmn. 1982-83), Am. Inst. Banking (bd. dirs. 1968-70), Soc. Real Estate Appraisers (treas. 1978-80), Linn County Bankers Assn (pres. 1979-80), Cedar Rapids Bd. Realtors, Cedar Rapids C. of C. (bus.-edn. com. 1986-91), Cedar Rapids Country Club. Lutheran. Avocations: travel, reading, walking. Home: 147 Ashcombe SE Cedar Rapids IA 52403-1700

WAX, PAUL MATTHEW, emergency medicine physician, educator, medical toxicologist; b. Hanover, N.H., Mar. 8, 1958; s. Sandor Harry and Edith Mae (Ellen) W.; m. Janet Ruth Reiser, Oct. 23, 1988; children: Rebecca Sasha, Sarah Elisa. BA, Dartmouth Coll., 1980; MD, Mt. Sinai Sch. Medicine, 1984. Diplomate Am. Bd. Emergency Medicine, Am. Bd. Med. Toxicology. Intern in gen. surgery U. Mich., 1984-86; resident in emergency medicine UCLA Med. Ctr., 1986-89; fellow in med. toxicology Bellevue Med. Ctr., 1989-91; instr. emergency medicine/surgery NYU, N.Y.C., 1989-91; asst. prof. emergency medicine U. Rochester, N.Y., 1991-96, assoc. prof. emergency medicine, 1996—. Asst. dir. Finger Lakes Poison Control Ctr., Rochester, 1991—; bd. dirs. Am. Bd. Emergency Medicine Subboard of Med. Toxicology, Lansing, Mich., 1997—. Contbg. author: (textbook) Goldfrank's Emergency Toxicology, 1994, revised edit. 98, Emergency Medicine, 1996; mem. editl. bd. Jour. Toxicology, Clin. Toxicology; contbr. articles to profl. jours. Fellow Am. Coll. Emergency Medicine, Am. Coll. Med. Toxicology (bd. dirs. 1998—); mem. Am. Acad. Clin. Toxicology, Soc. Acad. Emergency Medicine, Toxicology History Soc. Jewish. Avocations: photography, genealogy, jazz. Office: U Rochester Med Ctr 601 Elmwood Ave # Rochester NY 14642-0001 Home: 5431 E Cheryl Dr Paradise Valley AZ 85253-1136

WAX, WILLIAM EDWARD, photojournalist; b. Miami, Fla., Dec. 7, 1956, s. Ira and Rita (Gunshor) W. AS, Berry Coll., Rome, Ga., 1976; BS in Engring., U. Fla., 1983. With Ind. Fla. Alligator, Gainesville, Fla., 1977-79; staff photographer Gainesville (Fla.) Sun, 1979-87; photo cons. N.Y. Times regional newspapers, 1984—; freelance photographer Miami, 1987—; pres. Wax & Co. Inc., Miami Beach, Fla., 1989—, Waxcom, Miami Beach, 1996—. Owner Studio SoBe, Miami Beach, 1992—; guest lectr. various univs.; faculty So. Short Course in News Photography, 1985—. Named Photographer of Yr., NPPA/U. Mo. and Nikon, 1980, So. Photographer of Yr., 1980, Regional Photographer of Yr., 1979, 82, 85; recipient Mark of Excellence, Sigma Delta Chi, 1978, Best of Show award Atlanta Seminar on Photojournalism, 1982, Best of Show and Silver medal Hearst awards, 1978, Design Gold award Fla. Tech. Writers Assn., 1992, Design award, Gold award, Excellence award Soc. Tech. Comm. Internat. Tech. Art Competition, 1993, 94, 97, 98, 99, 2000-03, Best of Show, 1994, 98, 2001, Disting. Design award, 1993, 97, 99, 2000, 2001, 2002-03, Excellence Design award, 1993, 98, 99, 2 Design Excellence awards and award of merit, 1995, 2000, Best of Show award Ann. Report Fla. Pub. Rels., 1995, Silver and Bronze awards Fla. Mag. Assn., 1994, 96, 97, 98, 99, 2000, Gold, Silver and Bronze awards Fla. Mag. Assn., 1995-2003, Merit award STC, 1995, Apex Design awards 1996-2003, Global award/Ann. Report Photography, 1996, Maggie award Best Newsletter in the West, 2003, Healthcare Advt. award, 2003, 04; nominated for Pulitzer prize, 1979, 89, STC Internat. Design, 1996-97. Mem. Nat. Press Photographers Assn., Fla. Mag. Assn., Profl. Photographers Am., Nikon Profl. Svcs., Fla. Press Photographers Assn. Office: Wax & Co 350 Lincoln Rd Ste 516 Miami FL 33139-3148

WAXLER, BEVERLY JEAN, anesthesiologist, physician; b. Chgo., Apr. 11, 1949; d. Isadore and Ada Belle (Gross) Marcus; m. Richard Norman Waxler, Dec. 24, 1972; 1 child, Adam R. BS in Biology, No. Ill. U., 1971; MD, U. Ill., Chgo., 1975. Diplomate Am. Bd. Anesthesiology, Am. Bd. Pathology. Intern dept. pathology Northwestern U., Chgo., 1975-76, resident, 1976-79; instr. Rush Presbyn. St. Luke's Med. Ctr., Chgo., 1979-81; asst. prof. pathology Loyola U., Maywood, Ill., 1981-84; resident dept. anesthesiology Stroger Hosp. Cook County (formerly Cook County Hosp.), Chgo., 1984-87, attending anesthesiologist, 1987—; chmn. divsn. postanesthetic care Stroger Hosp. of Cook County, Chgo., 2004—; clin. asst. prof. U. Ill., Chgo., 1988-95; asst. prof. Rush Med. Coll., Chgo., 1996—. Contbr. articles to profl. jours. Grantee, Varlen Corp., 1982; Nat. Rsch. Svc. fellow, Nat. Cancer Inst., 1980. Mem.: AAAS, Ill. Soc. Anesthesiologists, Chgo. Soc. Anesthesiologists, Am. Soc. Anesthesiologists, Internat. Anesthesia Rsch. Soc. (B. B. Sankey Anesthesia Advancement award 1989), Sigma Xi. Office: Stroger Hosp Cook County Chicago IL 60612 Office Phone: 312-864-2140.

WAXMAN, ANITA, producer; Prodr. (plays) Mrs. Klein, Below the Belt, Wild Honey (Drama Desk award nomination), The Foreigner, Music Man, 2000-01, One Flew Over the Cuckoo's Nest, 2001, Noises Off, 2001-02, Top Dog/Underdog, 2002, The Elephant Man, 2002, Flower Drum Song, 2002-03, Gypsy, 2004, Bombay Dreams, 2004—; co-prodr. (plays) Present Laughter (Tony award nomination), Breaking the Code, Circle & Bravo, Long Day's Journey Into Night, Annie get Your Gun, Mr. & Mrs. Nobody. Office: Waxman Williams Entertainment c/o Four Corners Prodn 260 W 44th St Ste 500 New York NY 10036-3900*

WAXMAN, CHAIM I. sociology educator, researcher; b. N.Y.C., Feb. 26, 1941; s. Nissan and Sara R. W.; m. Chaya Lifshitz, June 12, 1962; children: Ari, Shani, Dani. MA, New Sch. for Social Rsch., N.Y.C., 1965, PhD, 1974; MHL, Yeshiva U., 1966. Asst. prof. sociology Ctrl. Conn. State Coll., New Britain, 1965-72, Bklyn. Coll. CUNY, 1972-75, Rutgers U., New Brunswick, N.J., 1975-78, assoc. prof., 1978-96, prof., 1996—. Mem. adv. com. Am Jewish Com., N.Y.C., 1975—, NEH, Washington, 1975—. Author: America's Jews in Transition, 1953, The Stigma of Poverty 2d edit., 1983, American Aliya, 1989, Jewish Baby Boomers, 2001; co-author: Historical Dictionary of Zionism, 2000; editor Israel Studies Bull., New Brunswick, 1993-2001; book rev. editor Society Mag., New Brunswick, 1975-82. Grantee Found. for Middle East Peace, Washington, 1984, Lucius Littauer Found., N.Y.C., 1987, Meml. Found. for Jewish Culture, 1989. Mem. Am. Sociol. Soc., Soc. for Sci. Study Religion, Assn. for Sociol. Study of Jewry (pres. 1979-81), Assn. for Jewish Studies, Assn. for Israel Studies. Jewish. Avocation: coin collecting/numismatics. Office: Rutgers U Dept Sociology 54 Joyce Kilmer Ave Piscataway NJ 08854-8045 E-mail: Waxmanci@rci.rutgers.edu.

WAXMAN, DAVID, internist, consultant, academic administrator; b. Albany, N.Y., Feb. 7, 1918; s. Meyer and Fannie (Strosberg) W.; m. Jane Zabel; children: Gail, Michael, Dan, Ann, Steve, Abby. BS, Syracuse U., 1942, MD, 1950. Intern Grace Hosp., Detroit, 1950-51; resident in medicine, fellow in cardiology Kans. U. Med. Ctr., Kansas City, 1958-61, instr. internal medicine, 1961-64; asst. prof. internal medicine Kans. City Med. Ctr., 1964-69, assoc. prof., 1969-77, prof., 1977—, dir. dept. medicine outpatient service, 1970-74, asst. dean, 1970-71, assoc. dean for student affairs, 1971-72, dean of students, 1972-74, vice chancellor for students, 1974-76, vice chancellor, 1976-77, exec. vice chancellor, 1977-83, spl. cons. to chancellor for health affairs, 1983-94; ret. Nat. cons. to surgeon gen. USAF. Contbr. articles to med. jours. Mem. Kans. State Bd. Healing Arts, 1984-88. Maj. gen. USAFR ret. Decorated D.S.M., Legion of Merit with one oak leaf cluster. Fellow ACP, Alpha Omega Alpha; mem. Kans. Med. Soc., Soc. Med. Cons. to the Armed Forces. Office: Kans U Med Ctr 39th and Rainbow Blvd Kansas City KS 66103

WAXMAN, DONALD, composer; b. Steubenville, Ohio, Oct. 25, 1925; s. Harold and Judy Waxman; m. Jho Wheeler, June 4, 1950; 1 child, Jordan. Cert. in Tchg., Composition, Peabody Conservatory, Balt., 1949; BS in Composition, Juilliard Sch. of Music, N.Y.C., 1950. Co-dir. The Music House Sch., Nyack, NY, 1955—82; mng. editor Galaxy Music Corp., N.Y.C., 1970—89. Composer: (composition) Trio for Flute, Oboe and Piano (Commn. from The Huntingdon Trio, 1986), Di vertimento for Flute, Clarinet, Violin, Cello and Piano (Delius Soc. Grand Prize for Chamber Music, 1998), Trio for two Flutes and Piano (N.Y. State Music Tchrs. Assn. Commn. and Composer of the Yr., 1985), Arabesques and Ostinato for Two Pianos (Calif. MTA Commn. and Composer of the Yr., 1993), Variations on a Waltz of Diabelli for Violin, Clarinet, Cello and Piano (Fla. Commn. and Composer of the Yr., 1997). With U.S. Army, 1944—45. Decorated Purple Heart, Bronze Star; recipient Klemm Composition award, Peabody Conservatory of Music, 1947—48, Gold Medal Award as first Composer in Residence at the Kang Nung (Korea) Music Festival; fellow Guggenheim fellow, Guggenheim Found., 1964—65. Mem.: ASCAP (ASCAP Spl. Awards 1980 - 2003). Home: 5667 Wind Drift Ln Boca Raton FL 33433 Home Fax: same (call in advance). Personal E-mail: jdjwaxman@adelphia.net.

WAXMAN, HENRY ARNOLD, congressman; b. L.A., Sept. 12, 1939; s. Louis and Esther (Silverman) W.; m. Janet Kessler, Oct. 17, 1971; children: Carol Lynn, Michael David. BA in Polit. Sci, UCLA, 1961, JD, 1964. Bar: Calif. 1965. Mem. Calif. State Assembly, 1969-74, U.S. Congress from 30th Calif. dist. (formerly 29th), 1975—; chmn. commerce subcom. on health and environment, 1979-94; ranking minority mem. govt. reform & oversight com. Pres. Calif. Fedn. Young Democrats, 1965-67. Mem. Calif. Bar Assn., Guardians Jewish Home for Aged, Am. Jewish Congress, Sierra Club, B'nai B'rith, Phi Sigma Alpha. Democrat. Office: US Ho Reps 2204 Rayburn Ho Office Bldg Washington DC 20515-0001

WAXMAN, MERLE, dean; b. Newark, Mar. 6, 1946, m. Stephen G. Waxman, June 25, 1968; children: Matthew Curtis, David Mitchell. BS, Boston U., 1968; MA, CUNY, 1972. Rsch. asst. MIT, 1977-78; coord. Peninsula French Am. Sch., Palo Alto, Calif., 1980-83; mng. editor Customer Survey, Palo Alto, CA, 1980-82; asst. ombudsman Stanford U. Med. Ctr., 1983-86; dir. office for women in medicine Yale U., 1986—; ombuds person Yale U. Sch. Medicine, 1992—, assoc. dean acad. devel., 1993—. Cons. conflict resolution, gender and profl. devel., mentoring; presenter in field. Editor: Women in Medicine Newsletter, 1986—; contbr. articles to profl. jours. Recipient: Womens Leadership award, Amer Assoc. Med Coll., 1996, Cole award, Yale U. Physicians Assoc., 1992. Mem. Am. Arbitration Assn., Am. Med. Women's Assn., Nat. Coun. Women's Health, Calif. Caucus U. and Coll. Ombudspersons, Assn. Women Sci.(trustee, 1992-94), Coun. Concerns Women on New England Colls. and Univs., Coun. Employee Respinsibilities and Rights (mem. edit. bd. Jour. 1987), Grad. Women in Sci., Soc. Profls. Dispute Resolution, The ombudsman Assn. Office: Yale U Sch Medicine 333 Cedar St PO Box 208012 New Haven CT 06520-8012 E-mail: merle.waxman@yale.edu.

WAXMAN, RONALD, computer engineer; b. Newark, Nov. 28, 1933; s. Benjamin and Rose (Lifson) W.; m. Pearl Latterman, June 19, 1955; children: David, Roberta, Benjamin. BSEE, N.J. Inst. Tech., 1955; MEE, Syracuse U., 1963. Engr. IBM, Poughkeepsie, N.Y., 1955-56, 58-64, East Fishkill, N.Y., 1964-70, Poughkeepsie and Kingston, N.Y., 1970-80, sr. engr. Manassas, Va., 1980-87; prin. scientist U. Va., Charlottesville, 1987-97; cons. pvt. practice, Reston, Va., 1997—. IEEE rep. and tech. advisor to Internat. Elec. Commn. U.S. tech. activities group for internat. design automation stds., 1994—98; mem. steering com. very high speed integrated circuits hardware description lang. VHDL Users Group, 1987—91; mem. panel for assessment of Nat. Inst. Stds. and Tech. Measurement and Stds. Labs. NRC, 2002—. Contbr. numerous articles to profl. jours. and tech. presentations. 1st lt. USAF, 1956-58. Fellow IEEE, IEEE Computer Soc. (bd. govs. 1989-94, 96-98, 2000-02, chmn. fellows evaluation com. 1995-96, chmn. audit com., 1997, founder, chmn. design automation stds. subcom. 1983-88, steering com. 1989—2003, chmn. design automation tech. com. 1988-90, steering com. 1991—, vice-chmn. tech. activities bd. 1991-92, 99, chmn. awards com. 1993, disting. visitor 1986-88, chmn. disting. visitor program 2004, v.p. mem. activities bd. 1994, v.p. tech. activities, 1998, Meritorious Svc. cert. 1988, Disting. Svc. cert. 1994, TAB Pioneer award 1989, 3d. Millennium medal 2000), Internat. Fedn. Info. Processing Orgns. TC5 (CS rep. 2000—, sec. tech. reps. com., 2000—, vice chmn., 2004—), Assn. for Computing Machinery (spl. interest group DA). Achievements include patents in field.

WAXMAN, SETH PAUL, lawyer; b. Hartford, Conn., Nov. 28, 1951; s. Felix H. and Frieda (Goodman) W.; m. Debra F. Goldberg, Mar. 20, 1977; children: Noah, Sarah, Ethan. AB summa cum laude, Harvard U., 1973; JD, Yale U., 1977. Bar: D.C. 1978, U.S. Dist. Ct. D.C., 1979, U.S. Ct. Appeals D.C Circuit, 1979, U.S. Supreme Ct. 1982, U.S. Ct. Appeals (1st cir.), 2000, (2d cir.), 1998, (3d cir.), 1983, (4th cir.), 1982, (5th cir.), 1997, (6th cir.), 1998, (7th cir.), 1998, (8th cir.), 1998, (9th cir.), 1989, (10th cir.), 1998, (11th cir.), 1989, U.S. Ct. Appeals Fed. Circuit, 1998. Law clk to Judge Gerhard A. Gesell, Washington, 1977-78; ptnr. Miller Cassidy Larroca & Lewin, Washington, 1978-94; assoc. dep. atty. gen. U.S. Dept. Justice, Washington, 1994-96, dep. solicitor gen., 1996-97, acting dep. atty. gen., 1997, solicitor gen. of the U.S., 1997-2001; partner Wilmer, Cutler & Pickering, 2001—. Disting. vis. from practice Georgetown U Law Ctr., 2001—; vis. prof. Georgetown U. Law Ctr., 2001; vis. fellow Harvard U. JFK Sch. Govt., 2001; dir. Supreme Ct. Inst., Georgetown U. Law Ctr. Prin. Coun. for Excellence in Govt.; trustee Supreme Ct. Hist. Soc.; director Nat. Found. for Jewish Culture; elected dir. Harvard Alumni Assn.; mem. com. to visit Harvard Coll. Harvard U.; trustee Bruce J. Ennis Found. Named hon. spl. agt., FBI, 2001; recipient Pro Bono Publico award, ABA, 1988, Edmund J. Randolph award, U.S. Dept. Justic, 2001, Benjamin L. Cardozo Cert. of Merit, Anti-Defamation League, 1987, Thomas Jefferson Found. medal in law, U. Va., 2002, Pursuit of Justice award, Internat. Assn. Jewish Lawyers and Jurists, 2001, BYU Rex Lee Advocacy Award, 2002; fellow Michael C. Rockefeller, Harvard U., 1973—74. Master: Edward Coke Appellate Inn Court; fellow: Am Acad. Appellate Attys., Am. Bar Found.; mem.: Am. Law Inst. Office Phone: 202-663-6800. E-mail: seth.waxman@wilmer.com.

WAXMAN, SHELDON ROBERT, lawyer; b. Chgo., Apr. 22, 1941; s. Henri and Ann (Sokolsky) W.; m. Katherine Slamski, Aug. 23, 1979; children: Josiah, Zoe. BA, U. Ill., 1963; JD, DePaul U., 1965. Bar: Ill. 1965, U.S. Supreme Ct. 1976, Mich. 1985. Staff atty. Argonne (Ill.) Nat. Lab., 1968-71; asst. U.S. Atty., Chgo., 1971-74; owner firm Waxman Tax & Legal Network, Chgo. and South Haven, Mich., 1976—. Owner Ind. Contractor Cons. Svcs. Author: In the Teeth of the Wind, 2002, All Anybody Needs to Know About Independent Contracting, 2003; (screenplays) Black Messiah Murders, 2003, Chicago Piranhas, 2003; co-author: Black Messiah Murders, A Sam Cohen Case Adventure, Number 1, 2003, Piranhas on the Loose, A Sam Cohen Case Adventure Number 2, 2003; editor-in-chief New Z Letter; contbr. articles to profl. jours. Founder Freedom Lawyers of Am., People for Simplified Tax Law, Nukes to the Sun. Office: PO Box 309 South Haven MI 49090-0309 Office Phone: 269-207-6219. E-mail: shelly@cybersol.com.

WAXMAN, STEPHEN GEORGE, neurologist, neuroscientist; b. Newark, Aug. 17, 1945; s. Morris and Beatrice (Levitch) Waxman; m. Merle Applebaum, June 25, 1968; children: Matthew, David. AB, Harvard U., 1967, PhD, 1970, MD, 1972; MA (hon.), Yale U., 1986. Rsch. fellow in neurosci. Albert Einstein Coll. Medicine, Bronx, NY, 1970—72; clin. fellow Boston City Hosp., 1972—75; asst. prof. neurology Med. Sch. Harvard U., Boston, 1975—77, assoc. prof., 1977—78; prof. Stanford (Calif.) U., 1978—86, vice chmn. dept. neurology, 1981—86, chmn. neurosci. program, 1982—86; chief neurology unit Palo Alto (Calif.) VA Hosp., 1978—86; chmn. dept. neurology Yale U., New Haven, 1986—, prof. neurology, neurobiology and pharmacology, 1986; chief neurology Yale-New Haven Hosp., 1986—. Vis. asst. prof. biology MIT, Cambridge, 1975—77, vis. assoc. prof., 1977—78; vis. prof. U. Coll. London, 1998—, Inst. Neurology, Queen Square, England, 1998—; vice chmn. dept. neurology Stanford U., 1981—86, chmn. neurosci. program, 1982—86; mem. adv. bd. Regeneration Programs VA, Washington, 1982—86; mem. sci. adv. com. Nat. Spinal Cord Injury Assn., 1982—87, Paralyzed Vets. Am., 1981—91; dir. Ctr. Rsch. Neurol. Disease VA Med. Ctr., West Haven, Conn., 1986—; mem. corp. Marine Biol. Labs., Woods Hole, Mass., 1988; mem. sci. adv. coun. Am. Paralysis Assn., 1988—92; mem. bd. sci. counselors NINDB, 1990—92; mem. bd. neurosci. and behavior Inst. Medicine, 1990; Geschwind vis. prof. Harvard U., 1996; dir. PVA/EPVA Neurosci. Rsch. Ctr. VA Hosp., West Haven, 1986—; numerous vis. lectureships. Author: Spinal Cord Compression, 1990, Correlative Neuroanatomy, 1995, 2d edit., 2000, The Axon, 1995, Diseases of the Spinal Cord, 2000, Form and Function in the Brain and Spinal Cord, 2001; editor: Physiology and Pathobiology of Axons, 1978; editor-in-chief: The Neuroscientist, assoc. editor: Muscle and Nerve, Jour. Neurol. Scis., mem. editl. bd.: Ann. Neurology, Brain Rsch., Internat. Rev. Neurobiology, Jour. Neurol. Rehab., Devel. Neurosci., Jour. Neurotrauma, Neurobiology of Disease, Cerebrovascular Disease, Synapse, Restorative Neurology and Neurosci. Named Nat. Multiple Sclerosis Soc. established investigator, 1987; recipient Trygve Tuve Meml. award, NIH, 1973, Rsch. Career Devel. award, 1975, Disting. Alumnus award, Albert Einstein Coll. Medicine, 1990; rsch. fellow, Univ. Coll., London, 1969. Fellow: NAS, Am. Acad. Neurology (Wartenberg award 1999, Dystel prize 2003), Am. Heart Assn. (stroke coun.), Royal Soc. Medicine (Gt. Britain), Inst. Medicine; mem.: Am. Univ. Profs. Neurology, Assn. Rsch. in Nervous and Mental Diseases (trustee, pres. 1992), World Fedn. Neurology, Am. Neurol. Assn. (councillor 1980), Soc. Neurosci., Internat. Brain Rsch. Orgn. (U.S. nat. com.), Dana Alliance for Brain Initiatives, Am. Soc. Cell Biology. Office: Yale U Sch Medicine 33 Cedar St New Haven CT 06519-2314 Business E-Mail: stephen.waxman@yale.edu.

WAY, BARBARA HAIGHT, dermatologist; b. Franklin, N.J., Dec. 27, 1941; d. Charles Padley and Alice Barbara (Haight) Shoemaker; m. Anthony Biden Way; children: Matthew Shoemaker Way, Sarah Shoemaker Way. AB in Music cum laude, Bryn Mawr Coll., 1962, postgrad., 1963-64; MD, U. Pa., 1968. Diplomate Am. Bd. Dermatology. Systems engr. IBM, Balt., 1962-63; mem. dean's staff Bryn Mawr (Pa.) Coll., 1963-64; med. intern U. Wis. Hosps., Madison, 1968-69, resident in dermatology, 1969-72; physician emergency rm. St. Francis Hosp., La Crosse, Wis., 1969-72, founder dept. dermatology, 1972; asst. prof. dept. dermatology Tex. Tech U. Sch. Medicine, Lubbock, 1972-73, from asst. clin. to assoc. clin. prof., 1973-74, asst. prof., assoc. chair, 1974-76, assoc. prof., chair, 1976-81, assoc. clin. prof., 1981-92; clin. prof. Tex. Tech. U. Health Scis. Ctr., Lubbock, 1995—, founder, dir. dermatology residency tng. program, 1978-81, pvt. practice, 1973-74, 81—; acting dir. Lubbock City Health Dept., 1982-83. Courtesy staff Covenant Hosp., Lubbock, subsect. chief, 1992, 94; courtesy staff Covenant Lakeside Hosp., Lubbock, mem. credentials com., 1990, 92, 94, 95, founding dir. phototherapy unit, 1990-91, 93, mem. exec. com., 1991, 93, 98, chief dermatology sect., 1991, 93, 98. Alumna admissions rep. Bryn Mawr Coll., 1972-75, 87-96; mem. selection com. outstanding physician Lubbock chpt. Am. Cancer Soc., 1991-94, chmn., 1991; bd. dirs. Tex. Tech. U. Med. Found., 1987-89, Double T. Connection, 1988-90. Fellow Am. Acad. Dermatology (reviewer jour.); mem. Tex. Dermatol. Soc. (chmn. roster com. 1980), Tex. Med. Assn. (mem. sexually transmitted diseases com. 1986-90, mem. coun. pub. health 1990-92, vice councillor dist. III 1992-98, councillor dist. III 1998-2000, chmn. reference com. fin. and orgnl. affairs ann. session 1992), Lubbock County-Garza County Med. Soc. (mem. various coms. 1980-2000, chmn. sch. and pub. health com. 1983, mem. bd. censors 1983-85, chair 1985, sec. 1986, v.p. 1987, liaison with Tex. Tech. U. Health Scis. Ctr. com. 1988-91, co-chmn. pub. rels. com. 1988-89, alt. Tex. Med. Assn. del. 1988-89, del. 1990-95, 98-2000, pres.-elect 1989, pres. 1990, chmn. ad hoc bylaws com. 1991-94, chmn. Hippocratic award 1991), Women's Dermatologic Soc. (founding sec.). Office: 4102 24th St Ste 201 Lubbock TX 79410-1801 Office Phone: 806-797-1892.

WAY, E(DWARD) LEONG, pharmacologist, toxicologist, educator; b. Watsonville, Calif., July 10, 1916; s. Leong Man and Lai Har (Shew) W.; m. Madeline Li, Aug. 11, 1944; children: Eric, Linette. BS, U. Calif., Berkeley, 1938, MS, 1940; PhD, U. Calif., San Francisco, 1942. Pharm. chemist Merck & Co., Rahway, NJ, 1942; instr. pharmacology George Washington U., 1943-46, asst. prof., 1946-48; asst. prof. pharmacology U. Calif., San Francisco, 1949-52, assoc. prof., 1952-57, prof., 1957-87, prof. emeritus, 1987—, chmn. dept. pharmacology, 1973-78. USPHS spl. rsch. fellow U. Berne, Switzerland, 1955-56, China Med. Bd.; rsch. fellow, vis. prof. U. Hong Kong, 1962-63; Sterling Sullivan disting. vis. prof. Martin Luther King U., 1982; hon. prof. pharmacology and neurosci. Guangzhou Med. Coll., 1987; mem. adv. com. Pharm. Rsch. Mfrs. Assn. Found., 1968-98; mem. coun. Am. Bur. for Med. Advancement in China, 1982; bd. dirs. Li Found., 1970—, pres., 1985-98, bd. dirs. Haight Ashbury Free Clinics, 1986-93; Tsumura prof. neuropsychopharmacology med. sch. Gunma U., Maebashi, Japan, 1989-90; sr. staff fellow Nat. Inst. on Drug Abuse, 1990-91; rschr. on drug metabolism, analgetics, devel. pharmacology, drug tolerance, drug dependence and Chinese materia medica. Editor: New Concepts in Pain, 1967, (with others) Fundamentals of Drug Metabolism and Drug Disposition, 1971, Endogenous and Exogenous Opiate Agonists and Antagonists, 1979; mem. editl. bd. Clin. Pharmacology, Therapeutics, 1975-87, Drug, Alcohol Dependence, 1976-87, Progress in Neuro-Psychopharmacology, 1977-91, Research Communications in Chem. Pathology and Pharmacology, 1978-91, Alcohol and Drug Dependence, 1986-91, Asian Pacific Jour. Pharm., 1985—, Jour. Chinese Medicine, 1993—; contbr. numerous articles and revs. to profl. pubs. Recipient Faculty Rsch. Lectr. award, U. Calif., San Francisco, 1974, San Francisco Chinese Hosp. award, 1976, Cultural citation and Gold medal, Ministry of Edn., Republic of China, 1978, Nathan B. Eddy award, Coll. on Problems in Drug Dependence, 1979, Mentorship award, 2004, Chancellor's award for pub. svc., U. Calif., 1986, Disting. Alumnus award, U. Calif., San Francisco, 1990, Asian Pacific Am. Systemwide Alliance award, 1993, Lifetime Achievement award, Chinese Hist. Soc., 2001. Fellow Am. Coll. Neuropsychopharmacology (life, emeritus), Am. Coll. Clin. Pharmacology (hon.), Coll. on Problems of Drug Dependence (exec. com. 1978-92, chmn. bd. dirs. 1978-82); mem. AAAS, Am. Soc. Pharmacology, Exptl. Therapeutics (bd. editors 1957-65, pres. 1976-77, Torald Sollman award 1992), Fedn. Am. Socs. Exptl. Biology (exec. bd. 1975-79, pres. 1977-78), Am. Pharm. Assn. (life, Rsch. Achievement award 1962), AMA, Soc. Aid and Rehab. Drug Addicts (Hong Kong, life), Western Pharmacology Soc. (pres. 1963-64), Japanese Pharm. Soc. (hon.), Coun. Sci. Soc. Pres.' (exec. com. 1979-84, treas. 1980-84), Chinese Pharmacology Soc. (hon.), Academia Sinica (academician). Office: U Calif Dept Cellular and Molecular Pharmacology 1210 S San Francisco CA 94143-0001

WAY, JACOB EDSON, III, museum director, realtor; b. Chgo., May 18, 1947; s. Jacob Edson Jr. and Amelia (Evans) W.; m. Jean Ellwood Chappell, Sept. 6, 1969; children: Sarah Chappell Quiroga, Rebecca Stoddard, Jacob Edson IV. BA, Beloit Coll., 1968; MA, U. Toronto, 1971, PhD, 1978. Instr. Beloit (Wis.) Coll., 1972-73, asst. prof., 1973-80, assoc. prof., 1980-85; dir. Logan Mus. Anthropology, Beloit, 1980-85, Wheelwright Mus. Am. Indian, Santa Fe, 1985-89; interim dir. N.Mex. Mus. Natural History, Albuquerque, 1990-91; exec. dir. Space Ctr. Internat. Space Hall of Fame, Alamogordo, N.Mex., 1991-94; dir. N.Mex. Farm and Ranch Heritage Mus., 1994-99; cultural affairs officer State of N.Mex., Santa Fe, 1997—; realtor Margo Cutler, Ltd., Santa Fe, 2003—. Evaluator Nat. Park Service, Denver, 1986. Contbr. articles to profl. jours. Mem. Nuke Watch, Beloit, 1983-84; cultural affairs officer State of N.Mex., 1997-2003. Research grants Wis. Humanities Com., 1984, NSF, 1981; grantee Cullister Found., 1978-84; fellow U. Toronto, 1971. Mem. Am. Assn. Mus., Am. Assn. Phys. Anthropology, Can. Assn. for Phys. Anthropology, N.Mex. Assn. Mus. (pres. 1994-96), Soc. Am. Archaeology, Wis. Fedn. Mus. (adv. bd. 1982-85). Mem. Soc. Friends. Avocations: camping, skiing, fishing, reading, horseback riding. Office Phone: 505-982-1700. E-mail: jeway@earthlink.net.

WAY, KENNETH L. motor vehicle seat manufacturing company executive; b. 1939; BS, Mich. State U., 1961, MBA, 1971. V.p. Lear Siegler, Inc., Southfield, Mich., 1966-88; chmn., CEO Lear Corp., Southfield, 1988-2000. With USAF, 1962-66. Office: Lear Corp 21557 Telegraph Rd Southfield MI 48034-4248

WAYANS, DAMON, actor; b. N.Y.C., 1961; m. Lisa Wayans, 1984 (div. 2000); children: Damon Jr., Michael, Cara Mia, Kyla. Actor: (TV appearances) Saturday Night Live, 1985—86, Triple Cross, 1985, Take No Prisoners: Robert Townsend and His Partners in Crime, 1988, The Mutiny Has Just Begun: Robert Townsend and His Partners in Crime, III, 1989; (TV series) One Night Stand, 1989, In Living Color, 1990—92 (Emmy Outstanding writing in variety program, 1990, 1991, Outstanding individual in variety program, 1991), Damon (also exec. prodr.), 1998, My Wife and Kids (also exec prodr., writer), 2001—; (films) Beverly Hills Cop, 1984, Hollywood Shuffle, 1987, Roxanne, 1987, Colors, 1988, I'm Gonna Git You Sucka, 1988, Punchline, 1988, Earth Girls Are Easy, 1989, Look Who's Talking Too (voice), 1990, The Last Boy Scout, 1991, Mo' Money (also prodr., writer), 1992, Last Action Hero, 1993, Blankman (also exec. prodr., writer), 1994, Major Payne (also exec. prodr., writer), 1995, Celtic Pride, 1996, Great White Hype, 1996, Bulletproof, 1996, The Great White Hype, 1996, Goosed, 1999, Harlem Aria (also prodr.), 1999, Bamboozled, 2000, Marci X, 2003. Office: Wife & Kids Productions 10202 West Washington Blvd Culver City CA 90232*

WAYANS, KEENEN IVORY, actor, producer; b. NYC, June 8, 1958; s. Howell and Elvira Wayans; m. Daphne Polk, June 2001; 5 children: Jolie Ivory Imani, Keenen Ivory Jr., Nala, Bella, Daphne Ivory. Student Tuskegee Inst., Ala. Actor: (films) Star 80, 1983, The Glimmer Man, 1996, (TV films) For Love and Honor, 1983, (TV series) For Love and Honor, 1983; actor, prodr. (films) Don't Be a Menace to South Central While Drinking Your Juice in the Hood, 1996; actor, writer: (films) Hollywood Shuffle, 1987; actor, dir., prodr.: (films) Scary Movie, 2000; actor, dir., writer: (films) I'm Gonna Git You Sucka, 1988, A Low Down Dirty Shame, 1994; actor, exec. prodr., writer: (films) Most Wanted, 1997; dir.: (films) Scary Movie 2, 2001; dir., writer, creator: (TV series) In Living Color, 1990-94 (Emmy award for outstanding variety, music or comedy series, 1990); dir., prodr., writer: (films) White Chicks, 2004; exec. prodr., host: (TV series) The Keenen Ivory Wayans Show, 1997-98; prodr., writer (TV films) Hammer, Slammer, & Slade, 1990, (comedy sketch) Eddie Murphy Raw, 1987; writer: (films) The Five Heartbeats, 1991.*

WAYANS, MARLON, actor, film producer, writer; b. NYC, July 23, 1972; s. Howell and Elvira Wayans; children: Amai Zachary, Shawn Howell. Student, Howard U. Actor: (films) I'm Gonna Git You Sucka, 1988, Mo' Money, 1992, Above the Rim, 1994, The Sixth Man, 1997, Senseless, 1998, Requiem for a Dream, 2000, (voice) The Tangerine Bear, 2000, Dungeons & Dragons, 2000, The Ladykillers, 2004; (TV series) In Living Color, 1990—94, (voice) Waynehead, 1996—97, (prodr., writer): (films) Don't Be a Menace to South Central While Drinking Your Juice in the Hood, 1996, Scary Movie 2, 2001, White Chicks, 2004, (dir., prodr., writer): (TV series) The Wayans Brothers, 1995—99; writer (films) Scary Movie, 2000, Scary Movie 3, 2003. Office: William Morris Agy One William Morris Place Beverly Hills CA 90212

WAYANS, SHAWN, actor, film producer, writer; b. NYC, Jan. 19, 1974; s. Howell and Elvira Wayans. Actor: (films) I'm Gonna Git You Sucka, 1988, New Blood, 1999; (TV series) In Living Color, 1990—94, (voice) Waynehead, 1996—97, (dir., prodr., writer) The Wayans Brothers, 1995—99, (prodr., writer): (films) Don't Be a Menace to South Central While Drinking Your Juice in the Hood, 1996, Scary Movie, 2000, White Chicks, 2004, (co-exec. prodr., writer) Scary Movie 2, 2001; writer (films) Scary Movie 3, 2003. Office: William Morris Agy One William Morris Pl Beverly Hills CA 90212

WAYBURN, EDGAR, internist, environmentalist; b. Macon, Ga., Sept. 17, 1906; s. Emanuel and Marian (Voorsanger) W.; m. Cornelia Elliott, Sept. 12, 1947; children: Cynthia, William, Diana, Laurie. AB magna cum laude, U. Ga., 1926; MD cum laude, Harvard U., 1930. Hosp. tng. Columbia-Presbyn. Hosp., N.Y.C., 1931-33; assoc. clin. prof. Stanford (Calif.) U., 1933-65, U. Calif., San Francisco, 1960-76; practice medicine specializing in internal medicine San Francisco, 1933-1985; mem. staff Pacific Presbyn. Med. Ctr., San Francisco, 1959-86, chief endocrine clinic, 1959-72, vice chief staff, 1961-63, hon. staff, 1986—. Editor: Man Medicine and Ecology, 1970, Your Land and Mine, 2004; contbr. articles to profl. and environ. jours. Mem. Sec. of Interior's Adv. Bd. on Nat. Park System, 1979-83, mem. world commn. on protected areas Internat. Union for Conservation Nature and Natural Resources; leader nat. campaigns Alaska Nat. Interest Lands Conservation Act; trustee Pacific Presbyn. Med. Ctr., 1978-86; bd. dirs. Garden Sullivan Hosp., 1965-80; chmn. People For a Golden Gate Nat. Recreation Area, 1971—; mem. citizens' adv. commn. Golden Gate Nat. Recreation Area, San Francisco, 1974-2003, leader nat. campaigns, 1955-90; prin. citizen advocate Redwood Nat. Park, 1968, 78; dir. The Antarctica Project, 1993-2003; mem. adv. bd. Pacific Forest Trust; hon. chmn. Tuolomne River Preservation Trust, 1983-1985; prin. adv. Enlargement of Mt. Tamalpais State Pk.; leader campaign to establish Golden Gate Nat. Recreation Area, 1972. Maj. USAF, 1942-46. Recipient Douglas award Nat. Pks. and Conservation Assn., 1987, Leopold award Calif. Nature Conservancy, 1988, Fred Packard award Internat. Union Conservation Nature, 1994, Laureate of Global 500 Roll of Honour award U.N. Environment Programme, 1994, 1st Conservation award Ecotrust, 1994, Albert Schweitzer prize, 1995, Presdl. Medal of Freedom, 1999. Fellow ACP (laureat); mem. AMA, Am. Soc. Internal Medicine, Calif. Med. Assn. (del. 1958-83, Recognition award 1986, Leadership and Quality awards 1986), San Francisco Med. Soc. (pres. 1965, Resolution of Congratulations 1986), Sierra Club (pres. 1961-64, 67-69, John Muir award 1972, hon. pres. 1993), Sierra Club Found. (dir. 1960-87, pres. 1971-78, hon. pres. 1998—), Fedn. Western Outdoor Clubs (pres. 1953-55). Avocations: exploration, hiking. Home: 1450 Post St Apt 1008 San Francisco CA 94109

WAYCASTER, BILL, chemical company executive; b. Feb. 8, 1939; BS, Miss. State. With Dow Chem. Co., until 1969, Tex. Olefins Co., Houston, 1969—, CEO, 1995; with Tex. Petrochems. Corp., Houston, 1969—; CEO, pres. Tex. Petrochems. Corps., Houston, 1992—. Address: Tex Petrochemicals Corp 3 Riverway Ste 1500 Houston TX 77056-1935

WAYLAND-SMITH, ROBERT DEAN, retired banker; b. Oneida, NY, July 2, 1943; s. Robert and Prudence Cragin W.-S.; m. Kathleen Anne Schultz, Aug. 24, 1968 (dec. Oct. 1999), m. Linda M. Amendola, July 21, 2002; children: Kristin, Debra. BA in Econs., U. Rochester, 1965. Mgr. equipment svc. Strong Meml. Hosp., Rochester, N.Y., 1965-67; mgmt. trainee Chase Lincoln First Bank, N.A., Rochester, 1967-68, mgr. mcpl. securities, 1968-81, mgr. portfolio mgmt. depart., 1981-84, mgr. fin. and investment svc. dept., 1984-87, mgr. trust and fin. svc. dept., 1987-88; pres. and CEO Rochester region Chase Manhattan Bank, N.A., 1988-93, upstate trust and investment divsn. exec., 1993-98; ret., 1998. Mem. adv. bd. Roberts Wesleyan Coll., Rochester, 1989-99; mem. adv. coun. J.W. Jones Sch. Bus. SUNY, Geneseo, 1990-99. Trustee Ctr. for Govtl. Rsch., 1985—; dir. Greater Rochester Visitors Assn., 1990-93, Rochester Downtown Devel. Corp., 1991-93, United Neighborhood Ctrs., Greater Rochester Found., 1992-2002; mem. fin. execs. adv. bd. Coll. Bus. Rochester Inst. Tech., 1994-97; mem. United Way Greater Rochester Corp., 1998-2003; bd. dirs. Oneida Cmty. Mansion House, 1988—; bd. dir. Via Health, 1999-2001; bd. govs. The Genesee Hosp., 1992-2001; mem. bd. trustees Rochester Inst. Tech., 2003—; chair coll. coun. SUNY Coll. Geneseo, 1999—; bd. dirs. Greater Rochester Enterprise, 2004—. Fellow: Assn. for Investment Mgmt. and Rsch.; mem.: Greater Rochester Met. C. of C. (bd. dirs. 1992—95), Greater Rochester Ind. Practice Assn. (bd. dirs. 2000—), Rochester Soc. Security Analysts, Oak Hill Country Club, Genesee Valley Club. Avocations: golf, gardening, reading. Office: JP Morgan Chase One Chase Sq Rochester NY 14643 Office Phone: 585-258-5517. Business E-Mail: robert.d.wayland-smith@chase.com.

WAYMAN, JOSEPH MCKELDEN, editor, researcher; b. Strasburg, Va., Mar. 22, 1927; s. Joseph McKelden Wayman and Cathryn Bernice Loomis. Def. contract classes, UCLA, 1964—67; BS, Va. Tech., 1952. Gen. duty assignments Am. Safety Razor Yorkville Paper Co., N.Y.C., 1952—54; statis. compiler U.S. Census Bur., Washington, 1954—56; mail distbn. U.S. Post Office, U.S. Gen. Svcs. Adminstrn., San Francisco, 1956—58; item mgr. USAF, San Bernardino, Calif., 1958—62, price analyst L.A., 1962—84; editor Grandstand Baseball Ann., Downey, Calif., 1985—. Contbr. book Total Baseball, 1991—2001, book Walter Johnson: Baseball's Big Train, 1995, book Cy Young: A Baseball Life, 2000. With USAF, 1945—47. Mem.: Baseball Reliquary, Inc., Pacific Coast League Hist. Soc., Soc. for Am. Baseball Rsch. (pub. pitching W-L records Nat. League, 1890-1999 1996). Democrat. Methodist. Avocations: stamp collecting/philately, walking, attending baseball functions. Office: Grandstand Baseball Ann PO Box 4203 Downey CA 90241

WAYMAN, ROBERT PAUL, computer company executive; b. Chgo., July 5, 1945; s. Lowell Roger and Dorothy Emma (Francke) W.; m. Susan O. Humphrey; children: Jennifer, Allison, Grant, Kirsten, Clayton. BS in Sci. Engring., Northwestern U., 1967, MBA, 1969. Cost acct. Hewlett-Packard Co., Loveland, Calif., 1969-71, mgr. cost accounts, 1971-73, div. controller, 1973-76; instrument group controller Palo Alto, Calif., 1976-83; corp. controller, 1983-84; CFO, 1984—. Mem. Fin. Execs. Inst., Council Fin. Execs., Private Sector Coun., dir. Hewlett-Packard, CNF Transportation Sybase. Office: Hewlett-Packard Co 3000 Hanover St Palo Alto CA 94304-1181

WAYMIRE, BONNIE GLADINE, nursing administrator; b. Williamsport, Ind., Dec. 16, 1954; d. Jackie Lee and Mary Lou (Jennings) W. LPN diploma, Danville Jr. Coll., 1978; diploma, Lakeview Sch. Nursing, 1986; BS in Bus. Mgmt., Ind. Inst. of Tech., 1996; postgrad., Lakeview Coll. Nursing. RN, Ind., Ill.; cert. vascular nurse, dir. nursing, 1996. Supr. evening shift Vermillion Manor, Danville, Ill., 1986; staff nurse, rsch. coord. VA Med. Ctr., Indpls., 1986-92; vis. nurse Vis. Nurse Svc., Indpls., 1992; charge nurse Eagle Valley Health Care, Indpls., 1992; dir. nursing svc. Vinewood Health Care, Plainfield, Ind., 1992-93, Records Autumn Care, Franklin, Ind., 1993, Bloomfield (Ind.) Health Care, 1993-94, Shakamak Good Samaritan, Jasonville, Ind., 1994-98, Provena United Samaritan Med. Ctr., 1998—2000; state long term care surveyor Ind. State Dept. Health Long Term Care Div., 2001; program dir., instr. CNA and QMA classes Nurse Aide Tng. Ctr., Indpls., 2001—03; night supr. Kendried Hosp., 2003; occupl. health nurse for interim occupl. healthcare GM Metal Fabrication, Indpls., 2003—. Co-author: Am. Jour. Vascular Surgery, 1992. Mem.: Nat. Assn. Dirs. Nursing Adminstr. in Long Term Care, Soc. Vascular Nursing (nursing standard and practice Acte com. 1988—92), Gen. Fedn. Womens' Clubs, Plainfield Jr. Women's Club, Fedn. Women's Clubs Ind., Gen. Fedn. Women's Club Ill., Am. Legion Aux., Women of the Moose (Acad. Friendship award 1992), VFW Aux. Roman Catholic. Avocations: collecting stamps, coins and star trek memorabilia. Home: 6429 Atlanta Dr Indianapolis IN 46241

WAYNE, ANDREW MARK, diversified financial services company executive; b. N.Y.C., Sept. 22, 1970; s. Robert Andrew and Charlotte Wayne; m. Nancy Ross, July 22, 2000; 1 child, Jordan Matthew. BA in Econ., U. Wis., 1992. Fin. cons. Merrill Lynch, N.Y.C., 1995—98, sr. fin. cons., 1998—2000; first v.p. investments Smith Barney, N.Y.C., 2000—. Avocations: golf, travel. Office: Smith Barney 666 Fifth Ave 13th Flr New York NY 10103 E-mail: andrew.m.wayne@smithbarney.com.

WAYNE, BARBARA ANN, music educator, classical guitar performer; b. Saskatoon, Sask., Can., Apr. 13, 1957; d. Samuel Peter and Winnifred May Becker; m. Raymond Francis Wayne, Jan. 18, 1992. MusB with great distinction, U. Sask., 1983; MusM in Music Theory, So. Meth. U., Dallas, 1990; MusM in Classical Guitar Performance, So. Meth. U., 1990. Classical guitar instr. Everett Larson's Music Coll., Saskatoon, Canada, 1972—75, Schoen's Music Sales, Saskatoon, 1979—82, Saskatoon, 1983—87, 1991; music theory tchg. asst. So. Meth. U., Dallas, 1987—89; classical guitar instr. Idaho Falls, Idaho, 1997—. Brigham Young U.-Idaho, Rexburg, 1998—. Mem. classical guitar trio Guitar Camerata, Saskatoon, 1983—87; numerous recitals, solo, ensemble and student Idaho Falls and Rexburg, 1998—; organizer master class Brigham Young U.-Idaho, 2001. Composer: (classical guitar solo) Cady's Dance, 2002, numerous compositions. Performer Playing for a Cure for Diabetes, Idaho Falls, 2000, Eagle Rock Art Mus., Idaho Falls, 2002. Recipient Univ. prize in music, U. Sask., 1983; Meadows Artistic scholar, So. Meth. U., 1987—89, S. J. and Mary Hay scholar, 1989—90. Mem.: Pi Kappa Lambda. Avocations: travel, gardening, cross country skiing, quilting. Office: Brigham Young Univ-Idaho #215 525 S Center St Snow Rexburg ID 83460

WAYNE, EARL ANTHONY, federal agency administrator; BA, U. Calif., Berkeley; MA, Princeton U., Stanford U.; MPA, Harvard U. Joined Fgn. Svc., 1975, various positions; spl. asst. to sec. of state U.S. State Dept., 1981—83; first sec. Embassy, Paris, 1984—87; nat. security corr. Christian Sci. Monitor, 1987—89; dir. regional affairs U.S. Amb. at Large for Counter-Terrorism, 1989—91; dir. Western European affairs Nat. Security Coun., 1991—93; dep. chief mission U.S. Mission to European Union, 1993—96; dept. asst. sec. for Europe U.S. Dept. of State, 1996—97, prin. dep. asst. sec. for European affairs, 1997—2000, asst. sec. of state for econ. and bus. affairs, 2000—. Office: US Dept of State Econ and Bus Affairs Bur 2201 C St NW Washington DC 20520

WAYNE, JIM, state representative; b. May 21, 1948; MSW social work, Smith College Sch. for Social Work; MA, Maryknoll Sch. of Theology; BA, Maryknoll Coll. State Rep. House of Rep., Dist. 35, Ky., 1990—; pres. Wayne and Assoc., Inc. Mem. State Gov., Appropriation & Rev.; Vice chair Local Gov. Mem.: KY Soc. for Clinical Soc. Work (past pres.), Louisville Forum, Louisville Coalition for the Homeless, Bd. mem., Smith Coll. Sch. for Soc. Work, Capital Campaign Comm., Jefferson County Adv. Coun. for Women. Democrat. Office: Capitol Capitol Annex, Rm 429E Frankfort KY 40601 also: Dist 1280 Royal Ave Louisville KY 40204

WAYNE, KYRA PETROVSKAYA, writer; b. Crimea, USSR, Dec. 31, 1918; arrived in U.S., 1948, naturalized, 1951; d. Prince Vasily Sergeyevich and Baroness Zinaida Fedorovna (Fon-Haffenberg) Obbolensky; m. George J. Wayne, Apr. 21, 1961; 1 child, Ronald George. BA, Leningrad Inst. Theatre Arts, 1939, MA, 1940. Actress, concert singer, Russia, 1939-46; actress, 1948-59; enrichment lectr. Royal Viking Line cruises, Alaska-Can., Greek Islands-Black Sea, Russia/Europe, 1978-79, 81-82, 83-84, 86-8, 88. Author: Kyra, 1959, Kyra's Secrets of Russian Cooking, 1960, 1993, The Quest for the Golden Fleece, 1962, Shurik, 1971, 1992, The Awakening, 1972, The Witches of Barguzin, 1975, Max, The Dog that Refused to Die, 1979 (Best Fiction award Dog Writers Assn. Am., 1980), Rekindle the Dreams, 1979, Quest for Empire, 1986, Li'l Ol' Charlie, 1989, Quest for Bigfoot, 1996, Pepper's Ordeal, 2000. Founder, pres. Clean Air Program, Los Angeles County, 1971—72; mem. Seattle Art Mus.; mem. women's coun. Sta. KCET-Ednl. TV; mem. Monterey County Symphony Guild, 1989—91, Monterey Bay Aquarium, Monterey Peninsula Mus. Art, Friends of La Mirada, Fresno Art Mus., Fresno Met. Mus., Valley Children's Hosp. Served to lt. Russian Army, 1941—43. Decorated Red Star, numerous decorations USSR; recipient award, Crusade for Freedom, 1955—56, Los Angeles County, 1972, Merit award, Am. Lung Assn. Los Angeles County, 1988, award of Merit, Congress Russian Ams., 1999. Mem.: Idyllwild Sch. Music, Carmel Music Soc. (bd. dirs. 1992—94), Authors Guild, Soc. Children's Book Writers, PEN, Fresno Philharm., L.A. Lung Assn. (life), UCLA Affiliates (life), UCLA Med. Faculty Wives (pres. 1970—71, dir. 1971—75), Art and Theatre Assn. (trustee 1987), Friends Lung Assn. (pres. 1988), Club 25, Los Angelenos Club (life). Home: 25875 Canyon Rd NW Poulsbo WA 98370 *Personal philosophy: I believe in total loyalty. Loyalty to one's family and friends, to one's colleagues and to one's country. In my case - to my chosen country, the U.S.A.*

WAYNE, LYNN, photographer, writer; d. Ralph Elmer and Pauline Davenport Wayne. BA, U. Mass., 1971. Adminstrv. dir, photographer, tchr. Hamilton Sch. Photography, L.A., 1980—82; owner, photographer Lynn Wayne Photography, Boston, 1989—. Author: Kindred Spirits of the Thirteenth Moon. Avocations: travel, music, writing, photography, swimming.

WAYNE, STEPHEN J. government educator, writer; b. N.Y.C., Mar. 22, 1939; s. Arthur G. and Muriel Wayne; m. Cheryl Beil, May 22, 1982; children: Jared B., Jeremy B. BA with honors, U. Rochester, 1961; MA, Columbia U., 1963, PhD, 1968. Instr. polit. sci. U.S. Naval Postgrad. Sch., 1963-65; instr. politics and govt. Ohio Wesleyan U., 1966-68; asst. prof. to prof. polit. sci. and pub. affairs The George Washington U., 1968—88; prof. govt. Georgetown U., Washington, 1989—. Presenter and lectr. in field. Author: The Legislative Presidency, 1978, The Road to the White House, 1980, 7th edit., 2004, (with George C. Edwards) Presidential Leadership: Politics and Policy Making, 1985, 6th edit., 2002 (with Cal MacKenzie, David O'Brien and Richard L. Cole) The Politics of American Government, 1995, 3d edit., 1999, Is This Any Way to Run a Democratic Election?, 2d edit., 2002; editor: Investigating the American Political System: Problems, Methods, and Projects, 1974, (with George C. Edwards) Studying the Presidency, 1983, (with Clyde Wilcox) The Quest for National Office, 1992, (with Wilcox) The Election of the Century and What It Tells Us About the Future of American Politics, 2002, Is This Any Way to Run a Democratic Government?, 2004; appeared on 3 one-hour programs on presidency Every Four Years, sta. WHYY-TV, PBS, 1980; election night analyst ARD-German TV, 1992; adv. editor Polit. Sci. McGraw Hill Coll. Divsn., 1982—; series editor Am. Political Institutions and Pub. Policy, M. E. Sharpe, Inc., 1990—; contbr. numerous articles, chpts. and book revs. to books and profl. jours. Office: Georgetown U Dept Govt 37th And O NW Washington DC 20057-0001 Office Phone: 202-687-5908.

WAYTE, ALAN (PAUL WAYTE), lawyer; b. Huntington Park, Calif., Dec. 30, 1936; s. Paul Henry and Helen Lucille (McCarthy) W.; m. Beverly A. Bruen, Feb. 19, 1959 (div. 1972); children: David Alan, Lawrence Andrew, Marcia Louise; m. Nancy Kelly Wayte, July 5, 1975. AB, Stanford U., 1958, JD, 1960. Bar: Calif. 1961, U.S. Dist. Ct. (so. dist.) Calif. 1961, U.S. Supreme Ct. 1984. Ptnr. Adams, Duque & Hazeltine, Los Angeles, 1966-85, Dewey Ballantine, Los Angeles, 1985—. Mem. L.A. County Bar Assn. (chmn. real property sect. 1981-82), Am. Coll. Real Estate Lawyers (bd. govs. 1989—, pres. 1994), Am. Coll. Mortgage Attys., Anglo-Am. Real Property Inst. (bd. govs. 1989-91), L.A. Philharm. Assn. (exec. com. bd. dirs. 1973—), Chancery Club, Calif. Club (L.A.), Valley Hunt Club (Pasadena). Home: 1745 Orlando Rd Pasadena CA 91106-4131 Office: Dewey Ballantine 333 S Hope St Los Angeles CA 90071-1406 E-mail: awayte@deweyballantine.com.

WAZ, JOSEPH WALTER, JR., government relations consultant, author; b. Meriden, Conn., Jan. 13, 1953; s. Joseph Walter and Rose Marie (Barillaro) W.; m. Ann Stookey, Sept. 25, 1981; 1 child, Joseph W. III. AB, Boston U., 1975; JD, U. Conn., 1978. Bar: Conn. 1978; D.C. 1979, U.S. Ct. Appeals D.C. 1980. Dep. dir. Telecommunications Research and Action Ctr., Washington, 1979-82; sr. assoc. govt. rels. Wexler, Reynolds, Harrison & Schule, Inc., Washington, 1983-86; gen. counsel Wexler, Reynolds, Fuller, Harrison & Schule, Inc., Washington, 1986-90, ptnr., 1989-90; sr. v.p. The Wexler Group, a unit of Hill and Knowlton, Inc., Washington, 1990-92, exec. v.p., 1993—; gen. counsel The Wexler Group, 1990—. Author (with S. Simon): Reverse The Charges, 1983 (Book of the Month Club pro bono selection 1983); editor Telematics jour., The Computer Lawyer; contbr. articles to communications trade publs. Polit. broadcasting advisor Californians for Recycling and Litter Clean-up, L.A., 1982, Dukakis for Pres. Campaign, Boston, 1987-88; comm. policy advisor Clinton/Gore campaign, 1992; founding trustee FCBA Found., treas., 1992-93; mem. Montgomery County Alcohol and Other Drug Abuse Adv. Commn., 1993—. Mem. ABA (steering com., electronic media div., forum com. on communications), D.C. Bar Assn., Fed. Communications Bar Assn. (chmn. CLE and legislation coms.). Democrat. Avocations: music, travel, team sports. Home: 46 Summit St Philadelphia PA 19118-2833 Office: The Wexler Group 1317 F St NW Ste 600 Washington DC 20004-1157

WAZZAN, A(HMED) R(ASSEM) FRANK, engineering educator, dean; b. Lattakia, Syria, Oct. 17, 1935; married, 1959; 3 children. BS, U. Calif., Berkeley, 1959, MS, 1961, PhD in Engring. Sci., 1963. From asst. prof. to assoc. prof. engring. UCLA, 1962-69, prof. engring. and applied sci., 1974—, assoc. dean Henry Samueli Sch. Engring. and Applied Sci., 1981-86, dean Henry Samueli Sch. Engring. and Applied Sci., 1986—2001. Cons. McDonnell Douglas Corp., 1962-71, Lawrence Radiation Lab., 1965-67, Westinghouse Electric Corp., 1974-76, N.Am. Aviation, 1975-78, Rand Corp., 1975—; Honeywell Corp., 1976-78; vis. scholar Electricité de France, Paris, Office of Commr. Atomic Energy, Saclay, France, 1973-79. Reviewer Applied Mech. Rev., 1971-87. Guggenheim fellow, 1966. Fellow Am. Nuclear Soc. Achievements include research in modeling of fuel elements for fast breeder reactor, stability and transition of laminar flows, thermodynamics of solids and of dense gases, and thermal hydraulics of pressurized water reactors. Office: UCLA Henry Samueli Sch Engring Sci Box 951592 6288 Boelter Hall Los Angeles CA 90095-1592

WEAGEL, DEBORAH FILLERUP, writer, composer; b. LA, Apr. 6, 1955; d. Francis McDonald Fillerup and Donna Virginia Mortenson; m. Edward Finlinson Weagel, Dec. 15, 1981; children: Elisabeth Susan children: Edward Michael, Joseph Robert, Arthur Frederick. BA, Brigham Young U., 1980; MusM, U. N.Mex, 1997, MA, 2001. Author: Interconnections: Essays on Music, Art, Literature, and Gender; composer: (piano solo) Homage to Georgia O'Keeffe; contbr. articles to profl. jours., to ency. Fellow, U. N.Mex, 1996—97; grantee, 1995—96, 2000—01, 2003; scholar, 2000—01; Hewlett Fellow, 2002. Mem.: Internat. Assn. Word and Music Studies, Société des Etudes Camusiennes, Rocky Mountain MLA, MLA, Am. Musicological Soc. Mem. Lds Ch. Avocations: ballet/dance, opera, travel, films. Home: PO Box 581 Corrales NM 87048 Office: Univ New Mexico Albuquerque NM 87131 Personal E-mail: dweagel@comcast.net.

WEAGRAFF, PATRICK JAMES, psychology educator, writer; b. Buffalo, May 27, 1940; s. Harry Edward and Donnabelle (O'Brien) W.; children from a previous marriage: Michael, Patrick Jr., Kim Marie, Susan Lynn; m. Sandra Weagraff, Sept. 19, 1993; 1 stepchild, Nicholas Turner. BS, SUNY, Buffalo, 1963; MEd, U. Md., 1965; EdD, UCLA, 1970, PhD, 1971. Cert. psychology, post secondary edn., secondary edn., ednl. adminstrn., drug and alcohol counseling. Assoc. dir. U.S. Peace Corps, Lagos, Nigeria, 1965-68; ednl. adminstr. Calif. Dept. Edn., Sacramento, 1971-75; assoc. commr. edn. Mass. Dept. Edn., Boston, 1975-76; psychologist Sierra View Mental Health, Auburn, Calif., 1978-81; chief clin. svcs. Calif. Dept. Mental Health, Sacramento, 1981-93; clin. dir. St. Joseph's Hosp., Stockton, Calif., 1993-95; prof. psychology Profl. Sch. Psychology, Sacramento, 1993-98; assoc. prof. Nat. U., Stockton, Calif., 1983-99; mng. SP Behavioral Health LLC. Author 9 books including Careers in Focus, 1993, Communications, 1993, Public Service Occupations, 1993, Construction Occupations, 1993, Decision Making, 1995, Making Decisions Work, 1997. Trustee Crossroads Inc., Sacramento, 1982-90; bd. dirs. Golden Empire Scouts, Sacramento, 1985-91; trustee Western Inst. Therapeutic Studies, 1996—. Edn. Profession Devel. Act fellow UCLA, 1970. Mem. Phi Delta Kappa, Epsilon Pi Tau. Jewish. Avocation: classic cars. Home: PO Box 25756 Miami FL 33102-5756 E-mail: p.j.weagraff@yahoo.com.

WEAKLAND, REMBERT G. retired archbishop; b. Patton, Pa., Apr. 2, 1927; s. Basil and Mary (Kane) Weakland. AB, St. Vincent Coll., Latrobe, Pa., 1948, DD (hon.), 1963, LHD (hon.), 1987; MS in Piano, Juilliard Sch. Music, 1954; postgrad., Columbia U., 1954—56, PhD in Musicology, 2000; LHD (hon.), Duquesne U., 1964, Belmont Coll., 1964, Cath. U. Am., 1975, Xavier U., Cin., 1988, DePaul U., 1989, Loyola U., New Orleans, 1991, Villanova U., 1992, Dayton U., 1993, Marian Coll., Fond du Lac, Wis., 1995, St. Anselm Coll., Manchester, N.H., 1996, St. Norbert Coll., De Pere, Wis., 1996, U. San Francisco, 1997, Scholastica Coll., 1998; HHD (hon.), St. Ambrose U., Davenport, 1990, Aquinas Inst. Theology, St. Louis, 1991, St Mary's Coll., Notre Dame, Ind., 1994; LLD (hon.), Cardinal Stritch Coll., Milw., 1978, Marquette U., 1981, Loyola U., Chgo., 1986, U. Notre Dame, 1987, Mt. Mary

Coll., Milw., 1989, John Carroll U., Cleve., 1992; LLD (hon.), Fairfield U., 1994; D of Sacred Music (hon.), St. Joseph's Coll., Rensselaer, Ind., 1979; DST of Sacred Music (hon.), Jesuit Sch. Theology, Berkeley, Calif., 1989; DST (hon.), St. John's U., Collegeville, Minn., 1991, Santa Clara U., 1991; DST (hon.), Yale U., 1993; DD (hon.), Lakeland Coll., Sheboygan, 1991. Ill. Benedictine Coll., Lisle, Ill., 1992, Regis Coll., Toronto, 1993, Trinity Coll., Hartford, 1996, Trinity Lutheran Sem., Columbus, Ohio, 1998; D of Ministry (hon.), Catholic Theol. Union, Chgo., 1999. Joined Benedictines Roman Cath. Ch., 1945, ordained priest 1951. Faculty music dept. St. Vincent Coll., 1957—63, chmn., 1961—63, chancellor chmn. of bd. of Coll., 1963—67; elected co-adjutor archabbot, 1963; abbot primate Benedictine Confederation, 1967—77; archbishop of Milw., 1997—2002. Mem.: Ch. Music Assn. Am. (pres. 1964—66), Am. Guild Organists. Roman Catholic. Office: PO Box 070912 Milwaukee WI 53207-0912

WEAKLEY, CLARE GEORGE, JR., insurance executive, theologian, entrepreneur; b. Dallas, Apr. 14, 1928; s. Clare George and Louise (Cunningham) W.; children: Clare George III, Carol J. (dec.), Charles E.; m. Jean C. Burrow, July 20, 1962. BBA, So. Meth. U., 1948, ThM, 1967. Ordained min. Christian Cmty., 1977. With Employers Ins., Dallas, 1948-52; owner Weakley & Co., Dallas, 1952-2001. Founder, pres. Am. Svc. Found., Inc., 1967—, The Christian Cmty., 19770172, Cornerstone Ministries, 1982—, Small Bus. Assn., Inc., 1988—; vis. prof. western bus. theory and Christian ethics Internat. Mgmt. Inst. (formerly Leningrad Internat. Mgmt. Inst.), St. Petersburg, Russia, 1990—; founder, leader The Christian Cmty., internat. ch. on World Wide Web. Author: In God We Trust, 1997, God 101, 1998; author, editor: The Wesley Library Series for Today's Reader, The Nature of the Kingdom, 1976, The Nature of Spiritual Growth, 1977, The Nature of Revival, 1987, The Nature of Salvation, 1988, The Nature of Holiness, 1988. Republican. Home: 13731 Goldmark Dr Apt 1207 Dallas TX 75240-4220 Office: Christian Cmty 13731 Goldmark Dr #1207 Dallas TX 75240

WEARN, WILSON CANNON, retired media executive; b. Newberry, S.C., Oct. 7, 1919; s. George F. and Mary (Cannon) W.; m. Mildred Colson, Feb. 21, 1948; children: Jean Wearn Held, Joan Wearn Gilbert, Wilson Cannon Jr. B.E.E., Clemson U., 1941. Engr. Westinghouse Electric Corp., Pitts., 1941, FCC, Washington, 1946-48; assoc. cons. electronic engr firm Weldon & Carr, Washington, 1948-50; ptnr. Vandivere, Cohen & Wearn (cons. engrs.), Washington, 1950-53; with Multimedia Broadcasting Co., Greenville, S.C., 1953-68, organizer of corp., 1953, became corp. officer, 1960, pres., 1966-77, Multimedia, Inc., Greenville, 1977-81, chief exec. officer, 1978-84, chmn. bd., 1981-89, chmn. emeritus, 1989-95. Instr. electronic engring. Clemson U., 1946. Mem. S.C. Hosp. Adv. Council, 1969-71; bd. dirs. Family and Children Service of Greenville County, 1967-69, pres., 1969; bd. dirs. Newspaper Advt. Bur., 1981-85; trustee Greenville Symphony Assn., 1960-62, 71-77, pres., 1977; trustee Greenville Hosp. System, 1964-70, chmn., 1968-70; trustee Broadcast Rating Council, 1969-73, chmn., 1971-73; trustee Clemson U. Found., 1973-79, pres., 1979; trustee Presbyn. Coll., F.W. Symmes Found. Served to capt. Signal Corps, AUS, 1941-45, PTO. Decorated Bronze Star; recipient Outstanding Alumni award Clemson U., 1972 Mem. Nat. Assn. Broadcasters (chmn. bd. 1975-77), S.C. Broadcasters Assn. (pres. 1967), Greater Greenville C. of C. (pres. 1972), Nat. Assn. Securities Dealers (bd. govs. 1985-88), Kiwanis (Greenville), Poinsett Club (Greenville), Augusta (Ga.) Nat. Golf Club. Presbyterian (elder). E-mail: mcwearn@msn.com.

WEARNE, SUSAN L, mathematical biology research scientist; d. Harold Neil and Romola Meers; m. Peter Hamilton Wearne. BA, U. of Sydney, Australia, 1985; M.Math., U. of NSW, Australia, 1999; PhD, U. of Sydney, Australia, 1993. Rsch. asst. prof. Dept. of Biomathematical Sciences, Mt. Sinai Sch. of Medicine, NY, 1999—2000, asst. prof., 2000—. Fishberg Rsch. Ctr. for Neurobiology, Mt. Sinai Sch. of Medicine, NY, 2000—. Recipient H. Tasman Lovell Meml. Medal, U. of Sydney, 1993. Mem.: NY Acad. of Sciences, Soc. for Neuroscience, Soc. for Indsl. and Applied Math., Am. Math. Soc. Office: Mount Sinai School of Medicine Box 1023 One Gustave L Levy Place New York NY 10029 Office Phone: 212-241-1521. E-mail: susan@camelot.mssm.edu.

WEART, SPENCER RICHARD, historian; b. Detroit, Mar. 8, 1942; s. Spencer Augustus and Janet (Streng) W.; m. Carole Ege, June 30, 1971; children: Lara Kimi, Spencer Gen. BA, Cornell U., 1963; PhD, U. Colo., 1968. Postdoctoral fellow Calif. Inst. Tech., 1968-71, U. Calif., Berkeley, 1971-74; dir. Ctr. for History Physics, Am. Inst. Physics, College Park, Md., 1974—. Author: Scientists in Power, 1979, Nuclear Fear, 1988, Never at War, 1998, Discovery of Global Warming, 2003; contbr. articles to profl. jours. Recipient Andrew Gemant award Am. Inst. of Physics, 1994 Fellow AAAS. Home: 12 Buena Vista Dr Hastings On Hudson NY 10706-1104 Office: Am Inst Physics One Physics Ellipse College Park MD 20740-3843 Office Phone: 301-209-3174. E-mail: sweart@aip.org.

WEARY, PEYTON EDWIN, retired medical educator; b. Evanston, Ill., Jan. 10, 1930; s. Leslie Albert and Conway Christian (Fleming) W.; m. Janet Edsall Gregory, Aug. 23, 1952; children: Terry, Conway Christian, Carolyn Fielder. BA, Princeton U., 1970; MD, U. Va., 1955. Diplomate: Am. Bd. Dermatology (dir. 1978-88, pres. 1987-88). Intern, case Western Res. U. Hosps., Cleve., 1955-56; rotating intern Univ. Hosp. Cleve., 1955-56; asst. resident dermatology U. Va., Charlottesville, 1958-60, resident dermatology, 1960-61, instr. dept. dermatology, 1961-62, asst. prof., 1962-65, asso. prof., 1965-70, prof., chmn. dept. dermatology, 1970-93; mem. staff Univ. Hosp., mem. cancer com., 1979—98, ret., 2001, prof. emeritus, 2001—. Univ. Hosp. house staff, 1960-61, clin. staff, 1965-66, pres. clin. staff, 1966-67; co-chair Nat. Coun. on Skin Cancer Prevention, Fed. Coun. on Skin Cancer Prevention, 1997-2001, Ctr. for Disease Control, 1997-2000. Mem. editorial bd. Jour. Am. Acad. Dermatology, 1978-87; editorial adv. bd. Skin and Allergy News, 1978—; contbr. articles to profl. jours. Bd. dirs. Lupus Found. Am., 1980-84; trustee, mem. exec. com. Dermatology Found., 1975-79; pres. Albermarle County unit Am. Cancer Soc., 1967-69. Served from 1st lt. to capt., M.C. U.S. Army, 1956-58. Recipient Walter Reed Disting. Achievement award U. Va. Alumni Assn., 2001 Master: Am. Acad. Dermatology (hon. bd. dir. 1973—76, pres. 1993—95, elected master in dermatology 2000, Gold medal 1990); mem.: Coun. Med. Splty. Socs. (bd. dir. 1989—92, sec. 1992—95), Am. Bd. Med. Spltys. (v.p. 1988, pres.-elect 1989, pres. 1990—92, Disting. Svc. award 1999), Raven Soc., So. Med. Assn., Med. Soc. Va. (Cmty. Svc. award 2001), Albermarle County Med. Soc., Dermatology Found., Am. Dermatol. Assn. (bd. dir. 1987—93, pres. 1992—93), Assn. Profs. Dermatology (sec.-treas. 1976—79), Soc. Investigative Dermatology (bd. dir. 1976—81, v.p. 1985, hon. mem. 1996), Va. Dermatol. Soc. (sec.-treas. 1965—71), Nat. Assn. Physicians Environ. (pres. 1995—97), Boar's Head Sports Club, Alpha Omega Alpha, Sigma Xi. Presbyterian. Home: 110 Magnolia Dr Charlottesville VA 22901-2015 Office: Dept Dermatology Univ Va Hosp Charlottesville VA 22908-0001

WEATHERBY, DONALD ALAN, telecommunications industry executive, writer; b. Columbus, Ohio, Dec. 11, 1954; s. Virgil Byron and Janet JoAnn Weatherby. Student, Columbus State C.C. Mainframe sys. adminstr. Contract to Bell Labs., Columbus, 1981—86; ops. mgr. AT&T Labs., Reynoldsburg, Ohio, 1996—. Sys. developer and implementation AT&T Labs., Reynoldsburg, 1996—2002. Author: (tech. mgmt.) Geekology 101: Managing the Aliens, Your Computer Support Staff, 1999, (novels) The Star Spangled Specter, 1995; composer: (jazz rock lit.fusion) Plush Hush CD - Generation Y, 2000. Recipient Vol. award, Ohio Legal Rights Svc. - State of Ohio, 1999. Mem.: MUFON (assoc.; data specialist 1999—2002, award for creation of MUFON Web database 2001). Unitarian Universalist. Avocations: writing macabre fiction, astronomy, UFO researcher, jazz-literary music. Home: 7485 E National Rd South Charleston OH 45368-8770 Personal E-mail: geekology@worldnet.att.net.

WEATHERFORD, DONNA P. library director, educator; b. Bklyn., Mar. 17, 1960; d. Donald Samuel and Dorothy Lee Hays; m. Terry Glenn Weatherford, Dec. 2, 1991; 1 child, Holly Marie. BS in Elem. Edn., U. Memphis, 1986. Tchr. 4th grade Our Lady of Sorrows Sch., Memphis; asst. dir. pre-sch. Our Lady of Sorrow Sch., Memphis; owner ednl. enrichment bus.; dir. summer program Munford Libr., Tenn. Author: The Pout Tree, 2004. Dir. children's choir Leawood Bapt. Ch., Memphis. Home: 763 Tracy Rd Millington TN 38053

WEATHERFORD, GEORGE EDWARD, civil engineer; b. Oakdale, Tenn., Jan. 8, 1932; s. Walter Clyde and Kathleen (Hinds) W.; m. Martha Jeannette Beck, July 9, 1960; children: Kathleen Jeannette, Elizabeth Lynn. BSCE, Ind. Inst. Tech., Fort Wayne, 1957; BS Engr. in Constrn., U. Mich., 1959; MSBA, St. Francis U., 1975. Registered profl. engr., Ind., Ga., Ohio, Iowa, S.C., Pa., Ill., Md., La., Tenn., Mich., Kans., Miss. Plant engr. Cen. Soya Co., Inc., Decatur, Ind., 1959, civil engr., 1959-64; county hwy. engr. Allen County Ind. Govt., Ft. Wayne, 1964-66; sr. civil engr. Cen. Soya Co., Inc., Fort Wayne, 1966-69, engring. mgr., 1969-77, prin. engr., 1977-97; cons. engr. Weatherford Engring., Ft. Wayne, Ind., 1997—. Ind. cons. 1964 . Author book chpts.; contbr. articles to profl. jours. Trustee Ft. Wayne YWCA, 1973-76, North Christian Ch. and Endowment Trust. Sgt. USMC, 1950-54. Mem. ASCE (state treas. 1957), NSPE, Am. Concrete Inst., Am. Inst. Steel Constrn., Nat. Grain & Feed Assn., Nat. Fire Protection Assn., Ill. Assn. Structural Engrs., Grain Elevator and Processing Soc. (edn. programming com.). Republican. Home: 3617 Delray Dr Fort Wayne IN 46815-6012 E-mail: george.weatherford@gte.net.

WEATHERHEAD, ALBERT JOHN, III, business executive; b. Cleve., Feb. 17, 1925; s. Albert J. and Dorothy (Jones) W.; m. Celia Scott, Jan. 1, 1975; children: Dwight S., Michael H., Mary H. AB, Harvard U., 1950, postgrad., 1951. Prodn. mgr. Yale & Towne, Stamford, Conn., 1951-54, Blaw-Knox, Pitts., 1954-56; plant mgr. Weatherhead Co., Cleve., 1957-59, gen. mgr., 1959-61, v.p., gen. mgr., 1962-66, gen. sales mgr., 1962-63, v.p. mfg., 1964-66; v.p., dir. Weatherhead Co. of Can., Ltd., 1960-63, pres., CEO, dir., 1964-66; treas. Weatherchem Corp., 1971-82, pres., dir., 1971—; also bd. dirs., 1987—. Bd. dirs. Weatherhead Co., Protane Corp., L.P.G. Leasing Corp, Leasepac Corp., Leasepac Can., Ltd., Creative Resources, Inc. Author: The New Age of Business, 1965; patentee in field. Mem. Harvard U. com. on univ. resources, Weatherhead Ctr. Internat. Affairs, vis. com.; trustee Case Western Res. U., mem. resources com., coun. on rsch. involving human subjects, trustee Michelson-Morley Centennial Celebration; mem. Univ. Sch. alumni coun., trustee Univ. Sch., hon. trustee for life Univ. Sch., Cleve., 1988—; trustee, adv. bd. Egyptian Studies Assn., U. S.C.; mem. vis. com. Ohio U., Athens; v.p. nat. adv. com. Rollins Coll., Winter Park, Fla.; adv. trustee Pinecrest Sch., Ft. Lauderdale, Fla.; mem. capital campaign steering com. Laurel Sch.; trustee Vocat. Guidance and Rehab. Svcs., Hwy. Safety Found., Arthritis Found.; v.p. Weatherhead Found., 1953-86, pres., 1987—; bd. dirs. New Directions Inc., Glenwillow, Ohio; mem. chancellor's coun. U. Tex. Sys.; founder Weatherhead Sch. Mgmt., Weatherhead East Asian Inst., Weatherhead Ctr. for Prevention and Reversal of Heart Disease at U. Tex. Col. CAF. With USAAF, 1943-46. Mem. Am. Newcomen Soc., Beta Gamma Sigma (hon.), Union (Cleve.), Country (Shaker Heights, Ohio), Ottawa Shooting (Freemont, Ohio), Ocean (Delray, Fla.), Everglades (Palm Beach, Fla.), Codrington (Oxford, Eng.). Home: 90 Falls Creek Trail Moreland Hills OH 44022 Office: 25825 Science Park Dr Beachwood OH 44122-7323 Office Phone: 216-292-7100. Business E-Mail: ajw@weatherchem.com.

WEATHERHEAD, LESLIE R. lawyer; b. Tacoma, Sept. 28, 1956; s. A. Kingsley and Ingrid A. (Lien) W.; m. Anali C. Torrado, June 24, 1985; children: Spencer, Madeleine, Audrey. BA, U. Oreg., 1977; JD, U. Wash., 1980. Bar: Wash. 1980, Oreg. 1996, U.S. Ct. Appeals (9th cir.) 1981, U.S. Dist. Ct. (ea. dist.) Wash. 1984, U.S. Ct. Internat. Trade 1984, Hawaii 1987, U.S. Dist. Ct. (we. dist.) Wash. 1989, Idaho 1989, U.S. Dist. Ct. Idaho 1989, U.S. Supreme Ct. 1994, Colville Tribal Ct. 1993, U.S. Ct. Appeals (10th cir.) 1995, U.S. Ct. Fed. Claims 1995, U.S. Ct. Appeals (fed. cir.) 1999. Asst. terr. prosecutor Territory of Guam, Agana, 1980-83; spl. asst. U.S. Atty. Dist. of Guam and No. Marianas, Agana, 1982-83; atty. Witherspoon, Kelley, Davenport & Toole, Spokane, 1984—. Lawyer-rep. 9th cir. jud. conf., 1989-95, lawyer-rep. chmn., 1995, 9th cir. adv. bd., 2001-04, chair, 2004—; adj. faculty Gonzaga U. Sch. of Law, 1994-95, 2001-04. Contbr. articles on Indian law, administrv. investigations and fed. jurisprudence to profl. jours. Bd. dirs. Spokane Opera Co., 1989-96, pres., 1992-94. Fellow Am. Coll. Trial Lawyers; mem. ABA, Fed. Bar Assn. (pres. ea. dist. 1996-97), Hawaii Bar Assn., Idaho Bar Assn., Wash. State Bar Assn., Oreg. State Bar Assn. Avocations: sailing, scuba, skiing. Office: Witherspoon Kelley Davenport & Toole 428 W Riverside Ave Spokane WA 99201-0301

WEATHERLEY-WHITE, ROY CHRISTOPHER ANTHONY, surgeon, consultant; b. Peshawar, India, Dec. 1, 1931; S. Roy and Elfreda (Milward) Boehm, m. Dorian Jeanne Freeman Weatherley-White, Dec. 27, 1961; children: Carl Christopher, Matthew Richard, Larissa Chantal. MA, Cambridge U., 1953; MD, Harvard U., 1958. Surgeon Biomedical Cons., Denver, 1970—; pres. Plastic Surgery Group, Denver, 1992-97. Chmn. Plastic Surgery Rsch. Coun., 1975-76; pres. Rocky Mountain Assn. Plastic Surgeons, 1973-74; v.p. Am. Cleft Palate Assn. Author: Plastic Surgery of the Female Breast, 1982; contbr. over 45 articles to profl. jours. Cons. Colo. Biomedical Venture Ctr., Denver, 1993—; chmn. bd. trustees Colo. Venture Ctrs., 1999—; bd. chairperson Operation Smile, Colo., 2000—. Recipient Rsch. award Am. Soc. Plastic Surgery, 1962, 64. Mem. Harvard Club of N.Y., Oxford-Cambridge Club, Denver Country Club, Denver Athletic Club. Episcopalian. Avocations: flying, skiing, scuba diving, archaeology. Home: 2101 E Hawthorne Pl Denver CO 80206-4116 Office: 2101 E Hawthorne Pl Denver CO 80206-4116

WEATHERLY, ALVIS MORRISON, JR., retired association developer; b. Atlanta, Nov. 19, 1925; s. Alvis Morrison and Frances Louise (Stocks) W.; m. Mary Elizabeth Hyndman, Dec. 27, 1947; children: Mary Ann Weatherly Cobb, Elizabeth Louise Weatherly Williamson, Alvis Morrison III. Student, Ga. Inst. Tech., 1942-44; BBA, U. Ga., 1947; LLB, Atlanta Law Sch., 1952. Treasury cashier for Ga. So. Bell Te. Co. (now BellSouth), Atlanta, 1948-82; devel. dir. Atlanta Area Coun. Boy Scouts Am., 1984-93. Author, editor: History of Georgia Jaycees 1921-1962, 1962. Club pres., dist. pres., state chmn., state treas., state historian Ga. Jaycees, 1955-63, past asst. coun. comm., coun. adv. bd.; instr. commr. conf. Boy Scouts Am., 1982, coun. commr. sci., wood badge, asst. course dir., nat. exec. tng. inst., pres. basic training course class, coun. encampment chief, 1976; past dean Coll. of Commr. Sci., 1980-1983; Jr. Achievement, Atlanta, 1951, 63; loaned exec. Atlanta United Appeal, 1964, 65; mem. Selective Svc. Bd., Atlanta, 1964-74; mem. staff Atlanta Olympics, 1996; del. 17th World Meth. Conf., Rio de Janeiro, 1996; bd. dirs., past pres. Ga., Nat. Meml. Day Assn. and Ave. of Flags; adminstrv. bd. mem., usher, past sec. fin. com., past tchr. youth Sunday sch., past pres. adult Sunday sch. class, trustee, past ch. sch. membership cultivation supt., past asst. ch. sch. supt., past mem. commn. on edn., past mem. evangelism commn., past ch. sch. greeter adminstrv. bd. Peachtree Rd. United Meth. Ch. Sgt. U.S. Army Air Corps, 1946, WWII; 1st lt. USAFR, 1961. Named Jaycee of Yr. North DeKalb chpt., Jaycees, Outstanding Dist. Pres.-Ga., Key Man of Ga., Hal Salfen Outstanding State Com. Chmn., M. Keith Upson Outstanding State V.P.; recipient Silver Beaver award, Boy Scouts Am., 1974, James E. West fellow, 1996, Whitney M. Young Jr. Svc. in Urban Scouting award, 1996, Scout Show honoree, 1996, Disting. Award of Merit, Disting. Commr. award, Vigil honor, Order of the Arrow, Spirit of Op. 1st class, 2001, Internat. Scouter's award, Daniel Carter Beard Masonic Scouter's award, Internat. Scouter's award, Willing Svc. banner, WSB Radio, Atlanta, 1974, 1976, Cert., Indian Creek Garden Club, Atlanta, Cross of Mil. Svc., United Daus. of the Confederacy, Cross and Flame award, Peachtree Rd. United Meth. Ch., Daiel Carter Beard Masonic Scouter's award 35 yr. vet. scouter. Master Mason (50 Yr. pin); mem. SAR- Sons Am. Revolution (past pres. Atlanta chpt., War Svc. medal, Meritorious Svc. medal), Rotary (bd. dirs., treas. Sandy Springs club, bd. dirs., sec., v.p. Smyrna-Cumberland club, sgt.-at-arms, bd. dirs., treas., sec., past pres. Buckhead Atlanta Club, Paul Harris fellow, Will Watt fellow, Otis Jackson fellow, Tom Slaughter fellow, Cmty. Svc. award, Svc. Above Self award, Rotarian of Yr., Rotarian Found. Dist. Svc. award, Buckhead (Atlanta) Boy of Yr.), Tel. Pioneers of Am., Shrine, 1st Families of Ga., Sons of Confederate Vets. (War Svc. medal), Mil. Order of Stars and Bars (past comdr.), Huguenot Soc. in Town of Manakin in Colony of Va. (past state pres.), Jamestowne Soc. (past 1st Ga. Co. Gov.), Sons and Daus. of the Pilgrims (past 2d dep. gov.), Sons and Daus. of Antebellum Planters (founding), Order of Indian Wars of U.S., Soc. of Descendents of Washington's Army at Valley Forge, Gen. Soc. War of 1812, Order of Washington, Magna Charta Barons, Magna Charta Dames and Barons (past state chmn.), Sovereign Colonial Soc., Mil. Officers Assn. Am., Ams. Royal Descent, Colonial Order of the Crown, Soc. Descendants of Knights of the Most Noble Order of the Garter, Plantagenet Soc., Old Guard of the Gate City Guard (past commandant col., Hancock medal, Charles Gavin Trophy, The Dr. George Turnbull Pursley award, Guardsman Yr. Award), Sigma Nu, Beta Gamma Sigma (past pres. Atlanta chpt.), Alpha Phi Omega, Delta Sigma Pi, Omicron Delta Kappa (alumni), Scabbard and Blade, Gridiron Secret Soc., Buckhead 50 Club, Am. Legion (Post 140). Home: 710 Starlight Ln NE Atlanta GA 30342-2838

WEATHERLY, ROBERT STONE, JR., banker; b. Birmingham, Ala., May 12, 1929; s. Robert Stone and Gladys (Manning) W.; m. Mary Anne Burr, May 1, 1954; children: Robert Stone, III, Henry, William. AB, Princeton U., 1950; LL.B., Harvard U., 1953, grad. advanced mgmt. program, 1972. Bar: Ala. 1953. Assoc. firm Burr, McKamy Moore & Thomas, Birmingham, 1955-62; asst. gen. atty. Vulcan Materials Co., Birmingham, 1962-69, v.p. chems. div. Wichita, Kans., 1969-71, treas., 1971-74, v.p. and controller, 1974-77, pres. metals div., 1977-87, pres. Middle East div., 1982-87; chmn., chief exec. officer Jefferson Fed. Savings, Birmingham, 1987-91; dir., sec. All Seasons Travel, Birmingham, 1991—. Disting. lectr.-practitioner U. Ga. Served with U.S. Army, 1953-55. Mem. Nat. Assn. Accts. (cert. mgmt. acct.), Beta Gamma Sigma. Clubs: Country of Birmingham, Chattooga (Cashiers, N.C.). Presbyterian. Home: 4608 Old Leeds Rd Birmingham AL 35213-1802 Office: All Seasons Travel 120 Office Park Dr Birmingham AL 35223-2422

WEATHERLY-MCWATERS, BARBARA CANNON, artist; b. Savannah, Ga., Mar. 27, 1927; d. John Respess and Irma Elizabeth (Murray) Cannon; m. William Earl Weatherly, Nov. 11, 1950 (dec. Jan. 1990); children: William Craig, Barbara Page; m. Roy McWaters, May 1, 1993. Student, U. Ga., 1946-48, High Mus. Sch. of Art, 1948-50, Continuing Art Edn. Workshops, 1960—. Mem. Gallery 209, Savannah, Ga., 1975, pres., 1986-87, 94-95. Scenery chief Cmty. Children's Theatre, Savannah, 1964-65; treas. Huntingdon Jr. Woman's Club, Savannah, 1964-65. Recipient First award Ga. Fedn. of Women's Clubs. Mem. DAR. Home: 929 N Hills Dr Dandridge TN 37725-4686

WEATHERS, MILLEDGE WRIGHT, retired economics educator; b. Augusta, Ga., May 11, 1926; s. Robert Edward Lee and Margaret Elizabeth (Johnson) W.; m. Anna-Maria Helene von Bertrab; children: Helene, Martin, Margarete, Benjamin. BA, George Washington U., 1949, MA, 1957; doctor oeconomiae publicae, U. Munich, 1961. Rsch. analyst U.S. Dept. Air Force, Washington, 1951-57, Gen. Electric Co., Santa Barbara, Calif., 1959-62; pvt. practice cons. Munich, 1962-64; cons. Gesellschaft fuer Anlagewerte, Munich, 1964-66; sr. staff analyst Lockheed-Ga. Co., Marietta, 1966-68; prof. econs. Adrian (Mich.) Coll., 1968-91. Contbr. articles to profl. jours. With U.S. Army, 1944-46. Mem. Am. Econs. Assn., Assn. for Evolutionary Econs., Nat. Tax Assn., Economists Allied for Arms Reduction, Kappa Sigma. Avocations: music, walking. Home: 930 Lincoln Ave Adrian MI 49221-3230 Personal E-mail: Mweathers@adrian.edu.

WEATHERSBY, GEORGE BYRON, business executive; b. Albany, Calif., Dec. 9, 1944; s. Byron and Fannie A. W.; m. Linda Rose Scheirer, June 29, 1979; children: Deborah Jane, Geoffrey Byron. BS, U. Calif., Berkeley, 1965, MS, 1966, MBA, 1967; MS, Harvard U., 1968, PhD, 1970; DHL (hon.), U. San Francisco, 1987; LLD (hon.), U. So. Ind., 1992. Mem. faculty, assoc. dir. analytical studies, dir. Ford Found. rsch. program U. Calif., Berkeley, 1969-72; spl. asst. to U.S. Sec. of State Washington, 1972-73; dir. rsch. Nat. Commn. on Financing Higher Edn., Washington, 1973-74; assoc. prof. mgmt. Harvard U., Cambridge, Mass., 1974-78; commr. higher edn. State of Ind., 1977-83; pres. Curtis Pub. Co., 1983-86, New UPI Inc., Washington, 1985-86; corp. v.p. fin. Ontario Corp., Muncie, Ind., 1986-88, pres., 1988-91, also bd. dirs.; ptnr. Founders Court Inc., Princeton, N.J., 1991-93; independant cons., 1995—; pres. Oxford Mgmt. Corp., 1993-98, Cambridge Parallel Processing, 1994-98, Electronic Retailing Sys. Internat., 1996-98; pres., CEO, bd. dirs. Am. Mgmt. Assn., N.Y.C., 1998—2002; chmn., CEO Genesys Corp., LLC, 2002—. CEO, Quisic, Inc., 2001-02; chmn. bd. dirs. Otis Conner Cos., 1984-86, Curtis Media Corp., 1984-86, Curtis Internat. Ltd., 1985-86, Prince Gardner, Inc., 1991-93, Alma Industries, 1992-93, Hanes Holding Co., 1992-93; bd. dirs. Holcim (US), Inc., Farm Fans Inc., Delta Consol. Industries, Cambridge Parallel Processing, Advanced Retail Mktg., ERS, Inc. Author: (books) Financing Postsecondary Education in the U.S, 1974, Colleges and Money, 1976; contbr. numerous articles to profl. jours., 1967—; cons. editor: Jour. Higher Edn., 1974—; exec. editor: Change mag., 1980-84. Bd. dirs. Nat. Ctr. for Higher Edn Mgmt. Sys., 1980-83, U.S.A. Group, 1989—; mem. steering com. Edn. Commn. of States, 1978-82; mem. Ind. Com. Humanities, 1981-87; trustee U. So. Ind., 1985-91, Park Tudor Sch. Indpls., 1986-91, Butler U., 1987-93; mem. adv. coun. Invest in New Zealand, 2001–. Calif. Regents scholar, 1963-65; NSF fellow, 1966-67; AEC fellow, 1966-67; Kent fellow, 1967-70; White House fellow, 1972-73; named 1 of 100 Outstanding Young Leaders in Higher Edn. Change Mag., 1978 Mem. Am. Mgmt. Assn., Am. Coun. Edn., Ops. Rsch. Soc. Am., Inst. Mgmt. Scis., Econometrica, Young Pres. Orgn. Republican. Office Phone: 609-466-0861. E-mail: gweathersby@genesysllc.com.

WEATHERSBY, KATHRYN, historian; b. Rangely, Colo., Aug. 7, 1951; d. Fred Elbert Weathersby and Betty Weathersby Webb; PhD, Ind. U., 1990. Asst. prof. of history Fla. State U., Tallahassee, 1989—95; sr. rsch. scholar Woodrow Wilson Internat. Ctr. for Scholars, Washington, 1999—. Rsch. fellow Norwegian Nobel Inst., Oslo, 1998; guest lectr. Royal Swedish Acad. of Mil. Sci., Stockholm, 1998, Ctrl. European U., Budapest, Hungary, 1998, Marine Corps U., Quantico, Va., 1999, Wash. and Lee U., Lexington, Va., 1999, John F. Kennedy Presdl. Libr., Boston, 1999, Colgate U., Hamilton, NY, 1999, Wis. Veterans' Mus., Wis., 2000, Ohio U., Athens, 2001, U. of Urbino, Italy, 2001, U. of Rome, 2001; coord., Korea Initiative Woodrow Wilson Internat. Ctr. for Scholars, Washington, 2001—; guest lectr. The Gramsci Inst., Rome, 2001; instr. Internat. Summer Sch., Pamporovo, Bulgaria, 2002; guest lectr. Harry S Truman Libr. and Mus., Independence, Mo., 2003, The Nat. War Coll., Washington, 2003, U. of Tenn., Knoxville, 2003, George Wash. U., Washington, 1994, U. of Md., College Park, 1997, Ohio U., Athens, 1997, Johns Hopkins Nanjing Ctr., Nanjing, China, 1997, East China Normal U., Shanghai, 1997, The Sorbonne, Paris, 1997, The U. of Oslo, Oslo, 1998; program cons. various pub. TV stas. Contbr. articles to profl. jours., chapters to books. Recipient U. Tchg. award, Fla. State U., 1991, Coll. Arts and Sci. Tchg. award, 1991; Postdoctoral fellow, Joint Com. Soviet Studies, Am. Coun. Learned Socs. and the Social Sci. Rsch. Coun., 1991—93, Advanced Rsch. grantee, Internat. Rsch. and Exchanges Bd., 1991, Joint Coun. Korean Studies, Social Sci. Rsch. Coun., 1994, Rsch. scholar, Kennan Inst. Advanced Russian Studies, 1995. Mem.: Soc. for Historians of Am. Fgn. Rels. (bernath lecture prize com. 1998—2000), Assn. for Asian Studies, Am. Assn. for the Advancement of Slavic Studies (mem., task force on archival affairs 1994), The Hist. Soc. (editl. bd., the jour. of the hist. soc. 1999—2004), Am. Hist. Assn. Achievements include research in program consultant, PBS Frontline, CNN The Cold War, BBC Korea, Russia's Secret War. Office Phone: 202-691-4000. Business E-Mail: coldwar1@wwic.si.edu.

WEATHERSPOON, JACKIE K. state legislator; b. N.Y.C., Oct. 12, 1951; m. Russell D. Weatherspoon; 4 children. BS, SUNY, Brockport, 1973; MPA, Harvard U., 1991. Mem. N.H. Ho. of Reps. (dist. 20), Concord, 1996—; mem. election law com. N.H. Ho. of Reps., Concord, 1996—. UN observer, 1994—; sub. tchr., assoc. dean. Cellist Phillips Exeter Acad. Orch.; mem. Ch. Women United. Episcopalian. Office: NH State Legis State House Concord NH 03301

WEATHERSPOON, TERESA GAYE, professional basketball player; b. Jasper, Tex., Dec. 8, 1965; Grad., La. Tech. Inst., 1988. Guard Blusto, Italy, 1988—89, 1990—93, Magenta, Italy, 1989—90, Como, Italy, 1996—97, CSKA, Russia, 1993—95, WNBA - N.Y. Liberty, N.Y.C., 1997—2003, L.A. Sparks, 2004—. Named, NCAA Women's Basketball Team Decade, 1980, La.

State Player of Yr., 1988, Kodak All-Am., 1987, 1988, WNBA defensive player of yr., 1997, 1998, WNBA All-Star, 1999—2002; named to All-WNBA 2nd team, 1997—2000; recipient Gold medals, World Championship, 1986, Goodwill Games, 1986, World Univ. Games, 1987, Broderick Cup, Wade Trophy. Achievements include first player in WNBA history to record 1,000 career assists. Office: c/o Los Angeles Sparks 555 N Nash St El Segundo CA 90245

WEATHERSTONE, SIR DENNIS, bank executive; b. London, Nov. 29, 1930; s. Henry Philip and Gladys (Hart) W.; m. Marion Blunsum, Apr. 4, 1959; children— Hazel, Cheryl, Gretel, Richard Paul Student, Northwestern Poly., London, 1946-49. Sr. v.p. Morgan Guaranty Trust Co. N.Y., N.Y.C., 1972-77, exec. v.p., 1977-79, treas., 1977-79, vice chmn., 1979-80, chmn. exec. com., 1980-86; pres. J.P. Morgan & Co., Inc. (formerly Morgan Guaranty Trust Co. N.Y.), N.Y.C., 1987-90, chmn., chief exec. officer, 1990-95. Bd. dirs. GM Corp., 1986-2001, Merck & Co., Inc., L'Air Liquide, NY Stock Exchange, 2003; mem. bd. banking supervision Bank of Eng. Decorated Knight Comdr. Order Brit. Empire.*

WEATHERUP, ROY GARFIELD, lawyer; b. Annapolis, Md., Apr. 20, 1947; s. Robert Alexander and Kathryn Crites (Hesser) W.; m. Wendy Gaines, Sept. 10, 1977; children: Jennifer, Christine. AB in Polit. Sci., Stanford U., 1968, JD, 1972. Bar: Calif. 1972, U.S. Dist. Ct. 1973, U.S. Ct. Appeals (9th cir.) 1975, U.S. Supreme Ct. 1980. Assoc. Haight, Brown & Bonesteel, LA, Santa Ana, 1972—78, ptnr., 1979—2003, Lewis Brisbois Bisgaard & Smith, LA, 2004—. Judge Moot Ct. UCLA, Loyola U., Pepperdine U.; arbitrator Am. Arbitration Assn.; mem. com. Book Approved Jury Instrns. LA Superior Ct. Mem. ABA, Calif. Acad. Appellate Lawyers, LA County Bar Assn., Town Hall Calif. Republican. Methodist. Home: 17260 Rayen St Northridge CA 91325-2919 Office: Lewis Brisbois Bisgaard & Smith 221 N Figueroa St Los Angeles CA 90012 Office Phone: 213-250-1800. E-mail: royweatherup@aol.com.

WEATHERUP, WENDY GAINES, graphic designer, writer; b. Oct. 20, 1952; d. William Hughes and Janet Ruth (Neptune) Gaines; m. Roy Garfield Weatherup, Sept. 10, 1977; children: Jennifer, Christine. BA, U. So. Calif., 1974. Lic. ins. agt. Freelance graphic designer, desktop pub., Northridge, Calif. Mem. NAFE, U. So. Calif. Alumni Assn., Alpha Gamma Delta. Republican. Methodist. Avocations: photography, travel, writing novels, computers. Home: 17260 Rayen St Northridge CA 91325-2919 E-mail: weatherw@aol.com.

WEAVER, AGNES JIN AI, medical/surgical nurse; b. Kuching, Sarawak, Malaysia, Aug. 28, 1954; arrived in U.S., 1981; d. Teck Kuan Ho and Nora Yu Yung Phoong; m. Cecil Wade Weaver, Jr., Nov. 30, 1984; 1 child, Stephanie Mei Li. Diploma in Pianoforte, London Coll. Music, 1974; diploma in Nursing, St.Charles' Hosp., London, 1977; diploma of licentiate in Pianoforte Tchg., Guildhall Sch. Music Drama, London, 1977; BS in Bus. Adminstrn. (cum laude), So. Adventist U., 1984; MBA, Andrews U., 1985. RN Ga. Staff nurse St.Charles' Hosp., London, 1977—78; piano tchr. Sandakan, Malaysia, 1978—81; tchr. piano Bowling Green, Ky., 1985—90; staff nurse Anderson Med. Ctr., Anderson, Ga., 1990—96, So. Regional Med. Ctr., Riverdale, Ga., 1996—2003, diabetes nurse educator, 2003—. Performance improvement unit coord. So. Regional Med. Ctr., Riverdale, Ga., 1997—2003, nurse preceptor, 1997—2003, co-chair of clin. practice coun., 2001—02; clin. instr. nursing Griffin (Ga.) Tech. Coll., 2000; piano tchr., Fayetteville, Ga., 1996. Scholar Ulmer scholar, So. Adventist U., 1983, E.A. Anderson Bus. scholar, 1983, 1984. Mem.: Malaysia Family Planning Assn., Am. Coll. Musicians, Ga. Music Tchrs. Assn., Nat. Assn. Orthop. Nurses, Delta Mu Delta. Office Phone: 770-991-8000 5630. Personal E-mail: jinai@aol.com.

WEAVER, ARTHUR LAWRENCE, rheumatologist, consultant; b. Lincoln, Nebr., Sept. 3, 1936; s. Arthur J. and Harriet Elizabeth (Walt) Weaver; m. JoAnn Versemann, July 6, 1980; children: Arthur Jensen, Anne Christine. BS (Regents scholar) with distinction, U. Nebr., 1958; MD, Northwestern U., 1962; MS in Medicine, U. Minn., 1966. Diplomate Am. Bd. Internal Medicine, Am. Bd. Rheumatology. Intern U. Mich. Hosps., Ann Arbor, 1962-63; resident Mayo Grad. Sch. Medicine, Rochester, Minn., 1963-66; practice medicine specializing in rheumatology and internal Lincoln, 1968—2002; med. dir. Arthritis Ctr. Nebr., 1968—2002; ret., 2002. Staff mem., chmn. rheumatology dept. Bryan Meml. Hosp., 1976—78, 1982—85, 1989—91, vice-chief staff, 1984—87; chmn. fin. com. Bryancare, 1995—96; courtesy staff St. Elizabeths Hosp., Lincoln Gen. Hosp.; cons. staff VA Hosp.; chmn. Juvenile Rheumatoid Arthritis Clinic, 1970—88; asst. prof. Internal Medicine Dept. U. Nebr., Omaha, 1976—88, assoc. prof., 1988—95, clin. prof. Rheumatology divsn., 1995—; med. dir. Lincoln Benefit Life Co., 1972—90; bd. dirs., med. dir. Assurity Life Ins. Co., 1995—2003; adv. com. Coop. Systematic Studies in Rheumatic Diseases III; bd. dirs. M.G.I. Pharma Inc., Internat. Rheumatology Network, Boston Healthcare Inc.; cons. in field. Contbr. articles to profl. jours. Mem. tech. cons. panel for rheumatology Harvard Resource Based Relative Value Study; trustee U. Nebr. Found., 1974—. Capt. med. corps U.S. Army, 1966—68. Recipient Outstanding Nebraskan award, U. Nebr., 1958, C.W. Boucher award, 1958, Philip S. Hench Rheumatology award, Mayo Grad. Sch. Medicine, 1966, Founders award Nebr. chpt., Arthritis Found., 1997. Fellow: ACP (Nebr. coun. 1983—85, Laureate award Nebr. chpt. 1996), Am. Coll. Rheumatology (bd. dirs. 1985—96, planning com. 1987—96, sec. 1991—93, pres. rsch. and edn. found. 1991—93, exec. com. 1991—96, 2d v.p. 1993—94, 1st v.p., pres.-elect 1994—95, pres. 1995—96, chmn. nominating com. 1996—97, master 2001, 1st Paulding Phelps award 1989), Am. Rheumatism Assn. (pres.-elect Ctrl. region 1983—84, com. on rheumatologic practice 1983—87, pres. Ctrl. region 1984—85); mem.: AMA (life), Minn. Med. Assn., Midwest Coop. Rheumatic Disease Study Group (chmn. exec. com. 1986—92), Nat. Soc. Clin. Rheumatology (program chairperson 1986—87, exec. com. 1987—92, program chairperson 1988), Arthritis Found. (life; profl. del.-at-large 1987—88, 1989, 1990, 1995—96, blue ribbon rsch. com. 1995—96, bd. dirs. Nebr. chpt., Nat. Vol. Svc. citation 1988, Founder award 1997), Arthritis Health Professions Assn. (com. on practice 1984—87), Nebr. Soc. Internal Medicine (Internist of Yr. 1988), Am. Soc. Internal Medicine (coord. com. phys. payment svcs. 1988—93), U. Minn. Med. Sch. Alumni Assn., U. Mich Med. Sch. Alumni Assn., Mayo Grad. Sch. Medicine Alumni Assn., Phi Rho Sigma, Pi Kappa Epsilon, Alpha Omega Alpha, Sigma Xi, Phi Beta Kappa. Republican. Presbyterian. Home and Office: 9914 Weavers Point Rd Pequot Lakes MN 56472-6472 Office Phone: 218-562-5351.

WEAVER, BARBARA FRANCES, librarian, consultant; b. Boston, Aug. 29, 1927; d. Leo Francis and Nina Margaret (Durham) Weisse; m. George B. Weaver, June 6, 1951; 1 dau., Valerie S. Clark. BA, Radcliffe Coll., 1949; MLS, U. R.I., 1968; EdM, Boston U., 1978. Head libr. Thompson (Conn.) Pub. Libr., 1961-69; dir. Conn. State Libr. Svc. Ctr., Willimantic, 1969-72; regional adminstr. Ctrl. Mass. Regional Libr. Sys., Worcester, 1972-78; asst. commr. of edn., state libr. State of N.J., Trenton, 1978-91; dir. R.I. Dept. State Libr. Svcs., Providence, 1991-96; chief info. officer State of RI, 1996—2001; govt. cons. in tech. mgmt., orgnl. devel. and libr. adminstrn., 2001—. Lectr. Simmons Coll., Boston, 1976-78. Mem. Conn. Libr. Assn.

WEAVER, CARLTON DAVIS, retired oil industry executive; b. Grantsville, W.Va., May 27, 1921; s. Arley Ezra and Grace (Davis) Weaver; m. Nancy Mason McIntosh, Mar. 21, 1951; 1 child, Nancy Mason. BS in Engr. Mines, W.Va. U., 1948. Office engr. E.I. du Pont de Nemours & Co., 1941-42, tech. service rep., 1948-51; with Ashland (Ky.) Oil, Inc., 1951-81, exec. asst., 1960-67, v.p., 1967-72, sr. v.p., 1972-81, group oper. officer, 1976-81, pres. Ashland Resources Co. div., 1970-74; chmn. bd. Ashland Coal, Inc., 1981-84, Ven-Black, Inc., 1983-86. Chmn. vis. com. Coll. Mineral and Energy Resources W.Va. U., 1967—80. Served to 1st lt. USMCR, 1942—46, served to maj. USMCR, 1952—53. Home: 64 Surfsong Rd Kiawah Island SC 29455-5753 also: PO Box 578 White Sulphur Springs WV 24986-0578 Office: 1409 Winchester Ave Ashland KY 41101-7555 E-mail: carltondweaver@bellsouth.net.

WEAVER, CHARLES HORACE, humanities educator; b. Statesville, N.C., Nov. 11, 1927; s. Lucius Stacy and Elizabeth Roderick (Hallyburton) W.; m. Nancy Jane Veale, June 24, 1955; 1 child, Charles Horace. BA, Wofford Coll., Spartanburg, S.C., 1951; MA, Columbia U., 1956; PhD, U. N.C., 1961. Tchr. English Oak Ridge Mil. Inst., N.C., 1951-54, High Point (N.C.) Cen. High Sch., 1954-56; asst. prin. Ferndale Jr. High Sch., High Point, 1956-58; prin. N.E. Jr. High Sch., High Point, 1959-60, Ferndale Jr. High Sch., High Point, 1960-62; asst. supt. Asheboro (N.C.) City Schs., 1962-65; supt. Elizabeth City (N.C.) pub. schs., 1965-69, Burke County Pub. Schs., Morganton, N.C., 1969-79; with State Dept. Pub. Instrn., Raleigh, N.C., 1979—, asst. state supt. aux. svcs., 1989-96; educator Shook Design, Charlotte, N.C., 1996—. Bd. dirs. We. Carolina Bank & Trust Co., Wilmington Food Sys., Inc., Greenville Food Sys., Inc. Contbr. articles to profl. ours. Bd. dirs. Burke County United Fund, Burke County Council on Alcoholism, We. Piedmont Mental Health Assn., We Piedmont Symphony. Mem. Am. Assn. Sch. Adminstrs., N.C. Assn. Sch. Adminstrs., Horace Mann League (pres. 1975-76), High Point Jr. C. of C. (bd. dirs.), Burke Country C. of C., Rotary, Asheboro Country Club, Raleigh Capital City Club. Democrat. Methodist. Avocations: reading, golf, antiques.

WEAVER, CHARLES LYNDELL, JR., institutional and manufacturing facilities administrator, management and marketing systems consultant; b. Canonsburg, Pa., July 5, 1945; s. Charles Lyndell and Georgia Lavelle (Gardner) W.; m. Ruth Marguerite Uxa, Feb. 27, 1982; children: Charles Lyndell III, John Francis. BArch, Pa. State U., 1969; cert. in assoc. studies, U. Florence, Italy, 1968. Registered architect, Pa., Md., Mo., Va., Mass., Ky., Ga.; cert. Nat. Coun. Arch. Registration Bd.; cert. designee, Design Build Inst. Am., 2002. With Celento & Edson, Canonsburg, part-time 1966-71; project architect Meyers & D'Aleo, Balt., 1971-76, corp. dir., v.p., 1974-76; ptnr. Borrow Assocs.-Developers, Balt., 1976-79, Crowley/Weaver Constrn. Mgmt., Balt., 1976-79; pvt. practice arch. Balt., 1976-79; cons., project mgr. U. Md., College Park, 1979-80; corp. cons. architect Bank Bldg. & Equipment Corp., Am., St. Louis, 1980-83; dir. archtl. and engrng. svcs. Ladue Bldg. and Engrng. Inc., St. Louis, 1983-84; v.p., sec. Graphic Products Corp.; pres. CWCM Inc. Internat., 1987-2000. Dir. K-12 Edn. Market Ctr. and sr. program mgr., Sverdrup Corp., 1989-95; prin. Benham Internat. Eurasia, 1995, v.p., dir. mktg. and bus. devel. The Benham Group, St. Louis, 1995-96; v.p. Chiodini Assocs., 1997-98; asst. lectr. Washington U., 1997-2000, 2001-; cons. Stifel Cap. Start Up Venture Capital Fund; ops. mgr., generations cons. Stifel Capco Venture Capital, 1998; dir. mktg. sys. The Maiman Co., 1998-99; dir. edn. program mgmt. The Integral Group, Atlanta, 1999-2001; vis. Alpha Rho Chi lectr. Pa. State U., 1983; vis. lectr. Washington U. Lindenwood Coll., 1987, Wentworth Inst., Boston, Am. Assn. Cost Engrs., So. Fla., 1994, with U. Houston, 2002; mem. panel Assn. Univ. Architects Conv., 1983; v.p. program mgmt. and ednl. facilities Kennedy Assoc. Inc.; participant K-12 Nat. Summit, San Diego, 2002; URS Corp. dep. project mgmt. Phila. Sch. Improvement Team, 2003-04; pro constrn. svcs. coord.-design/build Joseph, Jingoli and Sons; spkr. in field. Contbr. Planning Guide for Maintaining Facilities, U.S. Dept. Edn. Project bus. cons. Jr. Achievement, 1982-85, 2001-2003; mem. cluster com., advisor Explorer Program, 1982-85; mem. Design Build Inst. Am., 1998—, splty. contractor task force chmn., 2000-2002; presenter So. Ill. Econ. Devel. Conf., 1998. Recipient 5 brochure and graphic awards Nat. Assn. Indsl. Artists, 1973; 1st award Profl. Builder/Am. Plywood Assn., 1974; Honor award, 2 articles Balt. chpt. AIA, 1974; Better Homes and Gardens award Sensible Growth, Nat. Assn. Home Builders, 1975; winner Ridgely's Delight Competition, Balt., 1976. Mem. ASCD, BBC Credit Union (bd. dirs. 1983-85), AACE (conv. spkr. So. Fla. sect. 1994), Vitruvius Alumni Assn., Pa. State Alumni Assn., BOCA, NFPA, AIA, Constrn. Specifications Inst., Am. Assn. Sch. Adminstrs. (nat. coun., panel moderator 1994), Coun. Ednl. Facilities Planners, Assn. Sch. Bus. Ofcls. (Mehlville Mo. schs. program mgmt. 1992-94, Chelsea, Mass. 1993-95, Orange County, Fla. 1994-95, Macon, Ga. 1999-2000, Atlantic City, N.J. 2000-2001), Tex. Women's U., Dallas, 2002, Tex. So. U., Houston, 2002,South St. Louis,Ill. Mixed Fin. Housing Devel. Program, 2003, Alpha Rho Chi (nat. treas. 1980-82, dir. nat. found. treas. 1989-97), Optimists Internat. Office: Bldg 4 Ste 216 3131 Princeton Pike Lawrenceville NJ 08648 Office Phone: 609-896-3111. Business E-Mail: cweaver@jingoli.com.

WEAVER, CHRISTOPHER E. naval officer; BS, U.S. Naval Acad., 1971; MPA, George Washington U.; Disting. Grad., Indsl. Coll. of Armed Forces. Commd. ensign USN, 1971, advanced through ranks to rear adm.; various assignments to comdg. officer USS Spruance (DD 963), U.S. Naval Sta., Norfolk, Va.; Commandant Naval Dist., Washington; comdr. Navy Installations Command USN, Washington. Home: 712 Warrington Ave SE Washington DC 20003 Office: Comdr Navy Installations Command CP5 Ste 480 2000 Navy Pentagon Washington DC 20350-2000

WEAVER, CLIFFORD LEE, retired lawyer, winery owner; b. Chgo., Mar. 11, 1945; s. Thomas E. and Thera A. (Ramey) Cash; m. Donna Rae Florence, Aug. 20, 1966; 1 child, Megan R. AB with honors, U. Chgo., 1966, JD with honors, 1969. Bar: Ill. 1969, U.S. Dist. Ct. (no. dist.) Ill. 1969, U.S. Ct. Appeals (7th cir.) 1969, U.S. Supreme Ct. 1975. Sr. clk. U.S. Ct. Appeals, Chgo., 1969-71; assoc. Ross & Hardies, Chgo., 1971-75, ptnr., 1976-83, Burke, Weaver & Prell, Chgo., 1983-99, mng. ptnr., 1990-99; owner, operator Azienda Agricola Le Miccine vineyard and winery, 1996—. Gen. counsel N.W. Water Commn., 1978—99, DuPage Water Commn., DuPage County, Ill., 1987—99, Lake County (Ill.) Forest Preserve, 1991—99; village atty. Village of Bannockburn, Ill., 1977—99, Village of Northbrook, 1977—99, Village of Glencoe, Ill., 1978—99, Village of Hinsdale, Ill., 1985—99, Village of Libertyville, Ill., 1990—99. Co-author: Special Districts in Illinois, 1977, City Zoning, 1979; contbr. numerous articles to profl. jours. Trustee Kenilworth (Ill.) Libr. Dist., 1987-89; mem. Kenilworth Zoning Bd., 1988—. Mem.: ABA, Order of Coif, Phi Beta Kappa. Republican. Home: 144 Woodstock Ave Kenilworth IL 60043-1262

WEAVER, CONSTANCE, communications executive; Various mgmt. positions in product mgmt., mktg. and corp. planning McGraw Hill; exec. dir. unit Bus. Week; leadership positions with responsibility for investor rels. and fin. comms. Microsoft Corp., MCI Comms.; v.p. investor rels. AT&T Corp., Bedminster, NJ, 1996—2002, exec. v.p. pub. rels., mktg. comms. and brand, 2002—. Bd. dirs. Applied Digital Solutions, Inc.; former dir. PrimarkCorp.; bd. dirs. New Jersey Performing Arts Ctr., Somerset Hills YMCA, Atlanta Symphony Orch., Nat. Coun. La Raza; grant com. mem. Monterey Peninsula Found.; corp. rep. Ford's Theatre Bd. Gov's., Wash., DC. Bd. dirs. Somerset Hills YMCA, N.J. Performing Arts Ctr. Mem.: Nat. Investor Rels. Inst. (former dir.), NJ300, Fin. Women's Assn., Arthur W. Page Soc., The Wisemen. Office: AT&T Corp 1 AT&T Way Bedminster NJ 07921

WEAVER, DAVID HUGH, journalism educator, communications researcher; b. Hammond, Ind., Dec. 23, 1946; s. David W. and Josephine L. Weaver; m. Gail Shriver, June 28, 1969; children: Quinn David, Lesley Jo. BA, Ind. U., Bloomington, 1968, MA, 1969; PhD, U. N.C., 1974. Copy editor The Post-Tribune, Gary, Ind., 1968; wire editor, reporter The Courier-Tribune, Bloomington, Ind., 1968; wire editor The Chapel Hill Newspaper, N.C., 1973; asst. prof. journalism Ind. U., Bloomington, 1974-78, assoc. prof., 1978-83, prof., 1983-88, Roy W. Howard prof., 1988—. Author: Videotex Journalism, 1983; co-author: Newsroom Guide to Polls and Surveys, 1980, 90, Media Agenda-Setting, 1981, The American Journalist, 1986 (award Soc. Profl. Journalists 1987), 2d edit., 1991, The Formation of Campaign Agendas, 1991, Contemporary Public Opinion, 1991, The American Journalist in the 1990's, 1996 (award Soc. Profl. Journalists 1997); co-editor: Communication and Democracy, 1997; editor: The Global Journalist, 1998. Lt. U.S. Army, 1969-71. Fellow Midwest Pub. Opinion Rsch. (pres. 1986-87), Internat. Comm. Assn.; mem. Assn. for Edn. in Journalism and Mass Comm. (pres. 1987-88, Krieghbaum award 1983), Soc. Prof. Journalists. Avocations: guitar, music. Office: Ind U Sch Journalism Ernie Pyle Hall Bloomington IN 47405-7108

WEAVER, DELBERT ALLEN, lawyer; b. Shoshone, Idaho, May 28, 1931; s. Arlo Irving and Kate Rosamond (McCarter) W.; m. Jeanne Carol Alford, June 1959; children: Tobin Elizabeth, Michael Andrew, Matthew Stewart, Edward Malcolm. BA, U. Oreg., 1953, LLB, 1956. Bar: Oreg. 1956, U.S. Dist. Ct. Oreg. 1956, U.S. Ct. Appeals (9th cir.) 1968. Ptnr. Weaver & Oram, Eugene, Oreg., 1956-59; dep. atty. City of Portland, Oreg., 1959-68; assoc. Winfree, Latourette, Murphy, et al., Portland, 1968-71; stockbroker Dupont Glore Forgan, Portland, 1971-73; securities examiner corp. div. State of Oreg., Salem, 1973-75, dep. commr. corp. div., 1975-80; pvt. practice Portland, 1980-87; counsel Schwabe, Williamson & Wyatt, Portland, 1987-90, sr. ptnr., 1991-96; pvt. practice Portland, 1996-2000; counsel Dunn, Carney, Portland, 2000—. Office: Ste 1500 851 SW 6th Ave Portland OR 97204-1001 E-mail: daw@dunn-carney.com.

WEAVER, DIANNE JAY, lawyer; b. Kansas City, Mo., June 28, 1944; d. Thomas G. and Anna Jeanette Jay; m. Benjamin J. Weaver, Sept. 16, 1970; children: Jay, Jennifer, Scott, Elizabeth. BS, U. Kans., 1965; JD, Ind. U., 1970. Bar: Ind., Fla., Colo.; bd. cert. trial lawyer. Former ptnr. Weaver & Weaver, P.A., Ft. Lauderdale, Fla.; former of counsel Krupnick Campbell Malone Roselli Buser Slama & Hancock P.A., Ft. Lauderdale; ptnr. Harrell & Johnson, P.A., Jacksonville, 2002—. Speaker in field. Contbr. articles to profl. jours. Trustee Civil Justice Found.; bd. dirs. Trial Lawyers for Pub. Justice; chmn. publicity com. Civil Justice Found. Fellow Roscoe Pound Found. (life); mem. ATLA (bd. govs., sec.), Acad. Fla. Trial Lawyers (bd. dirs.), So. Trial Lawyers Assn. (bd. govs.), Fla. Bar Assn. (chair trial advocacy com.),. Fed. Bar Assn., Broward County Women Lawyers Assn. (founding pres.). Office: Harrell & Johnson PA 4735 Sunbeam Rd Jacksonville FL 32257*

WEAVER, DONNA L. engraver; Grad. in Fine Arts, Art Acad. Cin., 1966. Sculptor Kenner Toys, 1966—80; sculptor, engraver US Mint, 2000—. Avocation: bas-relief. Office: 801 9th St NW Washington DC 20220

WEAVER, ELIZABETH A. state supreme court justice; b. New Orleans; d. Louis and Mary Weaver. BA, Newcomb Coll.; JD, Tulane U. Elem. tchr. Glen Lake Cmty. Sch., Maple City, Mich.; French tchr. Leelanau Sch., Glen Arbor, Mich.; pvt. practice Glen Arbor, Mich.; law clk. Civil Dist. Ct., New Orleans; atty. Coleman, Dutrey & Thomson, New Orleans; atty., title specialist Chevron Oil Co., New Orleans; probate and juvenile judge Leelanau County, Mich., 1975—86; judge Mich. Ct. of Appeals, 1987—94; justice Mich. Supreme Ct., Lansing, 1995—. Chief justice Mich. Supreme Ct., 1999—2000; instr. edn. dept. Ctr. Mich. U.; mem. Mich. Com. on Juvenile Justice, Nat. Conv. State Adv. Groups on Juvenile Justice for U.S.; chair Gov.'s Task Force on Children's Justice, Trial Ct. Assessment Commn., Office Juvenile Justice and Delinquency Prevention; jud. adv. bd. mem. Law and Orgnl. Econs. Ctr. U. Kans.; treas. Children's Charter of Cts. of Mich. Chairperson Western Mich. U. CLE Adv. Bd.; mem. steering com. Grand Traverse/Leelanau Commn. on Youth; mem. Glen Arbor Twp. Zoning Bd.; mem. charter arts north Leelanau County; mem. citizen's adv. coun. Arnell Engstrom Children's Ctr.; mem. cmty. adv. com. Pathfinder Sch. Treaty Law Demonstration Project; active Grand Traverse/Leelanau Mental Health Found. Named Jurist of Yr., Police Officers Assn. of Mich.; named one of five Outstanding Young Women in Mich., Mich. Jaycees; recipient Eastern award, Warren Easton Hall of Fame, Lifetime Dedication to Children award, Mich. Champions in Childhood Injury Prevention, 2000, Recognition award for outstanding svc. to Mich. children and families, Gov. Engler and Family Independence Agy., 2000, Profls. award, Mich. Assn. Drug Cts., 2002, Mary S. Coleman award, Ctr. for Civic Edn. Through Law, 2002. Fellow: Mich. State Bar Found.; mem.: ABA, Antrim County Bar Assn., Leelanau County Bar Assn., Grand Traverse County Bar Assn., La. Bar Assn., Nat. Coun. Juvenile and Family Judges, Mich. Bar Assn. (chair CLE adv. bd., chair crime prevention ctr., chair juvenile law com.), Delta Kappa Gamma (hon.). Office: Mich Supreme Ct 3300 Grandview Plz 10850 E Traverse Hwy Traverse City MI 49684-1364

WEAVER, FRANKLIN THOMAS, retired newspaper executive; b. Johnstown, N.Y., Oct. 11, 1932; s. Edwin K. and Bertha J. (Wendt) W.; children: Thomas, James, Michael, David, Tammy, Kelly, Anna; m. Joyce W. Phelps, Oct. 23, 1991. BA with high honors in Journalism, Mich. State U., 1954. Advt. sales rep. Grand Rapids Press, Mich., 1955-64; controller Muskegon (Mich.) Chronicle, 1964-66; mgr. Bay City (Mich.) Times, 1966-73, Jackson (Mich.) Citizen Patriot, 1973-84, pub., 1984—99; ret. Mem.: Mich. Press Assn. (pres. 1991), Newspapers Assn. Am., Greater Jackson C. of C., Ella Sharp Mus. (pres. 1995—96), Jackson Country Club.

WEAVER, GAIL ELAINE, religious organization administrator, tax specialist, consultant; b. Detroit, July 20, 1954; d. Columbus and Mable Weaver. AA in Acctg., Jimmy Swaggart Bible Coll., 1987; BA in Religious Edn., Cornerstone Theol. Sem., 1990; D (hon.), Urban Bible Inst., 1996. Cert. tax cons., H & R Block, 1989; ordained Nat. Assn. Women Ministry, Detroit, 1990. CEO, prin. Ameri-Tax, 1987—; pres. Nat. Assn. Women Ministry, Detroit, 1990—. Author: My Praise To Thee, Eschewance Of Evil, Psalms. 1981, Lady Weaver, (children books) My House, Mister Sun, Father's Riches; composer: (songs) Saturday Afternoon. Independent. Achievements include design of Christian American Flag. Avocations: travel, bowling, piano, writing. Personal E-mail: weav3g@aol.com.

WEAVER, HOWARD C. newspaper executive; b. Anchorage, Oct. 15, 1950; s. Howard Gilbert and Lurlene Eloise (Gamble) W.; m. Alice Laprele Gauchay, July 16, 1970 (div. 1974); m. Barbara Lynn Hodgin, Sept. 16, 1978. BA Johns Hopkins U., 1972, MPhil Cambridge U., 1993. Reporter, staff writer Anchorage Daily News, 1972—76, columnist, 1979—80, mng. editor, 1980—83, editor, 1983—95; editor, owner Alaska Advocate, 1976—79; asst. to pres. McClatchy Newspapers, 1995—97, editor of editl. pages, 1997—2001; v.p. news The McClatchy Co., 2001—. Internat. co-chair Northern News Svc., 1989—94; disting. lectr. journalism U. Alaska, Fairbanks, 1991. Pulitzer Prize juror, 1988, 1989, 1994, 1995, 2002; bd. visitors John S. Knight Fellowship Stanford U.; Pulitzer Prize juror, 2003. Recipient Pulitzer prize, 1976, 1989, Headliner award, Press Club of Atlantic City, 1976, 1989, Gold medal, Investigative Reporters and Editors, 1989, Pub. Svc. award, AP Mng. Editor's Assn., 1976, 1989. Mem.: Investigative Reporters and Editors, Am. Soc. Newspaper Editors, Upper Yukon River Press Club (pres. 1972), Alaska Press Club (bd. dirs. 1972—84), Sigma Delta Chi (Nat. award 1989). Avocations: ice hockey, foreign travel, opera .

WEAVER, JACQUELYN KUNKEL IVEY, artist, educator; b. Richmond, Ky., Mar. 14, 1931; d. Marion David and Margaret Tabitha (Brandenburg) Kunkel; m. George Thomas IveySr., 1951 (dec. 1989); children: George Thomas Ivey Jr., David Richard Ivey; m. Harrell Fuller Weaver, 1991. BFA, Wesleyan Coll., 1987. Owner J. K. Ivey Art, Macon, Ga., 1974-91, J.K. Ivey Bookkeeping and Tax Svc., Macon, Ga., 1976-84, Ivey-Weaver Art Studio, Macon, 1991—. Tchr. drawing, painting and sculpture, 1991—. Exhibitions include Stofko-Dixon Fine Arts, Bolingbroke, Ga., 1996—2001, Self Family Art Ctr., Hilton Head Island, SC, 2001, Mus. Arts and Scis., Macon, 2002, Brazier Art Gallery, Richmond, Va., 2002, Gallery 51, Forsyth, Ga., 2003—04, Roundtree Gallery, Seaside, Fla., 2003—04, Monroe County Arts Alliance, Forsyth, 2004, Richard Schmid Fine Art, Richard Schmid Fine Art Aucton, Bellvue, Colo., 2004. Bd. dirs., treas. Mid. Ga. Art Assn., Macon, 1981-84, 92, publicity chmn., 1988-89, chmn. nominating com., 1997, mem. fin. com., 1998-99, audit com., 1998. Mem.: Monroe County Arts Alliance, Hilton Head Island Art League, Oil Painters of Am., Portrait Painters Am., Inc., Mid. Ga. Art Assn., Catherine Lorillard Wolf Art Club, Mus. Arts and Scis., Wesleyan Coll. Alumnae Assn., Nat. Mus. Women in Arts (charter). Presbyterian. Avocations: ballroom dancing, reading, walking, music. Office: Ivey-Weaver Art Studio 6183 Hwy 87 Macon GA 31210 Office Phone: 478-477-1385. Office Fax: 478-744-0983. Business E-Mail: jweav550@bellsouth.net.

WEAVER, JANET S. newspaper editor; m. Mark Weaver; children: Sam, Rachel. B in journalism, U. Mo., 1984. Reporter, asst. city editor Stuart (Fla.) News, 1986—89; from reporter to dep. mng. editor/features and sports Virginian-Pilot, Norfolk, Va., 1989—94; mng. editor The Wichita (Kans.) Eagle, 1994—97, Sarasota (Fla.) Herald-Tribune, 1997—99, exec. editor, 1999—2003; dean faculty Poynter Inst., St. Petersburg, Fla., 2003—04; mng. editor The Tampa Tribune, Fla., 2004—. Mem.: Am. Soc. Newspaper Editors (bd. dirs.). Office: Tampa Tribune 202 S Parker St Tampa FL 33606*

WEAVER, JOHN BORLAND, organist, composer; b. Palmerton, Pa., Apr. 27, 1937; s. David Williams and Bertha Brownlee (Borl) W.; m. Marianne Carol Gruhn, Apr. 30, 1942; children: Jonathan Kirk, Kirianne Elizabeth. Diploma, Curtis Inst. Music, Phila., 1959; M in Sacred Music, Union Theol. Sem., 1968; MusD (hon.), Westminster Coll., 1995, MusD (hon.), 1995, Curtis Inst. Music, 2003. Head organ dept. Curtis Inst. Music, 1972—2003; chmn. organ dept. Manhattan Sch. Music, 1983-84, Juilliard Sch. Music, N.Y.C., 1986—2004. Mem. faculty Westminister Choir Coll., Princeton, N.J., 1970-72, Union Theol. Sem. Sch. Sacred Music, 1970-73 Organist, choirmaster, Holy Trinity Lutheran Ch., N.Y.C., 1959-70, dir. music, Madison Ave. Presbyn. Ch., N.Y.C., 1970—, organist, Temple Beth-El, Manhattan Beach, N.Y., 1970-88; solo organ recitalist, U.S., Can., Western Europe, U.K., Brazil; composer: Psalm 100, 1958, Toccatafor Organ, 1959, Epiphany Alleluias, 1967, Rhapsody for Flute and Organ, 1968, Good Christian Men, Rejoice, 1978, Introit for Pentecost, Fantasia for Organ, Passacaglia on a Theme by Dunstable, all 1981, The Joyful Feast, 1988, Psalm 46, 1989, Dialogues for Flute and Organ, 1991, Prayer for Transfiguration Day, 1991, Prelude and Fugue in E Minor, 1994, Prayer From Psalm 139, 1995, Variations on Three Hymn Tunes, 1997, Restore Us, O Lord of Hosts, 1995; contbr. articles to jours. including Reformed Liturgy and Music. Served with AUS, 1961-63. Decorated Army Commendation medal; recipient Disting. Svc. in the Field of Music award Peabody chpt. Johns Hopkins U., 1989. Mem. N.Am. Acad. Liturgy, Am. Guild Organists, Presbyn. Assn. Musicians (pres. 1984-86). Clubs: St. Wilfrid (N.Y.C.). Presbyterian. Address: 921 Madison Ave New York NY 10021-3508 *By hard work and good fortune I have been able to do that which I decided, at age ten, to do with my life.*

WEAVER, JOHN H, research scientist, educator; BS, U. Mo., 1967; PhD, Iowa State U., 1972. Post doctoral fellow U. of Mo., 1973; rsch. assoc. U. of Wis., 1974—75; asst. scientist U. Wis., 1975—77; sci. assoc. Ames Lab., U.S. Dept. of Energy, Iowa, 1975—85; assoc. scientist U.of Wis., 1977—82; prof. U. of Minn., Dept. of Chem. Engring. and Materials Sci., 1982—99; prof. and head U. of Ill., Dept. of Sci. and Engring., 2000—. Adj. prof. U. Wis., 1981—82; faculty assoc. Argonne Nat. Lab., Ill., 1982—87; dir. grad. studies for materials science U. of Minn., 1982—87; faculty assoc. Argonne Nat. Lab., Ill., 1982—87; lectr. U. of Brasilia, Internat. Ctr. for Condensed Matter Physics; mem. rev. panel Dept. of Energy, 1993—; lectr., summer sch. Universidad Complutense de Madrid, 1994; u. prof. Tohoku U., Inst. for Materials Rsch., Japan, 1994; royal soc. Kan Tong Po prof. U. of Hong Kong, 1995; vis. scientist Fritz-Haber Inst. der Max Planck-Gesellschaft, Berlin, 1995; dir. grad. studies for materials science U. of Minn., 1997—99; judge Nottingham prize, 2000—, R&D 100 awards, 2000; mem. internat. adv. com. European Conf. on Surface Sci., 2001—; mem. internat. adv. bd. 6th Internat. Conf. on Atomically Controlled Surfaces, Interfaces and Nanostructures, 2000—. Reviewer, referee and arbiter Sci., Nature, Physics Today, Physics Reviews, Physics Reviews Letters, Jour. of Vacuum Sci. and Tech., Surface Sci., Jour. of Applied Physics, Applied Physics Letters, Jour. of Am. Chem. Soc., et. al., 1974—, mem. editl. bd. Jour. of Vacuum Science and Tech., 1989—93, Jour. of Materials Rsch., 1989—92, Chem. of Materials, 1991—95, Jour. of Electron Spectroscopy and Related Phenomena, 1991—2000, Fullerence Science and Tech., 1992—, Surface Science Reports, 1998—, Surface Rev. and Letters, 1998—, Royal Soc. of Chem. Electronic Jour. PhysChemComm, 1999—, R&D mag., 2000—, Surface Science, 2000—, mem. editl. adv. bd. CRC Book Series Chem. and Physics of Surfaces and Interfaces, 1993—, assoc. editor Nanostructured Materials, 1992—. Nominee outstanding rsch. award for studies of electronic interactions of hydrogen in metals, U.S. Dept. Energy, 1980; recipient G.J. Lapeyre award for synchotron radiation rsch. per Ardua ad Bremsstrahlung, 1982, spl. creativity award, Nat. Sci. Found., 1991—92, Nat. Science Found., 1995—96, Alexander von Humboldt sr. rsch. award, Alexander von Humboldt Found., 1995, scientist of the yr., R&D mag., 1997, disting. lectr., Am. Vacuum Soc., 1998—, Medard W. Welch award, 1999, 19th Peter. G. Winchell lectr., Purdue U., 2000. Fellow: Am. Physical Soc., Am. Vacuum Soc. (bd. dirs. 1990—91); mem.: Nat. Sci. Found. Office: Dept of Materials Sciences and Engring U of Ill at Urbana-Champaign 1304 W Green St Urbana IL 61801

WEAVER, KAREN LYNN, writer, performing arts educator, actress, poet; b. Boston, Mass., Mar. 9, 1970; d. Alfred George and Eileen Francis Weaver. Post Baccalaureate-Secondary English & Edn., Framingham State Coll., Mass., 1998; BS, Emerson Coll., Boston, 1991. Cert. tchr., Secondary English Fla. and Mass. Personal asst. to exec. prodr. Vin Di Bona Prod., Los Angeles, 1992; exec. asst. to v.p. Smith Barney, Beverly Hills, 1993—94; drama tchr., head of drama dept. Sarasota HS, 1998—2000, English tchr., 9th grade, 1998—2000; sr. casting agent Parker Agy., Sarasota, 2000—02; creator/head writer animated TV series, Heidi's World, Los Angeles, 2003—. Post-prod. TV movie, The Movie Break, Los Angeles, 2003; theater dir. Sarasota HS, 1998—2000, tutor, SAT prep and English, 1998—2000, student adv. bd., 1998—2000; liason Sarasota Film Festival, 2000—01. Author: (poem) Inner Darkness, 2004 (Editor's Choice Award, 2004), Shattered, 2004. Vol. AIDS Hospice for Men, Los Angeles, 1992—93; dir. of dramatic presentation United Nations Dev. Fund, Sarasota, 1998. Recipient Internat. Poet of Merit, Internat. Soc. of Poets, 2004, Outstanding Achievement in Poetry Silver Award/Cup, 2004. Mem.: Internat. Soc. of Poets (hon.), Alpha Upsilon Alpha, Kappa Delta Pi. Avocations: yoga, walking, hiking.

WEAVER, KARL E. psychiatrist; b. Lakewood, Ohio, July 1, 1950; m. Christine R. Weaver. BA in Psychology, Haverford (Pa.) Coll., 1972; MD, Case Western Res. U., 1978. Bd. cert., cert. in forensic psychiatry Am. Bd. Psychiatry and Neurology; lic. physician Calif. Flexible intern Mt. Sinai Hosp., Cleve., 1978-79; psychiatry resident Univ. Hosps. of Cleve., 1979-82; pvt. practice Cleve., 1982-94; staff psychiatrist Calif. Men's Colony, San Luis Obispo, 1994-95, sr. psychiatrist, supr., 1995, chief psychiatrist, 1995—. Chmn. dept. psychiatry St. John & St. John Westshore Hosps., Cleve., 1985-90, Fairview Gen. Hosp., Cleve., 1992-94; pres., bd. dirs. St. John & St. John Westshore Profl. Corp., 1989-90; contract psychiatrist San Luis Obispo County Mental Health, 1997—, TeleCare, Santa Maria, Calif., 1998—. Address: PO Box 12826 San Luis Obispo CA 93406-2826 Office: PO Box 8101 San Luis Obispo CA 93403-8101 E-mail: karlweaver@msn.com.

WEAVER, KENNETH NEWCOMER, geologist, state official; b. Lancaster, Pa., Jan. 16, 1927; s. A. Ross and Cora (Newcomer) W.; m. Mary Elizabeth Hoover, Sept. 9, 1950; children: Wendy Elaine, Matthew Owen. BS, Franklin and Marshall Coll., 1950; MA, Johns Hopkins U., 1952, PhD, 1954. Instr. geology Johns Hopkins, 1953- 54; ops. analyst Ops. Rsch. Office, Washington, 1954-56; chief geologist, then mgr. geology and quarry dept. Medusa Portland Cement Co., Wampum, Pa., 1956-63; dir., state geologist Md. Geol. Survey, Balt., 1963-92; chmn. Md. Land Reclamation Com., 1978-92. Gov.'s rep. Interstate Oil Compact Commn., Interstate Mining Compact Commn.; mem. outer shelf adv. com. U.S. Dept. Interior; chmn. Md. Topographic Mapping Com.; mem. com. on surface mining and reclamation NAS, 1978, vice chmn. com. on disposal of excess spoil, 1980-81, mem. com. on geologic mapping, 1983, liaison mem. bd. earth scis., 1982-88, mem. com. on water resources rsch., 1989-92, chmn. com. on abandoned minelands rsch. priorities, 1987; mem. subcom. on mgmt. of maj. underground constrn. projects Nat. Acad. Engring.; mem. Md. Commn. on Artistic Property, 1988-92. With U.S. Maritime Svc., 1944—46, with AUS, 1954—56. Recipient John Wesley Powell award USGS, 1994; named hdqr. bldg. The Kenneth N. Weaver Bldg. Md. Geol. Survey, 1994. Fellow Geol. Soc. Am. (sec. N.E. sect. 1985-2001), AAAS (sr.); mem. Assn. Am. Petroleum Geologists (Ea. sect., George V. Cohee Pub. Svc. award 1991), Am. Inst. Mining Engrs., Am. Inst. Profl. Geologists (editor 1983-84, Martin Van Couvering Meml. award 1992), Am. Geol. Inst. (governing bd. 1973, exec. com. 1989-90, medal in memory of Ian Campbell 2001), Am. Water Rsch. Assn., Geol. Soc. Washington, Assn. Am. State Geologists (pres. 1973, hon. mem. 1992), Johns Hopkins Club (Balt.). Republican. Presbyterian (elder). Home: 14002 Jarrettsville Pike Phoenix MD 21131-1409 Office: Md Geol Survey 2300 St Paul St Baltimore MD 21218-5210 Office Phone: 410-554-5532. E-mail: kweaver438@aol.com.

WEAVER, KITTY DUNLAP, author; b. Frankfort, Ky., Sept. 24, 1910; d. Arch Robertson and Rebecca (Johnson) Dunlap; m. Henry Byrne Weaver, June 29, 1933. Student, Sorbonne, Paris, summer 1930; AB, William and Mary Coll., 1932; MA, George Washington U., 1933; BS, U. Md., 1947; postgrad., Georgetown U., U. Pa., George Washington U., 1964-67, Moscow U., 1983; studied with Alfred Adler, Vienna, 1932. Jr. H.S. tchr., 1931-32; poultry farmer, 1947-55; author, 1970—. Author: Lenin's Grandchildren, 1971, Russia's Future, 1981, Bushels of Rubles, 1992. Mem. Aldie Hort. Soc., Chevy Chase (Md.) Club, Met. Club (Washington), Garden Club Am., Fauquier Loudoun Garden Club. Home: 40820 John Mosby Hwy Aldie VA 20105-2820

WEAVER, LEAH ANN, journalist, speech writer; b. Galion, Ohio, May 4, 1958; d. William Hiram and Virginia Louise (Reif) Weaver; m. Charles Lamont Hall, Jr., Apr. 14, 1990. BA, Malone Coll., Canton, Ohio, 1980; MA, Ohio State U., 1989. Program coord. editorial projects Ohio State U. Office of the Pres., Columbus, 1989-92, editorial coord., 1992-96, editor, 1996-99; copywriter Resource Marketing, Columbus, 1999-2001, Gerbig, Snell & Weisheimer Advt., Inc., Columbus, 2001; dir. comms Big Lots, Inc., 2001—. English tutor Creative Living, Columbus, 1987, 88. Author: (plays) Wilber and Wife, 1989, Dora Dodd, 1991; contbg. writer Univ. Comms., Columbus, 1993—; spl. assignment reporter The Lantern, Columbus, 1987-88; freelance scriptwriter Ctr. for Teaching Excellence, Columbus, 1989; contbr. articles to jours. Mem. Soc. Profl. Journalists, N.Y. Dramatists Guild (playwright and assoc. mem.), Authors League Am., League Am. Comm. Profls., Kappa Tau Alpha, Phi Kappa Phi. Avocations: playwrighting, freelance feature writing. E-mail: lweaver@biglots.com.

WEAVER, LINDA MARIE, pharmacist, education educator; d. John William and Lorraine Marie Miller; m. Daniel Jacob Weaver. BA in Edn. and Spanish, Western Mich. U., 1974, BS in Pharmacy, Ferris State U., 1984, PharmD, Midwestern U., Chgo. Coll. of Pharmacy, 2000. Registered Pharmacist Mich., 1984. Ambulatory pharmacist Perry Drugs, Midland, Mich., 1984—87, Revco Drugs, Tucson, 1987—89, Walgreens Drug, Tucson, 1989—93; compliance officer Ariz. State Bd. of Pharmacy, Phoenix, 1993—99; clin. hosp. pharmacist John C. Lincoln Hosp., Phoenix, 1999—2001; med. sci. liaison Wyeth Pharmaceuticals, Scottsdale, 2001—03; med. liaison Abbott Labs., Scottsdale, 2003—04, clin. sci. mgr., 2004—. Adj. faculty mem. Midwestern U. Coll. of Pharmacy, Glendale, Ariz.; instr. Rio Salado C.C., Phoenix, 1997—98, Ariz. Pharmacy Assn., 1998—2000; adv. bd. mem. SCP Comm., Inc., Phoenix, 2001—01. Vol. Am. Diabetes Assn., Scottsdale, 1994—2003, Am. Heart Assn., Scottsdale, 1994—2003, Am. Cancer Assn., Scottsdale, 1994—2003. Recipient Golden Key Nat. Honor Soc., Mich. State U., 1981, Rho Chi Honor Soc., Midwestern U., 2000. Mem.: Am. Soc. of Health Sys. Pharmacists (licentiate), Am. Colleges of Clin. Pharmacists (licentiate), Am. Pharmacists Assn. (licentiate; del. 2001—03), Ariz. Pharmacy Assn. (licentiate; co-chair profl. affairs com. 1999—2000, maricopa rep. 2001—02, 2nd v.p. 2002—03, cert. of appreciation for outstanding svc. to Ariz. pharmacy assn. 2000, exec. bd. mem. award 2003). Avocations: scuba diving, cooking, jazz, travel, wine tasting. Home: 6120 E Gold Dust Ave Scottsdale AZ 85253 Office: Abbott Laboratories 6120 E Gold Dust Ave Scottsdale AZ 85253 Office Phone: 480-951-0366. Personal E-mail: lwpharmd@juno.com.

WEAVER, LYNN EDWARD, academic administrator, consultant, editor; b. St. Louis, Jan. 12, 1930; s. Lienous E. and Estelle F. (Laspe) W.; m. JoAnn D., 1951 (div. 1981); children: Terry Sollenberger, Gwen, Bart, Stephen, Wes; m. Anita G. Gomez, Oct. 27, 1983. BSEE, U. Mo., 1951; MSEE, So. Meth. U., 1955; PhD, Purdue U., 1958. Devel. engr. McDonnell Aircraft, St. Louis, 1952-53; aerophysics engr. Convair Corp., Ft. Worth, 1953-55; instr. elec. engring. Purdue U., Lafayette, Ind., 1955-58; assoc. prof., then prof., dept. head U. Ariz., Tucson, 1959-69; assoc. dean coll. engring. U. Okla., Norman, 1969-70; exec. asst. to pres. Argonne Univs., Chgo., 1970-72; dir. sch. nuclear engring. and health physics Ga. Inst. Tech., 1972-82; dean engring., disting. prof. Auburn (Ala.) U., 1982-87; pres. Fla. Inst. Tech., Melbourne, 1987—2002, pres. emeritus, prof. elec. engring., 2002—. Cons. Ga. Power; bd. dirs. Oak Ridge Associated Univs., 1984-87, DBA Systems, Inc., Melbourne, Fla.; chmn. pub. affairs coun. Am. Assn. Engring. Soc., Washington, 1984-87; bd. advisors Ctr. for Sci., Tech. & Media, Washington; chmn. Ind. Colls. and Univs. of Fla., 1998. Author: (textbook) Reactor Dynamics & Control, State Space Techniques, 1968; exec. editor Annals of Nuclear Energy; contbr. numerous articles to tech. jours. U.S. rep. World Fedn., Engring. Orgn. Energy Com., 1981-86. Served to lt. USAF, 1951-53. Recipient Mo. Honors award for disting. svc. in engring., 1996. Fellow Am. Nuclear Soc.; mem. IEEE (sr.), Am. Soc. Engring. Edn., Sigma Xi (bd. dirs. 2004). Clubs: Eau Gallie Yacht. Republican. Roman Catholic. Avocations: tennis, jogging. Office: Fla Inst Tech 150 W University Blvd Melbourne FL 32901-6975

WEAVER, MARTHA, newscaster; Degree, St. Olaf Coll., 1990. Aide to Gov. Arne Carlson State Dept. Adminstrn., Minn., 1990—94; reporter, anchor Sta. WEYI-TV, Flint, Mich., 1994—95; anchor Sta. WRTV-TV, Indpls., 1995—. Office: WRTV TV 1330 N Meridian St Indianapolis IN 46202*

WEAVER, MICHAEL GLENN, pharmacist; b. Tuscola, Ill., Sept. 11, 1955; s. Glen H. and Margaret I. (Long) W.; m. Catherine A. (Paynic), Sept. 30, 1978; children: Jennifer L., Michelle R., Gregory M. BS, St. Louis Coll. of Pharmacy, 1978; MBA, So. Ill. U., 1989. Registered pharmacist, Ill. Clin. coordinator, staff pharmacist St. Elizabeth Med. Ctr., Granite City, Ill., 1975-87; dir. pharmacy Freeport (Ill.) Meml. Hosp. (now Freeport Health Network), 1987-92, dir. pharmacy and info. systems, 1992-97, dir. info. and telecom. svcs., 1997—2002; dir. pharmacy Freeport Health Network, 2002—; dir. Ill. Bd. Pharmacy, 1995-99, AeroComputing, Inc., 2001—02. Allocations com. United Way of N.W. Ill., 2000—. Mem.: Am. Coll. Healthcare Execs., Ill. Coun. Hosp. Pharmacists (dir. ednl. affairs 1991—94), Ill. Pharm. Assn., Am. Soc. Hosp. Pharmacists, Kiwanis (bd. dirs. Lincoln-Douglas chpt. 2002—, v.p. 2003—), Delta Sigma Theta, Beta Gamma Sigma, Phi Kappa Phi. Republican. Mem. United Church of Christ. Avocations: computer, music, tennis, swimming, racquetball. Home: 1346 Carriage Hill Ln Freeport IL 61032-6168 Office: Freeport Health Network 1045 W Stephenson St Freeport IL 61032-4899

WEAVER, MICHAEL JAMES, lawyer; b. Bakersfield, Calif., Feb. 11, 1946; s. Kenneth James and Elsa Hope (Rogers) W.; m. Valerie Scott, Sept. 2, 1966; children: Christopher James, Brett Michael, Karen Ashley. AB, Calif. State U., Long Beach, 1968; JD magna cum laude, U. San Diego, 1973. Bar: Calif., 1973, U.S. Dist. Ct. (so. dist.) Calif. 1973, U.S. Ct. Appeals (9th cir.) 1975, U.S. Supreme Ct. 1977. Law clk. to chief judge U.S. Dist. Ct. (so. dist.) Calif., San Diego, 1973-75; with Latham & Watkins, San Diego. Judge pro tem San Diego Superior Ct.; master of the Bench of the Inn, Am. Inns of Ct., Louis M. Welch chpt.; lectr. Inn of Ct., San Diego, 1981—, Continuing Edn. of Bar, Calif., 1983—, Workshop for Judges U.S. Ct. Appeals (9th cir.), 1990; mem. task force on establishment of bus. cts. sys. Jud. Coun. Calif., 1996-97. Editor-in-chief: San Diego Law Rev., 1973; contbr. articles to profl. jours. Bd. dirs., pres. San Diego Kidney Found., 1985-90; bd. dirs. San Diego Aerospace Mus., 1985-97; trustee La Jolla (Calif.) Playhouse, 1990-91. lt. USNR, 1968-74. Fellow Am. Coll. Trial Lawyers; mem. San Diego Assn. Bus. Trial Lawyers (founding mem., bd. govs.), San Diego Def. Lawyers Assn. (dir.), Am. Arbitration Assn., 9th Cir. Jud. Conf. (del. 1987-90), Calif. Supreme Ct. Hist. Assn. (bd. dirs. 1998—), Safari Club Internat. (San Diego chpt.), San Diego Sportsmen's Club, Coronado Yacht Club. Republican. Presbyterian. Avocations: reading, family activities, flying, skiing. Office: Latham & Watkins 600 West Broadway Ste 1800 San Diego CA 92101-8197 Business E-Mail: mike.weaver@lw.com.

WEAVER, MOLLIE LITTLE, lawyer; b. Alma, Ga., Mar. 11; d. Alfred Ross and Annis Mae (Bowles) Little; m. Jack Delano Nelson, Sept. 12, 1953 (div. May 1970); 1 dau., Cynthia Ann; m. 2d, Hobart Ayres Weaver, June 10, 1970; stepchildren: Hobart Jr., Mary Essa, Robert. BA in History, U. Richmond, 1978; JD, Wake Forest U., 1981. Bar: N.C. 1982, Fla. 1983; Cert. profl. sec.; cert. adminstrv. mgr. Supr., Western Electric Co., Richmond, Va., 1952-75; cons., owner Cert. Mgmt. Assocs., Richmond, 1975-76; sole practice, Ft. Lauderdale, Fla., 1982-86, Emerald Isle, N.C., 1986-89, Richmond, 1989—. Author: Secretary's Reference Manual, 1973. Mem. adv. coun. to Bus. and Office Edn., Greensboro, N.C., 1970-73, adv. com. to bus. edn. Va. Commonwealth U., Richmond, 1977. Recipient Key to City of Winston-Salem, N.C., 1963; Epps award for scholarship, 1978. Mem. ABA, N.C. Bar Assn., Fla. Bar Assn., Word Processing Assn. (v.p., founder Richmond 1973-75), Adminstrv. Mgmt. Soc. (com. chmn. Richmond, 1973-75), Phi Beta Kappa, Eta Sigma Phi, Phi Alpha Theta. Republican. E-mail: legal311@aol.com. Home: 12301 Renwick Pl Glen Allen VA 23059-6959

WEAVER, PAMELA ANN, hospitality research professional; b. Little Falls, N.Y., July 7, 1947; d. Floyd Aron Weaver and Norma May (Putnam) Hoyer; m. Ken Ward McCleary, Mar. 2, 1947; children: Brian Wilson, Blake McCleary, Ryan McCleary. AA, Fulton Montgomery C.C., Amsterdam, NY, 1968; BA, SUNY, 1970; MA, U. South Fla., 1973; PhD, Mich. State U., East Lansing, 1978. Mem. math. dept. Riviera Jr. H.S., Miami, Fla., 1970-72; grad. asst. Office Med., Edn. R & D Mich. State U., East Lansing, 1973-74, grad. asst. dept. mktg., 1974-75, instr. mktg.; asst. prof. mktg., hospitality svcs. administrn. Ctrl. Mich. State U., Mt. Pleasant, 1978-79, 1982-86, chair acad. senate, 1985-86, prof. mktg., hospitality svcs. administrn., 1986-89; prof. dept. hospitality and tourism mgmt. Va. Poly. Inst. and State U., Blacksburg, 1989—. Contbr. over 100 articles to profl. jours. Mem. Coun. on Hotel, Restaurant and Instl. Edn. (John Wiley & Sons, Inc. award for Lifetime Achievement to Hospitality Industry 1994). Office: Va Poly Inst and State U Wallace Hall Blacksburg VA 24061-0429 E-mail: weaver@vt.edu.

WEAVER, PAUL DAVID, lawyer; b. Chgo., Feb. 15, 1943; s. Paul Stanley and Margaret Elizabeth (Wurster) W.; m. Carol Lynne Homan, July 1, 1978; children: Paul Tyson, Samuel Lincoln. AB, Yale U., 1965; JD, U. Mich., 1971. Bar: Mass. 1971, Ohio 1972. Mgr. west coast Big 3 Industries, Houston, 1965-68, assoc. Goodwin, Procter & Hoar, Boston, 1971-78; sec., gen. counsel Houghton Mifflin Co., Boston, 1979-88, sr. v.p., gen. counsel, 1989—. Mem. Beverly (Mass.) Hosp. Corp., 1978—; town counsel Town of Wenham, Mass., 1976—, moderator, 1987—. Mem. ABA, Mass. Bar Assn., Boston Bar Assn., Assn. Am. Pubs. (chmn. lawyers com. 1985-86), Am. Soc. Corp. Secs., Mass. City Solicitors/Town Counsels Assn., Mass. Moderators Assn., Myopia Hunt Club (Hamilton, Mass.), Yale Club (N.Y.C.), Phi Delta Phi. Avocations: antiques, skiing. Home: 30 Monument St Wenham MA 01984-1611 Office: Houghton Mifflin Co 222 Berkeley St Fl 5 Boston MA 02116-3748

WEAVER, PEGGY (MARGUERITE MCKINNIE WEAVER), plantation owner; b. Jackson, Tenn., June 7, 1925; d. Franklin Allen and Mary Alice (Caradine) McKinnie; children: Elizabeth Lynn, Thomas Jackson III, Franklin A. McKinnie. Student, U. Colo., 1943-45, Am. Acad. Dramatic Arts, 1945-46, S. Meisner's Profl. Classes, 1949, Oxford U., 1990, 91. Actress, 1946-52; mem. staff Mus. Modern Art, N.Y.C., 1949-50; woman's editor radio sta. WTJS-AM-FM, Jackson, Tenn., 1952-55; editor, radio/TV Jackson Sun Newspaper, 1952-55; columnist Bolivar (Tenn.) Bulletin-Times, 1986—2000; chmn. Ho. of Reps. of Old Line Dist., Hardeman County, Tenn., 1985-91, 94-97. Pres. Hardeman County chpt. Assn. Preservation of Tenn. Antiquities, 1991—95; charter mem. adv. bd. Tenn. Arts Commn., Nashville, 1967—74, Tenn. Performing Arts Ctr., Nashville, 1972—; chmn. trustees br. Tenn. Libr. Assn., Nashville, 1973—74; Henry County regional chmn. Opera Memphis, 1979—91; mem. nat. coun. Met. Opera, N.Y.C., 1980—92, Tenn. Bicentennial Com., Hardeman County, 1993—96; bd. sec. Memphis Brooks Mus. League, 1997—98; founder Paris-Henry County (Tenn.) Arts Coun., 1965. Mem. DAR, Nat. Soc. Colonial Dames Am. (chmn. Memphis Town com. 2002-04), Oxford Alumni Assn. N.Y., English Speaking Union (London chpt.), Crescent Club, Summit Dilettantes. Methodist. Avocations: horseback riding, travel, theater. Office: 402 Heritage Plantation Hickory Valley TN 38042 Office Phone: 731-764-6009.

WEAVER, PETER DAVID, bishop, religious organization administrator; b. Greenville, Pa., Jan. 15, 1945; s. Adolph Peter and Dorothy Selina (Barbor) W.; children: Rebecca Hope, Sarah Joy, Rachel Faith. ThD, Boston U., 1975; MDiv, Drew U., 1969; BA, W.Va. Wesleyan U., 1966. Ordained deacon and elder United Meth. Ch. Pastor Whitaker (Pa.) U. Meth. Ch., 1971-77; sr. pastor Smithfield United Ch., Pitts., 1977-88, First United Meth. Ch., Pitts., 1988-96; bishop United Meth. Ch., Phila., 1996—2004, pres. coun. of bishops, 2003—, bishop, New Eng. conference, 2004—. Adj. faculty Drew U., Madison, N.J., 1980's, Pitts. Theol. Seminary, 1990's; co-founder, pres. Bethlehem Haven, Pitts., 1981-88; chair mission divsn. Gen. Coun. on Ministries United Meth. Ch., Dayton, Ohio, 1992-96. Bd. dirs. YMCA, Pitts., 1978-88, Goodwill Industries, Pitts., 1981-93, One Voice Against Racism, Pitts., 1990-96, Vintage Inc., Pitts., 1989-96; trustee W.Va. Wesleyan Coll., Buckannon, 1980-96, Drew U., 1996—, Wesley Coll., 1996—, Lebanon Valley Coll., 1996—. Avocations: woodworking, music, water sports. Office: United Meth Ctr PO Box 820 Valley Forge PA 19482-0820*

WEAVER, PHILIP G. tire company executive; BS, Bowling Green State U.; degree advanced mgmt. internat. sr. mgr. program, Harvard Bus. Sch. Cert. CPA. Principal, sr. mgr. Ernst & Young; tire divsn. contr. Cooper Tire & Rubber, 1990—94; v.p. Cooper Tire & Rubber Co., Tire Divsn., 1994—98; v.p., CFO Cooper Tire & Rubber Co., Findlay, Ohio, 1998—. Mem.: Blanchard Valley Health Assn., Blanchard Valley Reg. Health Ctr., Am. Inst. of CPAs, Ohio Soc. of CPAs, Toledo Chpt. Fin. Exec. Inst. Office: Cooper Tire & Rubber Co 701 Lima Ave Findlay OH 45840

WEAVER, REG, National Education Association president; b. Danville, Ill. BS, Ill. State U.; MS, Roosevelt U., Chgo. Local Nat. Edn. Assoc. (NEA) pres., Harvey, Ill., 1967—71; pres. Ill Edn. Assoc., 1981—87; mem. NEA exec. com., 1989—95; vice-pres. NEA, 1996—2002, pres. Mem. exec. bd. Nat. Coun. for Accreditation of Tchr. Edn.; chair IEA Political Action Com. for Edn. (IPACE); appointed to Ill. Commn. for Improvement of Elementary and Secondary Edn., Ill. Project for Sch. Reform Adv. Coun., Ill. Literacy Coun., Task Force on At-Risk Youth; mem. Ill. State Bd. of Edn. Blue Ribbon Comm. on Improvement of Tchg. as a Profession. Named One of the Outstanding Men of America; recipient Ebony Mag. Influential Black Educators award, Ill. Edn. Assoc. Human Relations award. Mem.: Nat. Parent Tchr. Assn. (hon.). Office: NEA 1201 16th St NW Washington DC 20036

WEAVER, RICHARD L., II, writer, speaker, educator; b. Hanover, N.H., Dec. 5, 1941; s. Richard L. and Florence B. (Grow) W.; m. Andrea A. Willis; children: Richard Scott, Jacquelynn Michelle, Anthony Keith, Joanna Corinne. AB, U. Mich., 1964, MA, 1965; PhD, Ind. U., 1969. Asst. prof. U. Mass., 1968-74; assoc. prof. speech communication Bowling Green State U., 1974-79, prof., 1979-96, dir., basic speech communication course, 1974-96. Vis. prof. U. Hawaii-Manoa, 1981-82, Bond U., Queensland, Australia, 1990, St. Albans, Melbourne, Australia, 1990, Western Inst., Perth, Australia, 1990. Author: (with Saundra Hybels) Speech/Communication, 1974, 2d edit., 1979, Speech/Communication: A Reader, 1975, 2d edit., 1979, Speech/Communication: A Student Manual, 1976, 2d edit., 1979, Understanding Interpersonal Communication, 1978, 2d edit., 1981, 3d edit., 1984, 4th edit., 1987, 5th edit., 1990, 6th edit., 1993, 7th edit., 1996, (with Raymond K. Tucker, Cynthia Berryman-Fink) Research in Speech Communication, 1981, Foundations of Speech Communication: Perspectives of a Discipline, 1982, Speech Communication Skills, 1982, Understanding Public Communication, 1983, Understanding Business Communication, 1985, Understanding Speech Communication Skills, 1985, Readings in Speech Communication, 1985, (with Saundra Hybels) Communicating Effectively, 1986, 2d edit., 1989, 3d edit., 1992, 4th edit., 1995, 5th edit., 1998, 6th edit., 2001, 7th edit., 2004, Skills for Communicating Effectively, 1985, 2d edit., 1988, 3d edit., 1991, 4th edit., 1993, rev. edit., 1995, (with Howard W. Cotrell) Innovative Instructional Strategies, 1987, 2d edit., 1988, 3d edit., 1989, 4th edit., 1990, 5th edit., 1992, 6th edit., 1993, (with Curt Bechler) Listen to Win: A Guide to Effective Listening, 1994, Study Guide to Accompany Communicating Effectively, 1995, 2d edit., 1998, Essentials of Public Speaking, 1996, 2d edit., 2001. Mem. emeritus Nat. Comm. Assn., Ctrl. States Speech Assn., Ohio Speech Assn. Home and Office: 9583 Woodleigh Ct Perrysburg OH 43551-2669 E-mail: WeaverII@wcnet.org., Rich-Too@hotmail.com., Richard@Weaverworks.net.

WEAVER, ROBERT COOPER, small business owner, volunteer; b. Talladega, Alabama, Dec. 29, 1927; s. William Kiser and Roberta (Cooper) Weaver. BA, Howard Coll., 1949. Pres. Wood Weaver, Inc., Talladega, Ala., 1950—. Prodr.: (series of 53 radio programs for Talladega C.C.) Let's Do More in '54, 1954; filmed: (movie) Youth Recreation in Talladega, 1958; prodr.: (singing the Lord's Prayer) by deaf and blind children, 1983—; author hundreds of graphic Sunday sch. lessons for deaf children; dir.: (Sunday night worship svc. for deaf children), 1991—; coord. (deaf and blind students singing with voice and sign language) Talladega Super Speedway and Nat. TV program, The Deaf Shall Hear, —, designed (USS Talladega Monument) Talladega County Courthouse, 2002. Organized world's first Fellowship of Christian Athletics Chpt. for the Deaf Ala. Sch. for the Deaf, 1981; organizer City Basketball League, Talladega, Ala., 1953; chmn. Turkey Festival Parade, Talladega, 1953; organizer $1 season tickets, increasing attendance by thousands per season Municipal Pool, Talladega, Ala., 1954; organizer Kiwi Baseball League, Talladega, Ala., 1960, Athletic Club Basketball League, Talladega, Ala., 1961, Ala. Sch. for the Deaf Boys Basketball League, 1970; mem. libr. bd., Talladega, Ala., 1972—75; organizer Flag Tag Football League, Talladega, Ala.; organized Ala. State Table Tennis Tournament; organized Sunday morning devotional programs AIDB Lunchroom workers, Talladega, Ala.; organizer Little League Baseball, Talladega, Ala., 1953; music leader area Ch. revivals, Ala.; dir. Cmty. Ch. for the Deaf, Ala., 1971—76; established, directed Helen Keller Sch. of Ala. Sunday Sch., 1976—85; established sixty-second-sermons ministries writing and distr. leaflets to Sunday workers and jails; dir. AIDB's Hawkins Chapel, Talladega, Ala., 1985—88; mem. First Bapt. Ch., Talladega, Ala.; bd. mem., treas. Greater Talladega C. of C., Ala.; bd. mem. North Talladega County United Way, Ala., North Talladega County Assn. for Retarded Citizens, Ala., 2004—. Recipient Talladega Citizen of the Yr. Notable Svc. Award, C. of C., 1955, first Lotus Award, Ala., 1982, Ouststanding Good Neighbor in Am., Good Neighbor Search in N.Y., Newsweek Mag., 1990, Civitan Svc. Award, 1963, Ala. Recreation Soc. Lay Award, 1965, Alablind Award, Alumni and Workers Assn., 1970, Ala. Assn. for Deaf Award, 1981, Ala. Inst. for the Deaf and Blind dormitory named Robert C. Weaver Cottage, 1983, Alablind Award, Alumni and Workers Assn., 1989, first AIDB Robert C. Weaver Vol. Award, 1995, Ala. Assn. for Deaf Award, 1997, Outstanding Talladegans of the Centuries 1834-2000 Award, 2000, many others awards. Mem.: Ala. Assn. for Deaf (Ala. Royal Amb. chair 2003), Talladega Jaycees (chmn. horse show 1952, orginated newsboy appreciation day 1953), Talladega Kiwanis Club. Achievements include invention of electronic Weaver bd. game for blind children, 1965; development of campus radio sta. at the Ala. Sch. for the Blind to aid blind students at wrestling matches, 1967; reading aids for pre-sch. deaf children, 1980; attracted more than 15,000 boy scouts from southeastern states to walk the Odum Scout Trail at Cheaha Mountain; design of trail medal and color brochure to promote the Odum Scout Trail. Office: Wood Weaver Inc 112 Ct Square E Talladega AL 35160 Office Phone: 256-362-4741. Personal E-mail: weaver52@bellsouth.net.

WEAVER, ROBIN GEOFFREY, lawyer, educator; b. Columbus, Ohio, Aug. 19, 1948; s. Eugene Rudolph and Lois Ann (Banks) W.; m. Valerie Cheryl Waller, June 28, 1980; children: Allyson, Lauren, Meridith. BA, Ohio State U., 1970; JD, U. Mich., 1973. Bar: Ohio 1974, U.S. Dist. Ct. (no. dist.) Ohio 1974, U.S. Ct. Appeals (6th cir.) 1980, U.S. Ct. Appeals (3d cir.) 1998, U.S. Ct. Appeals (2d, 7th, and 11th cirs.) 2002, U.S. Supreme Ct., 2002, U.S. Dist. Ct. (so. dist.) Ohio 2004. Assoc. Squire, Sanders & Dempsey, Cleve., 1973-83, ptnr., 1983—; mem. faculty Nat. Inst. for Trial Adv. Northwestern U., Chgo., 1983—. Mem. Ohio Supreme Ct. Bd. of Commrs. on Grievances and Discipline, chair, 1996, master commr., 2002-. With U.S. Army, 1974. Fellow Am. Coll. Trial Lawyers, Internat. Soc. Barristers; mem. Cleve. Bar Assn. (pres. 2002-03); mem. ABA, Ohio Bar Assn., Cleve. Assn. Trial Attys. (life), 8th Appellate Jud. Conf., Am. Inns of Ct. (master bencher Cleve. chpt.). Episcopalian. Office: Squire Sanders & Dempsey 4900 Key Tower Cleveland OH 44114 Office Phone: 216-479-8500.

WEAVER, SIGOURNEY (SUSAN ALEXANDRA WEAVER), actress; b. NYC, Oct. 8, 1949; d. Sylvester (Pat) Weaver and Elizabeth Inglish; m. Jim Simpson, 1984; 1 child, Charlotte. BA in English, Stanford U., 1971; MA in Drama, Yale U., 1974. Actress: (theatre) including Watergate Classics, 1973, The Frogs, 1974 The Nature and Purpose of the Universe, 1974, Daryl and Carol and Kenny and Jenny, The Constant Wife, 1975, Titanic, 1976, Das Lusitania Songspiel (also co-writer), 1976, Marco Polo Sings a Song, 1977, A Flea in Her Ear, 1978, Conjuring an Event, 1978, Beyond Therapy, 1981, As You Like It, 1981, Hurlyburly, 1984-85, Sex and Longing, 1996, The Merchant of Venice, 1986, The Guys, 2002, The Mercy Seat, 2002, Mrs. Farnsworth, 2004, (films) Annie Hall, 1977, Madman, 1978, Alien, 1979, Eyewitness, 1981, The Year of Living Dangerously, 1982, Deal of the Century, 1983, Ghostbusters, 1984, Une femme ou deux, 1985, Aliens, 1986 (Acad. Award nomination for best actress, 1987), Half Moon Street, 1986, Gorillas in the Mist: The Story of Dian Fossey, 1988 (Acad. Award nomination for best actress, 1989, Golden Globe for best actress - drama, 1989), Working Girl, 1988 (Acad. Award nomination for best supporting actress, 1989, Golden Globe for best supporting actress in a motion picture, 1989), Ghostbusters II, 1989, 1492: Conquest of Paradise, 1992, Dave, 1993, Death and the Maiden, 1994, Jeffrey, 1995, Copycat, 1995, Snow White: A Tale of Terror, 1997, The Ice Storm, 1997 (BAFTA Film Award for best supporting actress, 1998), A Map of the World, 1999, Galaxy Quest, 1999, Airframe, 1999, Company Man, 2000, Speak Truth to Power, 2000, Heartbreakers, 2001, Big Bad Love (voice), 2001, Tadpole, 2002, The Guys, 2002, Holes, 2003, The Village, 2004, Imaginary Heroes, 2004, (TV series) Somerset, 1976, (TV miniseries) The Best of Families, 1977, (TV movies) 3 by Cheever: The Sorrows of Gin, 1979, 3 by Cheever: O Youth and Beauty!, 1979; co-prodr., actress: (films) Alien 3, 1992, Alien: Resurrection, 1997. Recipient Star on the Walk of Fame, 1999, Lifetime Achievement award, Chicago Internat. Film Festival, 2001. Office: ICM 8942 Wilshire Blvd Beverly Hills CA 90211-1934*

WEAVER, STEVEN M. publishing executive; Pub., pres. The Tampa Tribune, 2001—. Office: 200 S Parker St Tampa FL 33606 Address: PO Box 191 Tampa FL 33601 Business E-Mail: SWeaver@tampatrib.com.

WEAVER, THOMAS JAY, music educator; b. Olean, N.Y., May 13, 1967; s. Donald Claude Weaver and Sharon Lee Hare; m. Gretchen Albright, Dec. 27, 1990; 1 child, Eric Jonathan. MusB, Bowling Green State U., 1991, MusM, 1995. Cert. tchr. music K-12. Band dir. Northmor Local Schs., Galion, Ohio, 1991—93, Firestone H.S., Akron, Ohio, 1995—. Mem.: Internat. Assn. Jazz Educators, Ohio Music Edn. Assn. Avocations: running, skiing. Home: 981 Highland Rd E Macedonia OH 44056-2301 Office: Firestone High Sch 333 Rampart Ave Akron OH 44313

WEAVER, TIMOTHY ALLAN, lawyer; b. Elkhart, Ind., Nov. 30, 1948; s. Arthur and Joan Lucile (Yoder) W.; m. Catherine Anne Power, Nov. 23, 1974; children: Daniel Timothy, Christopher Matthew, David Colwell. AB, Brown U., 1971; JD, U. Ill., 1974. Bar: Ill. 1974, Wis. 1999, U.S. Dist. Ct. (no. dist.) Ill. 1975, U.S. Ct. Appeals (7th cir.) 1975, U.S. Dist. Ct. (no. dist. trial bar) Ill. 1982, U.S. Dist. Ct. (ea. dist.) Wis. 1999. Asst. pub. defender Cook County Pub. Defender, Chgo., 1974-75; trial atty. Chgo. Transit Authority, 1975-78; assoc. Philip E. Howard Ltd., Chgo., 1978, Pretzel & Stouffer, Chartered, Chgo., 1978-82, ptnr., 1982—. Editor: Medical Malpractice, 1989, 92, 96; contbr. chpts. to books. Mem. ABA, Ill. State Bar Assn., Ill. Assn. Def. Trial Counsel, State Bar of Wis., Civil Trial Counsel of Wis., The Lawyers Club of Chgo. Office: Pretzel & Stouffer Chartered One S Wacker Dr #2500 Chicago IL 60606 E-mail: tweaver@pretzel-stouffer.com.

WEAVER, WILLIAM CHARLES, retired industrial executive; b. Nov. 10, 1941; s. Curtis D. and Mary (Yahres) W.; m. Karla Lee Kottas, June 13, 1964; children: Michael, Kelli. BS in Edn., Indiana U. of Pa., 1963; postgrad. in acctg., Tex. Christian U., 1964-65. CPA, Pa. With Price Waterhouse & Co., Pitts., 1965-73, audit mgr., 1970-73; corp. contr. Kennametal Inc., Latrobe, Pa., 1973-78, v.p., contr., 1978-83, v.p., treas., 1983-86, v.p., CFO, 1987-89; sr. v.p., CFO Oak Industries, Inc., Waltham, Mass., 1990-95; ret., 1995. Bd. dirs. Gemini Precision Products; chmn. bd. Weaver Enterprises, Inc., 1996—. Pres. Mountain View Parent Tchrs. Orgn., 1976—77; bd. dirs. East High Acres Civic Assn., 1976—77; treas. Greater Latrobe Hockey Club, 1982—87; chmn. bd. dirs., mem. adv. coun. Jr. Achievement, Latrobe, 1982—85; chmn. bd. trustees Latrobe United Way, 1988—89; trustee Hampton United Presbyn. Ch., 1972—73. 1st lt. U.S. Army, 1963—65. Mem.: AICPA, Fin. Execs. Inst., Pa. Inst. CPAs, Palmetto Dunes Club Inc. (pres. 1998—2001). E-mail: kweaver589@aol.com.

WEAVER, WILLIAM CLAIR, JR., (MIKE WEAVER), human resources development executive; b. Indiana, Pa., Apr. 11, 1936; s. William Clair and Zaida (Bley) W.; m. Janet Marcelle Boyd, Sept. 18, 1963 (div. 1978); 1 child, William Michael; m. Donna June Hubbuch, Feb. 10, 1984. B Aero Engring., Rensselaer Poly. Inst., 1958; MBA, Washington U., St. Louis, 1971; postgrad., Rutgers U.; grad., Armed Forces Indsl. Coll. Registered profl. engr. Engr. aerodynamics N.Am. Aviation, Los Angeles, 1959-60; engr. flight test ops. Boeing/Vertol, Phila., 1963-66; engr. flight test project Lockhead Electronics, Plainfield, N.J., 1966-69; project engr. advanced systems, sr. staff engr. Emerson Electric Co., St. Louis, 1969-72; pres. Achievement Assocs., Inc., St. Louis, 1972—. Founder, charter mem. Catalyst, 1978—; faculty mem. Leadership Mgmt., Inc.; spkr. in field. Author: Winning Selling, 1983; contbr. articles to profl. jours. Adv. com. Boy Scouts Am., Bridgeton, Mo., 1974, Mo. Athletic Club, Am. Soc. Tng. & Devel. Capt. USAF, 1960-63, USAFR. Mem. AIAA, NSPE, Cato Inst., Am. Soc. Tng. and Devel., Am. Soc. Bus. and Mgmt. Cons., Am. Ordnance Soc., Assn. MBA Execs., Air Force Assn., Am. Helicopter Soc., Acacia Frat., St. Louis C. of C., Mensa, Mo. Athletic Club, Beta Gamma Sigma. Republican. Lutheran. Avocations: photography, music, sports. Home and Office: 1016 Evergreen Rd Yardley PA 19067-1018 Office Phone: 215-428-3400.

WEAVER, WILLIAM MERRITT, JR., investment banker; b. Phila., Jan. 7, 1912; s. William Merritt and Frances (Jones) W.; m. Rosemary R. Fine, May 9, 1972; children by previous marriage: Judith (Mrs. Ross Campbell), Patricia (Mrs. Clarence Wurts), Wendy, Alison M. Grad., Phillips Exeter Acad., 1930; BA, Princeton, 1934. Ptnr. Nathan Trotter & Co., Phila., 1934-40; pres., dir. Frank Samuel & Co., Inc., Phila., 1945- 59, Haile Mines, N.Y.C., 1957-58; pres. Howmet Corp., N.Y.C., 1958-65, chmn. bd. dirs., 1965-66; ptnr. Alexander Brown & Sons, Balt., 1966-86, ltd. ptnr. emeritus, 1986—. Served to col. AUS, 1941-45. Decorated Legion of Merit, Bronze Star, Croix de Guerre (France and Belgium). Mem. Knickerbacker Club, River (N.Y.C.) Club, Lyford Cay (Nassau) Club, Country Club of Fairfield (Southport, Conn.), Phi Beta Kappa. Home: Lazy W Ranch Smith NV 89430

WEAVER, WILLIAM SCHILDECKER, retired electric power industry executive; b. Pitts., Jan. 15, 1944; s. Charles Henry and Louise (Schildecker) W.; m. Janet Kae Jones, Mar. 7, 1981. BA, Hamilton Coll., 1965; JD, U. Mich., 1968. Bar: Wash. 1968. Assoc. Perkins Coie, Seattle, 1968-74, ptnr., 1975-91; exec. v.p., CFO Puget Sound Power & Light Co., Bellevue, Wash., 1991-97; vice chmn., chmn. unregulated subs. Puget Sound Energy, 1997, pres., COO, 1997, pres., CEO, 1998—2002, chmn., 2001—02, ret. Bd. dirs. Kinetic Ventures, Chevy Chase, Md., 1998—2002. Bd. dirs. Wash. Rsch. Coun., Seattle, 1991-97, chmn., 1995-97; trustee Seattle Repertory Theatre, 1992-95, 99-2000, chmn., 2000-02, Corp. Coun. Arts, 1995-2002, Pacific Sci. Ctr., 1997-2002. Mem. ABA, Wash. State Bar Assn., Seattle Yacht Club, Flounder Bay Yacht Club.

WEAVER-STROH, JOANNE MATEER, education educator, consultant; b. May 21, 1930; d. Kenneth Hall and Jean (Weakley) Mateer; children: Karen; Mark, Laurie. BS in Edn., U. Pa., 1952, elem. and secondary prin. cert., 1979; MS in Psychology Reading, Temple U., 1968. Tchr. Paoli (Pa.) Sch., 1952-53, Somerville Sch., Ridgewood, N.J., 1953-55, Bryn Mawr (Pa.) Sch., 1955-57, Erdenheim Sch., Springfield, Pa., 1957-58; reading specialist Abington (Pa.) Sch. Dist., 1966-67, curriculum specialist, 1967-73, coord. human rels. programs, 1973-80; prin. Rydal Elem. Sch., Abington, 1980-88, Willow Hill Elem. Sch., 1988-96; ret., 1996. Cons., tchr. Marywood Coll., Scranton, Pa., 1972—; coord. drug and alcohol abuse program Abington Sch. Dist., 1989-96; cons. Conflict Resolution, 1996—. Chmn. Abington Human Rels. Adv. Coun., 1973-88; chmn. Cmty. Rels. Com. Abington Twp., 1978—; mem. Ea. Montgomery County Human Rels. Adv. Coun., 1981-83; chmn. No Place for Hate project Abington Twp., 2003-; mediator Abington Twp.; leader Stephen Ministry program Abington Presbyn. Ch. Named Citizen of the Week Times Chronicle Newspaper, 1976; recipient award Four Chaplains Temple U., 1979, Disting. Citizens award Roslyn Jr. C. of C., 1981, Citizens for Progress Humanitarian award, 1982, Cmty. award Abington YMCA, 1987, Dr. Martin Luther King Jr. award Abington Twp., 1989, East Montgomery County/Pa. State Human Rels. Intergroup award, 2000, Citizens That Care award Abington Cmty. Taskforce, 2003, Disting. Cmty. Svc. award Intersvc. Clubs of Glenside, 2003. Mem. ASCD, NASEP, Internat. Coop. Learning Assn., Pa. Assn. Elem. Prins., Phi Delta Kappa, Delta Kappa Gamma. Republican. Home: 109 Durham Ct Maple Glen PA 19002-2854 Office Phone: 215-793-9434. Personal E-mail: rwstroh@att.net.

WEBB, ANTHONY ALLAN, banker, director; b. Lincoln, Nebr., May 24, 1943; s. Robert McGraw and Ruth Irene (Good) W.; m. Micheline Touchette, July 10, 1971; children— Annie, Christian BA, U. Colo., 1965; B.Internat. Mgmt., Am. Grad. Sch. Internat. Mgmt., 1970. Various positions Royal Bank Can., Montreal and London, 1970-77, assoc. mgr. Toronto, Ont., Can., 1977-80, v.p., 1980-83, sr. v.p. merchant banking, 1983-84, dir. gen. Geneva, 1984-88, sr. v.p. personal fin. svcs. Montreal, 1988-93; chmn. Royal Bank Can. Suisse, Royal Bank Can., Channel Islands; pres., CEO Royal Trust, Toronto, 1993-99; chair The Exec. Com., 2000—. Served to lt. comdr. USNR, 1965-69 Home: 90 Binscarth Rd Toronto ON Canada M4W 1Y4

WEBB, BOBBIE JAMES, insurance broker; b. Detroit, Feb. 4, 1954; arrived in Canada; s. Bobbie J. Sr. and Jennell W.; m. Lillie Webb, March 13, 1972 (div. May 1979); children: Kevin, Bobbie III. Office: Webb Casino Gambling Inc 2257 Hurlbut St Detroit MI 48214-4048 Address: 8520 Lakeshore Buntchville MI 40059

WEBB, CARL B. banker; BA, W. Tex. State U., 1972; attended, Tex. Tech. U., Masters Bus.; grad., Southern Methodist U., 1981. Corp. banking divn. InterFirst Bank, Dallas; v.p., dir. Gerald Ford's First United Bank Group, 1983; pres., COO First Nat. Bank, Lubbock, Tex., 1983-88, First Gibraltar Bank, 1988-93, First Nationwide Bank, 1994-97, Ca. Federal Bank, 1997—. Office: Golden State Bancorp 135 Main St San Francisco CA 94105-1812

WEBB, CHARLES HAIZLIP, JR., retired university dean; b. Dallas, Feb. 14, 1933; s. Charles Haizlip and Marion (Gilker) W.; m. Kenda McGibbon, June 21, 1958; children: Mark, Kent, Malcolm, Charles Haizlip III. AB, MMus, So. Meth. U., 1955; DMus, Ind. U., 1964; DMus (hon.), Anderson Coll., 1979. Asst. to dean Sch. Music, So. Meth. U., 1957-58; mem. faculty Sch. Music, Ind. U., 1960-97, dean, 1973-97, Disting. prof., 1997—. Mem. Nat. Rec. Preservation Found., 2002—. Dir. Indpls. Symphony Choir, 1967-81; guest condr. chorus and orch. festivals throughout U.S.; duo-pianist with Wallace Hornibrook in U.S. and Australian tour, 1973; organist First Meth. Ch., Bloomington, 1961-, mem. hymnal revision com. Meth. Ch.; mem. jury Chopin competition; mem. jury internat. piano competitions in Munich, Budapest, South Africa, Paris, Chile, Warsaw, Bolzano, London, Cologne, Japan, Israel; mem. adv. bd. Classical Insites. Chmn. adv. bd. Internat. Music Festivals, Inc.; mem. Ind. Arts Commn., 1975-83, U.S.-USSR Commn. on Music Performance Edn., Am. Coun. Learned Socs./USSR Ministry of Culture; mem. adv. panel The Music Found.; mem. recommendation bd. Avery Fisher Prize Program; bd. dirs. Busoni Found.; mem. bd. advisors Van Cliburn Internat. Piano Competition; mem. nat. adv. bd. Am. Guild Organists; trustee Indpls. Symphony Orch.; mem. Nat. Recording Preservation Found., 2002; mem. adv. com. on cultural diplomacy U.S. Dept. State, 2004. With U.S. Army, 1955-57. Decorated D.S.M.; recipient Disting. Alumni award So. Meth. U., 1980, Sagamore of Wabash Gov. award, 1987, 89, 97, Thomas Hart Benton medal Ind. U., 1987, Disting. Alumni award Highland Park High Sch., Dallas, 1989, Ind. Gov. award for arts, 1989, Rocking Chair award, Ind. U., 1997, Sterling Patron award Mu Phi Epsilon Internat., 1989, Ind. Gen. Assembly House Resolution # 39 for meritorious svc., 1997, Pres.'s award Ind. U., 2000; subject of tribute in U.S. Congl. Record, 1997; Rockefeller scholar Bellagio Study Ctr., 1997; named Ind. Living Legend, 2004; Paul Harris fellow, Rotary Internat., 1997. Mem. Ind. Acad., Century Assn. of N.Y., Pi Kappa Lambda, Phi Mu Alpha, Phi Delta Theta. Home: 648 S Woodcrest Dr Bloomington IN 47401-5417

WEBB, CHARLES RICHARD, retired university president; b. Berkeley, Calif., Oct. 4, 1919; s. Charles Richard and Adele (McDaniel) W.; m. Andrée Bonno; 1 child, Charles Richard III. AB, U. Calif., Berkeley, 1942, MA, 1944, Harvard U., 1947, PhD, 1949. Faculty San Diego State Coll., 1949-64, prof., 1958-64, chmn. dept. history, 1956-58; dean acad. affairs Stanislaus State Coll., Turlock, Calif., 1964-66; prof. history San Diego State Coll., 1966-70; pres. Eastern Conn. State U., Willimantic, 1970-88; ret., 1988; former assoc. dean acad. planning Calif. State Colls., 1966-69, former dep. state coll. dean acad. planning. Author: Workbook in Western Civilization, 2 vols, 1959, Western Civilization vol. 1 (with Schaefer), vol. 2 (with Palm), 1958, (with Crosby) The Past as Prologue, 2 vols, 1973; contbr. articles to profl. jours. Mem. pers. com. Santa Rosa Symphony Assn., New Eng. Program, Windham Meml. Comty. Hosp., Sea Rsch. Found.; mem. Commn. on Conn.'s Future. With USNR, 1941-45. Mem. AAUP, Am. Hist. Assn., Am. Fedn. Musicians, Nat. Pks. and Conservation, Sonoma Land Trust, Sierra Club, Nature Conservancy, New Eng. Hist. Assn., Assn. Calif. State Coll. Profs. (v.p. 1958-60), Save the Redwoods League, Conn. Employees Assn., Am. Assn. State Colls. and Univs., Phi Alpha Theta, Kappa Delta Pi, Omicron Delta Pi, Alpha Delta Phi. Clubs: University (San Diego), Commonwealth of Calif., Willimantic Country, Saddle Club, Santa Rosa, Montecito Heights Health & Racquet Club, Santa Rosa. Home: 6495 Timber Springs Dr Santa Rosa CA 95409-5900

WEBB, DAN K. lawyer; b. Bushnell, Ill., Sept. 5, 1945; s. Keith L. and Phyllis I. (Clow) W.; student Western Ill. U., 1963-66; J.D., Loyola U., 1970; m. Laura A. Buscemi, Mar. 15, 1973; children— Jeffrey, Maggie, Michael, Melanie, Megan. Bar: Ill. 1970. Chief spl. prosecutions div. U.S. Atty.'s Office, Chgo., 1970-76; ptnr. firm Cummins, Decker & Webb, Chgo., 1976-79; dir., Ill. Dept. Law Enforcement, Chgo., 1979-80; ptnr. Pierce, Webb, Lydon & Griffin, Chgo., 1980-81; U.S. atty. No. Dist., IL, Chgo., 1981-84; ptnr. Winston & Strawn, Chgo., 1985—; instr. John Marshall Law Sch., 1975—, Loyola U. Sch. Law, 1980—. Vice chmn. Met. Fair and Expn. Authority, 1978—81; bd. advisers Mercy Hosp. and Med. Ctr.; mem. Chgo. Council on Arson. Recipient spl. commendation award U.S. Justice Dept., 1975; named 1 of 10 Outstanding Young Chicagoans, Chgo. Jaycees, 1979. Mem. ABA, Ill. Bar Assn., Chgo. Bar Assn., Fed. Bar Assn., Legal Club Chgo., Execs. Club Chgo., Nat. Inst. of Trial Advocacy, 1979-. Republican. Office: Winston & Strawn 35 W Wacker Dr Ste 4200 Chicago IL 60601-1695*

WEBB, DARRYL WILLARD, systems engineer; s. La Verne Willard and Jeraldine Marie Webb; m. Christina Denise Kowalski, Aug. 27, 1971; children: Shannon J., Meagan C. AA in Liberal Arts, Fullerton Coll., 1973; BA in Bus. Ops. Rsch., Calif. State U., Fullerton, 1974. Life cycle cost analyst Northrop Corp., Anaheim, Calif., 1975—79; exec. advisor Rockwell Internat., Anaheim, 1979—86; prin. investigator ACS, Inc., Tustin, Calif., 1986—91; project mgr. Boeing Co., Huntington Beach, Calif., 1991—2000; tech. dir. Econ Inc., Huntington Beach, 2000—01; mgr. western region Price Sys., Inc., El Segundo, Calif., 2001—03; mgr. cost sect. Aerospace Corp., El Segundo, 2003—. Mem. adv. bd. Cost Credibility Team NASA, Marshall Space Flight Ctr., Ala., 2002; presenter in field. Contbr. articles to profl. pubs. Cpl. USMC, 1968—70, Vietnam. Mem.: Soc. Cost Estimating and Analysis, Internat. Soc. Parametric Analysts (pres. So. Calif. chpt. 1981—83, bd. dirs. 1986—87, tech. dir. So. Calif. chpt. 1980, Freiman award 2003, Parametrician of Yr. 1984), Phi Tau Sigma. Avocations: collecting historical photography, music, research in technology. Office: The Aerospace Corp 2350 E El Segundo Blvd El Segundo CA 90245 Fax: 310-336-5581. Business E-Mail: darryl.w.webb@aero.org.

WEBB, DONALD ARTHUR, minister; b. Wales, May 4, 1926; came to U.S., 1958; s. Arthur and Emily W.; m. Renee Mowbray, May 18, 1946; children— Cheryl, Marian, Christopher, Alison, Ian. Student, Queen's Coll., Cambridge (Eng.) U., 1944-45; BA, Ohio Wesleyan U., 1960; MDiv, Methodist Theol. Sch. in Ohio, 1963; PhD, Drew U., 1966; postdoctoral, Lincoln Coll., Oxford (Eng.) U., 1969, 72; LLD, Centenary Coll. La., 1991. Ordained to ministry Methodist Ch., 1960. Insp. Brit. Social Services, 1953-58; pastor various chs. Ohio and N.J., 1958-68; dean admissions, asst. prof. theology and lit. Meth. Theol. Sch. in Ohio, 1968-75, v.p. adminstrn., 1975-77; pres. Centenary Coll. La., Shreveport, 1977-91; sr. pastor First United Meth. Ch., Shreveport, 1991-92, scholar-in-residence, 1992—. Author: The Flame and Dusty Miller, 1970, We Hold These Truths, 1960; author: Dostoevsky and Christian Agnosticism, 1971, Deep Calls to Deep, 1998. With Brit. Royal Navy, 1945-53. Mem. Shreveport C. of C. (bd. dirs. 1978-80). Home: 5709 Lakefront Dr Shreveport LA 71119-3913 Office: First United Meth Ch Head of Tex Shreveport LA 71165-1567

WEBB, DORIS MCINTOSH, human resources specialist; b. Aliquippa, Pa., May 26, 1930; d. Hayward Victor and Elaine Eloise (Kiernan) McIntosh; m. Alan D. Webb Sr. JD, Aug. 15, 1953 (dec. Sept. 1979); children: Alan D. Jr., Amy E. Webb-Burke. Student, Western Coll. for Women, 1949-51; BS in Bus. Adminstrn., Geneva Coll., 1953, tchr. cert., 1968; MEd, U. Pitts., 1972. Mgr. Crestmont Home Supply Co., Aliquippa, 1953-57; real estate mgr. McIntosh Constrn. Co., Aliquippa, 1957-62; tchr. bus. Rochester (Pa.) H.S., 1968-78; bus. tchr. adult edn. Alleghney C.C., Pitts., 1972-75, Draughon's Jr. Bus. Coll., Knoxville, Tenn., 1979—81, Hartford C.C., Bel Air, Md., 1981—85; corp. sec. McIntosh & Webb Inc., Cockeysville, Md., 1981-88; exec. dir., CEO housing authority City of Havre de Grace, Md., 1989-98; v.p. human resources, tng., devel. McIntosh and Webb Assocs., Charlottesville, Va., 1999—. Chmn. North Boroughs, WQED, Pitts., 1964-68; mem. fin. com. Housing Authority Risk Retention Corp. of Housing Authority Ins. Co., Cheshire, Conn., 1995-97, mem. fin. com. Housing Authority Ins. Co., 1995-97; housing cons. for pub. housing and modernization programs, 1989-97; Sect. 8 Fed. Housing insp., 1996—; owner Ebenezer House bed and breakfast, Rochelle, Va., 2003—. Recipient Geneva Coll. Alumni Disting. Svc. award, 1993. Mem.: ASTD, NAFE, AAUW, The Profl. Woman Network, Profl. Woman Spkrs. Bur., Colonial Williamsburg Found. Republican. Lutheran. Avocations: fox hunting, beagling, travel, remodeling homes, decorating. Personal E-mail: dmwebb@cstone.net.

WEBB, EMILY, retired plant morphologist; b. Charleston, S.C., Apr. 10, 1924; d. Malcolm Syfan and Emily Kirk (Moore) W.; m. John James Rosemond, Apr. 23, 1942 (div. 1953); 1 child, John Kirk; m. Julius Goldberg, Sept. 9, 1954; children: Michael, Judith. Student, Coll. Charleston, 1951—54; AB in Liberal Arts and Sci. with honors, U. Ill., Chgo., 1968, MS in Biol. Scis., 1972, PhD in Biol. Scis., 1985. Undergrad. fellow in bacteriology Med. Coll. S.C., Charleston, 1952-54; teaching asst. U. Ill., Chgo., 1969-72, 77-84, rsch. asst., 1977; teaching fellow W.Va. U., Morgantown, 1974, instr., 1974-75. Rsch. in N.Am. bot. needlework art, 1986—. Author: Studies in Several North American Species of Ophioglossum, 1986; translator Nat. Transl. Ctr., Chgo., 1976; contbr. articles to profl. jours. James scholar U. Ill., 1968-69. Mem. DAR, ACLU. Democrat. Episcopalian. Avocations: garden design, writing, money management. Home and Office: PO Box 25661 Chicago IL 60625-0661

WEBB, H. LAWRENCE, real estate executive; m. Janet Hadley; children: Laura, Emily. Pres. Calif. divsn. John Laing Homes; CEO, WL Homes LLC (merger John Laing Homes and Watt Homes), Irvine, Calif., 1996—. Bd. dirs. Orange County Housing Authority, Interval House. Mem. Nat. Assn. Home Builders (bd. trustees Nat. Sales and Mktg. Coun., inducted into Legends of Mktg. Hall of Fame). Office: WL Homes LLC 895 Dove St Newport Beach CA 92660

WEBB, IGOR MICHAEL, academic administrator; b. Malacky, Czechoslovakia, Nov. 8, 1941; came to U.S., 1952; s. Michael and Josephine (Nash) W.; m. Catherine Lamb (div. 1989); 1 child, Kelly Webb-Lamb; m. Marianne F. Walters, 1990; children: Rebecca Alice, Sarah Elizabeth, Benjamin Oliver,

Hannah Olivia. BA, Tufts U., 1963; MA, Stanford U., 1966, PhD, 1971. Asst. prof. English Loyola U. Montreal, Can., 1968-70, U. Mass., Boston, 1971-77, assoc. prof., 1977-78; chair div. humanities Richmond Coll., London, 1979-86; spl. asst. to pres. Adelphi U., Garden City, N.Y., 1986-87, acting provost, 1987-89, provost, 1989-97, sr. v.p., 1992-97, prof. English, 1997—, acting pres., 1997. Author: From Custom to Capital, 1981, Against Capitulation, 1984. Trustee North Shore Bd. Edn., 2003—. Creative Writing fellow Nat. Endowment for Arts, 1978. Mem. Phi Beta Kappa. Office: Adelphi U Garden City NY 11530 E-mail: webb@adelphi.edu.

WEBB, J. DAVID, lawyer; b. Providence, Apr. 12, 1938; s. Brainard T. and Loretta A. (Dwyer) W.; m. Carmen Rodriguez, July 3, 1976. B.A., Emory U., 1959, LL.B., 1963. Bar: Ga. 1962, U.S. Dist. Ct. (no. dist.) Ga., U.S. Ct. Appeals (11th cir.). Atty., Fed. Res. Bank of Atlanta, 1969-72; corp. counsel Trust Co. Ga., Atlanta, 1972— . Bd. dirs. Ctr. Rehab. Tech., Inc., Ga. Inst. Technology, Shepherd Spinal Ctr., Atlanta, 1978—, Ga. Easter Seal Soc., 1983—; trustee Met. Atlanta Crime Commn., 1979—; mem. Nat. Council on the Handicapped, 1980-82. Mem. ABA, Ga. State Bar Assn., Atlanta Bar Assn. Democrat. Roman Catholic. Office: 25 Park Pl NE Atlanta GA 30303-2900

WEBB, JACK M. lawyer; b. Monroe, La., Feb. 23, 1936; s. Sam L. and Lillian Etta (McCowen) W.; m. Diane Adele Waterman, Aug. 22, 1964; children: Julia Lillian Pogue, Kathryn Joy, Samuel Logan. BS in Geology, Centenary Coll. La., 1957; JD, Tulane U., 1960; student, JFK Sch. Govt. Harvard U., 1999. Bar: La. 1960, Tex. 1962. Atty. Standard Oil Co. Tex., Houston, 1961-66; staff atty. Trunkline Gas. Co., Houston, 1966-71; sr. atty. M.W. Kellogg Co., Houston, 1971-73; sec., asst. gen. counsel Gulf Resources & Chem. Corp., Houston, 1973-78, v.p. govt. rels., adminstrv. asst. to chmn. bd., 1978-82; pres. Jack M. Webb & Assocs., 1983—; U.S. spl. amb. to Bolivia, 1985, to Finland, 1986, to Haiti, 1991, to Angola, 1992, to Ghana, 1993; hon. consul of Ghana, 1995—. Bd. dirs. Bradmark, Inc., Am. Meridian Ins. Co., Scotia Pacific Holding Co., Techxas Ventures, Veri Med Rsch. Corp. Bd. dirs. U.S. Peace Corps, 1985 86, Nat. Park Found., 1986-92, Boy Scouts Am., 1975—. Capt. U.S. Army, 1960-61. Mem. Tex. Bar Assn., La. Bar Assn. Methodist. Home: 3434 Locke Ln Houston TX 77027-4139 Office Phone: 281-586-7166. E-mail: jackw@jackwebb.com.

WEBB, JAMES TAYLOR, physiologist, pilot; b. Yakima, Wash., Mar. 5, 1942; s. Kenneth LeRoy and Marjorie Charmaine Webb; m. Frances Jeanne Laue, May 27, 1989; m. Judy Marie Bound, Aug. 22, 1964 (div. Mar. 26, 1985); children: Susan Marie Russo, Michael Taylor. BS, U. Wash., 1965, MS, 1975, PhD, 1979. Airline Transport Pilot FAA, 1987. Commd. pilot USAF officer 2Lt, 1965; aircraft comdr. 336th Tactical Fighter Squadron USAF, Seymour Johnson AFB, NC, 1967—69, advanced through grades to maj., 1979, aircraft comdr. and flight lead 389th Fighter Squadron, 1970—70, pilot and aircraft comdr. 97th Mil. Airlift Squadron McChord AFB, Wash., 1971—79; dir. rsch. and assoc. prof. dept. biology USAF Acad., Colorado Springs, Colo., 1979—84; rsch. physiologist Crew Tech. Divsn. USAF, Brooks AFB, Tex., 1984—87; sr. scientist Wyle Labs., San Antonio, 1987—. Contbr. articles to profl. jours. Decorated DFC USAF, 9 Air Medals; recipient Harold V. Ellingson Literary award, 1992, Fred A. Hitchcock award for excellence in aerospace physiology, Aerospace Physiology Soc., 1996, Sidney D. Leverett Environ. Sci. award, Aerospace Med. Assn., 1999, Silver Snoopy award, NASA Astronauts, 2002, Paul Bert award for Aerospace Physiology Rsch., Aerospace Physiology Soc., 2003. Fellow: Aerospace Med. Assn. (cert. aerospace physiology 1986); mem.: Res. Officer Assn. (life), Sigma Xi, Daedalians (life). Achievements include contribution to new method of protection from decompression sickness by astronauts constructing the International Space Station; research in decompression sickness, exercise-enhanced prebreathe for decompression sickness protection; abrupt zero-preoxygenation altitude threshold for decompression sickness symptoms; unpredictability of fighter pilot G tolerance using antrhopometric and physiologic variables. Avocations: genealogy, cooking, gardening, golf. Office: Wyle Laboratories 2485 Gillingham Dr San Antonio TX 78235-5105 E-mail: james.webb@brooks.af.mil.

WEBB, JOHN, retired state supreme court justice; b. Rocky Mount, N.C., Sept. 18, 1926; s. William Devin and Ella (Johnson) W.; m. Martha Carolyn Harris, Sept. 13, 1958; children: Caroline Webb Smart, William Devin. Student, U. N.C., 1946-49; LLB, Columbia U., 1952. Judge Superior Ct., Wilson, N.C., 1971-77, N.C. Ct. Appeals, Raleigh, 1977-86; justice Supreme Ct. N.C., Raleigh, 1986-99; ptnr. Webb & Webb, Raleigh, N.C., 1998—. Served with USN, 1944-46. Mem. N.C. Bar Assn. Democrat. Baptist. Home: 808 Trinity Dr W Wilson NC 27893-2131 Office: Webb & Webb 19 W Hargett St Raleigh NC 27601-1391

WEBB, JOHN GIBBON, III, lawyer; b. Flint, Mich., June 1, 1944; s. John Gibbon Jr. and Martha W.; m. Fain Murphey, July 6, 1968; children: Jennifer Horn, Philip, Andrew Aidan, John Matthew. AB, Davidson Coll., 1966; JD, Vanderbilt U., 1970. Bar: N.Y. 1971, N.J. 1981. Assoc. Curtis, Mallet-Prevost, Colt & Mosle, N.Y.C., 1970—80; gen. counsel, v.p., sec. J.M. Huber Corp., Edison, NJ, 1980—95; pvt. bus. law practice Mt. Olive, NJ, 1996—. Episcopalian. Office: Ste 125 500 International Dr N Budd Lake NJ 07828 Office Phone: 973-426-8435. E-mail: webbgc@aol.com.

WEBB, JULIA JONES, elementary school educator, minister; b. Portsmouth, Va., Apr. 3, 1962; d. William Edward Jones Jr. and Fannie Ford Jones; m. Alexander Maurice Webb Sr., Nov. 17, 1990; children: Brittany Alexandria, Alexander Maurice II. BA in Early Childhood Edn., Norfolk State U., 1988; postgrad., Va. Union U., 2004—. Lic. early edn. Va. Educator Chesapeake (Va.) Pub. Shcs., 1988—. Assoc. minister First Bapt. Ch. Gilmerton, Chesapeake, 1999—2002, New Hope Bapt. Ch., Chesapeake, 2002—04. USAA All-Am. scholar, Norfolk State U., 1989. Mem.: Va. Edn. Assn. (del. 1990—91), Chesapeake Tchr. Forum. Democrat. Baptist. Avocations: coaching cheerleading, gardening, cooking, interior decorating, reading. Home: 2701 Dockside Ct Chesapeake VA 23323 Office: Southwestern Elem Sch 4410 Airline Blvd Chesapeake VA 23321 Office Phone: 757-465-6310.

WEBB, KARRIE, professional golfer; b. Ayr, Queensland, Australia, Dec. 21, 1974; Profl. golfer LPGA, 1995—. Won Weetabix Women's Brit. Open, 1995, 97, Healthsouth Inaugural, 1996, Sprint Titleholders Championship, 1996, SAFECO Classic, 1996, 97, ITT LPGA Tour Championship, 1996, Susan G. Koman Internat., 1997, Australian Ladies Masters, 1998, City of Hope: Myrtle Beach Classic, 1998, Wegman's Rochester Internat., 1999, Mercury Title-holders Championships, 1999, Standard Register PING, 1999, Australian Ladies Masters, 1999, 2000, The Office Depot, 1999, 2000, ier Classic, 1999, Nabisco Championship, 2000, Take Fuji Classic, 2000; recipient Vare Trophy LPGA, 1997; named Rolex Rookie of Yr., LPGA, 1996. Office: care LPGA 100 International Golf Dr Daytona Beach FL 32124-1082

WEBB, LAMAR THAXTER, architect; b. Hapeville, Ga., Sept. 13, 1928; s. Eugene Garnette and Sara Ethel (Moore) W.; m. Bettye Jayne Jackson, Dec. 6, 1957; children: Mark Maynard, Robin Lynn. BBA in Fin., U. Ga., 1950; BS, Ga. Inst. Tech., 1959, BArch, 1960. Reg. arch. Ga., Fla., Tenn. Intern architect Abreu and Robeson, Inc., Brunswick, Ga., 1960-66; architect, pres. Webb & Baldwin, Inc., St. Simons Island, Ga., 1966-72; pres., owner Lamar Webb, Arch., Inc., St. Simons Island, 1972—. 1st lt. USAF, 1953—55. Mem. AIA (State bd. dirs. 1985—, v.p. Golden Isles chpt. 1988-89, pres. 1989-90), Am. Soc. Interior Designers, Am. Soc. Landscape Architects (affiliate), Audubon Soc., Nat. Hort. Soc., Humane Soc. (local bd. dirs. 1985-87), Smithsonian Assocs., Coastal Alliance for Arts, Nat. Trust for Hist. Preservation, Ga. Trust for Hist. Preservation, Coastal Ga. Hist. Assn., Met. Mus. Art, Golden Isles Gourmet Club (bd. dirs.) Chien de Rotessieurs, G.I. Chap. Avocations: cooking, drawing, painting, travel. Home: Marshoaks Saint Simons Island GA 31522 Office: 13 Retreat Pl Saint Simons Island GA 31522 Home: Willow Creek 654 Brice Station Rd Silver Creek GA 30173

WEBB, MARGOT, writer; b. Halle, Germany, Aug. 28, 1927; d. Egmont and Ilse Lewin; widowed; children: Robert Dave, Peter Dave, Sandy Kyte; m. Ezra C. Levy. B, Calif. State U., 1960, M, 1964; PhD, U. So. Calif. Tchr. 6th grade L.A. Unified Sch. Dist., 1958-88. Lectr. in field. Author: Shadows at Noon, 1992, Coping With Street Gangs, Jewish. Avocations: classical music, Scrabble, walking, travel. Home: Pvt Mail Box 805 25852 Mcbean Pkwy Valencia CA 91355-2004

WEBB, MARTHA JEANNE, author, speaker, film producer; b. Grinnell, Iowa, Oct. 26, 1947; d. Frederick Winfield and Helen (Potter) W.; m. Bruce A. Clark; children: Marjorie, Paula, David. Student, St. Cloud State U., 1965-67, U. Minn., 1967-69, Coll. of St. Catherine, 1979-81. Personnel, pub. relations, drug abuse edn. NIH, 1967-77; account services Doremus & Co., Mpls., 1977-79; v.p. adminstrn. Webb Enterprises, Inc., Mpls., 1979-81; v.p. Russell-Manning Prodns., Mpls., 1981-86; pres. Clark Webb, Inc., Mpls., 1986-92. Pres. Minn. Film Bd., 1986-87, BCW Corp., 1988— Author: Dress Your House for Success, 1997, Finding Home, 1998; co-prodr. Hubert H. Humphrey: A Passion for Justice, Whitney Mus., 1998. Recipient Summit awards, 1999, Distinction Communicator awards, 1998, Silver award Internat. Film and TV Festival of N.Y., 1983, 84, 85, 86, 87, Golden Eagle award CINE Festival, 1985, Gold award Telly Awards, 1987.

WEBB, MARTY FOX, principal; b. Des Moines, July 15, 1942; d. Joseph John and Jean (Way) Fox; m. Andrew H. Rudolph, Aug. 17, 1963 (div. Jan. 1988); children: Kristen Ann, Kevin Andrew; m. Eugene J. Webb, Nov. 23, 1991. BS, U. Mich., 1964; MEd, Houston Bapt. U., 1982; EdD, U. San Francisco, 1993. Cert. adminstr., Tex., elem. and spl. edn. educator, Mich., Tex. Tchr. spl. edn. Hawthorn Cu., Northville, Mich., 1964-70; tchr. Bellaire (Tex.) Sch. for Children, 1977-80; prin. Corpus Christi Sch., Houston, 1980-97; founding head The Monarch Sch., Houston, 1997—. Spkr. in field. Bd. dirs. DeBusk Found. Recipient Elem. Sch. Recognition award U.S. Dept. Edn., 1989-90, Blue Ribbon Sch. award, 1990, Outstanding Doctoral Student award, 1994. Mem. ASCD, U. Mich. Alumni Assn. Avocations: reading, flyfishing, camping, hiking, bodybuilding. Home: 3531 Sun Valley Dr Houston TX 77025-4148 Office: The Monarch Sch 1231 Wirt Rd Houston TX 77055-6852 Office Phone: 713-479-0800. Business E-Mail: mwebb@monarchschool.org.

WEBB, MARY CHRISTINE, reading recovery educator, in-class reading specialist; b. Ames, Iowa, Jan. 3, 1947; d. Howard Darrell and Lorena Faye (North) Webb; m. Harlen DuWayne Groe, Dec. 29, 1989 (div. Oct. 1997). BS in Elem. Edn., Iowa State U., 1969, MS in Emotional Disabilities, 1980, MEd in Learning Disabilities, 1986. Cert. tchr. K-9, learning disabilities, behavioral disabilities, multicategorical, Iowa; cert. in reading endorsement, Iowa, 2001. 1st grade tchr. Holy Spirit Sch., Carroll, Iowa, 1970; severe behavior disabilities tchr. Area Edn. Agy 7, Waterloo, Iowa, 1979-85; tchg. and rsch. assistantship Iowa State U., Ames, 1985-86; multicategorical 3-8 self contained with integration tchr. Madrid Elem. and Jr. H.S., 1986-87; behavior disability self contained with integration tchr. Des Moines Pub. Schs., 1987-88, resource rm. tchr., 1988-95, multicategorical self contained with integration tchr., 1995-99, reading recovery tchr., behavior interventionist, 1999-2000, reading recovery tchr., title reading tchr., 2000—02, reading recovery tchr., reading specialist, 2002—. Active People to People Spl. Edn. Del. to Mainland China, 1993. Mem.: NEA, ASCD, Iowa State Edn. Assn., Des Moines Edn. Assn. Office: King Acad Math and Sci 1849 Forest Ave Des Moines IA 50314-1336

WEBB, MAYNARD, Internet company executive; BA, Fla. Atlantic U. With Quantum, Thomas Conrad, figgie Internat., IBM; sr. v.p., CIO Gateway, Inc.; pres. eBay Techs. Ebay Inc., San Jose, Calif., 1999—, COO. Office: eBay Inc 2145 Hamilton Ave San Jose CA 95125-5905

WEBB, O. GLENN, retired farm supplies company executive; b. 1936; married BS, U. Ill., 1957; PhD, So. Ill. U., 1973. With Growmark, Inc., Bloomington, Ill., 1966—2000, sec., 1968-72, v.p., 1972-80, pres., 1980—2000, chmn., 1980—2000; dir. Archer Daniels Midland Co., 1991—. Trustee, chmn. Am. Inst. Coop.; dir. St. Louis Farm Credit Banks, Farmers Export Co., Nat. Coop. Refinery Assn., Ill. Agr. Leadership Found.; trustee Grad. Inst. Coop. Leadership.

WEBB, ORVILLE LYNN, retired physician, pharmacologist, educator; b. Tulsa, Oklahoma, Aug. 29, 1931; s. Rufus Aclen and Berla Ophelia (Caudle) W.; m. Joan (Liebenheim), June 1, 1954 (div. Jan. 1980); children: Kathryn, Gilbert, Benjamin; m. Jeanne P. (Heath), Aug. 24, 1991. BS, Okla. State U., 1953; MS, U. Okla., 1961; PhD in Pharmacology, U. Mo., 1966, MD, 1968. Diplomate Nat. Bd. Med. Examiners, Am. Bd. Family Practice; cert. med. examiner, 1999. Rsch. assoc. in pharmacology U. Okla., 1959—61; rsch. fellow NIH, 1962—66; instr. pharmacology U. Mo., Columbia, 1966—68, asst. prof., 1968—69; intern U. Mo. Med. Ctr., 1968—69; family practice New Castle, Ind., 1969—89; med. dir. VA Clinic, Lawton, Okla., 1989—94, Comanche County Hosp., Lawton, Okla., 1994—98; pvt. practice medicine Lawton, Okla., 1998—2002; owner Comanche County Med. Clinic, Lawton, Okla., 1998—2002, Okla. Med. Clinic, Lawton, 1999—2004. Clin. assoc. prof. family medicine U. Okla. Coll. Medicine, 1989—; adj. assoc. prof. pharmacology U. Okla. Coll. Medicine, 1989—; mem. U. Okla. Medicine Admissions Bd., 1995-98; mem. staff Henry County Meml. Hosp., New Castle, Pa. 1969-89; guest prof. pharmacy and pharmacology Butler U. Coll. Pharmacy, Indpls., 1970-75; owner, dir. Carthage Clinic, 1975-89; clin. assoc. prof. family medicine Ind. U. Coll. Medicine, 1986-89; county physician, jail med. dir. Henry County, Ind., 1976-89. Author: (with Blissitt, Stanaszek, Lea, and Febiger) Clinical Pharmacy Practice, 1972; contbr. numerous articles to profl. journals. Bd. dir. Lawton Philharm., 1990-95. Recipient Cert. of Merit in Pharmacol. and Clin. Med. Rsch., 1970, Med. Student Rsch. Essay Award Am. Acad. Neurology, 1968. Fellow Am. Acad. Family Physicians, Am. Coll. Physician Exec.; mem. AMA (ann. award recognition 1975-2001), AAAS, Ind. State Med. Assn., Am. Coll. Sports Medicine, Am. Coll. Occupl. and Environ. Medicine, N.Y. Acad. Sci., Am. Soc. Contemporary Medicine and Surgery, Okla. State Med. Assn., Festival Chamber Music Soc. (bd. dirs. Indpls. 1981-87), Nat. Fraternity Eagle Scouts, Mensa, Columbia Club, Skyline Club, Country Club, Kiwanis, Elks, Sigma Xi, Phi Sigma. Home: 85 Quail Creek Dr NW Lawton OK 73507-9026

WEBB, PAUL, physiologist, educator, researcher, consultant; b. Cleve., Dec. 2, 1923; s. Monte F. and Barbara (Webb) Bourjaily; m. Eileen Whalen, Mar. 13, 1948; children: Shaun P., Paul S. Womacks. BA, U. Va., 1943, MD, 1946; MS in Physiol., U. Wash., 1951. Asst. prof. physiology U. Okla. Sch. Medicine, Oklahoma City, 1952—54; chief environ. sect. Aeromed. Lab., Wright-Patterson AFB, Ohio, 1954-58; prin. assoc. Webb Assocs., Yellow Springs, Ohio, 1959-82; vis. scientist INSERM, Paris, 1983; vis. prof. U. Limburg, Maastricht, The Netherlands, 1986, U. Uppsala, Sweden, 1988-89; clin. prof. Wright State U. Sch. Medicine, Dayton, Ohio, 1980—. Cons. aerospace and undersea medicine, energy balance and thermal physiology, Yellow Springs, 1980—. Author: Human Calorimeters, 1985; contbr. articles to profl. jours. Village councilman Village of Yellow Springs, Ohio, 1969-75; mem. Air Force Scientific Adv. Bd., Washington, 1984-88. Recipient Ely award Human Factors Soc., 1972. Fellow Aerospace Med. Assn. (Aerospace Indsl. Life Scis. Assn. award 1969), Am. Inst. Med. and Biol. Engring.; mem. Am. Physiol. Soc., Am. Soc. for Clin. Nutrition, Undersea Med. Soc. (oceaneering internat. award 1979, pres. 1980-81). Home and Office: 370 Orton Rd Yellow Springs OH 45387-1321

WEBB, PHARRON R. counselor, secondary school educator; s. Victoria Grayson Roquemour. AS cum laude, Darton Coll., 1996; BA summa cum laude, Albany State U., 1998, MEd in Mid Grades, 2001, EdS in Adminstrn., 2002, MEd in Counseling, 2003. Counselor at-risk males Dougherty County Sch. Sys., Albany, Ga., 1999—2003, Lee County Sch. Sys., Leesburg, Ga., 2003—. Mem. Mentorship 2000, Albany State U., 2000. Recipient ednl. stipend, Congl. Black Caucus Spouses' Edn. Fund, 1999—2001. Mem.: NEA, Nat. Dean's List, Ga. Assn. Educators, Psi Chi, Alpha Beta Gamma, Phi Theta Kappa. Democrat. Baptist. Avocations: coaching, swimming, community service.

WEBB, RICHARD C. engineering company executive; b. Omaha, Sept. 2, 1915; m. Virginia; 1 son. BSE.E., U. Denver, 1937, DSc (hon.), 1996; MSE.E., Purdue U., 1944, PhD, 1951; DSc (hon.), U. Denver, 1996. Registered profl. engr., Colo. Traffic engr. Mountain States Telephone and Telegraph Co., Denver, 1937-39; research engr. RCA Labs. Div., Princeton, N.J., 1945-53; pres., founder, tech. dir. Colo. Research Corp. (subs. Carrier Corp.), Syracuse, N.Y., 1956-61; pres., founder. tech. dir. Colo. Instruments, Inc., Broomfield, Colo., 1961-71; pres., gen. mgr. Colo. Instruments div. Mohawk Data Scis. Corp., Utica, N.Y.C., 1971-73; pres. Webb Engring. Co. (name changed to Data Ray Corp.), Boulder, Colo., 1973-85. Vis. lectr. U. Colo., 1962-82; prof. elec. engring. U. Denver, 1953-56, Iowa State Coll., 1950 Contbr. articles to profl. jours.; patentee in field. Recipient Disting. Engring. Alumnus award Purdue U., 1970, Profl. Achievement award U. Denver Alumni Assn., 1983, Outstanding Elec. Engr. award Purdue U., 1992. Fellow IEEE; mem. Soc. Motion Picture and TV Engrs., Acoustical Soc. Am., Inst. Aerospace Scis., Am. Ordnance Assn., Western Electronics Mfrs. Assn. (past v.p., dir.), Sigma Xi, Tau Beta Pi, Eta Kappa Nu. Home: PO Box 3078 Estes Park CO 80517-3078

WEBB, RICHARD GILBERT, financial executive, antique selling service executive; b. Tulsa, May 11, 1932; s. William Leslie and Cora (Kroshus) W.; m. Patricia S. Wagdin, Apr. 13, 1957 (div. Sept. 1974); children: Catherine, Andrea, Nicholas; m. Judith A. Burke, Jan. 12, 1980; stepchildren: Mara, Karen, Jennifer, Christopher. Student, U. Okla., 1950-52; BBA, So. Meth. U., 1954; MBA, Harvard U., 1956. CPA, Okla. Mgmt. cons. McKinsey & Co., N.Y.C., 1959-61; planning analyst Mobil Oil Co., N.Y.C., 1961-64; sub controller, treas. ITT, N.Y.C., 1964-66; v.p., mgr. corp. devel. Ill. Tool Works, Chgo., 1966-70; v.p. planning, treas., chief fin. officer Interstate Bakers, Kansas City, Mo., 1970-78; v.p., treas., chief fin. officer Gen. Host Corp., Stamford, Conn., 1979-81, Grolier, Inc., Danbury, Conn., 1981-89, fin. cons., 1989—2000; co-owner Antique Assocs., 2000—. Cons. to State Ill., Springfield, 1969; adj. prof. fin. dept. We. Conn. State U., 1984; adv. bd. Conn. Bank and Trust Co., Danbury, 1986-88. Fundraiser, bd. dirs. United Way, Danbury, Conn., 1982-86; bd. dirs. Danbury YMCA, 1983-89, treas., 1985-87, chmn. bd. dirs., 1987-89, chmn. bd. trustees, 1981-91, trustee, 1991-00; mem. bd. advisors dept. fin. U. Conn., 1984-88; trustee Conn. Pub. Expenditure Coun., 1986 88. 1st lt. U.S. Army, 1956-59. Mem. AICPA, Okla. Soc. CPAs, Greater Danbury C. of C. (bd. dirs. 1985-89, treas. 1986-88, chmn. bd.dirs. 1988-89, trustee 1989-2000, chmn. bd. trustees 1989-91), Universalist-Unitarian Soc. Stamford (chmn. fin. com., chmn. bldg. & grounds 1999-2003, pres. 2003—.). Republican. Avocations: swimming, reading, antiques, golf. Home and Office: 37 Saddle Ridge Rd Pound Ridge NY 10576-1111

WEBB, ROBERT DAVID, school system administrator; b. Eastland, Tex., Aug. 20, 1970; s. Billy John Webb and Betty Carol Sanders; m. Tandy Elizabeth Brown, Dec. 18, 1994; children: Robert Aaron, Tyler Stone, Caitlin Elizabeth. BA, Tex. Tech U., 1995, MEd, 2001. Secondary social studies edn. Tex., 1996, cert. prin. Tex., 2001. Psychiat. correctional officer iii Tex. Dept. Criminal Justice, Lubbock, Tex., 1995—96; tchr., coach Lefors ISD, 1997—97, Sinton ISD, 1997—98, Tahoka ISD, 1998—2002; prin., coach Spur ISD, 2002—03; prin. Tahoka ISD, 2003 - . Chmn. Lynn County Repubican Party, Tahoka, 1999—2002; tchr. First Bapt. Ch., 2003—05; den leader Pack 782 Boy Scouts of Am., 2003—03. With U.S. Army, 1989—92. Decorated Army Achievement medal U.S. Army, Good Conduct medal, Nat. Def. medal, Army Svc. medal. Mem.: Tex. State Guard (corr.; co. comdr. 2002—03), Assn. Tex. Profl. Educators (corr.), Tex. Elem. Principals and Supervisors Assn. (assoc.), Lion's Club (corr.), Phi Kappa Alpha (life). Baptist. Avocations: reading, golf, travel, hunting, camping.

WEBB, SHEILA MENZIES, art educator; b. Lansing, Mich., May 26, 1951; d. Lawrence Adelbert Webb and Sheila Menzies Murray Webb; children: Claire Isabel, Elana Grace. BA, U. Mich., 1973; MA, U. Wis., 1977, MFA, 1980, PhD, 2000. Educator Cleve. Mus. of Art, 1980—84; curator, educator Sioux City Art Ctr., Iowa, 1985—87; assoc. curator John Michael Kohler Arts Ctr., Sheboygan, Wis., 1987—88; adj. asst. prof., rschr. U. Wis., Madison, 1989—97; asst. prof. Marquette U., Milw., 1999—. Project mgr. graphic design ONline@UW, Madison, 1993—2002. Mem.: Orgn. Am. Historians, Assn. for Edn. in Jourl. & Mass Comm. Office: Marquette University PO Box 1881 Milwaukee WI 53201 E-mail: sheila.webb@marquette.edu.

WEBB, THEODORE STRATTON, JR., aerospace scientist, consultant; b. Oklahoma City, Mar. 4, 1930; s. Theodore S. and Helen (Klabzuba) W.; m. Cuba Evans, Sept. 2, 1952; children: Theodore S. III, Kelly Elizabeth. BS in Physics, Okla. U., 1951; PhD in Physics and Math., Calif. Inst. Tech., 1955. Engr. Ft. Worth div. Gen. Dynamics, 1955-62, program mgr., 1962-69, dir. aero. tech., 1969-75, v.p. rsch. and engring., 1975-80, v.p. F-16 programs, 1980-89; pvt. practice cons. Ft. Worth, 1989—. Mem. engring. adv. bd. U. Okla., Norman, 1983-87; mem. aerospace coun. Soc. Automotive Engrs., 1975-81. Bd. mem. Engring. Found. U. Tex., Austin, 1975-81, Found. for Sci. and Engring. So. Meth. U., Dallas, 1974-81, Tarrant County Day Care Assn., Ft. Worth, 1975-80, 89-96; All Saints Episcopal Hosp., 1989-2003, Goodwill Industries of Tarrant Country, 1989-96. Mem. AAAS, Am. Phys. Soc., Rivercrest Country Club. Home: 4901 Westridge Ave Fort Worth TX 76116-8222 Office: 6100 Southwest Blvd Ste 250 Fort Worth TX 76109-6902 E-mail: ted.webb@nationwide.net.

WEBB, THOMAS IRWIN, JR., lawyer, director; b. Toledo, Sept. 16, 1948; s. Thomas Irwin and Marcia Davis (Winters) W.; m. Polly S. DeWitt, Oct. 11, 1986; 1 child, Elisabeth Hurst. BA, Williams Coll., 1970; postgrad., Boston U., 1970—71; JD, Case Western Res. U., 1973. Bar: Ohio, Mich. Assoc. Shumaker, Loop & Kendrick, Toledo, 1973-79, ptnr., 1979—, chmn. corp. law dept., 1992-94, mgmt. com., 1994-99. Dir. Calphalon Corp., 1990-98, York Automotive Group, Inc. Mem. coun. Village of Ottawa Hills, Ohio, 1979-85, adviser Ohio Securities, 1979-85, Village of Ottawa Hills, 1999—; bd. dirs. Kiwanis Youth Found. of Toledo, 1982-2002, Toledo Area Regional Transit Authority, 1989-91, Arts Commn. Greater Toledo, 1993-2003, exec. com., 1994-99, v.p., 1994-96, pres., 1996-97; bd. dirs. Jr. Achievement of Northwestern Ohio, Inc., 1992—, Lourdes Coll. Found., 1995-2001, Toledo Orch. Assn., 1999—, Med. Coll. Ohio, 2001—, Lourdes Coll., 2001—. Mem. ABA, Ohio Bar Assn. (corp. law com. 1989—), Toledo Bar Assn., Mich. Bar Assn., Northwestern Ohio Alumni Assn. of Williams Coll. (pres. 1974-83), Toledo-Rowing Found. (trustee 1985-2001), Toledo Area C. of C. (trustee 1991-98, exec. com. 1993-98, fin. com. 1993—), Order of Coif, Crystal Downs Country Club, Toledo Country Club, The Toledo Club (trustee 1984-90, pres. 1987-90), Williams Club NY, Crystal Lake Yacht Club. Republican. Episcopalian. Office: Shumaker Loop & Kendrick 1000 Jackson St Toledo OH 43624-1573 Office Phone: 419-321-1237. Business E-Mail: twebb@slk-law.com.

WEBB, THOMAS J. utilities executive; b. Alexandria, Va., Oct. 3, 1952; m. Donna; 3 children. B in Fin. with honors, George Mason U.; MBA. Various fin. mgmt. positions Ford Motor Co. and subs.; controller Electronics divsn., Large Front-Wheel Drive Vehicle Ctr.; CFO Visteon Corp.; chief fin. info. officer Ford Motor Co.; exec. v.p., CFO Kellogg Co., Battle Creek, Mich., 2000—02, CMS Energy, Dearborn, Mich., 2002—. Bd. dirs. Conix, Can., Hall Climate Control, Korea, Halla Electronics, Korea, Samcor, South Africa, Yan Feng, China, Toledo (Ohio) Molding and Die, Climate Sys., India, others. Office: CMS Energy 1 Energy Plaza Dr Jackson MI 49201-2357*

WEBB, VERONICA, fashion model, journalist; b. Detroit, Feb. 25, 1965; d. Leonard Douglas and Marion (Stewart) W. Student, New Sch. Social Rsch., 1983; signed with, Ford Models, Inc., N.Y.C., 1992—. Contbg. editor, columnist Paper Mag., 1989—; contbg. editor features column Interview Mag., 1990—; spokesmodel Revlon, 1992-96. First featured on cover of Vogue, 1988; appearances incluce (films) Jungle Fever, 1991, Malcolm X, 1992, For Love or Money, 1993, Catwalk, 1995, 54, 1998, Holy Man, 1998, In Too Deep, 1999, The Big Tease, 1999. First African-Am. to receive exclusive cosmetics contract. Mem. Lifebeat (bd. dirs. 1994—). Office: United Talent Agy 9560 Wilshire Blvd Ste 500 Beverly Hills CA 90212

WEBB, WATTS RANKIN, surgeon; b. Columbia, Ky., Sept. 8, 1922; s. Frank Elbert and Susie Josephine (Rankin) W.; m. Frances Luella Cooke, Aug. 19, 1944; children: Michael Andrew, Paul Alan, Harvey Elbert, Gordon Lewis. BA, U. Miss., 1942; MD, Johns Hopkins U., 1945. Diplomate Am. Bd. Surgery, Am. Bd. Thoracic Surgery, Am. Bd. Surg. Critical Care. Intern Barnes Hosp., St. Louis, 1945-46; resident in surgery VA Hosp., Biloxi, Miss., 1946-48; resident in gen. and thoracic surgery Barnes Hosp., 1948-52; chief surgeon Miss. State Sanatorium, 1952-63; instr. surgery U. Miss., 1955-56, asst. prof. surgery, 1956-58, prof., 1958-63; prof., chmn. div. thoracic and cardiovascular surgery U. Tex. Southwestern Med. Sch., Dallas, 1964-70; prof., chmn. dept. surgery SUNY Upstate Med. Center, Syracuse, 1970-77; prof. surgery Tulane U., New Orleans, 1977-93, La. State U., New Orleans, 1993—; chmn. dept. Tulane U., New Orleans, 1977-89. Author: Pulmonary Problems in Surgery, 1974, Surgery in Acute Coronary Problems, 1974, Aneurysms, 1983, Cardiovascular Emergencies, 1986, Atlas of Pulmonary Resections, 1988, (with others) Surgical Management for Chest Injuries, Vol. VII, 1990; editorial bd.: Annals of Thoracic Surgery, 1968-79, Surg. Rounds, 1978-82, Surgery Clinics, 1980-82, Microcirculation, 1983-84, Brit. Jour. Surgery, 1981-89; contbr. over 450 articles to profl. jours. Recipient award Hadassah, 1965, Knockers Soc. Outstanding Tchr. award SUNY Upstate Med. Ctr., 1972, Owl Club Clin. Tchr. of Yr. award Tulane U. Med. Sch., 1978, 86, 88-93, Gloria P. Walsh award for best tchr. in Med. Sch., 1992, Aesculapian Tchr. of Yr. award La. State U., 1995, 96. Fellow ACS, Am. Coll. Chest Physicians; mem. AMA, Am. Assn. Thoracic Surgery, Am. Coll. Cardiology, Am. Fedn. Clin. Research, Am. Heart Assn. (Silver medal 1963), Am. Physiol. Soc., Am. Surg. Assn., Am. Thoracic Soc., Halsted Soc., La. Med. Soc., Orleans Parish Med. Soc., New Orleans Surg. Soc., Societe International de Chirurgie, Soc. Cryobiology, Soc. Thoracic Surgeons, Soc. Univ. Surgeons, Southeastern Surg. Congress, So. Med. Assn., So. Soc. Clin. Research, So. Surg. Assn. (Shipley medal 1961), So. Thoracic Soc., So. Thoracic Surg. Assn., Surg. Assn. La., Surg. Biology Club II, Internat. Soc. Heart Transplantation, Gulf Coast Vascular Soc., Sigma Xi, Alpha Omega Alpha, Pi Kappa Pi, Beta Beta Beta, Alpha Epsilon Delta. Methodist. Home: 21 Park Island Dr New Orleans LA 70122-1228 Office: La State U Dept Surgery 1542 Tulane Ave New Orleans LA 70112-2825 Office Phone: 504-568-6574. Personal E-mail: wattsrwebb@yahoo.com.

WEBB, WELLINGTON EDWARD, political organization administrator, former mayor; b. Chgo., Feb. 17, 1941; m. Wilma J. Webb; 4 children. BA in Edn., Colo. State Coll., 1964; MA in Edn., U. No. Colo., 1971. Tchr., 1964-76; mem. Colo. Ho. of Reps., 1973—77; regional dir. HEW, 1977-81; exec. dir., Dept. Regulatory agencies State of Colo., 1981-87; auditor City of Denver, 1987-91, mayor, 1991—2003; vice chair Democratic Nat. Com., 2004—. V.p. Nat. Conf. Dem. Mayors; bd. dir. Nat. League Cities, mem. adv. bd., Brookings Inst. Ctr. Urban and Met. Policy; mem. Nat. Infrastructure Assurance Coun.; mem. bd. dirs. Cenveo, Inc., 2004—. Pres. U.S. Conf. of Mayors, 1993—2003, Nat. Conf. Black Mayors, 2000—. Named One of Top 25 Mayors in Nation, Newsweek, 1996, Chevalier of the Legion of Honor, Country of France, 1999; recipient Nat. Wildlife Fedn. Achievement award, 1999, Govt. Leadership in the Arts award, Ams. for the Arts, 2001, Bridge Builders award, Disting. Pub. Svc. award, US Conf. of Mayors, 2003.

WEBB, WILLIAM DUNCAN, lawyer, mediator; b. Dayton, Ohio, Feb. 14, 1930; s. Herbert Henry and Dorothy (Chamberlain) W.; m. Nancy Helen Regester, June 12, 1953; children: Joseph Chamberlain (dec.), Mary Helen, Nancy Katherine, Sarah Elizabeth, Lucy Ellen. AB, U. Mich., 1952, JD, 1956. Bar: Mo. 1956, Kans. 1958, U.S. Supreme Ct. 1969. Assoc. Stinson, Mag, Thomson, McEvers & Fizzell, Kansas City, Mo., 1956-58; sec. Kansas City (Mo.) Power & Light Co., 1960-78, asst. treas., 1969-78, asst. v.p. communications, 1978-79, asst. v.p. fed. affairs, 1979-84; v.p. investments Paine Webber, 1984-98. Legal counsel Fellowship of Christian Athletes. Mem. city coun. Roeland Park, Kans., 1960-62; chmn. Kansas City Myasthenia Gravis Found., 1965-67; bd. dirs. Boys Club of Kansas City, Mo., 1969-74, Greater Kansas City YMCA, Greater Kansas City chpt. ARC; chmn. bd. councilors Avila Coll., 1969-70; trustee, asst. sec., 1970-89; bd. dirs. Rural Water Dist. # 7, Johnson County, Kans., 1992-94. Mem. Internat. Maine-Anjou Assn. (dir., sec.-treas. 1969-76), Theta Delta Chi, Phi Alpha Delta. Presbyterian. Home and Office: 37000 W 155th St Gardner KS 66030-9617 E-mail: webb37ooo@aol.com.

WEBB, WILLIAM H. consumer products company executive; Joined Philip Morris, Port Chester, N.Y., 1966, from various mgmt. positions to pres. Asia/Pacific region, 1966-93, COO N.Y.C., 1993—. Office: Philip Morris Internat 120 Park Ave New York NY 10017-5592

WEBB, WILLIAM LOYD, JR., army officer; b. Mineral Wells, Tex., Sept. 30, 1925; s. William Loyd and Francis (Mayer) W.; m. Muriel Emma Hinson, Dec. 27, 1947; children: George Sidney, William Loyd III, Lucinda Adrienne, Alicia Muriel. Student, Tex. A & M Coll., 1942-44; BS, U.S. Mil. Acad., 1947; MA, U. Pa., 1958. Commd. 2d lt. U.S. Army, 1947, advanced through grades to maj. gen., 1974; co. comdr. Korea, 1950, 1951-52, 1953-54; assoc. prof. English U.S. Mil. Acad., 1958-61; regimental comdr., dep. comdt. of cadets U.S. Mil. Acad., 1969-71; squadron comdr. 14th Armored Cavalry, 1963-64; mem. faculty U.S Army War Coll., 1965-68; comdr. support command 1st Inf. Div., 1969; dep. comdg. gen., 1971-73; ops. officer 8th Army, U.S. Forces Korea, UN Command, 1973-75; sr. mem. UN Command Mil. Armistice Commn., 1975; comdr. 1st Armored Div., U.S. Army Europe, 1975-78; dep. comdg. gen. V Corps, U.S. Army Europe, 1978; asst. dep. chief of staff for personnel Dept. Army, 1978-82. Decorated D.S.M., Legion of Merit with oak leaf cluster, D.F.C., Bronze Star medal with oak leaf cluster, Air medal with 5 oak leaf clusters, Army Commendation medal with 2 oak leaf clusters, Purple Heart. Mem. Assn. U.S. Army, Armor Assn. Episcopalian. Office: 10148 Hillington Ct Vienna VA 22182-2908

WEBB, WILLIAM TIMOTHY, mobile communications professional; b. Walton-on-Thames, U.K., May 4, 1967; s. Christopher David and Genebeth Carol W.; m. Alison Margaret Porter, June 17, 1995; children: Katherine, Hannah. B of Engring., U. Southampton, 1989, PhD, 1992; MBA, Southampton Mgmt. Sch., 1997. Chartered engr. Tech. dir. Multiple Access Technologies, Southampton, England, 1990—94; prin. cons. Smith System Engring., Guildford, England, 1994—98; dir. strategy Motorola, Schaumburg, Ill., 1998—2001; mng. cons. PA Cons., 2001—03; head R & D Ofcom, England, 2004. Mem. innovation awards judging panel Wall St. Jour.; vis. prof. U. Surrey, England, 2003—. Author: Modern Quadrature Amplitude Modultion, 1994, Introduction to Wireless Local Loop, 1998, Understanding Cellular Radio, 1998, The Complete Wireless Communications Professional, 1999, Single and Multi-Carrier QAM, 2000, Narrowband and Broadband Wireless Local Loop, 2000, The Future of Wireless Communications, 2001; contbr. articles to profl. jours. Fellow: Inst. for Elec. Engrs. (v.p. 2004—); mem.: IEEE (sr.). Office Phone: +44 20 7981 3770. E-mail: william.webb@ofcom.org.uk.

WEBB ANDERSON, JOANN MARIE, lawyer, community advocate; b. St. Louis, Nov. 19, 1942; d. Jeff and Nancy Mae (Harris) Webb; m. Clifton Earl Anderson, Dec. 30, 1966; children: Ronald James Anderson, Nancy D. Anderson Tayborn. Student, U. Mo., Columbia and St. Louis, 1960-62; BA in History, St. Louis U., 1967, JD, 1978; grad., Ind. U., 1974-75. Bar: Mo. 1979, U.S. Dist. Ct. (ea. dist.) Mo. 1979, U.S. Ct. Appeals (8th cir.) 1979, U.S. Ct. Appeals (3d cir.) 1982. Staff atty. Legal Svcs. Ea. Mo., St. Louis, 1979-80; staff atty., mng. atty. Legal Svcs. V.I., Christiansted, Frederiksted, 1980-81; asst. atty. gen. Govt. of V.I., St. Croix, 1981-83; supervising atty. civil divsn. Dept. of Justice, Office of Atty. Gen., St. Croix, 1984-85, acting chief, supervising atty., 1985-87; exec.dir. Navy Relief Soc./Japan Aux., Yokusuka, 1988-89; sole practitioner St. Louis, 1997—2002; ptnr. Anderson and Webb Anderson, LLP, 2002—. Music arranger, exec. dir. St. Croix Inspirational Singers, 1983-85. Bd. dirs. Archway Cmtys., Inc., St. Louis, 1998-2001, Child Ctr. of Our Lady, 2001—; polit. action com. Coalition of 100 Black Women, St. Louis, 1990; planning and focus group Hyde Park Neighbors/Trinity Sq., St. Louis, 1990—; cmty. adv. panel bd. Mallinkrodt Chemical Co., 1998—. Mem. Bar Assn. Met. St. Louis (econ. devel. com.), Jr. League of St. Louis, Caths. Against Capital Punishment, Blacks for Life/Mo. Right to Life, Lawyers for Life (bd. dirs. St. Louis chot.), Zeta Phi Beta. Roman Catholic. Avocations: neighborhood development, historical preservation, reading, grandparenting, international travel. Home: 1420 Bremen Ave Saint Louis MO 63107-2918 Office: 3920 Lindell Blvd Ste 207 Saint Louis MO 63108 E-mail: justmo60@worldnet.att.net.

WEBBER, CARL MADDRA, lawyer; b. Champaign, Ill., May 23, 1944; s. Charles Maddra and Lucille Ethelyn (Rankin) W.; children: Wendy Elizabeth, Christopher Maddra, Alexandra Sandeen. BS, Northwestern U., 1966; JD, U. Ill., 1973. Bar: Ill. 1974, U.S. Dist. Ct. (cen. dist.) Ill. 1974, U.S. Ct. Appeals (7th cir.) 1979. Pres. Webber & Thies PC, Urbana, Ill., 1974—. Adj. prof. Coll. Commerce U. Ill., 1987-90. Contbr. articles to profl. jours. Active Champaign County Jail Cts. Tech. Adv. Com., 1978-79, Downtown Devel. & Redevel. Commn., Urbana, 1978-79, U. Ill. Pres. Coun., 1984—; pres. Downtown Urbana Promotion Com., 1981-82; bd. dirs. Prairielands Coun. Boy Scouts Am., 1974—, v.p., 1979-82, pres., 1997-99; bd. dirs. U. Ill. Libr. Friends Bd., v.p., 1984-86, pres., 1986-88; bd. visitors U. Ill. Coll. Law, 1980—. Lt. USN, 1966-70. Recipient Appreciation award City of Urbana, 1980. Fellow Am. Bar Found., Ill. Bar Found.; mem. ABA, Urbana C. of C. (dir. 1978-81, 87-89, chmn. bd. 1989-90), Champaign County Bar Assn. (bd. dirs. 1980-83, pres. 1981-82), Ill. Bar Assn. (family law sect. coun. 1978-79, real estate sect. coun. 1983-87, co-chmn. contract drafting com. 1984-88), Rotary (dir. local club 1980-82). Home: 1910 Woodfield Rd Champaign IL 61822 Office: Webber & Thies PC 202 Lincoln Square PO Box 189 Urbana IL 61801

WEBBER, CHRIS, III, (MAYCE EDWARD CHRISTOPHER WEBBER), professional basketball player; b. Detroit, Mar. 1, 1973; s. Mayce and Doris Webber. Student, U. Mich., 1991—93. Drafted Orlando Magic, Fla., 1993; forward Golden State Warriors, San Francisco, 1993—94, Washington Bullets, 1994—98, Sacramento Kings, 1998—. Founder Timeout Found. Named Nat. H.S. Player of Yr., 1990—91, Mr. Basketball, State of Mich., 1991, Coca-Cola Classic NBA Player of Yr., 1994, Brut Bullets Player of Yr., 1994—95; named to NBA All-Rookie 1st team, 1994. Achievements include being drafted 1st round Orlando Magic, 1993. Avocation: collecting signed historical documents of prominent African-Am. Office: Sacremento Kings One Sports Parkway Sacramento CA 95834

WEBBER, DIANA L. management consultant executive, engineering educator; b. Sacramento, May 12, 1960; d. Ralph and Mary P. (Chace) Van Tuyl. BS, Tex. A&M U., Coll. Sta., Tex., 1980—83; M in Computer Systems Mgmt., Creighton U., Omaha, Nebr., 1984—87; PhD, George Mason U., Fairfax, Va., 1997—2001. Aerospace engr. USAF, Crystal City, Va., 1978—2001, Scitor Corp., Chantilly, Va., 1995—2001; adj. prof. George Mason U., Fairfax, Va., 2001—; sr. assoc. Booz Allen Hamilton, McLean, Va., 2001—. Author: (jour. article) Modeling Variability with the Variation Point Model in software product lines, (conf. article) modeling adaptive and evolvable software product lines using the variation point model, modeling variability with the variation point model. Capt. USAF, 1978—94, Pentagon. Mem.: ACM, IEEE Computer Soc. Democrat. Achievements include research in The Variation Point Model. Avocations: walking, reading, swimming. Office: Booz Allen Hamilton 8283 Greensboro Dr Mc Lean VA 20191 Office Phone: 703-902-4062. Personal E-mail: drwebber@comcast.net. Business E-Mail: webber_diana@bah.com.

WEBBER, HELEN, artist, designer; b. NYC; d. David and Frieda (Berlin) Ross; children: Joel Benjamin (dec.), Daniel Saul, Rachel Frieda. BA, Queens Coll., 1951; postgrad., Columbia U., 1953; MA, RI Sch. Design, 1963. Site specific artist/designer, product designer toys, books; tchr. in design dept. Calif. Coll. Arts, Oakland, 1982, 1984, 1987; lectr. U. Calif. Keynote spkr. ASID, San Diego and Kansas City, 1983, Nat. Home Furnishings League, San Ferancisco, 1980, Chgo., 1982; lectr., exhibitor Internat. Congress Women Archs., Paris, 1983, U. Calif., Santa Cruz, 1988, Commnwealth Club, San Francisco, 1989, guest lectr. RI Sch. Design Alumni Conf., 1996; instr. Hussian Coll. Art, Phila., 2003-04. Author, illustrator: Good-Night, Night, The Sea Is My Blanket, 1963, My Kite it the Magic Me, Summer Sun; prin. commissions in 5 media tapestry, clay, glass, metal and wood for 6 Carnival Cruise Line ships; Festival, Tropical Fantasy, Holiday, Celebration, Destiny, Pittsburg Calif. Civic Ctr., Metro Commerce Bank, San Francisco, Statendam/Holland Am. Cruise Lines, VA Med. Ctr., Cleve., Vets. Cemetery, Riverside, Calif., VA Hosp., Lyons, NJ, East Tex. Med. Ctr., Tyler, St. Patrick's Hosp., Lake Charles, La., Gatwick Penta Hotel, London, Jewish Home for the Aged, Houston, Jewish Home for Aging, Riverdale, NY, Betty Ford Pavilion, Palm Springs, Fla., Sphohn Hosp., Corpus Christi, Tex., St. Agnes Hosp., Fresno, Calif., Chevron Corp., San Ramon, Calif., Merck & Co., Rahway, NJ, Kodak, Kingsport, Tenn., Kaiser Permanente, Bristol Hosp., Conn., Sacramento and San Jose, Calif., Quail Lodge Resort, Carmel Valley, Calif., Episcopal Homes Found., San Francisco, Menorah Manor, Dunedin, Fla., Hyatt Regency, Phoenix, 1st United Meth. Ch., Wichita Falls, Tex., Ctrl. Maine Hosp., Lewiston; designer, artist textile, wallpaper, sheets, towels, children's games for Collins & Aikman, Burlington, Covington, Peerage of Eng., Edward Fields, Pastime Industries. Mem. Design Internat. (pres., co-founder San Francisco 1984-85), Women -in-Design Internat. (founder, pres. 1977-83, Outstanding Contbn. to Design award 1980), Urban Art Internat. (bd. dirs.). Studio: 103 S Village Ave Exton PA 19341 Office Phone: 610-363-9241. E-mail: helenwebber@comcast.com.

WEBBER, HOWARD RODNEY, computer company executive; b. Berlin, N.H., Oct. 20, 1933; s. Robert Alfred and Amelia (Rousseau) W.; m. Helen Margaret McCubbin, May 6, 1959; children: Benjamin James, Adam Brooks, Holly Isabella. AB, Dartmouth Coll., 1956; postgrad., Lehigh U., 1956-57. Editor in chief U. N.C. Press, Chapel Hill, 1960-63, Johns Hopkins Press, Balt., 1963-65; dir. Case Western Res. U. Press Cleve., 1965-70, MIT Press, Cambridge, 1970-74; v.p., gen. mgr., pub. Open Court Pub. Co., LaSalle, Ill., 1974-83; v.p., pub. Reference div. Houghton Mifflin Co., Boston, 1983-87; mgr. advanced devel. Groupware Systems Digital Equipment Corp., Nashua, N.H., 1987-95; chmn. FutureTense, Inc., Acton, Mass., 1995-99; cons. Open Market, Inc., Burlington, Mass., 1999—2000; info. and tech. cons., 2001—. Served with AUS, 1957-59. Mem. Phi Beta Kappa. Democrat. Episcopalian. Home and Office: 49 Wilson Rd Bedford MA 01730-1340 E-mail: h.r.webber@verizon.net.

WEBBER, JOHN BENTLEY, orthopedic surgeon; b. Morristown, N.J., Jan. 27, 1941; s. George Bentley and Gladys (Moody) W.; m. Mary Christina Thometz, Feb. 25, 1978; children: John Bentley, Edward Alan BA, Lehigh U., 1962; MD, Temple U., 1966. Intern Rochester Gen. Hosp., N.Y., 1966-67; resident Temple U. Med. Ctr., Phila., 1967-70; Stelrling Bunnell fellow in hand surgery Pacific Med. Ctr., San Francisco, 1971; practice medicine specializing in orthopedic surgery and surgery of hand Phila., 1973—; assoc. prof. orthopedic surgery and rehab. Hahnemann Med. Coll. and Hosp., Phila., 1973—, chief sect. on hand surgery, 1973—; attending surgeon St. Christopher's Hosp. for Children, Phila., 1996—. Cons. in hand surgery Mcpl. Med. Svcs., Phila., 1973-87, USPHS, Phila., 1973-76, burn ctr. St. Agnes Med. Ctr., Phila., 1973—, Phila. unit Shriners' Hosp. for Crippled Children, 1979-95, Served to maj. USAF, 1971-73. Fellow ACS (Pa. com. on trauma), Am. Acad. Orthopedic Surgeons; mem. AMA, Am. Soc. for Surgery of Hand, Bunnell Hand Club (pres. 1978-80), Assn. for Acad. Surgery, Eastern Orthopedic Soc., Pa. Med. Soc., Phila. Orthopedic Soc., Phila. Hand Soc. (pres. 1987-89), Phila. County Med. Soc., Phila. Coll. Physicians, Meigs Med. Assn., Rotary, Union Leauge, Riverside Yacht Club (fleet surgeon), Phila. Country Club, Delaware Valley Ducks Unltd. (chmn. 1983-88), U.S. Coast Guard (cert. master). Republican. Congregationalist. Home: 1139 Rock Creek Rd Gladwyne PA 19035-1439 Office: Feinstein Bldg 216-220 N Broad St Ste 200 Philadelphia PA 19102

WEBBER, PAMELA D. information technology executive; Sr. mgr. applications devel. eCommerce Arrow Electronics, Inc., Melville, NY. Mem.: The Computer Tech. Industry Assn. (bd. mem. electronics industry data exch. leadership 2003—). Office: Arrow Electronics 50 Marcus Dr Melville NY 11747*

WEBBER, PEGGY, actress, producer, director, writer; b. Laredo, Tex., Sept. 15, 1925; d. Mathew Edward and Margaret Ann (Pierce) Weber; m. Robert Sinskey, Aug. 8, 1951 (div. 1968); children: Teresa Dickinson, Patricia Wynn, Robert Marshall Jr.; m. Sean McClory, Mar. 17, 1983. Student, U. So. Calif., L.A., 1942-44; AA, CUESTA, 1973; student, Calif. Poly. U. Founder Calif. Artists Repertory and Radio Theatre, 1972—. Actress, writer, dir., prodr.: (TV series) Treasures of Literature (Outstanding Prodn. award Acad. TV Arts and Scis., 1948, 1949); writer, dir., prodr.: Calif. Artists Radio Theatre Series; (Nat. Pub. Radio series) Mysteries in the Air, 1987—2001; actress: over 8,000 network radio broadcasts, and 300 nat. TV telecasts; actor: (films) Orson Welles' Macbeth, Hitchcock's The Wrong Man, Farrow's Submarine Command, and others; exec. dir. 7 theaters: prodr., writer, dir. over 100 drama, lit., music prodns.: Nat. Pub. Radio, 1984—2002; contbr. Pres. Calif. Artists Radio Theatre Non-profit Corp., artistic dir. Named Silver award for best drama spl., Internat. Radio Festival, 2002; recipient Outstanding Radio Personality, Time Mag., 1946, Ray Bradbury Creativity award, Woodbury U., L.A., 1998, Double Gold award, Corp. for Pub. Broadcasting, 1992, Gold and Silver award, Internat. Radio Festival, 2001, 27 nat. and internat. awards, Spl. Cert. of Commendation for Cultural Contbns., L.A. City Coun. and Mayor, 2003, various other awards, Internat. Radio Festival. Mem.: SAG, AFTRA, Pacific Pioneer Broadcasters (former bd. dirs.), Actors Equity Assn. Avocations: walking, history, genealogy, archaeology. Office: Calif Artists Repertory and Radio Theatre 6612 Whitley Ter Los Angeles CA 90068-3221 E-mail: info4Peggy@cs.com.

WEBBER, RICHARD JOHN, lawyer; b. Mpls., July 27, 1948; s. Richard John and Mary Lee (Moore) W.; m. Susan Barbara Listerman, Jan. 8, 1972; children: Hillary, Joanna. BA, Princeton U., 1970; JD, U. Mich., 1973. Bar: D.C. Ct. Appeals 1974, U.S. Ct. Appeals (9th and D.C. cirs.) 1980, U.S. Dist. Ct. D.C. 1980, U.S. Claims Ct. 1974, U.S. Supreme Ct. 1980. Law clk. U.S. Ct. Claims, Washington, 1973-75; trial atty. U.S. Dept. Justice, Washington, 1975-80; assoc. Arent, Fox et al, Washington, 1980-85, ptnr., 1985—. Mem. ABA (chmn. fed. contract claims and remedies com. sect. pub. contract law 1986-91), Fed. Bar Assn. (chmn. govt. contracts sect. 1992-94, 1994-96, chmn. ADR sect. 2002-03). Office: Arent Fox Washington Sq 1050 Connecticut Ave NW Ste 500 Washington DC 20036-5303 Office Phone: 202-857-6254. E-mail: webberr@arentfox.com.

WEBBER, ROSS ARKELL, management educator; b. New Rochelle, N.Y., July 18, 1934; s. Richard and Muriel (Arkels) W.; m. Mary Louise Foradora, Sept. 29, 1956; children: Sarah Ruth, Judith Mary, Gregory Ross, Jennifer Louise, Stephen Andrew. BSE, Princeton U., 1956; PhD, Columbia U., 1966; MS (hon.), U. Pa., 1972. Indsl. engr. Eastman Kodak Co., Rochester, NY, 1959-61; instr. Columbia U., N.Y.C., 1961-64; lectr. Wharton Sch. U. Pa., Phila., 1964-65, asst. prof., 1965-70, assoc. prof., 1970-76, prof., 1976-2000, chmn. dept. mgmt., 1992-95, prof. emeritus, 2000—; v.p. U. Pa., Phila., 1981-86. Dir. Wharton-Industry Exec. Program, U. Pa., 1966 68, chmn. Wharton Internat. Bus. com., 1968-69, coord. Orgn. Behavior and Mgmt. Group, 1968-75, asst. dept. chmn., PhD com., 1972-75, coord. Orgnl. and Mgmt. Component, Advanced Mgmt. Program in Health Care Adminstrn., 1973-74, mem. Univ. Coun., 1975-77, adv. com. Pub. Mgmt. Unit, The Wharton Sch., 1977-81, chmn. Grad. Admissions com.; mem. editl. bd. The Wharton Mag.; bd. dirs. Arcadis N.V. Author: Organizational Behavior and the Practice of Management, 1968, 5th rev. edit., 1987; Spanish lang. edit., 1982, Culture and Management: Text and Reading in Comparative Management, 1969, Management: Basic Elements of Managing Organizations, 1979, 3rd rev. edit., 1984, Polish lang. edit., 1984, Management Pragmatics: Readings and Cases on Managing Organizations, 1979, Time is Money!: The Key to Managerial Success, 1980, Japanese lang. edit. 1983, Swedish edit. 1983, Spanish lang. edit., 1985, Portugese lang. edit., 1989, To Be a Manager, 1981, A Guide to Getting Things Done, 1984, Becoming a Courageous Manager: Overcoming Career Problems of New Managers, 1991, Breaking Your Time Barriers: Becoming a More Effective Strategic Time Manager, 1992; contbr. over 55 articles to profl. jours. Past mem. bd. dirs. United Way Southeastern Pa.; coach youth athletics, fund raiser for ch., religious educator. Lt. (jg) USN, 1956-59. Avocations: painting, tennis, skiing. Office: U Pa Wharton Sch 2000 Steinberg Hall Philadelphia PA 19104 Business E-Mail: webber@wharton.upenn.edu.

WEBBER, WILLIAM ALEXANDER, university administrator, physician; b. Nfld., Can., Apr. 8, 1934; s. William Grant and Hester Mary (Constable) W.; m. Marilyn Joan Robson, May 17, 1958; children— Susan Joyce, Eric Michael, George David. MD, U. B.C., Can., Vancouver, 1958; LLD, U. B.C., 2000. Intern Vancouver Gen. Hosp., 1958-59; fellow Cornell U. Med. Coll., N.Y.C., 1959-61; asst. prof. medicine U. B.C., 1961-66, assoc. prof., 1966-69, prof., 1969—99, dean faculty medicine, 1977-90, assoc. v.p. acad., 1990-96, dean emeritus, 1999—. Mem. B.C. Med. Assn., Can. Assn. Anatomists, Am. Assn. Anatomists. Achievements include research on renal structure and function. Home: 2478 Crown St Vancouver BC Canada V6R 3V8 Office: U BC 2177 Westbrook Mall Vancouver BC Canada V6T 1Z3 Office Phone: 604-822-3550. E-mail: webber@interchange.ubc.ca.

WEBER, ALAN J. insurance company executive; b. Rye Brook, N.Y., 1949; BS in Econs., U. Pa., 1970; MBA, Northwestern U., 1971. Various fin., ops. and tech. positions and consumer bus. Citibank, N.Y.C., from 1971, exec. v.p. fin. instns. and transaction svcs., until 1998, v.p., group fin. contr., sr. v.p. ops., country mgr., divsn. exec. consumer bus. for Asia Pacific region; chmn. Citibank Internat., N.Y.C., 1994-98; vice chmn. for strategy and fin., CFO Aetna Inc., Hartford, Conn., 1998—2002; CEO US Trust Corp., N.Y.C., 2002—. Office: US Trust Corp 114 W 47th St New York NY 10036

WEBER, ALBAN, association executive, lawyer; b. Chgo., Jan. 29, 1915; s. Joseph A. and Anna (von Plachecki) W.; m. Margaret Kenny, Dec. 29, 1951; children: Alban III, Peggy Ann, Gloria, Brian. AB, Harvard U., 1935, JD, 1937; MA, Northwestern U., 1962; LLM, John Marshall Law sch., 1967. Bar: Ill. 1938, Mich. 1985, Fla. 1997, U.S. Supreme Ct. 1946. Ptnr. Weber & Weber, 1937-41; gen. counsel Fgn. Liquidation Commn., State Dept., 1946; trust officer Lake Shore Nat. Bank, Chgo., 1952-55; univ. counsel Northwestrn U., Evanston, Ill., 1955-70; pres. Fedn. Ind. Ill. Colls. and Univs., Evanston, 1970-85; of counsel Schuyler, Roche & Zwirner, Evanston, 1984-94; pres. Benjamin Franklin Fund, Inc., 1965-75, Northwestern U. Press, Inc., 1961-65; chmn. State Assn. Execs. Coun., 1981. Pres. N.E. Ill. coun. Boy Scouts Am., 1970-71, dist. chmn. Gulfstream coun., 1994-95; alderman City of Chgo., 1947-51. Comdr. USNR, 1941-45, rear adm., 1969-75. Recipient Silver Beaver award Boy Scouts Am., 1946, Meritorious Svc. award Loyola U., 1978, Edn. for Freedom award Roosevelt U., 1984. Mem. Nat. Assn. Coll. and Univ. Attys. (pres. 1962), Harvard Law Soc. Ill. (pres. 1984), Navy League (pres. Evanston coun. 1967-70), Univ. Risk Mgmt. Assn. (pres. 1965), Naval Order U.S. (nat. comdr. 1970-72), Harvard Club, Port St. Lucie Rotary Club, Chgo. Yacht Club, White Lake Yacht Club, Kiwanis (lt. gov., pres. Port St. Lucie club), St. Lucie River Power Squadron (comdr.), Anchor Line Yacht Club (commodore). Home: 1627 S Lake St Whitehall MI 49461-9705 E-mail: StormyWeber2@aol.com.

WEBER, ALFONS, physicist; b. Dortmund, Germany, Oct. 8, 1927; s. Alexander and Ilona (Banda) W.; m. Jeannine K. Weber, Oct. 8, 1955; children: Karl, Louise, Paul. PhD, Ill. Inst. Tech., 1956. Instr. physics Ill. Inst. Tech., Chgo., 1953-56; from asst. prof. physics to prof. Fordham U., Bronx, N.Y., 1957-81, prof. physics and chemistry, 1976-81, chmn. dept. physics, 1964-70; rsch. physicist Nat. Inst. Stds. and Tech., Gaithersburg, Md., 1977-98, acting chief molecular spectroscopy divsn., 1980-81, chief molecular physics divsn., 1982-95, sr. scientist physics lab., 1995-98, scientist emeritus, 1999—; program mgr. condensed matter physics divsn., materials rsch NSF, 1998—2001, program dir. exptl. phys. chemistry, chemistry divsn., 2001—. With chem scis. divsn. U.S. Dept. Energy, 1991-92, chem. divsn. NSF, 1992-95. Editor: Raman Spectroscopy of Gases and Liquids, 1979; Structure and Dynamics of Weakly Bound Molecular Complexes, 1987, Spectroscopy of the Earth's Atmosphere and Interstellar Medium, 1992; former mem. editl. bd. Jour. of Raman Spectroscopy, Jour. Chem. and Phys. Reference Data. V.p. Union Free Dist. # 1 Sch. Bd., Eastchester, N.Y., 1970-73. Postdoctoral fellow NRC Can., U. Toronto, 1956-57. Fellow Am. Phys. Soc. (councillor 1987-91);

mem. AAAS, Optical Soc. Am., Coblentz Soc., Soc. Applied Spectroscopy, Am. Chem. Soc. Office: Optical Technology Division National Inst Standards and Technology 100 Bureau Dr Gaithersburg MD 20899

WEBER, ALOIS HUGHES, principal; b. Clay County, Mo., Dec. 19, 1910; d. William Swan and Nora Mildred (Elam) Hughes; m. Frank Thomas Ewing Weber, May 28, 1934 (dec. 1980); children: Patricia Katherine Weber Brusuelas, Susan Weber Mills. BA, William Jewell Coll., Liberty, Mo., 1932; MA, U. Mo., Kansas City, 1971. Elem. prin. Linden (Mo.) Sch. Dist. #72, 1931-34; elem. tchr. Eugene (Mo.) Sch. Dist., 1935-38, Sycamore Sch., Boone County, Mo., 1938-41; reserve tchr. Kansas City (Mo.) Schs., 1941-55, contract tchr., 1955-63; head tchr. Allen Sch., Kansas City, 1963-67; remedial reading tchr. Benjamin Franklin Sch., Kansas City, 1967-69; reading cons. Div. Urban Edn., Kansas City, 1969-73; coord. Title I Elem. Reading and Compensatory Edn., Kansas City, 1974-79; ret. Instr., trainer ARC, Am. Assn. Ret. Persons, Staying Healthy After Fifty, State of N.Mex., 1987-89, Growing Old with Health and Wisdom, 1989-95; tutor Literacy Vols. of Am., Inc., Rio Rancho, N.Mex., 1990-93; spkr. AARP Health Care Reform, Health Care Am., 1992—, Lovelace Sr. Adv. Group, 1993-98. Vol. Corrales Libr., 1980-88; bd. dirs. Read West, Literacy Vols. Am., Rio Rancho, 1989-92; bd. dirs. Adobe Comty. Theatre, Corrales, 1989-90; lectr. in field; mem. State of N.Mex. steering com. Growing Old with Health and Wisdom, 1989-95; asst. state coord. Am. Assn. Ret. Persons, Health Advocacy Svcs., N.Mex., 1995-98; pres. adv. bd. Meadowlark Sr. Ctr., Rio Rancho, 1997-2003. Recipient Area Cmty. Svc. award AARP, Nat. award for HAS Outstanding Project Achievement, 1993; Area Cmty. Svc. award State of N.Mex., 1988, Cert. of Appreciation, ARC, 1988, Cert. of Appreciation for outstanding cmty. svc. N.Mex. Legislature, State Senate, 1997, Cert. of Appreciation Rio Rancho, N.Mex. Dept. Pub. Safety Srs. and Law Enforcement Together, 1997; NSF grantee, 1973. Mem. AAUW, N.Mex. Assn. Edn. Retirees (exec. com. 1987-89), Albuquerque Assn. Edn. Retirees (exec. sec., bd. dirs. 1990-95), PEO (chpt. BD chaplain, 1990-94), West Mesa Assn. Ednl. Retirees (membership chmn. 1991, v.p. 1993, pres. 1994), Grad. Club Albuquerque. Democrat. Baptist. Avocations: bridge, reading, travel. Home: 3321 Esplanade Cir SE Rio Rancho NM 87124-2198

WEBER, ALVIN JULIAN, III, radiologist; b. Knoxville, Tenn., Apr. 3, 1936; s. Alvin Julian and Nancy Rhea (Freeman) W.; m. Judith Anne Rowe, Sept. 16, 1967; children: Alvin Julian IV, Philip Rowe. MD, U. Tenn., 1962. Cert. Am. Bd. Internal Medicine, Am. Bd. Nuclear Medicine, Am. Bd. Radiology. Chmn. credentials com. Meth. Hosps. Memphis, 1986—91, dir. dept. nuclear medicine, 1990—2000. Cons. in nuc. medicine, Va., 1976—79, Tenn., 1976—79, Tenn., 2001—02, Ala., 2001—02, Miss., 2001—. Lt. USN, 1963-66. Mem. ACP, Am. Coll. Radiology, Am. Coll. Nuc. Physicians, Radiol. Soc. N.Am. Baptist. Avocations: marksmanship, hiking, camping.

WEBER, ARNOLD I. lawyer; b. Little Cedar, Iowa, Oct. 4, 1926; divorced; children: Katherine Weber Hickle, Thomas, Margaret Weber Robertson. PhB magna cum laude, Marquette U., 1949; MA, Harvard U., 1950; JD, George Washington U., 1954, LLM, 1956. Bar: D.C. 1954, Md. 1961, Calif. 1962, U.S. Dist Ct. D.C. 1954, (no. dist.) Calif. 1962, (cen. dist.) Calif. 1992, U.S. Ct. Claims 1960, U.S. Tax Ct. 1965, U.S. Ct. Appeals (D.C. cir.) 1954, (9th cir.) 1962, (fed. cir.) 1991, U.S. Supreme Ct. 1959. Lawyer Housing and Home Fin., Washington, 1954; pvt. practice Washington, 1954-55; lawyer Tariff Commn., Washington, 1954-55, FCC, Washington, 1955-56, IRS, Washington, 1956-61; assoc. Brobeck, Phleger & Harrison, San Francisco, 1961-64; sr. gen. atty. So. Pacific Transp., San Francisco, 1964-84; western tax counsel Santa Fe Pacific Corp., San Francisco, 1985-88; pvt. practice San Francisco, 1988—. With USNR, 1944-54, PTO. Mem. ABA, Olympic Club, Bar Assn. San Francisco, State Bar of Calif. Office: 57 Post St Ste 502 San Francisco CA 94104-5020

WEBER, ARNOLD ROBERT, academic administrator; b. N.Y.C., Sept. 20, 1929; s. Jack and Lena (Smith) W.; m. Edna M. Files, Feb. 7, 1954; children: David, Paul, Robert. BA, U. Ill., 1951; MA, PhD in Econs., MIT, 1958. Instr., then asst. prof. econs. MIT, 1955-58; faculty U. Chgo. Grad. Sch. Bus., 1958-69, prof. indsl. relations, 1963-69; asst. sec. for manpower Dept. Labor, 1969-70; exec. dir. Cost of Living Council; also spl. asst. to Pres. Nixon, 1971; Gladys C. and Isidore Brown prof. urban and labor econs. U. Chgo., 1971-73; former provost Carnegie-Mellon U.; dean Carnegie-Mellon U. (Grad. Sch. Indsl. Adminstrn.), prof. labor econs. and pub. policy, 1973-80; pres. U. Colo., Boulder, 1980-85, Northwestern U., Evanston, Ill., 1985-95, chancellor, 1995-98, pres. emeritus, 1998—. Cons. union, mgmt. and govt. agys., 1960—; cons. Dept. Labor, 1965; mem. Pres.'s Adv. Com. Labor Mgmt. Policy, 1964, Orgn. Econ. Coop. and Devel., 1987; vice chmn. Sec. Labor Task Force Improving Employment Svcs., 1965; chmn. rsch. adv. com. U.S. Employment Svc., 1966; assoc. dir. OMB Exec. Office of Pres., 1970—71; chmn. Presdl. R.R. Emergency Bd., 1982; trustee Com. for Econ. Devel., Nat. Multiple Sclerosis Soc.; bd. dirs. Diamond Tech. Partners Inc.; asst. sec. manpower U.S. Dept. Labor, 1969—70. Contbr. articles to profl. jours. Laureate, Lincoln Acad. Ill.; Ford Found. Faculty Rsch. fellow, 1964-65. Mem. Am. Acad. Arts and Scis., Indsl. Rels. Rsch. Assn., Nat. Acad. Pub. Adminstrn., Comml. Club Chgo. (pres., civic com. 1995-2000), Econ. Club Chgo. (pres. 1995-97), Phi Beta Kappa. Jewish. Office: Northwestern U Office of Pres Emeritus 555 Clark St 209 Evanston IL 60208-0805 E-mail: arnold-weber@nwu.edu.

WEBER, ARTHUR, magazine executive; b. Chgo., Feb. 1, 1926; s. Philip and Mary (Arlinsky) W.; m. Sylvia Zollinger, Aug. 19, 1950; children—Randy, Lori. Student, Ill. Inst. Tech., 1943-44; BSEE, Northwestern U., 1946. Elec. design engr. Corn Products Refining Co., 1946-48, Naess & Murphy, archs. and engrs., Chgo., 1949-51, Ford Motor Co., 1952-53, Skidmore, Owings & Merill, Chgo., 1954-57, Shaw, Metz & Dolio, Chgo., 1958-59; pres. Consumers Digest mag., Chgo., 1959—; pub. Money Maker mag. (name changed to Your Money mag., 1991), 1979-97, pres., 1997—2003; pub. U. Chgo. Better Health Letter, 1995-96, pres., 1997—2003. Served with USNR, 1944-46. Served with USN, 1944—46, served with USNR, 1946—56.

WEBER, BECKY, state legislator; b. Sept. 24, 1954; Restaurant developer; ins. agt.; mem. Wis. State Assembly, Madison, 2002—, mem. budget rev. com., vice chair aging and long-term care com., mem. govt. ops. and spending limitations com., mem. ins. com., mem. rural affairs com., mem. small bus. com. Republican. Office: State Capitol Bldg Rm 115W PO Box 8953 Madison WI 53708 Address: 2811 Antier Trail Green Bay WI 54313

WEBER, CHARLES L. electrical engineering educator; b. Dayton, Ohio, Dec. 2, 1937; BSEE, U. Dayton, 1958; MSEE, U. So. Calif., 1960; PhD, UCLA, 1964. Tech. staff Hughes Aircraft Co., Calif., 1958-62; from asst. prof. to prof. elec. engring. U. So. Calif., 1964—. Fellow IEEE. Office: U So Calif Comm Scis Inst Dept Elec Engring Sys Los Angeles CA 90089-2565

WEBER, CHARLES WALTER, nutrition educator; b. Harold, S.D., Nov. 30, 1931; s. Walter Earl and Vera Jean (Scott) W.; m. Marylou Merkel Adam, Feb. 3, 1961; children: Matthew, Scott. BS, Colo. State U., 1956, MS, 1958; PhD, U. Ariz., 1966. Research asst. U. Ariz., Tucson, 1963-66, asst. prof., 1966-68, assoc. prof., 1969-72, prof. nutrition, 1973-97, prof. emeritus, 1997—. Cons. Hermosillo, Mex., 1970-74, Inst. of Health, Cairo, 1981-82, U. Fortaleza, Rio de Janiero, 1986. Contbr. articles to sci. jours. Served as cpl. U.S. Army, 1952-54. Mem. Am. Assn. Cereal Chemists, Am. Inst. Nutrition, Inst. Food Technologists, N.Y. Acad. Scis., Am. Soc. Clin. Nutrition, Poultry Sci. Assn., Ariz. Referees Assn., Sigma Xi. Clubs: Randolph Soccer (Tucson) (pres. 1976-79). Avocation: stamp collection. Home: 4031 E Calle De Jardin Tucson AZ 85711-3410

WEBER, EICKE RICHARD, physicist; b. Muennerstadt, Germany, Oct. 28, 1949; s. Martin and Irene (Kistner) W.; m. Monika Rähse, Aug. 28, 1999. BS, U. Cologne, Fed. Republic of Germany, 1970, MS, 1973, PhD, 1976, Dr.Habil., 1983. Sci. asst. U. Koeln, 1976-82; rsch. asst. U. Lund, Sweden, 1982-83; asst. prof. dept. material sci. U. Calif., Berkeley, 1983-87, assoc. prof., 1987-91, prof. materials sci., 1991—; prin. investigator Lawrence Berkeley Lab., 1984—. Vis. prof. Tohoku U., Sendai, Japan, 1990, Kyoto (Japan) U., 2000; cons. in field; internat. fellow Inst. for Study of Defects in Solids, SUNY, Albany, 1978-79; chmn. numerous confs.; mem. founding com. CAESAR Found., Bonn, 1995-97, mem. scientific coun. 1999—; lectr. in field. Editor: Defect Recognition and Image Processing in III-V Compounds, 1987, Imperfections in III-V Compounds, 1993; co-editor: Chemistry and Defects in Semiconductor Structures, 1989, others; series co-editor: Semiconductors and Semimetals, 1991—; contbr. numerous articles to profl. jours. Recipient IBM Faculty award, 1984, Humboldt U.S. Sr. Scientist award, 1994; rsch. grantee Dept. of Energy, 1984—, Office Naval Rsch., 1985—, Air Force Office Sci. Rsch., 1988—, NASA, 1988-90, Nat. Renewable Energy Lab., 1992—. Fellow: Am. Phys. Soc.; mem.: German Scholars Orgn. (pres. 2003—), Materials Rsch. Soc., IEEE, Alexander von Humboldt Assn. Am. (pres. 2001—03). Achievements include first identification of point defects formed by dislocation motion in silicon; determination of the energy levels of antisite defects in GaAs, of 3d transition metal solubility, diffusivity, and lattice site in silicon, of mechanism of internal gettering in silicon; research in defects formed in III/V thin films and interfaces; on growth and characterization of semiconductor nanostructures; in structure and electronic properties of metal GaAs heterostructures; in nature and electronic properties of defects in GaAs, GaN, and related compounds; in MBE growth of GaN and related compounds; in low-temperature MBE growth of As-rich GaAs; in transition metal gettering in silicon; multicrystalline silicon for photovoltaic applications; scanning tunneling microscopy of semiconductor thin films and interfaces; on electron paramagnetic resonance of defects in semiconductors. Office: U Calif Dept Materials Sci & Engring 374 Hearst Mining Bldg Berkeley CA 94720-1760 Office Phone: 510-642-0205. Business E-Mail: weber@socrates.berkeley.edu.

WEBER, ELSA KOENIG, pre-school educator; b. Chgo., Ill., Mar. 18, 1948, d. Robert Emil and Norma (Evans) Koenig; m. John Pitman Weber, 1971; children: Daniel Abraham, Alexander Samuel, Benjamin John. BA, Elmhurst Coll., 1970; MAT in Elem. Edn., Roosevelt U., 1972; PhD of Edn., U. Ill. Chgo., 1993. Cert. Elem. Edn. Ill., 1972, Early Childhood Edn. Ill., 1986. Tchr., dir. Erie Neighborhood Ho. Head Start, Chgo., 1972—73; tchr. Chgo. Pub. Schools, 1973—76, Northeastern Ill. U. Child Care, Chgo., 1978—88; asst. prof. U. Wis., Whitewater, 1992—96; assoc. prof. Purdue U. Calumet, Hammond, Ind., 1996—. Bd. dirs. Woodland Child Devel. Ctr., Hammond; mem. adv. bd. Charlotte Riley Child Ctr., Hammond, 1996—, Hammond Area Career Ctr., 1997—; pres. Koenig Ch. Edn. Consultants, Havertown, Pa., 1986—. Author: (curriculum book) Students' Rights; contbr. articles to profl. jours. Summer Rsch. Grant, U. Wis. Whitewater, 1994, Summer Faculty Rsch. Grant, Purdue U., 2002. Mem.: N.D. Study Group, Assn. Childhood Edn. Internat., Piaget Soc., Nat. Assn. for Edn Young Children, Phi Kappa Phi. Mem. United Ch. Christ. Achievements include research in Children's Social Development. Avocations: music, gardening. Office: Purdue University Calumet 2200 169th St Hammond IN 46323 Office Phone: 219-989-2385. E-mail: weber@calumet.purdue.edu.

WEBER, ERIC SCOTT, mathematician, educator; b. Edina, Minn., Dec. 5, 1972; s. Gordon Earl and Andrea Jean Weber; m. Jennifer Anne Brown; children: Emily Jean, Ryan Joseph. BA in Math., Gustavus Adolphus Coll., St. Peter, Minn., 1995; PhD in Math., U. Colo., 1999. Vis. asst. prof. Tex. A&M U., College Station, 1999—2002; asst. prof. U. Wyo., Laramie, 2002—03, Iowa State U., Ames, 2003—. Contbr. articles to profl. jours. Solo PI Rsch. grantee, NSF, 2002—. Mem.: Am. Math. Soc., Math. Assn. of Am. Avocations: golf, skiing, apologetics of the Christian faith. Office: Iowa State U Dept Math 400 Carver Hall Ames IA 50011-3036 E-mail: esw@math.iastate.edu.

WEBER, EUGEN, historian, educator, writer; b. Bucharest, Romania, Apr. 24, 1925; arrived in U.S., 1955; s. Emanuel and Sonia (Garrett) Weber; m. Jacqueline Brument-Roth, June 12, 1950. Student, Inst. d'études politiques, Paris, 1948-49, 51-52; BA, Emmanuel Coll., 1950; MA, Emmanuel Coll., Cambridge U., 1954, M.Litt., 1956. History supr. Emmanuel Coll., 1953—54; lectr. U. Alta., 1954—55; asst. prof. U. Iowa, 1955—56; from asst. prof. history to prof. UCLA, 1956—84, Joan Palevsky prof. modern European history, 1984—, chmn. dept., 1965—68; dir. study center U. Calif., France, 1968—70; dean social scis. UCLA, 1976—77, dean Coll. Letters and Scis., 1977—82. Frum Meml. lectr. Toronto U., 1999; Ford faculty lectr. Stanford U., 1965; Patten lectr. Ind. U., 1981; vis. prof. Collège de France, Paris, 1983; dir. d'ètudes Ecole des hautes ètudes, Paris, 1984—85; Christian Gauss lectr. Princeton U., 1990. Author: Nationalist Revival in France, 1959, The Western Tradition, 1959, Paths to the Present, 1960, Action Française, 1962, Satan Franc-Maçon, 1964, Varieties of Fascism, 1964; author: (with H. Rogger) The European Right, 1965; author: A Modern History of Europe, 1970, Europe Since 1715, 1972, Peasants into Frenchmen, 1976 (Commonwealth prize Calif., 1977), La Fin des Terroirs, 1983 (Prix de la Société des gens de lettres, 1984), France Fin-de-siècle, 1986 (Commonwealth prize Calif., 1987), The Western Tradition (WGBH/PBS TV Series), 1989, My France, 1990, Movements, Currents, Trends, 1991, The Hollow Years, 1994, La France des années trente, 1995, Prix M. Baumont, 1995, Prix Etats-Unis/France, 1995, Prix de l'Academie des Jeux Floraux, 1997, Apocalypses, 1999; adv. editor: Jour. Contemporary History, 1966—, French History, 1985—, French Cultural Studies, 1990—, Am. Scholar, 1992—98, Nuova Storia Contemporanea, 1999—. Capt. Brit. Army, 1943—47. Decorated Ordre Nat. des Palmes Academiques, France; recipient Luckman Disting. Tchg. award, UCLA Alumnae Assn., 1992; fellow, Fulbright Found., 1952, Rsch. fellow, Am. Philos. Soc., 1959, Am. Coun. Learned Soc., 1962, Guggenheim fellow, 1963—64, sr. fellow, NEH, 1973—74, 1982—83; grantee Fulbright fellow, 1982—83, Social Sci. Rsch. Coun., 1959—61. Fellow: Am. Philos. Soc., Am. Acad. Arts and Scis., Netherlands Inst. Advanced Studies, Assn. Française de Sci. Politique; mem.: Soc. French Hist. Studies, Soc. d'histoire moderne, Am. Hist. Assn. (scholarly distinction award 1999), Phi Beta Kappa (hon.; senator 1988—2000, Ralph Waldo Emerson prize 1977). Office: UCLA Dept History Los Angeles CA 90095-1473

WEBER, FRANCIS JOSEPH, archivist, museum director; b. Jan. 22, 1933; s. Frank J. and Katherine E. (Thompson) W. Student, L.A. Coll., 1953, St. Johns Coll., 1955, St. Johns Seminary, 1959, Cath. U. Am., 1962, Am. U., Washington. Ordained priest Roman Cath. Ch., 1959. Archivist Archdiocese L.A., 1962—; prof. history Queen Angels Sem., 1962-72; chaplain St. Catherine Mil. Sch., 1972-75; pastor San Buenaventura Mission, 1975-81; dir. Borromeo Guild, 1984-87; archivist Hist. Mus. Archival Ctr., Mission Hills, Calif. Dir. San Fernando Mission, 1981—. Editor The Tidings, 1990, Hoja Volante, 1984-95, Miniature Book Soc. Newsletter, 1995-97; contbr. articles to profl. jours. Pres. Zamorano Club, 1991-93; sheriff L.A. Corral Westerners, 1995; hist. rev. commn. Diocese of Monterey. Decorated Grand Cross Isabel la Catolica, 1993, Knighthood of The Holy Sepulchre; recipient Commendation award El Pueblo do L.A. State Historic Park, 1970, L.A. County Bd. Supr., 1972, L.A. City Coun., 1981, L.A. County Bd. Supr., 1992, Merit award Rounce and Coffin Club, 1969, 71, 75, 77, 79-80, 84-86, 88, 92-95, Archivist Excellence award Calif. Heritage Preservation Commn., 1995. Fellow Calif. Hist. Soc. (Merit award 1972, 83), Hist. Soc. So. Calif. (bd. dirs.); mem. Assn. Cath. Diocesan Archivists (pres. 1996-97), Santa Barbara Mission Archves (bd. dirs.), Assn. Cath. Diocesan Archives (bd. dirs.). Democrat. Roman Catholic. Office: Hist Mus Archival Ctr 15151 San Fernando Mission Blv Mission Hills CA 91345-1109

WEBER, FREDERICK EDWIN, management recruiter; b. Quincy, Ill., Aug. 9, 1924; s. Edwin Frederick and Minnie Catherine (Boschulte) W.; m. Wanda Lou Woody, Aug. 10, 1946; children: Barbara L., Marcia A. (dec. 1990), William F. BS in Indsl. Mgmt., U. Ill., 1948. Cert. personnel cons. Foreman US Rubber Co., Mishawaka, Ind., 1948-56, supt., 1956-59, plant mgr. Stoughton, Wis., 1959-65, Uniroyal Inc., Port Clinton, Ohio, 1965-67, mng. dir. Edinburgh, Scotland, 1968-70; factory mgr. Masland Duraleather, Phila., 1971-74; indsl. cons. J.L. Tunnel Co., Blue Bell, Pa., 1974-76; pres. Mgmt. Recruiters, Cedar Rapids, Iowa, 1976—. Farm mgr., 1993—; regional rep. Midwest Region Mgmt. Recruiters, 1994—. Mem. Iowa Job Svc. Adv. Coun., Des Moines, 1982-95, chmn., 1984, 87, 93; mem. Bd. Edn., Stoughton, Wis., 1962-65; pres. Iowa Assn. Pers. Cons., 1982-83. With USN, 1943-46, PTO. Mem. Am. Legion, Rotary (bd. dirs. 1980-83). Republican. Lutheran. Avocations: travel, golf, photography, poetry. Home: 360 Red Fox Rd SE Cedar Rapids IA 52403-2056 Office: Mgmt Recruiters 150 1st Ave NE Ste 400 Cedar Rapids IA 52401-1126

WEBER, FREDRIC ALAN, lawyer; b. Paterson, NJ, July 31, 1948; s. Frederick Edward and Alida (Hessels) W.; m. Mary Elizabeth Cook, June 18, 1983. BA in History, Rice U., 1970; JD, Yale U., 1976. Bar: Tex. 1976, U.S. Dist. Ct. (so. dist.) Tex. Assoc. Fulbright & Jaworski, Houston, 1976-80, participating assoc., 1980-83, ptnr., 1983—. Dir. Houston Symphony Soc., 1993—, v.p. devel., 2001-03. Mem. ABA, Am. Coll. Bond Counsel (treas. 2003—), Nat. Assn. Bond Lawyers (bd. dirs. 1988-89, treas. 1989-90, pres.-elect 1991, pres. 1991-92), Houston Bar Assn. Office: Fulbright & Jaworski LLP 1301 Mckinney St Ste 5100 Houston TX 77010-3095 E-mail: fweber@fulbright.com.

WEBER, GEORGE, oncology and pharmacology researcher, educator; b. Budapest, Hungary, Mar. 29; came to U.S., 1959; s. Salamon and Hajnalka (Arvai) W.; m. Catherine Elizabeth Forrest, June 30, 1958; children: Elizabeth Dolly Arvai, Julie Vibert Wallace, Jefferson James. BA, Queen's U., 1950, MD, 1952; MD (hon.), U. Chieti, Italy, 1979, Med. Faculty, Budapest, 1982, U. Leipzig, Fed. Republic of Germany, 1987, Tokushima (Japan) U., 1988, Kagawa (Japan) U., 1992. Rsch. assoc. Montreal Cancer Inst., 1953-59; prof. pharmacology Ind. U. Sch. Medicine, Indpls., 1959—; dir. Lab for Exptl. Oncology Sch. Medicine, Ind. U., Indpls., 1974—; Milan Panič prof. oncology Ind. U., Indpls., 1994—, Wellcome prof., 1995—; prof. Lab. for Exptl. Oncology Sch. Medicine, Ind. U., Indpls., 1974-90, disting. prof. Lab. for Exptl. Oncology, 1990—. Chmn. study sect. USPHS, Washington, 1976-78; sci. adv. com. Am. Cancer Soc., N.Y.C., 1972-76, 94—, Damon Runyon Fund, N.Y.C., 1971-76; mem. U.S. Nat. Com., Internat. Union Against Cancer, Washington, 1974-80, 90-94, NAS, Washington, 1974-80, 90-94, U.S. Army Med. Rsch. and Breast Cancer Rsch. Program, 1996-97; prof. Brit. cancer campaign U. Oxford, Oxford, Eng., 2001; vis. prof. U. Bologna, Italy, 2001-02, 03-04. Editor: Advances in Enzyme Regulation, Vols. 1-45, 1962—; assoc. editor Jour. Cancer Rsch., 1969-80, 82-89. Recipient Alecce Prize for cancer rsch. Tiberine Acad., Rome, 1971, Best Prof. award Student AMA, Indpls., 1966, 68, G.F. Gallanti prize for enzymology Internat. Soc. Clin. Chemists, 1984, Outstanding Investigator award Nat. Cancer Inst., NIH, 1986-94, Semmelweis medal & diploma Budapest, Hungary, 2001, medal Gastroenterological Soc., Aliga, Hungary, 2001, Prestigious External Award Recognition Ind. U., Indpls., Ind., 2002. Mem. Am. Soc. for Pharmacology and Exptl. Therapeutics, Am. Assn. Cancer Rsch. (G.H.A. Clowes award 1982), Russian Acad. Sci. (hon.), Hungarian Cancer Soc. (hon.), Hungarian Acad. Scis. (hon.), Acad. Scis. Bologna (Italy) (hon.). Home: 7307 Lakeside Dr Indianapolis IN 46278-1618 Office: Ind U Sch Medicine Lab Exptl Oncology 699 West Dr Indianapolis IN 46202-5119

WEBER, GEORGE RICHARD, financial and internet marketing executive, writer; b. The Dalles, Oreg., Feb. 7, 1929; s. Richard Merle and Maud (Winchell) W.; m. Nadine Hanson, Oct. 12, 1957; children: Elizabeth Ann Weber Katooli, Karen Louise Weber Zaro, Linda Marie. BS, Oreg. State U., 1950; MBA, U. Oreg., 1962. CPA, Oreg. Sr. trainee U.S. Nat. Bank of Portland (Oreg.), 1950-51; jr. acct. Ben Musa, CPA, The Dalles, Oreg., 1954; tax and audit asst. Price Waterhouse, Portland, 1955-59; sr. acct. Burton M. Smith, CPA, Portland, 1959-62; pvt. practice Portland, 1962-99; assoc. World Mktg. Alliance, 1996-99, Waterman and Assocs., 2000—01, Allstate Fin. Svcs., 2001—03. Lectr. acctg. Portland State Coll.; expert witness fin. and tax matters. Author: Small Business Long-term Finance, 1962, A History of the Coroner and Medical Examiner Offices, 1963, CPA Litigation Service References, 1991, Letters to a Friend, 1995; contbr. to profl. publs. and poetry jours. Sec.-treas. Mt. Hood Kiwanis Camp, Inc., 1965; exec. counselor SBA; mem. fin. com., powerlifting team U.S. Powerlifting Fedn., 1984, amb. People to People, China, 1987. Arty. officer AUS, 1951-53. Decorated Bronze Star. Mem. AICPA, Internat. Platform Assn., Oreg. Hist. Soc., Oreg. City Traditional Jazz Soc., Order of the Holy Cross Jerusalem, Order St. Stephen the Martyr, Order St. Gregory the Illuminator, Knightly Assn. St. George the Martyr, World Literary Acad., Portland C.S. Lewis Soc., Beta Alpha Psi, Pi Kappa Alpha. Clubs: Kiwanis, Portland Track, City (Portland); Multnomah Athletic; Sunrise Toastmasters. Republican. Lutheran. Home and Office: 3715 NE Alberta Ct Portland OR 97211-8144 Office Phone: 503-288-3328. E-mail: grweber@earthlink.net. *My basic beliefs are in faith, family and freedom through limited government and personal responsibility, with personal responsibility including development and use of capabilities.*

WEBER, GLORIA RICHIE, retired minister, retired state legislator; married; 4 children. BA, Washington U., St. Louis; MA, MDiv, Eden Theol. Sem., Webster Groves, Mo. Ordained to ministry Evang. Luth. Ch. Am., 1974. Family life educator Luth. Family and Children's Svcs. Mo.; mem. Mo. Ho. of Reps., 1993-94. Mo. state organizer, dir. comm. Mainstream Voters C.A.R.E., 1995. Editor: Interfaith Voices for Peace and Justice, 1996—. Exec. dir. Older Women's League, 1990—95. Named Woman of the Yr., Variety Club, 1978, Woman of Worth, Older Women's League, 1993; recipient Woman of Achievement award, St. Louis Globe-Dem., 1977, Unselfish Cmty. Svc. award, St. Louis Sentinel Newspaper, 1985, Faith in Action award, Luth. Svcs. St. Louis, 1994. Mem.: Assn. Lutheran Older Adults (mem. nat. bd. 2004—), N.Am. Interfaith Network (bd. dirs. 1993—2003), Nat. Assn. Luth. Older Adults (bd. dirs. 2004—), Phi Beta Kappa. Democrat. Office Phone: 314-892-1192. E-mail: gloriaweber9@aol.com.

WEBER, HANNO, architect; b. Barranquilla, Colombia, Sept. 24, 1937; came to U.S., 1952; s. Hans and Ester (Oks) W. BA magna cum laude, Princeton U., 1959, MArch, 1961. Registered arch., Ill., Fla., Mo., Pa., N.J., Va. Urban designer, rsch. assoc. Guayana project MIT and Harvard U., Caracas, Venezuela, 1961-63; project arch. Paul Schweikher Assocs., Pitts., 1963-67; asst. prof. architecture Princeton U., 1967-73; assoc. prof. architecture Washington U., St. Louis, 1973-80; sr. design arch., studio head, assoc. Skidmore, Owings & Merrill, Chgo., 1980-83; prin. Hanno Weber & Assocs., Chgo., 1984—. Vis. lectr. Escuela Nacional de Arquitectura Universidad Nacional de Mex., 1975; rsch. assoc. Rsch. Ctr. Urban and Environ. Planning, Princeton, N.J., 1967-70; project dir. The Cmty. Design Workshop, Washington U. Sch. Architecture, St. Louis, 1973-78; prof. architecture U. Wis., Milw., 1983—. Contbr. articles to profl. jours. Mem. Pres.'s Commn. on Education of Women Princeton U., 1968-69. Fellow NEH, 1970, Graham Found., 1973; 1st prize winner Flagler Dr. Waterfront Master Plan design competition, West Palm Beach, Fla., 1984; 1st prize winner Mcpl. Ctr. design competition, Leesburg, Va., 1987; finalist Okla. City Meml. Internat. design competition, 1997; Chgo. AIA Disting. Bldg. award Citation of Merit, Altamira, Terrace, Highland Park, Fla., 1987, Urban Design award Mcpl. Govt. Ctr., Leesburg, Va., AIA, 1992; finalist Green Homes for Chgo. design competition, 2000. Mem. Nat. Coun. Arch. Registration Bds., The Arch. Assn., Phi Beta Kappa. Office: Hanno Weber & Assocs 417 S Dearborn St Chicago IL 60605-1120 Office Phone: 312-922-5589. E-mail: weber@hannoweber.com.

WEBER, HEIDI AMELIA-ANNE, historian, educator; d. Frederic Gordon and Patricia Banghart Weber. BA, Upsala Coll., East Orange, N.J., 1994; MA, East Stroudsburg U., Pa., 1997; postgrad., Kent State U., Ohio. Adj. history prof. Lehigh Carbon C.C., Schnecksville, 1998—99, Hudson County C.C., Jersey City, 1998—2000, Warren County C.C., Washington, NJ, 1997—2000; grad. asst. Kent State U., Ohio, 2000—02; mil. history program curriculum reviewer Am. Coun. on Edn., Manassas Park, Va., 2001; U.S. history advanced placement history exam. grader Ednl. Testing Svc., San Antonio, 2002, 2004; adj. history prof. Sussex County C.C., Newton, NJ, 2000—, Kean U., Union, NJ, 2003, East. Stroudsburg U., Pa., 2003—. Author: (book review) America's Civil War, Civil War History; internet site reviewer (review - public history resource center) Soldiers and Sailors; author: (book review) Historians of the Civil War Western Theater Online Journal, The Military Book Review Online Journal, Journal of America's Military Past; contbr. articles to profl. jours. Recipient Disting. Svc. award, Phi Alpha Theta, 2001, Yount Windsor award, Am. Coun. on America's Mil. Past, 2001. Mem.: USMA, So. Hist. Assn., The

Rotary Club of Newton (Russian com. co-chair, historian, Newtarian editor), Coun. on America's Mil. Past (bd. dirs.), Phi Alpha Theta (Psi chpt. pres., Mil. History Summer Seminar 2004). Personal E-mail: haweber@kent.edu.

WEBER, HERMAN JACOB, federal judge; b. Lima, Ohio, May 20, 1927; s. Herman Jacob and Ada Minola (Esterly) W.; m. Barbara L. Rice, May 22, 1948; children: Clayton, Deborah. BA, Otterbein Coll., 1949; JD summa cum laude, Ohio State U., 1951. Bar: Ohio 1952, U.S. Dist. Ct. (so. dist.) Ohio 1954. Ptnr. Weber & Hogue, Fairborn, Ohio, 1952-61; judge Fairborn Mayor's Ct., 1956-58; acting judge Fairborn Mcpl. Ct., 1958-60; judge Greene County Common Pleas Ct., Xenia, Ohio, 1961-82, Ohio Ct. Appeals (2d dist.), Dayton, 1982-85, U.S. Dist. Ct. (so. dist.) Ohio, Cin., 1985—92, sr. judge, 1992—. Chmn. Sixth Cir. Dist. Judges Conf., 1988, Ohio Jud. Conf., Columbus, 1980-82; pres. Ohio Common Pleas Judges Assn., Columbus, 1975. Vice-mayor City of Fairborn, 1955-57, council mem., 1955-59. Served with USNR, 1945-46. Office: US Dist Ct 801 100 E 5th St Cincinnati OH 45202-3905

WEBER, JAMES STUART, management educator; b. Sayre, Pa., Apr. 8, 1947; s. Arthur William and Margaret (Jensen) W. BA in Math., Northwestern U., 1971; AM in Math., Loyola U., Chgo., 1973; MS in Math. Stats., U. Ill., Chgo., 1975, PhD in Policy Analysis, 1981. Teaching asst. Loyola U., Chgo., 1972-73; teaching and rsch. asst. dept. math. and polit. sci. U. Ill., Chgo., 1973-75, 76-81; vis. asst. prof. Roosevelt U., Chgo., 1981-82, asst. prof., 1982-88, program dir. MS degree MIS, 1982-86, grad. faculty, 1986-88. Vis. lectr. Loyola U. Chgo., 1989; vis. asst. prof. U. Wis., Milw., 1989-91, U. Ill., Chgo., 1991—. Co-editor: Business and Society, 1984-85; reviewer IEEE Software Engring.; Proc. editor Structured Devel. Forum, 1987; contbr. to profl. jours. Block capt. Waukegan (Ill.) Neighborhood Watch Program, 1982-85; mem. Waukegan Downtown Assn., 1986-88. Mem. AAUP, Ops. Rsch. Soc. Am. (full), London Math. Soc., Regional Sci. Assn., Acad. Mgmt., Am. Math. Soc., Am. Statis. Assn., Hill Sch. Alumni Assn., Northwestern U. Club, RROC (life), Informs (Chgo. chpt. treas. 1994—). Republican. Episcopalian. Office: PO Box 603 Gurnee IL 60031-0603

WEBER, JOHN BERTRAM, architect; b. Evanston, Ill., Oct. 15, 1930; s. Bertram Anton and Dorothea W.; m. Sally Ann French; children: Suzanne French Roulston, Jane Marie McCarthy, Patricia Ann Blodgett, Nancy B. AB in Architecture, Princeton U., 1953; postgrad., Ill. Inst. Tech., 1959. Lic. arch.; registered energy profl. Field engr. United Constrn. Co., Riverdale, N.D., 1952; draftsman Bertram A. Weber Arch., Chgo., 1947, 53, architect, 1958-1973; field engr. Atkinson United Constrn. Co., Greenup and Ashland, Ky., 1956-58; ptnr., proprietor Weber & Weber Arch., Chgo., 1973—84; pvt. practice Northbrook, 1984—94, Winnetka, Northfield, 1994—. Mem. Ill. Architecture Act Revision task force, 1982—89; del. Ill. Arch.-Engr. Coun., 1976—87, chmn., 1981—82. Prin. works include Prestwick Country Club, 3175 Commercial Ave. Bldg., Northbrook, med. office bldg. and additions to Bi-county hospital, Warren, Mich., additions and alterations to Detroit Osteopathic Hosp., addition to Duraclean Internat. Bldg., Deerfield, additions to The Admiral, Chgo., Villa Stresov, Borovets, Bulgaria, numerous pvt. residences, churches, comml., ednl., and recreational bldgs. Active Winnetka Cmty. Caucus, 1965, 74; mem. Mayor's adv. com. on bldg. codes, Chgo., 1975-80; chmn. bldg. com. Winnetka Cmty. House, 1977-81; active Winnetka Zoning Bd. Appeals, 1983-88, chmn., 1987-88; active Winnetka Ad Hoc Zoning Com., 1995-96, Winnetka Design Review Bd., 2002—, Winneka Forestry Commn., 2003—; deacon, elder Winnetka Presbyn. Ch. Officer USN, 1953—56. Fellow: Assn. Lic. Arch., Ill. Soc. Arch. (bd. dirs. 1969—84, pres. 1976—78, bd. dirs. 1991—99); mem.: VFW, AIA (health com. 1969—76), Constrn. Specifications Inst., Northbrook C. of C., Am. Legion, Exmoor Curling Club, Exmoor Country Club, Dairymen's Country Club, Old Willow Club (pres. 1983), Builders Club Chgo. (bd. dirs. 1966—, pres. 1973—74), Architects Club Chgo. (bd. dirs. 1976—86, pres. 1981, bd. dirs. 1994). Office: John B Weber Architect 415 Berkeley Ave Winnetka IL 60093-2109 *Do what you should do, not what you have to do. In the end, it is only the things that we do that impact on other people's and other living being's lives that have real meaning.*

WEBER, JOHN WALTER, insurance company executive; b. Rochester, N.Y., Jan. 10, 1959; s. Donald J. and Patricia M. (Mangon) W. BS, U. Conn., 1984. Claims supr. Hartford Ins. Group, Southington, Conn., 1986-90; regional claims mgr. Housing Authority Risk Retention Group, Cheshire, Conn., 1990—. Mem. U. Conn. Alumni Assn. Avocations: running, reading, softball, cooking. E-mail: jweber6@charter.net.

WEBER, JONATHAN, editor, journalist, educator; BA in Philosophy, Wesleyan U.; postgrad., Columbia U. Reporter The Times, San Francisco, N.Y.C.; Paris corr. Electronic News, MIS Week; founding sr. editor World Link; columnist, tech. editor L.A. Times, 1989—97; founding editor-in-chief The Industry Std., 1997—2001; T. Anthony Pollner disting. prof. U. Mont. Sch. Journalism, Missoula, 2002; exec. editor internat. rsch. OTA Off the Record Rsch., San Francisco. Recipient First Pl. award in bus. category, AP News Exec. Coun. in Calif./Nev., 1993. Office: Univ Mont 32 Campus Dr Missoula MT 59812*

WEBER, KENNETH J. hotel executive; b. 1946; With Arthur Young & Co., N.Y.C., 1968-71, ITT-Grinnell Corp., Providence, 1971-73, Farmbest Foods Internat., Jacksonville, 1973-74; regional contr. Marriott Corp., Washington, 1974-76, group contr., 1976-77, divsn. contr., 1977-79, pres., CEO Farrell's Ice Cream divsn., 1983-86; exec. v.p., CFO Isaly Co., Pitts., 1979-80; v.p., contr. Country Kitchens Internat. divsn. Carlson Cos., Inc., Mpls., 1980-81; sr. v.p. Poppin Fresh Restaurant divsn. Pillsbury Co., Mpls., 1981-83; sr. v.p., corp. contr. Red Lion Hotels Corp., Vancouver, Wash., 1987-92; sr. v.p., CFO Omni Hotels Corp., Hampton, N.H., 1992—; also v.p., treas. Omni Ctr. Corp., Richmond, Va.

WEBER, LARRY, public relations executive; Founder, pres. Weber Group, Inc., Cambridge, Mass., 1987—2000; chmn., CEO The Weber Group, Inc., Cambridge, Mass.; founder, chmn., CEO Weber Shandwick Worldwide, 2001—02; CEO, chmn. bd. MIMC, Advanced Mktg. Svcs., 2002—. Author, The Provocateur, 2002. Office: MIMC 43 Charles St Boston MA 02114

WEBER, LAVERN JOHN, retired marine science administrator, educator; b. Isabel, S.D., June 7, 1933; s. Jacob and Irene Rose (Bock) W.; m. Shirley Jean Carlson, June 19, 1959 (div. 1992); children: Timothy L., Peter J., Pamela C., Elizabeth T.; m. Patricia Rae Lewis, Oct. 17, 1992. AAS, Everett Jr. Coll., 1956; BA, Pacific Luth. U., 1958; MS, U. Wash., 1962, PhD, 1964. Instr. U. Wash., Seattle, 1964-67, asst. prof., 1967-69, acting state toxicologist, 1968-69; assoc. prof. Oreg. State U., Corvallis, 1969-75, prof., 1976—, asst. dean grad. sch., 1974-77, dir. Hatfield Marine Sci. Ctr. Newport, 1977—2002, supt. Coastal Oreg. Marine Exptl. Sta., 1989-98, assoc. dean Coll. Agrl. Sci., 1998—. Pres., trustee Newport Pub. Libr., 1991-92, Yaquina Bay Econ. Found., Newport, 1991-92; chmn. Oreg. Coast Aquarium, 1983-95. Recipient Pres. award Newport Rotary, 1984-85. Mem. South Slough Mgmt. Commn., Am. Soc. Pharm. and Exptl. Therapy, West Pharm. Soc., Soc. Toxicology, Soc. Exptl. Biol. Med. (n.w. divsn., pres. 1978, 82, 87), Pacific N.W. Assn. Toxicologists (chair 1985-86, coun. 1991-93), Nat. Assn. Marine Lab. (pres. elect 1998-99, 2000-02), Western Assn. Marine Lab. (pres. 1993). Avocations: woodworking, reading, walking, scuba, gardening. E-mail: lavern.weber@oregonstate.edu.

WEBER, LESLEY ELIZABETH, music educator; b. Abington, Pa., Dec. 2, 1955; d. Stacey William and Elizabeth Schraut Lloyd; m. Mark Douglas Weber, June 17, 1978; children: Matthew Douglas, Benjamin Mark, Jacob Lloyd. BS in music edn., Mansfield U., 1973—77. Music tchr. Mid. Twp. Pub. Schools, Cape May Ct. House, NJ, 1977—. Flutist Classically Jazz Flute/Guitar Duo, Cape May, NJ, 1990—; baritone horn player Congress St. Brass Band, Cape May, NJ, 1991—; cantor and flutist St. John of God Ch., No Cape May, NJ, 1987—. Mem.: So Jersey Band and Orch. Dir. Assn., Music Educators Nat. Conf. Roman Cath. Avocations: music, reading, boating, antiques, quilting. Home: 12 Wakefield Pl Cape May NJ 08204 Office: Middle Twp Elem #2 101 W Pacific Ave Cape May Court House NJ 08210 Office Phone: 609-465-1827 ext. 2143.

WEBER, LISA M. insurance company executive; BA in Psychology, SUNY. With Painewebber, 1988—98; sr. v.p. human resources Metlife, Inc., N.Y.C., 1998—2001, sr. exec. v.p., chief adminstrv. officer, 2001—. Bd. dirs. New Eng. Fin., Gt. Am. Fin.; bd. dirs. benefits com. Metlife, Inc.; mem. social responsibility com. Metlife Found. Bd. Mem.: Phi Beta Kappa. Office: Metlife Inc 1 Madison Ave New York NY 10010

WEBER, LYNN, sociology educator; BA in Sociology, Memphis State U., 1971, MA in Sociology, 1973; PhD in Sociology, U. Ill., Urbana, 1976. Asst. prof. Dept. Sociology and Social Work Memphis State U., 1976-81, assoc. prof. Dept. Sociology and Social Work, 1981-86, assoc. dir., co-founder Ctr. Rsch. on Women, 1982-88, prof. Dept. Sociology and Social Work, 1986—96; dir. Ctr. Rsch. on Women U. Memphis, 1988—96; dir. Women's Studies Program U. S.C., 1996—. Faculty devel. assignment Memphis State U., 1987-88; vis. scholar Dept. Health Edn. Temple U., 1987; faculty devel. assignment U. Memphis, 1994-95; disting. vis. prof. gender studies Dept. Sociology and Criminal Justice U. Del., 1994; mem. program com. Assn. for General and Liberal Studies, Memphis, 1993, Soc. for Applied Anthropology, 1992; coord. faculty rsch. seminar on race, class and gender MSU, 1988-90; cons. various founds. and orgns. Co-author: The American Perception of Class, 1987, Women of Color and Southern Women: A Bibliography of Social Research, 1988, 89, 91, 92, (on-line bibliographic database) Research Clearinghouse on Women of Color and Southern Women; adv. editor: The Sociological Quarterly, 1980-85, Gender & Society, 1991-94; reviewer: various scientific publs. including Social Science Quarterly, Am. Sociological Review, Social Problems, Signs: A Jour. of Women in Culture and Society, others; contbr. articles to profl. jours. Recipient numerous grants and fellowships including, NSF, 1988-91, 1995—, NIH, 1989-93, others. Mem. Am. Sociological Assn. (coun. sect. on racial and ethnic minorities 1987-90, dissertation award com. sect. on sex and gender 1990-92, chair 1992, com. on coms. 1991-93, Disting. Contbns. to Tchg. award 1993, Jessie Bernard award 1993), So. Sociological Soc. (program com. 1995), Sociologists for Women in Soc., Society for the Study of Social Problems, Alpha Kappa Delta. Home: 200 Windsor Point Rd Columbia SC 29223-1823 Office: Univ SC Womens Studies WOST Office 201 flinn Hall 1324 Pendleton St Columbia SC 29208

WEBER, MARK, clothing company executive; With Phillips-Van Heusen, N.Y.C., 1972—, sr. v.p., gen. mmerchandise mgr., exec. v.p. merchandising, 1995, pres., COO, 1998—. Office: Phillips-Van Heusen Corp 200 Madison Ave New York NY 10016-3903

WEBER, MARK F. medical executive; MS, Wash. U., St. Louis, 1981. Pres., CEO St. John's Mercy Med. Ctr., 1995—. Office: 615 S New Ballas Rd Saint Louis MO 63141-8221

WEBER, MARK R. electronics executive; B in Indsl. Engring., Kettering U.; M in Mgmt. (Sloan fellow), MIT, 1983. Various pers. and labor rels. pos. GM Fisher Body, Elyria, Ohio, 1971—78, adminstr. pers. svcs. Columbus, Ohio, 1978—79, pers. dir. Syracuse, NY, 1979—82; adminstr. exec. compensation GM Pers. and Devel. Staff, Detroit, 1982—83, dir., classified employee compensation, 1983—85; dir. gen. offices pers. Chevrolet-Pontiac-GM of Can. Group, Warren, Mich., 1985—88, dir. human resources, salaried pers., 1985—88, dir. indsl. rels., 1988—91; gen. dir. pers. Inland Fisher Guide, Warren, Mich., 1991—93, gen. dir. pers. and pub. affairs, 1993—98; v.p. in charge human resources Delphi Corp., Troy, Mich., 1998—2000, exec. v.p., ops., human resource mgmt. and corp. affairs, 2000—. Office: World Hdqrs Delphi Corp 5725 Delphi Dr Troy MI 48098-2815

WEBER, MARY ELLEN, astronaut; b. Cleve., Aug. 24, 1962; d. Andrew Jr. and Joan W.; m. Jerome Elkind. BS in Chem. Engring., Purdue U., 1984; PhD in Physical Chemistry, U. Calif., Berkeley, 1988. With Tex. Instruments, with SEMATECH; astronaut NASA, Houston, 1992—, with crew on STS-70 on space shuttle Discovery, 1995, with cres on STS-101 on space shuttle Atlantis, 2000. Patentee in field; legis. affairs liaison NASA Hdqs., Washington, chmn. procurement bd. for Biotech. Program contractor. Contbr. articles to profl. jours. Avocations: scuba diving, flying, sky diving, golf. Office: Astronaut Office/CB NASA Lyndon B Johnson Space Ctr Houston TX 77058

WEBER, MARY ELLEN HEALY, economist; b. San Francisco, May 28, 1943; d. Ignatius Bernard and Grace Marie (Hogan) Healy; m. Stephen Francis Weber, Dec. 21, 1971. BA, Dominican Coll., 1965; postgrad., Nat. U. Mex., 1967; vis. scholar, Stanford U., 1969-70; postgrad., Cath. U. Chile, 1970-71, U. Chile, 1971-72; PhD, U. Utah, 1974. Tchg. fellow U. Utah, 1965-68; asst. prof. Smith Coll., 1972-75; country economist World Bank, IBRD, 1975-76; sr. economist Internat. Rsch. & Tech. Corp., McLean, Va., 1976-78; dir. regulatory analysis, chief economist OSHA, U.S. Dept. Labor, Washington, 1979-84; pres. Weber Software Enterprises, 1984-86, Web-Wolf Data Systems, Inc., 1986-90; dir. econs., exposure and tech. divsn. Office of Pollution Prevention & Toxics US EPA, Washington, 1990—, acting dep. dir., 2000—. Social Sci. Rsch. Coun. fgn. area fellow, 1969-71. Mem. Sr. Execs. Assn., Exec. Women in Govt. Roman Catholic.

WEBER, MELISSA MURPHY, state representative; b. N.J., Sept. 26, 1969; m. Bob Weber. Dir. Montgomery County Weed and Seed Program; criminal justice task force Am. Legisl. Exch. Coun.; mem. Brehon Law Soc., Denison U. Alumni Recruiting Team. Mem.: Brehon Law Soc., Montgomery Bar Assn., Pa. Bar Assn., Montgomery County Commn. on Women and Families, Phila. Alumnae Chpt., Delta Gamma Nat. Soc. Republican. Roman Catholic. Office: 6 E Wing Harrisburg PA 17120-2020

WEBER, MICHAEL MATHEW, small business owner; s. Mathew Francis and Nadine Norma Weber; m. Bonnie Sue Hagle; children: Lori Lei Ishibashi, Matthew Alan. BS in History, Pepperdine U., 1979. Tech. rep. CSR Hydro Conduit, Sparks, Nev., 1982—90; tech. coord. Stantec Consulting, Reno, 1990—; owner Weber Enterprises, Reno, 1999—. Western regional v.p. Nat. Fedn. Rep. Assemblies, 1999—2001, sergeant at arms, 2003—04; nat. del. Rep. Nat. Conv., New Orleans, 1988, Houston, 1992, mem. nat. platform com., 1992, del. Phila., 2000, mem. nat. rules com., 2000; platform com. chmn. Nev. Rep. State Conv.; state com. mem. Nev. Rep. Ctrl. Com., 1998—2004; state del. Nev. Rep. State Conv., 1988—2004, platform com. chmn.; chmn. Washoe County Rep. Party, 1989—90; del. Rep. Nat. Con., N.Y.C., NY, 2004; mem. Nat. Rules Com., 2004. Mem.: Am. Pub. Works Assn. (assoc.; no. br. chmn. 1989—90), Associated Gen. Contractors (assoc.). Republican. Avocations: photography, motorcycle riding, Nascar auto racing. Home: 8580 Sopwith Blvd Reno NV 89506 Office: Stantec Cons 6980 Sierra Center Pkwy Ste 100 Reno NV 89511

WEBER, RALPH EDWARD, history professor; b. St. Cloud, Minn., Apr. 19, 1926; s. Andrew A. and Kathryn (Desmond) W.; m. Rosemarie Hoyt; children: Mary, Elizabeth, Ralph A., Anne, Catherine, Neil, Therese, Thomas, Andrew. AB, St. John's U., Collegeville, Minn., 1948; MS in Edn., U. Notre Dame, 1950, PhD, 1956. Instr. U. Notre Dame, South Bend, Ind., 1953-54; asst. to dean Marquette U., Milw., 1954-57, registrar, dir. admissions, 1958-61, assoc. prof. history, 1961-69, prof. history, 1969—, chmn. history dept., 1993-96, bd. dirs. Marquette U. Press, 1994—2001, prof. emeritus, 2002—. Scholar-in-residence CIA, Washington, 1987-88, Nat. Security Agy., Ft. Meade, Md., 1991-92; bd. visitors Les Aspin Ctr., Washington, 1994—2001. Author: Notre Dame's John Zahm, 1961, U.S. Diplomatic Codes and Ciphers, 1979 (Best Scholarly Intelligence Book award Nat. Intelligence Study Ctr. 1980), Masked Dispatches, 1993, Spymasters: Ten CIA Officers, 1999; co-author: Admission to College, 1963; editor: As Others See Us, 1972, From the Foreign Press, 2 vols., 1980, The Final Memoranda, 1988, Talking with Harry: Candid Conversations with President Harry S. Truman, 2001, Dear Americans Letters from the Desk of Ronald Reagan, 2003; co-editor: Voices of Revolution, 1972. With USN, 1944-46. Grantee Am. Philos. Soc., 1974, rsch. grantee Bradley Ctr., Milw., 1995, 98. Mem. Soc. for Historians Am. Fgn. Rels. (membership chmn. 1976-94), Am. Cath. Historians Assn. (exec. coun. 1972-75), Assn. Former Intelligence Officers (bd. dirs. 1994-2002), Am. Legion. Avocations: fishing, skiing, hunting, forestry, farming. E-mail: weber09@earthlink.net.

WEBER, RANDY, publishing executive; Assoc. pub. Consumers Digest and Your Money mags., pub., 1993—. Office: Consumers Digest 6th Fl 8001 Lincoln Ave Fl 6 Skokie IL 60077-3695

WEBER, RAY EVERETT, engineering executive, consultant; b. Kenton, Ohio, Dec. 11, 1946; s. Mervin Clarence and Phylis Jean Weber; m. Carolyn Antinoro, Aug. 16, 1980; children: David Charles, Stephen Ray. BS in Physics, Ohio State U., 1973. Lic. real estate agt. N.Y., 1992-1997. Project engr. Erie Lackawanna R.R., Hoboken, NJ, 1974—75; nuclear engring. adminstr. ASME, N.Y.C., 1975—78; cognizant engr. Burns & Roe Inc., Oradell, NJ, 1978—80; supervising engr. Impell Corp., Melville, NY, 1980—88; pres. Webtor Inc., Northport, NY, 1988—; owner Weber Real Estate, Northport, NY, 1978—. Pres. Forest Ventures Inc., Northport, N.Y., 1987—. Author: Nuclear Codes/Standards. With USN, 1966—70. Mem.: ASME (nuclear subcom.), Marco Island Yacht Club, Northport Yacht Club, Am. Legion. Avocations: boating, fishing, skiing, golf. Office: Forest Ventures Inc 115 Soundview Ter Northport NY 11768-1231 E-mail: rweber3@optonline.net.

WEBER, ROBERT CARL, lawyer; b. Chester, Pa., Dec. 18, 1950; s. Robert Francis and Lucille (Nobili) W.; m. Linda Brediger, June 30, 1972; children: Robert F., Mary Therese, David P., Joseph T. BA cum laude, Yale U., 1972; JD, Duke U., 1976. Bar: Ohio 1976, U.S. Dist. ct. (no. dist.) Ohio 1976, U.S. Ct. Claims 1980, U.S. Ct. Appeals (6th cir.) 1981, U.S. Ct. Appeals (5th cir.) 1995. Assoc. Jones, Day, Reavis & Pogue (now Jones Day), Cleve., 1976—83, ptnr., 1983—. Bd. dirs. United Way Svcs. of Cleve., 1992-2002. Fellow Am. Coll. Trial Lawyers, Internat. Acad. Trial Lawyers; mem. Ohio Bar Assn., Am. Law Inst., Product Liability Adv. Coun., Cleve. Bar Assn. (chmn. jud. selection com. 1985-86, trustee 1990-93, pres.-elect 1994-95, pres. 1995-96), Jud. Conf. for 8th Jud. Dist. Ohio (life), Order of Coif. Roman Catholic. Office: Jones Day 901 Lakeside Ave E Cleveland OH 44114-1190 Office Phone: 216-586-7252. E-mail: rcweber@jonesday.com.

WEBER, ROBERT MAXWELL, cartoonist; b. L.A., Apr. 22, 1924; p. Milton and Edith (Huston) W.; m. Marilyn Baum, Oct. 11, 1953 (div.); children— Peter, Lee; m. Debora Graves, Dec. 24, 1988. Student, Pratt Inst., 1945-48, Art Students League, 1948-50. Fashion illustrator, 1949-54; artist New Yorker mag., 1962—; work commd. by IBM, N.Y. Telephone, Am. Airlines, Mobil, Blue Cross/Blue Shield, U.S. Healthcare, Goodyear Co., J.C. Penney Co., Air Canada, Swissair, others; contbr. cartoons to nat. mags. Served with USCGR, 1942-45. Office: New Yorker 4 Times Sq New York NY 10036-6522

WEBER, SHARI, state legislator; b. Owatonna, Minn., July 1, 1953; m. Marvin E. Weber. Student, St. John;s Acad. and Coll., Moorhead State U. Dir. downtown devel. Herington (Kans.) Main St. Program, Herington, Kans., 1993-97; rep. Dist. 68 Kans. State Ho. of Reps., Topeka, 1995—2003. Henry Toll fellow, 2000. Address: 405 E Lewerenz Herington KS 67449 Office Phone: 785-271-1404. E-mail: sjweber@kansas.net.

WEBER, STEPHEN LEWIS, university president; b. Boston, Mar. 17, 1942; s. Lewis F. and Catherine (Warns) W.; m. Susan M. Keim, June 27, 1965; children: Richard, Matthew. BA, Bowling Green State U., 1964; postgrad., U. Colo., 1964-66; PhD, U. Notre Dame, 1969; EdD (hon.), Capital Normal U., China, 1993. Asst. prof. philosophy U. Maine, Orono, 1969-75, assoc. prof., 1975-79, asst. to pres., 1976-79; dean arts and scis. Fairfield (Conn.) U., 1979-84; v.p. acad. affairs St. Cloud (Minn.) State U., 1984-88; pres. SUNY Oswego, 1988-95; interim provost SUNY Albany, 1995-96; pres. San Diego State U., 1996—. Participant Harvard Inst. Ednl. Mgmt., Cambridge, Mass., 1985. Contbr. numerous articles on philosophy and acad. adminstrn. to profl. jours. Mentor Am. Coun. Edn. Fellowship Program, Am. Coun. on Edn., Commn. on Internat. Edn. and Commn. on Govtl. Rels.; bd. govs. The Peres Ctr. for Peace, San Diego Found.; bd. dirs. San Diego Regional Econ. Devel. Corp.; mem. internat. adv. bd. Found. for the Children of the Californias. Named Outstanding Humanities Tchr., U. Maine, 1975; Rsch. fellow U. Notre Dame, 1968-69. Mem. Am. Philos. Assn., Am. Assn. Higher Edn. Democrat. Avocations: art, woodworking, swimming, boating. Office: San Diego State Univ Office Pres 5500 Campanile Dr San Diego CA 92182-8000 E-mail: presidents.office@sdsu.edu.

WEBER, STEPHEN VANCE, physics researcher, astrophysicist; b. Wooster, Ohio, Oct. 31, 1951; s. Dale Sarge and Lucy June (Smith) W.; m. Marie Christensen, June 21, 1980; children: Erik, Kristina. AB in Physics, Princeton U., 1973; MA in Astronomy, U. Calif., Berkeley, 1974, PhD, 1978. Rsch. fellow Calif. Inst. Tech., Pasadena, 1978-80; asst. prof. Dartmouth Coll., Hanover, N.H., 1980-82; rsch. scientist, physicist Lawrence Livermore Nat. Lab., Livermore, Calif., 1982—. Contbr. articles to profl. jours. Mem. Am. Astronomical Soc., Am. Physical Soc. (excellence in plasma physics award 1995). Achievements include investigations of Rayleigh-Taylor instability and implosions in inertial confinement fusion. Office: Lawrence Livermore Nat Lab MS L16 PO Box 808 Livermore CA 94551-0808 Business E-Mail: svweber@llnl.gov.

WEBER, SUSAN A. lawyer; b. 1958; BA, Drake U., 1984; JD, MBA, SUNY, Buffalo, 1989. Bar: Pa. 1990, D.C. 1992, Ill. 1993, U.S. Ct. Appeals (4th cir.) 1990, U.S. Ct. Appeals (3d cir.) 1991, U.S. Ct. Appeals (7th cir.) 1992. Clk. to Justice Byron White U.S. Supreme Ct.; clk. to Judge James Sprouse U.S. Ct. Appeals (4th cir.); with Sidley Austin Brown & Wood, Chgo., 1993—, ptnr., 1997—. Office: Sidley Austin Brown and Wood One Bank Plz 10 S Dearborn St Chicago IL 60603

WEBER, THOMAS WILLIAM, chemical engineering educator; b. Orange, N.J., July 15, 1930; s. William A. and Dorothy (Negus) W.; m. Marianne S. Hartmann, June 4, 1966; children: Anne Louise, William Alois B.Chem. Engring., Cornell U., 1953, PhD, 1963; MS in Chem. Engring., Newark Coll. Engring., 1958. Registered profl. engr., N.Y. Chem. engr. econs. and planning Esso Research & Engring., Linden, N.J., 1955-58; instr. Cornell U., 1961-62; asst. prof. SUNY-Buffalo, 1963-66, assoc. prof. chem. engring., 1966-82, prof., 1982-2000, assoc. chmn. dept., 1980-82, chmn. dept., 1982-89, acting chmn., 1996-97, prof. emeritus, 2000—. Author: An Introduction to Process Dynamics and Control, 1973 Named Prof. of Yr., Tau Kappa Chi, 1965; recipient Chancellor's award for excellence in teaching, 1981, Tchr. of Yr. award Tau Beta Pi, 1982 Fellow AIChE (chmn. western N.Y. sect. 1969-70, Profl. Achievement award western N.Y. sect. 1978), Am. Soc. Engring. Edn. (chmn. instrumentation divsn. 1975-77, chmn. St. Lawrence sect. 1979-80, 92-94, chmn. divsn. experimentation and lab.-oriented studies 1985-86, chmn. Zone I 1999-2001, Outstanding Zone Campus Rep. award 1988, AT&T Found. award 1987-88); mem. Tech. Socs. Coun. Niagara Frontier (sec. 1973-75, pres. 1975-76, treas. 1978—), Swedish Club of Buffalo (pres. 1974-76), U.S. Masters Swimming Club, Sigma Xi, Phi Kappa Phi, Tau Beta Pi, Theta Xi. Presbyterian. Home: 52 Autumnview Rd Buffalo NY 14221-1602 Personal E-mail: twweber@eng.buffalo.edu.

WEBER, WALTER WINFIELD, JR., lawyer, director; b. Ramsey, N.J., Feb. 7, 1924; s. Walter W. and Mary Elizabeth (Collins) Weber; m. Margaret Gardner Wilson, May 12, 1951; children: Ellen, Anne. BS, Va. Mil. Inst., 1947; LLB, Columbia U., 1950. Bar: N.J. 1949, N.Y. 1952, U.S. Supreme Ct. 1966. Assoc. Weber, Muth and Weber, Ramsey, NJ, 1949—52, ptnr., 1953—95; of counsel Poff & Bowman LLC, 1995—. Judge Upper Saddle River Mcpl. Ct., 1955—56. Bd. mgrs. Bergen Pines County Hosp., 1972—76, v.p., 1976. With U.S. Army, 1943—45. Mem.: N.J. State Bar Assn. (chmn. pub. utility law sect. 1972—74), Bergen County Bar Assn., Antique and Classic Boat Soc. (dir. 1987—99), Joe Jefferson (Saddle River, N.J.), Masons. Republican. Dutch Reformed Ch. Address: 1 Cherry Ln Ramsey NJ 07446-1848

WEBER, WILFORD ALEXANDER, education educator; b. Allentown, Pa., Apr. 29, 1939; s. Alexander F. and Kathryn A. (Campbell) W.; children from previous marriage: Kendra L., Brad A.; m. Cheryl Angelo. BA, Muhlenberg Coll., 1963; EdD, Temple U., 1967. Tchr., counselor New Life Boys Ranch, Harleysville, Pa., 1963-65; rsch. asst. Temple U., Phila., 1965-67; asst. prof. Syracuse (N.Y.) U., 1967-71; prof. U. Houston, 1971—, chair dept. curriculum & instrn. Author approximately 165 books, monographs, papers and articles. Grantee, Syracuse U., U. Houston. Mem. Am. Ednl. Rsch. Assn., Assn. Tchr. Educators. Avocation: sports. Home: 2015 Swift Blvd Houston TX 77030-1213

WEBLEY, WILMORE CHRISTOPHER, microbiologist, researcher; b. Bellas Gate, Jamaica, Jan. 1, 1972; s. Clifford Webley and Kathleen Henry-Webley. Postgrad., U. Mass., 1998—2003, M in microbiology, 2000; PhD in microbiology (pathogenic bacteriology and immunology), U. Mass, 2003; BS in med. tech., Northern Caribbean U., Jamaica, 1994. Cert. med. technologist Ministry of Health, Jamaica. Assoc. instr. No. Caribbean U., Mandeville, Jamaica, 1994—98; grad. rsch. asst. U. Mass., Amherst, 2000—03, asst. prof. microbiology, 2003—. Contbr. articles various profl. jours. Co-founder Adventist Christians Together to Serve, Amherst, 2001. Fulbright scholar, 1998—2000. Mem.: AAAS, Am. Soc. for Apheresis, N.Y. Acad. Scis., Am. Soc. Microbiologists, Nat. Geog. Soc. 7th Day Adventist. Achievements include research in new entry pathway for chlamydia. Avocations: travel, cricket, mountain sight seeing. Office: U Mass Morrill IVN Rm 203 Amherst MA 01003 E-mail: wilmore@microbio.umass.edu.

WEBRE, SEPTIME, ballet company artistic director, choreographer; b. New Orleans, Dec. 7, 1961; s. Alfred L. and Juanita (Chisholm) Webre. BA, U. Tex., 1984. Dancer Merce Cunningham Dance Co., N.Y.C., 1991, Am. Repertory Ballet/Princeton (N.J.) Ballet, 1987—99, choreographer, 1988—99, artistic dir., 1993-99, The Washington Ballet, 1999—. Freelance choreographer with Les Grands Ballets Canadienne, 1988—, Pacific N.W. Ballet, 1988—, Sacramento Ballet, 1988—, N.C. Dance Theatre, 1988—, Columbia City Ballet, 1988—, Ballet Austin, 1988—, Dayton Ballet, 1988—, Eglevsky Ballet, 1988—, The Aspen Ballet, the Carslile Project, 1988—, others, 1988—; guest master tchr. various ballet cos., 1990—. Former mem. exec. bd. Young Dems. Am., Austin. Choreographic fellow, N.J. Coun. on Arts, 1992. Roman Catholic. Office: The Washington Ballet 3515 Wisconsin Ave NW Washington DC 20016-3085

WEBSTER, CHRISTOPHER R. chemist, physicist, research scientist; b. Anglesey, Wales, Mar. 3, 1953; arrived in U.S., 1979; s. Donald McLeod Webster, Pamela Lilian Webster; m. Julie C. Webster; children: Genevieve, Philip, Jeffrey Foster, John Foster. BSc with honors, Reading (Eng.) U., 1974; PhD, Bristol (Eng.) U., 1977. Sr. rsch. scientist Jet Propulsion Lab., Pasadena, Calif., 1981—. Contbr. articles to profl. jours. Office: Jet Propulsion Lab 4800 Oak Grove Dr Pasadena CA 91109 Business E-Mail: Chris.R.Webster@jpl.nasa.gov.

WEBSTER, CHRISTOPHER WHITE, foreign service officer; b. Boston, Oct. 30, 1953; s. Henry deForest and Marion (Havas) W. BA cum laude, Amherst Coll., 1975; MA, Johns Hopkins U., 1977. Asst. comml. attache Am. Embassy, Buenos Aires, 1977-79; econ. comml. officer Georgetown, Guyana, 1979-81; desk officer for Jamaica and Guyana Washington, 1982—84; econ. officer Office of Energy, Washington, 1984-86, fin. and devel. officer Lisbon, Portugal, 1986—89, econ. sect. chief Algiers, Algeria, 1989—92; dep. dir. Office of Pakistan, Afghanistan and Bangladesh Affairs, Washington, 1992—95; dep. chief of mission Khartoum, Sudan and Addis Ababa, Ethiopia, 1995-96; chief, developed Country Trade Divsn., Washington, 1996-98; dep. dir. Office of Ctrl. Am. and Panamanian Affairs, Washington, 1998-00, dep. chief of mission Dhaka, Bangladesh, 2000—03, Oslo, 2003—. Recipient Superior Honor award Dept. State, 1983, 91, 98-2000. Office: Am Embassy Oslo PSC 69 Box 1000 APO AE 09707 E-mail: webstercw@state.gov.

WEBSTER, DAVID ARTHUR, retired life insurance company executive; b. Downs, Ill., July 20, 1937; s. Harold Sanford and Carmen Mildred (Moore) W.; m. Anna Elizabeth Prosch, June 10, 1956; children: Theodore David, Elizabeth Anna, Arthur Lee, William Harold. BS, U. Ill., 1960. Actuarial asst. Mass. Mut. Life Ins. Co., Springfield, 1960-64; cons. actuary George Stennes & Assocs., Mpls., 1964-68; v.p., actuary Piedmont Life Ins. Co., Atlanta, 1968-72, Pacific Fidelity Life Ins. Co., Los Angeles, 1972-74; v.p., chief actuary U.S. Life Corp., N.Y.C., 1974-76, exec. v.p., 1976-78, dir., 1976-78; pres., dir. Beneficial Pension Svcs, BPS Agy., Inc.; v.p., treas., dir. Beneficial Assurance Co., 1978-82; asst. sec., dir. Beneficial Computer Svcs., Inc.; treas. Tel-Assurance Corp.; exec. v.p., dir. Beneficial Standard Life, 1978-82; pres., dir. U.S. Life Ins. Co. of Calif., 1982-84, Western World Fin. Group Inc., 1984-86; exec. v.p., COO R.W. Durham and Co., 1987-99. Fellow Soc. Actuaries. Home: 1150 Ladera Ln Paso Robles CA 93446 E-mail: SLODavidPaso@aol.com.

WEBSTER, DAVID MACPHERSON, lawyer; b. Chgo., June 22, 1950; s. Robert Fielden and Julia Orendorff (Macpherson) Webster; m. Lucia Maxwell Blair, Oct. 3, 1987; 1 child, Jessie Maxwell. BA in History magna cum laude with honors, Williams Coll., 1972; JD, U. Va., 1975; DD (hon.), Seabury-Western Theol. Sem., 2000. Bar: Ill. 1975. Assoc. Winston & Strawn, Chgo., 1975-81, ptnr., 1981-87; White House fellow Washington, 1987-88; spl. asst. to dir. FBI, Washington, 1988-89; asst. gen. counsel for multilateral negotiations U.S. Arms Control and Disarmament Agy., Washington, 1989—94; v.p., gen. counsel A.T. Kearney, Inc., Chgo., 1994—2002; of counsel Butler Rubin Saltarelli & Boyd, Chgo., 2002—. Mem. adv. com. Ill. Bus. Corp. Ill. Sec. of State, Chgo., 1982—87. Bd. dirs. Ill. Soc. Prevention Blindness, Chgo., 1980—87, 1997—, pres., 1999—2001; trustee Village of Winnetka, Ill., 2003—; bd. dirs. Better Govt. Assn., Chgo., 1997—99; trustee Episc. Charities and Profl. Svcs., Chgo., 1980—87; bd. dirs. WBEZ Alliance, Inc., Chgo., 1996—; chair bd. trustees Seabury-Western Theol. Sem., Evanston, Ill., 1993—96, trustee, 1988—96, 2002—. Mem.: Chgo. Coun. Fgn. Rels., Manuscript Soc., Chgo. Hist. Soc., Orgn. Am. Historians (assoc.), Am. Hist. Assn. (assoc.), Ill. State Hist. Soc. (life), White House Fellows Assn., Abraham Lincoln Assn., Law Club City of Chgo., Mid-Day Club (Chgo.), Phi Beta Kappa (mem. exec. com. Chgo. chpt. 1996—98). Episcopalian. Avocations: history, writing. Home: 596 Arbor Vitae Rd Winnetka IL 60093-2302 Office: Butler Rubin Saltarelli & Boyd 70 W Madison St Ste 1800 Chicago IL 60602 Business E-Mail: dwebster@butlerrubin.com. E-mail: davidmwebster@comcast.net.

WEBSTER, GERALD BEST, musician, music educator; b. Antioch, Calif., Jan. 6, 1944; s. Gordon Best and Anne Elizabeth Webster; 1 child, Jeffrey Gordon. MusB, Ind. U., 1965, MusM, 1966. Prof. trumpet Western Ill. U., Macomb, 1969—70, Washington State U., Pullman, 1970—94, Portland State U., 1994—; prin. trumpet Spokane (Wash.) Symphony, 1970—77; mem. Edward H. Tarr Brass Ensemble, U.S., Germany, 1978—90, Portland Baroque Orch., 1980, Boston Baroque Orch., 1985—, Pacific Baroque Orch., 1990—. Music dir. for Expo '74 World's Fair, Spokane, 1974. Author: Method for piccolo Trumpet, 1980, Method for Piccolo Trumpet II, 1987, Improving Intonation, 2003, (Groves article) Brass Embouchure, 2002. Served with U.S. Army, 1966-69. Ford Found. fellow Ind. U., 1966. Mem. Internat. Trumpet Guild, Music Educators Nat. Conf., Am. Fedn. Musicians, Pi Kappa Lambda (fellow 1965). Avocation: windsurfing. Home: 11405 SE 18th Cir Vancouver WA 98664-5428 Office: Portland State U Dept Music Portland WA 97207 Office Phone: 503-725-3124.

WEBSTER, GORDON VISSCHER, JR., minister; b. Huntington, N.Y., Oct. 2, 1947; s. Gordon Visscher and Marion Beatrice W.; m. Gloria Marie Farwagi, May 31, 1975; children: David Gordon, Daniel Farwagi, Diana Alexandra. AB, Hamilton Coll., 1969; postgrad., St. Andrews Div. Sch., 1970-71, McCormick Theol. Sem., 1982-87; MDiv, Union Theol. Sem., 1973. Ordained to ministry Presbyn. Ch. (USA), 1973. Staff assoc. Met. Ch. Bd., Syracuse, NY, 1973-75; assoc. pastor 1st Presbyn. Ch., 1975-83; missionary Mid. East Coun. of Chs., Limassol, Cyprus, 1983-84; missionary-in-residence Presbyn. Ch. (USA), Stony Point Center, NY, 1984-86; interim pastor 1st Presbyn. Ch., Oneida, 1988-89, United Presbyn. Ch., Cortland, 1989-91; pastor Ogden Presbyn. Ch., Spencerport, 1991-2001, Downtown United Presbyn. Ch., Rochester, 2001—. Exec. dir. Am. Coalition Mid. East Dialogue, Jamesville, N.Y., 1986-88, Common Good Planning Ctr. of Rochester Area Cmty. Found., 1998-2001; v.p. Greater Rochester Cmty. Chs., 1992-93, pres., 1994-97; chair Interfaith Forum Greater Rochester, 1995, 99; pres. Interfaith Alliance Rochester, 1998-99; mem. Mayor's Stewardship Coun. Comprehensive Planning, City of Rochester, 1996—; mem. Mayor's Commn. on Race and Ethnicity, 2000—; Presbyn. Commr. to Gen. Assembly of NCCCUSA, 2000—; mem. Martin Luther King Jr. Commn. of Monroe County, 1995—; mem. pub. policy commn. N.Y. State Cmty. Chs., 1996-99; mem. Presbytery Genesee Valley, 1991—, trustee, 2003-; commr. PC Gen Assembly, 2004; leader workshops on Mid. East, 1983-89; moderator Syracuse Mid. East Dialogue Group, 1981-83; mem. gen. coun. Presbytery of Utica, 1988-89. Gen. coun. Cayuga-Syracuse Presbytery, 1975-83; commr. 2004 PC (USA) Gen. Assembly. Grantee George Gund Found., 1987, Presbyn. Women's Opportunity Giving, 1987, Joan and Harold Feinbloom Supporting Found. of the Rochester Area Cmty. Found., 1998-2002. Mem. Witherspoon Soc. (steering com. 1974-76), Presbyn. Peace Fellowship (bd. advisors, nat. com. 1972-83). Democrat. Office: Downtown United Presbyn Ch 121 N Fitzhugh St Rochester NY 14614 Office Phone: 585-325-4000. E-mail: revgvw@aol.com.

WEBSTER, HENRY DE FOREST, neuroscientist; b. NYC, Apr. 22, 1927; s. Leslie Tillotson and Emily (deForest) W.; m. Marion Havas, June 12, 1951; children: Christopher, Henry, Sally, David, Steven. AB cum laude, Amherst Coll., 1948; MD, Harvard U., 1952. Intern Boston City Hosp., 1952-53, resident, 1953-54; resident in neurology Mass. Gen. Hosp., 1954-56, rsch. fellow in neuropathology, 1956-59, prin. investigator NIH rsch. grants, electron micros. studies peripheral neuropathy, 1959-69, mem. staffs; instr. neurology Harvard Med. Sch., Boston, 1959-63, assoc. in neurology, 1963-66, asst. prof. neuropathology, 1966; assoc. prof. neurology U. Miami Sch. Medicine, Fla., 1966-69, prof., 1969; chief sect. cellular neuropathology Nat. Inst. Neurol. Diseases and Stroke, Bethesda, Md., 1969-97; chief Lab. Exptl. Neuropathology, 1984-97; scientist emeritus NIH, 1997—; mem. staff Newton-Wellesley Hosp. Disting. scientist, lectr. dept. anatomy Tulane U. Sch. Medicine, 1973; Royal Coll. lectr. Can. Assn. Neuropathologists, 1982; Saul Korey lectr. Am. Assn. Neuropathologists, 1992; chmn. Winter Conf. on Brain Rsch., 1985, 86; head neuropathology del. to visit China in 1990, Citizen Amb. Program, People to People Internat.; mem. exec. com. rsch. group on neuromuscular disease World Fedn. Neurology, 1986-93. Author: (with A. Peters and S.L. Palay) The Fine Structure of the Nervous System, 1970, 76, 91; contbr. articles to sci. jours. Recipient Superior Svc. award USPHS, 1977, A. von Humboldt award Germany, 1985, Sci. award Peripheral Neuropathy Assn., 1994; named hon. prof. Norman Bethune U. of Med. Scis., Chanchun, China, 1991. Mem. Am. Assn. Neuropathologists (v.p. 1976-77, pres. 1978-79, Weil award 1960, Meritorious Contbns. to Neuropathology award 2001), Internat. Soc. Neuropathology (hon., councillor 1976-80, v.p. 1980-84, exec. com. 1980-84, 86-94, pres. 1986-90), Internat. Congress Neuropathology (sec. gen. VIII 1978), Peripheral Nerve Study Group (exec. com. 1975-93, chmn. 1977 meeting), Japanese Soc. Neuropathology (hon.), Am. Neurol. Assn., Am. Acad. Neurology, Royal Soc. Medicine, Am. Soc. Cell Biology, Soc. Neurosci., Rotary Internat., Ausable Club. Office: NIH Rm 4A 29 Bldg 36 Bethesda MD 20892-4123 E-mail: websterh@ninds.nih.gov.

WEBSTER, HUGH, state legislator, accountant; b. Caswell County, N.C., Aug. 6, 1943; m. Patricia; 2 children. BS, U. N.C., 1968, postgrad., 1969, U. Ill., 1970. CPA, N.C. Farmer, N.C, 1953-62; mem. N.C. Ho. of Reps., Raleigh, 1995—. Mem. agr., environ. and natural resources com., fin. com., ins. com., ways and means com., ranking minority mem. state and local govt. com. Republican. Methodist. Office: NC Senate 1101 Legis Bldg 16 W Jones St Raleigh NC 27601-1030 also: PO Drawer W Yanceyville NC 27379

WEBSTER, JAMES RANDOLPH, JR., physician; b. Chgo., Aug. 25, 1931; s. James Randolph and Ruth Marian (Burtis) W.; m. Joan Burchfield, Dec. 28, 1954; children: Susan, Donovan, John. BS, U. Chgo.-Northwestern U., 1953; MD, MS, Northwestern U., 1956. Diplomate: Am. Bd. Internal Medicine (sub bd. pulmonary disease and geriatrics). Intern Phila. Gen. Hosp., 1956-57; resident in medicine Northwestern U., 1957-60, NIH fellow in pulmonary disease, 1962-64; chief medicine Northwestern Meml. Hosp., Chgo., 1976—88; prof. medicine Northwestern U. Med. Sch., 1977—, chief gen. med. sect. dept. medicine, 1987-88; chief exec. officer Northwestern Med. Group Practice, 1978-88; dir. Buehler Ctr. on Aging Northwestern U. Med. Ctr., 1988-2000. Chief staff Northwestern Meml. Hosp., 1988-90; pres. Chgo. Bd. Health, 2002—, Inst. Medicine, Chgo., Ill., 2002-04, exec. dir., 2004—; chair Ill. Ad Hoc Com. to Defend Health Care. Contbr. chpts. to books, articles to med. jours. Capt. U.S. Army, 1960-62. Recipient Outstanding Clin. tchr. award Northwestern U. Med. Sch., 1974, 77, 84, 86, Alumni Merit award Northwestern U., 1979, Henry P. Russe-Inst. of Medicine award for exemplary compassion in health care, 1997, Aeschulapian award as Physician of Yr., Anti Defamation League, 1998. Master: ACP (gov. for Ill. 1988—92, chair sub-com. on aging 1993, Clayppole award 1994); mem.: Ill. Geriatrics Soc. (pres. 1992—94), Am. Geriatrics Soc., Inst. Medicine Chgo. (pres. 2002—04), Alpha Omega Alpha. Home: Apt 2206 222 E Pearson St Chicago IL 60611-7758 Office: Inst Medicine Chgo 332 S Michigan Ave 525 Chicago IL 60604 Office Phone: 312-663-0040. Business E-Mail: j.webster@northwestern.edu. *Life should best be measured not by how long you live, but how well you function.*

WEBSTER, JEFFREY LEON, graphic designer; b. Idaho Falls, Idaho, Nov. 23, 1941; s. Leon A. and Marjory M. (McAllister) W.; student Sch. Associated Arts, St. Paul, 1962; m. Judith Kess, Apr. 17, 1965; children: Eric J., Marjorie P. Sci. illustrator Mayo Clinic, Rochester, Minn., 1963-66; layout artist Brown & Bigelow, St. Paul, 1966; graphic designer U. Minn., Mpls., 1966-67, U. Calgary (Alta., Can.), 1967-68; sr. artist Control Data Corp., St. Paul, 1968-70; mem. Idaho State U. Meml. Lectureship Com.; graphic designer Idaho State U., 1970-78; owner, operator studio, Harmony, Minn.; mktg. and advt. cons. to 45 regional and nat. firms, 1978—. Mem. Idaho Civic Symphony Bd. Chairperson rub. rels. Unitarian Ch. Rochester, 1991—; bd. dirs. Gift of Life Transplant House, Rochester, Minn. 1996, Rochester Orch. and Chorale, 1996. Recipient Profl. citation Libr. Congress, 1976; 1st Pl. Best Trucking ad, Overdrive Mag., 1990. Mem. Sierra Club (nat. agrl. com. 2003--), Artist pub. ednl. exhibits. Home and Office: RR 1 Harmony MN 55939-9801

WEBSTER, JILL ROSEMARY, historian, educator; b. London, Sept. 29, 1931; arrived in Can., 1965; d. Harold James and Dora Elena (Andreini) W. BA in Hispanic Studies with honors, U. Liverpool, Eng., 1962, postgrad. cert. in edn., 1965; PhD in Spanish, U. Toronto, Can., 1969; MA in Spanish, U. Nottingham, Eng., 1964; BA in History with honors, U. London, Eng., 1978. Prof. U. Toronto, 1968-95, assoc. dean, 1978-81, dir. Ctr. for Medieval Studies, 1989-94, grad. chair dept. Spanish and Portuguese, 1993-94; prof. emeritus, 1995—. Author: Els Menorets: The Franciscans in the Realms of Aragon from St. Francis to the Black Death (1348), 1993, Per Déu o per diners - els mendicants i el clergat al pais valencià, 1998, Carmel in Medieval Catalonia, 1999, Els Franciscans Catalans a l'Edat Mitjana, 2000. Recipient Creu de Sant Jordi award, Generalitat de Catalunya, 1999. Fellow Royal Soc. Can.; mem. Secció Històrico-Arqueològica Inst. d'Estudis Catalans (mem. corr. 1996). Office: U Toronto St Michaels Coll 81 St Mary St Toronto ON Canada M5S 1J4 Business E-Mail: jill.webster@utoronto.ca.

WEBSTER, JOHN DANIEL, corporate financial executive; s. Kenneth Ray and Anastasia Webster; m. Gloria Jean Barkhimer, Aug. 7, 1971; children: Kimberly Ann Ruzickova, John Kenneth. BS, U. Md. CPA Md., 1972. Dep. asst. dir., fin. control and mgmt. Retirement and Ins. Programs, U.S. Office of Pers. Mgmt., Wash., DC, 1985—89; CFO Libr. of Congress, Wash., DC, 1989—. Mem., audit com. U.S. Arch. of the Capitol, Wash., DC, 2003—. Contbr. articles various profl. jours. Recipient Distinction in Payments Mgmt. award, U.S. Dept. Treasury, 1990, Achievement of the Yr. award, Wash. D.C. Chpt. Assn. of Govt. Accountants, 1997, Nat. President's award, Assn. of Govt. Accountants, 2000. Mem.: AICPA, Assoication of Govt. Accountants (nat. treas. 1999—2000, Nat. Treasurer's Award 2000). Office Phone: 202-707-5189. Office Fax: 202-707-2829.

WEBSTER, JOHN GOODWIN, biomedical engineer, researcher, biomedical engineer, educator; b. Plainfield, N.J., May 27, 1932; s. Franklin Folger and Emily Sykes (Boody) W.; m. Nancy Egan, Dec. 27, 1954; children: Paul, Robin, Mark, Lark BEE, Cornell U., 1953; MSEE, U. Rochester, 1965, PhD, 1967. Engr. North American Aviation, Downey, Calif., 1954-55; engr. Boeing Airplane Co., Seattle, 1955-59, Radiation Inc., Melbourne, Fla., 1959-61; staff engr. Mitre Corp., Bedford, Mass., 1961-62, IBM Corp., Kingston, N.Y., 1962-63; asst. prof. elec. engring. U. Wis., Madison, 1967-70, assoc. prof. elec. engring., 1970-73, prof. elec. and computer engring., 1973-99, prof. biomed. engring., 1999—2001, prof. emertius biomed. engring., 2001—. Author: (with others) Medicine and Clinical Engineering, 1977, Sensors and Signal Conditioning, 1991, 2d edit., 2001, Analog Signal Processing, 1999; editor: Medical Instrumentation: Application and Design, 3d edit., 1998, Clinical Engineering: Principles and Practices, 1979, Design of Microcomputer-Based Medical Instrumentation, 1981, Therapeutic Medical Devices: Application and Design, 1982; Electronic Devices for Rehabilitation, 1985; Interfacing Sensors to the IBM-PC, 1988, Encyclopedia of Medical Devices and Instrumentation, 1988, Tactile Sensors for Robotics and Medicine, 1988, Electrical Impedance Tomography, 1990, Teaching Design in Electrical Engineering, 1990, Prevention of Pressure Sores, 1991, Design of Cardiac Pacemakers, 1995, Design of Pulse Oximeters, 1997, The Measurement Instrumentation, and Sensors Handbook, 1999, Encyclopedia of Electrical and Electronics Engineering, 1999, Mechanical Variables Measurement, 2000, Minimally Invasive Medical Technology, 2001, Electrical Measurement, Signal Processing and Displays, 2004, Bioinstrumentation, 2004. Recipient Rsch. Career Devel. award NIH, 1971-76; NIH fellow, 1963-67; recipient Western Electric Fund award Am. Soc. Engring. Edn., 1978, Best Reference Work award, 1999, Theo C. Pilkington Outstanding Educator award, 1994. Fellow IEEE (3d Millenium medal 2000, IEEE-EMBS Career achievement award 2001), Am. Inst. Med. and Biol. Engring., Inst. Physics, Instrument Soc. Am. (Donald P. Eckman Edn. award 1974), Assn. for Advancement Med. Instrumentation (Found. Laufman-Greatbatch prize 1996). Office: Univ Wis Dept Biomed Engring 1550 Engineering Dr Madison WI 53706-1609 Office Phone: 608-263-1574. E-mail: webster@engr.wisc.edu.

WEBSTER, JOHN KIMBALL, investment executive; b. N.Y.C., June 7, 1934; s. Reginald Nathaniel and Lillian (McDonald) W.; m. Katherine Taylor Mulligan; children: John McDonald, Katherine Kimball. BA, Yale U., 1956; postgrad., Wharton Sch., U. Pa., 1957-58. With Dominick & Dominick, N.Y.C., 1961-73, v.p., 1968-73; v.p., sec. Dominick Fund, Inc., also Barclay Growth Fund, N.Y.C., 1971-73; v.p. Dominick Mgmt. Corp., N.Y.C., 1971-73, Monumental Capital Mgmt., Inc., Balt., 1974-75, Bernstein-Macaulay, Inc., N.Y.C., 1975-78; v.p., dir. Penmark Investments, Inc., Chgo., 1978-79, sr. v.p., 1979-80, exec. v.p., 1980-84, Trust Banking Group, Sun Banks, Inc., 1984-85; v.p. MPT Assocs., 1986-90, Value Line Asset Mgmt., N.Y.C., 1990-96, M&T Capital Advisors Group, 1996—99; cons. Citigroup Asset Mgmt., 2000—. Mem. no-load com. Investment Co. Inst., Washington, 1971-73; exec. com. No Load Mut. Fund Assn., N.Y.C., 1971-73; treas. No Load Mut. Fund Assn., 1972-73. Chmn. Nat. Telethon Com., Lawrenceville, Sch., 1986-88, chmn. Ann. Giving, 1988-89; vice chmn. Parents Fund Trinity Coll., Conn., 1987-90; mem. adv. com. Lawrenceville Fund, 1995—. Capt. USAF, 1958-61. Mem. Church Club (N.Y.C.), Yale Club (N.Y.C.), Rumson (N.J.) Country Club, Seabright (N.J.) Lawn Tennis Club, Baltusrol Golf Club, Summit Paddle Tennis Club. Episcopalian. Home: 46 Meadowview Ln Berkeley Heights NJ 07922-1308 Fax: 212-350-2168.

WEBSTER, LESLEY DANIELS, bank executive; married; 2 children. PhD in Econs., Stanford U. Asst. prof. Wash. U., 1977-83; with Chase Securities, 1983—90; mng. dir., head arbitrage trading group Union Bank Switzerland, N.Y.C., 1990-94; exec. v.p. market risk mgmt. Chase Manhattan Corp. (now JPMorganChase), N.Y.C., 1994—. Bd. dirs. United Way of N.Y.C., chair Women United in Philanthropy for N.Y.C. Named one of 25 Women to Watch, US Banker Mag., 2003. Mem.: Securities Industry Assn. (risk mgmt. com.). Office: Chase Manhattan Corp 270 Park Ave Fl 12 New York NY 10017-2036*

WEBSTER, LESLIE TILLOTSON, JR., pharmacologist, educator; b. N.Y.C., Mar. 31, 1926; s. Leslie Tillotson and Emily (de Forest) W.; m. Alice Katharine Holland, June 24, 1955; children: Katharine White, Susan Holland Webster Van Drie, Leslie Tillotson III, Romi Anne. BA, Amherst Coll., 1947, Sc.D. (hon.), 1982; student, Union Coll., 1944; MD, Harvard U., 1948. Diplomate: Am. Bd. Internal Medicine. Rotating intern Cleve. City Hosp., 1948-49, jr. asst. resident in medicine, 1949-50; asst. resident medicine Bellevue Hosp., N.Y.C., 1952-53; research fellow medicine Harvard and Boston City Hosp. Thorndike Meml. Lab., 1953-55; from demonstrator to instr. medicine Sch. of Medicine Western Res. U., 1955-60; research assoc. to sr. instr. biochemistry Case Western Res. U. Sch. Medicine, 1957—60, asst. prof. medicine, 1960-70, asst. prof. biochemistry, 1960-65, asst. prof. pharmacology, 1965-67, asso. prof., 1967-70, prof. pharmacology, 1976-92, chmn. pharmacology dept., 1976-91, prof. medicine, 1980-86, prof. emeritus pharmacology dept., 1992. Prof., chmn. pharmacology dept. Northwestern U. Med. and Dental Sch., 1970-76; dir. med. scientist tng. program Case Western Res. U. Sch. Medicine, 1979-92. Served to lt. med. corps. USNR, 1950-52. Russell M. Wilder fellow Nat. Vitamin Found., 1956-59; Sr. USPHS Research fellow, 1959-61; USPHS Rsch. Career Devel. awardee, 1961-69; Macy faculty scholar, 1980-81. Mem. ACP (life), Central Soc. Clin. Rsch. Coalition (emeritus), Am. Soc. Clin. Investigation, Am. Soc. Biochemistry and Molecular Biology (emeritus), Assn. Med. Sch. Pharmacology (emeritus), Am. Soc. Pharmacology and Exptl. Therapeutics (emeritus), Alpha Omega Alpha (hon.). Home: 12546 Cedar Rd No 4 Cleveland Heights OH 44106-3294 Office: Univ Hosps of Cleve Rainbow Babies and Childrens Hosp 2074 Abington Rd Cleveland OH 44106-2602 Office Phone: 216-844-3310. Personal E-mail: ltwjr@sbcglobal.net.

WEBSTER, LINDA JANE, clinical social worker, consultant; b. Whitinsville, Mass., Mar. 23, 1948; d. David and Erva Viola (Chesley) Longmuir; m. Barry Ward Webster, Dec. 16, 1988; 1 child, Jeffrey. BS magna cum laude, Springfield (Mass.) Coll., 1969; MEd, U. Hartford, 1971; M. in Social Work, U. Utah, 1981, PhD, 1997. Lic. clin. social worker Utah; diplomate Am. Bd. Examiners and Nat. Assn. Social Workers. Sch. psychologist Bd. Edn., New Britain, Conn., 1969-77; dir. Project React Capital Region Edn. Coun., Bloomfield, Conn., 1977-79; coord. acute and intensive treatment Valley West Mental Health Ctr., Salt Lake City, Utah, 1981-86; program dir. Western Inst. NeuroPsychiatry, Salt Lake City, 1986-88; social worker pvt. practice Murray, Utah, 1988—. Cons. Episcopal Social and Pastoral Ministries, Salt Lake City, 1986-88; adj. faculty U. Utah, Grad. Sch. Social Work, Salt Lake City, 1986-93. Vol. Episcopalian Ch., Salt Lake City, 1980—; mentor Murray (Utah) H.S., 1997. Mem. Nat. Assn. Social Workers (sec. Utah chpt. 1986-88), Alumni Assn. U. Utah Grad Sch. Social Workers, (pres. 1986-89), Phi Kappa Phi. Avocations: skiing, tennis, basketball, teddy bears, crafts. Office: PhD LCSW 111 E 5600 S Ste 314 Murray UT 84107-8167

WEBSTER, LOIS SHAND, association executive; b. Springfield, Ill., Sept. 25, 1929; d. Richings James and C. Odell (Gilbert) S.; m. Terrance Ellis Webster, Feb. 12, 1954 (dec. July 1985); children: Terrance Richings, Bruce Douglas, Andrew Michael. BA, Millikin U., 1951; cert. in libr. tech., Coll. Du Page County, Glen Ellyn, Ill., 1974; postgrad. libr. sci., No. Ill. U., 1977-82. Exec. asst. Am. Nuclear Soc., La Grange Park, Ill., 1973—. Contbr. articles and book chpts. to profl. publs. Field dir. Springfield coun. Girl Scouts U.S., 1951-54; libr. advisor Du Page County coun. Girl Scouts U.S., 1973-74. Recipient Octave J. Du Temple award Am. Nuclear Soc., 1989. Mem. Spl. Libr. Assn. (divsn. chmn. 1984-85, chmn. by-laws com. 1987-89, bd. dirs. 1989-92, sec. 1990-91, visioning com. 1992—), Coun. Engring. and Sci. Soc.

Execs., Am. Soc. Assn. Execs., Met. Chgo. Libr. Assembly (bd. dirs. 1982-85). Avocations: travel, genealogy. Home: 5383 Newport St Lisle IL 60532-4126 Office: Am Nuclear Soc 555 N Kensington Ave La Grange Park IL 60526-5535

WEBSTER, MICHAEL ANDERSON, experimental psychologist; b. Atlanta, Mar. 24, 1958; s. John Calvin and Evelyn Gayle (Cox) W.; m. Shernaaz Michael Irani, Aug. 6, 1983; children: Anjali Dianne, Menka Linda. Exch. student, Am. U., Cairo, 1978-79; BA in Psychology, U. Calif., San Diego, 1981; MA in Psychology, U. Calif., Berkeley, 1985, PhD in Psychology, 1988. Postdoctoral fellow dept. exptl. psychology U. Cambridge, Eng., 1988-94; assoc. prof. dept. psychology U. Nev., Reno, 1994—. Contbr. articles to profl. jours. NATO fellow NSF, Cambridge U., 1988. Fellow Nat. Eye Inst. (First award 1994); mem. We. Psychol. Assn. (Outstanding Rsch. award 1998), Rocky Mountain Psychol. Assn., Exptl. Psychology Soc. (Eng.), Assn. for Rsch. in Vision and Ophthalmology, Optical Soc. Am. Achievements include research in psychophysical studies of human color vision. Office: Univ Nevada Dept Psychology Reno NV 89557-0001

WEBSTER, MURRAY ALEXANDER, JR., sociologist, educator; b. Manila, Philippines, Dec. 10, 1941; s. M.A. and Patricia (Morse) W. AB, Stanford U., 1963, MA, 1966, PhD, 1968. Asst. prof. social rels. Johns Hopkins U., Balt., 1968-74, assoc. prof., 1974-76; prof. sociology, adj. prof. psychology U. S.C., Columbia, 1976-86; vis. prof. sociology Stanford U., 1981-82, 85, 88-89; sr. lectr. San Jose State U., 1987-89; dir. sociology program NSF, 1989-91,99-2000; prof. sociology U. N.C., Charlotte, 1993—. Author (with Barbara Sobieszek): Soruces of Self-Evaluation, 1974; author: Actions and Actors, 1975; author: (with Martha Foschi) Status Generalization: New Theory and Research, 1988; mem. editl. bd. Am. Jour. Sociology, 1976—79, Social Psychology Quar., 1977—80, 1993—, Social Sci. Rsch., 1975—. Recipient First Citizens Bank Scholars award, 2003; NIH fellow, 1966-68; grantee NSF, Nat. Inst. Edn. Mem.: N.Y. Acad. Scis., So. Sociol. Soc., Am. Sociol. Assn. Office: Univ NC Dept Sociology Charlotte NC 28223 Office Phone: 704-687-4079. E-mail: mawebste@uncc.edu.

WEBSTER, NORMAN ERIC, journalist, charitable foundation administrator; b. Summerside, P.E.I., Can., June 4, 1941; s. Eric and Elizabeth (Paterson) W.; m. Pat Roop, 1966; children: David, Andrew, Derek, Gillian, Hilary. BA, Bishop's U., Que., Can.; MA, St. John's Coll., Oxford, Eng. Corr. Globe and Mail, Que. and Ottawa, Ont., Can.; editor Globe Mag., Toronto, Ont.; corr. Globe and Mail, Peking, China, 1969-71, columnist Ont. affairs Toronto, European corr. London, editor-in-chief Toronto, 1983-89, Montreal (Que.) Gazette, 1989-93; pres. R. Howard Webster Found., Montreal, 1993—. Chancellor U. P.E.I.; chmn. North-South Inst., Ottawa, 1998-2000; bd. dirs. Internat. Press Inst., Vienna, Montreal Children's Hosp. Found., McGill U. Health Ctr. Found., Can. Inst. for Advanced Rsch., Bishop's U., Michener Found. Recipient Nat. Newspaper award for Peking corr., 1971, for editl. writing, 1988; Rhodes scholar; mem. Order of Can. Office: R Howard Webster Found Ste 2912 1155 Rene Levesque Blvd W Montreal QC Canada H3B 2L5

WEBSTER, OWEN WRIGHT, chemist; b. Devils Lake, N.D., Mar. 25, 1929; s. Daniel Milton and Maude May (Wright) W.; m. Lillian Brostek; children: Ellen, Anne, John, James, Mary. BS in Chemistry, N.D. U., 1951, DSc (hon.), 1986; PhD in Chemistry, Pa. State U., 1955. Research chemist E.I. Du Pont de Nemours, Wilmington, Del., 1955-74, group leader, 1974-79, research supr., 1979-84, research leader, 1984-95, Du Pont fellow, 1986-95; ret., 1995. Adj. prof. dept. chemistry U. Ala., 1999—. Patentee in field; contbr. articles to profl. jours. Recipient Chem. Pioneer award Am. Inst. Chemists, 1995. Mem. AAAS, Am. Chem. Soc. (chmn. Del. sect. 1975-76, Excellence in Research award 1987, Applied Polymer Sci. award 1993), Sigma Xi. Republican. Roman Catholic. Avocations: chess, bridge, golf. Home: 318 S Village Ln Chadds Ford PA 19317-7319 Personal E-mail: owwebster@aol.com.

WEBSTER, PETER BRIDGMAN, lawyer; b. Boston, Jan. 11, 1941; s. John Archibald and Mildred (Bridgman) W.; m. Elaine Gerber, Dec. 20, 1964 (dec.); children: Amy Elizabeth, Peter Bridgman, Timothy James. AB, Bowdoin Coll., 1962; LLB, Cornell U., 1965. Bar: Maine 1965, U.S. Dist. Ct. Maine 1965. Assoc., then sr. ptnr. Verrill & Dana, LLP, Portland, Maine, 1965—. Mem. grievance commn. Maine Bd. Bar Overseers, Augusta, 1979-88, chmn., 1984-88, mem. 1986-94, chmn. 1990-92; adj. prof. law U. Maine, Portland, 1981; mem. Maine Commn. on Ethics and Govtl. Practices, 1991-2002, chair 1997-2002, chair Lawyers' Fund for Client Protection, 1997—. Recipient Alumni Svc. award Bowdoin Coll., 1999. Home: 185 W Main St Yarmouth ME 04096-8400 Office Phone: 207-774-4000. E-mail: pwebster@verrilldana.com.

WEBSTER, PETER DAVID, judge; b. Framingham, Mass., Feb. 12, 1949; s. Waldo John and Helen Anne (Borovek) W.; m. Michele Page Hernandez, Jan. 13, 1989; 1 stepchild, Alana Perryman. BS, Georgetown U., 1971; JD, Duke U., 1974; LLM, U. Va., 1995. Bar: Fla. 1974, U.S. Dist. Ct. (mid. dist.) Fla. 1975, U.S. Ct. Appeals (5th cir.) 1975, U.S. Dist. Ct. (so. dist.) Fla. 1977, U.S. Dist. Ct. (no. dist.) Fla. 1978, U.S. Supreme Ct. 1978, U.S. Ct. Appeals (11th cir.) 1981. Law clk. U.S. Dist. Judge, Jacksonville, Fla., 1974-75; assoc. Bedell, Bedell, Dittmar, Smith & Zehmer, Jacksonville, 1975-78; ptnr. Bedell, Bedell, Dittmar & Zehmer, Jacksonville, 1978-85; cir. judge State Fla., Jacksonville, 1986-91; judge Dist. Ct. of Appeal, First Dist., State of Fla., Tallahassee, 1991—. Master of bench Chester Bedell Am. Inn of Ct., 1988-91, Tallahassee Am. Inn of Ct., 1992—; chmn. com. on standard jury instrns. in civil cases, chmn. court reporter cert. planning com.; mem. com. on trial ct. info. sys.; com. on confidentiality of records of jud. br. Fla. Supreme Ct. Contbg. author: Sanctions: Rule 11 and Other Powers, 1986, Florida Criminal Rules and Practice Manual, 1990. Bd. dirs. Jacksonville Area Legal Aid, Inc., 1978-82, River Region Human Svcs., Inc., Jacksonville, 1986-88; mem. adv. bd. P.A.C.E. Ctr. for Girls, Inc., Jacksonville, 1986-91; com. mem. Shawnee dist. North Fla. coun. Boy Scouts Am., 1974-78; mem. delinquency task force Mayor's Commn. on Children and Youth, City of Jacksonville, 1988-91; officer, mem. exec. bd. Suwanee River Area coun. Boy Scouts, 1991-96. Mem. Am. Judicature Soc. (bd. dirs. 2002—), Fla. Conf. Appellate Judges, Jacksonville Bar Assn., Tallahassee Bar Assn., Phi Beta Kappa, Phi Alpha Theta, Phi Eta Sigma. Office: 1st Dist Ct Appeal 301 Martin Luther King Blvd Tallahassee FL 32399-1850 Office Phone: 850-487-1000.

WEBSTER, ROBERT BYRON, lawyer; b. Mar. 9, 1932; s. Don B. and Glennie E. (Cole) W.; children: Anne Elizabeth, Allison Dee, Peter Hey, James Byron. BA, U. Mich., 1955; JD, 1957. Bar: Mich. 1958, U.S. Dist. Ct. (ea. dist.) Mich., 1958, U.S. Dist. Ct. (we. dist.) Mich. 1972, U.S. Ct. Appeals (6th cir.) 1958, U.S. Supreme Ct. 1972. Law clk. U.S. Dist. Ct., 1957-59; assoc., ptnr. Hill, Lewis, Adams, Goodrich & Tait, 1959-73; judge Cir. Ct., Oakland County, 1973—82; chief judge, 1977; chmn. Hill Lewis PC, 1982—95, Clark Hill PLC, 1995—2002; shareholder Cox, Hodgman & Giarmarco, PC, Troy, Mich., 2003—. Chmn. Supreme Ct. Com. to Revise Ct Rules, 1975-78; mem. Mich. Ct. Rule Adv. Com., 1984; chair, State Bar Appellate Task Force, 1993; trustee, chmn. Horizon Health Systems, 1983-2002; co-chair Legis. Commn. on Cts. in 21st Century, 1990. Chmn. Oakland Rep. Com., 1970-71, commr. Nat. Commn. on Uniform State Laws, 1995—; chmn. State Officers Compensation Commn., 1998-2002; trustee Family and Children Svcs. Oakland County, 1976-84; mem. Oakland Cmty. Mental Health Bd. 1971-73; trustee Henry Ford Health Sys., 1995-2002; mem. jud. qualifications com. State Bar, 1990—. With USAF, 1951-53. Fellow Am. Bar Found. (life), State Bar Mich. Found. (life), Am. Coll. Trial Lawyers; mem. ABA (mem. ho. dels. 1990-2004), Am. Law Inst., Fed. Bar Assn., State Bar Mich. (commr. 1982-90, v.p. 1987-88, pres. elect 1988-89, pres. 1989-90), Oakland Bar Assn. Republican. Unitarian Universalist. Office: 101 W Big Beaver Rd 10th Fl Troy MI 48084-5280 Office Phone: 248-457-7050. Personal E-mail: rbwebster@hotmail.com. Business E-Mail: rwebster@chglaw.com.

WEBSTER, ROBERT G. virologist, educator; b. Balclutha, New Zealand, July 5, 1932; BSc, Otago (New Zealand) U., 1955, MSc, 1957; PhD, Australian Nat. U., Canberra, 1962. Virologist New Zealand Dept. Agr., 1958—59; postdoctoral fellow (Fulbright scholar) dept. epidemiology U. Mich. Sch. Pub. Health, Ann Arbor, Mich., 1962—63; rsch. fellow dept. microbiology Australian Nat. U., John Curtain Med. Sch., Canberra, 1964—66, fellow dept. microbiology, 1966—67; assoc. prof. dept. microbiology U. Tenn. Med. Units, Memphis, 1968—69, 1969—74, prof. dept. microbiology, 1974—75, 1975—78; prof. dept. microbiology and immunology U. Tenn. Ctr. for Health Scis., Memphis, 1978—85; Rose Marie Thomas chair dept. virology and molecular biology St. Jude Children's Rsch. Hosp., Memphis, 1988—. Assoc. mem. lab. immunology St. Jude Children's Rsch. Hosp., Memphis, 1968—69, mem. labs. virology and immunology, 1969—74, Memphis, 1974—75, mem. divsn. virology, 1975—78; Fogarty internat. sr. fellow Nat. Inst. for Med. Rsch., Med. Rsch. Coun., London, 1978—79; mem. dept. virology and molecular biology St. Jude Children's Rsch. Hosp., Memphis, 1978—85, Memphis, 1985—88. Fellow: Royal Soc. Medicine, Royal Soc., London, Royal Soc., New Zealand (hon.); mem.: AAAS, Am. Soc. for Virology, Am. Soc. for Microbiology, Nat. Acad. Scis. of U.S. Achievements include research in emergence and control of influenza; viral immunology. Office: St Jude Children's Rsch Hosp 332 N Lauderdale St Memphis TN 38105-2794

WEBSTER, ROBERT KENLY, lawyer; b. N.Y.C., May 16, 1933; s. Francis Kenly and Mary Louise (Rathbone) W.; m. Sally Irene Stratton, Apr. 16, 1960; children: Timothy Kenly, Kimberly Anne. AB, Princeton U., 1955; LLB, U. Va., 1960. Assoc. Cadwalader, Wickersham & Taft, N.Y.C., 1960-65; asst. U.S. atty. Dept. of Justice, Washington, 1965-68; prin. dep. gen. counsel Dept. of Army, Washington, 1968-73; ptnr. Kennedy & Webster, Washington, 1973-81, Shaw, Pittman, Potts & Trowbridge, Washington, 1981-98; sole practice Washington, 1999—. Spl. investigator Iran FMS program Sec. of Def., Washington, 1977; advisor conflict of interest issues Watergate defendants Dept. Justice, Washington, 1977. Gen. counsel Princeton (N.J.) Project 55, Inc., 1989—. Lt. j.g. USN, 1955—57. Mem. ABA, ATLA, Fed. Bar Assn., Met. Club. Avocations: pottery, reading, travel, tennis. Fax: (202) 659-0084.

WEBSTER, ROBERT LEE, accounting educator, researcher; b. Little Rock, Oct. 4, 1946; s. Daniel and Mildred LaNette (Patishall) W.; m. Mary Katherine Fiske, Aug. 26, 1967; children: Elizabeth Ashley, Jessica Lee. BA, Ouachita Bapt. U., 1968; MBA, Syracuse U., 1975; MS, L.I. U., 1986; DBA, La. Tech. U., 1993. Cert. govt. fin. mgr. Commd. 2d lt. U.S. Army, 1968, advanced through grades to lt. col., 1985; dep. contr. U.S. Army Electronics R&D Command, Adelphi, Md., 1975-80; chief of ops., comms. security NATO, Mons, Belgium, 1980-83; asst. prof. acctg. and fin. U.S. Mil. Acad., West Point, N.Y., 1983-86; prof. mil. sci. Henderson State U., Arkadelphia, Ark., 1986-88; ret. U.S. Army, 1988; asst. prof. acctg. Henderson State U., 1988-91, chair dept. acctg., econs. and bus. edn., 1991-93; chair dept. acctg. Ouachita Bapt. U., Arkadelphia, 1993—, George Young chair bus., 1995—. Bd. dirs. Hospitality Care Ctr., Arkadelphia, 1992-93; speaker in field. Editor Jour. Bus. & Behavioral Scis., 1995; author articles. Army scholar Syracuse U., 1974-75; Exch. Educator to Republic of Kazakhstan, 1994-95; recipient Dean's award for acad. achievement L.I. U., 1986. Mem. Nat. Social Sci. Assn. (bd. govs. 1992—, Outstanding Conf. Paper award 1992), Am. Acctg. Assn., Assn. of Govt. Accts., Beta Gamma Sigma, Sigma Beta Delta. Avocations: coin collecting/numismatics, exercising. Home: 205 Forrest Park Dr Arkadelphia AR 71923-2811 Office: Ouachita Bapt U PO Box 3689 Arkadelphia AR 71998 E-mail: websterb@obu.edu.

WEBSTER, SHARON B. economist; b. Wildwood, Fla., Aug. 23, 1937; d. James McWilliams and Marion (Hallbrook) Boen. BA in Polit. Sci., Econ. and Psychology, U. Fla., 1959; vis. doctoral fellow, Princeton U., 1964—65; PhD, U. Va., 1965. Asst. prof. No. Mich. U., Marquette, 1962—64, U. Md., 1964—66, Hollins Coll., Roanoke, Va., 1966—71; prof. Fed. Exec. Inst., Charlottesville, Va., 1971—72; mgr. internat. program Dept. Treasury, Washington, 1972—74; economist Econ., Stats. and Coop. Svc. U.S. Dept. Agr., Washington, 1974—79; mem. Presdl. Commn. for Exec. Exch., 1979—80; dir. internat. econ. Occidental Petroleum Corp., L.A., 1980—83; investment banker, account exec. Johnston, Lemon and Co., Inc., Washington, 1983—88; fin. cons. Shearson Lehman Hutton, Washington, 1988—. Mem. adv. bd. Pres.'s Caribbean Basin Initiative, 1982; chmn. bd. dirs. NATA, Inc.; bd. dirs. Genta, Inc., NABE; pres., CEO A.A. Global; bd. advisors Sintal Comm. USA, Inc., Internat. Trade Coun.; bd. advisors Patterson Sch. Diplomacy and Internat. Commerce U. Ky.; bd. advisors Consumer Health and Svcs. Am., Inc. Contbr. articles to profl. jours. Recipient Presdl. award Pvt. Sector Iniative, 1982; NDEA fellow. Mem.: AAUP, Assn. Polit. Risk Analysts, Washington Soc. Money Mgrs., Soc. Internat. Devel., Internat. Studies Assn., Nat. Assn. Bus. Economists, Am. Polit. Sci. Assn., Am. Assn. Agrl. Economists, Internat. Assn. Energy Economists, Internat. Policy Inst. (v.p. 1977—), Fed. Exec. Inst. Alumni Assn., Pres.'s Exec. Exch. Assn., Nat. Coun. Career Women, Internat. Club, Army Navy Club, Capital Spkrs. Club. Home: The Winthrop # 602 1727 Massachusetts Ave NW Washington DC 20036-2153 Office: AA Global 9039 Furrow Ave Ellicott City MD 21042-1841 Office Phone: 202-232-4024.

WEBSTER, STEPHEN BURTIS, dermatologist, educator; b. Chgo., Dec. 3, 1935; s. James Randolph Webster and Ruth Marion (Burtis) Holmes; m. Katherine Griffith Webster, Apr. 4, 1959; children: David Randolph, Margaret Elizabeth, James Lucian. BS, Northwestern U., 1957, MD, 1960. Diplomate Am. Bd. Dermatology (bd. dirs. 1992—, v.p. 1997-98, pres.). Intern Colo. Gen. Hosp., Denver, 1960-61; resident Walter Reed Gen. Hosp., Washington, 1962-65; staff physician Henry Ford Hosp., Detroit, 1969-71, Gundersen Lutheran Med. Ctr., La Crosse, 1971—; assoc. clin. prof. U. Wis., Madison, 1976—; clin. prof. U. Minn., Mpls., 1978—. Lt. col. U.S. Army, 1962-69. Fellow Am. Acad. Dermatology (sec.-treas. 1985-88, pres. 1991); mem. AMA, Am. Dermatol. Assn. (pres. 1996-97), Am. Bd. Dermatology (v.p. 1997-98, pres. 1999-2000, assoc. exec. dir. 2001—), Wis. Med. Soc., La Crosse County Med. Soc., Soc. Investigative Dermatology, Alpha Omega Alpha. Republican. Congregationalist. Avocations: bagpipes, model trains. Home: N2062 Wedgewood Dr E La Crosse WI 54601-7175 Office: Gundersen Clinic Ltd 1836 South Ave La Crosse WI 54601-5494

WEBSTER, WILLIAM G., JR., army officer; b. Baton Rouge, La., July 3, 1951; BS, U.S. Mil. Acad., 1974. Commd. 2d lt. U.S. Army, 1974, advanced through grades to brig. gen., tank co. comdr., 1974—78, ops. and plans officer Seventh Army Combined Arms Tng. Ctr., 1979—82, ops. officer 3-64 Armor, 3d Inf. Divsn., 1979—82, asst. G-3 and brigade ops. officer 24th Inf. Divsn., 1984—87, joint staff War Plans Divsn. Washington, 1988—91, comdr. 3d bn., 77th armor in 4th inf. divsn., 1991-93; sr. armor observer contr. Cobra Team Nat. Tng. Ctr., Ft. Irwin, Calif., 1993-94; comdr. 1st brigade, 1st cavalry divsn. Ft. Hood, 1995-97; asst .divsn. comdr. 3d Inf. Divsn., Ft. Stewart, Ga., 1997-98; comdr. Ft. Irwin and Nat. Tng. Ctr., 1998—2000; deployed Ops. Desert Thunder U.S. Army, 1998, Army's dir. tng. Office Dep. Chief of Staff G-3, 2000—01, dep. J-3 U.S. Ctrl. Command Operation Enduring Freedom, 2001—02, dep. comdg. gen. for ops. Third U.S. Army, Combined Forces Land Component Command, Operation Iraqi Freedom, 2002—03, 2002—03, comdg. gen. 3d Inf. Divsn., 2003—. Decorated Legion of Merit with 4 oak leaf clusters, Air Assault badge, Parachutist badge, Def. Superior Svc. medal, Armed Forces Expeditionary medal; recipient Bronze Star. Office: 3d Infantry Divsn Ste 204 42 Wayne Pl Fort Stewart GA 31314*

WEBSTER, WILLIAM HEDGCOCK, lawyer; b. St. Louis, Mar. 6, 1924; s. Thomas M. and Katherine (Hedgcock) W.; m. Drusilla Lane, May 5, 1950 (dec. 1984); children: Drusilla Lane Busch, William Hedgcock, Katherine Hagee Roessle; m. Lynda Clugston, Oct. 20, 1990. AB, Amherst Coll., 1947, LLD, 1975; JD, Washington U., 1949, LLD, 1978; LLD (hon.), William Wood Coll., 1978, DePauw U., 1978, Drury Coll., Columbia Coll., U. Dayton, U. Notre Dame, Center Coll., Dickinson Coll., U. Miami, DePaul U., Am. U., John Jay Coll., Westminster Coll., Georgetown U., Rockhurst Coll., Pepperdine U. Bar: Mo. 1949, D.C. 1981. With Armstrong, Teasdale, Kramer and Vaughan (and predecessors), St. Louis, 1949-50, 52-59, 61-70; U.S. atty. U.S. Dist. Ct. (ea. dist.) Mo., 1960-61, judge, 1971-73; judge U.S. Ct. Appeals (8th cir.), 1973-78; dir. FBI, 1978-87, CIA, 1987-91; sr. ptnr. Milbank, Tweed, Hadley & McCloy, Washington, 1991—. Mem. Mo. Bd. Law Examiners, 1964-69, mem. adv. com. on criminal rules, 1971-78, mem. ct. adminstrs. com., 1975-78; bd. dirs. Anhauser-Busch Cos., Maritz Inc., Pinkertons Inc., T.L.C. Beatrice Internat. Holdings Inc., Nextwave, Inc. Trustee Washington U., 1974—; bd. dirs. Atlantic Coun., Nat. Legal Ctr. for Pub. Interest, Nat. Symphony Assn., Coun. on Fgn. Rels.; bd. dirs., chmn. Police Found; hon. life pres. Big Bros. Orgn. St. Louis; bd. dirs. Big Bros. Am., 1966, hon. bd. dirs., 1978—. Lt. USNR, 1943-46, 50-52. Recipient Disting. Alumnus award Washington U., 1977, Stein award Fordham U., Law award U. Va., Nat. Svc. medal Freedoms Found., Theodore Roosevelt award, Presdl. medal of Freedom, Nat. Security medal, Silver Buffalo award Boy Scouts Am., Disting. Svc. award Am. Legion; named Father of Yr., 1986, Man of Yr., St. Louis Globe Dem., 1980. Fellow Am. Bar Found.; mem. ABA (chmn. sect. on corp. banking and bus. law 1977-78), FBA, Mo. Bar Assn., St. Louis Bar Assn., Am. Law Inst. (mem. coun. 1978—), Wash. U. Alumni Fedn. (pres. 1956-57), Rotary, St. Louis Country Club, Noonday Club (St. Louis), Met. Club, Chevy Chase Club, Alfalfa Club, St. Alban's Tennis Club, Order of Coif, Psi Upsilon, Delta Sigma Rho, Phi Delta Phi. Office: Milbank Tweed Hadley & McCloy 1825 I St NW Ste 1100 Washington DC 20006-5492

WECHMAN, ROBERT JOSEPH, economist, educator; b. Sept. 23, 1939; s. David Samuel and Blanche (Udell) W.; m. Stephanie Helene Kellman, June 18, 1967; children: Craig Samuel, Evan Mitchell, Darren Max. BA, CUNY, 1961, MA, 1964, Columbia U., 1966; PhD, Syracuse U., 1970; postdoc., U. Pa., 1974. Tchr. history, econs., NYC, 1961-63; tchr. history, econs. Dobbs Ferry (NY) HS, 1963-66; instr. Elmira (NY) Coll., 1966-70; asst. prof. social sci. Hartwick Coll., NY, 1970—74; asst. v.p. Beavertown Mills, NYC, Nebr., 1976-80, v.p., 1980-90; prin., owner Robert J. Wechman, Cons., NYC, 1984-90, Verdin Assocs., Inc., NYC, 1982-88, Robert J. Wechman Assocs., Inc., NYC, 1990-93. Vis. lectr. SUNY, Corning, summers 1967, 1970; adj. prof. New Sch. U., SUNY, Rockland Cmty. Coll., 1974-80, Empire State Coll., 1974—, Bergen Cmty. Coll., 1976-80, Berkeley Coll., 1979, 99-2001, Pace U., 1980-86, St. Thomas Aquinas Coll., 1981-94, Dominican Coll., summer 1981; adj. prof. Econs., Bus. CUNY, 1981—; adj. prof. Econs. St. Peters Coll., 1998-2002; adj. prof. Econs., Fin. Ramapo Coll., 1999-01; cons. Choice Jour., 1972—. Author: The Eager Immigrants, 1972, The Economic Development of the Italian-American, 1983, Encountering Management, 1987, Essentials of American Business, 1990, Aspects of German Nationalism, 1994, Dictionary of Economics and Business, 1997; editor: Critical Issues in Modern American Life, 1968, The Crisis in Population, 1969, Urban America: A Guide to the Literature, 1971; reviewer for profl. jours. Mem. Oneonta Bd. Ethics, 1971-74, Oneonta Anti-Pollution commn., 1972-74, Rockland County Bd. Ethics, 1997-99; committeeman, dist. chmn. Rockalnd County Rep. com., 1978—, Heritage Found., Hudson Inst. U.S. Army, 1959 USAR, 1959—65. Recipient Marcus award Excellence Tchg. 1972, Outstanding Educators Am. award 1972, Pres. Appreciation award 1989, 90, 91, Congl. Cert. Appreciation award 1991, 93, Disting. Svc. award Rockland County, 1992, Cert. of Merit award NY State Senate, 1992, Appreciation award CUNY, 1993, Excellence in Tchg. Econs. award Found. Tchg. Econs., 1994, 95, Tchr. Recognition award Newsday, 1995. Mem. K.P. Club, Phi Alpha Theta, Delta Tau Kappa, Delta Pi Epsilon. Republican. Home: 9 Verdin Dr New City NY 10956-3707

WECHSLER, ANDREW ROBERT, international economic consultant; b. N.Y.C., Oct. 24, 1946; s. Herbert and Jennie (Epstein) W.; m. Christine Macfarlane, Sept. 21, 1991. BA cum laude, Yale U., 1969; MA, Stanford U., 1974, postgrad., 1976-79. Tchr., high schs., New Haven and Balt., 1969-72; lectr. Calif. State U., Hayward, 1973-74; guest researcher Nationalekononiska institutionen, Uppsala, Sweden, 1974-76; lectr. econs. San Francisco State U., 1976-77, Stanford U., Calif., 1978-79; sr. econ. adviser to chairwoman U.S. Internat. Trade Commn., Washington, 1979-87; sr. economist Economists Inc., Washington., 1987-89, sr. v.p., 1989-91; prin., mng. dir. LECG, Inc., 1991—. Contbr. articles to profl. jours. Yale U. Ranking scholar, 1964-65; Social Sci. Rsch. Coun. West European fellow, 1975-76; John F. Kennedy fellow Swedish Embassy, Washington, 1974; Stanford U. fellow, 1972-74; Grumman Aircraft Engrng. scholar, 1964-68; N.Y. State Regents scholar, 1968; recipient Elks Nat. Most Valuable Student award, 1964. Mem. Am. Econ. Assn., Nat. Assn. Bus. Economists, Swedish Am. Cultural Union (U.S.-New Zealand coun.). Clubs: Nat. Econs. Yale of Washington. Avocations: photography, travel, tennis. Home: 5114 Edgemoor Ln Bethesda MD 20814-2311

WECHSLER, ARNOLD, osteopathic obstetrician, gynecologist; b. N.Y.C., June 10, 1923; s. David and Eva (Kirsch) W.; m. Marlene Esta Jurnovoy, Sept. 11, 1955 (div. Sept. 1986); children: Diane, Paul, Stewart. Grad., Rutgers U.; DO, Phila. Coll. Osteo. Medicine, 1952. Diplomate Am. Bd. Osteo. Obstetricians and Gynecologists; lic. physician, Pa., N.Y., Fla. Intern Hosps. of Phila. Coll. Osteo. Medicine, 1952-53, resident in ob-gyn. and gen. surgery, 1953-56; lectr. in ob-gyn. Nursing Sch. Phila. Coll. Osteo. Medicine; founder, mem. staff Tri County Hosp., Delaware County, Pa., from 1960, chief staff, 1960-62, chief dept. ob-gyn. surgery, 1960-77, dir. med. edn., 1968-71; attending and cons. in ob-gyn. surgery Met. Hosp., Phila., 1956-60, 71-75; chief dept. ob-gyn. Humana Hosp.-South Broward, Hollywood, Fla., 1980-84; cons. and attending in gynecol. surgery Drs. Hosp. of Hollywood, 1982-86. Insp. for intern and resident tng. programs Bur. Hosps. of Am. Osteo. Assn., 1965-66; founder, med. dir. Women's Med. Svcs., 1973-77, Nutrients Inc., Phila., 1977-79, Supplements Inc., Phila., 1979-80, Alternative Lifestyle Ctr., Fla., 1983-86; founder, dir. A.W. Profl. Consultants, Inc.; cons. Practice Mgmt. Group, Med Temps Plus, Plantation, Fla.; provider ambulatory gyn. surgery for multiple gyn ctrs. in Dade, Broward and Palm Beach Counties, Fla. Author: Dr. Wechsler's New You Diet, 1978. Staff Sgt. Signal Corps, USAF, 1942-46, PTO, Japan. Fellow Am. Coll. Osteo. Obstetricians and Gynecologists, Internat. Coll. Applied Nutrition; mem. Am. Osteo. Assn., Pa. Osteo. Med. Assn., Philadelphia County Osteo. Soc., Fla. Osteo. Med. Assn., Fla. Med. Soc., Fla. Ob-Gyn. Soc., Broward County Osteo. Med. Assn., Am. Soc. Bariatric Physicians, Assn. Maternal and Child Welfare, Internat. Acad. Preventive Medicine, Inst. Food Technologists, Coun. for Responsible Nutrition, Internat. Coll. Gynecologic Laparoscopists, Assn. Reproductive Health Profls. Avocations: photography, sculpture, woodworking. Home: 10419 NW 2nd St Coral Springs FL 33071-7334

WECHSLER, GIL, lighting designer; b. N.Y.C., Feb. 5, 1942; s. Arnold J. and Miriam (Steinberg) W. Student, Rensselaer Poly. Inst., 1958-61; BS, NYU, 1964; MFA, Yale U., 1967. Lighting designer Harkness Ballet, N.Y.C., 1967-69, Pa. Ballet, Phila., 1969-70, Stratford Shakespeare Festival, Ont., Canada, 1969—78, light designer, 1997—2004; lighting designer Guthrie Theatre, Mpls., 1971, Lyric Opera, Chgo., 1972-76, Met. Opera, N.Y.C., 1976-96, Equus, Stratford Sheakespeare Festival, 1997, Macbeth, Stratford Festival, 2004. Tchr. NYU, Rensselaer Poly. Inst., 1998; guest lectr. Teatro Colon, Buenos Aires, 1985, Yale U., New Haven, 1980, Broadway Lighting Designers, 1994—98; guest lighting designer Am. Ballet Theatre, N.Y.C., 1980, Paris Opera, 1983, Chatelet Theatre, Paris, 1991; dean's adv. coun. Rensselaer Poly. Inst., Troy, NY. Cons. editor Opera Quar., 1983-90. Recipient Emmy award nominations, Illuminating Engring. Soc., United Scenic Artists. Avocations: collecting ocean liner memorabilia, gardening, kayaking. Home: 1 Lincoln Plz New York NY 10023-7129 E-mail: gillights@aol.com.

WECHSLER, JESSICA See JOSELL, JESSICA

WECHSLER, MARY HEYRMAN, lawyer; b. Green Bay, Wis., Jan. 8, 1948; d. Donald Hubert and Helen (Polcyn) Heyrman; m. Roger Wechsler, Aug. 1971 (div. 1977); 1 child, Risa Heyrman; m. David Jay Sellinger, Aug. 15, 1981; 1 stepchild, Kirk Benjamin; 1 child, Michael Paul. Student, U. Chgo., 1966-67, 68-69; BA, U. Wash., 1971; JD cum laude, U. Puget Sound, 1979. Bar: Wash. 1979. Assoc. Law Offices Ann Johnson, Seattle, 1979-81; ptnr. Johnson, Wechsler, Thompson, Seattle, 1981-83; pvt. practice Seattle, 1984-87; ptnr. Mussehl, Rosenberg et al, Seattle, 1987-88, Wechsler, Becker LLP, Seattle, 1988—. Mem. Bd. Ct. Edn., 1998—2004, sec., 2003—04; bd. dirs. U. Wash. Law Sch. Child Advocacy Clinic, 1996—99; mem. Wash. State Commn. on Jud. Selection, 1995—96, Wash. State Commn. on Domestic Rels., 1996—97, 1999—2004; chair edn. com. Access to Justice Bd., 1996—99, mem. pub. trust and confidence com., 2000—04; presenter in field; mem. Jud. Coll. Bd. Trustees, 2004. Author: Family Law in Washington, 1987, rev. edit., 1988, Marriage and Separation, Divorce and Your Rights, 1994; contbr. articles to legal publs. Mem. Wash. State Ethics Adv. Com., 1992-95; bd. dirs. Seattle LWV, 1991-92. Named one of Seattle's Top Lawyers, Seattle Mag., 2003. Fellow Am. Acad. Matrimonial Lawyers (Wash. state chpt.,

sec.-treas. 1996, v.p. 1997-98, pres. 1999-2000, nat. arbitration com. 1999-2000, nat. interdisciplinary com. 1999-2000, nat. admissions procedure com. 2000-02, nat. long range planning com. 2003, chair 2003—); mem. ABA (chmn. membership Wash. state 1987-88), Wash. State Bar Assn. (exec. com. family law sect. 1985-91, chair family law sect. 1988-89), profl. devel. com. 2002-03, media project com. 2001, ct. improvement com. 1998-2000, legs. com. 1991-96, Outstanding Atty. of Yr. family law sect. 1988, comms. com. 1997-98, disciplinary hearing officer 1998—), Wash. Women Lawyers, King County Bar Assn. (legis. com. 1985-2000, vice-chair 1990-91, chair family law sect. 1986-87, chair domestic violence com. 1986-87, trustee 1988-90, policy planning com. 1991-92, 2d v.p. 1992-93, 1st v.p. 1993-94, pres. 1994-95, long-range planning com. 1998-99, awards com. 1997-99, nominations com. 2003, co-chair Bench-Bar Conf. 2003, Outstanding Atty. award 1999), Nat. Conf. of Bar Pres., King County Bar Found. (trustee 1997-2000), Am. Judicature Soc. (v.p. Washington chpt. 2000-03, pres. 2003—). Office: Wechsler Becker LLP Ste 4550 701 5th Ave Seattle WA 98104-7097 Office Phone: 206-624-4900.

WECHSLER, SERGIO, automotive executive, consultant; b. Rio de Janeiro, Aug. 10, 1944; arrived in US, 1965; s. Michael and Gertrud (Putziger) W.; children: Mark, Andrew. Student, Mackenzie U., 1962, Kettering U., 1967; MBA in Internat. Bus., NYU, 1974; PhD in Internat. Bus., Kennedy-Western U., 1996. Quality supr. GM do Brasil, Sao Paulo, 1963-65, quality control supt., 1967-70; quality control mgr. Gillette Corp., Berlin, 1970-71; project mgr. GM, N.Y.C., 1971-76; plant mgr. GM de Portugal, Lisbon, 1976-79; project mgr. Adam Opel AG, Russelheim, Fed. Republic of Germany, 1979-81; quality dir. GM, Linden, N.J., 1981-85, dir. ops. and quality control Warren, Mich., 1985-93, mgr. internat. programs, 1985-95, program mgr. Cadillac Luxury Car divsn. Flint, Mich., 1995-96. Pres. Marswex Global Enterprises, St. Petersburg, Fla., 1982—, Hudson Plaza, 1984-99; chmn. Auto Exchange Club, Clearwater, Fla., 1997-2001, MSX Internat., Detroit, 1996-99, v.p. German ops., 1999-2001. V.P. Temple Beth Jacob, Pontiac, Mich., 1986, pres., 1987-89. Mem. Am. Soc. Quality Control (cert. quality engr. 1992), Radio Club. Republican. Avocations: amateur radio, travel, automobile restoration.

WECHTER, CLARI ANN, manufacturing executive; b. Chgo., June 1, 1953; d. Norman Robert and Harriet Beverly (Golub) W.; m. Gordon Jay Siegel, Feb. 10, 1980; 1 child, Alix Jessica. BA, U. Ariz., 1975; BE, Loyola U., Chgo., 1977. Cert. tchr., Ill. Saleswoman, v.p. sales Federated Paint Mfg. Co., Chgo., 1979—. Republican. Jewish. Avocation: travel. Home: 25 E Cedar St Chicago IL 60611-1109 Office: Federated Paint and Pioneer Powder Mfg Co 1521 N 31st Ave Melrose Park IL 60160 Office Phone: 708-345-4848 622.

WECHTER, IRA MARTIN, tax specialist, financial planner; b. Bkyn., June 26, 1947; s. Nathan Harris and Mollie (Bauer) W.; m. Myrna Ellen Rosenbaum, Dec. 22, 1968; 1 child, Megan Jill. BA, CCNY, 1969; MPA, Bernard Baruch Coll., 1973. CFP; cert. practitioner of taxation; accredited tax advisor; registered investment advisor; lic. gen. securities prin.; enrolled to practice before IRS; lic. gen. securities prin., life, health and disability ins., N.J., N.Y. Dir. adminstrv. svcs. N.Y.C. Dept. City Planning, 1971-77; dep. asst. budget dir. N.Y., N.Y.C. Office Mgmt. and Budget, 1977-81; dep. commr. N.Y.C. Dept. Environ. Protection, 1981-84; pres. Wechter Fin. Svcs., Inc., Parsippany, N.J., 1984—. Mem. Community Bd. No. 1 S.I., 1973-76, 1st v.p., 1976-77; treas. S.I. Coun. on Arts, 1974-75. Recipient Outstanding Citizenship award Borough Pres. of S.I., 1977. Mem. Nat. Assn. Enrolled Agts., Inst. Cert. Fin. Planners, Nat. Assn. Tax Practitioners, Nat. Soc. Tax Preparers, Nat. Soc. Pub. Accts. Republican. Jewish. Avocations: U.S. mint stamp collecting, organist. Office: Wechter Fin Svcs Inc 1719 State Rt 10 Ste 310 Parsippany NJ 07054-4507 also: 1719 Route 10 Ste 224 Parsippany NJ 07054-4507 Office Phone: 973-605-1448. Business E-Mail: wfs@wechterfinancial.com.

WECK, MARGARET A. science educator; b. Bismarck, ND, Apr. 21, 1958; d. Herman I. and Barbara D. (Fiola) Weck; m. James G. Laing, May 22, 1993. BS in life scis., U. Ill., 1980; MS in zoology, Idaho State U., 1983, ArtsD in biology, 1985. Asst. prof. biology Coll. of St. Rose, Albany, NY, 1985—88, Lake Superior State U., Sault Sainte Marie, Mich., 1988—92; assoc. prof. biology St. Louis Coll. of Pharmacy, St. Louis, 1992—. Author: (Instructor's Manual) Anatomy and Physiology, (Instr.'s Resource Guide Manual), (Instructors Manual) Essentials of Anatomy and Physiology. Pres., bd. of trustees First Unitarian Ch. St. Louis, St. Louis, 1999—2001; mem., bd. of trustees First Unitarian Ch. of St. Louis, 1998—2001. Fellow Mich. Partnership New Edn. fellowship in Sci. Edn., Mich. State U., 1990-91. Mem.: AAUW (instl. rep. 2001—04), Human Anatomy and Physiology Soc. (sec., treas. 1996—97, nat. conf. coord.). Independent. Office: St Louis Coll Pharmacy 4588 Parkview Pl Saint Louis MO 63110 E-mail: mweck@stlcop.edu.

WECKESSER, ERNEST PROSPER, JR., publisher, educator; b. Akron, Ohio, Mar. 23, 1933; s. Ernest Prosper and Sadie (Liken) Weckesser; m. Mary B. Hunter, Jan. 12, 1959; children: Jeffrey, Franz, Kathleen, Lynne. BA, Bowling Green State U., 1955, MA, 1960; PhD, Mich. State U., 1963. Asst. prof. speech SUNY-Oneonta, 1962-63, Kent State U., 1963-64; mem. faculty Purdue U., 1964-70, assoc. prof., 1968-70; prof. speech Montclair (N.J.) Coll., 1970-71; assoc. prof. speech Pa. State U., 1971-72; dir. Ernest Weckesser Assos.; chmn. bd. dirs. Green Tree Press, Inc., Dunkirk, N.Y.; pres. Bierhaus Internat., Inc., Erie, Pa. Author: The Radio Rhetoric of John L. Lewis, 1963, How To Succeed in College, 1971, Dollars in Your Mailbox, 1975, Alternatives: A Network of Small Business Opportunities, 1992; co-author: The Bradley-Cooper Smoke Cessation Program, 1995. Bd. dirs. Florence Crittenden Home, Erie, Erie County Ct. Apptd. Spl. Advocates for Children; mem. Pres.'s Coun. Gannon U.; mem. adv. bd. Villa Maria Coll. Served to capt. USAF, 1955—59, provost marshal, 1956—59, RAF Sta. Woodbridge, Eng. Named Disting. Pennsylvalian, William Penn Soc., 1983.

WECKSELL, ALAN, radiologist; b. N.Y.C., 1939; MD, N.Y. Med. Coll., 1965. Diplomate Am. Bd. Radiology. Intern L.I. Coll. Hosp., Bklyn., 1965-66, resident in radiology, 1966-69; hosp. staff radiology North Shore U. Hosp., Manhasset, NY, 1991—; asst. clin. prof. radiology NYU. Mem. AMA, Am. Roentgen Ray Soc., Radiol. Soc. of N.Am. Office: North Shore Hosp Radiology Manhasset NY 11030 Address: Irving Goldman Family Care Ctr 865 Northern Blvd Great Neck NY 11021

WEDDING, CHARLES RANDOLPH, architect; b. St. Petersburg, Fla., Nov. 16, 1934; s. Charles Reid and L. Marion (Whitaker) W.; m. Audrey Whitsel, Aug. 18, 1956 (div. Apr. 1979); children: Daryl L., Douglas R., Dorian B.; m. Vonnie Sue Hayes, June 22, 1984 (div. Dec. 1991); stepchildren: Stephanie W., Brian E.; m. June A. Free, Mar. 31, 1993; stepchildren: Gregory, Kristine. BArch, U. Fla., 1957. Registered arch., Fla., Ga., N.C., S.C., Del., Va., Tex., Ill., Ind., Kans., La., Mo., Okla., Tenn. Arch. in tng. Harvard & Jolly AIA, St. Petersburg, 1957-60; arch., prin., pres. Wedding & Assocs., St. Petersburg, 1960—. Mayor City of St. Petersburg, 1973-75; past chmn. Pinellas County Com. of 100, Bldg. Dept. Survey Team, City of St. Petersburg; trustee All Children's Hosp., 1968-70; sect. leader St. Petersburg United Fund, 1965-70; mem. city coun. Action Team for Pier Redevel., 1967-68; mem. exec. com. Goals for City of St. Petersburg, 1970-72; den leader Webelos, Boy Scouts Am., 1971-72; chmn., trustee Canterbury Sch. YMCA, 1968-72; mem. adv. com. Tomlinson Vocat. Sch., 1969-79; past trustee Mus. Fine Arts; past bd. dirs. Neighborly Ctr., Jr. Achievement Pinellas County; chair Downtown Partnership, 2001—. Served to 1st lt. U.S. Army, 1958-60. Fellow AIA (5 Silver Spike awards, Merit of Honor, Medal of Honor); mem. Am. Soc. Landscape Archs., St. Petersburg Assn. Archs. (past pres.), Fla. Assn. Archs. (8 Merit Design awards), St. Petersburg Yacht Club, Suncoasters Club. Republican. Episcopalian. Avocations: sailing, hunting, golf, tennis. Home: 6900 10th Ave N Saint Petersburg FL 33710-6152 Office: Wedding/Stephenson/Ibargüen Archs Inc 300 1st Ave S Saint Petersburg FL 33701-4209 Office Phone: 727-821-6610. Business E-Mail: randy@weddingarchitects.com.

WEDDINGTON, SARAH RAGLE, lawyer, educator, speaker, writer; b. Abilene, Tex., Feb. 5, 1945; d. Herbert Doyle and Lena Catherine Ragle. BS magna cum laude, McMurry Coll., 1965, hon. doctorate, 1979; JD, U. Tex., 1967; hon. doctorate, Hamilton Coll., 1979, Southwestern U., 1989, Austin Coll., 1993, Nova Southeastern U., 1999. Bar: Tex. 1967, D.C. 1979, U.S. Dist. Ct. (we., no. and ea. dists.) Tex., U.S. Ct. Appeals (5th cir.), U.S. Supreme Ct. Pvt. practice law, Austin, 1967-77; gen. counsel Dept. Agr., Washington, 1977-78; spl. asst. to U.S. pres. Washington, 1978—79; asst. to U.S. pres., 1979—81; chmn. Interdepartmental Task Force on Women, 1978-81; mem. Pres.'s Commn. on Exec. Exchange, 1981; Carl Hatch prof. law and pub. adminstrn. U. N.Mex., Albuquerque, 1982-83; pvt. practice law Austin, Tex., 1985—; dir. Tex. Office State-Fed. Rels., Austin, Washington, 1983-85. Vis. prof. govt. Wheaton Coll., Norton, Mass., 1981-83; sr. lectr. Tex. Woman's U., Denton, 1981-90, 93, U. Tex., Austin, 1986-1989, adj. assoc. prof. 1989-2001, adj. prof., 2001-. Author: A Question of Choice, 1992; contbr. articles to various mags.; contbg. editor Glamour mag., 1981-83. Mem. Tex. Ho. of Reps., 1973-77; named hon. chair San Francisco Bar Assn. Breast Cancer Hotline/Network, 2001, named hon. chair ann. benefit for Breast Cancer Rsch. Ctr., Austin, 2002, named lecture showcase presenter Nat. Assn. Campus Activities, 2003. Recipient Woman of Yr. award Tex. Women's Polit. Caucus, 1973, Time Mag. Outstanding Young Am. Leaders, 1979, Leadership awards Ladies Home Jour., 1980, spl. recognition Esquire mag., 1984, Elizabeth (Betty) Boyer award Equity Action League, 1992, Woman Who Dares award Nat. Coun. Jewish Women, 1993, Woman of Distinction award Nat. Conf. for Coll. Women Student Leaders, 1993, Colby award for Pub. Svc. Sigma Kappa, 1996, Hummingbird award Leadership Am., 1998, Tallest Texan award Houston Chronicle, 2000, Speaking Out for Justice award AAUW Legal Advocacy Fund, 2001, Speaking Out for Justice award AAUW Ednl. Found., 2001, Ally award Possible Woman Leadership Conf., 2001; named Lectr. of Yr. Nat. Assn. for Coll. Activities, 1990, Tex. Women's C. of C. Tex. Woman of Century, 1999, San Antonio Express News Face of Century, 1999, 2000; named One of the Most Influential Lawyers of the 20th Century, Tex. Lawyer, 2000; hon. chair of Sarah Weddington Leadership Conf. named in her honor, Tex. Woman's U., 2001, hon. chair San Francisco Bar Assn Breast Cancer Hotline/Network, 2001, Annual Benefit for Breast Cancer Rsch., Austin, Tex., 2002, Lectr. Showcase presenter Nat. Assn. Campus Activities, 2003. Mem. Tex. Bar Assn. Office: The Weddington Ctr 709 W 14th St Austin TX 78701-1707 E-mail: sw@weddingtoncenter.com.

WEDDINGTON, SUSAN, political party official; m. Bob Weddington; 1 child, Sean. BA in Comms. with honors, Trinity U. Tchr. photojournalism; owner three small bus.; dir. media rels. Tex. Conservative Coalition, rsch. analyst; legis. asst. Rep. state rep.; vice chmn. Rep. Party Tex., 1994, 96, state chmn., 1997—. Del. four State Rep. Convs.; Tex. del. Rep. Nat. Conv., San Diego, 1996, Tex. rep. Nat. Rules Com.; worked 76 in 96 Polit. Action Com.; RPT liaison Campaign for Rep. Leadership Polit. Action Com. Active Drug Stop, San Antonio Citizens Against Pornography, crisis pregnancy ctrs.; bd. dirs. Pray Tex.; mem. Castle Hills First Bapt. Ch., San Antonio; dir. comms., rsch. Tex. Pub. Policy Found. Mem. Nat. Coun. Women Advisors to Congress (charter), Bexar County Rep. Women's Forum, Daus. of Liberty Rep. Club, Bexar County Hispanic Rep. Women's Club. Office: Rep Party of Tex 900 Congress Ave, Ste 300 Austin TX 78701-3218

WEDDLE, LAURA MILDRED THOMAS, retired language educator; b. Keene, Ky., June 28, 1933; d. John Wesley and Elizabeth (Munson) Thomas; m. Leo Franklin Weddle, June 15, 1955; children: Laura Lynn, Leo Jeffrey. BA, Georgetown Coll., 1955; MA, U. Ky., 1959, Morehead State U., 1977, MA, 1986. Asst. prof. Campbellsville (Ky.) Coll., 1961—65, U. Ky. C.C., Somerset, 1965—66, assoc. prof. Prestonsburg, 1966—72, prof., 1972—94; ret. Adv. bd. Nat. Coun. Staff Devel., Washington, 1975—90, David (Ky.) Alternative Sch., 1980—90. Author short stories. Dir. Children's Theater, Prestonsburg, 1970—75; mem. Prestonsburg City Coun., 1973—74. Mem.: Penwomen Am. Avocations: reading, antiques, travel, swimming.

WEDEL-COWGILL, MILLIE REDMOND, secondary school educator, performing arts educator, communications educator, education educator; b. Harrisburg, Pa., Aug. 18, 1939; d. Clair L. and Florence (Heiges) Aungst; m. T.S. Redmond, 1956 (div. 1967); children: T.S. Redmond II; m. Frederick L. Wedel, Jr., 1974 (div. 1986); m. Paul R. Cowgill, May 19, 2001. BA, Alaska Meth. U., 1966; MEd, U. Alaska, Anchorage, 1972; postgrad. in comm., Stanford U., 1975-76. Lic. third class broadcasting, FCC. Profl. actress Charming Models & Models Guild of Phila., 1954-61; asst. dir. devel. in charge pub. rels. Alaska Meth. U., Anchorage, 1966, part-time lectr., 1966, 73; comm. tchr. Anchorage Sch. Dist., 1967-96; owner Wedel Prodns., Anchorage, 1976-86; cons. comms., media and edn., owner Cowgill Cons., 2003—. Pub. rels. staff Alaska Purchase Centennial Exhibit, U.S. Dept. Commerce, 1967; writer gubernatorial campaign, 1971; instr. Chapman Coll., 1990-93; adj. instr. U. Alaska, Anchorage, 1972, 77-79, 89-2001; cons. Cook Inlet Native Assn., 1978, No. Inst., 1979; judge Ark. Press Women's Writing Contest, 1990-91; sec. exec. bd. Alaska Dept. Edn. Profl. Tchg. Practices Commn., 1993-94. Bd. dirs. Sta. KAKM, Alaska Pub. TV, membership chmn., 1978-80, nat. lay rep. to Pub. Broadcasting Svc. and Nat. Assn. Pub. TV Stas., 1979; bd. dirs. Ednl. Telecom. Consortium for Alaska, 1979, Mid-Hillside Cmty. Coun., Municipality of Anchorage, 1979-80, 83-88, Hillside East Cmty. Coun., 1984-88, pres., 1984-85; rsch. writer, legal asst. Vinson & Elkins, Houston, 1981; v.p., bd. dirs. Inlet View ASD Cmty. Sch., 1994-95, pres., 1995-97; Valley Forge Freedoms Found., Murdoch Scholarships; bd. dirs. Rev. Richard Gay Trust, Alaska and Pa., 1992-2000. Recipient awards for newspapers, lit. mags.; award Nat. Scholastic Press Assn., 1981, 82, 83, 84; Alaska Coun. Econs., 1982, Merits award Alaska Dept. Edn., 1982-93, Legis. commendation State of Alaska, Nat. Blue Ribbon Outstanding Sch. award, 1993. Mem. NEA (AEA bldg. rep., state del. 70s, 80s, 94-95), Assn. Pub. Broadcasting (charter mem., nat. lay del. 1980), Indsl. TV Assn. (San Francisco and Houston 1975-81), Alaska Press Club (chmn. high sch. journalism workshops, 1968-69, 73, awards for sch. newspapers 1972, 74, 77), Alaska Fedn. Press Women (dir. 1978-86, 94-95, pres. 1995-96, h.s. journalism competition youth projects dir., award for brochures 1978, chair youth writing contest 1994-95), Internat. Platform Assn., World Affairs Coun., Chugach Electric (chair 1990, nomination com. for bd. dirs. 1988-90), Hood Coll. Alaska Alumni Assn., Stanford U. Alumni Club (Alaska pres. 1982-84, 90-92, 99-2000, v.p. 1998-99), Rotary Club of Naples (photographer and asst. program chair 2003), Imperial Golf Course Country Club, Club at Pelican Bay, Naples (Fla.) Philharm. League, Naples Players Theatre Guild, Pelican Bay Women's League, Naples Fla. Univ. of Pa. Club, Delta Kappa Gamma. Presbyterian. Office: PO Box 111489 Anchorage AK 99511-1489 also: PO Box 770662 Naples FL 34107-0662 Office Phone: 907-345-7793, 239-597-7308., 239-598-3770. Business E-Mail: wedelcowgill@gci.net.

WEDEPOHL, LEONHARD MARTIN, electrical engineering educator; b. Pretoria, South Africa, Jan. 26, 1933; s. Martin Willie and Liselotte B.M. (Franz) W.; m. Sylvia A.L. St. Jean; children: Martin, Graham. BSc in Engring., Rand U., 1953; PhD, U. Manchester, Eng., 1957. Registered profl. engr., BC. Planning engr. Escom, Johannesburg, 1957-61; mgr. L.M. Erricson, Pretoria, South Africa, 1961-62; sect. leader Reyrolle, Newcastle, England, 1962-64; prof., head dept. Manchester U., 1964-74; dean engring. U. Man., Winnipeg, Canada, 1974-79; dean applied sci. U. BC, Vancouver, Canada, 1979-85, prof. elec. engring., 1985-97, prof. emeritus, 1998—, dean applied sci. emeritus, 1998—. Mem. Sci. Rsch. Coun., London, 1968-74; dir. Man. Hydro, Winnipeg, 1975-79, BC Hydro, Vancouver, 1980-84, BC Sci. Coun., 1982-84; cons. Horizon Robotics, Saskatoon, 1986; chmn. implementation team Sci. Place, Can., 1985; cons. CEPEL, Rio de Janeiro; adv. Man. High Voltage DC Rsch. Ctr.; tech. advisor RTDS Techs., Inc., Winnipeg, 1994—; head protection devel. Rolls Royce Indsl. Power Group, 1995-96; adj. prof. U. Man., 2002-. Contbr. articles to sci. jours.; patentee in field. Named Hon. Citizen, City of Winnipeg, 1979. Fellow Instn. Elec. Engrs. (premium 1967), Engring. Inst. Can.; mem. Assn. Profl. Engrs. BC. Avocations: music, cross country skiing, hiking. Office: 1511 Chardonnay Pl Westbank BC Canada V4T 2P9 E-mail: wedepohl@shaw.ca.

WEDESWEILER (RAYE), CHERYL, writer; b. San Gabriel, Calif., Aug. 11, 1964; d. Virginia Arlene McCool and William Marcellus Wedesweiler. AA, Citrus C.C., 1982—84; BA, Calif. State U. Fullerton, 1984—87; Honors Grad., Calif. Scholarship Fedn., Glendora H.S., 1979—82. Author: (poem/motivation/spirit lifter) Crack the Code in Generations, (article/recipes) The Disabled Cook in the book from The Nat.Ataxia Found. Cooking For a Cause, (poem) Summer Born in Generations, My Agility Goes Slipping Away in Generations, The Hummingbird in Hodegepodge, (article) The Hungry Hummingbird in REAL KIDS. Motivator/spirit lifter The Nat. Ataxia Found., Mpls., 2002—04. Recipient Honor Soc., Calif. Scholarship Found., 1982. Mem.: The Nat. Ataxia Found. (corr.), Calif. Scholarship Fedn. (life). Personal E-mail: cherylshasta@aol.com.

WEDGE, CAROLE C. architectural firm executive; B in Environ. Design, U. Colo., 1981; student, Alliance Francaise, 1982; BArch, Boston Archtl. Ctr., 1990. With J. & W. Seligman & Co., 1983—86; joined Shepley Bulfinch Richardson & Abbott, Boston, 1986, assoc., 1996, sr. assoc., 1998, prin., 2000, pres., 2004—. Lectr. in field. Mem.: ALA, AIA, Soc. Coll. and Univ. Planners, Assn. Coll. and Rsch. Librs. Office: Shepley Bulfinch Richardson & Abbott 40 Broad St Boston MA 02109-4306

WEDGE, CHRIS, animation director, studio executive; b. 1958; Grad., SUNY, Purchase, 1981; MA, Ohio State U. Stop-motion animator; with MAGI/SynthaVision; v.p. creative devel., founder Blue Sky, Ossining, N.Y. Animator films Tron, 1992, Joe's Apt., 1996, Alien Resurrection, 1997, Bunny, 1998 (Best Animation Oscar award 1999); dir. Ice Age, 2002; creator ind. films The Daymaker, Tuber's Two Step, Balloon Guy. Office: c/o Jayson Engquist Blue Sky Studios Inc 44 S Broadway 17th Fl White Plains NY 10601 also: Blue Sky Prodns 100 Executive Blvd Ossining NY 10562 2557 Fax: (914) 259-6505. E-mail: christ@blueskystudios.com.

WEDGE, MICHAEL T. wholesale distribution executive; With BJ's Wholesale Club, Inc., Natick, Mass., 1988—, exec. v.p. club ops., 1994—2002, pres., CEO, 2002—. Office: BJs Wholesale Club Inc 1 Mercer Rd Natick MA 01760-2400 Fax: 508-651-6114.

WEDGEWORTH, ANN, actress; b. Abilene, Tex., Jan. 21, 1935; m. Rip Torn (div.); 1 child, Danae; m. Ernest Martin; 1 child, Dianna. Attended, U. Tex.; BA in Drama, So. Methodist U. Broadway debut in Make A Million, 1958; other Broadway appearances Chapter Two (Tony award), Thieves, Blues for Mr. Charlie, The Last Analysis; off-Broadway appearances Line, Chapparal, The Crucible, Days and Nights of Beebee Fenstermaker, Ludlow Fair, The Honest to God Shnozzola, A Lie of the Mind, Elba, The Aunts, The Debutante's Ball; premiers of In the Moonlight Eddie at Pasadena Playhouse, Natural Affection in Pheonix, The Dream in Phila.; toured with nat. cos. of The Sign in Sidney Brustein's Window and Kennedy's Children; appeared in TV series Three's Company, The Edge of Night, Another World, Somerset, Filthy Rich, Evening Shade; other TV appearances All That Glitters, The Equalizer, Roseanne, Bronk, Evening Shade, Twilight Zone, Trapper John, M.D.; TV film The War Between the Tates, Right to Kill, Cooperstown, Fight for Justice: The Nancy Conn Story, Bogie, A Stranger Waits; movies Handle With Care (Nat. Soc. Film Critics award), Thieves, Bang the Drum Slowly, Scarecrow, Catamount Killing, Law and Disorder, One Summer Love, Dragon-Fly, Birch Intervals, Soggy Bottom, USA, No Small Affair, Sweet Dreams, Mens Club, A Tiger's Tale, Made in Heaven, Far North, Miss Firecracker, Green Card, Steel Magnolias, Love and a 45, The Whole Wide World, The Hunter's Moon, Hard Promises, Andy, My Science Project; TV host Evening at the Improv, A&E. Address: 70 Riverside Dr Apt 6E New York NY 10024-5716

WEDGLE, RICHARD JAY, lawyer; b. Denver, Dec. 2, 1951; s. Joseph M. and Lillian E. (Brown) W.; m. Susan R. Mason, Oct. 17, 1987. BA, U. Calif., Berkeley, 1974; JD, U. Denver, 1978. Bar: Colo. 1978, U.S. Dist. Ct. Colo. 1978, U.S. Ct. Appeals (10th cir.) 1980. Ptnr. Cox, Wedgle & Padmore, P.C., Denver, 1978-85, Barnes, Wedgle & Shpall, P.C., Denver, 1986-87, Wedgle and Shpall, P.C., Denver, 1987-98, Wedgle and Friedman, P.C., Denver, 1998-2000, Wedgle and Assoc. P.C., 2000—02, Wedgle and Kukseja, P.C., 2002—. Vol. coord. Dick Lamm for Gov., 1974, citizen adv. office, 1975; bd. dirs. Cherry Creek Improvement Assn., 1985-88. Mem. ABA, Colo. Bar Assn., Denver Bar Assn., Jewish Cmty. Ctr. Avocations: running, biking, gardening. Home: 365 Marion St Denver CO 80218-3927 Office: Wedgle & Kukrejs PC 730 17th St Ste 230 Denver CO 80202-3546 Office Phone: 303-893-3111.

WEDGWOOD, RUTH, law educator, international affairs expert; b. N.Y.C. d. Morris P. and Anne (Williams) Glushien; m. Josiah Francis Wedgwood; May 29, 1982; 1 child, Josiah Ruskin Wedgwood. BA magna cum laude, Harvard U., 1972; fellow, London Sch. Econs., 1972-73; JD, Yale U., 1976. Bar: D.C., N.Y., U.S. Supreme Ct. Law clk. to judge Henry Friendly U.S. Ct. Appeals (2d cir.), N.Y.C., 1976-77; law clk. to justice Harry Blackmun U.S. Supreme Ct., Washington, 1977-78; spl. asst. to asst. atty. gen. U.S. Dept. Justice, Washington, 1978-80; asst. U.S. atty. U.S. Dist. Ct. (so. dist.) N.Y., N.Y.C., 1980-86; prof. law Yale U., New Haven, 1986—2002, fellow Inst. for Social and Policy Studies, 1989—; fellow Berkeley Coll., Yale U., 1989—; Edward B. Burling prof. internat. law and diplomacy Nitze Sch. Advanced Internat. Studies Johns Hopkins U., Washington, 2001—. Mem. Sec. of State's Adv. Com. Internat. Law, 1993—; sr. fellow for internat. orgns. and law Coun. Fgn. Rels., 1994—; Charles Stockton prof. internat. law U.S. Naval War Coll., Newport, RI, 1998—99; mem. Hart-Rudman Commn. on Nat. Security in the 21st Century, Nat. Sec. Study Group, Dept. Def. Adv. Comm., 1999—2001; mem. acad. adv. com. to spl. rep. UN Sec.-Gen. for Children and Armed Conflict, 1999—; dir. studies Am. Soc. Internat. Law, 2000—; guest scholar U.S. Inst. Peace, 2001—02; dir. studies Hague Acad. Internat. Law, 2001—02; elected U.S. mem. UN Human Rights Com., Geneva, 2002—; mem. Hist. Rev. Panel, adv. to dir. CIA, 2002—; mem. Def. Policy Bd., advisor to U.S. Sec. Def., 2002—; prof. du Droit Internat. U. Paris I (Sorbonne), 2004. Exec. editor Yale Law Jour., 1975-76; author: The Revolutionary Martyrdom of Jonathan Robbins, 1990, The Use of Force in International Affairs, 1992, American National Interest and the United Nations, 1996, Toward an International Criminal Court?, 1999, After Dayton: Lessons of the Bosnian Peace Process, 1999; mem. bd. editors Yale Jour. Law and Humanities, 1988-98, Am. Jour. Internat. Law, 1998-, World Policy Jour. (New Sch. Social Rsch.), 2001-; contbr. articles to profl jours. and popular publs. including N.Y. Times, Washington Post, Christian Sci. Monitor, Internat. Herald Tribune, Wall St. Jour., Washington Times, Fin. Times, L.A. Times, Die Zeit, Fgn. Affairs, Fgn. Policy, Nat. Interest, Time mag.; commentator for CNN, PBS, Fox, Nat. Pub. Radio, MSNBC, BBC, Lehrer News Hour, PBS. Prin. rapporteur U.S. Atty. Gen.'s Guidelines on FBI Undercover Ops., Informant Use and Racketeering and Gen. Crime Investigations, 1980; bd. dirs. Lawyers Com. for Human Rights, N.Y.C., 1988-94; mem. policy adv. com. UN Assn. U.S.A., 1998—; bd. dirs. Lawyers Alliance for World Security, 1999-, Freedom House, 2003-, UN Watch, 2004—. Recipient Israel Peres prize, 1976, Disting. Contbn. to Internat. Law award N.Y. State Bar Assn., 2000; Ford Found. Rsch. grantee; Rockefeller Found. fellow. Mem. ABA (standing com. on law and nat. security 2002-, coun. Internat. Law sect. 2003-), Am. Law Inst., Am. Soc. Internat. Law (exec. com. 1995-98), Internat. Law Assn. (v.p. 1994-, program chmn. Am. br. 1992), Assn. Am. Law Sch. (chmn. sect. internat. law 1995-96), Assn. Bar City N.Y. (chmn. arms control and internat. security affairs com. 1989-92, chmn. internat. affairs coun. 1992-95, exec. com. 1995-99), Union Internationale des Avocats, U.S.A. (chpt. bd. govs. 1993-98), Coun. on Fgn. Rels., Internat. Inst. for Strategic Studies, Elizabethan Club, Mory's Assn., Yale Club (N.Y.C.). Office: Johns Hopkins Sch Advanced Internat Studies 1619 Massachusetts Ave NW Washington DC 20036 Office Phone: 202-663-5618. Business E-Mail: rwedgwood@jhu.edu. *Notable cases include: U.S. vs. Kostadinov, involving a Bulgarian spy traded for 25 East Bloc detainees; U.S. vs. Kampiles, involving government employee who gave satellite secrets to the Soviet Union; U.S. vs. Gold, Orosz, Egerhazi and Kompar, involving a million dollar racketeering/landlord arson ring in N.Y.C. that defrauded Lloyd's of London Sasse Syndicate; U.S. vs. Kazemzadeh and DeVelasco, involving pub. corruption in N.Y.C. Health and Hospitals Corporation and the fed. WIC program.*

WEDNER, H. JAMES, physician, researcher; b. Pitts., May 12, 1941; s. Benjamin Mayer and Lucille Ruth (Jacobs) W.; m. Maureen Patricia Martin, June 18, 1978; children: Bryna Kimberly, Jason Oliver. BS, Cornell U., 1963; MD, Cornell Med. Coll., N.Y.C., 1967. Intern Barnes Hosp., St. Louis, 1967-68; resident internal medicine Washington U. Med. Sch., St. Louis, 1970-71, fellow allergy and immunology, 1971-73; lt. comdr. USPHS, Govenor's Island, NY, 1968-70; prof. medicine Washington U. Med. Sch., St. Louis, 1990—, dir. tng. program allergy and immunology, 1986-95, 2001—, chief clin. allergy and immunology, 1988—, med. dir. The Asthma and Allergy Ctr., 2000—, acting chief Divsn. Allergy and Clin. Immunology, 2001—02, chief, 2002—. Vis. prof. Am. Coll. of Allergy and Immunology, Little Rock, 1991, U. Buffalo Med. Sch., 1999; William Pierson vis. prof. Ea. Va. Med. Sch., 2003; prin. investigator psychosocial aspects of asthma, St. Louis Asthma Study Unit; chmn. steering com. Nat. Coop. Inner City Asthma Study; prin. investigator Fungal Alleries Innercity Homes. Editor: Allergy: Theory and Practice, 1984, 2d rev. edit., 1991; mem. editl. bd. Jour. Immunology, 1980-82, Jour. Allergy and Clin. Immunology, 1991-96; assoc. editor Anaphylaxis and Drug Allergy Current Allergy Reports, 2000—; sect. editor Anaplylaxis and Drug Allergy, Current Allergy and Asthma Reports Fellow Am. Acad. Allergy Asthma Immunology; mem. Internat. Soc. Immunopharmacology, Am. Coll. Allergy Asthma Immunology, Am. Assn. Immunology, Clin. Immunology Soc., European Acad. Allergology and Clin. Immunology. Achievements include initial description of Parthenium hysterophruis allergy; research on asthma and the psychosocial aspects of asthma, molecular characterization of plant and fungal allergens and the role of fungi in asthma. Office: Washington U Med Sch Campus Box 8122 660 S Euclid Ave Saint Louis MO 63110-1010 Office Phone: 314-454-7937. E-mail: jwedner@im.wustl.edu., wednerj@att.net.

WEE, ALVIN GERARD, dental educator; b. Singapore, Jan. 30, 1967; arrived in U.S., 1994; s. Yeow Chin and Carmen Doreen Wee; m. Lisa Amy Davidson, June 7, 1997; 1 child, Natalie Carmen. B in Dental Surgery, Nat. U. Singapore, 1992; grad. cert. prosthodontics, U. Iowa, 1996, MS, 1997; grad. cert. maxillofacial prosthetics, U. Pitts., 1998; grad. cert. clin. rsch., Ohio State U., 2002. Asst. prof. Ohio State U. Coll. Dentistry, Columbus, 1998—. Contbr. articles to profl. jours. Named Clin. Instr. of the Yr., The Alpha Omega Profl. Dental Frat., 2000; recipient Fixed Prosthodontic Jr. Faculty award, Am. Acad. Fixed Prosthodontics, 2003, Third Pl. - Deloitte Touche Bus. Plan Competition, Ohio State Fisher Bus. Coll., 2002; grantee, Am. Acad. Esthetic Dentistry, 1999, Academic Rsch. Enhancement award, NIH/Nat. Eye Inst., 2002—04, Editl. Coun. Jour. Prosthetic Dentistry, 2003—04; Multi-Year Ambassadorial scholar, Rotary Internat. Found., 1994—96, Student Rsch. grantee, Greater N.Y. Acad. Prosthodontics, 1996, Bloc Travel grantee, Am. Assn. Dental Rsch., 2003, Clin. Rsch. fellow, Ohio State U./NIH, 2001—02. Fellow: Am. Acad. Maxillofacial Prosthetics; mem.: Am. Coll. Prosthodontics, Internat. Assn. Dental Rsch., Internat. Coll. Prosthodontics. Roman Catholic. Achievements include research in evaluation of the accuracy of solid implant casts; use of low fusing alloys in dentistry; strategies to achieve fit in implant prosthodontics; comparison of impression materials for direct multi-implant impressions; utilization of the neutral zone technique for a maxillofacial pateient; evaluating procelain color match of different porcelain shade matching systems; accuracy and pourability of gypsum preweighed packages; accuracy of die systems for implant casts; variation in color between intended matched shade and fabricated shade of dental porcelain; prosthodontic complications of spline dental implants; a new and easy method of stabilizing casts with cyanoacrylate. Office: OSU College Dentistry PO Box 182357 305 West 12th Ave Columbus OH 43210-1241 E-mail: wee.12@osu.edu.

WEE, CHRISTINE DIJOS, elementary school educator; b. Honolulu, Jan. 8, 1968; d. Cosme Wayne and Victoria Amparo Dijos; m. Phillip Ying Kin Wee, July 15, 2000; 1 child, Deanna Rae Patacsil. BEd, U. Hawaii, Manoa, 1991. Cert. tchr. Hawaii, prof. diploma in elem. edn. Univ. Hawaii, 1992. Kindergarten tchr. Island Paradise Sch., Honolulu, 1992—93, Pauoa Elem. Sch., Honolulu, 1993—94, choral dir., 1997—2002, 6th grade tchr., 1994—2002, choral dir., 2003—, 5th grade tchr., 2003—04, 3d grade tchr., 2004—; spl. edn. summer sch. aide Wailupe Valley Elem. Sch., Honolulu; Challenger Ctr.-trained educator, NASA program Barber's Point Elem. Sch., Kapolei, Hawaii, 1996—2002. Regional conf. del. Sch.-to-Work, Honolulu, 1998; cadre mem. Roosevelt Complex Writing Inst., Honolulu, 1999, student svcs. coord., 2002—03; mem. music action rsch. team Hawaii State Dept. Edn., 1999—2001. Mem. coun. Sch. Cmty.-Based Mgmt. Coun., Pauoa Elem. Sch., 2001—03; vol., chmn. Honolulu Dist. Choral Festival, 1994—2002; mem. ch. choir; mem. Sweet Adelines Internat.; bd. dirs. Pauoa Elem. Sch. PTA, 1996—97. Mem.: Hawaii Music Educators Assn. (3d v.p. 2000—02, chmn. 2001—02), Hawaii state tchr. assoc. (union rep. 1995—96, 2000—01), Delta Kappa Gamma. Avocations: walking, collecting keychains and unicorns/Pegasuses. Home: 823 9th Ave Honolulu HI 96816 Office: Pauoa Elem Sch 2301 Pauoa Rd Honolulu HI 96813 E-mail: tiniwee86@hawaii.rr.com.

WEEBER, STAN C. sociologist, educator; b. Iowa City, Dec. 20, 1951; s. Woodrow I. and Evelyn C. Weeber; m. Julie Westby Weeber, Feb. 8, 1997; 1 child, Abigail Westby. BA, Simpson Coll., 1974; MA, Miss. State U., 1979; PhD, U. North Tex., 2000. Rsch. assoc. U. Tex. Med. Br, Galveston, 1992—94; tchg. fellow U. North Tex., Denton, 1994—96; instr. Tex. Wesleyan U., Ft. Worth.; academic adv. U. North Tex., Denton, 1998—2000; asst. prof. McNeese State U., Lake Charles, La., 2000—. Author: (books) Political Crime in the U.S., 1978, Lee Harvey Oswald, 2004; contbr. articles to profl. jours. Grantee Sherman rsch. fellow, McNeese State U., 2001; Simpson Honor scholar, Simpson Coll., Indianola, Iowa, 1973. Achievements include conducting one of the first sociological studies utilizing internet communications as primary data. Office: Dept of Social Science McNeese State U 4205 Ryan St Lake Charles LA 70609 Office Phone: 337-475-5168. Business E-Mail: sweeber@mail.mcneese.edu.

WEED, EDWARD REILLY, marketing executive; b. Chgo., Jan. 25, 1940; s. Cornelius Cahill and Adelaide E. (Reilly) W.; m. Lawrie Irving Bowes, Feb. 2, 1969. Student, Fordham U., 1959-61, Loyola U., 1961-62. Account exec. Leo Burnett Co., Chgo., 1961-71; pres., corp. officer GDC Ad Inc., Miami, Fla., 1971-74; v.p., account supr D'Arcy Mac Manus & Masius, Chgo., 1975; group v.p. mktg. Hart Schaffner & Marx (Hartmarx), Chgo.; pres. Hart Svcs., Inc., 1975-82; v.p mktg. Tishman, 1983-86; exec. v.p. Hannah Marine, 1986-87; exec. v.p., dir. U.S. Auction, 1988-92; v.p. mktg. Telemedia, 1992-95; mng. dir. Brochure Assocs./The Consultancy, Lake Geneva, Wis., 1996—. Dir. First Nat. Bank So. Miami; seminar instr. Grad. Sch. Notre Dame U., South Bend, Ind.; guest faculty Loyola U., Chgo., Fla. Internat. U. Author, publisher: Genealogical Family History, editor manuscript reviewer; several books; contbr. articles to profl. jours. Trustee Latin Sch. Found., 1976—, The Admiral, 1999—; bd. dirs. North Ave. Day Nursery, 1969-73, Santa for Poor, 1975-87, Off-the-Street Club, 1982-87, Chgo. Boys' and Girls' Clubs, 1983-87, Map Inc., 1988-98, Geneva Lake Conservancy, 1994—; adv. bd. Fiduciary Mgmt. Assocs., 1998—. With Ill. N.G. Recipient Chi Ad Club award. Mem.: Casino Club, Lake Geneva Country Club. Republican. Roman Catholic. Office: The Consultancy 3638 Snake Rd Lake Geneva WI 53147

WEED, LAWRENCE L. biochemist; b. Troy, N.Y., Dec. 26, 1923; married, 1952; 5 children. BA, Hamilton Coll., 1945; MD, Coll. Physicians & Surgeons, 1947. Asst. prof. medicine and pharmacology Sch. Medicine Yale U., 1954-56; dir. medicine edn. Eastern Maine Gen. Hosp., Bangor, 1956—60; asst. prof. microbiology Case Western Reserve U., 1961—64, prof. medicine, assoc. prof. microbiology, 1964—69; prof. medicine U. Vt., 1969—82, emeritus prof. Coll. Medicine, 1982—; pres. PKC Corp., 1984—. Prof. medicine, dir. outpatient clinic Cliv. Met. Gen. Hosp., 1964—69; dir. Promis Lab., 1969—81; chief scientist Promis Info. Sys., Inc., 1981—82. Recipient Gustav O. Lienhard award, 1995; hon. fellow, American Academy of Medical Administrators. Fellow: Am. Coll. Med. Informatics; mem.: ACP, Am. Soc. Microbiology. Achievements include research in problem oriented medical information system; nucleic acid chemistry. Address: 120 Irish Settlement Rd Underhill VT 05489-9774 Office: U Vt Med Coll E109 Given Bldg Burlington VT 05401*

WEED, MAURICE JAMES, composer, retired music educator; b. Kalamazoo, Oct. 16, 1912; s. Frank Eugene and Ella May (Britton) W.; m. Berneice Laverne Pope, Aug. 23, 1937; children: Allison Gilbert (Mrs. Walter D. Herrick), Laurice Ellen (Mrs. Samuel L. Rich). BA, Western Mich. U., 1934; MusB, Eastman Sch. Music, 1940, MusM, 1952, PhD, 1954. Supr. instrumental music pub. schs., Ionia, Mich., 1934-36, Three Rivers, Mich., 1937-43; asst. prof. music, dir. instrumental music, tchr. music theory Ripon Coll., 1946-51; tchr. Eastman Sch. Music, summer 1954; prof., head dept. music No. Ill. U., 1954-61, prof. music, 1961-74; adj. prof. music Western Carolina U., 1974-75; ret., 1975. Composer in residence, MacDowell Colony, 1961; performances include: Serenity for chamber orch. Eastman-Rochester Symphony, 1953, Symphony Number 1, Nat. Symphony Orch., Washington, 1956, Symphony of the Air, Carnegie Hall, 1957, Wonder of the Starry Night, 1st ann. symposium Contemporary Am. Music, U. Kans., 1959, Serenity and Fanfare for Two Trumpets and Organ, 8th ann. symposium Univ. Composers Exchange, Valparaiso, Ind., 1959; Sept Cinquains for Soprano Voice and chamber instrumental group, No. Ill. U., 1964, 67, Symphonie Breve, 6th ann. symposium Contemporary Am. Music U. Kans., 1967, Symphonie Breve, Oklahoma City Symphony Orch.; MBS broadcast, 1965, U. Redlands, 1964, Asheville (N.C.) Symphony Orch., 1979; condr. symposium of 8 sacred choral and 2 organ works by 6 coll., univ., high sch. and ch. choirs, Atlanta, 1975; Serenity, Asheville Symphony Orch., 1977; composer: over 65 works including Ships, Witchery (songs for soprano and piano), 1937, Rain, for contralto and piano, 1940, Three Preludes for Organ, 1945, Introduction and Scherzo, symphonic band, 1948, Gratitude, for contralto with organ, 1950, An After Easter Prayer, 1950, Serenity, for chamber orch., 1953, Wonder of the Starry Night, a capella choir, 1958, Symphonie Breve, 1959, Trio for violin, cello and piano, 1961, Concertino for cello and orch, 1962, Psalm XIII (mixed choir and organ), 1964, Hopkins Park, concert march, 1966, Triptych for Voices, a cappella choir, 1966, Vestigia Nulla Retrorsum, processional march, 1968, Praise Ye the Lord (mixed choir), 1968, A Wedding Song (soprano and organ), 1969, In the Midnight Hour (soprano and organ), 1970, In Te, Domini, Speravi (mixed choir), 1970, 4 Anthems for Mixed Choir, 1973, Postlude for Organ, 1974, The Catamounts, concert march for band, 1974, Duo for Viola and C Trumpet, 1977, Choral Fanfare No. 2, 1977, An Appalachian Celebration for Choir and Band, 1978; Celebration (hymn-anthem), 1981; 3 anthems for mixed voices Let All the People Praise Thee, 1980, Sing Praises to God, 1981, Praise Ye the Lord, 1982, The 3Bs-Brass Sextet, 1982, Voices of Appalachia, 1986; numerous others. Recipient 25th Anniversary award Nat. Symphony Orch., 1956, Ostwald award, 1959, J. Fisher & Bro. Centennial award, 1964, Pedro Paz award, 1966; Eastman Sch. Music teaching fellow, 1951-54. Mem. Nat. Assn. Composers U.S.A., Am. Music Ctr., Music Edn. Nat. Conf., N.C. Music Educators, Am. Soc. Univ. Composers, Phi Mu Alpha. Methodist. Home: Asheville Manor 308 Overlook Rd Rm 55 Asheville NC 28803-3319

WEED, ROGER OREN, rehabilitation services professional, educator; b. Bend, Oreg, Feb. 2, 1944; s. Chester Elbert and Ruth Marie (Urie) W.; m. Paula J. Keller BS in Sociology, U. Oreg., 1967, MS in Rehab. Counseling, 1969; PhD in Rehab. Counseling, U. Ga., 1986. Cert. rehab. counselor; cert. disability mgmt. specialist; lic. profl. counselor; cert. case mgr., cert. life care planner. Vocat. rehab. counselor State of Alaska, Anchorage, 1969-71; instr. U. Alaska, Anchorage, 1970-76; counselor Langdon Psychiat. Clinic, Anchorage, 1971-74; from asst. dir. to exec. dir. Hope Cottages, Anchorage, 1974-79; owner Profl. Resources Group, Anchorage, 1978-80; mng. ptnr. Collins, Weed & Assocs., 1980-84; assoc. dir. Ctr. for Rehab. Tech. Ga. Tech. U., Atlanta, 1986-87; catastrophic injury rehab. Weed & Assocs., Atlanta, 1984—; from asst. prof. to prof. Ga. State U., Atlanta, 1987—. Adj. faculty Ga. Inst. Tech.; courtesy faculty U. Fla., 1996—. Co-author: Vocational Expert Handbook, 1986, Transferable Work Skills, 1988, Life Care Planning: Spinal Cord Injured, 1989, 2d edit. 1994, Life Care Planning: Head Injured, 1994, Life Care Planning for the Amputee, 1992, Rehab Cons. Handbook, 1994, rev. edit., 2001; editor: Life Care Planning and Case Mgmt. Handbook, 1999 (rev., 2004); assoc. editor Jour. Lifecare Planning, 2002—; mem. editl. bd. Jour. of Pvt. Sector Rehab., 1986—, Jour. Forensic Vocational Analysis; contbr. articles to profl. jour. Recipient Gov.'s award Gov.'s Com. on Employment, Alaska, 1982, Goldpan Svc. award Gov.'s Com. on Employment, Alaska, 1978, Profl. Svc. award Am. Rehab. Counselors Assn., 1993. Fellow Nat. Rehab. Assn. (chmn. legis. com., bd. dir. met. Atlanta chpt. 1987-89, pres. Pacific region 1983-85, Pres.'s award Pacific region 1986), Internat. Assn. Rehab. Profls. (chmn. rsch. and tng. com. 1988-93, pres. 1994-95, Educator of Yr. 1991, 97), Internat. Acad. Life Care Planning, Nat. Brain Injury Assn., Pvt. Rehab. Suppliers Ga., Rehab. Engring. Soc. N.Am., Anchorage Amateur Radio Club; mem., bd. dir. Found. for Life Care Planning Rsch. Republican. Methodist. Avocations: sailing, skiing, bicycling, flying, computers. Office: Ga State U Coll Edn Dept Counseling/Psychol Svc 9th Fl Atlanta GA 30303

WEEDN, TRISH, state legislator; b. Oklahoma City, May 10, 1950; d. Carl R. and Teddeline (Morrell) Throckmorton; m. James A. Weedn; children: Marnie, Mindy. Assessor McClain County, Okla., 1979-88; mem. Okla. State Senate, 1989—. Former chmn. McClain County Dem. Com; sect./treas. Purcell Pentacostal Holiness Ch. Mem. Okla. Assn. Assessing Officers, S.W. Coll. Ministry. Democrat. Pentecostal. Office: Okla State Senate State Capitol Oklahoma City OK 73105

WEEKES, REY, theater educator; b. Cambridge, Mass., Nov. 12, 1950; d. Albert Roger and Elsie Elizabeth (Waters) Crimm; m. Adam Kevin Weekes, Aug. 4, 1978; children: Derek, Susan, Veronica. BA, Boston Coll., 1971; MFA, U. Notre Dame, 1975. Artistic dir. Full Moon Theatre, Rochester, NY, 1977—86; asst. prof. theatre St. Mary's Coll., 1987—89, assoc. prof. theatre, 1989—90; prof. Meriks Coll. Performing Arts, Buffalo, 1991—. Author: Dancing in the Rain, 2000, What Dreams May Come: A Career in Theatre, 2002. Roman Catholic. Avocations: board games, dance, hiking, matchbook collecting. Office: Meriks Coll Performing Arts 34 Cooke St Buffalo NY 14218-1309

WEEKLEY, DAVID, real estate developer; b. 1954; BA, Trinity Univ., 1975. General Homes, Inc., Houston, 1975-76; CEO David Weekley Homes, Houston, 1976—.

WEEKLEY, FREDERICK CLAY, JR., lawyer; b. San Antonio, Aug. 29, 1939; s. F. Clay and Topsy (Stevens) W.; m. Lynda Freeman; children: Amber Lee Carothers, Caroline Lee. BBA, Baylor U., 1962, JD, 1963; LLM, NYU, 1969. Bar: Tex. 1963. Ptnr. Bracewell & Patterson, Houston, 1974-90; trust counsel Bank One, Tex., N.A., 1990-98; ptnr. Shannon, Gracey, Ratliff & Miller, LLP, Ft. Worth, 1999—. Mem. coun. real property, probate and trust law sect., State Bar of Tex., 1987-90; mem. adminstrv. coun. trust divsn. Tex. Bankers Assn., 1992-95, chmn. legis. com., 1992-95. Editor: Texas Wills System, 1984. Mem. Commn. Probate Law Examiners, Tex. Bd. Legal Specialization, 1978-82. Fellow Am. Coll. Trust and Estate Counsel. Home: 1821 Mossy Oak St Arlington TX 76012-5619 Office: 777 Main St Fort Worth TX 76102

WEEKLEY, JUDY LIDDINGTON, special education educator; b. Tacoma, Wash., Dec. 18, 1956; d. William Raymond and Shirley Charlotte Liddington; m. John Weekley, June 27, 1980 (dec. Feb. 1996). BA, Southeastern La. U., 1978, MEd, 1984. Tchr. Jefferson Parish Pub. Sch. Sys., Harvey, La., 1978—2002, Individual Edn. plan specialist, 2002—; instr., lectr. Our Lady Holy Cross Coll., New Orleans, 1992—. Presenter in field; cons. in field. Dir. area games, coach Spl. Olympics, La., 1978—92. Recipient Excellence in Tchg. award, C. of C., 1988, 1990, Spl. Edn. Tchr. of Yr., 1999; grantee, Jefferson Parish Pub. Sch. Sys., 1990, 1995. Mem.: Coun. Exceptional Children (Tchr. of Yr. La. 2001), Phi Delta Kappa (bd. dirs. 1992—2003, editor 1992—2003). Methodist. Avocations: gardening, cooking, music, dance, computer and video creations. Home: 323 Coral Ave Gretna LA 70056 Office Phone: 504-349-8668.

WEEKLY, JOHN WILLIAM, insurance company executive; b. Sioux City, Iowa, June 21, 1931; s. John E. Weekly and Alyce Beatrice (Preble) Nichols; children: John William Jr., Thomas Patrick, Michael Craig, James Mathew, Daniel Kevin. Grad. high sch., Omaha. V.p. First Data Resources, Inc., Omaha, 1969-74, Mut. of Omaha/United of Omaha Ins. Co., Omaha, 1974-81, sr. exec. v.p., 1981-87, pres., COO, 1987-95, vice chmn., pres., COO, 1995, vice chmn., pres., CEO, 1996-97, vice chmn., CEO, 1997, chmn., CEO, 1998—. Chmn. bd. dirs. Companion Life Ins. Co., Mutual Omaha Investor Svcs., Inc.; bd. dirs. United World Life Ins. Co., Kirkpatrick Pettis, Midwest Airlines, Inc., 1995—. Bd. govs. Ak-Sar-Ben, 2001—; bd. dirs. Omaha Zool. Soc., 1998—. Mem.: Greater Omaha C. of C. (bd. dirs. 1991—96), Health Ins. Assn. Am. (bd. dirs. 1992—96, chmn. 1996), Am. Coun. Life Ins. (bd. dirs. 1995—98, 2001—). Avocations: fishing, hunting. Office: Mut Omaha Ins Co Mutual Omaha Plz Omaha NE 68175-0001

WEEKS, A. RAY, real estate company executive; Co-chmn., pres., COO Duke-Weeks Realty Corp., Indpls., 1994—. Office: Duke-Weeks Realty Corp Ste 100 600 E 96th St Indianapolis IN 46240-3792

WEEKS, ALBERT LOREN, author, educator, journalist; b. Highland Park, Mich., Mar. 28, 1923; s. Albert Loren and Vera Grace (Jarvis) W. Student, U. Mich., 1942-43; MA, U. Chgo., 1949; PhD, Columbia U., 1965; cert., Russian Inst., 1960. Reporter Chgo. City News Bur., 1946; polit. analyst U.S. Dept. State, 1950-53, Free Europe Com., Inc., 1953-56; editorial asst. Newsweek mag., 1957-58; Russian tech. glossary compiler McGraw-Hill Book Co., 1960-61; prof. continuing edn. NYU, 1959-89. Lectr. U.S. diplomatic history and soviet govt. Columbia U., 1951-52; mem. adv. coun. Nat. Strategy Info. Ctr., 1979-89; instr. Ringling Sch. Art and Design, 1991—; pub. spkr. S.W. Fla. Host: A Week's View of Red Press, Sta. WNBC, 1965-68; series Myths That Rule America, NBC-TV, 1979-82; author: Reading American History, 1963, The First Bolshevik: A Political Biography of Peter Tkachev, 1968, The Other Side of Coexistence: An Analysis of Russian Foreign Policy, 1970, Richard Hofstadter's The American Political Tradition and the Age of Reform, 1973, Andrei Sakharov and the Soviet Dissidents, 1975, The Troubled Detente, 1976, Solzhenitsyn's One Day in the Life of Ivan Denisovich, 1976, Myths That Rule America, 1980, War and Peace: Soviet Russia Speaks, 1983; editor/compiler Brassey's Soviet and Communist Quotations, 1987, The Soviet Nomenklatura, 1987-1991, Stalin's Other War: Soviet Grand Strategy 1939-1941, 2002, Russia's Life-Saver: Lend-Lease Aid to the USSR in World War II; internat. affairs editor Def. Sci. mag., 1982-85; columnist Def. Report, 1982-90; contbr. articles to N.Y. Times, New Republic, New Leader, Annals, Russian, Slavic revs., Christian Sci. Monitor, Problems of Communism, Survey, Mil. Intelligence, Strategic Rev., World War II mag., Air Univ. Rev., L.A. Times, Washington Times, Orbis, Global Affairs, Panorama, Sarasota Herald-Tribune, Bradenton Herald, Defense and Diplomacy, Am. Intelligence Jour., USA Today, Rossiiskiye Vesti, Vechernii Vladimir, CityTempo mag., Modern Age mag. Home: 4884 Kestral Park Cir Sarasota FL 34231-3369 E-mail: aweeks1@compuserve.com.

WEEKS, ARTHUR ANDREW, retired lawyer, law educator; b. Hanceville, Ala., Dec. 2, 1914; s. A.A. and Anna S. (Seibert) W.; m. Carol P. Weeks; children: John David, Carol Christine, Nancy Anna. AB, Samford U., 1936; LL.B., JD, U. Ala., 1939; LL.M., Duke U., 1950; LL.D. (hon.), Widener U., 1980. Bar: Ala. 1939, Tenn. 1948. Sole practice, Birmingham, Ala., 1939-41, 1946-47, 1954-61; dean, prof. law Cumberland U. Sch. Law, 1947-54; dean, prof. Samford U., 1961-72, prof. law, 1972-74, Cumberland Sch. Law, Samford U., 1984—, Del. Sch. Law of Widener U., Wilmington, 1974-82, dean, 1974-80, interim dean, 1982-83, dean emeritus, prof., 1983—. Served to capt. AUS, 1941-46. Mem. ABA, Tenn. Bar Assn., Ala. Bar Assn., Birmingham Bar Assn., Del. Bar Assn. (assoc.), Phi Alpha Delta, Phi Kappa Phi, Delta Theta Phi Home: 1105 Water Edge Ct Birmingham AL 35244-1437

WEEKS, BRIGITTE, publishing executive; b. Whitchurch, Hants, Eng., Aug. 28, 1943; came to U.S., 1965; d. Jack and Margery May (Millett) W.; m. Edward A. Herscher, Sept. 6, 1969; children— Hilary, Charlotte, Daniel. Student, Univ. Coll. of North Wales, Bangor, 1962-65. Asst. editor Boston Mag., 1966-70; editor Kodansha Internat., Tokyo, 1969-72, Resources for the Future, 1973-74; asst. editor The Washington Post Book World, 1974-78, editor, 1978-88; sr. v.p., editor-in-chief Book-of-the-Month Club, N.Y.C., 1988-94; editor-in-chief Guideposts Books, N.Y.C., 1994—2002, Crossings Book Club, N.Y.C., 2002—. Pres. Nat. Book Critics Circle, 1990. Office: Bookspan 1271 Ave of the Americas New York NY 10020-9991

WEEKS, CHARLES, JR., real estate executive, retired publishing company executive; b. Palo Alto, Calif., Apr. 25, 1919; s. Charles and Mary Alice (Johnson) W.; m. Patricia Anne Blair, Apr. 7, 1949; children: Patricia Alice, Charles Blair, Clayton Brian, Phyllis Anne. Student, U. Fla., 1936-38. Prin. Fla. Airmotive, Inc., Lantana, 1946-50; v.p., dir. Perry Publs., Inc., West Palm Beach, Fla., 1950-69; bd. dirs. Perry Oceanographics, Inc., Riveria Beach, Fla., 1969-84; dir. mgmt. bd. Flagler Nat Bank, West Palm Beach, 1992. Mem. Planning and Zoning Bd., Lantana, 1962-65; assoc. trustee John. F. Kennedy Hosp., Atlantis, Fla., 1985. Served as pilot USAF, 1943-46, ETO. Decorated Air medal; recipient Pilot Safety award Nat. Bus. Aircraft Assn., 1970, 74, 78. Mem. Quiet Birdman, Handersonville (N.C.) Country Club, Sailfish of Fla. (Palm Beach) Club. Episcopalian. Democrat. Home: PO Box 3411 Lantana FL 33465-3411 Office: Palermo-Long Realty Inc 223 E Ocean Ave Lantana FL 33462-3201

WEEKS, CLIFFORD MYERS, musician, educational administrator; b. N.Y.C., Apr. 15, 1938; s. Vernal C. and Adeline (Campbell) W.; m. Ethel Lynn Fleming, Oct. 26, 1963 (dec. 1982); children: Clifford M. Jr., Michele Lynn. Diploma in Arranging and Composition, Berklee Coll. Music, 1962; MusB magna cum laude, Boston Conservatory Music, 1963, MusM, 1975; cert. in edn. adminstrn., Boston State Coll., 1977. Cert. secondary sch. adminstr. and tchr. music, Mass. Tchr. music Boston Pub. Schs., 1964-74, condr. All-City Stage Band, 1972-79, adminstrv. asst. to asst. supt., 1974-75, coordinator instrumental music, 1975-79, asst. prin., 1979, adminstrv. asst. to asst. supt., 1979-96, acting community supt., 1983, cluster coord., 1996-2001, exec. asst. supt. office, 2001—03; ret., 2003. Arranger, composer, trombonist, 1963—; condr. Boston Coll. Jazz and Stage Band, Chestnut Hill, Mass., 1976-78. Composer Tryptych for tuba and piano, 1971, (oratorio) The King-Life and Teachings of Dr. Martin Luther King Jr., 1976; composer, arranger various jazz compositions, 1975. Mem. Medford (Mass.) Jaycees, 1975-76; adv. bd. Roxbury (Mass.) Boys and Girls Club, 1970—, Berklee Coll. Music, Boston, 1972. Recipient Mayor's Parkman Club award, 1999, Suskind Young at Art award Wang Ctr. Boston Theatres, 2001. Mem. Boston Assn. Sch. Adminstrs. and Suprs. (adminstrs. union 1997—), Boston Tchrs. Union, Black Educators Alliance Mass. (treas. 1972-76, award 1976), ASCAP, Adminstrv. Assts. Assn. (chmn. local chpt. 1982—), Assn. for Supervision and Curriculum Devel., Omega Psi Phi. Methodist.

WEEKS, GERALD, psychology educator; b. Morehead City, NC, Nov. 20, 1948; s. Marion G. and Ada (Willis) W. BA in Philosophy and Psychology, East Carolina U., 1971, MA in Gen. Psychology, 1973; PhD in Clin. Psychology, Ga. State U., 1979. Diplomate Am. Bd. Profl. Psychology (pres. 1987-88, bd. dirs. 1982-87), Am. Bd. Family Psychology, Am. Bd. Sexology; cert. marital and family therapist; lic. practicing psychologist, Nev., Pa. Intern in family therapy Harlem Valley Psychiat. Ctr., Wingdale, NY, 1978-79; assoc. prof. psychology U. N.C., Wilmington, 1979-85; dir. tng. Penn Coun. for Relationships, 1985—; clin. asst. prof. psychology Sch. Medicine U. Pa., Phila., 1985-87, clin. assoc. prof., 1988-98; chair, prof. dept. counseling U. Nev.-Las Vegas, 1999—. Pvt. practice Carolina Ob-gyn. Ctr., Wilmington, 1980-85. Author: Promoting Change Through Paradoxical Therapy, 1985, Treating Couples: The Intersystem Model of the Marriage Council of Philadelphia, 1989, Promoting Change through Paradoxical Therapy, 1991, (with L. L'Abate) Paradoxical Psychotherapy: Theory and Practice with Individuals, Couples, and Families, 1982, (with R. Sauber, L. L'Abate) Family Therapy: Basic Concepts and Terms, 1985, (with L. Hof) Integrating Sex and Marital Therapy: A Clinicians Guide, 1987, (with S. Treat) Couples in Treatment, 1992, rev. edit., 2001, Integrative Solutions: Treating Common Problems in Couple's Therapy, 1995, (with L. Hof) Erectile Dysfunction, 2000; (with N. Gambescia) Focused Genograms: Intergenerational Assessment of Individuals, Couples and Families, 1999, (with Gambiscia) Hypoactive Sexual Desire, 2002, Treating Infidelity; (with Gambescia and Jenkins) Handbook of Family Therapy, 2003; contbr. articles to profl. jours. Fellow Am. Assn. Marital and Family Therapy (clin. mem., nat. adv. bd., approved supr.);

mem. APA, Acad. Family Psychology, Interpersonal and Social Skills Assn. (founding mem.), Acad. Psychologists in Marital, Sex, and Family Therapy. Office: U Nev Dept Counseling PO Box 453045 4505 S Maryland Pkwy Las Vegas NV 89154-3045 Office Phone: 702-895-1392.

WEEKS, HELEN BALLARD, retail executive; CEO Ballard Designs, Inc., Atlanta, Ga., 1982—. Office: Ballard Designs Inc 1670 Defoor Ave NW Atlanta GA 30318-7562

WEEKS, J. STEPHEN, architecture educator; AB in Art History, Colby Coll., 1963; BArch with high distinction, U. Minn., 1973. Registered arch., Minn., Wis. Assoc. prof., dept. co-head and dir. grad. studies Coll. Arch. and Landscape Arch., U. Minn., Mpls. Invited juror regional masonry design revs.; participant masonry rsch. and edn. devel. confs. Recipient Progressive Arch. Rsch. award, McKnight Found., 1985. Office: Univ Minn CALA Rapson Hall 89 Church St SE Minneapolis MN 55455*

WEEKS, JOHN ROBERT, geographer, sociology educator; b. Sacramento, June 1, 1944; s. Robert Louis and Thelma Hope (Evans) W.; m. Deanna Jean Hosea, May 16, 1965; children: John Robert, Gregory, Jennifer. AB, U. Calif., Berkeley, 1966, MA, 1969, PhD, 1972. Asst. prof. sociology Mich. State U., East Lansing, 1971-74, San Diego State U., 1974-78, assoc. prof., 1978-81, prof., 1981-92, prof. geography, 1992—, chmn. dept., 1978-85; adminstrv. dir. Internat. Population Ctr., 1985—; clin. prof. family & preventive medicine U. Calif. Sch. Medicine, San Diego, 1998—. Vis. rsch. demographer U. Calif., Berkeley, 1972; cons. Allied Home Health Assn., 1978-80, Area Agy. on Aging, San Diego, 1979-81, Los Angeles Regional Family Planning Coun., 1986—, East County Econ. Devel. Coun., 1986—, UN Food and Agrl. Orgn., 2002—. Author: Teenage Marriages, 1976, Population, 8th edit., 2002, Aging, 1984, Demography of Islamic Nations, 1988, High Fertility Among Indochinese Refuges, 1989, Demographic Dynamics of the U.S.-Mex. Border, 1992. Grantee USPHS, 1983-84, 87-88, 88-89, 90—, U.S. Adminstrn. on Aging, 1979-80, U.S. Bur. of Census, 1988-89, Andrew W. Mellon Found., 1998-2001, NSF, 2001—; trainee USPHS, 1967-71 Mem. Population Assn. Am., Am. Sociol. Assn., Internat. Union for Sci. Study Population, Am. Assn. Geographers. Democrat. Office: San Diego State U Dept Geography San Diego CA 92182 E-mail: john.weeks@sdsu.edu.

WEEKS, LEE, hotel executive; Exec. mgr. Ritz-Carlton, Naples, Fla.; v.p. resort ops. Grand Wailea (Hawaii) Resort & Spa; v.p. ops. Atlantis Resort and Casino, Nassau, Bahamas; gen. mgr. LaPlaya Beach Resort, Naples, Fla.; pres., owner Coral Beach, Naples; pres., COO Coral Beach Hotels, Naples. Office: 9180 Galleria Ct Ste 600 Naples FL 34109-4385

WEEKS, MAURICE RICHARD, JR., educational consultant, academic administrator; b. Washington, Dec. 14, 1943; s. Maurice Richard Sr. and Etienetta Adina (Duurloo) W.; children: Maurice III, Carol-Anne, William. BS, Villanova U., 1965; MEd, Temple U., 1966; EdD, Rutgers U., 1978. Cert. elem. tchr., Pa., cert. secondary tchr., Pa.; cert. secondary prin., Pa. Tchr. Sch. Dist. Phila., 1965-74, prin., 1974-95; ednl. cons., 1995—. Bd. trustees PILOT Svcs., Inc., Voorhees, N.J., 1992—. Bd. trustees Moorestown Libr. Assn., N.J., 1978-85, Phila. Parent/Child Ctr., 1983-90; bd. dirs. YMCA Camp Ockanickon, Medford, N.J., 1995—; coach Moorestown Men's League, 1982—, Camden Over 35 League, N.J., 1982—, Willingboro Summer League, N.J., 1972-73. Mem. Am. Counseling. Assn., N.J. Assn. Sch. Adminstrs., Schoolman's Club Phila (v.p.), Alpha Phi Alpha. Democrat. Roman Catholic. Avocations: basketball, tennis, pinochle, bidwhist. Home: 724 Kimberly Dr Moorestown NJ 08057-4407

WEEKS, PATSY ANN LANDRY, librarian, educator; b. Luling, Tex., Mar. 3, 1930; d. Lee and Mattie Wood (Callihan) Landry; m. Arnett S. Weeks, Dec. 2, 1950; children: Patsy Kate, Nancy Ann, Janie Marie. BS, Southwest Tex. State U., San Marcos, 1951; MLS, Tex. Woman's U., Denton, 1979. Tchr. art, reading, math. Grandview Ind. Sch. Dist., Tex., 1950—52; tchr. phys. edn. Beaumont Ind. Sch. Dist., Tex., 1953; tchr. art, coll. algebra Cisco Jr. Coll., Tex., 1957—58; tchr. remedial reading Taylor County Schs., Tuscola, Tex., 1965—66, Anson Ind. Sch. Dist., Tex., 1971—73; libr. Bangs Ind. Sch. Dist., Tex., 1973—79, learning resources coord., 1979—90; dir. Heart of Tex. Ctr. for the Rev. and Exam. of Children's and Young Adults' Lit., 1988—2001; cons. Heart of Tex. Lit. Ctr., 2001—03. Bd. dirs. Anson Pub. Libr., Tex., 1971—72, Brownwood Pub. Libr., 2003—; mem. adv. com. Edn. Svc. Ctr., 1978—83; coord. Reading is Fundamental Program, 1978—83; counsilor Children's Round Table, 1993—; cons. Heart of Tex. Lit. Ctr., 2000—03, dir. projects, 2003—. Exhibitions include oil paintings, pastels various Tex. Fairs (1st prize, 1952, 1960). Mem.: ALA, Tex. Assn. Sch. Libr. Adminstrs., Teenage Libr. Assn. Tex. (chmn. audio-visual award com. 1984), Tex. Assn. Improvement Reading, Tex. Assn. Sch. Librs. (media prodns. award com. 1985—86), Tex. Libr. Assn. (mem. intellectual freedom and profl. responsibility com. 1979—81, mem. Tex. Bluebonnet award com. 1982—85, chair adv. com. 1987, chair children's round table 1987, sec. young adult round table 1991—92, publs. com. 1991—, round table coun. 1993—95), Intellectual Freedom Round Table, Am. Assn. Sch. Librs., Young Adult Libr. Svcs. Assn. (outstanding books for coll.bound-fine arts com., mem. publ.'s liaison com.), Assn. Libr. Svc. to Children (Caldecott award com. 1986, mem. Grosset and Dunlap Group award selection com. 1988, nominating com. 1989, chair 1989—91, Newbery award com. 1999, Disting. Svc. award com. 2002—, Disting. Svc. award com. chair 2003—, cons. priority gorup III profl. devel.), Tex. State Tchr. Assn. (life), Bangs Prog. Women's Club (pres. 1974—76), Delta Kappa Gamma, Beta Phi Mu, Alpha Chi, Kappa Pi, Phi Delta Kappa. Bapt. Office: Howard Payne Univ Sta Walker Memorial Library Heart of Tex Ctr Brownwood TX 76801 Office Phone: 325-649-8606. E-mail: pweeks@hptux.edu.

WEEKS, ROBERT ANDREW, materials science researcher, educator; b. Birmingham, Ala., Aug. 23, 1924; s. William Andrew and Annie Bell (Hammond) W.; m. Jane Sutherland, Mar. 20, 1948; children: Kevin Dale, Robin Dee, Loren Hammond, Kerry Andrew. BS, Birmingham-So. Coll., 1947; MS, U. Tenn., 1951; PhD, Brown U., 1966. Sr. physicist Union Carbide Corp., Oak Ridge, Tenn., 1951-84; rsch. prof. material sci. Vanderbilt U., 1984-99, prof. emeritus, 1999—. Disting. vis. prof. Am. U. in Cairo, 1970-71; invited prof. Ecole Poly. Fed. de Lausanne, Switzerland, 1981; vis. prof. Cath. U., Leuven, Belgium, 1983; cons. numerous pvt. corps. and fed. agys.; prin. investigator lunar materials, 1968-74; co-prin. investigator expdn. Western desert of Egypt to desert glass site, 1981; CEO Oak Ridge Cons., 1993—. Co-editor: Effects of Modes of Formation on Structure of Glass, 1985, 88, Editing the Refereed Scientific Journal, 1994; assoc. editor Jour. Geophys. Rsch., 1968-74; editor Jour. Noncrystalline Solids, 1988-98; conf. editor Jour. Non-Crystalline Solids, 1998-2000; contbr. numerous articles to profl. jours. Served with U.S. Army, 1943-46. Union Carbide fellow, 1964; Fulbright lectr., 1980; research fellow Reading U., 1971, USIA Am. participant Egypt, India, Nepal and Sri Lanka, 1986. Fellow Am. Ceramic Soc. (R. A. Weeks Symposium on Sci. and Tech. Si02 and Related Materials named in his honor, Honolulu 1993, George W. Morey award for contbns. to glass sci. 1998, Symposium dedicated to him 2004); mem. AAAS, Am. Phys. Soc., Sigma Xi. Avocation: photography. Home and Office: 331 Southshore Dr Greenback TN 37742-2301 E-mail: e1e2e4@aol.com.

WEEKS, ROLAND, JR., newspaper publisher; b. Knoxville, Tenn., July 8, 1936; BS, Clemson U., 1958. Sales engr. Metal Products, Inc., Greenville, S.C., 1961-63; mgmt. trainee, then bus. mgr. Columbia Newspapers, Inc.; pubs. The State and Columbia (S.C.) Record newspapers, 1963-68; pres., pub. Gulf Pub. Co., Inc.; pub. Biloxi-Gulfport (Miss.) Sun Herald, 1968—. Pres. Pine Burr area council Boy Scouts Am., 1980; chmn. Miss. Bd. Corrections, 1982-88. Served to 1st lt. USAF, 1958-61. Mem. Am. Newspaper Assn., So. Newspaper Pubs. Assn. (pres. 1981), Young Pres. Orgn., Gulf Coast C. of C. (pres. 1989). Presbyterian. Office: Gulf Pub Co Inc PO Box 4567 Biloxi MS 39535-4567

WEEKS, ROSS LEONARD, JR., museum executive; b. Jamestown, N.Y., Sept. 11, 1936; s. Ross Leonard and Cecile Forbes (Carrie) W.; m. Patricia Ann Earley, June 10, 1961 (div.); children: Susan Woodall, Ross Leonard III, William Andrew, David James. AB, Colgate U., 1958; MS, George Washington U., 1971; cert., Fed. Exec. Inst., 1988. Reporter Jamestown (Va.) Post-Jour., 1958-60, Richmond (Va.) News Leader, 1960-65; dir. pub. info. Coll. William and Mary, Williamsburg, Va., 1965-71, asst. to exec. v.p., 1971-74, asst. to pres., dir. univ. comms., 1974-81; exec. dir. Jamestown-Yorktown Found., 1981-91, Hist. Crab Orchard Mus., Inc., Tazewell, Va., 1992—2002; ret., 2002; pres. Blue Ridge Concepts, Ltd., 1999—2003. Grant reviewer U.S. Inst. Mus. Svcs., Va. Arts Commn. Editor William and Mary Alumni Gazette, 1966-81; author: Virginia's Tazewell County: A Last Great Place, 2000; editor: 'Cause I'm Colored-The Black Heritage of Tazewell County, 2001; columnist: Clinch Valley News, 1998-2004. Chmn. Williamsburg-James City Bicentennial, 1975-77; treas. Coalfield Regional Tourism Devel. Authority S.W. Va., 1993-97; Va. S.W. Blue Ridge Highlands, Inc., 1993-97, v.p., 1996-97, pres., 1997-99; sec., treas. Frontier Culture Found., 1982-86; exec. dir. Va. Independence Bicentennial Commn., 1981-83; trustee coun. Thirteen Original States, 1982-87; chair Tazewell County Tourism Devel. Commn., 1993-97; mem. regional grant panel Va. Com. on the Arts, 1998—; mem. Gov.'s Va. History Initiative, 1995-2002; mem. parish coun., parish adminstr. Theresa's and St. Elizabeth's parish cmtys., 2003—. Mem. Am. Assn. Mus. (mus. assessment cons. 1988—), Am. Assn. State and Local History, Masons, Rotary (Paul Harris fellow 1987), Clan Ross Assn., SAR (pres. Clinch Mountain Militia chpt. 2001-03), Sigma Delta Chi, Kappa Delta Rho (Ordo Honora 1986). Avocations: travel, landscaping, antiquities, historical research. Home: 205 View Hill Tazewell VA 24651 E-mail: blueridge@isp.com.

WEEKS, STEVEN WILEY, lawyer; b. Topeka, Mar. 7, 1950; s. Glen Wiley and Grace Aileen (West) W.; m. Lee Nordgren, Aug. 1, 1974 (div. 1985); 1 child, Kirstin Nordgren. BS summa cum laude, Washburn U., 1972; JD cum laude, Harvard U., 1977. Bar: Ohio. Project leader Nat. Sanitation Found., Ann Arbor, Mich., 1972; engr. Kans. Dept. Health and Environ., Topeka, 1972-74; ptnr. Taft, Stettinius & Hollister, Cin., 1977—. Dir. The Myers Y. Cooper Co., Cin.; adj. faculty Chase Coll. Law, 1987-88. Mem. adv. com. prosecuting atty., Hamilton County, Cin., 1992; mem. Hamilton County Rep. Ctrl. Com., 1994—. Mem. Ohio State Bar Assn., Cin. Bar Assn. Republican. Methodist. Avocations: computers, golf. Home: 3560 Traskwood Cir Cincinnati OH 45208

WEEKS, WENDELL P. opto-electronics executive; BS, Lehigh U., 1981; MBA, Baker Scholar, Harvard Bus. Sch., 1987. Restructuring controller, Controller Divn. Corning, Corning, N.Y., 1983-84, controller, internat., 1984-87, corp. bus. devel. mgr., 1987-88, market devel. mgr., 1988-89, bus. mgr., Video Products, 1989-90, bus. mgr., Worldwide Video, 1990-92, gen. mgr., Opto-Electronics Components Bus., 1992-94, divn. v.p., 1994-95, dep. gen. mgr., 1995-97, sr. v.p., gen. mgr., 1997-98, sr. v.p., 1998—. Office: Corning Inc 1 Riverfront Plz Corning NY 14831-0002

WEEKS, WILFORD FRANK, retired geophysics educator, glaciologist; b. Champaign, Ill., Jan. 8, 1929; married; 2 children. BS, U. Ill., 1951, MS, 1953; PhD in Geology, U. Chgo., 1956. Geologist mineral deposits br. U.S. Geol. Survey, 1952-55; glaciologist USAF Cambridge Research Ctr., 1955-57; asst. prof. Washington U., St. Louis, 1957-62; adj. prof. earth scis. Dartmouth Coll., Hanover, N.H., 1962-85; glaciologist Cold Regions Rsch. and Engring. Lab., Hanover, 1962-89; chief scientist Alaska Synthetic Aperture Radar Facility, Fairbanks, 1986-93; prof. geophysics Geophys. Inst. U. Alaska, Fairbanks, 1986-96. Cons. in field, 1996—; vis. prof. Inst. Low Temperature Sci. Hokkaido U., Sapporo, Japan, 1973; chair Arctic marine sci. USN Postgrad. Sch., Monterey, Calif., 1978-79; mem. earth sys. sci. com. NASA, Washington, 1984-87; advisor U.S. Arctic Rsch. Commn., divsn. polar programs NSF, Washington, 1987-88; chmn. NAS Com. on Cooperation with Russia in Ice Mechanics, 1991-92; mem. environ. task force MEDEA Cons. Group, 1992-2002. Capt. USAF, 1955-57. Recipient Emil Usibelli Prize for Rsch., 1996, U. Ill. Dept. Geology Alumni Achievment award, 1999. Fellow Arctic Inst. N.Am., Am. Geophys. Union; mem. NAE, Internat. Glaciological Soc. (v.p. 1969-72, pres. 1973-75, Seligman Crystal award 1989), Am. Polar Soc. (hon.). Avocation: contrabassist. Home and Office: 6533 SW 34th Ave Portland OR 97239-1077 Office Phone: 503-244-1695. E-mail: w-f-weeks@comcast.net.

WEEKS, WILLIAM RAWLE, JR., oil company executive; b. Denver, Oct. 23, 1920; s. William Rawle Sr. and Besse Elizabeth (Griffith) W.; m. June Suzanne Stephens, Jan. 22, 1944 (div. 1980); children: Stephen R., Tacy A. Weeks Hahn. BA, Stanford U., 1943. With book prodn. divsn. Stanford U. Press, 1948-49; advt. exec. Palo Alto, Calif., 1949-50; with CIA, 1951—; gen. ptnr. Weeks, Brewer & Assocs., 1971; CEO Fort Collins Consol. Royalties, Inc., Cheyenne, Wyo., 1983—. Author: Knock and Wait Awhile, 1957 (Edgar Allan Poe award 1958, Commonwealth award 1958). Nat. press and media advance man Muskie Vice Presdl. Campaign, 1968. 2nd lt. U.S. Army, 1943-46. Mem. Nat. Press Club, Denver Petroleum Club, Heather Ridge Country Club. Avocations: flying, skiing, golf, hiking. Office: Fort Collins Consol Royalties Inc 1508 Stillwater Ave Cheyenne WY 82009-7349 Home: 3070 E 4th Ave Denver CO 80206-4352

WEEMS, CARRIE MAE, photographer; BA, Calif. Inst. Arts, Valencia, 1981; MFA, U. Calif., San Diego, 1984; postgrad., U. Calif., Berkeley, 1984-87. Asst. prof. Hampshire Coll., Amherst, Mass., 1987-91, Calif. Coll. Arts and Crafts, Oakland, 1991-95; artist, prof. Harvard U., 1995—. Vis. prof. Hunter Coll., N.Y., 1988-89, Williams Coll., 2000, Harvard U., 2001. One-person shows include Inst. Contemporary Art, 1991, Trustman Gallery, Simmons Coll., Boston, 1991, The New Mus. Contemporary Art, N.Y., 1991, Matrix Gallery, Wadsworth Atheneum, Hartford, Conn., 1991, Albright Coll., Reading, Pa., 1991, Greenville County Mus. Art, S.C., 1992, San Francisco Art Inst., 1992, Linda Carthcart Gallery, Santa Monica, Calif., 1993, Rhonda Hoffman Gallery, Chgo., 1993, New Langton Arts, San Francisco, 1993, Hood Mus. Art, Dartmouth Coll., N.H., 1994, Mus. Modern Art, N.Y., 1995, The Bunting Inst., 1996, Contemporary Arts Mus., Houston, 1996, Everson Art Mus., Syracuse, N.Y., 1998, High Mus. Art, Atlanta, 2000, Internat. Ctr. Photography N.Y., 2000, Parrish Art Mus., 2001; group shows include Reframing the Family Artists Space, 1991, Whitney Mus. Am. Art, 1991, Mus. Modern Art, 1992, Randy Alexander, 1992, Artists of Conscience: 16 Years of Social and Polit. Commentary, Alt. Mus. N.Y., 1991-92, Through the Kitchen Door, NAME, 1991-92, Disclosing the Myth of Family, Art Inst. Chgo., The Betty Rymer Gallery, Chgo., 1992, The Theater of Refusal: Black Art and the Mainstream Criticism (traveling), 1993-94, States of Loss: Migration, Displacement, Colonialism and Power, Jersey City Mus., N.J., 1993-94, Gesture and Pose, Mus. Modern Art, N.Y., 1994, Bad Girls, Part 1, New Mus. Contemporary Art, N.Y., 1994, Who's Looking at the Family? Barbican Art Gallery, London, 1994, Equal Rights and Justice, High Mus. Art and Nat. Black Arts Fest, Atlanta, 1994, Imaging Families: Images and Voices, Smithsonian Instn., 1994-95, Black Male, Representations of Masculinity in Contemporary Am. Art, Whitney Mus. Am. Art, N.Y., 1994-95, Embedded Metaphor, Ringling Mus. Art, Sarasota, 1996, Alternate Cultures, Johannesberg Biennial, Africa, 1997, Changing Spaces, Detroit Inst. Art, 1998, Bearing Witness, Polk Mus. Art, 1998, Art Worlds in Dialog, Mus. Ludwig, Cologne, Germany, 1999, Paradise Now, Exit Art, N.Y., 2000, Collection in Context, Studio Mus. Harlem, N.Y., 2001. Office: PPOW Gallery 555 W 25th St New York NY 10001-5542

WEEMS, HELEN RACHEL, piano teacher, accompanist; b. Morgantown, W.Va., Dec. 12, 1962; d. David Burnola and Charys (Ford) Weems; m. Robert Raymond Provine, June 8, 1996. BA, Sch. of the Ozarks, Point Lookout, Mo., 1986; MM, Peabody Conservatory of Music, Balt., 1991; MA, U. Md. Baltimore County, Balt., 1996. Cert. piano tchr. Music Tchrs. Nat. Assn., 2004. Radio host Sta. KSOZ, Point Lookout, 1985-86, Sta. WJHU, Balt., 1994-96; freelance pianist, tchr., singer, 1975—. Balinese dancer UMBC Gamelan, Balt., 1993—96; coord. Harper's Glen Watch, Columbia, 1998—; Choir dir. St. Luke's Episcopal Ch., Brookeville, Md., 1997—. Neighborhood improvement grantee, Gov.'s Office of Crime Control and Prevention, 1999—2002. Mem.: Greater Columbia Music Tchrs. Assn. (v.p. 1997—2000), Howard County Music Tchrs. Assn. (pres. 1996—2003, concert mgr. 2002—). Democrat. Episcopalian. Avocations: running, gardening. Office: Helen R Weems Piano Studio 5473 Green Dory Ln Columbia MD 21044-1912

WEEMS, KERRY N. federal agency administrator; PhB, B in Mgmt., N.Mex. State U.; MBA, U. N.Mex., 1981. Staff mem. Senate Appropriations Com., dir. divsn. budget policy U.S. Dept. Health and Human Svcs., Washington, chief budget planning br., program analyst Office of Budget, program and budget analyst, acting asst. sec. for budget, tech. and fin., 2003—. Office: US Dept Health and Human Svcs Office Budget Tech and Fin 200 Independence Ave SW Washington DC 20201

WEERTMAN, JOHANNES, materials science educator; b. Fairfield, Ala., May 11, 1925; s. Roelof and Christina (van Vlaardingen) W.; m. Julia Ann Randall, Feb. 10, 1950; children: Julia Ann, Bruce Randall. Student, Pa. State Coll., 1943-44; BS, Carnegie Inst. Tech. (now Carnegie Mellon U.), 1948, DSc, 1951; postgrad., Ecole Normale Superieure, Paris, 1951-52. Solid State physicist U.S. Naval Rsch. Lab., Washington, 1952-58, cons., 1960-67; sci. liaison officer U.S. Office Naval Rsch., Am. Embassy, London, 1958-59; faculty Northwestern U., Evanston, Ill., 1959—, prof. materials sci. dept., 1961-68, chmn. dept., 1964-68, prof. geol. scis. dept., 1963—, Walter P. Murphy prof. materials sci. and engring. emeritus, 1999—. Vis. prof. geophysics Calif. Inst. Tech., 1964, Scott Polar Rsch. Inst., Cambridge (Eng.) U., 1970-71, Swiss Fed. Inst. Reactor Rsch., 1986; cons. Cold Regions Rsch. and Engring. Lab., U.S. Army, 1960-75, Oak Ridge (Tenn.) Nat. Lab., 1963-67, Los Alamos (N.Mex.) Sci. Lab., 1967—; co-editor materials sci. books MacMillan Co., 1962-76. Author: Dislocation Based Fracture Mechanics, 1996, (with Julia Weertman) Elementary Dislocation Theory, 1964, 2d edit., 1992; mem. editorial bd. Metal. Trans., 1967-75, Jour. Glaciology, 1972—; assoc. editor Jour. Geophys. Rsch., 1973-75, 2000-01; contbr. articles to profl. jours. With USMC, 1943-46. Honored with naming of Weertman Island in Antarctica.; Fulbright fellow, 1951-52; recipient Acta Metallurgica gold medal, 1980; Guggenheim fellow, 1970-71 Fellow Am. Acad. Arts and Scis., Am. Soc. Metals, Am. Phys. Soc., Geol. Soc. Am., Am. Geophys. Union (Horton award 1972, AIME Mathewson Gold medal 1977); mem. AAAS, NAE, Am. Inst. Physics, Internat. Glaciol. Soc. (Seligman Crystal award 1983), Arctic Inst., Am. Quaternary Assn., Explorers Club, Fulbright Assn., Sigma Xi, Tau Beta Pi, Phi Kappa Phi, Alpha Sigma Mu, Pi Mu Epsilon. Home: 834 Lincoln St Evanston IL 60201-2405 Office: Northwestern U Materials Sci Dept Evanston IL 60208-0001 Office Phone: 847-491-3197. E-mail: j-weertman2@northwestern.edu.

WEERTMAN, JULIA RANDALL, materials science and engineering educator; b. Muskegon, Mich., Feb. 10, 1926; BS in Physics, Carnegie-Mellon U., 1946, MS in Physics, 1947, DSc in Physics, 1951. Physicist U.S. Naval Rsch. Lab., Washington, 1952-58; vis. asst. prof. dept. materials sci. and engring. Northwestern U., Evanston, Ill., 1972-73, asst. prof., 1973-78, from asst. prof. to assoc. prof., 1973-82, prof., 1982-99, Walter P. Murphy prof., 1989, chmn. dept., 1987-92, asst. to dean grad. studies and rsch. Tech. Inst., 1973-76, Walter P. Murphy prof. emeritus, 1999—. Mem. various NRC coms. and panels. Co-author: Elementary Dislocation Theory, 1964, 1992, also pub. in French, Japanese and Polish; contbr. numerous articles to profl. jours. Mem. Evanston Environ. Control Bd., 1972-79. Recipient Creativity award NSF, 1981, 86; Guggenheim Found. fellow, 1986-87. Fellow Am. Soc. Metals Internat., Minerals, Metals and Materials Soc. (leadership award 1997); mem. NAE, Am. Acad. Arts and Scis., Am. Phys. Soc., Materials Rsch. Soc. (Von Hippel award 2003), Soc. Women Engrs. (disting. engring. educator award 1989, achievement award 1991). Home: 834 Lincoln St Evanston IL 60201-2405 Office: Northwestern U Dept Material Sci & Engring 2220 Campus Dr Evanston IL 60208-0876 Office Phone: 847-491-5353. Business E-Mail: jrweertman@northwestern.edu.

WEESE, BENJAMIN HORACE, architect; b. Evanston, Ill., June 4, 1929; s. Harry Ernest and Marjorie (Mohr) W.; m. Cynthia Rogers, July 5, 1963; children: Daniel Peter, Catharine Mohr. B.Arch., Harvard U., 1951, M.Arch., 1957; cert., Ecole des Beaux Arts, Fontainebleau, France, 1956. Assoc., Harry Weese & Assocs., Architects, Chgo., 1957-77; prin. Weese Langley Weese, Chgo., 1977—. Co-founder, pres. Chgo. Arch. Found., Glessner House, Chgo., 1966— Trustee Graham Found. for Advanced Studies in Fine Arts, 1988—, pres. 1995-99; mem. Commn. Chgo. Landmarks, 1998—. Fellow AIA; mem. Nat. Council Archtl. Registration Bds. Home: 2133 N Hudson Ave Chicago IL 60614-4522 Office: Weese Langley Weese Ltd 9 W Hubbard St Chicago IL 60610-4630 E-mail: bweese@wlwltd.com.

WEESE, BRUCE ERIC, sales executive; b. Chewelah, Wash., Mar. 22, 1942; s. Harry M. and Roberta B. (Carman) Weese; m. Elaine M. Smith, June 18, 1962 (div. July 1972); children: Sandra G., Michael D.; m. Vera B. Reed, Mar. 22, 1975 (div. Aug. 3, 2001); 1 adopted child, Trishele. BA in Edn., Ea. Wash. State U., Cheney, 1964; MBA, Pepperdine U., 1981. Tchr. Grant Joint Union HS Dist., Sacramento, 1964-70; pharm. sales McNeil Labs., San Jose, Calif., 1970-77, Adria Labs., San Francisco, 1977-83, Serono Labs., San Francisco, 1983-84, Boehringer Ingelheim, Santa Rosa, Calif., 1984-91, mgr. govt. affairs western states, 1991-97, area mgr. managed care, 1997-98; pharm. sales rep. Olympia, Wash., 2000—. Bd. dirs. Russian River Health Ctr., Guerneville, Calif., 1994—95, 1998—, Redwood Empire br. Am. Lung Assn., 1998—. Mem.: Sierra Club, Sequoia Paddlers, United Anglers, Santa Rosa Sailing Club. Democrat. Avocations: kayaking, sailing, fishing. Home and Office: 4013 Grove Rd NW Olympia WA 98502-3766

WEESE, CYNTHIA ROGERS, architect, educator; b. Des Moines, June 23, 1940; d. Gilbert Taylor and Catharine (Wingard) Rogers; m. Benjamin H. Weese, July 5, 1963; children: Daniel Peter, Catharine Mohr. BSA.S., Washington U., St. Louis, 1962; B.Arch., Washington U., 1965. Registered architect, Ill. Pvt. practice architecture, Chgo., 1965-72, 74-77; draftsperson, designer Harry Weese & Assocs., Chgo., 1972-74; prin. Weese Langley Weese Ltd., Chgo., 1977—; design critic Ball State U., Muncie, Ind., Miami U., Oxford, Ohio, 1979, U. Wis.-Milw., 1980, U. Ill.-Chgo., 1981, 85, Iowa State U., Ames, 1982, Washington U., St. Louis, 1984, U. Ill., Champaign, 1987-92, Kans. State U., 1992; dean sch. architecture Washington U., St. Louis, 1993—. Bd. regents Am. Architecture Found., 1990-93; bd. mem. Landmarks Commn. St. Louis.; mem. Mayor's Task Force Downtown Now, St. Louis, 1997—. Recipient Alpha Rho Chi award Washington U., 1965, Met. Chgo. YWCA Outstanding Achievement award, 1990. Mem. AIA (bd. dirs. Chgo. chpt. 1980-83, v.p. 1983-85, 1st v.p. 1986-87, pres. 1987-88, regional dir. 1990-92, Disting. Bldg. awards 1977, 81-83, 86, 91, 95, Interior Architecture award 1981, 90, 92, nat. v.p. 1993, chmn. urban design task force St. Louis 2004 1997—), AIA/ACSA Coun. on Archtl. Rsch. (chair 1991-92), AIA Found. (pres. Chgo. chpt. 1988-89), Soc. Archtl. Historians (bd. dirs. 1992-94), Chgo. Women in Architecture, Chgo. Network, Nat. Inst. Archtl. Edn. (bd. dirs. 1988-90), Chgo. Archtl. Club (pres. 1988-89), Washington U. Sch. Architecture Alumni (nat. coun. 1988-93), Lambda Alpha. Clubs: Arts, Chgo. Archtl. Democrat. Office: Washington U Sch Architecture PO Box 1079 Saint Louis MO 63188-1079

WEESE, JOHN AUGUSTUS, mechanical engineer, educator; b. Topeka, Kans., July 24, 1933; s. Ray Augustus and Margaret Maureen (Richmond) Weese; m. Betty Kay Dietrich, June 5, 1955; children: Carol Ann, Katherine Lynn. BSME, Kans. State U., 1955; MS, Cornell U., 1958, PhD, 1959. Asst. prof. USAF Acad., Colo., 1960-62; assoc. prof. mech. engring. U. Denver, 1963-67, prof., 1967-74, chmn. mech. sci. and environ. engring., 1968-70, dean engring., 1970-74, Old Dominion U., Norfolk, Va., 1974-83; dir. mech. engring. and applied mechanics NSF, Washington, 1983-85, dir. mechanics structures and materials engring., 1985-86; prof. mech. engring. Tex. A&M U., College Station, 1986—, head dept. engring. tech., 1986-97, coord. accreditation, regents prof., 1997—, interim head mech. engring. dept., 2001—03. Structural dynamics engr. Boeing Co., Wichita, Kans., 1959—60, rsch. specialist, 1962—63; rsch. engr. Martin-Marietta Corp., Denver, 1963; bd. dirs. ABET, Inc., 1994—98, 2002—. Co-author: (book) Mechanics of Materials, 4th edit., 1985; contbr. articles to profl. jours. Fellow: ASME (ad hoc visitor 1977—83, Ben C. Sparks medal 1994), Am. Soc. Engring. Edn.

(projects bd. engring. rsch. coun. 1982—85, chmn. publs. com. 1983—86, exec. com. 1984—90, chmn. engring. rsch. coun. 1988—90, v.p. pub. affairs 1995—97, pres.-elect 1998—99, pres. 1999—2000, Outstanding Educator mechanics divsn. 1989, Frederick J. Berger award 1997, W. Leighton Collins award 2004). Republican. Congregationalist. Avocations: fishing, photography. Home: 9300 Lake Forest Ct South College Station TX 77845-8763 Office: Tex A&M U Dept Mech Engring College Station TX 77843-3123

WEESE, MIRANDA, dancer; b. San Bernardino, Calif. Student, Sch. Am. Ballet, 1990. Apprentice N.Y.C. Ballet, 1991—93, mem. corps de ballet, 1993—94, soloist, 1994—95, prin., 1996—. Dancer (ballets) Apollo, Concerto Barocco, Divertimento No. 15, The Four Temperaments, Romeo and Juliet, Chiaroscuro, The Sleeping Beauty, others, PBS TV spl. Martins' Swan Lake Live from Lincoln Ctr. Fellow USA Dance fellow, Princess Grace Found., 1995—96. Office: NYC Ballet NY State Theatre 20 Lincoln Ctr Plz New York NY 10023-6913

WEETH, GEORGE WRIGHT, lawyer; b. Houston, Apr. 1, 1954; s. Charles and Betty Weeth; m. Karen Weeth, Mar. 14, 1981. BA cum laude, U. Tex., 1976, JD, 1981. Bar: N.Mex. 1981, U.S. Dist. Ct. N.Mex. 1981, Tex. 1982, U.S. Dist. Ct. (we. dist.) Tex. 1986, U.S. Ct. Appeals (10th cir.) 1987. Assoc. Modrall, Sperling, Albuquerque, 1981-82, Butt, Thornton & Baehr, Albuquerque, 1982-88; pvt. practice Weeth Law Office, Albuquerque, 1988—. Mem. instnl. rev. bd. St. Joseph Healthcare, Albuquerque, 1993-97; pres. Acad. Hills Neighborhood, Albuquerque, 1989-91; v.p. Eastdale Little League, Albuquerque, 1997. Mem. State Bar of N.Mex. (sec. rep. young lawyers divsn. 1984-90, bd. dirs. trial practice sect. 1985-90, chair trial practice sect. 1990-91, bd. dirs. solo and small firm practitioners sect. 1999—, chair 2001-2002), N.Mex. Trial Lawyers Assn. (editor Worker's Compensation jour. 1994—). Avocations: running, skiing. Office: PO Box 91478 Albuquerque NM 87199-1478 Office Phone: 505-828-1122.

WEFALD, JON, university president; b. Nov. 24, 1937; s. Olav and Walma (Ovrum) W.; m. Ruth Ann; children— Skipp, Andy. BA, Pacific Lutheran U., Tacoma, 1959; MA, Wash. State U., Pullman, 1961; PhD, U. Mich., Ann Arbor, 1965. Teaching asst. Wash. State U., Pullman, 1959—61; teaching fellow U. Mich., Ann Arbor, 1961—64; assoc. prof. Gustavus Adolphus Coll., St. Peter, Minn., 1965—70; commnr. agr. State of Minn., St. Paul, 1971—77; pres. Southwest State U., Marshall, Minn., 1977—82; chancellor Minn. State Univ. System, St. Paul, 1982—86; pres. Kans. State U., Manhattan, 1986—. Author: A Voice of Protest: Norwegians in American Politics 1890-1917, 1971. Mem. Mid-Am. Internat. Agri-Trade Council (pres. 1974-75), Midwest Assn. State Depts. of Agr. (sec.treas. 1976-77), U.S. Dept. Agr. Joint Council on Food and Agrl. Scis. Office: Kans State U Office of Pres 110 Anderson Hall Manhattan KS 66506-0100

WEFALD, SUSAN, state commissioner; m. Robert O. Wefald; children: Sarah, Kathryn, Tom. BA, U. Mich., 1969; postgrad., U. N.D. Licensed social worker; cert. consumer credit counselor. Elected mem. Bismarck Pub. Sch. Bd., pres.; commr. N.D. Pub. Svc. Commn. Mem. Energy Conservation Com., Com. Consumer Affairs Nat. Assn. Regulatory Utility Commrs.; sec. Mid Am. Regulatory Commn. Violinist, charter mem. Bismarck-Mandan Symphony Orch.; pres. Sakakawea Girl Scout Coun.; bd. dirs. Mo. Slope United Way. Office: ND Pub Svc Commn 600 E Boulevard Ave Bismarck ND 58505-0660 Fax: 701-328-2410.

WEFLER, WILSON DANIEL, management consultant; b. Rocky River, Ohio, Feb. 27, 1927; s. Wilson Daniel and Myra (Johns) W.; m. Bonnie Kistner, Feb. 9, 1952; children: Wendy, Nancy, Bonnie, Susan, John. BS in Journalism, Northwestern U., 1950, postgrad., 1950-51. Asst. editor, writer Standard Oil Co., Chgo., 1951-55; asst. editor Keeney Pub. Co., Chgo., 1955-56; pub. rep. Urban Farley & Co., Chgo., 1957-61; dir. alumni relations Northwestern U., Evanston, Ill., 1961-65; pres. Com. for Middle Western Bus. Devel., Inc., Chgo., 1965-75; sr. v.p. Unimark Internat., Chgo., N.Y.C., Milan, 1975-79; pres. Wefler & Assocs., Inc., Evanston, 1979—. Past pres. Assn. Profl. Design Firms, Bellevue, Wash., 1985-88, chmn. founding com., 1984; pub. Design Firm Directory, 1979-99. Editor Design Firm Mgmt., 1980-95. Bd. commrs. Lighthouse Park Dist., Evanston, 1992—, pres., 1999—. Recipient Service award Northwestern U. Alumni Assn., 1966. Mem. John Evans Club, Half Century Club (chmn. 2001). Home: 6 Milburn Park Evanston IL 60201-1744 Office: Wefler & Assocs Inc 6 Milburn Pk Evanston IL 60201-1744

WEG, JOHN GERARD, physician; b. N.Y.C., Feb. 16, 1934; s. Leonard and Pauline M. (Kanzleiter) W.; m. Mary Loretta Flynn, June 2, 1956; children: Diane Marie, Kathryn Mary, Carol Ann, Loretta Louise, Veronica Susanne, Michelle Celeste. BA cum laude, Coll. Holy Cross, Worcester, Mass., 1955; MD, N.Y. Med. Coll., 1959. Diplomate: Am. Bd. Internal Medicine. Commd. 2nd lt. USAF, 1958, advanced through grades to capt., 1967; intern Walter Reed Gen. Hosp., Washington, 1959-60; resident, then chief resident in internal medicine Wilford Hall USAF Hosp., Lackland AFB, Tex., 1960-64, chief pulmonary sect., 1964-66, chief inhalation sect., 1964-66, chief pulmonary and infectious disease service, 1966-67; resigned, 1967; clin. dir. pulmonary disease div. Jefferson Davis Hosp., Houston, 1967-71; from asst. prof. to assoc. prof. medicine Baylor U. Coll. Medicine, Houston, 1967-71; assoc. prof. medicine U. Mich. Med. Sch. Univ. Hosp., Ann Arbor, 1971-74, prof., 1974—2001, prof. emeritus, 2001—. Physician-in-charge pulmonary div., 1971-81, physician-in-charge pulmonary and critical care med. div., 1981-85; cons. Ann Arbor VA, 1971—, Wayne County Gen. hosps., 1971-84; mem. adv. bd. Washtenaw County Health Dept., 1973—; mem. respiratory and nervous system panel, anesthesiology Sect. Nat. Ctr. Devices and Radiol. Health, FDA, 1983—, chmn., 1985-88. Contbr. med. jours., reviewer, mem. editorial bds. Decorated Air Force Commendation medal; travelling fellow Nat. Tb and Respiratory Disease Assn., 1971; recipient Aesculpaius award Tex. Med. Assn., 1971 Master ACP (chmn. Mich. program com. 1974); fellow Am. Coll. Chest Physicians (chmn. bd. govs. 1976-79, gov. Mich. 1975-79, chmn. membership com. 1976-79, prof.-in-residence 1972—, chmn. critical care coun. 1982-85, chmn. ethics com. 1998, master fellow, 2002, master FCCP, 2002, master), Am. Coll. Chest Physicians and Internat. Acad. Chest Physicians (master, exec. council 1976-82, pres. 1980-81); mem. AAAS, Am. Fedn. Clin. Rsch., AMA, Am. Thoracic Soc. (sec.-treas. 1974-76), Am. Assn. Inhalation Therapy, Air Force Soc. Internists and Allied Specialists, Soc. Med. Consultants to Armed Forces, Internat. Union Against Tb, Mich. Thoracic Soc. (pres. 1976-78), Mich. Lung Assn. (dir., Bruce Douglas award 1981), Am. Lung Assn., Rsch. Club U. Mich., Assn. Advancement Med. Instrumentation, Central Soc. Clin. Rsch., Am. Bd. Internal Medicine (subsplty. com. on pulmonary disease 1980-86, critical care medicine test com. 1985-87, critical care medicine policy com. 1986-87), N.Y. Med. Coll. Alumni Assn. (medal of honor 1990), Alpha Omega Alpha. Home: 3060 Exmoor Rd Ann Arbor MI 48104-4132 Office: B I H 245 Box 0026 1500 E Medical Center Dr Ann Arbor MI 48109-0005 Office Phone: 734-936-5245. Business E-Mail: jweg@umich.edu.

WEG, KENNETH E. pharmaceutical executive; b. Phila., July 30, 1938; m. Carol. B in English Lit., Dartmouth Coll., 1960; MBA, Columbia U., 1962. Dir. long range planning internat. divsn. Bristol-Myers Co., 1969-87; group v.p., pres. Squibb Internat. Squibb Corp., 1987-88; pres. Squibb Pharm. Group, 1988-89; overseer ops. domestic and internat. pharm. bus. Bristol-Myers Squibb Co., 1989-93, pres. pharm. group, 1993-95, exec. v.p., 1995-96, responsible for consumer medicines ops., 1996—; also bd. dirs.; vice-chmn. Trustee Princeton Med. Ctr., U. Medicine and Dentistry N.J., Found. N.J. Pub. Broadcasting, Inc., 1993, reappt., 1996, mem. fin. com.; trustee Fox Chase Cancer Ctr., bd. dirs., 2000—; mem. corp. exec. com. Phila. Mus. Art; co-chair Gov. Christie Whitman's Save the Dome campaign. Office: Bristol-Myers Squibb Co World Hdqs 345 Park Ave New York NY 10154-0037

WEGELIN, JACOB ANDREAS, statistician; b. Eugene, Oreg., Dec. 14, 1954; s. Christof Andreas and Caroline (Locke) W. BA, BS, U. Wash., 1986, MS, 1989, PhD, 2001. With Shiloh Youth Revival Ctrs., Inc., Oreg., Wash., Calif., Ariz., Alaska, 1971-76, Eugene Hotel, 1976-78; deckhand fishing industry, Alaska, 1978-79; tech. writer, editor IBM Corp., San Jose, Calif. and, N.Y., Poughkeepsie, N.Y., 1985-86; cook, deckhand, bull cook Alaska Boat Co., Wards Cove Packing Co., 1991-93; instr. MathSoft, Seattle, 1995; statistician U. Wash., Seattle, 1996—2002, U. Calif., Davis, 2002—. Recipient Pres.'s medal U. Wash., 1986; NSF fellow, 1986-89. Mem. Am. Statis. Assn., Phi Beta Kappa. Office: U Calif Dept Epidemiology/Preventive Medicine 1 Shields Ave TB-168 Davis CA 95616-8638

WEGENAST, JUDY H. elementary school educator, consultant; b. Grafton, N.D., Aug. 4, 1944; d. Donald M. and Donna (Ramsey) Matter; m. Jerry G. Wegenast, May 28, 1966; children: Kim. L. Albrecht, Elisa D. Wegenast. EdB, Valley City State U., 1966; MS, N.D. State U., 1982. Tchr. St. John's, Wahpeton, N.D., 1967; remedial reading Wahpeton (N.D.) Indian Sch., 1968; tchr. West Fargo (N.D.) Pub. Sch., 1968-70, Fargo (N.D.) Pub. Schs., 1970-91, peer coach, 1991—. Instr. N.D. State U. Fargo, Grand Forks, N.D., 1986—; cons. SW Enterprises, fargo, N.D., 1985—. Bd. dirs. Yunder Farm Childrens Mus., Fargo, N.D., 1992—. Named Tchr. of Month, Fargo (N.D.) C. of C., 1989, Tchr. of Yr., IBM/Tech. and Learning, Fargo, N.D., 1992, Fargo Tchr. of Yr., 1992, N.D. Tchr. of Yr., 1992. Mem. Valley Reading Assn., N.D. Edn. Assn., Fargo Edn. Assn. NEA, ASCD, Alpha Delta Kappa. Avocations: painting, gardening, golf, reading, wood working. Office: Centennial Elem 4201 25th St S Fargo ND 58104-6800

WEGENER, MARK DOUGLAS, lawyer; b. Nov. 1, 1948; BA cum laude, Cen. Coll., Pella, Iowa, 1970; JD, Rutgers U., 1973. Assoc. Howrey & Simon, Washington, 1973-79; ptnr. Howrey Simon Arnold & White, Washington, 1979—. Office: Howrey Simon Arnold & White LLP 1299 Pennsylvania Ave NW Washington DC 20004-2400

WEGENER, PETER PAUL, engineering educator, author; b. Berlin, Aug. 29, 1917; came to U.S., 1946; naturalized, 1953. m. Annette Schleiermacher, Aug. 14, 1961; children: Paul, Christopher, Philip. Dr rer. nat., U. Berlin, 1943; MA (priv.), Yale U., 1960; Dr. Ing. (E.h.) (hon.), U. Karlsruhe, Germany, 1979. Researcher supersonic wind tunnels, Kochel, Germany, 1943-45; researcher gasdynamics, hypersonic wind tunnels U.S. Naval Ordnance Lab., 1946-53, Jet Propulsion Lab. Calif. Inst. Tech., 1953-60; prof. applied sci. Yale U., New Haven, 1960-72, Harold Hodgkinson prof. engring. and applied sci., 1972—, chmn. dept. engring, applied sci., 1966-71, prof. emeritus, 1987—. Sr. Am. scientist Humboldt Found., 1979 Author: (books) The Peenemünde Wind Tunnels: A Memoir, 1996, What Makes Airplanes Fly?, 1997; researcher and contbr. articles on hypersonics, condensation metastable state, chem. kinetics, flow systems real gases, bubbles to profl. jours. Inst. Advanced Study Berlin fellow, 1986. Fellow Am. Phys. Soc., Conn. Acad. Sci. & Engring. (charter). Home: 29 Montgomery Pkwy Branford CT 06405-5128

WEGLEITNER, MARK A. telecommunications industry executive; BA in Math., St. John's U., 1972; MS in Elec. Engring. & Comp. Sci., U. Calif., Berkeley, 1974. With Bell Telephone Labs., 1972—79, AT&T, 1979—83; chief tech. officer, v.p. tech. & engring. Bell Atlantic Network Svcs., 1983—2000; sr. v.p., chief tech. officer Verizon Comm., Inc., N.Y.C., 2000—. Office: Verizon Comm Inc 1095 Ave of Americas New York NY 10036-6797

WEGMAN, DANIEL R. retail executive; m. Stency Wegman; 2 children. Student, Harvard U. Joined Wegman's Food Markets, Rochester, NY, 1969, pres., 1976—. Chmn. bd. govs. Uniform Code Coun. Named Supermarket Impresario, Self Mag., 1998. Mem.: Food Mktg. Inst. (chmn. 1999—2001). Office: Wegmans Food Markets 1500 Brooks Ave Rochester NY 14624

WEGMAN, DAVID HOWE, health science educator, consultant; b. Balt., Mar. 13, 1940; s. Myron Ezra and Isabel (Howe) W.; m. Cynthia Heynen, June 18, 1962 (div. Aug. 1968); m. Peggy Nelson, June 7, 1969; children: Jesse Howe, Marya Nelson. BA, Swarthmore Coll., 1962; MD, Harvard U., 1966, MS in Physiology, 1972. Diplomate Am. Bd. Preventive Medicine. Intern Cleve. Met. Gen. Hosp., 1966-67; med. epidemiologist, N.Y.C Health Dept. Nat. Communicable Disease Ctr., USPHS, 1967-69; dir. indsl. health project Urban Planning Aid, Inc., Cambridge, Mass., 1969-71; occupational hygiene physician Mass. Dept. Labor and Industry, Boston, 1972-78; asst. prof. pub. health Harvard U., Boston, 1972-77, assoc. prof. pub. health, 1977-83; prof., dir. environ. occupational health scis. UCLA, 1983-87; prof., chair work environment Coll. Engring. U. Mass., Lowell, Mass., 1987—2003, dean Sch. Health and Environment, 2003—. Mem. com. role of practicing physicians in occupl. and environ. health Inst. Medicine, 1987-88, mem. com. to review health consequences during Persian Gulf War, 1994-96, chair com. on health and safety implications of child labor, 1997-98, mem. com. on gender differences in susceptibility to environ. factors, 1997-98, mem. com. on musculoskeletal disorders and the workplace, 1999-2001, mem. planning meeting for study on changing dimensions of older Am. workers and their occupl. health and safety needs, 1999, chair Nat. Rsch. Coun. com. on health and safety needs of older workers, 2002--; chair adv. com. on elimination of pneumoconiosis among coal mine workers Mine Safety and Health Adminstrn., 1996; mem. stds. adv. com. on metal working fluids dept. labor Occupl. Safety and Health Adminstrn., 1997-99; Jameson Parkinson Meml. lectr. Brit. Soc. Occpl. Medicine, 2003. Author, editor: Occupational Health, 1983, 4th edit., 2000; editor, manuscript reviewer various health publs.; contbr. numerous articles to profl. jours. Adv. Bd. mem. Working Women, 1981-85. Recipient Alfred L. Frechette award Mass. Pub. Health Assn., 1979, Harriet Hardy award New Eng. Coll. Occupl. and Environ. Medicine, 1994; Fulbright Sr. fellow, 1998. Fellow Am. Coll. Epidemiology, Am. Coll. Preventive Medicine; mem. APHA (panel environ. studies 1976-78, exec. bd. 1982, chmn. occupl. health and safety sect. 1976, governing coun. 1974-80, 83-85, mem. sci. bd. 2002—), The Nat. Acads. (nat. assoc.), Internat. Epidemiol. Assn. (treas. 1999—), Internat. Commn. Occupl. Health (mem. exec. bd. 1996—, chair sci. com. epidemiology in occupl. health 1993-96, sec. 1990-93), Am. Conf. Govtl. Indsl. Hygienists, Am. Occupl. Medicine Assn., Am. Coll. Epidemiology, Soc. Epidemiol. Rsch., Soc. Occupl. and Environ. Health. Avocations: hiking, swimming, camping. Home: 398 Wolcott St Auburndale MA 02466-1533 Office: U Mass Lowell Dean Sch Health and Environment 3 Solomont Way Ste 5121 Lowell MA 01854 Office Phone: 978-934-4510. E-mail: david_wegman@uml.edu.

WEGMAN, HAROLD HUGH, management consultant; b. Cin., June 29, 1916; s. Clarence H. and Lillian (de Tellem) W.; m. Ruth Ellen Volk, May 1, 1937; children— Susan Ruth (Mrs. Michael Manning), Sally Ann (Mrs. Jerry Fine). BBA, U. Cin., 1941; MBA, Xavier U., 1954. Band leader, studio mgr. Rudolph Wurlitzer Co., 1946-50; Tng. supr., then asst. to v.p. Gruen Watch Co., 1950-55; personnel dir., asst. to pres. Bavarian Brewing Co., Covington, Ky., 1955-59; dir. indsl. relations, asst. to pres. Howard Paper Co., Dayton, Ohio, 1959-62; v.p., gen. mgr. Elano Corp., Xenia, Ohio, 1962-64; v.p., dir. indsl. relations Champion Papers Inc., Hamilton, Ohio, 1964-67; v.p. U.S. Plywood Champion Papers, Inc., 1967-71, Champion Internat., 1971-72; pres. PEP Group, 1972—; dir. Mgmt. Center, Sacred Heart U., 1974—. Contbr. articles to profl. pubs. Trustee Foreman Found., 1965-71. Served to lt. (j.g.) USNR, 1944-46. Mem. Am. Soc. Personnel Adminstrs. (bd. dirs. 1969—, treas. 1970), Am. Soc. for Tng. and Devel., NAM, Am. Paper Inst., Am. Mgmt. Assn., Conn. songwriters assn., Lambda Chi Alpha. Home: 3150 N Highway A1A Ph 3-5 Hutchinson Island FL 34949-8871 E-mail: halwegman@aol.com.

WEGMAN, ROBERT B. food service executive; b. Rochester, NY, Oct. 14, 1918; m. Peggy Wegman; children: Daniel, Joan Profeta, Gail Tobin, Marie Kenton. BBA, Niagara Univ., 1947; degree (hon.), St. John Fisher Coll., Rochester, 1986; LHD (hon.), SUNY, Genesco, 1994. With Wegman's Food Markets, Inc., Rochester, 1936—42, 1946—50, pres., 1950—69, chmn., CEO, 1969—. Chmn. Super Market Inst., 1967—69, pub. policy sub. com. for Grocery Industry Devel. of Universal Prod. Code, 1970—74. With USMC, 1942-46. Named one of 50 Industry Visionaries, Supermarket News, 2002; recipient Sidney Rabb Award, Food Mktg. Inst., 1981, VandenBrul Entrepreneurial Award, Rochester Inst. Tech., 1991, Civic Medal Award, Rochester C. of C., 1994, Corning Award, Bus. Coun. N.Y. State, 1998. Office: Wegmans Food Markets Inc PO Box 30844 Rochester NY 14603-0844

WEGMAN, WILLIAM GEORGE, artist; b. Holyoke, Mass., Dec. 2, 1943; s. George W. and Eleanor (Vezina) W. BFA in Painting, Mass. Coll. Art, 1965; MFA, U. Ill., 1967. One-man shows include Galerie Sonnabend, Paris, 1971, Pomona Coll. Art Gallery, 1971, Sonnabend Gallery, N.Y.C., 1972, 77, Galerie Ernst, Hanover, Ger., 1972, Situation, London, 1972, Konrad Fischer Gallery, 1972, 75, 79, Courtney Sale Gallery, 1972, Tex. Gallery, Houston, 1973, 75, 79, L.A. County Mus. of Art, Calif., 1973, 112 Greene St., N.Y.C., 1974, Mayor Gallery, London, 1975, Galleria Alessandra Castelli, Milan, 1975, The Kitchen, N.Y., 1976, Bruna Soletti Gallery, Milan, 1977, 82, Rosamund Felsen Gallery, 1978, Holly Solomon Gallery, N.Y.C., 1979, 80, 82, 84, 86, 88, 90, 92, Arnolfini Gallery, Eng., 1979, U. Wis., Milw., 1979, U. Colo. Art Galleries, Boulder, 1980, Marianne Deson Gallery, Chgo., 1980, Vivianne Esders Gallery, Paris, 1981, Magnuson Lee Gallery, Boston, 1981, Robert Hull Fleming Mus., Burlington, Vt., 1981, Locus Solus, Genoa, Italy, 1982, Dart Gallery, Chgo., 1982, Fraenkel Gallery, San Francisco, 1982, 88, 90, 92, 93, James Corcoran Gallery, Los Angeles, 1982, 90, Nancy Drysdale Gallery, Washington, 1982, 87, 94, Walker Art Ctr, Mpls., 1982, Ft. Worth Art Mus., Tex., 1982, De Cordova & Dana Mus. & Park, Mass., 1982, Southeastern Ctr. for Contemporary Art, Winston-Salem, N.C., 1982, The Contemporary Arts Ctr., Ohio, 1982, Newport Harbor Mus., Calif., 1982, Inst. Contemporary Arts at Va. Mus., Richmond, 1983, Fine Arts Gallery, U. Mass., Amherst, 1983, Tex. Gallery, Houston, 1983, 86, Greenville County Mus. Art, 1984, Lowe Mus. Art, Miami, Fla, 1985, Cleve. Mus. Art, 1986, Honolulu Acad. Arts, 1987, Mass. Coll. Art, Boston, 1987, U. San Diego, La Jolla, Calif., 1988, Pace MacGill Gallery, N.Y., 1988, 90, 92, 93, San Francisco Mus. Modern Art, Calif., 1988, Galerie Durand-Dessert, Paris, 1989, Budoin Lebon, Paris, 1989, Maison de la Culture et de la Communication de Saint Etienne, France, 1989, Linda Cathcart Gallery, L.A., 1990, 92, 94, The Taft Mus. Cin., 1990, The Butler Inst., Ohio, 1990, Sperone Westwater Gallery, N.Y., 1992, Kunstmuseum, Lucerne, Switzerland, 1990, ICA, London, 1990, Stedelijk Mus., The Netherlands, 1990, Frankfurt Kunstverein, Germany, 1990, Pompidou Ctr., Paris, 1990, ICA, Boston, 1990, Ringling Mus., Fla., 1990, Whitney Mus., N.Y., Contemporary Arts Mus., Tex., 1990, Neuberger Mus., SUNY, 1991, Galerie Andreas Binder, Germany, 1992, Athenaeum Music & Arts Library, Calif., 1992, Lisa Sette Gallery, Phoenix, 1994, Greg Kucera Gallery, Seattle, 1994, George Eastman House: Internat. Mus. Photography and Film, 1995, Aspen Art Mus., ACC Galerie, Weimar, Germany, 1995, Pace Wildenstein, L.A., 1995, Anderson Gallery, Pitts., 1995, Pace/MacGill Gallery, N.Y., 1995, Tex. Gallery, Houston, 1996, Jay Gorney Gallery, N.Y., 1996, Galleri Larsen, Stockholm, 1996, Ehlers Caudill Gallery, Chgo., 1996, Gallery Art Point, Tokyo, 1997, Isetan Mus. Art, Tokyo, 1997, Saks 5th Ave., N.Y.C., 1998, Geral Peters Gallery, Dallas, 1998, Mass. Coll. Art, Boston, 1999, SOMA Gallery, La Jolla, Calif., 1999, ACC Gallery Weimar, Germany, 1999, Birmingham (Ala.) Mus. Art, 1999, Durant-Dessert Gallery, Paris, 1999, Springfield (Mass.) Mus., 1999, others; exhibited in group shows at Walker Art Ctr., Mpls., 1968, N.J. State Mus., Trenton, 1968, Detroit Inst. Art, 1969, Mus. Contemporary Art, Chgo., 1969, 77, Allen Meml. Mus., 1970, L.A. County Mus., Calif., 1971, Pasadena Art Mus., 1972, Contemporary Arts Mus., Houston, 1972, Whitney Mus. Am. Art, N.Y.C., 1973, 81, 89, Sonnabend Gallery, N.Y.C., 1974, Milw. Art Ctr., 1975, Sarah Lawrence Coll. Gallery, 1975, Phila. Mus. Art, 1976, San Francisco Mus. Modern Art, 1976, U. Calif.-Berkeley Art Mus., 1976, U. Chgo., 1976, Ringling Mus. Art, Sarasota, Fla., 1977, Walker Art Gallery, Eng., 1978, Holly Solomon Gallery, N.Y.C., 1978, 82, 87, Mus. Fine Arts, Houston, 1978, Aspen Ctr. Visual Arts, 1979, Santa Barbara Mus. Art, 1979, Mus. Modern Art, N.Y.C., 1980, 82, 83, Sidney Janis Gallery, 1981, Art Inst. Chgo., 1981, 82, Young Hoffman Gallery, Chgo., 1983, Inst. Contemporary Art, Boston, 1983, Castelli Graphics, N.Y.C., 1983, Queens Mus., N.Y., 1986, James. Madison U., Harrison, Va, 1987, Fay Gold Gallery, Atlanta, 1988, Hudson River Mus., 1989, Volcano Arts Ctr., 1989, Pace/MacGill, N.Y.C., 1990, The History of Travel, The Taft Museum, Cin., The Butler Inst. Youngstown, Ohio, 1990, William Wegman: Paintings, Drawings, Photographs, Videotapes, Kunstmuseum, Luzern, Stedelijk Museum, Amsterdam, Frankfurt Kunstverein Frankfurt, Centre Nat. d'Art et cle Culture Georges Pompidou, Paris, Inst. of Contemporary Art, London, Inst. of Contemporary Arts, Boston, Contemporary Arts Mus., Houston, J.M. Ringling Mus., Sarasota, Whitney Mus., of American Art, N.Y., 1990-92, Outdoor Photographs, Neuberger Mus., State U. of N.Y. at Purchase, 1991, William Wegman: L'oeuvre photographique, 1969-76, Fonds Regional d'Art Contemporary, Limousin, France, 1991, New Polaroids, Holly Solomon Gallery, N.Y.C., Early Black and White Photographs, Pace/MacGill Gallery, N.Y.C., New Paintings, Sperone Westwater Gallery, N.Y.C., 1992, Turner/Krull Galleries, L.A., 1993, Calif. Ctr. Arts, Escondido, 1994, Drawing Space, N.Y., 1995, Found. Cartier pour l'art Contemporain, Paris, 1996, Lance Fung Gallery, N.Y., 1997, Huntingdon Beach (Calif.) Art Ctr., 1998, Art: Concept, Paris, 1999, many others; contbr. articles to profl. jours.; videography: Reel 1, 1970-72, Reel 2, 1972, Reel 3, 1972-73, Reel 4, 1973-74, Reel 5, 1975, Reel 6, 1975-76, Reel 7, 1976-77, Reel 8, 1997-98, Reel 9, 1999, Spit Sandwich, 1970, Gray Hairs, 1974-75, World History, 1976, Man Ray, Man Ray, 1978, Accident, 1979, How to Draw, 1983, The World of Photography, 1985, Blue Monday Music Video, 1988, Alive From Off Center, 1988, Sesame Street Videos, 1989, 92, 93, 94, 95, 96, 97, 98, 99; film: Dog Baseball, 1986, The Hardly Boys in Hardly Gold, 1995; publications: Man's Best Friend, 1982, Everyday Problems, 1984, William Wegman: Paintings, Drawings, Photographs, Videotapes, 1990, Cinderella, 1993, Little Red Riding Hood, 1993, ABC, 1994, 1, 2, 3, 1995, Triangle, Circle, Square, 1995, Mother Goose, 1996, Farm Days, 1997, Puppies, 1997, My Town, 1998, What Do You Do?, 1999, Pup, 1999, Fay, 1999; represented in numerous pub. collections including Kunstaus, Zurich, Mpls. Inst. Art, Mus. Fine Art, Houston, Bklyn. Mus., L.A. County Mus. Art, Mus. Fine Art, Houston, St. Louis Mus. Modern Art, Walker Art Ctr., Mpls., Whitney Mus. Am. Art, N.Y., Albright-Knox Gallery, Buffalo, Austrlian Nat. Gallery, Canberra, others; exhibited in numerous film and video festivals. Recipient Creative Artists Pub. Svc. award, 1979; Guggenheim Found. fellow, 1975, 86, Nat. Endowment for the Arts grantee, 1976, 82.

WEGMANN, CYNTHIA ANNE, lawyer; b. New Orleans, July 12, 1949; d. Edward F. and Shirley (Caire) W.; m. James A. Babst, Nov. 17, 1973; children: Cynthia Morgan, James A. Jr. BFA, Sophie Newcomb Coll., 1971; LLB, Tulane U., 1973. Bar: La. 1973, U.S. Dist. Ct. (eas., mid. we. dists.) La. 1973, U.S. Dist. Ct. (so., no. dists.) Miss. 1995, U.S. Ct. Appeals (5th cir.) 1974, U.S. Supreme Ct. 1975. Assoc. Leach, Paysse & Baldwin, New Orleans, 1973-77, mem., 1977-84; ptnr. Wegmann & Wegmann, New Orleans, 1984-90; of counsel Terriberry, Carroll & Yancey, 1990—. Alumni editor Tulane Maritime Lawyer, New Orleans. Bd. dirs. Travelers Aid Soc. New Orleans, 1974-85, pres., 1983-85; bd. dirs. Vol. Info. Agy., Jr. League, United Way Greater New Orleans; mem. Jr. League New Orleans; chmn. Second Careers. Mem. ABA, Fed. Bar Assn., Maritime Law Assn. (proctor), Southeastern Admiralty Assn., Average Adjusters Assn. of U.S. Democrat. Roman Catholic. Office: Terriberry Carroll & Yancey 1100 Poydras St Ste 3100 New Orleans LA 70163-3101

WEGMANN, MARY KATHERINE, art director; b. New Orleans, Sept. 18, 1948; d. Joseph A. and Catherine (Lyons) W. BA in English lit., Spring Hill Coll., Mobile, Ala., 1970; MA in English Lit., U. New Orleans, 1972. Asst. mgr., actor, dir. La Mise En Scene Theatre, New Orleans, 1970-72; loan processor First Homestead Savs. and Loan, New Orleans, 1972-74; home improvement contractor Superior Distbrs., New Orleans, 1974-75; adminstr. Freeman-Anacker, Inc., New Orleans, 1975-77; assoc. dir. Contemporary Arts Ctr., New Orleans, 1978-91, acting dir., 1986-88, 88-89; owner MK Arts Co., New Orleans, 1991—; mng. dir. Junebug Prodns., 1993-99; pres., CEO Nat. Performance Network, 2001—. Cons. Junebug Prodn., New Orleans, 1985-93, Alternate Roots, Atlanta, 1986, 92, Cultural Arts Coun. Houston, 1988-89, Seven Stages Performing Arts Ctr., Atlanta, 1989, 91, Nat. Endowment Arts, Washington, 1983-93, Assn. Performing Arts Presenters, 1994, Arts Coun. New Orleans, 1991, 92, La. Philharm. Orch., New Orleans, 1992, Melanie Beene and Assocs., 1991-93, La. Divsn. Arts, 1992—, Arts Coun. New Orleans, 1991—; mem. various panels, juries and adv. coms., 1980—. Bd. dirs. Dog & Pony Theatre Co., New Orleans, 1993—; bd. dirs., treas. Junebug Prodns., 1985—, Nat. Performance Network, 1998—, Contemporary Arts Ctr., 1999—. Office: MK Arts Co PO Box 71914 New Orleans LA 70172-1914 E-mail: mkw@npnweb.org., mkarts@earthlink.net.

WEGNER, GARY ALAN, astronomer; b. Seattle, Dec. 26, 1944; s. Herbert Edward and Melba Jean (Gardner) W.; m. Cynthia Kay Goodfellow, June 25, 1966; children: Josef, Kurt, Christian, Peter-Jürgen, Emma. Student, Wash. State U., Pullman, 1963-65; BS, U. Ariz., 1967; PhD, U. Wash., Seattle, 1971. Fulbright fellow Mount Stromlo Obs., Camberra, A.C.T., 1971-72; departmental demonstrator in astrophysics Oxford U., Eng., 1972-75; sr. sci. rsch. officer South African Astron. Obs., Capetown, Republic of South Africa, 1975-78; Annie J. Cannon fellow U. Del., Newark, 1978-79; asst. prof. Pa. State U., State College, 1979-82; asst. prof. to assoc. prof. physics and astronomy Dartmouth Coll., Hanover, N.H., 1982-88, Margaret Anne and Edward Leede Disting. prof. physics and astronomy, 1988—; dir. Mich.-Dartmouth-MIT Obs., 1991-99. Vis. astronomer Cornell U., 1992; vis. fellow St. Catherine's Coll., Oxford, 2002. Editor: White Dwarfs, 1989; contbr. articles to jours. in field. Keeley fellow Wadham Coll., Oxford, 1992-93, vis. fellow in astrophysics Oxford U., 1992-93; vis. prof. Astron. Inst. Ruhr U. Bochum, Germany, 1993-94; recipient rsch. prize The Alexander von Humboldt Found., Germany, 1993-94, numerous grants NSF, NASA. Mem. Am. Astron. Soc., Internat. Astron. Union. Luthran. Office: Dartmouth Coll Dept Physics & Astronomy Wilder Lab Hanover NH 03755 E-mail: gary.wegner@dartmouth.edu.

WEGNER, JUDITH WELCH, law educator, former dean; b. Hartford, Conn., Feb. 14, 1950; d. John Raymond and Ruth (Thulen) Welch; m. Warren W. Wegner, Oct. 13, 1972. BA with honors, U. Wis., 1972; JD, UCLA, 1976. Bar: Calif. 1976, D.C. 1977, N.C. 1988, U.S. Supreme Ct. 1980, U.S. Ct. Appeals. Law clk. to Judge Warren Ferguson, U.S. Dist. Ct. for So. Dist. Calif., L.A., 1976-77; atty. Office Legal Counsel and Land & Natural Resources Divsn. U.S. Dept. Justice, Washington, 1977-79; spl. asst. to sec. U.S. Dept. Edn., Washington, 1979-80; vis. assoc. prof. U. Iowa Coll. Law, Iowa City, 1981; asst. prof. U. N.C. Sch. Law, Chapel Hill, 1981-84, assoc. prof., 1984-88, prof., 1988—, assoc. dean, 1986-88, dean, 1989-99; sr. scholar Carnegie Found. for Advancement of Tchg., 1999—2001; chmn. faculty U. N.C., 2003—. Spkr. in field. Chief comment editor UCLA Law Rev., 1975-76; contbr. articles to legal publs. Mem. ABA (chmn. planning com. African Law Sch. Initiative 1994, co-chmn. planning com. 1994 mid-yr. deans meeting sect. on legal edn. and admission to bar), N.C. Assn. Women Attys. (Gweneth Davis award 1989), N.C. State Bar Assn., Assn. Am. Law Schs. (mem. exec. com. sect. on law & edn. 1985-88, mem. exec. com. sect. on local govt. law 1989-92, mem. accreditation com. 1986-88, chmn. 1989-91, program chmn. 1992 ann. meeting, program chmn. 1994 ann. meeting, mem. exec. com. 1992-96, pres. 1995), Soc. Am. Law Tchrs., Nat. League Cities (coun.-mentor program 1989-91), Women's Internat. Forum, Order of Coif (nat. exec. com. 1989-91), Phi Beta Kappa. Democrat. Office: U NC Sch Law Van Hecke Wettach Hall Campus Box 3380 Chapel Hill NC 27599-3380 Office Phone: 919-962-1617. Business E-Mail: judith_wegner@unc.edu.

WEH, ALLEN EDWARD, aviation executive; b. Salem, Oreg., Nov. 17, 1942; s. Edward and Harriet Ann (Hicklin) W.; m. Rebecca Ann Roberton, July 5, 1968; children: Deborah Susan, Ashley Elizabeth, Brian Roberton. BS, U. N.Mex., 1966, MA, 1973. Asst. to chief adminstrv. officer Bank N.Mex., Albuquerque, 1973; pres. N.Mex. Airways, Inc., Albuquerque, 1974; dep. dir. N.Mex. Indochina Refugee Program, Santa Fe, 1975-76; dir. pub. affairs UNC Mining & Milling Co., Albuquerque, 1977-79; pres., CEO, CSI Aviation Svcs., Inc., Albuquerque, 1979—. Bd. dirs. N.Mex. Symphony Orgh., Albuquerque Conv. and Visitors Bur., 1982; mem. Albuquerque Police Adv. Bd., 1977-78; co-chmn. fin. com. Rep. Heather Wilson (Rep.-N.Mex.) Re-Election Campaign, 1999—; mem. state fin. com. G.W. Bush for Pres.; co-chmn. N.Mex. Victory, 2000; chmn. N.Mex. Rep. Party, 2004—; mem. nat. adv. bd. U. N.Mex. Anderson Sch. Bus.; elected del. GOP Nat. Conv., 2000; chmn. Nat. Com. for Employer Support of the Guard and Res., 2002-03. Capt. USMC, 1966-71, Vietnam; col. USMCR, 1971-97, Col. USMC, 1990-91, Persian Gulf, 1992-93, Somalia, 2003-04, Iraq. Decorated Silver Star, Legion of Merit, Bronze Star with V device, Purple Heart with two gold stars, Meritorious Svc. medal with gold star, Air medal. Mem. Marine Corps Res. Officers Assn. (life, bd. dirs. 1973, 86), Res. Officers Assn. U.S. (life), SCV (life), N.Mex. Retail Assn. (chmn. 1999-2000). Republican. Episcopalian. Home: 6722 Rio Grande Blvd NW Albuquerque NM 87107-6330 Office: CSI Aviation Svcs Inc 3700 Rio Grande Blvd NW Albuquerque NM 87107-2876

WEHLING, ROBERT LOUIS, retired household products company executive; b. Chgo., Nov. 27, 1938; s. Ralph Joseph and Rita Helen (Casey) W.; m. Carolyn Thierry Harmon, July 5, 1958; children: Susan, Mary, Jennifer, Linda, Karen, Sandra. BA magna cum laude, Denison U., 1960; LHD (hon.), U. Cin., 1998. Brand asst. Procter & Gamble Co., Cin., 1960, 63-64, asst. brand mgr., 1964-66, brand mgr., 1966-70, assoc. advt. mgr., 1970-74, advt. mgr. bar soap and household cleaning products div., 1974-77, div. mgr. gen. advt., 1977-84, assoc. gen. advt. mgr., 1984-87, gen. mktg. svcs. mgr., 1987-88, v.p. mktg. svcs., 1988-90, v.p. pub. affairs, 1990-94, sr. v.p. advt., market rsch. and pub. affairs, 1994-99, sr. v.p. advt., market rsch. and govt. rels., 1994-99, global mktg., market rsch., consumer and market knowledge and govt. rels. officer, 1999—2001. Sr. advisor James B. Hunt, Jr. Inst.; mem. edn. task force Bus. Roundtable, 1990—; mem. Advt. Coun. Bd. (vice chmn. 1994-96, chmn. 1997-98, hon. chair 1998-99); bd. dirs. Nat. Bd. Profl. Tchg. Stds. Pres. March of Dimes, Cin., 1981-84; mem. allocations com. Fine Arts Fund, Cin., 1987—; bd. dirs. Just Say No Internat., 1991-93; co-founder with USA Today, Coalition on Edn. Initiatives, 1991—; mem. Mayor's Commn. on Children, 1992—; vice chmn. Downtown Cin., Inc.; exec. com. Cin. Youth Collaborative; trustee United Way Cin., Ohio Schs. Devel. Corp.; bd. dirs. Edn. Excellence Partnership; participant Gov.'s Edn. Mgmt. Coun.; mem. Hamilton county Family and Children First Coun., 1993-94, Greater Cin. C. of C. (trustee 1994-97, chmn. Blue Chip campaign 1994-97, chmn. 1998); numerous other civic activities. Named Citizen of Yr., City of Wyoming, 1986, One of 200 Greater Cincinnatians, Cin. Bicentennial Commn., 1988, recipient award Nat. Coun. Negro Women, 1989, Field of Svc. Organization award United Way, 1991, Chairman's award Marketing Assn. of Am., 1991, Madison Square Boys and Girls Club award, 1991, Disting. Svc. award Ohio Assn. Colls. for Tchr. Edn., 1993, award Coun. for Acad. Excellence, 1994, U.S. Dept. Edn., 1994, The Seasongood Good Govt. award 1994, Nat. Vol. of Yr. Elaine Whitelaw award March of Dimes, 1994, Ohio Gov.'s award, 1995, Beech Acres Children's Advocate award, 1995, Nat. Govs.' Assn. Disting. Svc. award, 1995, Community Hero Torchbearer for the 1996 Olympic Torch Relay, 1996; Bob Wehling Vol. of Yr. award named in his honor March of Dimes Southwestern Ohio chpt., 1993, numerous others. Mem. Assn. Nat. Advertisers (Robert V. Goldstein award for Disting. Svc. 1993), Advt. Coun. (campaign dir. 1988—), Greater Cin. C. of C. (trustee, exec. com.), Queen City Club, Commonwealth Club, Phi Beta Kappa. Republican. Methodist. Avocations: running, reading, education, children's issues.

WEHMEIER, HELGE H. pharmaceutical executive; b. Goettingen, Germany, 1943; married; 2 children. Grad., Mgmt. Devel. Inst., Lausanne, Switzerland, INSEAD, Fontainbleau, France. Mem. staff Bayer AG, 1966-69, mem. staff Mobay, 1969-74, mgr. mktg. orgn. fibers divsn. for Scandinavia and Britain Leverkusen, Germany, 1974-78, gen. mgr. fibers divsn., 1978-80, mgr. organic chems. divsn., 1981-84, mgr. indsl. photography divsn. Agfa-Gevaert AG, 1984-87, bd. mgrs., 1987-89, pres., CEO Agfa Div. Ridgefield Park, N.J., 1989-91, bd. dirs., exec. com. Bayer USA Inc.; pres., CEO Bayer AG, bd. dirs. Bayer Corp., Ridgefield Park, N.J., 1991—. Bd. dirs. PNC Bank Corp., Pitts.; mem. The Conf. Bd., Trilateral Commn. Bd. dirs. Pitts. Symphony Soc., Bus. Com. for the Arts, Inc., N.Y.; trustee Carnegie Mellon U., Pitts.; officer, mem. exec. cvom. Allegheny Conf. on Cmty. Devel., Pitts. Mem. Chem. Mfrs. Assn. (bd. dirs., exec. com., bd. internat. com.). Office: Bayer Corp 100 Bayer Rd Pittsburgh PA 15205-9741

WEHR, DAVID ALLEN, musician, educator; b. Princeton, N.J., June 22, 1957; s. David A. and Nancy Stone Wehr. MusB, Univ. Kans., Lawrence, Kans., 1977, MusM, 1979. Artist in residence Ouachita Univ., Arkadelphia, Ark., 1994—2002, Hillman Disting. prof. piano, 2001—. Jury mem. Santander Internat. Piano Competition, Santander, Spain, 2002. Musician 1000 concerts in 30 countries, 9 commercial recordinds released by Connoissuer Soc. songs. Recipient Gold Medal, Paloma O'Shea Internat. Piano competition, 1987, Chopin prize, Kosciusko Found., 1975. Mem.: Music Tchrs. Nat. Assn., Nat. Fedr. of Music Clubs (life). Office: Mary Pappert Sch of Music Duquesne Univ 600 Forbes Ave Pittsburgh PA 15282 Office Phone: 412-396-5864. Office Fax: 412-396-5479, Business E-Mail: wehr@duq.edu.

WEHR, WILLIAM JAMES, judge; b. Covington, Ky., July 13, 1950; s. Robert F. and Margaret O. (Schmaeling) W.; m. Nancy Jean Harrison, Dec. 29, 1971; children: Laura Beth, Lindsay Ann. BA, U. Ky., 1972; JD, No. Ky. U., 1976. Bar: Ky. 1976, U.S. Dist. Ct. (ea. dist.) Ky., 1976, U.S. Supreme Ct. 1980. Assoc. Kaufman, Johnson and Blau, Newport, Ky., 1976-77; ptnr. Twehues, Verst & Wehr, Newport, 1978-88; asst. county atty. Campbell County, Newport, 1978-88; judge Campbell County Cir. Ct. Divsn. I, Newport, 1988—; also chief regional cir. judge No. Ky. Region, 1996—. Guest lectr. Chase Coll. Law, 1981-90, adj. faculty, 1991—. Bd. dirs. Sr. Citizens No. Ky., Inc., Covington, 1980-87, pres., 1984-85; bd. dirs. Hosea House Soup Kitchen, 1992—. Served with USCGR, 1968-74. Recipient Disting. Prosecutor award Citizens for Decency Through Law, Inc., 1981. Mem.: No. Ky. Bar Assn. (pres. 1984), Ky. Bar Assn. (ho. of dels. 1985—88), Elks. Roman Catholic. Office: Campbell County Courthouse Newport KY 41071

WEHRENBERG, WILLIAM BUSSE, agricultural studies educator; m. Jane E. Kurhajec, May, 1973. BS in Chemistry, Valparaiso (Ind.) U., 1973; MS in Biol. Sci., Purdue U., Ft. Wayne, Ind., 1975; PhD in Endocrinology-Reproductive Phys., U. Wis., 1978. Postdoctoral rsch. fellow Internat. Inst. for Study Human Reprodn., Columbia U., N.Y.C., 1978-80; asst. prof. Labs. for Neuroendocrinology, Salk Inst., San Diego, 1980 82, Andrew W. Mellon asst. prof., 1982-85; assoc. prof. dept. health scis. U. Wis., Milw., 1985-87, chmn. dept. health scis., 1988-89, prof., 1987-96, assoc. dean for rsch. Sch. Allied Health Professions, 1989-96; affiliate scientist Wis. Regional Primate Rsch. Ctr., U. Wis., Madison, 1986-96; prof. dept. biol. sci., dean Coll. Agr., Forestry, Life Sci. Clemson (S.C.) U., 1996—. Vis. prof. dept. medicine U. Geneva, Switzerland, 1986, 91; adj. prof. dept. physiology Med. Coll. Wis., Milw., 1988-96. Editl. bd. Trends in Endocrinology and Metabolism, 1993—, Growth, Devel. and Aging, 1988—, Endocrinology, 1987-90, 93—, Domestic Animal Endocrinology, 1994—, Neuroendocrinology, 1995—, Advances in Life scis.-Exptl. and Clin. Endocrinology 1995—; reviewer for over 20 sci. jours. annually; contbr. over 150 articles to profl. jours. Sec. Watertower Landmark trust, Milw., 1988-94; mem. coun. Lake Park Luth. Ch., Milw., 1990-91; block watch capt. Milw. Police Dept. Recipient Andrew W. Mellon Found. award, 1982, U. Wis.-Milw. Found./Grad. Sch. Rsch. award, 1987, Rsch. Career Devel. award NIH, 1988, Rsch. Incentive award U. Wis.-Milw., 1989, Award for Tchg. Excellence, U. Wis.-Milw. Alumni Assn., 1989, Valparaiso U. Disting. Alumni award, 1992; Fulbright Rsch. scholar, U. Bordeaux, France, 1991; recipient numerous grants from The Upjohn Co., Eli Lilly & Co., Genentech, Inc., Monsanto Agrl. Co., Medialanum Farmaceutici, Milan, Italy, Europeptides, Inc., Paris, Intervet Am., Inc., U. Wis.-Milw., Wis. Dept. Agr., NIH, NIDDK, USDA. Mem. AAAS, Internat. Soc. Neuroendocrinology, Am. Assn. for Lab. Animal Sci., Wis. Endocrine Soc., Endocrine Soc., Soc. for Study of reprodn., Internat. Fur Animal Sci. Assn. (alt. mem. bd. dirs.), Wis. Assn. Biomed. Rsch. and Edn. (treas., mem. bd. dirs.), Wis. Soc. for Neursci. (organizing com. for regional midwest meeting), Sigma Xi, Phi Kappa Phi. Office: Clemson Univ Coll Agr Forestry Life Sci PO Box 340303 Clemson SC 29634-0001

WEHRER, CHARLES SIECKE, business and education educator; b. Norfolk, Nebr., July 13, 1914; s. Charles C. and Ella (Augusta) W.; m. May Winther Hansen, Aug. 21, 1982 (dec. Oct. 27, 1991). BA, Nebr. State Tchrs. Coll., 1940; MA in Sch. Adminstrn., postgrad., U. Nebr., 1950, Columbia U., 1950, U. So. Calif., 1954-55; PhD without dissertation, Ohio State U., 1961; LHD (hon.), Sioux Empire Coll., 1967. Asst. commandant, basketball coach Black-Foxe Mil. Inst., Hollywood, Calif., 1945-46; coach, supt. local schs. Wood Lake, Nebr., 1947-49; prin. Scottsbluff (Nebr.) Jr. High Sch., 1950-51; grad. asst. in edn. U. Nebr., 1949-50, U. So. Calif., 1954-55; grad. asst. prof. elem. edn. Ohio State U., 1960; tchr. pub. schs. Paramount, Calif., 1953-54; tchr. Excelsior Adult Sch., Norwalk, Calif., 1953-57; supt. local schs. Shandon, Calif., 1956-57; assoc. prof. edn., supr. student teaching Ohio No. U., Ada, 1958-60; assoc. prof., supr. elem. student teaching Capital U., Columbus, Ohio, 1961-62; prin. Norwalk Iowa Elem. Jr. High Sch., 1962-63; prof. edn., dir. student affairs, asst. to pres. Grand View Coll., Des Moines, 1962-64; with depts. youth, TV, ednl. programming City of Des Moines, 1965; cons. program Iowa Civil Def./Health Dept., 1966; prof. edn. and psychology S.W. Community Coll., Creston, Iowa, 1967; acad. dean Sioux Empire Coll., Hawarden, Iowa, 1967-68; chmn. depts. edn., psychology, dir. tchr. edn. J.F. Kennedy Coll., Wahoo, Nebr., 1970-71; prodr., emcee youth radio/TV program Let's Listen to Youth, Lincoln, Nebr., 1971, Des Moines, Sioux City, Iowa, 1952-74, L.A., Columbus, Ohio, 1952-74; prof. edn. Concordia Coll., Seward, Nebr., 1973; tng. coord., dir. spl. tng. programs for mgmt. State of Nebr., 1974-75; prof. bus. Metro Tech., Omaha, 1976-82; prof. mgmt. tng. Bus. Devel. Ctr. U. Nebr., Omaha, 1976-82; prof. bus. Nebr. State Coll., Wayne, 1982-88, ret.; pres. Bus. Mgmt. Cons. Co., Wisner, Nebr., 1982-90. Lectr. in field. Author: Keep in Touch, My Students, 1966; contbr. articles to profl. jours. Phys. dir. YMCA, Norfolk, 1934-36, McCook, Nebr., 1937-38, L.A. Downtown Y, 1940-41; counselor, adv. Nebr. Boys' State, 1949-50; Nebr. del. White House Conf. on Children and Youth, 1950; chmn. Nebr. Com. on Juvenile Delinquency; mem. Gov.'s Com. on Youth, Calif., Nebr.; spl. youth cons. radio program Art Linkletter House Party, Calif., 1952; dir. dept. guest rels. NBC, Hollywood, Calif., 1952; dir. spl. project Iowa Dept. Health, 1965-66; contbr. to sub-com. on poverty-youth programs U.S. Congress, 1964-65; chmn. youth sect. Iowa Congress Parents & Tchrs., 1966-67; lay min. Protestant Chs., 1967—, past ch. official First Cong. United Ch. of Christ, Norfolk, Elkhorn Valley Hist. Soc. Capt. USAAF, 1941-45. Decorated Bronze Star, Soldiers medal, 3 Battle Stars, 15th AF Unit citation, Pres. Unit citation, others; recipient spl. awards/commendations for radio/TV programs State PTA and other civic and youth groups, 1960-75, numerous awards for tchg. and youth work; named Outstanding Sch. Adminstr. in Nebr. dept. sch. adminstrn. U. Nebr., Nebr. Dept. Edn., 1948-50; named to Hall of Honor, Nebr. Softball Assn., 1993, Norfolk H.S. Students honor as Sr. Citizens of Yr., 1995, Spl. Proclamation for Edn. and Youth Svcs. State of Nebr., 1994, Outstanding Noted Alumni award U. Nebr. Tchrs. Coll., 1998, Alumni Football Quarterback honor, 1998; named to Norfolk H.S. Close Up Club Unanimous Spl. Honor Selection to Wall of Fame. Mem. NEA (Spl. Commendation for tchr. edn. programs), AAUP, Am. Assn. Ret. Persons (pres. Norfolk chpt. 1997-98, Nebr. Sr. Citizen Spl. Commendation 1980-81), Assn. for Higher Edn., Nat. Assn. Sch. Adminstrs., Nat. Soc. for Study of Edn., Internat. Platform Assn. (spl. spkr. conv. 1970, spl. honors for Vets. Day, Meml. Day spkr. for 52 yrs.), Am. Legion, VFW (spl. commendation for helping veterans, sr. citizens and youth 1997), SCORE, Lions (bd. dirs., past pres.), Kiwanis (past pres.), Rotary (Norfolk Noon Rotary Club Cmty. Svc. award, Pres.'s award 1998), Delta Sigma, Phi Delta Kappa (Spl. Recognition award 1992), Sigma Tau Delta (past pres.). Home: 600 E Benjamin Ave Norfolk NE 68701-0830 *We are living in a dangerous world of unrest, a difficult time for all of us to adjust to the emotional and mental problems of this changing environmental world. If we can be of help to those who are in need of a friendly act then let us do our best to be of help and service to young and old alike as we may not pass this way again.*

WEHRING, BERNARD WILLIAM, nuclear engineering educator; b. Monroe, Mich, Aug. 3, 1937; s. Bernard Albert and Alma Christina (Graf) W.; m. Margaret Mary Robinson, Sept. 5, 1959; children: Mary Ann, James, Susan, Barbara. BSE in Physics, BSE. in Math, U. Mich., 1959; MS in Physics, U. Ill., 1961, PhD in Nuclear Engring, 1966. Asst. prof. nuc. engring. U. Ill., Urbana, 1966-70, assoc. prof., 1970-77, prof., 1977-84, asst. dean engring., 1981-82; prof. nuc. engring. N.C. State U., Raleigh, 1984-89; dir. nuc. reactor program NC State U., Raleigh, 1984-89; prof. mech. engring. U. Tex., Austin, 1989-2000, dir. Nuc. Engring. Tchg. Lab., 1989-2000; adj. prof. nuc. engring. NC State U., Raleigh, 2000—. Cons. Argonne and Los Alamos nat. labs.; mem. crosssect. evaluation working group Brookhaven Nat. Lab. Contbr. sects. to books, articles to profl. publs. AEC fellow, 1963-65; NSF grantee, 1968— Fellow Am. Nuc. Soc.; mem. Am. Nuclear Soc. (standards com.), Am. Phys. Soc. Achievements include contributing in the generation of basic nuc. data and develop. of new instruments and exptl. techniques. Home: 516 Westbrook Dr Raleigh NC 27615-7321 E-mail: bwwehrin@eos.ncsu.edu.

WEHRLE, HENRY BERNARD, III, electrical supply company executive; CEO McJunkin, Charleston, W.Va. Office: McJunkin 835 Hillcrest Dr E Charleston WV 25311-1627

WEHRLE, LEROY SNYDER, economist, educator; b. St. Louis, Feb. 5, 1932; s. Fred Joseph and Eleanor (Snyder) W.; m. JoAnn Griffith, Aug. 29, 1959; children— Chandra Lee, Lon Joseph. BS, Washington U., St. Louis, 1953; MA in Econs, Yale, 1956, PhD with honors, 1959. Asst. instr. Yale, 1958-59; with econ. sect. AID mission to Laos, 1960-61; sr. staff economist President's Council Econ. Advisers, 1961-62; spl. econ. adviser to U.S. Ambassador Unger, Vientianc, 1962; dep. dir. AID mission to Laos, 1963-64; asst. dir. AID mission, also econ. counsellor to U.S. ambassador, Saigon, 1964-67; asso. dir. AID Mission, Saigon, 1964-67; dept. asst. adminstr. Vietnam, AID, Dept. State, 1967-68; univ. fellow Harvard, 1968-69; sr. fellow Brookings Instn., 1969-70; dir. Ill. Inst. for Social Policy, Springfield, 1970-72; aide to Lt. Gov. Paul Simon, 1972; prof. economics Sangamon State U., 1972-88; founding ptnr., chief exec. officer Health Econs. and Mkt. Analysis Inc., Springfield, 1987-94; pres. Healthcare Cost Analysis, Inc., 1994—. Chmn. bd. Tie Collar, Ltd. Mem. spl. study group Alliance Progress, 1962; mem. Rockefeller Latin Am. Mission, 1969; chmn. study team world food and nutrition study Nat. Acad. Sci., 1976-77. Served with AUS, 1953-55. Recipient William A. Jump meml. award, 1966 Home and Office: 2001 S Bates Ave Springfield IL 62704-3304 E-mail: wehrle@springnet1.com.

WEHRWEIN, AUSTIN CARL, newspaper reporter, editor, writer; b. Austin, Tex., Jan. 12, 1916; s. George S. and Anna (Ruby) W.; m. Judith Oakes, 1950; children: Sven Austin, Paul, Peter, Joanna Judith. AB, U. Wis., 1937; LL.B., Columbia U., 1940; student, London Sch. Econs., 1948. Reporter Washington Bur., UP, 1941-43, 46-48; information specialist E.C.A., London, Copenhagen, Oslo, Stockholm, 1948-51; financial writer Milw. Jour., 1951-53; staff corr. Time, Inc., Chgo., 1953-55; reporter Chgo. Sun-Times, 1955-56, fin. editor, 1956-57; chief Chgo. bur. N.Y. Times, 1957-66; editorial writer Mpls. Star, 1966-82. Editor The Observer, 1984-87. Served with USAAF, 1943-45; mem. staff Stars and Stripes 1945-46, Shanghai, China. Recipient Pulitzer prize for internat. reporting, 1953; Disting. Journalism award U. Wis., 1963; cert. of merit ABA Gavel competition, 1968, 80; Gavel award, 1969, 71 Home and Office: 2309 Carter Ave Saint Paul MN 55108-1640

WEI, BENJAMIN MIN, engineering educator; b. Hebei, China, Aug. 11, 1930; s. Fu Shun and Yuan Qing (Zhang) W.; m. Diana Yun Dee; 1 child: Victor Mark. BSME, Chung Cheng Inst. Tech., 1953; MSME, Concordia U., 1970; PhD, Pa. State U., 1981. Mech. engr. Ordnance Corps Arsenal, Taipei, Taiwan, 1953-59; tchr. Wenshan High Sch., Taipei, 1960-61; teaching asst. New Brunswick (Can.) U., 1962-64; supr. Domtar Constrn. Materials Co., Can., 1964-66; computer programmer McGill U., Can., 1966-67, Montreal (Can.) U., 1967 68; tchr Pierrefond Comprehensive High sch., Que., 1970-73; prof. Norfolk (Va.) State U., 1974—. Hon. prof., cons. Taiyuan U. Polytech. Contbr. articles to profl. jours. Mem. Statistical Quality Control of China. Home: 1152 Janaf Pl Norfolk VA 23502-2631

WEI, FONG, nephrologist; b. Shanghai, May 2, 1941; came to U.S., 1941; s. Tseh Heen and Waling (Chung) W.; m. Theodora Mary Zopko, July 16, 1966; children: Christopher, Alexander. BA, Yale U., 1963; MD, Tufts U., 1967. Diplomate Am. Bd. Internal Medicine, Am. Bd. Nephrology; specialist in clin. hypertension. Intern Boston City Hosp., 1967-68, resident, 1968-69, Bronx (N.Y.) Mcpl., 1969-70; fellow in nephrology U. N.C., Chapel Hill, 1970-72; pvt. practice Princeton, N.J., 1974—. Clin. assoc. prof. Robert Wood Johnson Med. Sch., New Brunswick, N.J., 1975—; pres. med. staff Med. Ctr. Princeton, 1981-82; prin. investigator Bristol Myers Squibb, Princeton, 1984—, Merck and Co., Princeton, 1988—; cons. Princeton U., 1990—; pres. Princeton Med. Group, 1982—. Med. advisor Princeton Regional Homemakers Assn., 1975—. Fellow ACP; mem. Am. Soc. Nephrology, Internat. Soc. Nephrology, Am. Soc. Hypertension. Office: Princeton Med Group 419 N Harrison St Princeton NJ 08540-3521

WEI, JAMES, chemical engineering educator, academic dean; b. Macao, China, Aug. 14, 1930; came to U.S., 1949, naturalized, 1960; s. Hsiang-chen and Nuen (Kwok) W.; m. Virginia Hong, Nov. 4, 1956; children: Alexander, Christina, Natasha, Randolph (dec.). BS in Chem. Engring, Ga. Inst. Tech., 1952; MS, MIT, 1954, ScD, 1955; grad., Advanced Mgmt. Program Harvard, 1969. From rsch. engr. to rsch. assoc. Mobil Oil, Paulsboro, NJ, 1956-62, sr. scientist Princeton, NJ, 1963-68, mgr. corp. planning N.Y.C., 1969-70; Allan P. Colburn prof. U. Del., Newark, 1971-77; Sherman Fairchild distinguished scholar Calif. Inst. Tech., 1977; Warren K. Lewis prof. MIT, Cambridge, 1977-91, head dept. chem. engring., 1977-88; Pomeroy and Betty Smith prof. chem. engring. Princeton (N.J.) U., 1991—, dean Sch. Engring. and Applied Sci., 1991—2002. Vis. prof. Princeton, 1962-63, Calif. Inst. Tech., 1965; cons. Mobil Oil Corp.; cons. on motor vehicle emissions Nat. Acad. Sci., 1972-74, 79-80; mem. sci. adv. bd. EPA, 1976-79; mem. Presdl. Pvt. Sector Survey Task Force on Dept. Energy, 1982-83 Bd. editors Chem. Tech, 1971-80, Chem. Engring. Communications, 1972—; cons. editor chem. engring. series, McGraw-Hill, 1964—; editor-in-chief: Advances in Chemical Engineering, 1980; Contbr. papers, monographs to profl. lit., The Structure of Chemical Processing Industries, 1979. Trustee Am. U. Beirut, 1998—, Smith Coll., 1999—. Recipient Am. Acad. Achievement Golden Plate award, 1966. Mem. AIChE (dir. 1970-72, Inst. lectr. 1968, Profl. Progress award 1970, Walker award 1980, Lewis award 1985, v.p. 1987, pres. 1988, Founders award 1990), Am. Chem. Soc. (award in petroleum chemistry 1966), Nat. Acad. Engring. (nominating com. 1981, 96, peer com. 1980-82, membership com. 1983-85, Draper award com. 1995 97, chair chem. engring. sect. 1998-99), AAAS, Am. Acad. Arts and Scis., Academica Sinica of Taiwan, Sigma Xi. Home: 571 Lake Dr Princeton NJ 08540 Office: Princeton U Engring Quadrangle Princeton NJ 08544-5263 E-mail: jameswei@princeton.edu.

WEI, JOHN HUA-FANG, engineering executive; b. Shanghai, Oct. 11, 1963; s. Keming and Quanbao Tang W.; 1 child, John Tiger. BS, Shanghai Jiao Tong U., 1985; MS, Stanford U., 1989; PhD, Dartmouth Coll., 1992. CAD/CAM engr. Shanghai Rsch. Inst. Tool and Die Tech., 1985-87; assoc. MIT, Cambridge, 1992-93; tech. staff Sharp Microelectronics Tech. Inc., Camas, Wash., 1994; design engr. LSI Logic Corp., Milpitas, Calif., 1994-97; tech. staff Equator Techs. Inc., Campbell, Calif., 1997-98; prin. engr. NeoMagic Corp., Santa Clara, Calif., 1998-99; mgr. IC design and silicon architect PMC-Sierra, Inc., Santa Clara, Calif., 1999—. Contbr. articles to profl. jours. Mem. IEEE, Sigma Xi. Achievements include 4 patents in field. E-mail: hfwei@alumni.stanford.org.

WEI, QINGYI, cancer research educator; b. Nanjing, Jiangsu, China, Apr. 30, 1956; parents Yongxing Wei and Huifeng; m. Jingrong Yan, Oct. 1, 1983; children: Michael Yang, Herbie Hao. MD, Nanjing Med. Coll., 1983; MS, Chinese Acad. Preventive Med., Beijing, 1986; PhD, Johns Hopkins U., 1993. Rsch. assoc. Chinese Acad. Preventive Medicine, Beijing, 1986-87, Johns Hopkins U. Sch. Hygiene and Pub. Health, Balt., 1992-93; asst. prof. U. Tex. M.D. Anderson Cancer Ctr., Houston, 1993-98, assoc. prof., 1998—2003, prof., 2003—. Contbr. rsch. articles to profl. jours. Grantee, NIH, 1996—97, 2000—01, 2003. Avocations: reading, music, ping pong/table tennis.

WEI, YING, chemist; b. Harbin, China, Aug. 29, 1952; d. Wen-Jia Wei and Su-Zhen Xu; m. Jian-Ming Jiang, Jan. 28, 1981 (div. Feb. 1997); 1 child, Mike Jiang. BS in Chemistry, Hei Long Jiang U., China, 1982; MS, Rennes (France) I U., 1984, PhD, 1986. Postdoc. fellow A&M U., College Station, Tex., 1989—90, Lamar U., Beaumont, Tex., 1990—91; IT corp. lab. supr. IT Corp., Cosby, Tex., 1991—95; city lab. mgr. City of Houston/Water Prodn., 1996—. Contbr. articles to profl. jour. Mem.: Am. Water Works Assn. Home: 3414 Almond Creek Dr Houston TX 77059 Office: City of Houston 2300 Federal Rd Houston TX 77015 E-mail: ying.wei@cityofhouston.net.

WEIANT, ELIZABETH ABBOTT, retired biology educator; b. New Britain, Conn., July 4, 1913; d. William Armstrong and Flora (Abbott) W. BS, MS, Tufts U., 1943; MA, Radcliffe Coll., 1952; EdD, Boston U., 1970. Instr. biology Tufts Coll., Medford, Mass., 1943-56, asst. prof., 1957-61; asst. prof. biology Simmons Coll., Boston, 1961-71, assoc. prof., 1972-79, chmn. dept., 1977-79, ret., 1979; corr. Evening Citizen, Laconia, N.H., 1987-98, Franklin-Tilton Telegram, Franklin, N.H., 1990-2000. Rschr. OSRD, USPHS, NSF, 1943-61; sr. rsch. fellow Max-Planck Inst., Seewiesen, Fed. Republic Germany, 1958; physiologist for product validation Cordis Corp., Miami, Fla., 1970 Contbr. articles to profl. jours. Active Hist. Dist. Commn., Sanbornton, N.H., 1979-83; sec., Sanbornton Conservation Commn., 1979-83, Trustees of Trust Fund, Sanbornton, 1985-96; bd. dirs., sec. N.H. affiliate Am. Heart Assn., Manchester, 1981-85; bd. dirs., com. mem. Franklin (N.H.) Regional Hosp., 1984-91; pres. Sanbornton Hist. Soc., 1980-82; publicity chmn. Friends N.H. Music Festival; alumna trustee Tufts U., 1974-81. Recipient Disting. Svc. award Tufts U., 1970, Tower award Westbrook Coll., Portland, Maine, 1974, Woman of Yr. award Tilton-Northfield Bus. and Profl. Women, 1980, Heart of Gold award Am. Heart Assn., 1986, award for Pub. Svc. Belknap County Pomona Grange, 1990, Gov.'s Outstanding Vol. award, 1992. Mem.: Am. Inst. Biol. Scis., Grange, Sigma Xi (sec. Tufts U. chpt. 1947—59). Republican. Home: PO Box 11 Sanbornton NH 03269-0011

WEIBEL, CHARLES ALEXANDER, mathematician; b. Terre Haute, Ind., Oct. 28, 1950; s. Charles G. and Evelyn S. (Black) W.; m. Laurel A. Van Leer, June 28, 1986; children: Chad, Aubrey. BS, BA, U. Mich., 1972; SM, U. Chgo., 1973, PhD, 1977. Mem. Inst. Advanced Study, Princeton, NJ, 1977—78, 1985—86, 1999—2000; asst. prof. U. Pa., Phila., 1978-80, Rutgers U., New Brunswick, NJ, 1980-83, assoc. prof., 1983-89, prof. math., 1989—, mem. faculty coun., 2001—, grad. program dir., 2003—. Editor: Proceedings Ibadan Conf., 1987, K-theory, 2000—, Homology, Homology Applications, 1997—; editor Jour. Pure and Applied Algebra, 1983-89, mng. editor, 1990—; contbr. rsch. articles to numerous publs. Mem. Am. Math. Soc. Avocation: athletics. Office: Rutgers U Dept Math New Brunswick NJ 08903 Home: 3 Arbit Rd East Brunswick NJ 08816

WEICHER, JOHN CHARLES, federal agency administrator; b. Chgo., Mar. 8, 1938; s. John Jr. and Ruth Agnes (Waits) W.; m. Alice Jean Landt, Sept. 30, 1972; children: John Victor, Stephany Jean Ruth. AB, U. Mich., 1959; PhD, U. Chgo., 1968. Acting asst. prof. U. Calif., Irvine, 1965-67; assoc. and asst. prof. econs. Ohio State U., Columbus, 1967-77; with div. policy rsch. OEO, Washington, 1972-73; dir. div. econ. policy HUD, Washington, 1973-74, dep. asst. sec. econ. affairs, 1975-77; dir. econs. and fin. markets program Urban Inst., Washington, 1977-81; F.K. Weyerhaeuser scholar in pub. policy Am. Enterprise Inst, Washington, 1981-87; assoc. dir. econ. policy Office of Mgmt. and Budget, Washington, 1987-89; dir. urban polity studies Hudson Inst., Washington, 1993—2001; asst. sec. policy devel. and rsch. HUD, Washington, 1989—93, asst. sec. housing, commr. FHA, 2001—. Author: Urban Renewal: Federal Program for Local Problems, 1972, Housing: Federal Policies and Programs, 1980, Maintaining the Safety Net, 1984; contbr. articles to profl. jours. Presbyterian. Avocation: sports. Office: US Dept HUD Office of Housing & Fed Housing Admin 451 7th St SW Washington DC 20410-9000

WEICHSELBAUM, RALPH R. oncologist chairman; BS, U. Wis., 1967; MD, U. Ill., Chgo., 1971. Intern Alameda County Hosp., Oakland, Calif., 1971-72; resident in radiation therapy Harvard Med. Sch., Boston, 1972-75; assoc. prof. radiation therapy Harvard Med. Ctr., Boston, 1980-84; assoc. prof. dept. cancer biology Harvard Sch. Public Health, Boston, 1983-84; prof., chmn. dept. radiation and cellular omcology Pritzker Sch. Medicine U. Chgo., 1984—, Harold H. Hines Jr. prof., chmn., 1990; head Michael Reese/U. Chgo. Ctr. Radiation Therapy, 1984—. Contbr. articles to profl. jours. Office: Ctr for Radiation Therapy Pritzker Sch of Medicine 5841 S Maryland Ave Chicago IL 60637-1463

WEICK, CYNTHIA WAGNER, business educator; b. Lincoln, Nebr., Jan. 29, 1957; d. Richard and Gloria Jean (Larsen) W. PhD, The Wharton Sch. U. of Pa, Phila., PA, 1982—86; MS, The Ohio State U., Columbus, OH, 1979—80, BS, 1975—79. Prof. of bus. adminstrn. U. of the Pacific, Stockton, Calif., 1990—; corp. planner Pioneer Hi-Bred, Internat., Des Moines, Iowa, 1987—90; cons. United Nat. Devel. Program, Manhattan, NY, 1984—85; rsch. scientist Battelle Columbus Laboratories, Columbus, Ohio, 1980—82. Contbr. articles on mgmt. of tech. to profl. jours. Dean's fellow Wharton Sch., U. Pa., 1983-84. Mem. AAAS. Avocations: art, philosophy, kayaking. Office: Univ of the Pacific 3601 Pacific Avenue Stockton CA 95211 Office Phone: 209-946-2631. Personal E-mail: cwagner@uop.edu. E-mail: cwagner@uop.edu.

WEIDA, LEWIS DIXON, marketing analyst, consultant; b. Moran, Ind., Apr. 23, 1924; s. Charles Ray and Luella Mildred (Dixon) W.; student Kenyon Coll., 1943, Purdue U., 1946; B.S., Ind. U., 1948; M.S., Columbia U., 1950. Mgr. statis. analysis unit Gen. Motors Acceptance Corp., N.Y.C., 1949-55; asst. to exec. v.p. Am. Express Co., 1955-82. Served with USAAF, 1943-46; PTO. Mem. Internat. Platform Assn. Democrat. Club: Masons. Home: 25 Tudor City Pl New York NY 10017-6819

WEIDEMANN, CELIA JEAN, social scientist, management consultant, financial consultant; b. Denver, Dec. 6, 1942; d. John Clement and Hazel (Van Tuyl) Kirlin; m. Wesley Clark Weidemann, July 1, 1972; 1 child, Stephanie Jean. BS, Iowa State U., 1964; MS, U. Wis., Madison, 1970, PhD, 1973; post grad., U. So. Calif., 1983. Advisor UN FAO, Ibadan, Nigeria, 1973—77; ind. rschr. Asia and Near East, 1977—78; program coord., asst. prof., rsch. assoc. U. Wis., Madison, Wis., 1979—81; chief inst. and human resources US AID, Washington, 1982—85; team leader, cons. Sumatra, Indonesia, 1984; dir. fed. econ. program Midwest Rsch. Inst., Washington, 1985—86; founder, pres. emeritus Weidemann Assoc., Arlington, Va., 1986—2000; pres. Weidemann Found., Arlington, Va., 2000—. Cons. U.S. Congress, Aspen Inst., Ford Found., World Bank, Egypt, Nigeria, Gambia, Pakistan, Indonesia, AID, Thailand, Jamaica, Panama, Philippines, Sierra Leone, Kenya, Jordon, Poland, India, Egypt, Russia, Finnish Internat. Devel. Agy., Namibia, pvt. client Estonia, Lativa, Russia, Japan, Internat. Ctr. Rsch. on Women, Zaire, UN FAO, Ghana, Internat. Statis. Inst., The Netherlands, Global Exch., 1986-87, Asian Devel. Bank, Mongolia, Nepal, Vietnam, Bangladesh, Indonesia, Philippines; mem. bd. visitors Sch. Human Ecology, U. Wis., 2002—; peer reviewer NRC, NAS. Author: (book) Planning Home Economics Curriculum for Social and Econ. Develop., Agrl. Ext. for Women Farmers in Africa, 1990, Fin. Services for Women, 1992, Egyptian Women and Micro.: The Invisible Entrepreneurs, 1992, Small Enterprise Development in Poland: Does Gender Matter?, 1994, Micro. and Gender in India, 1995, Supporting Women's Livelihoods: Micro Fin. That Works for the Majority, 2002; contbr. chapters to books and articles to profl. journals. Am. Home Econ. Assn. Fellow, 1969-73; grantee Ford Found., 1987-89. Mem. Soc. Internat. Devel., Am. Sociol. Assn., Assn. for Women in Devel. (pres. 1989, founder, bd. dirs.), Women in Devel. (steering com.), Coalition for Women's Econ. Devel. and Global Equality, Internat. Devel. Conf. (bd. dirs., exec. com.), Internat. Platform Assn., Pi Lambda Theta, Omicron Nu. Avocations: mountain trekking, piano and pipe organ, canoeing, photography, poetry. Office: Weidemann Assoc. Inc 933 N Kenmore St Ste 405 Arlington VA 22201-2236 Office Phone: 703-599-5906. E-mail: jweidemann@aol.com.

WEIDEMANN, JULIA CLARK, retired principal, educator; b. Batavia, N.Y., May 21, 1937; d. Edward Thomas and Grace Eloise (Kenna) Clark; m. Rudolph John Weidemann, July 9, 1960 (dec.); 1 child, Michael John (dec.). BA in English, Daemen Coll., 1958; MS in Edn., SUNY, Buffalo, 1961, MEd in Reading Edn., 1973, postgrad, 1985-86. Cert. sch. adminstr., supr. Tchr Buffalo Pub. Schs., 1958-61, 66-67; remedial reading tchr. West Seneca (N.Y.) Cen. Sch. Dist., 1972-79, coord. chpt. I reading program, 1974-79, reading coord., 1980-87; prin. Parkdale Elem. Sch. East Aurora (N.Y.) Union Free Sch., 1987—. Adj. prof. edn. Canisius Coll., Medaille Coll., Daemen Coll.; tchr. cons. Scott Foresman Lang. Arts Textbooks; sch. support team mem. N.Y. State Edn. Dept.; chmn. elem. com. staff devel. West Seneca Ctrl. Sch., 1985-87; mem. adv. coun. Medaille Coll.; chmn. various confs.; lectr. in field. Author numerous poems; invited poet Women's Impact Gallery, Buffalo, N.Y., 1996, 97. Mem. West Seneca Dist. Computer Adv. Com., 1980-87, East Aurora Hist. Soc., 1990—; mem. cmty. adv. coun. SUNY, Buffalo, 1994—, Women's Health Initiative, 1994-96; mem. Women's Action Coalition of Buffalo, 1994; pres. Roycroft Wordsmiths; mem. steering com. Kids Voting N.Y., 1996-99. Scholar Rosary Hill Coll., 1954, N.Y. State Regents, 1954; recipient Reading Award Niagara Frontier Reading Coun., 1986. Mem. AAUW (life, pres. Buffalo br. 1994-95, exec. bd. dirs., named gift ednl. found., state bd. dirs. equity in edn. com. 1995—), Assn. Compensatory Edn. (pres. 1984-85, exec. bd. Region VI 1983-87, conf. chmn. Region VI 1985-87), Internat. Reading Assn. (acting chmn. 3d ea. regional reading conf. 1980), Niagara Frontier Reading Assn. (pres. 1979-80, fin. com. chmn., bd. dirs. 1973—), Daemen Coll. Alumni Assn. (bd. govs. 1987, chmn. alumni reunion weekend, chmn. sr. reception, Disting. Alumna 1989), Assn. Supervision and Devel., Assn. Tchr. Educators, Delta Kappa Gamma (pres., Ruth Fraser scholar 1986), Beta Zeta (pres.), Phi Delta Kappa (Buffalo-South chpt. 1989). Democrat. Roman Catholic. Home: 21 Nye Hill Rd East Aurora NY 14052-2651

WEIDEMEYER, CARLETON LLOYD, lawyer; b. Hebbville, Md., June 12, 1933; BA in Polit. Sci., U. Md., 1958; JD, Stetson U., 1961. Bar: Fla. 1961, D.C. 1971, U.S. Dist. Ct. (mid. dist.) Fla. 1963, U.S. Ct. Appeals (5th cir.) 1967, U.S. Ct. Appeals (D.C. cir.) 1976, U.S. Supreme Ct. 1966, U.S. Ct. Appeals (11th cir.) 1982. Rsch. asst. Fla. 2d Dist. Ct. Appeals, 1961-65; ptnr. Kalle and Weidemeyer, St. Petersburg, Fla., 1965-68; asst. pub. defender 6th Jud. Cir., Fla., 1966-69, 81-83; ptnr. Wightman, Weidemeyer, Jones, Turnbull and Cobb, Clearwater, Fla., 1968-82; pres. Carleton L. Weidemeyer, P.A. Law Office, 1982—; pres. So. Mcpl. Corp., 1997—. Guest lectr. Stetson U., 1978—80; lectr. estate planning seminars; bd. dirs. Watson Ctr. for the Blind, 1998—; trustee Tampa Bay Rsch. Inst., 2000—. Author: (handbook) Arbitration of Entertainment Claims, Baltimore County's Second District, The Emerging Thirties, 1990, Area History, Baltimore County, 1990, History of Musicians' Association of Clearwater, Local 729, AFM, 1999; editor Ad Lib mag., 1978-81; contbr. numerous articles to profl. jours. and geneal. pubs.; performer This Is Your Navy Radio Show, Memphis, 1951-52; leader Polka Dots, The Jazz Notes, 1976—; mem. St. Paul Ch. Orch., Fla. Hist. Soc., 1973—, Md. Hist. Soc., 1990—, Pinellas County Estate Planning Assn., 1997—; performer Clearwater Jazz Holiday, 1980, 81, co-chmn., 1981. Bd. advisors Musician Ins. Trust; trustee Francis G. Prasse Meml. Scholarship Trust, 1984—; mem. planned giving com. Upper Pinellas Assn. Retarded Citizens, 1996-2001; bd. trustees Tampa Bay Rsch. Inst., 2001—; adv. com. Fla. Sheriff Youth Ranches, 1997—2001; bd. dirs. Pinellas Ctr. for Visually Impaired, 1999-2000; bd. dirs. Watson Ctr. for the Blind, 2000—. Served with USN, 1951-54. Recipient Pres.'s award, Upper Pinellas Assn. Retarded Citizens, 1998, Patron of Jazz award, Suncoast Classic Jazz Soc., Inc., 2003. Mem. Musicians Assn. Clearwater (pres. 1976-81), Fla.-Ga. Conf. Musicians (sec., treas. 1974-76), NRA, ABA (sr. bar sect.), Fed. Bar Assn., Fla. State Hist. Soc., Md. Hist. Soc., Greater St. Petersburg Musicians Assn., Clearwater Bar Assn. (probate divsn.), Am. Fedn. Musicians (internat. law com. pres. so. conf. musicians 1979-80), Nat. Geneal. Soc., Clearwater Genealogy Soc., Md. Geneal. Soc., Augustan Soc., Lancaster (Pa.) Geneal. Soc., Pinellas (Fla.) Geneal. Soc. (lectr. 1995—), Carroll County (Md.) Geneal. Soc., Balt. County Geneal. Soc., Lancaster Mennonite Hist. Soc., Navy Hurricane Hunters, Sons Am. Revolution, Sons Union Vets. Civil War, Md. Hist. Soc., Catonsville (Md.) Hist. Soc., Am. Legion, German Am. Geneal. Assn., DAV Fleet Res., Masons, Scottish Rite (Tampa), Egypt Temple Shrine, Moose, Sertoma (bd. dirs. Clearwater chpt. 1984-2002, v.p. 1989-92), Phi Delta Phi, Sigma Pi, Kappa Kappa Psi. Home: 2261 Belleair Rd Clearwater FL 33764-2761 Office: Legal Arts Bldg Ste 1 501 S Fort Harrison Ave Clearwater FL 33756-5317

WEIDEN, PAUL LINCOLN, cancer researcher, oncologist, educator; b. Portland, Oreg., Aug. 21, 1941; BA, Harvard U., 1963, MD, 1967. Intern U. Hosps., Cleve., 1967-68, resident medicine, 1968-69; fellow hematology and oncology U. Wash., Seattle, 1971-73; med. dir. Nat. Marrow Donor Program Collection Ctr., 1988-2001, Dendreon Corp., Seattle, 2001—02; cons. Bartlett Regional Hosp., Juneau, Alaska, 2001—; dir. clin. oncology Sonus Pharmaceuticals, Bothell, Wash., 2002—04; cons. cancer clin. rsch., 2004—. Chmn. stem cell transplantation com. Virginia Mason Hosp., Seattle, 1991—2001, prin. investigator cmty. clin. oncology program, 1993—2001, med. dir. cancer clin. rsch. unit, 1995—2001, chmn. rsch. adv. com., 2000—01, emeritus physician, 2001—; clin. prof. U. Wash. Med. Sch., 1991—. Fellow ACP; mem. Am. Soc. Clin. Oncology, Am. Soc. Hematology, Am. Assn. Cancer Rsch., Am. Assn. Pharm. Physicians. Office Phone: 206-755-0915. E-mail: plweiden@aol.com.

WEIDENAAR, DENNIS JAY, economics professor; b. Grand Rapids, Mich., Oct. 4, 1936; s. John and Jennie (Beukema) W.; m. Kristin Andrews, July 14, 1943; children: Kaarin Jaye, John Andrews. AB, Calvin Coll., Grand Rapids, 1958; MA, U. Chgo., 1961; PhD, Purdue U., 1969. Asst. prof. econs. Purdue U., West Lafayette, Ind., 1966-72, assoc. prof., 1972-77, prof., 1977-83; interim dean Krannert Sch. of Mgmt., West Lafayette, 1983-84, assoc. dean, 1984-99; dean Krannert Grad. Sch. Mgmt., West Lafayette, 1990-99, prof. econs., 1999—. Cons. TRW, B.F. Goodrich, Ea. Panhandle; bd. dirs. Lafayette Ins. Co. Author: Economics. Contbr. articles to profl. jours. Bd. dirs. Ind. Coun. on Econ. Edn., Lafayette, 1974-83, Lafayette Ins. Co. Recipient The Leavey Awd for Excellence in Pvt. Enterprise Edn., Freedom's Found., Valley Forge, 1983, Distinguished Service Awd., Joint Council on Econ. Edn., N.Y., 1986, Golden Key Nat. Honor Soc., 1985. Mem. Assn. for Advancement of Collegiate Schs. of Mgmt. Internat., Rotary, Delta Sigma Pi, Beta Gamma Sigma (bd. dirs., pres. 2002—), Phi Delta Kappa. Presbyterian. Home: 217 Rosebank Ln West Lafayette IN 47906-8614 Office: Purdue U Krannert Sch Mgmt West Lafayette IN 47907

WEIDENAAR, GARY ALAN, music educator; b. Oak Park, Ill., July 15, 1958; s. Peter Dirk and Elsbeth Jean Weidenaar; m. Marla Ann Reierson; children: Mark Henry, David Alan. MusB, Western Mich. U., 1981; MusM, Mich. State U., 1988; D of Musical Arts, U. Kans., 2002. Choral music tchr. Walled Lake (Mich.) Western H.S., 1981—86; music tchr. John F. Kennedy Sch., Berlin, 1988—93, Internat. Sch. of Stavanger, Norway, 1993—97, Palm Springs (Calif.) H.S., 1997—98; asst. dir. choral activities No. Ariz. U., Flagstaff, 2002—. Coord. choral music Blue Lake Fine Arts Camp, Twin Lakes, Mich., 1984—85; musical dir. Faculty/Parent/Cmty. Choir, Berlin, 1988—93, Am. Mil. Sector Allied Choir, Berlin, 1989; grad. tchg. asst. choral music, music tech. U. Kans., Lawrence, 1998—2002; musical & artistic dir. Kaw Valley Cmty. Chorus, Bonner Springs, Kans., 1999—2002. Mem.: Assn. for Music in Internat. Schs., VoiceCare Network, Music Educators Nat. Conf., Am. Choral Dirs. Assn. (life; state chair repertoire and stds. youth and student activities 2002—). Avocations: computers, racquetball, water-skiing. Office: No Ariz U PO Box 6040 Flagstaff AZ 86011 Office Phone: 928-523-2642. E-mail: gary.weidenaar@nau.edu.

WEIDENBAUM, MURRAY LEW, economist, educator; b. Bronx, N.Y., Feb. 10, 1927; s. David and Rose (Warshaw) Weidenbaum; m. Phyllis Green, June 13, 1954; children: Susan, James, Laurie. BBA, CCNY, 1948; MA, Columbia U., 1949; MPA, Princeton U., 1954, PhD, 1958; LLD, Baruch Coll., 1981, U. Evansville, 1983, McKendree Coll., 1993. Fiscal economist Bur. Budget, Washington, 1949—57; corp. economist Boeing Co., Seattle, 1958—62; sr. economist Stanford Rsch. Inst., Palo Alto, Calif., 1962—63; mem. faculty Washington U., St. Louis, 1964—, prof., chmn. dept. econs., 1966—69, Mallinckrodt prof., 1971—, dir. Ctr. for Study Am. Bus., 1974—81, Washington U., St. Louis, 1982—95; chmn. Ctr. for Study Am. Bus. Washington U., St. Louis, 1995—2000; asst. sec. econ. policy Treasury Dept., 1969—71; chmn. Coun. of Econ. Advs., 1981—82; hon. chmn. Weidenbaum Ctr. on the Economy, Govt. and Pub. Policy, St. Louis, 2001—. Chmn. rsch. adv. com. St. Louis Regional Indsl. Devel. Corp., 1965—69; exec. sec. Pres.'s Com. on Econ. Impact of Def. and Disarmament, 1964; mem. U.S. Fin. Investment Adv. Panel, 1970—72; cons. various firms and instns.; chmn. U.S. Commn. to Rev. the Trade Deficit, 1999—2000. Author: Federal Budgeting, 1964, Modern Public Sector, 1969, Economics of Peacetime Defense, 1974, Economic Impact of the Vietnam War, 1967, Government-Mandated Price Increases, 1975, The Future of Business Regulation, 1980, Rendezvous With Reality: The American Economy After Reagan, 1988, Rendezvous With Reality: The American Economy After Reagan, paperback edit., 1990, Business, Government, and the Public, 1990, Small Wars, Big Defense, 1992, The Bamboo Network, 1996, Business and Government in the Global Marketplace, 2004; mem. editl. bd.: Publius, 1971—2004, Jour. Econ. Issues, 1972—75, Challenge, 1974—81, 1983—, Business and the Contemporary World, 1997—2000; author: One-Armed Economist, 2004. With U.S. Army, 1945. Named Banbury fellow, Princeton U., 1952—54; named to Free Market Hall of Fame, 1983; recipient Alexander Hamilton medal, U.S. Dept. Treasury, 1971, Disting. Writer award, Georgetown U., award for disting. tchg., Freedoms Found., 1980, award for best book in econs., Assn. Am. Pubs., 1993. Fellow: Assn. for Pvt. Enterprise Edn. (Adam Smith award 1986), City Coll. Alumni Assn. (Townsend Harris medal 1969), Soc. Tech. Comm., Nat. Assn. Bus. Economists, Cosmos. Office: Washington Univ Weidenbaum Ctr 1 Brookings Dr Saint Louis MO 63130-4899 Office Phone: 314-935-5662.

WEIDENFELD, EDWARD LEE, lawyer; b. Akron, Ohio, July 15, 1943; s. Sam and Beatrice (Cooper) W.; m. Sheila Rabb, Aug. 11, 1968; children: Nicholas, Daniel. BS, U. Wis., 1965; JD, Columbia U., 1968. Bar: N.Y. 1968, U.S. Supreme Ct. 1972, D.C. 1973. Pvt. practice, N.Y.C., 1969-71, 73-82, Washington, 1982—. Spl. cons. N.Y.C. Dept. Bldgs., 1967; counsel, dir. energy staff Com. on Interior and Insular Affairs, U.S. Ho. of Reps., 1971—73; mem. faculty Am. Law Inst.-ABA CLE Programs; mem. Internat. Del. to Observe Philippine Election, 1986, Internat. Del. to Observe Republic Korea Election, 1987, Pakistan Election, 1988, Chilean Election, 1989, Albanian Election, 1997; mem. D.C. Bar Task Force on the Omnibus Trusts and Estates Amendment Act of 2000, 1999—2001; lectr. to profl. groups. Editor in chief Atomic Energy Law Jour., 1975-76; contbg. author: Generations: Planning Your Legacy, 1999. Mem. Pres.'s Commn. on White House Fellowships, 1977; nat. chmn. Lawyers for Reagan/Bush, 1980; chief dep. counsel Reagan/Bush Campaign, 1980; chmn. Reagan/Bush '84 Legal Adv. Bd., 1984; mem. D.C. Rep. Com., 1984-92, vice chmn., 1984-88; mem. Coun. Adminstrv. Conf. of U.S., 1981-92, sr. fellow, 1992-95; overseer dep. def. regional ctrs., sec. Salvation Army Adv. Bd.; trustee Danny Kaye and Sylvia Fine Kaye Found.; chmn. bd. visitors The Nat. Def. U. Recipient medal of Peter the Great, Russian Fedn., 2000. Mem. ABA, D.C. Bar Assn., Am. Law Inst. (life), Assn. Bar City N.Y., Met. Club (Washington). Office: 1828 L St NW Ste 500 Washington DC 20036-3806 Office Phone: 202-785-2143. Business E-Mail: edward@weidenfeldlaw.com.

WEIDENFELD, SHEILA RABB, television producer, author; b. Cambridge, Mass., Sept. 7, 1943; d. Maxwell M. and Ruth (Cryden) Rabb; m. Edward L. Weidenfeld, Aug. 11, 1968; children: Nicholas Rabb, Daniel Rabb. BA, Brandeis U., 1965. Assoc. prodr. Metromedia, Inc., Sta. WNEW-TV, N.Y.C., 1965-68; talent coord. That Show with Joan Rivers, NBC, N.Y.C., 1968-71; coord. NBC network game programs, N.Y.C., 1968-71; prodr. Metromedia, Inc., Sta. WTTG-TV, Washington, 1971-73; creator/prodr. Take It From Here, NBC (WBC-TV), Washington, 1973-74; press sec. to first lady Betty Ford, spl. asst. to Pres. Gerald R. Ford, 1974-77; mem. Pres.'s Adv. Commn. on Hist. Preservation, 1977-81; TV prodr., moderator On the Record, NBC-TV, Sta. WRC-TV, Washington, 1978-79; pres. D.C. Prodns., Ltd., 1978; prodr., host Your Personal Decorator, 1987; mem. Sec. State's Adv. Commn. on Fgn. Svc. Inst., 1972-74; founding mem. Project Censured Panel of Judges, 1976—. Bd. dirs. First Star. Author: First Lady's Lady, 1979. Mem. U.S. Holocaust Meml. Coun., 1987-97; corporator Dana Hall Sch., Wellesley, Mass.; bd. dirs. Wolf Trap Found., Women's Campaign Fund, 1978-79; bd. dirs. D.C. Contemporary Dance Theatre, 1986-88, D.C. Rep. Ctrl. Com., 1984—, D.C. Preservation League, 1987-90; chmn. C&O Canal Nat. Hist. Park Commn., 1988—; bd. dirs. Am. Univ. Rome, 1988—, Friends of the Scuola San Rocco, 2002—. Recipient awards for outstanding achievement in the media AAUW, 1973, 74, Silver Screen award A Campaign to Remember for the U.S. Holocaust Meml. Coun., 1989, Bronze medal Internat. Film and Video Festival N.Y., 1990; named hon. consul gen. of Republic of San Marino to Washington; knighted by Order of St. Agatha, Republic of San Marino, 1986. Mem. NATAS (Emmy award 1972), Washington Press Club, Am. Newspaper Women's Club, Am. Women in Radio and TV, Cosmos Club, Consular Corps, Sigma Delta Chi. Home: 3059 Q St NW Washington DC 20007-3081 E-mail: Sheila.Weidenfeld@verizon.net.

WEIDENKOPF, THOMAS W. human resources specialist; b. 1959; married; 2 children. Grad., Cornell U. Various human resources positions Pepsi-Cola, Pizza Hut; mgr. orgn. and staffing GE, 1981—83; dir. global staffing and devel. Honeywell Internat., Inc., 1995—97; v.p. human resources Honeywell Aerospace, 1999—2002; sr. v.p. human resources and comm. Honeywell Internat., Inc., Morristown, NJ, 2002—. Office: Honeywell Internat 101 Columbia Rd Morristown NJ 07962

WEIDENTHAL, MAURICE DAVID (BUD WEIDENTHAL), educational administrator, journalist; b. Cleve., Nov. 26, 1925; s. William and Evelyn (Kolinsky) W.; m. Grace Schwartz, Apr. 14, 1957; 1 child, Susan Elizabeth Weidenthal Saltzman. BA, U. Mich., 1950. Mem. staff Cleve. Press, 1950-81, editorial writer, 1950-51, asst. city editor, 1956-58, edn. editor, 1958-81; v.p. public affairs Cuyahoga Community Coll. Dist., Cleve., 1981-88; dir. Urban Colls. Project RC-2000, New York City, NY, 1989—. Editor The Urban Report, Cleve., 1989—. Mem. pub. affairs com. Greater Cleve. Growth Assn., 1981-88; mem. bd. advisors Coun. for Advancement and Support of Edn., 1981-88, Nat. Coun. Mktg. and Pub. Rels., 1981—; alt. bd. dirs. St. Vincent Quadrangle, 1983-88; trustee Hebrew Free Loan Assn., 1975-86. With AUS, 1944-45. Decorated Air medal. Mem. Edn. Writers Assn., Soc. Profl. Journalists, (bd. dirs. 1996-2003), Cleve. City Club (bd. dirs. 1969-76), Cleve. Press Club. Home: 25858 Fairmount Blvd Cleveland OH 44122-2214 Office: 4250 Richmond Rd Cleveland OH 44122-6104 Personal E-mail: u2w@aol.com. Business E-Mail: bud.weidenthal@tri-c.edu.

WEIDER, JOSEPH, wholesale distribution executive; Chmn. bd., treas. Weider Health and Fitness, Woodland Hills, Calif., 1970—. Mem. chmn. bd. Weider Health and Fitness, Great Am. Foods. Office: Mens Fitness 21100 Erwin St Woodland Hills CA 91367-3712

WEIDMAN, JOHN CARL, II, education and sociology educator, consultant; b. Ephrata, Pa., Oct. 3, 1945; s. John Carl and Mary Elizabeth (Grube) W.; m. Carla Sue Fassnacht, Aug. 20, 1967; children: Jonathan Scott, Rebecca Mary. AB in Sociology cum laude, Princeton U., 1967; AM, U. Chgo., 1968, PhD, 1974. Acting asst. prof. edn. U. Minn., Mpls., 1970-74, asst. prof. edn., sociology and Am. studies, 1974-77; sr. rsch. assoc. Bur. Social Sci. Rsch., Inc., Washington, 1977-78; assoc. prof. edn. and sociology U. Pitts., 1979-86, prof. edn. and sociology, 1986—, chmn. dept. adminstrv. and policy studies, 1986-93, dir. Inst. for Internat. Studies in Edn., 2004—. Cons. Nat. Ctr. Adminstrv. Justice, Youthwork, Inc., Upper Midwest Tri-Racial Gen. Assistance Ctr., Acad. for Ednl. Devel., Asian Devel. Bank, Indonesia, Laos, Kyrgyz Republic, Uzbekistan, German Acad. Exch. Svc., Mongolia, Sema-Belgium, Uzbekistan; UNESCO chair higher edn. rsch. Maseno U. Coll., Kenya, 1993. Author: rsch. monographs; mem. editl. bd. Rev. of Higher Edn., 1984-88, Am. Ednl. Rsch. Jour., 1991-92, 96-98; co-author: Research on Higher Education in Developing Countries: Suggested Agendas and Research Strategies, 1991, Implementing a Faculty Assessment System: A Case Study of the University of Pittsburgh-USA, 1994, Higher Education Costs and Tuition, 1996, Higher Education in Korea: Tradition and Adaptation, 2000, Socialization of Graduate and Professional Students: A Perilous Passage?, 2001, Finance Higher Education, 2001; asst. editor Comparative Edn. Rev., 2003—; cons. editor Jour. Higher Edn., 1989—; contbr. chpts. to books, articles to profl. jours. Bd. dirs. Sch. Vol. Assn. Pitts., 1982-90, pres., 1984-87. Grantee U.S. Office Edn., 1971-73, Spencer Found., 1973-76, Nat. Inst. Edn., 1976-79, NEH, 1985-86, Asian Devel. Bank, Laos, 1995-96, Mongolia, 1997-2000, Indonesia, 2001, Krygyz Republic, 2003; Fulbright scholar U. Augsburg, Germany, 1986-87. Mem. Am. Ednl. Rsch. Assn. (sec. postsecondary divsn. 1987-89), Am. Sociol. Assn., Assn. Study of Higher Edn., Comparative and Internat. Edn. Soc., Sigma Psi, Phi Delta Kappa. Office: U Pitts 5S38 Posvar Hall 230 S Bouquet St Pittsburgh PA 15260

WEIDMAN, SHEILA, marketing professional; b. Bradenton, Fla., July 11, 1961; BS in Sci., Journalism and Comms., U. Fla., 1983. Comms. mgr. ASHRAE, 1983—88; mgr. corp. comms. Georgia-Pacific Corp., 1988—90, dir. external comms. and corp. advt., 1990—98, dir., spl. asst. to chmn. and CEO, 1998—2000, sr. dir. corp. mktg. and sales excellence, 2000—01, v.p. corp. mktg., 2001—02, v.p. corp. comms. and mktg., 2002—. Com. mem. Am. Heart Assn., Atlanta Hist. Soc.; mem. Leadership Atlanta, Class of 2004. Recipient Women of Achievement awards, YWCA, 1995. Mem.: Atlanta Sports Coun. (bd. dirs., chmn. mktg. com.), Atlanta CMO Roundtable, CMO Group of N.Am., Ga. Press Assn., Ga. State CMO Roundtable, Met. Atlanta C. of C. (vice chair chmn.'s campaign 2003), Mktg. Leadership Coun. (vice chair chmn.'s campaign 2004), Pub. Rels. Soc. Am., Sales and Mktg. Execs., Atlanta Press Club. Office: Georgia-Pacific Corp 133 Peachtree St NE Atlanta GA 30303

WEIDMANN, K. TIMOTHY, not-for-profit fundraiser, writer; b. Bronxville, NY, May 28, 1950; s. Carl Frederick and Kathryn Henrietta Weidmann; m. Deborah Ann Emanuel, Sept. 18, 1976; children: Sarah, Seth, Jesse Florea. AB, Harvard Coll., Cambridge, MA, 1972; MDiv, Yale Div. Sch., New Haven, CT, 1980—80. Mktg. rep. IBM, White Plains, NY, 1981—83; assoc. dir. Yale U., New Haven, 1983—87; assoc. v.p. Northwestern U., Evanston, Ill., 1987—2001; sr. cons. Marts & Lundy, Inc., Lyndhurst, NJ, 2001—. V.p. devel. ALS Les Turner Found., Chicago, Ill., 1990—95; chair of devel. com. Vt. Studio Ctr., Johnson, Vt., 2001—. Co-author: Lives and Legacies: An Encyclopedia of People Who Changed the World, 1999, contbr. articles to mags. Sr. warden St. John's Ch., New Haven, 1986—87; vestry mem. St. Mark's Ch., Evanston, Ill., 1990—92. Recipient Scholarship, Harvard Club of Westchester, 1968; fellow fellowship, Roothbert Fund, 1977-80, Leopold Schepp Found., 1977-80, Vt. Studio Ctr., 2000. Fellow: Timothy Dwight Coll., Yale (residential fellow 1985—87); mem.: Am. Healthcare Profls., Am. Fundraising Profls., Coun. on Aid and Support of Edn. Episcopalian. Achievements include built infrastructure for corporate philanthrophy at Yale; built infrastructure for grateful patient philanthrophy as basis of fund-=raising at Northwestern University Medical School. Avocations: reading, squash, travel, poetry. Home: 9018 Sleeping Bear Rd Skokie IL 60076 Personal E-mail: weidmann@martsandlundy.com.

WEIDNER, EDWARD WILLIAM, university chancellor, political scientist; b. Mpls., July 7, 1921; s. Peter Clifford and Lillian (Halbe) W.; m. Jean Elizabeth Blomquist, Mar. 23, 1944 (dec. Apr., 1997); children: Nancy Louise, Gary Richard, Karen, William; m. Marjorie M. Fermanich, June 6, 1998. BA magna cum laude, U. Minn., 1942, MA, 1943, PhD, 1946; postgrad., U. Wis., 1943-45; LHD (hon.), No. Mich. U., 1969; PhD (hon.), Linköping U., Sweden, 1975. Staff mem. Nat. Mcpl. League, 1944, research assoc., 1944-45; cons. govts. div. U.S. Bur. Census, 1945, statistician, 1946; lectr. U. Wis., Madison, 1945; instr. U. Minn., Mpls., 1945-47, asst. prof., 1947-49, asst. dir. research in inter-govtl. relations, 1946-53; asst. prof. UCLA, 1949-50; faculty Mich. State U., East Lansing, 1950-62, from assoc. prof., dir. govtl. research bur., to prof. polit. sci., 1952-62, chmn. polit. sci. dept., 1952-57; coordinator, chief adviser Vietnam Project, 1955-57; dir. Inst. Research on Overseas Programs, 1957-61; vice chancellor E.W. Ctr., 1962-65; prof. polit. sci., dir. ctr. for devel. change U. Ky., Lexington, 1965-67; chancellor U. Wis., Green Bay, 1966-86, prof. polit. sci., 1966-89, chancellor emeritus, prof. emeritus, 1989—, dir. Cofrin Arboretum, 1986-89. Planning dir. Weidner Ctr. for the Performing Arts, 1987-93; bd. dirs. Univ. Bank, Green Bay; cons. Fgn. Ops. Adminstrn., Vietnam, 1954-55, Baltimore County (Md.) Reorgn. Commn., 1953-54, Ford Found., Pakistan, 1956, Nat. Assn. Fgn. Student Advisers, 1959-60, Pres.'s Task Force Fgn. Econ. Assistance, 1961, Dept. State, 1962-63, AID, 1964-65, Lees Coll., 1971-72, Green Bay Bot. Garden, 1997-98; mem. Gov. Mich. Commn. Inter-Govtl. Rels., 1954-55. Author: (with William Anderson) American Government, 1951, State and Local Government, 1951, (with others) The International Programs of American Universities, 1958, Intergovernmental Relations as Seen by Public Officials, 1960, (with William Anderson, Clara Penniman) Government for the Fifty States, 1960, The World Role of Universities, 1962, Technical Assistance in Public Administration Overseas, 1964; editor: Development Administration in Asia, 1970. Mem. Wis. Gov.'s Commn. on UN, 1975-81; trustee Prairie Sch., 1969-91, mem. adv. bd., 1991—; bd. dirs. Inst. for Shipboard Edn., 1976-89; mem. Lab. Ornithology, Cornell U., bd. dirs. 1989-98; chmn. adv. bd. Lakeland chpt. ARC, 1981-84; mem. N.Am. adv. group UN Environ. Programme, 1983-90; bd. advisers Nature Conservancy Wis., 1984-91; bd. dirs. Heritage Hill Found., 1987-92, 95-97, pres. 1991-92; bd. dirs. Assn. Am. Colls., 1978-80, Brown County, Family Svc. Assn., 1988-93; chmn. Brown County Cultural Coun., 1991-94; mem. nat. coun. ASPA, 1947-50; mem. internat. coun. UN U., 1974-80; bd. dirs. Am. Coun. on Edn., 1971-74, sec. bd., 1971-72; mem. nat. coun. Am. Polit. Assn., 1950-52. Recipient Outstanding Achievement award U. Minn., 1975. Mem. Wis. Soc. Ornithology, Wilderness Soc., World Wildlife Fund, Interfaith Alliance, Common Cause, Nature Conservancy, Audubon Soc., Am. Birding Assn., Green Bay Area C. of C. (bd. dirs. 1970-74), Mcpl. Clks. Edn. Found. (bd. dirs. 1980-97), Phi Beta Kappa, Pi Sigma Alpha. Home: 1656 Twin Lakes Cir Green Bay WI 54311-4207 E-mail: osggg@netnet.net.

WEIDNER, LAUREN FINDER, lawyer; b. N.Y.C., Jan. 21, 1965; B in Commerce, McGill U., 1986; JD, U. Calif., Hastings, 1991. Bar: Calif. 1991, U.S. Dist. Ct. (no. and ctrl. dists.) Calif. 1991, U.S. Dist. Ct. (so. dist.) Calif. 1996. Assoc. Sedgwick, Detert, Moran & Arnold, San Francisco, 1991-95, Higgs Fletcher & Mack, San Diego, 1996-97, Gilbert, Kelly, Crowley & Jennett, San Diego, 1997—. Co-chair El Rancho del Ray Playground Renovation Com., Chula Vista, Calif., 1997-98; commr. City of Chula Vista Parks and Recreation, 1998— chair, 2000-02. Mem. San Diego Bar Assn. Office: Gilbert Kelly Crowley & Jennett 750 B St Ste 2600 San Diego CA 92101-8175

WEIDNER, ROBERT WRIGHT, musician, music educator, musicologist; b. Brookfield, Wis., Oct. 21, 1923; s. Oswald Frederick and Minnie Marie (Giencke) W.; m. Jean Dionne Rockwell; children: Robert Rockwell Weidner, Diane Jean Weidner. BS, Milw. State Tchrs. Coll., 1949; MA, Eastman Sch. of Music, 1951, PhD, 1960. Band dir., tchr. history North Divsn. H.S., Milw., 1949-50; music dir. Oostburg (Wis.) Pub. Schs., 1951-52; band dir., music prof. Ohio No. U., Ada, 1952-55; band dir., prof. music Tex. Luth. Coll., Seguin, 1955-56; dir. music Abbotsford (Wis.) Pub. Schs./Dorchester (Wis.) Pub. Schs., 1956-58; prof. music, dir. orchestra Nebr. Wesleyan U., Lincoln, 1959-62; prof. music, dept. head U. Dubuque (Iowa), 1962-65; coord. grad. studies in music Ea. Ill. U., Charleston, 1987-89, prof. music, 1965-93, retired, 1994. Composer Tex. Luth. Coll. alma mater, 1956; editor (book) Christopher Tye: The Instrumental Music, 1965, Tye's Actes of the Apostles, 1970. Bd. dirs. Charleston Civic Assn., Charleston, 1991-97. With U.S. Army, 1943-46, ETO. Mem. Am. Musicol. Soc. Mem. Dem. Socialists of Am. Avocation: reading. Home: 1002 Scovill St Urbana IL 61801-6874 E-mail: rwweidner@aol.com.

WEIERMILLER, KATHY, publishing executive; V.p., CFO Orange County Register, Santa Ana, Calif. Office: The Orange County Register 625 N Grand Ave Santa Ana CA 92701-4347

WEIERS, JIM, state representative; b. SD; m. Gina Weiers; 4 children. Pres., CEO BHF, Inc.; mem. Ariz. Ho. of Reps., 1995—, speaker, 2001—. Republican. Office: Speaker of the House 1700 W Washington St Phoenix AZ 85007 Business E-Mail: jweiers@azleg.state.az.us.

WEIERSTALL, RICHARD PAUL, retired pharmaceutical chemist; b. Jersey City, N.J., Nov. 5, 1942; s. William August and Emily (Haughey) W.; m. Gail Janet Thomsen, Aug. 17, 1968; children: Eric, Kurt, Karen. BS, Rutgers U., 1966, MS, 1969; PhD, U. Calif., San Francisco, 1973. Unit head drug metabolism Sandoz Pharm., East Hanover, N.J., 1973-74; dir. tech. svc. Banner Gelatin Products, Chatsworth, Calif., 1974-76; v.p. tech. svc. Banner Gelatin Prod., Chatsworth, Calif., 1976-81; dir. pharm. sci. Ayerst Labs Inc., Rouses Point, N.Y., 1981-87; asst. v.p. Wyeth Ayerst Rsch., Rouses Point, 1987-95, asst. v.p. quality assurance, 1995-99; ret., 1999. Mem. Am. Assn. Pharm. Sci., Am. Pharm. Assn. Home: 7 Stewart St Rouses Point NY 12979-1511 E-mail: rweiers@northnet.org

WEIGEL, OLLIE J. dentist, former mayor; b. Guthrie County, Iowa, Sept. 29, 1922; s. Verne Noble and Ethel Rebecca (Johnson) W.; m. Mary Kathryn Finnegan, June 3, 1944 (dec. Sept. 1999); children: John, Marilyn, Larry, Susan. DDS, U. Iowa, 1951. Practice dentistry, Ankeny, 1951-94; mayor City of Ankeny, 1974-93. Mem. Metro Planning Orgn., 1995-2000; bd. dirs. Neveln Resource Ctr., 1995-2000. Mem. Ankeny Bd. Adjustment, 1953-58, Ankeny Planning and Zoning Commn., 1953-65, Ankeny City Coun., 1966-73, Des Moines Area C.C. Found. Bd., 1993—, mem. emeritus; mem. Des Moines Area Metro Forum, 1985-93, found. bd. On With Life, 1994-2000; life mem. Ankeny Indsl. Devel. Corp.; bd. dirs. Ankeny Cmty. Dist. Sch. Found.; mem. adv. bd. dirs. Brenton Bank of Ankeny, 1994-2000; mem. Polk County Aviation Authority, 2001-2003. 1st lt. USAAF, 1943-45, ETO. Named to Mayors Hall of Fame, 1993—96; recipient Person of Vision award, Ankeny Indsl. Devel. Corp. (1st recipient), 2001. Mem. ADA (life), Iowa Dental Assn. (life), Des Moines Dist. Dental Assn., Ankeny C. of C. (charter mem., life, pres. 1953, 70, Outstanding Citizen 1976, 93), Mid Iowa Assn. Local Govts. (chmn. 1983), League of Iowa Municipalities (pres. 1976-77), Ctrl. Iowa Regional Govts. (pres. 1978), Am. Legion (life), Republican. Methodist. Avocation: fishing. Home and Office: 2506 NW 4th St Ankeny IA 50021-1002

WEIGEL, PAUL HENRY, biochemistry educator, researcher, consultant; b. N.Y.C., Aug. 11, 1946; s. Helmut and Jeanne Weigel; m. Nancy Shulman, June 15, 1968 (div. Dec. 1987); 1 child, Dana J.; m. Janet Oka, May 17, 1992. BA in Chemistry, Cornell U., 1968; MS in Biochemistry, Johns Hopkins U., Balt., 1969, PhD in Biochemistry, 1975. NIH postdoctoral fellow Johns Hopkins U., Balt., 1975-78; asst. prof. U. Tex. Med. Br., Galveston, Tex., 1978-82, assoc. prof., 1982—94, prof. biochemistry and cell biology, 1987-94, vice chmn. dept. human biol. chemistry and genetics, 1990-93, acting chmn. dept. human biology, chemistry and genetics, 1992-93; prof., chmn. dept. biochemistry and molecular biology U. Okla. Health Scis. Ctr., Oklahoma City, 1994—, George Lynn Cross rsch. prof., 2004—; co-founder Hyalose LLC, 2000—. Mem. NIH Pathobiochemistry Study Sect., Washington, 1985-87; cons. Teltech, Mpls., 1985—, Hyalose LLC 2000—. Contbr. articles to profl. jours.; patentee in field. Treas. Bayou Chateau Neighborhood Assn., Dickinson, Tex., 1981-83, v.p., 1983-84, pres., 1984-86. With U.S. Army, 1969-71. Grantee NIH, 1979—, Office Naval Rsch., 1983-87, Tex. Biotech., 1989-94, Okla. Ctr. Advancement Sci. and Tech., 2000-03; recipient Disting. Tchr. award U. Tex. Med. Br., 1989, Disting. Rsch. award, 1989. Mem. Am. Chem. Soc., Am. Soc. Cell Biology, Am. Soc. Biochemistry and Molecular Biology (mem. pub. affairs adv. com., 2000-03), Assn. Med. and Grad. Depts. Biochemistry (web master, bd. dirs., 2002—). Democrat. Lutheran. Avocations: raquetball, basketball card collecting, poetry, camping. Home: 817 Hollowdale Edmond OK 73003-3022 Office: U Okla Health Scis Ctr Dept Biochem & Mol Biology Bmsb Rm 860 Oklahoma City OK 73190-0001 Business E-Mail: paul-weigel@ouhsc.edu.

WEIGEL, RICHARD GEORGE, psychologist, educator; b. St. Louis, Feb. 23, 1937; s. George D. and Irene K. (Bretz) W.; Virginia Novis Weige, 1964 (div. 2003); children: Paul K., Laura K.; m. Jean Anderson. BA, DePauw U., 1959; MA, U. Mo., Columbia, 1962, PhD in Psychology, 1968. Diplomate in clin. psychology Am. bd. Profl. Psychology; lic. psychologist Utah. Counselor/asst. prof. psychology Oreg. State U., Corvallis, 1964-67, acting dir. Counseling Ctr., 1967; asst. prof. to prof. and chmn. counseling psychology program Colo. State U., Ft. Collins, 1967-78; sr. cons. psychologist Rohrer, Hibler & Replogle, Inc., Denver, 1978-90, mgr., 1981-86; dir. and adj. prof. psychology Student Counseling Ctr., Ill. State U., Normal, 1990-92; dir. Counseling Ctr. U. Utah, Salt Lake City, 1992—, clin. prof. psychology, ednl. psychology and psychiatry, 1992—, asst. v.p. student devel., 1996-97, interim v.p. for student affairs, 1997-99. Pvt. practice psychology, Ft. Collins, 1970-78; adj. prof. Denver U. Sch. Profl. Psychology, 1977-78, Counseling Psychology Program, Ctr. for Spl. and Advanced Programs of U. No. Colo., Greeley, 1975-78, vis. assoc. prof. counseling psychology program, summer 1975; lectr. continuing edn. for nurses Poudre Valley Meml. Hosp., Ft. Collins, 1975; selection psychologist Peace Corps, 1973-74; asst. prof. psychology divsn. continuing edn. Oreg. State Sys. Higher Edn., Salem, 1965; ind. practice marriage counseling, Corvallis, Oreg., 1965-67; clin. psychologist Mo. Tng. Sch. for Boys, summer 1964; instr. psychology U. Mo., Columbia, 1963-64; counselor Counseling Svc., Stephens Coll., Columbia, 1963-64, Univ. Testing and Counseling Svc., U. Mo., Columbia, 1961-62; instr. psychology, resident advisor George Williams Coll., Lake Geneva, Wis., summer 1961; tchg./rsch. asst. psychology U. Mo., 1960-61; rsch. asst. Purdue U., West Lafayette, Ind., 1960; VA clin. psychology trainee Indpls., 1959-60; vis. scientist/lectr. APA, Drury Coll., 1974; lectr. in field; condr. workshops in field; v.p. Bd. Psychologist Examiners State of Colo., 1973-76. Assoc. editor Cons. Psychology Jour.: Practice and rsch., 1991-93, editl. bd., 1990-97; editl. bd. Jour. Coll. Student Devel., 1970-73, 92—, Profl. Psychology: Rsch. and Practice, 1990-92, Group Dynamics: Theory, Research & Practice, 1999—; reviewer Jour. Counseling Psychology, 1976, 94-96, Counseling Psychologist, 1994-98, Jour. Cons. and Clin. Psychology, 1977; editl. cons. Wadsworth-Brooks/Cole Pub. Co., 1974-78, Univ. Park Press, 1976; contbr. numerous articles to profl. jours.; co-author: Innovative Psychological Therapies, 1975, Innovative Medical-Psychiatric Therapies, 1976. Bd. dirs. Mental Health Assn., Benton County, Oreg., 1966-67; mem. Soc. Indiana Pioneers, 1990—; mem. profl. adv. bd. Denver U. Sch. Profl. Psychology, 1976-78. NIMH grantee, 1977-82, Colo. State U. grantee, 1976-77, Oreg. State U. grantee, 1965-66, 66-67; Paul Harris fellow Rotary, 1981-86. Fellow APA (task force on revision of accreditation criteria 1977-78, vis. scientist 1974, divsn. cons. psychology pres.-elect 1995-96, pres. 1996-97, past pres. 1997-98, sec. 1993 95, exec. com. 1990-98, com. fellows 1989-93, chair 1991-93, program com. 1990, counseling psychology divsn. awards com. 1993-95, 98, edn. and tng. com. 1975-78, 91-93, coll. counseling interest group 19915, clin. psychology divsn., group psychology and group psychotherapy divsn. com. on fellows 1991-93, 95—, chair 1992-93, pres. 2000—), Am. Psychol. Soc.; mem. AAUP, Assn. Univ. and Coll. Counseling Ctr. Dirs. (governing bd. 1993-95), Rocky Mountain Psychol. Assn. (pres. 1973-74, treas. 1971-72, Disting. Svc. award 1987), Rsch. Consortium of Counseling and Psychol. Svcs. in Higher Edn. (bd. dirs. 1993-95), Internat. Assn. Counseling Svcs. (site visitor 1991-95), Am. Coll. Pers. Assn., Utah Psychol. Assn., Colo. State Bd. Psychologist Examiners (vice chmn. 1974-76, del. to Am. Assn. State Psychology Bds. 1976), Coun. of Counseling Psychology Tng. Programs (bd. dirs. 1974-79, liaison to Am. Assn. State Psychology Bds. 1979), Newcomen Soc. U.S., Sigma Xi, Psi Chi, Phi Gamma Delta, Phi Mu Alpha, Phi Kappa Phi (hon., Golden Key). Avocation: history. Office: Univ Utah 201 S 1460 East Rm 426 Salt Lake City UT 84112-9061 E-mail: rweigel@sa.utah.edu.

WEIGEL, THOMAS J. pediatrician, cardiologist; m. Donna Theresa Vlcek, Aug. 6, 1983; children: Marjorie, Shannon, Hannah, Zachary, Theresa. BS, U. Notre Dame, 1980; MD, U. Loyola, Maywood, Ill., 1984. Diplomate Am. Bd. Pediats. Resident Children's Meml. Hosp., Chgo., 1984—87; fellow Mayo Clinic, Rochester, Minn., 1987—90; pvt. practice pediat. cardiology Chgo., 1990—. Mem. med. adv. bd. Children's Heart Found., Naperville, Ill., 1996—; v.p. med. staff Children's Meml. Hosp., Chgo. Fellow: Am. Acad. Pediat., Am. Coll. Cardiology. Office: 2350 N Lincoln Ave Chicago IL 60614 Office Phone: 773-871-5800.

WEIGELE, RICHARD SAYRE, police officer; b. Passaic, N.J., Oct. 5, 1949; s. Louis Charles and Marjorie (Sayre) W. BA, Hope Coll., Holland, Mich., 1972; MPA, Kean Coll. N.J., Union, 1989. Police officer Summit (N.J.) Police Dept., 1973-80; mobile intensive care paramedic Overlook Hosp., Summit, 1977—; first response tng. coord. Union County Police acad., Scotch Plains, N.J., 1980—; police sgt., 911 mcpl. coord. Mountainside (N.J.) Police Dept., 1980—, commdr. Emergency Svcs. Unit, 1998—. Paramedic preceptor Overlook Hosp., 1980—, pre-hosp. trauma life support instr., 1993—, pediatric prehosp. emergency care instr., 1995—; CPR instr. Am. Heart Assn., Summit, 1978; police instr. Union County Police Acad., 1980—; EMS text reviewer Brady Publishing, 1996. Officer Summit First Aid Squad, 1975-80; vol. Overlook Hosp., 1974-81; mem. Liberty Corner First Aid Squad, 1993-98; instr. ARC, Somerville, N.J., 1992-98. With N.J. Army NG, 1972-78. Recipient Award of Merit N.J. State Police Benevolent Assn., 1974, Award of recognition, Union County Police Acad., 1990. Mem. Nat. Assn. EMT/Paramedics (charter), N.J. Police Honor Legion, Internat. Police Assn. (reception officer 1989—), Mountainside Police Benevolent Assn. (Police Officer of the Yr. 1986), Pi Alpha Alpha. Ref. Ch. of Am. Avocations: skiing, biking, computers, community service. Home: 268 Crabtree Ct Basking Ridge NJ 07920-3154 Office: Mountainside Police Dept 1385 Route 22 Mountainside NJ 07092-2699

WEIGEND, GUIDO GUSTAV, geographer, educator; b. Zeltweg, Austria, Jan. 2, 1920; came to U.S., 1939, naturalized, 1943; s. Gustav F. and Paula (Sorgo) W.; m. Areta Kelble, June 26, 1947 (dec. 1993); children: Nina, Cynthia, Kenneth. BS, U. Chgo., 1942, MS, 1946, PhD, 1949. With OSS, 1943-45; with mil. intelligence U.S. War Dept., 1946; instr. geography U. Ill., Chgo., 1946-47; instr. then asst. prof. geography Beloit Coll., 1947-49; asst. prof. geography Rutgers U., 1949-51, assoc. prof., 1951-57, prof., 1957-76, acting dept. chmn., 1951-52, chmn. dept., 1953-67, assoc. dean, 1972-76; dean Coll. Liberal Arts, Prof. geography Ariz. State U., Tempe, 1976-84, prof. geography, 1976-89, ret., 1989. Fulbright lectr. U. Barcelona, 1960-61; vis. prof. geography Columbia U., 1963-67, NYU, 1967, U. Colo., summer 1968, U. Hawaii, summer 1969; liaison rep. Rutgers U. to UN, 1950-52; invited by Chinese Acad. Scis. to visit minority areas in Chinese Cent. Asia, 1988; mem. U.S. nat. com. Internat. Geog. Union, 1951-58, 61-65; chmn. Conf. on Polit. and Social Geography, 1968-69 Author articles, monographs, bulls. for profl. jours.; contbr.: (4th edit.) A Geography of Europe, 1977; geog. editor-in-chief: Odyssey World Atlas, 1966. Bd. adjustment Franklin Twp., N.J., 1959; mem. Highland Park (N.J.) Bd. Edn., 1973-75, v.p., 1975; mem. Ariz. Coun. on Humanities and Pub. Policy, 1976-80; vice chmn. Phoenix Com. on Fgn. Rels., 1976-79, chmn., 1979-81; mem. exec. com. Fedn. Pub. Programs in Humanities, 1977-82; bd. dirs. Coun. Colls. Arts and Scis., 1980-83; bd. dirs. Phoenix Chamber Music Soc., 1995—, pres., 2000—; commr. N. Cen. Assn. Colls. and Schs., 1976-80, bd. dirs. commn. on instns. of higher edn., 1980-83. Research fellow Office Naval Research, 1952-55, Rutgers Research Council, 1970-71; grantee Social Sci. Research Council, 1956, Ford Found., 1966, Am. Philos. Soc., 1970-71, German Acad. Exchange Service, 1984; Fulbright travel grantee Netherlands, 1970-71. Mem. Assn. Am. Geographers (chmn. N.Y. Met. divsn. 1955-56, editl. bd. 1955-59, mem. coun. 1965-66, chmn. N.Y.-N.J. divsn. 1965-66), Am. Geog. Soc., Phoenix Chamber Mus. Soc. (bd. dirs. 1995-2003, pres. 2000-03), Sigma Xi (pres. Ariz. State U chpt 1989-91). Home: 2094 E Golf Ave Tempe AZ 85282-4046 Office: Ariz State U Dept Geography Tempe AZ 85287

WEIGENSBERG, IRVING JOSEPH, radiation oncologist; b. Newark, N.J., Aug. 14, 1931; s. Abraham and Frieda (Mintz) W.; m. Marilyn Bierman, June 14, 1953; children: Marc, Irene Fahrenwald, Paula Feynman, David. AB, Washington U., 1953, MD, 1956. Diplomate Am. Bd. Radiology. Intern Jewish Hosp., St. Louis, 1956-57; resident in radiology Hosp. U. Pa., Phila., 1960-64; instr. div. radiation therapy Wash. U. Sch. Medicine Dept. Radiology, St. Louis, 1964—66; med. dir. dept. radiation oncology Meth. Med. Ctr., Peoria, Ill., 1971—93; clin. asst. prof. radiology U. Ill. Coll. Medicine, Peoria, Ill., 1972—93; ret. Mem adv. com. dept. radiology U. Ill., Peoria, 1985-93; vis. prof. dept. radiation oncology Albert Einstein Med. Ctr., Phila., 1988, Loyola U. Med. Ctr., Chgo., 1988; vis. prof., spl. cons. divsn. radiation therapy U. Hosp. Eppendorf, U. Hamburg, Germany, 1996, 2000. Contbr. articles to med. jours.; contbr. chpt. to book Tumor Bd. Case Mgmt., 1997. Bd. dirs. Am. Cancer Soc., St. Louis and Peoria, 1968-86, Ill. divsn., 1975-81, pres. Peoria County unit, 1973-76; pres. Friends of the Gateway Festival Orch., 1965-70; mem. Gov.'s Adv. Coun. on Cancer, Ill., 1980-93. Mem. AMA, Am. Coll. Radiology, Am. Radium Soc., Am. Soc. Therapeutic Radiology and Oncology, Am. Brachytherapy Soc.

WEIGER, JOHN GEORGE, foreign language educator; b. Dresden, Germany, Feb. 6, 1933; came to U.S., 1938, naturalized, 1945; s. Willy and Elisabeth (Prinz) W.; m. Leslie Lawrence Carpenter, Dec. 28, 1955; children: Robert Boyden, Mark Owen, Heidi Elaine. BA, Middlebury Coll., 1955; MA, U. Colo., 1957; PhD (NDEA fellow), Ind. U., 1966. Instr. U. Colo., Boulder, 1955-57, Lawrence Coll., Appleton, Wis., 1957-58; instr. Romance langs. U. Vt., Burlington, 1958-62, asst. prof., 1964-67, assoc. prof., 1967-73, prof., 1973-98, prof. emeritus, 1998—, vice chmn. Romance lang. dept., 1964-68, chmn., 1994-98, asst. dean Coll. Arts and Scis., 1968-69, assoc. dean, 1969-71, dean, 1971-76; instnl. rep. for Rhodes scholarships, Danforth fellowships, Turrell Fund scholarships, 1971-76; program chmn. George Aiken lecture series, 1975; vis. lectr. U. Bologna, 1978, 87, U. Venice, Italy, 1987, U. Valencia, Spain, 1987; Cervantes lectr. Fordham U., 1990. Cons. Eirik Borve, Inc., 1979-80. Author: Introduction to the Youthful Deeds of the Cid, 1969, The Valencian Dramatists of Spain's Golden Age, 1976, Cristobal de Virues, 1978, Hacia la Comedia, 1978, The Individuated Self: Cervantes and the Emergence of the Individual, 1979, The Substance of Cervantes, 1985, In the Margins of Cervantes, 1988; editor: Las Hazañas del Cid, 1981, La Infelice Marcela, 1985; mem. editl. bd.: Bull. of Comediantes, 1978-2000; editl. bd.: Hispania, 1993-01; contbr. articles to profl. jours., also chpts. to books. U. Vt. Faculty Research fellow, 1967, 83, 86; Am. Council Learned Socs. grantee, 1978; U. Vt. Univ. scholar for the humanities, 1985-86. Mem. MLA (chmn. comedia sect. 1970-71), Renaissance Soc. Am., Am. Assn. Tchrs. Spanish and Portuguese (chmn. com. hon. mems. and fellows 1984), The Comediantes, Internat. Assn. Hispanists, Cervantes Soc. Am., Phi Beta Kappa, Phi Sigma Iota, Phi Eta Sigma (hon.). Home: 63 Woodbine Rd Shelburne VT 05482-6702 E-mail: jweiger@adelphia.net.

WEIGERT, ANDREW JOSEPH, sociology educator; b. N.Y.C., Apr. 8, 1934; s. Andrew Joseph and Marie Teresa (Kollmer) W.; m. Kathleen Rose Maas, Aug. 31, 1967; children: Karen Rose, Sheila Marie. BA, St. Louis U., 1958, PhL, 1959, MA, 1960; BTh, Woodstock (Md.) Coll., 1964; PhD, U. Minn., 1968. NIMH trainee U. Minn., Mpls., 1965-67; asst. prof. sociology U. Notre Dame, Ind., 1968-72, assoc. prof., 1972-76, prof., 1976—, chmn. dept., 1980-84, 88-89. Vis. assoc. prof. Yale U., New Haven, 1973-74; participant nat. and regional profl. meetings. Co-author: Family Socialization, 1974, Interpretive Sociology, 1978, Society and Identity, 1986; author: Everyday Life, 1981, Social Psychology, 1983, Life and Society, 1983, Mixed Emotions, 1991, Self, Interaction, and Natural Environment, 1997; adv. editor various sociology jours.; contbr. numerous articles to profl. jours., chpts. to books. Recipient tchg. awards, 1999, 2002; NSF grantee, 1969. Avocation: woodlot and prairie management. Office: U Notre Dame Dept Sociology Notre Dame IN 46556 Office Phone: 219-631-7408. E-mail: aweigert@nd.edu.

WEIGHT, ALEC CHARLES, retired management consultant; b. Plymouth, Eng., July 20, 1939; s. Charles William and Jean Stirling (Thomson) W.; m. Barbara Anne Carpenter, Mar. 10, 1962 (div. Oct. 1979); children: Glenn, Paul, Andrew; m. Mary-Linn Wright, July 19, 1980; children: Christopher, Matthew, Ryan. B of Chem. Engring., McMaster U., Hamilton, Can., 1961; MS, Waterloo (Can.) U., 1973. Registered profl. engr., Ont. Plant engr. Procter and Gamble, Hamilton, 1961-69, plant mgr., 1969-73; assoc. McKinsey and Co., Toronto, Can., 1973-78; ptnr. Booz Allen and Hamilton, N.Y.C., 1978-90, mng. ptnr. Wassenaar, The Netherlands, 1990-93, ptnr. Sydney, Australia, 1993-98; ret., 1998. Republican. Avocations: skiing, sailing, watercolors. Home: 2710 Broke Spoke Way Park City UT 84060

WEIGHT, DOUG, professional hockey player; b. Warren, Mich., Jan. 21, 1971; Student, Lake Superior State Coll., Mich. Center N.Y. Rangers, 1990-93, Edmonton Oilers, 1993—2001, St. Louis Blues, 2001—. Mem. U.S. Olympic Hockey Team, Nagano, Japan, 1998, Salt Lake City, 2002, Team U.S.A., World Cup of Hockey, 1996, 2004. Named to NHL All-Star Game, 1996, 1998, 2001, 2003. Achievements include mem. World Cup Champion Team U.S.A., 1996. Address: St Louis Blues Savvis Ctr Saint Louis MO 63101-2709*

WEIGHT, MICHAEL ANTHONY, lawyer, former judge; b. Hilo, Hawaii, Jan. 5, 1940; s. Leslie A. and Grace B. (Brown) W.; m. Victoria Noel; children: Rachael R., Elizabeth G., Thomas P. BA in History, U. Rochester, 1961; LLB, Vanderbilt U., 1967. Bar: Hawaii 1967, U.S. Ct. Appeals (9th cir.) 1968, U.S.

Supreme Ct. 1972. Pvt. practice, Honolulu, 1974-97; former judge Dist. Ct. (1st cir.) Hawaii; asst. fed. pub. defender Dists. of Hawaii and Guam, 1997—. Bd. dirs. Bishop Mus. Assn. 1st lt. USMC, 1961-63. Mem. Hawaii Bar Assn., Hawaii Assn. Criminal Def. Lawyers (pres. 1986). Office: Fed Pub Defenders Office 300 Ala Moana Blvd Honolulu HI 96850-0001

WEIGLE, MAURICE S. lawyer; b. Chgo., Dec. 2, 1912; s. Maurice and Grace M. (Stein) W.; m. Helen Rosenberg, June 22, 1937; children— Babs W. Maltenfort, Alice W. Kraus. Ph.B., U. Chgo., 1933, J.D., 1935. Bar: Ill. 1935. Assoc., then ptnr. Goldberg & Weigle, Chgo., 1936-74; ptnr. Jenner & Block, Chgo., 1974— . Served with USNR, 1945-46. Mem. ABA, Ill. Bar Assn., Chgo. Bar Assn., Chgo. Council Lawyers. Jewish. Clubs: Standard (Chgo.); Birchwood (Highland Park, Ill.). Office: Jenner and Block One IBM Plaza Chicago IL 60611

WEIGLE, PEGGY, information technology executive; BA in philosophy cum laude, U. Mass. V.p. N. Am. sales Arbor Software, 1996; v.p. worldwide field operations Hyperion (merged with Arbor Software), v.p., gen. mgr. performance mgmt. divsn.; CEO Perfecto Tech. (now Sanctum, Inc.), 1999—. Chmn. application sub-com. BENS Silicon Valley Cyber Security Working Group; mem. tech. sub-com. Silicon Valley Blue Ribbon Task Force on Aviation Security and Tech. Named one of 50 Most Powerful Women in Networking, Network World mag., 2003. Office: Sanctum Inc 2901 Tasmand Dr Ste 205 Santa Clara CA 95054

WEIGNER, BRENT JAMES, secondary school educator; b. Pratt, Kans., Aug. 19, 1949; s. Doyle Dean and Elizabeth (Hanger) W.; m. Sue Ellen Weber Hume, Mar. 30, 1985; children: Russell John Hume, Scott William Hume. BA, U. No. Colo., 1972; MEd, U. Wyo., 1977, PhD, 1984. Cert. Nat. Bd. for Profl. Tchg. Stds. Counselor, coach Olympia Sport Village, Upson, Wis., 1968; dir. youth sports F.E. Warren AFB, Cheyenne, 1973—74; instr. geography Laramie County Comm. Coll., Cheyenne, 1974-75; tchr. social sci. McCormick Jr. HS, Cheyenne, 1975—, Laramie County Sch. Dist. 1, Cheyenne, 1975—; head social studies dept. McCormick Jr. HS, 1987-99, 2001—02; curriculum adv. coun. chmn. Laramie County Sch. Dist. No. 1, 1988-89. Lectr. ednl. methods U. Wyo., 1989, clin. faculty, 1992-94; nat. chmn. Jr. Olympic cross-country com. AAU, Indpls., 1980-81; pres. Wyo. Athletic Congress, 1981-87; tchr. cons. Nat. Geog. Soc. Geography Inst., 1991, North Pole Marathon cons. Global Expdns.; South Pole marathon cons. and guide Adventure Network Internat., 2002-03; alt. cert. assessor Wyo. State Dept. Edn., 2002—; cons. Adventure Network Internat., 1999-2002; cons. North Pole marathon, Polar Running Adventures, 2003—; presenter, cons. in field. Fgn. exch. student U. Munich, 1971-72; head coach Cheyenne Track Club, 1976—, pres., 1980; race dir. Wyo. Marathon, 1978—; deacon 1st Christian Ch., Cheyenne, 1987-90, elder, 1991-93; rep. candidate gen. election Wyo. Legis., 1991; bd. dirs. United Med. Ctr. of Wyo. Found., 1995—, Cheyenne Boys and Girls Club, 1999—; keynote spkr., Okla. Marathon, 2002. Named Wyoming State bd. edn. Disting. Educator, Wyo. U.S. West Outstanding Tchr., 1989, Wyo. Coun. for the Social Studies K-8 Tchr. of Yr., 1994-95, Jr. High Coach of Yr., Wyo. Coaches Assn., 1996, Vol. of Yr., office Youth Alternatives, 2000; fellow Taft Found., 1976, Earthwatch-Hearst fellow, Punta Allen, Mex., summer 1987, Christa McAuliffe fellow, 1991-92, Wyo. Christa Mcauliffe Fellowship Selection Com., 1994, 95, 01; Fulbright grantee, Israel, summer 1984; Fulbright scholar Ghana and Senegal, 1990; People-to-People Internat. Ambassador to Vietnam, 1993; recipient Masons of Wyo. Disting. Tchr. award 1994. Mem. NEA, Nat. Network for Ednl. Renewal, Nat. Coun. Social Studies, Nat. Coun. Geog. Edn., Dominican Rep. Nat. Coun. for Geog. Edn. (Cram scholarship 1992), Wyo. Geog. Alliance (steering com., Amazon Workshop Fellowship 1998), Cheyenne Tchrs. Edn. Assn. (govtl. rels. com., instrn. and profl. devel. com.), U. No. Colo. Alumni Assn., Cheyenne C. of C., Wyo. Heritage Soc., Wyo. Edn. Assn. (World Book Ency. classroom rsch. project cons. 1976—, accountability task force 1989-90), Fulbright Alumni Assn. (life), U. Wyo. Alumni Assn. (life), Cheyenne Sunrise, Lions (bd. dirs. Cheyenne 1987, pres. 1995-96, 1st v.p. 1993-94, Melvin Jones Fellowship, 1995), Phi Delta Kappa (life, bd. dirs. Cheyenne 1989—, v.p., edn. award for rsch. 1990, pres. 1992-93, ednl. found. rep. 1993-94, area 4-D coord. 1994-95, Gerald Read Internat. Seminar scholar 1994; mem. outstanding doctoral dissertation com. 1994, 96), Phi Delta Kappa (Ed. award 2000). Achievements include first to run ultramarathon races on all seven continents, 1999; South Pole Ultramarathon champion, 2002; sr. men's nat. snowshoe champion, 2003; North Pole Ultramarathon champion, 2003; first person in the world to run ultramarathons at both the North Pole and the South Pole, 2003. Home: 402 W 31st St Cheyenne WY 82001-2527 Office: McCormick Jr HS 6000 Education Dr Cheyenne WY 82009-3991 Office Phone: 307-771-2650. E-mail: RunWyo@msn.com.

WEIHAUPT, JOHN GEORGE, geosciences educator, scientist, university administrator; b. La Crosse, Wis., Mar. 5, 1930; s. John George and Gladys Mae (Ash) W.; m. Audrey Mae Reis, Jan. 28, 1961. Student, St. Norbert Coll., De Pere, Wis., 1948-49; BS, U. Wis., 1952, MS, 1953, U. Wis.-Milw., 1971; PhD, U. Wis., 1973. Exploration geologist Am. Smelting & Refining Co., Nfld., 1953, Anaconda Co., Chile, S.Am., 1956-57; seismologist United Geophys. Corp., 1958; geophysicist Arctic Inst. N.Am., Antarctica, 1958-60, Geophys. and Polar Research Center, U. Wis., Antarctica, 1960-63; dir. participating Coll. and Univ. program, chmn. dept. phys. and biol. sci. U.S. Armed Forces Inst., Dept. Def., 1963-73; assoc. dean for acad. affairs Sch. Sci., Ind. U.-Purdue U., Indpls., 1973-78, prof. geology, 1973-78; asst. dean (Grad. Sch., prof. geoscis. Purdue U.), 1975-78; prof. geology, assoc. acad. v.p., dean grad. studies and research, v.p. Univ. Research Found., San Jose (Calif.) State U., 1978-82; vice chancellor for acad. affairs U. Colo., Denver, 1982-86, prof. geoscis., 1987—. Sci. cons., mem. sci. adv. bd. Holt Reinhart and Winston, Inc., 1967—; sci. editor, cons. McGraw-Hill Co., 1966—; hon. lectr. U. Wis., 1963-73; geol. cons., 1968—; editorial cons. John Wiley & Sons, 1968; editorial adv. bd. Dushkin Pub. Group, 1971— Author: Exploration of the Oceans: An Introduction to Oceanography; mem. editorial bd. Internat. Jour. Interdisciplinary Cycle Research, Leiden; co-discoverer USARP Mountain Range (Arctic Inst. Mountain Range), in Victoria Land, Antarctica, 1960; discoverer Wilkes Land Meteorite Crater, Antarctic. Mem. Capital Community Citizens Assn.; mem. Madison Transp. Study Com., Found. for Internat. Energy Research and Tng.; U.S. com. for UN Univ.; mem. sci. council Internat. Center for Interdisciplinary Cycle Research; mem. Internat. Awareness and Leadership Council; mem. governing bd. Moss Landing Marine Labs.; bd. dirs. San Jose State U. Found. Served as 1st lt. AUS, 1953-55, Korea. Mt. Weihaupt in Antarctica named for him, 1966; recipient Madisonian medal for outstanding community service, 1973; Outstanding Cote Meml. award, 1974; Antarctic medal, 1968 Fellow Geol. Soc. Am., Explorers Club; mem. Antarctican Soc., Nat. Sci. Tchrs. Assn., Am. Geophys. Union, Internat. Council Corr. Edu., Soc. Am. Mil. Engrs., Wis. Alumni Assn., Soc. Study Biol. Rhythms, Internat. Soc. for Chronobiology, Marine Tech. Soc., AAAS, Univ. Indsl. Adv. Council, Am. Council on Edn., Expdn. Polaire France (hon.), Found. for Study Cycles, Assn. Am. Geographers, Nat. Council Univ. Research Adminstrs., Soc. Research Adminstrs., Man-Environ. Communication Center, Internat. Union Geol. Scis., Internat. Geog. Union, Internat. Soc. Study Time, Community Council Pub. TV, Internat. Platform Assn., Ind., Midwest assns. grad. schs., Western Assn. Grad. Schs., Council Grad. Schs. in U.S., Wis. Alumni Assn. of San Francisco, Kiwanis, Carmel Racquet Club (Rinconada), The Ridge at Hiwan (Evergreen, Colo., pres. 1991-93). Achievements include discovery of the Wilkes Land Anomaly and of the USARP Mt. Range in Victoria Land, both in Antarctica; also credited with revision of the discovery date of Antarctic continent by 3 centuries. Home: 30296 Snowbird Ln Evergreen CO 80439-9469 Office: U Colo Campus Box 172 PO Box 173364 Denver CO 80217-3364

WEIHMULLER, PATRICIA ANN, retired minister, artist; m. Fred H. Weihmuller, Aug. 31, 1957; children: Fredric, Susan Smith, Steven, Amy Kovanda. Secretarial Diploma, Blair Bus.Coll., Colorado Springs, 1955; Mgmt. Cert., William Rainey Harper Coll., Palatine, Ill., 1992; leadership diploma, Stephen Ministries, St. Louis, 1993; cert., William Rainey Harper Coll., 1983. Cert. profl. sec. Profl. Secs. Internat., 1983. Exec. sec. State Farm Ins. Co., Dearborn, Mich., 1959—60; exec. sec. Unocal, Schaumburg, Ill., 1971—92, Motorola (temp.), Schaumburg, Ill., 1993—94; Stephen ministry leader Prince of Peace Luth. Ch., Schaumburg, Ill., 1993—98, Stephen min., 1991—2004; oil painter Hoffman Estates, Ill., 1996—2004. Mem. Star (Rep. orgn.), Schaumburg Township, 1967—2004; election judge Cook County Bd. of Elections, Schaumburg Twp., 1995—2004; exec. sec. Parish Planning Coun. Prince of Peace Luth. Ch., Ill., 1989—92, bible study leader, mem. Naomi Cir., 1967—2004. Avocations: bridge, painting, reading, sewing, travel. Personal E-mail: fpweih@aol.com.

WEIHRICH, HEINZ, management educator; b. Germany; came to U.S., 1959; s. Paul and Anna Weihrich; m. Ursula Weihrich, Aug. 3, 1963. BS, UCLA, 1966, MBA, 1967, PhD, 1973; Dr. (hon.), San Martin de Porres U., Peru, 2000. Assoc. Grad. Sch. Mgmt. UCLA, 1968-73; from asst. to assoc. prof. Ariz. State U., Tempe, 1973-80; prof. global mgmt. and behavioral sci. U. San Francisco, 1980—. Vis. prof. China Europe Internat. Bus. Sch., Shanghai, Grad. Sch. Bus. Adminstrsn., Switzerland, Peking U., Beijing; global mgmt. cons. in field. Author: (with Harold Koontz and Cyril O'Donnell) Management, 7th edit., 1980, Japanese, Chinese and Indonesian edits., 8th edit., 1984, Singapore edit., 1985, Indonesian edit., 1986, Philippines edit., Bengali edit., 1989, Taiwan edit., 1985 (with Harold Koontz) 9th edit., 1988, Singapore edit., 1988, Chinese edit., 1989, Spanish edit., 1990, best-seller Spanish speaking world, Korean edit., 1988, 90, Pengurusan (Malaysian) edit., 1991, Czech edit., 1993. Hungarian edit., 1992, Management: A Global Perspective, 10th edit. (with Harold Koontz), 1993, Spanish edit., 1993, best-seller Spanish speaking world, Chinese, 1998, Singapore edit., 1993, Korean edit., 1996, Croatian edit., 1995, Administración una perspectiva global, 11th edit., 1998 (best seller), Administracão Fundamentos da Teoriae da Cienca, Primeiro Volume 1986, Administracão Organizacão Planejamento e Controle, Segundo Volume, 1987, Administracão Recursos Humanos: Desenvolvimento de Administradores, Terceiro Volume, 1987, (with Harold Koontz and Cyril O'Donnell) Management: A Book of Readings, 5th edit., 1980, (with George Odiorne and Jack Mendleson) Executive Skills: A Management by Objectives Approach, 1980, (with Harold Koontz) Measuring Managers--A Double-Barreled Approach, 1981, (with Harold Koontz and Cyril O'Donnell) Essentials of Management, 3d edit. 1982, Taiwan, Philippines, Chinese and India edits., 4th edit., 1986, Singapore edit., 1986, 6th edit., 2004, (with Harold Koontz) Manajamen, Jilid 1, Indonesian edit., 1987, Manajamen, Jilid 2, 1986, Elementos de Administracion, 3d edit., 1983, 6th edit., 2002, Management Excellence--Productivity through MBO, 1985, Singapore edit. 1986, Japanese edit., 1990, Greek edit., Produttivita con L' Italian edit. 1987, Administracion, 1985, Management Basiswissen, German edit., 1986, Excelencia Administrativa (Mex.), Spanish edit., 1987, Chinese edit., 1997, (with Harold Koontz and Cyril O'Donnell) Adminstracion Moderna, Tomo 1, 1986, (with Harold Koontz) Management: A Global Perspective, internat. edit., 1993, Administración: Una Perspectiva Global, 1994, 12th edit., 2004 (best seller 1998, 2004), Korean edit., 1993, 96, Croatian edit., 1996, Czech edit., 1993, 96, Elementos de Administracion - Enfoque Internactional, Exta Edicion, 2002, Principles of Management, 2004; editor: (with Jack Mendleson) Management: An MBO Approach, 1978; contbr. numerous articles and papers to profl. jours. Grantee Am. Mgmt. Assn., 1970. Fellow Internat. Acad. Mgmt., mem. Acad. Mgmt., Assn. Mgmt. Excellence (trustee 1985-87), Assn. Bus. Simulation Exptl. Learning, Acad. Internat. Bus., Beta Gamma Sigma, Sigma Iota Epsilon. Roman Catholic. Office: U San Francisco 2130 Fulton St San Francisco CA 94117-1080 Office Phone: 415-422-6780.

WEIKEL, MALCOLM KEITH, healthcare company executive; b. Shamokin, Pa., Mar. 9, 1938; s. Malcolm J. and Marian Eleanor (Faust) Weikel; m. Barbara Joan Davis, Dec. 17, 1960; children: Richard, Kristin. BSc, Phila. Coll. Pharmacy and Sci., 1960; MSc, U. Wis., 1962, PhD, 1966. Mgr. Roche Labs., 1966—70; commr. health svcs. HEW, Washington, 1970—77; v.p. Am. Med. Internat., 1978—82, pres., CEO, 1982—84; exec. v.p., COO, Manor Healthcare Corp., Silver Spring, Md., 1984—86; exec. v.p. Health Care & Retirement Corp., Toledo, 1986—88, sr. exec. v.p., COO, 1988—98, sr. exec. v.p., 1998—. Recipient Sec.'s Spl. citation, HEW, 1975, 1977. Mem.: Am. Health Care Assn. (v.p. 1990—, chmn. multifacility group 1990—93). Office: Health Care & Retirement Corp PO Box 10086 Toledo OH 43699-0086

WEIKLE, PAUL EUGENE, JR., music educator, musician; b. Rockledge, Fla., May 27, 1963; s. Paul Eugene Sr. and Gwenyth Ray Weikle. BA in Music, U. Ctrl. Fla., 1986; MusM, Ind. U., 1988. Musician/supr. Universal Studios Brass Band, Orlando, Fla., 1992—99, Busch Gardens, Tampa, Fla., 1988—92; adj. prof. low brass Brevard C.C., Cocoa, Fla., 1992—96, U. North Fla., Jacksonville, 1994—2001, Fla. C.C., Jacksonville, 1995—99, prof. of instrumental music, 1999—; adj. prof. of tuba and euphonium U. Ctrl. Fla., Orlando, 1999—2000. Musician live and recorded performances. Mem.: Music Educators Nat. Conf., Am. Fedn. Musicians, Internat. Tuba and Euphonium Assn., Internat. Trombone Assn., Internat. Assn. Jazz Edn., Coll. Band Directors Nat. Assn., Fla. Bandmasters Assn. (assoc.). Home: 414 Cutter Ct Orlando FL 32835 Office: Florida CC 11901 Beach Blvd Jacksonville FL 32246 Personal E-mail: pweikle@yahoo.com. E-mail: pweikle@fccj.org.

WEIKSNER, SANDRA S. lawyer; b. Washington, Nov. 9, 1945; d. Donald B. and Dick (Cutter) Smiley; m. George B. Weiksner, Aug. 19, 1969; children: Michael, Nicholas. BA in Psychology, Stanford (Calif.) U., 1966, JD, 1969. Tchg. fellow Stanford U., 1969-70; assoc. Cleary, Gottlieb, Steen & Hamilton, N.Y.C., 1970-77, ptnr., 1978—2003, sr. counsel, 2004—. Vis. lectr. Yale Law Sch., 1991-92. Bd. dirs. N.Y. Law Sch.; mem. Union Theol. Sem. Fellow Am. Bar Found., Am. Coll. Trusts and Estates Counsel, Internat. Acad. Estate and Trust Law; mem. ABA, N.Y. State Bar Assn., Assn. Bar City of N.Y., Conn. Bar Assn. Democrat. Unitarian Universalist. Home: 164 E 81st St New York NY 10028-1804 Office: Cleary Gottlieb Steen & Hamilton 1 Liberty Plz Fl 43 New York NY 10006-1404

WEIL, ANDREW L. retired lawyer; b. Pitts., July 19, 1920; s. Ferdinand T. and Allene (Guthman) W.; m. Margaret G. Thompson, Aug. 11, 1949; children: Wendy T., Peter A. AB cum laude, Princeton U., 1943; LLB, U. Pitts., 1948, JD, 1968. Bar: Pa. 1949, U.S. Ct. Appeals (3d cir.) 1955, U.S. Supreme Ct. 1965. Solicitor Twp. of O'Hara, Pa., 1956-64; spl. att. assty. gen. Commonwealth of Pa., Pitts., 1964-76; ptnr. Weil, Vatz & Weil, Pitts., 1958-68, Cleland, Hurtt, Witt & Weil, 1975-79, Rose, Schmidt, Hasley & DiSalle, 1980—2002; ret., 2002. Bd. dirs. Mary Hillman Jennings Found., 1970—. Served to lt. col. U.S. Army, 1943-46, ETO. Decorated Purple Heart, Bronze Star. Mem.: ABA, Am. Counsel Assn. (pres. 1982—83), Allegheny County Bar Assn., Pa. Bar Assn., Pitts. Athletic Club. Republican. Presbyterian. Mailing: 108 White Gate Rd Pittsburgh PA 15238-2622 E-mail: alw3invest@aol.com.

WEIL, ANDREW LAWRENCE, lawyer; b. Highland Park, Ill., Dec. 19, 1960; s. Edward A. and Julie R. Weil. BA in Econs. with honors, Northwestern U., 1983, JD, 1986. Bar: Ill. 1986. Ptnr. Sonnenschein Nath & Rosenthal LLP, Chgo., 1986—. Corp. sec. Donnelley Enterprise Solutions Inc., Chgo., 1997-98. Note and comment editor: Northwestern U. Jour. Internat. Law and Bus., 1984-86. Mem. Phi Beta Kappa. Office: Sonnenschein Nath & Rosenthal LLP 8000 Sears Tower Chicago IL 60606

WEIL, ANDREW THOMAS, physician, educator; b. Phila., June 8, 1942; s. Daniel Pythias and Jenny (Silverstein) Weil. BA, Harvard U., 1964, MD, 1968. Intern Mt. Zion Hosp. Med. Ctr., San Francisco, 1968-69; assoc. Harvard Bot. Mus., Cambridge, Mass., 1971-84; fellow Inst. Current World Affairs, N.Y.C., 1971-75; lectr. U. Ariz., Tucson, 1983—, dir. program in integrative medicine, clin. prof. medicine, 1996—. Author: Natural Mind, 1972, Marriage of the Sun and Moon, 1980, From Chocolate to Morphine, 1983, Health and Healing, 1984, Natural Health, Natural Medicine, 1990, Spontaneous Healing, 1995, 8 Weeks to Optimum Health, 1997, Eating Well for Optimum Health, 2000, The Healthy Kitchen, 2002, (newsletter) Self-Healing, (website) drweil.com. Served to lt. USPHS, 1969-70. Fellow Linnean Soc. London; mem. Am. Acad. Achievement, Sigma Xi. Democrat. Buddhist. Avocations: gardening, backpacking. Home: 6700 S X9 Ranch Rd Vail AZ 85641-6202 Office: Ariz Health Scis Ctr PO Box 245153 Tucson AZ 85724-5153 Office Phone: 520-647-7865. E-mail: karen@x9ranch.com.

WEIL, BARRY, theater director, entertainer; b. LA, Calif., Apr. 30, 1969; s. Steven Myron and Rosalind Margolis Weil. BA in theatre, Hampshire Coll., Amherst, Mass., 1987—91. Theatre program coord. Levels Cultural Ctr., Gt. Neck, NY, 1992—, asst. dir., 2000—. Co-artistic dir. EVOLVE Co., New York, NY, 1999—. Actor: (films) The Return of the King, 1993; actor, author, designer: (plays) Claim to Fame, 1993; actor, prodr., co-author, dir.: (films) Crittervision, 1994 (Puppeteers Am. Nat. Festival Featured Attraction, 1995); actor, co-prodr., author, designer, dir. The Jack O'Lantern Lady, 1997; actor, author, co-dir., co-designer: (stage performance (puppetry) Evolution, 2000 (Puppeteers Am. Nat. Festival Featured Attraction, 2001). Mem.: UNIMA-USA, Puppetry Guild Greater NY, Puppeteers Am. Avocations: painting, music, travel, sculpting. Personal E-mail: crittermkr@aol.com.

WEIL, D(ONALD) WALLACE, business administration educator; b. Cleve., July 20, 1923; s. Laurence J. and Carol S. (Wallace) W.; m. Jane A. Bittel, Dec. 29, 1947; children— John Wallace, Charles Andrew, Margaret Jane, Carol Wyn. BA, Oberlin Coll., 1947; JD, Willamette U., 1950. Pres. James Foundry Corp., Fort Atkinson, Wis., 1960-70; faculty bus. adminstrn. U. Wis., Eau Claire, 1971-74, chmn. dept. bus. adminstrn., 1974-77, prof., 1985—2003, ret., prof. emeritis, 2003—; pres. Diversified Industries, Inc., St. Louis, 1977-81, UHI Corp., Los Angeles, 1981-85. Dir. U.H.I. Corp. Diversified Industries, Inc., St. Louis, Sales Investments, Mgmt. Inc., Elmwood, Wis., Jane B. Inc., Eau Claire Served with AUS, 1942-45. Mem. Am. Security Council, Nat. Council Small Bus. Mgmt. Devel., Phi Kappa Phi, Beta Gamma Sigma. Republican. Congregationalist. Home: 1530 Canfield St Eau Claire WI 54701-4018 Office: U Wis-Eau Claire Dept Bus Adminstrn Eau Claire WI 54701

WEIL, EDWARD DAVID, chemistry researcher, consultant, educator; b. Phila., June 13, 1928; s. Irving E. and Minna M. (Stainbrook) W.; m. Barbara Joy Hummel, Sept. 11, 1952; children: David L., Claudia E. BS in Chemistry, U. Pa., 1950; PhD in Organic Chemistry, U. Ill., 1953; MBA, Pace U., 1982. Chemist, supr. Hooker Chem. Co., Niagara Falls, N.Y., 1950-65; supr., sr. scientist Stauffer Chem. Co., Dobbs Ferry, N.Y., 1965-86; ind. cons., patent agt., propr. Intertech. Svcs., 1986—; dir. exploratory rsch. Adelphi Rsch. Ctr., Garden City, 1986-87; rsch. prof. Poly U., Bklyn., 1987—. Contbr. articles to Kirk-Othmer Ency., Ency. Polymer Sci., Rsch. Mgmt., others. Recipient IR-100 award Indsl. Rsch. Mag. Mem. Am. Chem. Soc. (chmn. profl. rels. com. N.Y. sect. 1980-95), Assn. Cons. Chemists and Chem. Engrs., Sigma Xi. Achievements include more than 220 patents for commercial flame retardants, processes, agricultural chemicals, others. Home: 200 E 57th St Apt 5L New York NY 10022-2864 Office: Polytechnic U 6 Metrotech Ctr Brooklyn NY 11201-3840 Office Phone: 718-260-3715. E-mail: eweil@poly.edu.

WEIL, FRANK A. investment banker, lawyer; b. Bedford, N.Y., Feb. 14, 1931; s. Sylvan and Ruth Alice (Norman) W.; m. Denie Sandison, Feb. 10, 1951; children: Deborah Weil Harrington, Amanda, Sandison, William. AB cum laude, Harvard U., 1953, LL.B., 1956. Bar: N.Y. 1956. Practiced in, N.Y.C., 1957-60; gen. partner Loeb, Rhoades & Co., N.Y.C., 1960-71; pres. Abacus Fund, Inc., 1968-72; chief fin. officer, dir. Paine, Webber, Jackson & Curtis, N.Y.C., 1972-77; asst. sec. industry and trade Dept. Commerce, Washington, 1977-79; partner firm, bd. chmn., Ginsburg, Feldman, Weil & Bress, Washington, 1979-83, Wald, Harkrader & Ross, Washington, 1983-85; chmn., chief exec. officer, dir., Abacus and Assocs., Inc., 1985—; chmn. bd. SyVox Corp., Exxel/Atmos, Inc. Dir. Geico, Dorr-Oliver, Inc., Stamford, Conn., 1968-77, Hamburg Savs. Bank, N.Y.C., 1975-77, J.B. Lippincott Co., Phila., 1975-77, Govt. Research Corp., 1975-77, 79-85; dir., pres. Norman Found., 1953-77, 79, 92, chmn. bd. trustee, Ednl. Alliance. Trustee Tchrs. Coll., Columbia U., 1976-79, Montefiore Hosp., 1960-77; trustee, vice chmn. No. Westchester Hosp., 1971-77; past vice chmn. bd. govs. Atlantic Inst. Internat. Affairs; past pres. Ednl. Alliance, trustee, 1957-77; trustee, sec. Fedn. Jewish Philanthropies, N.Y.C., 1965-77; trustee, chmn. Harvey Sch., 1969-76; trustee Hurricane Island Outward Bound Sch., 1974—, Washington Opera, 1984-85, Asia Soc., 1993—; bd. dirs., pres., vice chmn., Hickrill Found., Inc., 1953-77, 79—; chmn. bd. dirs. Coun. Excellence in Govt., 1984—, chmn., 1988-93, Am. Assembly, 1992—, Smithsonian Inst., 1994—, chmn., 1997—; mem. vis. com. Kennedy Sch. Govt., Harvard U., chmn., 1998—; chmn. tax com., mem. N.Y. State Econ. Devel. Bd., 1975-77, mem. Appleseed Found. bd., 1995—; chmn., mem. N.Y. State Bd. Equalization and Assessment, 1976-77; adv. bd. Sch. Advanced Internat. Studies, Johns Hopkins U., 1979-88; mem. N.Y. State Council on Fiscal and Econ. Priorities, 1985-89, N.Y. Coun. Fgn. Rels.; mem. N.Y. State Adv. Commn. on Liability Ins., 1986. Mem. Century Assn., Harvard Club, River Club, Met. Club. Home: 1516 28th St NW Washington DC 20007-3058 Office: Abacus & Assocs Inc 147 E 48th St # 3fl New York NY 10017-1223 Office Phone: 212-230-9801. Business E-Mail: fweil2@abacusny.com.

WEIL, GORDON LEE, energy executive, publishing executive; b. Mineola, N.Y., Mar. 12, 1937; s. Irving and Sadye (Gordon) Weil; m. Roberta Meserve, Apr. 6, 1962; children: Anne Inger, Richard Clement. AB magna cum laude, Bowdoin Coll., 1958; Diploma of Advanced European Studies, Coll. Europe, Belgium, 1959; PhD, Columbia U., 1961. Dir. UN Semester Drew U., N.Y.C. and Madison, N.J., 1962—63; dep. ofcl. spokesman EEC, Washington, N.Y.C., Brussels, 1963—66; contbr. Washington Post, Newsweek, Bus. Abroad, Brussels, 1966—68; rsch. assoc. Twentieth Century Fund, N.Y.C., 1968—70; exec. asst. Sen. George McGovern, Washington, 1970—72; vis. prof. govt. Bowdoin Coll., Brunswick, Maine, 1973—74; corr., prodr. WNET/13, N.Y.C., 1973—75; pres. Polit. Intelligence, Inc., Harpswell, Maine, 1974—79; commr. bus. regulation State of Maine, Augusta, 1979—80, pub. adv., 1981—82; dir. Maine Office Energy Resources, Augusta, 1980—82; pres. Weil and Howe, Inc./Std. Energy Co., 1982—, Weil Pub. Co., Inc., 1989—2001; chmn. Weil Cos., 2001—. Chmn. New Eng. Energy Dirs., 1982; staff chmn. Nat. Govs. Assn. Subcom. Energy Conservation and Renewable Resources, 1981—82; vice chmn. New Eng. Power Planning Com., 1982; chmn., bd. dirs. Energy Testing Lab. Maine, 1979—82; gen. mgr. Dirigo Elec. Coop., 1983—89; lectr. Am. govt. Colby Coll., Waterville, Maine, 1977; lectr. internat. trade Baruch Coll., CUNY, N.Y.C., 1969—70; prof. European instns. Coll. Europe, Bruges, Belgium, 1966—67; lectr. internat. law Am. U., Washington, 1963—64; lectr. Am. govt. Rutgers U., New Brunswick, NJ, 1962. Author: The European Convention on Human Rights, 1963, A Handbook on the European Economic Community, 1965, Trade Policy in the '70s, 1969, A Foreign Policy for Europe, 1970, The Benelux Nations, 1970; author: (with Ian D. Davidson) The Gold War: The Story of the World's Monetary Crisis, 1970; author: The Long Shot: George McGovern Runs for President, 1973, The Consumer's Guide to Banks, 1975, American Trade Policy: A New Round, 1975, Election '76: A Complete Guide to the Campaign, 1976, Sears, Roebuck, U.S.A., 1977, The Welfare Debate of 1978, 1978, America Answers Sneak Attack, 2003. Selectman, chmn. Town of Harpswell, Maine, 1997—2000, 2003—; bd. dirs. Am. Lung Assn. of Maine, 1987—93. With U.S. Army, 1961—62. Rockefeller Found. fellow, 1966—68. Mem.: Phi Beta Kappa (senator 1999—2003). Democrat. Office: PO Box 1990 150 Capitol St Augusta ME 04332-1990 Office Phone: 207-621-0029. Business E-Mail: info@weilpublishing.com.

WEIL, JACK BAUM, clothing manufacturing company executive; b. Denver, Nov. 13, 1928; s. Jack Arnold and Beatrice (Baum) W.; m. Elizabeth Fried, 1956 (div. 1969); children: Steven Eugene, Judith B. Weil Oksner; m. Candace Helene Taylor, 1973 (div. 1983). BA, Tulane U., 1952. V.p. Rockmount Ranch Wear Mfg. Co., Denver, 1954—, designer, sales mgr., 1957—. Designer western apparel. Head planning group Humboldt Island Hist. Dist., Denver; planning com. City of Denver Chessman Park, 1996—; chmn. Commty. Coll. Denver Found. bd. dirs.; committeeman Denver Rep. Party, 1974—; del. Rep. county, dist. and state convs., 1974—; sec. Rep. Party Com., 1st Congl. Dist. Colo., 1993-94, chmn. 1995-99; sec. Colo. Rep. State Ctrl. Com., 1999—; mem. Colo. State Rep. Exec. Com., 1996—; bd. dirs. 1st Universalist Ch., Denver; mem. admissions com. Tulane U., 1994—; del. Rep. Nat. Conv., 1992, 96, nat. credentials com. 1st lt. U.S. Army, 1952-54. Mem. West Coast Western Mktg. Assn., Midwest Western Wear and Equipment Assn. (bd. dirs.), N.W. Western Wear & Equipment Travelers Assn. (pres. Mpls.), S.E. Western, English and Equine Assn. (bd. dirs. Altanta), Denver Western Wear and Equipment Assn., Hat Inst. Am. (del. 1974—), Denver

Athletic Club, Town Club, Lincoln Club (bd. dirs. 1997—), Rump Club, Kappa Delta Phi. Avocations: painting, politics, physical fitness, travel. Home: 1025 Humboldt St Denver CO 80218-3121 Office: Rockmount Ranch Wear Mfg Co 1626 Wazee St Denver CO 80202-1314

WEIL, JEFFREY GEORGE, lawyer; b. Allentown, Pa., Apr. 28, 1951; s. Russel G.E. and Irene Marie (Kozlowski) W.; children: Michael, Stephen, Brooke, Lauren, Kristen. AB, Princeton U., 1973; JD, Harvard U., 1976. Bar: Pa. 1976, U.S. Dist. Ct. (ea. dist.) Pa. 1976, U.S. Ct. Appeals (3d cir.) 1976, U.S. Supreme Ct., 1988. Assoc. Dechert, Phila., 1976-84, ptnr., 1984—, chmn. firm hiring com., 1987-89, mem. firm exec. com., 1990-94. Chmn. com. United Way Southeastern Pa., Phila., 1982-85, trustee, 1983-89, funding policy com., 1987-90; participant Community Leadership Seminar Program, Phila., 1986; bd. dirs. Hawk Mountain Sanctuary, 1993-99, chmn. bd. dirs., 2000—; bd. dirs. Pa. Wildlife Fedn., 1996-99. Mem. ABA (vice-chmn. adminstrn. law com. on pub. advs. and pub. representation 1985-88, antitrust sect. pvt. litigation subcom. 1991-2002), Pa. Bar Assn., Phila. Bar Assn. (fed. cts. com. 1985—), Princeton U. Alumni Schs. Com., Phila. Athenaeum, Princeton Club Phila. Avocations: fly-fishing, reading. Home: 195 Shelbourne Ln Phoenixville PA 19460-5710 Office: Dechert LLP 1717 Arch St Lbby 3 Philadelphia PA 19103-2713 Office Phone: 215-994-2538. E-mail: jeffrey.weil@dechert.com.

WEIL, JOHN DAVID, financial executive; b. Chgo., Sept. 28, 1947; s. Leslie Joseph and Carlyne (Strauss) W.; m. Marcie Bornfriend, July 4, 1981; children: Jessica Lauren, Michael Brandon, Samantha Leigh. BS in Econs., U. Ill., 1969; MBA in Fin., Northwestern U., 1971. Asst. to chmn. bd. Stanwood Industries, Lake Forest, Ill., 1971-74; pres. Kent Paper Co., Ridgewood, N.Y., 1974-81; pres., CEO Am. Envelope Co., Chgo., 1982-94; operating affiliate McCown De Leeuw & Co., 1995—; dir. Dimac Holdings, 1998—2003. Pres., CEO U.S.A. Internat. Data Response Corp., Scottsdale, Ariz., 1998—99; CFO Dimac Holdings, 1999—2001; sec., bd. dirs. Dimac Holdings, 1999—2003; sr. v.p., CFO, sec., bd. dirs. On Stage Entertainment, 2001—. Mem. Envelope Mfrs. Am. (bd. dirs. 1986-94), Ancala Country Club.

WEIL, JOHN WILLIAM, technology management consultant; b. N.Y.C., Feb. 3, 1928; s. Frank Leopold and Henrietta Amelia (Simons) W.; m. Joan Leatrice Landis, June 15, 1950; children— Nancy Ellen, Linda Jill. BS, MIT, 1948; PhD, Cornell U., 1953. Various positions in nuclear reactors and computers Gen. Electric Co. (various locations), 1953-70; v.p. advanced systems and tech. Honeywell Info. Systems, Inc., Waltham, Mass., 1970-74; v.p., chief tech. officer Bendix Corp., Southfield, Mich., 1974-77, sr. v.p., chief tech. officer, 1977-83; v.p. advanced tech. and engring. Allied Corp., Southfield, 1983; pres. Modular Bio Systems, Inc., 1983-85, Weil Assocs., Inc., Bloomfield Hills, Mich., 1985-97. Founder Met. Detroit Sci. and Engring. Coalition, 1977, sec., 1977-80, pres., 1980-82; chmn. Mich. Biotech. Inst., 1981-85, trustee, 1985-92; mem. Army Sci. Bd., 1982-84. Contbr. articles to prof. jours. AEC fellow, 1950-51 Home and Office: 218 Guilford Rd Bloomfield Hills MI 48304-2737 E-mail: johnww@weilhome.com.

WEIL, LEONARD, banker; b. 1922; married With U.S. Dept. State, Vienna, Austria, 1946; with Union Bank, Los Angeles, 1946-62; pres., CEO Mfrs. Bank, Los Angeles, 1962-86, pres. emeritus, 1986—. Adj. asst. prof. fin. Anderson Grad. Sch. Mgmt., UCLA (ret.) Trustee UCLA Found.; bd. visitors UCLA Grad. Sch. Mgmt.; past pres. Town Hall; bd. dirs. Braille Inst. Served with U.S. Army, 1943-45 Mem. Calif. Bankers Assn. (bd. dirs., past pres.), Am. Mgmt. Assn., Am. Econs. Assn., Am. Bankers Assn. (past dir.). Office: PO Box 571150 Tarzana CA 91357-1150 Address: 4501 La Barca Pl Tarzana CA 91356-5029

WEIL, LOUIS ARTHUR, III, retired newspaper publishing executive; b. Grand Rapids, Mich., Mar. 14, 1941; s. Louis Arthur, Jr. and Kathryn (Halligan) W.; m. Mary Elizabeth Buckingham, Sept. 7, 1963 (div. June 1977); children: Scott Arthur, Christopher Davison, Timothy Buckingham; m. Daryl Hopkins Goss, Jan. 26, 1980. BA in English, Ind. U., 1963; DHL (hon.), Mercy Coll., Grand Valley State U. Various positions Times Herald, Port Huron, Mich., 1966-68; personnel dir., pub. Journal and Courier, Lafayette, Ind., 1968-73; gen. mgr., pub. Gannett Westchester Rockland Newspapers, White Plains, N.Y., 1973-74, pres., gen. mgr., 1974-77, pres., pub., 1977-79; v.p. devel. Gannett Co., Inc., N.Y.C., 1979-83, sr. v.p. planning and devel., 1982-86; chmn., pub. Gannett Westchester Rockland Newspapers, White Plains, 1984-86; pres. The Detroit News, 1986-89, pub., 1987-89; U.S. pub. Time Mag., 1989-91; pub., chief exec. officer, exec. v.p. Ariz. Republic, Phoenix Gazette, Ariz. Bus. Gazette, 1991-96; chmn., pres., CEO Central Newspapers, Inc., Phoenix, 1996-2000. Bd. dirs. Ctrl. Newspapers, Inc., Prudential. Trustee Grand Canyon Nat. Park Found., Am. Grad. Sch. Internat. Mgmt.; bd. dirs. Heard Mus.; campaign chmn. Valley of the Sun United Way, 1992; past chmn. Greater Phoenix Leadership; past pres. bd. trustees Phoenix Art Mus. With USN. Office: 15974 N 77th St #102 Scottsdale AZ 85260

WEIL, MAX HARRY, internist, cardiologist, educator, medical researcher; b. Baden, Switzerland, Feb. 9, 1927; came to U.S., 1937, naturalized, 1944; s. Marcel and Gretl (Winter) W.; m. Marianne Judith Posner, Apr. 1955; children: Susan Margot, Carol Juliet. AB, U. Mich., 1948; MD, SUNY, N.Y.C., 1952; PhD, U. Minn., 1957; DSc (hon.), SUNY Downstate Med. Ctr., 2004. Diplomate Am. Bd. Internal Medicine and Critical Care Medicine, Nat. Bd. Med. Examiners. Intern in internal medicine U. Cin. Med. Ctr., 1952-53; resident U. Minn. Hosps., Heart Hosp., VA Hosp., Mpls., 1953-55; rsch. fellow U. Minn., Mpls., 1955-56; sr. fellow Nat. Heart Inst., Mayo Clinic, Rochester, Minn., 1956-57; chief cardiology City of Hope Med. Ctr., Duarte, Calif., 1957-59; asst. clin. prof. U. So. Calif. Sch. Medicine, L.A., 1957-59, asst. prof., 1959-63, assoc. prof., 1963-71, prof., 1971-81; chmn. L.A. Com. on Emergency Med. Svcs., 1968-73; prof., chmn. dept. medicine, chief divsn. cargiology Chgo. Med. Sch., Finch U. Health Scis., North Chicago, Ill., 1981-91, disting. univ. prof., 1992-94, disting. univ. prof. emeritus, 1994—, Finch U. Health Scis., North Chgo., Ill., 1994—. Adj. prof. medicine Northwestern U. Med. Sch., Chgo., 1992—; prof. clin. med. bioengring. U. So. Calif., L.A., 1972-91, adj. prof. medicine, 1981-94, clin. prof. anesthesiology, 1995—, rsch. prof. surgeyr, 1996—; disting. univ. prof. Inst. Critical Care Medicine, Palm Springs, Calif., 1995—; Knowles Meml. lectr. Vet. Emergency Critical Care Soc., 2002. Sect. editor Archives Internal Medicine, 1983-86, JAMA, 1969-72; guest editor Am. Jour. Cardiology, 1982, Critical Care Medicine, 1985; mem. editl. bd. Am. Jour. Medicine, 1971-79, Chest, 1980-95, Jour. Circulatory Shock, 1979-92, Clin. Engring. Newsletter, 1980—, Methods of Info. in Medicine, 1977-91, Jour. Clin. Illness, 1986—, Clin. Intensive Care, 1989—; mem. editl. adv. bd. Emergency Medicine, 1978—, Issues in Health Care Tech., 1983-86; assoc. editor Critical Care Medicine, 1973-74, mem. editl. bd., 1973-91, 94-96, sr. editor, 1997; editor-in-chief Acute Care, 1983-90, Jour. Cardiovasc. Pharmacol. Theories, 2003–; contbr. over 1000 articles to profl. jours.; patentee in field. Pres. Temple Brotherhood, Wilshire Blvd. Temple, L.A., 1967-68; bd. dirs. Hollywood Presbyn. Med. Ctr., 1976-81, L.A. chpt. Met. Am. Heart Assn., 1962-67, Chgo. chpt. Met. Am. Heart Assn., 1982-88. With U.S. Army, 1946-47. Recipient prize in internal medicine SUNY, 1952, Alumni medallion SUNY, 1970; Disting. Svc. award Soc. Critical Care Medicine, 1984; numerous rsch. grants, 1959—; named Disting. Alumni Lectr., 1967, Oscar Schwindetzky Meml. Lectr. Internat. Anesthesia Rsch. Soc., 1978; recipient Lawrence R. Medoff award Chgo. Med. Sch., 1987, Morris L. Parker Rsch. award, 1989, Mission of Mercy award Israeli Nat. Emergency Svcs., 2001; Lilly scholar, 1988-89. Master ACP; fellow Am. Coll. Cardiology (chmn. emergency cardiac care com. 1974-81); master, fellow Am. Coll. Chest Physicians (coun. clin. cardiology, coun. critical care medicine), Am. Coll. Clin. Pharmacology, Am. Coll. Critical Care Medicine (Disting. Investigator award 1990, 96, A.S. Laerdal Achievement award 2000, Lifetime Achievement award 2001), Am. Heart Assn. (coun. circulation, coun. basic sci., coun. cardiopulmonary and critical care, coun. clin. cardiology, Dickinson W. Richards Meml. lectureship 1998, Emergency Cardiac Care Lifetime Achievement award 2000), Vet. Emergency Critical Care Soc. (Knowles Meml. lectr. 2002), N.Y. Acad. Sci., Chgo. Soc. Internal Medicine; mem. AMA (sect. editor jour. 1969-72), IEEE, L.A. County Med. Assn., Am. Physiol. Soc. Am. Soc. Pharmacology and Exptl. Therapeutics, Am. Soc. Echocardiography, Am. Soc. Nephrology, Am. Trauma Soc. (founding mem.), Assn. Computing Machinery, Assn. Am. Med. Colls., Vet. Emergency and Critical Care Soc. (Knowles Meml. lectr. 2002), Ctrl. Soc. Clin. Rsch., Chgo. Cardiol. Group (sec.-treas. 1986-88, chmn. 1988-90), Chgo. Soc. Internal Medicine, Lake County Heart Assn. (bd. govs. 1983-86), Intensive Care Soc. U.K., L.A. Soc. Internal Medicine, Soc. Exptl. Biology and Medicine, Western Soc. Clin. Rsch., Fedn. Am. Socs. Exptl. Biology, Am. Soc. Parenteral and Enteral Nutrition, Nat. Acad. Practice (disting. practitioner), Skull and Dagger, Sigma Xi, Alpha Omega Alpha. Jewish. Avocations: swimming, tennis, photography, philosophy-economics. Office: Inst Critical Care Medicine 1695 N Sunrise Way Bldg 3 Palm Springs CA 92262-5309 E-mail: weilm@911research.org.

WEIL, PETER HENRY, lawyer; b. N.Y.C., Nov. 20, 1933; s. Frank L. and Amelia (Simons) Weil; m. Helen Fay Kolodkin, Dec. 18, 1960; children: Karen W. Markus, Frank L. BA cum laude, Princeton U., 1954; LLB cum laude, Harvard U., 1957. Bar: N.Y. 1957, U.S. Dist. Ct. (so. and ea. dists.) N.Y. 1972. Assoc. Weil, Gotshal & Manges, N.Y.C., 1958-62; from assoc. to ptnr. Kaye Scholer, N.Y.C., 1962-95; ret., 1995. Lectr. SMU Inst. Comml. Financing, 1985—94, Banking Law Inst., 1987—89. Author: Asset Based Lending: An Introductory Guide to Secured Financing, P.L.I., 1989, 3d edit., 1996. Former chmn. N.Y. bd. overseers, former bd. govs. Hebrew Union Coll., Jewish Inst. Religion, Cin., N.Y.C., L.A., Jerusalem. With U.S. Army, 1957—58. Named U.S. Nat. champions as member of Ringwood Golden Master Volleyball Team, 1983. Mem.: ABA, Assn. Bar of City of N.Y. (mem. banking law com. 1975—78).

WEIL, RANDOLPH ALLEN, engineering executive; b. Champaign, Ill., Nov. 23, 1951; s. Nicholas Andrew and Audrey Florence W.; m. Susan Kay Rostad, Feb. 26, 1977; children: Alexandra, Aaron. BS in Econs., U. Ill., Chgo., 1973; MBA, U. Calif., Berkeley, 1974. Gen. sales mgr. Cummins Engrng. Co., Downers Grove, Ill., 1975-83; gen. mgr. ops. Sub of Cummins Engine. Co., Chgo., 1983-85; v.p., gen. mgr. Global Parts, Inc. The Budd Co., Dallas, 1985-87; dir. coastal ops. Allied Tube & Conduit, Harvey, Ill., 1987-88; dir. distbn. ops. Square D. Co., Florence, Ky., 1988-92; v.p. logistics AT&T Network Systems, Morristown, NJ, 1992-94; v.p. svc. logistics NCR Corp., Dayton, Ohio, 1994—2000; pres., COO IHS Engring., 2001—03; exec. v.p. IHS Group, 2003—. Dir. Jr. Achievement, Dayton, 1996-99, Boy Scouts Am., Columbus, 1978-80. Mem. Am. Prodn. & Inventory Control Soc., Coun. Logistics Mgrs. Avocations: bicycling, swimming, opera, remodelling, gardening.

WEIL, RICHARD, III, surgeon, medical educator; b. N.Y.C., Feb. 22, 1936; s. Richard Jr. and Allene (Hall) W.; m. Polly Edgar, Aug. 22, 1959; children: Wendy, Richard. AB, Princeton U., 1957; MD, Columbia U. Coll. Physicians and Surgeons, 1961. Diplomate Am. Bd. Surgery, Nat. Bd. Med. Examiners. Intern in surgery Presbyn. Hosp., 1961-62, asst. resident in surgery, 1962-63, 65-67, chief resident in gen. surgery, 1968; chief resident in pediat. surgery Babies Hosp., 1969, chief resident in vasc. surgery, 1969, asst. attending surgeon, chmn. surg. house staff com., 1970-74, dir. kidney transplantation, 1973-74; asst. in surgery Columbia U. Coll. Physicians and Surgeons, 1967-68, instr. surgery, 1969, asst. prof. surgery, 1970-74; fellow in transplantation surgery U. Minn., 1970; assoc. prof. surgery U. Colo., 1974 79, prof. surgery, 1979-87, dir. transplantation, 1980-87; prof. surgery, dir. transplantation NYU, 1987-93; assoc. dean medicine, prof. surgery Brown U., Providence, 1993-98. Cons. surgeon Manhattan VA Hosp., 1989-92, Denver VA Hosp., 1980-87, Denver Gen. Hosp., 1980-87, St. Anthony-Ctrl. Hosp. Denver, 1980-87; attending surgeon Bellevue Hosp. Ctr., 1989-93 Contbr. more than 130 articles to profl. jours. including Surg. Forum, Am. Jour. Surgery, Transplantation, Surgery, Jour. Pediat. Surgery, Surgery, Gynecology & Obstets., among others. Capt. U.S. Army Med. Corps, 1963-65, Germany. Mem. Am. Assn. Tissue Banks, ACS, Am. Fedn. Clin. Rsch., Am. Soc. Transplant Surgeons, Am. Soc. for Artificial Internal Organs, Am. Surg. Assn., Assn. for Acad. Surgery, Allen O. Whipple Surg. Soc. (recorder 1976-78), Ctrl. Surg. Assn., Clin. Immunology Soc., Denver Acad. Surgery, Harvey Soc., Intermountain End-Stage Renal Disease Network (exec. com. 1975-79), Internat. Cardiovasc. Soc., N.Y. Ctr. for Liver Transplantation, N.Y. Clin. Soc., N.Y. Regional Transplant Program (pres. 1991-92), N.Y. Surg. Soc., Rocky Mountain Vasc. Surg. Soc., Soc. Internat. de Chirurgie, soc. Univ. Surgeons, Transplantation Soc., Western Assn. Transplant Surgeons, United Network for Organ Sharing (councilor for Colo., Wyo., Nebr., Kans., Iowa, Mo. 1986-87).

WEIL, ROLF ALFRED, economist, university president emeritus; b. Pforzheim, Germany, Oct. 29, 1921; arrived in U.S., 1936, naturalized, 1944; s. Henry and Lina (Landauer) W.; m. Leni Metzger, Nov. 3, 1945; children: Susan Linda, Ronald Alan. BA, U. Chgo., 1942, PhD, 1950; D Hebrew Letters, Coll. Jewish Studies, 1967; DHL, Loyola U., 1970, Bowling Green (Ohio) State U., 1986; LHD, Roosevelt U., 1988. Rsch. asst. Cowles Commn. for Rsch. in Econs., 1942-44; rsch. analyst Ill. Dept. Revenue, 1944-46; mem. faculty Roosevelt U., Chgo., 1946—, prof. fin. and econs., also chmn. dept. fin., 1954-65, dean Coll. Bus. Adminstrn., 1957-64, acting pres., 1965-66, pres., 1966-88, pres. emeritus, 1988—. Past pres. Selfhelp Home for the Aged, Chgo.; cons. to non-profit orgns., 1988—. Author: Through these Portals-from Immigrant to College President, 1991; contbr. articles on fin. to profl. jours. Bd. dirs. trustees Roosevelt U., Selfhelp of Chgo., Inc. Mem. Am. Econ. Assn., Cliff Dwellers Club. E-mail: rweil@roosevelt.edu.

WEIL, STEPHEN EDWARD, retired museum official; b. NYC, June 24, 1928; s. Sidney and Beatrice (Sachs) W.; m. Rose Reicherson, Oct. 15, 1950 (div.); children: Rachel J., David N., Michael D.; m. Elizabeth Carbone, Sept. 7, 1974 (div.); m. Wendy Luke, Apr. 8, 1990. AB, Brown U., 1949; LL.B., Columbia U., 1956. Bar: NY 1956. Assoc. firm Rosenman, Colin, Kaye, Petschek & Freund, N.Y.C., 1956-63; v.p., gen. mgr. Marlborough-Gerson Gallery, N.Y.C., 1963-67; adminstr., sec., trustee Whitney Mus. Am. Art, N.Y.C., 1967-74; dep. dir., sec. Hirshhorn Mus. and Sculpture Garden, Smithsonian Instn., Washington, 1974-95, scholar emeritus, 1995—. Cultural property adv. com. USIA, 1995-2000; chair adv. com. Mus. Loan Network, 1995-04. Co-author: Art Works - Law, Policy, Practice, 1974, Art Law - Rights and Liabilities of Creators and Collectors, 1986; author: Beauty and the Beasts, 1983, Rethinking the Museum, 1990, A Cabinet of Curiosities, 1995, Making Museums Matter, 2002; editor: A Deaccession Reader, 1997; co-editor: Art Galleries and Museums, 1973. Mem. mus. adv. panel N.Y. State Coun. on Arts, 1974-78; mem. adv. panel Inst. for Mus. Scis.; trustee Brown U., 1989-95. Mem. Am. Assn. Mus. (treas., v.p., councilor), Am. Fedn. Arts (trustee 1988-95). Jewish. Home: 800 25th St NW Washington DC 20037-2207 Office: Ctr for Edn and Mus Studies Smithsonian Instn Washington DC 20560-0427 Office Phone: 202-357-3175. Business E-Mail: sweil@scems.si.edu.

WEIL, THOMAS ALEXANDER, electronics engineer, retired; b. N.Y.C., Jan. 22, 1930; s. Frank Leopold and Henrietta Amelia (Simons) W.; m. Dianne Isaacs; children: Deborah, Elizabeth, Alexander. BSEE, MIT, 1951. Engr. modulator sect. Raytheon Co., Watertown, Mass., 1951-55, sect. mgr. transmitters, 1955-69, dept. mgr. transmitters, 1969-77, staff scientist equipment devel. labs., 1972-95, lab. mgr. radar systems, 1977-79, lab. mgr. advanced devel., 1979-80, program mgr. oil shale program, 1980-84; cons. in field, 1995—. Contbr. 3 chpts. to books, 37 articles to profl. jours.; holder 10 patents in field. Recipient Excellence in Tech. award Raytheon co., 1990; Raytheon Co. fellow, 1989. Fellow IEEE (tech. papers com. Modulator Symposia, Microwave Tube Symposia, Germeshausen award 1994). Universalist-Unitarian. Avocations: classical music, photography, mountain climbing, cosmology. Home: 14 Lanark Rd Wellesley MA 02481-3029 *Evolution and survival of the fittest have left mankind aggressive and prone to make war. Peace depends on finding how to overcome this heritage. Shouldn't we be working on how to resteer mankind's instincts?.*

WEIL, THOMAS P. health services consultant; b. Mount Vernon, N.Y., Oct. 2, 1932; s. H.M. and Alice (Franc) W.; m. Janet Whalen, Feb. 13, 1965. BA, Union Coll., 1954; MPH, Yale U., 1958; PhD, U. Mich., 1964. S.S. Goldwater fellow Mount Sinai Med. Ctr., N.Y.C., 1957-58; assoc. cons. J.G. Steinle Assocs., Garden City, N.Y., 1958-61; asst. prof. UCLA, 1962-65; assoc. dir. Touro Infirmary, New Orleans, 1964-66; prof., dir. U. Mo., 1966—71; v.p. E.D. Rosenfeld Assocs., N.Y.C., 1971-75; pres. Bedford Health Assocs. Inc., N.Y., N.C., 1975-2000. Chmn. Health Edn. & Applied Rsch. Found., Washington, 1981-83; bd. dirs. Albany (N.Y.) Med. Ctr., Inc., 1974-77; cons. to numerous hosps., med. schs., health related orgs., 1958-2000. Contbr. articles profl. jours. Named vis. prof. W.K. Kellogg Found., Sydney, Australia, 1969; recipient svc. award Am. Assn. Healthcare Cons., 1982; Weil Disting. Prof. in Health Svcs. Mgmt., U. Mo. established in 1991. Fellow APHA (emeritus), Am. Assn. Healthcare Cons. (emeritus), Am. Coll. Healthcare Execs. (emeritus). Jewish. Avocations: Appaloosa and Quarter Horses, english cocker spaniels. Office Phone: 828-252-1616.

WEILAND, ANDREW J. orthopaedic surgeon; MD, Wake Forest U., 1968. Diplomate Am. Bd. Orthop. Surgery (pres. 1998-99). Resident in gen. surgery U. Mich., Ann Arbor, 1969-70; resident in orthop. surgery Johns Hopkins Hosp., Balt., 1972-75; attending orthopedist Hosp. for Spl. Surgery, NYC; prof. surgery (orthop. and plastic) Cornell U. Med. Coll., Ithaca, NY, 1990 . Contbr. over 250 articles to profl. jours.; editl. bd. Jour. Bone and Joint Surgery, Jour. Hand Surgery, Internat. Jour. Microsurgery. Recipient Kappa Delta award for outstanding rsch., 1986, 91, Joseph Boyes award 43rd Ann. Meeting of Am. Soc. Surgery of the Hand, 1988; ASIF fellow in internal fixation of fractures, Switzerland, 1974, Christine Kleinert Hand fellow, 1975; ABC Traveling Fellow, 1981. Mem. Am. Orthop. Assn. (pres. 1998-99), Am. Soc. Reconstructive Microsurgery (pres. 1991), Am. Soc. for Surgery of the Hand (pres. 1995), Am. Acad. Orthopedic Surgeons (treas. 2000-) Achievements include research in dupuytren's contractures, upper extremity joint replacement and free vascularized bone grafts. Office: Hospital for Special Surgery 535 E 70th St New York NY 10021-4898 Office Phone: 212-606-1575. Office Fax: 212-535-0426. Business E-Mail: weilanda@hss.edu.*

WEILAND, CHARLES HANKES, lawyer; b. Billings, Mont., Feb. 19, 1921; s. George Michael and Elizabeth (Hankes) W. AB cum laude, Johns Hopkins U., 1942; JD, Harvard U., 1948. Bar: Ill. 1949, U.S. Dist. Ct. (no. dist.) Ill. 1949, U.S. Ct. Appeals (7th cir.) 1949, U.S. Supreme Ct. 1968. Assoc. Lord, Bissell & Brook, Chgo., 1948-55, ptnr., 1956-83. Chmn. Cook County Inquiry Bd., Supreme Ct. Ill. Atty. Regis. and Disciplinary Commn., 1974-75 Served with AUS, 1942-46. Mem. Ill. Bar Assn., Chgo. Bar Assn. Clubs: The Lawyers Club of Chgo. Republican.

WEILAND, JULIETTE MARIE, public relations executive, freelance writer and photographer, freelance photographer, writer; b. St. Cloud, Minn., Oct. 5, 1944; d. Raymond Henry and Marie Julie (Fradette) Peterson; m. James Edward Weiland, Sept. 18, 1965; children: James Edward Jr., Timothy Paul, Kristin Juliette, Stephanie Marie. BS, U. Minn., 1967; student, U. Calif., Berkeley, 1978-83, Silvermine Sch. Art, New Canaan, Conn., 1987, Am. Mgmt. Assn., 1993. Cert. English tchr. Tchr. English Anoka Hennepin Sch. Dist., Coon Rapids, Minn., 1968-71, tutor ESL Anoka, Minn., 1971-73, Cherry Creek Sch. Dist., Englewood, Colo., 1975-76; pvt. tutor ESL Bethel, Conn., 1976-78; ptnr., owner, author Pamphleteers & Co., Wilton, Conn., 1986-96; pub. rels. dir. Nursing & Home Care, Wilton, Conn., 1988-95; owner Breathe Easy Environ. Assocs., Wilton, Conn., 1991-96. Freelance writer, Acton, Mass., 1982—84; newspaper columnist on polit., govt. issues, 1987—89; newspaper columnist on pub. rels. issues for small bus., 2000—04. Author: (short story) Somewhere There's A Child Waiting For Me, 1984; co-editor The Wilton Voter, Wilton LWV, 1994-95; photographer various newspapers, mags., reports; contbr. numerous articles to profl. jours.; contbr. columns to papers. Co-chair Open Door Soc. for Adoptive Parents, Acton, 1980-83; pub. rels. dir. LWV Conn., Hamden, 1986-88, comm. cons., 1988-89; publicity dir. Crop Walk for Hungry, Wilton, 1987-88; mem. Graffiti Task Force, Norwalk, 1998-99. Recipient Apex award of excellence for columns and editls., 2002, 2003, Communicator award of distinction, 2003. Mem. Pub. Rels. Soc. Am. (treas. 1998, v.p. 1999, chmn. job bank 1997-2000, pres. 2000, nominating chmn. 2001-02, chmn. hospitality com. 2003-04), Internat. Freelance Photographers Orgn., Nat. Fedn. Press Women, Fairfield County Pub. Rels. Assn., Conn. Press Club (pres. 2000-02, 3rd prize external ann. report for non-profits 1990, 2d prize 1991, 3d prize news photo 1991), Healthcare Pub. Rels. and Mktg. Soc. Greater N.Y., Wilton C. of C. Democrat. Roman Catholic. Avocation: photography. Home: 67 Signal Hill Rd Wilton CT 06897-1930 Office: Juliette Weiland & Co 67 Signal Hill Rd Wilton CT 06897-1930 E-mail: jweiland@optonline.net.

WEILAND, MARK BRADLEY, corporate lawyer; b. Hinsdale, Ill., June 15, 1956; s. William Sheplar and Dorothy (Costello) W.; m. Susan Jean Hill, Nov. 14, 1987; children: William, Abigail. BA, U. Ill. Champaign, 1978; JD, U. Chgo.-Kent Coll. Law, 1981. Asst. state's atty. Dupage Co., Ill., 1982-86; atty. William D. Lyman and Assocs., Oakbrook Terr., Ill., 1986-87; gen. counsel/v.p. and corporate sec. Profl. Svc. Industries, Inc., Lombard, Ill., 1987—. Chmn. Advocate's Assembly, Silver Spring, Md., 1993—, Lawyer's Roundtable. Mem. ABA, Ill. Bar Assn., Am. Soc. Testing and Materials (mem. com. D-18 1998—), Chgo. Bar Assn., Columbia Yacht Club. Republican. Roman Catholic. Avocations: fly fishing, boating, woodworking. Office: Ste 400 1901 S Meyers Rd Oakbrook Terrace IL 60181-5208 Fax: 630-691-1498. E-mail: mark.weiland@psiusa.com.

WEILAND, SCOTT RICHARD, singer; b. Santa Cruz, Calif., Oct. 28, 1967; m. Mary Forsberg, 2000 (div. 2003); children: Noah, Lucy Olivia. Founder, lead singer Mighty Joe Young (later renamed Stone Temple Pilots), 1987; lead singer Stone Temple Pilots, 1992—, Velvet Revolver, 2003—; founder Softdrive Records, 2003. Singer: (albums) (with Stone Temple Pilots) Core, 1992, Purple, 1994, Tiny Music...Songs From the Vatican Gift Shop, 1996, No. 4, 1999, Shangri-La Dee Da, 2001, Thank You, 2003, (solo) 12 Bar Blues, 1998, (with Velvet Revolver) Contraband, 2004; co-prodr.: (albums) Break Your Silence, Cinder, 2003. Office: RCA Records 1540 Broadway New York NY 10036*

WEILER, EDWARD J. federal agency administrator; b. Chgo., 1949; PhD, Northwestern U., 1976. Staff scientist, chief ultraviolet/visible and gravitational astrophysics NASA, 1979, chief scientist Hobble Space Telescope, 1979—96, dir. origins program, 1996—98, assoc. adminstr. space sci., 1998—. Office: NASA Hdqrs Mail Code S 300 E St SW Washington DC 20546

WEILER, JEFFRY LOUIS, lawyer; b. N.Y.C., Dec. 31, 1942; s. Kurt and Elaine (Kabb) W.; m. Susan Karen Goodman, June 8, 1964; children: Philip K., June M. BS, Miami U., Oxford, Ohio, 1964; JD, Cleve. State U., 1970. Bar: Ohio 1970, Fla. 1981; CPA, Ohio 1968; bd. cert. specialist in estate planning trust and probate law, Ohio; bd. cert. tax specialist, Fla., 1983—. Acct. Meaden & Moore, CPAs, Cleve., 1964-65; IRS agt. U.S. Dept. Treasury, Cleve., 1965-70; assoc. Ulmer & Berne, Cleve., 1970-71; ptnr. Benesch, Friedlander, Coplan & Aronoff, LLP, Cleve., 1971—. Adj. assoc. prof. Cleve.-Marshall Coll. Law, Cleve. State U., 1980-87. Contbr. to profl. pubs. Fellow Am. Coll. Trust and Estate Counsel; mem. ABA (sect. taxation, estate and gift tax subcom.), Ohio State Bar Assn. (bd. govs. estate planning trust and probate law sect. 1999—), Cleve. Estate Planning Inst. (chmn. 1980), Cleve. Tax Inst. (chmn. 1983), Cleve. Bar Assn. (treas. 1993-96, trustee 1988-91), Tax Club of Cleve. (sec. 1996-97, v.p. 1997-99, pres. 1999-2000). Avocations: photography, sailboat racing. Home: 24714 Maidstone Ln Beachwood OH 44122-1614 Office: Benesch Friedlander Coplan & Aronoff LLP 2300 BP Tower 200 Public Sq Cleveland OH 44114-2378 Office Phone: 216-363-4551. E-mail: jweiler@bfca.com.

WEILER, JOSEPH, law educator; BA, Sussex U., 1976; diploma in internat. law, The Hague Acad. Internat. Law, 1978; LLB, Cambridge U., 1977, LLM, 1982; PhD, Florence European U. Inst., 1982. Mem. dept. law European U. Inst., Florence, Italy, 1978—85; co-founder Acad. European Law, 1989; prof. law U. Mich. Law Sch., 1985—92; Manley Hudson prof., Jean Monet chair Harvard Law Sch., 1992—2001; Joseph Straus prof. law NYU Sch. Law, 2001—, European Union Jean Monnet chaired prof., 2001—, chair, faculty

dir. Hauser Global Law Sch. Program, 2002—. Founding editor: European Jour. Internat. Law, European Law Jour., World Trade Rev. Fellow: Am. Acad. Arts and Scis. Office: NYU Sch Law Vanderbilt Hall 40 Washington Sq South Rm 102 New York NY 10012-1099*

WEILER, PAUL CRONIN, law educator; b. Port Arthur, Ont., Can., Jan. 28, 1939; s. G. Bernard and Marcella (Cronin) W.; m. Florrie Darwin, 1988; children: Virginia, John, Kathryn, Charles. BA with honors, U. Toronto, 1960, MA with honors, 1961; LLB, Osgoode Hall Law Sch., 1964; LLM, Harvard Law Sch., 1965; LLD, U. Victoria, 1981, U. Toronto, 2000. Bar: Ont. Prof. law Osgoode Hall Law Sch., 1965-72; chmn. Labour Rels. Bd. B.C., 1973-78; Mackenzie King prof. Can. studies Harvard Law Sch., 1978-80, prof. law, 1980—, Henry J. Friendly prof. law, 1993—. Chief counsel U.S. Commn. Future of Worker-Mgmt. Rels.; prin. legal investigator Harvard U. Med. Practice Study Group; impartial umpire AFL-CIO; chief reporter Am. Law Inst. Tort Reform Project; cons. to U.S. Commn. on Comprehensive Health Care (Pepper Commn.); spl. counsel Govt. of Ont. Rev. of Workers' Compensation, 1980-88; mem. pub. rev. bd. UAW, chief counsel Pres.' commn. Future Worker-Mgmt. Rels., 1993-94; panelist, U.S./Can. Free Trade Agreement Softwood Lumber Arbitration, 1992-93. Author: Labor Arbitration and Industrial Change, 1970, In the Last Resort: A Critical Study of the Supreme Court of Canada, 1974; (with others) Labor Relations Law in Canada, rev. edit., 1974; (with others) Studies in Sentencing in Canada, 1974, Reconcilable Differences: New Directions in Canadian Labour Law, 1980, Reforming Workers Compensation, 1980, MEGA Projects: The Collective Bargaining Dimensions, 1981, Protecting the Worker from Disability, 1983, Governing the Workplace: The Future of Labor and Employment Law, 1990, (with others) Patients, Doctors, and Lawyers: Medical Injury, Malpractice Litigation and Patient Compensation, 1990, Medical Malpractice on Trial, 1991, (with others) A Measure of Malpractice, 1992, Text, Cases, and Problems on Sports & the Law, 1993, 2d edit., 1998, 3RD EDIT., 2004, Text, Cases, and Problems on Entertainment, Media, and the Law, 1997, 2d edit., 2002, Leveling the Playing Field, 2000; contbr. articles to profl. jours. Mem. Nat. Acad. Arbitrators, Nat. Acad. Social Ins., Nat. Acad. Sci., Inst. Medicine. Roman Catholic. Office: Harvard U Law Sch 1525 Massachusetts Ave Cambridge MA 02138-2903 Office Phone: 617-495-2955. E-mail: pweiler@law.harvard.edu.

WEIL-GARRIS BRANDT, KATHLEEN (KATHLEEN BRANDT), art historian; b. Surrey, Eng. d. Kurt Hermann and Charlotte (Garris) Weil; m. Werner Brandt (dec. 1983). BA with honors, Vassar Coll., 1956; postgrad., U. Bonn, Germany, 1956-57; MA, Radcliffe U., 1958; PhD, Harvard, 1966; MA, Oxford U., 1998. Asst. prof. NYU, N.Y.C., 1963-67, assoc. prof., 1967-72, prof., 1973—; asst. prof. NYU Inst. Fine Arts, N.Y.C., 1966-67, assoc. prof., 1967-72, prof., 1973—; vis. prof. Harvard U., Cambridge, Mass., 1980; editor in chief The Art Bulletin, N.Y.C., 1977-81; Slade prof. Oxford U., 1998. Cons. on Renaissance art Vatican Mus., 1987—; vis. fellow Bibliotheca Hertziana (Max-Planck Inst.) Rome. Author: Leonardo and Central Italian Art, 1974, Problems In Cinquecento Sculpture, 1977; author: (with J. d'Amico) The Renaissance Cardinal's Ideal Palace, 1981, (with C. d'Acidini, J. Draper, N. Penny) Giovinezza di Michelangelo, 1999-2000; contbr. numerous articles to profl. jours.; editor: Michelangelo: la Cappella Sistina: documentazione e interpretazione, vol. III, 1996. Mem. Am. com. Medici Archive Project, 1996—; bd. dirs. Raccolta Vinciana, 1997—. Decorated officer Order of Merit (Italy); recipient rsch. award Humboldt Found., 1985, Disting. Tchg. award Lindback Found., 1967, Golden Dozen Tchr. award NYU, 1993, Alumni Great Tchr. award, 1996; Guggenheim fellow, 1976; grantee Henkel Found., 1987, Samuel H. Kress Found., 1999. Mem. Coll. Art Assn. (bd. dirs. 1973-74, 77-81), Renaissance Soc. Am. (editl. bd. 1992—), Soc. Archtl. Historians, N.Y. Acad. Scis., Phi Beta Kappa (v.p. NYU chpt. 1979-81). Avocations: art films, conservation, music, dance. Office: NYU Inst Fine Arts 1 E 78th St New York NY 10021-0119 E-mail: kathleen.brandt@nyu.edu.

WEILL, GEORGES GUSTAVE, mathematics educator; b. Strasbourg, France, Apr. 9, 1926; came to U.S., 1956; s. Edmond and Germaine (Falck) W. Ed., Ecole Polytechnique, Paris, 1950; E.N.S., Telecom., Paris, 1952; Licence de Mathematiques, U. Paris, France, 1954, D.Sc. in Physics, 1955; PhD in Math, U. Calif. at Los Angeles, 1960. Research scientist Compagnie Generale de Telegraphie Sans Fil, France, 1952-56; research fellow dept. elec. engring. Calif. Inst. Tech., Pasadena, 1956-59; teaching asso. math. U. Calif. at Los Angeles, 1959-60; research fellow math. Harvard, 1960-62; lectr., research asso. Yale, 1962-64; vis. asst. prof. Belfer Grad. Sch. Sci., Yeshiva U., 1964-65; assoc. prof. math. Poly. U., Bklyn., 1964-65, prof., 1966-95, prof. math. emeritus, 1995—. Adj. prof. math. Cooper Union, N.Y.C. Mem. Am. Math. Soc., Societe Mathematique de France, IEEE (sr. mem.), Sigma Xi, Pi Mu Epsilon. Office: Polytechnic Univ 333 Jay St Brooklyn NY 11201-2990

WEILL, HANS, medical educator; b. Berlin, Aug. 31, 1933; came to U.S., 1939; s. Kurt and Gerda (Philipp) W.; m. Kathleen Burton, Apr. 3, 1958; children: Judith, Leslie, David. BS, Tulane U., 1955, MD, 1958. Diplomate: Am. Bd. Internal Medicine. Intern Mt. Sinai Hosp., N.Y.C., 1958-59; resident Tulane Med. Unit, Charity Hosp. La., New Orleans, 1959-60, chief resident, 1961-62, sr. vis. physician, 1972—; NIH research fellow dept. medicine and pulmonary lab. Sch. Medicine Tulane U., New Orleans, 1960-61, instr. medicine, 1962-64, asst. prof. medicine, 1964-67, assoc. prof., 1967-71, prof. medicine, 1971—, Schlieder Found. prof. pulmonary medicine, 1985-97; chief Environ. Medicine sect. Tulane Med. Center, 1980-96; dir. univ. Ctr. for Bioenviron. Rsch., 1989-93; dir. interdisciplinary research group in occupational lung diseases Nat. Heart, Lung and Blood Inst., 1972-92, mem. nat. adv. council, 1986-90, chmn. pulmonary disease adv. com., 1982-84; active staff Tulane Med. Center Hosp., 1976—; program dir. Nat. Inst. for Environ. Health Sci., 1992-96. Cons. pulmonary diseases Touro Infirmary, New Orleans, 1962—; cons. NIH, Nat. Inst. Occupational Safety and Health, Occupational Safety and Health Adminstrn., USN, NAS, EPA; lectr., participant workshops and confs. profl. groups in U.S., France, Can., U.K.; dir. Nat. Inst. Environ. Health Scis Superfund. Basic Rsch. Program, 1992-96. Mem. editorial bd. Am. Rev. of Respiratory Disease, 1980-85, CHEST, 1987-91; editor Respiratory Diseases Digest, 1981; guest editor Byssinosis conf. supplement, CHEST, 1981. Fellow Am. Acad. Allergy, Royal Soc. Medicine, ACP; mem. Am. Thoracic Soc. (pres. 1976), Am. Lung Assn. (bd. dirs. 1975-78), New Orleans Acad. Internal Medicine (sec., treas. 1973-75), Am. Coll. Chest Physicians (gov. for La. 1970-75), Am. Fedn. Clin. Research, So. Soc. Clin. Investigation, N.Y. Acad. Scis., Brit. Thoracic Assn., Internat. Epidemiol. Assn., Am. Heart Assn. (task force on environment and cardiovascular system 1978), Brit. Thoracic Soc., Phi Beta Kappa, Alpha Omega Alpha. Home and Office: 755 Hearthstone Dr Basalt CO 81621-8205

WEILL, SANFORD I. bank executive; b. N.Y.C., Mar. 16, 1933; s. Max and Etta (Kalika) W.; m. Joan Mosher, June 20, 1955; children: Marc P., Jessica M. BA, Cornell U., 1955, student Grad. Sch. Bus. and Pub. Adminstrn., 1954-55. Chmn. bd., chief exec. officer Carter, Berlind & Weill (name changed to CBWL-Hayden, Stone, Inc. 1970, to Hayden Stone Inc. 1972, to Shearson Hayden Stone 1974, to Shearson Loeb Rhoades), N.Y.C., 1960-84, dir., chmn. exec. com., 1981-83, pres., 1983-85, Am. Express Co., 1983—85, chmn., CEO Fireman's Fund Ins. Co. subs., 1984-85; chmn., CEO Am. Express Insurance Svcs., Inc., 1984—85; chmn., pres., chief exec. officer Comml. Credit Co., Balt., 1986—88; chmn., CEO Primerica Corp., N.Y.C., 1988—93, pres., 1988—92; chmn. Primerica Holdings Inc., N.Y.C.; chmn., CEO Travelers Group, N.Y.C., 1993—98, Citigroup, N.Y.C., 1998—2003, chmn., 2003—. Bd. dirs. Fed. Res. Bank N.Y., AT&T Corp., United Technologies Corp; vice chmn. adv. council The Johnson Grad. Sch. of Mgmt.; founder Acad. of Fin. Mem. bd. overseers Joan and Sanford I. Weill Med. Coll. and Grad. Sch. Med. Scis. of Cornell U. (formerly Cornell Med. Coll.), 1982-, chmn., 1986-; chmn. bd. trustees Carnegie Hall, N.Y.C.; trustee N.Y. Presbyn. Hosp.; bd. overseers Meml. Sloan-Kettering Cancer Ctr.; bd. dirs. Balt. Symphony Orch. Mem. N.Y. Soc. Security Analysts Clubs: Cornell (N.Y.C.), Century Country (Purchase, N.Y.), Harmonie (N.Y.C.). Office: 399 Park Ave New York NY 10022-4614 also: Citigroup 153 E 53rd St New York NY 10043-0001

WEIMANN, ROBERT BRUCE, retired surgeon; b. Camden, N.J., May 18, 1931; s. Max Ludwig and Ruth Elizabeth (Karl) W.; m. Carol Lee Cain, June 1, 1957; children: Robert Steven, Theodore Harrison, Lauren Lee. AB, Duke U., 1952; MD, Thomas Jefferson U., Phila., 1956. Diplomate Am. Bd. Gen. and Thoracic Surgeons. Intern Thomas Jefferson U. Hosp., Phila., 1956-57; resident surgery Temple U. Med. Ctr., Phila., 1957-61; resident thoracic surgery Baylor U. Affiliated Hosps., Houston, 1961-62; mem. staff Cooper Med. ctr., Camden; chief sect. surgery West Jersey Health Systems; prof. surgery emeritus U. Medicine and Dentistry N.J.-Rutgers; ret., 1994. Bd. mem. Am. Cancer Soc., Camden County, N.J., 1963-80. Mem. ACS, Am. Coll. Chest Surgeons, Pan-Pacific Surg. Assn., Del. Valley Vascular Surg. Soc., S. Jersey Vascular Soc. Republican. Methodist.

WEIMER, DAVID LEO, political science educator; b. Buffalo, N.Y., May 23, 1950; s. Leo Nickolas and Dorthy May (Tates) W.; m. Melanie Frances Manion, June 7, 1990. BS in Engring and BA in Urban Studies, U. Rochester, 1973; M of Pub. Policy, U. Calif., 1975, MA in stats., 1976, PhD, 1978. Grad. intern office rsch. and stats. Social Security Adminstrn., 1974; teaching asst. grad. sch. pub. policy U. Calif., Berkeley, 1975-76; instr. dept. polit. sci. U. Rochester (N.Y.), 1977-78, asst. prof., 1978-82; economist office of policy, planning and analysis U.S. Dept. Energy, 1980-81; assoc. prof. U. Rochester, 1982-86, deputy dir. pub. policy analysis program, 1982-89, prof. polit. sci., pub. policy analysis, 1986-2000; prof. dept. polit. sci. Robert M. La Follette Sch. Pub. Affairs U. Wis., Madison, 2000—. Chevron disting. vis. prof. faculty bus. adminstrn. Simon Fraser U., 1986; disting. vis., prof. Robert M. La Follette Inst. Pub. Affairs U. Wis., Madison, 1989-90; disting. pub. policy lectr. pub. policy program U. N.C., Chapel Hill, 1992; vis. prof. dept. polit. sci. and pub. adminstrn. Peking U., 1993; found. dir. Ctr. For Pub. Policy Studies LIngnan Coll., Hong Kong, 1994-95. Author: Improving Prosecution? The Inducement and Implementation of Innovations for Prosecution Management, 1980, The Strategic Petroleum Reserve: Planning, Implementation and Analysis, 1982, Policy Analysis and Economics: Developments, Tensions, Prospects, 1991; co-editor: Oil Price Stocks, Market Response and Contingency Planning, 1984, Responding to International Oil Crises, 1988, Policy Analysis: Concepts and Practice, 4th edit., 2004, Instl. Design, 1995, Cost Benefit Analysis, 1996, 2d edit., 2001, Political Economy of Property Rights, 1997, Organizational Report Cards, 1999; editor Jour. Policy Analysis and Mgmt., 1985-89; author articles. Dir. U.S. Go Congress, Rochester, 1991. Bridging fellow Dept. Pharmacology and Toxicology U. Rochester, 1983. Mem. Assn. Pub. Policy Analysis and Mgmt., Am. Soc. Pub. Adminstrn., Am. Polit. Sci. Assn., Am. Econ. Assn., Am. Risk and Ins. Assn., Am. Go Assn.(chair, bd. dirs., 2003), Phi Beta Kappa. Avocation: go (asian game). Office: Robert M La Follette Sch Pub Affairs U Wis Dept Polit Sci Madison WI 53706 Office Phone: 608-262-5713.

WEIMER, JOHN L. state supreme court justice; b. Thibodaux, Oct. 2, 1954; m. Penny Hymel; 3 children. BS (with honors), Nicholls State U., 1980; JD, La. State U., 1980. Pvt. practice law, 1980—95; judge 17th Judicial Dist. Ct., 1995—98, 1st Cir. Ct. of Appeal, Dist. 1, Divsn. B, 1998—2001; justice La. Supreme Ct., 2001—. Adj. prof. law Nicholls State U., 1982—97, prof. law, 1982—97. Mem. Thibodaux Vol. Fire Dept. Recipient Crimefighter's Outstanding Jurist award . Mem.: Lafourche Parish Student Govt. Day Program (creator, coord.), Citizens' Summit Justice Reform (regional co-chmn. 1997), Assumption C. of C., Houma-Terrebonne C. of C., Thibodaux C. of C., Nicholls State U. (mem. alumni bd., former vol. legal counsel), Lafourche Parish Bar Assn., La. State Bar Assn. (del.), Rotary Club. Achievements include development of Lafourche Parish Drug Treatment Court. Mailing: 301 Loyola Ave New Orleans LA 70112

WEIMER, PETER DWIGHT, retired mediator, lawyer, corporate executive; b. Grand Rapids, Mich., Oct. 14, 1938; s. Glen E. and Clarabel (Kauffman) W.; children: Melanie, Kim; m. Judith Anne Minor. BA, Bridgewater Coll., 1962; JD, Howard U., 1969. Assoc. counsel Loporto & Weimer Ltd., Manassas, Va., 1970-75; chief counsel Weimer & Cheatle Ltd., Manassas, 1975-79, Peter D. Weimer, P.C., Manassas, 1979-83; pres., mediator Mediation Ltd., Manassas, 1981—2002, ret., 2002. Pres. Citation Properties, Inc., Manassas, 1971-93; pres. Preferred Rsch. of No. Va., Inc., 1985-89, Pro Rsch. Inc., 1989-93, Pro Mgmt., Inc., 1990-2002; cons. Continental Title & Escrow, Inc., 1992-96. Address: PO Box 7474 Sebring FL 33872

WEIMER, ROBERT JAY, geology educator, energy consultant, civic leader; b. Glendo, Wyo., Sept. 4, 1926; s. John L. and Helen (Mowrey) W.; m. Ruth Carol Adams, Sept. 12, 1948; children: Robert Thomas, Loren Edward (dec.), Paul Christner, Carl Scott. BA, U Wyo., 1948, MA, 1949; PhD, Stanford U., 1953. Registered profl. engr., Colo. Geologist Union Oil Co. Calif., 1949-54; cons. geologist U.S. and fgn. petroleum exploration, 1954—; prof. geology Colo. Sch. Mines, 1957-83, prof. emeritus, 1983—, Getty prof. geology, 1978-83; vis. prof. U. Colo., 1961, U. Calgary, Can., 1970, Inst. Tech., Bandung, Indonesia, 1975. Fulbright lectr. U. Adelaide, South Australia, 1967; disting. lectr. and continuing edn. lectr. Am. Assn. Petroleum Geologists, Soc. Expl. Geophysicists; ednl. cons. to petroleum cos., 1964—; mem. energy rsch. adv. bd. Dept. Energy, 1985-90, Bd. on Mineral and Energy Resources, Nat. Rsch. Coun., 1988. Editor: Guide to Geology of Colorado, 1960, Symposium on Cretaceous Rocks of Colorado and Adjacent Area, 1959, Denver Earthquakes, 1968, Fossil Fuel Exploration, 1974, Studies in Colorado Field Geology, 1976, Petroleum System, Denver Basin, 1996. Trustee Colo. Sch. Mines Research Found., 1967-70; pres. Rockland Found., 1982-83; bd. dirs. Foothills Art Ctr., 1997-2003. With USNR, 1944-46. Recipient Disting. Alumnus award U. Wyo., 1982, Mines medal Colo. Sch. Mines, 1984, Brown medal, 1990, Parker medal Am. Inst. Profl. Geologists, 1986, Exemplary Alumni award U. Wyo., 1994, ISEM Hedberg award, 2001. Fellow Geol. Soc. Am. (chmn. Rocky Mountain sect. 1966-67, Sloss award 2003), AAAS; mem. Am. Assn. Petroleum Geologists (hon. pres. 1992, Sidney Powers medal 1983, Dist. Educator award 1996), Soc. for Sedimentary Geology (hon., sec.-treas. 1966-67, v.p. 1971, pres. 1972, Twenhofel medal 1995), Colo. Sci. Soc. (hon., pres. 1981), Rocky Mountain Assn. Geologists (hon., pres. 1969, found. bd. 1976-86, Scientist of Yr. 1982), Nigerian Mining and Geoscis. Soc. (hon.), Can. Soc. Petroleum Geologists (hon.), Wyo. Geol. Assn. (hon.), Colo. Sch. Mines Alumni Assn. (hon., Coolbaugh award 1996), Am. Geol. Inst. Found. (sec., treas. 1984-88), Geol. Soc. Am. Found. (bd. dirs. 1999-2004), Nat. Acad. Engring. (ch. sec. 11 1999), Northwoodside Inc. Land Conservancy Found. (v.p. 1995-96, pres. 1997—), Mt. Vernon Country Club (Golden, bd. dirs. 1956-59, 81-84, pres. 1983-84). Home: RR 3 25853 Mt Vernon Rd Golden CO 80401-9699 Business E-Mail: rweimer@mines.edu.

WEIN, ALAN JEROME, urologist, educator, researcher; b. Newark, Dec. 15, 1941; s. Isadore R. and Jeanette Frances (Abrams) W. AB cum laude, Princeton U., 1962; MD, U. Pa., 1966. Diplomate, trustee emeritus Am. Bd. Urology. Intern mixed surgery Hosp. U. Pa., Phila., 1966-67, resident surgery, 1967-68; resident urology U. Pa., Phila., 1969-72, fellow Harrison Dept. Surg. Rsch. Urology Sch. Medicine, 1968-69, asst. instr. surgery Sch. Medicine, 1967-68, asst. instr. urology, 1969-71, instr., 1971-72, asst. prof., 1974-76, assoc. prof., 1976-83, prof., 1983—, asst. chief urology, 1974-79, dir. Urodynamic Evaluation Ctr., 1974—, chmn. div. urology, 1981—, chief urology, 1981—. Dir. resident edn. com. div. urology Sch. Medicine U. Pa., 1976—, coord. program urologics oncology, 1976—; chief urology VA Hosp., Phila., 1974-82, attending urologist, 1982-96; asst. surgeon Children's Hosp. Phila., 1974—; cons. CDC Coun. Incontinence, 1990—; assoc. surgeon Pa. Hosp., Phila., 1977—; attending urologist Grad. Hosp., Phila., 1980-97. Author: (with D.M. Barrett) Controversies in Neuro-Urology, 1984, Voiding Function and Dysfunction: A Logical and Practical Approach, 1988, 2d edit., 1995, (with A.R. Mundy and T.P. Stephenson) Urodynamics: Principles, Practice and Application, 1984, 2d edit., 1994, (with P.M. Hanno) A Clinical Manual of Urology, 1987, 2d edit., 1994, (with Hanno, Staskin and Krane) Interstitial Cystitis, 1990, Common Problems in Urology: Comon Problems in Infertility and Impotence, 1990, (with Abrams) The Overactive Bladder: A Widespread and Treatable Concition, 1998, (with Abrams and Khourys) Incontinence, 1999, (with Flanigan and Resnick) Objectives for Urologic Residency Education, 2001, (with Walship, REtika, Vaughan) Campbell's Urology, 8th edit., 2002, others; editl. bd. asst. Urol. Survey, 1978-81; editl. bd. cons. Investigative Urology, 1978-81; mem. editl. bd. World Jour. Urology, 1982—, Am. Urol. Assn. Update series, 1983—, Urol. Survey, 1987—, Internat. Jour. Impotence Rsch.: Basic and Clin. Studies, 1989-99, Urology, 1991—; ad hoc reviewer Cancer, 1985—; cons. editor Sexuality and Disability, 1985—; asst. editor Jour. Urology, 1980-89, ad hoc reviewer clin. sect., 1989—, editl. bd. investigative sect., 1989—; assoc. editor Neurourlogy and Urodynamics, 1982—; contbr. over 600 articles and abstracts to profl. jours. Mem. coun. urology Nat. Kidney Found., Inc.; mem lectrs. bur. Am. Cancer Soc., 1984—; mem. adv. panel Nat. Assn. for Incontinence, 1987—; mem. adv. bd. Simon Found., 1987—; mem. med. adv. bd. Institial Cystitis Assn., 1987—; chmn. bladder health coun. Am. Found. Urologic Disease, 1990-95; trustee Am. Bd. Urology, 1990-96. Maj. MC, U.S. Army, 1972-74. Grantee VA, 1974-79, 79, 81, 81-84, 82-85, 85-88, 88-92, Eaton Labs., 1975-76, 78-80, McCabe Rsch. Fund, 1975-82, 87-88, Merrell Nat. Labs., 1979-82, 1980-82, Nat. Kidney Found., 1980-81, NIH, 1980-83, 83-88, 84-87, 87—, Roche Labs., 1981, Smith Kline and French Labs., 1982, 86-88, Eli Lilly Labs., 1986-88, 91, Found. Interstitial Cystitis, 1986-87, 87-88, Sterling Drug Co., 1991; recipient F. Brantley Scott award Am. Found. for Urologic Disease, 1996, Hugh Hampton Young award, 1997, AUA Disting. Svc. award, 2000, AUA Disting. Contbn. award, 2001, Legion of Honor Gold Medallion award Chapel of Four Chaplains, VAlley Forge, Pa., 2001. Fellow ACS; mem. AAAS, AMA (cons. com. drug evaluation 1977-90), Am. Acad. Clin. Neurophysiology, Am. Assn. Surgery of Trauma, Am. Assn. Clin. Urologists, Am. Assn. Genito-Urinary Surgeons, Am. Surg. Assn., Am. Soc. Pharmacology and Exptl. Therapeutics, Am. Soc. Andrology, Am. Soc. Clin. Oncology, Am. Urol. Assn. (chmn. practical cases urology 1982—, rsch. com. 1985—, editl. com. mid-Atlantic sect. 1988—, pub. rels. adv. bd. 1998—, Disting. Svc. award 2000), Assn. Acad. Surgery, Can. Urol. Assn., Clin. Soc. Genito-Urinary Surgeons, Ea. Coop. Oncologic Group, Endourol. Soc., Internat. Continence Soc., Nat. Assn. VA Physicians, N.Y. Acad. Scis., Coll. Physicians Phila., John Morgan Soc., Pa. Med. Assn., Pa. Oncologic Soc., Phila. Acad. Surgery, Phila. County Med. Soc., Phila. Profl. Standards Rev. Orgn., Phila. Urologic Soc. (pres. 1990-91), Ravdin-Rhoads Surg. Soc., Urol. Assn. Pa., Radiation Therapy Oncology Group (genitourinary working com. 1980—), Royal Soc. Medicine, Soc. Internat. d'Urologie, Soc. Basic Urologic Rsch., Soc. Sex Therapy and Rsch., Soc. Govt. Svc. Urologists, Soc. Pelvic Surgeons, Soc. Univ. Surgeons, Soc. Univ. Urologists (counselor 1996—, pres. 1999-2000), Soc. Urologic Oncology, Univ. Urologic Forum, Urodynamics Soc. (exec. com. 1980—, Lifetime Achievement award 1996), Urologic Rsch. Soc., Urologist's Corr. Club, Sigma Xi. Home: 1224 Mirabeau Ln Gladwyne PA 19035-1048 Office: Hosp U Pa 9 Penn Tower 34th and Civic Center Blvd Philadelphia PA 19104-4206

WEIN, GEORGE THEODORE, music festivals producer, pianist, singer; b. Boston, Oct. 3, 1925; s. Barnet M. and Ruth Wein; m. Joyce Alexander, 1959 BA, Boston U., 1950; hon. doctorate, Berklee Coll., 1976. Founder Storyville Records, Boston, 1956; jazz columnist Boston Herald, 1956-59; founder, CEO, Festival Prodns., Inc., N.Y.C., 1962—; founder, current prodr. Carnegie Hall Jazz Orch., N.Y.C. Played with Dixieland combos in Boston, 1940's; operator Storyville jazz club, Boston, 1950-60; producer ann. Newport Jazz Festival, 1954-60, 61—, Ohio Valley Jazz Festival, Cin., 1962—, Down Beat Jazz Festival, Chgo., 1965; created Newport Folk Festival and Found., 1963, founder, Newport Jazz Festival-N.Y., 1972, N.Y. Jazz Repertory Co., 1973, Grande Parade Du Jazz festival, Nice, France, 1974, New Orleans Jazz and Heritage Festival, Hawaii Jazz Fair, 1976, Munich Jazz Festival, 1979, Capital Radio Jazz Festival, London, 1979, Playboy Jazz Festival, Los Angeles, 1979; producer 1st opera festival with Met. Opera, Newport, 1966, Kool Super Nights, Kool Country on Tour, throughout U.S., 1979, White House Jazz Festival, 1978; overseas tours gen. festival in Berlin, other European major cities, U.S. Govt. sponsored presentations World Jazz Festival, Japan, 1964, Jazz Festival, Hampton Inst., ann. Kool Jazz festivals; rec. artist; performer with group Newport Jazz Festival All-Stars, 1982—; author (memoir) Myself Among Others: A Life in Music. Served with U.S. Army, World War II Recipient medal Order of Arts and Letters France, 1980; Frederic Douglass award N.Y. Urban League, 1980 Pioneer of corp. sponsorship of festivals and concerts. Address: Festival Prodns Inc 311 W 74th St New York NY 10023-1604*

WEINBACH, ARTHUR FREDERIC, computer company executive; b. Waterbury, Conn., May 3, 1943; s. Max and Winifred (Eckstein) Weinbach; m. Joanne Kaplan, Nov. 20, 1970; children: Michael Scott, Jonathan David. BS in Econs., U. Pa., 1965, MS in Acctg., 1966. CPA. With Touche Ross & Co., N.Y.C., 1966—75, ptnr. Stamford, Conn., 1976—79; from v.p. to pres. Automatic Data Processing, Inc., Roseland, 1980—98, CEO, 1996—, chmn., 1998—; also bd. dirs. Bd. dirs. Schering-Plough Corp., First Data Corp., N.J. Inst. Tech., N.J. Seeds. Bd. dirs. Boys Hope, 1991—2003, Overlook Hosp. Found., 1991—98, Metro N.J. U. Pa. Club, 1993—99, United Way of Tri-State, 1998—. Jewish. Office: ADP Inc 1 A D P Blvd Roseland NJ 07068-1786

WEINBACH, LAWRENCE ALLEN, computer company executive; b. N.Y.C., Jan. 8, 1940; s. Max N. and Winifred E. Weinbach; m. Patricia Leiter, Dec. 1961; children: Wendy, Peter, Daniel. BS in Econs., U. Pa., 1961. CPA. With Andersen Worldwide, N.Y.C., 1961-97, mng. ptnr. Stamford, Conn., 1974-80, N.Y.C., 1980-83, mng. ptnr. N.Y. Met. area, 1983-87, COO, 1987-89, mng. ptnr., CEO, 1989-97; pres. Unisys Corp., Blue Bell, Pa., 1997—2004, chmn., CEO, 1997—. Bd. dirs. Avon Products, Inc., Unisys Corp., UBS, AG. Trustee Carnegie Hall, U. Pa., Catalyst; mem bd. overseers Wharton Sch., U. Pa.; life trustee emeritus Northwestern U.; trustee cancer ctr. bd. U. Pa.; mem. adv. com. NYSE Listed Co., Nat. Security Telecomm. Mem. Harmonie Club, Beta Gamma Sigma, Beta Alpha Psi. Office: Unisys Corp Unisys Way Blue Bell PA 19424-0001*

WEINBAUM, BATYA, artist, writer; b. Ann Arbor, Mich., Feb. 2, 1952; d. Jack and Barbara Weinbaum; 1 child, Ola. BA, Hampshire Coll., 1976; MA, SUNY, Buffalo, 1986; PhD, U. Mass., Amherst, 1996. Asst. prof. English Cleve. State U., 1998—2003; self-employed artist, writer, editor. Working with a family learning cmty. Cleve. Heights, Ohio, 2003. Author: Curious Courtship of Women's Liberation & Socialism, 1978, Pictures of Patriarchy, 1984, Island of Floating Women, 1993, Islands of Women & Amazons, 2000; editor: Femspec, 1999—. Founder Feminist Mothers and Their Allies Task Force/Nat. Womens Studies. Grantee, Robert Fleming Fund, 1976, Rabinowitz Found., 1978. Mem.: Sci. Ficiton Rsch. Assn., Am./Popular Culture Assn., Nat. Assn. Women's Studies. Jewish. Avocations: swimming, music, dance, bicycling, meditation. Home: 1610 Rydal Mount Cleveland Heights OH 44118

WEINBAUM, PAUL OWEN, historian; b. Bklyn., Dec. 22, 1945; BA, CUNY, N.Y.C., 1967; PhD, U. Rochester, N.Y., 1977. Curator Statue of Liberty Nat. Monument, N.Y.C., 1973—80; historian Boston Nat. Hist. Pk., 1980—90; regional historian North Atlantic regional office Nat. Pk. Svc., Boston, 1990—95, lead historian Boston support office, 1995—2003, history program mgr. NE region, 2003—. Author: (rsch.) Mobs and Demagogues: The New York Response to Collective Violence in the Early Nineteenth Century, Hoosac Docks: Fgn. Trade Terminal. A Case of the Expanding Transp. Sys. of the Late Nineteenth Century. Fellow, Woodrow Wilson Nat. Fellowship Found., 1970—71. Mem.: Orgn. of Am. Historians. Home: 392 Washington St Norwood MA 02062 Office: Nat Park Svc 15 State St Boston MA 02109 Office Phone: 617-223-5057. E-mail: paul_weinbaum@nps.gov.

WEINBAUM, SHELDON, biomedical engineer; b. Bklyn., July 26, 1937; s. Alexander Weinbaum and Frances Clare (Stark) Colby; m. Alexandra Tamara Weinbaum, June 10, 1962; children: Alys Eve, Daniel Eden. BAE, Rennselaer Polytech. Inst., Troy, 1959; MS, Harvard U., 1960, PhD, 1963. Mem. rsch. staff Sperry Rand Rsch. Lab., Sudbury, Mass., 1963-64; prin. rsch. scientist Avco Everett Rsch. Lab., Everett, Mass., 1964, G.E. Space Sci. Lab., Valley Forge, Pa., 1964-67; assoc. prof. CCNY, 1967-72, H. Kayser Prof., 1980-85; CUNY Disting. Prof. N.Y.C., 1986—; dir. N.Y.C. Ctr. Biomed. Engring. CUNY, N.Y.C., 1994-99. Vis. prof. Imperial Coll. Sci. and Tech., London, 1973—74, MIT, 1980—81; Russell S. Springer vis. prof. U. Calif., Berkeley, 1979—80; sr. fellow Sci. Rsch. Coun. Gt. Britain, 1973—74. Chair legal action com. CUNY, 1992—96. Recipient Pub. Svc. award, Fund for City of N.Y., 1988, Rsch. award, European Soc. Biomechanics, 1994, Spl. Creativity award, NSF,

1985—87; fellow Gordon McKay prize, Harvard U., 1959—60, NSF, 1961—63, John Simon Guggenheim, 2002. Fellow: ASME (H.R. Lissner award 1994, Melville medal 1996, Classic Paper award Heat Transfer divsn. 2000), Nat. Acad. Sci. and Inst. of Medicine, Nat. Acad. Engring. (acad. adv. coun. 1998—2000), Am. Inst. Med. Bio. Engring., Am. Phys. Soc. (sr.); mem.: Biomed. Engring. Soc. (bd. dirs. 1989—92, Whitaker Disting. lectr. 1997). Achievements include contributions in the broad application of engineering principles to the understanding of biological and medical processes; including Weinbaum-Caro model for transport in artery wall, water and solute transport in capillary interendothelial clefts; new interpretation of Starling hypothesis, Weinbaum-Jiji bioheat equation, plasma skimmings and red cell screening in blood flow; leaky junction-cell turnover hypothesis, for LDL transport, model for intraocular fluid mechanics, transport models for the arterial intima and atherogenesis; fluid shear hypothesis for activation of osteocytes, mechanosensory mechanisms for bone growth and brush border microvilli in kidney, fundamental fluid mechanics; contributions include particle and boundary interactions at low Reynolds number, non-linear lubrication theory in highly compressible porous media, high altitude near wake, mechanics of skiing. Office: City Coll City of New York Convent Ave & 137th St New York NY 10031 E-mail: weinbaum@ccny.cuny.edu.

WEINBERG, ADAM D. museum director; b. N.Y.C., Dec. 10, 1954; s. James Lionel and Edith (Zickerman) W.; m. Lorraine Ferguson; 1 child, Zoë. BA, Brandeis U., 1977; MFA, SUNY, Buffalo, 1981. Dir. edn., asst. curator Walker Art Ctr., Mpls., 1981-88; dir., equitable ctr. Whitney Mus. Am. Art, N.Y.C., 1988-90; artistic and program dir. Am. Ctr., Paris, 1990—92; sr. curator, curator of permanent collection Whitney Mus. Am. Art, N.Y.C., 1993—99; dir. Addison Gallery of American Art, Andover, Mass., 1999—2003; mus. dir. Whitney Mus. Am. Art, N.Y.C., 2003—. Author: (catalog) On the Line: The New Color Photojournalism, 1986, (book and catalog) Vanishing Presence, 1989, (exhbn. catalogs) Aldo Crommelynck: Master Prints with American Artists, 1989, Contingent Realms, 1990. Mem. Am. Assn. Mus., Coll. Art Assn. Office: Whitney Mus Am Art 945 Madison Ave New York NY 10021*

WEINBERG, ALVIN MARTIN, physicist; b. Chgo., Apr. 20, 1915; s. J.L. and Emma (Levinson) W.; m. Margaret Despres, June 14, 1940 (dec 1969); children: David, Richard; m. Gene K. DePersio, Sept. 20, 1974. AB, U. Chgo., 1935, A.M., 1936, PhD, 1939; LL.D., U. Chattanooga, Alfred U.; D.Sc., U. Pacific, Denison U., Wake Forest U., Kenyon Coll., Worcester Poly. Inst., U. Rochester, Stevens Inst. Tech., Butler U., U. Louisville, U. Bridgeport. Research assoc. math. biophysics U. Chgo., 1939-41, Metall. Lab., 1941-45; joined Oak Ridge Nat. Lab., 1945, dir. physics div., 1947-48, research dir. lab., 1948-55, dir. lab., 1955-74; dir. Office Energy R&D, Fed. Energy Adminstrn., 1974, Inst. Energy Analysis, Oak Ridge, 1975-85; disting. fellow Oak Ridge Associated Univs., 1985—. Mem. Pres.'s Sci. Adv. Com., 1960-62, Pres.'s Medal of Sci. Com. Author: Reflections on Big Science, (with E.P. Wigner) Physical Theory of Neutron Chain Reactors, 1958, Continuing the Nuclear Dialogue, 1985, Nuclear Reactions: Science and Trans-Science, 1992, The First Nuclear Era: The Life and Times of a Technological Fixer, 1994; co-author: The Second Nuclear Era, 1985; co-editor: The Nuclear Connection, 1985, Strategic Defenses and Arms Control, 1987; editor: Eugene Wigner's Collected Works on Nuclear Energy. Recipient Atoms for Peace award, 1960, E.O. Lawrence award, 1960, U. Chgo. Alumni medal, 1966, Heinrich Hertz award, 1975, N.Y. Acad. Scis. award, 1976, Enrico Fermi award, 1980, Harvey prize, 1982, Eugene Wigner award in reactor physics, 1992. Mem. Nat. Acad. Scis. (applied sci. sect.), Am. Nuclear Soc. (pres. 1959-60, Alvin M. Weinberg award 1996), Nat. Acad. Engring., Am. Acad. Arts and Scis., Am. Philos. Soc., Royal Netherlands Acad. Sci. (fgn. asso.) Home: 111 Moylan Ln Oak Ridge TN 37830-5351 Office: Oak Ridge Associated Univs PO Box 117 Oak Ridge TN 37831-0117

WEINBERG, ARNOLD N. physician, educator; b. Bklyn., Sept. 30, 1929; m. Shirley Weinberg (div. 1986); children: Suzanne, Davida, Carolyn; m. Inge Toftgaard. BS, Cornell U., 1952; MD, Harvard U., 1956. Intern to resident Mass. Gen. Hosp., 1956—58, 1961—62; from instr. to prof. medicine Harvard U., Boston, 1971—; from asst. physician to physician Mass. Gen. Hosp., Boston, 1973—; chief of medicine Cambridge Hosp., 1971—75; med. dir. MIT, Cambridge, 1986—2000. Bd. dirs. Whitehead Inst. Biomed. Rsch., Cambridge, 1989—. Office: Dept Infectious Disease Mass Gen Hosp 55 Fruit St Boston MA 02114

WEINBERG, D. MARK, health insurance company executive; b. Aug. 4, 1952; s. Melvin Weinberg; m. Allyson Weinberg; children: Amanda, Sarah, Tiffany, Sean. BS in Elec. Engring., U. Mo., 1975. Gen. mgr. CTX Products div. Pet, Inc., St. Louis, 1975-81; prin. Touche-Ross and Co., Chgo., 1981-87; exec. v.p. Blue Cross of Calif., Thousand Oaks, 1987-92, Wellpoint Health Networks, Woodland Hills, 1992—. Pres. UNICARE, 1995—02 Contbr. articles to profl. jours. Bd. dirs. NCPFC, Pepperdine Ctr. for the Family, Lightforge Devel. Mem. Conejo Valley C. of C. (bd. dirs.). Address: Wellpoint #1 Wellpoint Way Thousand Oaks CA 91362-3800

WEINBERG, DALE GLASER, technical writer, consultant, trainer; b. N.Y.C., Oct. 21, 1948; d. Milton and Joyce I. (Litsky) Glaser; m. Howard Weinberg, June 20, 1971 (separated); 1 child, Tracy J. BS in English Edn., NYU, 1971; MS in English Edn., Iona Coll., New Rochelle, N.Y., 1975. Lic. secondary tchr. English, N.Y. Programmer, documentation adminstr. ITT Continental Baking, Rye, N.Y., 1971-78; owner, pres. Techically Write, Eastchester, N.Y., 1978—. Cons., course leader, tchr. writing seminars throughout U.S., Am. Mgmt. Assn., N.Y.C., 1980; designer, tchr. bus. writing Am. Mgmt. Assn.-Operation Enterprise, Hamilton, N.Y., 1998; ind. tech. writing and tng. cons., 1978—. Editor: Money Smarts, 1982, A Funny Thing Happened on the Way to the Interview, 1995; designer, editor, prodr. 3 major publs. Eastchester (N.Y.) Mid. Sch., 1993—; assoc. editor Calif. Ride Reporter, 1993—. Recipient Spl. Svc. award/citation for publs. Eastchester Mid. Sch., 1994. Mem. IEEE Profl. Comm. Soc. (assoc.), Soc. Tech. Comm. (sr.), Assn. Computing Machinery. Avocations: scuba diving, yoga, skiing, theater, reading, travel. Office: Technically Write 19 Soundview Dr Eastchester NY 10709-1526

WEINBERG, DAVID B. investor; b. Chgo., Feb. 19, 1952; s. Judd A. and Marjorie (Gottlieb) W.; m. Lynne Ellen Mesirow, July 6, 1980. AB cum laude, Harvard U., 1974; JD, Georgetown U., 1977. Bar: Ill. 1977, U.S. Dist. Ct. (no. dist.) Ill. 1977, U.S. Ct. Appeals (7th cir.) 1978. Law clerk to Hon. William G. Clark Supreme Ct. Ill., 1977-79; assoc. Lord, Bissell & Brook, Chgo., 1979-84, ptnr., 1985-89, Mayer, Brown & Platt, Chgo., 1989-96; chmn., CEO Judd Enterprises, Inc., Chgo., 1996—; pres. Digital BandWidth LLC, Chgo., 1996—; dir. NFR Security, Inc., Rockville, Md., 2001—. Ill. Supreme Ct. com. Profl. Responsibility, Chgo., 1984-94, chmn. subcom. lawyers certification. Chmn. bd. trustees Ravinia Festival Assn., Highland Park, Ill., 1998—2001; vice chmn. bd. trustees Northwestern U., 1999—. Mem. Chgo. Club, Econ. Club Chgo., Lake Shore Country Club, Arts Club Chgo., Comml. Club Chgo., Civic Com. Office: Judd Enterprises Bank One Plz 21 S Clark St Ste 3140 Chicago IL 60603-2090

WEINBERG, EUGENE DAVID, microbiologist, educator; b. Chgo., Mar. 4, 1922; s. Philip and Lenore (Bergman) W.; m. Frances Murl Izen, Sept. 5, 1949; children— Barbara Ann, Marjorie Jean, Geoffrey Alan, Michael Benjamin. BS, U. Chgo., 1942, MA, 1948, PhD, 1950. Instr. dept. microbiology Ind. U., Bloomington, 1950-53, asst. prof., 1953-57, asso. prof., 1957-61, prof., 1961—, head microbiology sect., med. sci. program, 1978—92. Mem. sci. adv. bd., chair publs. Iron Disorders Inst., 1998—. Served with AUS, 1942-45. Mem. AAAS, Am. Soc. Microbiology. Office: Ind U Biology Dept Jordan Hall Bloomington IN 47405 Fax: 812-855-6705. Office Phone: 812-336-5556. Business E-Mail: eweinber@indiana.edu.

WEINBERG, GERHARD LUDWIG, history professor; b. Hannover, Germany, Jan. 1, 1928; came to U.S., 1940, naturalized, 1949; s. Max Bendix and Kate Sarah (Gruenebaum) W.; m. Janet Kabler White, Apr. 29, 1989. BA, N.Y. State Coll. Tchrs., Albany, 1948; MA, U. Chgo., 1949, PhD, 1951; LHD honoris causa, SUNY, Albany, 1989; PhD (hon.), U. Hannover, 2001. Research analyst War Documentation project Columbia U., 1951-54; vis. lectr. history U. Chgo., 1954-55, U. Ky., Lexington, 1955-56; dir. project microfilming captured German documents Am. Hist. Assn., 1956-57; asst. prof. U. Ky., 1957-59; mem. faculty U. Mich., Ann Arbor, 1959-74, prof. history, 1963-74, chmn. dept., 1972-73; William Rand Kenan, Jr. prof. history U. N.C., Chapel Hill, 1974-99, prof. emeritus, 1999—, acting chmn. dept., 1989-90. Vis. prof. Bonn U., 1983, USAF Acad., 1990-91; Shapiro sr. scholar-in-residence U.S. Holocaust Meml. Mus., 2001-02; bd. dirs. World War II Studies Assn., 1968—; cons. in field. Author: Guide to Captured German Documents, 1952, Germany and the Soviet Union, 1939-41, 1954, The Foreign Policy of Hitler's Germany, 1933-36, 1970, The Foreign Policy of Hitler's Germany, 1937-39, 1980, World in the Balance: Behind the Scenes of World II, 1981, A World at Arms: A Global History of World War II, 1994, Germany, Hitler and World War II, 1995, co author: Soviet Partisans in World War II, 1964; editor: Hitlers zweites Buch, 1961, 95, Transformation of a Continent, 1975, Hitler's Second Book, 2003; bd. editors Jour. Modern History, 1970-72, Central European History, 1970-72, Kansas Humanities Series, 1987—, Internat. History Rev., 1990-2000, Jour. Intelligence History, 2001—. Chmn. Ann Arbor Democratic Com., 1961-63; mem. Mich. Dem. Central Com., 1963-67; mem. adv. com. on the air force history program Sec. of Air Force, 1987-90; mem. adv. com. army history program Sec. Army, 1996-2003, chmn., 1998-2003; mem. dept. defence Hist. Records Declassification Adv. Panel, 1996-02; chmn. hist. adv. panel to interagy. working group on Nazi War Crimes and Imperial Japanese Records Disclosure, 2000—. With AUS, 1946-47. Fellow Social Sci. Research Council, 1962-63; fellow Am. Council Learned Socs., 1965-66; fellow Guggenheim Found., 1971-72; fellow Nat. Endowment Humanities, 1978-79 Mem. Am. Hist. Assn. (George Louis Beer prize 1971, 95, v.p. rsch. 1982-84), So. Hist. Assn. (chmn. European sect. 1989), Conf. Group for Ctrl. European History (chmn. 1982), Coordinating Com. Women in Hist. Profession, German Studies Assn. (exec. com. 1989-92, Halverson prize 1981, v.p. 1994-96, pres. 1996-98), World War II Studies Assn., Am. Acad. Arts and Scis., Phi Beta Kappa. Jewish. Home: 1416 Mount Willing Rd Efland NC 27243-9646 E-mail: gweinber@email.unc.edu.

WEINBERG, H. BARBARA, art historian, educator, curator; b. NYC, Jan. 23, 1942; d. Max and Evelyn Kallman; m. Michael B. Weinberg, Aug. 30, 1964. AB, Barnard Coll., 1962; MA, Columbia U., NYC, 1964, PhD, 1972. Asst. prof., prof. art history Queens Coll. Grad. Sch., CUNY, 1972-94; curator Am. paintings sculpture Met. Mus. Art., NYC, 1990-98; Alice Pratt Brown curator Am. paintings sculpture Met. Mus. Art, NYC, 1998—. Author: The Decorative Work of John La Farge, 1977, The American Pupils of Jean-Léon Gérome, 1984, The Lure of Paris: Nineteenth-Century American Painters and Their French Teachers, 1991, Thomas Eakins and the Metropolitan Museum of Art, 1994, co-author: American Impressionism and Realism: The Painting of Modern Life, 1885-1915, 1994, American Drawings and Watercolors in The Metropolitan Museum of Art: John Singer Sargent, 2000, John Singer Sargent in The Metropolitan Museum of Art, 2000, Childe Hassam, American Impressionist, 2004; mem. editl. bd. Am. Art Jour., 1984—. Mem.: Phi Beta Kappa. Office: Met Mus Art 1000 5th Ave New York NY 10028-0198

WEINBERG, HERSCHEL MAYER, lawyer; b. Bklyn., Oct. 13, 1927; s. Jacob and Gertrude (Wernick) W. BA, Bklyn. Coll., 1948; LL.B., Harvard U., 1952. Bar: N.Y. 1952. Atty. firm Payne & Steingarten, N.Y.C., 1952-57, Jacobs, Persinger & Parker, N.Y.C., 1957-61; partner firm Rubin, Rubin, Weinberg, & Di Paola, N.Y.C., 1961-78, Weinberg Tauber & Pressman, 1979-90; pvt. practice N.Y.C., 1990—. Served with AUS, 1946-47. Mem. Assn. of Bar of City of N.Y., N.Y. State Bar Assn. Clubs: Harvard (N.Y.C.). Home: 50 Sutton Pl S New York NY 10022-4167 Office: 110 E 59th St New York NY 10022-1304

WEINBERG, HUBERT, plastic surgeon; b. Clermont-Ferrant, France, Feb. 2, 1950; came to U.S., 1955; s. Paul and Esther Weinberg; m. Rita Weinberg, June 24, 1974; children: Deborah, Nevin, Michael, Jennifer, Lauren, Aimee. BA, Yeshiva U., 1971; MD, Cornell U., 1975. Diplomate Am. Bd. Plastic Surgery. Intern, resident Mt. Sinai Hosp.; instr. Mt. Sinai Med. Ctr., N.Y.C., 1982-84, assoc. prof., 1984-97, prof., 1998-2000; clin. prof., 2000—; assoc. attending physician Mt. Sinai Med. Ctr., N.Y.C., 1984-97, dir. microsurgery rsch. dept., 1982-2000, attending physician, 1998—, Westchester Med. Ctr., Valhalla, N.Y., 2000—. Adj. prof. N.Y. Med. Coll., 2000—. Author: (with others) Musculoskeletal Oncology, 1992; contbr. articles to profl. jours. including Current Surgery, Plastic Reconstrn. Surgery, and Jour. Reconstructive Microsurgery. Recipient 2d pl. award Plastic Surgery Ednl. Found., 1983. Fellow ACS, N.Y. Acad. Scis. (1st prize awards 1987, 93); mem. Am. Soc. Plastic and Reconstructive Surgeons, Am. Assn. Plastic Surgeons. Avocations: computer graphics, gardening, landscaping. Office: Westchester Med Ctr Burn Ctr Macy Pavilion Valhalla NY 10595 E-mail: weinbh01@doc.mssm.edu.

WEINBERG, JEFFREY MITCHELL, dermatologist, researcher; b. Bklyn., Jan. 19, 1967; s. Barry Martin and Leslie Dann Weinberg; m. Caryn Robin Mermelstein, Nov. 18, 2001. BA summa cum laude, Columbia U., 1989; MD, U. Pa., 1993. Diplomate Am. Bd. of Dermatology. Intern Internal Medicine Columbia Univ. Coll. of Physicians and Suregeons, N.Y., 1993—94; resident, dermatology Univ. Pa., Phila., 1994—97; dir. divsn. of dermatology Jamaica (NY) Hosp. Med. Ctr., 1998; dir. clin. rsch. ctr. St. Luke's-Roosevelt Hosp. Ctr./Beth Israel Med. Ctr., New York, 1999—. Sr. assoc. editor Cutis; mem. internat. editl. bd. Am. Jour. of Clin. Dermatology. Contbr. articles to med. jours. Recipient Nelson Paul Anderson Meml. award, Pacific Dermatologic Assn., 1995, Johnson-Beerman award, Coll. of Physicians of Phila., 1997; NIH Cancer Edn. Rsch. fellow, NIH, 1992. Fellow: Am. Acad. Dermatology; mem.: Phi Beta Kappa. Jewish. Achievements include research in atopic dermatitis, acne, biologics for psoriasis. Home: 180 West 93 St Apt 4E New York NY 10025 Office: Dept Dermatology 1090 Amsterdam Ave Ste 11D New York NY 10025 Office Phone: 212-523-4366. E-mail: jmw27@columbia.edu.

WEINBERG, JOHN LEE, federal judge; b. Chgo., Apr. 24, 1941; s. Louis Jr. and Jane Kitz (Goldstein) W.; m. Sarah Kibbee, July 6, 1963; children: Ruth, Leo. BA, Swarthmore Coll., 1962; JD, U. Chgo., 1965. Bar: Ill. 1966, Wash. 1967, U.S. Dist. Ct. (we. dist.) Wash. 1967, U.S. Ct. Appeals (9th cir.) 1967. Law clk. to Hon. Henry L. Burman Ill. Appellate Ct., Chgo., 1965-66; law clk. to Hon. Walter V. Schaefer Ill. Supreme Ct., Chgo., 1966; law clk. to Hon. William T. Beeks U.S. Dist. Ct. Wash., Seattle, 1967-68; atty. Perkins Coie Law Firm, Seattle, 1968-73; magistrate judge U.S. Dist. Ct.; U.S. Magistrate judge Seattle, 1973—2003; ret., 2003. Author: Federal Bail and Detention Handbook, 1988. Mem. ABA, Am. Judicature Soc., Wash. State Bar Assn., Seattle-King County Bar Assn., Fed. Magistrate Judges Assn. (nat. pres. 1982-83). Avocations: sports and physical fitness activities, bridge. Office: US Magistrate Judge 12th Fl States Courthouse 700 Stewart St Seattle WA 98101

WEINBERG, JOHN LIVINGSTON, investment banker; b. N.Y.C., Jan. 5, 1925; s. Sidney James and Helen (Livingston) W.; m. Sue Ann Gotshal, Dec. 6, 1952; children: Ann K. (dec.), John, Jean. AB cum laude, Princeton U., 1948; MBA, Harvard U., 1950. With Goldman, Sachs & Co., N.Y.C., 1950—, ptnr., 1956-76, sr. ptnr., 1976-90, co-chmn. mgmt. com., 1976-84, sr. ptnr., chmn. mgmt. com., 1984-90, sr. chmn., 1990-2001. Sr. chmn. The Goldman Sachs Group, Inc., 2001—; mem. Conf. Bd.; hon. chmn. John L. Weinberg Ctr. Corp. Governance, U. Del. Dir. emeritus N.Y. and Presbyn. Hosps.; corp. governance program U. Del. 2d lt. USMCR, 1942-46, capt., 1951-52. Fellow AAAS; mem. Coun. on Fgn. Rels., Bus. Coun. (grad.), DeWitt Wallace Fund for Meml. Sloan Kettering Cancer Ctr. Office: Goldman Sachs Group Inc Ste 1002 375 Park Ave New York NY 10152 E-mail: john.l.weinberg@gs.com.

WEINBERG, JONATHAN T. law educator; b. Queens, N.Y., Dec. 5, 1958; s. Norman and Naomi Joan (Miller) W.; m. Jessica D. Litman, June 2, 1987. AB, Harvard U., 1980; JD, Columbia U., 1983. Bar: D.C. 1984. Law clk. to hon. Ruth Bader Ginsburg U.S. Ct. Appeals (D.C. cir.), Washington, 1983—84; assoc. Shea & Gardner, Washington, 1984-85, 87-88; law clk. to Justice Thurgood Marshall, U.S. Supreme Ct., Washington, 1985—86; vis. scholar U. Tokyo, 1986—87; asst. prof. Law Sch., Wayne State U., Detroit, 1988—93, assoc. prof., 1993—99, prof., 1999—; prof. in residence U.S. Dept. Justice, Washington, 1993—94. Scholar in residence U.S. FCC, 1997—98. Contbr. articles to legal jours. Fulbright grantee, Tokyo, 1986-87. Office: Wayne State U Law Sch 471 W Palmer Detroit MI 48202-3814

WEINBERG, LARRY, lawyer, labor union administrator; b. 1944; BA in Econs., U. Mich., JD, 1970. Bar: DC 1971. With FTC, Washington, Zwerdling, Washington, 1972—80; gen. counsel AFSCME, Washington, 1980—. Office: AFSCME 1101 17th St NW Washington DC 20036-4704

WEINBERG, LILA SHAFFER, writer, editor; d. Sam and Blanche (Hyman) Shaffer; m. Arthur Weinberg, Jan. 25, 1953; children: Hedy Merrill Cornfield, Anita Michelle Miller, Wendy Clare Rothman. Editor Ziff-Davis Pub. Co., 1944—53; assoc. chief manuscript editor jours. U. Chgo. Press, 1966—80, sr. manuscript editor books, 1980—98; mem. faculty Sch. for New Learning DePaul U., Chgo., 1973—89. Vis. faculty continuing edn. programs U. Chgo., 1984-92. Author: (with A. Weinberg) The Muckrakers, 1961 (selected for White House Library 1963), Verdicts Out of Court, 1963, Instead of Violence, 1963, Passport to Utopia, 1968, Some Dissenting Voices, 1970, Clarence Darrow: A Sentimental Rebel, 1980; contbr. articles and revs. to various publs. Bd. dirs. Hillel Found. U. Chgo., 1988-96. Recipient Friends of Lit. award Chgo. Found. Lit., 1980, Social Justice award Darrow Community Ctr., 1980, Disting. Body of Work award Friends of Midwest Authors, 1987, John Peter Altgeld Freedom of Speech award, 2001. Mem. Soc. Midland Authors (dir. 1977-83, pres. 1983-85, Best Midwest Biography award 1980), ACLU, Clarence Darrow Commemorative Com., YIVO, Authors' League, Work in Progress. Home: 5421 S Cornell Ave Chicago IL 60615-5646 E-mail: lilawein@aol.com.

WEINBERG, LORETTA, state legislator; b. N.Y.C., Feb. 6, 1935; d. Murray Isaacs and Raya Hamilton; m. Irwin S. Weinberg, July 25, 1960 (dec. Feb. 1999); children: Daniel J., Francine S. BA, UCLA, 1956. Former aide N.J. Assemblyman D. Bennett Mazur, Trenton; mem. N.J. Assembly, Trenton, 1992—. Mem. Teaneck Coun., 1990-94. Recipient Legis. Leadership award No. N.J. Chiropractic Assn., 1992, Woman of Achievement award Bus. and Profl. Women's Club of East Bergen, 1993, Carrie Chapman Catt award No. N.J. NOW, 1997, Ethical Recognition award Ethical Culture Soc. of Bergen County, 1998, Barbara Boggs Sigmund award, Women's Polit. Caucus, 2004, Legis. Recognition, Consumers for Civil Justice; named Citizen of Yr. N.J. Jewish War Vets., Legislator of Yr., N.J. State Nurse's Assn., 2000. Mem. Nat. Coun. Jewish Women (life mem., Hannah G. Solomon award 1995, Disting. Achievement award Women's Commn.). Democrat. Jewish. Office: State of NJ 545 Cedar Ln Teaneck NJ 07666-1740 Office Phone: 201-928-0100.

WEINBERG, LOUISE, law educator, author; b. N.Y.C. m. Steven Weinberg; 1 child, Elizabeth. AB summa cum laude, Cornell U.; JD, Harvard U., 1969, LLM, 1974. Bar: Mass. Sr. law clk. Hon. Chas. E. Wyzanski, Jr., Boston, 1971-72; assoc. in law Bingham, Dana & Gould, Boston, 1969-72; teaching fellow Harvard Law Sch., Boston, 1972-74; lectr. law Brandeis U., Waltham, Mass., 1974; assoc. prof. law Suffolk U., Boston, 1974-76, prof., 1977-80; vis. assoc. prof. law Stanford U., Palo Alto, Calif., 1976-77; vis. prof. law U. Tex., Austin, 1979; prof. law Sch. Law, U. Tex., Austin, 1980-84, Thompson prof. law, 1984-90, Andrews and Kurth prof. law, 1990-92; Fulbright and Jaworski regents rsch. prof. U. Tex., Austin, 1991-92, Angus G. Wynne, Sr. prof. civil jurisprudence, 1992-97, Fondren chair faculty excellence, 1995—, Eugene R. Smith Centennial rsch. prof. law, 1993-97, holder William B. Bates chair adminstrn. justice, 1997—. Vis. scholar Hebrew U., Jerusalem, 1989; Forum fellow World Econ. Forum, Davos, Switzerland, 1995—; pub. spkr., lectr. in field. Author: Federal Courts: Judicial Federalism and Judicial Power, 1994, and ann. supplements; co-author: Conflict of Laws, 1990, 2d edit., 2002; contbr. chpts. to books, articles to profl. jours. Bd. dirs. Ballet Austin, 1986-88, Austin Coun. on Fgn. Affairs, 1985—, Austin Civil War Round Table, 1998—. Recipient Disting. Educator award Tex. Exes Assn., 1996. Mem.: Supreme Ct. Hist. Soc., Am. Constn. Soc., Maritime Law Assn., Tex. Asian C. of C., Assn. Am. Law Schs. (chair sect. on conflict laws 1991—93, exec. com. sect. on fed. cts. 2001—02, program chair 2002—03, chair 2003—04, treas. sect. on admiralty 2003—04, program chmn. 2004—, acting chmn. 2004—, chair-elect), The Philos. Soc. Tex., Am. Law Inst. (consultative com. complex litigation 1989—93, consultative com. enterprise liability 1990—95, adv. group fed. judicial code revision project 1996—2001, mems.' consultative group, intellectual property 2004—, adv. group internat. jurisdiction and judgments 2004—), Phi Kappa Phi, Phi Beta Kappa. Office: U Tex Sch Law 727 Dean Keeton St Austin TX 78705-3224 Business E-Mail: lweinberg@mail.law.utexas.edu. *Personal philosophy: The right thing is usually also the humane and liberal thing.*

WEINBERG, MILTON, JR., cardiovascular and thoracic surgeon; b. Sumter, S.C., Aug. 8, 1924; s. Milton and Ethel (Harper) W.; m. Joan Ehrenstrom, Nov. 24, 1956; children: Caryl, Susan, Amy. Student, Duke U., 1941-43, MD, 1947. Diplomate Am. Bd. Surgery, Am. Bd. Thoracic Surgery. Attending surgeon Rush Presbyn.-St. Luke's Med. Ctr., Chgo., 1957-90, emeritus attending, 1990—; attending surgeon Cook County Hosp., Chgo., 1956-80, Luth. Gen. Hosp., Park Ridge, Ill., 1986—, mem. governing coun., 1996—2001; assoc. prof. Rush Med. Coll., Chgo., 1969-78, prof. surgery, 1978-90, emeritus prof., 1990—; clin. prof. U. Chgo., 1990-99. Chmn. dept. surgery Luth. Gen. Hosp., Park Ridge, 1988-94, vice-chmn. dept. surgery, 1994-2003; pres. med. staff Rush Med. Ctr., Chgo., 1977-79; presenter movies at mtgs. ACS. Mem. editorial bd. Annals of Thoracic Surgery, 1968-79; contbr. articles to profl. jours., chpts. to surg. textbooks. Trustee The Presbyn. Home, Evanston, Ill., 1984—; bd. dirs. Chgo. Symphony Orch., 1985-95; advocate Charitable Found. Bd., 1996-2002. Maj. U.S. Army, 1951-53. Decorated Bronze Star. Fellow ACS, Am. Coll. Chest Physicians, Am. Coll. Cardiology; mem. Am. Assn. Thoracic Surgery, Soc. Thoracic Surgeons, Soc. Vascular Surgery, Internat. Cardiovascular Soc., Ctrl. Surg. Soc. Avocations: fly fishing, fly rod building. Home: 983 Kirkhill Ln Lake Forest IL 60045-4209 E-mail: mw983@yahoo.com.

WEINBERG, MYRL, medical association administrator; Exec. Assn. for Retarded Citizens, Joseph P. Kennedy, Jr. Found., Am. Diabetes Assn.; pres. Nat. Health Coun. Office: Nat Health Coun 1730 M St NW Ste 500 Washington DC 20036

WEINBERG, NORBERT, rabbi; b. Bad Nauheim, Germany; arrived in U.S., 1940; s. Seligmann and Kaethe (Cohn) Weinberg; m. Susan B. Hirshkowitz; children: Judith Anna Eisenstock, Shira Shreier, Rena Gittel Rossman, Sharona Blank. BA, Yeshiva U., 1953; MEd, R.I. Coll., 1982. Ordained rabbi 1957. Rabbi Congregation Beth Shalom, Quebec City, Canada, 1957—59, Congregation Ahauath Achim, New Bedford, Mass., 1959—67, Congregation Adas Israel, Fall River, Mass., 1967—97, Congregation Bros. Joseph, Norwich, Conn., 1997—. Chaplain Mental Health Ctr., Fall River, Walpole State Prison. Author: The Essential Torah, Beyond the Wall, In the Footsteps, A Time to Tell. Scribe Rabbinical Ct. Mass., Boston, 1989—97. Home: 146 Eastbourne Rd Newton MA 02459 Office: Congregation Bros Joseph 17 Taylor Dr Norwich CT 06360 Office Phone: 860-899-3426. Personal E-mail: nswein@aol.com.

WEINBERG, ROBERT ALLAN, biochemist, educator; b. Pitts., Nov. 11, 1942; s. Fritz E. and Lore (Reichhardt) Weinberg; m. Amy Schulman Weinberg, Nov. 19, 1976; children: Aron, Leah Rosa. S.B., MIT, 1964, Ph.D, 1969; PhD (hon.), Northwestern U., 1984. Instr. Stillman Coll., Tuscaloosa, Ala., 1965—66; research fellow Weizmann Inst., Rehovoth, Israel, 1969—70, Salk Inst., LaJolla, Calif., 1970—72; from asst. prof. to assoc. prof. dept. biology & ctr. cancer rsch. MIT, Cambridge, 1973—82, prof. biology, 1982—, Daniel K. Ludwig prof. for cancer rsch., 1997—. Mem. Whitehead Inst., Cambridge, 1982—; rsch. prof. Amer. Cancer Soc., 1985; elected mem. Inst. of Medicine, 2000; mem. adv. bd. GM Cancer Rsch. Found. Contbr. articles to profl. jours. Recipient Bristol Myers award, 1984, Brown-Hazen award NY State Dept. Health, 1984, Sloan prize, GM Cancer Rsch. Found., 1987, Rsch. Recognition award, Samuel Roberts Noble Found., 1990, Gairdner Found. Internat. award, 1992, Harvey Prize, Technion, 1994, G.H.A. Clowes Meml.

award, 1996, Nat. Medal of Sci., 1997. Fellow: Am. Acad. of Arts & Sciences; mem.: NAS (sci. award 1984). Avocations: genealogy, house building. Office: Whitehead Inst 9 Cambridge Ctr Cambridge MA 02142-1479 E-mail: Weinberg@wi.mit.edu.*

WEINBERG, ROBERT LESTER, lawyer, law educator; b. N.Y.C., May 23, 1931; s. Abraham Matthew and Beatrice (Kohn) W.; m. Patricia Wendy Yates, Aug. 19, 1956; children: Susan Clare, David Hal, Jeremy Michael. BA, Yale U., 1953, LLB, 1960; PhD in Econs., London Sch. Econs., U. London, 1960. Bar: D.C. 1961, Conn. 1960, U.S. Supreme Ct. 1963, U.S. Ct. Appeals (D.C. and 2d cirs.) 1961, U.S. Ct. Appeals (3d and 7th cirs.) 1965, U.S. Ct. Appeals (6th cir.) 1968, U.S. Ct. Appeals (9th cir.) 1976, U.S. Ct. Appeals (10th cir.) 1977, U.S. Ct. Appeals (5th cir.) 1978, U.S. Ct. Appeals (4th cir.) 1982. Assoc. Law Offices of Edward Bennett Williams and successor firms, 1960-66; founding ptnr. Williams & Connolly, 1967-96, ret., 1996; vis. lectr. U. Va. Sch. Law, Charlottesville, 1965—; adj. prof. U. Tex. Sch. Law, summer 1986, George Washington U. Law Sch., 1999—; chmn. standing com. on pro bono matters D.C. Cir. Jud. Conf., 1980-96. Columnist No. Va. Sun, 1970s; contbr. articles to profl. jours. Pres. No. Va. Fair Housing, Inc., 1968-69; chmn. Arlington Pub. Utilities Commn. (Va.), 1968, Arlington County Dem. Com., 1969-71, 10th Congl. Dist. Dem. Com., No. Va., 1972-76; del. Dem. Nat. Conv., 1976; pres. Arlington County Civic Fedn., 1973-75; mem. governing coun. Am. Jewish Congress, 1984-96; Dem. nominee for Congress, 10th Congl. Dist., 1988, 96. Served with U.S. Army, 1957-59. Recipient Outstanding Citizen of Yr. award Washington Evening Star and Arlington County Civic Fedn., 1975, Servant of Justice award Legal Aid Soc. of D.C., 1996. Mem. ABA (ho. of dels. 1977-82, 93—), Bar Assn. D.C. (pres. 1994-95, Lawyer of Yr. award 2000), Conn. Bar Assn., D.C. Bar (pres. 1977-79), D.C. Bar Found. (pres. 1988-89, 91-92), Am. Assn. Jewish Lawyers and Jurists (pres.), Internat. Assn. Jewish Lawyers and Jurists (exec. com.), Nat. Jewish Dem. Coun. (bd. dirs.). Home: 4 Quaintance Rd Sperryville VA 22740-2412 Office: 5171 37th Rd N Arlington VA 22207-1825

WEINBERG, STEVEN, physics educator; b. N.Y.C., May 3, 1933; s. Fred and Eva (Israel) Weinberg; m. Louise Goldwasser, July 6, 1954; 1 child, Elizabeth. BA, Cornell U., 1954; postgrad., Copenhagen Inst. Theoretical Physics, 1954—55; PhD, Princeton U., 1957; AM (hon.), Harvard U., 1973; ScD (hon.), Knox Coll., 1978, U. Chgo., 1978, U. Rochester, 1979, Yale U., 1979, CUNY, 1980, Clark U., 1982, Dartmouth Coll., 1984, Columbia U., 1990, U. Salamanca, 1992, U. Padua, 1992, Bates Coll., 2002, McGill U., 2003; D (hon.), U. Barcelona, 1966, D (hon.), 1996; PhD (hon.), Weizmann Inst., 1985; DLitt (hon.), Washington Coll., 1985. Rsch. assoc., instr. Columbia U., 1957-59; rsch. physicist Lawrence Radiation Lab., Berkeley, Calif., 1959-60; mem. faculty U. Calif., Berkeley, 1960-69, prof. physics, 1964-69; vis. prof. MIT, 1967-69, prof. physics, 1969-73; Higgins prof. physics Harvard U., 1973-83; sr. scientist Smithsonian Astrophys. Lab., 1973-83; Josey prof. sci. U. Tex., Austin, 1982—; sr. cons. Smithsonian Astrophys. Obs., 1983—. Cons. Inst. Def. Analyses, Washington, 1960—73, ACDA, 1973; Sloan fellow, 1961—65; chair in physics Coll. de France, 1971; mem. Pres.'s Com. on Nat. Medal of Sci., 1979—82, Coun. of Scholars, Libr. of Congress, 1983—85; sr. adv. La Jolla Inst.; mem. Com. on Internat. Security and Arms Control, NRC, 1981, Bd. on Physics & Astronomy, 1989—90; adv. coun. Tex. Superconducting Supercollider High Energy Rsch. Facility, 1987; Loeb lectr. in physics Harvard U., 1966—67, Morris Loeb vis. prof. physics, 1983—; Richtmeyer lectr., 1974; Scott lectr. Cavendish Lab., 1975; Silliman lectr. Yale U., 1977; Lauritsen Meml. lectr. Calif. Inst. Tech., 1979; Bethe lectr. Cornell U., 1979; de Shalit lectr. Weizmann Inst., 1979; Cherwell-Simon lectr. Oxford U., 1983; Bampton lectr. Columbia U., 1983; Einstein lectr. Israel Acad. Arts and Scis., 1984; Hilldale lectr. U. Wis., 1985; Clark lectr. U. Tex., Dallas, 1986; Dirac lectr. U. Cambridge, 1986; Klein lectr. U. Stockholm, 1989; Brittin lectr. U. Colo., 1994; Sackler lectr. U. Copenhagen, 1994; Gibbs lectr. Am. Math. Soc., 1996; Bochner lectr. Rice U., 1997; Sanchez lectr. Tex. A&M Internat. U., 1998; Witherspoon lectr. Washington U., 2001; mem. Supercollider Sci. Policy Com., 1989—93; bd. dirs. Fedn. Am. Scientists. Author: Principles and Application of the General Theory of Relativity, 1972, The First Three Minutes: A Modern View of the Origin of the Universe, 1977, The Discovery of Subatomic Particles, 1982, revised edit., 2003; author: (with R. Feynman) Elementary Particles and the Laws of Physics; author: Dreams of a Final Theory, 1992, The Quantum Theory of Fields - Vol. I: Foundations, 1995, Modern Applications, Vol. II, 1996, Supersymmetry, Vol. III, 2000, Facing Up: Science and Its Cultural Adversaries, 2001, Glory and Terror: The Growing Nuclear Danger, 2004; rsch. and publs. on elementary particles, quantum field theory, cosmology, coeditor monographs on math. physics Cambridge U. Press, mem. adv. bd. Issues in Sci. and Tech., 1984—87, mem. sci. book bom. Sloan Found., 1985—91, editl. bd. Jour. Math. Physics, 1986—88, mem. bd. editors Daedalus, 1990—, Jour. Math. Physics, 1998—, mem. bd. assoc. editors Nuc. Physics B, —. Bd. advisors Santa Barbara Inst. Theoretical Physics, 1983—86; bd. overseers SSC Accelerator, 1984—86; bd. dirs. Headliners Found., 1993—. Recipient J. Robert Oppenheimer Meml. prize, 1973, Dannie Heineman prize in math. physics, 1977, Am. Inst. Physics U.S. Steel Found. sci. writing award, 1977, Nobel prize in Physics, 1979, Elliott Cresson medal, Franklin Inst., 1979, Madison medal, Princeton U., 1991, Nat. medal of Sci., NSF, 1991, Andrew Gemant prize, Am. Inst. Physics, 1997, Piazzi prize, Govts. Sicily and Palermo, 1998, Lewis Thomas prize, Rockefeller U., 1999. Mem.: NAS, Tex. Inst. Letters, Philos. Soc. Tex., Royal Soc. London, Am. Philos. Soc. (Benjamin Franklin medal 2004), Coun. Fgn. Rels., Internat. Astron. Union, Am. Phys. Soc., Am. Acad. Arts and Scis., Cambridge Sci. Soc., Headliners Club, Saturday Club (Boston), Tuesday Club (Austin), Phi Beta Kappa.

WEINBERG, SYDNEY STAHL, historian; b. N.Y.C., Oct. 2, 1938; d. David Leslie and Berenice (Jarvis) Stahl; divorced; children: Deborah Sara, Elisa Rachel; m. Gerald Tenenbaum, Mar. 23, 1996. BA, Barnard Coll., 1960, Columbia U., 1964, PhD, 1969. Instr. history N.J. Inst. Tech., 1967-69, asst. prof., 1969-72; assoc. prof. history Ramapo Coll. N.J., Mahwah, 1972-74, prof., 1974—, dir. MA program in liberal studies, 1994—. Dir. Garden State Immigration History Consortium, 1987-89. Author: The World of Our Mothers: The Lives of Jewish Immigrant Women, 1988; contbr. articles to profl. jours. Sec.-treas. Berkshire Conf. Women Historians, 1994-97. NEH fellow, 1977-78. Mem. Am. Hist. Assn., Orgn. Am. Historians, Am. Studies Assn., Jewish Studies Assn., Assn. Grad. Liberal Studies Programs. Home: 80 La Salle St Apt 19F New York NY 10027-4716 Office: Ramapo Coll MA Liberal Studies Program Office Mahwah NJ 07430

WEINBERG, SYLVAN LEE, cardiologist, educator, author, editor; b. Nashville, June 14, 1923; s. Abraham J. and Beatrice (Kottler) W.; m. Joan Hutzler, Jan. 29, 1956; children: Andrew Lee, Leslie. BS, Northwestern U., 1945, MD, 1948. From intern to resident, fellow Michael Reese Hosp., Chgo., 1947-51; attending physician Good Samaritan Hosp., Dayton, Ohio, 1953-99, chief of cardiology, 1966-99, founding dir. coronary care unit, 1967—; clin. prof. medicine Wright State U., Dayton, 1975—; dir. med. edn. Dayton Heart Hosp., 2000—. Former panelist Med. Affairs, nat. TV; pres. Weinberg Marcus Cardiomed. Group, Inc., 1970-99; pres. Arts & Comms. Internat., Inc., 1995—. Author: An Epitaph for Merlin and Perhaps for Medicine, 1983, The Golden Age of Medical Science and the Dark Age of Health Care Delivery, 2000; founding editor Dayton Medicine, 1980—, Heart & Lung, 1972-87, The American Heart Hosp. Jour., 2002—; contbr. articles to profl. jours. Capt. U.S. Army, 1951-53, Korea. Recipient Army Commendation medal, Richard A. DeWall MD award for excellence in cardiology, Am. Heart Assn., 2001, Outstanding Pub. Svc. award, Ohio State Senate, 1980. Fellow ACP (Ohio Laureate award 1997), Am. Coll. Cardiology (editor in chief jour. ACCEL 1985-2000, pres. 1993-94), Am. Coll. Chest Physicians (pres. 1984); mem. Montgomery County Med. Soc. (pres. 1980). Avocations: writing, travel, golf. Home: 4555 Southern Blvd Dayton OH 45429-1118 Office: Dayton Heart Hosp 707 S Edwin Moses Blvd Dayton OH 45408 E-mail: slwjal@aol.com.

WEINBERG, WILLIAM HENRY, chemical engineer, chemical physicist, educator; b. Columbia, S.C., Dec. 5, 1944; s. Ulrich Vivian and Ruth Ann (Duncan) W. BS, U. S.C., 1966; PhD in Chem. Engring, U. Calif., Berkeley, 1970; NATO postdoctoral fellow in phys. chemistry, Cambridge U., Eng., 1971. Asst. prof. chem. engring. Calif. Inst. Tech., 1972-74, assoc. prof., 1974-77, prof. chem. engring. and chem. physics, 1977-89, Chevron disting. prof. chem. engring. and chem. physics, 1981-86; prof. chem. engring. and chemistry U. Calif., Santa Barbara, 1989—, assoc. dean Coll. Engring., 1992-96; chief tech. officer Symyx Techs., Santa Clara, Calif., 1996—. Vis. prof. chemistry Harvard U., 1980, U. Pitts., 1987-88, Oxford U., 1991; Alexander von Humboldt Found. fellow U. Munich, 1982; cons. E.I. DuPont Co. Author: (with Van Hove and Chan) Low-Energy Electron Diffraction, 1986; editor 4 books in field; mem. editl. bd. Jour. Applications Surface Sci., 1977-85, Handbook Surfaces and Interfaces, 1978-80, Surface Sci. Reports, 1980—, gen. editor, 1992—, Applied Surface Sci., 1985—, Langmuir, 1990-96, Surface Sci., 1992—, Jour. Combinatorial Chemistry, 1998—; contbr. articles to profl. jours., chpts. to books. Recipient Giuseppe Parravano award Mich. Catalysis Soc., 1989, Disting. Teaching award Coll. of Engring., U. Calif. Santa Barbara, 1995; fellow NSF, 1966-69, Alfred P. Sloan Found., 1976-78, Camille and Henry Dreyfus Found., 1976-81. Fellow AAAS, Am. Phys. Soc. (Nottingham prize 1972), Am. Vacuum Soc.; mem. AIChE (Colburn award 1981), Am. Chem. Soc. (LaMer award 1973, Kendall award 1991, Arthur W. Adamson award 1995), N.Am. Catalysis Soc., Nat. Acad. Engring., Phi Beta Kappa. Office: Symyx Technologies 3100 Central Expy Santa Clara CA 95051-0801 Office Phone: 408-764-2000. Business E-Mail: hweinberg@symyx.com.

WEINBERGER, ADRIENNE, artist, appraiser; b. Washington, Apr. 28, 1948; d. Samuel Aaron and Marta (Barta) W.; m. Edward Herschel Egelman, Mar. 21, 1980; children: Serge Maurice, Liana Dora. BA, Goucher Coll., 1970; MEd, Johns Hopkins U., 1973; MA, Northwestern U., 1974; postgrad., Sch. of Mus. of Fine Arts, 1979-82. Lectr. Art Inst. Chgo., 1973-75; lectr., docent trainer Mus. of Fine Arts, Boston, 1978-82; mus. educator Yale Ctr. Brit. Art, Yale Art Gallery, New Haven, 1984-86; instr., coord. alumni coll. Albertus Magnus Coll., New Haven, 1987-89; instr. Mpls. C.C., 1989-94; propr. Studio 95, Edina, Minn., 1995-99, Charlottesville, Va., 1999—. Panelist New England Regional Confs., Am. Assn. Muss., Mass., Conn., 1976-77; mem., workshop leader New Haven Green Found., New Haven 350 Com., 1987-88; pres. Cmty. Art Fund., 2000—. Author, illustrator, pub.: New Haven Coloring Book, 1987, CulchaMan Visits New York City, 1988, CulchaMan Visits Washinton, D.C., 1988. Participant Edina Futures Forum, 1990; dir. Edina-Woodhill Assn., 1997—98; active State Affirmative Action Commn., 1996—98; del. chair, mem. nominating com. Dem. State Conv., St. Paul, 1994, del., chair Rochester, 1996, St. Cloud, 1998, del. Norfolk, 2000, Roanoke, 2004; active Dem. State Exec. Com., 1997—99; sec. Dem.-Farmer Labor Party, Edina, Eden Prairie, 1990—94, chair, 1994—96, treas. 3d Congl. Dist., 1996—99; mem. Dem. State Cen. Com., 1994—99; adv. bd. gifted edn. svcs. Edina Pub. Schs., 1993—96; bd. dirs. Consortium for Advancement of Arts, 2001—03, Leadership Charlottesville, 2002, Northwestern U. Alumni Club, 2003—, Northwestern U. Club Va. Recipient Juror's award Berkshire Mus., Pittsfield, Mass., 1981, New Haven Brush & Palette Club, 1985, Edina Art Ctr., 1991. Mem. Am. Soc. Appraisers (accredited sr. appraiser; sec. Twin Cities chpt. 1997-99, pres. Richmond chpt. 2000-01, 3d v.p. Richmond chpt. 2001-03), Charlottesville C. of C. (Amb. Corps. 2000, legis. action com., founder, pres. cmty. art fund 2000—), U. Va. Art Mus.(vol. bd. 2003-), Leadership Charlottesville, Northwestern U. Alumni Club Va. (bd. dirs. 2003—), Alumni Assn. Avocations: travel, reading, politics, advising on education. Office: Studio 95 3100 Waverly Dr Charlottesville VA 22901-9576 Office Phone: 434-297-0694. Business E-Mail: studio95@guanotronic.com.

WEINBERGER, ALAN DAVID, lawyer; b. Washington, July 31, 1945; s. Theodore George and Shirley Sunshine (Gross) W.; m. Lauren Myra Kaminski, Dec. 2, 1979; children: Mark Henry, Benjamin Charles. BA, NYU, 1967, JD, 1970; LLM, Harvard U., 1973. Bar: N.Y. 1971, D.C. 1978, U.S. Supreme Ct. 1980. Assoc. White & Case, N.Y.C., 1970-72; founding law prof. Vt. Law Sch., South Royalton, 1973-75; atty. SEC and Fed. Home Loan Bank Bd., Washington, 1977-81; founder, chmn. bd. dirs., CEO The ASCII Group Inc., Washington, 1984—; founder, chmn. bd. dirs. Tech. Net, Inc., Bethesda, Md., 1995. Adv. bd. Ashton Tate Inc., Torrance, Calif., 1986-87; sponsor, agt. All Union Fgn. Trade Acad., Acad. Nat. Economy of USSR in U.S.A., 1988-90; chmn. U.S. adv. bd. Moscow State U. of Commerce, 1992—; chmn. govt. affairs com. Computer Tech. Industry Assn., 1993-95; founder Artemis Channel Tech. Fund, Inc., 2004. Author: White Paper to Reform Business Education in Russia, 1996; law rev. editor NYU Sch. Law, 1970. Named one of Top 25 Most Influential Execs. in Computer Industry, Computer Reseller News, 1988; recipient CEO of Yr. award Cyber Chanels, 1999; named eInnovator of Yr. Cyber Channels Assn., 2000. Mem. Nat. Orgn. on Disability (CEO coun.), D.C. Bar Assn., Order of Coif, Kenwood Country Club. Avocation: tennis. Office: ASCII Group Inc 7101 Wisconsin Ave Bethesda MD 20814-4871 Business E-Mail: aw@ascii.com.

WEINBERGER, ARNOLD, retired electrical engineer; b. Bardejov, Czechoslovakia, Oct. 23, 1924; came to U.S., 1939; s. Henry C. and Bina (Shapira) W.; widowed; children: Paul I., Ronda B., Keith A. BSEE, CCNY, 1950. Engr. Nat. Bur. Standards, Washington, 1950-60; rsch. staff mem. IBM, Yorktown Heights, N.Y., 1960-66, engr., Poughkeepsie, N.Y., 1966-91, ret., 1991. Contbr. articles on computer arithmetic, logic, large-scale integration, system organization, memories, design automation. Patentee in field. With U.S. Army, 1944-46, ETO. Fellow IEEE (Outstanding sect. award 1981). Avocation: ping pong/table tennis.

WEINBERGER, CASPAR WILLARD, publishing executive, former secretary of defense; b. San Francisco, Aug. 18, 1917; s. Herman and Cerise Carpenter (Hampson) W.; m. Jane Dalton, Aug. 16, 1942; children: Arlin Cerise, Caspar Willard. AB magna cum laude, Harvard U., 1938, LLB, 1941; LLD (hon.), U. Leeds, Eng., 1989; LittD (hon.), U. Buckingham, 1995, Rensselear Poly., U. San Francisco. Bar: Calif., 1941, U.S. Ct. Appeals (D.C. cir.) 1990. Law clk. U.S. Judge William E. Orr, 1945-47; with firm Heller, Ehrman, White & McAuliffe, 1947-69, ptnr., 1959-69; mem. Calif. Legislature from 21st Dist., 1952-58; vice chmn. Calif. Rep. Ctrl. Com., 1960-62, chmn., 1962-64, Com. Calif. Govt. Orgn. and Econs., 1967-68; dir. fin. Calif., 1968-69; chmn. FTC, 1970; dep. dir. Office Mgmt. and Budget, 1970-72, dir., 1972-73; counsellor to the Pres., 1973; sec. HEW, 1973-75; gen. counsel, v.p., dir. Bechtel Power Corp., San Francisco, 1975-80, Bechtel, Inc., 1975-80, Bechtel Corp., 1975-80; sec. U.S. Dept. Def., Washington, 1981-87; counsel Law Firm of Rogers & Wells, Washington and N.Y.C., 1988-94; chmn. Forbes Magazine, New York, 1989—. Formerly staff book reviewer San Francisco Chronicle; moderator weekly TV program Profile, Bay Area, sta. KQED, San Francisco, 1959-68; Frank Nelson Doubleday lectr., 1974; co-host World Bus. Review, 1996-99. Author: Fighting for Peace: Seven Critical Years in the Pentagon, 1990; co-author (with Peter Schweizer): The Next War, 1996; co-author: (with Gretchen Roberts) In the Arena, A Memoir of the 20th Century, 2001. Chmn. Pres.'s Com. on Mental Retardation, 1973-75; former mem. Trilateral Commn.; former mem. adv. coun. Am. Ditchley Found.; former bd. dirs. Yosemite Inst.; former trustee St. Luke's Hosp., San Francisco, Mechanics Inst.; former chmn. nat. bd. trustees Nat. Symphony, Washington; former bd. govs. San Francisco Symphony; chmn. bd. USA-ROC Econ. Coun., 1991-94; co-chmn. Winston Churchill Travelling Fellowships Found., 1989-99; trustee Winston Churchill Meml. Trust, 1994—; bd. dirs. Chatham House Found., Inc., 1996—; mem. coun. on fgn. rels. Capt., inf. AUS, 1941-45; PTO. Decorated Bronze Star, Grand Cordon of Order of the Rising Sun (Japan), Hon. Knight Grand Cross Civil Div. Order of Brit. Empire, Order of Brillians Star with Grand Cordon, Taiwan; recipient Presdl. medal Freedom with distinction, 1987, Merite First Class, Mex., 1987, George Catlet Marshall medal, 1988, Civil award Hilal-i-Pakistan, 1989. Mem. ABA, State Bar Calif., D.C. Ct. Appeals, Century Club (N.Y.), Bohemian Club (San Francisco), Pacific Union Club (San Francisco), Harvard Club (Washington). Episcopalian (former treas. Diocese of Calif.). Office: Forbes Mag Office of Chmn 1101 17th St NW Ste 406 Washington DC 20036-4720 Office Phone: 202-835-8394.

WEINBERGER, DANIEL R. psychiatrist, neurologist; b. N.Y.C., May 24, 1947; married; 1 child. BA, Johns Hopkins U., 1969; MD, U. Pa., 1973. Diplomate Am. Bd. Psychiatry and Neurology. Intern L.A. County-Harbor Gen. Hosp., Torrance, Calif., 1973-74; grad. fellow in medicine UCLA Sch. Medicine, 1973-74; clin. fellow in psychiatry Harvard U., 1974-77; resident in psychiatry Mass. Mental Health Ctr., Boston, 1974-76, chief resident, 1976-77; assoc. in medicine, divsn. psychiatry Peter Bent Brigham Hosp., Boston, 1974-76; asst. clin. prof. psychiatry George Washington U., Washington, 1978-81, assoc. clin. prof., 1982, assoc. clin. prof. neurology and psychiatry, 1984; resident in neurology George Washington U. Med. Ctr., Washington, 1980-83; dir. rsch. ward adult psychiatry br., intermural rsch. program NIHM, Washington, 1977-78, staff psychiatrist, 1977-81; head clin. neuropsychiatry and neurobehavior unit NIMH/St. Elizabeth's Hosp., Washington, 1981-82, chief sect., 1983-86, chief clin. brain disorders br., 1986—; dir. movement disorder, dementia clinic, experimental therapeutics br. Nat. Inst. Neurol. Diseases and Stroke, Washington, 1983-86; dir. behavioral neurology svc. St. Elizabeth's Hosp., Washington, 1983-88. Part-time gen. practice Bridgewater Med. Ctr., East Bridgewater, Mass., 1974-76; emergency rm. physician Cardinal Cushing Gen. Hosp., Brockton, Mass., 1974-77; examiner Am. Bd. Psychiatry and Neurology; part-time gen. practice psychiatry and neurology, Washington, 1978—; scientists promotion review com. NIMH, 1984-87; elected to coun. Assembly of Scientists NIMH/Nat. Inst. Neurological Diseases and Stroke, 1985-88; Roerig vis. prof. U. N.Mex., 1990, U. Mich., 1992; adv. bd. Alzheimer Disease Found., 1990—, Adams Super Ctr. Brain Studies, Tel Aviv, 1993—; Neal Mysell lectr. Harvard Med. Sch., 1993; steering com. in vivo NMR Ctr., NIH, 1993—. Mem. editorial bd. Biol. Psychiatry, 1986—, Internat. Jour. Schizophrenia Rsch., 1987—, Jour. Neuropsychiatry and Clin. Neurosci., 1987—, Psychiatry, 1987—, Progress in Neuropsychiatry and Psychopharmacology, 1989—, Jour. Clin. Brain Imaging, 1989—, Psychiatry Research: Neuroimaging, 1990—, Jour. Psychiatry and Neurosci., 1990—, Neuropsychopharmacology, 1991—, Development and Psychopathology, 1991—, Harvard Review of Psychiatry, 1992—; contbr. articles to profl. jours.; patentee in field. Capt. USPHS, 1977-86. Recipient Morton Prince award Am. Psychopathol. Assn., 1984, Judith B. Silver award Nat. Alliance for Mentally Ill, 1985, Arthur S. Flemming award Washington Jaycees, 1986, Established Investigator award NARSAD, 1990, Lieber award, 1993, Dean award Am. Coll. Psychiatrists, 1994. Fellow Am. Coll. Neuropsychopharmacology (Joel Elkes internat. award 1989); mem. AMA, AAAS, Am. Psychiat. Assn. (Found. Fund prize for rsch. 1991), Am. Acad. Neurology (sci. program com. 1993—), Am. Neuropsychiatric Assn., Soc. Biol. Psychiatry (A.E. Benett Found. award clin. science 1981), Behavioral Neurology Soc., Soc. Neurosci. (pub. lectr. 20th ann. meeting 1990), Washington Neurology Soc., Washington Psychiat. Soc., Phi Beta Kappa, Alpha Omega Alpha, Inst. Medicine. Office: NIMH Clinical Brain Disorders Branch 10 Center Dr Rm 4S235 Bldg 10 Bethesda MD 20892-1379

WEINBERGER, FRANK, information management consultant; b. Chgo., Sept. 18, 1926; s. Rudolph and Elaine (Kellner) W.; m. Beatrice Natalie Fixler, June 27, 1953; children: Alan J., Bruce I. BSEE, Ill. Inst. Tech., Chgo., 1951; MBA, Northwestern U., 1959; DBA, U.S. Internat. U., San Diego, 1996. Registered profl. engr., Ill, Calif. Engr. Admiral Corp., Chgo., 1951-53; sr. engr. Cook Rsch., Chgo., 1953-59; mem. tech. staff Rockwell Internat., Downey, Calif., 1959-80, info. systems advisor, 1980-95; info. mgmt. cons., 1995—. Pres. Temple Israel, Long Beach, Calif., 1985-87, bd. dirs. 1973-85. With USN, 1944-46. Mem. Assn. for Computer Machinery. Democrat. Jewish. Avocation: microcomputers. Home and Office: 3231 Yellowtail Dr Los Alamitos CA 90720-5253 E-mail: weinberger@covad.net. *Don't ask "what can I do?" Instead, survey the needs, prepare the information, and give your best recommendation.*

WEINBERGER, HAROLD PAUL, lawyer; b. N.Y.C., Mar. 12, 1947; s. Fred and Elaine (Schonfeld) W.; m. Toby Ann Strassman, Dec. 15, 1968; children: James David, Karen Ellen. BA, CCNY, 1967; JD, Columbia U., 1970. Bar: N.Y. 1971, U.S. Dist. Cts. (so., ea., and no. dists.) N.Y. 1972, U.S. Ct. Appeals (2d cir.) 1972. Law clk. to presiding justice U.S. Ct. Appeals (2d cir.), N.Y.C., 1970-71; assoc. Kramer Levin Naftalis Frankel LLP, N.Y.C., 1971-77, ptnr., 1978—. Recipient John Ordronaux prize Columbia U. Law Sch., 1970. Mem. ABA (intellectual property law sect. 1999—), Assn. Bar City N.Y. (com. fed. legislation 1975-78, com. on products liability 1983-86, mem. com. on trademarks and unfair competition 1995-97). Democrat. Jewish. Home: 336 Central Park W New York NY 10025-7111 Office: Kramer Levin Naftalis & Frankel LLP 919 3rd Ave New York NY 10022-3902 E-mail: hweinberger@kramerlevin.com.

WEINBERGER, MARK, federal agency administrator; m. Nancy Weinberger; children: Rachel, Noah, Sean, Benjamin. Grad., Emory U.; MBA, Case We. Res.; LLM in Taxation, Georgetown U. Co-founder Washington Counsel, P.C. (merged with Ernst & Young); dir. U.S. nat. tax practice Ernst & Young LLP; asst. sec. treasury for tax policy U.S. Dept. Treasury, Washington, 2001—. Chief of staff, counsel Pres. Bipartisan Commn. on Entitlement and Tax Reform; sr. advisor Kemp Commn.; commr. Nat. Commn. on Retirement Policy; apptd. mem. Social Security Adv. Bd. Office: US Dept Treasury Tax Policy 1500 Pennsylvania Ave NW Washington DC 20220

WEINBERGER, MARTIN ANDREW, computer company executive; b. Santa Monica, Calif., Sept. 9, 1962; s. Tibor Weinberger and Katalin Klara Avedissian. BSEE, UCLA, 1984; postgrad. in computer engring., U. So. Calif. Microsoft cert. sys. engr.; Microsoft cert. product specialist; sun expert level 1000 engr.; Digital Equipment Corp. Network Product Bus. Unit Level II Engr. Sr. engr. Northrop Electronics, Hawthorne, Calif., 1985-87; sr. engr. data systems divsn. Litton Industries, Van Nuys, Calif., 1987-90; prin., owner, pres. Genesis Software Applications, Santa Monica, 1990—; device driver engr. Peerless Systems Corp., El Segundo, Calif., 1997-2000; 3d level engr. Unisource AT&T Internat., The Hague, Netherlands, 1997; chief software engr. I.N. Inc., Los Alamitos, Calif., 2000—. Developer: (software) MediSec. Democrat. Avocations: violin, skiing, ice skating, swimming. Office: Genesis Software Applications PMB 753 2118 Wilshire Blvd Santa Monica CA 90403-5784

WEINBERGER, MILES M. pediatrician, educator; b. McKeesport, Pa., June 28, 1938; divorced; 4 children; m. Leslie Kramer, Aug. 22, 1992. AB, U. Pitts., 1960, MD, 1965. Diplomate Am. Bd. Pediatrics, Am. Bd. Allergy and Immunology, Am. Bd. Pediatric Pulmonology. Intern U. Calif. Med. Ctr., San Francisco, 1965-66, pediatric resident, 1965-67; research assoc NIH, Bethesda, Md., 1967-69; allergy and pulmonary fellow U. Colo., Denver, 1969-71; staff Ross Valley Med. Clinic, Greenbrae, Calif., 1971-73; clin. pharmacology fellow U. Colo., Denver, 1973-75; divsn. dir. U. Iowa, Iowa City, 1975—; Cons. D.C.Hosp. for Sick Children, 1967-69, allergy and immunology Family Practice Program, Sonoma County Community Hosp., U. Calif. Sch. Medicine, 1972-73; clin. instr. pediatrics Georgetown U. Sch. Medicine, Washington, 1967-69; staff pediatrician part-time West Side Neighborhood Health Ctr., Denver, 1970-71; pediatric sr. staff mem. Nat.Jewish Hosp. and Research Ctr., 1973-75; clin. asst. U. Colo. Med.Ctr., 1974-75; assoc. prof. pediatrics, chmn. pediatric allergy and pulmonary div. U. Iowa Coll. Medicine, 1975-80, assoc. prof. pharmacology, 1975-79, dir. Cystic Fibrosis Ctr., 1977—, prof. pediatrics, 1980—, dir. pediatric allergy and pulmonary div., 1975—. Author: Managing Asthma, 1990; contbr. numerous articles to profl. jours., chpts. to books, also audio-visual materials, commentaries, pub. letters and presentations in field Recipient Clemens von Pirquet award Am. Coll. Allergy, 1974; grantee NIH, 1980-85, Cystic Fibrosis Ctr., Pharm. Mfrs. Assn. Fellow Am. Acad. Pediatrics (allergy sect. 1972, sect. on clin. pharmacology and therapeutics 1978, diseases of chest 1978); mem. Am. Acad. Allergy, Am. Soc. Clin. Pharmacology and Therapeutics, Soc. for Pediatric Rsch., Am. Thoracic Soc. (pres. Iowa Thoracic Soc. 1992-93), Camp Superkids of Iowa (adv. bd. 1981—), Am. Lung Assn. (pediatric pulmonbary ctr. task force com. 1984-86). Home: 7 Cottage Grove Dr NE Iowa City IA 52240-9171 Office: U Iowa Dept Pediatrics Iowa City IA 52242 Office Phone: 319-356-3485. E-mail: miles-weinberger@uiowa.edu.

WEINBERGER, MYRON HILMAR, medical educator; b. Cin., Sept. 21, 1937; s. Samuel and Helen Eleanor (Price) W.; m. Myrna M. Rosenberg, June 12, 1960; children: Howard David, Steven Neal, Debra Ellen. BS, Ind. U., Bloomington, 1959, MD, 1963. Intern Ind. U. Med. Ctr., Indpls., 1963-64, resident in internal medicine, 1964-66, asst. prof. medicine, 1969-73, assoc. prof., 1973-76, prof., 1976—, dir. Hypertension Research Ctr., 1981—; USPHS trainee in endocrinology and metabolism Stanford U. Med. Ctr.,

Calif., 1966-68, USPHS spl. fellow in hypertension, 1968-69. Contbr. articles to profl. jours. Recipient Tigerstedt award Am. Soc. Hypertension, 1996, Page-Bradley Lifetime Achievement award Am. Heart Assn. Coun. for High Blood Pressure Rsch., 1999. Fellow ACP, Am. Coll. Cardiology, Am. Coll. Nutrition, Am. Soc. for Clin. Pharmacology and Therapeutics; mem. AAAS, Am. Fedn. Clin. Research, AMA, Am. Heart Assn. (lifetime achievement award coun. for high blood pressure rsch. 1999), Am. Soc. Nephrology, Internat. Soc. Nephrology, Central Soc. Clin. Research, Endocrine Soc., Internat. Soc. Hypertension, Soc. for Exptl. Biology and Medicine Home: 135 Bow Ln Indianapolis IN 46220-1023 Office: Ind U Hypertension Research Ctr 541 Clinical Dr Indianapolis IN 46202-5233 Office Phone: 317-274-8153. Business E-Mail: mweinbe@iupui.edu.

WEINBERGER, PETER HENRY, lawyer; b. Cleve., Nov. 15, 1950; s. Eric and Eva (Grant) W.; m. Laurie Ann Novak, Aug. 26, 1972; children: Kelly, Adam. AB in Psychology, Syracuse U., 1972; JD, Case Western Res. U., 1975. Bar: Ohio 1975, U.S. Ct. Appeals (6th cir.) 1975, U.S. Ct. Appeals (4th cir.) 1986, Pa. 1995, U.S. Supreme Ct. 1995. Ptnr. Kube & Weinberger, Cleve., 1975-88, Spangenberg, Shibley & Liber, Cleve., 1988—. Lectr. to bar assns., Case Western Res. U. Sch. Law. Contbr. articles to legal jours. Chmn. Solon (Ohio) Cable TV Adv. Com., 1984-85; mem. Solon Civil Svc. Commn., 1985-87, vice chmn., 1986-87; bd. dirs. 1st Unitarian Ch. Cleve., pres., 1992-93. Fellow Am. Coll. Trial Lawyers; mem. ABA, Ohio Bar Assn., Cleve. Bar Assn. (chmn. young lawyers sect. 1980-81, charter mem. coun. litigation sect. 1987—), Cuyahoga Bar Assn. (pres. 1991-92, chmn. grievance com. 1984-86, trustee 1987—, cert. of appreciation 1985, 89, outstanding svc. award 1986), Assn. Trial Lawyers Am., Ohio Acad. Trial Lawyers (trustee 1999—), Cleve. Acad. Trial Attys. (pres. 1984-85, spl. merit award 1985), 8th Dist. Jud. Conf. (charter mem. commn. on pre-trials), Cuyahoga Bar Found. (pres. 1998—), Am. Bd. of Trial Advs. (adv.). Democrat. Unitarian Universalist. Home: 34910 Forest Ln Cleveland OH 44139-1441 Office: Spangenberg Shibley & Liber 2400 National City Ctr Cleveland OH 44114 E-mail: phw@spanglaw.com.

WEINBERGER, STEVEN, lawyer, educator; b. Bklyn., Apr. 13, 1953; s. Robert Ira and Elaine (Lichtenthal) W.; m. Maureen Susan Horan, Oct. 15, 1978 (div. 1998); children: John William, Matthew Lawrence; m. Maria DiBenedetto, Sept. 26, 1998. BA, SUNY, Binghamton, 1974; JD, U. Miami, 1977; MS, Hartford Grad. Ctr., 1989. Bar: N.Y. 1978, Conn. 1987, U.S. Dist. Ct. (no. dist.) N.Y. 1981, U.S. Dist. Ct. Conn. 1990. Legis. atty. N.Y. City Council, 1977-78; asst. atty. Westchester County, White Plains, N.Y., 1978-79; sr. asst. atty. Broome County, Binghamton, N.Y., 1979-81, dep. personnel officer, 1981-82; from labor rels. specialist to chief employee svcs. bur. State of Conn., Hartford, 1982-95, dir. retirement and benefit svcs. divsn., 1995—. Adj. prof. Teikyo Post U., Waterbury, Conn., 1984—, Albertus Magnus Coll., New Haven, 2000—. Mem. N.Y. State Bar Assn. Democrat. Jewish. Office: State of Connecticut Retirement & Benefit Svcs 55 Elm St Hartford CT 06106-1746 E-mail: steve.weinberger@po.state.ct.us.

WEINBLATT, CHARLES SAMUEL, university administrator, employment consultant; b. Toledo, Dec. 23, 1952; s. Morris and Clara (Volk) W.; m. Frances Barbara Auslander, Aug. 12, 1973; children: Brian J., Lauren M. BA, U. Toledo, 1974. Cert. edn. and tng. counselor, Ohio. Psychiat. counselor St. Vincent Hosp., Toledo, 1974-77; vocat., rehab. counselor Goodwill Industries, Toledo, 1977-85; employment cons., pvt. practice Toledo, 1985—; tng. counselor UAW Chrysler, Perrysburg, Ohio, 1987; dir. divsn. orgn. devel. and leadership U. Toledo, 1988—. Employment svcs. cons. Employers' Assn. Toledo, 1985-90; outplacement cons. Toledo Pub. Schs., 1986; spkr. in field of labor and mgmt. rels., employee involvement. Author: Job Seeking Skills for Students, 1987. Mem. Toledo Vision Com., 1989-90. Recipient Quality Improvement award Chrysler, 1987, cert. Am. Inst. Banking, 1989. Mem. ASTD, Ohio Continuing Higher Edn. Assn., Toledo Area Human Resource Assoc., World Future Soc. Jewish. Avocations: music, sports, gardening. Home: 5118 Brenden Way Sylvania OH 43560-2223 Office: U Toledo Seagate Campus 401 Jefferson Ave Toledo OH 43604-1063 E-mail: cweinbl@utnet.utoledo.edu.

WEINBRENNER, GEORGE RYAN, aeronautical engineer; b. June 10, 1917; s. George Penbrook and Helen Mercedes (Ryan) W.; m. Billie Marjorie Elwood, May 2, 1955. BS, MIT, 1940, MS, 1941; AMP, Harvard U., 1966; ScD (hon.), Mapua Inst. Tech., Manila, 1994. Commd. 2d lt. USAAF, 1939, advanced through grades to col., 1949; def. attaché Am. Embassy, Prague, Czechoslovakia, 1958-61; dep. chief staff intelligence Air Force Sys. Command, Washington, 1962-68; comdr. fgn. tech. divsn. USAF, Wright-Patterson AFB, Ohio, 1968-74; comdr. Brooks AFB, Tex., 1974-75; ret., 1975; exec. v.p. B.C. Wills & Co., Inc., Reno, 1975-84; chmn. bd. Hispaño-Technica S.A. Inc., San Antonio, 1977—. Lectr. Sch. Aerospace Medicine Brooks AFB, Tex., 1975-84; adv. dir. Plaza Nat. Bank, San Antonio; cons. Def. Dept., 1981, Dept. Air Force, 1975-84. Decorated D.S.M., Legion of Merit, Bronze Star, Air medal, Purple Heart, Ordre Nat. du Merite, Medaille de la Resistance, Croix de Guerre (France). Fellow AIAA (assoc.); mem. World Affairs Coun., Air Force Assn. (exec. sec. Tex. 1976-94), Assn. Former Intelligence Officers (nat. dir.), Air Force Hist. Found. (dir.), U.S. Strategic Inst., Nat. Mil. Intelligence Assn., Tex. Aerospace & Nat. Def. Tech. Devel. Coun., Am. Astron. Soc., Aerospace Ednl. Foun. (trustee), Disabled Am. Vets. (life), Mil. Order World Wars, Am. Legion, Assn. Old Crows, Army-Navy Club (Washington), Kappa Sigma. Roman Catholic. Home: 7400 Crestway Dr Apt 903 San Antonio TX 78239-3094 Office: AFA Texas 8406 Cadmus San Antonio TX 78214-3001 E-mail: afatexas@member.afa.org.

WEINBROT, HOWARD DAVID, English educator; b. Bklyn., May 14, 1936; s. William and Rose (Shapiro) W. BA, Antioch Coll., Yellow Springs, Ohio, 1958; MA with honors (Woodrow Wilson fellow 1959, grad. fellow 1959-63), U. Chgo., 1959, PhD, 1963. Teaching fellow U. Chgo., 1962-63; instr. English Yale U., 1963-66; asst. prof., then assoc. prof. U. Calif., Riverside, 1966-69; mem. faculty U. Wis., Madison, 1969—, prof. English, 1972-84, Ricardo Quintana prof., 1984-87, Vilas prof., 1987—. Andrew Mellon vis. prof. Inst. Advanced Studies, Princeton, N.J., 1993-94. Author: The Formal Strain, 1969, Augustus Caesar in Augustan England, 1978, Alexander Pope and the Traditions of Formal Verse Satire, 1982, Essays on 18th-Century Satire, 1988, Britannia's Issue, 1993; also numerous articles, revs.; editor: New Aspects of Lexicography, 1972, Northrop Frye and 18th Century Studies; co-editor: The 18th Century: A Current Bibliography for 1973, 1975, Poetry in English, An Anthology, 1987, Eighteenth-Century Contexts, 2001. NEH fellow, 1975-76; Guggenheim fellow, 1988-89. Mem. Am. Soc. 18th Century Studies (mem. editl. bd. 1977-80, exec. com. 96-99), Internat. Soc. 18th Century Studies UCLA (planning com. 2003), Johnsonians, Johnson Soc. (sec.-treas. 1970-75, v.p. 2000-01, pres. 2002-03), Midwest Am. Soc. Eighteenth Century Studies, Eighteenth Century Scottish Studies, Inst. Adv. Study (vis. 2002). Home: 1505 Wood Ln Madison WI 53705-1456 Office: U Wis English Dept 600 N Park St Madison WI 53706-1403 E-mail: weinbrot@facstaff.wisc.edu.

WEINCEK, CRAIG JAMES, communications educator, writer; b. Bay Shore, N.Y., Oct. 27, 1945; s. Floyd P. and Julaine Weincek; m. Betty Bucco, July 15, 1967. BA in English Edn., U. of Md., College Park, 1967, MFA, 1998. H.s. rugby coach, tchr. English Walt Whitman H.S., Bethesda, Md., 1968—70; head football coach Nassau (Bahamas) Marlins, West Indies, 1971—73; head rugby coach, asst. football coach, tchr. English Seneca Valley H.S., Germantown, Md., 1974—83; sports editor Potomac (Md.) Almanac, 1983—85; mng. editor The Express Newspapers, Germantown, 1985—89; assoc. prof. comm. and English Frederick (Md.) C.C., 1989—. Movie reveiwer The Express Newspapers, Germantown, 1980—95; movie reviewer The New Paper, Frederick, 1990—99, WAFY Radio, Frederick, 1996—99, Adelphia Cable Channel 10, Frederick, 1997—. Author: (novels) The Perfect Game. Advisor to student newspaper Frederick C.C., 1989—95, 1998—2003; coll. rep. Assn. for the Advancement of C.C. Tchg., Frederick, 2003—04. Named Two-Year Coll. Advisor of the Yr. Mem.: Coll. Media Advisors, Inc., Holly Hills Country Club (life). Democrat. Avocations: golf, rugby, travel, gardening, labradors. Office: Frederick C C 7932 Opossumtown Pike Frederick MD 21702 E-mail: cweincek@frederick, edu.

WEINER, ALAN E. accountant, lawyer; BBA, CCNY, NY, 1963; JD, Bklyn. Law Sch., Bklyn., 1968; LLM, NYU, NY, 1972. Bar: N.Y., 1969, U.S. Tax Ct. 1969, U.S. Supreme Ct., 1995; CPA, N.Y. 1967. Staff acct. Kamerman & Kamerman, N.Y.C., 1963-68; assoc. law firm Wien & Malkin, N.Y.C., 1968-69; tax mgr. Touche Ross & Co. (now Deloitte & Touche LLP), L.I., N.Y., 1969-75; tax dir. Wolf & Co., N.Y.C., 1975; sr. tax ptnr. Holtz Rubenstein & Co., LLP, L.I., 1975—. Instr., Hofstra U., 1973-76; lectr., Found. for Acctg. Edn., N.Y.C., 1974—, pres., 2000-2001. Columnist,Suffolk County Life Underwriters Assn., 1976-79; author: All About Limited Liability Companies and Partnerships, 1994, DFK International Worldwide Tax Overview, 2000; editl. adviser, The Tax Adviser, 1997-2001; editor: fed. tax column, The CPA Jour., 1983-85; mem. adv. bd., Financial Manager mag., 1988-90; contbr. articles to profl. jours. Pres. Estate Planning Coun. of Suffolk County (N.Y.), 1978-79, founder, chmn. L.I. Accts. Blood Drive, 1982-84; trustee L.I. chpt. Leukemia Soc. Am., 1987-98. Mem. AICPA (coun. 1997-2000), NY State Soc. CPAs (pres. 1999-2000, pres.-elect 1998-99, treas. 1995-97, bd. dirs. 1992-95, chmn. tax divsn. exec. com. 1993-95, chmn. tax simplification task force, 2003-04, chmn. Clinton tax proposals task force 1993, ltd. liability co. task force 1992, chmn. tax plenary session 1991, chmn. partnership tax com. 1989-91, chmn. fed. tax com. Nassau chpt. 1986-87, chmn. estate planning coun. Nassau chpt. 1973-74), Nassau County Bar Assn. (tax law com. 1973—), Am. Assn. Atty.-CPA's, Suffolk County Bar Assn. (tax law com. 1980—, chmn. bi-county com. atty./accts. 1990-91), DFK Internat. (exec. com. 2000—, v.p. of the Ams. 1997-2000, 2003—, chmn. internat. tax com. 1990-95). Office: Holtz Rubenstein and Co LLP 125 Baylis Rd Melville NY 11747-3823 Fax: 631-752-1742. Office Phone: 631-752-7400. E-mail: aeweiner@hrcpa.com.

WEINER, ANDREW JAY, lawyer; b. Hartford, Conn., Dec. 19, 1950; m. Debra Lewin, May 29, 1977; children: Joshua Isaac, Hannah Leah. BA, Yale Coll., 1972; JD, Harvard U., 1976. Bar: N.Y. 1977. Planner N.Y.C. Dept. City Planning, 1972-73; assoc. Shearman & Sterling, N.Y.C., 1976-84; ptnr. Gordon Hurwitz Butowsky Weitzen Shalov & Wein, N.Y.C., 1984-89, Morrison & Foerster LLP, N.Y.C., 1990—. Office: Morrison & Foerster LLP 1290 Avenue Of The Americas Fl 40 New York NY 10104-0050 Personal E-mail: aweiner@mofo.com.

WEINER, ANNE LEE, social worker; b. Chelsea-Malden, Mass., Nov. 2, 1932; d. Nathan and Edith E. (Sigel) Varnick; m. Paul J. Weiner, Jan. 25, 1959; children: Berdine R., Ronald M. Diploma in med. sec., Chandler Sch. for Women, 1952; AA in Social Work, Middlesex C.C., 1974; BSW, Salem Coll., 1987. Med. sec. New Eng. Med. - Boston U. Hosp., Boston, 1952-1960; social worker Lynn-Union Hosp., Lynn, Mass., 1968-1982; home care social worker Mass. Elder Care, Peabody, 1982-1987; nursing home social worker Logan Homes, Wingate Homes, Hill Haven Homes, Mass., 1987-99. Mem. region bd. Hadassah steering com. social work, Hadassah, Boston and Fla. Atlantic region, pres. Chessed, 2003—; active Hist. Soc. Peabody; organizer social work support groups Chessed, North Shore, Mass., 2003-04 Office: Lakes Delray # 114 Watersedge J Delray Beach FL 33484 Personal E-mail: lighthouselaw@bellsouth.net.

WEINER, ANTHONY DAVID, congressman; b. Bklyn., N.Y., Sept. 4, 1964; BA, SUNY, Plattsburgh, 1985. Washington DC and N.Y. aide to U.S. Congressman Charles Schumer; city councilman Dist. 48, N.Y.C., 1991-98, mem. pub. safety, consumet affairs, transp. coms., chmn. subcom. crime in pub. housing; mem. 106th-108th Congress from 9th N.Y. dist., 1999—; mem. judiciary com.; mem. sci. com., 1998—. Bd. dirs. Boys Town, Jerusalem, Shaare Zedek Hosp., Israel. Democrat. Office: 1901 Emmons Ave Ste 212 Brooklyn NY 11235-2700 also: US Ho of Reps 1122 Longworth Ho Office Bldg Washington DC 20515-3209

WEINER, CARL DORIAN, historian; b. N.Y.C., Mar. 26, 1934; s. Alexander and Ann (Goodson) W.; m. Ruth Ann Feinglass, Sept. 6, 1959; children— Nicholas, Kevin, Daniel BA, Queens Coll., 1955; postgrad., U. Wis., 1958-61; MA, Columbia U., 1959. Instr. U. Pitts., 1961-62; mem. faculty Carleton Coll., Northfield, Minn., 1964—2004, chmn. dept. history, 1974-77, 95-98, prof., 1982—2002, William H. Laird prof. emeritus, history and the liberal arts, 2002—04. Served with U.S. Army, 1957 Recipient 2d Century award Carleton Coll., 1968; Bush grantee, 1983-84 Jewish. Home: 403 Laurel Ave Saint Paul MN 55102-2015 Office Phone: 507-646-4209.

WEINER, CHARLES, historian, educator; b. Bklyn., Aug. 11, 1931; s. Louis and Minnie (Florman) W.; m. Shirley Marks (div. 1976); 1 child, Susan. BS, Case Inst. Tech., 1960, MA, 1963, PhD, 1965. Asst. editor Tooling and Production mag., Cleve., 1958-60, asso. editor, 1961; editor The Explorer, Cleve. Museum of Natural History, 1960-62; dir. Project on History of Recent Physics in the U.S., Am. Inst. Physics, N.Y.C., 1964-65, Center for History of Physics, 1965-74; prof. history of sci. and tech. Mass. Inst. Tech., 1974—, dir. oral history program, 1975—. Co-editor: The Legacy of George Ellery Hale, 1972, Robert Oppenheimer: Letters and Recollections, 1980; editor: Exploring the History of Nuclear Physics, 1972, History of 20th Century Physics, 1977; mem. editorial council: Bull. of Atomic Scientists, 1979-84. Mem. com. social orgn. sci. Social Sci. Research Council, 1968-71; adv. com. to Library of Congress on Nat. Union Catalog of Manuscript Collections, 1965-71; mem. editorial adv. bd. Joseph Henry Papers, Smithsonian Instn., 1968—; com. on history of recent biochemistry and molecular biology Am. Acad. Arts and Scis., 1968-80, project dir. com. history contemporary physics, 1966-74; mem. adv. bd. Center for the Study of Consumer Movement, Consumers Union; mem. humanities adv. bd. Sta. WGBH, Boston, 1978-79. Served with U.S. Army, 1951-53. Recipient Disting. Service citation Am. Assn. Physics Tchrs., 1974; Case fellow, 1961-64; Guggenheim fellow, 1970-71; NSF grantee, 1965, 68, 70, 73, 75, 77, 81, 86; Nat. Endowment Humanities grantee, 1976, 77, 81, 86. Fellow AAAS (council 1969-75, com. on meetings 1969-72), History of Sci. Soc. (council 1968-70, chmn. Met. N.Y. Sect. 1969-70), Am. Hist. Assn., Oral History Assn., Orgn. Am. Historians, Soc. for History of Tech. (adv. council 1977-79). Office: Mass Inst Tech Program in Sci Tech and Society Bldg E51-296 Cambridge MA 02139

WEINER, CHARLES R. federal judge; b. Phila., June 27, 1922; s. Max and Bessie (Chairney) W.; m. Edna Gerber, Aug. 24, 1947; children: William, Carole, Harvey. Grad., U. Pa., 1947, MA, 1967, PhD, 1972; LL.B., Temple U., 1950. Bar: Pa. bar 1951. Asst. dist. atty. Philadelphia County, 1952-53; mem. Pa. Senate from Phila. County, 1952-67, minority floor leader, 1959-60, 63-64, majority floor leader, 1961-62; U.S. dist. judge Eastern Dist. Pa., 1967—; now sr. judge. Mem. Phila. County Bd. Law Examiners, 1959— Mem. Pres.'s Adv. Commn. Inter-Govtl. Rels., Phila., Pub. Policy Com., Phila. Crime Prevention Assn., Big Bros. Assn.; mem. Pa. Bd. Arts and Scis.; trustee, exec. com. Fedn. Jewish Philanthropies of Phila., Allied Jewish Appeal of Phila.; bd. dirs. Mental Health Assn. of Pa., Phila. Psychiat. Ctr., Phila. Tribune Charities, Phila. Wharton Ctr. Parkside YMCA, Jewish Publ. Soc. Am., The Athenaeum, and others. With USN, 1942—46. Recipient Phila. Fellowship award; Founder's Day award Temple U.; Alumni award U. Pa.; Founder's award Berean Inst.; others. Mem. ABA, Pa. Bar Assn., Phila. Bar Assn., Am. Law Inst. Office: US District Ct 6613 US Courthouse Ind Mall W 601 Market St Philadelphia PA 19106-1713

WEINER, CLAIRE MURIEL, freelance writer; b. Bronx, N.Y., Dec. 18, 1951; d. David and Norma (Berry) W. BA, U. Miami, Coral Gables, Fla., 1973; MA, U. Md., 1980. Pub. rels. specialist Hialeah Recreation Div., Hialeah, Fla., 1974-77; freelance writer North Miami Beach, 1977-78, Germantown, Md., 1989—, Montgomery County, Md., 1981—. Govt. affairs liaison for new ednl. data base co. being formed, Montgomery County, 1982—; acting comm. dir. Ednl. Info. Svcs., 1996—. Contbr. articles to local newspapers; contbr. travel articles to profl. jours, mags. Active membership com. newsletter Greater Miami Jewish Fedn., 1974-77; charter mem. Women for Today chpt. B'nai B'rith Women, Washington, 1985-89. Named Hon. Citizen of Historic Williamsburg. Life fellow Am. Biog. Inst. Rsch. Assn., World Lit. Acad.; mem. NAFE, Internat. Platform Assn., Nat. Trust for Hist. Preservation. Jewish. Home: 18828 Sky Blue Cir Germantown MD 20874-5398

WEINER, CLAIRE ZUNDELL, theatrical director; b. Worcester, Mass., June 19, 1933; d. Edward A. and Mary (Abramson) Shapiro; children: Aaryn Anne, Elliot Michael. Student, Clark U., SUNY, Miami-Dade Coll. Instr. fundamentals of theatre Dade County (Fla.) Cmty. Sch. Sys., 1965-68; tchr. theatre arts Roberson Centre of the Arts, Binghamton, N.Y., 1969-70; artist-in-theatre Colgate U., Hamilton, N.Y., 1968-70; freelance feature writer Norwich (N.Y.) Eve. Sun, 1969-72; dir. Norwich Sr. High Theatre, 1968-72; dir. cultural activities for youth Norwich Youth Commn., 1969-72; resident dir., actress Gold Crown Dinner Theatre & Touring Co., Downey, Calif., 1972-76; dir. Theatre for Youth City of Santa Clara, Calif., 1979-80; dir. The Center Players, Long Beach, Calif., 1977-78; resident dir./playwright Arrowhead Theatre, San Jose, Calif., 1990—, resident dir./actor, Reader's Theatre for Original Plays, 1992-94. Mem. Miami Actor sCo., Miami, Fla., 1965-68, Gainesville (Fla.) Little Theatre, 1956-58, Jacksonville (Fla.) Little Theatre, 1958-62, Gallery Theatre, Coral Gables, Fla., 1961-62, Miami Beach Players, 1962-64, Arlington Players, Jacksonville, 1958-61, dir. Norwich Adult Weekly Summer Repertory Theatre, 1969-72, Norwich Weekly Children's Theatre in Mime, 1969-72; originator 1st area multi-sch. project Tino WorkShop Theatre, Fremont H.S. Dist., 1980—; guest dir. West Valley Civic Light Opera, 1982; advisor N.Y. State Coun. on Arts, 1968-70; tchr. theatre arts Norwich Bd. Edn. summer 1970, Met. Edn. Dist., San Jose, 1998. Author: The Rabbi's Daughter, 1987, Between the Night Shadows, 1989, Thresholds, 1990, Billington's, 1992, What Do I Wear Now? The Breast Cancer Legacy, 1995, Gettin On With It, 2001, The WaterStreet Diaries: a work in progress, 2001, (in pen name Claire Z. Cameron) The Home, a novel, 2003, Patterns of Life (inducted into Internat. Libr. Poets, anthology), 2003, New to America: A Family History, 2004; guest spkr., 1992—; animation voice-overs E.J. Sound/Hosca Prodn., Inc., San Jose; featured poet Norwich Sun, N.Y., 2000—. Youth leader B'nai B'rith; reader for the blind San Jose Pub. Libr. Mem. AFTRA, Am. Ednl. Theatre Assn., Internat. Platform Assn. Home: 5363 Joseph Ln San Jose CA 95118

WEINER, CLARE FRANCES, social worker, psychotherapist; b. Phila., Dec. 3, 1929; d. Jack and Jessie (Rosengarten) Weinbaum; m. George C. Wheeler, Jan. 21, 1978; children by previous marriage: Justin M., Kate J., Lucian J. BS, Temple U., 1951; MSW, U. Wis., 1967. Diplomate Am. Bd. Examiners in Clin. Social Work. Social worker Ohio Valley Mental Retardation Evaluation Unit, Athens, Ohio, 1968-69; social worker inpatient psychiat. svc. VA Hosp., Albany, N.Y., 1969-70; chief social worker Schenectady County Outpatient Mental Health Clinic, 1970-76; adult treatment team leader, supervising social worker Saratoga County Mental Health Ctr., N.Y., 1976-81; pvt. practice psychotherapy individuals, couples, families Schenectady, 1975—. Fellow N.Y. State Soc. for Clin. Social Workers, Nat. Assn. Social Workers (diplomate); mem. Gestalt Inst. Cleve., Burnt Hills Oratorio Soc. Avocations: music, hiking, quilting. Office: 29 Front St Schenectady NY 12305-1301 Office Phone: 518-346-6621.

WEINER, EARL DAVID, lawyer; b. Balt., Aug. 21, 1939; s. Jacob Joseph and Sophia Gertrude (Rachanow) W.; m. Gina Helen Priestley Ingoglia, Mar. 30, 1962; children: Melissa Danis Balmain, John Barlow. AB, Dickinson Coll., 1960; LL.B., Yale U., 1968. Bar: NY 1969. Assoc. Sullivan & Cromwell, N.Y.C., 1968-76, ptnr., 1976—. Adj. prof. Rutgers U. Sch. Law, 1987-88; bd. dirs. Solvay Techs. Inc., Hedwin Corp., The Acting Co., vice-chmn., 1992-2003, chmn., 2003—. Gov. Bklyn. Heights Assn., 1980-87, pres., 1985-87, adv. com., 1987—; gov. The Heights Casino, 1979-84, pres., 1981-84; trustee Bklyn. Bot. Garden, 1985—, chmn. 1998—; trustee Green-Wood Cemetery, 1986—, Bklyn. Hosp. Ctr., 1998—; bd. advisors Dickinson Coll., Carlisle, Pa., 1986-90, chmn., 1988-90, trustee, 1988-2002, vice chmn., 1998-2002; mem. adv. com. East Rock Inst., 1988—; bd. visitors U. Md. Ctr. for Environ. Sci., 2002—. Lt. USN, 1961-65. Fellow Fgn. Policy Assn. (sr.); mem. ABA, N.Y. State Bar Assn., Assn. Bar City N.Y. Office: Sullivan & Cromwell 125 Broad St Fl 28 New York NY 10004-2489

WEINER, EDWARD, civil engineer, federal agency administrator; b. Bklyn., Mar. 31, 1941; s. Abe C. and Elsie (Botwinick) W.; m. Joanne Jessen, Sept. 9, 1967 (div. Mar. 1988); children: Jennifer Lynn, Michael Andrew; m. Janis Lynn Wolford, Oct. 7, 1995. BA, BCE, NYU, 1963; MS in Civil Engring., Purdue U., 1964; MPA, U. So. Calif., 1978. Registered profl. engr. Hwy. rsch. engr. Bur. of Pub. Rds., then Fed. Hwy. Adminstrn., Washington, 1964—70; mgr. urban analysis program Office Sec. Transp., Washington, 1970—77, sr. policy analyst, 1978—2001, mobility and infrastructure team leader, 2001—. Sec. Task Force on Pub. Transp., Transp. Rsch. Bd., 1971-72, mem. Com. on Travel Behavior and Values, Oct. 1973—; group 1 coun., transp. sys. planning and adminstrn., 1984-90; mem. com. Intergovernmental Rels. and Policy Process, Telecom. and Travel Behavior; guest lectr. George Washington U., U. Va., Portland State U., U. Wis.; U.S. rep. internat. working groups on urban travel and sustainability. Co-editor: Emerging Transportation Planning Methods, 1978; author, co-author: Urban Transportation Planning in the U.S., 1987, revised edit., 1999, National Transportation System Initiative, 1999; (monographs) Role of Taxicabs in Urban Transportation, 1974, Glossary of Urban Public Transportation Terms, 1978, Modal Split, 1966; co-editor Internat. Assn. for Travel Behavior newsletter, 1985-88; contbr. over 80 articles to profl. jours. and books; mem. editl. adv. bd. Transp., 1978-80, 92-2000. Asst. troop leader Girl Scouts Am., Silver Spring, Md., 1981-82; v.p. Unitarian Universalist Ch. of Silver Spring, 1984, pres., 1985-86, v.p., 1998-99. Edn. for Public Mgmt. fellow U.S. Dept. Transp., 1978; recipient Bronze medal Dept. Transp., 1981, Spl. Achievement award, 1990, 95, 98, 99, 2000. Mem. ASCE, Transp. Rsch. Bd. Home: 16615 Harbour Town Dr Silver Spring MD 20905-4082 Office: US Dept Transp P 110 400 7th St SW Washington DC 20590-0001 Business E-Mail: ed.weiner@ost.dot.gov.

WEINER, EDWARD G. export company executive; CFO Transammonia Inc., N.Y.C. Office: Transammonia Inc 350 Park Ave New York NY 10022

WEINER, FERNE, psychologist; b. N.Y.C., June 14, 1928; d. Irving Kapp and Peggy (Finkelstein) Hessberg; m. Howard Weiner, July 20, 1948; children: Irving Kenneth, Laurie. BA, Skidmore Coll., 1965; MA, Sarah Lawrence Coll., 1971; PhD, U. Hawaii, 1975. Lic. psychologist, Calif., Hawaii. Asst. prof. West Oahu Coll. U. Hawaii, Honolulu, 1975—77; staff psychologist Cmty. Guidance Clinic, Manchester, Conn., 1978—83; chief cons. psychologist Consultation and Evaluation Ctr., Meriden, Conn., 1984—85; psychologist cons. Disability Determination Svcs., Hartford, Conn., 1986—87, Honolulu, 1988—; police psychologist Honolulu Police Dept., 1988. Pvt. practice, Greenwich, Conn., 1983-87, Honolulu, 1988—; cons. Adopt-A-Sch. Project, Honolulu, 1991-94; interviewer, therapist Sexual Abuse Treatment Team, Manchester, 1979-83; cons., trainer Conn. schs., day care, ch. groups, 1979-87. Contbr. articles to profl. jours. Active Disaster Assistance Mgmt. Team, Hawaii, 1994-95; v.p., sec. Queens Court at Kapiolani Bd., Honolulu, 1992-95; admissions rep. Hawaii Sarah Lawrence Coll., Honolulu, 1970-80; cons. to adoptees search Orphan Voyage, Conn., 1980-87; mentor Girl Scout Coun. Am., Oahu, 1993-94. Mem. Am. Psychol. Assn. (clin. psychotherapy and neuropsychology divsn.), Hawaii Psychol. Assn., Nat. Registry Health Svcs. Providers, Outrigger Canoe Club, Honolulu Club. Democrat. Jewish. Avocations: aerobics, interior design, property renovation, gourmet cooking, travel. Address: 9776 Claiborne Sq La Jolla CA 92037-1158 E-mail: wferne1@san.rr.com.

WEINER, FRANK H. architect, educator; BArch, Tulane U., 1980; MS in Arch. and Bldg. Design, Columbia U., 1987. Registered architect, N.Y. Dept. head and assoc. prof. dept. arch. Va. Inst. Tech., 2001—. Spkr. in field; invited panelist Practice Edn. Summit, Raleigh, NC, 1997; guest juror Sch. Arch. U. Va., 1996. Contbr. articles to profl. jours. Mem. planning com. Roanoke's Neighborhoods: A Design Competition for New Housing, 2000—01. Mem.: AIA. Office: 201 Cowgill Hall Blacksburg VA 24061

WEINER, GEORGE JAY, internist; b. Plainview, N.Y., Mar. 1, 1956; m. Teresa Emily Wilhelm, July 30, 1983; children: Aaron, Miriam, Nathan. BA, Johns Hopkins U., 1978; MD, Ohio State U., 1981. Resident in internal medicine Med. Coll. Ohio, Toledo, 1981-85; hematology/oncology fellow U. Mich., Ann Arbor, 1985-89; asst. prof. medicine U. Iowa, Iowa City, 1989-94,

assoc. prof., 1994-99, prof., 1999—, dir. Cancer Ctr., 1998—. Dir. Holden Comprehensive Cancer Ctr., U. Iowa. Achievements include devel. of new approaches to cancer immunotherapy. Office: Univ of Iowa 5970 JPP Iowa City IA 52242

WEINER, GERALD ARNE, stockbroker; b. Chgo., Dec. 20, 1941; s. Irwin S. and Lilyan (Stock) W.; m. Barbara I. Allen, June 18, 1967; children: Rachel Anne, Sara Naomi. BSS, Loyola U., Chgo., 1964; student, U. Vienna, 1962-63; MS, Georgetown U., 1966; postgrad., Ind. U., 1966-72, S.E. Asian Areas Cert., 1967. Pacification specialist AID, Laos, 1965; instr. polit. sci. Loyola U., Chgo., 1970-72; asst. v.p. A.G. Becker & Co., Chgo., 1973-78; sr. v.p. Oppenheimer & Co., Chgo., 1978-83, J. David Securities, Inc., Chgo., 1983-84, Morgan Stanley, Chgo., 1984—. Exec. edn. for securities industry Wharton Sch. Bus. U. Pa., 1988-90. Trustee Highland Park Police Pension Fund. Mucia fellow, 1969. Mem. Midwest Bonsai Soc., Multiplex Club. Republican. Jewish. Office: Morgan Stanley 70 W Madison St Ste 300 Chicago IL 60602-4278 Office Phone: 312-827-6834. Business E-Mail: gerald.weiner@morganstanley.com.

WEINER, HOWARD MARC, physician; b. Feb. 25, 1946; BSc, Marietta Coll., 1967; MD, U. Cin., 1971; MPH, Med. Coll. Wis., 1994. Diplomate Am.Bd. Allergy, Asthma and Immunology, Am. Bd. Preventive Medicine/Occupl. Medicine, Am. Bd. Ind. Med. Examiners. Intern in medicine Temple U. Hosp., Phila., 1971-72, resident in internal medicine, 1972-74; fellow in allergy and clin. immunology Hosp. of U. Pa., Phila., 1974-76; pres., physician Allergy & Asthma Assocs. West Boca, Boca Raton, Fla., 1988—; pres., med. dir. Med. Assessment Inst. Inc., Boca Raton, Fla., 1997—. Chmn. ethics com. Palm Beach County Med. Soc., West Palm Beach, Fla., 1994-97; bd. dirs. Primus Physicians Svcs., Inc., So. Fla. Mem. Omicron Delta Kappa Soc., Pi Kappa Epsilon. Office: 9980 Central Park Blvd N Boca Raton FL 33428-1762 Office Phone: 561-451-0200.

WEINER, IRVING BERNARD, psychologist; b. Grand Rapids, Mich., Aug. 16, 1933; s. Jacob H. and Mollie Jean (Laevin) W.; m. Frances Shair, June 9, 1963; children: Jeremy Harris, Seth Howard. BA, U. Mich., Ann Arbor, 1955, MA, 1957, PhD, 1959. Diplomate Am. Bd. Profl. Psychology. From instr. to prof. psychiatry and pediat. U. Rochester, N.Y., 1959-72; head divsn. psychology U. Rochester Med. Center, 1968-72; prof. psychology, chmn. dept. Case Western Res. U., 1972-77, dean grad. studies, 1976-79; vice chancellor for acad. affairs U. Denver, 1979-83, prof. psychology, 1979-85; v.p. for acad. affairs Fairleigh Dickinson U., Teaneck, N.J., 1985-89, prof. psychology, 1985-89; prof. psychiatry U. South Fla., Tampa, 1989—. Adv. editor John Wiley & Sons, 1967-93, 99—, Lawrence Erlbaum Assocs., 1993-99; psychology edn. rev. com. NIMH, 1977-81. Author: Psychodiagnosis in Schizophrenia, 1966, Psychological Disturbance in Adolescence, 1970, rev. edit., 1992, Rorschach Handbook, 1971, Child Development, 1972, Principles of Psychotherapy, 1975, rev. edit., 1998, Development of the Child, 1978, Child and Adolescent Psychopathology, 1982, Rorschach Assessment of Children and Adolescents, 1982, rev. edit., 1995, Adolescence, 1985, rev. edit., 1995, Handbook of Forensic Psychology, 1987, rev. edit., 1999, Principles of Rorschach Interpretation, 1998, rev. edit., 2003, Handbook of Psychology, 2003; editor: Readings in Child Development, 1972, Clinical Methods in Psychology, 1976, 83, Adult Psychopathology Case Studies, 2004, Jour. Personality Assessment, 1985-93, Rorschachiana, 1989-96; mem. editl. bd. Profl. Psychology, 1971-76, Jour. Adolescent Health Care, 1979-87, Children and Youth Svcs. Rev., 1979-91, Jour. Pediat. Psychology, 1981-87, Devel. and Behavioral Pediat., 1985-96, Studi Rorschachiani, 1985—, European Jour. Psychol. Assessment, 1985—, Jour. Adolescent Rsch., 1986-91, Jour. Personality Disorders, 1986-92, Psychol. Assessment, 1994—2003, Jour. Personality Assessment, 2003—, Assessment, 2004—. Recipient Disting. Profl. Achievement award Genesee Psychol. Assn., 1974 Fellow APA, Am. Psychol. Soc., Acad. Clin. Psychology, Acad. Forensic Psychology, Acad. of Assessment Psychology (Lifetime Achievement awrd 2001); mem. Assn. Advancement Psychology, Soc. Personality Assessment (pres. 1976-78, Disting. Contbn. award 1983), Assn. Internship Ctrs. (exec. com. 1971-76), Soc. Rsch. in Adolescence, Soc. for Rsch. in Child and Adolescent Psychopathology, Soc. for Exploration Psychotherapy Integration, Soc. Pediat. Psychology, Am. Psychol. Law Soc., Internat. Rorschach Soc. (pres. 1999—), Phi Beta Kappa, Sigma Xi, Phi Kappa Phi. Home and Office: 13716 Halliford Dr Tampa FL 33624-6903 Office Phone: 813-961-8032. Business E-Mail: iweiner@hsc.usf.edu.

WEINER, JEROME HARRIS, mechanical engineering educator; b. N.Y.C., Apr. 5, 1923; s. Barnet and Dora (Muchar) W.; m. Florence Mensch, June 24, 1950; children: Jonathan David, Eric Daniel. B. Mech. Engring., Cooper Union U., 1943; A.M., Columbia U., 1946, PhD, 1952. Mem. faculty Columbia U., N.Y.C., 1952-68, prof. mech. engring., 1960-68, acting chmn. dept., 1961-62; L. Herbert Ballou Univ. prof. Brown U., Providence, 1968-93; L. Herbert Ballou Univ. prof. emeritus, 1993—. Author: (with B.A. Boley) Theory of Thermal Stresses, 1960, Statistical Mechanics of Elasticity, 1983. Fulbright research scholar Rome, Italy, 1958-59, Haifa, Israel, 1965- 66; Guggenheim fellow, 1965-66 Mem. Am. Phys. Soc., Am. Math. Soc., ASME Home: 24 Taber Ave Providence RI 02906-4113 Office: Brown U 79 Waterman St Providence RI 02912-9079

WEINER, JOEL DAVID, retired consumer packaged goods products executive; b. Chgo., Aug. 27, 1936; m. Judith L. Metzger; children: Beth, David. BBA, Northwestern U. Dir. new products and household div. Alberto-Culver Co., Melrose Park, Ill., 1963-66; group mktg. mgr. Bristol Myers Co., N.Y.C., 1966-74; v.p. new products Carter Wallace Co., N.Y.C., 1974-78; exec. v.p. Joseph E. Seagram Corp., N.Y.C., 1979-84; exec. v.p. corp. mktg. Kraft, Inc., Glenview, Ill., 1984-89. Home: 550 Park Dr Kenilworth IL 60043-1095

WEINER, JONATHAN DAVID, writer; b. N.Y.C., Nov. 26, 1953; s. Jerome Harris and Ponnie (Mensch) W.; m. Deborah Heiligman, May 29, 1982; children: Aaron, Benjamin. BA cum laude, Harvard U., 1977. Asst. editor Moment, Boston, 1978; sr. editor The Sciences N.Y. Acad. of Scis., N.Y.C., 1978-84, contbg. editor, 1984—, columnist "Field Notes", 1984—. Columnist "Quanta", The Sciences; vis. fellow dept. molecular biology Princeton, 1995-97; McGraw prof. in writing Princeton U., 1998, prof., 1999; writer in residence Rockefeller U., 2000; John J. Rhodes chair Ariz. State U., 2001 Author: Planet Earth, 1986 (award Am. Geol. Inst. 1986), The Next One Hundred Years: Shaping the Fate of Our Living Earth, 1991, The Beak of the Finch: A Story of Evolution in Our Time, 1994 (L.A. Times Sci. Book prize 1994, Pulitzer prize for nonfiction 1995), Time, Love, Memory: A Great Biologist and His Quest for the Origins of Behavior, 1999 (Nat. Book Critics award for gen. nonfiction 2000). Recipient Rsch. grant, Alfred P. Sloan Found., 1995—97. Mem. Nat. Assn Sci. Writers, Linnean Soc.

WEINER, KAREN COLBY (KAREN LYNN COLBY), psychologist, lawyer; b. Oak Park, Ill., Oct. 28, 1943; d. Leonard L. and Mildred Irene (Berman) Colby; m. J. Laevin Weiner, July 26, 1964; children: Joel Laevin, Doren Robin, Anthony Justin. BA, Mich. State U., East Lansing, 1964; JD, U. Detroit, 1977, MA, 1986, PhD, 1988. Bar: Mich. 1977, D.C. 1978. Speech therapist Oak Park Sch. Dist., 1965-68; law clk. justice G. Mennen Williams Mich. Supreme Ct., Lansing, 1977-79; assoc. Dickinson, Wright, Moon, Van Dusen & Freeman, Detroit, 1979-83; intern in psychology Detroit Psychiat. Inst., 1986-88; psychologist Northland Clinic, Southfield, Mich., 1987-88, Counseling Assocs., Southfield, 1988—; postdoctoral intern Wyandotte (Mich.) Hosp. and Health Ctr., 1988-90; dir. psychol. svcs., quality assurance coord. Counseling Assocs., Southfield, 1991-99. Mem. ethics and stds. com., Internat. Coaching Fedn.; hearing panelist Atty. Discipline Bd., Detroit, 1982-95; hearing referee Mich. Civil Rights Commn., Detroit, 1983-91; mem. Mich. Bd. Psychology, 1999—, vice chair, 2004—; adj. prof. U. Detroit Mercy, 2001-03; mem. ethics com. Internat. Coaching Fedn., 2003—; grad., adj. prof. Inst. Life Coach Tng., 2004. Contbr. articles to profl. jours. Mem. adv. bd. Mich. chpt. Anti-Defamation League, 1981-90. Fellow Mich. Psychol. Assn. (mem. ethics com. 1992—, chmn. legis. com. 1993, chmn. ethics com. 1997-99); mem. APA, Internat. Coaching Fedn. (ethics and stds. com.), Mich. Soc. for Psychoanalytic Psychology (pres. 1995-97, sec. 1991-92, treas. 1992-94), Women Lawyers Assn. Mich. (pres. 1981-82, pres. Found. 1982-83), Mich. Bar Assn. (chmn. spl. com. for expansion under represented groups in law 1980-83). Jewish. Home: 2501 Long Lake Rd West Bloomfield MI 48323 Office: 29260 Franklin Rd Ste 115 Southfield MI 48034-1144 Office Phone: 248-353-1020. Personal E-mail: drkcw@comcast.net.

WEINER, KENNETH BRIAN, lawyer; b. N.Y.C., Oct. 13, 1954; s. Irwin I. and Elayne B. (Biffer) W.; m. Sandra Hong, Apr. 30, 2000; 1 child: Quinton. BSCE, Case Western Res. U., 1976; JD summa cum laude, N.Y. Law Sch., 1986. Bar: N.Y. 1986, Washington 1997; registered profl. engr., N.J. Quality control engr. Cosmic Constrn. Co., Newport News, Va., 1976-77; project engr., geotech. engr. Mueser Rutledge Cons. Engrs., N.Y.C., 1977-86; assoc. Olwine, Connelly, Chase, O'Donnel & Weyner, N.Y.C., 1986-91, Ballard Spahr Andrews & Ingersoll LLP, Washington, 1992, Reid & Priest LLP, Washington, 1992-95, ptnr., 1996-98, Thelen Reid & Priest LLP, Washington, 1998—. Contbr. articles to profl. jours. Mem. Aircraft Owners and Pilots Assn. Avocation: flying. Office: Thelen Reid & Priest LLP 701 Pennsylvania Ave NW Washington DC 20004-2608 Office Phone: 202-508-4347. Business E-Mail: kweiner@thelenreid.com.

WEINER, LAWRENCE, lawyer; b. Phila., Aug. 20, 1942; s. Robert A. and Goldie Weiner; m. Jane M. Coulthard, Feb. 28, 1976; 1 child, Kimberly. BS in Econs., U. Pa., 1964, JD, 1967. Bar: Pa. 1967, U.S. Dist. Ct. (ea. dist.) Pa. 1967, Fla. 1970, U.S. Dist. Ct. (so. dist.) Fla. 1976, U.S. Ct. Appeals (5th cir.) 1976, U.S. Tax Ct. 1984. Assoc., ptnr. Blank, Rome, Klaus & Comisky, Phila., 1967-71, 1975-77; ptnr. Weiner & Weisenfeld, P.A., Miami Beach, Fla., 1971-73, Pettigrew & Bailey, Miami, Fla., 1973-75; pres. Lawrence Weiner, P.A., Miami, 1977-83; ptnr. Spieler, Weiner & Spieler, P.A., Miami, 1983-89, Weiner & Cummings, P.A., Miami, 1989-94, Weiner, Cummings & Vittoria, Miami, 1994—. Lectr. Wharton Sch. U. Pa., Phila., 1968-70; instr. bus. law and acctg. Community Coll. Phila., 1967-70; lectr. estate planning various non-lawyer groups, Miami, 1972—. Mem. Fla. Bar (liaison non-lawyers groups 1980-87), Pa. Bar Assn., Phila. Bar Assn., Dade County Bar Assn. (chmn. ins. com. 1977-78, probate law com. 1992-2002). Democrat. Jewish. Office: Weiner Cummings & Vittoria 1428 Brickell Ave Ste 400 Miami FL 33131-3436

WEINER, LAWRENCE CHARLES, artist; b. Bronx, N.Y., Feb. 10, 1942; One-man shows include Hirshhorn Mus. and Sculpture Garden, Washington, 1990, San Francisco Mus. Modern Art, 1992, Walker Art Ctr., Mpls., 1994, Städtische Galerie Chemnitz, Germany, 1994, Phila. Mus. Art, 1994, Radio Düsseldorf, Germany, 1994, Leo Castelli Gallery, N.Y., 1994, N.Y. Pub. libr., 1995, Mus. Ludwig Köln, 1995, Mus. Boijmans Van Beuningen, Rotterdam, 1996, The Lawrence Weiner Poster Archive, Kunsthalle Nüurnberg, 1998, Yvon Lambert Gallery, Paris, 2003, Galleri Susanne Ottesen, Copenhagen, 2003, The Wrong Gallery, 2004; exhibited in group shows Mus. Modern Art, N.Y., 1970, Art Inst. Chgo., 1974, Tate Gallery, London, 1982, Mus. Contemporary Art, L.A., 1983, Deutsche Guggenheim, Berlin, 2000, Kunstmuseum Rolfsburg, 2000; represented in permanent collections Mus. Modern Art, N.Y., Guggenheim Mus., N.Y., Van Abbe Mus., Eindhoven, The Netherlands, Staatliches Mus. Mönchengladbach, Germany, Ctr. Georges Pompidou, Paris, Nat. Gallery Australia, Canberra, others. Recipient Arthur Köpcke prize, Copenhagen, 1991, Wolfgang Hahn prize, 1995, Skowhegan medal for painting, 1999; fellow Nat. Endowment Arts, 1976, 83; John Simon Guggenheim fellow, 1994. Home: 297 W 4th St New York NY 10014-2207

WEINER, LESLIE PHILIP, neurology educator, researcher; b. Bklyn., Mar. 17, 1936; s. Paul Larry and Sarah (Paris) W.; m. Judith Marilyn Hoffman, Dec. 26, 1959; children: Patrice, Allison, Matthew, Jonathan. BA, Wilkes Coll., 1957; MD, U. Cin., 1961. Diplomate Am. Bd. Psychiatry and Neurology. Intern in medicine SUNY, Syracuse, 1961-62; resident in neurology Johns Hopkins Hosp., Balt., 1962-65, fellow, 1967-69; resident Balt. City Hosp., 1962-63; fellow in virology Slow Virus Lab., Nat. Inst. Neurol and Communicative Disorders-Stroke, NIH, Balt., 1969; asst. prof. neurology Johns Hopkins U., 1969-72, assoc. prof., 1972-75; prof. neurology and microbiology U. So. Calif. Sch. Medicine, L.A., 1975—, chmn. dept. neurology, 1979—2003, Richard Angus Grant Sr. chair in neurology, 1987—. Chief neurologist U. So. Calif. Univ. Hosp., 1991-96, mem. bd. govs.; chief neurologist L.A. county-U. So. Calif. Med. Ctr., 1979-94,; chmn. U. So. Calif. Gen. Clin. Res. Ctr., 1994-95; bd. dirs. John Douglas French Found., L.A., 1987-2000; mem. neurosci. tng. study sect. NIH, 1990-93; chmn., mem. sci. adv. bd. Hereditary Disease Found., 1992—, chmn., 1994-96; mem. programs rsch. adv. com. Nat. Multiple Sclerosis Soc., 2000—. Contbr. over 120 articles on neurology, immunology and virology to med. jours., chpts. to books; assoc. editor: Neurobase, 1994-95, Neuronet; mem. editl. bd. Infectious and Geographic Neurol., 1994—; assoc. editor: Neurobase. Bd. dirs. Starbright Found., L.A., 1991—99. Capt. M.C. U.S. Army, 1965—67. Grantee, Conrad Hilton Found., 1995—97, Kenneth Norris Found., 1995—, NIH, 1999—, Race to Erase MS Nancy Davis Ctrs. Without Walls, 2000—, McDonald Found., Oxnard Found., Gogian Found., Heron Found. Fellow: Am. Acad. Neurology; mem.: AAAS, Nat. MS Soc. (mem. adv. com. rsch. program 2000—, grant 2000—), Coalition Advancement Med. Rsch., Assn. Univ. Profs. Neurology, L.A. Acad. Medicine, Johns Hopkins U. Soc. Scholars, Soc. Neurosci., Am. Neurology Assn., Am. Health Assistance Found., Alpha Omega Alpha. Democrat. Jewish. Avocations: collecting books, concerts, plays. Home: 625 S Rimpau Blvd Los Angeles CA 90005-3842 Office: 1975 Zonal Ave # Kam410 Los Angeles CA 90089-0105 Fax: 323-442-3015. E-mail: lweiner@hsc.usc.edu.

WEINER, LOWELL B. corporate communications executive; m. Leslie Weiner; 1 child. BM, Ind. U., 1972, MM, 1974; PhD, NYU, 1980. Formerly with Hill and Knowlton, Ketchum Pub. Rels.; formerly dir. pub. rels. and internat. comm. Schering-Plough Corp.; asst. v.p. pub. rels. Wyeth, Madison, NJ, 1995—. Trustee N.J. Symphony Orch. Office: Wyeth 5 Giralda Farms Madison NJ 07940-1027 E-mail: weinerl@wyeth.com.

WEINER, MARCIA MYRA, judge; b. Apr. 12, 1934; BA, St. Mary's U., San Antonio, 1965, JD, 1970. Bar: Tex. 1971. Atty-advisor HUD, San Antonio, 1971—84, chief counsel, 1984—97; elected justice of the peace Precinct 2 Pl., Bexar County, Tex., 2000—. Recipient Spl. Achievement awards, HUD, 1972, 1975, 1977, Hub Fed. Women's Program award, Leigh Curry award, Fed. Women's Program Coun. Mgmt. award, Outstanding Bus. Woman of Yr., 2000. Mem.: Coll. State Bar Tex., San Antonio Bar Assn., Bexar County Women's Bar Assn., Fed. Bar Assn., Tex. Bar Assn., Greyhound Pets of Am., Tex. Wanderers, Randolph Roadrunners, Alamo Unit #2 of Am. Legion Aux. Jewish. Office: Justice Ct Precinct 2 6715 Bandera Rd San Antonio TX 78238

WEINER, MAX, educational psychology educator; b. Hartford, Conn., May 7, 1926; s. Harry Sam and Gertrude (Cohen) W.; m. Gloria Sall, Feb. 24, 1960; children: William Ronald, Jennifer Sharon. BA, U. Conn., 1950; MA, Trinity Coll., 1953; PhD, Yale U., 1957. Sci. tchr. Meriden (Conn.) Pub. Schs., 1952-55; guidance dir. White Plains (N.Y.) Pub. Schs., 1956-59; assoc. prof. Bklyn. Coll., CUNY, 1959-68; prof. Grad. Sch. CUNY, 1968-81, acting univ. dean, tchr. edn., 1973-74, exec. officer PhD program edn. psychology, 1970-76, dir. Ctr. for Advanced Study Edn., 1970-78, acting dean rsch. Grad. Sch., 1978-79; dean edn. Fordham U., N.Y.C., 1981-93, prof. ednl. psychology, 1981-97, prof. and dean emeritus, 1997—. Cons. psychologist SUNY Health Sci. Ctr., Bklyn., 1967-89; mem. nat. commn. on excellence in edn. adminstrn. Univ. Coun. for Edn. Adminstrn., 1985-87; mem. nat. adv. commn. Coll. Bd. Equity 2000, 1993-2000. Contbr. articles to profl. jours. Treas. N.Y. Alliance for Pub. Schs., N.Y.C., 1987-93; mem. Mayor's Commn. on Spl. Edn., N.Y.C., 1984-85; bd. dirs. Arthritis Found., Atlanta, 1974-76; trustee Beth El Synagogue, New Rochelle, N.Y., 1985-2001, La Scuola, N.Y., 1986-2003; bd. visitors Scranton U. Sch. Edn., 1992-2002. Fellow Japan Soc. Promotion Scis., 1978. Fellow APA, Am. Psychol. Soc., N.Y. Acad. Scis.; mem. ACA (life), AAAS, Arthritis Health Professions Assn. (pres. 1974-75), Am. Ednl. Rsch. Assn., Assn. Colls. and Schs. Edn. in State Univs. and Land Grant Colls. and Affiliated Pvt. Univs. (mem. exec. com. 1986-89, 92-93), Assn. for Measurement and Evaluation in Guidance (senator 1966-72, sec. 1973-75), Nat. Coun. Measurement in Edn., Westchester Assn. Hebrew Schs. (pres. 1982-84), Sigma Xi, Phi Delta Kappa, Kappa Delta Pi. Office: Fordham U Grad Sch Edn Neparan Rd Tarrytown NY 10591 E-mail: maxglow22@aol.com.

WEINER, MORTON DAVID, banker, insurance agent; b. Balt., Aug. 19, 1922; s. Max and Rose (Wolfe) W.; children: Bruce, Lori, Julie, Jeff. BS, Towson State Coll., 1942; grad. exec. program, UCLA, 1959. Pres., dir. AVNET, Inc., N.Y.C., 1963-69; pres., owner Morton D. Weiner & Co., Inc., N.Y.C., 1969-70; dir. USLIFE Corp., 1968-70; chmn. bd. Nat. Investors Life Ins. Cos., 1970-77; exec. v.p. Norris Grain Co., 1971-78; pres., chief exec. officer Norin Corp., 1971-78; chmn. bd. Maple Leaf Mills, Ltd., Toronto, Ont., Can., 1974-78; chmn., dir. South Atlantic Fin. Corp., 1978-80, Atico Fin. Corp., 1980-81; chmn. Morton D. Weiner & Co., 1981—. Bd. dirs. City Nat. Bank Fla. Served to capt. Signal Corps, U.S. Army, 1942-46, CBI. Office: 362 Minorca Ave Coral Gables FL 33134

WEINER, RICHARD, public relations executive; b. Bklyn., May 10, 1927; s. George M. and Sally (Kosover) W.; m. Florence Chaiken, Dec. 9, 1956; children: Jessica Weiner Lampert, Stephanie Weiner Iosbaker. BS, U. Wis., 1949, MS, 1950. Pres. Creative Radio Assocs., Madison, Wis., 1951-52, Weiner-Morton Assocs., Madison, 1952-53; sr. v.p. Ruder & Finn, Inc., N.Y.C., 1953-68; pres. Richard Weiner, Inc., N.Y.C., 1968-86; pres. N.Y. divsn. Porter/Novelli, N.Y.C., 1987-88, sr. counselor, 1988—. Author: Professional's Guide to Public Relations Services, 1968, News Bureaus in the U.S., 1970, Syndicated Columnists, 1972, Professional's Guide to Publicity, 1979, Military Publications, 1979, College Alumni Publications, 1980, Investment Newsletters, 1981, Webster's New World Dictionary of Media and Communications, 1996. Bd. dirs. Shake-A-Leg Miami, Fla. Fellow Pub. Rels. Soc. Am. (accredited counselor, Silver Anvil award 1965, 84, 86, 87, John Hill award 1984, Gold Anvil award 1990). Jewish. Office Phone: 305-865-3262. E-mail: rweiner522@aol.com. *The essence of life is growth, adaptation, change. I hope to continue to succeed in living vigorously.*

WEINER, RICHARD DAVID, psychiatrist, researcher; b. N.Y.C., Nov. 25, 1945; BS, MIT, 1967; M of Systems Engring., U. Pa., 1969; MD, PhD, Duke U., 1973. Diplomate Am. Bd. Psychiatry and Neurology. Prof. psychiatry Duke U. Med. Ctr., Durham, N.C., 1997—, dir. electroconvulsive therapy program, 1991—; chief, mental health svc. line VA Med. Ctr., Durham, 1993—. Office: Duke U Med Ctr PO Box 3309 Durham NC 27702-3309

WEINER, ROBERT STEPHEN, federal agency administrator; b. Paterson, N.J., Apr. 3, 1947; s. Jess Joseph Weiner and Dorothea Violet (Slavin) Tabor. BA, Oberlin Coll., 1969; MA, U. Mass., 1974. Student coord. Hampshire County, dir. telephone bank Kennedy for U.S. Senate, Amherst, Mass., 1970; dir. nat. voter registration Young Dems. Am., Washington, 1971-72; dir. voter registration, media dir. get out the vote Dem. Nat. Com., Washington, 1972; legis. asst. Congressman Edward Koch, Washington, 1974-75; staff dir. subcom. health and long-term care U.S. Ho. of Reps., Washington, 1975-76, staff dir. com. aging, 1976-80; sr. assoc. Mgmt. Recruiters Internat., Springfield, Mass., 1981-83; dir. Robert Weiner Assocs., Amherst, 1983-86; media dir., press sec. com. narcotics U.S. Ho. of Reps., Washington, 1987-90, press sec./comms. dir. com. on govt. ops., 1990-95; dir. comm. Ho. Judiciary com. Minority and Cong. John Conyers Jr., 1995; dir. pub. affairs White House Drug Policy Office, Washington, 1995—2002; pres. Robert Weiner Assocs., Pub. Affairs and Issues, 2002—. Dir. gen. press rm. Dem. Nat. Conv., Atlanta, 1988, N.Y.C, 1992, Chgo., 1996, L.A., 2000, Boston, 2004; cons. Carter-Mondale Transition, Washington, 1976-77, Congressman Claude Pepper, Washington, 1975-89. Represented in permanent exhbns. Nat. Mus. Am. History, Smithsonian Instn., Washington; contbr. numerous articles to profl. jours. Dem. nominee for U.S. Congress, Mass., 1986; chmn. Road Runners Am. Nat. 10 Mile Championship, Amherst, 1984; vice chmn. Dem. Town Com., Amherst, 1984-87; legis. chmn. Pioneer Valley Gray Panthers, Amherst, 1981-87; nat campaign aide Kennedy for Pres., Washington, 1980. Named Communicator of Yr., Washington Crime News Svcs., 1988, 89, 90; 2d place U.S. Nat. Masters Track Championship, 1994, 97, 2003, 2004. Mem. Nat. Dem. Club (bd. govs. 2002—), Sugarloaf Mountain Athletic Club (pres. 1984-86), White House Athletic Ctr. (exec. bd. 1995-2001), Potomac Valley Track Club, Capitol Hill Runners (pres. 1991—). Avocations: running, attending performing arts, hiking. Home: 1104 Sanford Ln Accokeek MD 20607-2324 Office: PO Box 28271 1750 Pennsylvania Ave NW Washington DC 20038-8271 Office Phone: 202-329-1700.

WEINER, RONALD GARY, accounting firm executive; b. Newark, Nov. 24, 1945; s. Seymour and Beatrice (Goldberg) W.; m. Vicki Miles, Sept. 8, 1973; children: Jennie, Maureen. BSBA, Babson Coll., 1966; postgrad., NYU, 1968-69, Harvard U., 1982. CPA, N.Y., N.J., Pa. Mgmt. cons., acct., pres. Perelson Weiner LLP, N.Y.C., 1971—. Trustee Babson Coll., Citizens Budget Com., N.Y.C.; officer, bd. govs., Am. Jewish Com.; v.p., bd. dirs. Irvington Inst. Immunol. Rsch.; mem. adv. com. Nat. Polish Am. Jewish Am. Coun. Fellow Wexner Heritage Found., Adenauer Exch. Program. Mem.: AICPA, Internat. Group of Acctg. Firms (pres.), Chief Execs. Orgn. (bd. dirs.), N.Y. State Soc. CPAs, N.J. Soc. CPAs, Pa. Soc. CPAs, Mt. Ridge Country Club, Harvard Club, Harmonie Club, Econ. Club, Accts. Club Am. Office: Perelson Weiner LLP One Dag Hammarskjold Plz New York NY 10017-2286 Fax: (212) 605-3128. Office Phone: 212-605-3100. E-mail: ron@pwcpa.com.

WEINER, RONALD MARTIN, microbiology and cell biology educator, research scientist; BS, Bklyn. Coll., 1964; MS, L.I. U., 1967; PhD, Iowa State U., 1970. Instr. dept. bacteriology Iowa State U., Ames, 1969-70; asst. prof. dept. microbiology U. Md., College Park, 1970-75, assoc. prof. dept. microbiology, 1975-86, acting chmn. dept. microbiology, 1980-81, prof. dept. cell biology and molecular genetics, 1986—2001; joint appointment Ctr. Marine Biotech., College Park, 1987-93, prof. cell and molecular biology program, 1990—93; program dir. cell biology and microbial observatories NSF, 2001—03. Vis. scientist NIH, 1985—89; mem. panel granting agys.; svc. on numerous univ. and govt. coms. and commns.; spkr. in field; rschr. in field; mentor to more than 50 grad. students, postdoctoral fellows and vis. profs.; Gordon conf. invitee. Author 25 book chpts.; reviewer, mem. editl. bd. 10 jours.; contbr. over 90 articles to profl. jours.; multiple patents in field. Recipient Panhellenic Outstanding Tchr. award, 1997, Outstanding Faculty recognition, Kappa Delta, 1998, Ocean award, Pacific Congress of Marine Tech., 1998, Outstanding Svc. award, Am. Soc. for Microbiology, 2002, numerous grants in field; Fulbright scholar, 1990. Fellow Am. Acad. Microbiology (colloquium chair) Life Sci. Coun. (mem. strategic planning com.); mem. AAAS, Am. Soc. Microbiology (Svc. award 2000), Indsl. Microbiology Soc., Sigma Xi, Phi Kappa Phi. Office: Univ Md Microbiology Bldg Dept Cell Biology & Molecular Genetics College Park MD 20742-0001 Business E-Mail: RW19@umail.umd.edu.

WEINER, RUTH EILEEN BLOWER KASSEWITZ, retired public relations executive; b. Columbus, Ohio, May 15, 1928; d. E. Wallett and Helen (Daub) Blower; m. Jack Kassewitz, July 28, 1962 (dec.); m. Morton D. Weiner, Dec. 22, 2002. BS in Journalism-Mgmt., Ohio State U., 1951. Copywriter Ohio Fuel Gas Co., Columbus, 1951-55, Merritt Owens Advt. Agy., Kansas City, 1955-56; account exec. Grant Advt., Inc., Miami, 1956-59; account supr. Venn/Cole & Assocs., Miami, 1959-67; dir. comms. Ferendino/Grafton/Candela/Spillis Archs. & Engrs., Miami, 1967-69, Dade County dept. Housing and Urban Devel., Miami, 1969-72, Met. Dade County Govt., County Mgrs. Office, 1972-78; adminstr. pub. rels. U. Miami/Jackson Meml. Med. Ctr., 1978-90, ret., 1990. Bd. dirs. Girl Scouts USA, Tropical, Fla., 1974—76, 1981—83, Lung Assn. Dade-Monroe Counties, 1976—87, Met. YMCA, 1996—2003; exec. com. Miami-Dade C.C. Found., 1984—99; pres. Mental Health Assn. Dade County, 1982; mem. City of Miami Ecol. and Beautification Com. (now TREEmendous Miami, Ind.), 1978—2000; 1st vice-chmn., 1996—98; bd. govs. Barry U., Miami, 1981—83; trustee Nat. Humanities Faculty, 1981—83; treas., past chmn. Health, Edn., Promotion Coun., Inc.; adv. bd. Miami's For Me, 1987—88; mem. Coral Gables Cable TV Bd., 1983—86; cmty. adv. bd. Jr. League Greater Miami, Inc., 1989—92; founding mem. Nat. Honor Roll, Women in Pub. Rels., No. Ill. U., 1993; trustee emeritus United Protestant Appeal, 1992—99; ch. moderator Plymouth

Congl. Ch., 1986—88, trustee, 1995—99, co-pres. Women's Fellowship, 2001—02. Recipient Disting. Svc. award Plymouth Congl. Ch., Miami, 1979; Ann Stover award, 1983; Golden Image award Fla. Pub. Rels. Assn., 1987; named Woman of Yr. Plymouth Congl. Ch., U. Miami Med. Sch., 1991, Humanitarian of Yr. YMCA of Gtr. Miami, 1998; honoree Fla. Women of Achievement. Fellow Pub. Rels. Soc. Am. (pres. South Fla. chpt. 1969-70, nat. chmn. govt. sect. 1973-74, nat. dir. 1974-76; cont. edn. coun. 1981-83; Silver anvil award 1973, del Assembly 1970-73, 86-89, Paul M. Lund Pub. Svc. award 1993, Miami chpt. Lifetime Achievement award 1995); mem. Women in Comms. (pres. Gtr. Miami chpt. 1962-63; Clarion awards 1973, 75, Cmty. Headliner 1985), Miami Internat. Press Club (bd. dirs. 1986-87, treas. 1992), 200 Club Greater Miami (v.p. 1999-2000), Rotary Club of Miami (bd. dirs. 1988-97, pres. 1993-94, Disting. Rotarian of Yr. 1996, Rotarian of Yr. internat. dist. # 6990 1999), Delta Delta Delta (pres. Miami alumnae chpt. 1997-99). Home: 335 Costanera Rd Coral Gables FL 33143

WEINER, SHARON ROSE, public relations executive; d. Mike and Elaine (Feinberg) W.; m. William H. Stryker. BA, Northwestern U., 1965; MBA, U. Hawaii, 1975. Sales rsch. asst. WBBM-TV, Chgo., 1965-66; acct. exec. Pub. Relations Bd., Chgo., 1966-67; pub. relations mgr. Levi Strauss & Co., San Francisco, 1967-73, C. Brewer Co., Honolulu, 1975-76; v.p. Fawcett McDermott Cavanagh Inc., Honolulu, 1976-79; pres., chief exec. officer Stryker Weiner Co., Honolulu, 1979—. Bd. dirs. Hawaii Vis. Bur., Honolulu; v.p. bd. dirs. Aloha coun. Boy Scouts Am. Aloha United Way, Honolulu, Honolulu Symphony. Mem. Pub. Relations Soc. Am. (Gregg W. Perry award 1988), Soc. Am. Travel Writers, Pacific Area Travel Assn., Oahu Country Club, Pacific Club.

WEINER, STEPHEN ARTHUR, lawyer; b. Bklyn., Nov. 20, 1933; s. Joseph Lee W. and Ruth Lessall (Weiner); m. Mina Rieur, Sept. 1, 1958; children: Karen, James. BA summa cum laude, Harvard U., 1954; JD cum laude, Yale U., 1957. Bar: N.Y. 1958, U.S. Supreme Ct. 1963. Assoc. Winthrop, Stimson, Putnam & Roberts, N.Y.C., 1958-65, ptnr., 1968—2000, vice chmn. mgmt. com., 1984-97; acting prof. law U. Calif., Berkeley, 1965-68; ptnr. Pillsbury Winthrop, LLP, N.Y.C., 2001, sr. counsel, 2002— . Arbitrator NASD Dispute Resolution, 2002—; mem. com. on character and fitness 1st dept. appellate divsn. N.Y. Supreme Ct., 1998—, spl. master, 1999—; mem. N.Y. State Jud. Inst. on Professionalism in the Law, 1999—; adj. prof. law Bklyn. Law Sch., 2003—. Contbr. articles to legal publs.; comment editor Yale Law Jour., 1956-57. Fellow Am. Coll. Trial Lawyers, Am. Bar Found.; mem. Assn. of Bar of City of N.Y. (chmn. recruitment of lawyers com., chmn. com. on Stimson medal), Fed. Bar Coun. (chmn. com. on 2d cir. cts., trustee), Order of Coif, Phi Beta Kappa. Home: 190 Harbor Rd Sands Point NY 11050-2636 Office: Pillsbury Winthrop LLP 1540 Broadway New York NY 10036 Office Phone: 212-858-1749. E-mail: sweiner@pillsburywinthrop.com.

WEINER, STEPHEN MARK, lawyer; b. Boston, Mar. 20, 1943; s. Meyer and Esther (Lowenstein) W.; m. Roslyn G. Weiner, Dec. 19, 1967 (div. 1992); children: Jeremiah, Ben, Miriam, Isaac. AB magna cum laude, Harvard U., 1964; LLB, Yale U., 1968. Bar: Mass. 1968. Teaching fellow Boston Coll. Law Sch., Chestnut Hill, Mass., 1968-69; assoc. Goodwin, Proctor & Hoar, Boston, 1969-71; spl. asst. to Gov. Francis W. Sargent Commonwealth of Mass., Boston, 1971-74; chmn. Mass. Rate Setting Commn., Boston, 1972-78; assoc. prof. Boston U. Sch. Law, 1978-81, dir. Ctr. for Law and Health Scis.; mem. Goulston & Storrs, Boston, 1981-90, Mintz, Levin, Cohn, Ferris, Glovsky and Popeo, P.C., Boston, 1990—. Chair health law sect. Mintz, Levin, Cohn, Ferris, Glovsky and Popeo, P.C.; adj. prof. law Boston U. Sch. Law, 1993-94, Suffolk U. Sch. Law, 1997—; vis. lectr. Yale Law Sch., 1994-95; bd. dirs., pres. Health Wall Found., 2003—. Mem. editl. bd. New Eng. Jour. Human Svcs., 1979-81; adv. bd. Hosp. Risk Mgmt., 1979-83; contbr. articles to profl. jours. Legal adv. com. AIDS Action Com., Washington; dir., treas. AIDS Action Com., Mass., 1989—97; bd. dirs. GLAD, Inc., 1999—2000, Boston Film Video Found., 1986—2003; del. Mass. Easter Seal Soc.; trustee Beth Israel Hosp., Boston, 1979—95, Spaulding Rehab. Hosp., Boston, 1979—95, Corp. Ptnrs. Healthcare Sys., Inc., Boston, 1994—2001, Boston Ballet, treas., 2001—; overseer Boston Lyric Opera; dir. New Eng. Conservatory Lab. Charter Sch. Found.; trustee Huntington Theater Co., Boston; mem. govt. task force to evaluate Mass. Determination of Need Program, 1979—80; profl. adv. coun. Mass. Dept. Elder Affairs, 1979—81; Mass. atty. gen. Mass. Adv. Com. on Health Care and Tobacco Control. Mem. ABA, Nat. Health Lawyers Assn., Mass. Bar Assn., Boston Bar Assn. Home: 7 Beethoven Ave Walpole MA 02081 Office: Mintz Levin Cohn Ferris Glovsky and Popeo PC 1 Financial Ctr Boston MA 02111-2657 Office Phone: 617-348-1757. E-mail: sweiner@mintz.com.

WEINER, WALTER HERMAN, banker, lawyer; b. Bklyn., Aug. 29, 1930; s. Harry and Sylvia (Freifeld) W.; m. Nina Ester Avidar, Oct. 11, 1966; children: Thomas Field, Jon Michael. BA, U. Mich., 1952, JD, 1953. Bar: N.Y. 1953. Sr. ptnr. Kronish, Lieb, Weiner & Hellman, N.Y.C., 1965-79; chmn. exec. com., CEO Republic N.Y. Corp., 1980-81, pres., CEO, 1981-83, chmn. bd., CEO, 1983—; chmn. exec. com., CEO Republic Nat. Bank of N.Y., 1980-82, pres., CEO, 1981-86, chmn. bd., CEO, 1986-99, also bd. dirs.; pres. WHW Mgmt. Corp., N.Y.C. Bd. dirs. Republic N.Y. Corp., Republic Nat. Bank of N.Y. Assoc. editor U. Mich. Law Rev. Bd. dirs. Interant. Sephardic Edn. Found.; mem. N.Y. Holocaust Meml. Commn.; bd. visitors U. Mich. Law Sch. Recipient Humanitarian award NAACP, 1987, Human Rels. award Accts., Bankers, Factors and Fin. divsn. Am. Jewish Com., 1988, Man of Yr. award Bklyn. Sch. for Spl. Children, 1988, Good Scout award Greater N.Y. Couns./Boy Scouts Am., 1994, Jewish Theol. Sem.'s Louis Marshall award, 1994, numerous others. Mem. ABA, N.Y. State Bar Assn., Assn. of Bar of City of N.Y. Office: WHW Management Corp Ste 1401 477 Madison Ave New York NY 10022-5836

WEINER, WENDY L. elementary school educator, writer; b. Milw., Jan. 2, 1961; d. Kenneth J. and Jessie M. Weiner. AA, U. Wis. Washington County, West Bend; BS, MS, U. Wis., U. Wis., Milw., 1993; prin. lic., Marian Coll. Cert. nat. cert. early childhood edn. Nat. Bd. Profl. Tchg. Standards, tchr. Wis. Tchr. Milw. Pub. Schs. Contbr. articles to profl. jours. Mem. Milw. Pub. Mus. Tchr. Adv. Coun., TV and Tech. Com., Vision and Tech. Com., Learning Mag.'s Student Best Adv. Coun. Recipient Presdl. Award in Sci. Tchg. Excellence, AT&T Recognition in Sci. Tchg. Excellence, Wis. Aerospace Educator of Yr., Milw. Tchr. of Yr., Grad. Last Decade award U. Wis. Milw. Alumni Assn., Warner Cable-Tchg. Creativity with Cable award, Excellence in Sci. Tchg. award. Wis. Elem. Sci. Tchrs. Assn., Nat. Urban Tech. in Edn. award Coun. Great City Schs., Sen. Herb Kohl Tchr. Achievement award, Ameritech-Wis. Bell Gold Tchr. Recognition award, 1992, Presdl. award for elem. sci. tchg. excellence; grantee Greater Mil. Edn. Trust, Wis. Space Grant Consortium/NASA, NSF. Mem. PTA, Wis. Aerospace Edn. Assn. (instr. mag. adviser 1996-2000, Sam's Club Tchr. of Yr. 2002), YMCA-Young Astronauts, Nat. Arbor Day Assn., NSTA, Wis. Elem. Tchrs. Assn., Milw. Kindergarten Assn., Wis. Secondary Sci. Assn., Wis. Assn. Sch. Adminstrs., Milw. Reading Assn., Midwest Devel. Corp., Assn. Presdl. Awardees in Sci., Soc. for Elem. Presdl. Awardees, Coun. Elem. Sci. Internat., Civil Air Patrol (sr. officer). Avocations: crafts, walking. Office: Parkview Sch 4966 N 91st St Milwaukee WI 53225-4127

WEINER-HEUSCHKEL, SYDELL, theater educator; b. N.Y.C., Feb. 18, 1947; d. Milton A. and Janet (Kay) Horowitz; children: Jason, Emily; m. Rex Heuschkel, Sept. 3, 1992. BA, SUNY, Binghamton, 1968; MA, Calif. State U., L.A., 1974; postgrad., Yale U., 1968-70; PhD, NYU, 1986; MS, Calif. State U., Dominguez Hills, 1996. Lic. marriage and family therapist. Prof. theater arts, chmn. dept., dir. honors program Calif. State U. Dominguez Hills, Carson, 1984—. Guest lectr. Calif. Inst. Arts, 1988. Appeared in play Vikings, Grove Shakespeare Festival, 1988; dir. Plaza Suite, Brea (Calif.) Civic Theatre, 1982, Gypsy, Carson Civic Light Opera, 1990, Same Time Next Year, Muckehthaler, 1987, Slow Dance on the Killing Ground, Alternative Repertory Theatre, 1989; co-author: School and Community Theater Problems: A Handbook for Survival, 1978, (software) Public Speaking, 1991; contbr. Am. Jour. Psychotherapy, 1997, Jour. Clin. Psychology, 1998. Yale U. fellow, 1969; recipient Lyle Gibson Disting. Tchr. award, 1989. Mem. Screen Actors Guild, Am. Fedn. TV and Radio Artists, Calif. State U. Women's Coun. (treas. 1989-91), Phi Kappa Phi. Office Phone: 310-243-3534. E-mail: sweiner@csudh.edu.

WEINFURTER, DANIEL JOSEPH, business services executive; b. Milw., Apr. 16, 1957; s. Joseph Thomas and Betty E. (Stanton) W.; m. Martha Marie Brennan, May 14, 1983; children: Amy Jordan, Andrea Taylor. BSBA, Marquette U., 1979, MBA, 1984; postgrad., George Washington U., 1984-85. Account rep. Gen. Electric Info. Svcs., Milw., 1979-81, sr. account rep., 1982-84, project mgr. Rockville, Md., 1984-86; acting regional sales mgr. Gen. Electric Corp., Morristown, N.J., 1986, dist. sales mgr. Bensonville, Ill., 1986-87; regional sales mgr. Intelogic Trace, Inc., Schaumburg, Ill., 1987-89, area sales mgr., 1989; dir. bus. devel. Alternative Resources Corp., Lincolnshire, Ill., 1989-90, v.p. ops., 1990-93; pres. Alternative Resources Corp. Ventures, Lincolnshire, Ill., 1993—; CEO and founder Parson Group, Chgo., 1995—2002; CEO Capital H Group, Chgo., 2003—. Ad-hoc com. Riverwoods (Ill.) Village Coun., 1990—; mem. YMCA. Named number 1 of INC 500, INC Mag., 2000. Democrat. Avocations: running, raquetball, bicycling, golf, reading. Home: 201 Cumberland Ave Kenilworth IL 60043-1169 Office: Capital H Group 225 W Washington St Chicago IL 60606

WEINGARTEN, JOSEPH LEONARD, aerospace engineer; b. N.Y.C., June 5, 1944; s. Herman H. (dec.) and Irene Jane (Binzer) (dec.) W.; m. Cindy L. Carter; 1 child, Toby. B Mech. Engring., NYU, 1966; postgrad., Air War Coll., 1976. Chief engr. Air Transportability Test Loading Agy. Wright-Patterson AFB, Wright-Patterson AFB, Ohio, 1972-74; project engr. dept. engring USAF, Wright-Patterson AFB, 1966-72, sr. project engr. dept. engring., 1974-76, planning and project engr. dept. engring., 1976-81, chief mgmt. ops. dept. engring., 1981-83, sr. tech. planner dept. engring., 1983-92; tech. asst. DCS Engring. and Tech. Mgmt. Air Force Material Command, Wright-Patterson AFB, 1992-93; founder, CEO Huffman Wright Inst., 1993-98; cons. Main Net Inc., Urbana, Ohio, 1997—2002; exec. dir. MAC Reseller Assn., 2002—. CEO Weingarten Gallery, Dayton, Ohio, 1967—; pres., v.p., sec., treas., bd. dirs. Ohio Designer Craftsmen, Columbus; sec. Ohio Designer Craftsmen Enterprise, Columbus, 1982-90; chmn. continuing edn. design dept. Affiliate Socs. Coun., Dayton, 1971-74, chmn. edn. coord. com. Kettering Inst., Wright State U., 1974-76, chmn. scientist and engr. awards panel, 1990-91, mem., 1992-94. Contbr. articles on systems engring. to Aeronautical Sys. divsn. Mech. Engring. Jour. (1st place award nat. contest 1970), Procs. 4th Intersoc. Conf. on Transp., Air Force Sys. Command, USAF Spl. Purpose Report, Gems and Minerals, Friends Jour. USAF Mus., Ceramics Monthly, The Crafts Report, Macintosh Software. Scoutmaster Troop 81, Boy Scouts Am., Kettering, Ohio, 1985—91, com. mem., 1991—93, dist. chmn. Wright Bros. Dist., 2000—04, dist. chmn. Sequoia Dist. Miami Valley Coun., 1991—93, asst. coun. commr., 1993—2000, exec. bd. Miami Valley Coun., 2004—; pres. Friends of Montessori Sch., South Dayton, Ohio, 1978—94. Capt. USAF, 1967—71. Recipient Disting. Eagle award Boy Scouts Am., 1992, Silver Beaver award Boy Scouts Am., 1995, Pinnacle award Eastern Region Microage, Inc., 1999; named as one of 5 bus. execs. of yr. Miami Valley Bus. Advisor/Cox Pub., 1998. Mem. AIAA (sr. mem., air transport systems tech. com. 1976-78, 80-82, Lawrence Sperry award 1977), ASME (sr. mem.), Am. Nat. Standards Inst. (materials handling 5 com. 1968-70), Soc. Automotive Engrs. (aircraft ground support equipment com. 1969-75). Achievements include 11 patents for expendable air cargo pallet, mail container, collapsible air cargo container, process for reinforcing extruded articles, process for large scale extrusions, air flotation cargo handling system, integral aircraft barrier net, load distributive cargo platform, laminated plastic packaging material, computer printer paper support, and investment casting mold base; developments include 3g cargo restraint criteria used worldwide on aircraft/spacecraft/shuttles, rope extraction system for C-5A, system for large scale structural plastics extruxions, advanced planning documents for Air Force, report in new type of DOD procurement system; other achievements include the design and creation of jewelry sold in museums and retail stores. E-mail: mrmac@aol.com.

WEINGARTEN, RHONDA, lawyer; b. N.Y.C., Dec. 18, 1957; d. Gabriel and Edith (Appelbaum) W. BS, Cornell U., 1980; JD cum laude, Benjamin N. Cardozo Sch. Law, 1983. Bar: N.Y. 1984, U.S. Dist. Ct. (so. and ea. dists.) N.Y. 1984. Legis. asst. Labor Com. N.Y. State Senate, Albany, 1979-80; assoc. Stroock, Stroock and Lavan, N.Y.C., 1983-86; counsel to pres. United Fedn. Tchrs., N.Y.C., 1986—98; tchr. Clara Barton HS, Brooklyn, 1991—97; asst. sec. United Fedn. Teachers, N.Y.C., 1995, treas., 1997, pres., 1998—; v.p. Am. Fedn. Teachers. Bd. dirs. N.Y. State United Teachers; adj. instr. Cardozo Sch. Law, N.Y.C., 1986; mem. Mayor Bloomberg's transition com., N.Y.C., 2001. Mediator Bklyn. Mediation Ctr. Victim Services Agy., 1981-82 (outstanding achievement award, 1981); mem. N.Y. Com. Safety and Health, 1986, Park Slope Safe Homes Project, 1984—. Dem. Nat. Com.; bd. dirs. Justice Resource Ctr., Coun. for Unity, N.Y. Com. on Occupational Safety and Health, N.Y. Region Anti-Defamation League, United Way Greater N.Y., Internat. Rescue Com. Mem. ABA (labor and employment sect.), N.Y. State Bar Assn., Women's Bar Assn., Council N.Y. Law Assocs., Cardozo Sch. Law Alumni Assn. (treas., bd. dirs. 1983—). Democrat. Jewish. Office: United Fedn Tchrs 260 Park Ave S New York NY 10010-7214*

WEINGARTNER, H(ANS) MARTIN, finance educator; b. Heidelberg, Germany, Apr. 4, 1929; came to U.S., 1939, naturalized, 1944; s. Jacob and Grete Weingartner; m. Joyce Trellis, June 12, 1955; children— Steven M., Susan C. De La Paz, Eric H., Kenneth H. AB, SB, U. Chgo., 1950, AM, 1951; MS, Carnegie Mellon U., 1956, PhD, 1962. Economist Dept. Commerce, 1951-53; instr. Grad. Sch. Indsl. Adminstrn., Carnegie Mellon U., 1956-57; instr., then asst. prof. Grad. Sch. Bus., U. Chgo., 1957-63; assoc. prof. fin. Alfred P. Sloan Sch. Mgmt., Mass. Inst. Tech., 1963-66; prof. Grad. Sch. Mgmt., U. Rochester, N.Y., 1966-77; Brownlee O. Currey prof. fin. Owen Grad. Sch. Mgmt., Vanderbilt U., Nashville, 1977-98, Brownlee O. Currey Prof. of Fin., emeritus, 1998—; dir. Computer Consoles, Inc., 1974-89. Cons. to industry. Author: Mathematical Programming and the Analysis of Capital Budgeting Problems, 3d edit, 1974, (with George Benston and Dan Horsky) An Empirical Study of Mortgage Redlining, 1978; also articles.; Deptl. editor: Mgmt. Sci, 1967-73. Served with AUS, 1951-53. Mellon fellow, 1954-55; Ford Found. fellow, 1955-56, recipient first prize Dissertation Competition, 1963. Fellow: Inst. for Ops. Rsch. and the Mgmt. Scis.; mem.: Coun. Sci. Soc. Pres. (alumni mem.), Inst. Mgmt. Scis. (v.p. fin. 1978—84, pres. 1985—86), Beta Gamma Sigma. Home: 1616 Ash Valley Dr Nashville TN 37215-4202 Office: Vanderbilt U Owen Grad Sch Mgmt 401 21st Ave S Nashville TN 37203

WEINGARTNER, RUDOLPH HERBERT, philosophy educator; b. Heidelberg, Germany, Feb. 12, 1927; came to U.S., 1939, naturalized, 1944; s. Jacob and Grete (Kahn) W.; m. Fannia Goldberg-Rudkowski, Dec. 28, 1952 (dec. Nov. 1994); children: Mark H., Eleanor C.; m. Regitze E.G. Winkelhorn Hamburger, June 13, 1997. AB, Columbia U., 1950, MA, 1953, PhD, 1959. Fellow Inst. Philos. Research, San Francisco, 1953-55; instr. philosophy Columbia, 1955-59; from asst. prof. to prof., chmn. dept. philosophy San Francisco State Coll., 1959-68; prof. philosophy Vassar Coll., Poughkeepsie, 1968-74, chmn. dept., 1969-74, Taylor prof. philosophy, 1973-74, dean Coll. Arts and Scis.; prof. philosophy Northwestern U., Evanston, Ill., 1974-87; provost U. Pitts., 1987-89, prof. philosophy, 1987-94, chmn. dept. philosophy, 1991-93. Author: Experience and Culture: The Philosophy of Georg Simmel, 1962, The Unity of the Platonic Dialogue: The Cratylus, The Protagoras, The Parmenides, 1973, Undergraduate Education: Goals and Means, 1992 (Frederick W. Ness book award 1993), Fitting Form to Function: A Primer on the Organization of Academic Institutions, 1996, The Moral Dimensions of Academic Administration, 1999, Mostly About Me: A Path Through Different Worlds, 2003; editor: (with Joseph Katz) Philosophy in the West, 1965; exhibited sculptures in Mendelson Gallery, 1992, 94, UP Gallery, 1992, Assoc. Artists Pitts. Gallery, 2000, Internat. Images Gallery, 2002-03; contbr. articles to profl. jours. Bd. dirs. Chamber Music Chgo., 1982-87, pres., 1986-87; mem. bd. advisors Pitts. Symphony, 1991-2000, mem. bd. dirs., chmn. artistic com., mem. exec. com.; mem. adv. bd. Sch. Music Carnegie Mellon U., Pitts., 1992-2002. Social Sci. Rsch. Coun. fellow, 1958-59; Guggenheim fellow, 1965-66; Am. Coun. Learned Socs. fellow, 1971-72; residency Rockefeller Found. Study and Conf. Ctr. in Bellagio, 1994. Mem. Am. Philos. Assn., Assn. Am. Colls. (bd. dirs. 1985-89, task force on gen. edn. 1985-88, editorial bd. liberal edn. jours. 1986-94), Assoc. Artists Pitts. (artist mem.), Phi Beta Kappa. Home: 5448 Northumberland St Pittsburgh PA 15217-1129 Personal E-mail: rudywein@earthlink.net. Business E-Mail: rudywein@pitt.edu.

WEINGAST, MARVIN, laboratory executive; b. Bklyn., Jan. 1, 1943; s. Abe and Rose (Altein) W. BS, L.I. U., 1967, MS, 1971; postgrad., Poly. Inst., 1967-68. Analytic and pollution chemist Amerada Hess Corp., Pt. Reading, N.J., 1969-73; asst. lab. dir. Chem. Constrn., North Brunswick, N.J., 1973-74; dir. Indsl. Hygiene Lab. Nat. Starch and Chemical, Bridgewater, N.J., 1974—. Grant com. mem. Ctr. for Hazardous and Toxic Substance Mgmt., Newark, 1988—; mem. Sourland Regional Citizens Planning Coun., Neshanic, N.J., 1989—. Contbr. to book: Small Business Programs, 1980; contbr. articles to profl. jours. Recipient Chemistry Dept. award L.I. U., 1967, Teaching fellowship Poly. Inst., 1967, L.I. U., 1968. Mem. MENSA, Am. Chem. Soc., Am. Conf. Chem. Labeling, Soc. Toxicology. Achievements include development of improved system for identification of hazardous chemicals; organization of first global monitoring of indsl. workers to hazardous workplace chemicals. Office: Nat Starch & Chem Co 10 Finderne Ave Bridgewater NJ 08807-3355 E-mail: weingast@weingast.com.

WEINGEIST, THOMAS ALAN, ophthalmology educator; b. N.Y.C., Jan. 28, 1940; s. Samson and Fausta (Haim) W.; m. Carol Perera, Mar. 19, 1963 (div. Aug. 1977); children: Aaron P., Rachel; m. Catherine McGregor, Aug. 18, 1977; children: Robert M., David M. BA, Earlham Coll., 1963; PhD, Columbia U., 1969; MD, U. Iowa, 1972. Resident in ophthalmology U. Iowa, 1972-75, fellow in retina, 1976, asst. prof. ophthalmology, 1976-80, assoc. prof., 1980-83, prof., 1983—, prof., head dept. ophthalmology, 1986—; Francis Heed Adler lectr. U. Pa., 2004. DeVoe lectr. Columbia U., 2001; Doheny lectr. U. S.C., 2002. Mem. editl. bd. Documenta Ophthalmologica, The Netherlands, 1989-94, Ophthalmology World News, 1994-96; med. editor Argus/Ophthalmology's World News, 1996-98; med. editor EyeNet mag., 1999-2001. Named Eye Health Advocate, Iowa Acad. Opthalmology, 2003; recipient Lifetime Achievement Award, Am. Acad. Ophthalmology, 2003. Fellow: Am. Acad. Ophthalmology (editl. bd. jour. 1982—, assoc. sec. for self-assessment 1988—93, sec. continuing edn. 1993—, trustee 1993—, sr. sec. clin. edn. 1994—, pres. 2002, Honor award 1979, Sr. Honor award 1989); mem.: Assn. Univ. Profs. Ophthalmology (pres. 1995, bd. dirs.), Am. Medico-Legal Found., Vitreous Soc., Retina Soc., Macula Soc. Avocations: photography, tennis. Home: 3 Heather Ct Iowa City IA 52245-3226 Office: U Iowa Dept Ophthalmology Iowa City IA 52242

WEINGER, STEVEN MURRAY, lawyer; b. Chgo., Feb. 7, 1954; s. Paul and Joan (Taxay) W.; children: Blake, Paige, Haley. BA, Hampshire Coll., 1975; JD, U. Chgo., 1978. Bar: Fla. 1979, Ill. 1979, U.S. Dist. Ct. (so. dist.) Fla. 1979, U.S. Ct. Appeals (5th cir.) 1980, U.S. Ct. Appeals (11th cir.) 1981, U.S. Supreme Ct. 1982, U.S. Dist. Ct. (mid. dist.) Fla. 1989. Mem. faculty U. Miami Sch. Law, Coral Gables, Fla., 1978-79; ptnr. Kurzban, Kurzban & Weinger, P.A., Miami, Fla., 1979—. Bd. dirs. Sunrise Cmty. for Mentally Retarded, Miami, United Cerebral Palsy Tallahassee, Inc., Palmer-Trinity Sch., Miami, GobleStage, Inc., 1999—. Recipient Chmn.'s award Sunrise Cmty. for Mentally Retarded, 1987; honoree United Cerebral Palsy in South Fla., 1995, Fla. Assn. Rehab. Facilities, 1996, United Cerebral Palsy Assn., 1997. Mem. ABA, Assn. Trial Lawyers Am., Fla. Assn. Trial Lawyers. Office: Kurzban Kurzban & Weinger 2650 SW 27th Ave Fl 2D Miami FL 33133-3003 E-mail: swmiami@aol.com.

WEINGOLD, ALLAN BYRNE, obstetrician, gynecologist, educator; b. N.Y.C., Sept. 2, 1930; s. Irving and Evelyne (Gold) W.; m. Marjorie Nassau, Dec. 21, 1952; children: Beth, Roberta, Matthew, Daniel BA, Oberlin Coll., 1951; MD, N.Y. Med. Coll., 1955; DSc, George Washington, 1997. Diplomate Am. Bd. Ob-Gyn. Instr. N.Y. Med.Coll., N.Y.C., 1960-63, asst. prof., 1963-67, assoc. prof., 1967-70, prof., 1970-73; prof., chmn. dept. ob-gyn George Washington U., Washington, 1973-92, v.p. med. affairs and exec. dean, 1992-96, pres. health plan, 1992-2000, mem. partnership bd., 1997-99. Cons. NIH, Bethesda, Md., 1974-97, Walter Reed Army Med. Ctr., Washington, 1974-97. Author: Principles and Practices of Clinical Gynecology, 1988; editor: Monitoring the Fetal Environment, 1969, Surgical Complications of Pregnancy, 1984. Bd. dirs. Mayor's Adv. Bd. Maternal Health, Washington, 1981-87; mem. host com. John Glenn Campaign Com., Washington, 1983-85. Maj. U.S. Army, 1957-66. Recipient Alumni award N.Y. Med. Coll., 1974 Fellow Am. Coll. Obstetricians and Gynecologists (program chmn. 1975-77), Am. Gyn.-Ob. Soc. (coun. 1988-90); mem. Assn. Profs. Ob-Gyn. (sec. 1981-84, pres. 1985-86), Soc. Perinatal Rsch., Alpha Omega Alpha. Republican. Office: George Washington U 2300 I St NW Washington DC 20037-2336

WEINGROW, HOWARD L. financial executive, investor; b. NYC, Dec. 6, 1922; s. Nathan and Anna (Mintzes) W.; m. Muriel Corrine Franzblau, Nov. 24, 1946; children: Terry Vaccaro, Caron Abby Haim. Owner Legion Fluorescent Corp., N.Y.C., 1946-56; ptnr. Hechler & Weingrow, Inc., N.Y.C., 1956-58, Hechler, Lifton & Weingrow, Inc., N.Y.C., 1958-78; exec. v.p. Tanscontinental Investing Corp., N.Y.C., 1960-67, pres., 1967-70; prin. Lifton & Weingrow, N.Y.C., 1958—; co-chmn. Marcade Group, Inc., N.Y.C., 1986-91, bd. dirs., 1986-93; pres. Medis Techs., Ltd. (MDTL), 1992—, Stanoff Corp., 1980—, Wesak Internat., 1992-94; chmn. Wesak Chrysler, 1992-94; pres. Medis Techs. Ltd. Bd. dirs. Preferred Health Care, N.Y.C., Four Winds Inc., N.Y.C., Medis-El, Medis Techs. Ltd.; founder Ctr. for Chilhood Asthma Schneider Children's Hosp., 2002, Weingrow Family Pediatric Urology Lab., L.I. Jewish Hosp., 1989, The Howard L. and Muriel Weingrow Collection of Avant-Garde Art and Lit., Hofstra U., 1972; chmn. Vision Telemedia, Inc., 1995-98. Treas. Dem. Nat. Com., Washington, 1970-72; mem. bd. govs. Hofstra U. Law Sch., 1977-79; dep. fin. chmn. Pres. Carter, Washington, 1976, 80; trustee Hofstra U., Hempstead, N.Y., 1973-76, James S. Brady Presdl. Found., 1982, Children's Med. Fund, L.I. Jewish Children's Hosp., Lake Success, N.Y., 1986—, Am. Jewish Congress, 1988-96; treas. Nassau County Mus. Fine Arts, 1988—, North Shore, L.I. Jewish Hosp. Sys., 1999—; advisor to Pres. Lyndon Johnson, OEO, Washington; fin. advisor to the Govt. of Grenada and Office of Prime Minister Garry, 1977-79. Decorated DFC, Air medal, 2 bronze, 2 silver clusters; recipient Presdl. medal, Hofstra U. Office: Stanoff Corp 805 3rd Ave Fl 15 New York NY 10022-7513 Office Phone: 212-935-8484.

WEINHAGEN, ERIC JOHN, writer, musician; b. Cheverly, Md., Dec. 5, 1971; s. Robert Frederick and Michelle Marie Weinhagen. BA in Anthropology, George Mason U., 1993; profl. editing cert., USDA Grad. Sch., 1999. Fin. liaison U.S. House Rep., Washington, 1994—95. Author: Under A Blue Sky, 2002, To Cross A Stormy Sea, 2004; musician: An Evening with Eric Weinhagen, 2003. Avocations: guitar, bicycling, hiking, reading. Home: 1794 Duffield Ln Alexandria VA 22307 Address: 7515 Snowpea Ct Unit L Alexandria VA 22306

WEINHARDT, J. W. computer company executive; Chmn. bd. dirs., CEO SJW Corp., San Jose, Calif. Office: SJW Corp 374 W Santa Clara St San Jose CA 95113-1502

WEINHAUER, WILLIAM GILLETTE, retired bishop; b. N.Y.C., Dec. 3, 1924; s. Nicholas Alfred and Florence Anastacia (Davis) W.; m. Jean Roberta Shanks, Mar. 20, 1948; children: Roberta Lynn, Cynthia Anne, Doris Jean. BS, Trinity Coll., Hartford, Conn., 1948; MDiv, Gen. Theol. Sem., 1951, STM, 1956, ThD, 1970. Ordained to ministry Episcopal Ch., 1951. Pastor Episcopal parishes Diocese N.Y., 1951-56; prof. N.T. St. Andrews Theol. Sem., Manila, Philippines, 1956-60; asst. prof. N.T. Gen. Theol. Sem., 1961-71; rector Christ Ch., Poughkeepsie, N.Y., 1971-73; bishop Episcopal Diocese of Western N.C., Black Mountain, 1973-90, ret., 1990. Vis. prof. religion Western Carolina U., Cullowhee, N.C., 1991-98; adj. faculty Seabury-Western Theol. Sem., Evanston, Ill., 19991-94. Served with USN, 1943-46. Mem. Soc. Bibl. Lit. Episcopalian.

WEINHOLD, CLIFFORD LEE, photographer; b. Reading, Pa., May 13, 1957; s. Richard Allen and Arlene May Weinhold; m. Cindy Lou Batz (div.). BS Forest Mgmt., Wash. State U., Pullman, 1981. Freelance photographer Internat. Freelance Photo, Lewisville, NC, 1994—. Mem. Appalachian Trail Conf., Harpers Ferry, W.Va., 1977—. Author: (poems) The First Step to the Last Step, 2003; three-color screen, The Four Musicians, 1971 (First Place, State of Pa., 1971). Mem.: Internat. Freelance Photographers Orgn. (life), Clover Pk. Athletic Assn. (life). Republican. Lutheran. Achievements include hiking entire 2,100 miles of Appalachian Trail from Ga. to Maine 1977 and 2003. Avocations: photography, poetry, hiking, camping, computers. Home: 46 South Miller Street Shillington PA 19607 Office: Reading Equipment and Distribution 1363 Bowmansville Road Bowmansville PA 17507

WEINHOLD, LINDA LILLIAN, psychologist, researcher; b. Reading, Pa., Nov. 9, 1948; d. Aaron Zerbe Weinhold and Nancy Louise (Spotts) Weikel; m. Jack Wayne Prisk, Jan. 21, 1967 (div. 1969). Lic. practical nurse, AVTS, 1970; BS, Penn State U., 1975; MS, C.W. Post Ctr., 1982; PhD, Fordham U., 1986. LPN; cert. profl. counselor. Instr., asst. prof. Gettysburg (Pa.) Coll., 1985-86; post doc. fellow John Hopkins U., Balt., 1986-88; staff fellow NIH NIDA Addiction Rsch. Ctr., Balt., 1988-93; cons. NIH NIDA Medications Devel., Rockville, Md., 1993-94; soc. sci. program coord. Med. Ctr. NIDA Rsch., Washington, 1994-95; cons. The Clin. Cons. Group Antech, Inc., Balt., 1995; substance abuse counselor Hope Village, Inc., Washington, 1996—. Various presentations. Mem. Am. Psychological Assn., Phi Kappa Phi, Sigma Xi. Democrat. Avocations: singing, dance, painting, photography, reading. Home: 2611 Bowen Rd SE Apt 203 Washington DC 20020-6623 Office: Hope Village Inc 2840 Langston Pl SE Washington DC 20020-3241

WEINHOLD, VIRGINIA BEAMER, interior designer; b. Elizabeth, N.J., June 21, 1932; d. Clayton Mitchell and Rosemary (Behrend) Beamer; divorced; children: Thomas Craig, Robert Scott, Amy Linette. BA, Cornell U., 1955; BFA summa cum laude, Ohio State U., 1969; MA in Design Mgmt., Ohio State U., 1982. Freelance interior designer, 1969-72; interior designer, dir. interior design Karlsberger and Assocs. Inc., Columbus, Ohio, 1972-82; assoc. prof. dept. design Ohio State U., 1982—, grad. studies chairperson, 1986-89, 1995-96; lectr. indsl. design Ohio State U., 1972, 79-80. Trustee Found. for Interior Design Edn. and Rsch., 1991-97. Mem. Inst. Bus. Designers (chpt. treas. 1977-79, nat. trustee 1979-81, nat. chmn. contract documents com. 1979-84, chpt. pres. 1981-83), Constrn. Specifications Inst., Interior Design Educator's Coun. (nat. treas. 1989-93), Interior Design Educator's Coun. Found. (nat. treas. 1992-94), Illuminating Engring. Soc. (chpt. v.p. 1997-98), AIA (assoc.), Internat. Interior Design Assn. (nat. dir. 1994-97). Prin. works include Grands Rapids (Mich.) Osteo. Hosp., Melrose (Mass.) Wakefield Hosp., Christopher Inn, Columbus, John W. Galbreath Hdqrs., Columbus, Guernsey Meml. Hosp., Cambridge, Ohio, Trinity Epis. Ch. and Parish House, Columbus, Hale Hosp., Haverhill, Mass., Ohio State U. Dept. Indsl. Design Lighting Lab., others. Author: IBD Forms and Documents Manual, Interior Finish Materials for Health Care Facilities, Subjective Impressions: Lighting Hotels and Resturants, 1989, Effects of Lighting on The Perception of Interior Spaces, 1993. Home: 112 Glen Dr Columbus OH 43085-4010 Office: Ohio State U Dept Design 128 N Oval Mall Columbus OH 43210-1318

WEINKAUF, MARY LOUISE STANLEY, clergywoman; b. Eau Claire, Wis., Sept. 22, 1938; d. Joseph Michael and Marie Barbara (Holzinger) Stanley; m. Alan D. Weinkauf, Oct. 12, 1962 (dec. Nov. 2000); children: Stephen, Xanti. BA, Wis. State U., 1961; MA, U. Tenn., 1962, PhD, 1966; MDiv, Luth. Sch. Theology, Chgo., 1993. Grad. asst., instr. U. Tenn., 1961-66; asst. prof. English Adrian Coll., 1966-69; prof., head dept. English Dakota Wesleyan U., Mitchell, S.D., 1969-89; instr. Columbia Coll., 1989-91. Pastor Calvary Evang. Luth. Ch., Siloa Luth. Ch., Ontonagon Faith, White Pine, Mich., Gowrie, Iowa. Author: Hard-Boiled Heretic, 1994, Sermons in Science Fiction, 1994, Murder Most Poetic, 1996. Trustee The Ednl. Found., 1986-90; bd. dirs. Ontonagon County Habitat for Humanity, 1995-97; mem. bd. Luth. Campus Ministry for Wis. and Upper Mich., 1996—2002, Fortune Lake Bible Camp, 2003—. Mem. AAUW (divsn. pres. 1978-80), Nat. Coun. Tchrs. English, S.D. Coun. Tchrs. English, Sci. Fiction Rsch. Assn., Popular Culture Assn., Milton Soc., S.D. Poetry Soc. (pres. 1982-83), Delta Kappa Gamma (pres. local chpt., mem. state bd. 1972-89, state v.p. 1979-83, state pres. 1983-85), Sigma Tau Delta, Pi Kappa Delta, Phi Kappa Phi. E-mail: woodwork@nnex.net.

WEINKAUF, WILLIAM CARL, communications executive; b. Fond du Lac, Wis., Apr. 7, 1934; s. Carl Alfred and Erma Gertrude (Lueck) Weinkauf; m. Carole Jean Hill, May 3, 1958 (div.); children: Carl William, Mary Gretchen, Donald Hill; m. Jean Boyne Hawks, Sept. 10, 1988. BA, Ripon Coll., 1955; postgrad., U. Wis., 1954, 57-58. Dir. Wis. Ctrl. Lumber Co., 1959-63; with Carlton Films, Beloit, Wis., 1965-68; founder, pres. IMCO, Inc., Green Lake, Wis., 1968—, IMCO Pub. Co., Green Lake. Bd. dirs. Peterson Sys., Inc.; co-founder, chmn. Affluence Unlimited, Inc., Dallas, 1986; founder, pres. Weinkauf Techs., LLC, Dallas, 1996. Chmn. coun. Cub Scouts Am., 1968—69; mem. exec. com. County Reps., 1970—71; trustee United Ch. Christ, Green Lake, 1965—66, deacon Dallas, 1989—93, chmn. bd. deacons, 1992—93. Mem.: Nat. Sch. Supply and Equipment Assn. (bd. dirs. 1986—87), Nat. Audio Visual Assn. (chmn. legis. com. Wis. 1975—), Heroes of '76, U.S. Res. Officers Assn. (chpt. pres. 1966—70), Scotish Rite (32 deg.), Order Ea. Star (worthy patron Dallas 2001—), Sojourners, Masons (32d degree), Sigma Nu. Office: 2215 Commerce St Dallas TX 75201-4345

WEINKE, CHRIS, professional football player; b. St. Paul, Minn., July 31, 1972; Attended, Fla. State Univ. Quarterback Carolina Panthers, 2001—; winner Heisman Trophy. Achievements include ranking second in NFL history for passing yards as a rookie. Office: Carolina Panthers 800 S Mint St Charlotte NC 28202

WEINKOPF, FRIEDRICH J. lawyer; b. Bautsch, Germany, Feb. 17, 1930; Referendar, U. Marburg, Germany, 1954; LLM, U. Pa., 1958; JD, Chgo.-Kent Coll. Law, 1967. Bar: Ill. 1967. Ptnr. Baker & McKenzie, Chgo. Office: Baker & McKenzie 1 Prudential Plz 130 E Randolph St Fl 3600 Chicago IL 60601-6315

WEINMAN, DARYL GAIL, lawyer; b. North Tarrytown, N.Y., Dec. 22, 1967; d. Lawrence S. Weinman and Serena Negrin Michelson; m. Donald Paul Morehart, July 19, 1997; children: Nathan Daniel Morehart, Benjamin Jake Morehart. BA, Colgate U., 1988; JD, N.Y. Law Sch., 1993. Bar: Tex. 1994, U.S. Dist. Ct. (we. dist.) Tex. 1994, U.S. Ct. Appeals (5th cir.) 1995, U.S. Supreme Ct. 1997, bd. cert. family law: 2000. Pvt. practice, Austin, Tex., 1994—2000; ptnr. Morehart and Weinman, Austin, 2000—. Vol. Sidelines, Austin, 1999—; mem. Jewish Cmty. Ctr., Austin, 1998—; local coord. Stepmothers Internat., Austin, 1999—; founding fellow Travis Bar Found. Mem.: Tex. Acad. Family Specialists, Dist. 9A Grievance Com., Pro Bono Coll. State Bar, Coll. State Bar of Tex., State Bar Tex., Travis County Bar. Democrat. Jewish. Avocations: quilting, travel, children's activities. Office: Morehart and Weinman 316 W 12th St Ste 602 Austin TX 78701 Office Phone: 512-472-4040. Personal E-mail: darylesq@aol.com.

WEINMAN, GLENN ALAN, lawyer; b. NYC, Dec. 9, 1955; s. Seymour and Iris Rhoda (Bergman) W. BA in Polit. Sci., UCLA, 1978; JD, U. So. Calif., 1981. Bar: Calif. 1981. Assoc. counsel Mitsui Mfrs. Bank, LA, 1981-83; assoc. McKenna, Conner & Cuneo, LA, 1983-85, Stroock, Stroock & Lavan, LA, 1985-87; sr. counsel Buchalter, Nemer, Fields & Younger, LA, 1987-91; ptnr. Keck, Mahin & Cate, LA, 1991-93; sr. v.p., gen. counsel Western Internat. Media Corp., LA, 1993-96; v.p. gen. counsel and human resources, sec. Guess?, Inc., LA, 1996-2000, also bd. dirs.; chief adminstrv. officer Competitive Knowledge, Inc., 2000; v.p., gen. counsel, sec. Luminent, Inc., Chatsworth, Calif., 2000-01; exec. v.p., COO Insolvency Svcs. Group, Woodland Hills, Calif., 2001—03; v.p., gen. counsel, sec. Inter-Con Security Sys., Inc., Pasadena, Calif., 2003—. Mem. ABA (corp. banking and bus. law sect., com. on savs. instns., com. on banking law corp. counsel sect.), Calif. Bar Assn. (bus. law sect., com. fin. instns. 1989-91, com. consumer svcs. 1991-94), LA County Bar Assn. (corp. legal depts. sect., bus. and corps. law sect., subcom. on fin. instns.), Calif. Fashion Assn. (exec. bd. 1997-2000), Am. Apparel Mfrs. Assn. (govt. rels. com. 1997-2000), Legion Lex, U. So. Calif. Law Alumni Assn., Phi Alpha Delta. Avocation: tennis. Office: 210 S Delacey Ave Pasadena CA 91105 Personal E-mail: gaweinman@aol.com.

WEINMAN, HOWARD MARK, lawyer; b. N.Y.C., May 6, 1947; s. Joseph and Kate (Dorn) Weinman; m. Pamela Eve Brodie, Jan. 6, 1980; children: David Lewis, Nathaniel Saul. BA magna cum laude, Columbia U., 1969; MPP, JD cum laude, Harvard U., 1973; LLM with hons. in Taxation, George Washington U., 1981. Bar: D.C. 1973. Assoc. Fried, Frank, Harris, Shriver & Kampelman, Washington and N.Y.C., 1973—78; legis. atty. Joint Com. on Taxation U.S. Congress, Washington, 1978—80; assoc. Sachs, Greenebaum & Tayler, Washington, 1980—82, Crowell & Moring LLP, Washington, 1982—84, ptnr., 1984—. Adj. prof. internat. tax Georgetown U. Law Ctr., Washington, 1988—89. Contbr. articles to profl. jours. Mem.: ABA (taxation sect.), Kenwood Club, Phi Beta Kappa. Jewish. Home: 5404 Center St Chevy Chase MD 20815-7101 Office: Crowell & Moring LLP 1001 Pennsylvania Ave NW Fl 10 Washington DC 20004-2595

WEINMAN, IRVING, writer; b. Boston, Mass. s. Leon and Dora Weinman; m. Judith Pakenham; m. Zoe deRopp (div.); children: Zoe Hart, Michael. MLitt, DLitt. Founder/dir. Key West Writers' Workshop, Fla., 1996—; dir./vice pres. Key West Lit. Seminar. Author: (novels) Tailor's Dummy, 1986, Stealing Home, 2004, Hampton Heat, Virgil's Ghost, Easy Way Down, Stealing Home.

WEINMAN, STEVEN ALAN, emergency nurse, researcher, writer, educator, consultant; b. St. Louis, July 17, 1962; s. Stanley I. Weinman and Diana Raye (Kessler) Schrader; m. Carol Angela Daiber, July 27, 1986; children: Erin Elizabeth, Sarah Katherine. Diploma in Nursing, Jewish Hosp. of St. Louis, 1986; BSN, Webster U., Kansas City, 1996; postgrad., Webster U., 2001—. RN, Mo., NY, NJ; cert. emergency nurse. Emergency nurse Jewish Hosp. of St. Louis, 1986-87, Truman Med. Ctr.-West, Kansas City, Mo., 1987-93, clin. nurse mgr., 1987-93, clin. educator, 1993-95, St. Luke's Northland Hosp., Kans. City, Mo., 1996-97; prin. ptnr. Emergency Care Cons. Greater NY, Somerville, NJ, 1996—; instr. dept. emergency medicine NY Hosp.-Cornell Med. Ctr., NYC, 1997-2001; sr. dir. Med. Ed. and Custom Publ., Excepta Med. Elsevier, Hillsborough, NJ, 2001—02; dir. Office of Continuing Med. Edn. Elsevier Health Scis. Divsn., 2004—. Clin. rsch. assoc. Clin. Multiphase Rsch., Wilton, Conn., 1991—93, nurse rschr., 1991—2000; rsch. coord. dept. emergency medicine Truman Med. Ctr., Kansas City, 1991—96; mem. editl. adv. bd. Roadrunner Press/ENA, 1999—2001; per diem instr. in emergency and trauma care N.Y. Presbyn. Hosp.-Cornell Med. Ctr., N.Y.C., 2001—. Editor textbooks and monographs; mem. editl. bd. Clin. CORNERSTONE, Excerpta Medica, Inc.; contbg. author books and book chpt; contbr. articles to profl. jour. Mem. adv. bd. Kansas City chpt. ARC, 1991-94; chief nurse first aid Kansas City Spiritfest, 1989-95; emergency med. technician Somerville Rescue Squad, State of NJ, 2002, crew chief, 2004, edn. and tng. officer, 2003—. Recipient Spl. Recognition award Emergency Nursing Found. Mem.: Am. Orgn. Nurse Execs., NJ State Nurses Assn., Nat. Assn. EMS Educators, Global Alliance for Med. Edn., Alliance for Continuing Med. Edn., Soc. Trauma Nurses, Am. Trauma Soc., Emergency Nurses Assn. (treas. Greater Kansas City chpt. 1989—91, pres. 1994, state coun. exec. com. 1993—95, sec. 1991, state del. 1991—95, Recognition award 1991, 1993, 1994, 2000, 2001, Edn. award 1993, Educator of Yr. 1994, 1996, Disting. Svc. award 2000). Avocations: photography, writing, computers/electronics, travel. Home: 29 W Spring St Somerville NJ 08876-1627 Office: 105 Raider Blvd Ste 101 Hillsborough NJ 08844

WEINMANN, ERIC, retired lawyer; b. Teplice, Czech Republic, July 29, 1913; came to U.S., 1942; s. Ing Edmund and Josefine (Taussig) W.; m. Camilla Behn, May 4, 1946 (div. 1953); children: Edward Marvin, Gail Greenwood; m. Mary Ethel de Limur Carothers, Dec. 21, 1974. Diploma, Handelshochschule, Berlin, 1935; MA, Columbia U., 1943, JD, 1957; LLM, Georgetown U., 1963. Bar: N.Y. 1957, D.C. 1958, U.S. Supreme Ct. 1963. Assoc. counsel Legal & Monetary Subcom., Ho. of Reps., Washington, 1957-60; atty. SEC, Washington, 1960-63; counsel SBA, Washington, 1963-89; ret., 1989. Contbr. articles to profl. jours. Trustee emeritus Folger Shakespeare Libr., Washington, 1985. Mem. Met. Club City of Washington, City Tavern Assn., N.Y. Athletic Club. Avocations: skin diving, mountain climbing, dressage riding. Home: 3244 Nebraska Ave NW Washington DC 20016-2704

WEINMANN, JOHN GIFFEN, lawyer, diplomat; b. New Orleans, Aug. 29, 1928; s. Rudolph John and Mary Victoria (Mills) W.; m. Virginia Lee Eason, June 11, 1955; children: Winston Eason, Robert St. George Tucker, John Giffen Jr., Mary Virginia Lewis, George Gustaf. BA, Tulane U., 1950, JD, 1952. Bar: La. 1952. Pvt. practice law Phelps Dunbar and predecessor firm, New Orleans, ptnr., 1955-80, of counsel, 1981-83, 85-89, 1993—; gen. counsel Times-Picayune Pub. Corp., Rathborne Land Co., 1968-80; pres., dir. Waverly Oil Corp., 1981-89; amb. to Finland Am. Embassy, Helsinki, 1989-91; amb., chief of protocol of White House Dept. of State, Washington, 1991-93. Lectr. bills and notes New Orleans chpt. Am. Inst. Banking, 1958-59; bd. dir. Eason Oil Co., 1961-81, chmn., 1977; bd. dir. 1st Nat. Bank of Oklahoma City, 1978-84, Am. Life Ins. Co. of N.Y., 1981-88, Allied Investment Corp., 1985-88; asst. sec. Am. Bar Endowment, 1971-74, bd. dirs., sec., 1975-80 Mem. adv. bd. Tulane Law Rev., 1965-92. Bd. govs. Tulane Med. Ctr., 1968-81; bd. adminstrs. Tulane Ednl. Fund, 1981-98, emeritus, 99—, chmn. devel. com., 1985-89, co-chmn. Tulane Parents Fund, 1980-81, bd. chmn., 1993-98; nat. chmn. ann. giving Campaign for Tulane, 1983-85; bd. dirs. Coun. for Better La., 1987-89, Tulane Children's Ctr., 1981-84, WYES Ednl. TV Sta., 1981-82; trustee S.W. Legal Found., 1978-80, Metairie Park Country Day Sch., vice chmn., 1976-77, chmn., 1978-80, U.S. commr. gen. for 1984 La. World Expn., 1983-85; U.S. del. Bur. Internat. Expositions, Paris, 1984-85, chmn. del., 1985; state fin. co-chmn. George Bush for Pres., and Victory La. '88, 1987-89. Named Outstanding Law Alumnus Tulane U., 1985, Outstanding Alumnus Class of 1950, Tulane Coll., 2000, Disting. Tulane U. Alumnus, 2002; selected Rex, King of Carnival, New Orleans, 1996. Mem. ABA (chmn. jr. bar conf. 1963-64, mem. ho. dels. 1964-66, 70, 72-76, sec. com. ethics evaluation 1965, rep. to conv. Union des Jeunes Avocats de France, 1964, chmn. sect. bar activities 1969-70), La. Bar Assn. (sec. treas. 1965-67, Outstanding Young Lawyer award), La. Soc. Colonial Wars (gov. 1976), Swiss-Am. Cultural Exch. Found. (hon. com. 1994—), Phi Beta Kappa, Order of Coif, Delta Kappa Epsilon, Omicron Delta Kappa. Episcopalian. Home: 611 Hector Ave Metairie LA 70005-4415 Office: Waverly Enterprises 601 Poydras St Ste 2690 New Orleans LA 70130-6026

WEINMANN, RICHARD ADRIAN, lawyer, arbitrator; b. N.Y.C., Oct. 15, 1917; s. Randolph and Mae (Korber) W.; m. Bert Millicent Landes, Dec. 26, 1946; children: Harriet Joan, Elaine Anita; m. Ginger Grace Rich, 1999. LLB, Bklyn. Law Sch., 1948; LLM, NYU, 1953. Bar: N.Y. 1958, U.S. Dist. Ct. (so. dist.) N.Y. 1960; U.S. Dist. Ct. (ea. dist.) N.Y. 1960, U.S. Ct. Appeals (2d cir.) 1965, U.S. Supreme Ct. 1964. Ptnr. Sipser, Weinstock & Weinmann, N.Y.C., 1963-71; sole practice N.Y.C., 1972—. Guest lectr. seminars; mem. staff Cornell U. Sch. Indsl. and Labor Relations; panel arbitrator Fed. Mediation and Conciliation Svc. Am. Arbitration Assn. Suffolk and Nassau Counties Pub. Employment Relations Bds. N.Y. State; N.Y. State Employment Rels. Bd. Committeeman Nassau County (N.Y.), 1965—; former mem. legal adv. bd. Union Lawyers Ednl. Conf. Served with AUS, 1943-46. Mem. ABA, ACLU, VFW, N.Y. State Bar Assn., Indsl. Rels. Rsch. Assn., B'nai B'rith. Office Phone: 718-224-8928.

WEINMANN, ROBERT LEWIS, neurologist; b. Newark, Aug. 21, 1935; s. Isadore and Etta (Silverman) Weinmann; m. Diana Weinmann, Dec. 13, 1980 (dec. Dec. 1989); children: Paul, Chris, Dana, Paige. BA, Yale U., 1957; MD, Stanford U., 1962. Diplomate Am. Bd. EEG and Neurophysiology (v.p.), Am. Acad. Pain Mgmt., Am. Bd. Forensic Medicine. Intern Pacific Presbyn. Med. Ctr., San Francisco, 1962-63; resident in neurology Stanford (Calif.) U. Hosp., 1963-66, chief resident, 1965-66; pvt. practice San Jose, Calif., 1969—. Former clin. instr. neurology Stanford U. Chmn. editl. bd. Clin. EEG Jour., mem. editl. bd. Clin. Evoked Potentials Jour.; contbr. articles to various publs. Capt. M.C. U.S. Army, 1966—68. Recipient award, State of R.I., Santa Clara County Med. Soc., Calif. State Assembly, U.S. Congress, other orgns.; fellow, U. Paris, 1957—58. Fellow: Am. Coll. Forensic Medicine; mem.: Union Am. Physicians and Dentists (pres. 1990—, bd. dirs. 1972—, pres. Calif. fedn. 1990—). Avocations: softball, tennis, music, theater, martial arts. Office: Union Am Physicians & Dentists 1330 Broadway Ste 730 Oakland CA 94612-2589 Office Phone: 510-839-0193., 408-292-0802.

WEINREB, MICHAEL PHILIP, physicist; b. Lakewood, N.J., Feb. 2, 1939; s. Sol and Lillian (Bolotsky) W.; m. Alice Kogan, Aug. 28, 1966; children: Jenya, Elizabeth. BA, U. Pa., 1960; MA, Brandeis U., 1963, PhD, 1966. Physicist NASA, Cambridge, Mass., 1965-70, U.S. Dept. Transp., Cambridge, 1970, Nat. Oceanic and Atmospheric Adminstrn., Washington, 1970—2004, Gen. Dynamics Advanced Info. Sys., Washington, 2004—. Adj. prof. math. Am. U., Washington, 1984-85. Contbr. articles to profl. jours. Recipient Gold medal U.S. Dept. of Commerce, 1998, Bronze medal, 1994, 2003. Mem. Optical Soc. Am., Am. Meteorol. Soc., Am. Geophys. Union, Phi Beta Kappa. Avocation: music.

WEINREB, TZVI HERSH, religious organization administrator, rabbi; m. Chavi Taub, 1965; 3 children. MA in pyschology, New Sch.for Social Rsch.; PhD, U. Md., 1970. Asst. supervisor psychological services Prince George's County Public Schools; chief psychologist Potomac Found. Mental Health; private practice, psychotherapy; rabbi Congregation Shomrei Emunah, Balt., 1989—2002; exec. v.p. Orthodox Union, 2002—. V.p. Rabbinical Coun. Am.; rabbinic liaison N. Am. Network Orthodox Mental Heath Professionals; mem. ethics com. Veterans Admin. Hosp.; mem. rabbinic cabinet United Jewish Communities. Office: Orthodox Union 11 Broadway New York NY 10004 Office Phone: 212-563-4000. Office Fax: 212-564-9058.*

WEINRICH, ALAN JEFFREY, occupational hygienist; b. Passaic, N.J., Aug. 24, 1953; s. Erwin Hermann and Ann Elizabeth Weinrich; m. Nina Kathryn Hooker, Jan. 14, 1983; 1 child, Sheena Elizabeth Rochelle. BS with high honors, Rutgers U., 1975; MS, U. Iowa, 1988, postgrad., 1988-89. Cert. Am. Bd. Indsl. Hygiene, cert. environ. trainer Nat. Environ. Tng. Assn. Indsl. hygienist Tenn. Dept. Labor, Nashville, 1975-78; health info. specialist occupl. health program U. Tenn., Memphis, 1980-82; vol. tchr. Internat. Sch. Moshi, Tanzania, 1982-84; sr. rsch. asst. agrl. medicine rsch. facility U. Iowa, Iowa City, 1985-89; sr. indsl. hygienist PSI Energy, Inc., Plainfield, Ind., 1989-92; asst. dir. health & safety programs environ. mgmt. and edn. Purdue U., West Lafayette, 1992-94; assoc. dir. tech. affairs Am. Conf. Govtl. Indsl. Hygienists, Cin., 1994-97, dir. tech. affairs, 1997-99, dir. scientific affairs, 1999—. Co-editor book supplements: Documentation of the Threshold Limit Values and Biological Exposure Indices, 1996-98; editor, author ACGIH newsletter Today!; developer, editor CD-Rom publ. TLVs and Other Occupational Exposure Values. Mem. healthy cities com. Butler-Tarkington Neighborhood Assn., Indpls., 1992-94; mem. Greenways Com., City of Wyoming, Ohio. Mem. Am. Acad. Indsl. Hygiene, Am. Conf. Govtl. Indsl. Hygienists, Am. Indsl. Hygiene Assn. (v.p. Mid-South sect. 1981-82, bd. dirs. Iowa-Ill. sect. 1987-89, bd. dirs. Ind. sect. 1991-94, pres. Ind. sect. 1994-95), Internat. Occupl. Hygiene Assn., Am. Soc. Assn. Execs. Avocations: bicycling, family, reading, walking, softball. Office: Am Conf Govtl Indsl Hygienists 1330 Kemper Meadow Dr Cincinnati OH 45240-4147 E-mail: science@ACGIH.org.

WEINRICH, BARBARA DIANE, speech pathology/audiology services professional, educator; b. Hamilton, Ohio, July 25, 1947; d. Robert Earl and Pearl Edith (McDuffee) Derickson; m. Lancer Richard Weinrich, Jr. BS, Miami U., Oxford, Ohio, 1968; MA, U. Cin., 1973, PhD, 1997. Cert. speech pathologist, lic. Ohio. Sch. speech pathologist various schs., 1968—75; prof. speech-lang. pathology Miami U., Oxford, 1975—. Pvt. practice speech pathology, Middletown, Ohio, 1975—. Contbr. articles to profl. jours. Grantee Rsch. grantee, Miami U., U. Cin. Mem.: Southwestern Ohio Speech-Lang.-Hearing Assn., Ohio Speech-Lang.-Hearing Assn., Am. Speech-Lang.-Hearing Assn. Avocations: skiing, tennis, travel, reading. Office: Miami University Dept Speech Pathology 28 Bachelor Hall Oxford OH 45056

WEINRICH, BRIAN ERWIN, mathematician, computer scientist; b. Passaic, N.J., Jan. 8, 1952; s. Erwin H. and Ann E. (Gall) Weinrich. BS, Pa. State U., 1974, MA, 1978; MS, Shippensburg (Pa.) U., 1983; postgrad. in computer engring., U. Fla., 2002—. Mathematician U.S. Dept. Agr., Agrl. Rsch. Svc., University Park, Pa., 1974-80; instr. math and computer sci. Shippensburg U., 1980-84; assoc. prof. maths. and computer sci. California U. of Pa., 1984-97, assoc. prof. emeritus of mathematics and computer scis., 1997—. Cons. in field; mem. Wall St. Jour. Panel, 1990—; devel. articulation agreements in Malaysia California U. of Pa., 1992—2001; vis. sr. lectr. in computer sci. Inti Coll., Subang Jaya, Malaysia, 1993—2001; cons. in math., sys. and database programming, 1981—2002. Author (with A. S. Rogowski): (book) Water Movement and Quality on Strip-Mined Lands: A Compilation of Computer Programs, 1984; author: (with others) Surface Mining, 1990; contbr. articles to profl. jours. Mem. mission bd. Calvary Bapt. Ch., State College, Pa., 1975—80; visitation team Prince St. United Brethren Ch., Shippensburg, 1982—84; Bible study leader, asst. Sunday sch. tchr. Libr. Bapt. Ch., 1986—92. Fellow, U. Fla., 2002—; grantee, U.S. Dept. Age, 1982—89. Mem.: Assn. Computing Machinery, Math. Assn. Am., Am. Biog. Inst. (bd. advisors 1989—), Computer Soc. of IEEE. Republican. Home: 1001 SW 16th Ave Apt 67 Gainesville FL 32601 Office: U Fla Dept Computer and Info Sci and Engring PO Box 116120 Gainesville FL 32611 Office Phone: 352-392-1200. Personal E-mail: brianew@cise.ufl.edu.

WEINRICH, JOHNATHAN EDWARD, lawyer; b. NYC, Sept. 17, 1949; s. John Edward and Anne (Murray) W.; children: Joy Teresa, Johnathan Joseph; m. Evelyn; 1 child, Kristina Lynn. BA, SUNY, Binghamton, 1974; JD magna cum laude, Vt. Law Sch., 1977. Bar: N.Y. 1978, U.S. Dist. Ct. (ea. and so. dist.) N.Y. 1978, U.S. Tax Ct. 1981, U.S. Ct. Appeals (2d cir.) 1980. Sr. staff atty. Legal Aid Soc., N.Y.C., 1979-81; ptnr. Rutberg & Weinrich, N.Y.C., 1981-83; prin., owner Johnathan E. Weinrich Law Firm, N.Y.C., 1983—; sr. trial atty. appellate divsn. 2d dept. NYS Supreme Ct., 2004—. Legis. counsel N.Y.C. Councilman Ralph Colon, 1987-92, N.Y.C. Councilman David Rosado, 1992-96, N.Y.C. Councilman Federico Perez, 1997-98, N.Y. State Senator David Rosado, 1997-2000; mem. Gov.'s Metro Task Force on Correctional Services, N.Y.C., 1984; trustee Vt. Law Sch., 1975-76. Editor Vt. Law Rev., 1976-77. Counsel Excise Bonds, 1990—, Kings County Soc. Prevention Cruelty to Children, 1992—, Local One Security Officers Union, 1998—, South Bronx Housekeeping Vendors Assn., 1998—. Recipient State of N.Y. Legis. Resolution #759, 1989, N.Y. Coun. Proclaimation, 1992, N.Y. State Senate Resolution, 2000. Mem. ABA, ATLA, N.Y. State Trial Lawyers Assn., Bklyn. Bar Assn., Kings County Criminal Bar Assn., Ret. Detectives of N.Y., Rockland County Shields, Fraternal Order of Police (local #38), Legal Aid Alumni Assn., N.Y. State Defenders Assn., N.Y. State Assn. Criminal Def. Attys. (charter 1987—), Royal Order of Scotland, Knight York Cross of Honor, Masons. Democrat. Roman Catholic. Address: 15 Maiden Lane Ste 800 New York NY 10038 Office Phone: 212-344-8828.

WEINSCHEL, ALAN JAY, lawyer; b. Bklyn., Feb. 9, 1946; m. Barbara Ellen Schure, Aug. 20, 1967; children: Lawrence, Adam, Naomi. BA, Bklyn. Coll., 1967; JD, NYU, 1969. Bar: N.Y. 1970, U.S. Dist. Ct. (so. and ea. dists.) N.Y. 1973, U.S. Ct. Appeals (2d cir.) 1979, U.S. Ct. Appeals (9th cir.) 1986, U.S. Ct. Appeals (3d cir.) 1993, U.S. Ct. Appeals (7th cir.) 1996. Assoc. Breed, Abbott & Morgan, N.Y.C., 1969-74, Weil, Gotshal & Manges, N.Y.C., 1974-78, ptnr., 1978—. Lectr. Practising Law Inst., Ohio Legal Ctr., Am. Mgmt. Assn., Law Jour. Seminars, Law and Bus. Seminars, Glasser Legalworks, Insight Seminars, Mfrs.' Alliance. Author: Antitrust Intellectual Property Handbook, 2000. Trustee N.Y. Inst. Tech., Old Westbury, N.Y., 1969-76, Temple Sinai, Roslyn, N.Y., 1981-87, 89-95. Capt. U.S. Army res., 1969-74. Mem. ABA (editl. bd. Antitrust Devels. 1981-87), N.Y. State Bar Assn. (chmn. antitrust sect. 1993-95), Assn. Bar of City of N.Y. Office: Weil Gotshal & Manges 767 5th Ave New York NY 10153-0119

WEINSHENKER, NAOMI JOYCE, clinical psychiatrist, educator, researcher; b. Ridgewood, N.J., Mar. 28, 1961; d. Theodore and Anne Betty (Jaffe) W. BA summa cum laude, Yale U., 1983; MD, U. Pa., 1989 Diplomate Am. Bd. Psychiatry and Neurology. Rotating intern Overlook Hosp., Summit, N.J., 1989-90; resident in adult psychiatry Mass. Mental Health Ctr., Harvard U. Med. Sch., Boston, 1990-92, fellow in child and adolescent psychiatry, 1992-93, Boston Children's Hosp., Harvard U. Med. Sch., 1993-94; staff psychiatrist Choate Health Systems, Woburn, Mass., 1994-96; asst. prof. clin. psychiatry U. Medicine and Dentistry of N.J., Newark, 1996-2000; asst. prof. clin. psychiatry Sch. Medicine NYU, 2000—. Staff psychiatrist Univ. Behavioral HealthCare, Newark, 1996—97; asst.dir. Univ.Hosp. Psychiat. Outpatient Ctr., 1998—2000; mem. faculty NYU Child Study Ctr., 2000—; cons. child outpatient svcs. Tri City Mental Health and Retardation Ctr., Inc., Medford, Mass., 1996; dir., young adult inpatient program Tisch Hosp., 2000—04. Contbr. articles to profl. jours.; editl. asst. Emergency Medicine mag., 1983-84. Vol. psychiatry unit, coord. psychiatry vols., Yale-New Haven Hosp., 1979-83; vol. recruitment coord. Phila. Adult Spl. Olympics, 1985. Mem. Am. Psychiat. Assn., Am. Acad. Child/Adolescent Psychiatry, N.J. Psychiat. Assn. (Essex County rep. Tri-County chpt. 1997-98, treas. 1998-99, sec. 1999-00, v.p. 2000-2001, pres.-elect 2001-02), N.J. Coun. Child/Adolescent Psychiatry, Phi Beta Kappa, Sigma Xi. Democrat. Jewish. Avocations: singing, viola, musical theatre, nutrition and vegetarianism, weight training and aerobics. Office: NYU Child Study Ctr 577 First Ave New York NY 10016 Business E-Mail: Naomi.Wweinshenker@msnyuhealth.org.

WEINSHIENK, ZITA LEESON, federal judge; b. St. Paul, Apr. 3, 1933; d. Louis and Ada (Dubov) Leeson; m. Hubert Troy Weinshienk, July 8, 1956 (dec. 1983); children: Edith Blair, Kay Anne, Darcy Jill; m. James N. Schaffner, Nov. 15, 1986. Student, U. Colo., 1952-53; BA magna cum laude, U. Ariz., 1955; JD cum laude, Harvard U., 1958; Fulbright grantee, U. Copenhagen, Denmark, 1959; LHD (hon.), Loretto Heights Coll., 1985; LLD (hon.), U. Denver, 1990. Bar: Colo. 1959. Probation counselor, legal adviser, referee Denver Juvenile Ct., 1959-64; judge Denver Mcpl. Ct., 1964-65, Denver County Ct., 1965-71, Denver Dist. Ct., 1972-79, U.S. Dist. Ct. Colo., Denver, 1979—, sr. judge, 1998—. Precinct committeewoman Denver Democratic Com., 1963-64; bd. dirs. Crime Stoppers. Named one of 100 Women in Touch with Our Time Harper's Bazaar Mag., 1971, Woman of Yr., Denver Bus. and Profl. Women, 1969; recipient Women Helping Women award Soroptimist Internat. of Denver, 1983, Hanna G. Solomon award Nat. Coun. Jewish Women, Denver, 1986, Soaring Eagle award Colo. Womne's Leadership Conf., 1997; inducted into Colo. Women's Hall of Fame, 2000. Fellow Colo. Bar Found., Am. Bar Found.; mem. ABA, Denver Bar Assn., U. Ariz. Alumni Assn. (Disting. Citizen's award 1994), Colo. Bar Assn., Nat. Conf. Fed. Trial Judges (exec. com., past chair), Dist. Judges' Assn. of 10th Cir. (past pres.), Colo. Women's Bar Assn. (Mary Lathrop award 1995), Fed. Judges Assn., Denver Crime Stoppers Inc. (bd.dirs.), Denver LWV, Women's Forum Colo., Harvard Law Sch. Assn., Phi Beta Kappa, Phi Kappa Phi, Order of Coif (hon. Colo. chpt.). Office: US Dist Ct US Courthouse Rm 4-841 901 19th St Denver CO 80294-2500 Office Phone: 303-844-2784.

WEINSHILBOUM, RICHARD M. pharmacologist, educator, biomedical researcher; b. Eldorado, Kans., Mar. 31, 1940; s. Robert Saul and Rose Lazer Weinshilboum; m. Lily Shuling, June 4, 1965; children: Rebecca Y., David H. BA, U. Kans., 1962; MD, U. Kans., Kansas City, 1967; LLD (hon.), New Eng. U., 1995. Cert. bd. cert. in internal medicine, bd. cert. in clin. pharmacology. Rsch. assoc. NIMH, Bethesda, Md., 1969—71; resident in internal medicine Mass. Gen. Hosp., Boston, 1967—69, 1971—72; asst. to assoc. prof. pharmacology and medicine Mayo Med. Sch., Mayo Clinic, Rochester, Minn., 1972—79, prof. molecular pharmacology and exptl. therapeutics and medicine, 1979—. Contbr. articles to profl. jours. Burroughs-Wellcome in Clin. Pharmacology scholar, 1981—86. Mem.: Catecholamine Club (Julius Axelrod award 2003), Am. Soc. Pharmacology and Exptl. Therapeutics (Harry Gold award 2003), Am. Soc. Clin. Pharmacology and Therapeutics (Rawls-Palmer award 1979, Oscar B. Hunter award 1998). Jewish. Achievements include major contributions to the fields of pharmacogenetics and pharmacogenomics of drug metabolism. Avocation: tennis. Office: Mayo Clinic 200 First St SW Rochester MN 55905 Office Phone: 507-284-2790.

WEINSIER, ROLAND LOUIS, nutrition educator and director; BS, U. Fla., Gainesville; MD, Harvard U., 1968, MPH, 1971. Diplomate Nat. Bd. Med. Examiners, Am. Bd. Clinical Nutrition, Am. Bd. Preventive Medicine. Resident U. Va., Charlottesville, 1968-70; mem. field nutrition survey team INCAP, Guatemala, 1971; asst. in medicine Peter Bent Brigham Hosp., Boston, 1971-73; internal medicine/nutrition cons., flight surgeon USAF, Brooks AFB, Tex., 1973-75; asst. prof. medicine, dir. clin. nutrition U. Ala., Birmingham, 1975-77, assoc., then full prof. nutrition, chmn. dept. nutrition scis., 1975-99, prof., dir. clin. nutrition rsch. ctr., 2000—. Contbr. articles to profl. jours., chpts. to books. Fellow ACP, Am. Coll. Preventive Medicine, Am. Coll. Nutrition; mem. Am. Soc. Clin. Nutrition, Am. Soc. Parenteral and Enteral Nutrition, Soc. Nutrition Edn., North Am. Assn. Study of Obesity, Alpha Omega Alpha. Office: U Ala Birmingham Clin Nutrition Rsch Ctr 1675 University Blvd # 232 Birmingham AL 35294-0001

WEINSTEIN, ALAN EDWARD, lawyer; b. Bklyn., Apr. 20, 1945; s. John and Matilda W.; m. Patti Kantor, Dec. 18, 1965; children: Steven R., David A. AA, U. Fla., 1964; BBA, U. Miami, Fla., 1965, JD cum laude, 1968. Bar: Fla. 1968, U.S. Dist. Ct. (so. dist.) Fla. 1968, U.S. Ct. Appeals (5th cir.) 1969, U.S. Supreme Ct. 1973, U.S. Ct. Appeals (4th and 11th cirs.) 1981. Assoc. Cohen & Hogan, Miami Beach, Fla., 1968-71; pvt. practice Miami Beach, 1972-81; sr. ptnr. Weinstein & Preira, Miami Beach, 1981-92; prin. Law Offices of Alan E. Weinstein, Miami, 1992—. Lectr. in field. Mem. ABA (criminal and family law sect. 1968—, white collar crime commn. 1986—), Nat. Assn. Criminal Def. Lawyers, 1st Family Law Am Inn of Court, Fla. Bar Assn. (criminal and family law sect. 1968—, ethics com. 1987-88, bench/bar com. 1988-89, grievance com. 1999-2002, chmn. 2002, unlicensed practice of law com. 2002—), Fla. Criminal Def. Attys. Assn. (pres. 1978-79), Fla. Assn. Criminal Def. Lawyers (treas. 1989-90), Miami Beach Bar Assn., Soc. Wig and Robe, Phi Kappa Phi. Avocations: marlin fishing, reading, travel. Office: 1801 West Ave Miami FL 33139-1431 Office Phone: 305-534-4666. E-mail: defense1@bellsouth.net.

WEINSTEIN, ALLEN, educator, historian, non-profit administrator; b. N.Y.C., Sept. 1, 1937; s. Samuel and Sarah (Popkoff) W.; m. Adrienne Dominguez, June 14, 1995; children: Andrew Samuel, David Meier. BA, CCNY; MA, Yale U., PhD, 1967. Prof. history Smith Coll., Northampton, Mass., 1966-81; editl. staff The Washington Post, 1981; exec. editor, The Washington Quarterly Georgetown Ctr. for Strategic and Internat. Studies, Washington, 1981—83; univ. prof. Georgetown U., Washington, 1981—84; pres. Ctr. for the Study of Democratic Institutions, Santa Barbara, 1984; editor The Ctr. Magazine, 1984; prof. history Boston U., 1985-89; founder, pres. The Ctr. for Democracy, Washington, 1985—2003; sr. adviser for democratic institutions and dir. Internat. Found. for Elections Sys., Washington, 2003—. Author: Prelude to Populism, 1970, Freedom and Crisis, 1974, 3d edit., 1981, Perjury, 1978 (NISC award 1978), new edit., 1998, Between the Wars, 1978; co-author: The Haunted Wood: Soviet Espionage in America, 1999, The Story of America, 2002; editor: Am. Negro Slavery, 1968, 3d edit., 1981, HST and Israel, 1981. Exec. dir. The Democracy Program, Washington, 1982-83; acting pres. Nat. Endowment for Democracy, Washington, 1983-84; chmn. edn. com. U.S. Inst. Peace, Washington, 1986-2001; mem. U.S. Observer del., Feb., 1986 Philippines election, co-author report; vice chmn. U.S. del. UNESCO World Conf. on Culture, 1982, UNESCO/IPDC meeting, 1983; chmn. Internat. IMPAC/Dublin Lit. award, 1996-2003. Recipient Meade prize in history CCNY, 1960, Egleston prize Yale U., 1967, Binkley-Stephenson prize Orgn. Am. Historians, 1968, UN Peace medal, 1986, Coun. of Europe Silver medal, 1990, 96; Fulbright lectr., Australia, 1968, 71; Commonwealth Fund lectr. U.S. History, U. London, 1981; Fourth of July Orator Faneuil Hall, Boston, 1987. Fellow Woodrow Wilson Ctr., NEH; mem. Soc. Am. Historians, Cosmos Club. Democrat. Jewish. From 1982-84 directed the rsch. study which led to the creation of the Nat. Endowment for Democracy (NED). Home: 6021 Onondaga Rd Bethesda MD 20816 Office: Internat Found for Elections Sys 1101 15th Street NW Washington DC 20005

WEINSTEIN, ANDREW H. lawyer; b. Pitts., Oct. 5, 1943; s. Adolph J. and Meta I. (Schwarz) W.; m. Susan Balber, Aug. 11, 1968; children: Jodi L., Toby M., Jamie M. BSBA, Duquesne U., 1965; JD, U. Pitts., 1968; LLM in Taxation, NYU, 1969. Bar: Pa. 1969, U.S. Tax Ct. 1969, Fla. 1970, U.S. Dist. Ct. (so. dist.) Fla., U.S. Ct. Fed. Claims. Trial atty. IRS, L.A., 1969-70, Miami, Fla., 1970-73; ptnr. Glass, Schultz, Weinstein & Moss, Coral Gables, Fla., 1973-80, Holland & Knight, Miami, 1980—. Contbr. articles to profl. jours. Bd. dirs. New World Symphony, Miami, Zool. Soc. Fla. Fellow Am. Coll. Tax Counsel; mem. ABA (tax sect., bd. cert. tax law), ARC, Fla. Bar. Avocations: golf, travel. Office: Holland & Knight 701 Brickell Ave Ste 3000 Miami FL 33131-2898 Office Phone: 305-789-7755.

WEINSTEIN, BARRY ALAN, architect; b. Chgo., Oct. 31, 1943; s. Reuben and Dorothy (Weiss) W.; m. Margery Gail Spector, June 12, 1966; children: Scott Howard, Allison Beth. BArch, U. Ill., 1967. Architect-in-tng. C.F. Murphy Assocs., Chgo., 1967-69, Norman A. Koglin Assocs., Chgo., 1969-71; project mgr., tech. dir. R.M.M. Inc., Chgo., 1971-74; ptnr. Berger-Weinstein Assocs., Chgo., 1974-81; owner B. Weinstein Assocs., Chgo., 1981—. Instr. Harrington Inst. of Interior Design, Chgo., 1972-74, adj. prof. Triton Coll., 1988. Recipient Hon. award Am. Architecture State of the Art in the '80s, 1985. Mem.: BBB, AIA, ALA, Nat. Coun. Archtl. Registration Bds. Home and Office: 1166 Wade St Highland Park IL 60035-3451 Office Phone: 847-432-5183. Personal E-mail: bwa1166@comcast.net.

WEINSTEIN, EDWARD MICHAEL, architect, consultant; b. Bklyn., May 5, 1947; s. Hyman and Freda (Rochkes) W.; m. Melanie Jane Ross, June 22, 1969; children: Valerie, David. BS, CCNY, 1969. Registered architect; lic. N.Y., N.J. Jr. architect N.Y.C. Dept. Ports and Terminals, 1970-72, architect, 1972-75, sr. urban designer, 1975-80, dir. waterfront devel., 1980-84, asst. commr., 1984-87; pres. EMW Assocs., Hastings-On-Hudson, N.Y., 1984—; ptnr. The Hastings Design Group, Hastings-On-Hudson, 1987—2001; prin. Edward M. Weinstein, Planning and Architecture, 2001—02, Edward M. Weinstein, Architecture and Planning, P.C., 2002—. Adv. bd. Metro Marine Express Ltd., N.Y.C., 1989-91. Active Planning Bd., Hastings-on-Hudson, 1990-2000, Waterfront Ctr.; trustee Greenburgh Hebrew Ctr., Dobbs Ferry, N.Y., 1986-89, 92—; v.p. N.Y. Port Promotion Assn., N.Y.C., 1984-87; adv. com. on waterfront devel. N.Y. State Assembly; chair Village of Hastings-on-Hudson Waterfront Revitalization Com., 1999—. Recipient Gold Key award House Plan Assn., 1969. Mem. AIA, Am. Assn. Port Authority, N.Y. Soc. Architects, The Waterfront Ctr., CCNY Alumni Assn., Bklyn. Tech. H.S. Alumni Assn. (life), Am. Inst. of Cert. Planners, Mcpl. Art Soc. Democrat. Jewish. Avocations: tennis, art. Office: EMW Architecture and Planning PC 14 Spring St Hastings On Hudson NY 10706 Office Phone: 914-478-0800. E-mail: edward@emweinsteinpc.com.

WEINSTEIN, ELLEN, performing company executive; BFA in Dance, SUNY. Dancer Garden State Ballet, Savannah Ballet; tchr., choreographer Nat. Dance Inst., N.Y.C., 1985—89, assoc. artistic dir., 1989—94, artistic dir., 1995—. Cons. Nat. Dance Inst. Nat. Outreach Program. Choreographer (films) Disney, Polaroid's 50th Anniversary Celebration, Radio City Music Hall. Office: National Dance Institute 594 Broadway Rm 805 New York NY 10012

WEINSTEIN, GEORGE WILLIAM, retired ophthalmology educator; b. East Orange, N.J., Jan. 26, 1935; s. Henry J. and Irma C. (Klein) W.; m. Sheila Valerie Wohlreich, June 20, 1957; children: Bruce David, Elizabeth Joyce, Rachel Andrea. AB, U. Pa., 1955; MD, SUNY, Bklyn., 1959. Diplomate Am. Bd. Ophthalmology (bd. dirs. 1981-89). Intern then resident in ophthalmology Kings County Hosp., Bklyn., 1959-63; asst. prof. ophthalmology Johns Hopkins U., Balt., 1967-70; head ophthalmology dept. U. Tex., San Antonio, 1970-80; prof., Jane McDermott Shott chmn. W.Va. U., Morgantown, 1980-95, ret., 1999. Author: Key Facts in Ophthalmology, 1984; editor: Open Angle Glaucoma, 1986; editor Ophthalmic Surgery jour., 1971-81, Current Opinion in Ophthalmology jour., 1988—; contbr. articles to profl. jours. Served to lt. comdr. USPHS, 1963-65. Sr. Internat. fellow Fogarty Internat. Ctr. NIH, 1987. Mem. ACS (bd. govs. 1983-85, bd. regents 1987-92), Assn. Univ. Profs. Ophthalmology (pres. 1986-87, exec. v.p. 1994), Am. Acad. Ophthalmology (bd. dirs. 1980-92, chmn. long range planning com. 1986-89, pub. and profl. sec. 1983-89, pres.-elect 1990, pres. 1991, Honor award, Sr. Honor award), Alpha Omega Alpha (faculty 1987), Am. Ophthalmology Soc. (coun. 1992-97, chair 1996-97). Jewish. Avocations: jazz, banjo, photography, tennis, reading. Home: 1755 York Ave Apt 26B New York NY 10128-6872

WEINSTEIN, GERALD, former housing and building corporation executive; CFO Lefrak Orgn. Inc, Rego Park, N.Y., 1980-99, cons., 1999—. Office: Lefrak Organization Inc 97 77 Queens Blvd Rego Park NY 11374

WEINSTEIN, GERALD D. dermatology educator; b. N.Y.C., Oct. 13, 1936; m. Marcia Z. Weinstein; children: Jeff, Jon, Debbie. BA, U. Pa., 1957, MD, 1961. Diplomate Am. Bd. Dermatology. Intern Los Angeles County Gen. Hosp., 1961-62; clin. assoc. dermatology br. Nat. Cancer Instn. NIH, Bethesda, Md., 1962-64; resident dept. dermatology U. Miami, Fla., 1964-65; asst. prof. Dept. Dermatology U. Miami, Fla., 1966-71, assoc. prof., 1971-74, prof., 1975-79; prof., chmn. dept. dermatology U. Calif., Irvine, 1979—, acting dean Coll. Medicine, 1985-87. Attending staff VA Med. Ctr., Long Beach, Calif., 1979—, UCI Med. Ctr., Orange, Calif., 1979—, St. Joseph Hosp., Orange, 1980—. Contbr. articles to profl. jours., chpts. to books. Recipient Lifetime Achievement award Nat. Psoriasis Found., 1994; co-recipient award for psoriasis rsch. Taub Internat. Meml., 1971; NIH spl. postdoctoral fellow, 1965-67. Mem. Am. Acad. Dermatology (chmn. task force on psoriasis 1986—, bd. dirs. 1984-88). Office: U Calif Irvine Coll Medicine Dept Dermatology C340 Med Scis Bldg 1 Irvine CA 92697-0001

WEINSTEIN, HARRIS, lawyer; b. Providence, May 10, 1935; s. Joseph and Gertrude (Rusitzky) W.; m. Rosa Grunberg, June 3, 1956; children: Teme Ring, Joshua, Jacob. BS in Math., MIT, 1956, MS in Math., 1958; LLB, Columbia U., 1961. Bar: D.C. 1962. Law clk. to Judge William H. Hastie U.S. Ct. Appeals (3d cir.), Phila., 1961-62; with Covington & Burling, Washington, 1962-67, 69-90, 1993—; chief counsel Office of Thrift Supervision U.S. Dept. of Treasury, Washington, 1990-92; asst. to solicitor gen. U.S. Dept. Justice, 1967-69. Pub. mem. Adminstrv. Conf. of U.S., 1982-90; lectr. U. Va. Law Sch., 1996; mgmt. com. Undiscovered Mgrs., LLC, 1998-2001. V.p. Jewish Social Svc. Agy., 1995-98; mem. MIT Corp., 1989-95; bd. dirs. Jewish Cmty. Coun. of Greater Washington, 2004—. Mem. Nat. Press Club. Home: 7717 Georgetown Pike Mc Lean VA 22102-1411 Office: Covington & Burling 1201 Pennsylvania Ave NW Washington DC 20004

WEINSTEIN, HARVEY, film company executive, film producer; b. Buffalo, Mar. 19, 1952; s. Max and Miriam Weinstein. Co-chmn. (with Bob Weinstein) Miramax Films Corp., N.Y.C., 1979—. Dir. (films) Playing for Keeps (also writer), 1986, The Gnome's Great Adventure, 1987, Gandaharm, 1988; prodr. (films) The Burning, 1981, Deep End, 1985, Playing for Keeps, 1986, Shakespeare in Love, 1998 (Academy award best picture, 1998, Golden Globe award best picture, 1998, Golden Satellite award best picture, 1998, BAFTA award best picture, 1999), Malena, 2000, Gangs of New York, 2002; exec. prodr. (films) including Hardware, 1990, Strike It Rich, 1990, The Pope Must Die, 1991, Benefit of the Doubt, 1993, Map of the Human Heart, 1993, The Night We Never Met, 1993, The Hour of the Pig, 1993, Mother's Boys, 1994, The Road Killers, 1994, Pret-a-Porter, 1994, The Englishman Who Went Up a Hill But Came Down a Mountain, 1995, Things to Do in Denver When You're Dead, 1995, Smoke, 1995, The Crossing Guard, 1995, A Month by the Lake, 1995, Blue in the Face, 1995, Beautiful Girls, 1996, Flirting With Disaster, 1996, The Pallbearer, 1996, Emma, 1996, I Love You, I Love You Not, 1996, The Crow: City of Angels, 1996, The English Patient, 1996, Nightwatch, 1997, Addicted to Love, 1997, Robinson Crusoe, 1997, Air Bud, 1997, Cop Land, 1997, The Wings of the Dove, 1997, Good Will Hunting, 1997, Scream 2, 1997, Jackie Brown, 1997, Wishful Thinking, 1997, The Prophecy II, 1998, A Price Above Rubies, 1998, Phantoms, 1998, Senseless, 1998, Wide Awake, 1998, Ride, 1998, Velvet Goldmine, 1998, The Mighty, 1998, 54, 1998, Heaven, 1998, Rounders, 1998, Talk of Angels, 1998, The Faculty, 1998, She's All That, 1999, Teaching Mrs. Tingle, 1999, Mansfield Park, 1999, Music of the Heart, 1999, The Cider House Rules, 1999, Down to You, 2000, The Crow: The Salvation, 2000, Scream 3, 2000, Love's Labour's Lost, 2000, Reindeer Games, 2000, Scary Movie, 2000, Highlander: Endgame, 2000, Bounce, 2000, Chocolat, 2000, Dracula, 2000, Spy Kids, 2001, Texas Rangers, 2001, Daddy and Them, 2001, Scary Movie 2, 2001, The Others, 2001, Jay and Silent Bob Strike Back, 2001, The Lord of the Rings: The Fellowship of the Ring, 2001, Iris, 2001, The Shipping News, 2001, Kate & Leopold, 2001, Spy Kids 2: Island of Lost Dreams, 2002, Waking Up in Reno, 2002, The Lord of the Rings: The Two Towers, 2002, Chicago, 2002, Confessions of a Dangerous Mind, 2002, Spy Kids 3-D: Game Over, 2003, The Human Stain, 2003, Duplex, 2003, Kill Bill: Vol. 1, 2003, Scary Movie 3, 2003, Bad Santa, 2003, The Lord of the Rings: The Return of the King, 2003, Cold Mountain, 2003; co-exec. prodr. (films) including Scandal, 1989, The Lemon Sisters, 1990, Into the West, 1992, Pulp Fiction, 1994, Restoration, 1995, Jane Eyre, 1996, Scream, 1996, She's So Lovely, 1997, Mimic, 1997, Imposter, 2002; exec. prodr. (TV series) Clerks, 2000, Project Greenlight, 2001, Glory Days, 2002, Tokyo Pig, 2002; recipient BAFTA Britannia award (with Bob Weinstein, 1996, IFP Gotham Lifetime Achievement award (with Bob Weinstein), 1997. Office: Miramax Films Corp 375 Greenwich St Fl 4 New York NY 10013-2376*

WEINSTEIN, HELENE E. state legislator; b. N.Y.C., Sept. 6, 1952; BA, Am. Univ., 1973; JD, New Eng. Sch. Law, 1976. Assemblywoman dist. 41 N.Y. State Assembly, 1981—, chair standing assembly com. on judiciary, 1993—. Chair task force on women's issues N.Y. State Assembly, 1987-92, task force on food, farm & nutrition, 1987-88, ethics, ways and means, aging com., codes com., jud. com.; mem. facilities rev. bd. N.Y. State Ct. Mem. Legis. Women's Caucus, Bklyn. Women's Polit. Caucus, Jewish Women's Leadership Caucus. Mem. B'nai B'rith, Bklyn. Bar Assn. Home: 3520 Nostrand Ave Brooklyn NY 11229-5203 Office: NY State Capitol State Capital Albany NY 12207

WEINSTEIN, HERBERT, chemical engineer, educator; b. Bklyn., Mar. 10, 1933; s. Abraham and Pauline (Feldman) W.; m. Judith Cooper, Apr. 6, 1957; children: Michael Howard, Edward Marc, Ellen Rachel. B.Engring. in Chem. Engring, Coll. City N.Y., 1955; MS in Chem. Engring, Purdue U., 1957; PhD, Case Inst. Tech., 1963. Staff mem. Los Alamos Sci. Lab., 1956-58; research engr. NASA Lewis Research Center, Cleve., 1959-63; asst. prof. chem. engring. Ill. Inst. Tech., 1963-66, assoc. prof., 1966-72, prof., 1972-77; dir. Center for Biomed. Engring., 1973-77; prof. CUNY, 1977—, Herbert G. Kayser prof. of chem. engring., 1987—2003, dep. exec. officer PhD program, 2003—. Vis. rsch. assoc., mem. Med. Rsch. Inst. Michael Reese Hosp. and Med. Ctr., Chgo., 1965-77; vis. prof. mech. engring. Technion-Israel Inst. Tech., 1972-73; vis. prof. biomed. engring. Rush Med. Coll., Chgo., 1973-76; summer prof. Exxon Rsch. and Engring. Co., annually, 1981-92; Lady Davis vis. prof. Technion-Israel Inst. Tech., 1985; cons. to industry, rsch. labs. Mem.: Am. Inst. Chem. Engrs., Sigma Xi. Jewish. Achievements include research publs. and patents on fluidization, chem. reactor engring., fluid mechanics, biomed. engring. Office: CUNY Dept Chem Engring New York NY 10031 Business E-mail: weinstein@ccny.cuny.edu. E-mail: hweinst@chemail.engr.ccny.cuny.edu.

WEINSTEIN, I. BERNARD, oncologist, director, geneticist, educator; b. Madison, Wis., Sept. 9, 1930; married, 1952; 3 children. BS, U. Wis., 1952, MD, 1955, DSc (hon.), 1992. Nat. Cancer Inst. spl. rsch. fellow bacteriology/immunology Harvard Med. Sch./MIT, Boston, 1959-61; career scientist Health Rsch. Coun., City of N.Y., 1961-72; assoc. vis. physician Francis Delafield Hosp., 1961-66; from asst. attending physician to assoc. attending physician Presbyn. Hosp., 1967-81, attending physician, 1981—; from asst. to assoc. prof. medicine Columbia U. Coll. Phys. and Surg., N.Y.C., 1978-90; prof. medicine Columbia U., N.Y.C., 1973—, prof. pub. health, 1978—, prof. genetics and devel., 1990—, Frobe Jensen prof. medicine, 1990—, dir. comprehensive cancer ctr., 1985-96. Advisor Lung Cancer Segment, Carcinogenesis Program, Nat. Cancer Inst., 1971-74, Chem. and Molecular Biol. Segment, 1973-76; mem. interdisciplinary comm. program Smithsonian Inst., 1971-74, Pharmacology B Study Sect., NIH, 1971-75, numerous sci. and adv. coms. Nat. Cancer Inst., Am. Cancer Soc., 1976-88; advisor Roswell Park Meml. Inst., Buffalo, Brookhaven Nat. Lab., Divsn. Cancer Cause and Prevention, Nat. Cancer Inst., Coun. on Analysis and Projects, Am. Cancer Soc., Internat. Agy. for Rsch. on Cancer, WHO, Lyon, France; Nakasone vis. prof., Tokyo, 1987; GM Cancer Rsch. Found. vis. prof. Internat. Agy. Rsch. Cancer, Lyon, 1988; mem. adv. coun. Nat. Inst. Environ. Health Scis., 1995—; chmn. Bristol-Myers Squibb Cancer Awards, 1993-96; mem. adv. coun., GM Cancer Rsch. Found. Assoc. editor Cancer Rsch., 1973-76, 86-95, Jour. Environ. Pathology and Toxicology, 1977-84, Jour. Cellular Physiology, 1982-89, Oncogene, 1989-99, Clin. Cancer Rsch., 1998—. Named Louise Weissberger lectr., U. Rochester, 1981, Mary Ann Swetland lectr., Case Western Res. U., 1983, Daniel Laszlo Meml. lectr., Montefiore Med. Ctr., 1983, Samuel Kuna Disting. lectr., Rutgers U., 1985, Ester Langer lectr., U. Chgo., 1989, Harris Meml. lectr., MIT, 1989, Rufus Cole lectr., 1997, travel fellow, European Molecular Biology Orgn., 1970—71; recipient Meltzer medal, 1964, Clowes award, Am. Assn. Cancer Rsch., 1987, Silvio O. Conte award, Environ. Health Inst., 1990, Nakahara award, 1996, Anthony Dipple Carcinogenesis award, 2000, Disting. Achievement award, Am. Soc. Preventive Oncology, 2001, Am. Assn. Cancer Rsch./Am. Cancer Soc. award, 2001. Mem.: AAAS (coun. del. 1985—88), N.Y. Acad. Sci., Am. Soc. Clin. Investigation, Internat. Soc. Quantum Biology, Am. Soc. Microbiology, Am. Assn. Physicians, Am. Acad. Arts and Scis., Inst. Medicine/Nat. Acad. Sci., Am. Assn. Cancer Rsch. (pres. 1990—91). Achievements include research in cellular and molecular aspects of carcinogenesis, environmental carcinogenesis, molecular epidemiology, cancer prevention. Office: Cancer Ctr Columbia Univ 701 W 168th St New York NY 10032-2704 Office Phone: 212-305-6921. E-mail: ibw1@columbia.edu.

WEINSTEIN, JACK BERTRAND, federal judge; b. Wichita, Kans., Aug. 10, 1921; s. Harry Louis and Bessie Helen (Brodach) W.; m. Evelyn Horowitz, Oct. 10, 1946; children: Seth George, Michael David, Howard Lewis. BA, Bklyn. Coll., 1943; LLB, Columbia U., 1948; LLD (hon.), Bklyn. U., Yeshiva U., Albany U., Hofstra U., L.I. U., Yale U., NYU. Bar: N.Y. 1949. Assoc. Columbia Law Sch., 1948-49; law clk. N.Y. Ct. Appeals Judge Stanly H. Fuld, 1949-50; ptnr. William Rosenfeld, N.Y.C., 1950-52; mem. faculty Columbia Law Sch., 1952-67, prof. law, 1956-67, adj. prof., 1967-97; U.S. judge (Eastern Dist. N.Y.), 1967 93, chief judge, 1980-88; sr. judge Ea. Dist. N.Y., 1993—. Vis. prof. U. Tex., 1957, U. Colo., 1961, Harvard U., 1982, Georgetown U., 1991, Bklyn. Law Sch., 1988-97, others; counsel N.Y. Joint Legis. Com. Motor Vehicle Problems, 1952-54, State Sen. Seymour Halpern, 1952-54; reporter adv. com. practice and procedure N.Y. State Temp. Commn. Cts., 1955-58; adv. com. practice N.Y. Judicial Conf., 1963-66; adv. com. rules of evidence U.S. Jud. Conf., 1965-75, mem. com. jurisdiction, 1969-75, mem., 1983-86; mem. 2d Cir. Jud. Coun., 1982-88, U.S. Jud. Conf., 1983-86, others in past. Author: (with Morgan and Maquire) Cases and Materials on Evidence, 4th edit, 1965, (with Maguire, Chadbourne and Mansfield, 5th edit.), 1971, 6th edit., 1975, (with Mansfield, Abrams and Berger), 9th edit., 1997, (with Rosenberg) Cases and Materials on Civil Procedure, 1961, rev. edit, (with Smit), 1971, (with Smit, Rosenberg and Korn), 1976, (with Korn and Miller) New York Civil Procedure, 9 vols., rev. edit, 1966, Manual of New York Civil Procedure, 1967, Basic Problems of State and Federal Evidence, 1976, (with Berger) Weinstein's Evidence, 7 vols., 1967, rev. edit., 1993, Revising Rule Making Procedures, 1977, A New York Constitution Meeting Today's Needs and Tomorrow's Challenges, 1967, Disaster, A Legal Allegory, 1988, (with Greenawalt) Readings for Seminar on Equality and Law, 1979, (with Murphy) Readings for Seminar in Individual Rights in a Mass Society, 1990-91, (with Berger) Readings for Seminar in Science and Law, (with Feinberg) Mass Torts, 1992, 94, Individual Justice in Mass Litigation, 1995. Chmn. N.Y. Dem. adv. com. on Constl. Conv., 1955; bd. dirs. N.Y. Civil Liberties Union, 1956-62, Cardozo Sch. Law, Conf. on Jewish Social Studies, 1980-88; nat. adv. bd. Am. Jewish Congress, 1960-67, CARE, 1985-90, Fedn. Jewish Philanthropies, 1985-94; chmn. lay bd. Riverside Hosp. Adolescent Drug Users, 1954-55. Lt. USNR, 1943-46. Mem. ABA, N.Y. State Bar Assn., Assn.

of Bar of City of N.Y., Nassau County Bar Assn., Am. Law Inst., Soc. Pub. Tchrs. Law (Eng.), Am. Acad. Arts and Scis. Jewish. Office: US Dist Ct US Courthouse 225 Cadman Plz E Brooklyn NY 11201-1818

WEINSTEIN, JAY A. social science educator, researcher; b. Chgo., Feb. 23, 1942; s. Lawrence E. and Jacqueline L. (Caplan) W.; m. Diana S. Staffin, Sept. 16, 1961; m. Marilyn L. Schwartz, Nov. 25, 1972; children— Liza, Bennett. AB, U. Ill., 1963, PhD, 1973; MA, Washington U., St. Louis, 1965. Teaching fellow U. Ill., Urbana, 1963-64; teaching asst. McGill U., Montreal, Que., Can., 1966-68; instr. Sir George Williams U., Montreal, Que., Can., 1967-68; lectr. Simon Fraser U., Vancouver, B.C., Can., 1968; asst. prof. North Central Coll., Naperville, Ill., 1970-71, U. Iowa, 1973-77; prof. social sci. Ga. Inst. Tech., Atlanta, 1977-86; head dept. sociology Eastern Mich. U., 1986-90, 2004—, faculty rsch. fellow, 1990-91; grantee ednl. devel. project USIA-Soros Found., Albania, 1992—; dir. Applied Rsch. Unit, 1996—. Cons. World Bank Study Social and Econ. Vulnerability in Albania, 1997, World Bank Study on Closing the Vulnerability Gap, Albania, 1997—98; project dir. Ea. Mich.-U-Ypsilanti Cmty. Outreach Partnership Ctr.; cons. pvt. and pub. agencies; rschr. in field. Author: Madras: An Analysis of Urban Ecological Structure in India, 1974, Demographic Transition and Social Change, 1976, Sociology-Technology: Foundations of Postacademic Social Science, 1982, The Grammar of Social Relations: The Major Essays of Louis Schneider, 1984; editor: Paradox and Society, 1986; (with Vinod Tewari and V.L.S. Prakash Rao) Indian Cities: Ecological Perspectives, Social and Cultural Change: Social Science for a Dynamic World, 1997, 1987, The Holocaust: A Sociological Analysis, 1997, Demography: The Science of Population, 2000; Studies in Comparative International Development, 1978-88; mem. editorial bd. Social Development Issues, 1977-85; specialized contbr. Calcutta Mcpl. Gazette, 1979—; editor: Social and Cultural Change, 1974-75; ed. Michigan Soc. Review, 1997—, editorial reviewer Jour. Asian Studies, Social Devel. Issues, Tech. and Culture, Am. Sociologist, Technol. Forecasting and Social Change; contbr. chpts. to book, articles to profl. jours. Recipient Charles Horton Cooley award for outstanding contbns. to sociology in Mich., 1998; Fulbright prof. Ahmedabad, India, 1975-76, Hyderabad, India, 1981-82; grantee Ga. Tech. Found., 1981-82, World Order Studies Course, 1994-97, State of Mich. Rsch. Excellence Fund; Steinberg fellow, 1967. Mem. Am. Sociol. Assn., Soc. for Applied Sociology (v.p. 1998-99), mem. exec. bd. 2000, pres. 2002-03), Mich. Sociol. Assn. (pres. 1988-89, v.p. 1994-95), Sigma Xi. Jewish. Office: Eastern Mich U Sociology Dept Ypsilanti MI 48197 Office Phone: 734-487-0012. E-mail: weinst@aol.com., jay.weinstein@emich.edu.

WEINSTEIN, JOYCE, artist; b. June 7, 1931; d. Sidney and Rose (Bier) W.; m. Stanley Boxer, Nov. 28, 1952. Student, CCNY, 1948-50, Art Students League, 1948-52. Exec. coord. Women in Arts Found., Inc., 1975-79, 81-82, coord. bd., 1983-87. One-person shows include Perdalma Gallery, N.Y.C., 1953-56, L.I. U., Bklyn., 1969, U. Calif.-Santa Cruz, 1969, T. Bortolazzo Gallery, Santa Barbara, Calif., 1972, Dorsky Gallery, N.Y.C., 1972, 74, Galerie Ariadne, N.Y.C., 1975, Gloria Cortella Gallery, N.Y.C., 1976, Meredith Long Contemporary Gallery, N.Y.C., 1978, 79, 88-90, Martin Gerard Gallery, Edmonton, Alta., Can., 1981, 82, 84, Galerie Wentzel, Cologne, Fed. Republic of Germany, 1982, 87, Haber Theodore Gallery, N.Y.C., 1983, 95, Gallery One, Toronto, Ont., Can., 1983, 2002, Paul Kuhn Gallery, Calgary, 1985, Eva Cohn Gallery, Highland Park, Ill., 1985, Meredith Long & Co., Houston, 1988, 90, Alena Adlung Gallery, N.Y.C., 1989, Flanders Art Gallery, Mpls., 1999 Harmon-Meek Gallery, Naples, Fla., 2000, Gallery One, Toronto, 2002; exhibited in group shows at Marlborough Gallery, N.Y.C., 1968, Bula Mus. Art, Calcutta, India, 1970, Phoenix Gallery, N.Y.C., 1988, Provident Nat. Bank, 1988, Alena Adlung Gallery, 1989, 90, Edmonton Art Mus., 1975, 77, 83, 85, 89, Rose Fried Gallery, N.Y.C., 1970, Hudson River Mus., 1971, Dorsky Gallery, 1972, 94, Suffolk Mus., Stony Brook, N.Y., 1972, N.Y. Cultural Ctr., 1973, Stamford (Conn.) Mus., 1973, Landmark Gallery, N.Y.C., 1974, Women's Interart Ctr., N.Y.C., 1974, 75, 78, New Sch. Social Rsch., N.Y.C., 1975, Bklyn. Mus., 1975, Galerie Ariadne, 1975, Mus. of Modern Art, N.Y.C., 1981, The Queens Mus. N.Y., 1984, The Centre de Creacio Contemporania, Barcelona, Spain, 1987, Fairleigh Dickinson U., Hackensack, N.J., 1976, Gloria Cortella, Inc., 1976, Northeastern U., Boston, 1977, Lehigh (Pa.) U., 1977, Meredith Long Contemporary Gallery, 1977, 78, 79, 80, Galerie Wentzel, 1981-85, Martin Gerard Gallery, 1981-84, Gallery One, 1983, 84, Haber Theodore Gallery, 1982-85, Jerald Melberg Gallery, Charlotte, N.C., 1984, Richard Green Gallery, N.Y.C., 1986, Rosel Art Fair, Basel Switzerland, 1986, Meredith Long & Co., 1988-90, Broome St. Gallery, N.Y.C., 1991, 97, Andre Zarre Gallery, N.Y.C., 1990, Cork Gallery, N.Y.C., 1990, Chgo. Internat. Art Exbn., 1990, Queens Coll., N.Y.C., 1991, Miami Art Fair, 1993, Bklyn. Botanic Gardens, 1994, Dorothy Blau Gallery, Bay Harbor Islands, Fla., 1997-98, Harmon-Meek Gallery, Naples, Fla., 1998-99, Flanders Contemporary Art, Mpls., 1999, Hubert Gallery, N.Y.C., 2003; represented in permanent collections: Pa. Acad. Fine Arts, N.J. State Mus., Ciba-Geigy Corp., New Sch. Social Rsch., Bula Mus. Art, U. Calif., Mus. Modern Art, N.Y.C., McMullen Gallery, Edmonton, Ga., De Spisset Mus., U. Santa Clara, Edmonton Art Gallery Mus., The Hines Collection, Boston, others; represented by Smith Anderson Gallery, Palo Alto, Calif., Flanders Art Gallery, Harmon-Meek Gallery, Naples, Fla., Flanders Contemporary Art, Mpls., Dorothy Blau Gallery, Bay Harbor Island, Fla., Gallery One, Toronto. Recipient Lambert Fund award Pa. Acad. Fine Arts, 1955, Susan B. Anthony award NOW, 1983. Home: 46 Fox Hill Rd Ancramdale NY 12503-5311 Office Phone: 518-329-0614. E-mail: weinsteinjoyce@aol.com.

WEINSTEIN, MARTA, packaging services company executive; Founder iLogistix (formerly Logistix), Fremont, Calif., 1984—, co-chair, 1998—.

WEINSTEIN, MARTIN, aerospace manufacturing executive, materials scientist; b. Mar. 3, 1936; s. Benjamin and Dora (Lemo) W.; m. Sandra Rebecca Yaffie, June 5, 1961; children: Hilary Ann, Sarah Elizabeth, Joshua Aaron. BS in Metals Engring., Rensselaer Poly. Inst., 1957; MS, MIT, 1960, PhD, 1961. Mgr. materials sci. Tycolabs., Waltham, Mass., 1961-69; tech. dir. turbine support divsn. Chromalloy Am. Corp., San Antonio, 1968-71, v.p., asst. gen. mgr., 1971-74, pres., 1975-79, Chromalloy Compressor Techs., San Antonio, 1979-82; group pres. Chromalloy Gas Turbine, San Antonio, 1982-86, chmn., CEO N.Y.C., 1986—; vice chmn., exec. officer SEQUA Corp., N.Y.C., 2004—. Supervisory mng. dir. Turbine Support Europe, Tilburg, Netherlands, 1975—; bd. dirs. Turbine Support Thailand, Bankok, Chromalloy U.K., Nottingham, Eng., Internat. Coating Co., Tokyo, Japan, Chromalloy, France, Malichaud Orleans, France. Patentee diffusion coating of jet engine materials; contbr. articles to profl. jours. Bd. dirs. Jewish Fedn., 1981-85, Chamber Players of San Antonio, 1979-83, NCCJ, 1982-85, Sequa Corp., N.Y.C., 1999—, vice chmn., exec. officer, 2004; mem. vis. com. dept. metallurgy and materials sci. MIT, 1992-2001. Recipient Turner Meml. award Electrochem. Soc., 1963, Achievement award NASA, 1963; Am. Iron and Steel Inst. fellow, 1960. Mem. Am. Soc. Metals, Am. Inst. Metall. Engrs., N.Y. Acad. Sci., Sigma Xi. Home: 111 Sheffield San Antonio TX 78213-2626 Office: Chromalloy Gas Turbine Corp 200 Park Ave New York NY 10166-0005 E-mail: mw@chronalloy.com.

WEINSTEIN, MELVIN PHILLIP, physician educator; b. Long Branch, N.J., Apr. 27, 1944; s. Joseph and Selma Joyce (Nathanson) W.; m. Dustra Lee Anderson, July 13, 1969; children: Joanna Lee, Michael Jacob. BA in Zoology with distinction, Rutgers U., 1966; MD, George Washington U., 1970. Diplomate Nat. Bd. Med. Examiners, Am. Bd. Internal Medicine, Am. Bd. Infectious Diseases, Am. Bd. Pathology (Med. Microbiology). Intern Hartford (Conn.) Hosp., 1970-71, resident, 1973-75; fellow in infectious diseases U. Colo. Health Sci. Ctr., Denver, 1975-77, fellow in clin. microbiology, 1983; asst. prof. medicine U. Medicine and Dentistry N.J., New Brunswick, 1977-83, assoc. prof. medicine and pathology, 1983-91, prof. medicine and pathology, 1991—; staff Robert Wood Johnson U. Hosp., New Brunswick, 1977—. Cons. staff St. Peter's U. Hosp., 1998—; cons. Roosevelt Hosp., Edison, N.J., 1986-89; vis. assoc. prof. Rutgers U., New Brunswick, 1986-98; vis. prof. Rutgers U. Coll. Pharmacy, 1998—; trustee Am. Bd. Med. Microbiology, Washington, 1991-97; mem. area com. on microbiology, 1997-2003, mem. subcom. antimicrobial susceptibility testing Nat. Com. Clin. Lab. Stds., Wayne, Pa., 1993—, vice chair area com. on microbiology, 1998-2002; dir. Microbiology Lab., Robert Wood Johnson U. Hosp., New Brunswick, 1983—, HIV-Antibody Counselling and Testing Svc., 1985-87, 91—; chief divsn. of allergy, immunology and infectious diseases Robert Wood Johnson Med. Sch., 2001—; lectr. in field. Mem. editl. bd. Jour. Clin. Microbiology, 1984-99, Am. Jour. Infection Control, 1987-2000, Diagnostic Microbiology and Infectious Disease, 1989—, Clin. Microbiol. Rev., 2002-; sect. editor Clin. Infectious Diseases, Manual Clin. Microbiology, 8th and 9th edit.; contbr. chpts. to books, articles to profl. jours. Comdr. USPHS, 1971-73. Henry Rutgers Rsch. fellow, 1965-66. Fellow ACP, Infectious Diseases Soc. Am., Am. Acad. Microbiology; mem. Am. Fedn. Clin. Rsch., Am. Soc. Microbiology, Soc. Hosp. Epidemiologists Am., N.J. Infectious Disease Soc. (founding mem.), Alpha Omega Alpha. Avocation: golf. Office: Robert Wood Johnson Med Sch 1 Robert Wood Johnson Pl New Brunswick NJ 08901-1928 Office Phone: 732-235-7713.

WEINSTEIN, MICHAEL ALAN, political science educator; b. Bklyn., Aug. 24, 1942; s. Aaron and Grace (Sosin) W.; m. Deena Schneiweiss, May 31, 1964. BA summa cum laude, NYU, 1964; MA in Polit. Sci., Case Western Res. U., 1965, PhD, 1967. Asst. prof. polit. sci. Case Western Res. U., summer 1967, Va. Poly. Inst., 1967-68; asst. prof. Purdue U., 1968-70, assoc. prof., 1970-72, prof., 1972—; Milward Simpson disting. prof. polit. sci. U. Wyo., 1979. Author: (with Deena Weinstein) Living Sociology, 1974, The Polarity of Mexican Thought, 1976, The Tragic Sense of Political Life, 1977, Meaning and Appreciation, 1978, The Structure of Human Life, 1979, The Wilderness and the City, 1982, Unity and Variety in the Philosophy of Samuel Alexander, 1984, Finite Perfection, 1985, Culture Critique: Fernand Dumont and New Quebec Sociology, 1985, (with Helmut Loiskandl and Deena Weinstein) Georg Simmel's Scopenhauer and Nietzsche, 1986; (with Deena Weinstein) Deconstruction as Cultural History/The Cultural History of Deconstruction, 1990, La Déconstruction un Jeu Symbolique, 1990, (with Deena Weinstein) Georg Simmel: Sociological Flãmeur/Bricoleur, 1991, Photographic Realism as a Moral Practice, 1992, (with Deena Weinstein) Postmodern(ized) Simmel, 1993, (with Arthur Kroker) Data Trash: The Theory of the Virtual Class, 1994, Culture/Flesh: Explorations of Postcivilized Modernity, 1995, Peter Vierecki Reconciliation and Beyond, 1997, East/West: Globalizing Civilization, 2000, (with Deena Weinstein) Hail to the Shrub: Mediating the President, 2002; artist in residence Columbia Coll., 2002; mem. editl. bd. Humanitas, Social Philosophy Rsch. Book Series. Recipient Best Paper prize Midwest Polit. Sci. Assn., 1969; Guggenheim fellow, 1974-75; Rockefeller Found. humanities fellow, 1976; fellow Center Humanistic Studies, Purdue U., 1981, Lily Endowment Tchg. grant, 2001. Mem. Phi Beta Kappa. Home: 800 Princess Dr West Lafayette IN 47906-2038 Office: Dept Polit Sci Purdue U West Lafayette IN 47907 *And which is worse, to be arbitrary or to be contradictory? I have attempted to be the most consistent rationalist of all by refusing to harmonize what is irreconcilable in the name of reason.*

WEINSTEIN, MILTON CHARLES, health policy educator, decision scientist; b. Brookline, Mass., July 14, 1949; s. William and Ethel (Rosenbloom) W.; m. Rhonda Kruger, June 14, 1970; children: Jeffrey William, Daniel Jay. AB, AM, Harvard U., 1970, MPP, 1972, PhD, 1973. Asst. prof. John F. Kennedy Sch. Govt., Harvard U., Cambridge, Mass., 1973-76, assoc. prof., 1976-80; prof. policy and decision scis. Harvard Sch. Pub. Health, Boston, 1980-86, Henry J. Kaiser prof. health policy and mgmt., 1986—; prof. medicine Harvard Med. Sch., Boston, 1992—; v.p. Innovus Rsch. Inc., Medford, Mass., 1998—. Adj. prof. cmty. and family medicine Dartmouth Med. Sch., Hanover, N.H., 1981-87; vis. lectr. Intermountain Health Care, Salt Lake City, 1997—; cons. U.S. Office Tech. Assessment, 1979-87, HHS, 1979—, VA, 1984-86, EPA, 1983—, Smith Kline and French, 1984-87, Ciba-Geigy, 1987-98, New Eng. Med. Ctr., 1986-87, Intermountain Health Care, 1987—, Bristol Myers-Squibb, 1989-92, E.I. Dupont de Nemours Co., 1989-91, Schering-Plough Corp., 1991-98, Hoechst Marion Roussel, 1992-98, Pharmacia and Upjohn, Inc., 1992-98, Berlex Corp., 1992-98, Fournier Rsch., 1998; mem. adult treatment panel Nat. Cholesterol Edn. Program, NIH; co-chair Panel on Cost-Effectiveness in Health and Medicine, USPHS, 1993-96. Author: Clinical Decision Analysis, 1980, Hypertension: A Policy Perspective, 1976, Cost-Effectiveness in Health and Medicine, 1996, Decision Making in Health and Medicine, 2001; mem. editl. bd. Med. Decision Making, 1981-94, Jour. Environ. Econs. and Mgmt., 1986-88, Jour. Clin. Oncology, 1996-99; assoc. editor Med. Decision Making, 1994-2001. NSF fellow, 1972. Mem. Inst. Ops. Rsch. Mgmt. Scis., Inst. Medicine of NAS (com. on priorities for new vaccine devel., com. to evaluate the NIH artificial heart program), Soc. Med. Decision Making (trustee 1980-82, pres. 1984-85), Internat. Health Econs. Assn., Soc. Risk Analysis, Internat. Soc. Tech. Assessment in Health Care, Internat. Soc. Pharmacoens. and Outcomes Rsch., Am. Med. Joggers Assn., U.S. Speedskating (bd. dirs. 1996-2000), Phi Beta Kappa. Office: Harvard U Sch Pub Health Ctr for Risk Analysis 718 Huntington Ave Fl 2 Boston MA 02115-5924

WEINSTEIN, ROBERT, film company executive; b. Buffalo, 1953; m. Annie Clayton, 2000. Co-founder, co-chmn. (with Harvey Weinstein) Miramax Films Corp., NYC, 1979—. Prodr. (films) Playing for Keeps (also dir.), 1986, Gandahar, 1988, Mimic, 1997, Reindeer Games, 2000; exec. prodr. (films) Hardware, 1990, Strike It Rich, 1990, The Pope Must Die, 1991, Into the West, 1992, Benefit of the Doubt, 1993, Map of the Human Heart, 1993, The Night We Never Met, 1993, True Romance, 1993, Hour of the Pig, 1993, Mother's Boys, 1994, Road Killers, 1994, Prêt-à-Porter, 1994, The Englishman Who Went Up a Hill But Came Down a Mountain, 1995, Things to Do in Denver When You're Dead, 1995, Smoke, 1995, The Crossing Guard, 1995, A Month by the Lake, 1995, The Journey of August King, 1995, Blue in the Face, 1995, Beautiful Girls, 1996, Flirting with Disaster, 1996, The Pallbearer, 1996, Emma, 1996, I Love You, I Love You Not, 1996, The Crow: City of Angels, 1996, The English Patient, 1996, Scream, 1996, Sono pazzo di Iris Blond, 1996, Nightwatch, 1997, Addicted to Love, 1997, Robinson Crusoe, 1997, Mononoke-hime, 1997, Air Bud, 1997, Cop Land, 1997, Wings of the Dove, 1997, Good Will Hunting, 1997, Scream 2, 1997, Jackie Brown, 1997, Wishful Thinking, 1997, A Price Above Rubies, 1998, Phantoms, 1998, Senseless, 1998, Wide Awake, 1998, Ride, 1998, Velvet Goldmine, 1998, The Mighty, 1998, 54, 1998, Heaven, 1998, Rounders, 1998, Talk of Angels, 1998, The Faculty, 1998, Shakespeare in Love, 1998, Playing by Heart, 1998, She's All That, 1999, Guinevere, 1999, My Life So Far, 1999, Teaching Mrs. Tingle, 1999, Outside Providence, 1999, In Too Deep, 1999, Mansfield Park, 1999, Holy Smoke, 1999, Music of the Heart, 1999, Cider House Rules, 1999, Allied Forces, 1999, Down to You, 2000, Committed, 2000, The Crow: Salvation, 2000, Scream 3, 2000, Love's Labour's Lost, 2000, Takedown, 2000, The Yards, 2000, Boys and Girls, 2000, Scary Movie, 2000, Highlander: Endgame, 2000, Backstage, 2000, Malèna, 2000, Bounce, 2000, Chocolat, Dracula 2000, 2000, Spy Kids, 2001, Texas Rangers, 2001, Daddy and Them, 2001, Scary Movie 2, 2001, The Others, 2001, Shu shan zheng zhuan, 2001, Jay and Silent Bob Strike Back, 2001, Lord of the Rings: The Fellowship of the Ring, 2001, Shipping News, 2001, Kate & Leopold, 2001, Only the Strong Survive, 2002, Full Frontal, 2002, Spy Kids 2: Island of Lost Dreams, 2002, Below, 2002, Equilibrium, 2002, Waking Up in Reno, 2002, Lord of the Rings: The Two Towers, 2002, Gangs of New York, 2002, Chicago, 2002, Confessions of a Dangerous Mind, 2002, Spy Kids 3-D: Game Over, 2003, The Human Stain, 2003, Duplex, 2003, Kill Bill: Vol. 1, 2003, Scary Movie 3, 2003, Bad Santa, 2003, Lord of the Rings: The Return of the King, 2003, Cold Mountain, 2003, Ella Enchanted, 2004, Kill Bill: Vol. 2, 2004, Fahrenheit 9/11, 2004; co-exec. prodr. (films) Scandal, 1989, The Lemon Sisters, 1990, The Big Man, 1990, Dust Devil, 1992, Pulp Fiction, 1994, Victory, 1995, Jane Eyre, 1996, She's So Lovely, 1997, Halloween H20: 20 Years Later, 1998, B. Monkey, 1998, Halloween: Resurrection, 2002; prodr. (TV series) The Real Magees, 1973, Wasteland, 1999, Clerks, 2000, Project Greenlight, 2001, Glory Days, 2002, Tokyo Pig, 2002. Office: Miramax Films Corp 375 Greenwich St Fl 4 New York NY 10013-2376*

WEINSTEIN, ROBERT, hematologist, researcher; b. Bklyn., Aug. 10, 1949; s. Rachel Weinstein, George Weinstein; m. Brenda Leigh Laufs; children: Rebecca, Jessica. MD, NYU, 1975. Dir. Non-Invasive Vascular Lab. Caritas St. Elizabeth's MedCtr. of of Boston, 1987—96, chief hematology and transfusion medicine, 1994—. Mem. med. adv. com. ARC Blood Svcs. New Eng. Region, Dedham, Mass., 2000—. Co-editor: Apheresis, Principles and Practice, 1997 (Morton-Grove Rasmussen award Mass Assn. Blood Banks, 2000); editor-in-chief: Jour Clin. Apheresis, 2004—. Pres. Temple Beth Avodah, Newton Centre, Mass., 2000—02. Mem.: Mass. Med. Soc. (com. on stransusion medicine 1998—), Am. Soc. Hematology (chmn. com. on practice 2004—), Am. Assn. Blood Banks (chair hemapheresis com. 2001—03), Am. Soc. for Apheresis (pres. 1999—2000). Jewish. Office: Caritas St Elizabeths Med Ctr Boston 736 Cambridge St MMR 3 HEM Boston MA 02135 Office Phone: 617-789-3081. Office Fax: 617-789-3349. Business E-Mail: Robert_Weinstein_MD@cchcs.org.

WEINSTEIN, ROY, physics educator, researcher; b. N.Y.C., Apr. 21, 1927; s. Harry and Lillian (Ehrenberg) W.; m. Janet E. Spiller, Mar. 26, 1954 (dec. 1995); children: Lee Davis, Sara Lynn; m. Gail A. Birdsell, July 26, 1996. BS, MIT, 1951, PhD, 1954; ScD (hon.), Lycoming Coll., 1981. Rsch. asst. Mass. Inst. Tech., 1951-54, asst. prof., 1956-59, Brandeis U., Waltham, Mass., 1954-56; assoc. prof. Northeastern U., Boston, 1960-63, prof. physics, 1963-82, exec. officer, chmn. grad. div. of physics dept., 1967-69, chmn. physics dept., 1974-81; spokesman MAC Detector Stanford U., 1981-82; dean Coll. Natural Scis. and Math. U. Houston, 1982-88; prof. physics, 1982—; dir. Inst. Beam Particle Dynamics U. Houston, 1985-95; assoc. dir., spokesman Tex. Ctr. for Superconductivity, 1987-89. Vis. scholar and physicist Stanford (Calif.) U., 1966-67, 81-82; bd. dirs. Perception Tech., Inc., Winchester, Mass., Omniwave Inc., Gloucester, Mass., Wincom Inc., Woburn, Mass.; cons. Visidyne Inc., Burlington, Mass., Houston Area Rsch. Ctr., Stanford U., Hodotector Inc., Houston, Park Square Engring., Marietta, Ga., Harvard U., Cambridge, Mass., Cambridge Electron Accelerator, mem. adv. com., 1967-69; adv. com. and portfolio evaluation com. Houston Venture Ptnrs., 1990-99; chmn. bd. dirs. Xytron Corp., 1986-91; dir., mem. exec. com. Houston Area Rsch. Ctr., 1984-87; chmn. organizing com. Internat. Conf. on Meson Spectroscopy, 1974, chmn. program com., 1977, mem. organizing com., 1980; chmn. mgmt. group Tex. Accelerator Ctr., Woodlands, 1985-90; chmn. Tex. High Energy Physicists, 1989-91; keynote spkr. MIT Alumni series, 1988; permanent mem. exec. com. Large Vol. Detector (Underground Neutrino Telescope, Italy), 1988—; organizer session High Temperature Superconducting Magnets 3d and 4th World Congress on Superconductivity, Munich, 1993, Orlando, 1994. Author: Atomic Physics, 1964, Nuclear Physics, 1964, Interactions of Radiation and Matter, 1964; editor: Nuclear Reactor Theory, 1964, Nuclear Materials, 1964; editor procs.: 5th Internat. Conf. on Mesons, 1977; contbr. over 200 articles to profl. jours. Active Lexington (Mass.) Town Meeting, 1973-84; vice chmn. Lexington Coun. on Aging, 1977-83. With USNR, 1945-46. Recipient Founders award World Congress Superconductivity, 1988, Materials/Devices award Internat. Superconductivity Technology Ctr., Japan, and Materials Rsch. Soc., U.S., 1995, High Current award, 1997, Excellence award for great achievements in the field of bulk superconducting materials Internat. Program Com. Processing and Applications of Large Superconducting Rare Earth Grains Worshop, 1999, NSF Rsch. awards, 1961-96, Tex. Rsch. award, 1986-87, 90—, U.S. Dept. Energy award 1974, 77, 87-97, NASA award, 1990-98, ARO award, 1994—, Elec. Power Rsch. Inst. award, 1990-95, Welch Found. award, 1997—, Nat. Cancer Inst. award, 2000—; NSF fellow Bohr Inst., Copenhagen, 1959-60, Stanford U. 1969-70, Guggenheim fellow Harvard U., 1970-71. Fellow Am. Phys. Soc. (organizer session SSC and High Energy Physics 1984); mem. Am. Assn. Physics Tchrs., Masons, Sigma Xi, Phi Kappa Phi (chpt. pres. 1977-79, Nat. Triennial Disting. Scholar prize 1980-83), Pi Lambda Phi (pres. Theta chpt. 1949-50). Unitarian Universalist. Achievements include measurement of fine structure of positronium; first measurement of rho meson coupling to gamma rays, of phi meson decay to two muons; early observation of break down in SU3 symmetry; demonstration of electron-muon universality, discovery of non-applicability of Lorentz contraction to length measured by a single observer; disproof of splitting of A2 meson; independent discovery of upsilon meson (bottom quark); achievement of highest magnetic field for any permanent magnet, in YBa2Cu307, 10.1 Tesla; achievement of highest current density in textured superconductor, 0.3 megA/cm2. Home: 4368 Fiesta Ln Houston TX 77004-6603 Office: U Houston IBPD 632 SR1 Houston TX 77204-5005

WEINSTEIN, SIDNEY, retired university program director; b. N.Y.C., July 1, 1920; s. Jacob and Yetta W.; m. Celia Kahn, Mar. 6, 1943 (dec.); children: Risa, Jeri; m. Florence Landau, June 21, 1988. BA, Bklyn. Coll., 1951; MA, Columbia U., 1955; DPA, Indsl. Coll. Armed Forces, 1964. Contract adminstr. U.S. Corps Engrs., 1941-43; mgmt. analyst Dept. Army, N.Y.C., 1946-55; dir. data processing procurement GSA, 1956-68, dep. asst. commr. automated data mgmt. services, 1968-72, asst. commr. automated data and telecommunications, 1972-75; exec. dir. Assn. Computing Machinery, N.Y.C., 1975-85; assoc. prof., dir. affiliates program Ctr. Research Info. Systems, Leonard N. Stern. Sch. Bus. NYU, 1985-99, ret., 1999. Cons. to chmn. U.S. CSC Served with USAF, 1943-46. Recipient Exceptional service award U.S. Govt., 1975 Mem. ABA (arbitrator 1989—), Coun. Engring. and Sci. Soc. Execs. (dir.), N.Y. Soc. Assn. Execs., Assn. Indsl. Coll. Armed Forces, Assn. Fed. Execs. Inst., Assn. Computing Machinery, Soc. Info. Mgmt. Home: 360 E 72nd St New York NY 10021-4753 E-mail: s_weinstein@msn.com.

WEINSTEIN, SIDNEY, neuropsychologist; b. Apr. 27, 1922; s. Celia (Schneider) W.; children: Curt, Karen, Laura; m. Margaret Carla Diamond, July 28, 1968; children: Ethan, Ari. BS, CCNY, 1949; MA in Exptl. Psychology, NYU, 1950, PhD in Physiol. Psychology, 1952. Lic. psychologist, N.Y., Conn. Dir. neuropsychol. lab., rsch. assoc. prof. Albert Einstein Coll. Medicine, N.Y.C., 1958-66, rsch. asst. prof. dept. neurology, 1958-60, rsch. assoc. prof. dept. neurology, 1960-66; rsch. assoc. neuropsychology Bronx Mcpl. Hosp. Ctr., 1958-66; pres. NeuroCommunication Rsch. Labs., Inc., Danbury, Conn., 1974-77, CEO, 1977—. Vis. assoc. prof. NYU, 1958-64, adj. clin. prof. dept. neurology, 1975—; vis. assoc. prof. Yeshiva U., 1960-67; adj. prof. CUNY, 1966—; lectr. Mt. Sinai Sch. Medicine, 1966—; prof. dept. pediat. N.Y. Med. Coll., N.Y.C., 1967-80, prof., dir. neuropsychol. lab. N.Y. Med. Coll.-Flower and Fifth Ave. Hosps., 1967-73. Author: (with others) Somatosensory Changes After Penetrating Brain Wounds in Man, 1960; The Neuropsychology of Alcohol Ingestion, 1970; editor-in-chief Internat. Jour. Neuroscience; editor Neuroscience Monographs; contbr. articles to profl. jours. Bd. dirs. Neuropsychol. Rsch. Found., Danbury, 1974—. Decorated knight of honor and merit Imperial Order St. John Jerusalem Ecumenical. Mem. AAAS, APA (pres. divsn. physiol. and comparative psychology 1963), Internat. Coun. Psychologists; mem. AAUP, Eastern Psychol. Assn., Soc. Cosmetic Chemists, Am. Acad. Neurology, Psychonomic Soc., Acad. Aphasia (bd. govs. 1966-70), Internat. Neuropsychol. Soc. (bd. govs. 1980-82), Soc. Rsch. Child Devel., Assn. Am. Med. Colls., European Brain and Behavior Soc. (charter), Soc. Neuroscience (charter), Soc. Psychophysiol. Rsch., Internat. Soc. Bioengineering and Skin, Dermal Clin. Evaluation Soc. (charter), Conn. Pyschol. Assn., N.Y. Acad. Scis., N.Y. State Psychol. Assn. (mem. divsn. exec. com. 1965-68), N.Y. Brain Function Group (charter, scribe 1964), Sigma Xi, Psi Chi. Address: 2300 Cherry Laurel Ln Chapel Hill NC 27516-8306

WEINSTEIN, STANLEY, Buddhist studies educator; b. Bklyn., Nov. 13, 1929; s. Louis Arthur and Ruth (Appleson) W.; m. Lucie Ruth Krebs, Sept. 23, 1951; 1 son, David Eli. BA, Komazawa U., Tokyo, 1954-58; MA, U. Tokyo, 1960; PhD, Harvard U., 1966; MAH (hon.), Yale U., 1974. Lectr. Sch. Oriental and African Studies, London, 1962-68; assoc. prof. Buddhist studies Yale U., New Haven, 1968-74, prof., 1974—2003, prof. emeritus, 2003—, chmn. coun. East Asian studies, 1982-85. Author: Buddhism under T'ang, 1987. Served with U.S. Army, 1952-54. Ford Found. fgn. area fellow, 1958-62; NEH sr. fellow, 1974-75 Mem. Am. Oriental Soc., Assn. Asian Studies Home: 270 Ridgewood Ave Hamden CT 06517-1426 E-mail: stanley.weinstein@yale.edu.

WEINSTEIN, STEPHEN BRANT, communications executive, researcher, writer; b. N.Y.C., Nov. 25, 1938; s. Max S. and Evelyn A. (Brandt) W.; m. Judith Louise Benham, June 10, 1961; children: Brant M., Anna M. SB, MIT, 1960; MS, U. Mich., 1962; PhD, U. Calif. at Berkeley, 1966. Mem. tech. staff Philips Rsch. Labs., Eindhoven, The Netherlands, 1967-68, Bell Labs., Holmdel, N.J., 1968-79; v.p. tech. strategy Am. Express Co., N.Y.C., 1979-84; exec. dir. subscriber systems rsch. Bellcore, Morristown, N.J., 1984-93; fellow, mgr. comm. tech. rsch. C&C Rsch. Lab., NEC USA, Inc., 1994—2001; ptnr. Comm. Theory & Tech. Cons., 2002—. Editor-in-chief KICS Jour.

Comms and Networks, 1999-2001; adj. prof. Columbia U., 2002—. Author: Getting the Picture: A Guide to CATV and the New Electronic Media, 1986; co-author: Data Communication Principles, 1992; contbr. articles to profl. jours.; patentee in field. Fellow IEEE (div. III dir. 2002-03, chmn. Press 1979-82, Centennial medal 1984), IEEE Comms. Soc. (pres. 1996-97, v.p. tech. affairs 1994-95, dir. publs. 1990-93, editor-in-chief Comms. mag. 1984-89). Avocations: skiing, digital photography. Home and Office: 150 Woodland Ave Summit NJ 07901-2029 E-mail: s.weinstein@ieee.org.

WEINSTEIN, STEVEN WAYNE, lawyer; b. Hollywood, Calif., Dec. 13, 1966; s. Robert and Carolyn DeLois Weinstein; m. Lauren Weinstein, May 14, 1994; children: Rachel Leah, Adam Robert. BS in Pub. Adminstrn., U. So. Calif., L.A., 1990; JD, Whittier Law Sch., 1993; LLM in Taxation, So. Meth. U., Tex., 1994. Bar: Calif. 1993, Tex. 1994. Investigator Logan Clarke Internat., Hollywood, 1989; law clk. L.A. Dist. Atty. Office, 1991, L.A. City Atty.'s Office, 1992; clk. dist. coun. treas. dept. IRS, Dallas, 1994; atty. Roberts Law Group, Dallas, 1995—96, Ernst & Young, LLP, Dallas, 1996—97; atty., asst. vp N.Y. Life, Dallas, 1997—. Recipient Am. Jurisprudence Award in Estate Planning, Lawyers Coop. Pub., 1993. Personal E-mail: swwesq@comcast.net.

WEINSTEIN, SUSAN ANN, secondary school educator; b. Danville, Ill., Mar. 18, 1954; d. John Alan Winick and Joan Barbara Thiele-Winick; m. Eric Kent Hufford (div.); children: Alissa Michelle Hufford, Chad Eric Hufford; m. Mel Ira Weinstein. BA in English and Second Edn., Millikin U., 1988; MA in Comm., U. Ill., 2003. Cert. tchr. Ill. English tchr. Decatur (Ill.) Pub. Sch. Dist., 1988—. Elder First Presbyn. Ch., Decatur, 1988—91; pres. bd. dirs. dir. Unity Ch., Decatur, 2002—03. Mem.: Editl. Freelancers Assn., Assn. Women in Comm., Sigma Tau Delta. Avocations: writing, gardening, reading, spiritual practices. Office: Eisenhower HS S 16th St Decatur IL 62521 E-mail: sueweinstein@hotmail.com.

WEINSTEIN, TODD JAY, photographer; b. Detroit, June 13, 1951; s. Hyman and Pearl Weinstein; m. Isabelle Jud Weinstein, Jan. 4, 2002. One-man shows include Looking Glass Gallery, Detroit, 1981, UMA Gallery, N.Y.C., 1987, Union Sq. Gallery, 1991, Janice Charach Epstein Mus. Gallery, West Bloomfield, Mich., 1996, U. Mich. Hillel, 1997, Standmus. Synagogue, Grobzig, Germany, 1998—99, Inst. GEschichte DerJuden, Vienna, 1989, U. Mich. Hillel, Ann Arbor, 2000, Yeshiva U. Mus., N.Y.C., 2001, UJA Fedn., 2003, Holocaust Meml. Ctr., Detroit, 2004, German Ho., N.Y.C., 2004, exhibited in group shows at NYU, 1981, Midtown Y Gallery, 1982—83, Union Square Gallery, 1983, Paint Creek Ctr., Rochester, Mich., 1983, Focal Point Gallery, City Island, N.Y., 1984, Joseph E. Seagram & Sons Collection, N.Y.C., 1987, Burden Gallery, 1987, Pace/MacGill Gallery, 1987, U. Art Gallery, Loas Cruces, N.Med., 1988, Cork Gallery, Lincoln Ctr., N.Y.C., 1989, Ward-Nasse Gallery, 1990, N.Y. Pub. Libr., 1992, Maine Coast Artists Gallery, Rockport, Maine, 1993, Jersey City Mus., 1993, Detroit Inst. Arts, 1993, Photokina, Cologne, Germany, 1994—95, Leica Gallery, N.Y.C., 1994—95, Puffin Gallery, 1997, Ballroom Gallery, Berlin, 1997, Portland Mus. Art, 1998, Taranto Gallery, N.Y.C., 1999, Marion Meyer Gallery, Paris, 2000, Represented in permanent collections Bibliotheque Nationale, Bklyn. Mus., Detroit Inst. Arts., Getty Mus., L.A., Met. Mus. Art, N.Y.C., Mus. Photographic Art, San Diego, Joseph E. Seagram & Sons, N.Y.C., others. Home: 174 5th Ave New York NY 10010

WEINSTEIN-BACAL, STUART ALLEN, lawyer, educator; b. Stuttgart, Germany, May 23, 1948; s. Marvin Stuart and Mae (Beal) W.; m. Holly Laurette Thompson, Aug. 7, 1982; children: Rachel Lee, Maximillian II, Sarah Nicole. BA, U. Va., 1970, MEd, 1973; JD cum laude, U. Miami, 1979. Bar: D.C. 1979, Va. 1981, V.I. 1985, P.R. 1988. Tchr., pvt. tutor various schs., Conn., Fla., Costa Rica, 1973-76; mem. prof. staff Merchant Marine and Fisheries Com. U.S. Ho. of Reps., Washington, 1978; assoc. Cameron, Hornbostel & Adelman, Washington, 1979-80, Burch, Kerns & Klimek, PC, Washington, 1980-81; staff atty. C.A.C.I., Washington, 1982-83; sr. assoc. Dudley, Dudley & Topper, St. Thomas, U.S. Virgin Islands, 1984-85; v.p., gen. counsel Redondo Construction Corp., San Juan, PR, 1985-89; founder Indiano, Williams & Weinstein-Bacal, San Juan, PR, 1989-2000; owner Weinstein-Bacal & Assocs., P.S.C., Old San Juan, PR, 2000—. Contbr. articles to profl. jours. Capt. USAR, 1970-85. Mem. ABA, Am. Arbitration Assn. (pres., Caribbean region adv. coun. 1988—, arbitrator 1989—), Res. Officers Assn., Colegio de Abogados de P.R., U. Va. Alumni Assn., Nature Conservancy, Sovereign Order of the Oak (knight comdr.), Rotary Club of San Juan (bd. dirs. 1991-95), Middleburg Tennis Club, Bankers Club P.R., Phi Alpha Delta. Avocations: sailing, golf, tennis, riding, gourmet cooking, travel. Home: Villas Del Mar E # 7D Carolina PR 00979 also: Mallory Chase Farm 35919 Turkey Roost Rd Middleburg VA 20117-3401 Office: Gonzalez Padin Bldg-Penthouse 154 Rafael Cordero St Plz Armas Old San Juan PR 00901 E-mail: sawbacal@aol.com.

WEINSTOCK, DAVID MARC, bone marrow transplantation and infectious diseases physician, researcher; b. Washington, Sept. 26, 1973; s. Hal Jerome and Frances Barbara Weinstock; m. Julia Gianna Zuccotti, Sept. 16, 2001. BA, U. Chgo., 1993; MD, George Washington U., 1997. Diplomate in internal medicine and med. oncology Am. Bd. Internal Medicine. Resident N.Y. Presbyn. Hosp., N.Y.C., 1997—2000; fellow Meml. Sloan-Kettering Cancer Ctr., N.Y.C., 2000—04. Contbg author Med. Letter on Drugs and Therapeutics, New Rochelle, NY, 2001—, www.mdconsult.com, St. Louis, 2002—. Contbr. articles to profl. jours. Mem.: ACP (Outstanding Rsch. award 1997), AMA, AAAS, N.Y. Soc. Infectious Diseases, Infectious Disease Soc. Am., Am. Soc. Hematology, Am. Soc. Clin. Oncology, Alpha Omega Alpha, Alpha Delta Phi. Achievements include research in Recombination and translocation formation. Office: Meml Sloan-Kettering Cancer Center 1275 York Ave Box 109 New York NY 10021 E-mail: weinstod@mskcc.org.

WEINSTOCK, HAROLD, lawyer; b. Stamford, Conn., Nov. 30, 1925; s. Elias and Sarah (Singer) W.; m. Barbara Lans, Aug. 27, 1950; children—Nathaniel, Michael, Philip. BS magna cum laude, N.Y. U., 1947; JD, Harvard, 1950. Bar: Conn. bar 1950, Ill. bar 1950, Calif. bar 1958. Atty. SEC, Washington, 1950-52, IRS, 1952-56; tax atty. Hunt Foods & Industries, Inc., Los Angeles, 1956-58; pvt. practice Beverly Hills, Calif., 1958-71, Los Angeles, 1971—; mem. Weinstock, Manion, Reisman, Shore & Neumann (and predecessor firms), 1958—. Lectr. extension div., estate planning courses U. Calif. at Los Angeles, 1959—86; estate planning and taxation courses Calif. Continuing Edn. of the Bar, 1960-87. Author: Planning An Estate, 4th edit., 2002; contbr. articles to profl. publs. Nat. trustee Union Am. Hebrew Congregations, 1976-79; trustee Jewish Cmty. Found., L.A., 1993-99; adv. bd. Estate Planning Inst. UCLA Law Sch., 1979-92, NYU Inst. on Fed. Taxation, 1986-95. Mem. ABA, Calif. Bar Assn., Beverly Hills Bar Assn. (chmn. probate and trusts com. 1967-68), Los Angeles Bar Assn., Beverly Hills Estate Planning Council (pres. 1968-69), Estate Counselors Forum of Los Angeles (pres. 1963-64) Jewish (pres. temple 1974-76). Office: Weinstock Manion 1875 Century Park E Fl 15 Los Angeles CA 90067-2501

WEINSTOCK, JOEL VINCENT, immunologist; b. Detroit, Mar. 21, 1948; s. Herman and Esther B. (Frazein) W.; m. Allison Lee Rose, July 15, 1979; children: Lisa, Jeffrey, Andrew. BS, U. Mich., 1969; MD, Wayne State U., 1973. Diplomate Am. Bd. Internal Medicine, subspeciality gastroenterology; lic. physician, Mich., Iowa. Straight med. intern Univ. Hosp., Ann Arbor, Mich., 1973-74, resident internal medicine, 1974-76, fellow gastroenterology dept. internal medicine, 1976-78; asst. prof. internal medicine Wayne State U. Sch. Medicine, Detroit, 1978-83, assoc. prof., 1983-86, adj. assoc. prof. dept. immunology and microbiology, 1983-86, vice chief divsn. gastroenterology, 1984-86; assoc. prof., dir. gastroenterology divsn. U. Iowa, Iowa City, 1986-91, prof., dir., 1991—, dir. Ctr. Digestive Diseases, 1990—, dir. divsn. gastroenterology-hepatology, 1986—. Mem. exec. bd. Crohn's and Colitis Found. Am., N.Y.C., 1993—, mem. tng. awards rev. com., 1991-93, chmn., 1993—; chief sect. gastroenterology Hutzel Hosp., Detroit, 1978-84, dir. endoscopy unit, 1978-84, dir. nutritional support svc., 1980-84; vice chief gastroenterology dept. medicine Wayne State U. Sch. Medicine, 1984-86; dir. gastroenterology subspecialty unit Harper Hosp., Detroit, 1984-86, vice-chief gastroenterology, 1984-86; mem. sci. adv. ang grant rev. com. Crohn's and Colitis Found. Am., 1987—; mem. NIH Task force for developing nat. agenda for IBD rsch., 1989; mem. Lederle award selection com., 1989; mem. study sect. NIH Core Ctr. Rev. Com., 1990, 92; mem. abstract rev. com. ASCI, 1990; vis. prof. Washington U., St. Louis, 1990, U. Tex., Houston, 1991, Cleve. Clinic, 1992, U. Md., Balt., 1993; participant various conferences and meetings; mem. Digestive Diseases Ctr. Planning Com., 19886—; mem. Adult TPN Subcom., 1986—; chmn. coord. com. Ctr. Digestive Diseases, 1986—; mem. grant rev. coms. NIH, 1980—; mem. gastroenterology subspecialty coun. CSCR, 1993—. Mem. editl. bd. Autoimmunity Forum: Gastroenterology Edit., 1989-92; mem. internat. adv. bd. Alimentary Pharmacology and Therapeutics, 1990—; sect. editor Jour. Inflammatory Bowel Disease, 1994; reviewer Am. Jour Gastroenterology, Jour. Clin. Investigation, Jour. Immunology, Jour. Clin. Immunology, Gastroenterology, Digestive Diseases and Scis.; contbr. articles to profl. jours., chpts. to books. Rsch. grantee NIH, 1982—, Sandoz Pharm., 1993, Marion Merrell Dow, 1994, Centocor, 1995. Mem. AAAS, Am. Inst. Nutrition, Am. Soc. Clin. Nutrition, Ctrl. Soc. Clin. Rsch., Am. Soc. Gastrointestinal Endoscopy, Am. Assn. Study Liver Disease, Am. Fedn. Clin. Rsch., Am. Assn. Immunologists, Ileitis and Colitis Found. Am., Am. Soc. Clin. Investigation, Clin. Immunology Soc., Am. Gastroenterological Assn. (rsch. com. 1987-90, chmn. task force rsch. fellowship awards 1989-90, program evaluation com. 1990—), Midwest Gut Club (councillor 1990—), Alpha Omega Alpha. Achievements include research in elucidaiton of immunoregulatory circuits that control granulomatous inflammation; characterization of how neurokines help control inflammatory responses. Office: U Iowa College of Med Internal Medicine 4607JCP 200 Hawkins Dr Iowa City IA 52242-1009

WEINSTOCK, JUDITH, obstetrician/gynecologist; b. Mt. Vernon, N.Y., Mar. 30, 1952; MD, Baylor U., 1982. Diplomate Am. Bd. Ob-Gyn. Intern L.I. Coll. Hosp., Bklyn., 1982-83, resident in ob-gyn., 1983-86, attending physician, 1986—. Mem. Assn. Womens Surgeons, Bklyn. Gynecol. Soc., N.Y. Soc. Ob-gyn., N.Y. Med. Soc. Office: Bklyn Womens Health Care 9 Pierrepont St Brooklyn NY 11201-3302 also: 421 78th St Brooklyn NY 11209-3403

WEINSTOCK, LEONARD, lawyer; b. Bklyn., Aug. 18, 1935; s. Samuel Morris and Evelyn (Reiser) W.; m. Rita Lee Itkowitz, May 25, 1963; children: Gregg Douglas, Valerie Lisa, Tara Diane. BS, Bklyn. Coll., 1956; JD, St. John's U., Bklyn., 1959. Bar: N.Y. 1961, U.S. Supreme Ct. 1964, U.S. Ct. Appeals (2d cir.) 1963, U.S. Dist. Ct. (ea. and so. dists.) N.Y. 1963, U.S. Tax Ct. 1963. Assoc. Bernard Helfenstein law practice, Bklyn., 1962-63; supr. All State Ins. Co., Bklyn., 1963-64; atty. Hertz Corp., N.Y.C., 1964-65; ptnr. Nicholas & Weinstock, Flushing, N.Y., 1965-68; v.p., ptnr. Garbarini & Scher, P.C., N.Y.C., 1968—. Lectr. Practicing Law Inst., N.Y.C., 1975—; arbitrator Nassau County Dist. Ct., Mineola, N.Y., 1979—, U.S. Dist. Ct. (ea. dist.) N.Y. 1986—; mem. Med. Malpractice Mediation Panel, Mineola, 1978—. Legal counsel Massapequa Soccer Club, N.Y., 1981—; county committeeman Dem. Party, Massapequa Park, N.Y., 1979—. With U.S. Army, 1959-62. Mem. ABA, N.Y. State Bar Assn., Nassau County Bar Assn. (mem. med. jurisprudence ins. com. 1978), N.Y. Trial Lawyers Assn. Avocations: stamp collecting/philately, softball, racquetball. Home: 38 Barstow Rd Great Neck NY 11021-2218 Office: Garbarini and Scher PC 432 Park Ave S New York NY 10016-8013

WEINSTOCK, MICHAEL S. emergency physician, department chairman; b. Passaic, N.J., 1940; BS, Am. U., 1962; MD, U. Health Scis. Ctr./Chgo. Med. Sch., 1967. Bd. cert. emergency medicine, bd. cert. pediat. Intern Md. Hosp., Balt., 1967—68; resident pediat. L.I. Jewish Med. Ctr., 1968—70; fellow allergy/immunology Walter Reed Army Med. Ctr., Washington; chmn. dept. emergency medicine Lehigh Valley Hosp. and Health Network, Allentown, Pa. Recipient James D. Mills Outstanding Contbn. to Emergency Medicine award, Am. Coll. Emergency Physicians, 2000. Office: Lehigh Valley Physician group PO Box 689 Cedar Crest & I-78 Allentown PA 18105-1556 Office Phone: 610-402-4363. E-mail: michael.weinstock@lvh.com.

WEINSTOCK, ROBERT, physics educator; b. Phila., Feb. 2, 1919; s. Morris and Lillian (Hirsch) W.; m. Elizabeth Winch Brownell, Apr. 22, 1950; children: Frank Morse, Robert B. Weinstock-Collins. AB, U. Pa., 1940; PhD, Stanford (Calif.) U., 1943. Instr. physics Stanford U., 1943-44, instr. math., 1946-50, acting asst. prof. math., 1950-54; rsch. assoc. in radar countermeasures Radio Rsch. Lab. Harvard U., Cambridge, Mass., 1944-45; asst. prof. U. Notre Dame, Ind., 1954-58, assoc. prof. math., 1958-59; vis. assoc. prof. math. Oberlin (Ohio) Coll., 1959-60, assoc. prof., 1960-66, prof. physics, 1966-83, emeritus prof., 1983—. Author: Calculus of Variations, 1952; contbr. numerous tech. articles to profl. jours. Fellow AAAS, Ohio Acad. Sci.; mem. ACLU, Am. Assn. Physics Tchrs., Am. Phys. Soc., History of Sci. Soc., Brit. Soc. for the History of Sci., Sigma Xi. Avocations: concert going, reading, walking, travel, letter writing. Home: 37 Kendal Dr Oberlin OH 44074-1902 Office: Oberlin Coll Dept Physics and Astronomy Oberlin OH 44074 Office Phone: 440-775-8233. Business E-Mail: zweinsto@oberlin.net.

WEINSTOCK, WALTER WOLFE, systems engineer; b. Phila., Aug. 18, 1925; s. Abraham and Jeanne (Feldman) W.; m. Doris Alpert, Sept. 21, 1946; children— Steven Eric, Bruce Alan. BSE.E., U.Pa., 1946, MSE.E., 1954, PhD, 1964. Design engr. Philco, 1946-49; with RCA Corp., 1949-87; prin. scientist RCA Corp. (Missile and Surface Radar div.), Moorestown, N.J., 1979-87; cons., 1987—. Mem. planning and steering adv. group Surface Ship Security Panel, Dept. Navy, 1979-82 Contbg. author: Modern Radar, 1965, Practical Phased Array Antenna Systems, 1991; contbr. articles to profl. jours. Recipient David Sarnoff award for Outstanding Achievement in Enrging. RCA, 1972 Fellow IEEE (Pioneer Recognition award 2004); mem. Tau Beta Pi, Eta Kappa Nu, Sigma Tau, Pi Mu Epsilon. Achievements include patents in field. Home: 6 Beryl Rd Cheltenham PA 19012-1206 E-mail: walter.w.weinstock@lmco.com., walt1925@earthlink.net.

WEINSTOCK RAD, KATHERYN LOUISE, music educator; d. Henry Robert and Jeanallan Joyce Weinstock; m. Jalal Rad, Aug. 23, 1993. Aux. music study, U. Birmingham, England, 1983—84, U. Keele, Staffordshire/Newcastle, 1983—84; MusB, U. Tulsa, 1985, MusM, 1988. Cert. Okla. Tchr. Cert. State of Okla., 1988. Cellist Signature Symphony Okla. Sinfonia, Tulsa, 1982—, Tulsa (Okla.) Philharm., 1982—; adj. cello instr. Northeastern State U, Tahlequah, Okla., 1988—90; music tchr. Tulsa Pub. Sch., 1989—96; dir. of strings, tchr. Broken Arrow (Okla.) Pub. Sch., 1996—99; music curriculum coord. Tulsa Pub. Sch., 1999—2002; music coord. Tulsa Cmty. Music Sch., 2003; adj. cello instr. Performing Arts Ctr. Edn. Tulsa C.C., 2000—; fine arts coord. Cent. High Sch. Acad. Arts, 2003—. Mem. bd. fine arts task force Tulsa Pub. Sch., 1996—; adv. Barthelmes Conservatory, 2000—02; bd. mem. Chamber Music Tulsa(Okla.), 2001—; performer cellist Tulsa Philharmonic, Tulsa Signature Symphony, Okla. City Philharmonic; prin. cellist Light Opera Orchestra of Okla.; performer has performed with many classical, pop/rock, jazz and blues artists, including a live performance on NPR. Grandstand, judge Vet. Day Parade, Tulsa, 1999—2002; mem. Tulsa Now Task Force - Mayor Bill Fortune, 2002—; fundraiser raised over one half million dollars music programs Tulsa Pub. Schs. Recipient Tchr. Touching Tomorrow Award, Tulsa Pub. Sch., 1996, Superior Civilian Svc. Award, Dept. of the U.S. Army, 1999—2000; grantee VH-1 save the Music Grant, VH-1, 2001, U.S. Dept. Edn., 2002. Mem.: Hyetchka, Am. Federation of Musicians. Avocations: playing cello in variety of genres, cooking, exercise. Home: 630 Pioneer Rd Sapulpa OK 74066 Office Phone: 918-833-8492.

WEINTRAUB, ARTHUR E. health service association executive; b. N.Y.C., July 18, 1935; s. Jacob and Sarah (Jaffe) W.; m. Carole, Apr. 14, 1962; children: Jill, David. BA, Hunter Coll., 1956; M in Planning, NYU, 1965. Project planner U.S. Army Corps Engrs., N.Y.C., 1956-64; chief long range planning Tri-State Regional Planning Commn., N.Y.C., 1964-67; sr. v.p. Mid Hudson Pattern, Poughkeepsie, N.Y., 1967-78; exec. dir. Hudson Valley Health Sys. Agy., Tuxedo, N.Y., 1978-82; pres. No. Met. Hosp. Assn., Newburgh, N.Y., 1982—. Adj. faculty SUNY, New Paltz, 1982-91, New Sch. U., N.Y.C., 1992—; sr. lectr. N.Y. Med. Coll., Valhalla, 1992—. Contbr. articles to profl. jours. Trustee St. Luke's Hosp., Newburgh, 1972-78; pres. Bd. Edn., Newburgh, 1974-82; mem. health law adv. bd. Pace U. Law Sch., White Plains, N.Y., 1995—, Ch. Conf. Metro Hosp. Assns., 1997. NEH fellow Princeton U., 1977; recipient Disting. Cmty. Svc. award Orange County C. of C., 1970, Am. Red. Cross, 1996, Family Health Ctr., 1997, Arthritis Found., 2001. Office: No Met Hosp Assn 400 Stony Brook Ct Newburgh NY 12550-6522 Office Phone: 845-562-7520. E-mail: awein@normet.org.

WEINTRAUB, ELLEN L. commissioner; b. 1957; m. Bill Dauster; 3 children. BA cum laude, Yale Coll.; JD, Harvard Law Sch. Bar: NY, DC and Supreme Court. Chair Fed. Election Commn., Washington, 2002—03, vice chair, 2004—; of counsel Perkins Coie, Political Law Group; litigator Cahill Gordon & Reindel; counsel Com. on Stds. of Ofcl. Conduct for U.S. Ho. Reps. Office: 999 E St NW Washington DC 20463

WEINTRAUB, JOSEPH BARTON, publishing executive; b. Phila., Dec. 2, 1945; s. George and Edith (Lubner) W.; m. Denise Waters, June 14, 1974. BA, U. Pitts., 1966; MA, U. Chgo., 1967, PhD, 1973. Assoc. faculty U. Ind., Gary, Ind., 1970-74; mktg. specialist journalism div. U. Chgo. Press, 1974-75, sr. copywriter journalism div., 1975-78; periodical specialist ABA, Chgo., 1978-80, mktg. mgr., 1980-92, dir. publ. planning, 1992-97, dir. book publ., 1997-99; mgr. dir. mktg. U. Chgo. Press, 1999—. Writer You, 2000; contbr. essays, translations, plays, poems, short fiction to lit. revs. and small press anthologies. Recipient award Literary awards, Ill. Art Coun., 1984-2004, Barrington Art Coun. Mem. Phi Beta Kappa. Avocations: writing, language study, running. Office: U Chgo Press 1427 E 60th Street Chicago IL 60637-5418

WEINTRAUB, NEAL L. medical educator, cardiologist; Student, Tulane u., 1977-80, MD, 1984. Diplomate Am. Bd. Internal Medicine, Am. Bd. Cardiovasc. Diseases. Resident Emory U., Atlanta, 1984-86, U. Ill., Urbana-Champaign, 1986-87, clin. instr. medicine Coll. Medicine, 1987-88, asst. clin. prof. medicine Coll. Medicine, 1988-90; staff physician VA Med. Ctr., Danville, Ill., 1987-90, St. Louis, 1990-91; asst. prof. medicine Sch. Medicine St. Louis U., 1990-95, postdoctoral fellow clin. pharmacology, 1992-94; asst. cardiology divsn. U. Iowa Coll. Medicine, Iowa City, 1995-97, assoc. prof. cardiology, 1997—. Contbr. articles to profl. jours. Recipient Travel award Am. Coll. Cardiology/Bristol-Myers Squibb, 1994, Clinician Scientist award Am. Heart Assn., 1996. Mem. Alpha Omega Alpha. Achievements include research in vascular biology and physiology and lipid biochemistry. Office: U Iowa Coll Medicine CV Div Dept Internal Medicine 200 Hawkins Dr Iowa City IA 52242-1009

WEINTRAUB, RUSSELL JAY, lawyer, educator; b. N.Y.C., Dec. 20, 1929; s. Harry and Alice (Lieberman) W.; m. Zelda Kresshover, Sept. 6, 1953; children— Sharon Hope, Harry David, Steven Ross. BA, NYU, 1950; JD, Harvard U., 1953. Bar: N.Y. 1955, Iowa 1961, Tex. 1980. Tchg. fellow Harvard U. Law Sch., 1955-57; asst. prof. law U. Iowa, 1957-61, prof., 1961-65, U. Tex., 1965—, Marrs McLean prof. law, 1970-80, Bryant Smith chmn., 1980-82, John B. Connally chmn., 1982-98, Powell chmn., 1998—2003, emeritus, 2004—. Vis. prof. law U. Mich., 1965, UCLA, 1967, U. Calif., Berkeley, 1973-74, Bklyn. Law Sch., 1990, 95, Inst. Internat. Comparative Law, Paris, 1975, Florence, Italy, 1997, Barcelona, 1999, 2002, London, 2000, U. Houston, 1979-80, Inst. Internat. and Comparative Law, Oxford, Eng., 1982-83, 86-87, 92, 2003, Dublin, Ireland, 1991, La. State U., Aix-en-Provence, France, 1993, Tulane U., Spetses, Greece, 1998, Australian Nat. U., 2001; Ronald Graveson Meml. lectr. King's Coll., London, 2000, lectr. Hague Acad. Internat. Law, 1984; cons. U.S. Dept. State, 1995—; cons. in field. Author: International Litigation and Arbitration, 1994, 4th revised edit., 2003, ann. supplement; (with Eugene Scoles) Cases and Materials on the Conflict of Laws, 1967, 2d rev. edit., 1972, supplement, 1978, Commentary on the Conflict of Laws, 1971, 4th rev. edit., 2000, ann. supplement; (with Hamilton and Rau) Cases and Materials on Contracts, 1984, 2d rev. edit., 1992; (with Hay and Borchers) Cases and Materials on the Conflict of Laws, 12th rev. edit., 2004, annual supplement; contbr. articles to profl. jours. Trustee U. Iowa Sch. Religion, 1960-65. With U.S. Army, 1953-55. Recipient Disting. Prof. award U. Tex. Sch. Law, 1977, Teaching Excellence award, 1979, cert. of meritorious service Am. Bar Assn., 1977, cert. of meritorious service Tex. Bar Assn., 1978, Best Tchr. award U. Houston, 1980, Carl Fulda award scholarship in internat. law, 1993. Mem. Am. Law Inst., Am. Bar Found. (life), Tex. Bar Found. (life), Scribes. Jewish. Office: U Tex Sch Law 727 E Dean Keeton Austin TX 78705-3224 Office Phone: 512-232-1370. E-mail: rweintraub@mail.law.utexas.edu. *The only true happiness lies in useful work done to the best of your ability.*

WEINTRAUB, SAM, reading educator; b. St. Louis, Apr. 24, 1927; s. Julius and Jeannette (Schwartz) W.; 1 child, Robert. BA, Ohio State U., 1948, BS, 1950, MEd, 1954; EdD, U. Ill., 1960. Tchr. Wyandotte Pub. Schs., Mich., 1950-53, Campus Sch. Wis. STate Coll., La Crosse, 1953-54; asst. prof. Case Western Res. U., Cleve., 1960-61, U. Chgo., 1964-68; assoc. prof. Ind. U., Bloomington, 1968-74; prof. SUNY-Buffalo, Amherst, 1974-95, prof. emeritus, 1995—. Vis. prof. Tex. Woman's U., Denton, 1980-81; cons. in field. Author, editor: Ann. Summary of Investigations Relating to Reading, 1968-97; co-editor: Improving Reading Research, 1976; co-editor jour. Reading Rsch. Quar., 1969-79. Recipient Legacy Builder award Family and Children's Svc. of Niagara, Inc., 2003; named to Reading Hall of Fame. Fellow Nat. Conf. Rsch. in English (pres. 1978-79); mem. Internat. Reading Assn. (Spl. Svc. award 1987, Wm. S. Gray citation of merit 1997), Nat. Coun. Tchrs. English, Am. Ednl. Rsch. Assn., Niagara Frontier Reading Coun. (v.p. 1990-91, Spl. Svc. award 1990). Avocations: reading, travel.

WEINTRAUB, SIDNEY, economist, educator; b. N.Y.C., May 18, 1922; s. Reuben and Anna Weintraub; m. Gladys Katz, Aug. 11, 1946; children: Jeffrey, Marcia Weintraub Plunkett, Deborah Weintraub Chilewich. BBA, CCNY, 1943; B, MA in Journalism, U. Mo., 1948; MA in Econs., Yale U., 1958; PhD in Econs., Am. U., 1966. Commd. fgn. svc. officer Dept. State, 1949, dep. asst. sec. of state for internat. fin. and devel., 1969-74; asst. adminstr. for interagy. devel. coordination AID, 1974-75, exec. dir. interagy. devel. coordination com., 1974-75; ret., 1975; sr. fellow Brookings Instn., Washington, 1978-79; Dean Rusk prof. Lyndon B. Johnson Sch. Pub. Affairs, U. Tex., Austin, 1976-96, prof. emeritus, 1996, also co-dir. Program for U.S.-Mex. Policy Studies; William E. Simon chair in polit. economy Ctr. Strategic and Internat. Studies, 1993—. Disting. vis. scholar Ctr. for Strategic and Internat. Studies, Washington, 1990. Author: Free Trade with Mexico, 1984, A Marriage of Convenience: Relations Between Mexico and The United States, 1990, NAFTA: What Comes Next, 1994, NAFTA at Three: A Progress Report, 1997, Financial Decision-Making in Mexico: To Bet a Nation, 2000, Commentaries on International Political Economy: Constructive Irreverence, 2004; contbr. articles to profl. jours. Served with U.S. Army, 1943-46. Recipient Disting. Career Svc. award AID, 1975 Mem.: Am. Econ. Assn., Am. Fgn. Service Assn., Coun. on Fgn. Rels., Cosmos (Washington). Office: Ctr Strategic and Internat Studies 1800 K St NW Washington DC 20006-2202 Office Phone: 202-775-3292. Personal E-mail: sxw1@erols.com. *Once having been thrust into the Second World War, my main intellectual interest has been in foreign affairs. I had concluded, as President Kennedy did later, that domestic issues can hurt but misplaced foreign policy can kill. My drive has been to understand what motivates nations, what stimulates people within different nations, what is the U.S. national interest, and to become as expert as my talents would allow about such crucial issues as domestic security, international economic interaction, social mobility, and human development generally. This remains my ambition.*

WEINTRAUB, STANLEY, arts and humanities educator, writer; b. Phila., Apr. 17, 1929; s. Ben and Ray (Segal) W.; m. Rodelle Horwitz, June 6, 1954; children: Mark, David, Erica. BS, West Chester (Pa.) State Coll., 1949; MA, Temple U., 1951; PhD, Pa. State U., 1956. Instr. Pa. State U., University Park, 1953-59, asst. prof., 1959-62, assoc. prof., 1962-65, prof. English, 1965-70, research prof., 1970-86, Evan Pugh prof. Arts and Humanities, 1986-99, Evan Pugh prof. Emeritus, 2000—; dir. Inst. for Arts and Humanistic Studies, 1970-90. Vis. prof. U. Calif. at Los Angeles, 1963, U. Hawaii, 1973, U. Malaya, 1977, Nat. U. Singapore, 1982 Author: Private Shaw and Public Shaw, 1963, The War in the Wards, 1964, Reggie, 1965, The Art of William Golding, 1965, Beardsley, 1967, The Last Great Cause, The Intellectuals and the Spanish Civil War, 1968, Evolution of a Revolt: Early Postwar Writings of T.E. Lawrence, 1968, The Literary Criticism of Oscar Wilde, 1968, Journey to

Heartbreak, 1971, Whistler: A Biography, 1974, Lawrence of Arabia: the Literary Impulse, 1975, Four Rossettis, A Victorian Biography, 1977, Aubrey Beardsley: Imp of the Perverse, 1976, The London Yankees: Portraits of American Writers and Artists in England, 1894-1914, 1979, The Unexpected Shaw. Biographical Approaches to G.B. Shaw and His Work, 1982, A Stillness Heard Round the World: The End of the Great War, 1985, Victoria. An Intimate Biography, 1987, Long Day's Journey into War: December 7, 1941, 1991, Bernard Shaw: A Guide to Research, 1992, Disraeli: A Biography, 1993, The Last Great Victory-The End of World War II, July/August 1945, 1995, Shaw's People. Victoria to Churchill, 1996, Uncrowned King: The Life of Prince Albert, 1997, MacArthur's War: Korea and the Undoing of an American Hero, 2000, The Importance of Being Edward. King in Waiting, 1841-1901, 2000, Silent Night. The Remarkable 1914 Christmas Truce, 2001, Charlotte and Lionel: A Rothschild Love Story, 2003, General Washington's Christmas Farewell: A Mount Vernon Homecoming, 1783, 2003; editor: An Unfinished Novel by Bernard Shaw, 1958, C.P. Snow: A Spectrum, 1963, The Yellow Book: Quintessence of the Nineties, 1964, The Savoy: Nineties Experiment, 1966, The Court Theatre, 1966, Biography and Truth, 1967, Evolution of a Revolt: Early Postwar Writings of T.E. Lawrence, 1968, The Literary Criticism of Oscar Wilde, 1968, Shaw: An Autobiography 1856-1898, 1969, Shaw: An Autobiography, The Playwright Years, 1898-1950, 1970, Bernard Shaw's Nondramatic Literary Criticism, 1972, Directions in Literary Criticism, 1973, Saint Joan Fifty Years After: 1923/24-1973/74, 1973, The Portable Bernard Shaw, 1977, (with Anne Wright) Heartbreak House. A Facsimile of the Revised Typescript, 1979, (with Richard Aldington) The Portable Oscar Wilde, 1981, Modern British Dramatists, 1900-1945, 1982, The Playwright and the Pirate. Bernard Shaw and Frank Harris: A Correspondence, 1982, British Dramatists Since World War II, 1983, Bernard Shaw, the Diaries, 1885-1897, 1986, Bernard Shaw on the London Art Scene, 1885-1950, 1989, (with Rodelle Weintraub) Dear Young Friend. The Letters of American Presidents to Children, 2000, also editor Comparative Literature Studies, 1987-92, Shaw, The Ann. of Bernard Shaw Studies, 1956-89. Pres. Jewish Community Council of Bellefonte (Pa.) State Coll., 1966-67. Served to 1st lt. AUS, 1951-53, Korea. Decorated Bronze Star medal.; Guggenheim fellow, 1968-69; recipient Disting. Humanist award Pa. Humanities Council, 1985 Mem. The Authors' Guild, PEN. Home: 4 Winterfield Ct Newark DE 19711 Office Phone: 302-235-2859. E-mail: sqw4@psu.edu., sqw4@comcast.net. *I subscribe to Bernard Shaw's declaration in the Preface to Man and Superman that "This is the true joy in life, the being used for a purpose recognized by yourself as a mighty one; the being thoroughly worn out before you are thrown on the scrap heap; the being a force of Nature instead of a feverish selfish little clod of ailments and grievances complaining that the world will not devote itself to making you happy.".*

WEINTZ, JACOB FREDERICK, JR., retired investment banker; b. N.Y.C., June 27, 1926; s. Jacob Frederick and Grace (Cortelyou) W.; m. Elisabeth Hamlin Brewer, Nov. 26, 1955; children: Elizabeth Hunt Cerf, Polly Weintz, Eric Cortelyou, Karl Frederick. Student, Norwich U., 1943-44; BA, Stanford U., 1948; MBA, Harvard U., 1951. Salesman Vick Chem. Co., N.Y.C., 1948-49; assoc. buying dept. Goldman, Sachs & Co., N.Y.C., 1951-54, assoc. new bus. dept., 1954-65, ptnr., 1965-84; ltd. ptnr. Goldman, Sachs Group L.P., 1984—99, ret. ptnr., 1999. Pres., chmn. bd. dirs. Stonebridge Condominium Assn., Snowmass Village, Colo., 1978-85; trustee Pace U., 1981-97, Norwich U., Stanford U., 1985-95, Sierra Club Found., 1984-90, 92—98; trustee Harbor Lights Found., N.Y.C.; mem. Dept. . Population and Internat. Health, Harvard Sch. Pub. Health, Fin. and Audit and Investment com., 1997-, bd. vis., Stanford Inst. Internat. Studies; vice chmn. bd. dirs. Guiding Eyes for Blind, 1984-93; bd. dir. The Forum for World Affairs, Stanford, Conn., 1988-94; mem. Ctr. Internat. Security and Arms Control Stanford U.; pres. Harvard U. Bus. Sch. Alumni Assn., 1988-90; del. Coun. Governing Bds., Albany, N.Y.; chmn. bd. dirs. N.Y. Young Rep. Club, 1957-58; mem. exec. com. Greenwich Rep. Town Com., Conn., 1962-69, The Task Force on Def. Spending, The Economy and the Nation's Security, BENS-ED Commn. on Fundamental Def. Mgmt. Issues, 1991-92; mem. Stanford in Washington Coun.; mem. vis. com. Inst. Internat. Studies Stanford U. With USAAF, 1944-45. Recipient La Medaille de la Ville de Paris, 1990, Stanford Gold Spike award, 1992. Mem. Ambs. Round Table (Stamford), Bond Club (N.Y.), Newcomen Soc. N.Am., Down Town Assn., Harvard Club, Riverside Yacht Club, Flying Scot Sailing Assn. (pres. 1968-69), Theta Chi. Republican. Episcopalian. Home: Harbor Lights 43 Jones Park Dr Riverside CT 06878-2205 Office: c/o Markum and Kliegman LLP BCRS Group 100 Wall St New York NY 10005

WEIR, ALEXANDER, JR., utility consultant, inventor; b. Crossett, Ark., Dec. 19, 1922; s. Alexander and Mary Eloise (Field) W.; m. Florence Forschner, Dec. 28, 1946; children: Alexander III, Carol Jean, Bruce Richard BSChemE, U. Ark., 1943; MChemE, Poly Inst. Bklyn., 1946; PhD, U. Mich., 1954; cert., U. So. Calif. Grad. Sch. Bus. Adminstrn., 1968. Chem. engr. Am. Cyanamid Co., Stamford Rsch. Labs., 1943-47; with U. Mich., 1948-58; rsch. assoc., project supr. Engring. Rsch. Inst., U. Mich., 1948-57; lectr. chem. and metall. engring. dept. U. Mich., 1954-56, asst. prof., 1956-58; cons. Ramo-Woolridge Corp., L.A., 1956-57; mem. tech. staff, sect. head, asst. mgr. Ramo-Wooldridge Corp., L.A., 1957-60, incharge Atlas Missile Captive test program, 1956-60; tech. adv. to pres. Northrop Corp., Beverly Hills, Calif., 1960-70; prin. scientist for air quality So. Calif. Edison Co., L.A., 1970-76, mgr. chem. sys. R & D, 1976-86, chief rsch. scientist, 1986-88; utility cons. Playa Del Rey, Calif., 1988—. Rep. Am. Rocket Soc. to Detroit Nuc. Coun., 1954-57; chmn. session on chem. reactions Nuc. Sci. and Engring. Congress, Cleve., 1955; U.S. del. AGARD (NATO) Combustion Colloquium, Liege, Belgium, 1955; Western U.S. rep. task force on environ. R & D goals Electric Rsch. Coun., 1971; electric utility advisor Electric Power Rsch. Inst., 1974-78, 84-87; industry advisor dept. chemistry and biochemistry Calif. State U., L.A., 1981-88. Author: Two and Three Dimensional Flow of Air through Square-Edged Sonic Orifices, 1954; (with R.B. Morrison and T.C. Anderson) Notes on Combustion, 1955, also tech. papers; inventor acid rain prevention device used in 5 states. Sea scout leader, Greenwich, Conn., 1944-48, Marina del Rey, Calif., 1965-70; bd. govs., past pres. Civic Union Playa del Rey, chmn. sch., police and fire, nominating, civil def., army liaison coms.; mem. Senate, Westchester YMCA, chmn. Dads sponsoring com., active fundraising; chmn. nominating com. Paseo del Rey Sch. PTA, 1961; mem. L.A. Mayors Cmty. Adv. Com.; asst. chmn. advancement com., merit badge dean Cantinella dist. L.A. Area coun. Boy Scouts Am. Recipient Nat. Rsch. Coun. Flue Gas Desulfurization Industrials Scale Reliability award NAS, 1975, Power Environ. Achievement award EPA, 1980, Excellence in Sulfur Dioxide Control award EPA, 1985; named Arkansas Traveler by Gov. Bill Clinton, 1989. Mem. AIChE, Am. Geophys. Union, Navy League U.S. (v.p. Palos Verdes Peninsula coun. 1961-62), N.Y. Acad. Scis., Sci. Rsch. Soc. Am., Am. Chem. Soc., U.S. Power Squadron (hon. capt. of fleet 1997), St. Andrew Soc. So. Calif. (mem. bd. govs.), Clan Macnachtan Assn., Clan Buchanan Soc. Am., Clan Farquharson Assn., Clan Chattan of the U.S., Clan MacFarland Soc., Betty Washington Lewis Soc. of Children of Am. Revolution (past pres.), Ark. Soc. of Children of Am. Revolution (past pres.), Santa Monica Yacht Club (lifetime hon. cannoneer, chief of protocal, mem. marina mgmt. com.), Sigma Xi, Phi Kappa Phi, Phi Lambda Upsilon, Alpha Chi Sigma, Lambda Chi Alpha. Office: 8229 Billowvista Dr Playa Del Rey CA 90293-7807

WEIR, ANNE, writer; b. Boston, Feb. 9, 1942; d. John Weir and Martha (Kingman) Perry; children: Emily Weir, Sarah Noel, Katherine Joy. BA, Swarthmore Coll., 1964; MEd, U. Maine, 1984. Cert. elem. and secondary edn. tchr. Editor: Marlowe: Being In the Life of the Mind, 1996, A Book of Certainties, 1998, The Color Book, 1998, Marlowe, corrected and augmented, 1999, Christopher's Journey, Acts & Scenes, News, The Bird's Eye, 1996-2000, A Native Woman poems, 1999, American City, 2000, A Codebook for the Plays, 2000, Waking, An Academic Celebration, 2001, A Teacher's Holiday, "Streamlines" A Study in Bibliography, New Songs, 2001, The Reincarnation of Love, 2002, Literary Picture Notebooks, And in Aftertimes, 2003. Office: Marlowe Books PO Box 10364 Portland ME 04104-0364

WEIR, BRYCE KEITH ALEXANDER, neurosurgeon, neurologist, educator; b. Edinburgh, Scotland, Apr. 29, 1936; arrived in U.S., 1992; s. Ernest John and Marion Weir; m. Mary Lou Lauber, Apr. 25, 1976; children: Leanora, Glyncora, Brocke. BSc, McGill U., Montreal, Que., Can., 1958, MD, CM, 1960, MSc, 1963. Diplomate Am. Bd. Neurol. Surgery, Nat. Bd. Med. Examiners. Intern Montreal Gen. Hosp., 1960-61; resident in neurosurgery Neurological Inst., Montreal, 1962-64, 65-66, N.Y. Neurol. Inst., N.Y.C., 1964-65; neurosurgeon U. Alta., Edmonton, Can., 1967-92, dir. div. neurosurgery, 1982-86, Walter Anderson prof., chmn. dept. surgery, 1986-92; surgeon-in-chief U. Alta. Hosps., 1986-92; Maurice Goldblatt prof. surgery and neurology U. Chgo., 1992—2002, dir. Brain Rsch. Inst., 1993—2001, interim dean biol. scis. divsn. and Pritzker Sch. Medicine, v.p. med. affairs, 2001—02. Past pres. V Internat. Symposium on Cerebral Vasospasm; mem. neurology A study sect. NIH, 1991—93; invited speaker at over 135 profl. meetings; vis. prof. over 68 univs., including Yale U., Cornell U., Columbia U., Duke U., U. Toronto, U. Calif., San Francisco; 19 named lectureships, including White lectr., Harvard U.; 18 named lectureships, including Gainey lectr., Mayo Clinic. Author: Aneurysms Affecting the Nervous System, 1987, Subarachnoid Hemorrhage-Causes and Cures, 1998, Cerebral Vasospasm, 2001; co-editor: Primer on Cerebrovascular Diseases, 1997, Stroke: Pathophysiology, Diagnosis and Management, 4th edit., 2004; mem. editl. bd. Jour. Neurosurgery, chmn. bd. 1993—94, mem. editl. bd. Neurosurgery Quar., Jour. Cerebrovascular Disease, Neurosurgery; contbr. over 275 articles to profl. jours. Named Officer of the Order of Can., 1995. Fellow: ACS, Royal Coll. Surgeons Can., Royal Coll. Surgeons Edinburgh (hon.); mem.: Interurban Neurosurg. Soc. (chmn.), Nat. Acad. Scis., Inst. Medicine, Soc. Neurol. Surgeons (Grass gold medal 1992), Japan Neurosurg. Soc. (hon.), Am. Acad. Neurol. Surgeons, James. IV Assn. Surgeons, Am. Surg. Assn. Achievements include rsch. in cerebral vasospasm and the surgical management of intracranial aneurysms.

WEIR, EDWARD KENNETH, cardiologist, educator; b. Belfast, No. Ireland, Jan. 7, 1943; came to U.S. 1973; s. Thomas Kenneth and Violet Hilda (ffrench) W.; m. Elizabeth Vincent Pearman, May 29, 1971; children: Fergus G., Conor K. BA, U. Oxford, U.K., 1964; MA, BM, BCh, U. Oxford, Eng., 1967, DM, 1976. Diplomate Am. Bd. Internal Medicine. Intern Churchill Hosp., Oxford, Eng., 1968, Radcliffe Infirmary, Oxford, 1968, resident, 1970-71, Hammersmith Hosp., London, 1969, Groot Schuur Hosp., Cape Town, South Africa, 1969-70, registrar in cardiology, 1971-73; postdoctoral rsch. fellow U. Colo., Denver, 1973-75; cons. pediatric cardiologist U. Cape Town Med. Sch., 1975-76; cons. cardiologist U. Natal Med. Sch., Durban, South Africa, 1976-77; assoc. prof. medicine U. Minn., Mpls., 1978-85, prof. medicine, 1985—, prof. physiology, 1999—. Staff physician VAMC, Mpls., 1978—, chief of cardiology, 2000—; dir. Grover Confs. on Pulmonary Circulation, 1984-2000. Co-editor: Pulmonary Hypertension, 1984, The Pulmonary Circulation in Health and Disease, 1987, Pulmonary Vascular Physiology and Pathophysiology, 1989, The Diagnosis and Treatment of Pulmonary Hypertension, 1992, Ion Flux in Pulmonary Vascular Control, 1993, The Pulmonary Circulation and Gas Exchange, 1994, Nitric Oxide and Radicals in the Pulmonary Vasculature, 1996, Pulmonary Edema, 1998, Oxygen Regulation of Ion Channels and Gene Expression, 1998, The Fetal and Neonatal Pulmonary Circulations, 2000, Interactions of Blood and the Pulmonary Circulation, 2002. Fulbright scholar, 1973-75; Sr. Internat. Fogarty fellow, 1993. Fellow Am. Coll. Cardiology, Royal Coll. Physicians London; mem. Am. Heart Assn. (Minn. affiliate bd. dirs. 1989-93, Nat. Cardiopulmonary Coun. (exec. com. 1992-2003), Pulmonary Circulation Found. (treas. 1985-2001). Office: VA Med Ctr 1 Veterans Dr # 111C Minneapolis MN 55417-2300 *What you "achieve" in life is much less important than what you do for those around you. One hundred years after their death, very few people are remembered for what they achieved.*

WEIR, DAME GILLIAN CONSTANCE, concert organist, harpsichordist; b. Martinborough, New Zealand, Jan. 17, 1941; d. Cecil Alexander and Clarice M. Foy (Bignell) W. Grad., Royal Coll. Music, London, 1965; Mus D (hon.), U. Victoria of Wellington, New Zealand, 1983; DLitt (hon.), Huddersfield U., 1997; Mus D (hon.), Hull U., 1999, Exeter U., 2001; Doctorate (hon.), U. Ctrl. Eng., 2001; Mus D (hon.), Leicester Univ., 2003, U. Aberdeen, Scotland, 2004. Artist in residence numerous univs. including Yale U, Washington U., St. Louis, U. Western Australia, others; vis. lectr. Royal No. Coll. Music, Manchester, Eng., 1974-89; vis. prof. organ Royal Acad. Music, London, 1997-98; Prince Consort prof. Royal Coll. of Music, London, 1999—; spkr. BBC programs on music and performance; subject of Melvyn Bragg's TV documentary South Bank Show, 2000. Concert appearances with leading Brit. Orchs. and Boston Orch., Seattle Orch., Australian ABC Orch., Wurttemberg Chamber and other fgn. orch.; appeared in major internat. festivals including Edinburgh, Flanders, Aldeburgh, Bath, Proms, Europalia; appeared at concert halls including Royal Festival Hall, Royal Albert Hall, Lincoln Ctr., NY, Sydney Opera House; numerous radio and TV appearances in Brit. and world-wide including Royal Festival Hall Jubilee; organ cons.; adjudicator internat. competitions; contbr. The Messiaen Companion, 1995; contbr. articles to profl. jour.; recs. include complete organ works of Olivier Messiaen, others; TV documentary film on career, 1982, BBC TV programs The King of Instruments, 1989. Decorated comdr., dame comdr. Order Brit. Empire; recipient Turnovsky award 1985, Evening Std. award for outstanding solo performance, 1998-99, winner (1st prize)St. Albans Internat. Organ Competition, 1964. Fellow Royal Coll. Organists (hon., mem. coun. 1977—, mem. exec. 1981-85, pres. 1994-96, 1st Woman pres.), Royal Can. Coll. Organists (hon.), Royal Coll. Music (hon.); mem. Royal Acad. Music (hon.), Inc. Soc. Musicians (1st woman pres. 1992-93), Albert Schweitzer Assn. (Silver medal 1998), Soloists' Ensemble (pres. 1997). Office: care Karen McFarlane Artists 2385 Fenwood Rd Cleveland OH 44118-3803 Office Phone: 216-397-3345.

WEIR, MORTON WEBSTER, retired academic administrator, educator; b. Canton, Ill., July 18, 1934; s. James and Frances Mary (Johnson) W.; m. Cecelia Ann Rumler, June 23, 1956; children: Deborah, Kevin, Mark. AB, Knox Coll., 1955; MA, U. Tex., 1958, PhD, 1959. Rsch. assoc., asst. prof. child devel. U. Minn., Mpls., 1959; asst. prof. child devel. U. Ill., Urbana, 1960-64, assoc. prof., 1964-68, prof., 1968-93, prof. emeritus, 1993—, head dept. psychology, 1969-71, vice chancellor acad. affairs, 1971-79, v.p. acad. affairs, 1982-88, chancellor, 1988-93, chancellor emeritus, 1993—, sr. found. rep., 1993-99; dir. Boys Town Center Study Youth Development, 1979-80. Contbr. numerous articles to profl. jours. Trustee Knox Coll., 1984—, chmn., 1995—99. With AUS, 1960. NSF Predoctoral fellow, 1957-59 Fellow AAAS; mem. Soc. Rsch. in Child Devel. (chmn. bd. publs. 1971, chmn. fin. com. 1993-95), Sigma Xi, Phi Beta Kappa, Phi Kappa Phi. E-mail: mortweir@msn.com.

WEIR, PETER LINDSAY, film director; b. Sydney, Australia, Aug. 21, 1944; s. Lindsay Weir and Peggy Barnsley; m. Wendy Stites, 1966; 2 children. Educated, Scots Coll., Sydney, Vaucluse Boys H.S., Sydney U. Worked in real estate until 1965; worked as stagehand in TV, Sydney, 1967; dir. film sequences in variety show, 1968; dir. amateur univ. revs., 1967-69; dir. for Film Australia, 1969-73; made own short films, 1969-73, incl. feature film producer, dir. and writer, 1973—. Films include: Cars That Ate Paris, 1973, Picnic at Hanging Rock, 1975, The Last Wave, 1977, The Plumber (TV), 1978, Gallipoli, 1980 (Australian Film Inst. award for best dir., 1981), The Year of Living Dangerously, 1982, Witness, 1985, The Mosquito Coast, 1986, Dead Poets Society, 1989, Green Card, 1990, Fearless, 1993, The Truman Show, 1997 (David Lean award for best dir., BAFTA, 1999, London Critics Circle Film award for best dir., 1999), Master and Commander: The Far Side of the World, 2003. Raymond Longford Award, Australian Film Inst., 1990, Douglas Sirk Award, 1998. Mem. Australia A.M. Office: Creative Artists Agy care John Ptak 9830 Wilshire Blvd Beverly Hills CA 90212-1804*

WEIR, ROBERT H. lawyer; b. Dec. 7, 1922; s. Abraham and Beatrice (Stern) W.; m. Ruth Hirsch, July 2, 1954 (dec. Nov. 1965); children: Nicole F., Daniella F.; m. Sylvia T. Frias. Bar: Mass. 1948, Washington 1952, Calif. 1957. Spl. asst. to atty. gen. U.S. Dept. Justice, Seattle, 1953—56; pvt. practice San Jose and Palo Alto, Calif., 1957—. Instr. taxation of real estate U. Calif. at San Jose and San Francisco; lectr. U. So. Calif. Tax Inst.; CEO Villa Tita Group, 1974—2001; spkr. on taxation at ann. meetings Nat. Assn. Real Estate Bds., 1958—60. Author: Advantages in Taxes, 1960; tax columnist: Rural Realtor, 1959—; author: Taxes Working for You, 1966, How to Make the Most of Depreciation Write Off; contbr. articles to profl. jours. Bd. dirs. San Jose Light Opera Assn., Inc.; mem. prison com. Am. Friends Svc. Com. With U.S. Army, 1942—45. Mem.: ABA, Am. Judicature Soc., State Bar Calif., Santa Clara County Bar Assn. Address: 27743 Via Ventana Los Altos CA 94022-3241 Office Phone: 650-248-5262.

WEIR, SONJA ANN, artist; b. Hazleton, Pennsylvania, Oct. 12, 1934; d. Stephen and Anna (Prehatny) Tatusko; m. Richard Clayton Weir, Jan. 14, 1956; children: Robert, Carl, Donna, Lisa, and Nancy. Studied with Mary Ellen Silkotch, 1963—83; student, Art Students League, N.Y.C., 1985—87. Artist Knickerbocker Toy Co., Middlesex, NJ, 1980; represented by Agora Gallery, Soho, NY, 1999. Tchr. adult art edn. in Jointure, NJ., 2001-03; guest spkr. career day Bridgewater H.S., 1993-94. One-woman shows include Johnson & Johnson, Piscataway, N.J., 1992, Stillman, N.J., 2003 (Meml. award), Somerset County Libr., Bridgewater, N.J., 1992—94, Manville (N.J.) Pub. Libr., 1994—99, exhibited in group shows at Raritan Valley Art Assn., 1982—83, 1995, 1998 (Best in Show award, 1983, 2d prize, 1995, 1st pl. for oil, 1998), Ariel Gallery, N.Y.C., 1991, Am. Artists Profl. League, 1991, 1994, Barren Art Ctr., Woodbridge, N.J., 1993, Agora Gallery, N.Y.C., 1995—99, 2001, Somerset County Libr., 1998—99, Am. Artists Profl. League, 1999, Atrium Gallery, Morristown, N.J., 2001, Somerset County Cultural and Heritage Gallery, 2003, Johnson & Johnson, Stillman, N.J., 2003, Children's Specialized Hosp., N.J., 2003, Barrons Art Ctr., Woodbridge, N.J., 2003, Art Extraordinaire, Bernardsville, N.J., 2004, N.J. Soc. Watercolor Show, 2004 (award of excellence, 2004); featured in Artis Apectrum mag., vol. 11/6, 1999, Star Ledger, 2000; Star Ledger, 2003, Chronicle, Bound Brook, N.J., 2003, Represented in permanent collections N.W.B. Bank of South Bound Brook, N.J., Summit Bank. Recipient Peter Matulavage Award Salmagundi Club, Meml. Award Am. Artists Profl. League, N.Y.C., Samual Lightment Meml. Award Salmagundi Club, 2003; featured in Artis Spectrum mag., 1999, Star Ledger, 2003. Fellow: Nat. Am. Artists Profl. League (v.p. N.J. chpt. 1988—91, publicity com. 1988—91, show chmn. 1989—91, pres. N.J. chpt. 1992—95, editor newsletter 1992—99, nat. exec. bd. 1998—2000, show chmn. 2001—04, nat. pres. 2001—04); mem.: Miniature Art Soc. Fla., Raritan Valley Arts Assn. (pres. 1982—84), Nat. Miniature Assn. (assoc.), Nat. Mus. Women in the Arts. Home: 25 Madison St South Bound Brook NJ 08880-1244

WEIR, THOMAS ALBERT, education educator; b. St. Louis, July 30, 1915; s. Frank George and Mary Catherine Weir; m. Evelyn Mae Dobbin, Dec. 6, 1947; children: Pamela Jean, Larry James. BS, U. Ill., Urbana, 1939, MA, 1940; PhD, Ohio State U., Columbus, 1951. H.s. tchr. St. Louis Pub. Schs., 1941—42, chmn., social studies, 1946—47, rsch. scholar, 1950—51; prof., tchr. Harris-Stowe H.S., St. Louis, 1951—80; prof., secondary edn. Drury Grad. Sch., Springfield, Mo.; prof., edn. U. Okla., Norman. Staff sgt. Signal Svc., 1942—46, Pacific. Mem.: Mo. State Tchrs. Assn. (pres., St. Louis dist. 1969—70), St. Louis' Tchrs. Assn. (pres. 1969), Pub. Question Club (pres. 1951), Masonic Order. Avocation: swimming. Home: 6037 Tholozan Saint Louis MO 63109

WEIR, WILLIAM THOMAS, retired engineer, educator; b. Wildwood, N.J., Dec. 23, 1931; s. Willliam Thomas and Mildred Kendall Weir; m. Sarah McGowan Weir, June 5, 1954; children: William Thomas, Blair Stephen, Timothy Andrew, James Christopher. BSEE, Drexel U., 1954, MS in Physics, 1958; PhD in Sys. Engring. and Ops. Rsch., U. Pa., 1972. Registered profl. engr., Calif. Customer engr. IBM, 1950—53; component engr. RCA, 1954—57; prof. Drexel U., 1954—2002; mgr. sys. engring. lab. GE, 1958—73; pres., chmn. bd. dirs. Evaluation Assocs., 1973—89; prin. engr. PSEG, 1990—97. Mem. U.S. Sci. Del. to People's Republic of China, 1979. Fellow: IEEE. Home: PO Box 506 513 19th St Ocean City NJ 08226-0506

WEIS, JOSEPH FRANCIS, JR., federal judge; b. Pitts., Mar. 12, 1923; s. Joseph Francis and Mary (Flaherty) Weis; m. Margaret Horne Weis, Dec. 27, 1958; children: Maureen, Joseph Francis, Christine. BA, Duquesne U., 1947; JD, U. Pitts., 1950; LLD (hon.), Dickinson Coll., 1989. Bar: Pa. 1950. Pvt. practice, Pitts., 1950—68; judge Ct. Common Pleas, Allegheny County, Pa., 1968—70, U.S. Dist. Ct. (we. dist.), Pa., 1970—73, U.S. Ct. Appeals (3d cir.), Pitts., 1973—88, sr. judge, 1988—. Lectr. trial procedures, 1965—; adj. prof. law U. Pitts., 1986—; chmn. Fed. Cts. Study Com., Jud. Conf. Com. on Expt. to Videotape Trial Procs. within the 3rd Cir., Internat. Jud. Conf. the Joint Am.-Can. Appellate Judges Conf., Toronto, 1986, London, 85; futurist subcom. bicentennial com. Ct. Common Pleas, Allegheny County, Pa., 1988; participant programs legal medicine, Rome, London; mem. Am.-Can. Legal Exch., 1987; apptd. by Chief Justice Rehnquist U.S. Jud. Conf., Com. on Internat. Jud. Rels., 1998—2004; com. on adminstrn. bankruptcy sys., subcom. on jud. improvements Jud. Conf. U.S., 1983—87, chmn. civil rules com., 1986—87, chmn. standing com. rules of practice and procedure, 1988. Contbr. articles to profl. jours. Active Mental Health and Mental Retardation Bd., Allegheny County, 1970—73, Leukemia Soc., 1970—73, Disabled Am. Vets., Cath. War Vets, Mil. Order of the World Wars; trustee Forbes Hosp. Sys., Pitts., 1969—74; bd. adminstrn. Catholic Diocese Pitts., 1971—83. Capt. U.S. Army, 1943—48. Decorated Bronze Star, Purple Heart with oak leaf cluster; recipient St. Thomas More award, 1971, Phillip Amram award, 1991, Edward J. Devitt Disting. Svc. to Justice award, 1993, History Makers award, 1997. Fellow: Am. Bar Found., Internat. Acad. Trial Lawyers (hon.); mem.: ABA (chmn. appellate judges' conf. 1981—83), Inst. Jud. Adminstrn., Am. Judicature Soc., Acad. Trial Lawyers Allegheny County (past pres.), Allegheny Bar Assn. (past v.p.), Pa. Bar Assn., 4th Armored Divsn. Assn., Am. Legion, Knights of Malta, KC. Home: 225 Hillcrest Rd Pittsburgh PA 15238-2307 Office: US Ct Appeals US PO & Courthouse 7th & Grant St Rm 219 Pittsburgh PA 15219

WEIS, JUDITH SHULMAN, biology professor; b. N.Y.C., May 29, 1941; d. Saul B. and Pearl (Cooper) Shulman; m. Peddrick Weis; children: Jennifer, Eric. BA, Cornell U., 1962; MS, NYU, 1964, PhD, 1967. Lectr. CUNY, 1964-67; asst. prof. Rutgers U., Newark, 1967-71, assoc. prof., 1971-76, prof., 1976—. Congl. sci. fellow U.S. Senate, Washington, 1983—84; mem. grante rev. panel NSF, Washington, 1976—82, program dir., 1988—90; mem. rev. panel EPA, 1984—92; mem. NOAA Nat. Sea Grant Rev. Panel, 1997—; vis. scientist EPA Lab., Gulf Breeze, Fla., 1992. Mem. marine bd. NAS, 1991—94. Grantee NOAA, 1977—, N.J. EPA Rsch., 1978-79, 81-83, N.J. Marine Scis. Consortium Rsch., 1987—; NSF fellow, 1962-64, U.S. Geol. Survey, 1996—, NSF, 1998—. Mem.: NOW (pres. Essex County 1972), AAAS (chair biology sect. 1999), Assn. Women in Sci. (councilor 2002—, bd. dirs. 2003—), Ecol. Soc. Am., Estuarine Rsch. Fedn., Soc. Environ. Toxicology and Chemistry (bd. dirs. 1990—93), Am. Inst. Biol. Scis. (bd. dirs. 1986—88, 1989—91, 1997—99, pres.-elect 2000—01, pres. 2001), Sierra Club (bd. dirs. N.J. chpt. 1986—88). Avocations: choral singing, swimming, light opera. Office: Rutgers U Dept Biol Scis Newark NJ 07102 Business E-Mail: jweis@andromeda.rutgers.edu.

WEIS, MARGARET EDITH, writer, editor; b. Independence, Mo., Mar. 16, 1948; d. George Edward and Francis Irene (Reed) W.; m. Robert William Baldwin, Aug. 22, 1970 (div. 1981); children: David William (dec.), Elizabeth Lynn; m. Donald Bayne Stewart Perrin, 1996 (div. 2003). BA in Creative Writing, U. Mo., 1966-70. Proofreader Herald Pub. House, Independence, Mo., 1970-73, advt. dir., 1973-82; dir. div. Independence (Mo.) Press, 1977-82; editor TSR Inc, Lake Geneva, Wis., 1982-86. Freelance writer; co-owner Sovereign Press, Williams Bay, Wis., margaretweis.com. Author: (short story) The Test of the Twins, 1984, (books) The Endless Catacombs, 1984, Tower of Midnight Dreams, 1984, (with Tracy Hickman) The Dragonlance Chronicles, Vols. 1-3, 1984, 85, Dragonlance Legends, Vols. 1-3, 1985, 86, The Darksword Trilogy, Vols. 1-3, 1987, (with Roger Moore) Riddle of The Griffon, 1985, (under Margaret Baldwin) The Boys Who Saved The Children, 1982, Kisses of Death, 1983, (with Pat O'Brien) Wanted: Frank and Jesse James, The Real Story, 1981, (with Janet Pack) Children of The Holocaust, 1986, My First Thanksgiving, 1983, (with Gary Pack) Computer Graphics, 1984, Robots and Robotics, 1984, (short story) The Thirty Nine Buttons, 1987, (novella) (with Tracy Hickman) The Legacy, 1987, Wanna Bet?, 1987; editor: The Art of Dungeons and Dragons, 1985, Leaves of the Inn of the Last Home, 1987, The Art of Dragonlance, 1987, Dragonlance Tales, vol. 1, 2, 3, 1987, (with Tracy Hickman) The Rose of the Prophet, 1989, (with Tracy Hickman) Death's Gate, vol. 1, 1990, vols. 2, 3, 4, 5, 6, 7, Star of the

Guardian, vol. 1, The Lost King, 1990, King's Test vol. 2, 1991, King's Sacrifice Vol. 3, 1991, Ghost Legion Vol. 4, 1991, Dragons of Summer Flame, 1996, (with Don Perrin), Doom Brigade, 1997, Mag Force 7 novels, 3 vols., The Soulforge, 1998, Brothers in Arms, 1999, (with Tracy Hickman) Starshield, Vols. 1-3, 1997, Legacy of the Darksword, 1997, War of Souls, 3 vols., 2000; editor: Kender, Gully Dwarves and Gnomes, 1989, Love and War, 1991, Reign of Istar, 1993, Dragons of War, 1996, Dragons of Chaos, 1997, Relics and Omens, 1998, Sovereign Stone Role-Playing Games, 1999, Sovereign Stone novels, (with Tracy Hickman) vol. 1, Well of Darkness, 2000, vol. 2, Guardians of the Lost, 2001, Journey Into the Void, vol. 3, 2003, Mistress of Dragons, 2003, Draconian Measures, 2000, Dragon's Son, 2004, Ashes and Amber, 2004. Named to Writer's Hall of Fame, 2002, Adventure Gaming Hall of Fame, 2002; recipient Origins award, 2001. Avocations: role-playing games, flyball, agility.

WEIS, MERVYN J. physician, gastroenterologist; b. Chgo., June 9, 1940; s. Theodore A. and Anita (Stavins) W.; m. Myra Rubenstein, Nov. 26, 1966 (dec. Nov. 1990); children: Jonathan Mandel, Sari Tova; m. Anita Kaplan Sherbet, Oct. 1992. BA, Northwestern U., 1961, MD, 1965. Diplomate Am. Bd. Internal Medicine. Intern in internal medicine Michael Reese Hosp. and Med. Ctr., Chgo., 1965-66, resident in internal medicine, 1966-67, 69-70, attending physician, 1972-78; fellow in gastroenterology Northwestern U. Med. Ctr., Chgo., 1970-72; attending physician Ravenswood Hosp., Chgo., 1979-83, St. Francis Hosp., Evanston, Ill., 1984-88, Rush North Med. Ctr., Skokie, Ill., 1985-91, Louis A. Weiss Meml. Hosp., Chgo., 1972—, chmn. divsn. medicine, 1987-89, pres. med. staff, 1989-93, mem. bd. govs., 1987—. Cons. in gastroenterology VA Rsch. Hosp., Chgo., 1972-80 Contbr. articles to profl. jours. Capt. U.S. Army, 1967-69. Fellow ACP, Am. Coll. Gastroenterology, Am. Gastroenterologic Soc.; mem. AMA, Ill. State Med. Soc., Chgo. Soc. Gastroenterology, Chgo. Med. Soc., Am. Gastroenterol. Assn. (diplomate). Avocations: golf, jogging, computers. Office: 4640 N Marine Dr Ste C 6100 Chicago IL 60640-5719

WEIS, ROBERT FREEMAN, supermarket company executive; b. Sunbury, Pa. m. Patricia Ross; children: Jennifer, Colleen, Jonathan. Grad., Mercersburg Acad., 1937; BA, Yale U., 1941. With Weis Markets, Sunbury, Pa., 1946—, v.p., treas., bd. dirs., treas., 1995—, chmn. bd. dirs., 2002—. Chair steering com. capital campaign Susquehanna U., Selinsgrove, Pa., past vice chmn. bd. trustees; past pres. bd. trustees Sunbury Cmty. Hosp., trustee; bd. dirs. Lown Cardiovascular Rsch. Found., Brookline, Mass. Past pres. Sunbury C. of C.; past chmn. bd. dirs. First Nat. Trust Bank Sunbury, ereritus dir.; past dir. Susquehanna Bancshares; treas. Sunbury chpt. United Jewish Appeal. Office: Weis Markets Inc 1000 S 2d St PO Box 471 Sunbury PA 17801-0471

WEISBACH, LOU, advertising executive; Pres., CEO, founder Ha-Lo Industries, Inc., Niles, Ill., 1972-99, chmn., 1999—. Office: HALO Industries Inc 5800 W Touhy Ave Niles IL 60714

WEISBERG, DAVID CHARLES, lawyer; b. N.Y.C., June 25, 1938; s. Leonard Joseph and Rae M. (Kimberg) W.; m. Linda Gail Kerman, Aug. 27, 1975; children: Leonard Jay, Risa Beth. AB, U. Mich., 1958; LLB, Harvard U., 1961. Bar: N.Y. 1962, U.S. Dist. Ct. (so. and ea. dists.) N.Y. 1965, U.S. Supreme Ct. 1970. Assoc. Dreyer & Traub, Bklyn., 1962, Lee Franklin, Mineola, N.Y., 1962-65; pvt. practice, Patchogue, N.Y., 1965-67, 77-80; ptnr. Bass & Weisberg, Patchogue, 1967-77, Davidow, Davidow, Russo & Weisberg, Patchogue, 1981-82, Davidow, Davidow, Weisberg & Wismann, Patchogue, 1982-87, Davidow, Davidow & Wismann, Patchogue, 1988-92, Weisberg & Wismann, Patchogue, 1992-98; propr. The Lawyer's Equalizer, 2000—. Assoc. justice and justice Village of Patchogue, 1968-70, village atty., 1970-85; spl. asst. dist. atty. Suffolk County, Patchogue, 1970-85; assoc. estate tax atty., appraiser N.Y. State Dept. Taxation and Fin., Hauppauge, N.Y., 1975-85; lectr. estate tax Suffolk County Acad. Law, 1976-84, negligence law, 1994; cons. in field. Law chmn. Suffolk County Dem. Com., N.Y., 1975-85; bd. dirs. Temple Beth El of Patchogue. With USAR, 1961-62. Mem. ATLA, N.Y. State Bar Assn., Suffolk County Bar Assn., Nassau-Suffolk Trial Lawyers Sect., Lions (pres. Medford 1978-79, 2d v.p. 1984-85). Avocations: bicycling, skiing. Personal E-mail: dcw608@yahoo.com. Business E-Mail: dcw@lawyersequalizer.com.

WEISBERG, HERBERT FRANK, political science educator; b. Mpls., Dec. 8, 1941; s. Nathan R. and Jean (Schlessinger) W.; m. Judith Ann Robinson, Dec. 16, 1979; 1 child, Bryan Bowen. BA, U. Minn., 1963; PhD, U. Mich., 1968. Asst. prof. polit. sci. U. Mich., Ann Arbor, 1967-73, assoc. prof. polit. sci., 1973-74, Ohio State U., Columbus, 1974-77, prof. polit. sci., 1977—. Author: Central Tendency and Variation, 1992; co-author: Theory Building and Data Analysis, 1984, Controversies in Voting Behavior, 2001, Survey Research Polling and Data Analysis, 1996, Classics in Congressional Politics, 1999; editor: Political Science: Science of Politics, 1985, Democracy's Feast: Elections in America, 1995; co-editor Am. Jour. Polit. Sci., 1979-82, Great Theatre: The American Congress in the 1990's, 1998, Reelection 1996: How Americans Voted, 1999, Models of Voting in Presidential Elections, 2004. Mem.: Am. Polit. Sci. Assn. (program chmn. 1983), Midwest Polit. Sci. Assn. (pres. 2001—02), Phi Kappa Phi, Pi Sigma Alpha, Phi Beta Kappa. Home: 742 Gatehouse Ln Columbus OH 43235-1732 Office: Ohio State U Dept Polic Sci 2140 Derby Hall 154 N Oval Mall Columbus OH 43210-1330

WEISBERG, LEONARD R. retired engineering executive, researcher; b. N.Y.C., Oct. 17, 1929; s. Emanuel E. and Esther (Raynes) W.; m. Frances Simon, Mar. 23, 1980; children: Glenna Weisberg Andersen, Orren Weisberg Falk, Frances Weisberg Brookner. BA magna cum laude, Clark U., 1950; MA, Columbia U., 1952. Rsch. asst. Watson Labs. IBM, N.Y.C., 1953-55; with RCA Labs., Princeton, N.J., 1955-71, mem. tech. staff, 1955-66, head rsch. group, 1966-69, dir. semicondr. device rsch. lab., 1969-71; dir. materials rsch. lab. Itek Corp., Lexington, Mass., 1972-74, v.p., dir. ctrl. rsch. lab., 1974-75; dir. electronics tech U.S. Dept. Def., Washington, 1975-79; v.p. rsch. and engring. Honeywell Inc., Mpls., 1980-94, ret., 1994. Mem. adv. group on electron devices U.S. Dept. Def., 1981-99; bd. dirs. TimeLab Corp. Contbr. articles to profl. jours. Recipient award for initiating VHSIC program U.S. Dept. Def., 1979. Fellow IEEE; mem. Am. Phys. Soc., Sigma Xi Home: 1250 S Washington St # 202 Alexandria VA 22314-4455 Personal E-mail: LenW5678@aol.com.

WEISBERG, LOIS, arts administrator, city official; Commr. Chgo. Dept. Cultural Affairs, 1989—. Office: Chicago Cultural Center 78 E Washington St Chicago IL 60602-4816

WEISBERG, LYNNE WILLING, psychiatrist, consultant; b. N.Y.C., Apr. 11, 1948; d. Stanley S. and Pearl R. Willing. BA, Barnard Coll., 1969; PhD, U. Mich., 1972; MD, SUNY, Downstate, 1978. Diplomate Am. Bd. Psychiatry and Neurology, Am. Bd. Adolescent Psychiatry. Intern NYU Med. Ctr., 1978-79; resident in adult psychiatry Mt. Sinai Hosp., N.Y.C., 1979-81; fellow in child psychiatry Columbia Med. Ctr., 1981-83; staff psychiatrist Fair Oaks Hosp., Summit, N.J., 1983-85, asst. dir. child and adolescent psychiatry, 1985-88, assoc. dir. child and adolescent psychiatry, 1988-92; dir. child and adolescent outpatient psychiat. svcs. Psychiat. Assocs. N.J. at Fair Oaks Hosp., Summit, 1992—; pvt. practice Morris County, N.J., 1993—. Cons. Bonnie Brae Sch., Millington, N.J., 1984-92. Author: When Acting Out Isn't Acting, 1991. Horace Rackham Prize fellow, 1972. Mem. AMA, Med. Soc. N.J., Am. Soc. Clin. Psychopharmacology. Office: 135 Columbia Tpke Ste 201 Florham Park NJ 07932-2104

WEISBERGER, BARBARA, artistic director, educator, choreographer; b. Bklyn., Feb. 28, 1926; d. Herman and Sally (Goldstein) Linshes; m. Sol Spiller, Sept. 3, 1945 (div. 1948); m. Ernest Weisberger, Nov. 15, 1949; children: Wendy, Steven. BS in Edn., Psychology, Pa. State U., 1945; L.H.D. (hon.), Swarthmore Coll., 1970; D.F.A. (hon.), Temple U., 1973, Kings Coll., 1978, Villanova U., 1978, U. New England, 1996. Founder, dir., tchr. Wilkes-Barre (Pa.) Ballet Theater, 1953-63; founder, dir. Pa. Ballet, Phila., 1962-82, Carlisle (Pa.) Project, 1984—; artistic advisor Peabody Dance, Balt., 2001—. Vice chmn. dance panel Nat. Endowment for the Arts, Washington, 1975-79. Performed with Met. Opera Ballet, N.Y.C., 1937, 38, Mary Binney Montgomery Co., Phila., 1940-42, ballet mistress, choreographer, Ballet Co. of Phila. Lyric Opera, 1961-62; choreographic works include Italian Concerto, Bach, Symphonic Variations, Franck; also operas for, Phila. Lyric Opera Co. Named Disting. Dau. of Pa., 1972, Disting. Alumna, Pa. State U., 1972; recipient 46th ann. Gimbel Phila. award, 1978. Mem. Psi Chi. Home and Office: 571 Charles Ave Kingston PA 18704-4711 Office Phone: 570-287-8349.

WEISBERGER, JOSEPH ROBERT, retired judge; b. Providence, Aug. 3, 1920; s. Samuel Joseph and Ann Elizabeth (Meighan) W.; m. Sylvia Blanche Pigeon, June 9, 1951; children: Joseph Robert, Paula Ann, Judith Marie. AB, Brown U., 1942; JD, Harvard U., 1949; LLD (hon.), R.I. Coll., Suffolk U., Mt. St. Joseph Coll.; DCL (hon.), Providence Coll.; DHL (hon.), Bryant Coll.; LLD (hon.), Roger Williams Coll., 1992; LLD (hon.), Brown U., 1992, Constantine U., 1997; LLD, So. New England Sch. Law, 1998; DHL (hon.), Salve Regina U., 2001. Bar: Mass. 1949, R.I. 1950. With Quinn & Quinn, Providence, 1951-56; solicitor Glocester, R.I., 1953-56; judge Superior Ct. R.I., Providence, 1956-72; presiding justice R.I. Superior Ct., Providence, 1972-78; justice R.I. Supreme Ct., Providence, 1978—, chief justice, 1993—2001; ret., 2001. Adj. prof. U. Nev., 1986—; mem. faculty Nat. Jud. Coll.; vis. lectr. Providence Coll., Suffolk Law Sch., Roger Williams Coll.; chmn. New Eng. Regional Conf. Trial Judges, 1962, 63, 65, New Eng. Regional Commn. Disordered Offender, 1968-71, R.I. Com. Adoption on Rules Criminal Procedure, 1968-72, R.I. Adv. Com. Corrections, 1973; bd. dirs. Nat. Ctr. for State Cts., 1975-81. Chmn. editorial bd. Judges Jour., 1973-75. Pres. R.I. Health Facilities Planning Coun., 1967-70; chmn. Gov. R.I. Coun. Mental Health, 1968-73; moderator Town of East Providence, 1954-56; mem. R.I. Senate, 1953-56, minority leader, 1955-56; vice chmn. bd. trustee R.I. Hosp., 1968-92, St. Joseph's Hosp., trustee, 1962—. Lt. comdr. USNR, 1941-46. Recipient Erwin Griswold award Nat. Jud. Coll., 1989; named to R.I. Hall of Fame; Paul Harris fellow Rotary Internat. Fellow Am. Bar Found.; mem. ABA (ho. of dels., task force on criminal justice stds. 1977-79, exec. com. appellate judges' conf. 1979-95, nat. conf. state trial judges 1977-78, exec. com. appelate judges conf. 1979—, vice chmn., 1983-85, chmn., 1985-86), KC, R.I. Bar Assn., Am. Judges Assn. (gov.), Inst. Jud. Adminstrn., Am. Judicature Soc. (Herbert Harley award 1990), Am. Law Inst., Order of St. Gregory (knight comdr. with star 1989, Goodrich award for Svc. 1995), Phi Beta Kappa (past pres. Alpha chpt. Brown U.). Home: 60 Winthrop St Riverside RI 02915-2624 Office: RI Supreme Ct 250 Benefit St Ste 7 Providence RI 02903-2724 Office Phone: 401-222-7691. E-mail: jweisberger@courts.state.ri.us. *My professional life for the last 45 years has been occupied with judicial duties. I have been blessed with the opportunity to meet ever changing challenges and to attempt to solve a myriad of problems. These opportunities have been rewarding and absorbing. I consider judicial work to be a great privilege.*

WEISBIN, CHARLES RICHARD, nuclear engineer; b. Bklyn., Jan. 4, 1944; s. Alma (Schwartz) Lovitt; m. Alison Norma Weisbin, June 20, 1964; children: Daniel Mark, Amy Gayle. MS in Nuclear Engring., Columbia U., 1965, DSc in Nuclear Engring., 1969. Group leader Oak Ridge (Tenn.) Nat. Lab., 1977-80, sect. head, 1980-89, dir. robotics and intelligence sys., 1986-89, dir. Ctr. Engring. Sys. Advanced Rsch., 1982-89; mgr. telerobotics tech. Jet Propulsion Lab., Calif. Inst. Tech., Pasadena, 1991-92, mgr. robotic sys. and advanced computer tech. sect., 1989-93, mgr. rover and telerobotic tech., 1993-95, Mars program technologist, 1994-96, mgr. robotics and Mars exploration tech., 1995-98, dep. mgr. Cross Enterprise Tech. Devel. Program, thrust mgr. surface sys., 1999-2000, dep. program mgr. Strategic Sys. Tech. Program Office, 2001—. Mem. joint tech. panel on robotics DOD Joint Dirs. Labs., 1986—89; assoc. prof. computer sci. U. Tenn., Knoxville, 1984—89; program chmn. 2d Internat. Conf. on Artificial Intelligence IEEE Computer Soc., 1985; co-chmn. U.S. NASA Telerobotics Working Group, 1990—98; robotics and telepresence com. Space Tech. Interagy. Group, 1992—96. Author: Sensitivity and Uncertainty Analysis of Reactor Performance Parameters, 1982; contbr. Recipient Exceptional Svc. medal, NASA, 1993, 1999, Nova award, 1998, Thomas O. Paine award for advancement of human exploration to Mars, 1998, Outstanding Leadership in surface robotics award, 2000, Decadal Planning Team Achievement award, 2001, Lifetime Achievement award, World Automation Congress, 2004. Mem.: IEEE (Cert. Appreciation 1987), Robotics and Automation Soc., Am. Nuclear Soc. (program chmn. 1977—79), Tau Beta Pi, Sigma Chi. Republican. Jewish. Achievements include initiation of robotics and intelligent systems at Oak Ridge; research in sensitivity analysis, non-destructive assay of spent nuclear fuel, supervised inspection, emergency response robotics, and risk assessment for long-range, one-of-a-kind missions. Home: 775 Starlight Heights Dr La Canada Flintridge CA 91011-1854 Office: Jet Propulsion Lab Calif Inst Tech 4800 Oak Grove Dr Pasadena CA 91109-8099 Business E-Mail: Charles.R.Weisbin@jpl.nasa.gov.

WEISBLATT, BARBARA ANN, secondary school educator; b. New Brunswick, N.J., Mar. 21, 1958; d. Stanley Herman and Clara Armel Friedelbaum; m. Alan Joel Weisblatt, Dec. 27, 1992. BA in French/Spanish, Rutgers U., 1979, MAT in French, 1986, supr. cert., 1991. Cert. French, Spanish tchr. K-12 N.J. Tchr. Somerville (N.J.) H.S., 1980—; supr. Somerville Pub. Schs., 1993—94. Mem. Holocaust H.S. and Dist. Coms., Somerville, 1995—, Mid. States Steering Com., Somerville, 2000—02, H.S. Renaissance Com., Somerville, 2000—, H.S. Quality Coun., Somerville, 2002—. Author: (test) French Placement Test for Middle School Students, 1995. Mem. Hebrew HS bd. edn. Temple Sholom, Bridgewater, NJ, 1995—. Recipient Tchr. Recognition award, Gov. State of N.J., 2001; NEH grantee, Figaro Inst., 1991. Mem.: NEA, Assn. for Supervision and Cirriculum Devel., Fgn. Lang. Educators N.J., Am. Assn. Tchrs. French, Somerville Edn. Assn., N.J. Edn. Assn. Avocations: reading, photography, travel, exercise. Home: 85 Perrine Pike Hillsborough NJ 08844 Office: Somerville HS 222 Davenport St Somerville NJ 08876 Office Phone: 908-218-4157.

WEISBROD, BURTON ALLEN, economist, educator; b. Chgo., Feb. 13, 1931; s. Leon H. and Idelle C. (Chernoff) W.; m. Shirley Lindsay, Dec. 23, 1951; children: Glen, Linda. BS, U. Ill., 1951; MA in Econs, Northwestern U., 1952, PhD, 1958. Lectr. econs. Northwestern U., Evanston, Ill., 1954-55; instr. econs. Carleton Coll., Minn., 1955-57, Washington U., St. Louis, 1957-58, asst. prof. econs., 1958-62, assoc. prof. econs., 1962-64; vis. assoc. prof. Princeton (N.J.) U., 1962-63; sr. staff mem. Council of Econ. Advs., Pres. U.S., 1963-64; assoc. prof. dept. econs. U. Wis., Madison, 1964-66, prof., 1966-91, Evjue-Bascom prof. econs., 1985—91; dir. Ctr. for Urban Affairs and Policy Rsch. Northwestern U., Evanston, Ill., 1990-95, John Evans prof. econs., 1990—. Vis. prof. SUNY, Binghamton, 1972; sr. Fulbright lectr. U. Autonoma de Madrid, summer, 1970; vis. prof. Yale U., 1976-77; Ziskind vis. prof. Brandeis U., 1982-83; vis. scholar J.F. Kennedy Sch., Harvard U., 1982-83; mem. rsch. adv. com. Econ. Devel. Adminstrn., U.S. Dept. Commerce, 1967-69; mem. adv. com. Commn. on Pvt. Philanthropy and Pub. Needs, 1973-75; cons. various fed. and state govt. agys., 1964—; also IBM, Econ. Coun. Can., 1969, 71, 76, 78; mem. bd. econ. advs. Public Interest Econs. Ctr., 1973-86; mem. adv. com. med. care and med. econs. to 3d Nat. Cancer Survey, 1969-71; U.S. del. UN World Population Conf., Belgrade, Yugoslavia, 1965; bd. dirs. Nat. Bur. Econ. Rsch., Inc., 1979-90; vis. scholar Phi Beta Kappa Soc., 1998-99; mem. nat. rsch. resources coun. NIH, 1999-2003; mem. panel on nonmarket activity NRC, 2002-; chair com. on philanthropy and the nonprofit sector Social Sci.Rsch. Coun., 2002-. Author: Economics of Public Health, 1961, External Benefits of Public Education, 1964, (with W. Lee Hansen) Benefits, Costs, and Finance of Public Higher Education, 1969, (with Ralph L. Andreano) American Health Policy, 1974, The Voluntary Nonprofit Sector: An Economic Analysis, 1978, (with Joel F. Handler and Neil K. Komesar) Public Interest Law: An Economic and Institutional Analysis, 1978; contbg. author: (with others) Disease and Economic Development: The Case of Parasitic Diseases in St. Lucia, West Indies, 1974, Economics and Medical Research, 1983, The Nonprofit Economy, 1988; editor (with James Worthy) The Urban Crisis, 1997; author, editor: To Profit or Not to Profit, 1998; contbr. nearly 200 articles on econs. of edn., program evaluation, health care and econs. of pvt. non-profit sector to profl. jours.; mem. editl. bd.: Jour. Human Resources, 1966-86, Internat. Jour. Social Econs, 1972—, Jour. Public Econs, 1971-87, Pub. Fin. Rev., 1990—, Nonprofit and Voluntary Sector Quar., 1997—; assoc. editor: Public Fin. Quar, 1972-87. Guggenheim fellow, 1969-70; Ford Faculty fellow, 1971-72; Sr. research fellow Brookdale Inst., Jerusalem, 1978—; recipient Disting. Lifetime Rsch. award Assn. Rsch. Nonprofit Orgns. and Voluntary Assns., 1997; co-recipient Carl Taube award Disting. Rsch., APHA, 1992. Fellow AAAS; mem. Am. Econ. Assn. (exec. com. 1975-77, com. status of assn. jours. 1973-74, chmn. budget com. 1977), Midwest Econs. Assn. (pres. 1980-81), Nat. Acad. Scis. Inst. Medicine, Public Choice Soc., Internat. Inst. Public Finance, AAUP (exec. com. Washington U. chpt. 1961-62). Office: Northwestern U Econs Dept 2003 Sheridan Rd Evanston IL 60208-0826

WEISBROD, CARL, lawyer, public official; b. N.Y.C., Oct. 5, 1944; s. Walter and Hilda (Pelzer) W.; m. Jody Adams, Jan. 21, 1979; 1 child, William. BS, Cornell U., 1965; JD, NYU, 1968. Bar: N.Y., 1968; U.S. Dist. Ct. (so. dist.) N.Y., 1969, Asst. commr. N.Y.C. Housing Dept., 1970-72; counsel, chief exec. officer Wildcat Svc. Corp., N.Y.C., 1972-77, gen. counsel Manpower Demonstration Rsch. Corp., N.Y.C., 1977-78; dir. Mayor's Office of Midtown Enforcement, N.Y.C., 1978-84; exec. dir. City Vol. Corps, N.Y.C., 1984-86, N.Y.C. Planning Commn., 1986-87; pres. 42d St. Devel. Project, N.Y.C., 1987-90, pres., chief exec. officer N.Y.C. Econ. Devel. Corp., 1990-94; pres. Alliance for Downtown N.Y., 1995—; dir. Sept. 11 Fund, 2001—. Chmn. N.Y.C. Loft Bd., 1982-84; chmn. Wildcat Svc. Corp., 2002- . Contbr. articles to profl. jours. Trustee The Ford Found., 1996-, NYU Downtown Hosp., 1999—; dir. Tarragon Realty Advisors, Inc., 1995—; dir. Lower Manhattan Devel. Corp., 2002- . Office: Alliance for Downtown NY 120 Broadway New York NY 10271-0002 Business E-Mail: cwiesbrod@downtownny.com.

WEISBROD, JOHN, professional sports team executive; b. Syosset, N.Y., Oct. 8, 1968; Degree, Harvard U. Exec. v.p., dir. hockey ops., alt. gov. Albany (N.Y.) River Rats, 1993—97; v.p., gen. mgr. Orlando (Fla.) Solar Bears, 1997—2000; COO Orlando (Fla.) Magic, 2000—04, gen. mgr., 2004—. Mem. Nat. Championship Hockey Team, 1989. Recipient Donald Angier trophy, Harvard U. Mailing: 8701 Maitland Summit Blvd Orlando FL 32810*

WEISBUCH, ROBERT ALAN, English educator; b. Rochester, NY, Nov. 22, 1946; s. Irving Arthur and Ferne (Paull) W.; m. Susan Ann Remington, July 23, 1972 (div. 1979); 1 child, Max; m. Louise Wicks Freymann, Aug. 6, 1983 (div. 1994); children: Sarah, Michael; m. Candy Jaye Cooper, Aug. 27, 1994; 1 child, Gabriel. BA magna cum laude, Wesleyan U., Middletown, Conn., 1968; MPhil in English, Yale U., 1970, PhD in English, 1972. Asst. prof. English U. Mich., Ann Arbor, 1972-76, assoc. prof., 1976-85, prof., 1985—, assoc. chmn. dept. English, 1981-84, chmn., 1987-94, assoc. v.p. rsch., assoc. dean faculty programs Rackham Sch. Grad. Studies, 1994-95, assoc. v.p. rsch., 1994-95, interim dean Grad. Sch., 1995-96; pres. The Woodrow Wilson Nat. Fellowship Found., 1997—; dir. Mellon Fellowships Humanistic Studies, 1998—. Author: Emily Dickinson's Poetry, 1975, Atlantic Double-Cross, 1986; co-editor Dickinson and Audience, 1995. Am. Coun. Learned Socs. fellow, 1976-77, Rackham fellow, U. Mich., 1983; recipient Amoco teaching award U. Mich., 1986 Mem. Phi Beta Kappa. E-mail: bobweis@woodrow.org.

WEISBURGER, ELIZABETH KREISER, retired chemist; b. Greenlane, Pa., Apr. 9, 1924; d. Raymond Samuel and Amy Elizabeth (Snavely) Kreiser; m. John H. Weisburger, Apr. 7, 1947 (div. May 1974); children: William Raymond, Diane Susan, Andrew John. BS, Lebanon Valley Coll., 1944, DSc (hon.), 1989; PhD, U. Cin., 1947, DSc (hon.), 1981. Rsch. assoc. U. Cin., 1947-49; col. USPHS, 1951-89; postdoctoral fellow Nat. Cancer Inst., Bethesda, Md., 1949-51, chemist, 1951-73, chief carcinogen metabolism and toxicology br., 1972-75, chief Lab. Carcinogen Metabolism, 1975-81, asst. dir. chem. carcinogenesis, 1981-89, ret. Cons. in field; lectr. Found. for Advanced Edn. in Scis., Bethesda, 1980-95; adj. prof. Am. U., Washington, 1982-83. Asst. editor-in-chief Jour. Nat. Cancer Inst., 1971-87; mem. editl. adv. bd. Chem. Health and Safety, 1994-99, Jour. Applied Toxicology, 1996—; contbr. articles to profl. jours. Trustee Lebanon Valley Coll., 1970—, pres. bd. trustees, 1985-89. Recipient Meritorious Svc. medal USPHS, 1973, Disting. Svc. medal, 1985; Hillebrand prize Chem. Soc. Washington, 1981, Charles Gordon award, 1999. Fellow AAAS (nominating com. 1978-81); mem. Am. Chem. Soc. (Garvan medal 1981, Tillmanns-Skolnick award divsn. chem. health and safety 2001), Am. Assn. Cancer Rsch., Soc. Toxicology, Am. Soc. Biochem. and Molecular Biology, Royal Soc. Chemistry, Am. Conf. Govtl. Indsl. Hygienists (Herbert Stokinger award 1996, William Wagner award 2003), Grad. Women in Sci. (hon.), Iota Sigma Pi. Lutheran. Office Phone: 301-309-0078. Office Fax: 301-309-0078.

WEISBURGER, JOHN HANS, medical researcher; b. Stuttgart, Germany, Sept. 15, 1921; came to U.S., 1943, naturalized, 1944; s. William and Selma (Barth) W.; children: William, Diane, Andrew. AB, U. Cin., 1947, MS, 1948, PhD, 1949; MD (hon.), U. Umeå, Sweden, 1980. Officer USPHS, 1950-72; mem. staff Nat. Cancer Inst., NIH, Bethesda, Md., 1950-61, head carcinogen screening sect., 1961-72; dir. bioassay segment, Carcinogenesis Programs Nat. Cancer Inst., Bethesda, Md., 1971-72; v.p. rsch. Am. Health Found., Valhalla, N.Y., 1972-87; dir. Naylor Dana Inst. for Disease Prevention, Valhalla, 1972-87, dir. emeritus, sr. mem., 1987—; rsch. prof. pathology N.Y. Med. Coll., Valhalla, 1974—; pres. Weisburger Assocs., North White Plains, N.Y., 1987—. Mem. biochemistry and nutrition study sect. NIH, 1957—58; mem. interdepartmental panel on carcinogens FDA, USDA, USPHS, 1962—71; chmn. carcinogenesis subcom. Nat. Large Bowel Cancer Project, 1972—75; mem. expert panel on nitrites and nitrosamines USDA, 1973—77; mem. Nat. Cancer Inst. Clearinghouse on Environ. Carcinogens, 1976—78; co-chmn. organizing com. US-Japan Coop. Workshop on GI Tract Cancer, 1979; chmn. sci. rev. panel NJ State Commn. Cancer Rsch., 1988—90; co-chmn. internat. symposium on health effects of tea, NY, 1991; chmn. nutrition and cancer sect. 3d Anticarcinogenesis & antimutagenesis conf., Italy, 1991; chmn. study sect. NIH-Nat. Cancer Inst., Bethesda, Md., 1991; rsch. fellow Japanese Found. for Promotion of Cancer Rsch. Nat. Cancer Ctr. Rsch. Inst., Tokyo, 1992; adv. com. rev. RDA Food & Nutrition Bd. NAS, 1993; lectr. numerous lectures in field; chmn. numerous confs. national & internat. Assoc. editor Jour. Nat. Cancer Inst., 1960-62, Xenobiotica, 1971—, Archives of Toxicology, 1977-87, Internat. Jour. Toxicology, 1982-2002, Preventive Medicine, 1988—; mem. internat. editl. adv. bd. Food and Chem. Toxicology, 1967—; assoc. editor Cancer Rsch., 1969-80, mem. cover editl. bd., 1987-99; mem. editl. bd. Chemico-Biol. Interactions, 1969-88, Carcinogenesis, 1979-87, Inst. Sci. Info. Atlas of Sci., 1987-89, Cancer Epidemiology Biomarkers Prevention, 1991-98, Cancer Detection Prevention, 1994—; mem. guest editl. bd. Japanese Jour. Cancer Rsch., 1987 . With U.S. Army, 1944—46, (Italy, Austria). Decorated D.S.M., 1964; recipient Meritorious Svc. medal USPHS HEW, 1970, Outstanding Service award Westchester div. Am. Cancer Soc., 1984, Meyer and Anna Prentis award Mich. Cancer Ctr., 1987; named one of 1000 most cited scientists, ISI List, 1981. Leadership plaque N.J. State Commn. Cancer Rsch., 1990. Fellow N.Y. Acad. Scis., Am. Coll. Nutrition; mem. Am. Assn. Cancer Rsch. (hon. mem., rep. to European Assn. Cancer Rsch 1985-89), Am. Chem. Soc. (hon., com. environ. improvement 1992-94, chmn. lectr. chemistry and health 31st Middle Atlantic regional meeting 1997, chmn. symposium tea and health, N.Y., 2003), Am. Gastroent. Assn., Am. Soc. Biochem. Molecular Biologists, Am. Soc. Preventive Oncology (founding mem., bd. dirs. 1983-90, Disting. Svc. award 1990), Biochem. Soc. (London, emeritus), Environ. Mutagen Soc., European Assn. Cancer Rsch. (coun. 1985-90), Japan Cancer Assn. (hon. life), Soc. Exptl. Biol. Medicine, Soc. Toxicology (chmn. bd. publs. 1968-71, councilor 1972-74, amb. toxicology Mid-Atlantic divsn. 1990, hon. mem. 1995, Award of Merit 1981), Westchester Chem. Soc. (Disting. Scientist 1996), Sigma Xi, Alpha Chi Sigma (pres. Washington profl. chpt. 1967-68), Phi Lambda Upsilon. Achievements include research and over 570 publs. on lifestyle and chronic disease prevention, relevant mechanisms, and medical care cost reduction. Home: 4 Whitewood Rd White Plains NY 10603-1137 Office: Inst Cancer Prevention Am Health Found 1 Dana Rd Valhalla NY 10595-1599 Office Phone: 914-789-7141. Business E-Mail: jweisbur@ifcp.us. *In my lifetime a revolutionary change occurred in our knowledge of the causes and the mechanisms involved in the majority of premature killing diseases—heart disease, hypertension, stroke, many forms of cancer. These key advances stemmed from the partnership between the federal government, public-supported societies and academic institutions that encour-*

age health research. The impact of these diseases can be reduced in virtually all countries of the world provided their political bodies can agree that peaceful endeavors and cooperation in fostering better health for their people can be made a high priority goal. Medical science now can implement successful prevention efforts. I am glad I have lived through this period and have played a role in this development.

WEISEL, THOMAS W. investment company executive; Sr. ptnr., CEO Montgomery Securities, San Francisco; chmn., founder, CEO Thomas Weisel Ptnrs., San Francisco, 1998—. Office: Thomas Weisel Ptnrs 1 Montgomery St San Francisco CA 94104

WEISEMANN, CLAUS, pharmaceutical executive; b. Ulm, Germany, Nov. 9, 1957; arrived in U.S., 1999; s. Kurt and Elfriede Weisemann; m. Sabina Katrin Reiser, Apr. 15, 1982; children: Sina, Katja. Diplom in Chemistry, U. Ulm, 1983, PhD in Chemistry, 1987. Tchg. asst. U. Ulm, 1981—87; head coffee chemistry Jacobs Suchard, Bremen, Germany, 1987—91; mgr. structural rsch. Bayer AG, Leverkusen, Germany, 1991—94, product and lab. mgr. quality assurance devel., 1994—99; mgr. quality assurance validation Bayer Corp., Clayton, NC, 1999—2001, assoc. dir. quality assurance, 2001—03; dir., Regulatory Compliance Watson Pharm., Corona, Calif., 2003—. Contbr. articlels to profl. jours.; translator: articles to profl. jours. Pilot Civil Air Patrol, Hemel, Calif., 2001—. Scholar Scholar for gifted students, State of Bavaria, 1977; Grad. Study scholar, State of Baden-Wuerttemberg, 1984. Mem.: Gesellschaft Deutscher Chemiker, Internat. Soc. of Pharm. Engrs., Parenteral Drug Assn. Achievements include patents in field. Avocation: flying. Office: Watson Pharm 311 Bonnie Circle Corona CA 92878-1900

WEISENBECK, SHARON M. healthcare regulatory administrator; b. Durand, Wis., Mar. 18, 1941; d. William E. and Margaret Mary (Weiss) W. BS, Coll. St. Teresa, 1966; MS, U. Mich., 1970. Asst. prof. Coll. St. Teresa, Winona, Minn.; asst. chmn. dept. nursing East Cen. U., Ada, Okla.; edn. supr. State of Wis., Madison; exec. dir. Ky. Bd. Nursing, Louisville. Office: 312 Whittington Pky Ste 300 Louisville KY 40222-4925

WEISENBERG, ELLIOT, pathologist, educator; b. Chgo., Sept. 24, 1958; s. Bertram and Victoria Shuken Weisenberg; m. Clara E. Orban, PhD, June 16, 1985. MS, MD, Chgo. Med. Sch.; BA sociology, U of Chgo., 1980; MS sociology, U. of Chgo., 1989; MD, U of Chgo., 1989. Anatomic and Clin. Pathology Am. Bd. Pathology, 1994. Attending pathologist Adv. Ill. Masonic Med. Ctr., Chgo., 1994—. Vis. prof. pathology U. Ill., Chgo. Med. Ctr., Chgo., 2001—; assoc. prof. pathology Rosalind Franklin U. Health Scis., Chgo. Med. Ctr., North Chicago, 1998—. Contbr. articles to profl. jours. Sec., treas. Chgo. Pathology Soc., Chgo., 2001—04. Mem.: Alpha Omega Alpha. Office: Advocate IL Masonic Med Ctr-Pathology 836 W Wellington Chicago IL 60657 Office Phone: 773-296-5730. E-mail: elliot.weisenberg-md@advocatehealth.com.

WEISENBURGER, RANDALL J. retired company executive; b. 1958; With Coopers & Lybrand, 1980-85, First Boston Corp., 1987-88; mng. dir. to pres. & CEO Wasserstein Perella & Co., 1988-99; CEO Wickes Mfg. Co., Inc., Southfield, Mich., 1990-93; co-chmn. Collins & Aikman Corp., Charlotte, N.C., 1993-99; exec. v.p. & CFO Omnicom Group, Inc., N.Y.C., 1999—. Vice-chmn. Maybelline, Inc.; chmn. Yardley of London; bd. dirs. Alliance Entertainment Corp. Office: Omnicom Group Inc 437 Madison Ave New York NY 10022 also: 701 Mccullough Dr Charlotte NC 28262-3318

WEISENBURGER, THEODORE MAURICE, retired judge, poet, educator, writer; b. Tuttle, N.D., May 12, 1930; s. John and Emily (Rosenau) W.; children: Sam, Jennifer, Emily, Todd, Daniel, Dwight, Holly, Michael, Paul, Peter; m. Maylyne Chu, Sept. 19, 1985; 1 child, Irene. BA, U. N.D., 1952, LLB, 1956, JD, 1969; BFT, Am. Grad Sch. Internat. Mgmt., Phoenix, 1957. Bar: N.D. 1963, U.S. Dist. Ct. N.D. 1963. County judge, tchr. Bensen County, Minnewaukan, N.D., 1968-75, Walsh County, Grafton, N.D., 1975-87; trial judge Devils Lake Sioux, Ft. Totten, N.D., 1968-84, Turtle Mountain Chippewa, Belcourt, N.D., 1974-87; U.S. magistrate U.S. Dist. Ct., Minnewaukan, 1972-75; Justice of the Peace pro tem Maricopa County, Ariz., 1988-92; instr. Rio Salado C.C., 1992—. Tchr. in Ethiopia, 1958-59. Author: Poetry and Other Poems, 1991. 1st lt. U.S. Army, 1952-54. Recipient Humanitarian award U.S. Cath. Conf., 1978, 82, Right to Know award Sigma Delta Chi, 1980, Spirit of Am. award U.S. Conf. Bishops, 1982. Home: 4353 E Libby St Phoenix AZ 85032-1732 Office Phone: 602-992-0492. Personal E-mail: tweisenburger@cox.net.

WEISER, ERIK SAUL, materials research engineer, project manager; b. Quantico, Va., Feb. 8, 1972; s. Sidney Leon and Debbie B. Weiser; m. Andrea Sue Karlsberg, Jan. 31, 1973. BS in Materials Sci. and Engring., Ga. Inst. Tech., 1995, MS in Materials Engring., 1997; postgrad., Coll. of William and Mary. Sr. materials rsch. engr. NASA Langley Rsch. Ctr., Hampton, Va., 1992—. Program mgr. NASA Langley Rsch. Ctr., 1999—. Contbr. articles to profl. jours.; patentee in field. Republican. Avocations: sailing, jogging, weightlifting, travel. Office: 6A W Taylor St Rm 120B Hampton VA 23681-2102

WEISER, FRANK ALAN, lawyer; b. L.A., Dec. 12, 1953; s. Carl and Rose (Klein) W.; m. Susan Koenig, Aug. 12, 1983. BA, UCLA, 1976; JD, Southwestern U., L.A., 1979; LLM in Taxation, U. San Diego, 1986. Bar: Calif. 1979, U.S. Dist. Ct. (cen. dist.) Calif. 1981, U.S. Tax Ct. 1982, U.S. Ct. Appeals (9th cir.) 1982, U.S. Supreme Ct. 1987, U.S. Ct. Claims 1987, U.S. Ct. Mil. Appeals 1988, U.S. Ct. Appeals (fed. cir.) 1989, U.S. Ct. Internat. Trade 1989, U.S. Ct. Appeals Temporary Emergency Ct., 1989, U.S. Ct. Vets. Appeals 1990, U.S. Dist. Ct. (no. and so. dists.) Calif. 1993. Tax cons., advanced underwriter Transam. Occidental Life Ins. Co., L.A., 1979-80; assoc. Law Offices Herman English, 1980-81; atty., owner Frank A. Weiser-A Law Corp., L.A., 1981—. Judge pro tem L.A. County Mcpl. Ct., 1987—. Editor So. Calif. mag., 1987—; contbr. articles to profl. jours. Bd. suprs. Michael Antonovich Election Com., 1988; mem. World Affairs Coun., L.A.; mem. U.S. Ct. of Vets. Appeals, 1990; assoc. mem. Calif. Rep. Cen. Com. Recipient official resolutions from Calif. State Legislature, 1989, joint rules com. resolution for state assembly and sate senate, 1990, Calif. State Assembly and Senate, 1989, L.A. County Bd. of Suprs., 1989, City Coun. of L.A., 1987, Congressional Cert. of Appreciation; tribute to him placed into official Congl. record, 1989; Nat. Merit scholar, 1971. Mem. ABA (internat. labor com., arts control and disarmament com., internat. employment practices com., editorial advisor internat. law and practive sect. publs. com., internat. property, estate and trust com., fgn. investment in U.S. com.), Fed. Bar Assn. (internat. law com.), Inter-Am. Bar Assn., Am. Judicature Soc., Assn. Trial Lawyers Am., Calif. Trial Lawyers Assn., L.A. Trial Lawyers Assn., Internat. Bar Assn., World Affairs Coun. L.A., World Inst. Achievement, L.A. Athletic Club. Office: 3460 Wilshire Blvd Ste 903 Los Angeles CA 90010-2230

WEISER, RALPH RAPHAEL, oil industry executive; b. N.Y.C., May 25, 1925; children: Jane, Jeffrey. BA, NYU, 1947; JSD, Harvard U., 1950. Bar: N.Y. 1950. Ptnr. Lotterman & Weiser, Esq., N.Y.C., 1955-64; pres. Dragor Shipping Inc., N.Y.C., 1964-65; chmn. Nat. Equipment Rental, N.Y.C., 1965-67; exec. v.p. Am. Export Industries, N.Y.C., 1967-69; pvt. practice investment, 1970-84; chmn. World Fuel Svc. Corp. (NYSE-INT), Miami, Fla., 1984—. Sgt. USAAF, 1943-45, PTO. Office: World Fuel Services Corp 9800 NW 41st St Ste 400 Miami FL 33178

WEISER, SHERWOOD MANUEL, hotel and corporation executive, lawyer; b. Cleve., Mar. 9, 1931; s. Aaron A. and Helen (Scheiner) W.; m. Judith A. Zirkin, July 31, 1955; children: Douglas J., Warren P., Bradley A. BS, Ohio State U., 1952; LLB, Case Western Res. U., 1955. Bar: Ohio 1955. Ptnr. Weiser & Weiser, Attys., Cleve., 1955-65, Weiser & Lefton, Attys., Cleve., 1965-69; chmn., chief exec. officer TCC, Miami, Fla., 1970—. Bd. dirs. Mellon United Bank, Miami, Wyndham Hotels, Interstate Hotels, Watsco. Trustee Fla. Internat. U. Found., Miami, 1984-94, U. Miami, 1988—, New World Symphony, Miami, 1987—; trustee, chmn. bd. Ransom-Everglades Sch., Miami, 1974-84; co-chmn. bd. advisors Coconut Grove Playhouse, 1986-90; chmn. Performing Arts Ctr. Found., 1994—. Mem. Am. Hotel and Motel Assn., Cleve. Bar Assn., Soc. of Benchers, Order of Coif. Jewish. Avocations: tennis, sailing, art. Office: Continental Hospitality Holdings 3250 Mary St Miami FL 33133-5232

WEISERT, KENT ALBERT FREDERICK, lawyer; b. Passaic, N.J., Sept. 9, 1949; s. Frederick William and Waleska Anna Sophia (Bischoff) W.; m. Deborah Jean Searing, Mar. 12, 1983; 1 child, Christianna Lillian. BA magna cum laude, Rutgers U., 1971, JD, 1974. Bar: N.J. 1974, U.S. Dist. Ct. N.J. 1974, U.S. Tax Ct. 1975, U.S. Ct. Appeals (3d cir.) 1978, U.S. Supreme Ct. 1987. Adminstrv. asst. trust dept. Howard Savs. Bank, Newark, 1973-74; ptnr. Schwartz, Tobia & Stanziale, Montclair, NJ, 1975—2001; pvt. practice law Bloomfield, NJ, 2001—. Arbitrator U.S. Dist. Ct., Newark, 1985—. Contbr. chpt. to book New Jersey Transaction Guide, 1987. Pres. ch. coun. Holy Trinity Luth. Ch., Nutley, N.J., 1982-83; session mem., elder Watchung Presbyn. Ch., Bloomfield, N.J.; mem. Greater N.J. Estate Planning Coun.; trustee, v.p. Oakeside Bloomfield Cultural Ctr. Mem. N.J. State Bar Assn., Essex County Bar Assn., Rutgers Law Sch. Alumni Assn., Nat. Trust Hist. Preservation, N.J. Hist. Soc., Phi Beta Kappa, Phi Alpha Theta, Pi Delta Epsilon. Republican. Presbyterian. Avocations: classical music, antiques, mil. and gen. history, hist. preservation, tennis. Home and Office: Kent AF Weisert Esq 51 Fairway Bloomfield NJ 07003

WEISFELD, ERIC, newscaster; Degree, Ind. U. Anchor, reporter Sta. WWAG-TV, Hopkinsville, Ky., Sta. WEHT-TV, Evansville, Ind., Sta. WLFL-TV, Raleigh, NC; anchor Sta. WRTV-TV, Indpls., 2000—. Recipient Edward R. Murrow Regional award. Office: WRTV TV 1330 N Meridian St Indianapolis IN 46202*

WEISFELD, SHELDON, lawyer; b. McAllen, Tex., Feb. 20, 1946; s. Morris and Pauline (Horwitz) W.; m. Eve F. Weisfeld, Jan. 23, 1994; 1 child, Raquel Paolina. BBA, U. Tex., 1967; postgrad., Nat. U. Mex., Mexico City, 1969; JD, U. Houston, 1970. Bar: Tex. 1971, U.S. Dist. Ct. (so. dist.) Tex. 1978, U.S. Dist. Ct. (we. dist.) Tex. 1995, U.S. Dist. Ct. (ea. dist.) Tex. 2001, U.S. Ct. Appeals (5th cir.) 1978, U.S. Ct. Appeals (11th cir.) 1981, U.S. Supreme Ct. 1982. Pvt. practice, Austin, Tex., 1973-77; pvt. practice law Brownsville, Tex., 1980—. Asst. fed. pub. defender U.S. Dist. Ct. (so. dist.) Tex., Brownsville, 1977-80. Mem. Nat. Assn. Criminal Def. Lawyers (life), Tex. Criminal Def. Lawyers (dir.), ABA, Fed. Bar Assn., State Bar Tex., Cameron County (Tex.) Bar Assn., Hidalgo County (Tex.) Bar Assn., B'nai B'rith. Democrat. Office: 855 E Harrison St Brownsville TX 78520-7173 Fax: 956-544-7446. Office Phone: 956-546-2727. E-mail: isweisfeld@aol.com.

WEISFELDT, MYRON LEE, cardiologist, educator; b. Milw., Apr. 25, 1940; s. Simon Charles and Sophia (Price) W.; m. Linda Nan Zaremski, Dec. 29, 1963; children— Ellyn Joy, Lisa Janel, Sara Michelle Student, Northwester U., 1958-60; BA, Johns Hopkins U., 1962, MD, 1965. Intern and resident Columbia-Presbyn. Med. Ctr., N.Y.C., 1965-67; fellow in cardiology Mass. Gen. Hosp., Boston, 1970-72; asst. prof. medicine Johns Hopkins U., Balt., 1972-78, prof. medicine, 1978-91, Robert L. Levy prof. cardiology, 1979-91; Samuel Bard prof. medicine, chair dept. Columbia-Presbyn. Med. Ctr., N.Y.C., 1991—2001; William Osler prof. medicine, dir. dept. medicine Johns Hopkins Med. Sch., 2001—; physician in chief Johns Hopkins Hosp., 2001. Dir. cardiology Johns Hopkins Med. Inst., Balt., 1975-91, Peter Belfer Lab. for Johns Hopkins, Ischemic Heart Disease Spl. Ctr. Rsch., 1977-91; nat. pres. Am. Heart Assn., 1989-90; cardiology adv. com. Nat. Heart, Lung and Blood Inst., 1986-90, chmn., 1988-90; mem. adv. coun. Nat. Inst. on Aging, 1999-2002. Editor: The Aging Heart, 1980; editorial bd. Jour. Clin. Investigation, 1984-88, Circulation, 1980-86, 88—2004, Jour. Am. Coll. Cardiology, 1987-93, Jour. Molecular and Cellular Cardiology, 1975-80, 86-89, Circulation Rsch., 1988-94. Served with USPHS, 1967-69 NIH grantee, 1977-91; recipient Golden Heart award Am. Heart Assn., 1998, Harrick award, 2004. Fellow AAAS, ACP, Am. Coll. Cardiology; mem. Assn. Univ. Cardiologists, Am. Soc. Clin. Investigation, Assn. Am. Physicians, Assn. Prof. Medicine, Inst. of Medicine, Phi Beta Kappa, Alpha Omega Alpha, Interurban Clin. Club. Jewish. Office: Johns Hopkins Medicine 1830 E Monument St Ste 9026 Baltimore MD 21287 Home: 1002 Rolandvue Ave Baltimore MD 21204 Office Phone: 410-955-6642. Business E-Mail: mlw5@jhmu.edu.

WEISGALL, JONATHAN MICHAEL, lawyer; b. Balt., Mar. 17, 1949; s. Hugo David and Nathalie (Shulman) W.; m. Ruth Macdonald, June 3, 1979; children: Alison, Andrew, Benjamin. BA, Columbia Coll., 1970; JD, Stanford U., 1973. Bar: D.C. 1974, N.Y. 1974, U.S. Supreme Ct. 1982, Marshall Islands 1983. Law clk. to judge U.S. Ct. Appeals (9th cir.), San Francisco, 1973-74; assoc. Covington & Burling, Washington, 1974-79; from assoc. to ptnr. Ginsburg, Feldman, Weil & Bress, Washington, 1980-83; pvt. practice Washington, 1983-99; v.p. Legis. and Regulatory Affairs MidAmerican Energy Holdings Co., 1995—. Adj. prof. Georgetown U. Law Ctr. Author: Operation Crossroads: The Atomic Tests at Bikini Atoll, 1994; exec. prodr. documentary film Radio Bikini. Chmn. bd. dirs. Ctr. for Energy Efficiency and Renewable Techs.; trustee Arena Stage, Washington; bd. dirs. Meet the Composer, Geothermal Resources Coun. Mem. Geothermal Energy Assn. (past v.p., bd. dirs., pres.), Geothermal Resources Coun. (bd. dirs.), Phi Beta Kappa. Jewish. Home: 5309 Edgemoor Ln Bethesda MD 20814-1323 Office: Ste 300 1200 New Hampshire Ave NW Washington DC 20036-6812 E-mail: jweisgall@aol.com.

WEISKITTEL, RALPH JOSEPH, retired real estate broker; b. Covington, Ky., Jan. 1, 1924; s. Nelson I. and Hilda (Nieman) W.; m. Audrey Bushelman, June 19, 1948; children— Thomas, Carol Anne, Barbara Jane. Ev. student, Xavier U., Cin., 1946-47. Mem. staff Cin. Enquirer, 1942-43, 45, home sect. editor, 1958-63, bus. editor, 1963-77; v.p. corp. markets Koetzle Corp. (Realtors), 1977-79; v.p. Devitt and Assocs. (Realtors), 1979-90; v.p. sales and mktg. Toebben Cos., 1990-91; sr. v.p. The Chelsea-Moore Co., 1991-94; v.p. sales Cline Realtors, Cin., 1994-2001; comml. broker Huff Realty, Ft. Mitchell, Ky., 2001—, ret. Dir. New Comty. Developers, Inc. Mem. city council, Ft. Wright, Ky., 1960-68; mem. St. Agnes Parish Council, 1974-77; mem. bishop's adv. council Diocese of Covington. Served with AUS, 1943-46. Mem. Nat. Assn. Real Estate Editors, Soc. Am. Bus. Writers. Clubs: Cin. Athletic. Home: 1571 St Anthony Dr Covington KY 41011-3752 Office: Huff Realty 334 Beechwood Rd Fort Mitchell KY 41017

WEISL, EDWIN LOUIS, JR., foundation executive, lawyer; b. NYC, Oct. 17, 1929; s. Edwin L. and Alice (Todriff) W.; m. Barbara Butler, June 12, 1974; 1 child, by previous marriage, Angela Jane. AB, Yale, 1951; LL.B., Columbia, 1956. Bar: N.Y. 1956, D.C. 1968. Assoc. Simpson Thacher & Bartlett, N.Y.C., 1956-64, mem. firm, 1964-65, 69-73; adminstr. parks, recreation and cultural affairs, commr. parks City of N.Y., 1973-75; asst. atty. gen. of U.S. in charge of land and natural resources division, 1965-67; asst. atty. gen. in charge civil div., 1967-69; asst. spl. counsel, preparedness investigating com. U.S. Senate, 1957-58; former pres. Internat. Found. for Art Research. Dir. N.Y. State Dem. campaign, 1964; mem. The 1001, World Wildlife Fund; mem. vis. com. dept. European paintings Met. Mus. Art; bd. dirs. Robert Lehman Found.; mem. corp. Presbyn. Hosp., N.Y.C.; bd. dirs. Old Master Exhbn. Soc. N.Y.; mem. Villa I Tatti Coun, Harvard Ctr. for Renaissance Studies. Lt. (j.g.) U.S. Navy, 1951-53. Mem. Explorers Club, Warrenton Hunt Club, Century Assn., Fauquier Club. Office: 50 E 77th St New York NY 10021-1842

WEISMAN, AVERY, psychiatrist; b. Detroit, Dec. 13, 1913; s. Alec and Sadie Belle (Danto) W.; m. Erma Carman, Dec. 30, 1950 (dec. 1982); m. Lois London, July 8, 1988. AB, U. Mich., 1935, BS, 1936, MD, 1940. Diplomate Am. Bd. Psychiatry and Neurology. Intern Montefiore Hosp., Pitts., 1940-41; resident in Neurology Wayne County Gen., Eloise, Mich., 1941-42; resident in Neuropath and Neurology Boston City Hosp., 1942-44; resident in psychiatry to sr. psychiatrist Mass. Gen. Hosp., Boston, 1944—; instr. to prof. of psychiatry emeritus Med. Sch. Harvard U., Boston, 1944—. Disting. vis. prof. Northwestern U. Med. Sch., 1986-90; numerous vis. professorships; cons. Mass. Gen. Hosp., 1995. Author: Existential Core of Psychoanalysis, 1965, On Dying and Denying, 1972, Psychological Autopsy, 1968, Realization of Death, 1975, Coping Capacity, 1984, Coping with Cancer, 1989, Vulnerable Self, 1993, (novel) The Next Taboo, 2002; contbr. articles to profl. jours. Recipient Deutsch award Boston Psychoanalytic soc., 1950, Sutherland award Sloan Kettering Cancer Ctr., 1982, Disting. Svc. award Yeshiva U., 1983, Avery Weisman Lectureship Found. of Thanatology, 1988, Pollin Found. award 1989, Hackett award Acad. Psychosomatic Medicine, 1992. Fellow Am. Psychiat. Assn.; mem. Am. Psychoanalytic Assn., Am. Acad. Neurology, Psychosomatic Acad., Am. Assn. Suicidology (pres. 1977, Dublin award). Jewish. Home: 7476 E Beryl Ave Scottsdale AZ 85258-1019 Personal E-mail: averydw@aol.com.

WEISMAN, ERIC, music company executive; With Premier Artists Svcs., 1985, Bassin Distbr., 1985—90, Alliance Entertainment Corp., Minnetonka, Minn., 1990, pres., CEO, 1997—2003, CEO, 2003—. Office: Musicland Group 10400 Yellow Circle Dr Minnetonka MN 55343

WEISMAN, GARY ANDREW, biochemist; b. Bklyn., June 18, 1951; s. Joseph Herman and Elaine (Melman) W.; m. Sandra Kay Hille, Aug. 4, 1979; children: Laura Joanne, Pamela Michelle, Veronica Evelyn. BS, Polytechnic U., 1972; postgrad., U. Bordeaux, France, 1972-74; PhD, U. Nebr., 1980. Postdoctoral rsch. assoc. Cornell U., 1980-85; asst. prof. U. Mo., Columbia, 1985-92, assoc. prof., 1992-98, prof., 1998—. Spl. reviewer NIH; reviewer NSF, Jour. Membrane Biology and Eur. Jour. Cancer, Am. Jour. Physiology. Contbr. articles to profl. jours. Grantee USDA, 1987—, NIH, 1988—, CF Found., 1994—, Am. Diabetes, 1995—. Mem. AAAS, Am. Chem. Soc., Am. Soc. Biochem. and Molecular Biology, Am. Diabetes Assn., Am. Heart Assn., N.Y. Acad. Scis. Home: 1804 University Ave Columbia MO 65201-6004 Office: U Mo Dept Biochemistry M121 Med Scis Bldg Columbia MO 65212-0001 Business E-Mail: weismang@missouri.edu.

WEISMAN, JOEL, retired engineering educator; b. N.Y.C., July 15, 1928; s. Abraham and Ethel (Marcus) W.; m. Bernice Newman, Feb. 6, 1955; 1 child, Jay (dec.) B.Ch.E., CCNY, 1948; MS, Columbia U., 1949; PhD, U. Pitts, 1968. Registered profl. engr., N.Y. Plant engr. Etched Products, N.Y.C., 1950-51; from jr. engr. to assoc. engr. Brookhaven Nat. Lab., Upton, N.Y., 1951-54; from engr. to fellow engr. Westinghouse Nuclear Energy Systems, Pitts., 1954-59, from fellow engr. to mgr. thermal and hydraulic analysis, 1960-68; sr. engr. Nuclear Devel. Assocs., White Plains, N.Y., 1959-60; assoc. prof. nuclear engring. U. Cin., 1968-72, prof. nuclear engring., 1972-96, dir. nuclear engring. program, 1977-86, dir. lab. basic and applied nuclear research, 1984-94, prof. emeritus nuclear engring., 1996—. Co-author: Thermal Analysis of Pressurized Water Reactors, 1970, 2d edit., 1979, 3rd edit., 1996, Introduction to Optimization Theory, 1973, Modern Power Plant Engineering, 1985; editor: Elements of Nuclear Reactor Design, 1977, 2d edit., 1983; contbr. tech. articles to profl. jours.; patentee in field. Mem. Cin. Environ. Adv. Council, 1976-78; mem. Cin. Asian Art Soc., 1977—, v.p., 1980-82, pres., 1982-84; mem. exec. bd. Air Pollution League Greater Cin., 1980-90. Sr. NATO fellow, Winfrith Lab., U.K. Atomic Energy Authority, 1972; sr. fellow Argonne Nat. Lab., Ill., 1982; NSF research grantee, 1974-78, 82-85, 86-89; recipient Dean's award U. Cin. Coll. Engring., 1987. Fellow Am. Nuclear Soc. (v.p. Pitts. sect. 1957-58, mem. exec. com. thermal-hydraulics div. 1989-92); mem. Am. Inst. Chem. Engrs., Sigma Xi Democrat. Jewish. Avocation: Japanese art. Home: 3419 Manor Hill Dr Cincinnati OH 45220-1522 Office: U Cin Dept Mech Ind & Nuclear Engr Cincinnati OH 45221-0001

WEISMAN, JOHN, author; b. NYC, Aug. 1, 1942; s. Abner I Weisman and Syde (Lubowe) Kremer; m. Susan Lee Povenmire, Feb. 12, 1983. AB, Bard Coll., 1964. Mng. editor Coast mag., LA, 1969-70; staff writer Rolling Stone, San Francisco, 1971, Detroit Free Press, 1971-73; assoc. editor TV Guide, Radnor, Pa., 1973-77, bur. chief Washington, 1977-89; sr. fellow Annenberg Washington program Northwestern U., Washington, 1989-91; columnist Military.Com, 2003—. Author: (nonfiction) Guerrilla Theatre, 1973, Shadow Warrior, 1989, Rogue Warrior, 1992 (No 1 bestseller NY Times Book Rev), (novels) Evidence, 1980, Watchdogs, 1983, Blood Cries, 1987, Rogue Warrior II, Red Cell, 1994 (bestseller NY Times), Green Team, 1995 (bestseller NY Times), Task Force Blue, 1996 (bestseller NY Times), (anthology) Unusual Suspects, 1996, Designation Gold, 1997 (bestseller NY Times), The Best American Mystery Stories of 1997, 1997, SEAL Force Alpha, 1998 (bestseller NY Times), Option Delta, 1999, Echo Platoon, 2000, Detachment Bravo, 2001, SOAR, 2003 (bestseller Amazon.com), The Best Am. Mystery Stories of 2003, 2003, Jack in the Box, 2004; roving contbg. editor: Soldier of Fortune mag., 2004. Active Clarke County Rep Comt, Va. Mem.: AFIO, Internat. Defensive Pistol Assn., Bard Coll. Alumni Assn., Naval and Mil. Club (London), Cosmos Club, Army and Navy Club. Personal E-mail: blackops@johnweisman.com.

WEISMAN, LORENZO DAVID, investment banker; b. Guatemala, Central America, Apr. 22, 1945; arrived in U.S.A., 1957; s. Eduardo and Suzanne (Loeb) Weisman; m. Danielle Maysonnave, June 22, 1971; children: Melissa Anne, Alexia Maria, Thomas Alexander. BA in History and Lit. cum laude(hon.), Harvard U., 1966; postgrad., Conservatoire Nat. D'Art Dramatique, Paris, 1966—71; MBA in Fin., Columbia Univ., 1973. V.p. Dillon, Read, and Co., Inc., N.Y.C., 1977—80, sr. v.p., 1980—82, mng. dir. London, 1982—84; pres., CEO Dillon Read, Ltd., London, 1984—93; head Internat. Dillon, Read, and Co., Inc., N.Y.C., 1993—97; head L.Am. corp. fin. UBS Warburg, N.Y.C., 1997—2001; co-founder, mng. mem. Hill St. Capital, LLC, N.Y.C., 2002—. Com. univ. resources Harvard Univ., 1991, mem. adv. com. David Rockefeller Ctr. for L.Am. studies, 1995—; mem. bd. overseers Columbia Bus. Sch., 1992. Co-chairman and trustee Institut Français Alliance Française, N.Y.C., 1995. Mem. Harvard Club, N.Y.C., Travelers Club, Paris, Knickerbocker Club, N.Y.C. Office Phone: 212-326-2601. E-mail: lweisman@hillstreetcap.com.

WEISMANN, DONALD LEROY, art educator, artist, filmmaker, writer; b. Milw., Oct. 12, 1914; s. Friedrich Othello and Stela Priscilla (Custer) W.; m. M. Virginia Stant; children: Anne Wilder, Christopher Thomas. BS, U. Wis., Milw., 1935; PhM, U. Wis., Madison, 1940; PhD, Ohio State U., 1950. Asst. prof. art Ill. State U., Normal, 1940-42, 47-48, Wayne U., Detroit, 1949-51; prof., head dept. art U. Ky., Lexington, 1951-54; prof., chmn. dept. art U. Tex., Austin, 1954-58, Univ. prof. arts, 1959-81, prof. emeritus, 1981—. Cons. Ford Found., N.Y.C., 1958, 66, U.S. Nat. Com. UNESCO, 1953, Rockefeller Found., 1956, Nat. Council Arts., 1966-72; spl. cons. USIS, Forence, Italy, 1961-62 Author: Language and Visual Form, 1968, Visual Arts as Human Experience, 1970, Duncan Phyfe & Drum, 1984, Follow the Bus with the Greek License Plates, 1981, Frank Reaugh, Painter to the Longhorns, 1985, The Stuff of Stories, 1999, Artifacts, Fictions and Memory, 2001, An American Fugue, 2002; contbr. articles, poems, stories and revs. to profl. jours.; painter, collagist one-man shows, Cushman Gallery, Houston, Nye Gallery, Dallas, Petite Gallery, N.Y.C., Art Mus. U. N. Mex., group shows, Bocur Gallery, N.Y.C., Chgo. Art Inst., Dallas Mus. Fine Arts, Rockefeller Ctr., N.Y.C., Vanucci Gallery, Pistoia, Italy, Villa Monte Carlo Chapala, Jalisco, Mexico; film-maker numerous productions. Served to lt. (j.g.) USN, 1942-45, PTO. Recipient Letter of Commendation Pres. U.S., 1972; honoree for book Some Folks Went West, 12th Ann. Writers Conf., Austin, 1960; grantee U. Tex. Rsch. Inst., Italy, Eng., 1961-62, 71, Pub. Broadcast Corp., 1970, 72; named fine arts scholar Harvard U., 1941 Mem. Nat. Humanities Faculty Home: 4513 Edgemont Dr Austin TX 78731-5223 Office: Am Studies U Tex Austin TX 78712

WEISMANTEL, GREGORY NELSON, management consultant and software executive; b. Houston, Sept. 8, 1940; s. Leo Joseph and Ellen Elizabeth (Zudis) W.; m. Marilyn Ann Fanger, June 18, 1966; children: Guy Gregory, Christopher Gregory, Andrea Rose. BA in English, U. Notre Dame, 1962; MBA in Internat. Bus., Loyola U., Chgo., 1979. With mgmt. staff Gen. Foods Corp., White Plains, N.Y., 1966-80; pres., chief exec. officer Manor House Foods, Inc., Addison, Ill., 1980-82, Weismantel & Assocs., Downers Grove, Ill., 1982-84; v.p. perishable div. Profl. Marketers, Inc., Lombard, Ill., 1984-86, group v.p. sales and mktg. services, dir. corp. strategy, 1986-87; v.p. mng. prin. CPG Industry, Louis A. Allen Assoc. Inc., Palo Alto, Calif., 1987-88; pres., chief exec. officer The Vista Tech. Group, Ltd., St. Charles, Ill., 1989-2000, chmn. bd., 2001—. Bd. dirs. Epicurean Foods, Ltd., Chgo.; pres., CEO The Vista Tech. Group, Ltd., The Vista Mgmt. Group. Chmn. fin. St.

Edward's High Sch. Jubilee, Elgin, Ill., 1982-85; bd. dirs. Dist. 301 Sch. Bd., Burlington, Ill., 1980-84, St. Edward's Found., Elgin, 1982—. Capt. U.S. Army, 1962-66. Recipient ICP/Chgo. Software Assoc. Re-Engring. award, 1994-96; State of Ill. grantee, 1989, Build Ill. Investment Fund. Mem. Grocery Mfg. Sales Execs., Chgo. Software Assn., Chg. C. of C. (small bus. com.). Clubs: Merchandising Execs., Food Products, Am. Mktg. (Chgo.). Roman Catholic. *Success can only occur when a person realizes that life is not a rehearsal.*

WEISNER, DAVID, illustrator; b. Bridgewater, N.J. m. Kim Khang; 2 children. BFA in Illustration, R.I. Sch. Design. Illustrator Houghton Mifflin, N.Y.C. Author (illustrator): Freefall, 1988 (Caldecott Honor, 1989), Hurricane, 1990, Tuesday, 1991 (Caldecott medal, 1992), The Loathsome Dragon, 1987, Moo, 1996, Sector 7, 1997. Home: 730 E Hadley St Milwaukee WI 53212

WEISS, AL, hotel executive; m. Doreen Weiss; 1 child, Jason. Grad., U. Ctrl. Fla.; MBA, Rollins Coll. Pres. Walt Disney World Resort, Lake Buena Vista, Fla. Mem. Osceola County Tourist Devel. Coun., Metro Orlando Econ. Devel. Commn. Mid-Fla. Office: Walt Disney World Resort PO Box 10040 Orlando FL 32830

WEISS, ALLAN JOSEPH, transport company executive, lawyer; b. Boston, Nov. 1, 1932; s. Mark and Eve S. (Kane) W.; m. Sherrill Roecker, Feb. 18, 1973; children: Stephanie Eve, Mark Allan. BS, U.S. Mcht. Marine Acad., 1955; JD, Cornell U., 1961. Bar: N.Y. 1961, D.C. 1962, Calif. 1965, U.S. Supreme Ct. 1965. Trial atty. admiralty and shipping U.S. Dept. Justice, 1961-67, chief trial atty. admiralty office, 1967-74; Pacific counsel Sea-Land Service, Inc., Oakland, Calif., 1974-76, dep. gen. counsel, 1977-78, gen. counsel, 1978-82, sec., 1979-82; assoc. gen. counsel Sea-Land Industries, 1979-82; pres. Freights Unltd., Inc., 1982—; gen. counsel Toledo, Peoria & Western Rwy., 1991-96. Adj. prof. law McGeorge Sch. Law, 1974-76 Served with U.S. Navy, 1956-57. Mem. Fed. Bar Assn., Calif. Bar Assn., D.C. Bar Assn., San Francisco Bar Assn., Maritime Law Assn. U.S., Cornell U. Law Assn., Kings Point Alumni Assn. Home: 89 Loft Dr Martinsville NJ 08836-2246 Office: Freights Unlimited Inc 89 Loft Dr Martinsville NJ 08836-2246 Office Phone: 732-627-5007. Business E-Mail: freights@optonline.net.

WEISS, ALVIN HARVEY, chemical engineering educator, catalysis researcher and consultant; b. Phila., Apr. 28, 1928; s. Louis and Helen F. (Wilinsky) W.; children: Linda S., Louis B.; m. Devorah Schwartz, June 10, 1979. BSChemE, U. Pa., 1949, PhD in Phys. Chemistry, 1965; MSChemE, Newark Coll. Engring., 1955. Registered profl. engr., Mass., Del. Chem. engr. Fiber Chem. Corp., Cliffwood, NJ, 1949-51, Colgate-Palmolive Co., Jersey City, 1953-55, Houdry Process and Chems. Co., Linwood, Pa., 1956-63; rsch. assoc., lectr. U. Pa., Phila., 1963-66; prof. chem. engring. Worcester (Mass.) Poly. Inst., 1966-94, prof. emeritus, 1994—. Vis. prof. Northeastern U., Boston, 2000—02; NASA-ASEE summer faculty fellow Stanford U. Ames Rsch. Ctr., 1967—68; affiliate scientist Worcester Found. Exptl. Biology, 1972—74; Fulbright-Hays sr. faculty fellow to dept. chem. engring. Ben-Gurion U. of Negev, Beersheva, Israel, 1973—74, vis. prof. chem. engring., 1974; U.S. coord. U.S.-USSR Coop. Sci. Program in Chem. Catalysis, Topic IV, 1973—76, prin. investigator (with M.M. Sakharov), 1976—78; prin. investigator (with K.I. Ione) U.S.-USSR Coop. Sci. Program in Chem. Catalysis, Topic III, 1978—80; Fulbright-Hays vis. lectr. dept. chem. engring. Mid. East Tech. U., Ankara, Turkey, 1974, vis. prof., 91; vis. rsch. scientist dept. organic chemistry Weizmann Inst., Rehovoth, Israel, 1974; vis. lectr. Inst. Isotopes and Ctrl. Inst. Chemistry, Hungarian Acad. Scis., Budapest, 1976; vis. prof. Inst. Cultural Rels. and Inst. Isotopes, Hungarian Acad. Scis., 1978, 80; UNIDO chief tech. advisor to Petrochem Complex of Bahia Blanca, Argentina, 80; sr. rsch. fellow chem. sys. lab. Army Chem. Ctr., Md., 1981; UNIDO expert in chem. process devel. Rsch. Inst. for Chem. Industry, Beijing, 1982; UNIDO expert in catalysis to YARPET Petrochem. Complex, Yarimca, Turkey, 1986—87; bd. dirs. U.S. com. for sci. coop. with Vietnam; vis. lectr. Nat. Ctr. for Sci. Rsch., Hanoi Inst. of Indsl. Chemistry, Ho Chi Minh City, 1986; vis. prof., vis. scientist Ctr. for Advanced Microgravity Materials Processing, Northeastern U., Boston, 2000—02. Translator: (with M. Delleo, G. Dembinski and J. Happel) Catalysis by Non-Metals (O.V. Krylov), 1970; contbr. articles to profl. jours.; patentee in field. With U.S. Army, 1951-53. Recipient Sci. Achievement award Worcester Engring. Soc., 1984; rsch. grantee NSF, PRF, NASA, DOD, DOE. Fellow AIChE (rsch. com. 1968-80, symposia chmn. 1973-84); mem. AAUP, Catalysis Soc. (bd. dirs., sec. 1968-88), Catalysis Soc. New Eng. (founding pres. 1967-68, bd. dirs. 1968—), Am. Chem. Soc. (New Eng. petroleum divsn. rep. 1970-88, session chmn. 1973—), Deutsche Gesellschaft für Chemische Apparatwesen.

WEISS, ARMAND BERL, economist, association management executive; b. Richmond, Va., Apr. 2, 1931; s. Maurice Herbert and Henrietta (Shapiro) W.; m. Judith Bernstein, May 18, 1957; children: Jo Ann Michele, Rhett Louis. BS in Econs., Wharton Sch. Fin., U. Pa., 1953, MBA, 1954; DBA, George Washington U., 1971. Cert. assn. exec. Officer USN, 1954-65; spl. asst. to auditor gen. Dept. Navy, 1964-65; sr. economist Ctr. for Naval Analyses, Arlington, Va., 1965-68; project dir. Logistics Mgmt. Inst., Washington, 1968-74; dir. systems integration Fed. Energy Adminstrn., Washington, 1974-76; sr. economist Nat. Commn. Supplies and Shortages, 1976-77; tech. asst. to v.p. Sys. Planning Corp., 1977-78; chmn. bd., pres., CEO Assns. Internat. Inc., 1978—; chmn. bd. dirs., CFO Rail Digital Corp., 1988-91; v.p., treas. Tech. Frontiers, Inc., 1978-80; sr. v.p. Weiss Pub. Co., Inc., Richmond, 1960—. V.p. Condo News Internat., Inc., 1981; v.p., bd. dirs. Leaders Digest Inc., 1987-88; sec., bd. dirs. Mgmt. Svcs. Internat. Inc., 1987-88; adj. prof. Am. U., 1979-80, 89-90; vis. lectr. George Washington U., 1971; assoc. prof. George Mason U., 1984; treas. Dranesville (Va.) Dist. Dem. Com., 1989-93, 2003-, Fairfax County (Va.) Dem. Com., 1992-94, assisted Pres. Clinton, v.p. Gore transition at White House, 1993-; pres. Washington Mgmt. and Bus. Assn., 1993—; chmn. U.S. del., session chmn. NATO Symposium on Cost-Benefit Analysis, The Hague, Netherlands, 1969, NATO Conf. on Operational Rsch. in Indsl. Systems, St. Louis, France, 1970; pres. Nat. Coun. Assns. Policy Scis., 1971-77; chmn. adv. group Def. Econ. Adv. Coun. Dept. Def., 1970-74; resident assoc. Smithsonian Instn., 1973—; expert cons. Dept. State, GAO; undercover agt. FBI, 3 yrs. Co-editor: Systems Analysis for Social Problems, 1970, The Relevance of Economic Analysis to Decision Making in the Department of Defense, 1972, Toward More Effective Public Programs: The Role of Analysis and Evaluation, 1975; editor: Cost-Effectiveness Newsletter, 1966-70, Operations Rsch./Systems Analysis Today, 1971-73, Operation Rsch./Mgmt. Sci. Today, 1974-87, Feedback, 1969-93, Condo World, 1981, The Democrat, 1997-2000; assoc. editor Ops. Rsch., 1971-75; pub. IEEE Scanner, 1983-89, Spl. and Individual Needs Tech. (SAINT) Newsletter, 1987-88, Jour. Parametrics, 1984-88. Del. Pres.'s Mid-Century White House Conf. on Children and Youth, 1950; scoutmaster Japan, U.S.; leader World Jamborees, France, Can., U.S., 1945-61; Eagle scout, 1947; U.S. del. Internat. Conf. on Ops. Rsch., Dublin, Ireland, 1972; organizing com. Internat. Cost-Effectiveness Symposium, Washington, 1970; spkr. Internat. Conf. Inst. Mgmt. Scis., Tel Aviv, 1973, del., Mexico City, 1967; mem. bus. com. Nat. Symphony Orch., 1968-70, Washington Performing Arts Soc., 1974-88; bus. mgr. Nat. Lyric Opera Co., 1983—, Internat. Assn. Med. Sci. Educators, 1997-98, Data Adminstrv. Mgmt. Assn. Nat. Capital, 1992-2001, Potomac Pedalers Touring Club, 1990-2001, Am. Friends of London Sch. Econs., 1988-97; mem. mktg. com. Fairfax Symphony Orch., 1984-91; bd. dirs. McLean (Va.) Orch., 1992-94; exec. com. Mid Atlantic coun. Union Am. Hebrew Congregations, 1970-79, treas., 1974-79, mem. nat. MUM com., 1974-79; mem. dist. com. Boy Scouts Am., 1972-75; bd. dirs. Nat. Coun. Career Women, 1975-79; pres. Jewish temple, 1970-72; adminstr. Daniel Heumann Fund for Spinal Cord Rsch., 2000-; treas. Quest for the Cure, 2000-; mem. Coalition for Advancement of Med. Rsch., 2002-; del. UN Sci. Conf., 2004; mem. adv. bd. U. Pa. Mid. Atlantic Region, 2003-. Named Hero of Hope, Rutgers U. Spinal Cord Injury Project, 2004; recipient Silver medal 50-yard free style and half mile swimming meet, No. Va. Sr. Olympics, 1990, Gold, 2 Silver, 3 Bronze medals, 2001. Fellow AAAS, Washington Acad. Scis. (gov. 1981-92, v.p. 1987-88, pres.-elect 1989-90, pres. 1990-91, past pres. 1991-92), Va. Acad. Scis., Nat. Assn. Acad. Sci. (del. 1991-93), Ops. Rsch. Soc. Am. (chmn. meetings com. 1969-71, chmn. cost-effectiveness sect. 1969-70), Washington Ops. Rsch./Mgmt. Sci. Coun. (editor newsletter 1969-93, sec. 1971-72, pres. 1973-74, trustee 1975-77, bus. mgr. 1976-93, Moving Spirit award 1994), Internat. Inst. Strategic Studies (London), Am. Soc. Assn. Execs. (membership com. 1981-82, assn. mgmt. co. sect. coun. 1995-98, cert.), Inst. Ops. Rsch. and the Mgmt. Scis., Am. Econ. Assn., Wharton Grad. Sch. Alumni Assn. (exec. com. 1970-73), Nat. Eagle Scout Assn., VFW, Am. Legion, Navy League of U.S., Greater Washington Soc. Assn. Execs. (new ventures com. 1995-97), Alumni Assn. George Washington U. (governing bd. 1974-82, chmn. univ. publs. com. 1976-78, Alumni Svc. award 1980), Alumni Assn. George Washington U. Sch. Govt. and Bus. Adminstrn. (exec. v.p. 1977-78, pres. 1978-79), George Washington U. Doctoral Assn. (sr. v.p. 1968-69), Wharton Sch. Washington (sec. 1967-69, pres. 1969-70, exec. dir. 1987-2001, Joseph Wharton award 1991, Lifetime Svc. award 2000). Home: 6516 Truman Ln Falls Church VA 22043-1821 Office Phone: 703-237-1104. Personal E-mail: aiboss@aol.com.

WEISS, ARNOLD HANS, lawyer; b. Nurnberg, Germany, July 25, 1924; m. Artemis Lychos, May 5, 1956; children: Daniel L., Andrew A. BA, U. Wis., 1951, JD, 1952. Bar: Wis. 1953, DC 1958. Atty. advisor Office Gen. Counsel US Treasury, 1953 60; atty. Inter Am. Devel. Bank, 1960 61, dep. gen. counsel, 1961-70, gen. counsel, 1970-77; ptnr. Arent, Fox, Kintner, Plotkin & Kahn, Washington, 1977-90; cons. Chevy Chase, Md., 1991; sec., gen. counsel Emerging Markets Corp., Washington, 1992—. With US Army, 1942-47; served to lt. col. JAGC USAR, 1948-62. Decorated Bronze Star Mem.: ABA, Inter-Am. Bar Assn., Am. Soc. Internat. Law, Columbia Country Club (Chevy Chase, Md.), Army and Navy Club (Washington), Univ. Club D.C. Office: Emerging Markets Corp 2001 Pennsylvania Ave NW # 1100 Washington DC 20006-1850

WEISS, BARBARA G. artist; b. Phila., Mar. 14, 1917; d. Carl Jacob Greenspan, Nellie Ellen Moyed; m. Victor Hugo Jr., May 6, 1942 (div. Dec. 1945); m. John Weiss, Nov. 10, 1946; children: Warren P., Willard Eric. Student, Calif. Art Ctr., Los Angeles, 1962—64. Owner, creator Balema Hugo Studio, Phila., 1942—49; interior designer L.A., 1953—63. Organizer workshops Charles Reid and other Artists of note, Thousand Oaks, 1994—96; creator gallery City of Thousand Oaks Civic Arts Plaza, 1996; creator mo. art show Umbrella Artists, Westlake Village, 1997—. Represented in permanent collections, L.A., Tucson, San Francisco, Paris, Rome; dir.(show): (art) The Gallery/Bernscat Municpal Art Gallery, 1993—95, Heritage Gallery/Ventura County Adminstrn. Bldg., 1994—96; Exhibited in group shows at Viva Gallery, Los Angeles, 1996—97, collections, Still life, Corina/M. & Mme René BoeuF (Chagal collectors), A Cap Martin Morning on Santarini, Anne Murphy (Collects Calif. Arts), geometrics, Dr. Francoise Farneti, Rome, Le Lac, Pamela Peterson Gallery Dir., Rythmns, A LeMarché, Le Petit Pont, Mme Monique Salvie, Tuscon, Ar. Social chmn. San Fernando Valley for John F. Kennedy campaign, Pierre Salinger Senatorial Campaign; pres. Westlake Village Art Guild, Calif., 1994—96, program dir., 1993—2001; art show dir. Caruso Holdings Ltd., Westlake Village, Calabasas, Calif., 1997—. Recipient 1st prize, Westlake Village Art Guild, 1996, Best of Show, Dr. Winefrid Higgins, Judge, U. Calif./San Diego, 1998, 1st prize, Westlake Village Art Guild, 2000. Mem.: Valley Watercolor Soc. Home: 31756 Bedfordhurst Ct Westlake Village CA 91361

WEISS, BARRY, recording industry executive; Pres. Jive Records, N.Y.C. Office: Jive Records 137 W 25th St # 139 New York NY 10001-7200

WEISS, BERNARD, toxicology educator; b. N.Y.C., Ny, May 27, 1925; s. Max and Sadie (Albert) W.; m. Ann Bartlett, Oct. 10, 1950 (div. 1972); children: Wendy, Thomas; m. Susan Edelman, Dec. 16, 1978 (div. Dec. 2003). BA, NYU, 1949; PhD, U. Rochester, 1953. Exptl. pscyhologist USAF Sch. Aviation Medicine, San Antonio, Tex., 1954-56; asst. prof. Johns Hopkins Med. Sch., Balt., 1956-65; prof. U. Rochester (N.Y.) Med. Sch., 1965—. Mem. Sci. Adv. Bd., EPA, Washington, 1981—, Toxicology Study Sect., NIH, Bethesda, Md., 1982-86, Bd. Sci. Counselors Nat. Inst. Environ. Health Sci., Research Triangle Park, N.C., 1986-90, Nat. Acad. Scis. Com. on Neurotoxicology, Washington, 1986-91; Burroughs Wellcome vis. prof. U. Miss., 1986. Editor: Digital Computers in the Behavioral Laboratory, 1973, Behavioral Toxicology, 1975; contbr. 190 articles to profl. jours. Sgt. USAF, 1944-46, PTO. Staff sgt. Air Force, 1944—46, Pacific. Recipient Stokinger award Am Conf. Govt., Indsl. Hygienists, 1990; named Scientist of Yr., Assn. Children with Learning Disabilities. Fellow AAAS, Amer. Psychol. Assn. (pres. div. 28 1961-62); mem. Behavioral Toxicology Soc., (pres. 1984-86), Soc. Toxicology (neurology spl. sect. pres. 1990-91). Achievements include Scientist of the Year, 1986, Asso for Learning Disabilities; Stokinger Award, Am Conf Gov Industrial Hygienists. Office: U Rochester Med Ctr Box EHSC Rochester NY 14642 Office Phone: 585-275-1736. Business E-Mail: bernard_weiss@urmc.rochester.edu.

WEISS, CARL, aerospace company executive; b. Bklyn., Dec. 6, 1938; s. Morris Harold and Sonia B. (Botwinick) W.; m. Judith Fellner, Jan. 27, 1963; children: Daniel Oren, Jonathan Michael. BBA, CUNY, 1961, MBA, 1968; postgrad., Harvard U., Boston, 1971. CPA, NY. Acct. Joseph Warren & Co., NYC, 1965-68; asst. contr. Fisher Radio Corp., LI, NY, 1968-69; sr. v.p. Deutsch Relays, Inc., East Northport, NY, 1969-83; owner, exec. v.p. Logical Solutions, Inc., Melville, NY, 1983-92; owner, pres., COO G&H Tech., Inc., Camarillo, Calif., 1992—. Bd. dirs. Deutsch Dagan, Inc. With U.S. Army, 1961-67. Mem. AICPA (future issues com. 1985-88); NY Soc. CPA. Office: G & H Tech Inc 750 W Ventura Blvd Camarillo CA 93010-8382

WEISS, CHARLES, JR., educator; b. San Francisco, Dec. 20, 1937; s. Charles and Dorothy (Wilkes) W.; m. Edith Gayle Brown, July 24, 1969; children: Jed Ariel, Tamara Ginger. BA summa cum laude, Harvard U., 1959, PhD, 1965. Post-doctoral fellow U. Calif., Berkeley, 1967-69; chemist Lawrence Berkeley Lab., U. Calif., Berkeley, 1969; staff scientist IBM Watson Lab., Columbia U., N.Y.C., 1969-71; sci. and tech. advisor World Bank, Washington, 1971-86; prin. Internat. Tech. Mgmt. and Fin., 1987-91, Innovation Ptnrs., 1987-91; pres. Global Tech. Mgmt., 1991—. Lectr. U. Pa., Phila., 1986-90; vis. lectr. Woodrow Wilson Sch., Princeton U., 1989-94; professorial lectr. Sch. Advanced Internat. Studies, Johns Hopkins U., 1994-97; disting. prof., chair sci., tech. and internat. affairs Sch. Fgn. Svc., Georgetown U., 1997—; corp. bd. mem. Vols. in Tech. Assistance, Arlington, Va., 1974-85; mem. U.S. Nat. Climate Adv. Com., Washington, 1978-81, Coun. of Fgn. Rels., 1985—. Editor: Mobilizing Technology for World Development, 1979, Technology, Finance and Development, 1984, Choice and Management of Technology, 1987; contbr. articles to profl. jours. Land use chmn. Bannockburn Cmty. Assn., 1990-94. Capt. U.S. Army, 1965-67. Fellow NSF, 1959-62, NIH, 1962-65, Woodrow Wilson Found. (hon.). Fellow AAAS; mem. Internat. Orgn. Chem. Scis. for Devel. (exec. officer biotic exploration fund), Am. Chem. Soc., Soc. Internat. Devel., Phi Beta Kappa. Avocation: ethnographic art and music. Office: Sch Fgn Svc Georgetown Univ 37th & O Sts NW Washington DC 20057-0001 E-mail: weissc@georgetown.edu.

WEISS, CHARLES ANDREW, lawyer; b. Perryville, Mo., Jan. 24, 1942; s. Wallace Francis and Iola Francis Weiss; m. Marie Suzanne Desloge, June 10, 1972; children: Christopher, Robert, Julie, Anne. BJ with highest honors, U. Mo., 1964, AB with hons. in History, 1965; JD cum laude, Notre Dame U., 1968. Bar: Mo. 1968, U.S. Dist. Ct. (ea. dist.) Mo. 1968, U.S. Ct. Appeals (8th cir.) 1968, U.S. Supreme Ct. 1972, U.S. Ct. Appeals (9th cir.) 1974, U.S. Ct. Appeals (2d cir.) 1977, U.S. Ct. Appeals (1st cir.) 1987, U.S. Ct. Appeals (5th cir.) 1992, U.S. Ct. Appeals (fed. cir.) 2003, U.S. Ct. Appeals (7th cir.) 2003. Law clk. to chief judge U.S. Ct. Appeals (8th cir.), 1968; ptnr. Bryan Cave, St. Louis, 1969—. Lectr. St. Louis U. Law Sch., 1970-73; chmn. Legal Aid Mo. Statewide, Inc., 2003—. Supr. Red Cross Water Safety Program, Perry County, Mo., 1962-64; dir. Neighborhood Youth Corps., Perry County, 1965-66; pres. Perry County Young Democrats Club, 1965-67; committeeman Boy Scouts Am., 1982-86; mem. St. Louis Met. Sewer Dist. Civil Svc. Commn., 1999—; bd. dirs. United Way of Greater St. Louis, 1988-90. Fellow Am. Coll. Trial Lawyers; mem. ABA (ho. of dels. 1986-2002, 2004—), Met. Bar Assn. St. Louis (pres. 1984-85), Mo. Bar Assn. (bd. govs. 1985, v.p. 1994-95, pres.-elect 1995-96, pres. 1996-97), St. Louis Bar Found. (pres. 1983), Mo. Lawyers Trust Account Found. (pres. 1992), Mo. Athletic Club (St. Louis), The Riverlands Assn., Inc. (pres. 1991-93), Jefferson Nat. Parks Assn. (chmn. 1993-2000), Notre Dame Club St. Louis (dir. 1993—), Notre Dame Law Assn. (dir., pres. 1997—). Roman Catholic. Office: Bryan Cave 211 N Broadway Saint Louis MO 63102-2733 Office Phone: 314-259-2215. Business E-Mail: cweiss@bryancave.com.

WEISS, CHARLES MANUEL, environmental biologist; b. Scranton, Pa., Dec. 7, 1918; s. Morris and Fannie (Levy) W.; m. Shirley Friedlander, June 7, 1942. BS, Rutgers U., 1939, postgrad., 1939-40, Harvard U., 1940; PhD, Johns Hopkins U., 1950. Fellow in marine microbiology, research assoc. in marine biology Woods Hole Oceanographic Instn., Mass., 1939-47; chemist, biologist Balt. Harbor Project, Johns Hopkins U. Dept. San Engring., 1947-50; basin biologist div. water pollution control USPHS, N.Y.C., 1950-52; biologist med. labs. Army Chem. Ctr., Edgewood, Md., 1952-56; prof. environ. biology U. N.C., Chapel Hill, 1956-89, prof. emeritus, 1989—, creator/sponsor C. & S. Weiss Urban Livability program, 1992—. Cons. limnology Duke Power Co., 1980-94; mem. ad hoc panel waste treatment Space Sci. Bd., Nat. Acad. Sci., 1966-68, chmn. panel mgmt. of spacecraft solid and liquid wastes, 1968-69, subcom. atmosphere and water contaminants of manned spacecraft, 1971; mem. triennial water quality standards rev. com. N.C. Dept. Natural Resources and Community Devel., 1982-83; cons. Nat. Health Service, Santiago, Chile, 1971; mem. Grad. Edn. Advancement Bd., U. N.C., Chapel Hill, 2001—. Author: Water Quality Investigations, Guatemala: Lake Atitlan 1968-70, 1971, Water Quality Investigations, Guatemala: Lake Amatitlan 1969-70, 1971, The Trophic State of North Carolina Lakes, 1976, The Water Quality of the Upper Yadkin Drainage Basin, 1981, Water Quality Study, B. Everett Jordan Lake, N.C., 1981-85, 87; editor N.C. Conf. AAUP Newsletter, 1985-91. Mem. Chapel Hill Planning Bd., 1969-76, chmn., 1970-72, 75-76, trustee Chapel Hill Preservation Soc., 1972; bd. dirs. Triangle Opera, 1986, 89, 91-2002; mem. adv. coun. Santa Fe Chamber Music Festival, 1990-91, 97-98, trustee, 1991-97, 98—; bd. dirs. The Chamber Orch. of the Triangle, 1997—. Recipient Gifford Phillips award Santa Fe Chamber Music Festival, 2000; Bigelow fellow Woods Hole Oceanographic Instn., 1970—. Fellow AAAS, APHA, N.Y. Acad. Scis.; mem. AAUP (chpt. pres. 1980-81, pres. N.C. conf. 1982-83, William S. Tacey award Assembly of State Confs. 1992), Am. Chem. Soc., Am. Geophys. Union, Am. Fisheries Soc., Am. Soc. Limnology and Oceanography, Ecol. Soc. Am., Soc. Internat. Limnologie, Water Pollution Control Fedn. (chmn. rsch. com. 1966-71), Am. Water Works Assn. (chmn. subcom. water quality sampling for quality control in reservoirs 1978-80), Am. Soc. Microbiology, Sigma Xi, Delta Omega. Home: 750 Weaver Dairy Rd # 2114 Chapel Hill NC 27514-1483

WEISS, CHRISTOPHER JOHN, lawyer; b. Oswego, N.Y., Sept. 1, 1952; s. Robert Leo and Flora Elizabeth Weiss; m. Corinne Fratt, Mar. 28, 1973; children: Allison Ardis, Natalie Elizabeth, Christine Corinne, Kathryn Creigh. BS, Fla. State U., 1970, JD, 1977. Bar: Fla. 1977, U.S. Dist. Ct. (mid. and so. dists.) Fla. 1977, U.S. Supreme Ct. Ptnr. Holland and Knight (and predecessor firm), Orlando, Fla., 1977—. Lectr., author various constrn. litigation issues, 1977—. Mem. Orlando Rep. Com., 1975—. Mem. Fla. Bar, Orange County Bar Assn. (constrn. com. 1987—), Am. Arbitration Assn. (nat. panelist 1982—), Assoc. Gen. Contractors, Assoc. Builders and Contractors, Constrn. Fin. Mgrs Assn. Avocations: reading, travel. Office: Holland & Knight PO Box 1526 Orlando FL 32802-1526 Office Phone: 407-244-1110.

WEISS, DANIEL EDWIN, minister, educator; b. Kenosha, Wis., June 9, 1937; s. Edwin and Ruth J. (Stromquist) Weiss; m. Rachel A. Johnson, Aug. 9, 1958; children: Daniel E. Jr., Kirsten R. BA, Wheaton Coll., 1959, MA, 1962; MDiv, Gordon Conwell Theol. Sem., South Hamilton, Mass., 1962; PhD, Mich. State U., 1964; DD (hon.), Judson Coll., 1976, Franklin Coll., 1990; DHL (hon.), Ottawa (Kans.) U., 1997; STD (hon.), Linfield Coll., 2000. Ordained to ministry Am. Bapt. Ch., 1962. Prof. ministry Gordon Div. Sch., Wenham, Mass., 1964—69; v.p. Gordon Coll., 1969—73; pres. Eastern Coll., St. Davids, Pa., 1973—81, Eastern Bapt. Theol. Sem., Phila., 1973—81; exec. v.p. Pace U., N.Y.C., 1981—83; exec. dir. Am. Bapt. Bd. Edn. and Publ., Valley Forge, Pa., 1983—88; gen. sec. Am. Bapt. Chs. U.S.A., 1988—2000. Mem. ctrl. com. World Coun. Chs., Geneva, 1989—98; mem. gen. bd. Nat. Coun. Chs., N.Y.C., 1989—2000; mem. gen. coun. Bapt. World Alliance, Washington, 1985—2000.

WEISS, DAVID I. land developer, business executive, lawyer; b. Dallas, Tex., Feb. 24, 1961; s. Kurt George and Phyllis Lee Weiss; m. Lynn Alice Epstein, Apr. 5, 1987; 1 child, Alexander Jacob. BS in fin., U. Fla., Gainesville, 1979—83; JD, Nova Southeastern U., 1983—86. Bar: State Fla. Bar Assn. 1987, U.S. Dist. Ct. Fla. (so., mid. and no. dists.) 1987, U.S. Tax Ct. 1988, U.S. Ct. Appeals (11th cir.) 1988, U.S. Supreme Ct. 1990. Law clk. to Hon. Joe Eaton Sr. U.S. Dist. Judge, So. Dist. Fla., 1986—87; ptnr. Herzfeld & Rubin, Miami, 1988—95; CEO Am. Coastal Corp., Plantation, Fla., 1995—; v.p., gen. counsel Nat. Gen. Corp., Ft. Lauderdale, Fla., 1997—; pres. Hawks Landing, Plantation, 1997—; CEO Design Safety Corp., Plantation, 2000—; ptnr. SouthStar Storage LLC., Boca Raton, Fla., 2001—, Security Storage, Delray Beach, Fla., 2003—; pres. Bluewater Groves, Inc., Ft. Pierce, Fla., 2003—. Mem. bd. editors U.S. Dist. Ct. So. Dist. Digest, Miami, 1987; mem. appellate ct. com. ABA Jud. Adminstrn. Div., Chgo., 1989—90; dir. HLPOA, Plantation, 1998—; CEO Organon Wireless, Inc., Ft. Lauderdale, 2000—; bd. mem. City of Plantation Nat. US Girls 12 Clay Tournament, 2002—. Author: When I Was A Duck, 2004; co-author: (law review article) On the Differences Between Blood and Red Ink: Economic Loss Rule (Outstanding Law Review Article, Product Liablity Jour., 1996), Conflicts of Interest under ERISA (Outstanding Law Review Article, West Pub., 1986). Bd. dirs. youth tennis program City of Plantation, 2001—; chmn. UJA U. Fla., 1982—83, mem. UJA student adv. bd., 1983—85; bd. dirs. Soref Jewish Cmty. Ctr., 2004—. Recipient Outstanding Grad. Svc. award, Hillel Found. Am., 1983. Mem.: Fla. Bar Assn. (bd. govs. 1994), Dade County Bar Assn., Broward County Bar Assn., Fed. Bar Assn., South Fla. Leukemia and Lymphoma Soc. (bd. dirs. 2004—). Democrat. Achievements include patents in field of food, service, technology and medical testing including US patent #6, 230, 924 (lid closure mechanism); #6, 207, 100 (lid closure mechanism); #D469, 693 (lid closure design); #D468, 206 (lid closure design); #6, 273, 111 (retractable water protective device); patents pending for wireless interaction, meta and collection system-PageJump (TM); lid closure mechanisms (24 pending); 30 international patents awarded on lid closure design and utility patents. Avocations: swimming, running, tennis, weight training. Office: Design Safety Corporation 8751 W Broward Blvd Ste 209 Plantation FL 33324 Office Phone: 954-472-4000. Personal E-mail: dweiss@medscape.com. Business E-Mail: dweiss@design-safety.com.

WEISS, DIETER WALDEMAR, economics educator, consultant; b. Berlin, Dec. 2, 1935; s. Waldemar Weiss and Elsa Radke. Diploma in engring., Tech. U., Berlin, 1960, PhD, 1962. With policy planning sect. Fed. Ministry Econ. Cooperation, Bonn, Germany, 1962-65; chief Mid. East dept. German Devel. Inst., Berlin, 1965-80; prof. Freie U., Berlin, 1980—. John Foster Dulles vis. prof. Princeton U., 1994; mem. German econ. adv. mission to Pres. Anwar Sadat, Egypt, 1977. Author, co-author 10 books; contbr. over 120 articles to profl. jours. Named to Order of the Arab Republic of Egypt, Govt. Egypt, Cairo, 1977. Office: Freie U Berlin Goethestr 80 10623 Berlin Germany E-mail: prof.d.weiss@gmx.de.

WEISS, DONALD A. naval officer; b. Jamestown, N.D. Graduate, U.S. Naval Acad., 1968. Advanced through grades to rear adm. USN; naval aviator Kingsville, Tex., 1970; various assignments USS Independence, USS America; detailer Jr. Officer Aviation Assignment Branch, 1980-82; comdg. officer Gunslingers, 1982-85; attack/strike fighter readiness officer U.S. Atlantic Fleet, 1985—; comdg. officer USS Concord, 1989-91, USS Saratoga, 1992-94; dir. ops. Defense Spl. Weapons Agy., 1994-96; comdr. USS Carl Vinson Battle Group, 1996-98, U.S. Naval Forces, Japan, 1998-00; dir. Asian Pacific affairs officer U.S. Sec. Def., Washington, 2000-01. Govt. fellow Harvard U., 1995.

WEISS, DONALD S. real estate developer; b. St. Petersburg, Fla., Aug. 18, 1947; s. Jonas Weiss and Miriam Kahan; m. Anne M. Weiss, Feb. 1978 (div. Jan. 1991); children: Laurie Blumstein, Melissa, Jason. BSBA, U. Fla., 1969.

Lic. real estate broker N.Y. Asst. portfolio mgr. Chase Manhattan Bank, N.Y.C., 1969—70; office space leasing salesperson Williams & Co., N.Y.C., 1971—74, Sylvan Lawrence & Co., N.Y.C., 1974—78; pvt. real estate investor N.Y.C., 1978—; developer, creator Sugar Hill Art Ctr., N.Y.C., 2001—. Dir. Com. for Rational Housing Laws and Econ. Devel. in N.Y.C. and N.Y. State (CRHNYC.COM), 1995—, Com. for a New Am. (CFANA.COM). Exhibited in group shows. With U.S. Army, 1969—73. Avocations: skiing, bridge, photography. Home: 243-07 73 Ave Douglaston NY 11362 Office: 555 W 151 St #26 New York NY 10031 Office Phone: 212-283-1278.

WEISS, EARLE BURTON, physician; b. Waltham, Mass., Nov. 23, 1932; s. Murray E. and Ruth R. (Pill) W.; m. Ruth Lithwick, Dec. 1, 1963; children: Ilana, Joshua. BS with honors, Northeastern U., 1955; MS, MIT, 1957; MD, Albert Einstein Coll. Medicine, 1961. Intern King's County Hosp., Bklyn., 1961-62; resident Boston City Hosp., 1962-64, Nat. Heart Inst. fellow, 1964-66; assoc. chief of medicine Tufts Med. Svc., 1969-71; founder/first dir. respiratory ICU, physician pulmonary svc. Boston City Hosp., 1964-71; dir. divsn. respiratory diseases St. Vincent Hosp., Worcester, Mass., 1971-89, also acting med. dir., 1985-87; prof. medicine U. Mass. Med. Sch., 1977—; sr. pulmonary rsch. scientist, dept. anesthesia Rsch. Labs. Brigham and Womens Hosp., Boston, 1989—. Cons. FDA, 1975-77; cons. in physiology Norfolk County Sanitorium, 1966-69; lectr. medicine Tufts Med. Sch., 1978—; assoc. prof. life scis. Worcester (Mass.) Poly. Inst., 1976—; vis. prof. Faculty of Medicine, dept. of anesthesia Harvard Med. Sch., 1990-2002, vis. prof. U. Guadalajara, Mexico, 1973, 77; med. dir. Found. Rsch. in Bronchial Asthma and Related Diseases, 1980—; Tb cons. Commonwealth of Mass., 1972-89; dir. regional inpatient Tb and outpatient Tb clinic, Worcester County, 1972-89; vis. prof. U. Guadalajara, Mex., 1973, 77; prof. extraordinario faculty of medicine U. Guadalajara Med. Sch., 1977, 82. Author: Bronchial Asthma, 2d edit., 1976, 3d edit., 1993, Status Asthmaticus, 1978; contbr. (with artist Frank H. Netter) Ciba Collection: The Respiratory System and Clinical Symposia Bronchial Asthma; contbr. over 90 articles to profl. jours., abstracts, audio tapes and book chpts. Capt. USAFR, 1965-70. Recipient 1st Dr. J. McKeever Meml. award for outstanding med. educator, 1970, The Acad. Honor Soc., Tchg, and Patient Care award Boston City Hosp. (I-III), 1971. Fellow ACP, Am. Coll. Chest Physicians, Royal Coll. Physicians; mem. AAAS, AMA, Mass. Thoracic Soc. (pres. 1976-78, Chadwick medal for meritorious contbn. 1990), Am. Thoracic Soc. (co-founder clin. assembly, rep. councilor 1979-82, chmn. med. devices com. 1972-79, med. edn. com. 1972-74), Am. Assn. Clin. Scientists, Am. Soc. Internal Medicine, Soc. Free Radical Rsch., N.Y. Acad. Scis., Interasthma, Sigma Xi. Achievements include pioneering use of controlled mech. ventilation in acute respiratory failure of chronic lung disease, arterial blood gas profiles in status asthma, "cross-over" point in asthma, recording of breath sounds, the theory of the role of calcium and oxygen toxic products in causing asthma and airways reactivity 1979, and percutaneous lung biopsy for diagnosis of respiratory infections. Home: 57 South St Natick MA 01760-5526 Office: Brigham and Womens Hosp Dept Anesthesia Rsch L Boston MA 02115 Business E-Mail: eweiss@bics.bwh.harvard.edu. E-mail: drwe@comcast.net.

WEISS, ELAINE LANDSBERG, community development management official; b. N.Y.C. d. Louis and Sadie Blossum (Schoenfeld); divorced. BA in Philosophy and Polit. Sci., Bklyn. Coll., 1960; postgrad., NYU Law Sch., 1960-62; MA in Sociology, Hunter Coll., N.Y.C., 1969. Social investigator N.Y.C. Dept. Social Services, 1963-64; intern, fellow Eleanor Roosevelt Meml. Found., Nat. Assn. Intergroup Relations Ofcls., 1964-65; asst. dir. housing and asst. project dir. Operation Equality, Nat. Urban League, 1965-67; program assoc. housing div. ch. missions Am. Bapt. Home Mission Socs., 1967-70; pres. E.L. Weiss Assocs., 1970-76; exec. dir. Suffolk Community Devel. Corp., Coram, N.Y., 1976-89, E.L. Weiss Assocs., N.Y.C., 1990—, Grenadier Realty Corp., 1990-92; COO Morningside Heights Housing Corp., 1992-95; exec. dir. Fairmont Housing Corp. (N.J.) subsidiary YWCA Hudson County, 1995-97, Westchester Residential Opportunities, Inc., White Plains, N.Y., 1997-98, Saparn Realty, Inc., N.Y.C., 1998-2001, N.Y. Soc. Deaf, 2001—. Mem. citizens adv. com. N.Y.C. Dept. Housing Preservation and Devel.; exec. com. L.I. Community Devel. Orgn.; past 2d v.p. Suffolk Housing Task Force; chmn. Suffolk County Citizens Adv. Com., 1981-82. Recipient cert. of commendation L.I. Council Chs., 1981. Mem. Nat. Assn. Housing Ofcls., N.Y. State Assn. Housing and Redevel. Ofcls., Am. Contract Bridge League (life master). Home: PO Box 1532 East Quogue NY 11942-1333

WEISS, ERIC GLENN, physician; b. White Sands, N.Mex., Mar. 19, 1962; s. Richard Fred and Harriet (Stuart) W.; m. Debra R. Weiss, June 12, 1988; children: Morgan Rachel, Adam Howard, Brett Phillip. BS in Biochemistry, Pa. State U., 1984; MD, Temple U., 1988. Diplomate Am. Bd. Surgery, Am. Bd. Colon and Rectal Surgery. Resident in surgery Albert Einstein Med. Ctr., Phila., 1988-93; fellow in colorectal surgery Cleveland Clinic Fla., Ft. Lauderdale, 1993-94, staff colorectal surgeon, 1994—, assoc. residency program dir., 1998—, chmn. surg. endoscopy, 1996—, chmn. grad. med. edn., 1999—. Co-editor: Diagnosis and Treatment of Fecal Incontinence, 2000. Fellow ACS, Am. Soc. Colon and Rectal Surgeons; mem. Am. Coll. Gastroenterology. Office: Cleveland Clinic Fla 2950 Cleveland Clinic Blvd Weston FL 33331 E-mail: weisse@ccf.org.

WEISS, GAIL ELLEN, legislative staff director; b. N.Y.C., Apr. 11, 1946; d. Joseph and Elaine (Klein) W.; m. John A. Kelly. BA, U. Md., 1967. Staff asst. U.S. Office Econ. Opportunity/Job Corps, Washington, 1967-69; legis. asst. Hon. William L. Clay, Mem. Congress, Washington, 1969-72; rsch. asst. Rt. Hon. Roy Hattersley, Mem. Parliament, London, 1972-73; legis. asst. various coms. U.S. Ho. of Reps., Washington, 1973-90, staff dir. Com. on P.O. and Civil Svc., 1991-94, Dem. staff dir. Com. on Econ. and Ednl. Opportunities, 1995—. Mem. working group Pres.'s Task Force on Nat. Health Reform, 1993. Democrat. Jewish. Office: Com on Edn and the Workforce 2101 Rayburn Ho Office Bldg Washington DC 20515-0001

WEISS, GEORGE HERBERT, mathematician, consultant; b. N.Y.C., Feb. 19, 1930; s. Morris and Violet (Mayer) W.; m. Delia Esther Orgel, Dec. 20, 1961; children: Miriam Judith, Alan Keith, Daniel Jonathan. BA, Columbia U., 1951; MA, U. Md., 1953, PhD, 1958. Physicist USN, White Oak, Md., 1951-61; asst. prof. U. Md., College Park, 1959-63; fellow Rockefeller U., N.Y.C., 1963-64, Weizmann Inst., Rehovot, Israel, 1958-59; mathematician NIH, Bethesda, Md., 1964—. Cons. GM, IBM, GE. Author: Lattice Dynamics in the Harmonic Approximation, 1963, 2d edit., 1971, The Master Equation in Chemical Physics, 1977, Contemporary Problems in Statistical Physics, 1994, Aspects and Applications of the Random Walk, 1994, Introduction to Crystallographic Statistics, 1995. With U.S. Army, 1954-56. Recipient Disting. Svc. in Math. award Washington Acad. Sci., 1967, Disting. Svc. award NIH, 1970. Avocations: photography, music, chess, stamp collecting/philately. Office: NIH Bethesda MD 20892 Business E-Mail: ghw@helix.nih.gov.

WEISS, GERHARD HANS, German language educator; b. Berlin, Aug. 6, 1926; came to U.S., 1946; s. Curt Erich and Gertrud (Grothus) W.; m. Janet Marilyn Smith, Dec. 27, 1953; children: John Martin, Susan Elizabeth Weiss Spencer, James David. BA, Washington U., St. Louis, 1950, MA, 1952; PhD, U. Wis., 1956. Prof. German U. Minn., Mpls., 1956—98, assoc. dean, 1967—71, 1979, chmn. dept. German, 1987-95, prof. emeritus, 1998—, interim dir. Ctr. Austrian Studies, 1999-2001. Mem. German-Am. Textbook Commn., Braunschweig, Fed. Republic Germany, 1985-88. Author: Begegnung mit Deutschland, 1970; editor: Unterrichtspraxis, 1975-80, Minn. Monographs in the Humanities, 1964-70; contbr. articles to profl. jours. Served to lt. col. USAR, 1946-75. Recipient Cross Merit, Fed. Republic Germany, 1982. Mem. MLA, Am. Assn. Tchrs. German (pres. 1982-83, cert. of merit 1981, Disting. German Educator award 1991, elected hon. mem. 1995), German Studies Assn. (v.p. 1997-98, pres. 1999-00), Am. Coun. Tchg. Fgn. Langs. (Nelson Brooks award 1987). Methodist. Home: 4101 Abbott Ave S Minneapolis MN 55410-1004

WEISS, GERSON, reproductive endocrinologist, educator; b. N.Y.C., Aug. 1, 1939; s. Samuel and Lillian (Wolpe) W.; m. Linda Gordon, Dec. 24, 1959; children: Jonathan, David, Michele, Andrew. BA, NYU, 1960, MD, 1964. Diplomate Am. Bd. Ob-Gyn. (mem. divsn. reproductive endocrinology 1985-90, pres. bd. 1999-2002). Intern, fellow dept. medicine Johns Hopkins Sch. Medicine, 1964-65; resident ob-gyn NYU Med. Ctr., 1964-69; rsch. fellow physiology U. Pitts. Sch. Medicine, 1971-73; asst. prof. ob-gyn NYU Med. Ctr., 1971-76, asso. prof., 1976-80, prof., 1980-85; dir. div. reproductive endocrinology NYU Med. Center, 1975-85; prof. ob-gyn U. Med. and Dentistry N.J.-N.J. Med. Sch., 1986—, chmn. dept., 1986—; dir. divsn. reproductive endocrinology Hackensack (N.J.) U. Med. Ctr., 1996—2002. Rep. Am. Bd. Med. Specialists. Mem. editl. bd. Fertility and Sterility Jour., 1986-93, Gyn.-Ob. Investigation; contbr. rsch. articles reproductive endocrinology and gynecology to med. jours. Served to maj. MC U.S. Army, 1969-71. Rsch. grantee NIH, 1975—, United Cerebral Palsy Found., 1977-83, Mellon Found., 1982-85; John Polachek Found. Med. Rsch. fellow. Mem. ACOG, Am. Gyn-Ob. Soc., Am. Bd. Ob-Gyn. (bd. dirs., treas. 1997-98, pres. 1998-2002, chmn. 2002—, ob-gyn. residency rev. com. 1995-2000, coun. univ. chairs ob-gyn, pres.-elect, 1998-99, pres. 2000-02), Am. Bd. Med. Spltys. (coun. 2002—), Endocrine Soc., Soc. Gynecol. Investigation (pres.-elect 2004), N.Y. Obstet. Soc. (pres. 1990-91), N.Y. Gynecol. Soc. (pres. 1989-90), Soc. Study of Reprodn., Endocrine Soc., Phi Beta Kappa, Sigma Xi, Alpha Omega Alpha. Home: 390 1st Ave Apt 11D New York NY 10010-4935 Office: UMDNJ NJ Med Sch Dept Ob-Gyn 185 S Orange Ave Newark NJ 07103-2757

WEISS, GREGORY LEE, sociology educator; b. Canton, Ohio, Aug. 19, 1949; m. Janet S. Jonas. BA, Wittenberg U., 1971; MS, Purdue U., 1972, PhD, 1975. Fellow USPHS Purdue U., West Lafayette, Ind., 1971-75, instr. Sch. of Continuing Edn., 1974-75; asst. prof. sociology Roanoke Coll., Salem, Va., 1975-81, assoc. prof. sociology, 1981-87, prof., 1987—, chair dept. sociology, 1996-99, dir. assessment, 1999—2001. Dir. Ctr. for Cmty. Rsch., 1983-91. Author: The Sociology of Health Hearing and Illness, 1994, The Sociology of Health Hearing and Illness, 4th edit., 2002; co-author: Annual Research in the Spociology of Health Care; contbr. articles to profl. jours. Bd. dirs. Bradley Free Clinic, Roanoke, Planned Parenthood, Roanoke, League for Animal Protection, SPCA Pet Therapy. Recipient Outstanding Svc. award Bradley Free Clinic, 1981; Institutional Lab. Improvement grant NSF, Washington, 1994. Mem.: APHA, Va. Social Sci. Assn. (pres. 1985—86, scholar award 1982), So. Sociol. Soc., Am. Assn. Higher Edn., Am. Sociol. Assn. (cons. 1991—, Tchg. Endowment Fund grants 1997, Va. outstanding faculty mem. award 2004). Home: 182 Forest Dr Salem VA 24153-6860 Office: Roanoke Coll Dept Sociology Salem VA 24153 E-mail: weiss@roanoke.edu.

WEISS, JAMES LLOYD, cardiology educator; b. Chgo., Jan. 15, 1941; s. Edward Huhner and Ruth (Wingerhoff) W.; m. Susan Forscher Weiss. July 23, 1967; children: Ethan James, Lisa Fleur. BA, Harvard Coll., 1963; MD, Yale U., 1968. Intern, resident U. Mich. Hosp., Ann Arbor, 1968-70; staff fellow NIH, Bethesda, Md., 1970-72; resident medicine Johns Hopkins Hosp., Balt., 1972-73, fellow cardiology, 1973-75, dir. Heart Station, 1976—, asst. prof. Medicine, 1975-81, assoc. prof. Medicine, 1981-90, prof. Medicine, Cardiology, 1990—, Michael J. Cudahy prof. of cardiology, 1992—, assoc. dean admissions and acad. affairs, 1999—, dir. cardiology fellowship and tng. program, 1999—. Mem. editl. bd.: Johns Hopkins Med. Letter, 1991—, Jour. Am. Coll. Cardiology, 1995—; contbr. 120 articles to profl. jours. Recipient Harvard Book prize, 1959. Fellow Am. Coll. Cardiology, AHA Coun. on Circulation; mem. Harvard Club N.Y.C., Ctr. Club. Office: Cardiology Divsn Johns Hopkins Hosp 600 N Wolfe St Baltimore MD 21287-0005 Office Phone: 410-955-6834.

WEISS, JAMES MICHAEL, financial analyst, portfolio manager; b. Chgo., July 20, 1946; s. Harold Cornelius and Elizabeth Josephine (Jesse) W.; m. Kathleen Jane Postorino, July 18, 1970; children: Elizabeth, Ann, Jane, William. BA, Marquette U., 1968; MBA, U. Pa., 1972. CFA; chartered investment counselor. Credit analyst Provident Nat. Bank, Phila., 1972; ptnr., sr. portfolio mgr. Stein Roe & Farnham Investment Counsel, Chgo., 1972—87, 1st v.p., prin., sr. portfolio mgr., 1987—90, sr. v.p., prin., sr. portfolio mgr., 1991—92; exec. v.p., sr. portfolio mgr. IDS Adv. Group, Inc., Mpls., 1993—95; pres., chief investment officer IDS Equity Advisors, 1995; sr. v.p., dep. chief investment officer Equities, State St. Rsch. & Mgmt. Co., Boston, 1995—97, exec. v.p., mem. mgmt. com., dep. head of equities, 1998—99, exec. v.p. mem. mgmt. com., chief invest. officer, bd. dirs., 1999—2002; pres. Weiss Capital Mgmt., Inc., 2002—. Bd. dirs. Tropp & Co., Chgo.; v.p. Stein Roe Cash Reserves Fund, Chgo., 1982-87. Author: (with others) Handbook of Cash Flow and Treasury Management, 1987; contbr. articles to profl. jours. Commr. Glenview (Ill.) Zoning Bd., 1978-80; trustee Glenview Village Bd. Trustees, 1980-86; chmn. Marquette U. Exec. Senate, Chgo., 1984-87; mem. Glenview Bus. Area Redevel. Com., 1990-93; mem. bus. adv. coun. Elmhurst (Ill.) Coll., 1986-93; founding bd. dirs. Glenview Edn. Found., 1990-93; bd. trustees The Fenn Sch., Concord, Mass., 1996-2002; co-chmn. Fenn Sch. Capital Campaign, 1997-2000; bd. dirs. Gaining Ground, Concord, 2003—. With U.S. Army, 1968-70. Recipient Cert. Merit Village of Glenview, 1987. Mem.: Investment Counsel Assn., Fin. Analysts Fedn., Investment Analysts Soc., Marquette U. Alumni Assn. (nat. bd. dirs. 1989—91, liberal arts bd. 2000—, Nat. Svc. award 1995), Indian River Country Club (Vero Beach, Fla.), Boston Coll. Club, Wedgewood Pines Club (Stow, Mass.), North Shore Country Club (Glenview, Ill.). Avocations: golf, travel, writing. Office: Weiss Capital Mgmt PO Box 1128 Concord MA 01742-1128 Home: 251 Caterina Hts Concord MA 01742-4774 E-mail: jweiss6@earthlink.net.

WEISS, JEFFREY M. From sr. v.p. to pres., COO Am. Greetings Corp., Cleve., 1997—2003, pres., 2003—, COO, 2003—. Office: American Greetings Corp 1 American Rd Cleveland OH 44144-2398*

WEISS, JERRY KENNETH, sales executive, consultant, marketing professional; s. Charels and Gladys Weiss; m. Bonnie Goldner, Feb. 18, 1981; 1 child, Samantha. BA, State U. N.Y., Toledo; MA, State U. N.Y., Ohio, 1974; study in mktg. and advt., N.Y. U., 1976—80. Nat. field sales and mktg. mgr. Mego Toy Corp. Internat., N.Y.C., 1981—83; sales and mktg. mgr. Sharp Inc., Paramus, NJ, 1983—85; dir. sales Mattel, Inc., Hawthorne, Calif., 1985—87; sr. ptnr. Cutting Edge Enterprises, Inc, Cedarhurst, NY, 1988—. Bd. dirs. CE2, Inc., Cedarhurst, 1991—, Dover Automation, Inc., Clev., 1998—2002. Author: (audio cassette/cd) Sales Directions. Fundraisor Westchester Reform Temple, Scarsdale, NY, 1998—2003. Scholar, State U. Ohio. Fellow: Sigma Alpha Mo (sec.), Acad. Mktg. Sci. (assoc.); mem.: Phi Alpha Theta. Avocations: motorcycling, auto racing, white-water rafting.

WEISS, JOEL ALEXANDER, environmental and manufacturing executive; b. Washington; s. Jack Lawrence and Margaret (Siegal) W.; m. Sandra Jean Spaulding, July 6, 1969; children: Martin, Robert, Eric, Amy. B of Engring. Sci., Johns Hopkins U., 1969; AM, Harvard U., 1970, PhD, 1975. Rsch. physicist U.S. Naval Rsch. Lab., Washington, 1966-75; program mgr. U.S. Dept. Energy, Washington, 1975-78, exec. asst., 1978-80; mgr. Washington ops. Acurex Corp., Mtn. View, Calif., 1980-84; dir. tactical warfare Gould Inc., Glen Burnie, Md., 1984-87; mgr. rsch. & technology Martin Marietta Aero & Naval Systems, Balt., 1987-90; v.p. bus. devel. Marietta Tech. Svcs. Inc., Bethesda, Md., 1990-93; dir. strategic planning Sandia Nat. Labs., Albuquerque, 1993-95; v.p. bus. devel. Lockheed Martin Energy Programs, Bethesda, Md., 1995-2000; pres. Lockheed Martin Energy Techs., Inc., Bethesda, Md., 1999-2000; exec. v.p., prin. QuadraTech Group, LLC, Arlington, Va., 2001—; pres. EnergoTech, LLC, a QuadraTech Co., Arlington, 2001—. Patentee in field. Mem. Sigma Xi, Tau Beta Pi. Avocation: computers. Office: EnergoTech LLC 1803 Research Blvd Ste 503 Rockville MD 20850-3141 E-mail: joel.a.weiss@energotechllc.com.

WEISS, JONATHAN ARTHUR, lawyer; b. May 1, 1939; s. Paul and Victoria Brodkin Weiss. BA, Yale U., 1960, LLB, 1963; student, U. Chgo. Law Sch., 1960—61. Bar: NY 1967, DC 1994, Vet.'s Ct. (2d and 3d cirs.), U.S. Supreme Ct. 1967. Mng. atty. Neighborhood Legal Svcs., Washington, 1964-66, Mobilization for Youth Legal Svcs., N.Y.C., 1969-71; with Ctr. on Welfare Law, Columbia U. Law Sch., N.Y.C., 1967-69; dir. Legal Svcs. for Elderly, N.Y.C., 1971—. Lectr. Hebrew U., Jerusalem, 1966; vis. prof. Tex. So. U. Law Sch., Houston, 1971; adj. prof. Yeshiva U. Cardozo Law Sch., N.Y.C., falls 1983-85. Co-author, editor: The Law and the Elderly, 1976; co-author: Right and Wrong a Philosophical Dialogue and Between Father and Son, 1968; contbr. numerous articles and revs. to law and philos. jours. and newspapers, French and Russian transls. of novels, screenplay and play. Bd. dirs. N.Y. Civil Liberties Union, Disability Legal Def. Fund, World Trust Fund Inc. Recipient Disting. Scholar medal Hofstra U., 1972; Fulbright scholar, 1966. Mem. ABA (mem. Adv. Coun. ethics 2000 com.), Native Am. Bar Assn., N.Y. State Bar (internat. sect. human rights). Democrat. Office: Legal Svcs for Elderly 130 W 42d St New York NY 10036

WEISS, JULIE, costume designer; Costume designer: (stage) The Elephant Man, 1979 (Tony award nomination best costume design 1979); (films) I'm Dancing as Fast as I Can, 1982, Independence Day, 1983, Second Thoughts, 1983, Spacehunter: Adventures in the Forbidden Zone, 1983, Testament, 1983, The Mean Season, 1985, Creator, 1985, F/X, 1986, Cherry 2000, 1987, Masters of the Universe, 1987, The Whales of August, 1987, 1969, 1988, Tequila Sunrise, 1988, Steel Magnolias, 1989, Wicked Stepmother, 1989, The Freshman, 1990, Married to It, 1991, Honeymoon in Vegas, 1992, House of Cards, 1993, Searching for Bobby Fischer, 1993, Naked in New York, 1993, It Could Happen to You, 1994, 12 Monkeys, 1995 (Acad. award nominee for best costume design 1996), Marvin's Room, 1996, The Edge, 1997, Touch, 1997, A Simple Plan, 1998, Finding Graceland, 1998, Fear and Loathing in Las Vegas, 1998, Isn't She Great, 1999, American Beauty, 1999; (TV movies) The Gangster Chronicles, 1981, The Elephant Man, 1982 (Emmy award nominee for best costume design 1982), Little Gloria...Happy at Last, 1982 (Emmy award nominee for best costume design 1983), The Dollmaker, 1984 (Emmy award nominee for best costume design 1984), Do You Remember Love?, 1985, Evergreen, 1985 (Emmy award nominee for best costume design 1985), Conspiracy of Love, 1987, A Woman of Independant Means, 1994 (Emmy award for best costume design), Love She Sought, 1990, The Portrait, 1993. Office: c/o Costume Designers Guild 13949 Ventura Blvd Ste 309 Sherman Oaks CA 91423-3570

WEISS, KENNETH ANDREW, lawyer, law educator; b. New Orleans, Jan. 16, 1951; s. Irving and Julia (Mayer) W. BA, Tulane U., 1972, JD with honors, 1975; LLM in Taxation with highest honors, George Washington U., 1981. Bar: La. 1975, D.C. 1976. Editl. writer, Washington corr. The Times-Picayune, New Orleans and Washington, 1973-79; news editor Congl. Quarterly, Washington, 1979-81; mng. editor Reporters Com. for Freedom of the Press, Washington, 1981-82; assoc. McGlinchey Stafford, New Orleans, 1982-84, dir., 1984—. Prof. Tulane U. Law Sch., New Orleans, 1987—, La. State U. Law Sch., 2000—; mem. trust code com. La. Law Inst., Baton Rouge, 1993—, mem. successions and donations com., 1996—; mem. planning com. Tulane Tax Inst., 1996—; chair Tulane U. Law Sch. Ann. Estate Planning Seminar, 1995—2001, Tulane U. Estate Planning Inst., 2002—; dean's adv. coun. Tulane Law Sch., 2003—. Co-author: Bankers' Guide to Establishing, Managing and Operating Common Trust Funds, 1986, Business Uses of Life Insurance, 1986, Executive Compensation, 1990; assoc. editor Tulane Law Rev., 1974-75, mem. bd. adv. editors, 1992—; contbr. articles to profl. jours. Bd. dirs. Longue Vue House and Gardens Adv. Corp., 1993-95, bd. dirs. Longue Vue Found., 1995—2003; trustee Greater New Orleans Ednl. TV Found., Sta. WYES-TV, 1994-98; bd. dirs. So. Repertory Theatre, 1996-2001, pres., 1998-99; bd. advisors Project Lazarus, 1996-2000, pres. 1997-99; mem. profl. adv. com., Jewish Endowment Found., 1982—; mem. planned gifts adv. com. Tulane U., 1989—; active Met. Area Com. Leadership Forum, New Orleans, 1983; fellow Inst. Politics Loyola U., New Orleans, 1989-90; mem. devel. com. Greater New Orleans Found., 1995—. bd. dirs., Innocence Project New Orleans, 2002—, treas., 2002-04. Recipient Addy award for polit. advt., 1989, awards for investigative reporting; Phi Delta Phi scholar, 1972-73. Fellow Am. Coll. Trust and Estate Counsel; mem. La. State Bar Assn. (taxation sect., bd. cert. tax atty., bd. cert. estate planning and adminstrn. specialist), New Orleans Bar Assn. (chair taxation law com. 2003), Nat. Coun. Planned Giving (greater New Orleans chpt.), New Orleans Estate Planning Coun., Order of the Coif. Republican. Jewish. Office: McGlinchey Stafford 643 Magazine St New Orleans LA 70130-3477 Office Phone: 504-596-2751.

WEISS, LAWRENCE MARTIN, pathologist, researcher; s. Sidney and Esther Weiss; m. Tina Dianne Pasternack; children: Dina Emily, Tessa Simone. BS, U. Md., College Park, 1976; MD, U. Md., Balt., 1981. Diplomate Am. Bd. Pathology. Asst. prof. pathology Stanford (Calif.) U., 1985—89; dir. surg. pathology City of Hope Nat. Med. Ctr., Duarte, Calif., 1989—97, chmn. pathology, also bd. dirs. Bd. dirs. City of Hope Med. Group, Monrovia, Calif., 2000—. Editor: (textbooks) Modern Surgical Pathology, Tumors of the Lymph Nodes and Spleen, Hodgkin's Disease, Pathology of Lymph Nodes. Recipient Benjamin Castleman award, U.S.-Can. Soc. Pathologists, 1986, Young Investigator award, 1999, Clin. Oncology Career Devel. award, Am. Cancer Soc., 1987—89; fellow, Andrew Mellon Found., 1988—89. Mem.: L.A. Soc. Pathologists (pres. 2004—). Achievements include research in identiification of Epstein-Barr virus in Hodgkin's Disease and other neoplasms. Office: City of Hope Nat Med Ctr 1500 Duarte Rd Duarte CA 91010 E-mail: lweiss@coh.org.

WEISS, LAWRENCE N. lawyer; b. N.Y.C., Aug. 9, 1942; s. Joseph and Martha (Guggenheimer) W.; m. Osnat Gad. BA, CCNY, 1963; LLB summa cum laude, Columbia U., 1966. Bar: N.Y. 1966, U.S. Ct. Appeals (2d cir.) 1967, U.S. Dist. Ct. (so. and ea. dists) N.Y. 1968, U.S. Supreme Ct. 1971, U.S. Ct. Appeals (3d cir.) 1968, U.S. Ct. Appeals (6th cir.) 1980, U.S. Tax Ct. 1977. Assoc. Kaye, Scholer, Fierman, Hays & Handler, N.Y.C., 1966-67, 67-73; law clk. to judge N.Y. Ct. Appeals, Albany and N.Y.C., 1967; assoc. Botein, Hays, Sklar & Herzberg, N.Y.C., 1973-76, Weisman, Celler, Spett, Modlin & Wertheimer, N.Y.C., 1976, ptnr., 1977-79, counsel, 1979-81; prin. Lawrence N. Weiss, P.C., N.Y.C., 1981—, Pantaleoni & Weiss, N.Y.C., 1993—2003. Arbitrator Civil Ct., N.Y.C., 1985—; mediator U.S. Dist. Ct. (ea. dist.) N.Y. and N.Y. Supreme Ct. Mem. Assn. Bar of City of N.Y. (com. on legal edn. and admission to bar), N.Y. State Bar Assn. (chair com. CLE, com. on fed. judiciary, spl. com. on copyright, vice chair com. on UN, subcom. internat. cts., litig. sect., judiciary com.). Avocation: shakespearean studies. Home: 107 E 37th St New York NY 10016-3065 Office Phone: 212-213-3285. E-mail: larry@lweiss.net.

WEISS, LEONARD, mathematician, consultant; b. N.Y.C., Mar. 14, 1934; s. Max and Sadie (Albert) W.; m. Sandra Joyce Raynes, June 15, 1958; children: Madelyn, Eugene. B.E.E., CCNY, 1956; MS, Columbia U., 1959; PhD, Johns Hopkins U., 1962. Lectr. CCNY, 1956-59; staff scientist Research Inst. for Advanced Studies, Balt., 1962-64; asst. prof. Brown U., Providence, 1964-66, assoc. prof., 1966-68; prof. U. Md., College Park, 1968-78; legis. asst. to Senator John Glenn of Ohio, 1976-77; cons. Naval Research Lab., Washington, 1970-77; staff dir. Senate Subcom. on Energy, Nuclear Proliferation and Govt. Processes, 1977-86, Senate Com. Govtl. Affairs., 1987-99; cons. Lawrence Livermore Nat. Lab., 1999—. Editor: Ordinary Differential Equations, 1972; contbr. articles to profl. jours. and mags.; author legislation on nuclear proliferation, energy, health and safety, govt. orgn., and govt. mgmt. Alfred P. Sloan research fellow, 1966-68, IEEE Congl. fellow, 1976, Stennis Congl. fellow, 1997. Home and Office: 11701 Auth Ln Silver Spring MD 20902-1644

WEISS, LYNNE S. pediatrician, educator; MD, Hahnemann Med. Coll., Phila., 1974. Diplomate Pediatrics Am. Bd. Pediatrics, 1979, Pediatric Nephrology Am. Bd. Pediatrics, 1982. Intern in Pediatrics Michael Reese Hosp., Chgo., 1974—75, resident in Pediatrics, 1975—77, fellow in Nephrology (pediatric), 1977—79; physician divsn. Nephrology dept. Pediarics Robert Wood Johnson Univ. Med. Group, New Brunswick, NJ, 1985—. Prof. Pediatrics Robert Wood Johnson Univ. Hosp., New Brunswick, NJ, 1987—, dir. Pediatric Nephrology Ctr., 1987—. Office: Clin Acad Bldg Ste 6140 125 Paterson St New Brunswick NJ 08901-1977 Office Phone: 732-235-7880.

WEISS, MARK, public relations executive; b. N.Y.C., Mar. 5, 1950; BA in Psychology, Queens Coll., 1972; MA in Social Psychology, New Sch. for Social Rsch., 1975. With Multimedia Advt./Pub. Rels., 1970-74; account rep. Edward Baker, Inc., 1974-78; account exec. Rowland Co., 1978-81, v.p., 1980-84, sr. v.p., 1984-86, exec. v.p., 1986-90, sr. exec. v.p., COO, 1991-92, pres., CEO, 1992-98, Rowland Worldwide, 1998—2003. Office: Rowland Comm Worldwide 1675 Broadway Fl 34 New York NY 10019-5820*

WEISS, MARK ANSCHEL, lawyer; b. N.Y.C., NY, June 20, 1937; s. George and Ida (Galin) W.; m. Joan Roth, June 8, 1958; children: Rebecca, Sarabeth, Jonathan, Deborah. AB, Columbia U., 1958; LLB magna cum laude, Harvard U., 1961. Bar: N.Y. 1961, D.C. 1962, U.S. Supreme Ct. 1965. Assoc. Covington & Burling, Washington, 1961-66, 69-70, ptnr., 1970—; spl. asst. to Under Sec. Treasury Dept. Washington, 1966-68; spl. asst. to sec., 1968-69. Mem. editl. adv. bd. Electronic Banking Law and Commerce Report. Mem. ABA, D.C. Bar, Fed. Bar Assn. (chmn. banking law com.). Office: Covington & Burling 1201 Pennsylvania Ave NW Washington DC 20004-2401 Office Phone: 202-662-5308. Business E-Mail: mweiss@cov.com.

WEISS, MARTIN HARVEY, neurosurgeon, educator; b. Newark, Feb. 2, 1939; s. Max and Rae W.; m. R. Debora Rosenthal, Aug. 20, 1961; children: Brad, Jessica, Elisabeth. AB magna cum laude, Dartmouth Coll., 1960, BMS, 1961; MD, Cornell U., 1963. Diplomate Am. Bd. Neurol. Surgery (bd. dirs. 1983-89, vice chmn. 1987-88, chmn. 1988-89). Intern Univ. Hosps., Cleve., 1963-64, resident in neurosurgery, 1966-70; sr. instr. to asst. prof. neurosurgery Case Western Res. U., 1970-73; asso. prof. neurosurgery U. So. Calif., 1973-76, prof., 1976-78, prof., chmn. dept., 1978—, Martin H. Weiss chair in neurol. surgery, 1997—. Chmn. neurology B study sect. NIH; mem. residency rev. com. for neurosurg. Accreditation Commn. for Grad. Med. Edn., 1989—, vice chmn., 1991—93, chmn., 1993—95, mem. appeals coun. in neurosurg., 1995—; vis. prof. U. Mich, 1987; vis. prof. Med. Sch. Harvard U., 1988; vis. prof. U. Wash., 1988, U. Calif., San Francisco, 1994, U. Oreg., 1995, Tufts U., 1996, U. Melbourne, 1996, U. Sydney, 1996, U. Erlangen/Nurnberg, 1999, U. Geneva, 1999, U. Tex., 2004, U. Oreg., 2004; Afrox traveling prof. South African Congress Neurol. Surgeons, 1989; hon. guest Royal Coll. Physicians Endocrine Sect., London, 2001; lectr. in field. Author: Pituitary Diseases, 1980; editor-in-chief Clin. Neurosurgery, 1980-83; assoc. editor Bull. L.A. Neurol. Socs., 1976-81, Jour. Clin. Neurosci., 1981—; mem. editl. bd. Neurosurgery, 1979-84, Neurol. Rsch., 1980—, Jour. Neurosurgery, 1987—, chmn., 1995—, assoc. editor, 1996—. Served to capt. USAR, 1964-66. Spl. fellow in neurosurgery NIH, 1969-70; recipient Jamieson medal Australasian Neurosurg. Soc., 1996. Mem. ACS (adv. coun. neurosurgery 1985-88), Soc. Neurol. Surgeons (v.p. 1999, pres.-elect 2000—, pres. 2001-02), Neurosurg. Soc. Am., Am. Acad. Neurol. Surgery (exec. com. 1988-89, v.p. 1992-93), Rsch. Soc. Neurol. Surgeons, Am. Assn. Neurol. Surgeons (bd. dirs. 1988-91, sec. 1994-97, pres.-elect 1998-99, pres. 1999-2000, past pres. 2000-2001), Congress Neurol. Surgeons (v.p. 1982-83), Western Neurosurg. Soc., Neurosurg. Forum, So. Calif. Neurosurg. Soc. (pres. 1983-84), Phi Beta Kappa, Alpha Omega Alpha. Home: 357 Georgian Rd La Canada Flintridge CA 91011-3520 Office: 1200 N State St Los Angeles CA 90033-1029 Office Phone: 213-226-7421. Business E-Mail: weiss@email.usc.edu.

WEISS, MAX TIBOR, retired aerospace company executive; b. Hajduananas, Hungary, Dec. 29, 1922; came to U.S., 1929, naturalized, 1936; s. Samuel and Anna (Hornstein) W.; m. Melitta Newman, June 28, 1953; children: Samuel Harvey, Herschel William, David Nathaniel, Deborah Beth. BEE, CCNY, 1943; MS, MIT, 1947, PhD, 1950. Rsch. assoc. MIT, 1946-50; mem. tech. staff Bell Tel. Labs., Holmdel, N.J., 1950-59; assoc. head applied physics lab. Hughes Aircraft Co., Culver City, Calif., 1959-60; dir. electronics rsch. lab. The Aerospace Corp., L.A., 1961-63, gen. mgr. labs. div., 1963-67, gen. mgr. electronics and optics div., 1968-78, v.p., gen. mgr. lab. ops., 1978-81, v.p. engring. group, 1981-86; v.p. tech. and electronics system group Northrop Corp., L.A., 1986-91, v.p., gen. mgr. electronics systems div. Hawthorne, Calif., 1991-94; corp. v.p., dep. gen. mgr. electronics/systems integration Northrop Grumman Corp., Bethpage, N.Y., 1994-96, corp. v.p., 1996. Asst. mgr. engring. ops. TRW Systems, Redondo Beach, Calif., 1967-68; mem. sci. adv. bd. USAF; bd. dirs. Concorde Solutions, Inc., Concord, Calif. Contbr. articles to physics and electronics jours.; patentee in electronics and communications. With USNR, 1944-45. Fellow Am. Phys. Soc., IEEE (Centennial medal, 1983, Fredrik Philips award, 1993), AIAA, AAAS; mem. NAE, Sigma Xi. Business E-Mail: maxweiss@comcast.net.

WEISS, MELVYN I. lawyer; b. NYC, Aug. 1, 1935; s. Joseph and Jean Weiss; m. Barbara Joan Kaplan, Dec. 27, 1958; children: Gary Michael, Stephen Andrew, Leslie Caryn. BBA, CCNY, 1957; JD, NYU, 1959. Bar: NY 1960, US Dist. Ct. (so. dist.) NY, US Dist. Ct. (ea. dist.) NY, US Ct. Appeals (2d, 3rd, 5th, 6th, 8th, 9th, 10th adn 11th cirs.) 1975, US Supreme Ct. 1976. Assoc. Strasser, Spiegelberg, Fried & Frank, N.Y.C., 1959-61, Galef & Jacobs, N.Y.C., 1962-65; founding ptnr. Milberg Weiss Bershad Specthrie & Lerach LLP (now Milberg Weiss Bershad & Schulman LLP), N.Y., Boca Raton, L.A., Wilmington, D.C., Seattle, 1966—. Lectr. panelist univs., bar groups, continuing legal edn. orgns. Contbr. articles to profl. jours. Founder Melvyn and Barbara Weiss Pub. Interest Student Loan Repayment Found., NYU. Mem. ABA, Am. Coll. Trial Laywers, B'nai B'rith (Human Rels. award Anti Defamation League 1976), CCNY Alumni Assn. (Oustanding Alumni award 1982), NYU Sch. Law (trustee, Vanderbilt medal 1993), Glen Oaks Golf and Country Club, Boca Rio Golf Club. Office: Milberg Weiss Bershad & Schulman LLP Ste 4900 1 Pennsylvania Plz New York NY 10119-0165 Office Phone: 212-594-5300. E-mail: brudman@milbergweiss.com.

WEISS, MICHAEL ALLEN, retail executive; b. N.Y.C., Apr. 21, 1941; s. Robert and Estelle (Kirchner) W.; m. Arlene Markman, Dec. 25, 1962; children: Eloise Kyle, Katherine Jane. BA, Syracuse U., 1962. Buyer Abraham & Straus, Bklyn., 1965-72, Casual Corner, Enfield, Conn., 1972-74; merchandiser Apparel Industries, N.Y.C., 1974-81; pres., CEO Limited Express, Columbus, Ohio, 1981-93; vice chmn. The Limited, Inc., Columbus, 1993—. Bd. dirs. United Way of Franklin County, ARC. Mem. Winding Hollow Country Club, Capitol Club, New Albany Country Club.

WEISS, MITCH, journalist; Corr. AP, Ohio, 1986—98; state editor Block News Alliance (The Blade and The Pitts. Post-Gazette), 1998—. Recipient Pulitzer Prize for investigative reporting, 2004, medal winner, Investigative Reporters and Editors Inc., 2004. Office: The Blade 541 N Superior St Toledo OH 43660*

WEISS, MORRY, greeting card company executive; b. Czechoslovakia, 1940; m. Judith Stone. Grad., Wayne State U. Salesman, field mgr. Am. Greetings Corp., Cleve., 1961-66, advt. mgr., 1966-68, v.p., 1969-73, group v.p. mktg. and sales, 1973-78, formerly chief operating officer, from 1978, pres., 1978-92, also bd. dirs., chief exec. officer, 1987—, chmn., 1992—. Office: Am Greetings Corp 1 American Rd Cleveland OH 44144-2301

WEISS, MYRNA GRACE, management consultant; b. N.Y.C., June 22, 1939; d. Herman and Blanche (Stiftel) Ziegler; m. Arthur H. Weiss; children: Debra Anne Huddleston, Louise Esther Pennington. BA, Barnard Coll., 1958; MA, Hunter Coll., 1968; MPA, NYU, 1978; cert. in Mktg., U. Pa. Tchr., N.Y.C. and Vallejo, Calif., 1959-68; dir. admissions Columbia Prep. Sch., N.Y.C., 1969-72; dir. PREP counselling NYU, N.Y.C., 1973-74; dept. head Hewitt Sch., N.Y.C., 1974-79; mgr. Met. Ins. Co., N.Y.C., 1979-84; mktg. exec. Rothschild, Inc., N.Y.C., 1984-85; pres. First Mktg. Capital Group Ltd., N.Y.C., 1985—; mng. dir. Wrap Co. Internat. N.V., 1992-97; advisor Lared Group, N.Y.C., 1987-97; CEO, pres., bd. dirs. Ibnet, 1998—2002. Advisor Gov.'s Hwy. Safety Com., N.Y.C., 1985-88; pres. Fin. Women's Assn. N.Y., 1984-85. Bd. dirs. 92nd Y, N.Y.C., 1972-90, ARC, N.Y.C., 1989-96, 97—, asst. treas., 1993-96, 97—. Mem. Internat. Women's Forum (bd. dirs. 1990-92), Econ. Club N.Y., Women's Econ. Roundtable (bd. dirs. 1988-90). Office: 1st Mktg Capital Group Ltd 1056 5th Ave New York NY 10028-0112 E-mail: mzweiss@nyc.rr.com.

WEISS, NOEL S. epidemiologist; b. Chgo., Mar. 10, 1943; s. Sidney and Dorothy (Bloom) W.; m. Chu Chen, Oct. 12, 1980; children: Jessica, Jeremy. BA, Stanford U., 1965, MD, 1967; MPH, Harvard U., 1969, DrPH, 1971. Epidemiologist Nat. Ctr. for Health Stats., Rockville, Md., 1971-73; prof. U. Washington, Seattle, 1973—; epidemiologist Fred Hutchinson Cancer Rsch. Ctr., Seattle. Author: Clinical Epidemiology: The Study of the Outcome of Illness, 1996. Recipient Rsch. Career Devel. award Nat. Cancer Inst., 1975, Outstanding Investigator award Nat. Cancer Inst., 1985. Mem. Inst. of Medicine, Soc. for Epidemiol. Rsch., Am. Epidemiol. Soc. Democrat. Office: U Wash Sch Pub Health & Cmty Med Dept Epidemiology Box 357236 Seattle WA 98195-7236

WEISS, PAUL RICHARD, plastic surgeon; b. Bklyn., July 4, 1942; s. Marray and Belle (Edelman) W.; m. Linda Wayne, Aug. 23, 1964; children: Fredda Susan, Jonathan Michael. BS, Tufts U., 1964; MD, Tulane U., 1969. Diplomate Am. Bd. Plastic Surgery, 1977, Am. Bd. Surgery, 1975. Intern Bronx Muni Hosp Ctr., NY, 1969—70, resident surgery, 1970—72, Montefiore Hosp. Med. Ctr., NY, 1972—74, resident plastic surgery, 1974—76; attending plastic surgeon Montefiore Med. Ctr., NY, 1976—, Albert Einstein Coll. Med. Hosp., NY, 1976—, Beth Abraham Hosp., NY, 1976—, Jewish Home & Hosp., NY, 1976—, Beth Israel Med. Ctr., NY, 1986—; clin. prof. plastic surgery Albert Einstein Coll. Medicine, Bronx, NY, 1994—. Adv. bd. FOJP Medical Malpractice, N.Y.C., 1988—. Fellow ACS (Bronx chpt., pres. 1995-96); Am. Soc. Plastic Surgeons, Am. Assn. Plastic Surgeons, Am. Soc. Aesthetic Plastic Surgery, N.Y. Regional Soc. Plastic Surgeons (pres. 1992-93), Montefiore Med. Ctr. Staff Alumni Assn. (pres. 1994-97), Northeastern Soc. Plastic Surgeons, Harry Benjamin Soc. Jewish. Avocations: landscape gardening, vintage automobiles, stamp collecting/philately, collecting and restoring antique furniture. Home: 11 Ross Rd Scarsdale NY 10583-4425 Office: 1049 5th Ave Ste 2D New York NY 10028-0115 Office Phone: 212-861-8000. Office Fax: 212-861-8376. E-mail: weissclan@mindspring.com.

WEISS, PHILLIP MARION, philosopher, educator, head of religious order; b. Bronx, N.Y., June 21, 1951; s. Nathan and Diana Weiss; m. Naomi Davidson, June 27, 1982; children: Isaiah Kesem, Simon Elkanah. BA in Philosophy, Columbia Coll., 1973; MA in Philosophy, SUNY, 1979, PhD in Philosophy, 1985. Lectr. U. Mass., Lowell, Mass., 1979—81; instr. Bentley Coll., Waltham, Mass., 1981—82; lectr. Wheelock Coll., Boston, 1982—85, asst. prof., 1985—; darshan Cong. B'nai Brith, Somerville, Mass., 1985—. Author: Awesome! Sermons for Yamim Noraim, 1986-1990, 1991, More Awe! Sermons Through Bitter Times, 1991-1995, 1996, God-Awful! Sermons, 1996–2001, 2002. Mem.: AAUP, Am. Philos. Assn. Jewish. Home: 65 Pearson Rd Somerville MA 02144 Office: Wheelock College 200 The Riverway Boston MA 02215 Office Phone: 617-879-2172.

WEISS, PHILLIP W. social worker, writer; b. Bklyn., N.Y., July 12, 1949; s. Samuel and Lillie (Gottenberg) Weiss. BA, Bklyn. Coll., Bklyn., 1970; MSW, Hunter Coll., N.Y., 1978; MA, Bklyn. Coll., Bklyn., 1992. Cert. social worker N.Y., 1979, Fla., 1999. Case worker Dept Social Svcs., N.Y., 1970—80; social worker VA Med. Ctr., Syracuse, NY, 1980—81, Long Beach, Calif., 1981—84; sr. level social worker USAMEDDAC, Bremerhaven, Germany, 1984—87; social worker Bellevue Hosp., N.Y., 1988—2001, supr. social worker, 2001—. Dir. transfer ops. Assisted Outpatient Treatment Program, N.Y., 2004—. Author: History of Arcana Lodge No. 246, 2002, (poetry collections) Larry the Angry Turtle, 1999, (plays) Neville and Adolf in Munich-A One-Act Musical Event, 1998, Captain Dingleman's Great Adventure, 1998, Lesson for Life, Moishe and Mohammed, 2003. Founder Organ. for Fiscal Integrity, 1983. With USAR, 1969—75. Mem.: N.Y. C. Ctrl. Labor Coun. (del.), Acad. of Cert. Social Workers, Arcana Lodge No. 246. Avocations: photography, history, movies. Office: Box 82 149 East 23rd St New York NY 10010

WEISS, RANDALL A. television and radio producer, supermarket executive; b. Gary, Ind., Sept. 3, 1952; s. Arthur and Sylvia Weiss; m. Adrienne J. Weiss, Feb. 5, 1973; children: Benjamin, Caleb, Joshua, James, Abigail, Emma. AA, Coll. DuPage, 1977; BA, Dallas Bapt. U., 1993; MA in Religious Studies, Greenwich U., 1994; diploma of practical theology, Christ for the Nations Inst., 1993; PhD, Greenwich U., 1995; MS in Jewish Studies, Spertus Inst. Jewish Studies, 1996; DMin, Faraston Theol. Sem., 1996. Ordained to Ministry, Christ for Nations Alumni Ministers Fellowship. Gen. mgr. We Care Food Stores, Inc., Knox, Ind., 1975-84; pres., CEO We Care Food Stores, Inc. subs. Five Star Foods, Knox, Ind., 1984—; prodn. mgr. Excellence in Christian Broadcasting; comml. real estate developer Magnum Value Properties, LLC; TV sta. owner KUOT-Ca, Oklahoma City, Sta. KTAV-LP, Lancaster, Calif. Songwriter, pub. Lordship Music Pub., BMI; asst. prof. on adj. faculty Global U.; dean Jewish studies dept. Columbia Evang. Sem.; bd. regents Columbia Evangelical Sem. (formerly Faraston Theol. Sem.); Am. rep. Australian Christian Channel. Author: Jewish Sects of the New Testament Era, Does Jacob's Trouble Wear a Cross?: Christianity: A Jewish Religion, In Search of the Lost Jewish Atonement; writer, artist: (TV) Crosstalk, 1994—, Passover: The Jewish Connection to the Last Supper, Hanukkah: It's Not A Jewish Christmas, Days of Awe: The Jewish High Holidays, Father's Day, Beyond the Manger, Independence Day: Our Divine Right of Freedom; author (CD) Crosstalk Bible study software: Does Jacob's Trouble Wear a Cross?, Jewish Sects of the New Testament Era, The Passion Conspiracy: Did the Jews Kill Christ or Was Jesus the Victim of Identity Theft?; writer, prodr. albums Munchy Manna, Never Seen a U-Haul on a Hearse, Lead Me to the Rock: Worship in the Holy Land, Good News Jew's Blues; writer, prodr.: I Don't Need no Designer Jeans, Never Seen a U-Haul on a Hearse, Jesus is Lord, The Ballad of Jess B. Notwhite (NRB Program Showcase Music Video of Yr., 2004); radio host: Crosstalk; contbg. editor World Evangelism mag. Bd. dirs. World Missionary Evangelism. Nominated NRB Christian T.V. Program of Yr., 2000. Mem. Full Gospel Bus. Men's Fellowship Internat. (life, banquet spkr.), Soc. for Pentecostal Studies, Evang. Theol. Soc., Nat. Religious Broadcasters (exec. officer TV com.), Alliance for Cmty. Media, Fellowship of European Broadcasters. Avocations: fishing, travel, reading, music. Office: Five Star Foods 1209 S Heaton St Knox IN 46534-2398

WEISS, RENÉE KAROL, editor, musician; b. Allentown, Pa., Sept. 11, 1923; d. Abraham S. and Elizabeth (Levitt) Karol; m. Theodore Weiss. BA, Bard Coll., 1951; student, Conn. Sch. Dance; studied violin with, Sascha Jacobinoff, Boris Koutzen, Emile Hauser, Ivan Galamian. Mem. Miami U. Symphony Orch., 1941, N.C. State Symphony, 1942-45, Oxford U. Symphony, Opera Orchs., Eng., 1953-54, Woodstock String Quartet, 1956-60, Bard Coll. Chamber Ensemble, 1950-66, Hudson Valley Philharmonic, 1960-66, Hudson Valley String Quartet, 1965, Princeton Chamber Orch., 1980-93; orchestral, chamber work, 1966—. Participant Theodore and Renée Weiss poetry writing workshops Princeton U., 1985, Hofstra Coll., 1985, modern poetry workshop Cooper Union, 1988, Princeton Adult Edn.; tchr. modern dance to children Bard Coll., Kindergarten Tivoli, N.Y. Pub. Sch., 1955-58. Author: (children's books) To Win A Race, 1966, A Paper Zoo, 1968 (best books for children N.Y. Times, Book World 1968, N.J. Author's award 1968, 70, 88), The Bird From the Sea, 1970, Biography: David Schubert: Works and Days, 1984; co-editor, mgr. Quar. Rev. Lit., 1945—; author of poetry: (with Theodore Weiss) The Always Present Present, 2004; poetry readings (with Theodore Weiss) at various colls. in U.S. and abroad, including China. Mem. PEN (Nora Magid Lifetime Achievement award with Theodore Weiss 1997). Office: Q R L Poetry Series Princeton U 185 Nassau St Princeton NJ 08540-4914 Office Phone: 609-258-4703. E-mail: QRL@princeton.edu.

WEISS, RICHARD A. state official; b. Africa; m. Jan Weiss; 3 children. Grad. in liberal arts, Baylor U. Adminstr. Office of Budget, Dept. Fin. and Adminstrn., Little Rock, dep. dir., dir., 1994-97; CFO, State of Ark., Little Rock, 1994—; dir. Ark. Dept. Fin. and Adminstrn., Little Rock, 2001—. Office: Fin and Adminstrn Dept PO Box 3278 Little Rock AR 72203-3278 Office Phone: 501-682-2242. E-mail: richard.weiss@dfa.state.ar.us.

WEISS, ROBERT ALAN, surgeon; b. Chgo., Mar. 8, 1956; s. Harold Richard and Nancy (Rogoff) W.; m. Tina Haberer (dec.). MD, Chgo. Med. Sch., North Chicago, Ill., 1982. Diplomate Nat. Bd. Med. Examiners, Am. Bd. Ophthalmology, Am. Soc. Oculoplastic and Reconstructive Surgery. Flexible intern Cook County Hosp., Chgo., 1982-83; resident ophthalmology house staff Cornell U., N.Y. Hosp. & Meml. Sloan Kettering Cancer Ctr., N.Y.C., 1983-86, fellow ophthalmic oncology and orbital disease, 1986-87; fellow oculoplastic and reconstructive surgery Emory U. Med. Ctr., Atlanta, 1987-88; asst. clin. prof. ophthalmology Cornell U. Med. Ctr., N.Y.C., 1988-90; clin. assoc. prof. ophthalmology and neurosurgery U. Ill., Chgo. Med. Ctr., 1991—; attending oculoplastic surgeon Chgo. Eye Inst., 1991—. Asst. dir. Cornell Med. Ctr. Robert Ellsworth-Ophthalmic Oncology Ctr., N.Y.C., 1988-90; credentialled specialist U. Ill. Divsn. Svcs. Cripped Children, Chgo., 1991—; co-dir. U. Ill. Retinoblastoma Bd., Chgo., 1992—; vis. prof. Lions Club, Bolivian Am. Med. Soc., S.Am. Med. Soc., Israel, Bolivia, Columbia, Equador, Philippines, Egypt, 1991, 93, 94, 98, 99, 2000. Editor: Principles and Practice of Ophthalmic Plastic and Reconstructive Surgery, 1996. Recipient Golden Apple Tchg. award U. Ill., Chgo., 1994; named tchr. of yr. Chgo. Curriculum in Ophthalmology, 2000. Fellow Am. Soc. Oculoplastic and Reconstructive Surgery, Am. Acad. Ophthalmology, Alpha Omega Alpha. Avocations: gardening, photography, painting. Office: Chgo Eye Inst 3982 N Milwaukee Ave Chicago IL 60641-2703

WEISS, ROBERT EDWARD, urologist, educator; b. Manchester, Conn., Sept. 17, 1959; BS magna cum laude, Brown U., 1981; MD, NYU, 1985. Intern Mt. Sinai Med. Ctr., N.Y.C., 1985-86, resident surgery, 1986-87, resident urology, 1987-91; fellow urol. surgery Meml. Sloan-Kettering Cancer Ctr., N.Y.C., 1991-94; assoc. prof. urology R.W. Johnson Hosp. Med. Ctr., New Brunswick, NJ, 1994—. Fellow ACS; mem. Am. Urol. Assn., Soc. Urologic Oncology, Soc. Surg. Oncology, N.Y. Urol. Assn., N.J. Urol. Assn., Soc. of Basic Urologic Rsch. Office: RW Johnson Med Ctr 1 RW Johnson Pl CN-19 New Brunswick NJ 08903

WEISS, ROBERT FRANCIS, former academic administrator, religious organization administrator, consultant; b. St. Louis, Aug. 27, 1924; s. Frank L.G. and Helen M. (Beck) Weiss. BA, St. Louis U., 1951, Ph.L., MA, St. Louis U., 1953, S.T.L., 1961; PhD, U. Minn., 1964. Joined Soc. of Jesus, 1946; ordained priest Roman Catholic Ch., 1959; tchr. Rockhurst High Sch., Kansas City, Mo., 1953-56; adminstrv. asst. to pres. St. Louis U., 1961-62; asst. dean Rockhurst Coll., Kansas City, Mo., 1964-66, dean, v.p., asst. prof. edn., 1966-72, pres., 1977-88, St. Louis U. High Sch., 1973-77, interim pres., 1992; asst. for higher edn. and continuing formation Mo. Province S.J., St. Louis, 1989-92, 97—, treas., 1992—2003, asst. to treas., 2003—. Mem. Commn. on Govtl. rels. Am. Coun. Edn., 1985—87; bd. dirs. Kansas City Regional Coun. for Higher Edn., 1987—88, Boys Hope Girls Hope, 1977—. Contbr. chapters to books, articles to profl. jours. Trustee St. Louis U., 1973—87, 1991—2003, Loyola U., New Orleans, 1973—82, 1985—88, United Student Aid Funds, Inc., 1977—94, U. San Francisco, 1987—99, Marymount Coll., Salina, Kans., 1986—88, St. Louis U. H.S., 1989—99, 2003—, Fontbonne Coll., St. Louis, 1973—77, Sacred Heart Program, Radio and TV Apostolate, St. Louis, 1990—96, pres., 1992—96, bd. mem., 2000—; bd. dirs. Creighton U., Omaha, 1981—97, Our Little Haven, St. Louis, 1992—, St. Elizabeth Acad., St. Louis, 1997—2004, Loyola Acad., St. Louis, 2003—, Desmet Jesuit H.S., 2003—, St. John's Coll., Belize City, Belize, 2003—. 1st sgt. U.S. Army, 1943—46. Decorated Bronze Star. Mem.: Am. Assn. for Higher Edn., Vets. Assn. Rainbow divsn. (nat. chaplain 1976—84, 1988—90, pres.-elect 1990—91, pres. 1991—92, assoc. nat. chaplain 1992—, found. pres. 2003—), Alpha Phi Omega, Alpha Sigma Nu. Home and Office: 4511 W Pine Blvd Saint Louis MO 63108-2109 Office Phone: 314-361-7765. Business E-Mail: rweiss@jesuits-mis.org. *The only way for me to look at life is in the light of faith, which I consider one of God's greatest gifts. Life for me is an opportunity to serve God and as many of my neighbors as I can. I am basically an optimist. There is so much beauty around us, so many good people, so many marvels to behold— that I thank the Lord for giving me the ability to know and experience this life and to look forward to eternal life with God, the Source of all life. Any success I have had I attribute to taking advantage of the opportunities that God has put in my path.*

WEISS, ROBERT JEROME, psychiatrist, educator; b. West New York, N.J., Dec. 9, 1917; s. Harry and Dora (Samuels) W.; m. Minnie Thompson Moore, Apr. 21, 1945; children— Scott Tillman, James Woodrow, Elizabeth Thompson. Student, Johns Hopkins, 1937; AB, George Washington U., 1947; MD, Columbia, 1951; MA (hon.), Dartmouth, 1964. Intern Columbia div. Bellevue Hosp., 1951, asst. resident medicine, 1953; resident psychiatry N.Y. Psychiat. Inst., 1954-56; asst. attending Vanderbilt Clinic, 1957-58, Presbyn. Hosp., N.Y.C., 1958-59; chief psychiatry Mary Hitchcock Meml. Hosp., 1959-70; career tchr. trainee Nat. Inst. Mental Health, 1956-58; tchr., research Columbia Coll. Phys. and Surg., 1956-59; prof. psychiatry, founder, chmn. dept. Dartmouth Med. Sch., 1959-70; psychiatrist Beth Israel Hosp., 1988-90; attending physician Presbyn. Hosp., 1975-85, cons., 1985—. Vis. prof. cmty. medicine Harvard Med. Sch., 1970-75, assoc. dir. cmty. health, 1970-75, assoc. dean health care planning; prof. psychiatry and social medicine Columbia Coll. Physicians and Surgeons, 1975-86, also dir. Ctrs. for Cmty. Health, 1975-86; De Lamar prof. pub. health practice, dean Columbia U. Sch. Pub. Health, 1980-86, dean and De Lamar prof. of pub. health practice, prof. psychiatry, prof. social medicine, prof. emeritus, 1986—, dean emeritus, 1996—; vis. prof. cmty. medicine U. N.Mex. Med. Sch., 1986-89; adj. prof. arts and sci. U. Maine, Orono, 1997—; cons. Nat. Ctr. for Health Svcs. Rsch., 1975-86, NIMH, 1977-86; chmn. psychiatry tng. com. NIMH, 1967-68, mem. coord. panel, 1965-67, ad hoc com. interdisciplinary tng. program, 1966, mem. agenda com., 1966; cons. AT&T, 1990-92; chmn. bd. Academica, 1992, Employee Managed Care Corp., 1994-96; prin. Weiss, Baldacci & Fletcher. Co-editor: Columbia U. Coll. Physicians and Surgeons Complete Home Medical Guide, 1986, editor emeritus 2d and 3d edits., 1989; contbr. articles to profl. jours., chpts. to books. Founder dept. psychiatry Dartmouth Med. Sch., 1959. Served to maj. AUS, 1941-46. Recipient Bi-Centennial medal Columbia Coll. Phys. and Surg., 1967. Fellow Am. Psychiat. Assn. (life); mem. Am. Assn. Chmn. Depts. Psychiatry (pres. 1979-80). Achievements include first telemedicine 2-way transmission between medical centers; demonstrated social supports reduce disability due to mental illness; research in special health care delivery, health care preventive psychiatry. Home: 10 Cromwell Dr Orono ME 04473-3639

WEISS, ROBERT M. urologist, educator; b. N.Y.C., Jan. 13, 1936; s. David and Laura W.; m. Ilana Shemer, May 20, 1973; children: Erik Daniel, Dana Alexandra. BS magna cum laude, Franklin and Marshall Coll., Lancaster, Pa., 1957; MD, SUNY, Bklyn., 1960; MA (hon.), Yale U., 1976. Diplomate: Am. Bd. Urology, Nat. Bd. Med. Examiners. Intern Cornell Med. Divsn., Bellevue Hosp., N.Y.C., 1960-61; resident in gen. surgery Beth Israel Hosp., N.Y.C., 1961-62; resident in urology Squier Urol. Clinic, Presbyn. Hosp., N.Y.C., 1963-64, 65-67; vis. fellow Columbia U. Coll. Physicians and Surgeons, N.Y.C., 1964-65, adj. assoc. prof. pharmacology, 1975-77, adj. prof. pharmacology, 1977—; mem. faculty Yale U. Med. Sch., New Haven, 1967—, prof. urology, 1976-88, prof., chief sect. of urology, 1988—, interim chmn. dept. surgery, 1999-2001; attending urology Yale-New Haven Hosp., New Haven, 1967-88, head sect. of urology, 1988—, interim chief dept. surgery, 1999—2001. Cons. West Haven VA Hosp., Waterbury (Conn.) Hosp. Contbr. articles to med. publs. Trustee Am. Bd. Urology, 1998-2004. With USAR, 1962-63. Fellow ACS, Am. Acad. Pediat.; mem. AAAS, Am. Assn. Genito-Urinary Surgeons, Am. Surg. Assn., Am. Physiol. Soc., Soc. Gen. Physiologists, Assn. Univ. Urologists, Soc. Pediatric Urology, Am. Urol. Assn., Clin. Soc. Genito-Urinary Surgeons, Phi Beta Kappa, Sigma Xi. Office: Yale U Sch Medicine Dept Urology PO Box 208041 New Haven CT 06520-8041 Office Phone: 203-785-2815. E-mail: robert.weiss@yale.edu.

WEISS, ROBERT MICHAEL, dentist; b. Bklyn., June 5, 1940; s. Henry and Rena (Bluth) W.; m. Irene Marilyn Sternick, June 30, 1962; children: Lori Ann, Julie Lynn, Karen Michelle. Trustees scholar, L.I. U., 1958-61; DDS, NYU, 1965; postdoctoral cert., LD Pankey Inst. for Advanced Dental Edn., 1979. Pvt. practice dentistry, Avon, Conn., 1967—; pres. Avon Dental Group, P.C., 1972—; clin. prof. Coll. Dentistry U. Conn., 2000—. Nat. cons. Conn. Gen. Ins. Co. for ins. coverage for Gen. Electric Co., 1980—; advisor dental assisting program Briarwood Coll.; cons. CNA Ins. Co., 1988—; mem. mentorship program U. Conn. Coll. Dentistry; bd. dirs. Sentinel Bank; mentor program U. Conn. Coll. Dentistry. Chmn. Children's Dental Health Week, Hartford County, Conn., 1971; chmn. Jewish Adult Edn., West Hartford, Conn., 1986-87; trustee Temple Beth Israel, 1983—. Served to capt. USAF, 1965-67. Fellow Acad. Gen. Dentistry, Am. Acad. Gen. Dentistry, Pierre Fauchand Acad. (hon.); mem. ADA, Am. Soc. Preventive Dentistry (pres. Conn. chpt.), Acad. Osseointegration, Internat. Congress Oral Implantologists, Hartford Dental Soc. (exec. com. 1993—, chmn. centennial yr., chmn. 100th

anniversary 1996-97), Conn. State Dental Assn. (ho. of dels. 1992—), Chronic Fatigue Immune Dysfunction Syndrome (Conn. bd. dirs. 1992—), So. New Eng. Assn. Practice Adminstrn., Starnard Beach Assn. (pres. 1984-86), Avon Jr. C. of C. (pres. 1971-72), Masons, Alpha Omega, Sigma Alpha Mu. Home: 13 Alpine Meadow Ln Avon CT 06001-3935 Office: Avon Dental Group 20 W Avon Rd Ste 2 Avon CT 06001-3540

WEISS, ROBERT MICHAEL, dermatologist; b. N.Y.C. s. Leonard Seymour and Edith Rose (Levine) W.; 1 child, Michael Louis. Ba, U. Pa., 1970; MD, SUNY, Buffalo, 1974. Diplomate Am. Bd. Dermatology. Intern in internal medicine SUNY, Buffalo, 1974-75, resident in internal medicine, 1975-76, resident in dermatology, 1976-79; pvt. practice in dermatology Las Vegas, Nev., 1979—. Fellow Am. Acad. Derrmatology; mem. AMA. Office: Robert M Weiss MD 2300 S Rancho Dr Ste 106 Las Vegas NV 89102-4507

WEISS, ROBERT ORR, speech educator; b. Kalamazoo, Apr. 8, 1926; s. Nicholas John and Ruth (Orr) W.; m. Ann Lenore Lawson, Sept. 16, 1951; children: Elizabeth Ann, John Lawson, James Robert, Virginia Lenore. BA, Albion Coll., 1948; MA, Northwestern U., 1949, PhD, 1954. Instr. speech Wayne State U., Detroit, 1949-51; instr. pub. speaking Northwestern U., Evanston, Ill., 1954-55; mem. faculty DePauw U., Greencastle, Ind., 1955—2002, H.B. Gough prof. speech, 1965-97, head comm. arts and scis., 1963-78, 85-86, 93. Author: Public Argument, 1995; editor: Speaker and Gavel, 1968-75, Speaking Across the Curriculum, 1990—; co-editor: Current Criticism, 1971; contbr. articles to profl. jours. Served with AUS, 1945-46. Recipient Fred C. Tucker Disting. Career award, 1995, Lifetime award, Nat. Ednl. Debate Assn., 1997, Presdl. citation Nat. Communication Assn., 1999. Mem. AAUP (pres. DePauw U. chpt. 1961-62), Nat. Communication Assn. (legis. assembly 1966-68), Am. Forensic Assn. (sec.-treas. 1958-59), Ctrl. States Communication Assn., Phi Beta Kappa, Delta Sigma Rho-Tau Kappa Alpha (nat. v.p. 1981-83, pres. 1983-85), Sigma Nu. Home: 722 Highridge Ave Greencastle IN 46135-1402 Office Phone: 765-658-4490. Business E-Mail: robertweiss@depauw.edu.

WEISS, ROBERT STEPHEN, medical manufacturing company financial executive; b. Oct. 25, 1946; s. Stephen John and Anna Blanche (Lescinski) W.; m. Marilyn Annette Chesick, Oct. 29, 1970; children: Christopher Robert, Kim Marie, Douglas Paul. BS in Acctg. cum laude, U. Scranton, 1968. CPA, N.Y. Supr. KPMG (formerly Peat, Marwick, Mitchell & Co.), N.Y.C., 1971-76; asst. corp. contr. Cooper Labs., Inc., Parsippany, N.J., 1977-78; group contr. Coopen Vision, Inc., 1980; v.p., corp. contr. Cooper Labs., Palo Alto, Calif., 1981-83, The Cooper Cos., Inc. (formerly CooperVision, Inc.), Palo Alto, Calif., 1984-89; v.p., treas., CFO The Cooper Cos., Inc., Pleasanton, Calif., 1989—, sr. v.p., 1992-95, exec. v.p. fin., 1995—. Bd. dirs. The Cooper Cos., Inc., Pleasanton, Calif. With U.S. Army, 1969-70. Decorated Bronze Star with oak leaf cluster, Army Commendation medal. Mem. AICPA, N.Y. State Soc. CPAs. Home: 1775 Spumante Pl Pleasanton CA 94566-6478 Office: The Cooper Companies Inc Ste 590 6140 Stoneridge Mall Rd Pleasanton CA 94588 E-mail: rweiss@cooperco.com.

WEISS, RONALD L. lab administrator; MD, Creighton U.; MBA, U. Utah. Cert. in anatomic and clin. pathology, microbiology and hematology. Chief med. officer, dir. labs. ARUP Labs., Salt Lake City, 1993—2002, sr. v.p., dir., bus. devel., 2002—03, pres., COO, 2003—; prof., pathology U. Utah Sch. Medicine, Salt Lake City. Office: ARUP Labs 500 Chipeta Way Salt Lake City UT 84108*

WEISS, RONALD PHILLIP, lawyer; b. Springfield, Mass., Apr. 28, 1947; s. Kermit Paul and Fay Roslyn (Robinovitz) W.; m. Janet Faye Landon, June 15, 1969; children: Emily, Katherine. BA, Dartmouth Coll., 1968; JD, U. Pa., 1972. Bar: Mass. 1972, U.S. Dist. Ct. Mass. 1975, U.S. Tax Ct. 1979, U.S. Ct. Appeals (1st cir.) 2000. Assoc. Bulkley, Richardson and Gelinas, Springfield, Mass., 1972-78; ptnr. Bulkley, Richardson and Gelinas, LLP, Springfield, 1978—. Pres. Estate Planning Coun. Hampden County, 1979-81; trustee Mass. Continuing Legal Edn. Inc., 1978-81. Author: (with others) Drafting Wills and Trusts in Massachusetts, 1990, 92, 94; editor: (with others) Massachusetts Corporate Tax Manual, 1986; musician Pioneer Valley Symphony. Trustee Springfield Symphony Orch., 1986—, v.p., 1988—89, pres., 1989—91, chmn., 1991—94; bd. adv. U. Mass. Family Bus. Ctr., 1992—; adv. panel Hanson Initiative for Lang. and Literacy, MGH Inst. Health Professions, 2001—; counsel Cmty. Found. of Western Mass.; appropriations com. Town of Longmeadow, Mass., 1990—96, chmn., 1991—92, 1995—96; violinist Pioneer Valley Symphony; trustee Jewish Fedn. Greater Springfield, 1986—90. Mem. ABA, Mass. Bar Assn. (chmn. taxation sect. 1978-81, bd. dels. 1979-81), Mass. Bar Found., Hampden County Bar Assn., Rotary. Office: Bulkley Richardson and Gelinas LLP 1500 Main St Ste 2700 Springfield MA 01115-0001 Office Phone: 413-272-6259.

WEISS, SAMUEL ABRAHAM, psychologist, psychoanalyst; b. N.Y.C. m. Alice Langer, May 20, 1958; children: Benjamin Z., Naomi E., Susan J. BA, Yeshiva U., 1944; MA, NYU, 1948, PhD, 1957. Diplomate in clin. psychology, Am. Bd. Profl. Psychology. Intern Bellevue Psychiat. Hosp., N.Y.C., 1955-56; assoc. rsch. scientist NYU Med. Ctr., N.Y.C., 1956-59, rsch. scientist, 1959-68, assoc. dir. amputee psychology rsch., 1958-66; assoc. prof. psychology Yeshiva U., N.Y.C., 1961-71; psychol. cons. Stern Coll. for Women, Yeshiva U., N.Y.C., 1960-71; psychologist, psychotherapist, psychoanalyst in pvt. practice N.Y.C. Cons. N.Y. State Div. Vocat. Rehab., 1958-73. Contbr. articles to profl. jours. Fellow AAAS (Rosette award 1991), APA (editl. cons. rehab. psychology 1972-80), Am. Psychol. Soc. Jewish. Achievements include new research on medical factors in phantom limb pain and rehabilitation. Home: 80-40 Lefferts Blvd Kew Gardens NY 11415-1723 Office: 7 Park Ave Apt 66 New York NY 10016-4356

WEISS, SCOTT ALAN, commercial real estate consultant; s. Stuart Rollin Weiss and Sandy Carol Courson, Dan Christopher Courson; m. Corey Elizabeth Weilbacher, June 17, 2000. BA in Journalism, La. State U., 1997; postgrad. in law, South Tex. U., 2001—03. Cert. comml. investment mem. Editor: Constrn. Law Jour., 2002. Scholar, HBAI Constrn. Law Sect.; Blask Fed. fellow award for fed. interns. Mem.: Currents Internat. Trade Law (mng. editor 2002), South Tex. Law Rev. (asst. editor 2001—02). Avocations: running, reading. E-mail: scottalanweiss@yahoo.com.

WEISS, SHIRLEY F. urban and regional planner, economist, educator; b. NYC, Feb. 26, 1921; d. Max and Vera (Hendel) Friedlander; m. Charles M. Weiss, June 7, 1942. BA, Douglass Coll., Rutgers U., 1942; postgrad., Johns Hopkins U., 1949-50; M in Regional Planning, U. N.C., 1958; PhD, Duke U., 1973. Assoc. research dir. Ctr. for Urban and Regional Studies U. N.C., Chapel Hill, 1957-91, lectr. in planning, 1958-62, assoc. prof., 1962-73, prof., 1973-91, prof. emerita, 1991—; joint creator-sponsor Charles and Shirley Weiss Urban Livability Program, U. N.C., Chapel Hill, 1992—; research assoc. Inst. for Research in Social Sci., U. N.C., 1957-73; research prof. U. N.C., Chapel Hill, 1973-91, acting dir. women's studies program Coll. Arts and Scis., 1985, faculty marshal, 1988-91. Grad. edn. advancement bd. U. NC, Chapel Hill, 2001—, tech. com. Water Resources Rsch. Inst., 1976-79; adv. com. on housing for 1980 census Dept. Commerce, 1976-81; cons. Urban Inst., Washington, 1977-80; rev. panel Exptl. Housing Allowance Program, HUD, 1977-80; adv. bd. on built environ. Nat. Acad. Scis.-NRC, 1981-83, program coordinating com. fed. constrn. coun. of adv. bd. on built environ., 1982-83; mem. Planning Accreditation Bd., Site Visitation Pool, Am. Inst. Cert. Planners and Assn. Collegiate Schs. Planning, 1985—; discipline screening com. Fulbright Scholar awards in Architecture and City Planning, Coun. for Internat. Exchange of Scholars, 1985-88; N.Mex. adv. bd. Enterprise Found., Santa Fe, 1997-2002; governing bd. Acad. Freedom Fund, AAUP, 1997-2000. Author: The Central Business District in Transition: Methodological Approaches to CBD Analysis and Forecasting Future Space Requirements, 1957, New Town Development in the United States: Experiment in Private Entrepreneurship, 1973; co-author: A Probabilistic Model for Residential Growth, 1964, Residential Developer Decisions: A Focused View of the Urban Growth Process, 1966, New Communities U.S.A., 1976; co-author, co-editor: New Community Development: Planning Process, Implementation and Emerging Social Concerns, vols. 1, 2, 1971, City Centers in Transition, 1976, New Communities Research Series, 1976-77; mem. editl. bd.: Jour. Am. Inst. Planners, 1963-68, Rev. of Regional Studies, 1969-74, 82-92, Internat. Regional Sci. Rev., 1975-81. Trustee Friends of Libr., U. N.C., Chapel Hill, 1988-94, Santa Fe Chamber Music Festival, adv. coun., 1990-91, 97-98, trustee, 1991-97, 98—; bd. dirs. Triangle Opera, 1986-89, 91-2002, Chamber Orch. of the Triangle, 1997—. Recipient Cornelia Phillips Spencer Bell award U. NC, Chapel Hill, 1996, Disting. Alumni award Alumni Assn. Dept. City and Regional Planning, U. NC, Chapel Hill, 1996, Mary Turner Lane award Assn. Women Faculty, 1994, (with Charles M. Weiss) Gifford Phillips award Santa Fe Chamber Music Festival, 2000, Disting. Alumni and Alumnus award U. NC, Chapel Hill, 2003; Adelaide M. Zagoren fellow Douglass Coll., Rutgers U., 1994. Emeritus fellow Urban Land Inst. (sr. fellow, exec. group, cmty. devel. coun. 1978—); mem. Am. Inst. Planners (sec., treas. southeast chpt. 1957-59, v.p. 1960-61), Am. Inst. Cert. Planners, Am. Planning Assn., Am. Econ. Assn., So. Regional Sci. Assn. (pres. 1977-78), Regional Sci. Assn. (councillor 1971-74, v.p. 1976-77), Nat. Assn. Housing and Redevelopment Ofcls., Interamerican Planning Soc., Internat. Fedn. Housing and Planning, Town and Country Planning Assn., Internat. Urban Devel. Assn., Econ. History Assn., Am. Real Estate and Urban Econs. Assn. (regional membership chmn. 1976-82, 84-85, dir. 1977-80), AAUP (chpt. pres. 1976-77, pres. N.C. Conf. 1978-79, mem. nat. coun. 1983-86, William S. Tacey award Assembly of State Confs.), Douglass Soc., Order of Valkyries, Phi Beta Kappa. Home: 750 Weaver Dairy Rd # 2114 Chapel Hill NC 27514-1483

WEISS, STEPHEN J. medical educator, researcher, oncologist; MD. E. Giffert, Love Barnett Upjohn prof. internal medicine U. Mich., Ann Arbor, prof. cell and molecular biology divsn. Mem.: Nat Sci. Acad Inst. of Medicine. Office: Univ Mich Med Ctr Dept Medicine MSRB III 5220D 1150 LO Med Ctr Box 0640 Ann Arbor MI 48109-0640 E-mail: sjweiss@umich.edu.

WEISS, STEVEN GARY, physician; b. Gary, Ind., June 28, 1949; s. Morris Eugene and Edith (Wolinsky) W.; m. Irene Cohn, May 14, 1977; children: Leah Rose, Julia Inger, Mara Emily, Max martin. BA, Ind. U., 1971, MD, 1974. Intern Highland Gen. Hosp., Oakland, Calif., 1974; resident Mt. Zion Hosp. and Med. Ctr., San Francisco, 1977; fellow U. Chgo., 1982; Assoc. prof. U. South Fla. Coll. Medicine, Tampa, 1984—; physician pvt. practice, Clearwater, Fla., 1984—. Chief of med. staff Mease Hosps., Dunedin, Fla., 1991-92. Trustee Mease Health Care, 1991-94. Fellow Am. Acad. Allergy/Immunology, Am. Coll. Allergy.

WEISS, SUSAN, newspaper editor; Managing editor Life Section, USA Today, Arlington, Va. Office: USA Today 7950 Jones Branch Dr Mc Lean VA 22108-0001

WEISS, VOLKER, university administrator, educator; b. Rottenmann, Austria, Sept. 2, 1930; came to U.S., 1953, naturalized, 1960; s. Othmar and Pauline (Morianz) W.; m. Peg Hake, Sept. 14, 1957; children: Erick V., Christopher J. Dipl.Ing. Physics, Tech. U. Vienna; Dipl.Ing. Physics (Fulbright scholar), 1955; PhD in Solid State Sci. and Tech, Syracuse U., 1957. Rsch. metallurgist DEMKA Steel, Utrecht, The Netherlands, 1952; asst. prof. metallurgy Syracuse U., 1957-60, prof. materials sci., 1965—, prof. engrng. and physics, 1986—, chmn. solid state sci. and tech. program, 1960-77, assoc. dean sponsored programs, 1972-78; dir. Inst. Energy Rsch., 1976-80, v.p. rsch. and grad. affairs, 1978-86, dir. engrng physics program, 1988-99, chmn. dept. mechanical, aerospace, mfg. engrng., 1992-94, U.S.-Can. prof., 1993—99; prin. scientist JENTEK Sensors Inc., Waltham, Mass., 2003—. Cons. indsl. firms Dept. Transp.; bd. dirs., past pres. Syracuse Friends of Chamber Music, Tech. Club Syracuse; v.p., bd. dirs. Discovery Ctr. of Sci. and Tech., 1979—; NATO sr. scientist fellow, Germany and Gt. Britain, 1967-68. Editor: Sagamore Conf. Procs, 1962-86; contbr. articles on mech. behavior of materials and phys. metallurgy to profl. jours. Fellow Am. Soc. Metals; mem. ASME, ASTM, Am. Physical Soc., Sigma Xi. Home: 238 Scottholm Ter Syracuse NY 13224-1738 Office: Syracuse U 251 Link Hl Syracuse NY 13244-0001 Office Phone: 315-443-3918. E-mail: vweiss1@twcny.rr.com.

WEISS, WALTER STANLEY, lawyer; b. Newark, Mar. 12, 1929; s. Jack and Mollie (Orkin) W.; m. Misty M. Moore; children from previous marriage: Jack Stephen, Andrew Scott. AB, Rutgers U., 1949, JD, 1952. Bar: D.C. 1952, N.J. 1956, Calif. 1961. Trial atty. IRS, Phila., Los Angeles, 1957-62; asst. U.S. atty., chief tax div. Los Angeles, 1962-63; ptnr. firm Goodson & Hannam, Los Angeles, 1963-67; mng. ptnr. firm Long & Levit, Los Angeles, 1967-79; ptnr. firm Greenberg & Glusker, Los Angeles, 1979-81, Rosenfeld, Meyer and Susman, Beverly Hills, Calif., 1981-93; prin. Law Office of Walter S. Weiss, L.A., 1993—. Judge pro tem L.A. and Santa Monica (Calif.) Mcpl. Cts., 1994—. Contbr. articles to legal jours. Served to capt. JAGC USAF, 1953-56. Named Arbitrator Nat. Assn. Securities Dealers, 1974 Fellow Am. Coll. Trial Lawyers; mem. ABA, Los Angeles County Bar Assn., Beverly Hills Bar Assn. Home: 12349 Ridge Cir Los Angeles CA 90049-1183 Office: 12400 Wilshire Blvd Ste 1300 Los Angeles CA 90025-1055 Office Phone: 310-207-6679. E-mail: wsweiss@aol.com.

WEISS, ZEV, From sales dir. to exec. v.p., CEO Am. Greetings Corp., Cleve., 1994—2001, exec. v.p., 2001—, CEO, 2001—. Office: American Greeting Corp 1 American Rd Cleveland OH 44144-2398*

WEISSBACH, HERBERT, biochemist, researcher; b. N.Y.C., Mar. 16, 1932; s. Louis and Vivian (Ruhalter) W.; m. Renee Kohl, Dec. 27, 1953; children—Lawrence, Nancy, Marjorie, Robert BS, CUNY, 1953; MS, George Washington U., 1955, PhD, 1957. Chemist Nat. Heart Inst., Bethesda, Md., 1953-68; acting chief NIH, Bethesda, 1968-69; assoc. dir. Roche Inst. Molecular Biology, Nutley, NJ, 1969-83, dir., 1983-96; v.p. Hoffmann-La Roche, Nutley, 1983-96; disting. rsch. prof., dir. ctr. for molecular biology and biotech. Fla. Atlantic U., Boca Raton, 1997—. Adj. prof. George Washington U., 1964-69, Columbia U., 1969-85, U. Medicine and Dentistry N.J., Newark, 1981-93, Princeton U., 1984-85. Editor: Molecular Mechanisms of Protein Biosynthesis, 1977, Archives of Biochemistry and Biophysics; contbr. articles to profl. jours. Recipient Superior Svc. award HEW, 1968, Enzyme award Am. Chem. Soc., 1970, Disting. Alumni award George Washington U., 1994. Mem. Am. Chem. Soc., Am. Soc. Biol. Chemists, Am. Soc. Pharmacology and Exptl. Therapeutics, Am. Soc. Microbiology, Nat. Acad. Scis., AAAS Home: 8008 Desmond Dr Boynton Beach FL 33437-5011 Office: Fla Atlantic U 777 Glades Rd Boca Raton FL 33431-6424 E-mail: hweissba@fau.edu.

WEISSBARD, SAMUEL HELD, lawyer; b. N.Y.C., Mar. 3, 1947; children: Andrew Joshua, David S. BA, Case Western Res. U., 1967; JD with highest honors, George Washington U., 1970. Bar: D.C. 1970, U.S. Supreme Ct. 1974, Calif. 1998. Assoc. Fried, Frank, Harris, Shriver & Kampelman, 1970-73, Arent, Fox, Kintner, Plotkin & Kahn, 1973-78; prin. Weissbard & Fields, P.C., 1978-83; shareholder, v.p. Wilkes, Artis, Hedrick & Lane, Washington, 1983-86; ptnr. Foley & Lardner, Washington, 1986-97, L.A., 1997-98, co-chair creditors' rights workout and bankruptcy group Washington, 1992-95; sr. counsel Cox, Castle & Nicholson, L.L.P., Newport Beach, Calif., 1998—2001; exec. v.p., gen. counsel Makar Properties, LLC, Newport Beach, 2001—. Editor in chief George Washington U. Law Rev., 1969-70. Bd. dirs. Luther Rice Soc., George Washington U., 1985-87, Atlanta Coll. Art, 1993, Nat. Learning Ctr., 1993-96, Georgetown Arts Commn. and gen. counsel 1995-96; Chmn. steering com. of Lawyer's Alliance for Nat. Learning Ctr. and Capital Children's Mus., 1989-90; mem. steering com. DC/NLC Don't Drop Out Campaign, 1992,93, bd. dirs., 1994-96; devel. com. Shelter for the Homeless, 1998-99. Recipient John Bell Larner medal, 1970. Mem. ABA, D.C. Bar, Calif. Bar Assn., Orange County Bar Assn., Georgetown Bus. and Profl. Assn. (bd. dirs. 1993-96, sec., gen. counsel 1993-96), Orange County Bus. Assn. (legis. com. 1998-99), Order of Coif. Office: Makar Properties LLC 4100 MacArthur Blvd Ste 200 Newport Beach CA 92660-2063 E-mail: sweissbard@makarproperties.com.

WEISS-CORNWELL, AMY, interior designer; b. Mpls, Minn, Dec. 8, 1950; d. August Carl and Margaret Amelia (Wittman) Weiss; m. Dan Cornwell, July 31, 1995; 1 child, Emma Cornwell. AA in Home Econs., Cerritos Coll.; student, Long Beach State U., Santa Ana Jr. Coll. Asst. to interior designer Bobbi Hart at Pati Pfahler Designs, Canoga Pk., Calif., 1974-75; interior designer B.A. Interiors, Fullerton, Calif., 1976-78, Birns Co., Rancho Mirage, Calif., 1978-79; staff interior designer Assoc. Design Studios, Costa Mesa, Calif., 1979-81; interior designer Carole Eichen Interiors, Fullerton, 1981, Sears, Roebuck and Co., Alhambra, Calif., 1982-84; sr. corp. designer, mgr. design studio Barratt Am., Irvine, Calif., 1984-88; owner, retail designer Amy Weiss Designs, Coronado, Calif., 1988—; office, yacht designer, 1997—. Designer in residence San Diego Design Ctr., 1990—92; participant Pacific Design Ctr.; Designer on Call program, 1994—95. Prin. works include interior designs for residences, yachts; comml. interiors including lobbies and offices. Mem. Am. Soc. Interior Designers (Globe-Guilders steering com. 1989-92, chmn. Christmas party, co-chmn. Christmas on Prado 1989, 89, designer for ASID showcase house 1992, 93), Bldg. Industry Assn. (sales and mktg. coun. awards com. 1993, mem. sales and mktg. coun. 1986-88, mem. home builders coun. 1994, 2d place M.A.M.E. award 1987, 1st place M.A.M.E. award 1986, 2d place S.A.M. award 1987), Building Industry Assn. Remodeler's Coun., Nat. Kitchen and Bath Assn., Coronado C. of C., Coronado Cays Yacht Club. Office: Amy Weiss Designs 1123 Marysville Ave Chula Vista CA 91913 Office Phone: 619-216-6002. Fax: 619-482-0438. E-mail: amyweissdesigns@cox.net.

WEISSENBURGER, DAVID ALLEN, psychologist, educator, consultant; b. Anchorage, Sept. 7, 1953; s. Kenneth Albert and Dolores Jean Weissenburger; m. Barbara Jean Lyon, Nov. 28, 1998; m. Jan Elizabeth Stone, Aug. 20, 1977 (div. Sept. 15, 1997); children: Jon Eric, Caryn Ann. AA, Sauk Valley Coll., 1973; BS, Western Ill. U., 1975; MA, Stephen F. Austin State U., 1979; PhD, Tex. Woman's U., 1994. Lic. psychol. assoc. Tex. State Bd. Examiners of Psychologists, 1980; cert. comprehensive diagnosis and evaluation - psychology Tex., 1980, qualified mental retardation profl. Tex., 1980. Unit dir., psychologist Tex. Dept. MHMR, Denton, 1976—87; dir. mental retardation svcs. Denton County MHMR Ctr., 1987—88; v.p. assessment and rsch. Behavioral Scis. Rsch. Press, Dallas, 1991—94; assoc. prof. U. Ctrl. Tex., Killeen, 1994—99, Tarleton State U., Killeen, 1999—. Gen. ptnr. Weiss-Lyon Assocs., Copperas Cove, Tex., 1997—; faculty senate pres. Tarleton State U., Stephenville, Tex., 2002—03; v.p. West Tex. region Tex. Coun. Faculty Senates, Austin, 2002—04, pres.-elect, 2004—. Author: (psychological test) Weiss-Lyon Scale. Mem. Ctrl. Tex. Coop. Workshop Coun., Killeen, 2001—02; asst. scoutmaster Boy Scouts, Roanoke, Tex., 1989—95; dir., past pres., v.p. Families in Crisis, Inc., Killeen, 1997—; mem. Texan Club - Tarleton State U., Stephenville, 2000—; pres. Student Govt. Assn. - Sauk Valley Coll., Dixon, Ill., 1972—73. Fellow Sr. fellow, Tex. Higher Edn. Coordinating Bd., 2002; scholar, State of Ill., 1971—75. Mem.: APA, Nat. Assn. Sch. Psychologists, Southwestern Psychol. Assn., Am. Psychol. Soc., Phi Theta Kappa, Psi Chi.

WEISSKOPF, BERNARD, pediatrician, child behavior, development and genetics specialist, educator; b. Berlin, Dec. 11, 1929; came to U.S., 1939, naturalized, 1944; s. Benjamin and Bertha (Loew) W.; m. Penelope Allderdice, Dec. 26, 1965; children: Matthew David, Stephen Daniel. BA, Syracuse U., 1951; MD, U. Leiden, Netherlands, 1958. Diplomate Am. Bd. Med. Mgmt. Intern Meadowbrook Hosp., East Meadow, N.Y., 1958-59, resident, 1959-60, Johns Hopkins Hosp., Balt., 1962-64; fellow child psychiatry Johns Hopkins U. Sch. Medicine, Balt., 1962-64; asst. prof. pediatrics U. Ill. Coll. Medicine, Chgo., 1964-66; faculty U. Louisville, 1966—, prof. pediatrics, 1970-2000, emeritus prof. pediat., 2000—, assoc. in psychiatry, pathology and ob-gyn., 1966-2000, dir. Child Evaluation Ctr., 1966-2000. Chmn. Gov.'s Adv. Com. Early Childhood, Gov.'s Council on Early Childhood, Ky., 1986-88. Contbr. articles to profl. jours. Trustee Jewish Hosp., Louisville, 1974-77. Served to capt. USAF, 1960-62. Fellow Am. Acad. Pediatrics, Am. Assn. Mental Deficiency; mem. Am. Soc. Human Genetics, So. Soc. Pediatric Rsch., Am. Soc. Law and Medicine, Am. Coll. Physician Execs. Home: 6409 Deep Creek Dr Prospect KY 40059-9422 Office: Weisskopf Ctr Evaluation Children 571 S Floyd St Ste 100 Louisville KY 40202-3828 E-mail: bernweisul@aol.com.

WEISSLER, CHAVA (LENORE), religious studies educator; b. Washington, June 12, 1947; d. Alfred and Pearl Weissler. BA, Brandeis U., 1967; MS, Columbia U., 1970; PhD, U. Pa., 1982. Cataloger Libr. of Congress, Washington, 1970—75; reference librarian U. Pa. Librs., Phila., 1975—82; asst. prof. religion Princeton (NJ) U., 1982—88; vis. instr. women's studies Harvard Divinity Sch., Cambridge, Mass., 1986—87; assoc. prof. religion studies Lehigh U., Bethlehem, Pa., 1988—99, prof. religion studies, 1999—, Philip and Muriel Berman prof. Jewish civilization. Mem. acad. adv. bd. Ctr. for Jewish History, N.Y.C., 2001—. Author: Making Judaism Meaningful, 1989, Voices of the Matriarchs, 1998 (Best Book in Jewish History award, 99). Fellow, NEH, 1985, 2003, Annenberg Rsch. Inst., Phila., 1990—91; grantee, U. Penna, 2003; Koret Found. fellow, Ctr. Judaic Studies, U. Pa., 2003. Mem.: Am. Acad. Jewish Rsch., Am. Folklore Soc., Assn. Jewish Studies (bd. dirs. 1988—94, 2004—). Democrat. Jewish. Office: Lehigh U Dept Religion Studies 9 W Packer Ave Bethlehem PA 18015 E-mail: chava.weissler@lehigh.edu.

WEISSLER, FRAN, theatrical producer; Co-prodr. plays Othello, Medea, Zorba, My One and Only, Cabaret, Cat on a Hot Tin Roof, Gypsy, Fiddler on the Roof, Bye Bye Birdie, My Fair Lady, Falsettos, Chicago, Full Gallop; prodr. (play) Chicago. Co-recipient 3 Tony awards. Office: Shubert Theatre 225 W 44th St New York NY 10036-3991

WEISSMAN, IRVING L. medical researcher; b. Great Falls, Mont., Oct. 21, 1939; married, 1961; 4 children. BS, Mont. State Coll., 1960, DSc (hon.), 1992; MD, Stanford U., 1965. NIH fellow dept. radiology Stanford U., 1965—67, rsch. assoc., 1967—68, from asst. prof. to assoc. prof. dept. pathology, 1969—81, prof. pathology Sch. Medicine, 1981—, prof. devel. biology, 1989—; prof. pathology and devel. biology Stanford U. Sch. Medicine. James McGinnis Meml. lectr. Duke U., 1982; George Feigen Meml. lectr. Stanford U., 1987; Albert Coons Meml. lectr. Harvard U., 1987; Jame Stahlman lectr. Vanderbilt U., 1987; R. E. Smith lectr. U. Tex. Sys. Cancer Ctr., 1988; Chauncey D. Leake lectr. U. Calif., 1989; Harvey lectr. Rockefeller U., 1989; Rose Litman lectr., 90; sr. Dernham fellow Calif. divsn. Am. Cancer Soc., 1969—73; mem. immunobiology study sect. NIH, 1976—80; mem. sci. rev. bd. Howard Hughes Med. Inst., 1986—; mem. sci. adv. com. Irvington House Inst., 1987—; co-founder Systemix, Inc., 1988, bd. dirs., 1988—; Karel & Avice Beekhuis prof. cancer biology, 1987; 5th Ann. vis. prof. cancer biology U. Tex. Health Sci. Ctr., 1987; disting. lectr. Western Soc. Clin. Investment, 1990; chmn. U.S.-Japan Immunology Bd., 1992—94; chmn. sci. adv. com. McLaughlin Rsch. Inst., 1992—, trustee, 1992—; bd. govs. Project Inform, 1995—. Named Mont. Conservationist of Yr., Mont. Land Reliance, 1994, One of Top 100 Alumni, Mont. State U., 1993; recipient Pasarow award, 1989, Faculty Rsch. award, Nat. Am. Cancer Soc., 1974—78; scholar, Josiah Macy Found., 1974—75. Fellow: AAAS; mem.: NAS (steering com. NIOM AIDS panel 1985—86), Inst. Immunology, Am. Assn. Cancer Rsch., Am. Soc. Microbiology, Am. Assn. Pathologists, Am. Assn. Univ. Pathologists, Am. Assn. Immunologists (pres. 1994—95), Am. Acad. Arts and Scis. Office: Stanford U Sch Medicine B257 Beckman Ctr Stanford CA 94305-5323

WEISSMAN, JACK (GEORGE ANDERSON), retired editor; b. Chgo., June 6, 1921; s. Ben and Ida (Meyerson) W.; m. Bernice Platt, Nov. 13, 1949; children: Bruce, David, Ellen Weissman Montgomery. BA in Edn., Northwestern U., 1943, MS in Journalism, 1944. Asst. editor Bankers Monthly, Chgo., 1944-45; mng. editor Practical Knowledge, Chgo., 1945-50; with pub. relations dept. Roosevelt U., Chgo., 1947-50; editor Opportunity Mag., Chgo., 1950-89, ret. Author: Make Money at Home, 1963, How to Make Correct Decisions, 1964, Money Making Businesses You Can Start for $500 Or Less, 1965, Making It Big in Selling, 1987. Served to cpl. USAAF, 1945-46 Mem. Sigma Delta Chi, Phi Delta Kappa. Jewish.

WEISSMAN, MICHAEL LEWIS, lawyer; b. Chgo., Sept. 11, 1934; s. Maurice and Sue (Goldberg) Weissman; m. Joanne Sherwin, Dec. 19, 1961; children: Mark Douglas, Greg Steven, Scott Adam, Brett Anthony. Student White scholar, U. Chgo., 1951-52; BS in Econs, Northwestern U., 1954; MBA in Acctg., U. Pa., 1956; JD, Harvard U., 1958; postgrad. Fulbright scholar, U.

Sydney, Australia, 1958-59; postgrad., Hague Acad. Internat. Law, 1959. Bar: D.C. 1958, Ill. 1959. Asst. prof. bus. law Roosevelt U., Chgo., 1959-61; pvt. practice Chgo., 1959—; mem. firm Aaron, Aaron, Schimberg & Hess, 1969-78; sr. ptnr. Boorstein & Weissman, 1978-82, Weissman, Smolev & Solow, 1982-88, Foley & Lardner, 1988-92, McBride Baker & Coles, Chgo., 1992—2001; exec. v.p., gen. counsel Bridgeview Bank Group, Chgo.; of counsel Holland & Knight LLC, 2001—. Asst. prof. Roosevelt U., 1960—62; adj. prof. law John Marshall Law Sch., 2001—02; lectr. Lake Forest (Ill.) Coll., 1979—80; chmn. Banking Group, Union League Club Chgo.; panelist Robert Morris Assocs., Banking Law Inst., Midwest Fin. Conf., Greater O'Hare Assn., Miss. Law Inst., Bank Lending Inst., Chgo. Assn. Commerce and Industry, State of Art Seminars, Infocast Inc., SBA, Fed. Res. Bank Chgo., Lenders Ednl. Inst., Bank Adminstrn. Inst. Found., Lender's Forum, Clarion Legal. Author: (book) Lender Liability, 1988, Commercial Loan Documentation and Secured Lending, 1990, How to Avoid Career-Ending Mistakes in Commercial Lending, 1996, The Lender's Edge, 1997; mem. editl. bd.: Commercial Damages, 1985—; contbr. articles to profl. jours. Mem. adv. bd. Affective Disorders Clinic, U. Ill. Med. Sch., 1979—81; instr. mentor program Risk Mgmt. Assn. Scholar White, U. Chgo., 1951—52, Fulbright, U. Sydney, 1958—59. Mem.: ABA, Robert Morris Assn., Comml. Fin. Assn. Ednl. Found. (adv. bd.), Turnaround Mgmt. Assn. (steering com. Chgo. chpt.), Harvard Law Soc. Ill., Assn. Comml. Fin. Attys. (bd. dirs.), Ill. Inst. CLE (bd. dirs. 1989—2000, chmn. 2001—02), Ill. Bankers Assn. (mem. com. bank counsel 1987—88, vice chmn. 1988—89), Chgo. Bar Assn., Ill. Bar Assn., Beta Alpha Psi. Home: 2067 Old Briar Rd Highland Park IL 60035-4245 Office: Holland & Knight LLP 131 S Dearborn St 30th Fl Chicago IL 60603-5506 also: Bridgeview Bank Group 1970 N Halsted St Chicago IL 60614 Office Phone: 312-715-5767, 773-975-5308. Business E-Mail: michael.weissman@bridgeviewbank.com. E-mail: weissman@hklaw.com.

WEISSMAN, MORRIS, printing company executive; b. 1942; Grad., NYU, 1962. Assoc. Demou Morris Levin & Shein, 1965-70; mng. dir. Gen. Mortgage Investments, 1971; pres. Midwest, 1973-86; vice chmn. U.S. Banknote; chmn., chief exec. Am. Banknote Co. and Am. Banknote Holographics. Trustee UN Bus. Coun. Address: American Banknote Corp 410 Park Ave Fl 12 New York NY 10022-4407

WEISSMAN, MYRNA M. epidemiologist, researcher, medical educator; PhD in Chronic Disease Epidemiology, Yale U., 1974. Prof. psychiatry and epidemiology Yale U.; prof. epidemiology and psychiatry Coll. Physicians and Surgeons, Columbia U., N.Y.C. Chief divsn. clin. and genetic epidemiology N.Y. Psychiat. Inst., N.Y.C. Office: NY Psychiatric Inst Columbia U 1051 Riverside Dr Unit 24 New York NY 10032 Office Phone: 212-534-5880. Business E-Mail: mmw3@columbia.edu.

WEISSMAN, ROBERT EVAN, information services company executive; b. New Haven, May 22, 1940; s. Samuel and Lillian (Warren) W.; m. Janet Johl, Aug. 27, 1960; children: Gregory, Christopher, Michael BSBA, Babson Coll., Wellesley, Mass., 1964. Exec. v.p. Rediffusion Inc., Saugus, Mass., 1972-73; dir. corp. devel. Nat. CSS, Wilton, Conn., 1973-74, chmn., 1975-81; exec. v.p. Dun & Bradstreet Corp., N.Y.C., 1981-84, pres., 1985-93, chmn., CEO, 1994-96, Cognizant Corp., Westport, Conn., 1996-98; CEO IMS Health, Westport, Conn., 1998-99, chmn., 1999-2001. Bd. dirs. State St. Boston Corp., Gartner Group, Nielsen Media Rsch.; mem. adv. bd. N.Y. Stock Exch. Liste Co.; mem. bus. roundtable com. econ. devel. U.S.-Japan Bus. Coun. Vice chmn. bd. trustees Babson Coll. Mem. IEEE, Info. Tech. Assn. Am., Inst. Mgmt. Accts., Soc. Mfg. Engrs. (sr.). Office: IMS Health 1499 Post Rd Fairfield CT 06430-5940

WEISSMAN, WILLIAM R. lawyer; b. N.Y.C., Aug. 16, 1940; s. Emanuel and Gertrude (Halpern) W.; m. Barbra Phylis Gershman; 1 child, Adam; stepchildren: Eric, Jace, Julie Greenman. BA, Columbia U., 1962, JD cum laude, 1965. Bar: N.Y. 1965, D.C. 1969, U.S. Dist Ct. (no. dist.) Tex. 1965, U.S. Dist. Ct. (so. and ea. dists.) N.Y. 1977, U.S. Ct. Appeals (D.C. dir.) 1969, U.S. Ct. Appeals (9th cir.) 1973, U.S. Ct. Apeals (2d and 3d cirs.) 1974, U.S. Ct. Appeals (10th cir.) 1979, U.S. Ct. Appeals (11th cir.) 1981, U.S. Supreme Ct. 1968. News dir., progrm dir. WKCR-FM, N.Y.C., 1960-62; law clk. U.S. dist. judge, Dallas, 1965-66; trial atty. antitrust divsn. Dept. Justice, Washington, 1966-69; spl. asst. U.S. atty. Washington, 1967; assoc. Wald, Harkrader & Ross, Washington, 1969-72, ptnr., 1973-85, Piper & Marbury LLP, Washington, 1986-99, Piper Marbury Rudnick & Wolfe LLP, Washington, 2000—02, Piper, Rudnick, LLP, Washington, 2002—. Instr. D.C. Bar continuing legal edn. program Georgetown U. Law Sch., Washington, 1980-89; environ. regulation course Exec. Enterprises, Inc., 1985-95. Mem. editl. bd. Jour. Environ. Regulation, 1991-95, Environ. Regulation & Permitting, 1995-2000. Parliamentarian Arlington County Dem. Com., 1971-75; mem. Arlington (Va.) County Tenant-Landlord Commn., 1973-77, chmn. 1975-77. Mem. ABA, ASTM (E-50 com. environ. assessment 1996—, rec. sect., 1998-99, vice chmn. 2000—), Columbia U. Washington Club (bd. dirs. 1987-93). Jewish. Home: 3802 Lakeview Ter Falls Church VA 22041-1313 Office: Piper Rudnick LLP 1200 19th St NW Fl 7 Washington DC 20036-2430 Office Phone: 202-861-3878. Business E-Mail: william.weissman@piperrudnick.com.

WEISSMANN, GERALD, internist, medical educator, researcher, writer, editor; b. Vienna, Aug. 7, 1930; came to U.S., 1938; s. Adolf and Greta (Lustbader) W.; m. Ann Raphael, Apr. 1, 1953; children: Lisa, Andrew. BA with honors, Columbia U., N.Y.C., 1950; MD, NYU, 1954. Diplomate Am. Bd. Internal Medicine. Intern Mt. Sinai Hosp., N.Y.C., 1954-55, asst. resident medicine, 1957-58; chief resident medicine Bellevue Hosp., N.Y.C., 1959-60; fellow depts. biochemistry and medicine Arthritis and Rheumatism Fedn., NYU, 1958-59; rsch. asst. dept. medicine NYU Sch. Medicine, 1959-60, instr. medicine, 1959-62, asst. prof., 1962-65, assoc. prof., 1966-70, prof., 1970—, dir. div. cell biology, 1969-73, dir. div. rheumatology of dept. medicine, 1973-2000; dir. Ctr. Biotech. Studies, 2000—. USPHS spl. rsch. fellow dept. biophysics Strangeways Lab., Cambridge, Eng., 1960-61; sr. investigator Arthritis and Rheumatism Found., N.Y.C., 1961-65; career rsch. scientist Health Rsch. Coun. N.Y.C., 1966-71; instr. physiology Marine Biol. Lab., Woods Hole, Mass., 1973-77, investigator, 1970—, trustee, 1993—; vis. investigator ARC Inst. Animal Physiology, Babraham, Eng., 1964-69, Centre de Physiologie et d'Immunologie Cellulaires, Hosp. St. Antoine, Paris, 1973-74, William Harvey Rsch. Inst., London, 1987; mem. postdoctoral fellowships rev. com. Pfizer Internat., 1983-89; mem. scholarship selection com. Pew Scholars in Biomed. Scis., New Haven, 1984-94; lectr. Johns Hopkins U., 1976, 89, Med. Coll. Ga., Augusta, 1980, Med. Coll. Pa., 1988, William Harvey Rsch. Inst., London, 1987, others; nat. adv. bd. Ellison Med. Found, 1997—. Author: The Woods Hole Cantata, 1995, They All Laughed at Christopher Columbus, 1987, The Doctor With Two Heads, 1990, The Doctor Dilemma, 1992, Democracy and DNA, 1996, Darwin's Audubon, 1998, The Year of the Genome, 2001; editor-in-chief Inflammation, 1975-2001, Advances in Inflammation Rsch., 1979—, MD Mag., 1989-94; mem. editl. bd. Clin. Immunology and Immunopathology, 1972-88, Advances in Prostaglandin, Thromboxane and Leukotriene Rsch., 1975—, Am. Jour. Medicine, 1976-88, Tissue Reactions, 1979, Immunopharmacology, 1982; contbr. over 300 articles to profl. jours. Capt. M.C., U.S. Army, 1955-57. Recipient Allesandro Robecchi prize Internat. League Against Rheumatism, 1972, Marine Biol. Lab. award, 1974, 1979, U. Bologna medal, Italy, 1978, Lila Gruber Cancer Rsch. award Am. Acad. Dermatology, 1979, Solomon A. Berson Med. Alumni Achievement award NYU, 1980, Merit award NIH, 1987, Centennial award Marine Biol. Lab., 1988, C.M. Plotz award N.Y. Arthritis Found., 1993, Paul Klemperer award N.Y. Acad. Medicine, 1997, others; Guggenheim Found. fellow, N.Y.C., 1973-74. Fellow AAAS; mem. Am. Coll. Rheumatology (pres. 1982-83, Disting. Investigator award 1992, master 1996), Am. Fedn. Clin. Rsch., Soc. Exptl. Biology and Medicine, Am. Soc. Pharmacology and Exptl. Therapeutics, Am. Soc. Exptl. Pathology, Assn. Am. Immunologists, Am. Soc. Cell Biology, Am. Soc. Clin. Investigation, Am. Soc. Biol. Chemistry and Molecular Biology, Assn. Am. Physicians, Harvey Soc. of N.Y. (pres. 1981-82), Interurban Clin. Club, PEN Am. Ctr., Phi Beta Kappa, Alpha Omega Alpha, fgn. mem. Accademia Nazionale dei Lincei (Rome) Avocation: tennis. Office: NYU Med Ctr Dept Medicine BCD686 550 1st Ave New York NY 10016-6402

WEISSMANN, HEIDI SEITELBLUM, radiologist, educator; b. N.Y.C., Feb. 4, 1951; d. Louis and June (Joseph) Seitel Bloom; m. Murray H. Weissmann, June 16, 1973; 1 dau., Lauren Erica BS in Chemistry magna cum laude, Bklyn. Coll., CUNY, 1970; MD, Mt. Sinai Sch. Medicine, N.Y.C., 1974. Diplomate Nat. Bd. Med. Examiners. Intern Montefiore Med. Ctr. Bronx, N.Y., 1974-75, resident in diagnostic radiology, 1975-78; fellow in computerized transaxial tomography and ultrasonography N.Y. Hosp.-Cornell U. Med. Ctr., N.Y.C., N.Y., 1978-79; instr. in radiology and nuclear medicine Albert Einstein Coll. Medicine, Montefiore Med. Ctr., Bronx, N.Y., 1979-80; asst. prof. radiology and nuclear medicine Albert Einstein Coll. Medicine and Montefiore Med. Ctr., Bronx, N.Y., 1980-84, assoc. prof. nuclear medicine, 1984-94, assoc. prof. radiology, 1986-94; dir. Ctr. for Women, Medicine and Healthcare, Washington, 1994—. Adj. attending physician Montefiore Med. Ctr., 1979-87; chmn. Nuclear Medicine Grand Rounds: Greater N.Y., 1980-87; physician coord. Nuclear Medicine Technologist In-Service Tng. Program, 1982-86; cons. NIH, 1984-86, NIH Diagnostic Radiology, 1985-86 Assoc. editor Nuclear Medicine Ann., 5 vols., 1979-84, editor, 5 vols., 1985—; contbr. chpts. to books, articles to jours.; editor Jour. Sci. and Engring. Ethics, 1994—; reviewer Jour. of Radiology, 1981—, mem. editl. adv. bd., 1985-86, assoc. editor, 1986—; reviewer. Jour. of Nuclear Medicine, 1981—, Am. Jour. of Roentgenology, 1986—, Gastroenterology, 1986—, Western Jour. of Medicine, 1985—; contbr. audiovisual programs and films Recipient Saul Horowitz, Jr., Meml. award (Disting. Alumnus award), Mt. Sinai Sch. Medicine, 1980, Pres.' award, Am. Roentgen Ray Soc., 1979, Berta Rubinstein, M.D., Resident award, 1978, Cavallo award for moral courage, 1993, others. Mem. Radiol. Soc. N.Am. (mem. subcom. for nuclear medicine of program com., 1981, 82, 83, chmn. 1984, 85, 86), Soc. Nuclear Medicine (trustee 1983-87, 88—, sec.-treas. Correlative Imaging Council 1979 82, exec. bd. 1982-84, pres. 1984-86, exec. bd. 1986—, mem. acad. council 1980—, task force on interrelationship between nuclear medicine and nuclear magnetic resonance 1983-85, gov. Greater N.Y. chpt. 1983-85, treas., 1985-86, 86-87, 2d ann. Tetalman award of Edn. and Research Found. 1982, mem., vice chmn. coms. and subcoms.), Soc. Gastrointestinal Radiologists, Am. Inst. Ultrasound in Medicine, N.Y. Acad. Scis., Assoc. Alumni Mt. Sinai Med. Ctr., Nuclear Radiology Club (chmn. 1983—). Phi Beta Kappa. Home and Office: 14 Powder Hill Rd Saddle River NJ 07458-3215

WEISSTEIN, ULRICH WERNER, English literature educator; b. Breslau, Germany, Nov. 14, 1925; came to U.S., 1950, naturalized, 1959; s. Rudolf and Berta (Wende) W.; m. Elisabeth Rieckh; children: Cristina, Cecily, Eric Wolfgang, Anton Edward. Student, Goethe-Universität, Frankfurt, 1947-50, 51-52, U. Iowa, 1950-51; MA, Ind. U., 1953, PhD, 1954; Doctorate (hon.), U. Lund, Sweden, 1993. Instr. Lehigh U., Bethlehem, Pa., 1954—58, asst. prof., 1958; asst. prof. English and comparative lit. Ind. U., Bloomington, 1959-62, assoc. prof., 1962-66, prof. German and comparative lit., 1966-90, chmn. comparative lit. program, 1985-89; dir. Ind. U.-Purdue U. Studienprogramm U. Hamburg, 1981-82. Vis. prof. U. Wis., summer 1966, Middlebury Sch. German, summer 1970, U. Hamburg (Germany), spring 1971, spring 1982, U. Vienna, 1976, Stanford U., 1979, Graz U., Austria, 1985, 95, 96, U. Bologna, Italy, 1991, U. Antwerp, Belgium, 1992, U. Salzburg, 1997; external examiner comparative lit. U. Hong Kong, 1974-76. Author: Heinrich Mann, 1962, The Essence of Opera, 1964, Max Frisch, 1967, Einführung in die Vergleichende Literaturwissenschaft, 1968, English version: Comparative Literature and Literary Theory, 1973; Spanish version: Introduccion a la Literatura Comparada, 1975, Chinese version, 1987, Japanese version, 1976, Korean version, 1979; Forschungsbericht zur Vergleichenden Literaturwissenschaft, 1968-1977, 1981, Links und links gesellt sich nicht: Gesammelte Aufsätze zum Werk Heinrich Manns und Bertolt Brechts, 1985; editor: Literatur und Bildende Kunst: Ein Handbuch zur Theorie und Praxis eines komparatistischen Grenzgebiets, 1992; editor German sect. Twayne World Authors series, 1964-86, Yearbook of Comparative and General Literature, 1960-90, Oper Im Brennpunkt, 2001-, Expressionism as an International Literary Phenomenon, 1973; co-editor: Literature and the Other Arts, 1981, Texte und Kontexte: Festschrift für Norbert Fuerst, 1973, Intertextuality: German Literature and Visual Art from the Renaissance to the Twentieth Century, 1993, Musico-Poetics Today: Calvin S. Brown in Memoriam, 2000; translator: The Grotesque in Art and Literature (W. Kayser), 1963. Recipient Grosses goldenes Ehrenzeichen des Landes Steiermark, 1996; Guggenheim fellow, 1974-75; MLA grantee, 1958-59. Mem.: Gesellschaft der Freunde der Oper in Graz (pres. 1991—97, hon. pres. 2003—), Coun. Internat. Exchange Scholars (area com. for West Germany and Austria 1983—85), Internat. Comparative Lit. Assn. (exec. coun. 1979—85, sec. 1985—89). Home: Baiernstrasse 54/IV 8020 Graz Austria

WEISWASSER, STEPHEN, electronics manufacturing executive; b. Detroit, Nov. 21, 1940; BA, Wayne State U.; postgrad., Johns Hopkins U.; JD magna cum laude, Harvard U. Ptnr. Wilmer, Cutler & Pickering; sr. v.p. Capital Cities/ABC, Inc.; pres., CEO Americast, 1995-98; ptnr. Covington & Burling, Washington, 1998-99; exec. v.p., gen. counsel Gemstar Internat. Group Ltd., Pasadena, Calif., 1999—, also bd. dirs. Woodrow Wilson Nat. fellow Johns Hopkins U. Office Fax: 626-792-0257.

WEISZ, PAUL B(URG), physicist, researcher, chemical engineer; b. Pilsen, Czechoslovakia, July 2, 1919;, naturalized, 1946; s. Alexander and Amalia (Sulc) Weisz; m. Rhoda A.M. Burg, Sept. 4, 1943; children: Ingrid B., P. Randall. Student, Tech. U. Berlin, 0193—1939; BS, Auburn U., 1940; ScD, Swiss Fed. Inst. Tech., Zurich, 1965, ScD (hon.), 1980. Research physicist Bartol Research Found., Swarthmore, Pa., 1940—46, Mobil Oil Corp. (formerly Socony Mobil Oil Corp.), 1958—61, sr. scientist, 1961—69, mgr. process research sect., 1967—69; mgr. Central Research Lab. Mobil Research & Devel. Corp., Princeton, NJ, 1969—82, sr. scientist and sci. adv., 1982—84; Disting. prof. chem. and bio-engring. sci. U. Pa., 1984—90, prof. emeritus, 1990—. Adj. prof. Pa. State U., 1992—; cons. rsch. and tech. strategy; vis. prof. Princeton U., 1974—76, mem. adv. coun. dept. chem. engring., 1973—78; mem. adv. and resource coun. Princeton U. Sch. Engring., 1974—78; chmn. ctr. policy bd. Ctr. for Catalytic Sci. and Tech., U. Del., 1977—81; mem. energy rsch. adv. bd. U.S. Dept. Energy, 1985—90. Editor: Advances in Catalysis, 1956—93; editl. bd. Jour. Catalysis, 1962—83, Chem. Engring. Comms., 1972—78, Heterogeneous Chem. Revs., 1993—96, monthly columnist Sci. of the Possible, Chemtech, 1980—83, contbr. 180 articles to sci. jours., holder 80 patents. Recipient ann. award, Catalysis Club Phila., 1973, Lavoisier medal, Chem. Soc. France, 1983, Perkin medal, Soc. Chem. Industries, U.S. Nat. medal of Tech., 1992. Fellow: NAE, AIChE (R.H. Wilhelm award 1978), Am. Inst. Chemists (Chem. Pioneer award 1974), Am. Phys. Soc.; mem.: N.Y. Acad. Scis., Am. Chem. Soc. (sci. award South Jersey sect. 1963, E.V. Murphree award 1972, 1977, Chemistry of Contemporary Tech. Problems award 1986, Carothers award 1987), Nassau Club (Princeton). Mem. Soc. Of Friends. Fax: 814-237-3202. E-mail: pweisz@aol.com, pbweisz@mailaps.org.

WEISZ, RACHEL, actress; b. London, Mar. 7, 1971; BA, U. Cambridge, England. Motion picture and T.V. actress. Films include Chain Reaction, 1996, Going All the Way, 1997, Amy Foster, 1997, Land Girls, 1998, I Want You, 1998, The Mummy, 1999, Sunshine, 1999, Beautiful Creatures, 2000, Enemy at the Gates, 2001, The Mummy Returns, 2001, About a Boy, 2002, The Shape of Things, 2003 (also prodr.), Confidence, 2003, Runaway Jury, 2003, She Died on Canvas, 2003, others; (TV film) My Summer with Des, 1998. Office: c/o CAA 9830 Wilshire Blvd Beverly Hills CA 90212

WEITBERG, ALAN BARRY, physician, researcher; b. Phila., Mar. 2, 1950; s. Sidney and Esther Weitberg; m. Katherine Raphaela Bick, Sept. 6, 1975 (div. Apr. 1993); children: Allison Ross, Seth Raphael. AB, Cornell U., Ithaca, NY, 1972; MD, Univ. Medicine and Dentistry NJ, Newark, 1976; MEd (hon.), Brown U., Providence, 1992. Lic. MD RI, 1978, Mass., 1982, cert. Nat. Bd. Med. Examiners, 1977, Internal Medicine, 1980, Med. Oncology, 1987, Hematology, 1988. Resident and chief resident in medicine Roger Williams Med. Ctr. and Brown Med. Sch., Providence, 1976—80; hematology fellow Mass. Gen. Hosp. and Harvard U., Boston, 1980—82; instr. med. sch. Harvard Med. Sch., Boston, 1982—85; chief divsn. hematology, oncology Brown Med. Sch. and Roger Williams Med. Ctr., Providence, 1985—91; prof. and chmn., dept. medicine Roger Williams Med. Ctr. and Boston U. Sch. Medicine, Providence, 1991—. Dir. divsn. med. oncology Brown U., 1988—; prof. medicine Boston U. Sch. Medicine, 1988—. Author: Cancer of the Lung, 2002; contbr. more than 75 sci. papers to profl. jours., chapters to books, articles to over 60 profl. jours. Critical care, med. appraisal, med. audit, med. rec. Roger Williams Hosp., 1979—80, infection control, nutritional support, patient care/greivence, 1979—80, intern selection, clin. competence com., 1985—, chmn. cancer com., 1986—99, chmn. credentials com., 1987—91, transfusion com., 1988—92, physician's adv. com., 1989—, exec. com., 1991—, strategic planning com., 1992—, joint conf. com., 1992—, quality improvement steering coun., 1992—, oncology task force, 1995—, pres., med. assoc., 1996—, bd. trustees, 2002—, Univ. Med. Group, 1999—, exec. com. bd., 2001—; chmn. admissions com. for an integrated med. residency program Brown U., 1990—; com. sectional chiefs Boston U., 1997—. Nominee Ernesta Nuti Internat. prize for Cancer Rsch., Rome, 1992; named to Mu Eplison Delta Hon. Soc., Cornell U., 1971, Watts Scholarship Soc., Cornell Univ., 1971; recipient Dean Charles L. Brown award, Univ. Medicine and Dentistry NJ, 1976, Tchr. of Yr. award, Brown U. Sch. Medicine, 1992, Eminent Scientist award, Internat. Rsch. Promotion Coun.; Arts and Sci. Dean's scholar, Cornell U., 1969, over 30 rsch. grants from various colls. and univs. Fellow: ACP (exec. coun. RI chpt. 1992—); mem.: AAAS, Cancer Trials Support Unit, Assn. Acad. Med. Ctr., Clin. Oncology Group, Am. Soc. Hematology, Assn. Am. Med. Coll., Leukemia Soc. Am. (bd. dirs. 1989—), Am. Bd. Internal Medicine (recertification com. 1993—), Am. Soc. Cancer Rsch. (chmn. carcinogeneses sect. 1987—, state legis. com. 1992—), Am. Soc. Clin. Oncology (chmn. lung cancer sect. 1987—), Am. Cancer Soc. (chmn. nominating com. 1992, instl. rsch. grant rev. study sect. 1992—), Am. Fed. for Clin. Rsch. (chmn. hematology sect. 1993—), Internat. Soc. Free Radical Rsch., Sigma Xi Sci. Rsch. Soc. Avocations: painting, opera, running, reading. Office: Roger Williams Med Ctr Dept Medicine 825 Chalkstone Ave Providence RI 02908 Office Phone: 401-456-2070.

WEITZ, BRUCE (PETER WEITZ), actor; b. Norwalk, Conn., May 27, 1943; s. Alvin Weitz and Sybil Weitz Rubel; m. Cecilia Hart, 1973 (div. 1980) BA, MFA, Carnegie Inst. Tech. Performer Long Wharf Repertory Theater, Norwalk, 1967, Guthrie Theater, Mpls., 1967-69, Arena Stage, Washington, 1970-76, Shakespeare-in-the Park prodns., N.Y.C., 1976-80, others; star: (TV series) Hill Street Blues, 1981-87 (Emmy nominations 1981-83, Emmy award for best supporting actor 1984); actor: (TV films) including Every Stray Dog and Kid, 1981, Death of a Centerfold: The Dorothy Stratton Story, 1981, A Reason to Live, 1985, If It's Tuesday, This Must Be Belgium, 1988, The Baby "M" Story, 1988, A Deadly Silence, 1989, Rainbow Drive, 1990, Leona Helmsley: The Queen of Mean, 1990, Babe Ruth, 1991, The O.J. Simpson Story, 1995, Mixed Blessings, 1995, Her Hidden Truth, 1995, Sudden Terror: The Hijacking of School Bus #17, 1996, The Legend of the Ruby Silver, 1996, Justice for Annie: A Moment of Truth Movie, 1996, Breaking the Surface: The Greg Louganis Story, 1996, Joe and Max, 2002, (films) No Place to Hide, 1992, Molly & Gina, 1993, The Liars' Club, 1993, Windrunner, 1995, Prehysteria 3, 1995, Cops n Roberts, 1995, Coyote Summer, 1996, Velocity Trap, 1997, Deep Impact, 1998, The Landlady, 1998, Shattered Illusions, 1998, Memorial Day, 1998, Fool's Gold, 1998, Gut Feeling, 1999, Quality Time, 2000, Mach 2, 2000, The Entrepreneurs, 2000, Focus, 2001, Facing the Enemy, 2001, No Place Like Home, 2001, Half Past Dead, 2002, (Broadway plays) including Death of a Salesman, Norman, Is That You?, The Basic Training of Pavlo Hummel, 1978-80; TV series appearances include The White Shadow, Paris, Midnight Caller, Anything But Love, 1989, Byrds of Paradise, 1994. Office: care William Morris Agy 151 S El Camino Dr Beverly Hills CA 90212-2704

WEITZ, HARVEY, lawyer, educator; b. Bklyn., Aug. 16, 1933; AB, Bklyn. Coll.; JD, Bklyn. Law Sch. Bar: N.Y. 1954, U.S. Dist. Ct. (ea. and so. dists.) N.Y. 1956. Diplomate Am. Bd. Profl. Liability Attys. Ptnr. Schneider, Kleinick, Weitz, Damashek & Shoot, N.Y.C., 1966—; dean N.Y. State Trial Lawyers Inst.; adj. prof. Bklyn. Law Sch.; spl. master Supreme Ct., 1980-84. Author: A Compendium of the Art of Summation, Weitz on Automobile Litigation: The No-Fault Handbook, Vols. I & II; editor in chief Trial Lawyers Quar., 1972-80. Served with U.S. Army. Fellow Internat. Acad. Trial Lawyers, Internat. Soc. Barristers, Roscoe Pound Found.; mem. N.Y. State Trial Lawyers Assn. (bd. dirs.), Trial Lawyers for Pub. Justice (bd. dirs.), Am. Bd. Trial Advocates (nat. bd. mem.), ATLA (bd. govs. 1981-93, nat. sec. 1986-87), N.Y. State Trial Lawyers Assn. (pres. 1980-82), Bklyn. Law Sch. Alumni Assn. (bd. dirs.), Inner Circle of Advocates, Nat. Forensic Ctr. (mem. adv. panel), N.Y. State Bar (lectr.), Nat. Practice Inst. (lectr.), Assn. of the Bar, N.Y. County Lawyers Assn. (lectr.), N.Y.C. Trial Lawyers Assn. Office: Schneider Kleinick Weitz & Damashek 233 Broadway Fl 5 New York NY 10279-0050 E-mail: hweitz@lawyer1.com.

WEITZ, JEANNE STEWART, artist, educator; b. Warren, Ohio, Apr. 30, 1920; d. William McKinley and Ruth (Stewart) Kohlmorgan; m. Loyal Wilbur Weitz, Aug. 1, 1940 (dec. 1986); children: Gail, Judith, John, Marc. BS in Art and English, Youngstown U., 1944; MEd in Art, U. Tex., El Paso, 1964; postgrad., Tex. Tech U., 1976. Indsl. engr. Republic Iron & Steel, Youngstown, Ohio, 1942-43; art tchr. pub. schs., Bessemer, Pa., 1943-44, El Paso (Tex.) Independent Sch. Dist., 1944-50, 54-78, art. cons., 1978-87; art tchr. Hermosa Beach (Calif.) Independent Sch. Dist., 1950-53, El Paso Mus. Art, 1960-65; lectr. in art U. Tex., El Paso, 1963-66; instr. El Paso Community Coll., 1970-78; free-lance artist, lectr. El Paso, 1987-91; supr. student tchr. U. Tex., El Paso, 1989-91; mgr. Sunland Art Gallery, 1994-95. Represented in group exhibitions at Sun CarnivalExhbn., 1961, El Paso Mus. Art, 1962; author highsch. curriculum guide; exhibited at LVAA Shows, 1990 (5 First Places), Westside Art Guild, 1992, LVAA, 1992 (1st in Watercolor). Coordinator art edn. El Paso Civic Planning Coun., 1985-86; chmn. art edn., art resources dept. City of El Paso, 1982-83. Recipient Purchase award El Paso Art Assn. Spring Show, 1995, 1st pl. award KCOS (PBS), 1996, 1st pl. award Westside Art Guild, 1996, 2d pl. El Paso Art Assoc., 1998, 1st pl. award West Side Art Guild, 1998, 99, H.M. El Paso Pastel Soc. Show, 1998. Mem.: Pastel Soc. N.Mex. (v.p. 2001, pres. 2003), Rio Grande Art Assn., N.Mex. Watercolor Soc. (signature mem. 2004), Pastel Soc. El Paso (v.p. 1999—2000), Rio Bravo Watercolorists (sec. 1998), Nat. Soc. Am. Pen Women, Westside Art Guild (pres. 1993—95), Nat. Art Edn. Assn. (sec. 1988—93, two 1st place award LVAA shows 1989), Lower Valley Art Assn. (Hon. Mention award 1988), El Paso Mus. Art Guild, Nat. Soc. Arts and Letters (sec. El Paso chpt. 1988—), Tex. Art Edn. Assn. (local orgn. 1981, conf. planner, Hon. Mention award 1972). Republican. Presbyterian. Avocations: printmaking, travel. Home: 22 Canon Escondito Sandia Park NM 87047 Office Phone: 505-281-0881. Personal E-mail: jweitz@prodigy.net.

WEITZ, JOHN JEROME, JR., city planner; b. Mobile, Ala., Aug. 19, 1961; s. John J. and Marcheta (Knight) W.; m. Patricia L. Weitz, Oct. 20, 1990; 1 child, John Jerome III. AA, Oxford Coll. of Emory Univ., 1981; BA, Emory U., Atlanta, 1983; M City Planning, Ga. Inst. Tech., Atlanta, 1985; D Philosophy Urban Studies, Portland (Oreg.) State U., 1998. Cert. planner. Planner technician City of Roswell, Ga., 1985-87; planner II Fulton County Dept. Planning and Econ. Devel., Atlanta, 1987-88; zoning adminstr. Albany-Dougherty Planning Commn., Albany, Ga., 1988-89; sr. planner Ga. Mountains Regional Devel. Ctr., Gainesville, 1989-94; urban growth mgmt. specialist State of Oreg., Salem, 1994-97; cons. Benkendorf Assocs., Portland, 1994-96; planning divsn. mgr. Cowlitz Coun, Kelso, Wash., 1997-99; planning dir. City of Roswell, 1999-2000; pres. Jerry Weitz & Assocs., Inc., Alpharetta, 2001—; adj. asst. prof. pub. adminstrn. Kennesaw (Ga.) State U., 2001; asst. prof. pub. adminstrn. Troy State U., Atlanta, 2001—. Exec. com. Ga. Planning Assn., Atlanta, 1993—94, v.p. legislative affairs, 2000—03, pres. -elect, 2002—, pres., 2003—04; adj. faculty city and regional planning program Ga. Inst. of Tech., 2003—. Author: Sprawl Busting: State Programs to Guide Growth, 1999, Jobs-Housing Balance, 2003; co-author: Smart Growth Audits, 2002. Coun. mem. City of Gillsville, Ga., 1994; mem. design rev. bd. City of Beaverton, Oreg., 1997-99. Recipient Outstanding Achievement award Alpharetta Jaycees, 1986. Mem. Am. Planning Assn., Urban Affairs Assn., Internat. City/County Mgmt. Assn., Assn. Collegiate Schs. Planning, Ga. Planning Assn. (disting. profl. achievement in planning award 2000), ASPA, Am. Inst. for Cert. Planners. Avocations: fishing, camping, golf. Home: 1045 Mid Broadwell Rd Alpharetta GA 30004-1027 E-mail: jerryweitz@aol.com.

WEITZEL, JOHN PATTERSON, lawyer; b. Pitts., Aug. 24, 1923; s. Albert Philip and Elizabeth (Patterson) W.; m. Elisabeth Swan, Mar. 20, 1965; children: Mary Middleton, Paul Patterson. Student, Deerfield (Mass.) Acad., 1937-40; AB, Yale U., 1946; LL.B., Harvard U., 1949. Bar: Mass. 1949, U.S. Supreme Ct. 1960. Asso. Herrick, Smith, Donald, Farley & Ketchum (now Herrick & Smith), Boston, 1949-53, ptnr., 1961-86, Palmer & Dodge, Boston, 1986-93; of counsel, 1993—; spl. asst. to asst. sec. treasury, 1953-55; asst. to under sec. treas, 1955-56; asst. gen. counsel Treasury Dept., 1956-59, dep. to sec. treasury, 1959-60, asst. sec. treasury, 1960-61; U.S. exec. dir. World Bank, 1960-61. Mem. planning bd. NSC, 1959-61; cons. to sec. def., 1973. Mem. Mass. Council Arts and Humanities, 1966-71; overseer, dir. sec. Boys and Girls Clubs, Boston; mem. corp. Mass. Gen. Hosp., Boston Mus. Sci.; trustee Roxbury Latin Sch. Served with USAAF, 1943-45. Mem. Am., Boston bar assns., Am. Law Inst. Clubs: Harvard (Boston), Union Boat (Boston). Home: 45 Devon Rd Chestnut Hill MA 02467-1851 Office: Palmer & Dodge LLP 111 Huntington Ave Boston MA 02199-7613

WEITZEL, JOHN QUINN, bishop; b. Chgo., May 10, 1928; s. Carl Joseph and Patricia (Quinn) W. BA, Maryknoll (N.Y.) Sem., 1951, M of Religious Edn., 1953; PMD, Harvard U. Ordained priest Roman Cath. Ch., 1955. With ednl. devel. Cath. Fgn. Mission Soc. of Am., Maryknoll, 1955—63, nat. dir. vocations for Maryknoll, dir. devel. dept. and info. services, 1963—72, mem. gen. coun., 1972—78; asst. parish priest Cath. Ch., Western Samoa, 1979—81, pastor, vicar gen., 1981—86; consecrated bishop, 1986; bishop Cath. Ch., 1986—. Roman Catholic. Office: Diocese Samoa-Pago Pago PO Box 596 Pago Pago AS 96799-3594

WEITZEL, WILLIAM DAVID, psychiatrist; b. Detroit, Sept. 16, 1942; s. William Howard and Mary Ann (Buscanics) Weitzel; m. Joan Carol Heiser, June 8, 1968; children: Erica Marie, Jennifer Joan, Sarah Elizabeth. BS cum laude, Xavier U., 1964; MD, St. Louis U., 1968; postgrad. alcohol studies, Rutgers U., 1970; tng. family therapy, The Washington Sch. Psychiatry, 1971—72. Diplomate Am. Bd. Psychiatry and Neurology, Am. Bd. Forensic Psychiatry. Intern William Beaumont Gen. Hosp., El Paso, Tex., 1968—69; psychiat. resident Walter Reed Gen. Hosp., 1969—72; chief dept. psychiatry and neurology Moncrief Army Hosp., Columbia, SC, 1972—74; asst. prof. psychiatry and dir. Hosp. Inpatient Psychiatry Svc. Coll. Medicine, U. Ky., Lexington, 1974—78, assoc. prof. psychiatry, 1979, assoc. clin. prof. psychiatry, 1980—88, clin. prof. psychiatry, 1988—. Lectr. Coll. Law, 1977—82; supervising and cons. psychiatrist William S. Hall Psychiat. Inst., Columbia, 1973—74; psychiat. cons. Commn. on Ministry Episcopal Diocese of Lexington, 1975—87, Clin. Rsch. Ctr. Project, Ky. Bur. Health Svcs., Homestead Nursing Ctr., Lexington, 1978—88. Contbr. numerous articles to profl. jours. Mem. Ky. Gov.'s Task Force on Welfare Reform, 1978—79, Ky. Commn. on Corrections and Cmty. Svc., 1992—96. Maj. MC AUS, 1968—74. Fellow: Am. Psychiat. Assn. (pres. Ky. dist. br. 1979—80, co-author task force report on involuntary outpatient commitment 1987), Am. Coll. Psychiatrists; mem.: AAAS, Am. Acad. Psychiatry and the Law, Group for Advancement of Psychiatry. Office: Ste 128 1725 Harrodsburg Rd Lexington KY 40504-3628 Office Phone: 859-277-5419. E-mail: wweitzel@pol.net.

WEITZMAN, ARTHUR JOSHUA, English educator; b. Newark, Sept. 13, 1933; s. Louis I. and Cecele W.; m. Catherine Ezell, Aug. 8, 1982; children: Peter A., Anne E. BA, U. Chgo., 1956, MA, 1957; PhD, NYU, 1964. Instr. English, Bklyn. Coll., 1960-63; asst. prof. Temple U., Phila., 1963-69; assoc. prof. Northeastern U., Boston, 1969-72, prof., 1972—2002, prof. emeritus, 2002—; mem. faculty Brookline (Mass.) Adult and Cmty. Edn., 2003—, Cambridge (Mass.) Ctr. Adult Edn., 2003—. Editor: Letters Writ by a Turkish Spy (G.P. Marana), 1970; founder, co-editor: The Scriblerian, 1968—2004; co-editor: Milton and the Romantics, 1980-81; contbr.: revs. and articles to profl. jours. and newspapers including Los Angeles Times, Boston Globe, Miami Herald NEH fellow, 1972-73; Mellon fellow, 1976; research grantee Temple U.; research grantee Northeastern U. Mem.: MLA, Na. Assn. Scholars, Am. Soc. 18th Century Studies. Jewish. Home: 4 Bellis Ct Cambridge MA 02140-3240 E-mail: weitzman@neu.edu.

WEITZMAN, HERBERT D. real estate company executive; BA, U. Tex. Chmn., founder Cencor Realty Svcs., Inc., Dallas, 1989—. Office: Cencor Realty Svcs Inc 3102 Maple Ave Ste 500 Dallas TX 75201-1292*

WEITZMAN, ROBERT HAROLD, investment company executive; b. Chgo., July 15, 1937; s. Nathan and Selma Weitzman; m. Marilynn Beth Felzer, Sept. 5, 1965; children— Joshua C., Eliza S. BA in Bus., Econs., Grinnell Coll., 1959; JD, DePaul U., 1963. Bar: Ill 1963. Vice pres. Weitzman Enterprises, Chgo., 1955-63; assoc. Lissner, Rothenberg, Reif & Barth, Chgo., 1963-68; real estate counsel Continental Ill. Nat. Bank and Trust Co., Chgo., 1968-74; v.p., group head Continental Ill. Investment Trust, Chgo., 1974-76; founding ptnr. Group One Investments, Chgo., 1977—. Founding sponsor DePaul U. Real Estate Ctr., 2002—; lectr. in field. Editor: Real Estate Finance Handbook, 1979. Contbr. articles to profl. jours. Trustee, advisor Weitzman Found., 1963-77, mng. trustee, 1978—; cons., advisor Ill. chpt. Big Bros. Am. Orgn., 1969-72; trustee The Wis. Real Estate Investment Trust, 1980, 81. Recipient Outstanding Young Man Am. award U.S. Jaycees, 1973 Mem. Ill. Bar Assn., Chgo. Bar Assn., Nat. Assn. Rev. Appraisers and Mortgage Underwriters (charter mem. cert. rev. appraiser designation), Real Estate Securities and Syndication Inst. (bd. dirs. Ill. chpt. 1982-90, pres. 1984, regional v. p. 1988, specialist in real estate securities designation 1988, chmn. nat. com. on continuing edn. 1989, 90). Real Estate Investment Assn. (founding mem., Nat. bd. dirs. 1990—, exec. com. nat assn. and Ill. chpt. 1990—, chmn. nat. com. for advanced edn., 1990-95, nat. pres. 1996-98, nat. chmn. 1999—, specialist in real estate investment designation 1990), Am. Inst. Banking, Internat. Coll. Real Estate Cons. Profls., Internat. Real Estate Bd. Home: 535 Carriage Way Deerfield IL 60015-4534 Office: Group One Investments 77 W Washington St Ste 1005 Chicago IL 60602-2805 E-mail: r.weitzman@g1invest.com.

WEIXLMANN, JOSEPH NORMAN, JR., English educator, provost; b. Buffalo, N.Y., Dec. 16, 1946; s. Joseph Norman and Mary C. (Degenhart) W.; m. Sharron Pollack, Mar. 14, 1982; children: Seth Jacob, Adira Jenna, Benjamin Ari. AB, Canisius Coll., 1968; MA, Kans. State U., 1970, PhD, 1973. Instr. U. Okla., Norman, 1973-74; asst. prof. Tex. Tech U., Lubbock, 1974-76; from asst. prof. to prof. Ind. State U., Terre Haute, 1976—2001, assoc. dean, 1987-92, acting dean, 1992-94, dean, 1994—2001; prof. St. Louis U., 2001—, dean, 2001—02, provost, 2002—. Author: John Barth, 1976, American Short-Fiction Criticism, 1982; co-editor: Black American Prose Theory, 1984, Belief vs. Theory in Black American Literary Criticism, 1986, Black Feminist Criticism, 1988, Studies in Black Am. Lit. Ann., 1984-88; editor African Am. Rev. jour., 1976-2004; contbg. editor High Plains Lit. Rev., 1987-2002; adv. editor Langston Hughes Rev., 1982—. Fellow NDEA, 1970-72, NEH, 1980; Nat. Endowment for Arts grantee, 1988-95. Mem. MLA (exec. com. divsn. Black Am. Lit. and Culture 1985-2004), Coll. Lang. Assn., Langston Hughes Soc., Zora Neale Hurston Soc., Coun. Lit. Mags. and Presses (grantee 1977-96, Editor's grantee 1986), Coun. Editors Learned Jours. Office: Saint Louis U DuBourg Hall #106 Saint Louis MO 63103 Home: 6344 Wydown Blvd Saint Louis MO 63105-2213 Office Phone: 314-977-3078. E-mail: weixlmj@slu.edu.

WEJCMAN, LINDA, state legislator; b. Dec. 1939; m. Jim. Student, Iowa State U. Minn. State rep. Dist. 61B, 1991—; cons. Mem. local govt. and met. affairs com., energy, health and human svcs., housing and judiciary coms. Home: 3203 5th Ave S Minneapolis MN 55408-3248 Office: Minn Ho of Reps 203 State Capital Bldg Saint Paul MN 55155-0001

WEJMAN, JANET P. information technology executive, air transportation executive; BS, Northwestern U., Evanston, Ill. Programmer United Airlines; dir. sys. devel. Covia Technologies, 1988—92; with Chgo. & Northwestern R.R., 1992—96; sr. v.p. and chief info. officer Continental Airlines, Inc., Houston, 1996—. Office: Continental Airlines PO Box 4607 Houston TX 77210-4607

WEKSTEIN, DAVID ROBERT, physiology educator, researcher; b. Boston, Feb. 26, 1937; s. Abraham Jacob and Dorothy (Goldschmidt) W.; m. Merle Barbara Weiner, Aug. 31, 1958; children: Lauren Jane, Karen Gail, Debra Susan, Jeffrey Bruce. AB, Boston U., 1957, MA, 1958; PhD, U. Rochester, 1962. Instr. to assoc. prof. physiology U. Ky., Lexington, 1962—, prof. physiology, 1981—. Assoc. dir. Sanders-Brown Ctr. on Aging, Lexington, 1973—, Alzheimer's Disease Rsch. Ctr., Lexington, 1984—. Mem. AAAS, Am. Physiol. Soc., Am. Geriatrics Soc., Gerontol. Soc. Am., Soc. for Exptl. Biology and Medicine, Sigma Xi (pres. local chpt. 1985). Office: U Ky Sanders Brown Ctr On Aging Lexington KY 40536-0001 Office Phone: 859-323-6040. E-mail: dwekste@email.ky.edu.

WELBAUM, R(OME) EARL, lawyer; b. Miami, Feb. 4, 1932; s. Rome Lewis and Helen Louise (Richter) W.; m. Joan M. Tubridy, May 16, 1959; children: Karl Patrick, Michael Frederick, Carrie Kathleen. BBA, U. Miami, 1954, LLB, 1959. Bar: Fla. 1959, U.S. Dist. Ct. (so. dist.) Fla. 1959, U.S. Ct. Appeals (5th cir.) 1963, U.S. Ct. Appeals (11th cir.) 1983. Law clk. to presiding judge 3d Dist. Ct. Appeals Fla., 1959—61; from assoc. to ptnr. Welbaum, Guernsey, Hingston, Greenleaf & Gregory, LLP, Miami, 1961—. Pres. Hall of Fame com. U. Miami, 1990—91. Capt. USAF, 1954—62. Named to Sports Hall of Fame, U. Miami. Fellow: Am. Bar Found. (life); mem.: Internat. Assn. Def. Counsel (chmn. fidelity insured com. 1988—89), Fla. Bar Assn., Dade County Bar Assn. Office: 901 Ponce De Leon Blvd Miami FL 33134-3073 Office Phone: 305-441-8900. E-mail: ewelbaum@welbaum.com.

WELBORN, CARYL BARTELMAN, lawyer; b. Phila., Jan. 29, 1951; d. Raymond C. and Helen Ann Bartelman; m. Lucien Ruby, Apr. 11, 1987. AB, Stanford U., 1972; JD, UCLA, 1976. Bar: Ill. 1976, Calif. 1978. Assoc. Isham Lincoln & Beale, Chgo., 1976—78; from assoc. to ptnr. Morrison & Foerster, San Francisco and L.A., 1978—95; prin. Law Office of Caryl Welborn, 1995—2004; ptnr. Piper Rudnick LLP, San Francisco, 2004—. Lectr. real property law. Named Best Lawyers in America. Mem. ABA (chmn. com. on partnerships, real property sect. 1989-93), Am. Coll. Real Estate Lawyers (bd. govs. 1994-2002, pres. 2001). Office: Piper Rudnick LLP 333 Market St Ste 3200 San Francisco CA 94105-2150 Office Phone: 415-659-7100. Business E-Mail: caryl.welborn@piperrudnick.com.

WELBORN, R. MICHAEL, bank executive; Chmn., CEO Citibank Ariz., CEO, 1996—. Active Greater Phoenix Econ. Coun., Valley of the Sun United Way, Ariz. Bankers Assn. Recipient Torch of Liberty Humanitarian of the Yr. award Anti-Defamation League, 1996. Office: Bank One Ctr 201 N Central Ave Phoenix AZ 85073-0073 Fax: 602-221-4840.

WELBORNE, JOHN HOWARD, railway company executive, lawyer; b. July 24, 1947; s. William Elmo and Pauline Cornwell (Schoder) W.; m. Mary Martha Lampkin, Oct. 8, 1994. AB, U. Calif.-Berkeley, 1969; MPA, UCLA, 1974; JD, U. Calif.-Davis, 1977. Bar: Calif. 1977, D.C. 1980. Congl. intern Congressman John V. Tunney, Washington, 1969; assoc. firm Adams, Duque & Hazeltine, L.A., 1979-84, of counsel, 1984-96; gen. counsel Magnum Software Corp., Chatsworth, Calif., 1989-98. Mgmt. cons., 1971—; dir. Pueblo Viejo Devel. Corp., 1979-88, Union Hardware & Metal Co., 1981—98; pres. Angels Flight Railway Co., L.A., 1995—; COO Calif. Sesquicentennial Found., 1996-97; dir. Childrens Hosp. L.A. Centennial Celebration, 1998-2001. Contbr. articles to profl. jours. Mem. cen. bus. dist. project adv. com., downtown strategic plan adv. com., chmn. open space task force, mem. South Park task force City of L.A. Cmty. Redevel. Agy.; mem. L.A. Philharm. Men's Com., 1978-89; pres. L.A. County Host Com. for Olympic Games, 1984; mem. exec. com. Citizens's Task Force for Cen. Libr. Devel., L.A., 1981-83; bd. dirs. Children's Bur., L.A., 1982-88, El Pueblo Park Assn., 1983-89, L.A. Chpt. ARC, 1986-89, Angels Flight Rlwy. Found., 1995—, Friends of the USC Librs., 1999—2002, Inner City Law Ctr., 1992-95, Los Amigos del Pueblo, L.A. Libr. Assn., 1983-89, 1992-2002, Windsor Sq. Assn., 1980-87, 1999—, L.A. Beautiful, 1982-85, Pershing Sq. Restoration Campaign, 1986-87, Children's Bur. Found., 1997—; bd. dirs. In the Wings divsn. Music Ctr., Los Angeles County, 1982-86, pres. 1984-85; bd. dirs., officer L.A. 200 Com., 1978-91; bd. councilors U. So. Calif. Sch. Pub. Adminstrn., 1983-89; mem. adv. bd. The L.A. Conservancy, 1986—; trustee Windsor Sq-Hancock Park Hist. Soc., 1983-86, Nat. Trust Hist. Preservation, 1997—; fellow Amundsen Inst. U.S.-Mex. Studies, 1987. Capt. Adj. Gen.'s Corps., U.S. Army, 1970-71, USAR, 1972-79. Decorated Army Commendation medal with oak leaf cluster; Cross of Merit 1st class (Fed. Republic Germany). Mem. ABA, D.C. Bar Assn., State Bar Calif., Ordre des Coteaux de Champagne, Confrerie Saint-Etienne d'Alsace, Calif. Vintage Wine Soc. Episcopalian. Office: Angels Flight Railway PO Box 712345 Los Angeles CA 90071-7345

WELBURN, BRENDA LILIENTHAL, professional society administrator; Grad., Howard U.; postgrad., U. Pa. Social worker, Phila.; rsch. analyst U.S. Ho. Reps. Select Com. on Assassinations; legis. asst. to Senator Paul Tsongas Mass.; dir. govtl. affairs Nat. Assn. State Bds. Edn., Alexandria, Va., 1984—88, dep. exec. dir., 1988—93, exec. dir., 1993—. Presenter in field. Author: The American Tapestry: Educating a Nation; contbr. articles to profl. jours. Office: Nat Assn State Bds Edn 277 S Washington St Alexandria VA 22314

WELBURN, EDWARD T. automotive executive; b. Philadelphia, Pa., Dec. 14, 1950; BA, Howard U., 1972. Assoc. designer GM Advanced Design Studios, 1972, Buick Exterior Studio, 1973, Oldsmobile Exterior Studio, 1975—85, chief designer, 1989—98; dir. GM Corp. Brand Ctr., Warren, Mich., 1998—2001; exec. dir. design body-on-frame architecturs GM, 2002, v.p. design N. Am., 2003—. Designer Indianapolis 500 Pace Car, 1985. Recipient The Best Concept Truck, N. Am. Internat. Auto Show, 2003, Best Concept Car, Autoweek, 1995, Award of Design Excellence, Indsl. Designers Soc. Am., 1988. Office: GM Corp 300 Renaissance Ctr Detroit MI 48265-3000

WELCH, ASHLEY JAMES, engineering educator; b. Ft. Worth, May 3, 1933; married, 1952; 3 children. BS, Tex. Tech U., 1955; MS, So. Meth. U., 1959; PhD in Elec. Engring., Rice U., 1964. Aerophys. engr. Gen. Dynamics, Ft. Worth, 1957-60; instr. elec. engring. Rice U., 1960-64, from asst. to assoc. prof., 1964-68, dir. engring. computing facility, 1970-75, dir. biomed. engring. program, 1971-75, 95-96; prof. elec. and biomed. engring. U. Tex., Austin, 1975—, Marion E. Forsman Centennial prof. engring., 1985—, faculty advisor undergraduate biomedical engring. students, 2002—03. Contbr. more than 500 articles to profl. jours. Fellow: IEEE, Am. Inst. for Med. and Biol. Engring., Am. Soc. Lasers Surg. Medicine (bd. dirs. 1989—92, 1999—2002, W.B. Mark award 2002, Hocott award 2004). Achievements include research in laser-tissue interaction, application of lasers in medicine. Office: U Tex at Austin Dept Biomedical Engring Austin TX 78712 Office Phone: 512-471-1453.

WELCH, C. DAVID, ambassador; b. Munich, 1953; m. Gretchen Gerwe; children: Emma, Molly, Hannah. BA, Georgetown U., 1975; M, Fletcher Sch. Law and Diplomacy; student, London Sch. Econs., 1973—74. With Office of Under Sec. for Security Assistance, Sci. and Tech., 1977—79; polit. officer U.S. Embassy, Islamabad, Pakistan, 1979—81, officer responsible for Syria Washington, 1981—82, officer responsible for Lebanon, 1982—83, chief polit. sect. Damascus, Syria, 1984—86, polit. officer Amman, Jordan, 1986—88; mem. staff Nat. Security Coun. at White House, Washington, 1989—91; exec. asst. to under sec. polit. affairs U.S. Dept. of State, Washington, 1991—92; charge d'affaires U.S. Embassy, Riyadh, Saudi Arabia, 1992—94, dep. chief of mission, 1992—95; prin. dep. asst. sec. of state Bur. Near Eastern Affairs, Washington, 1996—97; asst. sec. of state for internat. orgn. affairs, 1998—2001; U.S. amb. to Egypt, 2001—. Mem.: Am. Fgn. Svc. Assn., Coun. Fgn. Rels. Office: 8 Sharia Kamal al-Din Salah Garden City Cairo Egypt

WELCH, CHARLES EDGAR, JR., retired English language educator, writer; b. Phila., July 20, 1918; s. Charles Edgar and Eva Dudley (Morris) W.; widower. BS in Edn., West Chester U., 1947; MA in Early Am. History, U. Pa., 1948, PhD in Folklore, 1970; cert. in 20th Century poetry, Oxford (Eng.) U., 1948. Cert. tchr., Pa. Lectr. English, Phila. Coll. Pharmacy and Sci., 1947-50, asst. prof., 1951-60, assoc. prof., 1960-69, prof., 1969-77, emeritus prof., 1977—, chmn. dept. langs. and social scis., 1950-77. Adj. prof. ESL, Temple U., Phila., 1977-96; part-owner Trevose Summer Theater, 1950-52; contbr., cons. Ledger Syndicate, 1950-70; actor, asst. stage mgr. New Angola (Pa.) Summer Theater, 1955; program dir. Folk Fair, Nationalities Svc. Ctr., Phila., 1955-75; contbr. to humanities program Thomas Jefferson U.; writer Milestones, Phila.; a host You and Your Health, Sta. WFIL-TV, 1958-70; folklorist for documentary on Phila. Mummers Parade Look Who's Having Fun, 1986. Author: Oh! Dem Golden Slippers: A History of the Philadelphia Mummers Parade, 1970, revised, 1993, (with A. Osol): A Sesquicentennial of Service 1821-1971 of the Philadelphia College of Pharmacy and Science; contbr. articles and book revs. to profl. jours., newspapers and mags. Stage mgr. fund raising program, fund raiser Erlanger Theater, Phila., Internat. House, Phila. Mem. Acad. Natural Scis., Pa. Hist. Soc., Pa. Acad. Arts, Nat. Mus. Women in Arts (charter). Republican. Avocation: writing. Home: 2423 Pine St Philadelphia PA 19103-6416

WELCH, CLAUDE (CLAUDE RAYMOND WELCH), theology educator; b. Genoa City, Wis., Mar. 10, 1922; s. Virgil Cleon and Deone West (Grenelle) W.; m. Eloise Janette Turner, May 31, 1942 (div. 1970); children— Eric, Thomas, Claudia; m. Theodosia Montigel Blewett, Oct. 5, 1970 (dec. 1978); m. Joy Neuman, Oct. 30, 1982. BA summa cum laude, Upper Iowa U., 1942; postgrad., Garrett Theol. Sem., 1942-43; BD cum laude, Yale U., 1945, PhD, 1950; DD (hon.), Ch. Div. Sch. of Pacific, 1972, Jesuit Sch. Theology, 1982; LHD (hon.), U. Judaism, 1976. Ordained to ministry Meth. Ch., 1947. Instr. religion Princeton (N.J.) U., 1947-50, asst. prof., 1950-51, vis. prof., 1962; asst. prof. theology Yale U. Div. Sch., New Haven, 1951-54, assoc. prof., 1954-60; Berg prof. religious thought, chmn. dept. U. Pa., Phila., 1960-71, assoc. dean Coll. Arts and Scis., 1964-68, acting chmn. dept. philosophy, 1965-66; prof. hist. theology Grad. Theol. Union, Berkeley, Calif., 1971—, dean, 1971-87, pres., 1972-82. Vis. prof. Garrett Theol. Sem., 1951, Pacific Sch. Religion, 1958, Hartford Sem. Found., 1958-59, Princeton Theol. Sem., 1962-63, U. Va., 1987; Fulbright sr. lectr. U. Mainz, Germany, 1968; Sprunt lectr. Union Theol. Sem., Richmond, Va., 1958; Willson lectr. Southwestern U., Georgetown, Tex., 1994; dir. study of grad. edn. in religion Am. Coun. Learned Socs., 1969-71; del. World Conf. on Faith and Order, 1963. Author: In This Name: the Doctrine of the Trinity in Contemporary Theology, 1952, (with John Dillenberger) Protestant Christianity, interpreted through its Development, 1954, 2d rev. edit., 1988, The Reality of the Church, 1958, Graduate Education in Religion: A Critical Appraisal, 1971, Religion in the Undergraduate Curriculum, 1972, Protestant Thought in the 19th Century, vol. 1, 1799-1870, 1972, vol. 2, 1870-1914, 1985; Editor, translator: God and Incarnation in Mid-19th Century German Theology (Thomasius, Dorner and Biedermann), 1965; Contbr. to publs. in field. Recipient decennial prize Bross Found., 1970; Guggenheim fellow, 1976; NEH research fellow, 1984, Fulbright research fellow, 1956-57. Mem. Am. Acad. Religion (pres. 1969-70), Coun. of Socs. for Study of Religion (chmn. 1969-74, 85-90), Soc. for Values in Higher Edn. (pres. 1967-71), Am. Soc. Ch. History, Am. Theol. Soc., Phi Beta Kappa. Methodist. Home: 123 Fairlawn Dr Berkeley CA 94708-2107 E-mail: claudew2@juno.com.

WELCH, DOMINIC, publishing consultant; Former pres., pub. The Salt Lake Tribune, Salt Lake City. Office: 400 Tribune Bldg 143 S Main St Salt Lake City UT 84111

WELCH, EDWIN HUGH, academic administrator; b. Balt., Apr. 11, 1944; s. Lester Kenneth and Catherine (Dodrer); m. Janet Gail Boggess, Nov. 22, 1977. BA, Western Md. Coll., 1965; STB, Boston U. Sch. Theology, 1968; postgrad., London Sch. Econs. and Polit. Sci., 1968-69; PhD, Boston U., 1971; EdD (hon.), Alderson-Broaddus Coll., 2003. Assoc. prof., chmn. W.Va. Wesleyan Coll., Buckhannon, 1971-75, Lebanon Valley Coll., Annville, Pa., 1975-79, dir. weekend coll., 1979-80; dean Lakeland Coll., Sheboygan, Wis., 1980-81; provost Wartburg Coll., Waverly, Iowa, 1981-89; pres. U. Charleston, W.Va., 1989—. Chmn. Iowa Deans Confs., Des Moines, 1984-89; title III evaluator Iowa Wesleyan Coll., Mt. Pleasant, 1983-85. Contbr. articles to edn. jours. Bd. dirs. Bus. and Indsl. Devel. Corp., Charleston Area Med. Ctr., Health Sys., Health, Edn. and Rsch. Inst.; mem. adv. bd. BB&T of W.Va.; creator, dir. Cmty. Leadership Devel. Program, Waverly, 1986-88; bd. dirs., pres. Lebanon (Pa.) Family Planning Assn., 1976-81. Named Tchr. of Yr., W.Va. Wesleyan Coll., 1974. Mem. W.Va. Ind. Colls. and Univs. (exec. com.) Balt. Conf. United Meth. Ch. (ordained), Appalachian Coll. Assn. (chair 2000-03), Coun. Ind. Colls., W.Va. Intercollegiate Athletic Conf. (pres. 1994-96), Rotary Internat. (past pres. Charleston chpt.). Democrat. Methodist. Office: U Charleston Office of Pres 2300 Maccorkle Ave SE Charleston WV 25304-1045

WELCH, JACK HAMILL, retired internist; b. Columbus, Ohio, July 14, 1915; s. John Orr and Evelyn (Bigger) Welch; m. Mary Elaine Childs, Apr. 25, 1943 (div. 1976); children: David, Pamela, Michael; m. Alice Elizabeth Welch, May 6, 1978. BA, Ohio State U., 1936; MD, Duke U., 1940. Diplomate Am. Bd. Internal Medicine, Nat. Bd. Med. Examiners. From intern to resident Henry Ford Hosp., Detroit, 1940-42, 46-48; pvt. practice internal medicine Columbus, 1948-50, Hollywood, Calif., 1950-52, San Fernando Valley, 1952-83; ret., 1983. Instr. medicine White Meml. Hosp. Loma Linda Sch. Medicine, L.A., 1954—56; moderator Nat. Issues Forum, 1985—91, participant, 1992—94; active supporter Calif. Proposition 186 Universal Health Care, Fresno, 1994. Author: (book) Battalion Surgeon WWII, 1996. Mem. Visions of Cmty., 1984—94, chair, 1990—92; initiator Peace and Justice com. United Ch. of Christ, Fresno, 1990—97; co-founder, bd. dirs. Fresno Ctr. for Non Violence, 1992—, Black.White Dialogue Group, Fresno, 1997—. With M.C. U.S. Army, 1942—45, ETO. Decorated Bronze Star; fellow, Ctrl. Calif. Inst., prog. pub. policy rsch. found., Fresno, 2003. Mem.: ACP, AMA, Fgn. Policy Assn., Physicians for Social Responsibility (ho. dels. 1987—88). Democrat. Avocations: singing, writing, walking, tv, golf. Home: 6432 N Dolores Ave Fresno CA 93711

WELCH, JAMES DOUGLAS, lawyer, engineer; b. Omaha, Dec. 4, 1945; s. James J. and Lois V. (Hibbs) W. BSEE, U. Nebr., 1969, JD, 1982, postgrad., 1993—; MS in Electronic Engring., U. Toronto, 1974. Registered profl. engr., Nebr.; bar: Nebr. 1982, U.S. Patent Bar 1984; lic. radio FCC. Technician Comm. Supply, Omaha, 1958-66; engr. Fed. Pacific Electric, Toronto, 1969-72; lab instr. Toronto U., 1972-74; lab technician Nebr. Med. Ctr., Omaha, 1975-76; engr. Omaha Pub. Power, 1977-78; pvt. practice lawyer and engr. Omaha, 1982—. Patentee in field. Grantee, U.S. Dept. Energy, 1993. Avocation: restoring 280z cars. Home and Office: 10328 Pinehurst Ave Omaha NE 68124-1870

WELCH, JASPER ARTHUR, JR., security company executive, consultant; b. Baton Rouge, Jan. 5, 1931; s. Jasper Arthur and Oramay Ballinger (Young) W.; m. Frances Carroll Wright, Mar. 28, 1953 (div. Nov. 1984); children: Jasper Arthur III, Carroll Welch Pawlikowski, Brent Ballinger; m. Jane Ann Alford Tudor, Dec. 31, 1985. BS in Physics, La. State U., 1952; MA in Physics, U. Calif., Berkeley, 1954, PhD in Physics, 1958. Commd. officer 2d lt. USAF, 1952, advanced through grades to maj. gen., 1975; chief analyst Hdqs. USAF, Washington, 1969—71; chief strategic analysis Office Sec. Def., Washington, 1971—74; chief strategic concepts Hdqs. USAF, 1974—75, asst. chief staff for analysis, 1975—79; coord. def. policy NSC, 1979—81; asst. dept. chief staff Hdqs. USAF, 1981—83; ret., 1983; tech. cons. Jasper Welch Assocs., Santa Fe, 1983—. Bd. dirs. Sci. Applications Intrnat. Corp., San Diego; mem. tech. adv. coun. Sikorsky Aircraft, Stratford, Conn., 1984—; mem. adv. coun. NASA, Washington, 1985-89; chmn. mil. adv. panel to dir. CIA, Washington, 1986-98; mem. nat. security panel U. Calif., 2000—. Author: Atomic Theory of Gas Dynamics, 1965; contbr. articles to sci. jours., including Phys. Rev., Strategic Rev. Youth dir. St. Matthews Epis. Ch., Pacific Palisades, Calif., 1969-74, St. Andrews Epis. Ch., Arlington, 1965-68; mem. found. bd. Santa Fe Chamber Music Festival, 1998—. Decorated D.S.M. with oak leaf cluster, Legion of merit with two oak leaf clusters. Mem. NAE (found. bd. 1999—), Am. Geophys. Union, Am. Phys. Soc., Coun. on Fgn. Rels. Avocations: music, theater, gardening, hiking, racing sailboats. Office: Sci Applications Internat Corp 1710 SAIC Dr Mc Lean VA 22102

WELCH, JEANIE MAXINE, librarian; b. L.A., Jan. 22, 1946; d. Howard Carlton and Roberta Jean (Dunsmuir) W. BA, U. Denver, 1967, MA, 1968; M of Internat. Mgmt., Am. Grad. Sch. Internat. Mgmt., 1981. Asst. libr. Am. Grad. Sch. Internat. Mgmt., Glendale, Ariz., 1968-83; reference libr. Lamar U., Beaumont, Tex., 1983-85, head reference, 1985-87, reference unit head U. N.C., Charlotte, 1988-98, asst. coord. reference svcs., 1998-2000, bus. ref. libr., 2000—. Author: The Spice Trade, 1994, The Tokyo Trial, 2002; contbr. articles to profl. jours. Chpt. pres. NOW, Beaumont, 1985-87, state sec., Tex., 1986; exec. bd. Ariz. State Libr. Assn., 1976-80. Rsch. grantee Tex. Libr. Assn., 1986; recipient Best Bibliographies in History, 2003; named Dun & Bradstreet Info. Svcs. Online Champion of Yr., 1996; recipient Highly Commended award Literati Club, 2000 Mem.: ALA, N.C. Libr. Assn., Phi Beta Delta. Democrat. Methodist. Office: U NC Atkins Libr Charlotte NC 28223 E-mail: jmwelch@email.uncc.edu.

WELCH, JERRY, oil company executive; b. Marion, Ohio, Mar. 13, 1963; s. Arthur Leroy and Donna R. (Ellwood) W.; m. Sharon Carol Lee, 1995; children: Joseph Peterson, Shellie Peterson, James Peterson. BA, U. Colo., 1984. Exec. Amoco Oil, Houston, 1984—; CEO Brit. Inc., Paris. Mem. Internat. Platform Assn. Republican. Avocations: auto racing, tennis, sailing, swimming. Home: 31650 Hwy 44 E Eustis FL 31650 also: PO Box 470512 Lake Monroe FL 32747-0512

WELCH, JOE BEN, academic administrator; b. Amite County, Miss., May 18, 1940; s. H.A. Joe and Mildred Pill (Bean) W.; m. Dorothy Louise Rostron, June 2, 1962; children: Wendi Jo Welch Sands, Robin Clare Welch Peveto, Sandra Tres Welch Dobbs, Roxana Merry Welch Blackwell. BS, La. Tech. U., 1963; MEd, Lamar U., 1967; EdD, McNeese State U., 1974. Instr. math., sci. Clinton (La.) High Sch., 1963-64; instr. math. Port Neches (Tex.) Groves H.S., 1964-67; acting head math. and sci. dept. Trinity Christian Coll., Baton Rouge, 1967-68; head math. and sci. dept. Mid-City Bapt. Jr. Coll., New Orleans, 1968-69; instr. math. Orange (Tex.) Extension Ctr., Lamar U., 1969-70, dir., 1970-75; dean Lamar U. Ctr.-Orange, 1975-81, provost, 1981-83, pres., 1983-89, Middle Ga. Coll., Cochran, 1989-98; chancellor River Parishes C.C., Sorrento, La., 1998—. Adv. bd. dirs. Bleckley Meml. Hosp., 1989—. Recipient Grateful Appreciation award West Orange-Cove Consol. Sch. Dist., 1976-82, Outstanding and Dedicated Svc. award ARC, Orange, 1985; named Citizen of Yr. C. of C., Orange, 1985. Mem. Am. Assn. Community and Jr. Colls., Cochran (Ga.) Bleckley C. of C., Macon City Club (bd. dirs. 1991—), Phi Delta Kappa. Baptist. Office: River Parishs Cmty Coll PO Box 310 Sorrento LA 70778-0310

WELCH, JOHN DANA, retired urologist; b. Canton, Ill., Mar. 14, 1938; m. Myrna Lee Loring, Dec. 23, 1962; children: Timothy Lance, Christina Dawn. BS, U. Ill., 1960, MD, 1963. Diplomate Am. Bd. Urology, Nat. Bd. Med. Examiners, Fla. Bd. Med. Examiners. Rotating intern Tampa (Fla.) Gen. Hosp., 1963-64, resident in urology, 1964-68; pvt. practice, Sarasota, Fla., 1970-98. Bd. dirs. Bay Area Renal Stone Ctr., 1986-98; chief surgery HCA Doctors Hosp., 1981, chief of staff, 1983, trustee, 1988-91. Bd. dirs. Asolo Ctr. for Performing Arts, 1982-95, 2003—, sec., 1989-90, v.p., 1990-93, pres., 1993-94; pres., founder Sarasota Film Festival, 1998—. Maj. USAF, 1968-70. Mem. Fla. Med. Assn., Sarasota County Med. Soc., Am. Urological Assn. (SE sect.), Fla. Urological Soc. (pres. 1986), Am. Lithotripsy Soc. Home and Office: 650 Mourning Dove Dr Sarasota FL 34236-1926 E-mail: SRQDOC@aol.com.

WELCH, JUDY ANN, language educator; b. Miami Beach, Fla., Nov. 16, 1965; d. Albert and Frances Blue Swain; m. Albert P. Welch, Dec. 18, 1999; children: Dominique, Brittany. BA in English, Spelman Coll., Atlanta, 1987; MS in English Edn., Nova Southeastern U., Fort Lauderdale, Fla., 2001, EdD, 2004. English tchr. Miami-Dade County Pub. Schs., Fla., 1989—2001; lang. arts tchr. Palm Beach Sch. Dist., Boca Raton, Fla., 2001—03; adj. prof., English Lynn U., Boca Raton, Fla., 2001—; mem. English faculty Miami Dade Coll., 2003—; adj. prof., English Broward Cmty. Coll., Boca Raton, Fla., 2001—. Mem. Hopewell Baptist Missionary Ch., Pompano, Fla., 2001—. Mem.: Zeta Phi Beta. Democrat. Baptist. Avocations: singing, dance, poetry. Home: 1320 SW 18th St Boca Raton FL 33486 Office: 11380 NW 27th Ave Miami FL 33167 Office Phone: 561-702-0112. Business E-Mail: jwelch@aiufl.edu. E-mail: professorjawelch@aol.com.

WELCH, LLOYD RICHARD, electrical engineering educator, communications consultant; b. Detroit, Sept. 28, 1927; s. Richard C. and Helen (Felt) W.; m. Irene Althea Main, Sept. 12, 1953; children: Pamela Irene Towery, Melinda Ann Bryant, Diana Lia Worthington. BS in Math., U. Ill., 1951; PhD in Math., Calif. Inst. Tech., 1958. Mathematician NASA-Jet Propulsion Lab., Pasadena, Calif., 1956-59; staff mathematician Inst. Def. Analyses, Princeton, N.J., 1959-65; prof. elec. engring. U. So. Calif., L.A., 1965-99, prof. emeritus, 1999—. Cons. in field of elec. comms. Contbr. articles to profl. jours. Served with USN, 1945-49, 51-52. Fellow IEEE (Shannon award Info. Theory Soc. of IEEE 2003); mem. Nat. Acad. Engring., Am. Math. Soc., Math. Assn. Am., Phi Beta Kappa, Sigma Xi, Phi Kappa Phi, Pi Mu Epsilon, Eta Kappa Nu Office: U So Calif Elec Engring Bldg 500A Los Angeles CA 90089-0001 E-mail: lloydwelch@earthlink.net.

WELCH, LYNNE BRODIE, nursing school dean; b. Norwalk, Conn., Oct. 19, 1941; d. John and Jeannette Brodie; m. C. William Welch, Aug. 1965 (div. Dec. 1980); children: John, Andrew. BS, U. Conn., 1963; MSN, Cath. U. Am., 1968; EdD, Columbia U., 1979. From staff nurse to instr. Sch. of Nursing Stamford (Conn.) Hosp., 1963-65; staff nurse, instr. Children's Hosp. Ctr., Washington, 1965-66; staff nurse CCU Washington Hosp. Ctr., 1966-67; staff nurse ICU/CCU Danbury (Conn.) Hosp., 1968-69; asst. prof. Western Conn. State U., Danbury, 1970-79; assoc. prof., chairperson Pace U., Pleasantville, N.Y., 1979-82; prof., dean Sch. Nursing So. Conn. State U., New Haven, 1982-86; prof., dean Coll. of Nursing and Allied Health U. Tex., El Paso, 1986-89; statewide dir. S.C. Area Health Edn. Consortium Med. U. of S.C., Charleston, 1989-91; prof., dean Sch. of Nursing Marshall U., Huntington, W.Va., 1991—98, dean Coll. Nursing & Health Professions, 1998—. Mem. joint bd. Kellogg Community Partnership, Morgantown, W.Va., 1991—; mem. bd. W.Va. Ptnrs. of the Americas, Charleston, 1992—; chairperson W.Va. Health Care Planning Commn. Task Force, Charleston, 1992—. Editor: Women in Higher Education: Changes and Challenges, 1990, Minority Women in Higher Education, 1992, Roles of Nursing Faculty in Higher Education, 1992, Strategies for Promoting Pluralism in Education and the Work Place, 1997. Mem. Leadership Tri State, Ashland, Ky., 1992, Leadership W.Va., 1993, Leadership El Paso, Class 10, 1988. Mem. ANA, Nat. League for Nursing, Am. Assn. Acad. Adminstrs. (state commr. 1979-92), Sigma Theta Tau, Phi Kappa Phi. Republican. Presbyterian. Avocations: gardening, cooking, travel. Home: 3200 Orchard Dr Huntington WV 25701-9534 Office: Marshall U Pritchard Hall 426 1 John Marshall Dr Huntington WV 25755-0003

WELCH, MARTHA GRACE, physician, researcher; b. Buffalo, June 21, 1944; d. Thomas Harris and Jane Elizabeth (Todd) W.; m. Anthony H. Horan, July 11, 1970 (div. May 1985); 1 child, Thomas Bramwell Welch Horan. BA, N.Y.U., 1966; MD, Columbia U., 1971. Diplomate Am. Bd. Psychiatry and Neurology. Intern Greenwich (Conn.) Hosp. Assn., 1971-72; resident Albert Einstein Coll. Med., Bronx, N.Y., 1972-74, fellow, 1974-77, instr., 1977-79; dir., founder The Mothering Ctr., Greenwich, 1978—; asst. clin. prof. psychiatry Columbia U., N.Y.C., 1997—. Author: Holding Time, 1989, (with others) Autistic Children, 1983; contbr. articles to profl. jours. Pres. alumni coun. Columbia U. Coll. Physicians and Surgeons, 2001-2002 Recipient Alumni Achievement award Middlebury (Vt.) Coll., 1995. Mem. Am. Psychiat. Assn., Internat. Soc. for Devel. Psychobiology, Soc. for Neuroscience. Avocations: reading, skiing, tennis, sewing, biking, music. Office: 15 E 91st St New York NY 10128-0648

WELCH, MARTHA LYNN, environmentalist, educator; d. Margaret Melvina Sandifer and Richard Charles O'Connell; m. John Tyler Welch II, Aug. 28, 1987. BA in Environ. Studies, U. N.C., 1983; MS in Edn., Old Dominion U., 1996; EdD, Fla. Internat. U., 2004. Asst. edn., exhibits coord. N.C. Aquarium, Ft. Fisher, 1984—86; owner, operator Manatee Tours, Inc., Islamorada, Fla., 1990—93; marine edn. specialist Coll. William and Mary, Va. Inst. Marine Sci., Gloucester Point, 1996—97; field leader, instr. Audubon Fla., Miami, 1999—2003; dir. edn. Fla. Flora and Fauna, Inc., Jupiter, 1999—. Cons. Sch. Dist. Palm Beach County, Fla., 2002—. Author: Mandy the Manatee Saves the Day; contbr. articles to profl. jours. Mem. Nat. Audubon Soc., N.Y.C., 2002—03, Fla. Marine Sci. Edn. Assn., Miami, 1999—2003. Mem.: NSTA (assoc.), Nat. Marine Edn. Assn. (assoc.), Am. Ednl. Rsch. Assn. (assoc.), Phi Kappa Phi. Avocations: travel, snorkeling, boating. Home: 103 South US Hwy 1 Suite F5 PMB 176 Jupiter FL 33477 Office: Florida Flora and Fauna Inc 103 South US Hwy 1 Suite F5 PMB 176 Jupiter FL 33477 Personal E-mail: mwelch01@fiu.edu. E-mail: mwelch01@fiu.edu.

WELCH, MARTIN E., III, investor, retail executive; b. Detroit, June 25, 1948; m. Anne Welch; children: Michele, James, Mary Beth, Brian. BS in Acctg., U. Detroit-Mercy, 1970, MBA, 1973. Audit mgr. Arthur Young & Co., Detroit, 1970-77; dir. mktg. acctg. Fruehauf divsn. Fruehauf Corp., Detroit, 1977-82; mgr. corp. acctg. Chrysler Corp., Highland Park, Mich., 1982-83, asst. contr., 1983-86, gen. auditor, 1987-88, asst. treas., 1988-91; CFO Chrysler Can., Windsor, Ont., 1986-87; sr. v.p., CFO Federal-Mogul corp., Southfield, Mich., 1991-95; exec. v.p., CFO Kmart Corp, Troy, Mich., 1995—2001; bus. advisor, dir. York Mgmt. Svcs., Somerset, NJ, 2002—; exec. v.p., CFO Oxford Automotive, Inc., Troy, Mich., 2003—04. Mem. nat. adv. bd. JP Morgan Bank, 1997—2000; bd. dirs. No. Group Retail, Ltd., Popular Club Plan, Inc. Bd. dirs. U. Detroit-Mercy. Mem.: Fin. Execs. Internat. E-mail: martywelch@yahoo.com.

WELCH, MICHAEL JOHN, chemistry educator, researcher; b. Stoke on Trent, Staffordshire, Eng., June 28, 1939; came to U.S., 1965; s. Arthur John W. and Mary (Welch); m. Teresa Jean Conocchiolli, Apr. 22, 1967 (div. 1979); children: Colin, Lesley. BA, Cambridge U., Eng., 1961; MA, Cambridge U., 1964; PhD, London U., 1965. Asst. prof. radiation chemistry in radiology Washington U. Sch. Medicine, St. Louis, 1967-70, assoc. prof., 1970-74, assoc. prof. dept. chemistry, 1971-75, prof. dept. chemistry, 1978—, prof. radiology, 1991—, prof. molecular biology and pharmacology, 1993—; prof. biomed. engring. program Washington U., St. Louis, 1996; co-dir. Mallinckrodt Inst. Dir. radiol. scis. dept. Washington U., 1990—; mem. diagnostic radiology study sect. NIH, 1986-89, chmn., 1989-91; mem. sci. adv. com. Whitaker Found., 1995-2003. Author: Introduction to the Tracer Methods, 1972; editor: Radiopharmaceuticals and Other Compounds Labeled with Shortlived Radionuclides, 1977; assoc. editor Jour. Nuclear Medicine, 1989—2003; contbr. chpts. to books, more than 400 articles to profl. jours. Recipient Georg Charles de Hevesy Nuclear Medicine Pioneer award, 1992; scholar St. Catharine Coll. Cambridge U., 1958-61. Mem. Soc. Nuclear Medicine (trustee, pres. 1984, Paul C. Aebersold award 1980, de Hevesy Nuclear Pioneer award 1992), Radiopharm. Sci. Coun. (pres. 1980-81), Am. Chem. Soc. (St. Louis award 1988, award for nuclear chemistry 1990, Mid-West award 1991), Chem. Soc. London, Radiation Rsch. Soc., Inst. of Medicine, Sigma Xi Office: Washington U Sch Medicine Edward Mallinckrodt Inst Radiology 510 S Kingshighway Blvd Box 8225 Saint Louis MO 63110-1016 E-mail: welchm@mir.wustl.edu.

WELCH, MICHAEL R. sociologist, educator; b. Ogdensburg, N.Y., Feb. 8, 1947; s. Carlton Curtis Welch and Eleanor (Francis) Caruso; m. Helena Rose Kleist, Jan. 29, 1966; children: Kristen Reynolds, Michael Jr., Scott, Brian. BA, LeMoyne Coll., 1972; MA, U. N.C., 1975, PhD, 1980. Asst. prof. Fla. Atlantic U., Boca Raton, 1976—80, U. Cin., 1980—81; assoc. prof. U. Notre Dame, 1981—. Contbr. articles to profl. jours. Mem.: Am. Soc. Criminology, Am. Sociol. Assn., Alpha Kappa Delta, Pi Gamma Mu. Roman Catholic. Office: Univ Notre Dame Sociology Dept 810 Flanner Hall Notre Dame IN 46556

WELCH, OLIVER WENDELL, retired pharmaceutical executive; b. Jacksonville, Tex., Jan. 9, 1930; s. Jackson Andrew and Annie Laura (Trapp) W.; m. Wanda Virginia Urrey, Nov. 14, 1948. BA, Tex. Tech U., 1952; MA, Columbia U., 1958. Pharm. rep., supr. mktg. rsch., manpower devel. Warner Lambert Co., Morris Plains, N.J., 1962-72; mgr. corp. devel. Boehringer Mannheim Corp., N.Y.C., 1972-75; v.p. Biomed. Data Co., N.Y.C., 1975-77; assoc. dir., dep. dir. regulatory affairs Sterling Winthrop Inc., N.Y.C., 1977-94; ret., 1994. Cons. Sanofi Winthrop, Inc., N.Y.C., 1995. Mem. Regulatory Affairs Profls. Soc., Drug Info. Assn., Order St. John of Jerusalem. Republican. Episcopalian. Avocations: music, travel, theater. *Pursue excellence. Pay attention to detail. Expect a positive result.*

WELCH, PATRICK, health insurance company executive; BS, Seattle U.; MS, MBA, U. Wash. Chmn., pres. and CEO GNA Corp., Gen. Electric Capital Corp.; chmn. bd. Sentinel Group Funds, Inc.; chmn., CEO and pres. Nat. Life Group; pres. CIGNA HealthCare, 2002—. Office: 1 Liberty Pl Philadelphia PA 19192

WELCH, PATRICK JAMES, economics educator, author, consultant; b. Chgo., Feb. 8, 1944; s. Lourde John and Regina Frances W.; m. Geraldine Frances Nasiatka, Apr. 15, 1968. BSBA, Marquette U., 1966, MA in Econs., 1968; PhD in Econs., U. Pitts., 1974. Instr. econs. St. Ambrose Coll., Davenport, Iowa, 1968-70; asst. prof. St. Louis U., 1974-78, assoc. prof., 1978-83, prof., 1983—, prof. sch. pub. health, 1985—, prof. pub. policy studies, 1987—. Vis. economist Fed. Res. Bank St. Louis, 1982; spl. asst. dir. strategic planning Ralston Purina Agri-Prod Group, St. Louis, 1983; cons. competitive analysis Monsanto Co., St. Louis, 1984-86; cons. antitrust and competitive analysis various clients, 1988—. Co-author: Economics: Theory and Practice, 7 edits.; editor: Forum for Social Economics, 1995—; contbr. articles to profl. jours. chpts. in books. Mem. Human Rights Commn. Archdiocese of St. Louis, 1992—99; bd. dirs. Epworth Children & Family Svcs., 2000—, pres-elect, 2004. Grantee NSF, 1973. Mem.: Assn. Social Econs. (bd. dirs. 1989—91, pres. 2004), Nat. Assn. Bus. Economists (pres. St. Louis chpt. 1992—93), Webster Grove Hist. Soc. (pres., bd. dirs. 2001—03). Avocation: jazz musician. Home: 320 S Gray Ave Saint Louis MO 63119-3608 Office: St Louis U Dept Econs 3674 Lindell Blvd Saint Louis MO 63108-3302 Office Phone: 314-977-3814.

WELCH, PEGGY, state representative; b. Fulton, Miss., Oct. 13, 1955; BS in Social Studies and Edn., Miss. Coll., 1977; ASN, Ivy Tech. State Coll., 1995; student, Ind. U., 1992—94. Substitute tchr. Monroe County Cmty. Sch. Corp., 1981—82, 1991; dir., probation officer Monroe County Cmty. Corrections Program, 1983—90; cert. childbirth educator Lamaze of Bloomington, Inc., 1983—94; grad. sec., dept. theater and drama Ind. U., Bloomington, 1991—94; RN, oncology Bloomington Hosp. CCU and Cancer Care Units, 1995—; state rep. dist. 60 Ind. Ho. of Reps., Indpls., 1998—, mem. human affairs, tech. R & D, and ways and means coms. Chair, nursing programs adv. bd. Ivy Tech. State Coll., Bloomington; adv. bd. Ind. U. Sch. Nursing. Named Ind. C. of C. Small Bus. Champion, 2003; recipient Heart of Ind. award, Am. Heart Assn., 2003, Child Safety Advocate award, Ind. Safe Kids Coalition, 2002, Legis. Leadership award, Ind. United Sr. Action, 2001, Meritorious Svc. award, Ind. Assn. Homes and Svcs. for the Aging, Inc., 2001, numerous other awards. Mem.: Ind. State Nurses Assn., Children's Organ Transplant Assn. (bd. dirs.), Fraternal Order of Police, NAACP, Women in Govt., Bloomfield C. of C., Greater Bloomington C. of C., Brown County C. of C., Local Coun. of Women, Ind. U. Theater Circle, RN Club, Monroe County Dem. Women's Club. Democrat. Office: Ind Ho of Reps 200 W Washington St Indianapolis IN 46204-2786

WELCH, PETER F. lawyer, state senator; b. Springfield, Mass., May 2, 1947; s. Edward and Mart (Tracy) W.; m. Joan Smith, Dec. 10, 1975; 5 children. A.B., Holy Cross Coll., 1969; LL.B., U. Calif.-Berkeley, 1973. Bar: Vt. Sole practice law; mem. State Senate, Vt., 1981—1988, 2001-, pres., 2003-Address: PO Box 858 White River Junction VT 05001-0858

WELCH, PHILIP BURLAND, electronics and office products company executive; b. Portland, Maine, Nov. 15, 1931; s. Philip Gerald Welch and Clara Jenny (Berry) Hawxwell; m. Sheila Mae Preston, May 19, 1960 (dec.); children: Jahna Holly Welch Roth, Victoria Preston Welch Johnsen. Student, Berklee Coll., 1955—58. Profl. trumpeter, arranger, composer, NYC, 1958—65; dist. sales mgr. Rheem Mfg. Co., Phila., 1965—66, regional sales mgr., 1966—70; nat. sales mgr. Akai Am. Ltd., Anaheim, Calif., 1970-73, BSR, USA, Blauvelt, NY, 1973-76; nat. sales and mktg. mgr. Philips High Fidelity Labs., Ft. Wayne, Ind., 1976-79; dir. mktg. Pioneer Electronics, Moonachie, NJ, 1979-82; pres. Schneider N.Am. Ltd., Dayton, NJ, 1982-83; v.p. Lyons & Assocs., Indpls., 1986-88; pres. Nat. Electric Mktg. Co., Jacksonville, Fla., 1975-88, Hemisphere Enterprises Corp., Jacksonville, 1988-91, Phil Welch Enterprises, Jacksonville, 1989-99, ret., 1999. Cons. ContraTech Corp., Portland, Oreg., 1986-87, Kukje Internat., NYC, 1986, FCI Inc., NJ, 1985, Multiform Products, Inc., Jacksonville, 1989-90, gen. mgr., v.p., 1990-96; pres. Atlantic Office Sources, Inc., Jacksonville, 1996-99, comdr. Am. Legion Post 372, Jacksonville, 2003, 04. Contbr. articles to profl. jours. Served with USAF, 1950—54. Named Man of Decade Audio/Video Cons. USA, 1982, Man of Yr. Soc. Audio Cons., 1974. Republican. Avocations: flying, golf. Home and Office: 12821 Julington Forest Dr W Jacksonville FL 32258-3454 Office Phone: 904-608-6073. E-mail: tinkersall@aol.com.

WELCH, RAQUEL, actress; b. Chgo., Sept. 5, 1940; d. Arm and Josepha (Hall) Tejada; m. James Westley Welch, May 8, 1959 (div.); children: Damon, Tahnee; m. Patrick Curtis (div.); m. Andre Weinfeld, July 1980 (div.). Actress: (films) including Fantastic Voyage, 1966, One Million B.C, 1967, The Biggest Bundle of Them All, 1968, Fathom, 1967, The Queens, 1967, 100 Rifles, 1969, Magic Christian, 1970, Bedazzled, 1971, Fuzz, 1972, Bluebeard, 1972, Hannie Caulder, 1972, Kansas City Bomber, 1972, Myra Breckinridge, 1970, The Last of Sheila, 1973, The Three Musketeers, 1974 (Golden Globe award for best actress), The Wild Party, 1975, The Four Musketeers, 1975, Mother, Jugs and Speed, 1976, Crossed Swords, 1978, L'Animal, 1979, Chairman of the Board, 1998, (TV movies) The Legend of Walks Far Woman, 1982, Right to Die, 1987, Scandal in a Small Town, 1988, Trouble in Paradise, 1989, Torch Song, 1993, Naked Gun 33 1/3, 1993, Folle d'elle, 1998; (Broadway debut) Woman of the Year, 1982; star Victor/Victoria (on Broadway), 1997; (TV series) Central Park West, 1995; author: The Raquel Welch Total Beauty and Fitness Program, 1984. Address: Innovative Artists 1999 Ave Of Stars Ste 2850 Los Angeles CA 90067-4612

WELCH, REED LYNN, political scientist, educator; b. Wichita Falls, Tex., Dec. 19, 1966; s. Robert Godfrey and Arlene Lynn Welch; m. Jennifer Laura Foess, June 27, 1989; children: Regan, Emily, William, Lindsey, Nathan. BA, Brigham Young U., 1990; PhD, Tex. A&M U., 1997. Instr. Tex. A&M U., Coll. Station, Tex., 1994—2000; prof. polit. sci. We.Tex. A&M U., Canyon, Tex., 2000—. Mem. Lds Ch. Office: West Texas A&M University WTAMU Box 60807 Canyon TX 79016-0001

WELCH, RHEA JO, special education educator; b. Jacksonville, Ill., Jan. 26, 1957; d. James Daniel and Bobbye Jo (Weatherford) W.; 1 child, James Alexander. BA, William Woods U., Fulton, Mo., 1980; cert., U. Ill., Springfield, 1981; postgrad., MacMurray Coll., 1985, 86, 88, So. Ill. U., 1990, 91. Cert. 6-12 tchr., spl. edn., Ill. Tchr. recreational skills Ill. Sch. for Visually Impaired, Jacksonville, 1984; cross categorical tchr. Sangamon Area Spl. Edn. Dist., Springfield, 1988-89; tchr.'s aid Four Rivers Spl. Edn. Dist., Jacksonville, 1981, substitute tchr. spl. edn., 1982-86, tchr. learning disabilities, 1987, tchr. students with severe behavioral disorders, 1989—. Mem. human rights com. Jacksonville Devel. Ctr., 1992—; pub. speaker; project dir. for community svc. programs Garrison Sch., Ill. Adv. Coun. on Voluntary Action-Serve Ill.; originator Class Time Community Svc. Volunteerism Four Rivers Spl. Edn. Dist.; coord. Spl. Olympics Ivan K. Garrison Sch., 1992-93; speaker Ill. Coun. Children With Behavior Disorders, 1997. Vol. ARC, instr. HIV-AIDS, CPR, First Aid. Named Staff Mem. of Month, Ivan K. Garrison Alternative Sch., 1992, 2001; recipient 2 Disting. Svc. citations, 1992; grantee, Kraft Food Co., 1991—92. Mem. Coun. for Exceptional Children, Nat. Soc. for Experiential Edn. Episcopalian. Office: Four Rivers Spl Edn Dist 936 W Michigan Ave Jacksonville IL 62650-3113

WELCH, RICHARD LON See ABELL, RICHARD

WELCH, ROBERT BOND, ophthalmologist, educator; b. Balt., May 24, 1927; s. Robert S.G. and Sally (Bond) W.; m. Elizabeth Truslow, May 30, 1953. AB, Princeton U., 1949; MD, Johns Hopkins U., 1953. Diplomate: Am. Bd. Ophthalmology. Intern in internal medicine Duke U. Hosp., 1953-54; resident in ophthalmology Wilmer Inst., Johns Hopkins U., 1954-57, chief resident in ophthalmology, 1959, co-dir. retina service, 1959-84, dir. retina service, 1984-85; retinal cons. in ophthalmology Walter Reed Army Hosp., 1961—2003, Bethesda Naval Hosp, 1976-99; assoc. prof. ophthalmology Johns Hopkins U.; chmn. dept. ophthalmology Greater Balt. Med. Ctr., 1985-91. Author: (with others) The Wilmer Institute 1925-1975, 1976; author: The Wilmer Opthalmological Institute 1925-2000, 2000; editor Transactions Am. Ophthal. Soc., 1984-91; mem. editorial staff Retina mag., 1980-86. Served with USNR, 1945-47. Recipient Disting. Alumnus award, Johns Hopkins U., 2001, Superior Civilian Svc. award, U.S. Army, 2004. Mem. Am. Ophthal. Soc. (v.p. 1992-93, pres. 1993-94, editor 1984-90), Retina Soc. (pres. 1981-83), Pan. Pacific Surg. Assn. (v.p. 1972-80), Md. Soc. Eye Physicians and Surgeons (pres. 1963-64), Md. Club., Elkridge Club, South River Club. Democrat. Episcopalian. Home: 4409 Atwick Rd Baltimore MD 21210-2811 Office: 86 State Cir Annapolis MD 21401-1906 Office Phone: 410-263-3492.

WELCH, RONNIE SCOTT, health facility administrator; b. San Diego, Oct. 1, 1959; s. Marvin and Evelyn Welch. Student, Brigham Young U., 1987—88; cert. in Bus. Adminstrn., AA in Bus. Adminstrn. with honors, Long Beach City Coll., 1994, AA in Social Scis. with honors, 1995, cert. in Gen. Bus., 2002; BA in Econ., Calif. State U., Long Beach, 2001, cert. in Entrepreneurship, 2002; cert. in Profl. Fiduciary Mgmt. for Conservators, Calif. State U., Fullerton, 2002; postgrad., Coll. Fin. Planning, Greenwood Village, Colo., 2001—; AA in Acctg. with high honors, cert. in Acctg., Long Beach City Coll., 2003. Cert. residential care facility for elderly adminstr., IRS enrolled agt., accredited bus. acct., accredited tax advisor, accredited tax preparer, registered fin. cons., cert. retirement counselor, retirement adminstr., bus. mgr. Adminstr., CEO, CFO Cerritos Manor, Inc., Long Beach, Calif., 1977—. Recipient Mayor's Cert. of Award for contbns. to elderly, City of Signal Hill, Calif., 1993. Mem.: Nat. Assn. Tax Profls., Nat. Soc. Accts., Internat. Assn. Registered Fin. Cons., Fin. Planning Assn., Am. Fin. Assn., Am. Tax Assn., Am. Acctg. Assn., Inst. Internal Auditors, Inst. Mgmt. Accts., Golden Key, Omicron Delta Epsilon (mem. Tau chpt.). Avocations: reading, writing, jogging, walking. Office: Cerritos Manor Inc 1046 East Fourth St Long Beach CA 90802-1634 E-mail: rscottwelch@cs.com.

WELCH, ROSS MAYNARD, plant physiologist, researcher, educator; b. Lancaster, Calif., May 8, 1943; s. Lloyd C. and Theda W. (Slane) W.; m. Jill Susanne Varley, Aug. 22, 1965; children: Renell Cherie, Brent Ross BS, Calif. Poly. U., 1966; MS, U. Calif., Davis, 1969, PhD, 1971. Plant physiologist Agrl. Rsch. Svc. USDA, Ithaca, NY, 1971—; rsch. assoc. Cornell U., Ithaca, 1971—75, asst. prof. plant nutrition, 1975—81, assoc. prof. plant nutrition, 1981—87, prof., 1987—, co-organizer food sys. for improved health program Coll. Agr. and Life Scis., 1994—2000. Disting. vis. scientist Murdoch U., Perth, Australia, 1980-81; vis. disting. scholar and lectr. U. Adelaide, Australia, 1991—. Editor: Crops as Sources of Nutrients for Humans, 1984; co-editor: Micronutrients in Agriculture, 2d edit., 1989; contbr. over 160 rsch. articles and 55 rev. articles to profl. jours. Recipient Outstanding Scientist of Yr. award, USDA Agrl. Rsch. Svc., 2003. Fellow: Soil Sci. Soc. Am., Am. Soc. Agronomy (rsch. award N.E. br. 1992); mem.: AAAS, Am. Soc. Agronomy, Corp. Sci. Soc. Am., Am. Soc. Assn., Am. Soc. Plant Physiologists, Masons (master 1984—85), Sigma Xi. Republican. Mem. United Ch. of Christ. Achievements include discovery that nickel is an essential element for all higher plants; discovery that zinc plays a role in maintaining the integrity of root-cell plasma membranes. E-mail. Home: 24 Hickory Cir Ithaca NY 14850-9673 Office: US Plant Soil & Nutrition Lab Tower Rd Ithaca NY 14853 Office Phone: 607-255-5434. Business E-Mail: rmw1@cornell.edu.

WELCH, STANTON, performing company executive; b. Melbourne, Australia, Oct. 15, 1969; s. Garth Welch and Marilyn Jones. Studied at, San Francisco Ballet Sch. Dancer to soloist Australian Ballet, 1989, resident choreographer, 1995—2003; artistic dir. Houston Ballet, 2003—. Artistic assoc. Ballet Met, Columbus, Ohio. Created commissions for many of the world's best companies including American Ballet Theater, Houston Ballet, San Francisco Ballet, Royal Danish Ballet, Australian Ballet et al. Avocations: country music, country and western dancing. Office: Houston Ballet 1921 W Bell St Houston TX 77019

WELCH, THOMAS ANDREW, international and domestic commercial arbitrator; b. Lincoln, Nebr., Dec. 22, 1936; s. Lawrence William and Edna Alberta (Tangeman) W.; m. Ann Reinecke, Sept. 12, 1959; children: Jonathan Thomas, Michael Andrew, Susan Jennifer. Student, Stanford U., 1955-56; BA, UCLA, 1959; JD, Harvard U., 1965. Bar: Calif. 1966, U.S. Dist. Ct. (no. dist.) Calif. 1966, U.S. Ct. Appeals (9th cir.) 1966, U.S. Supreme Ct. 1976. Assoc. Brobeck, Phleger & Harrison, San Francisco, 1965-71, ptnr., 1972-96; ret., 1996. Bd. dirs. Ctr. Internat. Dispute Resolution, Honolulu. Bd. dirs. Youth Law Ctr., San Francisco, 1990—. Lt. USNR, 1959-66. Mem. ABA, Calif. Bar Assn., Am. Law Inst., Am. Arbitration Assn. (large complex case panel of neutrals). Republican. Presbyterian. Home and Office: 449 S Clovercrest Lane San Ramon CA 94583-5505 E-mail: thomwelch@comcast.net.

WELCH, THOMAS ROBERT, pediatrician, educator; s. Robert Hart and Katherine O'Brien Welch; m. Carolyn Christine Sterling, June 24, 1972; children: Timothy Patrick, Elizabeth Kathleen. BA (suma cum laude), Princeton U., 1969; MD, CM, McGill U., Montreal, Que., 1973. Cert. Am. Bd. of Pediat., 1979, Pediat. Nephrology Am. Bd. of Pediat., 1988. Prof. of pediat., dir. pediatric nephrology Children's Hosp. Med. Ctr., Cin., 1981—2001; prof. and chair, dept. of pediat. Upstate Med. U., Syracuse, NY, 2001—. Nat. adv. bd. The Wilderness Edn. Assn., Bloomington, Ind., 2001—. Assoc. editor The Jour. of Pediats., 1995—. Recipient Recognition award, Med. Soc. of the County of Herkimer, N.Y., 1981, Louise M. Williams Professorship of Pediat., Cin. Children's Hosp. Med. Ctr., 1994. Fellow: Am. Acad. of Pediat.; mem.: Am. Assn. of Immunologists, Am. Pediatric Soc., Soc. for Pediatric Rsch., Wilderness Edn. Assn. (nat. adv. bd. 2001). Avocations: professional wilderness guiding, challenge (ropes) course facilitation, marathon running, scuba diving. Office: Upstate Med Univ 750 E Adams St Syracuse NY 13210 Office Phone: 315-464-7526. E-mail: welcht@upstate.edu.

WELCH, WILLIAM CHARLES, neurosurgeon; b. NYC, Mar. 24, 1961; s. William Barker and Carolyn W. (Ferrandino) Welch; m. Bonnie Katz, Apr. 18, 1998; children: Kimberly Carolyn, Rachel Lauren. BS, CCNY, 1983; MD, SUNY Downstate Med. Ctr., Bklyn., 1985. Intern gen. surgery, resident neurosurgery Stong Meml. Hosp., Rochester, NY, 1985-91; fellow neurosurgical oncology, spinal surgery Montefiore Med. Ctr., Bronx, NY, 1991-93; asst. prof. neurologic surgery U. Pitts. Presbyn. U. Hosp., 1993-98, co-dir. spine splty. ctr., 1995-2000, dir. neurosurg. spine svcs., 1997—, assoc. prof. neurologic, orthop. surgery, sch. rehab. scis., 1998—2004, dir. spine splty. ctr., 1999—2002, chief of neurol. surgery, 2002—, prof., 2004—; prof. neurologic orthopedic surgery U. Pitts. Presbyn. U. Hosp. Sch. Rehab. Scis., 2004—. Chief editor Operative Spine Surgery, 1999. Lt. comdr. USNR, 1988-98. Office: Dept Neurol Surgery U Pitts Presbyn Univ Hosp 200 Lothrop St Pittsburgh PA 15213-2546 Office Phone: 412-647-0987. E-mail: welchwc@upmc.edu.

WELCHER, ROSALIND, artist, author; b. NYC, Oct. 21, 1922; d. Peter and Ida (Rubenstein) W.; m. Fred M. Salvic, Nov. 14, 1945. BA, Hunter Coll., 1942. Editor Joan & Ginger's Mag., 1944; freelance illustrator various mags. including McCalls, Today's Woman, Glamour, 1944-46; co-organizer, art dir. Panda Prints, Inc., N.Y.C., 1946-77; art dir., ptnr. Fisher Hill Studios, Fitzwilliam, N.H., 1977—. Author, illustrator: The Runaway Angel Angel, 1963, The Split-Level Child, 1963, The Magic Top, 1965, It's Wonderful To Be in Love, 1966, Have You Ever Been Lonely, 1967, Somebody's Thinking of You, 1967, Please Don't Feel Blue, 1967, 68, I Wish You a Merry Christmas, 1967, Squeaking By, 1969, There is Nothing Like a Cat, 1968, When You're Away, 1969, Moonlight Cobwebs and Shadows, 1969, The Wonderful Season, 1970, Thank You for So Many Things, 1970, Do You Believe in Magic, 1971, Maybe the Sky is Falling, 1970, This Could Be Such a Beautiful World, 1970, It Must Be Hard to Be a Mother, 1971, I Want to Be Somebody's Cat, 1986, My Brother Says There's a Monster Living in Our Toilet, 1987, Dear Tabby, 1989, Social Insecurities, 1989, (video) When Nino Flew, 1997 (One of the Ten Best Videos 1997), The Fluffy Files, 2002, Cat People, 2003. Named to Hunter Coll. Hall of Fame. Mem. Phi Beta Kappa, Ocean Cruising Club (London), Stavenger Club (Norway), Yacht. Home and Office: Fisher Hill 572 Rhododendron Rd Fitzwilliam NH 03447-3039 Office Phone: 603-585-6883. Business E-Mail: rws@cheshirenet.com.

WELD, JONATHAN MINOT, lawyer; b. Greenwich, Conn., Feb. 25, 1941; s. Alfred White and Sally (Duggan) W.; m. Jane Paige, June 19, 1965; children: Elizabeth, Eric. AB in History cum laude, Harvard U., 1963; JD, Cornell U., 1967. Bar: NY 1967, U.S. Ct. Appeals (2d cir.) 1969, U.S. Dist. Ct. (ea. and so. dists.) NY 1970. Assoc. Shearman & Sterling, NYC, 1967-75, ptnr., 1976—, London, 1982-85. Bd. dirs. Bank of N.S. Internat.; chmn., bd. dirs. The Evergreens, Bklyn. Hosp. Bd. dirs. St. Ann's Sch., Bklyn. Bot. Garden, NY Presbyn. Healthcare Sys.; former bd. dirs. Bklyn. Home for Children, Harvard Coll. Fund, Winant and Clayton Vols. Mem.: ABA, NY State Bar Assn. Office: 599 Lexington Ave Fl C2 New York NY 10022-6030 Office Phone: 212-848-8075. Business E-Mail: jweld@shearman.com.

WELD, ROGER BOWEN, retired religious organization administrator; b. Greenfield, Mass., Dec. 1, 1953; s. Wayland Mauney and Luvycie (Bowen) W.; m. Patricia Ann Kaminski, June 7, 1978 (div. 1979); m. Cynthia Lou Lang, Apr. 15, 1995 (div. 2001). Grad., Sacred Acad. Jamilian U. of the Ordained, Reno, 1976-77, Seminary, 1978-82; student, U. Nev., 1983-85; postgrad., Sacred Coll. Jamilian Theology, 1988-90. Ordained to ministry Internat. Cmty. of Christ Ch. of Second Advent, 1977, appointed Rabim priest Internat. Cmty. of Christ, 1993. Adminstrv. staff Internat. Cmty. of Christ Ch. of Second Advent, Reno, 1977—, exec. officer dept. canon law, 1985—2001, exec. officer advocates for religious rights and freedoms, 1985—, exec. officer spkrs. bur., 1985—2001, exec. officer office pub. info., 1986—2001, mgr. Jamilian Univ. Press, 1987—, dir. advt. prodns., 1988—; founder, pres. Crown Rsch. Found., 1992—; now ret. Mem. Chamber of Concerned Christians for Separation of Ch. and State. Author: Twelve Generations of the Family of Weld: Edmund to Wayland Mauney, 1986, A Steamboat in the Desert--A History of Steamboat Springs, Nevada, 1998; dir. photography, supervising editor: (video documentary) Gene Savoy's Royal Roads to Discovery, 1993, The Gran Vilaya Expeditions, Reclaiming a Legendary Lost City From the High Jungles of Peru, 1996. Staff sgt. USAF, 1971-75. Named Life Mem., Sacred Oversee, 1991. Mem.: Nev. Clergyman's Assn., Andean Explorers Found. (Explorer's medal 1990), Ocean Sailing Club (exec. sec. 1988—94, v.p. 1994—2001, vice-commodore 2001—, Participant's Silver Medallion 1989, Survivors medal Feathered Serpent III Grand Ophir Sea Expedition 1998, Dolphin award 1999). Avocations: photography, cinematography, videography, print media. Office: Andean Explorers Found & Ocean Sailing Club 16026 S Virginia St Reno NV 89511 Office Phone: 775-853-2031. E-mail: rweld@aefosc.org. *In the volatile arena of international politics, mankind's hope rests upon the acceptance of its spiritual destiny, not dwelling on its material past.*

WELDEN, ARTHUR LUNA, biology professor; b. Birmingham, Ala., Jan. 27, 1927; s. Arthur Luna and Mary Woodson (Smith) W.; m. Frances Merkl Colvin, Aug. 19, 1950; children: Charles Woodson, Arthur Frederick. AB, Birmingham-So. Coll., 1950; MS, U. Tenn., 1951; PhD, U. Iowa, 1954. Asst. prof. Millikin U., Decatur, Ill., 1954-55; instr. in botany Tulane U., New Orleans, 1955-59, asst. prof., 1959-63, assoc. prof., 1963-68, prof. biology, 1968-79, Ida Richardson prof. botany, 1979-93, chmn. dept. biology, 1979-83, prof. emeritus, 1994—. Panel chmn. So. Assembly, Biloxi, Miss., 1970-71; program dir. Mesoam. Ecology Inst., New Orleans, 1982-87. Assoc. editor Tulane Studies in Zoology and Botany, 1966-78; contbr. articles to profl. jours. Served with U.S. Army, 1945-47. Grantee Am. Philos. Soc., 1957, NSF, 1960-75, NSF and Consejo Nacional de Mex., 1976-79, fellow AAAS, 1992; named to Socio Honorario, Sociedad Mexicana de Mex., 1982. Mem. Mycol. Soc. Am. (councilor 1967-69), Orgn. for Tropical Studies (life), Sigma Xi. Democrat. Home: 7826 Willow St New Orleans LA 70118-4056 Office: Tulane U Dept Biology 6823 Saint Charles Ave New Orleans LA 70118-5698

WELDON, DAVID BLACK, company director; b. London, Ont., Can., June 27, 1925; s. Douglas Black and Margaret (Black) W.; m. Ina G. Perry, July 7, 1951; children: Susan, Douglas, Anthony, Mardie, Kate BA with honors, U. Western Ont., London, 1947, LLD (hon.). With Midland Walwyn Inc. and predecessor cos., Toronto, Ont., 1950—; ret. Midland Doherty Fin. Corp. and predecessor cos., Toronto, Ont., 1989; chancellor U. Western Ont., 1984-88, chancellor emeritus, 1994—. Dir. Dover Industries Ltd., Toronto. Trustee Ont. Jockey Club; bd. dirs. Royal Agrl. Winter Fair, Toronto, 1970—, pres., 1980-82. Served with inf. Can. Army, 1944-45 Mem. Order of Can. Progressive Conservative. Anglican. Clubs: Toronto (bd. mgrs. 1983-85), York, Toronto Golf; London Hunt, London; Ristigouche Salmon (Quebec, Que., Can.); Griffith Island Avocations: breeding and racing standardbred horses; fishing; hunting. Home: Prospect Farms Arva ON Canada N0M 1C0 also: 18A Hazelton Ave Apt 408 Toronto ON Canada M5R 2E2

WELDON, DAVID JOSEPH, JR., congressman, physician; b. Amityville, N.Y., Aug. 31, 1953; s. David Joseph and Anna Weldon; m. Nancy Sourbeck, Aug. 18, 1979; children: Kathryn, David. BS, SUNY, Stony Brook, 1978; MD, SUNY, Buffalo, 1981. Intern Letterman Army Med. Ctr., 1981-82, resident in internal medicine, 1982-84; pvt. practice, Melbourne Internal Medical Assoc, 1987—94; mem. 104th Congress from 15th Fla. dist., Washington, 1995—. Pres. Space Coast Family Forum, Melbourne, 1988-91. Elder Zion Christian Fellowship, Palm Bay, Fla., 1991—. Maj. USAR, 1981—. Mem. AMA, ACP, Fla. Med. Assn. Republican. Office: US Ho of Reps 2347 Rayburn Ho Office Bldg Washington DC 20515-0915

WELDON, JEFFREY ALAN, lawyer; b. Billings, Mont., May 6, 1963; s. Richard Allen and Monica (Michaud) Weldon; m. Leslie Helen Boileau, July 7, 1990; 2 children. BA, U. Mont., 1986, MPA, 1994, JD, 1996. State senator, Mont., 1993-97; assoc. atty. Moulton Bellingham, Longo & Mather, P.C., Billings, Mont., 1997-2000; chief legal counsel Office of Pub. Instrn., State of Mont., Helena, 2000—03; legal counsel Billings Pub. Schs., 2003—. Office Phone: 406-247-3768.

WELDON, THEODORE TEFFT, JR., manufacturing executive; b. Evanston, Ill., July 19, 1932; s. Theodore Tefft and Dorothe Galbraith (Stover) W.; m. Barbara Ann Eskilson, Aug. 17, 1957; children: Lisa Courtney Weldon LeFevre, Theodore Tefft III, Margaret Helen, Weldon Wickstrom. BA, Dartmouth Coll., 1954. Retail store salesman Sears Roebuck & Co., Gary, Ind., 1954-58, retail advt. mgr. Kankakee, Ill., 1958-62, sales mgr. Craftsman Chgo., 1962-69, advt. mgr. Craftsman, 1969-70, mktg. mgr. tires, 1970-81, sr. buyer sporting goods, 1981-82, nat. gen. catalog mgr., 1982-86; dir. home TV shopping Sears/QVC, Chgo., 1986-92. Cons. Drake, Beam, Morin, Inc., Chgo., 1992-94, Focus Media, Inc., L.A., 1993-96, Std. Mktg. Corp., Naperville, Ill., 1993-98, King World Direct, L.A., 1993-97, Guthy-Renker, Las Vegas, 1997-98, Sears Roebuck and Co., 1997-2000, Ovation Group, Atlanta, 1997-2003, Home Depot, 1997-98, Kmart, 1997-98, Walmart, 1997-98, Pearle Vision, 1998, 3M, 1998, Tyee, Portland, Oreg., 1998-2000, Target Stores, 1998, Panasonic 1997-2000; v.p. mktg. Link Tools Internat., USA, 1998—, Content = Commerce Inc., 2001-03, pres. Weldon & Weldon, 1992-, pres. Weldon et Fille, 1996-, pres. Weldon & Son, 1998-. Mem. Jr. Achievemnt, Chgo., 1966-68; rep. Winnetka (Ill.) Village Caucus, 1972-74; advisor Children's Theatre of Winnetka, 1972—; pres. Sunset Improvement Assn., Winnetka, 1975—. Avocations: internat. travel, theatre, swimming, biking, golf. Home and Office: 426 Sunset Rd Winnetka IL 60093-4232

WELDON, THOMAS DAVID, medical products manufacturer; b. West Lafayette, Ind., Aug. 17, 1955; s. Norman Ross and Carol Janet (Warne) W.; divorced; children: Marijke Lee, David Joesph, Michael John; m. Cheryl R. Johnson, 2001. BS in Indsl. Enging., Purdue U., 1977; MBA, Ind. U., 1981. Indsl. engr. Sq. D Co., Cedar Rapids, Iowa, 1977-79; instr. Ind. U., Bloomington, 1981-82; corp. strategic planner Key Pharms., Miami, Fla., 1982-84; sr. cons. Arthur Young and Co., Miami, 1984-85, mgr., 1985-87; chmn. Novoste Corp., Atlanta, 1987—, also bd. dirs.; CEO, chmn. The Innovation Factory, Atlanta, 1999—; chmn., mng. ptnr. Accuitive Med. Ventures, 2004—. Pres. contest coordinator Nat. Jr. Achievement Inc., Bloomington, Ind., 1979-87, instr. applied econs., Miami chpt., 1984-87; trustee Bur. Univ., 2001—. Presbyterian. Avocations: collecting artwork and books, volleyball, sailing, tennis. Office: Innovation Factory Ste 200 2750 Premiere Pkwy Duluth GA 30097

WELDON, VIRGINIA V. retired corporate executive, pediatrician; b. Toronto, Sept. 8, 1935; came to U.S., 1937; d. John Edward and Carolyn Edith (Swift) Verral; children: Ann Weldon Doyle, Susan Weldon Mohart. AB cum laude, Smith Coll., 1957; MD, SUNY-Buffalo, 1962; LHD (hon.), Rush U., 1985. Diplomate Am. Bd. Pediat., Am. Bd. Pediatric Endocrinology and Metabolism, Nat. Bd. Med. Examiners (bd. dirs. 1987-89). Intern Johns Hopkins Hosp., Balt., 1962-63, resident in pediatrics, 1963-64; fellow pediatric endocrinology Johns Hopkins U., Balt., 1964-67, instr. pediatrics, 1967-68, Washington U., St. Louis, 1968-69, asst. prof., 1969-73, assoc. prof., 1973-79, prof., 1979-89, v.p. Med. Ctr., 1980-89, dep. vice chancellor med. affairs, 1983-89; v.p. sci. affairs Monsanto Co., St. Louis, 1989, v.p. pub. policy, 1989-93, sr. v.p. pub. policy, 1993-98; dir. Ctr. for Study Am. Bus., Washington U., 1998-99. Mem. gen. clin. rsch. ctrs. adv. com. NIH, Bethesda, Md., 1976—80, mem. rsch. resources adv. coun., 1980—84; advisor Monsanto Co., 1989—98. Contbr. articles to sci. jours. Mem. risk assessment mgmt. commn. EPA, 1992—97; commr. St. Louis Zool. Park, 1983—92; mem. Pres.'s Com. of Advisors on Sci. and Tech., 1994—2000; trustee Calif. Inst. Tech., 1996—, Whitaker Found., 1997—99, St. Louis Sci. Ctr.; bd. dirs., vice chmn., chmn. St. Louis Symphony Orch.; bd. dirs. United Way Greater St. Louis, 1978—90, St. Louis Regional Health Care Corp., 1985—91; mem. adv. com. on agrl. biotech. USDA, 2000—01. Fellow: AAAS, Am. Acad. Pediat.; mem.: St. Louis Med. Soc., Soc. Pediat. Rsch., Endocrine Soc., Am. Pediat. Soc., Assn. Am. Med. Colls. (disting. svc. mem., del., chmn. coun. acad. socs. 1984—85, chmn. assembly 1985—86), Nat. Acads. (nat. assoc.), Inst. Medicine, Knights of Malta, Equestrian Order of Holy Sepulchre, Alpha Omega Alpha, Sigma Xi. Roman Catholic. Home: 242 Carlyle Lake Dr Saint Louis MO 63141-7544

WELDON, W(AYNE) CURTIS (CURT WELDON), congressman; b. Marcus Hook, Pa., July 22, 1947; m. Mary Gallagher; children: Karen, Kristin, Kimberly, Curt, Andrew. BA in Humanities, West Chester State Coll., 1969; AAS in Fire Sci., Del. County C.C., Media, Pa., 1972; state instrn. cert., Cheyney State Coll.; postgrad., Cabrini Coll., Temple U., St. Joseph's U. Lic. tchr. Pa. From tchr. to head tchr. Walnut St. Sch., Darby-Colwyn-William Penn Sch. Dist., Pa., 1972-76; dir. tng. and manpower CIGNA (INA Corp.), Del. County, 1976-87; mayor City of Marcus Hook, 1977-81; councilman Del. County Council, 1981-87, from vice-chmn. to chmn., 1984-87; mem. U.S. Congress from 7th Pa. dist., Washington, 1987—; mem. armed svcs. com. and sci. com., homeland sec. com. Past chmn. Del. Valley Regional Planning Commn.; asst. dir. Elem. Secondary Edn. Act Title I Program, 1972-76; environ. specialist Project KARE, 1972-76; chmn. R&D House Nat. Security Com. Readiness; mem. Com. on Sci. Energy and Environ. Tech.; co-chmn. Congl. Fire Svcs. Caucus, Globe Ocean Protection Task Force, Congl. Missil Def. Caucus, US-FSU Energy Caucus. Named Man of Yr. Chester Bus. and Profl. Assn., Most Effective Freshman Legislator Am. Security Coun., Citizen of the Yr. Del. County C. of C., Clean Air Champion Sierra Club, Man of Yr. Internat. Soc. Fire Protection Engrs., 1988, taxpayers hero Citizen's Against Government Waste; recipient Outstanding Govt. Leadership award Nat. Recycling Coalition, Fed. Legis. award Pa. Dirs. Assn. Community Action Agys., Spirit of Enterprise award U.S. C. of C., Golden Bulldog Watchdogs of Treasury award. Republican. Office: US Ho of Reps 2466 Rayburn Ho Office Bldg Washington DC 20515-0001

WELDON, WILLIAM C. pharmaceutical executive; Grad. Quinnipiac U. With Johnson & Johnson and subs., 1971—92; pres. Ethicon Endo-Surgery, 1992, group chmn., 1995, chmn., pharm. group, 1998; vice-chmn., bd. dirs. Johnson & Johnson, New Brunswick, NJ, 2001—, CEO, 2002—. Mem. Bus. Coun., Bus. Roundtable; bd. dirs., exec. com. mem., treas. Pharm. Rsch. and Manufacturers of Am. Serves Liberty Sci. Center Chmn.'s Adv. Coun.; mem. Sullivan Commn. on Diversity in the Healthcare Workforce; trustee Quinnipiac Univ. Office: Johnson & Johnson 1 Johnson & Johnson Plaza New Brunswick NJ 08933

WELDON, WILLIAM FORREST, electrical and mechanical engineer, educator; b. San Marcos, Tex., Jan. 12, 1945; s. Forrest Jackson and Rubie Mae (Wilson) W.; m. Morey Shepard McGonigle, July 28, 1968; children: William, Embree, Seth Forrest. BS in Engring. Sci., Trinity U., San Antonio, 1967; MSME, U. Tex., 1970. Registered profl. engr., Tex. Engr. Cameron Iron Works, Houston, 1967-68; project engr. Glastron Boat Co., Austin, Tex., 1970-72; chief engr. Nalle Plastics Co., Austin, 1972-73; rsch. engr. U. Tex., Austin, 1973-77, tech. dir. Ctr. Electromechanics, 1977-85, dir. Ctr. Electromechanics, 1985-93, prof., 1985-2000, Josey Centennial prof. in energy resources, 1992-2000, Josey Centennial prof. emeritus, 2000—. Mem. permanent com. Symposium on Electromagnetic Launch Tech., 1978-97, vice chmn., 1995-98, naval rsch. adv. com., 1992-97, 2001-; cons. numerous cos. and govts., 1973—; chief scientist Office Naval Rsch.-Europe, 1998-99; tech. dir. Office Naval Rsch. Internat. Field Office, 1998-99. Contbr. over 285 articles to profl. publs. Bd. dirs. Water Control & Improvement Dist. No. 10, Travis County, Tex., 1984-97. Recipient Peter Mark medal Electromagnetic Launch Symposium, 1986, IR 100 award Indsl. Rsch. mag., 1983, Navy Superior Pub. Svc. award, 1998, 99. Fellow ASME; mem. IEEE (sr.), NSPE. Achievements include 38 patents for rotating electrical machines, pulsed power, and electromagnetic propulsion.

WELDON-LINNE, C. MICHAEL, pathologist, microbiologist; b. Danville, Ill., Dec. 25, 1953; s. Curtis Lane and A. Charline Linne; m. Madeleine Marie Weldon, Dec. 27, 1976; children: Aleksandra Patrice, Mariel Charline, Alyssa Faith. BS, Northwestern U., 1977, MD, 1978. Diplomate Am. Bd. Pathology, Am. Bd. Med. Examiners. Resident in pathology Evanston (Ill.) Hosp.-Northwestern McGaw Med. Ctr., 1978-81, chief resident in pathology, 1981-82; staff pathologist, dir. microbiology Adv. Ill. Masonic Med. Ctr., Chgo., 1982—, dir. virology, 1982—2002; assoc. chmn., chief divsn. clin. pathology Ill. Masonic Med. Ctr., Chgo., 1994—. Clin. asst. prof. U. Ill., Chgo., 1984—; mem. faculty Nat. Ctr. Advanced Med. Edn., Chgo., 1983—; bd. dirs. Metromed Health Sys., Inc., 1999- 2002; v.p., 2001— 2002. Contbr. chpts. to books, articles to profl. jours. Fellow Am. Soc. Clin. Pathologists, Coll. Am. Pathologists, Am. Soc. Microbiology, Inst. Medicine Chgo.; mem. AMA, Ill. Soc. Pathologists (sec., treas., bd. dirs. 1986-92), Alpha Omega Alpha. Roman Catholic. Avocations: painting, toy soldier collecting, gardening. Office: Adv Ill Masonic Med Ctr 836 W Wellington Ave Chicago IL 60657-9224 E-mail: michael.weldon-linne-md@advocatehealth.com.

WELDON-LINNE, MADELEINE MARIE, lawyer; b. Oak Park, Ill., July 3, 1954; d. William Glynn and Patricia Butler Weldon; m. C. Michael Weldon-Linne, Dec. 27, 1976; children: Aleksandra, Mariel, Alyssa. BS, Northwestern U., 1975; JD, DePaul U., 1981. Bar: Ill., Wis. Atty. Pretzel & Stouffer, Chgo., 1981-84; atty., ptnr. Bullaro & Carton, Chgo., 1984-96; founding ptnr., atty. Weldon-Linne & Vogt, Chgo., 1996—. Author (book rev.) Perspectives in Biology, 2000; contbr. articles to profl. jours. Mem. ABA, Wis. Bar Assn., Profl. Liability Underwriter Soc., Am. Soc. Hosp. Risk Mgmt., Trial Net. Roman Catholic. Office: Weldon-Linne & Vogt Ste 1400 105 W Madison St Chicago IL 60602

WELEBER, RICHARD GORDON, ophthalmologist, geneticist, medical educator, researcher; s. Frederick Joseph and Carolyn Ruth Weleber; m. Barbara Carolyn Berry, Apr. 6, 1968; children: Misha Gordon, Sasha Kristin. BS, Oreg. State U, Corvallis, Oreg., 1959—63; MD, Oreg. Health & Sci. U, Portland, Oreg., 1963—67; Rotating Internship, Mary Fletcher Hosp., U of Vt., Burlington, VT, 1967—68; Fellowship in Genetics, Oreg. Health & Sci. U, Portland, Oreg., 1971—72, Residency in Ophthalmology, 1972—75; Fellowship in Genetics, U of Colo. Med. Ctr., Denver, Colo., 1975—76. Diplomate Am. Bd. of Ophthalmology, 1976, Diplomate, Clinical Genetics Am. Bd. of Med. Genetics, 1981, Founding Fellow Am. Coll. of Med. Genetics, 1993. Instr. in ophthalmology Oreg. Health & Sci. U, Portland, Oreg., 1976—82, assoc. prof. of ophthalmology and molecular and med. genetics, 1982—88, prof. of ophthalmology and molecular and med. genetics, 1988—. Dir. of visual electrophys. svc. Oreg. Health & Sci. U, Portland, Oreg., 1976—, dir., Oreg. retinal degeneration ctr., 1984—, dir. of cataract services, 1978—2002, dir., ophthalmic genetics svc., 1976—. Author 130 peer-rev. jour. articles, 27 book chapt., 115 sci. abstracts. Mem. sci. adv. bd. Found. Fighting Blindness. Maj. US Army MC, 1968—71, Germany. Recipient Francheschetti Award and Lecture, Internat. Soc. for Genetic Eye Disease, 2001. Mem.: Internat. Soc. for Clin. Electrophys. of Vision (assoc.; sec. for the am., dir. of edn. 1998—2002). Avocations: classical music, sports, reading. Office: Casey Eye Inst 3375 SW Terwilliger Blvd Portland OR 97239-4197

WELGE, DONALD EDWARD, food manufacturing executive; b. St. Louis, July 11, 1935; s. William H. and Rudelle (Fritze) W.; m. Mary Alice Childers, Aug. 4, 1962; children: Robert, Tom. BS, La. State U., 1957. With Gilster-Mary Lee Corp., Chester, Ill., 1957—, pres., gen. mgr., 1965—. Dir. Buena Vista Bank of Chester; pres. Buena Vista Bankcorp. Former chmn. St. John's Luth. Bd. Edn. 1st lt. Transp. Corp, U.S. Army, 1958-63. Named So. Ill. Bus. Leader of Yr. So. Ill. U., 1988. Mem. Perryville C. of C. (pres. 1989), Chester, Ill. C. of C. (past pres.), Alpha Zeta, Phi Kappa Phi. Republican. Lutheran. Home: 5 Knollwood Dr Chester IL 62233-1416 Office: Gilster Mary Lee Co PO Box 227 Chester IL 62233-0227

WELK, RICHARD ANDREW, plastic surgeon; b. Aug. 9, 1956; BS, U. Mich., 1977, MD, 1981. Diplomate Am. Bd. Surgery, Am. Bd. Plastic Surgery. Resident gen. surgery, Grand Rapids, Mich., 1981-86; resident plastic surgery U. Calif., Irvine, 1986-88; plastic surgeon pvt. practice, Kirkland, Wash., 1988-91, Polyclinic, Seattle, 1991—. Mem. Am. Soc. Plastic & Reconstructive Surgery, Am. Soc. Aesthetic Plastic Surgery, Wash. State Med. Assn., Wash. Soc. Plastic Surgeons (pres. 1995-96). Office: Polyclinic 1145 Broadway Seattle WA 98122-4299

WELKER, JAMES ANTHONY, physician; b. Pitts., Oct. 27, 1969; s. James Edward and Janet Rachael Welker. BS, Ohio No. U., 1991; DO, Phila. Coll. Osteo. Medicine, 1995. Intern U. Medicine and Dentistry N.J., Stafford, 1995-96; resident in internal medicine Washington Hosp., 1996-99; dir. hospitalist sect., mem. tchg. faculty Harbor Hosp. Ctr., Balt., 1999—. Cons., software developer, Med. Info. Sys.; founding ptnr. real estate investment co.; prin. investigator multi-instnl. clin. trials.; presenter in field. Contbr. articles to profl. jours. Vol. physician Mobile Med. Care, Rockville, 1997-99. Med. scholar Frederick A. Pressott, M.D., 1992-95, Pa. Osteo. Med. Assn., 1994; recipient Preceptor award Am. Coll. of Gen. Practitioners, 1994. Roman Catholic. Avocations: exercising, outdoors. Office: Harbor Hosp Ctr Baltimore MD 21225 Office Phone: 410-350-3668. Personal E-mail: jimwelker@hotmail.com.

WELKOWITZ, WALTER, biomedical engineer, educator; b. Bklyn., Aug. 3, 1926; s. Samuel and Shirley (Rosenblum) W.; m. Joan Horowitz, June 17, 1951; children: David, Lawrence, Julie. BS, The Cooper Union, N.Y.C., 1948; MS, U. Ill., 1949, PhD, 1954. Profl. engr., N.J. Rsch. assoc. U. Ill., Urbana, 1948-54, Columbia U., N.Y.C., 1954-55; asst. to pres., gen. mgr. Gulton Industries, Inc., Metuchen, N.J., 1955-64; prof., chmn. elec. engring. Rutgers U., Piscataway, N.J., 1964-86, prof. biomed. engring., 1986—, chmn. biomedical engring., 1986-90. Cons. Gulton Industries, Metuchen, N.J., 1964-74. Author: Engineering Hemodynamics: Application to Cardiac Assist Devices, 1977, 2d edit., 1987; co-author: Biomedical Instruments: Theory and Design, 1976, 2d edit., 1992; author numerous chpts. in books; contbr. more than 100 articles to profl. jours. With U.S. Navy, 1944-46. Rutgers U. Rsch. Coun. fellow, 1974-75; recipient Centennial medal IEEE, 1984, Excellence in Rsch.

award Rutgers Bd. Trustees, 1985, IEEE Career Achievement award Soc. Engring. Med. Biology, 1991; Llewellyn Thomas vis. prof. U. Toronto, Can., 1989. Fellow IEEE (engring. in medicine and biol. soc. career achievement award 1991), N.Y. Acad. Medicine, Am. Inst. of Medicine and Biol. Engring. Achievements include 26 patents for Electron Tube, Ultrasonic Flowmeter, Ultrasonic Transducer, Piezoelectric Heart Assist Apparatus, Method and Apparatus for Non-Invasive Monitoring Dynamic Cardiac Performance, and others. Home: PO Box 2289 Lenox MA 01240-5289 Office: Rutgers U Biomed Engring PO Box 909 Piscataway NJ 08855-0909 E-mail: wwelkowitz@msn.com.

WELL, IRWIN, language educator; b. Cin., Apr. 16, 1928; s. Sidney and Florence (Levy) Weil; m. Vivian Max, Dec. 27, 1950; children: Martin, Alice, Daniel. BA, U. Chgo., 1948, MA, 1951; PhD, Harvard U., 1960; D (hon.), Nevsky Inst., Petersburg, Russia, 1999. Tchg. fellow Harvard U., Cambridge, Mass., 1955-58; asst. prof. Brandeis U., Waltham, Mass., 1958-65; assoc. prof. Northwestern U., Evanston, Ill., 1966-70, prof. Russian, Russian Lit., 1970—. Pres., bd. dirs. Am. Coun. Tchrs. Russian, Washington, 1967—. Author: numerous books in field; contbr. articles to scholarly jours. Recipient Pushkin medal, Internat. Assn. Russian Profs. Jewish. Avocations: music, singing. Office: Northwestern U Slavic Dept Evanston IL 60208-2163

WELLBERG, EDWARD LOUIS, JR., insurance company executive; b. Eagle Pass, Tex., June 5, 1945; s. Edward L. Wellberg and Nell L. (Kownslar) Walker; children: Elizabeth, Ashley, Jennifer; m. Yvonne Hill, Feb. 4, 1989. Student, St. Mary's U., San Antonio, 1978. CLU, Life Underwriters Tng. Coun. Fellow. Sales agt. Washington Nat. Ins. Co., San Antonio, 1969-82; ptnr. Mazur Bennett Wellberg Assocs., San Antonio, 1982-91; mktg. exec. Wellberg Assocs., San Antonio, 1991—. Bd. dirs. Tex. State Ins. Bd. Adv. Coun., Austin, 1988-94. Contbr. articles to profl. jours. Mem. Am. Soc. CLU's, Tex. Assn. Ins. and Fin. Advisors (bd. dirs. 1983-86, 92-93, pres. 1996, state nat. com. 1997-2000), Tex. Life Underwriters Polit. Action Com. (vice chmn. 1981-83, 88-90, chmn. 1990-92, state nat. committeeman 1997-2000), San Antonio Assn. Ins. and Fin. Advisors (pres. 1982). Home: 1746 Santa Fe Trail San Antonio TX 78232 Office: 14400 Northbrook Dr Ste 200 San Antonio TX 78232-5038 Office Phone: 210-490-1188. E-mail: ed@wellberg.net.

WELLBORN, CHARLES IVEY, science and technology business consultant; b. Houston, Dec. 9, 1941; s. Fred W. and Emily R. (Gladu) W.; m. JD McCausland, Aug. 14, 1965; children: Westly O., Kerry S. Phillips. BA in Econs., U. N.Mex., 1963, JD, 1966; LLM, NYU, 1972. Bar: N.Mex. 1966, U.S. Dist. Ct. N.Mex. 1966. Assoc. Neal & Matkins, Carlsbad, N.Mex., 1966-68, Robinson & Stevens, Albuquerque, 1969-71; ptnr. Schlenker, Parker, Payne & Wellborn, Albuquerque, 1971-76, Parker & Wellborn, Albuquerque, 1976-82, Modrall, Sperling, Roehl, Harris & Sisk, Albuquerque, 1982-95; pres., CEO Sci. & Tech. Corp. at U. N.Mex., Albuquerque, 1995-2000; pres. Wellborn Strategies LLC, Albuquerque, 2000—. Chmn. N.Mex. Tax Rsch. Inst., 2002—, N.Mex. Small Bus. Investment Corp., 2003—. Contbr. articles to law revs. Vice chair U. N.Mex. Found., Inc., 1990—94; mem. Econ. Forum, 1986—2002, chmn., 1995—96; mem. City-County Unification Charter Commn., 2002—03; bd. dirs. N.M. Assn. Commerce & Industry, 2003—, N.Mex. Symphony Orch., 1988—91, U. N.Mex. Anderson Schs. Mgmt. Found., 1989—94, N.Mex. First, 1989—93, 2000—04, Accion N.Mex., 1995—97, Outpost Performance Space, 2000—04; private equity investment adv. com. N.Mex. State Investment Coun., 1991—98; mem. Govs. Prayer Breakfast Com., 1991—2002, chair, 2000—02, N.Mex. Tax Rsch. Inst., 2002—; bd. dirs. Next Generation Economy Inc., 2002—, Sci. and Tech. Corp. at U. N.Mex., 2000—, SharedVision, Inc., 2002—; chair N.Mex. Small Bus. Investment Co., 2003—. Sgt. USAF, 1968—69, Korea. Mem.: ABA (ho. of dels. 1984—91), State Bar N.Mex. (pres. 1982—83), N.Mex. Bar Found. (pres. 1980—82), Albuquerque Bar Assn. (pres. 1977—78). Democrat. Roman Catholic. Office: Wellborn Strategies LLC 3819 La Hacienda Dr NE Albuquerque NM 87110-6115 E-mail: chuckwellborn@hotmail.com.

WELLEN, ROBERT HOWARD, lawyer; b. Jersey City, Aug. 19, 1946; s. Abraham Louis and Helen Rose (Krieger) W.; m. Anita Fass, June 16, 1968; children: Elizabeth, Judith Maria. BA, Yale Coll., 1968; JD, Yale U., 1971; LLM in Taxation, Georgetown U., 1975. Bar: Conn. 1971, D.C. 1972, Colo. 1982. Assoc. Fulbright & Jaworski, Washington, 1975-76, participating assoc., 1976-79, ptnr., 1979-93, Ivins, Phillips & Barker, Washington, 1993—. Adj. prof. law Georgetown U. Law Ctr., 1982-85. Contbr. articles to legal publs. Served to lt. JAGC, USNR, 1971-75. Mem. ABA (past asst. sec., past chmn. com. on corp. tax, sect. taxation, past supr. editor sect. taxation newsletter, vice chair law devel. com. on corp. tax), Fed. Bar Assn. (coun. taxation), Phi Beta Kappa. Jewish. Office: Ivins Phillips & Barker 1700 Pennsylvania Ave NW Washington DC 20006-4704 E-mail: rwellen@ipbtax.com.

WELLER, ELIZABETH BOGHOSSIAN, child and adolescent psychiatrist; b. Aug. 7, 1949; m. Ronald A. Weller, Feb. 18, 1978; children: Andrew, Christine. BS, Am. U., Beirut, Lebanon, 1971, MD, 1975. Lic. psychiatrist, Lebanon, Mo., Ohio, Pa. Intern Am. U. of Beirut, 1974-75; resident Renard Hosp./Washington U., St. Louis, 1975-78; fellow U. Kans. Med. Ctr., Kansas City, 1978-79; asst. prof. psychiatry U. Kans. Med. Sch., Kansas City, 1979-85; chief child/adolescent psychiatry Ohio State U., Columbus, 1985-94, assoc. chair dept. psychiatry, 1994-96; prof. psychiatry and pediat. U. Pa., 1996—, chair dept. psychiatry child and adolescent psychiatry, 1996-99, vice chair dept. psychiatry, prof. psychiatry/pediatrics, 1996—. Fred Allen chair dept. psychiatry Children's Hosp. of Phila., med. dir. Child Guidance Ctr., 1996-99; pres. Am. Bd. Psychiatry and Neurology, 2004. Co-author: Psychiatric Disorders in Child/Adolescent, 1990, Current Perspectives on Major Depressive Disorders in Children, 1984, Children's Interview for Psychiatric Syndromes, 1999. Fellow APA, Am. Acad. Child/Adolescent Psychiatry; mem. AMA, ACP, World Fedn. for Mental Health, Soc. Biol. Psychiatry, Pa. Psychiat. Assn. (pres. 1995). Office: 34th St and Civic Ctr Blvd Philadelphia PA 19104-4399 Office Phone: 215-590-7573. Business E-Mail: weller@email.chop.edu.

WELLER, GERALD C. congressman; b. Streator, Ill., July 7, 1957; s. LaVern and Marilyn Weller. Degree in Agriculture, U. Ill., 1979. Aide to U.S. Congressman Tom Corcoran, 1977-78; aide to U.S. Sec. of Agriculture John R. Block, 1981-85; active family farm, 1985-88; rep. State of Ill., 1988-94; mem. 104th-108th Congresses from 11th Ill. dist., 1994—; asst. majority whip; mem. ways and means com., 1996—; mem. Internat. Relations Com., 2003—. Rep. House Republican steering com.; mem. Newt Gingrich's policy com.; exec. com. NRCC, House Banking Com., House Veterans Affairs Com., House Transp. and Infrastructure Com. Mem. 1st Christian Ch. of Morris, Ill. Mem. Nat. Republican Legis. Assn. (nominated Legislator of Yr.). Republican. Office: US House Reps 1210 Longworth HOB Washington DC 20515-1311

WELLER, GUNTER ERNST, geophysics educator; b. Haifa, June 14, 1934; came to U.S., 1968; s. Erich and Nella (Lange) W.; m. Sigrid Beilharz, Apr. 11, 1963; children: Yvette, Kara, Britta. BS, U. Melbourne, Australia, 1962, MS, 1964, PhD, 1968. Meteorologist Bur. Meteorology, Melbourne, 1959-61; glaciologist Australian Antarctic Exps., 1964-67; from asst. prof. to assoc. prof. geophysics Geophys. Inst., U. Alaska, Fairbanks, 1968-72, prof., 1973-98, dep. dir., 1984-86, 90-98; prof. emeritus Geophys. Inst., U. Ala., Fairbanks, 1998—; project dir. NASA-UAF Alaska SAR Facility, Fairbanks, 1983-93. Program mgr. NSF, Washington, 1972-74; pres. Internat. Commn. Polar Meteorology, 1980-83; chmn. polar rsch. bd. NAS, 1985-90, Global Change Steering Com. Sci. com. on Antarctic Rsch., 1988-92; chmn. Global Change Working Group Internat. Arctic Sci. Com., 1990-97; dir. Ctr. for Global Change and Arctic Sys. Rsch., U. Alaska, 1990—; dir. Coop. Inst. Arctic Rsch., 1994—; exec. dir. Arctic Climate Impact Assessment, Arctic Coun., 2000—. Contbr. numerous articles to profl. jours. Recipient Polar medal Govt. Australia, 1969; Mt. Weller named in his honor by Govt. Australia, Antarctica; Weller Bank named in his honor by U.S. Govt., Arctic. Fellow AAAS (exec. sec. arctic divsn. 1982-93), Arctic Inst. N.Am.; mem. Internat. Glaciological Soc., Am. Meteorol. Soc. (chmn. polar meteorology com. 1980-83), Am. Geophys. Union. Home: PO Box 81024 Fairbanks AK 99708-1024 Office: U Alaska Coop Inst Arctic Rsch Fairbanks AK 99775-7740 E-mail: gunter@gi.alaska.edu.

WELLER, JONATHAN, real estate investment company executive; Degree, Williams Coll., Columbia U. Various positions to exec. v.p. Eastdil Realty, 1970-93; pres., CEO, trustee Pa. Real Estate Investment Trust, Phila., 1993—. Office: Pa Real Estate Investment Trust 200 S Broad St Ste 300 Philadelphia PA 19102-3803*

WELLER, MILTON WEBSTER, wetland ecologist, educator; b. St. Louis, May 23, 1929; m. Doris Laverne Leach; 1 child, Mitchel Wayne. AA, Harris Jr. Coll., 1949; BA, U. Mo., 1951, MS, 1954, PhD, 1956. Instr. dept zoology U. Mo., Columbia, 1956-57, asst. prof. zoology Iowa State U., Ames, 1957-61, assoc. prof., 1961-67, prof.-in-charge wildlife and fish, 1967-74; prof., head fish and wildlife U. Minn., St. Paul, 1974-82; prof., Kleberg chair wildlife Tex. A&M U., College Station, 1982-94, prof. emeritus, 1995—. Dir. Nat. Audubon Soc., N.Y.C., 1987-92; mem. Environ. Steering Com., Tex. Utilities, Dallas, 1990-99; assoc. editor Wetlands, Ann Arbor, Mich., 1988-92. Editor: Waterfowl in Winter, 1988; author: Wetland Birds, 1999; Freshwater Marshes, 1994, 3rd edit.; contbr. chpts. to Wetland Creation & Restoration, 1989, Habitat Use By Breeding Waterfowl, 1992; contbr. articles to profl. jours. Recipient Lifetime Achievement award Soc. Wetland Sci., 1996, Aldo Leopold Meml. award The Wildlife Soc., 1997. Fellow AAAS, Am. Ornithologist Union. Achievements include rsch. in wetland dynamics in relation to wildlife populations and regional biodiversity, wetland restoration and creation, waterbird ecology and management.

WELLER, PHILIP DOUGLAS, lawyer; b. Richmond, Ind., May 5, 1948; s. Lawrence E. and Barbara Jean (Hughes) W.; m. Kathryn Jean Deucker, Apr. 3, 1971; 1 child, Leigh Rachel. Student, Ohio U., 1966-67; BS, Bowling Green State U., 1970; JD, Bates Coll. Law, 1975. Bar: Tex. 1975. Assoc. Vinson & Elkins, Houston, 1975-79, ptnr. Houston, Dallas, N.Y.C., 1980—, Baker, Brown, Sharman, Wise & Stephens, Houston, 1979-80. Speechwriter. Mem. ABA, ACMA, AARPI, ICSC, ULI, Am. Coll. Real Estate Lawyers, Tex. Bar Assn., Houston Bar Assn., Dallas Bar Assn., D.C. Bar Assn., Assn. Bar City N.Y. Office: 2300 First City Tower 1001 Fannin St Houston TX 77002-6760 E-mail: pweller@velaw.com.

WELLER, ROBERT N(ORMAN), hotel executive; b. Harrisburg, Pa., Feb. 1, 1939; s. Charles Walter and Martha Ann (MacPherson) W.; m. Nancy M. Wood, June 21, 1975; children— Wendi Elizabeth, Terrie Lynn, Nikki Ann. BS, Cornell U., 1969. Mgr. Hall's Motor Transit Co., Harrisburg, 1961-65; market rsch. analyst Carrolls Devel. Corp., Syracuse, NY, 1970-72; asst. to pres. Econo-Travel Motor Hotel Corp., Norfolk, Va., 1972-74, dir. franchise sales, 1975, pres., dir., 1976-84, Econo-Travel Devel. Corp., Norfolk, 1977-84; pres. Internat. Data Bank Ltd., 1985-86; pres., dir. Econo Lodges of Am., 1986-90; group pres., exec. v.p. Choice Hotels Internat., Silver Spring, Md., 1990-91; with Hospitality Ventures, Virginia Beach, Va., 1991—93; pres. Super 8 Motels, Inc. divsn. Hospitality Franchise Systems, Parsippany, NJ, 1993—2001; group pres. hotel divsn. Cendant Corp., Parsippany, 2001—. Served in USMC, 1957-60. Home: 3027 Lynndale Rd Virginia Beach VA 23452-6233 Office: Cendant Hotel Group Inc One Sylvan Way Parsippany NJ 07054 Business E-Mail: bob.weller@cendant.com.

WELLER, SOL WILLIAM, chemical engineering educator; b. Detroit, July 27, 1918; s. Ira and Bessie (Wieselthier) W.; m. Miriam Damick, June 11, 1943; children: Judith, Susan, Robert, Ira BS, Wayne State U., 1938; PhD, U. Chgo., 1941. Asst. chief coal hydrogenation U.S. Bur. Mines, Pitts., 1945-50; head fundamental rsch. Houdry Process Corp., Linwood, Pa., 1950-58; mgr. propulsion rsch. Ford Aeronutronic Co., Newport Beach, Calif., 1958-61; dir. chem. lab. and materials rsch. lab. Philco-Ford Co., Newport Beach, 1961-65; prof. chem. engring. SUNY-Buffalo, 1965—; emeritus, 1989; C.C. Furnas prof. SUNY-Buffalo, 1983—. Vis. fellow Oxford U., 1989. Author numerous sci. papers, book chpts., ency. entries Fulbright lectr. Madrid, 1975, Istanbul, 1980 Mem. Am. Chem. Soc. (chmn. Orange County sect. 1964, H.H. Storch award 1981, E.V. Murphree award 1982, Schoellkopf medal 1984, Dean's award 1991), ASTM (founder com. D32 on catalysts). Achievements include patents in field. Office: SUNY Buffalo 305 Furnas Hall Buffalo NY 14260-4200

WELLER, THOMAS HUCKLE, physician, former educator; b. Ann Arbor, Mich., June 15, 1915; s. Carl V. and Elsie A. (Huckle) Weller; m. Kathleen R. Fahey, Aug. 18, 1945; children: Peter Fahey, Nancy Kathleen, Robert Andrew, Janet Louise. AB, U. Mich., 1936; MS, 1937, LL.D. (hon.), 1956; MD, Harvard, 1940; Sc.D., Gustavus Adolphus U., 1975, U. Mass., 1985; L.H.D., Lowell U., 1977. Diplomate Am. Bd. Pediatrics. Teaching fellow bacteriology Harvard Med. Sch., 1940—41, research fellow tropical medicine, pediatrics, 1947—48, instr. comparative pathology, tropical medicine, 1948—49, asst. prof. tropical pub. health Sch. Pub. Health, 1949—50, assoc. prof., 1950—54, Richard Pearson Strong prof. tropical pub. health, 1954—85, prof. emeritus, 1985—, head dept., 1954—81; intern bacteriology and pathology Children's Hosp., Boston, 1941, intern medicine, 1942, asst. resident medicine, 1946, asst. dir. research div. infectious diseases, 1949—55; mem. commn. parasitic diseases Armed Forces Epidemiol. Bd., 1953—72, dir., 1953—59. Contbr. articles to sci. jours. Maj. M.C. U.S. Army, 1942—46. Named Stern Symposium honoree, 1972; recipient Mead Johnson award for devel. tissue culture procedures in study virus diseases, Am. Acad. Pediats., 1953, Kimble Methodology award, 1954, Nobel Prize in physiology and medicine, 1954, George Ledlie prize, 1963, Weinstein Cerebral Palsy award, 1973, Bristol award, Infectious Diseases Soc. Am., 1980, Gold medal and diploma of honor, U. Costa Rica, 1984, First Sci. Achievement award, VZV Rsch. Found., 1993, Walter Reed medal, Am. Soc. Tropical Medicine, 1996. Fellow: Am. Acad. Arts and Scis., Royal Soc. Tropical Medicine and Hygiene (hon.); mem.: NAS Inst. Medicine, Am. Soc. Tropical Medicine and Hygiene, Assn. Am. Physicians, Am. Pediat. Soc., Am. Epidemiol. Soc., Harvey Soc., NAS, AMA, Alpha Omega Alpha, Sigma Xi, Phi Beta Kappa. Home and Office: 56 Winding River Rd Needham MA 02492-1025

WELLES, JUDITH, public affairs executive; b. N.Y.C., Jan. 15, 1946; d. John and Millicent (Richman) Welles; m. Alan M. Bekelman, 1966 (div. 1994); children: David Bekelman, Justin Bekelman; m. Timothy P. Shank, Apr. 18, 1998; 1 child, Jenica Shank. BA, Vassar Coll., 1963. Speechwriter, editor U.S. Dept. Interior, Washington, 1965-66; asst. to dir. VISTA, Washington, 1967-70; speechwriter to sec. HHS, Washington, 1971-76, mgr. pub. affairs, 1977-86; dir. comm. and pub. affairs Pension Benefit Guaranty Corp., Washington, 1987-2000; worklife editor, sr. reporter PlanetGov.com, Fairfax, Va., 2000—. Commr. County Health Planning Commn., Md., 1986-88. Recipient 1st place ann. report competition Fin. World, 1991, 92. Mem. Nat. Assn. Govt. Communicators (Gold Screen award 1992, award of Excellence 1994). Office: PlanetGov.com 14155 Newbrook Dr Chantilly VA 20151-2224 E-mail: Jwelles@planetgov.com.

WELLFORD, HARRY WALKER, retired federal judge; b. Memphis, Aug. 6, 1924; s. Harry Alexander and Roberta Thompson (Prothro) Wellford; m. Katherine E. Potts, Dec. 8, 1951; children: Harry Walker, James B., Buckner P., Katherine T., Allison R. Student, U. N.C., 1943—44; BA, Washington and Lee U., 1947; postgrad., U. Mich., 1947—48; LLD, Vanderbilt U., 1950. Bar: Tenn. 1950. Atty. McCloy, Myar & Wellford, Memphis, 1950—60, McCloy, Wellford & Clark, Memphis, 1960—70; judge U.S. Dist. Ct., Memphis, 1970—82, U.S. Ct. Appeals (6th cir.), Cin. and Memphis, 1982—92, sr. judge, 1992—2002, ret., 2002. Chmn. Tenn. Hist. Commn., Tenn. Constnl. Bicentennial Commn., 1987—88; charter drafting com. City of Memphis, 1967, Tenn. Am. Revolution Bicentennial Commn., 1976; com. on adminstrn. fed. magistrates sys. Jud. Conf. Subcom. Adminstrn. Criminal Law Probation; clk. session, commr. Gen. Assembly; campaign chmn. Senator Howard Baker, 1964—66; elder Presbyn. Ch.; moderator Memphis Presbytery, 1994. Recipient Sam A. Myar award, Memphis State Law U., 1963. Mem.: Omega Delta Kappa, Phi Beta Kappa.

WELLIN, KEITH SEARS, investment banker; b. Grand Rapids, Mich., Aug. 13, 1926; s. Elmer G. and Ruth (Chamberlin) W.; m. Carol D. Woodhouse, Sept. 5, 1951 (dec. 1970), m. Wendy C.H. Lane, Nov. 15, 2002; children: Cynthia Wellin Plum, Peter, Marjorie Wellin King. BA, Hamilton Coll., 1950; MBA, Harvard U., 1952. With E.F. Hutton & Co., Inc., Chgo., 1952-71, regional v.p., dir., 1962-66, pres., 1967-71, vice chmn., 1970-71; sr. v.p., treas., dir. Reynolds Securities Inc., 1971-74, pres., dir., 1974-78; exec. v.p., dir. Dean Witter Reynolds Orgn., from 1978; chmn. Dean Witter Reynolds Inter-Capital, from 1978; former vice chmn. Dean Witter Reynolds Inc. Chmn. bd. Moorco Internat., Houston; former gov., mem. exec. com. Assn. Stock Exchange Firms; mem. governing council Securities Industry Assn. Mem. investment com., trustee Hamilton Coll. Served to 2d lt., inf. AUS, 1945-47. Mem.: Knickerbocker (N.Y.C.); Clove Valley Rod and Gun (La Grangeville, N.Y.); Round Hill (Greenwich, Conn.); River Club. Home (Summer): Seaside Farm PO Box 335 Friendship ME 04547-0335 Office: c/o Dean Witter Reynolds 1345 Avenue Of The Americas New York NY 10105-0302 Home: John's Island 161 Coquille Way Vero Beach FL 32963

WELLIN, THOMAS, music director; m. Annette Wellin; children: Claire, Christopher, Patrick. BMus summa cum laude, Ind. U.; MMus, U. Maine; postgrad., Acad. Mus. Chigiana, Siena, Italy; studied with Julius Herford, Ruggiero Ricci, Franco Rerrara, Gustav Meier. Music dir., condr. Bismarck (N.D.)-Mandan Symphony Orch., 1990—. Guest condr. Fargo-Moorhead Symphony; lectr. in field. Condr. summer concerts Pops on the Prairie, New Year's Eve Viennese Gala, Dickinson State U., I-94 Music Festival, Beulah, N.D., 4th of July Spectacular on State Capitol Mall, (CD) Vivaldi's The Four Seasons. Performing Artists fellow N.D. Coun. Arts. Office: Bismarck-Mandan Symphony Orch PO Box 2031 Bismarck ND 58502 2031

WELLING, KATHRYN MARIE, editor; b. Ft. Wayne, Ind., Feb. 4, 1952; d. Arthur Russell Sr. and Genevieve (Disser) W.; m. Donald Robert Boyle, Oct. 21, 1978; children: Brian Joseph, Thomas Arthur. BS in Journalism, Northwestern U., 1974. Copy reader Dow Jones News Retrieval, N.Y.C., 1974-75; copy reader/reporter AP-Dow Jones, N.Y.C., 1975-76; copy editor Wall Street Jour., N.Y.C., 1976; reporter Barron's, N.Y.C., 1976-81, asst. to editor, 1981, mng. editor, 1982-92, assoc. editor, 1992—99; ltd. ptnr. Weeden & Co. L.P., Greenwich, Conn., 1999—; editor, pub. Welling@Weeden, Greenwich, 1999—. Columnist Welling's Acute Observations, Traders Magazine. Charter mem. Northwestern U. Coun. of One Hundred. Avocations: sailing, skiing. Office: Weeden & Co LP 145 Mason St Greenwich CT 06830 Office Phone: 203-861-7600. E-mail: welling@weedenco.com.

WELLINGTON, CAROL STRONG, law librarian; b. Altadena, Calif., Jan. 30, 1948; d. Edward Walter and Elizabeth (Leonards) Strong; m. David Heath Wellington, May 27, 1978; one child, Edward Heath. BA, Lake Forest Coll., Ill., 1969; MLS, Simmons Coll., 1973. Libr. Hill and Barlow, Boston, 1973—88, Peabody and Arnold, LLP, Boston, 1988—2002, Day, Berry, and Howard, LLP, Boston, 2002—. Mem.: Law Librs., Spl. Librs. Assn., Assn. Boston Law Librs. (v.p. 1979—80, pres. 1980—81), Am. Assn. Law Librs. Office: Day Berry and Howard LLP 260 Franklin St Boston MA 02110 Office Fax: 617 345 4745. Business E Mail: cswellington@dbh.com.

WELLINGTON, HARRY HILLEL, lawyer, educator; b. New Haven, Aug. 13, 1926; s. Alex M. and Jean (Ripps) W.; m. Sheila Wacks, June 22, 1952; children: John, Thomas. AB, U. Pa., 1947; LLB, Harvard U., 1952; MA (hon.), Yale U., 1960; LLD, N.Y. Law Sch. Bar: D.C. 1952. Law clk. to U.S. Judge Magruder, 1953-54, Supreme Ct. Justice Frankfurter, 1955-56; asst. prof. law Stanford U., 1954-56; mem. faculty Yale U., 1956—, prof. law, 1960—, Edward J. Phelps prof. law, 1967-83, dean Law Sch., 1975-85, Sterling prof. law, 1983-92, Sterling prof. emeritus law, 1992—, Harry H. Wellington prof. lectr., 1995—; pres., dean, prof. law N.Y. Law Sch., N.Y.C., 1992-2000, dean emeritus, prof., 2000—. Ford fellow London Sch. Econs., 1965; Guggenheim fellow; sr. fellow Brookings Instn., 1968-71; Rockefeller Found. fellow Bellagio Study and Conf. Ctr., 1984; faculty mem. Salzburg Seminar in Am. Studies, 1985; John M. Harlan disting. vis. prof. N.Y. Law Sch., 1985-86; review person ITT-SEC; moderator Asbestos-Wellington Group; cons. domestic and fgn. govtl. agys.; trustee N.Y. Law Sch.; bd. govs. Yale U. Press; mem. jud. panel, exec. com. Ctr. Public Resources Legal Program; Harry H. Wellington lectr., 1995—. Author: with Harold Shepherd) Contracts and Contract Remedies, 1957, Labor and the Legal Process, 1968, (with Clyde Summers) Labor Law, 1968, 2d edit., 1983, (with Ralph Winter) The Unions and the Cities, 1971, Interpreting the Constitution, 1990; contbr. articles to profl. jours. Mem. ABA, Bar Assn. Conn., Am. Law Inst., Am. Arbitration Assn., Am. Acad. Arts and Scis., Common Cause (nat governing bd.). Office: NY Law Sch 57 Worth St New York NY 10013-2959 also: Yale U Sch Law New Haven CT 06520

WELLINGTON, ROBERT HALL, manufacturing executive, director; b. Atlanta, July 4, 1922; s. Robert H. and Ernestine V. (Vossbrinck) W.; m. Marjorie Jarchow, Nov. 15, 1947; children: Charles R., Robert H., Christian J., Jeanne L. BS, McCormack Sch. of Engring. and Applied Scis. (formerly Northwestern Tech. Inst.), 1944; MSBA, MBA, U. Chgo., 1958. With Griffin Wheel Co., 1946-61; v.p. parent co. Amsted Industries, Inc., Chgo., 1961-74, exec. v.p., 1974-80, pres., chief exec. officer, 1981-88, chmn. bd., chief exec. officer, 1988-90. Served to lt. USN, 1943-46. Office: Amsted Industries Inc 205 N Michigan Ave Fl 44 Chicago IL 60601-5927

WELLINGTON, SHEILA WACKS, foundation administrator, psychiatry educator; b. N.Y.C., Feb. 24, 1932; d. Louis and Rose Feldman; m. Harry Hillel Wellington, June 22, 1952; children: John, Thomas. BA in Polit. Sci., Wellesley Coll., 1952; traineeship, USPHS, 1966-68; MUS, MPH, Yale U., 1968. Lectr. dept. psychiatry Sch. Medicine Yale U., New Haven, 1974-93; dir. Hill-West Haven div. Conn. Mental Health Ctr., 1977-80, Greater Bridgeport Community Mental Health Ctr., 1980-86; sec. Yale U., New Haven, Conn., 1987-93; pres. Catalyst, N.Y.C., 1993—. Mem. plan and rev. pnel Pres.'s Com. Mental Health; mem. exec. com. Conn. conf. Ind. Colls., Am. Coll. Mental Health Adminstrn.; fellow Berkeley Coll.; trustee Nuveen Select Portfolios. Contbr. articles to profl. jours. Bd. dirs. N.Y. Women's Agenda, Bus. Coun. N.Y. State, Inst. for Women's Policy Rsch. Recipient New Haven Mayoral Citation for Cmty. svc., 1981, Conn. Gov.'s Com. to Employ Handicapped Outstanding Svc. award, 1984, Ofcl. Citation Gen. Assembly of Conn., 1985, Spl. Citation for Pub. Svc. Gov. William O'Neill, 1986, New Haven YWCA Women in Leadership award, 1990, Marrakech Founders award, 1990, Elm Ivy award, 1993. Mem. Phi Beta Kappa. Home: 249 E 48th St Apt 16C New York NY 10017-1535 Office: Catalyst 120 Wall St Fl 5 New York NY 10005-3904

WELLINGTON, WILLIAM GEORGE, entomologist, ecologist, educator; b. Vancouver, B.C., Can., Aug. 16, 1920; s. George and Lilly (Rae) W.; m. Margret Ellen Reiss, Sept. 22, 1959; children: Katherine Jean, Stephen Ross. BA, U. B.C., 1941; MA, U. Toronto, 1945, PhD, 1947. Meteorol. officer Can. Meteorol. Svc., Toronto, 1942-45; rsch. entomologist Can. Dept. Agr., Sault Sainte Marie, 1946-51; head bioclimatology sect. Can. Dept. Forestry, Sault Sainte Marie, Ont., Victoria, 1951-67, prin. scientist Victoria, 1964-68; prof. ecology U. Toronto, Toronto, 1968-70; dir. Inst. Animal Resource Ecology, U. B.C., Vancouver, 1973-79, prof. plant sci. and resource ecology, 1970-86, hon. prof. dept. plant sci., 1986—, prof. emeritus, 1986—; Killam sr. rsch. fellow U. B.C., 1980-81. Inaugural lectr. C.E. Atwood Meml. Seminar Series, Dept. Zoology, U. Toronto, 1993; vis. prof. NC State U., 1972, 75, 81, San Diego State U., 1975, Laval U., 1981, U. Calgary, 1983, Simon Fraser U., 1987. Contbr. articles to profl. jours. Fellow Entomol. Soc. Can. (pres. 1976-78, Gold medal 1968), Royal Soc. Can., Explorers Club; mem. Am. Meteorol. Soc. (award 1969), Entomol. Soc. Am. (C. J. Woodworth award 1979), Japanese Soc. Population Ecology, Entomol. Soc. Ont., Am. Philatelic Soc. Club. Anglican. Home: 1010 W 42d Ave # 305 Vancouver BC Canada V6M 2A8 Office: U BC ARE and Dept Plant Sci Vancouver BC Canada V6T 1W5

WELLISZ, STANISLAW, economics professor; b. Warsaw, Mar. 28, 1925; came to U.S., 1941; s. Leopold and Jadwiga (Landau) W.; m. Anna Blaszkiewicz; children: Tadeusz, Krzyszrof. BA magna cum laude, Harvard

Coll., 1946, MA, 1949; postgrad., U. Cambridge, England, 1949-52; PhD, Harvard U., 1953; D (hon.), Warsaw U., 1998. Asst. prof. U. Chgo., 1957-60, assoc. prof., 1960-63; prof. Columbia U., N.Y.C., 1964-94, Kathryn and Shelby Cullom Davis prof. econs. & internat. affairs, 1994—. Vis. prof. Warsaw U., 1989-97; adv. Polish Minister Fin., 1989-91. Author: The Economics of the Soviet Bloc, 1964; co-author: The Political Economy of Growth, 1993; co-editor: Stabilization in Poland, 1993. NSF fellow, 1975, 82; named officer Polish Order Merit, Govt. Poland, 1997. Office: Columbia U Dept Econs New York NY 10027 Office Phone: 212-854-8033. Business E-Mail: SW11@columbia.edu.

WELLIVER, CHARLES HAROLD, hospital administrator; b. Wichita, Kans., Feb. 14, 1945; married. BA, Wichita State U., 1972; MHA, U. Mo., 1974. Asst. dir. St. Luke's Hosp., Kansas City, 1974-79, assoc. dir., 1979-80; adminstr. Spelman Meml. Hosp., Smithville, Mo., 1980-82; sr. adminstr., COO Good Samaritan Med. Ctr., Phoenix, 1982-86, v.p., CEO, 1989—, Thunderbird Samaritan Hosp., Glendale, Ariz., 1986-89; exec. vice-chmn., COO Good Samaritan Med. Ctr., Glendale. Office: Good Samaritan Regional Med Ctr 1441 N 12th St Phoenix AZ 85006-2837

WELLIVER, WARREN DEE, lawyer, retired state supreme court justice; b. Butler, Mo., Feb. 24, 1920; s. Carl Winfield and Burdee Marie (Wolfe) W.; m. Ruth Rose Galey, Dec. 25, 1942; children: Gale Dee (Mrs. William B. Stone), Carla Camile (Mrs. Dayton Stone), Christy Marie. BA, U. Mo., 1945; JD, U. Mo., 1948. Bar: Mo. 1948. Asst. pros. atty. Boone County, Columbia, 1948-54; sr. ptnr. Welliver, Atkinson and Eng, Columbia, 1960-79; tchr. law Law Sch. U. Mo., 1948-49; mem. Mo. Senate, 1977-79; justice Supreme Ct. Mo., Jefferson City, 1979-89. Mem. Gov. Mo. Adv. Coun. Alcoholism and Drug Abuse, chmn. drug coun., 1970-72; chmn. Task Force Revision Mo. Drug Laws, 1970-71; liaison mem. coun. Nat. Inst. Alcoholism and Alcohol Abuse, 1973-76; mem. Cen. Regional Adv. Coun. Comprehensive Psychiat. Svcs., 1990-92. Bd. dirs. Nat. Assn. Mental Health, 1970-76, regional v.p., 1973-76; pres. Mo. Assn. Mental Health, 1968-69, Stephens Coll. Assocs., 1965-79; pres. Friends of Libr., U. Mo., 1976, bd. dirs., 1979-92; chmn. Dem. Com., 1954-64; hon. fellow Harry S. Truman Libr. Inst., 1979—; bd. dirs. Supreme Ct. Hist. Soc., 1982—; vice chair adv. bd. U. Mo. Multiple Sclerosis Inst., 1992—; bd. curators Stephen's Coll., 1980-92. With USNR, 1941-45. Recipient Disting. Alumni medal and award U. Mo., 1994. Fellow Am. Coll. Trial Lawyers, Am. Bar Found., Mo. Bar Found.; mem. ABA, Mo. Bar Assn. (pres. 1967-68), Boone County Bar Assn. (pres. 1970), Am. Judicature Soc., Am. Legion (past post comdr.), Multiple Sclerosis Soc. (Gateway chpt. bd. dirs. 1986-92), Order of Coif, Country Club of Mo., Columbia Country Club (past pres.). Home: 3430 Woodrail Ter Columbia MO 65203-0926

WELLMAN, BARCLAY ORMES, furniture company executive; b. Jamestown, N.Y., May 13, 1936; s. Albert Austin and Leona (Greenlund) W.; m. Diane Taylor, July 2, 1960; children: Barclay Ormes Jr., Taylor A., Alexandra C. BA, Dartmouth Coll., 1959; grad., U.S. Army War Coll., 1982. Interior designer Wellman Bros., Inc., Jamestown, 1963-64, treas., 1964—, pres., 1978—. Trustee Lakeview Cemetery Assn., Jamestown, 1978—, Sheldon Found., Jamestown, 1981—. Maj. gen. U.S. Army, ret. Mem. Am. Soc. Interior Designers (v.p. 1972-74), Am. Appraisers Assn., Am. Legion, Res. Officers Assn., Sr. Army Res. Comdrs. Assn., Sportsmens Club, Moon Brook Country Club, Delta Kappa Epsilon. Republican. Presbyterian. Avocation: fishing. Home: 1235 Prendergast Ave Jamestown NY 14701-3146 Office: Wellman Bros Inc 130 S Main St Jamestown NY 14701-6623

WELLMAN, CARL PIERCE, philosophy educator; b. Lynn, Mass., Sept. 3, 1926; s. Frank and Carolyn (Heath) W.; m. Farnell Parsons, June 20, 1953; children: Timothy, Philip, Lesley, Christopher. BA, U. Ariz., 1949; MA, Harvard U., 1951, PhD, 1954; postgrad., U. Cambridge, Eng., 1951-52. Instr. Lawrence U., Appleton, Wis., 1953-57, asst. prof., 1957-62, assoc. prof., 1962-66, prof., chmn. dept. philosophy, 1966-68; prof. philosophy Washington U., St. Louis, 1968-88, Hortense and Tobias Lewin Disting. prof. humanities, 1988-99, Hortense and Tobias Lewin Disting. prof. emeritus, 1999—. Mem. rev. panel rsch. grants NEH, 1968—71. Author: The Language of Ethics, 1961, Challenge and Response: Justification in Ethics, 1971, Morals and Ethics, 1975, Welfare Rights, 1982, A Theory of Rights, 1985, Real Rights, 1995, An Approach to Rights, 1997, The Proliferation of Rights, 1999. Recipient Uhrig Distinguished Teaching award Lawrence U., 1968; Am. Council Learned Socs. fellow, 1965-66; NEH sr. fellow, 1972-73; Nat. Humanities Center fellow, 1982-83 Mem. Am. Philos. Assn., Internat. Assn. for Philosophy Law and Social Philosophy (hon. pres.). Home: 625 S Skinker Blvd # 902 Saint Louis MO 63105-2340 E-mail: cpwellma@artsci.wustl.edu.

WELLON, ROBERT G. lawyer; b. Port Jervis, NY, Apr. 18, 1948; s. Frank Lewis and Alice (Stevens) W.; m. Jan Montgomery, Aug. 12, 1972; children: Robert F., Alice Wynn. AB, Emory U., 1970; JD, Stetson Coll. Law, 1974. Assoc. Turner, Turner & Turner, Atlanta, 1974-78; ptnr. Ridley, Wellon, Schwieger & Brazier, Atlanta, 1978-86; of counsel Wilson, Strickland & Benson, Atlanta, 1987—2000; pvt. practice Atlanta, 2000—. Adj. prof. Atlanta Law Sch., 1981-94; adj. prof. law Emory U. Sch. of Law, 1995—. Gov.'s task force chmn. Atlanta 2000, 1978; exec. com., treas., 2nd v.p. Atlanta Easter Seals Soc., 1983-88; rep. Neighborhood Planning Unit, 1981-83; adminstrv. bd. Northside United Meth. Ch., 1996-99, Stephen min.; mem. Atlanta Sports Coun. Served with USAR, 1970-76. Recipient Judge Joe Morris award Stetson Coll. Law, St. Petersburg, 1974; named a. Super Lawyer, Atlanta Mag. Master: Charles Longstreet Weltner Family Law Inn of Ct. (founding pres. 1997—2000); fellow: Am. Bar Found.; mem.: Lawyers Found. of Ga., Atlanta Bar Found. (bd. dirs. 1996—), Am. Judicature Soc., Atlanta Bar Assn. (bd. dirs. 1978—88, pres. 1986—87, Atlanta continuing legal edn. bd. trustees 1994—97, del. to ho. of dels. 1999—, Charles E. Watkins Svc. award 1995), State Bar. of Ga. (professionalism com. 1994—), Fla. Bar, Atlanta Found. for Psychoanalysis, Inc. (bd. dirs. 1994—, exec. com. 1997—), Old War Horse Lawyers Club, Lawyers Club Atlanta. Methodist. Office: Ste 1900 Promenade II 1230 Peachtree St NE Atlanta GA 30309 Office Phone: 404-942-3505. E-mail: rgwlaw@earthlink.net.

WELLS, ALAN HILARY, biomedical researcher; b. N.Y.C., Dec. 15, 1958; AB, Brown U., 1979; D Med. Sci., Karolonska Inst., Stockholm, 1982; postdoctoral studies, Brown U., 1981—. Assoc. prof. Okayama (Japan) U. Med. Sch., 1983-84; postdoctoral fellow U. Calif., San Francisco, 1984-86; asst. prof. U. Ala., Birmingham, 1986—. Contbr. articles to profl. jours. Recipient ICRETT award Union Internat. Against Cancer, Geneva, 1980. Mem. AAAS, N.Y. Acad. Scis., Sigma Chi, Phi Beta Kappa, N.Y. Acad. Scis. Jewish. Avocations: hiking, skiing, reading, travel. Home: Brown Univ Med Program Box G Providence RI 02912-0001 Office: U Ala Dept Pathology Lmrb 531 Birmingham AL 35294-0001

WELLS, ANNIE, photographer; b. 1954; B in Sci. Writing, U. Calif., Santa Cruz; postgrad., San Francisco State U. Past photographer Herald Jour., Logan, Utah, Greeley (Colo.) Tribune, Associated Press, San Francisco; photographer Press Dem., Santa Rosa, Calif., 1989—97, L.A. Times, 1997—. Photographer (permanent collections) Nat. Mus. Women Arts, Washington. Recipient Pulitzer Prize spot news photography, 1997. Office: LA Times 202 West First St Los Angeles CA 90012 E-mail: annie.wells@latimes.com.

WELLS, ARTHUR STANTON, retired manufacturing company executive; b. Kingsport, Tenn., Jan. 8, 1931; s. Arthur Stanton and Blanche Welch (Duncan) W.; m. Ellen N. Blackburn, June 15, 1957; children: Arthur S., Thomas B., Emily B., Richard R. BS, Yale U., 1953; MBA, Harvard U., 1957. Fin. analyst Eastman Kodak Co., Kingsport, Tenn., 1957-65; mgr. profit analysis Xerox Corp., Rochester, N.Y., 1966-68, asst. treas. Stamford, Conn., 1969-76, treas., 1976-79; v.p. fin. Barnes Group Inc., Bristol, Conn., 1979-86, exec. v.p. fin., 1987-93, pres., CEO, 1994-96, also dir., 1994-96. Bd. dirs. Nash Engring. Co., Trumbull, Conn., 1995—98. Trustee, treas. Wilton (Conn.) Libr. Assn., 1972-78; trustee Lincoln Acad., Newcastle, Maine, 2002—; bd. dirs. New Eng. Opera Assn., 1972-78; assoc. bd. dirs. Conn. Bank and Trust Co., Hartford, 1984-90; chmn. bd. trustees, exec. com. Conn. Pub. Expenditure Coun., Inc., 1990-93. With AUS, 1953-55. Mem. Fin. Execs. Inst. Democrat. Home: 4 CCIA Rd South Bristol ME 04568-4710 E-mail: wellses@midcoast.com.

WELLS, BENJAMIN GLADNEY, lawyer; b. St. Louis, Nov. 13, 1943; s. Benjamin Harris and Katherine Emma (Gladney) W.; m. Nancy Kathryn Harpster, June 7, 1967; children: Barbara Gladney, Benjamin Harpster. BA magna cum laude, Amherst (Mass.) Coll., 1965; JD cum laude, Harvard U., 1968. Bar: Ill. 1968, Tex. 1973, U.S. Tax Ct. 1973, U.S. Ct. Claims 1975, U.S. Ct. Appeals (5th cir.) 1981, U.S. Dist. Ct. (so. dist.) Tex. 1985, U.S. Dist. Ct. (we. dist.) Tex. 1993. Assoc. Kirkland & Ellis, Chgo., 1968—69; assoc. to ptnr. Baker Botts, L.L.P., Houston, 1973—, chmn. firmwide tax dept., 2002—. Contbr. articles to profl. jours. Mem. planned giving com. St. John's Sch., Houston (chmn. 1987-98); Harvard Legal Aid Bureau, 1966-68. Capt. U.S. Army, 1969-72. Fellow Am. Coll. Tax Counsel; mem. ABA (chair corp. tax com. sect. on taxation 2001-02), Houston Tax Roundtable (pres. 1994-95), The Forest Club, The Houston Club, Phi Beta Kappa. Presbyterian. Office: Baker Botts LLP One Shell Plaza 910 Louisiana St Ste 3330 Houston TX 77002-4916 E-mail: benjamin.wells@bakerbotts.com.

WELLS, CAROL MCCONNELL, genealogist, retired archivist; b. Phila., Feb. 21, 1918; d. William Hugh McConnell and Edith Mary Lower; m. Tom Henderson Wells, Dec. 31, 1943 (dec.); children: Lucy, Sarah, Tom, Christopher, Julia, Peter. BA, Pa. State Coll., 1939; MA, Northwestern State U., 1973. Archivist Northwestern State U., Natchitoches, La., 1974-88; editor So. Studies, Natchitoches, 1982-88. Spkr. in field. Author: Williamson County, Tennessee: A Genealogical Abstract of the County Court Minutes, 1800-1804, 1987, 88, Davidson County, Tennessee, County Court Mnutes 1783-1792, 1990, Davidson County, Tennessee, County Court Minutes, 1792-1799, 1991, Davidson County, Tennessee, County Court Minutes 1799-1803, 1991, many others. Mem. Natchitoches Hist. Found., 1994—. Lt. (j.g.) USNR, 1942-44. Named Woman of Yr. C. of C., 1975; recipient Clio award Phi Alpha Theta, 1988. Mem. DAR, PEO Sisterhood, Phi Mu, Phi Beta Kappa, Phi Kappa Phi. Republican. Anglican Catholic. Avocation: gardening. Home: 607 Williams Ave Natchitoches LA 71457 E-mail: granny@cp-tel.net.

WELLS, CHARLES TALLEY, state supreme court justice; b. Orlando, Fla., Mar. 4, 1939; BA, U. of Florida, 1961, JD, 1964. Bar: Fla. 1965, U.S. Dist. Ct. (mid. dist.) Fla., U.S. Ct. Appeals (5th and 11th cirs.) 1966, U.S. Supreme Ct. 1969, U.S. Dist. Ct., U.S. Dist. Ct. (so. dist.) Fla. 1976, U.S. Ct. of Claims 1990. Trial atty. U.S. dept justice, Washington, 1969; pvt. practice Maguire, Voohris and Wells, PA, Orlando, Fla., 1965—68, 1970—75, Wells, Gattis, Hollowes & Carpenter, PA, Orlando, Fla., 1976—94; justice Fla. Supreme Ct., Tallahassee, 1994—. Methodist. Office: Fla Supreme Ct Supreme Ct Bldg 500 S Duval St Tallahassee FL 32399-1925

WELLS, DAMON, investment company executive; b. Houston, May 20, 1937; s. Damon and Margaret Corinne (Howze) W. BA magna cum laude, Yale U., 1958; BA, Oxford U., 1964, MA, 1968; PhD, Rice U., 1968. Owner, CEO Damon Wells Interests, Houston, 1958—; pres. Damon Wells Found., Houston, 1993—. Author: Stephen Douglas: The Last Years, 1857-61, 1971 (Tex. Writer's Roundup prize, 1971), paperback edit., 1990. Bd. dirs. Child Guidance Ctr. of Houston, 1970-73; trustee Christ Ch. Cathedral Endowment Fund, 1970-73, 84-88, chmn., 1987-88; trustee Kinkaid Sch., 1972-86, Camp Allen retreat of Episc. Diocese of Tex., 1976-78, Kinkaid Sch. Endowment Fund, 1981-86, Churchill Grave Trust, 2002—, Winston Churchill Found. U.S., 2003-; hon. friend of Somerville Coll., Oxford U., 1988—; mem. Sr. Common Room, Pembroke Coll., Oxford U., 1972—; founding bd. dirs. Brit. Inst. US, 1979-80; pres.'s coun. Tex. A&M U., 1983-89. Named Hon. Comdr. Most Excellent Order of Brit. Empire by Her Majesty Queen Elizabeth II, 1991, Outstanding Alumnus Yr. by Kinkaid Sch., 1994; fellow Jonathan Edwards Coll. (assoc.), Yale U., 1982—, Sterling fellow Yale U., 2000—, hon. fellow Pembroke Coll., Oxford U., 1984—. Mem. English-Speaking Union (nat. dir. 1970-72, v.p. Houston br. 1966-73), Coun. Fgn. Rels., Houston Country Club, Houston Club, Yale Club (N.Y.C.), United Oxford and Cambridge U. Club (London), Cosmos Club (Washington), Buck's Club (London), Coronado Club (Houston), Little Ship Club (London). Anglican. Home: 5555 Del Monte Dr Houston TX 77056-4100 Office: 2001 Kirby Dr Ste 806 Houston TX 77019-6088 Office Fax: 713-528-4832.

WELLS, DAVID LEE, professional baseball player; b. Torrance, Calif., May 20, 1963; Grad. high sch., San Diego. Pitcher Toronto Blue Jays, 1987—92, 1999—2001, Detroit Tigers, 1993-95, Cin. Reds, 1995, Balt. Orioles, 1996, N.Y. Yankees, 1997-98, 2002—03, Chgo. White Sox, 2001, San Diego Padres, 2004—. Named Am. League All-Star Team, 1995, 98, 2000; Perfect game thrown May 17th, 1999; mem. World Series champion Toronto Blue Jays, 1992, N.Y. Yankees, 1998. Office: c/o San Diego Padres PO Box 2000 San Diego CA 92112-2000*

WELLS, DENNIS J. dentist; DDS, U. Tenn., 1983. Dentist Nashville Ctr. for Aesthetic Dentistry. Dental cons. ABC's Extreme Makeover; clin. faculty PAC-Live, U. of the Pacific. Mem.: Am. Acad. Cosmetic Dentistry (examiner in accreditation process, chpt. pres.). Office: Nashville Ctr for Aesthetic Dentistry 105 Powell Ct Ste 101 Brentwood TN 37027

WELLS, GERTRUDE BEVERLY, psychologist; b. Haverhill, Mass., July 14, 1940; d. True Franklyn Wells and Priscilla Eleanor (Browne) Duerstling. BS, SUNY, Fredonia, 1962; MA, Coll. St. Rose, 1969; PhD, U. Mo., 1976; PhD in Clin. Psychology, The Fielding Grad. Inst., 1999. Tchr. speech pathology N.Y. Pub. Schs., Albany and Clifton Park, 1962-70; lectr. SUNY, Albany, 1970-73; asst. prof. Coll. St. Rose, Albany, 1975-77; assoc. prof. U. No. Iowa, Cedar Falls, 1977-78; prof. U. of La., Lafayette, 1978-85; prof., program dir. Calif. State U. Stanislaus, Turlock, 1985-87; prof. comm. Calif. State U., San Francisco, 1987—92; chief exec. officer West Coast Inst., 1992—2000; clin. psychologist, pvt. practice, 2001—. Author: Stuttering Treatment, 1987; contbr. articles to profl. jours. Health svc. provider Nat. Register of Health Svc. in Psychology. Mem.: APA, Calif. Psychol. Assn., Am. Acad. Health Care Providers in Addictive Disorders. Avocations: writing, bicycling, gardening. Office: 16 Joost Ave San Francisco CA 94137 Office Phone: 415-585-5212.

WELLS, GLADYSANN, library director; BA in English, Greensboro (N.C.) Coll., 1970; MLS, SUNY, Albany, 1972. Libr. Empire State Coll., 1972—73; legis. reference libr. N.Y. State Libr., Albany, 1973—78; with Senate Rsch. Svc., 1975—80; libr. Senate Libr., 1978—80; adminstr. N.Y. Stat eLibr., 1980—95; interim dir. N.Y.State Libr. Rsch. Libr., 1995—97; state libr. Ariz. State Libr., 1997—. Editor several books on the economy of the northeast; contbr. articles to profl. jours. Avocations: horseback riding, cross country skiing, hiking, snow shoeing. Office: Ariz State Libr 1700 W Washington Ste 200 Phoenix AZ 85007-2896

WELLS, HUEY THOMAS, JR., lawyer; b. Gadsden, Ala., Mar. 22, 1950; s. Huey Thomas Sr. and Ruth (Allison) W.; m. Jan McKenzie, Dec. 29, 1972; children: Lynlee, Trey. BA with honors, U. Ala., 1972, JD, 1975. Bar: Ala. 1975, U.S. dist. Ct. (no. dist.) Ala. 1975, U.S. Ct. Appeals (D.C. and 5th cirs.) 1977, U.S. Supreme Ct. 1981, U.S. Ct. Appeals (11th cir.) 1982. Assoc. Cabaniss, Johnston, Gardner, Dumas & O'Neal, Birmingham, Ala., 1977-82, ptnr., 1983-84, Maynard, Cooper & Gale P.C., 1984—. Chmn. adv. com. on civil justice reform U.S. Dist. (no. dist.) Ala., 1991-95. Legal co-chmn. championship Profl. Golf Assn., Birmingham, 1984, legal chmn., 1990; legal chmn. U.S. Amateur Golf Championship, Birmingham, 1986. Served to capt. USAF, 1975-77. Mem. ABA (standing com. profl. disciple 1985-88, standing com. on environ. law 1988-94, chmn. environ. litigation com. of litigation sect. 1988-91, chmn. ho. of dels. 2002-04, Ala. state del. 1991—, mem. coun. litigation sect. 1992-95, chair litigation sect. 1999-2000), Birmingham Bar Assn. (law day com., grievance com., divsn. dir. litigation sect. 1991-92), Ala. Bar Assn. (jud. liaison). Roman Catholic. Avocations: golf, softball, reading. Office: Maynard Cooper & Gale PC 2400 AmSouth/Harbart Plz 1901 6th Ave N Ste 2400 Birmingham AL 35203-4604 Office Phone: 205-254-1062. E-mail: twells@mcglaw.com.

WELLS, HUGH NEAL, IV, lawyer; b. L.A., Sept. 18, 1961; BA, Occidental Coll., 1983; JD, U. Pacific, 1986. Cert.: State Bar Calif. (workers' compensation specialist) 1992. Assoc. atty. Ibold & Anderson, L.A., 1987—89; ptnr. Hallett & McCormick, LLP, San Bernardino, Calif., 1989—. Chmn./workers' compensation sect. Orange County Bar Assn., Santa Ana, Calif., 1991—95; instr. Ins. Edn. Assn., Newport Beach, Calif., 1994—. Contbg. writer: Workers' Compensation Quarterly, 1998—. Trustee First Presbyn. Ch. Orange, 1992—95. Mem.: State Bar Calif. (pres. workers' compensation exec. com. 1997—2002).

WELLS, JAMES H. plastic surgeon; m. Karen Wells; children: Sara, Gregory. MD, U. Tex., 1966. Cert. Am. Bd. Plastic Surgery, 1978. Med. staff St. Mary's Med. Ctr., Long Beach, Calif., Los Alamitos Hosp., Hoag Prsbyn. Hosp., Newport Beach Hosp., Comm. Hosp., Long Beach; resident, gen. and plastic surgery Ochsner Found. Hosp., New Orleans, U. Va. med. Ctr., Charlottesville, Va.; currently pvt. practice Long Beach. Mem.: Am. Soc. Plastic Surgeons (pres. 2002—). Office: 2880 Atlantic Ave Ste 290 Long Beach CA 90806

WELLS, JAMES M., III, bank executive; b. 1946; Student, U. N.C., Rutgers U., U. Colo. Mgmt. trainee United Va. Bankshares, 1968-71, corporate adminstrv. officer, sec., 1971; br. officer, mgr. United Va. Bankshares/State-Planters, 1971-74; v.p. and treas. United Va. Mortgage Corp., 1974-79; pres., CEO United Va. Leasing Corp., 1974-79; exec. v.p. United Va. Bank, Norfolk, Va., 1979-83, pres. Ea. region, 1983-85, exec. v.p. corporate banking, 1985-86, exec. v.p. banking group, 1986-88; pres. Crestar Fin Corp, Richmond, Va., 1988—. Office: Crestar Fin Corp 919 E Main St PO Box 26665 Richmond VA 23261-6665

WELLS, JAMES ROBERT, pharmaceutical company executive; b. Moundsville, W.Va., Apr. 5, 1940; s. Robert H. and Maxine (Mason) W.; m. Lynne Holt, Mar. 28, 1981. BS, Wheeling Jesuit U., 1962; PhD, U. Pitts., 1967. Profl. and managerial positions in R&D DuPont Co., Wilmington, Del., 1967-76, prodn. supt. Orange, Tex., 1976-77, rsch. mgr. Wilmington, Del., 1977-79, mgr. strategic planning, 1979-87, mgr. external alliances, 1987-91; dir. external alliances DuPont Merck Pharm. Co., Wilmington, 1991-92, v.p. bus. devel., 1992-95, v.p. internat., 1995—. Bd. dirs. Dupont-Sankyo Pharm. Co., Ltd., Tokyo. Patentee in field. Pres. West Orange-Cove Sch. Bd., Orange, Tex., 1976-77. Mem. Am. Chem. Soc., Licensing Execs. Soc., Drug Info. Assn. Achievements include granting 2 U.S. patents, 1974, 1975. Home: 24 Drake Rd Chesapeake City MD 21915-1709 Office: DuPont Pharm Co 974 Centre Rd Wilmington DE 19805-1269 E-mail: jrwells@crosslink.net.

WELLS, JEFFREY S. retail executive, human resources specialist; Sr. v.p. Toys "R" Us, Inc., 1992—96; sr. v.p. human resources Circuit City, Richmond, Va., 1996—. Mem.: Vocat. Rehab. Coun. for the Blind, WorkForce One Richmond C. of C. Office: Circuit City 9950 Mayland Dr Richmond VA 23233-1464

WELLS, JERRY WAYNE, protective services official; b. Hodgenville, Ky., Dec. 17, 1950; s. Lawrence and Margaret Evelyn Wells. BA in History, Western Ky. U., 1973; postgrad., So. Police Inst., Louisville, 1987; MS in Criminal Justice Adminstrn., Ea. Ky. U., 1990; grad., FBI Nat. Acad., Quantico, Va., 1998. Cert. police officer, police mgmt. instr. Ky. Audio visual technician, police dispatcher Western Ky. U., Bowling Green, 1972-74, police officer, detective, sgt., 1975-76; police officer City of Bowling Green, 1976-83, police sgt., 1983-87, police capt., 1987-94, sector comdr., capt., 1994-99, capt. profl. stds. unit, 2000—02, maj., dep. chief support svcs. divsn., 2002—03, lt. col., dep. chief support svcs., 2003—. Part-time tchr. police related topics; legal mgmt. rschr. Mem., grad. Leadership Bowling Green, 1989. Mem.: FBI Nat. Acad. Assocs., Ky. Assn. Chiefs Police, Internat. Assn. Chiefs Police, Fraternal Order Police (treas. 1981—84, Svc. award 1979, 1981), Coll. Law Enforcement Alumni Assn., Leadership Bowling Green Alumni Assn., Eastern Ky. U. Alumni Assn., So. Police Inst. Alumni Assn., Western Ky. U. Alumni Assn. Republican. Baptist. Avocations: reading, bowling, golf, travel, historical research. Home: PO Box 684 Bowling Green KY 42102-0684 Office: Bowling Green Police Dept 911 Kentucky St Bowling Green KY 42101-2105 Business E-Mail: jerry.wells@bgky.org.

WELLS, JOHN MARCUM, producer, writer; b. Alexandria, Va., May 28, 1956; s. Llewellyn Wallace Jr and Marjorie Elizabeth (Risberg) Wells; m. Belinda Casas, Dec. 30, 1978 (div.). BFA in Drama, Carnegie-Mellon U., 1979; MFA in Cinema, U. So. Calif., 1982. Founder, artistic dir. Pitts. New Playwrights Festival, 1978-79; asst. to v.p. mktg. Paramount Pictures Corp., 1981-82; theatrical producer various plays, Los Angeles, 1982-85; producer, writer Warner Bros. TV, Los Angeles, 1987, co-exec. producer, writer, 1988, 89, 90; producer New World Pictures, Los Angeles, 1986-87; suprg. producer, creater Roughhouse, Los Angeles, 1988. Prodr.(writer): (plays) Balm In Gilead, She Also Dances, Battery, Judgement, Ground Zero, Steaming, Femme Fatale, Tanzi; (TV series) China Beach (George Foster Peabody award, 3 Writers Guild of Am. Nominations, 6 Emmy nominations), Angel Street, Just In Time, Shell Game, The Nightman; (films) Nice Girls Don't Explode, Interview With A Vampire, A Time To Kill, Wired. Assoc. producer nat. Dem. fundraising events, L.A., 1984, Carnegie-Mellon U. Endowment Drive, Pitts., 1986. Recipient Los Angeles Drama Critics Circle award, 1982, Los Angeles Weekly award, Drama-Logue mag. award, 1985, Writers Guild Am. award, 1989, Humanitas award, 1989, Peabody award, 1990, Golden Globe award, 1990; grantee Triseme Corp., 1982. Mem.: NATAS, Carnegie-Mellon U. West Coast Alumni Assn. (bd. dirs. 1982—, pres. 1986—90), Writers Guild Am. Democrat. Episcopalian. Office: 4000 Warner Blvd # 2 Burbank CA 91522-0001

WELLS, JON BARRETT, engineer; b. Sewickley, Pa., Oct. 21, 1937; s. Calvin and Martha Barrett (Byrnes) W.; m. Nancy Lou LaFrance, Nov. 18, 1967; children: James Jonathan, Tiffany Lynn. BSEE, Calif. Poly U., 1961. Various positions Bell & Howell Co. Datatape Div., Pasadena, Calif., 1961-73, chief engr., 1973-75, engring. mgr., 1975-87; remittance projects mgr. Lundy Fin. Systems, Rancho Cucamonga, Calif., 1987-92; engring. mgr. Recognition Internat. (formerly Lundy Fin. Systems), Irving, Tex., 1992-96; project mgr. BancTec (formerly Recognition Internat.), Irving, 1996—. Pres. Datatape Fed. Credit Union, Pasadena, 1978-93; v.p. Recognition Tech. Users Assn., Boston, 1987—; sec. Am. Nat. Standard Inst. X9B6, Washington, 1989-92. Patentee in field; contbr. articles to pubs. Sec., founder Pasadena Neighborhood Housing Svcs., Pasadena, 1976-80. Mem. IEEE, Pasadena IBM Personal Computer Users Group, U.S. Power Squadrons, Aircraft Owners and Pilots Assn., Internat. Underwater Explorers Soc. Republican. Avocations: flying, boating, scuba diving, computers. Office: Synergistic Solution Techs Inc 13740 Rsch Blvd Ste M-3 Austin TX 78750-1834 Home: 103 Neville Wood Ct Austin TX 78738-1712 Office Phone: 512-467-2100 29. E-mail: wellsjon@hotmail.com.

WELLS, JULIA ELIZABETH See DAME ANDREWS, JULIE

WELLS, KAREN KAY, medical librarian; b. Petaluma, Calif., Jan. 9, 1956; d. Albert Lee and Miyoko (Kay) W.; m. John Edward Guth, Aug. 4, 1979 (div. 1986). BS with honors, U. Colo., 1977; MEd with honors, U. Ill., 1980, MS with honors, 1982. Cert. tchr., Colo., Ill. Grad. asst. grad. libr. U. Ill., Urbana, 1981—82; asst. prof. med. libr. svcs. sch. medicine Mercer U., Macon, Ga., 1982—88; libr., head dept. Presbyn. Denver & St. Luke's Med. Ctr., 1983; instr., cons. dialog pharm. database AMI-St. Luke's Hosp. Health Scis. Libr., Denver, 1985—87; head libr. Manville Health, Safety and Environ. Libr., Denver, 1988—91; info. cons. Wells Info. Svc., Denver, 1989—91, sr. adminstrv. assessor, 1996—98; med. libr. Exemple Luth. Med. Ctr., Wheat Ridge, Colo., 2000—. Coord. Westend Consumer Health Info. Libr., 2000—. Mem. ALA, Med. Libr. Assn., Colo. Coun. Med. Librs. (cons. med.-sci.

databases 1984—), U. Colo. Alumni Assn., U. Ill. Alumni Assn., Beta Phi Mu, Kappa Delta Pi. Democrat. Presbyterian. Avocations: racquetball, diving. Office: Exempla Luth Med Ctr 8300 W 38th Ave Wheat Ridge CO 80033

WELLS, KENNETH B. medical educator; Prof. psychiatry & biobehavioral scis. UCLA Sch. Medicine, L.A. Address: 1700 Main St Santa Monica CA 90401-3208

WELLS, KIMBERLY K. not-for-profit organization executive; BA in Psychology, MA in Counseling Psychology. Dir. youth svcs., dir. program svcs., assoc. exec. dir. Home Sweet Home Mission, 1987—97; exec. dir. Corp. Alliance to End Prtnr. Violence, 1997—. Mem. Workplace Com. Nat. Task Force to End Sexual and Domestic Violence Against Women; chair Promotion Com., State of Ill.; mem. Gov.'s Commn. on Status of Women in Ill. Violence Reduction Group, Ill. Corp. Citizenship Initiative; mem. steering com. Ill. Family Violence Coordinating Coun.; mem. 11th Jud. Cir. Family Violence Coordinating Coun. Planning Com.; co-chair McLean County Domestic Violence Task Force Youth and Children Work Group; treas., bd. dirs. Ill. Ctr. for Violence Prevention; grad. Leadership Am. Am. Issues Forum, 1999; guest lectr. Ill. State U., Heartland C.C. Office: 2416 E Washington St Ste E Bloomington IN 61704-4472

WELLS, KITTY (MURIEL DEASON WRIGHT), country western singer; b. Nashville, Aug. 30, 1919; d. Charles Carey and Murtle Bell (Street) Deason; m. Johnnie Robert Wright, Oct. 30, 1937; children: Ruby Jean Wright Taylor, Bobby Wright, Carol Sue Wright-Sturdivant. Grad. high sch. Country music singer; sang gospel in chs. as a child; performed on radio, early 1930s; with John and Jack and the Tenn. Mountain Boys, late 1930's-early 1940's, regular on Grand Ole Opry, from 1952, now with Johnny Wright, Bobby Wright and the Tennessee Mountain Boys; songs include: Release Me, It Wasn't God Who Made Honky Tonk Angels, Making Believe; albums include Kitty Wells & Roy Drusky, Vol. 1 & 2, Back to Back Patsy Kline, 1995, (with Red Foley, Webb Pierce, others) Duets, 1995; author: Kitty Wells Cookbook. Bd. dirs. Nashville Meml. Hosp. Recipient award as number 1 female singer Cashbox Mag., 1953-62, Billboard 1954-65, award of yr. for top female country vocalist Record World mag. 1965, award for highest artistic achievement in rec. arts 1964, various awards Downbeat mag., award as all-time queen of country music Music Bus. mag. 1964, Woman of Yr. award 1974, named Top Female Artist of Decade, Record World mag. 1974, named to Country Music Hall of Fame 1976. Mem. Country Music Assn., Nat. Assn. Rec. Arts and Scis. Mem. Ch. of Christ. Achievements include being the first woman to hit No. 1 on the country charts with "It Wasn't God Who Made Honky Tonk Angels.".

WELLS, LESLEY, federal judge; b. Muskegon, Mich., Oct. 6, 1937; d. James Franklin and Inez Simpson Wells; m. Charles F. Clarke, Nov. 13, 1998; children: Lauren Elizabeth, Caryn Alison, Anne Kristin, Thomas Eliot. BA, Chatham Coll., 1959; JD cum laude, Cleve. State U., 1974; cert., Nat. Jud. Coll., 1983, 85, 87, cert., 89. Bar: Ohio 1975, U.S. Dist. Ct. (no. dist.) Ohio 1975, U.S. Supreme Ct. 1989. Pvt. practice, Cleve., 1975; ptnr. Brooks & Moffet, Cleve., 1975—78; dir., atty. ABAR Litigation Ctr., Cleve., 1979-80; assoc. Schneider, Smeltz, Huston & Ranney, Cleve., 1980-83; judge Ct. of Common Pleas, Cleve., 1983-94, U.S. Dist. Ct. (no. dist.) Ohio 6th Cir., Cleve., 1994—. Adj. prof. law and urban policy Cleve. State U., 1980-83, 90-93. Editor, author: Litigation Manual, 1980. Past pres. Cleve. Legal Aid Soc.; legal chmn. Nat. Women's Polit. Caucus, 1981-82; chmn. Gov.'s Task Force on Family Violence, Ohio, 1983-87; mem. biomed. ethics com. Case Western Res. U. Med. Sch., 1985-94; mem. N.W. Ordinance U.S. Constn. Commn., Ohio, 1986-88; master William K. Thomas Inn of Ct., 1989—, counselor, 1993, pres., 1998-99; trustee Rosemary Ctr., 1986-92, Miami U., 1988-92, Urban League Cleve., 1989-90, Chatham Coll., 1989-94. Recipient Superior Jud. award Supreme Ct. Ohio, 1983, J. Irwin award Womenspace, Ohio, 1984, award Womens City Club, 1985, Disting. Alumna award Chatham Coll., 1988, Alumni Civic Achievement award Cleve. State U., 1992, Golden Gavel award Ohio Judges Assn., 1994, Outstanding Alumni award Cleve. Marshall Law Alumni Assn., 1994, Greater Cleve. Achievement award YWCA, 1995. Mem. ABA (coun. litigation sect. 1996-99), Am. Law Inst., Ohio Bar Assn., Ohio Womens Bar Assn., Cleve. Bar Assn. (Merit Svc. award 1983), Cuyahoga County Bar Assn., Nat. Assn. Women Judges, Philos. Club Cleve. Office: 18-A US Court House 801 W Superior Ave Cleveland OH 44113-1836

WELLS, LINDA ANN, editor-in-chief; b. N.Y.C., Aug. 9, 1958; d. H. Wayne and Jean (Burchell) W.; m. Charles King Thompson, Nov., 1993. BA in English, Trinity Coll., 1980. Edit. asst. Vogue Mag., N.Y.C., 1980-83, assoc. editor beauty, 1983-85; style reporter New York Times, N.Y.C., 1985, beauty editor, food editor, 1985-90; founding editor, editor-in-chief Allure Mag., N.Y.C., 1990—. Spkr. Am. Womens' Econ. Devel., N.Y., 1988-89, Brand Futures Group, N.Y., 1999. Contbr. numerous articles to N.Y. Times Mag., Allure Mag., 1985—. Chmn. N.Y. Shakespeare Festival, 1993, 94; bd. fellows Trinity Coll., 1998—; bd. visitors Mary Inst. Country Day Sch., St. Louis. Recipient Fragrance Found. award 1991, 99, 2000, 2001, Nat. Mag. Design award, 1994, Legal Def. and Edn. Fund Equal Opportunity award NOW, 1994, Trinith Coll. Alumni Achievement award, 2000, Cosmetic Exec. Women Achiever award, 2001. Mem. Am. Soc. Mag. Editors (bd. dirs. 1993-97). Office: Allure Mag Conde Nast Publs 4 Times Sq Fl 10 New York NY 10036-6522

WELLS, LLOYD ALLAN, psychiatrist, educator; b. Providence, Mar. 4, 1948; s. Lloyd Alvin and Elizabeth Hunter Wells; m. Denise Marie Coutu, Dec. 15, 1973; children: Aynslee, Llyd, Ethan. BA, Harvard Coll., 8, 1968; PhD, U. Rochester, 1973, MD with distinction, 1974. Diplomate Am. Bd. Psychiatry and Neurology. Cons. Mayo Clinic, Rochester, Minn., 1974—2001, assoc. prof., 1983—, sect. head, 1980—91, vice-chmn. edn., 1999—. Contbr. articles to profl. jours. Active Olmsted County Task Force on Family Violence, Rochester, Minn., 1982—83, Olmsted County Task Force on Guidelines for Hospitalization, Rochester, Minn., 1989. Named Tchr. of Yr., Assn. for Acad. Psychiatry, 1998; named to Tchg. Hall of Fame, Mayo Graduate Sch. Medicine, 1987; recipient Fisher award, Internat. Hibernation Soc., 1969, Writing award, Perspectives in Biology and Medicine, 1976; fellow Falk fellow, Am. Psychiatric Assn., 1976—77, Laughlin fellow, Am. Coll. Psychiatrists, 1977. Fellow: Am. Psychiat. Assn. (psychiat. nursing com. 1977—80); mem.: Am. Acad. Child and Adolescent Psychiatry (com. on substance abuse 1988—93), Am. Assn. for the History of Medicine (Harvey Osler award 1972), Am. Assn. Dirs. of Psychiatry Residency Training Pprograms (child and adolescent caucus), Soc. Profs. of Child and Adolescent Psychiatry (edn. chmn. 2003—04), Assn. for the Advancement of Philosophy and Psychiatry, Am. Acad. Psychoanalysis (managed care com., edn. com. 1998—2002), Am. Soc. Adolescent Psychiatry (coun. on fellowships, treas., dir. ednl. resources 1990—94), Am. Bd. Psychiatry and Neurology, Inc. (assoc. examiner), Acad. Psychosomatic Medicine (ednl. dir. 1983), Minn. Psychiat. Soc. (nominating com. 1979, ethics com. 1989), Sigma Xi. Home: 623 8th Ave SW Rochester MN 55902 Office: Mayo Clinic Rochester MN 55905 Office Phone: 507-284-2933. Business E-Mail: wells.lloyd@mayo.edu.

WELLS, MARY ELIZABETH THOMPSON, minister; b. Dallas, Oct. 9, 1936; d. Owen Perry and Ruth Marie (Baker) Thompson; children: Tadd Whitney, Britony Ruth. BA in Sociology, Syracuse (N.Y.) U., 1958; MA in Child Devel., Tufts U., 1964, MEd in Counseling Psychology, 1974; postgrad. in theology, St. Vincent de Paul Sem., 1996—. Asst. dir. pub. relations Inst. for Crippled and Disabled, N.Y.C., 1958-59; head tchr. Eliot-Pearson Children's Sch., Tufts U., Medford, Mass., 1964-66; psychotherapist Mental Health Ctr. of Greater Cape Ann, Gloucester, Mass., 1974-89; deacon, chaplain, spiritual dir. St. Paul's Episcopal Ch., Delray Beach, Fla., 1998—. Mem. Am. Psychol. Assn., Am. Orthopsychiat. Assn., Gulfstream Bath & Tennis Club, Assn. Clinical Pastoral Educators, Assn. Profl. Chaplains, Spiritual Dirs. Internat. Home: 1183 Canoe Point Delray Beach FL 33444 Office: St Paul's Episcopal Ch 188 S Swinton Ave Delray Beach FL 33444-3698

WELLS, MELISSA FOELSCH, foreign service officer; b. Tallinn, Estonia, Nov. 18, 1932; emigrated to U.S., 1936, naturalized, 1941; d. Kuno Georg and Miliza (Korjus) Foelsch; m. Alfred Washburn Wells, 1960; children: Christopher, Gregory. BS in Fgn. Service, Georgetown U., 1956. Fgn. svc. officer Dept. State, Washington, 1958 61, consular officer, 1961-64, econ. officer mission OECD, Paris, 1964-66; econ. officer London, 1966-71; internat. economist, 1971-73; dep. dir. maj. export projects Dept. Commerce, 1973-75; comml. counselor Brazil, 1975-76; amb. to Guinea-Bissau and Cape Verde Dept. of State, 1976-77; U.S. rep. ECOSOC, UN, N.Y.C., 1977-79; resident rep. UNDP, Kampala, Uganda, 1979-81, dir. IMPACT program Geneva, 1982-86; amb. to Mozambique, 1987-90; amb. to Zaire, Kinshasa, 1991-93; under-sec. gen. for adminstrn. and mgmt. UN, N.Y., 1993-94; consul gen. Sao Paulo, Brazil, 1995-97; amb. to Republic of Estonia Dept. of State, 1998—2001. Bd. dirs. U.S.-Baltic Found. Mem. Am. Fgn. Service Assn. Office: Casa Wells Plz Leoncio Bento 7 38830 Agulo Gomera Canary Islands Spain

WELLS, PALMER DONALD, performing arts executive; b. Keokee, Va., Jan. 31, 1937; s. Lon S. Wells and Ada Mae (Russell) Craft. BA in Journalism, U. Ky., 1960. Co-founder, producing dir. Theatre in the Square, Marietta, Ga., 1982—. V.p. IBM Drama Club, White Plains, N.Y., 1976. Appeared in The Three Penny Opera, 1963; director plays The Glass Menagerie, 1965, Dark of the Moon, 1966, The Little Foxes, 1983, Tobacco Road, 1985, Mary Shelly's Frankenstein, 1988; director musicals The 1940's Radio Hour, 1987. Founder Lonesome Pine Players, Cumberland, Ky., 1960; mem. Cobb Landmarks Soc., Marietta, 1990. With U.S. Army, 1961-63. Democrat. Avocations: pottery, spanish. Home: 43 Mcdonald St Marietta GA 30064-3217 Office: Theatre in the Square 11 Whitlock Ave Marietta GA 30064-2321

WELLS, PETER NATHANIEL, judge, lawyer; b. Ogdensburg, N.Y., May 13, 1938; s. John Harris and Mary Theresa (Houlihan) W.; m. Diana Barry Wells, Apr. 8, 1967; childen: Mary, Sarah, Matthew. BS in Polit. Sci., Manhattan Coll., 1960; LLB, Boston Coll., 1963. Bar: N.Y. 1964, U.S. Dist. Ct. (no. dist.) N.Y. 1967, U.S. Dist. Ct. (we. dist.) N.Y. 1971, U.S. Ct. Appeals (d cir.) 1974, U.S. Ct. Appeals (3d cir.) 1978, U.S. Supreme Ct. 1974. Asst. atty. gen. State of N.Y., 1964-68; assoc. Costello, Cooney & Fearon, Syracuse, N.Y., 1968-70, ptnr., 1970-76, Williams, Micale & Wells, Syracuse, 1976-88, Mackenzie Smith Lewis, Michell & Hughes, Syracuse, 1988; surrogate ct. judge Onondaga County, 1989—. Mem. EPTL-SCPA Legis. adv. com. of N.Y. State. Editl. bd. Warren's Heaton on Surrogate Ct. Chmn. Dewitt Republican Com., 1976-87; town justice Dewitt, N.Y., 1987-88. Served with USAR, 1963-69. Mem. Onondaga County Bar Assn., Def. Rsch. Inst., Upstate Trial Lawyers Assn., N.Y. State Surrogates Assn. (pres. 1999-2001), Cavalry Club, Manlius Club (N.Y.). Roman Catholic. Home: 100 Downing Rd De Witt NY 13214-1503 Office: Surrogate Ct Chambers Onondaga County Courth Syracuse NY 13202 Office Phone: 315-671-2098. Business E-Mail: pwells@courts.state.ny.us.

WELLS, PETER SCOVILLE, retired marketing executive; b. N.Y.C., Apr. 25, 1938; s. Jonathan Godfrey and Eleanore Shannon (Scoville) W.; m. Patricia Ann Trent, Dec. 8, 1973; 1 child by previous marriage, Peter Scoville. Asst. to contr. Laird & Co., N.Y.C., 1961-63; asst. to ptnr. charge ops. Goldman Sachs, N.Y.C., 1963-64; mgr. new bus. dept. B.J. Herkimer Co., N.Y.C., 1964-67; divisional policy and procedures adminstr. Paine, Webber, Jackson & Curtis, Inc., N.Y.C., 1967-70, asst. to exec. cashier, 1970-73, asst. v.p., mgr. employment svcs., adminstr. equal employment opportunity, 1973-80; pers. officer, exec. recruiter N.Y. Stock Exch., 1980-86, mgr. employment; sr. v.p. Wesley Brown & Bartle, 1986-87; sr. v.p., dir. Alliance Mktg., Inc., 1987; ptnr. Richards & Wells, 1988-90, Brookman Assocs., Inc., 1990—2000; ret., 2000. With AUS, 1958-66. Mem. SAR, Vet. Corps Artillery, Mil. Order Loyal Legion, Knights of Malta (knight comdr.), Order of Lafayette, Knights Templar, L'Ordre Militaire, Phi Kappa Psi. Home: 449 E 78th St New York NY 10021-1649

WELLS, RAYMOND O'NEIL, JR., mathematics educator, researcher; b. Dallas, June 12, 1940; s. Raymond O. and Hazel (Rand) W.; m. Rena Schwarze, Aug. 1, 1963; children: Richard Andrew, René Michael. BA, Rice U., 1962; MS, NYU, 1964, PhD, 1965. Asst. prof. math. Rice U., Houston, 1965-69, assoc. prof., 1969-74, prof. math., 1974-2000, prof. edn., 1993-2000; chmn. dept. math., 1976-79; chmn. dept. edn. Rice U., Houston, 1994-98, dir. sch. math. project, 1987-2000, dir. computational math. lab., 1990-2000, prof. math emeritus, 2000—, asst. to pres., 2000-01; v.p. external affairs, prof. math. Internat. U., Bremen, 2001—. Vis. asst. prof. Brandeis U., Waltham, Mass., 1967-68; vis. prof. U. Göttingen, Germany, 1974-75, U. Colo., Boulder, 1983-84, U. Bremen, Germany, 1995-96, Internat. Univ. Bremen, 1998-2001; adj. prof. cmty. medicine Baylor Coll. Medicine, 1994—; active Inst. for Advanced Study, Princeton, N.J., 1970-71, 79-80; exch. visitor NAS, Sofia, Bulgaria, 1984; planning com. Internat. U., Bremen, 1997-99. Author: Differential Analysis on Complex Manifolds, 1973, Mathematics in Civilization, 1973, Twister Geometry and Field Theory, 1990, Wavelet Analysis: The Scaleable Structure of Information, 1998; editor: Mathematical Heritage of Herman Weyl, 1989, (book series) Expositions in Mathematics, 1988—2003, The Founding of International University Bremen: Perspectives for the Twenty First Century, 2003; contbr. numerous articles to sci. jours. Pres. Stages Repertory Theater, Houston, 1989-90. Recipient Alexander von Humboldt Sr. U.S. Scientist award U. Göttingen, 1974-75; Fulbright fellow, 1968, Guggenheim fellow, 1974. Fellow AAAS (coun. 1989—); mem. Am. Math. Soc. (coun., editor 1978-88), Carl Schurz Soc. (pres. 2002—), Cosmos Club Washington. Home: Lüder-von-Bentheim Str 12 28209 Bremen Germany Office: Internat Univ Bremen PO Box 750561 28725 Bremen Germany Office Phone: 49 421 200 4321. Business E-Mail: wells@iu-bremen.de.

WELLS, RICHARD A. manufacturing executive; BSBA, U. Wis., Madison, 1960; cert. in data processing, U. Wis., Milw. CPA, Wis. With Kohler (Wis.) Co., sr. v.p. fin., CFO, 1979-1999, also mem. exec. com., pension investment com., bd. dirs. Office: Kohler Co 444 Highland Dr Kohler WI 53044-1500

WELLS, ROGER STANLEY, software engineer; b. Seattle, Apr. 13, 1949; s. Stanley A. and Margaret W. BA, Whitman Coll., 1971; postgrad., U. Tex., Austin, 1973-74; BS, Oreg. State U., 1977. Software evaluation engr. Tektronix, Beaverton, Oreg., 1979-83; computer engr. Aramco, Dhahran, Saudi Arabia, 1983-84; software engr. Conrac Corp., Clackamas, Oreg., 1984-85, Duarte, Calif., 1985; software analyst Lundy Fin. Systems, San Dimas, Calif., 1986-89; pvt. practice Seattle, 1989-92; sr. project engr. Illuminet, Olympia, Wash., 1993-2000, mem. Exec. Yr. 2000 com., 1998-99; configuration mgr. New Edge Networks, Vancouver, Wash., 2000; sr. product engr. Wind River Systems, Beaverton, Oreg., 2000-01; tech. advisor E-corps Wash. Svc. Corps, 2002—. Bd. dirs. The Lydia Whitney Found., Collinsville, Conn. Bd. dirs. The Sci. Fiction Mus., Salem, Oreg., 1993—; co-founder, bd. dirs., pres. Oreg. Sci. Fiction Conv., 1979-81; vol. Americorps, Yakima, Wash., 2002-03, Pasco, Wash., 2003—. Mem. IEEE, Am. Philatelic Soc., Nat. Assn. Parliamentarians, Am. Inst. Parliamentarians (chpt. v.p. 1996-97, pres. 1997-98), Fantasy Amateur Press Assn., Portland Sci. Fiction Soc., N.W. Sci. Fiction Soc., Mensa, Assn. Computing Machinery, L.A. Sci. Fantasy Soc., Melbourne (Australia) Sci. Fiction Club, Toastmasters Internat. (club pres. 1980, v.p. edn. 1994-95, area gov. 1994-95, dist. 32 parliamentarian 1996-99), Internat. Platform Assn. (2d place Monologue contest 1997, conv. com. 1998-99, bd. govs. 1999-2000). Achievements include designing software program to transfer billing records for regional telephone companies. Avocations: travel, public speaking, science fiction, stamp collecting/philately. Home: PO Box 3786 Pasco WA 99302

WELLS, ROGER W. lawyer, food products executive; b. Sioux Falls, S.D., May 7, 1957; BSBA summa cum laude, Creighton U., 1979, JD summa cum laude, 1981. Bar: Nebr. 1981, U.S. Dist. Ct. Nebr. 1981, U.S. Tax Ct. 1981. With McGrath, North, Mullin & Kratz, P.C., Omaha; gen. counsel ConAgra, Omaha, 2002—. Mem. editl. staff: Creighton U. Law Rev., 1980—81. Mem.: ABA (mem. corp., banking and bus. sect., mem. taxation sect., mem. internat. law sect.), Omaha Bar Assn., Nebr. Bar Assn., Beta Gamma Sigma. Office: ConAgra 1 Center Park Plz Ste 1400 222 S 15th St Omaha NE 68102 also: McGrath North Mullin and Kratz PC Ste 3700 1st Nat Tower 1601 Dodge St Omaha NE 68102 Business E-Mail: rwells@mnmk.com.

WELLS, SAMUEL ALONZO, JR., surgeon, educator; b. Cuthbert, Ga., Mar. 16, 1936; s. Samuel Alonzo and Martha Steele W.; m. Barbara Anne Atwood, Feb. 13, 1964; children: Sarah, Susan. Student, Emory U., 1954—57, MD, 1961. Intern Johns Hopkins Hosp., Balt., 1961—62, resident in internal medicine, 1962—63; asst. resident in surgery Barnes Hosp., St. Louis, 1963—64; resident in surgery Duke U., Durham, NC, 1966—70; guest investigator dept. tumor biology Karolinska Inst., Stockholm, 1967—68; asst. prof. surgery Duke U., Durham, NC, 1970—72, assoc. prof., 1972—76, prof., 1976—81; clin. assoc. surgery br. Nat. Cancer Inst., NIH, Bethesda, Md., 1964—66, sr. investigator surgery br., 1970—72, cons. surgery br., 1975—; prof., chmn. dept. surgery Washington U., St. Louis, 1981—98, dir. ACS, Chgo., 1998—99; group chair, prin. investigator ACS Oncology Group, Chgo., 1998—. Dir. Duke U. Clin. Rsch. Ctr., 1978—81; mem. Residency Rev. Com. Surgery, 1987—93, chmn., 1991—93; mem. bd. regents ACS, 1989—98, vice chmn. bd. regents, 1998—; prof. surgery Duke U. Sch. Medicine, 2001—. Mem. editl. bd.: Annals of Surgery, 1975—93, Surgery, 1975—93, Jour. Surg. Rsch., 1981—93, editor in chief: World Jour. Surgery, 1983—92, Current Problems in Surgery, 1989—. Pres. GM Cancer Rsch. Found., 1996—. Lt. comdr. USPHS, 1964—66. Fellow: AAAS; mem.: ACS, Soc. Internationale de Chirurgie (pres. 2001), Soc. Surg. Oncology (pres. 1993—94), Halsted Soc. (pres. 1987), Nat. Cancer Adv. Bd., Inst. Medicine of NAS, Am. Soc. Clin. Investigation, Soc. Clin. Surgery (treas. 1980—86, v.p. 1986—88, pres. 1988—90), Soc. Univ. Surgeons (exec. coun. 1976—78), Am. Surg. Assn. (mem. coun. 1986—91, pres. 1995 96, recorder, Sci. Achievement medallion 2004), Am. Bd. Surgery (exec. com. 1986—89, vice chmn. 1987—88, chmn. 1988—89), Alpha Omega Alpha. Office: Dept Surgery Box 3627 Duke U Sch Medicine Durham NC 27710 Office Phone: 919-668-8435.

WELLS, SAMUEL FOGLE, JR., research center administrator; b. Mullins, SC, Sept. 13, 1935; s. Samuel Fogle and Mildred Inez (Meeks) W.; m. Novella R. Cloninger, June 15, 1957 (div. 1969); children: Lauren, Anthony (dec.), Jeffrey (dec.); m. Sherrill Perkins Brown, June 7, 1969; 1 child, Christopher Wentworth. AB, U. NC, 1957; MA, Harvard U., 1961, PhD, 1967. Instr. Wellesley (Mass.) Coll., 1963-65; asst. prof. U. NC, Chapel Hill, 1965-70, assoc. prof., 1970-78; dir. internat. security studies program Woodrow Wilson Ctr., Washington, 1977-87, assoc. dir., 1985-88, 99—, dep. dir., 1988-98. Cons. Office Sec. of Def., Washington, 1974-77; trustee Z. Smith Reynolds Found., Winston-Salem, NC, 1977-83. Author: The Challenges of Power: American Diplomacy, 1900-1921, 1990; editor and contbr. to books: Economics and World Power: An Assessment of American Diplomacy Since 1789, 1984, Limiting Nuclear Proliferation, 1985, Strategic Defenses and Soviet-American Relations, 1987, Security in the Middle East: Regional Change and Great Power Strategies, 1987, Superpower Competition and Security in the Third World, 1988, The Helsinki Process and the Future of Europe, 1990, New European Orders, 1919 and 1991, 1996, The Quest for Sustained Growth: Southeast Asian and Southeast European Cases, 1999; contbr. articles to profl. jours. Capt. USMC, 1957-60. Woodrow Wilson fellow, 1957, Danforth Found. fellow, 1957, Peace fellow Hoover Instn., 1972-73, Woodrow Wilson Internat. Ctr. for Scholars fellow, 1976-77. Mem. Am. Hist. Assn., Internat. Inst. Strategic Studies, Orgn. Am. Historians, Soc. for Historians of Am. Fgn. Rels., Internat. Studies Assn., Coun. on Fgn. Rels. Avocations: hiking, soccer. Home: 1509 Woodacre Dr Mc Lean VA 22101-2538 Office: Woodrow Wilson Internat Ctr 1300 Pennsylvania Ave NW Washington DC 20004-3027 Office Phone: 202-691-4208. Business E-Mail: wellssam@wwic.si.edu.

WELLS, STEVEN WAYNE, lawyer; b. Ft. Walton Beach, Fla., Sept. 8, 1960; s. H. Wayne and Shirley A. W.; m. Lisa Stieler, May 20, 1983; Robert, James, Jessica. BA in Comm., Mich. State U., 1982; JD with distinction, Detroit Coll. of Law, 1985. Bar: Mich. Asst. prosecutor Oakland County, Pontiac, Mich., 1985-88; mng. ptnr. Schnelz, Bondy & Wells, PC, Troy, Mich., 1988-93; shareholder, mng. ptnr. Cross Wrock, PC, Detroit, 1993-99; prin. shareholder Schnelz, Wells, Monaghan, Wells & Parry PC, Birmingham, Mich., 1999—. Lectr., presenter in field. Contbr. articles to State Bar Jour. Pres. Bloomfield Village Bd. Fellow Mich. Bar Assn.; ABA, ATLA, Detroit Bar Assn., Mich. Trial Lawyers Assn., Nat. Dist. Attys. Assn. Avocations: golf, tennis, coaching youth baseball, soccer. Address: 255 S Old Woodward Ave Ste 200 Birmingham MI 48009-6184

WELLS, THEODORE V., JR., lawyer; b. 1950; BA, Holy Cross, 1972; MBA, Harvard U., 1976; JD, Harvard Law Sch., 1976. Bar: N.J. 1977. Law clerk to Hon. John J Gibbons U.S. Ct. Appeals (3rd cir.), 1976-77; ptnr. Lowenstein, Sandler, Kohl, Fisher & Boylan P.C., Roseland, N.J. Mem. adj. faculty trade regulation Sch. Law, Seton Hall U., 1980-81; mem. faculty trial advocacy Practicing Law Inst., 1982—; mem. lawyers adv. com. U.S. Ct. Appeals (3rd cir.), 1982-85, 88—. Bd. trustees Coll. Holy Cross, 1977—, Newark Mus., 1979-82; bd. dirs. Essex County Urban League, 1979-88. Mem. ABA (antitrust law sect., state antitrust law subcom. 1980—), Assn. Crimiunal Def. Lawyers (trustee 1984—), N.J. State Bar Assn. (antitrust law com. 1980—). Office: Lowenstein Sandler Kohl Fisher & Boylan 65 Livingston Ave Ste 9 Roseland NJ 07068-1725

WELLS, THOMAS B. federal judge; b. 1945; BS, Miami U., 1967; JD, Emory U., 1973; LLM, NYU, 1978. Atty. Graham & Wells, Vidalia, Ga., Hurt, Richardson, Garner, Todd & Cadenhead, Atlanta, Shearer & Wells, Atlanta; city atty. City of Vidalia; county atty. Toombs County, Ga.; judge U.S. Tax Ct., Washington, 1986—, chief judge, 2000—. With USNR, 1967—70. Mem. ABA. Office: US Tax Ct 400 2nd St NW Washington DC 20217-0002

WELLS, VICTOR HUGH, JR., retired advertising agency executive; b. Bloomington, Ill., Apr. 19, 1924; s. Victor Hugh and Wilma Julia (Codlin) W.; m. Jacqueline L. Wade, Nov. 25, 1949; children— Victor Hugh, III, Polly Jo, Ken Douglas. BS, Bradley U., 1948. Copywriter Chgo. Tribune, 1949-54, Earle Ludgin & Co., Chgo., 1954-58, creative dir., 1959-64; group creative dir. Tatham-Laird, Chgo., 1958-59; founder, creative dir., pres. Rink Wells & Assos. (advt. agy.), Chgo., 1964-72; exec. v.p., dir. creative services N.W. Ayer Inc., Chgo., 1972-84, N.Y.C., 1984-86, also bd. dirs.; cons. N. W. Ayer Inc., N.Y.C., 1986-91; ret., 1991. Served to 2d lt. AC U.S. Army, 1943-45. Recipient various advt. creative awards, including Clio, Andy awards.

WELLS, ZELLA FAYE, school system administrator; b. Prestonsburg, Ky., Oct. 15, 1948; d. Robert Jackson and Nancy Jane (Stephens) Wallace; m. Frank Allen Wells Jr., Aug. 11, 1972 (div. Dec. 1992). AS, Prestonsburg C.C., 1968; BA, U. Ky., 1970, MA, 1973, Ed.D, 1999. Tchr. Floyd County Schs., Prestonsburg, 1970-72; tchr., instrnl. supr., asst. prin., asst. supt. Johnson County Schs., Paintsville, Ky., 1972—95, 1996—2001; disting. educator Ky. Dept. Edn., Frankfort, 1995-96; state mgr. Floyd County (Ky.) Sch. Sys. Adj. instr. Prestonsburg C.C., 1983-91. Mem. Ky. Edn. Profl. Stds. Bd., Frankfort, 1996-2000, Morehead State U. Big Sandy Adv. Bd., Prestonsburg, 1996—, Ky. Testing and Internship Adv. Bd., Frankfort, 1993-98, Ky. Edn. Assn. Pub. Edn. Task Force, Frankfort, 1996-98. Named Disting. Educator, Ky. Dept. Edn., Frankfort, 1993; recipient Disting. Svc. award Ky. Coun. Tchrs. of Math., 1993, Outstanding Math. Edn. Achievement award Ea. Ky. Coun. Tchrs. of Math., 1993. Mem.: ASCD, Ky. Assn. Sch. Supts., Ky. Assn. Sch. Adminstrs., Univ. Coun. for Edn. Adminstrn., Ky. Assn. Tchr. Educators, Nat. Coun. Tchrs. Math., Am. Ednl. Rsch. Assn., U. Ky. Alumni Assn., Sierra Club, Phi Delta Kappa. Avocations: canoeing, running, birding. Home: PO Box 1024 Paintsville KY 41240-5024 Office: Floyd County Bd Edn 106 N Front St Prestonsburg KY 41653

WELLS BRADLEY, CHARLENA RENEE, editor, writer; b. Cleve., Oct. 2, 1964; BA in Comm., Cleve. State U., 1988. Libr. asst., typist John Carroll U., University Heights, Ohio, summer 1982; asst. sociology dept., registration asst. Cleve. State U., 1985-88; project asst. Jones, Day, Reavis & Pogue, Cleve., 1988-94; asst. writer Righteousness Newsletter, Cleve., 1990-93; editor-in-chief, writer Holiness Inc., Cleve., 1993—; project asst. Jones, Day, Reavis & Pogue, 1988-94; adminstrv. exec. USA Mobile Comms., 1994; file

adminstrv. clk. Pioneer Stds. Electronics Inc., 1994; mktg. rep. APT Publs., 1996—; adminstrv./registration asst. MBA degree program Case Western Res. U., Cleve., 1996; telephone operator Roetzel & Andress, 1996; property asst. Trammell Crow Co., Cleve., 1997-98; counter mgr. lingerie dept. Dillard's, 1998-99, assoc., 1999; telemarketer Allied Capital Corp., 1999; sr. sec., outsourcing rep. Kaiser Permanente, Cleve., 2000; account mgr. MBNA Am. Bank, Beachwood, Ohio, 2001—; pres. Wells Bradley Film Prodn. Cons., 2001—. Outsourcing rep. CCS, Kaiser Permanente, Cleve., 2000—; radio asst. Sta. WABQ, Cleve., spring 1987; beauty advisor Fashion Fair Dilliards, 1998; selling specialist J.C. Penney, 1998; bus. builder Shaklee Products, 1998; sr. sec. Kaiser Permanente, 2000—; ind. beauty cons. Mary Kay Cosmetics, 2002—; sr. v.p., sec. Wells Creations. Nursing asst. St. Vincent Charity Hosp., Cleve., 1987; facilitator/exhibit guide Cleve. Children's Mus., 1986; guest spkr. AME Zion Ch., Cleve., 1993, Assembly Missionary Bapt. Ch., Cleve., 1994; lay min. St. Anthony Messenger, 2001; vol. child care ministry Mega Ch., 2001—; Christian actress, psalmist Parma Heights Bapt. Ch., 1998—; co-hostess Sta.-WCIN, Cin., 1991. Acad. scholar John Carroll U., 1982. Avocations: tennis, chess, singing, reading, writing. Home: 137 Ruth Ellen Dr #401k Richmond Heights OH 44143 also: 3203 Brunswick Ave Lawrenceville NJ 08648-2409 Office: MBNA 25875 Science Park Dr Beachwood OH 44122 also: Wells Creations 21936 Lakeshore Blvd Euclid OH 44132 Office Phone: 440-449-7012. E-mail: lena--7_5@hotmail.com.

WELLS-HENDERSON, RONALD JOHN, investment counselor; b. Jan. 28, 1934; s. William Noel and Sylvia Mary (Gowen) W.-H.; m. Kathleen Louise McDonnell, Sept. 14, 1957; children: Anne, John. BA, U. Wash., 1955; MBA, Northwestern U., 1957. CFA. Security analyst Continental Bank, Chgo., 1957—59; fin. analyst Boeing Co., Seattle; trust investment mgr. Seattle Trust, 1970—80; prin. KAS Investment Cons., Seattle, 1980—. Contbr. articles to profl. jours. Mem. Seattle Art Mus., Bellevue Art Mus., 1957—; treas. Civil Affairs Assn., 1975—79; curator-treas. Seattle King County Mil. History Soc., 1978—80. Lt. col. USAR, 1955—83. Named Gazzam Found. scholar, 1952—55. Mem.: Washington Water Trails Assn., CFA Inst. (charter holder), Seattle Soc. Fin. Analysts. Episcopalian. Home: 13005 SE 46th St Bellevue WA 98006-2042 Office: KAS Investment Cons PO Box 5617 Bellevue WA 98006-0117 Office Phone: 425-641-7645.

WELLS-MAXWELL, VIOLET, writer, artist; b. Redkey, Ind., Aug. 3, 1927; d. James William Philebaum and Etta Catherine Hunt; m. Paul Eugene Wells, Sept. 5, 1947 (dec. May 1975); children: Carol Parrott, Randy Wells, Joy Wells; m. Rudolph Neff Maxwell, Sept. 22, 1990 (dec. Aug. 2002). BBA, Olivet Nazarene U., 1949. Sec. Olivet Nazarene U., Kankakee, Ill., 1947-49; receptionist Speech Clinic Ohio State U., 1950-54; art and music instr. Ea. Nazarene Coll., Boston, 1955-69; art tchr., 1960-99; receptionist Office for Fin. Aid to Students Mt. Vernon (Ohio) Nazarene Coll., 1970-73; realtor assoc. Gtr. Ohio Realty, Mt. Vernon, 1974-76; real estate assoc. Century 21 Dalbec, Willsboro, N.Y., 1976-82; nutrition supr. Shaklee Products, Mt. Vernon, Ohio, 1990—2002. Exhbns. include Dixie Days Street Fair, Mt. Vernon, 1997, Dan Emmett Festival, 1994-96, Mt. Vernon (Ohio) News, 1988, Lake Holm Ch. Gallery, Mt. Vernon, 1988, Heritage Hall Gallery, Mt. Vernon, 1996-98. Mem. ch. choir, Mt. Vernon, 1970-75; active Celebration of the Arts high sch., middle sch., Mt. Vernon, 1992-99. Mem. Poetry Appreciation, Mt. Vernon Pub. Libr. Avocations: Mark Twain, poetry, singing, restoring art work. Studio: 500 N Gay St Mount Vernon OH 43050-1708 Personal E-mail: vwm76@earthlink.net.

WELNA, CECILIA, retired mathematics educator; b. New Britain, Conn., July 15, 1927; d. Joseph and Sophie (Roman) W. BS, St. Joseph Coll., 1949; MA, U. Conn., 1952, PhD, 1960. Instr. Mt. St. Joseph Acad., 1949-50; asst. instr. U. Conn., 1950-55; instr. U. Mass., Amherst, 1955-56; prof., chmn. dept. math. and physics U. Hartford, 1957-82, dean Coll. Edn., Nursing and Health Professions, 1982-91, prof. math., 1991—2004. Mem. Math. Assn. Am., Nat. Council Tchrs. Math., Assn. Tchrs. Math. Conn., Sigma Xi. E-mail: seawell31@aol.com.

WELNETZ, DAVID CHARLES, human resources executive; b. Antigo, Wis., Apr. 12, 1947; s. Francis P. and Marquette A. (Stengl) W.; m. Mary L. McCulley, Aug. 25, 1973; children: Andrew, Timothy. BS in Biology, U. Wis., Stevens Point, Wis., 1969; MS in Indsl. Rels., U. Wis. Madison, 1975. Mgr. coll. recruitment tng. Rexnord Inc., Milw., 1975-77, personnel mgr. Sarasota, Fla., 1977-80, corp. dir. employee rels. Milw., 1980-83; sr. cons. The Thompson Group, Brookfield, Wis., 1983-87, v.p., 1987-91; pres. Thompson Cons., Brookfield, 1991—. Adv. bd. SUNY, Buffalo, 1982-88; bd. dirs. Matarah Industries. Bd. dirs. Outplacement Internat., 1996—; bd. dirs. Matarah Ind., 1994—, Lutheran Social Svcs., Milw. Ctr. for Independence. Recipient Bronze Star U.S. Army, 1972. Mem. Pers. Indsl. Rels. Assn. (program com. 1988-91, chmn. pers. rsch. 1980-82), Human Resources Planning Soc., Human Resources Mgmt. Assn. Roman Catholic. Home: N54W 38928 Islandale Dr Oconomowoc WI 53066-2101 Office: Thompson Cons Ltd 17700 W Capitol Dr Brookfield WI 53045-2006

WELPOTT, JACK WARREN, photographer, educator; b. Kansas City, Kans., Apr. 27, 1923; s. Ray Calvert and Dolores (Davenroy) W.; m. Doris Jean Franklin, June 12, 1949; children— Jan Marie, Matthew David; m. Judy Dater, May 22, 1969; m. Wendy Brooke Gray, May 11, 1986. BS, Ind. U., 1949, MS, 1954, M.F.A., 1959. Mem. acad. staff Ind. U., 1949-59; mem. faculty San Francisco State U., 1959-93, ret., 1993. Artist in residence RISD, 1984; workshop leader Columbia Coll., 1985, Friends of Photo, 1985, Humboldt State U., 1985, Parsons Sch. Design, Paris, 1985, Volcano Hawaii, 1986, numerous others in France, England, Switzerland, Japan and Mexico. One man shows include, U. Calif., Davis, Art Inst. Chgo., 1972, Wall Street Gallery, Spokane, 1973, Gallery 113, Santa Cruz, Calif., 1974, San Francisco Mus. Art, 25 year retrospective, 1976, U. So. Calif., 25 year retrospective, 1977, Ind. U., 25 year retrospective, 1977, Silver Image Gallery, Seattle, 1977, Ohio State U., 1978, Center for Creative Photography, U. Ariz., 1979, Colo. Mountain Coll., 1980, Bard Coll., 1981, Jehu Gallery, San Francisco, 1981, Galerif Voor Fotografie, Antwerp, Belgium, 1983, R.I. Sch. Design, 1984, La Photographie Creative, Pavillon des Arts, Paris, 1984, New Sch. Social Research, N.Y.C., 1984, Foto Biennale Enschede, Netherlands, 1984, Vision Gallery, San Francisco, 1984, Min Gallery, Tokyo, 1987, Osaka (Japan) Cultrual Ctr., 1989, Retrospective Vision Gallery, San Francisco, 1992; two man shows include Musee Reattu, Arles, France, 1976, Photographers Gallery, Palo Alto, Calif., 1986, group exhbns. include Santa Barbara Mus., Mus. Modern Art, Mexico City, Photography in Am, Whitney Mus., N.Y.C., Photography in the 20th Century, George Eastman House, California Photography, Oakland Mus., San Francisco Mus. Art, U. Oreg. Commitment to Vision, 1986, U. Colo. Photographics, 1986, numerous others, Met. Mus. Art, N.Y.C., De Cordova Mus., Lincoln, Mass.; represented in permanent collections Graham Nash Collection, Mus. Modern Art, N.Y.C., Whitney Mus. Art, N.Y.C., Art Inst. Chgo., Biblioteque Nat, Paris, Tokyo Coll. Photography, Open U., London, Internat. Mus. Photography, Rochester, N.Y., San Francisco Mus. Art, Musee Reattu, Arles, Frances, Oakland (Calif.) Mus., U. Colo., Center Creative Photography, Tucson, U. N.Mex., Pasadena Art Mus., Australian Nat. Gallery, Houston Mus. Fine Arts, Fogg Art Mus., Cambridge, Mass., Gallery Van Haarlem, Netherlands; author: The Halide Conversion, 1989; contbr. photos to books. Served with USAAF, 1943-46. NEA fellow, 1979; grantee Polaroid, 1983, Marin Arts Coun., 1991. Home: PO Box 496 Inverness CA 94937-0496 E-mail: jax@svn.net.

WELSCH, FEDERICO, cancer researcher; b. Seville, Spain, Dec. 26, 1933; married; 4 children. BA, U. Barcelona, Spain, 1950; MD summa cum laude, U. Valencia, Spain, 1955, D of Med. Sci. in Biochemistry, 1957; MS in Biophysics, Ctr Rsch. and Advanced Studies, Mexico City, 1965; PhD in Molecular Biology, Dartmouth Coll., 1968. Med. clk. Hamburg (Germany)-Eppendorf Univ. Hosp., 1954-55; instr., then asst. prof. physiology and physiol. chemistry U. Valencia (Spain) Sch. Medicine, 1955-58; prof. physiology U. Autonoma de Guadalajara (Mex.) Sch. Medicine, 1958-60; prof. biochemistry and biophysics U. Chihuahua (Mex.) Sch. Medicine, 1960-63; rsch. scientist Ctr. for Rsch. and Advanced Studies, Mexico City, 1963-65; asst. prof. biochemistry, and USPHS postdoctoral fellow Dartmouth Coll. Sch. Medicine, Hanover, N.H., 1965-70; assoc. dir., then exec. dir. Worcester (Mass.) Found. for Exptl. Biology Inc., 1970-87; exec. officer to rsch. com. Harvard U.-MIT Divsn. Health Sci. and Tech., Cambridge, Mass., 1987-88; assoc. dir. for internat. affairs Nat. Cancer Inst., Bethesda, Md., 1988—. Mem. adv. bd. Fogarty Internat. Ctr., NIH, 1987-88; trustee Mass. Biotech. Rsch. Inst., Worcester, 1984-86; budget analyst del. for Basic Biomed. Rsch., Washington, 1977-88; dir. jt. PhD program in biomed. scis. Clark U.-U. Mass., Worcester Poly. Inst., Worcester Found. for Exptl. Biology, 1974-84; mem. gov.'s adv. coun. on comprehensive health planning Commonwealth of Mass., 1970-76; vis. prof. numerous univs. in Europe, Latin Am. and Asia, 1955—. Contbr. articles to profl. jours. Lt. Spanish Air Force, 1953-56. Fellow, grantee Spanish Rsch. Coun., 1958—, Rockefeller Found., 1963-64, Mex. Rsch. Coun., 1964-65, USPHS, NIH, 1966-68, 70-87, Am. Heart Assn., 1968-70, others. Office: 6130 Executive Blvd Ste 100 Rockville MD 20852-4910 E-mail: fw11x@nih.gov.

WELSCH, ROBERT LOUIS, anthropologist, curator; b. St. Louis, May 19, 1950; s. Russell Louis and Carmen Celia Welsch; m. Sarah Leslie Leslie, Oct. 15, 1988. BA, Northwestern U., 1972; MA, U. of Wash., 1976, PhD, 1982. Adj. curator of anthropology The Field Mus., Chgo., 1984—. Vis. prof. anthropology Dartmouth Coll., Hanover, NH, 1994—. Author: An American Anthropologist in Melanesia, 1998. Recipient Morton H. Fried prize, Am. Anthrop. Assn., 1992, Antiquity prize, Antiquity Jour., 1998; fellow Sylvan C. Coleman and Pamela Coleman Meml. Fund fellowship, Met. Mus. of Art, 2001; grantee, Fulbright Found., 1977—79, NSF, 1977—79, Fulbright Found., 1985—87, NSF, 1989—90, NEH, 1993—94, NSF, 1993—94, Mus. Planning grant, Nat. Endowment for the Humanities, 1999—2001, NSF, 2000—01. Mem.: Pacific Arts Assn. (treas. 1999—2001, spl. publs. editor 2001—). Office: Dartmouth Coll Dept Anthropology 6047 Silsby Hall Hanover NH 03755 Personal E-mail: robert.l.welsch@dartmouth.edu.

WELSER, WILLIAM, III, military officer; B in Biology, U. Buffalo, 1971; grad., Squadron Officer Sch., 1977, Air Command and Staff Coll., 1980; M in Pers. Mgmt., Webster U., 1981; grad., Armed Forces Staff Coll., 1982, Nat. War Coll., 1988; exec. devel. program, U. N.H., 1994. Commd. 2d lt. USAF, 1971, advanced through grades to maj. gen., 1998; F-4 br. chief, job control duty officer 8th Tactical Fighter Wing, Ubon Royal Thai AFB, Thailand, 1973-74; C-141 pilot, crew contrl. 20th Mil. Airlift Squadron, Charleston AFB, S.C., 1975-79; instr. pilot, asst. chief pilot 6th Mil. Airlift Squadron Airlift Wing, McGuire AFB, N.J., 1982-83; chief airlift mgmt., chief wing current ops. 438th Mil. Airlift Wing, McGuire AFB, 1983-85; ops. officer, comdr. 6th Mil. Airlift Squadron, McGuire AFB, 1985-87; spl. asst. for gen. and flag officer matters Office of Dir., Joint Staff, Washington, 1988-90; vice comdr. 443d Airlift Wing, Altus AFB, Okla., 1990-92; comdr. 436th Airlift Wing, Dover AFB, Del., 1992-94; vice comdr. Tanker Air Lift Control Ctr., Hdqs. Air Mobility Command, Scott AFB, Ill., 1994-95, comdr., 1995-97, Air Mobility Warfare Ctr., Ft. Dix, N.J., 1997-99; dir. ops. HQ Air Edn. and Tng. Command, Randolph AFB, Tex., 1999—. Decorated Def. Superior Svc. medal, Legion of Merit with oak leaf cluster, Meritorious Svc. medal with 2 oak leaf clusters. Office: USTRANSCOM TCJ 3/4 508 Scott Dr Scott Air Force Base IL 62225-5357

WELSER-MÖST, FRANZ, conductor; b. Linz, Austria, Aug. 16, 1960; Chief condr. Sinfonieorkester Norrköping, Sweden, 1986-91, Stadtorchester Winterthur, Switzerland, 1987-90; music dir. London Philharm., 1990—, The Cleve. Orch., 2002—. Conducting debut Salzburg Festival, Austria, 1985; Am. debut St. Louis, 1989; condr. Vienna Opera, 1987, Berlin Opera, 1991. Office: Severance Hall 11001 Euclid Ave Cleveland OH 44106

WELSH, SIR ALFRED JOHN, lawyer, international advisor; b. Louisville, May 10, 1947; s. Elvin Alfred and Carol (Kleymeyer) W.; m. Lee Mitchell, Aug. 1, 1970; children: Charles Kleymeyer, Kathryn Thomas. BA, Centre Coll., 1969; JD, U. Ky., 1972; LLM in Internat. Law cum laude, U. Brussels, 1973. Bar: Ky. 1972, U.S. Dist. Ct. (we. and ea. dists.) Ky. 1972, U.S. Ct. Appeals (6th cir.) 1972. Asst. atty. Ky. Atty. Gen. Office, Frankfort, 1973-74; legis. counsel to congressman Ho. of Reps., Washington, 1974-77; mng. ptnr. Adams, Hayward and Welsh, Louisville, 1977—, Boone Welsh and Hayward Internat. Law. Hon. counsel of Belgium, 1983—; econ. devel. advisor Kingdom of Belgium; mem. Ky. Econ. Adv. Coun., 1991-94; pres. Transcontinental Trading Cons., Ltd.; del. North African Mideast Econ. Summit Conf., Morocco, 1994; bd. dirs. Intervention Resources Ctr., Inc. Bd. dirs. Greater Louisville Swim Found., 1983-94, exec. com., 1994—; bd. dirs. Louisville com. Coun. Fgn. Rels., 1981—, also pres.; chmn. Louisville com. on Fgn. Rels.; bd. dirs. Jefferson County Alcohol and Drug Abuse Found., Louisville, 1986-98, Internat. Resolve, Louisville Internat. Cultural Ctr.; mem. econ. task force of Ky. Legis. Agts.; mem. Louisville Meml. Auditorium Commn., Am. Com. Fgn. Rels. Decorated knight Order of the Crown (Belgium). Mem. ABA (internat. law sect., commn. on impairment, com. on substance abuse), ATLA, Ky. Bar Assn. (bd. dirs. 1981-82, pres. young lawyers divsn. 1981-82), Ky. Acad. Trial Lawyers, Am. Judicature Soc., Louisville C. of C., Am. Ctr. Foreign Rels. (pres. Louisville com. on Foreign Rels.). Democrat. Presbyterian. Avocations: swimming, water polo, soccer. Office: Barristers Hall 1009 S 4th St Louisville KY 40203-3207 Office Phone: 502-584-8583. Business E-Mail: bwbh@earthlink.net.

WELSH, ANNE MARIE, theater critic, writer, educator; b. Batavia, N.Y., Apr. 17, 1946; d. Paul Patrick and Geraldine Driscoll Welsh; children: Adam Morawski, Martin Morawski, Casimir Morawski. BA with honors, Manhattanville Coll., Purchase, NY, 1967; MA, U. Rochester, NY, 1972; PhD, U. Rochester, 1976. Dance critic, theater writer Washington Star, 1976—81; arts writer San Diego Union, 1983—97; theater critic San Diego Union Tribune, 1997—. Vis. lectr. San Diego State U., 1985—, U. Calif., San Diego, 1989—; spkr. in field. Author: (book) Evaluating Plays on Film and Video, 2003; co-author: Longman Anthology of Modern Drama, 2003; editor: The Longman Anthology of World Drama and Theater, 2001, author eight poems; contbr. articles to profl. jours. Pres. La Jolla (Calif.) Elem. Found., 2001—02, San Diego Theater Critics Cir., 2002—04; co-pres. Friends La Jolla Schs. Found., 2001—02; cultural arts chair La Jolla Parent Tchrs. Assn. Nominee Pulitzer Prize for disting. criticism, 2001—03; recipient First Pl. Criticism, Cultural Commentary, Soc. Profl. Journalists, First Pl. Criticism, Arts Writing, Investigative Reporting, San Diego Press Club, Living Legacy award, Women's Internat. Ctr., 2004; fellow Creative Writing, Ragdale Found. Arts, 2002—03, Norcroft Wrtier's Found., 1995, Univ. fellow, U. Rochester, 1967—70. Mem.: Shakespeare Soc. San Diego, Com. Concerned Journalists, Am. Theater Critics Assn. Avocations: walking, piano. Home: 520 Westbourne St La Jolla CA 92037 Office: San Diego Union Tribune 350 Camino de la Reina San Diego CA 92112

WELSH, DIANE M. federal judge; BA in Polit. Sci. magna cum laude, Villanova U., 1976, JD, 1979. Bar: Pa. 1979, U.S. Dist. Ct. (ea. dist.) Pa. 1981, U.S. Ct. Appeals (3rd cir.) 1984, U.S. Supreme Ct. 1985. Legal counsel Pa. Senate Judiciary Com., 1980-81; dep. dist. atty. Bucks County Dist. Atty.'s Office, Pa., 1981-84; ptnr. Gold-Bikin Welsh & Assocs., 1984-94; magistrate judge U.S. Dist. Ct. (ea. dist.) Pa., Phila., 1994—. Spkr. in field. Contbr. articles to legal jours. Trustee Manor Jr. Coll., 1981-83, Norristown State Hosp., 1987-90. Mem. ABA, Fed. Bar Assn., Fed. Magistrate Judge Assn., Nat. Assn. Women Judges, Pa. Bar Assn., Montgomery County Bar Assn., Phila. Bar Assn., Brehon Law Soc. Office: US Courthouse 3029 US Courthouse 601 Market St Philadelphia PA 19106-1713

WELSH, DONALD EMORY, publisher; b. Youngstown, Ohio, Oct. 6, 1943; s. Edward Francis and Clevelle Rose W.; m. Elizabeth Bourne Floyd, June 25, 1966; children: Leah Bourne, Emory Philip. AB, Columbia U., 1965; JD, Cleveland Marshall Sch. Law, 1969. Bar: Ohio 1969. Trust devel. officer Cleve. Trust Co., 1968-70; advt. sales rep. Fortune mag., Time, Inc., N.Y.C., 1970-75; advt. dir. Rolling Stone mag., N.Y.C., 1975-77, v.p., assoc. pub., 1977-78; pub. Outside mag., N.Y.C., 1978-82; pub. Muppet mag. and pres. Lorimar Pub. Group (formerly Telepictures Publs., Inc.), 1982-87; pres. Welsh Pub. Group, Inc., 1987-94; exec. v.p. Marvel Comics Group, N.Y.C., 1994-96; chmn. Group XXVII Comms., N.Y.C., 1997-2000; pres. pub. group Digital Convergence Inc., N.Y.C., 2000-2001; chmn. Budget Living Commn., N.Y.C., 2001—. Trustee Outward Bound, U.S.A., Cousteau Soc.; former bd. dirs. Big Apple Circus. Mem. ABA, Mag. Pubs. Assn. (past bd. dirs.), Century Assn., Racquet and Tennis Club, Sharon Country Club (Conn.), Ocean Reef Club (Fla.), Brook Club (N.Y.C.). Home: 501 E 79th St New York NY 10021-0735 Office: Budget Living Commn 317 Madison Ave Ste 2300 New York NY 10017 E-mail: DonaldEWelsh@aol.com.

WELSH, DONALD S. government agency administrator; b. 1957; m. Joanne Welsh; 2 children. B in Polit. Sci., U. Pa. With region 3 US EPA, Phila., 1985—95, adminstr. region 3, 2001—; with Pa. Dept. Environ. Protection, 1995—2001, dep. sec. state/fed. affairs, 1997—2001. Office: US EPA Region 3 1650 Arch St 3PM52 Philadelphia PA 19103-2029

WELSH, DOUGLAS LEE, psychologist, researcher; b. Lumberton, N.C., Oct. 29, 1973; s. Jesse Luckey and Mary Peterson Welsh. BS, Furman U., Greenville, South Carolina, 1992—97; MA in Exptl. Psychology, U. Richmond, Va., 2000; MA in Applied Psychology, Columbia U. Tchr. Coll., N.Y.C., 2004; post grad. in Clin. Psychology, U. Louisville, 2004—. Rsch. asst. Furman U., Greenville, SC, 1996—97, U. Richmond, Va., 1997—2000, tchg. asst., 1997—99; project coord. U. Ala., Tuscaloosa, 2000—03, rsch. assoc., 2000—04, student therapist psychol. clinic, 2001—02, instr., 2001—02; student therapist Mary Stark Harper Ctr., 2001—02, Brewer Porch Children's Ctr., 2001—02; psychol. technician Riverside Med. Ctr., Tuscaloosa, Ala., 2002; student U. Louisville, 2004—. Student liaison Divsn. of Clin. Geropsychology, APA, Washington, 2000—01; presenter to profl. and academic confs. Author: (research) Age, Self-Efficacy, and Performance on Memory and Attention Tasks. (Outstanding Grad. Student Rsch. award, 2000); contbr. chapters to books, articles to profl. jours. Recipient Grad. Rsch. award, APA, 2000; grantee, Grad. Sch. of Arts and Sci. U. Richmond, 1997—2000. Mem.: APA (assoc.), Am. Soc. on Aging, Soc. for the Study of Human Devel. (assoc.), Am. Psychol. Soc. (assoc.), Gerontol. Soc. of Am. (assoc.), Am. Assn. of People with Disabilities, Kappa Delta Pi, Psi Chi. Home: 189 W 89th St 3N New York NY 10024 Office: Univ Louisville Dept of Psychol and Brain Scis Louisville KY 40292 Office Phone: 502-852-6068. Home Fax: 212-706-7650. Personal E-mail: dlw2101@columbial.edu. E-mail: dlwels03@louisville.edu.

WELSH, GEORGE FRANKLIN, plastic surgeon, educator, healthcare consultant; b. Charles City, Iowa, Oct. 13, 1940; s. George S. Welsh and Aldeen (Paris) Welsh Taylor; m. Rosemary Dahlen, June 23, 1973; children: Christopher Franklin, Penelope Cosette, Bradford Alexander. BA, Carleton Coll., 1962; BS, U. N.D., 1964; MD, Harvard U., Boston, 1966; M Health and Hosp. Adminstrn., Xavier U., Cin., 1994; Cert. in Horticulture, U. Cin., 2002. Diplomate Am. Bd. Surgery, Am. Bd. Plastic Surgery; cert. physician exec; Health Care Garden Design, Chgo., 2004. Commd. officer USAF, 1966, advanced through grades to lt. col., 1974; intern USAF Hosp., San Antonio, 1966—67; resident in surgery Mayo Clinic, Rochester, Minn., 1969—73; resident in plastic surgery U. Okla. Health Sci. Ctr., Oklahoma City, 1973—75; Maytag Fellow in plastic surgery U. Miami, Fla., 1976; plastic surgeon USAF, Dayton, Ohio, 1975—78, flight surgeon, dir. base med. svcs., 1991; ret. USAFR, 1996; pvt. practice Cin., 1978—. Cons. on healthcare adminstrn., Cin., 1994—; asst. clin. prof. surgery Wright State U. Sch. Medicine, Dayton, 1975-78; vol. asst. prof. surgery U. Cin. Sch. Medicine, 1978-2002. Contbr. articles to med. jours., including Surg. Clinics N.Am., Jour. Thoracic and Cardiovasc. Surgery, So. Med. Jour., Plastic and Reconstructive Surgery, Aesthetic Plastic Surgery, Brit. Jour. Plastic Surgery, Mil. Medicine, Health Care Fin. Mgmt., Jour. Health Care Fin., Quality Progress, Physician Exec. Mem. Leadership Cin., 1981; citizen amb. People to People Internat., Albania, Russia, 1994, Cuba, 2000, Egypt, 2003; mem. fin. and facilities Hamilton County Alcohol and Drug Addiction Svc. Bd., Cin., 1999—. Fellow ACS; mem. Am. Soc. Plastic Surgeons, Am. Soc. for Aesthetic Plastic Surgery, Millard Plastic Surg. Soc. (treas.), English Spkg. Union (past pres. Cin. br.), Soc. Colonial Wars (chmn. grants and contbns.), Harvard Alumni Assn. Avocations: medical missions, landscape design, fishing. Office: Aesthetic Plastic Surgery Ctr 6200 Pfeiffer Rd Ste 320 Cincinnati OH 45242-5861 Office Phone: 513-793-0302. E-mail: aestheticps@aol.com.

WELSH, JOHN BERESFORD, JR., retired lawyer; b. Seattle, Feb. 16, 1940; s. John B. and Rowena Morgan (Custer) W. Student, U. Hawaii, 1960, Georgetown U., 1960; BA, U. Wash., 1962; LLB, 1965. Bar: Wash. 1965. Staff counsel Joint Com. on Govtl. Cooperation, 1965-66; asst. atty gen. Dept. Labor and Industries, 1966-67; atty. Legis Counsel; acting as counsel Pub. Health Com., Labor Com., Pub. Employees Collective Bargaining Com., Com. on State Instns. and Youth Devel., State of Wash., 1967-73; sr. counsel Wash. Ho. of Reps., Ho. Com. on Social and Health Svcs., Olympia, WA, 1973-86; atty., spkr. Ho. of Reps., 1973; counsel Ho. Com. Human Svcs., 1987-91, 93-95, Ho. Com. on Health Care, 1987—2003, ret., 2003. Counsel Ho. Com. on Trade and Econ. Devel., 1995-98, Joint Select Com. on Nurse Delegation, 1995-98, Joint Select Com. on Oral Health, 1996. legal cons. Gov.'s Planning Commn. Vocat. Rehab., 1968, Gov.'s Commn. on Youth Involvement, 1969; envoy from Gov. Wash. to investiture of Prince of Wales, London, 1969, fac. Nat. Conf. State Legislatures, Denver, 1977, New Orleans, 1977; fac. Coun. Licensure, Enforcement and Regulation, San Francisco, 1984, Orlando, Fla., 1985, Denver, 1986, Kansas City, Mo., 1987, Washington, 1988, Indpls., 1989, Seattle, 1990, Ft. Lauderdale, Fla., 1991, Albuquerque, 1992, Boston, 1994, San Antonio, 1995, Norfolk, 1997; steering com., 1986-90, legis. issues com., 1986-88, Coun. of State Govts. com. on suggested state legis., 1988-95, subcom. scope and agenda, 1988-95. Vol. Hampton Rds. U.S. Naval Mus., mem. gov.'s state medal merit com., 1986-. Recipient Gov.'s award for excellence in state health care policy, 2002, Spkr. of House award for dedicated pub. svc., 2002, Sec. of State award for pub. svc. to state legislature and people of state of Wash., 2003, Sec. of Health award for creating meaningful health policy change, 2003. Mem. SAR, Wash. Bar Assn., Soc. des Amis du Musee de l'Armee, Paris, English Speaking Union, La Societe Napoleonienne (pres.), Sons of Union Veterans of the Civil War, Custer Battlefield Hist. & Mus. Assn., The Colonial Williamsburg Found., Jamestown-Yorktown Found., Napoleonic Alliance (bd. dirs., exec. v.p.), World Affairs Coun., Friends of Old Ft. Stevens (bd. dirs.), Friends of Willie & Joe, Northwest Hist. Assn. (pres., 2003), Sons of Am. Revolution. Home: 1700 Evergreen Park Lane SW Olympia WA 98502 E-mail: JBWelsh@comcast.net.

WELSH, JOHN FRANCIS, retired advertising executive; b. New Haven, May 19, 1916; s. Pierce Jerome and Irene (Kennedy) W.; m. Margaret Burke, Sept. 18, 1947; children: Peter Burke, Diana Margaret. BA, Yale U., 1937. With Warwick & Legler, Inc., N.Y.C, 1946-81; exec. v.p., mgmt. supr., mem. mgmt. com.; vice chmn. Warwick, Welsh & Miller, Inc., 1973-81. Served with AUS, 1941-45. Decorated Bronze Star, Croix de Guerre France). Mem.: Tokeneke (Darien). Home: 98 Ridge Acres Rd Darien CT 06820-2616

WELSH, KELLY RAYMOND, lawyer, former telecommunications company executive; b. Chgo., July 6, 1952; s. Raymond J. and Mary Jane (Kelly) W.; m. Ellen S. Alberding, June 28, 1985; children: Katherine A., Julia S. AB cum laude, Harvard U., 1974, JD magna cum laude, 1978; MA, Sussex U., Eng., 1975. Assoc. Mayer, Brown & Platt, Chgo., 1979-85, ptnr., 1985-89; corp. counsel City of Chgo., 1989-93; v.p., assoc. gen. counsel Ameritech Corp., Chgo., 1993-96, exec. v.p., gen. counsel, 1996-99; ret., 1999. Chmn. Met. Pier and Exposition Authority, Chgo., 1994—. Mem. ABA, Chgo. Bar Assn., Chgo. Coun. Lawyers, Chgo. Coun. Fgn. Rels. (mem. exec. com.), Legal Club Chgo. Office: Ameritec 225 W Randolph St Fl 27 Chicago IL 60606-1836

WELSH, MARY MCANAW, family mediator, educator; b. Cameron, Mo., Dec. 7, 1920; d. Francis Louis and Mary Matilda (Moore) McAnaw; m. Alvin F. Welsh, Feb. 10, 1944 (dec.); children: Mary Celia, Clinton F., M. Ann. AB, U. Kans., 1942; MA, Seton Hall U., 1960; EdD, Columbia U., 1971. Reporter Hutchinson (Kans.) News Herald, 1942-43; house editor Worthington Pump & Machine Corp., Harrison, N.J., 1943-44; tchr., housemaster, coord. Summit (N.J.) Pub. Schs., 1960-68; prof. family studies N.Mex. State U., Las Cruces, 1972-85; adj. faculty dept. family practice Tex. Tech Regional Acad. Health Ctr., El Paso, 1978-82, Family Mediation Practicce, Las Cruces, 1986—. Author: A Good Family is Hard to Found, 1972, Parent, Child and Sex, 1970; contbr. articles to profl. jours.; writer, presenter home econs. and family study

series KRWG-TV, 1974; moderator TV series The Changing Family in N.Mex./LWV, 1976. Mem. AAUW (pres. N.Mex. 1981-83), N.Mex. Coun. Women's Orgn. (founder, chmn. 1982-83), Delta Kappa Gamma, Kappa Alpha Theta. Democrat. Roman Catholic. Home and Office: 1975 Avenida Antigua Las Cruces NM 88005

WELSH, MICHAEL JAMES, medical educator, biophysicist, educator; b. Marshalltown, Iowa, Dec. 22, 1948; Student, Loras Coll., 1967-69; BS, U. Iowa, 1970, MD, 1974. Intern and resident internal medicine U. Iowa Coll. Medicine, Iowa City, 1974-77; clin. fellow internal medicine U. Calif. San Francisco, 1977-78; rsch. fellow cardiovasc. rsch. unit U. Calif., San Francisco, 1978-79; rsch. fellow physiology and cell biology U. Tex., Houston, 1979-80; asst. prof. medicine U. Iowa Coll. Medicine, Iowa City, 1981-84, assoc. prof. medicine, 1984-87, prof. medicine, 1987—, prof. physiology and biophysics, 1989—. Cons. VA Hosp., Iowa City, 1981—; investigator Howard Hughes Med. Inst., U. Iowa., Iowa City, 1989—. Contbr. chpts. to books and numerous articles to profl. jours. Recipient Doris F. Tulcin Cystic Fibrosis Rsch. award, 1992, Paul di Sant-Agnese Disting. Sci. Achievement award, 1993. Mem. Am. Fedn. for Clin. Rsch., Am. Physiol. Soc., Am. Thoracic Soc. (J. Burns Amberson award 1994), Iowa Thoracic Soc. Office: Howard Hughes Med Inst 500 EMRB Univ Iowa Coll Medicine Iowa City IA 52242

WELSH, MICHAEL LOUIS, business executive; b. Clayton, Ga., June 14, 1959; s. John F. and Mary Ann (Casimes) W.; m. Susie Googe, June 5, 1982; children: Sarah Alex, Daniel, Grace, Samuel BBA magna cum laude, U. Ga., 1981, MACC, 1986. Consolidation acct. Tex. Instruments, Dallas, 1981-82, fin. analyst, 1982-84; v.p. cons. MISA, Atlanta, 1986-87; consolidation analyst Coca-Cola Enterprise, Atlanta, 1987-88; mid-Atlantic supr., mgr. Coca-Cola Bottling Co., Columbia, Md., 1988-90; div. mgr. Coca-Cola Enterprises-North, Columbia, 1990-91; ops. controller Cott Beverages USA, Columbus, Ga., 1993-95; v.p. adminstrn. Thompson Hardwoods, Inc., Hazlehurst, Ga., 1995-98; owner MWelsh Co., LLC, Evans, Ga., 1998—. Acctg. and system implementation cons., Dallas and Athens, Ga., 1982-86. Youth leader Ascension Ch., Dallas, 1982-83, St. Michael's Ch., Stone Mountain, Ga., 1986-88, St. John's Episc. Ch., Ellicott City, Md., 1988-91; leader Approved Workers Are Not Ashamed, 1995-98, 2000-03, Altamaha Youth Soccer Assn., pres. 1996-98, co-founder; bd. trustees Westside Bapt. Ch., 2000-03; treas. Riverchase Homeowners Assn., 2002. Mem. U. Ga. Alumni Soc. (pres. Dallas chpt. 1983-84), Blue Key, Golden Key, Phi Kappa Phi, Beta Gamma Sigma, Phi Eta Sigma, Beta Alpha Psi, Phi Kappa Psi. Baptist. Avocations: sports, reading. Office: MWelsh Co LLC PO Box 1983 Evans GA 30809-1983

WELSH, PAUL PATRICK, retired lawyer; b. L.I., Dec. 13, 1941; s. Howard P. and Kathryn W.; m. Linda Franz, May 25, 1968; children: Sarah L., Carolyn A. AB, U. Pa., 1963, LLB, 1966. Bar: Pa. 1966, U.S. Dist. Ct. (ea. dist.) Pa. 1966, U.S. Dist. Ct. Del. 1970, U.S. Ct. Appeals (3d cir.) 1967, Del. 1968, U.S. Supreme Ct. 1972. Assoc. Morgan, Lewis & Bockius, Phila., 1966-67, Morris, Nichols, Arsht & Tunnell, Wilmington, Del., 1967-72, ptnr., 1972-99; Rep. candidate for Del. Senate, 2000. Mem. comty. adv. bd. Wilmington (Del.) News Jour., 1998—2000. Contbr. articles to profl jours. chpts to Lawyers Coop 3d cir. Practice Guide. Mem. Del. and Newark Rep. Orgns. Mem.: ADA, Del. Bar Assn. Unitarian Universalist. Home: 319 Cox Rd Newark DE 19711-3023

WELSH, PETER CORBETT, museum consultant, historian; b. Washington, Aug. 28, 1926; s. Arthur Brinkley and Susan Jane (Putney) W.; m. Catherine Beatrice Allen, Nov. 27, 1951 (div. 1969); children— Susan Jane, Peter Corbett; m. Caroline Levert Mastin, Sept. 8, 1970; 1 child, James Munson Corbett. BA, Mt. Union Coll., Alliance, Ohio, 1950; postgrad., U. Va., 1950-51; MA (Hagley fellow), U. Del., 1956. Research asst., fellowship coordinator Eleutherian Mills-Hagley Found., Wilmington, Del., 1956-59; assoc. curator dept. civil history Mus. History and Tech., Smithsonian Instn., 1959-61; curator Growth U.S., 1962-64, curator dept. civil history, 1964-69, asst. dir. gen. mus. of instn., 1969-70, dir. Office Mus. Programs, 1970-71; dir. N.Y. State Hist. Assn., Cooperstown, 1971-74; vis. prof. Cooperstown Grad. Program, N.Y. State Hist. Assn.; dir. Cooperstown Grad. Programs, 1971-74; dir. spl. projects N.Y. State Mus., Albany, 1975-76; dir. Bur. Mus., Pa. Hist. and Mus. Commn., 1976-84; pres. The Welsh Group, 1984-86; curator The Adirondack Mus., Blue Mountain Lake, N.Y., 1986-88, sr. historian, 1988-89; mus. cons., lectr., 1989—. Adj. prof. SUNY; cons. FDR Mus. and Little White House, Warm Springs, Ga., 1968-72; trustee Landon Sch., Bethesda, Md., 1964-70; bd. dirs., mem. exec. com. Ctr. for Conservation of Hist. Art and Artifacts, 1979-83; bd. dirs. Lake Placid Ctr. for the Arts, 1992-96; mem. publs. adv. com. The Adirondack Mus., 2002--. Author: Tanning in the United States: A Brief History, 1964, American Folk Art: The Art and Spirit of the People, 1967, Track and Road: The American Trotting Horse, 1820-1990, 1968, The Art of Enterprise: A Pennsylvania Tradition, 1983, Jacks, Jobbers and Kings: Logging the Adirondacks, 1850-1950, 1996; contbr. articles to profl. publs.; editor Smithsonian Jour. History, 1967-70. Served to 1st lt. AUS, 1951-54. Mem. Am. Hist. Assn., Am. Studies Assn., Am. Assn. Mus., N.Y. State Assn. Mus. (council 1971-75), Am. Assn. State and Local History (publ. com.), Soc. History of Tech., Sigma Nu. Clubs: Country of Harrisburg. Democrat. Roman Catholic. Office: 34 Second St Tupper Lake NY 12986-2011

WELSH, WILLIAM DANIEL, geriatric medicine family practice physician; b. Balt., May 18, 1950; s. Joseph Leo and Bessie Mary (Tangires) W.; m. Loraine Lynn Barkhaus, July 11, 1985; children: Sean William, Ryan Daniel. Student, Johns Hopkins U., 1971; BS in Biology cum laude, Fairleigh Dickinson U., 1972; DO, Coll. Osteo. Medicine-Surgery, Des Moines, 1975. Diplomate Nat. Bd. Osteo. Physicians; cert. ATLS; approved supr. physician assts. Osteopathic Med. Bd. Calif.; radiography and fluoroscopy x-ray supr., operator Calif. Intern Martin Place Hosp., Madison Heights, Mich., 1975-76, resident in internal medicine, 1976-77; pvt. practice Detroit, 1977-79; pvt. practice, Whittier, Calif., 1979—. Instr. ACLS, L.A., 1980-92; bd. dirs. Whittier Hosp. Med. Ctr., 1981, vice chief staff, 1982-84, med. dir. family asthma forum, 1979-88, med. dir. Summit Place alcohol treatment program, 1983-88; med. dir. Mirada Hills Rehab. Hosp., La Mirada, Calif., 1980-88; former clin. preceptor Coll. Osteo. Med. Pacific, Pomona, Calif., clin. assoc. prof. internal medicine; mem. dept. family practice, physician rev. com. Friendly Hills Regional Med. Ctr., La Habra, Calif., 1994-97; mem. staff Presbyn. Intercmty. Hosp., Whittier, Whittier Hosp. Med. Ctr., chmn. by laws com. 1999-2001, mem. exec. com. 1999-2001; med. dir. Royal Ct. Convalescent Hosp.; spkr. in field. Participant Calif. Beach Clean Up Day, 1996. Recipient Physician Recognition award AMA, 1991, 95, 96, Commn. of Merit Rep. Nat. Com., 1995. Mem. Am. Osteo. Assn., Am. Coll. Osteo. Family Physicians, Osteo. Physicians and Surgeons Calif., Am. Coll. Osteopathic Family Practitioners (bd. cert. family practice 1991, geriatrics 2000), L.A. County Osteopathic Med. Assn. Avocations: boating, skiing, reading, tennis. Home: 16871 Marina Bay Dr Huntington Beach CA 92649-2913 Fax: 562-592-4225. Office Phone: 562-945-9333. E-mail: wdwelsh@socal.rr.com.

WELSHIMER, GWEN R. state legislator, real estate broker, appraiser; b. Poughkeepsie, N.Y., Nov. 5, 1935; d. Freanor Ralph and Beulah M. (Reedy) Grant; m. Billy L. Blake (div. 1979); children: Donald E., Jerry A.; m. Robert E. Welshimer (dec. 1996). Student, Kans. State U., 1953-54; cert., Jones Real Estate Coll., Colorado Springs, Colo., 1975. Cert. real estate appraiser, 1993. Exec. sec. Coll. Bd. Trustees, Bellevue, Wash., 1967-69; exec. sec. to chmn. bd. dirs. Garvey Industries, Wichita, Kans., 1969-73, adminstrv. asst. pers. and pub. affairs, 1969-73; copywriter Walter Drake & Sons, Colorado Springs, 1973-75; real estate agt. UTE Realty, Colorado Springs, 1975-76; newspaper pub., owner Black Forrest News, Colorado Springs, 1976-79; real estate broker, appraiser Gwen Welshimer Real Estate, Wichita, 1979—; coord. Epic Real Estate Sch., Wichita, 1988—; legislator Kans. Ho. of Reps., Topeka, 1990—; mem. bus., commerce and labor, ethics and elections, health and human svcs., new economy nat. conf. state legislatures cultural and econ. devel. com., 2001—; mem joint health care reform legis. oversight com., 2001—. Dem. precinct committeewoman, Wichita; bd. dirs. United Meth. Urban Ministries, Wichita, 1990—, Counseling & Mediation Ctr., Wichita, Great Plains Comprehensive Agriculture & Med. Inst. Mem.: Women Dems., Lions Club Internat. Democrat. Methodist. Home: 6103 Castle Dr Wichita KS 67218-3601 Office: Kans Ho of Reps State Capitol Topeka KS 66612

WELSOME, EILEEN, journalist; b. NYC, Mar. 12, 1951; d. Richard H. and Jane M. (Garity) Welsome; m. James R. Martin, Aug. 3, 1983. BJ with honors, U. Tex., 1980. Reporter Beaumont (Tex.) Enterprise, 1980—82, San Antonio Light, 1982—83, San Antonio Express-News, 1983—86, Albuquerque Tribune, 1987—94, Westword Newspaper, Denver, 2000—01. Author: The Plutonium Files, 1999. Recipient Clarion award, 1989, News Reporting award, Nat. Headliners, 1989, John Hancock award, 1991, Mng. Editors Pub. Svc. award, AP, 1991, 1994, Roy Howard award, 1994, James Aronson award, 1994, Gold Medal award, Investigative Reporters and Editors, 1994, Sigma Delta Chi award, 1994, Investigative Reporting award, Nat. Headliners, 1994, Selden Ring award, 1994, Heywood Broun award, 1994, George Polk award, 1994, Sidney Hillman Found. award, 1994, Pulitzer Prize for nat. reporting, 1994, PEN/Martha Albrand award for first nonfiction, 2000, PEN/West Lit. award for rsch. nonfiction, PEN, 2000; John S. Knight fellow, Stanford U., 1991—92.

WELSTAD, KIRK, small business owner; b. Minot, N.D. m. Kim Welstad; children: Tyler, Dustin, Trey, Lindsey. Owner Connole and Somerville Heating and Air Conditioning, 1994—2003, Command Staffing and Labor, 2003—. Mem. N.D. Edn. Stds. and Practices Bd., 2001—, chmn., 2002—; mem. Minot Bd. Pub. Sch., 1993—. Mem.: N.D. Sch. Bd. Assn. (N.W. regional dir. 2002). Address: 1104 15th Ave SE Minot ND 58701 Business E-Mail: kwelstad@nglobe.com.

WELT, PHILIP STANLEY, lawyer, consultant; b. Freeport, NY, July 5, 1959; s. Morris and Rose (Offenberg) W.; m. Karen Teresa Gault, May 22, 1994. BBA summa cum laude, Hofstra U., 1983; MBA, Columbia U., 1988; JD cum laude, NYU, 1995. Bar: N.J. 1995, N.Y. 1995; U.S. Dist. Ct. N.J. 1995, U.S. Dist. Ct. (so. and ea. dists.) N.Y. 1996, U.S. Ct. Appeals (2d cir.), 1997, U.S. Ct. Appeals Armed Forces, 2000, U.S. Supreme Ct. 1999; CPA, N.Y. Sr. mgr. Deloitte & Touche, N.Y.C., 1983-92; assoc. Reboul MacMurray Hewitt Maynard & Kristol, N.Y.C., 1993, Davis Polk & Wardwell, N.Y.C., 1994, 1996-2001; jud. clk. U.S. Dist. Ct. N.J., Newark, 1995-96; special asst. dist. atty. Kings Co., NY, 1999—2001; asst. gen. counsel Am. Internat. Group, Inc., 2001—04; v.p. W.R. Berkeley Corp., Greenwich, Conn., 2004—, sr. counsel, 2004—. Bd. dirs., treas. Pub. Interest Law Found., N.Y.C., 1993-94; guest spkr. Boy Scouts Am., Nassau County, 1984-91, Nat. Assn. Accts., N.Y./N.J., 1988-92, others. Sr. editor Columbia Jour. World Bus., 1986-88; sr. exec. editor Ann. Survey Am. Law, 1993-95; contbr. articles to profl. jours. Vol. income tax asst. Dept. Treasury, IRS, N.Y.C., 1981-87; vol. Variety-The Children's Charity, N.Y.C., 1985-87; advisor Friends of Jon Kaiman, Nassau County, 1995. Provost's scholar Hofstra U., 1981-83, Deloitt & Touche fellow Columbia U., 1986-88; recipient Appreciation cert. Dept. Treasury, IRS, 1981-87, Variety, 1985-87, Bovenaan Outstanding Cmty. Svc. award Hofstra U., 1983, Orison S. Marden Moot Ct. Advocacy award NYU Sch. Law, 1993, Seymore A. Levy meml. award, 1995. Mem. ABA, AICPA, N.Y. State Bar Assn., N.Y. State Soc. CPAs, Beta Alpha Psi, Beta Gamma Sigma. Avocations: golf, rock climbing, photography, stamp collecting/philately, amateur radio. Home: 157 Mountain Wood Rd Stamford CT 06903-2107 Office: W R Berkeley Corp 475 Steamboad Rd Greenwich CT 06830 Office Phone: 212-629-3000. Business E-Mail: psw12@columbia.edu.

WELTE, A. THEODORE, chamber of commerce executive; b. Mankato, Minn., Feb. 11, 1944; s. Arthur William and Bernice (Town) M.; m. Kathleen P. Browne, May 3, 1969; 1 child, Jason N. BA in Sociology, Psychology, Mankato State U., 1966, MA in Econs., 1972; cert., U. Notre Dame, 1987; cert. mgmt., Stonehill Coll., 1990. Cert. chamber exec. Program officer, br. officer Peace Corp, Washington, 1968-69; rsch. dir. Tech. Found., W.Va. Tech., Montgomery, 1969-70; project dir. Self-Help, Inc., Brockton, Mass., 1972-73; regional planner, planning supr. Old Colony Planning Coun., Brockton, 1974-81; pres., CEO Metro South C. of C., Brockton, 1981-90, MetroWest C. of C., Framingham, Mass., 1990—. Trustee Brockton Regional Econ. Devel. Corp., 1982-90; treas. Brockton Area Pvt. Industry Coun., 1987-89. Cubmaster pack 68 Boy Scouts Am., Easton, Mass., 1989-90, com. chair troop 86, 1991-94, bd. dirs. Algonquin/Knox Trail coun., 1991—, v.p. exploring, 1996-99. Mem. New Eng. Assn. C. of C. Execs. (sec. 1990-91, 2d v.p. 1991-92, 1st v.p. 1992-93, pres. 1993-94), Mass. Assn. C. of C. Execs. (pres. 1988-89), Rotary (sec. Brockton 1988-90, v.p. Framingham 1990-92, pres. 1993-94). Presbyterian. Office: MetroWest C of C 1671 Worcester Rd Ste 201 Framingham MA 01701-5400 E-mail: ted@metrowest.org.

WELTER, WILLIAM MICHAEL, marketing and advertising executive; b. Evanston, Ill., Nov. 18, 1946; s. Roy Michael and Frances (DeShields) W.; m. Pamela Bassett, June 11, 1971; children: Barclay, Robert Michael. BS, Mo. Valley Coll., 1966. Account exec. Leo Burnett Co., Inc., Chgo., 1966-74; v.p., account supr. Needham Harper Worldwide, Chgo., 1974-80; v.p. mktg. Wendy's Internat., Inc., Dublin, Ohio, 1981, sr. v.p. mktg., 1981-84, exec. v.p., 1984-87; owner, chief exec. officer Haunty & Welter Advt. Agy., Worthington, Ohio, 1987-91; sr. exec. v.p. mktg. Rax Restaurants Inc., Dublin, 1992; exec. v.p. mktg. Metromedia Steakhouses, Inc., Dayton, 1992-93; sr. v.p. mktg. Metromedia Co., Dayton, 1993-95; exec. v.p., chief mktg. officer Heartland Foods Inc., Dublin, Ohio, 1995-96; exec. v.p. brand mgmt. Late Nite Magic, Inc., Las Vegas, Nev., 1996—99; pres., CEO W.M. Welter & Assocs., Las Vegas, 1996—; pres. Wings West LLC, Las Vegas, 1999—, Buffalo Wild Wings, Inc., Las Vegas, 2001—. Founder Santa's Silent Helpers, Columbus, Ohio, 1985 Mem. Advt. Fedn. Las Vegas, Spanish Trail Country Club. Avocations: golf, fishing. Home: 1517 Angelberry St Las Vegas NV 89117-1372 Office: 8084 W Sahara Las Vegas NV 89117 Fax: 702 360-8379. E-mail: billwingman@cs.com.

WELTERS, ANTHONY, health services executive, BA in economics, Manhattanville Coll.; JD, NYU. Atty. SEC; exec. asst. to Sen. Jacob Javits; sr.-level positions Amtrak and U.S. Dept. Transp.; chmn. bd., pres. CEO Americhoice (sub. of United Health Group), 1989—. Vice chmn. bd. Morehouse Sch. Medicine; mem. bd. Healthcare Leadership Coun., NYU Law Sch., Wolf Trap Found. Recipient Horatio Alger award, 1998. Office: Americhoice 8045 Leesburg Pike Ste 650 Vienna VA 22182*

WELTMAN, DAVID LEE, lawyer; b. Springfield, Mass., Jan. 12, 1933; s. Sol Walter and Esther (Ziskind) W.; m. Lois Handmaker, Sept. 2, 1956; children: John, Elizabeth, Herman, Sally. AB, Yale U., 1954; LLB, Harvard U., 1957; DHL (hon.), Newbury Coll., 2002. Bar: Mass. 1957. Assoc. Mintz, Levin & Cohn, Boston, 1957-60; v.p. Ansonia Mills, Inc., Taunton, Mass., 1960-63; assoc. Foley, Hoag & Eliot, Boston, 1963-67, ptnr., 1967—. Sec., clk. Charles River Assocs., Boston, 1965-97, Brigham Med. Group Found., 1972—, Siemens-Nixdorf Info. Systems, Burlington, Mass., 1979-94, Am. Brush Co., Clairmont, N.H., 1982-92. Chmn. leadership devel. coun. Jewish Fedn. and Welfare Funds, 1966-68; trustee New Eng. Med. Ctr., Boston, 1970-82, Combined Jewish Philanthropies, Boston, 1970—, Hebrew Coll., Boston, 1995-2002; chmn. Newbury Coll., Boston, 1972-2002, Lown Cardiovasc. Rsch. Found., 1993—; incorporator Mus. Sci., Boston, 1972-92, Boston U. Med. Ctr., 1965-96; pres. Beaver Country Day Sch., Chestnut Hill, Mass., 1975-80, Jewish Cmty. Ctr., Brookline and Newton, 1968-71; bd. overseers South Shore Hosp. Found., Weymouth, Mass., 1990—. Recipient Young Leadership award Combined Jewish Philanthropies, 1968, Class of 1954 award Yale U., 1989, Founders Day award Beaver Country Day Sch., 1991. Mem. ABA, Boston Bar Assn., Nat. Health Lawyers Assn., Cohasset Golf Club, Cohasset Yacht Club. Avocations: tennis, sailing, golf. Home: 90 Gammons Rd Cohasset MA 02025-1406 Office: Foley Hoag & Eliot 155 Seaport Blvd Boston MA 02210-

WELTON, SHARON MARIE, food service executive; b. Waterbury, Conn., Nov. 18, 1943; d. George Galvin Touponse and Catherine Marie Coon; m. Allen Richard Welton (div.); children: Catherine Welton-Pando, Douglas. AAS, Mattatuck Cmty. Coll., 1988; BS, U. Conn., 1996. Cert. dietary mgr. Nat. Dietary Managers Assn., 1992, instr. for Serv-Safe Course Nat. Restaurant Assn., 2002, food protection profl. 1996. Legal sec. Membrino/Fitzgerald, Waterbury, Conn., 1963—64; asst. mgr. Judy's Deli, Southbury, Conn., 1980—84; prin./mgr. Feasts by Sharon, Conn., 1981—2001; intern- affirmative action office Southbury Training Sch., Conn., 1995, supvr. food svc., 1984—. Cons./trainer State of Conn. Nutritional Work Group, 1999—2003, Southbury Training Sch., 1992—. Polit. action com. mem. Dietary Managers Assn., 1993—95; mem./leader Girl Scouts, Watertown, Conn., 1951—61, 1977—81; com. mem. Christmas Town Festival, Bethlehem, 1999. Recipient State Achievement award, Dietary Managers Assn., 1994—95. Mem.: Dietary Managers Assn. (legis. coord. 1992—98, 2003—, pres. 1994—95). Republican. Roman Cath. Avocations: sewing, swimming, wine tasting. Home: 143 Pine Hill Rd 22B Thomaston CT 06787 Office: Southbury Training Sch Rte 172 Southbury CT 06488 Office Phone: 203-586-2193.

WELTY, JOHN DONALD, academic administrator; b. Amboy, Ill., Aug. 24, 1944; s. John Donald and Doris (Donnelly) W.; m. Sharon Welty; children: Anne, Elisabeth, Bryan, Darren, Heather. BS, Western Ill. U., 1965; MA, Mich. State U., 1967; Ed.D., Ind. U., 1974. Asst. v.p. for student affairs SW State U., Marshall, Minn., 1973-74; dir. residences SUNY-Albany, 1974-77, assoc. dean for student affairs, 1977-80; v.p. for student and univ. affairs Indiana U. of Pa., 1980-84, pres., 1984-91, Calif. State U., Fresno, 1991—. Lectr. in field; chair Am. Humanics. Contbr. articles to profl. jours. Recipient Chancellor's award SUNY, 1977, Chief Exec. Leadership award Coun. for Advancement and Support of Edn., 1999, John Templeton Found. award for leadership in student character devel., 1999. Mem. Fresno Bus. Coun., Fresno Econ. Devel. Commn., Sunnyside Country Club. Lodges: Rotary. Roman Catholic. Office: Calif State U 5241 S Maple Ave Fresno CA 93725-9739 Business E-Mail: johnw@csufresno.edu.

WELU, JAMES A. art museum director; b. Dubuque, Iowa, Dec. 15, 1943; s. Andrew L. and Anna E. (Riley) W. BA, Loras Coll., 1966; MA, U. Notre Dame, 1967, MFA, 1968; PhD, Boston U., 1977. Instr. St. Mary-of-the-Woods (Ind.) Coll., 1968-70; asst. curator Worcester (Mass.) Art Mus., 1974-76, assoc. curator, 1976-80, curator, 1977-78, 80-81, chief curator, 1980-86, dir., 1986—. Instr. Clark U., Worcester, 1980. Panelist Mass. Coun. on Arts and Humanities, Boston, 1981-82, 90, Utilization of Mus. Resources Nat. Endowment for the Arts, 1988; trustee Williamstown Regional Art Conservation Lab., Inc., Mass., 1981-86; mem. panel Utilization Mus. Resources, NEA, 1988. Boston U. grantee, 1973, NEA Mus.' Profl. grantee, 1976-81; Samuel H. Kress Found. fellow, 1973; recipient Netherland-Am. Found. award Netherland Found., 1973, Disting. Alumni award Boston U. Grad. Sch., 1986. Mem.: Historians Netherlandish Art, New Eng. Mus. Assn., Am. Assn. Mus. (accreditation commr. 2000—), Coll. Art Assn. Am., Am. Fedn. Arts (trustee), Assn. Art Mus. Dirs. (pres. 1999—2000, trustee). Home: 10 Massachusetts Ave Worcester MA 01609-1649 Office: Worcester Art Mus 55 Salisbury St Worcester MA 01609-3196

WEMPNER, GERALD ARTHUR, engineering educator; b. Waupun, Wis. s. Paul Christian and Thekla Nelda (Jung) W.; m. Lorraine Bischel, Sept. 6, 1952 (div. Apr. 1983); children: Susan K., Paul J. BS, U. Wis., 1952, MS, 1953; PhD, U. Ill., 1957. Instr. U. Ill., Urbana, 1953-57, asst. prof., 1957-59; assoc. prof. U. Ariz., Tucson, 1959-62; prof. U. Ala., Huntsville, 1964-73, Ga. Inst. Tech., Atlanta, 1973-91, prof. emeritus, 1991—. Vis. prof. U. Calif., Berkeley, 1962-63. Author: Mechanics of Solids, 1973; co-author: Mechanics of Deformable Bodies, 1961, Mechanics of Solids, 1995, Mechanics of Solids and Shells, 2003; contbr. articles to profl. jours. With U.S. Army, 1946—48. NSF fellow, Stanford (Calif.) U., 1963-64, Sr. fellow Alexander von Humboldt Found., Germany, 1973, Killam fellow U. Calgary, Can., 1983. Fellow ASME (asssoc. editor 1976-83), Am. Acad. Mechanics. Avocations: art, sculpture, photography, woodwork. Home and Office: 3397 Hidden Acres Dr Doraville GA 30340-4445

WEN, GEORGE WALTER SUN, editor; b. Seattle, Wash., Jan. 22, 1948; s. Herbert Jack Hsiu-rui and Rena Sun (Hsing-fang) Wen. BA magna cum laude, Dartmouth Coll., 1970; BA hon., Cambridge (Eng.) U., 1973; postgrad., Harvard U., 1970—71; MA, Cambridge (Eng.) U., 1976; Licence-ès-Lettres, Univ. Paris-VII, 1979; MS in Journalism, Columbia U., 1986. Sr. lectr. Inst. d'Etudes Politiques de Paris, Paris, 1982—85; sr. editor Attenzione Mag., N.Y., 1986; editor N.Y. Mag., N.Y., 1987; mng. editor Henry Holt and Co., N.Y., 1990—. Trustee, bd. trustees Hemophilia Assn. of N.Y., 2002—. Yaddo residency, Saratoga Springs, NY, 2001, Reynolds scholar, 1972—73. Mem.: Phi Kappa Phi, Phi Beta Kappa. Office: Flatiron Bldg 175 Fifth Ave New York NY 10010 Office Phone: 212-886-9244.

WEN, GEYI, applied physics educator; b. Pingjiang, Hunan, China, Dec. 28, 1962; s. Zhiwu and Meiran Li Wen; m. Jun Yuan Wen, Jan. 22, 1988; 1 child, Lan. BS, Xidian U., Xian, China, 1982, MS, 1984, PhD, 1987. Lectr. S.E. U., Nanjing, China, 1988-90; assoc. prof. U. Electronic Sci. and Tech. China, Chengdu, 1990-92, prof., 1993—. Vis. rschr. U. Calif., Berkeley, 1992-93j; vice chmn. Inst. Applied Physics, U. Electronic Sci. and Tech. China, 1996-97, chmn., 1997—; vis. prof. U. Waterloo, Can., 1998; EM rschr. Rsch. in Motion, Can., 1998—. Author: Modern Methods for Electromagnetic Computation, 1996, Advances in Electomagnetic Theory, 1999; contbr. articles to profl. jours. Recipient Talent through Century award Sichuan Province, Chengdu, China, 1994, Sci. and Tech. Progress award China Soc. Sci. and Tech., 1996, Talent through Century award Nat. Edn. Com., Beijing, 1996. Mem. IEEE (editl. bd. IEEE Transactions on Microwave Theory & Techniques 1992—), China Soc. Computational Physics (mem. couns. 1992—), China Inst. Electronics (editl. bd. Jour. Electromagnetic Waves 1997—). Avocations: ping pong/table tennis, chinese chess. Office: Rsch in Motion 295 Phillip St Waterloo ON Canada N2L 3W8 E-mail: gwen@rim.net.

WEN, SHEREE, computer company executive; BS in Physics, Natural Tsiug Hua U, Taiwan; PhD, U. Calif., Berkeley, 1979. Rsch. divsn. staff IBM, 1979-81, dept. mgr. Materials, Characterization and Analysis, 1981-84, program mgr. Tech., 1984-86, sr. mgr of Optics, prog. mgr., tech. asst. to sr. v.p.; pres. WenLab USA Inc., N.Y.C. Patentee in field; Contbr. articles to profl. jours. Recipient John E. Dom Achievement award Am. Soc. for Metal, 1978, Outstanding tech. Achievement award, IBM, 1986, invention Achievement award, IBM, 1987; The Robert Lansing Hardy gold Metal The Metals, Materials & Minerals Soc. (TMS-AIME); the AIME as the most promising young Materials Scientist in Am., 1979 Mem. TMS-AIME's Process Monitor & Control Com. (chmn.), Materials Design & Mfg. Divsn. Award Com.; Indsl. Liaison for U. Calif. at Berkeley's ctr. for Materials. Office: WEN Tech Corp 999 Central Park Ave Yonkers NY 10704-1088 Fax: 914-376-7092.

WEN, SHIH-LIANG, mathematics professor; came to U.S., 1959; s. S.W. and C.F. (Hsiao) W.; m. Liang Tao; children: Dennis, Andy, Jue, Nannan. BS, Nat. Taiwan U., Taipei, 1956; MS, U. Utah, 1961; PhD, Purdue U., 1968. Assoc. research engr. The Boeing Co., Seattle, 1961-63; with dept. math. Ohio U., Athens, 1968—, successively asst. prof., assoc. prof. and prof., chmn. dept. math., 1985-93. Rsch. analyst Applied Math Rsch. Lab. USAF, Wright-Patterson AFB, Ohio, summer, 1972; vis. rsch. scientist Courant Inst. Math. Scis. NYU, 1978-79; hon. prof. Jiangxi U., People's Republic of China, 1985; disting. vis. prof. Lanzhou U., People's Republic of China, 1989. Mem. Am. Math. Soc., Soc. for Indsl. and Applied Math., Math. Assn. Am. Avocations: fishing, bridge, music. Office: Ohio Univ Dept Of Math Athens OH 45701

WENDEBORN, RICHARD DONALD, retired manufacturing company executive; b. Winnipeg, Man., Can. came to U.S., 1976; naturalized, 1988; s. Curtis and Rose (Lysecki) W.; m. Dorothy Ann Munn, Aug. 24, 1957; children: Margaret Gayle, Beverley Jane, Stephen Richard, Peter Donald, Ann Elizabeth. Diploma, Colo. Sch. Mines, 1952; grad. advanced mgmt. program, Harvard U., 1974. With Can. Ingersoll-Rand Co., Montreal, 1952—, gen. mgr., v.p., dir., 1968, pres., 1969-74, chmn. bd., 1976—; exec. v.p. Ingersoll-Rand Co., Woodcliff Lake, N.J., 1976-89; ret., 1989. Mem. Can Govt. Oil and Gas Tech. Exch. Program with USSR, 1972—, Minerals and Metals Mission to China, 1972—. Mem. Resource Fund Colo. Sch. Mines; past pres., dir. Town and River Civic Assn. Mem. Machinery and Equipment Mfrs. Assn. Can. (bd. dirs. 1974—, past chmn.), Royal Palm Yacht Club (commodore

1994), Internat. Order of Blue Gavel (past Commodore's Club, past pres. Royal Palm br. dist. 8), Useppa Island Club, Tau Beta Pi. Home: 9990 Cypress Lake Dr Fort Myers FL 33919-6020 E-mail: Dickandda@aol.com.

WENDEL, CHARLES ALLEN, lawyer; b. Lockport, N.Y., Aug. 13, 1942; s. Harold Henry and Doris Lillian (Gardner) W.; m. Helen W. Roberts, June 23, 1973; children: William Charles, Jonathan David. BChem Engring., Rensselaer Poly Inst., 1964; JD, Am. U., 1968. Bar: N.Y. 1969, Va. 1971, D.C. 1980, U.S. Ct. Appeals (fed. and 4th cirs.), U.S. Dist. Ct. (ea. and we. dists.) Va., U.S. Supreme Ct. Patent examiner U.S. Patent and Trademark Office, Washington, 1964—66; patent trainee Union Carbide Corp., Washington, 1966—68, patent atty. N.Y.C., 1968—70; assoc., then ptnr. Stevens, Davis, Miller & Mosher, Arlington, Va., 1970—83; ptnr. firm Wegner & Bretschneider, Washington, 1983—85; assoc. solicitor U.S. Patent and Trademark Office, 1985—88; assoc. Lyon & Lyon, Washington, 1988—90; founding ptnr. Parkhurst, Wendel & Rossi, Alexandria, Va., 1990—95. Contbr. articles to profl. jours. Mem. Va. State Bar (patent trademark copyright sect., chmn. 1977-78), Am. Intellectual Patent Law Assn., Patent Lawyers Club Washington (prs. 1982-83), Delta Theta Phi. Republican. Office: Parkhurst & Wendel LLP 1421 Prince St Ste 210 Alexandria VA 22314-2805 Office Phone: 703-739-0220.

WENDEL, JOAN AUDREY, music educator; b. N.Y.C., Dec. 1, 1931; d. Adam and Edna Sophia Wohlfart; m. Ralph Aurel Wendel, July 21, 1962 (dec. May 1998); 1 child, Tracy Lynn. BA summa cum laude, Dowling Coll., 1969; MA, Adelphi U., 1971. Cert. elem. tchr., N.Y. Sec. A.C. Edwards Inc., Sayville, N.Y., 1950-53; office mgr. John V. Potter Ins., East Islip, N.Y., 1953-59, Pilger Agy., Patchogue, N.Y., 1959-66; tchr. Connetquot CSD of Islip, Bohemia, N.Y., 1969-91; pvt. music tchr. Bohemia, 1979—; music dir. Christ Luth. Ch., Cape Coral, Fla., 1996—, Sounds of Fla., Cape Coral, 1999—2003. Mem. Music Tchrs. Nat. Assn., Music Educators Nat. Conf., Assn. Luth. Ch. Musicians, Ft. Myers Music Tchrs. Assn. (v.p. 1999), Order Eastern Star (worthy matron 1964, assoc. grand marshal 1973, grand musician 1987). Republican. Lutheran. Avocations: walking, golf, music, reading. Home: 2218 SE 10th Ter Cape Coral FL 33990-6217 Office: Christ Luth Ch 2911 Del Prado Blvd S Cape Coral FL 33904-7297 Office Phone: 239-542-2709.

WENDEL, JOHN FREDRIC, lawyer, professional sports consultant; b. Newark, Nov. 8, 1936; s. John J. and Margaret D. (Mortimer) W.; m. Barbara Vaughn Smith, Dec. 17, 1960 (dec. July 1978); children: David I., Stephen F.; m. Carlene M. Arnoldini, 1 child, Carlene Margaret. BA, U. Fla., 1958; JD, Stetson U., 1963. Bar: Fla. 1963, U.S. Dist. Ct (so. and mid. dists.) 1964, U.S. Ct. Appeals (5th, 9th, and 11th cirs.) 1964, U.S. Supreme Ct. 1968. Of counsel Wyte & Hirschboeck, Milw., 1989—90; pres., chmn. Wendel & Chritton Chartered and predecessor firms, Lakeland, Fla., 1965—. Town atty. Town of St. Leo, Fla., 1964-78, town judge, 1968; asst. mcpl. judge Lakeland, Fla., 1966; county atty. Citrus County, Fla., 1976-81; of counsel, Whyte and Hirschboeck, Milw., 1989-90, gen. counsel and spl. counsel to varous profl. baseball leagues, 1969-1998, Sun n Fun Fly-In, Inc., 1998-; vis. prof. law, dir. Nat. Sports Law Inst., Marquette U. Law Sch., Milw., 1989-90; adj. prof. law Marquette U. Law Sch., Milw., 1990-91, adj. prof. Stetson U. Coll. Law, 1992-93; adj. faculty mem. Fla. So. Coll., Lakeland, 1963-65; faculty mem. St. Leo Coll., 1963-73; del. 2d Internat. Conf. Ptnrs. for Alliance for Progress; mem. Fla. Columbia Alliance Coms. and Subco.; gen. counsel Sun 'n Fun Fly-In, Inc., 1998—. Mem. editorial bd. Sports Law and Fin., 1992-98. Active ARC; assoc. mem. counsel Fla. Sports Adv. Coun. Served to 1st lt. USMC, 1957-59. Named one of Lakeland's Five Outstanding Young Men, Jaycees, 1967. Mem. Am. Arbitration Assn. (arbitrator alternative dispute resolution to settle sports disputes), Sports Lawyers Assn. (pres. 1986-93, sec., v.p., bd. dirs. 1974—, pres. and dir. emeritus, Award of Excellence 1993), The Fla. Bar (exec. coun. entertainment, arts and sports law sect.), Lakeland Bar Assn. (gen. couns.), Fla. Assn. County Attys. (pres. 1981), Nat. Assn. of Profl. Baseball Leagues, Inc. (gen. counsel 1971-82, spl. counsel 1969-98), Lakeland Yacht and Country Club, KC. Republican. Roman Catholic. Office: Wendel & Chritton Chartered 5300 S Florida Ave PO Box 5378 Lakeland FL 33807-5378

WENDEL, RICHARD FREDERICK, economist, educator, consultant; b. Chgo., Apr. 29, 1930; s. Elmer Carl and Victoria Matilda (Jeffrey) W.; m. Leslie Jane Travis, June 15, 1957; children: John Travis, Andrew Stewart. AB, Augustana Coll., 1951; MBA, U. Pa., 1957, PhD (fellow 1962-64), 1966. Asst. to pres. Flexonics Corp., Maywood, Ill., 1957-59; sales rep., product mgr. Kordite div. Nat. Distillers Corp., Macedon, N.Y., 1959-62; instr. Wharton Sch., U. Pa., 1964-65; asst. prof. mktg. Grad. Sch. Bus. Adminstrn., Washington U., St. Louis, 1965-69; assoc. prof. U. Conn., 1969-74, prof., 1974-90, prof. emeritus, 1990. Mem. U.S. Census Field Adv. Commn., 1967-69; mem. acad. adv. commn. Bur. Labor Stats., U.S. Bur. Census Survey of Consumer Expenditures, 1971-76; mem. Conn. Export Devel. Council, Dept. Commerce, 1972-76; dir. Neon Software Inc. Author: (with M.L. Bell) Economic Importance of Highway Advertising, 1966; (with W. Gorman) Selling: Preparation. Persuasion. Strategy., 1983, 88; editor: Readings in Marketing, 1973-74, 75-76, 77-78, 78-79, 79-80, 80-81, (with C.L. Lapp) Add to Your Selling Know-How, 1968; editorial staff: jour. Mktg., 1965-74. Bd. dirs. Roper Center. Served with USAF, 1951-55. Center for Real Estate and Urban Econs. grantee, 1969-70 Mem. Am. Mktg. Assn., N.Y. Acad. Scis. Republican. Episcopalian. Home: 106 S Queen St Chestertown MD 21620-1522

WENDEL, SHIRLEY ANNE, college dean; Diploma, St. Mary's Hosp. Sch. Nursing, 1970; AA, Penn Valley Cmty. Coll., 1972; BSN, Avila Coll., 1974; MN, U. Kans., 1980; PhD, Kansas State U., 1998, U. Kans., 1999. Staff nurse St. Mary's Hosp., Kans. City, Kans., 1970-74, Unity Hosp., Fridley, Minn., 1974-76; nursing instr. Kans. City Kans. Cmty. Coll., 1976-80, dean nursing edn., 1980-98, dean of nursing and allied health, 1998—. Mem. adv. com. Johnson County Cmty. Coll. nursing program, Avila Coll. nursing program, Mid Am. Nazarene Coll. nursing program; asst. Den Mother Cub Scouts, 1985-87; active Annual Health Fair. Mem. Nat. League Nursing, Kans. Assoc. Degree Nursing Educators, Collegiate Nurse Educators Greater Kans. City, Sigma Theta Tau. Home: 12100 W 141st St Shawnee Mission KS 66221-2902 Office: Kansas City Kansas Community College 7250 State Ave Kansas City KS 66112-3003 E-mail: swendel@toto.net.

WENDELBURG, NORMA RUTH, composer, pianist, educator; b. Stafford, Kans. d. Henry and Anna Louise (Moeckel) W. MusB, Bethany Coll., 1943; MusM, U. Mich., 1947, Eastman Sch. Music, 1951, postgrad., 1964-65, 66-67, PhD in Composition, 1969; postgrad., Mozarteum, 1953-54, Vienna Acad. Music, 1955. Tchr. music edn., piano Wayne (Nebr.) State Coll., 1947-50; asst. prof. Bethany Coll., Lindsborg, Kans., 1952-53, U. Iowa, 1956-58; asst. prof. composition, theory, piano Hardin-Simmons U., Abilene, Tex., 1958-66, chmn. grad. com. Sch. Music, 1960-66, founder, chmn. ann. univ. festival contemporary music, 1959—; assoc. prof. music Dallas Bapt. Coll., 1973-75; rsch. asst. to dir. grad. studies Eastman Sch. Music, 1966-67; assoc. prof., chmn. dept. theory and composition S.W. Tex. State U., 1969-72; mem. faculty Friends Bible Coll., Haviland, Kans., 1977-83. Guest composer colls. including U. Ottawa, 1984; performed in Eng. and Prague; performed Am. Conservatory Mus., Charles Ives Ctr. for Am. Music, 1990—; various solo recitals and festivals. Composer: Symphony, 1967, Suite for Violin and Piano, 1965, Song Cycle for Soprano, flutes, Piano, 1974, Music for Two Pianos, 1985, Affirmation, 1982, Interlacings (organ), 1983, (recorded) Suite No. 2 for Violin and Piano, 1989, Fantasy for Trumpet and Piano, 1990, Sonata for Clarinet and Piano, Sinfonietta, 1994, Concerto for Clarinet and Orch.; performances Mosaic, Smetana Hall, Prague, 1999, Symphony Orch. of Prague, 1999, Symphony Hall, Boston, 1998, Concertino for Oboe and String Orch., Alice Tully Hall Lincoln Ctr., N.Y.C., 1999, Warsaw Rhapsody, Warsaw Philharm. Orch., Lutoslawski Hall, 1999, performed Warsaw Rhapsody, Warsaw, 1999, CD Mosaic, 2001. Recipient Meet the Composer award N.Y. State Coun. Arts, 1979; named Kans. Composer of Yr., Kans. Fed. Music Clubs, 2000; Composition scholar Composers' Conf. Middlebury (Vt.), 1950, Berkshire Ctr., 1953; Fulbright awardee, 1953-55; Resident fellow Huntington Hartford Found., 1955-56, 58, 61; MacDowell Colony fellow, 1958, 60, 70; Nat. Festival Performing Arts fellow, 1989. Mem. ASCAP (Composition awards 1988-2001), Music Tchrs. Nat. Conf., Am. Soc. Univ. Composers, Minn. Composers Forum, Am. Women Composers, Music Club (Hutchinson), Sigma Alpha Iota. Republican. Avocations: travel, photography, gardening. Address: 2206 N Van Buren St Hutchinson KS 67502-3738

WENDELSTEDT, HARRY HUNTER, JR., umpire; b. Balt., July 27, 1938; m. Cheryl Maher, Nov. 2, 1970; children: Harry III, Amy. Student, Essex Community Coll.; BS in Edn., U. Md. Profl. baseball umpire, 1962—; with minor leagues, Ga.-Fla., 1962, 1963, 1964, 1965, maj. leagues (Nat.), 1966-98; umpire All-Star Game, 1968, 76, 83, 92, Nat. League championship series, 1970, 72, 77, 80, 82, 84, 88, 90, 96, World Series, 1973, 80, 86, 91, 95; umpire supr. Nat. Baseball League, 1999—. Owner, operator Harry Wendelstedt Umpire Sch. Named Top Umpire in Maj. League Baseball Md. Profl. Baseball Players Assn., 1975, Best Umpire in Nat. League Chgo. Tribune, 1982, Best Ball and Strike Umpire Sports Illustrated, 1982, Major League Umpire of Yr., 1992, Fla. Diamond Club, 1993. Mem. Major League Umpires Assn. (4 term past pres.) Address: care Wendelstedt Sch for Umpires 88 S Saint Andrews Dr Ormond Beach FL 32174-3857

WENDER, IRA TENSARD, lawyer; b. Pitts., Jan. 5, 1927; s. Louis and Luba (Kibrick) W.; m. Phyllis M.Bellows, June 24, 1966; children: Justin B., Sarah T; children by previous marriage: Theodore M., Abigail A., John B. Swarthmore Coll., 1942-45; JD, U. Chgo., 1948; LLM, NYU, 1951. Atty. Lord, Day and Lord, N.Y.C., 1950-52, 54-59; asst. dir. internat. program in tax. Harvard U. Law Sch., 1952-54; lectr. N.Y. U. Sch. Law, N.Y.C., 1954-59; ptnr. Baker and McKenzie, Chgo., 1959-61; founding ptnr. N.Y.C. office, 1961-71; sr. ptnr. Wender, Murase & White, 1971-82; of counsel, 1982-86; chmn. C. Brewer and Co., Ltd., Honolulu, 1969-75; pres., CEO A. G. Becker Paribas Inc., 1978-82; chmn., CEO Sussex Securities Inc., 1983-85; of counsel Patterson, Belknap, Webb & Tyler, N.Y.C., 1986-87, ptnr., 1988-93; of counsel, 1994—. Chmn. Perry Ellis Internat., Inc., N.Y.C., 1994; bd. dirs. REFAC Corp., N.Y.C., Dime Bancorp, N.Y.C.; bd. mgrs. Swarthmore Coll, 1978-89; pres., bd. mgrs. PARC Vendome Condominium, 1990-94; trustee Putnet (Vt.) Sch., 1985-92, 93—, vice chmn., 1998—; trustee Brearley Sch., N.Y.C., 1980-85. Author: (with E.R. Barlow) Foreign Investment and Taxation, 1995. Dir., treas. Fountain House, Inc., N.Y., 1998—; dir. Am. Near East Refuge Aid, Washington; mem. Coun. on Fgn. Rels. Mem. ABA, N.Y. State Bar Assn., Assn. of Bar of City of N.Y. Home: 115 E 67th St New York NY 10021-5951 Office: Patterson Belknap Webb & Tyler LLP Ste 2200 1133 Avenue Of The Americas New York NY 10036-6731

WENDER, PAUL ANTHONY, chemistry professor; BS, Wilkes Coll., 1969; PhD, Yale U., 1973; PhD (hon.), Wilkes U., 1993. Asst. prof., assoc. prof. Harvard U., 1974-81; prof. chemistry Stanford U., 1981—; Bergstrom prof. chemistry, 1994—. Cons. Eli Lilly & Co., 1980—, lectr. Am. Chem. Soc. Recipient ICI Am. Chem. award Stuart Pharm., merit award NIH, Pfizer rsch. award, 1995. Fellow AAAS; mem. Am. Chem. Soc. (Arthur C. Cope Sholan award 1990, Guenther award, award for creative work in synthetic organic chemistry 1998). Office: Stanford U Mudd Bldg Rm 390 Mail Code 5080 Stanford CA 94305

WENDER, PHYLLIS BELLOWS, literary agent; m. Ira Tensard Wender; children: Justin Bellows, Sarah Tensard. BA, Wells Coll., 1956. Publicity dir. Grove Press, N.Y.C., 1958-61, Dell Pub. Co., N.Y.C., 1961-63; theatrical agt. Artists Agy. Inc., N.Y.C., 1963-68; agt. Wender & Assocs., N.Y.C., 1968-81; prin., agent, ptnr. Rosenstone/Wender, N.Y.C., 1981—. Bd. dirs. Just Women Inc., Bklyn., 1982, mem. adv. com., 1983-87; bd. dirs. Fortune Soc., N.Y.C., 1977-80; trustee Wells Coll., Aurora, N.Y., 1981-90. Mem. Women's Media Group (dir. 1988-90), Cosmopolitan Club. Office: Rosenstone Wender 38 East 29th St 10th Flr New York NY 10016

WENDLANDT, GARY E. insurance company executive; BS in applied math., computer sci., Wash. U., Mo. Various positions Mass. Mutual Life Ins. Co., 1972—92, exec. v.p., chief investment officer, 1992—99; chmn., CEO New York Life Investment Mgmt. LLC; exec. v.p., exec. mgmt. com. New York Life Ins. Co., 1999—. Fellow: Soc. of Actuaries; mem.: Am. Acad. of Actuaries. Office: NY Life Ins Co 51 Madison Ave New York NY 10010

WENDLER, M. CECILIA, nursing educator; b. Detroit, Jan. 27, 1954; d. William J. and Martha A. Kent; children: Zachary R., Andrew J. A in Nursing, Presentation Coll., 1977; BS in Nursing, Coll. St. Benedict, 1986; MA in Nursing, Coll. St. Scholastica, 1991; PhD of Nursing, U Colo. Health Sciences Ctr., 1999. Critical Care Registered Nurse (CCRN), AACN, 1982. Assoc. prof. of nursing U. of Wis.- Eau Claire, 1997—; mem. staff Fairview-U. Med. Ctr., Mpls., 1991—. Med./surg. nurse/critical care U.S. Army Reserves/Nat. Guard, Minneapolis, Minn., 1977—2002. Editor: (Book) The HeART of Nursing: Creative and Expressive Arts in Nursing, 2003 (nominated for an Am. Jour. of Nursing Book of the Yr. award, 2003). Lt. col. US Army Reserves, 1977—2002, Mpls. Mem.: Sigma Theta Tau, Internat. (immediate past pres., delta phi chpt. 1999—2002). Achievements include research in First nurse to publish research in the area of Tellington TTouch, a natural healing modality. Avocations: travel, writing, exercise, fishing, camping. Home: 1530 Thomas Lake Pointe Dr Apt 301 Eagan MN 55122-2555 Personal E-mail: mcewern@aol.com.

WENDORF, RICHARD HAROLD, library director, scholar; b. Cedar Rapids, Iowa, Mar. 17, 1948; s. Harold Albert and Jeanne Ellen (Hamblin) W.; m. Barbara Hilderman, 1970 (div. 1983); m. Diana Thanet French, 1984 (div. 1995); children: Reed Thanet Wendorf-French, Carolyn Thanet Wendorf-French; m. Elizabeth Morse, 1997. BA, Williams Coll., 1970; PhB, U. Oxford, Eng., 1972; MA, Princeton U., 1974, PhD, 1976. From asst. prof. English to assoc. prof. English Northwestern U., Evanston, Ill., 1976-86, assoc. dean, 1984-88, prof. English and art history, 1986-89; libr. dir. Houghton Libr., Harvard U., Cambridge, Mass., 1989-97; Stanford Calderwood dir. and libr. Boston Athenaeum, 1997—. Sr. lectr. fine arts Harvard U., 1990-97, acting libr. Fine Arts Libr., 1991-92; lectr. Phi Beta Kappa Assocs., 1992-96; dir. NEH summer seminars for coll. tchrs. Northwestern U., 1987, Harvard U., 1990, 92, 96, Boston Athenaeum, 2004; Robert Sterling Clark vis. prof. art history Williams Coll., 1993. Author: William Collins and Eighteenth-Century English Poetry 1981, The Elements of Life: Biography and Portrait Painting in Stuart and Georgian England, 1990, paperback edit., 1991, Sir Joshua Reynolds: The Painter in Society, 1996; editor: Articulate Images: The Sister Arts from Hogarth to Tennyson, 1983, Rare Book and Manuscript Libraries in the Twenty-First Century, 1993, (with Charles Ryskamp) The Works of William Collins, 1979; contbr. essays in field; mem. editl. bd. Studies in 18th Century Culture, 1985-89, Word and Image, 1992-2000, Yale edit. Writings of Samuel Johnson, Old-Time New Eng., 1996-99. Trustee Mus. Fine Arts, Boston. Rsch. grantee Folger Shakespeare Libr., Washington, 1976, Am. Philos. Soc., Phila., 1977, 82, Henry E. Huntington Libr., 1979, 2003, Yale Ctr. for Brit. Art, 1983, Brit. Acad., 2003; jr. rsch. fellow Am. Coun. Learned Socs., 1978-79; summer stipend NEH, 1979; sr. rsch. fellow Am. Coun. Learned Socs., 1981-82; NEH rsch. fellow Newberry Libr., Chgo., 1988-89; fellow John Simon Guggenheim Meml. Found., 1989-90. Mem.: The Johnsonians (chmn. 1994—95, 1997—98), Nat. Com. on Stds. in Arts, Colonial Soc. Mass., Soc. Brit. Art Historians, Coll. Art Assn., Am. Soc. 18th Century Studies (pres. Midwest regional soc. 1986, Annibel Jenkins Biography prize 1998), Am. Antiquarian Soc., Keats-Shelley Assn. Am. (bd. dirs. 1993—98), Signet Soc. (assoc.), Union Club Boston, Cambridge Sci. Club, Saturday Club, Grolier Club, Phi Beta Kappa (exec. bd. Chgo. 1984—87, nominating com. 1998—2002). Office: Boston Athenaeum 10 1/2 Beacon St Boston MA 02108-3777

WENDT, CHARLES WILLIAM, soil physicist, educator; b. Plainview, Tex., July 12, 1931; s. Charles Gottlieb and Winnie Mae (Bean) W.; m. Clara Anne Diller, Oct. 15, 1955; children: Charles Diller, John William, Elaine Anne, Cynthia Lynne. BS in Agronomy, Tex. A&M U., 1951, PhD in Soil Physics, 1966; MS in Agronomy, Tex. Tech U., 1957. Research asst. Tex. Tech Coll., 1953-55, instr. agronomy, 1957-61, asst. prof., 1961-63; research asst. soil physics Tex. A&M U., 1963-65, research assoc., 1965-66; asst. prof. Tex. A&M U. (Agrl. Research and Extension Center), Lubbock, 1966-69, assoc. prof., 1969-74, prof., 1974-91, prof. emeritus, 1991—. Cons. cotton prodn. Ministry of Agr. Sudan, summer 1960; cons. Irrigation Assn., 1977-81, Office of Tech. and Assessment, 1982, S.E. Consortium for Internat. Devel., 1989, Rhone Poulenc Agrl. Co., 1992-93; prin. backstop scientist U.S. AID West African Rsch. Program on Soil-Plant0Water Mgmt., 1982-91; chmn. agrl. sect. Southwestern and Rocky Mountain divsn. AAAS, 1982-83. Contbr. articles to profl. jours., chpt. to book. Del. Lubbock County Rep. Conv., 1978; elder Westminster Presbyn. Ch.; Tex. rep. to Great Plains Coun. 1 com. on evapotranspiration; bd. dirs. Presbyn. Ctr., Inc., 1999—. Land Use and Development, Boys and Girls Club of Lubbock, 2002—; bd. dirs. devsn. land use and devel. The South Plains Food Bank, 1999—, Presbyn. Women's Clinic, 1999—. 1st lt. U.S. Army, 1951-53. Named Outstanding Researcher High Plains Research Found., 1982; recipient Superior Achievement award for rsch., soil and crop scis. dept. Tex. A&M Univ., 1987, Vice Chancellors award in excellence as mem. TROPSOILS Rsch. team Tex. A&M U., 1996; grantee industry and water dists. Dept. Interior, U.S. AID, EPA. Mem. Soil Sci. Soc. Am., Am. Soc. Agronomy, Optimist Club (1st v.p., bd. dirs. 2001—). Home: 4518 22nd St Lubbock TX 79407-2515 Office: Texas Agrl Expt Station RR 3 Lubbock TX 79403-9803 E-mail: absendt@aol.com., absendt@cox.net.

WENDT, E. ALLAN, international affairs consultant; b. Chgo., Nov. 8, 1935; s. John Arthur Frederic and Dorothy Stephenson W. BA magna cum laude, Yale U., 1957; Certificat d'Etudes Politques, Institut d'Etudes Politques, Paris, 1959; MPA, Harvard U., 1967. Econ. comml. officer Am. Embassy, Saigon, Vietnam, 1967-71; fin. officer U.S. Mission to European Cmtys., Brussels, 1971-74; State Dept. fellow Coun. on Fgn. Rels., N.Y.C., 1974-75; dir. Office Internat. Commodities Dept. State, Washington, 1975-79; counselor for econ. and comml. affairs Am. Embassy, Cairo, 1979-81; dep. asst. sec. of state for internat. energy and resources policy Dept. State, 1981-86, sr. rep. for strategic tech. policy, 1987-92, with rank of amb., 1988-92, U.S. amb. to Republic of Slovenia Ljubljana, 1993-95, spl. rep. Internat. Donor Activities in Kosovo, 1998-2000; internat. affairs cons., 2000—. Councillor Atlantic Coun. of U.S.; mem. Coun. Fgn. Rels. Washington Inst. Fgn. Affairs.; mem. adv. bd Nat Youth Leadership Forum. Contbr. articles to profl. jours., radio stas. and newspapers. Recipient award for heroism Dept. State, 1968, Presdl. Meritorious Svc. award, 1986, Superior Honor award Dept. State, 1992. Episcopalian.

WENDT, ELIZABETH WARCZAK, retired insurance company executive; b. Chgo., Aug. 27, 1931; d. John George and Elizabeth Marion (Jankowski) Warczak; m. John Edward Wendt, Oct. 31, 1953 (div.); children: John Alan, Brian Arthur, James Michael. Student Loyola U., Chgo., 1951-52; BSBA, St. Mary-of-the-Woods Coll., 1980; postgrad. Chgo. Kent Coll. Law, 1981-82. Asst. to actuary Globe Life Ins. Co., Chgo., 1970-74; asst. compliance officer Globe Life/Ryan Ins. Group, Chgo., 1974-86; mgr. credit product devel., 1986-96; ret. 1996; mem. FLMI Soc. Chgo., 1983—; co. rep. Consumer Credit Ins. Assn., Chgo., 1983-89; co. rep., mem. Handout Com. Life & Health Compliance Assn., 1979-96. Election judge, 1984—. Mem. United Farm Workers Support Com., Chgo. Fellow Life Mgmt. Inst. Democrat. Roman Catholic.

WENDT, GARY CARL, finance company executive; b. Portage, Wis., Mar. 13, 1942; s. Walter Carl and Dorothy Mae (Neesam) W.; children: Sarah, Rachel. BS in Civil Engring., U. Wis., 1965; MBA, Harvard U., 1967. V.p. La. Co. Inc., Houston, 1967-71, Diversified Advisor, Miami, 1971-75, GE Credit Corp., Stamford, Conn., 1975-84, COO, 1984-86; pres., CEO GE Capital Svcs. (formerly Gen. Electric Credit Corp.), Stamford, 1986—; CEO, chmn., Conseco, Inc., Carmel, IN, 2000—. Trustee Boy's and Girl's Club of Stamford, past campaign chmn. capital fund campaign; past chmn. Stamford United Way; chmn. Conn. Bus. Edn. Coun.; trustee Outward Bound USA; chmn. corp. adv. com. Fairfield County Community Found. Recipient of His Royal Highness Prince Philips award, 1996, Corporate award for Outstanding Svs. to Outward Bound, Stamford Vol. Ctr Heart of Gold Soc. award, Herbert Hoover Humaniarian award, The Boys and Girl Club of Am., 1994, Recipirnt of The Nat. Ethnic Coalition Org. Ellis Island Medal, 1993, Recipient of the SACIA Walter H. Wheeler Jr. Business Leadership award, 1993, Disting Svs. Citation from The Coll. Engring. at U. Wis., Recipient of The Nat. Conf. of Christian and Jews Nat. Human Rels. award, 1990, Recipient of The Outward Bound Corp. Leadership award, 1990, The SACIA Excalibur Leadership award, 1990, Regional Plan Assn. Leadership award, 1990. Mem. Southwestern Area Commerce and Industry Assn. of Conn. (bd. dirs., past chmn.), The Regional Plan Assn. (mem. bd., past chmn.), mem nat. bd of governors, Boys and Girls Club of Am., mem. bd., of govs. for United Way of Tri State. Office: Conseco Inc 11825 N Pennsylvania St Carmel IN 46032

WENDT, GEORGE ROBERT, actor; b. Chgo., Oct. 17, 1948; m. Bernadette Birkette; children: Joshua, Andrew, Hilary, Joe, Daniel. BA in Econs., Rockhurst Coll., 1971. Mem. Second City comedy troupe, Chgo., 1974-81. Actor: (feature films) My Bodyguard, 1980, Somewhere in Time, 1980, Airplane II: The Sequel, 1982, Jeckyl & Hyde: Together Again, 1982, The Women in Red, 1984, Thief of Hearts, 1984, No Small Affair, 1983, Fletch, 1985, House, 1986, Plain Clothes, 1988, Guilt by Suspicion, 1991, Forever Young, 1992, Man of the House, 1995, Lakeboat, 2000, Teddy Bears' Picnic, 2002, My Dinner with Jimi, 2003, King of the Ants, 2003, (TV film) Alien Avengers, 1996, Star Truckers, 1997, (TV film) Price of Heaven, 1997, The Lovemaster, 1997, Rupert's Land, 1998, Pooch and the Pauper, 1999, (TV film) Alice in Wonderland, 1999, Outside Providence, 1999, My Beautiful Son, 2001, Robertson's Greatest Hits, 2001; guest-star: (TV shows) Alice, Soap, Taxi, Hart to Hart, The American Dream, Seinfeld, Wings, St. Elsewhere, Spin City, The Simpsons, The Larry Sanders Show, Madigan Men, 2000, Becker, 2002, Frasier, 2002, The Jamie Kennedy Experiment, 2002; regular (TV show) Cheers, 1982-1993, The George Wendt Show, 1995, The Naked Truth, 1995, Sabrina, the Teenage Witch, 2001-02; appeared in various commls.; appeared on stage with the Second City comedy troupe, also Wild Men, 1993.*

WENDT, HANS W. life scientist; b. Berlin, July 25, 1923; s. Hans O. and Alice (Creutzburg) W.; m. Martha A. Linger, Dec. 23, 1956 (div.); children: Alexander, Christopher, Sandra; m. Judith A. Hammer, June 25, 1988. MSc, U. Hamburg, Germany, 1949; PhD in Psychopharmacology, U. Marburg, Germany, 1953. Diplomate in psychology. Rsch. asst. U. Marburg, 1949-53; rsch. assoc. Wesleyan U. and Office Naval Rsch., Middletown, Conn., 1952-53; asst. prof., field dir. internat. project U. Mainz, Germany, 1955-59; engring. psychologist to prin. human factors scientist Link Aviation, Apollo Simulator Systems, Binghamton, N.Y., 1959-61; assoc. to prof. psychology Valparaiso (Ind.) U., 1961-68; prof. psychology Macalester Coll., St. Paul, 1968-93; sr. rsch. fellow Chronobiology Labs. U. Minn., 1980—; prin. investigator A.v. Humboldt Geomedicine Collaboration (astrobiology), 1994—. Cons. and reviewer, 1961—; hon. prof. sci. U. Marburg, Germany, 1971—; vis. prof. U. Victoria, B.C., Can., U. Marburg, U. Bochum, U. Bielefeld, U. Goettingen, all Germany, 1966-89. Contbr. articles to profl. jours., chpts. to books. Recipient Disting. Sr. Scientist award, Alexander von Humboldt Found., 1976. Home: 2180 Lower Saint Dennis Rd Saint Paul MN 55116-2831

WENDT, JOHN ARTHUR FREDERIC, JR., lawyer; b. Cleve. s. John Arthur Frederic and Martha Ann (Hunter) W.; m. Marjorie Rickard Richardson, Oct. 2, 1962; children: Eric A., John A. F. III, Hilary H.; m. Dorothy Fay Nuttall, Dec. 29, 1976. AB with honors, U. Mich., 1942; JD, U. Colo., 1951. Bar: Colo. 1951, U.S. Dist. Ct. Colo. 1951, U.S. Ct. Appeals (10th cir.) 1957, U.S. Supreme Ct. 1971. Assoc. Tippit, Haskell & Welborn, Denver, 1953-58; ptnr. Wendt & Kistler, Denver, 1958-62, Wendt Law Offices, Aspen, Colo., 1971-81, Delta, Colo., 1985—; dist. atty. 9th Jud. Dist. Colo., 1965-69; judge Pitkin County, Colo., 1971-78; dist. atty. 7th Jud. Dist. Colo., 1981-85; judge Cedaredge, Colo., 1986—2002. Contract mediator, Colo. Judiciary, 1995—. Chmn. Delta County Planning Comm., 1991-94. Maj. U.S. Army, 1942-46, 51-53. Decorated Purple Heart (2), Silver Star, Bronze Star (2). Mem. Am. Arbitration Assn., Acad. Family Mediators, Colo. Bar Assn. (gov. 1965-71, 82, 85, 87-96), Pitkin County Bar Assn. (pres. 1971-72), Delta County Bar Assn. (pres. 1986-89), 7th Jud. Dist. Bench-Bar Com., 187th Infantry (disting.), U.S. Equestrian Team (chmn. Colo. chpt. 1976-86), Masters of Fox Hounds Assn.,

M.F.H. Roaring Fork Hounds, U.S. Pony Clubs, Inc. (gov. 1996-2000), Phi Kappa Psi, Phi Delta Phi, Phi Beta Kappa. Republican. Episcopalian. Office: PO Box 94 540 Main St Delta CO 81416-1834 Home: PO Box 120 Austin CO 81410-0120

WENDT, MARILYNN SUZANN, elementary school educator, principal; b. Bay City, Mich., Oct. 6, 1939; d. Clarence Henry and Margaret Viola (Rugenstein) W. AA, Bay City Jr. Coll., 1959; BA, Ctrl. Mich. U., 1962, MA, 1964; EdD, Wayne State U., 1971. Cert. elem. adminstr., Mich. Tchr., teaching prin. Baxman Sch., Bay City, 1959-62; tchr., guidance counselor, dir. elem. edn. Essexville (Mich.)-Hampton Schs., 1962-66; tchr., dir. elem. edn., dir. curriculum rsch. Bloomfield Hills (Mich.) Schs., 1966-78; elem. prin., staff development trainer, learning improvement ctr. supr. Waterford (Mich.) Schs., 1978—. Consortium facilitator Mich. Dept. Edn. Exptl. & Demonstration Ctr., Lansing, 1975-76; part time faculty mem. Wayne State U., Detroit, 1972-78. Co-author: Rational Basis for Planning School Accountability, 1976; contbr. articles to profl. jours. Trustee, v.p. Waterford Twp. Libr., 1990-95; trustee St. Mark's Bd. Edn., West Bloomfield, Mich., 1991-95. Recipient Outstanding Educator award U.S. Office of Edn.-Harold Howe II, 1968, Disting. Svc. award Bloomfield Hills Schs., 1980. Mem. ASCD, Nat. Coun. Tchrs. English, Internat. Reading Assn., Mich. Reading Assn. (Celebrate Literacy award 1989, Adminstr. of Yr. 1991), Mich. ASCD (editor newsletter, conf. planner), Oakland County Reading Assn., Oakland County State & Fed. Program Specialists, Delta Kappa Gamma (v.p. 1990-93, Woman of Distinction 1982). Avocations: reading, swimming.

WENDT, RODERICK C. manufacturing executive; B, Stanford U.; JD, Willamette U. Corp. counsel JELD WEN, Inc., Klamath Falls, Oreg., 1980, v.p., corp. sec., sr. v.p., pres., 1992—. Office: JELD-WEN Inc 401 Harbor Isles Blvd Klamath Falls OR 97601

WENDT, THOMAS, finance executive; CPA, Wis. Auditor Coopers & Lybrand, Milw., 1973-75; supr. Conley, McDonald, Sprague & Co., Milw., 1975-80; CFO E. Cen./Select Sires, Waupun, Wis., 1981—, also rec. sec., bd. dirs. Bd. dirs. Moravian Homes Inc., Mueller Apts., Inc., Marquardt Meml. Manor, Inc., Watertown, Wis., 1985—, sec. and treas. bd. dirs., 1986—. Mem. Marquardt Found., 1988—; bd. dirs. Zinsendorf Hall, 1989—, sec., treas., 1989—, forward campaign chmn., 1988, pres. bd. trustees Watertown Moravian Ch., 1981-84, bd. elders, 1990-93, ch. sec., 2000-03; adv. del. Western Dist. Synod, Wis., 1982, 86, 90, 96; bd. dirs. Moravian Homes of Sturgeon Bay, 1991—; bd. dirs. Hus Apts., Inc., 1993—, sec., treas., 1993—. Mem. AICPA, Wis. Inst. CPAs, Milw. Art Mus. Office: E Central/Select Sires PO Box 191 Waupun WI 53963-0191

WENDZEL, ROBERT LEROY, political science educator; b. May 28, 1938; married; 3 children. BA in Polit. Sci. magna cum laude, Kalamazoo Coll., 1960; PhD in Polit. Sci., U. Fla., 1965. Assoc. prof. polit. sci. U. Maine, Orono, 1977-81, 82-83; prof. internat. affairs U.S. Air War Coll., Maxwell AFB, Ala., 1981-82, prof. internat. politics, 1986-87, ednl. advisor to the Commandant, 1987-2000, prof. internat. security studies, 2002—; asst. dean arts and scis., prof. polit. sci., coord. internat. affairs program U. Maine, 1984-86; Paschal P. Vacca prof. liberal arts U. Montevallo, Ala., 2001; Merrill prof. polit. sci. Utah State U., Logan, 2001. Internat. affairs com., U. Maine, 1970-86, budget adv. com., 1983-86, coord. internat. affairs program, 1984-86. Author: International Relations: A Policymaker Focus, Thai edit., 1989, Relacoes Internacionais, 1985, International Politics: Policymakers and Policymaking, 1981, International Relations: A Policymaker Focus, 1977, 2d edit., 1980; co-author: America's Foreign Policy in a Changing World, 1994, Defending America's Security, 1988, 2d edit., 1990, To Preserve the Republic: The Foreign Policy of the United States, 1985, Games Nations Play, 9th edit., 1996; contbr. articles to profl. jours. Mem. Phi Beta Kappa. Home: 160 Old Field Dr Montgomery AL 36117-3938 Personal E-mail: blw052838@aol.com.

WENEGRAT, SAUL S. arts administrator, art educator, consultant; b. Jersey City, Mar. 28, 1933; s. John and Tillie (Freeman) W. BA, Rutgers U., 1960; PhD, Harvard U., 1962; cert., London U., 1975. Dir. art program Port Authority of N.Y. & N.J., N.Y.C., 1962-95; prof. grad. divsn. Fashion Inst. Tech., N.Y.C., 1987-95; v.p. Forums Internat., 1995—; cons. arts advisor Voorsanger and Assocs., Archs., 2001—04. Pub. art panelist N.J. State Com. Arts, Trenton, 1985-95, Conn. State Com. Arts, Hartford, 1988, N.Y.C. Cultural Affairs, 1980-88, Met. Transit Authority, N.Y.C., 1994-95. Editor: Art for the Public, 1985. Capt. USAF, 1953-57. Recipient Doris Freedman award Mayor of N.Y.C., 1984, Merit cert. Mcpl. Art Soc., 1980, 85; Carnegie fellow, 1960, Fels fellow, 1960. Mem. Nat. Assn. Corp. Art Adminstrn. (chmn. bd. 1985-95), Internat. Assn. Art Advisors, Am. Assn. Museums, Harvard Club. Avocations: bridge, walking, museums. Home: 2 Beekman Pl New York NY 10022-8058

WENG, GEORGE JUENG-CIOUS, engineering educator; b. Oct. 8, 1944; s. Wan-Chung and Kuang-chieh (Hsieh) Weng; m. Jackie Li; children: Shawn, Cidney, Zoe; children from previous marriage: Bruce, Joyce. BS, Taiwan U., 1967; MPhil, Yale U., 1971, PhD, 1974. Rsch. fellow Delft (The Netherlands) U. Tech., 1973-74; postdoctoral fellow Yale U., UCLA, 1974-76; sr. rsch. engr. GM Rsch. Lab., Warren, Mich., 1976-77; asst. prof. mech. and aerospace engring. Rutgers U., New Brunswick, NJ, 1977-80, assoc. prof., 1980-84, prof., 1984-92, disting. prof., 1992—, grad. dir., 1995-98. Contbr. more than 140 articles to profl. jours.; editor Acta Mechanica, 1985—; tech. editor Jour. Engring. Materials and Tech., trans. ASME, 1992-97; editl. bd. Internat. Jour. Plasticity, 1985—, Acta Mechanica Solida Sinica, 1997—, JSME Internat. Jour., 1997-2002, Mechanics and Materials in Design, 2001—. NSF grantee, 1978—. Fellow ASME, Am. Acad. Mechanics. Achievements include work in mechanics of materials, micromechanics of composite materials, shape-memory alloys, ferroelectric ceramics, nano-grained materials. Home: 65 Sycamore Way Warren NJ 07059 Office: Sch Engring Rutgers U New Brunswick NJ 08903 Office Phone: 732-445-2223. Business E-Mail: weng@jove.rutgers.edu.

WENG, JUYANG JOHN, computer science educator, researcher; b. Shanghai, Apr. 15, 1957; came to U.S., 1983; m. Min Guo, 1985; children: Colin S., Rodney D. BS in Computer Sci., Fudan U., Shanghai, 1982; MS in Computer Sci., U. Ill., 1985, PhD in Computer Sci., 1989. Rsch. asst. U. Ill., Urbana, 1984-88; rschr. Computer Rsch. Inst. Montreal, Can., 1989-90; vis. asst. prof. U. Ill., 1990-92; asst. prof. Mich. State U., East Lansing, 1992-98, assoc. prof., 1998—2003, prof., 2003—. Author: (chpt.) Early Visual Learning, 1996; co-author: (chpt.) Handbook of Pattern Recognition and Computer Vision, 1993, Motion and Structures from Image Sequences, 1993, (chpt.) Visual Navigation, 1997. Mem. IEEE (Computer Soc., chair CIS Autonomous Mental Devel. Tech. Com., assoc. editor IEEE Transactions on Image Processing 1994-97; assoc. editor Transactions on Pattern Analysis and Machine Intelligence 2000—), CIS Autonomous Mental Devel. Tech. Com. (chair), Am. Soc. Engring. Edn., Sigma Xi, Phi Beta Delta. Achievements include contributions to understanding and computation of estimation of motion and structure from image sequences; co-inventor of Cresceptron, an experimental system for recognizing and segmenting objects from natural images; director of SHOSLIF project for a general framework for visual learning by computers; an originator of the developmental approach to artificial intelligence; dir. SAIL and DAV developmental robot projects. Office: Mich State Univ 3115 Engring Bldg East Lansing MI 48824 Office Phone: 517-353-4388.

WENG, WEN-KAI, oncologist, medical researcher; b. Taipei, China, Dec. 11, 1962; arrived in U.S., 1990; s. Hua-Min and Lee (Chu) W. MD, Chung-Shan Med. & Dental Coll., Taichung, China, 1988; PhD, U. Minn., 1996. Rsch. asst. U. Minn., Mpls., 1990-96; resident in internal medicine U. Tex./Houston Med. Sch., 1996-99; fellow in oncology Stanford U., Calif., 1999—2002, clin. instr. oncology, 2002—. Ad hoc reviewer Blood-Jour. Am. Soc. Hematology, 1996. Dir. acad. com. Minn. Chinese Soc. Biomed. Sci., Mpls., 1993-96; cons. Minn. Chinese Student Assn., Mpls., 1993-96. With Rep. of China Army, 1988-90. Recipient fellowship U. Minn. Grad. Sch., 1995-96, rsch. fellowship Lymphoma Rsch. Found., 2002-04, Nat. Rsch. Svc. award NIH, 1994-95. Mem. Chinese Med. Assn., Am. Soc. Hematology, Am. Assn. Cancer Rsch., Sigma Xi (Charles and Dorothy Andrew Bird award 1996). Avocations: wildlife photography, birding, rock climbing, computers. Office: Stanford U Divsn Oncology Medicine 1000 Welch Rd Ste 202 Palo Alto CA 94304-1808 Office Phone: 650-723-7621.

WENGER, GALEN ROSENBERGER, pharmacology educator; b. Sellersville, Pa., May 16, 1946; s. Warren Martin and Ethel (Rosenberger) W.; m. Carolyn Jean Liechty; children: Alyssa Nicole, Aaron Joseph. BA, Goshen Coll., 1968; PhD, Wa. Va. U., 1971. Postdoctoral fellow U. Colo. Med. Ctr., Denver, 1972-73, Harvard U. Med. Sch., Boston, 1973-75, instr., 1975-78; asst. prof. U. Ark. Med. Sci., Little Rock, 1978-81; assoc. prof. U. Ark. for Med. Scis., Little Rock, 1981-86, prof., 1986—; div. dir. U. Ark. Med. Scis., Little Rock, 1991—. Cons. VA Agt. Orange and Agt. Blue Rsch. Program, 1982, Nat. Inst. Environ. Health Scis., 1983, 84, 85, Nat. Ctr. Toxicol. Rsch., 1983-89, Health Effects Inst., Cambridge, Mass., 1986, Nat. Inst. Drug Abuse, 1988, Tox II study sect. NIH, 1991-94, ALTX-3, 2000-2003; rsch. coun. Coll. Medicine U. Ark. Med. Scis., 1979-85, others. Editorial bd. Neurotoxicology and Teratology, 1990-95, Neurotoxicology, 1995—; contbr. numerous articles to profl. jours. Grantee Nat. Inst. Occupl. Health and Safety, 1978-83, Nat. Inst. Drug Abuse, 1978—, NSF, 1981-86, EPA, 1982-85, NIAAA, 1999—; named to Outstanding Young in Am., 1981; recipient Golden Apple award for excellence in teaching, U. Ark., 1986-87. Mem. Am. Soc. Pharmacology and Exptl. Therapeutics, Soc. Toxicology, Coll. on Problems of Drug Dependence, Behavioral Pharmacology Soc., Behavioral Toxicology Soc., AAAS. Mennonite. Office: Pharmacology/Toxicology Dep U Ark Med Scis 4301 W Markham St Little Rock AR 72205-7101 Office Phone: 501-686-8040. E-mail: wengergalenr@uams.edu.

WENGER, JAY LAMAR, psychology educator; b. Hershey, Pa., Jan. 16, 1954; s. Melvin Sensenig and Janette Louise Wenger; m. Suzanne Marie Shenk; 1 child, Kira. BS in Math., Millersville U. of Pa., 1976, BA in Psychology, 1989; MS in Psychology, Pa. State U., 1991, PhD in Psychology, 1994. Tchr. math. Locust Grove Mennonite Sch., Smoketown, Pa., 1977—87; prof. psychology U. West Ala., Livingston, 1994—2004; prof. Harrisburg Area C.C., Lancaster, Pa., 2004—. Contbr. rsch. articles to profl. jours. Scholar Fulbright scholar, Tallinn (Estonia) Pedagog. U., 2001—02. Mem.: APA, Christian Assn. for Psychol. Studies, Southeastern Psychol. Assn. Avocations: travel, photography. Office: HACC Lancaster 1641 Old Philadelphia Pike Lancaster PA 17602 Business E-Mail: jlwenger@hacc.edu.

WENGER, LARRY BRUCE, law librarian, law educator; b. Everett, Wash., Dec. 21, 1941; s. Lester Edwin Wenger and Selma Marie (Norberg) W. Saterstrom; m. Marilyn Diane Watt, June 26, 1965; children: Bruce Daniel, Kathleen Marie. BA, U. Wash., 1964, JD, 1967; MLS, Simmons Coll., 1969. Reference libr. Sch. Law Harvard U., Cambridge, Mass., 1967-69; asst. law libr. SUNY, Buffalo, 1969-71, law libr., assoc. prof. law, 1971-76; law libr., prof. law U. Va., Charlottesville, 1976—. Cons. to law librs.; bd. dirs. Nat. Ctr. for Preservation Law. Editor: Marine Affairs Bibliography. Mem. Am. Assn. Law Librs., Internat. Assn. Law Librs. (pres. 1995-2001), Bibliog. Soc., Bibliog. Soc. Am. Home: 2630 Meriwether Dr Charlottesville VA 22901-9513 Office: U Va Law Libr 580 Massie Rd Charlottesville VA 22903-1739

WENGER, RONALD DAVID, surgeon; b. Phila., May 1, 1944; s. Christian Showalter and Helen Grace (Heisey) W.; m. Judith Kay Anderson, Jan. 24, 1970; children: Clayton, Lera. BA, Ohio Wesleyan U., 1966; MD, Case Western Res. U., 1970. Diplomate Am. Bd. Surgery. Intern U. Oreg. Med. Sch., Portland, 1970-71; fellow Mayo Clinic Surgery Dept., Rochester, Minn., 1973-77; clin. prof. surgery U. Wis. Med. Sch., Madison, 1977—; pvt. practice, Madison, 1977—; asst. chief surgery St. Mary's Hosp., Madison, 1980-00; chief surgery Dean Med. Ctr., Madison, 1988-93. Named one of Best Drs. in Dane County, Madison Mag., 2002. Mem. ACS (also Wis. chpt.), AMA, SAGES, Wis. State Med. Soc., Madison Surg. Soc., Wis. Surg. Soc., Soc. for Surgery of Alimentary Tract. Avocations: skiing, bicycling, sailing, travel, reading. Home: 726 Farwell Dr Madison WI 53704-6032 Office: 1821 S Stoughton Rd Madison WI 53716-2257 Office Phone: 608-260-6003.

WENGER, SHARON LOUISE, pediatrics educator, researcher, cytogeneticist; b. Washington, Sept. 25, 1949; d. William Fred and Lois Helen (Compton) W.; m. George E. Fromlak Jr., Jan. 10, 1976; children: Nicholas Edward, Holly Louise, Andrea Lee. BA in Biology, Thiel Coll., 1971; MS in Human Genetics, U. Pitts., 1973, PhD in Human Genetics, 1976. Asst. prof. Sch. of Medicine U. Pitts., 1980-89, assoc. prof. Sch. of Medicine, 1989—. Contbr. articles to profl. jours. Mem. Am. Soc. Human Genetics, Midwest Soc. for Pediatric Rsch. Achievements include research in association of sister chromatid exchange with rare fragile site Xq27 and support for imprinting in Fragile X syndrome by late DNA synthesis at Xq27 area. Office: Children's Hosp Pitts 3705 5th Ave Pittsburgh PA 15213-2524

WENGERT, TIMOTHY, church history educator, clergyman; b. Teaneck, NJ, Oct. 1, 1950; s. Norman Irving and Janet (Mueller) W.; m. Barbara Ann Farlow, Nov. 17, 1973 (dec. May 2001); children: Emily, David. AB, U. Mich., 1972, MA, 1973; MDiv, Luther Sem., St. Paul, 1977; PhD, Duke U., 1984. Ordained to ministry Evangel. Luth. Ch. in Am., 1977. Asst. pastor Luth. Ch. of the Master, Edina, Minn., 1977-78; pastor Cross Luth. Ch., Roberts, Wis., 1983-89; prof. Luth. Theol. Sem. Phila., 1989—. Author: Philip Melanchthon's Annotationes in Johannem, 1987, Human Freedom, Christian Righteousness, 1998, Law and Gospel, 1997; author: (with Gordon Lathrop) Christian Assembly, 2004; editor (with Charles Brockwell): Telling the Churches' Stories, 1995; editor: (with Robert Kolb) The Book of Concord, 2000; editor: Harvesting Martin Luther's Reflections, 2003; assoc. editor The Luth. Quar., 1997—. Grantee Deutscher Akademischer Austauschdienst, 1980-81, 95, Herzog August Bibliothek, 1991, 94, Lilly Theol. Rsch. grantee, faculty fellow, 1999—; recipient Melanchthon prize City of Bretten, Germany, 2000. Mem.: Soc. for Reformation Rsch., Sixteenth Century Studies Conf. Office: Luth Theol Sem 7301 Germantown Ave Philadelphia PA 19119-1726 Office Phone: 215-248-6377. Business E-Mail: twengert@ltsp.edu.

WENGLER, MARGUERITE MARIE, educational therapist; b. Kokomo, Ind., Nov. 18, 1943; d. Eugene Ferdinand and Flavia Marie (Marullo) Scalzo; m. James Burton Wengler, Oct. 4,1969; children: James Eugene, Dale Douglas, Lauren Christine. BS in Edn., Hofstra U., 1964; MA in Moderate Spl. Needs Edn., Assumption Coll., 1991. Cert. elem. tchr. N.Y., Mass., spl. needs tchr. Mass. Spl. needs dir. Montessori Primary and Upper Schs., Lexington, Mass.; spl. edn. tchr. Lincoln-Sudbury Pub. Schs., Sudbury, Mass., 1987-88; from assoc. lectr. to sr. lectr. Program Advanced Lng. Curry Coll., Milton, Mass., 1993—, outreach dir., 1997-98. Dir. Learning Success Helpline, Acton, Mass., 1984—; profl. devel. provider towards tchr. cert. Dept. of Edn. state of Mass. Author: 60 Minutes to Much Higher Grades, coll. edit., 1995, 60 Minutes to Much Higher Grades, H.S. edit., 1997; contbg. author A Closer Look, 1995; mng. editor Shared Visions of Teaching and Learning, 1997-2001. Del. People to People/Citizen Amb., China, 1994; dir., founder A Friend in Need, Acton, Mass., 1990-96, bd. dirs. Recipient Grant to Friend in Need United Way, 1991-94, Cmty. Chest, 1993; grantee State of Mass., 1989-91. Mem. AAUP, Learning Disabilities Network. Office: Program Advancement Lng Curry Coll Blue Hill Ave Milton MA 02186-2302 Office Phone: 617-333-2169. E-mail: learningsuccess@yahoo.com.

WENGLOWSKI, GARY MARTIN, economist; b. Rochester, N.Y., Sept. 2, 1942; s. Henry Bernard and Isabelle (Franc) W.; m. Joyce Richards, Oct. 3, 1964; children: Gary Martin, Catherine Jean. BS in Econs., U. Pa., 1964, MA, 1965, PhD in Econs., 1967. With Goldman Sachs & Co., N.Y.C., 1967—, v.p., dir. econ. rsch., 1972-78, ptnr., 1978-86, ltd. ptnr., 1986-99; ret. ptnr., 1999—. Adj. prof. Baruch Coll., 1998—; chmn. vis. com. econ. dept. U. Pa., 1985-98. Author: Industry Profit Forecasting, 1972, Industry Profit Forecasting—Progress Report, 1975. Trustee CARE Found., 1991—, Haystack Mountain Sch., 1993-2002. Named Best Economist on Wall St., Ann. Instnl. Investor Mag. Polls, 1976-86; NDEA fellow, 1965, 67. Fellow Nat. Assn. Bus. Economists; mem. Am. Econ. Assn., Deer Isle Yacht Club (vice commodore 1993-94, commodore 1994-2000). Home: 32 Partridge Ridge Rd Katonah NY 10536-3500

WENIGER-PHELPS, NANCY ANN, media specialist, photographer; b. Kingman, Kans., Sept. 4, 1948; d. Watson and Reva Jo (Schlup) W. BA in Phys. Edn., Ottawa (Kans.) U., 1970; MA in LS, U. Denver, 1980. Cert. K-12 media specialist, secondary phys. edn. tchr., Ariz. Phys. edn. tchr. Grand Junction (Colo.) Sch. Dist., 1970-73; dist. mgr. World Book Ency., 1973-74; personal sec. Younger Bail Bond Svc., Grand Junction, 1974-76; media specialist K-12, phys. edn. tchr. Kingman (Kans.) Unified Sch. Dist., 1976-78, Ovid (Colo.) Sch. Dist., 1980-82, Sargeant Sch. Dist., Monte Vista, Colo., 1982-84, Antonito Sch. Dist., Ovid, Colo., 1984-85; photographer's asst. Bill Westenberg Photography, Alamosa, Colo., 1985-86; sch. media specialist Window Rick (Ariz.) Unified Sch. Dist., 1986-96. Profl. photographer; trainer adult and student storytellers; head dist. lib. computer program. Author: Photographic Uses in the Library; exhibited in group shows Gallup (N.Mex.) Gallery, 1989, Window Rock Elem. Sch., 1989, Sunflower Shop, Wichita, Kans. 1989-90, 96-98, also Alamosa, Colo., 1985-87, 1st Nat. Bank, Kingman (Kans.), Fernley (Nev.) Phys. Therapy, 1993, Greatest Little Art Show in Reno, Nev., 2003, Moms Arts and Crafts Show, Reno, Nev., 2003; photo consignment Trout Creek Nursery, Trucker, Calif., 2003. Mem. Washoe County Friends of Libr., Reno, Nev., vol. book sorter, vol. book sale. Mem. AAHPERD, ALA, Am. Fedn. Tchrs., Internat. Platform Assn., Ariz. Fedn. Tchrs., Window Rock Fedn. Tchrs., Ariz. Edn. Media Assn., Assoc. Photographers Internat. Ariz. Edn. Assn., Alpha Delta Kappa. Home and Office: 5255 Tyrone Rd Reno NV 89502

WENK, EDWARD, JR., civil engineer, policy analyst, educator, writer; b. Balt., Jan. 24, 1920; s. Edward and Lillie (Heller) Wenk; m. Carolyn Frances Lyford, Dec. 27, 1941; children: Lawrence Shelley, Robin Edward Alexander, Terry Allan(dec.). BE, Johns Hopkins U., 1940, DEng, 1950; MSc, Harvard U., 1947; DSc (hon.), U. R.I., 1968; LHD (hon.), Johns Hopkins U., 1989. Registered profl. engr. Head structures div. USN David Taylor Model Basin, Washington, 1942-56; chmn. dept. engring. mechanics S.W. Research Inst., San Antonio, 1956-59; sr. specialist sci. and tech. Legis. Reference Service, Library of Congress, Washington, 1959-61, chief sci. policy research div., 1964-66; tech. asst. to U.S. President's sci. adviser and exec. sec. Fed. Council for Sci. and Tech., White House, Washington, 1961-64; exec. sec. Nat. Council on Marine Resources and Engring. Devel., Exec. Office of Pres., Washington, 1966-70; prof. engring. and pub. affairs U. Wash., Seattle, 1970-83, prof. emeritus, 1983—, dir. program in social mgmt. tech., 1973-79; tech. advisor to gov. State of Wash., 1993-96. Nat. Adv. Com. on Oceans and Atmosphere, 1972-73; vice chmn. U.S. Congress Tech. Assessment Adv. Coun., 1973-79; adviser Congress, GAO, NSF, EPA, NOAA, White House, UN Secretariat, Wash. State, Alaska, U.K., Australia, Sweden, The Philippines, Alaska Oil Spill Commn., 1989, Wash. State Marine Oversight Bd., 1992, pub. interest groups, 1997, US Dept. Transportation; vis. scholar Woodrow Wilson Internat. Ctr. for Scholars, 1970-72, Harvard U., 1976, Woods Hole Oceanographic Instn., 1976, U. Sussex, 1977, Bellagio Ctr., Rockefeller Found., 1977, 90; lectr., cons. in field. Author: The Politics of the Oceans, 1972, Margins for Survival, 1979, Tradeoffs-Imperatives of Choice in a High-Tech World, 1986, Making Waves—Engineering, Politics and the Social Management of Technology, 1995, The Double Helix: Technology and Democracy in the American Future, 1999; editor Exptl. Mechs. Jour., 1954-56, Engring. Mechs. Jour., 1958 60; mem. editl. bd. Tech. Forecasting, Tech. in Soc.; contbr. articles to profl. jours.; designer Aluminaut submarine. Bd. dirs. Human Interaction Rsch. Inst., 1980-90, Smithsonian Sci. Info. Exch., 1977-82, URS Corp., 1973-88; mem. Interfaith Alliance. Ensign USNR, 1944-45. Recipient Navy Meritorious Civilian Svc. award, 1946, authors prize Gov. Wash., 1974, ann. prize Edn. Press Assn., 1997; named Disting. Alumnus Johns Hopkins U., 1979, Tchr. of Yr., Wash. State Engrs., 1980, Tchr. of Yr., Students in Pub. Adminstrn., 1986, Disting. Alumnus, Balt. Poly. Inst., 1991; Ford Found. grantee, 1970; Rockefeller Found. Bellagio fellow, 1976, 90; 1st Stuckenburg lectr. Wash. U., 1988; Regents lectr. U. Calif., Berkeley, 1989, Woodrow Wilson award Johns Hopkins U., 2004. Fellow ASME (exec., Ralph Coats Roe medal 1999), AAAS; mem. ASCE, NSPE, LWV, Soc. Exptl. Stress Analysis (past pres. and William M. Murray lectr.), Internat. Assn. Impact Assessment (pres. 1981-82), NAE (chmn. com. on pub. policy 1970-75), Nat. Acad. Pub. Adminstrn., Am. Soc. for Pub. Adminstrn. (chmn. com. on sci. and tech. in govt. 1974-78), Assembly Engring. and Marine Bd. NRC, Nat. Oceanography Assn. (v.p. pub. affairs 1970-72), Cousteau Soc. (chmn. adv. bd. 1975-97), USA Club of Rome (bd. dirs. 1997-98), Cosmos Club (Washington), Explorers Club, Sigma Xi, Tau Beta Pi, Chi Epsilon. Home: 900 University St # 13L Seattle WA 98101 E-mail: future@u.washington.edu. *Each of us has the opportunity, indeed responsibility, to contribute to the human experience and to enrich the lives of future generations. In a world of change, cultural diversity and uncertainty, we must be ourselves and not merely slaves of conventional thought. We must act on the basis of what we believe to be right rather than only from the desire to be loved.*

WENKERT, DEBORAH, pediatric rheumatologist, researcher; b. Ames, Iowa, July 2, 1958; d. Ernest and Ann (Davis) W.; m. Roger Alan Young, Aug. 1988; children: Benjamin Sidney Young, Jonathan Davis Young, Nathaniel Theodore Young. BA, Rice U., 1979; MD, U. Tex., 1987. Diplomate Am. Bd. Pediat. and Pediatric Rheumatology. Technician, rschr. Baylor Coll. Medicine, Houston, 1979-81; intern Children's Hosp., St. Louis, 1987-88, resident, 1988-90; fellow New Eng. Med. Ctr., Boston, 1990-93; postdoctoral Harvard U., Cambridge, Mass., 1991-94; instr. Washington U. Med. Sch., St. Louis, 1994-98; v.p. Bench Master Inc., St. Louis, 1998—2002; from asst. clin. prof. to assoc. clin. prof. Med. Sch. St. Louis (Mo.) U., 1999—2004, assoc. clin. prof. Med. Sch., 2004—. Mem. courtesy staff Shriners Hosp. for Crippled Children, St. Louis, 2001—. Recipient Physician Scientist award, NIH, 1993; fellow, Cancer Rsch. Inst., 1991. Fellow Am. Acad. Pediat., Am. Coll. Rheumatology, Am. Soc. Bone and Mineral Rsch.

WENNBERG, JOHN E. epidemiologist; b. June 2, 1934; BA, Stanford U., 1956; MD, McGill Med. Sch., 1961; MPH, Johns Hopkins U., 1966. Intern DC Gen. Hosp., Washington, 1961-62; assoc. med. resident Johns Hopkins Hosp., Balt., 1962-63, fellow in renal disease & pharmacology, 1963-65; resident in chronic disease Balt. City Hosp., 1966-67; dir. No. New England Regional Med. Program, Burlington, Vt., 1967-71; interim dir. Coop. Health-care Info. Ctr., Burlington, 1972-73; sr. assoc. Harvard Ctr. Cmty. Health & Med. Care, Boston, 1973-75; from asst. prof. to prof. epidemiology Dartmouth Med. Sch., Hanover, N.H., 1975—. Dir. Ctr. Evaluation & Clin. Sci., Hanover, 1989—; bd. dirs. Am. Med. Rev. Rsch. Ctr., 1985—; physicians adv. group N.Y. Health & Hosps. Corp., 1988—. Mem. Am. Hosp. Assn. (coun. rsch. & devel. 1973-75), Johns Hopkins Soc. Scholars. Address: Dartmouth Med Sch Ctr Evaluative Clin Scis Hinman Box 7252 MML Bldg Hanover NH 03755-3871

WENNBERG, PAUL, chemist; BA, Oberlin Coll., 1985; PhD, Harvard U., 1994. Prof. Calif. Inst. Tech., 2001—. Contbr. articles to profl. jours. Recipient Presdl. Early Career award, 1999; fellow MacArthur Found., 2002. Office: Calif Inst Tech 110 N Mudd 1200 E Calif Blvd Pasadena CA 91125

WENNER, CHARLES RODERICK, lawyer; b. New Haven, Jan. 10, 1947; s. Charles Bellew and Joan Rhoda (Morrison) Wenner; m. Jovita C. Vergara, June 11, 1999; children: Abigail Jessica, Charles Roderick Jr. BS, Coll. Charleston, 1969; JD, U. Conn., 1973. Bar: Conn. 1974, DC 1977. Law clk. Conn. Superior Ct., Hartford, 1973-74; staff atty. SEC, Washington, 1974-76, spl. counsel to chmn., 1976—77; assoc. Fulbright & Jaworski, 1977—81, ptnr., 1981—. Lectr. law U. Conn. Sch. Law, 1973—74. Bd. dirs. Operation Friendship Internat., Inc., Washington, 1993—; trustee United Meth. Ch., Arlington, Va., 1993—95, 1997—98; counselor Gospel Mission Washington, 1991—. Recipient Am. Hist. award, DAR, 1969. Mem.: ABA, DC Bar Assn. Methodist. Avocation: running. Home: 1808 South Lynn St Arlington VA 22202 Office: Fulbright & Jaworski 801 Pennsylvania Ave NW Fl 3-5 Washington DC 20004-2623 Office Phone: 202-662-4575. Business E-Mail: cwenner@fulbright.com.

WENNER, DEBBY LINN, music educator, mezzo soprano; b. Cumberland, Md., Nov. 9, 1953; d. Raymond Calvin and Beatrice Linn Wenner; adopted children: Timothy Alan, Lois Linn. BS in Music, Frostburg State U., 1975; postgrad., W.Va. U., 1976, Cath. U. Am., 1977; MusM, George Washington

U., 1984. Pvt. voice instr., Alexandria, Va., 1975—; vocal instr. George Washington U., Washington, 1979—84, Foxes Music, Falls Church, Va., 1980—85, Olde Towne (Va.) Music, 1981—86; theory tutor Mary Baldwin Coll., 1984; voice/opera instr. St. Mary's (Md.) Coll., 1985—90; adj. prof. voice and pedagogy George Mason U., Fairfax, Va., 2000—. Alto soloist Rodef Shalom Temple, Falls Church, 1980—, Ch. of the Annunciation, Washington, 1995—; alto soloist, sect. leader Foundry United Meth., Washington, 1980—95. Singer: (world premiere) Carnegie Hall; soloist: Tidewater Music Festival, 1985—90, recitalist: Kennedy Ctr. Terr. Theater, Nat. Portrait Gallery. Vol., fundraiser Challenger Little League, Springfield, Va., 1992—; vol., coord. Eddies Club for Disabled Children, Springfield, 1993—. Recipient Washington Post/Maude Steward awards, Met. Opera Coun., N.Y.C., 1987, Study award, 1987, Outstanding Alumni award, Frostburg State U., 1992. Mem.: Associated Bd. Royal Schs. Musicians, Nat. Assn. Tchrs. Singing, Spina Bifida Assn. Democrat. Avocations: neuroscience, poetry, interior decorating, jazz, baseball. Home: 6524 Fairland St Alexandria VA 22312 Office: George Mason Univ Music Dept 4400 University Dr Fairfax VA 22030 Office Phone: 703-256-7225.

WENNER, GENE CHARLES, arts management executive; b. Catasauqua, Pa., Dec. 21, 1931; s. Clinton G. and Bertha (Taggert) W.; m. Carole Brunner, Aug. 15, 1953; children: Robert Larren, Laurel E. Wenner Carsell BS in Music, West Chester (Pa.) State Coll., 1953; M.Ed. in Music, Pa. State U., 1954. Tchr. music Phila. pub. schs., 1945-55, 56-60; assoc. prof. Kutztown (Pa.) State Coll., 1960-66, dir. coll. choir, 1960-66; fine arts adv. Pa. Dept. Edn., 1966-69, U.S. Office Edn., 1969-71; asst. dir. arts in edn. program John D. Rockefeller 3d Fund, 1971-78; arts edn. coordinator Office Commr., U.S. Office Edn., 1978-79; pres. Am. Music Conf., Wilmette, Ill., 1979-81; v.p. for programs Nat. Found. Advancement in Arts, Miami, Fla., 1983-87; pres. Arts and Edn. Cons., Inc., Reston, Va., 1987-91; sr. cons. Bus. & Industry for Arts Edn., 1990-91; exec. dir. Charlotte (N.C.) Community Sch. for the Arts, 1991-96; pres. Arts & Edn. Cons., Inc., Pittsfield, Mass., 1996—. Fund raising cons. Nat. Pub. Radio, Nat. Music Found., Mohawk Theater Capital Campaign, Goldman Meml. Band, Jacob's Pillow, Berkshire C.C. Non-Profit mgmt. Counsel, Mass. Coll. Liberal Arts; mus. dir. Allentown (Pa.) Mcpl. Oper, 1962-63, Allentown Civic Little Theatre, 1964, Little Theatre Alexandria, Va., 1971; dir. Hershey (Pa.) Little Theatre, 1967-68, Hershey Community Chorus, 1967-69 Composer: I'll Never Forget You, 1968, Chorale of Dedication, 1974, Great Things God Hath Done, 1986, In My ather's House, 1986; original music and script Adventures in the Arts, Hershey, 1968; also original TV music, I Am the Way, 1985, When You Remember, 1985; author papers, reports in field. Served with AUS, 1955-56. Named Best Mus. Dir. Little Theatre Alexandria Mem. Music Educators Nat. Conf., Network Performing and Visual Arts Schs. Clubs: Masons. Home and Office: 112 Doreen St Pittsfield MA 01201 Office Phone: 413-499-5311. E-mail: gwenner@berkshire.rr.com.

WENNER, JANN SIMON, editor, publisher; b. N.Y.C., Jan. 7, 1946; s. Edward and Ruth N. (Simmons) Wenner; m. Jane Ellen Schindelheim, July 1, 1968 (div. 1995); children: Alexander Jann, Theodore Simon, Edward Augustus. Student, U. Calif.-Berkeley, 1964—66. Co-founding editor, pub. Rolling Stone mag., NYC, 1967—; editor, pub. Record, NYC, 1981—86, Look mag., NYC, 1979, Men's Jour., 1992—; editor in chief Outside Mag., San Francisco, 1977—79, US Mag., NYC, 1985—, Men's Jour., 1992—; pub. Family Life, 1993—95; editor in chief Wenner Media Inc., 1993—; founder Cease Fire Inc., 1995—. Vice chmn. Rock & Roll Hall of Fame. Author: Lennon Remembers, 1971, Garcia, 1972; actor: (films) Perfect, 1985, Jerry Maguire, 1996, Almost Famous, 2000, Breakfast with Hunter, 2003. Bd. dirs. Robinhood Found. Recipient Disting. Achievement award, U. So. Calif. Sch. Journalism and Alumni Assn., 1976, Nat. Mag. award, 1970, 1977, 1986, 1987, 1988, 1989, Lifetime Achievement award, Rock and Roll Hall of Fame, 2004. Mem.: Am. Soc. Mag. Editors. Achievements include youngest editor to be inducted into the American Society of Mag. Editors Hall of Fame, 1997. Office: Rolling Stone Wenner Media Inc 1290 Avenue Of The Americas Fl 2 New York NY 10104-0295

WENNERSTROM, ARTHUR JOHN, aeronautical engineer; b. N.Y.C., Jan. 11, 1935; s. Albert Eugene and Adele (Trebus) W.; m. Bonita Gay Westenberg, Sept. 6, 1969 (div. Jan. 1989); children: Bjorn Erik, Erika Lindsay; m. Vicki Lynn Merrick, Feb. 17, 1990. BS in Mech. Engring., Duke U., 1956; MS in Aero. Engring., MIT, 1958; DSc of Tech., Swiss Fedn. Inst. Tech., Zurich, 1965. Sr. engr. Aircraft Armaments, Inc., Cockeysville, Md., 1958-59; rsch. engr. Sulzer Bros., Ltd., Winterthur, Switzerland, 1960-62; project engr. No. Rsch. and Engring. Corp., Cambridge, Mass., 1965-67; rsch. leader Air Force Aerospace Rsch. Lab., Dayton, Ohio, 1967-75, Air Force Aero Propulsion Lab., Dayton, 1975-91; dir. NATO Adv. Group for Aerospace R & D, Paris, 1991-94; engring. cons. Hillsborough, N.C., 1994-95, Hot Springs Village, Ark., 1995—2003, Henderson, Nev., 2003—. Mem. tech. adv. com., von Karman Inst. for Fluid Dynamics, Rhode-St-Genese, Belgium, 1988-94, bd. dirs.; lectr. in field. Contbr. articles to profl. jours. 1st lt., USAF, 1962-65. Recipient Cliff Garrett Turbo Machinery award Soc. Automotive Engrs., 1986; named Fed. Profl. Employee of Yr. Dayton C. of C., 1975; fellow Air Force Wright Aeronautical Labs., 1987; named Hon. Prof., Inst. Engring. Thermophysics, Chinese Acad. Scis. and Beijing U. Aeronautics and Astronautics, 1994. Fellow AIAA (assoc. editor 1980-82, Air Breathing Propulsion award 1979), ASME (chmn. turbomachinery com. gas turbine divsn. 1973-75, mem. exec. com. 1977-82, chmn. 1980-81, program chmn. internat. gas turbine conf. 1976, Beijing internat. gas turbine symposium 1985, mem. nat. nominating com. 1985-87, mem. TOPC bd. on rsch. 1985-88, mem.-at-large energy conversion group 1986-88, mem. bd. comm. 1989-91, editor Jour. Engring. for Gas Turbines and Power 1983-88, chmn. bd. editors 1989-91, founder, editor Jour. Turbomachinery 1986-88, mem. internat. adv. com. 1995-96, R. Tom Sawyer award 1993). Achievements include introduction of wide-chord integrally-bladed fan, introduction of swept blading into mil. aircraft turbine engines; 5 patents in field. Home and Office: 363 Marlin Cove Rd Henderson NV 89012-4829 Office Phone: 702-837-1344. E-mail: wennco1@cox.net.

WENRICH, JOHN WILLIAM, college president; b. York, Pa., June 8, 1937; s. Ralph Chester and Helen Louise (McCollam) W.; m. Linda Larsen, June 23, 1961 (dec. Sept. 1966); 1 child, Thomas Allen; m. Martha Gail Lofberg, Sept. 1, 1967; 1 child, Margaret Ann AB, Princeton U., 1959; MA, U. Mich., 1961, PhD, 1968. Fgn. service officer Dept. State, Washington, 1962-65; rep. Internat. Devel. Found., N.Y.C., 1965-66; project dir. U. Mich., Ann Arbor, 1966-69; asst. to pres. Coll. San Mateo, Calif., 1969-71; v.p. Ferris State U., Big Rapids, Mich., 1971-75, pres., 1984-88, Canada Coll., Redwood City, Calif., 1975-79, Santa Ana Coll., Calif., 1979-84; chancellor San Diego C.C. Dist., 1988-90, Dallas (Tex.) C.C., 1990—2003, chancellor emeritus, 2003—. Co-author: Leadership in Administration of Technical and Vocational Education, 1974, Administration of Vocational Education. Recipient Meritorious Service medal Dept. State, 1966; Hinsdale scholar Sch. Edn. U. Mich., 1968 Avocations: bridge; tennis; travel. Home: 3504 Springbrook St Dallas TX 75205-4337 Office: 4343 North Hwy 67 Mesquite TX 75150-2095 Office Phone: 972-860-7494. E-mail: bwenrich@dcccd.edu.

WENSINGER, ARTHUR STEVENS, language and literature educator, writer, translator; b. Grosse Pointe, Mich., Mar. 9, 1926; s. Carl Franklin and Suzanne (Stevens) W. Grad., Phillips Acad. Andover, 1944; BA, Dartmouth Coll., 1948; MA, U. Mich., 1951, PhD, 1958; postgrad., U. Munich, 1948, postgrad., 1950—51, U. Innsbruck, 1953—54. Instr., asst. prof., assoc. prof. Wesleyan U., Middletown, Conn., 1955-68, prof. German and humanities, 1968-93, Marcus Taft prof. German and humanities, 1977-93, prof. emeritus, 1994—, chmn. dept. German lang. and lit., 1971-93, also sr. tutor Coll. Letters; pres. Friends of Davison Art Ctr.; co-editor Higganum Hill Books, 2003—. Mem. selection com. German Acad. Exch. Svc., 1980-92. Author: Hogarth on High Life, 1970, Plays by Arthur Schnitzler, 1982-1983, 1995; translator, editor (with W. Gropius): The Theater of the Bauhaus, 1961, rev. edit., 1996, translator, editor: The Letters and Journals of Paula Modersohn-Becker, 1983, 2d edit., 1990, Querelle: The Film Book, 1983, Franz Kafka: Pictures of a Life, 1984; translator: Marlene Dietrich: Portraits, 1984, Shabbat (Peter Stefan Jungk), 1985, Hanna Schygulla and R.W. Fassbinder, 1986, Kaethe Kollwitz: The Work in Color, 1988, Niklas Frank, In the Shadow of the Reich, 1991, (plays) Arthur Schnitzler; co-translator: Kafka: The Sons, 1989, Günter Grass, Two States-One Nation?, 1990; editor: Stone Island (Peter S. Boynton), 1973; co-editor: Hesse's Siddhartha, 1962; continuing editor: Correspondence of Norman Douglas, 1868-1952, exhbn. and symposium catalog articles on: Norman Douglas, continuing translator: plays of Schnitzler, contbr.: Columbia U. Database CD-ROM for quotations, aphorisms, 1995—, contbr. (DVD): Munich 1948, 2004; contbr. articles to profl. jours. Wesleyan Ctr. for Humanities fellow, 1974, Reynolds fellow, 1950-51, Fulbright fellow, 1954-55, Danforth fellow, 1959, Ford Found. fellow, 1970-71; Inter Nations grantee, 1978, 82, NEH rsch. grantee, 1993. Mem. MLA, Am. Assn. Tchrs. German, Heinrich von Kleist Gesellschaft, Internat. Brecht Soc., Kafka Soc. Am., Auden Soc., Soc. Preservation New Eng. Antiquities, Conn. Acad. Arts and Scis., Yale Libr. Assocs., Haddam, Conn. Land Trust, Phi Beta Kappa, Phi Kappa Phi, Delta Tau Delta. Home: Candlewood Farm 95 Jacoby Rd Higganum CT 06441-4225 Office: Wesleyan U Fisk Hall Middletown CT 06459-6082 Office Phone: 860-685-3357. Business E-Mail: awensinger@wesleyan.edu.

WENSITS, DAVID L. aerospace executive; b. Sept. 19, 1947; AAS in Aviation Maintenance, Purdue U., 1968, BS in Indsl. Supervision, 1970. Supportability mgr. Rolls-Royce Corp., Indpls., 1970—. With U.S. Army, 1971-73. Recipient Aerospace Maintenance award AIAA, 1996. Office: Rolls-Royce Corp, SPEED Code S27C PO Box 420 Indianapolis IN 46206-0420 Office Phone: 317-230-4949. E-mail: david.l.wensits@rolls-royce.com., davewensits@comcast.net.

WENSKI, THOMAS GERARD, bishop; b. West Palm Beach, Fla., Oct. 18, 1950; s. Chester Stephen and Louise Mary (Zawacki) W. AA, St. John Vianney Sem., Miami, Fla., 1970; BA, St. Vincent De Paul Sem., Boynton Beach, Fla., 1972, MDiv, 1975; MA, Fordham U. Ordained priest Roman Cath. Ch., 1976. Assoc. pastor Corpus Christi Cath. Ch., Miami, 1976-79; assoc. dir. Haitian Cath. Ctr., Miami, 1979-84, dir., 1984-98; pastor Notre Dame d'Haiti Roman Cath. Ch., Miami, 1984-98, aux. bishop, 1997—. Episcopal vicar to cultural groups, Miami, 1990—; mem. Archdioces of Miami Presbyterial Coun., 1988—; host Cath. Focus, Religious TV, Miami, 1989-91. Editor Lavwa Katolik - Creole Lang., 1981—. Mem. Dade County Cmty. Rels. Bd., Miami, 1989—; chmn. Greater Miami United Krome Liaison Com., 1982. Recipient St. Vincent de Paul award, St. Vincent Sem., 1987. Home and Office: PO Box 1800 Orlando FL 32802

WENSTRUP, H. DANIEL, chemical company executive; b. Cin., Sept. 27, 1934; s. Carl D. and Lucille (Cahill) W.; m. Eileen O'Brien, Nov. 24, 1956; children: Gary, Julie, Patrick, Kevin, Katy, Greg. BSBA, Xavier U., 1956. Sales rep. Chemcentral Corp., Cin., 1958-66, sales mgr. Detroit, 1966-72, gen. mgr., 1972-75, v.p. regional mgr., 1975-82, v.p. dir. mktg. Chgo., 1982-86, pres., 1986—, pres., CEO, 1988-99, bd. dirs., chmn. of bd., 1998; ret., 1999. Bd. dirs. Prove Quim S.A. de C.V. Mem., supporter Mus. Sci. Industry, Chgo., 1991—, Ravinia Chgo. Symphony, 1991—, adv. com. Gov. Edgar. 1st lt. U.S. Army, 1956-58. Mem. Chem. Mfrs. Assn. (dir. 1990-92), Chem. Industry Coun. Ill. (dir. 1989-93, pres., chmn.), Nat. Paint & Coatings Assn., Nat. Petroleum Refiners Assn., Ill. Mfrs. Assn., Ill. C. of C., Medinah Country Club, Oak Brook Tennis Club, Am. Cancer Soc., NACD Edn. Found. (trustee). Republican. Roman Catholic. Avocations: golf, tennis, jogging, reading, theater.

WENTE, VAN ARTHUR, retired aerospace scientist; b. Johnston City, Ill., Jan. 11, 1925; s. Edward H. and Pauline Lucille (Barham) W.; m. Jane Van Derveer Updike, Sept. 22, 1962; children: Gretchen Jane, Robert Edward. BSChemE, Washington U., St. Louis, 1945; grad., Nat. Def. U., 1977. Chem. engr. Firestone Tire & Rubber Co., Pottstown, Pa., 1945-50, USN Research Lab., Washington, 1950-56; info. officer U.S. Atomic Energy Agy., Germantown, Md., 1956-59, sci. advisor, 1959-61; documentation head NASA, Washington, 1961-64, systems head, 1965-80, sci. and tech. info. dir., 1981-89, sr. exec. svc., 1983-89. Mem. adv. group on aerospace R & D info. NATO, 1983-89. Contbr. articles to profl. jours., chpts. to books. Chairperson ch. coun. Concord-St. Andrews United Meth. Ch., 2000-02; treas. Montgomery Interclub Sr. Tennis League, 1997—. Recipient Presdl. award Mgmt. Improvement, 1970. Fellow Nat. Fedn. Abstracting and Info. Svcs. (hon., bd. dirs. 1986-88); mem. AIChE, Am. Soc. for Info. Scis., Chem. Engrs. Washington (treas. 1957-58, sec. 1958-59), Kenwood Golf and Country Club (bd. govs. 1995-2000, chair tennis com. 1998-00), Mil. Officers Club, Omicron Delta Kappa, Sigma Xi. Avocations: tennis, music, photography. Home and Office: 5919 Gloster Rd Bethesda MD 20816-1144 E-mail: van.wente@att.net.

WENTWORTH, DIANA VON WELANETZ, author; b. L.A., Mar. 4, 1941; d. Eugene and Marguerite (Rufi) Webb; m. Frederic Paul von Welanetz, Nov. 2, 1963 (dec. Mar. 19, 1989); 1 child, Lexi Welanetz Bursin; m. Theodore S. Wentworth, Dec. 9, 1989; stepchildren: ChristinaWentworth Coyne, Kathryn Allison Wentworth Purdy. Student, UCLA, 1958-60. Ptnr. von Welanetz Cooking Workshop, L.A., 1968-85; host TV series New Way Gourmet, 1983-86; founder Inside Edge Found. Edn., Calif., 1985-93. Spkr. in field. Author: The Pleasure of Your Company, 1976 (Cookbook of Yr.), With Love from Your Kitchen, 1976, The Art of Buffet Entertaining, 1978, The Von Welanetz Guide to Ethnic Ingredients, 1983, L.A. Cuisine, 1985, Celebrations, 1985, Chicken Soup for the Soul Cookbook, 1995, Send Me Someone, 2001, Chicken Soup to Inspire The Body and Soul, 2003. Treas. Louise L. Hay Found., Carson, Calif., 1988—; advisor Women of Vision, Calif., 1995—. Mem. Internat. Food, Wine & Travel Writers Assn., Angels of Arts/Orange County Performing Arts Ctr., Ctr. Club. Avocations: painting, fine art, travel writing, design. Office: 4631 Teller Ave Ste 100 Newport Beach CA 92660-8105 E-mail: diana@sendmesomeone.com.

WENTWORTH, EARL JEFFREY, lawyer, realtor, state legislator; b. San Antonio, Nov. 20, 1940; s. Earl and Margaret Wentworth; m. Karla Whitsitt; children: Jason, Matthew. BA, Tex. A&M U., 1962; JD, Tex. Tech. U., 1972. Bar: Tex. 1971, DC. 1972. Staff mem. U.S. Congressman Bob Price; pvt. practice law San Antonio; mem. Tex. Ho. of Reps., 1988-92, Tex. Senate, 1993—. County commr. Bexar County, 1977-82; bd. regents Tex. State U. Sys., 1987-88. Spl. agt. U.S. Army Counterintelligence Corps, 1962—65. Republican. Office: PO Box 12068 Austin TX 78711-2068 also: 1250 NE Loop 410 Ste 720 San Antonio TX 78209-1525 Office Phone: 210-826-7800.

WENTWORTH, JACK ROBERTS, business educator, consultant; b. Elgin, Ill., June 11, 1928; s. William Franklin and Elizabeth (Roberts) W.; m. Rosemary Ann Pawlak, May 30, 1956; children: William, Barbara Student, Carleton Coll., 1946-48; BS, Ind. U., 1950, MBA, 1954, DBA, 1959. Coord. displays Cadillac divsn., Gen. Motors Corp., Detroit, 1954-56; asst. prof. bus., assoc. dir. research Sch. of Bus. Ind. U., Bloomington, 1957-60, assoc. prof., dir. rsch., 1960-70, prof., 1970-93, chmn. MBA program, 1970-76, chmn. dept., faculty rep. NCAA, 1978-85, dean Sch. of Bus., 1984-93, Arthur M. Weimer prof., 1993-97, Arthur M. Weimer prof. emeritus, 1997—. Mktg. cons., Bloomington, 1960—; bd. dirs. Kimball Internat., Jasper, Ind. Editor: (monograph) Marketing Horizons, 1965; exec. editor Bus. Horizons, 1960-70 Served to 1st lt. USAF, 1950-53 Recipient Teaching award MBA Assn., 1973, 78, 81, 84, 85, Svc. award Assn. for Bus. and Econ. Rsch., 1983; Disting. Alumni Svc. award Ind. U., 1999. Mem. Am. Mktg. Assn. (v.p. 1971-73), Grad. Mgmt. Admissions Coun. (chmn. bd. trustees 1977-78), Univ. Club, Masons, Beta Gamma Sigma (pres. Alpha of Ind. chpt. 1971-72, bd. govs. 1986-98, nat. pres. 1994-96). Republican. Methodist. Avocations: athletic events; travel; bicycling; model railroading; magic. Office: Indiana Univ Sch Bus Bloomington IN 47405

WENTWORTH, LYNN A. telecommunications industry executive; BSBA, Babson Coll.; MS in Taxation, Bentley Coll.; MBA Ga. State U. Various positions with numerous depts. including handling tax, strategic planning, investor rels. and finl. planning Bellsouth Corp., 1985—2003, v.p., treas., 2003—. Tutor C.W. Hill Elem. Sch., Atlanta. Mem.: AICPA, Ga. Soc. CPA's. Office: Bellsouth Corp 1155 Peachtree St NE Atlanta GA 30301-3610

WENTWORTH, MURRAY JACKSON, artist, educator; b. Boston, Jan. 18, 1927; s. Harold Squires and Mary Louise (Murray) W.; m. Elaine Magnuson, June 16, 1953; 1 child, Janet Louise. Diploma, Art Inst. Boston, 1950. Advt. artist Agy. Art Svcs., Boston, 1950-58; instr. Art Inst. Boston, 1958-78; artist, instr. Norwell, Mass., 1968—. Group shows, Allied Artists Am., 1980, 82 (Silver medal 1980), Allied Art Am., 1982 (Obrig prize 1982), Am. Watercolor Soc., 1980 (Dolphin fellow 1980), Rocky Mount Nat. Exhibition, 1982 (Grumbacher award 1982). Cpl. U.S. Army, 1945-47. Recipient Hudson Valley Art Assn. award, 1991, Whitney Meml. award, 1996, Guild Boston Artists award, 1992, Watercolor award Acad. Artists' Assn., 1997, Daler Rowney award, 1998, Hudson Valley Art Assn. Watercolor award, 1998. Mem. NAD (Pike Meml. award 1986, award of merit 1997), Allied Artists Am. (Mina Mora Meml. award for watercolor 1997), Am. Watercolor Soc., New Eng. Watercolor Soc. (Grumbacher gold medal 1989). Home: 116 Ridge Drive Oneonta NY 13820 Office Phone: 607-432-6322.

WENTWORTH, THEODORE SUMNER, lawyer; b. Bklyn., July 18, 1938; s. Theodore Sumner and Alice Ruth (Wortmann) W.; m. Sharon Linelle Arkush, 1965 (dec. 1987); children: Christina Linn, Kathryn Allison; m. Diana Webb von Welanetz, 1989; 1 stepchild, Lexi von Welanetz. AA, Am. River Coll., 1958; JD, U. Calif., Hastings, 1962. Bar: Calif. 1963, U.S. Dist. Ct. (no. and ctrl. dists.) Calif., U.S. Ct. Appeals (9th cir.), U.S. Supreme Ct.; cert. trial specialist; diplomate Nat. Bd. Trial Advocacy. Assoc. Adams, Hunt & Martin, Santa Ana, Calif., 1963-66; ptnr. Hunt, Liljestrom & Wentworth, Santa Ana, 1967-77; pres. Solabs Corp.; chmn. bd., exec. v.p. Plant Warehouse, Inc., Hawaii, 1974-82; ptnr. Law Offices of Wentworth, Paoli & Purdy, Newport Beach & Temecula, Calif.; judge pro tem Superior Ct. Attys. Panel Harbor Mcpl. Ct.; owner, CEO Home Guardens, Inc., Murrietta, Calif., 2000—. Owner Eagles Ridge Ranch, Temecula, 1977-2003. Author: Build a Better Spouse Trap, 2002. Pres., bd. dirs. Santa Ana-Tustin Cmty. Chest, 1972; v.p., trustee South Orange County United Way, 1973-75; pres. Orange County Fedn. Funds, 1972-73; bd. dirs. Orange County Mental Health Assn. Mem. ABA, Am. Bd. Trial Advs. (assoc.), State Bar Calif., Orange County Bar Assn. (dir. 1972-76), Calif. Trial Lawyers Assn. (bd. govs. 1968-70), Orange County Trial Lawyers Assn. (pres. 1967-68), Bahia Corinthian Yacht Club, Pacific Club, Newport. Achievements include research in vaidika principles, natural law, quantum physics and mechanics. Office: 4631 Teller Ave Ste 100 Newport Beach CA 92660-8105 also: 41530 Enterprise Cir S Temecula CA 92590-4816 Office Phone: 949-752-7711. E-mail: oclawfirm@aol.com., ted@homegardensinc.com.

WENTZ, CHARLES ALVIN, JR., environmentalist, chemical engineer; b. Edwardsville, Ill., Oct. 12, 1935; s. Charles Alvin and Frances Margaret (Bohm) W.; m. Sandra Niederecker, Dec. 11, 1961 (div. Jan. 1982); children: Sharon, Christopher, Suzanne, Sheila; m. Joan Domigan, Aug., 1983. BSChemE, U. Mo., Rolla, 1957, MSChemE, 1959; PhDChemE, Northwestern U., 1961; MBA, So. Ill. U., 1985; cert. in Culinary Arts, S.W. Ill. Coll., 2003. Registered profl. engr. Various exec. positions Phillips Petroleum Co., Bartlesville, Okla., 1961-82; pres. New Pk. Waste Treatment, Inc., New Orleans, 1982-83, ENSCO, Inc., El Dorado, Ark., 1983-84; pres., CEO Wentz Healthcare, Inc., Lebanon, Ill., 1984—; CEO Internat. Sci. Mgmt., Inc., Edwardsville, Ill., 1985—; mgr., waste and safety Argonne Nat. Lab., Ill., 1988-91; assoc. dean Chulalongkorn U., Bangkok, 1994; ptnr. Bohm Heirs Partnership, 2000—. Vis. prof. So. Ill. U., Edwardsville, 1984-86 Author: Hazardous Waste Management, 1989, 2d edit., 1995, (with others) Occupl. and Environ. Safety, 1990, Encyclopedia of Environ. Control Technology, vol. 5, 1992, Safety, Health and Environ. Protection, 1998; editor spl. issues Environ. Progress, 1988, 89, Chef Al's Gourmet Treasures, 2004; patentee in field; contbr. articles to profl. jour. Mem. adv. bd. Ill. Hazardous Waste Rsch. and Info. Ctr., 1989-91. Mem.: ACS, AIChE, Acad. Chem. Engr. U. Mo. Rolla Alumni Assn., Greater Edwardsville Area Cmty. Found. (treas.), Lincoln Sch. Alumni Found., Alpha Kappa Ednl. Found. (chair, pres.), Sigma Xi. Avocations: hunting, fishing, gardening, cooking. Office: Internat Sci Mgmt Inc 5953 Old Poag Rd Edwardsville IL 62025-7341 Office Phone: 618-692-1231. Personal E-mail: jdomigan@aol.com.

WENTZ, JEFFREY LEE, information systems executive; b. Philippi, W.Va., Nov. 29, 1956; s. William Henry and Edith Marie (McBee) W.; m. Phuong Thi Thanh, Nov. 17, 2001. AS in Data Processing, BS in Acctg., Fairmont (W.Va.) State Coll., 1978. Programmer/analyst U.S. Dept. Energy, Morgantown, W.Va., 1978-79; analyst Middle South Svcs., New Orleans, 1979-81; sr. analyst Bank of Am., San Francisco, 1981-83; pres., info. sys. cons. Wentz Cons. Inc., San Francisco, 1983-2000; dir. tech. solutions Charles Schwab & Co., San Francisco, 2000—.

WENTZ, SIDNEY FREDERICK, insurance company executive, foundation executive; b. Dallas, Mar. 27, 1932; s. Howard Beck and Emmy Lou (Cawthon) W.; m. Barbara Strait, Sept. 9, 1961; children: Eric, Jennifer, Robin. AB, Princeton U., 1954; LLB, Harvard U., 1960. Bar: N.Y. 1961. Atty. White & Case, N.Y.C., 1960-65, Western Electric Co., 1965-66, AT&T Corp., 1966-67; with Crum & Forster Inc., Morristown, N.J., 1967—, v.p., gen. counsel, 1967-71, sr. v.p., gen. counsel, 1971-72, exec. v.p., 1972, pres., 1972-87, chmn. bd., 1987-88, chmn. exec. com., 1988-90, also bd. dirs.; chmn. bd. Robert Wood Johnson Found., Princeton, N.J., 1989-99. Trustee Morristown Meml. Hosp., 1974-96, Drew U., 1991—. Served to lt. (j.g.) USNR, 1954-57. Mem. Morris County Golf Club, Sakonnet (R.I.) Golf Club, Baltusrol Golf Club, Jupiter Hills (Fla.) Golf Club, Loblolly Pines (Fla.) Golf Club, Carnegie Abby Golf Club (R.I.).

WENTZ, WENDELL FRANKLIN, columnist, writer; b. Eufaula, Ala., Mar. 24, 1939; s. Hermann Wendell and Johnnie Mae (Jones) W., children,Hermann Wendell Wentz, II AB, Mercer U., Macon, Ga., 1961. Pastor Liberty Bapt. Ch., Georgetown, Ga., 1956-57, Mitchell (Ga.) Bapt. Ch., 1957-70, Benton (Ala.) Bapt. Ch., 1970-77, First Bapt. Ch., Lowry City, Mo., 1977-79, Lakeland Bapt. Ch., Clinton, Mo., 1979-80; with material svcs. Kansas City Power & Light Co., Clinton, 1979—; columnist Clinton Daily Dem., 1989—. Freelance writer. Avocations: photography, gardening, reading. Office: Kansas City Power & Light 400 SW Highway P Clinton MO 64735-9093 Home: PO Box 451 Clinton MO 64735-0451

WENTZ, WILLIAM HENRY, JR., aerospace engineer, educator; b. Wichita, Kans., Dec. 18, 1933; BS in Mech. Engring. cum laude, Wichita State U., 1955, MS in Aeronautical Engring., 1961; PhD in Engring. Mechanics, U. Kans., 1969. Lic. profl. engr., Kans. Liaison engr. Beech Aircraft, 1952-53; propulsion engr. Boeing Co., Wichita, Kans., 1955; instr. mech. engring. Wichita State U., 1957-58; aerodynamicist Boeing Co., Wichita, 1958-63; from asst. prof. to assoc. prof. aeronautical engring. Wichita State U., 1963-75, prof. aeronautical engring., 1975-83, Gates-Learjet prof. aeronautical engring., 1983-86, disting. prof. aerospace engring., 1986-98, dir. Ctr. Basic and Applied Rsch. Inst. Aviation Rsch., 1986-89, exec. dir. Nat. Inst. Aviation Rsch., 1988-97; sr. fellow Nat. Inst. Aviation Rsch., 1997-98; disting. prof. emeritus aerospace engring., exec. dir. emer. Nat. Inst. Aviation Rsch., 1999; ret. Dir. rsch. projects Boeing Co., 1960, 61, NASA, 1964-66, 66-68, 70-71, 71-83, 86-87, 86-88, 82-87, Dept. of Def., 1986-88, Kans. Tech. Enterprise Corp., 1988-96, FAA, 1986-96. Contbr. articles to profl. jours. With USAF, 1955-57. Recipient Disting. Engr. Svc. award Wichita State U., 1999, Kans. Aviation Honors award Gov. Bill Graves, 1999; Sci. Faculty fellow NSF, 1967-68. Fellow AIAA (assoc., past chmn. Wichita sect., Outstanding advisor student chpt. 1964, 65, 70, Gen. Aviation award 1981, Engr. of Yr. award Wichita sect. 1992, Engr. of Yr. award Region V 1991-92; mem. Soc. Automotive Engrs. (Ralph R. Teeter award 1973), Sigma Gamma Tau, Tau Beta Pi.

WENTZEL, PAUL H., JR., state agency administrator; b. 1949; m. Kathy Wentzel; 1 child, Sally. BA in polit. sci., MA in polit. sci., East Stroudsburg U. Rsch. analyst House Bus. and Commerce Com.; exec. asst. Pa. Dept. Banking, 1981—2002, acting sec., 2002—. Office: 333 Market St 16th fl Harrisburg PA 17101-2290

WENZEL, BOB, federal agency administrator; b. Oak Park, Ill., Dec. 23, 1941; Dep. commr. ops. Dept. of the Treasury, 1998—. Office: Dept of Treasury 1111 Constitution Ave NW Washington DC 20224-0001

WENZEL, LOREN ALVIN, accounting educator; b. Dec. 12, 1945; s. Alvin Karl Gustav and Lois LaVonne (Kuechenmeister) W.; children: Lisa Anne (Wenzel) Szumilas, Karl Louis, Sara Kirsten Wenzel; m. Nylah Onalee. DBA, U. Memphis, 1990. Asst. prof. acctg. Wichita (Kans.) State U., 1987-88; prof. acctg. Mankato (Minn.) State U., 1988-98, U. Md. European Divsn., Heidelberg, Germany, 1996-97, Buena Vista U., Storm Lake, Iowa, 1998-99, Austin Peay State U., Clarksville, Tenn., 1999-2000, Marshall U., Huntington, W.Va., 2000—, prof., head divsn. accountancy and legal environment, 2000—, Elizabeth McDowell Lewis endowed chair Lewis Coll. Bus., 2000—. Contbr. articles to profl. publs. Named W.Va. Acctg. Educator of Yr., W.Va. Soc. CPAs, 2004. Office: Marshall U Lewis Coll Bus Div Acctancy/Legal Environ One John Marshall Dr Huntington WV 25545 Office Phone: 304-696-2660. Business E-Mail: wenzel@marshall.edu.

WENZEL, RICHARD PUTNAM, internist; b. Phila., Jan. 8, 1940; m. Jo Gail Wenzel; children: Amy, Richard. BS, Haverford (Pa.) Coll., 1961; MD, Jefferson Med. Coll., 1965; MSc, London U., 1986. Diplomate Am. Bd. Internal Medicine, Am. Bd. Infectious Diseases. Intern Phila. Gen. Hosp., 1965-66; resident in internal medicine U. Md. Hosp., Balt., 1966-68, fellowship infectious diseases, 1968-69, chief resident in internal medicine, 1969-70; asst. in medicine U. Md. Med. Sch., Balt., 1969-70; hosp. epidemiologist U. Va. Med. Ctr., Charlottesville, 1972-86; asst. prof. internal medicine U. Va. Sch. of Medicine, Charlottesville, 1972-76, assoc. prof., 1976-81, prof. internal medcine, 1981-86; dir. divsn. clin. epidemiology U. Iowa Coll. Medicine, Iowa City, 1986-89, prof. medicine, preventive medicine, 1986-95, dir. hosp. epidemiology and statewide epidemiology svcs., 1986-95, dir. divsn. gen. medicine, clin. epidemiology and health svcs. rsch., 1989-95; prof., chair dept. internal medicine Med. Coll. Va./Va. Commonwealth U., Richmond, 1995; pres. MCV Physicians (practice plan), 2002—. Founding chair dept. epidemiology MS degree granting program Grad. Sch. Arts and Scis., U. Va., Charlottesville, 1981-86; pres. ho. staff assn. of interns, residents and fellows U. Md. Hosp., 1968-69; cons. U.S. HO. Reps. Ethics Adv. Bd. Ethics Regarding Freedom of Info. and Infection Surveillance Data, Washington, 1979-80, NIH small bus. innovation rsch, 1988; infection control cons. U. Calif. Systemwide Task Force on AIDS, 1987; spl. cons. NIH Study Sect. Epidemiology and Disease Control (#2), 1987-92. Author: Assessing Quality Care: Perspective for Clinicians, 1992, Prevention and Control of Nosocomial Infections, 1987, 91, 97, 2003, Handbook on Hospital Acquired Infections, 1981; founding editor Infection Control and Hospital Epidemiology, 1979—, Clinical Performance and Quality Health Care, 1993—; editorial bd. Jour. of Hosp. Infection, London, 1984—, Enfermedades Infecciosas y Microbiologia Clinica, 1990—, New England Jour. of Medicine, 1992—, others; contbr. numerous articles to profl. jours. Recipient Sir Henry S. Wellcome medal prize, 1971, Major Louis Livingston Seaman prize, 1974, Burlington No. Found. Faculty Achievement award, 1990; Sr. Internat. fellowship, NIH, 1985-86. Fellow ACP, Infectious Diesease Soc. of Am. (coun. mem. 1988-91), Am. Coll. Epidemiology, Am. Acad. of Microbiology; sr. internat. fellow NIH, 1985-86; mem. Am. Assn. of Physicians, Am. Clin. and Climatological Assn., Am. Epidemiological Soc., So. Soc. for Clin. Investigation, Am. Fedn. for Clin. Rsch., Am. Soc. for Microbiology, Assn. for Practitioners in Infection Control, Surg. Infection Soc., Soc. for Epidemiologic Rsch., Hosp. Infections Soc. (Europe), Assn. Am. Physicians, Am. Soc. Clin. Investigation. Address: U Va Commonwealth Dept Internal Med PO Box 980663 Richmond VA 23298-0663 E-mail: rwenzel@hsc.vcu.edu.

WEPNER, SHELLEY BETH, education educator, software developer; b. Phila., Pa., Oct. 23, 1951; d. Bernard and Carole Frances (Abramson) Markovitz; m. Roy Henry Wepner, Aug. 3, 1974; children: Leslie Marcia and Meredith Susan (twins). BS magna cum laude, U. Pitts., 1972; MS, U. Pa., 1973, EdD, 1980. Cert. reading specialist, prin., supr., elem. tchr., N.J. Reading tchr. West Deptford Sch. Dist., NJ, 1973-74; reading resource tchr. Middletown Sch. Dist., 1974-75, Title I tchr., 1975-76; reading specialist Marlboro Sch. Dist., 1976-78, curriculum cons., 1978-80, supr. curriculum and instrn., 1980-82; prof. edn. William Paterson U., Wayne, 1989, chair dept. curriculum and instrn., 1991-94, asst. to dean, 1994-97; dir. ctr. edn., assoc. dean, prof. edn. Widener U., Chester, Pa., 1997—2004; dean sch. of edn. Manhattanville Coll., Purchase, NY, 2004—. Cons. Tchr. Support Software, Gainesville, Fla., 1988-99, East Brunswick (N.J.) Sch., 1989. Co-author: Using Computers in the Teaching of Reading, 1987, Moving Forward with Literature: Basals, Books, and Beyond, 1993; co-editor: Linking Literacy and Technology, 2000, The Administration and Supervision of Reading Programs, 1989, 2d edit., 1995, 3rd edit., 2002, Process Reading and Writing: A Literature Based Approach, 1992; author software Read-A-Logo, 1987 (Methods and Media award 1989), Reading Realities, 1989 (Top Five award, Methods and Media award), updated, 2001, Reading Realities Elem. Series, 1990 (Top 36 award, Methods and Media award), updated, 2001; co-author 45 lit. lesson booklets; contbr. over 100 articles to profl. jours. Chmn. gifted and talented Coles Sch. PTA, Scotch Plains, N.J., 1989-90. Mem. Am. Assn. Tchr. Educators (chair tech. and tchr. edn. com. 2001-2003), Pa. Assn. Colls. Tchr. Edn., Coll. Reading Assn., Am. Ednl. Rsch. Assn., Internat. Reading Assn., N.J. Reading Assn. (bd. dirs. 1982-85), Phi Delta Kappa, Phi Kappa Phi. Avocations: travel, walking, aerobics, reading, theater. Home: 20 Glenwood Ct Tenafly NJ 07670 Office: Manhattanville Coll Sch Edn 2900 Purchase St Purchase NY 10577

WEPRIN, BRADLEY, neurosurgeon; b. Chgo. m. Rebecca Weprin; 2 children. BA in Biology, Washington U., St. Louis, 1988; MD with honors, U. Tex. Southwestern Med. Sch., 1992. Diplomate Am. Bd. Neurol. Surgery, Nat. Bd. Med. Examiners, lic. physician Minn., Ala., Tex. Intern in gen. surgery U. Minn. Hosps. and Clinics, Mpls., 1992, resident in neurol. surgery, 1992—97; fellow in pediat. neurosurgery U. Ala. Birmingham-Children's Hosp. of Ala., 1998—99; asst. prof. neurol. surgery U. Tex. Southwestern Med. Sch., Dallas, 1999—. Attending neurosurgeon Children's Med. Ctr. Dallas, Med. City Dallas Hosp., Tex. Scottish Rite Hosp. for Children; presenter in field. Mem.: AMA, Joint Sect. Pediat. Neurosurgery, Alpha Omega Alpha. Office: Children's Med Ctr-Neurosurgery 1935 Motor St Dallas TX 75235

WERB, ZENA, cell biologist, educator; BSc in Biochemistry, U. Toronto, 1966; PhD in Cell Biology, Rockefeller U., 1971. Postdoctoral fellow in protein chemistry Strangeways Rsch. Lab., Cambridge, Eng., 1971-73, rsch. scientist, 1973-75; vis. asst. prof. medicine Dartmouth Med. Sch., Hanover, N.H., 1975-76; asst. prof. radiobiology and radiology U. Calif., San Francisco, 1976-80, asst. prof. anatomy, 1979-80, assoc. prof. anatomy and radiology, 1980-83, prof. anatomy, 1983—. Vis. prof. Sir William Dunn Sch. Pathology, U. Oxford, Eng., 1985-86. Mem. editl. bd. Jour. Cell Biology, 1982-85, Am. Jour. Physiology, 1982-87, Neoplasia, 1999—, Jour. Cell Scis., 1999—; adv. editor Jour. Exptl. medicine, 1985—; bd. reviewing editors Sci., 1990—; assoc. editor Matrix Biology, 1999—; contbr. numerous articles to profl. jours. Recipient Excellence in Sci. award Am. Soc. Exptl. Biology, Women's Excellence in Scis. award Fdn. Am. Socs. Exptl. Biology, 1996; U. Toronto scholar, 1963-66; John Simon Gugenheim Found. fellow, 1985-86, other grants and awards. Mem. AAAS, ASCB, ASIP, ASBMB, ISMB. Office: U Calif Dept Anatomy HSW 1320 513 Parnassus Ave San Francisco CA 94143-0001

WERBER, STEPHEN JAY, lawyer, educator; b. N.Y.C., Apr. 20, 1940; s. Murray H. and Teddie Werber; m. Mary Jo Weinberg (dec. June 1965); m. Joan C. Kirsh, May 30, 1968; children: David S., Lauren F. BA, Adelphi U., 1961; JD, Cornell U., 1964; LLM, NYU, 1970; MA in Judaic Studies, Siegal Coll. Sudaic Studies, 2003. Bar: N.Y. 1965, U.S. Dist. Ct (no. dist.) Ohio 1970, U.S. Supreme Ct. 1970, U.S. Dist. Ct. (so. dist.) Ohio 1980, U.S. Ct. Appeals (6th cir.) 1982. Atty. FCC, Washington, 1964-65; assoc. Sidney G. Hollander, N.Y.C., 1965-67, Herzfeld & Rubin, N.Y.C., 1967-70; asst. prof. law Cleve. State U., 1970-73, assoc. prof.law, 1973-76, prof. law, 1976—; of counsel Guren, Merritt, Feibel, Sogg & Cohen, 1979-84, Weston, Hurd, Fallon, Paisley & Howley, 1984-89, cons. spl. litigation, 1989—. Asst. dean Cleve. State U., 1973-74; sec., treas. Am. Inns of Ct. Harold H. Burton chpt., 1990-91, counsellor, 1991-92, pres., 1993-94; mem. Consultative Group for Restatement Torts: Products Liability. Contbr. numerous articles on product liability to profl jours. Former bd. dirs. NE Ohio Multiple Sclerosis Soc., Bur. Jewish Edn.; v.p. Temple Emanu-El, 1983-85; dir. continuing legal edn. programs Cleve.-Marshall Alumni Assn. Mem. ATLA, AAUP, ABA (litigation sect., com. on mfrs. liability), Fed. Bar Assn., Am. Arbitration Assn., N.Y. State Bar Assn., Ohio Bar Assn., Ohio Assn. Civil Trial Lawyers. Democrat. Avocations: bridge, golf. Home: 2560 Lafayette Dr Cleveland OH 44118-4608

WERBITT, WARREN, gastroenterologist, educator; b. Phila., Jan. 29, 1939; s. Saull Boris and Pearl (Weiner) W,; m. Drue Natalie Engman Werbitt, Aug. 30, 1964; children: Julie Michele, Jeffrey Brian. BS in Pharmacy, Temple U., 1960; D in Osteopathy, U. Osteo. Med. and Health Sci., Des Moines, 1966; MD, Drexel U., 1973. Diplomate Am. Osteo. Bd. Internal Medicine, also sub-splty. bd. Gastroenterology; diplomate Am. Bd. Internal Medicine, also sub splty. bd. Gastroenterology. Intern Doctor's Hosp., Columbus, Ohio, 1966-67, resident in internal medicine, 1967-68, Kennedy Meml. Hosps., Cherry Hill, N.J., 1968-69, Mercy Cath. Med. Ctr., Phila., 1969-70, Drexel U. Coll. Medicine, Phila., 1971—72, fellow in gastroenterology, 1970-71, 72-74, instr., 1973—, attending physician and cons. in gastroenterology, 1977-94; instr. Phila. Coll. Osteo. Medicine, Phila., 1973-75, chmn. divsn. gastroenterology, 1975-77; clin. assoc. prof. medicine U. Medicine and Dentistry, N.J., 1977—; attending physician and cons. in gastroenterology Vet. Adminstrn. Hosp., Phila., 1972-75; chmn. Div. Gastroenterology, Dept. Medicine Phila. Coll. Osteopathic Medicine, 1975-77; chmn. Dept. Medicine Kennedy Meml. Hosp. U. Med. Ctr., Cherry Hill, 1979-81, chmn. subsect. Gastroenterology, 1979-87. Contbg. editor The N.J. Jour. for Ostepathic Physicians and Surgeons, 1980—; mem. scientific adv. com. Phila. chpt. Nat. Found. Ileitis & Colitis, Inc., 1982—; contbr. articles to profl. jours. Recipient Profl. Svc. award Med. Soc. N.J., 1991. Fellow Am. Coll. Physicians, Am. Coll. Gastroenterology, Acad. Med. N.J.; mem. AMA, Am. Soc. Gastrointestinal Endoscopy, Am. Gastroenterology Assn., Am. Soc. Parenteral and Enteric Nutrition, Am. Inst. Ultrasound in Medicine, Am. Assn. Gynecologic Laparoscopists, Phila. Gastrointestinal Rsch. Forum, State Med. Soc. N.J., Camden County Med. Soc., N.J. Endoscopic Soc., Del. Valley Soc. for Gastrointestinal Endoscopy, South Jersey Gastroenterological Soc., Am. Osteopathic Assn., N.J. Soc. Osteopathic Physicians and Surgeons, Am. Coll. Osteopathic Internists, Camden County Osteopathic Assn., Am. Cancer Soc. (bd. dirs. N.J. chpt.), Crohn's and Colitis Found. Am. Inc. (Phila. and Del.), Pres.'s Circle Am. U., N.Y. Acad. Scis., John Sherman Myers Soc., Med. Club Phila., Lambda Omicron Gamma. Avocations: golf, running, music, reading, american history. Office: Profl Gastroenterology Assn 1939 Route 70 E Ste 250 Cherry Hill NJ 08003-4507 Office Phone: 856-429-4433. E-mail: progastro@comcast.net.

WERBOS, PAUL JOHN, neural net research director; b. Darby, Pa., Sept. 4, 1947; s. Walter Joseph and Margaret Mary (Donohue) W.; m. Ludmila Dolmatora, Dec. 7, 1998; children: Elizabeth, Alexander, Maia, Christopher. BA magna cum laude, Harvard U., 1967; MSc, London Sch. Econs., 1968; MA, Harvard U., 1969, PhD, 1974. Rsch. assoc. MIT, Cambridge, Mass., 1973-75; asst. prof. U. Md., College Park, 1975-78; math. statistician U.S. Census Bur., Suitland, Md., 1978-79; energy analyst U.S. Dept. Energy, Washington, 1979-88, 89; program dir. NSF, Washington, 1988, 89—. Author: The Roots of Backpropagation: From Ordered Derivatives to Neural Network & Political Forecasting, 1993; contbr. chpt. to Handbook of Intelligent Control, 1992. Regional dir., Washington rep. L-5 Soc. (merged with Nat. Space Soc.), Washington, 1980s. Mem. IEEE (sr.), Internat. Neural Network Soc. (pres. 1991-92, sec. 1990). Quaker-Universalist. Achievements include five patents on learning based control, nonlinear filtering, fuzzy logic; devised theory of intelligence; backwards-time of quantum theory (reviewed quant-ph 0008036). Home: 5304 1st Pl N Arlington VA 22203-1246 Office: NSF 4201 Wilson Blvd Rm 675 Arlington VA 22230-0001 E-mail: pwerbos@nsf.gov.

WERBOW, STANLEY NEWMAN, language educator; b. Phila., Apr. 19, 1922; s. Morris and Sadie (Newman) W.; m. Naomi Esther Ecker, June 1, 1952; children: Susan Linda, Emily Frances, Carol Martha. BA, George Washington U., 1946; postgrad., Middlebury Coll., 1946, 47, U. Mich., 1948; PhD, Johns Hopkins, 1953. Tchr. Ea. High Sch., Washington, 1946-47; research analyst specialist U.S. Dept. Def., Washington, 1952-53; mem. faculty U. Tex., Austin, 1953—, prof., 1965-69, 78-97, chmn. dept. Germanic langs., 1969-71, dean Coll. Humanities, 1971-78, acting dean Coll. Fine Arts, 1980-81, prof. emeritus, 1997—. Vis. prof. U. Marburg, 1963, U. N.Mex. German Summer Sch., 1984, 87, 89. Author: Martin von Amberg, 1957, (with Lehmann, Rehder, Shaw) Review and Progress in German, 1959; Editor: Formal Aspects of Medieval German Poetry, 1970. Served with Signal Corps AUS, 1943-45. Decorated Bronze Star medal; Bundesverdienstkreuz erster klasse W. Ger.; recipient Fulbright award to Netherlands, 1950-51; Guggenheim fellow, 1960; Fulbright research scholar Germany, 1960-61 Mem. Modern Lang. Assn. (pres. South Central assn. 1976—), Medieval Acad., Internat. Assn. Germanists, Phi Beta Kappa, Phi Kappa Phi, Delta Phi Alpha. Home: 4205 Prickly Pear Dr Austin TX 78731-2017 Office: Univ Texas Dept Germanic Studies Austin TX 78712 E-mail: s.werbow@mail.utexas.edu.

WERDEGAR, KATHRYN MICKLE, state supreme court justice; b. San Francisco; d. Benjamin Christie and Kathryn Marie (Clark) Mickle; m. David Werdegar; children: Maurice Clark, Matthew Mickle. Student, Wellesley Coll., 1954—55; AB with honors, U. Calif., Berkeley, 1957; JD with highest distinction, George Washington U., 1962; JD, U. Calif., Berkeley, 1990. Bar: Calif. 1964, U.S. Dist. Ct. (no. dist.) Calif. 1964, U.S. Ct. Appeals (9th cir.) 1964, Calif. Supreme Ct. 1964. Legal asst. civil rights divsn. U.S. Dept. Justice, Washington, 1962—63; rsch. atty., author Calif. State Study Commn. on Mental Retardation, 1963—64; assoc. U. Calif. Ctr. for Study of Law and Soc., Berkeley, 1965—67; spl. cons. State Dept. Mental Health, 1967—68; cons., author Calif. Coll. Trial Judges, 1968—71; dir. criminal law divsn. Calif. Continuing Edn. of Bar, 1971—78; assoc. dean acad. and student affairs, assoc. prof. Sch. Law, U. San Francisco, 1978—81; sr. staff atty. Calif. 1st Dist. Ct. Appeal, 1981—85, Calif. Supreme Ct., 1985—91; assoc. justice Calif. 1st Dist. Ct. Appeal, 1991—94, Calif. Supreme Ct., San Francisco, 1994—. Regents' lectr. U. Calif., Berkeley, 2000. Author: Benchbook: Misdemeanor Procedure, 1971, Misdemeanor Procedure Benchbook rev., 1975, Misdemeanor Procedure Benchbook, 1983; contbr. California Continuing Education of the Bar books; editor: California Criminal Law Practice series, Discovery, 1975, California Uninsured Motorist Practice, 1973, I California Civil Procedure Before Trial, 1977. Recipient Charles Glover award, George Washington U., 1962, J. William Fulbright award for disting. pub. svc., George Washington U. Law Sch. Alumni Assn., 1996, excellence in achievement award, Calif. Alumni Assn., 1996, Roger J. Traynor Appellate Justice of Yr. award, 1996, Justice of Yr. award, Consumer Attys. of Calif., 1998, Citation award, Boalt Hall Sch. Law U. Calif., Berkeley, 2002, also 5 Am. Jurisprudence awards, 1960—62. Mem.: Am. Law Inst., Nev./Calif. Women Judges Assn., Calif. Judges Assn., Nat. Assn. Women Judges, Calif. Supreme Ct. Hist. Soc. (bd. dir.), Order of the Coif. Office: Calif Supreme Court 350 McAllister St San Francisco CA 94102-4797 Office Phone: 415-865-7032.

WERDIGER, NORMAN, neurologist; b. Freeport, N.Y., May 15, 1952; s. David and Ilona Werdiger; m. Lucille A. Patrone. BS, SUNY, Albany, 1973; MD, Cornell U., 1977. Diplomate Am. Bd. Psychiatry and Neurology. Pvt. practice, New Haven, 1982—; instr. neurology Yale U. Sch. Medicine, New Haven, 1982—94, attending physician Yale New Haven Hosp., 1982—, asst. clin. prof. neurology, 1994—; asst. chief neurology Yale-New Haven Hosp., 2003—. Office: 2 Church St S New Haven CT 06519 Home: 43 Sage Hollow Rd Guilford CT 06437

WERESH, THELMA FAYE, sculptor, artist; b. Baca County, Colo., Mar. 15, 1919; d. William Lee Cotton and Myrtle Mae (Quiet) Cotton-Winston; m. Andrew Anthony Weresh, Jan. 28, 1939; children: Charlotte Maria, Catherine Ann. BA, Coll. St. Mary, 1967. Art tchr. Ralston (Nebr.) Pub. Schs., 1967-73, Father Flanagan's Boys Home, Boys Town, Nebr., 1973-75. Bd. dirs. Alliance of Arts Coun., Lincoln, Nebr., 1975; chmn. Visual Arts Commn., Loveland, Colo., 1990-91. One person exhibn. includes Ariel Gallery, N.Y., 1991; featured in Artist's Profile KRMA TV, 1995. Recipient SOHO Internat. 1st Place, 1990, 1st Place United Coun., 1990, 2nd Place, 1991, 1st Place George Lewis, 1991, 1st Place Southwest Art, 1992, 1st Place Women Artists, 1992, Spl. award Mus. N.W., 1992, First Annual Hall of Fame award Revue mag., 1996. Mem. Allied Artists Am., Loveland (Colo.) Sculpture Group. Home: 2009 Lakewood Dr Loveland CO 80538-3423

WERFEL, SANDRA DIANE, clinical social worker; d. Israel Harry and Charlotte; m. Mark Werfel, Oct. 25, 1970; children: Justin Keith, Erica Elizabeth. BA, Queens Coll., 1968; MSW, Simmons Coll., 1970. Diplomate in Clin. Social Work; lic. social worker, Va., Md., Washington, D.C. Staff social worker Child Guidance Ctr., Greater Lynn, Mass., 1970-73; supervising social worker Union Hosp. Cmty. Mental Health Ctr., Lynn, 1973-77; instr., supr. Boston U. Sch. Social Work, 1974-77; cons. Paragon Assocs., McLean, Va., 1980-82, Enterprise Sch., Vienna, 1982-83, Marriage and Family Clinic, Annandale, Va., 1982-85, Silver Hill Svcs. to Families and Children, Temple Hills, Md., 1984-87; founder, pres. Met. Stress Cons., Burke, Va., 1985-87, Burke Family Counseling and Consultation Ctr., 1987—. Mem. adv. com. Family Day Care Program, No. Va. Jewish Cmty. Ctr., Fairfax, 1984-87, Elem. Age Programs, 1987-88; mem. sch. com. Congregation Beth-El, Alexandria, Va., 1983-85; vol. Red Cross Mental Health, 2003-. Recipient Maida H. Solomon honorable mention citation Simmons Coll. Sch. Social Work, 1979; scholar NIMH, 1968, 69. Mem.: NASW, Obsessive-Compulsive Found., Anxiety Disorders Assn. Am., Greater Washington Soc. Clin. Social Work, Acad. Cert. Social Workers. Avocations: reading, music, needlecrafts, bike riding, travel. Office: Burke Profl Ctr 5206 Rolling Rd Ste B Burke VA 22015-1605

WERFELMAN, WILLIAM HERMAN, JR., public relations executive; b. Bridgeport, Conn., July 11, 1953; s. William H. and Helen D. (Rainier) W.; m. Patricia Aileen Maytrott, Aug. 28, 1977; children: Lauren Aileen, Juliana Aileen. BA in English, St. Bonaventure U., 1975; postgrad., Georgetown U., 1975—76. Staff writer Post-Telegram newspapers, Bridgeport, 1976—79; product publicity specialist Dictaphone Corp., Rye, NY, 1979—81; supr. press rels. GE, Fairfield, Conn., 1981—84; mgr. corp. pub. rels. Olin Corp., Stamford, Conn., 1984—90, dir. pub. rels./comm., 1990—94; v.p. external comms. Home Ins. Co., N.Y.C., 1994—95; v.p. media rels. N.Y. Life Ins. Co., N.Y.C., 1995—2003; first v.p. N.Y Life Ins. Co., N.Y.C., 2003—. Mem., chmn. Zoning Bd. Appeals, Redding, Conn., 1977-89, 92-99; party recruitment chmn. Rep. Town Com., Redding, 1976-90. Recipient Fin. World Bronze award for ann. report, 1992. Mem. Internat. Assn. Bus. Communicators (Best Pub. Rels. results 1982), Pub. Rels. Soc. Am., Nat. Assn. Investors (Best Ann Report 1988, 90). Republican. Roman Catholic. Avocations: fiction writing, investments. Home: 195 Gallows Hill Rd Redding CT 06896-1423 Office: NY Life Ins Co Rm 1600 51 Madison Ave New York NY 10010-1603

WERKHEISER, STEVEN LAWRENCE, financial executive; b. Oct. 6, 1945; s. Laverne Eugene and Dorothy M. W.; m. Michelle Sue Phelan; children: Steven Lawrence, Kirsten Elizabeth. Student, L.A. Pierce Coll., 1964-66; BA, UCLA, 1970, MS, 1971. Mcpl. bond trader/underwriter Blyth & Co., L.A., 1971-72, 1972-73, mgr. mcpl. bond dept., 1974; fin. analyst Northrop Corp., Hawthorne, Calif., 1974-75, fin. planning analyst, 1976-80; v.p. trading R.H. Moulton & Co., L.A., from 1980; divsn. fin. specialist, mgr. planning and adminstrn. Northrop Corp., Hawthorne; corp. fin. cons. L.A., 1975-92; bus. devel., treas., CFO Ticom Corp., Warren, Mich., 1992-95; also bd. dirs.; bus. devel. Northrop Grumman, 1995—98; CFO Italbiz, 2000—01, New Century Companies, Inc., 2001—. Bd. dirs. Monadnock Corp., Bridge Tech. With AUS, 1966-68. Mem.: UCLA Alumni Assn. (bd. dirs.), Assn. MBAs, In the Wings, Fin. Mgmt. Assn., L.A. Bond Club. Republican. Methodist. Home: 25102 Avenida Ignacio Valencia CA 91355-3033

WERKING, RICHARD HUME, librarian, historian, academic administrator; b. Charleston, S.C., Sept. 29, 1943; s F. Woody and Mary S. (Prissinger) W. BA, U. Evansville, 1966; MA in Am. History, U. Wis., 1967, PhD in Am. History, 1973; MA in Librarianship, U. Chgo., 1975. Instr. history Northland Coll., Ashland, Wis., 1967-68; pers. staffing specialist U.S. Civil Svc. Commn., Indpls., 1968-69; reference libr. Lawrence U., Appleton, Wis., 1975-77; head reference dept., asst./acting libr. dir. U. Miss., Oxford, 1977-81, asst. prof. history, 1977-81; assoc. libr. dir., asst. prof. history Trinity U., San Antonio, Tex., 1981-83, libr. dir., assoc. prof. history, 1983-91; libr. dir., assoc. dean, prof. history U.S. Naval Acad., Annapolis, Md., 1991—. Author: The Master Architects: Building the U.S. Foreign Service, 1977; contbr. articles to profl. jours., chpts. to books, also papers, monographs and revs. With Ind. Nat. Guard, 1961—65, with U.S. Army, 1962. Sparks fellow Phi Kappa Phi, 1966, postdoctoral fellow Coun. on Libr. Resources, 1974. Mem. ALA (chmn. coll. librs. sect. 1987-88), Orgn. Am. Historians. Office: US Naval Acad Nimitz Libr 589 Mcnair Rd Annapolis MD 21402-1323 Business E-Mail: rwerking@usna.edu.

WERKMAN, SIDNEY LEE, psychiatry educator; b. Washington, May 3, 1927; AB, Williams Coll., 1948; MD, Cornell U., 1952. Diplomate Am. Bd. Psychiatry and Neurology, Am. Bd. Child Psychiatry. Intern U. Va. Hosp., Charlottesville; resident in psychiatry Yale U., 1953-55, St. Elizabeth's Hosp., Washington, 1955-56; assoc. prof. psychiatry George Washington U., Washington, 1960-69; prof. U. Colo. Sch. Medicine, Denver, 1969-87; dir. div. adolescent psychiatry Children's Hosp. of Washington, 1965-69; clin. prof. Georgetown U. Sch. Medicine, Washington, 1989—; psychiatrist Capital Area Permanente Med. Group, Washington, 1990—. Cons. grants NIMH, Washington, 1982—, guest researcher, 1984-85 Author: The Role of Psychiatry in Medical Education, 1966, Only a Little Time: A Chronicle of Dying, 1972, Bringing Up Children Overseas, 1977 Bd. dirs. Med. U. So. Africa, Performing Arts Soc., Nat. Mus. Arts, Young Concert Artists Assn., Washington Concert Operas. Master sgt. U.S. Army. Fellow Commonwealth Fund, Florence, Italy, 1963-64, NEH, 1979 Mem. Am. Psychiat. Assn., Am. Acad. Child Psychiatry, Group for Advancement Psychiatry, Am. Orthopsychiat. Assn. (bd. dirs. 1970-73), Colo. Psychiat. Soc. Office: Ste AG 29 3636 16th St NW Ste Ag29 Washington DC 20010-8138 Office Phone: 202-483-4637.

WERLEIN, EWING, JR., federal judge; b. Houston, Sept. 14, 1936; s. Ewing and Ruth (Storey) W.; m. Kay McGibbon Werlein, June 29, 1963; children: Ewing Kenneth, Emily Kay. BA, So. Meth. U., 1958; LLB, U. Tex., 1961. Bar: Tex. 1961, U.S. Dist. Ct. (so. dist.) Tex. 1965, U.S. Dist. Ct. (ea. dist.) Tex. 1990, U.S. Ct. Appeals (5th cir.) 1970, U.S. Ct. Appeals (10th cir.) 1980, U.S. Claims Ct. 1985, U.S. Tax Ct. 1985, U.S. Supreme Ct. 1983. Ptnr. Vinson & Elkins, Houston, 1964-92; dist. judge U.S. Dist. Ct. (so. dist.) Tex., 1992—. Trustee So. Meth. U., Dallas, 1976-92, Asbury Theol. Sem., Wilmore, Ky., 1989—; mem. gen. bd. pub. United Meth. Ch., Nashville, 1974-84, chmn., 1980-84, chancellor Tex. ann. conf., 1977—; mem. exec. com. World Meth. Counh., 1981-96, treas, 1991-93. Capt. USAF, 1961-64. Fellow Am. Coll. Trial Lawyers, 1984, Internat. Soc. Barristers, 1987; recipient Disting. Alumni award SMU Alumni Assn., 1994. Fellow Am. Bar Found., Tex. Bar Found., Houston Bar Found.; mem. State Bar Tex. (dir. 1990-93), Nat. Conf. Bar Pres., Houston Bar Assn. (pres. 1988-89), Houston C. of C. (life), SAR, Order of Coif, Petroleum Club, Houston Club, Phi Beta Kappa. Office: US Dist Ct Tex US Courthouse 515 Rusk St Ste 9136 Houston TX 77002-2605

WERLIN, LAWRENCE B. obstetrician, gynecologist, reproductive endocrinologist; b. Albany, N.Y., 1948; s. Esther (Caplan) W.; m. Sally Rosso, Dec. 24, 1970; children: Rachel, Evan, Emma. BA, Boston U., 1970; MD, Mt. Sinai Sch. Medicine, N.Y.C., 1976. Diplomate Am. Bd. Ob-Gyn. Intern Harbor Gen. Hosp., Torrance, Calif., 1976-77, resident in ob-gyn., 1977-80; fellow in reproductive endocrinology NIH, Bethesda, Md., 1980-82; mem. staff Hoag Meml. Hosp., Newport Beach, Calif. Nat. Reproductive Medicine fellow, 1980-82. Mem. AAAS, Am. Soc. Reproductive Medicine, Soc. for Assisted Reproductive Tech., Pacific Coast Fertility Soc. Office: Coastal Fertility Med Ctr 4900 Barranca Pkwy Ste 103 Irvine CA 92604-8603 also: Ste 220 5 Journey St Aliso Viejo CA 92656 E-mail: werlmd@coastalfertility.com.

WERLY, JOHN MCINTYRE, retired historian, educator; b. Rochester, N.Y., Nov. 6, 1939; s. Berlyn McIntryre and Grace (Steinhauser) W.; m. Bonnie Windolf, July 8, 1961; children: Aric, Robyn, Scott. BA, Trinity Coll., Hartford, Conn., 1961, MA, 1966; PhD in U.S. History, Syracuse U., 1972. Instr. history Robinson Sch., West Hartford, Conn., 1963-68; teaching asst. U. S. history Syracuse (N.Y.) U., 1969-70; instr. U.S. history SUNY, Cortland, 1970-72; asst. prof. history Southeastern Mass. U., North Dartmouth, 1972-78, assoc. prof., 1978-84; prof. U. Mass., Dartmouth, 1984—2002, prof. emeritus, 2002—. Community lectr. in field. Contbr. articles to profl. jours. Trustee Saquish Found. Recipient Mass. Commonwealth Citation for Outstanding Performance, 1987. Mem. Orgn. Am. Historians. Home: 20 Stillman St South Dartmouth MA 02748-3540 Office: U Mass Dartmouth North Dartmouth MA 02747 E-mail: jwerly@umassd.edu.

WERMAN, DAVID SANFORD, psychiatrist, psychoanalyst, educator; b. N.Y.C., Jan. 1, 1922; s. Morris and Blanche (Heftel) W.; m. Marjolijn R. de Jager, Oct. 25, 1958 (div. 1975); children: Marco W., Claudia J. BA, Queens Coll., 1942; postgrad., Columbia U., 1946-47; MD, Cert. d'Etudes Medicales, U. Lausanne, Switzerland, 1952. Diplomate Am. Bd. Obstetrics and Gynecology, Am. Bd. Psychiatry and Neurology. Intern Beth Israel Hosp., N.Y.C., 1953-54, resident, 1954-57, Montefiore Hosp., Bronx, N.Y., 1964-67; pvt. practice specializing in ob-gyn. N.Y.C., 1957-64; faculty acad. psychiatry U. N.C., Chapel Hill, 1967-76, assoc. prof., instr. psychoanalytic tng. program, 1974—; prof. psychiatry Duke U. Med. Ctr., Durham, N.C., 1976—, supervising and tng. analyst psychoanalytic tng. program, 1981-97, Honored prof. psychiatry, 1990—, prof. emeritus, 1992—, supervising and tng. analyst emeritus, 1997—. Cons. Durham VA Hosp. Author: The Practice of Supportive Psychotherapy, 1984. Contbr. chpts. to books, articles to profl. jours. With AUS, 1943-45 Named Outstanding Tchr. psychiatry U. N.C., 1975, honored tchr. psychiatry Duke U., 1978, hon. prof., 1990. Fellow ACS, Am. Psychiat. Assn., Am. Coll. Psychoanalysts, others Home and Office: 1225 Park Ave New York NY 10128 Fax: 914-271-1358. Office Phone: 212-722-0744. E-mail: davidwerman@aol.com.

WERMAN, THOMAS EHRLICH, record producer; b. Newton, Mass., Mar. 2, 1945; s. Lester and Ruth (Ehrlich) W.; m. Susan Lynne Gould, Aug. 25, 1968; children: Julia Gould, Nina Eve, Daniel Lester. BA, Columbia U., 1967, MBA, 1969. Asst. account exec. Grey Advt., N.Y.C., 1969-70; asst. to dir. Epic Records Artistes and Repertoire, 1970-73; dir. talent acquisition Epic Records, 1973-76, staff producer, 1976-80; v.p., exec. producer CBS Records, Inc., L.A., 1980-81; sr. v.p. Elektra Records, 1981-82; pres. Julia's Music Inc., L.A., 1981—; v.p. artists and repertoire EMI-Capitol Entertainment Properties, L.A., 1997-98; owner, operator Stonover Farm Bed and Breakfast, Lenox, Mass., 2001—. Bd. trustees Berkshire Music Sch. Recipient N.Y.C. Civilian Commendation award for heroism, 1968, 14 platinum records awards Rec. Industry Assn. Am., 1977—, 10 Gold Record awards, 1977—. Mem.: Lenox C. of C. (bd. dirs.), Country Club of Pittsfield. Democrat. Jewish.

WERMUTH, PAUL CHARLES, retired English educator; b. Phila., Oct. 28, 1925; s. Paul C. and Susan (Manga) W.; m. Barbara Ethel Braun, Aug. 26, 1951; children— Geoffrey Paul, Paul Charles, Alan John, Stephen Mark. AB, MA, Boston U., 1951; PhD, Pa. State U., 1955. Instr. Clarkson Coll., Potsdam, N.Y., 1951-52; part-time instr., grad. asst. Pa. State U., 1952-55; asst. prof. Coll. William and Mary, 1955-57; mem. faculty Central Conn. State Coll., New Britain, 1957-68, assoc. prof. English, 1966-68; prof. English Northeastern U., 1968-90, prof. emeritus, 1990—, chmn. dept., 1968-75. Vis. prof. Middlebury Coll., 1963-64 Author: Modern Essays on Writing and Style, 2d edit, 1969, Essays in English, 1967, Bayard Taylor, 1974, Selected Letters of Bayard Taylor, 1997, also articles. Served with USAAF, 1943-46. Danforth summer study grantee, 1961 Mem. Modern Lang. Assn., AAUP, Mensa. Home: 73 Mostyn St Swampscott MA 01907-1616 Office: English Dept Northeastern Univ Boston MA 02115 E-mail: pwermuth@comcast.net.

WERNER, ARNOLD, psychiatrist; BS cum laude, Bklyn. Coll.; MD, U. Rochester. Diplomate Am. Bd. Psychiatry and Neurology in Psychiatry. Intern Vanderbilt U., Nashville, 1964; resident in psychiatry U. Rochester, NY, 1964—67, instr. psychiatry, 1966—67, Temple U., Phila., 1967—69; asst. prof. Mich. State U., East Lansing, Mich., 1969—72, assoc. prof., 1972—78, prof., 1978—2001, prof. emeritus, 2001—. Cons. Gratiot Co. Mental Health Ctr., Alma, 1972-96, Montcalm Ctr. for Behavioral Health, 1996—; coord. Psychosocial Curriculum, 1986-95, gen. practice psychiatry Temple U., 1967-69, Mich. State U., 1969—; dir. home vis. svc. Temple U., 1967-69, psychiat. svcs. Mich. State U. Health Ctr. 1969-78; dir. consultation liason psychiatry Ingham Med. Ctr., Lansing, 1983-85. Contbr. numerous articles and book reviews to profl. jours., syndicated newspaper columnist, 1969-76. Research grantee NIMH, 1970-71, undergrad. grant, 1980, psychiat. edn. grants. 1982-85; recipient Outstanding Faculty award Sr. Class Council Mich. State U., 1971. Fellow (dist. life) Am. Psychiat. Assn. (com. on pub. info. 1972-75, chmn. 1974-75, peer rev. com. 1975-76, joint commn. on pub. affairs 1976-82, com. on med. student edn., 1982-89, 1994-96, sci. program com. 1988-94); mem. Am. Psychosomatic Soc. Avocation: photography. Office: Mich State U B109 W Fee Hall East Lansing MI 48824-1316 Office Phone: 517-353-3070. Business E-Mail: werner@msu.edu.

WERNER, BILL, communication media executive; Capitol bur. chief UP Internat., Mpls., 1998—. Office: UP Internat 331 S 11th St Minneapolis MN 55404-1006

WERNER, BURTON KREADY, insurance company executive; b. St. Louis, Apr. 24, 1933; s. Elmer L. and Helen (Kready) W.; m. Joanna Catherine Hill, Oct. 17, 1959; children: Lisa Anne, Cynthia Catherine, Bradford Kready. AB cum laude, Amherst Coll., 1954; MBA, U. Pa., 1958. CPCU. Sec. Insurers Svc. Corp., St. Louis, 1958-65, exec. v.p., 1965-75, pres., also bd. dirs., 1975-88; v.p., bd. dirs. Safety Mut. Casualty Corp., St. Louis, 1958-76, pres., 1976-87, chmn., 1987-91; also bd. dirs.; chmn. Safety Nat. Casualty Corp., St. Louis, 1991-99, chmn. emeritus, 1999—. Chmn. SIG Holdings, Inc., St. Louis, 1991-96, Delphi Fin. Group, Inc., bd. dirs.; originator unemployment compensation reinsurance for non-profit orgns. under pub. law 91-373. Guarantor St. Louis Mcpl. Opera; trustee Churchill Sch., St. Louis Country Day Sch.; mem. Humane Soc. Mo., Arts and Edn. Coun. St. Louis, Associated Industries Mo., Mo. Bot. Garden, Mo. Hist. Soc., St. Louis Symphony Soc., City Art Mus., St. Louis Landmark Assn, Maui Meml. Med. Ctr. Found., Inc., Hui No'Eau Visual Arts Ctr., Maui Arts and Cultural Ctr. Capt. USAF, 1954—56. Named to Hon. Order Ky. Cols. Fellow: Truman Libr.; mem.: Better Bus. Bur. St. Louis, Am. Soc. CPCU, Nat. Assn. Safety and Claims Orgns., St. Louis McDonnell Planetarium, St. Louis Zoo Assn., Wailea Golf Club, Casa y Pesca Las Cruces Club, Windfall Club, Univ. Club, Racquet Club, Napili Kai Beach Club, Boone Valley Golf Club, Jupiter Hills Club, Delta Kappa Epsilon. Episcopalian. Office: Safety Nat Casualty Corp 2043 Woodland Pkwy Ste 200 Saint Louis MO 63146-4235 E-mail: bk.werner@sncc.com.

WERNER, DAVID A. paper company executive; BS, MBA, U. So. Calif. CPA. With Peat, Marwick, Mitchell & Co., 1974-78; various mgmt. positions Lear Siegler's Telecomms. divsns./subsidiaries, Anaheim, Calif., 1978-86, v.p. fin. and adminstrn., 1986-90; v.p., CFO Microdot Components Group, 1990-94; exec. v.p., dir. Kaynar Technologies Inc. (formerly Microdot Components), Orange, Calif., 1994-99; exec. v.p., CFO Day Runner, Irvine, 1999—. Office: 101 Oneil RD Sidney NY 13838-1055

WERNER, JANE, museum administrator; m. Robert Rutkowski; 2 children. B. Synaesthetic Edn., Syracuse U. With Buhl Sci. Ctr., Franklin Inst. and Sci. Mus.; dep. dir. Pitts. Children's Mus., exec. dir. Carnegie-Mellon U./Studio for Creative Inquiry fellow. Office: Pittsburgh Childrens Mus Allegheny Sq North Side 10 Childrens Way Pittsburgh PA 15212

WERNER, JOANNE LOUCILLE, financial executive; b. Midland, Mich., Jan. 20, 1940; d. Ewald George and Martha (Yuchlal) W. AAS, Ea. Nazarene Coll., Quincy, Mass., 1972; BAS, Boston U., 1977; MBA, Suffolk U., Boston, 1979. Prog. asst. Dept. Def., Washington, 1966-68, budget analyst, 1968-70, Dept. of Navy, Washington, 1970-72, GSA, Boston, 1972-77, sr. budget analyst, 1977-79; sr. fin. mgmt. specialist HUD, Boston, 1979-90; founder, dir., coord. Network Industry Leaders Internat., Quincy, Mass., 1990; ind. contractor courier svcs., 1994-95; data quality analyst South Shore Hosp., 2001. Exec. Gillette Co., Boston, 1995—97. Editor newsletter Baystatement, 1980-81. Vol. med. supplies mgr. Mass. Emergency Mgmt. Agy., Quincy, 1995. With USNR. Sioux Falls Coll. grantee, 1959; named Sailor of Yr. USNR, 1985. Mem. Am. Soc. Women Accts. (bd. dirs. 1986-88, 90-91), Habitat for Humanity Internat. (vol., family selection com., family partnership liaison 1997-98). Avocations: music, reading, nutrition, travel. Home and Office: 4514 Illicium Dr Palm Beach Gardens FL 33418

WERNER, LAWRENCE H. editor; BA in Journalism, Mich. State U., 1969. Reporter Courier-Jour., 1969—78; asst. features editor (Louisville) Courier-Jour., 1978—79; bus. editor Grand Rapids (Mich.) Press, 1979; consumer reporter Detroit Free Press, 1979—81; mng. editor features and sports Buffalo Courier-Express, 1981—82; features editor Dallas Times Herald, 1982—83; asst. mng. editor bus. Star Tribune, Mpls., 1983—95, reader involvement editor, 1995—. Mem.: Soc. Am. Bus. Editors and Writers (past pres.). Avocations: coaching youth soccer, travel, reading. Office: Star Tribune 425 Portland Ave Minneapolis MN 55488-0002 E-mail: werner@startribune.com.

WERNER, MARY ANN, lawyer; b. Latrobe, Pa., July 11, 1954; BA in English, Coll. of charleston, 1982; JD with highest honors, george Washington U., 1987. Bar: Pa. 1988, D.C. 1990, U.S. Ct. Appeals (D.c. cir.) 1990, Va. 1991, U.S. Dist. Ct. D.C. 1991. Law clk. to Hon. Spottswood W. Robinson III U.S. Ct. Appeals (D.C. cir.), 1987-88; v.p., counsel Washington Post, 1988—. Adj. prof. George Washington Nat. Law Ctr., 1990-92; mem. exec. com. Libel Def. Resource Ctr. Editor-in-chief George Washington Law Rev., 1986-87. Mem. ABA (1st amendment and media litigation coms.), D.C. Bar (publs. com., bd. editors Washington Lawyer), Newspaper Assn. Am. (legal affairs com.), Order of Coif. Office: Washington Post 1150 15th St NW Washington DC 20071-0002

WERNER, PATRICE (PATRICIA ANN WERNER), academic administrator; b. Jersey City, May 31, 1937; d. Louis and Ella Blanche (Smith) W. BA in French, Caldwell Coll., 1966; MA in French, McGill U., 1970; PhD in French, NYU, 1976; postgrad. Inst. Ednl. Mgmt., Harvard U., 1991. Joined Dominican Sisters of Caldwell, 1954. Sch. tchr. Archdiocesan Sch. Systems, N.J., Ala., 1954-62; tchr. French, Latin Jersey City, Caldwell, NJ, 1962-72; instr. French Caldwell (NJ) Coll., 1973-76, dir. continuing edn., 1976-79, chair dept. fgn. langs., assoc. prof. French, 1979-85, acad. dean, prof. French, 1985-94, pres., 1994—. Trustee Caldwell Coll.; mem. corp., trustee Providence Coll.; mem. Dominican Higher Edn. Coun. Recipient Caldwell Cup, Excellence in Edn. award, N. Essex C. of C. Found., 2003, Outstanding Woman in Am. History, DAR Maj. Joseph Bloomfield Chpt., The Archbishop T.E. McCarrick award for Disting. Svc. to the Ch., 2000, Cmty. Woman of Achievement, West Caldwell Hist. Soc. and West Essex Women's Club, 2000, Woman of Achievement award, N. N.J. Coun. of Boy Scouts of Am., 1999; scholar AATF Summer Grant. Mem.: Assn. Gov. Bds. of Univs. and Colls., N.J. C. of C., Assn. Cath. Colls. and Univs., Am. Assn. Higher Edn., Neylan Commn. (bd. dirs., sec.- treas.), Nat. Assn. Ind. Colls. and Univs. (bd. dirs., com. policy analysis and pub. relations), Coun. Ind. Colls. (bd. dirs., pub. info. com.), Ind. Coll. Fund. N.J. (bd. trustees, vice chmn. exec. com.), Assn. Ind. Colls. and Univs. in N.J. (chmn. bd. dirs.), N.J. Pres. Coun. Avocations: tennis, reading, avid sports fan, travel. Office: Caldwell Coll 9 Ryerson Ave Caldwell NJ 07006-6195 Office Phone: 973-618-3217. Business E-Mail: spwerner@caldwell.edu.

WERNER, ROBERT JOSEPH, dean, music educator; b. Lackawanna, N.Y., Feb. 13, 1932; s. Edward Joseph and Marian L. (Gerringer) W.; m. Sharon Lynne Mohrfeld, June 22, 1957; children: Mark J., Kurt M., Erik J. BME, Northwestern U., 1953, MusM, 1954, PhD, 1967. Dir. instrumental music Evanston (Ill.) Twp. H.S., 1956-66; assoc. prof. mus. Harpur Coll. SUNY, Binghamton, 1966-68, dir. Contemporary Music Project, 1968-73; dir. Sch. Mus. U. Ariz., Tucson, 1973-85, dean fine arts, 1981-82; dean Coll.-Conservatory of Music U. Cin., 1985-2000, dean emeritus, 2000—. Editor: Comprehensive Musicianship: An Anthology of Evolving Thought, 1971; contbr. articles to profl. jours. Mem. exec. bd. Tucson Symphony Orch., 1974-85; bd. dirs. Cultural Commn. Tucson, 1974-75, Cin. Symphony Orch., 1985-2000, Cin. Opera, 1985-2000, Cin. Ballet, 1985-2000; mem. artistic directorate Am. Classical Music Hall of Fame. With U.S. Army, 1954-56. Mem. Nat. Assn. Schs. Music (pres. 1989-91), Coll. Music Soc. (pres. 1977-78), Internat. Soc. for Music Edn. (pres. 1984-86, treas. 1986-97), Music Educators Nat.Conf., McDowell Soc., Coll. Music Soc., Psi Upsilon, Phi Mu Alpha Sinfonia, Sigma Alpha Iota. E-mail: wernerrj@uc.edu.

WERNER, ROBERT L. lawyer, consultant; b. NYC, Feb. 28, 1913; s. Abraham L. and Elsa (Ludwig) W.; m. Raye Davies, Oct. 13, 1945; children: William, John. AB, Yale U., 1933; LLB, Harvard U., 1936. Bar: N.Y. 1936, U.S. Supreme Ct. 1936, also various fed. cts. and adminstrv. agys. 1936. Spl. asst. to U.S. atty. So. Dist. N.Y., 1936, asst. U.S. atty, 1937-40, confidential asst., 1940-42; 1st asst. civil div. U.S. Dept. Justice, Washington, 1946-47; spl. asst. to atty. gen. U.S., 1946-47; mem. law dept. RCA, N.Y.C., 1947, v.p., gen. atty., 1951-62, exec. v.p., gen. atty., 1962-66, exec. v.p., gen. counsel, 1966-78, dir., 1963-79, cons., 1978-83. Mem. adv. bd. Internat. and Comparative Law Ctr. Southwestern Legal Found., Dallas, 1966—, treas., 1970-72, vice chmn., 1972-73, chmn. advisory bd., 1974-76, found. trustee 1976-88, hon. trustee 1988—; lectr. Conf. Bd., Practicing Law Inst., others; mem. nat. adv. council corp. law depts. Practising Law Inst., 1974-78; com. on restrictive bus. practices U.S. council Internat. C. of C., 1973-78; N.Y. Lawyers' Com. for Civil Rights under Law, 1972-78. Trustee Ithaca Coll., N.Y., 1968-88, hon. trustee, 1988—, chmn. bd., 1976-78; trustee Salisbury (Conn.) Sch., 1975-77, N.Y. Chiropractic Coll., 1986-89; bd. dirs. Midtown Arts Common at St. Peter's Ch., 1983-89. Capt. U.S. Army, 1942-44; to lt. col. USAAF, 1944-46, ETO. Recipient Disting. Service award Ithaca Coll., 1988. Fellow Am. Bar Found.; mem. Internat., Fed., Am., N.Y. State, City N.Y., FCC bar assns., IEEE (sr.), Am. Legion, Harvard Law Sch. Assn., Assn. Gen. Counsel (emeritus), U.S. Naval Inst., Internat. Law Assn. (Am. br.), Nat. Legal Aid and Defender Assn. (dir. 1974-79), Am. Judicature Soc., Newcomen Soc., N.Y. County Lawyers' Assn., Am. Soc. Internat. Law, Yale Club, Harvard Club N.Y., Nat. Lawyers Club, Army and Navy Club (Washington), Coral Beach Club (Bermuda). Home: 116 E 68th St New York NY 10021-5955

WERNER, ROBIN A. humanities educator; b. Phila., Jan. 21, 1973; d. Paul R. and Linda Fairfield (Fuhrmann) Werner. BA summa cum laude with honors, St. Lawrence U., 1995; MA, Tulane U., 1997, PhD, 2003. Adjunct instr., English Tulane U., New Orleans, 1996—2003; instr. English U. New Orleans, 2003—04. Presenter in field. Contbr. chapters to books, articles to profl. jours. Mem.: Modern Language Assoc., Rocky Mountain Modern Language Assoc. (assoc.), Phi Beta Kappa. Avocations: acting, horseback riding, skiing, cooking, travel. Office: U New Orleans New Orleans LA 70148

WERNER, SAMUEL ALFRED, physics and astronomy educator; b. Elgin, Ill., Jan. 5, 1937; s. Charles August and Frances Agnes (Tasch) W.; m. Laura Louise Reed, Sept. 1, 1961; 1 dau., Catherine Louise. AB, Dartmouth Coll., 1959, MS, 1961; PhD, U. Mich., 1965. Staff scientist physics dept. Ford Motor Co., Dearborn, Mich., 1964-75; adj. prof. nuclear engring. U. Mich., Ann Arbor, 1968-75; prof. physics U. Mo., Columbia, 1975-2000, chmn. physics dept., 1981-83, Millsap Disting. prof., 1986—, Curator's prof., 1992—, prof. emeritus, 2000—; scientific cons.physics lab. Nat. Inst. Standards Tech., Gaithersburg, Md., 2000—. Vis. scientist A.B. Atomenergi, Studsvik, Sweden, 1970, Institut Laue-Langevin, Grenoble, France, 1977, Argonne Nat. Lab., Oak Ridge Nat. Lab., Brookhaven Nat. Lab.; cons. Argonne Nat. Lab., 1968—, mem. solid scis. div. rev. com., 1972-77, chmn. spl. com. Intense Pulsed Neutron Source, 1978-82; cons. Nat. Acad. Scis., 1977, 83; vis. scientist Nat. Bur. Stds, 1983-84; vis. scientist Nat. Inst. Stds. and Tech., 1996—, chmn. com. on assessment of physics lab., 1992-95. Contbr. numerous articles to profl. jours. Grantee NSF; fellow Swedish Research Council; recipient outstanding alumni award U. Mich., 1980, Chancellor's award for Outstanding Research U. Mo., 1980, Presdl. Research award U. Mo., 1983 Fellow Am. Phys. Soc.; mem. Sigma Xi Home: 7620 Augustine Way Gaithersburg MD 20879-4587 Office: Reactor Bldg 235 NIST Mail Stop 8461 Gaithersburg MD 20899 Office Fax: 301-926-1604. Business E-Mail: swerner@nist.gov.

WERNER, THOMAS LEE, hospital administrator; b. Hazen, N.D., Dec. 8, 1945; married. BA, Union Coll., 1967; MA, U. Nebr., 1969. Asst. dir. pers. Portland (Oreg.) Adventist Med. Ctr., 1971-72; v.p. Verticare Ambulatory Care Program, Portland, 1972-73; adminstr. Tillamook (Oreg.) CountyGen. Hosp., 1973-77, Walla Walla (Wash.)Gen. Hosp., 1977-81; exec. v.p. Fla. Hosp. Med. Ctr., Orlando, 1981-85, pres., 1985-2000, Adventist Health Systems, Winter Park, Fla., 2000—. Office: Adventist Health Systems 111 N Orlando Ave Winter Park FL 32789-3675

WERNER, TOM, television producer, professional baseball team executive; m. Jill Werner; children: Teddy, Carolyn, Amanda. BA, Harvard Univ., 1971. With ABC Television, Inc., 1972-82; co-owner Carsey-Werner Co., Studio City, Calif., 1982—; chmn. San Diego Padres, 1991-94. Mem. bd. dirs. Old Globe Theatre, Sharp Hospital. Prodr.(co-exec): (TV series) Oh, Madeline, 1983, 3rd Rock from the Sun, Cosby, 1996; exec. prodr.: The Cosby Show, 1984—92 (Emmy awd. Outstanding Comedy Series, 1985). Office: Carsey Werner Prodns 4024 Radford Ave Bldg 3 Studio City CA 91604-2101

WERNER, WADE W. secondary school educator; b. Amherst, Ohio, Dec. 14, 1949; s. Norman M. and Lavonne J. Werner; m. Sharon L. Tinapple, July 3, 1976; 1 child, Leslie. BE, Bowling Green (Ohio) State U., 1971; MEd, Kent (Ohio) State U., 1979. Cert. ednl. adminstrn. Cleve. State U., 1982. 8th English tchr. Huron (Ohio) City Schs., 1971—72; English tchr. Lorain (Ohio) Cath. HS, 1972—73; 7th-9th English tchr. Burneston Jr. HS, Westlake, Ohio, 1974—94; English tchr. Westlake (Ohio) HS, 1994—. Football coach Burneson Jr. HS, Westlake, Ohio, 1974—79; basketball coach Westlake (Ohio) HS, 1994—99, lit. mag. adv., 1999—2004, English dept. chmn., 2001—04. Author: (newspaper article) Cleve. Plain Dealer, 1983—86. Recipient Westlake Tchr. of Yr., Westlake (Ohio) Bd. of Edn., 1979, Excellence award in edn., 2003. Mem.: NEA, Nat. Coun. Tchrs. of English. Avocations: reading, golf, writing. Home: 25795 Butternut Ridge Rd North Olmsted OH 44070 Office Phone: 440-899-3075. Personal E-mail: wern55@sbcglobal.net.

WERNER, WILLIAM ARNO, architect; b. San Francisco, Dec. 11, 1937; s. William Arno and Sophie (Menutis) W.; m. Wendy Rolston Wilson, Feb. 3, 1963 (div. Jan. 1983); 1 child, Christa Nichol. BA with honors, Yale U., 1959, BArch, 1962, MArch, 1963. Drafter Serge Chermayeff, Paul Rudolph and Charles Brewer, New Haven, 1961-63; project designer Johnson, Poole & Storm, San Francisco, 1963-64, Leo S. Wou & Assocs., Honolulu, 1965-66, v.p. of design, 1971-72; project architect John Tatom Assocs., Honolulu, 1965-66; sr. designer Skidmore, Owings & Merrill, San Francisco, 1968-71, assoc./project architect, 1972-76; prin. W.A. Werner Assocs., San Francisco, 1976-80; ptnr. Werner & Sullivan, San Francisco, 1980—. Mem. planning commn. City of Sausalito, Calif.; bd. govs. Yale U., New Haven; visitorship in architecture U. Auckland Found., New Zealand, 1994. Prin. works include Alameda Mcpl. Credit Union, Lane Pub. Co., Menlo Park, Calif., Pacific Data Images, Mountain View, Calif., Saga Corp., Menlo Park, Tiffany & Co., Union Square, San Francisco, Somerset Collection, Troy, Mich., Touche Ross & Co., Oakland, U.S. Post Office, San Francisco, (renovations) Fed. Express Co., San Francisco, KD's Grog N' Grocery, San Francisco, Jessie Street. Substation, San Francisco, Lakeside Tower Health Ctr./Mt. Zion Hosp., Qantas Bldg, San Francisco, Women's Care, San Francisco, Moon Residence, Dillon Beach, Calif., Shenkar Residence, San Francisco, Tacker Residence, Denver, Lasky Residence, San Francisco, Starring Residence, San Francisco, Whitehead Residence, Monte Rio, Calif., various laboratories, theatres and rsch. facilities, urban design. Recipient Progressive Architecture Design award Jessie St. Substation, 1980, DuPont Co. Design award Touche Ross & Co., 1983, award of Excellence Woodwork Inst. of Calif., 1989, USPS/NEA Nat. Honor award for Design Excellence, 1990, Tucker Design Excellence award Bldg. Stone Inst., Tiffany & Co., 1992. Mem. AIA (San Francisco chpt.), Found. for San Francisco's Architectural Heritage (hon.). Home: 213 Richardson St Sausalito CA 94965-2422 Office: Werner & Sullivan 207 Powell St Ste 800 San Francisco CA 94102-2209

WERNER DENADAI, MARY, architectural firm executive; Prin. John Miller Archs., Chadds Ford, Pa., 1977—. Bd. trustees Nat. Trust for Hist. Preservation; bd. dirs. Preservation Action, Cliveden, Preservation Pa.; v.p., mem. Hist. Preservation Bd. of Commonwealth of Pa. Recipient F. Otto Haas award, Pa., 1999; fellow, Am. Inst. of Archs., 2003. Office: John Miller Architects 104 Lakeview Dr Chadds Ford PA 19317

WERNER-JACOBSEN, EMMY ELISABETH, developmental psychologist; b. Eltville, Germany, May 26, 1929; came to U.S., 1952, naturalized, 1962; d. Peter Josef and Liesel (Kunz) W. BS, Johannes Gutenberg U., Germany, 1950; MA, U. Nebr., 1952, PhD, 1955; postgrad., U. Calif., Berkeley, 1953-54. Research asso. Inst. Child Welfare, U. Minn., 1956-59; vis. scientist NIH, 1959-62; asst. prof. to prof. human devel., rsch. child psychologist U. Calif., Davis, 1962-94, rsch. prof., 1995—. Sr. author: The Children of Kauai, 1971, Kauai's Children Come of Age, 1977; author: Cross-Cultural Child Development: A View from the Planet Earth, 1979, Vulnerable, but Invincible, 1982, 3d edit., 1998, Child Care: Kith, Kin and Hired Hands, 1984, Overcoming the Odds, 1992, Pioneer Children on the Journey West, 1995, Reluctant Witnesses: Children's Voices From the Civil War, 1998, Through the Eyes of Innocents: Children Witness World War II, 2000, Unschuldige Zeugen, 2001, Journeys From Childhood to Mid Life: Risk, Resilience and Recovery, 2001, A Conspiracy of Decency: The Rescue of the Danish Jews in World War II, 2002; contbr. articles to profl. jours. Fellow Am. Psychol. Soc., German Acad. Social Pediats. (hon.), Soc. for Rsch. in Child Devel.

WERNET, PATRICIA A. director; b. Chgo., Jan. 14, 1955; d. Lee and Norma Dascenzo; m. Todd Phillip Wernet, Dec. 6, 1956; children: Dan, Dana, Doug. BA in elem. edn., MA in multicategorical spl. edn., Governors State U.; EdD, Aurora U., 2004. Cert. Edn. Admin. Governors State U. Lang. arts, reading tchr. Evergreen Pk. (Ill.) Sch. Dist. 124, 1992—94, gifted coord., 1993—96, learning disabled behavior disordered tchr., 1994—96, acting interim spl. edn. dir., 1996, edn. instrnl. asst. to prin., 1997—98; asst. prin. Palos South Mid. Sch., Palos Pk., 1998—99, prin., 1999—2002; dir. tchg. and learning Palos Sch. Dist. 118, 2002—. Mem.: Assn. of Supr. and Curriculum, Ill. Prin. Assn., Ednl. League of Ill. Horace Mann Soc., Phi Delta Kappa. Office Phone: 708-448-4800.

WERNICK, RICHARD FRANK, composer, conductor; b. Boston, Jan. 16, 1934; s. Louis and Irene (Prince) W.; m. Beatrice Messina, July 15, 1956; children: Lewis, Adam, Peter (dec.). BA, Brandeis U., 1955; MA, Mills Coll., 1957. Instr. music U. Buffalo, 1964-65; asst. prof. music, dir. univ. symphony U. Chgo., 1965-68; conductor Pa. Contemporary Players, 1968-93; prof. music U. Pa., 1968-96, prof. emeritus, 1996—. Co-founder Community Youth Orch. of Delaware County; cons. Contemporary Music, The Phil. Orch., 1983-89, spl. cons. to the music dir., 1989-93; bd. dirs. Theodore Presser Co. Music dir. Royal Winnipeg Ballet Can., 1957-58; composer: Haiku of Basho, 1967, A Prayer for Jerusalem, 1971 (Naumburg award 1975), Moonsongs from the Japanese, 1972, Kaddish Requiem, 1973, String Quartet 2, 1973, Songs of Remembrance, 1974, Visions of Terror and Wonder, 1976 (Pulitzer prize 1977), Contemplations of the Tenth Muse, Book I, 1976, Book II, 1978, Introits and Canons, 1977, A Poison Tree, 1979, Concerto for Cello and Ten Players, 1980, In Praise of Zephyrus, 1981, Piano Sonata: Reflections of a Dark Light, 1982, Sonata for cello and piano: Portraits of Antiquity, 1982, The Oracle of Shimon bar Yochai, 1983, Concerto for Violin and Orch., 1983-84 (Friedheim 1st prize 1986); Oracle II for soprano, oboe and piano, 1985, Concerto for Viola and Orch., 1985-86, Musica Ptolemeica brass quintet, 1987, Symphony #1, 1988, String Quartet #3, 1988, Concerto for Piano and Orch. (Friedheim award 1992), 1989-90, Fragments of Prophecy, 1990, String Quartet #4, 1991 (Friedheim 1st prize 1991), Concerto for Saxophone Quartet and Orch., 1991, Cello Concerto #2, 1992, Symphony #2, 1993, ...and a time for peace, 1994, String Quartet #5, 1995, Cassation-Music Tom Jefferson

Knew, 1995, Trio for violin, cello, piano, 1996, Da'ase for solo guitar, 1996, Fagotton Memories for solo bassoon, 1997, Sonata for violin and piano, 1997, Duettino for violin and oboe, 1997, String Quartet 6, 1998, Musica da Camerata, 1999, Telino's Acrobats, 1999, Piano Sonata # 2, 2000, The Name of the Game, 2000, Duo for cello and piano, 2001, Quintet for Horn & String Quartet, 2002, Suite for Unaccompanied Cello, 2003, Sextet (for string quartet, double bass, piano), 2003. Recipient music award Nat. Inst. Arts and Letters, 1976, Nat. Endowment Arts grantee, 1975, 79, 82; Fellow Ford Found., 1962-64, Guggenheim Found., 1976. Mem. ASCAP. Democrat. E-mail: rfwernick@aol.com.

WERRIES, E. DEAN, food distribution company executive; b. Tescott, Kans., May 8, 1929; s. John William and Sophie E. Werries; m. Marjean Sparling, May 18, 1962. BS, U. Kans., 1952. With Fleming Foods Co., Topeka, 1955-89, exec. v.p., 1973-76, exec. v.p. Eastern ops. Phila., 1976-78, pres. Oklahoma City, 1978-81; pres., chief operating officer Fleming Cos., Inc., Oklahoma City, 1981-88, also dir., pres., chief exec. officer, 1988-89, chmn., CEO, 1989-93. Chmn. bd. Sonic Corp., 1995-99. Sec. of Commerce State of Okla., 1995. With U.S. Army, 1952-54, Korea. Mem. Nat. Am. Wholesale Grocers Assn. (bd. dirs. 1979-93), Food Mktg. Inst. (bd. dirs. 1984, chmn. 1989-91), Ind. Grocers Alliance (bd. dirs. 1984-94). Republican. Presbyterian.

WERRONEN, BETSY WARREN, political organization administrator; BA in Polit. Sci., Newton Coll. Sacred Heart, 1965. Legis. asst. to Sen. Thruston B. Morton, 1966-68; exec. asst. to Sen. Edward W. Brooke, 1968-75; dir. legis. nuclear energy and taxes Edison Electric Inst., 1979-81, chief lobbyist on nuclear power issues, 1979 81; dep. asst. sec. of state for legis. affairs Dept. of State, Washington, 1981-85, prin. dep. asst. sec. of state for legis. affairs, 1987-89; prin. dep. asst. sec. for congl., intergovtl., pub. affairs Dept. of Energy, Washington, 1985-86; founder, pres. Warren and Co., 1989—; fin. chmn. Rep. Com. DC Rep. Party, Washington, 1998-2000, chmn. Rep. Com., 2000—. Mem. nat. steering com., congl. steering com. Women for Bush/Quayle, 1992; co-chair Ward 2, 1996-98; alternate del. Rep. Nat. Conv., 1996, del., 2000, 04. Apptd. U.S. election observer, El Salvador, 1988; bd. dirs. Fgn. Student Coun., 1993-97. Mem. League of Rep. Women (1st v.p. 1997-99, pres. 1999-2000). Office: DC Rep Party 1275 K St, NW, Ste 102 Washington DC 20005 Office Phone: 202-289-8005.

WERT, JAMES JUNIOR, materials scientist, educator; b. Barron, Wis., Jan. 9, 1933; s. James Lewis and Bernice Janet (Walker) W.; m. Jane Alice Thornton, Aug. 16, 1958; children: Thaddeus Thornton, Melissa Jane. BS, U. Wis., 1957, MS, 1958, PhD, 1961; postgrad., Carnegie Tech. Inst., 1958-59. Assoc. engr. Westinghouse Electric Corp., Pitts., 1958-60; rsch. scientist A.O. Smith Corp., Milw., 1961-62; mem. faculty Vanderbilt U., Nashville, 1962—, prof. material sci. and engring., 1967—, chmn. dept., 1969, chmn. materials, mechanics and structures div., 1969-72, chmn. materials sci. dept., 1975-82, chmn. dept. mech. and materials engring., 1976-82, George A. Sloan prof. metallurgy, 1976-96, Sloan prof. metallurgy and profl. mech. engring. emeritus, 1997—; mayor City of Forest Hills, Tenn., 1990-95. Dir. Ctr. for Coatings Sci. and Tech., Vanderbilt U., 1969-74; co.-dir. Ctr. for Materials Tribology, 1987—; vis. prof. Cambridge U., 1974; sr. Fulbright lectr. Mid. East; cons. Avco, 1964-71, Temco, 1964-71, Arnold Engring. Ctr., Tullahome, Tenn., 1966-71, Nat. Acad. Scis., 1969-70; pres. Technology Assocs., Inc., Nashville, 1975-85; pres. James Wert & Assocs., 1985—. Contbr. articles to profl. jours.; patentee nuclear fuels and cladding materials. Served with AUS, 1953-55. Ampco fellow, 1957-58; Westinghouse-Bettis fellow, 1958-59; Foundry Edn. fellow, 1952-57; recipient Adams award Am. Welding Soc., 1969, Teaching award Tau Beta Pi, 1970, 78. Fellow ASME, ASM Internat.; mem. ASTM, AIME, Am. Welding Soc., Am. Soc. Metals, Hillwood Country Club, Vines Golf and Country Club, Sigma Xi, Tau Beta Pi, Phi Eta Sigma, Alpha Sigma Mu, Pi Kappa Alpha, Pi Tau Sigma, Omicron Kappa Delta Methodist. Home: 2510 Ridgewood Dr Nashville TN 37215-4518 E-mail: jimwert@worldnet.att.net.

WERT, JONATHAN MAXWELL, II, management consultant; b. Port Royal, Pa., Nov. 8, 1939; s. Jonathan Maxwell and Helen Leona (Leonard) Wert; m. Wendy J. Mast; children: Jonathan Maxwell III, Kimberly Dee, Jon Adam, Justin Tyler, Amanda Elizabeth, Gabriel Chadwick, Emily Lauren. BS in Biology, Austin Peay State U., 1966, MS in Biology, 1968; PhD in Adminstrn., U. Ala., 1974. Park supt., chief interpretive services Bur. State Parks Pa. Dept. Environ. Resources, Harrisburg, 1968-69; chief naturalist Bays Mountain Park Environ. Edn. Ctr., Kingsport, Tenn., 1969-71; environ. and energy edn. specialist TVA, Knoxville, 1971-75; cons. energy, environment, conservation U. Tenn., Knoxville, 1975; sr. assoc.-energy Energy Extension Svc., Coop. Extension Svc., Pa. State U., 1977-80; pres. Energy-Environ. Consultants, Port Royal, Pa., 1981-85, Mgmt. Diagnostics, Inc., Port Royal, 1985—. Author: Writing Environmental Education Grant Proposals, 1974, Environmental Education Study Projects for High School Students, 1974, Environmental Education Study Projects for College Students, 1974, Developing Environmental Study Areas, 1974, Developing Environmental Education Curriculum Material, 1974, Finding Solutions to Environmental Problems . . . A Process Guide, 1975, Assessing an Issue in Relation to Environmental, Economic, and Social Impact . . . A Process Guide, 1976, Energy Conservation Measures for Mobile Home Dwellers, 1978, Selected Energy Conservation Options for the Home, 1978, Selected Energy Management Options for Small Business and Local Government, 1978, Life Lines: A Book of Poetry, Prose, and Axioms, 1983, Survivorship and Growth in Employment: A Question and Answer Guide, 1983; mem. adv. bd.: Environ. Edn. Report, 1974—; cons. editor: Jour. Environ. Edn, 1975; contbr. articles to profl. jours. Counselor Boy Scouts Am., 1975. Served with USMC, 1958-61. Recipient Conservation award Am. Motors Co., 1976 Mem. U.S. Energy Assn., Inst. Mgmt. Cons., Orgn. Devel. Inst., Inst. of Mgmt. Cons. (cert. mgmt. cons.), The Cons. Bur. (profl. mgmt. cons.). Lutheran. Home: RR 5 Box 250 Mifflintown PA 17059-9576 Office: Mgmt Diagnostics Inc PO Box 240 Port Royal PA 17082-0240 E-mail: jwert@mdi-wert.com.

WERTENBAKER, CHRISTIAN T. neuro-ophthalmologist, writer; b. NYC, June 10, 1943; s. Charles Christian and Lael Tucker Wertenbaker; m. Marilyn Kirby Lundquist, Apr. 2, 1970 (div. Feb. 1986); m. Caroline Randolf George, May 25, 1986; children: Charles Christian, Josee Timberlake Elena. Student, Harvard U, 1964—67; MD, N.Y. U, 1967—71; post doc. in Neurophysiology, Albert Einstein Coll. of Med., 1971—73. Diplomate Nat. Md. of Med. Examiners, Am. Bd. Psychiatry and Neurology in Neurology, Am. Bd. Ophthalmology. Intern Montefiore Med. Ctr., Bronx, NY, 1973—74, dir. Evoked Response Lab., 1978—80, asst. attending dept. neurology, 1978—80, asst. attending dept. ophthalmology, 1978—80, attending in neuro-ophthalmology, 2002; resident in neurology Albert Einstein Coll. Med., Bronx, 1974—77, resident in ophthalmology, 1980—83, rsch. assoc. vision and aging dept. neurology, 1990—91; Neuro-ophthalmology Fellow Columbia Presbyn. Med. Ctr., NYC, 1977—78; physician Montefiore Hosp. Headache Unit, Montefiore Med. Ctr., Bronx, 1976—85; attending dept. ophthalmology Montefiore Med. Ctr., Bronx Mcpl. Hosp., attending dept. neurology, 1983—; pvt. practice Bronx, 1983—; dir. Ophthalmology and Neuro-ophthalmology In-patient Consultation Svc. Montefiore Med. Ctr., Bronx Mcpl. Hosp., 1987; attending in neuro-ophthalmology Cath. Med. Ctr. of Bklyn. and Queens NY, 1993—, Brookdale Hosp. Med. Ctr., 1996—2000, Bronx Lebanon Hosp. Ctr., 1997—. Lectr., reviewer in field. Editor: Donbas, 1965, Parabola Mag.; contbr. chapters to books, articles to profl. jours. Recipient Bertram M. Gessner Mem. award, 1971. Mem.: North Am. Neuro-ophthalmology Soc., N.Y. Neuro-ophthalmology Forum, Am. Acad. of Ophthalmology, Walsh Soc. Avocation: music. Home: 379 City Island Ave Bronx NY 10464 Office: Private Practice 379 City Island Ave Bronx NY 10464

WERTHAMER, NATHAN RICHARD, physicist; b. Milw., Feb. 9, 1935; BA, Harvard Coll., 1956; PhD in physics, U. Calif., 1961. Rsch. assoc. U. Calif., San Diego, 1961-62; mem. tech. staff Bell Labs, 1962-75; mem. corp. planning dept. AT&T, 1975-76; chmn. N.Y. State Energy Rsch. and Devel. Authority, 1976-78; sr. advisor sci. and tech. dept. Exxon Corp., 1978-83; exec. dir. Becton Dickinson Devel. Corp., 1983-89; exec. officer Am. Phys. Soc., 1990-93; mgmt. cons. Chelsea Technols, N.Y.C., 1993—. Fellow AAAS, Am. Phys. Soc. Office: Chelsea Technols 43 W 16th St Apt 7D New York NY 10011-6321

WERTHEIM, JAY PHILIP, lawyer; b. Lexington, Mass., Jan. 19, 1952; s. Richard M. and Marion F. (Glazier) W.; m. Jeanette M. Alexander. BS, MA, Stanford U., 1974; JD, U. Calif., San Francisco, 1979. Bar: Calif. 1979, U.S. Ct. Appeals (9th cir.) 1979, U.S. Dist. Ct. (ea. and no. dists.) Calif. 1979. Cons. Bank of Am., San Francisco, 1974-75; fin. analyst Assoc. Freight Lines, Oakland, Calif., 1975-78; assoc. Dinkelspiel & Dinkelspiel, San Francisco, 1980-88, Perkins Coie, L.A., 1988-95; assoc. gen. counsel Baxter Healthcare Corp., Irvine, Calif., 1995—; v.p., assoc. gen. counsel Edwards Lifescis. Corp., Irvine, Calif., 2000—; asst. sec. Edwards Lifesci Corp., 2004—. Instr. legal writing and rsch. U. Calif., San Francisco, 1983-85; judge pro tem Mcpl. Ct. of State of Calif. L.A. Judicial Dist., 1991. Mem. ABA, Assn. Data Processing Svc. Orgns. (mem. lawyers' com. 1982-86), Bar Assn. San Francisco (com. on arbitration of fee disputes), Stanford Alumni Assn. (pres., bd. dirs. San Francisco chpt. 1980-84), Am. Assn. Equipment Lessors, Am. Arbitration Assn. (arbitrator), L.A. County Bar Assn., Orange County Bar Assn., The Asia Soc., L.A. World Affairs Coun., Buchanan Flying Club (v.p. 1981-82). Office: Edwards Lifesciences Corp One Edwards Way Irvine CA 92614-5627 Office Phone: 949-250-6815. E-mail: jay_wertheim@edwards.com.

WERTHEIM, MARY DANIELLE, elementary education coordinator; b. N.Y.C. d. Daniel Leo and Helen Loretta (Sudimick) Conroy; m. Stanley Claude Wertheim, Mar. 9, 1963. BA in English with honors, CCNY, 1960, MA, 1979. Coord. English and lang. arts Horace Mann Lower Sch., Riverdale, N.Y., 1969—. Pvt. investor Wertheim Trust, N.Y.C., 1985—; pres. winner's cir. Horace Mann Investment Club, Riverdale, 1989—. Founder, advisor Horace Mann Lower Sch. Cmty. Svc. Group, Riverdale, 1980—; active Rep. nat. Com., 1980—. Mem.: ASCD, Nat. Assn. Investors Corp., The Internat. Netsuke Soc. (sec. N.Y. chapter), Priory Scholars, Am. Firm, Mensa, The Grolier Club. Avocations: desk top publishing, manuscript collecting, frogs, sherlock holmes. Home: 180 Cabrini Blvd New York NY 10033-1138 Office: Horace Mann Lower Sch 4440 Tibbett Ave Bronx NY 10471-3416 E-mail: herbieboo@aol.com.

WERTHEIM, MITZI MALLINA, technology company executive; b. N.Y.C. d. Rudolf and Myrtle B. (McGraw) Mallina; m. Ronald P. Wertheim, Feb. 25, 1965 (div. July 1988); children: Carter, Tiana. BA, U. Mich., 1960. Asst. dir. div. research Peace Corps, Washington, 1961-66; sr. program officer Cafritz Found., Washington, 1970-76; dep. undersec. navy, 1977-81; with Fed. Sector Div. IBM, 1981-94; v.p. enterprise solutions SRA Corp., 1994-98, CNA Corp., 1998—. Woodrow Wilson vis. fellow, 1979, 80 Bd. dirs. Nat. Coalition Sci. and Tech., 1983—86; mem. vis. com. MIT, 1983—89; bd. dirs. Youth Policy Inst., 1986—91, VITA, 1990—2000, Cebrowski Inst., Naval Post Grad. Sch.; founder MIT Seminar XXI, 1985—. Recipient Federally Employed Women award Def. Dept., 1980; Disting. Pub. Svc. medal Navy Dept., 1981; fellow Maxwell Sch. Syracuse U., 1996-97. Mem.: Naval Studies Bd., Coun. on Fgn. Rels. Episcopalian. Home: 3113 38th St NW Washington DC 20016-3726

WERTHEIM, ROBERT HALLEY, national security consultant; b. Carlsbad, N.Mex., Nov. 9, 1922; s. Joseph and Emma (Vorenberg) W.; m. Barbara Louise Selig, Dec. 26, 1946; children: Joseph Howard, David Andrew. Student, N.Mex. Mil. Inst., 1940-42; BS, U.S. Naval Acad., 1945; MS in Physics, M.I.T., 1954; postgrad., Harvard U., 1969. Commd. ensign U.S. Navy, 1945, advanced through grades to rear adm., 1972; assigned Spl. Projects Office, Washington, 1956-61, Naval Ordnance Test Sta., China Lake, 1961-62, Office Sec. Def., Washington, 1962-65; head Missile br. Strategic Systems Project Office, Washington, 1965-67, dep. tech. dir., 1967-68, tech. dir., 1968-77, dir., 1977-80; sr. v.p. Lockheed Corp., 1981-88; cons. nat. def., 1988—. Emeritus mem. Draper Lab., Inc.; mem. U. Calif. Pres. Adv. Coun.; mem. sci. adv. group Dept. Def., Dept. Energy, U.S. Strategic Command; mem. nat. security adv. Lawrence Livermore Nat. Lab. Decorated D.S.M. with cluster, Legion of Merit, Navy Commendation medal, Joint Svc. Commendation medal; recipient Rear Adm. William S. Parsons award Navy League U.S., 1971, Chmn. Joint Chiefs of Staff Disting. Pub. Svc. award, 1996, Sec. of Def. medal for outstanding pub. svc., 1996. Fellow AIAA, Calif. Coun. Sci. Tech.; mem. Am. Soc. Naval Engrs. (hon. mem., Gold medal 1972), Nat. Acad. Engring., U.S. Naval Inst., Bernardo Heights Country Club, Sigma Xi, Tau Beta Pi. Home: 17705 Devereux Rd San Diego CA 92128-2084 Office: Sci Applications Internat Corp 16701 W Berardo Dr MS RB-2 San Diego CA 92127-3608 E-mail: rhwertheim@aol.com.

WERTHEIM, SALLY HARRIS, academic administrator, dean, education educator, consultant; b. Cleve., Nov. 1, 1931; d. Arthur I. and Anne (Manheim) Harris; m. Stanley E. Wertheim, Aug. 6, 1950; children: Kathryn, Susan B., Carole J. BS, Flora Stone Mather Coll., 1953; MA, Case Western Res. U., 1967, PhD, 1970. Cert. elem. and secondary edn. tchr., Ohio. Social worker U. Hosps., Cleve., 1953-54; tchr. Fairmount Temple Religious Sch., Cleve., 1957-72; mem. faculty John Carroll U., Cleve., 1969—, chair dept. edn., 1979—86, dean Grad. Sch., 1986—99, dir. planning and assessment, 1999—, interim dean, Coll. Arts & Scis., 2004—. Cons. in field; cons. Jennings Found., Cleve.; chmn. sch. com. Cleve. Commn. on Higher Edn., 1987-99. Contbr. articles to profl. jours. Sec. Cuyahoga County Mental Health Bd., Cleve., 1978—82; pres. Montefiore Home for Aged, Cleve., 1987—90; bd. dirs. Mt. Sinai Med. Ctr., Cleve., 1984—93, Cleve. Edn. Fund, 1992—94; chair edn. com. Cleve. Found. Commn. on Poverty, 1988—93, Cleve. Cmty. Bldg. Initiative, 1993—95, United Way Svcs., 1994—2001; trustee Mt. Sinai Health Care Found., 1998, Gerson Found., 1998, Miller Found., 1998, Begun Found., 2001, Mandel Found., 2001; pres. Jewish Family Svc. Assn., Cleve., 1974—77; v.p. Jewish Cmty. Fedn., 1988—91, pres., 1994—97, trustee, 1975, life trustee, 1997—. Named One of 100 Most Influential Women, Cleve. mag., 1983, One of 29 Most Influential Women, Cleve. Mag., 1997; recipient award John Carroll U., Curtis Miles award for cmty. svc., 1997; grantee Jennings Found., 1984-87, Cleve. and Gund Found., 1987-90, Lilly Found., 1988; S.H. Wertheim scholarship and edn. excellence award established John Carroll U., 1997. Mem. Am. Assn. Colls. for Tchrs. Edn. (bd. dirs. 1982-85), Ohio Assn. Colls. for Tchrs. Edn. (pres. 1981-83), Coun. of Grad. Schs. Avocations: flower arranging, travel, antiques. Office: John Carroll U Planning & Assessment Cleveland OH 44118

WERTHEIM, STEVEN BLAKE, orthopedist; b. Apr. 1, 1956; m. Melinda Mitchell; children: Meredith, Julia, Eve. BA, Northwestern U., 1977; MD, Case Western Reserve U., 1981. Cert. Am. Bd. orthopaedic Surgery, Ga., 1989. Intern in Surgery Univ. Hosp. Cleve., 1981-82; resident in orthopaedics, 1982-86; fellow in Sports Medicine U. Pa., 1986-87; asst. prof. Orthopaedic Surgery U. Pa. Sch. Medicine, 1987-88; faculty U.S. Sports Acad., 1995—; clin. asst. prof. Orthopaedics Emory U. Sch. Medicine, 1989—. Bd. trustees Atlanta Jewish Fedn.; com. Am. Israeli Pub. Affairs; regional v.p. Macabah USA/Sports for Israel; team physician East Paulding H.S., 1993-94 Atlanta Fire Ants U.S. Profl. roller Hockey League, 1993-94; chmn. Promina Windy Hill Bd. Dirs. 1993, 94, Kennestone Hosp at Windy Hill, 1992, 93; chief of staff elect Kennestone Hosp. at Windy Hill, 1991, 92; chief of Orthopaedics Kennestone Hosp. at Windy Hill, 1989, 91; Ambulatory Care Com., Cobb Hosp. and Med. Ctr., 1989, 91; O.r. Com. Kennestone Hosp. at Windy Hill, 1989-92; team physician Phila. Flyers, Atlanta Knights, U. Pa. athletic teams; pres. Resurgens Orhtop.; physician Olympic Village, 1996. Numerous lectures and exhibits in field; contbr. articles to profl. jours. Recipient Jesse T. Nicholson award, U. Pa. Dept. Orthopaedics, 1988, James Scholar award Psychology, 1977, Bus. Atlanta Forty Under Forty award, 1993. Mem. AMA, Am. Acad. Orthopaedic Surgeons, Arthroscopy Assn. N.Am., U.S. Olympic Com. Sports Medicine Soc., Nat. Athletic Trainers Assn., Southern Orthopaedic Assn., Southern Med. Assn. Office: C/O Resurgens Orthopaedics Ste 700 5671 Peachtree Dunwoody Rd NE 700 Atlanta GA 30342-5007

WERTHEIMER, ESTHER, sculptor; b. Poland; Student, Montreal Mus. Fine Arts, 1958-63, Internat. Acad., Austria, 1966, Acad. Belle Arte, Florence, Italy, 1967-68; BA, Loyola of Montreal, 1973; MA, Goddard Coll., 1975. Sculptures installed at Maimonides Hosp., Montreal, Can., Recreation Ctr., Pt. St. Lucie, Fla., Itami City Cultural Hall, Hyogo Prefecture, Japan, Okaloosa-Walton C.C., Niceville, Fla., Upper Iowa U., Fayette, Okayama Mcpl. Ctr., Japan, Health Care Ctr., Kyoto, Japan, Royal Palm Plaza, Boca Raton, Fla., Hikifune Cultural Ctr., Sumida-ku, Tokyo, 21st Century forest Park, Fukushima, Japan, Yumeji Mus. Okayama, Katsushika Performing Art Ctr., Tokyo, City of Hamura, Tokyo, Fukuoka City Hall, Japan, Hakone Open-Air Mus., Kanagawa-ken, Sun Bank, Palm Springs, Calif., North Miami Beach, Fla., Atrium of Alcan Aluminum Ltd., Montreal, Glouster City Hall for Carling Park of Commerce, East Ottawa, Joliette Mus., Que., Carling Exec. Pk., Ottawa, Cote St-Luc City Hall and Libr., Montreal, Conf. Bd. of Can., Ottawa, Douglas Hosp., Montreal, Gordon Gramm, Goulder, Colo., Livermore (Calif.) Pub. Libr., City of Palm Desert, Calif., others. Recipient awards Montreal Mus. Fine Arts, 1956-63, Borsa di Studio, Italian Govt., 1967-68, Govt. Que. Bource de l'Enseignement Superieur, 1974, Gold medal INT Tourismo, Rome, EUR Europa Premio, Rome, B'nai B'rith Internat. Arts award, 1997, others; grantee Can. Coun. Travel, 1967, Elizabeth T. Greenshields Meml., 1969, Govt. Can., 1989, 94. Home: 6507 Brava Way Boca Raton FL 33433-8239 also: 145 Radcliffe Montreal QC H4X 1C1 Canada Fax: 561-392-0065. Office Phone: 561-392-3503. E-mail: ewertheimer@ewertheimer.com.

WERTHEIMER, FREDRIC MICHAEL, public policy advocate; b. Bklyn., Jan. 9, 1939; s. Irving Wertheimer and Mildred (Klein) Van Brink; m. Linda Cozby, June 15, 1969. BA, U. Mich., 1959; LL.B., Harvard U., 1962. Bar: N.Y. bar 1963, D.C. bar 1971. Atty. SEC, 1963 66; legis. counsel Congressman Silvio Conte, 1967-68; counsel House Small Bus. Com., 1969-70; lobbyist, legis. dir., v.p. Common Cause, Washington, 1971-81, pres., 1981-95; news polit. analyst CBS News, Washington, 1996; pres. Democracy 21, 1997—. Fellow Press Politics and Policy Ctr. Harvard U., 1996; J. Skelly Wright fellow, vis. lectr. Yale Law Sch., 1997; polit. analyst ABC News, 1999-2000. Author: Common Cause Manual on Money and Politics. With U.S. Army, 1962-63. Fellow Inst. Politics Harvard U., 1972. Jewish. Home: 3502 Macomb St NW Washington DC 20016-3162

WERTS, MERRILL HARMON, retired management consultant; b. Nov. 17, 1922; s. Mack Allen and Ruth Martha (Badger) Werts; m. Dorothy Wilson, Mar. 22, 1946 (dec. Jan. 15, 2003); children: Stephen M., Riley J., Todd J., Kelly M. BS, Kans. State U., 1947; MS, Cornell U., 1948. Beef sales mgr. John Morrell & Co., Topeka, Memphis, 1948-53; dir. mktg. Kans. Dept. Agr., Topeka, 1953-55; sec.-treas. Falley's Markets, Inc., Topeka, 1955-58; v.p. S.W. State Bank, Topeka, 1958-65; pres. First Nat. Bank, Junction City, Kans., 1965-78; pvt. practice mgmt. cons. Junction City, 1978-98; ret., 1998. Pres. Junction City CC, 1975—76. Mem. adv. com. U.S. Comptroller Currency, 1971—72; mem. Topeka Bd. Edn., 1957—61, Kans. Bank Mgmt. Commn., 1967—71, Kans. Pub. Employees Rels. Bd., 1989—94, Kans. Commn. Future Health Care, 1991—94; trustee Kans. State U. Found., 1958—2001, Kans. Synod Presbyn. Westminster Found., 1965—72, Kans. Pub. Policy Inst., 1995—99; pres. Junction City Indsl. Devel., Inc., 1966—72, Junction City-Geary County United Fund, 1967—68; chmn. Kans. WWII Commemoration Com., 1995—96, Kans. Commn. Vets. Affairs, 1995—98, Geary County Pub. Bldg. Commn., 1996—99; civillian aide Sec. Army for Kans., 1991—95; mem. Kans. Senate, 1978—88; bd. dirs. Kans. Hist. Soc., 1989—97. 1st lt. inf. U.S. Army, 1943—46. Decorated Bronze Star, Purple Heart; named Outstanding State legis., Am. Legis. Exch. Coun., 1988; named to Inf. Officer Candidate Hall of Fame, 1981. Mem.: DAV, VFW, Kans. Livestock Assn., Kans. Farm Bur., Kans. Bankers Assn., Assn. Army Kans. (bd. dirs., v.p. 1979—84), Kans. State U. Alumni Assn. (pres. 1957), Assn. U.S. Army (Gen. Creighton W. Abrams medal 1997), Junction City Country Club (past pres.), Rotary (dist. gov. 1973—74), Am. Legion, Masons, Jesters, Shriners, Sigma Phi Epsilon. Republican. Presbyterian. Address: 1228 Miller Dr Junction City KS 66441-3312

WERTSMAN, VLADIMIR FILIP, librarian, information specialist, author, translator; b. Secureni, Romania, Apr. 6, 1929; came to U.S., 1967; s. Filip and Anna Wertsman. LLM summa cum laude, U. A.I. Cuza, Romania, 1953; MLS, Columbia U., 1969. Judge lower and appellate cts., Romania, 1953-67; examiner stock certs. 1st Nat. City Bank, N.Y.C., 1967-68; reference libr. sci. div. Bklyn. Pub. Libr., N.Y.C., 1969-74, sr. libr. Canarsie br., 1974-77, sr. libr. Greenpoint br., 1977-80, sr. libr. Leonard br., 1980-82; sr. libr., Slavic and Romanian specialist Donnell Libr. Ctr. N.Y. Pub. Libr., 1982-86; sr. libr. Learner's Adv. and Job Info. Ctr., 1987-93. Author, editor: The Romanians in America, 1748-1974, 1974, The Ukrainians in America, 1608-1975, 1976, The Russians in America, 1727-1970, 1977, The Armenians in America, 1618-1976, 1978, The Romanians in America and Canada, 1980, Librarian's Companion: A Handbook of Thousands of Facts and Figures on Libraries/Librarians, 1987, 2d edit., 1996, Career Opportunities for Bilinguals and Multilinguals: A Directory of Resources in Education, Employment and Business, 1991, 2d eidt., 1994, What's Cooking in Multicultural America, 1996, New York: The City in Over 500 Memorable Quotations From American & Foriegn Sources, 1996, paperback edit., 1999, Romanians in the United States and Canada: A Guide to Ancestry and Heritage Research, 2002, Directory of Ethnic and Multicultural Publishers, Distributors and Resource Organizations, 3d edit., 1995, 4th edit., 1999, 5th edit., 2003; co-author: Ukrainains in Canada and United States, 1981, Five Voices in Russian Literature, 1950s-1980s, 1986; editl. cons. Harvard Ency. Am. Ethnic Groups, 1980; contbr. Books, Libraries and Information in Slavic and East European Studies, 1986, Immigrant Labor Press in North America, 1840s-1970s, 1987, Through American Eyes, 1989, Ency. of N.Y.C., 1995; mem. adv. bd., contbr.: Gale Ency. Multicultural Am., 1995, 99; contbr. articles, book revs. to profl. jours. Recipient Disting. Lit. Achievement award Am. Soc. Writers, 1977. Mem. ALA (chair multilingual libr. materials and svcs. com. 1976-88, chair pub. and multicultural material com. of Emic Round Table Ala. 1989—, ethnic and multicultural info. exchange roundtable, spl. merit award 1988, David Cohen Emiert Multicultural award 2003), Am. Assn. Advancement of Slavic Studies, Am. Romanian Acad. Arts & Scis., Delta Tau Kappa. Avocations: chess playing, travel, stamp collecting/philately, dance. Personal E-mail: vladimirw@aol.com. *America is by its very nature of historical formation and development a multiethnic, multicultural and multilingual society. And if variety is the spice of life then American ethno-linguistic and cultural mosaique is the spice of our society. America's pluralism is also a microcosm of the entire world its citizens representing virtually all continents.*

WERTZ, JOHN ALAN, retired secondary school educator; b. Mpls., May 28, 1945; s. John Edward and Florence (Carlson) W.; m. Margaret M. Schlangen, 1993. BS, Hamline U., 1967; MS, St. Cloud State Coll., 1973; postgrad., George Washington U., 1985. Tchr. social sci. St. Cloud Cmty. Schs., St. Cloud, Minn., 1967—2002; ret., 2002. Trainer and field rep. New Games Found., San Francisco, 1980-83; tchr.-coach Apollo H.S. Mock Trial team, 1987-2000. Mem. com. social action Minn. Synod, Luth. Ch. Am., 1971-74; chair social action com. Salem Luth. Ch. Coun., St. Cloud, 1974-76; mem. affirmative action com. St. Cloud Cmty. Schs., 1975-78, co-chair student assistance com., 1982-83, mem. site coun. Apollo H.S., 1994-96, co-chair site coun. Apollo H.S., 1995-96; chair St. Cloud Human Rights Commn., 1979-83; adv. Ctrl. Minn. Sexual Assault Ctr., 1981-83; bd. dirs. St. Cloud Area Tenants' Assn., 1975-77, St. Cloud Area Spl. Olympics, 1982-83, United Way St. Cloud Area, 1996-2001, Minn. Edn. Assn., 1996-99; bd. dirs. Great River Roundtable, 1997-2003, sec., 1997-98; mem. Edn. Minn. Transition Bd., 1998-99, Edn. Minn. Governing Bd., 1999-2002; mem. St. Cloud Area Disabilities Coun., 1995—, pres., 2002—; bd. dirs. St. Cloud Area Family YMCA, 2001-, bd. sec., 2002-03, pres., 2003—; candidate for Minn. State Legislature, 2000, 02; counselor Sr. Corps of Ret. Execs., 2002—, chpt. chmn. 2003—. Recipient Merit award St. Cloud Area Coun. for Handicapped, 1976; grad. St. Cloud Area Leadership Program, 1995. Mem. NEA, Edn. Minn., St. Cloud Edn. Assn. (chair govtl. rels. coun. 1978-83, 88-96), Am. Hist. Soc. Germans from Russia, St. Cloud Area C. of C. (edn. divsn. 1992-97, vice-chmn. PreK-12 com. 1993-94, chair edn. recognition com. 1994-96, Thayer Youth Leadership steering com. 1995-97). Avocations: theatre arts, travel. Home: 816 Rilla Rd Saint Cloud MN 56303-1037

WERTZ, KENNETH DEAN, real estate executive; b. Oklahoma City, July 14, 1946; s. Walter K. and Kathryn L. (Moore) W.; children: Adam Troy, Kirsten Paige. BS in Acctg., Okla. State U., 1968, MS in Acctg. and Econs., 1969; JD, U. San Francisco, 1978. CPA, Okla., Calif; lic. real estate broker, Okla. Sr. acct. Deloitte, Haskins & Sells, San Francisco, 1969-70, 71-75; v.p. acquisitions, mng. dir. Landsing Corp., Menlo Park, Calif., 1975-86; pres. Detrick Salsberry Mgmt. Inc., Tulsa, 1987-88; v.p. asset mgmt. Corporex Co., Cin., 1989-90; exec. v.p. real estate Brunner Cos., Dayton, Ohio, 1990-92; pres. Pillar Real Estate Advisors, Dayton, 1992—. Lt. col. Med. Svc. corps U.S. Army, 1968-98. Decorated Army Commendation medal with three oak leaf clusters, Meritorious Svc. medal. Mem. AICPA, Okla. Soc. CPAs, Calif. Soc. CPAs, Nat. Assn. Securities Dealers (fin. prin., registered sales rep.). Republican. Methodist. Avocations: bicycling, snow and water skiing, racquetball, camping, fishing. Home: 835 Huntersknoll Ln Cincinnati OH 45230-4343 Office: Pillar Real Estate Advisors 5335 Far Hills Ave Ste 318 Dayton OH 45429-2317 Office Phone: 937-434-4250. E-mail: kdeanw@juno.com.

WESBERRY, JAMES PICKETT, JR., financial management consultant, auditor, international organization executive; b. Columbia, S.C., Sept. 22, 1934; s. James P. and Ruby L. (Perry) W.; m. Lea Esdras Casteneda, June 13, 1975; children: Jonathan Jesse, Perry Latimer, Ruby Lee Nilda; children by previous marriage: James Pickett III, Elisa Marie, Lillian Sue, Paul Armand. BBA, Ga. State U., 1955; LLD (hon.), Atlanta Law Sch., 1967; MPA, Am. U., 1983. CPA, Ga.; cert. internal auditor, fraud examiner, govt. fin. mgr., fin. svcs. auditor. Page U.S. Ho. Reps., 1949-51; acct., mgmt. cons. Atlanta, 1956-67; v.p. fin. and adminstrn. Computer Tech. South, Atlanta, 1969-70; sr. cons. Inst. Pub. Adminstrn., N.Y.C., 1967-69, 70-76; cons. to comptr. gen. Peru, 1970-74, 1974-78; adv., prof. Latin Am. Inst. Auditing Scis. Peruvian and Ecuadorean Sch. Govtl. Auditing, 1971-78; dir. sys., stds. and procedures Days of Inns Am., Inc., 1979-80; chief auditor OAS, Washington, 1980-82; cons. World Bank, 1982-83; prin. advisor acctg. and auditing pub. sector Latin Am. and Caribean Region, 1994-97; dir. America's accountability/anti-corruption project Casals & Assocs., Alexandria, Va., 1997—2001, dir. accountability audit, anti-corruption project Project -ATLATL-Mex., 2001—03; dir. anti-corruption project si Se Puede, Mgmt. Sys. Internat., Quito, Ecuador, 2003—. Founder, pres. Accountability 21, 1998—2003; advisor to pres. of Latin Am. Orgn. of Supreme Audit Instn., 1993—2000; sr. adv. to comptr. gen. U.S., 1983—85; dir. internat. ops. Price Waterhouse, 1985—88; sr. fin. advisor U.S.AID, 1988—93; pres., CEO Inst. Pub. Adminstrn., 1993—94, trustee; dir. N.Y. Bur. Mcpl. Rsch., 1993—94; mem. panel of experts in acctg. and auditing UN, 1972—82; adj. prof. Am. U., Washington, 1981—85; founding dir. Internat. Consortium Govtl. Fin. Mgmt., 1977—88, 1994—97, pres., 1984—87; cons., tchr. all Spanish-speaking We. Hemisphere nations Brazil, Haiti, Jamaica, The Netherlands Antilles, Guyana, Peoples Republic China, The Philippines, Can., U.S. Co-author: UN Handbook on Government Auditing for Developing Countries; editor: Latin American Manual of Professional Auditing in the Public Sector, Spanish Lang. newsletter Pistas de Auditoria, 1985-92; mem. editl. bd. Pub. Budgeting and Fin. Mgmt., 1982-92, The Govt. Accts. Jour.; contbr. articles to profl. jours. Mem. Ga. Senate, 1962-67, Fulton County Dem. Exec. Com., 1962-66. Decorated Order of Merit (Peru), 1972, Comptr. Gen. Venezuela, 1998; recipient Outstanding Career Achievement award USAID, 1993, Most Meritorious Accountant of the Americas award Interamerican Accounting Assn., 2003. Mem. AICPA (hon. life, chmn. interam. com. 1988-95), Interam. Acctg. Assn. (cert. assoc., bd. dirs. 1989-95, chmn. pub. sector com. 1989-91, 2000-2001, exec. com. 1994-95, Vet. Acct. Am. award 1987, Lifetime Acct. of Am. 1995, Most Meritorious Acct. 2003), Am. Acctg. Assn., Assn. Govt. Accts. (Authors award 1981-82, 89-90, chmn. internat. affairs com. 1981-82, 89-91), Inst. Internal Auditors (v.p. Latin Am. 1978-79, internat. rels. com. 1977-82, 84-88, regional dir. Latin Am. 1986-88, chpt. bd. govs. 1981-87, v.p. 1982-84, pres. 1984-85, vice chmn. internat. membership com. 1989-90, chpt. Disting. Svc. award 1987, Bradford Cadmus Meml. award internat. orgn. 1989, Outstanding Author's award 1990), Honduras CPA Soc. (Hon. award 1990), Jr. Chamber Internat. (life senator), Quito (Ecuador) Inst. Internal Auditors (life bd. dirs.), Lima Coll. Pub. Accts. (hon.), Lima Jr. C. of C. (hon.), Pinchicha (Ecuador) Coll. Pub. Accts. (hon.), Ecuador Fedn. Pub. Accts. (hon.). Baptist. Home: PO Box 17-22-20297 Cumbaya Quito Ecuador Office: Mgmt Sys Internat 600 Water St SW Washington DC 20024 E-mail: jimwes@sisepuede.com.ec., jimwes@mis-ecu.com.

WESBROOK, FREDERIC P. health facility administrator, physician; MD, Ind. U. Sch. Medicine, Indpls., 1970. Bd. cert. in Internal Medicine 1975, lic. State of Wisc. Intern Ind. U. Hosp., Indpls., 1971; resident Fitzsimmons Army Med. Ctr., Denver, 1975; pres. Marshfield (Wis.) Clinic, 2000—. Mem.: State Med. Soc. Wis. Office: Marshfield Clinic 1000 N Oak Ave Marshfield WI 54449

WESBURY, STUART ARNOLD, JR., health administration and policy executive, educator; b. Phila., Dec. 13, 1933; s. Stuart Arnold and Jennie (Glazewska) W.; m. June Carol Davis, Feb. 23, 1957; children: Brian, Brent, Bruce, Bradford. BS, Temple U., 1955; MHA, U. Mich., 1960; PhD, U. Fla., 1972. Dir. health svcs. USPHS, 1955, served as adminstrv. officer, hosp. and clinic pharmacist, resigned, 1958; adminstrv. asst. Del. Hosp., 1960-61; asst. adminstr. Bronson Meth. Hosp., 1961-66; assoc. dir., asst. prof. U. Fla. Tchg. Hosp., 1966-67, dir., assoc. prof., 1967-69; v.p. Computer Mgmt. Corp., Gainesville, Fla., 1969-72; dir., prof. grad. studies in health svcs. mgmt. U. Mo., Columbia, 1972-78; pres. Am. Coll. Healthcare Execs., Chgo., 1979-91; sr. v.p. TriBrook Group, Inc., Westmont, Ill., 1992-94; prof. Sch. of Health Adminstrn. and Policy Ariz. State U., Tempe, 1994-2000, dir., exec. edn. programs Coll. Bus., 1996-2000, prof. emeritus, 2000—. Chmn. bd. trustees Blood Sys., Inc., Scottsdale, Ariz. Co-author: Why We Spend Too Much on Health Care; contbr. articles to profl. jours. Bd. dirs. Health Task, Inc., Atlanta, Boys Clubs, Gainesville, Heartland Inst.; chmn. bd. dirs. Mid-Am. chpt. ARC, 1988-91, DuPage County Dist., 1984-87; active Boy Scouts Am.; chmn. adminstrv. bd. Meth. Ch.; trustee Nat. Blood Found.; Rep. Congl. candidate Dist. 13, Ill. Fellow Am. Coll. Health Care Adminstrs. (hon.), Am. Coll. Healthcare Execs. (Silver Medal award 1991); mem. APHA, Am. Hosp. Assn., Hosp. Mgmt. Sys. Soc., Assn. Univ. Programs in Health Adminstrn. (chmn. 1977-78), Am. Assn. Healthcare Cons. (hon.), Rotary (past pres.). Home and Office: 950 Willow Valley Lakes Dr H-312 Willow Street PA 17584 Business E-Mail: stu.wesbury@asu.edu.

WESCHCKE, CARL LLEWELLYN, publishing executive; BS, Babson Coll., 1951. Pres., publisher Llewellyn Worldwide Ltd., St. Paul, 1957—. Mem. Pub. Roundtable Minn. Home: 16363 Norell Ave N Marine On Saint Croix MN 55047-9747 Office: Llewellyn Worldwide Ltd 84 Wabasha St S Saint Paul MN 55107-1803

WESCOTT, JOSEPH WARREN, II, academic administrator, education educator; b. Wilmington, N.C., July 19, 1959; s. James Warren and Delores (Pridgen) Wescott; m. Lisa Ann Blanton (div. Oct. 2002); children: Rachel, Joseph, Rose. BA, Wake Forest U., Winston-Salem, N.C., 1981; MS, N.C. State U., Raleigh, N.C., 1998; MA, Wake Forrest U., Winston-Salem, N.C., 2000; postgrad. in Edn., N.C. State U., 2003—04. Officer U.S. Army, Columbia, SC, 1984—87, U.S. Army Res., Garner, NC, 1987—94; dir. alt. learning ctr. Beulaville Mid. Sch., NC, 1988; bus. mgr. Associated Ins. Agy., Wallace, NC, 1989—96; dir. of grants and spl. projects Duplin County Hist. Assn., Rose Hill, NC, 1998—2000; coll. instr. James Sprunt C.C., Kenansville, NC, 1999—2001; fed. rels. analyst Duke U., Durham, NC, 2001—03. Assoc. AAU Coun. on Fed. Rels., Washington, 2002—03; U. rep. The Sci. Coalition, Washington, 2001—03; com. mem. Edn. Adv. Com. and Ind. Agts., Raleigh, NC, 1998—2002. Editor: (book) 1870 Fed. Census: The African Am. Population in Duplin County, 2000; author (contbr.): Ency. of N.C., 2002. Lay Pastor Town Creek Christian Ch., Winabow, NC, 1990—; bd. mem. Duplin County 250th Celebration, Kenansville, NC, 2000. Cap. U.S. Army, 1984—87, S.C. Rsch. grant, N.C. State U., 1998—2000, full fellowship, Wake Forest U., Winston-Salem, N.C., 1982—84. Mem.: Phi Alpha Theta, Phi Kappa Phi. Pentecostal. Avocations: reading, gardening, travel, public speaking. Home: 3225 Oxford Dr Durham NC 27707-3844 Office: Duke Univ Office Pub Rels Durham NC 27708 E-mail: history@post.com.

WESCOTT, WILLIAM BURNHAM, oral maxillofacial pathologist, educator; b. Pendleton, Oreg., Nov. 10, 1922; s. Merton Girard and Josephine (Creasey) W.; m. Barbara L., Dec. 31, 1944 (dec. June 12, 1969); children: William Douglas, Diane Elizabeth; m. Gloria Greer-Collins, Aug. 28, 1989. DMD, U. Oreg., Portland, 1951, MS, 1962. Asst. prof. to assoc. dean admin. U. Oreg. Dental Sch., Portland, 1953-72; co-dir. oral disease rsch. VA, Houston, 1972-75, dir. dental edn. ctr. L.A., 1980-85; acting dir. Reg. Med. Edn. Ctr., Birmingham, Ala., 1978-80; chief dental svc. Dept. of Veteran's Affairs, San Francisco, 1985-94; clin. prof. U. Calif., San Francisco, 1994—; cons. Northern System of Clinics Dept. Vets. Affairs, 1994—. Dental surgeon, Oreg. Air N.G., Portland, 1954-68; cons. Madigan Army Med. Ctr., Ft. Lewis, W. Va., 1971-74, VA Med. Ctrs., No. Calif., 1985—, prof. pathology Duke U. Med. Sch., 1977-79; cons. U. Med. Ctr., Fresno, 1998—. Contbr. 80 articles to profl. jours. and several chpts. to profl. books; 4 chpts. to books. Dist. chmn. Boys Scouts Am., Portland, 1965-67; bd. dirs. Am. Cancer Soc., Portland, 1964-67; comdr. Veterans Foreign Wars Post 5731, Gridley, Calif., 1994-95, comdr., 1996-98; chmn. Mil. Vets Ct. of Honor Meml., No. Calif., 1997—. With Oreg. N.G., 1938-40; with U.S. Army, 1940-42; lt. col. USAF, 1942-68. Decorated DFC with oak leaf cluster, USAF, Oreg. N.G. Merit Svc. Medal, Portland, Fedn. des Anciens Combattants Français medal, 1944. Fellow Am. Acad. Oral and Maxillofacial Pathology, Mil. Officers Assn. Am. (sec. 2000—), Omicron Kappa Upsilon, Sigma Xi. Avocations: woodworking, fishing. Home: 437 Justeson Ave Gridley CA 95948-9434 Office: U Calif Sch Dentistry S 512 San Francisco 3rd & Parnassus San Francisco CA 94143-0424 Office Phone: 415-476-4866. Business E-Mail: wesco@manznet.com.

WESELY, EDWIN JOSEPH, lawyer; b. N.Y.C., May 16, 1929; s. Joseph and Elizabeth (Peles) W.; children: Marissa Celeste, Adrienne Lee; m. Marcy Brownson, Sept. 23, 1992. Ed., Deep Springs Coll., 1945-47; AB, Cornell U., 1949; JD, Columbia U., 1954. Bar: N.Y. 1954, D.C. 1985, U.S. Supreme Ct. 1960, others. Law clk. to judge U.S. Dist. Ct. (so. dist.) N.Y., 1954-55; asst. U.S. atty. So. Dist. N.Y., 1955-57; assoc. Winthrop, Stimson, Putnam & Roberts, N.Y.C., 1957-63, ptnr., 1964-2000; sr. counsel Pillsbury Winthrop LLP, N.Y.C., 2001—. Spl. master numerous cases; chmn. spl. com. on effective discovery in civil cases U.S. Dist. Ct. (ea. dist.) N.Y., 1982-84, com. on civil caseflow, 1985-88, com. on civil litigation, 1988-2002, chmn. emeritus, 2002—, civil justice reform adv. group, 1990-95; mem. com. on pretrial phase civil cases Jud. Coun. 2d Cir., 1984-86, standing com. on improvement civil litigation, 1986-89; ex-officio Civil Justice Reform Act adv. group U.S. Dist. Ct. (so. dist.) N.Y.; pres. CARE, 1986-89, chmn., 1978-86, 89-90, internat. bd. dirs., 1981-90, pres., 1987-90; bd. dirs. Internat. Rescue Com., 1960-; bd. dirs., exec. com. Internat. Ctr. in N.Y., 1990—, chmn., 1998-2003, chmn. emeritus, 2003-. Trustee Deep Springs Coll., 1991-2000; vice-chair, 1998-2000. Decorated Order of Civil Merit (Republic of Korea); recipient World Humanitarian award Fgn. Press Assn., 1988, Commendation Bd. Judges U.S. Dist. Ct. (ea. dist.) N.Y., 1993, Deep Springs Medal, Deep Springs Coll., 2003. Fellow Am. Coll. Trial Lawyers; mem. ABA (spl. adv. com. on internat. activities 1990-93, litigation sect. chmn. com. on discovery 1977-78, spl. com. study discovery abuse 1977-82, chmn. task force on liaison with internat. profl. assns. on matters of mutual concern 1989-93, Civil Justice Reform Act task force 1991-93, task force on the state of the justice sys. 1993-95, fed. initiatives task force 1995-98, co-chmn. task force on fed. and local rules 1997-98), UN Assn. U.S.A. (bd. dirs. 1991—2004), Assn. of Bar of City of N.Y. (com. chmn., organized demonstration observation panel), Coun. on Fgn. Rels., River Club. Office: Pillsbury Winthrop LLP 1540 Broadway New York NY 10036-4039 Office Phone: 212-858-1712. Business E-Mail: ewesely@pillsburywinthrop.com.

WESELY, MARISSA CELESTE, lawyer; b. N.Y.C., Apr. 25, 1955; d. Edwin Joseph and Yolanda Teresa (Pyles) W.; m. Frederick Hamerman; 1 child, Emma Elizabeth Wesely Allen. BA magna cum laude, Williams Coll., 1976; JD cum laude, Harvard U., 1980. Bar: N.Y. 1981. Assoc. Simpson Thacher & Bartlett, N.Y.C., 1980-82, 84-88, ptnr., 1989—, assoc. London, 1982-84. Lectr., cons. Harvard Inst. Internat. Devel., Beijing, 1981, Jakarta, Indonesia, 1982; guest lectr. Yale Law Sch., New Haven, 1991; spkr. Am. Conf. Inst., Practicing Law Inst., Bankers Assn. for Fgn. Trade, N.Y. State Bar Assn. confs., 1993—. Bd. dirs. City Lore, N.Y.C. Mem. N.Y.C. Bar Assn., N.Y. State Bar Assn. (mem. exec. com. sect. internat. law and practice), Internat. Bar Assn., Phi Beta Kappa.

WESEMAN, VICKI LYNNE, elementary school educator; b. Hastings, Nebr., Oct. 29, 1954; d. Virgil John and Vera Lillie (Berg) Kennedy; m. Creighton Lee Weseman, May 28, 1988 (div. Oct. 1999); 1 child, Jason K. BS, U. Nebr., 1977, MA, 1988. Cert. elem. tchr. Nebr., profl. tchr. Nebr. Elem. tchr. Hanover Elem. Sch., Glenvil, Nebr., 1977—2003, Lincoln Elem. Sch., Grand Isle, Nebr., 2003—. Pres. Adams County Edn. Assn., Hastings, Nebr., 1996—97; team leader stds. Adams County Schs., Hastings, 2000—01. Oregon Trail rodeo pageant coord. Adams County Agrl. Soc., Hastings, 1992—. Named Miss Rodeo, Nebr., 1977, Com. Person of Yr., Oregon Trail Rodeo, Hastings, 1999. Mem.: Nebr. Edn. Assn. (mem. selection com. 2000), Women's Profl. Rodeo Assn. Democrat. Lutheran. Avocation: barrel racing in rodeo. Home: 835 Briggs Ave Hastings NE 68901 Office: Lincoln Elem 805 Beal St Grand Island NE 68801

WESKAMP, KELLEY S. loan account manager, real estate company executive; b. Boulder City, Nev., Jan. 9, 1964; d. Dale P. and Phyllis J. (Cooper) W. BA in English Lang. Lit. with distinction, Loretto Heights Coll., 1985. Cons. Ely Leadership Mgmt., Lakewood, Colo., 1985-88; budget asst. Bureau Reclamation, Denver, 1988-90; real estate owned technician FDIC, Denver, 1990-93; real estate specialist Westfall and Co., Westminster, 1993-95, account mgr., 1995-97, Castle Advisors subs. Chgo. Title, 1998-99; sr. account mgr. Litton Loan Servicing, Houston, 1999—. Participant Bench Mark Study, Pete Marwick Assocs., 1997. Contbr. article to mag. Democrat. Roman Catholic. Avocations: weaving, reading, travel, cooking. Home: 12080 W Mexico Ave Lakewood CO 80228-3909

WESLER, KEN, performing arts company executive; b. Phila., Apr. 3, 1964; s. Irwin Harvey and Marcia Elaine (Trilling) W.; m. Deborah Lee Rader, Nov. 2, 1986; children: Alexander, Samantha. BA, Temple U., 1994. Prodn. mgr. The Wilma Theatre, Phila., 1983-89; gen. mgr. Gretna Prodns., Inc., Mt. Gretna, Pa., 1989, 90, Walnut St. Theatre, Phila., 1989-95; exec. dir. The Grand Opera House, Wilmington, 1995—. Guest lectr. Cabrini Coll., Phila., 1988, Temple U., Phila., 1988—. Bd. dirs. MBNA Excellence in Edn. Found., Downtown Visions. Mem. The Wilma Theater. Office: The Grand Opera House 818 N Market St Wilmington DE 19801-3011 Office Phone: 302-658-7897. E-mail: kwesler2000@yahoo.com.

WESLEY, JOHN MERCER, artist; b. LA, Nov. 25, 1928; s. Ner Wesley and Elsa Marie (Patzwaldt) W.; m. Hannah Allen Green, Dec. 18, 1971; children: Christine Alice, Ner. Student, Los Angeles City Coll., UCLA, 1947-50. One-man shows include, Robert Elkon Gallery, N.Y.C., 1963-80, 84, Premio Internat., Instituto Torcuato di Tella, Buenos Aires, 1967, Documenta 5, Kassel, 1972, Carl Solway Gallery, Cin., 1972, 85, 89, Galerie Rudolf Zwirner, Cologne, 1973, Rush Rhees Gallery, U. Rochester, 1974, PS 1, N.Y.C., 1978, Reinhard Onnasch Ausstellungen, Berlin, 1982-83, 101 Spring St. Gallery, N.Y.C., 1987, fiction/non fiction, N.Y.C., 1990, 91, Chinati Found., Marfa, Tex., 1990, 98, Daniel Weinberg Gallery, Santa Monica, Calif., 1992, 98, Portikus, Frankfurt, 1993, Stedelijk Mus., Amsterdam, 1993, Kunstverein, Ludwigsburg, Germany, 1993, daad-Galerie, Berlin, 1993, Galerie Rolf Ricke, Cologne, 1994, José Freire Gallery, N.Y.C., 1994, Jessica Fredericks Gallery, N.Y.C., 1996, 98, 99, 2000, 01, 02, 03, Galerie Haus Schneider, Karlsruhe, Germany, 1996, Danese Gallery, N.Y.C., 1998, P.S.1 Contemporary Art Ctr., N.Y.C., 2000-01, Sert Gallery, Harvard U., 2001, Gagosian Gallery, London, 2001, Daniel Weinberg Gallery, L.A., 2002, 04; group exhbns. include, Whitney Mus., 1968, 69, 76, Indpls. Mus., 1976, Royal Academy, London, 1991, Mus. Contemporary Art, L.A., 1992-93, Mus. Beaux Arts, Montreal, 1992-93, Deichtorhallen, Hamburg, 1997, Kunsthaus, Zürich, 1997; represented in permanent collections Albright-Knox Mus., Buffalo, Mus. Modern Art, N.Y.C., U. Tex., Austin, Mpls. Soc. Fine Arts., Chinati Found., Marfa, Tex., Rose Art Gallery, Brandeis U., Waltham, Mass., U. Kentucky, Lexington, Kunstmuseum, Basel, Switzerland, Dayton (Ohio) Mus. Art, Portland (Oreg.) Art Mus., Whitney Mus., Stedelijk Mus., Speed Mus., Louisville, Ky. Guggenheim fellow, 1976; grantee Nat. Endowment Arts, 1989. Address: 27 Washington Sq N New York NY 10011

WESLEY, LATONYA RASHAWN, legislative assistant; b. Detroit, Oct. 22, 1974; Student, Spelman Coll., 1992-94; BA in Polit. Sci., Mich. State U., 1997; postgrad., U. Balt., 2002—. Legis. corrd. U.S. Senate, Washington, 1998-99; adminstrv. asst. APA, Washington, 1999-2000, legis. asst., 2000—. Contbr. to Psychol. Sci. Agenda. Legis. intern Mich. State Senate, Lansing, 1997; vol. Atlanta Project, 1993, Econ. Crisis Ctr., East Lansing, Mich., 1996, Debbie Stabenow Campaign for U.S. Ho. of Reps., East Lansing, 1996, Make a Difference Day, Ft. Meade, Md., 1998-99, AIDS Walk, Washington, Walk for Wellness-Am. Heart Assn., Balt., 1999, ARC, East Lansing, 1997; mentor, tutor Cornerstone Charter Sch., Washington, 1998; telefundraiser Am. Cancer Soc., East Lansing, 1997; mentor Brent Elem. Sch., Washington, 1998. Mem. Mich. State U. Alumni Assn., Zeta Phi Beta (grammateus 2000-02, Md. del. Rho Eta Zeta chpt. 2001, 2d anti-basileus, 2002—, fundraising chmn., 2001-02, fundraising co-chmn., 2002—), LEST Club. Office: APA 750 1st St NE Washington DC 20002 Home: 6537 Penn Ave #102 Forestville MD 20747 Fax: 202-336-6063. E-mail: lwesley@apa.org, rashawn74@netstorm.net.

WESLEY, NORMAN H. metal products executive; b. 1949; BA, MBA, U. Utah, 1973. With Crown Zellerbach Corp., San Francisco, 1973—83; pres., CEO, Fortune Brands Home & Office ACCO World Corp., Wheeling, Ill., 1983—99; pres. & COO Fortune Brands, Inc., Lincolnshire, Ill., 1999, chmn & CEO, 1999—. Office: Fortune Brands Inc 300 Tower Pkwy Lincolnshire IL 60069-3640

WESLEY, RICHARD C. federal judge; b. Canandaigua, N.Y., Aug. 1, 1949; s. Charles and Beatrice W.; m. Kathryn Rice; 2 children. BA summa cum laude, SUNY, Albany, 1971; JD, Cornell U., 1974. Assoc. Harris, Beach & Wilcox, 1974-76; assoc. atty. Welch, Streb & Porter, 1976-77; ptnr. Streb, Porter, Meyer & Wesley, 1977—87; asst. counsel to minority NY State Assembly, 1979—82; justice Supreme Ct. 7th Jud. Dist., 1987—94; supervising judge Criminal Cts. 7th Jud. Dist., 1991; judge appellate div. Supreme Ct. 4th Dept., 1994—96; assoc. judge N.Y. Ct. Appeals, Albany, 1997—2003; circuit judge U.S. Ct. Appeals, (2nd cir.), New York, NY, 2003—. Creator Felony Screening Program, 1993; lectr. in field; bd. trustees Ctr. Dispute Resolution, Pre-Trial Svcs. Corp. Editor: Cornell Law Rev. Asst. counsel to Assembly Rep. leader James L. Emery, 1979-1982; assemblyman N.Y. State 136th Assembly Dist., 1982-84, 84-86; chair Livingston County Alcohol and Drug Abuse Prevention Coun.; bd. trustees United Ch. Livonia, Chances and Changes, Charles Settlement House; bd. dirs. Myers' Found.; driver Livonia Vol. Ambulance. Named Legislator of Yr., Livingston-Wyoming Assn. Retarded Citizens, 1988; recipient Disting. SUNY Alumni award SUNY Alumni Assn., 1997. Fellow N.Y. State Bar Found.; mem. Livingston County Bar Assn. (sec.), Supreme Ct. Justices Assn. (pres. 7th jud. dist.). Office: 1702 US Courthouse 40 Centre St New York NY 10007-1561

WESLEY, STEPHEN BURTON, training professional; b. Louisville, July 13, 1949; s. Leon and Montie C. (Burton) W.; m. Kun Wanna Jarusin, May 22, 1972; 1 child, Thomas Jayson. AA, Somerset (Ky.) Coll., 1969; student, Community Coll. of Air Force, Maxwell, AFB, 1970-77; AA, Watterson Coll., 1977; student, U. Louisville, 1978-80. Cert. energy mgr., lighting efficiency profl. Electronics tech. Kegco, Somerset, 1973-74; instrument tech. Ky. Air Nat. Guard, Louisville, 1974-78; application engr. Johnson Controls, Inc., Louisville, 1978-81, sales engr., 1981-88, energy svcs. mgr., 1988-96; regional tng. dir. Excel Telecom., 1995—. Adv. bd. Ivy Tech Vocat. Sch., Jeffersonville, Ind., 1988-90. Inventor pitot tube removal tool. Lay dir. Walk to Emmaus, Elizabethtown, Ky., 1989. Sgt. USAF, 1969-73. Mem. Assn. Energy Engrs. Methodist. Avocations: fishing, reading, church work, investments, genealogy. Home and Office: 5304 Bloomfield Ln Louisville KY 40219-5191

WESLEY, VIRGINIA ANNE, real estate property manager; b. Seattle, Apr. 29, 1951; d. Albert William and Mary Louise (Heusser) W. BA in Speech, U. Hawaii, Hilo, 1978. Cert. property mgr. Mgr. office, traffic Radio Sta. KIPA, Hilo, 1972-74; reporter West Hawaii Today, Kailua-Kona, Hawaii, 1974; mgr. office U. Hawaii, Hilo, 1975-78; dir. property mgmt. First City Equities, Seattle, 1978-88, Winvest Devel. Corp., Seattle, 1988-89; with Quadrant Corp, Bellevue, Wash., 1992-98; dir. property mgmt. Fisher Properties, Inc., Seattle, 1998—2003; dir. investor rels. Shohomish County Econ. Devel. Coun., Everett, Wash., 2004—. Instr. Bellevue (Wash.) C.C., 1982-85. Bd. dirs. Mayor's Small Bus. Task Force, Seattle, 1981-83, 1st Hill Improvement Assn., Seattle, 1982—; active Goodwill Games, Seattle, 1990, Kauri Investments, Ltd., Seattle, 1991-92. Mem. Inst. Real Estate Mgmt., Internat. Coun. Shopping Ctrs., Bldg. Owners and Mgrs. Assn. (bd. trustees 2001—), Comml. Real Estate Women, Women's Bus. Exch., Seattle-King County Bd. Realtors, Big Island Press Club, Phi Kappa Phi. Home: 5143 S Wildwood Ln Seattle WA 98118-4252 Business E-Mail: gwesley@shoedc.org. E-mail: gingerwesley@msn.com.

WESLEY, WILLIAM MATTHEW, lawyer; b. Green Bay, Wis., Dec. 19, 1943; BEE, Marquette U., 1966; JD cum laude, Loyola U., Chgo., 1971. Bar: Ill. 1971, U.S. Dist. Ct. (no. dist.) Ill. 1982, U.S. Ct. Appeals (7th cir. and fed. cir.) 1976, U.S. Supreme Ct. 1992. Engr. Tex. Instruments, Motorola; ptnr. McAndrews, Held & Malloy, Ltd., Chgo. Hearing officer Ill. Pollution Control Bd., 1972-85. Named one of Leading Experts in Patent Law, Euromoney Mag., 1997-99. Mem. ABA, Chgo. Bar Assn., Am. Intellectual Property Law Assn., Fed. Cir. Bar Assn., Intellectual Property Law Assn. Chgo., Internat. Trade Commn. Trial Lawyers Assn. (exec. com. 1991—), Licensing Execs. Soc., Tau Beta Pi, Eta Kappa Nu, Alpha Sigma Nu. Office: McAndrews Held & Malloy Ltd 500 W Madison St Fl 34 Chicago IL 60661-2511 E-mail: bwesley@mhmlaw.com.

WESSEL, HARRY, political scientist, educator, director; b. Balt., Md., June 13, 1954; s. Harry and Lillan Elizabeth Wessel; 1 child, Jakob Harry. BA, U. Md., 1977; MA, SUNY, Buffalo, 1980, PhD, 1984. Lectr. SUNY, Buffalo, 1980—81; vis. asst. prof. U. Md., Balt., 1981—83, Colgate U., Hamilton, NY, 1983—84; asst. prof. Northeastern U., Boston, 1984—87; assoc. prof. Merrimack Coll., North Andover, Mass., 1987—, chair polit. sci. dept., 1994—, dir. comm. studies, 1997—. Contbr. chapters to books. Cons. Rep. John Turney for Congress, Salem, Mass., 1994—96. Unitarian Universalist. Avocation: running. Home: 17 Japonica St Salem MA 01970 Office: Merrimack Coll 315 Turnpike Rd North Andover MA 01845

WESSEL, HENRY, photographer; b. Teaneck, N.J., July 28, 1942; s. Henry and Jennie (Cincotta) W.; children by previous marriage: Nicholas, Rider. BA, Pa. State U., 1966; M.F.A., SUNY, Buffalo, 1972. Propr., mgr. comml. photog. studio, State Coll., Pa., 1966-68; cinematographer for documentary film Dept. HEW, 1967; instr. dept. art Pa. State U., Phila., 1967-69; prof. dept. photography San Francisco Art Inst., 1973-98, chmn. grad. program photography, 1977-78, chmn. dept. photography, 1987-93; asst. prof. San Francisco State U., 1974-75; vis. lectr. photography various colls. and art schs., 1967-81; propr., dir. Photographic Resources, Point Richmond, Calif., 1977—. Vis. artist Mills Coll., 1987-88 One-man show at Mus. Modern Art, N.Y.C., 1973, Mus. Contemporary Art, L.A., 1998; represented in permanent collections, Mus. Modern Art, N.Y.C., Phila. Mus. Art, Boston Mus. Fine Arts, Library of Congress, Am. Arts Documentation Center, Exeter, Eng., Nat. Gallery of Can., Ottawa; author: Henry Wessel, 1987, House Pictures, 1992, Night Walk, 2000, Odd Photos, 2002. Guggenheim fellow, 1971, 78; Nat. Endowment Arts fellow, 1975, 77, 78 Home: PO Box 475 Richmond CA 94807-0475

WESSEL, MORRIS ARTHUR, retired pediatrician; b. Providence, Nov. 1, 1917; s. Morris Jacob and Bessie (Bloom) Wessel; m. Irmgard Rosenzweig, June 1, 1952; children: David, Bruce, Paul, Lois. BA, Johns Hopkins U., 1939; MD, Yale U., 1943. Diplomate Am. Bd. Pediat. Intern Babies Hosp., NYC, 1943-44; fellow in pediat. Mayo Found., Rochester, Minn., 1947-48; rooming-in fellow in pediat. Yale U. Sch. Medicine, 1948-51; asst. dir. pediatric outpatient clinic Yale-New Haven Hosp., 1951-52, dir. pediatric outpatient clinic, 1952-57; staff pediatrician, collaboration project Yale U. Sch.

Medicine, 1957-62, instr. pediat., 1950-53, clin. asst. prof., 1963—71, clin. assoc. prof., 1961-75, clin. prof., 1975-97; ret., 1997. Bd. dirs. Clifford Beers Child Guidance Clinic, New Haven, 1950—55, cons. pediatrician, 1967—; bd. dirs. Women's Health Svc., New Haven, 1992—97, Child Welfare League, NYC, 1979—91. Author: Parents Book on Raising a Healthy Child, 1987. Maj. U.S. Army, 1944—47, ETO. Mem.: New Haven County Med. Soc., Conn. Med. Soc., Soc. Adolescent Medicine, Am. Acad. Pediatrics (Practitioner Rsch. award 1994, C. Anderson Aldrich award 1997). Office: Clifford Beers Clinic 93 Edwards St New Haven CT 06515 Fax: 203-387-1927. E-mail: mwessel@snet.net.

WESSELINK, DAVID DUWAYNE, finance company executive; b. Webster City, Iowa, Sept. 5, 1942; s. William David and Lavina C. (Haahr) W.; m. Linda R. DeWitt, Dec. 27, 1971; children: Catherine, Bill. BA in Bus., Ctrl. Coll., 1964; MBA, Mich. State U., 1970. Tchr. Peace Corps, Turkey, 1964-66, Karabuk Koleji, Turkey, 1967-68, Robert Koleji, Turkey, 1969-70; rsch. analyst Household Fin. Corp., Chgo., 1971-73, asst. dir. rsch., 1973-77, asst. treas. Prospect Heights, Ill., 1977, v.p., dir. rsch., 1977-82, group v.p., CFO, 1982-86, sr. v.p., CFO, 1986—; v.p., treas. Household Internat., Prospect Heights, 1988-93; sr. v.p., CFO Advanta Corp., 1993-98; exec. v.p., CFO Metris Cos., Saint Louis Park, Minn., 1998-2000, vice chmn., 2000—02, chmn., CEO, 2002— . Bd. dirs. CTC Internat., Chicago Heights, Ill., Am. Fin. Svcs. Assn., Saxon Capital Corp., Glen Allen, Va.; mem. U.S. regional bd. Mastercard Internat., 2003—. Bd. dirs. Ctrl. Coll., Pella, Iowa, 1990—. Mem.: Fin. Execs. Inst., Econ. Club Chgo. Office: Metris Cos 10900 Wayzata Blvd Minnetonka MN 55305 E-mail: david.wesselink@metriscompanies.com.

WESSELKAMPER, SUE, academic administrator; m. Tom Wesselkamper; 2 children. BA History, Govt., Edgecliff Coll.; M Social Work, U. Mich.; PhD Social Welfare, CUNY. Head cmty., social svs. program New River Cmty. Coll.; dir. social work field instrn. program Radford U., Va.; dean sch. arts and scis., assoc. prof. social work Coll. New Rochelle, NY; pres. Chaminade U. Honolulu, 1995—. Author: Enhancing Ethnic Identity Through Cross-Cultural Interaction, An Intercultural Approach to Contemporary Ethnicity, Issues in Implementing Cultural Diversity Content, Role of the Social Worker in Health Planning. Chmn. bd. dirs. Family Svcs. Westchester County, NY; mem. adv. com. Pew Charitable Trust 3d Black Colls. Project on Student Retention; mem. Hawaii Cath. Conf., Hawaii State Network of Am. Coun. on Edn.'s Women Leaders in Higher Edn. Avocations: reading, movies, hiking, travel. Office: Chaminade U of Honolulu 3140 Waialae Ave Honolulu HI 96816

WESSELMANN, GLENN ALLEN, retired hospital executive; b. Cleve., Mar. 21, 1932; s. Roy Arthur and Dorothy (Oakes) W.; m. Genevieve De Witt, Sept. 6, 1958; children: Debbie, Scott, Janet. AB, Dartmouth, 1954; MBA with distinction, Cornell U., 1959. Research aide Cornell U., Ithaca, N.Y., 1958-59; adminstrv. resident Meml. Hosp., N.Y.C., 1957-58, adminstrv. asst., 1959-61, asst. adminstr., 1961-65, asst. v.p., 1965-68; v.p. for adminstrn. Meml. Hosp. for Cancer and Allied Diseases, N.Y.C., 1968-79; exec. v.p., chief operating officer St. John Hosp., Detroit, 1979-84; pres., CEO St. John Health System, 1984-95, vice chmn., 1995-97; chmn., pres., CEO St. John Hosp. & Med. Ctr., 1984-94, ret., 1995. Mem. bus. adv. bd. City of Detroit, 1991-95, chmn., 1993-94; mem. exec. com. Greater Detroit Area Health Coun.; bd. dirs. Caymich Ins. Co. Ltd., Mich. Health Care Alliance, SelectCare, Detroit Econ. Growth Corp. Trustee Sisters of St. Joseph Health System 1981-94, Sisters of St. Joseph Health Svc., 1983-95, St. John Hosp. and Med. Ctr., 1979-95, St. John Health System, 1984-95, The Oxford Inst., 1984-95, Eastwood Clinics, 1992-95; pres. Providence Ch. Corp., Hilton Head Island, S.C., chmn. ch. fin. ocm., corp. pres. session; mem. bus. adv bd.! City of Detroit, 1991-95, chmn. 1993-94. Served with MC AUS, 1955-57. Fellow ACHE; mem. Am. Hosp. Assn., Internat. Hosp. Fedn., Mich. Hosp. Assn. (trustee, chmn. 1994-95, mem. exec. com.), Assn. Am. Med. Colls. (Coth rep.), Am. Cancer Soc. (regional adv. bd. 1994-95), Med. Group Mgmt. Assn., Soc. Health Service Adminstrs., Sigma Phi Epsilon. Home: 63 Big Woods Dr Hilton Head Island SC 29926-2604

WESSELS, BRUCE W. materials scientist, educator; b. N.Y.C., Oct. 18, 1946; m. Beverly T. Wessels; children: David, Kirsten. BS in Metallurgy and Materials Sci., U. Pa., 1968; PhD in Materials Sci., MIT, 1973. Tech. staff GE R&D Ctr., 1972-77, acting branch mgr., 1976; from asst. prof. to assoc. prof. Northwestern U., Evanston, Ill., 1977-83, prof. materials sci. and engring., 1984—, Walter P. Murphy prof., 1998—, prof. elec. and computer engring., 1987—. Vis. sci. Argonne Nat. Lab., 1978; mem. program com. Internat. Conf. Superlattices, Microdevices and Microstructures, 1987. Editor 5 books including (with G.Y. Chin) Advances in Electronic Materials, 1986; mem. editl. bd. Jour. Electronic Materials, 1982-88, 98—; contbr. articles to profl. jours.; patentee in field. Fellow ASM, Am. Phys. Soc., AIME (bd. trustees 1996-97); mem. TMS, The Minerals, Metals and Materials Soc. (chmn. electronic materials com. 1987-89, conf. program chmn. 1986-87, key reader Trans. of AIME 1985-92, bd. dirs. 1993-98, vice-chmn. exec. coun. electronic, magnetic and photonic materials divsn. 1991-92, chmn. 1993-95, v.p. 1995, pres. 1996), Electrochem. Soc. Materials Rsch. Soc. (symposium organizer 1993, 95), Optical Soc. Am., Sigma Xi, Tau Beta Pi. Office: Materials Science-Engring Northwestern U 2220 Campus Dr Evanston IL 60208-3108 E-mail: b-wessels@northwestern.edu.

WESSENDORF, MARKUS, theater educator; s. Werner and Margret Wessendorf; m. Cynthia Brodt, July 25, 1998; 1 child, Maxwell. Diploma in Applied Theatre Studies, Justus-Liebig-University, 1991; PhD in Applied Theatre Studies, Justus-Liebig-Univ., 1996. Asst. prof. Justus-Liebig-U., Giessen, Germany, 1992—97; adj. prof. Marymount Manhattan Coll., NYC, 1999—2001, Queens Coll./City U. of NY, 1999—2001, NY U., 2000; asst. prof. U. of Hawai'i at Manoa, Honolulu, 2001—. Vis. scholar U. of Queensland, Brisbane, Australia, 1997—98, NY U., 1994—95, Ctr. for Advanced Study in Theatre Arts, New York, NY, 2000; studied Kathakali with Prof. Govindan Kutty, Kalamandalam Calcutta, West Bengal, India, 1991. Dir.: (theatre production) Germania Death in Berlin (by Heiner Müller), 1989, Barking Dogs (by Norman Price), Curdom (by Cynthia Farar), The Robbers (by Friedrich Schiller); performance The Perfect Moment; author: The Stage as a Scene of Thinking: Richard Foreman's Ontological-Hysteric Theatre; editor: (anthology) Border-Crossings: Theatre and the Other Arts; author: essays on The Wooster Group, Richard Maxwell, Richard Foreman, Bertolt Brecht, William Forsythe, Ungunstraum, Ron Athey and Bob Flanagan., German Academic Exch. Program, 1994—95, 1997—98. Mem.: ATHE, Internat. Brecht Soc. Office: Dept of Theatre & Dance/UHM 1770 East-West Road Honolulu HI 96822

WESSLER, MELVIN DEAN, farmer, rancher; b. Dodge City, Kans., Feb. 11, 1932; s. Oscar Lewis and Clara (Reiss) W.; m. Laura Ethel Arbuthnot, Aug. 23, 1951; children: Monty Dean, Charla Cay, Virgil Lewis. Grad. high sch. Farmer, rancher, Springfield, Colo., 1950—. Dir., sec. bd. Springfield Co-op. Sales Co., 1964-80, pres. bd., 1980—; pres. Arkansas Valley Co-op Coun., SE Colo. Area, 1965-87, Colo. Co-op Coun., 1969-72, v.p. 1974, sec. 1980-86; cmty. com. chmn. Baca County, Agr. Stablzn. and Conservation Svc., Springfield, 1961-73, 79—, vice chmn. Baca County Com., 1980-90; mem. spl. com. on grain mktg. Far-Mar-Co; mem. com. for PROMARK, Hutchinson, Kans., 1978. Mem. adv. bd. Denver Bapt. Bible Coll., 1984-89; chmn. bd. dirs. Springfield Cemetery Bd., 1985—; apptd. spl. com. Farmland Industries spl. project Tomorrow, 1987—. Recipient The Colo. Cooperator award Colo. Coop. Coun., 1990. Mem. Colo. Cattlemen's Assn., Colo. Wheat Growers Assn., Southeast Farm Bus. Assn. (bd. dirs. 1991-95), Big Rock Grange (treas. 1964-76, master 1976-82), Southwest Kans. Farm Bus. Assn. (dir. 1996—, pres. 1999-2001). Address: 18363 County Road Pp Springfield CO 81073

WESSLER, STANFORD, physician, educator; b. N.Y.C., Apr. 20, 1917; S. Hugo and Minerva (Miller) W.; m. Margaret Barnet Muhlfelder, Dec. 17, 1942; children— John Stanford, Stephen Lawrence, James Hugh. Grad., Fieldston Sch., N.Y.C., 1934; BA, Harvard, 1938; MD, N.Y.U., 1942. From fellow to asst. prof. medicine Harvard U. Med. Sch., 1946-64; from resident to assoc. chief med. svc. Beth Israel Hosp., Boston, 1946-64; prof. medicine Washington U. Sch. Medicine, St. Louis, 1964-74, John L. and Adalaine Simon prof., 1966-74; prof. medicine, assoc. dean postgrad. programs NYU Sch. Medicine, 1974-90; physician in chief Jewish Hosp., St. Louis, 1964-74; assoc. physician Barnes Hosp., St. Louis, 1964-74; attending physician NYU Med. Center, Univ. Hosp., N.Y.C., 1974-90, Bellevue Hosp. Center, N.Y.C., 1974-90, Manhattan VA Hosp. Med. Ctr., 1974-90. Mem. coms. NRC, Inst. of Medicine, Nat. Heart, Lung and Blood Inst.; bd. dirs. N.Y. Heart Assn., 1980-86, pres. Council Continuing Med. Edn., N.Y., 1979-85. Contbr. articles on vascular disease.; mem. editorial bds. jours. in field. Served with M.C. AUS, 1943-46. Recipient James A. Mitchell award, 1972. Mem. Am. Physiol. Soc., Am. Soc. Clin. Investigation, Assn. Am. Physicians, Am. Heart Assn. (investigator 1955-59, bd. dirs. 1971-76, chmn. publs. com. 1972-76, chmn. coun. on thrombosis 1974-76, v.p. 1974-76, mem. sci. adv. com. 1986-90, Merit award 1978, Disting. Achievement award 1989), Alpha Omega Alpha. Home: 575 Osgood St #1202 North Andover MA 01845-1975

WESSLING, GREGORY JAY, retail executive; b. Chgo., Dec. 11, 1951; s. Robert J. and Doris (Tosch) W.; m. Mary Anne Richmond, Nov. 16, 1974; children: Douglas A., James R., Robert E. BBA, U. N.C., 1974; postgrad., Wake Forest U. Sch. Bus., 1974-76, MBA, 1987. Store mgr. Lowe's Co., Inc., Winston-Salem, N.C., 1973-76, mktg. mgr. North Wilkesboro, N.C., 1976—, dir. merchandising, 1978-80, v.p. merchandising, 1980-96, sr. v.p., gen. merchandise mgr., 1996—99, sr. v.p. store operations, southern division, 1999—. Bd. dirs. DJR Corp., Winston-Salem; mem. alumni coun., bd. visitors Babcock Grad. Sch. Mgmt., Wake Forest U. Mem. Home Ctr. Leadership Council. Republican. Methodist. Avocations: skiing, water-skiing. Office: Lowes Cos Inc PO Box 1111 North Wilkesboro NC 28659-1111

WESSLING, ROBERT BRUCE, retired lawyer; b. Chgo., Oct. 8, 1937; s. Robert Euans and Marguerite (Rickert) W.; m. Judith Ann Hanson, Aug. 26, 1961; children: Katherine, Jennifer, Carolyn. BA, DePauw U., 1959; JD, U. Mich., 1962. Bar: U.S. Ct. Appeals (9th cir.) 1965. Assoc. Latham & Watkins, L.A., 1962-70, ptnr., 1970-94; ret., 1995. Bd. govs. Fin. Lawyers Conf., Los Angeles, 1974-2000. Mem. World Affairs Coun., L.A., Town Hall, L.A.; trustee DePauw U. Mem. ABA, Los Angeles Bar Assn., Phi Beta Kappa, Phi Delta Phi, Phi Eta Sigma, Order of Coif. Democrat. Methodist. Avocations: tennis, travel. E-mail: bbwessling@aol.com.

WESSON, HERB J. state representative; b. Cleve. m. Fabian Wesson; children: Douglas, P.J., Herb III, Justin. BA in History, Lincoln U., Pa., 1999. Served as chief of staff LA County Supr. Yvonne Brathwaite Burke; served as chief dep. LA City Councilman Nate Holden; mem. Calif. State Assembly, 1998—, served on appropriations, health, utilities, and commerce com., served on bus. and professions com., chair govtl. orgn. com., speaker, 2002—. Mem. Mid-City C. of C., Culver City C. of C.; former mem. adv. bd. African Cmty. Resource Ctr.; bd. dirs. Martin Luther King, Jr. Gen. Hosp. Found., Second Dist. Edn. Found. Recipient Pub. Svc. award, Greater LA C. of C., Crusader State Leadership award, Calif. Alliance for Pride and Equality, Legis. of Yr. award, Youth Employment Sys., 1999—2000, Pub. Official award, Stonewall Dem. Club, 2000, Legis. of Yr. award, Planned Parenthood LA, 2001, Calif. Assessors' Assn., 2001. Democrat. Office: Speaker of the Assembly PO Box 942849 Sacramento CA 94249-0001

WEST, ALEXANDER BRIAN, pathologist; arrived in U.S., 1986; s. Timothy Roberts and Dorothy Trevor West; m. Lynda Tyrrell, June 25, 1970; children: Timothy Eoin, Stephanie Aoife. BA, U. Dublin, 1965, MB, BCh, BAO, 1979; MS, U. Calif., Davis, 1967. Cert. anatomic pathology Am. Bd. Pathology, 1989. Lectr. in zoology U. Dublin Trinity Coll., 1967—74, lectr. pathology, 1982—86; asst. prof. pathology Yale U., New Haven, 1988—91, assoc. prof. pathology, 1991—95, prof. pathology, 1995, U. Tex. Med. Br., Galveston, 1995—99, NYU, N.Y.C., 1999—. Fellow: Royal Coll. Pathologists, Royal Coll. Physicians Ireland; mem.: Binford-Dammin Soc. Infectious Disease Pathologists (pres. 2002—03), Gastrointestinal Pathology Soc. (pres. 1999—2000), US and Can. Acad. Pathology, Am. Assn. for the Study Liver Diseases, Am. Gastroent. Assn. Achievements include research in gastrointestinal, hepatic and pancreatic pathology; pathogenesis of infectious diseases. Avocation: fly fishing. Office: NYU Dept Pathology 560 First Ave (TH461) New York NY 10016

WEST, A(RNOLD) SUMNER, chemical engineer; b. Phila., Jan. 12, 1922; s. Arnold and Mary (Sumner) W.; m. Beverly Helen Lehman, Oct. 5, 1946; children: Barbara Ann, Richard Sumner. BSChemE, U. Pa., 1943; MS, Pa. State U., 1946. With Rohm and Haas Co., Phila., 1946—87, rsch. engr., 1946—62, rsch. supr., 1962—72, mgr. rsch. dept., 1972—77, sr. tech. specialist govt. and regulatory affairs, 1978—87; owner, prin. A.S. West Assocs., Huntingdon Valley, Pa., 1987—. Cons. dept. chem. engring. U. Pa., 1952-72; mem. indsl. and profl. adv. com. Coll. Engring., Pa. State U., 1978-84, chmn. chem. engring. divsn., 1980-81, chmn. com., 1982-83. Editor: AIChE Safety and Health News, 1996—. Mem. Lower Moreland Twp. (Montgomery County) Authority, 1970, sec., 1971—; vice-chmn. bd. dirs. Chemical Heritage Found., 1984-92; pres. United Engring. Trustees, 1986-87. Fellow Am. Inst. Chem. Engrs. (dir. 1964-66, treas. 1973-75, v.p. 1976, pres. 1977); mem. Engrs. Joint Council (dir. 1976-79), Am. Assn. Engring. Socs. (vice chmn. public affairs council 1981, chmn. council 1982-83), Am. Chem. Soc., Nat. Soc. Profl. Engrs., Soc. Automotive Engrs., Water Environ. Fedn. Clubs: The Valley (Huntingdon Valley). Home and Office: 3896 Sidney Rd Huntingdon Valley PA 19006-2347 Office Phone: 215-938-7181. E-mail: aswest@worldnet.att.net.

WEST, BENJAMIN B. advertising executive; b. 1951; BA, Washington and Lee U. With West Advt. & Mktg., Tampa, Fla., 1973-80; pres., CEO & founder WestGroup Inc, Tampa, Fla., 1980-96; pres. WestWayne Inc. (merger of WestGroup with Tucker Wayne/Luckie & Co.), Tampa, FL, 1996-99; CEO WestWayne Inc., Tampa, FL, 1999—. Office: WestWayne Inc 4018 Jackson St Ste 3600 Tampa FL 33602

WEST, BETSY, broadcast executive; m. Oren Jacoby. Grad., Brown U.; MS, Syracuse U. Reporter WHEN Radio, Syracuse, N.Y., 1974; writer, editor ABC Radio, 1975; writer ABC News World News Tonight, Chgo., 1978-82; sr. prodr. ABC News Nightline, 1983-89; sr. broadcast prodr. ABC News Turning Point, 1989-98; exec. prodr. ABC News; v.p. primetime news CBS, N.Y.C., 1998—. Recepient 19 Emmy awards, Christopher award, duPont-Columbia award. Mem. Phi Beta Kappa (trustee). Office: CBS News 524 W 57th St New York NY 10019-2924

WEST, BILL, writer, artist, photographer, composer; b. Chgo. s. Joseph James and Catherine Theresa W. AB in English, Loyola U., Chgo.; MA in English, PhD in English and Am. Literatures, Northwestern U., Evanston, Ill. Tchg. asst. Northwestern U., Evanston, Ill.; instr. in English Ill. Inst. Tech., Georgetown U.; asst. prof. in English Ill. Inst. Tech., Loyola U., Chgo., prof. emeritus. Author: Sacred Numbers, American Summer Suite, Kaimami, The Heians, The Sparrow with the Slit Tongue and Beautiful Oiwa: Ghost Tales of Old Japan; contbr. more than 1000 poems to anthologies and mags.; illustrator Canopy Mag., Iota Poetry Quar. Mag., Aabye's Baby Mag., The Inquirer Mag., NIH's Haiku 2000 Anthology, Presence Mag., Writer's Own Mag., Azami Mag., Prijatelj Mag., The Brobdingnagian Times Mag., Raw NerVZ Mag., Yumtzilob: Tijdschrift over den Ams. Mag., Calligraphy for Azami Mag., Iota Poetry Quar. Mag., Krax Mag., Presence Mag., Handshake Mag., Lotus Mag., Raw Nervz, Carlew; guest artist Hidden Oak mag, Inclement mag.; creative cons. Contemporary Ghazal. Mem. SAG, Poets and Writers, Internat. Artists and Writers Assn., Tanka Soc. Am. Avocations: tennis, bicycle riding, gardening.

WEST, BLAIR, investment banker, consultant; b. Toronto, Ont., Can., Dec. 10, 1965; s. Robert Scott and M. Ray (Marshal) W.; m. Ann Michele Byrne; children: Hunter Alexander, Madison Ann, Parker Alexander. BA, Wheaton Coll., 1987; MBA, U. Chgo., 1995. Lic. real estate broker, N.Y., NASD series 7, 24, 28, 63, and 66. V.p. Barnett Bank, Tampa, Fla., 1988-93, Credit Suisse First Boston, N.Y.C., 1995-2000; mng. dir., owner Crusader Securities, N.Y.C., 2000—. Mem. Met. Club, Penn Club. Avocations: golf, sailing, flying. Office: Crusader Investments 230 Park Ave Ste 1000 New York NY 10169

WEST, BOB, pharmaceutical executive; b. Ellenville, N.Y., Mar. 7, 1931; s. Harry and Elsie May Wicentowsky; m. Betty Parker, May 9, 1957 (div.); children: Debra Ellen, Elizabeth Ann, Sharon Lynn; m. Jacqueline Cutler, Jan. 3, 1982. BS, Union U., 1952; MS, Purdue U., 1954, PhD, 1956; postgrad. mgmt. seminar, U. Chgo., 1972. Pres., dir. research Food, Drug, Chem. Svcs., Stamford, Conn., 1975—; pres., dir. research Bob West Assocs., Inc., Stamford, 1975—. Pres. Drug Info. Assn., Phila., 1974-75; sci. adv. bd. Fountain Pharms., Inc., Largo, Fla., 1993—, Dovetail Techs., Inc., College Park, Md., 1996—, Phytopede, Inc., Sarasota, Fla., 1999—. Editorial bd. Drug Info. Assn. Jour., Phila., 1977-85; contbr. articles to profl. jours. Mem. ASPET, Soc. Toxicology, Acad. Pharm. Scis., Assn. Rsch. Dirs., Drug Info. Assn., Assn. Univ. Tech. Mgrs. Home and Office: Food Drug Chem Svcs 7925 Meadow Rush Loop Sarasota FL 34238-4319 Office Phone: 941-925-8958. Personal E-mail: bjwest22@verizon.net.

WEST, CAROL CATHERINE, law educator; b. Phila., May 23, 1944; d. Scott G. and Helen (Young) West. BA, Miss. U. for Women, 1966; MLS, U. So. Miss., 1984; JD, U. Miss., 1970. Pub. svcs. law libr. U. Va., Charlottesville, 1966-67; catalog law libr. U. Miss., Oxford, 1967-70; legis. reference libr. Miss. Legislature, Jackson, 1970-75; law libr. Miss. Coll., Jackson, 1975-94, prof. law, 1975—. Del. White House Conf. Libr. and Info. Svcs., 1991; cons. to Parliament of Armenia, 1995, Parliament of Tanzania, 1997; mem. bd. commrs. Miss. Libr. Commn., 1993—98; mem., sec. Miss. Task Force on Gender Fairness in the Cts. Mem.: ABA, Miss. Women's Polit. Network (bd. dirs. 1998—2000), Miss. Libr. Assn., Miss. Women Lawyers Assn. (bd. dirs. 1991—93), Hinds County Bar, Miss. Bar Assn. (Susie Blue Buchanan award 2001). Methodist. Office: Miss Coll Law Sch 151 E Griffith St Jackson MS 39201-1302

WEST, CAROLYN MARIE, psychologist, educator, writer; b. St. Louis, Mo., Jan. 14, 1964; d. Georgia Mae West. PhD, U. Mo., St. Louis, 1994. Predoctoral intern U. Notre Dame Counseling Ctr., South Bend, Ind., 1993—94; postdoctoral clin. and tchg. fellowship Ill. State U. Counseling Ctr./Psychology Dept., Normal, Ill., 1994—95; postdoctoral rsch. fellow U. N.H. Family Rsch. Lab., Durham, NH, 1995—97; assoc. prof., psychology U. Wash., Tacoma, 1997—. Author (editor): (book) Violence in the Lives of Black Women: Battered Black and Blue, 2002 (Nat. Inst. on Alcohol Abuse and Alcoholism Rsch. Supplement ($63, 443), 2003), essay. Rschr. Gov. Domestic Violence Action Group, Seattle, 2001—02; steering com. mem. Pierce County Commn. Against Domestic Violence, Tacoma, 2000—03. Recipient Outstanding Young Women of Am. Award, 1997, Outstanding Rsch. Award in the Field of Domestic Violence in the African Am. Cmty., U. of Minn., 2000. Mem.: APA, Psychology for Women in Psychology (governing bd. mem. 1993—96). Achievements include research in University of Washington, Tacoma Founder's Endowment Grant, 1998 ($5, 000). Office: Univ Wash Tacoma IAS Box 358436 1900 Commerce St Tacoma WA 98402

WEST, CHARLES CONVERSE, retired theologian; b. Plainfield, N.J., Feb. 3, 1921; s. George Parsons and Florence (Farish) W.; m. Ruth Floy Carson, Sept. 6, 1944; children: Russell Arthur, Walter Lawrence, Glenn Andrew. BA, Columbia U., 1942; B.D., Union Theol. Sem., N.Y.C., 1945; PhD, Yale U., 1955. Ordained to ministry Presbyterian Ch. U.S.A., 1946; missionary, fraternal worker Bd. Fgn. Missions Presbyn. Ch. U.S.A., 1946-56; instr., chaplain Cheeloo U., Hangchow, China, 1948-49; instr. Nanking Theol. Sem., 1949-50; indsl. mission work Gossner Mission, Mainz-Kastel, Germany, 1950-51; lectr. Kirchliche Hochschule, Berlin, 1951-53; Lectr. Hartford Sem. Found., 1955-56; asso. dir. Ecumenical Inst., Bossey, Switzerland under World Council Chs., 1956-61; chargé de cours U. Geneva, 1956-61; instr. Peking Nat. U., 1948; assoc. prof. Christian ethics Princeton Theol. Sem., 1961-63, Stephen Colwell prof. Christian ethics, 1963-91, prof. emeritus, 1991—, acad. dean, 1979-84. Mem. Commn. to Form Statement Faith U.P. Ch. U.S.A., 1961-67, chmn. internat. affairs adv. com., 1963-66; Chmn. U.S. Com. for Christian Peace Conf., 1965-72; chmn. working com. Dept. Studies in Mission, Evangelism World Council Chs., 1967-68; member Commn. on Internat. Affairs, Nat. Council Chs., 1968-73 Author: Communism and the Theologians, 1958, Outside the Camp, 1959, Ethics, Violence and Revolution, 1969, The Power to be Human, 1971, Perspective on South Africa, 1985, Power, Truth and Community in Modern Culture, 1999, Storm Front, 2003; editor: The Sufficiency of God, Essays in Honor of Dr. W.A. Visser't Hooft, 1963; assoc. editor: Religion in Eastern Europe, 1985—; translator: J. Hamel-A Christian in East Germany, 1960. Mem. Am. Soc. Christian Ethics (v.p. 1972-73, pres. 1973-74), Am. Theol. Soc. (v.p. 1982-83, pres. 1983-84), Presbytery N.Y.C., Ams. for Dem. Action., Christians Associated for Rels. with Eastern Europe (pres. 1988-92). Presbyterian. Home: 9 Hedge Row Rd Princeton NJ 08540-5047 Office: Princeton Theological Seminary CN821 Princeton NJ 08542 E-mail: c.c.west@att.net.

WEST, CHRISTOPHER EUGENE, military officer; b. Memphis, Tenn., Jan. 16, 1963; s. John Walter West, Sr. and Clara Lucille Block; 1 child, Christopher Gabriel. AS, S.W. Tenn. C.C., 1987; BA, U. Memphis, 1989. Patient care specialist Gorgas Army Hosp., Rep. of Panama, 1981-84; acad. tutor U. Memphis, 1986-89; co. exec. officer 1st/26th Inf. Regiment, Fort Jackson, S.C., 1989-93; dir. mktg. and pub. rels. Personnel Plus, Memphis, 1993-97; comdr. Hdqtrs. Co./467th Engr. Btn., Memphis, 1997—. Intern Office of U.S. Sen. Bill Frist, Memphis, 1996; cons. Office of Pub. Affairs, U.S. Army Corps of Engrs., Memphis, 2000. Editor: U.S. Army Engr. Mag./Helena, Vicinity Project. Pub. affairs dir. Memphis Police Ambs., 1996; civil mil. coord. Convoy of Hope, memphis, 2000. 1st lt. U.S. Army, 1989-93. Recipient Gen. Douglas MacArthur Leadership award, Washington, 2001, Outstanding Jr. Officer of Yr. award Res. Officers assn. of the U.S. Major Gen. Strom Thurmond, 1999; decorated Bronze Order of the De Fluery medal Army Engr. Assn., Hon. Order of St. Barbara. Mem. Pi Sigma Alpha. Republican. Baptist. Avocations: reading, writing, Internet, polit. sci. Office: HHC 467th Engr Btn 25262 Avery Ave Memphis TN 38112-4898 Home: 101 Heather Ct Radcliff KY 40160-9367

WEST, CLARK DARWIN, pediatric nephrologist, educator; b. Jamestown, N.Y., July 4, 1918; s. Clark Darwin and Frances Isabel (Blanchard) W.; m. Ruthann Asbury, Apr. 12, 1944 (div.); children: Charles Michael, John Clark, Lucy Frances; m. Dolores Lachenman, Mar. 1, 1986. AB, Coll. of Wooster, 1940; MD, U. Mich., 1943. Intern Univ. Hosp., Ann Arbor, Mich., 1943-44, resident in pediatrics, 1944-46; fellow in pediatrics Children's Hosp. Research Found., Cin., 1948-49, research asso., 1951-89, asso. dir., 1963-89, dir. div. immunology and nephrology, 1958-89; with cardiopulmonary lab. chest service Bellevue Hosp., N.Y.C., 1949-51; attending pediatrician Children's Hosp., 1951-89; asst. prof. pediatrics U. Cin., 1951-55, asso. prof., 1955-62, prof., 1962-89. Mem. coms. NIH, 1965-69, 1972-73 Mem. editorial bd.: Jour. Pediatrics, 1960-79, Kidney Internat., 1977-89, Clin. Nephrology, 1989-96; contbr. articles to profl. jours. Served to capt. M.C., AUS, 1946-47. Decorated Army commendation medal; recipient recognition award Cin. Pediat. Soc., 1980, Mitchell Rubin award, 1986, Henry L. Barnett award, 1995, Daniel Drake medal, 1996, John P. Peters award, 1996. Mem. Soc. Pediatric Research (sec.-treas. 1958-62, pres. 1963-64), Am. Pediatric Soc., Am. Soc. Pediatric Nephrologists (pres. 1973-74), Am. Physiol. Soc., Am. Assn. Immunologists, Am. Soc. Nephrology, Internat. Pediatric Nephrology Assn., Sigma Xi, Alpha Omega Alpha. Achievements include research on immunopathogenesis and treatment of glomerulonephritides and in the complement system. Home: 11688 Aristocrat Dr Harrison OH 45030-9753 Office: Children's Hosp Med Ctr Cincinnati OH 45229 Personal E-mail: CWest_2865@fwse.net.

WEST, CORNEL, humanities educator, writer; b. Tulsa, June 2, 1953; s. Clifton L. W.; 1 child from previous marriage, Clifton; m. Elleni Gebre Amlak. BA, Harvard U., 1973; PhD, Princeton U., 1977. Prof. religion Union Theol. Sem., N.Y., 1977-84, 87-88, Yale U. Divinity Sch., New Haven, 1984-87; prof. religion, dir. dept. Afro-Am. Studies Princeton (N.J.) U., 1988-94; prof. Afro-Am. studies, philosophy of religion Harvard U., Cambridge, Mass., 1994—99, Alphonse Fletcher jr. prof., 1999—2002; Class of 1943 Univ. prof. of religion Princeton U., 2002—. Am. cert. Le Monde Diplomatique; vis. prof. U. Paris; DuBois fellow Harvard U., 1994-99. Author: Prophesy Deliverance! An Afro-American Revolutionary Christianity, 1982, Prophetic Fragments, 1988, The American Evasion of Philosophy: A Genealogy of Pragmatism,

1990, Breaking Bread: Insurgent Black Intellectual Life, 1991, The Ethical Dimensions of Marxist Thought, 1991, Race Matters, 1993, Beyond Eurocentrism and Multiculturalism, Vol. I: Prophetic Thought in Postmodern Times, 1993, Vol. II: Notes on Race, Class and Power, 1993, Keeping Faith: Philosophy and Race in America, 1993, (with Paula Giddings) Regarding Malcolm X, 1994, (with Michael Lerner) Jews and Blacks: Let the Healing Begin, 1995, Future of the Race, 1996, Restoring Hope, 1997, The Cornel West Reader, 2000; co-prodr. (with Derek "D.O.A." Allen, Clifton West & Mike Daily) album, Sketches of my Culture, 2001. Recipient Literary Lion award N.Y. Pub. Libr., 1993. Office: Princeton U Dept Religion Hall Princeton NJ 08544-1066

WEST, DANIEL CHARLES, dentist; b. Trenton, N.J., July 23, 1955; s. Harry E. and Alma R. (Washburn) W.; m. Deborah L. Scott, May 28, 1977; children: Lauren Elizabeth, Colin Jeffrey, Aaron Samuel. BS, Ea. Nazarene Coll., 1977; DMD, U. Pitts., 1982; M, Acad. Gen. Dentistry, 2003. Min. youth/music South Hills Ch. of the Nazarene, Bethel Park, Pa., 1977-82; pvt. practice specializing in family dentistry Terre Hill, Pa., 1982-95; pvt. practice specializing in cosmetic, implant and reconstructive dentistry New Holland, Pa., 1995—. Mem. Internat. Gen. Bd. Ch. of Nazarene, Kansas City, Mo., 1989—2002, lay mem. dist. adv. bd. Phila. dist., Frazer, Pa., 1985—, coord. work and witness program, 1988—90, dir. compassionate ministries, 1990—; bd. dirs. Mission Am.; dir. Phila. Dist. IMPACT, 1982—89, 2001—; trustee Ea. Nazarene Coll., Wollaston, Mass., 1984—, mem. exec. com., chmn. dept. fin., chmn. bd. dirs., 2002—; mem. clin. faculty U. Pa. Sch. Dental Medicine, Med. U. Ukraine, Kiev, Pediat. Med. U., Moscow; mem. Mission Am. Bd., 1997—. Contbr. articles to jours. Bd. dirs. Garden Spot Village Retirement Cmty., 1996—97; interim min. music Fairview Village Ch. of Nazarene, 2001—02; mng. ptnr. CIS Partnership for Ministry, 1998—2002; chmn. bd. trustees Eastern Nazarene Coll., 2002—. Lt. USPHS, 1982—85. Recipient Alumni Achievement award, Eastern Nazarene Coll., 1996. Master Am. Acad. Gen. Dentistry; mem. ADA (Cert. Recognition for Internat. Svc. in a Fgn. County 1996), Am. Acad. Cosmetic Dentistry, Pa. Dental Assn., Lancaster County Dental Soc. Republican. Home: 1442 Hay Field Dr East Earl PA 17519-9685 Office: 650 E Main St New Holland PA 17557-1410 *The greatest joy I have is in serving others through ministry in the church, my dental practice, and especially in my home.*

WEST, DAVID WAYNE, mechanical engineer; b. Logansport, Ind., Mar. 20, 1955; m. Bernadette Mary Porsche, Oct. 25, 1980; children: Theresa Anne, John Porsche. BS, Purdue U., West Lafayette, Ind., 1979. Design engr. Square D Co., Peru, Ind., 1979—83; project engr. Panduit Corp., Tinley Park, Ill., 1983—. Mem.: ASME. Achievements include patents for trim clamp assembly; vent assembly and method of making it; portable cable tie tool; apparatus for testing a wire harness; locking head for a bundling strap; four piece cable tie. Avocations: Christmas nutcracker soldiers, woodcarving. Home: 215 Robin Hill Dr Naperville IL 60540 Office: Panduit Corp 17301 S Ridgeland Ave Tinley Park IL 60477-3091

WEST, DOE, bioethicist, social justice activist, researcher; b. Tucson, July 14, 1951; d. George Oliver and Dorothy Marie (Watson) W. AA, Dutchess C.C., 1975; BS, SUNY, New Paltz, 1977; BA, Logos Bible Coll., 1986, MDiv, 1993; MS, Boston U., 1980; PhD, Northeastern U., 2001. Dir. 504/compliance officer dept. health and hosp. City of Boston, 1979-81, commr. handicap affairs, 1981-84; pres. Myth Breakers, Inc., 1984—; pvt. practice psychotherapy, 2004—. Project coord. task force on human subject rsch. Fernald State Sch., 1994; sr. rsch. assoc. N.E. Family Study, Harvard Sch. Pub. Health, 2004—. Postdoctoral fellow Ctr. for Psychol. Rehab. Boston U., 1999-2002. Home: PO Box 985 Framingham MA 01701 E-mail: doewest@aol.com.

WEST, DOUGLAS M. automotive executive; m. Irene Ziebarth. Degree in Social Sci. and Pre-Law, Mich. State U., 1967; JD cum laude, Detroit Coll. Law, 1974. With U.S. Peace Corps, Jamaica, 1968—71; sr. law clk. hon. Ralph M. Freeman U.S. Dist. Ct. Ea. Dist. Mich.; atty. Office Gen. Counsel Ford Motor Co.; assoc. gen. counselor for product litigation Toyota Motor Sales, 1982—89, v.p., gen. counselor product law, 1989—93, group v.p., 1993—96, sr. v.p., chief adminstrv. officer, 1996—2002; sr. v.p. govt. and industry affairs Toyota Motor N.Am., 2002—. Trustee Claremont (Calif.) Grad. U. Office: Ste 600 1850 M St NW Washington DC 20036

WEST, DOUGLAS XAVIER, retired science educator; b. Tacoma, Wash., June 11, 1937; s. Raymond Idaho and Myrtle Agnes West; m. Gayl Lee Lucas, June 6, 1964; children: Gregory Joseph, Gabrial Douglas. AB, Whitman Coll., Walla Walla, WA, 1959; PhD, Wash. State U., Pullman, 1964. Instr. Upsala Coll., East Orange, NJ, 1964—65; asst. prof. Ctrl. Mich. U., Mt. Pleasant, 1965—68, assoc. prof., 1968—72, dir. U. honors programs, 1970—72, prof., 1972—75; chmn. and prof. inorganic chemistry Ill. State U., Normal, 1975—86, prof., 1986—93, disting. prof., 1993—2000; affiliate prof. U. of Wash., Seattle, 2000—02; prof. emeritus Ill. State U., Normal, 2000—. Contbr. articles to profl. journals. Grantee Instrumentation award, NSF, 1979, 1984, NATO, 1985-7, Am. Chem. Soc., 1988-1990, Indo-American fellowship, Coun. for the Internat. Exch. of Scholars, 1990, Am. Chem. Soc., 1990-1992, 1993-1995, 1997-1999, Dreyfus Scholar, Camille and Henry Dreyfus Found., 1994-1996, Sr. Scholar, 2000-2002. Master: Am. Contract Bridge League (life; pres. ea. Mich. bridge unit 1970—72); mem.: Am. Chem. Soc. Avocations: golf, surf fishing, razor clamming, hiking, beach walking. Home: Box 402 Long Beach WA 98631 Personal E-mail: westdx@hotmail.com.

WEST, FELTON, retired journalist, councilman; b. Houston, May 9, 1926; s. Felton Eber and Clara Viola (Ross) West; m. Jean Frances Osborn, Oct. 27, 1945; children: Bruce Eugene, Wade Osborn, Barbara Jean. Student, U. N.Mex., 1944-46; BS, U. Houston, 1952, MLitt, 1957. Mem. staff Houston Post, 1943-95, Washington corr., 1961-65, chief Austin (Tex.) capitol bur., 1966-85, columnist, 1985-93, editl. writer, 1993-95; ret., 1995; councilman City of Liberty Hill, Tex., 2002—04. With USNR. Mem.: Phi Kappa Phi. Home and Office: 209 Barrington Dr Liberty Hill TX 78642-4297 E-mail: few2@evi.net.

WEST, GAIL BERRY, lawyer; b. Cin. d. Theodore Moody and Johnnie Mae (Newton) B.; m. Togo D. West, Jr., June 18, 1966; children: Tiffany Berry, Hilary Carter. BA magna cum laude, Fisk U., 1964; MA, U. Cin., 1965; JD, Howard U., 1968. Bar: D.C. 1969, U.S. Supreme Ct. 1978. Staff atty. IBM, 1969-76; spl. asst. to sec. HUD, 1977-78; staff asst. to spl. asst. to Pres., Washington, 1978-80; dep. asst. sec. for manpower res. affairs installations Dept. Air Force, 1980-81; atty. AT&T, Washington, 1983-84; exec. dir. govt. affairs Bell Comm. Rsch. Inc., Washington, 1984-95; dir. govt. rels. Armstrong World Industries, Inc., Washington, 1995—2003, cons., 2003—. Mem. exec. com. ARC, Washington, 1974-85; bd. dirs. Family and Child Svcs., Washington, 1974-87; trustee Corcoran Gallery Art, 1983-2000, Arena Stage, 1992-99, Decatur House, 1994—, WETA, 1995-2001, Fisher House Found., Inc.; bd. dirs. Meridian House, 1994-2000; mem. D.C. Commn. Fine Arts, 2003-; mem. cathedral chpt. Nat. Cathedral. Ford Found. fellow, 1965-68. Mem. ABA, D.C. Bar Assn., Unified Bar D.C. Democrat. Episcopalian. Home: 4934 Rockwood Pkwy NW Washington DC 20016-3211

WEST, GLENN EDWARD, investment banking executive; b. Kansas City, Mo., Nov. 19, 1944; s. Ernest and Helen Cecil (Johnson) W.; m. Vicki Lynn Knox, May 22, 1970; children: Keele Kay, Kollen Chandler, Ashley Knox. BS in Acctg. and Mktg. cum laude, Northwest Mo. State U., 1966; student, U. Colo. Inst. Orgn. Mgmt., 1974, Notre Dame U. Acad. Orgn. Mgmt., 1977. Auditor Arthur Young & Co., Kansas City, 1966-68; sales mgr. Procter & Gamble, Kansas City, 1968-69; mgr. pub. rels. St. Joseph (Mo.) Area C. of C., Mo., 1969-71, mgr. econ. devel., 1971-74; exec. v.p. Lawrence (Kans.) C. of C., 1974-81, Greater Macon (Ga.) C. of C., 1981—; pres. Greater Austin Co. of C., 1987-99; mng. dir. Hoak Breadlove Wesneski & Co, Austin, 1999—. Contbr. articles to profl. jours. Chpt. chmn. ARC, Macon, 1984; pres. Quality of Life Found. Austin, Greater Austin Sports Found.; ctrl. campaign chair Capital Area United Way, 1995. Served with USNG, 1967-73. Recipient Leadership award Kiwanis, St. Joseph, 1974. Mem. Kans. Assn. Commerce and Industry (bd. dirs. 1977-79, leadership award 1981), Kans. C. of C. Execs. (bd. dirs. 1977-80, pres. 1979), Ga. C. of C. Execs. (bd. dirs. 1982—), Am. C. of C. Execs. (bd. dirs. 1979-81, 83-84, vice chmn. 1989—, chmn. 1991, cert. chamber exec. 1980), C. of C. of U.S. (adv. com. 1981-89, bd. dirs. 1995, U. Tex. IC2 fellow), Rotary, Barton Creek County Club. Republican. Methodist. Office: Breedlove Hoak Wesneski & Co 701 Brazos Ste 500 Austin TX 78701 E-mail: gwest@hbwco.com.

WEST, GREGORY ALAN, physician; b. Houston, Aug. 1, 1950; s. Wayne Garland and Frankie Onalita (Russell) W.; m. Catherine Ann Sharp, June 18, 1976 (div. Oct. 1980); 1 child, Benjamin M.; m. Linda French Lucas, Apr. 13, 1985 (div. 1994); children: Robert, Scott; m. Cynthia Lee Swainston, Apr. 30, 1997. BA, Austin Coll., 1972; PhD, U. Louisville, 1980, MD, 1982; MDiv, Louisville Presbyn. Theol. Sem, 1981. Diplomate Am. Bd. Pediat., 1987, Am. Bd. Emergency Medicine, 1990, 99, with additional cert. in pediat. emergency medicine, 1997. EMT Louisville Emergency Med. Svc., 1977-79; intern in pediatrics U. Louisville Affiliated Hosps., 1982-83, resident in pediatrics, 1983-85; staff physician emergency dept. St. Anthony Hosp., Louisville, 1985-86, King's Daus. Hosp., Madison, Ind., 1985-95, med. dir. emergency med. svcs., 1989-91; staff physician emergency dept. Tri-County Cmty. Hosp., La Grange, Ky., 1991-92, Hardin County Meml. Hosp., Elizabethtown, Ky., 1995-99, Harrison County Hosp., Corydon, Ind., 2000—03, Russell Co. Hosp., Ky., 2003. Contbr. articles to profl. jours. Recipient pediatric radiology award and chmn.'s achievement award U. Louisville Affiliated Hosps. Fellow Am. Acad. Emergency Medicine, Am. Acad. Pediatrics; mem. Omicron Delta Kappa. Episcopalian. Avocations: tae kwon do karate, scuba diving, travel.

WEST, HUGH STERLING, aircraft leasing company executive; b. Kansas City, Kans., Apr. 5, 1930; s. Gilbert Eugene and Dorothy (Johnson) W.; m. Willa Alden Reed, Jan. 16, 1954; children: Karen, Phillip, Susan. BS, U. Va., 1952; BS in Aero., U. Md., 1959; grad., U.S. Naval Test Pilot Sch., 1959. Commd. 2d lt. USMC, 1948, advanced through grades to maj., 1961; exptl. flight test pilot U.S. Naval Air Test Ctr., Patuxent River, Md.; resigned, 1961; program mgr. Boeing Aircraft Co., Seattle, Phila., 1961-66, dir. airworthiness, comml. airplane divsn., 1969-71; dir. aircraft sales Am. Airlines, Tulsa, 1971-76; v.p. equipment mgmt. GATX Leasing Corp., San Francisco, 1976-80; v.p. tech., ptnr. Polaris Aircraft Leasing Corp., San Francisco, 1980-85; v.p., co-founder U.S. Airlease, Inc. divsn. Ford Motor Co., 1986-96; ret., 1996. Pres. Hugh S. West & Assocs., Comml. Aircraft Cons. Mem. Soc. Exptl. Test Pilots, Army Navy Country Club. Republican. Episcopalian. Home and Office: 37464 Purple Shadow Rd Palm Desert CA 92211-1328

WEST, JAKE, labor union administrator; Pres. Internat. Assn. Bridge, Structural & Ornamental Iron Workers, Washington. Office: Internat Assn Bridge Structural & Ornamental Iron Workers 1750 New York Ave NW Ste 400 Washington DC 20006-5301

WEST, JAMES C., JR., lawyer; b. White Sulphur Springs, W.Va., Mar. 15, 1932; LLB, W.Va. U., 1959. Bar: W.Va. 1959. Law clk. to Hon. Herbert S. Boreman, Judge of 4th Cir. Ct. Appeals, 1958—59; atty. Clifford, Jones & Williams, Clarksburg, W.Va., 1960—89, West & Jones (formerly Clifford, Jones & Williams), Clarksburg, W.Va., 1989—. Fellow: Am. Bd. Trial Advs., Am. Coll. Trial Lawyers; mem.: ABA, Assn. Trial Lawyers Am., W.Va. Trial Lawyers Assn. (pres. 1971), Harrison County Bar Assn., W.Va. State Bar (bd. govs. 1975 1978), Phi Delta Phi. Office: West and Jones PO Box 2348 360 Washington Ave Clarksburg WV 26301

WEST, JAMES E. acoustical engineer; Mem. tech. staff dept. acoustics and audio comm. AT&T Bell Labs., now Lucent Technologies, Bell Labs, Murray Hill, N.J. Recipient Silver medal Acoustical Soc. Am., 1995. Mem. NAE. Office: Lucent Technologies Bell Labs Room 2D 338 600 Mountain Ave Rm 2d338 New Providence NJ 07974-2008

WEST, JAMES JOSEPH, lawyer; b. Tarentum, Pa., Nov. 26, 1945; s. Samuel Elwood and Rose (McIntyre) W.; m. Kathleen Geslak, Aug. 19, 1967; children: Joseph Allen, Yvonne Michelle, KaiLynn Ann. BS in Econs., St. Vincent Coll., 1967; JD, Duquesne U., 1970. Bar: Pa. 1971, U.S. Dist. Ct. (we. dist.) Pa. 1971, U.S. Ct. Appeals (3d cir.) 1971, U.S. Dist. Ct. (mid. dist.) Pa., 1980. Law clk. to presiding justice U.S. Dist. Ct., Pa., 1970-74; asst. U.S. atty. chief appellate sect. U.S. Atty.'s Office, Pitts., 1974-79; dep. dir. criminal law Pa. Atty. Gen.'s Office, Harrisburg, 1979-82; 1st asst. U.S. atty. U.S. Dist. Ct. (mid. dist.) Pa., Harrisburg, 1982-84, U.S. atty., 1984-93; assoc. Sprague & Sprague, Phila., 1993-95; pvt. practice Harrisburg, Pa., 1995—. Mem. Nat. Environ. Enforcement Council. Recipient Outstanding Performance award U.S. Dept. Justice, 1974-78, Commendation Gov. of Pa., 1981. Mem. Pa. Bar Assn., Allegheny County Bar Assn., Dauphin County Bar Assn. Republican. Roman Catholic. Home: 1222 Cardinal Way Rd Hummelstown PA 17036-8548 Office: James West 105 N Front St Harrisburg PA 17101-1483 E-mail: jwestlaw@aol.com.

WEST, JAMES REYENARD, dance educator, health educator; b. Jersey City, Nov. 28, 1960; s. James Albert and Juanita (Shorter) West; life ptnr. Dennis Milone. BA in Health Edn. summa cum laude, U. Palmers Green, London, 1983, MA in Social Work summa cum laude, 1985. Attendant U.S. Army Europe Terrace Officers Club, Frankfurt, Germany, 1984-85; mgr. King Creole's Restaurant, Frankfurt, 1985-86; asst. mgr. Dance Ctr. Frankfurt/Arthur Murray Dance Studio, 1986-97; coord. peer edn. AIDS Project R.I., Providence, 1997-2000, cons. youth programs, 1999—; instr. Burlington (Mass.) Sch. Dance, 1999—; dance dir. Authur Murray Dance Studio, N.Y.C. Cons. Dept. Human Svcs., Pitts., 1999. Founding mem., mem. adv. com. Gay Men of African Descent-N.E. Regional Capacity Bldg. Assistance Program, N.Y.C., 1999—; chmn. pub. rels. Enforcers, R.I., Providence, 1999; incorporator, exec. dir. Orgn. for Men of Ethnicity Geared to Advancement, Providence, 2000—. With USAF, 1981-83. Mem.: World Profl. Dance Tchrs. Assn. (master bachelor instr./adj.). Democrat. Moslem. Avocations: weight training, travel, reading, movies, theater. Office: Arthur Murray Dance Studio 677 5th Ave New York NY 10022 Home: 108-52 Union Hall St Jamaica NY 11433 Office Phone: 212-593-1633. Business E-Mail: blackmerc@nyc.rr.com.

WEST, JERRY ALAN, professional basketball team executive; b. Chelyan, W.Va., May 28, 1938; s. Howard Stewart and Cecil Sue (Creasey) West; m. Martha Jane Kane, May 1960 (div. 1977); children: David, Michael, Mark; m. Karen Christine Bua, May 28, 1978; 1 child, Ryan. BS, W.Va. Coll.; LHD (hon.), W.Va. Wesleyan Coll. Mem. L.A. Lakers, NBA, 1960—74, coach, 1976—79, spl. cons., 1979—82, gen. mgr., 1982—94, exec. v.p. basketball ops., 1994—2000; pres. basketball operations Memphis Grizzlies, 2002—; mem. first team Nat. Basketball Assn. All-Star Team, 1962—67, mem. second team, 1968—69. Mem. NBA champion L.A. Lakers, 1972. Author (with William Libby): Mr. Clutch: The Jerry West Story, 1969. Named capt., U.S. Olympic Basketball Team, 1960, Most Valuable Player NBA Playoff, 1969, All-Star Game Most Valuable Player, 1972, NBA Exec. of Yr., Sporting News, 1994—95, NBA Exec. of the Year, 1995, 2004; named to Naismith Meml. Basketball Hall of Fame, 1979, NBA Hall of Fame, 1980, NBA 35th Anniversity All-Time Team, 1980. Office: c/o Memphis Grizzlies 175 Toyota Plaza ste 150 Memphis TN 38103

WEST, JOHN BURNARD, physiologist, educator; b. Adelaide, Australia, Dec. 27, 1928; came to U.S., 1969; s. Esmond Frank and Meta Pauline (Spehr) W.; m. Penelope Hall Banks, Oct. 28, 1967; children: Robert Burnard, Joanna Ruth. MB, BChir, Adelaide U., 1951, MD, 1958, DSc, 1980; PhD, London U., 1960; DSc (hon.), U. Barcelona, Spain, 1987, U. Ferrara, 2004. Resident Royal Adelaide Hosp., 1952, Hammersmith Hosp., London, 1953-55; physiologist Sir Edmund Hillary's Himalayan Expdn., 1960-61; dir. respiratory rsch. group Postgrad. Med. Sch., London, 1962-67, reader medicine, 1968; prof. medicine and physiology U. Calif., San Diego, 1969—. Leader Am. Med. Rsch. Expdn. to Mt. Everest, 1981; U.S. organizer China-U.S. Conf. on respiratory failure, Nanjing, 1986; mem. life scis. adv. com. NASA, 1985-88, task force sci. uses of space sta., 1984-87, aerospace med. adv. com., 1988-89, chmn. sci. verification com. Spacelab SLS-1, 1983-92, commn. on respiratory physiol. Internat. Union Physiol. Scis., 1985—, commn. on clin. physiol., 1991—, commn. gravitation physiol., 1986—, study sect. NIH, chmn., 1973-75; prin. investigator Spacelabs SLS 1, 2, LMS, Neurolab, 1983—; co-investigator European Spacelabs, D2, Euromir, 1987—; external examiner Nat. U. Singpore, 1995; lectr. in field. Author: Ventilation/Blood Flow and Gas Exchange, 1965, Respiratory Physiology-The Essentials, 1974, Translations in Respiratory Physiology, 1975, Pulmonary Pathophysiology-The Essentials, 1977, Translations in Respiratory Physiology, 1977, Bioengineering Aspects of the Lung, 1977, Regional Differences in the Lung, 1977, Pulmonary Gas Exchange (2 vols.), 1980, High Altitude Physiology, 1981, High Altitude and Man, 1984, Everest-The Testing Place, 1985, Best and Taylor's Physiological Basis of Medical Practice, 1985, 91, Study Guide for Best and Taylor, 1985, High Altitude Medicine and Physiology, 1989, The Lung: Scientific Foundations, 1991, 2d edit., 1997, Lung Injury, 1992, Respiratory Physiology: People and Ideas, 1996, High Life: A History of High Altitude Physiology and Medicine, 1998; founder, editor-in-chief High Altitude Medicine and Biology, 2000-. Recipient Ernest Jung prize for medicine, Hamburg, 1977, Presdl. citation Am. Coll. Chest Physicians, 1977, Kaiser Tchg. award 1980; scholar Macy Found., 1974; Jeffries Med. Rsch. award AIAA, 1992. Fellow Royal Coll. Physicians (London), Royal Australasian Coll. Physicians, Royal Geog. Soc. (London), AAAS (med. sci. nominating com. 1987-93, coun. del. sect. med. scis.), Am. Inst. for Med. and Biol. Engring. (founding fellow 1992), Am. Heart Assn. (G.C. Griffith lectr. 1978, D.W. Richards lectr. 1980), Internat. Soc. for Mountain Medicine (pres. 1991-94); mem. NAS (com. space biology and medicine 1986-90, subcom. on space biology 1984-85, com. advanced space tech. 1992-94, panel on small spacecraft tech. 1994), Am. Assn. Thoracic Surgery (hon.), Nat. Bd. Med. Examiners (physiology test com. 1973-76), Am. Physiol. Soc. (pres. 1984-85, coun. 1981-86, chmn. sect. on history of physiology 1984-92, hist. pubs. adv. com., Reynolds prize for history 1987, Ray Daggs award 1998, Guyton Tchg. award 2002, Julius H. Comroe lectr. 2003), Am. Acad. Arts and Scis., Am. Soc. Clin. Investigation, Physiol. Soc. Gt. Britain, Am. Thoracic Soc. (Edward Livingston Trudeau medal 2002), Assn. Am. Physicians, Western Assn. Physicians, Russian Acad. Sci. (elected fgn. mem.), Explorers Club, Fleischner Soc. (pres. 1985), Harveian Soc. (London), Royal Instn. Gt. Britain, Royal Soc. Medicine (London), Hurlingham Club (London), La Jolla Beach & Tennis Club. Home: 9626 Blackgold Rd La Jolla CA 92037-1110 Office: U Calif San Diego Sch Medicine 0623 Dept Medicine La Jolla CA 92093 Office Phone: 858-534-4192. Business E-Mail: jwest@ucsd.edu.

WEST, JOHN GARRETT, political scientist, educator; b. Auburn, Wash., 1964; s. John G. and Sophie West; m. Sonja Elise Nutley. BA in Comm., U. Wash., 1986; PhD in Govt., Claremont Grad. U., 1992. Mng. editor Pub. Rsch., Syndicated, Monclair, Calif., 1986—89; lectr. Calif. State U., San Bernardino, 1989—89; adj. lectr. Azusa (Calif.) Pacific U., 1989—90; fellow Discovery Inst., Seattle, 1992—93, sr. fellow, 1993—, assoc. dir. Ctr. for Sci. and Culture, 1996—; asst. prof. polit. sci. Seattle Pacific U., 1994—99, assoc. prof. polit. sci., 1999—, chmn. dept. polit. sci., 2000—. Grant proposal reviewer U.S. Commn. on the Bicentennial of the Constn., 1990—91. Author: (book) The Disney Live-Action Productions, 1994 (Silver Angel, Excellence in Media, 1995), The Politics of Revelation and Reason: Religion and Civic Life in the New Nation, 1996, (monograph) Public Life in the Shadowlands: What C.S. Lewis Can Teach Us About Politics; editor: (reference book) The C.S. Lewis Readers Encyclopedia, 1998 (Gold Medallion, Best Biography/Autobiography, ECPA, 1999), The Encyclopedia of Religion in American Politics, 1999, Encyclopedia of the American Constitution, Supplement I, (book) The Theology of Welfare, 2001; asst. editor: Encyclopedia Am. Constrn., 1988—92, mem. editl. bd.: Jour. Markets and Morality, 1998—2003; editor: Celebrating Middle Earth: The Lord of the Rings as a Defense of Western Civiliation, 2002. Fellow, Earhart Found., 1988—89; Publius fellow, Pub. Rsch., Syndicated, 1985, Chevron Journalism-Economics scholar, U. Wash., 1985—86, Weaver fellow, Intercollegiate Studies Inst., 1987—88, Haynes Found. Dissertation grantee, Claremont Grad. U., 1990—91. Mem.: Am. Polit. Sci. Assn., Golden Key, Pi Sigma Alpha (pres. Claremont Coll. chpt. 1989—90), Phi Beta Kappa. Office: Seattle Pacific Univ 3307 Third Ave W Seattle WA 98119 E-mail: jwest@spu.edu.

WEST, JOHN MERLE, retired physicist, nuclear consultant; b. Stilwell, Okla., Jan. 18, 1920; s. James M. and Maude B. (Bacon) W.; m. Navlion Farmer, Oct. 5, 1945; children: J. Cornel, L. Clark. BS in Phys. Sci. and Math. with highest honors, Northeastern State U., 1939; MS in Physics, U. Iowa, 1941. Physicist, supr. Du Pont Co., Carney's Point, N.J., 1941-42, Pryor, Okla., 1942-43, U. Chgo. Manhattan Project, 1943-44, Hanford Works Manhattan Project, 1944-46, GE, Hanford Works, Richland, Wash., 1946-49; asst. dir. reactor engring., project mgr. Argonne Nat. Lab., Lemont, Ill., 1949-57; exec. v.p. Gen. Nuclear Engring. Corp., Dunedin, Fla., 1957-65; v.p. nuclear activities Combustion Engring. Inc., Windsor, Conn., 1965-84; sr. v.p. Nuclear Combustion Engring. Inc., Windsor, Conn., 1984-85. Nuclear cons., Cape Coral, Fla., 1985—. Contbr. numerous articles to profl. jours., papers at profl. meetings; holder numerous patents. Recipient Charles Coffin award GE, 1949. Fellow Am. Nuclear Soc. (charter mem., Walter Zinn award 1983); mem. NAE, Engrs. Club. Republican. Presbyterian. Home and Office: 1608 SE 40th Ter Cape Coral FL 33904-7467

WEST, KENNETH IRWIN, automotive executive; b. Aza Kuwae, Okinawa, Japan, July 1, 1966; (parents Am. citizens); s. Jackie Eugene and Ritsuko Maki West. Diploma in small engine repair, Foley-Belsaw Inst., Kansas City, Mo., 1983; A in Bus. and Auto/Diesel Tech., U. Northwestern Ohio, 1985; diploma in computer repair, Internat. Corr. Sch., 1991. Cert. automotive svc. excellence Bur. Automotive Repair. Gen. mgr. Great Bear Auto Ctr., Huntington Beach, Calif., 1987—. Avocations: building models, computer programming, computer graphics, multiplayer online gaming, building high performance street cars.

WEST, LEE ROY, federal judge; b. Clayton, Okla., Nov. 26, 1929; s. Calvin and Nicie (Hill) W.; m. MaryAnn Ellis, Aug. 29, 1952; children: Kimberly Ellis, Jennifer Lee. BA, U. Okla., 1952, JD, 1956; LL.M. (Ford Found. fellow), Harvard U., 1963. Bar: Okla. 1956. Individual practice law, Ada, Okla., 1956-61, 63-65; faculty U. Okla. Coll. Law, 1961-62; Ford Found. fellow in law teaching Harvard U., Cambridge, Mass., 1962-63; judge 22d Jud. Dist. Okla., Ada, 1965-73; mem. CAB, Washington, 1973-78, acting chmn., 1977; practice law Tulsa, 1978-79; spl. justice Okla. Supreme Ct., 1965; judge U.S. Dist Ct. (we. dist.) Okla., 1979-94; sr. judge U.S. Dist. Ct. (we. dist.), Okla., 1994—. Editor: Okla. Law Rev. Served to capt. USMC, 1952-54. Recipient Humanitarian award Nat. Conf. Cmty. and Justice, 2000, Jud. Excellence award Okla. Bar Assn., 2000. Mem. U. Okla. Alumni Assn. (dir.), Phi Delta Phi (pres. 1956), Phi Eta Sigma, Order of Coif. Home: 6500 E Danforth Rd Edmond OK 73034-7601 Office: US Dist Ct 3001 US Courthouse 200 NW 4th St Oklahoma City OK 73102-3027

WEST, MACDONALD, real estate executive; b. Bournemouth, Eng., July 15, 1943; arrived in U.S., 1968; s. Joseph Stanley and Maisie Siswick W.; m. Charlotte Denise Duvall, Nov. 1, 1980. Diploma, London U. Coll. Estate Mgmt., 1968; MBA, Columbia U., 1970. Trainee surveyor Navy Works Dept., Admiralty, London, 1960—64; sr. assoc. Robinson & Roods, London, 1965—68; dir. cost control Nat. Liberty Corp., Valley Forge, Pa., 1970—71; v.p., dir. Philipsborn Cos., Coral Gables, Fla., 1972—76, Allen Morris Co., Miami, 1976—89; sr. v.p., COO Allen Morris Constrn. Co., 1978—89, also sr. v.p. asset mgmt. divsn.; pres. Miami Lakes Devel., Inc., Fla., 1989—91; exec. v.p. The Graham Cos., Miami Lakes, 1989—91; pres., CEO The Macdonald West Co., Miami, 1991—; mng. dir. The Allen Morris Co., 2000—02. Deacon U. Bapt. Ch., Coral Gables, 1977—. Fellow Royal Instn. Chartered Surveyors; mem. Counselors Real Estate (pres. 1995), Nat. Assn. Realtors, Am. Arbitration Assn., Realtors Comml. Alliance (chair 2000, 2004-2005), Nat. Assn. Indsl. and Office Parks, Indsl. Assn. Dade County, Comml. Realtor Assn. Greater Miami (pres. 2000), Builders Assn. South Fla. (pres. 1996), Nat. Assn. Home Builders, Ocean Reef Club, Rotary (Miami). Republican. Home: 5325 Orduna Dr Coral Gables FL 33146-2640 Office: 1390 S Dixie Hwy Ste 2225 Miami FL 33146-2946

WEST, MARK OTTO, psychology educator; b. Omaha, Nebr., Jan. 16, 1948; s. Otto Cornelius and Cathryn Ann West; m. Carol Anne Christian, Aug. 12, 1984; children: Tivoli Anne, Heidi Cathryn, Whitney Caroline, Dane Mark, Skye Shannon, Dallas Kristin, Robert Edward. BS, U. of Calif., 1976; PhD, Wake Forest U., 1982. Postdoctoral rsch. assoc. U. of Tex. Southwestern Med. Sch., Dallas, 1982—86; prof. of psychology Rutgers U., New Brunswick, NJ, 1986—. Ad hoc reviewer NIH, Bethesda, Md., 1990—. Contbr. rsch. articles to sci. jours.; editl. reviewer: manuscripts for jours. With U.S. Army, 1968—69, Vietnam. Grantee, NSF, 1987—90, Nat. Inst. on Drug Abuse, 1987—92, 1990—93, 1992—97, 1993—97, 1997—2001, 2001—04. Mem.: Soc. for Neurosci. Achievements include discovery of functional reorganization of brain connections in basal ganglia in Parkinson's disease; First described somatotopic arrangement (functional organization) of the striatum in the basal ganglia of the rat brain; discovery of electrical activity in hippocampus that was correlated with updating (working) memory. Avocations: running, swimming, bicycling. Office: Rutgers U Busch Campus 152 Frelinghuysen Rd Piscataway NJ 08854 E-mail: markwest@rci.rutgers.edu.

WEST, MARY BETH, federal agency administrator; b. Wis., Nov. 20, 1944; BA with honors, U. Mich., 1966; JD, Stanford U., 1972. Bar: Calif. 1973, D.C. 1974. With Office Legal Adviser Dept. State, 1973-75, 82-88, 92-96; with Am. Indian Lawyer Tng. Program, 1975-78; with Office of Gen. Counsel NOAA, 1978-82; dep. asst. sec. of state for oceans, fisheries and space Bur. Oceans & Internat. Environ. and Sci. Affairs Dept.State, Washington, 1995—2003; prof., State Dept. chair Indsl. Coll. of Armed Forces, 2003—. Vis. prof. U. N.Mex. Sch. Law, 1988-92. Contbr. articles to profl. jours. Bd. dirs., bd. visitors Stanford Law Sch., 1989 91; bd. dirs. Trinity Forum, 1989-92, N.Mex. Mediation Assn., 1991-92, Coun. on Ocean Law, 1992-96, Am. Soc. Internat. Law Com. on State Responsibility, 1992-97; adv. bd. Univ. Va. Ctr., 2001-.

WEST, MICHAEL ALAN, retired hospital administrator; b. Waseca, Minn., Aug. 4, 1938; s. Ralph Leland and Elizabeth Mary (Brann) W.; m. Mary Thissen, Jan. 21, 1961; children— Anne, Nancy, Douglas. BA, U. Minn., 1961, MHA, 1963. Sales corr. Physicians and Hosps. Supply Co., Mpls., 1959-60; adminstrv. resident R.I. Hosp., Providence, 1962-63, adminstrv. asst., 1963-65, asst. dir., 1965-68; exec. asst. dir. Med. Center U. Mo., Columbia, 1968-70, assoc. dir., 1970-74, asst. prof. community health and med. practice, 1968-74; v.p. for adminstrn. Luth. Gen. Hosp., Park Ridge, Ill., 1974-80, exec. v.p., 1980-84; pres., CEO Akron Gen. Med. Ctr., Ohio, 1984-97, Akron Gen. Health Sys., 1997—2002. Bd. dirs. Vol. Hosps. Am. Inc.; chair VHA-Ctrl., Inc. Bd. dirs. Great Trails Coun. Boy Scouts Am. Mem. Am. Coll. Healthcare Execs., Akron Regional Hosp. Assn. (chmn.), Portage Country Club, Akron City Club, Catawba Island Club, Noreaster Club. Home: 495 Woodbury Dr Akron OH 44333-2780

WEST, MICHAEL G. semiconductor company executive; BS in Electronic Engring.; BS in Math., Oreg. State U.; MSEE, U. Ill. Integrated cir. designer Floating Point Sys., 1982—86; integrated cir. design engr. Bipolar Integrated Tech., 1986—87; chief scientist, sr. engr. In Focus Sys., 1988—96; co-founder, v.p. tech. Pixelworks, Inc., Tualatin, Oreg., 1997—, fellow, 2003—. Office: Pixelworks Inc Ste 300 8100 SW Nyberg Rd Tualatin OR 97062*

WEST, NANCY LEE, music educator, performance artist, entertainer; b. Evansville, Ind., Dec. 5, 1929; d. Harold Addison and Helen Beatrice (Roland) Hill; m. Owen L. West, Aug. 2, 1952; children: Gail Ann, Janet Lee, Robert Owen. BFA, Wesleyan U., Ill., 1952. Pvt. practice, Gibson City, Ill., 1952-57, Urbana, Ill., 1957-59, Buckhannon, W.Va., 1959-68, Eureka, Ill., 1968—; music tchr. Elliott (Ill.) Elem. Sch., 1953-54; piano soloist various events, hotels, restaurants in W.Va. and Ill., 1953—; dance orch. leader various parties, clubs, benefits, Ill., 1985—; piano accompanist various musical prodns., performances in W.Va. and Ill., 1953—. Cello player Symphony Orch., Bloomington, Ill., 1950-52. Mem. adv. bd. Ctrl. Ill. Youth Symphony, Peoria, 1969-78; mem. women's bd. Eureka Coll. Recipient Purchase award Walnut Grove Fine Arts Assn., Eureka, 1978, Best of Show award, Clarksburg, W.Va., 1966, One Person Show award Volkwein Music, Pitts., 1967; winner Grand prize Salem Coll., W.Va., 1965. Mem. Am. Coll. Musicians, Music Tchrs. Nat. Assn., Am. Fedn. Musicians, AAUW, Peoria Area Music Tchrs. Assn. Mem. Christian Ch. Avocations: sewing, crafts, reading, dance. Home and Office: 810 N Main St Eureka IL 61530-9412

WEST, NATALIE ELSA, lawyer; b. Greenwich, Conn., Mar. 11, 1947; AB, Smith Coll., 1968; JD, U. Calif., Berkeley, 1973. Bar: Calif. 1974. Counsel Calif. Fair Polit. Practices Commn., Sacramento, 1975-79; city atty. City of Berkeley, Calif., 1980-85, City of Novato, Calif., 1985-92, City of Brentwood, Calif., 1994-99; gen. counsel Livermore-Amador Valley Water Mgmt. Agy., 1996—2001; shareholder McDonough, Holland & Allen, Oakland, Calif., 1991—. Lectr. law U. Calif., Berkeley, 2000-01. Pres. city attys. dept. League of Calif. Cities, 1986-87, bd. dirs., 1995-97. Mem. State Bar Calif., Alameda County Bar Assn. Office: McDonough Holland & Allen 9th Fl 1901 Harrison St Oakland CA 94612-3582

WEST, NETTIE J.R. music educator; b. Schoharie, NY, Oct. 12, 1925; d. Everett C. and Christina M. Maria (Youngs) Ruland; m. J. Russell Langwig, Sept. 11, 1948 (div. 1976); children: J. Russell, John Everett, Christina; m. Robert L. West, Oct. 8, 1983; stepchildren: Elizabeth Ann, Kathleen Suzanne, Laurel Marie. BS, BM cum laude, Skidmore Coll., 1947; MA, U. Buffalo, 1968; cert. Suzuki tchg., Sch. for Strings, N.Y.C., 1983, Ithaca Coll., 1978-79. Music instr. Suzuki Sounds Violin Sch., Lagrangeville, NY, 1984—; orch. tchr. Hyde Park (N.Y.) H.S., 1983-84; Suzuki violin tchr. The Music Box, Poughkeepsie, 1997-99, Hudson Valley Philharm. Music Sch., Poughkeepsie, 1979-80; sub. tchr. Arlington Sch., Wappingers Dist., 1976-80; violinist Woodstock (N.Y.) Chamber Orch., 1983—; Suzuki violin instr. Dutchess Cmty. Coll. Music Sch., 2003—. Attendee internat. confs. Suzuki Method, Matsumoto, Japan, 1983, 89, 99, Alberta Canada, 1985, Berlin, Germany, 1987, Adelaide, Australia, 1991, Dublin, Ireland, 1995; instr. Dutchess C.C., 2003—. Mem. Religious Soc. Friends, Bulls-Head Oswego Meeting, 1980—, mem. worship group Green Haven Corr. Fac., 1980—; facilitator Alternatives to Violence Project, 1980—, coord. 1986-89; mem. Martha's Vineyard Hist. Assn. Mem. Suzuki Assn. Am., Inc., Music Educators Nat. Conf., N.Y. State Sch. Music Assn., Lagoon Pond Assn. Inc. of Martha's Vineyard. Avocations: swimming, skiing, bird watching, reading, attending concerts.

WEST, NORMAN ELLSWORTH, artist; b. Exeter, N.H., May 16, 1952; s. Norman Ellsworth and Alice Marie West. BS, Plymouth State Coll., 1976; BFA, Maine Coll. of Art, 1980. Leader color workshops regional schs., York County, 1981—; artist in residence Holderness Acad., Plymouth, N.H., 1989-91; set designer Shenanigans Prodns., Portland, Boston, 1993-96; tchr. Heartwood Coll. of Art, Kennebunk, Maine, 1994—. Dir. Heartwood Coll. Art Gallery, 2002. One person shows include West Kuhn Gallery, Cape Neddick, Maine, 1988, Van Ward Gallery, Ogunquit, Maine, 1994, 98; group shows include Currier Gallery, Manchester, N.H., 1988, 89, Barn Gallery, Ogunquit, 1988, Mast Core Galleries, Kennebunkport, Maine, 1988, 89, Ogunquit Art Assn., 1988—, Maine Coast Artists, Rockport, Maine, 1989, 90. Bd. dirs. Shellfish Commn., Ogunquit, Maine, 1996—; clam warden Town of Ogunquit, 1997-99. Mem. Ogunquit Art Assn. (curator invited sculptor's exhibit 1996—), Ogunquit Arts Collaborative (v.p. 2000—), Ogunquit Rotary Club. Home: PO Box 1560 Ogunquit ME 03907

WEST, PAUL NODEN, author, playwright; b. Eckington, Derbyshire, Eng., Feb. 23, 1930; arrived in US, 1961, naturalized, 1971; s. Alfred Massick and Mildred (Noden) W. Student, Oxford U., 1950-53; MA, Columbia U., 1953. Asst. prof. English Meml. U. Nfld., Canada, 1957-58, assoc. prof., 1958-60; faculty Pa. State U., Pa., 1962-95, prof. English and comparative lit., 1968-95; prof. emeritus, 1995—. Crawshaw prof. Colgate U., 1972; Melvin Hill disting. vis. prof. Hobart and William Smith Coll., 1973; vis. English prof. Cornell U., 1986; disting. writer in residence Wichita State U., 1982; vis. prof. English Brown U., 1992; fiction judge Creative Artists Pub. Svc. Program, NYC, 1974, 81; writer-in-residence U. Ariz., 1984; judge Katherine Ann Porter Prize for Fiction, 1984, Artists Found. Author: Byron and the Spoiler's Art, 1960, rev. edit., 1990, I Said the Sparrow, 1963, The Snow Leopard, 1965, Tenement of Clay, 1965, The Wine of Absurdity, 1966, Alley Jaggers, 1967, libretta for opera, 1968, I'm Expecting to Live Quite Soon, 1970, Words for a Deaf Daughter, 1970, Caliban's Filibuster, 1972, Colonel Mint, 1973, Gala, 1976, The Very Rich Hours of Count von Stauffenberg, 1980, Out of My Depths: A Swimmer in the Universe, 1983, Rat Man of Paris, 1986, theatrical version, 1987, Sheer Fiction, 1987, The Universe and Other Fiction, 1988, The Place in Flowers Where Pollen Rests, 1988, Lord Byron's Doctor, 1989, Portable People, The Women of Whitechapel and Jack the Ripper, 1991, Sheer Fiction: II, 1991, James Ensor, 1991, Love's Mansion, 1992, Tenement of Clay, 2d edit., 1993, Sheer Fiction, III, 1994, A Stroke of Genius, 1995, The Tent of Orange Mist, 1995 (memoir) My Mother's Music, 1996 (novel) Sporting with Amaryllis, 1996, Terrestrials, 1997, Life With Swan, 1999, O.K.: The Corral, The Earps, and Doc Holliday, 2000, The Dry Danube: A Hitler Forgery, 2000, The Secret Lives of Words, 2000, A Fifth of November, 2001, Master Class, 2001, Oxford Days, 2002, Cheops: A Cupboard for the Sun, 2002, (play) Any Old How, 2002, (radio play) The Sacrifice, 1955, The Immensity of the Here and Now, 2003, Sheer Fiction IV, 2004, Samuel Beckett: Born Astride A Grave, 2004; contbr. Washington Post and NY Times, 1962—, Harper's Mag., Paris Rev., Yale Rev., Parnassus, Agni, Conjunctions, War, Literature and the Arts, First Intensity, Tin Roof, tranlator Les Romanesques by Rostand, 1954 fiction judge NY Found. for the Arts, Nat. Book award, 1990. Served RAF, 1954—57. Decorated chevalier de l'Ordre des Arts et des Lettres (France); recipient Aga Khan Fiction prize, 1973, Hazlett Meml. award for Excellence in Arts (lit.), 1981, Lit. award Am. Acad. and Inst. Arts and Letters, 1985, Pushcart prize 1987, 91, 2003, The Best Am. Essays award, 1990, Outstanding Achievement medal Pa. State U., 1991, Grand Prix Halpérine Kaminsky award, 1992, Lannan Fiction award, 1993, Tchg. award Northeastern Assn. Grad. Sch., 1994, Art of Fact prize SUNY, 2000; named Lit. Lion NY Pub. Libr., 1987; Guggenheim fellow, 1963; NEA Creative Writing fellow, 1979, 84; nominated for Médicis, Femina and Meilleur Livre Étranger prizes, France, 1991, Lannan Lit. Videos 35, Nat. Book Critics award for fiction, 1996; named to Honor Roll The Yr. in Fiction, DLB Yearbook, 1996, Conf. on works of West, U. of Tours, France, 2003; manuscript collection at Pattee Libr., Pa. State U. Office: Elaine Markson Agy 44 Greenwich Ave Fl 3 New York NY 10011-8389 *The unexamined life may not be worth having, but the examined life is endurable only to an open mind, through which life holistically flows, keeping that mind as incomplete as our knowledge of the universe itself.*

WEST, RALPH LELAND, veterinarian; b. Grand Rapids, Minn., Apr. 23, 1915; s. Ralph Leland and Elsie (Wardall) W.; m. Mary Elizabeth Brann, June 14, 1937; children: Michael Alan, Janet Lee West Friedrich, Thomas James. DVM, Iowa State U., 1936; MS, Purdue U., 1972. Pvt. practice, Waseca, Minn., 1936-42, 46-70; grad. asst. Sch. Vet. Medicine Purdue U., West Lafayette, Ind., 1970-72; asst. dir. sci. activities Am. Vet. Med. Assn., Schaumburg, Ill., 1972-77, dir. sci. activities, 1977-87. Contbr. articles to jours. in field. Mem. Pk. Bd., Waseca, 1948-50, Youth Commn., 1948-52; mem., chmn. Waseca Hosp. Bd., 1954-64; trustee Sunny Acres Village Inc., Denver, 1988-95. Maj. U.S. Army, 1942-46, ETO. Recipient Stange award Iowa State U., 1983. Mem. AMVA (award 1990), Am. Assn. Ret. Vets. (dir. 1987-90), Am. Vet. History Soc., Colo. Vet. Med. Assn., Minn. Vet. Med. Assn., Iowa State U. Vet. Alumni Assn., Phi Zeta. Republican. Avocations: reading, tv sports, stock market. Home: 1719 E Bijou St Apt 611 Colorado Springs CO 80909-5751 E-mail: WDrwest1@aol.com.

WEST, REXFORD LEON, retired bank executive; b. Syracuse, N.Y., Feb. 18, 1938; s. Rexford A. and Nina (Crysler) W.; m. Grace Carlile, Apr. 24, 1999 (div.); children from previous marriage: Lisa, Julie, Gregory, Kristen. AAS, Auburn C.C., N.Y., 1957; BS magna cum laude, Syracuse U., N.Y., 1972; Advanced Mgmt. Program, Harvard Bus. Sch., Boston, 1984. Accountant Marine Midland Bank, Syracuse, N.Y., 1959-67, v.p., asst. treas., 1967-72; v.p., contr. Marine Midland Services Corp., Buffalo, N.Y., 1972-76; v.p. ops. divsn. Marine Midland Bank, N.A., Buffalo, N.Y., 1976-77, sr. v.p., sr. ops. officer, 1977-79, exec. v.p., sr. ops. officer, 1979-85, divsn. exec. ops., 1985-87, sector exec. ops. and fin. mgmt., 1987-90, sr. exec. v.p. corp. engring., 1990-92; exec. v.p. adminstrv. svc. Fleet Bank, Melville, N.Y., 1992-94; exec. v.p. loan servicing Fleet Mortgage Group, Columbia, S.C., 1994-96; ret., 1996. Served with U.S. Army, 1957-61

WEST, ROBERT GRADY, lawyer; b. Dallas, Aug. 13, 1947; s. Robert Sorrells and Thelma Grady W.; m. Marsha Lee Riegert, June 5, 1971; children: Kathryn Lee, Laura Elaine. BA, Midwestern State U., 1969; JD, U. Tex., 1972. Bar: Tex. 1972, U.S. Dist. Ct. (no. dist.) Tex. 1975, U.S. Ct. Appeals (5th cir.) 1976, U.S. Dist. Ct. (ea. dist.) Tex. 1992. Assoc. McGown, Godfrey, Decker, McMackin, Shipman & McClane, Ft. Worth, 1972-77, ptnr., 1977-88, Decker, McMackin & McClane, Ft. Worth, 1988-90, Decker, Jones, McMackin, McClane, Hall & Bates, Ft. Worth, 1990-93; assoc. Michener, Larimore, Swindle, Whitaker, et al, Ft. Worth, 1993-98, ptnr., 1999-2000, Whitaker, Chalk, Swindle & Sawyer, 2000—. Contbr. articles to profl. jours. Bd. regents Midwestern State U., Wichita Falls, Tex., 1992-98; dir. Grace Found., Dallas, 1990-92, Hist. Camp Bowie, Inc., Ft. Worth, 2002-; mem. Tex. Ctr. Legal Ethics and Professionalism, 1994—, Leadership Ft. Worth, 1984; elder, trustee Presbyn. Ch. Mem. ABA, Am. Assn. Profl. Landmen, State Bar Tex., Tarrant County Bar Assn. (chmn. real estate sect. 2001-02, 04-, spkr. CLE seminars). Avocations: travel, musical theatre, walking, volunteering. Office: Whitaker Chalk Swindle & Sawyer 3500 City Ctr Tower II 301 Commerce St Fort Worth TX 76102-4186 E-mail: rwest@whitakerchalk.com.

WEST, ROBERT LEE, JR., marketing professional; b. Wilmington, N.C., Oct. 5, 1958; s. Robert L. Sr. and Elsie S. (Skipper) W.; m. Shari H., Aug. 1, 1998. BSBA, U. N.C., Pembroke, 1981; postgrad., U. Pa., 1988—90. Divsn. controller Royster Co., Norfolk, Va., 1982-84; regional fin. mgr. Rohm & Haas Co., Phila., 1984-86; head Asian ops. Franklin Mint, Hone Kong, 1986-88, head corp. cost improvement Phila., 1988-89, head European ops. London, 1989-90; v.p. fin. & ops. Paradise Galleries, Inc., San Diego, 1990-91; v.p., chief fin. officer Georgetown Collection, Inc., Portland, Maine, 1992-95; v.p. worldwide ops. Nat. Media Corp., Phoenix, 1995-97; pres., founder DCA Internat., Phoenix, 1990—; CEO, pres. Georgetown Collection, Inc., Portland, Maine, 1997-98; chief oper. officer, pres. LL Knickerbocker, Lake Forest, Calif., 1998-99; v.p., gen. mgr. Chevrolet Catalog, San Diego, 1999—. Cons. to CEO J Crew, N.Y.C., 1990-91. V.p. Maxton (N.C.) Conservative Response, 1980-82; lay leader Good Shepherd Luth. Ch., Irvine, Calif. Named one of Top Exec. Leading Direct Mktg., Phila. Inquirer Mag. Mem. Am. Mgmt. Assn., Am. Fin. Assn., Inst. Mgmt. Accts., World Affairs Coun. Republican. Avocations: biking, church activities, model railroading, tennis, long distance running. Office: DCA Dynamic Cons Assocs Ste 300 4 Venture Irvine CA 92618 Address: 26741 Portola Pkwy Ste 1E Box 130 Foothill Ranch CA 92610

WEST, ROBERT LEWIS, financial planner; b. Springfield, Ohio, Aug. 18, 1951; s. Robert Leslie W. and Julia Belle (Early) Emmons; m. Helen Marie Israel, June 1982 (div. Dec. 1992); m. Deanne Kay Bender, Oct. 14, 1995; children: Christopher Robert, Amy Lynn. Cert. fin. planner; cert. sr. advisor designation. Ins. agt., Springfield, Ohio, 1973-77; fin. planner, sales mgr. Columbus, Ohio, 1977-84; stockbroker McDonald & Co., Dayton, Ohio, 1984-85; assoc. v.p. investments Prudential Bache Securities, Dayton, Ohio, 1985-87; v.p. investments Dean Witter Reynolds, Dayton & Cin., Ohio, 1987-90; fin. planner, investment advisor Dayton, 1990—; founder, CEO Estate Planning Strategies, Inc., dba EPS Invest. Adv., Dayton, 1992—. Republican. Lutheran. Avocations: hunting, fishing, wood working, sports cars. Office: Estate Planning Strategies Agy 3055 Rodenbeck Dr Beavercreek OH 45432

WEST, ROBERT MACLELLAN, science educator, consultant; b. Appleton, Wis., Sept. 1, 1942; s. Clarence John and Elizabeth Ophelia (Moore) West; m. Jean Sydow, June 19, 1965; 1 child, Christopher. BA, Lawrence Coll., 1963; SM, U. Chgo., 1964, PhD, 1968. Rsch. assoc. Princeton (N.J.) U., 1968-69; asst. prof. Adelphi U., Garden City, NY, 1969-74; curator geology Milw. Pub. Mus., 1974-83; dir. Carnegie Mus. Natural History, Pitts., 1983-87, Cranbrook Inst. Sci., Bloomfield Hills, Mich., 1987-91; prin. RMW Sci. Action, Washington, 1992-95; pres. Informal Sci., Inc., Washington, 1993-98, Informal Learning Experiences, Inc., Washington, 1999—. Adj. prof. U. Wis., Milw., 1974—83. Contbr. articles to profl. jours. Bd. dirs. Friends New Zoo, Pitts., 1984—87; treas. E. Mich. Environ. Action Coun., Birmingham, 1987—92. Named Man of the Yr. in Sci., Vectors Pitts., 1988; recipient Arnold Guyot prize, Nat. Geographic Soc., 1982; NSF fellow, 1965—68, NSF Rsch. grantee, 1970—82, Nat. Geographic Soc. Rsch. grantee, 1973, 1976, 1977, 1979, 1980, 1982. Mem.: Am. Assn. Mus., Mus. Group, Paleontology Soc., Geol. Soc. Am., Soc. Vertebrate Paleontology, Nepal Natural History Soc. (advisor 1992—), Nat. Ctr. Sci. Edn. (bd. dirs. 1984—88, 1992—), Rotary. Avocations: nature, history, sports. Office: Informal Learning Experiences Inc PO Box 42328 Washington DC 20015-0928 Office Phone: 202-362-5823. Business E-Mail: ile@informallearning.com.

WEST, ROBERT VAN OSDELL, JR., retired petroleum executive; b. Kansas City, Mo., Apr. 29, 1921; s. Robert Van Osdell and Josephine (Quistgaard) W.; divorced; children: Robert Van Osdell III, Kathryn Anne, Suzanne Small, Patricia Lynn; m. Helen L. Boecking, 1978. BS, U. Tex., 1942, MS, 1943, PhD, 1949. Registered profl engr., Tex. Petroleum engr. Slick Urschel Oil Co., 1949-56; pres. Slick Secondary Recovery Corp., 1956-59; v.p. Texstar Corp., 1959; pres. Texstar Petroleum Co. subs. Texstar Corp., 1959-64; founder Tesoro Petroleum Corp., San Antonio, 1964, chmn. bd. dirs., chief exec. officer, 1971-88, chmn. bd., 1989-92, chief exec. officer, 1964-92; retired. Bd. dirs. Frost Nat. Bank. Mem. engring. found. adv. coun. U. Tex., mem. at large and life Centennial Commm.; former bd. visitors McDonald Obs. and Astronomy; mem. devel. bd. U. Tex. San Antonio Health Sci. Ctr.; assoc. mem. bd. visitors U. Tex. M.D. Anderson Cancer Ctr., Houston; Trinity U. Assoc., San Antonio; mem. adv. coun., trustee St. Mary's U. Sch. Bus.; past trustee San Antonio City Public Service Bd.; trustee S.W. Research Inst.; past chmn. San Antonio Econ. Devel. Found.; bd. dirs. World Affairs Council, San Antonio; chmn. St. Luke's Luth. Hosp. Found., San Antonio; emeritus chmn. bd. trustees San Antonio Symphony; founder, former chmn. bd. dirs. Tiwanaku Archaeol. Found., Bolivia.; founder, former chmn. exec. com. Caribbean/L.Am. Action, Washington; trustee Ams. Soc. N.Y.; chmn. gen. campaign United Way of San Antonio and Bexar County, 1986, vice chmn. bd. trustees, 1988—; chmn. pub. sector campaign subcom. United Way of Am., 1988—. Named Disting. Grad., U. Tex. Coll. Engring., 1973; recipient People of Vision award Nat. Soc. Prevention of Blindness, 1982, Internat. Citizens award World Affairs Coun., 1986, Good Scout award Boy Scouts Am., 1987, Alexis de Tocqueville award United Way of San Antonio and Bexar County, 1990. Mem. Ind. Petroleum Assn. Am., Soc. Petroleum Engrs. (past chmn. San Antonio-Austin chpt.), 25 Yr. Club Petroleum Industry, Pvt. Enterprise Edn. (Herman W. Lay Meml. award 1986), Am.'s Soc., All-Am. Wildcatters Club, Sigma Chi (Significant Sig award 1979). Episcopalian. Office: 1250 NE Loop 410 Ste 805 San Antonio TX 78209-1533

WEST, ROBERTA BERTHA, writer; b. Saline County, Mo, Sept. 7, 1904; d. Robert and Amanda Melvina (Driver) Baur; m. Harold Clinton West, Aug. 27, 1932; children: Arle Faith W. Lohof, Lydia Ann (Lyda) F H. Hyde, Danna Rose F H. Burns. AB, William Jewell Coll., 1928; AM, U. Mo., 1930. Cert. tchr., Mo., Mont. Elem. and secondary sch. tchr. Mo. and Mont. Sch., 1922-47; supt. sch. Hogeland Sch., Mont., 1947-48, 55; prof. fgn. lang. Will Mayfield Coll., Marble Hill, Mo., 1930, columnist Quad County Star, Viburnum, Mo., 1982—; writer and rschr. ch. history, 1964-91. Cons. hist. com. Yellowstone Conf. Meth. Ch., 1971-84; compiler Mont. list of Meth. Mins. 1784-1984. Author: Northern Montana Methodist History, 3 vols., 1974, Faith, Hope and Love in the West, 1971; editor: Brother Van by Those Who Knew Him, 1975, reprinted, 1989,; also contbr. articles. Recipient 1st John M. Templeton prize, 1959, Wedgwood Jasper Plate 70th Anniversary of Class of 1927 Wm. Jewell Coll., 1997. Mem. Alpha Zeta Pi. Democrat. Achievements include first to At age 98, still writing weekly for the Star. Avocation: crocheting. Home: PO Box 583 Viburnum MO 65566-0583 Office: Quad County Star Viburnum MO 65566

WEST, ROYCE, lawyer, state legislator; b. Sept. 26, 1952; BA, MA, U. Tex., Arlington; JD, U. Houston. Sr. ptnr. Law Firm of West & Gooden, P.C.; mem. Tex. Senate, 1993—, mem. com. of the whole on legis. and congl. redistricting; mem. com. fin., health and human svs., jurisprudence; chmn. subcom. higher edn.; vice chmn. edn. Democrat. Address: 5787 S Hampton Rd Ste 385 Dallas TX 75232-6331 Office: PO Box 12068 Austin TX 78711-2068

WEST, STEPHEN ALLAN, lawyer; b. Salt Lake City, Mar. 23, 1935; s. Allan Morrell and Ferne (Page) W.; m. Martha Sears, Mar. 21, 1960; children: Stephen Allan, Jr., Page, Adam. JD, U. Utah, 1961, BS in Philosophy, 1962. Law clk. to judge U.S. Dist. Ct., Utah, 1961-62; assoc. Marr, Wilkins & Cannon, Salt Lake City, 1962-65, ptnr., 1965-67; atty. Jennings, Strouss, Salmon & Trask, Washington, 1967-68, Marriott Corp., Washington, 1968-71, asst. gen. counsel, 1971-74, v.p. and assoc. gen. counsel, 1974-87, v.p. and dep. gen. counsel, 1987-93; sr. v.p., gen. counsel Marriott Internat., Inc., Washington, 1993-94; pres. Tex. San Antonio mission Ch. of Jesus Christ of Latter-day Saints, 1995-98, Gen. Authority, 1998—. Mem. exec. bd. Interfaith Conf. Met. Washington, 1989-93, vice chmn., 1992-93; mem. exec. bd. Christa McAuliffe Inst. Task Force of Nat. Found. for Improvement Edn. Mem. ABA (exec. coun. young lawyers sect. 1964-65), Utah Bar Assn. (exec. com. young lawyers sect. 1962-67), D.C. Bar Assn., Utah Profl. Rels. Com., U. Utah Alumni Assn. (Disting. Alumni award 1971), Skull and Bones, Owl and Key, Phi Delta Phi, Sigma Chi. Office: Ch Jesus Christ Latter-day Saints 47 E South Temple Salt Lake City UT 84150-1700 Home: 1117 Fox Farm Rd Logan UT 84321-4807

WEST, STEPHEN KINGSBURY, lawyer, director; b. Pittsfield, Mass., Sept. 28, 1928; s. William Bradford and Ruth (Osteyee) W.; m. Ann Wick, Apr. 30, 1955; children: Timothy Wick, Lucy West Engebretson, Todd Kingsbury, Daniel Wick. BA, Yale U., 1950; LL.B., Harvard U., 1953. Assoc. Sullivan & Cromwell, N.Y.C., 1957-64, ptnr., 1964-97, of counsel, 1997—. Bd. dirs. Pioneer Mut. Fund, Boston, AMVESCAP Plc, London, Swiss Helvetin Fund, Inc. Served to lst lt. inf. U.S. Army, 1953-56. Mem. N.Y. State Bar Assn., Assn. Bar City N.Y. Office: Sullivan & Cromwell 125 Broad St Fl 28 New York NY 10004-2489

WEST, TERENCE DOUGLAS, furniture company design executive; b. Twin Falls, Idaho, Sept. 12, 1948; s. Clark Ernest and Elsie Erma (Kulm) W. BS, San Jose State U., 1971. Indsl. designer Clement Labs., Palo Alto, Calif., 1970-74, U.S. Govt., Washington, 1974-78; dist. mgr., arch., designer programs Steelcase, 1978-82, nat. mgr., arch., designer program, 1982-84, dir. indsl. design, 1984—92; dir. product devel. Steelcase Japan Ltd., 1992-94, Steelcase Asia Pacific Ltd., 1994-95; dir. market planning Steelcase Inc., 1995-97, dir. corp. strategy and devel., 1997-2000, dir. advanced concepts, R&D, 2000—. Guest lectr. San Jose State U., 1988, Lehigh U., 1988, Art Ctr. Coll. Design, Pasadena, Calif., 1989, Kendall Coll. of Design, 1990, Waseda U. Tokyo, 1994; Devos lectr., Grand Rapids, Mich., 1990; guest spkr. Mfg. Sys. Engring. for 21st Century Conf., 1989, Internat. Facilities Mgmt. Assn. Conf., 1989, Internat. Facilities Exec. Conf., 1991; mem. bd. advisors Art Ctr. Coll. Design, Pasadena, 1990—; design jurist Women's Archtl. League Portland, Oreg. Sch. Design, Portland chpt. AIA, 1979, Internat. Design Ann. Rev., 1991, Internat. Design mag., 1991. Contbr.: Behaviour and Information Technology, 1987; also articles and designs to profl. jours.; patentee sensor seating. Mem. com. San Jose Urban Coalition, 1971-72; mem. Mayor's Com. for Commemorative Sculpture, Grand Rapids, 1990-95; mem. bldg. com. Grand Rapids Art Mus. Fulbright fellow on design and design edn.; recipient numerous group design awards. Mem. Am. Ctr. For Design, Indsl. Designers Soc. Am. (guest spkr. Denver 1991), Design Mgmt. Inst. Democrat. Lutheran. Achievements include patents for RoomWizard Digital Appliance; sensor office seating. Home: 9655 Ravine Rdg SE Caledonia MI 49316-8243 Office: PO Box 1967 Grand Rapids MI 49501-1967

WEST, THOMAS JAMES, music educator; b. Pitts., Feb. 24, 1973; s. James Thomas and Elizabeth Rose West; m. Melissa June Shanahan, July 15, 2000; children: Daniel Raymond children: Michael Joseph. BS in Music Edn., The Pa. State U., 1998. Cert. tchr. Pa., 1998. Asst. summer band dir. Warren Jr. Mil. Band, Youngstown, Ohio, 1995—; music tchr. Muncy (Pa.) Sch. Dist., 1998—. Mem.: Lycoming County Band Dirs. Assn., Nat. Band Assn., Pa.

Music Edcators Assn., Music Educators Nat. Conf., Phi Mu Alpha Sinfonia (life; v.p. alpha zeta chpt. 1994—96). Roman Catholic. Avocations: video games, singing. Home: 290 S Main St Hughesville PA 17737 Office: Muncy Jr/Sr High School 200 West Penn St Muncy PA 17756 E-mail: twest@muncysd.k12.pa.us.

WEST, TOGO DENNIS, JR., lawyer, former cabinet member, former aerospace executive; b. Winston-Salem, N.C., June 21, 1942; s. Togo Dennis and Evelyn (Carter) W.; m. Gail Estelle Berry, June 18, 1966; children: Tiffany Berry, Hilary Carter. BSEE, Howard U., 1965, JD cum laude, 1968; LLD (hon.), Winston-Salem U., 1996, Gannon U., 1998. Bar: D.C. 1968, N.Y. 1969, U.S. Ct. Mil. Appeals 1969, U.S. Supreme Ct. 1978, U.S. Ct. Claims 1981. Elec. engr. Duquesne Light and Power Co., 1965; patent researcher Sughrue, Rothwell, Mion, Zinn and McPeak, 1966-67; legal intern U.S. EEOC, 1967; law clk. firm Covington & Burling, Washington, 1967-68, summer assoc., 1968, assoc., 1973-75, 76-77; law clk. to Judge Tyler U.S. Dist. Ct. for So. Dist. N.Y., 1968-69; assoc. dep. atty. gen. U.S. Dept. Justice, Washington, 1975-76; gen. counsel Dept. Navy, Washington, 1977-79; spl. asst. to sec. and dep. sec. Dept. Def., Washington, 1979-80, gen. counsel, 1980-81; ptnr. Patterson, Belknap, Webb & Tyler, Washington, 1981-90; sr. v.p. govt. rels. Northrop Corp., Washington, 1990-93; sec. of Army, Washington, 1993-98; chair Panama Canal Commn., 1997; sec. U.S. Dept. of Veterans Affairs, Washington, 1998—. Adj. prof. Duke U. Sch. Law, 1980-81; bd. cons. Riggs Nat. Bank, Washington, 1990-93; bd. dirs. Krispy Kreme Doughnuts, Inc., Bowater, Inc., Washington Hosp. Ctr.; mem. coun. trustees AUSA; bd. trustees Mitretek Sys., Inc., 2001—. Mng. editor: Howard Law Jour, 1968. Commr. D.C. Law Rev. Comm., 1982-89, chmn., 1985-89; mem. Nat. Council of Friends of John F. Kennedy Ctr. for Performing Arts, 1984-91, treas., 1987-91; bd. govs. Antioch U. Sch. Law, 1983-87, vice chmn., 1986-87; bd. visitors Wake Forest U. Sch. Law, 1991-94; chmn. Greater Washington Bd. Trade, legis. bur., 1987-89, bd. dirs., 1987-93, mem. exec. com. 1987-92; mem. fed. legis. com., 1990-93; chmn. Kennedy Ctr. Community and Friends Bd., 1991-2001; mem. Washington Lawyers' Com. Civil Rights Under Law, 1987-93, D.C. Com. on Pub. Edn., 1988-93, chmn., 1990-91; trustee The Aerospace Corp., 1983-90, Ctr. for Strategic and Internat. Studies, 1987-90, Nat. Lawyers Com. for Civil Rights Under Law, 1987-93, Inst. for Def. Analyses, 1989-91, Protestant Episcopal Cathedral Found., 1989-95, Shakespeare Theatre at The Folger, 1990-93, N.C. Sch. Arts, 1990-2002, Aerospace Edn. Found. of Air Force Assn., 1991-93; bd. dirs. D.C. Law Students in Ct. Program, 1986-92, World Affairs Coun., 1991-93, 2000—, Atlantic Coun., 1991-93, 2000—; mem. fin. com. Episcopal Diocese of Washington, 1989—, mem. standing com., 1990-92; sr. warden St. John's Ch., Lafayette Sq.; mem. Coun. Fgn. Rels., 1996—; chmn. trustee coun. YMCA Metro. Wash., 1990-92; mem. nat. adv. com. UN Assn. USA, 1991-93; D.C. Ct. Appeals Admissions Com., 1990-93; pres. Nat. Capital Area Coun. Boy Scouts Am.; chmn. Greater Washington Bd. of Trade; bd. trustees Assn. of U.S. Army, 2001—. Served to capt. Judge Adv. Gen. Corps U.S. Army, 1969-73. Decorated Legion of Merit; recipient Disting. Pub. Svc. medal Dept. Def., 1981, Eagle Scout award with Bronze Palm Boy Scouts Am., 1957, Disting. Eagle Scout award 1995, Svc. to Howard U. award, 1965, Meritorious Svc. medal, Medal of Merit, Brazil, Disting. Civil Svc. medal, 1998, Dept. Vet. Affairs, 2000, Silver Buffalo award, 2000, Silver Beaver award, 2003. Mem. ABA, Nat. Bar Assn., Washington Coun. Lawyers (dir. 1973-75), Sigma Pi Phi, Phi Alpha Delta, Omega Psi Psi, Alpha Phi Omega. Clubs: Metropolitan, University (Washington). Office: Covington & Burling 1201 Pennsylvania Ave NW Washington DC 20004

WEST, W. RICHARD, museum director; b. San Bernardino, Calif., Jan. 6, 1943; s. W. Richard Sr. and Maribelle (McCrea) W.; m. Mary Beth Braden, June 29, 1968; children: Amy Elizabeth, Benjamin Braden. BA magna cum laude in Am. History, U. Redlands, 1965; AM in Am. History, Harvard U., 1968; JD, Stanford U., 1971; LHD (hon.), Bacone Coll., 1992, Ottawa U., 1994, U. Okla., 1995. Bar: Calif., D.C., U.S. Ct. Appeals (8th cir.), U.S. Supreme Ct. Clk. to Hon. Benjamin C. Duniway U.S. Ct. Appeals (9th cir.), 1971-72; assoc. Fried, Frank, Harris, Shriver & Jacobson, Washington, 1973-79, ptnr., 1979-88; dir. direct support component Am. Indian Lawyer Tng. Program, Inc., 1976-77; ptnr. Gover, Stetson Williams & West P.C., Albuquerque, 1988-90; founding dir. Smithsonian Instn's Nat. Mus. Am. Indian, Washington, 1990—. Treas. Am. Indian Lawyer Tng. Program, Inc., 1973—; adj. prof. Indian law Stanford U., 1977. Mem. edit. bd. Am. Indian Historian, 1969-71; note editor Stanford Law Review, 1970-71; contbr. articles to profl. jours. Coord., treas. Native Am. Coun. Regents Inst. Am. Indian Arts, 1975-80; bd. visitors Stanford Law Sch., 1978-81; trustee Phelps Stokes Fund, 1981-87, Bush Found., 1991—, Bacone Coll., 1986-89, chmn., 1988-89, Morning Star Found., 1987-93, U. Redlands, 1991—, alumni bd., 1987-89, Ednl. Found. Am., 1993-96; bd. dirs. Amerindian Circle, Inc., 1981-88, Nat. Indian Justice Ctr., 1982-89; cultural edn. com. Smithsonian Inst., 1987-90; nat. support com. Native Am. Rights Fund, 1990—; adv. com. Winslow Found., 1991—; hon. coun. Wings Am., 1993—; mem. Environ. Def. Fund, bd. trustees, 1986—. Recipient Career Achievement award U. Redlands, 1987, Disting. Svc. award, 1992, award Appreciation and Recognition, Cheyenne and Arapaho Tribes Okla., 1990, Spirit of the People award Okla. Inst. Indian Heritage, 1990; named (with another) Amb. of Yr. Red Earth Indian Ctr. Okla., 1993. Mem. Am. Indian Bar Assn. (charter pres. 1976-77). Mem. Cheyenne and Arapaho Tribes Okla. Office: Nat Mus of Am Indian 470 Lenfant Plz SW Ste 7102 Washington DC 20024-2124*

WEST, WILLIAM ROBERT, history educator; b. Woodbury, N.J., Feb. 4, 1947; s. William Robert Sr. and Genevieve Jane (Cooper) West; m. Rhonda Gaye Foster, Apr. 4, 1981; children: Shaun Cooper Foster West, Ryan William Foster West. BA, Ky. Wesleyan Coll., 1970; MA, Western Ky. U., 1973; postgrad., U. Louisville, U. Shanghai, U. Denver, U. Wash., others. Ky. secondary cert. life. Tchr. Daviess County Pub. Schs., Owensboro, 1971-86; prof. history Ky. Cmty. Tech. Coll. Sys. (KCTCS)_, 1984—. Ky. C.C. faculty senate coun. rep. univ. studies; U. Ky. C.C.S. coun. mem., 1994-97; elected faculty rep. KCTCS Bd. of Regents, 2003—; parent rep. local sch. based coun. Mem. Leadership Owensboro Class of 1988, Leadership Ky. Class of 1997; exec. dir. Owensboro Sister Cities Program, 1990—; mem. state mgmt. team Ky. Sister Cities, 1991—; internat. rep. Shawnee Trails Coun. Boy Scouts Am. Recipient cert. of merit Ky. Ednl. TV-Ashland Oil Found., 1982, Internat. Scout award Boy Scouts Am., 2002; rsch. scholar Lyndhurst Found., 1984, scholar Japan Endowment at U. Wash., 1983, N.E. Asia Coun. of Assn. for Asian Studies, 1983; travel grantee U.S.-Japan Found., 1983. Mem. Am. Assn. Individual Investors, Nat. Geographic Soc., Nat. Trust Historic Preservation, Hon. Order Ky. Cols., U.S.-China Peoples Friendships Assn. (nat. bd. dirs. 1997-2001), UN Assn. U.S.A., Ky. C.C. Humanities Assn., The So. Hist. Assn. (European history sect.), others. Democrat. Unitarian Universalist. Avocations: reading, traveling, fostering internat. perspective through edn. Home: 5829 Jack Hinton Rd Philpot KY 42366-9641 Office: Owensboro Cmty and Tech Coll 4800 New Hartford Rd Owensboro KY 42303-1800

WESTALL, ANDREW JON, legislative staff member, urban planner; b. San Diego, Jan. 14, 1973; s. Frederick Charls and Janet (Robertson) W. BA in Polit. Sci.-Pub. Svc., U. Calif., Davis, 1996; MA in Urban Planning, UCLA, 1999. Acad. rsch. intern Office of City Councilmem. Deborah Ortiz, Sacramento, Calif., 1995-96; DC office intern Office of Andrew Cuomo, HUD, Washington, 1995; capitol office intern Office Assembly Mem. Carole Migden, Sacramento, 1996; viewpoint columnist The Daily Bruin, L.A., 1997; dist. cons. Office of Assembly Mem. Deborah Ortiz, Sacramento, 1997; pres. Grad. Students Assn., UCLA, 1997-98; adminstrv. asst. The Durfee Found., Santa Monica, Calif., 1996-98; campaign worker Working Families for Deborah Ortiz, State Senate, Sacramento, 1998; cons. Nat. Assn. Latino Elected and Apptd. Ofcls., L.A., 1998—; field rep., rschr. Office of Assembly Mem. Robert M. Hertzberg, Van Nuys, Calif., 1999—. Advisor Sacramento County Adult and Aging Commn., 1996. Author: Reapportionment, Redistricting and the Latin Community Toward 2000, 2000. Recipient award U. Calif. Pres. Washington Ctr., 1995. Mem. ACLU, Am. Planning Assn., U. Calif. Davis Alumni Assn., Chi Pi (pres. Sigma Delta chpt. 1995). Democrat. Episcopalian. Avocations: hiking, basketball. Office: Office Assembly Mem Robert M Hertzberg 6150 Van Nuys Blvd Ste 305 Van Nuys CA 91401-3345 E-mail: Andrew.Westall@asm.ca.gov.

WESTBERRY, DAVID M. executive search consultant; b. Savannah, Ga., Aug. 26, 1951; s. John R. and Marianne (Stopfer) W.; m. Carolyn Diane Manton, Apr. 27, 1987. AA, Pensacola Jr. Coll., 1976; BA in Acctg., U. West Fla., Pensacola, 1978. CPA, Fla. Sr. acct. KPMG Peat Marwick, Jacksonville, Fla., 1979-81; v.p. Robert Half Internat., Jacksonville, 1981-82, Pierce Catterton, Houston, 1983; sr. mgr. exec. search KPMG Peat Marwick, Dallas, 1983-89; mng. dir. Ward Howell Internat., Dallas, 1989-95, exec. com., 1992-95; ptnr. LAI, Dallas, 1995-98; mng. dir. Korn Ferry Internat., Dallas, 1998—. Mem. adv. coun. U. West Fla. Coll. Bus., Pensacola, 1992—. Trustee U. West Fla. Found., Pensacola, 1994—. Sgt. USAF, 1971-74, South Korea. Home: 6429 Pemberton Dr Dallas TX 75230-4126

WESTBERRY, JOHN ELLIOTT, mathematics professor; b. Knoxville, Tenn., Aug. 8, 1922; s. John Elliott and Annie (Richardson) W.; m. Gaynelle Hines, July 8, 1942 (dec. May 1992); 1 child, Larry; m. Maxine Willis, Mar. 18, 1993. BS, Livingstone Coll., 1941; MS, Atlanta U., 1949; MA, U. Mich., 1954. Asst. prof. Tex. Coll., Tyler, 1949-50, Tex. State U., Houston, 1950-54; registrar, dir. admissions Tex. So. U., Houston, 1954-94, assoc. prof., 1975—. Tech. sgt. U.S. Army, 1942-45, ETO. Named one of 100 Most Influential Blacks, Ebony mag., 1974, 75, 76, Am.'s Best Tchrs. Ednl. Comms., Inc., 1998. Mem. Am. Assn. Coll. Registrars and Admissions Officers (sec.-treas. 1980-83), Math. Assn. Am., Tex. Assn. Coll. Registrars and Admissions Officers (pres. 1982), Phi Beta Sigma (pres. 1974-76). Democrat. Avocations: reading, speaking. Home: 5306 Stuyvesant Ln Houston TX 77021-3145 Office: Tex So U 3100 Cleburne St Houston TX 77004-4501

WESTBIE, BARBARA JANE, retired graphics designer; b. Little Rock, Nov. 3, 1946; d. Freeman Bryant Davis and Virginia Lee Thompson; children: Suzanne Michelle, Derrek Christopher. Grad. in graphic design, U. Calif., Davis, 1992; student, Miramar Coll., San Diego, 1976, Chabot Coll., Hayward, Calif., 1974. Exec. dir. Ambiance, Danville, Calif., 1980—84; dir. Lake Gallery, Tahoe City, Calif., 1985—87; art cons. Reed Gallery, Tahoe City, 1988—90; ret., 1990. Art dir., creative cons. Associated Students Re-Entry Ctr. Chico State U., Calif., 2001—03. Inventor Fat Fuzzy/Iknonotrisc Family, 1981, artist (poster/logo) Project Mana Fundraising Event, 1988, (brochure/media kit) Chocolate Festival, 1989. Vol. crisis intervention counselor CIS/Tahoe Women's Svcs., Kings Beach, 1989—91; lead counselor Emotions Anonymous 12-Step Program, North Lake Tahoe Area, 1990—93; vol. pk. svc. Washoe Lake State Pk., Carson City, Nev., 1993—94; coord. new vols. ARC, Chico, 2000—01, vol. Butte County, 2000—, Emergency Animal Rescue Svcs., 2002—. Named Vol. of Yr., Tahoe Women's Svcs., 1989; recipient Disting. Svc. award, CIS/Tahoe Women's Svcs., 1989—90. Mem.: Smithsonian Instn. (assoc.). Protestant. Avocations: skiing, reading, gardening, writing, painting.

WESTBROOK, BILL, advertising executive; Internat. pres. Fallon-McElligott, Mpls., 1999—. Office: Fallon-McElligott 901 Marquette Ave Ste 3200 Minneapolis MN 55402-3232

WESTBROOK, DON ARLEN, minister; b. Clinton, N.C., June 2, 1941; s. Ennis and Geneva (Gainey) W.; m. Carrol Ann Holder, Sept. 15, 1963; children: Felisha Ann, Neal Vance. Student, Logos Bible Coll./Grad. Sch., 1989. Ordained to ministry Full Gospel Fellowship Chs. and Mins. Internat., 1965. Pastor Bethel Christian Ctr., Durham, N.C., 1969—. V.p. Full Gospel Fellowship Chs. and Mins. Internat., Dallas, 1982—; missionary to India, Nicaragua and Haiti, 1990; leader Durham In Prayer, 1999—. Chmn. Concerned Citizens for Moral Govt., Durham, 1989. Home: 5311 Emeraldwood Dr Durham NC 27705-7170 Office: Bethel Christian Ctr 3518 Rose Of Sharon Rd Durham NC 27712-3306

WESTBROOK, GARY WAYNE, music educator, consultant; b. Burlington, N.C., June 29, 1966; s. Betty Briggs Smith. MusB, East Carolina U., 1989; MusM, U. N.C., 1996, DPhil Music Edn., 2002. Dir. bands So. Nash High Sch., Spring Hope, NC, 1989—90, Blenheim Mid. Sch., Blenheim, SC, 1990—92, South Florence High Sch., Florence, 1992—95; dir. athletic bands and percussion studies Concord Coll., Athens, W.Va., 2001—03; asst. prof. music, asst. dir. bands La. Tech. U., Ruston, 2003—. Percussionist Florence Symphony Orch., Florence, 1990—94; instr./arranger percussion Liberty High Sch., Bedford, 1995—; drummer Necessary Jazz Combo, Tazewell, 2000—; dir. corps ops. and program coord. Carolina Gold Sr. Drum and Bugle Corps, Raleigh, NC, 2001—; Member, Pit Section Leader Bridgemen Drum and Bugle Corps, Bayonne, NJ, 1986—87; adj. instr. percussion Pfeiffer U., Meisenheimer, 1999—2001, Concord Coll., 1999—2001. Contbr. articles to profl. jours. Mem.: Music Educators Nat. Conf., Music Tchrs. Nat. Assn., Percussive Arts Soc., Internat. Assn. Jazz Edn. Pentecostal. Avocations: hiking, bicycling, swimming, basketball. Home: 604 Eastland Ave Ruston LA 71270 Office: Concord Coll Department of Music Athens WV 24712 Office Phone: 304-384-6041. Personal E-mail: Blwinkl@stargate.net.

WESTBROOK, JAMES EDWIN, lawyer, educator; b. Camden, Ark., Sept. 7, 1934; s. Loy Edwin and Helen Lucille (Bethea) W.; m. Elizabeth Kay Farris, Dec. 23, 1956; children: William Michael, Robert Bruce, Matthew David. BA with high honors, Hendrix Coll., 1956; JD with distinction, Duke U., 1959; LLM, Georgetown U., 1965. Bar: Ark. 1959, Okla. 1977, Mo. 1982. Assoc. Mehaffy, Smith & Williams, Little Rock, 1959-62; asst. counsel, subcom. of U.S. Senate Jud. Com., Washington, 1963; legis. asst. U.S. Senate, Washington, 1963-65; asst. prof. law U. Mo., Columbia, 1965-68, asst. dean, 1966-68, assoc. prof., 1968-70, prof., 1970-76, 80—, James S. Rollins prof. law, 1974-76, 80—, Earl F. Nelson prof. law, 1982-99, emeritus prof., 1999—, interim dean, 1981-82; dean U. Okla. Coll. Law, Norman, 1976-80. George Allen vis. prof. law, U. Richmond, 1987; vis. prof. law Duke U., 1988, Washington U., St. Louis, 1996, 2001; reporter Mid-Am. Assembly on Role of State in Urban Crisis, 1970; dir. Summer Internship Program in Local Govt., 1968; cons. various Mo. cities on drafting home-rule charters; mem. Gov.'s Adv. Coun. on Local Govt. Law, 1967-68, Fed. Practice Com. U.S. Dist. Ct. (we. dist.) Mo., 1986-90; chmn. Columbia Charter Revision Commn., 1973-74; mem. spl. com. labor relations Mo. Dept. Labor and Indsl. Rels., 1975; mem., chmn. subcom. on domestic violence Task Force on Gender and Justice, Mo. Jud. Conf., 1990-93; mem. com. to rev. govtl. structure of Boone County, Mo., 1991. Author: (with L. Riskin) Dispute Resolution and Lawyers, 1987, supplement, 1993, 2d edit., 1997, abridged edit. of 2d edit., 1998; contbr. articles to profl. jours. Chair search com. for chancellor U. Mo., Columbia, 1992, chair search com. for provost, 1998; mem. fin. com. Roman Cath. Diocese of Jefferson City, 2003—, mem. investment com. Mem. ABA, Nat. Acad. Arbitrators, Assn. Am. Law Schs. (chmn. local govt. law round table com. 1972), Ctrl. States Law Sch. Assn. (pres. 1982-83), Mo. Bar Assn. (vice chmn. labor law com. 1986-87, chmn. 1987-88, Spurgeon Smithton award 1995), Order of Coif, Blue Key, Alpha Chi. Roman Catholic. Home: 3609 S Woods Edge Rd Columbia MO 65203-6606 Office: U Mo Sch Law Columbia MO 65211-0001 Office Phone: 573-882-6540.

WESTBROOK, JAY LAWRENCE, law educator; b. Morristown, NJ, Dec. 11, 1943; s. Joel W. and Elaine Frances (Summers) W.; m. Pauline June Travis, Feb. 15, 1969; 1 child, Joel Mastin. BA in Polit. Sci./Philosophy, U. Tex., 1965, JD, 1968. Bar: Tex. 1968, D.C. 1969, U.S. Ct. Appeals (D.C. cir.) 1969, U.S. Supreme Ct. 1976, U.S. Ct. Appeals (4th cir.) 1978, U.S. Ct. Appeals (2d cir.) 1979. Assoc. Surrey & Morse (name now Jones, Day, Reavis, Pogue), Washington, 1969-74; ptnr. Surrey & Morse (name now Jones, Day, Reavis, Pogue, Surrey & Morse), Washington, 1974-80; mem. law faculty U. Tex., Austin, 1980—, Benno C. Schmidt Chair Bus. Law, 1991—. Vis. prof. U. London, 1990, Harvard Law Sch., 1991-92; advisor Tex. Internat. Law Jour., 1985-91; reporter Am. Law Inst. Transnat. Insolvency Project, 1994-2000; co-leader U.S. delegation to UN Commn. on Internat. Trade Law Working Group on Model Law Internat. Insolvency, 1995-97, 99; sr. advisor Nat. Bankruptcy Rev. Com., 1997; mem. State Dept. Adv. Com. on Pvt. Internat. Law, 1997-2000; vis. scholar Humboldt U., Berlin, 2002. Co-author: As We Forgive Our Debtors: Bankruptcy and Consumer Credit in America, 1989 (Silver Gavel award ABA 1989), The Law of Debtors and Creditors: Text, Cases and Problems, 4th edit., 2001, Teacher's Manual, The Law of Debtors and Creditors, 4th edit., 2001, The Fragile Middle Class: Americans in Debt, 2000(Ann. Writing award Am. Coll. Consumer Fin. Svcs. Lawyers); contbr. articles to profl. jours. Grantee U. Tex. Law Sch. Found., 1982, U. Rsch. Inst., 1982-83, NSF, 1983-86, Policy Rsch. Inst., Lyndon Johnson Sch. Pub. Affairs, 1984, Tex. Bar Found., 1985, Nat. Inst. Child Health and Human Devel., 1986, Nat. Conf. Bankruptcy Judges, 1991, 93, Am. Coll. Banker, 2004. Mem. ABA (bus. bankruptcy com., vice chair internat. bankruptcy subcom. 1999—, Meyer rsch. grant 1986), Am. Law Inst., Am. Coll. Bankruptcy, Nat. Bankruptcy Conf., State Bar Tex. (governing coun. internat. sect. 1987-89), Internat. Bar Assn., Internat. Bankruptcy Com. (com. J), Internat. Acad. Comml. and Consumer Law, Order of Coif. Office: U Tex Sch Law 727 E Dean Keeton St Austin TX 78705-3224

WESTBROOK, KENT COLEMAN, surgeon, educator; b. Hot Springs, Ark., Feb. 13, 1940; MD, U. Ark., 1965. Diplomate Am. Bd. Surgery. Intern U. Ark. Hosp., Little Rock, 1965-66, surg. resident, 1966-70; fellow in surg. oncology M.D. Anderson Tumor Inst., Houston, 1970-72; staff U. Ark. Hosp. Prof., U. Ark. Sch. Medicine. Mem. AMA, Southwestern Surg. Congress. Office: Univ Ark Med Ctr Slot 520 4301 W Markham St Little Rock AR 72205-7101

WESTBROOK, LARRY, electric power industry executive; CFO Southern Co, Atlanta. Office: Southern Co 270 Peachtree St NW Atlanta GA 30303-1247

WESTCARR, LINTON ANTHONY, nurse, pharmacist, writer; b. Spanish Town, Jamaica, Dec. 22, 1956; s. Oswald George and Ivy Maud Westcarr; m. Audrey Denise Kirby-Westcarr. RN, Kingston Sch. Nursing, Jamaica, 1980; diploma in pharmacy, U. Jamaica, 1988. Cert. pharmacist Jamaica, 1988; nutritional cons., Can. Sch. Nutrition, Ontario, 1992, RN Ontario, Can., Fla. Crisis counsellor Corp. Health Cons., 1995—99; RN Joseph Brant Hosp., Burlington, Canada, 1997, Trillium Health Ctr., Mississauga, 1999—2003; mental health home care cons. Spectrum Health Care, Toronto, 2000; trama nurse Bayfront Med. Ctr., St. Petersburg, Fla., 2003; ER psychiat. nurse St. Anthony's Hosp., 2003—. Mem.: Coll. of Nurses of Ontario. Avocations: sewing, music, gardening, bicycling, decorating.

WESTCOTT, JOAN CLARK, poet; b. Union City, Pa., Feb. 8, 1919; d. William Clyde and Marjorie (Clark) W. BA, Vassar Coll., 1941; grad., Katherine Gibbs Sec. Sch., Boston, 1942. Clk. Boston Port Embarkation, 1942—43; sec. Harvard U., Cambridge, Mass., 1943-45, Players Theater, Sarasota, Fla., 1947-49, AEC, UCLA, 1950-52; sec. to John Loveton L.A., 1953-54; sec. to J. West Arch., Sarasota, 1955-60. Author: (poetry) Fragments of Stained Glass, 1967, More Fragments of Stained Glass, 1968, Bits of Chaff, 1970, Taffeta and Lace, 1976, Ribbon of Light, 1980, Fragments of Stained Glass III, 1988, Homeward Bound, 1997. Poetry books plus papers in Rare Books and Spl. Collections Libr., U. Fla., Gainesville. Mem. Planetary Soc., Habitat Nat. Wildlife Fedn., Women in the Arts, Union of Concerned Scientists. Avocations: gardening, reading, needlepoint, working on autobiography from diaries. Home: 4100 E Fletcher Ave Tampa FL 33613-4863

WESTEN, BRODIE CURTIS, lawyer; b. Champaign, Ill., Nov. 10, 1960; s. Brodie Curtis and Sarah Jane (Mullen) W.; m. Sue Lynn Heubner, Nov. 21, 1987. BS, Western Ill. U., 1982, MBA, 1983; JD, U. Calif., Berkeley, 1986. Bar: Ill. 1986. Fin. analyst Nat. Credit Union Adminstrn., Washington, 1983; assoc. Lord, Bissell & Brook, Chgo., 1986—92; joined QualMed, 1992; v.p. adminstrn. Found. Health Systems, Inc. (now Health Net, Inc.), Woodland Hills, Calif., 1993—94, sr. v.p., gen. counsel and sec., 1993—94, 1995—. Mem. ABA, Ill. Bar Assn., Chgo. Bar Assn. Avocation: golf. Office: Health Net Inc 21650 Oxnard St Woodland Hills CA 91367-4901

WESTER, AARON MICAH, web production manager, consultant; b. Orlando, Fla., Mar. 14, 1974; s. Chenevert Forbes Gary (Stepfather) and Diane Birchea't; m. Jeannette Gwynn-Ellen Shafran, June 11, 1976; 1 child, Matthew Wester Winter Wester. Carnegie Business Training Calif., 2004. Web devel. cons. Deloitte & Tousche Tohmatsu, Long Beach, Calif., 1998—99; dir. web devel. US Congress - 27th Calif. Dist., Pasadena, Calif., 1998—99; ui designer Idealab!, Pasadena, Calif., 1999—2000; mgr. web prodn. United Online, Westlake Village, Calif., 2000—. Dir. web devel. Amro Fabrication Corp., City of Industry, Calif., 2002—. Author: (novels) Becoming a Web Designer; co-author (with John Dvorak): Online!. Varsity coach - boy scouts of am. LDS Ch., Thousand Oaks, Calif., 2003—04. Sgt. Army JROTC, 1991—92, Lemon Grove. R-Liberal. Church Of Jesus Christ Of Latter Day Saints. Avocations: amatuer astronomy, video gaming, travel, camping, running. Home: 843 Calle Ciruelo Thousand Oaks CA 91360 Office: United Online 2555 TownsGate Rd Westlake Village CA 91361 Office Phone: 805-418-2144. Personal E-mail: aaronix@netzero.net. E-mail: awester@corp.untd.com.

WESTER, R. GLEN, music educator, director; b. Wichita Falls, Tex., Oct. 7, 1938; s. George Odus and Minnie Mae Wester; m. Theresa Lois Ward, Nov. 27, 1968; children: Suzanne, Karen, George. MusB in edn., Midwestern State U., Wichita Falls, Tex., 1961; MusM in edn., U. of North Tex., Denton, 1968. Cert. piano and voice (nat.) Nat. Music Tchrs. Assn. Instr. music Southeastern Christian Coll., Winchester, Ky., 1971—72, Vernon (Tex.) Regional Jr. Coll., 1972—74; choral dir. Springlake - Earth HS, Earth, Tex., 1975—76, Leander (Tex.) HS, 1976—80, La Marque (Tex.) HS, 1980—82; instr. music San Jacinto Coll., Pasadena, Tex., 1982—. Judge Nat. Piano Guild, 1985—2002. Bd. dir. Comty. Concerts, Vernon, Tex., 1973—75. With USN, 1961—65. Named one of Most Prominent Music Tchers. in Tex., 1983; named to Hall of Fame, Nat. Piano Guild. Mem.: Nat. Assn. of Tchrs. of Singing (sec. 1986—), Pasadena Music Teachers (v.p. 1984—, Tchr. of the Yr. 1993), Nat. Music Tchrs. (v.p. 1982—). Avocations: bicycling, gardening. Home: 4201 Kelvin Deer Park TX 77536

WESTERBERG, ARTHUR WILLIAM, retired chemical engineering educator; b. St. Paul, Oct. 9, 1938; s. Kenneth Waldorf and Marjorie Claire (Darling) W.; m. Barbara Ann Dyson, July 14, 1963; children: Kenneth (dec.), Karl. BS, U. Minn., 1960; MS, Princeton U., 1961; PhD, Imperial Coll., London, 1964. Pres. Farm Engring. Sales Inc., Savage, Minn., 1964-65; sr. analyst Control Data Corp., San Diego, 1965-67; asst. prof., assoc. prof., prof. U. Fla., Gainesville, Fla., 1967-76; prof. chem. engring. Carnegie-Mellon U., Pitts., 1976—2004, chmn. dept., 1980-83, Swearingen prof., 1982—2004, dir. Design Research Ctr., 1978-80, Univ. prof., 1992—; dir. Engring. Design Rsch. Ctr., 1986-89. Co-author: Process Flowsheeting, 1979, Systematic Methods of Chemical Process Design, 1997. Recipient Murphree award Am. Chem. Soc., 1997, Steven J. Fenves Sys. Engring. award Carnegie Mellon, 1998, Engring. Disting. Prof. award, 2002, Robert E. Doherty Edn. award, 2003. Fellow AIChE (lectr. 1989, Computers and Sys. Tech. divsn. award 1983, Walker award 1987, McAfee award 1990, Founders Outstanding Contbns. Chem. Engring. award 1995); mem. NAE, Am. Soc. Engring. Edn. (chem. engring. divsn. lectr. 1981, GE Sr. Rsch. award 1999, Computer Aides Chem. Engring. and Edn. Excellence in Chem. Engring. Edn. award 2003). Home: 5564 Beacon St Pittsburgh PA 15217-1972 Business E-Mail: a.westerberg@cmu.edu.

WESTERBERG, LARS, automotive safety systems company executive; b. 1948; MBSS, Royal Instl Tech., Stockholm, 1972; MBA, U. Stockholm, 1978. With ASEA (now ABB), from 1972; various positions Esab AB, welding machine co.; pres. N.Am. subs. Esab AB welding machine co., 1984-87, pres., CEO, 1991—94, Granges AB, aluminum and plastics co., 1994—99, Autoliv Inc., Stockholm, 1999—. Office: Autoliv Inc World Trade Ctr Klarabergsviadukten 70 SE-10724 Stockholm Sweden Office Phone: 46-858720620. E-mail: lars.westerberg@autoliv.com.

WESTERDAHL, JOHN BRIAN, nutritionist, health educator; b. Tucson, Dec. 3, 1954; s. Jay E. and Margaret (Meyer) W.; m. Doris Mui Lian Tan, Nov. 18, 1989; 1 child, Jasmine Leilani. AA, Orange Coast Coll., 1977; BS, Pacific Union Coll., 1979; MPH, Loma Linda U., 1981; PhD, Pacific Western U., 2001. Registered dietitian, master herbalist; cert. nutrition specialist; bd. cert. anti-aging health practitioner. From nutritionist, health educator to dir. Castle Med. Ctr., Kailua, Hawaii, 1981—89, dir. wellness and lifestyle medicine and

nutritional svc., 1998—; dir. nutrition and health rsch. Health Sci., Santa Barbara, Calif., 1989-90; sr. nutritionist, project mgr. Shaklee Corp., San Francisco, 1990-96; dir. nutrition Dr. McDougall's Right Foods, Inc., South San Francisco, 1996—98; mem. faculty staff, dir. continuing edn. Am. Acad. Nutrition, 1996—; staff nutritionist Millennium Restaurant, San Francisco, 1995—. Radio talk show host Nutrition and You KGU Radio, Honolulu, 1983—89, KWAI Radio, Honolulu, 1999—; nutrition com. mem. Hawaii div. Am. Heart Assn., Honolulu, 1984—87; mem. nutrition study group Gov.s Conf. Health Promotion and Disease Prevention, Hawaii, 1985. Author: Medicinal Herbs: A Vital Reference Guide, 1998, The Millennium Cookbook: Extraordinary Vegetarian Cuisine, 1998; editor: Nourish Mag., 1995-96; nutrition editor: Veggie Life Mag., 1995—. Mem.: Seventh-day Adventist Dietetic Assn., Hawaii Dietetic Assn., Hawaii Nutrition Coun. (v.p. 1983-86, pres.-elect 1988-89, pres. 1989), Inst. Food Technologists, Am. Soc. Pharmacognosy, Am. Coll. Nutrition, Am. Dietetic Assn. (Hawaii coord. vegetarian nutrition dietetic practice group), Am. Acad. Anti-Aging Medicine, Am. Coll. Sports Medicine, AAAS. Republican. Seventh-Day Adventist. Avocations: swimming, scuba diving. Office: Castle Med Ctr Wellness & Lifestyle Med Ctr 642 Ulukahiki St Ste 105 Kailua HI 96734 *Personal philosophy: "Beloved, I wish above all things that thou mayest prosper and be in health, even as thy soul prospereth." 3 John 2.*

WESTERFIELD, CAROLYN ELIZABETH HESS, city planner; b. New Haven, Conn., May 3, 1933; d. Orvan Walter and Carol Woodruff (Maurer) Hess; m. Holt Bradford Westerfield, Dec. 17, 1960; children: Pamela Bradford Bingham, Leland Avery. BA, Wellesley Coll., 1954; postgrad., Yale U., 1954-55, M of City Planning, 1959. Planner, office mgr. Tech. Planning Assocs., New Haven, 1955-57, 61-62; assoc. planner City Plan Dept., New Haven, Conn., 1956-59; planner, editor State of Conn. Devel. Commn., 1959-61; cons., 1962—; prin. planner South Cen. Conn. Planning Region, 1979-87; asst. plan dir. Town of Fairfield (Conn.), 1987; planning and zoning adminstr. Town of North Branford (Conn.), 1987-89. Devel. pvt. programs New Haven Hosp.-Boston City Hosp., 1952-54; lectr. city planning U. New Haven, 1988-2003. Mem. alumni bd. Yale U. Sch. Architecture, 1964-76, 85-96, pres., 1993-95; bd. dirs. alumni orgns. Prospect Hill Sch., New Haven, St. Thomas Day Sch.; class officer Wellesley Coll.; mem. Econ. Devel. Commn. Consortium, Hamden, Conn., mem. design rev. com.; clk. Ethics Commn. Mem. Am. Planning Assn., Am. Inst. Cert. Planners, Conn. Women in Planning and Devel., Alliance for Architecture (steering com. 1995—), New Haven Colony Hist. Soc., Jr. League New Haven (various exec. position), Watch Hill Improvement Soc. (pres. 1971-73), Conn. Child Welfare Assn., Yale U. Women's Orgn. (pres. 1979-81). Avocations: music, arts, sports, cultural exchange. Home and Office: 29 Old Orchard Rd North Haven CT 06473

WESTERFIELD, HOLT BRADFORD, political scientist, educator; b. Rome, Mar. 7, 1928; s. Ray Bert and Mary Beatrice (Putney) W.; m. Carolyn Elizabeth Hess, Dec. 17, 1960; children: Pamela Bradford, Leland Avery. Grad., Choate Sch., 1944; BA, Yale U., 1947; MA, Harvard U., 1951, PhD, 1952. Instr. govt. Harvard U., 1952-56; asst. prof. polit. sci. U. Chgo., 1956-57; mem. faculty Yale U., 1957—, prof. polit. sci., 1965-2000, chmn. dept., 1970-72, Damon Wells prof. internat. studies, 1985-2000; prof. emeritus, 2000—; rsch. assoc. Washington Center Fgn. Policy Research, Johns Hopkins Sch. Advanced Internat. Studies, 1965-66. Vis. prof. Wesleyan U., Middletown, Conn., 1967, 71; bd. visitors U.S. Joint Mil. Intelligence Coll., Washington, 1998—. Author: Foreign Policy and Party Politics: Pearl Harbor to Korea, 1955, The Instruments of America's Foreign Policy, 1963; editor: Inside CIA's Private World: Declassified Articles from the Agency's Internal Journal, 1955-92, 1995. Sheldon traveling fellow Harvard, 1951-52; Henry L. Stimson fellow Yale, 1962, 73; sr. Fulbright-Hays scholar, 1973; hon. vis. fellow Australian Nat. U., 1973. Mem. Am. Polit. Sci. Assn. (Congl. fellow 1953-54), Internat. Polit. Sci. Assn., Internat. Studies Assn. Home: 115 Rogers Rd Hamden CT 06517-3541 Office: Yale Univ Dept Polit Sci PO Box 208301 New Haven CT 06520-8301

WESTERFIELD, PUTNEY, management consulting executive; b. New Haven, Feb. 9, 1930; s. Ray Bert and Mary Beatrice (Putney) W.; m. Anne Montgomery, Apr. 17, 1954; children: Bradford, Geoffrey, Clare. Grad., Choate Sch., 1942-47; BA, Yale, 1951. Co-founder, v.p. Careers, Inc., N.Y.C., 1950-52; mgr. S.E. Asia Swen Publs., Inc., Manila, Philippines, 1952; mem. joint adv. commn. Korea, 1953-54; polit. officer Am. embassy, Saigon, Vietnam, 1955-57; asst. to pub. Time mag., N.Y.C., 1957-59, asst. circulation dir., 1959-61, circulation dir., 1961-66, asst. pub., 1966-68, Life mag., N.Y.C., 1968; pub. Fortune mag., N.Y.C., 1969-73; pres. Chase World Info. Corp., N.Y.C., 1973-75; v.p. Boyden Assocs. Internat., San Francisco, 1976-80, sr. v.p., western mgr., 1980-84, pres., chief exec. officer N.Y.C. and San Francisco, 1984-90, mng. dir., 1990—. Chmn. bd. dirs. Upside Media Inc. Bd. dirs. Urban League, N.Y.C., 1969-71, Children's Village, 1968-71, Mediterranean Sch. Found., 1969-71, Nat. Boys Club, 1970-73, U.S. -S. Africa Leaders Exch. Program, 1971—, Bus. Coun. for Internat. Understanding, 1974-76, Yale-China Assn., 1975-78, East Meets West Found., 1991—; trustee Choate Sch., Wallingford, Conn., 1967-76, Westover Sch., Middlebury, Conn., 1975-79, Watch Hill Chapel Soc., 1963-77, Assn. Yale Alumni, 1972-75, 80-83. Mem. Burlingame Country Club, Pacific Union Club, Bohemian Club. Home and Office: 10 Greenview Ln Hillsborough CA 94010-6424 E-mail: putneyw@pacbell.net.

WESTERFIELD, RANDOLPH W. university dean, business educator; BA in econs., UCLA, 1963, MA in econs., 1965, PhD in fin., 1968. Asst. prof. fin. The Wharton Sch., U. Pa., Phila., 1968-73, assoc. prof. fin., 1973-81, sr. rsch. assoc., Rodney L. White Ctr. Fin. Rsch., 1977-88, prof. fin., 1981-88, chair fin. dept., 1986-88; Charles B. Thornton prof. fin., bus. econs. chair U. So. Calif. Sch. Bus. Adminstrn., L.A., 1988-93; dean, Robert R. Dockson chair in bus. adminstrn. Marshall Sch. Bus., U. So. Calif., L.A., 1993—2004. Bd. dirs. William Lyon Homes, 2000-, Health Mgmt. Assocs. Inc., 2000-, Nicholas Applegate Growth Equity Fund; vis. prof. fin. U. Nova de Lisbon, Portugal, 1981, Stanford U., Palo Alto, Calif., 1981-82, Claremont (Calif.) Grad. Sch., 1983; mem. trust com. Continental Bank, Phila., 1979-88; mem. pension rsch. coun., The Wharton Sch., 1979-88; mem. editl. adv. bd. John Wiley & Sons (Asia) Pte Ltd., 1996; mem. authors adv. coun., Times Mirror-Irwin Co., 1987-97; chmn. Consortium for Grad. Study in Mgmt., 1997; past cons. AT&T, Mobil Oil, UN, U.S. Depts. Labor and Justice. Co-author: (with Stephen A. Ross, Jeffrey Jaffe) Corporate Finance, 1988, 90, 93, 96 (including Can., Australian and internat. edits.), (with Stephen A. Ross, Bradford D. Jordan) Fundamentals of Corporate Finance, 1992, 93, 95, 97 (including South African, Can., Australian, Chinese, Dutch and Spanish edits.), (with Stephen A. Ross, Bradford D. Jordan) Essentials of Corporate Finance, 1996; author monographs; contbr. chpts. to books, numerous articles to profl. jours. and conf. procs.; assoc. editor Fin. Rev., 1985-92. Mem. Nat. Assn. Corp. Bds. (mem. bd. L.A. chpt. 1996). Office: Marshall Sch Bus Adminstrn U So Calif Hoffman Hall 800 701 Exposition Blvd Los Angeles CA 90089-0001

WESTERFIELD, RICHARD, music director; BA in Music, Yale Coll., 1979; MMus, Yale Sch. Music, 1986; MBA, Dartmouth U., 1990. Condr. N.Y. Philharmic, 1993; assoc. condr. Boston Symphony Orch.; music dir. Ala. Symphony Orch., Birmingham, Harrisburg Symphony; asst. prof. Brown U. Guest condr. NY Philharm., Pitts. Symphony, Buffalo Philharm., Montreal Symphony, Netherlands Radio Symphony, Melbourne Symphony, Sydney Symphony, Adelaide Symphony, NY Chamber Symphony, San Diego Symphony, L'Orchestre de Bretagne, Augsburg Philharm. Orchester, Heidelberg Symphony, BBC Symphony, Wales, Edmonton Symphony, Tapiola Sinfonietta, Oreg. Bach Festival, Balt. Symphony, Phoenix Symphony, Kansas City Symphony, Tucson Symphony, Colo. Symphony, Indpls. Symphony, Grand Rapids Symphony, Pacific Symphony, Chgo.'s Grant Park Festival Orch., Can. Nat. Arts Ctr. Orch., Kitchener-Waterloo Symphony, Minn. and Fla. Orchs., Orch. of St. Luke's, New World, Jacksonville, Fla., West Coast and Colo. Springs Symphonies, R.I. and Tulsa Philharm. Orchs., Aukland Philharmonia, Singapore Symphony, Japan's Osaka Century and Hiroshima Symphonies, Bucharest, Cluj and Moldova Philharm. Orchs., Finland's Koupio and Oulu Symphonies, Mexico City Camerata Nacional. Office: Ala Symphony Orch 3621 6th Ave S Birmingham AL 35222-2407

WESTERGAARD, GEORGE HENRY, secondary school educator; b. Sumas, Wash., Aug. 4, 1942; s. Henry C. and Mary T. Westergaard; m. Donna M. Westergaard, June 20, 1964; 1 child, Kristen. BA in Edn., Ctrl. Wash. State Coll., 1964; MS in Interdisciplinary Studies, U. Oreg., 1969; DA in History, Carnegie Mellon U., 1976. Cert. secondary edn. tchr., Wash. Tchr. social studies and English Woodrow Wilson Jr. H.S., Yakima, Wash., 1964-67, Cal Young Jr. H.S., Eugene, Oreg., 1967-73; mem. staff, asst. rsch. historian Carnegie Mellon U., Pitts., 1971-73; tchr. social studies, counselor Thomas Jefferson Jr. H.S., Eugene, 1973-83; tchr. govt., econs., global studies, and psychology South Eugene H.S., 1983-88, tchr. social scis., chair social studies dept., 1988-94, tchr. advanced placement govt. and politics, 1994-99; tchr. advanced placement psychology, comp. govt., politics Sammamish H.S., Bellevue, Wash., 1999—. Cons. AP Govt. and Politics workshops, 1990—; adj. prof. edn. U. Oreg., summer 1991; mem. social studies task force State of Oreg., 1997-99; nat. reader, question leader AP Gov. and Politics; adj. prof. Pacific Luth. U., 2001-03; editor, writer govt. and politics curricula and texts. Mem. budget rev. com. Bellevue Sch. Dist. Fellow Ind. Study in the Humanities, 1986. Avocations: photography, fishing, hiking, boating. Home: 2323 167th Ave NE Bellevue WA 98008

WESTERHAUS, CATHERINE K. social worker; b. Corydon, Ind., Oct. 13, 1910; d. Anthony Joseph and Permelia Ann (Mathes) Kannapel; m. George Henry Westerhaus, Apr. 15, 1950. BEd in Music, Kans. U., 1934; MSW, Loyola U., Chgo., 1949. Cert. Acad. Cert. Social Workers. Clin. social worker Friendly Acres Home of Aged, Newton, Kans.; county welfare dir., state adult svcs. supr. Newton-Harvey County, State of Kans.; vol. cert. social worker Newton. Project dir.: Memories of War Years, 1995, The War Years Including Veterans of Harvey County, Kansas, 1995; contbr. articles to profl. jours. Vol. to veterans, home-bound and disabled people, residents in nursing homes, patients in hospitals. With USNR, 1945-46. Named Kans. Social Worker of Yr., 1975, Kans. 5th Dist. Legionnaire of Yr., 1998. Mem. NASW (cert.), Kans. Soc. Cert. Social Work, Am. Legion (comdr. Wayne G. Austin post 1981-82, del Nat. Conv. 1997, Legionnaire of Yr. Dept. Kans. 1998). Home: 20215 SE 30th Ave Pratt KS 67124-8371

WESTERHAUS, DOUGLAS BERNARD, lawyer; b. Marion, Kans., Jan. 11, 1951; s. Edwin Gerard and Bernadine (Ullman) W.; m. Susan Elizabeth Scott, Aug. 20, 1973 (div. Jan. 1979); m. Karen Sue Giersch, Sept. 20, 1980 (div. Aug. 1997); children: John Joseph, Jamie Lynn, Jeffrey Michael; m. Victoria Lee Ruhga, March, 1998; 1 child: David Burton. BSBA, Kans. U., 1973, JD, 1976. Bar: Kans. 1976, U.S. Dist. Kans. 1976, U.S. Supreme Ct. 1980. Assoc. Harper & Hornbaker, Junction City, Kans., 1976-78, ptnr., 1978-80; prin. Westerhaus Law Office, Marion, Kans., 1980-86; pres. Hydrogen Energy Corp., 1986-91, also bd. dirs.; staff atty. THORN Ams., Inc., dba Rent-A-Ctr., Wichita, Kans., 1991-95, chief counsel human resources, 1995-96, assoc. gen. counsel, 1996-97; dir. Field Human Resources, 1997-98; exec. v.p. Mr. Goodcents Franchise Sys., Inc., 1999—2001, sr. v.p. and gen. counsel, 2001—02; pres. DVW Properties LLC, 2002—. Atty. City of Grandview Plaza, Kans. 1977-80, City of Lehigh, Kans. 1980-86, Marion County, 1981-85; gen. counsel The Hydrogen Energy Corp., Kansas City, Mo. 1984-86, Marion Die & Fixture, 1980-86. Bd. dirs. St. Luke's Hosp., Marion, 1985-86. Mem. ABA, Kans. Bar Assn. (chmn. Lawyer Referral Commn. 1979-84, Outstanding Service award 1984), Marion County Bar Assn. (pres. 1985), Johnson County Bar Assn. Republican. Lutheran. Home: 12813 King St Overland Park KS 66213-4416 Office Phone: 913-814-8200. E-mail: dwesterhaus@everestkc.net.

WESTERHOFF, GARRET PETER, environmental engineer, executive; b. Fairlawn, N.J., Oct. 12, 1935; s. Garret Peter and Elizabeth (Ullmer) W.; m. Helga Ann Kasch, May 31, 1958; children: Garret Peter, Eric John, Paul Keith. BS in Civil Engring., N.J. Inst. Tech., 1957, MS in Sanitary Engring., 1967. Registered profl. engr., N.J., N.Y., Ohio, Va., Ariz., Calif., Md., Fla., Ala., La., Maine, Mass., Nebr., N.Mex., Nev., N.C., Pa., Wash.; cert. profl. planner; diplomate Am. Acad. Environ. Engrs. Loss prevention engr. Factory Mutual Engring. Co., 1960-64; project engr. Jersey Engring. Assocs., 1964-65; from v.p. to chmn., CEO Malcolm Pirnie, Inc., White Plains, N.Y., 1967—. Mem. rsch. adv. coun. Nat. Water Rsch. Inst.; internat. rapporteur on water quality and treatment in U.S. Internat. Water Supply Assn., World Congress, Budapest, 1993, Durban, S. Africa, 1995; tech. cons. Office Drinking Water U.S. EPA; presenter in field. Contbr. articles to profl. jours. 1st lt. USAF, 1957-60. Mem. ASCE, NAE, NSPE, Am. Water Works Assn. (former stds. coun., chmn. Internat. Water Supply Assn. N.Am. com., former chmn. water supply planning and coord. com., former trustee engring. and constrn. divsn., former chmn. water reuse com., former chmn. water treatment plant wastes disposal com., former chmn. alum recovery rsch. adv. com., rsch. adv. coun. Rsch. Found.), Water Environment Fedn. Avocations: fishing, photography, writing. Office: Malcolm Pirnie Inc 104 Corporate Park Dr Ste 1 White Plains NY 10604-3335 E-mail: gwesterhoff@pirnie.com.

WESTERHOFF, JOHN HENRY, III, clergyman, theologian, educator; b. Paterson, N.J., June 28, 1933; s. John Henry and Nona Celia (Walsh) W.; m. Alberta Louise Barnhart, Dec. 27, 1955 (div. 1991); childen: Jill Louise, John Jeffrey, Beth Anne; m. Caroline Askew Hughes, Oct. 27, 1991. BS, Ursinus Coll., 1955; STB, Harvard U., 1958; EdD, Columbia U., 1974; DD, Ursinus Coll., 1990. Ordained to ministry United Ch. of Christ, 1958, Episcopal Ch., 1978; pastor Congl. Ch., Presque Isle, Maine, 1958-60, assoc. pastor Needham, Mass., 1960-64; pastor 1st Congl. Ch., Williamstown, Mass., 1964-66; edn. sec., editor Colloquy (United Ch. Bd. for Homeland Ministries), N.Y.C., 1966-73; Lentz lectr. Harvard U. Div. Sch., 1973-74; prof. Duke U. Div. Sch., Durham, N.C., 1974-94; dir. Inst. Pastoral Studies, Atlanta, 1992—2003; interim rector St. Bartholomew Episcopal Ch., Atlanta, 1993-94; theologian in residence St. Lukes Episcopal Ch., Atlanta, 1994—. Author: Values for Tomorrows Children, 1970, A Colloquy on Christian Education, 1972, Generation to Generation, 1974, Tomorrow's Church, 1976, Will Our Children Have Faith?, 1976, McGuffey and His Readers, 1978, Who Are We?, 1978, Learning Through Liturgy, 1978, Inner Growth-Outer Change, 1979, The Church's Ministry in Higher Education, 1979, Liturgy and Learning Through the Life Cycle, 1980, Christian Believing, 1980, Bringing Up Children in The Christian Church, 1980, A Faithful Church, 1981, The Spiritual Life: Learning East and West, 1981, Building God's People, 1983, A Pilgrim People, 1984, Living the Faith Community, 1985, On the Threshold of God's Future, 1986, Living Into Our Baptism, 1990, Schooling Christians, 1992, The Spiritual Life: Foundation for Preaching and Teaching, 1994; A People Called Episcopalians, 1995, Holy Baptism: A Guide for Parents and Godparents, 1996, Grateful and Generous Hearts, 1997, To Love and to Cherich Till Death Do Us Part, 1998, Sensing Beauty, 1998, A People on a Pilgrimage, 1999, Will Our Children Have Faith?, 2000; editor: Religious Edn, 1979-89. Mem. Assn. Profs. and Researchers in Religious Edn., Religious Edn. Assn. Democrat. Episcopalian. Office: Saint Luke's Episcopal Ch 435 Peachtree St NE Atlanta GA 30308-3228 Office Phone: 404-873-7624.

WESTERHOUT, GART, retired astronomer; b. The Hague, The Netherlands, June 15, 1927; arrived in U.S., 1962, naturalized, 1969; s. Gerrit and Magdalena (Foppe) W.; m. Judith Mary Monaghan, Nov. 14, 1956; children: Magda C., Gart T., Brigit M., Julian C. Drs., Leiden U., Netherlands, 1954, PhD, 1958. Asst. Leiden U. Observatory, 1952-56, sci. officer, 1956-59, chief sci. officer, 1959-62; prof., dir. astronomy U. Md., 1962-73, chmn. div. math. and phys. scis. and engring., 1972-73, prof. astronomy, 1973-77; sci. dir. U.S. Naval Observatory, Washington, 1977-93; vis. astronomer Max Planck Inst. Radio Astronomy, Bonn, Germany, 1973-74, mem. adv. bd., 1976-79. Mem. astronomy adv. bd. NSF, 1963-67; vice chmn. divsn. phys. sci. NRC, 1969-73; mem. com. on radio frequencies, 1971-92; trustee Assoc. Univs. Inc., 1971-74; mem. Inter Union Commn. on Allocation of Frequencies, 1974-82; mem. sci. coun. Stellar Data Ctr., Strasbourg, France, 1978-84, chmn., 1981; chmn. working group on astrometry, astronomy survey com. NAS, 1979-81; mem. adv. bd. Haystack-N.E. Radio Obs. Consortium, 1974-77; mem. Arecibo adv. bd. Nat. Astronomy and Ionosphere Ctr., 1977-80, chmn., 1979-80; mem. U.S. nat. com. CODATA, 1985-91. Contbr. on radio astronomy, spiral structure of our Galaxy and astrometry to profl. jours. Recipient citation for teaching excellence Washington Acad. Scis., 1972; U.S. Sr. Scientist award Alexander von Humboldt Stiftung, Ger., 1973; NATO fellow, 1959. Mem. Internat. Astron. Union (chmn. working group on astron. data 1985-91), Internat. Sci. Radio Union (pres. commn. on radio astronomy 1975-78), Am. Astron. Soc. (councillor 1975-78, v.p. 1985-87), Royal Astron. Soc. Roman Catholic. Home: 811 W 38th St Baltimore MD 21211-2203

WESTERMAN, LIANE MARIE, research scientist executive; b. Long Branch, NJ, June 20, 1949; d. Charles Wilson and Edith Doris (Johnson) Case; m. S. Thomas Westerman; children: David Aaron, Charles Paul. BA in Psychology, Monmouth U., West Long Branch, N.J., 1972; MA in Teaching, Coll. of N.J., 1979. Cert. tchr. of handicapped, N.J. Tchr. spl. edn., dir. afternoon program S.E.A.R.C.H., Ocean, N.J., 1972-74; tchr. spl. edn. Jackson (N.J.) Twp. Sch. System, 1974-79; exec. dir. Otologic Edn., Inc., Shrewsbury, N.J., 1980-88; dir. clin. rsch. Nat. Patent Analytical Systems, Inc., Roslyn Heights, N.Y., 1983-86, v.p. rsch., 1986-88; pres. Westerman Rsch. Assocs., Inc., Shrewsbury, N.J., 1988—. Participant numerous convs., profl. organs. and spl. interest groups, U.S.A., Israel and The Netherlands, 1974—; software devel. expert to knowledge engr. for Visual Perceptual System, 1984—; v.p. Otologic Edn., Inc., Shrewsbury, 1988—. Co-contbr. articles and chpts. to profl. publs.; U.S. and Can. patentee computer-aided drug-abuse detection. Fundraiser Am. Heart Assn., 1991; active MADD; activist Nat. Audubon Soc. Mem. Am. Acad. Otolaryngology, Head and Neck Surgery (assoc.), Internat. Regulatory Affairs Profls. Soc., Nat. Graphic Soc., Assn. Clin. Pharmacologists, Regulatory Affairs Profls. Soc., Monmouth County Assn. Children with Learning Disabilities, Psi Chi, Sigma Xi. Avocations: travel, classical music, creative writing. Office: Westerman Rsch Assocs Inc 170 Ave at the Common Ste 6 Shrewsbury NJ 07702-4003

WESTERMAN, ROSEMARY MATZZIE, nurse, administrator; b. Sewickley, Pa., May 20, 1949; d. Joseph Edward and Martha (Aquino) Matzzie; m. Philip M. Westerman, Aug. 7, 1971. BSN, Duquesne U., 1971, MSEd, 1975. RN Pa. Head nurse Dept. Vet. Affairs VA Med. Ctr., Pitts., 1982-83; assoc. chief, nursing svc., edn. W. S. Middleton Meml. VA Hosp., Madison, Wis., 1983-85, Dept. VA Affairs VA Med. Ctr., Chilicothe, 1985-91, assoc. chief nursing svc., long term. care, 1991-93; assoc. chief nurse VA Med. Ctr., Augusta, Ga., 1993-97, chief nurse Muskogee, Okla., 1997—; clin. program mgr. Office of the Med. Inspector Vet. Health Adminstrn., Washington. Active Literacy Vol. of Am. Mem. ANA (cert. nursing adminstrn. advanced), Assoc. Am. Coll. Health Care Execs. Nursing Orgn. of VA, Sigma Theta Tau. Home: 4001 Olney Laytonsville Rd Olney MD 20832-1801

WESTERMANN-CICIO, MARY LOUISE, academic administrator, library studies educator; b. N.Y.C., Mar. 11, 1953; d. A. Louis and Anne U. (Skelly) Morse; m. Edward L. Cicio, June 20, 1998. BS in Biology, L.I. U., 1975, MS in Libr. Sci., 1976, MPA in Health Care Adminstrn., 1986; MA in History, SUNY, Stony Brook, 1992, PhD, 2001. Con. med. libr. Nassau-Suffolk Health Systems Agy., Melville, N.Y., 1976-77; dir. John N. Shell Libr. Nassau Acad. Medicine, Garden City, NY, 1977—88; instr. L.I. U., Greenvale, N.Y., 1977-88, adj. prof., 1983-88; assoc. prof. Palmer Grad. Libr. Sch., 1988-95, asst. dean, 1995—. Trustee L.I. Libr. Resources Coun., 1986-91; mem. adv. bd. Sr. Connections Program, Adelphi U., 1987-92; bd. dirs. Nassau County coun. Girl Scouts, 2002. Recipient E. Hugh Behymer award L.I. U., 1976, Disting. Alumni award Palmer Sch. L.I. U., 1993, Jackson Turner Maid award SUNY at Stony Brook, 1993. Mem. ALA, Med. Libr. Assn. (sec. med. socs. sect. 1981-82, instr. continuing edn. 1982, chmn. med. soc. sect. 1986-87; cert. health scis. librianship, Murry E. Gottlieb award 1998), Acad. Health Info. Professions, Spl. Librs. Assn. (sec. L.I. chpt. 1978-80, bd. dirs. 1982-84, pres. elect 1988, pres. 1989-90), Cath. Libr. Assn. (instr. workshop, Libr. of Yr. award 1992), Suffolk-Nassau on-Line Retrievers (chmn. 1981), Med. and Sci. Librs. of L.I. (pres. 1980-81), Nassau County Libr. Assn. (chmn. health svcs. com. 1978-81, 83-93, bd. dirs. 1990-92), Beta Beta Beta, Beta Phi Mu (bd. dirs. Beta Mu chpt. 1987-89, Golden Anniversary award 1999), Pi Alpha Alpha. Office: LI Univ CW Post Campus Palmer Sch Libr and Info Scis Greenvale NY 11548 Office Phone: 514-299-2866. E-mail: westerma@liu.edu.

WESTERMEYER, JOSEPH JOHN, psychiatrist; b. Chgo., Apr. 8, 1937; m. Rachel Moga; children: Michelle, Joseph; 5 foster children. Student, U. Notre Dame and St. Thomas Coll., 1955-57; BS in Biology and Chemistry, U. Minn., 1959, MD, 1961, MA in Anthropology, 1969, MPH, PhD, 1970. Diplomate Am. Bd. Psychiatry and Neurology, Am. Bd. Family Practice. Rotating intern St. Paul-Ramsey Hosp., 1961-62; gen. practice medicine Payne Ave. Med. Clinic, St. Paul, 1962-65; dep. chief divsn. pub. health AID, Laos, 1965-67; resident in psychiatry U. Minn., Mpls., 1967-70, instr., 1970-71, asst. prof., 1971-74, assoc. prof., 1974-78, prof. psychiatry, 1978—, prof., chair, 1989, adj. prof. anthropology, 1979—89, 1993—, adj. prof. psychology, 1979—89, dir. med. student edn. dept. psychiatry, 1976-82; mem. psychiatry staff, outpatient psychiat. practice U. Minn. Hosps. and Clinics, Mpls., 1970-89; prof., chmn. dept. psychiatry and behavioral sci. Okla. U. Med. Ctr., Oklahoma City, 1989—92; founder, dir. acute in-patient service U. Minn. Hosps. and Clinics, Mpls., 1970-72, founder, dir. day hosp., 1971-73, cons. primary care clinic, 1970-83, founder, dir. outpatient clinic for refugees from S.E. Asia, 1977—89, founder, dir. program for alcohol and drug dependence, 1982—89, founder, dir. internat. clinic dept. psychiatry, 1984—89; chief psychiatry, dir. mental health Mpls. VA Med. Ctr. Mem. ad hoc com. on Indochinese refugees Minn. Dept. Pub. Welfare, 1980-82; cons. methadone program Minn. VA Hosp., 1977-84, dept. psychiatry Mpls. VA Hosp., 1978-85; mem. case devel. com. for computer-based exam. Nat. Bd. Med. Examiners, 1983-88; mem. com. on mental and behavioral assessment and disorder in pilots FAA and AMA, 1984-85; chmn., co-editor devel. of a teaching manual on drug/alcohol dependence WHO, 1982-85, chmn., co-editor task force and report on methadone treatment in opiate dependence, 1982-85, research cons. internat. collaborative study of drug dependence intervention and treatment in primary health care, 1982-85; cons. in field; vis. prof. various colls.; lectr. in field. Author: A Primer on Chemical Dependency: A Clinical Guide to Alcohol and Drug Problems, 1976, Poppies, Pipes and People: A Study of Opium and Its Use in Laos, 1983, (with C. Williams) Refugees Mental Health Issues in Resettlement Countries, 1986, A Clinical Guide to Drug and Alcohol Problems, 1986; (with A. Arif) A Manual for Substance Abuse Education, 1988, An Update on Methadone, 1988; The Psychiatric Care of Migrants, 1989; editor: Anthropology and Mental Health, 1976; co-editor: (with E. Foulks, R. Wintrob and A. Favazza) Transcultural Psychiatry, 1977; contbr. revs. and articles to profl. jours., chpts. to books; mem. editorial bd. Am. Jour. Drug and Alcohol Abuse, 1973—, Jour. Operational Psychiatry, 1977-86, Am. Jour. Pub. Health, 1980-83, 83-87, Advances in Alcohol and Substance Abuse, 1980—, Alcoholism: Clin. and Exptl. Research, 1980-86, Alcohol and Research World, 1981—; social sci. editor Substance Abuse Newsletter, 1979-83; rev. reader Am. Jour. Psychiatry, 1978—, Transcultural Psychiat. Revs., 1980-84, Archives Gen. Psychiatry, 1981—, White Cloud Jour., 1981—, Jour. Nervous and Mental Disease, 1977—, Current Anthropology, 1979, 83, 85, Culture, Medicine and Psychiatry, 1979-80, various others. Recipient Meritorious Service award U.S. AID, 1967; Ginzburg fellow Group for Advancement of Psychiatry, 1969-70, NIH summer fellow Grad. Session in Epidemiology, U. Minn. Continuation Ctr., 1970, 72, 78; research grantee Office Internat. Programs, U. Minn., 1974-75, 78, 81; NIMH, 1973-74, 80-81, 82-84, Nat. Inst. Alcohol Abuse and Alcoholism, 1974-77, 78-79, Grad. Sch. U. Minn., 1977-78, Office Drug Abuse Prevention, U. Minn., 1977-78, Minn. Med. Found., 1974-75, 81, 82-83, Nat. Inst. Drug Abuse, 1977-78, 83-85, State Minn., 1979-80, Ctr. Urban and Regional Affairs, U. Minn., 1982-83, career tchr. grantee Alcohol, Drug Abuse and Mental Health Adminstrn., HEW, 1973-75, Biomed. research support grantee U. Minn. Med. Sch., 1977-78, Minn. Med. Found., 1977, tng. grantee Office Alcohol and Other Drug Abuse Programming, U. Minn., 1979-83, Indochinese Health Professionals, 1979-81, Archie; recipient numerous other research grants. Fellow Am. Anthropol. Assn., Am. Assn. Family Practice, Am. Psychiat. Assn. (com. on drug abuse 1985—); mem. World Psychiat. Assn. (transcultural sect.), Am. Soc. Social Psychiatry, Soc. Med. Anthropology, Assn. Med. Educators and Researchers in Substance Abuse (award for disting. contributions to the field 1987), AAAS, Assn. Behavioral Sci. and Med. Edn., Assn. Acad. Psychiatrists, Am. Pub. Health Assn., Research Soc. on Alcoholism, World Psychiat. Assn. (sect. on transcultural psychiatry), Soc. for Study of Psychiatry and Culture (steering com. 1979—,

secretariat 1984-85), Am. Med. Soc. on Alcoholism (state chmn. 1979—), Am. Acad. Psychiatrists in Alcoholism and Addictions, Soc. Traumatic Stress Studies, Minn. Psychiat. Assn. (mem. chem. dependency subcom. 1979—, mem. Minn. mental health interdisciplinary interest group rep. 1980-85, pres. 1984-86), Minn. State Med. Assn. (resource group on alcoholism and other chem. dependencies 1976-81), Alpha Omega Alpha. Home: 1935 Summit Ave Saint Paul MN 55105-1430 Office Phone: 612-725-2037. Business E-Mail: joseph.westermeyer@med.va.gov.

WESTERVELT, CHARLES EPHRAIM, JR., lawyer; b. Columbus, Ohio, Mar. 10, 1922; s. Charles Ephraim and Winifred Reed (Wells) W.; m. Melba Louise Kuhlman, Mar. 3, 1946 (dec.); children: John Charles (dec.), Kirk Thomas, Todd William, Reed Matthew. BA, Ohio State U., 1943, LLB and JD, 1948. Ptnr. Graves & Westervelt, Columbus, 1948-53; chief right of way atty. Ohio Turnpike Commn., Columbus, 1953-55, asst. to exec. dir., 1956; pvt. practice C.E. Westervelt Jr., Westerville, Ohio, 1956—. Trustee Westerville Pub. Libr., 1958-75; twp. clk. Geona Twp. Del. County, Ohio, 1960-72, mem. vol. fire dept., 1970-95; various offices Westerville Hist. Soc., 1948—. With USAAF, ETO, 1943-46. Decorated Air medal with 4 oak leaf clusters. Mem. Phi Beta Kappa. Republican. United Methodist. Avocations: reading, gardening, camping, fishing, genealogy. Home: 7974 Africa Rd Westerville OH 43082-8818 Office: 18 W College Ave Westerville OH 43081-2176 Office Phone: 614-882-2339.

WESTERVELT, JAMES JOSEPH, retired insurance company executive; b. Bklyn., July 8, 1946; s. Cornealius V. and Regina Elizabeth (May) W.; m. Sue Jane Brubaker, Aug. 5, 1972; children: Kevin K., Natalie M. BBA, Manhattan Coll., 1967. Mgr. auditing Peat, Marwick & Mitchell, N.Y.C., 1967-78; dir. auditing City Investing, N.Y.C., 1978-81; asst. v.p., asst. contr. The Hartford Financial Svcs. Group, Inc., Conn., 1981-89, v.p., group contr., 1989-94, sr. v.p., group contr., 1994—2001; group contr. Hartford Fin. Svc. Group, 1998-99; sr. v.p., CFO Himco, 1999—2001; sr. v.p. Hartford Fin. Svc., Inc.; ret., 2002—. With U.S. Army, 1968-69. Mem. AICPA, Hawaii Soc. CPAs, Conn. Soc. CPAs, Am. Ins. Assn. Roman Catholic. Avocations: skiing, wine tasting, tennis, chess, electronics.

WESTFALL, CONSTANCE COURTNEY, lawyer; b. Plainview, Tex., Nov. 29, 1960; d. M.H. and Carolyn Courtney; m. Monte Jay Westfall, Jan. 3, 1998; children: William, John. BS, U. Tex., 1982, JD, 1985. Bar: Tex., U.S. Dist. Ct. (we. and no. dists.) Tex., U.S. Dist. Ct. (we. and ea. dists.) Ark., U.S. Dist. Ct. (we. dist.) Okla., U.S. Ct. Appeals (5th and 8th cirs.) Tex. Com. clk. Natural Resources Com., Tex. Ho. of Rep., 1979; legis. staff to hon. Buck Florence Tex. Ho. of Rep., 1980-82; law clk. to hon. Jerre Williams U.S. Ct. Appeals (5th cir.), 1985-86; assoc. Thompson & Knight, Dallas, 1986-92, Brown McCarroll, Dallas, 1992-94; ptnr. Hutcheson & Grundy, Dallas, 1994-98, Strasburger & Price, Dallas, 1998—. Contbr. articles to profl. jours. Moderator So. Meth. U. Sch. Law Environ. Career Seminar, 1989-2000. Mem.: ABA, State Bar Coll., State Bar Tex. (mem. law sch. com. 1988—97, chmn. outreach com. environ. sect. 1989—92, chmn. law sch. com. 1997—2003, chmn. environ. and natural resources sect. 2003—). Office: Strasburger & Price 901 Main St Ste 4300 Dallas TX 75202-3724

WESTFALL, DAVID, lawyer, educator; b. Columbia, Mo., Apr. 16, 1927; s. Wilhelmus David A. and Ruth (Rollins) W.; children: Elizabeth Stewart, William Beatty, Thomas Curwen, Katharine Putnam. AB, U. Mo., 1947; LLB magna cum laude, Harvard U., 1950. Bar: Ill. 1950, Mass. 1956. Assoc. Bell, Boyd, Marshall & Lloyd, Chgo., 1950-55; asst. prof. law Harvard Law Sch., 1955-58, prof., 1958—, John L. Gray prof., 1983—, Carl F. Schipper Jr. prof., 1996—. Author: Estate Planning Cases and Text, 1985, Every Woman's Guide to Financial Planning, 1984, Family Law, 1993; co-author: Estate Planning Law and Taxation, 4th edit., 2001; co-editor: Readings in Federal Taxation, 1983. Served as 1st lt. JAGC, AUS, 1951-53. Fellow Am. Coll. Trust and Estate Counsel (acad.); mem. ABA, Mass. Bar Assn., Am. Law Inst., Phi Beta Kappa, Phi Delta Theta. Office: 1525 Massachusetts Ave Cambridge MA 02138-2903 Office Phone: 617-495-4630. Business E-Mail: dwestfal@law.harvard.edu.

WESTFALL, JEFFREY N. education educator; s. Lillian Neal; m. Ginne Ryan, Mar. 2, 2002. MA, U. of Iowa, 1980. Prof. Skyline Coll., San Bruno, Calif., 1996—. Personal E-mail: westfall@smccd.net.

WESTFALL, MORRIS, state legislator; b. Apr. 5, 1939; s. Raymond Earl and Ethel Faye (Neill) W.; m. Sharon Kay Douglas, Dec. 19, 1964; children: Craig Lin, Christi Dawn. BS, U. Mo., 1962. Mem. Mo. Ho. of Reps., Jefferson City, 1971-81; minority whip, 1977—80; asst. minority floor leader, 1981; mem. Mo. Senate from 28th dist., Jefferson City, 1994—2002; chmn. Senate Majority Caucus, 2001—02. State exec. dir. agrl. stabilization conservation svc. USDA, Mo., 1981-93. Mem. U. Mo. Alumni Assn., Saddle Club. Office: State Capitol Building Jefferson City MO 65101-1556 E-mail: morris_westfall@senate.state.mo.us.

WESTFIELD, FRED M. economics professor; b. Essen, Germany, Nov. 7, 1926; came to U.S., 1940; s. Dietrich and Grete (Stern) W.; m. Joyce A. Horwitz Nochlin, Nov. 15, 1968; stepchildren: Steven Nochlin, Keith Nochlin. BA magna cum laude, Vanderbilt U., 1950; PhD in Indsl. Econs., MIT, 1957. Teaching asst., instr. MIT, Cambridge, 1952-53; lectr. Northwestern U., Evanston, Ill., 1953-57, asst. prof., 1957-60, assoc. prof., 1960-65; prof. econs. Vanderbilt U., Nashville, 1965-98, mem. faculty coun. Coll. Arts and Sci., 1974-76, mem. faculty senate, 1979-82, 94-95, dir. undergrad. studies dept. econs. and bus. adminstrn., 1984-87, mem. grad. faculty coun., 1991, prof. econs. emeritus, 1998—. Vis. prof. U. Colo., summers 1973-74; condr. seminars, lectr., participant univs. and rsch. orgns.; Fulbright sr. lectr. U. Nac. del Sur, Argentina, 1986; cons. Coun. Econ. Advisers, Exec. Office Pres., 1968, World Bank and Water and Power Devel. Authority, Pakistan, 1970-72, World Bank and East African Power and Light Co., Kenya, 1975, NSF, 1975, FTC, 1976-78, World Bank, UN Devel. Program and Econ. Planning Bd. South Korea, 1975-76; expert witness Tenn. Pub. Svc. Commn., 1980-89, Consumer Advocate Tenn. Atty. Gen., 1994; also others. Mem. editl. bd. Utilities Policy, 1990—2002, mem. bd. editors So. Econ. Jour., 1973—75, editl. referee Am. Econ. Rev., Jour. Polit. Economy, Econometrica, So. Econ. Jour., Econ. Inquiry; contbr. articles and book revs. to profl. jours. With U.S. Army, 1945-46. Fellow Gen. Edn. Bd., MIT, Ford Found., 1958-59. Mem. Am. Econ. Assn., Econometric Soc. (program com. 1967, chmn. conf. sessions), So. Econ. Assn. (v.p. 1976-77, chmn. conf. sessions), Phi Beta Kappa. Home: 1097 Lynnwood Blvd Nashville TN 37215-4540

WESTHAVER, LAWRENCE ALBERT, electronics engineer, consultant; b. Washington, Oct. 24, 1936; s. James Waldo and Hattie Virginia (Bush) W.; m. Jo Ann Turner, Jan. 5, 1957; children: Lawrence Albert Jr., Wendy Jo Westhaver Burke, Bonnie Jo Westhaver Green. Cert. engring., U. Va., 1966. Electronic design, cons. Westhaver Assocs., Inc., Laurel, Md., 1971—; engring. draftsman Office Rsch. and Devel. Nat. Security Agy., Arlington Hall, Va., 1955-57, engring. technician Office Rsch. and Engring. Ft. G.G. Meade, Md., 1958-66, electronic engr. Office Rsch. and Engring., 1967-82, sr. engr. Office of Rsch. and Engring., 1982-84; sr. engr. Communications Systems Support Group, Laurel, Md., 1984-93. Patentee method for photographic aperture control, photographic light integrator, switching current regulator, photographic test equipment, electronic tuner for stringed musical instruments, microcomputer-based Ni-Cd battery charger, and color-correcting filter for underwater photography. Avocations: scuba diving, snorkeling, biking, hiking, bird watching. Home: 8609 Portsmouth Dr Laurel MD 20708-1819 Personal E-mail: larry@westhaver.com.

WESTHEIMER, DAVID KAPLAN, novelist; b. Houston, Apr. 11, 1917; s. Adolf and Esther (Kaplan) W.; m. Doris Gertrude Rothstein, Oct. 9, 1945; children: Fred, Eric. BA, Rice Inst., Houston, 1937. Successively asst. amusement editor, radio editor, mag. editor, TV editor Houston Post, 1939-41, 45-46, 50, 53-60, columnist, 1984-88. Columnist: SeniorWomen Web (seniorwomen.com); author: Summer on the Water, 1948, The Magic Fallacy, 1950, Watching Out for Dulie, 1960, Von Ryan's Express, 1964, My Sweet Charlie, 1965, Song of the Young Sentry, 1968, Lighter Than a Feather, 1971, Over the Edge, 1972, Going Public, 1973, Tha Avila Gold, 1974, The Olmec Head, 1974, Rider on the Wind, 1979, Von Ryan's Return, 1980, The Great Wounded Bird, and other poems, 2000, (with John Sherlock) The Amindra Gamble, 1982, Sitting It Out, 1992, Death Is Lighter Than a Feather, 1995, Delay En Route, 2002, (with Karen Westheimer) LoneStar Zodiac, 1995, (play) My Sweet Charlie, 1966, (TV films) Trouble Comes to Town, 1972, A Killer Among Us, 1990. Served to capt. USAAF, 1941-45, ETO; served to capt. USAF, 1950-53; lt. col. USAF; ret. Decorated Air medal, D.F.C. Mem. ACLU, Writer's Guild Am. West, Ret. Officers Assn., Calif. Writers Club. Democrat. Avocation: reading. Home and Office: 11722 Darlington Ave Apt 2 Los Angeles CA 90049-5525 E-mail: dwestheime@aol.com.

WESTHEIMER, FRANK HENRY, chemist, educator; b. Balt., Jan. 15, 1912; s. Henry Ferdinand and Carrie (Burgunder) Westheimer; m. Jeanne Friedmann, Aug. 31, 1937; children: Ruth Susan, Ellen. AB, Dartmouth Coll., 1932, ScD (hon.), 1961; MA, Harvard U., 1933, PhD, 1935; ScD (hon.), U. Chgo., 1973, U. Cin., 1976; ScD (hon.), Tufts U., 1978, U. N.C., 1983, Bard Coll., 1983, Weizmann Inst., 1987; ScD (hon.), U. Ill., Chgo., 1988. Rsch. assoc. U. Chgo., 1936—37, instr., 1937—41, asst. prof., 1941—44, assoc. prof., 1946—48, prof. chemistry, 1948—53; vis. prof. Harvard U., 1953—54, prof. chemistry, 1954—82, sr. prof., 1982—83, prof. emeritus, 1983—, chmn. dept., 1959—62; Overseas fellow Churchill Coll., U. Cambridge, England, 1962—63. Mem. Pres.'s Sci. Adv. Com., 1967—70; rsch. supr. Explosives Rsch. Lab., Nat. Def. Rsch. Com, 1944—45; presenter in field. Mem. editl. bd.: Jour. Chem. Physics, 1942—44, 1952—54, 1960—69; contbr. articles to profl. jours. Recipient Naval Ordnance Development award, 1946, Army-Navy cert. of appreciation, 1946, James Flack Norris award in phys.-organic chemistry, 1970, Willard Gibbs medal, 1970, Theodore W. Richards medal, 1976, Richard Kokes award, 1980, Charles Frederick Chandler medal, 1980, Rosenstiel award, 1981, Nichols medal, 1982, Robert A. Welch award, 1982, Cope award, 1982, Ingold medal, 1983, Nat. Medal of Sci., 1986, Paracelsus medal, 1988, Priestley medal, 1988, Repligen award, 1992, Nakanishi award, 1997, Westheimer medal, Harvard U. Dept. Chemistry, 2003; fellow, Columbia U. NRC, 1935—36, Guggenheim Found., 1962—63, Fulbright-Hays Found., 1974, Japan Soc. Promotion of Sci., 1982; Exchange fellow, NAS, China, 1982. Mem.: Royal Soc., Am. Acad. Arts and Scis. (sec. 1985—90), Am. Philos. Soc. (council 1981—84), Nat. Acad. Sci. (council 1971—75, 1976—79, chmn. com. survey chemistry 1964—65, award in chem. scis. 1980). Home: 3 Berkeley St Cambridge MA 02138-3409 E-mail: westheimer@chmistry.harvard.edu.

WESTHEIMER, GERALD, optometrist, educator; b. Berlin, May 13, 1924; naturalized, 1944, came to U.S., 1951; s. Isaak and Ilse (Cohn) W. Optometry diploma, Sydney (Australia) Tech. Coll., 1943, fellowship diploma, 1950; BSc, U. Sydney, 1947; PhD, Ohio State U., 1953; DSc (hon.), U. NSW, Australia, 1988; ScD (hon.), SUNY, 1990. Practice optometry, Sydney, 1945-51; research fellow Ohio State U., 1951-53; prof. physiol. optics U. Houston, 1953-54; asst. prof., then assoc. prof. physiol. optics Ohio State U., 1954-60; postdoctoral fellow neurophysiology Marine Biol. Lab., Woods Hole, Mass., 1957; vis. researcher Physiol. Lab., U. Cambridge, Eng., 1958-59; mem. faculty U. Calif. at Berkeley, 1960—, prof. physiol. optics, 1963-68, chmn. group physiol. optics, 1964-67, prof. physiology, 1968-89, prof. neurobiology, 1989—, head div. neurobiology, 1987-92; adj. prof. Rockefeller U., N.Y., 1992—. Sackler lectr. Tel Aviv U. Med. Sch., 1988, D.O. Hebb lectr. McGill U., 1991, Grass Found. lectr. U. Ill., 1991, Wertheimer lectr. U. Frankfort on the Main, 1998; mem. com. vision NRC, 1957-72; mem. visual scis. study sect. NIH, 1966-70, chmn. visual scis. B study sect., 1977-79; mem. vision, research and tng. com. Nat. Eye Inst., NIH, 1970-74, chmn. bd. sci. counselors, 1981-83; mem. exec. council com. vision NAS-NRC, 1969-72; mem. communicative scis. cluster Pres.'s Biomed. Rsch. Panel, 1975. Author rsch. papers; editor: Vision Rsch., 1972-79; editl. bd. Investigative Ophthalmology, 1973-77, Exptl. Brain Rsch., 1973-89, Optics Letters, 1977-78, Spatial Vision, 1985—, Ophthalmic and Physiological Optics, 1985—, Vision Rsch., 1985-92, Jour. of Physiology, 1987-94. Recipient Von Sallman prize Columbia U., 1986; Prentice medal Am. Acad. Optometry, 1986, Bicentennial medal Australian Optometric Assn., 1988. Fellow AAAS, Royal Soc. London (Ferrier lectr. 1992, editl. bd. procs. 1990-96, 2000—), Am. Acad. Arts and Scis., Optical Soc. Am. (Tillyer medal 1978, assoc. editor jour. 1980-83), Am. Acad. Optometry; mem. Royal Soc. New So. Wales, Soc. Neurosci., Assn. Rsch. in Vision and Ophthalmology (Proctor medal 1979), Internat. Brain Rsch. Orgn., Physiol. Soc. Gt. Britain, Sigma Xi. Home: 582 Santa Barbara Rd Berkeley CA 94707-1746 Office Phone: 510-642-4828. E-mail: gwest@socrates.berkeley.edu.

WESTHEIMER, RUTH SIEGEL (KAROLA WESTHEIMER), psychologist, television personality; b. Frankfurt, Fed. Republic Germany; came to U.S., 1956; m. Manfred Westheimer; children: Miriam, Joel. Grad. psychology, U. Paris Sorbonne; Master's degree, New Sch. for Social Research, N.Y.C., 1959; EdD, Columbia U., 1970. Research asst. Columbia U. Sch. Pub. Health, N.Y.C., 1967-70; assoc. prof. Lehman Coll., Bronx, N.Y., 1970-77; with Bklyn. Coll., West Point Milit. Acad.; counsellor, radio talk show hostess Sexually Speaking Sta. WYNY-FM, N.Y.C., 1980-90; hostess TV series Good Sex, Dr. Ruth Show, Ask Dr. Ruth, 1987-92; pvt. practice, 1976—. Adj. assoc. prof. NYU; leader seminars for residents and interns in pediats. on adolescent sexuality Brookdale Hosp. Author: Dr. Ruth's Guide to Good Sex, 1983, First Love: A Young People's Guide to Sexual Information, 1985, Dr. Ruth's Guide for Married Lovers, 1986, (autobiography) All In a Lifetime, 1987, Sex and Morality: Who is Teaching Out Sex Standards?, 1988, Dr. Ruth's Guide to Erotic and Sensuous Pleasures, 1991, Dr. Ruth's Guide to Safer Sex, 1992, Dr. Ruth Talks to Kids, 1993, The Art of Arousal, 1993, Dr. Ruth's Encyclopedia of Sex, 1994, Heavenly Sex, 1995, Sex for Dummies, 1995, The Value of Family, 1996; co-author: (with Steven Kaplan) Surviving Salvation; contbr. articles to mags.; appeared in film A Woman or Two, 1986; appeared on TV show Quantum Leap, 1993, Play Boy Making Love Series (video), 1996, All New Dr. Ruth Show (nominated 5 times by Ace awards, Ace award for excellence in cable TV, 1988), What's Up, Dr. Ruth (gold medal Internat. Film and TV Festival for excellence in ednl. TV), You're on the Air with Dr. Ruth, Never Too Late, 1992—, Dr. Ruth's House, (calendar) Dr. Ruth's Good Sex Night-to-Night Calendar, 1993, 94, (boardgame) Dr. Ruth's Game of Good Sex; exec. prodr. documentary on Ethiopian Jews Surviving Salvation, 1991; columnist Ask Dr. Ruth. Pres. YMHA, Washington Heights. Recipient Mother of Yr. award Nat. Mother's Day Com., Liberty medal City of N.Y. Fellow N.Y. Acad. Medicine. Office: Pierre A Lehu Comms Connection 145 W 45th St Ste 1009 New York NY 10036-4008

WESTHEIMER, RUTH WELLING, retired management consultant; b. Detroit, May 17, 1922; d. Benjamin Dennis and Elsa (Friedenberg) Welling; m. Robert Irvin BA, U. Wis., 1944. V.p., bd. dirs. Stepping Stones Ctr., Cin., 1976-85; chmn., developer Vol. Action Ctr., Cin., 1979-82; trustee United Way Community Chest, Cin., 1980-88; organizer Cooporate Voluntarism Council, Cin., 1982-85; v.p., exec. com. United Way Community Chest, Cin., 1983-85; chmn. Evaluation Com. United Way, Cin., 1985-88; advisor YWCA Career Women Achievement, Cin., 1981—; bd. dirs. Cancer Family Care, Cin., 1986—; chmn. United Way Agy. Partnership Devel., Cin., 1988—. Treas. Workum Scholarship Found., Cin., 1969-86; chmn. Fine Arts Fund, Trustee Cin. Psychoanalytic Found., 1974-78, Ohio Citizens Coun., Columbus, 1967-70; bd. dirs. Planned Parenthood Assn., Cin., 1991—. Mem. Woman's City Club, League of Women Voters (treas. 1959-68); bd. of trustees, American Classical Music Hall of Fame, Cincinnati. Avocations: tennis, golf, horticulture, travel.*

WESTLEY, JOHN RICHARD, economist; b. Fairmont, Minn., Feb. 25, 1939; s. Richard and Margaret (Kindschi) W.; m. Sidney Kathryn Bohanna, Mar. 26, 1966(div. Sept. 1977); children: Elizabeth Laura, Karen Margaret, Marian Bohanna; m. Joan Nancy Ehrlich, Apr. 12, 1980; 1 child, Katherine Matthea. BA in Philosophy, Yale U., 1961; MA in Econs., Columbia U., 1966; PhD in Econs., Am. Univ., 1983. Internat. economist U.S. Dept. Treasury, Washington, 1966-69; loan officer U.S. AID, Addis Ababa, Ethiopia, 1970-72, economist Nairobi, Kenya, 1973-75, Washington, 1976-78, program officer New Delhi, 1979-84, dir. mission to Bangladesh Dhaka, 1985-87, assoc. asst. adminstr. bur. Africa Washington, 1987-90, dir. mission to Kenya Nairobi, 1990-94; dir. Mission to Egypt US AID, Cairo, 1994-98; v.p. Internat. Fund Agrl. Devel., Rome, 1998—2002; adj. assoc. prof. econs. John Cabot U., Rome, 2002—. Author: Agriculture and Equitable Growth, 1986. With U.S. Army, 1961-64. Mem. Am. Econ. Assn., Phi Beta Kappa. Presbyterian. Office: John Cabot Univ Via Della Lungara 233 00165 Rome Italy E-mail: jwestle@tin.it.

WESTLING, JON, university administrator; b. Yakima, Wash., June 7, 1942; s. Norman L. and Jean R. (Bergamini) W.; m. Elizabeth A. Wüthrich, Oct. 14, 1977; children: Emma E., Matthew R., Andrew N. BA, Reed Coll., 1964; postgrad., St. John's Coll. Oxford (Eng.) U., 1964-67, UCLA, 1971-74. Instr. history Centre Coll., Danville, Ky., 1967-68; asst. prof. history and humanities Reed Coll., Portland, Oreg., 1968-71; assoc. dir. Boston Univ. Prodns., 1974-76; asst. to pres. Boston U., 1976-79, assoc. provost, 1979-83, provost ad interim, 1983-84, provost, 1984-88, exec. v.p., 1988-90, interim pres., 1990, exec. v.p., provost, 1991-95, provost, pres.-elect, 1995-96, pres., 1996—2002, pres. emeritus, 2002—. Bd. dirs. Century Bank. Bd. dirs. Jobs for Mass., Inc., 1998—, Boston 2000, 1987—2000; trustee Boston Mus. Sci., 1990—; mem. corp. Nat. Braille Press, Inc., 1998—; trustee Am. Coll. Greece, 1998—; bd. dirs. Boston History Collaboration, 2000—, treas., 2001—. Gen. Motors Nat. scholar, 1960-64, Rhodes scholar, 1964-67. Home: 135 Ivy St Brookline MA 02446-3904 Office: Boston U Office Pres 147 Bay State Rd Boston MA 02215-1708 also: Boston University 121 Bay State Road Boston MA 02215

WESTLUND, MARIBETH, secondary school educator; b. Chgo., Apr. 29, 1961; d. Francis Joseph and Catherine Marie Balda. BS, Ill. State U., 1983; MEd, DePaul U., 1993. Cert. ednl. adminstr., tchr. Ill. Tchr. Our Lady of Knock Cath. Sch., Calumet City, Ill., 1985—86; dept. chair of social studies, tchr. Schaumburg H.S., Schaumburg High School, Ill., 1986—. Bd. dirs. N.W. Ctr. Against Sexual Assault. Nominee Golden Apple Educator Nominee, Golden Apple Found., 2002. Mem.: AAUW, NOW, Nat. Coun. Social Studies. Avocations: travel, hiking, bicycling, tennis. Office: Schaumburg HS 1100 W Schaumburg Rd Schaumburg IL 60194 Personal E-mail: mbwestlund@yahoo.com. E-mail: mwestlund@d211.org.

WESTMAN, CARL EDWARD, lawyer; b. Youngstown, Ohio, Dec. 12, 1943; s. Carl H. and Mary Lillis (Powell) W.; m. Carolyn J., July 17, 1965; children: C. Forrest, Stephanie A. BBA, Sam Houston State U., 1966; JD, U. Miami, 1969, LLM in Taxation, 1972. Bar: Fla. 1969. Ptnr. Frost & Jacobs, 1983-93, Roetzel & Andress, 1993-98; adminstrv. ptnr. Steel, Hector & Davis, Naples, Fla., 1999—2004, Cohen & Grigsby, 2004—. Active S.W. Fla. coun. Boy Scouts Am. Eagle Bd. of Rev., 1987—; chmn. planned giving com. Audubon of Fla. for S.W. Fla.; trustee David Lawrence Found. for Mental Health, Inc., 1976-86, chmn. 1985-86; trustee Pikeville Coll., 1993—; trustee, vice chmn., NCH Healthcare Sys. Inc., 1995—, chmn. profl. capabilities com. physician credentialing, 1998—; trustee, chmn. Naples Cmty. Hosp.; past pres. bd. trustees, elder Moorings Presbyn. Ch. Master lic. capt. USCG. Mem. ABA, Fla. Bar Assn., Collier County Bar Assn., Estate Planning Coun., Useppa Island Club, Marco Island Yacht Club (bd. dirs.). Home: 1952 Crayton Rd Naples FL 34102-5070 Office: Collier Place I 3003 Tamiami Trail N Ste 3003 Naples FL 34103-2718 Office Phone: 239-430-1800. E-mail: cwestman@cohenlaw.com.

WESTMAN, JUDITH ANN, clinical geneticist; b. Columbus, Ohio, Nov. 7, 1957; d. Paul Marshall and Anna Marie (Stahly) Whetstone; m. David Arthur Westman, Apr. 12, 1980; children: Matthew, Joel, Rachel, Deborah. BA, Ohio No. U., 1978; MD, Ohio State U., 1981, MS, 1987. Diplomate Am. Bd. Pediatrics, Am. Bd. Med. Genetics. Resident in pediatrics Children's Hosp. Ohio State U., Columbus, 1981-84, chief resident, 1984-85, fellow clin. genetics, 1985-87, clin. asst. prof., 1987-95, clin. assoc. prof., 1995—, assoc. dean admissions and student affairs, 1996-99, assoc. dean student and med. edn., 1999—. Chair admissions com. Ohio State U. Coll. Medicine, 1990-96. Contbr. articles to profl. jours. Mem. adv. bd. Coll. Arts and Scis., Ohio No. U., Ada, 1988-97, trustee, 1997—; trustee Malone Coll., Canton, Ohio, 1988-94. Grantee FDA, 1987, NCI, 2001. Fellow Am. Acad. Pediatrics, Am. Soc. Human Genetics. Republican. Mem. Ch. of God (Anderson). Avocations: music, church activities. Office: 260 Meiling Hall 370 W 9th Ave Columbus OH 43210-1238

WESTMAN, STEVEN RONALD, rabbi; b. Chgo., Sept. 16, 1945; s. Kurt S. and Hilda (Schmoller) W.; m. Sherri, Nov. 30, 1980; children: Rachel Dara, Emily Nicole, Molly Sarah Levin. BA, U. Ill., 1967; B of Hebrew Letters, Hebrew Union Coll., 1969, MA in Hebrew Letters, 1972, DDiv., 1997. Ordained rabbi, 1972. Asst. rabbi Congregation Rodeph Shalom, Phila., 1972-75; rabbi Temple Israel, Stroudsburg, Pa., 1975-83, Temple Beth Torah, Wellington, Fla., 1983-95, Temple Beth El Israel, Ft. Pierce, Fla., 1995-00, Temple Beth El, West Palm Beach, 2000—. Mem. Commn. for Jewish Edn., West Palm Beach, Fla., 1990-94; bd. dirs. Jewish Cmty. Day Sch., West Palm Beach, 1988-91, Jewish Cmty. Ctr., 1987-89; pres. Palm BEach County Bd. Rabbis, 1989-92. Bd. dirs. Palms West Hosp., Loxahatchee, Fla., 1986-91, Pocono Hosp., East Stroudsburg, Pa., 1979-83; found. bd. dirs. Hospice of Monroe County, East Stroudsburg, 1978-83; bd. dirs. Palm Beach Liturgical Culture Soc., West Palm Beach, 1986-95. Recipient Tower of David award State of Israel Bonds, 1988, Leadership award Jewish Fedn. of Palm Beach County, 1985. Mem. Cen. Conf. of Am. Rabbis, Rotary. Home: 5170 Foxhall Dr S West Palm Beach FL 33417 Office: Temple Beth El 2815 N Flagler Dr West Palm Beach FL 33407 E-mail: rabbiwestman@bellsouth.net. *The theme and spirit of my rabbinate are found in the words of Pirkey Avot, the ethics of the Fathers: "Be of the disciples of Aaron, loving peace and pursuing peace, loving your fellow creatures and bringing them close to the Torah." (Avot 1:12).*

WESTMORE, MICHAEL GEORGE, make-up artist, writer; b. Hollywood, Calif., Mar. 22, 1938; s. Montague George and Edith Adeline Westmore; m. Marion Christine Bergeson, Dec. 4, 1966; children: Michael George, Michele, McKenzie. BA, U. Calif., Santa Barbara, 1961. Apprentice make-up artist Universal City Studios, Universal City, Calif., 1961-63, staff make-up artist, 1964, asst. head dept. make-up lab., 1965-71; freelance make-up artist various studios, Hollywood, Calif., 1971-87; make-up supr. and designer Paramount Studios, Hollywood, 1987—. Instr. theatre arts dept. Los Angeles Valley Coll., 1966—71; pres. Cosmetic Control Ctrs., Inc., 1971—76, Hollywood Magic Cosmetics, 1985—87; rsch. cons., lectr. therapeutic cosmetics for med. assns. Author: The Art of Theatrical Make-Up for Stage and Screen, 1971, also chpts. in books; co-author: Star Trek Makeup FX Journal, Star Trek-Aliens & Artifacts; make-up artist TV spls. Eleanor and Franklin (emmy award NATAS, 1976), Why Me? (Emmy award 1984, 1984), Three Wishes of Billy Grier (Emmy award, 1985), Star Trek (Emmy award, 1988, 1992, 1993, 1995, 1996), Amazing Stories (Emmy award, 1987), make-up artist films 2010 (Acad. award nomination Acad. Motion Picture Arts and Scis., 1985), Mask (Acad. award, 1986), Clan of the Cave Bear (Acad. award nomination, 1987), Star Trek First Contact (Acad. award nomination, 1996). Served with AUS, 1956. Recipient Best Spl. Effects Make-up on TV for Geppetto award, Hollywood Make-up Artists Guild, 2001, Order of Achievement award, Lambda Chi Alpha. Mem.: Archive of Am. TV, Internat. Alliance Theatrical Stage Employees, Knights of the Vine, Soc. Make-up Artists, Vikings of Scandia, Lambda Chi Alpha (life). Address: 4616 Balboa Blvd Encino CA 91316-4105

WESTMORELAND, THOMAS DELBERT, JR., chemist; b. near Vivian, La., June 2, 1940; s. Thomas Delbert and Marguerite Beatrice (Moore) W.; m. Martha Verne Beard, Jan. 1, 1966; children: Anne Laura, Kyle Thomas. BS, U. North Tex., 1963, MS, 1965; PhD, La. State U., 1971, postdoctoral fellow, 1971-72. Tchr., rsch. dir. Lewisville (Tex.) H.S., 1964; summer devel. program student Tex. Instruments, Inc., Dallas, 1966; sr. exptl./analytical engr. Power Systems divsn. United Technologies, South Windsor, Conn., 1972-76; sr. rsch. chemist Pennzoil Co., Shreveport, La., 1976-82, rsch. assoc., 1983-93; sr. environ. engr. Pennzoil Products Co. Tech. Ctr., The Woodlands, Tex., 1993-96; lectr. U. Houston, 1996-98; adj. prof. Tomball (Tex.) Coll., 1997, Montgomery Coll., Conroe, Tex., 1997-2000; health and safety officer Lexicon Genetics Inc., The Woodlands, 1998—2000, mgr. corp. safety, 2001—.

Contbr. sci. articles to profl. jours.; patentee in field. Recipient E.I. duPont Tchg. award La. State U., 1968-69. Mem. Nat. Fire Protection Assn., Am. Chem. Soc. (treas. 1978-79, chmn. 1979-80), Assn. Rsch. and Enlightenment, Soc. Automotive Engrs., Jaycees (state dir. Conn. 1976, gov.'s civic leadership award Conn. 1975-76, C. William Brownfield Meml. award 1976), Masons (Scottish Rite, 32nd degree), Sigma Xi (sec.), Phi Eta Sigma (pres. 1959-60), Alpha Chi Sigma, Kappa Mu Epsilon. Home: 588 Melmont St Conroe TX 77302-3116 Office: 8800 Technology Forest Pl The Woodlands TX 77381-1160 Office Phone: 281-863-3172. Business E-Mail: twestmoreland@lexgen.com.

WESTMORELAND, TIMOTHY M. education educator; b. Omaha, Apr. 6, 1954; s. Roger James and Peggy Mae (Hall) Westmoreland; life ptnr. Nicholas Ian James Olcott, 1979. BA, Duke U., Durham, N.C., 1976; JD, Yale U., New Haven, Conn., 1996. Counsel subcom. on health and environ. U.S. Ho. of Rep., Washington, 1979—95; sr. policy fellow Georgetown U. Law Ctr., Washington, 1995—99; dir. Ctr. for Medicaid and State Ops., Dept. of Health and Human Svcs., Washington, 1999—2001; counsel Com. on Govt. Reform Dem. Staff, Washington, 2001—; rsch. prof. Georgetown U. Health Policy Inst., Washington, 2001—; vis. prof. Georgetown U. Law Ctr., Washington, 2001— Fellow Investigator in Health Services Rsch. Fellowship, Robert Wood Johnson Found., 2001-2004. Office: Georgetown Univ #525 2233 Wisc Avenue NW Washington DC 20007

WESTOFF, CHARLES FRANCIS, demographer, educator; b. N.Y.C., July 23, 1927; s. Frank Barnett and Evelyn (Bales) Westoff; m. Joan P. Uszynski, Sept. 11, 1948 (div. Jan. 1969); children: David, Carol; m. Leslie Aldridge, Aug. 1969 (div. Feb. 1993); m. Jane DeLung, May 1997. AB, Syracuse U., 1949, MA, 1950; PhD, U. Pa., 1953. Instr. sociology U. Pa., 1950—52; rsch. assoc. Milbank Meml. Fund, N.Y.C., 1952—55; rsch. assoc. Office Population Rsch. Princeton (NJ) U., 1955—62, Maurice P. During '22 prof. demographic studies and sociology, 1962—99, prof. emeritus, 1999—, sr. rsch. demographer, 1999—, chmn. dept. sociology, 1965—70, assoc. dir. Office Population Rsch., 1962—75, dir., 1975—92; assoc. prof. sociology N.Y.U., also chmn. dept. sociology Washington Sq. Coll., 1959—62; vis. sr. fellow East-West Population Inst., Honolulu, 1979—81; Disting. vis. prof. Am. U., Cairo, 1979; mem. vis. com. Harvard-MIT Joint Ctr. for Urban Studies, 1980—83. Exec. dir. Commn. Population Growth and Am. Future, 1970—72; mem. adv. com. on population stats. U.S. Bur. Census, 1973—79; chmn. Nat. Com. for Rsch. on 1980 Census, 1981—88; bd. dirs. Alan Guttmacher Inst., 1977—88, 1989—97; sr. tech. advisor Demographic Health Surveys, 1984—; bd. dirs. Population Resource Ctr., 1985—, Population Ref. Bur., 1988—94, Population Commns. Internat., 1992—98; com. on population NAS, 1983—88. Co-author: Family Growth in Metropolitan America, 1961, The Third Child, 1963, College Women and Fertility Values, 1967, The Later Years of Childbearing, 1970, From Now to Zero, 1971, Reproduction in the United States, 1965, 1971, Toward the End of Growth: Population in America, 1973, The Contraceptive Revolution, 1976, Demographic Dynamics in America, 1977, Mass Media and Reproductive Behavior in Africa, 1997, Replacement of Abortion by Contraception in Three Central Asian Republics, 1998, Unmet Need at the End of the Century, 2002, Reproductive Preferences in Developing Countries at the Turn of the Century, 2002, Trends in Marriage and Early Childbearing in Developing Countries, 2003; contbr. articles on demography and sociology to profl. jours. Recipient Irene Taeuber award for Outstanding Rsch. Contbns., 1995. Fellow: Am. Acad. Arts and Scis.; mem.: Internat. Union Sci. Study Population, Population Assn. Am. (bd. dirs. 1960—62, 1968—70, 1st v.p. 1972—73, pres. 1974—75), Planned Parenthood Fedn. Am. (dir. 1978—81), Inst. Medicine-NAS. Home: 1 Highland Rd Princeton NJ 08540 Office: Princeton U Wallace Hall Princeton NJ 08544 Business E-Mail: westoff@princeton.edu.

WESTON, ARTHUR WALTER, chemist, scientific and business executive; b. Smith Falls, Ont., Can., Feb. 13, 1914; came to U.S., 1935, naturalized, 1952; s. Herbert W. and Alice M. (Houghton) W.; m. V. Dawn Thompson, Sept. 10, 1940; children: Roger L., Randall K., Cynthia B. BA, Queen's U., Kingston, Ont., 1934, MA, 1935; PhD, Northwestern U., 1938. Postdoctoral fellow Northwestern U., Evanston, Ill., 1938-40; with Abbott Labs., North Chgo., Ill., 1940-79, dir. rsch. and devel., 1959-61, v.p. rsch. and devel., 1961-68, dir. company, 1959-68, v.p. sci. affairs, 1968-77, v.p. corp. licensing, 1977-79; v.p., dir. San-Abbott, Japan, 1976-79; cons. Abbott Labs., North Chgo., Ill., 1979-85; pres. Arthur W. Weston & Assocs., Lake Forest, Ill., 1979—. Contbr. profl jours. and books. Patentee in field. Mem. Office Sci. Rsch. and Devel., War Manpower Commn., 1942-45; mem. exec. com. indsl. chemistry, div. chemistry and chem. tech. NRC, 1961-65; mem. indsl. panel on sci. and tech. NSF, 1974-80; mem. ad hoc com. chem. agts. Dept. Def., 1961-65. Mem. Rsch. Dirs. Assn. Chgo. (pres. 1965-66), Am. Chem. Soc. (trustee Chgo. 1965—, dir. Chgo. sect. 1952-59, nat. com. corp. assocs. 1967-72), Dirs. Indsl. Rsch., Indsl. Rsch. Inst. (bd. dirs. 1970-73), Phi Beta Kappa, Sigma Xi, Phi Lambda Upsilon. Home and Office: 349 Hilldale Pl Lake Forest IL 60045-3031 Personal E-mail: awweston@aol.com.

WESTON, DAWN THOMPSON, artist, researcher; b. Joliet, Ill., Apr. 15, 1919; d. Cyril C. and Vivian Grace Thompson; m. Arthur Walter Weston, Sept. 10, 1940; children: Roger Lance, Randall Kent, Cynthia Brooke. Student, Penn Hall Jr. Coll., Chambersburg, Pa., 1937—38; BS, Northwestern U., 1942; student, Art Inst. Chgo., 1954, Pestalozzi-Froebel, Chgo., 1955; postgrad., Northwestern U., 1960—61; student, Phila. Inst. for Achievement Human Potential, 1963; postgrad., U. Ill., 1964; MA in Ednl. Adminstrn., Northwestern U., 1970. Cert. tchr./adminstr. Ill. Therapist USN Hosp., Great Lakes, Ill., 1940—45; tchr. Holy Child and Waukegan (Ill.) High Schs., 1946—54, Lake Forest (Ill.) H.S., 1966—69; elem. and jr. high art dir. Lake Bluff (Ill.) Schs., 1954—58; pioneer ednl. dir. Grove Sch. for Brain-Injured, Lake Forest, 1958—66, life mem., treas. corp., chmn. bd., 1982—. Ind. rschr., lectr. on shifting visual imagery due to trauma, 1982—99; rschr. on uneven growth, 1969—. One-woman shows include Evanston Woman's Club, Northwestern U., Deerpath Gallery, Lake Forest, The Hein Co., Waukegan, numerous group shows, 1939—76, Represented in permanent collections ARC, Victory Meml. Hosp., Waukegan, Sierra Assocs., Chgo., numerous pvt. collections U.S., Can., Japan, Africa, works include:, Poisonous Plants of Midwest set of etchings for Country Gentleman mag., 1956, Clouds mural, 1981. Mem. 1st found. bd. for srs. in Lake Forest, 1999; chair Grove Sch. Inc., 1996—; chmn. July 4th parade 100th Anniversary Child-Serve Greater Chgo., 1994; mem. Presdl. Gold Chain, Trinity Coll., 1979; mem. alumni bd. leadership com. Northwestern U., 2003; del. ann. conf. Meth. Ch., 1982—90; lay leader Grace United Meth. Ch., Lake Bluff, 1990—93. Named Citizen of Yr., Grove Sch., 1978, rm. at sch. named in her honor, 1982; scholar, Penn Hall Jr. Coll., 1937—38. Mem.: Deerpath Art League (bd. dirs.), Penn Hall Alumni Assn. (Chgo. pres. 1938—40), Art Inst. Chgo., Pi Lambda Theta. Home and Office: 349 E Hilldale Pl Lake Forest IL 60045-3031

WESTON, FRANCINE EVANS, secondary school educator; b. Mt. Vernon, N.Y., Oct. 8, 1946; d. John Joseph and Frances (Fantino) Pisaniello. *Dr. Weston voiced her gratitude to her maternal grandfather by dedicating "Beautifully Old" to him in 1984. She fondly acknowledges here: The paternal grandparents who allowed her to spend what seemed like hours happily, though cacophonously, "playing" their piano, the various aunts who took her to Radio City, Horn-N-Hardart and for wheelbarrow rides, the godparents who took her to the rodeo, and especially the maternal grandmother for whom she picked raspberries, who typed her first essay contest entry (three times), and who was the only person who could make "You're just like your father," sound like a compliment.* BA, Hunter Coll., 1968; MA, Lehman Coll., 1973; cert., Am. Acad. Dramatic Arts, N.Y.C., 1976; PhD, NYU, 1991. Cert. elem., secondary tchr., N.Y. Tchr. Yonkers (N.Y.) Bd. Edn., 1968—; aquatic dir. Woodlane Day Camp, Irvington-on-Hudson, N.Y., 1967-70, Yonkers Jewish Community Ctr., 1971-75. Creative drama tchr. John Burroughs Jr. H.S., Yonkers, 1971-77; stage lighting designer Iona Summer Theatre Festival, New Rochelle, N.Y., 1980-81, Yonkers Male Glee Club, 1981-89, Roosevelt H.S., 1980-97; freelance, 1998—; rsch. specialist Scholarship Locating Svc., 1992-94, Yonkers Civil Def. Police Aux., 1994—; master electrician NYU Summer Mus. Theatre, 1979-80; appointed program developer for Cadet Acad. of Police & Fire Scis., Pub. Safety Magnet, Roosevelt H.S., 2001, program dir., 2004-. *Although an explosion at school on 3/10/97 changed Dr. Weston's life forever by substantially impairing her hearing, she resumed her professional life as an outstanding educator and active member of Yonkers' volunteer citizenry. Fortified with hearing aids and 300 hours of speechreading exercises, she stalwartly returned to the classroom and to the auxiliary police. Her volunteer responsibilities are restructured to administrative duties, but her contribution and value to the Yonkers Public School System remains unchanged. Never a clockwatcher, she continues to provide expert instruction, emotional support, tutorial help, guidance and inspiration as a Teacher/Program Developer and activities sponsor.* Actress in numerous comty. theater plays including A Touch of the Poet, 1979; dir. stage prodns. including I Remember Mama, 1973, The Man Who Came to Dinner, 1975; author: A Descriptive Comparison of Computerized Stage Lighting Memory Systems With Non-Computerized Systems, 1991, (short stories) A Hat for Louise, 1984, Old Memories: Beautiful and Otherwise, 1984; lit. editor: (story and poetry collection) Beautifully Old, 1984; editor: Command Post Dispatch quar., 1997—. Mem. Yonkers Civil Def. Police Aux., 1994—, adminstrv. asst. to commanding officer, 1996—, capt. adminstrn., 2002—; steering com. chairperson Roosevelt H.S.-Middle States Assn. of Schs. and Colls. Self-Evaluation, 1985—88. Named Tchr. of Excellence, N.Y. State English Coun., 1990, 95, 2000; recipient Monetary award for Teaching Excellence, Carter-Wallace Products, 1992; named to Arrid Tchrs. Honor Roll, 1992. Republican. Roman Catholic. Avocations: swimming, animal related activities, anything theatrical. Office: Roosevelt High Sch Tuckahoe Rd Yonkers NY 10710

WESTON, I. DONALD, architect; b. Bklyn., Feb. 16, 1928; s. Martyn N. and Betty (Lash) W.; m. Sylvia Stone, Oct. 23, 1952; children: Suzanne, Pamela. BArch, MIT, 1950; MArch, Pratt Inst., 1959, M in City and Regional Planning, 1981. Cert. Nat. Coun. Archtl. Regis. Bd.; lic. architect N.Y., Mass. Ptnr., prin. Martyn & Don Weston Architects, Bklyn., 1956—. Dir. Bklyn. Arts Coun., 1998—. Co-authored 2 studies for determining methods of reducing the cost of pub. housing, 1960. Mem. Mayor's Blue Ribbon Panel to Investigate the Bldg. Process in N.Y.C., 1987-88; pro bono pub. mem., sec. Cadman Plz. Co-op., Bklyn., 1972-78. Fellow AIA (mem. Bklyn. chpt. 1954—, chmn. urban design com. Bklyn. chpt. 1994—, pres. 1964-65); mem. Architects Coun. of N.Y.C. (pres. 1970-72), N.Y.C. Art Commn.; mem. Nat. Sculpture Soc. (v.p. 1990-94), Fine Arts Fedn. N.Y. (v.p. 1981—, pres. 1984-87, 90-91, hon. v.p. 1992—), Art Commn. Assocs. (pres. 1991-92). Avocations: tennis, golf, community activism. Office: Martyn & Don Weston Arch 100 Remsen St Brooklyn NY 11201-4256

WESTON, JANE SARA, plastic surgeon, educator; b. Oceanside, N.Y., May 21, 1952; m. Jan K. Horn; children: Jonathan Spencer Horn, Jennifer Danielle Horn. MD, Stanford U., 1975-79. Diplomate Am. Bd. Plastic Surgery. Resident gen. surgery Sch. Medicine Stanford (Calif.) U., 1979-82, resident plastic surgery Sch. Medicine, 1982-83; fellow craniofacial surgery Hopital des Enfants Malades, Paris, 1983-84; plastic surgeon Kaiser Permanente Med. Group, San Jose, Calif., 1985-90; pvt. practice Palo Alto, Calif., 1990—. Mem. faculty Stanford U. Med. Sch., 1994-95. Active Leadership Palo Alto, 1993. Fellow ACS; mem. Am. Soc. Plastic and Reconstructive Surgeons (chair women plastic surgeons com. 1993-96, chair ethics com. 1998-99). Avocation: harp. Office: Ste 201 3351 El Camino Real Atherton CA 94027-3802

WESTON, SIR JOHN (SIR PHILIP JOHN WESTON), company non-executive director, retired diplomat; b. Apr. 13, 1938; s. Philip George and Edith Alice Bray (Ansell) W.; m. Margaret Sally Ehlers, 1967; 3 children. Grad. with 1st class honors, Worcester Coll., Oxford (Eng.) U.; student Chinese lang., Hong Kong, 1964-66, Peking, China, 1967-68. Joined diplomatic svc. Govt. of Gt. Britain, 1962, served Fgn. Office, 1962-63, 69-71, with Treasure Ctr. for Adminstrv. Studies, 1964, permanent rep. to EEC, 1972-74, asst. pvt. sec. to sec. state fgn. affairs and commonwealth affairs, 1974-76, counsellor, head EEC presidency secretariat Fgn. and Commonwealth Office, 1976-77, counsellor Brit. Embassy, 1978-81, head def. dept. Fgn. and Commonwealth Office, 1981-84, asst. under-sec. state Fgn. and Commonwealth Office, 1984-85, min. Brit. Embassy, 1985-88, dep. sec. to cabinet Cabinet Office, 1988-89, dep. under-sec. state def. Fgn. and Commonwealth Office, 1989-90, polit. dir. Fgn. and Commonwealth Office, 1990-92, amb., permanent rep. to NATO, also accredited to Western European Union, 1992-95; U.K. amb. to UN, U.K. permanent rep. UN Security Coun., N.Y.C., 1995-98. Non-exec. dir. Brit. Telecom, 1998-2002, Rolls-Royce plc, 1998-2004, Hakluyt & Co. Ltd., 2001—; vis. fellow Old Souls Coll., Oxford (Eng.) U., 1977-78; hon fellow Worcester Coll., Oxford, 2003. Chmn. governing body Sherborne Sch., 2001-04; trustee Nat. Portrait Gallery; Am. assoc. Royal Acad., 1999-2004; bd. govts. Ditchley Found., 2000-04; mem. coun. Internat. Inst. Strategic Studies, 2001—; hon. pres. Cmty. Found. Network, 1999—. Served Royal Marines, 1956-58. Decorated knight comdr. St. Michael and St. George (Eng.); Order of Merit with star (Fed. Republic Germany). Address: 13 Denbigh Gardens Richmond Surrey TW10 6EN England

WESTON, JOHN FREDERICK, business educator, consultant; b. Ft. Wayne, Ind., Feb. 6, 1916; s. David Thomas and Bertha (Schwartz) W.; children: Kenneth F., Byron L., Ellen J. BA, U. Chgo., 1937, MBA, 1943, PhD, 1948. Instr. U. Chgo. Sch. Bus., 1940-42, asst. prof., 1947-48; prof. The Anderson Sch. UCLA, 1949—, Cordner prof. The Anderson Sch., 1981-94, prof. emeritus recalled The Anderson Sch., 1986—, dir. rsch. program in competition and bus. policy, 1969—, dir. Ctr. for Managerial Econs. and Pub. Policy, 1983-86. Econ. cons. to pres. Am. Bankers Assn., 1945-46; disting. lecture series U. Okla., 1967, U. Utah, 1972, Miss. State U., 1972, Miami State U., 1975. Author: Scope and Methodology of Finance, 1966, International Managerial Finance, 1972, Impact of Large Firms on U.S. Economy, 1973, Financial Theory and Corporate Policy, 1979, 2d edit., 1983, 3d edit., 1988, Mergers, Restructuring and Corporate Control, 1990, Takeovers, Restructuring and Corporate Governance, 3d edit., 2000, Managerial Finance, 9th edit, 1992; assoc. editor: Jour. of Finance, 1948-55; mem. editorial bd., 1957-59; editorial bd. Bus. Econs., Jour. Fin. Rsch., Managerial and Decision Econs.; manuscript referee Am. Econ. Rev., Rev. of Econs. and Statistics, Engring. Economist, Bus. Econs., Fin. Mgmt. Bd. dirs. Bunker Hill Fund. Served with Ordnance Dept. AUS, 1943-45. Recipient Abramson Scroll award Bus. Econs., 1989-94; McKinsey Found. grantee, 1965-68; GE grantee, 1967; Ford Found. Faculty Rsch. fellow, 1961-62. Fellow Nat. Assn. Bus. Economists; mem. Am. Finance Assn. (pres. 1966, adv. bd. 1967-71), Am. Econ. Assn., Western Econ. Assn. (pres. 1962), Econometric Soc., Am. Statis. Assn., Royal Econ. Soc., Fin. Analysts Soc., Fin. Mgmt. Assn. (pres. 1979-80) Home: 258 Tavistock Ave Los Angeles CA 90049-3229 Office: UCLA 258 Tavistock Ave Los Angeles CA 90049-3229

WESTON, JOSH S. retired data processing company executive; b. Bklyn., Dec. 22, 1928; married. BS, CCNY, 1950; MA, U. New Zealand, 1951. Exec. v.p. Popular Svcs., Inc., 1955—70; v.p. planning adminstrn. Automatic Data Processing, Inc., Roseland, NJ, 1970—75, exec. v.p., 1975—77, pres., 1977—; hon. chmn. ADP, Inc., 1997—. Bd. dirs. Gentiva Health Svcs., Russ Berrie Co. Inc., J. Crew Inc.

WESTON, LAURIE BETH, psychiatrist; b. Washington, Oct. 4, 1951; d. Burt H. Weston and Doreen Elizabeth Berger; m. Craydon Dean McDonald, Dec. 4, 1982; children: Ian Cameron McDonald, Brendan Roarke McDonald, Tavis Hunter McDonald, Morgynne Elizabeth McDonald. BA, Kalamazoo Coll., 1974; MD, Med. Coll. Va., 1982. Diplomate Nat. Bd. Med. Examiners, Am. Bd. Psychiatry and Neurology, added qualification in geriatric psychiatry, Am. Bd. Adolescent Psychiatry. Med. dir. Unified Counseling Svcs., Lancaster, Wis., 1987-88; psychiatrist Lakeland Counseling Ctr., Elkhorn, Wis., 1988-93; psychiatrist, med. dir. Drs. McDonald, Weston and Assocs., Lake Geneva, Wis., 1991-93, Dr. McDonald, Weston Assoc., Flagstaff, Ariz., 1993—; univ. psychiatrist No. Ariz. U., Flagstaff, 1993-95; med. dir., psychiatrist Mt. Vista Family Health Ctr., Flagstaff, 1994-96. Counseling psychiatrist Ariz. Divsn. Devel. Disabilities, Flagstaff, 1995—, Geriatric Svcs. of Cen. Mass., Worcester, 1986-87. Asst. scoutmaster Boy Scouts Am., Flagstaff, 1998—, asst. Cub Scout leader, 1993-97; pres. Med. Sch. class Med. Coll. Va., 1979-80. Mem. Am. Psychiat. Assn., Phi Sigma, Phi Kappa Phi. Democrat. Avocations: camping, hiking, swimming, genealogy, travel. Office: Drs McDonald Weston and Assocs 1100 N San Francisco St Ste C Flagstaff AZ 86001-3260

WESTON, MICHAEL C. retired lawyer; b. Asheville, N.C., Aug. 13, 1938; m. Mary Ann Damme; two children. AB in English, Brown U., 1960; JD, U. Mich., 1963. Bar: Mich. 1964, Ill. 1973. Assoc. Clark Hill, Detroit, 1963-68; from sec. to pres. corp. and indsl. consortium Econ. Devel. Corp. of Greater Detroit, 1969-73; chief staff atty. Northwestern U., Evanston, Ill., 1973-81, v.p. legal affairs, 1981-89; v.p. and gen. counsel, 1990-2001. Lectr. minority bus. devel. Inst. Continuing Legal Edn., conflicts of interest Nat. Coun. Univ. Rsch. Adminstrs. Contbr. articles to profl. jours. Chmn. Univ. Gallery Com., 1982-85; bd. dirs. Northwestern U. Press. Mem. ABA (sec. taxation, com. on exempt orgns., ho. of dels., lectr. Inst. on Minority Bus. Devel.), Chgo. Coun. Lawyers, Nat. Assn. Coll. and Univ. Attys. (lectr. fed. tax matters, outside activities faculty mems. univ.-cmty. rels., med. risk mgmt., bd. dirs. 1985-88, 92-97, pres. 1995-96). E-mail: m-weston@northwestern.edu.

WESTON, PHYLLIS JEAN, art gallery director; b. Cleve., Mar. 17, 1921; d. Armin and Wilma H. (Wasserman) Hornstein; m. Leo F. Weston, Oct. 18, 1963; children: H. Todd Cobey, John Cobey. Student, Yale U. Dir. Phyllis J. Weston Art Gallery at Clossons, Cin., v.p., 1964—; instr. I.L.R., U. Cin., 1995—2001. Art cons. Proctor & Gamble Co., Cin., 1983—; cons., lectr. in art. Curator Ohio Gov. Residential Found. Bd. dirs. Cin. Opera Guild, Internation Visitors Ctr., Inc., Cin. Chamber Orch., C.A.S.A., Chinese Music Soc.; founder Enjoy the Arts, Cin. Commn. on the Arts, The Post Corbett awards, adv. judge Congl. Art Competition Sch. Creative and Performing Arts; founder Cin. Ballet; mem. Citizens Against Substance Abuse, Cin. Symphony, Women's Comm., others. Recipient Post Corbett award, 1989, Prima award, 1999; named Woman of the Yr. Cin. Enquirer, 1987. Home: 4 Taft Road Ln Cincinnati OH 45206-1805 Office: 2643 Erie Ave Cincinnati OH 45208

WESTON, REBECCA LYNN, forensic educator; b. Waren, Pa., Aug. 22, 1949; BS in Criminology, 1995. Sgt. Union Co. prosecutor office, Elizabeth, NJ, 1981—2000; instr. Warren Co. Cmty. Coll., Washington, NJ, 1996—.

WESTON, ROGER LANCE, banker; b. Waukegan, Ill., Mar. 2, 1943; s. Arthur Walter and Vivian Dawn Weston; children: Cynthia Page, Kent Andrew, Arthur Eladio, Rebecca Dawn, Alice Sinclair, Elliot Churchill, Evan Walter, Spencer Lance. BS, MacMurray Coll., 1965; MBA, Washington U., St. Louis, 1967. Investment adviser Harris Trust & Savs. Bank, Chgo., 1967-69; sr. investment counselor Security Suprs., Chgo., 1969-70; gen. ptnr. Sierra Capital Group, Chgo., 1970-85; exec. v.p., treas., chief fin. officer Telemed Corp., Hoffman Estates, Ill., 1971-79; vice chmn. Bank Lincolnwood, Ill., 1979-85; pres., CEO, GSC Enterprises, Lincolnwood, 1979-85; chmn. bd. dirs., pres., CEO, GreatBanc, Inc., Aurora, Ill., 1986—. Mem. Barrington Hills (Ill.) Zoning Bd. Appeals, 1987-2003, com. Asian art Art Inst. Chgo., 1987; mem. nat. coun., mem. Hatchery devel. com. John M. Olin Sch. Bus., Washington U. Mem. Washington U. Eliot Soc. (Chgo. nat. com., chmn. membership com. 1996-92), Univ. Club. Republican. Presbyterian. Office: Great Banc Inc 1 N Wacker Dr Ste 4075 Chicago IL 60606

WESTON, SAUNDRA OLIVIA (SAUNDRA LAIDLAW), quality assurance professional, minister; b. Loiret, France, Sept. 23, 1954; arrived in U.S., 1957; d. Cleophus Hamiter, Olivia Hamiter; m. Michael LaRay Laidlaw, Nov. 22, 2001. AAS, Milw. Tech. Coll., 1996; B in Elective Studies, St. Cloud State U., 2002. Ordained evangelist Minn., 1992, ordained to ministry Minn., 1999. Data entry operator Blue Cross & Blue Shield United Wis., Milw., 1987, acctg. technician, 1987—89, microcomputer technician, 1989—93, microcomputer project analyst II, 1993—96, sys. adminstr., 1996—99; software programmer EMR Innovations, St. Cloud, Minn., 1999—2001, quality assurance analyst, 2001—. Cons., Milw., 1992—99. Author: (book) One That Got Away, 2002. V.p. Overcomers Internat., St. Cloud, 2002; pastor Temple Faith Ch., St. Cloud, 2000—. Finalist State Amb., Milw. Area Tech. Coll., 1996; recipient Lamp of Knowledge, 1996. Pentecostal. Avocation: travel. Office Phone: 320-252-0234. Home Fax: 320-354-0026. E-mail: slaidlaw@tds.net.

WESTON, W. GALEN, SR., diversified holdings executive; b. Eng., Oct. 29, 1940; s. W. Garfield Weston and Reta L. Howard; m. Hilary Frayne, 1966; 2 children. BA, LLD (hon.), U. Western Ont. Chmn. bd. Wittington Investments, Ltd., George Weston Ltd., Toronto, Ont., Can., Holt, Renfrew & Co. Ltd., Loblaw Cos. Ltd., Weston Foods Ltd. Bd. dirs. Fortnum and Mason PLC (U.K.); bd. dirs. Assoc. Brit. Foods PLC (U.K.), Can. Imperial Bank Commerce, Brown Thomas Group Ltd. (Ireland). Hon. trustee The Upper Can. Coll. Found.; mem. internat. adv. bd. Columbia U. Officer Order of Can. Mem. Badminton and Racquet Club, York Club, Toronto Club, Windsor Club (Fla.), The Brook Club (N.Y.), White's Club (U.K.), Sunningdale Golf. (U.K.), Toronto Lawn Tennis, Windsor Club (Fla.), Toronto Golf Club, Rosedale Golf Club (Toronto). Office: George Weston Limited 22 St Clair Ave E Ste 2001 Toronto ON Canada M4T 2S3

WESTON, WILLIAM LEE, dermatologist; b. Grand Rapids, Minn., Aug. 13, 1938; s. Eugene and Edith Kathryn (Lee) W.; m. Janet J. Atkinson, June 9, 1964; children: Elizabeth Carol, William Kemp. AB, Whitman Coll., 1960; B in Med. Sci., U. S.D., 1963; MD, U. Colo., 1965. Resident in pediatrics U. Calif., San Francisco, 1967-68; intern, then resident in pediatrics U. Colo., Denver, 1965-67, resident in dermatology, 1970-72, asst. prof. dermatology and pediatrics, 1972-76, prof., 1976—, chmn. dept. dermatology, 1976—. Author: Practical Pediatric Dermatology, 1979, rev. edit., 1985, Color Textbook of Pediatric Dermatology, 1991, rev. edit., 1996; editor-in-chief Current Problems in Dermatology, 1988-93. With AUS, 1968-70. Mem. Soc. Pediatric Dermatology (founder, sec.-treas. 1975-80, pres. 1984-85), Colo. Dermatol. Soc. (pres.), Soc. Investigative Dermatology (bd. dirs.), Am. Acad. Dermatology (bd. dirs.). Methodist. Home: 8550 E Ponderosa Dr Parker CO 80138-8233 Office: 4200 E 9th Ave Denver CO 80220-3706

WESTPHAL, JOSEPH W. academic administrator; m. Linda Westphal; 4 children. PhD in political, Univ. Mo.; BA, Adelphi Univ. Chancellor Univ. Maine Sys., 2002—; sr. policy adv. U.S. Environment Protection Agency; exec. dir. Congressional Sunbelt Caucus, 1988—95; spl. asst. Dept. Interior; prof. Okla. State Univ., head political sci. dept. Served House Com.; adj. prof. Georgetown Univ. Contbr. articles to jours. Acting sec. U.S. Army, asst. sec. U.S. Army, 1998. Mem.: Patton Boggs, LLP (sr.), Wash. Law Firm (sr.). Office: U Maine Sys 107 Maine Ave Bangor ME 04401

WESTPHAL, KLAUS WILHELM, university museum director; b. Berlin, Mar. 20, 1939; came to U.S., 1969; s. Wilhelm Heinrich and Irmgard (Henze) W.; m. Margaret Elisabeth Dorothea Wagner, May 16, 1969; children: Barbara, Marianne, Christine. BS in Geology, Eberhard-Karls Universität, Tübingen, Germany, 1960, MS, 1964, PhD in Paleontology, 1969. Dir. geology mus. U. Wis. Madison, 1969—. Bd. dirs. natural history coun. U. Wis. Madison, 1973—, Friends of Geology Mus., Inc., 1977—; nat. speaker on paleontology Outreach, 1977—; instr. paleontology U. Wis., 1977—; leader expeditions fossil vertebrates including dinosaurs, 1977—. Participant various tchr.-tng. projects Wis. Pub. Schs. Lutheran. Home: 3709 High Rd Middleton WI 53562-1003 Office: U Wis Geology Mus 1215 W Dayton St Madison WI 53706-1600 E-mail: westphal@geology.wisc.edu.

WESTPHAL, PAUL, professional basketball coach; b. Torrance, Calif., Nov. 30, 1950; m. Cindy Westphal; children: Victoria, Michael Paul. Degree in phys. edn., U. So. Calif., 1972. Player Boston Celtics, 1972-75, Phoenix Suns, 1975-80, 83-84, Seattle Supersonics, 1980-81, NY Knicks, 1981-83; coach SW Coll., Phoenix, 1985-86, Grand Canyon Coll., 1986-88; asst. coach. Phoenix Suns, 1988-92, head coach, 1992—95; coach high sch., 1995—98; head coach Seattle Supersonics. Named All-Star 5 times, Comeback Player of Yr.; uniform number retired by Suns, 1989. Office: Seattle Supersonics 351 Elliott Ave W Seattle WA 98119-4101

WESTWOOD, ALBERT RONALD CLIFTON, management consultant, researcher; b. Birmingham, Eng., June 9, 1932; came to U.S., 1958, naturalized, 1974; s. Albert Sydney and Ena Emily (Clifton) W.; m. Jean Mavis Bullock, 1956; children: Abigail, Andrea. BS with honors, U. Birmingham, 1953, PhD in Phys. Metallurgy, 1956, D.Sc. in Materials Sci., 1968. Chartered engr. and physicist, U.K. Tech. officer research dept., metals div. Imperial Chem. Industries, Birmingham, 1956-58, successively scientist, sr. scientist, assoc. dir., head materials sci. dept., dep. dir., 1958-74; dir. Martin Marietta Labs., Balt., 1974-84, corp. dir. R & D, 1984-87; v.p. R & D Martin Marietta Corp., Bethesda, Md., 1987-90, v.p. sci., 1990, v.p. rsch. and tech., 1990-93; v.p. rsch. and exploratory tech. Sandia Nat. Labs. divsn. Lockheed Martin Corp., Albuquerque, 1993-96; v.p. emeritus Sandia Nat. Labs.; chmn., chief exec. Cen. Lab. of Rsch. Couns., U.K., 1998-2000; internat. cons. R. and D. Mgmt. Mem. numerous govt. and univ. adv. coms. including Office Sci. and Tech. Policy, NASA, NRC, NAS, NAE, NSF, Nat. Inst. Stds. and Tech., U. Md., U. Fla., MIT, Ga. Inst. Tech., Coun. on Competetiveness; bd. dir. Martin Marietta Energy Systems, Assn. Ind. Rsch. and Tech. Orgns. U.K., U.S. Civilian R&D Found.; mem. European rsch. coun. informatics and math. resources bd. Brit. Nat. Space Sci. Ctr.; mem. R&D coun. European Spallation Source; mem. coun. Found. Tech. Innovation and Soc. U.K.; lectr. in field. Contbr. over 100 articles to profl. jours. Chmn. Md. Humanities Coun., N.Mex. Humanities Coun., N.Mex. Symphony Orch.; bd. dirs. Santa Fe Opera; adv. com. Musica Russia Found. Recipient disting. young scientist award Md. Acad. Scis., 1966, centennial award U. Md., 1994, Beilby gold medal Royal Inst. Chemistry, 1970, J. Herbert Holloman award Acta Metallurgica, 1996, Tewksbury lectr. U. Melbourne, 1974, Wenk lectr. Johns Hopkins U., 1995. Fellow AAAS (chmn. indsl. sci. sect.), Am. Soc. Metals Internat. (Burgess lectr. 1984, Campbell meml. lectr. 1987, disting. lectr. materials and soc. 1995), Inst. of Physics, Inst. of Materials, The Minerals, Metals and Materials Soc. (dir., fin. officer, pres. 1990, Krumb lectr. 1988, leadership award 1992); mem. NRC (chmn. com. engring. and tech. sys.), ASME (disting. lectr. 1989), NAE (elected), Royal Swedish Acad. Engring. Scis. (elected), Russian Acad. Engring. (elected), Royal Acad. Engring. (elected, U.K.), Md. Acad. Scis. (coun.), Md. Inst. Metals (pres.), Indsl. Rsch. Inst. (bd. dirs., pres. 1989-90). Home: 13539 Canada Del Oso Pl NE Albuquerque NM 87111-8045

WESTWOOD, JAMES NICHOLSON, lawyer; b. Portland, Oreg., Dec. 3, 1944; s. Frederick Alton and Catherine (Nicholson) W.; m. Janet Sue Butler, Feb. 23, 1980; children: Laura, David. BA, Portland State U., 1967; JD, Columbia U., 1974. Bar: Oreg. 1974, U.S. Dist. Ct. Oreg. 1974, U.S. Ct. Appeals (9th cir.) 1978, U.S. Supreme Ct. 1981, U.S. Ct. Appeals (fed. cir.) 1984, U.S. Ct. Appeals (D.C. cir.) 1997. Assoc. Miller, Anderson, Nash, Yerke & Wiener, Portland, 1974-76, 78-81; asst. to pres. Portland State U., 1976-78; ptnr. Miller, Nash, Wiener, Hager & Carlsen, Portland, 1981-99, Stoel Rives LLP, Portland, 1999—. Recipient Disting. Svc. award Portland State U. Found., 1984, Outstanding Alumni award Portland State U., 1992. Mem. ABA (chmn. forest resources com. 1987-89), Oreg. Bar Assn. (chmn. appellate practice sect. 1996-97), Am. Acad. Appellate Lawyers, Univ. Club (bd. govs. 1994), City Club (pres. 1991-92), Park Blocks Found. (pres. 1999—). Republican. Unitarian Universalist. Home: 3121 NE Thompson St Portland OR 97212-4908 Office: Stoel Rives LLP 900 SW 5th Ave Ste 2600 Portland OR 97204-1268 E-mail: jnwestwood@stoel.com.

WESTWOOD, LEE, professional golfer; b. Worksop, England, Apr. 24, 1973; Profl. golfer, 1993—. Winner Peter McEvoy Trophy, Brit. Youth's Championship; winner Volvo Scandinavian Master, 1996, Visa Taiheijo Masters, 1996; Volvo Masters, 1997; Australian Open, 1997; Loch Lomond Invitational, 1998; European TPC, 1998; English Open, 1998; Freeport-McDermott Classic, 1998, Deutsche Bank-SAP Open TPC of Europe, 2000. Avocations: films, snooker, cars. Office: care PGA 100 Avenue Of Champions Palm Beach Gardens FL 33418

WESTWOOD, MELVIN NEIL, horticulturist, pomologist; b. Hiawatha, Utah, Mar. 25, 1923; s. Neil and Ida (Blake) W.; m. Wanda Mae Shields, Oct. 12, 1946; children: Rose Dawn, Nancy Gwen, Robert Melvin, Kathryn Mae. Student, U. Utah, 1948-50; BS in Pomology, Utah State U., 1952; PhD in Pomology, Wash. State U., 1956. Field botanist Utah State U., Logan, 1951-52, supt. Howell Field Sta., 1952-53; rsch. asst. State Coll. Wash., 1953-55; rsch. horticulturist Agrl. Rsch. Svc. USDA, Wenatchee, Wash., 1955-60; assoc. prof. Oreg. State U., Corvallis, 1960-67, prof., 1967-80, prof. emeritus, 1986—; rsch. dir. Nat. Clonal Germplasm Repository, Corvallis, 1980-83, nat. tech. advisor, 1984-86. Author: Deciduous Fruit and Nut Production, 1976, Temperate-Zone Pomology: Physiology and Culture, 1978, 3d edit., 1993, Contract Military Air Transport: From the Ground Up, 1995, Pear Varieties and Species, 1996; author: (with others) Cherry Nutrition, 1966, Pear Rootstocks, 1987, Management and Utilization of Plant Germplasm, 1988, Maintenance and Storage: Clonal Germplasm, 1989, Genetic Resources of Malus, 1991; contbr. articles to profl. jours. With U.S. Air Transport Command, 1943-45, USAAF, 1946-47. Grantee NSF, 1966; recipient Hartman Cup award Oreg. Hort. Soc., 1989, Earl Price Excellence in Rsch. award Oreg. State U., 1983. Fellow Am. Soc. Hort. Sci. (bd. dirs. 1974-75, chmn. com. environ. quality 1971, adv. coun. 1974-79, mem. pomology sect. 1967-74, publs. com. 1971-74, pres. Western region 1974, Joseph Harvey Gourley award for Pomology 1958, 77, Stark award for Pomology 1969, 77, Outstanding Rschr. award 1986); mem. AAAS, Am. Soc. Plant Physiologists, Am. Pomological Soc. (mem. adv. bd. 1970-75, mem. exec. bd. 1980-84, Paul Howe Shepard award 1968, 82, Wilder medal 1980), UN Assn. USA, Ams. United for Separation of Ch. and State, Amnesty Internat., Phi Kappa Phi, Gamma Sigma Delta. Baptist. Achievements include patent for Autumn Blaze ornamental pear; research on Pyrus (pear), Malus (apple) and Prunus (plum, cherry, peach) and on the physiology of rootstock genera. Office: Oreg State U Dept Horticulture Corvallis OR 97331

WETEKAM, DONALD J. career officer; BS, USAF Academy, Colorado Springs, 1973; M in Engring. Adminstrn., U. Utah, 1978. Commd. 2d lt. USAF, 1973, advanced through grades to brigadier gen., 1999; officer in charge 4th Munitions Maintenance Squadron, Seymour Johnson AFB, N.C., 1974-75, 635th Munitions Maintenance Squadron, U-Tapao Royal Thai Naval, Airfield, Thailand, 1975-76; munitions svc. officer, officer in charge 388th Tactical Fighter Wing, Hill AFB, Utah, 1976-79; officer in charge 313th Aircraft Maintenance Unit, Hahn Air Base, Germany, 1981-84; maintenance staff officer HQ Tactical Air Command, Langley AFB, Va., 1984-86; comdr. 56th Equipment Maintenance Squadron, MacDill AFB, Fla., 1986-89; F-15 and standard avionics logistics program mgr. HQ USAF, Pentagon, 1989-93; comdr. 49th Logistics Group, Holloman AFB, N.M., 1994-95; dir. aircraft mgmt. directorate Oklahoma City Air Logistics Ctr., Tinker AFB, 1995-97, vice comdr., 1997-98; dir. logistics Hdqrs. Pacific Air Forces, Hickam AFB, Hawaii, 1998—2000; dep. dir. combat weapons systems Hdqrs. Air Combat Command, Langley AFB, Va., 2000, dir. maintenance and logistics, 2000—02; comdr. Warner Robins AFB, Ga., 2002—.

WETENHALL, JOHN, museum director; b. June 1, 1957; s. Jack Wetenhall and Jane (Rinaud) Keating. AB cum laude, Dartmouth Coll., 1979; MA, Williams Coll., Williamstown, Mass., 1982, Stanford U., 1985, PhD, 1988; MBA, Vanderbilt U., 1999. Fellow Smithsonian Instn., Washington, 1986-87, 88-89; lectr. Santa Clara (Calif.) U., 1985, U. Minn., Mpls., 1988; curator painting and sculpture Birmingham (Ala.) Mus. Art, 1989-95; dir. Checkwood Mus. Art, Nashville, 1995-2001; exec. dir. John and Mable Ringling Mus. Art, Sarasota, Fla., 2001—; dean Fla. State U., 2001—. Founder Thomas Art Projects, Birmingham, 1992-95, Carell Woodland Sculpture Trail, Nashville, 1996-99; cons. Vietnam Women's Meml. Project, Washington, 1988-89, U. So. Calif. Pub. Art Program, 1991. Author: (with Karal Ann Marling) Iwo Jima: Monuments, Memories and the American Hero, 1991, (with David Cass) (catalogue) Italian Paintings, 1850-1910, 1982; editor: (catalogue) Splendors of the American West, 1990; contbr. articles to profl. jours.; appearance in Am. Masters: Alexander Calder, PBS, 1998. Chair Livelier City Ctr. com. Ops. New Birmingham, 1994—95, chair cultural dist. forum, 1992—94; nat. register peers, design excellence program Gen. Svcs. Adminstrn., 1998—; chair Nashville Rotary Adopt-A House Program; mem. Leadership Manatee, 2002, Leadership Fla., 2003. Recipient Award of Excellence Tenn. Assn. Mus., 1996, 2001, Gold and Silver medals for ednl. programming Southeastern Mus. Conf., 1999; B. Gerald Cantor fellow, 1986, Nat. Endowment for the Arts grantee, 1991, Lyndon Baines Johnson Found. Moody Travel grantee, 1986, John F. Kennedy Libr. Found. grantee, 1986, Inst. Mus. and Libr. Svcs. grantee. Mem. Am. Tchrs. Assn. of the Martial Arts (sensei), Rotary (Paul Harris fellow), Kiwanis, Beta Gamma Sigma, Assn. Art Mus. Dirs. Avocations: white water kayaking, flying, aiki ju jitsu (blackbelt). Office: Ringling Mus of Art 5401 Bay Shore Rd Sarasota FL 34243 Business E-Mail: jwetenhall@ringling.org.

WETHERALL, ROBERT SHAW, librarian; b. Jesup, Ga., Aug. 18, 1944; s. Robert and Elizabeth (Shaw) W; m. Cynthia Jane Campbell, July 31, 1976; children— Robert G., Gerritt C. B.A. in History, U. Del., 1966, M.A. in History, 1968; M.L.S., Drexel U., 1973. Cert. profl. libr., N.J. Libr. Cumberland County Libr., Bridgeton, N.J., 1973-76; asst. dir., 1976-80, dir., 1981-89; dir. Dover (Del.) Pub. Libr., 1989—; mem. Cumberland County Audio-Visual Aids Commn., Bridgeton, 1981-89; pres. South Jersey Regional Libr. Coop., Inc., 1986-88, treas., 1988-89. Served with USAF, 1968-72. Mem. ALA, Del. Libr. Assn. (pres. 1992-93, action implementation com.). Office: Dover Pub Libr 45 S State St Dover DE 19901-7311

WETHERBEE, JAMES D. astronaut; b. Flushing, N.Y., Nov. 27, 1952; s. Dana A. and Wetherbee; m. Robin DeVore Platt; 2 children. BS in Aerospace Engring., U. Notre Dame, 1974. Commd. ensign USN, 1975, advanced through grades to capt.; naval aviator Attack Squadron 72, USS John F. Kennedy, 1977—80; with Systems Engring. Test Directorate; project officer, test pilot; with Strike Fighter Squadron 132; astronaut NASA, Houston, 1984—, dir. Flight Crew Ops. Directorate. Mem.: Soc. Exptl. Test Pilot. Achievements include logged over 5,000 hours flying time; 345 carrier landings in over 20 different types of aircraft; logged over 1,262 hours in space; pilot STS-32 Columbia (1990); mission comdr. STS-52 Columbia (1992), STS-63 Discovery (1995), STS-86 Atlantis (1997) and STS-102 Discovery (2001). Office: Astronaut Office/CB NASA Johnson Space Ctr Houston TX 77058

WETHERBY, IVOR LOIS, retired librarian; b. Louisville, May 22, 1924; d. Luther Silas and Clara Marders (Hite) W.; m. Herbert Charles Howard, July 4, 1947; children: Ivor Jane, Elizabeth Wetherby, John Allen, Luther Hite, Ann Dell. AB, Ky. Wesleyan Coll., 1944; MS in Library Sci., Fla. State U. 1965; SEd, Fla. Atlantic U., 1984; EdD Fla. Internat. U., 1992. Various clerical and secretarial positions, 1944-50; tchr. Our Lady of Mercy Acad., Louisville, 1963-64; librarian Palm Beach Jr. Coll., Lake Worth, Fla., 1966-78; head librarian Sebring (Fla.) Pub. Library, 1978; health scis. reference librarian Miami (Fla.)-Dade CC, Med. Ctr. Campus, 1978-87; librarian med. library Moncrief Army Cmty. Hosp., Ft. Jackson, S.C., 1987-89; ref. libr. Fla. Internat. U., 1992, ret., 1992. Active New Life Alliance Ch., West Palm Beach, Fla., Pleasant Grove Bapt. Ch., Louisville. Mem. DAR, Palm Beach County Geneal. Soc., Daus. of Founders and Patriots of Am., Nat. Soc. Colonial Dames XVII Century, Nat. Soc. of U.S. Daus. of 1812, Holland Soc. NY, Nat. Huguenot Soc., Nat. Soc. Daus. Union 1861-65. Home: 232 Orange Tree Dr Lantana FL 33462-1130

WETHERELL, DAVID S. communications executive; BA, OH Wesleyan U. Chmn., CEO CMG Info. Svcs. (now CMGI Inc.), Andover, Mass., 1986—. Office: 425 Medford St Charlestown MA 02129-1408

WETHERELL, MICHAEL E. lawyer; b. Redding, Calif., Mar. 2, 1945; s. Robert Miles and Rose Clair (Hart) W.; m. Karen Lansdowne Mackenzie, Aug. 16, 1969; children: Kelly Mackenzie, Kristen Michelle, Katherine Marie. BS in Edn., U. Idaho, 1967; JD, George Washington U., 1972. Bar: Idaho 1972, U.S. Dist. Ct. Idaho 1972, U.S. Ct. Appeals (9th cir.) 1984. Copywriter KBOI-AM-FM-TV, Boise, Idaho, 1965-67; legis. asst. Senator Frank Church, Washington, 1967-72, chief legal counsel, 1972-74, adminstrv. asst., 1975-76; sole practice Boise, 1977-78; assoc. Martin, Chapman & Hyde, Boise, 1978-82; ptnr. Hyde & Wetherell, Boise, 1982-85, Hyde, Wetherell, Bray & Haff, Boise, 1985-93, Hyde, Wetherell, Bray, Haff & French, A Profl. Co., Boise, 1993—98, Hyde Wetherell and Haff PLLC, 1998—2002; dist. judge Idahois 4th Jud. Dist., 2003—. Author: The Worker's Compensation Law of Idaho, 1989, 2d edit. 1991, 3rd edit. 1993, 4th edit. 1996, 5th edit. 2001; contbr. articles to profl. jours. Dem. candidate for Idaho atty. gen., 1978; pres. Boise City Coun., 1988-92, 2002-03; mem. human welfare com. Mountain State Tumor Inst., Boise, 1985-2002, St. Lukes Regional Med. Ctr. (co-chmn. 1997-2002); bd. dirs. Epilepsy Found. am., 1980-87, United Way of Ada County, Boise, 1982-88, Idaho Epilepsy League, Boise, 1977—; chmn. Idaho State Dem. Party, 1991-93, mem. exec. com. Nat. Dem. Party, 1992-93; candidate for Idaho Supreme Ct., 1998; mem. Idaho Supreme Ct. Criminal Jury Instrn. Com., 2003—. Recipient Outstanding Personal Achievement award Epilepsy Found. Am., 1987. Mem. ABA, Idaho State Bar Assn. (Outstanding Service to Handicapped award 1981), Assn. Trial Lawyers Am., Idaho Trial Lawyers Assn. (editor Idaho Trial Lawyers Mag. 1978-85, bd. govs. 1979-85, Outstanding Svc. award 1990), Kiwanis (pres. 1985-86), Delta Chi. Roman Catholic. Avocations: sailing, camping, photography, woodworking. Home: 1292 Candleridge Dr Boise ID 83712-6504 Office: 4th Jud Dist Ada County Courthouse 200 W Front St Boise ID 83702-7300 Office Phone: 208-287-7541.

WETHERELL, THOMAS KENT, college president; m. Virginia B. Wetherell; children: Kent, Blakely, Page. BS in Social Studies, Fla. State U., 1967, MS in Social Studies, 1968, PhD in Adminstrn., 1974. Pres. Wetherell Enterprises, Inc.; acad. counselor Fla. State U.; dir. housing and adminstrn., asst. v.p., asst. dean housing U. Ctrl. Fla.; assoc. prof. Bethune-Cookman Coll.; exec. asst. to pres. to dean of instrn. Daytona Beach C.C., v.p., provost acad. and univ. transfer programs, dist. v.p., planning and devel.; pres. First Am. Mortgage and Investments, Inc., Ind. Colls. and Univs. of Fla., Tallahassee C.C., 1975—. Mem. Fla. Ho. of Reps., spkr. 1990-92, chair appropriations com., 1989-90, chair appropriations edn. com., 1986-88, chair higher edn. com., 1984-86, majority fl. leader, 1982-84, chair Volusia county legis. delegation, 1981-83, 86-87. Bd. dirs. Econ. Devel. Coun., ARC, Canaveral Nat. Seashore Park, Southern Scholarship Found., United Way. Mem. Tallahassee C. of C. (bd. dirs.), Lions, Kiwanis, Blue Lodge, Shriners, Bahia Temple. Office: Tallahassee Cmty Coll 444 Appleyard Dr Tallahassee FL 32304-2895

WETHERILL, EIKINS, lawyer, investment company executive; b. Phila., Oct. 3, 1919; s. A. Hecksher and Edwina (Brunner) W. LL.B., U. Pa., 1948. Practiced in, Phila., 1948-55, Norristown, 1955-98; assoc. firm Evans, Bayard & Frick, 1948-50; ptnr. Reilly, Hepburn, Earle & Wetherill, 1950-55; firm Henderson, Wetherill, O'Hey & Horsey, 1955-98; pres. Phila. Stock Exchange, Inc., 1965-81. Bd. dirs. Germantown Savs. Bank; fin. commentator CBS-TV News, 1966-68; chmn. bd. Sta. WHYY-TV, 1970-76, dir., 1976-90; dir. 1st Pa. Corp., 1st Pa. Bank, solicitor to lt. gov. Pa., 1951-55, asst. U.S. atty. gen., 1953-55, treas., Montgomery County, 1956-59; pres. Montgomery County Bd. Commrs., 1960-63; chmn. Pa. Securities Commn., 1963-65; commr. Delaware Valley Regional Planning Commn., 1965—, chmn., 1968-69, 70-71, 78-79. Former bd. dirs. Greater Phila. Partnership; chmn. Phila Drama Guild, 1975-80, dir., 1980-87; trustee Davis and Elkins Coll., 1973-91. Served to capt., cav. Signal Corps, OSS, AUS, 1941-45. Mem. Am., Phila. bar assns., Delta Psi. Clubs: Phila. (Phila.), Racquet (Phila.). Episcopalian.

WETHERILL, GEORGE WEST, geophysicist, planetary scientist; b. Phila., Aug. 12, 1925; s. George West and Leah Victoria (Hardwick) Wetherill; m. Phylliss May Steiss, June 17, 1950 (dec. 1995); children: Rachel, George, Sarah; m. Mary Bailey, 1998. PhB, U. Chgo., 1948, SB in Physics, 1949, SM, 1951, PhD in Physics, 1953. Mem. staff dept. terrestrial magnetism Carnegie Inst., Washington, 1953—60; prof. geophysics and geology UCLA, 1960—75, chmn. dept. planetary and space sci., 1968—72; dir. dept. terrestrial magnetism Carnegie Inst., Washington, 1975—91, mem. sci. staff, 1991—2001, dir. emeritus, 2001—. V.p. Snickersville Gen. Store, Inc., Bluemont, Va., 1976—80; cons. NASA, NSF, NAS. Editor Ann. Rev. of Earth and Planetary Sci., 1981—96, assoc. editor, 1972—80, Meteoritics and Planetary Sci., Icarus; contbr. articles to profl. jours. With USN, 1943—46. Recipient G.K. Gilbert award, Geol. Soc. Am., 1984, Profl. Achievement citation, U. Chgo. Alumni Assn., 1985, Nat. medal of Sci., 1997; Henry Norris Russell Lectureship, Am. Astronomical Soc., 2003. Fellow: Meteoritical Soc. (v.p. 1971—74, 1981—83, pres. 1983—85, Leonard medal 1981), Am. Geophys. Union (pres. planetology sect. 1970—72, H.H. Hess medal 1991), Am. Acad. Arts and Scis.; mem.: NAS (J. Lawrence Smith award 2000), Am. Astron. Soc. Divsn. Planetary Scis. and Dynamic Astronomy (Russell lectr. 2003, G.P. Kuiper prize 1986), Internat. Astron. Union, Internat. Assn. Geochemistry and Cosmochemistry (pres. 1977—80), Geochem. Soc. (v.p. 1973—74, pres. 1974—75), Am. Philos. Soc., Internat. Soc. Study of Origin of Life, Religious Soc. Free Quakers. Episcopalian. E-mail: wetherill@dtm.ciw.edu. *Seek him that maketh the Pleiades and Orion, and turneth the shadow of death into morning. Amos 5:8.*

WETHINGTON, CHARLES T., JR., academic administrator; AB, Ea. Ky. U., 1956; postgrad., Syracuse U., 1958-59; MA, U. Ky., 1962, PhD, 1965. Instr. edn. psychology U. Ky., Lexington, 1965-66; dir. Maysville (Ky.) C.C., 1967-71; asst. v.p. c.c. system U. Ky., Lexington, 1971-81, v.p. c.c. system, 1981-82, chancellor c.c. system, 1982-88, chancellor c.c. system and univ. rels., 1988-89, interim pres., 1989-90, pres., 1990—2001, pres. emeritus, 2001—. Chmn. legis. com. State Dirs. Community and Jr. Colls., 1983-85, chmn. nat. coun., 1985-86; commn. on colls. So. Assn. Schs. and Colls., 1978-84, vice chmn. exec. commn., 1984, trustee, 1986-89; mem. So. Regional Edn. Bd., 1988-2000, mem. exec. com., 1989-93, vice-chmn., 1991-93; pres. Southeastern Conf., 1993-95, chair exec. com. NCAA, 1999-2001. Bd. dirs. Bluegrass State Skills Corp., 1984-91, vice-chmn. bd. dirs., 1986-87; bd. visitors C.C. Air Force, 1986-90; jud. nominating commn. 22nd Jud. Dist., Fayette County, Ky., 1988-91, So. Growth Policies Bd., 1990-2000; bd. dirs. NCAA Found., 1999—; active Bus.-Higher Edn. Forum, 1999-2001. With security svc. USAF, 1957-61. Home: 2926 Four Pines Dr Lexington KY 40502 Office: U Ky 5-52 Wm T Young Libr Lexington KY 40506-0456 E-mail: cwething@email.uky.edu.

WETHINGTON, JOHN ABNER, JR., retired nuclear engineering educator; b. Tallahassee, Apr. 18, 1921; s. John Abner and Mary McQueen (Hale) W.; m. Kathryn Kemp Greene, Aug. 19, 1943; 1 son, John Abner III. AB, Emory U., 1942, MA, 1943; PhD, Northwestern U., 1950. Vis. research asst. Princeton, 1943-44; chemist Fercleve Corp., Oak Ridge, 1944-46; chemist to sr. chemist Oak Ridge Nat. Lab., 1949-53; asst. prof. to prof. nuclear engring. U. Fla., 1953-85, prof. emeritus, 1985-98; on leave as fellow Lawrence Livermore Lab., Calif., 1971-72; vis. scientist P.R. Nuclear Center, 1962-63, Oak Ridge Nat. Lab., 1979-80; retired. U.S. del. to Radiation Congress, Haregate, Eng., 1963, 2d Internat. Conf. Peaceful Uses of Atomic Energy, Switzerland, 1958; faculty participant Oak Ridge Sch. Reactor Tech., 1957-58; owner tree farm. Contbr. articles to profl. jours. Recipient Fla. Tree Farmer of Year, 1984. Fellow AAAS; mem. Am. Chem. Soc., Am. Nuclear Soc., Phi Beta Kappa, Sigma Xi, Alpha Chi Sigma. Democrat. Methodist. Home: 109 NW 22nd Dr Gainesville FL 32603-1426

WETHINGTON, NORBERT ANTHONY, medieval scholar; b. Dayton, Ohio, Sept. 14, 1943; s. Norbert and Sophie Lillian W.; m. Martha M. Vannice, Aug. 13, 1966. BA, U. Dayton, 1965; MA, John Carroll U., 1967; postgrad., Baldwin Wallace Coll., 1968—70; PhD, U. Toledo (Ohio), 1997. Grad. asst., tchg. assoc. John Carroll U., Cleve., 1965—67; English tchr. Padua Franciscan High Sch., Parma, Ohio, 1967—70; instr., chmn. dept. tech. writing and speech N. Ctrl. Tech. Coll., Mansfield, Ohio, 1978—80, dir. pub. and cmty. svc. technologies, 1980—94; dir. humanities Terra State C.C., 1994—96, assoc. dean of instr., 1996—97; affiliate scholar Oberlin Coll., 1998—. Cons. in field. Contbr. articles. V.p. Sandusky County Bd. Health, 1979—80. Mem.: Nat. Coun. Tchrs. English, Ohio Vocat. Assn. (pres. tech. edn. divsn. 1985—86, Disting. Svc. award 1987), Am. Vocat. Assn., Nat. Coalition Ind. Scholars, MLA. Democrat. Roman Catholic. Mailing: PO Box 842 Fremont OH 43420-0842

WETLE, TERRIE FOX, gerontologist, educator, dean; b. Bremerton, Wash., Nov. 7, 1946; d. Gerald Lee and Elinor Myrle (Martindale) Todd; m. Richard W. Besdine, July 2, 1981; children: Sarah, Molly. BS in Psychology, Portland State U., 1968, MS in Psychology, 1971, PhD of Urban Studies, 1976. Asst. prof. Portland (Oreg.) State U., 1976-78; social policy analyst Dept. Health, Edn. and Welfare, Washington, 1978-79; asst. prof. Yale U., New Haven, 1979-81, Harvard U., Boston, 1981-88; dir. Braceland Ctr., Hartford, Conn., 1988-95; assoc. prof. U. Conn. Health Ctr., Farmington, 1989—95; dep. dir. Nat. Inst. Aging, NIH, Bethesda, Md., 1995-2000; assoc. dean medicine, prof. cmty. health Brown U. Med. Sch., Providence, 2000—. Bd. dirs. Armed Forces Retirement Home, Washington. Editor: Older Veterans, 1984, Handbook of Geriatric Care, 1982; contbr. articles to profl. jours. Pres. Alzheimer's Assn. Greater Hartford, 1993-95; apptd. Alzheimer's Coalition Conn., 1991-95. Fellow: Gerontol. Soc. Am. (chair com.); mem.: APHA (del., governing coun.), Am. Soc. Aging. Office: Brown U Sch Medicine 97 Waterman St G-A2 Providence RI 02912

WETMORE, KEITH CHIDESTER, lawyer; b. Valparaiso, Ind., Oct. 17, 1956; s. Leonard Leander and Dorisann (Chidester) W. BA, Northwestern U., 1977; JD magna cum laude, U. Mich., 1980. Bar: Calif. 1981, U.S. Dist. Ct. (no. dist.) Calif. 1981. Law clk. to Hon. J. Edward Lumbard U.S. Ct. Appeals (2d cir.), 1980-81; assoc. Steinhart & Falconer, San Francisco, 1981-82, Morrison & Foerster LLP, San Francisco, 1982-86, ptnr., 1986—. Articles editor U. Mich. Law Rev. 1980-81. Mem. ABA, Calif. Bar Assn., Bay Area Lawyers for Individual Freedom, San Francisco Bar Assn. Methodist. Office: Morrison & Foerster LLP 425 Market St San Francisco CA 94105-2482 E-mail: kwetmore@mofo.com.*

WETSCH, JOHN ROBERT, information systems specialist; b. Dickinson, ND, Aug. 27, 1959; s. Joseph John (dec.) and Florence Mae (Edwards) W.; m. Laura Jean Johnson, Aug. 29, 1981; children: Julie Elizabeth, Katherine Anne, John Michael, Joseph Harold. BS, Excelsior Coll., Albany, 1984; MA, Antioch U., 1989; PhD, Nova Southeastern U., 1994; BS, U. N.D., 2001; M in Astronomy, U. Western Sydney, 2002; Grad. Cert of Arts in Theology, Australian Cath. U. Radiation physics instr. Grand Forks (N.D.) Clinic, 1983-85; sr. programmer PRC, Inc., Cavalier Air Force Sta., N.D., 1987-91, PARCS project-SAFEGUARD sys.; pres. Dakota Sci. Inc., Langdon, N.D., 1988-95; instr. U. N.D.-Lake Region, Devils Lake, 1988-91; systems adminstr. U.S. Courts Nat. Fine Ctr., Raleigh, N.C., 1991-94; project leader U.S. Postal Svc., Raleigh Integrated Bus. Sys. Solution Ctr., 1994—2001, program mgmt. info. tech. enabling portfolio, 2001—03; sr. tech. fellow Litton/PRC, 1997—2002; tech. fellow Northrop Grumman Info. Tech., 2002—, sys. engr., 2004—. Cons. on Wave Obs./N.D. Proposal, Gov.'s Office, Bismarck, 1991; founder, developer Dakota Sci., Inc., Langdon, 1988-95; instr. divsn. continuing edn. Wake Tech. C.C., 1993-99; adj. faculty computer info. systems N.C. Wesleyan Coll., 1997—; adj. faculty N.C. State U., 1999-2000, Capella U., Mpls., 2000—, U. Phoenix, 1998-2001. Author: Distributed UNIX System Administration, 1998; (with others) COMPUTE!'s 2nd Book of Amiga, 1988; contbr. articles to COMPUTE! Jour. of Progressive Computing, 1987, other profl. jours. Program coord. Lake Region Outreach, U. N.D., Cavalier Air Force Sta., 1988—91; mem. bd. alumni trustees USNY-Regents Coll., Albany, 1995—2000, v.p., 1996—97, pres., 1997—2000, ex-officio mem. bd. overseers, 1997; pres. Zeta Rho chpt. Pi Kappa Alpha, Grand Forks, 1981; pres. Alumni Assn. Excelsior Coll., 1999—2001; ex-officio voting Excelsior Coll. Bd. Trustees, 1999—2001, bd. trustees, 2001—. Named Larimore-Mathews scholar, U. N.D., Grand Forks, 1978, N.D. Acad. Sci. scholar, 1978, SMITS scholar, N.D. Acad. Sci., 1990; recipient Westinghouse Sci. Talent Search award, 1978, Nova Southeastern U. Leadership award, Internat. Alumni Assn., 1998. Mem.: IEEE Computer Soc., IEEE, AAAS, Internat. Coun. on Sys. Engring., N.Y. Acad. Sci., Dakota Astron. Soc. (pres. 1987—91, co-founder), Assn. for Computing Machinery. Republican. Roman Catholic. Achievements include rsch. in missile simulation; microcomputer short range weather forecasting algorithm, study in astronomy and culture, astronomy information systems, large scale sys. integration to govt. info. sys. Office: 12005 Sunrise Valley Dr Reston VA 20191 Office Phone: 703-620-8795. Business E-Mail: drwetsch@msn.com.

WETSCH, LAURA JOHNSON, lawyer; b. Fargo, N.D., Nov. 18, 1959; d. Ronald Lee Johnson and Jacqualene Lee (Goudie) Johnson Trefz; m. John Robert Wetsch, Aug. 29, 1981; children: Julie Elizabeth, Katherine Anne, John Michael. Joseph Harold. AA, Bismarck (N.D.) State Coll., 1980; BA, U. N.D., 1982, JD, 1985. Bar: N.D. 1985, N.C. 1992. Law clk. to Hon. Patrick A. Conmy, U.S. Dist. Ct. for N.D., Bismarck, 1985-88, pvt. practice, Langdon, ND, 1988-91; assoc. Jordan Price Wall Gray Jones & Carlton, PLLC, Raleigh, NC, 1992-99; dir., v.p. legal affairs Hytec Cons., Inc., Cary, NC, 1999—2003; of counsel Joyce L. Davis & Assocs., Raleigh, 1999—. Instr. bus. and criminal law U. N.D.-Lake Region, Cavalier, 1990-91; instr. paralegal studies Ctrl. Carolina C.C., Sanford, N.C., 1991-92; instr. bus. law Wake Tech. C.C., Raleigh, 1992-93. Author, editor (pamphlet) Crime Survivors Handbook, 1996; editor N.D. Women Lawyers Assn. Newsletter, 1990-91; contbr. articles to profl. jours. Vol. mediator and arbitrator Burleigh County Housing Authority, Bismarck, 1986-88; concessions co-chmn. Sanderson H.S. Band Boosters, 1996-2000; curbside cons. in employment law, N.C. Ctr. for Nonprofits, 1998. Mem. Nat. Employment Lawyers Assn., N.C. Bar Assn. (citizen edn. com. young lawyers divsn. 1994-96, chmn. membership svcs. com. young lawyers divsn. 1996-97), N.C. Acad. Trial Lawyers, Wake County Bar Assn. (fee arbitration com. 2001—). Democrat. Roman Catholic. Office: 2 Hannover Sq Ste 1730 Raleigh NC 27601-1767 E-mail: lwetsch@jldavis.com.

WETSCHLER, ED, editor; b. N.Y.C., Nov. 3, 1946; s. Herman and Elsie (Singer) W.; m. Carol M. Loftus, Jan. 24, 1988. AB, U. Rochester, 1968; MA, CUNY, 1973. Tchr. Erasmus Hall High Sch., Bklyn., 1968—84; freelance writer, theatre critic Entertainment, N.Y.C., 1980—84; assoc. editor Diversion Mag. (Hearst), N.Y.C., 1984—89, sr. editor, 1989—95, exec. editor, 1995—2001, editor-in-chief, 2002—. Contbg. author: Berlitz Guide to New York. Mem.. N.Y. Travel Writers Assn., Am. Soc. Mag. Editors. Avocations: gardening, skiing, music. Office: Diversion 888 Seventh Ave F12 New York NY 10019 Personal E-mail: ewetschler@juno.com.

WETSEL, WILLIAM DAVID, literature educator; b. Sweetwater, Tex., May 28, 1949; s. W.B. Wetsel and Elizabeth Heriot Evans. BA with highest honors, U. Tex., 1971; MDiv, U. Chgo., 1989; PhD, Brandeis U., 1978. Author: Scripture and the Rest: Pascal's Pensées in the Exegetical Tradition of Port-Royal, 1983, Pascal and Disbelief: Catechesis and Conversion in the Pensées, 1995; editor: N.Am. Soc. Seventeenth Century French Literature Tempe Acta, 6. vol., 2003 (Acad. Palms award French Govt., 2004), Pascal Translation Project. Faculty co-ordinator Gay and Lesbian Student Caucus Ariz. State U. Recipient Fulbright scholarship, U. Paris, 1982—83, Andrew Mellon fellowship, U. Pitts., 1980—81; fellow, Fulbright Found., 1971—72, Woodrow Wilson Found., 1972; grantee, Am. Coun. of Learned Societies, 1979. Mem.: N.Am. Soc. for Seventeenth-Century French Lit. (pres. 2000—02), Phi Beta Kappa. Democrat. Episcopal. Achievements include research in French 17-th century studies, Cajun French language, gay studies in France. Avocations: religious art, minority languages. Home: 3508 N Pueblo Way Scottsdale AZ 85251 Office: Arizona State U Dept Langs Tempe AZ 85287-0202 Office Phone: 480-994-8942., 480-213-4006. Personal E-mail: wdwetsel@aol.com.

WETSTONE, JANET MEYERSON, designer, journalist; b. Spartanburg, S.C., 1928; d. Louis Alexander and Ella (Levinson) Meyerson; m. Richard J. Wetstone, Sept. 21, 1947 (div. Dec. 1973); children: John B., Gregory S., Linda Wetstone Sherman. Student, U. Mo., 1945-47, Ga. State U., 1970, 80. Interior designer Jan's Interiors, Atlanta, 1965-68; pres. Wetstone Crafts Co., Atlanta, 1968—, Jan Westone Crafts Co., 1998—. Instr. women in bus. Emory U., 1972; cons. Plaid Enterprises Inc. Author: Rags to Riches with Mod-Podge, 1969; Specially Yours Decorating With Sheets, 1977; Needle-Podge Book, 1976; Creative Frame Maker, 1972; prin. works include Fast-Cast Designs Arts Kits for QVC Network., Home Shopping Networks, 1999; guest on Rosie O'Donnell Show, 2002; patentee craft paint Mod-Podge, frame-maker. Pres., founder Experts at Sea, Inc.; pres. edn. guild Ringling Mus., Sarasota, Fla., 1963-64, chair 1st creative art carnival, 1963-64; decorating chair Jimmy Carter Election Night, Atlanta, 1976. Nominee Fla. State Legis., 1988; dir. comms. Carter-Mondale 1980 campaign, Atlanta, 1980; chmn. visual arts Sarasota Centennial, 1985-86. Mem. United INventors and Scientists Am., Women in Film (v.p. 1982-83), Fla. Assn. Realtors, Million Dollar Club, Phi Sigma Sigma. Democrat. Avocations: painting, photography. Home: 3969 Glen Oaks Manor Dr Sarasota FL 34232-1045 E-mail: janwetstone@msn.com.

WETTACK, F. SHELDON, academic administrator; AB, San Jose State U., 1960, MA, 1962; PhD, U. Tex., Austin, 1967. From asst. prof. to prof. Hope Coll., Holland, Mich., 1967-82, dean nat. and social scis., 1974-82; dean faculty arts and scis. U. Richmond, 1982-89; pres. Wabash Coll., Crawfordsville, Ind., 1989-93; v.p., dean of faculty Harvey Mudd Coll., Claremont, Calif., 1993—. Office: Harvey Mudd Coll 301 E 12th St Claremont CA 91711-5901 E-mail: sheldon_wettack@hmc.edu.

WETTERAU, MARK S. food products/distributor executive; BA, Westminster Coll. Chmn., CEO, pres. Golden State Foods, Irvine, Calif., 1998—. Office: Golden State Foods Ste 1100 18301 Von Karman Ave Irvine CA 92612

WETTER-KUBECK, DAISY FISHER, dietitian, consultant; b. Lubbock, Tex., Jan. 27, 1936; d. Arthur Frederick and Margaret Elizabeth Fisher; m. John Francis Wetter, Aug. 24, 1958 (div. June 1975); children: James Robert, Jeffrey Mark; m. Edmund Kubeck, Nov. 29, 1997. BS cum laude, Linfield Coll., McMinnville, Oreg., 1956; MS, Purdue U., 1959. Cert. surveyor healthcare fin.; registered dietitian; lic. dietitian, Tex. Coop. rsch. agt. USDA, West Lafayette, Ind., 1957-59; grad. tchg. asst. Purdue U., West Lafayette, 1957-59, dietitian Women's Resident Halls, 1958-59; instr. food, nutrition, advanced nutrition North Ctrl. Coll., Naperville, Ill., 1960-61; mgr. sch. lunch program/jr. h.s. tchr. Geneva (Ill.) Pub. Schs., 1961-64; long-term care unit nutritionist, surveyor Tex. dept. Human Svcs., San Antonio, 1986-96; dietary cons. San Marcos, 1996—. Contbr. articles to profl. jours. Mem. com. for halfway houses Tex. Youth Commn., Austin, 1984; vol. dietitian Sr. Citizens Ctr./Meals on wheels, San Marcos, Tex., 1982; mem. parent adv. com. San Marcos H.S., 1981-85; mem. citizens adv. coun., exec. bd. Parkway Sch. dist., Chesterfield, Mo., 1973-74, PTA exec. bd., v.p., 1972-74; exec. bd., treas., cmty. projects chmn., yearbook chmn. Oak Tree Farms, Mo. Garden Club, 1969-75; mem. ch. bd. Manchester United Meth. Ch., 1972-73. Mem. Am. Dietetic Assn. (bd. dirs. gerontol. nutrition dietetic practice group 1998—), Am. Heart Assn. (nutrition com. 1997-98), Tex. Nutrition Coun. (co-chmn. statewide workshops, v.p., parliamentarian, nominating chmn.), San Antonio Dietetic Assn. (presenter in field), Tex. Dietetic Assn. (gerontol. practice group 1984—, cons. dietitians in health care facilities practice group 1981—), Omicron Nu, Pi Gamma Mu, Mu Phi Epsilon. Democrat. Avocations: gardening, travel. Home and Office: 126 Algarita St San Marcos TX 78666-2504

WETTSTEIN, SHANNON LEIGH, music educator; b. Ft. Scott, Kans., June 16, 1968; d. Walter Lee and Dorothe Ann Wettstein. MusB, U. Kans., 1990; MusM, New Eng. Conservatory Music, 1992; D in Musical Arts, U. Calif., San Diego, 2000. Summer session artist faculty New Eng. Conservatory, Boston, 1998—; asst. prof. music Bemidji (Minn.) State U., 2000—; artist-in-residence Walden Sch. Musician: (compact disc) Shannon Wettstein Performs Music of Chopin, Berg, Ferneyhough and Debussy, 2003, Catfish and Disciplines, Including Performances of Music By Applebaum. Grantee Commn. grant, Am. Composers Forum, 2004; Merle Montgomery fellow, Mu Phi Epsilon, 1999, Individual Artist grantee, Minn. Region 2 Arts Coun., 2001. Mem.: Am. Composers Forum, Coll. Music Soc. Avocations: exercise, cooking, reading. Office: Bemidji State Univ Box 16 1500 Birchmont Dr NE Bemidji MN 56601 Office Phone: 218-755-3997. E-mail: swettstein@bemidjistate.edu.

WETZEL, HEINZ, foreign language educator; b. Ziesar, Germany, May 11, 1935; immigrated to Can., 1965; s. Ernst and Katharina (Jentzsch) W.; m. Marianne Dummin, Mar. 19, 1957; children: Andreas, Suzanne, Claudia. Staatsexamen, Free Univ., Berlin, 1960; Dr. phil., U. Göttingen, Fed. Republic Germany, 1967. Asst. prof. German dept. Queen's U., Kingston, Canada, 1965-69; assoc. prof., grad. sec. German dept. U. Toronto, 1969-72, prof. German dept., 1972—2000, prof. emeritus, 2000—, chmn. German dept., 1984-89. Vis. prof. U. Calif., San Diego, 1973, Technische U. Braunschweig, Germany, 1973, Humboldt U. Berlin, 1995, 97, 99. Author: Konkordanz zu den Dichtungen Georg Trakls, 1971, Klang und Bild in den Dichtungen Georg Trakls, 2d edit., 1972, Banale Vitalitaet und laehmendes Erkennen, Drei vergleichende Studien zu T.S. Eliots, The Waste Land, 1974; editor: Seminar: A Journal of Germanic Studies, 1980-85; contbr. 50 articles on German and comparative lit. to profl. jours. Fellowships and grants from Social Scis. and Humanities Rsch. Coun. of Can. Mem. MLA of Am., Can. Assn. Univ. Tchrs. German. E-mail: h.wetzel@rogers.com.

WETZEL, JODI (JOY LYNN WETZEL), history and women's studies educator; b. Salt Lake City, Apr. 5, 1943; d. Richard Coulam and Margaret Elaine (Openshaw) Wood; m. David Nevin Wetzel, June 12, 1967; children: Meredith (dec.), Richard Rawlins. BA in English, U. Utah, 1965, MA in English, 1967; PhD in Am. Studies, U. Minn., 1977. Instr. Am. studies and family social sci. U. Minn., 1973-77, asst. prof. Am. studies and women's studies, 1977-79, asst. to dir. Minn. Women's Ctr., 1973-75, asst. dir., 1975-79; dir. Women's Resource Ctrs. U. Denver, 1980-84, mem. adj. faculty history, 1981-84, dir. Am. studies program, dir. Women's Inst., 1983-84; dir. Women in Curriculum U. Maine, 1985-86, mem. coop. faculty sociology, social work and human devel., 1986; dir. Inst. Women's Studies and Svcs. Met. State Coll. Denver, 1986—, assoc. prof. history, 1986-89, prof. history, 1990—. Speaker, presenter, cons. in field; vis. prof. Am. studies U. Colo., 1985; mem. judges panel nominations rev. Nat. Women's Hall of Fame, Seneca Falls, N.Y., 2002, 03, 04. Co-author: Women's Studies: Thinking Women, 1993; co-editor: Readings Toward Composition, 2d edit., 1969; contbr. articles to profl. publs. Del. at-large Nat. Women's Meeting, Houston, 1977; bd. dirs. Rocky Mountain Women's Inst., 1981-84; treas. Colo. Women's Agenda, 1987-91. U. Utah Dept. English fellow, 1967; U. Minn. fellow, 1978-79; grantee NEH, 1973, NSF, 1981-83, Carnegie Corp., 1988; named to Outstanding Young Women of Am., 1979. Mem. Am. Hist. Assn., Nat. Assn. Women in Edn. (Hilda A. Davis Ednl. Leadership award 1996, Sr. Scholar 1996), Am. Assn. for Higher Edn., Am. Studies Assn., Nat. Women's Studies Assn., Golden Key Nat. Honor Soc. (hon.), Alpha Lambda Delta, Phi Kappa Phi. Office: Met State Coll Den Campus Box 36 PO Box 173362 Denver CO 80217-3362 Office Phone: 303-556-8441. Business E-Mail: wetzelj@mscd.edu.

WETZEL, LAURA REISER, educator; BS, Beloit Coll., 1990; PhD, Wash. U., St. Louis, 1997. Asst. prof. Eckerd Coll., St. Petersburg, Fla., 1997—. Mem. Friends of Boyd Hill Nature Pk., St. Petersburg, 2003. Office: Eckerd Coll 4200 54th Avenue South Saint Petersburg FL 33711

WETZEL, ROBERT CHARLES, lawyer; b. Hackensack, N.J., Sept. 27, 1952; s. George August and Gertrude Ruth (Dilba) W.; m. Nancy Archibald, July 24, 1976; children: Justin, Brian. BA, Wittenberg U., 1975; JD, Widener U., 1980. Bar: Va. 1981, Va. Supreme Ct. 1981, U.S. Ct. Appeals (4th cir.) 1981. Law editor Michies, Charlottesville, Va., 1980; claims adjustor Nationwide Insurance Co., Lynchburg, Va., 1980-81, trial atty., claim atty., 1981-87, sr. claims atty., 1987—; private practice Lynchburg, 1981—. Dir., legal counsel Campbell County Humane Soc., Rustburg, Va., 1982—. Home: 88 Mountain Dr Lynchburg VA 24504-9752 Office: Nationwide Ins Co 116 Nationwide Dr Lynchburg VA 24502-0669

WETZEL, ROBERT GEORGE, botany educator; b. Ann Arbor, Mich., Aug. 16, 1936; s. Wilhelm and Eugenia (Wagner) W.; m. Carol Ann Andree, Aug. 9, 1959; children: Paul Robert, Pamela Jeanette, Timothy Mark, Kristina Marie. BS, U. Mich., 1958, MS, 1959; PhD, U. Calif. at Davis, 1962; PhD (hon.), U. Uppsala, Sweden, 1984. Rsch. assoc. Ind. U., Bloomington, 1962-65; asst. prof. botany Mich. State U., East Lansing, 1965-68, assoc. prof., 1968-71, prof., 1971-86, U. Mich., Ann Arbor, 1986-90; Bishop prof. biology U. Ala., Tuscaloosa, 1990—2001; prof. environ. scis. U. N.C., Chapel Hill, 2001—03, W. Kenan Disting. prof., 2003—. Cons. Internat. Biol. Program, London, 1967-75; chmn. Internat. Seagrass Commn., 1974-75; founding mem. Internat. Lake Environment Com., 1986—. Author: Limnology, 1975, 3d rev. edit., 2001, Limnological Analyses, 1979, 3d rev. edit., 2000, To Quench Our Thirst: Present and Future Freshwater Resources of the United States, 1983, Freshwater Ecosystems: Revitalizing Educational Programs in Limnology, 1996; editor: Periphyton of Freshwater Ecosystems, 1983, Wetlands and Ecotones, 1993, Recent Studies on Ecology and Management of Wetlands, 1994, Wetland Ecology, 1995, Lake Okeechobee: A Synthesis, 1995, Limnology of Developing Countries, vol. 1 1995, Limnology of Developing Countries, Vol. 2, 1999, Vol. 4, 2004, Watershed Management for Potable Water Supply, 2000, Confronting Climate Change in the Gulf Coast Region, 2001, The Missouri River Ecosystem, 2002; contbr. numerous articles on ecology and freshwater biology sys. to profl. jours.; mem. editl. bd. Aquatic Botany, 1975—, Jour. Tropical Freshwater Ecology, 1987—, Internat. Jour. Salt Lake Resources, 1991—, Biogeochemistry, 1993—, Lakes and Reservoirs, 1995—, Aquatic Ecology, 1996—, Boreal Environment Rsch., 1996—, Jour. Limnology, 1999—; N.Am. editor Archiv für Hydrobiologie, 1989—. Served with USNR, 1954—62. Recipient First T. Erlander Nat. professorship Swedish Nat. Research Council and U. Uppsala, 1982-83, award of Distinction U. Calif. at Davis, 1989; AEC grantee, 1965-75; NSF grantee, 1962—; ERDA grantee, 1975-77; Dept. Energy grantee, 1978— Fellow AAAS; mem. Royal Danish Acaad. Scis. (elected fgn. mem. 1986), Am. Acad. Arts and Scis. (elected 1993), Am. Inst. Biol. Scis., Am. Soc. Limnology and Oceanography (edtl. bd. 1971-74, v.p. 1979-80, pres. 1980-81, G.E. Hutchinson medal 1992), Aquatic Plant Mgmt. Soc., Ecol. Soc. Am., Internat. Assn. Ecology, Freshwater Biol. Assn. U.K., Internat. Assn. Theoretical and Applied Limnology (gen. sec. treas. 1968—, editor-in-chief 2001-04, Baldi Meml. award 1989, Naumann-Thienemann medal 1992), Hungarian Acad. Scis. (fgn. mem.), Internat. Phycological Soc., Mich. Acad. Scis., N.Am. Benthological Soc., Phycological Soc. Am., Internat. Assn. Great Lakes Rsch., Internat. Consortium Salt Lake Rsch. (editl. bd. 1991—), Japanese Soc. Limnology (editl. bd. 2001—), Mich. Bot. Soc., Internat. Assn. Aquatic Vascular Plant Biologists (founder, pres. 1979-91), Water Assn. Finland (editl. bd. 1990—), Asociacion Argentina de Limnologia (hon.), Brazilian Soc. Limnology, Finnish Limnological Soc. (editl. bd. 1989—), Internat. Lake Environ. Comm. Found. (exec. bd. 1986—), Netherlands Soc. Aquatic Ecology (editl. bd. 1996—), Soc. Wetland Scientists (Lifetime Achievement award 2000), Sigma Xi, Phi Sigma. Home: 102 Songbird Ln Chapel Hill NC 27514-2650 Office: U North Carolina Dept Environ Scis-Engring Chapel Hill NC 27599-7431 Office Phone: 919-843-4916.

WETZEL, VOLKER KNOPPKE, law educator; BA, Wayne State U., 1966; MA, Goethe U., Franfurt, Fed. Republic Germany, 1967; LLD, U. Wis.-Madison, 1971. Bar: Wis. 1971, U.S. Dist. Ct. Wis. 1971, U.S. Supreme Ct. 1971. Asst. prof. law U. Wis.-Madison, 1971-74; vis. prof. law Bielefeld U., Fed. Republic Germany, 1974-76; dir. criminal justice U. West Fla., Pensacola, 1976-77; assoc. prof. law Vt. Law Sch., Royalton, 1977-81; dir. jud. edn. Wis. Supreme Ct., Madison, 1981—; cons. German Ministry Justice, Bonn, 1977—. Author: Defense of Criminal Cases in Wisconsin, 1974. Co-editor: Wis. Jud. Benchbooks, 1982. Contbr. articles to profl. jours. Bd. dirs. Ctr. for Comparative Law and Social Scis., Madison, 1982—. Russell Sage fellow, 1967-69; NEH fellow, 1980. Mem. Nast. Assn. State Jud. Educators (pres. 1994-95), Wis. Bar Assn., Internat. Sociol. Assn., Sociology of Law Rsch. Com. Address: Dir Judicial Edn Wis Supreme Ct 408 S Page St Stoughton WI 53589-2168

WETZEL-WILLIAMS, KIMBERLY, lawyer; b. Ulysses, Kans., Jan. 27, 1958; d. Herbert O. and Manetta V. Wetzel; m. Robert E. Williams; 1 child, Matthew Williams. BS in Bus. Adminstrn., U. Kans., 1979, JD, 1982. Bar: Kans. 1982. Assoc. Mustaine & Newman, Kansas City, Kans., 1982—83; staff atty. Hyatt Legal Svcs., Kansas City, 1983—85; asst. dist. atty. Wyandotte County, Kansas City, 1985—2002; pvt. practice, 2002—. Adv. to youth officers Wyandotte County 4-H Coun., Kansas City, 2001—; cmty. club leader Brauer Beavers 4-H Club, Kansas City, 2000—03, Nearman 4-H Club, Kansas City, 2004—; chmn. Wyandotte County Ext. Coun., Kansas City, 2000—02; bd. dirs. Kans. State Ext. Adv. Coun., Manhattan, 2001—04. Mem.: Kansas Bar Assn., Wyandotte County Bar Assn. Roman Catholic. Avocations: photography, gardening, gourmet cooking, working with youth. E-mail: kimwetzelwilliams@yahoo.com.

WEVERS, JOHN WILLIAM, retired Semitic languages educator; b. Baldwin, Wis., June 4, 1919; emigrated to Can., 1951; s. Bernard and Wilemina (Te Grootenhuis) W.; m. Grace Della Brondsema, May 22, 1942; children: Robert Dick, John William, Harold George, James Merritt. AB, Calvin Coll., Grand Rapids, Mich., 1940; ThB, Calvin Sem., 1943; ThD, Princeton Theol. Sem., 1945; DD (hon.), Knox Coll., Toronto, 1973; DHC (hon.), Leiden U., 1985. Lectr., then asst. prof. O.T. and Semitic langs. Princeton Theol. Sem., 1946-51; mem. faculty U. Toronto, Ont., Can., 1951—, prof. Near Eastern studies, 1963—, prof. emeritus, 1984—, grad. chmn., 1972-75, chmn. dept., 1975-80. Chmn. adminstrv. council Presbyn. Ch. Can., 1960-65 Author: Commentary on the Book of Ezekiel, 1969, Septuaginta Vetus Testamentum Graecum: Genesis, 1974, Deuteronomium, 1977, Numeri, 1981, Leviticus, 1986, Exodus, 1991; also text histories, 1974, 78, 83, 86, 92, Notes on the Greek Text of Exodus, 1990, Genesis, 1993, Deuteronomy, 1995, Leviticus, 1997, Numbers, 1998. Bd. govs. Ctrl. Hosp., Toronto, 1963-96, chmn., 1967-80; chmn. Hosp. Coun. Met. Toronto, 1974-75; bd. govs. Ont. Hosp. Assn., 1974-84, pres., 1978-79. Recipient Queen's Jubilee medal, 1978 Fellow Royal Soc. Can.; mem. Oriental Club Toronto, Internat. Orgn. Septuagint and Cognate Studies (pres. 1972-80, hon. pres. 1989—), Can. Bibl. Studies (hon. life), Akademie Wissenschaften Goettingen (corr.), Arts and Letters Club (Toronto). Home: 116 Briar Hill Ave Toronto ON Canada M4R 1H9 Office: U Toronto Near and Middle East Civs Toronto ON Canada M5S 1A1 E-mail: j.wevers@utoronto.ca.

WEXELBAUM, MICHAEL, lawyer; b. Bklyn., Aug. 12, 1946; s. Joseph and Beatrice (Skurnick) W.; m. Cynthia Debra Schorr, Apr. 15, 1973 (dec. 1984); children: Joshua David, Stephanie Faye; m. Joan Brenda Math, Aug. 21, 1994; stepchildren: Jonathan David Kaye, Matthew Lawrence Kaye, Julie Dana Kaye. BA in Econs., Bucknell U., 1968; JD, NYU, 1971. Bar: N.Y. 1972, U.S. Dist. Ct. (so. and ea. dists.) N.Y. 1973, U.S. Dist. Ct. (ea. dist.) Wis. 1998. Assoc. Sherman, Citron & Karasik, P.C., N.Y.C., 1972-80, ptnr., head litigation dept., 1980-2001; ptnr. litigation dept. Snow Becker Krauss P.C., N.Y.C., 2001—, co-chair litigation dept., 2003—. Arbitrator Nat. Arbitration Forum, 1999—. Arbitrator Am. Arbitration Assn. and Gen. Arbitration Coun. of Textile and Apparel Industries, N.Y.C., 1982—. Mem. Bankruptcy Lawyers Bar Assn., Lawyers Assn. Textile and Apparel Industries (bd. govs.), Am. Arbitration Assn. (arbitrator), Nat. Arbitration Forum (arbitrator), Assn. Comml. Fin. Attys. Democratic. Jewish. Avocations: tennis, skiing, biking, theater. Home: 85 Norrans Ridge Dr Ridgefield CT 06877-4237 Office: Snow Becker Krauss PC 605 Third Ave New York NY 10158-0125 Office Phone: 212-455-0486. Office Fax: 212-455-0455. Personal E-mail: jmwex@hotmail.com. Business E-Mail: mwexelbaum@sbklaw.com.

WEXLER, ALLAN, architect, art educator; BFA, R.I. Sch. Design, 1971, BArch, 1972; MArch, Pratt Inst, 1976. Asst. prof. Sch. Arch. N.J. Inst. Tech., 1974—83; mem. faculty environ. design Parsons Sch. Design, 1983—94; assoc. adjunct prof. Sch. Arch. Pratt Inst., 1994—; arch., designer Ronald Feldman Fine Arts, N.Y.C. Mem. faculty Brown U. Sch. Art, 1986, Temple U. Tyler Coll. Art, 1989, Cooper Union Sch. Fine Arts, 1989; artist-in-residency U. Calif., San Diego, 1991; vis. prof. R.I. Sch. Design, Sch. Arch., 1992, Hochschule der Kunste, Berlin, 1994; vis. critic in sculpture SUNY, Purchase, 1993. One-man shows include Albright Coll., Freedman Gallery, Reading, Pa., 1985, Brown U., List Art Ctr., Providence, 1985, Ronald Feldman Fine Arts, N.Y.C., 1985, 1988, 1990, 1992, 1994, 1998, Temple U. Gallery, Phila., 1986, McIntosh/Drysdale Gallery, Washington, 1986, The Jewish Mus., N.Y.C., 1988, Univ. Gallery, U. Mass., Amherst, 1989, Inst. Contemporary Art, U. Pa., 1989, Horace Richter Gallery, Old Jaffa, Israel, 1990, San Diego Mus. Contemporary Art, La Jolla, Calif., 1991, U. Gallery, U. Mass., Amherst, 1991, The Forum Gallery, St. Louis, 1991, De Cordova Mus. and Sculpture Park, Lincoln, Mass., 1992, Karl Ernst Osthaus Mus., Hagen, Germany, 1993, Hochschule der Kunste, Berlin, 1994, Three Rivers Art Festival, Pitts., 1995, Md. Inst. Coll. Art, Balt., 1996, Parsons Sch. Design, Dept. Arch. and Environ. Design, 1997, Stadtgalerie Saarbricken, Germany, 1997, Gallery Joe, Phila., 1997, Atlanta Coll. Art Gallery and City Gallery at Chastain, Atlanta, 1999, Stephen Wirtz Gallery, San Francisco, 2000, Forum for Contemporary Art, St. Louis, 2000, San Francisco Mus. Modern Art, 2001, Ronald Feldman Fine Arts, NYU, 2002, Parrish Art Mus., Southampton, N.Y., 2002, exhibited in group shows at Arlene Bujese Gallery, East Hampton, N.Y., 1995, N.J. Ctr. Arts, Summit, 1995, Davis Mus. and Cultural Ctr., Wellesley (Mass.) Coll., 1996, Calif. Ctr. Arts. Mus., Escondido, 1996, Gallery Joe, Chgo., 1997, Union Brauerei/Dortmunder U., Germany, 1998, White Box, N.Y., 1999, Aldrich Mus. Contemporary Art, Ridgefield, Conn., 2000, 2002, Wave Hill Glyndor Gallery, Bronx, N.Y., 2000, Apex Art, N.Y.C., 2001, Westfalischen Landesmuseum, Munster, Germany, 2001, Hallwalls Contemporary Arts Ctr., Buffalo, N.Y., 2001, Yeshiva U., N.Y.C., 2002, Wilhelm-Hack Mus. and Kunstverein Ludwigshafen, Germany, 2002, Denver Art Mus., 2002, Karl Ernst Osthaus-Mus., Hagen, Germany, 2002, Ronald Feldman Fine Arts, N.Y.C., 2002, Mus. Contemporary Arts, Chgo., 2002, numerous others, commns. include, Vera List, Greenwich, Conn., 1990, Parson's Sch. Design, 1993, ARTWALK, 1995, others, NYC Bd. Edn., 1999, Schneider Vineyard, 2000—, Expo 2000, Hannover, Germany, 2000, Met. Transp. Authority, NYC, 2001—, Hudson River Park, 2002—. Recipient First prize The City as a Significant Environment Competition, Milan and Casabella Mag., 1972, First prize Birch Burdette Long Competition, Archtl. League, 1975, Bessie award 40 Under 40, Interiors Mag., 1986, Sponsored Project award N.Y. State Coun. on Arts, 1989, Chrysler award for design innovation, 1997, George Nelson Design award, Interiors mag., 1999; fellow, N.Y. Found. Arts, 1985, 1990; grantee, Archtl. League, 1975. Office: 305 W 20th St New York NY 10011*

WEXLER, ANNE, government relations and public affairs consultant; b. N.Y.C., Feb. 10, 1930; d. Leon R. and Edith R. (Rau) Levy; m. Joseph Duffey, Sept. 17, 1974; children by previous marriage: David Wexler, Daniel Wexler. BA, Skidmore Coll., 1951, LLD (hon.), 1978; DSc in Bus. (hon.), Bryant Coll., 1978. Assoc. pub. Rolling Stone mag., 1974-76; personnel adviser Carter-Mondale transition planning group, 1976-77; dep. undersec. regional affairs Dept. Commerce, 1977-78; asst. to Pres. of U.S., Washington, 1978-81; pres. Wexler and Assocs., Washington, 1981-82; govt. relations and pub. affairs cons., chmn. Wexler, Reynolds, Harrison & Schule, Inc., Washington, 1981-90; vice chmn. Hill and Knowlton PA Worldwide, Washington, 1990-92; chmn. The Wexler Group, 1992—. Bd. dirs. Methanex, Dreyfus Index Funds, Wilshire Mut. Funds, Dreyfus Family of Funds. Bd. dirs. Washington Econ. Club, WETA. Decorated officer Order of Australia; named Outstanding Alumna Skidmore Coll., 1972, recipient most disting. alumni award, 1984, Bryce Harlow award, 1989. Mem. Coun. on Fgn. Rels., Nat. Women's Forum. Jewish. Office: Wexler Group 1317 F St NW Ste 600 Washington DC 20004-1157

WEXLER, HASKELL, film producer, cameraman; b. Chgo., 1922; s. Simon Wexler; m. Nancy Ashenhurst (div.); two children; m. Marian Witt (div.); 1 son, Mark; m. Rita Taggart. Ednl. documentaries, Chgo., for eleven years; cinematographer films: The Hoodlum Priest, The Best Man, America America, The Loved One, In the Heat of the Night, Who's Afraid of Virginia Woolf? (Acad. award), The Thomas Crown Affair, American Graffiti, One Flew Over the Cuckoo's Nest, Introduction to the Enemy, Bound for Glory (Acad. award), Coming Home, Colors, Three Fugitives, 1988, Blaze, 1989, Lookin' to Get Out, Matewan, Other People's Money, The Babe, Mulholland Falls, 1995, Rich Man's Wife, 1995, (with others) Days of Heaven, (with others) Rolling Stones-IMAX, The Secret of Roan Inish, Canadian Bacon, Limbo, 1999, HBO 61—, 2001, Silver City, 2004; writer, dir., photographer: Medium Cool, 1969; wrote and directed Latino, 1985, feature documentary Bus Riders Union, documentary Five Days in March. Received star on Hollywood's Walk of Fame, 1996. Mem. Acad. Motion Picture Arts and Scis. (bd. govs. cinematographers br.). Office: Skouras Agy 631 Wilshire Blvd Ste 2C Santa Monica CA 90401-1513 E-mail: perigol@aol.com.

WEXLER, HERBERT IRA, retail company executive; b. Newark, Sept. 6, 1916; s. Irving and Jeanette (Lesser) W.; m. Elaine L. Ellis, Oct. 10, 1948; children: Susan, Peter, Toni. Student, Rutgers U., 1939-41; student Advanced Mgmt. Program, Harvard U., 1956. From stock boy to asst. buyer L. Bamberger & Co., 1935-47; from buyer appliances to sr. v.p., exec. com., dir. R.H. Macy & Co., N.Y.C., 1947-73; pres., CEO, chmn. bd. dirs. Marcade Group Inc., N.Y.C., 1973-86, cons., bd. dirs., 1987-97. Vice chmn. Greater N.Y. coun. Boy Scouts Am.; organizer, fundraiser Yale Grace New Haven Hosp.; mem. Gov. Harriman's Com. to Investigate Fraud and Misrepresentation in Consumer Products; mem. adv. coun. to bd. trustees Greens Farms Acad., Westport, Conn.; gen. chmn. State of Israel Bond Drive, 1980, testimonial, 1978; gen. chmn. N.Y. Cmty. Svc. Soc.; chmn. N.Y. sect. for fundraising Denver Jewish Hosp; dir. Children's Blood Found. N.Y. Hosp. Capt. U.S. Army, 1941—46. Named Key Man of Yr. Am. Jewish Com. and B'nai B'rith, 1957; named B'nai B'rith Man of Yr., 1976; recipient Disting. Service award Am. Jewish Com. and Anti-Defamation League, 1960, Award of Honor Fedn. Jewish Philanthropies of N.Y., 1961, Scroll of Honor United Jewish Appeal of Greater N.Y., 1964, Man of Yr. award Conn. Digestive Disease Soc., 1973 Mem. Harvard Club, Birchwood Country Club. Home: Greenfield Hunt 49 Palmer Brg Fairfield CT 06430-7830

WEXLER, NANCY SABIN, clinical neuropsychology educator; b. Washington, July 19, 1945; d. Milton and Leonore Wexler. AB cum laude, Radcliffe Coll., 1967; PhD in Clin. Psychology, U. Mich., 1974; DHL (hon.), N.Y. Med. Coll., 1991; DSc (hon.), U. Mich., 1991. Lic. psychologist, N.Y. Psychol. intern, teaching fellow U. Mich., 1968-74; asst. prof. psychology grad. faculty New Sch. Social Rsch., N.Y.C., 1974-76; pvt. practice psychology N.Y.C., 1974-76; health sci. adminstr. Nat. Inst. Neurol., Comm. Disorders and Stroke, NIH, 1978-83; pres. Hereditary Disease Found., Santa Monica, Calif., 1983—; prof. neuropsychology Coll. Phys. and Surgeons, Columbia U., N.Y.C., 1985-92, prof. clin. neuropsychology, 1992—. Mem. Ctr. for Brain and Behavior Coll. Phys. and Surgeons of Columbia U., 1985; mem. adv. com. Human Genome Ctr., Lawrence Berkeley Labs. and U. Calif., 1988—; mem. external adv. com. Ctr. for Human Genome Studies, Los Alamos Nat. Labs., 1990—; co-chairperson ethical, legal and social issues com. Human Genome Orgn., 1991—, mem. dir. search Nat. Ctr. for Human Genome Rsch., NIH, 1992; chairperson Joint NIH/Dept. of Energy Ethical, Legal, Social Issues Working Group on Human Genome, 1989—. Contbr. articles to profl. jours. Trustee Nat. Huntington's Disease Assn., 1983-85, Marine Biol. Lab., 1984-86, Eleanor Roosevelt Inst. Cancer Rsch., 1985-91, Found. for Care and Cure of Huntington's Disease, 1988—. Fulbright scholar U. West Indies, Jamaica, 1967-68; fellow The Hastings Ctr., 1990—; recipient award Robert J. and Claire Pasarow Found., 1987, Living Legacy award Women's Internat. Soc., 1988, Alumnae Athena award Alumnae Coun. U. Mich., 1989, award Gov.'s Office, Zulia, Venezuela, 1989, Venezuelan Presdl. award, 1990, Legis. Commendation N.Y. State, 1990, Disting. Svc. award Nat. Assn. Biology Tchrs., 1993, Nat. Med. Rsch. award Nat. Health Coun., 1993, Albert Lasker Pub. Svc. award, 1993. Mem. AAAS (bd. dirs. 1993—), APA, Am. Soc. Law and Medicine, Soc. Neurosci. (chairperson social issues com. 1988-90, organizing com. Neurobiology of Human Diesease Workshop 1980—), Am. Psychol. Soc., Am. Soc. Human Genetics, World Fedn. Nuerology, Rsch. Group on Huntington's Disease, Am. Neurol. Assn. Office: Columbia U Coll Phys & Surg NY State Psychiat Inst 1051 Riverside Dr Unit 6 New York NY 10032-1013 also: Ste 511 2444 Wilshire Blvd Santa Monica CA 90403-5826

WEXLER, PATRICIA SUSAN, dermatologist, surgeon; b. 1951; MD, U. Libre de Bruxelles, Belgium, 1979. Cert. Am. Bd. Internal Medicine 1983, Am. Bd. Dermatology 1986. Intern Beth Israel Med. Ctr., NY, 1979—80, resident internal medicine, 1980—82, fellowship infectious disease, 1982—83, attending physician, Mt. Sinai Hosp., NY; private practice Wexler Dermatology, Manhattan, NY. Tchr. Beth Israel Med. Ctr. Dermatology Surgery Clinic; asst. clin. prof. Albert Einstein Sch. Medicine, Bronx, NY; cons. in the develop. of several skin care and make-up lines. Author medical rsch. publs. Recipient Am. Acad. Cosmetic Surgery award for Excellence in Cosmetic Surgery. Fellow: Am. Soc. Dermatologic Surgery. Office: 145 E 32nd St 7th Fl New York NY 10016-6055 Office Phone: 212-684-2626.*

WEXLER, RANDY, medical educator; b. Columbus, Ohio, July 20, 1964; s. Joyce Wexler; m. Claudia O'Leary, May 23, 1992. MD, MD-Wright State U., 1990; M in pub. health, Ohio State U., 1993. Lic. Am. Bd. of Family Practice, 1999, Diplomate Nat. Bd. of Med. Examiners, 1991. Staff physician Mt. Carmel Health, Columbus, Ohio, 1994—2000, chief med. dir., 1998—2000; asst. prof., clin. family medicine Ohio State U., Columbus, 2000—. Team physician Columbus Pub. Schools, Ohio, 1992—; del. Ohio State Med. Assn., Columbus, 1998—; bd. mem. Ohio Occupl. Therapy, Phys. Therapy, and Athletic Trainers Bd., Columbus, 1998—2003; legislative vice chair Ohio Acad. of Family Physicians, Columbus, 1999—; quality intervention panel Med. Bd., State of Ohio, Columbus, 2001—. Recipient Hon. Membership in the Ohio Athletic Trainers Assn., Ohio Athletic Trainers Assn., 2003, President's award, Ohio Acad. of family Physicians, 2003. Mem.: Ohio Acad. of family Physicians (legislative vice chair 1999—2003), Ohio Acad. of Family Physicians (bd. mem. 1998—2003), Ohio State Med. Assn. (del. 1998—2003), Ohio Athletic Trainers Assn. (hon.), Delta Omega, Phi Kappa Phi. Office: Ohio State U 21 E State St Ste 250 Columbus OH 43215 Home Fax: N/A.

WEXLER, RICHARD LEWIS, lawyer; b. Chgo., June 19, 1941; s. Stanley and Lottie (Pinkert) W.; m. Roberta Seigel, June 13, 1962; children: Deborah (Mrs. Jonathan Sokobin), Joshua, Christine, Jonathan, Amie. Student, U. Mich., 1959-1962; JD cum laude, John Marshall Law Sch., 1965. Bar: Ill. 1965, U.S. Dist. Ct. (no. dist.) Ill. 1967. Gen. counsel Metro. Planning Council, Chgo., 1965-67; ptnr. Wexler, Kane, Rosenzweig & Shaw, Chgo., 1967-71, Taussig, Wexler & Shaw, Chgo., 1971-78, Wexler, Siegel & Shaw, Ltd., Chgo., 1978-83, Sachnoff & Weaver, Ltd., Chgo., 1983-91, chair real estate dept., 1985-91, mng. ptnr., 1985-90; ptnr., chmn. real estate dept. Lord Bissell & Brook, Chgo., 1991-97, mem. compensation com., 1995. Legal counsel Zoning Laws Study Commn., Ill. Gen. Assembly, Springfield, 1969-71, Urban Counties Study Commn., Springfield, 1971-72; legal counsel Ill. Coastal Zone Mgmt. Program, Springfield, 1979-81, Northeastern Ill. Planning Commn., Chgo., 1969—. Contbr. numerous articles to profl. jours. Chmn. Jewish Fedn. Met. Chgo., 1986-88, mem. numerous coms., also bd. dirs., 1978-90; chmn. Jewish United Fund, 1986-88; bd. dirs. Coun. Jewish Fedns., 1980, mem. exec. com., 1985—, v.p., 1988—, chmn. planning steering com., 1990-95, chmn. fedn./agy. rels. com., 1988-90; co-chmn. Task Force on Poverty and Low Income, 1985-87; nat. vice-chmn. United Jewish Appeal, 1988, nat. chmn., 1996-98, regional allocations chmn., 1987-88, chmn. region II, 1988-90, budget com., 1989-92, allocations com., 1990-91, campaign exec., 1991-2000; chmn. Operation Exodus II, 1993-94, chmn. nat. mktg. com., 1994-95, chmn. 1997 campaign planning and budget com., nat. chmn., 1997-98, pres. bd. trustees, 1998-2000; co-chair United Jewish Appeal Fedns. N.Am., 1998-2000; bd. dirs. Jewish Edn. Soc. N.Am., 1982-85, Hebrew Immigrant Aid Soc., 1988—, Nat. Conf. on Soviet Jewry, 1989-95, vice chmn., 1989-92, nat. chmn., 1992-94; bd. dirs. Nat. Jewish Cmty. Rels. Adv. Coun., 1988-90, vice chmn., 1988-92; chmn. Jewish Com. Rels. Coun. Chgo., 1988-89. Fellow Eta Lambda; mem. ABA, Ill. State Bar Assn. (Lincoln award, Legal Writing, 1966). Avocations: tennis, reading, travel. Office: Lord Bissell & Brook 115 S La Salle St Ste 3400 Chicago IL 60603-3801 Office Phone: 312-443-1751. Business E-Mail: rwexler@lordbissell.com.

WEXLER, ROBERT, university administrator; Pres. U. of Judaism, L.A. Office: U Judaism 15600 Mulholland Dr Los Angeles CA 90077-1599

WEXLER, ROBERT, congressman; b. Queens, Jan. 2, 1961; m. Laurie Wexler; children: Rachel, Zachary, Hannah. BA in Polit. Scis., U. Fla., 1982; JD, George Washington U. Law Sch., 1985. Mem. Fla. State Senate, 1990-96, U.S. Congress from 19th Fla. dist., 1997—; mem. internat. rels. com., judiciary com. Recipient Senatorial Leadership award Fla. Prosecutor's Assn.; named Legis. of the Year Palm Beach Police Benevolent Assn., Top Environ. Senator Fla. Leagues Conservation Voters, 1996. Democrat. Office: Ho Rep 213 Cannon Ho Office Bldg Washington DC 20515-0919

WEXMAN, VIRGINIA WRIGHT, English language educator; b. Winnipeg, Man., Can., Apr. 2, 1941; d. Douglas Wright and Jean Swinton Hine; m. Todd Ellis Wexman, July 25, 1960 (div. 1979); children: Kimberly, Todd; m. John W. Huntington, Jr., Aug. 28, 1982. BA, U. Chgo., 1970, MA, 1971, PhD, 1976. Producer Office of Radio-TV, U. Chgo., 1971—75; asst. prof. U. Ill., Chgo., 1975—82, assoc. prof., 1982—92, prof. dept. English, 1992—, assoc. vice-chancellor for acad. affairs, 1997—99. Vis. assoc. prof. U. Chgo., 1990; vis. prof. U. Mich., 1999; seminar leader Lilly Endowment Workshop on Liberal Arts, Colo. Springs, 1988—94. Editor: Cinema Jour., 1982—87, Film and Authorship, 2002; mem. editl. bd.: U. Ill. Press, 1991—94, 2003—; author: Roman Polanski, 1984, Creating the Couple, 1993; co-author: Robert Altman, 1984, A History of Film, 2002; co-editor: Letter from an Unknown Woman, 1986; contbr. articles to profl. jours. Mem.: MLA (chair film divsn. 1981—82, exec. coun. 1998—2002), Soc. for Cinema Studies (pres. 1993—95, Svc. award 2003). Democrat. Home: 711 S Dearborn St Apt 808 Chicago IL 60605-3821 Office: Univ Ill at Chgo Dept English # 162 601 S Morgan St Chicago IL 60607-7100 Office Phone: 312-413-2246.

WEXNER, LESLIE HERBERT, retail executive; b. Dayton, Ohio, 1937; BSBA, Ohio State U., 1959, HHD (hon.), 1986; LLD (hon.), Hofstra U., 1987; LHD (hon.), Brandeis U., 1990; PhD (hon.), Jewish Theol. Sem. Founder, pres., chmn. bd. The Limited, Inc., fashion chain, Columbus, 1963—. Dir., mem. exec. com. Banc One Corp., Sotheby's Holdings Inc., vis. com. Grad. Sch. Design Harvard U.; mem. bus. adminstrn. adv. coun. Ohio State U.; chmn. Retail Industry Trade Action Coalition. Bd. dirs. Columbus Urban League, 1982-84, Hebrew Immigrant Aid Soc., N.Y.C., 1982—; co-chmn. Internat. United Jewish Appeal Com.; nat. vice chmn., treas. United Jewish Appeal; bd. dirs., mem. exec. com. Am. Jewish Joint Distbn. Com., Inc.; trustee Columbus Jewish Fedn., 1972, Columbus Jewish Found., Aspen Inst., Ohio State U., Columbus Capital Corp. for Civic Improvement; former trustee Columbus Mus. Art, Columbus Symphony Orch., Whitney Mus. Am. Art, Capitol South Community Urban Redevel. Corp.; former mem. Governing Com. Columbus Found.; founding mem., first chair The Ohio State U. Found; exec. com. Am. Israel Pub. Affairs Com. Decorated cavaliere Republic of Italy. Named Man of Yr. Am. Mktg. Assn., 1974. Mem. Young Presidents Orgn., Sigma Alpha Mu. Clubs: B'nai B'rith. Office: Limited Inc PO Box 16000 3 Limited Pkwy Columbus OH 43230-1450

WEXO, ALEX, actor; s. John and Pamela Wexo. Student, Creighton U., London, 1975—81, Edinburgh U., Scotland, 1982—83. Actor: (TV series) A Few Good Men, 1993, The Pretender, 1996—2000, The Invisible Man, 2000—02; prodr.: espionage tng. films. Sgt. USMC, 1985—89.

WEYAND, WILLIAM J. engineering executive; BBA, Nichols Coll., 1966. Exec. v.p. Measurex Corp.; pres., CEO SDRC, Milford, Ohio, 1997—, also chmn. bd. dirs. Bd. dirs. U. Maine. Office: SDRC 2000 Eastman Dr Milford OH 45150-2740

WEYER, DIANNE SUE, health facility administrator; b. Anchorage, Aug. 15, 1954; d. Vernon H. and Myrtle M. Larson; m. Merlin D. Weyer; 1 child, Alison. BSW magna cum laude, Augustana Coll., Sioux Falls, S.D., 1976; MPA, U.S.D., Vermillion, 1989. LCSW 1996. Program dir. Threshold, Sioux Falls, SD, 1976—78; policy analyst S.D. Divsn. Law Enforcement Assistance, Pierre, SD; youth projects coord. Mountain Plains Youth Svcs. Coalition, Pierre, SD, 1980—82; social worker S.D. Dept. Social Svcs., Pierre, SD, 1983—85; child and adolescent program specialist S.D. Divsn. Mental Health, Pierre, SD, 1985—96; Social Services Manager St. Mary's Healthcare Ctr., Pierre, SD, 1996—2000, outreach dir., 2002—. Social work adv. bd., adj. faculty Augustana Coll., Sioux Falls, SD, 1977—79; interagy. coord. coun., state bd. mem. S.D. Dept. Edn., Pierre, SD, 1989—96; state rep. for children and youth Nat. Assn. State Mental Health Program Dirs., Washington, 1985—96; chair S.D. Interagy. Coordination Network Coun., Pierre, SD, 1991—96; social work adv. bd. Presentation Coll., Aberdeen, SD; adj. faculty Capital U., Pierre, SD, 2000—01; exec. bd., past pres. S.D. Social Work Leaders in Health Care, Sioux Falls, SD, 1999—2001. Healthcare com. Pierre C. of C., 1999—2003; tchr., confirmation guide Luth. Meml. Ch., Pierre, 1985—2001; bd. dirs. Missouri Shores Resource Ctr., Pierre, 1980—82; exec. bd. Healthy Cmtys./Healthy Youth, Pierre, 1999—. Recipient Spl. Recognition award, Capitol Area Counseling Svc., 2001, S.D. Family-Based Svcs. Assn., 1994, Outstanding svc. award, S.D. Corrections Assn., 1990; grantee S.D. CASSP-Local Infrastructure Demonstration, Ctr. Mental Health Svcs., 1993—96, Rural Mental Health Demonstration, NIH, 1987—89, HHS Adminstrn. Children, Youth and Family Svcs., 1987—90. Mem.: NASW, S.D. Alliance for the Mentally Ill, S.D. Social Work Leadership in Healthcare (sec., v.p., pres. 1998—2001, Spl. Recognition award 0196), Nat. Social Work Leadership in Healthcare. Home: 1217 Hilgers Dr Pierre SD 57501 Office: St Mary's Healthcare Ctr 800 E Dakota Pierre SD 57501 Personal E-mail: MWDW1234@aol.com. Business E-Mail: dianneweyer@chi-midwest.org.

WEYERHAEUSER, GEORGE H., JR., paper manufacturing company executive; b. w; B in Philosophy/Maths., Yale U., 1976; MS, MIT, 1986. Tech. forester, contract logger adminstr., sawmill supr. Weyerhaeuser Co., Dierks, Ark., 1978-80, v.p., mill mgr. Containerboard Valliant, Okla., 1981-90, v.p. mfg. pulp & paper bus. Federal Way, 1990-93, pres., CEO Can. divsn., 1993-98, sr. v.p. technology, 1998—. Office: Weyerhaeuser Co PO Box 2999 Tacoma WA 98477-2999

WEYERS, LARRY LEE, energy executive; b. Nebr. BA, Doane Coll., 1967; ME, Columbia U., 1971; MBA, Harvard U., 1975. Registered profl. engr. Pres., CEO WPS Resources Corp. Holding Co., Green Bay, 1989-98; chmn., pres., CEO WPS Resources Corp., Green Bay, 1998—. Office: WPS Resources Corp PO Box 19001 Green Bay WI 54307-9001

WEYGAND, BOB A. former congressman; b. Attleboro, Mass., May 10, 1948; BA in Fine Arts, U. R.I., 1971, BS in Civil and Environ. Engring., 1976. Project mgr. R.I. Dept. Nat. Resources, 1973-82; owner Weygand, Orciuch & Christie, Inc., 1982-92; mem. R.I. Ho. of Reps. from 84th dist., 1985-93; lt. gov. State of R.I., 1993-97; mem. 105th-106th Congress from 2d R.I. dist., 1997—2001; pres., CEO New England Board Higher Edu., Boston, 2001—. Mem. budget com., banking and fin. svcs. com.; chmn. R.I. house com. on corps., 1990; chmn. E. Providence Planning Bd., 1979-84, R.I. Small Bus. Advocacy Coun., 1993-97, R.I. Long Term Care Coord. Coun., 1993-97, R.I. Delegation/White House Conf. on Aging, 1995; presdl. appointee White House Conf. on Small Bus., 1995. Bd. dirs. Save the Bay, 1984-87, United Way, 1993—, Meeting St. Ctr., 1993—, Big Bros. of R.I.; pres., bd. dirs. R.I. Parks Assn., 1983-92; chmn. R.I. Land Use Commn., 1987-92. Recipient Legislator of Yr. award R.I. League Cities and Towns, 1988, Exceptional Pub. Svc. award FBI, 1992, Disting. Svc. Star State of R.I., 1992. Mem. Am. Soc. Landscape Architects; Am. Planning Assn. (Outstanding Pub. Svc. award New Eng. chpt. 1992, Leadership award 1992). Office: New England Board Higher Edu 45 Temple Pl Boston MA 02111 E-mail: rweygand@nebhe.org.

WEYHENMEYER, CONSTANZE ELISABETH, environmental scientist, researcher; b. Bonn, Germany, Mar. 1, 1966; BSc, Albert-Ludwigs-U., Freiburg, Germany, 1988; MSc, Trent U., Peterborough, Can., 1992, Scripps Inst. Oceanography, La Jolla, Calif., 1996; PhD, U. Bern, Switzerland, 2000. Postdoctoral rschr. U. Bern, Switzerland, 2000—02; rsch. scientist Lawrence Livermore Nat. Lab., Calif., 2002—; prof. Syracuse U., NY, 2004—. Contbr. scientific papers to rsch. jours. (Outstanding Student Paper Award (AGU), 1998), articles to profl. jours. Musician Symphony Orch., Berkeley, Calif., 2002. Recipient Best PhD Thesis, U. Bern, 2000, Best Poster prize, Swiss Global Change Day 2000; scholar Can. Govt. award, Deutscher Akademischer Austausch Dienst, 1989-1992. Mem.: Internat. Assn. of Hydrogeologists, Am. Geophys. Union. Achievements include research in scientific expeditions to Greenland, Antarctica, Sultanate of Oman. Home: Apt 604 2525 Stuart St Berkeley CA 94705 Office: Lawrence Livermore Nat Lab 7000 East Avenue L-397 Livermore CA 94550 Personal E-mail: weyhen@gmx.de.

WEYHER, HARRY FREDERICK, III, merchant banker; b. N.Y.C., Mar. 9, 1956; s. Harry F. and Barbara (McCusker) W.; m. Anda Gailitis, July 7, 1984; children: Harry F. IV, Jesse D. BA, Middlebury Coll., 1977. Treas. Bunge Corp., N.Y.C., 1977-90; v.p. fin. Gerald Metals Inc., Stamford, Conn., 1990-96; ptnr. Littlejohn & Co., LLC, Greenwich, Conn., 1996-01; pres. Vy Capital LLC, Westport, Conn., 2001—. Mem. Racquet & Tennis Club, L.I. Wyandanch Club. Home: 215 Ridgefield Rd Wilton CT 06897-2432 Office: Vy Capital LLC 181 Post Rd W Westport CT 06880

WEYL, TOM F. advertising executive; b. 1943; Creative dir. Am. Acad. Art, 1963-68; with Campbell-Mithun Inc., Mpls., 1968-73; pres., sec., CCO Martin-Williams Inc., Mpls., 1973—.

WEYMAN, STEVEN ALOYSIUS, retired military officer; b. Fort Thomas, Ky., May 31, 1957; s. Edward Joseph Weyman and Carol Jean (Steffen) Jackson; m. Kathleen Anne Bradford, June 2, 1990; 1 child, Jennifer Elizabeth. BS in Math., No. Ky. U., 1978; MS in Comm. Sys. Tech., Naval Postgrad. Sch., 1988. Commd. 2d lt. U.S. Army, 1978, advanced through grades to lt. col., 1995; bn. signal officer 8th Engr. Bn., 1st Cav. Divsn., Ft. Hood, Tex., 1979-81, 2nd M.I. Bn., Pirmasens, Germany, 1982-85; co. comdr. B Co., 307th M.I. Bn., Ludwigsburg, Germany, 1985-86; signal combat devel. project officer Combined Arms Command, Ft. Leavenworth, Kans., 1988-91; student U.S. Army Command Gen. Staff Coll., Ft. Leavenworth, 1991-92; bn. exec. officer 123rd Signal Bn., 3rd Inf. Divsn., Kitzingen, Germany, 1992-94; asst. divsn. signal officer 3rd Inf. Divsn., Wuerzburg, Germany, 1994-95; operational readiness evaluation team chief 5th U.S. Army (West), Ft. Lewis, Wash., 1995-97; def. info. sys. network deployed program mgmt. chief Def. Info. Sys. Agy., Arlington, Va., 1997-2000; student Armed Forces Staff Coll., Norfolk, Va., 1998; ret. Def. Info. Sys. Agy., Arlington, Va., 2000; student Armed Forces Staff Coll., Norfolk, Va., 1998; tech. acct. mgr. Intel Online Svcs., 2000—01; teleport installation program mgr., prin. engr. Arrowhead Global Solutions Inc., 2001—03; network sys. lead engr. Mitre Corp., 2003—. Decorated Legion of Merit. Mem. U.S. Signal Corps Assn. (Bronze Order of Mercury 1995), Armed Forces Comm. Electronics Assn. Avocations: computers, travel, reading, sports. Home: 43921 Felicity Pl Ashburn VA 20147-4860 E-mail: steve@weyman.net., sweyman@mitre.org.

WEYMOUTH, ELIZABETH (LALLY) GRAHAM, editor, columnist; children: Katharine Scully, Pamela Bass. BA in Am. History and Lit. with honors, Harvard U. Freelance writer, reporter Boston Globe, 1966—76; freelance journalist, contbg. editor numerous publs. including NY Times Mag., Esquire, Atlantic Monthly, Parade, LA Times, New York, 1977—83; contbg. editor LA Times, 1983—86; sr. editor, spl. diplomatic corr. Newsweek Mag. Interviewer Washington Post, 1986—; mem. Coun. Fgn. Rels. Author: America in 1876, The Way We Were, 1976; editor, compiler Thomas Jefferson: The Man, His World, His Influence, 1973.

WEYRAUCH, PAUL TURNEY, retired army officer, retired principal; b. Alpine, Texas, July 22, 1941; s. Paul Russell and Margaret Fischer (Fletcher) W.; m. Nancy Virginia (Haight), Dec. 18, 1965; children: Julie Lynn, Paul C. BS, U.S. Mil. Acad., West Point, NY., 1963; MBA, Tulane U., 1976; Tchg. Cert., South West. Tex. State U., 1995; EdM, South West Tex. State U., 1997, prin. cert., 1998. Comdr. 2d lt. U.S. Army, 1963, brig. gen.; bn. comdr. U.S. Army, first bn., fifth F.A., Ft. Riley, Kans., 1978-80; asst. chief of staff U.S. Army, first inf. div., Ft. Riley, Kans., 1980-81; comdr. U.S. Army, first cav. div. arty., Ft. Hood, 1982-85; chief of staff U.S. Army, F.A. Ctr., Ft. Sill, Okla., 1985-86; asst. chief of staff for plans and policy Allied Forces South Europe, Naples, Italy, 1986-89; chief of staff U.S. Army, III Corp and Ft. Hood, 1989-91; ret. U.S. Army, 1991; planning and zoning commr. City of Georgetown, Tex., 1994-96, chmn. planning and zoning commn., 1995-96; tchr. math. Richarte H.S., Georgetown, Tex., 1995-97, prin., 1997—2003; ret., 2003. Sunday sch. tchr. local Protestant ch.; pres. chapel coun., leader, coord. Bible studies. Decorated D.S.M., Def. Superior Svc. medal; Legion of Merit; Bronze Star medal with V. device; Bronze Star medal with 1 oak leaf cluster; Meritorious Svc. medal with 3 oak leaf clusters. Mem. First Cav. Div. Assn. Avocations: running, collecting mil. insignia. Home: 320 S Ridge Cir Georgetown TX 78628-8213

WEYRAUCH, WALTER OTTO, law educator; b. Lindau, Germany, Aug. 27, 1919; came to U.S., 1952; s. Hans Ernst Winand and Meta Margarete (Lönholdt) W.; m. Jill Carolyn White, Mar. 17, 1973; children from previous marriages: Kurt Roman (dec.), Corinne Harriet Irene, Bettina Elaine (dec.). Student, U. Freiburg, 1937, U. Frankfurt Main, Germany, 1940-43, Dr. iur, 1951; LL.B., Georgetown U., 1955; LL.M., Harvard, 1956; J.S.D., Yale, 1962; Golden Dr. diploma (hon.), U. Frankfurt Main, 2001. Referendar, Frankfurt, Germany, 1943-48; atty. German cts. U.S. Ct. Appeals, Allied High Commn., Frankfurt, 1949-52; expert on trade regulations, visit in U.S. under auspices Dept. State, 1950; Harvard U. Dumbarton Oaks Library and Collection, Washington, 1953-55; asst. in instrn. Law Sch., Yale, 1956-57; assoc. prof. law U. Fla., Gainesville, 1957-60, prof., 1960-89, Clarence J. TeSelle prof. law, 1989-94, Stephen C. O'Connell chair, 1994—, disting. prof. law, 1998—; hon. prof. law Johann Wolfgang Goethe U., Franfurt Main, 1980—. Vis. cons. U. Calif. at Berkeley, Space Scis. Lab., 1965-66; vis. prof. law Rutgers U., 1968; vis. prof. polit. sci. U. Calif. at Berkeley, 1968-69; vis. prof. law U. Frankfurt, 1975; cons. Commn. of Experts on Problems of Succession of the Hague Conf. on Pvt. Internat. Law, U.S. Dept. State, 1968-71; Rockefeller Found. fellow, Europe, 1958-59; Richard G. Huber disting. lectr. Law Sch. Boston Coll., 1999. Author: The Personality of Lawyers, 1964, Zum Gesellschaftsbild des Juristen, 1970, Hierarchie der Ausbildungsstätten, Rechtsstudium und Recht in den Vereinigten Staaten, 1976, Gestapo V-Leute: Tatsachen und Theorie des Geheimdienstes, 1989, 2nd edit., 1992; author: (with Sanford N. Katz) American Family Law in Transition, 1983; author: (with Katz and Frances E. Olsen) Cases and Materials on Family Law: Legal Concepts and Changing Human Relationships, 1994; author: Das Recht der Roma und Sinti: Ein Beispiel autonomer Rechtsschöpfung, 2002; author, editor: Gypsy Law: Romani Legal Traditions and Culture, 2001; contbr. Clinical Law Training-Interviewing and Counseling, 1972, Law, Justice, and the Individual in Society-Psychological and Legal Issues, 1977, Marriage and Cohabitation in Contemporary Societies: Areas of Legal, Social and Ethical Change_An International and Interdisciplinary Study, 1980, Dutch transl., 1981, Group Dynamic Law: Exposition and Practice, 1988, The Living Law of Nations: Essays on Refugees, Minorities, Indigenous Peoples and the Human Right of Other Vulnerable Groups, 1996, Law, Morality, and Religion: Global Perspectives, 1996. Mem. Law and Soc. Assn., Internat. Soc. on Family Law, Assn. Am. Law Schs. (chmn. com. studies beyond 1st degree in law 1965-67), Order of Coif. Home: 2713 SW 5th Pl Gainesville FL 32607-3113 Office: U Fla Coll Law Gainesville FL 32611 Business E-Mail: weyrauch@law.ufl.edu.

WEYRICH, PAUL MICHAEL, political organizations executive; b. Racine, Wis., Oct. 7, 1942; s. Ignatius A. and Virginia M. (Wickstrom) W.; m. Joyce Anne Smigun, July 6, 1963; children: Dawn, Peter, Diana, Stephen, Andrew. AA, U. Wis., 1962. Ordained deacon Melkite Greek Eparchy, 1990. News dir., announcer, program dir. SLIP, WAXD-FM, Kenosha, Wis., 1960-63; reporter Milw. Sentinel, 1963-64; polit. reporter, newscaster CBS, Milw., 1964-65; news dir. Sta. KQXI, Denver, 1966; press sec. U.S. Sen. Gordon Allott of Colo., 1967-73; spl. asst. to Sen. Carl T. Curtis, Nebr., 1973-77; founder, pres. Heritage Found., 1973-74; nat. chmn. Free Congress PAC, Coalitions for Am., 1987—, BOD, Amtrak, 1987-93. Founder, pres. Free Congress Found.; pres. Krieble Inst. of Free Congress Found., 1989-96, America's Voice, 1991-97; nat. editor Transport Central, 1968-71; treas. Coun. Nat. Policy, 1981-92; bd. dirs. All News Radio WEEI, Boston, 1984-90, Krieble Inst. Russia; nat. chmn. Com. for Effective State Govt., 1985-87; chmn. bd. Yorktownuniversity.com, 1999—. Author: The Role of Rails series, 1964; pub. Polit. Report, 1975-89, The New Electric Rwy. Jour., 1988-96, Spotlight on Congress, 1989-93; host (daily talk show) Direct Line, 1993-98; co-host The New Electric Rwy. Jour., 1994-96, Ways & Means, 1994—. Recipient Youth of Yr. award Racine Optimist Club, 1960, Excellence in Reporting citation Milw. Common Council, 1964, Documentary of Yr. award for Wis. TV, 1965, Crystal Ball award for predicting outcome 1996 presdl. election Washington Post, 1996, Thomas Jefferson award for servant leadership Coun. Nat. Policy, 1997. Mem. Ctrl. Electric Railroaders Assn., Internat. Policy Forum (chmn. 1983-84); former

mem. HUD Adv. Commn. on Regulatory Barriers to Affordable Housing. Greek Catholic. Home: 12615 Lake Normandy Ln Fairfax VA 22030-7262 Office: Free Congress Found 717 2nd St NE Washington DC 20002-4368 E-mail: paulwey@free.congress.org.

WHACK, RITA COBURN, television producer, writer; b. Harvey, Ill., June 13, 1958; d. Charlie Guss and Willie Essie Coburn; m. Harold Lee Whack Sr., June 25, 1983; children: Harold Lee Jr., Christine Coburn. Student, Ill. State U., 1976, Columbia Coll., 1977; BA in Comm., Northwestern U., 1980. Field prodn. coord. Hour Mag., Chgo., 1980; news writer Satellite News Channel, Stamford, Conn., 1981; rsch./prodn. coord. The Dr. Ruth Show WNEW-TV, N.Y.C., 1982—83; freelance prodr., publicist, and writer Pitts., 1983—91; segment prodr. The Jenny Jones Show, Chgo., 1991—92; ind. writer and prodr. RCW Prodns., Inc., Chgo., 1992—; prodr. DANNY!, Chgo., 1995; sr. prodr. WBEZ-91.5 Chgo. Pub. Radio, 1996—98; series prodr. WYCC-20 Chgo. Pub. TV, 2001—03. Author: Meant To Be, 2002. Office Phone: 708-957-4806. Personal E-mail: RitaCoburnWhack@aol.com.

WHALE, ARTHUR RICHARD, retired lawyer; b. Detroit, Oct. 28, 1923; s. Arthur B. and Orpha Louella (Doak) W.; m. Roberta Lou Donaldson, Oct. 29, 1949; children: Richard Donaldson, Linda Jean. BSChemE, Northwestern U., 1945; LLB, George Washington U., 1956. Bar: D.C. 1957, Mich. 1957, Ind. 1977, U.S. Patent and Trademark Office 1957. Chem. engr. Ansul Chem. Co., Marinette, Wis., 1946-47, Parke, Davis & Co., Detroit, 1947-50, writer med. lit., 1950-52; chem. engr. Bur. Ships, U.S. Dept. Navy, Washington, 1952-55, dep. sect. head, indsl. gas sect., 1954-55; patent engr. Swift & Co., Washington, 1955-56; patent atty. Upjohn Co., Kalamazoo, 1956-65; asst. mgr. organic chems. sect. patent dept. Dow Chem. Co., Midland, Mich., 1965-66, mgr., 1967-73, mng. counsel, 1973-75; asst. sec., gen. patent counsel Eli Lilly & Co., Indpls., 1975-86; of counsel Miller, Morriss & Pappas, Lansing, Mich., 1986-89, Baker & Daniels, Indpls., 1987—2003; ret., 2003. Lectr. Practicing Law Inst., John Marshall Law Sch. Contbr. articles to profl. jours. Pres. Nat. Inventors Hall of Fame Found., 1978-79; bd. dirs. Holcomb Rsch. Inst., Indpls., 1982-86. Served to lt. (j.g.) USNR, 1943-46. Mem. State Bar Mich. (chmn. patent trademark copyright sect. 1967-69), D.C. Bar Assn., Midland County Bar Assn. (pres. 1974-75), Am. Bar Assn. (mem. patent trademark copyright sect.), Assn. Corp. Patent Counsel, Nat. Coun. Patent Law Assns. (chmn. 1979-80), Am. Intellectual Property Law Assn. (pres. 1974-75), Ashlar Lodge, Masons, Shriners. Republican. Presbyterian. Avocation: golf. Office: Baker & Daniels Ste 2700 300 N Meridian St Indianapolis IN 46204-1782 Office Phone: 317-237-1437.

WHALEN, CHARLES WILLIAM, JR., author, business executive, educator; b. Dayton, Ohio, July 31, 1920; s. Charles William and Colette (Kelleher) W.; m. Mary Barbara Gleason, Dec. 27, 1958; children— Charles E., Daniel D., Edward J., Joseph M., Anne E., Mary B. BS, U. Dayton, 1942, HHD (hon.), 1980; MBA, Harvard U., 1946; postgrad., Ohio State U., 1959-60; LLD, Central State U., Ohio, 1966. Vice pres. Dayton Dress Co., 1946-52; faculty U. Dayton, 1952-66; mem. 90th-95th Congresses 3d Dist. Ohio; pres. New Directions, Washington, 1978-79; fellow Woodrow Wilson Internat. Center for Scholars, 1980; adj. prof. Sch. Internat. Service, Am. U., 1981. Mem. Ohio Ho. of Reps., 1954-60, Ohio Senate, 1960-66; mem. Internat. Vol. Svcs., Inc., 1985-95; v.p. Washington Inst. Fgn. Affairs, 1982-98, mem. U. Dayton adv. bd. Ctr. for Internat. Studies, 1990-96; bd. dirs. Harvard Bus. Sch., Washington, 1982-84, 91-94. 1st lt. AUS, 1943-46. Recipient Disting. Alumnus award U. Dayton Alumni Assn., 1975, Alumni Lifetime Achievement award U. Dayton Sch. Bus. Adminstrn., 2001. Mem.: Dayton Bicycle Club, Kenwood Country Club, Capitol Hill Club. Roman Catholic.

WHALEN, JOHN PHILIP, retired educational administrator, clergyman, lawyer; b. Troy, N.Y., Jan. 4, 1928; s. Philip Joseph and Mary Catherine (Doyle) W. BA summa cum laude, St. Mary's Sem. and Univ., Balt., 1949; STL, Cath. U., 1953, MA, 1954, STD summa cum laude, 1965; JD, George Washington U., 1976; postgrad., Johns Hopkins U., 1959-60, U. Md., College Park, 1958-59, Fordham U., 1953-54; LHD (hon.), Marymount U., 1987. Ordained priest Roman Cath. Ch., 1953. Instr. Mater Christi Sem., Albany, 1953-58; asst. prof. Mt. St. Mary's Coll., Emmitsburg, Md., 1959-61; assoc. prof. Cath. U. Am., Washington, 1961-67, acting pres., 1968-69; pastor St. Mary's Ch., Oneonta, N.Y., 1970-72; pres. Consortium of Univs. of Washington area, 1972-88; mng. editor New Cath. Ency., 1963-67; pres., editor-in-chief Corpus Publs., 1967-94, ret., 1994. Cons. 12 colls. and univs.; founder, chmn. Univ. Support Svcs., Inc., 1986-94, pres., CEO, founder; cons. student loans, capital access trust, capital loans to colls., 1999-2000; founder, prin. Power Systems, Inc.; founder Whalen Holdings, LLC; founder prin. Full Measure, LLC, Whalen Holdings, LLC, JMJ Whalen Found., Inc.; bd. dirs. U.S. Fund for Improvement Postsecondary Edn., 1988-91. Mem. editl. bd. Law and Edn.; weekly columnist Evangelist, Albany; contbr. to Nat. Geog. mag.; contbr. articles to edn. and theol. jours. Pres. Univ. Extension Ednl. Corp., 1974—94; mem. Fed. City Coun., 1982—, Coun. for Ct. Excellence, 1984—90; chmn. Ctr. Advanced Studies of the Ams., 1984—90; bd. dirs. Sta. WETA-TV, 1968—69, Washington Ctr. for Met. Studies, 1968—69, Cath. U. Am., 1968—69, Nat. Shrine of Immaculate Conception, 1968—69, Dunbarton Coll., 1970—72, Trinity Coll., 1969—72, St. Mary's Coll., South Bend, Ind., 1970—74, St. Anselm's, 1979—85, Mt. Vernon Coll., 1982—84, CBR Found., 2001—, Met. Bd. Trade, Washington, 1975—90, sec bd. dirs., 1983—85. Named Man of the Yr., 1984; recipient Disting. Alumnus award George Washington U., 1988. Mem. Nat. Cath. Edn. Assn., Cath. Theol. Soc. Am. (dir. 1966-68), Higher Edn. Group Washington (pres. 1974-75), Tired Hands Club (pres. 1982-84), Cosmos Club (Washington), City Club, Rotary. Office: 1614 Parham Rd Silver Spring MD 20903-2256 E-mail: jwhalen@erols.com.

WHALEN, JOHN SYDNEY, management consultant; b. Moncton, N.B., Can., Sept. 26, 1934; s. Harry Edward and Sarah Maude (Bourgeois) W.; m. Margaret Joan Carruthers, May 3, 1958; children: Bradley Graham, Elizabeth Ann. Grad., Can. Inst. Chartered Accts., 1959. Chartered acct. Coopers & Lybrand (formerly McDonald, Currie & Co.), St. John, N.B., 1954-63; with Kaiser Services, Oakland, Calif., 1963-75, telecommunications mgr., 1966-69, asst. controller, 1969-70, controller, 1970-74; mgr. corp. acctg. Kaiser Industries Corp., Oakland, 1975; controller Kaiser Engrs., Inc., Oakland, 1975-76, v.p. fin. and adminstrn., 1976-82; mgmt. cons., owner Whalen & Assocs., Inc., Alamo, Calif., 1983—. Pres. Round Hill Holdings, Inc., 1993-99. Mem. Commonwealth Club, Rancho Cañada Golf Club. Home: 2216 Nelda Way Alamo CA 94507-2004 Office: 3195 Danville Blvd Ste 4 Alamo CA 94507-1920 Office Phone: 925-820-3506. E-mail: sydwhalen@aol.com.

WHALEN, LORETTA THERESA, religious educational administrator; b. Bklyn., May 21, 1940; d. William Michael and Loretta Margaret (Malone) Whalen; children: Ann Lindsay, Margaret Force. RN, St. Vincent's Hosp., N.Y.C., 1960; BSN, U. Pa., 1965; MA in Edn., Fordham U., 1971; cert. in sociology religion, Louvain U., Belgium, 1974; PhD in Global Edn., The Union Grad. Sch., 1994. Staff nurse Holy Family Hosp., Atlanta, 1967-69; Latin Am. communication dir. Med. Mission Sisters, Maracaibo, Venezuela, 1969-71; intensive care nurse St. Vincent's Hosp., N.Y.C., 1971-72; mem. ministry team Med. Mission Sisters, various locations, 1972-74, dir. communications Phila., 1974-77; asst. to exec. Interreligious Peace Colloquium, Washington, 1977; freelance writing, photography Ch. World Svc., N.Y.C., 1978-79; dir. Office Global Edn. Nat. Council Chs., N.Y.C., 1980-99. Co-author: Make a World of Difference: Creative Activities for Global Learning, 1990, Tales of the Heart: Affective Approaches to Global Education, 1991; mem. editorial bd., rev. editor Connections Mag., 1984-87; contbr. articles to profl. jours. Mem. Peace and Justice Commn., Archdiocese of Balt., 1985-89. Mem. Amnesty Internat., Bread for the World, NOW, World Wildlife Fund, Greenpeace, Sigma Theta Tau. Democrat. Roman Catholic. Avocations: photography, writing, racquetball, interior design, travel.

WHALEN, LUCILLE, retired academic administrator; b. Los Angeles, July 26, 1925; d. Edward Cleveland and Mary Lucille (Perrault) W. BA in English, Immaculate Heart Coll., Los Angeles, 1949; MSLS, Catholic U. Am., 1955; DLS, Columbia U., 1965. Tchr. elem. and secondary parochial schs., L.A., Calif., 1945—52; tchr., libr. Conaty Meml. H.S., L.A., 1950—52; reference/serials librarian, instr. in library sci. Immaculate Heart Coll., 1955-58; dean Immaculate Heart Coll. (Sch. Library Sci.), 1958-60, 65-70; assoc. dean, prof. SUNY, Albany, 1971-78, 84-87, prof. Sch. Info. Sci. and Policy, 1979-87; dean grad. programs, libr. Immaculate Heart Coll. Ctr., Los Angeles, 1987-90; ref. libr. (part-time) Glendale Community Coll., 1990—. Dir. U.S. Office Edn. Instn. Author, editor (with others): Reference Services in Archives, 1986, author, editor (with Nina Redman): (with Nina Redman), 2nd edit., 1998; author: Human Rights: A Reference Handbook, 1989; author: (with Nina Redman) 2d edit., 1998. Mem. ACLU, Common Cause, Amnesty Internat. Democrat. Roman Catholic. Home: 320 S Gramercy Pl Apt 101 Los Angeles CA 90020-4542 Office: Glendale CC 1500 N Verdugo Rd Glendale CA 91208-2809 Personal E-mail: lucillew@aol.com.

WHALEN, SARAH EVE, professional soccer player; b. Greenlawn, N.Y., Apr. 28, 1976; Student in psychology, U. Conn. Mem. U.S. Nat. Women's Soccer Team, 1996—, including Nike Victory Tour, 1995, U.S. Women's Cup, 97. Named 1997 Soccer Am. Player of Yr. Achievements include holder U.Conn. career record for games played (99). Office: US Soccer Fedn 1801-1811 S Prairie Ave Chicago IL 60616

WHALEN, THOMAS EARL, psychology educator; b. Toledo, June 26, 1938; s. T. Mylo and Alice E. (Tallman) W.; m. Carolyn Margaret Lapham, Dec. 24, 1960; children: Jennifer Susan, Holly Elizabeth. BA, UCLA, 1960; MA, San Diego State U., 1967; PhD, U. Conn., 1970. Cert. secondary tchr., Calif. Secondary tchr. San Diego City Schs., 1964-68; rsch. assoc. Southwest Regional Lab., Inglewood, Calif., 1969; prof. Calif. State U., Hayward, 1970—, chair ednl. psychology dept., 1977-79, assoc. dean sch. edn., 1987-89, 95 96, prof. emeritus, 1997. Rsch. con. Evaluation Assocs., San Sanfrancisco Bay Area Schs., 1971-88, Lawrence Livermore (Calif.) Nat. Lab., 1982-83. Author: (text book) Ten Steps to Behavioral Research, 1989; contbr. articles to profl. jours. Lt. USN, 1960-63. U.S. Office of Edn. fellow U. Conn., 1968-70, post doctoral scholar Am. Edn. Rsch. Assn., U. Iowa, 1972. Mem. Am. Ednl. Rsch. Assn., APA, Calif. Ednl. Rsch. Assn. (bd. dirs. 1982-84), Bay Area Coun. on Measurement and Evaluation in Edn. (pres. 1976-77), United Profs. of Calif. (exec. bd. Calif. State U. Hayward 1975-76). Avocations: golf, travel, gardening. Home: 325 Conway Dr Danville CA 94526-5511 Office: Calif State U 25800 Carlos Bee Blvd Hayward CA 94542-3001

WHALEN, THOMAS J. lawyer; b. Jersey City, July 29, 1938; s. Arthur and Mae (Cavannagh) W.; m. Anne Marie Donovan, Sept. 5, 1970; 1 child, Honore. B.A., St. Peter's Coll., Jersey City, 1960; J.D., Georgetown U., 1963. Bar: N.J. 1964, D.C. 1964, N.Y. 1968. Law sec. to judge U.S. Ct. Appeals (3d cir.), Newark, 1963-64; assoc. firm Condon & Forsyth, N.Y.C. and Washington, 1967-75, ptnr., 1975—; author, spkr. on airline regulatory and liability law. Served to capt. JAGC, U.S. Army, 1964-67; Vietnam. Mem. ABA, Fed. Bar Assn., Univ. Club (Washington). Democrat. Roman Catholic. Address: Condon & Forsyth 1016 16th St NW Ste 700 Washington DC 20036-5724 E-mail: twhalen@condonlaw.com.

WHALEN, WAYNE W. lawyer; b. Savanna, Ill, Aug. 22, 1939; s. Leo R. and Esther M. (Yackley) W.; m. Paula Wolff, Apr. 22, 1970; children: Amanda, Clementine, Antonia, Nathaniel, Daniel. BS, U.S. Air Force Acad., 1961; JD, Northwestern U., 1967. Bar: Ill. 1967, US Ct. Appeals (7th cir.) 1968, US Supreme Ct. 1972. Commd. 1st lt. USAF, 1961, ret., 1964; assoc. Mayer, Brown & Platt, Chgo., 1967-74, ptnr., 1974, Skadden, Arps, Slate, Meagher & Flom LLP, Chgo., 1984—. Bd. dir. Van Kampen Funds, Oak Brook, Ill. Author: Annotated Illinois Constitution, 1972. Del. 6th Ill. Constitutional Conv., 1969-70, chmn. style drafting and submission com. Named Outstanding Young Lawyer, Chgo. Bar Found., 1970. Mem. Chgo. Club. Office: Skadden Arps Slate Meagher & Flom LLP 333 W Wacker Dr Ste 2100 Chicago IL 60606-1220

WHALEY, CHARLES HENRY, IV, communications company executive; b. Elmhurst, N.Y., Jan. 15, 1958; s. Charles Henry III and Edna Mae (Squires) W.; m. Jeanette Marie Smith, Sept. 26, 1987. AAS in Electrical Tech., Queensborough Community Coll., Bayside, N.Y., 1979. Testing engr. GTE/Telenet, Mount Laurel, NJ, 1979-81; field service engr. Gen. Dynamics Communications Co., St. Louis, 1981-82; ops. engr. United Techs. Communications Co., Pine Brook, NJ, 1982-84, sr. ops. engr. N.Y.C., 1984-85, ops. supr., 1985-86; project mgr. Telex Computer Products, N.Y.C., 1986; pres. Pertel Comms. of N.E., Hartford, Conn., 1990—, Metrocom Tech. Svcs., N.Y.C., 1997—. Democrat. Presbyn. Avocations: computers, classic automobiles, contemporary music, U.S. history, study of industrial/mechanical evolution. Office: Pertel Comm of NE Inc 750 Main St Hartford CT 06103 also: 350 Fifth Ave New York NY 10018 Office Phone: 212-760-1339. E-mail: cwhaley@pertelne.com.

WHALEY, MARVIN, food products executive; B in polit. sci., U. Md. Mgr. trainee McDonald's Corp., 1973—80, dir. ops., 1980—83, regional v.p., Atlanta, 1983—93; pres. McDonald's China Development Co., 1994—98; sr. v.p. and internat. relationship ptnr People's Republic of China, Hong Kong, Macau, Korea and Taiwan, 1998—2000; pres., North Asia divsn. McDonald's Corp., 2000—03, pres., Asia/Middle East/Africa region, 2003—. Adv. dir. McDonald's Bd. of Dirs., 1996—97. Mem. Ronald McDonald House, Ronald McDonald's Children's Charities; Atlanta Tip Off Club. With U.S. Army, 1967—70. Office: McDonalds Corp McDonald's Plaza Oak Brook IL 60523

WHALEY, ROBERT HAMILTON, judge; m. Lucinda Schilling Whaley; 3 children. BA, Princeton U., 1965; JD, Emory U., 1968. Litigator land and natural resources divsn. Dept. Justice, 1969-71; asst. U.S. atty. U.S. Dist. Wash. (ea. dist.), 1971-72; assoc. Winston & Cashatt, Spokane, Wash., 1972-76, ptnr., 1976—; judge Spokane County Superior Ct., 1992-95, U.S. Dist. Ct. (ea. dist.) Wash., Spokane, 1995—. Office: US Dist Ct Ea Dist Wash PO Box 283 920 Riverside Ave W Spokane WA 99210

WHALEY, ROSS SAMUEL, environmentalist, educator; b. Detroit, Nov. 7, 1937; s. Lyle John and Margaret Nielson (Semple) W.; m. Beverly Mae Heemstra, June 14, 1958; children: Heather Jean, Susan Lesli, Lindsay John. BS, U. Mich., 1959, PhD, 1969; MS, Colo. State U., 1961. Asst. prof., assoc. prof., prof. Utah State U., Logan, 1965—70, dept. head, 1967—70; assoc. dean Colo. State U., Ft. Collins, 1970—73; dept. head U. Mass., Amherst, 1973—76, dean, 1976—78; dir. econ. research USDA Forest Service, Washington, 1978—84; pres. SUNY Coll. Environ. Scis. and Forestry, Syracuse, 1984—2000, prof., 2000—; chair Adirondack Park Agy., 2003—. Cons. UN FAO, Rome, 1983-84, UN, Budapest, Hungary, 1974, U.S. Peace Corps., South Am., 1972, Geddes, Brecher, Qualls & Cunningham, Denver, 1971-72; chmn. Adirondack Pk. Agy. Contbr. articles to profl. jours. Bd. dirs. Glynwood Ctr., Paul Smith's Coll.; trustee Paul Smiths Coll. Fellow Soc. Am. Foresters (pres. 1991). Mem. Christian Ref. Ch. Avocations: reading, swimming, hiking, fly fishing, cross country skiing. Office: SUNY/ESF 326 Marshall Hall 1 Forestry Dr Syracuse NY 13210

WHALEY, STORM HAMMOND, retired government official, consultant; b. Sulphur Springs, Ark., Mar. 15, 1916; s. Storm Onus and Mabel Etta (Prater) W.; m. Jane Florence Bucy, Oct. 6, 1935; children: Carroll Jean Whaley Anderson, Ann Marie Whaley Adams, Rebecca Glenn Whaley Dyess. BA, John Brown U., 1935; LL.D. (hon.), 1959; postgrad., Am. U. Law Sch., 1954; D.Sc. hon., U. Ark. for Med. Scis., 1983. Mgr. Sta. KUOA, Siloam Springs, Ark., 1935-53, Sta. KGER, Long Beach, 1948-53, KOME, Tulsa, 1951-53; asst. to Congressman J.W. Trimble, 1953-54; asst. to pres. U. Ark., 1954-59, acting pres., 1959-60, v.p. health scis., 1960-70; assoc. dir. communications NIH, Bethesda, Md., 1970-92; retired, 1992. Mem. U.S. del. World Health Assembly, 1962, 63, 64; mem. nat. adv. health council USPHS, 1963-66; chmn. ad hoc com. Report to Pres. and Congress Regional Med. Programs, 1967; mem. U.S. Sr. Exec. Service, 1979 Author: They Call It, 1951. Del. Democratic Nat. Conv., 1940, 44, 48, 52. Recipient Superior Service award HEW, 1974, SES Performance award, 1982, Superior Service award USPHS, 1987; named Outstanding Alumnus, John Brown U., 2001. Fellow AAAS; mem. Broadcast Pioneers, Ark. Broadcasters Assn. (life), NIH Alumni Assn., Nat. Press Club, Masons (33d deg.), Omicron Delta Kappa, Lambda Chi Alpha. Home and Office: 4400 E West Hwy Bethesda MD 20814-4524

WHALEY, WALLACE W. military officer; b. NC; BSCE, The Citadel, 1968; postgrad., Air Command and Staff Coll., 1980. Commd. USAF, 1968, advanced through grades to maj. gen., 1995; provider pilot 311th Tactical Airlift Squadron, Da Nang Air Base, Vietnam, 1969—70; starlifter pilot, instr. 14th Mil. Airlift Squadron, Norton AFB, Calif., 1970—72; galaxy simulator instr., flight examiner 3d Mil. Airlift Squadron, Charleston AFB, SC, 1972—73; command post duty officer, C-5 flight examiner, pilot 436th Mil. Airlift Wing, Dover AFB, Del., 1973—74; res. C-5 and C-141 pilot, asst. squadron ops. officer 349th Mil. Airlift Wing, Travis AFB, Calif., 1974—83; WC-130 pilot, dep. comdr. ops. 920th Weather Reconnaissance Group, Keesler AFB, Miss., 1983; pilot, dep. comdr. ops. 446th Mil. Airlift Wing, McChord AFB, Wash., 1983—84; comdr. 928th Tactical Airlift Group, O'Hare Air Res. Forces Facility, Chgo., 1984—86; vice comdr. 446th Mil. Airlift Wing, McChord AFB, Wash., 1986 88; comdr. 349th Mil. Airlift Wing, Travis AFB, Calif., 1988—90; dep. to chief of AF Res. Hdqrs. USAF, Washington, 1990—93; comdr. 14th AF, AF Res. Command, McClellan AFB, Calif., 1993—98, March AFB, Calif., 1998—2000; dir. ops. Hdqrs. AF Res. Command, Robins AFB, Ga., 2000—. Decorated SDM, Legion of Merit with oak leaf cluster, DFC, Air medal with four oak leaf clusters. Mem.: Assn. of The Citadel, Res. Officers Assn., Air Force Assn. Office: Robbins AFB Robins AFB GA 31098-5009

WHALIN, ROBERT W. physicist; B in Physics, U. Ky.; M in Physics, U. Ill.; PhD of Phys. Oceanography, Tex. A&M U. Registered Profl. Engr. Dir. Army Rsch. Lab. Army Rsch. Lab., Adelphi, Md., 1998—; dir. U.S. Army Engr. Waterways Experiment Sta., Vicksburg, Miss., 1992—98; tech. dir. U.S. Army Engrs. Waterways Experiment Sta., Vicksburg, Miss., 1985—92, U.S. Army Corps Engrs. Coastal Engring. Rsch. Ctr., Fort Belvoir, Va., 1982—85. Adj. prof. Miss. State U., Tex. A&M U., U. Miss.; mem. external rsch. adv. com. Miss. State U.; engring. adv. coun. mem. U. Fla.; rsch. adv. com. for Army High Performance Computing Rsch. Ctr. U. Minn.; adv. bd. mem. Dept. Civil Engring. U. New Orleans. Contbr. numerous articles to profl. jours. Mem.: ASCE, Sr. Exec. Assn., Army Engr. Assn., Soc. Am. Mil. Engrs., Tsunami Soc., Permanent Internat. Assn. Navigation Congresses, Am. Soc. Engring. Edn., Sigma Xi, Phi Kappa Phi, Phi Eta Sigma. Office: US Army Rsch Lab AMSRL-VS-EA-PA 2800 Powder Mill Rd Adelphi MD 20783-1197

WHALIN, W. TERRY, writer, editor; b. Huntington, W.Va., Aug. 12, 1953; s. Wallace Eugene and Rose Terry (Estill) W.; children: Jonathan David, Timothy Benjamin; m. Christine Elizabeth Johnson, May 3, 1995. BA, Ind. U., 1975; cert., Multnomah Sch. of Bible, 1977; MA, U. Tex., Arlington, 1984. Linguist Wycliffe Bible Translators, Huntington Beach, Calif., 1975-85, mng. editor In Other Words, 1985-93; assoc. editor Decision mag. Billy Graham Evangelistic Assn., Mpls., 1993-94; CEO, pres. Whalin & Assocs., Colorado Springs, Colo., 1994—. Instr. Inst. of Children's Lit., 1997—. Author: When I Grow Up, 1992, Never Too Busy, 1993, A Strange Place to Sing, 1994, Chuck Colson, 1994, Today's Heroes Series, 1994, The Brave But Gentle Shepherd, 1996, Samuel Morris, Heroes of the Faith series, 1997, Sojourner Truth Heroes of the Faith Series, 1997, Luis Palau, Men of Faith Series, 1996, Billy Sunday, Young Reader's Christian Libr., 1996, John Perkins, 1996, Today's Heroes Series, 1996, Luis Palau, Young Reader's Christian Libr., 1998, Pocket Prayer Companion series: Prayers for My Son, Prayers for My Daughter, Prayers for My Wife, Prayers for My Husband, 1999, Lighthouse Psalms, 1999, Love Psalms, 1999, Billy Graham, Men of Faith Series, 2000; co-author: One Bright Shining Path, 1993, Ayacucho Para Cristo, 1995, Bottom-Line Faith, Ten Characteristics of Committed Christians, 1995, Let the Walls Fall Down, 1996, The World at Your Door, 1997, Better Men on the Path to Purity, 1998, The Book of Prayers: A Man's Guide to Reaching God, 1998, Sharing God with Others, 1998, Lessons from the Pit, 1999, Money for Life, 1999; ghostwriter (books): Seeking Christ, 1994, Freedom From Addiction, 1996, Pathway to His Prescence, 2000; contbr. articles to profl. publs. and mags. Treas. Evangelical Press Assn., Earlysville, Va., 1992-94. Mem. Evangelical Press Assn., Am. Soc. Journalists and Authors, Soc. Children's Book Writers and Ilustrators. Republican. Office: 445 E Cheyenne Mtn Blvd #C-368 Colorado Springs CO 80906-4570

WHALLEY, TOM, recording industry executive; Various positions Interscope/Geffen/A&M, 1989—, pres., 1997—. Office: Interscope Records 2220 Colorado Ave Santa Monica CA 90404-3574

WHALLON, WILLIAM, humanities educator; b. Richmond, Ind., Sept. 24, 1928; s. Arthur J. and Adelaide (Wheeler) Whallon; m. Joanne Holland; children: Andrew, Nicholas. BA, McGill U., 1950; PhD, Yale U., 1957. Prof. Mich. State U., East Lansing, 1963—. Author: Formula, Character, and Context, 1969, Problem and Spectacle, 1980, Inconsistencies, 1983, A Book of Time, 1990, The Oresteia/Apollo & Bacchus, 1997, The Jesus Rule, 2002. Home: 1655 Walnut Heights Dr East Lansing MI 48823-2943

WHAM, DAVID BUFFINGTON, secondary school educator; b. Evanston, Ill., May 25, 1937; s. Benjamin and Virginia (Buffington) W.; m. Joan Field Wilber, Mar. 9, 1968 (div. May, 1972); children: Benjamin, Rachel. AB cum laude, Harvard U., 1959; MA, So. Ill. U., Carbondale, 1967. Instr. U. Wyo., Powell, 1963-65, So. Ill. U., Carbondale, 1965-67; legis. asst. U.S. Congress, Washington, 1969-78; freelance writer Chgo., 1980-89; tchr. Chgo. Pub. Schs., 1994—. Speechwriter Adlai Stevenson for Gov. campaign, 1986, Dawn Netsch for Gov. campaign, 1994. Author: My Farewell to Bohemia, 1968, The Comic Genuflection, 1984, A Wave of Bright Boys, 1994. With U.S. Army, 1959-62. Recipient fiction award Columbia Pacific U., 1994. Mem. Harvard Club Chgo. (interviewer 1984—), Spee Club Harvard, Hasty Pudding Club Harvard. Democrat. Episcopalian. Home: 860 Hinman Ave # 724 Evanston IL 60202 Office: 125 S Clark St Chicago IL 60603-5200

WHAM, GEORGE SIMS, retired publishing executive; b. Laurens, S.C., Jan. 27, 1920; s. George Sims and Nellie (Melette) W.; m. Beth Keeler, Sept. 13, 1947; children— Norman Brent, Bonnie Beth, Barry Keeler. BS, Clemson U., 1941; MS, U. Tenn., 1947; PhD, Pa. State U., 1951. Textile technologist USDA, 1947-49; research assoc. Sch. Chemistry and Physics, Pa. State U., 1949-51; prof., asst. dean Tex. Women's U., 1951-54; sr. editor Good Housekeeping mag., N.Y.C., 1954-60, v.p., tech. dir., 1961-87; tech. cons., 1987-98. Disting. vis. prof. U. N.C., 1987-88; dir. R&D, Phillips Van Heusen, Inc., 1960-61; guest lectr. Purdue U., U. Md., Ariz. State U., U. Conn., U. Del., Clemson U., U. R.I., Mich. State U.; leader U.S. del. Internat. Standards Confs., 1968, 71, 86, 87. Contbr. articles to profl. jours. Pres. Governing Council, Hightstown, N.J., 1960-62; mem. Bd. Edn., Hightstown, 1959-61. Served to maj. AUS, 1941-46. Decorated Silver Star, Purple Heart. Mem. Am. Assn. Textile Chemists and Colorists (past pres., Harold C. Chapin award), Am. Nat. Standards Inst. (chmn. bd. dirs. 1986-88, chmn. textile standards bd. 1966-68, Howard Coonley medal 1985, George S. Wham Leadership medal 1990), Consumer Coun. (chmn. 1985), Sigma Xi, Phi Psi, Omicron Nu. Home: 19 Meadow Lakes 08 Hightstown NJ 08520-3313

WHAM, WILLIAM NEIL, publisher; b. N.Y.C., Dec. 28, 1934; s. William and Jessie (Neill) W.; m. Lynn McCorvie, Mar. 6, 1966; children: McCorvie, Avery. BS, Syracuse U., 1956. Salesman Mut. N.Y., N.Y.C., 1959-61; regional sales mgr. Doubleday Pub. Co., N.Y.C., 1961-64, Reinhold Pub. Co., N.Y.C., 1964-68; sales mgr. United Bus. Publs., N.Y.C., 1968; pres., pub. jours. Internat. Scientific Communications, Inc., Shelton, Conn., 1968—. Founder: sci. jours. Am. Lab., Internat. Lab., Am. Biotech. Lab., Am. Clin. Lab., Internat. Biotech. Lab., Am. Lab. News, European Clin. Lab., Internat. Lab. News, Am. Environ. Lab., Mng. The Modern Lab., UK Lab., Jour. of Capillary Electrophorisis and Microchip Tech. Served with AUS, 1956-58. Home: 157 Pinewood Trl Trumbull CT 06611-3312 Office: Internat Sci Communications Inc 30 Control Dr Shelton CT 06484-6111

WHANG, SUKOO JACK, pathologist, microbiologist; b. Seoul, South Korea, Feb. 3, 1934; arrived in U.S., 1963, naturalized; m. Chung A. Park, Nov. 30, 1963; children: Selena, Stephanie, John. BS, Oreg. State U., 1957; MS, UCLA, 1960, PhD, 1963; MD, Korea U., Seoul, 1972. Diplomate Am. Bd. Tropical Medicine, Am. Bd. Forensic Medicine, Am. Bd. Pathology, Am. Bd. Med. Microbiology. Intern Good Samaritan Hosp., Dayton, Ohio, 1973—74; resident White Meml. Med. Ctr., L.A., 1974—77, clin. pathologist, 1977—90, chmn. infection control com., 1977—87, dir. Sch. Med. Tech., 1977—87; dep. med. examiner L.A. County Coroner's Dept., L.A., 1991—2000; med. dir. Dimensions Med. Lab., Northridge, Calif., 1990—. Recipient Physician's Recognition award, AMA, 1980—. Fellow: ACP, Coll. Am. Pathologists (Pathology Continuing Med. Edn. award 1984—), Am. Coll. Forensic Medicine, Am. Coll. Tropical Medicine, Am. Soc. Clin. Pathologists. Republican. Seventh Day Adventist. Avocations: swimming, reading. Home: 1325 Via Del Rey South Pasadena CA 91030

WHANGER, PHILIP DANIEL, biochemistry educator and researcher, nutrition educator; b. Lewisburg, W.Va., Aug. 30, 1936; married, 1964; 2 children. BS, Berry Coll., 1959; MS, W.Va. U., 1961; PhD in Nutrition, N.C. State U., 1965. From asst. to assoc. prof. Oreg. State U., Corvallis, 1966-78, prof. nutrition & biochemistry, 1978—. Rsch. assoc. biochemistry Mich. State U., 1965-66; mem. assoc. staff Harvard Med. Sch., 1972-73; vis. scientist Gen. Acad. Exch. Svc., U. Tubingen, 1986, Commonwealth Sci. & Industry Rsch. Orgn., Wembley, Western Australia, Acad. Preventive Medicine, Beijing, 1988. Rsch. fellow NIH, 1966-67, Spl. fellow, 1972; Internat. fellow NSF, 1980-81; Rsch. grantee Oreg. State U., 1968—. Mem. Am. Inst. Nutrition, Am. Soc. Animal Sci., Internat. Bioinorg Scientists, Soc. Environ. Geochemistry and Health. Achievements include research in altered metabolic pathways under selenium deficiency, relationships of vitamin E and selenium in myopathies, biochemical properties of selenium and cadmium metalloproteins, metabolic pathways for incorporation of selenium into proteins, selenium and gluthathione peroxidise in human blood fractions, selenium deficiencies in primates, selenium intake on human blood and urine fractions. Office: Oreg State U Dept Agrl Chemistry Corvallis OR 97331

WHARAM, MOODY DEWITT, JR., physician, medical educator; b. Washington, July 22, 1941; s. Moody DeWitt Wharam Sr. and Ethyl May Wharam; m. Sheila Mairead Reese, June 22, 1968; children: Julia M., J. Franklin, Anne M. BA, Harvard U., 1963; MD, U. Va., 1969. Diplomate Am. Bd. Radiology. Intern in medicine and pediatrics Georgetown U. Med. Ctr., Washington, 1969-70; NIH fellow in radiation oncology U. Calif. Med. Ctr., San Francisco, 1970-73, resident, clin. instr., 1973-74; asst. prof. radiology Sch. Medicine Duke U., Durham, N.C., 1974-75; asst. prof. oncology and radiol. sci. Sch. Medicine Johns Hopkins U., Balt., 1975-80, assoc. prof. oncology, radiol. sci., pediatrics and neurosurgery, 1980-93, prof., 1993—. Acting dir. Radiol. Oncology divsn. Johns Hopkins Oncology Ctr., Balt., 1991—93, dir. Radiol. Oncology divsn., 1994—2000. Lt. (j.g.) USNR, 1963—65. Fellow: Am. Coll. Radiology; mem.: Internat. Soc. Pediat. Oncology, Am. Soc. Clin. Oncology, Am. Soc. Therapeutic Radiology and Oncology. Roman Catholic. Office: Johns Hopkins Hosp 401 N Broadway Rm 1460 Baltimore MD 21231-2410 Office Phone: 410-955-7312.

WHARTON, DANNY CARROLL, zoo biologist; b. Ontario, Oreg., Mar. 13, 1947; s. Carroll Curtis and Norma (Grigg) W.; m. Marilyn Christine Hoyt, Sept. 22, 1973; children: Amanda, Catherine, Margaret, Arcadio. BA in Psychology, Coll. Idaho, 1969; MA in Internat. Adminstrn., Sch. for Internat. Tng., 1975; PhD in Biology, Fordham U., 1990. Rsch. assoc. Foresta Inst., Carson City, Nev., 1973-74; curatorial asst. Woodland Park Zool. Garden, Seattle, 1974-79; asst. curator N.Y. Zool. Soc./The Wildlife Conservation Soc., Bronx, 1979-85; assoc. curator N.Y. Zool. Soc., Bronx, 1985-89, curator, 1989—; dir. Ctrl. Pk. Wildlife Ctr., N.Y.C., 1994—; adjunct sci. faculty Columbia U. Chmn. Internat. Advisors Internat. Snow Leopard Trust, Seattle, 1986; mem. US-USSR Environ. Agreement of U.S. Fish and Wildlife Svc., 1983. Contbr. articles to profl. jours.; editor Jour. Zoo Biology, 1996-98, exec. editor, 1998—. Vol. U.S. Peace Corps., Ecuador, 1969-71. Fulbright scholar, U. Münster, Fed. Republic Germany, 1976-77. Fellow Am. Assn. Zool. Parks and Aquariums (chmn. gorilla species survival plan 1992—, chmn. snow leopard species survival plan 1986—, co-chmn. marsupial and monotre,e taxon adv. group 1990-94; mem. Soc. for Conservation Biology, Internat. Union for Conservation of Nature/Species Survival Commn. (mem. captive breeding specialist group). Office: Wildlife Conservation Soc Ctrl Park Wildlife Ctr 830 5th Ave New York NY 10021-7001 E-mail: dwharton@wcs.org.

WHARTON, LENNARD, engineering company executive; b. Boston, Dec. 10, 1933; s. Nathaniel Philip and Deeda (Levine) W.; m. Judith R. Gordon, Dec. 26, 1957; children: Ruth, Rebecca, Nathaniel. BS in Chem. Engring, MIT, 1955; BA, MA, Cambridge U., 1957; A.M., Harvard U.; A.M. (NSF fellow 1957-60), 1960, PhD (Jr. fellow Soc. of Fellows 1960-63), 1963. Registered profl. engr., N.J., Ill. Prof. dept. chemistry U. Chgo., 1963-80; v.p. engring. ITE Imperial Corp., 1972-73; v.p. tech. Studebaker-Worthington, Barrington, Ill., 1978-79, McGraw Edison Co., Rolling Meadows, Ill., 1979-80, v.p. engring. and tech. Worthington group Mountainside, N.J., 1980-85; corp. v.p. tech. Material Research Corp., Pearl River, N.Y., 1985-87; v.p. Packer Engring. Inc., Naperville, Ill., 1987-95, chmn. bd., 1994-95; pres. Evidentia Engring. Inc., Short Hills, N.J., 1995—. Sloan fellow, 1964-66; named Outstanding Young Man of Chgo. Chgo. Jr. Assn. Commerce and Industry, 1968 Mem. IEEE (sr.), Nat. Fire Protection Assn., Am. Inst. Chem. Engrs. Office: 10 Park Pl Short Hills NJ 07078-2826

WHARTON, RALPH NATHANIEL, psychiatrist, educator; b. Boston, June 15, 1932; s. Nathaniel Philip and Deeda (Levine) W.; children: Naida, Philip, Laura. AB cum laude, Harvard U., 1953; MD, Columbia U., 1957, degree in psychoanalysis, 1970. Intern Cornell divsn. Bellevue Hosp., N.Y.C., NY, 1957—58; resident Columbia-Presbyn. Med. Ctr., 1961—64; pvt. practice psychiatry/pharm., 1964—; assoc. psychiatry Coll. Physicians and Surgeons, 1964—69, asst. prof. clin. psychiatry, 1969—72, assoc. prof., 1972—83, prof., 1984—; sr. rsch. psychiatrist N.Y. State Psychiat. Inst., 1964—70; assoc. attending psychiatry Columbia-Presbyn. Hosp., NY, 1970—. Ex-officio mem. bd. trustees Columbia-Presbyn. Med. Ctr., pres. soc. practitioners, 1980—82, attending, 1984—; exec. dir. Wharton Fund for Brain Rsch.; med. dir. Black Sea project Macalester Coll., 1994—98; co-dir. Ctr. for Behaviour and Psychosomatic Rsch. Columbia U. Med. Ctr., 2004—. Author: Landmark Papers, Lithium Carbonate for Affective Disorders, 1966; contbr. numerous papers and publs. in profl. jours. Mem. alumni coun. Coll. Physicians and Surgeons, Columbia U., 2001—. Served to capt. M.C., U.S. Army, 1958-61. Named one of Best Drs. N.Y. mag. Fellow: Am. Coll. Psychoanalysts (pres. 1996, bd. dirs. 1996—), Am. Psychiat. Assn., N.Y. Acad. Medicine; mem.: AMA (mem. legis. action com.), Internat. Assn. Study of Pain (founder), Royal Soc. Medicine, Soc. Biol. Psychiatry, Soc. Practitioners (exec. com. 1990—), Harmonie Club, Harvard Club (class agent 1953—), Salon de Virtuosi (founding bd. mem. 1991—, treas. 1991—), Lotos Club. Office: Columbia-Presbyn Med Ctr Atchley Pavilion Ste 209 161 Ft Washington Ave New York NY 10032-3713 also: 1070 Park Ave 1D New York NY 10128-1000 Office Phone: 212-860-2666. Business E-Mail: rnw1@columbia.edu.

WHARTON, THOMAS WILLIAM, medical products executive; b. St. Louis, Nov. 20, 1943; s. Thomas William and Elaine Margaret (Bassett) Wharton; children from previous marriage: Thomas William, Christopher John. BSc in Econs., U. Mo., 1967; M in Health Adminstrn., U. Ottawa, Ont., Can., 1978. Asst. to exec. dir. Ottawa Civic Hosp., 1978-80; exec. dir. Cariboo Meml. Hosp., Williams Lake, Canada, 1980-83; dir. clinic and rehab. services Workers' Compensation Bd., Vancouver, B.C., 1983-89; dir. Conquistador Gold Mines, Vancouver, 1989-98; pres. Diagnostic and Health Cons., Vancouver, 1989—; dir. Citrine Holdings, Ltd., Vancouver, Can., 1994-98; v.p. corp. devel. and med. affairs MTI Corp., Vancouver, Canada, 2000—. Bd. dirs. Moving Bytes Corp., Emeryville, Calif., Innexus Med. Corp, Vancouver. Named Lord of the Manors of Wharton and Kirkby Stephen, Eng., 1991; recipient Founder award, Cariboo Musical Soc., 1983. Avocations: music, art.

WHATLEY, JACQUELINE BELTRAM, lawyer; b. West Orange, NJ, Sept. 26, 1944; d. Quirino and Eliane (Gruet) Beltram; m. John W. Whatley, June 25, 1966 (dec. July 1998). BA, U. Tampa, 1966; JD, Stetson U., 1969. Bar: Fla. 1969, Alaska 1971; cert. real estate law splst. Assoc. Tucker, McEwen, Smith & Cofer, Tampa, Fla., 1969-71; pvt. practice Anchorage, Alaska, 1971-73; ptnr. Gibbons, Tucker, Miller, Whatley & Stein, P.A., Tampa, 1973—; pres., 1981—. Bd. dirs. Travelers Aid Soc., 1982-94; trustee Humana Women's Hosp., Tampa, 1987-93, Keystone United Meth. Ch., 1986-89, 99—. Mem. ABA, Fla. Bar Assn. (real estate cert. com. 1993-95), Alaska Bar Assn., Tenn. Walking Horse Breeders and Exhibitors Assn. (v.p. 1984-87, dir. Fla. 1981-87, 90-93, 97-99, adv. com. Tenn. Walking Horse Celebrateion 1994-97), Fla. Walking and Racking Horse Assn. (bd. dirs. 1988-89, pres. 1980-82), Athena Soc. Republican. Methodist. Home: PO Box 17595 Tampa FL 33682-7595 Office: 101 E Kennedy Blvd Ste 2190 Tampa FL 33602-5146 Office Phone: 813-228-7841. E-mail: whatley@gte.net.

WHATMORE, GEORGE BERNARD, physician, scientist, clinical neurophysiologist; b. Seattle, Aug. 31, 1917; s. Harry Joseph and Delia (Frolich) Whatmore; m. Frances Maxwell Beatty, May 28, 1942; children: Pamela Frances, David Blake, Nancy Janice. BS, U. Wash., 1940, MS, 1941; PhD, U. Chgo., 1946, MD, 1948. Intern King County Hosp., Seattle, 1948—49, resident, 1949—50, Lab. Clin. Physiology, Chgo., 1950—51; pvt. practice and rsch. in internal medicine, clin. neurophysiology, functional disorders Seattle, 1951—. Mem. staff Virginia Mason Hosp., Seattle, 1951—, Swedish Hosp., Seattle, 1951—, Med.-Dental Bldg. Hosp., Seattle, 1951—, Eastern State Hosp., Medical Lake, Wash., 1955—58; prin. investigator Pacific N.W. Rsch. Found. and Inst., Seattle, 1966—. Author (with Daniel R. Kohli): Dysponesis: A Neurophysiologic Factor in Functional Disorders, 1968, The Physiopathology and Treatment of Functional Disorders, 1974; author: A Scientist Looks at Religion, Based on Evidence Plus Logic, 3d edit., 2002, De-contaminating The New Testament, Based On Lessons Learned From The Galileo Scandal, 2004; contbr. articles to profl. jours. Recipient Ginsburg award, U. Chgo., 1946; Univ. fellow, 1941—45, Rawson fellow, 1945—46, Sheldon fellow, 1945—46. Mem.: AMA, AAAS (life), Western Acad. Beaux Arts, King County Med. Soc., Wash. State Med. Assn., Assn. for Applied Psychophysiology and Biofeedback, Acad. Psychosomatic Medicine, Behavior Therapy and Rsch. Soc., Biofeedback Rsch. Soc., Internat. Stress and Tension Control Assn., Am. Physicians Soc. for Physiologic Tension Control, NY Acad. Sci., Sigma Xi. Home and Office: 10524 SE 27th St Bellevue WA 98004-7231 Office Phone: 425-454-7273.

WHAYNE, THOMAS FRENCH, JR., cardiologist, educator; b. Ft. Leavenworth, Kans., Aug. 25, 1937; s. Thomas French and Mary Lutenia (Porter) W.; m. Eugenia McDonald Ingram, June 22, 1963; children: Thomas French III, James Givens, Katherine Ingram. AB in Chemistry, U. Pa., 1959, MD, 1963; PhD in Biochemistry, U. Calif., San Francisco, 1970. Intern in medicine The N.Y. Hosp., 1963-64, resident in medicine, 1964-66; fellow in cardiovascular disease Cardiovascular Rsch. Inst., San Francisco, 1966-69, U. Toronto, Ontario, Can., 1969-70; asst. prof. medicine Ohio State U., Columbus, 1970-72; assoc. prof. medicine U. Okla., Oklahoma City, 1972-77; clin. prof. medicine U. Ky., Lexington, 1977-98, prof. medicine cardiovascular medicine, 1998—. Assoc. mem. Okla. Med. Rsch. Found., 1972-77; staff cardiologist Lexington Clinic, 1977-98. Named man of yr, Okla. Heart Assn., 1975-76. Fellow ACP, Am. Coll. Cardiology, Am. Heart Assn., Coll. Physicians of Phila. Presbyterian. Avocations: spanish, golf, scuba diving, communications. Office: Divsn Cardiovascular Medicine 326 Wehington Bldg 900 S Limestone Lexington KY 40536-0200 Office Phone: 859-323-5479. E-mail: twhayn0@uky.edu.

WHEALEY, LOIS DEIMEL, humanities scholar; b. N.Y.C., June 20, 1932; d. Edgar Bertram Deimel and Lois Elizabeth (Hatch) Washburn; m. Robert Howard Whealey, July 2, 1954; children: Richard William, David John, Alice Ann. BA in History, Stanford U., 1951; MA in Edn., U. Mich., 1955; MA in Polit. Sci., Ohio U., 1975. Tchr. 5th grade Swayne Sch., Owyhee, Nev., 1952-53; tchr. 7th grade Ft. Knox (Ky.) Dependent's Sch., 1955-56; tchr. adult basic edn. USAF, Oxford, 1956-57; tchr. 6th grade Amerman Sch., Northville, Mich., 1957-58; tchr. 8th grade English, social studies Slauson Jr. High Sch., Ann Arbor, Mich., 1958-59; adminstrv. asst. humanities conf. Ohio U., Athens, 1974-76, 83. Part-time instr. Ohio U., Athens, 1966-68, 75, VISTA with Rural Action, 1996-98. Contbr. articles to profl. jours. Mem. Athens County Regional Planning Commn., 1974—78, treas., 1976—78; mem. Ohio coord. com. Internat. Women's Yr., 1977; v.p. Black Diamond Girl Scout Coun., 1980—86; chair New Day for Equal Rights Amendment, 1982; mem. Athens City Bd. Edn., 1984—90, v.p., 1984, pres., 1985; mem. Tri-County Vocat. Sch. Bd., Nelsonville, Ohio, 1984—90, v.p., 1988—89; mem. adv. com. Ohio River Valley Water Sanitation Commn., 1986—95; Ohio outreach liaison Nat. Town Meeting for Sustainable Am., 1999; bd. dirs. Ohio Environ. Coun., 1984—90, sec., 1986—90; bd. dirs. Ohio Alliance for Environ., 1994—98, v.p., 1998; bd. dirs. Organize Ohio, 1999—, bd. pres., 2001—; bd. dirs. Ohio Women, Inc., 1995—, sec., 1997—; bd. dirs. Unitarian Universalist Svc. Com., 2001—03, Ohio Meadville Dist. Unitarian-Universalist Assn., 1975—81; co-chair nat. vol. network Unitarian Universalist Svc. Com., 2003—. Recipient Unsung Unitarian Universalist award Ohio-Meadville Dist. Unitarian Universalist Assn., 1984, Thanks badge Black Diamond Girl Scout Coun., 1986, How-to award Ednl. Press Assn. Am., 1990, Donna Chen Women's Equity award Ohio U., 1994, Cmty. Svc. award Athens County Cmty. Svcs. Coun., 1998, award for an individual contbn. over a lifetime Ohio Alliance for Environment, 2002; named Woman of Achievement, Black Diamond Girl Scout Coun., 1987, Peacemaker Appalachian Peace and Justice Network, 1998, Outstanding Feminist, Athens Herstory Celebration, 2002. Mem. AAUW (pres. Athens br. 1969-70, 89-90, 93-2001, AAUW/Ohio bd. 1995-2004), LWV (pres. 1975-77), Phi Lambda Theta (life). Democrat. Avocations: classical music, genealogy. Home: 14 Oak St Athens OH 45701-2605

WHEALY, MICHAEL THOMAS, data processing company executive, lawyer; b. Sioux Falls, S.D., Apr. 29, 1952; s. Donald Stuart and Elaine Helen Whealy; m. Brenda L. Whealy, May 18, 1974; children: Andrew, Michael. BSChemE with highest honors, S.D. Sch. Mines & Tech., 1974; JD cum laude, Harvard U., 1977. Bar: Mass. 1977, Nebr. 1981, Ga. 1988. Asst. to gen. counsel Dept. Army, Washington, 1977-81; from assoc. to ptnr. Kutak Rock, Omaha, 1981-91; staff atty. First Data Corp., Omaha and Atlanta, 1991-97, gen. counsel Atlanta, 1998—, exec. v.p., chief adminstrv. officer, 1998—. Lt. col. USAR, 1974-96. Avocations: hunting, fishing, hiking. Office: First Data Corp 5660 New Northside Dr NW Atlanta GA 30328-5800 E-mail: mike.whealy@firstdatacorp.com.

WHEAT, BRENT DOUGLAS, music educator; s. Douglas Wheat; m. Donna Elaine Colburn, Sept. 18, 1976; children: Courtney Elizabeth, Gillian Alexandra. MusB, Ithaca Coll., 1972. Cert. tchr. NY. Jr. high band dir. Ithaca (NY) City Sch. Dist., 1972—73; h.s. band dir. Cairo-Durham Ctrl. Sch., Cairo, NY, 1973—82, Ravena (NY)-Coeymans-Selkirk Ctrl. Sch., 1982—. Mem.: NY State Alliance for Arts Edn., NY State Coun. Adminstr. Music Edn.; Percussive Arts Soc., Internat. Assn. Jazz Educators Assn., Internat. Trumpet Guild, NY State Band Directors Assn., NY State Sch. Music Assn., Music Educators Nat. Conf., Masons, Phi Mu Alpha. Republican. Avocations: investing, golf, reading, travel.

WHEAT, MYRON WILLIAM, JR., cardiothoracic surgeon; b. Sapulpa, Okla., Mar. 24, 1924; s. Myron William and Mary Lee (Hudiburg) W.; m. Erlene Adele Plank, June 12, 1949 (div. June 1970); children: Penelope Louise, Myron William III, Pamela Lynn, Douglas Plank; m. Carol Ann Karmgard, June 18, 1970 (div. Apr. 1996); 1 child, Christopher West. AB, Washington U., St. Louis, 1949; MD cum laude, Washington U., 1951. Diplomate Am. Bd. Surgery, Am. Bd. Thoracic Surgery. Instr., clin. fellow Washington U., St. Louis, 1956-58; asst. prof. surgery U. Fla., Gainesville, 1958-65, prof. surgery, 1965-72; dir. profl. svcs., chief clin. physician U. Fla. Shands Teaching Hosp., Gainesville, 1968-72; prof. surgery, dir. thoracic and cardiothoracic surgery U. Louisville Sch. Medicine, 1972-75; clin. prof. surgery U. Louisville Sch. of Medicine, 1975—; cardiothoracic surgeon Cardiac Surg. Assocs., P.A., St. Petersburg, Fla., 1975-91; cons., thoracic surgery Bay Pine VA Hosp., St. Petersburg, Fla., 1994—; clin. prof. surgery U. So. Fla. Sch. Medicine, Tampa, 1995—; cardiothoracic surgeon Cardiac Surg. Assocs., P.A., Clearwater, Fla., 1991—. Clin. prof. surger U. South Fla., 1995—; cons. Bay Pines VA Hosp., St. Petersburg, Fla., 1991—. Author (with others) 14 books; contbr. over 100 articles to profl. jours.; developed drug therapy for acute dissecting aneurysms of the aorta. 1st lt. USAF, 1943-46, ETO. Named First Howard W. Lillenthal Meml. lectr. Mt. Sinai Hosp., 1963; recipient DFC Air medal, Presdl. Citation. Fellow Am. Coll. Cardiology (chmn. bd. govs. 1968-69), Am. Coll. Surgeons (gov.); mem. Am. Surg. Assn., Am. Assn. for Thoracic Surgery, So. Surg. Assn., So. Thoracic Surg. Assn., Soc. Thoracic Surgeons, Soc. Thoracic Surgeons Great Britain and Ireland, Alpha Omega Alpha. Republican. Avocation: field trials-bird dogs. Home and Office: PO Box 136 Largo FL 33779-0136 Office Phone: 727-446-4637. E-mail: myronwheat@msn.com.

WHEAT, ROBERT E. museum director; b. Bogalusa, La. With Orleans Levy Dist., 1986—92; chief of police Dept. Culture Recreation and Tourism, Office of State Mus., 1992; dep. dir. La. State Mus., New Orleans, 1992—2004, interim dir., 2003—. Master sgt. USAF. Office: La State Mus 751 Chartres New Orleans LA 70116*

WHEATER, MICHELLE KURPAKUS, biologist, educator; b. Arcadia, Calif., June 8, 1959; d. Paul B. and Magdalene M. Kurpakus; m. Bryan David Wheater, Mar. 16, 1958; 1 child, Ryan David. BS, Ind. U. of Pa., 1982; PhD, Iowa State U., 1987. Postdoctoral fellow Med. Sch. Northwestern U., Chgo., 1987—91; assoc. prof. Sch. Medicine Wayne State U., Detroit, 1991—. Dir. of grad. recruitment Sch. of Medicine Wayne State U. Grantee, Nat. Eye Inst., NIH, 1989—96, 1999—2003. Mem.: Am. Soc. for Cell Biology, Assn. for Rsch. in Vision and Ophthalmology (Travel fellowship 1992). Avocation: travel. Office: Wayne State University School of Medicin 540 E Canfield Avenue Detroit MI 48201 E-mail: mkurpaku@med.wayne.edu.

WHEATLAND, RICHARD, II, fiduciary services executive, museum executive; b. Boston, Nov. 25, 1923; s. Stephen and Dorothy (Parker) W.; m. Cynthia McAdoo, Feb. 13, 1954; 1 child, Sarah Wheatland Fisher. AB, Harvard U., 1944, postgrad., 1946-47; JD, Columbia U., 1949. Various positions with Marshall Plan adminstrn. Office Spl. Rep. in Europe, Dept. State, Paris, 1950-53; v.p. N.Y. Airways, N.Y.C., 1953-68; pres. Acadia Mgmt. Co., Inc., Boston, 1968-93, chmn., 1993—. Bd. dirs., v.p. Pingree Assocs., Bangor, Maine. Mem. Mayor's Com. Insl. Leaders for Youth, N.Y.C., 1963-66; mem. corp. New Eng. Forestry Found.; mem., former chmn. Fund for Preservation of Wild Life and Natural Areas, Boston, 1980-92, bd. dirs. 1980-91; trustee Penobscot Marine Mus., Searsport, Maine, 1968-90, hon. trustee, 1990—.; bd. dirs. Friends of Pub. Garden, Boston, 1972-89, 90-96, 97—, Beacon Hill Civic Assn., Boston, 1985-89, Boston Natural Areas Fund, 1987—, asst. treas., 1993-94, treas. 1994-96, bd. dirs. 1997, acting chair, 1997—; treas. Frank Hatch for Gov. com., Boston, 1977-78; chmn., bd. trustees & overseers Peabody Essex Mus. (formerly Peabody Mus. of Salem), Salem, Mass., 1992—, trustee, 1972-92, pres., 1983-92. Lt. (j.g.) USN, 1943-46, PTO. Mem. Am. Assn. Mus. (bd. dirs. trustee com. 1976-86, govt. affairs com. 1985-89), Mus. Trustee Assn. (founder, bd. dirs. 1986—, sec. 1986-92), City Club Corp. (former bd. mgrs., former treas.). Avocations: jogging, sailing, travel. Office: Acadia Mgmt Co Inc 31 Milk St Ste 1104 Boston MA 02109-5129

WHEATLEY, CHARLES HENRY, III, education and technology company executive, lawyer; b. Balt., Aug. 11, 1932; s. Charles Henry Jr. and Rebecca W. (Cloud) Wheatley; m. Charlotte Beryl Davis, June 11, 1955; children: Charles H. IV, Craig A., Cheryl L.W. Wilhelm. BA in Polit. Sci.(hon.), Western Md. Coll., 1954; JD (hon.), U. Md., 1959. Bar: Md. 1960, DC 1981, US Supreme Ct. 1964. Tchr. Carroll County Pub. Sch., Westminster, Md., 1955-56; officer, missiles, judge adv. U.S. Army, 1957-62; law clk. assoc. judge William R. Horney Md. Ct. Appeals, Annapolis, 1959-60; pvt. practice Md. and Washington, 1960—; mem. Md. Ho. of Del., Annapolis, Md., 1962-66; pres., COO, advisor corp. rels., dir. Cell Works, Inc., Balt., 1997—2002. SOI Assoc.,real estate, ins. exec. AID Realty & Ins. Co., Balt., 1960—; adj. coll. instr. Western Md. Coll., Westminster, 1963-65, Villa Julie Coll., 1980-86, Balt. Cmty. Coll., 1966-72; mem. adv. bd. Balt. C.C., 1986—; chmn. bd., CEO Regional Mfg. Inst., Balt., 1993-96; nat. del. White House Conf. on Small Bus., Washington, 1985; pres. Fish Am., Inc., 1990—, Replex, Inc., 1986—, Life, Inc., 1994—; spkr. in field. Contbr., editor: (weekly newspaper) Maryland Teacher, 1974-77; guest News Makers program WJZ-TV, 1985; contbr. articles to profl. jours. Md. del. Md. State Constitutional Convention, Annapolis, 1967-68; councilman Balt. City Coun., 1971-74. 1st lt. Missile Brigade, JAG US Army, 1957-62. Received Cell Works Co. Computerworld-Smithsonian Science Innovation laureate award, 1999. Mem.: Md. State Tchrs. Assn. (exec. sec. 1974—77), Supreme Ct. Bar, Dist. Columbia Bar Assn., Md. State Bar Assn., Md. Commn. Mfg. Competitiveness, Order of Coif, Pi Gamma Mu. Methodist. Avocations: education, music, writing, photography, health. Office: 707 Wheatley Dr Westminster MD 21157

WHEATLEY, GEORGE MILHOLLAND, medical administrator; b. Balt., Mar. 21, 1909; s. William Francis and Teresa Genevieve (Milholland) W.; m. Eleanor Dodge, June 28, 1933 (dec. June 1969); children: George Milholland, Jr., Mary Ellen Rausch, Sarah Grinnell Nichols, William Bradford; m. Virginia Connelly Garling, Feb. 21, 1970 (dec. 1997); m. Lady Lorna Doone Snow, Sept. 6, 1997 (dec. Nov. 1998). BS, Cath. U., 1929; MD, Harvard U., 1933; MPH, Columbia U., 1942. Diplomate Am. Bd. Pediatrics, Am. Bd. Preventive Medicine. Intern Hartford Hosp., Conn., 1933-35; house officer pediatrics Johns Hopkins Hosp., Balt., 1935-36; rsch. fellow N.Y. Post. Grad. Hosp., N.Y.C., 1936-37; prin. pediatrician Health Dept., N.Y.C., 1937-40; asst. med. dir. Met. Life Ins. Co., N.Y.C., 1940-45, asst. v.p., 1945-69, v.p., chief med. dir., 1969-74; med. dir. Dept. Social Svcs., Hauppauge, N.Y., 1974-95; ret., 1995. Founder, 1st chmn. com. for joint action with Am. Coll. Surgeons, Assn. Surgery of Trauma, and Nat. Safety Coun.; 1st chmn. accident prevention com. Am. Acad. Pediatrics. Author: Health Observation of School Children, 3d edit., 1965; contbr. articles to profl. jours. Bd. dirs. Med. Alert Found. Internat., Calif., 1974-84. Recipient Disting. Svc. award Am. Heart Assn., 1968. Fellow Am. Acad. Pediatrics (pres. 1960-61, trustee Partnership for Child Health 1987—, Clifford Grulee award 1964, Injury and Poison Prevention award 1993); mem. Union League Club, Piping Rock Club. Avocations: civil war history, water-color painting. E-mail: georgewheatley@aol.com.

WHEATLEY, JOSEPH KEVIN, physician, urologist; b. N.Y.C., Jan. 5, 1946; s. Patrick Owen and Catherine (Malloy) W.; m. Anne Johanna Foody, Aug. 22, 1970; children: Joseph, Thomas. BSChemE, Manhattan Coll., 1967; MSChemE, U. Del., 1969; MD, N.J. U. of Medicine, 1974. Diplomate Am. Bd. Urology. Rsch. engr. NASA, Houston, 1965, 66, Exxon, Florham Park, N.J., 1968-69; urology resident Emory Univ., Atlanta, 1975-79, assoc. prof. urology, 1979—; clin. urology practice Urology Assocs., Atlanta, 1986—; chief of urology Kennestone Hosp., Marietta, Ga., 1990-93. Medicare care cons. Ga. Found. med. Care, Atlanta, 1982—; tchr. Atlanta VA Med. Ctr., Atlanta, 1979—; mem. hosp. exec. com. Kennestone Hosp., Marietta, 1990-93. Contbr. chpts. to books and articles to profl. jours. Active various Rep. actitives, 1992—. Named Top Drs. in Atlanta Atlanta Mag., 1995-96. Fellow ACS; mem. AMA, Urol. Assn., Urodynamics Soc., Am. Fertility Soc., Soc. of Reproductive Surgeons, Lithotripsy Soc. Roman Catholic. Avocations: skiing, hiking, biking trips, tennis, computers. Home: 692 N Saint Marys Ln NW Marietta GA 30064-1454 Office: Urology Assocs 55 Whitcher St NE Ste 250 Marietta GA 30060-1169 Office Phone: 770-428-4475. Personal E-mail: jkwheatley2000@comcast.net.

WHEATLEY, KATHERINE HOLBROOK, federal official; AB, Harvard, 1976, JD, 1979. Asst. gen. counsel Fed Res. Bd., Washington. Office: Fed Res Bd 20th And C Sts NW Washington DC 20551-0001

WHEATLEY, MELVIN ERNEST, JR., retired bishop; b. Lewisville, Pa., May 7, 1915; s. Melvin Ernest and Gertrude Elizabeth (Mitchell) W.; m. Lucile Elizabeth Maris, June 15, 1939; children: Paul Melvin, James Maris, John Sherwood (dec.). AB magna cum laude, Am. U., 1936, DD, 1958; BD

summa cum laude, Drew U., 1939; DD, U. of Pacific, 1948. Ordained to ministry Meth. Ch., 1939. Pastor area Meth. ch., Lincoln, Del., 1939-41; assoc. pastor First Meth. Ch., Fresno, Calif., 1941-43; pastor Centenary Meth. Ch., Modesto, Calif., 1943-46, Cen. Meth. Ch., Stockton, Calif., 1946-54, Westwood Meth. Ch., L.A., 1954-72; bishop Denver Area, 1972-84; ret., 1984. Instr. philosophy Modesto Jr. Coll., 1944; summer session instr. Hebrew-Christian heritage U. of Pacific; instr. Homiletics U. So. Calif., So. Calif. Sch. Theology, Clarement; lectr. St. Luke's Lectures, Houston, 1966; mem. Bd. of Ch. and Soc., Commn. on Status and Role of Women, United Meth. Ch., 1976-84; condr. European Christian Heritage tour, 1961, Alaska and Hawaii Missions, 1952, 54, Israel in behalf of Stockton Jewish Congregation, 1951. Author: Going His Way, 1957, Our Man and the Church, 1968, The Power of Worship, 1970, Family Ministries Manual, 1970, Christmas Is for Celebrating, 1977; contbr. articles to profl. jours. Chmn. Community Rels. Conf. So. Calif., 1966-69; pres. So. Calif.-Ariz. Conf. Bd. Edn., 1960-68; hon. trustee Iliff Sch. Theology; hon. dir., active mem. Parents and Friends of Lesbians and Gays, 1980—. Recipient Disting. Alumnus award Am. U., 1979, Ball award Meth. Fedn. Social Action, 1984, Prophetic Leadership award The Consultation on Homosexuality, Tolerance and Roman Cath. Theology, 1985, Human Rights award Universal Fellowship of Met. Community Congregations, 1985, award for social justice Calif.-Pacific Meth. Fedn. for Social Action, 2000, Lifetime Achievement award Denver Parents, Families and Friends of Lesbians and Gays, 2000, Outstanding Svc. award Parents Reconciling Network, 2000. Home: 859 Ronda Mendoza Unit A Laguna Hills CA 92653-5940 E-mail: lmwheatley@webtv.net.

WHEATLEY, STEVEN CHARLES, educational association administrator; b. Washington, D.C., July 19, 1952; s. Charles Howard Wheatley and Elisabeth Mary Hamilton; m. Linda-Marie Delloff, Oct. 23, 1982. BA, Columbia U., 1974; MA, U. Chgo., 1975, PhD, 1982. Asst. to dean, divsn. social scis. U. Chgo., 1982—84, dean of students, com. on pub. policy, 1984—86; dir., Am. Studies program Am. Coun. Learned Socs., N.Y.C., 1986—94, program dir., 1994—98, dir. programs, 1998—2000, v.p., 2000—. Mem. governing coun. Rockefeller Archive Ctr., Pocantico Hills, NY, 1997—. Author: Politics of Philanthropy, 1988; co-editor: Constitutionalism and Democracy, 1993. Mem.: Am. Studies Assn., Orgn. Am. Historians. Home: 387 Park Slope Mountainside NJ 07092 Office: Am Coun Learned Socs 633 Third Ave New York NY 10017

WHEATLEY, WILLIAM ARTHUR, architect, musician; b. Knoxville, Tenn., Sept. 23, 1944; s. Arthur Cornwallis and Inda Mary (Benway) W.; m. Celeste Ann George, Mar. 25, 1970 (div.); children: Charles Arthur, James Harris Giddings; m. Rosaria Giovanna Cilia, June 10, 1995. Student, Rice U., 1962-66; BA, U. St. Thomas, 1972. Registered architect, Pa., Md., N.J. Design draftsman W.W. Alexander, Houston, 1966-70; chief prodn. W.W. Scarborough, Houston, 1970—72; project arch. Ronald H. Waldie & Assocs., Houston, 1972-74; pres. Wheatley & Assocs., Inc., Houston, 1974-81; project arch. Brooks Assn., Houston, 1977—79; mgr. design Stone Bldg. Systems, Inc., Houston, 1979-81; project arch. Bechtel, Houston, 1981—84; prin. Wheatley & Assocs., Houston, 1984-87; project mgr. STV/Sanders & Thomas, Pottstown, Pa., 1987-88, MDC Sys. Divsn. Day & Zimmermann Internat., Inc., Phila., 1988-97; prin., exec. v.p. MDC Sys., Inc., 1997-2000; chmn. MDC Sys. UK Ltd., Aberdeen, Scotland, 1999—2001; pres. Wheatley US Ltd., Bala Cynwyd, Pa., 2000—; chmn. Wheatley UK Ltd., London, 2002—; mem., mng. dir. ICS Group LLC, 2003—. Composer piano solos, chorales, oratorio and cantata, 1961—; contbr. articles to profl. jours. Del. Tex. Rep. Convs., 1980, 82, 84; bd. dirs. Found. for Anglican Cath. Tradition. Mem. AIA, ABA (assoc.), AAAS, Am. Coll. Forensic Examiners, Royal Archtl. Inst. of Can., Am. Arbitration Assn., Pa. Soc. Architects, Am. Assn. for Advancement of Sci., Internat. Code Coun., The Mastersingers (bd. dirs. 1989-92, treas. 1990-91), Archeol. Inst. Am., Choral Soc. Montgomery County (bd. dirs. 1990-96, pres.1992-95). Anglican. Avocations: writing music, poetry and fiction, drawing, painting, sculpture. Office: Wheatley US Ltd Two Bala Plz Ste 300 Bala Cynwyd PA 19004-1501 also: Wheatley UK Ltd II Thistle Pl Aberdeen AB10 1UZ Scotland Office Phone: 610-658-0579.

WHEATON, DAVID, professional tennis player; b. Mpls., Minn., June 2, 1969; s. Bruce and Mary Jane W. Student, Stanford U. 9th in USTA rankings, 1992, 95; 210th in USTA rankings, 1999. Host David Wheaton Show, KKMS-AM, Mpls.; bd. dir. US Tennis Assn. U.S. Jr. Titles: Open Jr. Singles, 1987, 19 Clay Singles, 1987, 18 Natl. Doubles (with Jeff Tarango) 1987, 18 Hard Court Doubles (with Tarango) 1985; Career Pro Tour Singles Titles, 1990, U.S. Clay Courts, 1991, Grand Slam Cup, 1994, Newport. Office: US Tennis Assn 70 W Red Oak Ln White Plains NY 10604-3602*

WHEATON, DOUGLAS B. lawyer; b. Milw., July 21, 1972; s. Frank and Doreen Wheaton. BS in criminal justice, Carroll Coll., 1994; JD, Marquette U. Law Sch., 1998; MA in polit. sci., Marquette U. Grad. Sch., 1999; attended program of inst. for law, Harvard Law Sch., 2000. Bar: Wis. 1998, US Ct. of Appeals, 7th Circuit, US Dist. Ct., Ea. Dist. Wis., US Dist. Ct., Western Dist. Wis. Jud. intern Milw. County Circuit Ct., 1996; Congl. intern US Congress, Wash., 1996; atty. Bailey Law Office, LLC, Milw., 1999; leg. asst. Wis. State Senate, Madison, 1999—2002; govt. affairs dir. Wis. Realtors Assn., Madison, 2002—. Mem., bd. of vis. Ave Maria Sch. of Law, Ann Arbor, Mich., 2000—; alumni career asst. network Marquette U. Law Sch., Milw., 2004—. Contbr. articles various profl. jours. Bd. of elders St. Paul's Ch., Franklin, Wis., 2002—. Recipient CALI Excellence for the Future award, Ctr. for Computer Assisted Legal Instr., 1997, Outstanding Svc. award, Kenosha Realtors Assn., 2003. Mem.: Acad. of Polit. Sci., Racine County Bar Assn., Seventh Cir. Bar Assn., Marquette U. Alumni Assn., Am. Enterprise Inst., Am. Polit. Sci. Assn., Federalist Soc. Achievements include first to law student to ever complete grad. studies at Marquette U. Aspin Ctr. for Govt., Wash. DC, 1996. Avocations: travel, reader of fgn. affairs. Office: Wis Realtors Assn 4830 Indian Hills Dr 204 Racine WI 53406 Office Phone: 262-633-9085, 262-633-9085. Office Fax: 262-633-3687. Business E-Mail: dwheaton@wi.rr.com.

WHEATON, M. GENE, investigator, consultant; b. Pawnee, Okla., May 19, 1935; s. Bert Albert Wheaton and Ruth Savannah Bartlett; m. Theresa Joyce Bryant, Nov. 23, 1956; children: Gary B., Denise M., Anita L. BS in Law Enforcement, U. Nebr., Omaha, 1969; MA in Pub. Adminstrn., Webster U., 1975. Cert. polygraph examiner U.S. Army Polygraph Sch., Farsi linguist Def. Lang. Inst., bd. cert. police comdr. Internat. Assn. Chiefs of Police. Police officer Tulsa (Okla.) Police Dept., 1957—58; spl. agt. Office Spl. Investigations USAF, 1958—66; spl. agt. Criminal Investigations Divsn. U.S. Army, 1966—75; dep. dir. Pub. Safety Dept., Kish Island, Iran, 1976—77; exec. asst. to v.p. Rockwell Internat., Tehran, Iran, 1977—79; v.p. Nat. Airlines, Calif., 1985—86, 1985—86. Police/counter-terrorism advisor to Shah of Iran, 1971—73, 1975—79; mem. adv. bd. Nat. Security Inst., Framingham, Mass., 1986—93; cons. in field, 1986—. Mem. exec. bd. Homeowners Assn., Winchester, Calif., 2000. Sgt. USMC, 1953—56, chief warrant officer U.S. Army, 1966—75. Decorated Bronze star U.S. Army, Vietnam, Legion of Merit U.S. Army, Iran, Meritorious Svc. medal U.S. Army. Mem.: VFW (life; former vice comdr.), CID Agts. Assn., Alpha Kappa Delta. Avocations: swimming, shooting, exercising.

WHEATON, MARILYN, music educator, pianist, organist; b. Warren, Ohio, Feb. 1, 1933; d. Russell and Donabelle Irene Donehue; m. Warren Randall Wheaton, June 20, 1953; 1 child, Janean Renee Vaupel-Wilson. BS in Music Edn. cum laude, Kent State U., 1955. Cert. Yamaha music instr. Pvt. piano and organ tchr., Ohio and Ariz., 1950—; profl. pianist, organist, accompanist, 1946—; elem. music supr. Austintown Pub. Schs., Youngstown, Ohio, 1955-61. Founder, dir. Potter's Clay Christian singing group, Phoenix, 1981-85; choir dir., organist, pianist at various chs., Ohio and Ariz., 1942—; rep. for elem. music texts and programs Mahoning County Schs., Youngstown, 1959-60; tchr., organizer student trips to numerous concerts; tchr., dir. choirs and soloists for dist. and state competitions, 1955—. Composer (poems to music) Seven Last Words of Christ, also anthems, introits, reponses; arranges music for beginning and handicapped students. Dir., accompanist Terry's Variety Show, Austintown, 1951, Potter's Clay, 1980-85. Kent State U. and Youngstown U. scholar, 1951-55. Mem. Music Tchrs. Nat. Assn., Delta Omicron (life, charter mem., pres. Delta Upsilon chpt.). Avocations: travel, camping, reading, walking. Home and Office: 3245 W Yucca St Phoenix AZ 85029-4133

WHEDON, GEORGE DONALD, medical administrator, researcher; b. Geneva, N.Y., July 4, 1915; s. George Dunton and Elizabeth (Crockett) W.; m. Margaret Brunssen, May 12, 1942 (dic. Sept. 1982); children: Karen Anne, David Marshall. AB, Hobart Coll., 1936, ScD (hon.), 1967; MD, U. Rochester, 1941, ScD (hon.), 1978. Diplomate Am. Bd. Internal Medicine, Am. Bd. Nutrition. Intern in medicine Mary Imogene Bassett Hosp., Cooperstown, N.Y., 1941-42; asst. in medicine U. Rochester Sch. Medicine; also asst. resident physician medicine Strong Meml. Hosp., Rochester, 1942-44; instr. medicine Cornell U. Med. Coll., 1944-50, asst. prof. medicine, 1950-52; chief metabolic diseases br. Nat. Inst. Arthritis, Diabetes, Digestive and Kidney Diseases, NIH, Bethesda, Md., 1952-65, asst. dir., 1956-62, dir., 1962-81, sr. sci. adv., 1981-82; sr. assoc., dir. conf. program Kroc Found., Santa Ynez, Calif., 1982-84; adj. prof. medicine (endocrinology) UCLA Sch. Medicine, 1982-84; dir. med. rsch. programs Shriners Hosps. for Crippled Children, Tampa, 1984-91. Mem. subcom. on calcium, com. dietary allowances Food and Nutrition Bd., NRC, 1959-64; cons. to office manned space flight NASA, 1963-78, chmn. Am. Inst. Biol. Scis. med. program adv. panel to, 1971-75, chmn. NASA life scis. com., 1974-78, mem. space program adv. coun., NASA, 1974-78; cons. on endocrinology and metabolism adv. com. Bur. Drugs, FDA, 1977-82; mem. subcommn. on gravitational biology Com. on Space Rsch., Internat. Union Physiol. Scis., 1979-85; mem. rsch. adv. bd. Shriners Hosps., 1981-84; mem. subcom. spacecraft maximum allowable concentrations, com. toxicology, bd. on environ. studies and toxicology Commn. on Life Scis. NRC, 1989-99; cons. in medicine Wadsworth Gen. Hosp. VA Ctr., L.A., 1982-84; mem. U.S. Del. of U.S.-Japan Coop. Med. Sci. Program, 1984-93; mem. Internat. Soc. Gravitational and Space Physiol., 1991—. Mem. editorial bd. Jour. Clin. Endocrinology and Metabolism, 1960-67; adv. editor Calcified Tissue Rsch., 1967-76; contbr. articles to profl. publs. Mem. med. alumni coun. Sch. Medicine, mem. trustees' coun. U. Rochester, 1971-76, vice chmn. trustees' coun., 1973-74, chmn., 1974-75; trustee Dermatology Found., 1978-82; bd. dirs. Osteogenesis Imperfecta Found., 1991-97, med. adv. coun., 1993-96. Recipient Superior Svc. award USPHS, 1967, Alumni citation U. Rochester, 1971, Alumni citation Hobart Coll., 1986, Hobart Medal of Excellence, 1998, Exceptional Sci. Achievement medal NASA, 1974, NASA award of Merit, 1996. Fellow Royal Soc. Medicine; mem. AAAS, Am. Fedn. Med. Rsch., Assn. Am. Physicians, Aerospace Med. Assn. (Arnold D. Tuttle Meml. award 1978), Internat. Bone and Mineral Soc., Md. Acad. Scis. (sci. coun. 1964-70, 81-82), Endocrine Soc. (Robert H. Williams Disting. Leadership award in endocrinology 1982, Ayerst award 1974), Am. Physiol. Soc., Am. Inst. Nutrition, Am. Acad. Orthopaedic Surgeons (hon.), Am. Soc. Bone and Mineral Rsch., Orthopaedic Rsch. Soc., Am. Soc. Gravitational/Space Biology (Founders award 1994), Internat. Soc. Gravitational Physiology, Theta Delta Chi. Episcopalian. Home: 880 Mandalay Ave Apt N1014 Clearwater FL 33767-1257

WHEDON, RALPH GIBBS, manufacturing executive; b. Elizabeth, N.J., Aug. 10, 1949; s. Ralph Gibbs and Jane (MacMaster) W.; m. Lorna Jean Neebe, June 3, 1972; children: Deborah, David. Student, Clarkson Coll., 1968-70; BS, St. Lawrence U., 1972; student, Rensselaer Polytech. Inst., 1978; MBA, De Paul U., 1985. CPA, Ohio. Credit rep. Internat. Harvester Credit Corp., Albany, N.Y., 1972-75, ops. supr., 1975-79; mgr. export ops. Internat. Harvester Co., Chgo., 1979-86; treas. Pettibone Corp., Des Plaines, Ill., 1986-91; mgr. cash resources Bailey Controls Co., Wickliffe, Ohio, 1991-95, acting dir. treas., 1992-95, mgr. adminstrn., 1993-95; dir. MIS HMI Industries, Cleve., 1995-97; project mgr. Unum Am., Portland, Maine, 1997-98; mgr. Unum Provident, 1998—2003; CFO ProActivHealth, 2002—; info. sys. audit mgr. U. Maine System, 2004—. Sec. Tube Form, 1995-97; sec. Bliss Mgg., 1995-97; sec. Newton Falls Holding Co., 1995-97. Bd. dirs. Naperville (Ill.) Cmty. Chorus, 1985-87; trop leader Boy scouts Am., Naperville, 1985-91; mem. adv. coun. United Way, 1993-95; mem. adv. coun. Cleve. Treas. Club, 1992-97, bd. dirs., 1994-96; pres. Brightwood Lakes Assn., 1996-97; treas. S.J.E.C. Found., 1996-97. Episcopalian. Avocations: sailing, flying. Home: 82 Curtis Rd Portland ME 04103-2924 also: 7 Fairwind Way Ellsworth ME 04605-2935

WHEELAN, BELLE S. educational association administrator; 1 child, Reginald. BA in Psychology and Sociology, Trinity U.; MA in Devel./Ednl. Psychology, La. State U.; D in Ednl. Adminstrn., U. Tex., 1984. Asst. prof. psychology, dir. devel. edn., dir. acad. support svcs. San Antonio Coll., 1974—87; dean student svcs. Thomas Nelson C.C., Hampton, Va., 1987—89; provost Tidewater C.C., Portsmouth, Va., 1989—92; pres. Ctrl. Va. C.C., 1992, No. Va. C.C., 1998—2001; sec. of edn. Commonwealth of Va., Richmond, 2002—. Mem. Jobs for Va. Grads. Bd., Am. Coll. Testing Bd., Nat. Commn. on NAEP 12th Grade Assessment and Reporting, 2003—. Recipient Outstanding Alumnus award, Trinity U., 2002, Strong Men and Women award, 2003. Mem.: Nat. Coun. on Black Am. Affairs (mem. pres. roundtable). Office: Sec of Edn Ninth St Office Bldg 5th Fl 202 N 9th St Richmond VA 23219 also: PO Box 1475 Richmond VA 23218 Office Phone: 804-786-1151. E-mail: belle.whelan@governor.virginia.gov.

WHEELAN, R(ICHELIEU) E(DWARD), lawyer; b. N.Y.C., July 10, 1945; s. Richard Fairfax and Margaret (Murray) W. BS, Springfield (Mass.) Coll., 1967; MS, Iona Coll., 1977; JD, Pace U., 1981. Bar: N.Y. 1982, Minn. 1983, Colo. 1989, Tex. 1990, U.S. Dist. Ct. (no dist.) Calif. 1982, (so. dist.) Tex. 1991, U.S. Internat. Trade 1982, U.S. Ct. Appeals (2d cir.) 1982, (9th cir.) 1983, (5th cir.) 1993, U.S. Supreme Ct. 1994, U.S. Tax Ct. 1998, U.S. Dist. Ct. (no. dist.) Tex. 2003, U.S. Dist. Ct. (ea. dist.) Tex. 2004; bd. cert. criminal law, trial advocacy. Lt. of detectives White Plains (N.Y.) Police Dept., 1969-81; area counsel IBM, Armonk, N.Y., 1981-89; gen. counsel Kroll Assocs. (Asia), Hong Kong, 1989-91; pvt. practice, Houston, 1991—. Abogado consultor Mex. Consulate. Mem.: ABA (mem. sentencing guidelines com.), Tex. Assn. Criminal Def. Lawyers, Pro Bono Coll. State Bar Tex., New York County Lawyers Assn., N.Y. State Bar Assn., Coll. of State Bar Tex., Nat. Assn. Criminal Def. Lawyers (life; mem. death penalty com., Champion adv. bd.). Office: 440 Louisiana St Houston TX 77002-1639 Office Phone: 713-225-1300. E-mail: defensecounsel@houston.rr.com.

WHEELER, ALBIN GRAY, retired military officer, retail executive, educator; b. Huntington, W.Va., Mar. 16, 1935; s. Harvey Gray and Hattie Benson (Weddle) W.; m. Beatrice Thomas, May 17, 1958; children: Dianne, Michelle, Patrice. BA, Marshall U., 1958; MBA, Pepperdine U., 1975; student, Army War Coll., 1976, Harvard U., 1990; DHL (hon.), Marshall U., 2004. Enlisted U.S. Army, 1952, commd. 2d lt., 1959, advanced through grades to maj. gen., 1982; comdr. divsn. spt. command, chief of staff 1st Inf. Divsn., Ft. Riley, Kans., 1978-80; dep. comdr. U.S. Army Logistics Ctr., Ft. Lee, Va., 1980-81; chief exec. officer Army AF Exch. Svc.-Europe, Munich, 1981-83; comdr. 2d Spt. Command, VII U.S. Corps, Germany, 1983-85; pres. Indsl. Coll. Armed Forces, Washington, 1985-89; dir. human resources Army Materiel Command, Washington, 1989-91; CEO Army and Air Force Exch. Svc., Dallas, 1991-93; ret. U.S. Army, 1993; exec. dir. Arent Fox Kitner Plotkin & Kahn, Washington, 1993-96. Bd. dirs. Yeager Scholars, Marshall U., 1986—; pres. bd. advisors Army Quartermaster Found.; bd. dirs. Army Distaff Found. Decorated Def. and Army D.S.M., Bronze Star with two oak leaf clusters, Legion of Merit with two oak leaf clusters; inducted into Army Quartermaster Hall of Fame, 1999. Mem. Marshall U. Alumni Assn. (disting. alumnus 1983).

WHEELER, BARBARA MONICA, lawyer; b. Chgo., Mar. 20, 1947; d. John Benjamin and Elizabeth (Keife) Wheeler. BA, St. Dominic Coll., 1969; cert. Lewis U. Sch. Paraprofl. Studies, 1976; JD, DePaul U., 1980. Bar: Ill. 1980. Gen. supt. Md. Manor Devel. Co., Chgo., 1970-74; v.p. Omega Constrn. Co., Chgo., 1974-78; asst. state's atty. Cook County, Ill. Mem. Bd. Edn., Community High Sch. Dist. 99, DuPage County, 1974-76, pres., 1976—; mem. Ill. Assn. Sch. Bds., dir.-at-large Tri County div., 1976-77, dir. DuPage div., 1977-78, state dir., 1982-83, v.p., 1985-87, mem. exec. com., 1984-87; bd. dirs. Sch. Mgmt. Found. Ill., 1983; mem. task force on purposes of edn. in eighties Nat. Sch. Bds. Assn. Mem. ABA, Ill. Bar Assn., Chgo. Bar Assn., Am. Mgmt. Assn., Phi Alpha Delta. Roman Catholic. Office: Nat Bd Professional Teaching Standards 1525 Wilson Blvd Ste 500 Arlington VA 22209-3276

WHEELER, BURTON M. literature educator, higher education consultant, college dean; b. Mullins, S.C., Mar. 12, 1927; s. Paul and Elizabeth (Cleveland) W.; m. Jacquelyn Mulkey, Aug. 20, 1950; children— Paul, Geoffrey, Kristin AB, U. S.C., 1948, MA, 1951; PhD, Harvard U., 1961. Teaching fellow Harvard U., Cambridge, Mass., 1953-56; mem. faculty Washington U., St. Louis, 1956-96, prof., 1974-96; prof. emeritus, 1996—; dean Coll. Arts and Scis. Washington U., St. Louis, 1966-78, interim dean univ. librs., 1988-89. Cons., panelist Danforth Found., St. Louis, 1958-82; mem. GPEP panel Assn. Am. Med. Colls., Washington, 1981-84; cons.-evaluator North Cen. Assn., Chgo. Author: Close to Me, But Far Away, 2001; contbr. articles to profl. jours. Mem. spkrs. bur. Alzheimers Assn. Eli Lilly Found. fellow, 1965-66 Mem. Alzheimer's Assn., Phi Beta Kappa (senator 1992-2004, chmn. qualifications com., chmn. com. on chpts.). E-mail: bwheeler@artsci.wustl.edu.

WHEELER, C. HERBERT, architect, consultant, educator; b. Merchantville, N.J., June 6, 1915; s. Clarence Herbert and Louise Emma (Pennell) W.; m. Cicely Pointer, Aug. 29, 1940; children: Pamela, Janet, Betsy. BArch, U. Pa., 1937; MArch, MIT, 1940, postgrad., 1953, 56, Alexander Hamilton Inst., 1947. Registered architect N.Y., N.J., Pa., Mich.; cert. Nat. Council Archtl. Registration Bds. Archtl. designer Austin Co., N.Y.C., 1938-41; from architect to chief architect J.G. White Engring. Co., N.Y.C., 1941-55; mgr. engring. Stran Steel Corp., Detroit, 1955-58; mgr. environ. sys. Curtiss-Wright Corp., Quehanna, Pa., 1958-64; prof. archtl. engring. Pa. State U., University Park, 1964-80, prof. emeritus, 1980—. Author: Public Organizations and Public Architecture, 1987; co-author: Emerging Techniques of Architectural Practice, 1966, Emerging Techniques of Architectural Programming, 1969. Served to maj. C.E., U.S. Army, 1942-46. Decorated Commendation Ribbon U.S. Army CE, 1945. Fellow AIA (emeritus, internat. relations com. 1981-84, v.p. Central Pa. chtp. 1984), Union Internat. des Architects Paris (permanent sec. profl. devel. work group 1980-85, coll. dels. 1981-85), mem. Am. Soc. Engring. Edn. (emeritus, chmn. archtl. engring. div. 1970), constrn. Specifications Inst., Ret. Officers Assn., Theta Xi (v.p. St. Louis 1953-54). Republican. Episcopalian/Methodist. Avocations: travel, precanceled stamp collecting, geography, literature. Home: 638 Franklin St State College PA 16803-3459 Office: PA State U 104 Engring A Unit University Park PA 16802

WHEELER, CATHY JO, federal agency administrator; b. Birmingham, Ala., Feb. 14, 1954; d. Charles Edwin and Hazel Josephine Wheeler; m. David Arthur Tate, 1994. BA, U. Montevallo, 1975; postgrad., U. Ala., 1982-84. With Social Security Adminstrn., Birmingham, 1975—, sr. employment devel. specialist, 1983-85, mgr. tech. tng. dept., 1985-91, mgmt. analyst, 1991—2000, staff advisor to asst. regional commr. Process Ctr. Ops., 2000-01, fin mgmt specialist, 2001—. V.p. Fed. Women's Program, Birmingham, 1984—85; treas., charter mem. Federally Employed Women, Birmingham, 1984—88. Mem. Art Alumni Adv. Bd., 1997—2001, v.p., 1998—2000; bd. dirs. U. Montevallo Found., 2002—. Mem.: ASTD (treas. 1987—88, pres. elect 1989, pres. 1990, asst. regional dir. 1991—92), Ala. Designer-Craftsmen, Soc. Govt. Meeting Planners (v.p. 1989—90, sec. 1990—91), U. Montevallo Nat. Alumni Assn. (bd. dirs. 1991—94, v.p. fin. 1994—98, pres.-elect 1998—2000, pres. 2000—02, parliamentarian 2002—04), Riverchase Women's Club, Jaycees (v.p. mgmt. devel. Hoover Ala. chpt. 1988—89), Chi Omega Alumni Assn. (treas. 1991, advisor 1991—). Avocations: photography, reading, travel. Home: 4001 Fairchase Ln Birmingham AL 35244-1300 Office: Social Security Adminstrn 2001 12th Ave N Birmingham AL 35285 Personal E-mail: cathyjowheeler@bellsouth.net.

WHEELER, CHRIS D. investment company executive; Degree in applied physics with honors, Calif. Inst. Tech., 1978; MBA, Harvard U., 1980. Various positions including group mng. ptnr. Trammell Crow Residential, 1982-98; sr. v.p. strategic initiatives Gables Residential Trust, Atlanta, 1998-99, pres., CEO, 1999—. Office: Gables Residential Trust 2859 Paces Ferry Rd SE Ste 1450 Atlanta GA 30339-5716*

WHEELER, CLAYTON EUGENE, JR., dermatologist, educator; b. Viroqua, Wis., June 30, 1917; s. Clayton Eugene and Vesta Beulah (Heal) W.; m. Susie Brooks Overton, Oct. 11, 1952; children: Susan Brooks, Margaret Ann, Elizabeth Clayton. BA, U. Wis., 1938, MD, 1941. Diplomate Am. Bd. Internal Medicine, Am. Bd. Dermatology (dir. 1970-79, vice pres. 1977-78, pres. 1978-79). Intern Cin. Gen. Hosp., 1941-42; resident in internal medicine U. Mich. Hosps., 1942-44, research fellow endocrinology and metabolism, 1947-48, resident in dermatology, 1948-51; from asst. prof. to prof. dermatology U. Va. Med. Sch., 1951-62; prof. dermatology U. N.C. Med. Sch., Chapel Hill, 1962—, chmn. div., 1962-72, chmn. dept., 1972-87, chmn., exec. com. Med. Faculty Practice Plan, 1986-90. Cutaneous commn. Armed Forces Epidemiol. Bd., 1961-72; dermatology tng. grants com. NIAMD, 1963-67, residency rev. com. dermatology, 1973-79, chair, 1975-79; chair task force ednl. programs faculty Nat. Program Dermatology, 1969-74; trustee Dermatology Found., 1975-79. Author: Practical Dermatology, 3d edit, 1967, also articles. Served to maj. M.C. AUS, 1944-47. Recipient U. N.C. Med. Alumni Disting. faculty award, 1986, Disting. Svc. award U. N.C. Med. Alumni, 1997; honored with establishment of Clayton E. Wheeler Jr. Professorship of Dermatology position, 1991, recipient David Martin Carter Mentorship Award, 2002. Mem. Soc. Investigative Dermatology (bd. dirs. 1970-73, pres. 1974-75, Rothman award 1979, hon. mem. 1993), Assn. Profs. Dermatology (bd. dirs. 1969-71, 76-79, sec.-treas. 1971-74, pres. 1975-76), Am. Dermatol. Assn. (pres. 1982-83, hon. mem. 1997), Am. Acad. Dermatology (past dir., pres.-elect 1983-84, pres. 1984-85, past pres. 1985-86, hon. mem. 1988, masters in dermatology 1993, Gold medal 1993), Am. Skin Assn. (David Martin Carter award 2002), Phi Beta Kappa, Alpha Omega Alpha. Methodist. Home: 2120 N Lakeshore Dr Chapel Hill NC 27514-2027 Office: U NC Cb # 7287 Chapel Hill NC 27599-0001 E-mail: spryor@med.unc.edu.

WHEELER, DANIEL SCOTT, management executive, editor; b. Richmond, Virginia, Apr. 23, 1947; s. Arthur Bruce Jr. and Lavinia (Akers) W.; m. Kathy E. (Wheeler); children: Matthew, Beth Marie, Jennifer Lynne, Brandy, and Jennifer Ann. Attended, Va. Commonwealth U., 1966-69, Butler U., 1981, Ind. U., 1984-85. Spl. agt. Northwestern Mut. Life, Richmond, 1969-71; enlisted U.S. Navy, 1971, resigned, 1979; editor Am. Legion Mag., Indpls., 1979-85, pub., editor-in-chief, 1985-95; exec. dir. The Am. Legion, Indpls., 1995—; pub., editor in chief The Am. Legion Mag., Indpls., 2003—. Bd. dir. HPC/PM Direct. Pres. Citizen's Flag Alliance, Inc. Mem. Am. Legion, Mensa. Republican. Avocation: painting. Home: 4518 Fairhope Dr Indianapolis IN 46237-2951 Office: Am Legion PO Box 1055 Indianapolis IN 46206-1055

WHEELER, DAVID LAURIE, university dean; b. Saginaw, Mich., July 30, 1934; s. Clayton Final and Blanche Beatrice (Hunt) W.; m. Jane Louise Manchester, Sept. 6, 1958; children: Elizabeth, Anne. AB, U. Mich., 1956, AM, 1958, PhD, 1962. Asst. dean student service Ill. State U., Normal, 1967-68, assoc. dean, 1968-69, assoc. dean grad. sch., 1969-72; dean grad. sch. West Tex. State U., Canyon, 1972-79, Ball State U., Muncie, Ind., 1979-96, dean emeritus, 1996—. Cons. McGraw-Hill Pub. Co., N.Y.C., Van Nostrand Reinhold Pub. Co., N.Y.C. Editor: The Human Habitat: Contemporary Readings, 1971. Woodrow Wilson fellow, 1961; recipient Commdrs. Pub. Svc. award Dept. of Army, 1996. Mem. Assn. Am. Geographers, Nat. Coun. Univ. Rsch. Adminstrs., Western History Assn., Tex. State Hist. Assn., U.S. Army War Coll. Found., Rotary, Sigma Xi, Phi Kappa Phi, Kappa Sigma. Republican. Presbyterian. E-mail: wheeler2@onlinecol.com.

WHEELER, DENNIS EARL, mining company executive, lawyer; b. Wallace, Idaho, Dec. 17, 1942; s. Earl L. and Virginia (Rice) W.; m. Jacquline Rae, May 16, 1971; children: Michelle, Maura, Wendy, Brad. BS in Bus., U. Idaho, 1965, JD, 1967. Bar: Idaho 1967. Ptnr. Hull, Hull & Wheeler, Wallace, 1967-78; sr. v.p., gen. counsel Coeur d'Alene (Idaho) Mines Corp., 1978-80, pres., 1980-86, CEO, 1986—, chmn., 1992—. Bd. dirs. Sierra Pacific Resources; vice chmn., dir. Ctr. for Democracy; dir. World Gold Coun.,

Geneva, 1994—. Pres. Idaho Bd. Edn., 1984-87; founder Jobs Plus, Coeur d'Alene, 1987—; bd. dirs. Ctr. for Democracy, Washington, 1992—, Children's Village, Coeur d'Alene, 1994—, Wildlife Habitat Enhancement Coun., Silver Spring, Md., 1992—, Idaho chpt. Nature Conservancy, Sun Valley, Idaho, 1992—; mem. exec. bd. Boy Scouts Am., Coeur d'Alene, 1994—,=. Recipient Environ. Conservation Disting. Svc. award Soc. for Mining, Metallurgy and Exploration, 1993. Mem. ABA, Idaho Bar Assn., Silver Inst. (pres. 1992-94), Am. Mining Congress (chmn. western bd. govs. 1993—), Elks, Sigma Chi (Significant Sig award 1992). Avocations: fishing, skiing, boating. Office: Coeur D'Alene Mines Corp PO Box 1 Coeur D Alene ID 83816-0316

WHEELER, DIANA D. educational consultant; b. Athol, Mass., July 12, 1959; d. Donald Francis and Lorraine Doris Bachelder; 1 child, Nicholas Henry. MusB in Edn., Anna Maria Coll., Paxton, Mass., 1983; MEd, Worcester State Coll., 1999. Cert. tchr. Mass., 1983, credit union devel. educator. Music supr./tchr. Petersham Ctr. Sch., Mass., 1987—95; music tchr. St. Josephs Elem. Sch., Fitchburg, Mass., 1993—95; childrens svc. ch. pianist Starrett Meth. Ch., Athol, Mass., 1994—2002; promotions mgr. Wal*Mart, Orange, Mass., 1995—98; youth svcs. coord. GFA Fed. Credit Union, Gardner, Mass., 1997—2001; ch. pianist Unitarian Ch., Athol, Mass., 1999—2001; edn. specialist Digital Fed. Credit Union, Marlborough, Mass., 2001—. N.E. regional coord. Nat. Youth Involvement Bd., 1998—, treas., 1999—2002, sec., 2002—, fin. literacy com. chmn., 2002—; bd. mem. Mass. Credit Union League Youth Involvement Com., Southborough, 2001—. Contbr. articles to profl. jours. Recipient Leading Classroom Presenter award, Nat. Youth Involvement Bd., 1998, 1999, 2000, Outstanding Vol. award, Jr. Achievement, 2002, All Star Vol. award, 2004. Mem.: Sch. Bus. Com. C. of C. (assoc.). Avocation: Boy Scouts. Home: 627 Pleasant St Athol MA 01331 Office: Digital Fed Credit Union 220 Donald Lynch Blvd Marlborough MA 01752 Office Phone: 800-328-8797 9429. Business E-Mail: dwheeler@dcu.org.

WHEELER, DOLORES, food products executive; married. Pres., CEO Gossner Foods, Logan, Utah. Bd. dir. Bus. and Econ. Delvel., Logan, Utah. Office: Gossner Foods 1051 N 1000 W Logan UT 84321-6852 Fax: 435-752-3147.

WHEELER, DOUGLAS LANPHIER, history educator, writer; b. St. Louis, July 19, 1937; s. Russell Charles and Lucille (Wengler) W.; m. Katherine Wells Wheeler; children: Katherine Gladney, Lucille Lanphier. AB in History, Dartmouth Coll., 1959; MA in History, Boston U., 1960, PhD in History, 1963; postgrad., Lisbon U. (Portugal), 1961-62. Vis. asst. prof. Morgan State Coll., Balt., 1965; from asst. prof. to prof. U. N.H., Durham, 1965—2002, chair dept. history, 1971-74, Prince Henry the Navigator prof. of Portuguese History and the Discoveries, 1995—2002, prof. history emeritus, 2002—. Vis. asst. prof. U. Coll. Rhodesia, Salisbury, Richard Welch Meml. fellow in Advanced Rsch. Intelligence, Harvard U., Cambridge, 1984-85. Author: Republican Portugal, 1978, Ditadura Militar Portuguesa, 1988, Historical Dictionary of Portugal, 1993, 2d edit., 2002; co-author: Angola, 1971; co-editor: In Search of Modern Portugal, 1983; editor Portuguese Studies Newsletter, 1976-91, Portuguese Studies Rev., 1991—; bd. editors European Studies Quarterly, 1983—; mem. editorial bd. Mediterranean Studies. Moderator Community Ch. of Durham, 1983-84, com. mem. 1969—; bd. mem. Mill Pond Ctr., Arts Ctr. Durham, 1982-98, Theatre by the Sea, Portsmouth, N.H., 1981-85; dir. N.H. Coun. World Affairs, Durham, 1974—. 1st Lt. USAR, 1963-65. Decorated grand officer Order of Prince Henry The Navigator (Portugal), 1993, Order of Liberty (Portugal), 2004; Fulbright grantee, Fulbright Commn., U. Lisbon, 1961-62, Fulbright Hays Faculty Rsch., U.S. Govt., 1969-70, Gulbenkian Found., Lisbon, 1972—; recipient Cert. Achievement, U.S. Army Intelligence Sch., Md., 1965. Mem. Internat. Conf. Group on Portugal (coord. 1978—), Soc. for Spanish and Portuguese Hist. Studies (gen. sec. 1981-84), Nat. Mil. Intelligence Assn., Assn. Former Intelligence Officers, Nat. Intelligence Studies Ctr. Democrat. Avocations: reading, travel abroad, tennis, amateur theatricals, playwriting. Home: 27 Mill Rd Durham NH 03824-3006 Personal E-mail: DougWheeler2@aol.com.

WHEELER, DOUGLAS PAUL, conservationist, government official, lawyer; b. Bklyn., Jan. 10, 1942; s. Robert S. and Lottie (Neubauer) W.; m. Heather A. Campbell, Aug. 28, 1965; children— Clay Campbell, Christopher Campbell. AB in Govt. with honors, Hamilton Coll., Clinton, N.Y., 1963; LLB, Duke U., 1966. Bar: N.C. 1966, D.C. 1999. Assoc. Levine, Goodman & Murchison, Charlotte, N.C., 1966-69; legis. atty. to asst. legis. counsel U.S. Dept. Interior, Washington, 1969-72, dep. asst. sec. Fish and Wildlife and Pks., 1972-77; exec. v.p. Nat. Trust for Hist. Preservation, Washington, 1977-80; pres. Am. Farmland Trust, Washington, 1980-85, now life mem.; exec. dir. Sierra Club, San Francisco, 1985-86; v.p. Conservation Found., Washington, 1986-88, exec. v.p., 1989-91; sec. for resources State of Calif., 1991-99; ptnr. Hogan & Hartson LLP, Washington, 1999—. Vis. lectr. Duke U. Sch. Law; mem. Trade and Econ. Adv. Coun.; U.S. Trade Rep. Hon. life mem. bd. visitors Duke U. Sch. of Law; chair bd. visitors Bren Sch. Environ. Mgmt., U. Calif., Santa Barbara, Tahoe-Baikal Inst.; candidate N.C. Ho. of Reps., 1968; mem. D.C. Rep. Ctrl. Com., 1984-85; chmn. Am. Farmland Trust; mem. adv. coun. The Conservation Fund; mem. biodiversity conservation working group N.Am. Commn. for Environ. Cooperation; chmn. adv. bd. Nat. Park Sys. Lt. JAGC, USNR, 1969-75. Recipient commendation U.S. Dept. Interior, 1976, Achievement award, 1980, Conservation award Gulf Oil Corp., 1985, Charles S. Murphy award for pub. svc, 1995, Presdl. award for sustainable devel., 1996, Nat. Conservation Leadership award The Conservation Fund, 1997. Mem. ABA, D.C. Bar Assn., N.C. Bar Assn., Sierra Club (life), Am. Farmland Trust (life). Episcopalian. Home: 4541 45th St NW Washington DC 20016-4473 E-mail: dpwheeler@hhlaw.com.

WHEELER, EDWARD NORWOOD, chemical consultant; b. Yancey, Tex., Oct. 11, 1927; s. Wilber Basel and Clara Clementine (Stafford) W.; m. Luella Jean Brossette, Nov. 21, 1950; children: Gordon A., Sterling R., Darrell S., Charlotte, Murray H. BS, Tex. A&I U., 1947, BSChemE, 1949; MA, U. Tex., 1951, PhD, 1953. Rsch. chemist Celanese Chem. Co., Corpus Christi, 1953-55, group leader, 1955-62, section mgr., 1962-67, dir. rsch., 1967-72, dir. devel., 1972-74, planning dir. N.Y.C., 1974-75, dir. rsch. devel. planning, 1975-76, v.p. rsch. devel. planning, 1976-79, v.p. rsch. & devel. Dallas, 1979-83; cons. and expert witness White and Case, Hong Kong and N.Y.C., 1986-91. Mem. adv. coun. U. Tex. Natural Sci. Found. Contbr. articles to profl. jours., patentee 14 inventions. Treas. Dallas Bethlehem Ctr., 1985-89; hon. life mem., mem. adv. coun. U. Tex. Coll. Natural Sci. Found.; bd. trustees Tex. A&M U.-Kingsville Found., 1994-98; pres. North Tex. Conf. Coun. on Fin. and Adminstrn., United Meth. Ch., 1992-96. Recipient Disting. Alumnus award Tex. A&I U., Kingsville, 1981. Mem. Am. Chem. Soc., Indsl. Rsch. Inst., Synthetic Organic Chem. Mfrs. Assn. (bd. govs. 1977-81), Littlefield Soc. U. Tex. Methodist. Avocations: gardening, genealogy, cooking. Home and Office: 9238 Moss Haven Dr Dallas TX 75231-1412

WHEELER, ELTON SAMUEL, financial executive; b. Salinas, Calif., Oct. 25, 1943; s. Luther Elton and Naomi E. (Beatty) W.; m. Moretha Jean Miller, June 17, 1995; children: Pamela Kathleen, Leslie Elizabeth-Anne, Deborah Suzanne, Jonathan Samuel. BS, Calif. State U., 1966. CPA, Calif. Acct. Pricewaterhouse Coopers, Oakland, Calif., 1967-70, Adams Properties, Inc., San Francisco, 1970-71, treas., 1972-75, v.p., CFO, 1976-77, Adams Capital Mgmt. Co., San Francisco, 1977-79, pres., CEO, 1979-87; pres., CEO, bd. dirs. Calif. Real Estate Investment Trust, 1980-88, Franklin Select Real Estate Income Trust, 1989-2000, Franklin Advantage Real Estate Income Trust, 1990-96. With USMCR, 1966-72. Mem. Nat. Assn. Real Estate Investment Trusts, Inc. (sec., treas., bd. govs. 1984-89), Am. Inst. CPAs, Calif. Soc. CPAs, United Way of Tuolumne-Calaveras Counties (pres., dir., treas. 1989-98), Rotary (Sonora, Calif., pres. 1994-95), Rotary Internat. (dist. 5220 dir. 1998-99, asst. gov. 2000-2001, dist. conf. chair 2001-2002). Home: 16399 Crestridge Ave Sonora CA 95370-8752 Office: PO Box 3718 Sonora CA 95370-3718 E-mail: swheeler@samwheelercpa.com.

WHEELER, FLOYD LARRY, education educator; b. Reagan County, Tex., Aug. 25, 1947; s. Floyd L and Rita Marie Wheeler; m. Pamela Sue Wilkerson, Aug. 2, 1969; children: Melissa Dawn, Andrew Lawrence. BA, Austin Coll., 1969; MABS, Dallas Theol. Sem., 1983. Commn. tech. USN, 1970—74; assoc. pastor Marsh Lane Bapt. Ch., Dallas, 1975—81; carpenter Calvin Justice Corp., Lewisville, Tex., 1981—84; instr. Wayland Bapt. U., Plainview, Tex., 1984—88; asst. prof. Hardin Simmons U., 1988—. Lighting/set design cons. First Bapt. Ch., Plainview, Tex., 1984—88, Elmcrest Bapt. Ch., Abilene, Tex., 1988—95, Pioneer Dr. Bapt. Ch., Abilene, 1995—, Abilene Opera Assn., Abilene, 1988—93. E-5 USN, 1970—74, Iceland, Spain. Recipient Cullen Tchg. award, Hardin Simmons U., 1995. Mem.: Am. Univ. Prof. Assn. Republican. Bapt. Office: Hardin Simmons U Box 14864 Abilene TX 79698 Office Phone: 325-670-1511.

WHEELER, FRANK KNOWLES BLASDELL, retired military officer, business consultant; b. Mpls., Oct. 29, 1912; s. Walter Hall and Eva Maude (Blasdell) W.; widowed, Oct. 1991; children: Mary Ann Wheeler Masher, Frances Blasdell Wheeler Kindle, Charles Knowles. BSME, U.S. Naval Acad., 1935, PhD (Equivalent) Electronics, 1944. Registered profl. engr., Calif. Commd. ensign USN, 1935, advanced through grades to capt., 1954; commdg. officer U.S.S. Kearney, 1944-46; mem. various fleets/electronics staffs USN, 1946-60, ret., 1960; mfg. mgr. Hewlett Packard Co., Palo Alto, Calif., 1960-70; co. mfg. mgr. Fairchild, Mountain View, Calif., 1970-72; pres., bus. cons. Wheeler & Assocs., Los Altos Hills, Calif., 1972—. Mem. IEEE. Republican. Presbyterian. Avocations: electronics, preparing historical video productions. Home and Office: 27174 Elena Rd Los Altos Hills CA 94022

WHEELER, GEORGE CHARLES, JR., materials and processes engineer; b. Balt., Oct. 9, 1923; s. George Charles and Julia Elizabeth (Watrous) W.; m. Dorothy W. Whittemore, Sept. 13, 1947; children: Scott, Craig, Mark, Matthew, Tracy, Bruce; m. Clare Frances Weiner, Jan. 21, 1978. BS in Metall. Engring., Lehigh U., 1944. Various engring. and supervisory positions GE, Mass. and N.Y., 1944-62; mgr. materials, welding and nondestructive test engring. Knolls Atomic Power Lab., G.E., Schenectady, N.Y., 1962-68; mgr. nondestructive testing G.E. Power Sys., Schenectady, N.Y., 1968-85; pres., CEO Wheeler Nondestructive Testing, Inc., Schenectady, 1985-95, Materials and Processes Cons., Schenectady, 1995—; mgr. tech. svcs. Am. Soc. for Nondestructive Testing, Columbus, Ohio, 1993-94. Cons. UN, N.Y.C., 1985-98, IAEA, Vienna, Austria, 1985-98, ASNT, 1997—, others; guest lectr. Rensselaer Poly. Inst., Troy, N.Y., Union Coll., Schenectady, 1978-87; mem. math. sci. and tech. com. Schenectady County C.C., 1978-85, adj. prof., 1987-97; U.S. del. Internat. Stds. Orgn., com. TC 135/SC7 NDT Pers. Qualification, 1987-97, convenor working group #2, ISO-9712; mem. ASNT Cert. Mgmt. Bd., 1994-98, chmn. 1976-80, 86-89. Author: Guide to Personnel Cert., 1990, rev. edit., 2003, Guide to Developing Certification Exams, 1992; Level II Study Guide: Radiographic Testing, 1998, Level II Study Guide: Ultrasonic Testing, 1999; contbg. editor JMaterials Evaluation, Jour. of ASNT; tech. editor Nondestructive Testing Handbook, 3d edit., vol. 3. Fellow Am. Soc. Nondestructive Testing (hon. life mem., bd. dirs. 1976-85, pres. 1983-84, chmn. 1984-85, chmn. cert. com. 1976-80, 86-89); mem. ASTM (com. internat. stds., com. nondestructive testing), NRA (life), Am. Soc. Metals (life), Nature Conservancy (life), Adirondack Mountain Club, Adirondack Forty-Sixers. Avocations: mountain climbing, flying, firearms, photography, cross country skiing, golf. Personal E-mail: geocharles@aol.com., sirbuzzard@bigfoot.com.

WHEELER, GERALDINE HARTSHORN, historian, writer; b. Pomona, Calif., Feb. 5, 1919; d. Albion True and Beatrice Osa (Barnes) Hartshorn; m. Lloyd Franklyn Wheeler, Dec. 2, 1938 (dec. Mar. 1996); children: Russell Lloyd, Robert Gerald. AA, Santa Barbara (Calif.) C.C., 1950's. Co-owner Atheling's, Santa Barbara, Calif., 1971-76, Pomona, 1976-90; chmn. bd. trustees Atheling Heritage Trust, Claremont, Calif., 1994—. Pub., editor: mag. Athling's, 1974—75, newsletter Grand Priory of America Order of St. Lazarus, 1974—86; editor: St. Margaret's Jour., 1975—; author: (essays) A World Full in 1891, 1975—, President John Adams - A Profile, 1975—, Ralph Waldo Emerson--A Profile, 1975, The Many Masks of Communism, 1975, A Tale of St. Nicholas, 1995, Post Cards and Postal Cards, 1996, Pocahontas Kinships, 1996. Vol. PTA, Fontana and Santa Barbara, 1945-60; active Hist. Soc. Pomona Valley, 1950—; mem. various coms. and choir First Congl. Ch., Santa Barbara, 1952-72; leader Cub Scouts Am., Santa Barbara, 1953-56; grey lady unit chmn. Santa Barbara chpt.-ARC, 1958-62; women's project bd. v.p., activities chmn., active various coms. Santa Barbara Hist. Soc., 1960-74; exec. sec. 1960 Nixon for Pres. Campaign, Santa Barbara, 1960; mem. spkrs. bur. Nixon for Gov. Campaign, Santa Barbara, 1962; mem. Rep. state ctrl. com. State of Calif., 1962-64; blitz chmn. Rockefeller for Pres. Campaign, Santa Barbara, 1964; coord. vol. svcs. Office of Civil Def., City of Santa Barbara, 1965-76; coord. tv series on earthquakes Sta. KEYT, Office of Civil Def., Santa Barbara, 1968; bd. dirs. Calif. Ctrl. Coast Area, U.S.O., 1968-76, treas. bd., 1970-76; supporter Vis. Nurses and Hospice Assn., 1994—; others. Decorated Dame of Grace, Mil. and Hospitaller Order of St. Lazarus of Jerusalem, Cert. of Merit, 1973, The Alan Weaver Hazelton award; recipient Cert. of Merit, Santa Barbara Jr. Coll., 1954-55, Medal of Appreciation SAR, 1972, Cert. of Award Nat. Soc. Daus. of Founders and Patriots of Am., 1977. Mem. Calif. Hist. Soc., New Eng. Hist. and Geneal. Soc., The Pomona Ebell (pres. 1998-2000), Wilson Ctr. Assocs., Smithsonian Assocs., Nat. Trust for Hist. Preservation, Am. Farmland Trust, Nat. Woman's History Mus., Nat. Mus. Women in the Arts, Nat. Arbor Day Found. Republican. Avocations: book collecting, reading, genealogy, classical music, needlecrafts. Home: 1047 E Baseline Rd Claremont CA 91711-1577

WHEELER, GRACE R. retired market researcher; b. Phila., May 17, 1927; d. Norman F.S. Russell and Ella Dewees Eisenbrey; m. Philip Price Sharples, Oct. 9, 1954 (div.); children: Martha Sharples Daniels, Grace Sharples Cooke, Russell Price Sharples; m. Alexander Bowman Wheeler, Aug. 16, 1980 (dec.). BA, Bennington Coll., 1948; MBA, Temple U., 1968. Rsch. analyst ARCO, Phila., 1948-51, Alderson & Sessions, Phila., 1951-54; owner Gen. Rsch. Assn., Bryn Mawr, Pa., 1974-88; ret., 1988. Contbr. (sch. history): ...better than riches..., 1989; author, editor exhibit catalog, 1976. Adv. bd., Montessori Genesis II, Phila., 1980—; founder Gladwyne (Pa.) Montessori Sch., 1960; mem. William Penn Charter Sch. Bd., 1973—, head of bd., 1975-85; mem. bd., Darby Creek Valley Assn., Drexel Hill, Pa., 1998—. Republican. Mem. Soc. Of Friends. Avocations: land stewardship, gardening. Home: 3824 Darby Rd Bryn Mawr PA 19010

WHEELER, HAROLD H. state legislator, utility contractor; b. Noble County, Ind., Sept. 4, 1929; m. Darlene Adamson; children: Johnna, Tara, Kim. Grad., N. Webster High Sch., 1947. Mem., trustee Etna-Troy Twp, 1963-70; mem. Columbia City Joint High Sch. Bd., 1964-70; commissioner Whitley County, 1973-76; mem. Ind. Senate from 17th dist., Indpls., 1983—; majority caucus chmn. govtl. affairs; pres., CEO M.C. Wheeler & Sons, Inc., Columbia City. Trustee Etna-Troy (Ind.) Twp., 1963-70; commr. Whitley County (Ind.), 1973-76; bd. dirs. Columbia City (Ind.) Joint High Sch., 1964-70, Whitley County Hosp., 1977-83; chmn. Appointments & Claims. Mem. Fraternal Order Elks, Fraternal Order Moose, Fraternal Order Eagles, Masons, Scottish Rite, Mizpah Shrine Methodist. Home: 6370 N State Road 5 Larwill IN 46764-9716 Office: Ind Senate Dist 17 200 W Washington St Indianapolis IN 46204-2728

WHEELER, HEWITT BROWNELL, surgeon, educator; b. Louisville, July 21, 1929; s. Arville and Lois (Vance) W.; m. Elizabeth Jane Maxwell, July 21, 1956; children: Stephen, Elizabeth, Jane, Mary. Student, Vanderbilt U., 1945-48; MD, Harvard U., 1952. Diplomate Am. Bd. Surgery (bd. dirs. 1984-90). Cushing fellow Harvard Med. Sch., Boston, 1953, Peters fellow, 1956, research fellow, 1959-60, instr. surgery, 1961-64, clin. assoc. surgery, 1964-67, asst. clin. prof. surgery, 1967-70, assoc. prof. surgery, 1970-71; asst. in surgery Peter Bent Brigham Hosp., Boston, 1959-60, jr. assoc. surgery, 1961-64, assoc. surgery, 1964-69, sr. assoc. surgery, 1969-71; asst. chief surgery Roxbury VA Hosp., Boston, 1961-62, chief surgery, 1962-71, chief of staff, 1968-71; cons. surgery U. Mass. Med. Sch., Worcester, 1966-71; prof., chmn. dept. surgery U. Mass. Med. Sch. at Worcester, 1971-96, Harry M. Haidak disting. prof. surgery, 1985-98, prof. emeritus, 1998—; chief staff U. Mass. Hosp., 1974-76, surgeon-in-chief, 1976-96; exec. dir. Ctr. for Advanced Clin. Tech., 1995—; affiliate prof. biomed. engring. Worcester Poly. Inst., 1974—; lectr. surgery Harvard Med. Sch., 1974-96; chief surgery St. Vincent Hosp., Worcester, 1971-75. Cons. Meml. Hosp., Worcester City Hosp., 1970-96, Worcester Hahnemann Hosp., 1974-94, Peter Bent Brigham Hosp., 1973-96; chmn. surg. research program com. VA, Washington, 1965-67, nat. participant surg. cons., 1965-69, chmn. ad hoc adv. com. surgery, 1969-71. Pres. Mass. Compassionate Care Coalition, 2000—; trustee Ctrl. Mass. Health Care Found., 1975—77, Worcester Found. for Biomed. Rsch., 1996—, Hospice Ctrl. Mass. Inc., 1997—2000, U. Mass. Meml. Found., 1998—, Boston Med. Libr., 1996—. 1st lt. M.C. AUS, 1953—55. Mem. ACS (bd. govs. 1984-90, coun. Mass. chpt. 1973-76, pres. 1980), AAAS, AMA, Am. Surg. Assn., Soc. Univ. Surgeons, Internat. Cardiovascular Soc., New Eng. Surg. Soc. (treas. 1977-84, v.p. 1986-87, pres. 1989-91), Boston Surg. Soc. (pres. 1995-96), Worcester Surg. Soc. (pres. 1973-75), Transplantation Soc., Mass. Med. Soc. (100th Shattuck lectr. 1990), Worcester Dist. Med. Soc. (sec. 1996-99, v.p. 1999-00, pres. 2000-01), New Eng. Vascular Soc. (v.p. 1985-86, pres. 1988-89). Achievements include rsch. in exptl. transplantation, blood vessel surgery, method to detect blood clots, improving end-of-life care. Home: 52 Cloyster Rd South Portland ME 04106-5110 E-mail: bwheele1@maine.rr.com.

WHEELER, HOYT NOLAND, finance educator; b. Ravenswood, W.Va., Jan. 21, 1937; s. Harold Lee and Virginia Laura Wheeler; m. Elizabeth Scrivener Scrivener, May 30, 1996; children: Jeffrey Smith, Jonathan Philip. BA cum laude, Marshall U., Huntington, W.Va., 1958; JD, U. of Va., 1961; PhD, U. of Wis., 1974. Bar: W.Va. 1961, Wyo. 1974. Assoc. Kay, Casto & Chaney, Charleston, W.Va., 1961—65, ptnr., 1966—70; instr. in bus. adminstrn. U. of Wyo., Laramie, 1973—74, asst. prof. of bus. adminstrn., 1974—76; assoc. prof. of indsl. rels. U. of Minn., Mpls., 1976—81; prof. of mgmt. U. S.C., Columbia, 1981—. Labor arbitrator, Columbia, SC, 1974—. Author: (scholarly book) Workplace Justice Without Unions, (scholarly/trade book) The Future of the American Labor Movement, (scholarly book) Workplace Justice: Employment Obligations in International Perspective, Workplace Justice Without Unions, Industrial Conflict: An Integrative Theory. Mem.: Internat. Indsl. Rels. Assn., Internat. Soc. for Labor Law and Social Security (exec. bd. 2003—04), Nat. Acad. of Arbitrators (chair, rsch. com. 2003—04), Indsl. Rels. Rsch. Assn. (pres. 1996—97). Episcopalian. Avocations: tennis, reading, swimming. Home: 109 Saluda View Ct West Columbia SC 29169 Office: Moore School of Bus University of South Carolina Columbia SC 29208 Office Phone: 803-777-5959. Office Fax: 803-777-6782. Business E-Mail: hwheeler@sc.edu.

WHEELER, JOHN ARCHIBALD, physicist, educator; b. Jacksonville, Fla., July 9, 1911; s. Joseph Lewis and Mabel (Archibald) Wheeler; m. Janette Hegner, June 10, 1935; children: Isabel Letitia Wheeler Ufford, James English, Alison Christie Wheeler Lahnston. PhD, Johns Hopkins U., 1933; ScD (hon.), Western Res. U., 1958, U. N.C., 1959, U. Pa., 1968, Middlebury Coll., 1969, Rutgers U., 1969, Yeshiva U., 1973, Yale U., 1974; PhD (hon.), U. Uppsala, 1975; ScD (hon.), U. Md., 1977, Gustavus Adolphus U., 1981, Cath. U. Am., 1982, U. Newcastle-upon-Tyne, 1983, Princeton U., 1986, U. Conn., 1989, U. Maine, 1992, Tufts U., 1992; LLD (hon.), Johns Hopkins U., 1977; LittD (hon.), Drexel U., 1987. NRC fellow, N.Y., Copenhagen, 1933—35; from asst. prof. to assoc. prof. physics U. N.C., 1935—38; asst. prof. physics Princeton U., 1938—42, assoc. prof., 1945—47, prof., 1947—76, Joseph Henry prof. physics, 1966—76, Joseph Henry prof. physics emeritus, 1976—; prof. physics and dir. Ctr. for Theoretical Physics, U. Tex., Austin, 1976—86; Ashbel Smith prof. U. Tex., Austin, 1979—86, Blumberg prof., 1981—86, Smith and Blumberg prof. emeritus, 1986—. Cons. and physicist on atomic energy projects Princeton U., 1939—42, U. Chgo., 1942, E.I. duPont de Nemours & C, Wilmington, Del., Richland, Wash., 1943—45, Los Alamos, 1950—53; dir. Project Matterhorn (H-bomb) Princeton U., 1951—53; Guggenheim fellow, Paris and Copenhagen, 1949—50; summer lectr. U. Mich., U. Chgo., Columbia U; Lorentz prof. U. Leiden, 1956; Fulbright prof. Kyoto U., 1962; vis. fellow Clare Coll., Cambridge U., 1964; Ritchie lectr. Edinburgh, 1958; vis. prof. U. Calif.-Berkeley, 1960; Battelle prof. U. Wash., 1975; I.I. Rabi vis. prof. Columbia U., 1983; sci. advisor U.S. Senate del. to 3d ann. conf. NATO Parliamentarians, Paris, 1957; mem. adv. com. Oak Ridge Nat. Lab., 1957—65, U. Calif., Los Alamos and Livermore, 1972—77; v.p. Internat. Union Physics, 1951—54; chmn. joint com. on history of theoretical physics in 20th century Am. Phys. Soc. and Am. Philos. Soc., 1960—72; sci. adv. bd. USAF, 1961—62; chmn. Dept. Def. Advanced Rsch. Projects Agy. Project 137 (now Project Jason), 1958; mem. U.S. Gen. Adv. Com. Arms Control and Disarmament, 1969—72, 1974—77. Author: Geometrodynamics, 1962; author: (with others) Gravitation Theory and Gravitational Collapse, 1965; author: Spacetime Physics, 1966; author: (with E. Taylor) Spacetime Physics, 2d edit., 1992; author: (in German) Einstein's Vision, 1968; author: (with C.W. Misner and K.S. Thorne) Gravitation, 1973; author: (with M. Rees and R. Ruffini) Black Holes, Gravitation Waves and Cosmology, 1974; author: Frontiers of Time, 1979, A Journey into Gravity and Spacetime, 1990, At Home in the Universe, 1994; author: (with I. Ciufolini) Gravitation and Inertia, 1995; author: also translations, 1991—92; author: (with Kenneth Ford) Geons, Black Holes and Quantum Foam: A Life in Physics, 1998; editor (with W. Zurek): Quantum Theory and Measurement, 1983; contbr. 375 articles to profl. jours. Trustee Battelle Meml. Inst., 1959—89, S.W. Rsch. Inst., San Antonio, 1977—92, Unitarian Ch., 1965. Recipient A. Cressy Morrison prize for work on nuc. physics, N.Y. Acad. Scis., 1947, Albert Einstein prize, Strauss Found., 1965, Enrico Fermi award, AEC, 1968, Franklin medal, Franklin Inst., 1969, Nat. medal of Sci., 1971, Herzfeld award, 1975, Outstanding Grad. Tchg. award, U. Tex., 1981, Niels Bohr Internat. Gold medal, 1982, Oersted medal, Am. Assn. Physics Tchrs., 1983, J. Robert Oppenheimer Meml. prize, 1984, Matteucci medal, Nat. Acad. Sci. Rome, Soc. of the Forty, 1994, Wolf Found. prize in Physics, Jerusalem, 1997. Fellow: AAAS (dir. 1965—68), Am. Phys. Soc. (pres. 1966, Einstein prize 2003); mem.: NAS, Royal Danish Acad. Scis., Royal Soc. (London), Accademia Nazionale dei Lincei, Internat. Union Physics (v.p. 1951—54), L'Academie Internationale de Philosophie des Sciences (v.p. 1987—90), Tex. Philos. Soc., Royal Acad. Sci. (Uppsala, Sweden), Philos. Soc. of Tex., Am. Philos. Soc. (councillor 1963—66, v.p. 1971—73, councillor 1976—79, Franklin medal 1989), Am. Acad. Arts and Scis., Internat. Astron. Union, Am. Math. Soc., Princeton Club (N.Y.C.), Century Assn. (N.Y.C.), Sigma Xi, Phi Beta Kappa. Unitarian Universalist. Office: Princeton U Dept Physics Princeton NJ 08544-0001 E-mail: jawheeler@pupgg.princeton.edu. *We will first understand how simple the universe is when we recognize how strange it is.*

WHEELER, JOHN CRAIG, astrophysicist, writer; b. Glendale, Calif., Apr. 5, 1943; s. G.L. and Peggy Wheeler; m. Hsueh Lie, Oct. 29, 1967; children: Diek Winters, J. Robinson. BS in Physics, MIT, 1965; PhD in Physics, U. Colo., 1969. Asst. prof. astronomy Harvard U., Cambridge, Mass., 1971-74; assoc. prof. U. Tex., Austin, 1974-80, prof., 1980—, Samuel T. and Fern Yanagisawa Regents prof. astronomy, 1985—, chmn. astronomy dept., 1986-90. Vis. fellow Joint Inst. Lab. Astrophysics, Boulder, Colo., 1978-79, Japan Soc. for Promotion of Sci., 1983; 1st vis. prof. Assn. Univs. for Rsch. in Astronomy, 1990; vis. sr. scientist Inst. for Theoretical Physics, U. Calif., Santa Barbara, 1997; gen. mem. Aspen (Colo.) Ctr. for Physics; mem. exec. com. Tex. Symposium on Relativistic Astrophysics; mem. NRC Space Studies Bd., 2002--, mem. com. on the origin and evolution of life, 2002--. Author: The Krone Experiment, 1986, Cosmic Catastrophes, 2000; editor: Accretion Disks in Compact Stellar Systems, 1993, Supernovae, 1990, Disk Instabilities in Close Binary Systems, 1999, Proceedings of the 20th Texas Symposium on Relativistic Astrophysics. Recipient awards U. Tex., 1984, 86, 99, Pres.'s Assocs. Tchg. Excellence award, 1999; Fulbright fellow, Italy, 1991; Dads Assn. Centennial Tchg. fellow U. Tex., 1999. Mem. Internat. Astron. Union, Am. Astron. Soc. (v.p. 1999-2002), Acad. Disting. Tchrs., Sigma Xi. Avocations: running, writing, reading. Office: U Tex Dept Astronomy Austin TX 78712

WHEELER, JOHN ERNEST, JR., oil company executive; b. Leonardtown, Md., Nov. 28, 1952; s. John Ernest and Margaret Louise (Johnson) W.; m. Catherine Maria McConville, Oct. 21, 1978; children: Justin, Christian. BA in Acctg., Loyola Coll., Balt., 1974, MBA in Fin., 1985. CPA, Md. Staff acct.

Ernst & Young, Balt., 1974-76; auditor Crown Cen. Petroleum, Balt., 1976-77, sr. auditor, 1977-78, acctg. mgr., 1978-79, div. contr., 1979-81, contr., 1981—, v.p., 1984—; treas. Crown Cen. Petroleum Corp., Balt., 1991-98, exec. v.p., CFO & treas., 1998—. Treas. Crown Cen. Polit. Action Com., 1985—; bd. dirs. Easter Seals of Md., 1989—. Mem. AICPA, Md. Assn. CPA's, Fin. Execs. Inst., KC. Roman Catholic. Office: Crown Cen Petroleum Corp One N Charles St Baltimore MD 21201-3740

WHEELER, JOHN HARVEY, political scientist, writer; b. Waco, Tex., Oct. 17, 1918; m. Norene Burleigh; children: David Carroll, John Harvey III, Mark Jefferson. BA, Ind. U., 1946, MA, 1947; PhD, Harvard U., 1950. Instr. dept. govt., asst. dir. Summer Sch., Harvard U., 1950; asst. prof. Johns Hopkins U., 1950-54; assoc. prof. Washington and Lee U., 1954-56, prof. polit. sci., 1956-60; fellow in residence Ctr. for Study Dem. Instns., 1960-69; program dir., 1970-75; chmn., pres. Inst. Higher Studies, Carpinteria, Calif., 1975—. Martha Boaz rsch. prof. in acad. info. systems U. So. Calif. Libr. Systems, 1986—, Martha Boaz disting. rsch. prof., 1987—; cons. Fund for Republic, 1958-61; adj. prof. New Sch., 1986—, ISIM, 1989—; founder, bd. dirs. The Virtual Acad., 1987; mem. faculty Western Behavioral Scis. Inst., 1990—; mem. BESTnet, Nat. Rsch. and Edn. Network; pres. C-Mode Inst., 1992—; bd. dirs. Silicon Beach Comm. Author: The Conservative Crisis, 1958, (with Eugene Burdick) Fail-Safe, 1962, repub., 1999 (film 1962) asst. exec. prodr., (TV re-make 2000), Democracy in a Revolutionary Era, 1968, The Politics of Revolution, 1971, The Virtual Library, 1987, The Virtual Society, 1988, 2d edit., 1992, Atlantoz 2005, 2002; editor, contbg. author: Beyond Punitive Society, 1973, Structure of Ancient Wisdom, 1983, Bioalgebra of Judgment, 1986, Fundamental Structures Human Reflexion, 1990; editor: (with George Boas) Lattimore, The Scholar, 1953; co-founder, joint chief editor: (with James Danielli) Jour. Social and Biol. Structures, 1973-95; joint editor Goethe's Science, 1986; developed computer-mediated "Freshman Academy", 1993; contbr. articles on constitutionalism and Francis Bacon to profl. jours. Keynote spkr. Subiaco Writing Festival, 2002. Served with AUS, 1941-46. Recipient Mouton Tor award, 2001. Office: Inst Higher Studies PO Box 704 Carpinteria CA 93014-0704 E-mail: verulan@mindspring.com.

WHEELER, JOHN OLIVER, geologist; b. Mussoorie, India, Dec. 19, 1924; s. Edward Oliver and Dorothea Sophie (Danielsen) W.; m. Nora Jean Hughes, May 17, 1952; children: Kathleen Anna Wheeler Hunter, Jennifer Margaret Wheeler Crompton. BASc in Geol. Engring., U. B.C., 1947, DSc (hon.), 2000; PhD in Geology, Columbia U., 1956. Geologist Geol. Survey Can., Ottawa, 1951-61, Vancouver, 1961-65, rsch. scientist, 1965-70, rsch. mgr. Ottawa, 1970—, chief regional and econ. geology divsn., 1970-73, dep. dir. gen., 1973-79; rsch. scientist Geol. Survey Can. (Cordilleran divsn.), Ottawa, 1979-90, rsch. scientist emeritus, 1990—. Gen. editor: Geology of Canada, 8 vols., 1989-98; compiler of regional geol. maps of we. Can., Can. and no. N.Am. and Greenland; contbr. articles to profl. jours. Recipient Queen's Silver Jubilee medal, 1977, Can. 125 medal, 1994, Earth Sci. Sector and Dept. awards Nat. Resources Can., 1996, Spl. award of B.C.-Yukon Chamber of Mines for outstanding contbn. to Can. Cordilleran geology, 2000, Massey medal Royal Can. Geog. Soc., 2002. Fellow Royal Soc. Can., Geol. Assn. Can. (pres. 1970-71, Logan medal 1983, Disting. fellow 1996), Geol. Soc. Am. (councillor 1971-74), Can. Geosci. Coun. (pres. 1981); mem. Can. Inst. Mining and Metallurgy, Can. Geol. Found. (pres. 1974-79), Can. Alpine Club, Am. Alpine Club. Anglican.

WHEELER, JOHN WATSON, lawyer; b. Murfreesboro, Tenn., Sept. 11, 1938; s. James William and Grace (Fann) W.; m. Dorothy Anita Pressgrove, Aug. 5, 1959; children: Jeffrey William, John Harold. BS in Journalism, U. Tenn., 1960, JD, 1968. Bar: Tenn. 1968, U.S. Dist. Ct. (ea. dist.) Tenn. 1968, U.S. Dist. Ct. (mid. dist.) Tenn. 1968, U.S. Dist. Ct. (we. dist.) Tenn. 1968, U.S. Supreme Ct. 1974, U.S. Ct. Appeals (6th cir.) 1975. Editor The Covington (Tenn.) Leader, 1963-65; adminstrv. asst. to lab. dir. UT-AEC Rsch. Lab., Oak Ridge, Tenn., 1965-68; assoc. Hodges, Doughty & Carson, Knoxville, Tenn., 1968-72, ptnr., 1972—. Mem. commn. to study Applellate Cts. in Tenn.; chair U.S. magistrate merit selection panel, U.S. Dist. Ct. (ea. dist.) Tenn., 1991, 2002, 03, mem. bankruptcy judge merit selection panel, 1992-94; chmn. hist. soc., U.S. Dist. Ct. (ea. dist.) Tenn., 1993-2004. Mem. organizing com. Tenn. Supreme Ct. Hist. Soc. Lt. U.S. Army, 1961-63, capt. Res. Fellow Am. Bar Found. (life, Tenn. chair 1999—), Tenn. Bar Found. (life); mem. ABA (ho. of dels. 1986-2000), Tenn. Bar Assn. (pres. 1989-90, bd. govs. 1981-91), Nat. Conf. Bar Pres., Am. Inns. of Ct. (master of bench, emeritus), Internat. Assn. Def. Counsel, So. Conf. Bar Pres., 6th Cir. Jud. Conf. (life), Fox Den Country Club (bd. dirs. 2001-04). Republican. Lutheran. Avocations: golf, travel. Home: 12009 N Fox Den Dr Knoxville TN 37922-2540 Office: Hodges Doughty & Carson PO Box 869 Knoxville TN 37901-0869 Office Phone: 865-546-9611. Business E-Mail: jwheeler@hdclaw.com.

WHEELER, KARLA, education educator; d. Kristine and George Bloechl; m. Robert Wheeler, May 11, 1996. BA in art history, MA in pub. history, U. of WI - Milw.; Assoc. in bus. mgmt., Milw. Area Tech. Coll. Curatorial asst. Waukesha County Mus., Wis., 1998—2000, dir. of pub. edn., 2000—02; curator of edn. Logan Mus. of Anthropology, Beloit, Wis., 2002—; asst. prof. Beloit Coll., Wis., 2002—. Grad. student rep. UW-Milw., Dept. of History, 2001. Mem.: Nat. Coun. for History Edn., Mus. Edn. Roundtable, Nat. Coun. on Pub. History, Assn. of Midwest Museums, Am. Assn. of Museums, Nat. Vocat. and Tech. Honor Soc. (life). Avocation: travel. Office: Beloit College 700 College St Beloit WI 53511 E-mail: wheelerk@beloit.edu.

WHEELER, KATHERINE WELLS, retired state legislator; b. St. Louis, Feb. 8, 1940; d. Benjamin Harris and Katherine (Gladney) Wells; m. Douglas Lanphier Wheeler, June 13, 1964; children: Katherine Gladney, Lucille Lanphier BA, Smith Coll., 1961; MA, Washington U., St. Louis, 1966. Founder auction N.H. Pub. TV, Durham, 1973-76; pub. mem. N.H. Pub. Broadcasting Coun., Durham, 1975-80; founding mem. bd. govs. N.H. Pub. TV, 1980-88; elected N.H. Ho. of Reps., Concord, 1988, 90, 92,94; mem. N.H. Senate, 1966—98, 1998—2000, 2000— 02, chmn. health & human svcs. com. Coord. internat. visitors program N.J. Coun. World Affairs, 1981-95. Bd. dirs. Planned Parenthood No. New England, 1989-95, Gt. Bay Svcs., Newington, N.H., 1989-97, Behavioral Health and Devel. Svcs. Strafford County, Inc., 1991—; vice chairperson Strafford County Legis. Del., 1993-94; active Commn. on Health, Human Svcs. and Elderly Affairs N.H. Ho. of Reps., Concord, 1988-96; bd. dirs. N.H. Pub. Health Assn., 1996—, pres., 2003--; bd. dirs. NAMI N.H., 2002--, NARAL N.H. Found., 1998-- Named Woman of Yr., Union Leader Newspaper, 1984, Citizen of Yr., Homemakers of Strafford County, 1990, N.H. sect. NASW, 1993, Legislator of Yr., N.H. Nurses Assn., 1996, N.H. Acad. Pediat., 1996; recipient Elizabeth Campbell Outstanding Pub. TV Vol. award Nat. Friends Pub. Broadcasting, 1984, Meritorious Svc. award N.H. Women's Lobby, 1992, Dist. Contbn. award N.H. Psychol. Orgn., Inc., 1994, Cert. of Achievement for Outstanding Legis. Leadership N.H. Citizen Action, 1994; Fleming fellow Leadership Inst., Ctr. for Policy Alternatives, Washington, 1997-98. Mem. AAUW, LWV, Am. Assn. Ret. Persons, Order of Women Legislators, N.H. Smith Coll. Club (v.p. 1974-76, pres. 1976-78, v.p. class of 1961, 1991-96), N.H. Assn. Social Workers (Legislator of Yr. 1993), N.H. Psychol. Orgn. Inc. (Disting. Contbn. award 1994). Democrat. Mem. United Ch. of Christ. Home and Office: 27 Mill Rd Durham NH 03824-3006

WHEELER, LAWRENCE JEFFERSON, art museum director; BA cum laude in History and French, Pfeiffer Coll., 1965; MA in European History, U. Ga., 1969, PhD in European History, 1972; cert., Fed. Execs. Inst., Charlottesville, Va., 1977, U. N.C., 1982. Asst. prof. European history Pfeiffer Coll., Misenheimer, N.C., 1970-74; dep. sec. N.C. Dept. Cultural Resources, Raleigh, 1977-85; asst. dir. mus. and dir. devel. Cleve. Mus. Art, 1985-94; staff liaison for bldg. and staffing N.C. Mus. Art, Raleigh, 1977-83, dir., 1994—. Cons. on fundraising and pub. rels. N.C. Mus. History, Raleigh; coord. 400th anniversary celebration Sir Walter Raleigh's voyages festival, 1984. Bd. dirs. Am. Arts Alliance, 1991-92. Named N.C. Man of Yr., News and Observer newspaper, Raleigh, N.C. . Mem. Am. Assn. Mus. (chmn. dvel. and membership profl. com. 1990-92, sr. reviewer mus. assessment program 1992—), Inst. Mus. Svcs. (reviewer 1988—), Art Mus. Devel. Assn. (pres. 1987-88). Home: 44 Cedar St Chapel Hill NC 27514-2712 Office: NC Mus Art 4630 Mail Service Ctr Raleigh NC 27699-4630 Fax: 919-733-8034.

WHEELER, M. CASS, health science association administrator; b. Texas; BA in advertising, U. Texas, Austin, 1963. Stockbroker NY Stock Exch. firm, Dallas, 1969—73; with AHA, Austin, Tex., 1973—82, COO Dallas, 1982, sr. v.p., field ops., 1996, CEO, 1997—. Guest lecturer Harvard U. Sch. of Bus. & Pub. Health, U. Texas Sch. of Mgmt., Dallas, U. Texas Lyndon B. Johnson Sch. of Pub. Affairs, Austin; former bd. chmn. Nat. Health Coun.; bd. mem. Partnership for Prevention, Research! Am., Nat. Ctr. for Tobacco-Free Kids, Nat. Assembly of Health and Human Service Organizations; advisory bd. mem. Discovery Health Media, Inc.; mem. Citizens Advisory Council for the Campaign for Med. Rsch.; former mem. President's Commn. on Improving Econ. Opportunity in Communities Dependent on Tobacco Production While Protecting Pub. Health Avocations: running, skiing, bicycling. Office: Am Heart Assn 7272 Greenville Ave Dallas TX 75231-5129*

WHEELER, MALCOLM EDWARD, lawyer, educator; b. Berkeley, Calif., Nov. 29, 1944; s. Malcolm Ross and Frances Dolores (Kane) W.; m. Donna Marie Stambaugh, July 25, 1981; children: Jessica Ross, M. Connor. SB, MIT, 1966; JD, Stanford U., 1969. Bar: Calif. 1970, Colo. 1992, U.S. Dist. Ct (cen. dist.) Calif. 1970, U.S. Ct. Appeals (9th cir.) 1970, U.S. Ct. Appeals (10th cir.) 1973, U.S. Dist. Ct. (no., so., ea. and cen. dists.) Calif. 1975, U.S. Ct. Appeals (11th cir.) 1987, U.S. Ct. Appeals (D.C. cir.) 1987, U.S. Supreme Ct. 1976, U.S. Ct. Appeals (3d cir.) 1989, (4th cir.) 1992, (8th cir.) 1993, (5th cir.) 1995, (Fed. cir.) 1998. Assoc. Howard, Prim, Smith, Rice & Downs, San Francisco, 1969-71; assoc. prof. law U. Kans., Lawrence, 1971-74; assoc. Hughes Hubbard & Reed, Los Angeles, 1974-77, ptnr., 1977-81, 83-85, cons., 1981-83; ptnr. Skadden, Arps, Slate, Meagher & Flom, Los Angeles, 1985-91; dir. Parcel, Mauro, Hultin & Spaanstra P.C., Denver, 1991-98, Wheeler Trigg & Kennedy, P.C., Denver, 1998—. Vis. prof. U. Iowa, 1978, prof., 1979; prof. U. Kans., Lawrence, 1981-83; chief counsel U.S. Senate Select Com. to Study Law Enforcement Undercover Activities, Washington, 1982-83. Mem. editl. bd. Jour. Products Liability, 1984-90, Fed. Litigation Guide Reporter, 1986-90; contbr. articles to profl. jours. Fellow Am. Coll. Trial Lawyers; mem. ABA, Calif. Bar Assn., Colo. Bar Assn., Am. Law Inst. Home: 100 Humboldt St Denver CO 80218-3932 Office Phone: 303-292-2525. E-mail: wheeler@wtklaw.com.

WHEELER, MELANIE ELAINE, administrative assistant, realtor; b. Washington, Pa., Jan. 31, 1955; d. Charles Edward and Shirley Ann Wheeler. AA in civil Engring. with an archtl. maj., Stark State Coll. of Tech., 1994—2000; comml. art vocat., Timken Vocat. Highschool, 1969—73. Realtor Ohio, 2001, New Home Specialist Designation Ohio, 2002, Residential Investment Specialist Certification Ohio, 2002. Advt. layout and comml. artist Ray C. Crowl & Associates Advt. Agy., Canton, Ohio, 1973—74; artist and photgraphy labratory technician Buckeye Color Lab, North Canton, Ohio, 1974—2002; math tudor Stark State Coll. of Tech., North Canton, Ohio, 1997; realtor Realty One Real Estate Brokerage, Canton and Eastlake, Ohio, 2001—; civil engr. estimator and asst. T.A.B. Equipment & Supply, Inc., Canton, Ohio, 2002; adminstrv. asst. Spherion at The Goodyear Tire & Rubber Co., Akron, Ohio, 2002—. Profl. services committe mem. cons. Stark County Assn. of REALTORS, Canton, Ohio, 2004—. Watercolor painting, My Neice Abigail (Placement in the state-wide Touring Exhbn. of the Ohio Watercolor Soc., 1993). Litergist United Meth. Ch., Canton, Ohio, 1998. Recipient Award of Distinction Upon Graduation for Comml. Art, State Bd. of Edn. of Ohio, 1973, A Gold and Diamond Ring as a 15 Yr. Anniversity, Buckeye Color Lab, 1989, Cert. of Recognition, Canton Mus. of Art, 1992. Mem.: Ohio Assn. of REALTORS (licentiate; realtor 2001—04), No. Ohio Regional Multiple Listing Svc. (corr.; realtor 2004), Centralized Real Estate Info. Svc., Inc. (corr.; realtor 2001—04), The Cleve. Assn. of REALTORS (assoc.; realtor 2004), Stark County Assn. of REALTORS (assoc.; realtor of profl. services 2004). Avocations: quilting, writing, painting, sewing, walking. Office: Realty One Real Living 34001 Vine St Eastlake OH 44095 E-mail: m.wheeler@realtyone.com.

WHEELER, MIKE, retail food store corporate executive; CFO Hy-vec Food Stores Inc., West Des Moines, Iowa, 1998. Office: Hy-vec Food Stores Inc 5820 Westown Pkwy West Des Moines IA 50266-8223

WHEELER, OTIS BULLARD, retired English educator and university official; b. Mansfield, Ark., Feb. 1, 1921; s. Clarence Charles and Georgia Elizabeth (Bullard) W.; m. Doris Louise Alexander, Jan. 17, 1943; children: Ann Carolyn, Ross Charles; m. Anne Carol Loveland, Mar. 23, 1991. BA, U. Okla., 1942; MA, U. Tex., 1947; PhD, U. Minn., 1951. Mem. faculty La. State U., Baton Rouge, 1952—, prof. English, 1965-81, prof. emeritus, 1981—, chmn. dept., 1974, asst. dean grad. sch., 1962-67, vice chancellor for acad. affairs, 1974-80, acting chancellor, 1981. Fulbright-Hayes lectr. U. Innsbruck, Austria, 1968-69 Author: The Literary Career of Maurice Thompson, 1965; photographer: (with R.W. Heck) Religious Architecture in Louisiana, 1995, (with Anne C. Loveland) From Meetinghouse to Megachurch, 2003. Served with U.S. Army, 1942-46, 51-52. Decorated Bronze Star medal. Mem. Phi Kappa Phi, Omicron Delta Kappa. Democrat. Methodist. Home: 657 Highland Oaks Dr Baton Rouge LA 70810-5348

WHEELER, RAYMOND LOUIS, lawyer; b. Ft. Sill, Okla., Feb. 10, 1945; s. Raymond Louis and Dorothy Marie (Hutcherson) W.; m. Priscilla Wheeler, July 1, 1966 (div. 1982); children: Jennifer, Hilary; m. Cynthia Lee Jackson, July 14, 1984 (div. 1994); children: Matthew Raymond, Madeline Elizabeth; m. Freddie Kay Park, June 10, 1995. BA, U. Tex., 1967; JD, Harvard U., 1970. Bar: Calif. 1972, U.S. Dist. Ct. (no., cen., ea., so. dists.) Calif., U.S. Ct. Appeals (9th cir., 7th cir.), U.S. Ct. Appeals (7th cir.), U.S. Supreme Ct. Law clk. to hon. Irving L. Goldberg U.S. Ct. Appeals 5th cir., 1970-71; assoc. Morrison & Foerster, San Francisco, 1971-76, ptnr., 1976-90, Palo Alto, Calif., 1990—. Chmn. labor and employment law dept. Morrison & Foerster, San Francisco, 1984-88, 92—; lectr. labor and EEO law. Exec. editor Harvard Law Rev., 1969-70; editor in chief The Developing Labor Law; mem. nat. adv. bd. Berkeley Jour. Employment and Labor Law, 1980—; contbr. articles to law jours. Fellow Coll. Labor and Employment Lawyers; mem. ABA (chmn. com. on law devel. under labor rels. act 1990-93, coun. mem. sect. labor and employment 1994-02). Republican. Office: Morrison & Foerster 755 Page Mill Rd Palo Alto CA 94304-1018 E-mail: rwheeler@mofo.com.

WHEELER, R(ICHARD) KENNETH, lawyer, educator; b. Washington, July 25, 1934; s. Nathaniel Dudley and Ruth Lee (Matthews) W.; m. Christine Kandris, Jan. 11, 1990; children by previous marriage: Jennifer L., Ruth E. BA, Emory and Henry Coll., U. Richmond, 1957; LLB, U. Richmond, 1964. Bar: Va. 1963, D.C. 1977, U.S. Tax Ct. 1978. Assoc., then ptnr. Hunton, Williams, Gay, Powell & Gibson and successor firms, Richmond, 1963-88; sr. ptnr. Kane, Wheeler, Fenderson & Jeffries, Richmond, 1988-90; counsel Durrette, Irvin, Lemons & Fenderson, P.C., Richmond, 1990-94; sr. ptnr. Wallace, Harris & Wheeler, Richmond, 1994-95. Adj. prof. law T.C. Williams Sch. Law, U. Richmond, 1966, 83, bd. dirs., 1977-79; adj. prof. law Va. Commonwealth U., 1970; lectr. trial practice U. Va., 1981-82, 85, 87; arbitrator Am. Arbitration Assn. Served to capt. USMCR, 1957-61. Williams scholar U. Richmond, 1961-63. Mem. Am. Law Inst., Va. State Bar (chmn. com. liaison with law schs. 1977-78, chmn. com. legal edn. and admission to bar 1978-80, spcl. com. on professionalism 1987-88), Web Soc., McNeill Law Soc., Marine Corps League (life), Rector's Club (U. Richmond, life), Pi Sigma Alpha, Phi Delta Phi, Omicron Delta Kappa (hon.).

WHEELER, RICHARD PAUL, English educator, dean; b. Newton, Iowa, Sept. 9, 1943; s. Clifford Don and Irene Maxine Wheeler; m. Pat Gill, Mar. 28, 1997. BA, Cornell Coll., 1965; MA, SUNY, Buffalo, 1967, PhD, 1970. From asst. prof. to assoc. prof. U. Ill., Urbana, 1969-87, prof., 1987—, head English dept., 1987-89, dean grad. coll., 1989—, head anthropology. Evaluator English dept. U. Oreg., Eugene, 1996, U. Minn., Mpls., 1997, U. Tenn., Memphis, 1998. Author: Shakespeare's Development and the Problem Comedies, 1981; co-author: The Whole Journey: Shakespeare's Power of Development, 1986; editor: Creating Elizabethan Tragedy, 1988, Critical Essays on Shakespeare's Measure for Measure, 1999. Mem. MLA, Shakespeare Assn. Am., Coun. Grad. Schs., Assn. Grad. Schs., Coun. Rsch. Policy and Grad. Edn. Democrat. Home: 512 W Springfield Champaign IL 61820 Office: U Ill 801 S Wright St Champaign IL 61820-6210 Fax: 217-333-8019. E-mail: rpw@uiuc.edu.

WHEELER, ROBERT CHANNING, JR., health maintenance organization executive; b. Evanston, Ill., Mar. 4, 1952; s. Robert Channing Wheeler and Mary M. (Whitmire) Brown; m. Elizabeth Joan Mellor, June 1, 1951; children: Joy Carolyn, Anne Miriam. BA, BS, Stanford U., 1977, MA, 1978; MBA, UCLA, 1983. Program assoc. Community Cancer Control L.A., 1979-80; dir. prevention UCLA Cancer Ctr., Westood, 1980-83; sr. staff mgr. FHP Inc., Fountain Valley, Calif., 1983-84; dir. provider rels. Maxicare Health Plans, L.A., 1984-85, v.p., exec. dir., 1985-86, regional v.p., 1987—89; various executive positions CIGNA Healthcare, 1989—94; CEO UnitedHealth Group (Northeast Region), 1995—98, Uniprise (sub. UnitedHealth group), 1998—. Bd. dirs. Maxicare Calif. Corp., L.A., Gen. Med. Health Plan, Orange, Calif. Author: Preventing Lung Cancer in Los Angeles, 1983. Bd. dirs. Ladera Heights Community Hosp., L.A., 1987-88. Republican. Episcopalian. Avocations: scuba diving, sailing. Office: 450 Columbus Blvd Hartford CT 06115

WHEELER, RURIC E. mathematics professor; b. Clarkson, Ky., Nov. 30, 1923; s. Mark H. and Mary (Sullivan) Wheeler; m. Joyce Ray, May 31, 1946; children: Eddy Ray, Paul Warren. AB, We. Ky. U., 1947; MS, U. Ky., 1948, PhD, 1952. Instr. math. U. Ky., Lexington, 1948—52; asst. prof. stats. Fla. State U., 1952—53; assoc. prof. math. Samford U., 1953—55, prof., head math. dept., 1955—65, chmn. natural scis. divsn., 1965—67, asst. to dean, 1967—68; dean Howard Coll. Arts and Scis., 1968—70, v.p. acad. affairs, 1970—87, univ. prof., 1987—94, rsch. prof., 1994—. Cons. in field; dir. NSF Inst., 1961, Ala. Vis. Scientist Program, 1962—67. Author: Modern Math., 1966, 11th edit., 2002, Fundamental Concepts of Math, 1968, 2d edit., 1976, Modern Math for Business, 1969, 4th edit., 1986, A Programmed Study of Number Systems, 1972, Finite Mathematics, 1974, 3d edit., 1985, Intuitive Geometry, 1975, Mathematics, an Everyday Language, 1979, Student Activities Manual, Elementary Mathematics, 1984, Finite Mathematics (A Problem Solving Approach), 1991, Mathematicas un Lenguaje Cotidiano, 1982, Activities Manual for Elementary School Teachers, 1988, Introduccion a los Conjuntos Numericos, 1976, Modern Mathematics for Elementary School Teachers, 1994, College Mathematics (a Graphing Calculator Approach), 1996, Brief Calculus (a Graphing Calculator Approach), 1996, Chinese Translation of Brief Calculus, 1997, (novels) All Because of Polly, 2002. Mem. Birmingham Manpower Area Planning Coun., 1972—75; trustee Gorgas Found., 1968—94, chmn., 1988—92; mem. Jefferson County Ednl. Consortium, 1981—93, pres., 1986—90; mem. Com. to Upgrade Jefferson County Schs., 1982—86; deacon Bapt. Ch. Lt. USAAF, 1943—46. Mem.: Conf. Acad. Deans So. States (pres. 1985—86), So. Conf. Deans Faculties and Acad. V.P. (pres. 1982), Am. Conf. Acad. Deans, Am. Assn. Univ. Adminstrs. (exec. com. Ala. sect. 1972—74, v.p. 1974—76, pres. 1976—77), Assn. Ala. Coll. Adminstrs. (exec. com. 1976—80, pres. 1978—79), Am. Assn. Higher Edn., Ala. Acad. Sci. (pres. 1967—69), Assn. So. Bapt. Colls. and Schs. (sec. 1973, v.p. 1974, pres. 1975, deans sect.), Assn. Math Tchrs. Ala. (pres. 1963), Nat. Coun. Tchrs. Math., Am. Math. Assn. (chmn. SE sect. 1966—67, vis. lecture program 1989—93), Am. Math. Soc., Am. Edn. Assn., Rotary (pres. of Vestavia rotary club 1983—84). Home: 1347 Badham Dr Birmingham AL 35216-2939 Office Phone: 205-726-2389. E-mail: rewheele@samford.edu.

WHEELER, STEPHEN FREDERICK, legal administrator; BA in Polit. Sci., Mt. Union Coll., Alliance, Ohio, 1968; MS in Adminstrn. of Justice, Am. U., 1974. Probation officer 19th Dist. Juvenile and Domestic Rels. Ct. Prince William County, Manassas, Va., 1972-75; ct. systems planner Office of Jud. Planning Ky. Jud. Coun., Frankfort, 1975-76; co-dir. Ky. pretrial svcs. Adminstrv. Office of Cts. Ky. Ct. of Justice, Frankfort, 1976-81; ct. adminstr. Jud. Dist. 27A, Gastonia, N.C., 1982-87, Colorado Springs (Colo.) Mcpl. Ct., 1987—. Ct. systems cons. Nat. Criminal Justice Collaborative, Sea Island, Ga., 1981-85. Office: City of Colorado Springs Mcpl Ct PO Box 2169 Colorado Springs CO 80901-2169 Office Phone: 719-385-6301. E-mail: swheeler@springsgov.com.

WHEELER, STEVE DEREAL, neurologist; b. Chgo., Sept. 15, 1951; s. Clarence and Tommie L. (Andrews) W.; m. Debra B. Buckingham; children: Winter N., Ryan S., Gabrielle S. Student, Mich. State U., 1970-73; MD, Dartmouth Coll., 1976. Diplomate Am. Bd. Psychiatry and Neurology, Nat. Bd. Med. Examiners; lic. Mich., Ohio, Fla. Intern Thomas Jefferson U., Phila., 1976-77; emergency physician River Dist. Hosp. Emergency Cons., Inc., St. Clair, Mich., 1977-78; fellow Dartmouth Med. Sch., 1978; resident U. Miami, Fla., 1978-81; fellow Washington U., St. Louis, 1981-82; instr. in neurology Med. Coll. Pa., Phila., 1982-83; electroencephalograph reader, attending neurologist VA Med. Ctr., Phila., 1982-83; asst. neurologist, attending neurologist Muscle Clinic U. Hosps. Cleve., 1983-86; electromyographer Rainbow Babies and Children's Hosp., U. Hosps. Cleve., 1983-86; chief neuromuscular diseases divsn., asst. prof. neurology Case Western Res. U., Cleve., 1983-86, co-dir. muscle disease ctr. and lab., 1985-86; clin. assoc. prof. of neurology U. Miami, 1987-89; pvt. practice Miami, 1987—; dir., co-founder Ryan Wheeler Headache Treatment Ctr., Miami, 2001—. Lectr. Myasthenia Gravis Found., Vermillion, Ohio, 1984, Cleve., 1983—86; vol. assoc. prof. U. Miami Sch., 1992—97, 2004—, vis. lectr., 1993—2001; chief headache divsn. Neurologic Ctr. for South Fla.; neurology cons. Low Back Pain Team U. Hosps. Cleve., 1984—86; mem. quality assurance com. Coral Reef Hosp., Miami, 1987—88; cons. dir. planning Bapt. Headache Clinic Bapt. Hosp., Miami, 1993—95; mem. adminstrv. com. Deering Hosp. Pain Mgmt. Ctr., Miami, 1993—94; mem. sleep diagnostic ctr. com. Bapt. Hosp., 1990—92, 1994—98, advisor to headache support group, 1995—; lectr. in field; co-founder, dir. Ryan Wheeler Headache Treatment Ctr. Author: (chpt.) Intensive Care For Neurological Trauma and Disease, 1982, (chpt.) Migraine and the Primary Headaches, 2002; mem. editl. bd.: Headache, 2001—02, ad hoc reviewer:, 2000—02, Cephalalgia, 1999—, Jour. Nat. Med. Assn., 2001—. Named Internat. Man Yr., 1991-92; recipient Celebration Excellence Black Achiever award Family Christian Assn. Am., 1992. Fellow Royal Soc. Medicine, Am. Acad. Neurology; mem. ACP, Am. Headache Soc., So. Med. Assn. (chmn. psychiatry and neurology sect. 2000-02), Nat. Headache Found., Internat. Headache Soc., Fla. Med. Assn., Fla. Soc. Neurology, Fla. Soc. Internal Medicine, N.Y. Acad. Scis., Muscular Disease Soc. Northeastern Ohio (trustee 1984-86), Dade County Med. Assn., So. Pain Soc., Internat. Assn. Study of Pain, Dartmouth Club Greater Miami, Am. Coun. for Headache Edn. Achievements include research in plasmaphereses in treatment of acute Guillain-Barre Syndrome; repeat neuroimaging in headache when first study normal, migraine with cluster features, hemicrania continua. Office: Ryan Wheeler Headache Treatment Ctr 20601 Old Cutler Rd Miami FL 33189 Office Phone: 305-235-2243.

WHEELER, STEVEN M. lawyer; b. Evanston, Ill., Jan. 5, 1949; AB, Pricneton U., 1971; JD with distinction, Cornell U., 1974. Bar: Ariz. 1974. Mem. Snell & Wilmer, Phoenix, ptnr., 1980—. Mng. editor Cornell Law Review, 1973-74; contbr. articles to profl. jours. Mem. ABA, Order Coif, Phi Kappa Phi. Office: Snell & Wilmer 1 Arizona Ctr Phoenix AZ 85004-0001

WHEELER, THEODORE K., JR., small business owner; b. Edwards AFB, Mojav, Calif., Dec. 29, 1962; s. Theodore K. Wheeler, Sr. and Shirley Ann Rogness. Owner Base Cards, Post Falls, Idaho, 1986—2004, R.R.T.V.C., Post Falls, Idaho, 1998—2004, Studio's-P.F.M., Post Falls, Idaho, 1999—2004. U.S.T.-Treasury Notes Base Cards, 1995—2002. Avocations: water sports, hiking, swimming, music. Home and Office: Base Cards 3560 W Hudlow Drive Post Falls ID 83854 Office Phone: 208-773-8502.

WHEELER, THOMAS EDGAR, former telecommunications executive; b. Redlands, Calif., Apr. 5, 1946; s. Charles Taylor and Martha (Edgar) W.; married; children: Nicole Pierce, David Maxwell. BS, Ohio State U., 1968. Asst. dir. Ohio State U. Alumni Assn., Columbus, 1968-69; v.p. Grocery Mfrs. Am., Inc., Washington, 1969-76; exec. v.p. Nat. Cable TV Assn., Washington, 1976-79, pres., chief exec. officer, 1979-85, NABU: The Home Computer Network, 1985-86; chmn., chief exec. officer NuCable Resources Corp.,

Washington, 1986-94; pres., CEO Cellular Telecom. Industry Assn., Washington, 1992—2003; pres. Shiloh Group, LLC, 2003—. Author: Leadership Lessons from the Civil War, 1999. Bd. trustees John F. Kennedy Ctr. for Performing Arts; bd. dirs. Pub. Broadcasting Svc., Earthlink, Telephia, SmartBrief, InPhonic; pres. Found. for Nat. Archives. Democrat. Office: Shiloh Group LLC 1250 Connecticut Ave NW Ste 200 Washington DC 20036-2655 Office Phone: 202-737-3770.

WHEELER, W(ILLIAM) SCOTT, composer, conductor, music educator; b. Washington, Feb. 24, 1952; s. Malcolm Frederick and Aurora Dorothy (Anas) W.; m. Christen Struthers Frothingham, Jan. 5, 1985; children: Margaret Lee, Catherine Elizabeth. BA, Amherst Coll., 1973; MFA, Brandeis U., 1978, PhD, 1984. Artistic dir. Dinosaur Annex Music Ensemble, Boston, 1975—; dir. Cambridge (Mass.) Chorale, 1976-78; tchr. music, condr. Emerson Coll., Boston, 1978—. Composer (choral) A Babe is Born,,1979, (chamber) Winter Hills, 1987 (Somerville Arts Coun. Commn.), (symphony) Northern Lights, 1987 (Koussevitzky commn.), (opera) The Construction of Boston (libretto by Kenneth Koch), 1989, (choral) The Angle of the Sun, 1994 (Nat. Endowment for the Arts). Guggenheim fellow, 1988-89. Mem. Am. Music Ctr., ASCAP. Episcopalian. Home: 6 Sunset Ave North Reading MA 01864-1427 Office: Emerson Coll Div Performing Arts 120 Boylston St Boston MA 02116-4624 Office Phone: 617-824-8385. E-mail: scott_wheeler@emerson.edu.

WHEELER, WILMOT FITCH, JR., diversified manufacturing company executive; b. Southport, Conn., June 5, 1923; s. Wilmot Fitch and Hulda Day (Chapman) W.; m. Barbara Rutherfurd, Sept. 30, 1944 (dec. Sept. 1971); children: Wilmot Fitch III, James Alexander, John R. (dec.), Susan; m. Nonnye Landers, Dec. 20, 1973; children: Tracy Lynne, Alexa Margaret. BA, Yale U., 1945; postgrad., NYU, 1947-48; LLD honoris causa, Sacred Heart U., 1999. Staff engr. Stevenson, Jordan & Harrison, Inc. (mgmt. cons.), 1946-51; with Am. Chain & Cable Co., Inc., N.Y.C., 1951-76, pres., chmn., CEO, 1966-76; chmn., dir. Jelliff Corp., Southport, Conn., 1976—; prin. Case & Co. Inc. (mgmt. cons.), 1977-82; trustee Dollar Savs. Bank, 1974-83, chmn., CEO, 1982-83; chmn., trustee, CEO Dollar Dry Dock Savs. Bank, 1983-84. Vice chmn., chmn., bd. dirs., CEO Manhattan Nat. Corp., 1986-90; v.p. William T. Morris Found., 1976—; bd. dirs. Am. Mut. Liability Ins. Co., 1969-89, Am. Policyholders Ins. Co., 1969-89, Am. Dist. Telegraph Co., 1968-88, Bristol Co. of Can. Ltd., 1955-76, Brit. Wire Products Ltd. (Eng.), 1955-76, Cables Automotrices, S.A. (Mexico), 1955-76, Dominion Chain Co. Ltd., 1955-76, FATA, SpA (Italy), 1975-76, Hersey Products Corp., 1976-86, Instrumentos Bristol, S.A. (Mexico), 1955-76, Manhattan Life Ins. Co., 1972-93, Arthur G. McKee & Co., 1972-79, Parsons Controls Ltd., 1955-76, People's Bank, 1988-98, People's Mut. Holdings, 1975-98, Pratt-Read Corp., 1978-85, Pujol y Tarrago S.A. (Spain), 1969-85, Sormir Petroleum, Inc., 1994-98, Union Ctrl. Life Ins. Co., 1990-93, Wilmot F. Wheeler Found., 1944—. Trustee Am. Farm Sch., 1981-93, Bridgeport Hosp., 1977-94, U. Bridgeport, 1978-88. With AUS, 1943-46. Decorated Bronze Star. Mem. Yale Club (N.Y.C.), Country Club Fairfield. Episcopalian. Home: PO Box 429 Southport CT 06490-0429 Office: Jelliff Corp PO Box 758 354 Pequot Ave Southport CT 06490-1369

WHEELESS, LEON LUM, pathology educator; b. Jackson, Miss., Nov. 6, 1935; s. Leon Lum and Frances (King) W.; m. Waldine Marie Jones, Aug. 27, 1957; children: Susan, Diane, Linda. SB, MIT, 1958; MS, U. Rochester, 1962, PhD, 1965. Scientist Bausch & Lomb Corp., Rochester, N.Y., 1958-69, dir. biomed. rsch., 1969-71; assoc. prof. pathology and elec. engring. U. Rochester, 1971-84, prof. elec. engring., 1984-91; dir. analytical cytology divsn. U. Rochester Med. Ctr., 1975-97, prof. pathology and lab. medicine, 1984-97, prof. urology, 1989-97, prof. oncology, 1996-2001, emeritus prof. pathology and lab. medicine and urology, 1997—. Cons. NIH, 1976-2000. Patentee in field. Frequent NIH grantee, 1972-2000; recipient Gest Lectureship award Am. Soc. Cytology, 1975. Mem. IEEE (sr., Centennial award 1984), Internat. Soc. Analytical Cytology (charter, pres. 1982-84, Disting. Svc. award 1996), Engring. in Medicine and Biology Soc. (pres. 1974-75), Sigma Xi. Avocations: sailing, skiing, camping. Home: 47 Woodcliff Ter Fairport NY 14450-4208 Office: Univ Rochester Med Ctr Dept Pathology Rochester NY 14642-0001 Office Phone: 585-275-1580. E-mail: leonw@rochester.rr.com.

WHEELOCK, ARGIL J. urologist, medical company executive; Pvt. practice, Chattanooga, 1979—96; CEO HealthTronics Surgical Svcs., 1996—. V.p. lithotripsy svcs. Coram Healthcare, 1991—94; with Phymatrix, 1994—96; mng. gen. ptnr. TennGa Stone Group Two; chief mgr. Tenn-Ga Prostate; chmn., pres. Fla. Lithology, Inc. Office: 1841 W Oak Pkwy Ste A Marietta GA 30062

WHEELOCK, DONALD F. music educator, composer; b. Stamford, Conn., June 17, 1940; s. Ralph Douglas and Cynthia (Doliber) W.; children: Ingrid, Sarah, Benjamin; m. Anne Hunter, Feb. 8, 1997. AB, Union Coll., Schenectady, N.Y., 1962; MMus, Yale U., 1966. Instr. music Colgate U., Hamilton, NY, 1966—69; asst. prof. music Amherst (Mass.) Coll., 1969—74; faculty Smith Coll., Northampton, Mass., 1974—, prof. music, 1985—95, Alper Glass prof. music, 1995—. Composer 2 symphonies, 4 string quartets, many solo instrumental, ensemble and orchestral works. Office: Smith Coll Music Dept Northampton MA 01063

WHEELOCK, KEITH WARD, retired consulting company executive, educator; b. Phila., Oct. 17, 1933; s. Ward and Margot Trevor (Williams) W.; m. Susan Bowen Kimball, June 15, 1956 (div. Nov. 1975); children: Helen Fraser, James Voorhees; m. Bente Lorentzen Ott, July 1978 (div. June 1988); m. Georgia Whidden, May 17, 1997. BA, Yale U., 1955; MA, U. Pa., 1957; MS, MIT, 1972. Fgn. svc. officer Dept. State, Washington, 1960-69; dir. programs and policy divsn. N.Y.C. Housing and Devel. Adminstrn., 1970-71; devel. officer Moody's Investors Svc., Inc., N.Y.C., 1972-74, v.p. internat. ops., 1974-75, exec. v.p., 1975-76; pres. The Fantus Co., Millburn, N.J., 1976-83; mem. Sr. Dun & Bradstreet Mgmt. Group, 1979-83; prin. Wheelock Cons., 1983-88; project dir. Mng. Growth in N.J., 1986-90; assoc. prof. Raritan Valley C.C., 1992—. Rsch. asst. Fgn. Policy Rsch. Inst., U. Pa. Author: Nasser's New Egypt, A Critical Analysis, 1960, New Jersey Growth Management, 1989. Mem. Montgomery (N.J.) Twp. Com., 1986-88; pres. adv. coun. Eisenhower Exch. Fellowship. Sloan fellow MIT, 1972. Home: 325 Mountain View Rd Skillman NJ 08558-2412 E-mail: kwheelock@rcn.com.

WHEELOCK, KENNETH STEVEN, chemist; b. Kansas City, Mo., Sept. 18, 1943; s. Kenneth Lewis and Clara Mae (Hanenkratt) W.; m. Mary Corinne Percy, June 30, 1972; children: Michael Steven, Celeste Marie. BSc, U. Mo., Kansas City, 1965; PhD, Tulane U., New Orleans, 1970; JD magna cum laude, Western New Eng. Coll., 1998. Bar: Mass.; registered patent atty. Chemist Exxon Rsch. & Devel. Labs., Baton Rouge, 1969-72, rsch. chemist, 1972-77, staff chemist, 1977-83, sr. staff chemist, 1983-86; assoc. prof. physics La. State U., Baton Rouge, 1987; sr. rsch. chemist Phillips Petroleum Co., Bartlesville, Okla., 1987-91; chmn. Prakti Katalysts, Bartlesville, 1992-93; patent agt. GE Advanced Materials, Pittsfield, Mass., 1993-98, counsel intellectual property, 1998—. Cons. dept. chemistry Tulane U., New Orleans, 1970—75. Advisor Jr. Achievement, Baton Rouge, 1971; sec. Baton Rouge Orchid Soc., 1983, Bartlesville Gifted and Talented, 1989; vestry St. Stephen's, Pittsfield, 1999-2002. NDEA trainee, Tulane U., New Orleans, 1965-67, NASA fellow, 1967-69. Fellow Am. Inst. Chemists (profl. rels. com. 1991, 92, patents com. 1992); mem. ABA, Am. Chem. Soc. (program chmn. petroleum divsn. 1976-77, Snyder award Legal Ethics 1998), Am. Intellectual Property Law Assn., Mass. Bar Assn., NY Acad. Sci., Sigma Xi. Episcopalian. Achievements include 20 patents; preparation and determination of crystal structure of (211) phase of 123 superconductors; invention of randomly cross-linked smectites, of high surface area supported perovskite catalysts and method for preparation; selective auto exhaust catalysts; theory of finely divided metals; bonding model for zerovalent acetylene and olefin complexes; fluidized catalytic cracking catalysts, sulfur tolerant catalytic reforming. Office: GE Advanced Materials One Plastics Ave Pittsfield MA 01201 Office Phone: 413-448-4606. Business E-Mail: steve.wheelock@berkshire.net.

WHEELOCK, LARRY ARTHUR, retired engineer, consultant; b. Chgo., Nov. 20, 1938; s. Preston J. and Rozella (Schonert) W.; m. Ruth E. Pruess (div. Sept. 1975); children: John P., J. Robert, William D., Thomas K.; m. Norma Jane Fair, Oct. 22, 1984. BSEE, U. Evansville, 1962. Registered profl. engr., Ind.; cert. instrument rated comml. pilot, airframe and powerplant mechanic with inspection authorization, FAA. Co-op student engr. Naval Avionics Facility, Indpls., 1958-59, Naval Weapons Support Ctr., Crane, Ind., 1959-62, elec. engr., 1963-78, Delco Electronics, Kokomo, Ind., 1962-63; sr. mfg. eng. Ford Aerospace & Comm., Bedford, Ind., 1979-80; plant engr. Ethyl Corp., Terre Haute, Ind., 1980-81; plant mgr. Tredegar Industries/Ethyl Corp., Terre Haute, Ind., 1981-91. Cons. in field. Patentee in field. Bd. dirs. Hulman Regional Airport Authority, 1991-95, pres., 1992; pres. Greene County Airport Bd. Commrs., Bloomfield, Ind., 1972-81. Mem. IEEE, Aircraft Owners & Pilots Assn., Exptl. Aircraft Assn., AntiquAircraft Assn., Internat. Flying Farmers, Flying Engrs. Internat. (pres. 1994, 95), Mensa, Internat. Assn. Flying Rotarians, Rotary Internat. Avocations: aviation, agriculture, mechanics, amateur radio, computers. Home: 7480 State Road 42 Terre Haute IN 47803-9778 also: PO Box 309 Raymondville TX 78580-0309

WHEELOCK, PAM, financial executive; BA in History, Coll. St. Catherine; MA in Applied Econs., Marquette U. Exec. budget officer Minn. Dept. Fin., 1988—92; budget dir. City of St. Paul, 1992—94, dep. mayor, 1994—96, dir. dept. planning and econ. devel., 1996—99; commr. Minn. Dept. Fin., 1999—2002; sr. v.p., CFO Minn. Sports and Entertainment, 2002—. Office: Minn Wild 317 Washington St Saint Paul MN 55102

WHEELON, ALBERT DEWELL, physicist; b. Moline, Ill., Jan. 18, 1929; s. Orville Albert and Alice Geltz (Dewell) W.; m. Nancy Helen Hermanson, Feb. 28, 1953 (dec. May 1980); children: Elizabeth Anne, Cynthia Helen; m. Cicely J. Evans, Feb. 4, 1984. BSc, Stanford U., 1949; PhD, MIT, 1952. Tchg. fellow, then rsch. assoc. physics MIT, Boston, 1949-52; with Douglas Aircraft Co., 1952-53, Ramo-Wooldridge Corp., 1953-62; dep. dir. sci. and tech. CIA, Washington, 1962-66; with Hughes Aircraft Co., L.A., 1966-88, chmn., CEO, 1987-88. Vis. prof. MIT, 1989; mem. Def. Sci. Bd., 1968-76; mem. Pres.'s Fgn. Intelligence, 1983-88; mem. Presdl. Commn. on Space Shuttle Challenger Accident, 1986; trustee Aerospace Corp., 1990-93, Calif. Inst. Tech., Rand Corp., 1993-. Author Electromagnetic Scintillation: Vol. 1 and 2, 2001, 03; contbr. 36 papers on radiowave propagation and guidance systems. Recipient R.V. Jones Intelligence award, 1994. Fellow IEEE, AIAA (Von Karman medal 1986, Goddard Astronautics award 1997), Am. Phys. Soc.; mem. NAE, Sigma Chi. Episcopalian. Independent. Address: 181 Sheffield Dr Montecito CA 93108-2242

WHELAN, DANIEL J. communications company executive; b. Phila. married; 3 children. BA in Philosophy, LaSalle Coll., 1968; JD cum laude, Temple U., 1974. Bar: Pa. Atty. Bell of Pa., 1977; gen. atty. state and fed. arenas Bell of Pa. and Bell Atlantic Corp., v.p. Keystone ops., 1988-91, v.p. regulatory and govtl. rels., 1991-95; pres., CEO, Bell Atlantic-Md., Inc., Balt., 1995-97; also pres. bd. dirs. Bell Atlantic Pa., 1997—. Editor-in-chief Temple U. Law Rev., 1973-74. Bd. dirs. Greater Balt. Com., Md. Bus. Roundtable for Edn.; bd. govs. Nat. Aquarium, Balt. Mem. Md. C. of C. (bd. dirs.). Office: Bell Atlantic Pa 1717 Arch St Fl 17 Philadelphia PA 19103-2713

WHELAN, JAMES ROBERT, communications executive, international trade and investment consultant, author, educator, mining executive; b. Buffalo, July 27, 1933; s. Robert and Margaret (Southard) W.; children from previous marriage: Robert J., Heather Elizabeth; m. Guadalupe Aguirre, 1990 (div. Feb. 2004); m. Isabel Margarita Gomez, 2004. Student, U. Buffalo, 1951-53, U. R.I., 1955-57; BA, Fla. Internat. U., 1974. Staff corr., fgn. corr., country mgr., divsn. mgr. UPI, Buffalo, 1952-53, staff corr., fgn. corr., country mgr., div. mgr. Providence, 1955-57, Boston, 1957-58, Buenos Aires, Argentina, 1958-61, Caracas, Venezuela, 1961-66, San Juan, P.R., 1966, 68; regional dir. corp. rels., then v.p. ops. ITT World Directories, ITT, San Juan, 1968-70; Latin Am. corr. Scripps-Howard Newspaper Alliance, Washington, 1970-71; mng. editor Miami (Fla.) News, 1971-73; free-lance writer, 1973-74; pres., editor, pub. Hialeah (Fla.) Pub. Co., 1975-77; v.p., editl. dir. Panax Corp., Washington, 1977-80; v.p., editor Sacramento Union, 1980-82; editor, pub. Washington Times, 1982-84; mng. dir. CBN News, 1985-86; pres. Capital Comm. Internat., 1986—; editor-in-chief Conservative Digest, 1988-89; vice chmn. Inter-Am. Found., Arlington, Va., 1991-94; external affairs advisor Inter-Am. Investment Corp., 1992-93; dir. strategic planning Cocetel Holding, Santiago, Chile, 1993-94; pres. Minera Silver Standard S.A., 1994—, Silver Std., Mex., 1995—. Freelance writer; guest lectr. ednl. instns., including Boston U., U. Miami, Ctrl. U., Venezuela, Cath. U., Andrès Bello U., Chile, U. Chile, U. Tex., Austin, U. Concepcion, U. Santiago; guest prof. U. Fla., 1973; adj. prof. U. Md., 1992—93; vis. prof. Polit. Sci. Inst., U. Chile, 1993—95; assoc. prof. Finis Terrae U., 1993—; scholar World Assn. Internat. Studies, Stanford U., 1999—; adj. scholar Inst. of World Politics, Washington, 2003—. Author: Through the American Looking Glass; Central America's Crisis, 1980, Allende: Death of a Marxist Dream, 1981, Catastrophe in the Caribbean: The Failure of America's Human Rights Policy in Central America, 1984, The Soviet Assault on America's Southern Flank, 1988, Out of the Ashes: Life, Death and Transfiguration of Democracy in Chile, 1833-1988, 1989, Hunters in the Sky, 1991, Desde las Cenizas: Vida, Muerte y Transfiguracion de la Democracia en Chile, 1833-1988, 1993, 2d edit., 1995. Bd. dirs. Christian Community Service Agy., Miami, 1973, Hialeah-Miami Springs (Fla.) C. of C., 1976-77, Wolf Trap Found., 1984-87; bd. dirs. Nat. Council for Better Edn.; chmn. print media div. United Way campaign, Sacramento, 1981; bd. govs. Council on Nat. Policy, Washington, 1981-87; del. Commn. of Californias, 1981; chmn. Council for Inter-Am. Security Ednl. Inst., 1986-90; mem. spl. task force on pub. safety Greater Washington Bd. Trade; mem. Nat. Commn. on Free and Responsible Media, 1983-84; bd. dirs. Nat. Bus. Consortium for Gifted and Talented Children, 1985-87; bd. govs. Internat. Policy Forum, 1985—; mem. Presdl. Bd. Fgn. Scholarships (Fulbright Commn.), 1986-92, exec. planning com., 1987-92. With Signal Corps U.S. Army, 1953-55. Nieman fellow Harvard U., 1966-67; recipient citation of excellence Overseas Press Club, 1971, Unity award Lincoln U., 1976, Golden Press award Am. Legion Aux., 1977, Freedom award Valley Forge Found., 1981, Bernardo O'Higgins award Chilean Govt., 1990, presented at Chilean Embassy by Amb. Octavio Errazuriz. Mem.: Instituto O'Higginiano de Chile, Harvard Club (N.Y.C.), Cosmos Club, Georgetown Club.

WHELAN, JOSEPH L. neurologist; b. Chisholm, Minn., Aug. 13, 1917; s. James Gorman and Johanna (Quilty) W.; m. Gloria Ann Rewoldt, June 12, 1948; children: Joe, Jennifer. Student, Hibbing Jr. Coll., 1935-38; BS, U. Minn., 1940, MB, 1942, MD, 1943. Diplomate Am. Bd. Psychiatry and Neurology. Intern Detroit Receiving Hosp., 1942-43; fellow neurology U. Pa. Hosp., Phila., 1946-47; resident neurology U. Minn. Hosps., Mpls., 1947-49; chief neurology svc. VA Hosp., Mpls., 1949; spl. fellow electroencephalography Mayo Clinic, Rochester, Minn., 1951; practice medicine specializing in neurology Detroit, 1949-73, Petoskey and Gaylord, Mich., 1973-87; asst. prof. Wayne State U., 1957-63. Chief neurology svcs. Grace Hosp., St. John's Hosp., Bon Secour Hosp., Detroit; cons. neurologist No. Mich. Hosps., Charlevoix Area Hosp.; instr. Med. Sch. U. Minn., 1949; com. USPHS, Detroit Bd. Edn. Contbr. articles to profl. jours. Founder, mem. ad hoc Com. to Force Lawyers Out of Govt. Fellow Am. Acad. Neurology (treas. 1955-57), Am. Electroencephalography Soc.; mem. AMA, AAAS, Assn. Rsch. Nervous and Mental Diseases, Soc. Clin. Neurologists, Mich. Neurol. Assn. (sec.-treas. 1967-76, Disting. Physician award 1988), Mich. Med. Soc., No. Mich. Med. Soc., Grosse Pointe (Mich.) Club. Address: 9797 N Twin Lake Rd NE Mancelona MI 49659-9203

WHELAN, MARY KATHLEEN, marketing professional, consultant; d. Thomas Edward and Grace O'Leary Whelan; m. Nicholas G. Nyary, Aug. 16, 1980; 1 child, Miklos Whelan Nyary. BS, St. Peter's Coll., Jersey City, 1971. V.p. pub. rels., strategy and new and advanced svcs. AT&T, Bridgewater, NJ, 1995—97; v.p. product mktg. AT&T Internet Svcs., Bridgewater, 1997—99; v.p. global market ops. Lucent Techs., Warren, NJ, 1999—2000, v.p. ebusiness, 2000—01; pres. eMarkets Group, Basking Ridge, NJ, 2001—; v.p. mktg. BioElectronics Corp., Frederick, Md., 2002—, also bd. dirs. Mem. adv. bd. i360, Washington, 2001—02. Prodr.: (video) 10 Decades of Change (U.S. Indsl. Film Festival, 1982). Campaign mgr. Councilman Campaign, Jersey City, 1977—77. Recipient Recognition for Excellence in Sci. Writing, Ford Found., 1966; grantee, NSF, 1966. Mem.: N.Y. New Media. Office: BioElectronics Corp 23 Crest Dr Basking Ridge NJ 07920-2802 E-mail: mkwhelan@bioelectronicscorp.com.

WHELAN, RICHARD J. retired academic administrator; b. Emmett, Kans, June 23, 1931; s. Richard Joseph and Margaret Alma (Cox) W.; m. Carol Ann King, Nov. 21, 1959; children— Mark Richard, Cheryl Lynne BA, Washburn U., 1955; Ed.D., U. Kans., 1966. Dir. edn. Menninger Clinic, Topeka, 1959-62; dir. edn. children's rehab. unit U. Kans. Med. Ctr., Kansas City, Kans., 1966-99; prof. spl. edn. and pediatrics, chmn. dept. spl. edn. U. Kans., Lawrence, 1966-72, 78-80, 83-88, assoc. dean grad. studies and outreach, 1988-94, Ralph L. Smith disting. prof. child devel., 1968-99, dean sch. edn., 1992-94, prof. emeritus, 1999—; div. dir. U.S. Office Edn., Washington, 1972-74; cons. Blue Valley Sch. Dist., Overland Park, Kans., 1999—; complaint investigator Kans. Bd. of Edn., 2000—. Cons. colls. and univs., state and fed. agys.; chmn. policy bd. Evaluation Tng., Kalamazoo, 1975-81 Author, editor: Promising Practices..., 1983, Emotional and Behavioral Disorders, 1998; cons. editor Ednl. Research Ency., 1982; contbr. articles to profl. jours., chpts. to books Chmn. adv. bd. Kans. Bd. Edn., Topeka, 1982-92; mem. adv. bd. Shawnee Mission Sch. Dist., Kans., 1984-92; mem. Gov.'s Task Force on Early Childhood, 1984-92; hearing officer various sch. dists. Kans. Bd. Edn., Bur. Indian Affiars; mediator and trainer Kans. Superior Ct. Mem. Soc. for Learning Disabilities (pres. 1980-81), Council for Exceptional Children, Assn. for Persons with Severe Handicaps (bd. dirs. 1975-79), Kans. Council for Exceptional Children (pres. 1963-64, Service award 1978, award for excellence 2000), Phi Kappa Phi Avocations: reading, music, golf, flying. Home: 7400 West 148th St Overland Park KS 66223 E-mail: rwhelan@kumc.edu.

WHELAN, ROGER MICHAEL, lawyer, educator; b. Montclair, NJ, Nov. 12, 1936; s. John Leslie and Helen Louise (Callahan) W.; m. Rosemary Bogdan, Aug. 26, 1961; children: Helen, Theresa, John, James, Kathleen (dec.), Julie, Jennifer. AB cum laude, Georgetown U., 1959, JD, 1962. Bar: DC 1962, U.S. Dist. Ct. DC 1962, U.S. Ct. Appeals (DC cir.) 1962, U.S. Supreme Ct. 1968, U.S. Dist. Ct. Md. 1985. Assoc. Fried, Rogers & Ritz, Washington, 1961—66; ptnr. Doctor & Whelan, Washington, 1967—72; judge U.S. Bankruptcy Ct., Washington, 1972—83; sr. mem. Verner, Liipfert, Bernhard, McPherson & Hand, Chartered, Washington, 1984—89; ptnr., sr. counsel Shaw, Pittman, Potts & Trowbridge, Washington, 1989—2000; outside counsel to several Washington & Md. law firms, 2000—; resident scholar Am. Bankruptcy Inst., 2004. Dir. Lincoln Ctr. for Legal Studies, Arlington, Va., 1974-84; disting. lectr. Columbus Sch. Law, Cath. U. Am., Washington, 1975—; bd. govs. Conf. on Consumer Fin. Law, 1995—; resident scholar Am. Bankruptcy Inst., 2004. Sec. local campaign com., Alexandria, Va., 1964; trustee YMCAA, Silver Spring, Md., 1972-74. Recipient award DC Cir. Jud. Conf., 1984. Fellow: Am. Coll. Bankruptcy (bd. regents 1989—95, bd. dirs. 1995—2002); mem.: FBA (chmn. bankruptcy subcom. 1988, exec. com. 1993—96, pres. 1999—2000), Assn. Former Bankruptcy Judges (sec.-treas. 1996—), Am. Bankruptcy Inst. (bd. dirs. 1991—97, chmn. legis. com. 1991—99, exec. com. 1993—95, apptd. resident scholar 2004), Walter Chandler Inn of Ct. (master emeritus 1990—). Republican. Roman Catholic. Avocations: fishing, hunting, boating. Home: 17908 Ednor View Ter Ashton MD 20861-9757 Office Phone: 301-260-7707. E-mail: rmwhelan@msn.com.

WHELAN, SUSAN, member of parliament; b. Windsor, Ont., Can., May 5, 1963; d. Elizabeth and Eugene Whelan. Degree in commerce, U. Windsor, B in Laws, 1988; JD, U. Detroit. Bar: Ont. 1990. Assoc. Yuffy, Roberts, Goldstein, Manzocco, Windsor, 1988-93; M.P. for Essex-Windsor House of Commons, 1993—, parliamentary sec. to Min. Nat. Revenue, 1993-96, mem. standing com. pub. accouts, 1994-96, assoc. mem. standing com. on fin., 1994-96, vice chair fin. com., 1996-97, mem. justice subcom. on draft regulations on firearms, 1996-97, mem. subcom. on rev. of spl. import measures act, 1996, chair industry com., 1997—2002, min. internal cooperation, 2002—03. Former dir. Essex Region Conservation Found., Alzheimer Soc. Windsor and Essex County. Named "Hon. Susan E. Whelan", Minister for Internat. Coop., 2002. Mem. Law Soc. Upper Can., Can. Bar Assn., Essex County Law Assn. Office: 46 Fox St N8M2S2 Essex ON Canada

WHELCHEL, ANITA E. publishing executive; d. Andrew Jackson and Sandra Jane Whelchel. Receptionist Nat. Writers Assn., Aurora, Colo., 1995—97; pub. intern Write Way Pub., Aurora, Colo., 1997, Nat. Writers Press, Aurora, Colo., 1997, mgr., 1998—. Conf. coord. Nat. Writers Assn. Found., Aurora, Colo., 1998—; coll. dean Colo. Ind. Publishers Assn., Denver, 2001—01. Author: (poetry) Writer's World Magazine, Treasured Poems of America. Recipient Best How-To Profl., Colo. Ind. Publishers Assn., 2000, Second Pl. Entrepreneurship Event, FCCLA-HERO State Conf., 1997, Outstanding HERO Employee, Ponderosa H.S. FCCLA-HERO, 1997. Mem.: Nat. Writers Assn. Avocations: travel, snowboarding, gourmet cooking. Office: National Writers Press 3140 South Peoria St #294 Aurora CO 80014 Office Phone: 720-851-1944.

WHELCHEL, SANDRA JANE, writer; b. Denver, May 31, 1944; d. Ralph Earl and Janette Isabelle (March) Everitt; m. Andrew Jackson Whelchel, June 27, 1965; children: Andrew Jackson, Anita Earlyn. BA in Elem. Edn., U. No. Colo., 1966; postgrad., Pepperdine Coll., 1971, UCLA, 1971. Elem. tchr. Douglas County Schs., Castle Rock, Colo., 1966-68, El Monte (Calif.) schs., 1968-72; br. libr. Douglas County Librs., Parker, Colo., 1973-78; zone writer Denver Post, 1979-81; reporter The Express newspapers, Castle Rock, 1979-81; history columnist Parker Trail newspapers, 1985-93; columnist Authorship Mag., 1991—, Gothic Jour., 1994; writing tchr. Aurora Parks and Recreation, 1985-91; writing instr. Arapahoe C.C., 1991-2000; exec. dir. Nat. Writers Assn., 1991—. Lectr. on writing and history Durango Writer's Workshop, 1996-97, Estes Park Writer's Retreat, 1996-97, Pikes Peak Writer's Workshop, 1997, Sinipee Writer's Workshop, 1998, Oasis for Seniors, 2000, Denver Women's Press Club, 1999, Rocky Mountain Gold Conf., 1999, Colo. Writers Fellowship, 2000, Colo. Ind. Publishers, 2000; spkr. Internat. Olympiad of Mind, Paris, 2000, Art Cafe, 2003; motivational spkr. various Optomist groups in Denver area; hist. tours, Parker, Colo. Editor Authorship mag., 1992-98; lit. agent NWLA, 1996-99; contbr. short stories and articles to various publs. including: The Writer, Writer's Open Forum, Writer's Jour., Reunions, Fresno Bee, Ancestry Newsletter, Calif. Horse Rev., Host mag., Jack and Jill, Child Life, Children's Digest, Peak to Peak mag.; author (non-fiction books): Your Air Force Academy, 1982, A Guide to the U.S. Air Force Acad., 1990, Parker, Colorado: A Folk History, 1990, The Beginning Writer's Writing Book, 1996, A Folk History of Parker and Hilltop, 1996, (treatment writer documentary) Wild Blue, 2003; co-author: The Writer's Office, 1998, The Register, 1989, (coloring books) A Day at the Cave, 1985, A Day in Blue, 1984, Pro Rodeo Hall of Champions and Museum of the American Cowboy, 1985, Pikes Peak Country, 1986, Mile High Denver, 1987. Mem.: Nat. Writers Assn. (pres. 1990, 1991, 2003—04), Colo. Author's League (awards com. 1999—2000, who's who com. 2001), Parker Area Hist. Soc. (pres. 1987—89), Nat. Writer's Club (treas. Denver Metro chpt. 1985—86, v.p. membership 1987, sec, 1990, bd. dirs., pres. 1990—91, v.p. programs 1992, v.p. membership 2002, bd. dirs., pres. 2003). Office Phone: 303-841-0246. *Personal philosophy: Tenacity and perseverance are keys to success. Optimism and self-belief open the door. The goals achieved through these elements are the most thrilling and savory.*

WHELDEN, CRAIG B. retired army officer; b. Ind., Oct. 8, 1951; m. Karen Lusk; children: Scott, Holly. BA, Purdue U.; MA, Webster U. Commd. 2d lt. U.S. Army, 1973, advanced through grades to maj. gen.; comdr. 98th area Support Group, Wuerzburg, Germany, 1994-95; chief of staff 3d Inf. Divsn., 1995-96; dep. dir. for ops. Nat. Mil. Command Ctr., Pentagon, Washington, 1996-98; comdg. gen. Cmty. and Family Support Ctr., Alexandria, Va., 1998—2000; dep. comdr. U.S. Army Pacific, Ft. Shafter, Hawaii, 2000—04; ret.; ind. sales assoc. Pre-Paid Legal Svcs., Inc., Celebration, Fla. Bd. mem. World Trade Ctr.-Orlando, Army's Morale, Welfare and Recreation Exec. Com. Decorated Legion of Merit, Army Commendation medal, others. Home and Office: 1250 Celebration Ave Celebration FL 34747*

WHELESS, ALBERT EUGENE, lawyer; b. Timmonsville, S.C., Feb. 15, 1935; s. Albert B. and Marie (Martin) W.; m. Celeste Graham, Sept. 6, 1958; children— Al, Art, Ann Marie. BA, Wofford Coll., 1959; JD, U. S.C., 1969. Bar: S.C. 1969. Assoc. John W. Jenrette, North Myrtle Beach, S.C., 1969, ptnr. Jenrette & Wheless, North Myrtle Beach, 1970-75, Jenrette, Wheless, McInnis & Breeden, North Myrtle Beach, 1976-79, Wheless & McInnis, North Myrtle Beach, 1980—; city recorder North Myrtle Beach, 1970-71, city atty., 1972-79. Mem. ABA, S.C. Bar Assn., Horry County Bar Assn. (pres. 1982-84), ATLA, S.C. Trial Lawyers Assn., S.C. Def. Attys. Assn. Office: 457 Main St North Myrtle Beach SC 29582-3023

WHELESS, JAMES WARREN, neurologist; b. Glens Falls, N.Y., Apr. 18, 1956; s. True and Adelphine Ada (Bump) W.; m. Annette Carolyn Hyland, Apr. 7, 1984; children: Catherine Elizabeth, Margaret Caroline. BS, U. Okla., Oklahoma City, 1978, MD, 1982. Diplomate Am. Bd. Pediatrics, Am. Bd. Psychiatry and Neurology with spl. qualification in child neurology, with spl. qualification in clin. neurophysiology. Intern, then pediatric resident U. Okla.-Tulsa Med. Coll., 1982-85; fellow in child neurology Northwestern U., Chgo., 1985-88; fellow in clin. neurophysiology/epilepsy Med. Coll. Ga., Augusta, 1988-89; asst. prof. neurology and pediatrics U. Tex., Houston, 1989-95, dir. epilepsy monitoring unit, 1989—, assoc. prof. neurology and pediatrics, 1995-2000, prof. neurology and pediats., 2000—; dir., dir. pedia. epilepsy sect., head clin. EEG Tex. Comprehensive Epilepsy Program, 1998—. Exec. bd. internat. epilepsy consortium Nat. Tuberous Sclerosis Assn. Contbr. articles to profl. jours., chpt. to book; mem. editl. bd.: Jour. of Child Neurology, The Stroke Interventionalist, Formulary. Camp physician Kamp Kleidoscope, Livingston, Tex., 1995—; mem. profl. bd. Nat. Tuberous Sclerosis Assn., Citizens United for Rsch. in Epilepsy; mem. exec. bd. Internat. Epilepsy Consortium. Pres.'s Fund grantee U. Tex.-Houston, 1990, Children's Miracle Network Telethon grantee Hermann Children's Hosp.; rsch. grantee NIH. Fellow Am. Acad. Neurology, Child Neurology Soc.; mem. AMA, Am. Epilepsy Soc., Am. Acad. Pediatrics, Epilepsy Assn. of Houston/Gulf Coast (chmn. profl. adv. bd. 1992-94). Avocations: running, camping, hiking, travel, reading. Office: U Tex-Houston Dept Neurology 6431 Fannin St Ste 7044 Houston TX 77030-1501 Office Phone: 713-500-7117.

WHELIHAN, ALAN STUART, real estate developer, automotive executive; b. Phila., Sept. 17, 1932; s. John Franklin and Dorothy Dodge W.; m. Joan Murrell, June 20, 1959; children: Pamela, Deborah, Linda, Jacqueline. BS in Engring., Princeton U., 1954; MBA, U. Pa., 1960. Elect. engr. Philco Corp., Phila., 1954-55; product line mgr. govt. and indsl. divsn. RCA, Camden, N.J., 1959-65; gen. mgr. Chem. Micromilling Co., Pensauken, N.J., 1965-66; mgmt. cons. Peat Marwick Mitchell & Co., Washington, N.J., 1966-72; asst. commr. Fed. Supply Svc., Arlington, Va., 1973-79; dir. planning and coordination U.S. Metric Bd., Arlington, Va., 1979-82; dir. metric program U.S. Dept. Commerce, Washington, 1983-94; pres. VAW, LLC, Frederick, Md., 1994—, W Properties, L.L.C., Frederick, 1994. Dir. Am. Nat. Stds. Inst., 1973-75, Am. Nat. Metric Coun., Washington, 1990-92. Lt. Comdr. USNR, 1955-57. Mem. IEEE (life), Soc. Automotive Engrs. (metric adv. bd. 1990—), Congl. Country Club. Republican. Avocation: collecting antique automobiles. Office: W Properties LLC Stanford Indsl Park 4975 Winchester Blvd Frederick MD 21703-7400 Home: PO Box 221 Adamstown MD 21710-0221

WHELPLEY, DENNIS PORTER, lawyer; b. Mpls., Feb. 16, 1951; s. John Olsen and Harriet Marie (Porter) W.; m. Patricia Jan Adamy, Nov. 27, 1976; children: Heather Nicolle, Christopher Eric. BA, U. Minn., 1973, JD magna cum laude, 1976. Bar: Minn. 1976. Assoc. Oppenheimer Wolff & Donnelly, St. Paul, 1976-83, ptnr., 1983—. Mem. Order of Coif (Minn. chpt.), Phi Beta Kappa (Alpha of Minn. chpt.), Psi Upsilon (Mu chpt.), Dellwood Hills Golf & Country Club. Avocations: golf, tennis, squash, bridge. Home: 49 Locust St Mahtomedi MN 55115-1542 Office: Oppenheimer Wolff & Donnelly 45 S 7th St Ste 3300 Minneapolis MN 55402-1614 Office Phone: 612-607-7397. E-mail: dwhelpley@oppenheimer.com.

WHETSELL, PAUL W. hotel executive; Grad., Davidson Coll. Various positions to v.p. Quality Inns; v.p. devel. Lincoln Hotels, Dallas; founder, chmn., pres., CEO CapStar Hotel Co., Washington, 1987—; chmn. & CEO MeriStar Hotels & Resorts, Inc., MeriStar Hospitality Corp, Washington, D.C. Bd. dirs. Cystic Fibrosis Found. of Nat. Capitol Area; bd. govs. Marriott Hospitality H.S. NAREIT. Office: Meristar Hospitality Corp #800 4501 Fairfax DR Arlington VA 22203-1656 Fax: 202-295-2230.

WHETTEN, JOHN D. food products executive; b. Chgo., June 8, 1940; s. Lester and Kate (Allred) W.; m. Becky Pearse; children: Carma, Rebecca, Mary Coza. BS, Brigham Young U., 1965; MBA, U. Calif., Berkeley, 1967. Advt. and mktg. mgr. The Clorox Corp., Oakland, Calif., 1967-79; pres., CEO Challenge Dairy Products, Inc., Dublin, Calif., 1982—; CEO DairyAmerica, Inc., Dublin, Calif., 1995-98. U.S. rep. Internat. Dairy Mktg. and Promotion Ann. Meeting, 1996. Co-chair U.S. Butter Task Force, 1990—97; mem. nat. steering com. Brigham Young U. Sch. Mgmt., 1992—95; mem. nat. adv. coun. Utah Valley State Coll., 2001—; bd. dirs. U.S. Dry Export Coun., 1995—98, Epidermolysis Bullosa Med. Rsch. Found., 1991—. Mem.: Western Assn. Milk Mktg. Coop. (bd. dirs. 1992—2002, sec. 1994—2002), Barbecue Industry Assn. (dir. 1974—79, pres. 1977—78), Dairy Mktg. Coop. Fedn. (pres. 1992—), Dairy Export Incentive Program Coalition (pres. 1994—), Am. Dairy Products Inst. (bd. dirs. 1982—98, hon. life dir. 1999—), Am. Butter Inst. (bd. dirs. 1982—, v.p. 1995—99, pres. 1999—2001, Pres.'s Disting. Svc. award 1991). Office: Challenge Dairy Products Inc 11875 Dublin Blvd Ste B230 Dublin CA 94568-2818 E-mail: john@challengedairy.com.

WHETTEN, LAWRENCE L. international relations educator; b. Provo, Utah, June 12, 1932; s. Lester B. and Kate (Allred) W.; m. Gabriele Indra, Oct. 28, 1974 (dec. May 1985). BA, Brigham U., 1954, MA, 1955; PhD with honors, NYU, 1963. Sr. polit. analyst Hdqrs. USAFE, Wiesbaden, Fed. Republic Germany, 1963-70; resident dir. grad. program in internat. relations U. So. Calif., Munich, Fed. Republic Germany, 1971-78, dir. studies USC/SIR grad. program in Germany, 1978-86; Erich Voegelin Gast prof. Munich U., 1987-88; lectr. Boston U., 1988—; lectr. Profl. Assoc. Ctr. Def. and Strategic Studies S.W. Mo. State U., Springfield, 1991—. Cons. Fgn. Policy Inst., Phila., 1969-71, 76-79, R & D Assocs., Munich, 1977; prof. Hochschule für Politik, Munich U.; adj. prof., profl. assoc. Ctr. for Def. and Strategic Studies, S.W. Mo. State U., 1991—. Author: Germany's Ostpolitik, 1971, Contemporary American Foreign Policy, 1974, The Canal War: Four Power Conflict, 1974, Germany East and West, 1981. Author, editor: Present State Communist Internationalism, 1983, The Interaction of Political Reforms Within the East Block, 1989. Served to capt. USAF, 1960-63 Penfield fellow NYU, 1957-59; grantee Ford Found., 1970, Royal Inst. Internat. Affairs, London, 1970, Thyssen Found., Cologne, Germany, 1974-82, 89, Volkswagen Found., 1982-85 Mem. Am. Acad. Polit. and Social Scis., Internat. Inst. Strategic Studies, Am. Assn. Advancement of Soviet Studies, Gesellschaft für Auslandskunde, German Am. Assn. Home: Widenmayerstrasse 41 80538 Munich Germany

WHICHARD, WILLIS PADGETT, law educator, retired state supreme court justice; b. Durham, N.C., May 24, 1940; s. Willis Guilford and Beulah (Padgett) W.; m. Leona Irene Paschal, June 4, 1961; children: Jennifer Diane, Ida Gilbert. AB, U. N.C., 1962, JD, 1965; LLM, U. Va., 1984, SJD, 1994. Bar: N.C. 1965. Law clk. N.C. Supreme Ct., Raleigh, 1965-66; ptnr. Powe, Porter, Alphin & Whichard, Durham, 1966-80; assoc. judge N.C. Ct. Appeals, Raleigh, 1980-86; assoc. justice N.C. Supreme Ct., Raleigh, 1986-98; dean and prof. law Campbell U. Instr. grad. sch. bus. adminstrn. Duke U., 1978; vis. lectr. U. N.C. Sch. Law, 1986-98. Contbr. articles to profl. jours. Rep. N.C. Ho. of Reps., Raleigh, 1970-74; senator N.C. Senate, 1974-80, chair numerous coms. and commns.; N.C. legis. rsch. commn., 1971-73, 75-77, land policy coun., 1975-79; bd. dirs. Sr. Citizens Coordinating Coun., 1972-74; chair local crusade Am. Cancer Soc., 1977, state crusade chair, 1980, chair pub. issues com., 1980-84; pres., bd. chmn. Downtown Durham Devel. Corp., 1980-84; bd. dirs. Durham County chpt. ARC, 1971-79; Durham county campaign dir. March of Dimes, 1968, 69, chmn., 1969-74, bd. dirs. Triangle chpt., 1974-79; bd. advisors Duke Hosp., 1982-85, U. N.C. Sch. Pub. Health, 1985-96, U. N.C. Sch. Social Work, 1989—; bd. visitors N.C. Ctrl. U. Sch. Law, 1987—; mem. law sch. dean search com. U. N.C., 1978-79, 88-89, self-study com., 1985-86; pres. N.C. Inst. Justice, 1984-94; bd. dirs. N.C. Ctr. Crime and Punishment, 1984-94. Staff sgt. N.C. Army NG, 1966-72. Recipient Disting. Service award Durham Jaycees, 1971, Outstanding Legis. award N.C. Acad. Trial Lawyers, 1975, Outstanding Youth Svc. award N.C. Juvenile Correctional Assn., 1975, named Citizen of Yr. Eno Valley Civitan Club, Durham, 1982, Faith Active in Pub. Life award N.C. Coun. of Churches, 1983, Outstanding Appellate Judge award N.C. Acad. Trial Lawyers, 1983; named to Durham H.S. Hall of Fame, 1987. Mem. ABA, N.C. Bar Assn. (v.p. 1983-84, 2001-02), Durham County Bar Assn., U. N.C. Law Alumni Assn. (pres. 1978-79, bd. dirs. 1979-82), Nat. Guard Assn. (judge adv. 1972-73, legis. com. 1974-76), Order of Golden Fleece, Order of Grail, Order of Old Well, Amphoterothen Soc., Order of Coif, Phi Alpha Theta, Phi Kappa Alpha, Durham-Chapel Hill Torch Club (pres. 1984-85), Watauga Club (Raleigh, pres. 1994-95). Democrat. Baptist. Home: 84402 Winslow Chapel Hill NC 27517 Office: Wiggins Sch Law Campbell Univ PO Box 158 Buies Creek NC 27506-0158 Office Phone: 910-893-1750. E-mail: Whichard@law.campbell.edu., whichoo1@earthlink.net.

WHIDDEN, STANLEY JOHN, physiologist, physician; b. Oct. 10, 1947, s. Stanley Graham and Maybell (Van Houten) W.; m. Jan Venable Whidden, 1987. AS, Delgado Coll., 1969; BS, Southeastern La. U., 1971, MS, 1973; PhD, Auburn U., 1979; MD, U. Autono. de Ciudad Juarez, Mex., 1984; postgrad., Hyperbaric Physicians Ctr., NOAA, Nat. Def. U., 1986, Naval War Coll., 1996, Army War Coll., 1998. Asst. head ops. Nuclear Sci. Ctr., Auburn U., Ala., 1976-78; lectr. physiology U. Wis., Madison, 1978-79; asst. prof. U. New Orleans, 1980-82; rsch. med. staff JESM Baromed. Inst., New Orleans, 1984-86; asst. prof. rsch. physiology dept. La. State U. Med. Ctr., New Orleans, 1988-89; mgr. program Dept. Justice, Nat. Inst. Justice; intern Naval War Coll., Preventive Medicine, U.S. Army Ctr. Health. Contbr. chpts. to books: Handbook of Shock and Trauma, 1983, Physiological Basis of Decompression Sickness, 1987, Active Duty Army Combat Operation "Just Cause" Panama, 1990. Col. USAR, 1966—, Desert Storm/Shield, Saudi Action, 1991, Op. Provide Hope, Somalia, 1993. Decorated Bronze star; recipient Meritorious Svc. medal, Acom medal, UN medal, 1994; named to Hon. col. La. Gov. Staff, 1985; named one of Outstanding Young Men of Am., 1986; USAF fellow, Sch. Aero Medicine, Brooks AFB, Tex., 1986, 87, NASA fellow, Johnson Space Ctr., 1987; recipient Md. Gov.'s Citation, 1991. Mem. AAUP, AAAS, Am. Physiology Soc., Soc. Neurosci., Am. Chem. Soc., Aerospace Med. Assn., Aerospace Physiol. Soc., Am. Vet. Physiology and Pharmacology Soc., Am. Burn Assn., N.Y.Acad. Sci., Shock Soc., Undersea Med. Soc., Spl. Forces Assn. (New Orleans, pres. 1983-84, pres. Washington chpt. 1996-98). Achievements include research in underlining trial medical requirements during clinical research. Office: La Inst Clin Trial Mgmt 2917 Prytania St New Orleans LA 70115-3313 E-mail: swhidden@aol.com.

WHIDDON, THOMAS E. retail executive; BS in Acctg. magna cum laude, U. Ala., 1974. Tax ptnr. KPMG Peat Marwick, Tampa, Fla.; various positions to v.p. and treas. Eckerd Corp.; sr. v.p., treas. Zale Corp., 1994-95, sr. v.p., CFO, 1995-96; exec. v.p., CFO, Lowe's Cos., Inc., North Wilkesboro, N.C., 1996-2000, exec. v.p. logistics and tech., 2000—. Office: Lowe's Cos Inc PO Box 1111 North Wilkesboro NC 28659-1111

WHIFFEN, JAMES DOUGLASS, surgeon, educator; b. N.Y.C., Jan. 16, 1931; s. John Phillips and Lorna Elizabeth (Douglass) W.; child from a previous marriage, Gregory James; m. Sally Vilas Runge, Aug. 21, 1993. BS, U. Wis., 1952, MD, 1955. Diplomate: Am. Bd. Surgery. Intern Ohio State U. Hosp., 1955-56; resident U. Wis. Hosp., 1956-57, 59-61; instr. dept. surgery U. Wis. Med. Sch., 1962-64, asst. prof., 1964-67, assoc. prof., 1967-71, prof., 1971-96, vice chmn. dept., 1970-72, acting chmn., 1972-74; asst. dean Med. Sch., 1975-96; prof. emeritus U. Wis. Med. Sch., 1996—; mem. exam. council State of Wis. Emergency Med. Services, 1974-77. Bd. dirs. Wis. Heart Assn. Served to lt. comdr. USNR, 1957-59. John and Mary R. Markle scholar in acad. medicine, also; Research Career Devel. award NIH, 1965-75 Fellow A.C.S., Am. Soc. Artificial Internal Organs. Clubs: Maple Bluff Country. Achievements include research publs. on biomaterials, thrombo-resistant surfaces and the physiology of heart-lung bypass procedures. Home: 17 Cambridge Ct Madison WI 53704-5906 Office: 600 Highland Ave Madison WI 53792-0001 E-mail: jwhiffen@wisc.edu.

WHIGHAM, MARK ANTHONY, computer scientist; b. Mobile, Ala., Jan. 14, 1959; s. Tommie Lee Sr. and Callie Mae (Molette) W. BS in Computer Sci., Ala. A&M U., 1983, MS in Computer Sci., 1990; postgrad., Ala. A&M Univ., 1995—. Computer programmer U.S. Army Corps of Engrs., Huntsville, Ala., 1985-88; programmer analyst, coord. acad. computing Ala. A&M U., Normal, Ala., 1988-89, programmer analyst II, DEC systems coord., instr. part-time computer sci. dept., 1989-91; systems engr. Advanced Bus. Cons. Inc.-La. div. Dow Chem. Co., 1991-93; owner Whigham's Computer Cons., 1990—; sys. engr. DOW Chem. Co.-USA La. Divsn., Plaquemine, La., 1991-93; instr. computer info. system Calhoun C.C., Decatur, Ala., 1993-97; network specialist/cons. Ala. A&M U., Normal, 1994—; computer info. sys. instr. Calhoun C.C., Decatur, Ala., 1994—; mgmt. info. sys. dir., CIO J.F. Drake Tech. Coll., Huntsville, Ala., 1997-98; software engr. Colsa Corp., Huntsville, Ala., 1998—99; dir. info. tech. Lane Coll., 1999—2000; instr. computer sci. Lawson State CC, 2000—. Instr. computer sci. dept. Ala. A&M U., 1989-91; network specialist, cons. Ala. A&M U., Normal, 1994—. Active Huntsville Interdenominational Ministerial Fellowship, Huntsville, 1984. Mem. Nat. Assn. Sys. Programmers, Ala. Coun. for Computer Edn., Assn. for Computing Machinery, Huntsville Jaycees, Nat. Soc. Black Engrs., Assn. Info. Tech. Profls., So. Poetry Assn., Nat. Arts Soc., Internat. Black Writers and Artists Assn., Optimists, U.S. Chess Fedn. (cert. chess coach), Future Bus. Leaders of Am.-Phi Beta Lambda, Sigma Tau Epsilon, Alpha Phi Omega. Baptist. Avocations: chess, skating, reading, playing piano. Office: Lawson State CC 3060 Wilson Rd Birmingham AL 35209-1542 Home: Apt 202 917 Valley Ridge Dr Birmingham AL 35209-1542 Business E-Mail: mwhigham@cougar.ls.cc.al.

WHINERY, MICHAEL ALBERT, physician; b. Watsford, Eng., June 30, 1951; s. Leo Howard and Doris Eileene W. and Alma Piper; m. Tatjiana Dunnebier, 1976 (dec. Jan. 1981); m. Judy Renee Wright, Apr. 30, 1982; children: Rhiannon Daire Eileene, Terron Rae Lee. BS, Okla. U., 1976; D of Osteopathy, Okla. State U., 1980. Diplomate Am. Bd. Family Practice. Intern Hillcrest Health Ctr., Oklahoma City, 1980-81; with McLoud Clinic, McLoud, Okla., 1981-98; staff physician Okla. Vets. Ctr., Claremore, 2000—. House physician McLoud Nursing Ctr., 1988—; med. examiner Pottawatomie County Health, McLoud, 1983—. Author: Poetic Voices of America, 1991; composer lyrics and music at Stella Gospel Rec. Studio, 2000, A Solder Last Prayer. Mem. Presdl. Order Merit Nat. Repub. Senatorial Com., Washington, 1991, Presdl. Task Force, 1983—, Senatorial Commn. Repub. Senatorial Inner Circle, Washington, 1991; mem. U.S. Congrl. Adv. Bd., 1993. Served with USMC, Vietnam era. Recipient Acknowledgement of Outstanding Contbn. in Clin. Rsch. award SANDOZ Labs., 1992, Rep. Presdl. Legion of Merit, 1994, Rep. Majority medal, U.S. Senate, 1997, Rep. Task Force medal of merit, 1997. Mem. Am. Legion, C. of C., Jr. C. of C., U.S. Senatorial Club (preferred mem.), U.S. Congressional Act Bd. (state advisor 1990-91). Baptist. Avocations: fishing, music, composing songs, poetry and writing lyrics. Office: PO Box 988 3001 W Bluestarr Claremore OK 74018 Office Phone: 918-342-5432. E-mail: MWhinery@ODVA.State.OK.US.

WHINNERY, JOHN ROY, electrical engineer, educator; b. Read, Colo., July 26, 1916; s. Ralph V. and Edith Mable (Bent) Whinnery; m. Patricia Barry, Sept. 17, 1944; children: Carol Joanne, Catherine, Barbara. BS Elec. Engring., U. Calif., Berkeley, 1937, PhD, 1948. With GE, 1937—46; part-time lectr. Union Coll., Schenectady, 1945—46; assoc. prof. elec. engring. U. Calif., Berkeley, 1946—52, prof., vice chmn. div. elec. engring., 1952—56, chmn., 1956—59, dean Coll. Engring., 1959—63, prof. elec. engring., 1963—80, Univ. prof. Coll. Engring., 1980—. Rsch. sci. electron tubes Hughes Aircraft Co., Culver City, 1951—52; vis. mem. tech. staff Bell Tel. Labs., 1963—64; mem. sci. and tech. com. Manned Space Flight, NASA, 1963—69; chmn. Commn. Engring. Edn., 1966—68; standing com. controlled thermonuclear rsch. AEC, 1970—73; mem. Pres.'s Com. on Nat. Sci. Medal, 1970—73, 1979—80. Author (with Simon Ramo): Fields and Waves in Communication Electronics, 1944; author: (with Ramo and Van Duzor) Fields and Waves in Communication Electronics, 3rd edit., 1994; author: (with D.O. Pederson and J.J. Studer) Introduction to Electronic Systems, Circuits and Devices; contbr. tech. articles. Named to Hall of Fame, Modesto (Calif.) H.S., 1983, ASEE Hall of Fame, 1993; recipient Lamme medal, Am. Soc. Engring. Edn., 1975, Centennial medal, 1993, Engring. Alumni award, U. Calif.-Berkeley, 1980, Nat. Medal of Sci., NSF, 1992;, Guggenheim Fellow, 1959. Fellow: IRE (bd. dirs. 1956—59), IEEE (life; bd. dirs. 1969—71, sec. 1971, Edn. medal 1967, Centennial medal 1984, Medal of Honor 1985), Am. Acad. Arts and Scis., Optical Soc. Am.; mem.: IEEE Microwave Theory and Techniques Soc. (disting. lectr. 1989—92, Microwave Career award 1977, Okawa prize in info. and telecom. 1997), NAS, NAE (Founders award 1986), Eta Kappa Nu (eminent mem.), Tau Beta Pi, Sigma Xi, Phi Beta Kappa. Congregationalist. Home: 1804 Wales Dr Walnut Creek CA 94595-2472 Office: U Calif Dept Elect Engring Berkeley CA 94720-1770

WHIPPLE, DEAN, federal judge; b. 1938; BS, Drury Coll., 1961; postgrad., U. Tulsa, 1961-62; JD, postgrad., U. Mo., Kansas City, 1965. Pvt. practice, Lebanon, Mo., 1965-75; cir. judge div. II 26th Jud. Cir. Mo., 1975-87; judge U.S. Dist. Ct., Kansas City, Mo., 1987-2000, chief judge, 2000—. Prosecuting atty. Laclede County, Mo., 1967-71. Mem. Cen. United Meth. Ch., Kansas City. With Mo. N.G., 1956-61; USAR, 1961-66. Mem. Mo. Bar Assn. (mem. pub. info. com. 1971-72, mem. judiciary com. 1971-72, mem. bd. govs. 1975-87, mem. exec. com. 1983-84, 86-87, mem. planning com. for ann. meeting 1985, 87, chmn. 1986, mem. selection com. for Lon Hocker award 1986), Mo. Trial Judges Assn., 26th Jud. Bar Assn., Laclede County Bar Assn. (pres. 1968-69, 72-73), Kansas City Met. Bar Assn., Kansas City Inn of Ct. (instr. 1988-93), Mo. Hist. Soc., Phi Delta Phi. Office: US Courthouse 400 E 9th St Kansas City MO 64106-2607

WHIPPLE, HARRY M. newspaper publishing executive; b. Tulsa, June 30, 1947; children: Garth, Erin. Student, Ind. U., 1965-68, U. Evansville, 1965-68, Ark Poly. Coll., 1965-68. Gen. mgr. Mt. Vernon (Ind.) Pub. Co., 1972-75; asst. pub. Pioneer Newspapers (formerly Scripps League Newspapers), Monongahela, Pa., 1975-77; asst. dir. Rockford (Ill.) Morning Star and Register Republic, 1977-81; pres., pub. Valley News Dispatch, The Herald, North Hills News Record, Tarentum, Pa., 1981-84; v.p., regional mgr. Midwest Gannett Media Sales/Gannett Nat. Sales, Chgo., 1984-87; pres. TNI Ptnrs., Tucson, 1987-92; pres., pub. The Cincinnati Enquirer, 1992—2003; ret. The Cin. Enquirer, 2003—. Co-chair adv. bd. Nat. Underground R.R. Freedom Ctr. Mem. Greater Cin. C. of C. (chmn. bd. trustees). Home: 5640 Windridge Court Cincinnati OH 45243

WHIPPLE, JUDITH ROY, editor; b. N.Y.C., May 14, 1935; d. Edwin Paul and Elizabeth (Levis) Roy; m. William Whipple, Oct. 26, 1963. AB, Mount Holyoke Coll., 1957. Head libr. Am. Sch. Lima (Peru), S.A., 1957-59; asst. editor children's books G.P. Putnam's Sons, N.Y.C., 1959-62; assoc. editor W.W. Norton & Co., Inc., N.Y.C., 1962-68; editor Four Winds Press, 1968-75; editor-in-chief Scholastic Gen. Book Divsn., 1975-77; pub. Four Winds Press subs. Scholastic Inc., N.Y.C., 1977-82; pub., v.p. Macmillan Pub. Co., N.Y.C., 1982-89, exec. editor, 1989-94; editl. dir. Cavendish Children's Books, Tarrytown, NY, 1994—2002. Mem. PEN, Children's Book Coun. (pres. 1977, bd. dirs. 1970-79), Women's Nat. Book Assn., Soc. Children's Book Writers and Illustrators. Avocations: gardening, swimming, piano, travel. E-mail: jrwhipple@stny.rr.com.

WHIPPLE, KENNETH, utilities executive; b. 1934; BS, MIT, 1958. With Ford Motor Co., Dearborn, Mich., 1958—, systems mgr. Ford Credit, 1966-69, mgr. mgmt. svcs. dept. fin. staff, 1969-71, systems analysis mgr. fin. staff, 1971-74, asst. contr. internat. fin. staff, 1974-75, v.p. fin. Ford Credit, 1975-77, exec. v.p. Ford Credit, 1977-80, pres. Ford Credit, 1980-84, v.p. corp. strategy, 1984-86; v.p. chmn. Ford of Europe, 1986-88; exec. v.p., pres. Ford Fin. Svcs. Group, Dearborn, 1988—99; chmn. bd., CEO CMS Energy, Dearborn, Mich., 2002—. Office: CMS Energy 1 Energy Plaza Drive Jackson MI 49201

WHIPPLE, MARY MARGARET, state legislator; b. Watsela, Ill., May 26, 1940; BA, Am. U.; MA, George Washington U. Mem. Va. State Senate, 1996—, mem. agrl., conservation & natural resources com., mem. local govt. com., mem. privileges & elections com., mem. transp. com. Democrat. Presbyterian. Office: Gen Assembly Bldg 910 Capitol St Rm 430 Richmond VA 23219-3400

WHIPPLE, WILLIAM, JR., government policy consultant, writer; b. Cinclare, La., Feb. 4, 1909; s. William and Genevieve (Randolph) W.; m. Dixie Ancrum, Mar. 30, 1935 (dec. Oct. 1955); children: Anne Calhoun, William III, Claire Randolph; m. Renée Pauline Exiga, July 21, 1956 (div. May 1974); 1 child, Philip; m. Frances Edith Cheek, June 1, 1974 (dec. July 1983); m. Alice Terry Goodloe, Dec. 1, 1984. BS, U.S. Mil. Acad., 1930; BA, Oxford (Eng.) U., 1933, MA, 1937; Civil Engr., Princeton U., 1936. Registered profl. engr., N.J. Commd. 2d lt. Corps Engrs., U.S. Army, 1930, advanced through grades to brig. gen., ret., 1960; chief engr. N.Y. World's Fair Corp., Flushing Meadow, N.Y., 1960-64; pvt. practice cons. engr. N.Y.C., 1964-65; dir. Water Resources Rsch. Inst. Rutgers U., New Brunswick, N.J., 1965-79, rsch. prof. Coastal and Environ. Inst., 1979-81; asst. dir. divsn. water resources Dept. Environ. Protection, Trenton, N.J., 1981-89, coord. nonpoint cource control program divsn. water resource, 1989-90; prin. Greeley Polhemus Group, Chester, Pa., 1990-2000; pvt. practice cons. Princeton, N.J., 1999—. Author: New Perspectives on Water Supply, 1994, Comprehensive Water Planning and Regulation, 1996, Water Resource: A New Era for Coordination, 1998; contbr. articles to publs. on water resources. Chmn. Flood Control Com., Princeton, N.J., 1975-81; adv. coun., Revision of N.J.'s Water Supply Master Plan, 2001. Recipient Trustees award N.J. inst. Tech., 1985, govt. award Water Resource Assn. of Delaware River Basin, 1987, Toulmin award for best articles Mil. Engr., 1975, Formal Commendation from Pres. of U.S., 1971. Fellow AAAS, ASCE (life, chmn. urban water resources rsch. coun. 1973-75, Lifetime Achievement award Inst. Environment and Water Resources 2001), Soc. Am. Mil. Engrs. (life), Am. Water Resources Assn. (pres. 1993, Icko Iben award 1978, William Ackerman medal 1989, Boggess award; mem. Am. Acad. Environ. Engrs. (diplomate), Univs. Coun. on Water Resources (chmn. 1976-78), Sigma Xi. Avocation: history and biography. Home and Office: 2 Hedge Row Rd Princeton NJ 08540-5055

WHIPPLE, WILLIAM PERRY, foundation administrator; b. Cedar Rapids, Iowa, Nov. 1, 1913; s. Robert Milo and Jeanette (Fry) W.; m. Gayle Schroeder, Sept. 18, 1937; children: John William, Robert Milo. BA, Coe Coll., 1935, PhD (hon.), 1996. Prin. Whipple Ins. Agy., Cedar Rapids, 1935-57; pres. Whipple and Winterberg, Cedar Rapids, 1957-71; chmn. Frank B. Hall of Iowa, Inc., Cedar Rapids, 1971-74; pres. Hall Found., Inc., Cedar Rapids, 1974-95, also bd. dirs.; chair Hall-Perrine Found., Cedar Rapids, 1995—. Exec. in residence Colo. State U., Fort Collins, 1973; bd. dirs. Fire Mark Cir. of Ams., Chamblee, Ga., Interocean Reins. Corp., Cedar Rapids, 1st Fed. Savs. and Loan, Cedar Rapids, Nissen Corp., Cedar Rapids, 1966-72, Banks of Iowa, Inc., Des Moines, 1982-85. Trustee Cedar Rapids Pub. Library, Coe Coll., chmn.; hon. bd. dirs. Methwick Manor, Cedar Rapids, Linn County ARC, Greater Cedar Rapids Found. Recipient Outstanding Layman award YMCA, Cedar Rapids, 1986, Alumni Achievement award, Coe Coll., 1990, Founders Day award Coe Coll., 2001, First Community Svc. award, Cedar Rapids Rotary, 1993. Mem. Rotary (Paul Harris fellow 1987), Elks. Presbyterian. Avocations: signevierist, stamp collecting/philately. Home: 1224 13th St NW Cedar Rapids IA 52405-2404 Office: Hall-Perrine Found 115 3d St SE Cedar Rapids IA 52401-1222

WHIPPLE, WOODROW THOMAS, artist, educator; b. Brattleboro, Vt., June 5, 1944; s. Howard Woodrow Whipple and Anna Mastelar; m. Tina Sue Huggins, Dec. 31, 1992 (div. Apr. 24, 1996); m. Evelyn Crowley, May 9, 1967 (div. June 29, 1988); 1 child, Lori Michelle Pate. Student, Columbus Sch. of Art, 1963—65. Graphic artist Dept. of Def., Ft. Benning, Ga., 1971—74; gallery owner, art instr. Le Gallerie, Columbus, Ga., 1974—78; visual info.

specialist Dept. of Def., Ft. Benning, Ga., 1978—95; art instr., graphic designer, cons. Visual Imagery Prodns., Columbus, Ga., 1995—99; instr. graphic arts Ga. Dept. of Corrections, Pulaski State Prison, Hawkinsville, 1999—; owner, founder BackYard Woodys Grill-N-Sauces, Bonaire, Ga., 2000—. Author (illustrator): Wing Ding Party Book; painting, Gunboat Chattahoochee (Purchase award for Ga. Bicentenial Top 10 Ga. Artist, 1975), Savannah Pier (Purchase award for permanet exhbn. collection in the Bradley Mus. of Art, 1975), exhibit, CISM XXIV Internation Shooting Championships Norway (Outstanding Contibution, 1985). Mem.: Ga. Correctional Edn. Assn., Lower Chattahoochee Archaeological Soc. (pres. 1985—86), Sports Car Club of Am. (regional exec. 1966—67), U.S. Power Squardron (comdr. 1987—88), Columbus Artist Guild. Republican. Episcopalian. Avocations: fine art, photography, cooking, travel. Home: 110 Chipper St Bonaire GA 31005 Office: Ga Dept of Corrections PSP Rte 2 Upper River Rd Hawkinsville GA 31036 Personal E-mail: gdcwhip@aol.com.

WHIPPS, EDWARD FRANKLIN, lawyer; b. Columbus, Ohio, Dec. 17, 1936; s. Rusk Henry and Agnes Lucille (Green) W.; children: Edward Scott, Rusk Huot, Sylvia Louise, Rudyard Christian. BA, Ohio Wesleyan U., 1958; JD, Ohio State U., 1961. Bar: Ohio 1961, U.S. Dist. Ct. (so. dist.) Ohio 1962, U.S. Dist. Ct. (no. dist.) Ohio 1964, U.S. Ct. Claims 1963, U.S. Supreme Ct. 1963, Miss. 1965, U.S. Ct. Appeals (6th cir.) 1980. Assoc. George, Greek, King & McMahon, Columbus, 1961-66; ptnr. George, Greek, King, McMahon & McConnaughey, Columbus, 1966-79, McConnaughey, Stradley, Mone & Moul, Columbus, 1979-81, Thompson, Hine & Flory, Columbus, 1981-93; prin. Edward F. Whipps & Assocs., Columbus, 1993-94, 2000—; ptnr. Whipps & Wistner, Columbus, 1995-99. Founder, trustee Creative Living, Inc., 1969—; trustee, v.p. Unverferth House, Inc., 1989; trustee Eagle Scholarship Trust. Host: (TV) Upper Arlington Plain Talk, 1979-82, Bridging Disability, 1981-82, Lawyers on Call, 1982—, U.A. Today, 1982-86, The Ohio Wesleyan Experience, 1984— . Mem. Ohio Bd. Psychology, 1992—, pres. 2001-02; active Upper Arlington (Ohio) Bd. Edn., 1971-80, pres., 1978-79; bd. alumni dirs. Ohio Wesleyan U., 1975-79; trustee Walden Ravines Assn., 1992-96, pres. 1993-96. Mem. ABA, Columbus Bar Assn., Ohio State Bar Assn., Assn. Trial Lawyers Am., Ohio Acad. Trial Lawyers, Franklin County Trial Lawyers Assn., Am. Judicature Soc., Columbus Bar Found., Ohio Bd. Pscyhology, Columbus C. of C., Upper Arlington Area C. of C. (trustee 1978—), Lawyers Club, Barrister Club, Columbus Athletic Club, Nat. Football Found. & Hall of Fame, Columbus Touchdown Club, Downtown Quarterback Club, Ohio State U. Faculty (Columbus) Club, Ohio State U. Golf Club, Highlands Golf Club (dir. 2001—), Delta Tau Delta (nat. v.p. 1976-78). Republican. Home: 51 Highland Ct Pataskala OH 43062-8910 Office: Edward F Whipps & Assocs 500 S Front St Columbus OH 43215-7619 *Personal philosophy: Commitment to personal growth, the development of interpersonal relationships, the rule of law and a firm belief in the unique value of every individual in a holographic universe are the primary factors seen in my approach to life.*

WHISENHUNT, DONALD WAYNE, history educator; b. Meadow, Tex., May 16, 1938; s. William Alexander Whisenhunt and Beulah (Johnson) King; m. Betsy Ann Baker, Aug. 27, 1960; children: Donald Wayne Jr., William Benton. BA, McMurry Coll., 1960; MA, Tex. Tech U., 1962, PhD, 1966. Tchr. Elida (N.Mex.) High Sch., 1961-63; from asst. to assoc. prof. history Murray (Ky.) State U., 1966-69; assoc. prof., chmn. dept. Thiel Coll., Greenville, Pa., 1969-73; Dean Sch. Liberal Arts and Scis., Ea. N.Mex. U., Portales, 1973-77; v.p. acad. affairs U. Tex., Tyler, 1977-83; v.p., provost Wayne (Nebr.) State Coll., 1983-91, interim pres., 1985; prof. history, chmn. dept. Western Wash. U., Bellingham, 1991—. Fulbright lectr. Peoples Republic of China, 1995, Republic of Korea, 1994, Belarus, 2004. Author: Environment and American Experience, 1974, Depression in the Southwest, 1979, Chronological History of Texas, Vol. 1, 1982, Vol.2, 1987, Texas: Sesquicentennial Celebration, 1984; editor: Encyclopedia USA, 1988—, Poetry of the People: Poems to the President, 1929-1945, 1996, Tent Show: Arthur Names and His Famous Players, 2000, It Seems to Me: Selected Letters of Eleanor Roosevelt, 2001. Democrat. Methodist. Home: PO Box 1032 Murray KY 42071-1032 Business E-Mail: donw@wwu.edu.

WHISENHUNT, LIVIA L. marketing executive; b. Auburn, Ala., Oct. 15, 1958; d. Jack McKee and Fabiola (Tirado Plata) Whisenhunt; m. Dewey W. Johnson, Oct. 6, 1990. Grad. high sch. Proprietor Covington Gas & Grocery, Atlanta, 1980-81; gen. mgr. Petroleum Mktg. Co. of Ga., Atlanta, 1981-84; v.p. Ballenger-Hunt Investment Corp., Atlanta, 1984-86; pres. Petroleum Source & Systems Group, Atlanta, 1986—. Mem. Assn. Energy Engrs., Nat. Minority Purchasing Coun. Republican. Roman Catholic. Avocations: golf, tennis, orienteering, fishing, bird hunting.

WHISENNAND, CYNTHIA SIMMONS, librarian; b. Dallas, Oct. 29, 1956; d. Mickey Thorne Simmons and Diane Katherine (Gale) Neel; m. Dietrich P. Whisennand, June 28, 1980; 1 child, Matthew William. BA, So. Meth. U., 1979; MLS, North Tex. State U., 1985. Cert. tchr. Tex. Tchr. Dallas Ind. Sch. Dist., 1979—83; libr. Irving (Tex.) Ind. Sch. Dist., 1985—. Maj., dir. Tex. wing aerospace edn. CAP Aux. USAF; mem. dist. com. Mustang Dist. Cir. 10 coun. Boy Scouts Am., Dallas, 1980—; Solar Sys. amb., 2004. Recipient Dist. award of Merit, Boy Scouts Am., 1983, Wood badge, 1986, Silver Beaver award, 1991. Mem.: ALA, Tex. Assn. Profl. Educators, Am. Assn. Sch. LIbrs., Tex. Libr. Assn., Alpha Phi Omega. Republican. Mem. Christian Ch.(Disciples Of Christ). Avocations: Judo, photography, music, shooting, computers. Office: MacArthur HS 3700 MacArthur Blvd Irving TX 75061 E-mail: cswhiz@whisennand.net.

WHISLER, JAMES STEVEN, lawyer, mining and manufacturing executive; b. Centerville, Iowa, Nov. 23, 1954; s. James Thomas and Betty Lou (Clark) W.; m. Ardyce Dawn Christensen, Jan. 20, 1979; children: James Kyle, Kristen Elyse. BS, U. Colo., Boulder, 1975; JD, U. Denver, 1978; MS, Colo. Sch. Mines, Golden, 1984, DSc (hon.), 2001; AMP, Harvard Bus. Sch., 1998. Bar: Colo. 1978; CPA, Ariz. Assoc. gen. counsel, sec. Western Nuc., Inc., Denver, 1979-81; exploration counsel Phelps Dodge Corp., N.Y.C., 1981-85, legal and adminstrv. mgr. Phoenix, 1985-87, v.p., gen. counsel, 1987-88, sr. v.p., gen. counsel, 1988-91, pres., COO, 1997-99, chmn., pres., CEO, 2000—03, chmn., CEO, 2003—; pres. Phelps Dodge Mining Co., 1991-98. Bd. dirs. Phelps Dodge Corp., Burlington No. Santa Fe Corp., Am. West Holdings Corp., Copper Devel. Assn., Internat. Copper Assn., Nat. Mining Assn.; mem. Bus. Coun. Mem.: AIME, AICPA, Mining and Metall. Soc. Am., Colo. Bar Assn., Soc. Mining Engrs., Links Club. Office: Phelps Dodge Corp One N Central Ave Phoenix AZ 85004-2306

WHISNAND, REX JAMES, association housing executive; b. Van Nuys, Calif., Jan. 2, 1948; s. Harold Theodore Whisnand and Laura Fay Brigham Whisnand; m. Cathy Ladeane Bennett, Apr. 1, 1978; 1 child, Bryce James. BS in Agrl. Bus. Mgmt., Calif. Poly State U., San Luis Obispo, 1970; BSBA, Calif. State U., Sacramento, 1976; MPA in Housing Adminstrn., U. San Francisco, 1985; grad., U.S. Naval Submarine Sch., New London, Conn., 1972; postgraduate, Inst. for Organization Mgmt.; EdD in Orgn. and Leadership, U. San Francisco, 2000. Generalist W & W Hardware Store, Orcutt, Calif., 1964-70; state park ranger Calif. Dept. Parks and Recreation, Lompoc and Sacramento, 1969-75; exec. asst. Constrn. Industry Legis. Coun., Sacramento, 1974-75; dir. assn. svcs. Bldg. Industry Assn. Superior Calif., Sacramento, 1976-79; exec. v.p. West Bay divsn. Bldg. Industry Assn. No. Calif., Redwood City, 1980-84; exec. v.p. Bldg. Industry Assn., Tacoma/Pierce County, 1984-86; supr. Lumberjack Store, Lodi, Calif., 1988-90; exec. v.p. Rental Housing Owners Assn. of So. Alameda County, Hayward, Calif., 1990-96; field ops. supv., crew leader census 2000 Am. Housing Survey, 1997-98, crew leader, 2000; field rep. Westat survey U.S. Pub. Health Svc., 2000—02; exec. dir. Housing Conservation and Devel. Corp., San Francisco, 2002—. Com. mem. Calif. Bldg. Industry Assn., Sacramento, 1976-84; mem. exec. officers coun., local govt. com. Calif. Apt. Assn., 1991-96; mem. Alameda County Housing Rsch. Adv. Bd., Hayward, Calif., 1990-93; adj. faculty U. San Francisco; guest svc. rep. Oakland Athletics, 1997-2004. Editor Pierce County Builder, 1984-86 (Assn. Achievement award Nat. Assn. Home Builders 1984-85), Superior California Builder Mag., 1978-80. Active 20-30 Club Internat. #1, Sacramento, 1976-80, officer, 1981-82; mem. South Sacramento Area Cmty. Planning Adv. Bd., 1978-79; grad. Pleasanton Leadership, 1995; chmn. Coastside Coalition for Safe Hwys., Half Moon Bay, 1983-84; bd. congregations Family Emergency Shelter Coalition Alameda County, 1995-96; active Pleasanton Gen. Plan Econ./Fiscal Growth Com., 1994-96, Bay Area Indsl. Edn. Coun., 1995-96, Hayward Coalition for Youth, 1995-96, San Francisco Coun. Cmty. Housing Orgns., 2002—; mem. San Francisco Planning and Urban Rsch. Assn.-Homeless Taskforce, Housing Com., 2002-04, Non-Profit Housing Assn. No. Calif., 2002—, Pleasanton Housing Commn., 2003—, Pleasanton Housing Authority, 2003—; officer Half Moon Bay C. of C., 1982-84; cert. basketball coach Nat. Youth Sports Assn., 1994-97. With USNR, 1970-76, U.S. Army, N.G., 1990-92. Named Outstanding Young Man. in Am., Jr. C. of C., Foster City, Calif., 1983. Mem. Internat. Assn. Bus. Communicators (pres. Sacramento chpt. 1979, pres. Peninsula chpt. 1981), Am. Soc. Assn. Execs. (cert.), No. Calif. Soc. Assn. Execs. (bd. dirs. 1994-97, com. chmn. 1993-95), Pleasanton C. of C. (econ. devel. com. 1990-96), Wash. State Home Builders Assn. (pres. exec. officers coun. 1985), Western Conf. Assn. Execs. (com. mem. 1995-96), Hayward C. of C. (govt. rels. coun. 1990-95), Calif. Vocat. Indsl. Clubs Am. (bd. dirs. 1977-80), Calif. Polytech. Alumni Assn., World Future Soc., San Francisco Comprehensive Ho. (affordable strategy com. 2002-04), Alpha Gamma Rho (charter, com. chair 1969-99). Episcopalian. Avocations: dog training, genealogy. Home: 5435 Black Ave Ste 3 Pleasanton CA 94566-5966

WHISNANT, C. GENE, state representative, retired military officer; b. Caroleen, N.C., Dec. 8, 1943; s. Cleatus and Melba Jolly Whisnant; m. Josie Coffeey, Apr. 24, 1986; 1 child, Todd. BA in Journalism, U. N.C., Chapel Hill; MS in Internat. Affairs, U. Ark. With USAF; treas. Deschutes County Rep. Party, 1997—2000, chmn., 2000—; state rep. for dist. 53 Oreg., 2003—. Mem. Deschutes County Commn. on Children & Families, 1999—. Mem. Homeless Leadership Coun., 2000—. Decorated Legion of Merit, Bronze Star Medal, Meritorious Svc. Medal with two Oak Leaf Clusters, Air Medal, Air Force Commendation Medal with one Oak Leaf Cluster, Joint Svc. Achievement Medal, Vietnam Svc. Medal, German Fed. Armed Forces Commendation in Silver. Mem.: Sunriver Owners Assn. (bd. dirs. 1997—2000, v.p. 2000), Military Officers Assn. Am. (legis. affairs com. chair), Rotary, Am. Legion, VFW. Republican. Episcopalian. Office: 18160 Cottonwood Rd Sunriver OR 97707-9317 Home: PO Box 3565 Sunriver OR 97707

WHISNANT, JACK PAGE, neurologist; b. Little Rock, Oct. 26, 1924; s. John Clifton and Zula I. (Page) W.; m. Patricia Anne Rimmey, May 12, 1944; children: Elizabeth Anne, John David, James Michael. BS, U. Ark., 1948, MD, 1951; MS, U. Minn., 1955. Intern Balt. City Hosp., 1951-52; resident in medicine and neurology Mayo Grad. Sch. Medicine, Rochester, Minn., 1952-55, instr. neurology, 1956-60, asst. prof., 1960-64, asso. prof., 1964-69, prof., 1969—; Meyer prof. neurosci. Mayo Med. Sch.; chmn. dept. neurology Mayo Clinic, Mayo Med. Sch., Mayo Grad. Sch. Medicine, 1971-81; chmn. dept. health scis. research Mayo Clinic and Mayo Med. Sch., 1987-93. Cons. neurology Mayo Clinic, 1955-96, head sect. neurology, 1963-71; dir. Mayo Cerebrovascular Clin. Research Center, 1975-96. Contbr. articles on neurology and cerebrovascular disease to med. jours. Trustee YMCA, Rochester, pres., 1977. With USAAF, 1942-45. Decorated Air medal. NIH grantee, 1959-96. Fellow Am. Heart Assn., Am. Acad. Neurology (pres. 1993-95); mem. AMA, Am. Neurol. Assn. (pres. 1981-82), Am. Bd. Psychiatry and Neurology (bd. dirs. 1983-90, pres. 1989), Zumbro Valley Med. Soc., Minn. Med. Assn., Minn. Soc. Neurol. Scis., Ctrl. Soc. Neurol. Rsch. (pres. 1964), Alumni Assn. Mayo Found. Presbyterian. Office: Mayo Found Dept Health Scis Rsch 201 1st St SW Rochester MN 55905-0001 Home: 211 2nd St NW Apt 716 Rochester MN 55901-2813 Business E-Mail: whisnant@mayo.edu.

WHISTLER, ROY LESTER, chemist, educator, industrialist; b. Morgantown, W.Va., Mar. 31, 1912; s. Park H. and Cloe (Martin) W.; m. Leila Anna Barbara Kaufman, Sept. 6, 1935 (dec. 1994); 1 child, William Harris. BS, Heidelberg Coll., 1934, D.Sc. (hon.), 1957; MS, Ohio State U., 1935; PhD, Iowa State U., 1938; D.Litt. (hon.), St. Thomas Inst., 1982; D.Agr., Purdue U., 1985. Instr. chemistry Iowa State U., 1935-38; research fellow Bur. Standards, 1938-40; sect. leader dept. agr. No. Regional Rsch. Lab., 1940-46; prof. biochemistry Purdue U., 1946-76, Hillenbrand distinguished prof., asst. dept. head, 1974-82, Hillenbrand disting. prof. emeritus, 1982—; chmn. Inst. Agrl. Utilization Research, 1961-75; pres. Lafayette Applied Chemistry Inc., 1980-96. Vis. lectr. U. Witwatersrand, South Africa, 1961, South Africa, 65, South Africa, 77, South Africa, 85, Acad. Sci., France, 1975, Vladivostock Acad. Sci., Russia, 1976, numerous other countries; lectr. Bradley Polytech. Inst., 1941—42; adj. prof. Whistler Ctr. Carbohydrate Chemistry (named by Purdue U. 1984), advisor, bd. dirs.; indsl cons. dir. Pfanstiehl Lab., Inc., 1940—2000, Greenwich Pharm., Inc., 1946—52, Larex, 1999—. Author: Polysaccharide Chemistry, 1953, Industrial Gums, 1959, 2d rev. edit., 1976, 3d rev. edit., 1992; rev. edit.: Methods of Carbohydrate Chemistry, series, 1962—; co-author: Guar, 1979, Carbohydrates for Food Scientists, 1997; editor: Starch-Chemistry and Technology, 2 vols., 1965, 67, rev. edit., 1984, 3d edit. 1999; editl bd. Jour. Carbohydrate Research, 1960-91, Starchs Chemistry and Technology, 1985; bd. advisors: Advances in Carbohydrate Chemistry, 1950-96, Organic Preparations and Procedures Internat., 1970—, Jour. Carbo-Nucleosides-Nucleotides, 1973-77, Stärke, Starch, 1979-99; contbr. numerous articles to profl. jours. Recipient Sigma Xi rsch. award Purdue U., 1953, Medal of Merit, Japanese Starch Tech. Soc., 1967, German Saare medal, 1974, Thomas Burr Osborne award Am. Assn. Cereal Chemists, 1974, Sterling Henricks award USDA, 1991, 93, Nicholas Appert award Inst. Food Technologists, 1994; Roy L. Whistler internat. award in carbohydrates established in his hon., Rsch. bldg. named in his honor Purdue U., 1997; Fred W. Tanner lectr., Chgo., 1994; Named Hillenbrand Disting. prof. Fellow AAAS, Am. Chem. Soc. (chmn. Purdue sect. 1949-50, carbohydrate divsn. 1951, cellular divsn. 1962, nat. councilor 1953-87, bd. dirs. 5th dist. 1955-58, chmn. com. edn. and students, chmn. sub-com. polysaccharide nomenclature, symposium dedicated in his honor 1979, hon. fellow award cellulose divsn. 1983, Hudson award 1960, Anselme Payen award 1967, Carl Lucas Alsburg award 1970, Spencer award 1970, 75, Disting. Svc. award 1983, named one of 10 outstanding chemists Chgo. sect. 1948), Am. Inst. Chemists (pres. 1982-83, Gold medal 1992), Am. Assn. Cereal Chemists (pres. 1978), Internat. Carbohydrate Union (pres. 1972-74); mem. Lafayette Applied Chemistry (pres. 1970-94), Argentine Chem. Soc. (life), Rotary (pres. 1966), Sigma Xi (pres. Purdue sect. 1957-59, nat. exec. com. 1958-62, hon. life mem. 1983—), Phi Lambda Upsilon, Rotary (pres. 1966). Office: Whistler Ctr for Carbohydrate Rsch 1160 Food Sci Bldg Lafayette IN 47907

WHITACRE, CAROLINE CLEMENT, immunologist, researcher; b. Cin., Nov. 4, 1949; d. Richard Soteldo and Rosalyn (Wilson) W.; m. Michael Francis Para, June 28, 1975: 1 child, Alexander. BA, Ohio State U., 1971, PhD, 1975. Postdoctoral fellow Northwestern U., Chgo., 1975-78, instr., 1978-81; asst. prof. Ohio State U., Columbus, 1981-87, assoc. prof., 1987-92, prof. of microbiology and immunology, 1992—, interim chair, 1992-94, chair, 1994—. Mem. com. on fellowship awards Nat. Multiple Sclerosis Soc., 1992-97, com. air, 1995-97, chair com. on gender and autoimmunity, 1997-99. Contbr. articles to profl. pubs. Nat. Insts. for Allergy and Infectious Diseases grantee, 1987—, NIH-Nat. Insts. for Neurol. Disorders and Stroke grantee, 1991—, Nat. Multiple Sclerosis grantee, 1991—. Mem. AAAS, NIH (spl. study sect. 1987-91, neurol. disorders com. 1991-95), Am. Assn. Immunologists, N.Y. Acad. Scis. Presbyterian. Achievements include discovery that experimental autoimmune encephalomyelitis can be suppressed by the oral administration of myelin basic protein due to the anergy or deletion of myelin basic protein specific T lymphocytes; research on multiple sclerosis and the animal model, experimental autoimmune encephalomyelitis,sex differences in autoimmune diseases, and effects of stress on immune function. Office: Ohio State U 2078 Graves Hall 333 W 10th Ave Columbus OH 43210-1239 E-mail: whitacre.3@osu.edu.

WHITACRE, EDWARD E., JR., telecommunications executive; b. Ennis, Texas, Nov. 4, 1941; BS in Indsl. engring., Tex. Tech U., 1964. With Southwestern Bell Tel. Co., 1963-85, various positions in ops. dept., pres. Kans. divsn., 1982-85; group pres. Southwestern Bell Corp., 1985-86, v.p. revenues and pub. affairs, vice-chmn., chief fin. officer, 1986-88, pres., COO, 1988-89, chmn., CEO, 1990—, bd. dir. Mem. adv. coun. Nat. Security Telecomm.; bd. dirs. Anheuser Busch, Inc., May Dept. Stores, Burlington No. Santa Fe, Inc., Emerson Electric. Pres. Boy Scouts Am., 1999—2000; campaign chmn. United Way, San Antonio, 1998; mem. gov. bus. coun. State of Tex.; chmn. bd. regents Tex. Tech U. Health Sci., Lubbock, Tex., 1992—98; bd. govs. S.W. Found. Bio Med. Rsch. Recipient Internat. Citizen of Yr. award World Affairs Coun. San Antonio, 1997; Spirit of Achievement award Nat. Jewish Med. and Rsch. Ctr., 1998; Freeman award San Antonio C. of C., 1997; named to Tex. Bus. Hall of Fame, 1997. Presbyterian. Office: SBC Comm Inc 175 E Houston St San Antonio TX 78205-2255

WHITAKER, ARTHUR LUTHER, retired minister, psychologist; b. Malden, Mass., July 23, 1921; s. Robert William and Elizabeth Arveen (Hinton) W.; m. Virginia Aileene Carter, June 6, 1948; children: Ronald, Paul, Mark, Keith. BA, Gordon Coll., 1949; BD, Harvard U., 1952; MST, Andover Newton Theol. Sem., 1954, D in Ministry, 1973. Ordained to ministry Baptist Ch., 1951; lic. counseling psychologist and health provider, Mass.; diplomate Internat. Acad. Behavioral Medicine, Am. Bd. Forensic Examiners and Medicine, Am. Coll. Forensic Examiners, Am. Bd. Psychol. Svcs. Pastor Calvary Bapt. Ch., Haverhill, Mass., 1950-55; field rep. Am. Bapt. Home Mission, N.Y.C., 1955-56; pastor Mt. Olivet Bapt. Ch., Rochester, N.Y., 1956-66, Pilgrim Bapt. Ch., St. Paul, 1966-70; assoc. exec. min. Am. Bapt. Chs. Mass., Boston, 1970-78; exec. min. Am. Bapt. Chs. N.Y., Syracuse, 1978-83; Protestant chaplain VA Med. Ctr., Syracuse, 1984-86; ret. exec. min. Am. Bapt. Chs. USA-N.Y. State Region, 1986—; counselor, vis. lectr. Harvard U. Divinity Sch., Cambridge, Mass., 1990-2000, Interfaith Counseling Svcc. Inc., Newton, Mass., 1990-92. Lectr. social psychology U. Rochester, 1958-66; cons. U.S. Commn. Civil Rights, U.S. Govt., Rochester, 1964, Nat. Office NAACP, Rochester, 1964-65; vis. prof. Afro-Am. studies Gordon Coll., Wenham, Mass., 1972; trustee Colgate Rochester Divinity Sch., Gordon Coll., Keuka Coll. Contbr. articles and revs. to profl. jours. Active Mass. Dem. Party, Boston; hon. mem. nat. steering com. Gore 2000; contbg. mem. Dem. Nat. Com., 1995—; keynote spkr. 7th ann. Martin Luther King, Jr. Meml. Luncheon, North Shore Black Women's Assn., 2000; preacher Dr. Martin Luther King Jr. Chapel, Hanscom AFB, Mass., 2002, Historic First Bapt. Ch. of Boston, Mass.; sr. guest min. Friendship Bapt. Ch., Charlotte, NC, 2003. Tech. sgt. U.S. Army, 1943-46, ETO. Named Alumnus of Yr., Gordon Coll. Alumni Assn., Wenham, 1972; named to World War II: War Meml., Washington, 2004; recipient Whitaker Hall named in honor, Mt. Olive Bapt. Ch., Rochester, N.Y, 1991, Arthur L. Whitaker award, Am. Bapt. Chs. Mass., 1992. Mem. APA, Mass. Psychol. Assn., Harvard Divinity Sch. Alumni Assn. (sec. 1990-92, Outstanding Svc. award 1998, commemorative luncheon spkr. Dr. Martin Luther King Jr. celebration, miniature 1775 Minuteman statue recipient, African-Am. heritage com.), Andover Newton Theol. Sch. Alumni Assn. (pres. 1996-97). Avocations: music, spectator sports, drama, swimming, reading. Home: 292 Chestnut W # 27-E Randolph MA 02368-2331

WHITAKER, BRUCE EZELL, college president; b. Cleveland County, N.C., June 27, 1921; s. Oreor E. and Fay A. Whitaker; m. Esther Adams, Aug. 22, 1947; children: Barry Eugene, Garry Bruce. BA, Wake Forest U., 1944; BD, So. Bapt. Theol. Sem., 1947, ThM, 1948, PhD, 1950; postgrad., George Peabody Coll., 1952; DL, Wake Forest U., 1987. Ordained to ministry Bapt. Ch., 1945; pastor Smithfield, Ky., 1945-49; instr. sociology and philosophy Ind. U., 1947-50; prof. religion Cumberland U., Lebanon, Tenn., 1950-51, Belmont Coll., Nashville, 1951-52; prof. sociology, asst. to pres. Shorter Coll., Rome, Ga., 1952-53; asso. pastor, minister edn. Atlanta, 1953-54; state sec., student dept. Bapt. State Conv., N.C., 1954-57; pres. Chowan Coll., Murfreesboro, N.C., 1957-89, pres. emeritus, 1989—. Mem. adv. com. to Nd. Higher Edn., 1962-66; to N.C. Commn. Higher Edn. Facilities, 1964—; pres. N.C. Conf. Social Svc., 1965-67, Assn. Governing Bds., 1973-82, Assn. So. Baptist Colls. and Schs., 1967-68, Assn. Eastern N.C. Colls., 1968-69; bd. dirs. Regional Edn. Lab. for Carolinas and Va. Pres. bd. trustees N.C. Found. Church-Related Colls., 1970-74; bd. dirs., v.p. Nat. Coun. Ind. Jr. Colls., 1974-75, pres., 1975-76; mem. adv. coun. presidents Assn. Governing Bds., from 1973; mem. N.C. Bd. Mental Health, from 1966; bd. dirs. Am. Assn. Cmty. and Jr. Colls., 1976-82; pres. N.C. Assn. Colls. and Univs., 1977-78; chmn. N.C. Commn. Mental Health/Mental Retardation Sers., 1978-81; mem. N.C. Commn. on Mental Health, Developmental Disabilities, and Alcohol and Drug Svcs., 1995—. V.p. Bapt. State Conv. N.C., 1989-91. Named Tarheel of Week Raleigh News and Observer, 1962, Boss of Year N.C. Jaycees, 1972; tribute paid in Congl. Record, 1962, 89; Whitaker Libr. at Chowan Coll. named for him; Whitaker Sch. at Butner, N.C. named for him; selected one of nation's 18 most effective coll. pres. in 1985, funded study Exxon Found.; featured in We the People of North Carolina, 1989. Mem. N.C. Lit. and Hist. Assn. (pres. 1970-71), Am. Acad. Polit. and Social Scis., NEA, Am. Assn. Community and Jr. Colls. (dir. 1976-82, Leadership Recognition award 1989), Nat. Assn. Ind. Colls. and Univs. (dir. 1977-78, 81-85), Am. Assn. Higher Edn., Am. Coun. Edn. (bd. dirs. 1985-89), Internat. Platform Assn., Omicron Delta Kappa. Clubs: Capital City (Raleigh, N.C.), Capitol Club (Raleigh); Rotary (chmn. dist. student exchange com. 1969-72, Paul Harris fellow); Optimist; Beechwood Country (Ahoskie, N.C.); Harbor (Norfolk, Va.). Office: 2553 Bent Green St Raleigh NC 27614-6920

WHITAKER, EILEEN MONAGHAN (EILEEN MONAGHAN), artist; b. Holyoke, Mass., Nov. 22, 1911; d. Thomas F. and Mary (Doona) Monaghan; m. Frederic Whitaker. Ed., Mass. Coll. Art, Boston. Annual exhibits in nat. and regional juried shows; represented in permanent collections, Frye Mus., Seattle, NA, Hispanic Soc., N.Y.C., High Mus. Art, Atlanta, U. Mass., Norfolk (Va.) Mus., Springfield (Mass.) Mus. Art, Reading (Pa.) Art Mus., Nat. Acad., U. Mass., Okla. Mus. Art, St. Lawrence U., Wichita State U., San Diego Mus. Art, Retrospective show, Founders Gallery U. San Diego, 1988, invitational one-person show Frye Art Mus., 1990; included in pvt. collections; featured in cover article of American Artist mag., Mar. 1987, in article Art of Calif. mag., July 1991; invitational Am. Realism Exhbn. Cir. Gallery, San Diego, 1992, Challenging Tradition: Women of the Academy, 1826-2003 Exhbn., 2003; author: Eileen Monaghan Whitaker Paints San Diego, 1986. Recipient numerous major awards, including Allied Artists Am., Am. Watercolor Soc., 1st prize Providence Water Color Club, Wong award Calif. Watercolor Soc., De Young award Soc. Western Artists, 1st award Springville (Utah) Mus., Ranger Fund purchase prize, Orbrig prize NA, Walter Biggs Meml. award, 1987; silver medal Am. Watercolor Soc., Watercolor West; fellow Huntington Hartford Found., 1964. Mem. Nat. Acad. Design (Academician NA, William P. and Gertrude Schweitzer prize for excellence in watercolor 171st Annual Exbhn. 1996); mem. Am. Watercolor Soc. (Dolphin fellow), Watercolor West (hon.), San Diego Watercolor Soc. (hon.), Providence Watercolor Club (award), Phila. Watercolor Club. Home: 1579 Alta La Jolla Dr La Jolla CA 92037-7101 E-mail: fandemwhitaker@aol.com.

WHITAKER, ELIZABETH, lawyer; b. Washington, Feb. 20, 1953; BA magna cum laude, Wehaton Coll., 1975; JD with honors, So. Meth. U., 1980. Bar: Tex. 1980. Fellow: Dallas Bar Found., Tex. Bar Found.; mem.: Order of Coif, Coll. of State Bar Tex., State Bar Tex. (chair continuing legal edn. com. 1996—97, bd. dirs. 1996—99, chair bd. dirs. 1998—99). Office: Hankinson & Whitaker LLP 2305 Cedar Springs Ste 230 Dallas TX 75201

WHITAKER, EWEN ADAIR, retired astronomer; b. London, June 22, 1922; arrived in US, 1958; s. George Frederick and Gladys Emily (Johnstone) Whitaker; m. Beryl Joyce Horswell, June 22, 1946; children: Malcolm John, Graham David, Fiona Carolyn. Higher Nat. Cert. in Mech. Engring., Woolwich Polytechnic, Eng., 1944. Spectrographer Siemens Bros. & Co. Ltd., London, 1940—49; asst. exptl. officer Royal Greenwich Obs., London, 1949—58; rsch. assoc. U. Chicago, Yerkes Obs., Williams Bay, Wis., 1958—60; assoc. rsch scientist U. Arizona, Lunar & Planetary Lab., Tucson, 1960—87; retired, 1987. Cons. Air Force Chart & Info. Ctr., St. Louis, 1958—72; co-experimenter NASA Ranger Lunar Missions, 1963—66; team mem. NASA Lunar Surveyor TV, 1965—68, NASA Apollo Orbital Sci. Photog. Team, 1970—73. Author: Mapping & Naming the Moon, 1999, The University of Arizona's Lunar & Planetary Laboratory - Its Founding & Early Years, 1985; co-author: Orthographic Atlas of the Moon, 1960—61, Rectified Lunar Atlas, 1963, Consolidated Lunar Atlas, 1967. Recipient Goodacre Gold Medal & Gift, British Astron. Assoc., 1982. Fellow: Royal Astron. Soc.; mem.: Internat. Astron. Union, Natl. Assoc. of Watch & Clock Collectors. Achievements include first to be able to produce differential bi-spectral imagery of

moon; use of coronagraphic techniques to stars; discovery of orbital inclination and eccentricity of Uranus' satellite Miranda; chose impact location for Ranger 7, NASA's first successful moonshot; discovery of landing location of Surveyor 3 on the moon to which Apollo 12 was later targeted; received international approval for choosing two separate groups of 7 craters in the lunar farside Apollo basin to receive the names of the deceased Challenger and Columbia Space Shuttle astronauts; asteroid 7948 named Whitaker for contributions to NASA lunar programs and lunar science, Internat. Astron. Union. Avocation: clock repair and restoration. Home: 4332 E 6th St Tucson AZ 85711

WHITAKER, FOREST, actor, director, producer; b. Longview, Tex., July 15, 1961; m. Keisha Nash, 1996; children: Ocean Alexander, Sonnet, True Isabella, Autumn. Student voice, U. So. Calif. Pres. Spirit Dance Entertainment. Stage appearances (London) Swan, Romeo and Juliet, Hamlet, Ring Around the Moon, Craig's Wife, Whose Life Is It Anyway?, The Greeks; other stage appearances include Patchwork Shakespeare, Beggar's Opera, Jesus Christ Superstar; TV appearances include Amazing Stories, Hill Street Blues, Cagney and Lacey, Trapper John, M.D., The Fall Guy, Different Strokes, Feast of All Saints, 2001, The Twilight Zone, 2002; TV movies Hands of a Stranger, 1987, Criminal Justice, 1990, Last Light, 1993, Rebound: The Legend of Earl "The Great" Manigault, 1996, The Split, 1998, (TV) Witness Protection, 1999, Light It Up, 1999, Ghost Dog, 1999, Four Dogs Playing Poker, 1999, Deacons for Defense, 2003; mini-series North & South, Parts I and II; films: Fast Times at Ridgemont High, 1982, Vision Quest, 1985, The Color of Money, 1986, Platoon, 1986, Stakeout, 1987, Good Morning, Vietnam, 1987, Bloodsport, 1988, Bird, 1988 (best actor Cannes Festival 1988), Johnny Handsome, 1989, Downtown, 1990, (also co-prodr.) Rage in Harlem, 1991, Article 99, 1992, Diary of a Hit Man, 1992, Consenting Adults, 1992, Body Snatchers, 1993, The Crying Game, 1993, Blown Away, 1994, Jason's Lyric, 1994, Prêt-à-Porter, 1994, Species, 1995, Smoke, 1995, Phenomenon, 1996, The Split, 1997, Battlefield Earth, 2000, Four Dogs Playing Poker, 2000, Green Dragon, 2001, The Fourth Angel, 2001, Panic Room, 2002, Phone Booth, 2002; dir.: (films) Strapped (Toronto Film Festival award for best new dir.), Waiting to Exhale, 1995, Hope Floats, 1998; dir., exec. prodr.: (TV pilot) Black Jaq, 1998. Office: care DGA 7920 W Sunset Blvd Los Angeles CA 90046-3300*

WHITAKER, FREDA N. trust company executive; BS, U. Mo., Kansas City. With Patrons Bank (now NationsBank), Olathe, Kans., Johnson County Bank (now Firstar); exec. v.p. The Midwest Trust Co., Overland Park, Kans. Mem.: Ea. Kans. Estate Planning Coun., Estate Planning Soc. Kansas City (past pres.). Office: The Midwest Trust Co 10740 Nall Ave Ste 100 Overland Park KS 66211

WHITAKER, GILBERT RILEY, JR., academic administrator, business economist; b. Oklahoma City, Oct. 8, 1931; s. Gilbert Riley and Melodese (Kilpatrick) W.; m. Ruth Pauline Tonn, Dec. 18, 1953; children: Kathleen, David Edward, Thomas Gilbert. BA, Rice U., 1953; postgrad., So. Methodist U., 1956-57; MS in Econs., U. Wis., Madison, 1958, PhD in Econs. (Ford Found. dissertation fellow), 1961. Instr., Sch. of Bus. Northwestern U., 1960-61, asst. prof. bus. econs., Sch. of Bus., 1961 64, asso. prof., Sch. of Bus., 1964-66, research assoc. Transp. Center, Sch. of Bus., 1962-66; asso. prof. Washington U., St. Louis, 1966-67, prof., 1967-76, adj. prof. econs., 1968-76, asso. dean Sch. Bus. Adminstrn., 1969-76; dean, prof. bus. econs. M.J. Neeley Sch. Bus., Tex. Christian U., 1976-79; dean U. Mich., 1979-90; prof. Sch. Bus. Adminstrn. U. Mich., 1979-97; provost, v.p. acad. affairs U. Mich., Ann Arbor, 1990-93, provost, exec. v.p. acad. affairs, 1993-95; sr. advisor Andrew W. Mellon Found., 1996—; dean Jesse Jones Graduate Sch. of Mgmt. Rice U., Houston, 1997—. Dir. Am. Assembly of Collegiate Schs. of Bus., 1984-91, v.p., pres.-elect, 1988-89, pres., 1989-90, dir. Washington campus, 1980-89, chmn., 1985-88; bd. dirs. Lincoln Nat. Corp., 1986-2002; Johnson Controls, Inc., 1985-2001; Structural Dynamics Rsch. Corp., 1986-2001; sr. economist banking and currency com. U.S. Ho. of Reps., 1964; mem. Grad. Mgmt. Admissions Coun., 1972-75, chmn., 1974-75; bd. dirs. Washtenaw County United Way, 1990-96. Author: (with Marshall Colberg and Dascomb Forbush) Business Economics, 6th edit., 1981; (with Roger Chisholm) Forecasting Methods, 1971. Bd. trustees, sec.-treas. JSTOR, 1995-2002. With USN, 1953-56. Mem.: Am. Econ. Assn., Ft. Worth Boat Club. Office: Rice U Jesse Jones Grad Sch of Mgmt PO Box 2932 Houston TX 77252-2932

WHITAKER, HERBERT LOYD, retired special education educator; b. Paintsville, Ky, Jan. 20, 1953; s. John and Mildred Whitaker; m. Delorse Kaye Dotson, Oct. 8, 1971; children: Herbert Wesley, Rebecca Kay. AA, Prestonburg Cmty Coll., Ky., 1970—72; BA, Morehead State Univ., Ky., 1972—75; Master's, Morehead State U., Ky., 1977—79. Tchr./coach Scott County Schools, Scottsburg, Ind., 1975—77; tchr./dept. head Johnson County Schools, Paintsville, Ky., 1977—2001. Recipient Ky. Col., Gov./Commonwealth of Ky., 1991. Avocations: reading, fishing, music, building musical instruments. Home: 3629 Little Paint Road East Point KY 41216 Personal E-mail: webeck@foothills.net.

WHITAKER, JOEL, publisher, editor, elected public official; b. Indpls., May 27, 1942; s. Quincy Myers and Sigur Elizabeth (Moore) W.; m. Donna Kay, Apr. 27, 1986. BS in Bus. Journalism, Ind. U., 1964, MA in Journalism, 1971; JD, Temple U., 1979. Reporter St. Petersburg (Fla.) Times, 1964, copy editor, 1966-68, Wall St. Journal, N.Y.C., 1968-73; bus. news editor Phila. Evening and Sunday Bull., 1973-78; law clk. Fellheimer, Krakower & Eiclen, Phila., 1978—79; mng. editor Bank Letter, N.Y.C., 1979-80; editor, pres. Whitaker Newsletters Inc., Fanwood, N.J., 1980—. Chmn. Fanwood Planning Bd., 1981-85; trustee Fanwood cmty. Found. 1998—; mem. Downtown Redevel. Comm., Fanwood, 1983-85; mem. Union County (N.J.) local adv. commn. on alcoholism and drug abuse, 1993-97, chmn., 1994-95, vice chmn. 1997; councilman Borough of Fanwood, 1998-2003, coun. pres., 2000-2003. Mem. Newsletter Publishers Assn. (bd. dirs. 1983-92, found. trustee 1986—, treas. 1989-93), Soc. Profl. Journalists (treas. N.J. profl. chpt. 1997—), Nat. Press Club (Washington), Rotary (bd. dirs. Fanwood-Scotch Plains club 1996-98), Army and Navy Club (Washington). Republican. Roman Catholic. Office: Whitaker Newsletters Inc 313 South Ave Fanwood NJ 07023-1364 Office Phone: 908-889-6336. Personal E-mail: joelwhitaker@verizon.net.

WHITAKER, JOHN KING, economics professor; b. Burnley, Lancashire, Eng., Jan. 30, 1933; came to U.S., 1967; s. Ben and Mary Whitaker; m. Sally Bell Cross, Aug. 24, 1957; children: Ann Elizabeth, Jane Claire, David John. BA in Econs., U. Manchester, 1956; AM, Johns Hopkins U., 1957; PhD, Cambridge U., 1962. Lectr. U. Bristol, England, 1960-66, prof., 1966-69; vis. prof. U. Va., Charlottesville, 1967-68, prof. econs., 1969-86, chmn. dept. econs., 1979-82, Paul Goodloe McIntire prof. of econs., 1986-92, Georgia Bankard prof. of econs., 1992—2003, Georgia Bankard prof. of econs. emeritus, 2003—. Author: The Early Economic Writings of Alfred Marshall, 1867-1890, 2 vols., 1975, The Correspondence of Alfred Marshall, Economist, 3 vols., 1996. Mem. Am. Econ. Assn., Royal Econ. Soc., History of Econs. Soc. Home: 1615 Yorktown Dr Charlottesville VA 22901-3544

WHITAKER, KAY, poet; b. Tipton, Okla., Oct. 25, 1941; d. Joe Bob Whitaker and Helen Lorene Martin; m. Gene Randolph Shreve, Jan. 1965 (div. Aug. 1972). BA in Journalism, U. Okla., 1964. Society editor Okla. Daily, Norman, 1963—64; police reporter Daily Ardmoreite, Ardmore, Okla., 1964—65; polit. writer Cambridge (Mass.) Chronicle, 1965—68; asst. city editor Dallas Morning News, 1969—70. Author: (poetry) Spirit Matters, 1998, Wind Shadows, 2000, Autumn Twilight, 2002, Stirrings, 2002. Vol. Terrell (Tex.) State Hosp., 1998—, Integrated Health Svcs., 1999—. Named to Internat. Poetry Hall of Fame; recipient award of recognition, Famous Poets Soc., 1998, cert. of recognition, 2000, Editor's Choice award, Nat. Libr. Poetry, 1997. Mem.: Theta Sigma Phi (libr. 1963—64), Kappa Tau Alpha. Avocation: comparative religion. Home: 207 Laurel Tr Terrell TX 75160

WHITAKER, LINTON ANDIN, plastic surgeon; b. Navasota, Tex., Nov. 16, 1936; s. Ira Andin and Lena Rivers (Stedman) W.; m. Renata Grasmanis, Dec. 20, 1963; children: Derek Andin (dec.), Ingrid Marlena, Brandon Andrew. BA, U. Tex., 1958; MD, Tulane U., 1962. Diplomate Am. Bd. Surgery, Am. Bd. Plastic Surgery. Founder, dir. ctr. human appearance U. Pa. Med. Ctr., Phila., 1988—; resident in gen. surgery Dartmouth Affiliated Hosps., Hanover, N.H., 1965-69; resident in plastic surgery U. Pa. Hosp., Phila., 1969-71; chief plastic surgery Grad. Hosp., 1971-77, U. Pa. Hosp., Phila., 1987 , attending surgeon, 1971—; chief plastic surgery Children's Hosp. Phila., 1981—2001, attending surgeon, 1971—; v.p. med. staff Children's Hosp., Phila., 1992-94, pres. med. staff, 1994-96; attending physician VA Hosp., 1971—, Phila. Gen. Hosp., 1971-77; assoc. in plastic surgery Sch. Medicine, U. Pa., Phila., 1971-73, asst. prof. in plastic surgery, 1973-76, assoc. prof., 1976-81, prof., 1981—; founder, dir. ctr. human appearance U. Pa. Med. Ctr., Phila., 1988—. Vis. prof. South Australia Craniofacial Unit, Adelaide, Australia and New Zealand, 1981, U. Hawaii, 1983, Brown U., Providence, 1983, Mass. Gen. Hosp., Boston, 1984, U. Utah, Salt Lake City, 1984, U. B.C., Vancouver, 1986, U. Pitts., 1988, U. Calif., San Diego, 1992, Ohio Valley Soc. for Plastic and Reconstructive Surgery, 1992, N.Y. U., 1994; Curts vis. prof. Dartmouth U. Med. Ctr., Hanover, N.H., 1990, Kazanjian vis. prof. Mass. Gen. Hosp., Boston, 1990; First Seiichi Ohmori Meml. lectr. All Asiatic Congress on Aesthetic Surgery, Tokyo, 1988; vis. speaker Inst. Cosmotology and Inst. Stomatology, Moskow, Russia, 1985, vis. prof. Seoul Nat. U. and vis. speaker Korean Soc. for Plastic Surgeons, 1994; hon. vis. spkr. Chinese Plastic Surgery Soc., Beijing, 1996; lectr., speaker at univs., assns. in field. Co-author: Atlas of Cranio-maxillofacial Surgery, 1982, Aesthetic Surgery of the Facial Skelton, 1992; editor (with P. Randall): Symposium on the Reconstruction of Jaw Deformity, Clinics in Plastic Surgery, 1987, 1991; co-editor: Yearbook of Plastic and Reconstructive Surgery, 1980—97; assoc. editor: Seminars in Complementary Medicine, 2001—, mem. editl. bd.: Jour. Cutaneous Aging and Cosmetic Dermatology, 1988—; contbr. articles to profl. jours. Capt. M.C., U.S. Army, 1963-65. Foederer fellow Foederer Fund for Excellence, 1985-88; NIH grantee, 1976-79, 81-87, 82-85, 89, Plastic Surgery Edn. Found. Rsch. grantee, 1980-82; recipient James IV Surg. Traveller award, 1979. Fellow ACS, Am. Soc. Ophthalmic Plastic and Reconstructive Surgery (hon.); mem. AMA, Am. Assn. Plastic Surgeons (mem. program com. 1988, chmn. 1989, Rsch. grantee 1984-85), Am. Surg. Assn., Am. Alpine Workshop in Plastic Surgery (founding mem.), Am. Cleft Palate Assn. (chmn. com. classification craniofacial anomalies 1976-80, mem. program com. for 1978 mtg. 1977, mem. long-range planning com. 1980, mem. coun. 1981-84, chmn. internat. rels. com. 1981-83), Am. Cleft Palate Ednl. Found. (bd. dirs. 1975-84, chmn. rsch. com. 1975-78, chmn. instrl. courses 1980-81), Am. Soc. Aesthetic Plastic Surgery, Am. Soc. Craniofacial Surgery (mem. coun. 1992—), Am. Soc. Maxillofacial Surgeons (Spl. Honors 2003, bd. dirs. 2003—), Am. Soc. Plastic and Reconstructive Surgeons, mem. plastic surgery speakers bur. 1977—), Am. Soc. Plastic and Reconstructive Surgeons Ednl. Found. (chmn. ednl. assessment com., maxillofacial truama and craniofacial anomalies 1975-78, mem. clin. symposia com. 1978-82, chmn. clin. symposia com. 1981-82), Internat. Cleft Palate & Related Craniofacial Anomalies Soc., Internat. Soc. Aesthetic Surgery, Internat. Soc. Craniofacial Surgeons (founding mem., organizer, mem. exec. com. 1987—, sec and treas. 1993-95, pres. 1995-97), Phila. Med. Soc., Phila. Acad. Surgery, Coll. Physicians Phila., Assn. Acad. Surgery, Northeastern Soc. Plastic Surgeons N.Y. (chmn. program com. 1987, mem. programcom. 1988), Plastic Surgery Rsch. Coun., John Morgan Soc., Robert H. Ivy Soc., The Columbian Soc. Plastic, Maxillofacial and Hand Surgery (hon.), Academia Medica Lombarda (Italy, hon.), Sociedad Jamie Planas de Cirugia Plastica (Spain, hon.), Mt. Kenya Safari Club (hon.), Japan Soc. Craniomaxillofacial Surgeons (hon.), Asian Pacific Craniofacial Assn., Japan Soc. Plastic and Reconstructive Surgery (hon.), Phila. Club, Merion Cricket Club. Avocations: mountain climbing, skiing, wines. Office: U Pa Med Ctr 10 Penn Tower 3400 Spruce St Philadelphia PA 19104-4206 Office Phone: 215-662-2048. Business E-Mail: linton.whitaker@uphs.upenn.edu.

WHITAKER, MARK THEIS, magazine editor; b. Lower Merion, Pa., Sept. 7, 1957; s. Cleophus Sylvester and Jeanne (Theis) W.; m. Alexis Lynn Gelber, May 5, 1985; children: Rachel Eva, Matthew Edward. BA summa cum laude, Harvard U., 1979; postgrad., Oxford (Eng.) U., 1979-81; LLD (hon.), Wheaton Coll. Assoc. editor Newsweek mag., NYC, 1981-83, gen. editor, 1983, sr. writer, 1984-86, sr. editor, bus. editor, 1987-91, asst. mng. editor, 1991-95, mng. editor, 1996-98, editor, 1998—. Marshall scholar Brit. Marshall Fund, Oxford U., 1979-81. Mem. Nat. Assn. Black Journalists, Am. Soc. Mag. Editors (bd. dirs., 1999-, pres., 2004), Coun. on Fgn. Rels., Century Assn., Phi Beta Kappa. Office: Newsweek 251 W 57th St New York NY 10019-1802

WHITAKER, MARSHA JONES, author, educator; b. Balt., Nov. 12, 1959; d. Arthur John Jones Jr. and Joyce Irene Jones Smith; m. Marvin J. Whitaker Sr., May 31, 1991; 1 child, Marvin J. Jr. AA, U. Md., 1985, BS, 1996. Coord., legal writer State of Md., Office of State's Atty., Balt., 1986—; owner, prin. Learning By Reading Inc., Balt., 1998—. Author, editor: Marvin's Adventure in the Owl, 1997, Marvin's Adventures in the Talking, 1997, Marvin's Adventures in the Universe, 1998, Marvin's Adventures in Learning About Cells, 2000, Marvin's Adventures in Learning About Mammals, 2001. Recipient Editor's Choice award Nat. Libr. of Poetry, 1995, 96, 97, 98, Golden Apple award Balt. Pub. Schs., 1998, Cir. Ct. Cronicle Inspiration award, 2002. Democrat. Avocations: poetry, books, lyrics, music. Home and Office: Apt 6112 20 Estates CT Pikesville MD 21208-3774 E-mail: marshawhitaker3@att.net.

WHITAKER, MATTHEW GEORGE, prosecutor; JD, MBA, U. Iowa, 1995. U.S. atty. (so. dist. Iowa) U.S. Dept. Justice, Des Moines, 2004—. Office: US Courthouse Annex Ste 286 110 E Ct Ave Des Moines IA 50309*

WHITAKER, MICAL ROZIER, theater director, educator; b. Metter, Ga., Feb. 10, 1941; s. Ellis and Alma Mical Whitaker; m. Georgenia Lyons Whitaker, Sept. 1, 1978 (div. June 0, 1991); 1 child, Mical Anthony. BFA, NC A&T State U., Greensboro, 1989. Founder and dir. East River Players, New York, NY, 1964—76; prodr. Ossie Davis and Ruby Dee Story Hour, New York, NY, 1975—77; asst. prof. Ga. So. U., Statesboro, Ga., 1981—. Cons. Children's TV Producations Sesame St., 1969; artistic dir. Richard Allen Ctr. Culture and Art, 1978—82; writer and dir. Teleprompter Cable TV, New York, NY, 1971; founder and coord. Lincoln Ctr. St. Theatre Festivals, New York, NY, 1979—81. Dir.: (festival) Words from the Renaissance, (birthday pageant) A Place of Sunshine, (tragedy) Othello, (ceremony) The Audelco Awards, (historical drama) The Drinking Gourd, (tragi-comedy) The Real Queen of Hearts Ain't Even Pretty, (fables for children) Story Theatre, (comedy) I'm Not Rappaport, The Last Night at Ballyhoo, The Foreigner, Purile Victorious, (musical) Tambourines to Glory, Before the Flood, Everyman and Roach, The Fantasticks; (plays) A Glance From God, To Be Young, Gifted and Black, Shades of Harlem, Eyes, One More Sunday, Black Nativity, Home, On the Brink of the Mountaintop, Ceremonies in Dark Old Men, High on People, The Importance of Being Earnest, St. Louis Woman, Boochie, From the Mississippi Delta, Spunk, Maricella de la Luz, Long Day's Journey into Night, Stairs to the Roof, Jitney; actor: As You Like It; dir.: (dramas) Agamemnon, The Miracle Worker, The Biko Inquest, In Splendid Error, Who's Afraid of Virginia Woolf, The Piano Lesson, The Amen Corner, Johnny Moonbeam and the Silver Arrow, A Christmas Carol; actor: (plays) Everyman and Roach, Merlin, The Bloodknot, Ma Rainey's Black Bottom, The Piano Lesson, I'm Not Rappaport, Twelfth Night, The Cherry Orchard. Recipient Dir. Musical, Audelco Awards, 1975, Emmy, Seattle Chpt., 1979-1980, G.S.C. Masquers award, G.S.C., 1982, Jefferson citation Directing, Kuumba Theatre, 1979, Spl. award St. Theatre, NYC, 1973, Renaissance and Cultural Devel. award, Black Image Awards, 2000, YMCA Little Theatre Award Set Design, YMCA, 1963, AUDELCO award St. Theatre, AUDELCO, 1977, AUDELCO award Directing, 1979; fellow Nat. Endowment Humanities fellowship, Duke U., 1991, Fulbright-Hays and U.S. Dept. Edn. fellowship, Ga. Consortium, 1992. Mem.: NAACP. Achievements include founding of Candler County Cultural Center committee. Avocations: travel, reading, home decorating, theater. Home: 515 Washington Street Metter GA 30439 Office: Georgia Southern University Po 8091 Statesboro GA 30460 E-mail: mrwhit@gasou.edu.

WHITAKER, PERNELL (SWEET PEA WHITAKER), professional boxer; b. Jan. 2, 1964; Olympic Gold Medalist, boxing, lightweight divsn., L.A., 1984; lightweight champion Internat. Boxing Fedn., 1989; jr. lightweight champion World Boxing Coun., welterweight champion, 1993—97; lightweight champion World Boxing Assn., 1990, middleweight champion, 1995. Named pound for pound best boxer in the world, Ring mag., 1995; recipient Gold medal boxing lightweight divsn., Olympics, 1984, record 6 world championship titles in 4 weight classes, 1995. Office: care Main Events 390 Murray Hill Pkwy East Rutherford NJ 07073-2109

WHITAKER, RUTH REED, state legislator, retired newspaper editor; b. Blytheville, Ark., Dec. 13, 1936; d. Lawrence Neill and Ruth Shipton (Weidemeyer) Reed; m. Thomas Jefferson Whitaker, dec. 29, 1961; children: Steven Bryan, Alicia Morrow. BA, Hendrix Coll., 1958. Copywriter, weather person KTVE TV, El Dorado, Ark., 1958-59; nat. bridal cons. Treasure House, El Dorado, 1959; bridal cons. Pfeifers of Ark., Little Rock, 1959-60; dir. of continuity S. M. Brooks Advt. Agy., Little Rock, 1960-61; layout artist C. V. Mosby Co., St. Louis, 1961-62; editor, owner Razorback Am. Newspaper, Ft. Smith, Ark., 1979-81; ret., 1981; mem. from dist. 3 Ark. State Senate, 2000—. Host Crawford Conversations TV show; contbr. author indsl. catalog, 1979 (Addy award). State sec. Rep. Party of Ark., 1992-94, mem. Ark. Electoral Coll., 1996, del. Rep. Nat. Conv., 1996;; mem. Ben Geren Regional Park Commn., Sebastian County, Ark., 1984-89, pres., 1990; past pres. Jr. Civic League; mem. Ft. Smith Orchid Com.; mem. com. of 21 United Way; publicity chmn. Sebastian County Rep. Com., 1983-84; state press officer Reagan-Bush Campaign, 1984; exec. dir. Ark. Dole for Pres., 1995-96; pres. Women's Aux. Sebastian County Med. Soc., 1974; mem. Razorback Scholarship Fund; class agt. alumni fund Hendrix Coll., 1990, 91, 92; mem. Sparks Woman's Bd.; 1st vice chmn. 3d Dist. Rep. Party; state committeewoman Rep. Party Ark.; chmn. Crawford County Rep. Com.; apptd. by Gov. of Ark. to Commr. Ark. Ednl. TV Network Commn., sec. 1998-99; mem. city coun. City of Cedarville, Ark., 1998; dist. panelist NOW in Bux., 2003. Recipient Disting. Vol. Leadership award Nat. Found. March of Dimes, 1973, Appreciation award Ft. Smith Advt. Fedn., 1977, 78, Recognition award United Cerebral Palsy, 1980, Hon. Parents of Yr. award U. Ark., 1984, Firekeeper award Sparks Hosp. Women's Ctr., 2003. Mem. AAUW, Alden Soc. Am. (life), Ft. Smith C. of C., Ark. Nature Conservancy, Am. Legion Aux., Frontier Rschrs. Soc. (pres. 1995-96), Daus. Union Vets. Presbyterian. Avocations: philanthropy, genealogy, writing, photography, ornithology. Home: PO Box 349 Cedarville AR 72932-0349

WHITAKER, SCOTT, federal agency administrator; m. Michelle Whitaker; 2 children. B in Polit. Sci., Palm Beach Atlantic Coll.; M in Govt., Johns Hopkins U. Legis. asst. Senate Asst. Majority Leader Don Nickles, 1994—97, policy adviser, 1997—2001; asst. sec. for legislation US Dept. HHS, Washington, 2001—03, chief of staff, 2003—. Republican. Office: Dept HHS 200 Independence Ave SW Rm 615F Washington DC 20201*

WHITAKER, SUSANNE KANIS, veterinary medical librarian; b. Clinton, Mass., Sept. 10, 1947; AB in Biology, Clark U., 1969; MS in Library Sci., Case Western Res. U., 1970. Regional reference librarian Yale Med. Library, New Haven, 1970-72; med. librarian Hartford Hosp., Conn., 1972-77; asst. librarian Cornell U., Ithaca, N.Y., 1977-78; vet. med. librarian Coll. Vet. Medicine, Cornell U., 1978-98, vet. pub. svcs. libr., 1998—. Mem. Med. Libr. Assn. (sec.-treas. vet. med. librs. sect. 1983-84, chmn. 1984 85, chmn. pub. rels. com. 2000—), Med. Libr. Assn. (upstate N.Y. and Ont. chpt.), Acad. Health Info. Profls. Home: 23 Wedgewood Dr Ithaca NY 14850-1064 Office: Cornell U Coll Vet Medicine Flower-Sprecher Libr Ithaca NY 14853-6401 Office Phone: 607-253-3499. Business E-Mail: skw2@cornell.edu.

WHITAKER, THOMAS BURTON, agricultural engineer, educator; b. Asheville, N.C., May 16, 1939; BS, N.C. State U., 1962, MS, 1964; PhD in Agrl. Engring., Ohio State U., 1967. From asst. prof. to assoc. prof. N.C. State U., 1967-76, prof. biol. and agrl. engring., 1976—. Agrl. engr. USDA, 1967—. Recipient Golden Peanut Rsch. award Nat. Peanut Coun., 1980. Mem. Am. Soc. Agrl. Engrs., Am. Peanut Rsch. and Edn. Soc. (Bailey award 1976), Sigma Xi. Office: Dept Biol and Agrl Engring 124 Weaver Hall PO Box 7625 Raleigh NC 27695-0001

WHITAKER, THOMAS PATRICK, lawyer; b. Washington, Sept. 22, 1944; s. Thomas J. and Mary K. (Finn) W.; m. Donna Mae Brenish, Feb. 16, 1974; children: Laura, Kevin. BA, George Washington U., 1966, MPA, 1973, JD, 1979; postgrad., Naval War Coll., 1984. Bar: Va. 1979. Staff asst. Adminstrn. Office of U.S. Cts., Washington, 1972-73, analyst, 1975-77; cons. Planning Research Corp., McLean, Va., 1973-75; mgmt. analyst CAB, Washington, 1977-82; program analyst Social Security Adminstrn., Falls Church, Va., 1982—. Served to lt. (j.g.) USNR, 1966-71, Vietnam, capt. with Res. 1983-97. Asst. U.S. Naval Attache, Egypt, 1988, Malaysia, 1992. Mem. Res. Officers Assn. Home: 9817 Days Farm Dr Vienna VA 22182-7306 Office Phone: 703-605-8292. Personal E-mail: twhitake@hotmail.com.

WHITAKER, VICTORIA MANUELA KATZ, publisher, public relations executive, educator, consultant; b. N.Y.C., Mar. 12, 1941; d. Isaac William and Sylvia (Katz) Penner; m. Ronald Mark Katz, Sept. 8, 1974 (dec. Dec. 1996); m. Roger B. Whitaker, Nov. 11, 2000. BA in Journalism, Hofstra Coll., 1962. Sr. editor real estate, fin. Long Island (N.Y.) Comml. Review, 1962-72; freelance writer, publicist N.Y., 1972-74; managing editor North Shore News Group, Smithtown, N.Y., 1974-88; dir. u. news svcs. SUNY, Stony Brook, 1988-99; v.p., dir. midwest ops. Cordes Public Relations, N.Y., 1999—. Dir. Long Island Bus. Inc., Ronkonkoma, N.Y., 1965-98; adj. journalism prof. C.W. Post, Greenvale, N.Y., 1986-88, Hofstra Coll., Hempstead, N.Y., 1987. Author: (study) Smithtown Minorities, 1983. Trustee Harbor County Day Sch., St. James, N.Y., 1977-93, mktg. and pub. rels. com. mem. United Way, L.I., 1988-98; program com. mem. Mus. at Stony Brook, 1990-93; mem. Investigative Reporters & Editors; bd. dirs. Springfield Area Arts Coun. Recipient Media award for govtl. reporting Press Club L.I., 1987, 88. Mem. AAUW (past v.p.), Pub. Rels. Soc. Am. (chair steering com. L.I. chpt. 1996-97), Soc. Profl. Journalists (nat. bd. dirs., co-chair chpt. health and welfare com., regional dir. 1994-98, 2000—), Press Club L.I. Chpt. Soc. Profl. Journalists (pres. 1974, treas. 1985-93, 98-99, Deadline Club bd. 1994, program co-chair 1993, v.p. 1995-99), Headline Club (Chgo.), Am. Women in Journalism (v.p., sec. Springfield chpt.). Home: 2944 S Douglas Ave Springfield IL 62704-4912 E-mail: vkatz@racoon.com.

WHITBECK, ROGER JAMES, scriptwriter, lyricist; b. Gloversville, NY, Apr. 11, 1961; s. Robert Clifton and Ethel Georgia Whitbeck. H.S. Diploma, Riverview H.S., 1976—79. Mechanical Drafting, Sarasota County Tech. Inst., 1996; Insurance License Fla. Dept. of Fin. Services, 2002. Exec. trustee Hallelujah Creative Services Trust, Sarasota, Fla., 1997—. Dep. dir. gen. Internat. Biog. Ctr., Cambridge, England, 2000—; dep. gov. Am. Biog. Inst., Raleigh, NC, 2000—. Author: (film script) The Rifle Woman, (song lyrics) Puppy Pounders, Glory, Big Honey, The Heart Keeper, Happy Rocking, (novel) Live Free and Hurt Evil People, (screenplays) The Beautiful, the Righteous and the Holy, Captain Louie, Good Girls, Beyond Money, Streets of Righteousness, Beyond the Chase, Dead Fools, (song lyrics) True Hearts. Vol. dist. dir. Americans for Fair Taxation, Houston, 1999—2004. Recipient Internat. Order of Merit, Internat. Biog. Ctr., 2000, Outstanding Intellectuals of the 20th Century award, 2000; fellow, Am. Biog. Inst., 2000. Mem.: Am. Soc. of Composers, Authors and Publishers (life). R-Consevative. Christian. Avocations: swimming, weightlifting, automotive mechanics, composing, musicianship. Home: 4349 McIntosh Rd Sarasota FL 34233-1336 Office: Hallelujah Creative Services Trust 4349 McIntosh Rd Sarasota FL 34233-1336 Personal E-mail: holylife@comcast.net. E-mail: holylife@comcast.net.

WHITBREAD, THOMAS BACON, English educator, author; b. Bronxville, N.Y., Aug. 22, 1931; s. Thomas Francis and Caroline Nancy (Bacon) W. BA, Amherst Coll., 1952; A.M., Harvard U., 1953, PhD, 1959. Instr. English, U. Tex. at Austin, 1959-62, asst. prof., 1962-65, assoc. prof., 1965-71, prof., 1971—. Vis. asso. prof. Rice U., 1969-70; mem. lit. adv. panel Tex. Commn. on Arts and Humanities, 1972-76 Author (poetry): Four Infinitives, 1964, Whomp and Moonshiver, 1982; contbg. author: Prize Stories, 1962, The O. Henry Awards, 1962; editor: Seven Contemporary Authors, 1966. Recipient third Aga Khan prize for fiction Paris Rev., 1960, Lit. Anthology Program award Nat. Endowment for Arts, 1968, Outstanding Freshman Tchr. award Phi

Eta Sigma, 1972-73 Mem. AAUP, Tex. Inst. Letters (Poetry award 1965, 83), Nat., Am. amateur press assns., Phi Beta Kappa. Democrat. Home: 1014 E 38th St Austin TX 78705-1835 Office: U Tex Dept English Austin TX 78712 E-mail: whitbread@mail.utexas.edu.

WHITBURN, GERALD, insurance company executive; b. Wakefield, Mich., July 12, 1944; s. Donald and Ruby E. (Nichols) W.; m. Charmaine M. Heise, May 3, 1969; children: Bree, Luke. BS, U. Wis., Oshkosh, 1966; MA, U. Wis., Madison, 1968; postgrad., Harvard U., 1988, 00, U. Pa., 1997. Aide Gov. Warren P. Knowles, Wis., 1966-69; personal asst. USN sec. John H. Chafee, Washington, 1969-72; automoble dealer, real estate developer Merrill, Wis., 1973-80; exec. asst. to Senator Robert W. Kasten U.S. Senate, Washington, 1981-87; dep. sec. Wis. Dept. Adminstrn., Madison, 1987-89; sec. Wis. Dept. Industry, Labor and Human Rels., Madison, 1989-91, Wis. Dept. Health and Social Svcs., Madison, 1991-95; sec. exec. office of health and human svcs. Commonwealth of Mass., Boston, 1995-96; pres., CEO, dir. Ch. Mut. Ins. Co., Merrill, Wis., 1996—; dir. Property Casualty Insurers Assn. of Am., Wis. Manufacturers and Commerce, Wis. Ctr. for Academically Talented Youth. Mem. U.S. Labor Sec.'s Commn. on Achieving Necessary Skills, Washington, 1990-92. Contbr. articles to newspapers. Del. Rep. Nat. Conv., 1988, 92, 2004. Recipient Disting. Alumni award U. Wis., Oshkosh, 1991. Home: W7146A Village Rd Merrill WI 54452 Office: Ch Mut Ins Co 300 Schuster Ln Merrill WI 54452

WHITBURN, MERRILL DUANE, English literature educator; b. Mpls., Apr. 29, 1938; s. George and Marie Ellen (Carlstedt) W.; m. Diane Robertson, June 15, 1960; children: Stephen, Mark, Elizabeth. AB, U. Mich., 1960, AM, 1968; PhD, U. Iowa, 1973. With Western Electric Co., N.Y.C. and Indpls., 1965-67; asst. prof. Tex. A&M U., College Station, 1973-77, assoc. prof., 1977-79; assoc. prof. English Rensselaer Poly. Inst., Troy, N.Y., 1979-83, prof., 1983-89, Louis Ellsworth Laflin prof., 1989—, chmn. dept., 1979-85, 88-95; rsch. fellow Yale U. Divinity Sch., New Haven, 2003. Co-owner Pride and Prejudice Books, Ballston Lake, N.Y., 1985—. Author: Rhetorical Scope and Performance: The Example of Technical Communication, 2000; co-author: (booklet) Guide for Departments of English, 1985; contbr. articles to profl. publs. Recipient Disting. Svc. award Tex. A&M U., 1976, Disting. Teaching award, 1979, Jay R. Gould award for excellence in tchg. tech. comm. Soc. Tech. Comm., 1995, Trustee's Outstanding Tchr. award Rensselaer Poly. Inst., 2002; grantee Fund for the Improvement of Postsecondary Edn., 1983. Mem. Nat. Coun. Tchrs. English (best article in tech. writing award 1981), Coun. for Programs in Tech. and Sci. Communication.

WHITCOMB, JAMES HALL, geophysicist, foundation administrator; b. Sterling, Colo., Dec. 10, 1940; s. Clay Thane and Julia Melvina Whitcomb; m. Sandra Lynn McMurdo, July 13, 1965 (div. 1978); m. Teresa R. Idoni, Feb. 3, 1989; children: Lisa Michelle, Marisa Giulia, Sabina Maria. Geophysics engrng. degree, Colo. Sch. of Mines, 1962; MS in Oceanography, Geophysics, Oreg. State U., 1964; PhD in Geophysics, Calif. Inst. Tech., 1973. Grad. rsch. asst. dept. oceanography Oreg. State U., Corvallis, 1962-64; geophysicist ctr. astrogeology U.S. Geol. Survey, Flagstaff, Ariz., 1964-66; Fullbright-Hayes program rsch. fellow seismol. inst. U. Uppsala, Sweden, 1966-67; grad. rsch. asst. seismol. lab. Calif. Inst. Tech., Pasadena, 1967-73, sr. rsch. fellow seismol. lab., 1973-79; assoc. prof. attendant rank dept. geol. scis. U. Colo., Boulder, 1979-82, fellow Coop. Inst. Rsch. in Environ. Scis., 1979-84; v.p. technical applications and mktg. ISTAC, Inc., Pasadena, 1984-88; program dir. seismology NSF, Washington, 1989-99, acting dep. divsn. dir., 1999—2002, spl. projects sect. head, 2002—. Expert witness U.S. Ho. Reps. Com. on Sci. and Tech., 1977; mem. geodynamics rev. bd. Jet Propulsion Lab., 1980-82, com. on geodesy Nat. Acad. Scis., 1982-85; pres. Boulder Systems, Inc., Pasadena, 1987-88. Recipient Outstanding Achievement award U.S. Geol. Survey, 1964, Dir.'s award for mgmt. excellence NSF, 1995-2003; scholar State of Colo., 1958-62, Mobil Oil Co., 1960; fellow Sweden-Am. Found., 1966. Mem. AAAS, Am. Geophysical Union, Seismol. Soc. Am., Soc. Exploration Geophysicists (scholar 1963), Tau Beta Pi, Phi Kappa Phi, Sigma Xi. Office: Nat Sci Found Geosciences 4201 Wilson Blvd Arlington VA 22230-0002

WHITCOMB, JAMES HOWARD, JR., investment banker; b. Bryn Mawr, Pa., Nov. 15, 1954; s. James Howard, Sr. and Eleanor (Keady) Whitcomb; m. Havilande Bayard Brown, Oct. 11, 1986; children: James Howard III, Ashton Bayard, Christiana Prescott. BA with honors, Williams Coll., 1976; MBA, U. Va., 1981. Sr. v.p. Lehman Bros., N.Y.C., London, 1981-93; mng. dir. Chem. Securities, N.Y.C., 1995-97; sr. v.p. NatWest Markets, N.Y.C., 1997-98; prin. Shattuck Hammond Ptnr. LLC, N.Y.C., 1998—2003; mng. dir. The Chart Group, N.Y.C., 2003—. Trustee Southport Conservancy, 2000—, Southport Conglist. Ch., 1998—2000. Fellow: Fgn. Policy Assn.; mem.: Yale Club (N.Y.C.), Fairfield County Hunt Club, Pequot Yacht Club. Avocations: foreign relations, sailing, skiing, travel. Office: 70 E 55th St New York NY 10022

WHITCOMB, JAMES STUART, videographer, photographer, production company executive; b. Buffalo, May 7, 1957; s. C. Stuart and Helen Nancy (O'Reilly) W. BA in Journalism/Broadcasting, SUNY, Buffalo, 1983. Cert. master herbalist, iridologist. Pres., owner Ad Astra Prodns., Williamsville, N.Y., 1987—; co-owner, videographer, photographer STB Prodns., Williamsville, 1989—; owner legal books and computer software co. JSW Pub., Williamsville, 1997—. Videographer, editor nature/stress reduction Videos A Celebration of the Four Seasons, 1991, Autumn on Cape Code and Martha's Vineyard, 1993, Gardens, Blossoms & Blooms, 1994, A Walk Through St. Francis Woods, 1994, Nantucket Noel: Christmas on Nantucket, 1994, Reflections: Nature's Watercolors, 1995, Autumn in Vermont, 1995, A Day On the Farm, 1995, Window Shopping, 1995, Singalong with your Old Favorites, 1997, A Celebration of the Four Seasons II: Seasons of the Seashore, 1997, Kids and Animals, 1998; videographer, writer promotion video Internat. Modeling and Talent Assn., 1990; videographer numerous prodns. for modelling, fashion, and spl. interest. Supporter St. Joseph's Indian Sch., Chamberlain, S.D, supporter Inerlink Resources, Taraz, Kazakhstan. Mem. People for Ethical Treatment of Animals, Wilderness Soc., Am. Hiking Soc., Nat. Audubon Soc., Farm Sanctuary, Best Friends Animal Sanctuary, Assn. for Rsch. and Enlightenment, Adirondack Mountain Club. Avocations: skiing (former instr.), hiking (former mountain guide). Home: 71 Rinewalt St Williamsville NY 14221-5736 Office: Ad Astra and STB Prodns PO Box 1725 Williamsville NY 14231-1725 Office Phone: 716-626-5319.

WHITCOMB, RICHARD TRAVIS, aeronautical consultant; b. Evanston, Ill., Feb. 21, 1921; s. Kenneth Frederick and Gladys (Travis) Whitcomb. BS in Aero. Engring., Worcester Poly. Inst., 1943, DEng (hon.), 1956; DSc (hon.), Old Dominion U., 1985. Aero. rsch. scientist Langley Rsch. Ctr. NASA, Hampton, Va., 1943—58, head transonic aerodynamics br., 1958—80, disting. rsch. assoc., 1980—85; pvt. practice aero. cons. Hampton, 1980—90. Patentee aero. equipment. Named to Nat. Inventors Hall of Fame, 2003; recipient Collier Trophy, Nat. Aero. Assn., 1955, Nat. Medal for Sci., Office of the Pres. U.S., 1973, Wright Bros. trophy, Nat. Aero. Assn., 1974, award in Aero. Engring., NAS, 2000. Fellow: AIAA (hon. Reed award 1969, Daniel Guggenheim medal 2002); mem.: NAE. Avocations: music, reading, exercise.

WHITCRAFT, JAMES RICHARD, JR., accountant; b. Jan. 27, 1947; s. James R. and Hazel V. (Garner) Whitcraft; m. Pamela D. Imel, July 29, 1977; children: Christopher K., Kelle D. BS, Ball State U., 1969, MBA, 1972. Sr. staff acct. Arthur Andersen & Co., Indpls., 1969—77; audit mgr. Holdeman, Fulmer, Elkhart, Ind., 1977—81; owner Dick Whitcraft, CPA, Elkhart, 1981—84; mng. ptnr. Whitcraft & Pletcher, LLP, CPAs, Elkhart and Goshen, Ind., 1984—. Treas. Life Recovery Ctr., Inc., 1985—92; bd. dirs., treas. Elhart County YMCA, 1989—; pres. Big Bros./Big Sisters of Elkhart County, 1977—78; treas. Presbyn. Ch., 1985—87. With U.S. Army, 1969—71. Mem.: AICPA, Elkhart C. of C. (com. chmn. 1979—89), Ind. Assn. CPAs, Elcona Country Club, Optimists (pres. Elkhart chpt. 1981—82, 1984), Blue Key, Sigma Chi (life). Republican. Home: 19148 Calvin Hill St Cassopolis MI 49031-9542 Office: Whitcraft & Pletcher LLP CPAs 1832 W Lincoln Ave Goshen IN 46526

WHITE, ALAN EDWARD, computer company executive; b. Logan, W.Va., July 24, 1949; s. William Edward and Annabel White; m. Susan Rader, May 20, 1972; children: Megan, Elissa, Andrew. BS in Physics, W.Va. Tech., Montgomery, 1971. With tech. sales Preiser Sci., St. Albans, W.Va., 1972-75, Process Instruments Inc., Charleston, W.Va., 1975-76; v.p. Std. Instrumentation, Charleston, W.Va., 1976-80; sys. engr. Warren Tech. Assocs., Circleville, Ohio, 1984-87; mgr. engring. BH-F Sys. Ltd., Toledo, Ohio, 1987-91; v.p. engring. Advanced Control Solutions, Inc., Sylvania, Ohio, 1991—. Asst. scoutmaster Boy Scouts Am., 1994—. With W.Va. N.G., 1971-77. Recipient Alumnus of Yr. award W.Va. Tech., 1999. Mem. Toledo Astronomical Assn., Instrument Soc. Am., Nat. Eagle Scout Assn. Republican. Mem. Christian Ch. (Disciples Of Christ). Avocations: backpacking, trap shooting, restoring vintage bmws, building telescopes, watersports. Office: Advanced Control Solutions Inc 8750 Resource Park Dr Sylvania OH 43560

WHITE, ALAN FREDERICK, academic administrator; b. Evansville, Ind., Dec. 17, 1937; s. Hubert Ruben and Nota Lizzee (Culver) W.; m. Patricia Lynn Townsend, Nov. 7, 1959; children: Gregory Townsend, Samuel Townsend. AB, Miami U., Oxford, Ohio, 1963; MS, MIT, 1971. Dir. U. Hawaii Ctr. Crossculture Tng. and Rsch., Hilo, 1967-70, exec. asst. to pres. Honolulu, 1971-73; Alfred P. Sloan fellow MIT, Cambridge, 1970-71, assoc. dir. exec. edn., 1973-78, dir. exec. edn., 1978-85, assoc. dean for exec. edn., 1985-95, sr. assoc. dean, COO, lectr., 1991. Cons. AT&T, Brit. Petroleum, Alcoa Young Pres. Orgn.; bd. dirs. Ceridian Corp., SBS Tech., Internat. Consortium for Exec. Edn. Rsch.; bd. advisors The StartupAvenue.com, Toffler Assoc., Lingnan U., China; mem. Internat. Mgmt. Devel., 1985—. Contbr. articles to profl. jours. Mem. Consortium of Univ. Dirs. of Exec. Edn., Japan Mgmt. Inst. (adv. bd.), Mgmt. Scis. for Health (bd. dirs.). Avocations: painting, tennis, swimming, golf, gardening. Home: 13 Pickman Dr Bedford MA 01730-1009 Office: MIT Mit 50 Memorial Dr Cambridge MA 02139 Office Phone: 617-253-7189.

WHITE, ALFRED KENNETH, JR., lawyer; b. Pitts., Jan. 6, 1929; s. Alfred Kenneth Sr. and Mira Carlotta (Frey) W.; m. Virginia Ann Schwering, Sept. 1, 1956; children: Christopher F., Derek S. BA cum laude, Gettysburg (Pa.) Coll., 1951; JD, Yale U., 1957. Bar: N.Y. 1959, U.S. Dist. Ct. (so. and ea. dists.) N.Y. 1967. Atty. Vick Chem. Co., N.Y.C., 1957-59; gen. atty., sec. L. E. Waterman Pen Co. Ltd./Barker Automation, Inc., N.Y.C., 1959-62; spl. atty. Procter & Gamble Co., Cin., 1962-66, counsel internat. div., 1966-90, gen. counsel-internat., 1990-91, v.p., gen counsel-internat., 1991-94; of counsel Douglas M. Case Law Firm, Cin., 1995—. Vice chmn. Internat. & Comparative Law Ctr., Southwestern Legal Found., Dallas, 1985-90, symposium chmn., 1991-94; adv. bd. U.S./Can. Law Inst., Cleve. Maj. USAR, 1946-48, 51-54. Mem. ABA, Internat. Bar Assn., Cin. Bar Assn., Camargo Hunt Club (sec. 1997—), Bankers Club, The Camargo Club. Republican. Episcopalian. Avocations: equestrian, antique silver and furniture, travel. Home and Office: 8885 Spooky Ridge Ln Cincinnati OH 45242-7350 E-mail: white8885@fuse.net.

WHITE, ALICE ELIZABETH, physicist, researcher; b. Glen Ridge, N.J., Apr. 5, 1954; d. Alan David and Elizabeth Joyce (Jones) W.; m. Donald Paul Monroe, Oct. 13, 1990; children: Ellen Elizabeth White Monroe, Janet Clare White Monroe. BA in Physics, Middlebury (Vt.) Coll., 1976; MA in Physics, Harvard U., 1978, PhD in Physics, 1982. Postdoctoral mem. tech. staff AT&T Bell Labs., Murray Hill, N.J., 1982-84, mem. tech. staff, 1984-88; dir. Bell Labs Lucent Technologies, Murray Hill, N.J., 1988—. Contbr. over 100 articles to profl. pubs.; patentee in field. Recipient Alumni Achievement award Middlebury Coll., 1994; Bell Labs. fellow, 2001. Fellow Am. Phys. Soc. (Maria Goeppert-Mayer award 1991); mem. IEEE, Optical Soc. of Am., Phi Beta Kappa. Office: Bell Labs Lucent Technol Rm 1D-339 PO Box 636 New Providence NJ 07974-0636

WHITE, ALICE VIRGINIA, college campaign program administrator; b. Wichita, Kans., June 30, 1946; d. Harry Houston White and Margaret V. Milligan. BA in Russian with distinction and Spanish, U. Kans., 1967; MS in Counseling, Ft. Hays State U., 1973; PhD in Journalism, U. Tex., 1991. Tchr. Russian and Spanish Ingalls Sch. Dist., Kansas City, Mo., 1967-72; instr. Dodge City (Kans.) C.C., 1972-73, 84; tchr. Arrowhead West, Inc., 1984-85; asst. dir. Ctr. for Bus. & Industry Dodge City (Kans.) Community Coll., 1984-85, dir. community rels. and resource devel., 1985-87; co-founder, treas. Breitenbach Farms, Inc., Dodge City, 1970-79, pres., 1979-85; asst. to dean for devel. Coll. Comm., U. Tex., Austin, 1990-93, asst. instr. journalism, 1988-90, lectr. pub. rels., 1992; asst. coord. Shots Across Tex. coord. Tex. Dept. Health, Austin, 1993-95, coord. spl. health initiatives, 1995-96; mgr. Tex. Vol. Health Corps, 1996—2002; liaison Tex. Alliance for Healthy Communities, 1999—2002; program dir. Coll. for Texans Campaign, Austin, 2002—. Media judge Headliners Found., Austin, 1989, Tex. Hosp. Assn., 1990, 91; dir. job placement Kans. Elks Tng. Ctr. for Handicapped, 1984-85; mgr. dental office, 1973-83; bd. dirs. Dispute Resolution Ctr., 1992-93; adv. bd. N.E. Caregivers of Austin, 2002-. Treas. Ford County Hist. Soc., 1972-77, Ofcl. Bicentennial Com. Ford County, 1975-77; active Leadership Kans., 1986, Leadership Austin, 1990-91; co-founder Leadership Dodge, 1987, Tex. Leadership Inst. Colo. River Authority, 1999-; founder Walk-a-Dog project Williamson County SPCA, Austin State Sch., 1991-92; media judge Tex. PTA, 1992, Tex. Med. Assn., 1993; mem. chancellors coun. U. Tex. Sys.; mem. endowment com. United Way Capital Area, 1994—; mem. Ready Teddy, the Emergency Med. Svcs. Bear-A-Medic Mascot, 1994-2001; mem. Gov.'s Blue Ribbon Selection Com. for Tex. Vol. awards, 1998, 99; mem. Vols. of Yr. selection com. Tex. Commn. on Volunteerism and Cmty. Svcs., 2000—; mem. Gov.'s Unified State Planning/Cmty. Svc. Com., 1997, 98; mem. Leadership Tex., 1999; 2d v.p. Pub. Health Mus. of Tex., 1999-2002, bd. dirs., 2003—; treas. Pet Helpers, Inc., 2000—; mem. Animal Trustees of Austin's Vol. Spotlight, 2000, Tex. Youth Commn., 2001, 02; mem. selection com. for Tex. vol. awards Tex. Dept. Human Svcs., 2001; hon. laboratorian Tex. Dept. Health, 2000-; 5th grade mentor Gullett Elem. Sch., 2001—; mem. foudning adv. bd. Women's Giving Network, 2003—. Recipient Most Creative Vol. Project award Tex. Mental Health and Mental Retardation, 1992, Athena winner Women's C. of C., 1987, Kans. PRIDE honoree, 1988; U. Tex. fellow, 1987-89; named of one of 100 Best-Managed Farms in U.S., Farm Futures Mag., 1983; named endowments at Austin Cmty. Found., Wichita (Kans.) Cmty. Found., Arthur E. and Cornelia Scroggins Found., Dodge City, Kans. Mem. AAUW (treas. 1977-78, pres. Kans. 1979-81, gift honoree 1973, 81, 91), Nat. Assn. Individual Investors (life), Pub. Rels. Soc. Am. (mentor, profl. advisor U. Tex. 1987-93), Tex. Pub. Rels. Soc. (bd. dirs. 1993), Women in Comm. (liaison to student chpt. 1989-91), Tex. Exes Alumni Assn. (life), U. Kans. Alumni Assn. (nat. bd. dirs. 1977-82), Austin C. of C., U. Tex. Pres.' Assocs., U. Tex. Littlefield Soc., U. Kans. Chancellor's Club, Austin-Travis County Humane Soc. (life), Waterloo Benevolent Soc. of United Way Capital Area, Leave a Legacy Tex. Style, KLRU Pub.-TV Prodrs. Circle, Lone Star Cir. (State Employee Charitable Campaign 2001, 02), Phi Beta Kappa (treas. Austin Alumni Assn. 2001-02), Phi Kappa Phi, Chi Omega, Chi Omega Alumnae. Home: 1861 Coronado Hills Dr Austin TX 78752-2116 Office: Tex Higher Edn Coordinating Bd 1200 E Anderson Ln Austin TX 78752 E-mail: alice.white@thecb.state.tx.us.

WHITE, ALISA, communications educator, consultant; PhD, U. Tenn. Assoc. prof. advt. and pub. rels. U. Tex., Arlington, 1998—. Bd. dirs. Ad Club Ft. Worth. Contbr. articles to profl. jours. Mem.: Assn. for Edn. in Journalism and Mass Comm. Office: Univ Tex Arlington Box 19107 Arlington TX 76019-0107

WHITE, AUGUSTUS AARON, III, orthopedic surgeon; b. Memphis, June 4, 1936; s. Augustus Aaron and Vivian (Dandridge) W.; m. Anita Ottemo; children: Alissa Alexandra, Atina Andrea, Annica Akila. AB in Psychology cum laude, Brown U., 1957; MD, Stanford U., 1961; PhD, Karolinska Inst., Sweden, 1969; Advanced Mgmt. Program, Harvard U., 1984; DHL (hon.), U. New Haven, 1987; DMS (hon.), Brown U., 1997; DS (hon.), So. Conn. State U., 2000. Diplomate Nat. Bd. Examiners, Am. Bd. Orthopaedic Surgery. Intern U. Mich. Hosp., Ann Arbor, 1961-62; asst. resident in gen. surgery Presbyn. Med. Center, San Francisco, 1962-63; asst. resident in orthopaedic surgery Yale Med. Center, New Haven, 1963-65, sr. instr., resident orthopaedic surgery, 1965-66; asst. prof. orthopaedic surgery Yale Med. Sch., 1969-72, assoc. prof., 1972-76, prof., 1977-78, dir. biomech. research dept. orthopedics, 1970-78; prof. orthopedic surgery Harvard Med. Sch., 1978—; orthopedic surgeon-in-chief Beth Israel Deaconess Med. Ctr., Boston, 1978-92, orthopedic surgeon-in-chief emeritus, 1996—2001; sr. assoc. orthopedic surgery Children's Hosp. Med. Ctr., Boston, 1979-89; assoc. in orthopedic surgery Brigham & Women's Hosp., Boston, 1980-89; cons. div. surgery Sidney Farber Cancer Inst., Boston, 1980—; Ellen and Melvin Gordon prof. of med. edn., prof. orthopedic surgery Harvard Med. Sch., 2002. Rschr. biomechanics lab. Beth Israel Deaconess Med. Ctr.; chair sci. adv. bd., dir. OrthoLogic, Inc., Phoenix; sci. adv. bd. Am. Shared Hosp. Svcs., San Francisco; chair sci. adv. bd., bd. dirs. Zimmer Holding, Inc.; cons. orthop. surgery West Haven (Conn.) VA Hosp., 1970—78, Hill Health Ctr., New Haven, 1970—78; chief orthop. surgery Conn. Health Care Plan, 1976—78; adv. coun. Nat. Inst. Arthritis, Metabolism and Digestive Disease, NIH, 1979—82; mem. admissions com. Yale Med. Sch., 1970—72; presenter, moderator Symposium on Cervical Myelopathy, San Francisco, 1987; chmn. grant rev. com. NIH, 1985; founding mem., bd. overseers Brown U. Sch. Medicine, 1996—; bd. overseers WGBH Radio/TV, Boston, 1996—98, trustee, 1998—; Alfred R. Shands Jr. lectr. Am. Orthop. Assn., 2001; Pres. guest lectr. Scoliosis Rsch. Soc., 2001; chair com. culturally competence care Harvard Med. Sch., 2002. Author: Clinical Biomechanics of the Spine, 1978, 2d edit., 1990, (with M. Panjabi) Biomechanics in the Musculoskeletal System, 2001, Symposium on Idiopathic Low Back Pain, 1982, Your Aching Back-A Doctor's Guide to Relief, 1983, rev. edit., 1990, translated in German, 1992; guest editor Clin. Orthop. and Related Rsch., 1999; contbr. articles to profl. jours., chpts. to books. Trustee Brown U., Providence, 1971-76, bd. fellows, 1981-92, fellow emeritus, 1992—, chmn. corp. com. on minority affairs, 1981-86, chmn. corp. com. on med. edn., 1989-96, chmn. vis. com. on diversity; trustee Northfield Mt. Hermon Sch., Northfield, Mass., 1976-81; bd. dirs. The Partnership, Boston, 1984—. Capt. AUS, 1966-68. Decorated Bronze Star medal; named one of 10 Outstanding Young Men U.S. Jr. C. of C., 1969, Selected for Exceptional Black Scientist poster series CIBA-GEIGY Corp., 1982; recipient Martin Luther King, Jr. Med. Achievement award, 1972, Kappa Delta award, nat. prize for outstanding research in orthopaedics field, 1975; nat. award for spinal research Eastern Orthopaedic Assn., 1980, Disting. Service award Northfield Mt. Hermon Sch. Alumni Assn., 1983; William Rogers award Associated Alumni Brown U., 1984, Outstanding Achievement award Delta Upsilon, 1986, Brown Bear award Brown Alumni Assn.; Am.-Brit.-Canadian Travelling fellow Am. Orthopedic Assn., 1975. Master Oliver Wendell Holmes Soc.; fellow Am. Acad. Orthopaedic Surgeons (chmn. diversity com. 1997—), Scoliosis Rsch. Soc.; mem. Orthopaedic Rsch. Soc., Cervical Spine Rsch. Soc., Internat. Soc. for Study Lumbar Spine, Internat. Soc. Orthopaedic Surgery and Traumatology, Nat. Med. Assn. (Orthopaedic Scholar award 1994), Cervical Spine Rsch. Soc. (pres. 1988), N.Am. Spine Soc., Acad. Orthopaedic Soc. (co-chmn. com. on diversity), Clin. Orthopedic Soc. (Nix Ethics award 2002), J. Robert Gladden Orthopaedic Soc. (pres. 2000-03), Fedn. of Spine Assns. (pres. 1998), Sigma Xi, Sigma Pi Phi, Delta Upsilon (pres. Brown U. chpt. 1956).

WHITE, B. JOSEPH, former dean, business educator; BS, Georgetown U., 1969; MBA, Harvard U., 1971; PhD, U. Mich., 1975. Dean bus. adminstrn. U. Mich., Ann Arbor, 1991—2001, interim pres., 2001—, Wilbur K. Pierpont Collegiate prof. leadership in mgmt. edn. and prof. bus. adminstrn. Bus. Sch., 2002—. Mng. dir. Fred Alger Mgmt., Inc., N.Y.C. Office: U Mich Bus Sch 701 Tappan St Ann Arbor MI 48109-6354 Business E-Mail: bjwhite@umich.edu.

WHITE, BARBARA LEE, education educator; b. New Orleans, La., Oct. 7, 1936; d. Lee J. and DeLaura (McElhenny) Adams; m. Raymond Lovance White, Sept. 7, 1955 (div. June 15, 1969); children: Rayond Lovance Jr., Ronald Nathaniel. BA, Austin Peay State U., Clarksville, Tenn., 1961; MA, Austin Peay State U., Clarksville, Tenn., 1968; PhD, Bowling Green State U, Ohio, 1984. Vice chmn. exec. com. Internat. Visitors Ctr., Jackson, Miss.; adj. prof. Jackson State U.; tchr. Sch. Dist. Fed. Republic Germany, Wiesbaden and Baumholder; asst. supt. Jackson Pub. Sch. Dist. Mem. planetarium adv. bd. Jackson (Miss.) Arts Soc. Author: (Book) The Motley Crew, 2000; contbr. articles to education jours. Campaign mgr. for 1st black candidate to run for lt. gov. in Miss. Mem.: Phi Delta Kappa, Kappa Delta. Achievements include First Black to graduate from Austin Peay State U., 1961, First Black anchor on WLOX, Gulfport, Miss., 1972. Avocations: piano, writing. Home: 119 Chastity Dr Gulfport MS 39503

WHITE, BENJAMIN STEVEN, mathematician, researcher; b. Boston, Sept. 29, 1945; s. Norman Kenneth White and Mildred Ruth (Silverman) Stahl; m. Helen Katherine Frazer, June 12, 1966; children: Adam Frazer, Ethan Abraham. SB, MIT, 1967; MA, U. Ariz., 1968; PhD Courant Inst., NYU, 1974. Sr. mathematician Raytheon Co., Newport, R.I., 1969-70; sys. analyst Time-Sharing Resources, N.Y.C., 1970-71; vis. mem. Courant Inst., NYU, 1974-75; instr. applied math. Calif. Inst. Tech., Pasadena, 1975-78; mem. tech. staff Jet Propulsion Lab., Pasadena, 1978-81; corp. rschr. Exxon Rsch. and Engring. Co., Annandale, N.J., 1981-91, head applied math. group, 1986-89; sr. rsch. assoc. Exxon Mobil Corp. Strat. Rsch., 1999—2002, disting. rsch. assoc., 2003—. Instr. NYU, Bronx, 1971-72; v.p. Perceptive Systems, Inc., Pasadena, 1981. Contbr. articles to profl. jours. Mem. AAAS, Soc. Indsl. and Applied Math., Am. Math. Soc. Democrat. Home: 345 Shunpike Rd Chatham NJ 07928-1633 E-mail: benjamin.s.white@exxonmobil.com.

WHITE, BERTRAM MILTON, chemicals executive; b. Boston, Nov. 17, 1923; s. Samuel Louis and Jennie Anne (Cohen) W.; m. Bernice Hannah Ginns; children: Mark Alan, Leland Jeffrey. BS, Lowell Inst. Tech., Cambridge, Mass., 1943. Product mgr. Philipps Bros. Chems. Inc., Holbrook, Mass., 1952-65, Sobin Chems. Inc., South Boston, 1965-69; pres. Solvent Chems. Co., Inc., Malden, Mass., 1969-73; v.p. I.C.C. Chems. Inc., N.Y.C., 1973-80; sr. v.p. Asoma Chems. Inc., Boston, 1980-83, Laporte Chems. USA, Hackensack, N.J., 1983-84; pres. Gen. Plastics and Chems. Co., Natick, Mass., 1984-91, GFI Chems. Inc., Sudbury, Mass., 1991-93; vice chmn. E & F King & Co. Inc., Norwood, Mass., 1994-96; cons. Holtrachem Inc., 1997-2000. Bd. dirs. Sudexco N.V., Brussels, Recochem Inc., Montreal, Que., Can.; cons. Holtrachem Inc., Natick, 1996-2000, Lithium Co., LLC, White Plains, N.Y., 1997-2000, BMW Chems. Inc., 1998—, Salvage.com, Houston, 2000-01; pres. BMW Chems., Inc., Natick, Mass., cons. for SalvageSale.com., Houston. Served with Corps of Engring. U.S Army, 1943-46, ETO. Decorated Purple Heart. Mem. Drug Chem. and Allied Trades Assn., New Eng. Chemists Club, N.Y.C. Chemists Club, Salesmen's Assn. of Am. Chem. Industry. Jewish. Avocations: tennis, golf, boating. Office Phone: 508-650-5800. Office Fax: 508-651-0294.

WHITE, BETTY, actress, comedienne; b. Oak Park, Ill., Jan. 17, 1922; m. Allen Ludden, 1963 (dec.). Student pub. schs., Beverly Hills, Calif. Appearances on radio shows This Is Your FBI, Blondie, The Great Gildersleeve; actress: (TV series) including Hollywood on Television, The Betty White Show, 1954-58, Life With Elizabeth, 1953-55, A Date With The Angels, 1957-58, The Pet Set, 1971, Mary Tyler Moore Show, 1974-77, The Betty White Show, 1977, The Golden Girls, 1985-92 (Emmy award for best actress 1986), The Golden Palace, 1992-93, Maybe This Time, 1995—, The Story of Santa Claus, 1996, A Weekend in the Country, 1996; (TV miniseries) The Best Place to be, 1979, The Gossip Columnist, 1980, (films) Advise and Consent, 1962, Dennis the Menace 2, 1998, Hard Rain, 1998; guest appearances on other programs; summer stock appearances Guys and Dolls, Take Me Along, The King and I, Who Was That Lady?, Critic's Choice, Bells are Ringing. Recipient Emmy award NATAS, 1975, 76, 86; L.A. Area Emmy award, 1952. Mem. AFTRA, Am. Humane Assn., Greater L.A. Zoo Assn. (dir.). Office: c/o William Morris Agy Betty Fanning 151 S El Camino Dr Beverly Hills CA 90212-2704

WHITE, BEVERLY JANE, cytogeneticist; b. Seattle, Oct. 9, 1938; Grad., U. Wash., 1959, MD, 1963. Diplomate Nat. Bd. Med. Examiners, Am. Bd. Pediatrics, Am. Bd. Med. Genetics; lic physician and surgeon, Wash., N.J., Calif. Rsch. trainee dept. anatomy Sch. Medicine U. Wash., Seattle, 1960-62, pediatric resident dept. pediatrics, 1967-69; rotating intern Phila. Gen. Hosp., 1963-64; rsch. fellow med. ob-gyn. unit Cardiovascular Rsch. Inst. U. Calif. Med. Ctr., San Francisco, 1964-65; staff fellow lab. biomed. scis. Nat. Inst. Child Health and Human Devel. NIH, Bethesda, Md., 1965-67, sr. staff fellow, attending physician lab. exptl. pathology Nat. Inst. Arthritis, Metabolism and

Digestive Diseases, 1969-74, acting chief sect. cytogenetics, 1975-76, rsch. med. officer, attending physician sect. cytogenetics lab. cellular biology and genetics, 1974-86, dir. cytogenetics unit, interinstitute med. genetics program clin. ctr., 1987-95; dir. cytogenetics Corning Clin. Labs., Teterboro, N.J., 1995-96; assoc. med. dir. cytogenetics Nichols Inst.-Quest Diagnostics, San Juan Capistrano, Calif., 1996-97, med. dir. cytogenetics, 1998—2000, med. dir. genetics divsn., 2000—02, med. dir. cytogenetics and genetic counseling, 2002—. Vis. scientist dept. pediat. divsn. genetics U. Wash. Sch. Medicine, 1983-84; intramural cons. NIH, 1975-95; cons. to assoc. editor Jour. Nat. Cancer Inst., 1976; cons. dept. ob-gyn. Naval Hosp., Bethesda, 1988-89; lectr., presenter in field. Recipient Mosby Book award, 1963, Women of Excellence award U. Wash. and Seattle Profl. chpt. Women in Comm., 1959, Reuben award Am. Soc. for Study Sterility, 1963. Fellow Am. Coll. Med. Genetics (founding), Am. Acad. Pediatrics; mem. AMA, Am. Soc. Human Genetics, Assn. Genetic Technologists (program com. 1989). Home: 14 Toulon Laguna Niguel CA 92677 Office: Nichols Inst Quest Diagnostics Inc Dept Cytogenetics San Juan Capistrano CA 92690-6130 Office Phone: 949-728-4301. E-mail: bjwsur@aol.com

WHITE, BLAINE C, medical educator, researcher, emergency physician; MD. Prof. emergency medicine, physiology, molecular medicine and genetics Wayne State U., Detroit, vice chair dept. emergency medicine. Dir. Basic Sci. Rsch. and Fellowship Wayne State U., Detroit. Fellow: Am. Coll. Emergency Physicians; mem.: Emergecy Medicine Found. (First Nat. Ctr. of Excellence award 1993), Nat. Acad. Scis., Instn. of Medicine. Office: Detroit Recieiving Hosp Dept Emergency Medicine 4201 St Antoine 2Q3 Detroit MI 48202 E-mail: bwhite@wayne.edu.

WHITE, BRETT, real estate company executive; Sales trainee, indsl. salesperson CB Richard Ellis, L.A., 1984—91, sales mgr., 1991—2001, mng. dir. Newport Beach, 1991—2001, regional mgr. L.A., 1991—2001, pres. brokerage, 1991—2001, chmn. The Ams., 1991—2001, pres., 2001—, also bd. dirs., mem. exec. com. Office: CB Richard Ellis 34th Fl 865 S Figueroa St Los Angeles CA 90017*

WHITE, BRUCE DAVID, law and ethics educator, consultant; b. Elizabethton, Tenn., Jan. 10, 1951; s. Darold S. and Anna Ruth (Lewis) W.; m. Sarah Jo Pugh, Dec. 28, 1974; children: Sarah Elizabeth, Meredith Ruth, Rebecca Mae. BS in Pharmacy, U. Tenn., 1974, JD, 1976; DO, North Tex. State U., Tex. Coll. Osteo. Medicine, 1985. Bar: Tenn. 1977, U.S. Dist. Ct. (we. dist.) Tenn. 1979; diplomate Am. Bd. Pediats. Asst. prof. U. Tenn. Health Scis. Ctr., Memphis, 1977-81, assoc. prof., 1981; lectr. U. Miss., Oxford, 1980-81; asst. prof. North Tex. State U., Tex. Coll. Osteo. Medicine, Ft. Worth, 1981-85; ptnr. Swafford & White, Memphis, 1979-81; resident in pediats. U. Louisville, 1985-88; asst. prof. pediatrics. Meharry Med. Coll., 1988-93; asst. prof., asst. dir. Ctr. Clin. Rsch. Ethics, Vanderbilt U. Med. Ctr., 1988-94; fellow clin. med. ethics U. Chgo., 1989-91; dir. Clin. Ethics Ctr. St. Thomas Hosp., Nashville, 1993-98; prof. McWhorter Sch. Pharmacy, Samford U., Birmingham, Ala., 1994—; of counsel Moody Whitfield & Castellarin, 1999—. V.p. Integrity Svcs., L.L.C., Nashville, 1998-99; of counsel Moody Whitfield & Castellarin, 1999—; dir. Healthcare Ethics and Law Inst. Samford U., Birmingham, 1998—. Author: (with H. Wetherbee) Cases and Mateials on Pharmacy Law, 1980; (with W.B. Swafford) Tennessee Pharmacy Law Handbook, 1980, Mississipi Pharmacy Law Handbook, 1981. Fellow Am. Soc. Pharmacy Law, Am. Coll. Legal Medicine, Masons. Office: 95 White Bridge Rd Ste 509 Nashville TN 37205-1490

WHITE, CALVIN JOHN, zoo executive, zoological association executive, financial manager; b. Twillingate, Nfld., Can., Feb. 28, 1948; s. Harold and Meta Blanche (Abbott) W.; m. Lorna Joan Maclachlan; children: Chelsea Elizabeth, Evan Alexander. B in Commerce, U. Toronto, Ont., Can., 1971. Fin. analyst Can. GE Co. Ltd., Toronto, 1971-72, Ford Motor Co. Can., Oakville, Ont., 1972-74; sr. fin. analyst Municipality of Met. Toronto, 1974-77, asst. dir. budget and ops. analysis, 1977-81, dir. budget analysis and internal control, 1981-86; CEO Toronto Zoo, 1986—. Bd. dirs. Borealis Hydro Elec. Holdings Inc., Toronto Conv. and Visitors Assn., Can. Mus. Assn., Can. Assn. Zoos and Aquariums, Ctr. for Endangered Reptiles, 1989-91, Rouge Pk. Alliance, Toronto Chongqing Assn. Fellow Am. Zoo and Aquarium Assn.; mem. Am. Assn. Zoo Keepers, Inst. Pub. Adminstrn. Can. (bd. dirs. 1989-91), Toronto Zoo Found. (bd. dirs. 1991—, CEO 1994—), World Conservation Union, World Zoo Orgn., Toronto Sportmen's Assn., Mensa. Office: Toronto Zoo 361A Old Finch Ave Scarborough ON Canada M1B 5K7 E-mail: cwhite@torontozoo.ca.

WHITE, CALVIN LAMONT, engineer; b. Chico, Calif., Nov. 14, 1947; s. Calvin Hardy White and Jean Elizabeth (Detree) Hardy; m. Elsie Jean, June 28, 1968; 1 child: Calvin Frederick. BS in Mech. Engr., U. Calif., Davis, 1969; MS in Mater. Sci., U. Minn., 1971; PhD, Mich. Tech. U., Houghton, 1974. Mem. rsch. staff Oak Ridge (Tenn.) Nat. Lab., 1974-86; prof. Mich. Tech. U., Houghton, 1986—, chair dept. materials sci. and engring., 1996—2002. Recipient Material Sci. Rsch. award U.S. Dept. of Energy, 1984. Fellow ASM Internat.; mem. Am. Welding Soc., Materials Rsch. Soc., The Metall. Soc. Inc. (bd. dirs. 1988-91), Sigma Xi. Avocations: hunting, fishing. Office: Mich Tech U Materials Sci and Engring Houghton MI 49931 E-mail: cwhite@mtu.edu.

WHITE, CARL EDWARD, JR., pharmaceutical administrator; b. Huntington, W.Va., Apr. 4, 1955; s. Carl Edward Sr. and Peggy Joan (Church) W.; m. Denise Karen McDaniel, May 26, 1979; children: Daniel Aaron, David Kenton, Caitlin Ruth. BS, Purdue U., 1977; MBA, Ga. State U., 1996. Profl. sales rep. Ciba-Geigy Pharms., Huntington, 1977-85, dist. sales mgr., 1985-93, area bus. dir Atlanta, 1993-94; dist. bus. mgr. Atlanta, 1994-98; sr. dist. mgr. Novartis Pharms., Roswell, Ga., 1998—. Bd. dirs. Coventry Homeowners' Assn., Peachtree City, Ga., 1991, Park Brooke Homeowners' Assn., Alpharetta, Ga., 1996; chmn. deacons First Bapt. Ch., Peachtree City, 1992. Republican. So. Bapt. Avocations: computers, singing, gardening. Home: 3905 Brookline Dr Alpharetta GA 30022-6436

WHITE, CECIL RAY, librarian, consultant; b. Hammond, Ind., Oct. 15, 1937; s. Cecil Valentine and Vesta Ivern (Bradley) W.; m. Frances Ann Gee, Dec. 23, 1960 (div. 1987); children: Timothy Wayne, Stephen Patrick. BS in Edn., So. Ill. U., 1959; postgrad., Syracuse U., 1961; MDiv, Southwestern Bapt. Sem., 1969; MLS, No. Tex. State U., 1970, PhD, 1984. Libr. Herrin (Ill.) H.S., 1964-66; acting reference libr. Southwestern Sem., Ft. Worth, 1968-70, asst. libr., 1970-80; head libr. Golden Gate Bapt. Sem., Mill Valley, Calif., 1980-88, West Oahu Coll., Pearl City, Hawaii, 1988-89; dir. spl. projects North State Coop. Libr. System, Yreka, Calif., 1989-90; dir. libr. St. Patrick's Sem., Menlo Park, Calif., 1990—. Library cons. Hist. Commn., So. Bapt. Conv., Nashville, 1983-84, Internat. Bapt. Sem., Prague, Czech Republic, 1996; mem. Thesaurus Com., 1974-84; adv. bd. Cath. Periodical and Lit. Index, 1995—. Bd. dirs. Hope and Help Ctr., 1986-88, vice chmn., 1987-88. With USAF, 1960-64. Lilly Found. grantee Am. theol. Assn., 1969. Mem. ALA, Am. Theol. Libr. Assn. (coord. cons. svc. 1973-78, program planning com. 1985-88, chmn. 1986-88), Nat. Assn. Profs. Hebrew (archivist 1985—), Assn. Coll. and Rsch. Librs., Cath. Libr. Assn. (mem. exec. bd. 1999—), Phi Kappa Phi, Beta Phi Mu. Democrat. Baptist. Home: 229 Rome Place Hayward CA 94544 Office: St Patricks Sem 320 Middlefield Rd Menlo Park CA 94025-3563 Office Phone: 650-321-5655. E-mail: cecilrwhite@hotmail.com, stpats@ix.netcom.com. *Personal philosophy: Except for the gift of life and faith, the best gift that has been given to me, and which I can give, is the unique gift of oneself in friendship. No one else can give it, and it cannot be bought at any price.*

WHITE, CHARLES B. academic administrator; b. Oct. 21, 1943; BA, MS, San Diego State U., 1969; PhD, U. Ga., 1974. Prof. psychology Trinity U., San Antonio, Tex., 1980—, assoc. v.p., 1989-98, v.p. info. resources adminstrv. affairs, 1999—. Office: 715 Stadium Dr San Antonio TX 78212-3104 E-mail: cwhite@trinity.edu.

WHITE, CHARLES OLDS, aeronautical engineer; b. Beirut, Apr. 2, 1931; s. Frank Laurence and Dorothy Alice (Olds) W.; m. Mary Carolyn Liechty, Sept. 3, 1955; children— Charles Cameron, Bruce Blair. B.S. in Aero. Engring., MIT, 1953, M.S., 1954. Aero. engr. Douglas Aircraft Long Beach, 1954-60, aero. engr. Ford Aerospace & Communication Corp., Calif., 1960-79, sr. engr. specialist, 1979-80, staff office of gen. mgr. DIVAD div., 1980-81, tech. mgr. DIVAD Fuzes, 1981-82, supr. design and analysis DIVAD div., 1982-85; tech. mgr. Advanced Ordnance Programs, 1985-87, PREDATOR Missile, 1987-90, cons. 1990-93; engring. tech. prin. Aerojet Corp., 1993-94; tech. prin. OCSW Ammunition Olin Ordinance, 1994-97, cons., 1997—. Mem. AIAA, AAAS, Nat. Mgmt. Assn., Am. Aviation Hist. Soc., Sigma Gamma Tau. Republican. Presbyterian. Clubs: Masters Swimming, Newport Beach Tennis. Contbr. articles to profl. jours.

WHITE, CHARLES R. former mayor; b. Boston, Mass. m. Maria White; 4 children. Grad., Riverside CC. Mayor City of Moreno Valley, 1997. Mem. Moreno Valley City Coun., 1996—; mem. So. Calif. Assn. Govt., Regional Coun., Transp. & Comm. Policy Com., Magnetic Levitation Task Force, Growth Visioning Com.; bd. Riverside Transit Agency; mem., chmn. March Joint Powers Commn., 1999, vice chmn., 2001, chmn., 02. Served Planning Commr., Redevelopment Project Area Com., Traffic Safety Adv. Com., Disaster Preparedness Com., Mayor's Drug Task Force; treasurer Friends Moreno Valley Sr. Ctr.; pres. Moreno Valley Elks Lodge; vice comdr. Moreno Valley VFW Post; jr. deacon Moreno Valley Masonic Lodge; pres. Sunnymead Little League; v.p. Sunnymead PTA; co-founder Moreno Valley Youth Fedn. Served USAR. Mem.: Idylwild Am. Legion Post (life). Office: 14177 Frederick St PO Box 88005 Moreno Valley CA 92552

WHITE, CHARLES SIDNEY JOHN, retired humanities educator; b. New Richmond, Wis., Sept. 25, 1929; s. Ferne Rosemary Holt. BA in English with honors, U. Wis., 1951; MA magna cum laude, U. de las Am. Mexico City Coll., 1957; MA, U. Chgo., 1962, PhD with distinction, 1964. Pub. rels. and advt. staff Wallace Supplies Mfg. Co., Chgo., 1957—61; asst. prof. Indian studies U. (Madison) Wis., 1965—66; asst. prof. religious thought U. Pa., 1966—71; assoc. prof. philosophy and religion Am. U., Wash., 1971—78, prof. philosophy and religion, 1978—94, prof. emeritus philosophy and religion, 1995—, dir. Asia Ctr. Sch. Internat. Svc., 1976—78, chmn. dept. philosophy and religion, 1984—87, 1988—94. Vis. lectr. history of religions Princeton (N.J.) U., 1968; vis. prof. world religions Lakehead U., Thunder Bay, Ont., Canada, 1974—88; vis. prof. Wesley Seminary, 1985, 86; lectr. in field; vis. prof. Hindu studies faculty theology Oxford U., England, 2002. Author: The Caurāsī Pad of Śrī Hit Harivamś, 1977, Ramakrishna's Americans, 1979, The Adyar Library, The Institute for Vaisnava Studies and The American University Microfilm Collection of Vaisnava Literature, 2001, Teaching Saranagati: A Dialogue with HH Sri Sathguru Swami Gnanananda Sarasvathi, 2002, Catalogue of Vaisnava Literature, 2004; co-author: The Religious Quest, 1983, 1985, Joseph Campbell: Transformations of Myth Through Time, 1990; contbr. chapters to books, articles to profl. jours. With USN, 1951—55. Fellow, Hindi-Urdu U., Chgo., 1961—64, Am. Inst. Indian Studies, India, 1964, 1968, 1974, 1978, 1995; grantee, Smithsonian Instn., India, 1982—83. Mem.: Am. Inst. Indian Studies (exec. com. 1988—90).

WHITE, CHRISTINE ALLEN, elementary school educator; b. Steubenville, Ohio, Nov. 19, 1973; d. John Llanson and Jeanne Beard Allen; m. Charles Aaron White, Aug. 5, 1995; children: Connor Aaron, Alita Louise. MusB in Music Edn. and Music Therapy, East Carolina U., 1995. Cert. Nat. Bd. for Profl. Tchg. Stds., 2002. Elem. music tchr. Banks Elem. Sch., Kinston, NC, 1996—. Mentor Lenoir County Pub. Schs., Kinston, NC, 2001—, co-developer Lenoir county support group for nat. bd. candidates, 2003—. Recipient Tchr. of Yr., Banks Elem. Sch., 1997—98, 2003—04, Student participants in the NC Elem. Honors Chorus, NC Music Educators' Assn., 1997, Student participants in the NC Elem. Honors Chorus, 2002, 2003, Video Clip in the World's Largest Concert, Music Educators' Nat. Conf., 2002. Mem.: N.C. Music Educators' Assn., Music Educators' Nat. Conf., Omicron Delta Kappa (life), Sigma Alpha Iota (life; coll. chpt. pres. 1993—94). Christian. Avocations: reading, scrapbooking, music, knitting.

WHITE, CHRISTOPHER TODD, language educator; b. Columbia, Mo., Dec. 7, 1965; s. Eric B. and Barbara K. White. BA, U. Nebr., Lincoln, 1990; MA, U. Mo., Kansas City, 1994, U. Nev., Las Vegas, 1998; PhD, U. So. Calif., L.A., 1998—. Adj. lectr. Rockhurst Coll., Kansas City, Mo., 1994—95; editl. asst. BkMk Press, Kansas City, 1993—95; adj. lectr. English U. Mo., Kansas City, 1993—95; acad. advisor Ednl. Talent Search, Las Vegas, Nev., 1995—96; asst. prof./lectr. U. Nev., Las Vegas, 1996—98; instr. Glendale C.C., Calif., 1998—; tchr., rsch. asst. dept. anthropology U. So. Calif., L.A., 1998—. Dir. Homosexual Info. Ctr., L.A., 2001—, ONE Inst. and Archives, L.A., 2001—02. Editor: San Dieguito and La Jolla: Collected Papers of Claude N. Warren and Colleagues, 2003; asst. editor Before Stonewell: Activists for Gay and Lesbian Rights in Historical Context, 2002; editor: U. Nev.-Las Vegas Jour. Anthropology, 1995—; contbr. articles to profl. jours.; editl. adv. bd. Collegiate Press, 2002, referee Popular Culture Rev. Recipient Patricia Roccio Award in Anthropology, U. Nev.-Las Vegas, 1997; scholar Hal Call Mattachine scholar, Inst. for Study of Human Resources, 2000—01. Mem.: Homosexual Info. Ctr. (sec.-treas. 2001—), Southwestern Anthropol. Assn., Soc. of Lesbian and Gay Anthropologists (sec.-treas. 1998—), Soc. of Linguistic Anthropology, Am. Anthropol. Assn., Am. Fedn. Tchrs. Democrat. Buddhist. Avocations: camping, book collecting, piano, running, bicycling. Home: 4622 Charmion Ln Encino CA 91316 Office: Univ Southern Calif Dept Anthropology Los Angeles CA 90089-0661

WHITE, CONSTANCE BURNHAM, state official; b. Odgen, Utah, July 2, 1954; d. Owen W. and Colleen (Redd) Burnham; m. Wesley Robert White, Mar. 18, 1977. BA in English magna cum laude, U. Utah, 1976, postgrad., 1977, Boston Coll., 1979; JD, Loyola U., 1981. Law clerk Kruse, Landa, Zimmerman & Maycock, Salt Lake City, 1979; law clerk legal dept. Bell & Howell, Lincolnwood, Ill., 1980; clerk, assoc. Parsons, Behle & Latimer, Salt Lake City, 1981-82; assoc. Reynolds, Vance, Deason & Smith, Salt Lake City, 1982-83; chief enforcement sect. Utah Securities Divsn., Salt Lake City, 1984-87, chief licensing sect., 1988, asst. dir., 1989-90; legal counsel Utah Dept. Commerce, Salt Lake City, 1990-92, exec. dir., 1993-95, commr. pub. svc. div., 1995. Mem. Gov.'s Securities Fraud Task Force, 1984; spl. asst. atty. gen., 1986-88; spl. asst. U.S. atty., 1986—. Mem. North Am. Securities Adminstrs. Assn. (vice chair market manipulation com. 1988-89, penny stock/telecom. fraud com. 1989-90, chair uniform examinations com. 1990-92, chair forms revision com. 1992), Utah State Bar (securities adv. com. 1991—, task force on community-based mediation 1991—, chair securities sect. 1992-93). Office: Utah Pub Svc Commn 160 East 300 South Salt Lake City UT 84111

WHITE, DALE ANDREW, journalist; b. Jacksonville, Fla., Feb. 17, 1958; s. John Andrew and Jeannelle Corinne White. B in Journalism, U. Fla., 1983. Reporter UPI, Miami, Fla., 1980, Orlando (Fla.) Sentinel Star, 1981; corr. Fla. Times-Union, Gainesville, 1982; reporter, columnist, editl. writer, editor Sarasota Herald-Tribune, Fla., 1983—. Contbr. short stories to profl. publs. Recipient Chmn.'s award N.Y. Times, 1987, 2004, 3d place Editorial Writing award Fla. Soc. Newspaper Editors, 1993, 1st place Ind. Reporter Media award Fla. Sch. Bds. Assn., 1996. Office: PO Box 1695 Bradenton FL 34206-1695

WHITE, DANIEL BOWMAN, lawyer; b. Charlotte, N.C., Apr. 12, 1948; s. William Garner and Elizabeth (Bowman) W.; m. Sarah de Saussure Peterson, May 29, 1976; children: Bentley Parker, Sarah de Saussure. AB, Davidson Coll., 1970; JD, U. S.C., 1976. Bar: S.C. 1976, U.S. Dist. Ct. S.C. 1976, U.S. Ct. Appeals (4th cir.) 1978, U.S. Ct. Appeals (fed. cir.) 1990. Ptnr. Gallivan, White & Boyd P.A., Greenville, S.C., 1976—. Mem. Fed. Cir. Jud. Conf. Comments editor U. S.C. Law Rev., 1975-76. Commr. Greenville Zoning Commn., 1980-85; mem. Supreme Ct. Bd. Commrs. on Grievances and Discipline, 1988-91. 1st lt. U.S. Army, 1971-73. Decorated Bronze Star; Dana scholar Davidson Coll., N.C., 1966-70. Mem.: Assn. Def. Trial Attys., Internat. Assn. Def. Counsel, Nat. Assn. R.R. Trial Counsel, S.C. Bar (ho. dels. 1986—, bd. govs. 1992—95, chmn. ho. dels. 2000—02, bd. govs. 2000—, sec. 2002—03, treas. 2003—04, pres. elect 2004—), Def. Rsch. Inst., Greenville Young Lawyers Club (pres. 1981). Episcopalian. Office: Gallivan White & Boyd PO Box 10589 Greenville SC 29603-2804 Office Phone: 864-271-5342. E-mail: dwhite@gwblawfirm.com.

WHITE, DANIEL ERNEST, headmaster, educator, consultant; b. New Haven, Conn., July 25, 1947; s. Joseph Ray and Ruth Braem White; m. Judith Barker White, Sept. 16, 1967. BA, U. Calif., 1968; MA, U. Wash., 1969; PhD, U. Calif., 1973. Dir., student info. and rels. with schools U. Calif., 1973—78; asst. v.p., acad. affairs U. of So. Colo., 1978—79; acad. dean. Webb. Sch. of Calif., 1979—84; headmaster Webb Sch. of Calif., 1984—89, Sacramento Country Day Sch., 1989—98, Seabury Hall, 1998—2001; owner Non-Profit Ventures Hawaii, 2001—. Chmn., editl. adv. bd. Comstock's Mag., Sacramento, 1995—98; trustee Hawaii Assn. of Ind. Schools, 1998—2001; mem. accrediting commn. Western Assn. of Schools and Colleges, 1992—98. Author: (book) So Help Me God, 1995. Mem.: Kearnalai Congregational Ch., Rotary Club of Sacramento, Phi Beta Kappa.

WHITE, DAVID CALVIN, electrical engineer, energy educator, consultant; b. Sunnyside, Wash., Feb. 18, 1922; s. David Calvin Sr. and Leafie Eloise (Scott) W.; m. Glorianna Guilii, July 30, 1949 (dec. Dec. 1965); 1 child, Julie Anne White Coman (dec.); m. Margot Ann Fuller, June 4, 1966; 1 child, Constance Anne. BS, Stanford U., 1946, MS, 1947, PhD, 1949. Registered profl. engr. Elec. engr. Kaiser Industries, Vancouver, Wash., 1941-42, 43-45; assoc. prof. elec. engring. U. Fla., Gainesville, 1949-52; asst. prof. elec. engring. MIT, Cambridge, 1952-54, assoc. prof., 1954-58, prof., 1958-62, Ford prof. engring., 1962-92, dir. energy lab., 1972-89, Ford prof. engring. emeritus, 1992—. Pres., dir. Energy Conversion, Inc., 1961-64; cons. Gulf Oil, 1976-84, Johnson Controls, 1980-98; sr. advisor and vis. prof. Birla Inst., India, 1968-70; mem. council U. Benin, Nigeria, 1972; trustee Lowell Tech. Inst., Mass., 1972-74; mem. corp. Woods Hole Oceanographic Inst., Mass., 1977-84; mem. research coordinating panel Gas Research Inst., Chgo., 1977-85; chmn. adv. council Electric Power Research Inst., Palo Alto, Calif., 1984-86, mem., 1980-87. Author: (with others) Electromechanical Energy Conversion, 1959 Commr. Electric Light Plant, Concord, Mass., 1959-64, Kalmia Woods Water Dist., Concord, 1960-63 Named hon. prof. Instituto Politecnico Nacional, Mex., 1961 Fellow IEEE; mem. Nat. Acad. Engring., Am. Acad. Arts and Scis., Am. Soc. Engring. Edn. (George Westinghouse award 1961), New Seabury Country Club, Country Club Boca Raton, Phi Beta Kappa, Sigma Xi, Tau Beta Pi, Eta Kappa Nu. Republican. Avocations: golf, boating. Home: 8 Chart Way Popponesset Island Mashpee MA 02649 also: PO Box 809 Mashpee MA 02649-0809 Office: MIT 77 Massachusetts Ave Rm E40-473 Cambridge MA 02139-4307 also: 23401 Water Circle Boca Raton FL 33486 Personal E-mail: dcmfwhite@aol.com.

WHITE, DAVID CLEAVELAND, microbial ecologist, environmental toxicologist; b. Moline, Ill., May 18, 1929; s. Frederick Berryhill and Dorothy (Cleaveland) W.; m. Sandra Jean Shoults, July 7, 1957; children: Winifred Shoults, Christopher Cleaveland, Andrew Berryhill. AB magna cum laude, Dartmouth Coll., 1951; MD, Tufts U., 1955; PhD, Rockefeller U., 1962. Rotating intern Hosp. of U. Pa., 1955-56; asst. prof., assoc. prof., then prof. biochemistry U. Ky., Lexington, 1962-72; prof. biol. sci. Fla. State U., Tallahassee, 1972-86; disting. scientist U. Tenn./Oak Ridge Nat. Lab., Knoxville, 1986—; prof. microbiology, ecology U. Tenn., Knoxville, 1986—; prin. investigator Oak Ridge (Tenn.) Nat. Lab., 1988—. Mem. adv. com. Ctr. Theol. Inquiry, Princeton (N.J.) U., 1986-91; exec. dir. Ctr. for Environ. Biotech., 1991-2000; dir. Ctr. for Biomarker Analysis, 2001—; founder Inst. Applied Microbiology, Knoxville, 1986-91; mem. sci. adv. panel Mich. State Ctr. Microbial Ecology, Lansing, 1989-92, Mont. State Ctr. for Biofilm Engring., Bozeman, Mont., 1991-95; mem. sci. adv. bd. Nat. Water Rsch. Inst., 1993—; mem. Naval Rsch. Adv. Commn., 1995-96; dir. Microbial Insights, Inc., Knoxville, 1992-95; Wellcome vis. prof. U. Okla., Norman, 1984-85; spkr. profl. confs.; disting. vis. scientist Jet Propulsion Lab., Pasadena, 1998-99. Author: Sex, Drugs and Pollution, 1983, 2d edit., 1985; founding editor-in-chief Jour. Microbiol. Methods, 1985—; author numerous refereed sci. publs. Lt. M.C. USN, 1956-58. Recipient P.R. Edwards award S.E. br. Am. Soc. Microbiology, 1981, Procter & Gamble Applied and Environ., Microbiology award Am. Soc. Microbiology, 1993, Applied and Environ. Microbiol. award ASM, 1993, Antarctic Svc. medal USN/NSF, 1984, Sci. and Tech. Achievement award EPA, 1987, Athalie Richardson Clarke prize in water sci. and tech. Nat. Water Rsch. Inst., 1995. Presbyterian. Achievements include discovery of signature biomarker technique for microbial biomass, community structure and nutritional status from environmental samples, microbial ecology of deep subsurface, tropical and antarctic sediments, microbial biofilms in microbial influenced corrosion, biosensors environmental biotechnology, planetary protection in mans sample return missions, analysis of breath aerosols for regulatory lipids as harbingers of pulmonary pathobiology. Office: Ctr for Bomarker Analysis 10515 Research Dr Ste 300 Knoxville TN 37932-2572 E-mail: milipids@aol.com., dwhite1@utk.edu.

WHITE, DAVID HYWEL, physics educator; b. Cardiff, Wales, June 4, 1931; came to U.S., 1959, naturalized, 1966; s. William Richard and Bessie (Morgan) W.; m. Frances Mary Shearman, July 23, 1954; children: Richard Gerwyn, Christopher David. BS, U. Wales, 1953; PhD, Birmingham U., 1956. Asst. lectr. Birmingham U., 1958-59; asst. prof. U. Pa., 1961-64; asso. prof. Cornell U., Ithaca, N.Y., 1964-69, prof., 1969-78; sr. physicist, head exptl. facilities div. Isabelle Project, Brookhaven Nat. Lab., Upton, L.I., N.Y., 1978-86; group leader nuclear and particle physics rsch. P divsn. Los Alamos (N.Mex.) Nat. Lab., 1986-88, lab. fellow, 1998—. Cons., 1967-69, 76-78, 99—. Author: Elementary Electronics, 1967; Editor: Scintillation Counters, 1966. NSF sr. postdoctoral fellow, 1970; JSPS fellow, 1981 Fellow Am. Phys. Soc., AAAS. Home: 913 Calle Vistoso Santa Fe NM 87501-1031

WHITE, DEAN, advertising executive; b. Norfolk, Nebr., 1923; m. Barbara White; 4 children. Student, U. Nebr.; grad., U.S. Merchant Marine Acad. Pres. Whiteco Industries, Inc., Merrillville, Ind., 1953-98, chmn. bd., CEO, 1998—. Chief officer Merchant Marines, Navy. Office: Whiteco Industries Inc 1000 E 700N Merrillville IN 46410-5675

WHITE, DEBRA SAUNDERS, technology executive; b. Mason City, Iowa, Jan. 8, 1957; d. Roger Allen and Irene Boone Saunders; children: Elizabeth Paige, Cecil III. BA, U. Va., 1979; MBA, Coll. William and Mary, 1993; PhD, George Washington U., 2004—. Account mgr. IBM, Norfolk, Va., 1979-93; chief info. officer St. George's Sch., Newport, R.I., 1993-98, Hampton (Va.) U., 1999—. Mem. Va. Rsch. Tech. Adv. Commn., Hampton; chairperson Internet com. Advanced Network Minority Serving Inst., Washington. Coord. HBCU Com. ANMSI; program com.mem. Educause. Recipient Indpls. Minority Bus. Leader award City of Indpls., 1989; recognized Cyberstar, Black Issues in Higher Edn., 2002. Mem. Alpha Kappa Alpha. Avocation: skiing. Home: 21 Sarfan Dr Hampton VA 23664 Office: 130 E Tyler St Hampton VA 23669-5403 E-mail: debra.white@hamptonu.edu.

WHITE, DENNIS L. political organization administrator; b. 1954; Franklin County chmn. Ohio Dem. Party, 1994—2002, chmn., 2002—; CEO Transport Consol. Office: Ohio Dem Party 271 E State St Columbus OH 43215

WHITE, DIANE O'DONNELL, retired librarian; b. Petersburg, Alaska, Dec. 4, 1944; d. John James O'Donnell, Vera Gertrude O'Donnell; m. Max A. White. BA in German Lang. and Lit., U.Oregon, 1967, MLS, 1970; media specialist, Western Oreg. State U., 1989. Cert. tchr. grades K-12. Serials cataloger U. Oreg., Eugene, 1970—75; adult svcs. libr. Kern County Libr., Bakersfield, Calif., 1986—87; coord. Oregon Index Oreg. State Libr., Salem, 1987—88; media specialist Harrisburg (Oreg.) Elem. Sch., 1989—92; reference libr. Albany (Oreg.) Pub. Libr., 1992—96, supervising libr., 1997—2000, libr. dir., 2001—02, ret., 2002. Mem.: Oreg. Libr. Assn., Greater Albany Rotary, Alpha Lambda Delta, Phi Beta Kappa. Presbyterian. Avocations: jogging, singing, dance, animal rights. Office: Albany Pub Libr 1390 Waverly Dr SE Albany OR 97321

WHITE, DONALD HARVEY, physics educator emeritus; b. Berkeley, Calif., Apr. 30, 1931; s. Harvey Elliott and Adeline White; m. Beverly Evalina Jones, Aug. 8, 1953; children: Jeri, Brett, Holly, Scott, Erin. AB, U. Calif., Berkeley, 1953; PhD, Cornell U., 1960. Rsch. physicist Lawrence Livermore (Calif.) Nat. Lab., 1960-71, cons., 1971-90; prof. physics Western Oreg. U., Monmouth, 1971-95; ret. Vis. rsch. scientist Inst. Laue-Langevin, Grenoble, France, 1977-78, 84-85, 91-92. Author: (with others) Physics, an Experimental Science, 1968, Physics and Music, 1980. Pres. Monmouth-Independence Cmty. Arts, 1983. DuPont scholar, 1958; Minna-Heineman Found. fellow, Hannover, Germany, 1977. Mem. Am. Phys. Soc., Oreg. Acad. Sci. (pres. 1979-80), Phi Kappa Phi (pres. West Oreg. chpt. 1989-90) Democrat. Presbyterian. Home: 1450 SW Bridlewood Dr #13 Dallas OR 97338

WHITE, DONNA C, music educator, director; b. Columbus, Ohio, Dec. 17, 1955; d. George F and Madelyn B Clark; m. Robert G White, Aug. 12, 1978; children: Aaron R, Andrew J, Jill K. BA, Capital U., 1978. Cert. tchr. of music 2003. Subsitute tchr. Davison City Schools, Mich., 1979—80; choir dir. Brandon Christian Ch., Fla., 1989—90; subsitute tchr. Hilliard City Schoo.ls, Ohio, 1991—98; organist/music dir. St. Andrew Christian Ch., Dublin, Ohio, 1998—2003, So. Md. Faith Cmty. Ch., 2003—. Pvt. piano tchr., Columbus, Ohio, 1977—78, Cleveland, 1981—83, Medina, Ohio, 1983—87, Valrico, Fla., 1988—90, Hilliard, Ohio, 1991—2003, Lexinton Pk., Md., 2004—. Mem.: Nat. Guild Piano Teachers (judge 2003—), Md. State Music Teachers Assn. (dist. pres. 2004—), Ohio Music Teachers Assn. (dist. v.p. of student activities 2002—03), Music Teachers Nat. Assn. Avocations: gardening, reading, walking, birdwatching. Home: 46860 Hilton Dr #1721 Lexington Park MD 20653 Office: Donna C White Piano Studio 21815 Three Notch Rd Ste E Lexington Park MD 20653 Office Phone: 301-737-5570.

WHITE, DOUG, state legislator; b. 1943; m. Shirley White; children: Steve, Jenny. BS, Ohio State U. Commr. Adams County, 1985-90; mem. Ohio Ho. of Reps from 77th & 88th dists., Columbus, 1990-96; owner, operator livestock and crop farm; mem. Ohio Senate from 14th dist., Columbus, 1996—, pres., 2002—. Mem. Ohio Cattlemen's Assn. (pres.), Ohio Beef Coun. (former treas.), Adams County Rep. Club, Ohio 4-H Found., Manchester Lions, Ohio Farm Bur. Office: Ohio Senate State House Rm 201 Columbus OH 43215

WHITE, DOUGLAS JAMES, JR., lawyer; b. N.Y.C., Mar. 20, 1934; s. Douglas James and Margaret (Stillman) W.; m. Denise Beale, May 28, 1960; children: Brian Douglas, James Roderick. BA, U. Oreg., 1955; LLB, Willamette U., 1958. Bar: Oreg. 1958. Law clk. to assoc. justice Oreg. Supreme Ct., Salem, 1958-59; assoc. Schwabe, Williamson & Wyatt (formerly known as Mautz, Souther, Spaulding, Kinsey & Williamson), Portland, Oreg., 1959-69; shareholder, gen. ptnr. Schwabe, Williamson & Wyatt, P.C. (formerly known as Schwabe, Williamson, Wyatt, Moore & Roberts), Portland, Oreg., 1969-79, sr. ptnr., 1979-93; shareholder, 1994-98; of counsel, 1999—. Trustee Jesuit H.S., Beaverton, 1991-94; bd. dirs. St. Vincent de Paul Child Devel. Ctr., Portland, 1979-90, Portland Coun., Soc. St. Vincent de Paul, 1989-92, Portland House of Umoja, 1995—; bd. dirs., officer Maryville Nursing Home, Beaverton, 1993-99, St. Vincent de Paul Conf. of St. Thomas More, Portland, 1966—; adv. bd. Saturday Acad., Portland, 1982—. Mem.: Oreg. State Bar Assn. (real estate and land use sect. exec. com. 1984—85), Flyfisher Club Oreg., Multnomah Athletic Club. Republican. Roman Catholic. Avocations: fly fishing, bridge, walking and hiking, travel. Home: 6725 SW Preslynn Dr Portland OR 97225-2668 Office: Schwabe Williamson & Wyatt 1211 SW 5th Ave Ste 1800 Portland OR 97204-3713 Office Phone: 503-222-9981.

WHITE, DOUGLAS RICHIE, anthropology educator; b. Mpls., Mar. 13, 1942; s. Asher Abbott and Margaret McQuestin (Richie) W.; m. Jayne Chamberlain (div. Feb. 1971); m. Lilyan Amdur Brudner, Mar. 21, 1971; 1 child, Scott Douglas. BA, U. Minn., 1964, MA, 1967, PhD, 1969. Asst. prof. U. Pitts., 1967-72, assoc. prof., 1972-76, U. Calif., Irvine, 1976-79, prof., 1979—. Dep. dir. Lang. Attitudes Rsch. Project, Dublin, 1971—73; vis. prof. U. Tex., Austin, 1974—75, Ecole des Hautes Etudes en Sci. Sociales, Paris, 1999—2002, Inst. Nat. d'Etudes Démographique, 2000; chmn. Linkages: World Devel. Res. Coun., Md., 1986—, pres., Md., 1986—90. Co-editor: Research Methods in Social Networks, 1989, Anthropology of Urban Environments, 1972, Kinship, Networks and Exchange, 1998; founder, gen. editor World Cultures Jour., 1985-90; author sci. software packages; contbr. articles to profl. jours. Recipient Sr. Disting. U.S. Scientist award, Alexander von Humboldt Stiftung, Bonn, Germany, 1989—91, Bourse de Haute Niveau award, Ministry Rsch. and Tech., Paris, 1992; fellow, Ctr. for Advanced Studies, Western Behavioral Sci. Inst., La Jolla, Calif., 1981—84. Mem. Social Sci. Computing Assn. (pres. elect 1991, pres. 1992.), Santa Fe Inst. (mem. working groups 1999, 2000, 2001, external faculty 2004-). Democrat. Home: 8633 Via Mallorca Unit C La Jolla CA 92037 Office: U Calif School Social Sci Irvine CA 92697-0001 Office Phone: 949-824-5893.

WHITE, EDWARD ALFRED, lawyer; b. Elizabeth, N.J., Nov. 23, 1934; BS in Indsl. Engring., U. Mich., 1957, JD, 1963. Bar: Fla. 1963, U.S. Ct. Appeals (5th cir.) 1971, U.S. Ct. Appeals (11th cir.) 1981, U.S. Supreme Ct. 1976. Assoc. Jennings, Watts, Clarke & Hamilton, Jacksonville, Fla., 1963-66, ptnr., 1966-69, Wayman & White, Jacksonville, Fla., 1969-72; pvt. practice Jacksonville, Fla., 1972—. Mem. aviation law com. Fla. Bar, 1972-94, chmn., 1979-81, bd. govs., 1984-88, admiralty com., 1984—, chmn., 1990-91, chmn. pub. relations com., 1986-88, exec. coun. trial lawyers sect., 1986-91, chmn. admiralty cert. com., 1995-97. Fellow Am. Bar Found.; mem. ABA (vice chmn. admiralty law com. 1995—), Fla. Bar Assn. (bd. cert. civil trial lawyer, bd. cert. admiralty lawyer), Jacksonville Bar Assn. (chmn. legal ethics com. 1975-76, bd. govs. 1976-78, pres. 1979-80), Assn. Trial Lawyers Am. (sustaining mem. 1984—), Acad. Fla. Trial Lawyers (diplomate), Fla. Coun. Bar Assn. Pres.'s, Lawyer-Pilots Bar Assn., Am. Judicature Soc., Maritime Law Assn. (proctor in admiralty), Southeastern Admiralty Law Inst. (bd. dirs. 1982-84, chmn., pres. 1994), Am. Bd. Trial Advocates. Home: 1959 Largo Rd Jacksonville FL 32207-3926 Office: 901 Blackstone Bldg 233 E Bay St Jacksonville FL 32202-3452 Fax: 904-356-6508. Office Phone: 904-356-6500. E-mail: cwitherwax@damato-lynch.com.

WHITE, EDWARD ALLEN, electronics company executive; b. Jan. 1, 1928; s. Joseph and Bessie (Allen) W.; m. Joan Dixon, Dec. 22, 1949 (div. Aug. 1978); children: Dixon Richard, Leslie Ann; m. Nancy Rhoads, Oct. 6, 1979. BS, Tufts U., 1947. Vice chmn. White Electronic Designs Corp., Phoenix, 1951—. Pres. Ariz. Digital Corp., Phoenix, 1975—91, Interactive Digital Corp., Phoenix, 1992—. Patentee in field. Bd. dirs. Gov.'s Coun. Children, Youth and Families, Phoenix, 1982-84, Planned Parenthood Fedn. Am., 1984-88; pres., bd. dirs. Planned Parenthood Ctrl. and No. Ariz., 1984-88; trustee Internat. House, N.Y.C., 1973-75, Tufts U., 1973-83. Recipient Horatio Alger award, 1962. Mem.: World Pres.'s Orgn., Paradise Valley Country Club, Tau Beta Pi. Home: 5786 N Echo Canyon Cir Phoenix AZ 85018-1242 Office: White Electronic Designs Corp 3601 E University Dr Phoenix AZ 85034-7254 Office Phone: 602-437-1520 x111. Business E-Mail: ewhite@whiteedc.com.

WHITE, ELIZABETH G. music educator; b. Marshall, Mo., Sept. 4, 1929; d. Everett Gill, Jr. and Rachel Truex; m. Donald A. White, Oct. 13, 1956; children: Mac Donald, Dorothy Rachel Albritton. MusB, New Eng. Conservatory, 1952, MusM, 1954. Tchg. fellow New Eng. Conservatory Prep., Boston, 1952—54; organist various chs., Richmond, Va., 1954—56, Arlington (Va.) Forest Meth. Ch., 1956—58, Auburndale Bapt. Ch., Louisville, 1958—61; piano tchr. U. Louisville Prep., 1958—61, So. Bapt. Theol. Sem., Louisville, 1958—61; pvt. piano tchr. Bowie, Md., 1965—; organist Grace Bapt. Ch., Bowie, 1985—, Belcroft Bible Ch., Bowie, 1978—84, Belair Bapt. Ch., 1969—76. Freelance piano accompanist/collaborator, Washington, 1956—58, Washington, 1965—. Mem.: Md. State Music Tchr.'s Assn. (cert.), Music Tchr.'s Nat. Assn. (cert.), Music Tchrs. Assn. Bowie (pres. 1968—70, 2000—02), Friday Morning Music Club (performing mem. 1956—58, 1980—), Mu Phi Epsilon (pres. Washington alumni chpt. 1994—96, dir. dist. A-2 2002—04). Home: 2605 Chapel Lake Dr #314 Gambrills MD 21054

WHITE, EMMET, JR., retirement community administrator; b. Newark, Oct. 18, 1946; s. Emmet, Sr. and June (Howlett) White; m. Betty Orr, June 7, 1970; children: Benjamin, Suzanne, George. BA, Lafayette Coll., 1968; JD, Coll. William and Mary, 1971. Bar: Hawaii 1972; nursing home adminstr., Hawaii. Law ptnr. Mau and White, AAL, Honolulu, 1975-83, White and Tom, AAL, Honolulu, 1983-95; pres., CEO Arcadia Retirement Residence, Honolulu, 1996—. Trustee Ctrl. Union Ch., Honolulu, 1980-84, chmn. 1983-84, moderator, 1987, also deacon; mem. Health Planning Coun. Honolulu. Col. USAR, 1968-94. Mem.: Nat. Commn. Employer Spt. of Guard and Res. (ombudsman), Hawaii Long Term Care Assn. (chmn. 2001—03), Hawaii Bar Assn. Avocations: family activities, physical activities. Office: Arcadia Retirement Residence 1434 Punahou St Honolulu HI 96822-4754 E-mail: ewhite@arcadia-hi.org.

WHITE, EUGENE A. retired physician, neuroradiologist; b. Birmingham, Ala., Oct. 29, 1935; s. Roger O. and Gregory C. (Durr) W.; m. June Ardis Johnson, Feb. 6, 1965 (dec. Oct. 18, 2003); children: Theodore O., Forrest E., Darlene E. BA summa cum laude, Fisk U., 1956; MD, Case Western Res. U., 1964. Diplomate Am. Bd. Radiology. Postdoctoral fellow dept. neuroradiology Karolinska Hosp., Stockholm, 1969-70; radiologist Forest City Hosp., Cleve., 1970-72, Luth. Hosp., Cleve., 1972-73; from instr. to asst. prof. radiology Case Western Res. Med. Sch., Cleve., 1973-77, asst. clin. prof. radiology, 1977-99; neuroradiologist in pvt. practice Drs. Hill & Thomas Inc., Beachwood, Ohio, 1977-99, ptnr., v.p. neuroradiology svcs., 1988-99, also bd. dirs. Mng. dir. Assoc. Med. Enterprises, Beachwood, 1980-87; clin. cons. Technicare Corp., Solon, Ohio, 1984-86. Contbr. articles to profl. jours. Bd. dirs. League Park Ctr., Cleve., 1976-82, Murtis Taylor Cmty. Ctr., 1986-92, Fisk U., Nashville, 1988—, Adrienne Kennedy Soc., 1989-95, Great Lakes Theatre Festival, Cleve., 1992—, Cleve. Internat. Program, 1994-2004, Geric Found., 1996—; chmn. bd. dirs. Creative Writing Workshop, 1995—, Duffy-Lit Dance and Spirituals Ensemble, 2001--; trustee Coun. Internat. Programs, 1999--, chmn. bd., 2002. Mem.: NAACP (life), Internat. Symposium Neuroradiology, Am. Roentgen Ray Soc., Am. Coll. Neuroradiology, Am. Coll. Radiology, Cleve. Coun. on World Affairs, Cleve. Com. on Fgn. Rels., Rowfant Club, Pasteur Club, Cleve. Skating Club, Hermit Club, City Club of Cleve., Phi Beta Kappa, Alpha Phi Alpha (life). Avocations: music, tennis, theater, international relations, philosophy. Home: 3199 Van Aken Blvd Shaker Heights OH 44120 E-mail: eaw5@stratos.net.

WHITE, EUGENE VADEN, retired pharmacist; b. Cape Charles, Va., Aug. 13, 1924; s. Paul Randolph and Louise (Townsend) W.; m. Laura Juanita LaFontaine, Aug. 28, 1948; children: Lynda Sue, Patricia Louise. BS in Pharmacy, Med. Coll. Va., 1950; PharM (hon.), Phila. Coll. Pharmacy and Sci., 1966; DSc (hon.), Shenandoah U., 2001. Pharmacist McKim & Huffman Drug Store, Luray, Va., 1950, Miller's Drug Store, Winchester, 1950-53; pharmacist, ptnr. Shiner's Drug Store, Front Royal, 1953-56; pharmacist, owner Eugene V. White, Pharmacist, P.C., Berryville, 1956-98; ret., 1998. Sturmer lectr. Phila. Coll. Pharmacy and Sci., 1979; Lubin vis. prof. U. Tenn. Sch. Pharmacy, Memphis, 1974; mem. bd. visitors Sch. Pharmacy, U. Pitts., 1969. Author: The Office-Based Family Pharmacist, 1978; created first office practice in community pharmacy, 1960, developed patient medication profile record, 1960. 2d lt. USAAC, 1943-45. Recipient Nat. Leadership award Phi Lambda Sigma, 1979, Outstanding Pharmacy Alumnus award Med. Coll. Va. Sch. Pharmacy Alumni Assn., 1989; Eugene V. White scholarship named in his honor Shenandoah U. Sch. Pharmacy, 1996, Eugene V. White Disting. Lecture Series established by Delta Xi chpt. Kappa Psi Pharm. Fraternity, Shenandoah U. Sch. Pharmacy, 1998. Fellow Am. Coll. Apothecaries (J. Leon Lascoff award 1973); mem. Am. Pharm Assn. (Daniel B. Smith award 1965, Remington Honor medal 1978), Va. Pharm. Assn. (Pharmacist of Yr. award 1966, Outstanding Pharmacist award 1992). Methodist. Avocations: reading, woodworking, computer. E-mail: evwhite@visuallink.com.

WHITE, EVELYN, human resources administrator; With U.S. Postal Svc. Corp., Dept. of Energy, Office of Personnel Mgmt.; asst. and dep. dir. personnel USDA, dir. human resources, 1994; dep. asst. sec. human resources Office of Human Resources, Washington, 1997—. Chair Sec.'s Welfare to Work and Office of Sec. Quality of Work Life Initiatives. Named to Washington Carver Hall of Fame. Office: Office of Human Resources 200 Independence Ave SW Washington DC 20201-0004

WHITE, FREDERICK ANDREW, physics educator, physicist; b. Detroit, Mar. 11, 1918; s. Andrew Bracken and Mildred (Witzel) W.; m. Dorothy Janet Sibley, Nov. 7, 1942 (dec.); children: Wendell William, Lawrence Sibley, Eric Sibley, Roger Randolph (dec.). BS, Wayne State U., 1940; MS, U. Mich., 1941; postgrad., U. Rochester, 1943-46; PhD, U. Wis., 1959. Insp. U.S. Army Ordnance, Rochester, N.Y., 1941-43; rsch. asst. Manhattan project U. Rochester, 1943-45; grad. instr. rsch. Manhattan project U. Rochester, 1946; rsch. asst., rsch. assoc., cons. physicist Gen. Electric Co. Knolls Atomic Power Lab., Schenectady, 1947-62; adj. prof. nuclear sci. Rensselaer Poly. Inst., Troy, N.Y., 1961-62, prof. nuclear engrng. and environmental engrng., indsl. liaison scientist, 1962-81, prof. emeritus, 1981—; rsch. and liaison scientist Rochester Gas & Electric Co., N.Y., 1978-96; adj. prof. physics SUNY, Albany, 1981-88. Cons. NASA, 1965-80; organist and acoustic cons., 1952—2001. Author: American Industrial Research Laboratories, 1961, Mass Spectrometry in Science and Technology, 1968, Our Acoustic Environment, 1975; Mass Spectrometry: Applications in Science and Engineering, 1986. Mem. AIAA, IEEE, Optical Soc. Am., Am. Guild Organists. Achievements include developing mass spectrometric instrumentation and its uses in measurements relating to nuclear and atomic physics; co-discoverer last naturally-occurring stable isotope. Home: 2456 Hilltop Rd Niskayuna NY 12309-2405 E-mail: whitef@taconic.net.

WHITE, GARY RICHARD, electrical engineer; b. Detroit, Nov. 15, 1962; s. Thomas Richard and Davene (Reynolds) W. BSEE, Wayne State U., 1986. Electronics engr. U.S. Army Info. Sys. Engring. Command, Ft. Belvoir, Va., 1987-88, Ft. Shafter, Hawaii, 1988-92; elec. worker U.S. Navy Pub. Works Ctr., Pearl Harbor, Hawaii, 1992-96, plant operator helper, 1996—. Mem. IEEE, NRA, NSPE, Assn. Computing Machinery, Am. Assn. Individual Investors, Am. Mgmt. Assn. Avocations: weightlifting, biking, hardware and software, rock concerts, movies. Office: PO Box 19055 Honolulu HI 96817-8055 Office Phone: 808-474-2202.

WHITE, GAYLE CLAY, aerospace company executive; b. Wyandotte, Mich., Sept. 28, 1944; s. John Leonard and Irene Frances (Clay) W.; m. Sharon Wong, June 8, 1968; children: Lai Jean, Quinn Yee. BBA, Ea. Mich. U., 1967; MBA, Utah State U., 1971; MPA, Auburn U., 1976; postgrad., Nova U., 1985-99. Computer system analyst USAF Logistics Command, Odgen, Utah, 1967-71, U.S.-Can. Mil. Officer Exec., Ottawa, Ont., 1971-73; mgr. software devel. USAF Data System Design Ctr., Montgomery, Ala., 1973-77; data base adminstr. Supreme Hdqrs. Allied Powers Europe, Casteau, Belgium, 1977-81; mgr. software configuration System Integration Office, Colorado Springs, Colo., 1981-83; mgr. computer ops. N.Am. Aerospace Def. Command, Colorado Springs, 1983-84; dir. ops. 6 Missile Warning Squadron, Space Command, Cape Cod, Mass., 1984-86, comdr., 1986-87; mgr. program devel. Rockwell Internat., Colorado Springs, 1987-96; mgr. bus. devel. The Boeing Co., Colorado Springs, 1996-99; ret. Mem. faculty computer sci. and bus. Regis U., Colorado Springs, 1981—97; sr. mem. exec. staff Computer Scis. Corp., 1999—. V.p. European Parents, Tchrs. and Students Assn., 1979—81; mem. Pikes Peak Regional Workforce Investment Bd., 2002—, vice chmn., 2004—; treas. Christian Ctr. Ch., Colorado Springs, 1989—95. Recipient Mil.-Civilian Rels. award, Otis Civilian Adv. Coun., 1987, cert., Data Processing Mgmt. Assn., 1973, Significant Service award, Nat. Def. Indsl. Assn., 1998, Gold medal, 2003. Mem.: C. of C. Mil. Affairs Com., Christian Businessmen's Assn., Nat. Security Indsl. Assn. (bd. dirs. Rocky Mountain chpt. 1990—97, bd. dirs. space divsn. 1993—2003, vice chmn. ctrl. region 1996—97, chpt. pres. 1997—99, exec. vice chmn. 1999—2000, chmn. nat. space com. 2000—02, sr. advisor 2003—, Significant Svc. award 1998, Exceptional Svc. award 2001, Gold medal 2003), SHAPE Officers Assn., Air Force Assn. (v.p. membership Lance Sijan chpt. 2000—02, chmn. Space Symposium com. 2003, pres. Lance Sijan chpt. 2003—, Chpt. Exceptional Svc. award 2001, 2002, chpt. Star award 2003), Global Positioning Sys. Internat. Assn., Inst. Nav. (treas. Rocky Mountain sect. 1996—97), Armed Forces Comm. Electronics Assn., Colo. Air Force Assn. (medal of merit 2001, exceptional svc. award 2002), Woodmoor Pines Golf Club, Alpha Kappa Psi. Republican. Avocations: racquetball, camping, coin collecting/numismatics. Office: Computer Scis Corp 460 Wooten Rd Ste 144 Colorado Springs CO 80916 Personal E-mail: gwhite22@csc.com.

WHITE, GEORGE COOKE, theater director, foundation executive; b. New London, Conn., Aug. 16, 1935; s. Nelson Cooke and Aida (Rovetti) W.; m. Elizabeth Conant Darling, July 5, 1958; children: George Conant, Caleb Ensign, Juliette Darling. Student, U. Paris, 1956; BA, Yale U., 1957, MFA, 1961; student, Shakespeare Inst., 1959; ArtsD (hon.), Conn. Coll., 1994. Stage mgr. Imperial Japanese Azumakabuki Co., 1955; asst. mgr. Internat. Ballet Festival, Nervi, Italy, 1955; prodn. coordinator Talent Assos., 1961-63; adminstrv. v.p. score prodns. Paramount Pictures, 1963-65; founder, pres. Eugene O'Neill Meml. Theatre Found., 1965—2000; adviser, dir. Theatre One, Conn. Coll. Women, 1967-70; exec. dir. The Johnny Mercer Found., 1999; regional theater cons. Nat. Ednl. TV Network; guest lectr. Wagner Coll., 1970; acting dir. Hunter Coll. Hunter Arts, 1972-73; chmn. Florence Acad. Art, 2004—. Adj. prof. U. N.C.; prof. theater adminstrn. program Yale U., 1978-91; co-chmn. Yale Drama Sch.; mem. exec. com. Theatre Libr. Assn., 1967; bd. govs. Am. Playwrights Theatre; mem. bd. ANTA, 1967-68; mem. Mayor N.Y.C.'s. Theatre Adv. Com.; advisory bd. Internat. Theatre Inst.; panel mem. Exptl. Theatre; U.S. State Dept. cultural exchange grantee to Australia; guest adminstr. Australian Nat. Playwrights Conf., 1973; U.S. del. Internat. Theatre Inst. Congress, Moscow, 1973; mem. Conn. Commn. on Arts, 1978-93, mem. exec. com., 1979-83, vice chair, 1992-93; co-founder Caribbean-U.S. Theatre Exchange; dir. Actors Theatre St. Paul, 1979, 80, 82, 83, 86, Hartman Repertory Theatre, 1980; guest dir. Chinese Theater Assn., Beijing, 1984, 87, Hedgerow Theatre, 1986; mem. nominating com. Antoinette Perry Awards, 1984-86, 88, 94-96, 98-2002, adminstrv. com. Am. Theater Wing, 1997; dir. Anna Christie Beijing Cen. Dramatic Theater, 1984, 87; bd. dirs. New London Day. Appeared in TV series Citizen Soldier, 1959-61; appeared in off-Broadway prodn. John Brown's Body. Trustee Goodspeed Opera House, 1966-68, Nat. Theatre Conf., 1973—, Eastern Conn. Symphony, Dance Arts Coun., Conn. Opera Assn., Conn. Pub. TV, 1973-83, Mitchell Coll., 1994—, Arts & Bus. Coun., 1994—, Arts Internat., 2001, 02, Boston Conservatory, 2000--; trustee Conn. Edn. Telecommunications Corp., 1973-83, chmn., 1982; mem. planning bd. Op. Rescue; bd. dirs. Rehearsal Club, Centre for Inter-Am. Rels., Theater of Latin Am., Manhattan Theatre Club, 1970-80, Met. Opera Guild; Performance mag.; exec. com. Yale Drama Alumni, 1963-73; mem. Yale Alumni Bd.; bd. overseers drama dept. Brandeis U.; adv. bd. Am. Musical Theatre Program, Hartford Conservatory, Bd. Arts & Bus. Coun., Brandeis Creative Arts Award Jury, Theater and New Music Theatre Works Panel, NEA; mem. Waterford (Conn.) Rep. Town Meeting, 1975-77, 2001—; presdl. appointment to Nat. Coun. NEA, 1992; mem. Nat. Coun. Arts, 1992-97; trustee Arts Internat.; bd. dirs. Day Pub. Co., RKO Pictures, American Acad. Dramatic Arts; mem. Coast Guard Auxillary, Crew mem. U.S. Coast Guard Barque Eagle. Served with AUS, 1957-59; Flotilla Cmdr, U.S. Coast Auxillary, 1998-99. Named Officer first class, Royal Swedish Order of Polar Star; recipient spl. citation, New England Theatre Conf., 1968, 1998, Margo Jones award, 1968, Pub. Svc. award, New London County Bar Assn., 1975, Disting. Citizen's award, Town of Waterford, 1976, Distin. Svc. award, Conn. mag., 1981, Contbns. to State award, 1981, Lifetime Contbn. to Theatre award, Am. Theater Assn., 1989, Contbn. to Conn. Arts award, Quinnipiac Coll., 1989, Medal of Arts, Russian Federation, Chevalier des artes et des lettres (France), 1983, gold medal, Cairo Internat. Experimental Theater Festival; grantee Internat. Communications Agy. cultural exch. grantee to People's Republic of China, 1980. Fellow Royal Soc. Arts, Coll. of Am. Theatre; mem. Chinese Theatre Assn. (hon.). Clubs: Century; Cosmos (Washington); Thames (New London); White's Point Yacht. Office: O'Neill Theater Ctr 305 Great Neck Rd Waterford CT 06385-3825 Home: 30 Sutton Pl New York NY 10022 Office Phone: 212-382-2790. Personal E-mail: whitebg@att.net.

WHITE, GEORGE EDWARD, law educator, lawyer; b. Northampton, Mass., Mar. 19, 1941; s. George LeRoy and Frances Dorothy (McCafferty) W.; m. Susan Valre Davis, Dec. 31, 1966; children: Alexandra V., Elisabeth McC. BA, Amherst Coll., 1963; MA, Yale U., 1964, PhD, 1967; JD, Harvard U., 1970. Bar: D.C. 1970, Va. 1975, U.S. Supreme Ct. 1973. Vis. scholar Am. Bar Found., 1970-71; law clk. to Chief Justice Warren U.S. Supreme Ct., 1971-72; asst. prof. law U. Va., 1972-74, assoc. prof., 1974-77, prof., 1977-86, John B. Minor prof. law and history, 1987—2003, disting. univ. prof., John B. Minor prof. law and history, 1992—2003, David and Mary Harrison disting. prof. law, 2003—. Vis. prof. Marshall-Wythe Law Sch. spring 1988, N.Y. Law Sch., fall 1988. Author: The American Judicial Tradition, 1976, 2nd edit., 1988, Tort Law in America: An Intellectual History, 1980 (Gavel award ABA, 1981), ed edit., 2003, Earl Warren: A Public Life, 1982 (Gavel award ABA, 1983), The Marshall Court and Cultural Change, 1988, 2nd edit., 1991 (James Willard Hurst prize, 1990), Justice Oliver Wendell Holmes: Law and the Inner Self, 1993 (Gavel award ABA, 1994, Scribes award, 1994, Littleton-Griswold prize, 1994, Triennial Order of the Coif award, 1996), Intervention and Detachment: Essays in Legal History and Jurisprudence, 1994, Creating the National Pastime: Baseball Transforms Itself, 1903-1953, 1996, The Constitution and the New Deal, 2000, Alger Hiss's Looking-Glass Wars, 2004, others; editor: Studies in Legal History, 1980—86, Delegate in Law, 1986—97. Mem. AAAS, Am. Law Inst., Am. Soc. Legal History (bd. dirs. 1978-81), Soc. Am. Historians. Office: Law Sch U Va 580 Massie Rd Charlottesville VA 22903-1789 Office Phone: 434-924-3455. Business E-Mail: gew@virginia.edu.

WHITE, GEORGE EDWARD, pedodontist, educator; b. Jamestown, N.Y., July 31, 1941; s. Gordon Ennis and Margaret (Appleyard) W. AB, Colgate U., 1963; DDS, SUNY, Buffalo, 1967; PhD, MIT, 1973; DBA, Century U., 1982. Intern, then resident Children's Hosp., Buffalo, 1967-69; prof., chmn. dept. pediat. dentistry Tufts U. Sch. Dental Medicine, Boston, 1973—; chief dept. oral pediat. New Eng. Med. Center Hosp., Boston, 1973-80; pvt. practice pedodontics, Boston, 1974—; lectr. MIT, 1975-80; cons. Abcor, Inc.; nat., internat. lectr. Nat. Inst. Dental Rsch. grantee, 1973—. Author: Dental Caries: A Multifactorial Disease, 1975, To Stand Alone, 1979; co-author: Maxillofacial Orthopedics: For the Growing Child, 1983; founder, editor-in-chief Jour. Pedodontics, 1976, now named Jour. Clin. Pediat. Dentistry; editor: Clin. Oral Pediatrics, 1979, founder, editor-in-chief Mastering Clin. Pediat. Dentistry, 1993-98; editor-in-chief Protocols for Clin. Pediat. Dentistry; contbr. articles to profl. jours. Master Acad. Gen. Dentistry; fellow Am. Acad. Pediat. Dentistry, Internat. Coll. Dentistry, Am. Coll. Dentistry; mem. Am. Assn. Dental Editors, Fedn. Dentaire Internationale, Sigma Xi, Omicron Kappa Upsilon. Office: Tufts U Sch Dental Medicine Dept Pediat Dentistry 1 Kneeland St Boston MA 02111-1527

WHITE, GEORGE MALCOLM, architect; b. Cleve., Nov. 1, 1920; m. Susanne Neiley Daniels, Apr. 21, 1973; children: Stephanie, Jocelyn, Geoffrey, Pamela. BS, MS, MIT, 1942; MBA, Harvard, 1948; LL.B., Case Western Res. U., 1959. Design engr. Gen. Electric Co., Schenectady, 1942-47; practice architecture and law Cleve., 1948-71; Architect of Capitol, Washington, 1971-95; vice chmn. Leo A. Daly, Washington, 1996—. Bd. dirs. 3D Internat. Works include First Unitarian Ch., Cleve., 1959, Preformed Line Products Co. Office Bldg., Cleve., 1960, Mentor Harbor Yacht Club, 1968, restoration, Old Senate and Supreme Ct. Chambers, U.S. Capitol, 1975, Libr. of Congress James Madison Meml. Bldg., 1979, U.S. Capitol Power Plant Extension, 1979, master plan for U.S. Capitol, 1981, Hart Senate Office Bldg., 1982, restoration of the west cen. front U.S. Capitol Bldg., 1987, Thurgood Marshall Fed. Judiciary Bldg., 1992, U.S. Capitol west terr. restoration and courtyard addt., 1993. Former mem. D.C. Zoning Commn., U.S. Capitol Police Bd., U.S. Capitol Guide Bd., U.S. Ho. of Reps. Page Bd., Adv. Coun. on Hist. Preservation, Internat. Ctr. Com., Nat. Conservation Adv. Coun., Nat. Capital Meml. Commn., art adv. com. Washington Met. Area Transit Auth.; former acting dir. U.S. Bot. Garden; former mem. bd. dirs., chmn. design com. Pennsylvania Ave. Devel. Corp.; former bd. dirs. Nat. Bldg. Mus.; former trustee Fed. City Coun.; mem. bd. regents Am. Archtl. Found; former chmn. archtl. adv. com. Restoration of Statue of Liberty; chmn. com. for Statue of Liberty Mus.; mem. nat. panel arbitrators Am. Arbitration Assn.; former mem.

vis. com. dept. architecture and planning MIT; mem. bd. cons. Nubian monuments at Philae, Egypt; mem. internat. com. cons. for Egyptian Mus., Cairo; chmn. rev. com. Nat. Capital Devel. Commn. for Canberra, Australia. Recipient Gold medal Archtl. Soc. Ohio, 1971, Burton award for Disting. Pub. Svc. Cleve. Club, 1991. Fellow AIA (Thomas Jefferson award 1992), ASCE (hon.), Nat. Soc. Profl. Engrs., Nat. Acad. Forensic Engrs.; mem. Sigma Xi, Eta Kappa Nu, Lambda Alpha, Tau Beta Pi. Office: Leo A Daly 1201 Connecticut Ave NW Washington DC 20036-2683 Address: 3 Chalfont Ct Bethesda MD 20816-1805

WHITE, GEORGE WASHINGTON, automotive consultant; b. Monticello, Ga., June 18, 1918; s. George W. and Julia A. (Preston) W.; m. Annie L. White, Mar. 18, 1938 (div. July 1944); m. Fannie C. White, Nov. 1, 1944 (dec.); children: Walter A. Martin, Patricia Ann, Ernest George. Grad. high sch., Rome, Ga., 1935. Aircraft engine maintenance worker Allison Engring. Autonautical div, GM, Indpls., 1940-43, Wright Patterson AFB, Ohio, 1943-47, with rsch. and devel., 1947-57, with engines rsch. devel., 1949-57; salesman Davis Buick Co., Dayton, Ohio, 1957-73; pres. George White Olds Inc., Cin., 1973-80; cons. Ernest White Ford-Lincoln-Mercury, Delaware, Ohio, 1980-86; pres., cons. G.W. Cons. Inc., Worthington, Ohio, 1983—. Pres. Frontiers Internat. Inc., Dayton, 1947-68; mem. Pres.'s Club, Dayton, 1967-72, NAACP, 1946-73. Democrat. Christian Methodist. Avocations: bowling, golfing, sr. citizen activities. Home: 8818 Greenburg Dr Powell OH 43065-9214

WHITE, GERALD ANDREW, retired chemical company executive; b. L.I., N.Y., Aug. 2, 1934; s. Charles Eugene and Grace Mary (Trojan) W.; m. Mary Alice Turvey, June 8, 1957; children— Kevin, Patricia, Timothy, Megan B in Chem. Engring., Villanova U., 1957; cert. advanced mgmt. program, Harvard Bus. Sch., 1975. Staff engr. Air Products and Chems., Inc., Allentown, Pa., 1962-65, mgr. systems devel., 1965-66, group controller, 1969-72, corp. controller, 1974-76, v.p. planning, 1977-82, v.p. fin., chief fin. officer, 1982-92, sr. v.p. fin., chief fin. officer, 1992-95. Pres. United Way in Lehigh County, 1981; bd. dirs. Pa. Coun. on Econ. Edn., 1981-95; trustee, treas. Allentown Art Mus., 1984; trustee, chmn. bd. trustees De Sales U, Center Valley, 1983. Lt. USN, 1957-62. Recipient J. Stanley Morehouse Meml. award Villanova U. Coll. Engring., 1983 Mem. AIChE, Fin. Execs. Inst. (pres. northeastern Pa. chpt. 1974-75), Fin. Execs. Rsch. Found. (trustee 1992-96), Tau Beta Pi. Avocation: squash.

WHITE, GILBERT F(OWLER), geographer, educator; b. Chgo., Nov. 26, 1911; s. Arthur E. and Mary (Guthrie) W.; m. Anne Elizabeth Underwood, Apr. 28, 1944; children: William D., Mary, Frances; m. Claire Sheridan, July 18, 2003. BS, U. Chgo., 1932, SM, 1934, PhD, 1942; LLD (hon.), Hamilton Coll., 1951, Swarthmore Coll.; LL.D. (hon.), Earlham Coll., Richmond, Ind., Mich. State U., Augustana Coll.; ScD (hon.), Haverford Coll.; hon. degree, Northland Coll. Geographer Miss. Valley Com. of P.W.A., 1934, Nat. Resources Bd., 1934-35; sec. land and water com. Nat. Resources Com. and Nat. Resources Planning Bd., 1935-40; with Exec. Office Pres., Bur. Budget, 1941-42; asst. exec. sec. Am. Friends Service Com., 1945-46; relief adminstr. in France, 1942-43; interned Baden-Baden, 1943-44; sec. Am. Relief for India, 1945-46; pres. Haverford Coll., 1946-55; prof. geography U. Chgo., 1956-69; prof. geography, dir. Inst. Behavioral Sci., U. Colo., Boulder, 1970-78, Gustavson disting. prof. emeritus, 1979—; dir. Natural Hazards Info. Ctr., 1978-84, 92-94; exec. editor Environment mag., 1983-93. Vis. prof. Oxford U., 1962-63; cons. Investigations Lower Mekong Basin, 1961-62, 70; U.S. mem. UNESCO adv. com. on arid zone research, 1954-55; mem. mission Am. Vol. Agys. Relief Germany, 1946; vice chmn. Pres.'s Water Resources Policy Commn., 1950; mem. com. natural resources Hoover Commn., 1948; chmn. UN Panel Integrated River Basin Devel., 1956-57; chmn. Task Force Fed. Flood Control Policy, 1965-66; sci. adv. to adminstr. UN Devel. Program, 1966-71; chmn. adv. bd. Energy Policy Project, 1972-74; chmn. Am. Friends Service Com., 1963-69; chmn. com. on man and environment IGU, 1969-76; chmn. steering com. High Sch. Geography com., 1964-70; mem. Tech. Assessment Adv. Council, 1974-76; chmn. environ. studies bd. NRC, 1975-77; pres. Sci. Com. on Problems of Environment, 1976-82; chmn. bd. Resources for Future, 1973-79; co-chmn. U.S.-Egypt Joint Consultative Com. on Sci. and Tech., 1981-86; mem. adv. group on greenhouse gases World Meteorol. Orgn., Internat. Council of Scientific Unions, UN Environ. Program., 1986-90; chmn. tech. rev. com. Nev. Nuclear Waste Project, 1987-93; mem. adv. group on water UN Environ. Program, 1989-93, working group for Action Plan for Aral Sea Basin, USSR, 1990-93; chmn. nat. rev. com. Status U.S. Floodplain Mgmt., 1989; bd. dirs. Am. Soc. Flood Plain Mgrs. Found., 1996—. Author: Human Adjustment to Floods, 1942, Science and Future of Arid Lands, 1960, Social and Economic Aspects of Natural Resources, 1962, Choice of Adjustment to Floods, 1964, Strategies of American Water Management, 1969; co-author: Drawers of Water, 1972, Assessment of Research on Natural Hazards, 1975, Flood Hazard in the United States, 1975, The Environment as Hazard, 1978; editor: Natural Hazards: Local, National and Global, 1974, Environmental Aspects of Complex River Development, 1977; co-editor: Environmental Issues, 1977, The World Environment, 1972-1982, 1982, Environmental Effects of Nuclear War, 1983, Water for Life, 2003. Reicpient Daly medal Am. Geog. Soc., 1971, Eben award Am. Water Resources Assn., 1972, Caulfield medal, 1989, Alumni medal U. Chgo., 1979, Outstanding Achievement award Nat. Coun. for Geog. Edn., 1981, Sasakawa UN Evniron. prize, 1985, Tyler prize, 1987, Laureat d'Honneur award Internat. Geog. Union, 1988, Vautrin Lud Internat. Geog. prize, 1992, Hubbard medal Nat. Geog. Soc., 1994, Volvo Environment prize, 1995. Mem. AAAS, NAS (commn. on natural resources 1973-80, chmn. 1977-80, chmn. com. on water 1964-68, chmn. com. on sustainable water supplies of Middle East 1996-99, Environ. award 1980, Pub. Welfare medal 2000), Assn. Am. Geographers (pres. 1962, Outstanding Achievement award 1955, 74, Anderson medal 1986, US Nat. Medal Sci 2000, Lifetime Achievement award 2002), Internat. Coun. Sci. Unions (steering com. on study of environ. consequences of nuclear war 1983-87, adv. com. on environ. 1990-96), Internat. Water Resources Assn. (Millenium award 2000), Russian Geog. Soc. (hon.), Royal Geog. Soc. (hon.), Russian Acad. Scis. (fgn.), Am. Philos. Soc., Cosmos Club (Washington, award 1993), Sigma Xi, Mem. Soc. Friends. Home: 624 Pearl St Apt 302 Boulder CO 80302-5072 E-mail: gilbert.white@colorado.edu.

WHITE, GORDON ELIOT, historian; b. Glen Ridge, N.J., Oct. 25, 1933; s. Maurice Brewster and Sarah Fullilove (Gordon) W.; m. Nancy Johnson, 1955 (div. 1957); m. Mary Joan Briggs, Aug. 6, 1960 (dec. Nov. 1987); children: Sarah Elizabeth and Gordon O'Neal Brewster (twins), David McIntyre; m. Francis C. Barrineau, 1989 (div. 1996); m. Angela Tyler, Mar. 27, 1999. BA, Cornell U., 1955; MS in Journalism, Columbia U., 1957. Lic. master mariner USCG; lic. pilot FAA. Stringer Nassau Daily Rev.-Star, Rockville Centre, L.I., NY, 1948-50, Freeport (N.Y.) Leader, 1949-50; sports writer Morris County (N.J.) Citizen, 1950-51; stringer Ithaca (N.Y.) Evening News, 1951-55; photo editor, editl. writer Cornell Daily Sun, 1951-55; copy editor Am. Banker, N.Y.C., 1958; Washington corr. Chgo. Am., 1958-61; chief Washington bur. Deseret News, Salt Lake City, 1961-88. Also corr. in Europe, U.S. and Antarctic for WJR, Detroit; KSL-KSL-TV, Salt Lake City, also KGMB, Honolulu; free lance writer with U.S. Navy, Army and Air Force, 1959; cons. Nat. Air and Space Mus.; auto racing, mil. aviation electronics historian. Author: Offenhauser, the Legendary American Racing Engine and the Men Who Built It, 1996, The Indianapolis Racing Cars of Frank Kurtis, 1940-1963, 2000, Kurtis-Kraft: Masterworks of Speed & Style, 2001, Lost Race Tracks, 2003, The Marvelous Mechanical Designs of Harry A. Miller, 2004. Advisor auto racing Nat. Mus. Am. History, Smithsonian Instn., 1989—; curator Miller-Offenhauser Archive of historic race engine blueprints. Recipient 1st prize for newsphoto Sigma Delta Chi, 1954; Raymond Clapper Meml. award White House Corrs. Assn., 1978; award for excellence in reporting Exec. Dept. and White House; award for excellence in reporting Nat. Press Club, 1979; Nat. Sigma Delta Chi award for disting. work as Washington Corr., 1979; Roy W. Howard award for outstanding pub. svc. by a newspaper corr., 1979; award for disting. investigative reporting Investigative Reporters and Editors, 1980; Reser-Tuthill award for writing on history of automobile racing, Indpls., 1985. Mem. Nat. Press Club (Washington), Sigma Delta Chi, Pi Kappa Phi, Pi Delta Epsilon. Episcopalian. Home and Office: PO Box 129 Hardyville VA 23070 Office Phone: 804-776-7947. E-mail: gewhite@crosslink.net.

WHITE, GREGORY A. lawyer; b. Nov. 1949; BA in Criminal Justice and Police Adminstrn., Kent State U., 1973; JD magna cum laude, Cleveland Marshall Coll., 1976. Atty. Wilcox and White Law Firm, 1977—84; law dir. City of Elyria, 1979; prosecutor Lorain County, Ohio, 1981—2002; U.S. atty. No. Dist. Ohio, 2003—. With USMC, Vietnam. Office: 1800 Bank One Ctr 600 Superior Ave E Cleveland OH 44114

WHITE, GRETCHEN NANCE, education educator, writer; d. Virginia Lee Nance; m. Ronald Craig White (dec.); children: Loronzo De'Warren, David Lee, Mark Du'Pree, Paul Keith, Anthony O'Lunte, Michelle Ja'Nesse Jefferson. Diploma in child daycare, ICS, Pa., 1995; diploma in mgmt. in health care, Calif. Coll. of Health Scis., 1998, diploma in bus. comm., 2001. Cert. ordination Tex., 2001, Tex. Notary Pub. Commn. Pvt. duty nurses asst. Meth. Hosp., Houston, 1984—87; vocat. coord. Richmond (Tex.) State Sch., 1988—. Founder, pres. White's Internat. Scholarship Inc., Wharton, Tex., 2001—; adv. bd. mem. St. James Missionary Bapt. Ch., Wharton, Tex., 2002—. Author: (book) It's Vision Time, 2000, The Four F''s/Faith, Fear, Failure, Forgiveness, 2000, A Nation on the Rise to Be Educated or Not to Be Educated, 2003. Youth pastor St. James Missionary Bapt. Ch., 2000—. Grantee, Wal-mart Super Ctr., 2004. Avocations: cooking, reading, health glider, sports. Office: Whites Internat Scholarship Inc PO Box 1283 Rosenberg TX 77471 Office Phone: 281-844-2078. E-mail: gretwhite@academicplanet.com.

WHITE, HAROLD JACK, pathologist; b. Bklyn., Jan. 4, 1920; s. Abraham and Jennie (Warshawsky) W.; m. Lucette Darby, July 19, 1962; children: Elizabeth, Darby, Matthew, Esther. BS, Harvard U., 1941; MD, U. Geneva, 1952. Diplomate Am. Bd. Pathology. Intern, resident in pathology Yale U. Sch. Medicine, New Haven, 1953-58, fellow, 1957-58; assoc. pathologist Brigham and Women's Hosp., Boston, 1962-66; chief lab. svc. VA Hosp., West Roxbury, Mass., 1962-66, Little Rock, 1966-80; sr. scientist, acting head biomed. sci. dept. GM Rsch. Labs., Warren, Mich., 1980-85, cons., 1985—. Prof. pathology, microbiology U. Ark. Med. Sch., Little Rock, 1966—; vis. scientist dept. comparative medicine, MIT, Cambridge, 1988—. Contbr. over 100 articles, abstracts in pathology, microbiology, immunology, toxicology, biomedicine to profl. jours. 1st lt. USAAF, 1942-46. Fellow Coll. Am. Pathologists, Internat. Coll. Pathology. Home: 24 Bass Rocks Rd Gloucester MA 01930-3276 Office: 35 Main St Gloucester MA 01930-5730 Office Phone: 978-281-3531. E-mail: hswriverrun@aol.com.

WHITE, HARRY EDWARD, JR., lawyer; b. Menominee, Mich., Apr. 26, 1939; s. Harry Edward and Verena Charlotte (Leisen) W.; m. Mary P.A. Sheaffer, June 7, 1980. BS in Fgn. Svc., Georgetown U., Washington, 1961; LLB, Columbia U., 1964. Bar: N.Y. 1965, U.S. Supreme Ct. 1970, U.S. Dist. Ct. (so. dist.) N.Y. 1979, U.S. Tax Ct. 1980. Assoc. Milbank, Tweed, Hadley & McCloy, N.Y.C., 1964-65, 67-73, ptnr., 1974—. Contbr. chpts. to books, articles to legal jours. Served with M.I., U.S. Army, 1965-66, Vietnam. Decorated Bronze Star. Mem. ABA, Internat. Bar Assn., N.Y. State Bar Assn. (chmn. taxation com. internat. law practice sect. 1987-90, co-chmn. exempt orgns. com. tax sect. 1987-88), Internat. Law Assn., ssn. Bar City N.Y., Internat. Fiscal Assn., The Players. Republican. Roman Catholic. Home: 333 E 55th St New York NY 10022-8316 Office: Milbank Tweed Hadley & McCloy 1 Chase Manhattan Plz Fl 47 New York NY 10005-1413 Office Phone: 212-530-5092. E-mail: hwhite@milbank.com.

WHITE, HARRY HOUSTON, neurologist; b. Batesville, Ark., Jan. 21, 1934; s. Harry H. and Margaret V. White; m. Serena Rankin, Dec. 21, 1957; children: Rebecca, David, Maria. AB, U. Kans., 1955, MD, 1958. Diplomate Am. Bd. Psychiatry and Neurology (examiner 1970—). Asst. prof. neurology U. Kans., Kansas City, 1965-69, assoc. prof. neurology, 1969-72; prof. neurology U. Mo., Columbia, 1972-75, 88—; attending neurologist Menninger Found., Topeka, 1975-80; pvt. practice Durango, Colo., 1980-84, Columbia, 1984-88. Capt. U.S. Army, 1962-64. Markle Found. scholar, 1969. Fellow Am. Acad. Neurology; mem. Am. Neurol. Assn., Alpha Omega Alpha. Office: Truman VA Hosp 800 Stadium Dr Columbia MO 65201

WHITE, HELENE NITA, federal judge; b. Jackson Heights, N.Y., Dec. 2, 1954; d. Frank William and Ruth (Gruber) White. AB, Columbia U., 1978; JD, U. Pa., 1978. Bar: Pa. 1979, Mich. 1979. Law clk. to justice Mich. Supreme Ct., Southfield, 1978—80; judge Common Pleas Ct., Detroit, 1981, 36th Dist Ct., Detroit, 1981—83, Wayne Cir. Ct., Detroit, 1983—92, Mich. Ct. Appeals, Detroit, 1992—. Bd. dirs., chmn. bylaws com. Met. Detroit YWCA, 1986—87, Coalition Temporary Shelter, 1986—, chmn. nominating com., 1988—; program com. bus. and profl. divsn. Jewish Welfare Fedn., 1987—; bd. advisors Sojourner Found., 1988, Detroit Women's Forum, 1988—. Mem.: ABA, Women Lawyers Assn. Mich., Nat. Assn. Women Judges (chmn. publicity 1984, membership com. 1985—), Detroit Bar Assn., Pa. Bar Assn. Jewish.

WHITE, HELENE R. sociologist, educator; b. Paterson, NJ, July 11, 1949; d. Sidney and Madeleine Beck Raskin; m. Larry H. White, June 18, 1972. BA, Douglass Coll., 1971; MPhil, Rutgers U., 1975, PhD, 1976. From asst. prof. to prof. Rutgers U., New Brunswick, 1975—. Co-prin. investigator Nat. Inst. Drug Abuse, Washington, 1978—; grant reviewer NIH, Washington, 1992—; prin. investigator Alcoholic Beverage Med. Rsch. Found., Balt., 1992—2002; behavioral and social adv. coun. Alcoholic Beverage Med. Rsch. Found., Balt., 1997—2003; prin. investigator Robert Wood Johnson Found., Princeton, NJ, 1997—. Editor: Alcohol, Science and Society, 1982, Society, Culture and Drinking Patterns Re-examinned, 1991; guest editor (journ.) Journal of Drug Issues, 1996; contbr. articles to profl. jours., chapters to books. Recipient Pub. Svc. Award, Criminal Justice Alcoholism Coalition. Mem.: Am. Soc. Criminology, Discovery Inst. (bd. dirs., v.p.), Am. Sociol. Assn. (chair info. alcohol and drugs sect. 1991—92, chair alcohol and drugs sect. 2002—03). Avocations: golf, cooking, exercise. Office: Rutgers U Ctr Alcohol Studies 607 Alison Rd Piscataway NJ 08854-8001 Business E-Mail: hewhite@rci.rutgers.edu.

WHITE, HERBERT SPENCER, research library educator, university dean; b. Vienna, Sept. 5, 1927; came to U.S., 1938, naturalized, 1944; s. Leon and Ernestine (Lichteneger) Hochweis; m. Mary Virginia Dyer, Feb. 19, 1953 (dec.); 1 son, Jerome; m. Nancy J. Cornell, May 1, 2002. BS in Chemistry, CCNY, 1949; MSLS, Syracuse U., 1950; PhD in Humane Letters (hon.), Ind. U., 2003. Intern Libr. of Congress, Washington, 1950, mem. tech. info. divsn., 1950-53; tech. libr. AEC, Oak Ridge, Tenn., 1953-54; organizer, mgr. corp. libr. Chance Vought Aircraft, Dallas, 1954-59; mgr. engring. libr. IBM Corp., Kingston, N.Y., 1959-62, mgr. tech. info. ctr. Poughkeepsie, N.Y., 1962-64; exec. dir. NASA Sci. and Tech. Info. Facility, College Park, Md., 1964-68; v.p. info. mgmt. Leasco Systems & Rsch. Corp., Bethesda, Md., 1968-70; sr. v.p. Inst. Sci. Info., Phila., 1970-74, corp. dir., 1971-74; pres. Stechert-Macmillan, Inc., Pennsaucken, N.J., 1974-75; prof., dir. Rsch. Ctr. Grad. Libr. Sch. Ind. U., Bloomington, 1975-80, dean Sch. Libr. and Info. Scis., 1980-90, disting. prof., 1991-95; prof. emeritus, 1995—. Adj. prof. U. Ariz. Sch. Libr. Scis., 1995—; vis. prof. Alberta, San Jose State, Hawaii; cons., lectr. Author: Librarianship Quo Vadis?, 2000, others; contbr. articles to profl. publs.; columnist Libr. Jour. Mem. Pres.'s Adv. Com. for Adminstrn. Title II-B Higher Edn. Act, 1965-68, Libr. Rsch. Planning Com. for 1980s, U.S. Dept. Edn., v.p. Green Valley Cmty. Coordinating Coun., 1997—; grant reviewer Inst. Mus. and Librs., 1998—. Spl. honoree, U. of Essen (Germany) Conf., 1992. Fellow Spl. Libraries Assn. (pres. 1969-70, J.C. Dana award 1985, Hall of Fame 1994); mem. ALA (councillor 1988-92, planning com. 1989-91, Dewey medal 1987), Am. Soc. Info. Sci. (pres. 1973-74, W. Davis award 1977, award of merit 1981, named Pioneer, 1987), Assn. Libr. and Info. Sci. Edn. (chmn. govtl. rels. com. 1980-88), Am. Fedn. Info. Processing Socs. (dir. 1972-78), Federation Internationale de Documentation (Netherlands, bd. dir. 1976-78, treas. 1978-82), Soc. for Scholarly Pub. (bd. dirs. 1981-82), Assn. Rsch. Libraries (com. on libr. edn, 1983-85), Coun. Libr. Resources (rsch. priorities task force 1984-88, Ind. Libr. Lifetime Achievement award 1990), Beta Phi Mu (Svc. award 1995). Address: 5950 N Fountains Ave #7102 Tucson AZ 85704-7863

WHITE, HOWARD D. information science educator; PhD, U. Calif., Berkeley, 1974. Joined, Coll. of Information Sci. and Tech. Drexel U., Phila., 1974, prof. libr. sci., disting. prof., 1998—2002, prof. emeritus. Co-author (with Marcia Bates and Patrick Wilson): For Information Specialists: Interpretations of Reference and Bibliographic Work, 1992; author: Brief Tests of Collection Strength, 1995; contbr. articles to profl. publs. Office: Drexel U Coll Info Sci & Tech Rush Bldg 421 33rd and Market St Philadelphia PA 19104 Office Phone: 215-895-2484. Office Fax: 215-895-2494. Business E-Mail: whitehd@mail.drexel.edu.

WHITE, HUGH VERNON, JR., lawyer; b. Suffolk, Va., July 24, 1933; s. Hugh Vernon and Mary Lois (Claud) W.; m. Mary Margaret Flowers, Nov. 25, 1961; children: Hunter, William, John. BS in Civil Engring., Va. Mil. Inst., 1954; LLB, Washington & Lee U., 1961. Bar: Va. 1961. Engr. E.I. DuPont de Nemours & Co., Parlin, N.J., 1954-55; exec. dir. Va. Legis. Study Commn., Richmond, Va., 1961-63; assoc. Hunton & Williams, Richmond, 1963-69, ptnr., 1969-99, sr. counsel, 1999—. Bd. dirs. Chesapeake Corp., Richmond, Va. Mem. Richmond First, 1966—, pres., 1971; bd. trustees Va. Hist. Soc., 1997—, Randolph-Macon Woman's Coll., 1997—, YMCA of Greater Richmond, 1996—, chmn. 2000-01. Lt. USAF, 1955-58. Mem. ABA, Va. Bar Assn., Richmond Bar Assn., Phi Beta Kappa, Omicron Delta Kappa. Clubs: Commonwealth, Country (Richmond). Presbyterian. Home: 512 S Gaskins Rd Richmond VA 23233-5710 Office: Hunton & Williams Riverfront Plaza East Tower PO Box 1535 Richmond VA 23218-1535

WHITE, JAMES, JR., psychiatric, mental health nurse, consultant; b. Muskogee, Okla., Nov. 24, 1944; s. James Sr. and Mary Bd. (Brassfield) W.; children: Stacie R., Stephen W. BA, Northeastern State U., 1969; MS, Pittsburg State U., 1972, BSN, 1982; PhD, Columbia Pacific U., 1984. Diplomate Am. Bd. Forensic Examiners, Soc. for Study of Neuronal Regulation; CSW, advance register nurse practitioner, cert. rehab. counselor, cert./lic. psychologist, nationally bd. cert. counselor. Exec. dir. Sanilac County Mental Health, Sandusky, Mich., 1975-78, Crawford County Mental Health, Pittsburg, 1978-80; psychologist Psychol. and Ednl. Svcs., Pittsburg, 1982—84; psychiatric practitioner Family Counseling and Resource Ctr., Joplin, 1983-86; pvt. practice Joplin, 1986-88; med. sociologist Mich. Health Ctr., Detroit, 1988-91; psychiatric practitioner Wayne County Sheriff and Sinai Hosp. Psychiatry, Detroit, 1990—; clin. coord. Detroit Health Care for Homeless, 1991—. Chmn. recipient right com. Lafayette Clinic, Detroit, 1991—, coun. mem., 1990—. Lt. U.S. Army, 1969-82. Mem. ANA for Nurses in Advanced Practice, Am. Psychatric Nurses Assn., Am. Acad. Nurse Practitioners (Mich. State Rep. 1991—), Am. Bd. Med. Psychotherapists (cert., clin. assoc.), Coun. Psychiatric and Mental Health Nursing, Am. Acad. Pain Mgmt. Avocations: biking, swimming, boating. Home: 42029 Utah Dr Sterling Heights MI 48313-2965 Office: Inst for Inner Resource 75 W Square Lake Rd Troy MI 48098-2929 E-mail: info@expertsinmind.com.

WHITE, JAMES ALFRED, lawyer; b. Bay City, Mich., Jan. 5, 1939; s. Gerald J. and Clara E. (Barnes) White; m. Barbara J. White, Feb. 14, 1980. BA cum laude, Alma Coll., 1961; JD, U. Mich., 1964. Bar: Mich. 1964. Assoc. Foster, Swift, Collins & Coey, Lansing, Mich., 1964—69, ptnr., 1969—88, White, Schneider, Young & Chiodini PC, Okemos, Mich., 1988—. Counsel Mich. Edn. Assn., 1966—; mem. labor arbitrator labor panel Am. Arbitration Assn. Bd. dirs. Big Bros. and Big Sisters of Greater Lansing, Inc., 1972—80. Mem.: ABA, Ingham County Bar Assn., Mich. Bar Assn., Met. Flying Club (pres.). Home: 2410 Emerald Lake Dr East Lansing MI 48823 Office Phone: 517-347-7208. E-mail: jwhite@wsbyc.com.

WHITE, JAMES BOYD, law educator; b. Boston, July 28, 1938; s. Benjamin Vroom and Charlotte Green (Conover) W.; m. Mary Louise Fitch, Jan. 1, 1978; children: Emma Lillian, Henry Alfred; children by previous marriage: Catherine Conover, John Southworth. AB, Amherst Coll., 1960; AM, Harvard U., 1961, LLB, 1964. Assoc. Foley, Hoag & Eliot, Boston, 1964-67; asst. prof. law U. Colo., 1967-69, assoc. prof., 1969-73, prof., 1973-75; prof. law U. Chgo., 1975-83; Hart Wright prof. law and English U. Mich., Ann Arbor, 1983—. Vis. assoc. prof. Stanford U., 1972 Author: The Legal Imagination, 1973, (with Scarboro) Constitutional Criminal Procedure, 1976, When Words Lose Their Meaning, 1981, Heracles' Bow, 1985, Justice as Translation, 1990, "This Book of Starres", 1994, Acts of Hope, 1994, From Expectation to Experience, 1999, The Edge of Meaning, 2001. Sinclair Kennedy Traveling fellow, 1964-65; Nat. Endowment for Humanities fellow, 1979-80, 92; Guggenheim fellow, 1993; vis. scholar Phi Beta Kappa, 1997-98. Mem. AAAS, Am. Law Inst. Office: U Mich Law Sch 625 S State St Ann Arbor MI 48109-1215

WHITE, JAMES C. science educator, consultant; b. Hodge, La., July 7, 1936; s. Clarence Bud and Verda Houston White; m. Donna Aileene Hightower, July 13, 1957; 1 child, Laura White Lewis; 1 child, James Donald. BS, La. Tech. U., 1959; MS, La. State U., 1960, PhD, 1963. Instr. S.E. La. U., Hammond, 1963—65; asst. prof. to assoc. prof. La. Tech. U., Ruston, 1965—69, prof., 1970—95, assoc. dean Coll. Life Sci., 1988—90, prof. biol. sci., 1990—95, ret., 1995. With Viator's Ag Cons. Svc., New Iberia, La., 1975—80; owner White's Ag Cons. Svc., La., 1981—96; dir. rsch. Soil Enterprise Corp., Leland, Miss., 1993; owner Tomato Greenhouses, Ruston, 1996—2000. Author: Withstanding Storms That Surround, 2002. Bd. dirs., mem. bldg. com. Salem United Meth. Ch., Lincoln, La., 1996; chair programs com. for meth. men Grace United Meth. Ch., Ruston, 2003. Methodist. Avocations: pen and ink drawing, pencil sketches, hunting, fishing. Home: 412 Savannah Ruston LA 71270

WHITE, JAMES EDWARD, III, historian, educator; b. Kinston, N.C., Apr. 24, 1949; s. James E. White Jr. and Nina (Gilgo) White; m. Nancy Brinson, Aug. 4, 1973; children: James E. White IV, M. Jason, Jerry L. AA, Louisburg Coll., 1969; AB, U. N.C. Chapel Hill, 1971; MEd, E. Carolina U., 1978, EdS, 1985. Cert. tchr. N.C., prin. N.C., supt. N.C. Tchr. Pamlico Jr. H.S., Bayboro, NC, 1972—75, Arapahoe Elem. Sch., Arapahoe, NC, 1975—80; prin. Tyrrell Elem. Sch., Columbia, NC, 1980—85, Bridgeton Elem. Sch., Bridgeton, NC, 1986—93; tchr. West Craven H.S., Vanceboro, NC, 1993—2002, Pamlico C.C., Grantsboro, NC, 2002—. Author: Gilgoes of Portsmouth Island, 1979, Whichcotes of Maryland, 1982, Craven County Honor Roll 1861, 1980. Recipient Outstanding Young Men Am., Jaycees, 1981. Mem.: New Bern Hist. Soc., Assn. Colonial Historians, Assn. So. Historians, Masonic Lodge St. John #3. Episcopalian. Avocations: history, Civil War reenacting. Home: 405 W Wilson Creek Dr New Bern NC 28562 Office Phone: 252-249-1851. E-mail: jewhite3@earthlink.net.

WHITE, JAMES PATRICK, law educator; b. Iowa City, Sept. 29, 1931; s. Raymond Patrick and Besse (Kanak) W.; m. Anna R. Seim, July 2, 1964. BA, U. Iowa, 1953, JD, 1956; LLM, George Washington U., 1959; LLD (hon.), U. Pacific, 1984, John Marshall Law Sch., 1989, Weidner U., 1989, Campbell U., 1993; Jur D (hon.), Whittier Coll., 1992; LLD (hon.), Campbell U., 1993, Southwestern U., 1995, Quinnipiac U., 1995, Calif. Western Law Sch., 1997; LLD, Roger Williams U., 1999, New England Sch. of Law, 2001, Seattle U., 2001, We. New Eng. Coll., 2002. Bar: Iowa 1956, D.C. 1959, U.S. Supreme Ct. 1959. Teaching fellow George Washington U. Law Sch., 1958-59; asst. prof. U. N.D. Law Sch., Grand Forks, 1959-62, asso. prof., acting dean, 1962-63, prof., asst. dean, 1963-67; dir. agrl. law rsch. program, prof. law Ind. U. Law Sch., Indpls., 1967—2002, also dir. urban legal studies program, 1971-74, prof. emeritus, 2002—; dean acad. devel. and planning, spl. asst. to chancellor Ind. U., Indpls., 1974-83. Mem. for N.D., Commn. on Uniform State Laws, 1961-66; cons. legal edn. ABA, Indpls., 1974-2001, cons. emeritus, 2001—. Contbr. papers to tech. lit. Trustee Butler U., John Marshall Law Sch., Atlanta, Indpls. Mus. Art. 1st lt. JAGC, USAF, 1956-58. Recipient Thomas More award, St. Mary's U., 1965, Sagamore of the Wabash award, State of Ind.; Carnegie postdoctoral fellow, U. Mich. Ctr. for Study Higher Edn., 1964—65. Fellow: Soc. for Advanced Legal Studies (Eng.) (chair Fulbright com. awards in law 1989—92), Indpls. Bar Found. (disting. fellow), Am. Bar Found. (life); mem.: ABA (Kutak award medal 2001), Indpls. Bar Assn., Am. Law Inst. (life), Iowa Bar Assn., Ind. Bar Assn., Woodstock Club

(Indpls.), Order of Coif. Roman Catholic. Home: 7707 N Meridian St Indianapolis IN 46260-3651 Office: Ind U 530 W New York St Indianapolis IN 46202-3225 Office Phone: 317-278-9690. Business E-Mail: jwhite@iupui.edu.

WHITE, JAMES RICHARD, lawyer; b. McKinney, Tex., Jan. 22, 1948; s. James Ray and Maxine (Brown) W.; children: Nicole Olivia, Mandi Leigh, James Derek. BBA, So. Meth. U., 1969, MBA, 1970, JD, 1973, LLM, 1977. Bar: Tex. 1973, US Tax Ct. 1975, US Supreme Ct. 1989, US Ct. Appeals (5th cir.) 1989); cert. Comml. Real Estate Law Tex. Bd. Legal Specialization; The Best Lawyers in Am., 2003-04. Assoc. Elliot, Meer, Vetter, Denton & Bates, Dallas, 1973-74, Atwell, Cain & Davenport, Dallas, 1974-75; atty. Sabine Corp., Dallas, 1975-77; assoc. Brice & Barron, Dallas, 1977-79; ptnr. Millard & Olson, Dallas, 1979-82, Johnson & Swanson, Dallas, 1982-83, Winstead, Sechrest & Minick P.C., Dallas, 1983—, hiring ptnr., 1987-2001, exec. com., 2000-01. Mem. staff Southwestern Law Jour., Dallas, 1971-73; mem. So. Meth. U. Moot Ct. Bd., Order Barristers, Dallas, 1972-73; prof. North Lake Coll., Dallas, 1985; bd. dirs. Tex. Assn. Young Lawyers, Austin, 1980-82; sec. bd. dirs. Dallas Assn. Young Lawyers, 1976-80. Contbr. articles to profl. jours. Chmn. bd. dir. Tex. Lawyers Credit Union, Austin, 1980-82; pres. North Tex. Premier Soccer Assn., Dallas, 1979-81; v.p. Lake Highlands Soccer Assn., 1995-96, pres., 1996—; North Tex. State Soccer Assn., Volunteer of the Year, 2003; mem. regional mobility task force Real Estate Coun., City of Dallas, 1991-92, mem. downtown revitalization com., 1995-97; mem. Dallas Indsl. Devel. Bd., 1992-93, Dallas Higher Edn. Authority Bd., 1994-96; spkr.'s bur. and accreditation divsn. World Cup USA '94; mem. exec. coun. Recreational Interleague Assn. Dallas, 2002—; pres. Storm Soccer Club, 2003—. Named Vol. of the Yr., North Tex. State Soccer Assn., 2003. Mem. ABA (mem. title ins. and survey, mortgage loan origination and structure com., mortgage financing and opinion, non-traditional comml. real estate fin. coms.), Tex. Bar Assn. (cert. 1973, mem. mortgage loan opinion com.), Tex. Coll. Real Estate Attys., Coll. State Bar Tex., Storm Soccer Club (pres. 2003—). Methodist. Avocations: soccer, golf, skiing, racquetball. Home: 8003 Hundley Ct Dallas TX 75231-4728 Office: Winstead Sechrest & Minick 5400 Renaissance Tower 1201 Elm St Ste 5400 Dallas TX 75270-2199 Office Phone: 214-745-5400. E-mail: jrwhite@winstead.com.

WHITE, JAN TUTTLE (MRS. BENJAMIN WINTHROP WHITE), information technology executive; b. Bridgeport, Conn., Nov. 5, 1943; d. Michael and Jennie Agnes (Leko) Soltis; m. David Dustin Tuttle, Oct. 7, 1972 (div. Apr. 1988); m. Benjamin Winthrop White, May 6, 1989. BS in Math., Bates Coll., 1965; MBA in Mktg. and Ops. Rsch., Columbia U., 1967. Cert. comml. real estate broker, Mass. With corp. staff IBM Corp., Armonk, N.Y., 1966, sys. engr. N.Y.C., 1967-69, mktg. rep. to Harvard U., corp. staff, sys. engr., Harvard U. account mgr. Cambridge, Mass., 1969-72; asst. to dir. info. processing svcs. MIT, Cambridge, Mass., 1972-75; mng. dir. Tuttle Family Trust, Cambridge, Mass., 1975-81; VAX product mktg. mgr., then sr. product mgr. Digital Equipment Corp., Marlborough, Mass., 1981-86, artificial intelligence market devel. mgr., 1986-87, fin. sys. group market devel. mgr., 1987-90, market devel. mgr. banking/investments group, 1990; program mgr. MIT Internat. Fin. Svc. Rsch. Ctr., Hudson; med. sys. mgr. Beth Israel Deaconess Med. Ctr., Boston, 1990—. Spkr. in field; sponsor Harvard Host Family Program. Appeared in Disney channel documentary film Silver Men, 1987, Boston Mus. Sci. introductory film for opening of Mugar Omni Theatre, 1987; contbr. (books) An Olde Concord Christmas, 1980, Boston Symphony Orch. Cookbook, 1983, Boston Cooks, 1991. Chmn. Concord Coun. Boston Symphony Orch., assoc. assn. vols., supporter Tanglewood scholarship programs, capt. Centennial Major Gifts campaign; active guild bd. Opera Co. Boston, patron Fledrmaus Ball; life mem., chmn. Emerson Hosp. Aux.; trustee, mem. mgmt. rev. com. Women's Ednl. and Indsl. Union; edn. com. chmn. Ladies Assn.; life mem., bd. Concord Antiquarian Mus., nom. com. edn. long-range planning com., chmn. edn. com., costumes and textiles com., exhbt. designer An Old Concorde Christmas, established family meml. fund; bd. adv. Sci. Mus. Exhibit Collaborative, Garden Club Concord, Boston Mus. Sci.; life mem. Mus. of Fine Arts, Boston, Nat. Trust for Scotland, Friends of Loch Lomond, Friends of the Beth Israel Med. Ctr, Harvard Neighbors; mem. fin. com. Trinitarian Congl. Ch.; trustee, life mem. Women's Ednl. and Indsl. Union; bd. dirs., life mem. Hannah Duston Garrison House Assn., Mus. Fine Arts, Boston; life mem. Friends of the New Eng. Deaconess Hosp., Boston, Friends of the Beth Israel Deaconess Med. Ctr., Boston; patron mem. Friends of Music at the Mus. of Fine Arts, Boston; mem. Isabella Stewart Gardner Mus.; invitational alumni Hurricane Island (Maine) Outward Bound Sch., underwriter Silver Anniversary video 1987; water safety instr., sr. life saving instr., First Aid instr. Red Cross Nat. Aquatic Sch., 1964. Recipient numerous industry achievement awards; nominated White House fellow, 1971; honoree Nat. Women's Day, 1987. Mem. Am. Assn. Artificial Intelligence, Inst. for Mgmt. Scis., Ops. Rsch. Soc. Am., MIT Faculty Club, Hannah Duston Garrison house Assn. (life, bd.), Harwich Hist. Assn. (life), Stratford Hist. Soc. (life), Cambridge Hist. Soc., Bates Coll. Class 1965 (sec., treas., reunion chmn., com. chmn. 25th reunion major gifts), Columbia U. Grad. Sch. Bus. Alumni Assn. (nat. chmn. membership, bd. dirs.), Mass. Hort. Soc., Conn. Soc. Genealogists, Nat. Assn. Underwater Instrs. (cert. scuba diver), So. Mass. Yacht Racing Assn., Columbia Bus. Club Boston (founding dir., bd. dirs.), Columbia U. Club New Eng. (founding dir.), Columbia Club N.Y., Concord Country Club, Harvard Club (Boston, N.Y.C.), Harvard Neighbors, Harvard U. art Mus., MIT Faculty Club, Harvard Faculty Club, Stone Horse Yacht Club, Women's City Club (com. membership), Royal Scottish Automobile Club, So. Mass. Yacht Racing Assn., Friends of Loch Lomond (life), Mass. Hort. Soc., Arnold Arboretum Harvard U., Housatonic Boat Club. Republican. Avocations: the arts, sports, horticulture, environmental preservation, genealogy. Home: 20 Chapel St Ste C101 Brookline MA 02446-5445 Office: Beth Israel Deaconess Med Ctr 110 Francis St Ste 9-A Boston MA 02215-5501 Fax: (617) 566-8165. E-mail: janwhite20@aol.com.

WHITE, JASPER, food service executive; b. N.J. m. Nancy White; children: Jasper Paul, Mariel, Hayley. Diploma, Culinary Inst. Am., 1973. Chef, owner Jasper's Restaurant, Boston, 1983—95, Summer Shack, Cambridge, Mass., 2000—. Named Best Chef, James Beard Found., 1990. Office: Summer Shack 149 Alewife Pky Cambridge MA 02140

WHITE, JEANETTE K. state senator, health facility administrator; b. Thief River Falls, Minn., May 2, 1943; m. William White; 2 children. BS in Polit. Sci. and Sociology, U. Iowa, 1965; MS in Cmty Develop., So. Ill. U., 1972; postgrad., U. Bt. Health adminstr. Sojourns Cmty. Health Clinic, Westminister, Vt.; senator State of Vt., 2003—. Mem. Putney Selectboard, United Way, Leadership S.E. Vt., Vt. Cmty. Develop. Bd., So. Vt. Area Health Edn. Ctr. Office: 35A Old Depot Rd Putney VT 05346

WHITE, JEANNETTE LEE, information technology executive; BA in econ. with honors, George Wash. U.; exec. edn., Dartmouth; YPO/MIT Pres. Seminar on eBusiness, MIT, Cambridge. Sys. mgr. Employee Benefit Rsch. Inst., Wash. DC; regulatory analysis staff Office Mgmt. and Budget, Exec. Office of the Pres.; founder, CEO Sytel, Inc., 1987—. Bd. trustees George Mason U. Found.; bd. vis. U. Md. Sch. Pub. Affairs; chpt. officer Young Pres. Orgn.; chairwoman Montgomery United Way; served on Gov. apptd. bd. Md. Tech. Devel. Corp. (Tedco); bd. dirs. High Tech Coun. Md. Named Exec. Yr., High Tech Coun. Md., 1998; named one of 100 Most Powerful Women in Wash., Washingtonian mag., 2001; recipient Nat. Entrepreneur award in innovative bus. strategies category, Working Woman mag., 2000. Office: Sytel Inc 6430 Rockledge Dr Ste 400 Bethesda MD 20817 Office Phone: 301-530-1000. Office Fax: 301-530-1032.

WHITE, JEFFREY GEORGE, healthcare consultant; b. Lawrence, Mass., Apr. 16, 1944; s. Alfred James and Ruth Virginia (Maylum) W.; children: Jennifer L., Tracy E. AB in Econs., Bowdoin Coll., 1966; MBA, U. N.H., 1985. Asst. pers. dir., then asst. adminstr. Maine Med. Ctr., Portland, 1967-71; asst. adminstr. Regional Meml. Hosp., Brunswick, Maine, 1971, adminstr., 1971-74; assoc. dir. Elizabeth Ann Seton Hosp. (now Mid-Maine Med. Ctr.), Waterville, 1974-75; assoc. adminstr. Mid-Maine Med. Ctr., 1975-79, v.p. ops., 1979-83; asst. dir. Wentworth-Douglass Hosp., Dover, N.H., 1983-85; exec. v.p. Frisbie Meml. Hosp., Rochester, N.H., 1985-89, pres., 1989-92; sr. cons., prin. Helms & Co., Inc., Concord, N.H., 1992—. Interim pres., CEO New London (NH) Hosp., 2002-03; preceptor dept. health mgmt. and policy U. NH, Durham, 1985-92, adj. asst. prof., 1991-93, asst. prof., 1993-97, dean's leadership coun. sch. health human svcs., 1998—; bd. dirs. Riverwoods at Exeter, 2000-2003. Vol. pub. TV sta.; bd. dirs. Greater Seacoast United Way, 1991-94, chmn. comty. campaign, 1993; pres. Greater Rochester C. of C., 1990. Fellow Am. Coll. Healthcare Execs. (past regent for N.H.); mem. N.H. Hosp. Assn. (trustee emeritus). Republican. Avocations: tennis, skiing, reading, travel. Home: 37 Mill Pond Rd Durham NH 03824-2722 Office: Helms & Co Inc 1 Pillsbury St Concord NH 03301-3556 Office Phone: 603-225-6633. E-mail: jwhite@helmsco.com.

WHITE, JEFFREY MUNROE, lawyer; b. Lewiston, Maine, Jan. 16, 1948; BS in Applied Physics magna cum laude, Tufts U., 1970; JD, Boston Coll., 1975. Bar: Maine 1975, U.S. Ct. Appeals (1st cir.) 1979. Semiconductor engr. Fairchild Semiconductor, 1970-72; ptnr., head antitrust and trade regulation group Pierce, Atwood, Portland, Maine. Lectr., contbr. to profl. publs. on antitrust, litig., and intellectual property topics. Chmn. Cape Elizabeth Sch. Study Com., 1990-91. Mem. ABA (mem. antitrust, intellectual property and litigation sects.), N.E. Bar Assn. (dir. 1982-85), Maine State Bar Assn. (co-chmn. com. continuing legal edn. 1981-83), Maine Trial Lawyers Assn., Cumberland County Bar Assn. Office: Pierce Atwood Monument Sq Portland ME 04101 Office Phone: 207-791-1100. E-mail: jwhite@pierceatwood.com.

WHITE, JENNIFER PHELPS, counselor; b. Palo Alto, Calif., Aug. 31, 1943; d. Delmer Frank and Luella Elizabeth (McHugh) Phelps; m. Charles Evan White, Oct. 29, 1965; children: George Kevin, Colleen Elizabeth. AA in Liberal Arts, Foothill Jr. Coll., 1964; BA in Sociology & Anthropology, U. N.Mex., 1967, MPA, 1987. Lic. profl. mental health counselor N.Mex. Counseling and Therapy Bd. Sales clk. Barron Park Pharmacy, Palo Alto, 1960-64; caseworker State of N.Mex., Albuquerque, 1968-70; info. sys. coord. City of Albuquerque, 1971-75; rsch. specialist Pub. Interest Rsch. Group, 1976-77; interviewer Sandia Market Rsch., 1980-81; acad. adviser, counselor U. N.Mex., 1981-88; rehab. specialist Intracorps, 1988-89; dir. career svcs. ctr. YWCA, 1989-96; athletic advisor U. N.Mex., Albuquerque, 1996—. Mem. women in transition Planning Commn. State of N.Mex., Albuquerque, 1990—; mem. career guidance project adv. com. Commn. on Status of Women, Albuquerque, 1993-95; employment cons. Genesis Project, Albuquerque, 1989-91; mem. steering com. United Staff U. N.Mex., 1996—, staff coun., 2000—. Chair women's affirmative action coun. City of Albuquerque, 1976-82; mem. steering com. Choice Pac, Albuquerque, 1984—; mem. Human Rights Coalition, 1995—. Named Outstanding N.Mex. Women, Office of Gov., State of N.Mex., 1994; recipient Grassroots Accomplishment award Nat. Coun. Negro Women, Las Mujeres de Lulac, 1994, Human Rights award City of Albuquerque, 1995. Mem. NOW (mem. Albuquerque and N.Mex. chpts., bd. dirs., pres., coord. 1975—, lobbyist N.Mex. State Legislature 1978-87), Nat. Abortion Rights Action League/Right to Choose (bd. dirs. 1980-93), Career Devel. Assn., Women Work! Nat. Network (Svc. awards 1994-95), Women's Housing Coalition (bd. dirs., pres., v.p. 1989—, project change bd. dirs. 1996—). Democrat. Avocations: political activist, pre-columbian anthropology, sewing. Home: 416 Montclaire Dr SE Albuquerque NM 87108-2630 Office: Univ NMex Athletic Dept Main Campus Albuquerque NM 87131-0001

WHITE, JESSE, state official; b. Alton, Ill., 1934; BS, Ala. State U., 1957. With Chgo. Cubs; tchr., adminstr. Chgo. Pub. Sch. Sys.; mem. Ill. Gen. Assembly, Springfield, chmn. com. on human svcs., mem. edn. com., mem. select com. on children and aging; recorder of deeds State of Ill., Springfield, 1992-98, sec. of state, 1999—. Founder Jesse White Tumbling Team, 1959; Dem. committeeman 27th Ward, Chgo., 1996—; libr. State of Ill. State Libr.; archivist State of Ill.; mem. Ill. N.G. With USAF. Recipient Archbishop Richard Chenevix Trench award, 1999; Inductee Southwestern Athletic Conf. Hall of Fam, 1995, Chgo. Pub. League Basketball Coaches Assn. Hall of Fame, 1995. Democrat. Office: 213 State Capitol Springfield IL 62706

WHITE, JILL CAROLYN, lawyer; b. Santa Barbara, Calif., Mar. 20, 1934; d. Douglas Cameron and Gladys Louise (Ashley) W.; m. Walter Otto Weyrauch, Mar. 17, 1973. BA, Occidental Coll., L.A., 1955; JD, U. Calif., Berkeley, 1972. Bar: Fla. 1974, Calif. 1975, U.S. Dist. Ct. (no. and mid. dists.) Fla., U.S. Ct. Appeals (5th and 11th cirs.), U.S. Supreme Ct. Staff mem. U.S. Dept. State, Am. Embassy, Rio de Janeiro, 1956-58; with psychol. rsch. units Inst. Human Devel., Inst. Personality Assessment and Rsch., U. Calif., Berkeley, 1961-68; adj. prof. criminal justice program U. Fla., Gainesville, Fla., 1976-78; pvt. practice immigration and nationality law, Gainesville, 1976—2002. Contbr. articles to profl. jours. Mem.: Fla. Bar (immigration and nationality law cert. com. 1994—99, chmn. cert. com. 1997—98, cert. in immigration and nationality law 1995—), Bar Assn. 8th Jud. Cir. Fla., Am. Immigration Lawyers Assn. (bd. dirs. Ctrl. Fla. chpt. 1985—94, 1995—96, 1997—2000, chmn. Ctrl. Fla. chpt. 1988—89, co-chmn. so. regional liaison com. 1990—92, nat. bd. dirs. 1988—89), Altrusa. Democrat. Office Phone: 352-380-9122. E-mail: jwhite49@earthlink.net.

WHITE, JOE LLOYD, soil scientist, educator; b. Pierce, Okla., Nov. 8, 1921; s. Claud Amos and Alta Maurice (Denney) W.; m. Wanita Irene Robertson, May 29, 1945; children— Lerrill, Darla, Ronna, Bren, Janeil Student, Connors State Agrl. Coll., 1940-42; BS, Okla. State U., 1944, MS, 1945; PhD, U. Wis., 1947. Asst. prof. agronomy Purdue U., West Lafayette, Ind., 1947-51, assoc. prof., 1951-57, prof., 1957-88. Cons. Bancroft Co., William H. Rorer Co., Chattem Chem. Co., Merck Sharp & Dohme Rsch. Lab. Patentee in field Fellow NSF, 1965-66, Guggenheim Found., 1972-73; Fulbright scholar, 1973; recipient Sr. U.S. Scientist award Alexander von Humboldt Found., 1980-81 Fellow AAAS, Am. Soc. Agronomy, Am. Inst. Chemists, Soil Sci. Soc. Am., Mineral Soc. Am., Royal Soc. Chemistry; mem. Am. Chem. Soc., Clay Minerals Soc. (disting.), Am. Pharm. Assn., Coblentz Soc., Geochem. Soc., Internat. Soil Sci. Soc., Internat. Assn. Colloid and Interface Scientists, N.Y. Acad. Sci., Royal Soc. Chemists (chartered chemist), Soc. Petroleum Engrs. of AIME, Internat. Zeolite Assn., Soc. Applied Spectroscopy, Sigma Xi, Phi Kappa Phi, Phi Lambda Upsilon Mem. Ch. of Christ Achievements include patents for use of zeolites in ruminant nutrition, for stable dried aluminum hydroxide gel, for method and composition for treatment of hyperphosphatemia; establishment of the role of carbonate in inhibiting crystallization of aluminum hydroxide; definitive characterization of aluminum-containing adjuvants used in vaccines. Home: 2505 Roselawn Ave Lafayette IN 47904-2319 Office: Purdue U Dept Agronomy West Lafayette IN 47907

WHITE, JOHN DAVID, composer, theorist, cellist; b. Rochester, Minn., Nov. 28, 1931; s. Leslie David and Millie (Solum) W.; m. Marjorie Manuel, Dec. 27, 1952; children: Jeffrey Alan, Michele Kay, David Eliot. BA magna cum laude, U. Minn., 1953; MA, U. Rochester, 1954, PhD, performance cert., U. Rochester, 1960. Mem. faculty Kent (Ohio) State U., 1956-58, 60-63, 65-73, prof. music, assoc. dean Grad. Sch., 1967-73; asst. prof. U. Mich., 1963-65; dean Sch. Music, Ithaca (N.Y.) Coll., 1973-74; vis. prof. U. Wis., 1975-78; chmn. music dept. Whitman Coll., 1978-80; prof. U. Fla., 1980-97, prof. emeritus, 1997—; prof. U. Innsbruck, 1994; dist. chair U. Vienna, 2003—. Prin. cellist Eastman Philharmonia, 1959, Akron Symphony Orch., 1969-73; cellist Fla. Baroque Ensemble, 1980-97, Fla. Arts Trio, 1986-93; dir. Fla. Musica Nova, 1991-97; author: (with A. Cohen) Anthology of Music for Analysis, 1965, Understanding and Enjoying Music, 1968 (pub. in Japanese 1978), Music in Western Culture, 1972, The Analysis of Music, 1976, 2d edit., 1984, Guidelines for College Teaching of Music Theory, 1981, 2d edit., 2002, Comprehensive Musical Analysis, 1994, Theories of Musical Texture in Western History, 1995, New Music of the Nordic Countries, 2002; editor: Music and Man; editl. bd. Jour. for Musicological Research, Jour. Music Theory Pedagogy; contbr. articles to profl. jours.; Composer: Symphony No. 2, 1960, Blake Songs, 1961; (for flute, violin and viola) Divertimento, 1961; opera The Legend of Sleepy Hollow, 1962; Three Choruses From Goethe's Faust, 1965, Three Joyce Songs, 1966, Ode to Darkness, 1967, Cantos of the Year, 1969; (for clarinet and piano) Variations, 1971, Whitman Music, 1970, Three Madrigals, 1971, Russian Songs for Voices and Winds, 1972, Prayer (Solzhenytsin), 1973, String Quartet 1, 1975, Variations, 1976, Suite, 2001; Ode on the Morning of Christ's Nativity (Donne), 1977, Music for Oriana, 1978, Pied Beauty, 1980; (for cello and piano) Sonata, 1981, Zodiac, 1981, Music for violin and piano, 1982, The Soft Voice, 1983, Concerto for Flute and Wind Ensemble, 1983, Dialogues, 1984, Sonata, 2001, Symphony for Wind Band (3rd Symphony), 1985, Concerto da Camera, 1985, Symphony for a Saint (4th Symphony), 1986, Music for Cello and Percussion, 1988, Songs of the Shulamite, 1989, Mirrors, 1990, But God's Own Descent (5th Symphony), 1991, Music of the Open Road, 1993, Daylight and Moonlight, 1993, O Sing to the Lord a New Song, 1993, Illusions for Three, 1994, Tryptich, 1994, Ars Poetica, 1995, Colors of Earth and Sky (6th Symphony), 1995, Summer Storm Madrigals, 1996, Time and the Water, 1996, O Sing to the Lord a New Song, 1997, Maria Laudata, 1998, God's Own Descent, 1998, The Song of Ruth, 1999, Symbolic Interaction for Orchestra, 1999; (for harpsichord) Suite, 1999, The Heavens are Telling, 1999, Flower Songs, 2000, Concerto, 2000, Sonata de Camera for Piano, 2001, Music for 2 Cellos, 2002, Pindar Hymns for Choir and Orch., 2003, Olympiad for Chorus, Brass, Percussion and Piano, 2004, Nocte Surgentes, 2004; recs. on Advent, Mark, Capstone and Opus One Labels. With AUS, 1954-56. Recipient Benjamin award, 1960, award Nat. Fedn. Music Clubs, 1962, internat. composition award U. Wis.-Oriana Trio, 1979, composition award Am. Choral Dirs. Assn., 1984; grantee NEA; Fulbright rsch. fellow, 1995-96; Fulbright Disting. Lectr., 2003-04. Fellow Am. Scandinavian Found., 1997; mem. ASCAP (awards 1965—), Soc. Composers, Inc. (nat. coun. 1987-89, 93-96), Soc. Music Theory, Pi Kappa Lambda, Delta Omicron, Phi Mu Alpha, Phi Beta Delta. Home: 1555 California St Apt 608 Denver CO 80202-4276 Personal E-mail: jwhite48@earthlink.net.

WHITE, JOHN JOSEPH, surgery and pediatrics educator; b. Mt. Vernon, N.Y., Nov. 22, 1932; s. John Joseph and Bernice (Kilduff) W.; m. G. Andrea Melanson, May 14, 1966; children: Melanie Lara, Timothy Andrew. BA, Fordham U., 1953; MD, CM, McGill U., Montreal, Can., 1957. Demonstrator anatomy McGill U., 1962-63; asst. prof. surgery Johns Hopkins U., Balt., 1967-70, assoc. prof. surgery, 1970-76, assoc. prof. oncology, 1975-76; prof. surgery and pediatrics, chief pediatric surgeon Albany (N.Y.) Med. Coll., 1976-87, Loma Linda (Calif.) U., 1987-92; clin. prof. surgery and pediats. Mercer U. Sch. Medicine. Contbr. articles to profl. jours. Bd. dirs. Ronald McDonald House, Albany, 1981-87; active Gov's. Traffic Safety Commn., 1981-82. With USPHS, USCG, 1958-60. Mem. ACS, Am. Acad. Pediatrics, Am. Pediatric Surg. Assn. (charter, publ. com. 1976, 87, vice chmn. 1988, practice and cost concerns com. 1985, vice chmn. 1986, del. to AMA), Soc. Univ. Surgeons, Am. Soc. for Artifical Internal Organs, Brit. Assn. Pediatric Surgeons, Pacific Coast Surg. Assn., Pacific Assn. Pediatric Surgeons, So. Thoracic Surgery Assn., Nu Sigma Nu. Office: 840 Pine St Ste 700 Macon GA 31201-7526

WHITE, JOHN JOSEPH, III, lawyer; b. Darby, Pa., Nov. 23, 1948; s. John J. Jr. and Catherine (Lafferty) W.; m. Catherine M Staley, Dec. 9, 1983. BS, U. Scranton, 1970; MPA, Marywood U., 1977; JD, Loyola U., New Orleans, 1983. Bar: Pa. 1983, U.S. Dist. Ct. (ea. dist.) Pa. 1983, N.J. 1984, U.S. Ct. Appeals (3d cir.) 1983, U.S. Dist. Ct. N.J. 1984, U.S. Tax Ct. 1984, D.C. 1985, U.S. Supreme Ct. 1987. Exec. dir. Scranton (Pa.) Theatre Libre, Inc., 1973-77; pub. Libre Press Inc., Scranton, 1977-83; pvt. practice Phila., 1983—. Founder, publ. Metro Mag., 1977—83; pres. eMercury, Inc., Lansdowne, Pa., 1987—; N.Am. agt. Palacky U. Med. Sch., Olomouc, Czech Republic, 1995—2001. Founder, Scranton Pub. Theatre, 1976; exec. dir. Scranton Theatre Libre, Inc., 1973. Capt. USAF, 1970-73; lt. col. Res., 1973-89, col. ANG, 1999-2000, ret. 2000. Mem.: ABA, N.G. Assn., Phila. Bar Assn., Nat. Acad. Elder Law Attys., Mil. Order of Fgn. Wars, Air Force Assn. (chpt. pres. 1975—), Phi Delta Phi Internat. Legal Frat. Democrat. Roman Catholic. Avocations: jogging, art collecting. Office Phone: 215-732-2000. Personal E-mail: lawfirmusa@aol.com.

WHITE, JOHN KENNETH, politics educator; b. Providence, Oct. 10, 1952; s. Harold Allison and Margaret Mary (Morrissey) W.; m. Yvonne J. Prevost, July 1, 1995; 1 child, Jeannette Brigitte. BA, U. R.I., 1975; MA, U. Conn., 1976, PhD, 1980. Assoc. prof. SUNY, Potsdam, 1980-88; prof. Cath. U., Washington, 1988—. V.p. Ctr. for Party Devel., 1992-99; co-chair Com. for Party Renewal, 1994-99. Author: The Fractured Electorate, 1983, The New Politics of Old Values, 1990, Still Seeing Red, 1998; (with Daniel M. Shea) The Values Divide: American Politics and Culture in Transition, 2002, New Party Politics: From Hamilton and Jefferson to the Information Age, 2003. Roman Catholic. Office: Dept Politics Cath Univ Am Washington DC 20064-0001 Office Phone: 202-319-5128. E-mail: white@cua.edu.

WHITE, JOHN MICHAEL, chemistry educator; b. Danville, Ill., Nov. 26, 1938; married, 1960; 3 children. BS, Harding Coll., 1960; MS, U. Ill., 1962, PhD in Chemistry, 1966. From asst. to assoc. prof. U. Tex., Austin, 1966—76, prof. chemistry, Hackerman prof. chemistry, 1985—2000, Robert A. Welch chair chemistry, dir. Materials Chem. Ctr., 2001—. Mem. Am. Chem. Soc., Am. Phys. Soc. Achievements include research in surface and materials chemistry. Office: U Tex Dept Chemistry Welch Hall 3-310 Austin TX 78712

WHITE, JOHN P, federal agency administrator; BS in Indsl. and Labor Rels., Cornell U.; MA in Econs., PhD in Econs., Syracuse U. Sr. v.p. nat. security rsch. programs Rand Corp., 1968-77; asst. sec. Def. Manpower, Res. Affairs, and Logistics, 1977-78; dep. dir. Office Mgmt. and Budget, 1978-81; CEO, chmn. bd. dirs. Interactive Sys. Corp., 1981-88; gen. mgr. integration and sys. products divsn., v.p. Eastman Kodak Co., 1988-92; faculty dir. Ctr. for Bus. and Govt. Harvard U. Kennedy Sch. Govt., 1992-95; dep. sec. Dept. of Def., Washington, 1995-97; faculty Harvard U. Kennedy Sch. Govt., 1998—; sr. ptnr. Global Tech. Ptnrs., Washington, 1998—. Officer USMC. Office: Kennedy Sch Gov Harvard U 79 SFK St Cambridge MA 02138 Also: Global Tech Partners 99 Summer St Ste 1820 Boston MA 02110

WHITE, JOHN PATRICK, lawyer; b. Boston, Oct. 14, 1946; s. John Marion and Margaret Patricia (Gannon) W.; m. Gemma Mary Flattly, Feb. 9, 1980; 1 son, John Myles. BS in Chem. Engring., Columbia U., 1968, MA in Biochemistry, 1971, MPh in Molecular Biology, 1975; JD, Fordham U., 1977. Bar: N.Y. 1978, U.S. dist. ct. (ea. and so. dists.) N.Y. 1978, U.S. Ct. Customs and Patent Appeals 1979, U.S. Ct. Appeals (Fed. cir.) 1982. Legis. dir. Cmty. Coun. Greater N.Y., 1971-77; assoc. Cooper, Dunham, Clark, Griffin & Moran, N.Y.C., 1977-81, ptnr., 1981-88, Cooper & Dunham, LLP, N.Y.C., 1988—. Owner Shallow Brook Farm, Stillwater, N.J.; breeder Reg Angus Cattle, Ringneck Pheasants and Carriage Horses; dir. Oncogene Sci., Inc., BioTech. Gen. Corp.; instr. Practicing Law Inst. Contbr. articles to sci. and legal jours. Democratic dist. leader, 1975-81; vice chmn. Dem. Com. N.Y. County, 1977-81; jud. del. 1st jud. dept., 1975, 76, 77, 79; adminstr. screening panel 2d Mcpl. Ct. Dist.; pub. mem. Columbia U. Recombinant DNA Biosafety Com. Columbia U. faculty fellow, 1969-71; NIH grantee, 1969-71. Mem. ABA, Am. Chem. Soc., Am. Intellectual Property Law Assn., N.Y. Intellectual Property Law Assn., Assn. Bar City N.Y., Fed. Bar Coun. (com. patents), Club: Columbia of N.Y.C, Four In Hand Club, Upperville, Va. Office: Cooper & Dunham Ste 2200 1185 Avenue Of The Americas New York NY 10036-2615

WHITE, JOHN VINCENT, surgeon, consultant; b. Chgo., May 7, 1952; BS, Northwestern U., 1974; MD, Columbia U., 1978. Diplomate Am. Bd. Surgery. Instr. surgery Columbia U., N.Y.C., 1982-83; asst. prof. surgery Temple U., Phila., 1984-88, assoc. prof. surgery, 1988-94, prof. surgery, 1994-99; chmn. dept. surgery Luth. Gen. Hosp., Park Ridge, Ill., 1999—. Adj. sr. fellow Sch. Health Econs. U. Pa., Phila., 1994—; tech. cons. Boston Scientific Corp., Natick, Mass., 1995—; surg. cons. Dept. of Health N.Y. State, 1993; surg. tech. cons. Congl. Office of Tech. Assessment, Washington, 1995; laser tech. cons. Office of Naval Rsch., Washington, 1993-97. Editor: Hemodilution in Patient Care, 1989, Alternatives to Open Vascular Surgery, 1995, Surgical Clinics of North America, 1998; founding editor: Jour. Laparoendoscopic Surgery, 1990. Recipient Samuel D. Gross award Phila. Acad. Surgery, 1992. Mem. Am. Soc. Laser Medicine and Surgery, Soc. Univ. Surgeons (mem. found. bd. dirs. 1994-98), Del. Valley Vascular Soc. (pres. 1995—), Soc.

Vascular Surgery (mem. com. outcomes analysis 1994—), Alpha Omega Alpha. Office: Lutheran Gen Hosp 1775 Dempster St Park Ridge IL 60068-1173 Fax: (847) 696-3394. E-mail: john.white-md@advocatehealth.com.

WHITE, JOHN WESLEY, JR., retired academic administrator; b. Nashville, Oct. 20, 1933; s. John W. and Ernestine (Engle) W.; m. Martha Ellen Bragg, June 24, 1956; children: Marcus Wesley, Michelle Suzanne. Student, Martin Jr. Coll., 1952-54; BA, Vanderbilt U., 1956, BD, 1959; MA, George Peabody Coll., 1966, PhD, 1968; LHD, U. Nebr., 1983; LLD, Kwansai Gakuin U., Japan, 1991. Dean admissions, dir. student affairs Martin Coll., 1960-65; asst. to acad. v.p. George Peabody Coll., 1965-67; assoc. dean for humanities Oklahoma City U., 1968-70, dean Coll. Arts and Scis., 1970-77, assoc. prof. English, 1968-73, prof., 1973-77; pres. Nebr. Wesleyan U., 1977-97, chancellor, 1997-98, pres. emeritus, 1998—. Cons., spkr. in field; bd. dirs. Assurity Life Ins. Co.; chmn. Nebr. Ednl. Temecom. Commn., 1996-97. Past pres. U. Senate, United Meth. Ch.; bd. dirs. Cooper Found. Eli Lilly Sr. scholar Vanderbilt U., 1959. Mem. Nat. Assn. Ind. Colls. and Univs. (bd. dirs. 1989-93, 95-97), Lincoln C. of C. (bd. dirs. 1990-93), Rotary (pres. West Oklahoma City 1976), Kappa Delta Pi, Phi Kappa Phi, Alpha Mu Gamma, Blue Key. *Two principles have been paramount in my life: One, related to the attitude toward myself, is that we can help to shape life, not simply endure it. We are "creative" creatures, not just "surviving" creatures. The second principle, related to the attitude toward others, is that communication is essential to coexistence; and only as we make a real effort to hear what is meant, rather than simply what is said or written, are we able to communicate effectively.*

WHITE, JOSEPH B. reporter; b. N.Y.C., July 7, 1958; Attended, Harvard U. Reporter The Wall St. Jour., 1998, bur. chief, 1998—. Co author (with Paul Ingrassia): (book) Comeback: The Fall and Rise of the American Automobile Industry, 1994. Recipient Pulitzer Prize for beat reporting, 1993. Office: The Wall Street Journal Detroit Bureau 500 Woodward Ave Ste 1950 Detroit MI 48226-5497

WHITE, JOSEPH CHARLES, manufacturing and retailing company executive; b. Toronto, Ont., Can., Aug. 14, 1922; s. Joseph Cleveland and Edith Parker (Johnson) W.; m. G. Evelyn Vipond, July 15, 1944; children— Ronald, Richard, JoAnne. Chartered acct., Queens U., Kingston, Ont.; B.Commerce, U. Toronto. Vice-pres., dir. Agnew-Surpass, Inc., Brantford, Ont., Can., 1964-78; v.p., dir. Genesco Can., Inc., Cambridge, Ont., Can., 1978-82, exec. v.p., dir., 1982-87, pres., gen. mgr. retail op., 1986-87. Dir., v.p. Genesco Group Inc.; dir. Genesco Fin. Ltd.; pres. Brantford Art Gallery, 1994-95, Brantford Probus Club, 1995-96. Chmn. Ross MacDonald Found., Brantford, Ont., 1983-86; pres. YMCA, Brantford, 1968-69; chmn. Brant County Post-Secondary Edn. Corp., Brantford, 1973-76. Served with Royal Can. Air Force, 1943-45 Mem. Ont. Inst. Chartered Accts., Can. Council Distbn. (pres. 1972-73), Brant County C. of C. (treas. 1966-68) Mem. United Ch. of Can. Avocations: downhill skiing, tennis. Office: Genesco Can Inc 401 Fountain St Cambridge ON Canada N3H 4V5 Home: 40 Museum Drive Unit 420 Orillia ON L3V 7T9 Canada

WHITE, JOYCE LOUISE, librarian; b. Phila., June 7, 1927; d. George William and Louisa (Adams) W. BA, U. Pa., 1949; MLS, Drexel U., 1963; MA in Religion, Episc. Sem. S.W., 1978. Head libr. Penniman Libr. Edn. U. Pa., Phila., 1960-76; archivist St. Francis Boys' Home, Salina, Kans., 1982-84; libr. Brown Mackie Coll., Salina, 1983-86; libr., dir. St. Thomas Theol. Sem., Denver, 1986-95; libr., dir. Archbishop Vehr Theol. Libr. Archdiocese of Denver, 1995-96. Author: Biographical and Historial Yarnall Library, 1979, Colorado Episcopal Clergy in the 19th Century: A Biographical Register, 2003; asst. editor: Women Religious History Sources, 1983; contbr. articles to profl. jours. and chpts. to books. Vol. libr. St. John's Cath., Denver, 1993—. Mem. Ch. and Synagogue Libr. Assn. (life, founding, pres. 1969-70, exec. sec. 1970-72, exec. bd. 1967-76, ann. conf. chair 1996). Avocations: gardening, cats, church libraries. Office: St John's Cathedral Libr 1350 Washington St Denver CO 80203-2008

WHITE, JUDITH LOUISE, social worker, counselor; b. Lodi, Ohio, Feb. 27, 1939; d. Henry and Charlotte Virginia (Spahr) Schmelzer; m. Downer Dale White, Sept. 4, 1959; children: Mark, Kelly, Kristy, David. AA, Northland Pioneer Coll., 1980; postgrad., No. Ariz. U., 1984—, Ariz. State U., 1985—; BS in Human Svcs., Prescott Coll., 1992. Tchr. White Mountain Apache Heart Start Program, Whiteriver, Ariz., 1976-80, child svcs. coord., 1976-80; cons. Nat. Indian Head Start, 1980—; family svcs. coord. Whiteriver Elem. Sch., 1987—. Trainer Indian Child & Family Conf., Phoenix and Albuquerque, 1982-86, Fetal Alcohol Syndrome-Indian Health Services, Whiteriver, 1984—; cons. White Mountain Apache Head Start Resource Access Project, 1984—; assoc. tchr. Northland Pioneer Jr. Coll., Holbrook, Ariz., 1985—; trainer pilot parent program; coord. Whiteriver Pilot Parents. Mem. Coalition for Chronically Ill Children, Phoenix, 1985—, White Mt. Apache Child Protective Team, Kinishba Coun. Prevent Child Abuse. Mem. NASW (presenter conf. 1990), Coun. Exceptional Children, Nat. Assn. Edn. Young Children, White Mt. Assn. Edn. Young Children. Avocations: music, reading, theater, art. Home and Office: 660 N Spring Creek Trail Cornville AZ 86325 E-mail: whitejudith@myway.com.

WHITE, JUNE MILLER, mathematics professor, educational consultant; b. E. Bernstadt, Ky., June 13, 1938; d. James Fulton and Ida Mae (Hansel) Miller; m. Richard Allen White, Aug. 27, 1960; children: Jennifer Lynn, Richard Allen Jr. BS with high honors, Denison U., 1960; MA, U. Rochester, 1969; PhD, Bryn Mawr Coll., 1980. Engring. asst. AT&T, Kansas City, Mo., 1960-61; math. tchr. William Chrisman H.S., Independence Pub. Schs., Independence, Mo., 1961-62, Brighton (N.Y.) H.S., 1962-69, Conestoga H.S., Tredyffrin-Easttown Pub. Schs., Berwyn, Pa., 1970-72; chair math. dept. Hill Top Prep. Sch., Rosemont, Pa., 1972-76, curriculum coord., 1976-81; instr. math. St. Petersburg Jr. Coll., Clearwater, Fla., 1982-84, dir. math. program, 1984—2002, prof. math. edn., 2002—. Presenter at various confs. Author: A Collection of Mathematics Applications for College Students, 1989; editor SPECTRUM, 1983-95; contbr. articles to profl. jours. Elder Northwood Presbyn. Ch., Clearwater, 1986-90; chmn. blood drive ARC, King of Prussia, Pa., 1973-74; chmn. citizens adv. com. Upper Merion Pub. Schs., King of Prussia, 1975-76. Mem. Am. Math. Assn. of Two Yr. Colls., Math. Assn. Am. (v.p. Fla. and Caribbean sect. 1988-91, sec. 1994-99, pres.-elect 1999, pres. 2000), Nat. Coun. Tchrs. Math., Fla. Assn. Cmty. Colls., Rsch. Coun. for Diagnostic and Prescriptive Math., Pinellas County Assn. for Children and Adults with Learning Disabilities (bd. dirs. 1987-88), Phi Beta Kappa. Avocations: camping, sailing, travel. Home: 4951 Bacopa Ln S Unit 103 Saint Petersburg FL 33715-2617 E-mail: whitejune@spjc.edu.

WHITE, KAREN RUTH JONES, information systems executive; b. Ft. Meade, Md., Oct. 8, 1953; d. Frank L. Jones and Inge H. Lesser; m. M. Timothy Heath, Apr. 23, 1973 (div. Aug. 1976); m. Carl W. White, May 30, 1993. AS in Electronic Data Processing, N.H. Tech. Inst., Concord, 1977; BS in MIS with high honors, Northeastern U., Boston, 1984, MS in Info. Sys., 1997. Profect mgmt. prof. Project Mgmt. Inst., 2001. Programmer Chubb Life Ins. Co., Concord, N.H., 1977-79, Retailers Electronics Account Processing, Woburn, Mass., 1979-82; sr. programmer, analyst N.H. Ins. Group, Manchester, 1982-84; prin. systems analyst Wang Labs., Inc., Lowell, Mass., 1984-89; project mgr. TASC, Inc., Reading, Mass., 1989-2000; dir. consulting svcs. PM Solutions, Havertown, Pa., 2000—. Bd. dirs. Brandywyne Common Assn., Derry, N.H., 1991-94; mem. St. Paul's Sch. Advanced Studies Pgm Alumni Assn., Concord, N.H. With U.S. Army Res., 1974-84. Decorated Army Commendation medal, 1980. Mem.: NAFE, IEEE (program chair 5th reengring. forum 1996, mem. exec. adv. bd. 1996—99, dep. conf. chair 6th reengring. forum 1998, computer soc., tech. com. in software engring.), Project Mgmt. Inst. (Mass. Bay chpt. program dir. 1992—93, project chair PMI '96 1994—96, dir. seminars/symposium 1996—98, PMI 2000 adv. group 1999—2000, ethics rev. com. 2000—02, awards rev. com. 2001—03, chair ethics rev. com. 2003—, ethics stds. rev. com. 2004—), Sigma Epsilon Rho. Home: 50 Merrill Rd Weare NH 03281-4708 Office: PM Solutions 50 Merrill Rd Weare NH 03281-4708 Office Phone: 603-529-5849.

WHITE, KATE, editor-in-chief; m. Brad Holbrooke; 2 children. BA, Union Coll. Editor Child mag., 1988—89; editor-in-chief Working Woman mag., N.Y.C., 1989—91, McCall's mag., N.Y.C., 1991—94, Redbook, N.Y.C., 1994—98, Cosmopolitan mag., 1998—. Author: Why Good Girls Don't Get Ahead and Gutsy Girls Do, Nine Secrets of Women Who Get Everything They Want, If Looks Could Kill, 2002, A Body to Die For, 2003. Recipient Matrix award, Women in Comms., 2003—. Office: Cosmopolitan Hearst Magazines 224 W 57th St New York NY 10019-3299

WHITE, KATHERINE ANN, artist; b. New Haven, Conn., July 26, 1970; d. Jeffery Prosser Robinson and Deborah Ann Marenna, Frederick John Marenna (Stepfather); m. Verlon Lee White, May 20, 1995; 1 child, Alden Vander. BS, So. Conn. State U., New Haven, 1985. Tchr. pvt. child care, Niantic, Conn., 2003—; writer self employed, Niantic, Conn., 1988—, artist, 1978—. Consulting, Niantic, Conn., 1999—; spkr. in field. Author: (book) Book Smart: How I Taught My Son To Read Before Age Three, Fish Tale; painting, Mother and Child, Speckled Trout, Etc. Mem.: Delta Mu Delta. Achievements include on a nat. level, educating parents about the fun and advantage of tchg. their children to read before they start sch., 2003-; tchg. son to read by age 2 1/2 by inventing games. Avocations: painting, interior designing, playing sports, fishing, cooking. Office: Katherine White 11 King Arthur Dr #5M Niantic CT 06357 E-mail: readby3@yahoo.com.

WHITE, KATHERINE E. law educator; BSE elec. engring. and computer sci., Princeton U., 1988; JD, U. Wash., 1991; LLM in Intellectual Property, George Washington U., 1996. Bar: Mich. 1996, U.S. Supreme Ct, U.S. Ct. Appeals (fed. cir.), U.S. Ct. Appeals Armed Forces, U.S. Army Ct. Mil. Rev., U.S. Patent and Trademark Office, Wash. 1992. Intellectual property counsel U.S. Army Corps Engrs., Washington, 1992—95; jud. law clk. for Hon. Randall Rader U.S. Ct. Appeals (fed. cir.), 1995—96; assoc. prof. Wayne State U. Law Sch., Detroit, 1996—. Adj. prof. George Washington U. Law Ctr., Washington, 1994—96; regent U. Mich., Ann Arbor, 1999—; mem. patent pub. adv. com. U.S. Patent and Trademark Office, 2000—02. Actor: Intellectual Property Litigation, Pretrial Practice Guide, 1999; co-author (with Eric Dobrusin): Intellectual Property Litigation, Pretrial Practice Guide, 1999; contbr. articles to profl. publs. CPT JAG U.S. Army, 1992—95, maj. JAG USAR, 1995—. Recipient Fulbright Sr. Scholar award, Max-Planck Inst. for Fgn. Internat. Patent, Copyright and Competition Law, 1999—2000; grantee, Max-Planck-Inst. for Fgn. Internat. Patent, Copyright and Competition Law, 2000; scholar, ROTC, Washington Law Found., 1988—91; Shaw fellow, 1994—96, White House Fellow, special coun. to the sec. of agr., 2001—02. Mem.: AAUP, ABA, Wolverine Bar Assn., Wash. State Bar Assn., Nat. Bar Assn., Mich. Patent Lawyer's Assn., Am. Intellectual Property Law Assn., Am. Assn. Law Schs., State Bar Mich. (mem. coun. intellectual property law sec., co-chmn. student liaison com., co-chmn. com. pattent issues in legislation), Princeton Club Mich. Office: Wayne U Law Sch 471 W Palmer Detroit MI 48202

WHITE, KATHY BRITTAIN, medical association executive; BS, MS, Ark. State U.; PhD in Mgmt., U. Memphis. Various sr. positions with AlliedSignal Corp., Guilford Mills, Inc.; chief info. officer Baxter Internat., 1995-96; chief info. officer, sr. v.p. Allegian Corp. (now merged with Cardinal Health), 1996-99; exec. v.p., chief info. officer Cardinal Health, Dublin, Ohio, 1999—. Bd. dirs. MECON, Inc., San Ramon, Calif., Children's Meml. Med. Ctr./Children's Meml. Hosp., Children's Meml. Found., Chgo.; former assoc. prof. info. technology U. N.C., Greensboro. Bd. dirs. Lake Forest Grad. Sch., Ill. Mem. ACHE. Office: Cardinal Health 7000 Cardinal Pl Dublin OH 43017-1091

WHITE, KELVIN LEWIS, historian, researcher; s. Nathaniel Lewis Lewis and Joyce Marie White. PhD, UCLA, 2001. Rschr. UCLA, 2001—. Missionary Campus Christian Ministry, Houston, 1995—2000. Sgt U.S. Army, 1990—94. Decorated ARCOM US Army, AAM; fellow Libr. Scholars Program, UCLA, 2004—; Diversity fellow, 2002, Cota Robles, 2004—, Hispanic Culture scholar, Soc. Latino Culture, 2001. Mem.: Orgn. Am. Historians, Am. Hist. Assn., Phi Alpha Theta (pres. 2000—02), Golden Key Intenational Honor Soc. (life; v.p. 2001—02). Conservative. Evangelical. Achievements include research in Analysis of African American Comic Strip Characters in the Black Press. Avocation: missionary. Office: Ucla 405 Hilgard Los Angeles CA 90095 Personal E-mail: klwyte@ucla.edu.

WHITE, KERR LACHLAN, retired hygiene and tropical medicine physician, medical educator, foundation administrator; b. Winnipeg, Man., Can., Jan. 23, 1917; s. John Alexander and Ruth Cecelia (Preston) Stevenson; m. Isabel Anne Pennefather, Nov. 26, 1943; children: Susan Isabel, Margot Edith. BA with honors (Oliver Gold medal), McGill U., 1940, MD, CM, 1949; DM (hon.), U. Leuven, 1978; postgrad., London Sch. Hygiene and Tropical Medicine, 1960; DSc (hon.), McMaster U., 1983. Intern, resident in medicine Mary Hitchcock Meml. Hosp., Hanover, NH, 1949—52; Hosmer fellow McGill U. and Royal Victoria Hosp., Montreal, Canada, 1952—53; asst. prof. medicine U. N.C. Sch. Medicine, Chapel Hill, 1953—57, assoc. prof. medicine and preventive medicine, 1957—62; Commonwealth advanced fellow Med. Rsch. Coun., Social Medicine Rsch. unit London Hosp., 1959—60; chmn., prof. epidemiology and community medicine U. Vt., Burlington, 1962—64; prof. Sch. Hygiene and Pub. Health Johns Hopkins U., Balt., 1965—76, chmn. dept. health care orgn., 1965—72; dir. Inst. Health Care Studies United Hosp. Fund N.Y., 1977—78; dep. dir. health scis. Rockefeller Found., N.Y.C., 1978—97, ret., 1997. Chmn. U.S. Nat. Com. Vital and Health Stats., 1975—79; mem. health adv. panel Office of Tech. Assessment, U.S. Congress, 1975—82; cons. Nat. Ctr. Health Stats., 1967—83, WHO, 1967—. Editor: Manual for Examination of Patients, 1960, Medical Care Research, 1965, Health Care: An International Study, 1976, Epidemiology as a Fundamental Science, 1976, Task of Medicine, 1988, Healing the Schism, 1991; mem. editl. bd.: Med. Care, 1962—73, Inquiry, 1967—79, Internat. Jour. Epidemiology, 1971—81, Internat. Jour. Health Svcs., 1971—; contbr. chapters to books, articles to profl. jours. Trustee Case-Western Res. U., 1974—79; bd. dirs. Found. for Child Devel., 1969—80. With Can. Army, 1942—45. Recipient Pew Primary Care Achievement award, 1995, Baxter Found. award, 1996, Wood award for lifetime contbns. to primary care rsch., 1999. Fellow: APHA (gov. coun. 1964—68, 1971—73, coun. med. care sect. 1962—65), NAS (Inst. Medicine coun. 1974—76, chmn. membership com. 1975—77), ACP, AAAS, Am. Heart Assn., Am. Acad. Preventive Medicine, Royal Soc. Medicine (hon.); mem.: AMA, Kerr L. White Inst. Health Svcs. Rsch. (hon. dir. 1995—), Internat. Epidemiol. Assn. (hon.; life, pres. 1974—77, treas., exec. com. 1964—71, 1974—77, coun. 1971—81), Am. Hosp. Assn. (adv. coun. ednl. and rsch. trust 1965—68), Assn. Tchrs. Preventive Medicine (coun. 1963—68), Century Club (N.Y.C.), Cosmos Club (Washington), Alpha Omega Alpha, Sigma Xi. E-mail: klw2j@virginia.edu.

WHITE, K(ING) PRESTON, JR., systems engineering educator, researcher, consultant; b. Dec. 31, 1948; s. K. Preston and Rosamond (Conley) White; m. Charlotte Rebekah O'Cain, Apr. 9, 1977 (dec.); 1 child, William Preston. BSE, Duke U., 1970, MS, 1972, PhD, 1976. Grad. tchg. and rsch. asst. Duke U., Durham, NC, 1970—75; asst. prof. dept. ops. rsch. and sys. analysis Poly. Inst. NY, Bklyn., 1975—77; asst. prof. dept. mech. engring., dept. engring. and pub. policy Carnegie-Mellon U., Pitts., 1977—79; asst. prof. sys. engring. U. Va., Charlottesville, 1979—85, dir. undergrad. studies, 1983—96, assoc. prof., 1985—2000, prof., 2000—, interim dept. chmn., 1996, Capstone program dir., 1996—; executive Masters prog., 1999—. Fac. in res. Newport News Shipping and Drydock, 1986; v.p. ERICA, Inc., Charlottesville, 1993; disting. vis. prof. SEMATECH, Austin, 1993—94; rschr., cons. in field; jour. referee; bd. dirs. Va. Modeling, Analysis and Simulation Ctr.; sec. bd. dirs. Winter Simulation Conf., 2002, vice chmn. bd. dirs., 03; chmn. Winter Stimulatoin Conf., 2004; chmn. bd. dirs. Univ. of Va., Inst. for Microelectronics, 2000—02. U.S. editor: Internat. Abstracts in Ops. Rsch., assoc. editor: IEEE Transactions on Electronics Packaging Mfg.; contbr. chapters to books Ency. of Systems and Control, McGraw-Hill Ency. of Sci. and Tech., articles to profl. jours. Recipient Outstanding Educator award, Boeing, 2001, award for ednl. innovation, Accreditation Bd. for Engring. and Tech., 1990. Mem.: IEEE (sr.), Inst. for Ops. Rsch. and Mgmt. Sci., Sys., Man and Cybernetics Soc., Inst. Indsl. Engrs. (sr.), Pi Tau Sigma, Sigma Xi, Omega Rho (charter), Tau Beta Pi. Home: 1033 Findlay Mountain Rd Shipman VA 22971-9801 Office: U Va Dept Systems Engring PO Box 400747 151 Engineers Way Charlottesville VA 22904-4747 Office Phone: 434-982-2070. Business E-Mail: kpwhite@virginia.edu.

WHITE, LARRY D. retired political science educator; b. Paola, Kans., Nov. 22, 1937; s. Carl B. and Elsie I. White; m. Marilee A. Foster, Jan. 22, 1966. AA, Independence (Kans.) C.C., 1957; BS in Edn., Pittsburg (Kans.) State U., 1959, MS in Polit. Sci., 1960; ArtsD in Govt., Econs., Sociology, Idaho State U., 1974. Instr., coach Highland (Kans.) C. Coll., 1960-65, Prestonsburg (Ky.) C.C., 1965-68; from instr. to asst. prof. polit. sci. U. Wis. Colls., Rice Lake, 1969-82, assoc. prof. polit. sci. Menasha, 1982-98, prof. polit. sci., 1998—2000, dept. chmn., 1988-92, 95-98; ret., 2000. E-mail: ldwhite@c212.com.

WHITE, LAWRENCE EDWARD, treasurer, financial executive; b. Pitts., Mar. 5, 1950; s. Edward A. and Dolores C. (Cole) W.; m. Marjorie Claire Ertle, July 29, 1972; children: Matthew E., Christopher L. BS in Chem. Engring., Carnegie-Mellon U., 1972, MS in Indsl. Adminstrn. with distinction, 1976. Product devel. engr. Eastman Kodak Co., Rochester, 1972-74; fin. analyst, supr. Ford Motor Co., Dearborn, Mich., 1976-82; mgr. fin. analysis Lone Star Techs., Dallas, 1982-85, mgr. corp. acctg., 1985-87; dir. fin. analysis and planning, corp. treas. TGI Friday's Inc., Dallas, 1987-89; v.p., treas. Metromedia Steakhouses, Inc., Dayton, Ohio, 1989—. Active YMCA Youth Orgns., local ch. fin. com. Mem. Assn. for Corp. Growth., Fin. Execs. Inst., Carnegie-Mellon Univ. Alumni Assn. Republican. Methodist. Office: Metromedia Steakhouses Inc PO Box 578 Dayton OH 45401-0578 Home: 9432 Timber Ridge Ct Brentwood TN 37027-8629

WHITE, LAWRENCE GILBERT, state legislator, insurance company executive; b. Oklahoma City, Apr. 19, 1964; s. Richard Francis and Marilyn Sue (Gorman) White. BA, Duquesne U., Pitts. V.p. Paull Assocs., Wheeling, W.Va., 1987—; del. W.Va. Ho. Dels., Wheeling, 1990—. Republican. Roman Catholic. Office: Paull Assocs 1311 Chapline St Wheeling WV 26003

WHITE, LAWRENCE J. economics professor; b. N.Y.C., June 1, 1943; s. Martin H. and Florence M. (Meiman) W. AB, Harvard U., 1964, PhD, 1969; MS in Econs., London Sch. Econs., 1965. Econ. adviser Harvard Devel. Adv. Svc., Pakistan and Indonesia, 1969-70; asst. prof. econs. Princeton U., N.J., 1970-76; mem. faculty Stern Sch. Bus., NYU., 1976—; prof. econs. Stern Sch. Bus., NYU, 1979—, chmn. dept., 1990-95; sr. staff economist U.S. Council Econ. Advisers, 1978-79; dir. econ. policy office, antitrust div. Dept. Justice, Washington, 1982-83. Mem. Fed. Home Loan Bank Bd., 1986-89; cons. in field. Author: The Automobile Industry Since 1945, 1971, Industrial Concentration and Economic Power in Pakistan, 1974, Reforming Regulation: Processes and Problems, 1981, The Regulation: Processes and Problems, 1981, The Regulation of Air Pollutant Emissions from Motor Vehicles, 1982, The Public Library in the 1980s: The Problems of Choice, 1983, International Trade in Ocean Shipping Services. The U.S. and the World, 1988, The S&L Debacle: Public Policy Lessons for Bank and Thrift Regulation, 1991; editor or co-editor: The Deregulation of the Banking and Securities Industries, 1979, Mergers and Acquisitions: Current Problems in Perspective, 1982, Technology and the Regulation of Financial Markets: Securities, Futures and Banking, 1986, Private Antitrust Litigation: New Evidence, New Learning, 1988, The Antitrust Revolution, 1989, Bank Management and Regulation, 1992, Structural Change in Banking, 1993, The Antitrust Revolution: The Role of Economics, 2d edit., 1994, The Antitrust Revolution: Economics, Competition, and Policy, 3d edit., 1999, 4th edit., 2004; N.Am. editor Jour. Indsl. Econs., 1984-87, 90-95; co-editor Rev. of Indsl. Orgn., 2003-04, gen. editor, 2004-. NSF fellow, 1965—69. Mem. Am. Econ. Assn., Phi Beta Kappa. Office: NYU Stern Sch Bus 44 W 4th St New York NY 10012-1126 Office Phone: 212-998-0880.

WHITE, LEEANNE J. music educator; d. William O. and Nancy E. Gilman; m. David A. White, Sept. 7, 1991; children: Annalyn M., Sarah G. Music Edn. - Piano/Voice, Bob Jones U., Greenville, SC, 1978—81; Bible (Assoc.), Evang. Inst. of Greenville, Greenville, SC, 1983—85; Cert. of Practical Knowledge in French, Ecole de Langue Francaise d'Albertville, France, 1986. First time registration sec. Inst. in Basic Youth Conflicts, Oak Brook, Ill., 1981—83; music editor Evang. Inst., Greenville, SC, 1983—85; missionary Gt. Commn., France, 1986—87; legal sec. Van Riper, Temple & Mann, Greenville, SC, 1987—88; ho. staff Rydal Hall Cmty. & Conf. Ctr., England, 1988—89; legal sec. Horton, Drawdy, Ward & Johnson, Greenville, SC, 1989—90; asst. to assoc. vp Clemson U. Found./Devel. Office, Clemson, SC, 1991—94; dir. of music Pickens Presbyn. Ch., Pickens, SC, 1993—96; piano/voice tchr. White's Music Studio (Pvt. Studio), Pickens, SC, 1996—; ch. pianist, choral dir. Covenant Presbyn. Ch., Easley, SC, 2001—. Mem./soloist Chorale d'Albertville, Albertville, France (incl. Monaco), 1985—86; organist St. Mary's Rydal, Rydal, England, 1988—89; mem./soloist Foothills Chorale, Clemson, SC, 1997—99. Editor: (hymnal) Hymns For Worship and Praise, 1984; author: (musical plays) God's Covenants, 2000, The Life of Brother Andrew, 2002; editor: (newsletter) Taxpayer News; author: (piano curriculum) The Church Pianist; contbr. Fiction Clemson Chronicle. Vol. leader Pickens County 4-H Club, Pickens, SC, 2003—; head libr. Covenant Presbyn. Ch., Easley, SC, 2002—; sec./treas./founding mem./hon. bd. mem. Pickens County Taxpayers Assn., Pickens, SC, 1994—2002; vol. leader/founding mem. Pickens Christian Home Educators, Pickens, SC, 2001—03. Mem.: Nat. Fedn. of Music Clubs, Greenville Music Tchrs. Assn., Fiber Friends Spinning Group. Presbyn. Avocations: writing, cello, spinning, theology, reading, piano. Home and Office: Leeanne J White PO Box 921 Pickens SC 29671

WHITE, LEON SAMUEL, college administrator; b. West Palm Beach, Fla., Mar. 31, 1946; s. Edward Julius and Carmeta Francis (Ferguson) W.; m. Anne Fryer, Sept. 29, 1969; children: Nigel, Kanika Pele. BS, Tuskegee Inst., 1969, MEd, 1973; PhD, Ohio State U., 1976; cert. in journalism, Columbia U., 1970. Rsch. assoc. Ohio State U., Columbus, 1974—76; coord. counseling St. Augustine's Coll., Raleigh, NC, 1976—77, dean of students, 1977—81, Savannah (Ga.) State Coll., 1981—84; vice chancellor student affairs Elizabeth City (N.C.) State U., 1984—96; ednl. cons. Thomas White, PA Consultants, West Palm Beach, 1996-97, Hertford, NC, 1996—97; v.p. student affairs Cheyney U. of Pa., 1997-2000; counselor Elizabeth City (N.C.) Middle Sch., 2000—01, RCCDC YouthBuild Program, Elizabeth City, 2001—. Contbr. articles to profl. jours. Psychol. cons. Franklin County Drug Treatment Program, Columbus, Ohio, 1975-76; mentor Boys Club of Raleigh, 1978-81; vol. counselor Tidelands Cmty. Mental Health, Savannah, 1982-84. Tuskegee Inst. scholar, 1963, grad. internship, 1971. Mem. So. Assn. Coll. Student Pers., Nat. Assn. Pers. Workers, Am. Assn. Counseling and Devel., Phi Delta Kappa. Democrat. Methodist. Avocations: writing, gardening, swimming, tennis, running. Home: PO Box 2502 Elizabeth City NC 27906-2502 Office: RCCDC YouthBuild 303 W Ehringhaus St Elizabeth City NC 27909 E-mail: dr_leonswhitee@hotmail.com.

WHITE, LERRILL JAMES, clinical pastoral educator; b. Lafayette, Ind., Mar. 13, 1948; s. Joe Lloyd and Wanita Irene (Robertson) W.; m. Deborah June Brown, Dec. 27, 1969; children: Krister Colin Brant, Kourtney Cassidy Benay. BA, Abilene Christian U., 1970, MS, 1973; MDiv, Princeton Theol. Sem., 1975; postgrad., Pa. State U., 1980-89. Ordained to ministry Ch. of Christ, 1975. Clin. chaplain Ft. Logan Mental Health Ctr., Denver, 1975-76, Meml. Med. Ctr., Corpus Christi, Tex., 1976-78; sr. pastor Centre Community Ch. of Christ, State Coll., Pa., 1978-87; assoc. dir. pastoral care Geisinger Med. Ctr., Danville, Pa., 1983-87; dir. pastoral care Yuma (Ariz.) Regional Med. Ctr., 1987-95; pastor Mohawk Valley Cmty. Ch., Roll, Ariz., 1995-99; asst. dir. clin. pastoral edn. St. Luke's Episcopal Hosp., Houston, 2000—. Pres. well i b enterprises inc., 1995-2001; author, presenter tng. courses, 1978—. Contbr. articles to profl. jours.; creator interview instrument P.C. Ranking Instrument, 1981. Bd. dirs. Behavioral Health Svcs., Yuma, 1991-96; bd. dirs., treas. Internat. Pastoral Care Network for Social Responsibility, Inc., 1983—. Recipient Shalom award, IPCNSR, 2003. Mem. Assn. Clin. Pastoral Edn. (supr. 1983—), Assn. Profl Chaplains (bd. cert. 1983), Ariz. Chaplain's

Assn. (exec. com. 1988-93, pres. 1989-90), Cola-Gila Kiwanis (pres. 2000). *Making choices about how we live our lives in a responsible and meaningful way is ultimately what life is about and becomes our legacy for generations to come.*

WHITE, LILLIAS, actress; Appeared in Broadway plays Titanic, Cats, Once on This Island, Dreamgirls, Rock 'n' Roll: The First 5000 Years, Barnum, How to Succeed in Business..., The Life (Tony award 1997); (off-Broadway) Waiting for Godot, The Princess and The Black-eyed Pea, Antigone Africanus, Romance in Hard Times (Obie award); (nat. and internat. tour) Ain't Misbehavin', The Wiz, Tintypes, Dreamgirls (Drama-Logue award); (TV series) Sesame Street (Emmy award), Law & Order, NYPD Blue; (film) (voice) Hercules; concert appearance include Carnegie Hall, Lincoln Ctr., The White House. Office: Don Buchwald & Assocs 10 E 44th St Fl 2 New York NY 10017-3654

WHITE, LINDA DIANE, lawyer; b. N.Y.C., Apr. 1, 1952; d. Bernard and Elaine (Simons) Schwartz; m. Thomas M. White, Aug. 16, 1975; 1 child, Alexandra Nicole. AB, U. Pa., 1973; JD, Northwestern U., 1976. Bar: Ill. 1976. Assoc. Walsh, Case, Coale & Brown, Chgo., 1976-77, Greenberger & Kaufmann (merged into Katten, Muchin), Chgo., 1977-82, ptnr., 1982-85, Sonnenschein Nath & Rosenthal LLP, Chgo., 1985—. Mem. trustees coun. Penn Women; mem. Samuel Zell and Robert Lurie Real Estate Ctr., Wharton Sch., U. Pa. Mem.: ABA (mem. real property fin. com., mem. comml. leasing com., mem. real property, probate and trust law sect. 1987—), Practicing Law Inst. (chmn. program negotiating comml. leases 1995—99, mem. real estate law adv. com.), Chgo. Bar Assn., Ill. Bar Assn. Office: Sonnenschein Nath & Rosenthal LLP 8000 Sears Tower 233 S Wacker Dr Ste 8000 Chicago IL 60606-6491 Office Phone: 312-876-8950. Business E-Mail: lwhite@sonnenschein.com.

WHITE, LINDA LEE LOCY, secondary educator; b. Detroit, Sept. 12, 1943; d. John Lorenzo and Vivian Bethia (Greenlee) Locy. BA, Western Mich. U., 1965; MA in Speech Comm., San Francisco State U., 1982. Cert. secondary tchr., Calif. English tchr. Hillside Jr. H.S., Kalamazoo, 1965-67, Sinaloa Jr. H.S., Novato, Calif., 1975-83; mentor tchr. Novato Unified Sch. Dist., 1993-96, program overseer-at-risk student tutorial, 1997—99, English tchr., Journalism tchr., 1968—73, 1983—93. Bd. dirs. Hear Me & Co., San Francisco, 1997-98, Bay Area Women's Resource Ctr., San Francisco, 1977-78; grief counselor Marin Cmty. Counseling, San Rafael, 1991—; active Internat. Women's Conf., Nairobi, Kenya, 1985. Tech. grant Calif. State Dept. of Edn., 1987; learning fellowship Buck Inst. for Edn., 1997. Avocations: hiking, reading, golf. Home: 634 Plum St Novato CA 94945-2561

WHITE, LORAY BETTY, TV talk show host, writer, television producer, vocalist, actress, television director; b. Houston, Nov. 27, 1934; d. Harold White and Joyce Mae (Jenkins) Mills; m. Sammy Davis Jr., 1957 (div. 1958); 1 child, Deborah R. DeHart. Student, UCLA extension, 1948-50, 90-91, Nichiren Shoshu Acad., 1988-92; AA in Bus., Sayer Bus. Sch., 1970; study divsn. mem. dept. L.A., Calif. Study Group of Japan, 1970-86. Editor, entertainment writer L.A. Community New, 1970-81; exec. sec. guest rels. KNBC Prodns., Burbank, Calif., 1969-75; security specialist Xerox X10 Think Tank, L.A., 1975-80; exec. asst. Ralph Powell & Assocs., L.A., 1980-82; pres., owner, producer LBW & Assocs. Pub. Rels., L.A., 1980—; owner, producer, writer, host TV prodn. co. Pub. Pub. Rels., L.A., 1987—. Dir., producer L.B.W. Prodn. "Yesterday, Today, Tomorrow, L.A., 1981—; with CBS news dept./Bogey's Corner, The Vol. Brigade Corps, KCBS News, 1999. Actor: (films) Ten Commandments, 1956; singer: (films) The Jazz Review, 1960—65; headline singer Radio City Music Hall, N.Y.C., 1961, Can Can Cafe Concert in Mex., 1967—75, feature singer Hilton Hotel Mex., featured singer Hotel Maria Isabel, Acapulco, Disneyland, Calif.; singer: TV, 1981—, (Broadway plays) Joy Ride; appearances in the following (endorsements) Budweiser Beer, Old Gold Cigarettes, Salem Cigarettes, TV commls. including Cheer, Puffs Tissue, Coca Cola, Buffern, others, entertainment editor (newspaper) L.A. Community News, 1970—73, writer (column) Balance News, 1980—82. Vol. ARC, 1995, L.B.W. & Assocs., Ltd. Ann. Prodn. of Mother and Daughter of the Yr. Tribute, 1999, L.B.W. & Assocs., United Peace and Cultural Exch. Dinner and Awards Show, 1999; mem. Habitat for Humanity Internat, Nat. Com. Preserve Soc. Sec. and Medicare, 1998-99, Nat. Black Network Assn., AARP, So. Calif. Com. Sr. Citizens, re-elect Scott Wildmen Rep. campaign; mem. resident adv. bd. Burbank Housing Authority, HUD, 2002—; mem. Com. to Reelect Ted McConkey to Burbank City Coun., 1999; bd. dirs. Chamblee Found. of Calif., 1998-; apptd. area coord. San Fernando Valley area; exec. prodr. The Fifth L.B.W. and Assocs. Internat. Ann. Achievement Awards Show, 1999. The Sixth L.B.W. and Assocs. Internat. Ann. Achievement Awards Show, 2000. Recipient Cert. of Honor, ARC, 1984, Internat. Orgn. Soka Gakkai Internat. of Japan, Cmty. Vols. of Am. award, 1994, Mother and Daughter of Yr. Tribune, 2000-01, 6th Internat. Achievement award L.B.W. and Assoc.; named Performer of Yr. Cardella Demillo, 1976-77. Mem. ARC (planning, mktg., prodn. event com. 1995), UCLA Alumni Assn., Lupus Found. Am. (So. Calif. chpt.), Nat. Fedn. Blind, Myohoji-Hokkeko Internat.as a mem. of the USA, 2002. Attended Tozon Internat. with 56 countries, 300,000 mem. participated in "The 750th Anniv. of Nichiren Shoshu Head Temple Taisekiji" in Japan (area coord. 2004), Libr. of Congress Assoc. (charter). Buddhist. Avocations: singing, acting, tv writing and producing. Office Phone: 818-955-7728. Office Fax: 818-955-7728. Personal E-mail: lbwbootsie@aol.com. *Accepting challenges in life is a choice. The choice is always yours. I've chosen never to give up-to always give my best. To constantly keep a growing and open mind. To remember to strengthen and reinforce the quality of my integrity no matter what. Be a winner to yourself.*

WHITE, MARGUERITE, writer; b. Norwich, Conn., Aug. 6, 1937; d. Raymond Tenney and Louise Bradford; children: Amy Elizabeth, Richard Allan. Student, Memphis Coll. Art, 1965. Author: Over the Rainbow, 2002, Inspirational Poems to Live By, 2001, (poetry) The Power of God's Word, 2003; composer: (CD) Songs for Praise and Worship, A Few Minutes with Him, Set Me Free, (songs) Just You and Me Lord, The Whisper of Your Voice, Our Walk with God, Draw Me Closer to You Lord, America, In God We Trust, A Proud American, The Peaceful Place. Recipient Editor's Choice award, Internat. Libr. Poetry, 2002, 2000, 2001. Avocations: sewing, knitting, drawing, painting, writing. Home: 2139 Scenic Cove Southaven MS 38671

WHITE, MARILYN DOMAS, information science educator; b. Franklin, La., Aug. 16, 1940; d. George Julian and Norma Domas; m. Roger Stuart White, Aug. 31, 1968; 1 child, Joshua Stuart. BA, Our Lady of the Lake Coll., San Antonio, 1962; MS, U. Wis., 1963; PhD, U. Ill., 1971. Dir. Commerce Libr. U. Wis., Madison, 1963-65; head Social Sci./Bus. Libr. So. Ill. U., Edwardsville, 1965-67; cons. So. Ill. U./U.S. AID Adv. Team, South Vietnam, 1967; asst. prof. SUNY, Buffalo, 1972-74; lectr., vis. asst. prof. U. Md., College Park, 1976-77, asst. prof. info sci., 1977-82, assoc. prof. info. sci., 1982—. Cons. USIA, Washington and abroad, 1977-83, Inst. for Def. Analyses, Bowie, Md.,Supercomputing Rsch. Ctr., 1990-91, Am. Health Care Assn., Washington, 1990-92, Am. Coun. on Edn., 1995. Contbr. articles to Libr. Quar., Libr. & Info. Sci. Rsch., to Jour. Documentation, Jour. Am. Soc. for Info. Sci., others; editor (rev. editor): (Jours.) Libr.& Info. Sci. Rsch. James Lyman Whitney grantee ALA, 1983, Spl. Libr. Assn. rsch. grantee, 1993-94, Coun. Libr. Resources grantee, 1995-96, Info. Sci. Abstracts grantee, 1997-98. Mem. Am. Soc. for Info. Sci., Spl. Libr. Assn. Office: U Md Coll Info Studies Hornbake 4117F South Wing College Park MD 20742-0001 E-mail: whitemd@umd.edu.

WHITE, MARTHA VETTER, allergy and immunology physician, researcher; b. Richmond, Va., Oct. 23, 1951; d. Robert Joseph and Miriam Ernestine (Thomas) Vetter; m. Frederick Joseph Kozub, Oct. 11, 1975 (div. June 1982); m. John Irving White, Feb. 18, 1984; children: Josh, Christie. Student, Vanderbilt U., Nashville, 1969-71; BA, U. Richmond, 1973; MD, Va. Commonwealth U., Richmond, 1978. Cert. m. Bd. Pediatrics, Am. Bd. Allergy and Immunology. Pediatric intern and resident Va. Commonwealth U., Richmond, 1978-81; locum tenens Pub. Health, Richmond, Va., 1981-82; fellow Allergy and Immunology U. Southern Calif., L.A., 1983-84, Georgetown U., 1983-84; sr. staff fellow Food and Drug Adminstrn., Bethesda, Md., 1984-85; NSRA fellow Nat. Inst. Allergy and Infectious Diseases, Bethesda, Md., 1985-88; sr. staff fellow, 1988-93; rsch. dir. Inst. for Asthma and Allergy, Wheaton, Md., 1993—. Cons. Sandoz Pharms., Marion Merrell Dow, Glaxo, Boehringer Ingleheim, Ciba-Geigy, Miles Genentech; rschr. Glaxo, Abbott, Pfizer, Marion Merrell Dow, Miles, Rhône Poulenc Rhoen, Sanofi, Adams, Astra, Merck, Neurbiol. Techs., 3M, Zeneca, Wyeth, Smith-Kline Beecham; bd. dirs. Allery & Asthma Network/Mothers of Asthmatics, 1987—; med. editor MA Report, 1986—; assoc. editor Allergy, Asthma and Immunology Guide, 1989-90. Contbr. numerous scientific papers, abstracts, chpts. and reviews in field. Recipient Norwich Eaton Rsch. award, 1987; Merrell Dow scholar in allergy, 1989; Geigy fellow, 1984. Mem.: Soc. Prin. Investigators (pres. 2002—03), Am. Thoracic Soc., Am. Coll. Allergy and Immunology, Adm. Acad. Allergy and Immunology, Am. Acad. Pediat., Am. Assn. Immunologists, Gamma Sigma Epsilon, Psi Chi, Beta Beta Beta. Office: Inst Asthma and Allergy 11160 Viers Mill Rd # 414 Wheaton MD 20902

WHITE, MARTIN ARTHUR, utilities company executive; b. Whitehall, Mont., Aug. 3, 1941; s. Stewart E. and Sylvia J. (Olson) W.; m. Kathy Francis Harrington, Aug. 1965 (div. Nov. 1969); m. Sheila Mary McMahon, Aug. 24, 1973; children: Matthew Thomas, Jonathan Lewis. BS in Math. and Econs., Mont. State U., 1966; AMP, Harvard U., 1980. Acctg. clk. Mont. Power Co., Butte, 1966-67; acct. Western Energy Co., Butte, Mont., 1967-72, asst. gen. mgr., 1972-74; project mgr. Colstrip, Mont., 1974-1979; v.p., gen. mgr. Butte, 1979-83; pres., chief exec. officer Entech, Inc. (formerly Western Energy Co.), Butte, 1983—; also bd. dirs. Chmn. bd. dirs. Northwestern Resources Co., MSE, Inc., Mont. State U. Endowment and Alumni Found.; bd. dirs. Mont. Bank, Butte, EnTech, Inc., Sunlight Devel., Inc., MERDI, Inc. Mem. exec. com. Mont. Internat. Trade Commn. Served with U.S. Army, 1966-70. Mem. Nat. Coal Council (exec. com. mem., adv. panel to dept. of energy), U.S. High Altitude Speed Skating Found, Inc. (pres.), Mont. Amateur Speed Skating Assn. (v.p.). Lodges: Elks. Lutheran.

WHITE, MARTIN CHRISTOPHER, academic administrator; b. Anderson, S.C., Oct. 16, 1943; s. Jesse Martin and Christine Freida (Powell) W.; m. Linda Ann Fleming, July 31, 1965; children: Martin Lynn, Andrew Christopher. AB, Mercer U., 1965; MDiv, So. Bapt. Theol. Sem., 1968; PhD, Emory U., 1972. Prof. Elon Coll. (N.C.), 1972-76, dean acad. affairs, 1976-82, v.p. for acad. and student affairs, 1982-86; pres. Gardner-Webb U., Boiling Springs, N.C., 1986—. Cons. So. Assn. Colls. and Schs., Atlanta, 1982—. Contbr. articles in field. Bd. dirs. United Way, Shelby, N.C., 1987. Woodrow Wilson fellow, 1971. Mem. Soc. Bibl. Lit., Nat. Assn. Bapt. Profs. of Religion, N.C. Ind. Coll. Assn., Alpha Chi, Omicron Delta Kappa. Lodges: Rotary (bd. dirs. Burlington, N.C. chpt. 1986). Democrat. Baptist. Avocations: golf, tennis, music, travel. Office: Gardner-Webb U Campus Mail Dept Boiling Springs NC 28017 Home: 100 Jones Drive Murfreesboro NC 27855-1800

WHITE, MARY JO, state legislator, lawyer; b. Chgo., Dec. 27, 1941; d. Joseph and Patricia White; m. H. William White, Mar. 6, 1966; children: H. William III, David, Alison. BA, Quincy U., 1963; JD, U. Pitts. Mem. Pa. Senate, Dist. 21, Harrisburg, 1996—; vice chmn. comms. and tech. com. Pa. Senate, Harrisburg, mem. aging and youth com., mem. appropriations com., mem. cmty. and econ. devel. com., mem. intergovtl. affairs com., mem. jud. com., mem. pub. health and welfare com.; former defender Venango County Pub. Defender's Office, 1974-76; past v.p. environ. govtl. affairs Quaker State Corp. Past chmn. Am. Petroleum Inst.'s Used Oil Workshop Gruop; bd. dirs. N.W. Regional Planning and Devel. Corp., Pa. Environ. Coun.; mem. Venango County Assn. for the Blind, Venango Cmty. Found.; chair nursing adv. com. Clarion U.; mem. Barrow Civic Theatre Found., Cmty Health Action Team. Office: Pa State Senate Senate Box 203021 168 Capitol Bldg Harrisburg PA 17120-3021 also: 248 New Castle Rd Butler PA 16001-2561

WHITE, MATTHEW C. advertising executive; m. Maria White; children: Lauren, Ashley. Pres. E. James White Comms., Herndon, Va. Mem. Am. Assn. of Advt. Agencies (bd. govs.), Am. Soc. of Travel Agts. (allied mktg. com.), Am. Passenger Rail Coalition (bd. dirs.), Travel Industry of Am., Assn. of Travel Mktg. Execs. Office: E James White Comms Ste 150 13665 Dulles Technology Dr Herndon VA 20171

WHITE, MEG (MEGAN MARTHA WHITE), musician, vocalist; b. Grosse Pointe, Mich., 1974; m. John Gillis, 1996 (div. 2000). Drummer, vocalist The White Stripes, 1997—; toured with Pavement and Sleater-Kinney, 1999, 2000. Performer: (albums) The White Stripes, 1999, De Stijl, 2000, White Blood Cells, 2001, Maximum, 2002, Elephant, 2003. Mailing: Monotone Inc 8932 Keith Ave Los Angeles CA 90069

WHITE, MICHAEL DENNIS, food manufacturing company executive; b. Norwood, Mass., Jan. 11, 1952; s. Thomas Michael and Sally (Davenport) W.; m. Susan Lee Burns, June 30, 1972; children: Larissa, Paul, Jennifer. BA, Boston Coll., Newton, Mass., 1974; cert. of proficiency, Leningrad (USSR) State U., 1974; MA in Internat. Rels., Johns Hopkins U., 1976. CPA, Mass. Cons. Arthur Andersen & Co., Mgmt. Info. Cons. Div., Washington, Boston, 1976-80, mgr., 1980-81; cons. Bain & Co., Boston, 1981-84, mgr., 1984-86; v.p. planning, devel. Avon Products, N.Y.C., 1986-87, v.p. retail devel., 1987-88; sr. v.p., gen. mgr. internat. Parfums Stern Inc. (subs. Avon Products), N.Y.C., 1988-90; v.p. planning Frito-Lay Inc., Plano, Tex., 1990—91, sr. v.p. fin., CFO; exec. v.p., CFO PepsiCo, Intern. Snack div.; sr. v.p., CFO Pepsi-Cola Co., 1996—98, PepsiCo Inc., 1998—2000; pres., CEO Frito-Lay, Europe/Africa/Middle East division, 2000—03; chmn., CEO PepsiCo International, 2003—. Active Tri-State United Way, N.Y.C.; v.p. Westport (Conn.)-Weston United Way, 1988-90. Office: PepsiCo International 700 Anderson Hill Rd Purchase NY 10577

WHITE, MICHAEL JAMES, healthcare facilities administrator; b. Malone, N.Y., May 19, 1950; s. Lyle J. and Patricia M. (Finnegan) W. AAS in Nursing, SUNY, Canton, 1973; BSN, Case Western Res. U., 1978; MS in Healthcare Mgmt., LaSalle U., 1988; PhD, Kennedy-Western U., 1996. Cert. case mgr. Adminstrv. supr. The Inst. for Rehab. & Rsch., Houston, 1978-81; regional dir. NSI Svcs., Inc., Houston, 1981-85; dir. home care Tulane U. Med. Ctr., New Orleans, 1985-88; supr. case mgmt. Sanus/N.Y. Life Health Plan, Houston, 1988-91; lectr. 3d party reimbursement and medicare Sch. of Nursing U. Tex. Health Sci. Ctr., 1988-96; dir. splty. svcs. Vis. Nurse Assn., Houston, 1992; mng. ptnr. Sills, White and Assocs., managed care cons., Houston, 1988-96; dir. quality and resource mgmt. Bayshore Med. Ctr., Pasadena, Tex., 1994-96; group dir. clin. operations Columbia/HCA Healthcare Corp., Nashville, 1996-98; v.p. clin. ops. LifePoint Hosps., Inc., Nashville, 1998—. Chmn. nurses campaign United Way, Houston; adv. bd. ARC, Houston. Mem. ANA (rep. nat. ho. of dels.), Tex. Nurses Assn. (numerous local offices including pres., bd. dirs., state level rep. ho. of dels., coms.), Assn. Rehab. Nurses (local and state bd. dirs., state sec.-treas.), Case Mgmt. Soc. Am. (pres. local chpt., sec.-treas. state chpt.), Sigma Theta Tau. Home: 209 Rising Sun Ln Old Hickory TN 37138 Office: LifePoint Hosps Inc 103 Powell Ct Ste 200 Brentwood TN 37027

WHITE, MICHAEL R. secondary school educator, consultant; b. Sellersville, Pa., Mar. 3, 1953; s. Robert G. White and F. June Cressman; m. Lucille M. Stracka, July 12, 1980; children: Kristin A., Gary S. BS, Millersville U., 1975; MEd, Lehigh U., 1981. Cert. secondary edn. tchr. Pa. Tchr. Pennridge Sch. Dist., Perkasie, Pa., 1978—. Cons. Coll. Bd., Phila., 1993—. Named to Ponnridge Wall of Fame; recipient Siemens award for Advanced Placement, Siemens Corp., 2002—03, Pa. Student Coun. Advisor of the Yr., 2004, Advisor of Yr., Nat. Assn. Studen Couns., 2004. Mem.: Advanced Placement Com. Calculus, NCTM. Avocations: student council, sports, travel. Home: 112 Dublin Way Perkasie PA 18944-2301 Office: Pennridge HS 1400 North Fifth St Perkasie PA 18944

WHITE, MICHAEL REED, former mayor; b. Cleve., Aug. 13, 1951; s. Robert and Audrey (Silver) W. BA, Ohio State U., 1973, MPA, 1974. Spl. asst. Columbus (Ohio) Mayor's Office, 1974-76; adminstrv. asst. Cleve. City Coun., 1976-77; sales mgr. Burks Electric Co., Cleve., 1978-84; state senator Ohio Senate, Columbus, 1984-89; mayor Cleve., 1990—2001. Minority whip Ohio Senate Dems., 1987-89. City councilman City of Cleve., 1978-84; bd. dirs. Glenville Devel. Corp., Cleve., 1978—, Glenville Festival Found., Cleve., 1978—, United Black Fund, Cleve., 1986, Greater Cleve. Dome Corp., 1986; trustee U.S. Conf. Democratic Mayors. Named one of Outstanding Young Men Am., 1985, Outstanding Svc. award Cleve. chpt. Nat. Assn. Black Vets., 1985, Cmty. Svcs. award East Side Jaycees, Pres.'s award, 1993, named Black Profl. of Yr., 1993, Humanitarian award, 1994, Pub Svc. award Am. Pub. Power Assn., 1995. Mem. Nat. Conference Dem. Mayors. Democrat. Home: 1057 East Blvd Cleveland OH 44108-2972 Office: Office of Mayor City Hall 601 Lakeside Ave Cleveland OH 44114-1015

WHITE, MICHELLE JO, economics professor; b. Washington, 1945; d. Harry L. and Irene Rich; m. Roger Hall Gordon, July 25, 1982. AB, Harvard U., 1967; MSc in Econs., London Sch. Econs., 1968; PhD, Princeton U., 1973. Asst. prof. U. Pa., Phila., 1973-78; from assoc. prof. to prof. NYU, N.Y.C., 1978-83; prof. econs. U. Mich., Ann Arbor, 1984—2001, dir. PhD program in econs., 1992—94, 1998—99; prof. econs. U. Calif., San Diego, 2000—. Vis. asst. prof. Yale U., New Haven, 1978; vis. prof. People's U., Beijing, 1986, U. Warsaw, 1990, U. Wis., Madison, 1991, U. Munich, Germany, 1992, 2002, Tilburg U., The Netherlands, 1993, 95, U. Chgo., 1993, Copenhagen Bus. Sch., 1995, Uppsala U., Sweden, 1997, Hebrew U., Israel, 1997, U. Calif. Law Sch. Berkeley, 1999, Harvard Law Sch., 2004; rsch. assoc. Nat. Bur. Econ. Rsch., 2002—; cons. Pension Benefit Guaranty Corp., Washington, 1987, World Bank, 1999; chmn. adv. com. dept. econs. Princeton U., 1988-90. Editor: The Non-profit Sector in a Three Sector Economy, 1981, Financial Distress and Bankruptcy: Economic Issues, 1997; contbr. numerous articles to profl. jours. Bd. dirs. Com. on Status of Women in Econs. Profession, 1984-86. Resources for Future fellow, 1972-73; grantee NSF, 1979, 82, 88, 91, 93, 96, 2002, Sloan Found., 1984, Fund for Rsch. in Dispute Resolution, 1989; Fulbright scholar, Poland, 1990. Mem. Am. Econ. Assn., Am. Law and Econ. Assn. (bd. dirs. 1991-92, 2001-04, chair nominating com. 2002), Am. Real Estate and Urban Econs. Assn. (bd. dirs. 1992-95), Social Scis. Rsch. Coun. (bd. dirs. 1994-2000, treas. 1996-2000), Midwest Econs. Assn. (1st v.p. 1996-97). Office: U California-San Diego Dept Economics 9500 Gilman Dr La Jolla CA 92093-0508

WHITE, MILES D. pharmaceutical company executive; b. Minneapolis, MN; B in Mech. Engring., MBA, Stanford U. Mgmt. cons. McKinsey & Co.; with Abbott Labs., 1984—, v.p. diagnostic sys. and ops., 1993-94, sr. v.p. diagnostic ops., 1994-98, exec. v.p., dir., 1998-99, CEO, chmn., 1999—. Bd. trustee Field Mus., Chicago, Northwestern U., Joffrey Ballet, Chicago, Culver Ednl. Found.; dep. chmn. Fed. Reserve Bank of Chgo.; mem. Stanford Grad. Sch. of Bus. Adv. Coun., Stanford Adv. Coun. on Interdisciplinary Biosciences. Mem.: Econ. Club of Chgo., Executives' Club of Chgo. (chmn.). Office: Abbott Labs 100 Abbott Park Rd Abbott Park IL 60064-6400

WHITE, MORRIS FRANCIS, biochemistry educator; b. Detroit, Mar. 25, 1955; BS in Chemistry, U. Mich., 1977, MS in Biochemistry, 1979, PhD, 1981. Postdoctoral scholar dept. biol. chemistry U. Mich., Ann Arbor, 1981-82; rsch. fellow in medicine rsch. divsn. Harvard Med. Sch., Boston, 1982-85, instr. in medicine, 1985-87, asst. prof. biochemistry dept. medicine, 1987-92, assoc. prof. biol. chemistry, 1992—; assoc. investigator Howard Hugher Med. Inst., Boston. Investigator rsch. divsn. Joslin Diabetes Ctr., Boston, 1985—; mem. grant rev. study sects. Juvenile Diabetes Found., 1993—, Am. Diabetes Assn., 1992—, NIH, 1994; speaker in field. Mem. editl. bd. Jour. Biol. Chemistry, 1988-93, Diabetes, 1992—, Molecular Endocrinology, 1994—; contbr. articles to profl. jours. Pew scholar in biomed. scis. Pew Charitable Trusts Phila., 1987-91; recipient Individual Nat. Rsch. Svc. award NIH, 1983-85; Angell scholar U. Mich., 1977. Mem. Am. Diabetes Assn. (Balodimos award 1985-86), Am. Soc. for Biochemistry and Molecular Biology, Endocrine Soc., Juvenile Diabetes Found. Internat. Achievements include research in insulin receptor biochemistry, signal transmission by protein tyrosine kinases, src homology-2 domain proteins, phospatidylinositol 3'-kinase in signal transmission, and amino acid and glucose transport. Office: Howard Hughs Med Inst Joslin Diabetes Ctr 1 Joslin Pl Rm 620 Boston MA 02215-5306 E-mail: Morris.White@joslin.harvard.edu.

WHITE, MORRIS FRED, JR., physicist; b. Richmond, Va., June 26, 1957; s. Morris Fred Sr. and Alma (Liggins) W.; m. Gloria Hicks; 1 child, Samantha Sevynne. BS, Hampton U., 1980; MS, Va. State U., Petersburg, 2001. Physicist E.I. duPont, Aiken, S.C., 1981-85, Philip Morris U.S.A., Richmond, 1985—. Contbr. articles to profl. jours. Mem. Soc. Physics Students. Republican. Presbyterian. Achievements include 3 patents for novel cigarette filters. Office: Philip Morris USA PO Box 26583 Richmond VA 23261-6583 E-mail: morris.f.white@pmusa.com.

WHITE, MORTON GABRIEL, philosopher, historian; b. N.Y.C., Apr. 29, 1917; s. Robert and Esther (Levine) Weisberger; m. Lucia Perry, Aug. 29, 1940 (dec.); children: Nicholas Perry, Stephen Daniel; m. Helen Starobin, June 30, 1997. BS, CCNY, 1936; L.H.D., CUNY, 1975; A.M., Columbia U., 1938, PhD, 1942. Instr. philosophy Columbia U., 1942—46; instr. physics CCNY, 1942—43; asst. prof. philosophy U. Pa., 1946—48, Harvard U., 1948—50, assoc. prof., 1950—53, prof., 1953—70, chmn. dept., 1954—57, acting chmn. dept., 1967—69; prof. Inst. Advanced Study, 1970—87; prof. emeritus, 1987—. Guggenheim research fellow, 1950-51; vis. prof. Tokyo U., 1952, 60, 66, U. Oslo, 1977-78; Neesima lectr. Doshisha U., Kyoto, 1985, CUNY, 1968-69, Rutgers U., 1987-88, 88-89 Keio U., Tokyo, 2002-03; mem. Inst. Advanced Study, 1953-54, 62-63, 67-68, 68-69. Author: The Origin of Dewey's Instrumentalism, 1943, Social Thought in America, 1949, The Age of Analysis, 1955, Toward Reunion in Philosophy, 1956, Religion, Politics, and the Higher Learning, 1959, (with Lucia White) The Intellectual Versus the City, 1962; Editor: (with Arthur M. Schlesinger, Jr.) Paths of American Thought, 1963, Foundations of Historical Knowledge, 1965, Science and Sentiment in America, 1972, Documents in the History of American Philosophy, 1972, Pragmatism and the American Mind, 1973, The Philosophy of the American Revolution, 1978, What Is and What Ought to Be Done, 1981, (with Lucia White) Journeys to the Japanese, 1952-79, 1986, Philosophy, The Federalist and the Constitution, 1987, The Question of Free Will, 1993, A Philosopher's Story, 1999, A Philosophy of Culture, 2002. Fellow Center Advanced Study Behavioral Scis., 1959-60; fellow Am. Council Learned Socs., 1962-63 Mem. Am. Acad. Arts and Scis., Am. Antiquarian Soc., Am. Philos. Soc. Office: Inst for Advanced Study Princeton NJ 08540

WHITE, NANCY ELIZABETH, psychologist, artist; b. San Angelo, Tex., Feb. 8, 1935; d. John William and Vivian Olive (Harrison) Whitten; m. Kirkwood Coulter Myers, Nov. 25, 1954 (dec.); children: Kirkwood Coulter, Nancy Elizabeth; m. Robert Arthur White, Apr. 25, 1959 (dec. Oct. 1977); children: Mark Hadley, John Bradford. BFA, U. Houston, 1976, MA, 1978; PhD in Clin. Psychology, Union Inst., Cin., 1985. Diplomate Am. Bd. Sexology (clin. supr.), Nat. Registry Neurofeedback Providers; lic. marriage and family therapist, chem. dependency therapist; cert. neurotherapist; diplomate quantitative EEG. Profl. artist, Houston, 1970-77; art therapist Galveston County Hosp., Texas City, 1976-77; psychotherapist Houston, 1978—. Nat. seminar leader Practical Application Intimate Relationship Skills, Houston, 1989—; owner, dir. The Meta Ctr., Houston, 1989-99; pres. The Tex. Meta Corp., 1980-99; owner, dir. The Enhancement Inst., 2000—; mem. field faculty Norwich U.; bd. adv. Practical Application Intimate Relationship Skills Found. Fay Sch., The Lumatron Corp., The Pairs Found., The Quantitative EEG Cert. Bd. One-woman shows include Erdon Gallery, Houston, 1971-72, Houston Bar Ctr., 1971; group shows include: Alfred Lee Gallery, Houston, 1975, Sol Del Rio Gallery, San Antonio, 1976; cons. editor Jour. Neurotherapy; contbr. articles to profl. jours., chpts. to books. Recipient merit award S.W. Watercolor Soc., 1976; 1st prize Jewish Cmty. Ctr., 1976; citation Tex. Fine Arts, 1977; merit award Watercolor Art Soc. Houston, 1977. Fellow Am. Acad. Clin. Sexologists, Am. Bd. Sexology; mem. Am. Assn. Marriage & Family Therapy (clin.), Am. Assn. Sex Educators, Counselors & Therapists (cert.), Internat. Acad. Profl. Counseling and Psychotherapy, APA (clin.), Acad. Cert. Neurotherapists (cert.), Internat. Soc. Neuronal Regulation (sec. 1994-96), advanced addiction counselor, mem. neurotherapy and biofeedback cert. bd., peak performance exec., mem. adv. bd., Watercolor Art Soc.

Houston, Profit Seekers Investment Club (treas. 1965-70). Home: 9023 Briar Forest Dr Houston TX 77024-7220 Office Phone: 713-961-5243. Business E-Mail: nancywhite@enhancementinstitute.com.

WHITE, NICHOLAS L. legal educator; b. 1925; AB, Ohio Wesleyan U., 1950; JD, U. Cin., 1956. Bar: Ohio 1956, Ind. 1971, Tenn. 1978. Assoc. Taft, Stettinius & Hollister, Cin., 1956-65, ptnr., 1965-70; asst. dean adminstrn. Ind. U., Bloomington, 1970-73, prof. law, 1970-77, assoc. dean, 1974-77; dean, prof. law Memphis State U., 1977-84; prof. law U. Memphis, 1985—. Vis. prof. McGeorge Sch. of Law, Sacramento, Calif., 1984-85; cons. EPA Water Planning Divsn., 1974-77, Nat. Commn. Water Quality, 1975. Served with USMC, 1943-46. Mem. Phi Beta Kappa, Order of Coif, Omicron Delta Kappa. Office: U Memphis School of Law Memphis TN 38152 E-mail: nlwhite@memphis.edu.

WHITE, NORA LIZABETH, language educator; d. Ralph Senter and Carol L. Hay; m. Donald S. McSheehy; children: Daniel Stuart McSheehy, Luke Adam. BA, Urbana (Ohio) U., 1982; MA, Ohio State U., 1989, PhD, 1992. Cert. tchr. State Of Ohio Dept. of Edn., 1989. Postdoctoral rsch. fellow U. of Western Sydney, Penrith, Australia, 1997—99; assoc. prof. U. of Alaska, Fairbanks, 1992—2000, Tex. Woman's U., Denton, Tex., 2000—. Coord. grad. lang. and literacy edn. program U. of Alaska, Fairbanks, 1999—2000, coord. elem. edn. program, 1992—95, coord. Russian far east student exch. program, 1992—94. Contbr. articles to profl. jours. Field coun. rep. Nat. Reading Conf., Alaska, 1992—99, internat. com. mem., 2001—03. Recipient Vol. award, Newton Rayzor Elem. Sch., 2002, Outstanding Vol. award, Denton Ind. Sch. Dist., Adopt a Sch. Program, 2002, 2004; grantee, Alaska Schools Rsch. Project, 1995, 1992, Lang. Australia, 1999. Mem.: Denton Reading Coun., Australian Literacy Educator's Assn., Am. Anthrop. Assn., Nat. Coun. of Teachers of English, Am. Ednl. Rsch. Assn., Internat. Reading Assn., Nat. Reading Conf., Family, Sch., Cmty. Partnership Spl. Interest Group (newsletter editor 2002—), Phi Delta Kappa. Avocations: travel, reading, writing, swimming. Office: Texas Woman's U PO Box 425769 Denton TX 76204-5769 Home: 5201 W Oak Shores Dr Crossroads TX 76227 E-mail: nwhite@mail.twu.edu.

WHITE, NORVAL CRAWFORD, architect; b. NYC, June 12, 1926; s. William Crawford and Caroline Ruth (Taylor) W.; m. Joyce Leslie Lee, May 24, 1958 (div.); children: William Crawford, Thomas Taylor, Gordon Crawford, Alistair David; m. Camilla Cecilia Crowe, June 7, 1992. BS, Mass. Inst. Tech., 1949; student, Sch. Fine Arts, Fontainbleau, 1954; M.F.A., Princeton, 1955. Designer, assoc. Lathrop Douglass (Architect), 1955-59; prin. Norval C. White (Architect), N.Y.C., 1959-62, 66-67; partner Rowan & White (Architects), N.Y.C., 1962-66, Gruzen & Partners, N.Y.C., 1967-70; prin. Norval C. White & Assos., N.Y.C., 1970-74; ptnr. Levien, Deliso & White, 1974-80, Levien Deliso White Songer, 1980-86. Asst. prof. architecture Cooper Union, 1961-67; prof. architecture City Coll., CUNY, 1970-95, prof. emeritus, 1995—, chmn. dept. 1970-77. Author (with E. Willensky): AIA Guide to New York City, 1968, AIA Guide to New York City, 4th edit., 2000; author: The Architecture Book, 1976, New York: A Physical HIstory, 1987, The Guide to the Architecture of Paris, 1991; prin. works include Seiden House, Tenafly, N.J., 1960, Essex Terrace (housing), Bklyn., 1970, N.Y.C. Police Hdqrs., 1973, Brookhaven Parks (L.I.) Sanitary Landfill, 1971, Forsgate Indsl. Park, South Brunswick, N.J., 1978—86, Del Vista Condominiums, Miami, 1981, 61 Christopher Street, Greenwich Village, 1987, White House, Salisbury, Conn., 1998. Trustee Bklyn. Inst. Arts and Scis., 1973-82, Bklyn. Pub. Libr., 1993-96; gov. Bklyn. Mus., 1973-82, adv. com., 1982—; mem. N.Y.C. Art Commn., 1975-86, sec., 1975-77, v.p., 1978-80. Served with USNR, 1944-46. Fellow AIA; mem. Soc. Archtl. Historians, N.Y. State Assn. Architects. Clubs: Century Assn. (N.Y.C.). Democrat. Home and Office: Village 32310 Roques France E-mail: norval.white@wanadoo.fr.

WHITE, OWEN, research scientist; BS in Biotechnology, U. Mass., 1985; PhD in Molecular Biology, N.Mex. State U., 1992. Postdoctoral fellow genome informatics dept. Inst. for Genomic Rsch., Rockville, Md., 1992—94, collaborative investigator dept. bioinformatics, 1994—97, asst. investigator dept. bioinformatics, 1997—98, dep. dir., assoc. investigator bioinformatics, 1998—2000, dir. bioinformatics, assoc. investigator, 2000—. Contbr. articles to profl. jours. Office: Inst for Genomic Rsch 9712 Medical Center Dr Rockville MD 20850

WHITE, PAMELA JANICE, lawyer; b. Elizabeth, NJ, July 13, 1952; d. Emmet Talmadge and June (Howlett) W. BA, Mary Washington Coll., 1974; JD, Washington and Lee U., 1977. Bar: Md. 1977, U.S. Dist. Ct. Md. 1978, D.C. 1979, U.S. Dist. Ct. D.C. 1979, U.S. Ct. Appeals (4th cir.) 1979, U.S. Ct. Appeals (D.C. cir.) 1981, U.S. Ct. Claims 1981, U.S. Ct. Appeals (2d cir.) 1983, N.Y. 1983, U.S. Dist. Ct. (so. dist.) N.Y. 1983, U.S. Ct. Appeals (9th cir.) 1988, U.S. Supreme Ct. 1981. Assoc. Ober, Grimes & Shriver, Balt., 1977-84; prin. Ober, Kaler, Grimes & Shriver, Balt., 1985—. Chair Employment Group, 1994—; mem. Md. Bd. Law Examiners, 1986-94, Md. Judiciary Pub. Trust and Confidence Com., 2001-04; select com. on Gender Equality, 1989-2000, chair, 1997-99, spl. com. on ethics 2002-04; mem. fed. dist. ct. adv. group Civil Justice Reform Act, 1990; exec. com. Md. Inst. for Continuing Profl. Edn. Lawyers, 2000-02; adv. bd. Md. Mediation and Conflict Resolution Ctr., 2001-02; equal justice coun. Legal Aid Bur., 2000—. Note and comment editor Washington and Lee Law Rev. 1976-77, Washington and Lee Law Council 1983-87, pres. 1991-92. Mem. Fed. Ct. Bicentennial Com., 1988-90; vol. Profl. Gov.'s Drug-Free Workplace Initiative, 1990-93; bd. trustees Washington and Lee U., 1995-2004. Named Disting. Alumna, Washington and Lee U., 1994, Disting. Alumna, Mary Washington Coll., 2001; named among Md. Top 100 Women, 2000, 04. Fellow Am. Bar Found., Md. Bar Found. (award for excellence 1996, bd. dirs. 2000-02); mem. ABA (chair tort and ins. practice employer/employee rels. com. 1999-2000, del. 2000-02), Am. Arbitration Assn. (arbitrator, mediator employment and comml., large complex case panels), Balt. Bar Found. (bd. dirs. 2003—), Fed. Bar Assn., Md. State Bar Assn. (coun. legal edn. sect. 1987-96, chmn. 1992-93, labor sect. coun. 1992-96, professionalism com. 1991—, chmn. 1994-97, bd. govs. 1993-95, 1998-2003, exec. com. 1994-95, 99-2001, pres. 2001-02, immediate past pres. 2002-03, task force on professionalism chair 1996-97), D.C. Bar Assn., Balt. City Bar Assn. (exec. coun. 1995-96, 1997-98), Women's Bar Assn. Md. (treas. 1986-87, v.p. 1987-88, pres.-elect 1988-89, pres. 1989-90, bd. dirs. 1984-86, Rita C. Davidson award 2000), Md. Assn. Def. Counsel, Pro Bono Resource Ctr. (exec. com. 2000-02, bd. trustees 2002-03, Leaders of Equal Justice award 2002), Order of Coif, Phi Beta Kappa (hon. alumni). Presbyterian. Avocation: baseball. Office: Ober Kaler Grimes & Shriver 120 E Baltimore St Ste 800 Baltimore MD 21202-1643 Office Phone: 410-347-7323. E-mail: pjwhite@ober.com.

WHITE, PATRICIA DENISE, dean; b. Syracuse, N.Y., July 8, 1949; d. Theodore C. and Kathleen (Cowles) Denise; m. Nicholas P. White, Feb. 20, 1971 (div. 1997); children: Olivia Lawrence, Alexander Cowles. BA, U. Mich., 1971, MA, JD, 1974. Bar: D.C. 1975, Mich. 1988, Utah 1995. Assoc. Steptoe & Johnson, Washington, 1975-76; vis. asst. prof. Coll. of Law U. Toledo, 1976-77; assoc. Caplin & Drysdale, Washington, 1977-79; asst. prof. Law Ctr. Georgetown U., 1979-84, assoc. prof. Law Ctr., 1985-88; vis. prof. Law Sch. U. Mich., Ann Arbor, 1988-94; prof. U. Utah, Salt Lake City, 1994-98; counsel Parsons, Behle and Latimer, Salt Lake City, 1995—98; dean, prof. Ariz. State U. Coll. Law, 1999—. Counsel Bodman, Longley and Dahling, Detroit, Ann Arbor, 1990-95. Contbr. articles to profl. jours. Office: Ariz State U Coll Law McAllister & Orange Sts PO Box 877906 Tempe AZ 85287-7906 Office Phone: 480-965-6188.

WHITE, RAE ALISON, artist, writer; b. Jamestown, NY, Oct. 9, 1947; d. Kermit John White and Gertrude "Trudy" Mary Claire Watkins. BFA, State U. NY, Buffalo, 1965—69; MFA in visual design, So. Mass. U./U. Mass. N. Dartmouth, 1970—73. Graphic designer RI Dept. Health, Providence, 1974—80; illustrator Providence Jour. Bulletin, 1970—82, Channel 10 TV News, Providence, 1971—83; graphic designer/illustrator Blackstone Valley Tourism Coun., Cumberland, RI, 1982—94; graphic designer RI Dept. Econ. Devel., Providence, 1982—86. Lectr. in field. Logo design, for Women, Infant and Children's Food Program, Indsl. Graphics Internat., 1973. Mem.: Nat. Carousel Assn. Home: 515 Newland Ave Jamestown NY 14701 E-mail: rawhiteart@aol.com.

WHITE, RALPH EDWARD, chemical engineer, educator; b. Clovis, N.Mex., Nov. 6, 1942; s. Wilford Weldon and Fannie (Edens) W.; m. Carolyn Jean McDaniel, Feb. 24, 1969 (div. Oct. 1981); 1 child, David Stewart; m. Marjorie Nicholson, Oct. 13, 1981; children: Robert Edward, Priscilla Anne, Lillian Leigh, Samuel Joseph. BS in Engring., U. S.C., 1971; MS in Chem. Engring., U. Calif., Berkeley, 1973, PhD in Chem. Engring., 1977. Registered profl. engr., Tex. Asst. prof. Tex. A&M U., College Station, 1977-81, assoc. prof., 1981-85, prof., 1985-92, assoc. head dept. chem. engring., 1990-92; prof., chmn. dept. chem. engring. U. S.C., Columbia, 1993—2000, disting. scientist, 1993—, dir. Ctr. Electrochem. Engring., 1995—2000, dean Coll. Engring. & Info. Tech., 2000—. Cons. Dow Chem. Co., Freeport, Tex., 1979-93, Exxon Corp., 1981-82, GM Corp., Dearborn, Mich., 1984-87, Allied Corp., 1985-86. Editor: Comprehensive Treatise on Electrochemistry, 1981-84, Modern Aspects of Electrochemistry, 1982-; ECS Proc. of Symposiums, 1986-94. Recipient Silver Medal award Jour. Am. Electroplaters and Surface Finishers Soc., 1993, Sci. Achievement award, 1999. Fellow Electrochem. Soc. (nat. treas. 1990-94, Electrodeposition Divsn. Rsch. award 1992, Battery Divsn. Rsch. award 1991). Achievements include patent on electrochemical method for producing hydrogen and sulfur. Home: 5 Brandywine Ln Columbia SC 29206-1366 Office: Univ of South Carolina Dept Chem Engring Swearingen 3C01 Dean's Office Columbia SC 29208-0001 Office Phone: 803-777-3270. Business E-Mail: white@engr.sc.edu.

WHITE, RALPH PAUL, automotive executive, consultant; b. Watertown, Mass., Aug. 1, 1926; s. Irving William and Margaret Sarah (McGowan) W.; m. Shirley Irene Christie, Nov. 22, 1947; children: Karin Ann, Eric John. BS in Indsl. Engring., Columbia U., 1951; postgrad., Yale U., 1958-59. Instr. engring. mechanics U. Conn., Torrington, 1956-57; mgr. data processing. B.F. Goodrich Co., Shelton, Conn., 1956—61; ptnr., mgmt. cons. Bavier, Bulger & Goodyear, New Haven, 1961-66; v.p. Davidson Rubber Co., Dover, N.H., 1966-69, pres., 1969-80; group v.p. parent co. Ex-Cell-O, Troy, Mich., 1980-83; pres. Troy (N.H.) Mills Inc., 1983-86, chief exec. officer, 1983-89, chmn., 1987-89. Bd. dirs. J.A. Wright Co., Keene, NH, J.D. Cahill Co., Hampton, NH, Exeter Trust Co, D.G. O'Brien Co., Seabrook, NH. Mem. N.H. Indsl. Devel. Authority, 1972-80, 85-88, Pease Devel. Authority, State of N.H., 1990-93, N.H. Bus. Fin. Authority, 1992-2004; exec. bd. Whittemore Sch. Bus., U. N.H., Durham, 1984-2002. Mem. Am. Inst. Indsl. Engrs., Soc. Automotive Engrs., N.H. Bus. and Industry Assn. (bd. dirs. 1970-80, pres. 1972-73, vice chmn. 1984-86), Abenaqui Country Club, Rye Beach Club, Coral Beach Club. Republican. Roman Catholic. Avocations: skiing, golf. Home: 70 Woodland Rd # 667 North Hampton NH 03862-2234 Office Phone: 603-964-9758. Personal E-mail: rpw99@aol.com.

WHITE, RAYMOND BURTON, former insurance executive; b. Clarksburg, W.Va., Jan. 22, 1943; s. Joseph C. and Glendine Agnes (Saucer) W.; children: D. Andrew, Christopher B.; m. Cherry Semple; children: Fraser M., H. Hollyday. BS in Fin., U. W.Va., 1965; grad., Coll. of Ins., N.Y.C., 1970; postgrad., Columbia U., 1992. Lic. casualty, property broker. With U.S. Fidelity & Guaranty Co., Charleston, W.Va., 1965-66, Travelers Indemnity Co., Pitts., 1966-69, surety underwriter Hartford, Conn., 1969-70; trainee Johnson & Higgins, N.Y.C., 1970-71, mgr. fin. svcs. Pitts., 1971-76, mgr. sales dept., 1976-79, mgr. mid. market dept., 1979-83, mgr. benefits dept., 1983-85, mgr. nat. assn. dept. Washington, 1985-86, sr. acct. mgr., mgr. health group Pitts., 1986-95, sr. v.p., 1991, prin., 1991; CEO The Watson Inst., 1999. Pres. Margaret H. W. Watson Found., 1998. Bd. dirs. Craig House, Pitts., 1987-93, pres., 1992-93, Boyd Cmty. Ctr., Pitts., 1988-89; vestryman local Episcopal Ch., Pitts., 1975-78; mem. Calvary Episcopal Ch.; pres. Pitts. Philharm. Soc., 1987-88; bd. dirs. Pitts. Symphony Soc., 1994—, D.T. Watson Health Svcs., 1994-98; active visiting com. W.Va. U. Coll. Bus. & Econs. With USAR, 1965-70. Mem. W.Va. U. Alumni (pres. 1978-81), Duquesne Club, Allegheny Country Club, Rolling Rock Club. Republican. Avocations: golf, travel, civic involvement.

WHITE, RAYMOND LESLIE, geneticist; b. Orlando, Fla., Oct. 23, 1943; s. Lawrence and Marjorie White; m. Joan Palmer Distin, June 1, 1968; children: Juliette, Jeremy. BS in Microbiology, U. Oreg., 1965; PhD in Microbiology, MIT, 1971; postdoctoral studies, Stanford. Rsch. assoc., instr. MIT, Cambridge, 1971-72; postdoctoral fellow Sch. Medicine Stanford (Calif.) U., 1972-75; asst. prof. Dept. Microbiology U. Mass. Sch. Medicine, Worcester, 1975-78, assoc. prof. Dept. Microbiology, 1978-80; investigator Howard Hughes Med. Inst. U. Utah Med. Ctr., 1980-94; assoc. prof. Dept. Cellular, Viral and Molecular Biology U. Utah Sch. Medicine, 1980-84, co-chmn. Dept. Human Genetics, 1984-94, prof. Dept. Oncological Scis., 1985—; prof. Dept. of Human Genetics U. Utah Sch. of Medicine, 1985—; chmn. Dept. Oncological Scis. U. Utah Sch. Medicine, 1994—, dir. Huntsman Cancer Inst., 1994—2000; chief sci. officer DNA Scis., Inc., 2000—. Ad hoc mem. NIH Gen. Med. Sci. Inst. Coun., 1984, mem. NIH study sect., 1979-83. Consulting editor Jour. Clin. Investigation; subject area editor Genomics, 1987-90; contbr. articles to profl. jours. Woodrow Wilson fellow, 1965-66, NIH grad. fellow, 1966-71, Jane Coffins Childs Found. fellow, 1971-75; Nat. Cancer Inst. Cancer Ctr. Support grantee, 1995—; recipient Sword Hope award Am. Cancer Soc., 1995, Lewis S. Rosenstiel award Disting. Work Basic Med. Scis., Brandeis U., 1992, Rosenblatt award for excellence, 1993, Nat. Med. Rsch. award Nat. Health Coun., 1991, Friedrich von Recklinghausen award Nat. Neurofibromatosis Found., 1990, Charles S. Mott prize Gen. Motors Cancer Rsch. Found., 1990, Raymond Bourfine award, Paris, 2002. Mem. NAS, Am. Soc. Human Genetics (Allen Cancer Rsch. award 1989, assoc. editor Cancer Rsch.), Utah Acad. Scis. Achievements include the development of a new technology for mapping and ultimately identifying human genes causing disease and the discovery of fundamental genes and genetic mechanisms important in the inherited and cellular pathways to cancer. Office: DNA Scis Inc 6540 Kaiser Dr Fremont CA 94555-3613

WHITE, RAYMOND PETRIE, JR., dentist, educator, dean; b. N.Y.C., Feb. 13, 1937; s. Raymond Petrie and Mabel Sarah (Shutze) White; m. Betty Pritchett, Dec. 27, 1961; children: Karen Elizabeth, Michael Wood. Student, Washington and Lee U., 1955—58; DDS, Med. Coll. Va., 1962, PhD, 1967. Diplomate Am. Bd. Oral and Maxillofacial Surgery. Postdoctoral fellow anatomy Med. Coll. Va., Richmond, 1962—67, resident in oral surgery, 1964—67; asst. prof. U. Ky., Lexington, 1967—70, assoc. prof., 1970—71, chmn. dept. oral surgery, 1969—71; prof., asst. dean adminstrn. Va. Commonwealth U., Richmond, 1971—74; prof. Sch. Dentistry U. N.C., Chapel Hill, 1974—, Dalton L. McMichael disting. prof., 1993—, dean Sch. Dentistry, 1974—81, assoc. dean Sch. Medicine, Sch. Dentistry, 1981—92. Mem. staff U. N.C. Hosps., mem. exec. com., 1974—98, sec., 1977—78, assoc. chief staff, 1981—92; mem. adv. panel on dentistry U.S. Pharmacopial Conv., 1985—; sr. program cons. The Robert Wood Johnson Found., 1982—90. Author (with E.R. Costich): Fundamentals of Oral Surgery, 1971; author: (with Bell and Proffit) Surgical Correction of Dentofacial Deformities, 1980; author: (with W.R. Proffit) Surgical Orthodontic Treatment, 1990; author: (with M.R. Tucker, B.C. Terry, J.E. Van Sickels) Rigid Fixations for Maxillofacial Surgery, 1991; co-editor: Internat. Jour. Adult Orthodontics and Orthodontic Surgery, 1985—2002; asst. editor: Jour. Oral and Maxillofacial Surgery, 1993—; author (with W.R. Profit, R.P. Jr., and D. Sarver): Contemporary Treatment of Dentofacial Deformity, 2002; contbr. sci. articles to profl. jours. Bd. dirs. Am. Fund for Dental Health, 1978—86, v.p., 1982—85. Recipient Disting. Svc. award, Am. Fund Dental Health, 1987, Dental Found. N.C., 1981, John C. Brauer award for acad. distinction, U. N.C. Alumni Assn., 2000, Daniel M. Laskin award, 2002, Rsch. Excellence award, Oral and Maxillofacial Surgery Found., 2003. Mem.: AAAS, ADA, N.C. Assn. Oral and Maxillofacial Surgeons, Am. Assn. Oral and Maxillofacial Surgeons (gen. chmn. sci. sessions com. 1974—76, chmn. strategic planning com. 1990—96, Outstanding Svc. award as committeeman 1976, William Gies award 2000, Disting. Svc. award 2003), Chalmers J. Lyons Acad. Oral Surgery, Inst. Medicine of NAS, Internat. Assn. Dental Rsch. (pres. Ky. sect. 1970), N.C. Dental Soc., Sigma Xi, Omicron Kappa Upsilon, Sigma Zeta, Alpha Sigma Chi, Delta Tau Delta, Psi Omega. Roman Catholic. Home: 1506 Velma Rd Chapel Hill NC 27514-7601 Office: U NC Sch Dentistry Dept Oral/Maxillofacial Surgery Chapel Hill NC 27599-7450

WHITE, REBECCA E. advocate; b. Washington, Nov. 17, 1945; d. Edward and Anna Pendleton White. BS, D.C. Tchrs. Coll., 1971; postgrad., Pepperdine U., 1993, Calif. State U., 2003—. Cert. tchr., D.C., Calif. Tchr. English D.C. Pub. Schs., Washington, 1971-73; paralegal specialist U.S. Dept. Justice, Washington, 1973-81; adminstr. U.S. Dept. Vet. Affairs VA Med. Ctr., L.A., 1982-89, 94-96, Sepulveda, Calif., 1992-94; patient/employee advocate U.S. Dept. Vet. Affairs, L.A., 1982-89, 92-96; tchr. English L.A. Unified Sch. Dist., 1989-91, children's advocate, 1989—; tchr. English Inglewood (Calif.) Unified Sch. Dist., 1996-97, children's advocate, 1996-98; tchr. spl. edn. Gladstone St. Elem. Sch., Azusa, Calif., 2003—04. Cmty. advocate Baldwin Hills Cmty., L.A., 1983—; children's advocate L.A. County Schs., 1999—; mem. L.A. World Affairs Coun., 1999—. Mem. NEA, Calif. Tchrs. Assn. Avocations: writing, hiking, entertaining, reading.

WHITE, REBECCA T. lawyer; b. Asuncion, Paraguay, May 16, 1973; d. David A. Herman and Janet Towle Hall; m. James J. White, July 26, 1999; children: Christian James, Jacob Alexander. JD, U. Oreg., 1996. Bar: Wash. 1997. Assoc. Mikkelborg, Broz, Wells & Fryer, Seattle, 1997—2003; ptnr. Law Offices of White & White, Vashon/Seattle, Wash., 2003—. Unitarian. Office: Law Offices of White & White 1001 4th Ave Ste 3200 Seattle WA 98070 E-mail: rebeccawhite@attorneysww.com.

WHITE, RHEA AMELIA, information scientist, consciousness researcher; b. Utica, NY, May 6, 1931; d. John Raymond and Rhea Jane (Parry) White. BA, Pa. State U., 1953; MLS, Pratt Inst., Bklyn., 1965; postgrad., SUNY, Stony Brook, 1990-92. Rsch. fellow Parapsychology Lab. Duke U., Durham, N.C., 1954-58; editor Jour. Am. Soc. Psychical Rsch., N.Y.C., 1959-62, 84-00, editor-in-chief, 2001—; libr. dept. psychiatry Maimonides Med. Ctr., Bklyn., 1965-67; dir. info. Am. Soc. Psychical Rsch., N.Y.C., 1965-80; reference libr. East Meadow (N.Y.) Pub. Libr., 1965-95; founder, dir. Parapsychology Sources of Info. Ctr., Dix Hills, N.Y., 1981-90; editor Rsch. in Parapsychology, Metuchen, N.J., 1981-85, Theta, Durham, N.C., 1981-86; founder, editor Parapsychology Abstracts Internat., Dix Hills, 1983-89, Exceptional Human Experience, Dix Hills, 1990—, founder, producer PsiLine Database, Dix Hills, 1983—; mng. editor Advances in Parapsychol. Rsch., N.Y.C., 1977; founder, dir. Exceptional Human Experience Network, New Bern, 1990-94, 95—; with Exceptional Human Experience News, 1994—2002. Rsch. fellow Menninger Found., Topeka, 1963-65; abstractor Psychol. Abstracts, Washington, 1967-91; cons. Scarecrow Press, Metuchen, NJ, 1980-85; referee Jour. Parapsychology, Durham, 1981-85; sr. rsch. cons. Ctr. Sci. Anomalies Rsch., 1981—; chmn., keynote spkr. conf. on women and parapsychology Parapsychology Found., Dublin, Ireland, 1991; keynote speaker Acad. Religion and Psychical Rsch. Conf., 1992; founder, editor EHE News, Dix Hills, 1994, New Bern, 1995—; instr. exceptional human experience course Portland (Oreg.) State U., 1999. Author: Parapsychology: Sources of Information, 1973, Surveys in Parapsychology, 1975, Parapsychology: New Sources of Information, 1990; (with M Murphy) The Psychic Side of Sports, 1978, parapsychology book reviewer Libr. Jour., NYC, 1974-86, Reprint Bull., 1974-79, (with Michael Murphy) In the Zone, 1995; regional editor European Jour. Parapsychology, 1975-90; mem. editl. bd. Advances in Parapsychol. Rsch., 1980-85, Archaeus, 1985-93, 3 books on key aspects of the transformative potential of non-ordinary exceptional hum. experiences; contbr. over 100 articles to profl. jours. Recipient Hans Peter Luhn award Am. Soc. Info. Sci., N.Y.C. chpt., 1965; Coll. Human Scis. hon. fellow Internat. Inst. Integral Human Scis. Mem.: Soc. Psychical. Rsch., Am. Anthrop. Assn., Soc. Sci. Study of Religion, Assn. Near-Death Studies, Acad. Religion and Psychical Rsch. (mem. bd. 1982—84, publs. com. 1982—97), Parapsychology Assn. (mem. coun. 1958, 1962—63, 1982—85, pres. 1984, dir. 1986, Lifetime Outstanding Rsch. award 1992, conf. spkr. 1993), Ctr. for Psychology and Social Change, Spiritual Frontiers Fellowship, Internat., Internat. Assn. Religion and Parapsychology, Found for Shamanic Studies, Internat. Soc. for Study Subtle Energies and Energy Medicine, Inst. Noetic Scis., Soc. for Anthropology of Consciousness, Penn State Alumni Assn. Coll. Liberal Arts. Avocations: hiking, gardening, animals, reading, listening to music. Home and Office: 414 Rockledge Rd New Bern NC 28562-9553 E-mail: ehenwhite@cox.net.

WHITE, RICHARD BOOTH, management consultant; b. N.Y.C., Aug. 26, 1930; s. Frank K. and Doris (Booth) W.; m. Mary Kane Russell, Dec. 9, 1961; children: Katherine Learned, Richard Booth (dec.), Anne Tristram, Leslie Russell. BA, Yale U., 1952. Asst. account exec. Batten, Barton, Durstine & Osborn, N.Y.C., 1955, account exec., 1956-58, account supr., 1958-63, v.p., 1959-70, mgmt. supr., 1963-76, sr. v.p., 1970-76, exec. v.p., 1976-83, also dir., chmn. exec. com.; dir. BBDO Internat. Inc.; sr. dir., ptnr. Spencer Stuart & Assocs., N.Y.C., 1984-98; ind. cons., 1998—. Mem. New Canaan (Conn.) Town Coun.; bd. dirs. Waveny Care Ctr., New Canaan. 1st lt. USMCR, 1952-55. Mem. Yale Club (N.Y.C.), Country Club of New Canaan, Beta Theta Pi. Presbyterian. Home: 27 Bank St New Canaan CT 06840-6202

WHITE, RICHARD EDMUND, marketing executive; b. Reading, Pa., June 8, 1944; s. Carl Marshall and Miriam Elizabeth (Curry) W.; m. Kristen Margaret Lloyd, June 17, 1967; children: Ross, Peter, Andrew. BS in Econs., U. Pa., 1967; MBA with distinction, U. Mich., 1968. Gen. mgr. mktg. H. J. Heinz Co., Pitts., 1970-81; dir. mktg. Seven Up Co., St. Louis, 1981-83; v.p. mktg. & sales Herr Foods, Inc., Nottingham, Pa., 1984—. Bd. dirs. Conard-Pyle Co. Chmn. fin. com. Sewickley Borough Coun., Pa., 1977—81; pres. So. Chester County Devel. Found., Jennersville, Pa., 1988—94, So. Chester County YMCA, West Grove, Pa., 1988—93, bd. mgrs., 1988—93, Avon Grove United Way, 1988—93, pres., 1988—93; chmn. So. Chester County Med. Ctr., 1988—2001, bd. dirs., 1988—2001, Brandywine YMCA Assn.; chmn. bd. dirs. Jenners Pond, 2001—, Health and Welfare Found. So. Chester County, pres.; chmn. Health and Welfare Found. of So. Cheser County. Mem. Am. Mgmt. Assn. (mktg. coun.). Republican. Avocations: physical fitness, reading. Home: 7 Sullivan Chase Dr Avondale PA 19311-9347 Office: Herr Foods Inc PO Box 300 Nottingham PA 19362-0300 E-mail: richard.white@herrs.com.

WHITE, RICHARD MANNING, electrical engineering educator; b. Denver, Apr. 25, 1930; s. Rolland Manning and Freeda Blanche (Behny) W.; m. Chissie Lee Chamberlain, Feb. 1, 1964 (div. 1975); children: Rolland Kenneth, William Brendan. AB, Harvard U., 1951, AM, 1952, PhD in Applied Physics, 1956. Rsch. assoc. Harvard U., Cambridge, Mass., 1956; mem. tech. staff GE Microwave Lab., Palo Alto, Calif., 1956-63; prof. elec. engring. U. Calif., Berkeley, 1963—, Chancellor's prof., 1996-99. Chmn. Grad. Group on Sci. and Math. Edn., U. Calif. at Berkeley, 1981-85; co-dir. Berkeley Sensor and Actuator Ctr., 1986—, Co-author: Solar Cells: From Basics to Advanced Systems, Microsensors, 1991, Electrical Engineering Uncovered, 1997, Acoustic Wave Sensors, 1997; editor ElectroTechnology Rev.; patentee in field. Guggenheim fellow, 1968. Fellow AAAS, IEEE (Cledo Brunetto award 1986, Achievement award 1988, Disting. lectr. 1989, Cady award 2000, Rayleigh award 2003); mem. Nat. Acad. Engring., Acoustical Soc. Am., Am. Phys. Soc., Phi Beta Kappa, Sigma Xi. Avocations: photography, hiking, skiing, running, music. Office: U Calif Sensor & Actuator Ctr EECS Dept Ctr Berkeley CA 94720-1774

WHITE, RICHARD THOMAS, radiologist; b. Binghamton, N.Y., May 10, 1941; s. William Joseph and Winifred (Murphy) W.; 1 child by previous marriage, Kevin Michael; m. Rory Lynn Leyman. BS, SUNY, Binghamton, 1967; DO, Chgo. Coll. Osteo. Medicine, 1972. Intern Bi County Hosp., Warren, Mich.; staff radiologist Bi-County Hosp., 1977-79; resident Detroit Hosp., Children's Hosp., Detroit, 1973-76; fellow Johns Hopkins Hosp., Balt., 1976; asst. prof. radiology Mich. State U., East Lansing, 1980-84, cons. ultra-sound rsch., 1980-83, cons. nuclear magnetic rsch., 1982-83; asst. prof. radiology U. Tex., Houston, 1984-85, U. Ill., Chgo., 1985-88; chief radiology VA Med. Ctr., Bath, N.Y., 1988—; clin. prof. radiology U. Rochester (N.Y.) Sch. Medicine and Dentistry, 1989—. Cons. varsity sports, 1980-84, handicapped athletes Spl. Olympics, Washington, 1978-84, Detroit Red Wings hockey team, 1977-84; cons. in radiology St. James Hosp., Hornell, N.Y.,

1989—. Med. dir. Mich. Spl. Olympics Ctrl. Mich. U., Mt. Pleasant, 1977-84; bd. dirs. Spl. Olympics, Mich., 1980-84, N.Y. Spl. Olympics, 1996-2000; med. advisor Amateur Hockey Assn. USA, Colorado Springs, Colo., 1980-84. With U.S. Army, 1960-66; lt. col. USAR, 1990-96, ret. Recipient Outstanding Contbn. award Spl. Olympics, 1980; named Team Physician U.S. Nat. Hockey Team, Mich. Amateur Hockey Assn., 1979, 81, 83. Mem. AMA, Am. Osteo. Assn., Am. Osteo. Coll. Radiology, Assn. Mil. Physicians and Surgeons, Am. Osteopath Assn., Radiol. Soc. N.Am., Am. Coll. Radiology, Am. Inst. Ultrasound in Medicine, Am. Acad. Sci., Soc. Med. Cons. to U.S. Armed Forces, Kiwanis, Am. Legion. Office Phone: 607-664-4408.

WHITE, RICK, lawyer, former congressman; b. Nov. 6, 1953; BA in Govt. and French, Dartmouth Coll., 1975; postgrad., Pantheon-Sorbonne; JD, Georgetown U., 1980. Mem. 104th to 105th Congresses from 1st Wash. dist., 1995—98; mem. house commerce com.; ptnr. Perkins Coie LLP, Seattle, 1999—. Founder Congl. Internet Caucus, Books for Kids. Republican. Office: Perkins Coie LLP Ste 4800 1201 3d Ave Seattle WA 98101-3099

WHITE, RICK, publishing executive; Founder Strategic Merchandising Assn., N.Y.C.; past gen. mgr. subs. brands Nike Inc.; U.S. pres., CEO Reed Exhbn. Cos., Norwalk, Conn., 1999—. Office: Reed Exhbn Cos 383 Main Ave Norwalk CT 06851-1543

WHITE, ROBERT BROWN, medical educator; b. Ennis, Tex., Jan. 5, 1921; s. Robert Brown and Willia Elizabeth (Latimer) W.; m. Jimmiee Estelle Sims, Oct. 18, 1942; children: Robert B., Canelia White Layton, Margaret White Gilbert. BS, Tex. A & M Coll., 1941; MD, U. Tex., 1944; cert., Western New Eng. Psychoanalytic Inst., 1959. Intern Phila. (Pa.) Gen. Hosp., 1944-45; psychiat. residency John Sealy Hosp., Galveston, Tex., 1945-46, 48-49; psychiatry fellow Austen Riggs Ctr., Stockbridge, Mass., 1949-51, staff psychiatrist, 1951-62; assoc. prof. U. Tex. Med. Br., Galveston, 1962-67, prof., 1967—, Marie Gale prof. of psychiatry, 1981-93; prof. emeritus, 1993—; tng. analyst New Orleans (La.) Psychoanalytic Inst., 1966-76. Tng. analyst Houston-Galveston Psychoanalytic Inst., 1974-94; analyst emeritus, 1994—. Author: Elements of Psychopathology, 1975; contbr. chpts. to books and articles to profl. jours. Capt. U.S. Army, 1946-48. Recipient David Rapaport prize Western New Eng. Psychoanalytic Inst., New Haven, 1959; Ohio State award Ohio State Univ., 1976. Fellow Am. Psychiat. Assn., Am. Coll. Psychiatrists, Am. Coll. Psychoanalysts (bd. regents 1988-91); mem. Am. Psychoanalytic Assn., Alpha Omega Alpha. Democrat. Avocations: photography, carpentry. Home: 1013 Harbor View Dr Galveston TX 77550-3109 Office: Univ Tex Med Br Galveston TX 77550

WHITE, ROBERT C. air transportation executive; b. 1943; Student, Wake Forest U., 1961-65. With Procter & Gamble, Columbus, Ohio, 1971-73; asst. dir. Shreveport (La.) Airport Authority, 1973-75; airport mgr. Gainesville (Fla.) Regional Airport, 1975-78; dep. dir. aviation Jacksonville (Fla.) Port Authority, 1978-80; exec. dir. Peninsula Airport Commn., Newport News, Va., 1980-82; dir./cons. Lockheed Air Terminal, Burbank, Calif., 1982—; exec. dir. Reno Tahoe Internat. Airport, 1988—. With USN, 1966-71. Office: Reno Tahoe Internat Airport PO Box 12490 Reno NV 89510-2490

WHITE, ROBERT DENNIS, pediatrician, director; b. South Bend, Ind., Dec. 29, 1949; s. Alfred Butler and Mary Ruth (Gibbens) White; m. Kathy Lynn Samuels, Aug. 15, 1970; children: Luke Alfred, James Samuels, Kieran Claire, Benjamin Robert. Student, U. Notre Dame, 1967-69; BA, John Hopkins U., 1969-70, MD, 1970-74. Diplomate Am. Bd. Pediatrics. Resident in pediatrics Johns Hopkins Hosp., Balt., 1974-76, fellow in neonatology, 1976—77; sr. rsch. scientist Wellcome Rsch. Labs., London, 1980; dir. regional newborn program Meml. Hosp., South Bend, 1981—. Clin. asst. prof. pediat. Ind. U. Sch. Medicine, 1983—; adj. prof. psychology U. Notre Dame, 1989—; chmn. Recommended Stds. Newborn ICU Design, 2003. Co-editor: (book) Lifespan Perspectives on Health and Illness, 1999. Fellow: Am. Acad. Pediat. Office: Meml Hosp 615 N Michigan St South Bend IN 46601-1087

WHITE, ROBERT JAMES, newspaper columnist; b. Mpls., Nov. 6, 1927; s. Robert Howard and Claire Lillian (Horner) W.; m. Adrienne Hoffman, Sept. 24, 1955; children: Claire, Pamela, Sarah. BS, U.S. Naval Acad., 1950. V.p. White Investment Co., Mpls., 1957-67; editl. writer Mpls. Tribune, 1967-73, assoc. editor, 1973-82; editor editl. pages Mpls. Star Tribune, 1982-93, columnist, 1993-95, contbg. columnist, 1996—. Recipient cert. of excellence Overseas Press Club, 1981. Mem. Coun. Fgn. Rels., Mpls. Club. Congregationalist. Home: Summit House 400 Groveland Ave #2212 Minneapolis MN 55403 E-mail: rjw823@aol.com.

WHITE, ROBERT JOEL, lawyer; b. Chgo., Nov. 1, 1946; s. Melvin and Margaret (Hoffman) W.; m. Gail Janet Edenson, June 29, 1969 (div. Dec. 1982); m. Penelope K. Bloch, Dec. 22, 1985. BS in Accountancy, U. Ill., 1968; JD, U. Mich., 1972. Bar: Calif. 1972, N.Y. 1985, U.S. Dist. Ct. (ctrl., ea., so. dists.) Calif. 1972, U.S. Ct. Appeals (9th cir.) 1978, U.S. Ct. Appeals (5th cir.) 1983, U.S. Ct. Appeals (6th cir.) 1984, U.S. Supreme Ct. 1977. Staff auditor Haskin & Sells, Chgo., 1968-69; assoc. O'Melveny & Myers, L.A., 1972-79, ptnr., 1980-2001, chair reorgn. and restructuring dept., 1986—; CEO O'Melvey Cons. LLC, 2001—. Vis. lectr. U. Mich. Law Sch., Ann Arbor, 1986; lectr. Profl. Edn. Sys., Inc., Dallas, 1987, L.A., 1987, 89, Phoenix, 1990, Practicing Law Inst., San Francisco and N.Y.C., 1989-93, 2001-, Southwestern Legal Found., Dallas, 1991, UCLA Bankruptcy Inst., 1993, UCLA, 1993; mem. L.A. Productivity Comm., 1993-96. Contbr. articles to profl. jours. Active Constl. Rights Found., 1980—; active Am. Cancer Soc., 1989—, mem. L.A. bd. dirs., 1995—, vice chair, partnership com., 2003-; mem. exec. com. Nat. Bankruptcy Conf., 1999-2002. Fellow Am. Coll. Brankruptcy; mem. ABA (litig. sect., mem. comml. law and bankruptcy com. 1972—), L.A. County Bar Assn. (comml. law and bankruptcy sect., chmn. fed. cts. com. 1981-82, exec. com. 1982—), Assn. Bus. Trial Lawyers (bd. govs. 1983-85), Fin. Lawyers Conf. (bd. govs. 1986—, pres. 1990-91), Am. Bankruptcy Inst. Avocations: skiing, running, U.S. history. Office: O'Melveny & Myers 1999 Ave of Stars Los Angeles CA 90067-6035 Business E-Mail: rwhite@omm.com.

WHITE, ROBERT LEE, electrical engineer, educator; b. Plainfield, NJ, Feb. 14, 1927; s. Claude and Ruby Hemsworth Emerson (Levick) W.; m. Phyllis Lillian Arlt, June 14, 1952; children: Lauren A., Kimberly A., Christopher L., Matthew P. BA in Physics, Columbia U., 1949, MA, 1951, PhD, 1954. Assoc. head atomic physics dept. Hughes Rsch. Labs., Malibu, Calif., 1954-61; head magnetics dept. Gen. Tel. and Electronics Rsch. Lab., Palo Alto, Calif., 1961-63; prof. elec. engring., materials sci. and engring. Stanford U., Palo Alto, 1963, chmn. elec. engring. dept., 1981-86, William E. Ayer prof. elec. engring., 1985-88, prof. emeritus, 1988—; exec. dir. The Exploratorium, San Francisco, 1987-89; dir. Inst. for Electronics in Medicine, 1973-87, Stanford Ctr. for Rsch. on Info. Storage Materials, 1991—2003. Initial ltd. ptnr. Mayfield Fund, Mayfield II and Alpha II Fund, Rainbow Co-Investment Ptnrs., Halo Ptnrs.; vis. prof. Tokyo U., 1975, Nat. U. Singapore, 2002; Sony sabbatical chair, 1994; cons. in field. Author: (with K.A. Wickersheim) Magnetism and Magnetic Materials, 1965, Basic Quantum Mechanics, 1967; contbr. numerous articles to profl. jours. With USN, 1945-46. Fellow Guggenheim Oxford U., 1969-70, Canton Hosp., Swiss Fed. Inst. Tech., Zurich, 1977-78, Christensen fellow Oxford U., 1986, IEEE Magnetics Soc. Disting. lectr., 1998. Fellow IEEE, Am. Phys. Soc.; mem. Sigma Xi, Phi Beta Kappa. Home: 450 El Escarpado Stanford CA 94305-8431 Office: Stanford U Dept Material Sci Engr Stanford CA 94305 Office Phone: 650-723-4431. Business E-Mail: white@ee.stanford.edu.

WHITE, ROBERT LESLIE GORDON, JR., aerospace company executive; b. Orange, NJ, Dec. 20, 1941; s. Robert L.G. and Gertrude Marie (Wilson) W.; m. Joan Adam, May 9, 1970; children: Robert L.G. III, Sonya Lynn. BS in Metallurgical Engring., Lafayette Coll., 1964. Sr. engr. Crucible Steel Co., 1964-68; various positions Curtiss-Wright Corp., Woodridge, N.J., 1968-76, plant mgr. nuclear facility, 1976-80, dir. gas turbine overhaul, 1980-83; v.p., gen. mgr. Curtiss-Wright/Marquette, Inc., Fountain Inn, S.C., 1983-87; pres. GEC-Marconi Aerospace Inc., Whippany, N.J., 1987-94, Breeze-Eastern, Union, N.J., 1994-98; pres. aerospace products group Transtechnology Corp., Union, NJ, 1998—2003, pres., CEO, 2003—. Office: Transtechnology Corp 700 Liberty Ave Union NJ 07083-8198

WHITE, ROBERT M., II, newspaper executive, editor, publisher; b. Mexico, Mo., Apr. 6, 1915; s. L. Mitchell and Maude (See) W.; m. Barbara Whitney Spurgeon, Aug. 19, 1948 (dec. Feb., 1983); children: Barbara Whitney, Jane See, Laura L., Robert M. III. Grad., Mo. Mil. Acad., 1933; AB, Washington and Lee U., 1938, LL.B. (hon.), 1972. Writer of newspaper articles, Australia, Africa, S.Am., Europe, USSR, 1966, 86, 1972, 77; reporter Mexico (Mo.) Eve. Ledger, 1938-39, editor, pub., 1945; vis. prof. Sch. Journalism, Mo. U., 1968-69; reporter UP Bur., Kansas City, 1939-40; pres. Ledger Newspapers, Inc., Mexico, Mo., 1945-86. Spl. cons. to pub. Chgo. Sun-Times, 1956-58; pres. See TV Co., Mexico, 1966-81; editor, pres., bd. dirs. N.Y. Herald Tribune, 1959-61; juror Pulitzer prize journalism, 1964-65; bd. dirs. World Press Freedom Com. Co-author: A Study of the Printing and Publishing Business in the Soviet Union. President Gen. Douglas MacArthur Found., 1981-91. Lt. col. AUS, 1940-45. Decorated Bronze Star; recipient nat. disting. service award for editorials Sigma Delta Chi, 1952, 68; editorial award N.Y. Silurians, 1959; Disting. Service to Journalism award U. Mo., 1967; Pres. award of merit Nat. Newspapers Assn., 1967; Ralph D. Casey Minn. award disting. service in journalism, 1983; finalist Journalist in Space 1986—. Mem. Am. Soc. Newspaper Editors (dir. 1968-69, chmn. freedom of info. com. 1970-72), Am. Newspaper Pubs. Assn. (nat. treas. 1963, dir. 1955-63, chmn. internat. group 1982-86), Washington Inst. Fgn. Affairs, Inland Daily Press Assn. (chmn. bd. 1958-59, pres., past sec., v.p.), Mo. Press Assn. (dir., v.p. 1981-83, pres. 1983-84, Hall of Fame 1998), Mo. Press-Bar Commn. (chmn. 1972-74), Internat. Press Inst. (chmn. Am. com. 1982-85), Nat. Press Club, Bohemian Club, Burning Tree Club, Cosmos Club, Sigma Delta Chi (nat. pres. 1967, pres. found. 1968), Beta Theta Pi. Office: 3700 S Lenoir St Apt 214 Columbia MO 65201-3366

WHITE, ROBERT MARSHALL, physicist, government official, educator; b. Reading, Pa., Oct. 2, 1938; s. Carl M. and Miriam E. White; m. Sara Tolles; children: Victoria, Jonathan. BS in Physics, MIT, 1960; PhD, Stanford U., 1964. Vis. scientist Osaka (Japan) U., 1963; NSF postdoctoral fellow U. Calif., Berkeley, 1965-66; asst. prof. physics Stanford U., Palo Alto, Calif., 1966-70; NSF sr. postdoctoral fellow Cambridge U., England, 1970-71; mgr. solid state rsch. area XEROX PARC, 1971-78, mgr. storage tech., 1978-83, prin. scientist, 1983-84; v.p. rsch. and tech. Control Data Corp. Data Storage Products Group, Mpls., 1984-86; chief tech. officer, v.p. rsch. and engring. Control Data Corp., Mpls., 1986-89; v.p., dir. advanced computer techs. Microelectronics & Computer Tech. Corp., Austin, Tex., 1989-90; undersec. of commerce for tech. Dept. Commerce, Washington, 1990-93; prof., head dept. electrical and computer engring. Carnegie Mellon U., Pitts., 1993-99, dir. Data Storage Sys. Ctr., 1999—2004. Vis. scientist Ecole Polytechnique, Paris, 1976-78, U. Pernambuco, Brazil, 1978, Max Planck Inst., Stuttgart, 1981; cons. prof. applied physics Stanford U., 1982-93; adj. prof. dept. physics U. Minn., 1987-89; bd. dirs. Found. Nat. Medals Sci. and Tech., Silicon Graphics, STMicroelectronics, ENSCO; mem. sci. adv. bd. Data Storage Inst., Singapore, 2002—; mem. adv. bd. Pacific Enterprise Capital, LLC; mem. Nat. Adv. Com. on Semicondrs., 1990-92, Mfg. Forum, 1991, Nat. Critical Techs. Panel, 1990-91. Author: Quantum Theory of Magnetism, 1970 (Russian transl., 1972, Polish transl., 1979); Long Range Order in Solids, 1979 (Russian transl., 1982); Quantum Theory of Magnetism, 1983; Introduction to Magnetic Recording, 1985. Contbr. articles to profl. jours. Recipient Alexander von Humboldt prize, Fed. Republic of Germany, 1981. Fellow AAAS, IEEE (disting. lectr. Magnetics Soc., mem. editl. bd. SPECTRUM, IEEE Disting. Pub. Svc. award 1993), Am. Phys. Soc. (George E. Pake prize 2004); mem. NAE, NRC (mem. nat. materials adv. bd., chmn. com. magnetic materials 1984, material sci. and engring., vice chmn. IUPAP commn. on magnetism), Conf. Magnetism and Magnetic Materials (adv. com. 1976-78, 80-95, program com. 1973-75, chmn. 1981, chmn. Intermag. Conf. 1991), Internat. Conf. Magnetism (program chmn. 1985). Office: Carnegie Mellon U Elec & Computer Engring Dep Pittsburgh PA 15213-3890

WHITE, ROBERT MAYER, meteorologist; b. Boston, Feb. 13, 1923; s. David and Mary (Winkeller) W.; m. Mavis Seagle, Apr. 18, 1948; children: Richard Harry, Edwina Janet. BA, Harvard, 1944; MS, Mass. Inst. Tech., 1949, Sc.D., 1950; D.Sc. (hon.), L.I. U., 1976, Rensselaer Poly. Inst., 1977, U. Wis., Milw., 1978; ScD (hon.), U. Bridgeport, 1984, U. R.I., 1986, Clarkson U.; PhD (hon.), Johns Hopkins U., 1982, Drexel U., 1985, Ill. Inst. Tech., 1994. Project scientist Air Force Cambridge Research Center, 1950-58, chief meteorol. devel. lab., 1958-59; asso. dir. research dept. Travelers Ins. Co., 1959-60; pres. Travelers Research Center, Inc., 1960-63; chief U.S. Weather Bur., 1963-65; adminstr. Environ. Sci. Services Adminstrn., 1965-70, NOAA, 1970-77; pres. Joint Oceanographic Inst., Inc., 1977-79; chmn. Climate Research Bd., exec. officer Nat. Acad. Scis., 1977-79; Washington; adminstr. Nat. Research Council, 1979-80; pres. Univ. Corp. Atmospheric Research, 1980-83, Nat. Acad. Eng., 1983-95; Karl T. Compton lectr. MIT, Cambridge, 1995-96; sr. fellow Univ. Corp. Atmospheric Rsch., 1995—. Sr. fellow H. John Heinz III Ctr. for Sci., Econs. and Environment, 1996—2000; pres. Wash. Adv. Group, 1996—. Author: articles in field; mem. editl. bd.: Am. Soc. Engring. Edn. Jour. Bd. overseers Harvard U., 1977—79; mem. vis. com. Kennedy Sch. Govt., Harvard U.; bd. dirs. Resources for the Future, 1980—. Capt. USAF, World War II. Decorated Legion of Honor France; recipient Godfrey L. Cabot award, Aero Club Boston, 1966, Cleveland Abbe award, Am. Meteorol. Soc., 1969, Jesse L. Rosenberger medal, U. Chgo., 1971, Rockefeller Pub. Svc. award, 1974, David B. Stone award, New Eng. Aquarium, 1975, Neptune award, Am. Oceanic Orgn., 1977, Matthew Fontaine Maury award, Smithsonian Instn., 1976, Internat. Conservation award, Nat. Wildlife Fedn., 1976, Internat. Meteorol. Orgn. prize, 1980, Tyler prize for Environ. Achievement, U. Calif., 1992, Vannevar Bush award, Nat. Sci. Bd., 1998, Centenary medal, Australia, 2003, Milennium award, Australian Acad. Engring., 2003. Fellow: Am. Acad. Arts and Scis., Australian Acad. Tech. Scis. and Engring., Am. Geophys. Union, World Acad. Art and Scis., AAAS, UCAR (sr.), Am. Meteorol. Soc. (coun. 1965—67, 1977—, pres. 1980, Charles Franklin Brooks award1978); mem.: Royal Acad. Engring. (U.K.), Russian Acad. Engring., Royal Acad. Engring. (hon.), Engring. Acad. Japan (fgn. assoc.), Am. Philos. Soc., Finnish Acad. Tech. (fgn.), Nat. Action Coun. Minorities in Engring. Inc., Coun. Fgn. Rels., Marine Tech. Soc., NAE (coun. 1977, pres. 1983—95), Cosmos Club (Washington). Home: Somerset House II 5610 Wisconsin Ave Apt 1506 Bethesda MD 20815-4439 Office: 1275 K St NW Ste 1025 Washington DC 20005-4089 Business E-Mail: rmw@theadvisorygroup.com.

WHITE, ROBERT ROY, retired chemical engineer; b. Bklyn., Mar. 1, 1916; s. Laurance S. and Grace A. (Diffin) W.; m. Elizabeth R. Clark, July 2, 1940; children: Robert Roy, William Wesley, Elizabeth Ann, Margaret. BS, Cooper Union Inst. Tech., 1936; postgrad., Bklyn. Poly. Inst., 1936-37; MS (Horace H. Rackham predoctoral fellow 1938), U. Mich., 1938; PhD, 1941; postgrad., DePaul U. Law Sch., 1940-41, MIT, 1962. Jr. chem. engr. Calco Chem. Co., Bound Brook, N.J., 1936-37; rsch. chem. engr. Dow Chem. Co., 1937-38; chem. engr. Stnd. Oil Co. Calif., 1940, Universal Oil Products Co., 1940-42; faculty U. Mich., 1942-60, prof. chem. engring., 1945-60, assoc. dean Horace H. Rackham Sch. Grad. Studies, 1958-60; assoc. dean U. Mich. Coll. Engring., 1958-60; dir. U. Mich. Inst. Sci. and Tech., 1959-60; v.p., gen. mgr. R & D Atlantic Refining Co., Phila., 1960-62; sr. staff mgmt. svc. divsn. Arthur D. Little, Inc., 1962; v.p. devel. Champion Papers, Inc., Hamilton, Ohio, 1962-66; pres. rsch. divsn. W.R. Grace & Co., 1966-67; dean Sch. Mgmt., Case Western Res. U., Cleve., 1967-71; mng. dir. Karl Kroyer S.A., Denmark, 1970; spl. asst. to pres., dir. forum Nat. Acad. Sci., Washington, 1971-1981. Adj. prof. chem. engring. U. Md., 1982-85, Cath. U. Am., Am. U.; v.p. JC Tech., 1986—; cons. in field. Author: (with others) Unit Operations, 1950; Contbr. articles to profl. jours. Recipient Henry Russell award U. Mich., 1945; teaching award Phi Lambda Upsilon chpt. U. Mich., 1949; sesquicentennial award U. Mich., 1967; prof. award Cooper Union Inst., 1975; McCormack-Freud hon. lectr. Ill. Inst. Tech. Mem.: SAR, AIChE (Jr. award 1945, Presentation award 1951, Profl. Progress award 1956), AAAS, Am. Soc. Engring. Edn. (George Westinghouse award 1955), Am. Chem. Soc., Founders and Patriots Soc., Order Crown of Charlemagne, St. Andrews Soc., Baron Magna Charta, Nat. Yacht Club, Cosmos Club, Iota Alpha, Tau Beta Pi, Phi Kappa Phi, Phi Lambda Upsilon, Alpha Chi Sigma, Sigma Xi. Office: 2440 Virginia Ave NW Washington DC 20037-2601 Fax: 202-467-4002. E-mail: robroy82@erols.com.

WHITE, ROBERT STEPHEN, physics educator; b. Ellsworth, Kans., Dec. 28, 1920; s. Byron F. and Sebina (Leighty) W.; m. Freda Marie Bridgewater, Aug. 30, 1942; children: Nancy Lynn, Margaret Diane, John Stephen, David Bruce. AB, Southwestern Coll., 1942, DSc hon., 1971; MS, U. Ill., 1943; PhD, U. Calif., Berkeley, 1951. Physicist Lawrence Radiation Lab., Berkeley, Livermore, Calif., 1948-61; head dept. particles and fields Space Physics Lab. Aerospace Corp., El Segundo, Calif., 1962-67; physics prof. U. Calif., Riverside, 1967-92, dir. Inst. Geophysics and Planetary Physics, 1967-92, chmn. dept. physics, 1970-73, prof. emeritus physics dept., rsch. physicist, 1992—. Lectr. U. Calif., Berkeley, 1953-54, 57-59. Author: Space Physics, 1970, Why Science?, 1998; contbr. articles to profl. jours. Officer USNR, 1944-46. Sr. Postdoctoral fellow NSF, 1961-62; grantee NASA, NSF, USAF, numerous others. Fellow AAAS, Am. Phys. Soc. (exec. com. 1972-74); mem. AAUP, Am. Geophys. Union, Am. Astron. Soc. Home: 5225 Austin Rd Santa Barbara CA 93111-2905 Personal E-mail: stevewhite2@cox.net.

WHITE, ROGER L., JR., graphic designer, art director; b. Ft. Lauderdale, Fla., Feb. 16, 1961; s. Roger Lee and Bonnie Sue (Brooks) White. Cert. in Art History, Am. Coll. Paris, 1982; BFA, Parsons Sch. of Design, 1983. Designer, art dir. Late Show with David Letterman, N.Y.C., 1985—; art dir. Late Night with David Letterman, N.Y.C., 1993—; illustrator Saturday Night Live, N.Y.C., 1987-94, N.Y. Times, 1993; designer Between the Lions PBS, N.Y.C., 1999—, Court TV, N.Y.C., 1999; illustrator Newsweek Mag., N.Y.C., 1999—; web designer Uproar.com, N.Y.C., 1997-98. Instr. The Mac Learning Ctr., N.Y.C., 2001-2003, Tony Randall's Nat. Actors Theatre, N.Y.C., 1997-2003. Prin. works include theater marquee Ed Sullivan Theater, 1993, logo design Late Show with David Letterman, 1993, 5 Questions, Title Animation, Late Late Show with Craig Kilborn, CBS, 2001. Recipient Emmy Contribution award Acad. TV Arts & Scis., 1986, 87; nominee Emmy award, 1994. Mem. Assn. for Computing Machinery, Art Students League, Broadcast Designers Assn. Avocations: painting, skiing. Office: White Lie Design 160 W End Ave Apt 3K New York NY 10023-5603 E-mail: whiteLied_2000@yahoo.com.

WHITE, ROGER STUART, economist; b. Moline, Ill., June 21, 1942; s. Alvin Charles and Elsie White; m. Marilyn Domas White, Aug. 31, 1968; 1 child, Joshua Stuart. BA, Knox Coll., Ill., 1967; PhD, U. of Ill., 1971. Asst. prof. U. of Conn., Storrs, 1971—75; economist Congl. Rsch. Svc., Washington, 1975—81, asst. chief and specialist in econ. policy, 1981—98, coord. mgmt. studies and specialist in econ. policy, 1998—2004, assoc. dir. rsch., sr. specialist econs. policy, 2004—. Author: Spl. Studies for Congl. Coms. With U.S. Army, 1962—65. Mem.: Assn. for Pub. Policy Analysis and Mgmt., Am. Economics Assn. (life). Office: Congl Rsch Svc Library of Congress Washington DC 20540

WHITE, RONALD JOSEPH, life and biomedical researcher, physiologist, educator; b. Opelousas, La., Dec. 4, 1940; s. John Wesley and Alma Louise (LaSalle) White; m. Margaret Helen Launey, June 8, 1963; children: Joseph LaSalle, Angela Alma, Margaret Leslie. BS in Chemistry, U. S.W. La., 1963; PhD in Phys. Chemistry, U. Wis., 1968. NSF postdoctoral fellow in theoretical chemistry U. Oxford, England, 1967-68; rsch. assoc. Bell Tel. Labs., Murray Hill, NJ, 1968-70; from asst. prof. to assoc. prof. math. U. S.W. La., Lafayette, 1970—76, prof. math., dir. Univ. Honors Program, 1976—80; rsch. assoc. dept. physiology and biophysics U. Miss. Med. Ctr., Jackson, 1973-75; sr. scientist GE Co./Mgmt. and Tech. Svcs. Co., Washington and Houston, 1980-85; chief scientist Life/Biomed. Scis. and Applications Divsn. NASA, Washington, 1985—96; rsch. prof. physiology Uniformed Svcs. U. Health Scis., Bethesda, Md., 1985—96; prof. dept. otorhinolaryngology Baylor Coll. Medicine, Houston, 1996—2003; assoc. dir. Nat. Space Biomed. Rsch. Inst., 1997—2003; sr. fellow Univs. Space Rsch. Assn., Houston, 2003—. Editor (assoc. life scis.): Simulation, 1974—75; editor: (spl.) Medicine and Sci. in Sports and Exercise, 1996; contbr. numerous chpts. to books, papers to profl. jours. Vice pres. Assn. Gifted and Talented Students, La, 1977-80; pres. La. Collegiate Honors Coun., 1978-79. Recipient NASA traineeship, 1963-66, Woodrow Wilson fellowship (hon.), 1963, Am. Inst. Chemists award, 1963, Dist. Prof. award, 1978, Med. Info. Processing Best Paper award 15th ann. Hawaii Internat. Conf. on Systems Scis., 1982, Hon. Mem. award Soc. NASA Flight Surgeons, 1992, Exceptional Achievement medal NASA, 1992. Mem.: Internat. Acad. Astronautics (bd. trustees 1997—, chair life scis. 2001—, commr. space life scis. 2001—03, Luigi Napolitano Lit. award 1996), Am. Soc. for Gravitational and Space Biology (charter mem.), Am. Phys. Soc., Aerospace Med. Assn., Sigma Xi (rsch. award 1976), Phi Kappa Phi. Home: 1303 Primrose Ln Seabrook TX 77586-4718 Office: USRA Divsn Space Life Scis 3600 Bay Area Blvd Houston TX 77058 Office Phone: 281-244-2025. Business E-Mail: white@dsls.usra.edu.

WHITE, RONALD LEON, financial management consultant; b. West York, Pa., July 14, 1930; s. Clarence William and Grace Elizabeth (Gingerich) W.; m. Estheranne Wieder, June 16, 1951; children: Bradford William, Clifford Allen, Erick David. BS in Econs, U. Pa., 1952, MBA, 1957. Cost analysis supr. Air Products & Chem. Corp., Allentown, Pa., 1957-60; cost control mgr. Mack Trucks, Inc., Allentown, 1960-64; mgmt. cons. Peat, Marwick, Mitchell & Co., Phila., 1964-66; mgr. profit planning Monroe, The Calculator Co. (divsn. Litton Industries), Orange, N.J., 1966-67, contr., 1967-68; v.p. fin. Bus. Sys. Group of Litton Industries, Beverly Hills, Calif., 1968-70; pres. Royal Typewriter Co. divsn., Hartford, Conn., 1970-73; exec. v.p., COO, treas., dir. Tenna Corp., Cleve., 1973-75, pres., dir., 1975-77; v.p. fin. Arby's, Inc., Youngstown, Ohio, 1978-79; exec. v.p., dir. Roxbury Am., Inc., 1979-81; v.p. fin., treas. Royal Crown Cos., Inc., Atlanta and Miami Beach, Fla., 1981-86, TDS Healthcare Sys. Corp., Atlanta, 1987-88; v.p. Corp. Fin. Assocs., Atlanta, 1988-90; prin. The Janelle Co., Atlanta, 1991—. Vice chmn. Ga. Mental Health, Mental Retardation, Substance Abuse Regional Bd. #6, 1994-2002, chmn. leadership coun., 1999-2000; v.p. and dir. Ga. Alliance for Mentally Ill, 1997-2003; instr. acctg. Wharton Sch. U. Pa., 1952-53, instr. industry, 1953-54. Deacon area United Ch. of Christ. Lt. USNR, 1954-57. Mem. Am. Mgmt. Assn., Inst. Mgmt. Accts., Nat. Assn. Corp. Dirs., Fin. Execs. Internat., Acacia, Masons, Rotary. Office: The Janelle Co 2362 Kingsgate Ct Atlanta GA 30338-5931 Office Phone: 770-451-8763. E-mail: rlwcfo@mindspring.com.

WHITE, RONNIE L. state supreme court justice; AA, St. Louis C.C., 1977; BA, St. Louis U., 1979; JD, U. Mo., Kansas City, 1983. Bar: Mo. Law intern Jackson County Prosecutors Office; legal asst. U.S. Def. Mapping Agy.; trial atty. Office of Pub. Defender; mem. Mo. Ho. of Reps., 1989-93; judge Mo. Ct. Appeals, 1994; spl. judge Mo. Supreme Ct., 1994-95, justice, 1994-95, assoc. justice, 1995—. Adj. faculty Washington U. Sch. Law, 1997—. Office: PO Box 150 Jefferson City MO 65102-0150

WHITE, ROY BERNARD, theater executive; b. Cin. s. Maurice and Anna (Rudin) W.; m. Sally White, June 17, 1951; children: Maurice, Barbara Dee, Daniel Robert. BA, U. Cin., 1949. Sales staff Twentieth Century Fox Films, Cin.; pres. Mid-States Theatres; dir. Nat. Assn. Theatre Owners, nat. pres., exec. com., chmn. bd. Mem. film adv. panel Ohio Arts Coun.; bd. dirs. Will Rogers Meml. Fund, Found. Motion Picture Pioneers, Inc.; mem. media arts panel Nat. Endowment for Arts. Served with USAAF, 1944-45. Named Exhibitor of Year Internat. Film Importers and Distbrs. Am. Mem. Nat. Assn. Theater Owners (pres.), Am. Film Inst. (trustee 1972-75, exec. com. 1972-75), Fedn. Motion Picture Pioneers (v.p.), Masons, Queen City Racquet, Amberley Village (Ohio) Tennis Club (pres. 1972-73), Bankers Club, Quail Creek Country Club, Bay Colony Country Club, Bay Colony Golf Club. Home: 1274 Waggle Way Naples FL 34108-1994

WHITE, RUSSELL, publishing executive; b. Ill., Sept. 17, 1940; BS, U. Ill., 1962; MA, Stanford (Calif.) U., 1965. Mgr. McGraw Hill Thomson, N.Y.C., 1980-95; pres. Elsevier Sci. Inc., N.Y.C., 1995—. Bd. dirs. Copyright Clearance Ctr. Commn. Office: Elsevier Sci Inc 655 Avenue of Americas New York NY 10010 Home: PO Box 455 Bernardsville NJ 07924-0455

WHITE, SANDRA MARIE, retired artist; b. Ft. Wayne, Ind., Aug. 20, 1947; d. William Rutherford and Alice Ruth White. AS, Ind. U., 1994. Paraprofl. tchr. Adult Basic Edn., Ft. Wayne, 1970—79; clk. Lincoln Life Ins. Co., Ft. Wayne, 1979—80; asst. libr. to head libr. Coll of the Scriptures, Louisville, 1980 81; clk. Dept. of Pub. Welfare, Ft. Wayne, 1984; freelance artist. Bd. dirs. Legal Svcs. Maumee Valley, Inc., Ind., 1999—2004. Contbr. articles to newspapers; exhibitions include The Three Rivers Festival, Ft. Wayne, 1970—90, Avante Guard Art Gallery, 2003—04, Coll. of the Scriptures, Ky., 1980. Mem. missionary Turner Chapel African Meth. Episcopal Ch., Ft. Wayne, 1990—2004; vol. pub. access TV Allen Co Pub. Libr, Ft. Wayne, 1986—94; vol. artist Ft. Wayne Mus. Art, 1987—94. Scholar, Ft. Wayne Art Inst., 1962—96, 1965, Ind. U., 1990. Methodist. Avocations: Scrabble, writing, crafts, sewing, reading.

WHITE, SHANON KATHLEEN, accountant, consultant; b. Hackensack, NJ, July 25, 1953; d. Patrick William Carr, Trudy McFarland; m. Chester Haines White, II; 1 child, Tiffany. Associate of Arts in Accounting, Community College of Aurora, Aurora, Colorado, 1982—84. Acct. Denver Cascade, Inc, Denver, 1984—86, MDC, Inc, Denver, 1986—86; owner Jacqueline, Too, Denver, 1986—86; contr. Michael's Constrn. Co., Kans. City, Kans., 1987—87; acctg. mgr., sys. mgr. Walton Constrn. Co, Inc, Kans. City, Mo., 1987—93; owner Profit Enhancement Profls., Olathe, Kans., 1993—98; acctg. mgr. Mark One Electric Co, Inc, Kans. City, Mo., 1998—99; owner Shanon White Cons., Kans. City, Mo., 1999—2002. Selection Com. Kans. City Fairness in Constrn. Bd., Kans. City, 1991—92; Bd. Pres. Greater Kans. City NAWIC Scholarship Found., Kans. City, 1992—95. Treas. Romanelli West Homes Assoc., Kans. City, 1999—2002. Mem.: Nat. Assn. of Women in Constrn. (pres. 1991 92), Greater Kansas City Timberline Users Group (organizer, local coord. 2001—03). Avocation: Traveling, Dining, Reading. Office: Shanon White Consulting 10500 Meadow Ln Leawood KS 66206 Business E-Mail: scarrwhite@earthlink.net.

WHITE, SHELBY KATHRYN, music educator; b. Little Rock, Aug. 5, 1975; d. David Larry and Beverly Louise Joyner Staggs; m. James David White, Dec. 15, 1994. B Music Edn, Harding U., 1996, MEd, 2000. Cert. tchr. Ark., 1996. Choral dir. Bryant H.S., Ark., 2000—04; assoc. prof. voice Ark. State U., 2004—. Supr./mentor tchr. Bryant Pub. Schs., Ark., 2000—04, choral music dept. chairperson, 2003—04. Soprano Ark. Chamber Singers, Little Rock, 2002 , Coram Deo Music Ministries, North Little Rock, 1998—2004; v.p. for choral music Ark. Music Educators Assn., 2002—. Mem.: Am. Choral Dirs.' Assn. (assoc.), Music Educators Nat. Conf. (assoc.). Church Of Christ. Avocations: interior design, reading.

WHITE, STANLEY ARCHIBALD, research electrical engineer; b. Providence, Sept. 25, 1931; s. Clarence Archibald White and Lou Ella (Givens) Arford; m. Edda María Castaño-Benítez, June 6, 1956; children: Dianne, Stanley Jr., Paul, John. BSEE, Purdue U., 1957, MSEE, 1959, PhD, 1965. Registered profl. engr., Ind., Calif. Engr. Rockwell Internat., Anaheim, Calif., 1959-68, mgr., 1968-84, sr. scientist, 1984-90; pres. Signal Processing and Controls Engring. Corp., 1990—2000; pvt. practice San Clemente, Calif., 2000—. Adj. prof. elec. engring. U. Calif., 1984-97; cons. and lectr. in field; bd. dirs. Asilomar Signals, Systems and Computers Conf. Corp., 1988-2002. Contbr. chpts. to books; articles to profl. jours.; holder 80 patents in field. With USAF, 1951-55. N.Am. Aviation Sci. Engring. fellow, 1963-65; recipient Disting. Lectr. award Nat. Electronics Conf., Chgo., 1973, Engr. of Yr. award Orange County (Calif.) Engring. Coun., 1984, Engr. of Yr. award Rockwell Internat., 1985, Leonardo da Vinci Medallion, 1986, Sci. Achievement award, 1987, Disting. Engring. Alumnus award Purdue U., 1988, Meritorious Inventor's award Rockwell Internat. Corp., 1989, Outstanding Elec. Engr. award Purdue U., 1992, Boeing N.Am. Aviation Top Inventor award, 1998. Fellow AAAS (life), AIAA, IEEE (life; Centennial medal, Millenium medal, chair of ICASSP and ISCAS, Signal Processing Soc. disting. lect. and founding chmn. L.A. coun. chpt., Circuits and Sys. Soc. Tech. Achievement award 1996, Golden Jubilee medal 1999), Inst. for Advancement Engring., N.Y. Acad. Scis. (life); mem. VFW (life), Air Force Assn. (life), Am. Legion (life), Sigma Xi (life; founding pres. Orange County chpt., pres. 1988-2000), Eta Kappa Nu (disting. fellow, internat. dir. emeritus), Tau Beta Pi. Avocation: choral music. Office Phone: 949-498-5519. E-mail: stan.white@ieee.org.

WHITE, STEPHEN HALLEY, biophysicist, educator; b. Wewoka, Okla., May 14, 1940; s. James Halley and Gertrude June (Wyatt) W.; m. Buff Ertl, Aug. 20, 1961 (div. 1982); children: Saill, Shell, Storn, Sharr, Skye, Sunde; m. Jackie Marie Dooley, Apr. 14, 1984. BS in Physics, U. Colo., 1963; MS in Physics, U. Wash., 1965, PhD in Physiology and Biophysics, 1969. USPHS postdoctoral fellow biochemistry U. Va., Charlottesville, 1971-72; asst. prof. physiology and biophysics U. Calif., Irvine, 1972-75, assoc. prof. physiology and biophysics, 1975-78, prof. physiology and biophysics, 1978—, vice chmn. physiology and biophysics, 1974-75, chmn. physiology and biophysics, 1977-89. Guest biophysicist Brookhaven Nat. Lab., Upton, L.I., N.Y., 1977-99. Contbr. numerous articles to profl. jours. Served to capt. USAR, 1969-71. Recipient Research Career Devel. award USPHS, 1975-80, Kaiser-Permanente Tchg. award, 1975, 92; fellow Biophysical Soc., 2002; grantee NIH, 1971—, NSF, 1971—. Mem. NSF (adv. panel for molecular biology 1982-85, mem. nat. steering com. advanced neutron source 1992-95), Internat. Union Pure and Applied Biophysics (U.S. nat. com. 1997—, chmn. 2000-04), Fedn. Am. Soc. for Exptl. Biology (bd. dirs. 1998-2002), Biophys. Soc. (chmn. membrane biophysics subgroup 1977-78, acting sec., treas. 1979-80, coun. 1981-84, exec. bd. 1981-83, program chmn. 1985, ann. meeting, sec. 1987-95, pres. 1996-97, Disting. Svc. award 1999), Am. Physiol. Soc. (editl. bd. 1981-93, membership com. 1985-86, publ. com. 1987-91), Assn. Chmn. Depts. Physiology (rep. to coun. acad. socs. 1981-82, councilor 1982-83, pres. 1986-87), Soc. Gen. Physiologists (treas. 1985-88), The Protein Soc. (electronic pub. coord. 1993—). Avocations: skiing, cooking, travel. Office: U Calif Dept Physiology & Biophysics Med Sci I-D346 Irvine CA 92697-4560

WHITE, TERRENCE HAROLD, academic administrator, sociologist; b. Ottawa, Ont., Can., Mar. 31, 1943; s. William Harold and Shirley Margaret (Ballantine) W.; m. Susan Elizabeth Hornaday; children: Christine Susan, Julie Pamela. PhD, U. Toronto, 1972. Head dept. sociology and anthropology U. Windsor, Canada, 1973-75; prof., chmn. dept. sociology U. Alta., Edmonton, Canada, 1975-80, dean faculty of arts, 1980-88; pres. T.H. White Orgn. Rsch. Svcs. Ltd., Edmonton, 1975—, Brock U., St. Catharines, 1988-96, U. Calgary, Alta., 1996—2001, pres. emeritus, prof. bus., 2001—. Author: Power or Pawns: Boards of Directors, 1978, Human Resource Management, 1979; editor: Introduction to Work Science, 1981, QWL in Canada: Case Studies, 1983. Bd. dirs. Progressive Conservative Assn., Edmonton South, 1976-81, 1st v.p., 1981-85, pres., 1985-87; bd. dirs. Tri-Bach Festival Found., Edmonton, 1981-88, Alta. Ballet Co., 1985-88, Edmonton Conv. and Tourism Authority, Arch Enterprises, 1984-88, Niagara Symphony Soc., YMCA, St. Catharines, 1988-92; chair United Way Campaign St. Catharines, 1992, Fox Found., 1990-96, Can. Summer Games 2001 Bid Com.; bd. dirs. Edmonton Symphony Soc., v.p., 1986-88; bd. govs. U. Alta., 1984-88, Brock U., 1988-96, Ridley Coll., 1990—, Alta. Heritage Found. for Med. Rsch.; active Calgary R & D Authority, 1997; divsn. chair Calgary United Way Campaign, Calgary Econ. Devel. Authority, 1997-2000, McMahon Stadium Soc., Calgary Children's Initiative, Ctr. for Affordable Water and Sanitation; nat. bd. gov.'s Scouts Can., 2003- Recipient Can. 125 Commemorative medal Govt. of Can., Queen's Golden Jubilee medal. Mem. Calgary Petroleum Club, Ranchmen's Club, Rotary (pres. Edmonton South 1981-82), Delta Tau Kappa, Alpha Kappa Delta. Home: Box 68028 28 Crowfoot Terr NW Calgary AB Canada T3G 3N8 Office: U Calgary 2500 University Dr NW Calgary AB Canada T2N 1N4

WHITE, TERRY EDWARD, physician; b. Springfield, Mo., May 30, 1954; s. Roy Edward and Eselean (Moffis) W.; m. Susan Marie Peters, Aug. 16, 1981. BA, Drury Coll., 1976; MD, U. Mo., 1980. Diplomate Am. Bd. Physical Medicine and Rehab. Physician Lakeshore Hosp., Birmingham, Ala., 1983-86; clin. instr. U. Ala., Birmingham, 1984-86; physician Thomas Rehab., Asheville, N.C., 1986-97, chief staff, 1994-97, vice-chief staff, 1992-94; physician Rehab. Solutions Western N.C., Asheville, 1998—; attending physician Mission Hosp., 1986—. Alternate Medicare State Carrier adv. com., Greensboro, N.C., 1993; bd. dirs. Nationwide Post Polio Support Group, Dallas, N.C., 1992-94; vice chmn. Western N.C. Health Care Provider Coun., 1995-96, chmn., 1996-97; mem. editl. adv. com. Stroke Rehabilitation. Author: A Patient's and Physician Guide to Late Effects of Polio, 1995; mem. editl. staff Stroke Rehabilitation-Patient Education Guide, 1995. Named Rehab. Physician Yr., N.C. Med. Soc., 1993. Fellow Am. Acad. Phys. Medicine and Rehab.; mem. N.C. Soc. Phys. Medicine and Rehab. (v.p. 1989-91, pres. 1991-93). Republican. Mem. Christian Ch. Avocations: gardening, woodwork, metal work, reading, music. Office: Rehab Solutions Western NC 4 Doctors Park Ste C Asheville NC 28801-4523 Office Phone: 828-285-9795.

WHITE, THOMAS E. former federal agency administrator; Degree in ops. rsch., Naval Postgrad. Sch., Monterey, Calif., 1974; postgrad., U.S. Army War Coll., 1984; grad., U.S. Mil. Acad., 1967. Exec. assist. to chmn. Joint Chiefs, Washington, 1989—90; commd. 2d lt. U.S. Army, 1967, advanced through grades to brigadier gen., 1990, ret., 1990; various sr. exec. positions Enron, 1990—2001; sec. of Army Dept. Def., Washington, 2001—03.

WHITE, THOMAS EDWARD, lawyer; b. N.Y.C., July 11, 1933; s. Thomas Aubrey and Gladys Mary (Piper) W.; m. Joan Carolyn Olsen, Dec. 2, 1967 (dec.); children: Charles Garret, Nancy Carolyn, Linda Marie, Penelope Lindsay, Elizabeth Ann. AB, Princeton U., 1955; LLB, Columbia U., 1960; BA summa cum laude, SUNY-Purchase Coll., 2002; student, NYU Inst. Fine Arts, 2002—. Bar: N.Y. 1961. Atty. Seward & Kissel, N.Y.C., 1960-69; gen. counsel Howmet Corp., N.Y.C., 1969-70; v.p., gen. counsel, sec. Howmedica, Inc., N.Y.C., 1970-74, sr. v.p., dir., 1974-83; pvt. practice N.Y.C., 1983-97. Ptnr. Westmed Venture Ptnrs. (formerly Integrated Med. Venture Ptnrs.), N.Y.C., 1987 99; chmn. Shoreside Cons. Ltd., Miami, Fla., 1987-98. Mem. Mamaroneck Town Coun., 1971-75; mem. vestry Episcopalian Ch., 1987-90, mem. diocesan coun. Episcopal Ch. N.Y., 2001--. Served to 1st lt. U.S. Army, 1955-57. Mem.: Larchmont (N.Y.) Yacht; Princeton (N.Y.C.). Republican. Home: 260 Barnard Rd Larchmont NY 10538-1941

WHITE, THOMAS RAEBURN, III, law educator, consultant; b. Phila., Aug. 18, 1938; s. Thomas Raeburn Jr. and Charlotte (Gerhard) W.; m. Margaret Bardwell, Dec. 12, 1960 (div. June 1975); children: Elizabeth Krusenstjerna, Kathleen White, Thomas Ray IV; m. Maria Llanes, Oct. 19, 1975. BA, Williams Coll., 1960; LLB, U. Pa., 1963. Bar: Pa. 1964, Va. 1971. Assoc. White and Williams, Phila., 1963-65; atty.-advisor TLC U.S. Treasury Dept., Washington, 1965-67; assoc. prof. U. Va., Charlottesville, 1967-70, prof. law, 1970-96, John C. Stennis prof., 1996—. Legis. atty. Joint Com. on Tax U.S. Congress, Washington, 1973-75; cons. adminstrn. conf. IRS Project, Washington, 1975-76; vis. prof. NYU Law Sch., N.Y.C., 1978-79. Mem. ABA (com. chmn. tax sect. 1987-87, 96-98), Am. Coll. Tax Counsel, Va. Bar Assn., Va. State Bar Assn., Phila. Bar Assn., Charlottesville-Albemarle Bar Assn. Home: 12 Deer Path Charlottesville VA 22903-4707 Office: U Va Sch Law 580 Massie Rd Charlottesville VA 22903-1738 Office Phone: 434-924-3896. Business E-Mail: trw@virginia.edu.

WHITE, TIMOTHY PAUL, brokerage house executive; b. Ft. Sill, Okla., Jan. 9, 1963; s. Paul R. and Lucille (Mattison) White; m. Susan Gertrude Foreman, Dec. 29, 1984; children: Jessica Lynn, Rebecca Anne, Kathleen Marie. BS in Fin., Pa. State U., 1985. Cert. fin. planner Colo. Assoc. planner, agt. Pa. Fin. Group, Harrisburg, Pa., 1988-92; mgr. mktg. and sales Meridian Securities, Inc., Reading, Pa., 1992-96; v.p. products and sales mgr. Core States Securities Corp., Reading, 1996-98; regional sales mgr. First Union Brokerage Svcs. Inc., 1998-2001; fin. advisor First Union Securities Inc., 2001—02; pres. Investors Ctrl. Comm. Inc.; mng. dir. Guidon, LLC, 2001—; fin. advisor Wachovia Securities Inc., 2002—. Spkr. Nat. Mut. Fund Conf., 1995, Cmty. Bank Investment Program Symposium, 1996, Nat. Investment Products Conf., 1996. Author: Money Smart Records, 2002; contbg. editor: Bank Securities Jour.; contbr. articles to profl. jours. Program cons. Jr. Achievement, Lancaster, Pa., 1990—91; pres. Adamstown Recreation Bd., 1996. 1st lt. U.S. Army, 1985—88, with USAR, 1989—92. Decorated Commendation medal, Achievement medal; recipient George C. Marshal award, U.S. Army, 1985; scholar ROTC, 1980—84. Mem.: Ctrl. Pa. Soc. Inst. CFP (bd. dirs. 1996—, pres.-elect 1998, pres. 1999), U.S. Cav. Assn. (fundraising com. 1994—96), Inst. CFP. Republican. Lutheran. Avocations: military and political history, reading, gardening, woodworking. Office: Wachovia Securities Inc 12 E Market St York PA 17401 Office Phone: 717-852-5214.

WHITE, TOM WILLINGHAM, private investor; b. McAllen, Tex., Feb. 16, 1943; s. Louis Thomas and Leota Faye (Grimm) W.; m. Lauryn G. Longwell, Mar. 8, 1968; children: Brad Edward, Parker Thomas, Landon Allen. BBA, U. Tex., 1965. Acct. Haskins & Sells, CPAs, Houston, 1965-67, Paul Veale, CPA, McAllen, Tex., 1967-68; pvt. practice acctg. Corpus Christi, Tex., 1969-79; pres. Miller of Dallas, Inc., 1980—94; chmn. White Capital Mgmt., Inc., Dallas, Brushy Creek Timber Co., Inc., Dallas. Mem. chancellor's coun. U. Tex. Sys.; mem. investment com. St. Mark's Sch. of Tex. Mem.: World President's Orgn., Am. Inst. CPA's, U. Tex. Bus. Sch., Hermes Soc., Cooper Fitness Ctr., Brookhollow Golf Club. Home: 10111 Strait Ln Dallas TX 75229 Office: 6370 LBJ Fwy Ste 278 Dallas TX 75240 Office Phone: 972-386-4200.

WHITE, TOMMI A. human resources firm executive; Grad., Oakland U. Dir. sys. Ryder; asst. v.p., project dir. br. automotion Nat. Bank Detroit; divsn. v.p. Automated Data Processing, N.J.; exec. v.p., chief adminstrn. & technology officer Kelly Svcs., Inc., Troy, Mich., 1998—. Office: Kelly Svcs 999 W Big Beaver Rd Troy MI 48084-4716

WHITE, VANCE R.(RANDY), medical company executive; Exec. v.p. ops. Nat. Health Labs, Ind. cons., with Am. Med. Labs, Inc., exec. v.p. tech. opns and R&D; CEO, dir. Nanogen, Inc., San Diego. Office: Nanogen Inc 10398 Pacific Center Ct San Diego CA 92121

WHITE, W. ROBIN, writer; b. Kodaikanal, Madras, India, July 12, 1928; came to U.S., 1944; s. Emmons Eaton and Ruth Esther (Parker) W.; m. Marian Lucille Biesterfield, Feb. 3, 1948 (dec. Mar. 1983); children: Christopher, Parker, Shelley. BA, Yale U., 1950; MA, Calif. State Poly. U., 1991. Instr. writers program UCLA, 1985-93; lectr. Calif. State Poly. U., Pomona, 1985-93. Exec. officer Calif. State Regional Ctrs., Ukiah, Calif., 1973-79. Author: Elephant Hill, 1959 (Harper prize), House of Many Rooms, 1958, Men and Angels, 1961, Foreign Soil, 1962, All in Favor Say No, 1964, His Own Kind, 1967, Be Not Afraid, 1972, The Special Child, 1978, The Troll of Crazy Mule Camp, 1979, Moses the Man, 1981, The Winning Writer: Studies in the Art of Self-Expression, 1997; anthologies include: Best American Stories, O. Henry Prize Stories, Best Modern Short Stories, Seventeen's Stories, others; contbr. numerous mags. including Harper's, The New Yorker, New York Times, L.A. Times, Harper's Bazaar, Saturday Evening Post, Ladies' Home Jour., Seventeen, Nat. Wildlife, Mademoiselle, The Reporter; author poetry (Poetry award 1993, 94, 95); editor-in-chief Per/Se Internat. Quar., 1965-69; fiction editor UCLA West/Word, 1989-90. Class rep. Kodai-Woodstock Found., 1986-2000; elder Presbyn. Session, Claremont, Calif., 1988-91; mem. libr. commn. Pasadena Presbyn. Ch., 1996-99. Recipient Disting. Achievement award Ednl. Press Assn., 1974, North Coast Regional Ctr., Ukiah, 1978, Harper prize Harper & Bros., 1959, O. Henry award Doubleday, 1960, New Century Writers award, 2000; Bread Loaf fellow Middlebury Coll., 1956, Stegner fellow Stanford U., 1956-57. Mem. Calif. State Poetry Soc., Authors Guild, Am. Acad. Poets. Democrat. Presbyterian. Avocations: backpacking, gardening, photography, birds. Home: 1940 Fletcher Ave South Pasadena CA 91030-4625 E-mail: romarwrite@aol.com.

WHITE, WARREN WURTELE, retired retailing executive; b. McKeesport, Pa., Feb. 29, 1932; s. Jay Leonard and Elizabeth Katherine (Fehr) W.; m. Marjorie Ada Shuman, Mar. 20, 1954; 1 dau., Laura Lynn. BS, Duquesne U., 1954; M.Retailing, U. Pitts., 1957. With Strawbridge & Clothier, Phila., 1957-97, buyer, 1960-67, budget store divisional mdse. mgr., 1968-70, Clover Div. gen. mdse. mgr., 1970-76, v.p. for mdse. and sales promotion, 1977-79, exec. v.p., 1979-96, also dir., 1981-97; gen. mgr. Strawbridge & Clothier (Clover Div.), 1979-96; pvt. retailing cons. Haddonfield, N.J., 1997-98, Naples, Fla., 1998—. Bd. dirs. Ea. Star Charity Found. N.J., 1978-83. Served to 1st lt. arty. U.S. Army, 1954-56. Mem. Internat. Mass Retail Assn. (officer 1987-93, bd. dirs. 1981-96, chmn. bd. 1991-93), South Jersey C. of C. (bd. dirs. 1991-96), Am. Lung Assn. (bd. dirs. Phila. chpt. 1991-94), Masons, Kensington Golf and Country Club, Quail Creek Country Club. Republican. Presbyterian. Home: 11349 Longshore Way East Naples FL 34119

WHITE, WILL WALTER, III, public relations consultant, writer; b. Glen Ridge, NJ, July 3, 1930; s. Will Walter and Miriam Chandler (Milburn) W.; m. Phyllis Marcia DuFlocq, Dec. 28, 1951 (div. 1971); children: Will Walter IV, Scott, Alan; m. Anne Elizabeth Levenson, Nov. 21, 1971 (div. 1992); children: Duncan, Christopher; stepchildren: Michael, Susan; m. Catherine Laur, Aug. 26, 1992. BA, Cornell U., 1952. Supr. Union Carbide Corp., N.Y.C., 1954-59; account exec. Ketchum, MacLeod & Grove, N.Y.C., 1959-62; sr. v.p. Wilson, Haight & Welch, Hartford, Conn., 1962-72; chmn., chief exec. officer Lowengard & Brotherhood, Hartford, 1972-83; pres., chief exec. officer Harland & Tine & White, Hartford, 1983-87; chmn. Donahue Inc., Hartford, 1987-89; ptnr. Laur White & White, Heathsville, Va., 1992—2000; owner Omega Cubed Press, 1996—. Exec. com. Conn. Dist. Export Council, 1979-88. Author: The Sunfish Book, 1983, 96; contbg. editor Mid-Gulf Sailing mag., 1994-95. Mem. exec. com. Hartford Stage Co., 1982-86; pres. Vis. Nurse Assn., Hartford, 1979; fin. chmn. Vis. Nurse and Home Care, Inc., Hartford and Waterbury, 1982-91; mem. pub. rels. com. Fairfield County Rep. Com., 1961; chmn. S.W. Fla. Regional Harbor Bd., 1995-2000. 1st lt. U.S. Army, 1952-54. Nat. champion Sunfish Racing Class, 1966, 68 Mem. Pub. Rels. Soc. Am. (accredited, chmn. investor rels. sect. 1983, charter mem. Hall of Fame 1990), Bus. Profl. Advt. Assn. (cert. bus. communicator), Nat. Investor Rels. Inst., U.S. Sunfish Class Assn. (pres. 1985-88, charter mem. Hall of Fame 1991), Boaters Action and Info. League (exec. v.p. 1992-2000), Hist. Soc. Sarasota County (bd. dirs. 1995-2000). Address: 3220 S E Hansel Ave Arcadia FL 34266-3143

WHITE, WILLIAM, III, retail executive; BBA, Southwestern Meth. U., 1971. Ter. oper. mgr. Sears Roebuck and Co., 1988—89, nat. mktg. mgr., automotive, 1990—91, nat. mgr., product svc., 1991—93, regional v.p., southwest, 1993—99, sr. v.p., gen. mgr., automotive group, 1999—2003, exec. v.p., store ops., 2003—. Office: Sears Roebuck and Co 3333 Beverly Rd Hoffman Estates IL 60179

WHITE, WILLIAM BLAINE, geochemist, researcher; b. Huntingdon, Pa., Jan. 5, 1934; s. William Bruce and Eleanor Mae (Barr) W.; m. Elizabeth Loczi, Mar. 27, 1959; children: Nikki Elizabeth White Vezendi, William Brion (dec.). BS, Juniata Coll., 1954; PhD, Pa. State U., 1962. Rsch. assoc. Mellon Inst., Pitts., 1954-58; asst. prof. Pa. State U., University Park, 1963-67, assoc. prof., 1967-72, prof. geochemistry, 1972—2002, emeritus prof., 2002—, chmn. grad. program in materials, 1990-93. Assoc. editor Am. Mineralogist, 1972-75, Materials Rsch. Bull., 1979-93, Jour. Am. Ceramic Soc., 1985-93, Water Resources Bull., 1992-93; editor earth scis. Nat. Speleological Soc. Bull., 1964-94; author: Geomorphology and Hydrology of Karst Terrains, 1988, (with Elizabeth L. White) Karst Hydrology: Concepts from the Mammoth Cave Area, 1989, (with Susan Barger) Daguerreotype: Nineteenth-Century Technology and Modern Science, 1991, (with David C. Culver) Encyclopedia of Caves, 2004; contbr. articles to profl. jours. Home: 4538 Miller Rd Petersburg PA 16669-2711 Office: Pa State U Materials Rsch Lab University Park PA 16802 Office Phone: 814-865-1152.

WHITE, WILLIAM H. mayor; married; 3 children. BS in Econs. magna cum laude, Harvard U., 1976; JD, U. Tex., 1979. Atty. Susaman Godfrey LLP, Houston, 1979—93; instr. antitrust law and voting rights U. Tex., Austin; dep. sec., COO Dept. Energy, Washington, 1993—95; chmn. Howe-Baker Internat., Tyler, Tex., 1997—2000; pres., CEO The Wedge Group, Houston, 1997—2003; mayor City of Houston, 2004—. Office: City Hall 901 Bagby St 3rd Fl Houston TX 77002 also: PO Box 1562 Houston TX 77251 Office Phone: 713-247-2200. E-mail: mayor@cityofhouston.net.*

WHITE, WILLIAM NELSON, lawyer; b. Balt., Sept. 8, 1938; s. Nelson Cardwell and Ellen Atwell (Zoller) W.; m. Mary Kathleen Bitzel, Sept. 2, 1960 (div. 1971); children: Craig William, Jeffrey Alan, Colin Christopher; m. Christine Lewin Hanna, July 8, 1978. LLB, U. Md., 1968, JD, 1969. Bar: Md. 1972, U.S. Ct. Appeals (4th cir.) 1975, U.S. Dist. Ct. Md. 1976, U.S. Supreme Ct. 1976. Asst. state's atty., Balt., 1972; assoc. Brooks & Turnbull, Balt., 1973—76; pvt. practice Balt., 1977—. Counsel St. Andrews Soc. Balt., 1989—; counsel, bd. dirs. St. George's Soc. Former elder, pres. deacons, trustee Roland Park Presbyn. Ch.; former mem. worship, music and sacrament coun., former elder Second Presbyn. Ch. Mem. Md. Bar Assn., Baltimore County Bar Assn., U. Md. Alumni Assn. for Greater Balt. (pres. 1977), SAR (chancellor for Md. Soc.). Avocations: history, philosophy, classical music, tennis, sailing.

WHITE, WILLIAM NORTH, chemistry professor; b. Walton, N.Y., Sept. 16, 1925; s. George Fitch and Frances (Peck) W.; m. Hilda R. Sauter, Sept. 8, 1951; children: Carla Ann, Eric Jeffrey. AB, Cornell U., 1950; MA, Harvard U., 1951, PhD, 1953. NRC postdoctoral fellow Calif. Inst. Tech., Pasadena, 1953-54; asst. prof. Ohio State U., Columbus, 1954-59, asso. prof., 1959-63; prof. chemistry U. Vt., Burlington, 1963-76, 77-95, prof. emeritus, 1995—, chmn. dept., 1963-70, acting chmn. dept., 1975-76; prof. chemistry U. Tex. at Arlington, 1976-77, chmn. dept., 1976-77. NSF sr. postdoctoral fellow Brookhaven Nat. Lab., Upton, N.Y., 1963-64, Harvard U., 1965; vis. scholar Brandeis U., 1974-75; chmn. arrangements com. Nat. Organic Chemistry Symposium, 1966-67. Contbr. articles on organic chemistry profl. jours. Selectman Town of Shelburne, Vt., 1968-74, water commr., 1973-74, justice of the peace, 1981-, sewer commr., 1991-93, Natural Resources and Conservation com., 2004-; mem. Chittenden County Regional Planning Commn., 1983-91; mem. bd. suprs. Winooski (Vt.) Natural Resources Conservation Dist., 1999-2004. With AUS, 1943-46. Recipient Outstanding Forest Stewardship award Winooski Conservation Dist., 1997. Mem. Am. Chem. Soc. (chmn. Western Vt. sect. 1966-67), Royal Soc. Chemistry, New Eng. Assn. Chemistry Tchrs., AAAS, N.Y. Acad. Scis., Phi Beta Kappa, Sigma Xi, Phi Kappa Phi, Phi Lambda Upsilon. Home: 226 Pierson Dr Shelburne VT 05482

WHITE, WILLIAM RICHARD, manufacturing engineer, consultant; b. Muncie, Ind., May 4, 1948; s. William Richard and Barbara Ann White; m. Sandra Jo VanNatter; children: Matthew Shaw, Amy, Roxanne Lynnette Alcazar, Michael James. BA, Ball State U., Muncie, Ind., 1975, MA, 1978; PhD, Walden U., Mpls., 1998—2002. Cert. shainin journeyman. Kaizen mgr. New Venture Gear, Muncie, Ind., 1998—2000, mfg. engring. supr., 2000—. Cons. White's Consulting Svcs., Albany, Ind., 2000—03. Sgt USAF, 1968—72, Crete. Mem.: Acad. Mgmt., Epsilon Pi Tau. Home: PO Box 63 Albany IN 47320 Personal E-mail: billwh87@aol.com.

WHITE, WILLIAM SAMUEL, foundation executive; b. Cin., May 8, 1937; s. Nathaniel Ridgway and Mary (Lowndes) W.; m. Claire Mott, July 1, 1961; children: Tiffany Lowndes, Ridgway Harding. BA, Dartmouth Coll., 1959, MBA, 1960; LL.D. (hon.), Eastern Mich. U., 1975; hon. degree, GMI Engring. & Mgmt. Inst., 1996. With Barrett & Williams, N.Y.C., 1961-62; sr. assoc. Bruce Payne & Assos., N.Y.C., 1962-71; v.p. C. S. Mott Found., Flint, Mich., 1971-75, pres., 1976—, trustee, 1971—, also chmn. bd. dirs. Chmn. bd. dirs. U.S. Sugar Corp.; bd. dirs. Am. Water Works, 1999—2003. Exec. com. Daycroft Sch., Greenwich, Conn., 1966-70; bd. dirs. Flint Area Conf., 1971-84, Coun. on Founds., 1985-90, Independent Sector, 1994-99, 2004—, Am. Friends Czech. Republic, 1999-, European Found. Centre, 1994—, Civicus, 1995-2001; citizens adv. task force U. Mich., Flint, 1974-79; chmn. Coun. of Mich. Founds., 1979-81, Flint Area Focus Coun., 1988—, After-school Allstars, 2004-; mem. Pres.'s Task Force on Pvt. Sector Initiatives, 1982; trustee GMI Engring. and Mgmt. Inst., 1982-86, Network European Founds., 2000—, The Czech Rep., 2000—, Afterschool Allstars, 2004—. With U.S. Army, 1960-62. Office: C S Mott Foundation 1200 Mott Foundation Bldg Flint MI 48502-1807

WHITE, WILLIAM THOMAS, curator, historian, educator; b. Emporia, Kans., June 3, 1948; s. Larry Ernest and Jeanne Eunita White; m. Marilyn Kay Dietrich; children: Alisha Rae, Zachary Marty, Elizabeth Kim Dietrich Schultz, Andrew Lee Dietrich Schultz. BS in polit. science and history, U. of Mont., 1970, MA in history, 1975; PhD in history, U. of Wash., 1981. Vis. asst. prof. Dept. of History, U. of Minn., 1987, Dept. of History, St. Cloud State U., 1995; cmty. faculty Dept. of History, Met. State U., Minn., 1994—; curator James J. Hill Libr., St. Paul, 1981—. Cons. U. Publications of Am., Frederick, Md., 1983—85; mem., Solon J. Buck and Theodore C. Blegen awards com. Minn. Hist. Soc., 1991. Mem. adv. bd. Jour. Of The West, 2001—03, guest editor Railroads And The American West; author, editor: over 45 articles to profl. jours.; also microfilm pubs.; book reviewer for over 40 reviews on publications with the history of bus., labor, politics, and the Am. N.W., 1984—, manuscript referee/reviewer several publications. Chmn., commentator, and/or presenter 52 sessions of profl. hist. orgns., 1973—; proposal reviewer Nat. Endowment for the Humanities, Washington, 1989—91, Idaho Dept. of Edn., 1989—92. Doctoral Rsch. grant, Dept. of History, U. of Wash., 1980, Daughters of the Pioneers award, 1977, Academic advisor, 1979—81, Tchg. asst., 1976—77, Dept. of History, U. of Mont., 1972—74. Mem.: Lexington Group in Transp. History, Bus. History Conf., Bus. History Assn., Minn. Hist. Assn., Orgn. of Am. Historians, Wash. State Hist. Soc., Am. History Association-Pacific Coast Br., Western History Assn. Protestant. Achievements include obtained, opened and promoted nationally significant manuscript collections for the study of business activitiy and its implications for the larger society, coupled with research and publication. Avocations: tennis, travel, stamp collecting/philately. Office: James J Hill Library 80 West Fourth St Saint Paul MN 55102 E-mail: twhite@jjhill.org.

WHITE, WILLIS SHERIDAN, JR., retired utilities company executive; b. nr. Portsmouth, Va., Dec. 17, 1926; s. Willis Sheridan and Carrie (Culpepper) W.; m. LaVerne Behrends, Oct. 8, 1949; children: Willis Sheridan III, Marguerite Spangler, Cynthia D.W. Haight. BS, Va. Poly. Inst., 1948; MS, Mass. Inst. Tech., 1958. With Am. Electric Power Co. Inc., 1948-91; chmn., chief exec. officer Am. Electric Power Co., Inc. and its subs., N.Y.C., 1976-90, chmn., 1991, mem. bd. dirs., 1972-92. Pres., bd. dirs. Ohio Valley Electric Corp., Ind.-KTV Electric Corp., 1977-91. Trustee Battellle Meml. Inst., Grant/Riverside Meth. Hosp., Columbus. With USNR, 1945-46. Sloan fellow, 1957-58 Mem. IEEE, NAE, Eta Kappa Nu, Omicron Delta Kappa. Methodist.

WHITE, YMISTYE LAYMONDE, artist, composer, publishing executive; d. William Henry White and Rhussus (White) Shelby. Pres. Sun Glow Pub., Tuskegee Institute, 1981—. Composer: Extended Dimensions, 1994; author: Ymistye White an Autobiography, 2000. Recipient Golden Poet award, World of Poetry, 1988. Mem.: Sound Exch. Home and Studio: 3406 W Martin Luther King Hwy Tuskegee Institute AL 36088 Personal E-mail: ymistyewhite@webtv.ne.

WHITE BUFFALO, CHARLES DEAN, social studies educator, consultant; b. Bullhead, S.Dak., Aug. 7, 1957; children: Tyrel, Tabor. AA in Phys. Edn., Ctrl. Wyo. Coll., 1989; AA in Lakota Studies, Oglala Lakota Coll., 1993, BA in Lakota Studies, 1995, MA in Lakota Leadership and Mgmt., 2004. Instr. Lakota Studies Oglala Lakota Coll., Kyle, SD, 1994—. Office: Oglala Lakota College PO Box 490 Kyle SD 57752

WHITEHEAD, ALFRED K. labor union administrator; Gen. pres. Internat. Assn. Fire Fighters, Washington. Office: Internat Assn Fire Fighters 3d Fl 1750 New York Ave NW 3d Fl Washington DC 20006-5301

WHITEHEAD, CLAY THOMAS, economist; b. Neodesha, Kans., Nov. 13, 1938; s. Clay Bell and Helen Whitehead; m. Margaret Mahon, May 19, 1973; children: Abigail Walton, Clay Cother. BS, Mass. Inst. Tech., 1960, MS in Elec. Engring, 1961, PhD in Mgmt, 1967. Cons. def. studies RAND Corp., 1961-63, economist, 1967-69; mem. Pres.-Elect's Task Force on Budget Policies, 1968-69; spl. asst. to Pres. Nixon, 1969-70; dir. U.S. Office Telecommunications Policy, 1970-74; organized Pres. Ford transition, 1974; fellow Harvard Inst. Politics Mass. Inst. Tech. Center for Internat. Studies, 1974-76; pres. Allison Tech. Services, Santa Monica, Calif., 1976-78, Hughes Communications Inc., Los Angeles, 1979-83; founder SES Astra, 1983-85; pres. Nat. Exch. Inc., 1985—, Clay Whitehead Assocs., McLean, 1985—. Served with AUS, 1963-65. Office: PO Box 8090 Mc Lean VA 22106-8090

WHITEHEAD, COLSON, writer; b. NYC; BA, Harvard U., 1991. Author: The Intuitionist, 1998, John Henry Days, 2001. Recipient Whiting Writers' award, 2000, Young Lion's Fiction award, NY Pub. Libr., 2002. Office: c/o Random House 1745 Broadway New York NY 10019

WHITEHEAD, COREY ENNIS, music educator; b. Spruce Pine, N.C., June 22, 1969; s. Loren Stanley and Doris Marie Whitehead; m. Laila Arabi Whitehead, Feb. 8, 1997. MusB, U. Ariz., 1991, MusM, 1993, D of Music Arts, 2002. Prof. music Va. Commonwealth U., Richmond, 1994, Pima C.C., Tucson, 1994, The Levine Sch. Music, Washington, 2000—01, Duke Ellington Sch. Arts, 2000—02; lectr. music Calif. State U., Fresno, 2003—. Author: Sonata Para Guitarra by Antonio Jose, An Analysis, Performers Guide, 2002, The Flamenco Classical Tradition Vol. I: A Tech. Guitar Method and Intro. to Music, 2004, The Art of Flamenco Improvisation, 2003. Mentor Acad. Preparation for Excellence, Tucson, 1988. Mem.: Tucson Guitar Soc. (pres. 1996—97), Washington Guitar Soc. (editor 2000—02), San Joaquin Valley Guitar Soc. (v.p. 2003—), Guitar Found. Am., Calif. Music Educators Assn. Avocation: surfing. Home: 43 Robinson Ave Pittsburg CA 94565 Office: Calif State U Dept Music 2380 E Keats Ave MS MB77 Fresno CA 93740-8024 Office Phone: 559-278-2670.

WHITEHEAD, DAVID BARRY, lawyer; b. San Francisco, Oct. 14, 1946; s. Barry and Fritzi-Beth (Bowman) W.; m. René Dayan, May 26, 1990. AB in History, Stanford U., 1968, JD, 1971. Bar: Calif. 1972, U.S. Dist. Ct. (no. dist.) Calif. 1972, U.S. Ct. Appeals (9th cir.) 1972, U.S. Dist. Ct. (cen. dist.) Calif. 1974. Assoc. Cullinan Hancock Rothert & Burns, San Francisco, 1972-74, Cullinan Burns & Helmer, San Francisco, 1975-77, ptnr., 1977-78, Burns & Whitehead, San Francisco, 1979-85, Whitehead & Porter, San Francisco, 1986-97, Whitehead, Porter & Gordon LLP, San Francisco, 1998—. Bd. dirs. Rainbow Music, Inc., San Francisco, ITP, Inc., Sunnyvale, Calif.; founding dir. A. Lincoln High Sch. San Francisco, 1989—. Mem. San Francisco Rep. Steering Com., 1984—89; bd. dirs. Enterprise for High Sch. Students, San Francisco, 1982—86; bd. dirs. San Francisco chpt. Easter Seal Soc., 1986—90; bd. dirs. Opera West Found., San Francisco, 1986—90, Traveler's Aid Soc., San Francisco, 1989—, Hosp. de la Familia, 1995—2000, Gold Rush Trail Found., 1998, Calif. Hist. Soc. Found., 1998. Mem. ABA, Calif. Bar Assn., San Francisco Bar Assn., Calif. Scholarship Fedn. (life) Family Club San Francisco (bd. dirs. 1986-89, 93-95), World Trade Club, Abraham Lincoln High Sch. San Francisco Alumni Assn. (founding dir.). Roman Catholic. Avocations: tenor, writer, director, actor. Home: 1896 Pacific Ave Apt 502 San Francisco CA 94109-2302 Office: Whitehead Porter & Gordon LLP 220 Montgomery St Fl 18 San Francisco CA 94104-3402

WHITEHEAD, EDGAR DOUGLAS, urology educator; b. Galashiels, Scotland, Aug. 24, 1939; 1 child, Robin Stacey. BA, Vanderbilt U., 1961; MD, Ind. U., 1965; postgrad., U. London, 1972. Diplomate Am. Bd. Urology; med. lic. Ind., Ill., N.Y., Calif., N.J. Surgery intern Mount Sinai Hosp., N.Y.C., 1965-66; resident in surgery Presbyn.-St. Luke's Hosp., Chgo., 1966-67; resident in urology N.Y.U. Med. Ctr., 1969-73; clin. assoc. urology Mount Sinai Sch. Medicine, N.Y.C., 1973-77, sr. clin. instr. urology, 1977-80, asst. clin. prof. urology, 1980-92; pvt. practice, N.Y.C., 1973—; assoc. clin. prof. urology Mount Sinai Sch. Medicine, 1992-94, Albert Einstein Coll. of Medicine, 1994—; attending NYU Downtown Hosp. Assoc. attending Beth Israel Med. Ctr., N.Y.C.; mem. advisor Impotence Anonymous & Jr., Diabetes Self-Mgmt., 1983-85, Jour. Urol. Nursing; editl. adv. bd. The Female Patient, Med. Aspects of Human Sexuality; mem. med. adv. bd. Colostomy Soc., N.Y., Inc.; investigator Protocol 2560 (alfus) Alfuzosin study, 1998; cons. and speaker in field. Author: Viagra--The Wonder Drug for Peak Performance; editor: Current Operative Urology, 1975, 2d rev. edit., 1984, ann. edits., 1989-92, Mgmt. Impotence and Infertility, 1994, Sex Over Forty, 1990-2000, Atlas Surgical Techniques in Urology, 1997; contbr. articles to profl. jours.; patentee in field. Grantee U.S.P.H., Clin. Research Ctr. Fellow ACS, Clin. Soc. Am. Diabetes Assn., N.Y. Diabetes Affiliate; mem. AMA, AAAS, Am. Urol. Assn., Soc. Internat. Urology (diplomate), Sexual Medicine Soc. N.Am., Am. Assn. Clin. Urologists, N.Y. State Urol. Assn., Am. Acad. of Phalloplasty Surgeons (pres., bd. dirs.), Internat. Soc. for Artificial Organs, Am. So. Nephrology, Am. Assn. Sex Educators, Counselors and Therapists, Soc. for the Sci. Study of Sex, Soc. for Sex Therapy and Rsch., Sex Info. and Edn. Coun. of the U.S. Coalition on Sexuality and Disability, Am. Cancer Soc., Nat. Kidney Found., Am. Geriatric Soc., N.Y. Acad. Sci., N.Y. Acad. Medicine, N.Y. Urodynamic Soc., Internat. Continence Soc., Soc. Genitourinary Reconstructive Surgeons, Assn. Male Sexual Dysfunction (dir.), N.Y. Phalloplasty (dir.). Office: 24 E 12th St Ste 2-1 New York NY 10003-4403 Office Phone: 212-879-3130. Business E-Mail: info@drwhitehead.com.

WHITEHEAD, IAN, insurance company executive; CEO, pres. London PCF Lf & Annuity Co., Sacramento, now vice chmn., sec. London.

WHITEHEAD, J. RENNIE, science consultant; s. William and Beatrice Cora (Fenning) W.; m. Nesta Doone James, Nov. 1, 1944; children— Valerie Lesley (dec.), Michael James Rennie. B.Sc. in Physics, Manchester U., Lancashire, Eng., 1939; PhD in Phys. Chemistry, Cambridge U., Eng., 1949. Cert. profl. engr., Ont.; chartered engr., U.K. Sci. officer TRE (UK Radar), Eng., 1939-51; assoc. prof. McGill U., Montreal, P.Q., Can., 1951-55; dir. research RCA Victor Co Ltd., Montreal, 1955-65; prin. sci. adviser Govt. of Can., Ottawa, Ont., 1965-75; sr. v.p. Philip A. Lapp Ltd., Ottawa, 1975-82; pvt. practice sci. cons. Ottawa, 1982-86. Bd. dirs. Hancock-Lapp Assocs., Ottawa, 1986-89; bd. dirs. Found. for Internat. Tng., Toronto, 1976-86. Author: Superregenerative Receivers, 1949. Fellow Royal Soc. Can., Inst. Physics, Instn. Elec. Engrs., Can. Aeronautics and Space Inst., Can. Assn. for Club of Rome (chmn. 1976-81, editor and pub. newsletter and procs. 1987-99). Anglican. Avocations: automobiles, stamp collecting/philately, carpentry, computers. Home and Office: 1368 Chattaway Ave Ottawa ON Canada K1H 7S3 E-mail: drrennie@sympatico.ca.

WHITEHEAD, JANICE, secondary school educator; d. Warren W. and Betty Ostrom; m. Glen Whitehead, Jan. 28, 1978; children: Dustin, Sarah, Joshua. Assoc. degree, Blinn Coll., 1997—2000; attended, U. Houston-Downtown, 2000—02. Adult edn. instr. Brenham ISD, Tex., 1998—2003; secondary instr. Faith West Acad., Katy, Tex., 2002—. Exec. dir. Sealy C. of C., Tex., 1999—99. R-Consevative. Baptist. Avocations: swimming, travel. Office Phone: 281-391-5683.

WHITEHEAD, JOHN CUNNINGHAM, bank executive, diplomat, philanthropist; b. Evanston, Ill., Apr. 2, 1922; s. Eugene C. and Winifred W.; m. Helene E. Shannon, Sept. 28, 1946 (div. Dec. 1971); children: Anne Elizabeth, John Gregory; m. Jaan W. Chartener, Oct. 22, 1972 (div. 1986); 1 child, Sarah; m. Nancy Dickerson, 1989 (dec. 1997). BA, Haverford Coll., 1943; MBA, Harvard U., 1947; LLD (hon.), Pace. U., Rutgers U., Haverford Coll., Harvard U., Amherst Coll., Seton Hall U. With Goldman, Sachs & Co., N.Y.C., 1947-84, ptnr., 1956-76, sr. ptnr., co-chmn., 1976-84; dep. sec. Dept. State, Washington, 1985-89; chmn. Lower Manhattan Devel. Corp., 2001—. Past chmn. Fed. Res. Bank of N.Y. Trustee Haverford Coll., Rockefeller U., Lincoln Ctr. Theater; past pres. bd. overseers Harvard U.; past chmn. trustees coun. Nat. Gallery Art; co-chmn. greater N.Y. coun. Boy Scouts Am.; past chmn. Internat. Rescue Com., UN Assn. U.S.A.; chmn. emeritus Internat. House, Brookings Inst., Youth for Understanding, Andrew Mellon Found. With USNR, 1943-46. Mem. Coun. on Fgn. Rels., Links Club, Univ. Club. Office: 65 E 55th St New York NY 10022-3219

WHITEHEAD, JOHN WAYNE, law educator, organization administrator, author; b. Pulaski, Tenn., July 14, 1946; s. John M. and Alatha (Wiser) W.; m. Virginia Carolyn Nichols, Aug. 26, 1967; children: Jayson Reau, Jonathan Mathew, Elisabeth Anne, Joel Christofer, Joshua Benjamen. BA, U. Ark., 1969, JD, 1974. Bar: Ark. 1974, U.S. Dist. Ct. (ea. and we. dists.) Ark. 1974, U.S. Supreme Ct. 1977, U.S. Ct. Appeals (9th cir.) 1980, Va. 1981, U.S. Ct. Appeals (7th cir.) 1981, U.S. Ct Appeals (4th and 5th cirs.). Spl. counsel Christian Legal Soc., Oak Park, Ill., 1977-78; assoc. Gibbs & Craze, Cleve., 1978-79; sole practice law Manassas, Va., 1979-82; pres. The Rutherford Inst., Charlottesville, Va., 1982—, also bd. dirs. Frequent lectr. colls., law schs.; past adj. prof. O.W. Coburn Sch. Law. Author: Schools on Fire, 1980, The New Tyranny, 1982, The Second American Revolution, 1982, The Stealing of America, 1983, The Freedom of Religious Expression in Public High Schools, 1983, The End of Man, 1986, An American Dream, 1987, The Rights of Religious Persons in Public Education, 1991, Home Education: Rights and Reasons, 1993, Religious Apartheid, 1994, Slaying Dragons, 1999, Grasping For the Wind, 2001, others; writer, dir.: (video series) Grasping for the Wind (Silver World medal N.Y. Film Festival), 1998-99; contbr. articles to profl. jours., chpts. to books. 1st lt. U.S. Army, 1969-71. Named Christian Leader of Yr. Christian World Affairs Conf., Washington, 1986; recipient Bus. and Profl. award Religious Heritage Am., 1990, Hungarian Freedom medal, Budapest, 1991. Mem. ABA, Ark. Bar Assn., Va. Bar Assn. Office: The Rutherford Inst PO Box 7482 Charlottesville VA 22906-7482 Office Phone: 434-978-3888. Business E-Mail: johnw@ritherford.org.

WHITEHEAD, KENNETH DEAN, author, translator, retired federal government official; b. Rupert, Idaho, Dec. 14, 1930; s. Kenneth Christian and May Bell (Allen) W.; m. Margaret Mary O'Donohue, Aug. 2, 1958; children: Paul Daniel, Steven Francis, Matthew Patrick, David Joseph. BA in French, U. Utah, 1955; postgrad., U. Paris, 1956-57; cert. in Arabic and Middle East studies, Fgn. Service Inst., Beirut, 1962; LittD (hon.), Franciscan U., Steubenville, Oho, 2003. Instr. English U. Utah, Salt Lake City, 1955-56; fgn. service officer Dept. State, Rome, Beirut and Tripoli, Libya, 1957-65; chief Arabic service Voice of Am., Washington, 1965-67; dep. dir. fgn. currency program Smithsonian Instn., Washington, 1967-72; exec. v.p. Caths. United for Faith Inc., New Rochelle, N.Y., 1972-81; dir. Ctr. for Internat. Edn. U.S. Dept. Edn., Washington, 1982-86, dep. asst. sec. for higher edn. programs, 1986-88, asst. sec. for postsecondary edn., 1988-89. Author: Respectable Killing: The New Abortion Imperative, 1972, Agenda for the Sexual Revolution, 1981, Catholic Colleges and Federal Funding, 1988, DOA: The Ambush of the Universal Catechism, 1993, Political Orphan? The Prolife Cause after 25 Years of Roe v. Wade, 1998, One, Holy, Catholic, and Apostolic: The Early Church Was the Catholic Church, 2000; co-author: The Pope, The Council and the Mass, 1981, revised edit., 2004, Flawed Expectations: The Reception of the Catechism of the Catholic Church, 1996; sr. editor: World Almanac Book of Dates, 1982, Macmillan Concise Dictionary of World History, 1983; editor: Marriage and the Common Good, 2001, Pope John Paul II--Witness to Truth, 2001, The Catholic Imagination, 2003; co-editor: The Battle for the Catholic Mind, 2001; translator 18 books from French, German, Italian, 1980—. Bd. dirs. Notre Dame Inst. for Advanced Study, Arlington, Va., 1986-95, Philosophy Edn. Soc., 1995—, Christas Magister Found., 1997—. Fulbright scholar U.S. Dept. State, 1956-57. Mem. Fellowship Cath. Scholars (bd. dirs. 1990-2000), Brent Soc. Cath. Profls. (bd. dirs. 1992-98), Cath. League for Religious and Civil Rights (bd. dirs. 1992—), KC. Republican. Home: 809 Ridge Pl Falls Church VA 22046-3631 Fax: (703) 534-3015. E-mail: whiteheadz@msn.com.

WHITEHEAD, MICHAEL ANTHONY, chemistry professor; b. London, June 30, 1935; emigrated to Can., 1962; s. Francis Henry and Edith Downes (Rotherham) W.; 1 son, Christopher Mark. B.Sc. in Chemistry with honors, Queen Mary Coll., U. London, 1956, PhD, 1960, D.Sc., 1974. Asst. lectr. Queen Mary Coll., U. London, 1958-60; postdoctoral fellow U. Cin., 1960, asst. prof., 1961; asst. prof. theoretical chemistry McGill U., Montreal, Que., Can., 1962-66, asso. prof., 1966-74, prof., 1974-99, prof. emeritus, 1999—. Vis. prof. U. Cambridge, Eng., 1971-72, U. Oxford, Eng., 1972-74; vis. professorial fellow Univ. Coll. Wales, Aberystwyth, 1980, U. Oxford, 1990-91; invited prof. U. Geneva, 1983-84; life guest prof. Nat. U. Def. Tech., Changsha, People's Republic of China; vis. Erskine fellow chemistry dept. U. Canterbury, Christchurch, N.Z., co-chair history and advanced in quantum chemistry 84th conf., Montreal, 2001; mem. Internat. Com. on Nuclear Quadrupole Resonance.; co-chmn. 7th Internat. Symposium on Nuclear Quadrapole Resonance, Kingston, Ont., Can., 1983 Contbr. articles to profl. jours. Parish coun. St. John the Evangelist; exec. coun. Canadian Scientific and Christian Affiliation. Fellow Royal Chem. Soc., Chem. Inst. Can., Royal Soc. Arts; mem. Am. Chem. Soc., Am. Phys. Soc., James McGill Soc. (pres. 1993-95), Sigma Xi (pres. McGill chpt. 1971-72, 81-82, 92-95, 97-99, dir. Can. and internat. constituency group 2000—, chair awards com. 2001—, ad hoc mem. internat. com., 2001-), Phi Lambda Upsilon. Anglican. Office: McGill U Dept Chemistry 801 Sherbrooke St W Montreal QC Canada H3A 2K6 Office Phone: 514-398-6239. E-mail: tony.whitehead@mcgill.ca. *My faith in God and belief in Christ.*

WHITEHEAD, NEHEMIAH, III, music educator; b. Ft. Hood, Tex., Nov. 8, 1955; s. Nehemiah and Robbie Mae Whitehead; m. Brenda Joice Morris, Oct. 17, 2003; children: Scotty Nehemiah, Earnest T. MusB, Tex. A&I, 1977. Cert. tchr. Tex., detention officer Tex. Band dir. Mabank (Tex.) Sch. Dist., 1977—80, Chilton (Tex.) Sch. Dist., 1981—84; tchr., detention officer Bell County Juvenile Detention, Belton, Tex., 1986—95; band dir. Dallas Sch. Dist., 1995—. Exec. bd. mem. Tex. Juvenile Detention Assn., 1990—95. Mem.: Tex. Music Educators Assn., Nat. Assn. Music Educators, NEA, Classroom Tchrs. Assn., Phi Mu Alpha, Kappa Kappa Psi. Democrat. Baptist. Avocations: saxophone, music, preaching gospel. Office Fax: 972-223-2343.

WHITEHEAD, PAUL, lawyer, labor union administrator; b. 1951; BA, U. Wis.; JD, Harvard U. Asst. gen. counsel United Steelworkers Am., Pitts., 2001—. Office: United Steelworkers Am 5 Gateway Center Pittsburgh PA 15222

WHITEHEAD, WENDY LEE, special education educator; b. Wabash, Ind., Mar. 1, 1955; d. John Francis and Virginia Mae (Ritzi) W. BS, Ball State U., 1977, MS, 1981; cert. in visually impaired edn., Ind. U., Ft. Wayne, 1987. Cert. spl. edn. tchr., Ind. Tchr. of primary severe disabilities Sharp Creek Elem. Sch., Met. Sch. Dist., Wabash, Ind., 1977—. Active locla sch. dist. Assistive Tech. Team. Mem. Coun. for Exceptional Children (human rights com.). Republican. Roman Catholic. Avocations: reading, bowling, cross-stitch. Office: Sharp Creek Elem Sch 264 W 200 N Wabash IN 46992-9136

WHITEHEAD, WILLIAM J. advertising executive; With Bates Can., Toronto, chmn., CEO; regional dir. L.Am. network Bates; exec. dir. worldwide client svcs. Bates Worldwide, 1992; COO Bates N.Am., 1994; pres., COO Bates USA, 1995; CEO Bates N.Am. Bd. dirs. CCG. Mem. Advt. Coun. (bd. dirs.). Avocation: competitive horsemanship. Office: Bates NAm 405 Lexington Ave New York NY 10174-0002

WHITEHILL, ANGELA ELIZABETH, artistic director; b. Leeds, Yorkshire, Eng., Oct. 21, 1938; came to U.S., 1952, naturalized, 1995; d. Donald Paul and Audrey May (Clayforth) Warner; m. Norman James Whitehill, Dec. 23, 1959; children: Norman James III, Pamela Elizabeth; m. William Parker Noble, Dec. 27, 1998. Student, Arts Ednl. Sch., London, 1955-59. With corps de ballet Ballet Paris, 1958-59; dir. London Sch. Ballet, St. Thomas, V.I., 1960-63; asst. dir. Ocean County Ballet Co., Toms River, N.J., 1965-68; founder, dir. Shore Ballet Sch., Toms River, 1968-76; artistic dir. Shore Ballet Co., Toms River, 1971-76; artist in residence Castleton State Coll., Rutland, Vt., 1977-79; founder, artistic dir. Burklyn Ballet Theatre, Johnson, Vt., 1977—; dir. Ballet Umbrella, Dance Coun., Burklyn Designs, 2003—. Vis. prof. Colby Sawyer Coll., New London, N.H., 1978-79; resident designer Atlanta Ballet Co., 1982-83; designer, pub. relations N.J. Ballet Co., Orange, 1983-85; artistic dir. Vt. Ballet Theatre, Burlington, 1985-94; master tchr. 1st Congress Internat. de Ballet Classico Contemporaneo, Mex., 2000. Choreographer Arensky Dances, 1983, A Deux, 1984, 4 Plus 2, 1986, Twins From A Time Gone By, 1987, Heart of the Island, 2002; co-author: Parent's Book of Ballet, 1988, 2d edit., 2003, The Young Professional's Book of Ballet, 1990, The Dancer's Book of Ballet, 2000, Ballet Magic, The Burklyn Story, 2001, Nutcracker Backstage, 2004. Dir. Vt. Ballet Theatre Found., Calledonia County, 1993-96. Recipient Francis Hopkins award Ocean County, N.J., 1976, Woman of Achievement award Vt. Woman, 1989, Author's award N.J. Inst. Tech., 1989. Mem. Vt. Council on the Arts, Regional Dance Am. Mem. Soc. Of Friends. Home: 218 Ocean Ave Island Heights NJ 08732 Home (Winter): PO Box 907 Island Heights NJ 08732-0907 Office: Burklyn Ballet Theatre PO Box 302 Johnson VT 05656-0302 Office Phone: 732-288-2660. E-mail: awhitehill@aol.com.

WHITEHOUSE, ANNE CHERNER, writer; d. Marvin and Leona Roth Cherner; m. Stephen Compton Whitehouse, June 24, 1979; 1 child, Claire Landau. BA magna cum laude, Harvard U., 1972—76; MFA in Writing, Columbia U., 1976—79. Freelance journalist, 1988—; special projects mgr. Dorot, NYC, 1997—. Devel. cons. Am. Opera Projects, Bklyn., 1995—. Author: (novels) The Surveyor's Hand, 1981, Fall Love, 2001. Mem.: Phi Beta Kappa. Home: 340 Riverside Dr New York NY 10025 Office: Dorot 171 W 85th St New York NY 10024 E-mail: awhitehouse@dorotusa.org.

WHITEHOUSE, DAVID BRYN, museum director; b. Worksop, Nottinghamshire, Eng., Oct. 15, 1941; came to U.S., 1984; s. Brindley Charles and Alice Margaret (Dobson) W.; m. Ruth Delamain Ainger, 1963; children: Sarah, Susan, Peter; m. Elizabeth-Anne Ollemans, 1975; children: Julia, Simon, Nicola. BA, Cambridge U., 1963, MA, 1965, PhD, 1967. Dir. Brit. Inst. Afghan Studies, Kabul, Afghanistan, 1973-74, Brit. Sch., Rome, 1974-84; chief curator Corning Mus. Glass, NY, 1984-87, dep. dir., 1988-92, dir., 1992-99, exec. dir., 1999—. Dir. Siraf expdn. Brit. Inst. Persian Studies, Tehran, Iran, 1966-73. Author: (with Ruth Whitehouse) Archaeological Atlas of the World, 1975, (with David Andrews and John Osborne) Aspects of Medieval Lazio, 1982, (with Donald B. Harden and others) Glass of the Caesars, 1987, Glass of the Roman Empire, 1988, (with Richard Hodges) Mohammed, Charlemagne and the Origins of Europe, 1983, Glass: A Pocket Dictionary, 1993, English Cameo Glass, 1994, Roman Glass in The Corning Museum of Glass, Vol. 1, 1997, Vol. 2, 2001, Vol. 3, 2003, Excavations at ed-Dur (Umm al-Qaiwan, UAE), Vol. 1, The Glass Vessels, 1998, The Corning Museum of Glass, A Decade of Glass Collecting, 1990-1999, 2000, (with Stefano Carboni) Glass of the Sultans, 2001; contbr. numerous articles and revs. to profl. jours. Wainwright Fellow, Oxford U., 1966—73. Fellow Soc. Antiquaries (London), Royal Geog. Soc., Pontificia Accademia Romana di Archeologia; mem. Accademia Fiorentina delle Arti del Disegno, Accademia di Archeologia, Lettere e Belle Arti di Napoli, Deutsches Archaeologisches Inst., Internat. Assn. for the History of Glass (pres. 1991-95), Athenaeum Club (London). Office: Corning Mus of Glass 1 Mus Way Corning NY 14830-2253 Office Phone: 607-974-8424.

WHITEHOUSE, FRANK, JR., microbiologist, educator; b. Ann Arbor, Mich., Nov. 20, 1924; s. Frank and May Belle (MacIntire) Whitehouse; m. Helen Alice Schimkat; children: Lynne, Beth Ann, Frank Scott, Kim Elaine. AB, U. Mich., Ann Arbor, 1953; MD, 1953. Intern Blodgett Hosp., Grand Rapids, Mich., 1953—54; faculty U. Mich. Med. Sch., Ann Arbor, 1954—95, emeritus faculty, 1995—. Vis. scientist Queen Victoria Hosp., East Grinstead, England. Contbr. articles to profl. jours.; composer: (songs) (CD) Here's to you Maize and Blue, (Operas) Dr. Chase. Scoutmaster Boy Scouts Am. 1st lt. USAF, 1942—46. Decorated Air medal; named Sr. Fulbright lectr., Bahrain, 1979—80; recipient Univ. Hopwood Lit. award, Ann Arbor, 1947. Mem.: Assn. Am. Med. Colls. (mem. group student affairs), Nat. Bd. Med. Examiners, Nat. Assn. Advisors Health Professions (founder, 1st exec. dir.), Am. Soc. Microbiology, Gilbert and Sullivan Soc. and Choral Union. Avocations: secular and religous musical compositions and their public presentations, stamp collecting/philately. Home: 3411 Woodland Rd Ann Arbor MI 48104-4257 Office: U Mich Box 0620 Ann Arbor MI 48109-0620 Office Phone: 734-764-4372.

WHITEHOUSE, FRED WAITE, endocrinologist, researcher; b. Chgo., May 6, 1926; s. Fred Trafton Waite and Grace Caroline (Peters) W.; m. Iris Jean Dawson, June 6, 1953; children: Martha, Amy, Sarah. Student, Northwestern U., 1943-45; BS, U. Ill., Chgo., 1947, MD, 1949. Diplomate Am. Bd. Internal Medicine; cert. endocrinology and metabolism. Intern, then resident Henry Ford Hosp., Detroit, 1949-53, staff physician, 1955—, chief divsn. metabo-

lism, 1962-88, chief divsn. endocrinology and metabolism, 1988-95; divsn. head emeritus, 1995—; fellow Joslin Clinic, Boston, 1954-55. Cons. FDA, Washington, 1980—; mem. Coalition on Diabetes Edn. and Minority Health, 1989-91. Contbr. articles to profl. jours. Bd. dirs. Wheat Ridge Found., 1984-93. Lt. USNR, 1951-53. Master ACP; mem. NIH (nat. diabetes adv. bd. 1984-88), Am. Diabetes Assn. (pres. 1978-79, Banting medal 1979, Outstanding Clinician award 1989, Outstanding Physician Educators award 1994), Detroit Med. Club (pres. 1976), Detroit Acad. Medicine (pres. 1991-92). Lutheran. Avocations: bicycling, gardening. Home: 1265 Blairmoor Ct Grosse Pointe Woods MI 48236-1230 Office: Henry Ford Hosp 2799 W Grand Blvd Detroit MI 48202-2689 Fax: (313) 916-8343. Office Phone: 313-916-2131.

WHITEHOUSE, GARY, industrial engineer, educator; b. Trenton, N.J., Aug. 13, 1938; s. Edward Ernest and Lorraine Lee Etta (Baker) W.; m. Marian Greenhalgh, Aug. 24, 1963; children: Gail W. DePuy, Glenn Alan. BS in Indsl. Engring., Lehigh U., 1960, MS in Indsl. Engring., 1962; PhD, Ariz. State U., 1966. Registered profl. engr., Fla. Instr. indsl. engring. Lehigh U., Bethlehem, Pa., 1961—63; instr. Ariz. State U., Tempe, 1963—65; asst. prof. Lehigh U., Bethlehem, 1965—69, assoc. prof., 1969—74, prof., 1974—78; dept. chmn. U. Ctrl. Fla., Orlando, 1978—83, prof., 1983—87, acting dean, 1987—88, dean, 1988—93, provost, v.p. acad. affairs, 1993—2003, disting. univ. prof., 2003—, provost emeritus, 2003—. Cons. Air Products and Chem., Allentown, Pa., 1965-78, Martin-Marietta, Orlando, 1986-92. Author: Analysis and Design of Systems using Network Techniques, 1973, Applied Operations Research, 1976, Practical Partners (Outstanding I.E. Publ. award), 1985; co-author: Computer Tools, Models and Techniques for Project Management, 1989; editor: Software for Engineers and Managers, 1984, Softcover Software-28 Programsfor the IE and Manager, 1985, Proceedings of the 7th Annual Computers and Industrial Engring Conf., 1985, Software for Engineers and Managers Volume II, 1987; co-editor: Proceedings of the 8th Annual Conference on Computers and Industrial Engineering, 1986, Proceedings of the 9th Annual Conference on Computers and Industrial Engineering, 1986; editor I.E. Micro column, 1980-92; assoc. editor Computers and I.E. jour., 1983-89; contbr. articles to profl. jours. Fellow Inst. Indsl. Engrs. (dir. 1976-78, H.B. Maynard award 1978, Computer and Info. Systems Divsn. award 1982), Am. Soc. Engring. Educators (Western Electric award 1976). Democrat. Avocations: biking, music, sports. Home: 9967 Sweetleaf St Orlando FL 32827 Office: U Ctrl Fla Indsl Engring and Mgmt Sys Dept PO Box 162450 Orlando FL 32816-2450 also: 54 Mountain Dr Biltmore Lake NC 28715 Business E-Mail: whitehse@mail.ucf.edu.

WHITEHOUSE, JOHN HARLAN, JR., systems software consultant, diagnostician; b. Lakewood, Ohio, Sept. 12, 1951; s. John Harlan and Frances Elizabeth (Nation) W.; divorced; 1 child, John Harlan III. BA magna cum laude, Ohio Wesleyan U., 1973; postgrad., U. Chgo., 1974; MBA, Cleve. State U., 1976; PhD, Columbia Pacific U., San Rafael, Calif., 1988; postgrad., Vedic U. of Am., 1996—. Cert. computing profl.; cert. info. sys. auditor; cert. in Visual Basic. Programmer San Antonio Express-News, 1977; programming mgr. S.W. Info. Mgmt. Sys., San Antonio, 1977, Utility Data Corp., Houston, 1978; sr. data sys. auditor Nat. City Corp., Cleve., 1978-81; sys. programmer Std. Oil Co., Cleve., 1981-84; adv. sys. engr. IBM, Cleve., 1984-92; pres. Semiotica Corp., 1992—. Mem. exams. edtl. coun. Inst. for Cert. Computer Profls., Des Plaines, 1990—, test deployment mgr., 1996-2001, dir. certification, 1999—. Author: CICS Problem Determination Workshop, 1990; co-author: ICCP Guidelines for Recertification, 1990, ICCP Official Study Guide, 1991-95; editor Clifton-Gaston Allen Light, 1994—; also numerous articles, columnist. Mem. Assn. for Computing Machinery (chmn. Greater Cleve. chpt. 1982-83, Svc. Recognition award 1984), Assn. of Inst. for Cert. Computer Profls. (regional dir. 1989-93, nominating com. 1991), Masons (dist. edn. officer 2001-02, dist. dep. Grand Master 2002-), Philalethes Soc., Phi Beta Kappa. Unitarian Universalist. Home: 22291 Berry Dr Rocky River OH 44116-2013 Office: Semiotica Corp PMB 241 25935 Detroit Rd Westlake OH 44145-2449 Office Phone: 440-356-8738. E-mail: consultx@ix.netcom.com.

WHITEHOUSE, SHELDON, lawyer, former state attorney general; b. N.Y.C., Oct. 20, 1955; s. Charles Sheldon and Mary (Rand) Whitehouse; m. Sandra Christine Thornton, Sept. 20, 1986; 2 children. BA, Yale U., 1978; JD, U. Va., 1982. Bar: W.Va. 1982, R.I. 1983, U.S. Dist. Ct. R.I. 1984, U.S. Supreme Ct. 1986, U.S. Ct. Appeals (1st cir.) 1984. Atty., Providence, 1983—84; spl. asst. atty. gen., 1985—90; chief regulatory unit, 1988—90; asst. atty. gen., 1989—90; exec. counsel Office of Gov., 1991, dir. gov. policy office, 1991—92; dir. Dept. Bus. Regulation, 1992—94; U.S. atty for dist. of R.I., 1994—98; atty. gen. State of R.I., 1999—2003. Democrat.

WHITEHURST, BROOKS MORRIS, chemical engineer; b. Apr. 9, 1930; s. David Brooks and Bessie Ann (Lowry) W.; m. Carolyn Sue Boyer, July 4, 1951; children: Garnett, Anita, Robert. BS, Va. Poly. Inst. and State U., 1951. Registered profl. engr., N.C. Sr. process asst. Am. Enka Corp., Lowland, Tenn., 1951-56; sr. process devel. engr. Va.-Carolina Chem. Corp., Richmond, Va., 1956-63; project engr. Texaco Inc., Richmond, 1963-66; mgr. engring. svcs. Texasgulf, Inc., Aurora, N.C., 1967-80, mgr. spl. projects, long range planning, 1980-81; pres. Whitehurst Assocs., Inc., New Bern, N.C., 1981—. Instr., lectr., cons. alt. sources of energy cmty. colls. and univs.; presenter paper Solar World Forum, Brighton, Eng., 1981. Co-chmn. N.C. state supt. task force on secondary edn., 1974—; mem. N.C. state adv. com. on trade and indsl. edn, 1971-77; chmn. Gov.'s Task Force Vols. in Workplace, 1981; chmn. State Adv. Coun. Career Edn., 1977—; gov.'s liaison for edn. and bus., 1978-79. Recipient commendation Pres. U.S., 1981. Mem. AIChE, Am. Inst. Chemists (cert., bd. dirs. 1980-84), N.C. Inst. Chemists (pres. 1975-77), Nat. Soc. Profl. Engrs., N.C. Soc. Profl. Engrs., Royal Soc. Chemistry. Achievements include patents and current work on biodegradable chelate systems, municipal yard waste disposal, micronutrients for agriculture, waste rubber recycling, conversion of industrial by-products containing manganese and phosphorous to useful non-toxic materials for use in agriculture for environmental clean-up; development of environmentally friendly products for forest fertilization. Home: 1983 Hoods Creek Rd New Bern NC 28562-9103 Office: PO Box 3335 New Bern NC 28564-3335

WHITEHURST, GROVER JAY, federal official, psychologist and educator; b. Washington, N.C., Sept. 28, 1944; s. Grover J. and Dixie (Daniel) W.; m. Janet E. Fischel, June 7, 1981; children: Owen E., Adam E. BA, East Carolina U., Greenville, 1966; MA, U. Ill., 1968, PhD, 1970. Lic. psychologist, N.Y. Asst. prof. SUNY, Stony Brook, 1970—74, assoc. prof., 1975—79, prof. psychology, 1981—2002, chair dept. psychology, 1998—2002; sr. lectr. U. N.S.W., Sydney, Australia, 1974—75; acad. v.p. Merrill-Palmer Inst., Detroit, 1979—81; dir. Inst. of Edu. Sciences, 2002—. Author: Child Behavior, 1977; editor Developmental Rev., 1981-2000; contbr. over 100 articles to profl. jours. Grantee NIH, 1985, Smith Richardson Found., 1990, Pew Charitable Trusts, 1992, U.S. Adminstrn. Children and Families, 1996, 2000. Fellow APA, Am. Assn. Profl. and Applied Psychology; Nat. Rsch. Coun. (commn. early childhood); Head Start, Nat. Adv. Bd. on Rsch. Avocation: sailing. Mailing: Dir Inst Educ Sciences US Dept Edu 555 New Jersey Ave NW Washington DC 20208-5500

WHITEHURST, MARY TARR, artist, poet, writer; b. Norfolk, Va., Nov. 20, 1923; d. Henry Bennitt and Martha Ida Tarr; m. Jerry Rutter Whitehurst, Dec. 24, 1943; children: Henry Armistead, Jeffrey Tarr, Martha W. Bryant. Student, Coll. William & Mary, 1940-42, Wytheville C.C., 1968, Sullins Coll., 1976-80, Va. Western C.C., 1988. Docent Mus. Fine Arts, Roanoke, Va., 1973-75. Dir., endowing mem. Fine Arts Ctr. of New River Valley, Pulaski, Va., 1980-93; charter, endowing mem. Bristol Mus. Fine Arts, Va./Tenn., 1975-80; benefactor, mem. Arts Found. Radford U., Va., 1991—. One-woman shows include Mus. Fine Arts, Roanoke, Va., 1977, Emory & Henry Coll., Emory, Va., 1982, Radford U. Art Gallery, Va., 1991, Ashland Area Art Gallery, Ky., 1993, Va. Polytech. Inst. & State U., Blacksburg, 1985—, New River C.C. Found., 1985—, Coll. William & Mary, Williamsburg, 1995; endowment Poly. Inst. & State U., Blacksburg, Va., 1998; author: (poetry) Silent As Birds, 1997. Endowing mem. Va. Polytech. Inst. & State U., Blacksburg, 1985—, New River C.C. Found., 1985—, Coll. William & Mary, Williamsburg, 1995; mem. Va. Polytech. Found., Blacksburg, Va. Recipient Clement Gueenberg award of distinction Mus. Fine Arts, Roanoke, 1976, Grumbacher Gold medal Soc. Water Color Artists, 1995; art dept. named in honor New River C.C., Dublin, Va., 1994. Mem. Catharine Lorillard Wolfe Art Club (Joyce Williams water color award 1985), Midwest Transparent Water Color Soc. (signature mem.), Va. Water Color Soc. (dir. 1994), Ala. Water Color Soc., Blacksburg Regional Artists Assn., Allied Artists (assoc.), So. Water Color Soc. (two awards 1997, Blue Ribbon winner 2000). Avocations: travel abroad, art collection, history, philanthropy. Home: Painters Wood 2492 Forest Hill Dr Draper VA 24324-3224

WHITEHURST, WILLIAM OSCAR, lawyer; b. Ardmore, Okla., Oct. 23, 1945; s. William Oscar and Freddie Elizabeth (Ormsby) W.; m. Stephanie Anne Evans, June 22, 1968; children: Emilee Dawn, Rebecca Danielle. BS in Pharmacy, U. Okla., 1968; JD, U. Tex., 1970. Bar: Tex. 1971, U.S. Dist. Ct. (we. dist.) Tex. 1971, U.S. Ct. Mil. Appeals 1971, U.S. Ct. Appeals (5th cir.) 1971, U.S. Supreme Ct. 1971. Assoc. Fulbright & Jaworski, Houston, 1971; counsel, staff dir. jud. affairs com. Tex. Ho. Reps., Austin, 1975; sr. shareholder Whitehurst, Harkness, Ozmun & Brees, P.C., Austin, 1975—. Mem. Senate-House Select Com. on the Judiciary, 1983-84, subcom. on Svc. Delivery, subcom. on Jurisdiction; faculty law U. Tex., 1979-86, 88, Tex. Coll. Trial Adv., 1984—. Served to capt. JAGC, USAF, 1971-75. Fellow Am. Bar Found., Tex. Bar Found. (chmn. bd. trustees 1992-93), Internat. Acad. Trial Lawyers (sec. internat. rels. 2002-03, 2002-2005); mem. ABA (chmn. standing com. legal aid and indigent defendants), Nat. Conf. Bar Pres. (exec. coun. 1992-95), Tex. Bar Assn. (pres. 1986-87, exec. com. 1981-84, 85-88, bd. dirs. 1981-84, active various coms.), Travis County Bar Assn. (sec. 1980-81, bd. dirs. 1979-81), Am. Bd. Trial Advs., Tex. Young Lawyers Assn. (pres. 1982-83, bd. dirs. 1979-84), Austin Young Lawyers Assn. (pres. 1978-79), Tex. Trial Lawyers Assn. (pres. 1995), Am. Soc. Pharmacy Law, Am. Soc. Law and Medicine, Order of Barristers, Univ. Club, Austin Country Club. Democrat. Presbyterian. Avocations: flying, skiing, water-skiing, travel. Home: 2703 Westlake Dr Austin TX 78746-1909 Office: Whitehurst Harkness et al 1122 Colorado St Austin TX 78701-2100 Office Phone: 512-476-4346.

WHITEHURST, WILLIAM WILFRED, JR., management consultant; b. Balt., Mar. 4, 1937; s. William Wilfred and Elizabeth (Hogg) Whitehurst; m. Linda Joan Potter, July 1, 1961; children: Catherine Elizabeth, William Wilfred III. BA, Princeton U., 1958; MS with distinction, Carnegie Inst. Tech., 1963. Mathematician Nat. Security Agy., Fort George G. Meade, Md., 1961—63; mgmt. cons. McKinsey & Co., Inc., Washington, 1963—66; ptnr. L.E. Peabody & Assocs., Washington, 1966—69, exec. v.p., dir. Lanham, Md., 1969—82, pres., dir., 1983—86; pres. W.W. Whitehurst & Assoc., Inc., Cockeysville, Md., 1986—. Contbr. Code of Fed. Regulations 49 C.F.R. Sect. 1157. Comdr. USNR, 1958—65. Recipient Diploma De Honor 14th Pan Am. Rwy. Congress. Mem.: Washington Soc. Investment Analysts, Assn. for Investment Mgmt. and Rsch., Am. Rwy. Engring. Assn. Home and Office: 12421 Happy Hollow Rd Cockeysville Hunt Valley MD 21030-1711 Office Phone: 410-252-2422.

WHITELAW, CHRISTINE CAPPELLE, pediatrician, aesthetic medicine educator; b. DePere, Wis., Mar. 18, 1960; d. Aloyiosus Jules and Audrey Mae (Jacques) Cappelle; m. Grady Lightfoot Whitelaw, Oct. 29, 1994; children: Conlon Arthur, Robert Dean, Hayden Keith, MacKenzie Vesennia. Student, Baylor U., 1978-79; BS in Biology, U. Notre Dame, 1982; MD, St. George's U., Grenada, West Indies, 1989. Diplomate Am. Bd. Pediatrics. Intern and resident in pediat. Pitt County Meml. Hosp. E. Carolina U., Greenville, N.C., 1989-91; resident in pediat. Children's Hosp. King's Dau. E. Va. Med. Sch., Norfolk, 1991-92; fellow in pediatric emergency medicine U. Louisville, 1992-94, clin. instr., 1994-95, asst. prof., 1995-99, clin. prof., 1999—. Contbr. articles to profl. jours. Mem. sci. coun. cardiopulmonary and critical care Am. Heart Assn.; camp physician Beber Camp, Mushwonaka, Wis., 1999. Alliant Cmty. Trust Fund grantee, 1997. Mem. European Resuscitation Coun., Am. Acad. Pediat., Jefferson County Med. Soc. Avocations: tennis, skiing. Office: U Louisville Dept Pediat 235 E Chestnut St Louisville KY 40292 E-mail: cgwhitelaw@email.msn.com.

WHITELEY, BENJAMIN ROBERT, retired insurance company executive; b. Des Moines, July 13, 1929; s. Hiram Everett and Martha Jane (Walker) W.; m. Elaine Marie Yunker, June 14, 1953; children— Stephen Robert, Benjamin Walker BS, Oreg. State U., 1951; MS, U. Mich., 1952; postgrad. advanced mgmt. program, Harvard U.; DHL (hon.), Pacific U., 2001. Clk. group dept. Standard Ins. Co., Portland, Oreg., 1956-59, asst. actuary group dept. then asst. actuary actuarial dept., 1959-63, asst. v.p., asst. actuary, 1963-64, asst. v.p., assoc. actuary, 1964-70, v.p. group ins. adminstrn., 1970-72, v.p. group ins. div., 1972-80, exec. v.p. group ins., 1980-81, exec. v.p., 1981-83, pres., CEO, 1983-92, chmn. bd. dirs., CEO, 1993-94, chmn. bd. dirs., 1994—98; ret., 2000. Bd. dirs. Gunderson, Inc., Portland, The Greenbriar Cos. Past pres. Columbia Pacific coun. Boy Scouts Am.; past chmn. bd., trustee Pacific U., Forest Grove, Oreg.; past chmn. Oreg. Health Scis. Found., Oreg. Trail Coordinating Coun., Portland Opera Assn.; trustee Oreg. Cmty. Found., 1998—, chmn., 2004; campaign chair, bd. dirs. United Way Portland, 1994. 1st lt. USAF, 1952-55. Recipient Silver Beaver award Cascade Pacific coun. Boy Scouts Am., 1993, Harvey and Emiline Clark medal Pacific U., 1991, Alumni fellow award Oreg. State U., 1991, Aubrey R. Watzek award Lewis and Clark Coll., 1994, Lifetime Achievement award Bus. Youth Exch., Portland, Oreg., 1995. Fellow Soc. Actuaries; mem. Arlington Club (pres. 1991), Waverley Country Club, Multnomah Athletic Club. Republican. Methodist. E-mail: eorbwhiteley@earthlink.net.

WHITELEY, H. E. dean; BS in Animal and Vet. Medicine, U. Maine, 1973; DVM, Purdue U., 1977; PhD in Pathology, Colo. State U., 1984. Diplomate Am. Coll. Vet. Pathologists. Dir. vet. diagnostic lab., interim dir. Office Animal Rsch. Svcs., mem. Ctr. for Biochem. Toxicology U. Conn.; prof., dept. head Conn., 1995—; faculty mem. dept. vet. pathobiology U. Ill. Coll. Vet. Medicine, Urbana, 1984—95, interim dept. head, 1994, dean, 2001—, dir., Ctr. for Zoonoses Rsch. Office: U Ill Urbana-Champaign 3505 Veterinary Medicine Basic Scis Bldg 2001 S Lincoln Ave Urbana IL 61802 Business E-Mail: hwhite@uiuc.edu.*

WHITELEY, HENRY HOWARD, religious studies educator, minister; b. Roswell, N.Mex., Oct. 31, 1928; s. Alford and Ruth Henrich Whiteley; m. Yvonna Margaret Cornell, Feb. 28, 1953; children: Emma Lachelle Whiteley Yoder, Lynn Howard. BS in Music Edn., John Brown U., Siloam Springs, Ark., 1961; postgrad., West Tex. State U., 1963. Tchr., band dir. K-12 Gravette Pub. Schs., Ark., 1960—62, Balko Pub. Schs., Okla., 1962—63; minister Galena, Kans., Hardesty, Okla., Logan, Okla., Baxter Springs, Kans.; prof. music, bibl. studies Apostolic Faith Bible Coll., Baxter Springs, 1965—68, 1984—88, 1995—, supt., 1977—78; pastor Pampa Chapel of Apostolic Faith, Tex., 1988—95. Founder, dir. Cantatas cmty. choir, 1965—70. Editor: Apostolic Faith Report, 1964—72. Dir. Ann. Nat. Ch. Camp, Laverne, Okla., 1973; pres. Ministerial Alliance, Pampa, 1990, sec. Baxter Springs, Kans., 1999—2000; dir. Ann. Youth Camp, Baxter Springs, 1965—69, 1996—, Ann. Nat. Ch. Camp, Baxter Springs, 1965—69, Ann. Youth Camp, Laverne, Okla., 1973—75; adv. bd. Salvation Army, Pampa, 1993—95; bd. dirs. Apostolic Faith Bible Coll., 1977—79. Cpl. U.S. Army, 1948—51. Trinity Apostolic Faith. Avocations: reading, music, travel. Mailing: 2353 Washington Baxter Springs KS 66713

WHITELEY, JOHN FREDERICK, education educator, consultant; b. Paterson, NJ, July 18, 1950; s. Wilfred Edward Whiteley and Elizabeth Johanna DeJonge; m. Elizabeth Jane Davis, Nov. 1, 2001; m. Marian Elizabeth Robley, July 26, 1980 (div.); 1 child, Meredith Ray. BS in marine transp., U.S. Merchant Marine Acad., 1972; diploma, U.S. Naval War Coll., 1998. Ships officer various worldwide locations, 1979—2001; faculty Young Meml. Coll., Morgan City, La., 2001, Marshall U., Huntington, W.Va., 2002—. Officer U.S. Coast Guard, NYC, San Juan, 1972—79; dir. Tri-State Maritime Tng. Ctr., St. Albans, W.Va., 2003; owner Whiteley Global, LLC, St. Albans, 2001—03. Dist. exec. Boy Scouts of Am., Chattanooga, 1991—94, scoutmaster, 2003, vol. leader, 1983—2003; exec. Girl Scouts of the USA, Chattanooga, 1994—95. Lt. U.S. Coast Guard, 1972—79. Recipient Silver Beaver, Boy Scouts of Am., 2003, Def. Meritorious Svc. medal, U.S. Trans. Command, 1999. Avocations: hiking, bicycling, photography. Office: Whiteley Global LLC PO Box 342 Saint Albans WV 25177 Office Phone: 304-610-3321.

WHITELEY, ROSE MARIE, city clerk, treasurer; b. Benkelman, Nebr., Mar. 26, 1942; d. Alvin James and Grace Rebecca (Alsbury) W. BS, Nebr. State U., Kearney, 1963; MS, Colo. State U., 1968. Cert. home cons./bus. secondary tchr. Home econs. instr. Deuel County H.S., Chappell, Nebr., 1963-66; adult ednl. cons. McCalls Patterns, N.Y.C., 1967-70; exec. dir. Nebr./Iowa chpt. Nat. Multiple Sclerosis Soc., Omaha, 1971-78; grant writer, fundraising dir. Omaha Theatre, 1978-94; city clk., treas. City of Benkelman, 1994—. Cons. Fundraising/Grantwriting, Omaha, 1982-94, 94—. Contbr.: The Harvest Gardener, 1992. Treas. Prevention Policy Bd., 1994—, Dundy County Resource Ctr., 1994-2001, pres., 2001--; mem. Benkelman Tree Bd., 1994—. Mem. S.W. Clks. Assn. (pres.), Nebr. Mcpl. Clks. Assn., Internat. Inst. of Mcpl. Clks., Kappa Omicron Phi. Avocations: gardening, gourmet cooking. Home: HC 64 Box 58 Benkelman NE 69021-9156 Office: City of Benkelman PO Box 347 Benkelman NE 69021-0347

WHITEMAN, DOUGLAS E. publisher; b. Emporia, Kans., Mar. 4, 1961; s. Floyd E. and Phyllis E. (Troyer) W.; m. Susan R. Anderson, Sept. 14, 1985; 1 child, Aaron Anderson Douglas. BSBA, U. Kans., 1983. With Putnam Pub. Group, Denver and N.Y.C., 1983—, dir. trade sales and mktg., internat. sales mgr. N.Y.C., 1987—89, v.p. sales and mktg., 1989—94; sr. v.p. pub. Putnam and Grosset Book Group, N.Y.C., 1994—95, pres., pub., 1995—97; pres. Penguin Putnam Books for Young Readers, N.Y.C., 1997—; exec. v.p. Penguin Group, 1998—. Vice chmn., bd. dirs. Eric Carle Mus. of Picture Book Art, 2001—; pres. Publishers Lunch Club, 2004—; bd. dirs. Children's Book Coun., 2004—. Mem.: Pub.'s Lunch Club N.Y.C. Methodist. Avocations: literature, tennis, fantasy baseball. Office: Penguin Putnam Inc 345 Hudson St Fl 14 New York NY 10014-4592 E-mail: doug.whiteman@us.penguingroup.com.

WHITEMAN, JOSEPH DAVID, retired lawyer, manufacturing company executive; b. Sioux Falls, S.D., Sept. 12, 1933; s. Samuel D. and Margaret (Wallace) W.; m. Mary Kelly, Dec. 29, 1962; children: Anne Margaret, Mary Ellen, Joseph David, Sarah Kelly, Jane. BA, U. Mich., 1955, JD, 1960. Bar: D.C. 1960, Ohio 1976. Assoc. Cox, Langford, Stoddard & Cutler, Washington, 1959-64; sec., gen. counsel Studebaker group Studebaker Worthington, Inc., N.Y.C., 1964-71; asst. gen. counsel United Telecommunications, Inc., Kansas City, Mo., 1971-74; v.p., gen. counsel, sec. Weatherhead Co., Cleve., 1974-77, Parker Hannifin Corp., Cleve., 1977-98; ret., 1998. Immediate past chmn. bd. dirs. St. Lukes Med. Ctr. Served as lt. USNR, 1955-57. Mem. ABA, Beta Theta Pi, Phi Delta Phi. Republican. Roman Catholic. Home and Office: 2508 Robinson Springs Rd Stowe VT 05672

WHITEMAN, RICHARD FRANK, architect; b. Mankato, Minn., Mar. 24, 1925; s. Lester Raymond and Mary Grace (Dawald) W.; m. Jean Frances Waite, June 20, 1948 (dec. May 1980); children: David, Sarah, Lynn, Ann, Carol, Frank, Marie, Steven; m. Mavis Patricia Knutsen, May 30, 1982. BArch, U. Minn., 1945; MArch, Harvard U., 1948. Registered architect, Minn. Designer Ellerbe Co., St. Paul, Minn., 1946; architect Thorshov and Cerny, Mpls., 1948-53; ptnr. Jyring and Whiteman, Hibbing, Minn., 1953-62; pres. AJWM Inc., Hibbing and Duluth, Minn., 1963-72, Architects Four, Duluth, 1972-83; owner Richard Whiteman, Duluth, 1983-95; sr. architect U. Minn., Duluth. Chmn. Architect Sect. Registration Bd., Minn., 1972-80. Prin. works include Washington Sch., Hibbing, 1957 (Minn. Soc. Architects Design award 1957), Whiteman Summer Home, Pengilly, Minn. (Minn. Soc. Architects Design award 1959), Bemidji State Coll. Phys. Edn. Bldg. (Minn. Soc. Architects Design award 1960), Whiteman Residence, Griggs Hall UMD, 1990. Pres. U. for Srs., 1993-94, 2000-01; active Duluth Housing Authority, 2001—, Duluth Housing Commn., 2002; chmn. Brownlee Endowment Fund, 2004. With USNR, 1945. Mem. Minn. Soc. Architects (pres. 1972), Northeast Minn. Architects (pres. 1962), Minn. Designer Selection Bd. (chmn. 1990). Clubs: Kitchi Gammi (Duluth). Lodges: Kiwanis. Democrat. Roman Catholic. Avocations: photography, fishing, cross country skiing, travel. Home: 3500 E 3rd St Duluth MN 55804-1812

WHITEMIRE, STEVE L. judge; b. Ft. Payne, Ala., Oct. 13, 1972; s. Steven Lamar Whitmire and Vicki Renee Green; m. Heather Anique Muldock, May 30, 1998; children: Wesley Garrett, Trace Allen. AS, Snead State C.C., 1993; BA, Auburn U., 1995; JD, U. Ala., 1997. Atty. pvt. practice, Rainesville, Ala., 1998—2003; judge DeKalb County Dist. Ct., Ft. Payne, 2003—. Mem.: DeKalb County Dem. Club, Ft. Payne Optimist Club, Rainesville Civitans. Avocation: horseback riding. Office: DeKalb County Dist Ct 300 Grand Ave SW Ste 101 Fort Payne AL 35967

WHITENER, CAROLYN RAYE, artist; b. Corpus Christi, Texas, Feb. 2, 1941; d. Rayburn N. and Alice G. Hamilton; m. Howard Dwain Whitener; children: Mark Dwain, Rynn Rayna. Student, U. Sci. and Arts Okla., 1981-85. Co-owner Honk'n'Holler's, Stillwater, Okla., 1962-75; owner Clynn's Designs, Okla. City, 1969—; co-owner W&W Cattle Ranch, Okla., 1973—; comml. artist, co-owner Colorvision, Inc., Okla. and Tex., 1979—. Cons. Tele-Weight, Buena Vista, Colo., 1985-92, Craig Versus Boren, 1972-76; comml. design cons. for one and two dimensional rendering drawings Rynn's Lawncare & Landscaping, Oklahoma City, 1997—. Active Grady County Environ. Coalition, 1991—92; adv. mem. Gov.'s Okla. Commn. on Status of Women, 2000—. Recipient Outstanding Cmty. Svc. award, 1992, One Person Who Made a Difference LWVOK, 1997, Pres. Prestigious award Okla. State U., 1996, First Adv. award Okla. Commn. on Status of Women, 2001, Gov. Commendation award Gov. Frank Keating, 2001, State of Okla. Citation award Rep. Richard Phillips and Sen. Mike Fair, 2001; named Woman of Yr. Okla. City Coun. of Beta Sigma Phi, 1997-98. Mem. Okla. Assn. Family Cmty. and Edn., Grady County Ext. Homemakers, Oklahoma City Newcomer's Club, Beta Sigma Phi (Woman of Yr. award 1997-98, Outstanding Svc. award 1992, Evening Lions Homecoming Window Design awards, 1966-68). mem. adv. coun., Status of Okla. Woman, 2001-. Democrat. Methodist. Avocations: art, sewing, cooking, travel, meeting new people. Home: 12324 St Lukes Ln Oklahoma City OK 73142 E-mail: CrWhitener@aol.com.

WHITENER, GORDON D. textile manufacturing company executive; Sr. v.p. sales and mtkg. Interface Flooring Systems, Inc., 1993-94; sr. v.p. Interface, Inc., Atlanta, 1994—; pres., CEO Interface Americas Inc., Atlanta, 1994—. Bd. dirs. Interface, Inc. Office: Interface Americas Inc 2859 Paces Ferry Rd SE Ste 2000 Atlanta GA 30339-6216

WHITENER, WILLIAM GARNETT, dancer, choreographer; b. Seattle, Aug. 17, 1951; s. Warren G. and Virginia Louise (Garnett) Whitener. Student, Cornish Sch. Allied Arts, Seattle, 1958-69. Dancer N.Y.C. Opera, 1969, Joffrey Ballet, N.Y.C., 1969-77, Twyla Tharp Dance, N.Y.C., 1978-87; asst. to choreographer Jerome Robbins for Robbins' Broadway, N.Y.C., 1988; artistic dir. Les Ballets Jazz de Montréal, 1991-93, Royal Winnipeg Ballet, 1993-95, Kansas City Ballet, 1996—. Coord. dance dept. Concord Acad., Mass., 1988; vis. artist U. Wash., 1989—91; tchr. Harvard U. Summer Dance, 1989—90, NYU, 1985. Dancer (Broadway plays) Dancin', 1978, choreographer Princeton Ballet, Joffrey II, John Curry Ice Theatre, Ballet Hispanico of N.Y., Boston Ballet Internat. Choreography Competition, Tommy Tune, Martine Van Hamel/Kevin McKenzie, Ann Reinking, Seattle Repertory Theatre, Am. Ballroom Theatre, N.Y.C., Hartford Ballet, Conn., On the Boards with Bill Irwin, PBS-TV Alive From Off Center, (Operas) A Little Night Music, Pacific Northwest Ballet, Rusalka, Seattle Opera, (Operas) Aida, dancer (films) Amadeus, Zelig, (TV films) The Catherine Wheel, Dance in America; performer: Garden of Earthly Delights, 1988. Bd. trustees DanceUSA, 2000—. Ford Found. scholar, 1963—64. Mem.: Am. Guild Musical Artists, Actor's Equity. Office: Kansas City Ballet 1601 Broadway St Kansas City MO 64108-1207

WHITESCARVER, JACK EDWARD, federal agency administrator; b. Palestine, Tex., May 16, 1937; s. A.B. and Elizabeth Lorraine (Kimball) W. BS, Sam Houston State U., 1959, MS, 1965; PhD, U. Medicine Dentistry N.J.,

1974. Rsch. assoc. Harvard U. Sch. Pub. Health, Boston, 1976-77; grants assoc. NIH, Bethesda, Md., 1977-78; spl. asst. to dir. NIH/NIAID, Bethesda, 1978-84; asst. dean R&D Emory U. Sch. Medicine, Atlanta, 1984-86, asst. prof. pathology, 1985-88, assoc. dean, 1986-88; dep. dir. NIH/Office AIDS Rsch., Bethesda, 1988—99, acting dir., 1999—2002, dir., 2002—. Contbr. articles to Jour. Infectious Diseases, Jour. Investigative Dermatology, Tex. Reports Biol. Medicine. Fellow Albert Soiland Cancer Found., 1967-70; recipient Alumnus of Yr. award U. Medicine and Dentistry N.J., 1991. Mem. Am. Acad. Allergy and Immunology, Am. Soc. for Microbiology, Infectious Diseases Soc. Am., Internat. AIDS Soc., Royal Soc. Medicine. Office: Office AIDS Rs 9000 Rockville Pike Bldg 1 Bethesda MD 20892-0001*

WHITESELL, JOHN EDWIN, retired motion picture company executive; b. DuBois, Pa., Feb. 23, 1938; s. Guy Roosevelt and Grace Ethlyn (Brisbin) W.; m. Amy H. Jacobs, June 12, 1960; 1 child, Scott Howard; m. Martha Kathlyn Hall, Sept. 3, 1975; m. Phyllis Doyle, May 8, 1993. *Scott graduated from Los Angeles City College Drama Academy Summa Cum Laude and was the winner of the "Irene Ryan Acting Award." He makes his living as a children's entertainer in Los Angeles. Phyllis holds a BFA in Ballet from Texas Christian University (TCU) and an MA in Humanities from the University of Texas at Dallas (UTD). In 1974, she held the title of Miss Texas. She spent many years as a dancer, choreographer, actress, and model. Her work is seen in commercials, print ads, industrials, stage shows, television and film.* BA, Pa. State U., 1962. Asst. mgr. non-theatrical div. Columbia Pictures Corp., N.Y.C., 1963-66; with Warner Bros., Inc., 1966—2003, nat. sales mgr. non-theatrical div., 1968-75, v.p., 1975-76; v.p. internat. sales adminstrn. Warner Bros. Internat. TV Distbn., 1976-2001, cons., 2001—03, ret., 2003. Bd. dirs. Mastermedia Internat. Inc.; past bd. dirs. Found. for Entertainment Programming in Higher Edn.; mem. self-study com. Nat. Entertainment Conf., 1974-75. *At Columbia Pictures, started Royal-16-International, a new division distributing feature films to colleges and universities. After moving to Warner Bros., started Warner Bros. Film Gallery, which quickly became the nation's leading distributor serving this market. Also responsible for licensing motion pictures to a national network of 32 sub-distributors and various branches of the U.S. Government. Conceived and implemented the WB-NEC Film Project, a joint educational program between Warner Bros. and the National Entertainment Conference, enabling 20-film oriented college students selected by NEC to intern at Warner Bros. Studio each summer. Served last 25 years of career as Vice President, International Sales Administration, Warner Bros. International Television Distribution. In this capacity finalized agreements with virtually all TV stations outside of the U.S.* Served with USNR, 1956-58. Recipient Alumni Fellow award Pa. State U., 2001, Outstanding Alumnus award Pa. State U. DuBois Campus, 1995, Founders award Nat. Entertainment Conf., 1975. Mem. Nat. Audio-Visual Assn. (motion picture coun. 1973-76, exec. com. film coun. 1969-76, edn1. materials producers coun. 1970-76), Acad. TV Arts and Scis., Nat. Assn. Media Educators (adv. com. 1973-76)

WHITESELL, PATRICK, agent; Previously with Intertalent; agt. United Talent Agy.; with Creative Artists Agy., 1995—2000, co-head motion picture talent dept., 2000—01; ptnr. Endeavor Agy., Beverly Hills, Calif., 2001—. Office: Endeavor Agy 9701 Wilshire Blvd 10th Flr Beverly Hills CA 90212

WHITESELL, STEPHEN ERNEST, parks and recreation director; BS in Environ. Resources, Calif. State U., Sacramento, 1973; M in Landscape Architecture, Harvard U., 1977. Landscape architect, planner Denver Svc. Ctr., Lakewood, Colo., 1977-80, Ind. Dunes Nat. Lakeshore, Porter, Ind., 1980-83; chief maintenance Apostle Islands Nat. Seashore, Bayfield, Ind., 1983-84; supt. Longfellow, John F. Kennedy, Frederick Law Olmsted Nat. Hist. Sites, Cambridge, Mass., 1984-87; supt. Sandy Hook Unit Gateway Nat. Recreation Area, Albuquerque, N.Mex., 1987-91; supt. Petroglyph Nat. Monument, San Antonio, 1991-95, San Antonio Missions Nat. Hist. Park, 1995—. Bd. dirs. Cultural Alliance of San Antonio Area Tourism Coun., City Year San Antonio. Recipient Award of Merit Boston Soc. Landscape Architects, 1985, U.S. Dept. Interior Superior Svc. Honor award, 1998. Mem. Boy Scouts Am., Rotary Club San Antonio, South San Antonio C. of C. (adv. dir.), Los Compadres de San Antonio Missions (adv. bd.), San Antonio Tourism Coun. (bd. dirs.). Avocations: golf, fishing, gardening. Office: San Antonio Missions Nat Hist Park 2202 Roosevelt Ave San Antonio TX 78210-4919 Fax: 210-534-1106.

WHITESIDE, CAROL GORDON, foundation executive; b. Chgo., Dec. 15, 1942; d. Paul George and Helen Louise (Barre) G.; m. John Gregory Whiteside, Aug. 15, 1964; children: Brian Paul, Derek James. BA, U. Calif., Davis, 1964. Pers. mgr. Emporium Capwell Co., Santa Rosa, 1964-67; pers. asst. Levi Strauss & Co., San Francisco, 1967-69; project leader Interdatum, San Francisco, 1983-88; with City Coun. Modesto, 1983-87; mayor City of Modesto, 1987-91; asst. sec. for intergovtl. rels. The Resources Agy., State of Calif., Sacramento, 1991-93; dir. intergovtl. affairs Gov.'s Office, Sacramento, 1993-97; pres. Great Valley Ctr., Modesto, Calif., 1997—. Trustee Modesto City Schs., 1979-83; nat. pres. Rep. Mayors and Local Ofcls., 1990. Recipient Lifetime Achievement award League of Calif. Cities, 2002; named Outstanding Woman of Yr. Women's Commn., Stanislaus County, Calif., 1988, Woman of Yr., 27th Assembly Dist., 1991; Toll fellow Coun. of State Govts., 1996. Republican. Lutheran. Office: Great Valley Ctr 201 Needham St Modesto CA 95354-0903 Office Phone: 209-522-5103. E-mail: carol@greatvalley.org.

WHITESIDE, CHARLES B., III, investment company executive; b. Ft. Smith, Ark., Mar. 17, 1941; s. Charles B. Jr. and R. Evelyn cindy Whiteside; m. Catherine Ware, Jan. 29, 1966; children: Carrie H., Charles B. IV. BSBA, U. Ark., 1963. 1st v.p. Merrill Lynch & Co., Little Rock, 1965—. Trustee Ark. Children's Hosp., 1974—, chmn., treas., 1983—88; vice chmn. bd. dirs. Ark. Children's Hosp. Found., 1983—; trustee Ark. Children's Rsch. Inst., 1989—2000, chmn., 1990—; trustee, treas. Lyon Coll., Batesville, Ark., 1992—; bd. dirs. U. Ark. Nat. Devel., Fayetteville, 1997—. 1st lt. U.S. Army, 1963—65. Recipient Outstanding Vol. Fundraising award for State of Ark., Nat. Soc. Fund Raising Execs., 2000; Sr. Paul Harris fellow, Rotary. Mem.: Kappa Sigma Alumni Assn. (pres. bd. dirs. 1974—). Episcopalian. Avocations: hunting, fishing. Office: Merrill Lynch 2200 Rodney Parham Ste 300 Little Rock AR 72212

WHITESIDE, WILLIAM ANTHONY, JR., retired lawyer; b. Phila., Feb. 23, 1929; s. William Anthony and Ellen T. (Hensler) W.; m. Eileen Ann Ferrick, Feb. 27, 1954; children: William Anthony III, Michael P., Eileen A., Richard F., Christopher J., Mary P. BS, Notre Dame U., 1951; LLB, U. Pa., 1954. Bar: Pa. 1955. Assoc. Speiser, Satinsky, Gilliland & Packel, Phila., 1956-58, ptnr., 1958-61, Fox, Rothschild, O'Brien & Frankel, Phila., 1961—2001; ret., 2001. Chmn. Police Athletic League, Phila.; trustee Am. Coll. Mgmt. and Tech., Dubrovnik, Croatia; chmn. emeritus bd. trustees, emeritus trustee, Rochester Inst. of Tech.; trustee C.C. Phila. Found., LaSalle Coll. H.S., Phila.; pres. adv. coun. U. Notre Dame; emeritus trustee Germantown Acad., past pres. 1st lt. USAF, 1954-56. Named Man of Yr., Notre Dame Club Phila., 1967. Mem.: ABA, Pa. Soc., Phila. Bar Assn., Pa. Bar Assn., Wissahickon Skating Club, Union League Club Phila. Republican. Roman Catholic. Home: 7808 Cobden Rd Glenside PA 19038-7256 also: 901 Gardens Plz Ocean City NJ 08226-4719 Office: Fox Rothschild O'Brien & Frankel 2000 Market St Ste 10 Philadelphia PA 19103-3231 Office Phone: 215-299-2032.

WHITESIDES, GEORGE MCCLELLAND, chemistry professor; b. Louisville, Ky., Aug. 3, 1939; m. Barbara Breasted; children: George Thomas, Benjamin Haile. AB, Harvard U., 1960; PhD, Calif. Inst. Tech., 1964; D Honoris Causa (hon.), U. Twente, The Netherlands, 2001. Asst. prof. dept. chemistry MIT, Cambridge, 1963—69, assoc. prof., 1969—71, prof., 1971—75, Arthur C. Cope prof., 1975—80, Haslam and Dewey prof., 1980—82; prof. dept. chemistry Harvard U., Cambridge, 1982—86, Mallinckrodt prof., 1986—. Recipient Pure Chemistry award, Am. Chem. Soc., 1975, Harrison Howe award, Rochester sect., 1979, Arthur C. Cope award, 1995, James Flack Norris award, 1994, Remsen award, 1983, Arthur C. Cope Scholar award, 1989, Disting. Alumni award, Calif. Inst. Tech., 1980, Def. Advanced Rsch. Projects Agy. award, 1996, Madison Marshall award, Am. Chem. Soc., 1996, Nat. Medal of Sci., 1998, von Hippel award, Material Rsch. Soc., 2000, World Tech. award for materials, World Tech. Network, 2001, Rschr. of Yr. award, Small Times Mag., 2002, Pitts. Analytical Chemistry award, Soc. Analytical Chemists of Pitts., 2003, Kyoto prize for advanced tech., Inamori Found., 2003; Alfred P. Sloan fellow, 1968. Fellow: AAAS; mem.: NAS, Am. Philos. Soc., Am. Acad. Arts and Scis. Office: Harvard U Dept of Chemistry 12 Oxford St Cambridge MA 02138-2902 Office Phone: 617-495-9430. Business E-Mail: gwhitesides@gmwgroup.harvard.edu.

WHITESIDES, LAWSON EWING, JR., investment management executive; b. Cin., Dec. 31, 1946; s. Lawson Ewing and Elizabeth Igler Whitesides; m. Jane Grissom Whitesides, Sept. 29, 1973; children: Lawson Ewing III, Ellen Elizabeth, Margaret Mary. BSE, Princeton U., 1968; SM in Chem. Engring., MIT, 1971; MBA, Harvard U., 1973. Chartered fin. analyst. Assoc. Stein Roe & Farnham, Chgo., 1973-80, ptnr., 1981-86; 1st v.p. Stein Roe & Farnham, Inc., Chgo., 1986-87, sr. v.p., 1988-95; v.p., chief investment officer Miami Corp., Chgo., 1995-98, exec. v.p., chief investment officer, 1999-2000, pres., 2001—, also bd. dirs. Bd. dirs. Cutler Oil & Gas Corp., Chgo., 2000—. Mem. Soc. Colonial Wars (Ill.), Assn. for Investment Mgmt. and Rsch., Investment Analyst Soc. Chgo., The Casino, Indian Hill Club, Chgo. Club, Tau Beta Pi, Sigma Xi. Episcopalian. Office: Miami Corp 410 N Michigan Ave Chicago IL 60611

WHITE-THOMSON, IAN LEONARD, retired mining executive; b. Halstead, Eng., May 3, 1936; came to U.S., 1969; s. Walter Norman and Leonore (Turney) W-T.; m. Barbara Montgomery, Nov. 24, 1971. BA with 1st class honors, New Coll., Oxford U., 1960, MA, 1969. Mgmt. trainee Borax Consol. Ltd., London, 1960-61, asst. to sales mgr., 1961-64, asst. to sales dir., 1964; comml. dir. Hardman & Holden Ltd., Manchester, Eng., 1965-67, joint mng. dir., 1967-69; v.p. mktg. dept. U.S. Borax Inc., Los Angeles, 1969-73, exec. v.p. mktg., 1973-88, pres., 1988-98, also dir., chmn., 1996-99; group exec. Pa. Glass Sand Corp., Ottawa Silica Co., U.S. Silica Co., 1985-87; exec. dir. L.A. Opera, 2000—01. Bd. dirs. Canpotex Ltd., chmn. bd., 1974-76. Bd. dirs. L.A. Master Chorale, Colburn Sch.; bd. dirs. Thornton Sch. U. So. Calif. Served with Brit. Army, 1954—56. Named Mfr. of Yr., Calif. Mfrs. Assn., 1997. Mem. Can. Potash Prodrs. Assn. (v.p. 1976-77, dir. 1972-77), Chem. Industry Coun. of Calif. (bd. dirs. 1982-85, chmn. 1984), Am. Mining Congress (bd. dirs. 1989), RTZ Borax and Minerals (bd. dirs. 1992, chief exec. 1995-99), Kerr-McGee Corp. (bd. dirs. 1999—), Calif. Club, Valley Hunt Club. Home: 1897 Braemar Rd Pasadena CA 91103-3712

WHITE-WHITFIELD, LISA DENISE, social worker, grant writer; b. L.A., June 11, 1968; d. Charles L. White and Martha Jackson, Burrell Jackson (Stepfather); m. Ervin L. Whitfield, Apr. 25, 1992 (div. Oct. 1, 1995); 1 child, Alexis Ximara. BS in Bus. Adminstrn., Calif. State U., Long Beach, 1992; postgrad., Calif. State U., Carson, 2000. Tchg. credential Calif. Bank teller Wells Fargo Bank, Lakewood, Calif., 1987—88; proof operator Bank of Am., Long Beach, 1988—89; spl. edn. tchrs. asst. Inglewood (Calif.) Unifield Sch. Dist., 1989—91; adminstrv. asst. Remax Realtors, Carson, 1991—92; substitute tchr. Compton (Calif.) Unified Sch. Dist., 1992—93; acctg. clk. United Airlines, El Segundo, Calif., 1993—94; social worker LA County Dept. Pub. Social Svcs., 1994—. Mentor Welfare-to-Work Career Mentor Program, El Monte, CALIF., 2002—. Vol. March of Dimes, L.A., 1994—2000; vol., bd. mem. The Dance Connection Dance Acad., L.A., 2002; vol. Redeemer Christian Acad., L.A., 1999, West Angeles Ch. of God in Christ, L.A., 1996—2002. Scholar, Calif. Regional Purchasing Com., 1986. Mem.: ASPA, Dominguez Pub. Adminstrn. Assn., Assn. County Administrs., Calif. State U. Long Beach Alumni Assn. Avocations: marathon running, social research, volunteering, travel, hiking. Office: Los Angeles County Dept Social Svcs 10728 S Central Ave Los Angeles CA 90059

WHITE-WINTERS, JILL MARY, nursing educator; b. Milw., June 30, 1955; d. John Paul Gabor and Ann Lorraine (Ladish) Gordy; m. Jack Mark Winters; children: Jeffrey, Eric, David, Michael. BSN, U. Wis., Milw., 1978; MS in Nursing, Marquette U., 1991; PhD, U. Wis., 1996. Nurse various hosps., Milw., 1978—85, Peck Foods Corp., Milw., 1985-88; prof. U. Wis., Milw., 1996—2001, Marquette U., Milw., 2001—. Contbr. chpts. to books, articles to profl. jours. Grantee, Nat. Inst. Nursing Rsch., Wis. Women's Health Found., Nat. Inst. Disability and Rehab. Rsch. Mem. AACCN (grantee 1997), ANA, Midwest Nursing Rsch. Soc., Sigma Theta Tau (v.p. local chpt. 1997-99). Roman Catholic. Avocation: golf. Home: 10320 N Provence Ct Mequon WI 53092-5228 Office: Marquette U Coll Nursing PO Box 1881 Milwaukee WI 53201-1881 Office Phone: 414-288-3848. E-mail: jill.winters@marquette.edu.

WHITFIELD, EDWARD (WAYNE WHITFIELD), congressman; b. Hopkinsville, Ky., May 25, 1943; m. Constance Harriman; 1 child, Kate. BS in Bus., U. Ky., 1965; JD, U. Ky. Coll. of Law, 1969. Mem. Ky. Ho. of Reps., 1974-75; pvt. practice law, 1970-79; govt. affairs counsel Seaboard Sys. R.R. subs. CSX Corp., 1979-83, counsel to pres., 1983-85; v.p. state rels. CSX Corp., 1986-88, v.p. fed. r.r. affairs, 1988-91; legal counsel to chmn. Interstate Commerce Commn., 1991-93; mem. U.S. Congress from 1st Ky. dist., 1995—; mem. energy and commerce com. 1st lt. USAR. Republican. Office: US Ho of Reps 301 Cannon Hob Washington DC 20515-1701

WHITFIELD, GRAHAM FRANK, orthopedic surgeon; b. Cheam, Surrey, Eng., Feb. 8, 1942; arrived in U.S., 1969, naturalized, 1975; s. Reginald Frank and Marjorie Joyce (Bennett) W. BSc, King's Coll., U. London, 1963; PhD, Queen Mary Coll., U. London, 1969; MD, NY Med. Coll., 1976. Rsch. scientist Unilever Rsch. Lab., England, 1963-66; postdoctoral fellow dept. chemistry Temple U., 1969-71, instr., 1971-72, asst. prof., 1972-73; resident in surgery NY Med. Coll. Affiliated Hosps., NYC, 1976-78, resident in orthopedics, 1978-79, sr. resident in orthop. surgery, 1979-80, chief resident, 1980-81; attending orthop. surgeon Good Samaritan Hosp., West Palm Beach, Fla., 1981-87, JFK Med. Ctr., Lake Worth, Fla., 1981—, Palms Wellington Surg. Ctr., West Palm Beach, 1994-96, Wellington Regional Med. Ctr., West Palm Beach, 1996—, Bethesda Health City, Boynton Beach, Fla., 1996—, Palms West Hosp., Loxahatchee, Fla., 1997—2004, Columbia Hosp., West Palm Beach, 1997—2002. Instr. health professions divsn. Nova Southeastern U., North Miami, Fla., 1994-95, clin. asst. prof. dept. surgery, Coll. Osteo. Medicine, Nova Southeastern U., Ft. Lauderdale, Fla., 1995—. Author: (with Joseph Cohn and Louis Del Guercio) Critical Care Readings, 1981; editl. bd., contbg. editor Hosp. Physician, 1978-82; cons. editor Physician Asst. and Health Practitioner, 1979-82; orthop. cons. Conv. Reporter, 1980-82; assoc. editor-in-chief Critical Care Monitor, 1980-82; editl. bd. Complications in Orthopedics, 1986-96; practice panel cons. in orthop. surgery Complications in Surgery, 1982-96. Recipient N.Y. Med. Coll. Surg. Soc. award, 1976. Fellow Internat. Coll. Surgeons; mem. AMA, Fla. Med. Assn., Palm Beach County Med. Soc., Royal Inst. Chemistry (Eng.), So. Orthop. Assn., Fla. Orthop. Soc., Brit. Schs. and Univs. Club, Soc. the Four Arts, Soc. Sons of St. George (NYC), Explorer's Club (NYC), Rotary, Sigma Xi. Office: 2150 S Congress Ave West Palm Beach FL 33406-7604 Office Phone: 561-965-5200. Personal E-mail: GFW2150@aol.com.

WHITFIELD, ROY A. pharmaceutical executive; b. Crewe, England; BS in math.with first class honors, Oxford U.; MBA with distinction, Stanford U. Cons. Boston Consulting Group; various positions Technicon Instrument Corp. (formerly CooperBiomedical, Inc.), 1984-89; pres. Ideon Corp. subs. Invitron Corp., 1989-91; CEO IncyteGenomics (formerly Incyte Pharms., Inc.), Palo Alto, Calif., 1993—, dir., 1991—, pres., 1991-97, treas., 1991-95; dir. Aurora Biosci. Corp. Office: Incyte Genomics Inc 3160 Porter Dr Palo Alto CA 94304-1212 Fax: 650-855-0555.

WHITFIELD, SCOTT BURWICK, physics educator; b. Denver, Colo., Sept. 30, 1959; s. Julian Dale Whitfield and Jacqulyn Carole Burwick; m. Diane Lelani Wylie, Aug. 24, 1989; children: Heather Lehua, Kyle Kanoa. BA in Physics, U. of Colo., 1982; MS in Physics, PhD in Physics, U. of Oreg., 1988. Postdocorate U. Ctrl. Fla., Orlando, 1989—92; Humboldt fellow Fritz-Haber-Inst. der Max-Planck-Gesellschaft, Berlin, 1992—94; postdocorate U. of Nev., Las Vegas, 1995—96; physics prof. U. of Wis., Eau Claire, 1997—. Vis. prof. physics. U. South Ala., Mobile, 1996—97; mem. NSF, 2003—05. Contbr. articles to sci. jours. Grantee, Rsch. Corp., 2000—02. Mem.: Alexander Humboldt Found. of Am., Am. Phys. Soc. Achievements include research in fundamental investigations of atom photon interactions in open-shell atoms; fundamental interactions in nature, the interaction of light (photons) and matter; experimental investigation of this interaction in open-shell atoms where there is still, in many instances, very little data. Avocations: hiking, classical guitarist, backpacking. Home: 2905 Eisenhower St Eau Claire WI 54701 Office: U Wis - Eau Claire 105 Garfield St Eau Claire WI 54702 E-mail: whitfisb@uwec.edu.

WHITFIELD, SIMON, Olympic athlete; b. Kingston, Ont., Can., May 16, 1975; Can. Triathlon champion, Winnipeg, 1998—99, 2001; 1st place winner ITU World Cup, 2001; Bronze medallist Pan Am. Game, Winnipeg, 1999; completed and placed 10th (jr.) World Championships, Cancun, Mexico, 1995, completed and placed 9th Perth, Australia, 1997, completed and placed 7th Montreal, 1999, completed and placed 6th Edmonton, 2001; Gold medallist, flag bearer Can. Olympic Team Olympic Games, Sydney, Australia, 2000; Gold medallist Commonwealth Games, 2002. Spokesperson Multiple Sclerosis Soc., 2001. Named Triathlete of Yr., Triathlon Can., 2000; named to B.C. Sports Hall of Fame, 2001; recipient David Foster Olympic Achievement award. Office: c/o Michelle Comeau IMG Canada 175 Bloor St E Ste 400 S Tower Toronto ON Canada M4W 3RB

WHITFORD, DENNIS J. military officer; BS, U.S. Naval Acad., 1972; MS, Naval Postgrad. Sch., 1979, PhD, 1988. Commd. ensign USN, 1972, advanced through grades to capt., 1994; officer-in-chg., staff oceanographer Naval Oceanography Cmd Detachment, Moffett Field, Calif., 1982-84; comdg. officer Oceanographic Unit Four aboard USNS Chauvenet, 1985; dir. numerical models dept. Fleet Numerical Oceanography Ctr., Monterey, Calif., 1988-89; comdg. officer Naval Oceanography Command Facility, San Diego, 1989-91; dir. Operational Oceanography Ctr., Stennis Space Ctr., Miss., 1991-93; exec. officer Naval Oceanographic Office, Stennis Space Ctr., Miss., 1993-95; chmn. dept. oceanography U.S. Naval Acad., Annapolis, Md., 1995—2002, permanent mil. prof., 1998—2002; full prof. U. Md., U. Coll. and U.S. Naval Acad., 2002—. Contbr. articles to profl. jours. Named Outstanding Young Men of Am., 1982; Adm. Burke PhD fellow, 1972. Mem.: Am. Geophys. Union, Sigma Xi. Office: UMC Sch Undegrad Studies 3501 Univ Blvd East Adelphi MD 20783-8080

WHITING, ALBERT NATHANIEL, former university chancellor; b. Jersey City, July 3, 1917; s. Hezekiah Oliver and Hildegarde Freida (Lyons) W.; m. Charlotte Luck, June 10, 1950; 1 dau., Brooke Elizabeth. AB, Amherst Coll., 1938; student, Columbia, summer 1938, U. Pitts., 1938-39; MA in Sociology, Fisk U., 1941, L.H.D. (hon.), 1980; PhD in Sociology, Am. U., 1952; LL.D., Amherst Coll., 1968, Western Mich. U., 1974, Duke, 1974, Kyung Hee U., Seoul, Korea; L.H.D., N.C. Central U., 1983. Research and teaching asst. Fisk U., 1939-41; instr. sociology, dir. rural community study Bennett Coll., Greensboro, N.C., 1941-43, 46-47; asst. prof. sociology Atlanta U., 1948-53; dean coll., prof. sociology Morris Brown Coll., Atlanta, 1953-57; asst. dean coll. Morgan State Coll., Balt., 1957-59, dean of college, 1960-67; pres. N.C. Central U., Durham, 1967-72, chancellor, 1972-83. Mem. bd. regents U. Md. Sys., 1988-95. Contbr. articles profl. jours. Bd. dirs. Am. Coun. Edn., Edn1. Testing Svc.; bd. dirs., past pres. Assn. State Colls. and Univs.; v.p. Internat. Assn. Univ. Pres.; bd. dirs. Research Triangle (N.C.) Inst.; mem. Md. Higher Edn. Commn., 1995-98. 1st lt. AUS, 1943-46. Episcopalian. Home: 11253B Slalom Ln Columbia MD 21044-2810

WHITING, ANTHONY, executive search consultant; b. Saigon, Indochina, Nov. 6, 1951; s. Dinty Warmington and Lorraine (Yarborough) W. BA summa cum laude, Tulane U., 1973; MA with honors, Columbia U., 1974, MPhil, 1977, PhD, 1984. V.p. Columbia Consulting Group, N.Y.C., 1987-92; partner Johnson, Smith, and Knisely, N.Y.C., 1993-99; mng. dir. Illsley Bourbonnais, N.Y.C., 1999-2000; mng. ptnr. The Waterman Group, N.Y.C., 2000—. Vis. scholar Columbia U., 2001—03. Author: The Never Resting Mind: Wallace Stevens' Romantic Irony, 1996, Edward Thomas, 1996; contbg. author: Wallace Stevens: Comprehensive Research and Study Guide, 2003. Mem. Soc. of Mayflower Descendants, Order of Crown of Charlemagne, Baronial Order of Magna Carta, Soc. of the Cinn., Hereditary Order of Descendants of Colonial Govs., Soc. of Order of Founders and Patriots of Am., Soc. of Descendants of Colonial Clergy, Sons of Am. Revolution, Phi Beta Kappa. Office: 267 Fifth Ave New York NY 10016

WHITING, BRIAN CHRISTOPHER, hospitality consultant; b. Bronxville, N.Y., Aug. 14, 1969; s. William Gordon Whiting and Doris Edna (Chubb) Whiting Simmons. BA, U. R.I., 1990. Dir. The Ams. and Asia Pacific Commonweath of Mass./Dept. Econ. Devel./Office Travel & Tourism, Boston, 1996—99; mgr./dir. internat. mktg. Europe and Mid. East Travel Industry Assn. Am., London, 1999—2000; travel and tourism practice leader, mgr. sports conv. and tourism PricewaterhouseCoopers LLP, N.Y.C., 2000—03; pres. & CEO Providence Warwick Conv. & Visitors Bur., Providence, 2003—. Chmn. bd. dirs. RI Festival of Trees; mem. RI Sports Commn., RI Transit and Urban Transp. Subcom.; mem. dean's adv. coun. U. R.I. Coll. Arts and Scis. Named Student of the Yr., DAR. Mem.: NY Soc. Assn. Execs., Internat. Assn. Conv. and Visitors Burs., Am. Soc. Assn. Execs., Profl. Conv. Mgmt. Assn., Travel Industry Assn. Am., Skal Club Internat., Assn. Travel Mgmt. Execs., New Eng. Soc., The Boston Athenaeum, Bronxville Field Club, Newport Jaycees (founding mem.), Racquet and Tennis Club, The Downtown Assn., Masons, Sigma Alpha Epsilon (pledge class pres. 1987—88). Republican. Avocations: travel, shooting, racquet sports, sailing, reading. Office: Providence Warwick Conv & Visitors Bur One W Exchange St Providence RI 02903 Office Phone: 401-274-1636. Business E-Mail: bwhiting@goprovidence.com.

WHITING, ELLIS EUGENE, retired research scientist; b. Springview, Nebr., Apr. 2, 1931; s. George E Whiting and Zollie Rose Whiting (Cornett); m. Clara Lavawn Brantz, Nov. 14, 1952 (div. Sept. 20, 1987); children: Vicki Jo Silverman, Cheryl Marie Toivola. B in mech. engring., U. of Colo., 1951—55; M in aero. engring., Stanford U., 1958—61; PhD in physics, York U., 1969—73. Rsch. engr. NASA, Ames Rsch. Ctr., Moffett Field, Calif., 1958—62; project devel. Honeywell, Mpls., 1962—63; rsch. scientist NASA, Ames Rsch. Ctr., Moffett Field, Calif., 1963—77, br. chief, 1977—79; chief scientist NASA, Office of Aeronautics and Space Tech., Washington, 1979—82; rsch. scientist Eloret Corp., Sunnyvale, Calif., 1986—. Author (coauthor): (understanding interest rates.) Interest Rates are Dynamite; author: (book and computer code about stocks) TickerPlot, (book and flash cards on math facts) Math Facts, the Missing Link to Math Excellence. Vol. and bd. of dirs. Friends Outside Nat. Office, San Jose, Calif., 1990—2000, Friends Outside Santa Clara County, San Jose, Calif., 1964—89. Liutenant j.g. Navy Air, 1955—58, San Diego CA and over sea's. Achievements include research in how to determine atmospheric composition during a planetary entry mission; how to calculate accurate Honl-London factors for any multiplicity in diatomic molecules; defined how to specify consistent electronic transition moments in diatomic molecules; a major contributor to the improvement of a first principles computer code for calculating the non equilbrium radiation that occurs during atmospheric entry. Avocations: racquetball, reading, hiking, backpacking. Office: NASA Ames Rsch Ctr Building 230 Moffett Field CA 94035

WHITING, GORDON JAMES, investment banker; b. Bronxville, N.Y., Nov. 17, 1965; s. William Gordon Whiting and Doris (Chubb) Whiting Simmons; m. Cornelia Conway Cabot, Aug. 30, 2003. BS, Cornell U., 1988; MBA, Columbia U., 1994. Sales and mktg. mgr. Epcot Ltd., Tsim Sha Tsui, Kowloon, Hong Kong, 1989-90; mng. dir. Stapenhurst Ltd., Victoria, Hong Kong, 1990-92; acquisitions assoc. W. P. Carey & Co. LLC, N.Y.C., 1993-94, 2d v.p., 1994-95, v.p., 1995-97, 1st v.p., 1997-98, sr. v.p., 1998-2000, dep. dir. of acquisitions, 1999—2003, exec. dir., 2000—; exec. v.p. and portfolio mgr. Corp. Property Assocs.: 14 Inc., N.Y.C., 1998-2000, pres. and portfolio mgr., 2000—. Bd. dir. Ret. Thrift Investment Bd.; mem. coun. Cornell U., 2002—. Local bd. mem. Selective Svc. Sys., Eagle Scout. Mem. Profl. Assn. Diving Instrs., Bronxville Field Club, Constant Spring Golf Club (Jamaica), Holland Lodge No. 8 F&AM, Leander Club (U.K.), The Camp Fire Club Am.,

Mashomack Preserve Club (Pine Plains, N.Y.), The Order of St. John, The Pilgrims, Hon. Order Ky. Cols., Racquet and Tennis Club, Royal Hong Kong Yacht Club, Sigma Chi. Republican. Episcopalian. Avocations: fly fishing, golf, scuba diving, skiing, squash. Home: 136 E 55th St Apt 3P New York NY 10022-4518 Office: W P Carey & Co LLC 50 Rockefeller Plz New York NY 10020-1605 E-mail: gwhiting@wpcarey.com.

WHITING, LUCILLE DRAKE, retired elementary school educator, consultant; b. San Diego, Dec. 17, 1929; d. Robert Emmett and Helen Anglim; m. C. George Hewitt (div.); m. V. Edward Drake (div.); m. Erle Francis Whiting, Mar. 27, 1982; 1 child, Cecilie Anne. BA, U. Calif.-Santa Barbara, 1951; MEd, LaVerne (Calif.) U., 1975. Cert. Miller-Unruh reading specialist, spl. edn. specialist, elem. sch. tchr., adult edn. tchr., Calif. Owner, dir. Little Buckaroo Nursery Sch., Santa Barbara, Calif., 1956-65; tchr. various sch. dists. Calif., 1951-72; Title I resource tchr. Oxnard (Calif.) Sch. Dist., 1972-73, reading specialist, 1973-86; extension instr. Calif. Luth. Coll., Thousand Oaks, 1978-84, U. Calif.-Santa Barbara, 1976-82; ind. ednl. cons. Ventura, Calif., 1976-86, Cromberg, Calif., 1986—. Ind. ednl. cons. Active Plumas County Arts Commn., Quincy, Calif., 1987—, bd. dirs., 1989-90; life mem. Plumas County Mus.; bd. dirs. Quincy br. Friends of Plumas County Libr., 1990-1992, life mem.; bd. dirs. Plumas County Literacy Program, 1992-1996, founding com., v.p. 1994-1995, tutor 1992-98, advisor 1992—; vol. Cromberg Cmty. Com., 1987—; mem. Plumas County Rep. Women's Club; pres. joint com. on learning disabilities Santa Barbara and Ventura Counties, 1978-81. Mem. AAUW, Calif. Reading Assn. (ex-officio 1978-81, exemplary svc. award 1982, founding com. chair disabled reader spl. interest grou 1980), Ventura County Reading Assn. (pres. 1979-80), Reading Specialists of Calif., Orton Dyslexia Soc. (mem.-at-large Tri Counties exec. bd. 1982-85), Calif. Assn. Neurology Handicapped Children (v.p. Ventura County chpt. 1976-78), Tri-Counties Assn. Nursery Edn. (pres. 1960, adv. bd. 1961), Calif. Assn. Nursery Edn. (bd. dirs. Santa Barbara chpt. 1960-1962), Ventura County Panhellenic Assn. (v.p. 1970-72), Ben Franklin Stamp Collecting Club (leader 1989-92), Chi Omega, Phi Delta Kappa, Delta Phi Epsilon (pres. Santa Barbara chpt. 1964). Republican. Avocations: photography, travel, walking, hiking, wildflower preservation.

WHITING, MARTHA COUNTEE, retired secondary education educator; b. Marshall, Tex., Mar. 24, 1912; d. Thomas and Nannie Selena (Yates) Countee; m. Samuel Whiting, June 8, 1937; children: Jacqueline Dostic, Sammie Ellis, Nan Broussard, Tommye Casey, Martha Goddard. BA in Sci., Bishop Coll., 1934; M of Secondary Edn., Tex. So. U., 1959, postgraduate, 1962; postgrad., U. Colo., 1963. Tchr., sci., math. Houston Ind. Sch. Dist., 1942-73; researcher, local history Houston, 1973—. Lectr. in field. Mem. exec. com. (life mem.) Houston YWCA, 1977; advisor Preservation 4th Ward, Houston, 1991—; trustee Antioch Missionary Bapt. Ch., Houston, 1977; instrumental in getting the Antioch Missionary Bapt. Ch. in Christ Inc. on the Nat. Register of Hist. Places, 1976; presented Queen Elizabeth II with miniature history of Antioch Missionary Bapt. Ch. in Christ, 1991; author nomination form for Tex. hist. marker Antioch Missionary Bapt. Ch. in Christ, 1994; presenter to Harris County Heritage Soc. of Jack Yates House, the only house built by a former slave to be maintain ed by a U.S. city, and chmn. Pathfinder presentation of achievements of 64 Negro pioneers in Harris County, 1966-1986. Named Woman Courage, Houston Radcliffe Club, 1985, Black Womens Hall Fame Mus. Africal Am. Life, Dallas, 1986; recipient Friend of the Soc. award Harris County Heritage Soc., 1994. Mem. Tex. Ret. Tchrs. Assn., Houston Mus. Fine Arts, Harris County Heritage Soc. (exec. com. 1984), Bluebonnet Garden Club (pres. 1968), Jack & Jjll Am. (pres. Houston chpt. 1955-57), Smithsonian, Nationwide Trust for Historic Preservation. Avocations: writing, gardening, travel, sewing, singing. Home: 3446 Southmore Blvd Houston TX 77004-6349

WHITING, MEREDITH ARMSTRONG, public affairs executive; b. Cin., Nov. 28, 1937; d. Arthur Elmer and Laura Mae (Handley) W.; m. Raymond E. Armstrong, Jan. 20, 1956 (div. Aug. 1968); m. John D. Whiting, Sept. 7, 1985; children: Holly R. Wood, Lucinda Parker, Eric Armstrong, Robert Armstrong, India Leclef. BA, U. Cin., 1969. Pub. rels. dir. U. No. Ky., Alexandria, Ky., 1972-76, Cin. Symphony Orch., 1976-79; pub. affairs dir. Young & Rubicam Cin., 1979-80; dir. pub. liaison Dept. Commerce, Washington, 1980-81; dir. congl. and press affairs Office of V.P., Washington, 1980-85; pres. Whiting & Co., Washington, 1985—. Sr. fellow govt. affairs The Conf. Bd., N.Y.C., 1987—; mem. White House Working Group on Universal Basic Edn., Washington, 2000-2002. Author: Public/Private Partnerships, 1997, Land Conservation Partnerships, 2001, Sustainability, 2002, Best Practices in Safety, 2003. Chairwoman Goose Creek Assn., Middleburg, Va., 1999—. Republican. Home: 5423 Free State Rd Marshall VA 20115 Office: The Conf Bd 1255 34th St NW Washington DC 20007 E-mail: mwhiting@whitingcom.com.

WHITING, RICHARD ALBERT, lawyer; b. Cambridge, Mass., Dec. 2, 1922; s. Albert S. and Jessie (Coleman) W.; m. Marvelene Nash, Feb. 22, 1948 (div. 1984); children— Richard A. Jr., Stephen C., Jeffrey D., Gary S., Kimberly G.; m. Joanne Sherry, Oct. 14, 1984 AB, Dartmouth Coll., 1944; JD, Yale U., 1949. Bar: D.C. 1949. Assoc. Steptoe & Johnson, Washington, 1949-55, ptnr., 1956-86, of counsel, 1987—. Adj. prof. Vt. Law Sch., South Royalton, 1985-90; mem. exec. com. Yale Law Sch. Assn., New Haven, 1985-88; mem. adv. bd. The Antitrust Bull., N.Y.C., 1975-99. Contbr. articles to profl. jours. Trustee Colby-Sawyer Coll., 1987-97. 1st lt. U.S. Army, 1945-46. Mem. ABA (council mem. Antitrust Law sect. 1977-85, del. to Ho. Dels. 1982-83, chmn. 1984-85) Presbyterian. Home: PO Box 749 Grantham NH 03753-0749 Office: 1330 Connecticut Ave NW Washington DC 20036-1704 Office Phone: 202-429-8080. Business E-Mail: whiting@srnet.com.

WHITING, SUSAN D. marketing professional; BA in Econs. cum laude, Denison U. Mgmt. devel. program Neilsen Media Rsch., Dunedin, Fla., 1979-86, v.p. Nielsen Homevideo Index, 1986-87, mktg. mgr., 1987-93, sr. v.p., dir. mktg., 1993-97, gen. mgr. nat. svcs. & emerging markets, 1997—. Mem. Cable Television Adminstrv. and Mktg. Assn., Women in Cable & Telecomm., Conn. Women's Forum (v.p.), N.Y. Radio and TV Rsch. Coun. (past pres.). Office: Nielsen Media Rsch 375 Patricia Ave Dunedin FL 34698-8190

WHITING DOBSON, LISA LORRAINE, video production educator, producer, director; b. Lansing, Mich., July 22, 1959; d. Lowell Stanton and Ruth Lorraine (Gregory) Whiting. BS in Psychology, Mich. State U., 1981, BA in Telecom. cum laude, 1984, MA in Telecom., 1988; AA in Dance magna cum laude, Lansing C.C., 1984. Prodr., dir. Cath. Diocese Lansing, 1984—; video instr., prodr., dir. dept. telecom., info. studies and media Mich. State U., East Lansing, 1987—; instr. media tech. Lansing C.C., 1999—. Dance instr. Synergy, 2002—. Mem. Jr. League of Lansing. Office: Mich State U Dept Telecom 409 Communication Arts Bldg East Lansing MI 48824-1212 E-mail: whiting3@msu.edu.

WHITINGTON, PETER FRANK, pediatrics educator, pediatric hepatologist; b. Memphis, May 8, 1947; s. Frank Everett and Mary Lena (Hollingsworth) Whitington; m. Susan Maurine Hoagland, June 6, 1967; children: Helen Frances Josephic, Mary Louise, Katherine Daphne, Patrick M. BA in Econs., Tulane U., 1968; MD, U. Tenn., Memphis, 1971. Diplomate Am. Bd. Pediat., Am. Bd. Pediatric Gastroenterology. Resident in pediat., then chief resident U. Tenn. Ctr. for Health Scis., 1972—74, instr., 1975, asst. prof., 1978—81, assoc. prof., 1981—84, chief divsn. pediatric gastroenterology, 1978—84; rsch. fellow in gastroenterology Johns Hopkins Hosp., Balt., 1975—77; rsch. fellow in gastroenterology dept. pediatrics U. Wis., Madison, 1977—78; assoc. prof. dept. pediat. U. Chgo. Pritzker Sch. Medicine, 1984—87, assoc. prof. depts. pediat. and medicine, 1987—92, prof., 1992—97; prof. pediat. Northwestern U. Med. Sch., 1997—, Sally Burnett Searle prof. pediat. and transplantation; dir. divsn. gastroenterology, hepatology & nutrition Children's Meml. Hosp., Chgo., 1997—, dir. organ transplantation, Siragusa Transplantation Ctr., 1997—; co-dir. Northwestern U. Affiliated Transplant Ctrs., 1997—. Chief gastroenterology LeBonheur Children's Med. Ctr., Memphis, 1978—84; numerous invited lectures and guest spkr. at profl. meetings, workshops, symposia, hosps., confs.; mem. pediatric transplantation com. United Network for Organ Sharing, Nat. Organ Procurement and Transplantation Network, 1992—94; reviewer numerous med. jours. including New Eng. Jour. Medicine, Gastroenterology, Hepatology, Jour. Pediat., Digestive Diseases and Scis., Pediat., Transplant. Editl. bd. Jour. Pediatric Gastroenterology and Nutrition, 1991—96, Liver Transplantation, 1994—, Pediatric Transplantation, 1997—, sect. editor Birth Defects Compendium, 1987—90, contbr. numerous articles and abstracts to med. jours. Mem. sci. adv. bd. Mid-South chpt. Nat. Found. for Ileitis and Colitis, Memphis, 1983—84; chmn. med. adv. com. Ill. chpt. Am. Liver Found., 1996—, mem., med. adv. on bd. dirs., 1993—; med. dir. The Johnny Genna Found., Chgo., 1987—; bd. dirs. Parents for Ctrl. H.S., Memphis, 1983—84, Liver/Organ Transplant Fund, Memphis, 1983—84. Recipient Cmty. Svc. award, NCCJ, Memphis, 1983; fellow postdoctoral rsch. NIH, 1977. Mem.: Am. Assn. Transplantation, N.A.m Soc. for Pediatric Gastroenterology and Nutrition, Soc. for Pediatric Rsch., Am. Gastroenterol. Assn., Gastroenterology Rsch. Group, Am. Assn. for Study of Liver Diseases. Avocations: making fine furniture, fly fishing. Home: 5490 S South Shore Dr Apt 8 Chicago IL 60615-5984 Office: Childrens Meml Hosp Box 57 2300 Childrens Plaza Chicago IL 60614-3394 Business E-Mail: p-whitington@northwestern.edu.

WHITLEY, JOE DALLY, lawyer; b. Atlanta, Nov. 12, 1950; s. Thomas Youngie and Mary Jo (Dally) W.; m. Kathleen Pinion, Sept. 27, 1975; children: Lauren Jacqueline, Thomas McMillan. BA, U. Ga., 1972, JD, 1975. Bar: Ga. 1975, U.S. Supreme Ct. 1989. Assoc. Kelly, Denney, Pease & Allison, Columbus, Ga., 1975-78; asst. dist. atty. Chattahoochee Jud. Cir., Columbus, 1978-79; assoc. Hirsch, Beil & Partin, P.C., Columbus, 1979-81; U.S. atty. Dept. Justice, Macon, Ga., 1981-87, dep. asst. atty. gen., Criminal Div. Washington, 1987-88, dep. assoc. atty. gen., 1988-89, acting assoc. atty. gen., 1989; ptnr. Smith, Gambrell & Russell, Atlanta, 1989-90; U.S. atty. Dept. of Justice, Atlanta, 1990-93; ptnr. Kilpatrick Stockton, Atlanta, 1993-97, Alston & Bird, Atlanta, 1997—2003; gen. counsel U.S. Dept. Homeland Security, Washington, 2003—. Mem. atty. gen.'s adv. com. Dept. Justice, Washington, 1982-85; chmn. organized crime and violent crime subcom. Atty. Gen.'s Adv. Com., 1990-93, mem. investigative subcom., chmn. white collar crime subcom., 1993-99. Treas. Muscogee County Young Reps., Columbus, 1979-80. Mem. Ga. Bar Assn., Macon Bar Assn., Young Lawyers Club (pres. Columbus chpt. 1980-81), Lawyers Club of Atlanta. Republican. Presbyterian. Office: Naval Security Sta Nebraska and Mass Ave NW Washington DC 20393 E-mail: joe.whitley@dhs.com.

WHITLOCK, BENNETT CLARKE, JR., retired association executive; b. Charleston, S.C., June 10, 1927; s. Bennett C. and Isabel Price (Beckman) W.; m. Elizabeth Darley Marshall, July 18, 1959; children: Mary Elizabeth, Bennett C. III. AB, Presbyn. Coll., 1946; LL.B., U. S.C., 1949. With Am. Trucking Assns., Inc., Washington, 1949-89, asst. to mng. dir., 1961-70, asst. to pres., 1970-73, v.p., 1973-75, exec. v.p., chief oper. officer, 1975-76, pres., 1976-84, spl. adviser, pres., 1984-89; ret., 1989. Bd. dirs Braddock Road Boys Club, Mary Washington Coll. Found., 1998—; bd. visitors Mary Washington Coll., 1985-93, vice rector, 1986-88, rector, 1990-92 Mem. Hwy. Users Fedn. for Safety and Mobility (dir.), Country Club of Fairfax, Kiawah Island Govs. Club, Blue Key, Pi Kappa Alpha. Episcopalian. Personal E-mail: emwhitlock@aol.com.

WHITLOCK, BETTY, retired secondary school educator; b. Somerset, Ky., Mar. 17, 1942; d. Rual Robert and Hazel Ellen (Biers) Wilson; m. L. Craig Whitlock, June 12, 1962 (dec. 2002); children: Michael Craig, Jeffrey Robert, Katherine Elizabeth. BA, Georgetown Coll., 1964; MA, Miss. Coll., 1980, EdS, 1982; postgrad., U. So. Miss., 1986. Nat. bd. cert. tchr. Adolescence and Young Adulthood/English Lang. Arts. Tchr. kindegarten First Bapt. Ch. Kindergarten, Clinton, Miss., 1970-72, Northside Bapt. Ch. Kindegarten, Clinton, Miss., 1972-73; tchr. high sch. Miss. Bapt. H.S., Jackson, 1973-75, Clinton H.S., 1975—. Bd. dirs. Miss. Youth Congress, 1985—; chmn. com. Lit. Map of Miss., 1985—; cons. Miss. H.S. Activities Assn., 1991—. Co-author: Mississippi Writers: An Anthology, 1987, Mississippi Writers: Reflections on Childhood and Youth, 1988, (textbook) Dramatic Interpretation, 1994. Tchr. Sunday sch. First Bapt. Ch., Clinton, 1969—. Mem. Nat. Coun. Tchrs. English, Nat. Forensic League, Miss. Coun. Tchrs. English (chmn. maps 1975—, Outstanding Tchr. award 1992), Miss. Speech Communication Assn. (dir. congress 1973—), Miss. Profl. Educators, Miss. Forensic League (chmn. 1988-99), Jackson Cath. Forensic League (moderator 1991-93), Miss. Coll. Faculty Wives, Phi Delta Kappa. Republican. Baptist. Avocation: writing. Home: 100 Hannah Dr Clinton MS 39056-5107 Office: Clinton High Sch 401 Arrow Dr Clinton MS 39056-3108 Office Phone: 601-924-5656. Personal E-mail: nanawhit@aol.com.

WHITLOCK, CHARLES PRESTON, former university dean; b. Highland Park, N.J., June 19, 1919; s. Frank Boudinot and Rosena Craig (Foster) W.; m. Patricia Hamilton Hoey, Mar. 10, 1960; children: Carol Foster, Adam Hoey, Susan Boudinot, Matthew Fitzsimmons, Beth Brewer. BA, Rutgers U., 1941; MA, Harvard U., 1947. Assoc. dir. Bur. Study Counsel Harvard U., 1948-52, Allston Burr sr. tutor, 1952-58, lectr. social psychology, 1955-72, asst. to pres., 1958-70, assoc. dean of coll., 1970-72, dean of coll., 1972-76, assoc. dean faculty, 1976-82, master Dudley House, 1976-82. Dir. Cambridgeport Savs. Bank.; Mem. Mass. Higher Edn. Facilities Commn. Co-author: Harvard University Reading Films. Trustee Charity of Edward Hopkins, Lesley Coll.; bd. corporators New Eng. Deaconess Hosp.; treas. Annisquam Village Ch. Col. USAF. Decorated Silver Star, D.F.C., Air medal. Mem. Phi Beta Kappa. Home: 9 Barberry Heights Rd Gloucester MA 01930-1201 Office: Harvard U Cambridge MA 02138

WHITLOCK, DAVID C. retired military officer; b. Little Rock, Ark., Jan. 24, 1935; m. Rosemarie Binik (dec.); children: D. Patrick, David D.; m. Dagmar Gattung. B Bus., U. Nebr., 1962; grad., Squadron Officer Sch., 1965; MA Speech and Drama, U. Colo., 1966, PhD Communication, 1970; grad., Air Command and Staff Coll., 1978, Air War Coll., 1983. With USAF, 1952-62, tech. sgt., 1962, audiovisual tng. officer, 2d lt., 1st lt. Hdqs. N. Am. Air Defense Command, 1962-67; from English, speech intr., asst., dir. forensics, capt. to prof., major USAF Acad., 1967-74, prof. English, Speech, dir. Forensics, lt. col., 1979, pres. Tenure Coun., 1981-82; dir. Disting. Visitors Bureau Hdqs. USAF, Ramstein AFB, Germany, 1982-84; assoc. dean Civilian Inst. programs, col. AF Inst. Tech., Ohio, 1984-86; base comdr. 26th Combat Support Group Zweibrucken AFB, Germany, 1986-88; dean Civilian Inst. Programs Wright Patterson AFB, Ohio, 1989, commandant emeritus AF Inst. Tech. Air U., 1992-93. Recipient Legion of Merit, Meritorious Svc. medal with four oak leaf clusters, Air Force Commendation medal with two oak leaf clusters. Achievements include qualified parachutist. Home and Office: 441 Green Vista Dr Enon OH 45323-1340

WHITLOCK, GARY L. energy executive; b. Houston, 1950; B of Bus. Adminstrn. Acctg., Sam Houston State U., 1972. CPA. V.p. fin., CFO Dow AgroScis. subs. Dow Chem. Co., 1998—2001; exec. v.p., CFO delivery group Reliant Energy, 2001—02; exec. v.p., CFO CenterPoint Energy, Houston, 2002—. Mem.: AICPA, Inst. Mgmt. Accts. Office: CenterPoint Energy PO Box 4567 Houston TX 77210-4567

WHITLOCK, JOHN JOSEPH, museum director; b. South Bend, Ind., Jan. 7, 1935; s. Joseph Mark and Helen Marcella (Cramer) W.; m. Sue Ann Kirkman, June 10, 1956; children: Kelly Ann, Michele Lynn, Mark. BS in Art, Ball State U., 1957, MA in Art, 1963; EdD, Ind. U., 1971. Tchr. art Union City (Ind.) Pub. Schs., 1957-59; tchr. art, art dir. Madison (Ind.) City Schs., 1959-64; prof. art, dir. gallery Hanover (Ind.) Coll., 1964-69; dir. Burpee Art Mus., Rockford, Ill., 1970-72; prof. art and humanities Elgin (Ill.) Community Coll., 1970-72; dir. Brooks Meml. Art Gallery, Memphis, 1972-78; prof. mus. studies Southwestern Coll., Memphis, 1973-78; adj. asst. prof. art and museology Memphis State U., 1976-78; dir. Univ. Mus., mem. grad. faculty So. Ill. U., Carbondale, 1978-2000, emeritus dir., 2000—, also dir. mus. studies, 1978-2000, adj. assoc. prof. anthropology, 1978-2000, adj. assoc. prof. polit. sci., 1988—, adj. assoc. prof. history, 1994—, dir. mus. studies, 1989—, mem. ROTC acad. avc. coun., 1988—, mem. president's coun., 1988-93, adj. assoc. prof. art Univ. Mus., 1978-99, vis. emeritus prof., 2000—. Chmn. bd. Nat. Coal Mus., 1983-85; mem. Newsfront adv. bd. NC Broadcast News, Washington, 1982-85; sr. cons. Marine Mil. Acad. Mus., 1988—, mem. bd. advisors, 1991-97. Mem. Rockford Human Rels. Commn., 1971-72; mem. pres.'s coun. Southwestern Coll., 1973-78; vol. Carbondale Police Dept., 2000—, com. resources, forensics records and acad.; bd. dirs. Carbondale Crime Stoppers, 2000—, DARE, 2000—, Carbondale Fire and Police Commn., 2003—; univ. club bd. So. Ill. U., 2000—, univ. mus. amb., 2000—. Mem. Am. Assn. Mus., Internat. Coun. Mus., Midwest Assn. Mus., Assn. Art Mus. Dirs., Marine Corps League (commandant Shawnee detachment 1994-96, 99-2001, comdr. USCG Aux. 1994-95), Dept. Ill. Marine Corps League (trustee rank and file 1994-99, judge advocate 1999—), Semper Fi Soc. (faculty adviser So. Ill. U. 1995—). Office: So Ill U 605 W Walnut St Carbondale IL 62901-2615

WHITLOCK, JOHN L. lawyer; b. New Orleans, Oct. 24, 1946; s. John Bert and Virginia Katherine (Marzolf) W.; m. Dorothy Florence Oeste, Sept. 13, 1969; children: Sarah Katherine, Thomas John. AB, Harvard U., 1968, JD, 1973. Bar: Mass. 1973, U.S. Dist. Ct. Mass. 1974, U.S. Ct. Appeals (1st cir.) 1975. Assoc. Herrick & Smith, Boston, 1973-80, ptnr., 1981-86, Palmer & Dodge LLP, Boston, 1986—. Mem. ethics rules adv. com. Mass. Supreme Jud. Ct., 1996—. Bd. dirs., sec. Harvard-Radcliffe Collegiate Mus. Found., Inc., 1978—; treas. The Boston Cecilia, Inc., 1974-85, 98—, bd. dirs., 1974-86, 94—, pres., 1994-98 . With U.S. Army, 1968-70. Mem. Boston Bar Assn. (coun. 1996-97). Lutheran. Avocation: singing. Office: Palmer & Dodge LLP 111 Huntington Ave Boston MA 02199-7613 Office Phone: 617-239-0284. Business E-Mail: jwhitlock@palmerdodge.com.

WHITLOCK, PRENTICE EARLE, retired mathematics educator, clergyman; b. Pacolet Mills, S.C., Nov. 19, 1922; s. Carl French and Bertha Cleo Patra (Cook) W. BS, U.S. Mil. Acad., 1946; BA, Wofford Coll., 1950; MA, Columbia U., 1951, 65; PhD, Fordham U., 1974; MA, Princeton Theol. Sem., 1980; MDiv, Drew U., 1983, STM, 1992, postgrad., 1980; PhD, NYU, 1985; postgrad., Westminster Choir Coll. Ordained to ministry United Meth. Ch., 1983. Commd. 2d lt. U.S. Army, 1946; resigned, 1950; tchr. elem. schs., Spartanburg, S.C., jr. high sch., Teaneck, N.J., 1956-68, Dobbs Ferry, N.Y., 1958-61; prof. math. dept. N.J. City U., Jersey City, 1963-92, prof. emeritus, 1992—; min. music Hicksville (N.Y.) United Meth. Ch., 1983—. Mem. Nat. Math. Tchrs. Assn., N.J. Math. Assn., West Point Soc. N.Y., Organ Guild N.Y.C. and Nassay County, Univ. Club (N.Y.C.), N.Y. Athletic Club. Republican. Avocation: playing the organ. Home: 97 W Cherry St Hicksville NY 11801-3856

WHITLOCK, VERONICA P. interior designer, educator; b. N.Y.C., Sept. 29, 1961; d. Emmet and Gloria Welch Whitlock; children: Alexander M. Laughlin, III, Julia W. Laughlin. BA in Studio Art and Art History cum laude, Duke U., 1983; BFA in Interior Design with distinction, N.Y. Sch. Interior Design, 1989. Cert. Nat. Coun. Interior Design Qualification, lic. interior designer Conn., cert. N.Y. Adminstrv. asst. William Doyle Galleries, N.Y.C., 1984—86; assoc. Timmins-Munn, Inc., N.Y.C., 1987—98; interior designer V.W. Interiors, Greenwich, Conn., 1994—; tchr. N.Y. Sch. Interior Design, N.Y.C., 2001—. Vol. Jr. League, Greenwich, 1999—. Mem.: Interior Designers for Licensing N.Y. (bd. mem. 0001), Am. Soc. Interior Designers (profl.), Decorators Club. Home and Office: 25 Halsey Dr Old Greenwich CT 06870

WHITLOW, LILLIAN, retired elementary school educator, poet; d. James Cooper and Clemmie McCowen; m. Leo Whitlow, July 1, 1951 (dec. Mar. 1989); children: Leo Perry, Leon Terry, Leona Marie. BA, Langston U., Okla., 1951; MA, Okla. U., 1957. H.s. music and English tchr. Okla. Pub. Schs., Hugo, 1951—56, Rural Paris Pub. Schs., Tex., 1960—66; h.s. music tchr. Grant Pub. Schs., Okla., 1966—70; tchr. music Portland Pub. Schs., Oreg., 1970—88; ret. Editor: KUUMBA, 1992—98; contbr. articles, poems to profl. jours. Vol. tutor Ockley Green Mid. Sch., Portland, 1996—98. Recipient John Jackson award, 2000, Woman of Excellence in Arts and Lit. award, Delta Sigma Theta, 1997, Plaque for outstanding contbn. to African Am. Lit., 1992. Mem.: Internat. Soc. Poets (Disting. Mem. plaque 1996), Portland Fedn. Women's Clubs (pres. 2000—), Maya Angelou Writers Guild (pres. 1997—), Multnomah Woman's Club (pres. 1987), Portland Woman's Club (pres. 1998—), Alpha Kappa Alpha. Democrat. Roman Catholic. Avocations: walking, exercise, reading, sewing, writing. Home: 5714 NE 23d Ave Portland OR 97211 E-mail: lilwhi@msn.com.

WHITLOW, STACEY MATAXIS, English educator, university educator; b. Fort Beining, GA, Feb. 13, 1975; d. Theodore Christopher Mataxis, Kirby Jones Mataxis; m. Jeffrey Kenneth Whitlow. Master of Arts, North Carolina State University, Raleigh, North Carolina, 1999—2001; Bachelor of Arts, Universtity of North Carolina-Greensboro, Greensboro, NC, 1993—96. English Instructor Durham Technical Community College, Durham, NC, 2001—; High School English Teacher Pinecrest High School, Southern Pines, NC, 1996—99. Home: 6714 Lipscomb Dr Durham NC 27712-9289

WHITLOW, WILLIAM LA FOND, minister, theology school planter; b. Mpls., Oct. 20, 1932; s. George Lester and Wanona Nadine (Ridgeway) W.; m. Donna Mae Magnuson, June 13, 1953; children: Debra, Cathleen, Lisa Mae. Ministerial diploma, Eugene (Oreg.) Bible Coll., 1953; postgrad., Seattle Pacific U., 1961; BTh, ThM, Internat. Sem., Orlando, Fla., 1981, ThD summa cum laude, 1986, DD (hon.), 1984; LittD, Evangel Christian U. Am., 1992. Ordained to ministry Open Bible Standard Chs., 1954, Biltmore Bible Ch., 1988. Asst. and pastor Oreg. chs., 1949-55; dean pers. Calif. Open Bible Inst., Pasadena, 1957-58; pres., island supt. Bible Inst., Montego Bay, Jamaica, 1958-59, San Fernando, Trinidad, 1960-65; sr. pastor Biltmore Bible Ch., Phoenix, 1967—; pres. Biltmore Bible Sch. Theology, Phoenix, 1982-86. Extension sch. rep. Internat. Sem., Orlando, 1984-91; adj. faculty mem. Evang. Theol. Sem., Dixon, Mo., 1989-91; affiliate prof. Vision Christian U., Ramona, Calif., 1991. Author, compiler: Basic Bible School Builder, 1986—; also numerous Bible tng. courses. Recipient Outstanding Acad. Achievement award Internat. Sem., 1987. Office: Biltmore Bible Christian Ctr 3330 E Camelback Rd Phoenix AZ 85018-2310 Office Phone: 602-956-9266. E-mail: WLWhitlow@msn.com.

WHITMAN, CHRISTINE TODD, former governor; b. Sept. 26, 1946; d. Webster Bray and Eleanor Schley Todd; m. John Whitman, 1974; children: Kate, Taylor. BA in Govt., Wheaton Coll., 1968. Former freeholder Somerset County, N.J.; former pres. State Bd. Pub. Utilities; host radio talk show Sta. WKXW, Trenton, N.J.; gov. State of N.J., 1994-2001; adminstr. EPA, Washington, 2001—03. Chmn. Com. for an Affordable N.J.; bd. dirs. Texas Instruments Inc., 2003-, Millennium Challenge Corp., 2004-. Columnist newspapers. Bd. freeholders Somerset County, N.J., 1982-87; bd. pub. utilities, 1988-89; Rep. candidate for senator State of N.J., 1990. Republican. Achievements include first female governor in N.J.; delivered Republican response to President Clinton's 1995 State of the Union address.

WHITMAN, DALE ALAN, lawyer, law educator; b. Charleston, W. Va., Feb. 18, 1939; m. Marjorie Miller: 8 children. Student, Ohio State U., 1956-59; BES, Brigham Young U., 1963; LLB, Duke U., 1966. Bar: Calif. 1967, Utah 1971. Assoc. O'Melveny & Myers, Los Angeles, 1966-67; asst prof., then assoc prof. sch. law U. N.C., Chapel Hill, 1967-70; prof. law UCLA, 1970-71; dep. dir. Office Housing and Urban Affairs Fed. Home Loan Bank Bd., Washington, 1971-72; sr. program analyst FHA, HUD, Washington, 1972-73; prof. law Brigham Young U., 1973-78, 92-99; vis. prof. law U. Wash., 1978—82, U. Mo., Columbia, 1976; prof. law, assoc. dean U. Mo. Sch. Law, Columbia, 1982-88, prof., 1988—91, 1998—. Cons., lectr. in field; reporter Am. law Inst. Co-author: Cases and Materials on Real Estate Finance and Development, 1976, Real Estate Finance Law, 1979, 4th edit., 2001, Cases and Materials on Real Estate Transfer, Finance and Development. 1981, 6th edit., 2003, Land Transactions and Finance, 1983, 3d edit., 1997, The Law of Property, 1984, 3d edit., 2000, Contemporary Property, 1996, 2d edit., 2002, Restatement of Property (Mortgages), 1997; contbr. articles to profl. jours. Fellow Am. Bar Found.; mem. Am. Law Inst., Am. Coll. Real Estate Lawyers, Am. Coll. Mortgage Attys., Assn. Am. Law Schs. (pres. 2002). Home and Office: 2505 Black Cherry Ct Columbia MO 65201-3539 E-mail: whitmand@missouri.edu.

WHITMAN, GREGORY THEODORE, neurologist; b. Lansdale, Pennsylvania, Oct. 16, 1966; s. Steven and Sheila Whitman. BA, Cornell Univ., Ithaca, NY, 1985—89; MD, Univ. of Conn., Farmington, 1990—94. Cert. in Neurology Am. Bd. of Psychiatry and Neurology, 2000. Medicine intern Boston City Hosp., Boston Univ., 1994—95, neurology resident, 1995—97, Tufts Univ., Boston, 1997—98; clin. instr. neurology Univ. Calif., Los Angeles, 1998—2000, asst. prof. of neurology Irvine, 2000—. Neurology residency program dir. Univ. of Calif., Irvine, 2002—. Co-author: (journal articles) Neurology, Archives of Neurology, Jour. of Neuroimaging, Stroke, Neurobiology of Aging. Mem.: Am. Acad. of Neurology. Office Phone: 714-456-2324.

WHITMAN, HOMER WILLIAM, JR., retired investment counseling company executive; b. Sarasota, Fla., Jan. 8, 1932; s. Homer William and Phoebe (Corr) W.; m. Anne Virginia Sarran, May 8, 1954; children: Burke William, Michael Wayne. BA in Econs. optime merens, U. South, 1953; grad., U.S. Naval Officer Candidate Sch., 1953; postgrad., Emory U., 1969. Served to group v.p. 1st Nat. Bank Atlanta, 1956-72; pres., dir. Palmer 1st Nat. Bank & Trust Co., Sarasota, 1973-74, Hamilton Bank & Trust Co., Atlanta, 1974-76; v.p. Lionel D. Edie & Co., Atlanta, 1976-78, Mfrs. Hanover Trust Co., Atlanta, 1978-85; sr. v.p. Montag & Caldwell, Inc., Atlanta, 1985—2002, ret., 2001. Dir. Asolo State Theatre. Trustee Selby Found., 1973-74, West Paces Ferry Hosp., Ringling Sch. Art, St. Stephens's Sch.; bd. vis. Emory U.; mem. Leadership Atlanta. Lt. j.g. USNR, 1953-56. Named Hon. French Consul, Atlanta, Atlanta's Outstanding Young Man of Yr., 1963. Mem. Govt. Fin. Officer's Assn., Gla. Govt. Fin. Officers Assn., Ga. Govt. Fin. Officers Assn., Assn. Investment Mgmt. Sales Execs., Atlanta Soc. Fin. Analysts, Healthcare Fin. Mgmt. Assn., Fla. Pub. Pension Trustees Assn., Assn. Pvt. Pension and Welfare Plans (regional chmn.), Am. Cancer Soc. (dir. Atlanta city unit), Newcomen Soc., 300 Club, Atlanta C. of C. (life mem.), Piedmont Driving Club, Peachtree Golf Club, Commerce Club, Buckhead Club (bd. govs.), Union League Club (N.Y.), Breakfast Club, Sarasota U. Club (bd. dirs.), Farmington Country Club, Rotary, Mid Ocean Club. Episcopalian. Home: 12 Mooregate Sq NW Atlanta GA 30327-1539

WHITMAN, JAMES QUICK, education educator; b. N.Y., Apr. 29, 1957; s. Martin Jacob and Lois Quick Whitman; m. Gillian Stern, Dec. 22, 1996; 1 child, Lucien Stern; m. Deborah Marion Weiss (div.). BA; MA, Columbia Univ., N.Y., 1982; PhD, Univ. Chgo., Chgo., 1987; JD, Yale Univ., New Haven, Conn., 1988. Jud. clk. U.S. Ct. of Appeals, 2d Cir., New Haven, 1988—89; assoc. prof. law Stanford Univ., Stanford, Conn., 1989—94; prof. law Yale Univ., New Haven, 1994—, Ford prof. law, 1996—; vis. prof. law Harvard Univ., Cambridge, Mass., 1995, Université De Paris II, Paris, 2001—02, Université Di Roma III, Rome, 2002. Author: Harsh Justice, 2003, Legacy of Roman Law, 1990; contbr. articles pub. to profl. jour. Berlin Prize Fellow, Am. Acad., Berlin, 2000, Jean Monnet Fellow, European Univ. Inst., 1998. Mem.: Soc. D'Historie Droit, Am. Soc. for Legal History. Avocation: piano. Office: Yale Law Sch PO Box 208215 New Haven CT 06521

WHITMAN, JEFFREY PAUL, philosophy educator; b. Scranton, Pa., Mar. 25, 1955; s. Paul Ralph and Arlene Ruth (Morris) W.; m. Susan Linn Shuler, June 10, 1978; children: Laura Linn, Kevin Paul. BS, U.S. Mil. Acad., 1977; MA, Brown U., 1987, PhD, 1991. Commd. 2d lt. U.S. Army, 1977, advanced through grades to maj., 1989; philosophy prof. U.S. Mil. Acad., West Point, N.Y., 1987-95, ret., 1995; philosophy prof. Susquehanna U., Selinsgrove, Pa., 1995—. Ethics cons. Geisinger Med. Ctr., Danville, Pa., 1996—. Author: Power and Value of Philosophical Skepticicsm, 1996; contbr. articles to profl. jours. Pres. Sharon Luth. Ch. Coun., Selinsgrove, 1997-99; sch. bd. dirs. Selinsgrove Sch. Dist., 1999—. Mem. Am. Philos. Assn., Am. Assn. of Philosophy Tchrs., Assn. Practical and Profl. Ethics, Joint Svcs. Conf. on Profl. Ethics, Ea. Paralyzed Vets. Assn. Lutheran. Avocation: wheelchair sports and recreation. Office: Susquehanna U 514 University Ave Selinsgrove PA 17870-1164 Office Phone: 570-372-4168. E-mail: Whitman@susqu.edu.

WHITMAN, JULES ISIDORÉ, lawyer; b. N.Y.C., Apr. 30, 1923; s. Louis and Jenny (Mednitzky) W.; m. Aileen Epstein Whitman; children: David, Douglas. BBA, CCNY, 1943; LLB, NYU, 1948, LLM in Taxation, 1950. Bar: N.Y. 1948, Pa. 1950. Assoc. Otto A. Samuels, N.Y.C., 1948-50; trial atty. IRS, Phila., 1950-56; sr. ptnr., head tax dept. Dilworth, Paxson, Kalish & Kauffman, Phila., 1956-91, mng. ptnr., 1969-91; of counsel, Dilworth, Paxton, Kalish & Kauffman, Phila., 1992—; dir. U. Pa. Tax Conf., Phila.; lectr. Villanova U. Law Sch., Pa., 1980-81, NYU. Contbr. articles to profl. jours. Pres. Phila. chpt. Am. Jewish Com., 1977-79, chmn. bd., 1980-81, nat. gov., N.Y.C., 1981-84; bd. dirs. Citizens Crime Commn., Phila., 1980-92; trustee Rodeph Shalom Synagogue, Phila., 1980-86. Recipient Human Relations award Am. Jewish Com., 1983. Mem. ABA, Fed. Bar Assn., Pa. Bar Assn., Phila. Bar Assn. Jewish. Club: Locust (Phila.). Office: Dilworth Paxson Kalish & Kauffman 3200 Mellon Bank ctr 1735 Market St Philadelphia PA 19103-7501

WHITMAN, MARA ARDEN, publishing executive; b. NYC, Oct. 7, 1964; d. Robert and Edith Helen (Cybul) Whitman; m. Marc Stefan Edrich; children: Franklin Graham Whitman Edrich, Samantha Allison Whitman Edrich, Douglas Griffin Whitman Edrich, Mallory Sloan Whitman Edrich. BS in Bus., Skidmore Coll., 1986; MSLS, Simmons Coll., 1988; JD, U. Conn., 1992. Asst. librarian Warner & Stackpole, Boston, 1986—87; med. reference librarian Countway Library of Medicine Harvard U., 1987—88; law librarian New Eng. Sch. Law Library, 1987—88, Day, Berry & Howard, Hartford, Conn., 1988; asst. librarian U. Conn. Law Sch., 1988; law librarian Conn. Atty. Gen.'s Office, 1988—91; summer assoc. law clk. Lublin, Wolfe, Kantor & Silver, East Hartford, 1989; law libr. Tyler, Cooper & Alcorn, Hartford, 1992—97. Dir. The Grad. Group, 1987—. Sustainer Jr. League, Hartford. Grassroots grantee Jr. Mem. Roundtable Baker & Taylor, 1988: Starr fellow, 1989; Am. Assn. Law Librs. Mead Data Cen. scholar, 1989. Mem. ALA, Am. Assn. Law Librs., Spl. Libr. Assn., Student Bar Assn. (rep.), Jewish Law Students Assn. (pres.), Student Libr. Assn., New Eng. Libr. Assn., So. New Eng. Law Libr.'s Assn., Mass. Libr. Assn., Assn. Boston Law Librs., Hartford Assn. Law Librs., Skidmore Coll. Alumni Assn., Delta Delta Delta. Democrat. Avocations: travel, skiing, fishing, swimming, reading. Home: 86 Norwood Rd West Hartford CT 06117-2236 Personal E-mail: graduategroup@hotmail.com.

WHITMAN, MARGARET C. (MEG WHITMAN), internet company executive; b. N.Y., 1957; m. Griffith R. Harsh IV; children: Griff, Will. B in Econs., Princeton U., 1977; MBA, Harvard U., 1979. Brand asst. Procter & Gamble, 1979—81; v.p. Bain & Co., 1982—89; with Walt Disney Co. most recently as sr. v.p. mktg. consumer products divsn., 1989—92; with Stride Rite Corp., 1992—95, corp. v.p. strategic planning, 1992—93, exec. v.p. Keds divsn., pres. Stride Rite Divsn.; pres., CEO Florists' Transworld Delivery (FTD), 1995—97; gen. mgr. preschool divsn. Hasbro, 1997—98; pres., CEO eBay, Inc., San Jose, Calif., 1998—. Dir. Procter & Gamble. Bd. trustees Princeton U. Office: eBay Inc 2145 Hamilton Ave San Jose CA 95125*

WHITMAN, MARINA VON NEUMANN, economist, educator; b. N.Y.C., Mar. 6, 1935; d. John and Mariette (Kovesi) von Neumann; m. Robert Freeman Whitman, June 23, 1956; children: Malcolm Russell, Laura Mariette. BA summa cum laude, Radcliffe Coll., 1956; MA, Columbia U., 1959, PhD, 1962; LHD (hon.), Russell Sage Coll., 1972; LLD (hon.), Cedar Crest Coll., 1973, Hobart and William Smith Coll., 1973; LHD (hon.), U. Mass., 1975, N.Y. Poly. Inst., 1975; LLD (hon.), Coe Coll., 1975, Marietta Coll., 1976. Mem. faculty U. Pitts., 1962-79, prof. econs., 1971-73, disting. pub. svc. prof. econs., 1973-79; v.p., chief economist Gen. Motors Corp., N.Y.C., 1979-85, group v.p. pub. affairs, 1985-92; disting. vis. prof. bus. adminstrn., pub. policy U. Mich., Ann Arbor, 1992-94, prof. bus. adminstrn., pub. policy, 1994—. Bd. dirs. Unocal; mem. Trilateral Commn., 1973-84, 88-95; mem. Pres. Adv. Com. on Trade Policy and Negotiations, 1987-93; mem. tech. assessment adv. coun. U.S. Congress Office of Tech. Assessment, 1990-95; mem. Consultative Group on Internat. Econs. and Monetary Affairs, 1979—; mem. U.S. Price Commn., 1971-72, Coun. Econ. Advisers, Exec. Office of Pres., 1972-73. Author: Government Risk-Sharing in Foreign Investment, 1965, International and Interregional Payments Adjustment, 1967, Economic Goals and Policy Instruments, 1970, Reflections of Interdependence: Issues for Economic Theory and U.S. Policy, 1979, New World, New Rules: The Changing Role of the American Corporation, 1999; bd. editors: Am. Econ. Rev., 1974-77; mem. editl. bd. Fgn. Policy; contbr. articles to profl. jours. Trustee Nat. Bur. Econ. Rsch., 1993—, Princeton U., 1980-90, Inst. Advanced Study, 1999—; bd. dirs. Inst. for Internat. Econs., 1986—, Salzburg Seminar, 1994—, Eurasia Found., 1992-95; bd. overseers Harvard U., 1972-78, mem. vis. com. Kennedy Sch., 1992-98. Fellow Earhart Found., 1959-60, AAUW, 1960-61, NSF, 1968-70, Social Security Rsch. Coun.; recipient Columbia medal for excellence, 1973, George Washington award Am. Hungarian Found., 1975. Mem. Am. Econ. Assn. (exec. com. 1977-80), Am. Acad. Arts and Scis., Coun. Fgn. Rels. (dir. 1977-87), Phi Beta Kappa. Office: U Mich Gerald Ford Sch Pub Policy 411 Lorch Hall Ann Arbor MI 48109-1220 Office Phone: 734-763-4173. E-mail: marinaw@umich.edu.

WHITMAN, MARLAND HAMILTON, JR., lawyer; b. Balt., Oct. 13, 1947; s. M. Hamilton and Josephine Lee (Chatard) W.; m. Susan Zimmerman, Mar. 21, 1976; children: Elizabeth Miles, Hannah Minor. AB, Princeton U., 1969; JD, U. Va., 1976. Bar: Md. 1976, U.S. Supreme Ct. 1982, U.S. Ct. Appeals (3d cir.) 1986, (4th cir.) 1979, U. S. Ct. Internat. Trade 1985, U.S. Dist. Ct. Md. 1977. From assoc. to ptnr. Ober, Kaler, Grimes & Shriver, Balt., 1976-98, shareholder, 1998—. Contbr. chpt. (book) Construction Litigation: Strategies and Techniques, 1990. Lt. USN, 1969-73. Mem. ABA, Maritime Law Assn. of U.S. (proctor 1977—), Md. State Bar Assn., Bar Assn. of Balt. City, Propeller Club of U.S. Pt. of Balt. Office: Ober Kaler Grimes & Shriver 120 E Baltimore St Baltimore MD 21202-1643

WHITMAN, MARTIN J. portfolio manager; b. N.Y.C., Sept. 30, 1924; s. Irving and Dora (Cukier) W.; m. Lois M. Quick, Mar. 10, 1956; children: James Q., Barbara E., Thomas I. Chartered fin. analyst. Rsch. analyst, buyer Shearson Hammill & Co., N.Y.C., 1950—56; analyst William Rosenwald Co., N.Y.C., 1956—58; head rsch. Ladenburg, Thalmann & Co., N.Y.C., 1958—60; gen. ptnr. Gerstley Sunstein & Co., Phila., 1960—67; v.p., dir. Blair & Co., Inc., N.Y.C., 1967—68; pres., founder M.J. Whitman & Co. (now Inc.), N.Y.C., 1969—84; pres., CEO Equity Strategies Fund, Inc., N.Y.C., 1984—90; founder, chmn. Third Ave. Value Fund, Inc. (now Third Ave. Mgmt. LLC), N.Y.C., 1990—. CEO Third Ave. Value Fund, 1990—; dir. Nabors Industries, Inc., Danielson Holding Corp., past chmn. bd.; chmn. bd. Stewart Info. Svc., Inc.; Disting. Mgmt. Fellow in Fin. Yale U., New Haven, 1972—; adv. bd. Yale Sch. Mgmt., New Haven, 1994—99; cons. disclosure study SEC, 1968; cons. Pres.'s Commn. on Accident at Three Mile Island, 1979; prof. sch. bus. Columbia U., N.Y.C., 2001—. Author: Value Investing: A Balanced Approach, 1999; co-author: The Agressive Conservative Investor, 1979; contbr. articles to profl. pubs. Chmn. 3d Ave. Fund, 1991. Served with USNR, 1942-46. Named in his hon. Martin J. Whitman Sch. of Mgmt., Syracuse Univ. named its bus. sch., 2003. Mem. N.Y. Soc. Security Analysts, Phila. Econ. Soc. Jewish. Home: 285 Central Park W New York NY 10024-3006

WHITMAN, MEREDITH ELLIS, music educator; b. Rutland, Vt., Jan. 12, 1976; d. Gregory H. and Susan H. Ellis; m. Marc Aaron Whitman, Dec. 21, 2002. MusB in Edn., Ind. U., Bloomington, Indiana, 1994—98. Cert. Kodaly Level III Hartt Sch. Music, Conn., 2003. Music tchr. Rutland City Pub. Schs., Vt., 1999—; pvt. voice instr. Rutland, Vt., 2000—. Gen. music co-chair Vt. Music Educators' Assn., Vt., 2003—. Mem.: Music Educators Nat. Conf. Avocations: singing, reading, canine recreation.

WHITMAN, ROBERT VAN DUYNE, civil engineer, educator; b. Pitts., Feb. 2, 1928; s. Edwin A. and Elsie (Van Duyne) W.; m. Elizabeth Cushman, June 19, 1954; children: Jill Martyne Whitman Marsee, Martha Allerton (dec.), Gweneth Giles Whitman Kaebnick. BS, Swarthmore Coll., 1948, DSc (hon.), 1990; SM, MIT, 1949, ScD, 1951. Faculty MIT, 1953—, prof. civil engring., 1963-93, head structural engring., 1970-74, head soil mechanics divsn., 1970-72; prof. emeritus, 1993—. Vis. scholar U. Cambridge, Eng., 1976-77; cons. to govt. and industry, 1953—; mem. adv. com. for nat. earthquake hazard reduction program Fed. Emergency Mgmt. Agy., 1991-94, mem. commn. engring. and tech. systems NRC, 1992-97. Author: (with T. W. Lambe) Soil Mechanics. Mem. Town Meeting Lexington, Mass., 1962-76, 85—, mem. permanent bldg. com., 1968-75, mem. bd. appeals, 1979-81, 84-2000. Lt. (j.g.) USNR, 1954-56. Recipient U.S. Scientist award Humboldt Found., 1984-90; Norwegian Geotech. Inst. Rsch. fellow, 1984. Mem. NAE, ASCE (Rsch. award 1962, Terzaghi Lecture 1981, Terzaghi award 1987, C. Martin Duke Lifeline Earthquake Engring. award 1992, James Croes medal 1994), Boston Soc. Civil Engrs. (Structural Sect. prize 1963, Desmond Fitzgerald medal 1973, Ralph W. Horne Fund award 1977), Internat. Soc. Soil Mechanics and Found. Engrs., Mex. Soc. Soil Mechanics (hon., Nabor Carrillo lectr. 2000), Earthquake Engring. Rsch. Inst. (dir. 1978-81, 84-88, v.p. 1979-81, pres. 1985-87, Disting. lectr. 1994, hon. 1997—). Achievements include research in in soil mechanics, soil dynamics, earthquake engring. and earthquake loss estimation. Home: 1010 Waltham St # 557 Lexington MA 02421 Office: MIT Dept Civil & Environ Engring Cambridge MA 02139

WHITMER, EUGENE ROGER, minister, retired secondary school educator; b. Shawnee, Ohio, July 2, 1925; s. John and Edith Goldie Whitmer; m. Mabel Jane Hoops, Oct. 21, 1949; children: Gloria, Sharon, John, Joy. BA, Ohio U., 1950, MEd, 1964; MDiv, Winebrenner Theol. Sem., 1972. Ordained min. Ch. of the Nazarene, 67; cert. secondary sch. tchr. Ohio. H.S. tchr., Junction City, Ohio, 1956—57, Athens, Ohio, 1957—67, Northmor and Galion, Ohio, 1967—72; pastor Ch. of the Nazarene, Crestline, Ohio, 1967—72, Lexington, Ohio, 1972—76, Fulton, Ohio, 1976—88, interim pastor, sr. adult tchr. Mansfield, Ohio, 1996—2003; ret., 2003. Contbr. articles to newspapers. With USN, 1944—46, PTO. Avocations: farming, writing, preaching, woodworking. Home: 1082 Bellaire Dr Mansfield OH 44907-3005

WHITMER, FREDERICK LEE, lawyer; b. Terre Haute, Ind., Nov. 5, 1947; s. Lee Arthur and Ella (Diekhoff) W.; m. Valeri Cade; children: Caitlin Margaret, Meghan Connors, Christian Frederick. BA, Wabash Coll., 1969; JD, Columbia U., 1973. Bar: N.Y. 1975, U.S. Dist. Ct. (so. dist.) N.Y. 1975, N.J. 1976, U.S. Dist. Ct. N.J. 1976, U.S. Ct. Appeals (3d cir.) 1977, U.S. Ct. Appeals (fed. cir.) 1983, U.S. Ct. Appeals (2d cir.) 1987, U.S. Supreme Ct. 1988, U.S. Ct. Appeals (7th cir.) 1994. Assoc. Kaye, Scholer, Fierman, Hays & Handler, N.Y.C., 1973-76, Pitney and Hardin, Morristown, NJ, 1976—78; ptnr. Pitney Hardin LLP, Morristown, 1979—2004, Brown, Raysman, Millstein, Felder & Steiner, N.Y.C., 2004—. Mem. ABA, N.J. Bar Assn., Phi Beta Kappa. Republican. Episcopalian. Home: 190 Hurlbutt St Wilton CT 06897-2706 Office: Brown Raysman Millstein Felder & Steiner LLP 900 3d Ave New York NY 10022 Office Phone: 212-895-2593. E-mail: fwhitmer@brownraysman.com.

WHITMER, LESLIE GAY, federal official; b. Lexington, Ky., July 31, 1941; s. Leslie Allen and Gaynelle Kimbrell (McPherson) W.; m. Patricia Ann Welch, July 5, 1969; 1 child, Mary Gay. BS, U. Ky., 1963, JD, 1965. Bar: Ky. 1966, U.S. Dist. Ct. Ky. 1972, U.S. Supreme Ct. 1972. Atty. advisor gen. Office of Gen. Counsel, U.S. Dept. Agr., Chgo., 1966-69; dir. bar counsel Ky. Bar Assn.; editor Ky. Bar Jour., 1974-83; registrar Supreme Ct. Ky., 1975-83; clk. U.S. Dist. Ct. (ea. dist.) Ky., 1983—, mem. civil justice reform act adv. group, 1992—. Adj. prof. law U. Ky. Coll. Law, 1980, 82; mem. Gov.'s Task Force on Office Pub. Advocacy, 1982; exec. dir. Ky. Bar Ctr., 1979-83; sec.-treas. Ky. Bar Title Ins. Agy. Inc., 1973-83; asst. sec.-treas. Ky. Bar Found., 1979-83; exec. dir. Ky. Fed. Jud. Selection Commn., 1978-83; bd. dirs., sec.-treas. Ky. Legal Services Plan, Inc., 1978-83. Contbr. articles to legal jours. Recipient Recognition of Merit award U. Ky. Coll. Law Alumni Assn., 1983. Mem. Nat. Soc. Arts and Letters, Ky. Bar Assn. (bd. dirs., bar counsel, treas. 1973-83, discipline com. 1987-98), Fed. Bar Assn. (bd. dirs. 1998—), Psi Chi, Phi Alpha Delta, Spindletop Hall Club. Office: Federal Courthouse Lexington KY 40507

WHITMER, RICHARD E. insurance company executive; BS in Political Science, W. Mich. U., 1963; JD, U. Mich. Law School, 1965. Legislative counsel Gov. of Mich.; dir. Mich. Dept. of Commerce; sr. v.p., gen. counsel Blue Cross Blue Shield Mich., Detroit, 1977—87, pres., CEO, 1987—. Bd. mem. Greater Detroit Chamber of Commerce, Detroit Renaissance, United Way of Southeastern Mich., Detroit Economic Growth Corp.; chmn. New Detroit, 1991—93. Office: Blue Cross Blue Shield Mich 600 E Lafayette Blvd Detroit MI 48226-2927 Office Phone: 313-225-9000.*

WHITMORE, BRUCE G. lawyer; BA, Tufts U., 1966; JD, Harvard U., 1969. Bar: N.Y. 1970, Calif. 1973, Pa. 1979. Gen. atty. ARCO Transp. Co., 1985-86; assoc. gen. counsel corp. fin. ARCO, 1986-90; v.p., gen. counsel ARCO Chem. Co., 1990-94; sr. v.p., gen. counsel, corp. sec. Atlantic Richfield Co., L.A., 1995-2000. Mem. ABA.

WHITMORE, DONALD CLARK, retired engineer; b. Seattle, Sept. 15, 1932; s. Floyd Robinson and Lois Mildred (Clark) W.; m. Alice Elinor Winter, Jan. 8, 1955; children: Catherine Ruth, William Owen, Matthew Clark, Nancy Lynn, Peggy Ann, Stuart John. BS, U. Wash., 1955. Prin. engr. The Boeing Co., Seattle, 1955-87, ret., 1987. Developer, owner mobile home pk., Auburn, Wash., 1979—. Author: Towards Security, 1983, (monograph) SDI Software Feasibility, 1990, Characterization of the Nuclear Proliferation Threat, 1993, Rationale for Nuclear Disarmament, 1995. Activist for arms control, Auburn, Wash., 1962—; chmn. Seattle Coun. Orgns. for Internat. Affairs, 1973, Auburn Citizens for Schs., 1975; v.p. Boeing Employees Good Neighbor Fund, Seattle, 1977, Spl. Svc. award, 1977; pres. Abe Keller Peace Edn. Fund, 1998—, v.p., 2000—; pres., founder Third Millennium Found., 1993—; founder abolishnukes.com. Recipient Human Rights award, Seattle chpt. UN Assn., 2001. Avocations: hiking, travel, collecting. Home and Office: 16202 SE Lake Moneysmith Rd Auburn WA 98092-5274 Personal E-mail: 3rdm@gte.net.

WHITMORE, DOUGLAS MICHAEL, physician; b. Cambridge, Mass., Oct. 30, 1947; s. Donald Herbert and Marcela (Klein) W.; m. Ana Maria Lopez. BS, MS in Physics, U. Ill., Champaign-Urbana, 1969; MS in Physics, Stanford U., 1970, PhD in Physics, 1975; MD, U. Miami, 1978. Diplomate Am. Bd. Internal Medicine, Am. Bd. Pulmonary Disease, Am. Bd. Critical Care Medicine, Am. Bd. Geriatric Medicine. Physician Holy Cross Hosp., Ft. Lauderdale, Fla., 1983—. Pres. med. staff Holy Cross Hosp., 1996-97, chief of medicine, 1995-98. Trustee Holy Cross Hosp., 1995-98. Fellow ACP, Am. Coll. Chest Physicians; mem. AMA, Caducean Med. Soc. (pres. 1996-97), Am. Thoracic Soc., Royal Soc. Medicine. Office: Med Complex West 1930 NE 47th St Ste 205 Fort Lauderdale FL 33308-7728

WHITMORE, FRANK CLIFFORD, JR., geologist; b. Cambridge, Mass., Nov. 17, 1915; s. Frank Clifford and Marion Gertrude (Mason) W.; m. Martha Burling Kremers, June 24, 1939; children: Geoffrey, John, Katherine, Susan. BA, Amherst Coll., 1938; MS, Pa. State U., 1939; MA, Harvard U., 1941, PhD, 1942. Instr. geology R.I. State Coll., Kingston, 1942-44; geologist U.S. Geol. Survey, Washington, 1944-84, scientist emeritus, 1984—; mem. com. rsch. and exploration Nat. Geog. Soc., 1970-96, vice chmn., 1990-96, emeritus, 1997—; rsch. assoc. dept. paleobiology Smithsonian Instn., Washington, 1967—97. Sci. cons. U.S. Army, Philippines, Japan, Korea, 1945-46; mem. adv. bd. Ctr. for Study of Early Man, U. Maine, Orono, 1985-90. Editor: Resources for 21st Century, 1982; contbr. articles to profl. jours. Bd. dirs. Prince Georges County Boys Clubs, Md., 1954-56; mem. program com. Nat. Capital coun. Girl Scouts U.S.A., Washington, 1967-69; pres. Thornton Soc., Washington, 1977-84. Recipient medal of Freedom U.S. Army, 1946, spl. achievement award U.S. Geol. Survey, 1980, Meritorious Svc. award U.S. Dept. Interior, 1981, Arnold Guyot Meml. award Nat. Geog. Soc., 1993, Thomas Jefferson medal Va. Mus. Natural History, 2002; Tchg. fellow Harvard U., Cambridge, 1940-42. Fellow AAAS, Geol. Soc. Am.; mem. Soc. Vertebrate Paleontology (hon. life, exec. com. 1960-62), Midriver Club, Harvard Club. Democrat. Avocation: architectural history. Home: 20 Woodmoor Dr Silver Spring MD 20901-2447

WHITMORE, GEORGE MERLE, JR., management consulting company executive; b. Tarrytown, N.Y., Jan. 1, 1928; s. George Merle and Elizabeth Helen (Knodel) W.; m. Priscilla Elizabeth Norman, Mar. 30, 1963; children: Elizabeth Whitmore Lippincott, George Norman, Stephen Bradford. BE, Yale U., 1949; MBA, Harvard U., 1951. Test engr. Gen. Electric Co., Bridgeport, Conn., Erie, Pa., 1949; rsch. assoc. Harvard Bus. Sch., Boston, 1951-52; assoc. Cresap, McCormick and Paget Inc., N.Y.C., 1954-59, prin., 1959-61, ptnr., 1961-69, v.p., dir., 1969-79, mng. dir., CEO, 1979-81; mng. dir. Ayers, Whitmore & Co. Inc., N.Y.C., 1981-88, Ayers, Whitmore divsn. A.T. Kearney, Inc., N.Y.C., 1988-90, Whitmore & Co., Greenwich, Conn., 1990—. Bd. dirs. Carroll Enterprises, Inc., Worcester, Mass. Pres. N.E. Greenwich Assn. Inc., 2001—; hon. trustee, former bd pres. Hackley Sch., Tarrytown; former trustee, chmn. bd. Greenwich Acad.; former trustee, treas. Salisbury (Conn.) Sch.; pres. Northeast Greenwich Assn., Inc., 2001—. With USAF, 1952—53. Mem. Inst. Mgmt. Cons. (founding mem.), Newcomen Soc., Stanwich Club (former dir.), Yale Club (N.Y.C.), Tau Beta Pi. Presbyterian. Home and Office: 7 Wyngate Rd Greenwich CT 06830-4032 E-mail: whitpen@aol.com.

WHITMORE, MENANDRA M. librarian; b. Ancash, Peru; d. Rafael and Jacinta (Moreno) Mosquera; m. Jacob L. Whitmore III, Jan. 7, 1965; children: Jacqueline Grace, Michelle Jacinta. Degree in social work, U. Catolica del Peru, 1967; MLS, U. P.R., 1974, Catholic U. Am., 1984. Social worker Cornell U., Vicos, Peru, 1960-62, Servicio de Extension Agricola del Peru, 1962-63, Am. Friends Svc. Com., Mex. and Peru, 1963-65; libr. Colegio Maria Auxiliadora, P.R., 1971, Country Day Sch., San Jose, Costa Rica, 1974-76, Colegio San Ignacio, P.R., 1976-77; dir. libs. Am. Coll. P.R., 1977-80; libr. Lib. Gov. Printing Office, 1981-84; chief acquisitions sect., mgr. Hispanic employment program Pentagon Libr., Washington, 1984-99, chief tech. and stds. divsn., 1999—2002, acting dir., 2002—03, dir., 2003—. Author: (all pub. under name Menandra Mosquera) Bibliography on Hypsipyla, 1976, Bibliography of Forestry of Puerto Rico, 1984, Useful Trees of Tropical North America, 1998. Recipient commendation Dept. Def., 1987-98. Mem. ALA, Soc. for Acquisition Latin Am. Libr. Materials, Reforma (treas. Washington chpt. 1988, pres. 1989-91, 95-99, nat. ways and means chair 1991-92). Office Phone: 703-695-2006.

WHITNEY, CAROL MARIE, securities sales professional; b. Torrington, Conn., Mar. 31, 1946; d. Charles Lester and Emily Mae (Orr) W. BA in French, Wells Coll., 1968; 5th yr. cert., So. Conn. State Coll., 1971; postgrad., N.Y. Inst. Fin., 1976; MS in Mgmt., Rensselaer Poly. Inst., 1992, MBA in Internat. Mgmt., 1997. Trainee/investment exec. Blyth-Eastman Dillon, Hartford, Conn., 1976-77; licensee ins. fixed, variable, life and health, various cos., 1977—; account exec./registered rep. Bache Halsey-Stuart Shields, Hartford, Danbury, Conn., 1977-81, Advest, Inc., Hartford, 1981-88; registered securities rep. West Hartford, Conn., 1988-91; internat. fin. con., investment analyst, pres. Ask My Assoc., Collinsville, Conn., 1988—; v.p. registered rep. E.T. Andrews & Co. Inc., Hartford, Conn., 1991-92; v.p. Conn. Fin. Network, 1991-92; v.p., registered prin. Buell Securities Corp., Wethersfield, Conn., 1992—, br. mgr. Torrington office, 1993-95. Sec. Internat. Assn. for Fin. Planning, Hartford, 1982-83, pub. rels. Conn. chpt., Hartford, 1983-85, ethics chairperson Conn. chpt., Hartford, 1985-86. Exhibited 5 paintings in State Cultural Mus., Karelia, Russia, 1999, 16 paintings in The Cultural Mus., Petrozavodsky, Russia, 2000; solo exhibit Cultural Mus., Petrozarodsk, Russia, 2000; prodr. (CD) Guennady Vavilov, 1999; author: Global Corporate Derivatives, 1997. Performing mem. Farmington Valley chpt. Sweet Adelines, Simsbury, Conn., 1976-82; founder, exec. dir. Lydia Whitney Found Inc.; exec. dir. for classical composers concert, The Bushnell, Hartford, 1998—. Named for Effective Speaking and Human Rels., Dale Carnegie, West Hartford, 1985. Mem. DAR, Internat. Platform Assn. (3rd prize Washington 1995 Katyn Forest, World Tour 1997 for 5 paintings, 1st prize 1997), World Affairs. Republican. Episcopalian. Avocations: international travel, cooking and baking, writing, russian language studies. Home: PO Box 462 Collinsville CT 06022-0462

WHITNEY, CRAIG RICHARD, journalist; b. Milford, Mass., Oct. 12, 1943; s. A. Gordon and Carol Alma (Kennison) W.; m. Heidi Witt, May 11, 1974; children: Alexandra Kennison, Stefan Robert. AB, Harvard, 1965. Reporter New York Times, Washington, 1965-66, N.Y.C., 1969-70, Saigon, Vietnam, 1971-72, Bonn, West Germany, 1973-77, Moscow, USSR, 1977-80,

dep. fgn. editor, 1980-82, fgn. editor, 1982-83, asst. mng. editor, 1983-86, Washington Bur. chief, 1986-88, London bur. chief, 1988-92, European diplomatic corr., 1992-2000, asst. mng. editor, 2000—. Author: Spy Trader, 1993, All the Stops, 2003. Served with USNR, 1966-69. Mem. Coun. Fgn. Rels., Harvard Club (N.Y.C.). Home: 1 Pierrepont St Brooklyn NY 11201-3302 Office: The NY Times 229 W 43rd St New York NY 10036-3959 Office Phone: 212-556-3909. E-mail: whitney@nytimes.com.

WHITNEY, DAVID See MALICK, TERRENCE

WHITNEY, DOUGLAS EDGAR, SR., lawyer; b. Malden, Mass., May 1, 1939; s. Edgar Gordon and Jennie (Johnson) Whitney; m. Carol Annette Moore, July 31, 1965 (div. 1994); children: Douglas Jr., James A., Charles B.; m. Helleke Nieterink, May 11, 1996. BChem. Engring., Cornell U., 1962; JD, Columbia U., 1965. Bar: N.Y. 1965, Mass. 1970, Del. 1973, U.S. Dist. Ct. (so. dist.) N.Y. 1966, U.S. Dist. Ct. Mass. 1969, U.S. Dist. Ct. Del. 1973, U.S. Ct. Appeals (fed., 1st, 2d and 3d cirs.), U.S. Supreme Ct. 1972. Patent agt. Mobil Oil Corp., N.Y.C., 1963-65; assoc. Davis, Hoxie, Faithfull & Hapgood, N.Y.C., 1965-69; ptnr. Russell & Nields, Boston, 1969-72, Morris, Nichols, Arsht & Tunnell, Wilmington, Del., 1972—. Bd. dirs. U.S. Orienteering Fedn., St. Louis, 1981-84, Tech. Properties, Inc., Ft. Worth, 1992-2000. Mem. ABA, Am. Intellectual Property Assn., Del. Bar Assn. Democrat. Congregationalist. Home: 10 Hickory Ln Chadds Ford PA 19317-9715 Office: PO Box 1347 1201 N Market St Wilmington DE 19899 E-mail: dewsr@att.net., dwhitney@mnat.com.

WHITNEY, EDWARD BONNER, retired investment banker; b. Glen Cove, N.Y., June 6, 1945; s. Edward Farley and Millicent Bonner (Bowring) W.; m. Martha Congleton Howell, Aug. 17, 1974; children: William Howell, John Howell. BA, Harvard U., 1966, MBA, 1969. Systems engr. IBM, Cambridge, Mass., 1966-67; assoc. Dillon, Read & Co. Inc., N.Y.C., 1969-74, v.p., 1975-79, sr. v.p., 1980-83, mng. dir., 1984-97, also bd. dirs.; mng. dir. UBS Warburg, London, 1997—2002. Bd. dirs., chair Investor Responsibility Rsch. Ctr.; bd. dirs., 2d vice chmn. Am. Rivers. Mem. Harvard Club NYC E-mail: Nedwhitney@aol.com.

WHITNEY, FRANK D. prosecutor; b. N.C., Nov. 22, 1959; s. A. Grant and Lillian (DeArmon) Whitney; m. Catherine Whitney; children: Anne Stone, Francis Hunter. BA, Wake Forest U., 1982; MBA, JD, U. N.C., 1987. Bar: N.C. 1987, D.C. 1988. Asst. U.S. atty. We. Dist. N.C., U.S. Dept. Justice, Charlotte, 1990—2001; counsel Kilpatrick Stockton LLP, Charlotte, 2001—02; assoc. McKenna Conner Cuneo, Washington, 1987—90; law clk. to Hon. David B. Sentelle U.S. Ct. Appeals (D.C. cir.), 1988—89; U.S. atty. Ea. Dist. N.C. U.S. Dept. Justice, Raleigh, 2003—. Presbyterian. Office: Ea Dist NC Fed Bldg 310 New Burn Ave Ste 800 Raleigh NC 27601-1461

WHITNEY, JANE, foreign service officer; b. July 15, 1941; d. Robert F. and Mussette (Cary) W. BA, Beloit Coll., 1963; CD, U. Aix, Marseille, France, 1962. Joined Fgn. Svc., U.S. Dept. State, 1965; vice consul Saigon, Vietnam, 1966—68; career counselor, 1968—70; spl. asst. Office of Dir. Gen., 1970—72; consul Stuttgart, Fed. Rep. Germany, 1972-74, Ankara, Turkey, 1974—76; spl. asst. Office of Asst. Sec. for Consular Affairs, 1976—77; mem. Bd. Examiners Fgn. Svc., 1977—78, 1979—81; consul Munich, 1978—79, Buenos Aires, 1981—82; ethics officer Office of Legal Adviser, 1982—85; advisor Office of Asst. Sec. for Diplomatic Security, 1985—86; dep. prin. officer, consul Stuttgart, 1986—90; prin. officer, consul gen. Perth, Australia, 1990—91. Mem. Presbyterian Ch. Recipient awards U.S. Dept. State, 1968, 70, 81, 85, 87, 90.

WHITNEY, JOHN DENISON, English educator, writer; b. Pasadena, Calif., Sept. 23, 1940; s. John Keshishyan Whitney and Nathalie Adams Crane; children: Barbara, Joanne, Roger, David, Douglas, Suzanne, Michael. BA, U. Mich., 1962, MA, 1966. Prof. English U. Wis., Platteville, 1966-69, Wausau, 1969—, Coll. of Menominee Nation, Keshena, Wis., 1993—2003. Author: (poems) The Nabisco Warehouse, 1971, Word of Mouth, 1986, sd, 1988, What Grandmother Says, 1995, 3d edit., 2001, sd and done, 1995. Writing fellow Wis. Arts Bd., 1976, Creative Writing fellow Nat. Endowment for Arts, 1994. Avocations: tai chi, motorcycling. Home: 3926 Riverview Dr Wausau WI 54403-2250 Office: U Wis Marathon County 518 S 7th Ave Wausau WI 54401-5362 E-mail: jdwhitne@uwc.edu.

WHITNEY, PATRICK FOSTER, design educator; b. Edmonton, Alta., Can., Sept. 5, 1951; came to U.S., 1974; s. Gordon and Geraldine (Walker) W.; m. Cheryl Kent. BFA in Design with distinction, U. Alta., 1974; MFA in Design, Cranbrook Acad. Art, Bloomfield Hills, Mich., 1976. Designer RVI Corp., Chgo., 1976-79; chmn. Div. of Design Mpls. Coll. Art and Design, 1979-83; chmn. Inst. of Design, Ill. Inst. Tech., Chgo., 1983-87, dir., 1987—, Steelcase/Robert C. Pew Prof. Design. Mem., disting. advisor bd. Assn. Computing Machinery's Special Interest Group in Computer Human Interaction. Editor: Design in the Information Environment, 1984; author numerous published articles on design and communications. Mem. Am. Ctr. for Design (bd. dirs. 1984-86, v.p. 1986-90, pres. 1992-94), Arts Club. Office: Ill Inst Tech Inst Design Chicago IL 60616*

WHITNEY, PHYLLIS AYAME, author; b. Yokohama, Japan, Sept. 9, 1903; d. Charles J. and Lillian (Mandeville) W.; m. George A. Garner, July 2, 1925 (div. 1945); m. Lovell F. Jahnke, 1950 (dec. 1973). Grad., McKinley High Sch., Chgo., 1924. Instr. dancing, San Antonio, 1 yr; tchr. juvenile fiction writing Northwestern U., 1945; children's book editor Chgo. Sun, 1942-46, Phila. Inquirer, 1947, 48; instr. juvenile fiction writing N.Y.U., 1947-58; leader juvenile fiction workshop Writers Conf., U. Colo., 1952, 54, 56. Pres. exec. bd. 5th Ann. Writers Conf., Northwestern U., 1944. Author: A Place for Ann, 1941, A Star for Ginny, 1942, (vocat. fiction for teenage girls) A Window for Julie, 1943, (mystery novel for adults) Red Is for Murder, 1943, The Silver Inkwell, 1945, Willow Hill, 1947, Writing Juvenile Fiction, 1947, Ever After, 1948, Mystery of the Gulls, 1949, Linda's Homecoming, 1950, The Island of Dark Woods, 1951, Love Me, Love Me Not, 1952, Step to the Music, 1953, A Long Time Coming, 1954, Mystery of the Black Diamonds, 1954, The Quicksilver Pool, 1955, Mystery on the Isle of Skye, 1955, The Fire and The Gold (Jr. Lit. Guild), 1956, The Highest Dream (Jr. Lit. Guild), 1956, The Trembling Hills (Peoples Book Club), 1956, Skye Cameron, 1957, Mystery of the Green Cat (Jr. Lit. Guild), 1957, Secret of the Samurai Sword (Jr. Lit. Guild), 1958, The Moonflower, 1958, Creole Holiday, 1959, Thunder Heights, 1960, Blue Fire, 1961, Mystery of the Haunted Pool, 1961 (Edgar award Mystery Writers Am.), Secret of the Tiger's Eye, 1961, Window on the Square, 1962, Mystery of the Golden Horn, 1962, Seven Tears for Apollo, 1963, Mystery of the Hidden Hand, 1963 (Edgar award Mystery Writers Am. 1964), Black Amber, 1964, Secret of the Emerald Star, 1964, Sea Jade, 1965, Mystery of the Angry Idol, 1965, Columbella, 1966, Secret of the Spotted Shell, 1967, Mystery of the Strange Traveler, 1967, Silverhill, 1967, Hunter's Green, 1968, Secret of Goblin Glen, 1968, Mystery of the Crimson Ghost, 1969, Winter People, 1969, Secret of the Missing Footprint, 1970, Lost Island, 1970, The Vanishing Scarecrow, 1971, Listen for the Whisperer, 1971, Nobody Likes Trina, 1972, Snowfire, 1973, Mystery of the Scowling Boy, 1973, The Turquoise Mask, 1974, Spindrift, 1975, Secret of Haunted Mesa, 1975, The Golden Unicorn, 1976, Secret of the Stone Face, 1977, The Stone Bull, 1977, The Glass Flame, 1978, Domino, 1979, Poinciana, 1980, Vermilion, 1981, Guide to Fiction Writing, 1982, Emerald, 1983, Rainsong, 1984, Dream of Orchids, 1985, Flaming Tree, 1986, Silversword, 1987, Feather on the Moon, 1988, Rainbow in the Mist, 1989, The Singing Stones, 1990, Woman Without a Past, 1991, The Ebony Swan, 1992, Star Flight, 1993, Daughter of the Stars, 1994, Amethyst Dreams, 1997; sold first story to Chgo. Daily News; later wrote for pulp mags., became specialist in juvenile writing, now writing entirely in adult field. Spent first 15 years of life in Japan, China and P.I. (father in shipping and hotel bus.). Recipient Friends of Lit. award for contbns. to children's lit., 1974; Reynal and Hitchcock prize in Youth Today contest for book Willow Hill; Today's Woman award Coun. Cerebral Palsy Auxs., 1983, Agatha award Malice Domestic, 1990, Rita award Romance Writers Am., 1990, Lifetime award Romance Writers Am., 1990, Midland Authors award for a lifetime of literary achievement, 1995. Mem. Mystery Writers Am. (pres. 1975, Grandmaster award for lifetime achievement 1988), Am. Crime Writers League, Sisters in Crime, Authors League of Am., Authors Round Table (pres. 1943-44). Address: care McIntosh and Otis 353 Lexington Ave New York NY 10016-0941 *A learning period must be allowed for any talent. The accidental success is unfortunate because the person who achieves it doesn't really know how it happened. This does not mean that it ever becomes easy, even with learning. There is always work involved-long hours and dedication to that work-before a book is ready for publication. Any success demands a price, and the time and effort, and sometimes anguish a successful person gives to his work is that price. For me, the satisfactions have been worth it.*

WHITNEY, RALPH ROYAL, JR., financial executive; b. Phila., Dec. 10, 1934; s. Ralph Royal and Florence Elizabeth (Whitney) W.; m. Fay Wadsworth, Apr. 4, 1959; children: Lynn Marie, Paula Sue, Brian Ralph. BA, U. Rochester, 1957, MBA, 1972. Spl. agt. Prudential Ins. Co., Rochester, N.Y., 1958-59, divsn. mgr., 1959-63; gen. agt. Nat. Life Vt., Syracuse, 1963-64; contr. Wadsworth Mfg. Assocs. Inc., Syracuse, 1964-65, v.p., 1965-68, pres., 1968-71, Warren (Pa.) Components Corp., 1968-72; chmn. Hammond Kennedy Whitney & Co., N.Y.C., 1972—. Chmn. Reinhold Industries; chmn., CEO Grobet File Co.; bd. dirs. Baldwin Tech. Corp., First Tech., Ltd., M. Mossberg & Son, Inc., MedTek Inc., Wyo. Bus. Coun., Relm Wireless Comms. Inc., 1st Internet Bank, Seneca Printing, Inc., Dura Automobile Sys. Inc., Polytwine Inc., Maine Rubber Co. Bd. trustees U. Rochester. Mem. N.Y. Yacht Club, Lotus Club (N.Y.C.), Century Club (Syracuse), Merion Cricket Club, Princeton Club. Episcopalian. Home: 3441 Highway 34 Wheatland WY 82201-8714 E-mail: rrw@hkwinc.com.

WHITNEY, RAY, professional hockey player; b. Saskatchewan, Alta., Can., May 8, 1972; s. Floyd and Wendy W. Stick boy Edmonton Oilers, 1986-87, 87-88, player, 1997, Spokane Chiefs, 1988-91, 90-91, San Jose Sharks, 1991—97, Edmonton Oilers, 1997—98, Fla. Panthers, 1998—2001, Columbus Blue Jackets, 2001—. Named most valuable player WHL, 1988-91, 90-91, Most Valuable Player All-Star Game IHL, 1992. Avocation: golf. Office: Columbus Blue Jackets JMAC Hockey Suite 230 150 E Wilson Bridge Rd Worthington OH 43085

WHITNEY, RICHARD BUCKNER, lawyer; b. Corpus Christi, Tex., Mar. 1, 1948; s. Franklyn Loren and Betty Wolcott (Fish) Whitney; m. Chantal Marie Gindt, Aug. 18, 1972; children: Jennifer L, James R, Katherine F. BA in Polit. Sci., Union Coll., 1970; JD, Case Western Res. U., 1973. Bar: Ohio 1973, N.Y. 1998, US Ct Appeals (6th cir) 1974, US Ct Appeals (3d cir) 1987, US Dist Ct (so dist) NY 2000, U.S. Dist. Ct. (no. dist.) Ohio 1974. From assoc. to ptnr. Jones Day, Cleve., 1973—. Trustee Hospice of the We. Res., Roots of Am. Music. Mem.: Am Inns of Ct., Cleve. Bar Assn., Order of Coif. Home: 2750 Southington Rd Shaker Heights OH 44120-1603 Office: Jones Day 901 Lakeside Ave Cleveland OH 44114-1190 E-mail: rbwhitney@jonesday.com.

WHITNEY, WILLIAM ELLIOT, JR., advertising agency executive; b. Albany, N.Y., Feb. 22, 1933; s. William Elliot and Louise E. (Goldsmith) W.; m. Nancy B. Bivings, Mar. 1, 1958; children— Susan, James, Douglas. BA cum laude, Amherst Coll., 1954; MBA, Harvard U., 1956. Account exec. McCann-Erickson, N.Y.C., 1956-58, Marschalk Co., N.Y.C., 1958-60; v.p., then sr. v.p. Ogilvy & Mather, N.Y.C., 1960-80, sr. v.p., mng. dir. Chgo., 1980-85, exec. v.p., 1985-87, pres., 1987-89, chmn., 1990-91; cons. ptnr. Redirections, Inc., 1991-98. Lectr. U. Chgo. Grad. Sch. Bus., 1991-98. Bd. dirs., v.p. Chgo. Coun. Boy Scouts Am., 1978-81, 88—, Off-the-St. Club, Chgo., 1979—, pres., 1988-89; bd. dirs. Hinsdale (Ill.) Cmty. House, 1981, King-Bruwaert House, 1988—; v.p. civic adv. bd. Hinsdale Hosp., 1989-93; bd. dirs. Exec. Svc. Corps of Chgo., 1996—; trustee Village of Hinsdale, 1993-97, pres., 1997-2001; bd. dirs. Hinsdale Area United Way, 2001-. Mem. Econs. Club, Hinsdale Golf Club. Home: 736 S Park Ave Hinsdale IL 60521-4646

WHITSEL, RICHARD HARRY, retired biologist, entomologist; b. Denver, Feb. 23, 1931; s. Richard Elstun and Edith Muriel (Harry) W.; m. Laurie Pearson, May 25, 1997; children by previous marriages: Russell David, Robert Alan, Michael Dale, Steven Deane. BA, U. Calif., Berkeley, 1954; MA, San Jose State Coll., 1962. Sr. rsch. biologist San Mateo County Mosquito Abatement Dist., Burlingame, Calif., 1959—72; mgr. environ. program, chief watershed mgmt., chief planning, chief wetlands planning office Calif. Regional Water Quality Control Bd., Oakland, 1972—2000; ret., 2000. Trustee Alameda County Mosquito Abatement Dist., 1999-2001; mem. grad. faculty water resource mgmt. U. San Francisco, 1987-89. Served with Med. Svc. Corps, U.S. Army, 1954-56. Mem. Soc. Wetland Scientists, Entomol. Soc. Am., Calif. Alumni Assn., The Benjamin Ide Wheeler Soc., Nat. Parks and Conservation Assn. (life), Sierra Club. Democrat. Episcopalian. Home: 11552 Side Hill Cir Nevada City CA 95959 Personal E-mail: lwhitsel@sbcglobal.net.

WHITSELL, HELEN JO, lumber executive; b. Portland, Oreg., July 20, 1938; d. Joseph William and Helen (Cornwell) Copeland; m. William A. Whitsell, Sept. 2, 1960; 2 children. BA, U. So. Calif., 1960. With Copeland Lumber Yard Inc., Portland, 1960—, pres., chief exec. officer, 1973-84, chmn., chief exec. officer, 1984—. Office: Copeland Lumber Yards Inc PO Box 80769 Portland OR 97280-1769

WHITSELL, JOHN CRAWFORD, II, general surgeon; b. St. Joseph, Mo., Dec. 21, 1929; s. Ora Earl and Lorena (Spratt) W. AB, Grinnell Coll., 1950; MD, Washington U., St. Louis, 1954. Diplomate Am. Bd. Surgery, Am. Bd. Thoracic Surgery. From instr. to clin. prof. surgery Cornell U. Med. Ctr., N.Y.C., 1963-70; from asst. attending to attending in surgery N.Y. Hosp., N.Y.C., 1964-70; surg. dir. Rogosin Kidney Ctr. N.Y. Hosp.-Cornell Med. Ctr., N.Y.C., 1973-75; attending in surgery N.Y. Hosp., 1970-98, hon. attending surgeon, 2001—; clin. prof. surgery Cornell Med. Coll., 1970-98, clin. prof. surgery emeritus, 1998. Surg. cons. Rogosin Kidney Ctr., 1975—, Sharon (Conn.) Hosp., 1976-2001; hon. attending surgeon, N.Y. Hosp., 2001—. Contbr. articles to profl. jours. Capt. USAF, 1961-63. Eng. Fellow ACS; mem. Transplantation Soc., N.Y. Surg. Soc., Am. Soc. Transplant Surgeons, N.Y. Soc. for Thoracic Surgery, Soc. Thoracic Surgeons, N.Y. Acad. Medicine, N.Y. Soc. Cardiovascular Surgery, Harvey Soc., Union Club of N.Y., Phi Beta Kappa. Avocations: golf, fishing, auto racing, antique cars.

WHITSETT, JEFFREY ALLEN, pediatric educator; b. Cleve., May 19, 1947; s. William F. and Kathryn A. (Gilletly) W.; m. Dorinda Dew, May 3, 1975; children: Sarah, Anna, Margaret, David. BA, Colgate U., 1969; MD, Columbia U., 1973. Diplomate Am. Bd. Pediatrics, Am. Bd. Neonatology. Intern and resident Mt. Sinai Hosp., N.Y.C., 1973-76; fellow U. Cin. Children's Hosp., 1976-78, prof. pediatrics, pharmacology, cell biophysics, 1978—, dir. pulmonary biology, 1988—. Contbr. articles to sci. publs.; patentee in field. Recipient E. Mead Johnson award Bristol-Meyers Co., 1988; Human Embryololgy Devel. and Study Sect. grantee NIH, 1987-91. Mem. Soc. for Pediatric Rsch. (coun. 1989-91), Am. Soc. Cell Biology, Am. Soc. Clin. Investigation, Inst. Medicine, 2004). Office: U Cin Childrens Hosp 231 Bethesda Ave Cincinnati OH 45229-2827 E-mail: jeff.whitsett@cchmc.org.

WHITSON, ELIZABETH TEMPLE, graphics designer; b. Washington, D.C., Oct. 1, 1959; d. Norman Burkey Musselman, Elizabeth Temple (Henry) Musselman; m. William Stuart Whitson, Dec. 21, 1985; 1 child, Ian Alexander. BA, Va. Tech. U., 1982. Artist, office asst. Artisan Graphics, Alexandria, Va., 1983—84; graphic artist, office asst. Gestalt Assocs., Alexandria, 1984—86; graphic artist, sales rep., prodn. mgr. Gestalt Prodns., Herndon, Va., 1986—89, ImageMatrix, Inc., Falls Church, Va., 1989—91; graphic designer, publ. dept. head CompuSlides, Vienna, Va., 1991—94, New Media Comms., Vienna, 1994—95; graphic designer, owner Port City Prodns., Inc., Alexandria, 1993—. Editor (illustrator): "Highlights of the Alexandria Com.", 1988—. Mem. Brookville/Seminary Valley Civic Assn., Alexandria, 1988—2002; vol. Torpedo Factory Art Ctr.; active mem. The Alexandria Libr. Co.; com. vol., tchr., mem. Old Presbyn. Meeting House. Mem.: DAR (corr. sec. 1995—98, chmn. two coms. Mt. Vernon chpt.), The Old Presbyterian Meeting House (worship com. 1995—97, childcare com. 2000—03, childhood edn. com. 2003—), Friends of Gunston Hall, The Alexandria Assembly, Nat. Soc. Colonial Dames of Am. (rec. sec. 1999—2002, directory chmn. 2002—, vice chmn. 2004—). Presbyterian. Avocations: remodeling, gardening, painting, illustration, piano. Home and Office: 1701 Sherwood Hall Ln Alexandria VA 22306

WHITSON, JAMES NORFLEET, JR., retired diversified company executive; b. Clinton, Okla., Mar. 14, 1935; s. James Norfleet and Georgia (Webb) W.; m. Lyda Lee Gibson, Apr. 19, 1956; 1 child, James Mark. BBA, Tex. Tech U., 1957. With LTV, Inc., Dallas, 1960-70; v.p. fin. Omega-Alpha, Inc., 1970-73; pres. Sammons Comm., Inc., Dallas, 1973-89; exec. v.p., coo Sammons Enterprises, Inc., Dallas, 1989-98, also bd. dirs.; ret., 1998. Bd. dirs. Seligman Group Investment Cos., CommScope, Inc. Mem. Alpha Tau Omega. Home: 6606 Foresthire Dr Dallas TX 75230-2856

WHITSON, JAMES P. automotive executive; B in Econs., Davidson Coll., 1966; MBA, Harvard U., 1971. V.p., asst. treas., dir. taxes ITT, 1980—98; chief tax officer Delphi Corp, Troy, Mich., 1998—. Mem.: Internal Fiscal Assn., Fin. Execs. Inst. (mem. com. on taxation), Tax Execs. Inst., Am. Inst. Cert. Pub. Accts. Office: Delphi Corp World Headquarters 5725 Delphi Dr Troy MI 48098-2815

WHITSON, LISH, lawyer; b. Washington, Oct. 13, 1942; s. I. Lish and Clytie B. (Collier) W.; m. Barbara Lee Sullivan, Sept. 16, 1965; children: L. Richard, Kimberly S. BA in Philosophy, Pa. State U., 1965; JD, U. Wash., 1972. Bar: Wash. 1973, Oreg. 2002, U.S. Dist. Ct. (we. dist.) 1973, U.S. Dist. Ct. (ea. dist.) 1977, U.S. Supreme Ct. 1977. Assoc. Seattle-King County Pub. Defender Assn., 1972-76, Helsell, Fetterman, Martin, Todd & Hokanson, Seattle, 1976-81, ptnr., 1981-98; of counsel Badgley Mullins, Seattle, 1998-2000, Lish Whitson PLLC, Seattle, 2000—03, Stokes Lawrence PS, 2003—. Bd. dirs., past chmn. Downtown Emergency Svc. Ctr., Seattle, 1981-97; bd. dirs. Allied Arts, 1988-96, pres., 1994-96; mem. Allied Arts Found., 1997—; trustee Seattle Youth Symphony Orch., bd. dirs., 1986-95; mem. alumni bd. U. Wash. Law Sch., 1993-2001, treas., 1997-99, pres., 1999-2001; bd. dirs., teas. Little Bit Therapeutic Riding Ctr., 2002—. Fellow Am. Bar Found., Am. Coll. Trial Lawyers; mem. ABA (young lawyers divsn. rep. to exec. coun. 1979, mem. standing com. on lawyer referral svc. 1990-96, chmn. 1992-96, commn. on women in the profn. 1998-2001, mem. task force model defination of practice of law 2003, chair standing com. pub. oversight 2001-2004), ATLA, Am. Bd. Trial Advocates (assoc., mem. nat. bd. 2003—), Wash. State Bar Assn. (gov. 1995-98, spl. hearing officer 1999—, jud. rev. com. 2000—, chmn. 2003), King County Bar Found. (mem. pres. coun.), King County Bar Assn. (pro bono com. chmn. 1981-84, bd. dirs. 1988-91, young lawyers sect. 1977-79, chmn. 1979, Pro Bono Svc. award 1993, Atty. of Yr. 2000), Fed. Bar Assn., Am. Judicature Soc. (bd. dirs. 1981-86, sec. Wash. chpt. 2002—), Seattle Pub. Def. Assn. (bd. dirs. 1982-86), Seattle C. of C., Wash. Athletic Club. Office: StokesLawrence PS 800 5th Ave Ste 4000 Seattle WA 98104 Office Phone: 206-626-6000. E-mail: lwhitson@stokeslaw.com.

WHITT, GREGORY SIDNEY, evolution educator; b. Detroit, June 13, 1938; s. Sidney Abram and Millicent (Ward) W.; m. Dixie Lee Dailey, Aug. 25, 1963. BS, Colo. State U., 1962, MS, 1965; PhD, Yale U., 1970. Asst. prof. zoology U. Ill., Urbana, 1969-72, asso. prof. genetics and devel., 1972-77, prof., 1977-87, prof. ecology, ethology and evolution, 1987-2000, prof. animal biology, 2000—. Affiliate Ill. Natural History Survey, 1981—; mem. NIH study sect., 1975-76 Co-editor: Isozymes: Current Topics in Biological and Medical Research, 1977-87; editor: Isozyme Bull., 1978-81; mem. editl. bd. Biochem. Genetics, 1975—, Devel. Genetics, 1978-83, Jour. Molecular Evolution, 1979-2000, Molecular Biology and Evolution, 1983-93, Molecular Phylogenetics and Evolution, 1992-2000; contbr. articles to profl. jours. Fellow AAAS; mem. Am. Soc. for Microbiology, Soc. for Protection of Old Fishes, Internat. Soc. Molecular Evolution, Archaeological Inst. of Am. Home: 1510 Trails Dr Urbana IL 61802-7052 Office: U Ill Dept Animal Biology 515 Morrill Hall 505 S Goodwin Ave Urbana IL 61801-3707

WHITT, RICHARD ERNEST, reporter; b. Greenup County, Ky., Dec. 15, 1944; s. Walter Charles and Irene (Hayes) W.; m. Terri Bellizzi; children: Hayes Chadwick, Emily Catherine, Christen Leigh McCollough. Student, Ashland (Ky.) Community Coll., 1966-68; BA in Journalism, U. Ky., 1970. Reporter Middlesboro (Ky.) Daily News, 1970-71; asst. state editor Waterloo (Iowa) Courier, 1971-72; city editor Kingsport (Tenn.) Times, 1972-76; No. Ky. bur. chief Courier-Jour., Louisville, 1977, Frankfort bur. chief, 1977-80, spl. projects reporter, 1980-89; investigative reporter Atlanta Jour. & Constn., 1989—. Served with USN, 1962-66. Decorated Air medal; recipient Pulitzer prize for coverage of Beverly Hills Supper Club fire, 1978; named Outstanding Ky. Journalist, 1978; recipient John Hancock award for excellence, 1983; named to U. Ky. Journalism Hall of Fame, 1995. Democrat. Office: Atlanta Jour & Constn 72 Marietta St NW Atlanta GA 30303-2804

WHITTAKER, BILL DOUGLAS, minister; b. Bowling Green, Ky., June 14, 1943; s. Ewing A. and Lois (Jenkins) W.; m. Rebecca Kaye Howard, June 18, 1966; children: John, Karen, Mary. BA, Western Ky. U., 1965; MDiv, So. Bapt. Theol. Sem., Louisville, 1969, D of Ministry, 1974; MA, Union Coll., 2004. Ordained to ministry So. Bapt. Conv., 1964. Pastor 1st Bapt. Ch., Sturgis, Ky., 1969-76, Murray, Ky., 1976-82; missionary Internat. Mission Bd., So. Bapt. Conv., The Philippines, 1983-86; pastor Downtown Bapt. Ch., Orlando, Fla., 1986-88; pres. Clear Creek Bapt. Bible Coll., Pineville, Ky., 1988—. Author: Preparing to Preach, 1999, Korean edit. 2002; columnist Western Recorder newspaper, 1988—; editor: Ky. Bapt. Heritage, 2001—. Bd. dirs. Coalition for the Homeless, Cen. Fla. YMCA, Orlando, 1986-88; mem. Ky. Bapt. Archives Adv. Bd. Mem. Assn. Bible Colls. (accredited, del. 1988—), Assn. So. Bapt. Colls. and Schs. (del. 1988—), So. Assn. Coll. and Schs. (del. 1999—), Kiwanis (pres. Pineville chpt. 1994-95, dist. 6 lt. gov. 1997-98), Ky. Bapt. Conv. (pres. 1980). Baptist. Home and Office: 300 Clear Creek Rd Pineville KY 40977-9752 Office Phone: 606-337-1530. Business E-Mail: bwhittaker@ccbbc.edu.

WHITTAKER, JEANNE EVANS, former newspaper columnist; b. Detroit, Jan. 1, 1934; d. Alfred Heacock and Margaret (Evans) W.; m. Charles Martin Hines Jr., Sept. 29, 1962 (div. Feb. 1970); children: Charles M. Hines III, Margaret Helen Whittaker Zimmerman. Student, Northwestern U., 1952-53; BS in History, U. Mich., 1956. Clubmobile worker UN forces ARC, Republic of Korea, 1956—58; staff programmer ARC France, Chaumont, 1958—61; dir. Bexar County chpt. youth ARC, San Antonio, 1961—62; staff writer/columnist Detroit Free Press, 1970—75; editor Mich. Social Register, 1975—77; Lifestyle editor Observer and Eccentric newspapers, Birmingham, Mich., 1977—87; staff writer, columnist Detroit News, 1987—91; cons. in field, 1992—. Bd. dirs. Wayne State U. Press. Contbr. articles to mags. Bd. dirs. Detroit chpt. ARC, 1989-92; Mem. Univ.-Liggett Sch. Aumni Bd., 2003—; mem. adv. bd. Greenfield Village Antiques Show, 2000—. Recipient Penney-Mo. award U. Mo., 1984; 1st place lifestyles/Family award Mich. Press Assn., 1982, 84, Gen. Excellence award 1982, 86; Gen. Excellence award Suburban Newspaper Assn., 1979. Mem. Detroit Hist. Soc. (bd. dirs. 1986-91), Detroit Inst. Arts Women's Assn. Episcopalian. Avocations: writing, reading, travel. Home: 552 Cadieux Rd Grosse Pointe MI 48230-1508 E-mail: jeannewhittaker@aol.com.

WHITTAKER, JUDITH ANN CAMERON, lawyer; b. N.Y.C., June 12, 1938; d. Thomas Macdonald and Mindel (Wallman) Cameron; m. Kent E. Whittaker, Jan. 30, 1960; children: Charles Evans II, Catherine Cameron. BA, Brown U., 1959; JD, U. Mo., 1963. Bar: Mo. 1963, U.S. Dist. Ct. (we. dist.) Mo. 1963, U.S. Ct. Appeals (8th cir.) 1965, U.S. Supreme Ct. 1980, D.C. 1987. Assoc. and ptnr. Sheffrey, Ryder & Skeer, Kansas City, Mo., 1963-72; asst. and assoc. gen. coun., exec. v.p. gen. coun. Hallmark Cards, Inc., Kansas City, 1972—2004; dir., v.p., gen. coun. Univision Holdings, Inc., Kansas City, 1988-92; sec., bd. dirs. Crown Media Holdings, Inc., 2000—04; of counsel Shook, Hardy & Bacon, Kansas City, Mo., 2004—. Bd. dirs. Am. Arbitration Assn., 1997—. Trustee Brown U. Providence, 1977-83, U. Mo. Law Found., Kansas City, 1977-90; dir. Kansas City (Mo.) Indsl. Devel. Authority,

1981-84, Legal Aid Kansas City, 1971-77, De La Salle Sch. Episcopalian. Avocations: reading, skiing, hiking, piano, golf. Office: Shook Hardy & Bacon 2555 Grand Blvd Kansas City MO 64198-2613

WHITTELL, POLLY (MARY KAYE WHITTELL), editor, journalist; b. Washington, Oct. 20; d. Alfred Whittell Jr. and Mary Halsey (Patchin) Hopper. BA in English, U. Calif., Berkeley; postgrad., Radcliffe Coll.; postgrad. in journalism, Columbia U. Rschr. Nat. Rev. Mag., N.Y.C., 1970-71; asst. to presdl. speech writer The White House, Washington, 1971-72; asst. editor TravelAge East Mag., Dun & Bradstreet Publs., N.Y.C., 1973-75; copy editor Ski Mag. Skier's Guides, Times Mirror Mags. and Am. Express, N.Y.C., 1975-76; asst. editor to sr. editor Hearst Mags., Motor Boating & Sailing Mag., N.Y.C., 1977-2000; contbg. editor Powerboat Mag., 2000—01, Hearst Mags., 2002—. Contbg. author: (anthology) Against the Sea, 1998; contbr. articles to other nat. and internat. consumer mags. Mem. charity benefit com. Youth Counseling League, N.Y.C., 1975-85, Am. Cancer Soc., 1998-99, and others; v.p. Knickerbocker Rep. Club, N.Y.C., 1979-80; elected mem. N.Y. Rep. County Com., N.Y.C., 1980-84. Mem. Boating Writers Internat. (award for environ. article 1995), Soc. Profl. Journalists, Princeton Club (N.Y.), SandBar Beach Club (v.p. membership 1980-82). Episcopalian. Avocations: photography, travel, boating, skiing. E-mail: pollywhitt@aol.com.

WHITTEMORE, ALICE, biostatistician; b. N.Y.C., July 5, 1936; BS, Marymount Manhattan Coll., 1958; MA, Hunter Coll., 1964; PhD in Mathematics, CUNY, 1967. From asst. prof. to assoc. prof. math. Hunter Coll., N.Y.C., 1967-74; adj. assoc. prof. environ. med. N.Y.U., 1974-76, mem. faculty dept. statistics, 1976-87; prof. epidemiology dept. health rsch. and policy Stanford U., Palo Alto, Calif., 1987—. Recipient Sloan Found. rsch. grant, Soc. Ind. and Applied Math. Inst. Math and Soc., 1974-76, Rockefeller Found rsch. grant 1976-77. Mem. NAS Inst. Medicine, AAAS, Soc. Indsl. and Applied Math, Am. Math Soc., Math Assn. Am., Sigma Xi Office: Stanford U Sch Medicine Dept Health Rsch and Policy HBP Redwood Bldg Stanford CA 94305-5092

WHITTEMORE, ANTHONY DUNSTER, vascular surgeon; b. Boston, Nov. 5, 1944; s. Anthony Rogers Whittemore and Kathryn Gansevoort Binnian Howe; m. Rhoda Belknap Stetson, June 18, 1966; children: Anthony Rogers, Joshua Stetson, Sarah Belknap. BS, Trinity Coll., 1966; MD, Columbia U., 1970. Resident in surgery Columbia Presbyn. Med. Ctr., 1970-76; research assoc. Columbia U., N.Y.C., 1972-73, NIH trainee, 1975-76; vascular fellow Peter Bent Brigham Hosp., Boston, 1976-77; chief vascular surgery Naval Regional Med. Ctr., Portsmouth, Va., 1977-79; instr. surgery Harvard Med. Sch/Peter Bent Brigham Hosp., Boston, 1979-80; asst. prof. surgery Harvard U., Boston, 1981-87, assoc. prof. surgery, 1987-93, prof. surgery Harvard Med. Sch., 1993—; dir. surg. tng. program Harvard Med. Sch./Brigham & Women's Hosp., 1979; joined med. staff, Brigham and Women's Hosp., 1982, chief divsn. vascular surgery, 1990-1999, apptd. dir. Vascular Ctr., 1991, chief medical officer, 1999—; cons. Bard CardioSurgery, Billerica, Mass., 1982—, Meadox Medicals, Oakland, N.J., 1983—, instrumentation Labs., North Andover, Mass., 1980—; investigator grants NIH, 1979, 83. Contbr. articles to profl. jours. Served to lt. comdr. USN, 1977-79. Recipient Commendation USN, 1979. Fellow ACS; mem. Assn. Acad. Surgery, Am. Surg. Assn., Am. Soc. for Artificial Internal Organs (program com. 1982—), Am. Surg. Soc., Soc. U. Surgeons, Boston Surg. Soc., Internat. Cardiovascular Soc., Soc. Vascular Surgery, New Eng. Surg. Soc., New Eng. Soc. Vascular Surgery, Soc. Internat. de Chirurgie, The Country Club; patents in field. Home: 148 Farm Rd Sherborn MA 01770-1622 Office: Brigham & Women's Hosp 75 Francis St Boston MA 02115-6106

WHITTEMORE, EDWARD REED, II, poet, retired educator; b. New Haven, Sept. 11, 1919; s. Edward Reed and Margaret Eleanor (Carr) W.; m. Helen Lundeen, Oct. 3, 1952; children: Catherine Carr, Edward Reed III, John Lundeen (dec.), Margaret Goodhue. AB, Yale U., 1941; postgrad., Princeton U., 1945-46; Litt.D., Carleton Coll., 1971. Mem. faculty Carleton Coll., 1947-67, prof. English, 1962-67, chmn. dept., 1962-64; program assoc. Nat. Inst. Pub. Affairs, 1966-68; cons. in poetry Libr. of Congress, 1964-65, 84-85; Bain-Swiggett lectr. Princeton, 1967; prof. U. Md., 1968-84, prof. emeritus, 1984—; poet laureate State of Md., 1985-88. Lit. editor New Republic, 1969-74. Author: Heroes and Heroines, 1947, An American Takes a Walk, 1956, The Self-Made Man, 1959, The Boy From Iowa, 1962, The Fascination of the Abomination, 1963, Poems, New and Selected, 1967, From Zero to the Absolute, 1967, 50 Poems 50, 1970, The Mother's Breast and the Father's House, 1974, William Carlos Williams: Poet from Jersey, 1975, The Poet as Journalist, 1976, The Feel of Rock, 1982, Pure Lives, 1988, Whole Lives, 1989, The Past, the Future, the Present, 1990, Six Literary Lives, 1993; editor: Furioso, 1939-53, Browning, 1960, Carleton Miscellany, 1960-64, Delos mag., 1988-91. Capt. USAAF, 1941-45. Decorated Bronze star, 1945. Home: 4526 Albion Rd College Park MD 20740-3610

WHITTEMORE, JOHN DOUGLAS, soccer coach, writer; b. Little Rock, Ark., Feb. 17, 1979; s. Roxana Harsh (Whitner) and Donald Howard Whittemore. B.A. in English, York Coll., 2001. Youth min. Chenal Valley Ch., Little Rock, 2001—02; asst. men's soccer coach York Coll., Nebr., 2002—, assoc. head coach women's soccer, 2002—. Recipient Eagle Scout, Boy Scouts of Am., 1997. Avocations: photography, outdoors, travel. Personal E-mail: sour-blue@excite.com.

WHITTEMORE, LAURENCE FREDERICK, private banker; b. Bangor, Maine, Mar. 7, 1929; s. John Cambridge and Elizabeth Payson (Prentiss) Whittemore; m. Sarah Lee Arnold, Aug. 9, 1958; children: Arianna, Gioia, Lia, Nike. BA, Yale U., 1951; MBA, Harvard U., 1953; student, Balliol Coll., Oxford U., Eng., 1950. Account mgr. Brown Bros. Harriman, N.Y.C., 1956-72, gen. mgr., 1972-74; ptnr. Brown Bros. Harriman & Co., N.Y.C., 1974—2003, ltd. ptnr., 2004—. Dir. Manhattan Life Ins. Co., N.Y.C., Albany Ins. Co., N.Y.C.; mem. investment adv. com. Union Investment GmbH, Frankfurt, Germany, 1973—2002; mem. Chgo. Stock Exch., 1975—2003. Trustee Sarah Lawrence Coll., 1988-2000, hon. trustee, 2001—; trustee Am. Inst. Contemporary German Studies, 1994—2002, Asia Soc., 1998—; mem. Nat. Com. on U.S. China Rels., N.Y.C., 1982—, Chgo. Coun. on Fgn. Rels., 1980—; del. Assn. Yale Alumni, New Haven, 1982-86; chmn. Yale 35th Reunion Gift Drive, 1983-86; gov. Opportunity Internat., 1996—; mem. Bus. Execs. for Nat. Security, 1996—, New Eng. Air Mus., 1999—. Fellow Sterling fellow, Yale U., 2001—. Mem.: Chgo. Club, India House Club (N.Y.C.), Yale Club, Links Club. Republican. Episcopalian. Office: Brown Bros Harriman & Co 140 Broadway New York NY 10005-1101

WHITTEMORE, LINDA GENEVIEVE, clinical psychologist; b. Ft. Bragg, N.C., Nov. 1, 1948; d. James and Nancy (Caudill) White; children: Trevor Johnson, Dylan Lane. BA in Anthropology, East Carolina U., 1972, MA in Clin. Psychology, 1980. Rehab. svcs. coord. Social Center, Fairfax, Va., 1978-79; site coord. Mental Health Assn. of N. Va., Annandale, 1979-80; program asst. Alliance to Save Energy, Washington, 1981-82; ednl. psychology officer APA, Washington, 1984-88; exec. mktg. dir. I.D.N., Provo, Utah, 1989-93; supr. 24th Dist. Ct. Svcs. Unit, Lynchburg, Va., 1994-96; psychologist Ctrl. Va. Tng. Ctr., Lynchburg, 1996—2001; clin. coord. children and family svc. City of Lynchburg, Va., 2001—02; program mgr. ednl. support svcs. Child and Family Ctr., Lynchburg, 2002—. Prof. Benjamin Franklin U., Washington, 1986-87. Editor: Activities Handbook for the Teaching of Psychology, Vol. 2, 1987, Vol. 3, 1990. Mem.: Va. Counseling Assn., Dante Alighieri Soc. Va., Noetic Soc. Avocations: culinary arts, poetry, opera, travel, herb gardening. Home: Villa Mozart 517 Washington St Lynchburg VA 24504-2619

WHITTEMORE, PAUL BAXTER, psychologist; s. Harry Ballou and Margaret B. Whittemore; m. Jane Moore, Apr. 22, 1995. BA in Religion, Ea. Nazarene Coll., 1970; MDiv., Nazarene Theol. Sem., 1973; MA in Theology, Vanderbilt U., 1975, PhD in Theology, 1978; PhD in Clin. Psychology, U. Tenn., 1987. Cert. in clin. psychology Am. Bd. Profl. Psychology, lic. psychologist Calif. Asst. prof. philosophy and edn. Trevecca Nazarene Coll., Nashville, Tenn., 1973-76; asst. prof. philosophy and theology Point Loma Coll., San Diego, Calif., 1976-80; asst. prof. philosophy Mid. Tenn. State U., Murfreesboro, 1980-83; clin. psychology intern. Los Angeles County/U. So. Calif. Med. Ctr., L.A., 1986-87; coord. behavior health ctr. Calif. Med. Ctr., L.A., 1987-88; clin. asst. prof. family medicine U. So. Calif. Sch. Medicine, L.A., 1988—; pvt. practice psychologist Newport Beach, Calif., 1989—. Mem. behavioral sci. faculty Glendale Adventist Family Practice Residency Program, Glendale, Calif., 1989—90; inpatient group therapist Ingleside Hosp., Rosemead, Calif., 1990—92; founder, pres. Date Coach, 1992—2000. Contbr. articles to profl. jours. Recipient Andrew W. Mellon Postdoctoral Faculty Devel. award, Vanderbilt U., 1981. Mem.: AAUP (chp. v.p. 1982—83), APA, Orange County Psychol. Assn. (bd. dirs. 1996—2001), Calif. Psychol. Assn. (media divsn. sec.-treas. 1997—98), Am. Philos. Assn., Am. Acad. Religion. Achievements include discovery of link between phenylthiocarbamide tasting and depression. Office: 1001 Dove St Ste 145 Newport Beach CA 92660-2123

WHITTEMORE, RONALD PAUL, hospital administrator, retired army officer, nursing educator; b. Saco, Maine, Aug. 10, 1946; s. Ronald B. and Pauline L. (Larson) W.; m. Judy D. McDonald, Feb. 17, 1967; 1 child, Leicia Michelle. BGS, U. S.C., 1974, MEd, 1977; BSN, Med. Coll. Ga., 1975. Enlisted U.S. Army, 1968, advanced through ranks to maj., 1985, ret., 1991; adult/oncology nurse practitioner Martin Army Cmty. Hosp.; asst. head nurse SICU, infection control practitioner Moncrief Army Cmty. Hosp.; infection control practitioner U.S. Army Hosp., Seoul, Republic of Korea; chief nurse 2nd Combat Support Hosp., Ft. Benning, Ga.; cmty. health nurse Brooke Army Med. Ctr., Ft. Sam Houston, Tex.; comty. health nurse Giessen (Germany) Mil. Cmty.; clin. instr. Eisenhower Army Med. Ctr., Ft. Gordon, Ga.; chief nursing adminstrn. E/N Frankfurt (Germany) Army Med. Ctr.; adminstr., dir. quality improvement Gracewood (Ga.) State Sch. and Hosp., 1995-97. Instr. Augusta (Ga.) Tech. Inst.; nurse epidemiologist Med. Coll. Ga., Augusta. Mem. ANA, Ga. ANA (3rd Dist. honoree, pres. 1983-85), Assn. Practitioners in Infection Control, Am. Holistic Nurses Assn., Nat. Assn. Health Care Quality Profls., Assn. for Profls. in Infection Control and Epidemiology, Sigma Theta Tau. Office: Med Coll Ga Office Nurse Rschr Augusta GA 30901-3196

WHITTEN, CHARLES ALEXANDER, JR., physics educator; b. Harrisburg, Pa., Jan. 20, 1940; s. Charles Alexander and Helen (Shoop) W.; m. Joan Emann, Nov. 20, 1965; 1 son, Charles Alexander III. BS summa cum laude, Yale U., 1961; PhD in Physics, Princeton U., 1966. Research asso. A.W. Wright Nuclear Structure Lab., Yale U., 1966-68; asst. prof. physics UCLA, 1968-74, assoc. prof., 1974-80, prof., 1980—, vice chmn. physics dept., 1982-86. Vis. scientist Centre d'Etudes Nucléaires de Saclay-Moyenne Energie, 1980-81, 86-87. Contbr. articles to profl. jours. Mem. Am. Phys. Soc., Sigma Pi Sigma, Phi Beta Kappa. Home: 9844 Vicar St Los Angeles CA 90034-2719 Office Phone: 310-225-1691. E-mail: whitten@physics.ucla.edu.

WHITTEN, DAVID OWEN, economics professor; b. Nov. 30, 1940; s. Paul Harry and Bula (Owens) Ehrenbergh. BS, Coll. Charleston, 1962; MA, U. S.C., 1963; PhD, Tulane U., 1970. Instr. econs. and fin., U. New Orleans, 1965—68; asst. prof. econs. Auburn U., Ala., 1968—74, assoc. prof., 1974—82, prof., 1982—. Cons. U.S. Army C.E., New Orleans, 1964—65. Contbr. articles to profl. jours.; author: Andrew Dumford: A Black Sugar Planter in Antebellum Louisiana, 1981 (La. honor award, 1982), Emergence of Giant Enterprise, 1983, A History of Economics and Business at Auburn University, 1992; co-author: Democracy in Desperation: The Depression of 1893, 1998 (Choice Outstanding Acad. Title, 2000); editor (with Bessie E. Wten): Manufacturing: A Historiographical and Bibliographical Guide, 1990; editor: Two-Hundred Years of Eli Whitney's Cotton Gin, 1994, Andrew Durnford: A Black Sugar Planter in the Antebellum South, 1995, Extractives, Manufacturing and Services, 1992, Infrastructure and Services, 2000, Contbns. in Econ. and EEcon. History, 1980—2002, Wall St. Rev. of Books, 1981—89, Bus. Libr. Rev., 1990—2002, Essays in Econ. and Bus. History, 2004—. With USMC, 1957—63. Fellow, Tulane Edn. Found., 1964—65. Mem.: Rexford G. Tugwell Internat. Inst. for Great Depression Era Studies (v.p., treas., dir. 1992—), Econ. and Bus. Hist. Soc. (v.p. 1988—91, pres. 1991—92, CEO 2000—01), Bus. History Conf., So. Econ. Assn., Econ. History Assn., Agrl. History Soc., Am. Econ. Assn. Home: 102 Kimberly Dr Auburn AL 36832-6712 Office: Auburn U Dept Econs Bus Bldg 209 Auburn AL 36849 Office Phone: 334-844-2928. E-mail: DWhitten@Business.Auburn.edu.

WHITTEN, JERRY LYNN, chemistry professor; b. Bartow, Fla., Aug. 13, 1937; s. John Graves and Dorothy Iola (Jordan) W.; m. Mary Hill (div. Sept. 1977); 1 child, Jerrard John; m. Adela Chrzeszczyk, June 21, 1980; 1 child, Christina. BS in Chemistry, Ga. Inst. Tech., 1960, PhD, 1964. Cert. chemist. Rsch. assoc. to instr. Princeton (N.J.) U., 1963-65; asst. prof. chemistry Mich. State U., East Lansing, 1965-67, SUNY, Stony Brook, 1967-68, assoc. prof., 1968-73, prof., 1973-89, chmn. chemistry dept., 1985-89; prof. chemistry, dean Coll. Phys. and Math. Scis. N.C. State U., Raleigh, 1989-99. Vis. prof. Centre Européen de Calcul Atomique et Moléculaire, Orsay, France, 1974-75, Univ. Bonn and Wuppertal, Fed. Republic Germany, 1979-80, Eidgenossische Technische Hochschule, Zurich, Switzerland, 1984. Contbr. more than 160 articles to profl. jours. Bd. dirs. N.C. Sch. Sci. and Math Found., chair; bd. dirs. Burroughs Wellcome Fund. Recipient Alexander von Humboldt U.S. Sr. Scientist award, 1979; grantee Petroleum Rsch. Fund, 1966-67, 74-76, 77-81, NSF, 1967-72, U.S. Dept. Energy, 1977—; SDIO/ONR grantee, 1991-92; Alfred P. Sloan fellow, 1969-71. Mem. AAAS, Am. Phys. Soc., Am. Chem. Soc., N.Y. Acad. Scis., Sigma Xi (pres. N.C. chpt.), Phi Beta Kappa, Phi Kappa Phi. Democrat. Episcopalian. Avocations: boating, tennis, skiing. Office: NC State U Coll Dept Chemistry PO Box 8204 Raleigh NC 27695-0001 E-mail: j_whitten@ncsu.edu.

WHITTEN, LESLIE HUNTER, JR., author, newspaper reporter, poet; b. Jacksonville, Fla., Feb. 21, 1928; s. Leslie Hunter and Linnora (Harvey) W.; m. Phyllis Webber, Nov. 11, 1951; children: Leslie Hunter III, Andrew, Daniel, Deborah Wilson Engle. BA in Journalism/English magna cum laude, Lehigh U., 1950, LHD, 1989. Journalist Radio Free Europe, 1952-57, I.N.S., 1957-58, U.P.I., 1958, Washington Post, 1958-63; with Hearst Newspapers, 1963-66, asst. bur. chief, 1966-69; sr. investigator Jack Anderson's Washington Merry-Go-Round, 1969-92; pres. Athanor Inc., 1977-93. Vis. assoc. prof. Lehigh U., 1967-69; adj. prof. So. Ill. U., 1984. Author: Progeny of the Adder, 1965, Moon of the Wolf, 1967, Pinion the Golden Eagle, 1968, The Abyss, 1970, F. Lee Bailey, 1971, The Alchemist, 1973, Conflict of Interest, 1976, Washington Cycle, 1979, Sometimes a Hero, 1979, A Killing Pace, 1983, A Day Without Sunshine, 1985, The Lost Disciple, 1989, The Fangs of Morning, 1994, Sad Madrigals, 1997, Moses, the Lost Book of the Bible, 1999; contbr. numerous poems to anthologies and other publs. Vol. Hospice, 1987-2003. Served with AUS, 1946-48. Recipient hon. mention pub. service Washington Newspaper Guild, 1963, Edgerton award ACLU, 1974 Home and Office: 114 Eastmoor Dr Silver Spring MD 20901-1507 Office Phone: 301-593-5943. Personal E-mail: lhwhitjr@aol.com.

WHITTEN, MARY LOU, nursing educator; b. Vandalia, Ill., Apr. 8, 1946; d. Otto M. and Lucille (Mattes) Elam; m. Dennis L. Whitten, Aug. 27, 1966; children: Michael, Christopher, Andrew. BSN, Baylor U., 1968; MS in Nursing, So. Ill. U., 1990. RN, Ill. Instr. health occupations Okaw Vocat. Sch., Vandalia, Ill.; head nurse med.-surg. Fayette County Hosp., Vandalia; DON Kaskaskia Coll., Centralia, Ill. CPR instr. Am. Heart Assn. Vol. ARC. Mem. Am. Assn. of Women in C.C. Ill., Ill. Coun. Dirs. of Nursing, Phi Kappa Phi. Home: RR 3 Box 848 Vandalia IL 62471-9204 Office: Kaskaskia Coll 27210 College Rd Centralia IL 62801-7800 Office Phone: 618-545-3331. E-mail: mwhitten@kc.cc.il.us.

WHITTENBERG, IRA ORVILLE, lawyer; b. Ft. Worth; s. Ira Orville and Thyra Finch Whittenberg; m. Emma Jo Noland, Apr. 14, 1962; children: Ira Grant, Cheryl Lynn, Wendy Ann. BS in Indsl. Engring., So. Meth. U., 1957, LLB, 1961, LLM, 1977. Bar: Tex. 73. Contract mgr., corp. counsel Bell Helicopter Textron, Ft. Worth, 1961—89; dir. contracts, corp. counsel Murdock Engring., Irving, Tex., 1989—91; pvt. practice cons., mediator Colleyville, Tex., 1991—. Capt. USAF, 1955—57. Fellow: Nat. Contract Mgmt. Assn. (pres. 1962—); mem.: State Bar Tex. (award 2002), Toastmasters Internat. (chpt. pres. 1982—). Republican. Presbyterian. Avocations: sailing, bicycling. Home and Office: 3607 Cliffwood Dr Colleyville TX 76034

WHITTERS, JAMES PAYTON, III, lawyer, university administrator; b. Boston, Oct. 23, 1939; s. James P. Jr. and Norene (Jones) W.; m. Elizabeth Robertson, July 19, 1969; children: James P. IV, Catharine A. BA in History, Trinity Coll., Hartford, Conn., 1962; JD, Boston Coll., 1969; MA in Am. Studies, U. Mass., Boston, 2002. Bar: Mass. 1969, U.S. Dist. Ct. Mass. 1970, U.S. Ct. Appeals (1st cir.) 1972. Assoc. Ely, Bartlett, Brown & Proctor, Boston, 1969-74, Gaston Snow & Ely Bartlett, Boston, 1974-79, ptnr., 1979-88, Gaston & Snow, Boston, 1988-91; of counsel Peabody & Brown, Boston, 1991-95; dir. Office Career Devel., Suffolk U. Law Sch., Boston, 1995—, adj. prof. Am. legal history, 1997—. Bd. dirs., sec. Robertson Factories, Inc., Taunton, Mass., 1979—; v.p. Alkalol Co., Taunton, 1976-97, sr. v.p., 1997—; vis. tchr. Groton (Mass.) Sch., 1993-94; mem. Mass. Conflict Intervention Mediation Team, 1995—. Bd. dirs. New Eng. com. NAACP Legal Def. Fund, 1982—, Beacon Hill Nursery Sch., 1976-78, Mass. Appleseed Ctr. Law and Justice, 1997—; chmn. Mass. Outdoor Advt. Bd., Boston, 1975-81; vice chmn. Mass. Jud. Nominating Coun., Boston, 1983-87; trustee Trinity Coll., 1984-95; trustee, sec. Hurricane Island Outward Bound Sch., 1977-87; bd. dirs. Mass. affiliate Am. Heart Assn., 1979-98, chmn., 1989-91; bd. dirs. Greater Boston Legal Svcs., 1982-84, 93-99, Mass. Assn. Mediation Programs and Practitioners, 1993-98; founder Beacon Hill Seminars, 2000-2001, bd. dirs., 2001-02; facilitator Boston City Wide Dialogues on Racial and Ethnic Diversity, 2003-. Lt. (j.g.) USN, 1962-65. Recipient Alumni Excellence award Trinity Coll., 1987. Mem.: ABA, Boston Bar Assn. (standing com. on work-life balance, children's outreach task force, pub. svc. and criminal justice task force), Mass. Bar Assn., The Country Club (Brookline, Mass.). Democrat. Unitarian Universalist. Avocations: reading history, mountain climbing & jogging. Home: 44 Mount Vernon St Boston MA 02108-1302 Office Phone: 617-573-8093.

WHITTINGHAM, CHARLES ARTHUR, publisher, library administrator; b. Chgo., Feb. 11, 1930; s. Charles Arthur and Virginia (Hartke) W.; m. Jean Bragger Whittingham, June 4, 1955; children: Mary Elizabeth, Charles Arthur III, Philip Alexander, Leigh Ann. BS in English Lit. cum laude, Loyola U., Chgo., 1951. With McCall Corp., Chgo., 1956-59, Time, Inc., Chgo., 1959-62; pub.'s rep. Fortune mag., Time, Inc., N.Y.C., 1962-65, mgr. San Francisco, 1965-69; asst. to pub. Fortune, N.Y.C., 1969-70, asst. pub., 1970-78; pub. Life mag., N.Y.C., 1978-88; sr. v.p. N.Y. Pub. Libr., 1989-92; exec. prodr. Kunhardt Prodns., Inc., 1995—. Lt. j.g. USNR, 1951—55. Named to Athletic Hall of Fame Loyola U., Loyola Acad. Mem. Century Assn., Brook Club, The Pilgrims. Home and Office: 1 E 66th St 13D New York NY 10024 also: 5584 Bartram St Boca Raton FL 33433

WHITTINGHAM, HARRY EDWARD, JR., retired banker; b. Albany, N.Y., Dec. 25, 1918; s. Harry E. and Mary (Baer) Whittingham; m. Gladys D. Willstaedt, Sept. 2, 1942; children: Jeffrey A., Neal E. Grad., Stonier Grad. Sch. Banking, 1961. With Schenectady Trust Co., 1947-84, pres., chief exec. officer, 1974-82, chmn., chief exec. officer, 1982-84. Author (with Purdy, Schneider, Aldom): Automation in Banking, 1962. Vestryman Episcopal Ch. With AUS, 1941—46. Home: 2025 Cockrell Pt NW Kennesaw GA 30152

WHITTINGHAM, M(ICHAEL) STANLEY, chemist; b. Nottingham, Eng., Dec. 22, 1941; came to U.S., 1968, naturalized, 1980; s. William Stanley and Dorothy Mary (Findlay) W.; m. Georgina Judith Andai, Mar. 23, 1969; children: Jenniffer Judith, Michael Stanley. BA in Chemistry, Oxford U., 1964, MA, DPhil, 1968. Rsch. assoc., head solid state electrochemistry group Materials Ctr., Stanford U., 1968-72; mem. staff Exxon Rsch. Co., Linden, N.J., 1972—; group head solid state chem. physics, 1975-78; dir. solid state scis., 1978-80; mgr. chem. engring. tech., 1980-84; dir. phys. scis. Schlumberger Co., Ridgefield, Conn., 1984-88; prof. chemistry, dir. The Inst. for Materials Rsch., SUNY, 1988—; vice provost for rsch. SUNY, 1994-2000; vice-chair bd. dirs. Rsch. Found., 1995-2001. Cons., lectr. in field; JSPS fellow U. Tokyo. Author, editor papers in field; author 5 books. Recipient Gas Coun. scholarship, Oxford U., 1964-67. Mem. Electrochem. Soc. (Young Author award 1971, N.Y. chmn. 1980-81, Battery Rsch. award 2002, fellow 2004), Am. Chem. Soc. (chmn. solid state sect. 1987, chmn. Binghamton sect. 1991), Am. Phys. Soc., Materials Rsch. Soc. Achievements include patents in field; reversible (rechargeable) lithium batteries and methods for making intercalation batteries; method for making TiS2 mixed material cathodes, high briteness luminescent displays. Home: 396 Meeker Rd Vestal NY 13850-3230 Office: SUNY Dept Chemistry Binghamton NY 13902 E-mail: stanwhit@binghamton.edu.

WHITTINGTON, ANNE ELIZABETH, diabetes educator; b. Berea, Ohio, Apr. 4, 1957; d. Richard Murphy and Eleen Elizabeth (Cooney) Whittington. ADN, Sante Fe Coll., 1979; BSN, U. N.C., 1983; MSN, Med. Coll. Ga., 1990; MBA, Brenau U., 1997. Tchr. Nat. Cert. Bd. for Diabetes Educators; cert. water aerobics instr. Staff nurse U. Fla. Teaching Hosp., Gainesville, 1979-80, New Hanover Meml. Hosp., Wilmington, N.C., 1980-81, Cape Fear Meml. Hosp., Wilmington, 1983-84; home health nurse New Hanover Home Health Agy., Wilmington, 1984-85, Comprehensive Home Health Care, Augusta, Ga., 1985; coord. outreach edn. for Ga. Dept. of Human Resources Grant, Augusta, 1990—2000; dir. diabetes programs Naval Med. Ctr., San Diego, 2001—. Docent Augusta Richmond County Mus., 1987-91; dir. Our Lady of Peace Choir, North Augusta, 1990—; co-founder Cen. Savannah River Area Arthritis Support Group, Augusta, 1991—; Cath. chaplaincy Augusta Correctional Instn., 1991—. Recipient Woman of Excellence award Cen. Savannah River Area, 1992; named Outstanding Diabetes Educator, GADE, 1992, Outstanding Alumnus, Med. Coll. Ga. Sch. Nursing, 1992, Outstanding Diabetes Educator, Am. Assn. Diabetes Edn., 1993; torchbearer Atlanta Olympics, 1996. Mem.: Arthritis Health Profl. Assn., Ga. Nurses Assn., U. N.C. Sch. Nursing Alumni Assn. (bd. dirs. 1989—93), Am. Diabetes Assn., Am. Assn. Diabetes Educator (sec. visual impaired preson speciality practice group 1994—97, chair visual impaired person speciality group 1997—2000, bd.dirs. 1999—2002, treas. 2002—), Greater Augusta Diabetes Educators (chmn. profl. edn. 1991—2000, pres. 1995—97), ANA, Sigma Theta Tau (Grad. Student of Yr. 1991). Democrat. Roman Catholic. Avocations: music, water aerobics. Mailing: Attn: Health Promotion Dept 34800 Bob Wilson Dr Ste 301 San Diego CA 92134-1301 E-mail: aewhittington@nmcsd.med.navy.mil.

WHITTINGTON, CATHY DEE, chemist; b. Upland, Pa., Oct. 29, 1955; d. Frank Adam and Virginia Helen (Keil) W. AA in biology, Widenen Univ., 1984, BA, 1996. Asst. mgr. McDonald's, Brookhaven, Pa., 1973-75; blood lab. tech. CCMC, Chester, Pa., 1976-77; environmental tech. Scott Paper Internat., Chester, Pa., 1979-83; paramedic V AmbulCare Ambulance, Phila., 1984-96; sr. rsch. assoc. Scott Paper Corp. R&D, Phila., 1996-97; rsch. cons. Kimberly Clark Corp., Chester, Pa., 1997; process specialist HIA Cons., Chester, 1997-99; chemist Novell Inc., Provo, Utah, 1999—. Network engr. Novell, Inc., Provo, Utah, Scott Paper House of Quality, team orgn. Scott Paper R&D. Amb. lt. Parkside Vol. Fire Co., Parkside, Pa., 1977—. Recipient Military History Excellence award Daughter's of Founders & Patriots of Am., 1977, tech. excellence award, 1987-91. Mem. Tech. Orgn. of Pulp & Paper Ins., Nat. Archieves (assoc.). Republican. Baptist. Avocations: walking, hiking, reading. Home: 139 W Roland Rd Brookhaven PA 19015-3217 Office: Novell Inc 301 W Germantown Pike Bldg 1 Norristown PA 19403-4227

WHITTINGTON, FELICIA TRENISE, social services administrator, educator; b. New Orleans, Feb. 2, 1971; d. Audrey Mea Whittington-Simmons. MA, Jackson (Miss.) State U., 1996. Exec. dir. Family Life Ctr. Tougaloo (Miss.) Coll., 1996—, asst. dir. Owens Health & Wellness Ctr., 2002—. Adj. prof. dept. criminal justice Jackson State U., 1997—. Mem. youth adv. bd. United Way, Jackson, 2000—02; dir. Family and Cmty. Violence Prevention Program. Named one of Outstanding Young Women of Am., 1997; grantee, Office of Minority Health Family and Cmty. Violence Prevention Program, 1995—, Target Stores, 2002, Dept. Edn., 2001, 2002. Mem.: Delta Sigma Theta. Avocations: community service projects, reading. Office: Tougaloo Coll Family Life Ctr 500 W County Line Rd Tougaloo MS 39174 E-mail: felicia.whittington@tougaloo.edu.

WHITTINGTON, FREDERICK BROWN, JR., business administration educator; b. Sept. 22, 1934; m. Marjorie Ann Babington; children: Frederick Brown III, Marjorie Ellen, Lisa Anne. SB, MIT, 1958; MBA, Tulane U., 1965; PhD, La. State U., 1969. Staff economist Miss. Rsch. Commn., Jackson, 1961-64; sr. assoc. econ. rsch. Gulf South Rsch. Inst., Baton Rouge, 1966-69; asst. prof. bus. adminstrn. Emory U., Atlanta, 1969-73, assoc. prof., 1973-79, prof., 1979-96, prof. emeritus, 1997—, dir. customer bus. devel. track, 1991-94. Bd. dirs. Gwinnett Industries, Inc.; mem. forecasting panel Fed. Res. Bank Atlanta; vis. prof. Johannes Kepler U., Linz, Austria, 1983, 84, 89, 95-20034 guest lectr. Austrian Univs., Linz, Vienna, Innsbruck and Klagenfurt; presenter workshops; cons. in field. Contbr. articles and reports to profl. jours. Mktg. plan, mgmt. audit State of Miss., Park Commn.; past chmn., bd. deacons Decatur Presbyn. Ch.; mem. adv. bd. DeKalb/Rockdale Svc. Ctr., ARC. Capt. USNR, ret., 1994. Recipient Badge of Hon., Austrian Mktg. Rsch. Soc., 1996, recipient Trauner prize for ednl. innovation Upper Austrian Econ. Chamber, 1997; Sears Roebuck Found. fellow, 1965-66. Mem. Am. Mktg. Assn., Nat. Assn. Purchasing Mgmt., So. Mktg. Assn., Coun. for Logistics Mgmt., Warehousing Edn. and Rsch. Coun., Omicron Delta Kappa, Beta Gamma Sigma, Delta Tau Delta. Office: Emory U Goizueta Bus Sch Atlanta GA 30322-0001 E-mail: brown_whittington@bus.emory.edu.

WHITTINGTON, LORIN DALE, music educator; b. Balt., Nov. 1, 1951; s. Cicero Edward Whittington and Dorothy Virginia Peters. MusB, Appalachian State U., 1979. Cert. tchr. music k-12 N.C. Tchr. Hall Fletcher Mid. Sch., Asheville, NC, 1979—81, Hill St. Mid. Sch., Asheville, 1979—81, Owen H.S., Swannanoa, NC, 1981—97, Owen Mid. Sch., Swannanoa, 1997—. Chorus master Mid-Atlantic Opera Co., Asheville, 1985—86. Composer: (sound recording) Rochelle, 1972. Mem.: Music Educators Nat. Conf. Avocations: genealogy, art, computer graphics, guitar, travel. Home: 19 Clairmont Ave Asheville NC 28804 Office: Owen Mid Schl 730 Old US 70 Swannanoa NC 28778 Personal E-mail: vytiense@appleisp.net.

WHITTINGTON, RALPH EDWARD, curator, librarian; b. Washington, D.C., Jan. 13, 1945; s. Ralph John and Mildred May Whittington; m. Jennifer Kay Rutland, June 7, 1969 (div.); 1 child, Amanda Anne. Grad., Surrattsville H.S., Clinton, Md., 1963. Deck attendant Libr. of Congress, Washington, 1963—76, searcher libr. materials locator, 1976—85, curator main reading rm., 1985—2000; cons. Mus. Sex, N.Y.C., 2001—. Avocation: vinyl record collector. Home: 9204 Greenfield Ln Clinton MD 20735

WHITTINGTON, STEPHEN LUNN, museum director; b. Washington, Jan. 31, 1956; s. Charles Lunn and Alice Marie (Doyle) W.; m. Christine Ann Carlson, Aug. 18, 1979; children: Daniel, Joseph. AB in Anthropology, U. Chgo., 1977; MA, Pa. State U., 1981, PhD, 1989. Dir. Proyecto Arqueologico Ostuman, Copan, Honduras, 1989, U. Maine Hudson Mus., 1991—2002, Teozacoalco Archaeol. Project, 2002—; asst. curator collections Wyo. Hist. and Geol. Soc., Wilkes-Barre, Pa., 1989-90; cooperating assoc. prof. dept. anthropology U. Maine, 1991—2002. Dir. Iximche Osteological Project, 1992—95; adj. assoc. prof. dept. anthropology Wake Forest U., dir. Mus. Anthropology, 2002—. Author: Archaeology and Ethnohistory of Iximche, 2003; editor: Bones of the Maya, 1997; contbr. articles to profl. jours. Active Maine State Mus. Commn., 1998—2002. Grantee Wenner-Gren Found. for Anthrop. Rsch., 1992-93, NSF, 1989, Inst. Internat. Edn., 1988, Found. for the Advancement of Mesoamerican Studies, 1995, 99, 2002, NEH, 1997. Mem. Am. Assn. Mus., N.C. Mus. Coun., Soc. for Am. Archaeology, Southeastern Mus. Conf. Avocations: jogging, fencing. Home: 1307 Brookwood Dr Winston Salem NC 27106 Office: Wake Forest Univ Mus Anthropology PO Box 7267 Winston Salem NC 27109 Office Phone: 336-758-5827. E-mail: whittisl@wfu.edu.

WHITTINGTON, THOMAS LEE, lawyer; b. Waukesha, Wis., July 14, 1943; s. Floyd Leon and Winifred Carol (McDonald) W.; m. Ashley J. Whittington; children: Erin Elizabeth, Hilary Ann. BA, Coll. of Wooster, 1965; JD, U. Mich., 1967. Bar: Trust Terr. of Pacific Islands 1967, Mich. 1969, Wash. 1974, U.S. Dist. Ct. (we. dist.) Wash. 1974. Vol. Peace Corps, Micronesia, 1967-69; staff asst. legis. office Dept. Interior, Washington, 1969-74; ptnr. Thomas, Whittington, Anderson, Bergan & Studebaker, Issaquah, Wash., 1974—2000, Scottsdale, Ariz., 2000—. Home: 27684 N 72d Way Scottsdale AZ 85262

WHITTLE, MACK IRA, JR., bank executive; b. Columbia, S.C., Nov. 5, 1948; s. Mack Ira and Eleanor (Howell) Whittle; m. Jennifer Ann Mooney, May 28, 2000; children from previous marriage: Quincy Nye, Patricia Cameron, Lee Forester. BS, U. S.C., 1971, MBA, 1975; grad. Banking Sch. South, La. State U., 1979. Trust officer Bankers Trust S.C. (formerly State Bank and Trust Co.), Greenville, from 1974, v.p. comml. bus. devel., to 1979, v.p. city exec. Myrtle Beach, 1979-82; sr. v.p., regional officer N.C. Nat. Bank (formerly Bankers Trust S.C.), Greenville, 1982-86; pres. & CEO Carolina First Corp., Greenville, 1986—; also bd. dirs. Carolina First Bank, 1991—. Bd. dirs. Carolina First Corp., Carolina First Savs. Bank, R.L. Bryan & Co. Trustee U. S.C., Columbia, 1984; bd. dirs. campaign, cabinet Greenville United Way, 1984-85; bd. dirs. Community Found. Greater Greenville, Met. Arts Coun., Greenville Tech. Coll. Found., Carolina Piedmont Found., Inc.; trustee U. S.C.; bd. dirs., v.p., treas. Mus. Assn. Greenville/County Mus. Art; chmn. bd. dirs. Greenville Urban League; adv. bd. Peace Ctr.; chmn. Christ Ch. Endowment Corp., Greenville, 1989—; mem. ch. sch. bd. visitors Christ Episcopal Ch. Recipient Disting. Alumnus award U. S.C. Coll. Bus. Adminstrn., 1994; named Outstanding Young Banker S.C., 1988. Mem. S.C. Bankers Assn. (bd. dirs. 1989—, pres. 1993-94), Am. Bankers Assn., Ind. Banks S.C., Ind. Bankers Assn. Am., S.C. C. of C. (bd. dirs. 1989—), U. S.C. Alumni Assn. (past pres., Entrepreneur of Yr. in Fin. Industry 1993). Episcopalian. Avocations: running, reading. Office: Carolina First Bank PO Box 1029 Greenville SC 29602

WHITTLESEY, JUDITH HOLLOWAY, public relations executive; b. Bartlesville, Okla., Dec. 28, 1942; d. Harry Haynes and Suzanne (Arnote) Holloway; m. Dennis Jeffrey Whittlesey, Aug. 3, 1968; children: Kristin Arnote, Kevin Jeffrey. BA, U. Okla., 1964; postgrad., Tulsa U., 1965, U. Va., 1971-72. Staff aide Office of the V.P. of U.S., Washington, 1979-81, Com. for Future of Am., Washington, 1981-82; dep. dir. scheduling and advance Mondale-Ferraro Campaign, Washington, 1982-84; dir. media rels. Susan Davis Internat., Washington, 1986-87, v.p., 1987-88, exec. v.p., 1988—. Bd. dir. Cultural Alliance of Greater Washington, 1983-93, Washington Project for the Arts, 1987-93, Levine Sch. Music, 1993-98, Food Rsch. and Action Ctr., 1993—; bd. dir. Decatur House, Suited For Change. Chevy Chase Presbyn. Ch., Washington, Leadership Washington, 2004. Avocation: art/contemporary. Office: Susan Davis Internat 1000 Vermont Ave NW Washington DC 20005-4903 Office Phone: 202-408-0808. E-mail: jwhittlesey@susandavis.com.

WHITTY, JEFF, playwright, actor; b. 1972; s. John Whitty. BA, U. Oregon, 1993; MFA, NYU Tisch Sch. of the Arts. Actor: (TV series) As the World Turns; author: (plays) The Plank Project, Suicide Weather, Balls, The Hiding Place, (Broadway plays) Avenue Q, 2003 (Tony award best book of a musical, 2004, Drama Desk nom. for outstanding book of a musical, 2004); actor: (plays) Freedomland, The Beard of Avon. Office: John Golden Theatre 252 W 45th St New York NY 10010*

WHITWAM, DAVID RAY, appliance manufacturing company executive; b. Stanley, Wis., Jan. 30, 1942; s. Donald R. and Lorraine (Stoye) Whitwam; m. Barbara Lynne Peterson, Aug. 13, 1963; children: Mark, Laura, Thomas. BS, U. Wis., 1967. Gen. mgr. sales So. Calif. divsn. Whirlpool Corp., Los Angeles, 1975-77, mdse. mgr. ranges Benton Harbor, Mich., 1977-79, dir. builder mktg., 1979-80, v.p. builder mktg., 1980-83, v.p. whirlpool sales, 1983-85, vice-chmn., chief mktg. officer, 1985-87, chmn., pres., CEO, 1987-99, chmn., CEO, 1999—2004. Bd. dirs. Combustion Engring. Inc., Stamford, Conn. Mem. Nat. Council Housing Industry, Washington; pres. bd. dirs. The Soup Kitchen, Benton Harbor, 1980. Capt. U.S. Army. Fellow: Aspen Inst.; mem.: Point O'Woods Club (Benton Harbor). Republican. Lutheran.*

WHITWORTH, CAMILLE, newscaster; b. Houston; BA in Mass Comm., Hampton U., 1993. Reporter WAVE 3 TV, Louisville; gen. assignment reporter NBC 17, Raleigh, NC. Creator, co-host WAVE 3 Step Awards; reporter Winter Olympics for NBC 17, 2002. Vol. Nat. Assn. Black Journalists, NAACP, ARC; active Louisville Ballet. Nominee Spot News coverage, Ohio Valley Regional Emmy Award; recipient numerous awards, AP, award for excellence in reporting, Ky. chpt. Nat. Press Photographers Assn. Office: NBC 17 Studios 1205 Front St Raleigh NC 27609

WHITWORTH, HALL BAKER, forest products company executive; b. St. Paul, N.C., Feb. 15, 1919; s. A. Frederick and Maude Ethel (Baker) W.; m. Mary Margaret Mease, May 18, 1946; children: Hall Baker, Laura Ellen, David Allen. Student, Miss. So. Coll., 1942, U. N.C., 1957. With Champion Internat., Canton, N.C., 1936-62, mgr. materials, 1956-62, dir. materials packages div. Chgo., 1962-65, dir. purchase U.S. Plywood-Champion Papers, Inc. (now champion Internat. Corp.) Hamilton, Ohio, 1965-68, dep. dir. corporate materials services, 1966, v.p., dir. purchase, 1968-75, v.p. materials Stamford, Conn., 1975—, dir., 1975—, now ret.; v.p., dir. So. Agrl. Co., 1985—; pres., dir. H. Whitworth Enterprises, Cin., 1985—. Dir. Pathfork-Harlan Coal Co. Served with U.S. Army, 1942-46. Recipient Thomas award Carolina-Va. Purchasing Agts. Assn., 1963 Mem. Am. Paper Inst. (chmn. energy subcom.), Am. Mgmt. Assn. (v.p. purchasing, transp. and phys. distbn. div. council) Clubs: Canton Toastmakers (founder, 1st pres.). Lodges: Elks; Lions. Methodist. Home and Office: 3350 Brookwater Cir Orlando FL 32822-5800 E-mail: hall_whitworth@msn.com.

WHITWORTH, HORACE ALGERNON, mechanical engineer; b. Kingston, Jamaica, W.I., Mar. 24, 1953; came to U.S., 1967; s. Egbert Leopold and Violet Cecilia (Trouth) W. BSME, U. Mass., 1975; MS, George Washington U., 1977, DSc, 1983. Asst. prof. Howard U., Washington, 1983-89, dir. grad. studies dept. mech. engring., 1988-96, assoc. prof. mech. engring., 1989-99, prof. mech. engring., 1999—, chmn. dept. mech. engring., 2004—. Contbr. articles to profl. jours. Bd. dirs. Jamaica Support Found., Washington, 1991-95. Recipient Sr. Fellows Found. award Pacific Telesis Found., 1988, Prof. Acad. award Honeywell Corp., 1992; rsch. grantee in field. Mem. ASME (bd. dirs. Washington chpt. 1994—, Instr. of Yr. student chpt. 1985-86, 87-89), Am. Soc. Metals, Soc. for Exptl. Mechanics. Democrat. Methodist. Achievements include development of mathematical models to evaluate fatigue damage development in fibrous composite materials. Office: Howard U 2300 6th St NW Washington DC 20059-2323 Office Phone: 202-806-6600. Business E-Mail: hwhitworth@howard.edu.

WHITWORTH, J. BRYAN, JR., former oil company executive, lawyer; b. Baton Rouge, Aug. 14, 1938; s. Jennings Bryan Sr. and Virginia Ann (Calvert) W.; m. Sue Alice Walters, July 15, 1961 (Jan. 1982); children: Catherine Ann, Elizabeth, Suzanne Virginia; m. Donna Axum, Mar. 1, 1984. BS Pre-Law, U. Ala., 1961, LLM, 1964. Assoc. Cabaniss, Johnston, Gardner & Clark, Birmingham, Ala., 1964-66; gen. AT&T, Washington and N.Y.C., 1966-71; atty. Phillips Petroleum Co., Bartlesville, Okla., 1971-77, sr. counsel, 1977-79, assoc. gen. counsel, 1979-81, v.p. govt. relations, 1981-95, sr. v.p., gen. counsel and govt. relations, 1995—2003. Bd. dirs. Salk Inst. Biotechnology/Industry Assn. Inc., San Diego; mem. policy devel com. Am. Petroleum Inst., Washington, 1982—, Gov.'s Task Force on Higher Edn. in Okla. and the Council for Regrn. of State Govt., Oklahoma City, 1985-87; bd. dirs. First Nat. Bank & First Bancshares Inc., Bartlesville. Former editor-in-chief Ala. Law Rev., U. Ala. Mem. Okla. Bar Assn., N.Y. Bar Assn., D.C. Bar Assn., Bartlesville Area C. of C. (v.p., bd. dirs. 1985-87, pres. 1987-88). Lodges: Rotary.

WHITWORTH, KATHRYNNE ANN, professional golfer; b. Monahans, Tex., Sept. 27, 1939; d. Morris Clark and Dama Ann (Robinson) W. Student, Odessa (Tex.) Jr. Coll., 1958. Joined tour Ladies Profl. Golf Assn., 1959—. Mem. adv. Square Two Golf Co. Named to Hall of Fame Ladies Profl. Golf Assn., Tex. Sports Hall of Fame, Tex. Golf Hall of Fame, World Golf Hall of Fame; Capt. of Solhiem Cup, 1990-92. Mem. Ladies Profl. Golf Assn. (sec. 1962-63, v.p. 1965, 73, 88, pres. 1967, 68, 71, 89, 1st mem. to win over $1,000,000). Office: care Ladies Profl Golf Assn 2570 Volusia Ave Daytona Beach FL 32114-8144

WHITWORTH, WENDY WALKER, cable network executive; b. Bronxville, N.Y. m. Ralph Whitworth; children: Amaya, Walker. BA, LLD (hon.), Hollins Coll. TV prodr. White House CNN, 1980-93, sr. v.p., sr. exec. prodr. Larry King Live (TV), 1993—. Sr. event prodr. super-power summits CNN, 1984, 88, 92, presdl. inaugurations, 1989, 93. Recipient Houston Internat. Film Festival award, 1988, Best Talk Show Series award CableAce, 1993; named one of 20 Most Fascinating Women in Politics by George Mag., Named One of the Most Influential People, Brills Content, 1999. Office: One CNN Ctr 1 Cnn Ctr NW Atlanta GA 30303-2762

WHITWORTH, WILLIAM A. magazine editor; b. Hot Springs, Ark., Feb. 13, 1937; s. William C. and Lois Virginia (McNabb) W.; m. Carolyn Hubbard, Dec. 27, 1969; children— Matthew, Katherine. BA, U. Okla., 1960. Reporter Ark. Gazette, Little Rock, 1960—63; reporter N.Y. Herald Tribune, 1963—65; staff writer The New Yorker, 1966—72, assoc. editor, 1973—80; editor-in-chief The Atlantic Monthly, Boston, 1981—99, editor emeritus, 1999—; editor-at-large The American Scholar, Washington, 2002—04. Office: Atlantic Monthly 77 N Washington St Ste 500 Boston MA 02114-1916 Personal E-mail: ww131@comcast.net.

WHORISKEY, ROBERT DONALD, lawyer; b. Cambridge, Mass., May 9, 1929; s. John Joseph and Katherine Euphemia (MacDonald) W.; m. Martha Beebe Poutas, Apr. 16, 1966; children: Alexandra, Jonathan, Eliza. AB, Harvard U., 1952; JD, Boston Coll., 1958; LLM, NYU, 1960. Bar: Mass. 1958, NY 1963, U.S. Tax Ct. 1961, U.S. Claims Ct. 1969, U.S. Dist. Ct. (so. dist.) NY 1969, U.S. Ct. Customs 1971, U.S. Ct. Appeals (2d cir.) 1972, U.S. Supreme Ct. 1974, U.S. Ct. Appeals (3d cir.) 1983, U.S. Ct. Appeals (DC cir.) 1991. Sr. trial atty. Office Chief Counsel, IRS, NYC, 1960-67; assoc. Curtis, Mallet-Prevost, Colt & Mosle, NYC, 1967-70, ptnr., 1970-2000, of counsel, 2001—, exec. com., 1978-82, chmn. tax dept., 1982-87. Bd. dirs. InterNat. Tax Inst., v.p., lectr., 1980-84, chmn. bd., pres., lectr., 1985-87; lectr. Practicing Law Inst., World Trade Inst., Tax Execs. Inst., Am. Mgmt. Assn., Coun. for Internat. Tax Edn.; bd. dirs. Life Ins. Co. of Boston and NY, Inc. Author: Foreign Trusts, 1977, Annual Institute on International Taxation, 1966, 80, 81, (with Sidney Pine, Ralph Seligman) Tax and Business Benefits of the Bahamas, 1986; contbg. author: International Boycotts, CCH Federal Tax Service, 1988, CCH Smart Tax CD-ROM: Third Party Information, John Wiley and Sons, Inc.'s Transfer Pricing, 1993, Transfer Pricing Under IRC & 482: Overview and Planning, Part I, 1996, Accuracy Related Penalty Regulations for Transfer Pricing, Part II, 1997, Third Party Information, Part III, 1997, U.S. Taxation of International Operations, Warren, Gorham Lamont, 1998; mem. editl. adv. bd. Corp. Bus. Taxation Monthly, 2000—. Trustee, treas. Montessori Sch. Westchester, 1974-77; mem. bd. ethics Village of Larchmont, NY, 1988—. With U.S. Army, 1952-54. Mem. ABA (com. on alternative tax sys. tax sect. 1994—, com. on ct. procedure tax sec. 1997—), NY State Bar Assn. (com. on practice and procedure tax sect. 1990—), Harvard Club, Larchmont Yacht Club. Democrat. Roman Catholic. Office: Curtis Mallet-Prevost Colt & Mosle 101 Park Ave 35th Fl New York NY 10178-0061 Office Phone: 212-696-6031. E-mail: rwhoriskey@cm-p.com., rwhoriskey@aol.com.

WHORTON, M. DONALD, occupational and environmental health physician, epidemiologist; b. Las Vegas, N.Mex., Jan. 25, 1943; s. R. H. and Rachel (Siegal) Whorton; m. Diana L. Obrinsky, Apr. 9, 1972; children: Matthew Richard, Laura Elizabeth, Julie Hannah. Student, U.S. Naval Acad., 1961—62; B of Biology, N.Mex. Highlands U., 1964; MD, U. N.Mex., 1968; MPH, Johns Hopkins U., 1973. Intern Boston City Hosp., 1968—69; resident in pathology U. N.Mex., Albuquerque, 1969—71; instr., resident in medicine Balt. City Hosp., 1972—74; instr. Johns Hopkins U., Balt.; assoc. dir. divsn. emergency medicine Balt. City Hosps., 1974—75; clin. asst. prof. divsn. ambulatory and cmty. medicine U. Calif. Sch. Medicine, San Francisco, 1975—77; lectr. U. Calif. Sch. Pub. Health, San Francisco, 1975—79; med. dir. labor occup. health program Inst. Indsl. Rels., Ctr. for Labor Rsch. and Edn., 1975—79, assoc. clin. prof. occup. medicine, 1979—87; prin. Environ. Health Assocs., Inc., Oakland, 1978—88; v.p. ENSR Health Scis., 1988—94; pvt. practice Alameda, Calif., 1994—2001; with WorkCare, 2001—. Chmn. adv. com. for hazard evaluation svc. and info. system Indsl. Relations Dept., State of Calif., 1979—84; cons. in field; chmn. statewide adv. com. on occupl. and environ. health U. Calif. Ctrs., 1996—. Contbr. articles to profl. jours. Recipient Upjohn Achievement award, 1968; scholar, Robert Wood Johnson Found., 1972—74. Fellow: Am. Coll. Occupl. and Environ. Medicine, Am. Coll. Epidemiology; mem.: Inst. of Medicine of NAS, Calif. Med. Assn. (adv. panel on occupl. and environ. medicine), Soc. for Occupl. and Environ. Health, APHA, Alpha Omega Alpha. Office: WorkCare 1320 Harbor Bay Pkwy # 115 Alameda CA 94502-6556 Office Phone: 510-748-6900 201. Personal E-mail: whobrin@lmi.net. Business E-Mail: dwhorton@workcare.com.

WHYBARK, DAVID CLAY, business educator, researcher; b. Tacoma, Sept. 18, 1935; s. Clay Alfred and Irene (Stanton) W.; m. Neva Jo Richardson, July 6, 1957; children: Michael David, Suzanne Marie (dec.). BS, U. Wash., 1957; MBA, Cornell U., 1960; PhD, Stanford U., 1967. Rsch. assoc. Stanford (Calif.) U., 1962-67; asst. prof. Ariz. State U., Tempe, 1965-66; assoc. prof. Purdue U., West Lafayette, Ind., 1967-76; prof. Ind. U., Bloomington, 1976-90; Macon G. Patton disting. prof. U. N.C., Chapel Hill, 1990—. Vis. prof. Shanghai Inst. Mech. Engring., 1986-87, Chinese U. of Hong Kong, 1996, Victoria U., New Zealand, 1996, Canterbury U., New Zealand, 1996; adj. prof. Inst. for Mgmt. Devel., Lausanne, Switzerland, 1981-82, 85-90; dir., founder Global Mfg. Rsch. Group, 1990—, cons. in field. Author: Master Production Scheduling: Theory and Practice, 1979, Manufacturing Planning Control Systems, 1984, International Operations Management, 1989, Integrated Production and Inventory Management, 1993, Why ERP?, 2000, Manufacturing Planning and Control Systems for Supply Chain Management, 2004; editor: Internat. Jour. Prodn. Econs., 1991-95, Global Manufacturing Practices, 1993. Recipient Lilly Alumni MBA Tchg. Excellence award, 1990, Disting. Rsch. award Kenan-Flagler Sch., 1998. Fellow Decision Scis. Inst. (past pres., Disting. Svc. award 1984), Pan Pacific Bus. Assn. (mem. coun.); mem. Am. Prodn. Inventory Control Soc., Internat. Soc. Inventory Rsch. (mem. coun., pres. 2000-02). Avocations: travel, winemaking. Office: U NC Kenan-Flagler Sch Chapel Hill NC 27599-3490 Office Phone: 919-962-3206. E-mail: clay_whybark@unc.edu.

WHYBROW, PETER CHARLES, psychiatrist, educator, director, author; b. Hertfordshire, Eng., June 13, 1939; U.S. citizenship, 1975; s. Charles Ernest and Doris Beatrice (Abbott) W.; children: Katherine, Helen. Student, Univ. Coll., London, 1956-59; MB BS, Univ. Coll., 1962; diploma psychol. medicine, Conjoint Bd., London, 1968; MA (hon.), Dartmouth Coll., 1974, U. Pa., 1984. House officer endocrinology Univ. Coll. Hosp., 1962, sr. house physician psychiatry, 1963-64; house surgeon St. Helier Hosp., Surrey, Eng., 1963; house officer pediatrics Prince of Wales Hosp., London, 1964; resident psychiatry U. N.C. Hosp., 1965-67, instr., research fellow, 1967-68; mem. sci. staff neuropsychiat. research unit Charshalton, Surrey, 1968-69, dir. residency tng. psychiatry Dartmouth Med. Sch., Hanover, N.H., 1969-71, prof. psychiatry, 1970-84, chmn. dept., 1970-78, exec. dean, 1980-83; prof., chmn. dept. psychiatry U. Pa., Phila., 1984-96, Ruth Meltzer prof. psychiatry, 1992; psychiatrist-in-chief Hosp. U. Pa., 1984-96; prof. psychiatry and biobehavioral scis., chmn. dept. psychiatry Sch. Medicine UCLA, 1996—, dir. Neuropsychiatric Inst., 1996—, physician-in-chief Neuropsychiatric Hosp., 1996-99, Judson Braun Prof. of Psychiatry, 1999—. Dir. psychiatry Dartmouth Hitchock Affiliated Hosp., 1970-78; vis. scientist NIMH, 1978-79; cons. VA, 1970—, NIMH, 1972—; chmn. test com. Nat. Bd. Med. Examiners, 1977-84; researcher psychoendrocrinology. Author: Mood Disorders: Toward a New Psychobiology, 1984, The Hibernation Response, 1988, A Mood Apart, 1997; editor: Psychosomatic Medicine, 1977; mem. editl. bd. Cmty. Psychiatry, Psychiat. Times, Directions in Psychiatry, Neuropsychopharmacology, Depression; contbr. articles to profl. jours. Recipient Anclote Manor award psychiat. rsch. U. N.C., 1967, Sr. Investigator award nat. Alliance for Rsch. into Schizophrenia and Depression, 1989; Josiah Macy Jr. Found. scholar, 1978-79; fellow Cen. for Advanced Studies in Behavioral Sci., Stanford, 1993-94; recipient Lifetime Investigator award NDMDA, 1996; decorated Knight of Merit, Sovereign Order of St. John of Jerusalem, 1993. Fellow AAAS, Am. Psychiat. Assn., Royal Coll. Psychiatrist (founding mem.), Am. Coll. Psychiatrists, Ctr. Advanced Study of Behavioral Scis. (hon.), Soc. Psychosomatic Rsch. London (hon.); mem. Am. Assn. Chmn. Depts. Psychiatry (pres. 1977-78), Royal Soc. Medicine, Am. Psychopath Assn., Am. Coll. Neuropsychopharmacology, Soc. Biol. Psychiatry, N.Y. Acad. Scis., Soc. Neurosci., Sigma Xi, Alpha Omega Alpha. Office: UCLA Sch Medicine Neuropsychiat Rsch Inst 760 Westwood Plz Los Angeles CA 90095-8353 Address: UCLA Psychr & Biobehav Sci NPI & H Box 951759 C7-463NPI Los Angeles CA 90095-1759 Fax: 310-825-3942. Business E-Mail: pwhybrow@mednet.ucla.edu.

WHYTE, BRUCE LINCOLN, management executive, marketing professional; b. NYC, Mar. 13, 1941; s. Lincoln Dodge and Louise (Connor) W. BS, Fordham U., NY, 1962; MS, NYU, 1963. Editor corp. planning Am. Airlines, NYC, 1963-65; sr. mktg. analyst Ea. Airlines, NYC, 1965-67; v.p. Deckcraft Corp., NYC, 1967-69; founder, pres. Original Print Collectors Group, NYC, 1972; chmn. bd. OPCG (Subs. Reader's Digest), NYC, 1980-84; pres. Bruce Whyte Enterprises, internat. fine arts bus., NYC, 1984-92, Bruce Whyte Bus. Devel. Co., 1998—, Bruce Whyte Cons., 1998—. Cons. mktg. The Prudential Co., NYC, 1986, Am. Express, NYC, 1987; sr. mktg. cons. A.R.T. Corp., NYC, 1988; bus. cons. Mystic Seaport Mus., 1990-; Am. Art liaison Dr. of the World, Paris, 1992; chmn. Bus. Incubator Group Corp. Kingston, NY, 1993-; gen. mgr. Sherpa's Pet Trading Co., NYC, 1996; exec. v.p. Sanctuary, Inc., NYC, 1996-99, chmn. nat. bd. advisors, 2000-, v.p. bd. dirs., 2004-; cons. NY State coun. on the Arts, 1996-97; registered expert witness Dept. Treasury, 1983-; mng. dir. Venture Capital Forum, 1995-96; tech. assistance program cons. NY State Govt., 1996-; trustee Integrity Global Asset Mgmt., 1999-; gen. devel. dir. First Alert, Rockville Centre, NY, 1998-2002; pres. disaster recovery plans and response devel. Disaster Recovery Experts, Inc., Rockville Centre, 1999—; trustee Dow Jones Internet Index Fund/Dow Jones, Global Biotech. Index Fund, Dow Jones Global Wireless Commn. Fund Index, Wakefield, RI, 1999-2001; hon. chmn. Congl. Bus. Adv. Coun., 2002, spkr. Congress, 2003—; dep. dir. gen. Am.'s Internat. Biog. Ctr., 2000—. Editor: Art Newsletter OPCG Newsletter, 1972-84 (Best award in U.S.A. 1983-84). Sr. advisor U.S. Congl. Adv. Bd., Washington, 1981-83; chmn. Com. U.S. Senatorial Bus. Adv. Bd., Washington, 1981-83, 2002—; advisor NY Dept. State, 1993; trustee, v.p. Hist. Preservation Soc., NYC 1986-92, U.S. art liaison Found. Mitterand (The Universal Declaration of Human Rights) on behalf of Amnesty Internat., UN, UNESCO, High Commn. on Refugees, Nat. Mus., Heads of State, Paris, NYC, 1989; consumer art protection legis. advisor, atty. gen. NY State Senate and Assembly, 1981; pres. Ulster Arts Alliance, 1993-96; chmn. Kingston Carnegie Libr./Pub. Mus., 1993, Mus. Arts and Tech. Old City Hall, 1994-95; trustee Entrepreneurial Catalyst Forum, 1994-96; advisor Congl. Bus. Commn., 2002—, sustaining hon. chmn., 2003—; Comn. Congl. Com. voting del. to U.S. Congress, The White House and IRS, 2002—; mem. nat. adv. bd. Am. Security Coun., 1981-2004; dep. dir. gen. Ams. Internat. Biog. Ctr., 2002-, presenter of NYC homeland security awards to former NYC police commr. Bernard Kerrick on behalf of Sept. 11 disaster recovery efforts, 2002, and police commr. Raymond Kelly, 2003; dep. dir. gen. for Americas of the Internat. Biog. Ctr., Eng., 2002-; hon. co-chmn. Ann. Formal Pres.'s Dinner, 2003, Ann. Bus. Adv. Coun. Bd. Meeting honoring Pres. George W. Bush, 2003. Recipient Best of Art Catalogues award, Sroge Colorado Springs, 1983, Gold medal Congress Majority Whip Tom DeLay, 2002-03, Internat. Order of Merit, 2003; named to U.S. Congl. Bus. Honor Roll, 2002, Nat. Rep. Exec. Com. Congl. Spkrs. Cir., 2002; Artist fellow, 1988-, U.S. Businessman of Yr. Nat. Rep. Congl. Com. CC U.S., 2003. Mem. Fine Arts Publ. Assn. (bd. dirs. 1984—), Nat. Arts Club (gov., treas. 1972-74, 86—), U.S. C. of C. Office Phone: 203-367-0629.

WHYTE, NANCY MARIE, performing arts educator; b. Myrtlepoint, Oreg., Mar. 12, 1948; d. Lawrence Edward and Carol Elizabeth (Johnson) Guderian; m. Anthony John Whyte, Aug. 7, 1967 (div. Sept. 1968); 1 child, Charles Lawrence; m. Douglas Brian Graff, June 27, 1971 (div. Oct. 1974); m. Lawrence Hanson, Mar. 12, 1976 (div. Aug. 1984); m. Joseph Paul Deacon, Aug. 10, 1985; 1 child, Nina Alexandra. Student, U. Wash., 1969-72, Am. Sch. Dance, 1972; BA, Evergreen State Coll., 1987. Owner, dir. Nancy Whyte Sch. Ballet, Bellingham, Wash., 1969—; artistic dir. Garden Street Dance Players, Bellingham, 1969-72, MT Baker Ballet, Bellingham, 1975—, Alpha and Omega Worship Dancers, 2003—; co-dir. Exptl. Performance Workshop, Bellingham, 1975-77; instr. creative dance St. Paul's Primary Sch., Bellingham, 1993-97; facilitator dance workshop Allied Arts/Whatcom Co., Bellingham, 1995—. Guest lectr. Western Wash. U., Bellingham, 1976—83, Bellingham, 1996—; guest faculty Dance Theatre N.W., Tacoma, 1995—; liturgical dance cons. Assumption Cath. Sch., 2001—; artistic dir. Alpha and Omega Worship Dancers, 2003—. Author: Memoirs of a Child of Theatre Street, 1993; soloist Raduga Folk Ballet/N.Y. Character Ballet, N.Y.C., 1978-79; choreographer numerous ballets, 1972—. Mem. Nat. Dance Assn., Dancers Over 40, Sacred Dance Guild, Vancouver Ballet Soc. Democrat. Avocations: voice, writing. Office: MT Baker Ballet 1412 Cornwall Ave PO Box 2393 Bellingham WA 98227-2393 Office Phone: 360-734-9141.

WHYTE, RICHARD IAN, surgeon; b. Brighton, England, United Kingdom, July 4, 1958; MD, U. Of Pitts., 1979—83. Head, divsn. of thoracic surgery Stanford U. Med. Ctr., 1997—, med. dir. of oper. rooms, 2001—. Office: Cvrb 205 300 Pasteur Dr Stanford CA 94305 E-mail: riwhyte@stanford.edu.

WHYTE, RONALD M. judge; b. 1942; BA in Math., Wesleyan U., 1964; JD, U. So. Calif., 1967. Bar: Calif. 1967, U.S. Dist. Ct. (no. dist.) Calif. 1967, U.S. Dist. Ct. (cen. dist.) Calif. 1968, U.S. Ct. Appeals (9th cir.) 1986. Assoc. Hoge, Fenton Jones & Appel, Inc., San Jose, Calif., 1971-77, mem., 1977-89; judge Superior Ct. State of Calif., 1989-92, U.S. Dist. Ct. (no. dist.) Calif., San Jose, 1992—. Judge pro-tempore Superior Ct. Calif., 1977-89; lectr. Calif. Continuing Edn. of Bar, Rutter Group, Santa Clara Bar Assn., State Bar Calif.; legal counsel Santa CLara County Bar Assn., 1986-89; mem. county select com. Criminal Conflicts Program, 1988. Bd. trustees Santa Clara County Bar Assn., 1978-79, 84-85. Lt. Judge Advocate Gen.'s Corps, USNR, 1968-71. Recipient Judge of Yr. award Santa Clara County Trial Lawyers Assn., 1992, Am. Jurisprudence award. Mem. Calif. Judges Assn., Assn. Bus. Trial Lawyers (bd. govs. 1991-93), Santa Clara Inn of Ct. (exec. com. 1993—), San Francisco Bay area Intellectual Property Inn of Ct. (exec. com. 1994—). Office: US Courthouse 280 S 1st St Rm 2112 San Jose CA 95113-3002

WIANT, SARAH KIRSTEN, law library administrator, educator, director; b. Waverly, Iowa, Nov. 20, 1946; d. James Allen and Eva (Jorgensen) W.; m. Robert E. Akins. BA, Western State Coll., 1968; MLS, U. North Tex., 1970; JD, Washington & Lee U., 1978. Asst. law libr. Tex. Tech. U., 1970-72, 020, Washington & Lee U., Lexington, Va., 1972—, dir., 1978—, asst. prof. law, 1978-83, assoc. prof. law, 1984-92, prof. law, 1993—. Participant Conf. on Fair Use, NII, 1995-98. Co-author: Copyright Handbook, 1984, Libraries and Copyright: A Guide to Copyright Law in the 1990s, 1994, Legal Research in the District of Columbia, Maryland and Virginia, 1995, 3d edit., 2004, UCITA Encyclopedia of Lib. and Information Science, 2d edit., 2003; contbr. chapters to books; mem. adv. bd. Westlaw, 1988—93, 2003—. Mem.: ABA (com. on librs. 1987—93), U.S. Trademark Assn., Maritime Law Assn., Spl. Librs. Assn. (chair copyright com. 1990—96, John Cotton Dana award 1997), Am. Assn. Law Schs. (chmn. sec. on librs. 1990—92, accreditation com. 1991—94), Am. Assn. Law Librs. (mem. exec. bd. 1981—84, mem. copyright com. 1990—94, chmn. 2003—, copyright office rep., Pres.' award 2001, Spl. Dist. Svc. award Southeastern chpt. 1997). Office: Washington & Lee U Law Libr Lewis Hall Lexington VA 24450 Office Phone: 540-458-8540. Business E-Mail: wiants@wlu.edu.

WIATER, RICHARD M. manufacturing executive; b. Green Bay, Wis., Jan. 21, 1936; s. Adam Frank and Evelyn Catherine (Griakowski) W.; m. Eleanor G. Wiater, Mar. 17, 1987. Acctg. degree, Xavier U., 1961. Acct. P&G, Cin., 1957-62, various, 1963-66; mgr. auditing Aircraft Engine Group-GE, Cin., 1967-70, mgr. mfg. fin. analysis resource planning, 1971-78, mgr. fin. analysis overseas mfg., 1978-85; dir. Tusas Engine Industries, Aircraft Engine-GE, Turkey, 1986-89; mgr. GE90 fin. and bus. planning Aircraft Engine Group-GE, Cin., 1990-95; bus. cons. Cin., 1996-98; pres. Tactical Vehicle Sys. divsn. Stewart & Stevenson Svc., Inc., Sealy, Tex., 1999-2000, COO Specialty Wheeled Vehicle divsn. Houston, 2001—. Mem. AUSA, NDIA. Avocations: history, woodworking. Home: 1640 E T C Jester Blvd Apt 1017 Houston TX 77008-2578

WIATT, JAMES ANTHONY, theatrical agency executive; b. L.A., Oct. 18, 1946; s. Norman and Catherine (Sonners) W.; m. Randie Laine. BA, U. So. Calif., 1969. Campaign coord. Tunney for Senate, L.A., 1969-71; adminstrv. asst. Senator John V. Tunney, L.A., 1972-75; agt. FCA, L.A., 1976-78; lit. agt. Internat. Creative Mgmt., L.A., 1978-81, motion picture agt., 1981-83, head of motion picture dept., 1983-85, pres., COO, from 1985, co-chmn., co-CEO Beverly Hills, Calif., to 1999; pres., co-CEO William Morris Agy., Beverly Hills, 1999—. Office: William Morris Agy 151 S El Camino Dr Beverly Hills CA 90212-2775

WIBERG, DONALD MARTIN, electrical engineering educator, consultant; b. Battle Creek, Mich., Sept. 20, 1936; s. Martin and Lina (Havstein) W.; children: Erik M., Kristin A., Kenneth C. BS, Calif. Inst. Tech., 1959, MS, 1960, PhD, 1965. Registered profl. engr., Calif. Sr. design engr. Convair, San Diego, 1964-65; asst. prof. elec. engring. UCLA, 1965-71, assoc. prof., 1971-77, prof., 1977-94, prof. anesthesiology, 1979-94, vice chmn. dept. elec. engring., 1985-86, prof. emeritus 1994-2001; prof. emeritus dept. elec. engring. U. Calif., Santa Cruz, 2001—, rsch. prof. Ctr. for Adaptive Optics, 2002—. Cons. in field; vis. prof. German Rsch. Orgn. for Air and Space Flight, Munich, 1969-70, dept. elec. engring. and computer sci. U. Newcastle, Australia, 1989-90, Inst. for Systems Rsch., U. Md., College Park, 1994. Author: State Space and Linear Systems, 1971; co-editor: Regulation of Breathing, 1983. Mem. adv. bd. Parthenia Sch., Los Angeles, 1971-74. Sr. NATO research fellow KFZ Karlsruhe, W.Ger., 1973; sr. Fulbright fellow, Copenhagen, 1976-77, Trondheim, Norway, 1983-84 Fellow IEEE (applications assoc. editor Trans. on Automatic Control 1983, assoc. editor-at-large 1987-89, 92-94, named Congl. fellow legis. asst. office Senator Tom Harkin, D-IA 1995), Am. Physiol. Soc. (assoc. editor Modelling Methodology Forum 1980-91), Sigma Xi. Home: 2395 Delaware Ave #153 Santa Cruz CA 95060-5716 E-mail: wiberg@ee.ucla.edu.

WIBERG, LARS-ERIK, occupational compatibility consultant; b. Wakefield, Mass., June 1, 1928; s. Sverker Claesson and Ingrid (Heurlin) W.; m. Elizabeth Margaret (Allenbrook), Oct. 18, 1957; children: Kirsten, Margaret, Brenda. BS in Geology, MIT, 1950; MAT, Harvard U., 1952. From engr. to dir. corp. comm. EG and G Inc., Boston and Bedford, Mass., 1956—69; from asst. v.p. to v.p. compensation, orgnl. planning and ombudsman for officers First Nat. Bank of Boston, 1969—81; cons. Rockport, Mass., 1981—. Lectr. human resources mgmt., Boston U., 1988-92; lectr. job search and career planning, U. Karlstad, Sweden, 1992. Author: It's Your Move, 1991; inventor in the field of Occupl. Compatibility; interviewed in Rockport Recollected. Mem. Gov. John A. Volpe's Mgmt. Engring. Task Force, 1965; mem. planning bd., Rockport, 1965-72, chmn., 1969-72; pres. ch. coun. Swedenborg Chapel, Cambridge, Mass., 1984—; dir. Mass. New Ch. Union, 1990-2004; mem. zoning bd. appeals, Rockport, 1986—, mem. site rev. com., 1999-2001; 1st lt., USAF, 1953-55. Mem. Affiliated New Eng. Cons. (founding mem. Lexington, Mass. 1985), Life Ext. Found., Heritage Found., Swedenborg Sci. Assn. Avocations: ch. work, home repair, music, cooking, reading. Home and Office: 90 South St Rockport MA 01966-1916

WIBISONO, MAKARIM, diplomat; b. Mataram, Indonesia, May 8, 1948; married; 3 children. Degree in internatl rels., Gajahmada U., Jogjakarata, Indonesia, 1970; MS in Internat. Studies, Johns Hopkins U., 1984; MA in Polit. Economy, Ohio State U., 1986, PhD, 1987. Editor Express News Mag., Jakarta, Indonesia, 1970-72; head U.S. desk Dept. Fgn. Affairs, Indonesia, 1972-76, head N.Am. sect., 1976-77; head info. and cultural divsn. Indonesian Embassy, Brasilia, Brazil, 1977-81; dep. dir. trade and exhbns. Fgn. Affairs Dept., Indonesia, 1977-81, dep. dir. info. affairs, 1987-88; head info. divsn. Indonesian Embassy, Washington, 1988-91; min. counsellor, head econ. divsn. Indonesia UN Mission, 1991-93; dir. multilateral econ. coop. Dept. Fgn. Affairs, Indonesia, 1993-94; dep. permanent rep. from Indonesia UN, 1994-97; permanent rep. to UN Govt. Indonesia, N.Y.C., 1997—2001; dir.-gen. for fgn. econ. rels. Dept. Fgn. Affairs, Republic of Indonesia, UN, 2001—02; dir. gen. for Asia Pacific and Africa Affairs Indonesia Mission, UN, 2002—. Office: Permanent Mission Rep Indonesia to UN 325 E 38th St New York NY 10016-2745*

WICH, DONALD ANTHONY, JR., lawyer; b. Apr. 13, 1947; s. Donald Anthony and Margaret Louise (Blatz) W. BA with honors, Notre Dame U., Ind., 1969; JD, Notre Dame U., 1972. Bar: Fla. 1972, U.S. Dist. Ct. (so. dist.) Fla. 1972, U.S. Ct. Appeals (5th and 11th cirs.) 1982, U.S. Supreme Ct. 1976; cert. civil trial lawyer, 1983. Assoc. VISTA, Miami, Fla., 1972-74; atty. Legal Svcs., Miami, 1973-75; adj. prof. law U. Miami, 1974-75; ptnr. Wich, Wich & wich, P.A., Ft. Lauderdale, Fla., 1992—. Pres., dir. Legal Aid of Broward, Ft. Lauderdale, 1976-82; mem. 17th Cir. Jud. Nominating Commn., 1998-02; spl. prosecutor, grievance chmn. The Fla Bar, 1982-90; chmn. UPL Standing Com., 2001-2004 Bd. dirs. St. Thomas More of So. Fla., 1989-. Mem. ATLA, Am. Arbitration Assn., North Broward Bar Assn. (pres. 1983-84), Acad. Fla. Trial Lawyers Assn. (sustaining mem.), Broward County Trial Lawyers Assn. (pres. 1988-89, sustaining mem.), Broward Bar Assn. (chmn. legis. com. 1984-85, exec. com. 1986-92, 94-98, chmn. bench-bar com. 1993-94, chmn. clk.-bar com. 1993-95, mem. 1998-99, pres. 1997-98), Tex. Trial Lawyers Assn., N.Y. Trial Lawyers Assn., Pompano Beach C. of C. (pres. 1989-90, dir. 1984-87, 92-95, govtl. affairs chmn. 1983-84, art show chmn. 1984-85, seafood festival chmn. 1986-90), Notre Dame Frederick Sorin Soc., Rotary (bd. dirs. 1987-91), Woodhouse (bd. dirs. 1990-91). Office: Wich Wich & Wich PA # 620 2400 E Commercial Blvd Fort Lauderdale FL 33308-4030 E-mail: wich3@msn.com.

WICHA, MAX S. oncologist, educator; b. N.Y.C., Mar. 24, 1949; m. Sheila Crowley; children: Jason, Allyson. BS in Biology summa cum laude with honors, SUNY, Stony Brook, 1970; MD, Stanford U., 1974. Diplomate Am. Bd. Internal Medicine; lic. physician, Mich., Ill. Intern in internal medicine U. Chgo. Hosps. and Clinics, 1974-75, jr., sr. resident in internal medicine, 1975-77; rsch. assoc. lab. pathophysiology Nat. Cancer Inst./NIH, Bethesda, Md., 1977-79, fellow in clin. oncology, 1978-80, investigator lab. pathophysiology, 1979-80; asst. prof. internal medicine divsn. hematology and oncology U. Mich., Ann Arbor, 1980-83, assoc. prof., 1983-88, prof., 1988—, mem. tumor metastasis, extracellular matrix, reproductive endocrinology programs, 1982—, dir. divsn. hematology and oncology, dir. Simpson Meml. Rsch. Inst., 1984-93, mem. program in cellular and molecular biology, 1984—, dir. Comprehensive Cancer Ctr., 1987—. Mem. cancer rsch. com. U. Mich., 1981—, sci. adv. bd. dental rsch. inst., 1983—, dean's adv., 1988—, reproductive endocrinology selection com., breast care ctr. exec. com., 1988—, exec. dir.'s adv. coun., 1992—, chair instl. rev. com. gene therapy program project., 1992—, dean's adv. com. Howard Hughes Med. Inst., 1992—, strategic planning policy and organizational com. health scis. info. tech. and networking, 1992—; vis. prof. Mich. State U., 1985, Harvard U., Boston, 1986, Wash. State U., 1986, Boston U., 1986, Wayne State U./Harper Grace Hosps., 1987, U. Ill., 1987, Med. Coll. Wis., 1987., U. Chgo., 1987, Eppley Inst. for Rsch. in Cancer and Allied Diseases, Omaha, 1988, U. Nebr., Omaha, 1988, U. Minn./Minn. VA Hosp., 1988, MD Anderson Cancer Ctr., Houston., Mt. Sinai Med. Ctr., N.Y.C., Am. Cancer Soc., Kalamazoo, 1989, Gainesville, Fla., 1990, Orlando, Fla., 1990, Pezcoller Symposium, Rovereto, Italy, 1990, Prince Henry's Hosp., Melbourne, Australia, 1990, Northwestern U. Med. Ctr., Chgo., 1990, Meml. Sloan-Kettering Cancer Ctr., N.Y.C., 1990, Tex. S.W. U., Dallas, 1990, Mich. State U., 1991; lectr. U. Mich., 1990; mem. NIH Site Visit team U. Calif. Cancer Rsch. Lab., Berkeley, 1985; ad hoc mem. cell biology and physiology study sect. NIH, 1985, 86, study sect., Bethesda, 1991; mem. NCI Site Visit team Norris Cotton Dartmouth Cancer Ctr, 1989, Howard U., Wash., 1989, Howard U. Parent Com., 1989, MD Anderson Cancer Ctr., Houston, 1992; sci. advisor U. Colo. Cancer Ctr., Denver, 1990, Samuel Waxman Cancer Rsch. Found., Mt. Sinai Med. Ctr., N.Y.C., 1988-93; mem. NCI Adv. Panel, Bethesda, 1991; mem. sci. adv. com. U. Tex. San Antonio Cancer Ctr., U. Miami Sylvester Cancer Ctr., Mich. State U., East Lansing, Norris-Cotton Cancer Ctr., Dartmouth-Hitchcock Med. Ctr., Hanover, N.H., Mich. Cancer Found., Detroit, V. T. Lombardi Cancer Rsch. Ctr., Georgetown U., Washington, 1992—, MD Anderson Cancer Ctr., Houston, 1992—; mem. extramural sci. adv. bd. UCI Clin. Cancer Ctr., U. Calif. Irvine, Orange, 1992—; mem. NCI SPORE in Prostate Cancer Study Sect., 1992; chair NCI Cancer Ctr. Support Rev. Com., 1993; NCI Site Visit chair Jefferson Cancer Ctr., Phila., 1992, Worcester (Mass.) Cancer Found., 1993, Duke U. Cancer Ctr., Durham, N.C., 1993, Lineberger Comprehensive Ctr., Chapel Hill, N.C., 1993; mem. NCI Comprehensive Cancer Ctrs. Review, 1993, chmn. parent com. Cancer Ctr. Support Rev. Com., 1992—; cons. Warner Lambert Co., 1980—. Assoc. editor: Molecular and Cellular Differentation, 1993; co-editor: The Hematopoietic Microenvironment, 1993; mem. editorial bd. Blood, Molecular and Cellular Differentiation, Jour. Lab. and Clin. Medicine, Cancer Rsch., 1993—, Oncology, Cancer Prevention Internat.; reviewer Nature, Science, Proceedings of NAS, Jour. Clin. Investigation, Jour. Cell Biology, Exptl. Cell Rsch., Exptl. Hematology, Cancer., Clin. and Exptl. Metastasis, Jour. Nat. Cancer Inst., Tissue & Cell, Am. Inst. Biol. Scis., Am. Jour. Pathology, Jour Immunology, Jour. Med. Scis., NSF, Oncology Rsch., Lab. Investigation, Breast Cancer Rsch. and Treatment; contbr. over 110 articles and to profl. jours., chpts. to books.; invited lectr. in field. With USPHS, 1977-80. Recipient NSF RSch. award SUNY, 1969, Eli Luke and David Jacob Rsch. award Stanford U. Sch. Medicine, 1974, Upjohn Achievement Excellence in Medicine award, Outstanding Med. Resident award U. Chgo. Hosps., 1977, Jerome Conn Excellence in Rsch. award, 1983; grantee NIH, 1991—, 93—, Am. Cancer Soc., 1992—, Suntory Rsch. Inst., 1992-93. Mem. AAASN, Am. Assn. for Cancer Rsch. (state legis. com. 1992—, finance com. 1992—), Am. Fedn. for Clin. Rsch. (selections com. midwest sect. 1986—, comm. com., 1986—, awards com., 1986—), Am. Soc. for Cell Biology, Am. Soc. Hematology (com. on publs. 1991-93), Assn. Am. Cancer Insts. (bd. dirs. 1993—), Am. Soc. for Clin. Investigation, Am. Soc. Clin. Oncology (award selection com. 1992—), Ctrl. Soc. for Clin. Rsch., Mich. Soc. Hematology and Oncology, Southwest Oncology Group, Assn. Community Cancer Ctrs. Achievements include patents for antibodies to human mammary cell growth inhibitor and methods of production and use, human mammary cell growth inhibitor and methods of production and use; research in regulation of cell growth and differentiation, molecular mechanisms of tumor metastasis. Mailing: 6302 CCGC 0942 1500 E Medical Ctr Dr Ann Arbor MI 48109

WICHERN, DEAN WILLIAM, business educator; b. Medford, Wis., Apr. 29, 1942; s. Arthur William and Rebecca Ann (Ambler) W.; m. Dorothy Jean Rutkowski, Dec. 7, 1968; children: Michael, Andrew. BS in Math., U. Wis., 1964, MS in Stats., 1965, PhD in Stats., 1969. Instr. Sch. Bus. U. Wis., Madison, 1967-69, asst. prof., 1969-72, assoc. prof., 1972-76, prof., 1976-84, chmn. quantitative analysis dept., 1975-78; prof. Mays Bus. Sch. Tex. A&M U., 1984—, head info. and ops. mgmt. dept., 1984—88, 1997—98, 2004—, assoc. dean, 1988-95, John E. Pearson prof. bus. adminstrn., 1985—. Vis. prof. Math. Rsch. Ctr., 1978-79. Co-author: Intermediate Business Statistics, 1977, Applied Multivariate Statistical Analysis, 5th edit., 2002, Business Statistics: Decision Making With Data, 1997, Business Forecasting, 8th edit., 2005; mem. edit. bd. Jour. Bus. and Econ. Stats., 1983—91. Mem. Royal Statis. Soc., Am. Statis. Assn., Inst. Oper. Rsch. and Mgmt. Sci., Internat. Inst. of Forecasters, Beta Gamma Sigma, Phi Kappa Phi. Home: 9217 Riverstone Ct College Station TX 77845-8333 Office: Tex A&M U Mays Bus Sch 4217 TAMU College Station TX 77843-4217 E-mail: d-wichern@tamu.edu.

WICHMANN, HENRY, JR., accounting educator, researcher; b. Bemidji, Minn., Sept. 14, 1939; s. Henry and Bethel (Wells) W.; m. Nilda Oca, May 25, 1990; children: Holly Brittany, Henry William. BSBA in Mktg., U. Denver, 1962; MA in Bus. Edn., Colo. State Coll., 1965; PhD in Bus. Tchg., U. No. Colo., 1972. CPA, Wis. Asst. buyer May Co. Dept. Stores, Colo., 1962-63; distbributive edn. coord. Newburgh (N.Y.) Free Acad., 1963-64; instr. in bus. adminstrn. and mid-mgmt. Dawson Coll., Mont., 1964-68; tchg. asst. acctg. U. No. Colo., Greeley, 1969-71; instr. mid. mgmt. Casper (Wyo.) Coll., 1971-72; asst. prof. acctg. U. Wis., Eau Claire, 1972-77, U. Wyo., Laramie, 1977-80; assoc. prof. U. Alaska, Anchorage, 1980-85; prof. U. Alaska, Fairbanks, 1986—, head acctg. and info. sys. dept., 1996—. Advisor Mktg. Club, Glendive, Mont., 1964-68; advisor Christmas promotion Laramie C. of C., 1978-80; dir. small bus. inst. U. Alaska, Anchorage, 1980-85; manuscript dir. Nat. Acctg. Assn., Anchorage, 1980-85; bd. dirs. JW Trading Co., Taichung, Taiwan; presenter in field. Contbr. articles to profl. jours. Recipient Keller Trophy, Nat. Assn. Acctg., 1981-82, Pres.'s award Nat. Assn. Acctg., 1985-86, At-Large Achiever Rsch. award Assn. of Govt. Accts., 1991-92, Disting. Theoretical Paper award Inst. Decision Sci., 1982. Mem. AICPA, Am. Acctg. Assn., Nat. Soc. Pub. Accts., Wis. Soc. CPAs, Assn. Govt. Accts., Inst. Mgmt. Accts. (bd. dirs.), Beta Alpha Psi, Beta Gamma Sigma, Alpha Kappa Psi (historian, dist. dir. 1978-80). Baptist. Avocations: hunting, fishing, camping. Home: 1965 Weston Dr Fairbanks AK 99709-6535 Office: U Alaska Sch Mgmt PO Box 756080 Fairbanks AK 99775-6080 E-mail: FFHW@uaf.edu.

WICK, DOUGLAS, producer; m. Tracy Fisher; 3 children. Grad. cum laude, Yale U. Owner Red Wagon Prodns., Culver City, Calif. Assoc. prodr. Starting Over; prodr. Hush, The Craft, Wolf, Working Girl (six Acad. Award Nomiations, five Golden Globes including Best Picture), Stuart Little, Girl, Interrupted, Gladiator, The Hollow Man, Memoirs Of A Geisha. Office: Red Wagon Prodns 10202 Washington Blvd Culver City CA 90232-3119 Fax: 310-244-1480.

WICK, HILTON ADDISON, lawyer; b. Mt. Pleasant, Pa., Feb. 11, 1920; m. Barbara G. Shaw; children: James H., William S., B. Jane, Ann W., Julia A. BA, Maryville Coll., 1942; JD, Harvard U., 1948. Bar: Vt. 1948. Practiced in, Burlington; ptnr. Wick, Dinse & Allen, 1949-72; CEO Chittenden Bank, Chittenden Corp., 1969—85; bd. dirs. Sentinel Funds, 1970—76; of counsel Dinse, Allen & Erdmann, Burlington, 1972-80; bd. dirs. Nat. Life Ins. Co., 1976—92; of counsel Wick & Maddocks, Burlington, 1980—; state senator Vt., 1989-91; COO Gifford Med. Ctr., Inc., Randolph, 1993-95. Bd. dirs. Blue Cross/Blue Shield Vt., Beach Properties, Inc., Vt. Pub. Radio, chmn., 1990-96. Trustee Middlebury Coll., 1969-85, Champlain Coll., 1974-94, Maryville Coll., 1981-86, Shelburne Mus., 1985-94, Ethan Allen Homestead, 1989-96, Vt. Assn. for Blind and Visually Impaired, 1992-2001; pres. Coll. St. Congl. Ch., 1996-98; bd. dirs. Vt. divsn. Am. Cancer Soc., 1979-93, Intervale Found.; pres. bd. trustees Vt. Law Sch., 1975-95; chmn. bd. trustees Vt. Cmty. Found., 1985-91; chancellor Vt. State Colls., 1984-85; chmn. bd. dirs. Middlebury Coll., 1981-84. Mem. ABA, Vt. Bar Assn. (pres. 1967-68), Chittenden County Bar Assn. (pres. 1963-64), Internat. Soc. Barristers, Am. Bankers Assn. (bd. dirs. 1975-76), Vt. Bankers Assn. (pres. 1973-74), Ethan Allen Club, Harvard Club (Boston and N.Y.C.), Phi Kappa Delta. Home: Two Appletree Point Ln Burlington VT 05401 Office: 308 College St Burlington VT 05401-8319 Office Phone: 802-658-3037. E-mail: hiltbarb@aol.com.

WICK, SISTER MARGARET, former college administrator; b. Sibley, Iowa, June 30, 1942; BA in Sociology, Briar Cliff Coll., 1965; MA in Sociology, Loyola U., Chgo., 1971; PhD in Higher Edn., U. Denver, 1976. Instr. sociology Briar Cliff Coll., Sioux City, Iowa, 1966-71, dir. academic advising, 1971-72, v.p., acad. dean, 1972-74, 76-84, pres., 1987-99, Colls. of Mid-Am., 1985-87. Mem. adv. bd. Nations Bank, Sioux City. Bd. dirs. Mary J. Treglia Cmty. House, 1976-84, Marian Health Ctr., 1987-97, Iowa Pub. TV, 1987-95. Mem. North Ctrl. Edn. Assn. (cons.-evaluator for accrediting teams 1980-84, 89—), Siouxland Initiative (adv. bd.), Quota Internat., Rotary. Home: 3390 Windsor Ave Dubuque IA 52001-1326 Office: Briar Cliff Coll Office of the President 3303 Rebecca St Sioux City IA 51104-2324

WICK, MICHAEL M. biotechnology executive; MD, PhD in Chemistry, Harvard U. Chief melanoma clinic and lab. molecular dermatol. oncology Dana Farber Cancer Inst., Boston, 1980—92; assoc. prof. Harvard Med. Sch., Boston, 1981—94; exec. dir. oncology/immunology and clin. rsch. Lederle Labs. (divsn. Am. Cyanamid), 1990—95; sr. v.p. rsch. CV Therapeutics, 1995—97, cons., 1997; bd. dirs. Telik, Inc., South San Francisco, Calif., 1997—, exec. v.p. R&D, COO, 1997—98, pres., 1998—, CEO, 1999—, chmn. bd. dirs., 2000—. Office: Telik Inc 3165 Porter Dr Palo Alto CA 94304-1213

WICK, MITCHELL A. physician; b. N.Y.C., July 15, 1954; s. Edwin and Doris Wick. BA in Chemistry, U. South Fla., 1976; postgrad., U. Miami, Coral Gables, Fla., 1972—73; D.O., Kirksville Coll. Osteo. Medicine, Mo., 1980. Diplomate Am. Osteo. Bd. Family Physicians, Am. Acad. Pain Mgmt., Am. Assn. Integrative Medicine. Intern Southeastern Med. Ctr., N. Miami, Fla., 1980—81; resident Parkview Hosp., Toledo, 1981—83; staff physician Walk-in Family Medicine Ctr., Boynton Beach, Fla., 1983—86; physician Davie-Dania Med. Ctr., Fla., 1986—96; staff physician Meml. Pembroke Hosp., Pembroke Pines, Fla., 1991—. Author: Megaphysics, A New Look at the Universe, 2003. Mem.: Fla. Osteo. Med. Assn., Am. Osteo. Assn. Achievements include research and copywrite on physics theory regarding the fractal nature of spacetime manifolds and how matter and energy interact with thereof utilizing string theory. Avocations: physics, tensor calculus. Home: 831 SW 87th Ter Plantation FL 33324

WICK, PHILIP, wholesale distribution executive; CEO Les Schwab Tire Ctrs., Prineville, Oreg. Office: PO Box 667 Prineville OR 97754-0667

WICK, ROBERT THOMAS, retired supermarket executive; b. St. Louis, Nov. 26, 1927; s. Robert Berninger and Katherine (Burke) W.; m. Virginia Rose Allen, Sept. 6, 1952; children: Susan, Patrick, Nancy, Robert J. BS, St. Louis U., 1955; cert. in food distbn., Mich. State U., 1956. Sales mgr. Nat. Tea Co., St. Louis, 1966-68, asst. div. mgr., 1968-69, div. mgr. Sioux City, Iowa, 1969-71, Milw., 1971-73, Chgo., 1973-74; v.p., gen. mgr. A&P Food Stores, Indpls., 1975-77; div. v.p. Colonial Food Stores- Grand Union, Norfolk, Va., 1977-79; pres., chief exec. officer Bonnie Be-Lo Markets, Inc., Norfolk, 1979-90, ret., 1990. Bd. dirs. Virginia Beach (Va.) Community Svcs. Bd., 1985-89; mem. adv. bd. Straight, Inc., Chesapeake, Va., 1987-91; dir. Community Alternatives, Inc., Virginia Beach, 1991-92. Tech. cpl. U.S. Army, 1946-48. Recipient Citizen of Yr. award St. Louis Argus Newspaper, 1968. Mem. Food Mktg. Inst. (bd. dirs. 1982-89), Va. Food Dealers Assn. (bd. dirs. 1981-87), Tidewater Retail Mchts. Assn. (pres., bd. dirs. 1981-91). Conservative. Roman Catholic. Avocations: travel, golf. Home: 801 Winthrope Dr Virginia Beach VA 23452-3940 E-mail: rwick@cox.net.

WICK, TAMARA, photographer, artist, writer; b. July 15, 1966; d. James Alan and Maxine Evelyn (Tankersley) W.; m. John E. Kulukundis, 1986. BA in Comm./Broadcasting, Ariz. State U., 1984; grad., Am. Acad. Dramatic Arts, N.Y.C. Asst. to exec. prodr. video devel. Columbia Pictures Industries, N.Y.C., 1986-87; pub. rels. coord., asst. to Estée Lauder Estée Lauder Cos., N.Y.C., 1987-90; founder, creative dir. Imagination Enterprises, Inc., N.Y.C., 1993—; founder, photographer Santa Paws, N.Y.C., 1993—. Active Met. Mus. Art, N.Y.C. Merit scholar U. Ariz., 1976. Mem. NAFE, U.S. Equestrian Team, N.Y. Women in Comm., N.Y. Zool. Soc., N.Y. Young Reps. Club, Ariz. State U. Alumni, Kappa Kappa Gamma Alumnae. Episcopalian. Avocations: showed horses on english circuit, tennis, skiing, watercolor painting, photography. Home: 150 W 56th St Apt 3010 New York NY 10019-3842

WICK, WILLIAM SHINN, clergyman, chaplain; b. West Chester, Pa. s. William R. and Barbara (Shinn) W.; m. Debra R. Smith, Apr. 1, 1989; 1 child, Christopher R. BA, Trinity Internat. U., Deerfield, Ill., 1975; MDiv, Trinity Evang. Div. Sch., Deerfield, 1978. Ordained to ministry Evang. Free Ch. Am., 1978. Pastor Bradford (Vt.) Evang. Free Ch., 1978-85, Cornerstone Evangelical Fee Ch., Vt., 1985-89, Grace Evang. Free Ch., Northfield, Vt., 1989-96; chaplain Norwich U., Northfield, 1989—; interim pastor First Bapt. Ch., Barre, Vt., 2001—03, Resurrection Bapt. Ch., Montpelier, Vt., 2003—04. Mem. bd. govs. Trinity Western U., Langley, B.C., Can., 1999—. Mem. Evangelical Free Ch. Am. Avocations: alpine skiing, racquetball, tennis, scuba

diving, sailing. Home: 763 S Main St Northfield VT 05663-5601 Office: White Chapel Norwich U 158 Harmon Dr Northfield VT 05663-1000 Office Phone: 802-485-2128. E-mail: chaplain@norwich.edu., theskiingrev@hotmail.com.

WICKE, DALLAS CLYDE, retired aerospace engineer; b. Atwood, Kans., Nov. 18, 1940; s. Ernest William and Edith (Wimer) W. BS in Aerospace Engrng., U. Kans., 1962; MS in Aerospace Engrng., U. So. Calif., 1968. From assoc. engr. to sr. prin. engr. McDonnell Douglas Corp., Huntington Beach, Calif., 1962—97; sr. prin. engr. The Boeing Co., Anaheim, Calif., 1997—2001; ret., 2001. Patentee in field. Mem. AIAA (sr., adv. bd., sect. tech. com. for guidance, navigation, dynamics and control), U. Kans. Alumni Assn., U.S. Ski Assn., Tau Beta Pi, Sigma Tau, Sigma Gamma Tau.

WICKENS, DONALD LEE, engineer executive, consultant, rancher; b. Oklahoma City, Aug. 11, 1934; s. Claude Preston and Idora Bell (Wainscott) W.; m. Sylvia Ann Knopp, Aug. 25, 1957; children: Julia Ann, Donna Sue. BS, Okla. State U., 1957, MS, 1962. Engr. HTB Inc., Oklahoma City, 1961-65; chief structural engr. The Benham Group, Oklahoma City, 1965-70, prin. structural engr., 1970-75, sr. v.p. indsl., 1975-80, pres. Houston divsn., 1980-82, pres. St. Louis divsn., 1982-88, pres., 1988—, chmn., chief exec. officer, pres., 1991—, The Benham Cos., Oklahoma City, Benham Internat., Oklahoma City, 1999; ret. Chmn. bd. dirs. B-Vision Products, Oklahoma City, Benham-Electrosynthesis, Oklahoma City, Benham Internat.-Far East, Benham Internat. U.K.; bd. dirs. Benham Internat. Investments, Oklahoma City, Benham Internat. Eurasion, Moscow, Stainless Equipment and Sys. Co., Atlanta, Benham Internat. Pacific, Oklahoma City, Benham Real Estate and Devel., Oklahoma City, Stewart & Bottomleg, Tulsa; chmn. Gov.'s Internat. Team. Bd. visitors Sch. Arch., U. Okla. Named to Hall of Fame Coll. Engring., Arch. and Tech. Oklahoma State U., 1997. Mem. NSPE, ASCE, Am. Soc. Mil. Engrs., So. U.S. Japan Assn., Phi Delta Theta, Sigma Tau, Chi Epsilon. Republican. Lutheran. Home: 2604 Charleston Rd Edmond OK 73003-1623 Office: The Benham Group 9400 N Broadway Ext Ste 200 Oklahoma City OK 73114-7400

WICKER, DENNIS A. lawyer; b. Sanford, N.C., 1952; s. J. Shelton and Clarice (Burns) W.; m. Alisa O'Quinn; children: Quinn Edward, Jackson Dennis, Harrison Lee. BA in Econs. with honors, U. N.C., 1974; JD, Wake Forest U., 1978. Atty. Love & Wicker, 1978-92; mem. N.C. Ho. of Reps., 1981-92; lt. gov. State of N.C., 1993—2000; atty. Smith Helms Mulliss & Moore, LLP, Raleigh, 2000—01; attorney Helms, Mulliss & Wicker, PLLC, Raleigh, NC, 2001—. Chmn. law enorcement com., 1983, house com. cts. and adminstrn. justice, 1985, house jud. com., 1987; chmn. N.C. Small Bus. Coun., 1993—, N.C. State C.C. Bd., 1993—, N.C. State Health Purchasing Alliance Bd., 1993—, Gov.'s Task Force on Driving While Impaired, 1994—, N.C. Local Govt. Partnership Coun.; mem. N.C. Capitol Planning Com., 1993—, N.C. Coun. of State, 1993, N.C. Commn. on Bus. Laws and The Economy. Chmn. N.C. Local Govt. Partnership Coun.; chmn. Gov.'s Task Force on Driving While Impaired. Named Legis. of Yr., Children's Learning Disability Assn. N.C.; recipient Jane Alexander Pub. Svc. award MADD, 1993, Pres.'s award N.C. Assn. Educators, Legis. Leadership award Nat. Commn. Against Drunk Driving, 1994; listed among 10 most effective legis. N.C. Ctr. Pub. Policy Rsch. Mem. Phi Beta Kappa. Democrat. Methodist. Office: Helms, Mulliss & Wicker 2600 Two Hannover Sq Raleigh NC 27601

WICKER, ROGER F. congressman, lawyer; b. Pontotoc, Miss., July 5, 1951; m. Gayle Long; children: Margaret, Caroline, McDaniel. BA in Polit. Sci. and Journalism, U. Miss., 1973; JD, Ole Miss Law Sch., 1975. Judge advocate USAF, 1976—80; mem. staff rules com. Staff of U.S. Rep. Trent Lott, 1980-82; pvt. practice, 1982—; mem. Miss. State Senate, 1987—95, U.S. Congress from 1st Miss. dist., 1995—; mem. house appropriation com, 1995; mem. House Task Force for a Drug Free America, Rep. Policy Com., 2001, subcommittee on labor, health and human svcs. and edn., subcommittee on energy and water development, subcommittee on foreign operations, budget com. With USNR, 1980—. Republican. Office: US House Reps 2455 Rayburn HOB Washington DC 20515-2401

WICKER, THOMAS CAREY, JR., judge; b. New Orleans, Aug. 1, 1923; s. Thomas Carey and Mary (Taylor) W.; children: Thomas Carey III, Catherine Anne; m. Jane Anne Trepanier, Dec. 29, 1995. BBA, Tulane U., 1944, LLB, 1949, JD, 1969. Bar: La. 1949. Law clk. La. Supreme Ct., New Orleans, 1949-50; asst. U.S. Atty., 1950-53; practiced in New Orleans, 1953-72; mem. firm Simon, Wicker & Wiedemann, 1953-67; partner firm Wicker, Wiedemann & Fransen, 1967-72; dist. judge Jefferson Parish (La.), 1972-85, judge, Court of Appeal 5th cir., 1985-98, mem. faculty Nat. Jud. Coll., 1979-93, Tulane U. Sch. Law, 1978-83. Past bd. visitors Tulane U.; bd. dirs. La. Jud. Coll.; past pres. Sugar Bowl. Author: (with others) Judicial Ethics, 1982, (with others) Modern Judicial Ethics, 1992; editor Tulane Law Review, 1949. Lt. (j.g.), USNR, 1944-46. Mem. ABA (jud. div. council), La. (chmn. jr. bar sect. 1958-59, gov. 1958, mem. ho. of dels. 1960-72), Jefferson Parish, bar assns., Tulane U. Alumni Assn. (past pres.), Am. Judicature Soc., La. Dist. Judges Assn. (past pres.), Order of Coif, Beta Gamma Sigma, Pi Kappa Alpha. Episcopalian. Clubs: Rotary (pres. 1971-72), Metairie (La.) Country. Avocations: golf, photography, military history.

WICKER, THOMAS GREY, retired journalist; b. Hamlet, N.C., June 18, 1926; s. Delancey David and Esta (Cameron) W.; m. Neva Jewett McLean, Aug. 20, 1949 (div. 1973); children: Cameron McLean, Thomas Grey; m. Pamela Abel Hill, Mar. 9, 1974. AB in Journalism, U. N.C., 1948. Exec dir. Southern Pines (N.C.) C. of C., 1948-49; editor Sandhill Citizen, Aberdeen, N.C., 1949; mng. editor The Robesonian, Lumberton, N.C., 1949-50; pub. info. dir. N.C. Bd. Pub. Welfare, 1950-51; copy editor Winston-Salem (N.C.) Jour., 1951-52, sports editor, 1954-55, Sunday feature editor, 1955-56, Washington corr., 1957, editorial writer, city hall corr., 1958-59; assoc. editor Nashville Tennesseean, 1959-60; mem. staff Washington bur. N.Y. Times, 1960-71, chief bur., 1964-68; assoc. editor N.Y. Times, 1968-85, columnist, 1966-91. James K. Batten vis. prof. pub. policy Davidson Coll., 1977; vis. scholar First Amendment Ctr., Nashville, 1998; vis. prof. Journalism Middle Tenn. State U, 1999, U So. Calif., 1999. Author: (novels) The Kingpin, 1953, The Devil Must, 1957, The Judgment, 1961, Facing the Lions, 1973, Unto This Hour, 1984, Donovan's Wife, 1992, Easter Lilly, 1998, (non-fiction) Kennedy without Tears, 1964, JFK and LBJ: The Influence of Personality upon Politics, 1968, A Time to Die, 1975, On Press, 1978, One of Us: Richard Nixon and the American Dream, 1991, Tragic Failure: Racial Integration in America, 1996, Keeping the Record, 2001, Dwight D. Eisenhower, 2002. Served to lt. (j.g.) USNR, 1952-54. Nieman fellow Harvard, 1957-58, fellow Joan Shorenstein Barone Ctr. on the Press, Politics and Pub. Policy Harvard, 1993. Mem. Soc. Nieman Fellows, Century Assn., Soc. Am. Historians, Writers guild of Am. East.

WICKES, GEORGE, English literature educator, writer; b. Antwerp, Belgium, Jan. 6, 1923; came to U.S., 1923; s. Francis Cogswell and Germaine (Attout) W.; m. Louise Westling, Nov. 8, 1975; children by previous marriage: Gregory, Geoffrey, Madeleine (dec.), Thomas, Jonathan. BA, U. Toronto, Ont., Can., 1944; MA, Columbia U., 1949; PhD, U. Calif., Berkeley, 1954. Asst. sec. Belgian Am. Ednl. Found., N.Y.C., 1947-49; exec. dir. U.S. Ednl. Found. in Belgium, 1952-54; instr. Duke U., Durham, N.C., 1954-57; from asst. prof. to prof. Harvey Mudd Coll. and Claremont Grad. Sch., Calif., 1957-70; prof. English and comparative lit. U. Oreg., Eugene, 1970—, dir. comparative lit., 1974-77, head English dept., 1976-83. Lectr. USIS, Europe, 1969, Africa, 1978, 79; vis. prof. U. Rouen, France, 1970, U. Tübingen, Germany, 1981, U. Heidelberg, Germany, 1996. Editor: Lawrence Durrell and Henry Miller Correspondence, 1963, Henry Miller, Letters to Emil, 1989, Henry Miller and James Laughlin: Selected Letters, 1995; Author: Henry Miller, 1966, Americans in Paris, 1969, The Amazon of Letters, 1976; translator: The Memoirs of Frederic Mistral, 1986. Served with U.S. Army, 1943-46. Fulbright lectr. France, 1962-63, 66, 78; sr. fellow Ctr. for Twentieth Century Studies, U. Wis.-Milw., Milwaukee, 1971, Creative Writing fellow Nat. Endowment Arts, 1973, Camargo fellow, 1991. Mem. PEN. Office: U Oreg English Dept Eugene OR 97403

WICKESBERG, ALBERT KLUMB, retired management educator; b. Neenah, Wis., Apr. 2, 1921; s. Albert Henry and Lydia (Klumb) W.; m. Dorothy Louise Ahrensfeld, Oct. 28, 1944; children— Robert, William, James. BA, Lawrence Coll., 1943; MBA, Stanford U., 1948; PhD, Ohio State U., 1955. Staff accountant S.C. Johnson & Son, Inc., Racine, Wis., 1948-50; asst. prof. Sacramento State Coll., 1950-51; prof. U. Minn., Mpls., 1953-86, prof. emeritus, 1987—, chmn. dept. bus. adminstrn., 1959-62, dir. grad. studies, 1963-66, chmn. dept. mgmt. and transp., 1971-77. Author: Management Organization, 1966. Served with AUS, 1943-46, 51-52. Soc. Advancement Mgmt. fellow, 1972 Mem. Acad. Mgmt., Soc. Advancement Mgmt. (pres. Twin Cities chpt. 1961-62). Congregationalist. Home: 4501 Roanoke Rd Minneapolis MN 55422-5268

WICKFIELD, ERIC NELSON, investment company executive; b. Bryn Mawr, Pa., Feb. 14, 1953; s. Paul Gilbert Jacobs and Patricia Ruth (Nelson) Davies; m. Kristine Margaret Erickson, June 21, 1974 (div. 1976); m. Sara Lou Datt, July 23, 1977 (div. 1990); 1 child, Eric N. Jr.; m. Leslie Walsh Willingham, June 8, 1990; 1 child, Douglas N. BS, Rochester Inst. Tech., 1974; MBA, Boston U., 1990. Project mgr. Flight Safety Internat., Wichita, Kans., 1976-82; v.p. Aufleger-Garrett, Stillwater, Okla., 1982-86; demonstration pilot citation div. Gen. Dynamics, Wichita, 1986-87; pres. Prompt Fin. Inc., Concord, Mass., 1987—, bd. dirs.; adj. faculty Boston U. Grad. Sch. Mgmt., 1997—. Co-author: Sustaining High Performance, 1990; editor: 421 Pilot's Training Manual, 1981; author: Financial Users Network User's manual, 1997, Losing Situational awareness, 2001, Communicating the Loss of SA, 2004. Bd. dirs. Groton Ctr. for The Arts. Mem. Internat. Operator's Coun., Aircraft Owner's & Pilot's Assn., Aero Club New Eng. (bd. dirs.). Republican. Methodist. Avocation: skiing. Office: Prompt Fin Inc 30 Monument Sq Concord MA 01742-1858

WICKHAM, DIANNE, nursing administrator; b. Dillon, Mont., Feb. 26, 1952; d. William Byron Wickham and Margaret Dewalt (Lovell) Starkweather. ADN, No. Mont. Coll., 1974; BSN, Mont. State U., 1978, MSN, 1980. RN, Mont. Clin. dir. St. Patrick Hosp., Missoula, Mont., 1980-81; asst. prof. Lewis Clark State Coll., Lewiston, Idaho, 1981-83, Mont. State U., Bozeman, Mont., 1983-86; home health nurse West Mont. Home Health, Helena, 1986-87, dir. clin. svcs., 1987-90; critical care nurse St. James Hosp., Butte, Mont., 1986-87; exec. dir. Mont. State Bd of Nursing, Helena, 1990—. Mem. long term care com. Gov. Task Force on Aging, Helene, Mont., 1993-95, mem. task force to devel. investigator tng. Nat. Com. of State Bds. Nursing, Chgo., 1993—, mem. adj. faculty Mont. State U., Bozeman, 1993—, cons. in field, 1994—. Judge Soroptomists scholarship award, 1993, JC Penneys Golden Rule award, Helena, 1995. Recipient State award for excellence Am. Acad. Nurses Practitioners, 1994. Office: Mont State Bd Nursing 111 N Jackson St Helena MT 59601-4140

WICKHAM, JOHN ADAMS, JR., retired army officer; b. Dobbs Ferry, N.Y., June 25, 1928; s. John Adams and Jean Gordon (Koch) W.; m. Ann Lindsley Prior, June 18, 1955; children: Lindsley, John Adams, Matthew. BS, U.S. Mil. Acad., 1950; MA, Harvard U., 1955, M.P.A., 1956; grad., Nat. War Coll., 1967. Commd. 2d lt. U.S. Army, 1950, advanced through grades to gen., 1979; asst. prof. social scis. U.S. Mil. Acad., 1956-60; bn. comdr. 1st Cavalry Div., Republic of Vietnam, 1967; brigade comdr., chief of staff 3d Inf. Div., Fed. Republic of Germany, 1969-70; army mem. chmn.'s staff group Office of Chmn. Joint Chiefs of Staff, Washington, 1970-71; dep. chief of staff for econ. affairs Mil. Assistance Command, Republic of Vietnam, 1971-73; dep. chief, negotiator U.S. del. Four Party Joint Mil. Commn., Republic of Vietnam, 1973; sr. mil. asst. to Sec. Def. Washington, 1973-76; comdr. 101st Airborne Div. (Air Assault), Ft. Campbell, Ky., 1976-78; dir. Joint Staff Orgn. Washington, 1978-79; comdr. in chief UN Command, Republic of Korea-U.S. Combined Forces Command, Korea, 1979-82; vice chief of staff U.S. Army, Washington, 1982-83, chief of staff, 1983-87, ret., 1987; pres., chief exec. officer Armed Forces Communications and Electronics Assn., Fairfax, Va., 1987-92. Bd. dirs. Cooper Inst. for Aerobic Rsch., Xsirius, Inc., Honeywell Fed. Sys., Advanced Photonics, Nortel Inc. Author: Korea on the Brink, 2000. Pres. Sun City Town Coun., 1996—99, Sun City Found., 2001—03; elder St. Andrews Presbyn. Ch., 2001—. Decorated D.S.M. (8), Silver Star (2), Legion of Merit (4), Bronze Star with V device, Air medal (11), Purple Heart, Legion of Honor (France), Order of Mil. Merit (Rep. of Korea), Royal Order of Polar Star (Sweden). Mem. Assn. U.S. Army, 101st Airborne Assn., Retired Officers Assn. Home: 13590 N Fawnbrooke Dr Tucson AZ 85737

WICKHAM, MICHAEL W. transportation executive; b. 1946; With Roadway Express, Inc., Akron, Ohio, 1968—, terminal mgr., 1971-77, dist. mgr., 1977-81, v.p. N.E. divsn., 1981-85, v.p. western divsn., 1985-88, v.p. adminstrn. and fin., 1988-89, exec. v.p. adminstrn. and fin., 1989-90, pres., CEO, 1990-99, CEO, 1999—. Office: 1077 Gorge Blvd Akron OH 44310-2408

WICKIZER, CINDY LOUISE, retired elementary school educator; b. Pitts., Dec. 12, 1946; d. Charles and Gloria Geraldine (Cassidy) Zimmerman Sr.; m. Leon Leonard Wickizer, Mar. 20, 1971 (div. Oct. 2003); 1 child, Charlyn Michelle. BS, Oreg. State U., 1968. Tchr. Enumclaw (Wash.) Sch. Dist., 1968-99, ret., 1999. Mem. Wash. State Ret. Tchrs. Assn., Am. Rabbit Breeders Assn. (judge, chmn. scholarship found. 1986-87, pres. 1988-94, 96-98, dist. dir. 1994-96, 2003—, Disting. Svc. award 1987, Hall of Fame 1998), Wash. State Rabbit Breeders Assn. (life, Pres.'s award 1983, 94, sec., dir., v.p. 1995-97), Vancouver Island Rabbit Breeders Assn., Wash. State Rabbit and Cavy Shows Inc. (sec. 1994—), Evergreen Rabbit Assn. (sec., v.p., pres.), Alpha Gamma Delta, Women of Vision (bd. dir. 2004-), Sons/Daughters Pearl Harbor Survivors. Home: 20825 Star Rte 410 E PMB 196 Sumner WA 98390 E-mail: CindyWick@aol.com.

WICKIZER, STEPHEN WESLEY, pharmacist; b. Oklahoma City, Mar. 1, 1952; s. James and Virginia (Harris) W.; m. Joyce Baugher, Nov. 12, 1980; children: Alison, Stephanie. BS, U. Tenn. Ctr. Health Scis., 1975; D in Pharmacy, U. Md., 1996. Joined USPHS, 1977, advanced through grades to capt.; staff pharmacist Dept. Vets. Affairs, 1975-77; clin. pharmacist NIH, Bethesda, 1977-80; from dept. chief pharmacy to staff pharmacist USPHS Indian Health Svc., Okla, N.C., 1980-87; from pharmacist to health programs coord. FDA, Rockville, Md., 1987-91; adminstrv. officer Office of Surgeon Gen. Pub. Health Svc., Rockville, 1991-92; dep. dir. Office of Drug Pricing HRSA, Bethesda, Md., 1992-98; health sci. adminstr. sci. rev. divsn. Agency HealthCare Rsch. and Quality, Rockville, Md., 1998—2001; tech. transfer specialist NIH, NCI, TTB, Frederick, Md., 2001—. Clin. instr. U. Md. Sch. Pharmacy, Balt., 1997—. Disaster relief vol. Commd. Corps Readiness Force, USPHS. Fellow Am. Pharmacist Assn. Mem.: Commd. Officers Assn. of USPHS, Aircraft Owner's and Pilots Assn., Food and Drug Pharm. Soc., Am. Pharm. Assn., Expt. Aircraft Assn., Assn. Mil. Surgeons U.S., Fed. Health Care Execs. Inst. Methodist. Avocations: flying, diving, skiing, substance abuse prevention counseling. Office: NIH NCI Frederick Tech Transfer Br 1003 W 7th St Fairview Ctr Ste 502 Frederick MD 21701-1201 E-mail: wickizes@mail.nih.gov.

WICKLAND, J. AL, JR., petroleum product executive, real estate executive; CEO Wickland, to 1995, chmn. emeritus, 1995—. Office: Wickland Corp 3600 American River Dr Ste 145 Sacramento CA 95864-5997 also: PO Box 13648 Sacramento CA 95853-4648

WICKLEIN, JOHN FREDERICK, journalist, educator; b. Reading, Pa., July 20, 1924; s. Raymond Roland and Parmilla Catherine (Miller) W.; m. Myra Jane Winchester, July 31, 1948 (dec. 2002); children: Elizabeth, Peter, Joanna. LittB, Rutgers U., 1947; MS in Journalism, Columbia, 1948. Reporter Newark (N.J.) Evening News, 1947-51; news mng. editor Elec. World (McGraw-Hill weekly), N.Y.C., 1951-54; reporter, editor N.Y. Times, 1954-62; news dir. Sta. WNET-TV, N.Y.C., 1962-64; exec. producer news Sta. WABC-TV, N.Y.C., 1964-67; exec. producer Washington Bur. chief Pub. Broadcast Lab. (Nat. Ednl. TV), 1967-70; mng. news and pub. affairs broadcasts Sta. WCBS-TV, N.Y.C., 1970-71; gen. mgr. Sta. WRVR, N.Y.C., 1971-74; prof. journalism and broadcasting Boston U., 1974-80; dean Sch. Public Communication Boston U., 1974-78; vis. prof. communication Meth. U., São Paulo, Brazil, 1979; program officer for news and pub. affairs programs Corp. for Pub. Broadcasting, 1980-84; Willard M. Kiplinger chair in pub. affairs reporting, dir. Kiplinger mid-career program for journalists Ohio State U., 1984-89; Fulbright rsch. scholar Charles Sturt Univ., Bathurst, NSW, Australia, 1990. Lectr., cons. Rutgers U. Media Resources Ctr., Cracow, Poland, 1992, 94; Ayers vis. prof. journalism Jacksonville (Ala.) State U., 1992-93; prodr. news documentaries for pub. and comml. TV; ind. writing, reporting and editing coach for newspapers including Washington Post, Buffalo News, Memphis Comml. Appeal, 1994—; coord. Working Group for Pub. Broadcasting, 1987-89; spl. com. on regulation of media ACLU, 1988-92; adj. faculty Poynter Inst. for Media Studies, 1988; adj. prof. journalism for rsch. Ohio State U., 1991-93; media ethics com. Nat. Coun. Chs., 1975-92; fellow Inst. Dem. Comm. Boston U., 1975-78; newsroom trainers group Poynter Inst., 1995—; lectr., cons. in field. Author: (with Monroe Price) Cable Television: A Guide for Citizen Action, 1972, Electronic Nightmare: The New Communications and Freedom, 1981; editor: Investigative Reporting: The Lessons of Watergate, 1975; contgb. editor The Washington Monthly, 1969-72; contbr. to Am. Journalism Review, The Progressive, TV Quar., Atlantic Monthly, Columbia Journalism Rev., Archeology, Quill, Australian Journalism Rev., others. Recipient George Polk award, 1963, documentary award, Venice Film Festival, 1968, DuPont award, 1973, Brechner Freedom Info. prize, 1987. Mem.: ACLU, Amnesty Internat. USA, Phi Beta Kappa. Democrat. Home and Office: 23200 Wilderness Walk Ct Gaithersburg MD 20882-2732 Office Phone: 301-916-4494. Personal E-mail: fwicklein@comcast.net.

WICKLINE, MARIAN ELIZABETH, former corporate librarian; b. St. Louis, Feb. 18, 1915; d. William Anderson and Grace B. (Gooding) W. BA, Mills Coll., 1935; postgrad., U. Calif., Berkeley, 1935-37. Tech. files asst. Shell Devel. Co., San Francisco, 1938-45; libr. western div. Dow Chem. Co., Pitts. and Walnut Creek, Calif., 1945-75; ret., 1975. Mem. Planning Commn., Danville, Calif., 1982—86, El Dorado County Libr. Commn., Placerville, Calif., 1989—92, mem. policy adv. com. gen. plan, 1989—92, mem. commn. on aging, 2000—02; bd. dirs. Greenstone Country Cmty. Svcs. Dist., 1994—98. Named Woman of Yr. San Ramon Valley C. of C., Danville, Calif., 1983. Mem. AAUW (Gift Honoree 1982, 84), Am. Chem. Soc., Spl. Libr. Assn. (pres. San Francisco Bay region chpt. 1973-74, chair chemistry divsn. 1970-71). Avocation: gardening. Home: 5474 Comstock Rd Placerville CA 95667-8712

WICKLINE, SAMUEL ALAN, cardiologist, educator; b. Huntington, W.Va., Oct. 23, 1952; BA in Philosophy cum laude, Pomona Coll., 1974; MD, U. Hawaii, 1980. Diplomate Am. Bd. Internal Medicine, Am. Bd. Cardiology. Intern, resident in internal medicine Barnes Hosp. Barnes/Washington U. Sch. Medicine, St. Louis, 1980-83, clin. fellow in cardiology, 1983-85, rsch. fellow in cardiology, 1985-87; asst. prof. medicine Sch. Medicine Washington U. Sch. Medicine, St. Louis, 1987-93, assoc. prof., 1993—, adj. asst. prof. physics, 1990, adj. assoc. prof. physics, 1994, attending cardiologist, dir. echocardiology Jewish Hosp., 1992—, prof. medicine and physics, 1997, dir. divsn. cardiology, 1993—. Reviewer Jour. Clin. Investigation, Circulation, Arteriosclerosis and Thrombosis, Hypertension, Ultrasound in Medicine and Biology; contbr. over 100 articles to med. and sci. jours., chpts. to books on topics related to basic rsch. in cardiovascular biophysics and acoustics/ultrasonics. Grantee NIH, Am. Heart Assn., Whitaker Found. Fellow Am. Coll. Cardiology (reviewer jour.); mem. IEEE Soc. Ultrasonics, Ferroelectrics and Frequency Control, Am. Heart Assn. (coun. on radiology and clin. cardiology, Clinician-Scientist award 1988-93, Established Investigator award 1993—), Am. Soc. Clin. Investigation, Am. Inst. Ultrasound in Medicine, Acoustical Soc. Am., Alpha Omega Alpha. Home: 11211 Pointe Ct Saint Louis MO 63127-1741 Office: Jewish Hosp Cardiology 216 S Kingshighway Blvd Saint Louis MO 63110-1026

WICKLUND, DAVID WAYNE, lawyer; b. St. Paul, Aug. 7, 1949; s. Wayne Glenwood and Elna Katherine (Buresh) W.; m. Susan Marie Bubenko, Nov. 17, 1973; children: David Jr., Kurt, Edward. BA cum laude, Williams Coll., 1971; JD cum laude, U. Toledo, 1974. Bar: Ohio 1974. Assoc. Shumaker, Loop & Kendrick, Toledo, 1974-80, ptnr., 1981—. Adj. instr. law, U. Toledo, 1988. Editor-in-chief U. Toledo Law Rev. 1973-74. Mem.: ABA, Toledo Bar Assn., Ohio State Bar Assn. (bd. govs. antitrust sect. 1994—2001), U. Toledo Coll. Law Alumni Assn. (pres. 1999—2000), Inverness Club. Office: Shumaker Loop & Kendrick N Courthouse Sq 1000 Jackson St Toledo OH 43624-1573 Office Phone: 419-321-1213. Business E-Mail: dwicklund@slk-law.com.

WICKMAN, JOHN EDWARD, librarian, historian; b. Villa Park, Ill., May 24, 1929; s. John Edward and Elsie (Voss) W.; m. Shirley Jean Swanson, Mar. 17, 1951; children— Lisa Annette, Eric John. AB, Elmhurst Coll., 1953; A.M., Ind. U., 1958, PhD, 1964; LL.D., Lincoln Coll., 1973. Instr. history Hanover (Ind.) Coll., 1959-62, Southeast Campus, Ind. U., Jeffersonville, 1962; asst. prof. history Northwest Mo. State Coll., Maryville, 1962-64; asst. to Gov. William H. Avery of Kans., Topeka, 1964-65; asst. prof. history Regional Campus, Purdue U., Fort Wayne, Ind., 1965-66; dir. Dwight D. Eisenhower Libr., Abilene, Kans., 1966-89; ret., 1989. Contbr. articles on Am. West, archival mgmt., adminstrv. history, oral history to profl. publs. Served with U.S. Army, 1953-55. Nat. Ctr. for Edn. in Politics faculty fellow, 1964-65; Am. Polit. Sci. Assn. Congl. fellow, 1975-76 Mem. Oral History Assn. (v.p. 1971-72, pres. 1972-73), Western History Assn. (coun. 1972-75), Kans. Hist. Soc. (2d v.p. 1974-75, pres. 1976-77, dir.). Home: 411 W 4th St PO Box 325 Enterprise KS 67441-0325

WICKMAN, PETER M. sociologist, educator; b. Sault Ste Marie, Mich., Feb. 23, 1923; s. John Silas and Estelle (MacAdam) W.; m. Helen L. Colborne, Mar. 19, 1949 (div. 1964); 1 child, Stephen B.; m. Winona Moore Marsh, Sept. 1, 1984; 1 child, Matthew L. Marsh. BA in History, Greenville Coll., 1948; MA, Northwestern U., 1949; EdD, Mich. State U., 1960. Instr. soc. sci. John Wesley Coll., Owosso, Mich., 1950-54; asst., assoc. prof. Greenville (Ill.) Coll., 1954-60; asst. prof. U. Fla., Gainesville, 1960-63; assoc. prof. Nassau Comm. Coll., Garden City, N.Y., 1963-67; prof. in soc. and crim. SUNY, 1967-92, emeritus prof. sociology crim. and pub. policy; instr. Coll. Within Prison Walls, Colo., Ariz., 1992-94. Vis. prof. Troy (Ala.) State U., 1961, dir., cons. St. Law Regional, Canton N.Y., 1971-72, evaluation rschr. Assoc. Coll., Potsdam, N.Y., 1974-75, conf. organizer SUNY EEOP, 1969, Internat. White Collar Cr. 1980, rschr. UUP & SUNY Sabbatic, 1983-84; spkr. in field; adj. prof. sociology and criminology, SUNY Oswego and Canton, 1995-98; dir. rsch. Housing of Aging, N.Y., 1971, Regional Cmty. Corrections, Study, LEAA, 1971-72; evaluation field rschr. Kircshner Assocs., Albuquerque, 1973-80; rsch. of prisons reform in Nordic countries, 1974-75; participant in combind Congress of Japanese Soc. Control of Internat. Social Assn., Hiroshima, 1976. Editor: Readings in Soc. Prob's, 1973-76, Soc. Prob's Con' Per's, 1977, co-editor: Readings in Criminology, 1978, White Collar Crime, 1982, Contemporary Perspectives on Social Problems, 1977, others; co-author: Criminology Perspect's, 1980, Perspectives on Crime: Readings in Criminology, 1979; USIA Symposium lectures Am. Justice Sys., Estonia Nat. Pub. Svc. Acad., Nov. 1993; contbr. articles to profl. jours. Mem. bd. dirs. Potsdam Food Co-op, 1977-79, St. Francis Acad., Lake Placid, 1985-92, Reach-Out Crisis Line, Potsdam, N.Y., 1986-89; WWII vet. Mem. Am. Soc. of Criminology. Episcopalian. Avocations: tennis, reading, hiking, mountain climbing, travel. Home: 4 Somerset Dr Potsdam NY 13676-1635

WICKRAMASEKARA, SUJEEV, physicist, educator; s. W. K. and C. Wickramasekara. BS in Physics summa cum laude, U. Calif., 1993; PhD, U. Tex., 1999. Vis. scientist Erwin Scroedinger Inst., Vienna, 2000; postdoctoral fellow, lectr. U. Tex., Austin, 2000—03; asst. prof. St. Olaf Coll., Northfield, Minn., 2003—. Dir. conf. on irreversible quantum dynamics Internat. Ctr. Theoretical Physics, Trieste, Italy, 2002; spkr. in field. Contbr. more than 20 articles to profl. jours. Trustee scholar, U. So. Calif., 1990—93, Tuition fellow, U. Tex., 1996, 1997, 1999. Mem.: Internat. Ctr. Theoretical Physics (mem. referee com. 2002), Sigma Xi. Achievements include research in theoretical

and mathematical physics. Home: 1020 Ensley Ave #88 Northfiled MN 55057 Office: St Olaf Coll Physics Dept 1520 St Olaf Ave Northfield MN 55057 Personal E-mail: wickrama@stolaf.edu.

WICKRAMASEKERA, IAN EDWARD, psychophysiologist, psychology educator; b. Colombo, Ceylon, Oct. 23, 1938; s. Harry S. and Maude (Robinson) W.; m. Judy Wickram; children: Melissa, Ian Edward II. BA, Friend's U., Wichita, Kans., 1961; MA, Roosevelt U., Chgo., 1966; PhD, U. Ill., 1969. Diplomate Am. Bd. Profl. Psychology; diplomate in exptl. hypnosis Am. Bd. Psychol. Hypnosis. Assoc. prof. psychiatry Coll. Medicine U. Ill., 1974-80; prof. Ea. Va. Med. Sch., Norfolk, 1981-95, prof. family medicine, 1995—; clin. prof. psychiatry Med. Sch. Stanford (Calif.) U., 1995—; prof. psychology Saybrook Inst., San Francisco, 1995—. Author: Clinical Behavioral Medicine, 1988; editor: Biofeedback, Behavior Therapy and Hypnosis, 1976; contbr. over 100 articles to med. and sci. jours. Recipient Morton Prince award Am. Bd. Profl. Hypnosis, 1992. Mem. APA (pres. divsn. 30F hypnosis 1996-97), Assn. for Applied Psychophysiology (pres. 1998-99, Salvador Dali award 1991), Va. Hypnosis Soc. (pres. 1987-88). Roman Catholic. Home: 4055 Oak Pointe Dr Gulf Breeze FL 32563-8510 E-mail: iwickram@saybrook.edu.

WICKRAMASINGHE, HEMANTHA KUMAR, electrical engineer, physicist; b. Colombo, Sri Lanka, May 31, 1949; naturalized U.S. citizen, 1996; s. Percival Herbert and Therese Elizabeth (Soysa) W.; m. Sophie Marie de La Porte, Nov. 17, 1973; children: Lucille Samantha, Anita Elizabeth. BSc in Electronic Engring., U. London, 1970, PhD in Electronic and Elec. Engring., 1974. Assoc. rsch. asst. dept. electronic and elec. engring. U. Coll. London, 1974-75, lectr. dept. electronic and elec. engring., 1978-83; rsch. assoc. E.L. Ginzton Lab. Stanford (Calif.) U., 1975-78; mgr. phys. measurements IBM, T.J. Watson Rsch. Ctr., Yorktown Heights, NY, 1984-96, chief scientist mfg. rsch., 1992-94, mgr. imaging sci. and measurement tech., 1996—2002, IBM fellow, 2000—; sr. mgr. nanoscale and quantum studies IBM Almaden Rsch. Ctr., San Jose, Calif., 2002—. Cons. Hirst Rsch. Ctr. GE Co., London, 1980-83, U.K. Atomic Energy Authority, Harwell, Eng., 1980-82; adj. prof. Poly. Inst. N.Y., Bklyn., 1985-87; mem. editl. bds. Nanotech., 1991-96, Advances in Nanoscale Physics, electonics and Engring., 1991—, Rev. of Sci. Instruments, 1996—. Editor: Scanned Probe Microscopy, 1992; co-editor: Determining Nanoscale Properties of Materials by Microscopy and Spectroscopy, 1994; contbr. over 150 articles to profl. jours.; holder numerous patents in field. Recipient V.K. Zworykin premium, Inst. Elec. Engrs., 1983, Disting. Corp. Inventor award, Nat. Inventors Hall of Fame, 1998, Morris E. Leeds award, IEEE, 1992, Joseph F. Keithley award, Am. Phys. Soc., 2000. Fellow: IBM, Royal Microscopical Soc., Inst. of Physics, IEEE, Am. Phys. Soc. (centennial spkr. 1999); mem.: Nat. Acad. Engring. Achievements include first introduction of atomic force microscopes into manufacturing lines, first deployment of a magnetic force microscope capable of imaging nanometer scale magnetic properties, work in areas of optics, acoustics, photoacoustics, metrology and scanning probe microscopy. Home: 1261 Echo Valley Dr San Jose CA 95120 Office: IBM Almaden Rsch Ctr 650 Harry Rd San Jose CA 95120 E-mail: hkwick@us.ibm.com.

WICKS, DAVID O., JR., communications executive; b. Boston, May 17, 1941; s. David O. and Elizabeth L. Wicks; m. Joan Gagnebin, Sept. 7, 1963; children: Perrin, Sara. BA, Trinity Coll., Hartford, Conn., 1963; MBA, U. Va., 1968. With nat. divsn. Chem. Bank, 1963—66; specialist in venture capital and cable TV Warburg Paribas Becker, NYC, 1968—83, mng. dir., 1979—83; gen. ptnr. Becker Venture Assoc., Becker Comms. Assoc. II; sr. ptnr. Criterion Venture Ptnr., Houston, 1983—88. Mng. dir. Criterion Investments, Inc., 1983-88; pres. Criterion Investments, Inc., 1985-88; v.p. Cablevision Sys. Corp., Bethpage, NY, 1996-2002; pres. Devonshire Comms. Assocs. Cons., 2002—, ptnr. The Alwyn Group, LLC, exec. NASA Mid Continent Tech. Transfer Ctr., 1992-95; bd. dir. Matrix Enterprises Inc.; expert witness on cable TV, US Congress and state regulatory bodies. Contbr. articles to profl. jour. Bd. dir. Adult Literacy Media Alliance, Vis. Nurse Assn. NY; chmn. Cable Positive, Inc., 2003—, Interactive TV Assocs.; elected pioneer CATV, 2000. Recipient Vanguard award Nat. Cable TV Assn., 1978. Mem.: Univ. Club (NYC). Office Phone: 516-695-2951.

WICKS, JOHN R. lawyer; b. Ottumwa, Iowa, Dec. 8, 1937; m. Nedra Morgan, Mar. 27, 1940; children: Catherine, John. BSC, U. Iowa, 1959, JD, 1964. Bar: Iowa 1964, Minn. 1966. Assoc. Dorsey & Whitney, Mpls., 1966-71; ptnr. Dorsey & Whitney LLP, Rochester, Minn., 1972-2000, of counsel Mpls., 2001—. Fellow: Am. Coll. Trusts and Estates Counsel; mem.: Minn. State Bar Assn. (probate and trusts law coun. 1989—92). Office: Dorsey & Whitney LLP 50 S 6th St Minneapolis MN 55402-1498 E-mail: wicks.john@dorseylaw.com.

WICKS, WILLIAM WITHINGTON, retired public relations executive; b. Chgo., Dec. 20, 1923; s. William and Alice (Withington) W.; m. Frances M. Horner, Nov. 29, 1947; children: Barbara Anne, Christine Frances. BNS, U. Notre Dame, 1944, AB in Journalism magna cum laude, 1947. Staff corr. United Press Assn., Milw., 1947; pub. rels. mgr. Internat. Harvester Co., Louisville, 1948-58; mgr. field svcs. pub. rels. Std. Oil Co. (Ind.), Chgo., 1959—60; v.p. pub. rels. Griswold-Eshleman Co., Chgo., 1961-68; dir. pub. rels. G. D. Searle & Co., Chgo., 1968-74; dir. pub. rels./investor rels. Kimberly-Clark Corp., Neenah, Wis., 1974, staff v.p., 1974-80, v.p. Neenah (hdqrs. relocated to Dallas in 1985), 1980-89, v.p. and asst. to CEO, 1989-92. Chmn. pub. relations sect. Pharm. Mfrs. Assn., Washington, 1974. Pres. Jr. Achievement Neenah-Menasha, 1978-81; bd. mem. Friends of the Irving Pub. Libr., 1997-99. Served to lt. (j.g.) USNR, 1942-46, PTO. Recipient Silver Anvil award Pub. Rels. Soc. Am., 1963, 79. Mem. PRSA (founder, pres. Bluegrass chpt. 1957-58), Optimist (pres. South End Club in Louisville 1957), Publicity Club of Chgo. (pres. 1967-68), Las Colinas Sports Club (Irving), USN Meml. Found. (plank owner), Navy League U.S., Patrol Craft Sailors Assn. Republican. Roman Catholic. Home: 1312 Travis Cir S Irving TX 75038-6243

WICKSTED, JAMES PETER, physicist, educator, research scientist; b. N.Y.C., June 4, 1953; s. James Crease and Helen Maria Wicksted; m. Carol Jean Amess, May 19, 1990; children: Kelly Sullins, Jill Elaine England. BA, NYU, 1975; MA, CCNY, 1978; PhD, CUNY, 1983. Postdoctoral rschr. Brookhaven Nat. Lab., Upton, NY, 1983—85; from asst. prof. to prof. physics, Noble rsch. fellow Okla. State U., Stillwater, 1985—, dir. Ctr. Sensors and Sensor Tech., 1997—2003, interim dir. Ctr. Laser and PHotonics Rsch., 2003, interim head dept. physics, 2003. Vis. assoc. prof. biomed. laser and spectroscopy program dept. surgery U. Tex. Med. Br., Galveston, 1992—94, collaborator and cons. Biomed. Engring. Ctr., 1995—; presenter, spkr. in field. Contbr. articles to profl. jours. Noble fellow in optical materials, Noble Found., 1987—, George Granger Brown scholar, 1974. Mem.: AAAS (vice-chair, phys. sciences sect. Southwestern and Rocky Mountain 1995—96), Optical Soc. Am., Am. Phys. Soc. (editor divsn. laser sci. newsletter 1995—97), Pi Mu Epsilon, Sigma Pi Sigma. Democrat. Achievements include patents pending for implantable biosensor from stratified nanostructured membranes; design of optical system to diagnosis eye related problems; research in optical storage in glass materials; water-induced changes in the cornea of the eye. Avocations: reading, jogging, travel. Home: PO Box 1284 Stillwater OK 74076 Office: Okla State U Physics Dept 145 PS 2 Stillwater OK 74078-3072 Office Phone: 405-744-5807. Personal E-mail: jpw519@yahoo.com. E-mail: jpw519@okstate.edu.

WICKSTROM, JON ALAN, telecommunications executive, consultant; b. San Antonio, Apr. 17, 1949; s. Stanley Alan and Louise W.; m. Mary Carmen Sparkman, Jan. 25, 1969 (div. Jan. 1978); children: Dana Marie, Jon Alan Jr.; m. Jane Bielbey Slawson, June 19, 1988. BS, Tex. Tech. U., 1975; MS, U. Tex., 1998. Ptnr. Hensley & Assocs., Albuquerque, 1976-78; dealer svcs. mgr. Gulf States Toyota, Houston, 1978-80; comms. mgr. Hughes Tool Co., Houston, 1980-85; network svcs. mgr. Tenneco Oil Co., Houston, 1986-89; comms. mgr. Clarke Am., San Antonio, 1989-94; info/tech. planner USAA, San Antonio, 1994-96; sr. mgr. MMC Ernst & Young LLP, San Antonio, 1996-2000, Cap Gemini Ernst & Young, 2000—02; prin. Comm. Tech. Cons., Houston, 1980—96, 2002—. Author: (reference) 1976 Population Estimates for Bernallio County, New Mex., 1976. Rep. precinct chmn. Bexar County, Tex., 1992-94; cons. Houston Symphony Orch., 1988. Mem. Alamo Area Telecomms. Assn. (bd. dirs 1990-94, pres., 1992-93), S.W. Comms. Assn. (bd. dirs. 1981-85, pres. 1982-84), Tex. Telecomms. Conf. (bd. dirs. 1982-84, chmn. 1983), Am. Mensa. Avocations: sailing, golf, music, investing. E-mail: wickstrom@sbcglobal.net.

WICKUS, JAMES D. food service executive; m. Judee Wickus; 3 children. BSBA, Spencerian Bus. Coll., 1964. Various positions Baraboo Food Products (now Sysco Food Svcs.), Wis., 1964—78; pres. ops. Sysco Corp., 1978—96, pres., CEO, 1996—2003, sr. v.p. food svc. ops. Canton, Mich., 2003—. Office: Sysco Corp 41600 Van Born Rd Canton MI 48188-2797

WICKWIRE, PATRICIA JOANNE NELLOR, psychologist, educator; d. William McKinley and Clara Rose (Pautsch) Nellor; m. Robert James Wickwire, Sept. 7, 1957; 1 child, William James. BA cum laude, U. No. Iowa, 1951; MA, U. Iowa, 1959; PhD, U. Tex., Austin, 1971; postgrad., U. So. Calif., 1951-66, UCLA, 1951-66, Calif. State U., Long Beach, 1951-66. Lic. ednl. psychologist, marriage, family and child counselor, Calif. Tchr. Ricketts Ind. Schs., Iowa, 1946-48; tchr., counselor Waverly-Shell Rock Ind. Schs., Iowa, 1951-55; reading cons., head dormitory counselor U. Iowa, Iowa City, 1955-57; tchr., sch. psychologist, adminstr. S. Bay Union H.S. Dist., Redondo Beach, Calif., 1962-82, dir. student svcs. and spl. edn. Cons. mgmt. and edn.; pres. Nellor Wickwire Group, 1981—; mem. exec. bd. Calif. Interagy. Mental Health Coun., 1968-72, Beach Cities Symphony Assn., 1970-82; chmn. Friends of Dominguez Hills, Calif., 1981-85. Contbr. articles in field to profl. jours. Pres. Calif. Women's Caucus, 1993-95, 2003—. Mem. APA, AAUW (exec. bd., chpt. pres. 1962-72), Nat. Career Devel. Assn. (media chair 1992-98), Am. Assn. Career Edn. (pres. 1991—), L.A. County Dirs. Pupil Svcs. (chmn. 1974-79), L.A. County Pers. and Guidance Assn. (pres. 1977-78), Assn. Calif. Sch. Adminstrs. (dir. 1977-81), L.A. County SW Bd. Dist. Adminstrs. for Spl. Edn. (chmn. 1976-81), Calif. Assn. Sch. Psychologists (bd. dirs. 1981-83), Am. Assn. Sch. Adminstrs., Calif. Assn. for Measurement and Evaluation in Guidance (dir. 1981, pres. 1984-85, 98-2000), ACA (chmn. Coun. Newsletter Editors 1989-91, mem. com. on women 1989-92, mem. com. on rsch. and knowledge 1994—, chmn. 1995—, mem. and chmn. bylaws com. 1998-2001, rep. to joint com. on testing practices 2001—), Assn. Measurement and Eval. in Guidance (Western regional editor 1985-87, conv. chair 1986, editor 1987-90, exec. bd. dirs. 1987-91), Calif. Assn. Counseling and Devel. (exec. bd. 1984—, pres. 1988-89, jour. editor 1990—), Nat. Assn. for Ind.-Edn. Coop. (bd. dirs. 2002—), Internat. Career Assn. Network (chair 1985—), Pi Lambda Theta, Alpha Phi Gamma, Psi Chi, Kappa Delta Pi, Sigma Alpha Iota. Office: The Nellor Wickwire Group 2900 Amby Pl Hermosa Beach CA 90254-2216 Office Phone: 310-376-7378.

WIDAMAN, GREG, financial executive, accountant; b. St. Louis, 1955; s. Raymond Paul and Louise Agnes Widaman. BS in Bus. and Econs. cum laude, Trinity U., 1978. CPA, Tex. Sr. auditor Arthur Andersen LLP, Houston, 1978-82; sr. cons. Price Waterhouse, Houston, 1983-85; fin. advisor to segment pres. Teledyne, Inc., Century City, Calif., 1985-95; sr. mgr. ops. planning for consumer products ABC Broadcasting/TV The Walt Disney Co., Burbank, Calif., 1995-97; v.p. internal audit and spl. projects Hilton Hotels Corp., Beverly Hills, Calif., 1997—. Cons. Arthur Andersen LLP, Price Waterhouse, Teledyne, Walt Disney Co., Hilton Hotels Corp. Mem. AICPAs, Calif. Soc. CPAs, Christian Bus. Mens com. of U.S.A., World Affairs Coun., MIT/Calif. Tech. Enterprise Forum. Republican. Avocations: white water rafting, water and snow skiing, camping, business, chess. Office: Hilton Hotels Corp World Hdqrs 9336 Civic Center Dr Beverly Hills CA 90210-3604 Office Phone: 310-205-4578.

WIDDER, KENNETH JON, pathologist, educator; b. Chgo., Jan. 14, 1953; s. Alan A. and Edith Widder. BS, Carleton Coll., 1974; MD, Northwestern U., Evanston, Ill., 1979. Intern Duke U., Durham, N.C., 1979-80, resident in pathology, 1980-81; asst. clin. prof. pathology U. Calif., San Diego, 1981-84, assoc. clin. prof., 1984—; chmn., chief exec. officer Molecular Biosystems, Inc., San Diego, 1981—. Cons. Eli Lilly & Co., Indpls., 1978-83; mem. adv. com. Congl. Sci. and Tech. Com., Washington, 1986-88. Editor: Methods in Enzymology: Drug and Enzyme Targeting, 1985; patentee in field. Recipient Wiley J. Forbus award N.C. Sco. Pathology, 1981. Mem. AAAS, Am. Soc. Clin. Pathologists, Young Pres. Orgn., Sigma Xi. Office: Santarus Inc 10590 W Ocean Air Dr Ste 200 San Diego CA 92130

WIDDICOMBE, RICHARD PALMER, librarian; b. Paterson, N.J., Apr. 12, 1941; s. Robert Lord and Elvira Barbara (Guttilla) W.; m. Martha Elizabeth Bruyn, Feb. 26, 1972 BA, Alfred U., 1963; MS L.S., Syracuse U., 1964. Asst. librarian Yonkers Pub. Library, N.Y., 1964-65; asst. librarian Cooper Union, N.Y.C., 1965-66, Stevens Inst., Hoboken, N.J., 1966-72, dir. library, 1973—. Trustee Alfred U., NY; trustee, chmn. bd. Hoboken Hist. Mus., 2002—. Episcopalian. Home: 1 Castle Point Ter S1342 Hoboken NJ 07030-5906 Office: SC Williams Libr Stevens Inst Hoboken NJ 07030 Office Phone: 201-216-5421. E-mail: rpw@stevens.edu.

WIDEMAN, JOHN EDGAR, English literature educator, novelist; b. Washington, June 14, 1941; married; 3 children. BA, U. Pa., 1963; BPhil, Oxford U., Eng., 1966; postgrad., U. Iowa Writers Workshop, 1967; DLitt (hon.), U. Pa., 1985, Rutgers U. Mem. faculty U. Wyo., Laramie, prof. English, 1974—85, U. Mass., Amherst, Mass., 1986—. USIS lectr. in Ea. Europe. Author: A Glance Away, 1967, Hurry Home, 1969, The Lynchers, 1973, Hiding Place, 1981, Damballah, 1981, Sent for You Yesterday, 1983 (PEN Faulkner award for fiction, 84), Brothers and Keepers, 1984, Reuben, 1987, Fever, 1989, Philadelphia Fire, 1990 (PEN Faulkner award for fiction, 91), The Homewood Books, 1992, The Stories of John Edgar Wideman, 1992, All Stories Are True, 1993, Fatheralong, 1994, The Cattle Killing, 1996; contbr. numerous articles and revs. to profl. jours., mags. Recipient Lannan award, 1991; fellow Kent fellow, MacArthur fellow, 1993; grantee, Nat. Endowment for Humanities; scholar Ben Franklin scholar, Rhodes scholar. Mem.: MLA, Am. Acad. Arts Scis., Am. Studies Assn. (mem. coun. 1980—81), Am. Assn. Rhodes Scholars (dir.). Office: Univ Mass Dept English Bartlett Hall Amherst MA 01003-0515

WIDEN, DENNIS CHARLES, music educator; b. Corwith, Iowa, Mar. 22, 1949; s. Charles Thomas Widen and Doris Marie Weiland. MusB in Edn., Drake U., 1967—71, MusM in Piano Performance, 1971—73; PhD in Music Edn., U. of Okla., 1994—99. Instr. of music Western Mont. Coll., Dillon, Mont., 1973—80; dir. NE Iowa Acad. of Music, Monticello, Iowa, 1980—90; adj. instr. of music Kirkwood C.C., Cedar Rapids, 1990—93; asst. prof. of music Southwestern Okla. State U., Weatherford. Mem.: Music Educators Nat. Conf., Music Teachers Nat. Assn., Phi Mu Alpha Sinfonia. Democrat. Roman Catholic. Office: Southwestern Okla State U 100 Campus Dr Weatherford OK 73096 Office Phone: 580-774-3216. E-mail: dennis.widen@swosu.edu.

WIDENER, HIRAM EMORY, JR., judge; b. Abingdon, Va., Apr. 30, 1923; s. Hiram Emory and Nita Douglas (Peck) Widener; children: Molly Berendt, Hiram Emory III. Student, Va. Poly. Inst., 1940—41; BS, U.S. Naval Acad., 1944; LLB, Washington and Lee U., 1953, LLD, 1977. Bar: Va. 1951. Pvt. practice, Bristol, Va., 1953—69; judge U.S. Dist. Ct. (we. dist.) Va., Abingdon, 1969—71, chief judge, 1971—72; judge U.S. Ct. of Appeals (4th cir.), Abingdon, 1972—. U.S. commr. Western Dist. Va., 1963—66; mem. Va. Election Laws Study Commn., 1968—69. Chmn. Rep. 9th Dist., Va., 1966—69; state exec. com. Va. Rep. State Ctrl. Com., 1966—69. Lt. (j.g.) USN, 1944—49, lt. USNR, 1951—52. Decorated Bronze Star with combat V. Mem.: Va. State Bar, Va. Bar Assn., Am. Law Inst., Phi Alpha Delta. Republican. Presbyterian. Office: US Courthouse 180 E Main St Rm 123 Abingdon VA 24210-2839 Office Phone: 276-628-3138.

WIDENER, PERI ANN, business development executive; b. Wichita, Kans., May 1, 1956; d. Wayne Robert and LuAnne (Harris) W. BS, Wichita State U., 1978; MBA, Fla. Tech., 1992. Advt. intern Associated Advt., Wichita, 1978; pub. rels. asst. Fourth Nat. Bank, Wichita, 1978-79; mktg. communications rep. Boeing Co., Wichita, 1979-83, pub. rels. rep. Huntsville, Ala., 1983-85, pub. rels. mgr., 1985-92; sr. pub. rels. mgr. Boeing Mil. Airplanes, Seattle, 1992-95; bus. devel. mgr. Boeing Defense & Space Group, Washington, D.C., 1995-97, mem. exec. devel. program, 1993—, dir. Airborne Laser activities, 1997—; dir. bus. devel. The Boeing Co., Washington, 1998—, Info. Space and Def. Sys., Washington; dir. Lasers & ElectroOptics, Washington Office, 1998. Preston Huston scholar, Wichita State U., 1978; recipient Best Electronic Ad award Def. Electronics mag., 1982, Best Total Pub. Rels. Program award Huntsville Press Club, 1985, Huntsville Media awards, 1986, 87, 88, 89, 90, 91, Huntsville Advt. Fedn. Addys, 1988. Mem. Pub. Rels. Soc. Am. (Seattle chpt.), Women in Communications, Pub. Rels. Coun. Ala. (bd. dirs. 1985-92, state pres. 1992, officer Huntsville chpt. 1984-91, pres. No. Ala. chpt. 1989, Excellence award 1986-91, Achievement award 1986-91, Pres.'s award Huntsville chpt. 1985, State Practitioner of Yr., 1989, PRCA Medallion award excellence, numerous others), Internat. Assn. Bus. Communicators (D2 Silver Quills award 1985, 91, D6 Silver Quills 1993, 94), Pub. Rels. Soc. Am. (accredited 1989—), So. Pub. Rels. Fedn. (practitioner of yr. 1991, Excellence award 1986-91, Lantern award 1991), Huntsville-Madison County C. of C. (pub. rels. adv. com. 1987-92), Huntsville Press Club (bd. dirs. 1989-92), Sigma Delta Chi (pres.'s award 1991). Office: The Boeing Co 1200 Wilson Blvd Arlington VA 22209-2305

WIDERA, GEORG ERNST OTTO, mechanical engineering educator, consultant; b. Dortmund, Germany, Feb. 16, 1938; arrived in U.S., 1950; s. Otto and Gertrude (Yzermann) Widera; m. Kristel Kornas, June 21, 1974; children: Erika, Nicholas. BS, U. Wis., 1960, MS, 1962, PhD, 1965. Asst. prof. then prof. dept. materials engring. U. Ill., Chgo., 1965-82, prof. mech. engring., 1982-91, head dept., 1983-91, acting head indsl. sys. engring. dept., 1985-86, dir off-campus engring. programs, 1987-88; prof., chmn. mech. and indsl. engring. dept. Marquette U., Milw., 1991—2002, dir. Ctr. Joining and Mfg. Assembly, 2002—, dir. Discovery Learning Ctr., sr. assoc. dean Coll. Engring., 2001—, interim dean Coll. Engring., 1998—99, 2003. Gastdozent U. Stuttgart, Germany, 1968; vis. prof. U. Wis.-Milw., 1973—74, Marquette U., Milw., 1979—80; cons. Ladish Co., Cudahy, Wis., 1967—76, Howmedica, Inc., Chgo., 1972—75, Sargent & Lundy, 1970—88, Nat. Bur. Stds., 1980, bd. dirs.; cons. Engrs. and Scientists Milw., 1996—98; vis. scientist Argonne Nat. Lab., Ill., 1968. Editor: Procs. Innovations in Structural Engring., 1974, Pressure Vessel Design, 1982; assoc. editor: Pressure Vessel Tech., 1977—81, 2003—, Applied Mechanics Revs., 1987—94, Mfg. Rev., 1991—95, mem. editl. adv. bd.: Acta Mechanica Sinica, 1990—, mem. editl. bd.: Pressure Vessels and Piping Design Technology, 1982, tech. editor: Jour. Pressure Vessel Tech., 1982—93; co-editor: SME Handbook of Metalforming, 1985, 1994, Design and Analysis of Plates and Shells, 1986. Fellow Std. Oil Co. Calif., 1961—63, NASA, 1966, von Humboldt, Fed. Republic Germany, 1968—69. Fellow: WRC (chmn. subcom. design procedures for shell intersections 1983—87, chmn. com. reinforced openings and external loads 1987—91, vice chmn. com. polymer pressure components 1991—99, chmn. com. shells and ligaments 1994—97, pressure vessel rsch. coun.), ASCE (sec.-treas. structural divsn. Ill. sect. 1972—73, chmn. divsn. 1976—77, chmn. peer rev. com., tech. coun. rsch. 1984, coun. structural plastics), ASME (chmn. machine design div. Chgo. sect. 1967—68, exec. com. Chgo. sect. 1970—73, editor newsletter Chgo. sect. 1971—73, chmn. jr. awards com. applied mechanics divsn. 1973—76, chmn. design and analysis com. pressure vessel and piping divsn. 1980—83, chmn. pressure vessel rsch. com. 1982—87, bd. editors 1983—93, mem. exec. com. and program chmn. pressure vessel and piping divsn. 1985—89, vice-chmn., sec. pressure vessel and piping divsn. 1989—90, mem. bd. pressure tech. codes and stds. 1989—94, chmn. 1990—91, mem. materials and structures group 1990—91, historian, senate pressure vessel and piping divsn. 1992—93, honors and awards chmn. Milw. sect. 1992—95, mem. coun. engring. 1992—96, v.p., materials and structures group 1993—96, mem. tech. execs. com. 1993—96, Pressure Vessel and Piping medalist 1995), Wis. Mfg. Curriculum Com. (vice-chmn. exec. com. 1998—2002), 2d China Nat. Stds. Com. Pressure Vessels (hon. cons. 1989—94), Internat. Coun. Pressure Vessel Tech. (chmn. Am. regional com. 1988—, internat. chmn. 1992—96, 2003—), Am. Soc. Engring. Edn., Soc. Mfg. Engrs. (sr.), French Pressure Vessel Assn.; mem.: Wis. Assn. Rsch. Mgrs. (v.p. 2003—04, pres. 2004—). Achievements include research in mechanics of composite materials, plate and shell structures, stress analysis (including FEM), pressure vessels, mechanics of deformation processing. Office: Marquette U Coll Engring PO Box 1881 Milwaukee WI 53201-1881 Office Phone: 414-288-6720. E-mail: geo.widera@mu.edu.

WIDGER, CHRIS, professional baseball player; b. Wilmington, Del., May 21, 1971; m. Theresa Kidwell, Dec. 27, 1996. Student, George Mason U. Catcher Seattle Mariners, 1992—95, Montreal Expos, 1996—. Office: The New York Yankees Yankee Stadium 161st St and River Ave Bronx NY 10451 Address: 95 Fort Mott Rd Pennsville NJ 08070-2839

WIDGOFF, MILDRED, physicist, researcher; b. Buffalo, Aug. 24, 1924; d. Leo Widgoff and Rebecca Shulimson; children— Eve Widgoff Shapiro, Jonathan Bernard Widgoff Shapiro. BA, U. Buffalo, 1944; PhD, Cornell U., 1952. Rsch. assoc. Brookhaven Nat. Lab., Yaphank, N.Y., 1952-54; rsch. fellow Harvard U., Cambridge, Mass., 1955-58; asst. prof. rsch. Brown U., Providence, 1959-66, assoc. prof. rsch., 1966-74, prof. physics, 1974-95; prof. rsch., 1995—. Fellow Am. Phys. Soc.; mem. Sigma Xi, Phi Beta Kappa, Phi Kappa Phi. Office: Brown U Dept Physics PO Box 1843 Providence RI 02912-1843

WIDLUND, OLOF BERTIL, computer science educator; b. Stockholm, Feb. 11, 1938; s. Sten O. and Dagmar W.; m. Nadine H. Taub, June 13, 1972. MS in Engring., Royal Inst. Tech., Stockholm, 1960, PhD, 1964; Sc.D., Uppsala U., Sweden, 1966. Asst. prof. NYU, N.Y.C., 1968-72, assoc. prof., 1972-75, prof. computer sci., 1975—, chmn. dept. computer sci., 1980-86. Author articles and monograph on the numerical solutions of partial differential equations. Achievements include research in numerical solutions of partial differential equations. Office: NYU Courant Inst 251 Mercer St New York NY 10012-1110 Business E-Mail: widlund@cims.nyu.edu.

WIDMAN, DOUGLAS JACK, lawyer; b. Neptune, N.J., Feb. 28, 1949; s. Leonard and Phyllis (Rose) W.; m. Jill Rosenblad; children: Phyllis, Jared Leonard, Sarah. BA in Polit. Sci. cum laude, Syracuse U., 1971, JD, 1973. Bar: N.J. 1973, U.S. Dist. Ct. N.J. 1973, U.S. Supreme Ct. 1979, D.C. 1981, N.Y. 1990. Legal planner Syracuse-Onondaga (N.Y.) County Planning Agy., 1971-73; law sec. to presiding judges N.J. Superior Ct., 1973-74; dep. atty gen. State Enforcement Bur. Div. Criminal Justice, Trenton, NJ, 1974; ptnr. Widman, Cooney & Wilson, Oakhurst, NJ, 1976—. Assoc. editor Syracuse Jour. Internat. Law & Commerce. Syracuse U. Coll. Law scholar, 1971-73; Syracuse U. Grad. Research fellow, 1972. Mem. N.J. Bar Assn. (life), Phi Alpha Delta, Alpha Phi Omega, Pi Sigma Alpha. Office: Widman Cooney & Wilson 1803 Hwy 35 Oakhurst NJ 07755-2911

WIDMAN, GARY LEE, lawyer, former government official; b. Fremont, Nebr., June 1, 1936; s. Benjamin H. and Alice C. (Negley) W.; m. Mary Margaret Donnelly, Mar. 5, 1972(div. 1988); children: Andrew Scott, Natalie Claire. BS, U. Nebr., 1957; JD, Hastings Coll. Law U. Calif., 1962; LLM, U. Mich., 1966. Bar: Calif. 1962, D.C. 1982. Assoc. Thelen, Marrin, Johnson & Bridges, San Francisco, 1962-65; assoc. prof. law U. Denver, 1966-69; prof., dir. resource and environ. law program Hastings Coll. Law, U. Calif., San Francisco, 1969-80; gen. counsel Coun. Environ. Quality, Exec. Office Pres., Washington, 1974-76; lectr. U. Calif. at Davis, 1978, Boalt Hall, 1977-79; assoc. solicitor Dept. Interior, Washington, 1980-81; of counsel Fulbright & Jaworski, 1981-85; dir. staff attys. U.S. Ct. of Appeals (9th cir.), San Francisco, 1985-87; atty. Bronson, Bronson & McKinnon, San Francisco, 1988-95; chief counsel State Dept. Parks and Recreation, Sacramento, 1995-96; prof. law Santa Clara (Calif.) U. Law Sch., 1998-99; sr. mediator Concur Inc., Berkeley, Calif., 2001—04. Trustee Rocky Mountain Mineral Law Found., 1969-74, 77-80; apptd. by gov. P. Wilson to Bay-Delta Oversight Coun., 1993-95. Author and project dir.: Legal Study of Oil Shale on Public Lands, 1969. Bd. dirs. Sustainable Bus. Inst. Served with U.S. Army, 1957-59. Mem. ABA (coun. sect. natural resources 1975-77, spl. com. energy law 1977-82, coun. lawyers and scientists 1984-90), Fed. Bar Assn. (chmn. com.

natural resources 1977), Calif. Bar Assn., Trout Unltd. Calif. (pres. 1986-90), Calif. Heritage Coun. (exec. v.p. 2001—). Home: 28 Marinero Cir Apt 31 Tiburon CA 94920-1644 Business E-Mail: gwidman@mindspring.com.

WIDMAN, PAUL JOSEPH, insurance agent; b. DeSmet, S.D., Dec. 18, 1936; s. Warren Clay and Lorraine (Coughlin) W.; m. Elizabeth Ann Healy, July 30, 1959; children: Cynthia, Susan, Shelly, Richard, Mark. BS, Dakota State Coll., Madison, 1959; M in Comm., S.D. State U., 1968. Tchr. Clark (S.D.) Pub. Sch., 1959-60, Henry (S.D.) Pub. Sch., 1960-64, Custer (S.D.) Pub. Sch., 1964-66; ins. agt. Horace Mann Ins., Mitchell, S.D., 1966-77, Universal Underwriters, Mitchell, S.D., 1980-87, NGM Ins. Assn., Mitchell, S.D., 1987-91, Reginald Martin Agy., Mitchell, S.D., 1991—; state rep. State of S.D., 1993—; gen. agt., ins. sales agt. Reginald Martin Agy., Mitchell, 1992—. City coun. mem. Mitchell City Coun., 1972-76; state legislator S.D. Ho. of Reps., 1993-94. Sgt. U.S. Army N.G., 1955-61. Mem. Elks, Mitchell Jaycees (pres., v.p. 1968-70, Outstanding Jaycee 1970), S.D. Jaycees (v.p., regional dir. 1969-70). Democrat. Roman Catholic. Avocations: golf, bowling, hunting. Office: Reginald Martin Agy 510 W Havens St Mitchell SD 57301-3935

WIDMAN, PHILLIP C. machinery manufacturing executive; Fin. and opers. positions Asea Brown Boveri Ltd., 1987—98, v.p., CFO, supply mgmt., 1997—98; exec. v.p., CFO Philip Svcs. Corp., 1998—2001, ind. cons., 2001—02; sr. v.p., CFO Terex Corp., Westport, Conn., 2002—. Office: Terex Corp 500 Post Rd E Ste 320 Westport CT 06880*

WIDMAR, RUSSELL C. airport executive; V.p. airport svcs. Lockheed Air Terminal Inc., 1980-94; dir. Burbank-Glendale-Pasadena Airport, 1984; dir. ops. airport sys. divsn. Hughes Aircraft Co., Fullerton, Calif., 1994-96; exec. dir. aviation Salt Lake City Airport Authority, 1996-99; aviation dir. Kansas City Aviation Dept., 2000—. Office: Dir of Aviation 601 Brasila Ave Kansas City MO 64153

WIDMARK, RICHARD, actor; b. Sunrise, Minn., Dec. 26, 1914; s. Carl H. and Ethel Mae (Barr) W.; m. Ora Jean Hazlewood, Apr. 5, 1942; 1 dau., Anne Heath. BA, Lake Forest (Ill.) Coll., 1936, D.F.A. (hon.), 1973. Instr. drama dept. Lake Forest Coll., 1936-38; Pres. Heath Prodns., 1955—; v.p. Widmark Cattle Enterprises, 1957—. Actor various radio networks, N.Y.C., 1938-47; Broadway appearances include Kiss and Tell, 1943, Get Away Old Man, 1943, Trio, 1944, Kiss Them for Me, 1944, Dunnigan's Daughter, 1945, Dream Girl, 1946-47; summer stock appearances include The Bo Tree, 1939, Joan of Lorraine, 1947; motion picture appearances include Kiss of Death, 1947, Street with No Name, 1948, Yellow Sky, 1948, Roadhouse, 1948, Down to the Sea in Ships, 1949, Night and the City, 1949, No Way Out, 1949, Panic in the Streets, 1950, Slattery's Hurricane, 1949, Halls of Montezuma, 1950, The Frogmen, 1950, Price of Gold, 1954, Co Blue, 1954, Broken Lance, 1954, Backlash, 1955, St. Joan, 1956, Time Limit, 1957, Warlock, 1958, The Alamo, 1959, Judgement at Nuremberg, 1961, Flight from Ashiya, 1962, How the West Was Won, 1962, The Long Ships, 1963, Cheyenne Autumn, 1963, Bedford Incident, 1964, Alvarez Kelly, 1965, The Way West, 1966, Madigan, 1967, Patch, 1968, Talent for Loving, 1968, The Moonshine War, 1969, When the Legends Die, 1971, Murder on the Orient Express, 1974, The Sellout, 1975, To the Devil, A Daughter, 1975, The Twilight's Last Gleaming, 1976, The Domino Principle, 1976, Roller Coaster, 1976, Coma, 1978, The Swarm, 1977, Hanky Panky, 1982, The Final Option, 1983, Against All Odds, 1984, True Colors, 1990; NBC TV appearance in Vanished, 1971, TV series Madigan, 1972; TV appearance in Benjamin Franklin, 1974, Mr. Horn, 1979, Bear Island, 1979, All God's Children, 1980, A Whale for the Killing, 1981, Blackout, 1985, A Gathering of Old Men, 1986, Once Upon a Texas Train, 1987, Cold Sassy Tree, 1989. True Colors, 1990. Bd. dirs. Hope for Hearing. Named Comdr. of Arts and Letters (France), 1987. Mem. Century Club (N.Y.C.).

WIDNALL, SHEILA EVANS, aeronautical educator, former secretary of the airforce, former university official; b. Tacoma, July 13, 1938; d. Rolland John and Genievieve Alice (Krause) Evans; m. William Soule Widnall, June 11, 1960; children: William, Ann. BS in Aero. and Astronautics, MIT, 1960, MS in Aero. and Astronautics, 1961, DSc, 1964; PhD (hon.), New Eng. Coll., 1975, Lawrence U., 1987, Cedar Crest Coll., 1988, Smith Coll., 1990, Mt. Holyoke Coll., 1991, Ill. Inst. Tech., 1991, Columbia U., 1994, Simmons Coll., 1994, Suffolk U., 1994, Princeton U., 1994. Asst. prof. aeros. and astronautics MIT, Cambridge, 1964-70, assoc. prof., 1970-74, prof., 1974-93, head divsn. fluid mechanics, 1975-79; dir. Fluid Dynamics Rsch. Lab., MIT, Cambridge, 1979-90; chmn. faculty MIT, Cambridge, 1979-80, chair com. on acad. responsibility, 1991-92, assoc. provost, 1992-93; sec. USAF, 1993-97; Inst. prof. MIT, Cambridge, 1997—. Trustee Sloan Found., 1998—; bd. dirs. Gen. Corp., Chemfab Inc., Bennington, Vt., Aerospace Corp., L.A., Draper Labs., Cambridge, Gencorp; past trustee Carnegie Corp., 1984-92, Charles Stark Draper Lab. Inc.; mem. Carnegie Commn. Sci., Tech. and Govt, mem. Columbia Accident Investigation Bd, 2003-. Contbr. articles to profl. jours.; patentee in field; assoc. editor AIAA Jour. Aircraft, 1972-75, Physics of Fluids, 1981-88, Jour. Applied Mechanics, 1983-87; mem. editorial bd. Sci., 1984-86. Bd. visitors USAF Acad., Colorado Springs, Colo., 1978-84, bd. chair, 1980-82; trustee Boston Mus. Sci., 1989-93. Named to Nat. Women's Hall of Fame, 2003; recipient Washburn award, Boston Mus. Sci., 1987. Fellow AAAS (bd. dirs. 1982-89, pres. 1987-88, chmn. 1988-89), AIAA (bd. dirs. 1975-77, Lawrence Sperry award 1972, Durand Lectureship for Pub. Svc. award 1996, pres. 2000-01), Am. Phys. Soc. (exec. com. 1979-82); mem. ASME (Applied Mechs. award 1995, Pres. award 1999), NAE (coun. 1992-93, v.p. 1998—), NAS (panel on sci. responsibility), Am. Acad. Arts and Scis., Soc. Women Engrs. (Outstanding Achievement award 1975), Internat. Acad. Astronautics, Seattle Mountaineers. Office: MIT Bldg 33-411 77 Massachusetts Ave Cambridge MA 02139

WIDNER, RALPH RANDOLPH, retired civic executive; b. Phila., Oct. 21, 1930; s. Ralph Litteer and Viola (Cunningham) W.; m. Joan Sundelius Ziegler, July 9, 1955; children: Jennifer Anne, Wendy Widner Ducharme. BA, Duke U., 1952; postgrad., NYU, 1957, Georgetown U., 1958; DHL (hon.), Union Coll., Ky., 1970, Capital U., Columbus, Ohio, 1971. Journalist Paterson (N.J.) Evening News, 1955-56, N.Y. Times, 1956-58; Congressional fellow Am. Polit. Sci. Assn., 1958; dir. pub. affairs Pa. Dept. Forests and Waters, 1959-60; asst. dir. Pa. Planning Bd., 1960-62; legis. asst. to U.S. Senator Clark, 1962-65; exec. dir. Appalachian Regional Commn., 1965-71; pres. Acad. for contemporary problems, 1971-82; adj. prof. pub. adminstrn. and city planning Ohio State U., 1971-82; pres. Nat. Tng. and Devel. Service for State and Local Govt., 1979-81; staff v.p. Urban Land Inst., 1982-83; exec. dir. Greater Phila. First Corp., 1983-88; chmn. Fairfax House Internat., Alexandria, Va., 1988—. Fellow Nat. Acad. Pub. Adminstrn. (sr.). Democrat. Methodist. Home: 2210 Belle Haven Rd Alexandria VA 22307-1100 Office: PO Box 7517 Alexandria VA 22307-0517 Office Phone: 703-960-9626. E-mail: fxhouse@compuserve.com.

WIDNER, ROBERT LEE, JR., psychologist, educator; s. Robert Lee and Josephine Estella Widner; m. Gloria Chavez; children: David Yisrael, Joshua Moshe stepchildren: Able Irad Chavez, Edward Elieu Chavez. BS, U. Md.; MS, U. Tex., Arlington; PhD, Tex. A&M U., 1994. Rsch. assoc. Dept. of Edn., El Paso, 1988—91; asst. rsch. scientist NYU, N.Y.C.; rsch. fellow NSF, N.Y.C., 1995—97; asst. prof. U. Colo., Colorado Springs, 1997—2001, rsch. assoc. Boulder, 1997—2001; asst. prof. Minn. State U., Mankato, 2001—. Cons. U.S. Dept. of Edn., College Station, Tex., 1992; civilian rschr. USAF Acad., Colorado Springs, Colo., 1997—2001; vis. rsch. scientist Lackland AFB, San Antonio, 1999, U. Tex., Arlington, 2000; faculty affiliate Ctr. Neuroscience, Boulder, 2001; vis. fellow Mass. Gen. Hosp., Boston, 2001; Minn. area geriatric edn. ctr. fellow U. Minn., Mpls., 2002; vis. scholar MIT, Cambridge, Mass., 2003. Contbr. articles to profl. jours. Rep. Fed. Edn. Advocacy Coordinator's Network, Washington, 2003—. Recipient Tech. Workshop award, Nat. Inst. Aging, 1997, Advanced Tng. award, APA, 2001; grantee, NSF, 1995—97, Southeastern Ctr. Applied Cognitive Aging Rsch., 1995, Air Force Office Sci. Rsch., 1998—99; Tex. Tuition scholar, Tex. A&M U., 1992—94, Grad. Student Travel grantee, NSF, 1993, Minority Postdoctoral Rsch. fellow, 1995—97, Starter grantee, 1998—2000, NSF Rsch. fellow, Ga. Inst. Tech., 1994—95, Presdl. Tchg. Scholar fellow, Minn. State U., 2002—03. Mem.: AAAS, APA (assoc.), Cognitive Neuroscience Soc., Ea. Psychol. Assn., Soc. Applied Rsch. Memory and Cognition, Cognitive Sci. Soc., Rocky Mountain Psychol. Assn., Am. Psychol. Assn., Minn. Acad. Scis., N.Y. Acad. Scis., Psychonomics Soc. (assoc.). Office: Minn State U Armstrong Hall #23 Mankato MN 56001 Office Phone: 507-389-5822. Personal E-mail: robert.widner@mnsu.edu. E-mail: robert.widner@mnsu.edu.

WIDOM, BENJAMIN, chemistry professor; b. Newark, Oct. 13, 1927; s. Morris and Rebecca (Hertz) W.; m. Joanne McCurdy, Dec. 21, 1953; children: Jonathan, Michael, Elisabeth. AB, Columbia U., 1949; PhD, Cornell U., 1953; DSc (hon.), U. Chgo., 1991; Doctor honoris causa, U. Utrecht, 1999. Rsch. assoc. U. N.C., Chapel Hill, 1952-54; instr. chemistry Cornell U., Ithaca, N.Y., 1954-55, asst. prof., 1955-59, assoc. prof., 1959-63, prof., 1963-83, Goldwin Smith prof., 1983—; van der Waals prof. U. Amsterdam, The Netherlands, 1972; vis. prof. Harvard U., Cambridge, Mass., 1975; IBM vis. prof. Oxford (Eng.) U., 1978. Lorentz prof. U. Leiden, The Netherlands, 1985; vis. prof. Kath. U. Leuven, Belgium, 1988, U. Aix Marseille, France, 1995; Kramers/Debye prof. U. Utrecht, 1999. Author: (with J.S. Rowlinson) Molecular Theory of Capillarity, 1982. With U.S. Army, 1946-47. Recipient Clark disting. tchg. award Cornell U., 1973, Dickson prize for sci. Carnegie-Mellon U., 1986, Hirschfelder Prize in Theoretical Chemistry U. Wis., 1991, Bakhuis Roozeboom medal Royal Netherlands Acad. Arts & Scis., 1994, Onsager medal U. Trondheim, Norway, 1994, Boltzmann medal Internat. Union of Pure and Applied Physics, Commn. on Statis. Physics, 1998. Fellow Am. Phys. Soc., Am. Acad. Arts and Scis., N.Y. Acad. Scis. (Boris Pregel award for chem. physics rsch. 1976); mem. NAS, Am. Philos. Soc., Am. Chem. Soc. (Langmuir award in chem. physics 1982, Hildebrand award in theoretical and exptl. chemistry of liquids 1992, Theoretical Chemistry award 1999). Home: 204 The Parkway Ithaca NY 14850-2247 Office: Cornell U Chemistry Dept Ithaca NY 14853 Office Phone: 607-255-3363. Business E-Mail: bw24@cornell.edu.

WIDYOLAR, SHEILA GAYLE, dermatologist; b. Vancouver, B.C., Can., June 11, 1939; d. Walter Herbert and Olive Louise (O'Neal) Roberts; Kithi K. Widyolar, 1960 (div. 1979); 1 child, Keith. BS, Loma Linda U., 1962; MD, Howard U., 1972. Resident U. Calif., Irvine, 1973-76; dermatologist pvt. practice, Laguna Hills, Calif., 1976—. Clin. instr. U. Calif. Sch. Medicine, 1978-86. Chmn. bd. dirs. Opera Pacific, Costa Mesa, Calif., 1996-97. Fellow Am. Acad. Dermatology, Am. Soc. Dermatopathology; mem. AMA, Calif. Med. Assn., Dermatol. Soc. Orange County (pres. 1983), Alpha Omega Alpha. Avocations: music, travel. Office: Ste 403 23911 Calle de Mag Dalena Laguna Hills CA 92653 Office Phone: 949-452-3814.

WIE, MICHELLE SUNG, amateur golfer; b. Honolulu, Haw., Oct. 11, 1989; d. Byung-Wook and Hyun-Kyong Sung Wie. Played in major LPGA Tournaments US Women's Open, 2003, Kraft Nabisco Championship, 2003, 2004; winner Jennie K. Wilson Invitational, 2001, Haw. State Women's Stroke Play Championship, 2001, USGA Women's Amateur Pub. Links Championship, 2003. Mem.: Haw. State Jr. Golf Assn. Achievements include youngest player to win Haw. State Women's Stroke Play Championship, Jennie K. Wilson Internat., and US Amateur Pub. Links Championship; youngest player to make an LPGA cut, playing in the Kraft Nabisco Championship. Avocations: reading, drawing, computers. Office: 100 Internat Golf Dr Daytona Beach FL 32124-1092

WIEAND, JEFFREY SCOTT, lawyer; b. Harrisburg, Pa., Jan. 3, 1954; s. Richard Wilson and Annetta E. (Younker) W.; m. Janet G. Silver, Sept. 25, 1954; children: Douglas Leo, Roger Galvin. BA, Middlebury Coll., 1976; PhD, U. Chgo., 1981; JD, Harvard U., 1985. William Rainey Harper instr. U. Chgo., 1981-82; assoc. Hill & Barlow, Boston, 1985-87; mem. Hutchins, Wheeler & Dittmar, Boston, 1987-98; coun. Lane, Altman & Owens, Boston, 1998—99. Editor Boston Bar Jour., 1998-2001; contbr. articles to profl. jours. Bd. appeals Town of Concord, 1990-97; bd. dirs. Civic Symphony Orch., Boston, 1990-97; trustee Concord Open Land Found., 1998—, Hist. Dists. Commn., Public Works Commn., Town of Concord, 1999-2004. Mem. ABA, Nat. Bus. Aviation Assn., Am. Philosophical Assn., Mass. Bar Assn. Office: Boston JetSearch Inc Civil Air Terminal Hanscom Field Bedford MA 01730

WIEBE, LEONARD IRVING, radiopharmacist, educator; b. Swift Current, Sask., Can., Oct. 14, 1941; s. Cornelius C. and Margaret (Teichroeb) W.; m. Grace E. McIntyre, Sept. 5, 1964; children: Glenis, Kirsten, Megan BSP, U. Sask., 1963, MS, 1966; PhD, U. Sydney, Australia, 1970, DSc, 2002; D.Pharm.Sci (hon.), Meiji Pharm. U., Japan, 2002, Health Sci. U. Hokkaido, 2003. Pharmacist Swift Current Union Hosp., 1963-64; sessional lectr. U. Sask., Can., 1965-66; asst. prof. U. Alta., Can., 1970-73, assoc. prof., 1973-78, prof., 1978—, dir. Slowpoke Reactor Facility, 1975—89, 2001—02, asst. dean rsch., 1984-87, assoc. dean, 1990-99; prof. dept. exptl. oncology, 1999—; sessional lectr. U. Sydney, Australia, 1973; pres. Internat. Bionucleonics Cons. Lts., 1991—, BioCyDex Inc., 2003—. Rsch. assoc. Cross Cancer Inst., Edmonton, 1978—, Med. Rsch. Coun. Can.; vis. prof. Royal P.A. Hosp., Sydney, 1983-84, Searle vis. profl., 1986; MRC vis. prof., Toronto, 1987; PMAC vis. prof., 1988; McCalla prof. U. Alta, 1993-94; radiopharmacy cons. Australian Atomic Energy Commn., Sydney, 1983-84; mem. MRC standing com. on sci. and rsch., 1995-98; cons. IAEA, 2001, 03; hon. liason prof. Peoples U. Bangladesh. Editor: Liquid Scintillation: Science and Technology, 1976, Advances in Scintillation Counting, 1983; guest editor Jour. of Radioanalytical Chemistry, 1981; editor Internat. Jour. Applied Radiation Instrumentation Sect. A, 1988-90; regional editor Internat. Jour. Nuclear Biology and Medicine, 1992-95; mem. editl. bd. Jour. Pharmacy & Pharm. Sci., Jour. Applied Radiation Isotopes, 1995—. Recipient Janssen-Ortho Rsch. award, 1998, McNeil award, 1988; Commonwealth Univs. Exchange grantee, 1966; Alexander von Humboldt fellow, 1976-79, 82. Mem. Pharm. Bd. of New South Wales, Sask. Pharm. Assn., Soc. Nuclear Medicine, Assn. Faculties of Pharmacy of Can. (McNeil Rsch. award 1988), Can. Radiation Protection Assn., Can. Assn. Radiopharm. Scientists, Am. Pharm. Assn., Am. Assn. Pharm. Sci., Internat. Assn. Radiopharmacy (exec. sec. 1991-95), Can. Assn. Pharm. Scis. (founding), Univ. Club (Edmonton) (pres. 1985). Mem. Mennonite Ch. E-mail: leonard.wiebe@ualberta.ca.

WIEBENSON, DORA LOUISE, architectural historian, editor, author; b. Cleve., July 29, 1926; d. Edward Ralph and Jeannette (Rodier) W. BA, Vassar Coll., 1946; MArch, Harvard U., 1951; MA, NYU, 1958, PhD, 1964. Architect, N.Y., 1951-66; lectr. Columbia U., 1966-68; assoc. prof. U. Md., 1968-72, prof., 1972-77; vis. prof. Cornell U., 1974; prof. U. Va., Charlottesville, 1977-92, prof. emeritus, 1992—, chmn. div. archtl. history, 1977-79, assoc. fellow U. Va. Ctr. Advanced Studies, 1982-83; pres. Archtl. Publs., N.Y.C., 1982—; editor-in-chief Centropa, 2000—. Editor: Marsyas XI: 1962-64, 1965, Essays in Honor of Walter Friedlaender, 1965; Architectural Theory and Practice from Alberti to Ledoux, 1982, rev., 1983, Spanish transl., 1988; Guide to Graduate Degree Programs in Architectural History, 1982, rev., 1984, 86, 88, 90; co-editor: The Architecture of Historic Hungary, 1998, Hungarian transl., 1998; author: Sources of Greek Revival Architecture, 1969, Tony Garnier: The Cité Industrielle, 1969, Japanese transl., 1983, The Picturesque Garden in France, 1978, Mark J. Millard Architectural Collection, Vol. I: French Books: Sixteenth through Nineteenth Centuries, 1993; contbr. articles to profl. jours. Student fellow Inst. Fine Arts, 1961-62, 62-63; grantee Am. Philos. Soc., 1964-65, 70, Samuel H. Kress Found., 1966, 72-73, 98, Gen. Rsch. Fund, U. Md., 1969, 74, 76, NEH, 1972-73, Am. Coun. Learned Socs., 1976, 81, 85, Ctr. Advanced Studies, U. Va., 1980, 81, 97, Graham Found. Advanced Studies Fine Arts, 1982, 93, Archtl. History Found., 1996; fellow Yale Ctr. Brit. Art, 1983; sr. rsch. fellow NEH, 1986-87. Mem. Soc. Archtl. Historians (bd. dirs. 1974-77, 80-83, chair edn. com. 1976-90), Coll. Art Assn., Am. Soc. Eighteenth Century (mem. exec. bd. 1991-94).

WIECEK, BARBARA HARRIET, advertising executive; b. Chgo., Mar. 30, 1956; d. Stanley Joseph and Irene (Zagajewski) W. AA, Am. Acad. of Art, Chgo., 1977. Illustrator Clinton E. Frank Advt., Chgo., 1977-78, art dir., 1978-80, assoc. creative dir., 1980-84, v.p.; instr. Am. Acad. of Art, Chgo., 1977-80; assoc. creative dir. Tatham, Laird & Kudner, 1984—, ptnr., 1986—, creative dir., 1987—, sr. ptnr., 1995—, exec. creative dir., 1996. Recipient Silver Awd. Internat. Film Festival of N.Y., 1981, Gold Awd. Internat. Film Festival of N.Y., 1981. Roman Catholic. Avocations: painting, writing, gardening, remodeling, bicycling. Office: Tatham Euro RSCG 36 E Grand Ave Chicago IL 60611-3506

WIECHA, JOSEPH AUGUSTINE, linguist, educator; b. Chorzów II, Poland, Sept. 20, 1926; came to U.S., 1955, naturalized, 1958; s. Karol and Gertruda (Rudzki) W.; m. Mary Ruth Moore, 1953; children: Joseph Damian, Charles Francis, John Moore. BA with honors, Nat. U. Ireland, 1950; PhD with distinction, NYU, 1963. Instr. fgn. langs. U.S. Third Air Force, London, 1951-55; instr. German and Spanish U. Md., London, 1951-55; tchr. Spanish and math. Bklyn. Friends Sch., 1955-56; instr. German NYU, N.Y.C., summer, 1958; lectr. German and humanities Harvard U., Boston, 1959-63; lectr. German lit. Colby Coll., summer 1963; prof. German SUNY, Oswego, 1963-69, chmn. dept. fgn. langs. and lit., 1963-69, chmn. dept. Germanic and Slavic langs. and lit., 1969-72, disting. teaching prof., 1973-92, disting. tchg. prof. emeritus, 1992—; chmn. SUNY Fgn. Studies Ctr., 1972-73. Lectr. and cons. methodology of tchg. fgn. langs., 1959—; condr. seminars tchg. methodology fgn. langs. Nat. U. Pedro Enriquez Ureña, Santo Domingo, 1973, U. Pisa, Italy, 1974, Moscow State Pedagogical Inst.; Fgn. Langs., USSR, 1976; vis. prof. U. Wroctaw, Poland, 1977. Developed Wiecha Progressive-Reflex method of teaching fgn. langs. Served as officer 2d Polish Corps Brit. VIII Army, 1944-47. Decorated Bronze medal Polish Army, Brit. Def. medal; French Star; Star of Italy; recipient diploma of spl. recognition U. Nat. Pedro Enriquez Ureña, 1973; Galileo medal U. Pisa, 1974; Ogden Butler fellow, 1958-59, Fels fellow, 1956-59, Kosciuszko Found. fellow, 1959. Mem. MLA, N.Y. State Assn. Fgn. Lang. Tchrs. (dir. 1975-78, Disting. Tchr. award 1975, Disting. Bd. Dirs. award 1978, Spl. Contbn. to Teaching Fgn. Langs. award 1979), Am. Assn. Tchrs. of German, Polish Inst. Arts and Scis. in Am., Nat. Spanish Honors Soc. (hon.), Am. Coun. on Edn. (nat. honor roll), Delta Phi Alpha (hon.), Dobro Slovo (hon.) Home: 710 Copa De Oro Marathon FL 33050-5406 also: 22 Bayside Rd Northport ME 04849-4435

WIECHERT, ALLEN LEROY, educational planning consultant, architect; b. Independence, Kans., Oct. 25, 1938; s. Norman Henry and Serena Johanna (Steinke) W.; m. Sandra Swanson, Aug. 19, 1961; children: Kristin Nan, Brendan Swanson, Megan Ann. BArch, Kans. State U., 1962. Lic. arch., Kans.; cert. Nat. Coun. Archtl. Registration Bds. Arch. in tng. McVey, Peddie, Schmidt & Allen, Wichita, Kans., 1962 63; arch. Kivett & Myers, Kansas City, Mo., 1963-68; asst. to vice chancellor plant planning and devel. U. Kans., Lawrence, 1968-74, assoc. dir. facilities planning, 1974-78, univ. dir. facilities planning, 1978-92, univ. arch., 1993-95; campus planner Gould Evans Assocs., Lawrence, 1995-96; code enforcement officer City of Prairie Village, Kans., 1997-2001; ret.; project mgr. subs. corp. Kans. Bd. Regents, 2003—04; retired, 2004. Mem. long range phys. planning com. Kans. Bd. Regents, 1971-95; designer, archtl. programmer ednl. facilities; bd. dirs. Kans. U. Fed. Credit Union, 1972-81, pres. bd., 1974. Editor, contbr.: Physical Development Planning Work Book, 1973. Chmn. horizons com. Lawrence Bicentennial Commn.; designer Kaw River Trail, 1976; mem. Action 80 Com., 1980-81, Lawrence-Douglas County Horizon 2020 Task Group, 1993-95; mem. standing com. Kans. Episcopal Diocese, 1976-80, pres. com., 1981, mem. diocesan coun., 1982 84, chmn. coll. work com., 1982-84, commn. on ch. arch. and allied arts, 1986-99, long range planning com., 1988; sr. warden Trinity Episc. Ch., Lawrence, 1978-80, 2001-02, mem. vestry, 1997-99; trustee Kans. Sch. Religion, 1973-80, 82-95, v.p., 1984-85, pres., 1986-92, trustee friends of the dept. of religious studies, 1995—; mem. adv. bd. Salvation Army, 1990—; bd. dirs. Trinity Group Care Home, 1973-79; advancement chmn. troop com. Boy Scouts Am., 1981-87, dist. com. Pelathe dist., 1984—, vice chmn., 1984, chmn., 1985-87; exec. bd. Heart of Am. Coun., 1985-87. 1st lt. Kans. Air N.G., 1961-67. Recipient Dist. Award of Merit, Boy Scouts Am., 1988, Silver Beaver award, 1991, Follow Me Boys award, 2002. Mem. AIA, Assn. Univ. Archs. (sec.-treas. 1986-87, v.p. 1987-88, pres. 1988-89), Nat. Hist. Trust, Kans. U. Endowment Assn. (sec. 1981-85, founder, exec. bd. Hist. Mt. Oread Fund divsn.), Nat. Cathedral Assn. (regional co-chairperson 1993—). Home: 813 Highland Dr Lawrence KS 66044-2431

WIECHMANN, ERIC WATT, lawyer; b. Schenectady, N.Y., June 12, 1948; s. Richard Jerdone and Ann (Watt) W.; m. Merrill Metzger, May 22, 1971. BA, Hamilton Coll., 1970; JD, Cornell U., 1974. Bar: Conn. 1975, U.S. Dist. Ct. (so. and ea. dists.) N.Y. 1975, U.S. Dist. Ct. Conn. 1975, U.S. Dist. Ct. D.C. 1981, U.S. Ct. Appeals (2nd cir.) 1975, U.S. Ct. Appeals (9th cir.) 1980, U.S. Ct. Appeals D.C. 1982, U.S. Ct. Appeals (5th cir.) 1986, U.S. Ct. Appeals (10th cir.) 1989, U.S. Supreme Ct. 1978. Assoc. Cummings & Lockwood LLC, Stamford, Conn., 1974—82, ptnr., 1982—2003, mng. ptnr. Hartford office, bd. dirs., 1996—, bus. clients exec. com., 2003; ptnr. McCarter & English LLP, Hartford, Conn., 2003—, mng. ptnr., Hartford office, 2003—, mem. exec. com., 2003—. Spl. pretrial master U.S. Dist. Ct. Conn. 1984—; state atty. trial referee, 1986—, mem. evidence code oversight com.; civil task force, 1995-, civil jury instrn. com. Conn. Superior Ct., 1996-2000, docket control com., 2001-; comml. arbitrator Am. Arbitration Assn. Contbr. articles to profl. jours. Mem. Zoning Bd. Appeals, New Canaan, Conn., 1984-85; bd. dirs. Conn. Rivers coun. Boy Scouts Am., trustee, 2001—. Mem. ABA (vice-chmn. toxics and hazardous law com. TIPS sect.), Def. Rsch. Inst., Internat. Assn. Def. Counsel (mem. faculty Def. Trial Acad. 1996, chmn. toxic and hazardous substance com. 1998-99, chmn. CLE bd. 2000-02, bd. dirs. 2004), Internat. Soc. Barristers, Conn. Bar Assn. (exec. com. antitrust sect. 1982—, ct. rules adv. com, chmn. 1991-93), Conn. Bar Found., Golf Club Avon. Republican. Episcopalian. Home: 10 Langley Park Farmington CT 06032-1541 E-mail: ewiech@yahoo.com., ewiechmann@mccarter.com.

WIED, GEORGE LUDWIG, physician; b. Carlsbad, Czechoslovakia, Feb. 7, 1921; came to U.S., 1953, naturalized, 1960; s. Ernst George and Anna (Travnicek) W.; m. Kayoko Y. Yamauchi, 1980; 1 child, George. MD, Charles U., Prague, 1945, Hon. Med. Degree, 1995. Intern County Hosp., Carlsbad, Czechoslovakia, 1945; intern U. Chgo. Hosps., 1955; resident in ob-gyn U. Munich, Fed. Republic Germany, 1946-48; practice medicine specializing in ob-gyn West Berlin, 1948-53; asst. ob-gyn Free U., West Berlin, 1948-52; assoc. chmn. dept. ob-gyn Moabit Hosp., Free U., West Berlin, 1953; asst. prof., dir. cytology U. Chgo., 1954-59, assoc. prof., 1959-65, prof., 1965-91, mem. bd. adult edn., 1964-68, prof. pathology, 1967-91, Blum-Riese prof. ob-gyn, 1968-91, acting chmn. dept. ob-gyn, 1974-75. Editor-in-chief Jour. Reproductive Medicine, Acta Cytologica, Analytical and Quantitative Cytology, Clinical Cytology; editor: Introduction to Quantitative Cytochemistry, Automated Cell Identification and Cell Sorting, Compendium on Clinical Cytology, Compendium on the Computerized Cytology and Histology Laboratory, Compendium on Quality Assurance in Clinical Cytology; sr. editor Gen. and Diagnostic Pathology. Hon. dir. Chgo. Cancer Prevention Ctr., 1959-83; chmn. jury Maurice Goldblatt Cytology award, 1963-92. Recipient Cert. of Merit, U.S. Surgeon Gen., 1952, Maurice Goldblatt Cytology award, 1961, George N. Papanicolaou Cytology award, 1970, Masubuchi Gold Medal award 13th Internat. Cytology Congress, 1998, Kazumsa Masubuchi Lifetime Achievement award, 1998. Mem. Am. Soc. Cytology (pres. 1965-66), Mex. Soc. Cytology (hon.), Spanish Soc. Cytology (hon.), Brazilian Soc. Cytology (fgn. corr.), Indian Acad. Cytology (hon., Lifetime Achievement award 1998), Latin-Am. Soc. Cytology (hon.), Japanese Soc. Cytology (hon.), Internat. Acad. Cytology (pres. 1977-80), German Soc. Cytology (hon.), Ctrl. Soc. Clin. Rsch., Chgo. Path. Soc., Chgo. Gynecol. Soc. (hon.), Am. Soc. Cell Biology, German Soc. Ob-Gyn, Bavarian Soc. Ob-Gyn, German Soc. Endocrinology, Russian Assn. Cytologists (hon.), Swedish Soc. Medicine (hon.), Austrian Soc. Clin. Cytology (hon.), Sigma Xi. Home and Office: 1640 E 50th St Chicago IL 60615-3161 E-mail: wied@cytology.

WIEDEMANN, CHARLES LOUIS, dentist; b. Belvidere, N.J., May 6, 1936; s. Charles and Clothilde Paulina (Fischer) W.; m. Jacqueline Burdzy, June 11, 1960; children: Lorraine Carol, Julie Patricia. BA in Biol. Sci., Rutgers U., 1957; DDS with honors, Fairleigh Dickinson U., 1962; grad., U.S. Army Med. Field Svc. Sch., 1962; postgrad. student, Inst. for Grad. Dentists, 1968-69, St. Clare's Hosp. Continuing Edn., N.J., 1972—, U. Pa., 1974-75, Boston U. Sch. Grad. Dentistry, 1991. Pvt. practice dentistry, Hackettstown, N.J., 1966—. Mem., founder dental sect. staff dept. surgery Hackettstown Cmty. Hosp., chief dentistry, 1973-75, 77-78, chief of staff dental sect. dept.

surgery, 1974, 80, 85; dental health dir. Clarence W. Sickles Med. Ctr., Hackettstown, 1970-90; co-dir. Stargazer, Bd. of Edn., Online Mag. telecomm. sys., 1985-86; pres. Rexxcom Sys. Electronic Pub. and Computer Software, Co., 1990—; lectr. Morris County Coll., dental socs.; designer giant talking toothbrush, talking molar. Author: The Now Philosophy for Dentistry, 1972, Fantastic Facts About Dental Health, 1975, (computer software) The Format Machine, 1987, Autofont, 1990, Autofont, rev. edit., 1996, The Magic Font Machine (Magifont, Magivue, Magishow), 1990, News 1, 1991, Digipad, 1993, The Autofont Titler (for electronic books), 1994; co-author: Autodoc, 1990, Autodoc, rev. edit., 1993, Font Mania, 1991, Font Mania, rev. edit., 1996, XL1000, 1993, XL2000, 1993, XL2001, 1994, XL2001, rev. edit. (the XL book edit.), 1995, E-Z Book, 1995, Autofont Titler, 1995; author, designer: electronic publishing software Rexxcom., 1987—, editl. adv. panel: Dental Econs. Jour., 1979—80; editor: DPA News, 1993—95; contbr. articles to profl. jours. and mags.; editor: electronic books, 1995—; columnist: Hackettstown Gazette, 1983—85. Chmn. Bd. of Health, Washington Twp., Morris County, N.J., 1975-78; co-dir. telecomm. sys. Hunterdon Ctrl. Regional H.S., 1989-98; presentations to Morris, Warren, and Sussex Counties, N.J. elem. schs. ann., 1966-93. Capt. Dental Corps., U.S. Army, 1962-65. Recipient cert. Stuart L. Isler Found. for Preventive Dentistry, 1986. Fellow Acad. Gen. Dentistry, Am. Endodontic Soc. (Harold Katz Meml. award 1983); mem. ADA (panel on quar. survey of pvt. practitioners 1990-93), Digital Pub. Assn. (founder, bd. dirs.), Am. Analgesia Soc., Internat. Analgesia Soc., N.J. Dental Assn., Warren-Sussex Dental Soc., Tri-County Dental Soc. (tchr. dental practice adminstrn. 1970-71), Hackettstown Dental Study Group (co-founder 1974—), Found. for Motivation in Dentistry (founder, chmn., bd. dirs.). Republican. Achievements include co-inventor Electronic Pub. and e-books, 1990; design of computer fonts, modules, graphics simulations; first to develop electronic publishing software; invention of Rexxcom character set, 1992; development of new method for painless dental injections, 2002. Office: 110 Mill St Hackettstown NJ 07840-2343

WIEDEN, DAN G. advertising executive; b. 1945; m. Bonnie Wieden. BS journalism, Univ Oreg., 1967. With Georgia-Pacific Corp., Portland, Oreg., 1967-72; free-lance writer, 1972-78; with McCann-Erickson, Portland, 1978-80, William Cain, Portland, 1980-82; pres., exec. creative dir. Wieden & Kennedy Internat., Portland, 1982—. Named to Hall of Achievement, Sch. Journalism and Comm., Univ. Oreg., 2000. Office: Wieden & Kennedy Internat. LLC 224 NW 13th Ave Portland OR 97209-2953*

WIEDER, BRUCE TERRILL, lawyer, electrical engineer; b. Cleve., Dec. 9, 1955; s. Ira J. and Judith M.W. BSEE, Cornell U., 1978; MBA, U. Tex., 1980, JD with honors, 1988. Bar: Tex. 1988, U.S. Dist. Ct. (we. dist.) Tex. 1989, U.S. Patent and Trademark Office 1989, U.S. Ct. Appeals (fed. cir.) 1990, D.C. 1991, U.S. Supreme Ct. 1992, U.S. Dist. Ct. (no. dist.) Tex. 1995, Va. 1997, U.S. Dist. Ct. (ea. dist.) Va. 1997. Engr. Motorola, Inc., Austin, Tex., 1979-85; assoc. Arnold, White & Durkee, Austin, 1988-90; law clk. U.S. Ct. Appeals (Fed. cir.), Washington, 1990-91; assoc. Burns, Doane, Swecker & Mathis, Alexandria, Va., 1991-97, ptnr., 1998—. Adj. prof. Georgetown U. Law Ctr., 1998—. Mem. IEEE, ABA, Am. Intellectual Property Law Assn., Alpha Phi Omega (life), Beta Gamma Sigma (life). Office: Burns Doane Swecker & Mathis 1737 King St Ste 500 Alexandria VA 22314-2727 Office Phone: 703-836-6620.

WIEDERHORN, SHELDON M. materials engineer; Sr. fellow materials sci. and engring. lab. Nat. Inst. Stds. and Tech., Gaithersburg, Md. Recipient Gold medal U.S. Dept. Commerce, 1982. Mem. NAE. Office: Nat Inst Stds & Tech Materials 223 Rm A357 100 Bureau Dr Stop 8500 Gaithersburg MD 20899-8500 Office Phone: 301-975-5772.

WIEGAND, SYLVIA MARGARET, mathematician, educator; b. Cape Town, South Africa, Mar. 8, 1945; came to U.S., 1949; d. Laurence Chisholm and Joan Elizabeth (Dunnett) Young; m. Roger Allan Wiegand, Aug. 27, 1966; children: David Chisholm, Andrea Elizabeth. AB, Bryn Mawr Coll., 1966; MA, U. Wash., 1967; PhD, U. Wis., Madison, 1972. Mem. faculty U. Nebr., Lincoln, 1967—, now prof. math.; program dir. Nat. Sci. Found., 2002—03. Vis. assoc. prof. U. Conn., Storrs, 1978-79, U. Wis., Madison, 1985-86; vis. prof. Purdue U., 1992-93, Spring 1998, Mich. State U., Fall 1997. Editor Communications in Math., 1990-2004, Rocky Mountain Jour. Math., 1991-2004; contbr. rsch. articles to profl. jours. Troop leader Lincoln area Girl Scouts U.S., 1988-92. Grantee NSF, 1985-88, 90-93, 94-96, 97-2002, NSA, 1995-97, 2002, 03-; Vis. Professorship for Women, 1992, Nat. Security Agy., 1995-97. Mem. AAUP, Assn. Women in Math (pres.-elect 1995-96, pres. 1997-99), London Math. Soc., Math. Assn. Am., Am. Math. Soc. (mem. coun. 1994-96, chmn. policy com. on meetings and confs. 1994-96, mem. nominating com. 1997—), Can. Math. Soc. (bd. mem. at large 1997—). Avocations: running, family activities. Office: U Nebr Dept Math Lincoln NE 68588-0130 Office Phone: 402-472-7248. E-mail: swiegand@math.unl.edu.

WIEGEL, ROBERT LOUIS, consulting engineering executive; b. San Francisco, Oct. 17, 1922; s. Louis Henry and Antionette L. (Decker) W.; m. Anne Pearce, Dec. 10, 1948; children: John M., Carol E., Diana L. BS, U. Calif. at Berkeley, 1943, MS, 1949. Mem. faculty U. Calif. at Berkeley, 1946—, prof. civil engring., 1963-87, prof. emeritus, 1987—, asst. dean Coll. Engring., 1963-72, acting dean, 1972-73; dir. state tech. svcs. program for Calif. U. Calif., 1965-68, sec. acad. senate, 1988-89; vis. prof. Nat. U. Mex., summer 1965, Polish Acad. Sci., 1976, 88, U. Cairo, 1978; sr. Queen's fellow in marine sci. Australia, 1977; cons. to govt. and industry, 1946—. Chmn. U.S. com. for internat. com. oceanic resources, mem. marine bd. Nat. Acad. Engring., 1975-81; pres. Internat. Engring. Com. on Oceanic Resources, 1972-75, hon. mem., 1988; mem. coastal engring. research bd. Dept. Army, 1974-85; mem. IDOE adv. panel NSF, 1974-77, Gov. Calif. Adv. Commn. Ocean Resources, 1967, Calif. Adv. Commn. on Marine and Coastal Resources, 1967-73, Tsunami Tech. Adv. Council, Hawaii, 1964-66; U.S. del. U.S.-Japan coop. sci. programs, 1964, 65 Author publs. in field; editor Shore and Beach jour., 1988-96; patentee in field. V.p., bd. dirs. Am. Shore and Beach Preservation Assn., 1988-95, dir. emeritus, 1995—; mem. Nat. Rsch. Coun. com. on Beach Nourishment and Protection, 1992-95. Recipient Outstanding Civilian Svc. medal Dept. Army, 1985, Berkeley citation U. Calif., 1987, Joe W. Johnson Outstanding Beach Preservation award Calif. Shore and Beach Preservation Assn., 1993, Coastal Zone Found. award, 1993, Morrough P. O'Brien award Am. Shore and Beach Preservation Assn., 1995; Robert L. Wiegel scholar, 2001—. Fellow AAAS; mem. NAE, ASCE (hon., chmn. exec. com. waterways, harbors, coastal engring. div. 1974-75, vice chmn. coastal engring. rsch. coun. 1964-78, chmn. 1978-92, chmn. task com. wave forces on structures 1960-67, chmn. com. on coastal engring. 1970-71, Rsch. prize 1962, Moffatt-Nichol Coastal Engring. award 1978, Internat. Coastal Engring. award 1985), Japan Soc. Civil Engrs. (hon.), Sigma Xi. Home: 1030 Keeler Ave Berkeley CA 94708-1404 Office Phone: 510-642-7340.

WIEGENSTEIN, JOHN GERALD, retired physician; b. Fredericktown, Mo., June 22, 1930; s. John Joseph and Dorothy Faye (Mulkey) W.; m. Dorothy Iris Scifers, Dec. 27, 1952; children: Mark, Barbara, Paula, Cynthia. BS, U. Mich., 1956, MD, 1960. Intern Tripler Army Gen. Hosp., Honolulu, 1960-61; chmn. Emergency Medicine Ingham Regional Med. Ctr., Lansing, 1975-95; pres. profl. staff Mich. Capital Med. Ctr., Lansing, 1996-98; prof. emergency medicine Mich. State U., 1982-97, prof. emeritus, 1997—; founder Internat. Rsch. Inst. for Emergency Medicine, pres., 1983-85; v.p. occupl. health Emergency Cons., Inc., 1997-99, pres.; ret. Founder Am. Bd. Emergency Medicine, 1976, bd. dirs., 1976-86, pres., 1982-83; pres. Physician Assocs., P.C., 1976-96; chmn. bd. Occupl. Medicine Assocs., P.C., 1989-98; owner Health Care Info. Svcs., Inc., 1989-97. With USAF, 1951-53; M.C., U.S. Army, 1960-63. Recipient Disting. Achievement award, U. Mich. Med. Ctr. Alumni Assn., 2003. Mem. AMA (Disting. Svc. award 2001), Am. Coll. Emergency Physicians (founder, pres., chmn. bd. 1968-71, bd. dirs. 1968-76, John G. Wiegenstein Leadership award named in his honor), Mich. State Med. Soc. (award 1971, 82), Ingham County Med. Soc., Galens Hon. Med. Soc., Soc. Acad. Emergency Medicine (hon.). Home: 466 Eden Bay Dr Naples FL 34110-7073 Personal E-mail: jwiegen@aol.com.

WIEGLEY, ROGER DOUGLAS, lawyer; b. Buffalo, Dec. 8, 1948; s. Richard John and Georgianna (Eggleston) W. BA, SUNY, Buffalo, 1970; JD magna cum laude, U. Wis., 1977. Bar: Wis. 1977, Hawaii 1978, N.Y. 1982, D.C. 1982, Calif. 1986. Spl. asst. U.S. atty. U.S. Justice Dept., Honolulu, 1978-81; spl. asst. to gen. counsel Dept. of the Navy, Washington, 1981-82; assoc. Sullivan & Cromwell, Washington, 1982-88; ptnr. Sidley & Austin, Washington, 1988-94, Winthrop, Stimson, Putnam & Roberts, Washington, 1994-98; dir. Credit Suisse First Boston, N.Y.C., 1999—2001, Winterthur Ins. Group, N.Y.C., 2001—. Arbitrator nat. panel Am. Arbitration Assn., 1988—. Co-author: Trade and Export Finance, 2d edit., 2000; contbr. numerous articles to profl. jours. Served with USN, 1973-82. Mem. Assn. of Bar City of N.Y. (chmn. banking law com. 2000-03). Office: Winterthur Group 11 Madison Ave New York NY 10010-3629

WIEGMAN, EUGENE WILLIAM, minister, former college administrator; b. Fort Wayne, Ind., Oct. 27, 1929; s. A. Henry and E. Catherine (McDonald) W.; m. Kathleen Wyatt, Apr. 26, 1952; children: Kathryn, Rose Marie, Mark, Jeanine, Gretchen, Matthew. BS, Concordia Coll., 1953; MS, U. Kans., 1956, EdD, 1962; grad., Pacific Luth. Theol. Sem., 1985. Tchr., coach Trinity Luth. Sch., Atchison, Kans., 1954-58; prin. tchr. St. John's Coll., Winfield, Kans., 1958-61; prof. Concordia Coll., Seward, Nebr., 1961-65; adminstrv. asst. to Rep. Clair Callan, Lincoln, Nebr., 1965-66; asst. to adminstr. fed. extension service Dept. Agr., Washington, 1966-67; dean community edn. Fed. City Coll., Washington, 1967-69; pres. Pacific Luth. U., Tacoma, 1969-75, Independent Colls. Wash., 1975-76; dir. Wash. Office Community Devel., 1977-78; commr. Dept. of Employment Security, 1978-81; exec. dir., pres., CEO emeritus Family Counseling Service of Tacoma and Pierce County, Wash., 1987-97; assoc. pastor Luther Meml. Ch., Tacoma, 1987-90; pastor Gethsemane Luth. Ch., Tacoma, 1990-98, Luther Meml. Ch., Tacoma, 1998—2002; dean clin. pastoral edn. Grad. Sch. of Korea, 1992—. Mem. Wash. State Employment and Tng. Council; mem. cabinet Gov. of Wash., 1977-81. Candidate for U.S. Congress from 6th dist. Wash., 1976; mem. Council on Washington's Future; exec. bd. dirs. Pacific Harbors Coun. Boy Scouts Am.; bd. dirs. Tacoma Area Urban Coalition; past chmn. Wash. Friends Higher Edn.; bd. dirs. Tacoma Urban League, Bellarmine Prep. Sch., Tacoma, Camp Brotherhood, Nativity House; trustee Tacoma Gen. Hosp., Pacific Sci. Center; mem. Commn. on Children, Youth and Families for Tacoma and Pierce County; mem. com. Faith Homes for Young Women; pres. Second City chamber of Tacoma. Recipient Disting. Teaching award City Winfield, Kans., 1960, Freedom Found. Teaching award, 1961, Disting. Eagle Scout award, 1982, Pres. award St. Martins Coll., 1980. Mem. Kiwanis, Phi Delta Kappa. Home: 405 N Stadium Way Tacoma WA 98403-3228

WIEGNER, ALLEN WALTER, biomedical engineering educator, researcher; b. Bethlehem, Pa., July 22, 1947; s. Howard Jay and Anna (Strouse) W.; m. Sandra A. Waddock, Aug. 26, 1978; 1 child, Benjamin Waddock. SB, SM, MIT, 1970, PhD, 1978. Rsch. assoc. Harvard U. Med. Sch., Boston, 1978-87, asst. prof. neurology (biomed. engring.), 1987—; asst. biomed. engr. Mass. Gen. Hosp., Boston, 1980—. Cons. rsch. svc. VA Med. Ctr., 1984—, biomed. engr., 1987-96, computer specialist, 1996—. Contbr. articles, book chpts. to profl. publs. Lt. USPHS, 1970-72. Mem. IEEE (sr.), Soc. for Neurosci. Office: VA Boston HCS 1400 VFW Parkway Boston MA 02132

WIEGNER, EDWARD ALEX, multi-industry executive; b. Waukesha, Wis., Dec. 13, 1939; s. Roy Edwards and Margaret (Kuehnlein) Wiegner; m. Cathryn J. Mullens, Oct. 16, 1970; children: Carlin, Ryan; 1 child from previous marriage, Christine. BBA, U. Wis., 1961, MS in Econs., 1965, PhD in Econs., 1969. Asst. prof. bus. adminstrn. Marquette U., Milw., 1965-71; assoc. prof U. Wis., Madison, 1972-73; sec. Wis. Dept. Revenue, Madison, 1971-74; sr. v.p. fin., bd. dirs. Wis. Power and Light Co., Madison, 1974-76, sr. v.p. consumer, pub. and fin. affairs, dir., 1976-80, exec. v.p., bd. dirs., 1980-82; sr. v.p., CFO, bd. dirs. Am. Natural Resources Co., 1982-85, exec. v.p., chief adminstrv. officer, bd. dirs., 1985-86; sr. v.p. Coastal Corp., 1985-86; sr. v.p., chief fin. officer Household Internat., Inc., 1986-88; exec. v.p., CFO Progressive Corp., Mayfield Heights, Ohio, 1988-91, pres. fin. svcs. div., 1989-93; gen. ptnr. Aurora Ptnrs., 1994-96; vice chmn. 1st Am. Ins. Co., Kansas City, Mo., 1994-97; chmn., CEO First Am. Fin. Corp., 1997-98; chmn. Geologix, Inc., Placerville, Calif., 1998—, Ins. Distbn. Solutions, LLC, Jacksonville, Fla., 1999—. Contbr. articles to profl. jours. Mem.: Grand Harbor Country Club. Home and Office: 151 Shores Dr Indian River Shores FL 32963 E-mail: edward@wiegner.com.

WIEHE, FRED, writer; b. Cin., Ohio, Apr. 15, 1955; s. Fred Wiehe and Elizabeth Elfers; m. Suzanne Brenner, Nov. 25, 1989; children: Jesse Brenner-Wiehe, Ian Brenner-Wiehe. BA, U. Cin., 1974—78. Case mgr. Zonta Children's Ctr., San Jose, Calif., 1984—86; tchr. Children's Health Coun., Palo Alto, Calif., 1986—91; author San Jose, Calif. Author: (novels) Strange Days, 1993, Starkville, 1996, 2001, Night Songs, 2001, The Burning, 2003. Mem.: Horror Writers Assn. Personal E-mail: fwiehe@yahoo.com.

WIEHOFF, JOHN P. trucking executive; With Arthur Anderson, 1984—92; contr., treas. C.H. Robinson Worldwide, 1992—98, sr. v.p., CFO, 1998—99, pres., 1999—, CEO, 2002—. Office: 8100 Mitchell Rd Eden Prairie MN 55344

WIELAND, GILBERT DARRYL, health facility administrator, researcher; b. Hagerstown, Md., Oct. 31, 1951; s. Gilbert Hugh and Joan Kanaga Wieland; m. Manhal A. Wieland, Apr. 26, 1980; 1 child, Christopher. BA, Am. U., 1972; PhD, U. Rochester, 1982; MPH, UCLA, 1983. Sr. rsch. scientist VA Geriatric Rsch., Edn. and Clin. Ctr., Sepulveda, Calif., 1982—96; rsch. dir. Beverly Found., Pasadena, Calif., 1987—90; assoc. rsch. prof. divsn. geriat. UCLA, 1991—96; prof. U.S.C. Sch. Medicine, Columbia, 1996—; rsch. dir. geriat. Palmetto Health Richland, Columbia, 1998—. Fellow: Gerontol. Soc. Am. (chair pub. policy com. 2000—02, chair rsch. taskforce), Am. Geriatrics Soc. (mem. rsch. com. 2000—03). Office: Palmetto Health Richland Nine Medical Park #630 Columbia SC 29204 Office Phone: 803-434-4330. E-mail: darryl.wieland@palmettohealth.org.

WIELAND, GUALTERIO, automotive executive; Grad, U. Nacional de Buenos Aires. Dist. sales mgr. GM Argentina, 1968—74; sales mgr. GM Uruguay, 1974—78; mgr. sales ops. GM Argentina, 1978—80; dir. sales and mktg. GM Colmotores, Bogota, 1982—86; dir. sales mktg. GM Brasil; mng. dir. GM Colmotores, 1990—93, GM Venezolana, 1993—95; exec. dir. GM Andean Region, Latin Am., Miami, 1995—2000; pres. mng. dir. GM Brasil, 2000—. Office: GM Corp 300 Renaissance Ctr Detroit MI 48265-3000

WIELAND, JOHN, real estate executive; m. Sue Wieland; 2 children. BA magna cum laude, Amherst Coll., 1958; MBA with high distinction, Harvard Bus. Sch., 1964; LHD (hon.), Amherst Coll., 1993. Chmn., CEO, John Wieland Homes and Neighborhoods, Inc., Atlanta, 1970—. Bd. dirs. Fed. Res. Bank Atlanta. Internat. bd. dirs. Habitat for Humanity; bd. dirs. Ga. Trust Fund for Homeless, Atlanta Neighborhood Devel. Partnership; former chmn. High Mus. Art; former vice chmn. Woodruff Arts Ctr.; chmn. Adv. Coun., Emory U. Ctr. Ethics. Mem. Nat. Assn. Home Builders (life bd. dirs.), Atlanta (Ga.) C. of C. (mem. exec. com), Phi Beta Kappa. Office: 1950 Sullivan Rd Atlanta GA 30337-5706 Business E-Mail: john.wieland@jwhomes.com.

WIELAND, WILLIAM DEAN, healthcare consulting executive; b. Peoria, Ill., Feb. 15, 1948; s. George William and Virginia Lee (Delicath) W.; m. Joyce Lumia; 1 child, William Michael. BBA, Bradley U., 1971. Asst. adminstr. Galesburg (Ill.) Cottage Hosp., 1973-74; v.p. Anton & Damian, Iowa City, 1975-76; mgr. Clifton, Gunderson & Co., Peoria, 1977-80; v.p. OHMS Health Mgmt. Services, Columbus, 1980-84; dir., cons. VHA Cons. Svcs., Tampa, Fla., 1984-88; divsn. mgr. VHA, Inc., Tampa, Fla., 1988-95; sr. cons. mgr. Cost Sys. Group, Inc., Tampa, Fla., 1995-96; prin. Medifax Assocs., Tampa, Fla., 1997-98; managed care systems analyst U. Cmty. Hosp., Tampa, Fla., 1998—. Small bus. cons. Clifton, Gunderson & Co., 1977-80; cons. OHMS Health Mgmt. Svcs., Columbus, 1980-84. Mem.: Healthcare Info. and Mgmt. Sys. Soc., Am. Bus. Club, Sigma Nu (Zeta Phi chpt.). E-mail: wweland@tampabay.rr.com.

WIELER, SCOTT ALAN, investment banker; b. N.Y.C., Mar. 10, 1958; s. Richard Joseph and Valerie Helen (Straight) W.; m. Mary McCord Baily, Aug. 24, 1985; children: Alexander Evans, James Baily. AB in Econs. magna cum laude, Boston Coll., 1981; MBA, U. Pa., 1987. Mng. dir. BT Securities Corp., N.Y.C., 1981—94, Alexander Brown & Sons. Inc., Balt., 1994—99; with Deutsche Bank Alex Brown, Balt., 1999—2002; pres., CEO Signal Hill Capital Group, LLC, Balt., 2002—. Mem. Rockaway Hunt Club, Lawrence Beach Club (bd. dirs. 1985—), Elkridge Hunt Club, Balt. Republican. Avocations: tennis, golf. Office: Signal Hill Capital Group LLC 6225 Smith Ave Baltimore MD 21209-3630

WIELGUS, CHARLES JOSEPH, information services company executive; b. Hadley, Mass., Jan. 2, 1923; s. Joseph John and Anna Mary (Armata) W.; m. Irene Helen Graham, Jan. 1, 1949; children: Charles, Paul, Martha Jane. BS summa cum laude in Bus. Adminstrn, Bryant Coll., 1947, D.S. in Bus. Adminstrn. (hon.), 1977. With Bigelow-Sanford Carpet Co., Enfield, Conn. and N.Y.C., 1947-56; with Reuben H. Donnelley Corp. (subs. Dun & Bradstreet Corp.), Chicago and N.Y.C., 1956-71; v.p. personnel Dun & Bradstreet, Inc. (subs.), 1971-73, Dun & Bradstreet Corp., 1973-76, sr. v.p. human resources, 1976-82, exec. v.p. human resources and communications, 1983-88, ret., 1988; nature photographer, 1989—. Adj. faculty New Sch. Social Research, 1977-88, mem. adv. com. Masters program in human resources, 1977-88, ret., 1988; mem. adv. council on mgmt. edn. N.Y.C. C. of C., 1975-80; mem. bus. edn. adv. com. N.Y.C. Bd. Edn., 1977-88; dir. Nat. Ctr. Career Life Planning, 1986—; mem. adv. council on human resources mgmt. Nat. Conf. Bd., 1987-88. Bd. dirs. United Cerebral Palsy Assn. Westchester, 1966-75; trustee Operation Hope, Inc., 1966-75, active local and state Republican orgns., 1965-75. Served in USAF, 1943-46. Mem. Am. Arbitration Assn. (arbitrator 1988-98), Nat. Alliance Bus. (dir., steering com.), Lions, K. of C. Clubs: Univ, Larchmont Shore. Home: 151 Rockingstone Ave Larchmont NY 10538-1512 also: 7 Hummingbird Ct Hilton Head Island SC 29926

WIEMAN, CARL E. physics educator; b. Corvallis, Oreg., Mar. 26, 1951; m. Sarah Gilbert. BS, MIT, 1973; PhD, Stanford U., 1977; DS (hon.), U. Chgo., 1997. Asst. rsch. physicist dept. physics U. Mich., Ann Arbor, 1977—79, asst. prof. physics, 1979—84; assoc. prof. physics U. Colo., Boulder, 1984—87, prof., 1987—97, disting. rsch. prof., 1997—; fellow Joint Inst. for Lab. Astrophysics, Boulder, 1985—. Loeb lectr. Harvard U., 1990—91; Rosenthal Meml. lectr. Yale U., 1988, Columbia U., 1988; Cherwell-Simon Meml. lectr. Oxford U., 1999; vis. scholar Phi Beta Kappa, 1999—2000. Recipient Ernest Orlando Lawrence Meml. award, U.S. Dept. Energy, 1993, Einstein medal for laser sci., Soc. Optical and Quantum Electronics, 1995, Fritz London prize for low temperature physics, 1996, Newcomb Cleveland prize, AAAS, 1996, King Faisal Internat. prize for Sci., 1997, Sci. award, Bonfils Stanton Found., 1998, Lorentz medal, Netherlands Royal Acad. Sci., 1998, Benjamin Franklin Medal in Physics, 2000, The Nobel Prize in Physics, 2001, Nat. Sci. Found. Dir. Award for Dist. Teaching Scholars, 2001. Fellow: Guggenheim, 1990-1991, Hertz Found., 1973-1977, Am. Phys. Soc. (Davisson-Germer prize 1994, Schawlow prize in laser sci. 1998); mem.: NAS, 1995, Am. Physical Soc. (fellow, 1990), Am. Acad. Arts and Sci., 1998, Am. Assn. Physics Tchrs. (Richtmyer lectr. award 1996), Optical Soc. Am. (R.W. Wood prize 1999). Achievements include first to achieve Bose-Einstein condensation, 1995. Office: Dept of Physics and JILA CB440 U Colo Boulder CO 80309-0440

WIEMANN, MARION RUSSELL, JR., (BARON OF CAMSTER), biologist; b. Sept. 7, 1929; s. Marion Russell and Verda (Peek) W.; 1 child from previous marriage, Tamara Lee (Mrs. Donald D. Kelley). BS, Ind. U., 1959; PhD (hon.), World U. Roundtable, 1991; ScD (hon.), The London Inst. Applied Rsch., 1994, ScD (hon.), 1995, World Acad., Germany, 1995. Ordained hon. min., 1998; cert. hypnotist. Histo-rsch. technician U. Chgo., 1959, rsch. asst., 1959-62, rsch. technician, 1962-64; tchr. sci. Westchester Twp. Sch., Chesterton, Ind., 1964-66; with U. Chgo., 1965-79, sr. rsch. technician, 1967-70, rsch. technologist, 1970-79; prin. Marion Wiemann & Assocs., cons. R&D, Chesterton, Ind., 1979-89. Advisor Porter County Health Bd., 1989-91; mem. consultive faculty World U., 1991-99, SkyWarn, Nat. Weather Svc., 1993—. Author: Tooth Decay, Its Cause and Prevention Through Controlled Soil Composition, 1985, The Mechanism of Tooth Decay, 1985; contbr. articles to profl. jours. and newspapers. Vice-chmn. The Duneland 4th of July Com., 1987-91; v.p. State Microscopical Soc. Ill., 1969-70, pres., 1970-71. With USN, 1951-53. Recipient Disting. Tech. Communicator award Soc. for Tech. Communication, 1974, Internat. Order Merit (Eng.), 1991; ennobled Royal Coll. Heraldry, Australia, 1991, Highland Laird, Scotland, 1995; named Sagamore of the Wabash Gov. Ind., 1985; McCrone Rsch. Inst. scholar, 1968; named Prof. of Sci. Australian Inst. for Co-Ordinated Rsch., Australia, 1995, knight corps Diplomatique The Sovereign Military Templar Order, 1994; recipient Scouters Key award Boy Scouts Am., 1968, Arrowhead honor, 1968, Albert Einstein Silver medal, Huguenin, Le Locke, Switzerland, Henri Dunant Silver medal with silver bars, 1995, Henri Dunant Silver medal, 1995, medal of honor, England, 1996. Fellow: Australian Inst. Co-Ordinated Rsch., World Lit. Acad.; mem.: Can. Soc. Dowsers, Am. Soc. Dowsers, World Explorers Club, Akademie MIDI, Maison Internat. des Intellectuels, Internat. Graphoanalysis Soc., Order Internat. Fellowship, World Acad., Assn. Masters Universe, Internat. Soc. Soil Sci., Govs. Club, VFW (charter mem., bd. dirs., post judge adv. 1986—99, apptd. post adj. 1986—99, Cross of Malta 1986). Achievements include demostration that radiation does not produce dental caries; proved that soil calcium, magnesium, potassium and phosphorous, with soil PH, controls population size and longevity of earthworms and humans and the incidence of dental caries; demonstrated that flouride neither reduces or prevents dental caries. Address: PO Box 1016 Chesterton IN 46304-0016 *Personal philosophy: Leadership founded upon trust, perpetuated by participation, example and instruction, dedicated to wise use, protection or improvement of health and environment. If you put in an hour of real work you get an hour of results. There is no other way to do it.*

WIEMELS, JAMES R. automotive executive; b. Cleveland, Ohio, Apr. 15, 1946; BS in Mech. Engring., Kettering U., 1969; M in Bus. Mgmt., Ctrl. Mich. U., 1978. Plant mgr. GM, Flint Pressed Metal Plant, 1980—84, GM of Can. Group, Marion, Ind., 1984—87, mfg. mgr., 1987—91, gen. dir. tech. ops., 1991—92; mfg. mgr. Lansing Auto. Divsn., 1992—94, gen. mgr., v.p., 1994—97; chmn., mng. dir. Holden Ltd., 1997—99; v.p. mfg. GME, Zurich, Switzerland, 1999—2002, v.p. global mfg., 2002—, v.p., gen. mgr. metal fabricating, 2003—. Office: GM Corp PO Box 300 300 Renaissance Ctr Detroit MI 48265-3000

WIEMER, ROBERT ERNEST, film and television producer, writer, director; b. Highland Park, Mich., Jan. 30, 1938; s. Carl Ernest and Marion (Israelian) W.; m. Rhea Dale McGeath, June 14, 1958; children: Robert Marshall, Rhea Whitney. BA, Ohio Wesleyan U., 1959. Ind. producer, 1956-60; dir. documentary ops. WCBS-TV, N.Y.C., 1964-67; ind. producer of television, theatrical and bus. films N.Y.C., 1967-72; exec. producer motion pictures and TV, ITT, N.Y.C., 1973-84, pres. subs. Blue Marble Co., Inc., Telemontage, Inc., Alphaventure Music, Inc., Betaventure Music, Inc., 1973-84; founder, chmn., chief exec. officer Tigerfilm, Inc., 1984—; chmn., bd. dirs. Golden Tiger Pictures, Hollywood, Calif., 1988—; pres, CEO Tuxedo Pictures Corp., Hollywood, Calif., 1993—. Bd. dirs., v.p. prodn. Las Vegas Internat. Film Festival; v.p. prodn. Cinevegas. Writer, prodr., dir.: (feature films) My Seventeenth Summer, Witch's Sister, Do Me a Favor, Anna to the Infinite Power, Somewhere, Tomorrow, Night Train to Kathmandu; exec. prodr.: (children's TV series) Big Blue Marble (Emmy and Peabody awards); dir. (TV episodes) New York Undercover, seaQuest DSV, Star Trek: The Next Generation, Deep Space Nine, The Adventures of Superboy; composer (country-western ballad) Tell Me What To Do. Capt. USAF, 1960-64. Recipient CINE award, 1974, 76, 77, 79, 81, Emmy award, 1978. Mem. NATAS, ASCAP, Info. Film Producers Assn. (Outstanding Producer award), Nat. Assn. TV Programming Execs., Am. Women in Radio and TV, N.J. Broadcasters Assn., Dirs. Guild Am., v.p., bd. mem. CineVegas The Las Vegas Internat. Film Festival. Office: Golden Tiger Pictures 3896 Ruskin St Las Vegas NV 89147-1097

WIEMKEN, PATRICIA E. music educator, consultant; d. Harold G. and Dorothy E. Weber; m. Brian L. Wiemken, Sept. 16, 1995. Bachelor, Bowling Green State U., 1994. Vocal dir. Liberty Center Schs., Ohio, 1995—2002; music tchr. Northeastern Local Schs. Tinora, Defiance, Ohio, 2002—. Staff Ohio State Fair Youth Choir, Columbus, 1989—92. Youth tchr. First Ch. of Christ, Napoleon, Ohio, 1998—2004. Mem.: MENC, OMEA, OEA. Avocations: scrapbooking, gardening, piano, travel. Office: Northeastern Local Schs 5921 Domersville Rd Defiance OH 43512

WIENER, ARTHUR C. textiles executive; b. 1938; With menswear divsn. Burlington Industries, Inc., 1966-75, pres. menswear divsn., 1973-75, group v.p., pres. blended divsn., 1984-88; pres. apparel fabrics mktg. divsn. Dan River, Inc., 1975-84; pres., CEO Galey & Lord, Inc., N.Y.C., 1988—, chmn. bd., 1992—. Office: Galey & Lord Inc 980 Ave of the Americas New York NY 10018-5401 Office Fax: 212-465-3025.

WIENER, HESH (HAROLD FREDERIC WIENER), publisher, editor, consultant; b. Bklyn., July 20, 1946; s. Jesse Leonard and Regina (Rappaport) W. BS in Polit. Sci., MIT, 1969; LLB with honors, Open U., London, 2002. Mem. staff systems devel. Data Gen. Corp., Southboro, Mass., 1969-70; dir. computer edn. project U. Calif., Berkeley, 1970-72; editor Computer Decisions Mag., Rochelle Park, N.J., 1973-78; editor, pub. Tech. News Am., N.Y.C., 1976-88; pres. Tech. News of Am. Co., Inc., N.Y.C., 1982—; mng. dir. Tech. News Ltd., London, 1992—. Webmaster, tech-news.com, 1996—, primrosehill.com, 1998—, luminum.com, 2000—; pub. Computer and Comms. Buyer Newsletter, 1979-95, Mainstream Newsletter, 1980-82, Infoperspectives Newsletter, 1982 , Storage Tech. Monitor, 1984-87, Infoperspectives Internat. (U.K.), 1989—, (Mid. East), 1991—, The Four Hundred Newsletter (U.K.), 1990-97, The Four Hundred Newsletter (U.S.), 1990-97; editor Infoperspectives Internat. (Italy), 1991-98, The Four Hundred Newsletter (Italy), 1995—; pub. U.S. edit. Computergram Internat. Newsletter, 1985-90; corr. Processeurs mag., 1989-99; cons. Hewlett-Packard Co. (Paris), 1971-72, Xerox Corp., 1972-73; advisor NSF, 1975; columnist 451.com, 2000—. Author: Big Blue and You, The IBM Atlas, The Mainframe; corr. Computer Weekly, U.K., 1975-81, Computable, Amsterdam, 1976-87, Computing Can., 1977-78, Ordinateurs, Paris, 1977-89, Data News, Brussels, 1979-86, Informatics, U.K., 1981-85, Datanytt, Copenhagen, 1982-89, Mgmt. Tech. mag., 1983-85; editor BusinessWeek Newsletter for Info. Execs., 1987-90, Datamation Mag., 1983-90, Infoperspectives Internat. (Milan), 1991—; contbg. editor Bus. and Soc. Rev., 1978-85; contbr. N.Y. Times Syndicate, Los Angeles Times Syndicate, N.Am. Newspaper Alliance Wireservice, Newsday, Manhattan, Inc., Rom Mag., Informatique (Paris), The Economist (London), Dun's Bus. Month, Software News, Intermedia, Digital News, Data Communications, Bus. Week Newsletter for Info. Execs., Bus. Strategy Internat., Nikkei Watcher on IBM (Tokyo), 1989-96; contbg. editor Midrange Svc. Pubs., 2002—. Mem.: Overseas Press. Home: 246 6th Ave Brooklyn NY 11215-2103 Office: Tech News Am 123 7th Ave Brooklyn NY 11215-1383

WIENER, JACQUES LOEB, JR., judge; b. Shreveport, La., Oct. 2, 1934; s. Jacques L. and Betty (Eichenbaum) Wiener; m. Sandra Mills Feingerts; children: Patricia Wiener Shifke, Jacques L. III, Betty Ellen Wiener Spomer, Donald B. BA, Tulane U., 1956, JD, 1961. Bar: La. 1961, U.S. Dist. Ct. (we. dist.) La. 1961. Ptnr. Wiener, Weiss & Madison, Shreveport, 1961—90; judge U.S. Ct. Appeals (5th cir.), New Orleans, 1990—. Mem. coun. La. State Law Inst., 1963; master of the bench Am. Inn of Ct., 1990—98. Pres. United Way N.W. La., 1975, Shreveport Jewish Fedn., 1969—70. Fellow: La. Bar Found., Am. Bar Found., Am. Coll. Trust and Estates Counsel; mem.: ABA, Am. Law Inst., Shreveport Bar Assn. (pres. 1982), La. Bar Assn., Internat. Acad. Estate and Trust Law (academician). Avocations: fly fishing, upland game bird hunting, photography, travel. Office: Court of Appeals Building 600 Camp St Rm 244 New Orleans LA 70130-3425

WIENER, JOEL HOWARD, historian, educator; b. N.Y.C., Aug. 23, 1937; s. Philip Wiener and Elizabeth Weissman; m. Suzanne Wolff Wiener, Sept. 4, 1961; children: Paul, Deborah, Jane. BA, NYU, 1959; postgrad., U. Glasgow, Scotland, 1961—63; PhD, Cornell U., 1965. Asst. prof. history Skidmore Coll., Saratoga Springs, NY, 1964—67, CUNY, 1967—71, assoc. prof. history, 1972—78, prof. history, 1978—2000, emeritus prof. history, 2000—. Dir. study abroad program in Eng. CUNY, 1971—73, prof. history doctoral program, 1980—2000, chmn. dept. history, 1981—85; cons., advisor Cornell U. Press, U. N.C. Press, Victorian Studies, NEH, English Lit. in Transition, 1880-1920, Princeton U. Press, Greenwood Press, U.K. Social Sci. Rsch. Coun., Ill. U. Press, Victorian Periodicals Rev., Am. Journalism, Albion, Jour. Brit. Studies, Rutgers U. Press, PSC-CUNY, Dictionary Labour Biography, Harvester Press. Author: The War of the Unstamped, 1969, A Descriptive Finding List of Unstamped British Periodicals, 1830-1836, 1970, William Lovett, 1989, Radicalism and Freethought in Nineteenth-Century Britain, 1983; editor: Great Britain: Foreign Policy and the Span of Empire, 4 vols., 1972, Great Britain: The Lion at Home, 4 vols., 1974, Innovators and Preachers, 1985, Papers for the Millions, 1988; contbr. articles to profl. jours.; assoc. editor Dictionary of National Biography, 1999—2004. Grantee, Oxford Bibliog. Soc., 1971—72, Am. Philos. Soc., 1971—72. Fellow: Royal Hist. Soc.; mem.: Am. Journalism Historians Assn. (rsch. com. 1998—), Rsch. Soc. for Victorian Periodicals (v.p., pres. 1981—85). Avocations: travel, theater, cinema. Home: 267 Glen Ct Teaneck NJ 07666 Home Fax: 201-837-8658. E-mail: jwiener267@aol.com.

WIENER, JON, history professor; b. St. Paul, Minn., May 16, 1944; s. Daniel N. and Gladys (Aronsohn) Spratt. BA, Princeton U., 1966; PhD, Harvard U., 1971. Acting asst. prof. UCLA, 1973-74; asst. prof. history U. Calif.-Irvine, 1974-83, prof., 1984—. Plaintiff Freedom of Info. Lawsuit against FBI for John Lennon Files, 1983—. Author: Social Origins of the New South, 1979; Come Together: John Lennon in His Time, 1984, Professors, Politics, and Pop, 1991, Gimme Some Truth: The John Lennon FBI File, 2000; contbg. editor The Nation mag.; contbr. articles to profl. jours. including The New Republic and New York Times Book Rev. Mem. Am. Hist. Assn., Nat. Book Critics Circle, Orgn. Am. Historians, Liberty Hill Found. (bd. dirs.). E-mail: wiener@uci.edu.

WIENER, JOSEPH, pathologist; b. Toronto, Sept. 21, 1927; arrived in U.S., 1949, naturalized, 1960; s. Louis and Minnie (Salem) W.; m. Judith Hesta Ross, June 20, 1954; children: Carolyn L., Adam L. MD, U. Toronto, 1953. Intern Detroit Receiving Hosp., 1953-54; resident to chief resident pathology Mallory Inst. Pathology, 1954-55, 57-60; from asst. to assoc. prof. pathology Columbia U., N.Y.C., 1960-68; prof. pathology N.Y. Med. Coll., N.Y.C., 1968-78, Wayne State U., Detroit, 1978—, chmn. dept., 1978-90. Cons. NIH, 1970— Served to capt. M.C. U.S. Army, 1955-57. Grantee Heart, Lung and Blood Inst., 1971-93; fellow Coun. for High Blood Pressure Rsch., 1982. Fellow Am. Heart Assn.; mem. AAAS, Am. Soc. Investigative Pathology, Am. Soc. Cell Biology, Mich. Path. Soc., Internat. Acad. Pathology, Am. Heart Assn., U.S./Can. Acad. Pathology, Am. Stroke Assn., Mich. Heart Assn. (dir.), Internat. Soc. Hypertension. Achievements include rsch. on cellular/molecular biology of experimental hypertension. Office: 540 E Canfield St Detroit MI 48201-1928 Office Phone: 313-577-1157. Business E-Mail: jwiener@med.wayne.edu.

WIENER, LEONARD, journalist; b. NYC, Sept. 23, 1940; s. Isidore and Ethel (Berkowitz) W.; m. Edith Herman, June 16, 1974. BA, U. Mich., 1962, MA, 1964. Reporter Milw. Jour., 1964-67; reporter bus. news Chgo. Daily News, 1967-71, Chgo. Tribune, 1971-79; assoc. editor U.S. News and World Report, Washington, 1979-88, sr. editor personal taxes, personal finance, 1988—2003, contbg. editor, 2003—. Home: 5501 Burling Ct Bethesda MD 20817-6309 Office: U S News and World Report 1050 Thomas Jefferson St NW Washington DC 20007-3837

WIENER, MALCOLM HEWITT, historian, writer; b. Tsingtao, China, July 3, 1935; (parents Am. citizens); s. Myron and Ethel (Zimmerman) W.; m. Carolyn Talbot Seely, June 8, 1990; children: Kate, Elizabeth, Thomas, Jonathan. BA, Harvard U., 1957, JD, 1963; LittD (hon.), U. Sheffield, 1997; PhD (hon.), Eberhard-Karl U., Tübingen, Germany, 1998; Doctorate (hon.), U. Athens, Greece, 1998. Bar: N.Y. 1964. Atty., N.Y.C., 1963-71; pvt. practice investing, 1971-98; chmn. Millburn Corp., N.Y.C., 1977-98; chmn. bd. trustees Malcolm Hewitt Wiener Found., N.Y.C., 1984—. Columnist Newsday. Co-dir. Aegean Bronze Age Colloquium, NYU Inst. Fine Arts, 1975—; founder, exec. dir. Inst. Aegean Prehistory, 1982-89, pres., 1990—; trustee Am. Sch. Classical Studies in Athens, Metro. Mus. Art; mem. adv. bd. Malcolm Wiener Ctr. for Social Policy, Kennedy Sch. Govt. Harvard U.; mem. Coun. Fgn. Rels., chmn. Indep. Task Force Non-lethal Tech. Mil. Implications and Options, 1995. With USN, 1957-60. Fellow: AAAS, Soc. Antiquaries London, Archaeol. Inst. Am. (life); mem.: ABA, Chevalier de l'Ordre des Arts et des Lettres, Osterreichische Akademie Wissenschaften (corr.), Royal Swedish Acad. Letters, History and Antiquities (corr.), Austrian Archaeol. Inst. (corr.). Office: Villa Candia 66 Vista Dr Greenwich CT 06830 Office Phone: 203-862-9334. Business E-Mail: cpadgett@instap.org.

WIENER, MARVIN S. rabbi, editor, executive; b. N.Y.C., Mar. 16, 1925; s. Max and Rebecca (Dodell) W.; m. Sylvia Bodek, Mar. 2, 1952; children: David Hillel, Judith Rachel. BS, CCNY, 1944, MS, 1945; BHL, Jewish Theol. Sem. Am., 1947, MHL, Rabbi, 1951, DD (hon.), 1977. Registrar, sec. faculty Rabbinical Sch., Jewish Theol. Sem. Am., 1951-57; cons. Frontiers of Faith TV Series, NBC, 1951-57; dir., instr. liturgy Cantors Inst.-Sem. Coll. Jewish Music, Jewish Theol. Sem. Am., 1954-58; faculty coord. Sem. Sch. and Women's Inst., 1958-64; dir. Nat. Acad. for Adult Jewish Studies, United Synagogue Am., N.Y.C., 1958-78; editor Burning Bush Press, 1958-78, United Synagogue Rev., 1978-86; dir. com. congrl. stds. United Synagogue Am., 1976-86, cons. cmty. rels. and social action, 1981-82, editor, exec. joint retirement bd., 1986—. Mem. Joint Commn. on Rabbinic Placement, 1951-57, Joint Prayer Book Commn., 1957 62; mem. exec. coun. Rabbinical Assembly, 1958-86; editl. cons. N.Y. Bd. Rabbis, 1987-89; trustee joint retirement bd. Jewish Theol. Sem. Am. Rabbinical Assembly and United Synagogue Am., 1959-86, sec. 1968-76, 84-85, vice chmn., 1976-82, 85-86, chmn. 1982, treas., 1983-84; co-chmn. Jewish Bible Assn., 1960-64; chmn. bd. rev. Nat. Coun. Jewish Audio-Visual Materials, 1968-69; mem. exec. com. Nat. Coun. Adult Jewish Edn., 1966—; mem. exec. bd., editl. adv. bd., v.p. Jewish Book Couns., 1976-96; chmn. Internat. Conf. Adult Jewish Edn., Jerusalem, 1972. Editor: Nat. Acad. Adult Jewish Studies Bull., 1958-78, The High Holy Days, Book I (Herman Kieval), 1959, The Jewish Dietary Laws (Samuel H. Dresner and Seymour Siegel), 1959, Past and Present: Selected Essays (Israel Friedlaender), 1961, Heart of Wisdom, Book I (Bernard S. Raskas), 1962, Book II, 1979, Judaism: Profile of a Faith (Ben Zion Bokser), 1963, The Wisdom of Solomon Schechter (Bernard Mandelbaum), 1963, Jewish Tract Series, 1964-78 (15 titles), Foundations of A Faith (Simon Greenberg), 1967, Judaism and the Christian Predicament (Ben Zion Bokser), 1967, The Maturing of the Conservative Movement (Bernard Mandelbaum), 1968, The Sabbath (Samuel L. Dresner), 1970, Adult Jewish Edn., 1958-78, Talmudic Law and the Modern State (Moshe Silberg), 1973, Self-Incrimination in Jewish Law (Aaron Kirschenbaum), 1970, Sex and the Family in the Jewish Tradition (Robert Gordis), 1970; contbr. articles to numerous periodicals. Mem. Am. Acad. Jewish Rsch., Assn. Jewish Studies, N.Y. Bd. Rabbis, Rabbinical Assembly. Home: 67-66 108th St Apt D-46 Forest Hills NY 11375-2974 Office: Joint Retirement Bd 7 Penn Plz Ste 720 New York NY 10001-3900

WIENER, RONALD MARTIN, lawyer; b. Phila., June 1, 1939; s. William V. and Sylvia Wiener; children: Carol Jan, Alan Mark. AB, U. Pa., 1961; JD magna cum laude, Harvard U., 1964. Bar: DC 1965, Pa. 1966. Law clk. U.S. Tax Ct., 1964-66; assoc. Wolf, Block, Schorr and Solis-Cohen, LLP, Phila., 1966-72, ptnr., 1972—. Mem. commr.'s adv. group IRS, 1992—93. Fellow: Am. Coll. Tax Counsel (regent 3d cir. 1996—2003); mem.: ABA, Phila. Bar Assn. (chair tax sect. 1989—90), Pa. Bar Assn. Office: Wolf Block Schorr and Solis-Cohen LLP 1650 Arch St 22d fl Philadelphia PA 19103-2678 Office Phone: 215-977-2266. E-mail: rwiener@wolfblock.com.

WIENER, RUSSELL WARREN, environmental scientist, researcher; b. N.Y.C., June 23, 1952; s. Max and Rhoda (Bruntil) W.; m. Martha E. Smith, Sept. 5, 1982; children: Benjamin, Victoria. Student, Rensselaer Poly. Inst., 1970—71; BS in Biology, Emory U., 1974, MS in Environ. Sci., 1978; PhD in Environ. Health, U. Cin., 1987. Rsch. technician U. N.C., Chapel Hill, 1978-79; aerosol tech. GE, Cin., 1984-86; chief atmospheric methods and monitoring br. U.S. EPA, Research Triangle Park, NC, 1987—2002, project dir. Nat. Homeland Security Rsch. Ctr., 2002—. Adj. asst. prof. U. N.C., Chapel Hill, 1989—, N.C. State U., Raleigh, 1994—. Mem. Am. Assn. for Aerosol Rsch. (chair indoor air 1988-94), Am. Indsl. Hygiene Assn. (chair aerosol tech. com. 1997), Am. Acad. Indsl. Hygiene. Avocations: swimming, tennis.

WIENER, SOLOMON, writer, consultant, former city official; b. N.Y.C., Mar. 5, 1915; s. Morris David and Anna (Pinchuk) W.; m. Gertrude Klings, Feb. 24, 1946; children: Marjorie Diane, Willa Kay Ehrlich. BS, Cornell, 1936; MPA, NYU, 1946. Exam. asst. N.Y.C. Dept. Pers., 1937-42, civil svc. examiner, 1946-55, asst. divsn. chief, 1955-59, divsn. chief, 1959-67, asst. dir. exams, 1967-70, dir. exams, 1970-72, asst. pers. dir. for exams., 1972-75; author, cons., 1975—. Tchr. Washington Irving Evening Adult Sch., N.Y.C., 1949-60, tchr.-in-charge, 1960-67. Author: A Handy Book of Commonly Used American Idioms, rev. edit., 1981, Manual de Modismos Americanos Más Comunes, rev. edit., 1981, A handy Guide to Irregular Verbs and the Use and Formation of Tenses, 1959, Guia Completa de Los Verbos Irregulares en Inglès yel uso y Formación de los Tiempos, 1959, Questions and Answers on American Citizenship, rev. edit., 1982, Clear and Simple Guide to Business Letter Writing, rev. edit., 1978, The College Graduate Guide for Scoring High on Employment Tests, 1981, The High School Graduate Guide for Scoring High on Civil Service Tests, 1981, How to Take and Pass Simple Tests for Civil Service Jobs, 1981, Officer Candidate Tests, 5th edit., 2000, Military Flight Aptitude Tests, 4th edit., 2000; co-author Practice for the Armed Forces Test, ASVAB, 16th edit., 1999, Practica para el Examen de las Fuerzas Armadas, ASVAB en Español, 1989; contbr. to ARCO ROTC Coll. Guide, 1988. Served with AUS, 1942-46, PTO. Decorated Bronze Star. Mem. ASPA, Internat. Pers. Mgmt. Assn. for Human Resources, Authors Guild, Res. Officers Assn., Mil. Officers Assn. Am., Assn. of U.S. Army, Nat. Def. Indsl. Assn., Marines Meml. Assn. Home: 523 E 14th St Apt 4F New York NY 10009-2931

WIENER, THOMAS ELI, lawyer; b. Dallas, Nov. 29, 1940; s. Samson and Fan (Gardner) W.; m. Felice Gloria Goodwin, Jan. 24, 1970; children: Gary Allen, Debra Roslyn, Allison Beth, Todd David. BA, U. Tex., 1962, JD with honors, 1968. Bar: Tex. 1968, D.C. 1969, Pa. 1972, U.S. Supreme Ct. 1972. Atty.-advisor office chief counsel IRS, Washington, 1968-72; assoc. Pepper Hamilton & Scheetz, Phila., 1972-74, Abrahams & Loewenstein, Phila., 1974-76, Goodis, Greenfield, Henry & Edelstein, Phila., 1976-77, Mesirov, Gelman, Jaffe, Cramer & Jamieson, Phila., 1977-78; prin. Franklin, Margulies & Huntington, 1978-91, Riley & DeFalice, P.C., Phila., 1991-92, Wiener & Caplan, P.C., Phila., 1992-95; pvt. practice Bala Cynwyd, Pa., 1995—. Bd dirs. Lufkin (Tex.) Industries, Inc. Author: (with others) Tax Problems of Fiduciaries, 1977. Trustee Golden Slipper Club; pres. Main Line Reform Temple, 1992-94, pres. brotherhood 1981-83; pres. Rotary Gundaker Found., 1986-87; 1st v.p. N. Am. Fedn. Temple Brotherhoods, 1999-2001; v.p. Phila. Fedn. Reform Synagogues, 1993-98; chmn. Synagogue Fedn. Coun. of Phila., 1994-97; trustee Union Am. Hebrew Congregations, 1995—, exec. com., 2001-, ARZA/World Union N.Am. Mem. D.C. Bar Assn., Pa. Bar Assn., Tex. Bar Assn., Phila. Bar Assn., Am. Law Inst., Order of Coif, Masons (32 degree K.C.C.H., past master), Rotary (pres. chpt. 1985-86). Home: 1233 Remington Rd Wynnewood PA 19096-2329 Office: One Belmont Ave Ste 605 Bala Cynwyd PA 19004-1609 Office Phone: 610-667-8999. Personal E-mail: twiener@aol.com.

WIENER, VALERIE, state senator, writer, positioning strategist, communications executive; b. Las Vegas, Nev., Oct. 30, 1948; d. Louis Isaac Wiener and Tui Ava Knight. BJ, U. Mo., 1971, MA, 1972, U. Ill., Springfield, 1974; postgrad., McGeorge Sch. Law, 1976—79. Prodr. Checkpoint Sta. KOMU-TV, Columbia, Mo., 1972-73; v.p., owner Broadcast Assocs., Inc., Las Vegas, 1972-86; pub. affairs dir. First Ill. Cable TV, Springfield, 1973-74; editor Ill. State Register, Springfield, 1973-74; prodr. and talent Nev. Realities Sta. KLVX-TV, Las Vegas, 1974-75; account exec. Sta. KBMI (now KFMS), Las Vegas, 1975-79; nat. traffic dir. six radio stas., Las Vegas, Albuquerque and El Paso, Tex., 1979-80; exec. v.p., gen. mgr. Stas. KXKS and KKJY, Albuquerque, 1980-81; exec. adminstr. Stas. KSET AM/FM, KVEG, KFMS and KKJY, 1981-83; press sec. U.S. Congressman Harry Reid, Washington, 1983-87; adminstrv. asst Friends for Harry Reid, Nev., 1986; press sec. U.S. Senator Harry Reid, Washington, 1987-88; owner Wiener Comm. Group, Las Vegas, 1988—; mem. Nev. Senate, Dist. 3 Clark County, 1996—; Senate Dem. Whip, 2001—; owner PowerMark Pub., 1998—. Author: Power Communications: Positioning Yourself for High Visibility (Fortune Book Club main selection 1994, Money Book Club selection 1995), Gang Free: Friendship Choices for Today's Youth, 1995, 2d edit., 1996, The Nesting Syndrome: Grown Children Living at Home, 1997, Winning the War Against Youth Gangs, 1999, Power Positioning: Advancing Yourself as The Expert, 2000 (Nat. award), Power-Master HandBook Series, 2000— (several nat. awards); contbg. writer The Pacesetter, ASAE's Comm. News. Sponsor Futures for Children, Las Vegas, Albuquerque, El Paso, 1979—83; mem. El Paso Exec. Women's Coun., 1981—83; media chmn. Gov.'s Coun. Small Bus., 1989—93; mem. Clark Coun. Sch. Dist. and Bus. Cmty. PAYBAC Spkrs. and Partnership Programs, 1989—, chair legis. com. on juv. justice, 1999—2000; chair Commn. on Sch. Safety and Juvenile Violence, 1999—2000; various state and nat. legis. commns. and coms.; vice chmn. Congl. Awards Coun., 1989—93, Gov.'s Commn. on Postsecondary Edn., 1992—96; mem. Nev. Technol. Crimes Task Force, 1999—, Nev. Drug Commn., 1997—, Nev. Commn. on Aging, 1997—, Nev. Anti-Bullying Task Force, 2001—03, Govs. Task Force on Corrections, 2002; chair legis. com. on obesity, 2003—; Senate Minority Whip, 2001, 2003; mem. VIP bd. Easter Seals, El Paso, 1982; med. dir. 1990 Nev. Gov.'s Conf. on Women; bd. dirs. BBB So. Nev., 1994—, Pub. Edn. Found., 1997—; steering com. Youth Recovery Network, 2001—02. Named Outstanding Vol., United Way, El Paso, 1983, SBA Nev. Small Bus. Media Adv. of Yr., 1992, Disting. Sr. Athlete in Nev., 2000, So. Nev. Health Care Policy Hero, 2003; named one of 27 Healthy Sch. Heroes in U.S., 2002; recipient Outstanding Achievement award, Nat. Fedn. Press Women, 1991, Disting. Leader award, Nat. Assn. Cmty. Leadership, 1993, Gold medal in fitness and weightlifting, Nev. Sr. Olympics, 1998—2003, Outstanding Women Adv. for Edn. award, Va. Commonwealth U., 2000, Internat. Cmty. Svc. award, Internat. New Thought Alliance, 2001, Gold medals in swimming, Nev. Sr. Olympics, 2002—03, 150 Comms. awards, 1989—. Mem. Nat. Assn. of Women Bus. Owners (media chmn., nat. rep. So. Nev. 1990-91, Nev. Adv. of Yr. award 1992), Nev. Press Women, Nat. Spkrs. Assn., Small Pubs. Assn. N.Am., Dem. Press Secs. Assn., El Paso Assn. Radio Stas., U.S. Senate Staff Club, Las Vegas C. of C. (Circle of Excellence award 1993), Soc. Profl. Journalists. Democrat. Avocations: reading, writing, fitness and weighlifting training and competition, public speaking, community involvement. Office: 1500 Foremaster Ln Ste 2 Las Vegas NV 89101-1150

WIENS, ARTHUR NICHOLAI, psychology educator; b. McPherson, Kans, Sept. 7, 1926; s. Jacob T. and Helen E. (Kroeker) W.; m. Ruth Helen Avery, June 11, 1949; children: Barbara, Bradley, Donald. BA, U. Kans., 1948, MA, 1952; PhD, U. Portland, 1956. Diplomate: Am. Bd. Examiners Profl. Psychology. Clin. psychologist Topeka State Hosp., 1949-53; sr. psychologist outpatient dept. Oreg. State Hosp., Salem, 1954-58, chief psychologist, 1958-61, dir. clin. psychology internship program, 1958-61; clin. instr. U. Oreg. Med. Sch., Portland, 1958-61, asst. prof., 1961-65, assoc. prof., 1965-66; prof. med. psychology, 1966—96; prof. emeritus med. psychology, 1997—. Field assessment officer Peace Corps, 1965; cons. psychologist Portland Ctr. for Hearing and Speech, 1964—67, Dammasch State Hosp., 1967—69, Raleigh Hills Hosp., 1968—84, Oreg. Vocat. Rehab. Divsn., 1973—2001, mem. state adv. com., 1976—93; cons. William Temple Rehab. House, Episcopal Laymen's Mission Soc., 1968—88; chmn. State Oreg. Bd. Social Protection, 1971—84, State of Oreg. Bd. Psychologist Examiners, 1963—66, 1974—77; v.p. bd. dirs. Raleigh Hills Rsch. Found., 1974—80. Contbr. articles to profl. jour. Fellow AAAS, APA (chmn. com. on vis. psychologist program 1972-76, chmn. accreditation com. 1978, mem. task force edn. and credentialing 1979-84); mem. Am. Assn. State Psychology Bd. (pres. 1978-79), Nat. Register Health Svc. Providers in Psychology (bd. dirs. 1985-92, chmn. 1989-92), Profl. Exam. Svc. (bd. dirs. 1982-88, 90-96, chmn. 1986-88), Sigma Xi. Home: 74 Condolea Way Lake Oswego OR 97035-1010 Office: Oreg Health Scis U Portland OR 97201 Business E-Mail: wiensa@ohsu.edu.

WIENS, BEVERLY JO, psychology professor; b. Oildale, Calif., Oct. 2, 1947; d. Ernest and Irene Josephine (Klassen) Bartel; m. Gary D. Wiens, Aug. 19, 1967; children: Nicole Marie Wiens Cook, Katie Lyn Wiens. BA, San Jose State U., 1969, MA, 1971, Santa Clara U., 1992; PhD, No. Calif. Grad. U., 2001. Lic. counselor, Calif. Tchr. West Valley Coll., Saratoga, Calif., 1971-76, San Jose (Calif.) City Coll., 1974-75, San Jose State U., 1978; marriage, family therapist Coalition of Counseling Centers, Los Gatos, Calif., 1982-86; assoc. prof. San Jose Bible Coll., 1982-87; prof., dept. chair, counseling psychology San Jose Christian Coll., 1988—. Lectr. in field. Mem. Am. Assn. Christian Counselors, Am. Counseling Assn., Assn. Religious Value in Counseling, Assn. Counselor Training, Supervision, Calif. Assn. Marital Family Therapists. Republican. Mem. Mennonite Brethren. Office: San Jose Christian Coll 790 S 12th St San Jose CA 95112-2304 Business E-Mail: bwiens@jessup.edu.

WIENS, HAROLD J. electronics executive; b. Dallas, Oreg. BS in Mech. Engring., Mich. Tech. U., 1968. Exec. v.p., indsl. and consumer markets 3M Co., 1998—99, exec. v.p., indsl. and electro markets, 1999, exec. v.p., indsl. markets, 1999—2002. Mem. nat. adv. bd. Mich. Tech. U. Named to Acad. of Mech. Engring.-Engring. Mechanics, Mich. Tech. U., 1999. Mem.: QIC, Nat. Assn. of Mfrs. (bd. mem., chair, trade and tech. com.). Office: 3M Co 3M Ctr Saint Paul MN 55144

WIER, DARA, poet, English language educator; b. New Orleans, Dec. 30, 1949; d. Arthur Joseph and Grace Cecile (Barrois) Dixon; children: Emily Caitlin, Guy Gerard. Student, La. State U., 1967-70; BS, Longwood Coll., 1971; MFA, Bowling Green U., 1974. Asst. prof. Hollins (Va.) Coll., 1975-80; assoc. prof. U. Ala., Tuscaloosa, 1980-85; assoc. prof. English, U. Mass., Amherst, 1985-87, prof., 1988—. Vis. poet U. Tex., Austin, 1982; Richard Hugo prof. U. Mont., Missoula, 1992. Author: (poem collections) The Book of Knowledge, 1988, Blue for the Plough, 1991, Our Master Plan, 1999, Voyages in English, 2001, Hat on a Pond, 2002. Fellow Nat. Endowment for Arts, 1980, Guggenheim Found., 1991-92, Mass. Cultural Coun., 2001. Mem. Acad. Am. Poets, Poetry Soc. Am., Assoc. Writing Programs (bd. dirs. 1977-81, pres. 1980). Office: U Mass Program for Poets and Writers Amherst MA 01003 E-mail: daraw@hfa.umass.edu.

WIER, PATRICIA ANN, publishing executive, consultant; b. Coal Hill, Ark., Nov. 10, 1937; d. Horace L. and Bridget B. (McMahon) Norton; m. Richard A. Wier, Feb. 24, 1962; 1 child, Rebecca Ann. BA, U. Mo., Kansas City, 1964; MBA, U. Chgo., 1978. Computer programmer AT&T, 1960-62; lead programmer City of Kansas City, Mo., 1963-65; with Playboy Enterprises, Chgo., 1965-71, mgr. systems and programming, 1971; with Ency. Britannica, Inc., Chgo., 1971—; v.p. mgmt. svcs. Ency. Britannica USA, 1975-83, exec. v.p. adminstrn., 1983-84; v.p. planning and devel. Ency. Britannica, Inc., 1985, pres. Compton's Learning Co. divsn., 1985; pres. Ency. Britannica (USA), 1986-91, Ency. Britannica N.A., 1986—94; exec. v.p. Ency. Britannica, Inc., 1986-94; pres. Ency. Britannica N.Am., 1986—94; mgmt. cons. pvt. practice, Chgo., 1994—. Cons. pvt. practice, Chgo., 1994—; bd. dirs. NICOR, Inc., Mannatech, Inc., Alcas Corp., Mannatech, Inc. Life mem. coun. Grad. Sch. Bus., U. Chgo.; mem. bd. regents Lewis U.; chmn. bd. dirs. San Miguel Sch. Mem. Direct Selling Assn. (bd. dirs. 1984-93, chmn. 1987-88, named to Hall of Fame 1991), Women's Coun. U. Mo. Kansas City (hon. life) Com. 200, The Chgo. Network. Roman Catholic. Office: Patricia A Wier Inc 175 E Delaware Pl Apt 8305 Chicago IL 60611-7748

WIER, RICHARD ROYAL, JR., lawyer; b. Wilmington, Del., May 19, 1941; s. Richard Royal and Anne (Kurtz) W.; m. Anne E. Edwards, Nov. 25, 1978; children— Melissa Royal, Emma Kurtz; children from previous marriage: Richard Royal, III, Mimi Poole. BA in English, Hamilton Coll.,

1963; LLB, U. Pa., 1966; postgrad., Temple U., 1981-82. Bar: D.C. 1967, Del. 1967, Pa. 1980, U.S. Dist. Ct. Del., U.S. Ct. Appeals (3d cir.), U.S. Supreme Ct. Assoc. Connolly, Bove & Lodge, Wilmington, 1966-68; dep. atty. gen. State of Del., Wilmington, 1968-70; state prosecutor Del. Dept. Justice, Wilmington, 1970-74; atty. gen. State of Del., Wilmington, 1975-79; ptnr. Prickett, Jones, Elliott, Kristol & Schnee, Wilmington, 1979-92; pvt. practice Wilmington, 1993—. Lectr. criminal and labor law various instns. Active United Way campaign, 1976-77; supervisory bd. Gov.'s Commn. on Criminal Justice; bd. dirs. Del. Coun. Crime and Justice, 1982-89; adv. coun. Diabetes Control, 1990-92; dir. Project Assist, 1992-95, Commn. on Outreach, 1994—. Recipient Law Enforcement award Newark Police Dept., 1974; Law Enforcement Commendation medal Nat. Soc. SAR, 1976; Ideal Citizen award Am. Found. for Sci. Creative Intelligence, 1976; Commendation Del. Gen. Assembly Senate, 1976-77, 80; named one of Top Labor/Employment Attys. in Del., Del. Today, 1999—. Mem. ABA, Nat. Dist. Attys. Assn. (state dir.), Del. Bar Assn. (chmn. criminal law sect. 1987-91, co-chmn. on drug crisis 1993—, vice chmn. labor law sect. 1987-88, chmn. 1989-90), Pa. Bar Assn., D.C. Bar Assn., Nat. Assn. Attys. Gen. (hon. life, exec. com.), Soc. Attys. Gen. Execs. (emeritus), Am. Judicature Soc., Am. Del. Trial Lawyers Assn., Nat. Assn. Extradition Ofcls. (hon. life, regional v.p., exec. dir.), Italian Radio/TV Assn. (hon., Outstanding Achievement award), Internat. Platform Assn., Pi Delta Epsilon. Achievements include inventor in field. Office: 1220 N Market St Ste 600 Wilmington DE 19801-2598 E-mail: rwier@wierlaw.com.

WIERENGA, WENDELL D. biotechnology company executive; BA, Hope Coll.; PhD Chemistry, Stanford U. From dir. cancer and infectious diseases rsch. to exec. dir. drug discovery rsch. The Upjohn Co., Kalamazoo, 1974—90; sr. v.p. rsch. Parke-Davis Rsch. & Devel., 1990—97; CEO, dir. Syrrx, Inc., San Diego; adj. prof. chemistry U. Mich. Office: Syrxx Inc 10450 Sci Ctr Dr Ste 100 San Diego CA 92121

WIERMAN, JOHN CHARLES, mathematician, educator; b. Prosser, Wash., June 30, 1949; s. John Nathaniel and Edith Elizabeth (Ashley) W.; m. Susan Shelley Graupmann, Aug. 13, 1971; 1 child, Adam Christopher. BS in Math., U. Wash., 1971, PhD in Math., 1976. Asst. prof. math. U. Minn., Mpls., 1976-81; asst. prof. Johns Hopkins U., Balt., 1981-82, assoc. prof., 1982-87, prof., 1987—, chmn. math. scis. dept., 1988-2000, dir. entrepreneurship and mgmt. program, 1996—, dir. Ctr. for Leadership Edn., 2004—. Sr. rsch. fellow Inst. Math. and Its Applications, Mpls., 1987—88; Navy ASEE fellow Naval Surface Warfare Ctr., 2001—02. Co-author: First-Passage Percolation on the Square Lattice, 1978; contbr. articles to profl. jours. Grad. fellow, NSF, 1971—74, NSF rsch. grantee, 1976—93, sabbatical fellow, Navy-ASEE, 2001—02. Fellow Inst. Math. Stats. (organizer spl. session on percolation theory 1982, organizer spl. session on probability and math. stats. 1986); mem. Am. Soc. Quality, Inst. Math. Stats., Am. Math. Soc., Am. Statis. Assn., Math. Assn. Am., Sigma Xi, Phi Beta Kappa. Office: Johns Hopkins U Dept Math and Stats 34th & Charles Sts Baltimore MD 21218 Business E-Mail: wierman@jhu.edu.

WIERNIK, PETER HARRIS, oncologist, educator; b. Crocket, Tex., June 16, 1939; s. Harris and Molly (Emmerman) W.; m. Roberta Joan Fuller, Sept. 6, 1961; children: Julie Anne, Lisa Britt, Peter Harrison. BÅ with distinction, U. Va., 1961, MD, 1965; Dr. h.c., U. Republic, Montevideo, Uruguay, 1982. Diplomate Am. Bd. Internal Medicine, Am. Bd. Med. Oncology (mem. writing com. 1981-87). Intern Cleve. Met. Gen. Hosp., 1965—66, resident, 1969—70; resident Osler Svc. Johns Hopkins Hosp., Balt., 1970—71; sr. asst. surgeon USPHS, 1966, advanced through grades to med. dir., 1976; sr. staff assoc. Balt. Cancer Rsch. Ctr., 1966—71, chief sect. med. oncology, 1971—76, chief clin. oncology br., 1976—82, dir., 1976—82; assoc. dir. divsn. cancer treatment Nat. Cancer Inst., 1976—82; assoc. dir. Albert Einstein Cancer Ctr., Bronx, 1982—98, prof. medicine, 1983—98, prof. radiation oncology, 1996—98, head divsn. med. oncology. Asst. prof. medicine U. Md. Sch. Medicine, Balt., 1971-74, assoc. prof., 1974-76, prof., 1976-82; prof. medicine radiation oncology NY Med. Coll., 1998—; cons. hematology med. oncology Union Meml. Hosp., Greater Balt. Med. Ctr., Franklin Sq. Hosp.; bd. dirs. Balt. City unit Am. Cancer Soc., 1971-78; chmn. patient care com., 1972-75, mem. profl. edn. grants com., NYC divsn., 1983-90, mem. nat. clin. fellowship com., 1984-96; mem. med. adv. com. Nat. Leukemia Assn., 1976-88, chmn. med. adv. com., 1989—; chmn. adult leukemia com. Cancer Leukemia Group B, 1976-83; prin. investigator Ea. Coop. Oncology Group, 1982-94, 96—; chmn. gynecol. oncology com., 1986-88, chmn. leukemia com., 1988-94; sci. cons. Vt. Regional Cancer Ctr., 1987—; dir. OLM Comprehensive Cancer Ctr., NY Med. Coll., 1998—. Editor: Controversies in Oncology, 1982, Supportive Care of the Cancer Patient, 1983, Neoplastic Diseases of the Blood, 1985, 4th edit., 2003, Adult Leukemias, 2001; editor: (assoc.) Medical Oncology and Tumor Pharmacotherapy, 1987—91; editor: (sr.), 1991—; editor: (assoc.) (jour.) American Jour. Therapeutics, 1994—; co-editor: Year Book of Hematology, 1986—98, Handbook of Hematologic and Oncologic Emergencies, 1988—98, Bone Marrow Transplantation (textbook), 1995, (jour.) American Jour. of Medical Scis., 1976—81; editor (N. Am.): Jour. of Cancer Rsch. and Clin/Oncology, 1986—89; mem. editl. bd. Cancer Treatment Reports, 1972—76, Leukemia Rsch., 1977—86, 1991—, Leukemia, 1986—2003, Cancer Clin. Trials, 1977—, Jour. of Therapeutic Rsch., 1994—, Hospital Practice, 1979—, Jour. of Clin. Oncology, 1989—91, PDQ National Cancer Inst., 1987—94, Cancer Investigation, 1998—; editor (sect. antineoplastic drugs): (jour.) Jour. of Clin. Pharmacology, 1985—; contbr. articles to profl. jours., chapters to books. Recipient Z Soc. award U. Va., 1961, Byrd S. Leavell Hematology award U. Va. Sch. Medicine, 1965, Gold medal 1st Polish Congress of Oncology, 2002. Fellow AAAS, ACP, Am. Coll. Clin. Pharmacology (awards com. 1999—), Internat. Soc. Hematology, Royal Soc. Medicine (London), NY Acad. Medicine; mem. Am. Soc. Clin. Investigation (instl. rep. 1997—), Am. Soc. Clin. Oncology (chmn. edn. tng. com. 1976-79, 84, subcom. clin. investigation 1980-82, program com. 1990, pub. issues com., 1990-95, com. rsch. awards 1996-2000, com. health svcs. rsch. 2000-2003), Am. Assn. Cancer Rsch. (clin. cancer rsch. com. 2002—), Am. Soc. Hematology, Am. Fedn. Clin. Rsch., Am. Acad. Clin. Toxicology, Internat. Soc. Exptl. Hematology, NY Acad. Sci., Am. Soc. Hosp. Pharmacy, Am. Soc. Clin. Pharmacology Therapeutics, Am. Radium Soc. (program com. 1987-93, exec. com. 1988-95, publ. com. 1988-92, sec. 1990-91, pres.-elect, 1992-93; pres. 1993-94, Janeway medalist, 1996), Polish Oncology Soc. (hon., finalist Gold medal), Harvey Soc., Uruguayan Hematology Soc. (hon.), Acad. Medicine Uruguay (corr.), European Assn. Cancer Rsch., European Soc. Hematology, Phi Beta Kappa (assoc.), Sigma Xi, Alpha Omega Alpha, Phi Sigma (award 1961). Office: Comprehensive Cancer Ctr Our Lady Mercy Med Ctr 600 E 233rd St Bronx NY 10466-2604 Office Phone: 718-920-1100. Personal E-mail: pwiernik@aol.com. Business E-Mail: wiernik@jimmy.harvard.edu. E-mail: pwiernik@olmhs.org. *Always remember why you entered a profession in the first place. Leave the politics to those who have forgotten.*

WIERSBE, WARREN WENDELL, clergyman, author, lecturer; b. East Chicago, Ind., May 16, 1929; s. Fred and Gladys Anna (Forsberg) W.; m. Betty Lorraine Warren, June 20, 1953; children: David, Carolyn, Robert, Judy. B.Th., No. Baptist Sem., 1953; D.D. (hon.), Temple Sem., Chattanooga, 1965, Trinity Ev-Div. Sch., 1986; LittD (hon.), Cedarville U., 1987. Ordained to ministry, Bapt. Ch., 1951. Pastor Central Bapt. Ch., East Chicago, 1951-57; editl. dir. Youth for Christ Internat., Wheaton, Ill., 1957-61; pastor Calvary Bapt. Ch., Covington, Ky., 1961-71; sr. min. Moody Ch., Chgo., 1971-78; bd. dirs. Slavic Gospel Assn., Wheaton, 1973-87; columnist Moody Monthly, Chgo., 1971-77; author, conf. minister, 1978-80; pres. ScripTex, Inc., Lincoln, Nebr., 1982—. Vis. instr. pastoral theology Trinity Div. Sch., Deerfield, Ill.; gen. dir. Back to the Bible Radio Ministries, Lincoln, Nebr., 1984-89; writer-in-residence Cornerstone Coll., Grand Rapids, Mich.; disting. prof. preaching Grand Rapids Bapt. Sem. Author: over 150 books including William Culbertson, A Man of God, 1974, Live Like a King, 1976, Walking with the Giants, 1976, Be Right, 1977, (with David Wiersbe) Making Sense of the Ministry, 1983, Why Us? Why Bad Things Happen to God's People, 1984, Real Worship: It Can Transform Your Life, 1986, The Integrity Crisis, 1988, Be What You Are, 1988, The New Pilgrim's Progress, 1989, Living With the Giants, 1993, Preaching and Teaching with Imagination, 1994, Be Myself, 1994, The Bible Exposition Commentary, 6 vols., 2004. Home and Office: 441 Lakewood Dr Lincoln NE 68510-2419

WIERSEMA, HAROLD LEROY, aerospace engineer; b. Erie, Ill., Sept. 17, 1919; s. Clarence John and Tena (Griede) W.; m. Joanne Kearney, Mar. 19, 1955; children: Roger Kent, Marilyn Tena. BS, U. Ill., 1949. Aerospace engr. Space Div. Rockwell Internat., Downey, Calif., 1953-78; sr. spl. engr. Boeing Mil. Airplane Co., Wichita, Kans., 1978-86; aerospace engr., avionics cons. Long Beach, Calif., 1986-94. Com. chmn. Boy Scouts Am., Lynwood, Calif., 1968-70; pres. Compton (Calif.) Pacific Little League, 1966-69; deacon Presbyn. Ch., Southgate, Calif., 1942-70. Col. USAF, World War II, Korea. Decorated D.F.C., Air medal (5); recipient Mach Buster award N.Am. Aviation, Edwards AFB, 1963, Order of Arrow, Boy Scouts Am., 1967. Mem. IEEE (life), U.S. Air Force Assn. (life), 388th Bomb Group/8th Air Force Assn. (life), Nat. Geog. Soc., UCLA Alumni Assn., Shriners. Democrat. Presbyterian. Home: 5451 Jonesboro Way Buena Park CA 90621-1615

WIERSMA, G. BRUCE, dean, forest resources educator; b. Paterson, N.J., Oct. 26, 1942; s. George and Marjorie (Zeedyk) W.; m. Ann Becker, Aug. 15, 1964; children: Heather, Robin, Jennifer, Joshua. BS, U. Maine, 1964; MF in Forestry, Yale U., 1965; PhD Coll. Environ. Sci. & Forestry, SUNY, 1968. Teaching asst., 1965-66; rsch. biologist Coll. Environ. Sci. and Forestry SUNY, 1968; combat devels. staff officer U.S. Army Inst. Land Combat, Alexandria, Va., 1968-70; head monitoring sect. EPA, Washington, 1970-72, chief ecol. monitoring branch, 1972-74, chief pollutant pathways br. Las Vegas, Nev., 1974-79, sr. ecologist, 1979-80; mgr. environ. earth scis. group, Idaho Nat. Engring. Lab. EG&G Idaho, Inc., 1980-87; instr. Idaho Falls Campus of Higher Edn. U. Idaho, 1981-90, affiliate grad. faculty Coll. Forestry Wildlife and Range Scis., 1988-90; mgr., dir. Ctr. Environ. Monitoring and Assesment Environ. Sci. and Tech. Group, 1989-90; dir. Ctr. Environ. Monitoring and Assesment Idaho Nat. Engring. Lab., EG&G Idaho, Inc., Idaho Falls, 1988-90; dean Coll. Forest Resources, assoc. dir. Maine Agrl. Experiment Sta., prof. Forest Resources U. Maine, Orono, 1991-93, dean Coll. Natural Scis., Forestry and Agr., dir. Maine Agrl. and Forest Exptl. Sta., 1993—. Dir. Ctr. Environ. Monitoring and Assessment, Idaho Falls, Idaho, 1980-90; mem. ad-hoc task force to plan global environ. monitoring sys., 1993-95; trustee Nature Conservancy, 1993-95; mem. UN ad hoc task force to plan global terrestrial observing sys., 1993-95; bd. dirs. Maine Forest Products Coun., 1993—; U.S. Nat. Com. on Data for Sci. and Tech., 1990-92; chmn. com. on databased NRC, 1990-94, mem. com. on marine monitoring, 1986-90; mem. forest resources adv. com. U.S. Sec. Agr., 1998—; mem. Gov. Maine's Com. on Sawmill Biomass Conversion, 1999. Contbr. chpts. to books, articles to profl. jours; editor, founder Jour. Environ. Monitoring and Assesment. Pilot, Maine wing CAP. Capt. U.S. Army, 1968-70. Recipient numerous rsch. grants from various orgns. Mem. NRC (chair com. on databases, 1990-94, com. on marine monitoring, 1986-90, Nat. Assn. Profl. Forestry Schs. (exec. com. 1993-98), Assn. Expt. Sta. Dirs. (exec. com. N.E. region 1996-2000, chmn. 1998-99, com. on policy 1997—). Avocations: jogging, swimming, cross country skiing, backpacking. Home: 103 Wildwood Estates Dr Holden ME 04429-7344 Office: Univ of Maine/Coll Natural Scis Forestry and Agr 5782 Winslow Hall Orono ME 04469-5782 Office Phone: 207-581-3202. E-mail: wiersma@maine.edu.

WIERSMA, KEVIN, lab administrator; Various positions, fin. and opers. mgmt. Medtox Scientific, Inc., St. Paul, 1992—98, v.p., 1998—, COO, lab. divsn., 2000—. Office: Medtox Scientific Inc 402 W County Rd D Saint Paul MN 55112*

WIES, BARBARA, editor, publisher; b. Dec. 5, 1939; BA, U. Conn., 1961; student, New Sch. for Social Rsch., 1961-62. Product devel. Fearn Soya, Melrose Park, Ill., 1973-75; product devel. Modern Products, Milw., 1973-75; editor, pub. Bestways Mag., Carson City, Nev., 1977-89; pub. The Healthy Gourmet Newsletter, 1989-91, Fine Wine-Good Food Newsletter, 1991—; publicity dir. Nev. Artists Assn., 1994—; owner Gualala (Calif.) Galleries, 1989-90; assoc. pub., mgr. Edn. Range Mag., 1998—. Owner, operator cooking sch. Greensboro N.C. 1969-73; instr. Very Spl. Arts Nev., 1997. Author: Natural Cooking, 1968, Wok and Tempura, 1969, Japanese Home Cooking, 1970, The Wok, 1971, Super Soy, 1973, The Health Gourmet, 1981, International Healthy Gourmet, 1982; editor: Desert News, 2004—; one-woman show paintings Dolphin Gallery, Gualala, Calif., 1990, River Gallery, Reno, 1994; 2 women show 1992, 94, 96, Dolphin Gallery, Calif., 1994, solo exhbn. Nev. Artists Assn. Gallery, 1993, 95, 96, 97; featured artist Nev. State Libr., 1996, Silver State Gallery, Reno, 1998, West Nev. C.C., 1996, art show judge, 1997; restaurant critic Reno Gazette Jour., 1995-2001. Performer Nev. Arts sponsored Tumblewords, 2000—; del. Nev. Episcopal Diocese Convention, 2002, Vestry St. Peter's Episcopal Ch., 2003—. Grantee Nev. Arts Coun., 2002; recipient First Place adult fiction Nev. State Lit. Co., 1995, First Place fiction State Lit. Comp., 1998, 2d Place fiction Writers Block; Nev. Arts Coun. fellow, 1999-2000. Mem. Nat. League Am. Pen Women (chair 1st and 2d ann. lit. competition Reno br., chairperson 1st Nat. Lit. award), Inst. Food Technologists, Pastel Soc. of the West Coast, Inst. Am. Culinary Profls.

WIESCHAUS, ERIC F. molecular biologist, educator; b. June 8, 1947; BS, U. Notre Dame, 1969; PhD in Biology, Yale U., 1974. Rsch. fellow Zool. Inst., U. Zurich, Switzerland, 1975-78; group leader European Molecular Biol. Lab., Germany, 1978-81; from asst. prof. to assoc. prof. Princeton (N.J.) U., 1981-87, prof. molecular biology, 1987—. Fellow Lab. de Genetique Moleculaire, France, 1976; vis. rschr. Ctr. Pathobiology, U. Calif., Irvine, 1977; mem. sci. adv. coun. Damon Runyon-Walter Winchell Cancer Fund, 1987-92. Contbr. articles to profl. jours. Recipient Nobel prize in physiology or medicine, 1995. Fellow Am. Acad. Arts and Scis.; mem. NAS. Office: Princeton U MOF 435 Dept Molecular Biology Washington Rd Princeton NJ 08544-0001*

WIESE, DANIEL EDWARD, marketing and communications researcher; b. Cedar Rapids, Iowa, June 16, 1936; s. Erwin Edward and Bernice Virginia (Cristy) W.; m. Mary Virginia Smith, Nov. 3, 1958 (div. 1982); children: Anne, John, Amy; m. JoBeth Kuehl, Aug. 6, 1982; children: Jamie, Jill, Eric. BS, Iowa State U., 1958. Agy. assoc. ConnGen Life Ins., Hartford, Conn., 1959—61; rsch. assoc. Meredith Pub. Co., Des Moines, 1961—65; rsch. dir. Popular Sci. Pub. Co., N.Y.C., 1965—66; assoc. rsch. dir. Reader Digest Assn., N.Y.C., 1966—67; rsch. dir. Successful Farming divsn. Meredith Corp., Des Moines, 1967—77; mgr. Agtrack divsn. Chilton Rsch. Svcs., Radnor, Pa., 1977—80; v.p., dir. rsch. svcs. Creswell, Munsell, Fulta & Zirbel, Inc., Cedar Rapids, Iowa, 1980—86; pres. Dan Wiese Mktg. Rsch., Cedar Rapids, Iowa, 1986—. Mem. editl. adv. bd. Agrimarketing mag., 1989. Bd. dirs. Plymouth Congl. Nursery Sch., Des Moines, 1975; mktg. com. Cedar Rapids Symphony, 1984; mem. adv. bd. Cedar Rapids Better Bus. Bur., Area Mktg. Task Force, Linn County I-Club Bd., 1991-92; bd. dirs., exec. com., chmn. mktg. com. Witwer Sr. Ctr., 2001—. Capt. U.S. Army, 1959.mem. Celebration of Agr. com., 1999— Mem. Nat. Agri-Mktg. Assn. (chmn. mktg. rsch. com. 1982-83, Cornbelt chpt. bd. 1995-2001), Advt. Fedn. Cedar Rapids (1st v.p. 1988-89, pres. 1989-90, bd. dirs. 1987-90, mem. adv. bd. 2002—, inducted Hall of Fame 2003), Cedar Rapids C. of C. (agr.-bus. com.), Ag-Maizing Cedar Rapids (exec. com. 1998-99), Rotary. Home and Office: 2108 Greenwood Dr SE Cedar Rapids IA 52403-2727 Office Phone: 319-364-2866. Business E-Mail: danwiese@mchsi.com.

WIESE, WOLFGANG LOTHAR, physicist, researcher; b. Tilsit, Germany, Apr. 21, 1931; came to U.S., 1957; naturalized, 1965; s. Werner Max and Charlotte (Donath) W.; m. Gesa Ladehoff, Oct. 12, 1957; children: Margrit, Cosima. BS, U. Kiel, Fed. Republic Germany, 1954, PhD, 1957, PhD (hon.), 1993. Rsch. assoc. U. Md., College Park, 1958-59; rsch. physicist Nat. Bur. Standards, Gaithersburg, Md., 1960-62, chief plasma spectrosc. sect., 1962-77, chief atomic and plasma radiation div., 1978-91, chief atomic physics div., 1991—. Lectr. U. Calif., 1963, 64. Author: Atomic Transition Probabilities, Vol. I., 1966, Vol. II, 1969, Vol. III, 1988, Vol. IV, 1988, Atomic Transition Probabilities for C, N, and O, 1996, Spectral Data for Highly Ionized Atoms, 2000. Recipient Silver Medal award Dept. Commerce, 1962, Gold Medal award, 1971, Humboldt award, 1986, A.S. Fleming award U.S. C. of C., 1971, Disting. Career in Sci. award Wash. Acad. Sci., 1992, Disting. Postdoctoral award U. Md., 2003; Guggenheim fellow, 1966. Fellow Am. Phys. Soc., Optical Soc. Am., Wash. Acad. Sci.; mem. Internat. Astron. Union. Lutheran. Home: 8229 Stone Trail Dr Bethesda MD 20817-4555 Office Phone: 301-975-3201. E-mail: wiese@nist.gov.

WIESEL, ELIE, writer, educator; b. Sighet, Romania, Sept. 30, 1928; arrived in Paris, 1945; came to U.S., 1956, naturalized, 1963; s. Shlomo and Sarah (Feig) W.; m. Marion Erster, 1969; 1 child, Shlomo Elisha. Student, The Sorbonne, Paris, 1948-51; LittD (hon.), Jewish Theol. Sem., N.Y.C., 1967, Marquette U., 1975, Simmons Coll., 1976, Anna Maria Coll., 1980, Yale U., 1981, Wake Forest U., 1985, Haverford Coll., 1985, Capital U., 1986, L.I. U., 1986, U. Paris, 1987, U. Conn., 1988, U. Cen. Fla., 1988, Wittenberg U., 1989, Wheeling Jesuit Coll., 1989, Fairleigh Dickenson U., 1993; LHD (hon.), Hebrew Union Coll., 1968, Manhattanville Coll., 1972, Yeshiva U., 1973, Boston U., 1974, Coll. of St. Scholastica, 1978, Wesleyan U., 1979, Brandeis U., 1980, Kenyon Coll., 1982, Hobart/William Smith Coll., 1982, Emory U., 1983, Fla. Internat. U., 1983, Siena Heights Coll., 1983, Fairfield U., 1983, Dropsie Coll., 1983, Moravian Coll., 1983, Colgate U., 1984, SUNY, Binghamton, 1985, Lehigh U., 1985, Coll. of New Rochelle, 1986, Tufts U., 1986, Georgetown U., 1986, Hamilton Coll., 1986, Rockford Coll., 1986, Villanova U., 1987, Coll. of St. Thomas, 1987, U. Denver, 1987, Walsh Coll., 1987, Loyola Coll., 1987, Ohio U., 1988, Concordia Coll., 1990, N.Y.U., 1990, Fordham U., 1990, Conn. Coll., 1990, Upsala Coll., 1991, Duquesne U., 1991, Roosevelt U., 1991; PhD (hon.), Bar-Ilan U., 1973, U. Haifa, 1986, Ben Gurion U., 1988; LLD (hon.), Hofstra U., 1975, Talmudic U. Fla., 1979, U. Notre Dame, 1980, La Salle U., 1988, Bates Coll., 1995; HHD (hon.), U. Hartford, 1985, Lycoming Coll., 1987, U. Miami, 1988, Brigham Young U., 1989; D of Hebrew Letters, Spertus Coll. Judaica, 1973; DSc (hon.), U. Health Scis./Chgo. Med. Sch., 1989; ThD, U. Åbo Akadem, 1990; LHD (hon.), Hunter Coll., 1992, Susquehanna U., 1992, Am. U., 1992, Millersville U., 1993; hon. degree, U. Dayton, 1993, U. Mich., 1993; LHD (hon.), U. Bordeaux, 1993, Gustavus Adolphus Coll., 1994, McGill U., 1994, Mt. Sinai Med. Sch., 1994, Spelman Coll., 1995; Doctorat (hon.), U. Catholique de Louvain, 1995; LHD (hon.), Sacred Heart U., 1995; D (hon.), U. Buenos Aires, 1995; Docteur (hon.), U. de Picardie Jules Verne, Amiens, France, 1996, U. Paris, Sorbonne, 2001; LHD (hon.), Briar Cliff Coll., 1996, Clark U., 1996, Phila. Coll. Textiles, 1996, U. Mass., Dartmouth, 1997, U. South Fla., 1997, Fla. Atlantic U., 1997, U. R.I., 1997, U. Mass., Lowell, 1997; LLD (hon.), U. Guelph, 1997; LHD (hon.), De Paul U., 1997, Seton Hall U., 1998; LittD (hon.), St. John's U., 1998; LHD (hon.), Eckerd Coll., 1998, Appalachian State U., 1998, Merrimack U., 1998; D. in Pub. Svc. (hon.), Cedar Crest Coll., 1998; LHD (hon.), Gettysburg Coll., 1998, Loyola U., Chgo., 1999; HHD (hon.), Mich. State U., 1999; Doutor (hon.), U. do Estado do Rio de Janeiro, 1999; Docteur (hon.), U. Montreal, 1999; LHD (hon.), St. Norbert Coll., 1999, St. Joseph's U., 2000, U. Fla., 2000, Hebrew Coll., 2001; PhD (hon.), Hebrew U., 2000, U. Bologna, 2000; EdD (hon.), Regis U., 2001. Disting. prof. Judaic studies CCNY, 1972-76; Andrew W. Mellon prof. in the humanities Boston U., 1976—, prof. religious studies and univ. prof., 1976—, prof. philosophy, 1988—. Disting. vis. prof. Henry Luce, 1982-83, Yale U.; lectr. Andrew W. Mellon Ann. Lecture Series Boston U., 92d St. YMHA, YWHA Ann. Lectr. Series, ann. radio broadcast series Eternal Light for Jewish Theol. Sem. Am., advisory bd. Rena Costa Ctr. for Yiddish Studies at Bar-Ilan U., 1994, advisory coun. Carnegie Commn. on Preventing Deadly Conflict, 1994; chmn. U.S. Pres.'s Commn. on the Holocaust, 1979-80, U.S. Holocaust Meml. Coun., 1980-86; hon. chmn. Holocaust Studies Ctr. of Bronx H.S. Sci., Nat. Jewish Resource Ctr., N.Y.C., 1983, Holocaust Meml. Commn., Vancouver Holocaust Ctr. Soc., 1992—, Ctr. Christian-Jewish Understanding, Sacred Heart U., Am. Friends of Ghetto Fighter's House; co-chmn. Children of Chernobyl/Children at Heart, 1995—; steering com. The Balkan Inst., 1996—; mem. Nat. hon. com. Darius Milhaud Soc.; mem. coun. Ethic Accord Project on Ethic Rels., (hon.) Am. Friends of Neve Shalom/Wahat al-Salam, 1996—; leadership coun. Tanenbsum Ctr. Interreligious Understanding, 1997—; founder Elie Wiesel Found. for Humanity, 1987; founding pres. Paris-based Universal Acad. Cultures, 1993; pres. Am. Friends Kiryat Ungvar-Jerusalem, 1990—; hon. pres. Comité Français Pour "Yad Vashem," Am. Gathering of Jewish Holocaust Survivors, 1985, Am. Kurdish Info. Network, 1997, adv. bd., 1997; v.p. Internat. Rescue Com., 1985—; adv. bd. The Raoul Wallenberg Commn. of U.S., 1981—, Friends of LeChambon, 1982, Boston U. Inst. for Philosophy & Religion, 1986, Boston U. Students for a Free Tibet, Nat. Inst. Against Prejudice & Violence, Internat. Ctr. in N.Y., 1986—, Friends of Akim USA, 1991, Sholom Aleichem Meml. Found., Nat. Jewish Law Students Assn., 1995—, AmeriCares, 1995, React Take Action Awards, 1996—, No Greater Love, 1996—, Inst. Study of Violence, 1996—, Global Lawyers and Physicians: Working Together for Human Rights, 1997; internat. adv. bd. Elmhurst Coll. Holocaust Edn. Project, 1996—; Am. bd. adv. The Moscow Ctr.; adv. coun. U.S. Com. Refugees, 1996—, Nat. Endowmet for Democracy, 1996—; Helsinki adv. com. Human Rights Watch; bd. govs. Haifa U., (mem. emeritus) Tel Aviv U. 1976—, Massuah - Inst. Study of Holocaust, Israel; bd. dirs. Nat. Com. on Am. Fgn. Policy, Elaine Kaufman Cultural Ctr., Humanitas, Am. Assocs. Ben-Gurion U. of the Negev, Mut. of Am., France Libertés; hon. dir. HIAS; bd. trustees Annenberg Rsch. Inst., 1983-89, Am. Jour. World Svc., 1985—, Haifa U., Tel-Aviv U., Yeshiva U., 1977—, Am. Jewish Heritage Ctr., Mus. Jewish Heritage, N.Y.; patron Internat. Peace U., Berlin, 1995—; colleague Cathedral St. John the Divine, 1975—; mem. jury Neustadt Internat. Prize Lit., 1984; mem. Task Force Apprehending Indicted War Criminals, 1998—. Author: Night, 1960, Dawn, 1961, The Accident, 1962, The Town Beyond the Wall, 1964, The Gates of the Forest, 1966, The Jews of Silence, 1966, Legends of Our Time, 1968, A Beggar in Jerusalem, 1970, One Generation After, 1970, Souls on Fire, 1972, The Oath, 1973, Ani Maamin, 1973, Zalmen, or the Madness of God, 1974, Messengers of God, 1976, A Jew Today, 1978, Four Hasidic Masters, 1978, The Trial of God, 1979, The Testament, 1980, Le Testament D'Un Poète Juif Assassiné (France's Prix Livre-Inter 1980, Bourse Goncourt, 1980, Prix des Bibliothécaires, 1981), 1985, Images from the Bible, 1980, Five Biblical Portraits, 1981, Somewhere A Master, 1982, Paroles d'Étranger, 1982, The Golem, 1983, The Fifth Son (Grand Prix de la Littérature, City of Paris), 1985, Signes d'Exode, 1985, Against Silence (3 vols., ed. Irving Abrahamson), 1985, Job ou Dieu dans la Tempête, 1986, A Song for Hope, 1987, The Nobel Address, 1987, Twilight, 1988; (essays) Silences et Mémoire d'hommes, 1989, L'Oublié, 1989, From the Kingdom of Memory, 1990, Célébration Talmudique, 1991, Sages and Dreamers, 1991, The Forgotten, 1992, (with John Cardinal O'Connor) A Journey of Faith, 1990, (with Albert Friedlander) The Six Days of Destruction, 1988, (dialogues with Philippe-Michaël Saint-Cheron) Evil and Exile, 1990, commentaries to A Passover Haggadah, 1993, All Rivers Run To The Sea (a memoir), 1995, (with Jorge Semprun) Setaire est Impossible, 1995, (with François Mitterand) Memoir in Two Voices, 1996, Et la Mer N'est Pas Remplie, Memoirs II, 1996, Célébration Prophétique, Portraits et Légendes, 1998, Les juges, 1999, King Solomon and His Magic Ring, 1999, And the Sea is Never Full (English transl. of Et la mer n'est pas remplie, Memoirs II 1999), The Judges, 2002, (dialogues with Michael de Saint Cheron) Le Mal et L'Exil/Dix ans après, 1999, (essays) D'où viens-tu? (pub. by Le Seuil), 2001, After the Darkness, 2002, Wise Men and Their Tales, 2003; editorial and adv. bds. Midstream, Religion and Lit. (U. Notre Dame), Sh'ma: Jour. of Responsibility, Hadassah Mag., Acad. of the Air for Jewish Studies, Holocaust and Genocide Studies: An Internat. Jour., Passages, Religion and the Arts; subject of more than 50 books; journalist Israeli, French and Am. newspapers. Chmn. adv. bd. World Union Jewish Students, 1985—; comité d'Honneur Ligue International Contre le Racisme et l'Antisemitisme, 1985—; founder Nat. Jewish Ctr. Learning and Leadership, 1974; mem. soc. fellows Ctr. Judaic Studies, U. Denver, 1980, bd. overseer Bar-Ilan U., 1970—. Recipient Prix Rivarol, 1963, Prix de l'Universite de la langue Francaise, 1963, Ingram Merrill award, 1964, Jewish Heritage award, Haifa U., 1975, Remembrance award, 1965, Prix du Souvenir, 1965, Nat. Jewish Book Council award, 1965, 73, Prix Médicis, 1968, Prix Bordin French Acad., 1972, Eleanor Roosevelt Meml. award, N.Y. United Jewish Appeal, 1972, Am. Liberties medallion Am. Jewish Com., 1972, Martin Luther King Jr. medallion, CCNY, 1973, Annual award for Disting. Service to Am. Jewry, Nat. Fedn. of Jewish Men's Clubs, 1973, Faculty Disting. Scholar award Hofstra U., 1974, Rambam award Am. Mizrachi Women, 1974, Meml. award N.Y. Soc. Clin. Psychologists, 1975, First Spertus Internat. award, 1976, Myrtle Wreath award Hadassah, 1977, King Solomon award, 1977, Liberty award HIAS, 1977, Jewish Heritage award, B'nai B'rith, 1966, Avodah award, Jewish Tchrs. Assn., 1972,

Humanitarian award, B'rith Sholom, 1978, Joseph Prize for Human Rights, Anti-Defamation League, 1978, Zalman Shazar award State of Israel, 1979, Presdl. Citation, NYU, 1979, Inaugural award for Lit., Israel Bonds Prime Minister's Com., 1979, Jabotinsky medal, S.Y. Agnon medal, State of Israel, 1980, Rabbanit Sarah Herzog award Emunah Women of Am., 1981, Le Grand Prix Littéraire du Festival Internat. Deauville, 1983, Internat. Lit. prize for Peace, Royal Acad. Belgium, 1983, Lit. Lions award N.Y. Pub. Library, 1983, Jordan Davidson Humanitarian award Fla. Internat. U., 1983, Anatoly Scharansky Humanitarian award, 1983, Grand Officer, Legion of Honor, France, Congressional gold medal, 1985, Voice of Conscience award Am. Jewish Congress, 1985, Remembrance award, Israel Bonds, 1985, Anne Frank award, 1985, 4 Freedoms award FDR 4 Freedoms Found., 1985, Medal of Liberty award Statue of Liberty Presentation, 1986, Nobel Peace Prize, 1986, First Herzl Lit. award, First David Ben-Gurion award, Nat. UJA, Gov.'s award, Shaarei Tzedek, Internat. Kaplun Found. award Hebrew U. Jerusalem, Scopus award, 1974, Am.-Israeli Friendship award, Disting. Writers award Lincolnwood Library, 1984, First Chancellor Joseph H. Lookstein award Bar-Ilan U., 1984, Sam Levenson Meml. award Jewish Community Relations Council, 1985, Comenius award Moravian Coll., 1985, Henrietta Szold award Hadassah, 1985, Disting. Community Service award Mut. Am., 1985, Covenant Peace award Synagogue Council Am., 1985, Jacob Pat award World Congress Jewish Culture, 1985, Humanitarian award Internat. League Human Rights, 1985, Disting. Foreign-Born Am. award Internat. Ctr. N.Y., Inc., 1986, Freedom Cup award Women's League Israel, 1986, First Jacob Javits Humanitarian award UJA Young Leadership, 1986, Boston City Coun. Commendation, 1986, medal of Jerusalem, 1986, Freedom award Internat. Rescue Com., 1987, Achievement award Artist and Writers for Peace in the Middle East, 1987, La Grande Médaille de Vermeil de la Ville de Paris, 1987, La Médaille de la Chancellerie de l'Université de Paris, 1987, La Médaille de l'Université de Paris, 1987, First Eitinger Prize, U. Oslo, 1987, Lifetime Achievment award Present Tense mag., 1987, Spl. Christopher award The Christophers, 1987, Achievement award State Israel, 1987, Sem. medal Jewish Theol. Sem. Am., 1987, Metcalf Cup and Prize for Excellence in Teaching, Boston U., 1987, Spl. award Nat. Com. on Am. Fgn. Policy, 1987, Grã-Cruz da Ordem Nacional do Cruzeiro do Sul, Brazil's highest distinction, 1987, Profiles in Courage award B'nai B'rith, 1987, Centennial medal U. Scranton, 1987, Citation from Religious Edn. Assn., 1987, Golda Meir Sr. Humanitarian award, 1987, Spl. Christopher award The Christophers, 1987, Profiles in Courage award B'nai B'rith, 1987, Presdl. medal Hofstra U., 1988, Human Rights Law award Internat. Human Rights Law Group, 1988, Bicentennial medal Georgetown U., 1988, Hofstra U. Presdl. medal, 1988, Human Rights Law award Internat. Human Rights Law Group, 1988, Janus Korczak Humanitarian award INTERPHIL, 1989, Count Sforza award in Philanthropy Am. Hungarian Found., 1989, Lily Edelman award for Excellence in Continuing Jewish Edn. B'nai B'rith Internat., 1989, George Washington award NAHE, Kent State U., 1989, Bicentennial medal N.Y.U., 1989, Humanitarian award Human Rights Campaign Fund, 1989, Internat. Brotherhood award C.O.R.E., 1990, Frank Weil award for Disting. Contbn. to Adv. of N.Am. Jewish Culture Jewish Community Ctrs. Assn. N.Am., 1990, 1st Raoul Wallenberg medal U. Mich., 1990, Award of Highest Honor Soka U., 1991, Facing History and Ourselves Humanity award, 1991, La Médaille de la Ville de Toulouse, 1991, 5th Centennial Christopher Columbus medal City of Genoa, 1992, 1st Internat. Primo Levi award, 1992, Lit. Arts award Nat. Found. for Jewish Culture, 1992, Ellis Island Medal of Honor, 1992, Guardian of the Children award AKIM USA, 1992, Bishop Francis J. Mugavero award for religious and racial harmony Cath. Newman Ctr. Queens Coll., 1994, Golden Slipper Humanitarian award, 1994, Interfaith Coun. on the Holocaust Humanitarian award, 1994, Crystal award Davos World Economic Forum, 1995, First Niebuhr award, Elmhurst Coll., 1995, Mathilde Schecter award Women's League Conservative Judaism, 2000, Manhattan award Nat. Arts Club, 2000, Benediction medal The Delbarton Sch., 2001; named Humanitarian of the Century Coun. Jewish Orgns., Presdl. medal Freedom, 1992; Beth Hatefutsoth hon. fellow, 1988; honors established in his name: Elie Wiesel award for Holocaust Rsch., U. Haifa, Elie Wiesel Chair in Holocaust Studies, Bar-Ilan U., Elie Wiesel Endowment Fund for Jewish Culture, U. Denver, 1987, Elie Wiesel Disting. Svc. award, U. Fla., 1988, Elie Wiesel awards for Jewish Arts and Culture B'nai B'rith Hillel Founds., 1988, Elie Wiesel Chair in Judaic Studies Conn. Coll., 1990, Disting. Libery award N.Y.C. Refugee Employment Project, 1995, Freedom award Nat. Civil Rights Mus., 1995, Humanitarian award Queensborough Comty. Coll./Holocaust Resource Ctr. Archives, 1995, Socio Honorario de la Sociedad Hebrai ca Argentina, 1995, Pres. award Quinnipac Coll., 1996, Golden Plate award Am. Acad. Achievement, 1996, Lotos medal of Merit, The Lotos Club, 1996, Guardian of Zion award Ingeborg Rennert Ctr. Jerusalem Studies, Bar-Ilan U., 1997, Eisenhower Leadership prize Eisenhower World Affairs Inst. Gettysburg Coll., 1997, Canterbury medalist Becket Fund for Religious Liberty, 1998, ABA ann. award, 1998, Rabbi Marc H. Tanenbaum award for Advancement Interreligious Understanding, 1998, Yitzhak Rabin Peacemaker award Merrimack Coll., 1998, Aesop prize Children's Am. Folklore Soc. for King Solomon and His Magic Ring (Children's Folklore sect. 1999), Raoul Wallenberg Internat. Humanitarian award The Am. Jewish Joint Distbn. Com., 1999. Fellow Jewish Acad. Arts and Scis., Am. Acad. Arts and Letters (dept. lit.), Am. Acad. Arts & Scis., Modern Lang. Assn. Am. (hon.), Timothy Dwight Coll., Yale U.; mem. Fgn. Press Assn. (hon. life), Amnesty Internat., PEN (New England coun. 1993—), Writers & Artists for Peace in Middle East, Writers Guild of Am. East, The Author's Guild, Royal Norwegian Soc. Scis. and Letters, Soc. des auteurs Paris, European Acad. of Arts, Sci. and Humanities, Albert Einstein Soc. (hon., Phila.), Phi Beta Kappa (Assocs. award 1994). Office: Boston U Univ Profs Program 745 Commonwealth Ave Boston MA 02215-1401

WIESEL, SAM W. medical educator, academic administrator; b. Birmingham, Ala., July 7, 1945; MD, U. Pa., 1971. Intern Hosp. U. Pa., 1971—72, fellow in orthopedics, 1972—73, resident in orthopedics, 1973—76; exec. v.p. health studies, exec. dean sch. medicine Georgetown U. Med. Ctr., Washington, 1996—2002, sr. v.p., dean clin. affairs, 2002—, chmn. dept. orthop. surgery sch. medicine. Office: Georgetown U Main Campus and Med Ctr 37th and O St NW Washington DC 20057*

WIESEL, TORSTEN NILS, neurobiologist, educator; b. Upsala, Sweden, June 3, 1924; arrived in U.S., 1955; s. Fritz Samuel and Anna-Lisa Elisabet (Bentzer) Wiesel; 1 child, Sara Elisabet. MD, Karolinska Inst., Stockholm, 1954; D Medicine (hon.), Karolinska Inst, Stockholm, 1989; AM (hon.), Harvard U., 1967; D Medicine (hon.), Linköping U., 1982; ScD (hon.), NYU, 1987, U. Bergen, 1987. Instr. physiology Karolinska Inst., 1954—55; asst. dept. child psychiatry Karolinska Hosp., 1954—55; fellow in ophthalmology Johns Hopkins U., 1955—58, asst. prof. ophthalmic physiology, 1958—59; assoc. in neurophysiology and neuropharmacology Harvard U. Med. Sch., Boston, 1959—60, asst. prof. neurophysiology and neuropharmacology, 1960—64, asst. prof. neurophysiology, dept. psychiatry, 1964—67, prof. physiology, 1967—68, prof. neurobiology, 1968—74, Robert Winthrop prof. neurobiology, 1974—83, chmn. dept. neurobiology, 1973—82; Vincent and Brooke Astor prof. neurobiology, head lab. Rockefeller U., N.Y.C., 1982—98, pres., 1991—98, pres. emeritus, 1998—, dir. Shelby White and Leon Levy Ctr. for Mind, Brain & Behavior, 1998—; sec. gen. Human Frontier Sci. Program, 2000—. Ferrier lectr. Royal Soc. London, 1972, NIH lectr., 75; Grass lectr. Soc. Neurosci., 1976; lectr. Coll. de France, 1977; Hitchcock prof. U. Calif.-Berkeley, 1980; Sharpey-Schafer lectr. Phys. Soc. London; George Cotzias lectr. Am. Acad. Neurology, 1983; chmn. bd. govs. NY Acad Scis., 2001—. Contbr. numerous articles to profl. jours. Recipient Jules Stein award, Trustees for Prevention of Blindness, 1971, Lewis S. Rosenstiel prize, Brandeis U., 1972, Friedenwald award, Assn. Rsch. in Vision and Ophthalmology, 1975, Karl Spencer Lashley prize, Am. Philos. Soc., 1977, Louisa Gross Horwitz prize, Columbia U., 1978, Dickson prize, U. Pitts., 1979, Nobel prize in physiology or medicine, 1981, W.H. Helmerich III award, 1989. Mem.: AAAS, Royal Swedish Acad. Scis. (fgn.), Royal Soc. (fgn.), Soc. Neurosci. (pres. 1978—79), Swedish Physiol. Soc., Nat. Acad. Arts and Scis., Am. Acad. Arts and Scis., Am. Philos. Soc., Am. Physiol. Soc., Physiol. Soc. (Eng.) (hon.). Office: Rockefeller U 1230 York Ave New York NY 10021-6399 E-mail: wiesel@mail.rockefeller.edu.*

WIESEN, DONALD GUY, retired diversified manufacturing company executive; b. N.Y.C., July 4, 1928; s. Benjamin and Grace (Heath) W.; m. Patricia Ann Elfers, Apr. 29, 1950; children: Mara, Caitlin, Elizabeth, Anne, Megan. BS, Columbia U., 1948, MS, 1954. C.P.A., N.Y. Sr. tax specialist Price Waterhouse & Co., N.Y.C., 1950-58; with Chesebrough-Pond's Inc., Greenwich, Conn., 1958-87, gen. mgr. ops. Europe, 1965-70, treas., 1970-72, group v.p., chief fin. officer, 1972-77, group v.p., internat., 1977-82, sr. group v.p., 1982-84, vice chmn., chief fin. officer, 1984-87, also dir., ret., 1987. Bd. dirs. Skandia Am. Corp., 1985-91. Trustee Greenwich Libr., 1974-80; bd. govs. St. Bernard Coll., Cullman, Ala., 1973-75; rep. Columbia U. Alumni, Geneva, 1968; bd. dirs. Inner-City Found. for Charity and Edn., Bridgeport, Conn., 1992-93. Capt. USMC, 1951-54. Mem. AICPA, Indian Harbor Yacht Club, Univ. Club (N.Y.). Roman Catholic.

WIESEN, S. JONATHAN, historian, educator; b. Cambridge, Mass., June 26, 1968; s. David Stanley and Ellen Elizabeth Wiesen; m. Natasha Patricia Zaretsky, July 15, 2001. BA, U. Calif., 1990; MA, PhD, Brown U., 1997. Asst. prof. history So. Ill. U., Carbondale, 1998—. Vis. asst. prof. history Colgate U., Hamilton, NY, 1997—98. Author: West German Industry and the Challenge of the Nazi Past, 1945-1955 (Hagley Mus. prize best Book Bus. History, 2002). Recipient Clare Gregorian Presdl. award for Excellence in Tchg., Brown U., 1997; fellow, Social Sci. Rsch. Coun., 1995—96, J. Walter Thompson Rsch. fellow, Duke U., 2000; grantee, German Acad. Exch., 1994—95, German Academic Exch., 2002. Mem.: German Studies Assn., Am. Hist. Assn. Avocations: travel, music. Home: 506 W Pecan St Carbondale IL 62901 Office: Southern Ill U Dept History Carbondale IL 62901 Office Phone: 618 453 7873.

WIESENBERG, JACQUELINE LEONARDI, social sciences educator; b. West Haven, Conn., May 04; d. Curzio and Filomena Olga (Turrinziani) Leonardi; m. Russel John Wiesenberg, Nov. 23; children: James Wynne, Deborann Donna. BA, SUNY, Buffalo, 1970; postgrad., 1970-73, 80—. Interviewer, examiner U.S. Dept. Labor, New Haven, 1948-52; sec. W.I. Clark Co., Hamden, Conn., 1952-55; acct. VA Hosp., West Haven, 1956-60; acct.-commissary USAF Missle Site, Niagara Falls, N.Y., 1961-62; tchr. Buffalo City Schs., 1970-73, 79; acct. Erie County Social Svcs., Buffalo, 1971-73; lectr., 1973—. Contbr. articles to CAP, USAF mag. Capt., Nat. Found. March of Dimes, 1969—, com. mem. telethon, 1983-86; vol. VA, 1973—; den mother Boy Scouts Am., 1961-68; chmn. Meals on Wheels, Town of Amherst, 1975-76; leader, travel chmn. Girl Scouts U.S., 1968-77; mem. Nat. Congress Parents and Tchrs., 1957—; heart fund vol. Heart Assn., 1960-86; rep. Am. Diabetes Assn., 1994—, vol. diabetes collection, 1994-95; mem. Humane Soc. U.S., ASPCA, N.Y. Srs. Coalition. Mem. AAUW, NAFE, Internat. Platform Assn., Nat. Pks. and Conservation Assn., Am. Astrol. Assn., Nat. Arbor Day Found., Western N.Y. Conf. Aging, Nat. Geog. Soc., Wilderness Soc., Nat. Wildlife Fedn., Nat. Trust for Hist. Preservation, Nature Conservancy, Ctr. for Marine Conservation, Internat. Funds Animal Welfare, North Shore Animal League, The Nature Conservancy, The Libr. Congress, U. Buffalo Found., Pvt. Land Conservancy-Nat. Park Trust, Blue Planet Soc., U. Buffalo Alumni Assn., Epsilon Delta Chi, Alpha Iota. Home: 14 Norman Pl Amherst NY 14226-4233

WIESENBERG, RUSSEL JOHN, statistician; b. Kaukauna, Wis., Apr. 9, 1924; s. Emil Martin and Josephine (Appelbaker) W.; m. Jacqueline Leonardi, Nov. 23; children: James Wynne, Deborann Donna. BS, U. Wis., 1951; postgrad. Cornell U., 1960-61, U. Mich., 1969, George Washington U., 1976. Analyst, GE, West Lynn, Mass., 1951-56; specialist Internat. GE, Rio de Janeiro, 1956-59; statistician Gen. Motors Corp., Lockport, NY, 1959-65, sr. statistician, Harrison Radiator divsn., 1965-78, sr. reliability engr., 1978-82, sr. reliability statistician, 1982-87 . Auditor Cmty. Chest Fund, 1952-55; umpire Little League Baseball, 1962-65; committeeman Buffalo Area coun. Boy Scouts Am., 1962—, Cub Scout committeeman, 1962-64, Webelos cubmaster, 1963-64; mem. Nat. Congress Parents and Tchrs., 1963—; heart fund Vol. Heart Assn., 1968; tournament dir. Am. Legion Baseball, 1975; vol. United Way campaign, 1983, nat. telethon March of Dimes, 1983-84. Served with AUS, 1943-46. Decorated Bronze Star. Mem. AAAS, Am. Statis. Assn., Nat. Register Sci. and Tech. Pers., U. Wis. Alumni Assn., Artus, Internat. Platform Assn., Phi Kappa Phi. Lutheran. com.). Contbr. articles to profl. jours. Home: 14 Norman Pl Buffalo NY 14226-4233

WIESENFELD, BESS G. interior designer; b. Elizabeth, N.J., May 6, 1915; d. Morris and Rebecca (Sokolov) Gazevitz; m. Benjamin Wiesenfeld, Oct. 23, 1938 (dec.); children: Myra Judith Wiesenfeld Lewis, Elaine Phyllis Wiesenfeld Livingston, Ira Bertram (dec.), Sarah Ann Wiesenfeld Wasserman. BFA, N.Y. Sch. Interior Design, 1982. Pres. Anasarca Corp., 1958—; real estate devel. Colonia, N.J., 1961—; pres. Carolier Lns., Inc., 1986—, BGW LLC, Bess & Co. Patron Met. Opera; sustaining mem. N.J. Symphony Orch. Mem.: AAUW, Am. Soc. Interior Designers (allied mem.), Friends of Music at Princeton, Friends of Art Mus. of Princeton, N.J., Mus. Modern Art, Met. Mus. Art. Jewish. Home: 374 New Dover Rd Colonia NJ 07067-2713 also: 2600 S Ocean Blvd Palm Beach FL 33480-5484

WIESENFELD, JOHN RICHARD, chemistry professor; b. N.Y.C., July 26, 1944; s. Walter and Trude (Rosenberg) W. Stokes fellow, Pembroke Coll., Cambridge, Eng., 1971-72; BS with honors, CCNY, 1965; PhD, Case Inst. Tech., Cleve., 1969; MA, U. Cambridge, Eng., 1970. Asst. prof. Cornell U., Ithaca, N.Y., 1972-77, assoc. prof., 1978-84, prof., 1984-95, chair dept. chemistry, 1985-88, dep. v.p. for rsch., 1988-90, v.p. for plan, 1990-94, v.p. academic programs and planning, 1994-95; prof. Fla. Atlantic U., Boca Raton, 1995—, dean of sci., 1995-2001. Vis. scholar Stanford U. Calif., 1978-79, U. Wash., 1988; cons. E.I. DuPont, Wilmington, Del., 1975, Phys. Dynamics, La Jolla, Calif., 1980-82, U.S. Dept. Energy, Pitts., 1982, NIH, 1994; bd. dirs. Associated Univs., 1989-92. Contbr. more than 100 sci. articles to profl. jours. Sloan Found. research fellow, 1975; recipient Tchr.-Scholar award, Dreyfus Found., 1975. Fellow AAAS; mem. Am. Chem. Soc., Coun. Chem. Rsch. (governing bd. 1987-90). Home: 8012 Kiawah Trace Port Saint Lucie FL 34986-3023 Office: Fla Atlantic U PO Box 3091 Boca Raton FL 33431-0991 E-mail: jwiesenf@fau.edu.

WIESENTHAL, ROBERT S. corporate financial executive; BA in Polit. Sci., U. of Rochester, 1987. Mem., mergers & acquisitions group First Boston, 1986—93, mem., media group, 1993—99; mng. dir. to mng. dir. of credit Credit Suisse First Boston, 1999—2000; exec. v.p. & CFO Sony Corp. of Am., 2000—; exec. v.p. & chief strategy officer Sony Broadband Entertainment, 2000—. Bd. mem. Panavision, Inc. Bd. mem. Hamptons Internat. Film Festival. Office: Sony Corp of Am 550 Madison Ave New York NY 10022

WIESER, SIEGFRIED, planetarium executive director; b. Linz, Austria, Oct. 30, 1933; came to Can., 1955; s. Florian Wieser and Michaela Josepha (Kaufmann) Wieser-Burgstaller; m. Joan Xaven Quick, Sept. 8, 1962; children: Leonard Franz, Bernard Sidney. BS in Physics, U. Calgary, Alta., Can., 1966. Lead chorus singer, dancer Landes Theatre, Linz, 1949-53; project engr. EBG, Linz, 1952-54; with Griffith Farms Ltd., Eng., 1954-55; seismic computer operator Shell Can., Calgary, 1956-61; GTA systems analyst U. Calgary, 1961-66; planetarium dir. Centennial Planetarium, Calgary, 1966-84, exec. dir., 1984-91; exec. dir. emeritus Alberta Sci. Ctr., 1991—. Cons. Electro Controls, Salt Lake City, 1978-79. Contbr. articles to profl. publs. Recipient Violet Taylor award U. Calgary, 1964, Immigrant of Distinction Arts and Culture award, 2002; Queen Elizabeth scholar Province Alta., 1961; Paul Harris fellow Rotary Internat. Mem. Calgary Region Arts Found. (pres. 1999-2000), Alberta Coll. of Art Alumni Assn. (pres. 1991-92). Anglican. Avocations: swimming, hiking, astronomy, lecturing. E-mail: sigwies@shaw.ca.

WIESLER, JAMES BALLARD, retired banker; b. San Diego, July 25, 1927; s. Harry J. and Della B. (Ballard) W.; m. Mary Jane Hall, Oct. 3, 1953; children: Tom, Ann, Larry. BS, U. Colo., 1949; postgrad., Stonier Sch. Banking, Rutgers U., 1962, Advanced Mgmt. Program, Harvard U., 1973. With Bank of Am., NT & SA, 1949-87; v.p., mgr. main office San Jose, Calif., 1964-69; regional v.p. Cen. Coast adminstrn., 1969-74; sr. v.p., head No. European Area office Frankfurt, Fed. Republic of Germany, 1974-78; exec. v.p., head Asia div. Tokyo, 1978-81; exec. v.p., head N.Am. div. Los Angeles, 1981-82; vice chmn., head retail banking San Francisco, 1982-87; ret., 1987. Bd. dirs. Visa USA, Visa Internat., Sci. Applications Internat. Corp.; bd. dirs., chmn. Bank Adminstrn. Inst., 1986-87. Pres. Santa Clara County United Fund, 1969, 70, San Jose C. of C., 1968; fin. chmn. Santa Clara County Reps., 1967-74; bd. dirs. San Diego Armed Svcs., YMCA, Sidney Kimmell Cancer Ctr.; mem. bd. of trustees Borrego Cmty. Health Found.; trustee, chmn. bd. dirs. Sharp Meml. Hosp.; hon. consul-gen. for Japan, 1990-95. With USN, 1945-46. Mem. San Diego Hosp. Assn. (bd. dirs., treas.), San Diego Zool. Soc., Greater San Diego C. of C. (pres., CEO 1998-99), Bohemian Club, DeAnza Country Club, San Diego Yacht Club. Presbyterian. Home: 605 San Fernando St San Diego CA 92106-3312 Office: Bank Am Nat Trust & Savs 450 B St San Diego CA 92101-8001

WIESNER, CAROL A. financial services company executive; BS in Bus. Adminstrn., Pa. State U., 1960. CPA, Calif. Sr. auditor Price Waterhouse & Co., 1960-67; various positions Litton Industries, Inc., Woodland Hills, Calif., 1967-88, v.p., treas., 1988-94, v.p., controller, 1994—2000; ret. Mem. AICPA, Calif. Soc. CPA. Office: 21240 Burbank Blvd Woodland Hills CA 91367-6675

WIESNER, DAVID, illustrator, children's writer; Author (illustrator): (books) Free Fall, 1988 (Caldecott Honor book), Hurricane, 1990, Tuesday, 1991 (Caldecott medal, 1992), June 29, 1999, 1991 (Reading Rainbow book), Sector 7, 1999, Three Pigs, 2001 (Caldecott medal, 2002); illustrator (books) Kite Flier, 1986, The Sorcerer's Apprentice, 1989, The Rainbow People, 1989, Tongues of Jade, 1991, Man From the Sky, 1992, Night of the Gargoyles, 1994, creator (CD-ROM) The Day the World Broke; one-man shows include Nat. Ctr. for Children's Illustrated Lit., Abilene, Tex., 1999. Home: 2917 Moravian Ave Allentown PA 18103-6525 Office: Houghton Mifflin 222 Berkeley St Boston MA 02116 Address: 8700 Cheltenham Ave Glenside PA 19038-7124

WIESNER, JOHN JOSEPH, retail chain store executive; b. Kansas City, Mo., Mar. 31, 1938; s. Vincent A. and Jane Ann (Hagerty) W.; m. Georgiana Schild, Oct. 15, 1960; children: Susan, John V., Gretchen. BS in Bus. Adminstrn., Rockhurst U., 1960. Vice pres., contr. Fisher Foods, Cleve., 1970-77; asst. corp. contr. Richardson Vicks, N.Y.C., 1960-70; sr. exec. v.p. Pamida, Inc., Omaha, 1977-85, vice chmn., chief exec. officer, 1985-87; CEO C.R. Anthony Co., Oklahoma City, 1987-97, chmn., CEO, 1992-97; dir. Stage Stores, 1997—. Bd. dirs. Elder Beerman, Dayton, Lamonts, Inc., Kirkland, Wash. Bd. dirs. Omaha Area Council on Alcohol and Drug Abuse, 1983—; bd. dirs. Fontenelle Forest, Omaha, chmn., 1983, 84, A Chance to Change Fedn.; mem. bd. regents Rockhurst U, Okla. City Golf & Country Club, Oklahoma City, Kansas City, Mo. Named Bus. Assoc. of Yr., Am. Bus. Women's Assn., 1983. Mem. Nat. Assn. Accts. Republican. Roman Catholic. Home: 1476 S San Joaquin Dr Palm Springs CA 92264-8685

WIESNET, DONALD RICHARD, retired hydrologist; b. Buffalo, Feb. 7, 1927; s. Charles Anthony Wiesnet and Rose Elizabeth Nee Hildenbrand; m. Evelyn Elaine Jordan, Dec. 27, 1952; children: Peter Christopher, Ellen Elaine, Andrew John, Elizabeth Ann. AS, Syracuse U., 1947; BA in Geology, SUNY, Buffalo, 1950, MA in Geology, 1951. Teaching Certificate NY State Bd. Regents, 1952. Geologist US Geol. Survey, Washington, 1952—61, hydrogeological map editor, 1961—64; rsch. hydrologist US Naval Oceanog. Office, Suitland, Md., 1967—71; sr. rsch. hydrologist NOAA / Nat. Environ. Satellite Svc., Camp Springs, Md., 1971—80; chief, land sciences br. NOAA / Nat. Environ. Satellite Data & Info. Svc., Camp Springs, Md., 1980—82; CEO Satellite Hydrology, Inc., Vienna, Va., 1982—90. Author: (book) Satellite Hydrology; contbr. (book) Manual of Remote Sensing, V. II, Manual of Photographic Interpretation, Facets of Hydrology. Del. White Ho. Conf. on Aging, Washington, 1995—95; silver rep. (11th, va) Nat. Silver Haired Congress, Alexandria, Va., 1996—2004. Capt. USNR - Ret., 1965—87. NY State Veterans' Scholarship, NY State, 1951, Govt. Employee Grad. Scholarship, US Geol. Survey, 1964, Monetary Grant - Antarctic Mapmaking, NSF, 1978. Fellow: Am. Soc. Photogrammetry & Remote Sensing, Geol. Soc. of Am.; mem.: Nat. Assn. Ret. Fed. Employees (chpt. pres. 1993—94). Roman Catholic. Achievements include pioneer in the application of remote-sensing techniques and satellite data to snow measurements, river basin parameters, flood mapping, ocean currents, and estuarine tidal flows. Avocation: ornithology. Home: 601 McKinley St NE Vienna VA 22180

WIESSLER, DAVID ALBERT, news correspondent; b. Cambridge, Mass., July 20, 1942; s. Albert Francis and Vivian Mary Wiessler; m. Mary Judith Burton, Dec. 28, 1968. AB, Princeton U., 1964; MA, U. Tex., 1968. Editor UPI, Dallas, N.Y.C., Washington, 1966-82; assoc. editor U.S. News & World Report, Washington, 1982-84; Washington Bur. chief UPI, Washington, 1984-90, sr. polit. editor, 1990-93; news editor Bloomberg News Svc., 1994-95; editor nat. news Reuters, Washington, 1995-98, sr. Wash. corr., 1998—. Recipient Best Feature Writer award, Dallas Press Club, 1970. Mem.: Washington Gridiron Club. Avocations: reading, travel, cooking.

WIEST, DIANNE, actress; b. Kansas City, Mo., Mar. 28, 1948; Student, U. Md. Appeared in numerous plays including Ashes (off-Broadway), 1976, Leave It to Beaver is Dead, The Art of Dining (Obie award, 1979, Theatre World award 1983), Bonjour La Bonjour, Three Sisters, Serenading Louie (Obie award, 1983), Othello, After the Fall, Heartbreak House, Our Town, and Hunting Cockroaches, 1987, In the Summer House, 1993, Blue Light, 1994; appeared in films including It's My Turn, 1980, I'm Dancing as Fast as I Can, 1982, Independence Day, 1982, Footloose, 1984, Falling in Love, 1984, The Purple Rose of Cairo, 1985, Hannah and Her Sisters, 1986 (Acad. award for Best Supporting Actress 1987), Radio Days, 1987, Lost Boys, 1987, September, 1987, Bright Lights, Big City, 1988, Parenthood, 1989 (Acad. award nominee), Cookie, 1989, Edward Scissorhands, 1990, Little Man Tate, 1991, Cops and Robbersons, 1994, The Scout, 1994, Bullets Over Broadway, 1994 (Golden Globe award Best Supporting Actress-Drama 1995, Acad. award for Best Supporting Actress 1995), Drunks, 1995, The Birdcage, 1996, The Associate, 1996, Practical Magic, 1998, The Horse Whisperer, 1998, Portofino, 1999; TV appearances include The Wall, 1982, The Face of Rage, 1983, Simple Life of Noah Dearborn, 1999, The 10th Kingdom, 2000.

WIETING, GARY LEE, federal agency executive; b. Huron, SD, Apr. 24, 1937; s. LeRoy Charles and Edna Lorraine (Crawley) W.; m. Nancy Lou Clark, July 9, 1961 (div. 1991); children: Kevin Clark, Brian David; m. Julia Gladys Eli, Dec. 31, 1998. BA, U. Ill., 1961; MBA, Lake Forest Sch. Mgmt., 1983; travel and tourism diploma, Heritage Coll., Las Vegas, Nev., 1997. Logistics mgr. U.S. Army, Vietnam, 1967-68, NATO/Shape Support Group, Belgium, 1968-72, 8th U.S. Army, Korea, 1972-73, U.S. Army Readiness Region, Ft. Sheridan, Ill., 1973-77, U.S. Army Recruiting Command, Ft. Sheridan, Ill., 1977-83; rsch. and devel. logistics mgr. Belvoir Rsch. and Devel. Ctr., Ft. Belvoir, Va., 1983-85, 88-90; personal svcs. logistics mgr. Hdqrs. Dept. of Army, Washington, 1985-88; logistics mgr., assoc. program mgr. for adv. automation FAA, Washington, 1990-94; ret., 1994. Travel counselor, 1997; mem. So. Nev. Area Mil. Retiree Coun., 1998. Capt. U.S. Army, 1957-77, ret. lt. col., 1986. Decorated Army Commendation medal, Bronze Star medal; recipient Comdr. Award for Civilian Svc., U.S. Army, 1988. Mem.: Delta Sigma Phi. Avocations: collecting art, U.S. and internat. travel, playing bridge. Home: 2421 Flower Spring St Las Vegas NV 89134-1822

WIG, ROBERT CURTIS, retired music educator, conductor; b. Montevideo, Minn., Oct. 10, 1934; s. Emil Corneilius and Melda Dena Wig; m. Marilyn Ruth Berg, Oct. 16, 1960; children: Curtis, Karen, Kathleen. BS, St. Cloud State U., 1957, MS, 1963. Registered music educator Music Educators Nat. Conf., Washington, 1991. Music tchr. Dassel (Minn.) Pub. Sch., 1957—64, Milaca (Minn.) Pub. Sch., 1964—93, Pease (Minn.) Christian Sch., 1999—2000; ret. Mem., past condr. St. Cloud (Minn.) Mcpl. Band, 1957—; mem. Bell Choir, Trinity Luth., Milaca, 1977—; dir. Alleluia Singers, Milaca, 1993—. Recipient Commendation Mcpl. Band, City of St. Cloud, 1986.

Mem.: NEA (life), Assn. Concert Bands, Ret. Edn. Assn. Minn. (life), Minn. Edn. Assn. (life), Windjammers Unlimited Inc., Lions Club (past pres.). Lutheran. Avocations: gardening, golf, bowling, music. Home: 525 2nd Ave SW Milaca MN 56353

WIGAN, GARETH, film company executive; b. London, Dec. 2, 1931; m. Patricia Wigan. Agent MCA, London, 1957—60, John Redway & Associates, 1960—61, Gregson & Wigan, 1961—68; co-founder London Internat., 1968—70; independent film prodr., 1971—75; v.p. creative affairs 20th Century Fox, Los Angeles, 1975—76, v.p. production, 1976—83; co-founder W.W. Productions, 1983—87; production consultant Columbia Pictures, 1987—93, exec. v.p., 1993—97; co-vice chair Sony Pictures Entertainment, 1997—98, Columbia Tristar Motion Picture Group, 1998—. Office: Columbia TriStar Motion Picture Group 10202 Washington Blvd Culver City CA 90232-3119*

WIGDALE, JAMES B. bank executive; Chmn., chief exec. officer Marshall & Ilsley Bank, Milw., vice chmn. holding co., also bd. dirs. Office: Marshall & Ilsley Corp 770 N Water St Milwaukee WI 53202-3509

WIGFIED-PHILLIP, RUTH GENIVEA, genealogist, author, researcher; b. Couer d' Alene, Idaho, Dec. 1, 1918; d. Arthur and Jenivea Caroline (Crisp) Wigfield; m. Milton Fred Phillip, May 14, 1942 (dec. Nov., 1984); children: Rochelle Ruth, Gloria Genivea, Nancy Lenore, Douglas Fred, Andrea Arleen. BA, U. Montana, Missoula, 1939; registered genealogist, Augustine Genealogy Sch., Torrance, Calif., 1985, Desc. of William the Conquerer, Desc. of Companion of William Conquerer, Augustine Genealogy Sch., Torrance, Calif., 1997. Med. technician Deaconess Hosp., Great Falls, Mont., 1939-42; social worker Mont. State Welfare Dept., Helena, 1944-46; musical instr. Mont. Music Tchrs. Assn., Great Falls, 1947-62, Missoula, 1962-72; genealogy rschr. Phillip Heritage House, Missoula, 1962-66, writer, author, 1972—. Author, editor: (5 newsletters on genealogy) Wigfield Genealogy, 1972—, Crisp Genealogy, 1981—, Lipscomb Genealogy, 1981, Martin Genealogy, 1981, New Race, 1985—. Mem. Immanuel Luth. Ch., Sunday sch. supt., 1965-72; sec. Mont. State Music Tchrs. Union, 1969-71. Recipient music scholarship Harlowtown Music Dept., Harlowtown, Mont., 1932-35. Mem. DAR (regent Bitterroot chpt. 1973-75, state Indian chmn. 1976-90, 25 yr. h on. award Bitterroot chpt. 1997), Guild of St. Margaret of Scotland (grand dame Mont., 1986—), Eastern Star (organist), Rebecca Lodge (organist). Avocations: bridge, garden club, travel, fishing, golf. Home and Office: Phillip Genealogy Heritage House 605 Benton Ave Missoula MT 59801-8633

WIGFIELD, RITA L. elementary school educator; b. Mpls., Dec. 14, 1945; d. Willard Ernest and Bernice Eleanor (Peterson) Ahlquist; m. Vernon Carter Wigfield, Oct. 9, 1982. BS, U. Minn., 1967; grad., St. Thomas Coll.; postgrad., Hamlin U. Cert. elem. educator, Minn. Tchr. Alice Smith Sch., Hopkins, Minn., 1967-80, Meadowbrook Sch., Hopkins, 1980-86, Gatewood Sch., Hopkins, 1986—. Owner Swede Country, Minnetonka, Minn., 1983—; elem. team leader Prin.'s Adv. Bd.; chmn. bldg. tech. com. Hopkins Sch. Dist., past supr. bldg. sch. patrol; coop. tchrs. Gustavus Adolphus Coll.; cons. and presenter in field. Author: We Love Literature, 1991 (Grand Prize Scholastic Inc., 1991). Mem. Wooddale Choir Evang. Christian Ch., decorating com., Mission commn., organizer fellowship dinners; mem. Loaves and Fishes, Minn. Landscape Arboretum. Recipient Hon. Mention Learning Mag., 1990, Nat. Coun Econ. edn./Internat. Paper Col. Found., 1992, 2d pl. Minn. Coun. Econ. Edn., 1992, Ashland Oil award, 1994; named Minn. Tchr. of Yr., 1992. Mem. ASCD, Nat. Assn. Miniature Enthusiasts, Am. Quilting Soc., Internat. Reading Assn., Minn. Edn. Assn., Hopins Edn. Assn. (bldg. rep., treas.), Delta Kappa Gamma (pres. Beta Beta chpt.), Kappa Delta Pi. Avocations: miniatures, quilting, flowers, cross-stitch, antiques. Home: 4719 Diane Dr Hopkins MN 55343-8785 Office: Gatewood Elem Sch 14900 Gatewood Dr Minnetonka MN 55345-6731

WIGGER, JARREL L. lawyer; b. Wiesbaden, Germany, May 12, 1963; s. Philip Lee and Ervinetta (Maxey) W.; m. Rose Marie Riley, Aug. 1, 1987; children: Amy Elizabeth, Jordan Lee. BA in English, The Citadel, 1985; JD, Wake Forest U., 1988. Bar: S.C. 1988, U.S. Dist. Ct. S.C. 1993, U.S. Ct. Mil. Appeals 1991, U.S. Supreme Ct. 1998. Student prosecutor Forsyth County Dist. Atty. Office, Winston-Salem, N.C., 1988; assoc. Drose, Davidson & Bennett, Charleston, S.C., 1992-94, jr. ptnr., 1995-98; ptnr. Davidson, Bennett & Wigger, Charleston, 1999—. Real estate cons. Co-editor, author: U.S. Navy Mass Casualty Handbook, 1991; co-editor: Law School for Nonlawyers Handbook, 1995. Lt. USN, 1986-92. Mem. ABA, ATLA, S.C. Trial Lawyers Assn., S.C. Bar Assn., Charleston County Bar Assn., Claimant Assn. for Workers Compensation (bd. govs.), Assn. Citadel Men (life), Citadel Brigadier Found., Charleston Area Citadel Club, Citadel Old Timers Wrestling Club (pres. 1996—), Sigma Tau Delta. Avocations: running, guitar, wrestling, coaching. Office: 8086 Rivers Ave North Charleston SC 29406

WIGGERS, CHARLOTTE SUZANNE WARD, magazine editor; b. Cleve., Dec. 14, 1943; d. Raymond Paul and Irene Mary (Knapp) W.; m. John Houston Black, Feb. 1975 (div. 1980). AB, Smith Coll., 1966. Asst. editor The Hudson Rev., N.Y.C., 1966-76; assoc. editor The Print Collector's Newsletter, N.Y.C., 1977-79; copy editor Electronics mag., McGraw-Hill, N.Y.C., 1979-81; sr. copy editor Spectrum mag., N.Y.C., 1981-85; mng. editor Essence mag., N.Y.C., 1985—. Active St. Thomas Ch. Fifth Ave. Avocations: swimming, writing, photography, tennis. Home: 50 W 85th St Apt 5 New York NY 10024-4572 Office: Essence Magazine 1500 Broadway Ste 600 New York NY 10036-4015

WIGGIN, KENDALL FRENCH, state librarian; b. Manchester, N.H., Aug. 21, 1951; s. Ralph M. Jr. and Frances (Miltimore) W.; m. Elaine M. Elliott, June 2, 1973 (div. Jan. 1989); children: Sara, Douglas; m. Laura A. Larson, May 26, 1990; children: Lindsey, Tess. BA, U. N.H., 1974; MS in LS, Simmons Coll., 1975. Libr. Litchfield (N.H.) Pub. Libr., 1975; dir. Merrimack (N.H.) Pub. Libr., 1975-83; coord. tech. svcs. Manchester City Libr., 1983-90; state libr. N.H. State Libr., Concord, 1990-99, Conn. State Library, Hartford, 1999—. Mem. ALA, New Eng. Libr. Assn., N.H. Libr. Assn., Chief Officers State Libr. Agys., Chief Officers State Libr. Agys. in N.E., N.H. Writers and Publishers Project. Republican. Presbyterian. Avocations: stamp collecting/philately, gardening. Office: 231 Capitol Ave Hartford CT 06106

WIGGINS, BARBARA SUE, pharmacy clinical specialist, educator; b. St. Louis, Va., Mar. 5, 1969; d. Earl Leonard and Carrie Sue Pigg; m. John Wesley Wiggins, Nov. 4, 1962; children: Luke James, Lauren Grace. BS in Pharmacy, St. Louis Coll. Pharmacy, 1992; PharmD, Va. Commonwealth U./Med. Coll. Va., 1998. Bd. cert. pharmacoltherapy specialist with added qualifications in cardiology. Clin. specialist - cardiology U. Wash. Med. Ctr., Seattle, 1999—2002; clin. instr. U. Wash. Sch. Pharmacy, Seattle, 1999—2002; ACLS instr. Am. Heart Assn., Seattle, 1999—2002; pharmacy clin. specialist-cardiology U. Va. Health Sys., Charlottesville, 2002—; clin. instr. Sch. Nursing U. Va., Charlottesville, 2002—; ACLS instr. Am. Heart Assn., Richmond, Va., 2002—; clin. instr. Sch. Medicine U. Va., 2003. Contbg. editor and reviewer Springhouse (Pa.) Pub., 1998. Contbr. chapters to books, articles to profl. jours. Chair profl. affairs Wash. Soc. Health Sys. Pharmacists, Seattle, 2002—02. Lt. USN, 1993—99. Recipient Merck Award for Clin. Rsch., 1998. Mem.: Am. Soc. Health Sys. Pharmacists, Va. Soc. Health Sys. Pharmacists (assoc.), Am. Heart Assn. (assoc.), Rho Chi. Achievements include 1996 United States Olympic Marathon Trials Qualifier. Avocations: running, tennis, bicycling, hiking. Office: Univ Va PO Box 800674 Charlottesville VA 22908-0674 E-mail: bsw4v@virginia.edu.

WIGGINS, CELESTINE K. state legislator; b. Newport, N.H., Nov. 29, 1929; m. Frank Wiggins; 4 children. Student, U. N.H., 1947-48, Keene State Coll., 1967-71, Vt. State Coll., 1982-83. Postmaster U.S. Postal Svc., ret., 1992; mem. dist. 4 N.H. Ho. of Reps., Concord, 1996—, mem. criminal justice and pub. safety com., 1996—. Clk. Newport (N.H.) Sch. Dist.; chmn. Sullivan County Dem. Orgn., 1996—; chmn. Newport Revitalization Commn., 1994-96; bd. dirs. Sullivan County chpt. United Way, 1993—. Mem. Nat. League Postmasters (vice chmn. nat. legis. com. 1984-91). Roman Catholic. Office: NH State Legis State House Concord NH 03301

WIGGINS, CHARLES HENRY, JR., lawyer; b. Balt., July 15, 1939; s. Charles Henry and Kathryn Wilson (Walker) W.; m. Wendy Jane Horn, June 20, 1964 (div. 1996); children: Charles Hunter, Rebecca Rae, Melinda Marie; m. Karen Ann Kowal, Apr. 26, 1997 (div. 2002). BSEE, U. Ill., Urbana, 1962; JD with honors, U. Ill., 1965. Bar: Ill. 1965, U.S. Dist. (no. dist.) Ill. 1970, U.S. Tax Ct. 1974, U.S. Ct. Appeals (7th cir.) 1983. Assoc. Vedder, Price, Kaufman & Kammholz, Chgo., 1969-73, ptnr., 1974—. Mem. zoning bd. appeals Village of Indian Head Pk., Ill., 1984-91. Capt. U.S. Army, 1965-68. Mem. Chgo. Bar Assn., University Club (Chgo.), Edgewood Valley Country Club (LaGrange, Ill., bd. dirs. 1991-98), SAR. Avocations: golf, tennis, bridge. Office: Vedder Price Kaufman & Kammholz 222 N La Salle St Fl 26 Chicago IL 60601-1003

WIGGINS, JAMES BRYAN, religion educator; b. Mexia, Tex., Aug. 24, 1935; m. Elizabeth R. Wiggins, May 27, 1995; children: Bryan, Karis. BA, Tex. Wesleyan U., 1957; BD, So. Meth. U., 1959; PhD, Drew U., 1963; postgrad., Tübingen U., Fed. Republic Germany, 1968-69. Ordained to ministry Meth. Ch., 1959. Instr. humanities Union Jr. Coll., Cranford, N.J., 1960-63; asst. prof. religion Syracuse (N.Y.) U., 1963-69, assoc. prof., 1969-75, prof., 1975—, dir. grad. studies, 1975-80, chair dept., 1980—, Eliphalet Remington prof. religion, 1999—2001; exec. dir. Am. Acad. Religion, 1983-91, dir., 1973-75, 83-91; exec. dir. Interreligious Coun. of Ctrl. N.Y., Syracuse, 2002—. Cons. in field; People to People del. leader to former Soviet Union, 1992. Author: The Embattled Saint, 1966, Foundations of Christianity, 1970; editor: Religion as Story, 1975, Christianity: A Cultural Perspective, 1987, In Praise of Religious Diversity, 1996; contbr. articles to profl. jours. Trustee Scholars Press, Atlanta, 1983-91, chmn., 1986-91; chair, bd. dirs. Onondaga Pastoral Counseling Ctr., 1997-99; bd. dirs. Inter-religious Coun. Ctrl. N.Y., 1997-2001. Rockefeller Found. fellow, 1962-63; Lilly Endowment rsch. grantee, 1992-93. Fellow Soc. for Arts (bd. dirs. 1976—), Religion and Culture; mem. AAUP, Am. Acad. Religion. Democrat. Methodist. Avocations: golf, tennis, music, reading, travel. Office: 3049 E Genesee St Syracuse NY 13244-0001 Office Phone: 315-449-3552. E-mail: jwiggins@twcny.rr.com.

WIGGINS, JAMES L. lawyer; b. Savannah, Ga., Aug. 13, 1946; BS in Criminal Justice, Armstrong State Coll., 1972; JD, Mercer U., 1975. Pub. defender Oconee Jud. Cir. Ga., 1978—80, dist. atty., 1981—84; U.S. atty. for mid. dist. Ga. U.S. Dept. Justice, Macon, Ga., 1994-96; ptnr. Almand & Wiggins, Macon. Mem.: Macon Bar Assn., Ga. State Bar (bd. govs. Oconee jud. cir. 1989—). Office: Almand & Wiggins 1922 Forsyth Street PO Box 1605 Macon GA 31202-1605*

WIGGINS, KIM DOUGLAS, artist, art appraiser, art dealer; b. Roswell, N.Mex., Apr. 8, 1959; s. Walton Wray Wiggins and Barbara Jo (Chesser) Ortega; m. Mary Allison Raney, Sept. 4, 1977 (div. May 1984); children: Rebekah, Mona; m. Maria C. Trujillo, June 17, 1995; children: Gianna Josiah, Elisha Douglas, Eden Renee. Student, Ea. N.Mex. U., Roswell, 1977, 83-84, San Antonio Coll., 1978-79, Ind. Bapt. Coll., Dallas, 1982-83, Santa Fe Inst. Fine Art, 1989. Dir. Clarke-Wiggins Fine Art, Palm Springs, Calif., 1986-89; owner, mgr. Wiggins Fine Art, Santa Fe, 1989-93, Wiggins Studio, Roswell, 1991—; owner Print & Promise, Roswell, 1996—. Cons. Mus. N.Mex., Santa Fe, 1992—, Cline Fine Art, Santa Fe, 1993—; lectr. in field. One man shows at Altermann Morris Galleries, Houston, Dallas, Santa Fe, 1992-2004, Studio Gallery, Laguna Beach, San Diego, 1998; exhibited in group shows Pa. Acad. Fine Art, Phila., 1992-96, M.H. DeYoung Mus., San Francisco, 1993-96, Autry Mus. Western Heritage, L.A., 1999-2004, Desert Caballeros Western Mus., Wickenburg, Ariz., 2000, The Denver Art Mus., 2000, The Corcoran Gallery of Art, 2001, Joslyn Art Mus., 2002, Art Inst. Chgo., 2003; represented in permanent collections Mus. of N.Mex., Sante Fe, Anschutz Collection, Denver, Staples Ctr., L.A., Autry Mus. Western Heritage, L.A., Booth Western Art Mus., Atlanta; editor: K. Douglas Wiggins: Sense of Spirit, 1993; pub., contbr.: Art of the American West, 1999, Painters and the American West, 2000, The Trail of Painted Ponies, 2001, Gathered by Grace, 2002. Mem. NRA, HOG, CMA, Internat. Platform Assn., Soc. Am. Impressionists, Coun. for Art of West, Gladney Ctr., Assurance Home, Other Side of the West. Republican. Avocations: printmaking, poetry, motorcycles, scuba diving, fencing. Home: 6 El Arco Iris Dr Roswell NM 88201-7711 Studio: Altermann Galleries 225 Canyon Rd Santa Fe NM 87501-2755

WIGGINS, MARIANNE, writer; b. Lancaster, Pa., 1947; m. Salman Rushdie, 1988 (div. 1993); 1 child. Author: (novels) Babe, 1975, Went South, 1980, Separate Checks, 1984, Herself in Love and Other Stories, 1987, John Dollar, 1989, Bet They'll Miss Us when We're Gone: Stories, 1991, Eveless Eden, 1995 (nominee Orange prize, 1991), Almost Heaven, 1998, Evidence of Things Unseen (nominee for Nat. Book award, 2003). Recipient Whiting award, Nat. Endowment for the Arts Grant, Janet Heidinger Kafka prize. Home: P O Box 461597 Los Angeles CA 90046-9597

WIGGINS, MARY ANN WISE, small business owner, educator; b. Coushatta, La., Dec. 25, 1940; d. George Wilkinson and Maitland (Allums) Wise; m. Gerald D. Paul (div. Nov. 1977); children: John Barron, James Gordon, Brenda Michelle; m. Billy J. Wiggins, Oct. 3, 1981; children: Marshall Wade, Brian David, William Joshua, George Justin; stepchildren: Joseph James, Winona Gail. BA, Northwestern State U., Natchitoches, La., 1964, postgrad., 1994, Weatherford Coll., 1967, North Tex. State U., 1968. Lic. ins. agt., real estate agt., La., pvt. pilot. Tchr. U.S. Army Schs., Nuremberg, Germany, 1964—66, Mineral Wells Ind. Sch. Dist., 1967—70; bookkeeper Wise Dept. Store, Coushatta, La., 1966—67; amb. of good will Vietnam, 1971; owner, mgr. Mary Ann's Furniture & Hardware, Coushatta, 1977—97; tchr. Springville Mid. Sch., 1994—96, Red River Parish Alternative Sch., 1996—98, tchr. Ware Youth Ctr., 1998—. Com. mem. Instrn. and Profl. Devel. Com. La. Assn. Educators, 1998-2000, vice chmn. 1999-2002; v.p. La. Juvenile Detention Tchrs. Assn., 1999—; tchr. leader La. Tech., 2002-03. Chmn. Am. Cancer Soc., Conway, Ark., 1972, Red River Parish United Way, Coushatta, 1985; treas., bd. dirs. Hall Summit United Meth. Ch.; pres. Red River Parish Assn. Educators Polit. Action Com. Recipient German-Am. hospitality award Orgn. German-Am. Women, Nuremberg, 1965. Mem. NEA, La. Assn. Educators (chmn. legis. com.), Red River Assn. Educators (v.p. 1994, pres. 1998-2001), U.S. C. of C., Coushatta-Red River C. of C. (charter), Pi Kappa Sigma, Sigma Kappa. Democrat. Methodist. Avocations: gardening/landscaping, swimming, horseback riding, computers, week-enders with family. Home: 2217 E Carrol St Coushatta LA 71019-8567

WIGGINS, NANCY BOWEN, real estate broker, market research consultant; b. Richmond, Va., Oct. 9, 1948; d. William Roy and Mary Virginia (Colson) Bowen; m. Samuel Spence Saunders, Aug. 16, 1969 (div. 1977); m. Edwin Lindsey Wiggins, Jr., Apr. 16, 1983 (div. 1999); children: Neal Bowen, Mark Edwin. AA, St. Mary's Coll., Raleigh, N.C., 1968; postgrad., Trinity U., 1968-69; BA, U.S. Internat. U., San Diego, 1970; MA, U. Tex., Arlington, 1975; postgrad., Tulane U., 1976-77. Cert. comml. investment mem. Bank teller Bank of Am., San Diego, 1971-72; lectr. U. Tex., Arlington, 1974-76; instr. Johnson C. Smith U., Charlotte, N.C., 1977-78; human svcs. planner Centralina Coun. of Govt., Charlotte, 1978-80; mktg. rsch. analyst First Union Nat. Bank, Charlotte, 1980-81; mktg. rep. Burroughs Corp., Charlotte, 1981-83; ptnr., mktg. researcher George Selden & Assocs., Charlotte, 1983-84; pres., broker Bowen Wiggins Co., Charlotte, 1984-92; pres. WRB, Inc. (merger Bowen Wiggins Co. and W. Roy Bowen Co., Inc.), Charlotte, 1992-96; mgr., prin. Nancy Wiggins, LLC, Charlotte, 1996—; ptnr. Buster & Wiggins Internat., Myrtle Beach, S.C. Instr. U. N.C., Charlotte, 1984-85, 87-90, Winthrop U., Rock Hill, S.C., 1985-86, 91-92; bd. dirs. Roy Bowen, Inc., Frogmore, S.C., v.p., sec., 1990. Contbr. articles to profl. jours. Vice chmn. United Cerebral Palsy Coun., Charlotte, 1984; chmn. bd. dirs. Carriage House Condominium Assn., Charlotte, 1980-82; mem. Charlotte Mayor's Budget Adv. Com., 1980-81, Charlotte-Mecklenburg Planning Commn., 1994-99, mem. planning com., 1994-95, zoning com., 1995-97, vice-chmn. zoning com., 1997, planning com. 1998, vice chmn. planning com. 1998—, exec. com., 1997—; pres. Mecklenburg Dem. Women's Club, 1990; mem. state exec. com. N.C. Dem. Party, 1991-95, 99-2000; mem. Mecklenburg County Solid Waste Adv. Bd., 1991-92, chmn. recycling com., 1991-94, 95-96; mem. Comml. Investment Real Estate Inst., 1997-98, bd. dirs. N.C. chpg., 1999. Mem. AAUW, Charlotte Region Comml. Bd. Realtors, N.C. Assn. Appraisers (bd. dirs., pres. 1989-90), Internat. Coun. Shopping Ctrs., Internat. Real Estate Fedn. (Paris, U.S. del. Retail Conf. at World Congress 1998, U.S. vice chair trade missions, sec.-gen. exch. com. 1999-2000), Am. Planning Assn., Charlotte C. of C. (bd. advisors 1997), Multimillion Dollar Club, Tournament Players Club Piper Glen, Rose Soc., Good Friends, Nat. Assn. Realtors, FIABCI, Paris, Internat. Trade Mission Com. (sec. gen. internat. exch. com.), N.C. Citizens for Bus. and Industry, NAR Charlotte (region comml. bd.), CCIM (N.C. chpt. bd. dirs.), Pi Sigma Alpha. Democrat. Episcopalian. Avocations: gardening, art collecting. Home: 6919 Seton House Ln Charlotte NC 28277-4517 Office: Ste 300 501 N Church St Charlotte NC 28202-2207

WIGGINS, NORMAN ADRIAN, university administrator, legal educator; b. Burlington, N.C., Feb. 6, 1924; s. Walter James and Margaret Ann (Chason) W.; m. Mildred Alice Harmon. AA, Campbell Coll., 1948; BA, Wake Forest Coll., 1950, LLB, 1952; LLM, Columbia U., 1956, JSD, 1964; Exec. Program, U. N.C., 1968-69; LLD, Gardner-Webb Coll., 1972. Deacon Wake Forest Baptist Ch., Winston-Salem, N.C., 1963-66, Buies Creek (N.C.) Bapt. Ch., 1973—; deacon, tchr. Sunday sch., 1952—; lay preacher, 1953—; pres. N.C. Found. of Ch.-Related Coll., 1969-70, Campbell U., Buies Creek, 1967—, prof. law, 1976—. Author: Wills and Administration of Estates in North Carolina, 1964—, (with Gilbert T. Stephenson) Estates and Trusts, 1973; Editor: N.C. Will Manual, 1958—, Trust Functions and Services, 1978; Contbr. articles to legal jours. Chmn. Gov.'s Task Force Com. on Adjudication of the Com. on Law and Order, 1969-71; mem. Com. on Drafting Interstate Succession Act for N.C., 1957-59; mem. Com. for Revision of the Laws Relating to the Adminstrn. of Descs.' Estates, 1959-67, chmn., 1964-67; trustee Sunday Sch. Bd., So. Bapt. Conv., 1975—, chmn. bd. trustees, 1978—, nominations com., 1988—; pres. Bapt. State Conv. N.C., 1983-85; bd. dirs. N.C. Cititzens for Bus. and Industry, 1982—. Recipient Outstanding Civilian Svc. award Dept. Army, 1985, Patriotic Civilian Svc. award U.S. Dept. Army, 1998, award for longest tenure as univ. pres. Coalition Christian Colls. and Univs., 1998, The Order of the Long Leaf Pine award, 1998, John J. Parker award, 1999; Campbell Law Sch. renamed in his honor the Norman Adrian Wiggins Sch. of Law, 1989; recognized for outstanding svc. to high edn. and legal edn. Newcomen Soc. U.S., 1993; Comdr.'s award for Pub. Svc., 1995, Internat. Freedom of Mobility award, 1995; named to List of 100 Influential Bapt. Leaders in 20th Century, 2000. Mem. ABA, Nat. Assn. Coll. and Univ. Attys. (pres. 1972-73, Disting. Svc. award 1991), Am. Assn. Presidents Ind. Colls. and Univs. (pres. 1981-83), N.C. Assn. Colls. and Univs. (exec. com. 1980—, pres. 1984-85), N.C. Assn. Ind. Colls. and Univs. (pres. 1970-72, exec. com. 1980-81), N.C. Bar Assn., Harnett County Bar Assn., Nat. Fellowship Baptist Men (pres. 1987-90), Jay Waugh Evang. Assn. (dir./pres. 1970-72), Dunn Area C. of C., Wake Forest Alumni Assn., Rotary (hon. mem. Dunn club), Phi Alpha Delta, Phi Kappa Phi, Omicron Delta Kappa. Office: Campbell U PO Box 127 Buies Creek NC 27506-0127 E-mail: btrd@webster.campbell.edu.

WIGGINS, PATRICIA ANN, computer systems analyst, state legislator; b. Pasadena, Calif., Apr. 19, 1940; d. Ralph Curtis and Grace Lucille (Alpeter) W.; m. Yosef Pilch, Aug. 10, 1971 (div. July 1977); m. Guy Reed Conner, Mar. 13, 1983; stepchildren: Stephen Silverman, James Silverman. BA in English, UCLA, 1977. Bookkeeper Europa Motors Ltd., Studio City, Calif., 1959-62, Volvo Imports, North Hollywood, Calif., 1962-64, George Pope Assets, San Francisco, 1964-69; client rels. coord. Property Rsch. Corp., L.A., 1969-72; computer systems analyst Sys. Devel. Corp., Santa Monica, Calif., 1977-83, Fireman's Fund Ins., San Rafael, Calif., 1984; computer systems analyst, ptnr. Peer Protocols, Ltd., Costa Mesa, Calif., 1984-89; campaign mgr. Sen. Mike Thompson, Napa, Calif., 1990; field rep. Assemblywoman Valerie Brown, Santa Rosa, Calif., 1992-94; coun. mem. City of Santa Rosa, Calif., 1994—; computer cons. CW Assoc., Santa Rosa, 1990—. Mem. Calif. State Assembly, 1998—. Recipient Vol. Recognition, County of Sonoma, 1996. Mem. NOW, Bus. & Profl. Women, Nat. Women's Polit. Caucus (v.p. 1996), Sonoma Land Trust (bd. mem. 1993-97). Democrat. Avocations: reading, walking. Home: 315 Carrillo St Santa Rosa CA 95401-5111

WIGGINS, RITA CASSIDY, poet; b. Chgo., Oct. 2, 1926; d. Thomas Francis Cassidy and Anastacia Charlotte Higgins; m. John Lawson Wiggins, Aug. 16, 1947 (dec. Sept. 27, 2002); children: Laura, John, Thomas, Martha, Caroline, Paul, James, Edward. Degree in English lit., Barat Coll., 1947. Sales rep. Marshall Field's, Chgo., 1948, Bloomingdale's, NJ, 1968—70; owner Which-Crafts, NJ, 1972—74; fin. dir. Fashion Inst. of Design and Merchandising, San Francisco, 1981—83. Author: (poetry) Shedding Light, 2000, Art Scan - Napa Valley, 2000, Love, Honor and Value, 2002. Bd. dirs. Calistoga (Calif.) Caregivers, 2000—02; mem. Fair Housing, L.A., 1965—; mem. bd. Warren (Ill.) Pub. Libr., 1980—82. Recipient Hon. Mention award, Jassamyn West, Napa, Calif., 1991, 2d prize, Napa Arts Coun., 1995. Mem.: Nat. League Am. Pen Women. Democrat. Roman Catholic. Avocations: writing, travel, theater, music. Home: 1329 Madrona Ave Saint Helena CA 94574 E-mail: naparita@aol.com.

WIGGINS, ROGER C. internist, educator, researcher; b. Tetbury, Eng., May 26, 1945; BA, Cambridge U., Eng., 1968; BChir, Middlesex Hosp. Med. Sch., London, 1971, MB, MA, 1972. House physician dept. medicine The Middlesex Hosp., London, 1971-72; house surgeon Ipswich (Eng.) and East Suffolk Hosps., 1972; sr. house officer Hammersmith Hosp., The Middlesex Hosp., Brompton Hosp., London, 1972-74; rsch. registrar The Middlesex Hosp. Med. Sch., London, 1975-76; postdoctoral fellow Scripps Clinic and Rsch. Found., La Jolla, Calif., 1976-78, rsch. assoc., 1978-79, asst. mem. 1, 1979-81; asst. prof. U. Mich., Ann Arbor, 1981-84, assoc. prof., 1984-90, prof., 1990—, chief nephrology, 1988—, dir. O'Brien Renal Ctr., 1988—, dir. NIH Nephrology Tng. Program, 1988-96. Lectr., speaker in field. Author chpts. to books; assoc. editor: Jour. Am. Soc. Nephrology, Clin. Sci.; contbr. articles to profl. jours. First Broderip scholar, 1971, Harold Boldero scholar, 1971, James McIntosh scholar, 1971, The Berkeley fellow Gonville and Caius Coll., 1976; recipient Leopold Hudson prize, 1971, The William Henry Rean prize, 1971, Disting. Rsch. Jerome W. Conn award, 1984. Fellow Royal Coll. Physicians (U.K.); mem. Am. Assn. Pathologists, Am. Assn. Immunologists, Am. Soc. Nephrology, Fedn. Clin. Rsch., Am. Soc. Clin. Investigation, Ctrl. Soc. Am. Fedn. Clin. Rsch., Assn. Am. Physicians. Office: U Mich Nephrology Div 3914 Taubman Ctr Ann Arbor MI 48109

WIGGINS, SARAH, assistant principal, secondary school educator; d. Irvin and Sarah Johnson; m. Chester Wiggins, Apr. 6, 1946; children: DéMon, Marland. BA in English, Shaw U., 1968; MS in Edn. Adminstrn., N.C. Agrl. and State U., 1990. Tchr. English Person Sr. H.S., Roxboro, NC, 1968—95, asst. prin., 1995—98, 1998—. Mem. state assistance team div. sch. improvement Dept. Pub. Instrn., Raleigh, NC, 2000, H.S. English cons. div. sch. improvement, 2000—03. Dir. minority recruitment program Person County, Roxboro, 1993; co-dir. dept. youth Yan Ch., Yanceyville, 2002. Mem.: N.C. Tchrs. English, Nat. Coun. Tchrs. English (mem. secondary sect. steering com. 1994—97, mem. testing and evaluation com. 1998—99, State Farm Good Neighbor award 1990, Minority Tchr. Recruitment grantee 1991). Home: PO Box 1041 Yanceyville NC 27379

WIGGINS, STEPHEN EDWARD, physician, medical association administrator; b. Phila., May 7, 1951; s. Ralph Cannon and Bernice J. (Maslovitz) W.; m. Rebecca del Carmen, Oct. 3, 1992; children: Daniel Stephen, Elizabeth Rebekah. BA, Rutgers U., 1973; MD, Med. Coll. Va., 1977. Diplomate Am. Bd. Family Practice. Resident in family practice Riverside Hosp., Newport News, Va., 1977-80; staff emergency physician North Arundal Hosp., Glen Burnie, Md., 1980-81, So. Md. Hosp. Ctr., Clinton, 1982-84; med. dir. Convenient Health Care, Waldorf, Md., 1984—. Ptnr. Old Line Med. Partnership, Waldorf, 1990-97, Convenient Health Care Mgmt., Waldorf, 1989-97; instr. family practice Georgetown U. Sch. Medicine, Washington, 1995—; pres. 640 Old Line Ctr. L.P., 1997—; pres. Old Line Med. Svcs. P.C., 1997—.

Vol. physician and citizen diplomat Gesundheit Inst., Russia, 1991; citizen diplomat U.S.-China Peoples Friendship Assn., China, 1988; vol. physician March of Dimes Walk-a-thon, Md., 1985-86. William Demarest scholar, Rutgers U., New Brunswick, N.J., 1969-73. Fellow Am. Acad. Family Physicians; mem. Med. and Chirurg. Faculty of the State of Md., Md. Acad. Family Physicians, Charles County Med. Soc. Avocation: scuba diving. Office: Convenient Health Care 12090 Old Line Ctr Waldorf MD 20602-2556

WIGGINTON, ADAM, marketing professional; BSc in Zoology, U. Aberdeen; MBA in Fin., City U. With Unilever; prin. assoc. mgmt. consultancy divsn. Coopers & Lybrand; v.p. strategic planning Reed Travel Group, 1994-98, sr. v.p. of bus. devel. and circulation mktg., 1998—. Office: OAG Worldwide 2000 Clearwater Dr Oak Brook IL 60523-1955

WIGGINTON, LISA BENDERMAN, elementary school educator; b. Corinth, Miss., Nov. 7, 1963; d. Harvey Thomas and Betty Moore Benderman; m. Kirk Eugene Wigginton, Sept. 21, 1985; children: Kristy Lynn, Jennifer Leigh, Thomas Eugene. B in Elem. Edn., Blue Mt. Coll., 1989; M in Ednl. Adminstrn., U. North Ala., 2002, postgrad., 2003—. Cert. tchg. and adminstr. Miss., 1990. Tchr. Alcorn Sch. Dist., Corinth, Miss., 1990—. Mem.: Nat. Assoc. Elem. Sch. Principals (assoc.). Democrat-Npl. Baptist. Avocation: showing and raising registered angus cattle. Home: 4227 CR 200 Corinth MS 38834 Office: Alcorn Ctrl Elem Sch 20 CR 254 Glen MS 38846 Personal E-mail: liwi010@aol.com.

WIGGLEWORTH, MARGARET, property manager; b. Potomac, Md. Student, U. Md. Staff mem. judiciary com. and govtl. affairs com. Senator Charles McC. Mathias, Jr., Md., 1980—85; asst. dir. nat. affairs NPR, 1985—87, exec. dir. U.S. Coalition Svc. Industries, Inc., 1987—98; pres., CEO Colliers Internat. Property Consultants USA Inc., Boston, 1998—. Office: Colliers Internat Property Consultants USA Inc 20th Fl 50 Milk St Boston MA 02109*

WIGGS, EUGENE OVERBEY, ophthalmologist, educator; b. Louisville, Apr. 27, 1928; s. Eugene Overbey and Marie Helen (Martin) W.; children: Susan, Christopher, Karen, Mark. AB, Johns Hopkins U., 1950; MD, Duke U., 1955. Intern Denver Gen. Hosp., 1955-56; resident in ophthalmology Wilmer Inst. Johns Hopkins Hosp., 1956-59; ophthalmic plastic fellow Byron Smith, MD, N.Y.C., 1969; pvt. practice specializing in oculoplastic surgery Denver, 1961—. Clin. prof. U. Colo. Med. Ctr.; lectr. ophthalmic plastic surgery various med. ctrs. Contbr. articles to med. jours. With USNR, 1959-61. Mem. AMA, Denver Med. Soc., Colo. Med. Soc., Am. Soc. Ophthalmic Plastic and Reconstructive Surgery, Am. Acad. Ophthalmology (svc. award 1982), Colo. Ophthalmology Soc. Republican. Roman Catholic. Office: 2005 Franklin St Denver CO 80205-5401

WIGGS, SHIRLEY JOANN, retired secondary school educator; b. Johnston County, N.C., Nov. 6, 1940; d. William H. and Sallie P. (Barden) W. BA, Atlantic Christian Coll., 1963; postgrad., Duke U., 1966, East Carolina U., 1979-80; grad., Newspaper Inst. Am. Tchr. pub. schs., South Hill, Va., 1963-64; tchr. lang. arts and social studies Glendale Chapel H.S., Kenly, N.C., 1964-65, Benson (N.C.) H.S., 1965-69; tchr. advanced placement English, lang. arts, journalism South Johnston H.S., Four Oaks, N.C., 1969-96, chairperson dept. lang. arts, 1971-83; ret., 1996; historian, 2003—04. Evaluator profl. books Allyn and Bacon, Inc., 1974, 79; yearbook judge Columbia Scholastic Press Assn., 1986-92, yearbook advisor, 1980-94. Sunday Sch. tchr. 1st Bapt. Ch., Smithfield, N.C., 1964-66, assoc. supt. young people's dept., 1964-67, scholarship chair, 1987-91, ch. libr., 1992-2004, tutor, 2000, Clothes' Closet dir., 2004; chmn. Keep Johnston County Beautiful, 1979-81. Named Woman of Yr., Atlantic Christian Coll., 1962; recipient Internat. Cheerleading Found. award 1972, Acad. Booster Club award, 1986. Mem. NEA, Nat. Coun. Tchrs. English, Assn. Supervision and Curriculum Devel., N.C. Assn. Educators), N.C. English Tchrs. Assn. (dir. dist. 12, 1980-85), Johnston County Assn. Educators (pres. 1979), Johnston Co. Retired Tchrs Assn. (historian 2003—). Home: 102 E Sanders St Smithfield NC 27577-4211

WIGHT, JONATHAN B. economist, educator; b. Washington, Nov. 5, 1953; s. William L. and Joanne M. Wight; m. Jean McNall, June 19, 1999. BA, Duke U., 1976; MA, Vanderbilt U., 1980, PhD, 1982. Vol. Jesuit Vol. Corps, Portland, Oreg., 1976—77; instr. Vanderbilt U., Nashville, 1980; asst. prof. econs. U. Richmond, Va., 1982—88, assoc. prof. econs., 1989—97, assoc. prof. econs. and internat. studies, 1997—. Vis. prof. econs. U. Pitts. Semester-at-Sea, 1991; cons. The World Bank, Washington, 1984, Inter Am. Devel. Bank, Washington, 1993. Author: Saving Adam Smith, 2002; co-author: The Medical Offset Effect and Public Health Policy, 1989. Bd. officer Guatemala Highland Support Project, Richmond, 1993—; pres. Unity South Ch., Richmond, 1988—90. Recipient Paxton award, Internat. Assn. Torch Clubs, 2001. Mem.: The Torch Club (bd. mem. 2002—). Avocations: tennis, camping. Office: Univ Richmond Robins Sch Bus Richmond VA 23173

WIGHTMAN, ALEC, lawyer; b. Cleve., Jan. 23, 1951; s. John and Betty Jane (Follis) W.; m. Kathleen A. Little, June 19, 1976; children: Nora, Emily. BA, Duke U., 1972; JD, Ohio State U., 1975. Bar: Ohio 1975, U.S. Tax Ct. 1982, U.S. Ct. Appeals (6th cir.) 1983. Assoc. Krupman, Fromson & Henson, Columbus, Ohio, 1975-77; ptnr. Krupman, Fromson, Bownas & Wightman, Columbus, 1978-82; assoc. Baker & Hostetler, Columbus, 1982-83, ptnr., 1984—, exec. ptnr., 2004—. Bd. trustees The Arthur G. James Cancer Hosp., Richard J. Solove Rsch. Inst.; bd. dirs. Cleve. Rock & Roll., Inc. Mem. ABA, Ohio Bar Assn., Columbus Bar Assn., Ohio Oil and Gas Assn. Avocation: tennis. Office: Baker & Hostetler 65 E State St Ste 2100 Columbus OH 43215-4260

WIGHTMAN, ARTHUR STRONG, physicist, researcher; b. Rochester, N.Y., Mar. 30, 1922; s. Eugene Pinckney and Edith Victoria (Stephenson) W.; m. Anna-Greta Larsson, Apr. 28, 1945 (dec. Feb. 11, 1976); 1 child, Robin Letitia (dec. Mar. 2, 2001); m. Ludmilla Popova, Jan. 14, 1977. BA, Yale U., 1942; PhD, Princeton U., 1949; DSc, Swiss Fed. Inst. Tech., Zurich, 1969, Göttingen U., 1987. Instr. physics Yale, 1943-44; from instr. to asso. prof. physics Princeton, 1949-60, prof. math. physics, 1960-92; prof. emeritus, 1992—; Thomas D. Jones prof. math. physics Princeton, 1971-92. Vis. prof. Sorbonne, 1957, École Polytechnique, 1977-78. Served to lt. (j.g.) USNR, 1944-46. NRC postdoctoral fellow Inst. Teoretisk Fysik, Copenhagen, Denmark, 1951-52; NSF sr. postdoctoral fellow, 1956-57; recipient Dannie Heineman prize math. physics, 1969, Poincaré prize Internat. Assn. Math. Physics, 1997. Fellow NAS, Am. Acad. Arts and Scis., Royal Acad. Arts, Am. Phys. Soc.; mem. AAAS, Am. Math. Soc. Office: Princeton U 350 Jadwin Hl Princeton NJ 08544-0001 Business E-Mail: wrightman@princeton.edu.

WIGHTMAN, LUDMILLA G. POPOVA, language educator, foreign educator, translator; b. Sofia, Bulgaria, Sept. 29, 1933; came to U.S., 1977; d. Genko Mateev and Liliana (Kusseva) Popov; m. Ivan Todorov Todorov, Aug. 13, 1957 (div. 1976); 1 child, Todor; m. Arthur Strong Wightman, Jan. 14, 1977. MS, U. Sofia, 1956. Cons. Nat. Libr., Sofia, 1956-58; rsch. assoc. Joint Inst. for Nuclear Rsch., Moscow, 1958-65; lectr. Russian Rutgers U., New Brunswick, N.J., 1969-70; editor Bulgarian Ency., Sofia, 1973-77; tchr. lang. Princeton (N.J.) Lang. Group, 1977—2001. Libr. Firestone Libr., Princeton U., 1983-87. Translator: Introduction to Axiomatic Field Theory, 1975, New Eng. Rev., Bread Loaf Quar., 1987, Mr. Cogito, 1989, N.Y. Rev. Books, 1990, Poetry East, 1990-91, Literary Rev., 1992, US1 Worksheets, 1992-2003, Visions International, 1993-2002, Partisan Rev., 1996, Shifting Borders: East European Poetries of the Eighties, 1993, Internat. Quarterly, 1999, Cry of a Former Dog, 2000, Forbidden Sea, 2000, Frost Flowers, 2001, Scars, 2002, Capriccio for a Goya, 2003, Memory of a Dream, 2003.. Avocations: bird watching, music, photography, travel. Home and Office: 16 Balsam Ln Princeton NJ 08540-5327 Office Phone: 609-921-7779. E-mail: l.p.wightman@mac.com.

WIGINGTON, RONALD LEE, retired chemical information services executive; b. Topeka, May 11, 1932; s. Oscar and Virginia C. (Ritchie) W.; m. Margaret E. Willey, Aug. 17, 1951; children: Linda (dec.), Carol, David, Brian. BS in Engring. Physics, U. Kans., 1953; MEE, U. Md., 1959; PhD in Elec. Engring., U. Kans., 1964; postgrad., Harvard Bus. Sch., 1976-77. Tech. staff Bell Telephone Labs., Murray Hill, N.J., 1953-54; divsn. chief Dept. Def., Washington, 1956-68; dir. R & D Chem. Abstracts Svc., Am. Chem. Soc., Columbus, Ohio, 1968-84; dir. Washington ops. Am. Chem. Soc., 1984-86; CEO, dir. Chem. Abstracts Svc., Am. Chem. Soc., Columbus, 1986-91; dir. info. tech. Am. Chem. Soc., Columbus, 1991-94. Chmn. bd. Online Computer Libr. Ctr., Dublin, Ohio, 1985-87, trustee, 1978-92; lectr. Am. U., Washington, 1967-68; adj. assoc. prof. Ohio State U., 2969-78. Contbr. chpts. to books; contbr. articles to profl. jours. Pres., various positions PTA Prince George's County, Md., 1966-68; moderator, treas. Cmty. Assn. Upper Arlington (Ohio) Schs., 1970-74; mem. Upper Arlington Civic Orch., 1970-84, pres., 1973-76; bd. dirs. Ohio Ctr. of Sci. and Industry, 1988-93; trustee Health Coalition of Ctrl. Ohio, Columbus, 1991-99, treas., 1994-99, vice-chmn., 1996-99. With U.S. Army, 1954-56. Named Honor Man of U. Kans, 1953; named to, Topeka H.S. Hall of Fame, 2001; recipient Nat. Capital award, D.C. Coun. Engring. and Archtl. Socs., 1967, Meritorious Civilian Svc. award, Dept. Def., 1967; Summerfield scholar, U. Kans., 1949. Fellow: IEEE (sr.), Nat. Fedn. Abstracting and Info. Svcs. (hon.; exec. bd. 1986—94, treas. 1992—94, bd. dirs. 1987—94, 1979—84, pres. 1982—83); mem.: Material Property Data Network, Internat. Coun. Sci. and Tech. Info., Am. Chem. Soc., Sigma Xi. Avocations: gardening, music, genealogy. Home: 2470 Wimbledon Rd Columbus OH 43220-4212

WIGINTON, JAY SPENCER, sales executive; b. Lubbock, Tex., Sept. 21, 1941; s. Clarence Elbert and Faye (George) W.; m. Billye Kay Freitag, Nov. 28, 1968 (div. Feb. 1993); children: Lauren, Lindsay; m. Laverne Shook, June 18, 1993. BS, Tex. Tech. U., 1963, MS, 1968. Sales rep. West Tex. ter. Syntex Labs., Lubbock, 1968 70, regional sales rep., 1970-72, Far East regional mgr. Des Moines, 1972-73, dir. mtkg., 1973-74; regional sales mgr. Zoecon Corp., Dallas, 1974-76; nat. account mgr. Custom divsn., 1976-78; gen. mgr. V.A. Snell & Co. divsn. Gt. Plains Chem. Co., San Antonio, 1978-83, Southwest regional mgr., 1983-84, dir. field devel., 1984-85; dist. mgr. Agri-Sales Assocs., Inc., San Antonio, 1985-87; sales mgr. western region Allflex U.S.A., Inc., 1987-91; gen. mgr. Pro. Vet. S., 1991-93; equine sales specialist Merial Ltd., 1993—. With AUS, 1964-66, Vietnam. Mem. Tex. Grain and Feed Assn., Tex. Cattle Feeders Assn., Tex. Chem. Assn., Kappa Sigma. Mem. Christian Ch. (Disciples Of Christ).

WIGLESWORTH, MICHAEL BLAND, advertising executive; b. Balt., Apr. 13, 1949; s. Reginal A. and Janice (Peppler) W.; m. Barbara Atkinson, Aug. 5, 1972 (div. Apr. 1980); m. Shari Kulik, Dec. 7, 1997. BS, Va. Commonwealth U., 1975. Account exec. Richmond (Va.) Newspapers, 1973—75; v.p. mktg. Bunch & Laughon Advt., Richmond, 1975—76; pres. Collier & Wiglesworth, Inc., Richmond, 1976—80; v.p. account svcs. Brand Edmonds Bolio, Richmond, 1980—82; v.p. sales promotion Eisner & Assocs., Balt., 1983—85; dir. promotion J. Walter Thompson, L.A., 1985—87; mgmt. supr. Einson Freeman, Paramus, NJ, 1987—89; sr. v.p., mgmt. supr. SAI/Earle Palmer Brown Promotions, Phila., 1989—94; sr. v.p. acct. svc. Hadley, N.Y.C., 1994—96; ptnr. Allegis Mktg., 1996—2000; sr. v.p. acct. svcs. SAI Mktg., 1996—2000; v.p. promotional mktg. Marketsource, Cranbury, NJ, 2000—01; group dir., relationship mktg. Carlson Mktg. Group, Phila., 2001—03; sr. v.p. Mastermind Mktg., Phila., 2003—. Pres. M & W Ventures, Richmond, 1977-83; ptnr. Recreation Unltd., Inc., Richmond, 1979-80. Recipient best in Show award Am. Newspaper Assn., N.Y.C., 1979, Maxi award Direct Mail Assn., 1992, Reggie award Promotional Marketers Assn. Am., 1993, Pro award Coun. of Sales Promotion Agencies, 1994. Mem. Am. Advt. Fedn. (Retail Advt. award 1979), Am. Mktg. Assn. (Effie award 1980, Spire award 1992), Phi Kappa Sigma. Republican. Avocations: jogging, skiing, scuba diving, travel, music. Home: 520 Station Ave Glenside PA 19038-1419 Office: Mastermind Mktg 1450 W Peachtree St NW Atlanta GA 30309 E-mail: mike.wiglesworth@mastermindmarketing.com., mwiglesworth@comcast.net.

WIGLEY, MARK ANTONY, architecture educator; BArch, U. Auckland, New Zealand, 1979; PhD, 1987. Interim dean, prof. arch. Columbia U., 2003—04, dean Grad. Sch. of Architecture, Planning & Preservation, 2004—. Actor:; author: The Architecture of Deconstruction: Derrida's Haunt, 1993, White Walls, Designer Dresses: The Fashioning of Modern Architecture, 1995, The Architectural Cult of Synchronization, 2000, Network Fever, 2001; editor (with Catherine de Zegher): The Activist Drawing: Retracing Situationist Architectures from Constant's New Babylon to Beyond, 2001. Recipient Internat. Com. Archtl. Critics Triennial award for archtl. criticism, 1990; grantee, Graham Found., 1997; Resident fellow, Chgo. Inst. for Arch. and Urbanism, 1989. Office: Columbia Sch Architecture, Planning & Preservation 402 Avery MC 0358 2960 Broadway New York NY 10027-6902*

WIGMORE, BARRIE ATHERTON, investment banker; b. Moose Jaw, Sask, Canada, Apr. 11, 1941; came to U.S., 1970; s. Fred Henry and Pauline Elizabeth (Atherton) W.; m. Deedee Dawson, Aug. 24, 1964 BEd, U. Sask., Can., 1962, BA, 1963; MA, U. Oreg., 1964; BA, Oxford U., Eng., 1966, MA, 1971; LLD (hon.), U. Saskatchewan, 2002. Investment banker Goldman Sachs Group Inc., NYC, 1970—. Author: The Crash and Its Aftermath, A History of U.S. Securities Markets 1929-33, 1985, Securities Markets in the 1980s, 1997. Chmn. Am. Friends of Worcester Coll. (Oxford U.) Inc.; trustee Metropolitan Mus. Art. Hon. fellow Worcester Coll., Oxford. Avocations: financial history, golf. Home: 1 W 72nd St New York NY 10023-3486 Office: Goldman Sachs Inc 85 Broad St New York NY 10004-2456 Office Phone: 212-902-5272. Personal E-mail: barrie.wigmore@gs.com.

WIGMORE, JOHN GRANT, lawyer; b. L.A., Mar. 14, 1928; s. George Theodore and Mary (Grant) W.; m. Dina Burnaby, July 27, 1968 (dec. 1994); children: Alexander Trueblood, Adam Trueblood, John G. Jr., Mary. BS in Geology, Stanford U., 1949; JD, UCLA, 1958. Geologist Western Geophys., Calif., Colo., Mo., 1953-55; assoc. Lawler, Felix & Hall, L.A., 1958-62, ptnr., 1963-86, Pillsbury, Madison & Sutro, L.A., 1986-90; ret. Lectr. in field. Contbr. articles to profl. jours. Trustee L.A. County Mus. Natural History, 1970—; participant various local & state election campaigns, 1965-80. Officer USN, 1950-53. Fellow Am. Coll. Trial Lawyers, Am. Bar Found.; mem. ABA (chair litigation com. antitrust sect. 1970-74), Calif. State Bar (L.A. County bar del. 1965-75), L.A. County Bar Assn. (exec. com. trial sect. 1965-68), L.A. County Bus. Trial Lawyers (exec. com. 1984-87), Barristers (exec. com. 1960-65). Home: 870 Neptune Ave Encinitas CA 92024-2062

WIGSTON, DAVID LAWRENCE, biologist, dean; b. London, Dec. 12, 1943; came to U.S., 1993; s. Frederic Roland Wigston and Joan Mavin; m. Patricia Anne Werner, May 25, 1991; 1 child, Alexa Joan Dobinson. BSc with 1st class honors, U. Exeter, Eng., 1965; PhD in Forest Ecology, U. Exeter, 1972. Lectr. in biology Exeter Coll., 1967-69; sr. lectr. biology Coventry (Eng.) U., 1970-74; reader environ. sci. Plymouth (Eng.) U., 1974-82; prof., chair dept. forestry Papua New Guinea U. Tech., Lae, 1982-86; prof. environ. sci. No. Territory U., Darwin, Australia, 1986-93, dean faculty of sci., 1986-92; rsch. prof. U. Fla., Gainesville, 1993-96; rsch. assoc. dean U. Mich., Flint, 1996—. Vis. fellow St. Cross Coll. Oxford (Eng.) U., 1980; cons. Swedish Biomass Energy Program, 1981-82; chief wildlife scientist No. Territory (Australia) Govt., 1992-93. Narrator (symphonic works) Peter & The Wolf, Jungle Book, Hassan, 1961—. Cons. Internat. Convention Biodiversity, Australia, 1992-93; pres., bd. dirs. Gainesville Symphony Orch., 1994-96. Fellow Australian Inst. Biology (sec. No. Territory br. 1987-93); mem. Ecol. Soc. Am., Soc. Human Ecology, Soc. Econ. Botany. Avocations: music, theater, art, literature. Office: U Mich 303 Kearsley St Flint MI 48502

WIGTON, CHESTER MAHLON, family physician; b. Pueblo, Colo., Jan. 12, 1928; s. Washington Irving and Bessie Marie (Ramsey) W.; m. Marjorie Chanak, Aug. 29, 1953 (dec. Jan. 1981); children: Robin, Renee, Kent, Lance, Bruce, Scott; m. Anita Kay Nelson, July 4, 1993; children: Sallie Michelle Short, Sadie Kay Short. BS cum laude, Colo. Coll., 1950; MD, U. Colo., Denver, 1954. Diplomate Am. Bd. Family Practice. Intern Swedish Hosp., Seattle, 1954-55; pvt. practice family medicine, Durango, Colo., 1957—; emeritus active Med. Mercy Hosp., Durango, 1990—, v.p. staff, 1970-73. Med. dir. Hacienda Nursing Home, Bloomfield, N.Mex., 1992-95. Pres. CAMP Inc., Durango, 1970, CEOW Inc., Durango, 1964; treas. Tamarron Owners Assn. Bd., Durango, 1986-95; sec. Durango Sch. Bd., 1969-73; dir. San Juan Devel., Durango, 1971. Lt. (j.g.) USPHS, 1955-57; sec. Cmty. Hosp. Bd., Durango, 1986-92. Fellow Am. Acad. Family Practice; mem. Durango C. of C. (pres. 1965-66), Durango Rotary Club (pres. 1968), Electra Lake Sporting Club (pres. 1982-85), Delta Epsilon, Sigma Nu, Nu Sigma Nu. Republican. Presbyterian. Avocations: skiing, tennis, golf, fishing, hunting. Home: 151 Riverview Dr Durango CO 81301-4349 Office: 3575 Main Ave Durango CO 81301-4028 Office Phone: 970-247-3513.

WIJNBERG, SANDRA S. professional services company executive; BA English, UCLA; MBA, U. So. Calif., L.A. With Morgan Stanley & Co. Inc.; joined PepsiCo as v.p., treas., 1994; sr. v.p., CFO KFC Corp. Divsn.; sr. v.p., treas. Tricon Global Restaurants Inc, 1997—2000; sr. v.p., CFO Marsh & McLennan Cos., N.Y.C., 2000—. Bd. dirs. Pvt. Sector Coun., 2001—, Tyco Internat. Ltd., 2003—. Corp. adv. bd. N.Y.C. Ballet. Office: Marsh & McLennan Co 1166 6th Ave New York NY 10036*

WIKE, D. ELAINE, small business owner; b. Ridgecrest, Calif., Sept. 26, 1954; d. Robert G. and Jimmie Mae (Sallee) Field; m. Mike Wike, Oct. 14, 1978; children: Mike II, Angelina Elaine, William V., Danielle Elizabeth, Edward Lawrence, Windy Gale. Student, U. Houston, 1975—77. Legal sec. Morgan, Lewis & Bockius, Washington, 1977—78; legal asst. Alfred C. Schlosser & Co., Houston, 1972—77, 1978—81, Jerry Sadler, atty., Houston, 1982—83; founder, owner DEW Profl. & Bus. Svcs., Houston, 1979—; office mgr. Law Offices Mike Wike, Houston, 1983—. Contbr. poetry to publs. including Internat. Libr. of Poetry, 2001. Treas. Wilhelm Schole Parents Orgn, 1981—82, mem. Free, Inc.; vol. campaign worker Ron Paul for Congress and Reagan for Pres., 1975, 1976. Recipient 3d place, Nassau Bay Tex. Christmas Boat Lane Parade First Ann. Photography Contest, 1990. Mem.: Nat. Paralegal Assn., Am. Soc. Notaries, Nat. Assn. Female Execs., Nat. Notary Assn., Young Ams. for Freedom. Republican. Libertarian. Mem. Christian Ch. Office: 2421 S Wayside Dr Houston TX 77023-5318

WIKMAN, MICHAEL RAYMOND, advertising executive; b. Mpls., Dec. 28, 1950; s. Charles Pierce and Jeanne Elizabeth W.; m. Carrie Brandt, Feb. 7, 1981; children: Caroline Celeste, Charles Michael. B in Elected Studies, U. Minn., 1973. Analyst, supr. media services Cambell-Mithun Advt., Mpls., 1973-77, account mgr., 1977-80; pres. MWA Direct, Mpls., 1980—. Mem. Direct Mktg. Assn. (Echo award 1987), Midwest Direct Mktg. Assn. (Art, Response and Copy award 1987). Avocations: art collecting, downhill skiing, tennis, sailing. Home: 6929 Mark Terrace Cir Minneapolis MN 55439-1622 Office: MN Painting & Decorating Apprentices 5775 Wayzata Blvd #680 Saint Louis Park MN 55416-2649

WIKTOROWICZ, ANDREW CHARLES, engineer; b. Valevade, India, Nov. 25, 1945; came to U.S., 1951; s. Janusz Stanislaus and Kristina (Dziedzic) W.; m. Karen Wolff, Aug. 15, 1993; children by previous marriage: Tanya, Daniel, Dustin. BS in Physics, Ill. Inst. Tech., 1967. Instrument physicist CPC Internat., Argo, Ill., 1967-70; project engr. Fluor Corp., Irvine, Calif., 1970-73; engring. group leader Bechtel Power Corp., Norwalk, Calif., 1973-74; engr. chief controls Ameron Process Systems Div., Santa Ana, Calif., 1974-76; v.p. J.P.W. Industries, Orange, Calif., 1976-78; pres. Automated Dynamics Corp., Laguna Hills, Calif., 1978-85; v.p. Nova Power, Inc., Santa Ana, 1985-89; pres. Unigen Corp., Thousand Oaks, Calif., 1990—; exec. dir. Western Coun. of Constrn. Consumers, Torrance, Calif., 1995—; pres. Electronic Resource Ctr., Thousand Oaks, Calif., 1997—. Bd. dirs. Unigen, Mission Viejo, Calif., 1987—; prof. engring. Calif. Dept. Consumer Affairs, Sacramento, 1975, 78. Co-author: Instrument Engineers' Handbook-Programmable Controllers, 1985; contbr. articles to profl. jours. Expert examiner control systems Calif. Dept. Consumer Affairs-Bd. Profl. Engring., Sacramento, 1976—; trustee welfare fund Internat. Brotherhood of Electrical Workers, Orange, 1976-80. Undergrad. research grantee NSF, Washington, 1966. Mem. Instrument Soc. Am. Internat. (v.p. 1981-83, bd. dirs. 1981-83, fin. com. 1983—, dir. publs., 1983—, long-range planning com. 1988—), Orange County Instrument Soc. Am., Western Coun. Constrn. Consumers (program com. 1987, exec. dir. 1995—), Am. Soc. Engrs. and Architects (pres. 2003—). Republican. Roman Catholic. Avocations: racquetball, horseback riding, golf, tennis, chess. Home and Office: Unigen 1941 Coventry Ct Thousand Oaks CA 91362-1810 Office Phone: 805-379-9777. E-mail: andy@wccc.org.

WILBANKS, JAN JOSEPH, retired philosopher; b. Lynchburg, Ohio, Dec. 17, 1928; s. James Odell and Bernice Elizabeth (Daugherty) W.; m. Alice Ramona Pacheco, Nov. 14, 1953; children— Elise, Anita, Jennifer. BS, Cin. Coll. Pharmacy, 1951; PhD in Philosophy, Ohio State U., 1964. Instr. philosophy Purdue U., 1961-64; mem. faculty Marietta (Ohio) Coll., 1964-89, prof. philosophy, 1973-89. Author: Hume's Theory of Imagination, 1968, also articles. With AUS, 1951-53. Home: 122 High St Marietta OH 45750-2636

WILBER, DAVID JAMES, cardiologist; b. Wis., Apr. 1, 1951; s. Howard Spencer and Leona (Von Reuden) W.; m. Sandra Irene Reynertson, June 28, 1992. BS, U. Wis., 1973; MD, Northwestern U., 1977. Intern medicine Northwestern Meml. Hosps., 1977-80; fellow cardiology U. Mich., 1982-84; fellow electrophysiology Mass. Gen. Hosp., Boston, 1984-86; asst. prof. medicine Loyola U., Maywood, Ill., 1986-90, assoc. prof. medicine, 1990—94; prof. medicine Loyola U. Med. Ctr., Maywood, Ill., 2002—, dir. divsn. cardiology; prof. medicine U. Chgo., 1994—. Fellow Am. Coll. Cardiology, Am. Heart Assn. Office: Loyola U Chgo Divsn Cardiology 2160 S First Ave Maywood IL 60153-

WILBER, ROBERT EDWIN, trade association administrator; b. Boston, Dec. 15, 1932; s. Charles Edwin and Mary Charles (Gay) Wilber; m. Bonnie Marilyn Jones; children: Debra, Kathleen, Robert Jr., Thomas, Jeffrey, Mark, Matthew. BSBA in Acctg., Bowling Green State U., 1954. CPA, Mass., Tex. Sr. acct. Peat, Marwick, Mitchell and Co., Boston, 1954-58; gen. mgr. Door Controls Inc., Boston, 1958-59; asst. controller MKM Knitting Mills Inc., Manchester, N.H., 1959-63; internal audit supr. Raytheon Co., Lexington, Mass., 1963; asst. treas. Glens Falls (N.Y.) Ins. Co., 1963-66; controller Pnobscott Co., Boston, 1966-67; v.p. fin. and adminstrn. S.S. Pierce Co., Boston, 1967-73; v.p. Samson Ocean Systems Inc., Boston, 1973-78; v.p., chief acctg. officer Enserch Corp., Dallas, 1978-88; pres. Trade U.S.A., 1990—. Mem. AICPAs, Nat. Assn. Trade Exchanges, Mass. Soc. CPAs, Fin. Execs. Inst., BANC, Pres.'s Club (Bowling Green, Ohio). Home: 5804 Goliad Ave Dallas TX 75206-6818 Office: 5019 McKinney Ave Ste 110 Dallas TX 75205 Office Phone: 214-528-6626.

WILBER, ROGER ALAN, library supervisor, writer; b. Ravena, N.Y., Sept. 14, 1946; s. John Henry Wilber, Jr. and Sarah Frances (Krom) Wilber; m. Cyndy Michele Borowski, July 21, 1969; children: Roger Alan Wilber, Jr., Ami Leah Mosher. Diploma, A.P. Bible Sch., 1975, Moody Bible Inst. Corr. Sch., 1975; tchg. cert., Albany Bible Inst., 1978—79. Cert. C.P.R. Instr. ARC, 1982. Supr. libr. clk. III N.Y.S. Edn. Dept., Albany, 1981—. Deacon Apostolic Pentecostal Ch., Glenmont, NY, 1976—77; head deacon U.C.C. Ch., Ravena, NY, 1991—92; co-sec., treas. Capital Dist. Friends of Jung, Albany, 1994—96; facilitator Parallel Orgn. N.Y.S. Libr., Albany, 2000—; N.Y.S. libr. rep. Collections Stewardship Team Cultural Edn. Ctr., Albany, 2000—, floor marshal for Tenant Safety Orgn., 2001—. Author: (historical book) Teacher, Soldier, Doctor - The Life of John H. Wilber, M.D. (Copyrighted, 2003), William W. Wilber & the 113th Regiment - N.Y. Volunteers - 7th Heavy Artillery, NY in the Civil War (Copyright, 2004), Call To Duty - The Town of Coeymans in The Civil War (Copyright, 2004); editl. bd. and contbg. author: newsletter NYS Library Staff Information Bulletin, 1997—2000, NYS Library Information Bulletin, 2000—; contbg. author Schoharie County Hist. Review, 2003, (mag.) Boom Mag., 2004. Book repair instr. Ravena Free Libr., NY, 1992—92; adult bible study tchr. Ravena, Glenmont, & Albany, NY, 1970—2004. CTA 2 USN, 1966—68. Decorated Nat. Def. Svc. Medal U.S. Navy; recipient Commr. Richard P. Mills cert., N.Y.S. Edn. Dept., 2003, 30 Yrs, Svc. award, 2000, 25 Yrs. Svc. award, 1995, 20 Yrs. Svc. award, 1990. Mem.: editorial bd. NYS Library Info. Bulletin. Independent. Achievements include New York State Merit Awards in 1974, 1977, 1983, 1984. Avocations:

coin collecting/numismatics, paper clip collecting, writing, historical research, fishing. Home: 3 Jefferson Avenue Ravena NY 12143-1120 Office: New York State Rsch Libr Cultural Education Center Albany NY 12230

WILBUR, BARBARA MARIE, elementary school educator; b. Homer City, Pa., Dec. 1, 1945; d. Nicholas and Ann (Bender) Hrebik; m. Samuel Scime, Nov. 21, 1970 (div. Jan. 1974); m. Frederick Layton Wilbur, June 21, 1986 (dec. June 1989). BS in Elem. Edn., SUNY, Buffalo, 1967, EdM in Guidance Counseling, 1971; postgrad., Harvard U., 1969; grad., John Robert Powers Modeling Sch., Buffalo, 1974. Cert. permanent elem. sch. tchr., N.Y. Elem. tchr. Buffalo Pub. Schs., 1967-70, 94—, Diocese of Ft. Lauderdale, Fla., 1971-72, Diocese of Buffalo, 1973-94. Mem. Internat. Platform Assn., State U. Buffalo Alumni Assn., State U. Coll. Buffalo Alumni Assn. (Outstanding Svc. award 1982), Buffalo State Coll. Alumni Assn. (bd. dirs. 1980-87, active various coms.). Republican. Roman Catholic. Avocations: modeling, volleyball, ice skating, tennis. Home: 20 Schimwood Ct Amherst NY 14068 Office: Buffalo Pub Schs Sch # 11 100 Poplar Ave Buffalo NY 14211

WILBUR, COLBURN SLOAN, foundation consultant and trustee, former executive; b. Palo Alto, Calif., Jan. 20, 1935; s. Blake Colburn and Mary (Sloan) W.; m. Maria Grace Verburg, Sept. 1, 1961; children: Marguerite Louise, Anne Noelle. BA in Polit. Sci., Stanford U., 1956, MBA, 1960. Asst. cashier United Calif. Bank, San Francisco, 1960-65; v.p. Standata, San Francisco, 1965-68; adminstrv. mgr. Tab Products, San Francisco, 1968-69; exec. dir. Sierra Club Found., San Francisco, 1969-76, David and Lucile Packard Found., Los Altos, Calif., 1976—. Bd. dirs. Colo. Coll., Colorado Springs; sr. fellow Coun. on Founds., Washington. Bd. dirs. Philanthropic Ventures Found.; former bd. dirs., mem. adv bd. Global Fund Women, Palo Alto, Calif.; past bd. dirs. Big Bros. San Francisco, Calif. Confederation Arts, Peninsula Grantmakers, Women's Fund Santa Clara; former bd. dirs., pres. Big Bros. Peninsula, North Fork Assn., Peninsula Conservation Ctr.; past bd. dirs., chmn. No. Calif. Grantmakers; bd. dirs., mem. adv. bd. Sierra Club Found., Stanford Theater Found., Palo Alto, U. San Francisco/Inst. Nonprofit Orgn. Mgmt. With U.S. Army, 1957-58. Mem. Commonwealth Club (bd. advisors). Office: David & Lucile Packard Found 300 2nd St Los Altos CA 94022-3694 E-mail: c.wilbur@packfound.org.

WILBUR, E. PACKER, investment company executive; b. Bridgeport, Conn., Sept. 9, 1936; s. E. Packer and Elizabeth (Wells) Wilbur; m. Laura Mary Ferrier, Sept. 17, 1965; children: Alison Mary Thompson, Andrew Packer, Gillian Elizabeth Stratmann. BA, Yale U., 1959; MBA, Harvard U., 1965. Cons. McKinsey & Co. Inc., N.Y.C., 1964-67; dir. corp. planning Am. Express Co., N.Y.C., 1967-69; v.p. Van Alstyne Noel & Co., N.Y.C., 1969-70; exec. v.p., dir., mem. exec. com. Newburger Loeb & Co. Inc., N.Y.C., 1970-73; pres. E. P. Wilbur & Co., Inc., Southport, Conn., 1973—, Southport Fin. Corp., 1986—. Chmn. bd. dirs. Criterion Mgmt., Inc., Trend Mgmt., Inc., Fairfield Advisors, Inc., EPW Securities, Inc.; gen. ptnr. Grandland Realty Assocs., Embankment Properties Ltd., London, Autumn Woods Assocs., others; former allied mem. N.Y. Stock Exch., N.Y.C. Contbr. articles to fin. jours. Bd. dirs. Mus. Art, Sci., Industry, Bridgeport, Wakeman Meml. Boys/Girls Club, Southport, Greater Bridgeport Jr. Hockey League, Pequot Libr., Southport, Northfield-Mt. Hermon Sch.; mem. dean's coun. John F. Kennedy Sch. Govt., Harvard U. With U.S. Army, 1959—60. Mem.: Yale Club (N.Y.C.), Country Club Fairfield, Pequot Running Club (Southport) (chmn.), Pequot Yacht Club (Southport). Office: 2507 Post Rd Southport CT 06890-1259 Home: PO Box 669 Southport CT 06890

WILBUR, KATHLEEN, state agency administrator; m. Tom Wilbur; children: Thomas, William, Samuel, Raymond. BA, Mich. State U. Chief staff State Senator William Sederburg, Lansing, 1983-90; dir. Mich. Dept. Licensing, Regulation, Lansing, 1991, Mich. Dept. Occupational Profl. Regulation, Lansing, 1991-95; deputy dir. Mich. Dept. Commerce, Lansing, 1991-95, acting dir., 1995-96, dir., 1996, Mich. Dept. Consumer Industry Svcs., Lansing, 1996—. Chmn. MERRA Bd. Trustees, 1996—; mem. Mich. Investment Advisory Com, 1996—; bd. dirs. Mich. State Housing Authority, Mich. Municipal Bond Authority, Mich. State Fair, Women's Caring Program, Mich. Festival. Mem. Mich. State U. Alumni Assn., East Lansing Area Zonta Club. Office: Michigan Dept Consumer & Industry Services PO Box 30004 Lansing MI 48909-7504

WILBUR, RICHARD PURDY, writer, educator; b. NYC, Mar. 1, 1921; s. Lawrence L. and Helen (Purdy) W.; m. Mary Charlotte Hayes Ward, June 20, 1942; children: Ellen Dickinson, Christopher Hayes, Nathan Lord, Aaron Hammond. AB, Amherst Coll., 1942, AM, 1952, DLitt (hon.), 1967; AM, Harvard U., 1947; LHD (hon.), Lawrence Coll., Washington U., Williams Coll., U. Rochester, SUNY, Potsdam, 1986, Skidmore Coll., 1987, U. Lowell, 1990; LHD (hon.), Mass. Coll. Liberal Arts, 2002; DLitt (hon.), Clark U., Am. Internat. Coll., Marquette U., Wesleyan U., Carnegie-Mellon U.; DLitt. (hon.), Lake Forest Coll., 1982, Smith Coll., 1996, Sewanee U., 1996; DD (hon.), St. Mary's Sem. and U., 2001. Jr. fellow Harvard U., Cambridge, Mass., 1947-50, Asst. prof. English, 1950-54; assoc. prof. Wellesley Coll., 1955-57; prof. Wesleyan U., 1957-77; writer in residence Smith Coll., 1977-86. Author: The Beautiful Changes, 1947, Ceremony, 1950, A Bestiary, 1955, reprint, 1993, Things of This World, 1956, Poems 1943-56, 1957, Advice to a Prophet, 1961, Poems of Richard Wilbur, 1963, Walking to Sleep, 1969, The Mind-Reader, 1976, Seven Poems, 1981, The Whale, 1982, New and Collected Poems, 1988 (Pulitzer prize for poetry, 1989), Bone Key and Other Poems, 1998, Mayflies: New Poems and Translations, 2000, Collected Poems 1943-2004, 2004, (children's books) Loudmouse, 1963, Opposites, 1973, More Opposites, 1991, A Game of Catch, 1994, Runaway Opposites, 1995, The Disappearing Alphabet, 1998, Opposites, More Opposites and Some Differences, 2000, The Pig in the Spigot, 2000, (criticism) Responses, 1976, expanded edit., 2000, (prose pieces) The Catbird's Song, 1997; co-author (with Lillian Hellman): (comic opera) Candide, 1957; co-author: (with William Schuman) (cantata) On Freedom's Ground, 1986; translator (Moliere): The Misanthrope, 1955, Tartuffe, 1963 (co-recipient Bollingen Translation prize, 1963), The School for Wives, 1971, The Learned Ladies, 1978, Four Comedies, 1982; translator: (Racine) Andromache, 1982, Phaedra, 1986, The Suitors, 2001; translator: Moliere's The School for Husbands, 1992, Imaginary Cuckold, 1993, Molière's Amphitryon, 1995, Don Juan, 1998, Molière's The Bungler, 2000; editor: Complete Poems of Poe, 1959, Poems of Shakespeare, 1966, Selected Poems of Witter Bynner, 1978, Edgar Allen Poe: Peoms and Poetics, 2003. Decorated chevalier Ordre des Palmes Academiques; recipient Harriet Monroe prize Poetry mag., 1948, Oscar Blumenthal prize, 1950, Prix de Rome, Am. Acad. Arts and Letters, 1954, Edna St. Vincent Millay Meml. award, 1957, Nat. Book award, 1957, Pulitzer prize, 1957, Sarah Josepha Hale award, 1968, Bollingen prize, 1971, Brandeis U. Creative Arts award, 1971, Prix Henri Desfeuilles, 1971, Shelley Meml. award, 1973, Harriet Monroe Poetry award, 1978, St. Botolph's Club Found. award, 1983, Drama Desk award, 1983, Aiken-Taylor award, 1988, Bunn award, 1988, Washington Coll. Lit. award, 1988, St. Louis Lit. award, 1989, Grand Master award Birmingham-So. Coll., 1989, Gold Medal for Poetry, Am. Acad. Inst. Arts and Letters, 1991, Edward MacDowell medal, 1992, Nat. Arts Club Medal of Honor for Lit., 1994, PEN/Manheim Medal for Translation, 1994, Milton Ctr. prize, 1995, Acad. Am. Achievement award, 1995, Robert Frost medal Poetry Soc. of Am., 1996, T.S. Eliot award, 1996, Wallace Stevens award, 2003; Guggenheim fellow, 1952-53, 63, Ford fellow, 1960-61, Camargo Found. fellow, 1985; named U.S. Poet Laureate, Libr. Congress, 1987, Nat. Medal of the Arts, 1994; named to Theater Hall of Fame, 2003. Fellow: MLA (hon.); mem.: PEN (Transl. award 1983), ASCAP, AAAL (pres. 1974—76, chancellor 1976—78, 1980—81), Dramatists Guild, Acad. Am. Poets (chancellor emeritus), Am. Acad. Arts and Scis. Home: 87 Dodwells Rd Cummington MA 01026-9705 also: 715R Windsor Ln Key West FL 33040

WILBUR, RICHARD SLOAN, physician, executive; b. Boston, Apr. 8, 1924; s. Blake Colburn and Mary Caldwell (Sloan) Wilbur; m. Betty Lou Fannin, Jan. 20, 1951; children: Andrew, Peter, Thomas. BA, Stanford U., 1943, MD, 1946; JD, John Marshall, 1990. Intern San Francisco County Hosp., 1946—47; resident Stanford Hosp., 1949—51, U. Pa. Hosp., 1951—52; postgrad. tng. U. Mich. Hosp., 1957, Karolinska Sjukhuset, Stockholm, 1960; staff Palo Alto (Calif.) Med. Clinic, 1952—69; dep. exec. v.p. AMA, Chgo., 1969—71, 1973—74; asst. sec. for health and environment dept. def., 1971—73; sr. v.p. Baxter Labs., Inc., Deerfield, Ill., 1974—76; exec. v.p. Council Med. Splty. Socs., 1976—91, sec. accreditation coun. for continuing med. edn., 1979—91; assoc. prof. medicine Georgetown U. Med. Sch., 1971—77, Stanford Med. Sch., 1952—69; pres. Nat. Resident Matching Plan, 1991—92. Chmn. bd., CEO Inst. for Clin. Info., 1994—99; sr. v.p. healthcare Buckeye Corp. Pte. Ltd., Singapore, 1997—2000; CEO Medic Alert, 1992—94; pres. Am. Bd. Med. Mgmt., 1992; mem. Am. Bd. Electrodiagnostic Medicine, 1993—98; chmn. med. adv. bd. Med. City, Bangalore, India, 1997—2000; bd. vis. Drew U. Postgrad. Med. Sch. Contbr. articles to profl. jours. Bd. govs. ARC; chmn. Mid-Am. Blood Svcs. Bd., Lifesource Blood Bank, 1996—98; Vice-chmn. Rep. Cen. Com. Santa Clara County, Calif., 1966—89; bd. dirs. Nat. Adv. Cancer Coun., Nat. Health Coun., 1993—95; chmn. bd. dirs. Medic Alert Found.; chmn. bd. Calif. Med. Assn., 1968—69, Calif. Blue Shield, 1966—68, Am. Medico-Legal Found., 1987—; pres. Royal Soc. Medicine Found., 1998—. With USNR, 1942—49. Recipient Disting. Svc. medal, Dept. Def., 1973, Scroll of merit, Nat. Med. Assn., 1971. Fellow: ACP, Am. Coll. Physician Execs. (bd. regents 1985—89, pres.-elect 1987, pres. 1988—89), Am. Coll. Legal Medicine (treas. 2004—), Internat. Coll. Dentistry (hon.); mem.: Am. Soc. Internal Medicine, Am. Gastroent. Assn., Santa Clara County Med. Soc. (hon.), Lake County Med. Soc., Ill. Med. Assn., Inst. Medicine, Union League Phila., Cedars Club, Pacific Interurban Clin. Club, Alpha Omega Alpha, Phi Beta Kappa. Home: 985 Hawthorne Pl Lake Forest IL 60045-2217 Office: APT Management Inc 207 E Westminster Rd # 201 Lake Forest IL 60045-1881 E-mail: aptmgmnt@aol.com.

WILBURN, JOHN, editor; B in Govt., Coll. William and Mary; M in History, George Mason U. Fact checker Reader's Digest; joined Houston City Mag., 1979; founder San Antonio Light's Viva Mag., 1983; editor Dallas Morning News' Sunday mag. Dallas Life, 1985, Houston Press, 1989—93; assoc. prodr. David Frost's PBS TV Interview Program, 1993—97; exec. prodr. The Houston Sidewalk website, 1997—2000; news and ops. mgr. KHOU-TV website, 2000—02; asst. mng. editor Houston Chronicle, 2002—03, interim mng. editor, 2003—04, mng. editor, 2004—. Office: Houston Chronicle 11430 Bissonnet St Houston TX 77099*

WILBURN, MARY NELSON, retired lawyer, translator, poet; b. Balt., Feb. 18, 1932; d. David Alfred and Phoebe Blanche (Novotny) Nelson; m. Adolph Yarbrough Wilburn, Mar. 5, 1957; children: Adolph II, Jason David. AB cum laude, Howard U., 1952; MA, U. Wis., 1955, JD, 1975; cert. in translation, Georgetown U., 1997. Bar: Wis. 1975, U.S. Supreme Ct. 1981. Commr. Nat. Coun. of Negro Women Commn. on Edn., 1986—2000; English lang. officer U.S Dept. of State, Washington, 1999—. Vol. One Ch. One Addict, 1995—, bd. dirs., 1997—; mem. bd. Office Employee Appeals, D.C., 1997—2001; vol. Black Revolutionary War Patriots' Found., 1998—; judge NAACP ACT-SO Competition, 1994—, Leadership Am., 1991—; bd. dirs. Remington Ctr. Endowment Inc., U. Wis. Law Sch.; mem. bd. edn. Cath. Archdiocese of Washington, 1995—2000. Mem. Internat. Fedn. Women Lawyers (exec. coun. 1996—), Internat. Fedn. Women Lawyers (mem. coun. 1996—, UN rep. 2000-02, internat. sec. 2002—), Am. Translators Assn, Links, Inc., Leadership Greater Washington (bd. dirs. 1992-94, v.p. 1995-96), Zonta Internat., Friends of Remington Ctr. Endowment, Law Sch., U. of Wis. (bd. dirs.).

WILCHER, LARRY K. lawyer; b. Lebanon, Ky., July 19, 1950; s. Dwain LaRue and Juanita (Tungate) W.; m. Mary Jo Hayden, Aug. 21, 1971; children: Emily Jane, Joseph Keith. BS in Pharmacy, St. Louis Coll. Pharmacy, 1973; JD, No. Ky. U., 1984; program of instrn. for lawyers, Harvard U., 1987, 91, 94. Dir. real estate SuperX Drugs Corp., Cin., 1975-84; dir. real estate, real estate counsel Dollar Gen. Corp., Goodlettsville, Tenn., 1984-85, gen. counsel, 1985—2002; dir. U.S. Bank, 1995—; pres. Nations Title Co., Inc., 1999—2002; ptnr. Wyatt, Tarrant & Combs, 2002—. Contbr. to book: Kentucky Business Organizations, 1989; presenter in field. Sec., dir. Scottsville-Allen County Indsl. Devel. Authority, Inc., 1991—, Scottsville-Allen County Leasing Corp., 1992—; dir. Leadership Ky., 1994—2000, mem. exec. com., 1997—2000; dir. Bowling Green-We. Ky. U. Symphony Orch., 1998—2000; mem. internat. bus. adv. coun. Gordon Ford Coll.; chmn. Warren County Young Reps, Bowling Green, Ky., 1979, Scottsville-Allen County Planning Commn., 1997—. Named to Hon. Order Ky. Cols., 1968, One of Outstanding Young Men of Am., U.S. Jaycees, 1978; recipient Johnson & Johnson award St. Louis Coll. Pharmacy, 1973, Thurston B. Morton Leadership award Ky. Young Rep. Fedn., 1979. Mem. ABA, Nat. Assn. Corp. Dirs., Ky. Bar Assn. (recognition award 1987), Def. Rsch. Inst. Republican. Baptist. Office: Wyatt Tarrant & Combs LLP 918 State St Bowling Green KY 42101 Office Phone: 270-842-1050. E-mail: lwilcher@wyattfirm.com.

WILCHINS, HOWARD MARTIN, lawyer; b. Paterson, N.J., Mar. 6, 1945; s. Philip Aaron and Esther (Blake) Wilchins; m. Margaret Mandon, Sept. 6, 1970 (dec. July 2001); children: Julie, Daniel. AB, Mich. State U., 1966; JD, U. Chgo., 1969. Bar: D.C. 1969, U.S. Supreme Ct. 1975. Trial atty. FPC, Washington, 1969-70; spl. asst. to N.Y. Public Service Commn., Albany, 1970-72; dep. sect. chief AEC, Washington, 1972-75; dep. gen. counsel-litigation U.S. Ry. Assn., Washington, 1975-81, gen. counsel, 1981-84; dep. chief enforcement div. FCC Common Carrier Bur., Washington, 1984-90; v.p. Arnold S. Tesh Advisors, Washington, 1990-92; sr. litigation atty. Office Nuclear Safety Enforcement, U.S. Dept. Energy, Washington, 1992—. Mem. faculty Trial Practice Inst., U.S. CSC, 1977-79 Bd. dirs. United Jewish Appeal Greater Washington, 1984-90, 92-96; bd. dirs. Charles E. Smith Jewish Day Sch., 1983—, v.p., 1986-88, pres., 1988-90; mem. Hillel of Greater Washington, 1990—, v.p., 1992-94, pres., 1994-96; bd. dirs., mem. Capital Camps, 1990-96; bd. dir. Jewish Edn. Svc. N.Am., 1996—, asst. treas., 2000-03, treas., 2004—; bd. dirs. Tikvat Israel Congregation, Rockville, Md., 2000—. Mem. ABA, D.C. Bar Assn., Fed. Bar Assn. (co-chmn. com. on arbitration and mediation 1991-94), Am. Arbitration Assn. Home: 10308 Snowpine Way Potomac MD 20854-3940 Office: US Dept Energy Office Nuclear Safety Enforc Washington DC 20585-0001 E-mail: howard.wilchins@hq.doe.gov.

WILCHINS, SIDNEY A. gynecologist; b. Paterson, NJ, Feb. 2, 1940; s. Philip Aaron and Esther (Blake) W.; m. Carole Diane Brill, June 23, 1963, (div. Mar. 1985); children: Joan Helen, Edward Victor; m. Estelle Angel, Mar. 15, 1985; children: Jacqueline, Susan. BA in Biol. Scis., Rutgers U., 1961; MD, Georgetown U., 1965. Diplomate Am. Bd. Ob Gyn. Clin. instr. N.J. Med. Sch., Newark, 1971—73, clin. asst. prof., 1973—78, clin. assoc. prof., 1978—; med. dir. Cryosurgical Sys., 1999—. Adj. rsch. prof. NJ Inst. Tech., Newark, 1978—; assoc. dir. Pilgrim Med. Ctr., Montclair, NJ, 1982-93; med. dir. Ultrasound Diagnostic Sch., Union, NJ, 1989-91, NJ Menopause Found., 1992-98, Gynchoices Cen. Jersey, 1994—; gynecol. cons. Organon/Akzo, 1991—; program dir. ob-gyn. Phila. Coll. Trinitas Hosp., Elizabeth, NJ. Author, editor: Cryosurgery and Medicine, 1990; contbr. articles to profl. jours. Pres. Soc. Forensic Obstetricians & Gynecologists, 1994-96. Lt. USNR, 1965-69. Fellow ACOG, ACS, N.Y. Acad. Medicine; mem. ATLA, N.Y. Acad. Scis., Forensic Soc. Ob-Gyn. (pres. 1994-95), Peer Rev. Orgn. N.J., Colonia Country Club. Achievements include patent pending on Intraperitoneal Hyperthermia Device, pregnancy conducto for labor software copyright; application of chaost level to analysis of labor physiology. Home: 154 Devon Rd Colonia NJ 07067-3205 Office: 240 Williamson St Ste 503 Elizabeth NJ 07207 Office Phone: 908-354-5995. E-mail: guynee@aol.com.

WILCOX, ADAM BENJAMIN, medical researcher, educator; s. Blaine Hawkes and MarJean Clark Wilcox; m. Amy Susanne Hawkins, Nov. 6, 1993; children: Gregory Blaine, Matthew Hudson. PhD, Columbia U., NY, 1995—2000. Rsch. asst. U. Utah, Salt Lake City, 1993—95; asst. prof. U. Utah, 2001—; rsch. scientist Columbia U., New York, 2000—01; med. informaticist Intermountain Health Care, 2001—; interpreter FBI, 2003—04. Grant reviewer Nat. Libr. Medicine, Bethesda, Md., 2003—03. Contbr. scientific papers (First Prize, Student Paper Competition, AMIA, 2000, Richard P Covert Grad. Scholarship, 2000). Recipient Outstanding Physics Student, Soc. Physics Students, 1995; fellow Tng. Fellowship, Nat. Libr. Medicine, 1998-2000; grantee John A. Hartford Foundation grant. Mem.: Am. Med. Informatics Assn. Lds. Avocation: running. Office: Intermountain Health Care 4646 W Lake Park Blvd Salt Lake City UT 84120

WILCOX, BENSON REID, cardiothoracic surgeon, educator; b. Charlotte, NC, May 26, 1932; s. James Simpson and Louisa (Reid) W.; m. Lucinda Holderness, July 25, 1959 (div. June 2003); children: Adelaide, Alexandra, Melissa, Reid. BA, U. N.C., 1953, MD, 1957. Diplomate Am. Bd. Surgery, Am. Bd. Thoracic Surgery (chmn. 1991-93). Resident Barnes Hosp., St. Louis, 1958-59, N.C. Meml. Hosp., Chapel Hill, 1959-60, 62-64; clin. assoc. Nat. Heart Inst., Bethesda, Md., 1960-62; instr. U. N.C., Chapel Hill, 1963-65, asst. prof., 1965-68, assoc. prof., 1968-71, chief divsn. of cardiothoracic surgery, 1969-98, chief emeritus, 1998—, prof. of surgery, 1971—. Cons. NIH Grant Com., Bethesda, 1986—89; pres. Atlantic Coast Conf., Greensboro, NC, 1980—81; dir. Am. Bd. Thoracic Surgery, 1983—93, chmn., 1991—93; mem. coun. for grad. edn., 1993—; bd. dirs. Nat. Residency Matching Program, 1998—, pres., 2001—02, vice chmn. res. rev. com. for thoracic surgery, 2001—03, sec., treas., 2003—. Author (with others): Atlas of the Heart, 1988, Surgical Anatomy of the Heart, 1992, 3d edit., 2004; contbr. articles to profl. jours. Recipient Samaritan's Purse award, 1999; Markle scholar John and Mary Markle Found., 1967; recipient Hadassah Myrtle Wreath award, 1979, Disting. Alumnus award Darlington Sch., Rome, Ga., 1997. Mem.: ACS (mem. adv. coun. cardiothoracic surgery 1992—, chmn. 1998—2002), Grad. Med. Edn. (coun. 1993—), Womack Soc. (pres. 1991—93), Thoracic Surgery Dirs. Assn. (pres. 1985—87), So. Surg. Assn., Soc. Univ. Surgeons, Soc. Thoracic Surgeons (treas. 1980—86, pres. 1994—95), Am. Surg. Assn., Am. Assn. Thoracic Surgery, CTS Net Corp. (bd. dirs. 1999—). Democrat. Presbyterian. Avocations: medical history, golf, hiking. Office: U NC Med Sch Divsn Cardiothoracic Surgery 354 Wing C U NC Hosps CB 7065 Chapel Hill NC 27599-0001 Business E-Mail: benson@med.unc.edu.

WILCOX, BRIAN JAMES, military analyst; b. Corry, Pa., May 19, 1971; s. Shirley and Robert Wilcox. BS, Pa. State U., 1992—96. Ops. rsch. analyst/cost analyst US Army Tank-automotive and Armaments Command, Warren, Mich., 1997—99; mgmt. analyst US Army Material Command, Alexandria, Va., 1999—2000; ops. rsch. analyst US Army Force Mgmt. Support Agy., Ft. Belvoir, Va., 2000—03, U.S. Army G-I, Pentagon, 2003—. Mem.: INFORMS, Am. Soc. of Mil. Comptrollers, Mil. Ops. Rsch. Soc., Toastmasters Internat.

WILCOX, CHARLES JULIAN, geneticist, educator; b. Harrisburg, Pa., Mar. 28, 1930; s. Charles John and Gertrude May (Hill) W.; m. Eileen Louise Armstrong, Aug. 27, 1955; children: Marsha Lou, Douglas Edward. BS, U. Vt., 1950; MS, Rutgers U., 1955, PhD, 1959. Registered animal scientist. Dairy farm owner, operator, Charlotte, Vt., 1955-56; prof. U. Fla., Gainesville, 1959-95; prof. emeritus, 1995—. Cons. in internat. animal agrl. Gt. Britain, France, Sudan, Pakistan, Can., Mex., El Salvador, Ecuador, Brazil, Bolivia, Peru, Colombia, Venezuela, Dominican Republic, Saudi Arabia, Sweden, Norway. Mem. editl. bd.: Genetics and Molecular Biology, 1979—; editor: Large Dairy Herd Management, 1978, 1993; author (with others): Animal Agriculture, 1973, Animal Agriculture, 2d edit., 1980, Improvement of Milk Production in Tropics, 1990. 1st Lt. U.S. Army, 1951—53, Korea. Decorated Combat Infantry Badge; recipient award of merit jr. faculty, Gamma Sigma Delta, 1968, award of merit sr. faculty, 1984, Disting. Svc. award, Fla. Purebred Dairy Cattle Assn., 1986, Internat. award for Disting. Svc. for Agr., Gamma Sigma Delta, 1987, Sr. Rsch. Scientist award, Sigma Xi, 1994, 3 Korean Campaign medals. Mem.: Fla. Hostein Assn. (pres. 1979), Am. Registry Profls. Animal Sci. (examining bd. 1987—95), Am. Soc. Animal Sci., Am. Dairy Sci. Assn. (mem. editl. bd. 1999—), Fla. Guernsey Cattle Club. (pres. 1974—76), Fla. Jersey Cattle Club (bd. dir.). Republican. Avocations: spectator sports, baseball, football, basketball, tennis. Office: Univ Fla Animal Sci Dept Gainesville FL 32611-0920 E-mail: cjwgenetic@aol.com.

WILCOX, DAVID ERIC, electrical engineer, educational consultant; b. Cortland, NY, Sept. 4, 1939; s. James A. and Lucille (Fiske) C.; m. Phyllipa Ann Wilcox, Jan. 23, 1977; children: Terri L., Cinda A., Jana L. 0postgrad., Syracuse U., 1965; BSEE, U. Buffalo, 1961; 0postgrad., Marist Coll., Rutgers U.; MS, U. Bridgeport, 1977. Registered profl. engr., N.Y. Rsch. engring. mgr. input/output devices Rome (NY) Air Devel. Ctr., 1966—70; dir. sales Mercom Inc., Winsooki, Vt., 1970-73, dir., 1972—73; pres. Wilcox Tng. Sys., Newburgh, NY, 1973—98; pres., CEO Global Skills Exch., Alexandria, Va., 2003—. Exec. dep. dir., Nat. Skill Stds. Bd., 1998-2003, bd. dirs.; prin. Exec. Effectiveness, Inc., NYC; instr. Dale Carnegie courses. Author: Information System Sciences, 1965; contbr. articles to profl. jours.; patentee in field. Pres. N.Y. State Jaycees, 1972-73, chmn., 1973-74; dir. U.S. Jaycees, 1970-71; bd. dirs., v.p. N.Y. State Spl. Olympics, 1972-73; bd. dirs., treas. Family Counseling Svc., Inc.; mem. Orange County Pvt. Industry Coun., N.Y. State Excelsior Examiner, 1995. Lt. USAF, 1961-65. Mem. IEEE, Soc. Info. Display, N.Y. State Soc. Profl. Engrs., Internat. Transactional Analysis Assn., Internat. Platform Assn., Am. Soc. Quality Control. Methodist. Home: 528 Tobacco Quay Alexandria VA 22314 also: 30 W 60th St New York NY 10023-7902 Office: Global Skills Exch 1410 King St Alexandria VA 22314 Business E-Mail: dwilcox@gskillsxchange.com.

WILCOX, DIANE MARIE, educational psychologist, software designer; b. Cin., June 26, 1957; d. Herbert Arthur and Doris Ann Beard; m. Thomas Minshull Wilcox, Sept. 18, 1982; children: Alexandra Frances, Annika Marie. BBA in Bus. Mgmt., Coll. William and Mary, 1979; MA in Ednl. Psychology, U. N.C., 1994, PhD in Ednl. Psychology, 1997. Sales and tech. support corr. Tax Mgmt., Inc., Washington, 1980-82; dist. rep. Bur. Nat. Affairs, Inc., Washington, 1982-86; freelance computer graphic designer, editor Diane Wilcox & Assocs., San Rafael, Calif., 1986-91; instr. psychology King's Coll., Charlotte, N.C., 1995; pres. Mindforge, Inc., Burlington, N.C., 1996-98, Wilcox Instrnl. Media, LLC, Hillsborough, N.C., 1998—; instnl. design mgr. Autodesk, Inc., San Rafael, 2000—. Designer ednl. CD-ROM Mindforge Fractions, 1998. Cons. for gifted and talented programs River Mill Charter Sch., Saxapahaw, N.C., 1999-2000; vol. art instr. Grady Brown ELem. Sch., Hillsborough, N.C., 1997-98. Mem. APA, Am. Ednl. Rsch. Assn., Internat. Soc. for Performance Improvement. Avocations: art, music, dance. E-mail: drwilcox@wilcoxmedia.com.

WILCOX, GREGORY B. lawyer; b. Des Moines, Sept. 22, 1954; s. Lawrence R. and Mary T. Wilcox; m. Melinda S. Vande Lune, Sept. 4, 1976; children: Andrew, Austin, Morgan. BBA, U. Iowa, 1976; JD, Drake U., 1982. Bar: Iowa, 1982. V.p. Wilcox Enterprises, Inc., West Des Moines, Iowa, 1976-79; atty. Nyemaster Law Firm, Des Moines, 1982—, shareholder, dir., 1987—. Mem. bd. couns. Drake U. Law Sch., 1990-96, chair admissions com., 1992-93, exec. com., 1992-93. Assoc. articles editor Drake Law Sch., 1981-82; contbr. articles to profl. jours. Dir. Iowa State Chpt. March Dimes, Des Moines, 1993—; dir., sec. Iowa Sports Found., Des Moines, 1996—. Mem. ABA, Iowa State Bar Assn. (chair forms com. 1988-91, chair profl. corp. com. 1993-95), Polk County Bar Assn., Order of the Coif. Office: Nyemaster Law Firm 700 Walnut St Ste 1600 Des Moines IA 50309-3899

WILCOX, HARRY HAMMOND, retired medical educator; b. Canton, Ohio, May 31, 1918; s. Harry Hammond and Hattie Estelle (Richner) W.; m. D. June Freed., June 21, 1941; children: Joyce L. Wilcox Graff, Margaret J. (Mrs. Grayson S. Smith), James Hammond. BS, U. Mich., 1939, MS, 1940, PhD, 1948. Asso. prof. biology Morningside Coll., Sioux City, Iowa, 1947-48; asso. in anatomy U. Pa., 1948-52; mem. faculty U. Tenn. Center for Health Scis., 1952-83, Goodman prof. anatomy, 1966-83, emeritus prof. anatomy, 1983—. Assoc. editor: Anat. Record, 1968-83. Served with AUS, 1945-46. Mem.: AAAS, Soc. for Integrative and Comparative Biology, Am.Assn. Anatomists, Sigma Xi. Home: 1031 Marcia Rd Memphis TN 38117-5513

WILCOX, HARRY WILBUR, JR., retired corporate executive; b. Phila., Feb. 13, 1925; s. Harry Wilbur and Justine Elizabeth (Doolittle) W.; m. Colleen Ann Cerra, Apr. 6, 1946; children: Justine, Harry Wilbur III. BS, Yale U., 1949. With Gen. Electric Co., N.Y.C., 1949-50; mfg. supt. Sylvania Electric Products, 1951-67; v.p., gen. mgr. Granger Assocs. (electronics), Palo Alto, Calif., 1967-70; gen. mgr. ITT-Cannon Electric Co., Phoenix, 1970-72; pres. Hills McCanna Co., Carpentersville, Ill., 1972-75, VSI, and group v.p. IU Internat. Corp., 1975-78; exec. v.p. ITT-Grinnell, 1978-85; pres. ITT Indsl. and Constrn. Divsn., Lancaster, Pa., 1985-88. Dir. Meyer Industries, Nat. Temperature Control Centers, Paul N. Howard Co.; former chmn. VSI, VSI-UK. Patentee in electroluminescence. Mem. adv. com. Town of Sherborn,

Mass. Served with U.S. Army, 1943-46. Decorated Bronze star. Mem. Yale Club of Treasure Coast, Grand Harbor Golf and Beach Club (Vero Beach). Home: 1135 Harbor Links Cir Vero Beach FL 32967 also: 10310 Snowpine Way Potomac MD 20854 E-mail: harcon13@comcast.net.

WILCOX, HARVEY JOHN, lawyer; b. Elyria, Ohio, Nov. 1, 1937; s. Hubbard Clyde and Sylvia (Wahter) W.; m. Leslie Louise Coleman, Apr. 11, 1970. BA cum laude, Amherst Coll., 1959; LLB, Yale U., 1962. Bar: Ohio 1962, Va. 1994. Mem. firm Wilcox & Wilcox, 1962-78; with office gen. counsel Dept. Navy, Washington, 1966-94, asst. to gen. counsel, 1969-72, counsel Naval Air Systems Command, 1972-76, Navy dep. gen. counsel, 1976-94, cons. atty., arbitrator, 1994—. Guest lectr. U.S. Army Logistics Mgmt. Center; mem. Navy Contract Adjustment Bd., 1968-72 Designed Arlington County (Va.) flag, 1983. Bd. dirs. Navy Fed. Credit Union, 1974-77, sec.-treas., 1974-75, 2d v.p., 1975-77; mem. Def. Adv. Panel on Streamlining Acquisition Laws, 1991-92. Lt. USNR, 1963-66. Recipient Meritorious Exec. rank 1980, Disting Exec. rank, 1981, 89, Navy Disting. Civilian Svc. award, 1989, Defense Disting. Civilian Svc. award, 1994. Mem. Ohio Bar Assn., Va. State Bar, Charlottesville-Albemarle Bar Assn., Nat. Trust Hist. Preservation, Nature Conservancy, Piedmont Environ. Coun. Home: PO Box 338 Turner Mountain Rd Ivy VA 22945-0338 E-mail: wilcox@ivpc.net.

WILCOX, JEFF, dentist; b. Huntington, W.Va., Feb. 9, 1951; s. James Fleming and Jacqueline Rae Wilcox; m. Trilva Kay Brumfield, Feb. 2, 2000; 1 child, Chris. DDS, W.Va. U., 1978. Author: Acid Attack - The Real Causes of Dental Problems and How to Avoid Them, 2004. Missions trip dental trainer Xenos Christian Fellowship, Brazil, 1990, 1991, 1992. Avocations: photography, bass guitar, off-road motorcycles, snowboarding. Home: 426 Howland Dr Gahanna OH 43230 Office: Jeff Wilcox DDS 1345S Hamilton Rd Columbus OH 43227 Office Phone: 614-235-6064. E-mail: info@jefdds.com.

WILCOX, JOHN CAVEN, lawyer, corporate consultant; b. N.Y.C., Nov. 12, 1942; s. Daniel A. and Jessie Alexandra (Caven) W.; m. Vanessa Guerrini-Maraldi, Sept. 30, 1983; children Daniel D.G., William G.M., Julia G.M. BA magna cum laude, Harvard U., 1964; MA, U. Calif., Berkeley, 1965; JD, Harvard U., 1968; LLM, NYU, 1981. Bar: N.Y. 1973. Account exec. Georgeson & Co. Inc., N.Y.C., 1973-79, mng. dir., 1979 90, chmn., 1990 99; vice chmn. Georgeson Shareholder Comm., Inc., 1999—. Dir. GSC Proxitalia S.p.A.; bd. govs. Internat. Corp. Governance Network, chair ICGN com. on cross-border voting practices. Trustee Woodrow Wilson Nat. Fellowship Found., 1996, vice chmn., 1996—; trustee Bennington Coll., 1998—. With U.S. Army, 1968-70, Vietnam, trustee Family Dynamics, Inc., N.Y.C., 1979-1996. Woodrow Wilson fellow. Mem. ABA, NYSE (mem. shareholders comm. com. 1989-95), Am. Soc. Corp. Secs., Nat. Assn. Security Dealers (mem. issuer affairs com 1990—), The Brook, Downtown Assn., Harvard Club (N.Y.C.), Phi Beta Kappa. Democrat. Home: 580 West End Ave New York NY 10024-1723 Office Phone: 212-440-9800. E-mail: jwilcox@georgeson.com.

WILCOX, JOHN P. publishing executive; b. Pamona, Calif. Pub. Ventura (Calif.) County Star; exec. v.p., gen. mgr. Memphis (Tenn.) Comml. Appeal, 2000—02, pub., 2002—. Avocations: hiking, skiing, gardening, reading. Office: The Commercial Appeal PO Box 364 Memphis TN 38101-0364

WILCOX, JON P. state supreme court justice; b. Berlin, Wis., Sept. 5, 1936; m. Jane Ann; children: Jeffrey, Jennifer. AB in Polit. Sci., Ripon Coll., 1958; JD, U. Wis., 1965. Pvt. practice Steele, Smyth, Klos and Flynn, LaCrosse, Wis., 1965-66, Hacker and Wilcox, Wautoma, Wis., 1966-69, Wilcox, Rudolph, Kubasta & Rathjen, Wautoma, 1969-79; mem. Wis. State Legislature, 1969—75; elected judge Waushara County Cir. Ct., 1979-92; apptd. justice Wis. Supreme Ct., 1992-97, elected justice 10-yr. term, 1997. Commr. Family Ct., Waushara County, 1977-79; Wis. state legislator, 1969-75; del. Wis. Conservation Congress, 1975-80; vice chmn., chmn. Wis. Sentencing Commn., 1984-92; chief judge 6th Jud. Dist., 1985-92; mem. State-Fed. Jud. Coun., 1992-99, Jud. Coun. Wis., 1993-98; mem. Prison Overcrowding Task Force, 1988-90; mem. numerous coms. Wis. Judiciary; mem. faculty Wis. Jud. Coll., 1986-97; chmn. Wis. Chief Judges Com., 1990-92; co-chair comm. on judiciary as co-equal br. of govt. Wis. State Bar, 1995-97; lectr. in field. Contbr. (with others): Wisconsin News Reporters Legal Handbook: Wisconsin Courts and Court Procedures, 1987. Bd. visitors U. Wis. Law Sch., 1970—76. Lt. U.S. Army, 1959—61. Named Outstanding Jaycee Wautoma, 1974; recipient Disting. Alumni award Ripon Coll., 1993. Fellow Am. Bar Found.; mem. ABA (com. on continuing appellate edn.), Wis. Bar Assn. (bench bar com.), Wis. Law Found. (bd. dirs.), Tri-County Bar Assn., Dane County Bar Assn., Trout Unltd., Ducks Unltd., Rotary, Phi Alpha Delta. Office: Supreme Court State Capitol PO Box 1688 Madison WI 53701-1688

WILCOX, MARK DEAN, lawyer; b. May 25, 1952; s. Fabian Joseph and Zeryle Lucille (Tase) W.; m. Catherine J. Wertjes, Mar. 12, 1983; children: Glenna Lynn, Joanna Tessie, Andrew Fabian Joseph. BBA, U. Notre Dame, 1973; JD, Northwestern U., 1976; CLU, Am. Coll., 1979, ChFC, 1992. Bar: Ill. 1976, U.S. Dist. Ct. (no. dist.) Ill. 1976, Trial Bar 1982, U.S. Ct. Appeals (7th cir.) 1987, U.S. Supreme Ct. 1989. Staff asst. Nat. Dist. Attys. Assn., Chgo., 1974-75; trial asst. Cook County States Atty., Chgo., 1975; intern U.S. Atty. No. Dist. Ill., Chgo., 1975-76; assoc. Lord, Bissell & Brook, Chgo., 1976-85, ptnr., 1986—. Mem. YMCA Met. Chgo., Trinity United Meth. Ch., No Bats Baseball Club, Irving Park YMCA; venue ofcl. Internat. Spl. Olympics. Mem. ABA (tort and ins. practice sect.), Am. Soc. CLU and ChFC, Chgo. Bar Assn. (ins. law com.), Nat. Assn. Ins. and Fin. Advisors, Def. Rsch. Inst., Soc. Fin. Svc. Profls., Trial Lawyers Club Chgo., Notre Dame Nat. Monogram Club, Union League Club, Chgo. Lions Rugby Football Club, Beta Gamma Sigma. Office: Lord Bissell & Brook 115 S La Salle St Chicago IL 60603-3902 Office Phone: 312-443-0422.

WILCOX, MARY REBA, music educator; d. John Ruel Bohanan and Mary Gertrude Schmidt; m. Archie P. Wilcox, Jr. (dec.); 1 child, Sandra Wilcox Dunn. Cert. approval, U. Houston, 1957. Pres., v.p., sec.-treas. Galveston (Tex.) Bay Area Music Tchrs. Assn., 1968—72; piano adjudicator Am. Coll. Musicians, Austin, Tex., 1969—2003; pres., v.p., program chair Galveston Musical Club, 1972—74; dist. pres. Tex. Fedn. Music Clubs Dist. 8, 1975—76; cert. chmn. Houston Music Tchrs. Assn., 1978. Officer LWV, LaMarque, Tex., 1950—52. Named Music Tchr. of Yr., Galveston Bay Area Music Tchrs. Assn., 1968, 1970. Mem.: Tex. Music Tchrs. Assn., Nat. Guild Piano Tchrs. (Hall of Fame 1964—2003), Music Tchrs. Nat. Assn. Avocations: bridge, dance, music, reading, sewing. Home: 304 Meadowlakes Dr Meadowlakes TX 78654

WILCOX, MAUD, editor; b. N.Y.C., Feb. 14, 1923; d. Thor Fredrik and Gerda (Ysberg) Eckert; m. Edward T. Wilcox, Feb. 9, 1944; children: Thor (dec.), Bruce, Eric, Karen. AB summa cum laude, Smith Coll., 1944; A.M., Harvard U., 1945. Teaching fellow Harvard U., 1945-46, 48-51; instr. English Smith Coll., Northampton, Mass., 1947-48, Wellesley Coll., Mass., 1951-52; exec. editor Harvard U. Press, 1958-66, humanities editor, 1966-73, editor-in-chief, 1973—89; freelance editorial cons. Cambridge, 1989—; ret. Cons., panelist NEH, Washington, 1974-76, 82-84; cons. Radcliffe Pub. Course, 1991. Mem. MLA (com. scholarly edits. 1982-86), Assn. Am. Univ. Presses (chair com. admissions and standards 1976-77, v.p. 1978-79, chair program com. 1981-82), Phi Beta Kappa. Democrat. Episcopalian. Home and Office: 63 Francis Ave Cambridge MA 02138-1911 E-mail: maudwilcox@post.harvard.edu.

WILCOX, RAND ROGER, psychology educator; b. Niagara Falls, N.Y., July 6, 1946; s. Howard Clinton and Phyllis Hope (Stevens) W.; m. Karen Lesley Thompson, Apr. 25, 1986; children: Quinn Alexander, Bryce Colin. BA, U. Calif., Santa Barbara, 1968, MA in Math., PhD in Ednl. Psychology, U. Calif., Santa Barbara, 1976. Sr. rsch. assoc. UCLA, 1976-81; prof. psychology U. So. Calif., L.A., 1981—. Author: New Statistical Procedures for Social Sciences, 1987, Statistics for Social Sciences, 1996, Robust Estimation and Hypothesis Testing, 1997, Fundamentals of Modern Statistical Methods, 2001, Applying Contemporary Statistical Techniques, 2003; assoc. editor Psychometrika, Computational Stats. and Data Analysis.: mem. editorial bd. 4 jours; also numerous articles . Recipient T.L. Saaty award Am. Jour. Math. & Mgmt. Scis., 1984. Fellow Am. Psychol. Soc., Royal Statis. Soc.; mem. Psychometric Soc., Am. Statis. Assn., Inst. Math. Stats., Am. Ednl. Rsch. Assn. Achievements include research on improved methods for comparing groups and measuring achievement; resistant measures of correlation and regression; substantial gains in power when testing hypotheses. Office: U So Calif Dept Psychology Los Angeles CA 90089-0001 Office Phone: 213-740-2255.

WILCOX, RAYMOND I. oil industry executive; b. Mar. 19; BSME cum laude, U. MIch., 1968; postgrad., London Bus. Sch., 1994. Design and constrn. engr. Chevron, 1968—81, mem. fgn. ops. staff, 1981—86, ops. supt., 1986—90; mng. dir. Chevron Asiatic, Melbourne, Australia, 1990—96; v.p., gen. mgr. marine transp. Chevron Shipping Co., San Ramon, Calif., 1996—99; gen. mgr. asset mgmt. Chevron Nigeria Ltd., 1999—2000, chmn., mng. dir., 2000—01; mng. dir. Nigeria/Mid-Africa strategic bus. unit ChevronTexaco Corp., 2001—02; pres. ChevronTexaco Exploration and Prodn. Co., 2002—. Bd. dirs. Dynergy Inc. Bd. dirs. Spindletop Charities; chmn. Century divsn. United Way of Tex. Gulf Coast, 2003. Mem.: Am. Petroleum Inst. (mem. upstream com.). Office: Chevron Texaco Corp 6001 Bollinger Canyon Rd San Ramon CA 94583-2324

WILCOX, RHONDA V. media studies educator; d. Zeb Marshall and June Lee Wilcox; m. Richard John Gess, Oct. 30, 1982; 1 child, Jefferson Patrick Gess; m. Ralph Gerald Nelms (div.). PhD, Duke U., 1982. Prof. English Gordon Coll., Barnesville, Ga., 1985—. Co-editor: (book-collection of essays) Fighting the Forces: What's at Stake in Buffy the Vampire Slayer; contbr. foreword to book-collection of essays, book-reference work, book-collection of essays, articles to profl. jours.; co-editor (and co-founder): Slayage: The Online Internat. Jour. of Buffy Studies, 2001—. Recipient Whatley award, 1993. Mem.: Internat. Assn. Fantastic in the Arts, Popular Culture Assn., South Atlantic MLA (sect. chair, discussion group chair 1997—2002), Popular Culture Assn. South (pres., program co-chair 1989—2003). Office: Gordon College 419 College Drive Barnesville GA 30204 Personal E-mail: wilcox@slayage.tv. E-mail: rhonda_w@gdn.edu.

WILCOX, ROBERT KALLEEN, journalist; b. Indpls., July 21, 1943; s. Jacob Guire and Agnes Louise (Kalleen) W.; m. Begoña de Amezola, June 1, 1970; children: Robert, Amaya Begoña. BS in Journalism, U. Fla., 1966. Reporter, editor Miami (Fla.) News, 1967-72; freelance author, 1972—. Author: The Mysterious Deaths at Ann Arbor, 1977, Shroud, 1977, Fatal Glimpse, 1981, Japan's Secret War, 1985, paperback edit., 1995, Scream of Eagles: The True Story of Top Gun, 1990, paperback edit., 1991, Wings of Fury, 1997, paperback edit., 1998, 2d edit. 2004, Black Aces High, 2002, paperback edit., 2004, First Blue, 2004; (film, TV) Simon and Simon, 1985, God's Order, 1986, Frank's Place, 1987, Legend, 1994; writer TV pilots; staff story editor Famous Teddy Z, 1988-89, The New WKRP in Cin., 1990-93; sr. editor eStar, 1999—2000; contbr. to newspapers, mags. With USAF, 1967-72. Recipient William Randolph Hearst award Gainesville Sun, 1967, Cine Golden Eagle award, 1981, 82, Gold medal Venice Internat. Film Festival, 1982, Supple Meml. award Religious Newswriters Assn., 1970. Mem. Author's Guild, Writer's Guild Am. West. Avocations: history, sports. Personal E-mail: robkwilcox@aol.com.

WILCOX, SHIRLEY JEAN LANGDON, genealogist; b. Arcata, Calif., Dec. 10, 1942; d. Elmore Harold and Alberta May (Starkey) Langdon; m. Wayne Kent Wilcox, June 22, 1963; 1 child, Harold Bonner. BS, U. Md., 1964. Cert. Bd. for Certification of Genealogists. Tchr. Prince George's County (Md.) Sch. System, 1964-67, substitute tchr., 1968-73; profl. genealogist Lanham, Md., Arlington, Va., 1973—; genealogy tchr. Fairfax County Pub. Schs., 1995-99. Level II coord. Mid-Atlantic Genealogy and History Inst., George Mason U., Fairfax, Va., 1986; trustee bd. for Certification of Genealogists, 2000—. Editor: A Bibliography of Published Genealogical Source Records, Prince George's County, Maryland, 1975, Prince George's County Land Records, Vol. A, 1696-1702, 1976, 1850 Census Prince George's County, Maryland, 1978, 1828 Tax List Prince George's County, Maryland, 1985; author: The National Genealogical Society: A Look at Its First One Hundred Years. Elder Presbyn. Ch., 1970-73, 95-98. Fellow Nat. Geneal. Soc. (chmn. conf. program subcom. 1990, 2d v.p. 1990-94, councilor 1994-96, pres. 1996-2000); mem. DAR (libr. Belle Air chpt. 1985—, Outstanding Jr. Mem. award 1979), Assn. Profl. Genealogists (pres. 1991-93, pres. Nat. Capital area chpt. 1994-96, Grahame Thomas Smallwood Jr. award of merit 1995), Va. Geneal. Soc. (gov. 2001—), Prince George's County Geneal. Soc. (pres. 1973, 75-76, book rev. editor 1976-96, Jane Roush McCafferty award of excellence 1985), Fairfax Geneal. Soc. (pres. 1986-89), Soc. Mayflower Descs. in D.C., Paperweight Collectors Assn. (pres. Md.-D.C.-Va. chpt. 1988-90), Clay Family Soc. (dir. 2002—), numerous others. Avocation: collecting paperweights. Home: 1500 23rd St S Arlington VA 22202-1523

WILCOX, T.J. filmmaker; b. Seattle, 1965; BFA, Sch. Visual Arts, N.Y., 1989; MFA, Art Ctr. Coll. Design, Pasadena, 1995. Filmmaker: (one-man shows include) Gavin Brown's Enterprise, 1996, 1997; Daneil Buccholz, 1997; Inst. Contemporary Arts, 1993; Walker Art Ctr., 1998; Henry Art Gallery, 1999; (group shows include) Art Ctr. Coll. Design, 1994, 1995; Pasadena Plaza, 1994; Guggenheim Gallery, Chapman U., 1995; Bradbury Bldg., 1995; Marc Foxx Gallery, 1996; LACE, 1996; L.A. Ctr. Photographic Studies, 1996; Kunsthalle, 1996; Kunstlerhaus Bethanien, 1996; David Zwirner Gallery, 1996; Venice Biennale, 1997; Mus. of Art, 1997; Armand Hammer Mus. Art, UCLA, 1997; Whitney Mus. Am. Art, 1997; Mus. Abteilberg, 1998. Office: c/o Gavin Brown's Enterprise Corp 620 Greenwich St New York NY 10014-3304

WILCOXSON, KATHLEEN LOUISE, state legislator, educator; b. Lawton, Okla., Jan. 2, 1948; d. Lloyd and Susan McCullough; m. Lunden Wilcoxson; 1 child, Stacy. BS in Elem. Edn., MS in Spl. Edn., EdD in Curriculum and Instrn. Former tchr.; mem. Okla. State Senate, 1997—, mem. Edn. Com., Fin. Com., Tourism Com., Vets. Affairs Com. Mem. C. of C., Am. Bus. Women's Assn., Rep. Women's Club. Avocations: gardening, reading. Office: State Capitol Bldg 2300 N Lincoln Blvd Rm 533 Oklahoma City OK 73105-4805

WILCOXSON, ROY DELL, plant pathologist, researcher, educator; b. Columbia, Utah, Jan. 12, 1926; m. Iva Wall, 1949; children: Bonnie, Paul, Karren, John. BS, Utah State U., 1953; MS, U. Minn., 1955, PhD in Plant Pathlogy, 1957. Asst. prof., 1957-66; prof. plant pathology U. Minn., St. Paul, 1966-91, prof. emeritus, 1991—. Spl. staff mem. Rockefeller Found.; vis. prof. Indian Agrl. Rsch. Inst., New Delhi; dir. Morocco project U. Minn., 1983-87; adj. prof. Inst. Agronomy and Vet. Medicine, Hassan II, Rabat, Morocco, 1985—. Fellow Am. Phytopath Soc., Indian NAS, Indian Phytopath Soc., AAAS. Achievements include research in diseases of forage crops and cereal crops; cereal rust diseases. Office: 1669 County Road 8230 West Plains MO 65775-5766 Address: Dept Plant Path U Minn Saint Paul MN 55101

WILCUTT, TERENCE W. astronaut; b. Russellville, Ky., Oct. 31, 1949; BA in Math., Western Ky. U., 1974; grad. with distinction, U.S. Naval Test Pilot Sch., 1986. Math. tchr., 1974—76; commd. 2d lt. USMC, 1976, advanced through grades to col.; with VMFAT-101, VMFA-235, Kaneohe, Hawaii; F/A-18 fighter weapons and air combat maneuvering instr. VFA-125, Lemoore, Calif.; test pilot/project officer Strike Aircraft Test Directorate, Naval Aircraft Test Ctr., Patuxent River, Md.; astronaut NASA, Houston, 1990—, mem. astronaut support personnel team Kennedy Space Ctr., with Astronaut Office Ops. Devel. Br., dir. ops. Yuri Gagarin Cosmonaut Tng. Ctr., Star City, Russia, chief Astronaut Office Shuttle Ops. Br. Decorated DFC, Navy Commendation medal. Mem.: Soc. Exptl. Test Pilots. Achievements include logged over 4,400 flight hours in over 30 different aircraft; logged over 1,007 hours in space; pilot STS-68 (1994), STS-79 (1996); mission comdr. STS-89 (1998), STS-106 (2000). Avocations: flying, running, weightlifting, woodworking. Office: Astronaut Office/CB NASA Johnson Space Ctr Houston TX 77058

WILCZEK, FRANK ANTHONY, physics educator; b. Mineola, N.Y., May 15, 1951; s. Frank John and Mary Rose (Cona) W.; m. Elizabeth Jordan Devine, July 3, 1973; children: Amity, Mira. BS in Math., U. Chgo., 1970; MA in Math., Princeton U., 1971, PhD in Physics, 1973. Instr. Princeton (N.J.) U., 1973-74, asst. prof., 1974-76, assoc. prof., 1978-79, prof., 1980-81, Inst. for Theoretical Physics, Santa Barbara, Calif., 1981-88, Inst. for Advanced Study, Princeton, 1989—. Vis. fellow Inst. for Advanced Study, Princeton, 1977-78; vis. prof. Harvard U., 1987-88, J. Robert Oppenheimer prof. Inst. for Advanced Study, 1997-2000; Herman Feshbach prof. MIT, 2000—. Author: Longing for the Harmonies, 1988, Geometric Phases in Physics, 1989, Fractional Statistics and Anyon Superconductivity, 1990; editor-in-chief Annals of Physics, 2000—; contbr. articles to profl. jours. Trustee U. Chgo., 1998—. Recipient J.J. Sakurai prize Am. Phys. Soc., 1986, Dirac medal UNESCO, 1994, Michelson prize Case Western Res. U., 2002, Lorentz medal Netherlands Acad., 2002, Lilienfeld prize Am. Physics Soc., 2003, Europhysics prize, 2003; A.P. Sloan fellow, 1975-77, MacArthur fellow, 1982-87, Huttenback prof. U. Calif., Santa Barbara, 1984-88, Lorentz prof. Leiden U., 1998. Fellow Netherlands Acad. Sci.; mem. NAS, Am. Acad. Arts & Scis. Avocations: chess, music, logic puzzles. Home: 4 Wyman Rd Cambridge MA 02138-2218 Office: MIT 77 Massachusetts Ave 6-305 Cambridge MA 02139 E-mail: wilczek@mit.edu.

WILCZYNSKI, JANUSZ S. packaging technology executive, retired physicist; b. Warsaw, May 12, 1929; came to U.S., 1962; m. Brahna Lauger. Diploma in Indsl. Mechanics, Mining Acad., Cracow, Poland, 1954; MSc in Physics, Jagellonian U., Cracow, Poland, 1957; PhD in Physics and Optics, Imperial Coll. U. London, 1961. Physicist Watson, Ltd., London, 1961-62, research staff mem. T.J. Watson Research Ctr., IBM, Yorktown Heights, N.Y., 1962-63, mgr. tech. optics, 1963-83, 2d level mgr., 1983-84, sr. mgr., 1984-86, dir., 1986-93; gen. ptnr. Wilc Instruments LLP, 1995. Contbr. over 60 articles to profl. jours. Recipient 13 Invention awards, 1966-98, 7 Outstanding Innovation awards IBM, 1968-91; IBM fellow, 1981. Fellow Optical Soc. Am. (Richardson medal 1988); mem. NAE. Avocation: astron. optics. Home: PO Box 790 Sandia Park NM 87047-0790 Office Fax: 505-286-8273. Personal E-mail: wilczyn@swcp.com.

WILD, JAMES ROBERT, biochemistry and genetics educator; b. Sedalia, Mo., Nov. 24, 1945; s. Robert Lee and Frances Elleta (Wheeler) W.; m. Ann Lynn Brenner, Aug. 1, 1973; 1 child, Kalli Ann. BA in Zoology, U. Calif., Davis, 1967; PhD in Cell Biology, U. Calif., Riverside, 1971, post doctoral fellow, 1972. From asst. to assoc. prof. genetics and biochemistry Tex. A&M U., Coll. Sta., Tex., 1975-84, prof., chair genetics faculty, 1984-87, prof. biochemistry & genetics, 1984—2000, head biochemistry and biophysics dept., 1986-90; exec. assoc. dean Coll. Agriculture & Life Scs., Tex. A&M U., Coll. Sta., 1987-92, prof., head dept. biochemistry and biophysics, 1994-2000. Fellow faculty Tex. Agrl. Experiment Sta., 1999. With USN, 1972-75. Recipient So. Regional award for excellence in coll. anduniv. tchg. in food and agrl. scis., Higher Edn. program USDA, 1992. Fellow AAAS. Methodist. Office: Tex A&M U 2128 Biochemistry Bldg Rm 332 College Station TX 77843-2128 E-mail: j-wild@tamu.edu.

WILD, NELSON HOPKINS, lawyer; b. Milw., July 16, 1933; s. Henry Goetseels and Virginia Douglas (Weller) W.; m. Joan Ruth Miles, Apr. 12, 1969; children: Mark, Eric; m. Diana Morris, Sept. 7, 2002. AB, Princeton U., 1955; LL.B., U. Wis., 1961. Bar: Wis. 1962, Calif. 1967; cert. specialist in probate, estate planning and trust law State Bar of Calif. Research assoc. Wis. Legis. Council, Madison, 1955-56; assoc. Whyte, Hirschboeck, Minahan, Harding & Harland, Milw., 1961-67, Thelen, Marin, Johnson & Bridges, San Francisco, 1967-70; sole practice law San Francisco, 1970—. Mem. State Bar Calif. Client Trust Fund Commn., 1983, mem. exec. com. conf. dels., 1985-88. Contbr. articles to legal jours. Bd. dirs. Neighborhood Legal Assistance Found., San Francisco, 1974-85, chmn. bd., 1978-81. Served with USAF, 1956-58. Mem. ABA, Calif. Bar Assn., San Francisco Bar Assn., Am. Bar Found., Lawyers of San Francisco Club (gov. 1975, treas. 1981, v.p. 1982, pres.-elect 1983, pres. 1984), Calif. Tennis Club (bd. dirs. 1995-97, pres. 1997). Office: 332 Pine St Ste 710 San Francisco CA 94104-3230 Office Phone: 415-399-1600.

WILD, RICHARD P. lawyer; b. N.Y.C., Aug. 13, 1947; s. Alfred P. and Harriet C. (Hoffman) W.; m. Deirdre L. Felbin, June 15, 1969; children: Nicholas B., Daniel M. AB, Columbia U., 1968; JD, Yale U., 1971. Bar: Pa. 1971, U.S. Dist. Ct. (ea. dist.) Pa. 1971, U.S. Tax Ct. 1973, U.S. Claims Ct. 1977. Assoc. Dechert Price & Rhoads, Phila., 1971-78, ptnr., 1978—. Mem. Phila. Bar Assn. (tax sect.). Office: Dechert Price & Rhoads 4000 Bell Atlantic Tower 1717 Arch St Philadelphia PA 19103-2793

WILD, ROBERT ANTHONY, university president; b. Chgo., Mar. 30, 1940; s. John Hopkins and Mary Dorothy (Colnon) Wild. BA in Latin, Loyola U., Chgo., 1962, MA in Classical Lang., 1967; STL, Jesuit Sch. Theology, Chgo., 1970; PhD in Study of Religion, Harvard U., 1977. Ordained priest 1970. From asst. to assoc. prof. Marquette U., Milw., 1975—83; vis. prof. Pont. Istituto Biblico, Rome, 1983—84; dir. Jesuit philosophate program Loyola U., Chgo., 1984—85, assoc. prof. theology, 1985—92; provincial superior Chgo. Province S.J., 1985—91; pres. Weston Jesuit Sch. Theology, Cambridge, Mass., 1992—96, Marquette U., Milw., 1996—. Trustee Jesuit Sch. Theology, Berkeley, 1985—90, Weston Sch. Theology, Cambridge, Mass., 1985—96, Marquette U., 1990—, St. Louis U., 1994—2002, Milw. Rsch. Park, 2002—, Wis. Assn. Ind. Colls. and Univs., 1996—, chmn., 2001—, St. Joseph's U., Pa., 2004—. Author: Water in the Cultic Worship of Isis and Sarapis, 1981; co-editor: Sentences of Sextus, 1981; contbr. articles to profl. jours. Mem.: Cath. Bibl. Soc., Soc. Bibl. Lit. Office: Marquette Univ O'Hara Hall PO Box 1881 Milwaukee WI 53201-1881 Office Phone: 414-288-7223.

WILD, ROBERT WARREN, lawyer; b. Syracuse, N.Y., Mar. 25, 1942; s. Robert Sumner and Evelyn I. (Yorman) W.; m. Elizabeth Trowbridge, Sept. 5, 1965; children: Robert Mason, Alexander Lewis, Elizabeth Anne. BS, MIT, 1964; JD, Cornell U., 1970. Bar: N.Y. 1971, D.C. 1973. Engr. Smithsonian Astrophysical Obs., Cambridge, Mass., 1965-67; atty., advisor U.S. Dept. Justice, Washington, 1970-72; law clk. to Hon. Justice William H. Rehnquist U.S. Supreme Ct., Washington, 1972-73; ptnr. Nixon Peabody LLP, Rochester, N.Y., 1973—. Mem. Monroe County Bar Assn. (trustee 1990-91, 92-94, treas. 1992-94, counsel 1994—). Office: Nixon Peabody LLP Clinton Sq PO Box 31051 Rochester NY 14603-1051 Office Phone: 585-263-1302. Business E-Mail: rwild@nixonpeabody.com.

WILD, STEPHEN KENT, securities broker, dealer; b. Omaha, Nov. 18, 1948; s. Roger Charles and Marguerite Mae W.; m. Cheryl Katherine Sparano, June 5, 1971; children: Deric Justine, Drew Ian. Student, Ottawa U., 1967-68, U. Nebr., Omaha, 1968-71. Internal auditor Kirkpatrick, Pettis, Smith and Polian, Omaha, 1971-75; fin. planner First Fin. Planning Group, Omaha, 1975-80; mng. gen. agt. E.F. Hutton Life Ins. Co., Omaha, 1980-81; chmn. bd. Fin. Dynamics, Omaha, 1981-98, Securities Am., Inc., 1984—. Bd. dirs. Am. Express Fin. Advisors, 1998; chmn. bd. Quantum Alliance, 1998—. Trustee U. Nebr. Found.; bd. dirs. Child Saving Inst., U. Nebr., Omaha, Neb. Children & Families Found.; mem. hockey orgnl. com.; councillor Knights of Ak-Sar-Ben Found. Recipient Outstanding Alumni award U. Nebr. at Omaha, 1994, Omaha Family of Yr. award Family Svcs., 1998. Mem. Internat. Assn. Fin. Planners, Securities Industry Assn. (ind. firms com.). Baptist. Home: 14025 Lafayette Cir Omaha NE 68154-5118 Office: One Valmont Plz 4th Fl Omaha NE 68154-5203

WILD, VICTOR ALLYN, prosecutor, educator; b. Logansport, Ind., May 7, 1946; s. Clifford Otto and Mary E. (Helvey) Wild; 1 child, Rachel. BS in Pub. Adminstrn., U.Ariz., 1968, JD, 1974. Bar: Ariz. 1975, U.S. Dist. Ct. Ariz. 1975, Mass. 1984, U.S. Dist. Ct. Mass. 1984, U.S. Ct. Appeals (1st cir.) 1985, U.S. Ct. Appeals (9th cir.). Chief escrow officer Lawyers Title Co., Denver, 1971-72, escrow officer Tucson, 1970-71; law clk. Pima County Atty., Tucson, 1973-75, dep. county atty., 1975-81, chief criminal dep., 1981-84; asst. U.S. Atty. Dist. of Mass., Boston, 1984—. Chief gen. crimes unit U.S. Atty.'s Office, Boston, 1986—89; seminar instr. Mass. Continuing Legal Edn.,

Internat. Assn. Law Enforcement Investment Analysts, Dept. Justice Office Internat. Affairs, Employee Benefits Security Adminstrn., Dept. Labor, FBI, U.S. Postal Svc., Internat. Assn. Fin. Criminal Investigators, Secret Svc., State Bar Ariz., Tucson, Phoenix; instr. U. Ariz., Tucson, 1981—84, Pima CC, Tucson, 1981—84. Mem. editl. bd.: Episcopal Times, 1988—. Active Boston Ctr. Internat. Visitors, 1989—; bd. dirs. Crime Resistors, Inc., Tucson, 1983, CODAC, Tucson, 1983, 88-Crime, Inc., Tucson, 1983, Marblehead Seaport Trust, 1987—89, Old and Hist. Oversight Com., 1999—2000, Davenport House Child Enrichment Ctr., Marblehead, 1986—89, Marblehead Citizenship Scholarship Found., 1997—, Marblehead Sch. Master Plan Com., 2000—; chmn. Marblehead Capital Planning Commn., 1989—; mem. vestry St. Michael's Episc. Ch., Marblehead, Mass., 1986—90, lay Eucharistic min., 1988—, parish warden, 1992—96; mem. PhD rev. com. Law Policy and Soc. Northeastern U., 1991—92. With USAF, 1968—70. Named Prosecutor of the Yr., Office Insp. Gen., U.S. Dept. Labor, 1986; recipient Commendation award, Dept. Labor, Dept. State, USCG, USIA, U.S. Postal Svc., Dept. Treasury, EOUSA Rev., Software Pub. Assn., Mass. Ins. Fraud Bur., Spl. Achievement award, Dept. Justice. Master: Boston Inn of Ct.; mem.: Mass. Bar Assn., Ariz. Bar Assn., Phi Kappa Delta, Delta Sigma Pi, Tau Kappa Epsilon. Office: US Attys Office Ste 9200 US Courthouse One Courthouse Way Boston MA 02210 Office Phone: 617-748-3145. Business E-Mail: victor.wild@usdoj.gov.

WILDASIN, DAVID E(ARL), economics educator; b. Willimantic, Conn., Dec. 2, 1950; m. Kathleen Ann Preslin, Aug. 10, 1973. BA in Econs., U. Va., 1972; PhD Econs., U. Iowa, 1976. Asst. prof. U. Ill., Chgo., 1976—79, Ind. U., Bloomington, 1979—82, assoc. prof., 1982—86, prof. econs., 1986—93, prof. West European studies, 1993; prof. econs. Vanderbilt U., Nashville, 1993—2000; endowed prof. pub. fin. Martin Sch. Pub. Policy and Adminstrn., prof. econs. U. Ky., Lexington, 2000—. Cons. World Bank, 1992-2002, long-term cons. policy rsch. dept. pub. econs. divsn., 1995-96; vis. assoc. prof. Queen's U., Kingston, Ont., Can., 1982-83; vis. prof. U. Cath. Louvain, Louvain-la-Neuve, Belgium, 1986-87, Sch. of Higher Studies in Social Scis., Marseille, France, 1995; summer fellow U. Bonn, Germany, 1990; vis. scholar Interuniv. Ctr. for Econ. Studies, Gadjah Mada U., Indonesia, 1990, Ctr. for Econ. Studies U. Munich, 1991, U. B.C., Can., 1992; lectr. Helsinki (Finland) U., 1993, Norwegian Sch. Econs. and Bus. Adminstrn., 1994, European Econ. Assn., San Domenico di Fiesole, Italy, 1995; econ. policy rsch. unit Copenhagen Bus. Sch., 1996; lectr. Nordic doctoral program in econs. Uppsala U., 1997; cons. Dept. Fin., Can., 1990, Midwest U., Consortium for Internat. Activities, 1990, Human Resources Devel. Can., 2002-2003. Author: Urban Public Finance, 1986; co-author: Public Sector Economics, 1984; editor: Fiscal Aspects of Evolving Federations, 1997; assoc. editor: Regional Sci. and Urban Econs., 1987—, Jour. Regional Sci., 1989—, Jour. Urban Econs., 1991—, Internat. Tax and Pub. Fin., 1993—, Rev. Internat. Econs., 1994—, Nat. Tax Jour., 1998—, Jour. Pub. Econ. Theory, 1999—, Jour. Pub. Econs., 1999—2003, Papers in Regional Sci., 1999—2001, German Econ. Rev., 2000—, Finanzarchiv, 2000—, CESifo Econ. Studies, 2003—; referee: profl. jours.; contbr. over 80 articles to Am. Econ. Rev., Econ. Jour., others. Grantee, NSF, 1978—81; Ameritech fellow, Ind. U., 1988—89, Rsch. fellow, Ctr. for Ops. Rsch. and Econometrics, U. Cath. de Louvain, Belgium, 1986—87, U. Bonn, Germany, 1990, Rsch. fellow, Ctr. for Econ. Studies (CESifo), U. Munich, 1999—, Inst. for Study of Labor, U. Bonn, Germany, 2000—. Mem. Am. Econ. Assn., Econometric Soc., Nat. Tax Assn., Tax Inst. Am. Office: U Ky Martin Sch Pub Policy Lexington KY 40506-0027 Office Phone: 859-257-2456.

WILDE, CARLTON D. lawyer; b. Houston, Apr. 11, 1935; s. Henry Dayton and Louise (Key) W.; m. Martha Cloyes, July 26, 1958; children: Carlton D. Jr., Jennifer. Student, Coll. of William and Mary, 1953-55; BA, U. Tex., 1957, JD, 1959. Assoc. Bracewell & Patterson, Houston, 1959-62, ptnr., 1962-67, 85—; mng. ptnr., 1967-85. Trustee Presbyn. Sch. Fellow Am. Bar Found., Tex. Bar Found., Houston Bar Found.; mem. ABA, State Bar Tex., River Oaks Country Club, Coronado Club (Houston), Biltmore Forest Country Club (Asheville, N.C.). Republican. Home: 3105 Reba Dr Houston TX 77019-6209 Office: Bracewell & Patterson 2900 S Tower Pennzoil Pl 711 Louisiana St Ste 2900 Houston TX 77002-2781 E-mail: cwilde@bracepatt.com

WILDE, DANIEL UNDERWOOD, computer engineering educator; b. Wilmington, Ohio, Dec. 27, 1937; s. Arthur John and Ruby Dale (Underwood) W. BSEE, U. Ill., 1960; MS, M.I.T., 1962, PhD, 1966. Research instr. medicine Boston U. Med. Sch., 1964-66; asst. prof. info. adminstrn. U. Conn., 1966-69, assoc. prof., 1970-75, prof., 1976-85; assoc. dir. New Eng. Rsch. Application Ctr., Storrs, Conn., 1966-72, dir., 1973-85, NASA Indsl. Application Ctr., 1972-91; pres. NERAC, Inc., Tolland, Conn., 1985-99. Cons. NERAC Inc., 1999-2004; trustee Engring. Index, Inc.; cons. Am. Soc. Metals, 1973-76; bd. dirs. Internat. Coun. Sci. Info. Author: Author: Introduction to Computing: Problem Solving, Algorithms and Data Structures, 1973; contbr. articles to profl. jours. Served with USAF. Recipient NASA Public Service award, 1975 Fellow Nat. Fedn. Abstracting and Indexing Svcs. (hon.), Internat. Coun. Sci. Info. (hon.); mem. IEEE, Am. Soc. Info. Sci., Assn. Computing Machinery, Assn. Info. and Dissemination Centers (sec.-treas. 1976-79, pres. 1979-81).

WILDE, HAROLD RICHARD, college president; b. Wauwatosa, Wis., May 14, 1945; s. Harold Richard and Winifred (Wiley) W.; m. Benna Brecher, Feb. 4, 1970; children: Anna, Henry, Elizabeth Tey. BA, Amherst Coll., 1967; MA, PhD, Harvard U., Cambridge, Mass., 1973. Spl. asst. to gov. Office of Gov., State of Wis., Madison, 1972-75; ins. commr. Office of Commr. of Ins., State of Wis., Madison, 1975-79; spl. asst. to pres. U. Wis. System, Madison, 1979-81; v.p. for external affairs Beloit (Wis.) Coll., 1981-91; pres. North Ctrl. Coll., Naperville, Ill., 1991—. Bd. dirs. Ctr. for Pub. Representation, Inc., Madison, 1981-87, Beloit Community Found., 1988-91, Budget Funding Corp., 1993-99, Naperville Devel. Partnership, 1996—. Mem. Phi Beta Kappa. Home: 329 S Brainard St Naperville IL 60540-5401 Office: North Ctrl Coll 30 N Brainard St Naperville IL 60540-4607 Office Phone: 630-637-5454. E-mail: hrwilde@noctrl.edu.

WILDE, JOHN, artist, educator; b. Milw., Dec. 12, 1919; s. Emil F. and Mathilda (Lotz) W.; m. Helen Ashman, July 1943 (dec. Dec. 1966); children: Jonathan, Phoebe; m. Shirley Miller, 1969. BS, U. Wis., 1942, MS, 1948. Mem. faculty U. Wis., 1948—, prof. art, 1960—, chmn. dept. art, 1960-62, Alfred Sessler Distinguished prof. art, 1969-82, prof. emeritus, 1982—. Elected mem. Nat. Acad. Design, 1994. Works exhibited Met. Mus. Art, Mus. Modern Art, Whitney Mus. Am. Art, Corcoran Mus. Art, Mpls. Art Mus., San Francisco Mus. Art, Whitney Mus. Am. Art, 1978-80, Nat. Portrait Gallery, Smithsonian Instn., 1980, Nat. Gallery, Washington, 1988; drawing retrospective Elvehjem Mus. Art, U. Wis., 1984-85; 3-man retrospective (with Curry and Bohrod), Milw. Art Mus., 1982, 55 Yr. Retrospective Eluehjem Mus. of Art, U. Wis., Madison drawings and paintings, 1999-2000, others; represented in permanent collections, Pa. Acad. Art, Detroit Inst. Fine Art, Worcester Art Mus., Wadsworth Atheneum, Whitney Mus. Am. Art, Carnegie Inst., Nat. Collection Art, Smithsonian Instn., Yale U. Art Gallery, Butler Inst. Am. Art, Art Inst. Chgo., Sheldon Meml. Art Gallery, U. Nebr., Zimmerli Mus. Art, Rutgers U., N. Brunswick, N.J., Mus. Contemporary Art, Chgo., others, also extensive exhbns. abroad; subject of book WildeWorld, The Art of John Wilde, 1999. Recipient numerous awards for painting and drawing in regional and nat. exhbns. including, Childe Hassam purchase award Am. Acad. and Inst. Arts and Letters, 1968, 81, 87, Richard Florsheim Art Purchase award, 1994, Henry LeGrand Cannon prize Nat. Acad. Design, 2001; E.D. Found. grantee, 1995. Office Phone: 608-882-5352.

WILDE, MARY, secondary school educator; BS, Concordia Tchrs. Coll.; MS, U. Mo.; specialist degree, West Ga. Coll. Elem. tchr.; mid. sch. tchr. Booth Mid. Sch., Peachtree City, Ga., 1983—. Coach team Sci. Olympiad. Named Outstanding Earth Sci. Tchr., 1992. Mem. Ga. Sci. Tchrs. Assn. (pres.-elect). Office: Booth Mid Sch 250 Peachtree PkySouth Peachtree City GA 30269-1740

WILDE, NORMAN TAYLOR, JR., investment banking company executive; b. Phila., Sept. 13, 1930; s. Norman Taylor and Elizabeth (Duthie) W.; m. Ruth Nancy Osterndorf, Sept. 26, 1959; children: Karen, Suzanne, Norman Taylor III. BS, U. Pa., 1953. Vice pres. Janney, Montgomery, Scott, Inc., Phila., 1966-69; pres. Janney, Montgomery, Soctt, Inc., Phila., 1969-99, co-chmn., 2000—. Chmn. NASDAQ Stock Market, 1984. Bd. dirs. Abington Meml. Hosp. Served lt. USN, 1953-55. Mem.: Securities Industries Assn. (gov. 1979—82), Nat. Assn. Security Dealers (chmn. 1983—), Phila. C. of C. (bd. dirs. 1989—), Sunnybrook Golf Club, Phila. Cricket Club, Pine Valley Golf Club. Office: Janney Montgomery Scott Inc 1801 Market St Lbby 11 Philadelphia PA 19103-1602

WILDE, PATRICIA, retired artistic director; b. Ottawa, Ont., Can., July 16, 1928; m. George Bardyguine; children: Anya Bardyguine, Youri Bardyguine. Dancer Am. Concert Ballet, Marquis de Cuevas Ballet Internat., N.Y.C., 1944-45, Ballet Russe de Monte Carlo, N.Y.C., 1945-49, Roland Petit's Ballet Paris, Met. Ballet Britain, London, 1949-50; prin. ballerina N.Y.C. Ballet, 1950-65; dir. Harkness Sch. Ballet, N.Y.C., 1965-67; ballet mistress, tchr. Am. Ballet Theatre, N.Y.C., 1969-77; dir. Am. Ballet Theatre Sch., N.Y.C., 1977-82; artistic dir. Pitts. Ballet Theatre, 1982-97, artistic adviser, master tchr., 1997—. Tchr. Am. Ballet Theatre, 1969—79, Joffrey scholarship program, N.Y.C. Ballet, 1968—69; established Sch. of Grand Theatre of Geneva, 1968—69; adjudicator Regional Ballet in Am. S.E. and S.W., 1969—82; choreographer N.Y. Philharmonic; guest tchr. various ballet cos. and colls.; trustee Dance U.S.A.; panelist Nat. Choreographic Project. Recipient Leadership award in Arts and Letters YWCA, 1990, Pitts. Woman of Yr. in Arts award, 1993, Cultural award for outstanding contbns. to cultural climate of region Pitts. Ctr. for Arts, 1997, History Makers award in arts and letters Sen. John Heinz History Ctr. and the Hist. Soc. Western Pa., 1999. Office: Pitts Ballet Theatre 2900 Liberty Ave Pittsburgh PA 15201-1511

WILDE, ROBERT, lawyer; b. Salt Lake City, Aug. 31, 1947; s. H. Gordon and Helen (Ross) W.; m. Deanne Henriksen, Feb. 13, 1973; 6 children. BS in Math., U. Utah, 1971; MA in Econs., U. N.H., 1977; JD, U. Utah, 1979. Bar: Utah 1979, U.S. Ct. Appeals (10th cir.). Pvt. practice, Salt Lake City. Mem. adv. com. on rules of evidence Utah Supreme Ct., 1991—; mem. admissions com. Utah State Bar, 2001—. Contbr. articles to profl. jours. Asst. dist. chmn. Boy Scouts Am., Salt Lake City, 1996-97, explorer scout leader, 1992-96, scoutmaster, 1989-92, 2001-04. Col. USAFR, 1971-2001. Mem. ATLA, Utah Employment Lawyers Assn. (pres. 1994-96), Utah Trial Lawyers Assn. (pres. 1980-81, bd. govs. 1979-95), Nat. Employment Lawyers Assn. Achievements include listed in Best Lawyers in Am. Office: PO Box 71922 Salt Lake City UT 84171-0922

WILDE, THOMAS ANDREW, state legislator, home remodeler, writer; b. Mpls., Feb. 11, 1956; m. Melinda Wilde. BA, U. Minn. Mem. Oreg. Legislature, Salem, 1996—, vice chair agr. and natural resources com., mem. pub. affairs com., vice chair rev. com., mem. water and land use com., mem. subcom. on natural resources. Democrat. Office: 16635 SE Baxter Rd Portland OR 97236-5224 E-mail: wilde.sen@state.or.us.

WILDE, WILLIAM KEY, lawyer; b. Houston, May 3, 1933; s. Henry Dayton and Louise (Key) w.; m. Ann Jeannine Austin, Aug. 3, 1957; children— William Key, Austin, Adrienne, Michael AB, Coll. William and Mary, Williamsburg, Va., 1955; JD, U. Tex., Austin, 1958. Bar: Tex. 1958. Assoc. Bracewell & Patterson, Houston, 1958-61, ptnr., 1961—. Bd. dirs. Goodwill Industries Houston, 1972—; elder 1st Presbyn. Ch.; trustee Presbyn. Found. U.S.A., Ky., 1983-91; chmn. bd. trustees Schriener Coll., 1991-2000. Fellow ABA, Am. Bar Found., Am. Coll. Trial Lawyers; mem. Tex. Bar Assn. (bd. dirs. 1984-87), Houston Bar Assn. (pres. 1982-83), Houston Club (pres. 1981-82), Houston Country Club (bd. dirs., pres. 1989-90). Republican. Avocations: golf, skiing, scuba diving. Home: 6206 Woods Bridge Way Houston TX 77007-7041 Office: Bracewell & Patterson 2900 S Tower Pennzoil Place Houston TX 77002

WILDE, WILSON, insurance company executive; b. Hartford, Conn., Sept. 24, 1927; s. Philip Alden and Alice Augusta (Wilson) W.; m. Joanne Gerta Menzel, June 19, 1953; children— Stephen W., David W., Elisabeth L., Richard A. Student, Swarthmore Coll., 1945-46; BA, Williams Coll., 1949. Sales agt. Conn. Gen. Life Ins. Co., Hartford, 1949-53; with Hartford Steam Boiler Inspection & Ins. Co., 1953-70, exec. v.p., 1970-71, pres., CEO, 1971—, from chmn., CEO to chmn. emeritus, 1993-98, chmn. emeritus, 1998—. Corporator Inst. Living, Hartford; hon. bd. dirs. Hartford Stage Co., 1973—; Jr. Achievement, Old State House Assn., 1976—; trustee Loomis-Chaffee Sch., 1974—, chmn. bd., 1988-98. With USNR, 1945-47, 51-53. Office: PO Box 5024 Hartford CT 06102-5024

WILDEMANN, GREGG NYLUND, writer; b. Hartford, Conn., Sept. 19, 1956; s. Michael Nylund and Diana L. Wildemann. Student, Georgetown U., 1978—80; AA, Tompkins-Cortland CC, 1984; BA, SUNY, Albany, 1985. Press aide NY State Assembly, Albany, NY, 1985—89. Author: Love Letters from Cherr's, 1997, The Jerusalem Crusade, 2003; author: (under pseudonym) The Rag and Bone Shop, 2001, Letters From an Age of Reason, 2001, The Sound of Trees, 2002, Scorched Earth, 2002; author numerous poems. Recipient Medal of Honor, 2003; Baker scholar. Mem.: Hudson Valley Writer's Guild. Democrat. Methodist. Home: 32 Robin St Albany NY 12206-2917 E-mail: aquametaphors@yahoo.com.

WILDENTHAL, BRYAN HOBSON, university administrator; b. San Marcos, Tex., Nov. 4, 1937; s. Bryan and Doris (Kellam) W.; m. Joyce Lockhart; children: Rebecca, Bryan, Lora; m. Adele Sutton; children: Kerry, Andrea. BA, Sul Ross State Coll., 1958; PhD, U. Kans., 1964. Rsch. assoc. Rice U., Houston, 1964-66; AEC postdoctoral fellow Oak Ridge (Tenn.) Nat. Lab., 1966-68; asst. prof. physics Tex. A&M U., College Station, 1968-69; assoc. prof. physics Mich. State U., East Lansing, 1969-72, prof. physics, 1972-83; head physics and atmospheric sci. Drexel U., Phila., 1983-87; dean arts and scis. U. N.Mex., Albuquerque, 1987-92; v.p. acad. affairs U. Tex., Dallas, 1992-94, provost, v.p. acad. affairs, 1994-99, exec. v.p., provost, 1999—. Cons. Los Alamos (N.Mex.) Nat. Lab., 1987-92; sr. U.S. prof. Humboldt Found., Germany, 1973. Fellow J.S. Guggenheim Found., 1977. Mem. Phi Beta Kappa. Home: 3002 Cross Timbers Ln Garland TX 75044-2008 Office: U Tex Office Academic Affairs Richardson TX 75083

WILDENTHAL, BRYAN HOBSON, II, law educator; s. Bryan Hobson Wildenthal Sr. and Joyce Fay Lockhart Wildenthal. AB, Stanford U., 1986; JD, Stanford Law Sch., 1989. Bar: Mich. 1990. Law clk. Judge Frank M. Johnson, Jr U.S. Ct. Appeals, 11th Circuit, Montgomery, Ala., 1989—90; law clk. Chief Justice Michael F. Cavanagh Mich. Supreme Ct., Lansing, 1990—92; assoc. Wilmer, Cutler & Pickering, Washington, 1992—94; vis. prof. IIT Chgo.-Kent Coll. of Law, 1994—96; prof. Thomas Jefferson Sch. Law, San Diego, 1996—. Author: Native American Sovereignty on Trial. Liberal. Unitarian Universalist. Avocations: reading, travel, outdoors. Office: Thomas Jefferson School of Law 2121 San Diego Ave San Diego CA 92110 Office Phone: 619-297-9700 1509. E-mail: bryanw@tjsl.edu.

WILDENTHAL, C(LAUD) KERN, physician, educator; b. San Marcos, Tex., July 1, 1941; s. Bryan and Doris (Kellam) W.; m. Margaret Dehlinger, Oct. 15, 1964; children: Pamela, Catharine. BA, Sul Ross Coll., 1960; MD, U. Tex. Southwestern Med. Ctr., Dallas, 1964; PhD, U. Cambridge, Eng., 1970. Intern Bellevue Hosp., N.Y.C., 1964-65; resident in medicine, fellow cardiology Parkland Hosp., Dallas, 1965-67; rsch. fellow Nat. Heart Inst., Bethesda, Md., 1967-68; vis. rsch. fellow Strangeways Rsch. Lab., Cambridge, 1968-70; asst. prof. to prof. internal medicine and physiology U. Tex. Southwestern Med. Ctr., Dallas, 1970-76, prof., dean grad. sch., 1976-80, prof., dean Southwestern Med. Sch., 1980-86, prof., pres., 1986—. Hon. fellow Hughes Hall, U. Cambridge, 1994—. Author: Regulation of Cardiac Metabolism, 1976, Degradative Processes in Heart and Skeletal Muscle, 1980; contbr. articles to profl. jours. Bd. dirs. Dallas Ctr. Performing Arts, Dallas Symphony, Dallas Opera, Dallas Mus. Art, Dallas Citizen's Coun., Am. Friends Cambridge U., Greater Dallas C. of C. Recipient rsch. career devel. award NIH,

1972; spl. rsch. fellow USPHS, 1968-70; Guggenheim fellow, 1975-76. Mem. AMA, Inst. Medicine/NAS, Am. Soc. Clin. Investigation, Am. Coll. Cardiology, Royal Soc. Medicine Gt. Britain, Am. Physiol. Soc., Internat. Soc. Heart Rsch. (past pres. Am. sect.), Am. Fedn. Clin. Rsch., Assn. Am. Med Colls., Assn. Am. Physicians, Am. Heart Assn. (past chmn. sci. policy com.), Assn. Acad. Health Ctrs. (past chmn. sci. policy com.), Brit. N.Am. Com. Home: 4001 Hanover Ave Dallas TX 75225-7010 Office: U Tex Southwestern Med Ctr 5323 Harry Hines Blvd Dallas TX 75390-7208 Office Phone: 214-648-2508.

WILDER, C. JOHN, energy industry executive; b. Mo. m. Susan Burford; three children. BS in Bus. Adminstrn., S.E. Mo. State U., 1980; MBA, U. Tex. 1994. With Royal Dutch/Shell Group of Cos., asst. treas.; dir. econs. and fin. Shell Exploration and Prodn. Co.; asst. treas. Shell Oil Co.; CEO Shell Capital, 1998; exec. v.p., CFO Entergy Corp., New Orleans, 1998—2004; pres., CEO TXU Corp., 2004—. Office: TXU Corp Energy Plz 1601 Bryan St Dallas TX 75201-3411

WILDER, DAVID RANDOLPH, materials engineer, consultant; b. Lorimor, Iowa, June 11, 1929; s. Rex Marshall and Ethel Marie (Busch) W.; m. Donna Jean Moore, June 17, 1951; children: Susan, Michael, Margaret, Bruce. BS, Iowa State U., 1951, MS, 1952, PhD, 1958. Registered profl. engr., Iowa (inactive). Engr. Ames Lab., 1951-81; faculty mem. dept. materials sci. and engring. Iowa State U., Ames, 1955—, prof. engring., chmn. dept., 1961-89, prof. engring., 1989-91, prof. emeritus, 1991—; cons. to various industries, fed. agys. 1955—. Contbr. numerous tech. paper to profl. lit.; patentee in field. Fellow Am. Ceramic Soc., Accreditation Bd. for Engring. and Tech.; mem. Nat. Inst. Ceramic Engrs., Am. Soc. for Engring. Edn., Keramos. Home: 1214 Ridgewood Ave Ames IA 50010-5208

WILDER, DWIGHT SAFFORD, academic administrator; b. Plainfield, N.J., Dec. 24, 1946; s. Glenn Safford and Marion Seaver (Fiske) W.; children: Thomas, Douglas; m. Margaret Ruth Holland, Sept. 9, 1995. BA, Johns Hopkins U., 1969; postgrad., Harvard U., 1969-70; MBA, So. N.H. U., 1981; postgrad., Rivier Coll., 2002—03. Mem. faculty Hebron (Maine) Acad., 1969-70; assoc. dir. continuing edn. N.H. Coll., Manchester, 1975-78, seminar adminstr., 1978-80, asst. to dean, 1980-84; program design specialist N.H. Job Tng. Council, Concord, 1984-89; apprentice program mgr. Portsmouth Naval Shipyard, 1989-92; coord. Seacoast Tech. Prep. Consortium, 1992-96; sch.-to-career coord. Timberlane Sch. Dist., Plaistow, N.H., 1996—. Mng. editor Jour. Ednl. Computing Research, 1983-84. U.S. rep. Old Johannian Assn., 2001—; mem. Cold River Camp Com., 1999—; pres. Chatham Trails Assn., 2002—. Mem. Am. Soc. Tng. and Devel., Appalachian Mountain Club (vol. educator and cons., 1975—, sec. North Country bd. 1980-87), N.H. Personnel and Guidance Assn., Navy Brunswick Toastmasters (pres. chpt. 1973-74), Toastmasters of Manchester (pres. 1982-83) Avocations: hiking, backpacking, painting. Home: 15 Pinecrest Dr Somersworth NH 03878 Office: Timberlane Sch Dist 36 Greenough Rd Plaistow NH 03865 E-mail: dwilder@timberlanehs.com.

WILDER, ELEANOR MARIE (NORA ROBERTS WILDER), writer; b. Washington, Oct. 10, 1950; d. Bernard Edward Robertson and Eleanor Margaret Harris; m. Ronald Eugene Aufdem-Brinke, Aug. 17, 1968 (div. 1985); children: Daniel, Jason; m. Bruce Allen Wilder, July 6, 1985. Grad. high sch., Silver Spring, Md.; writer, 1979—. Author: Homeport, 1998, The Reef, 1998, River's End, 1999, Carolina Moon, 2000, others; (writing as J.D. Robb) Judgement in Death, 1990, Conspiracy in Death, 1999, Witness in Death, 2000. First inductee Romance Writers of Am. Hall of Fame, 1986; recipient Waldenbooks award, 1985, 86, 88, 91, 92, 94, B. Dalton award, 1990, 91, 92, Centennial award, Waldenbooks Lifetime Achievement award. Mem. Washington Romance Writers, Romance Writers Am. (Lifetime Achievement award), Mystery Writers Am. Democrat. Roman Catholic. Avocations: dancing, reading, films.

WILDER, EUNICE, city official; BA, Howard U., 1959. Treas. Office of Treas., City of Richmond, Va. Office: City of Richmond Office of the Treas Rm 107 900 E Broad St City Hall Richmond VA 23219 also: PO Box 26505 Richmond VA 23261-6505 E-mail: ewilder@ci.richmond.va.us.

WILDER, GENE, actor, film director, writer; b. Milw., June 11, 1935; s. William J. and Jeanne (Baer) Silberman; m. Mary Joan Schutz, Oct. 27, 1967 (div. 1974); 1 child, Katharine Anastasia; m. Gilda Radner, 1984 (dec.); m. Karen Boyer, Sept. 8, 1991. BA, U. Iowa, 1955; postgrad., Bristol Old Vic Theatre Sch., 1955-56. Appeared in Broadway play: The Complaisant Lover, 1962 (Clarence Derwent award); appeared in London production of Laughter on the 23rd Floor, 1996; appeared in motion pictures: Bonnie and Clyde, 1966, The Producers, 1967 (Acad. award nom. best supporting actor), Start the Revolution Without Me, 1968, Quackser Fortune Has a Cousin in the Bronx, 1969, Willy Wonka and the Chocolate Factory, 1970, Everything You Always Wanted to Know about Sex, 1971, Rhinoceros, 1972, Blazing Saddles, 1973, The Little Prince, 1974, Silver Streak, 1976, The Frisco Kid, 1979, Stir Crazy, 1980; Hanky Panky, 1982, See No Evil, Hear No Evil, 1989, Funny About Love, 1990, Another You, 1991; (TV films) Murder in a Small Town, 1999, Alice in Wonderland, 1999, The Lady in Question, 1999; dir., writer, actor film: The Adventures of Sherlock Holmes' Smarter Brother, 1975, The World's Greatest Lover, 1977, Sunday Lovers, 1980, The Woman in Red, 1984, Haunted Honeymoon, 1986; actor, co-writer film: Young Frankenstein, 1974 (Acad. award nomination); TV appearances include: The Trouble With People, 1973, Marlo Thomas Spl., 1973, The Scarecrow, 1972, Thursday's Games, 1973, (series) Something Wilder, 1994-95; guest appearances TV series The Defenders, 1962, The DuPont Show of the Week, 1962-63, The Frank Skinner Show, 1997, Will & Grace, 2002-03 (Emmy award best guest actor 2003). Campaigned with Elaine May and Rene Taylor for Eugene McCarthy, Allard Lowenstein and Paul O'Dwyer, 1968. Served with U.S. Army, 1956-58. Actors Equity Assn., Am. Federation of Television & Radio Artists, DGA, WGA. Office: c/o Innovative Artists 1505 10th St Santa Monica CA 90401*

WILDER, GINGER, newscaster; B in Broadcast News, U. Ga. Intern Fitzgerald Herald Leader; anchor, reporter CNN Affiliate, Athens, Ga.; edn. reporter Channel 4-Cables News, Cumming Ga.; reporter WSAV-TV, Savannah, Ga., 2000—. Avocations: reading, travel, family, pets. Office: WSAV-TV3 1430 E Victory Dr Savannah GA 31404

WILDER, JAMES EDWARD, resident manager; b. Washington, Dec. 28, 1948; s. Nathaniel Everett and Marie Inez Wilder; m. Barbara Anne Tracey, Aug. 13, 1973; 1 child, Huan. B of Ministry magna cum laude with high honors, Andersonville Bapt. Sem., Camilla, Ga., 1999. Cert. resident mgr. RM801484, D.C. Dept. Consumer and Regulatory Affairs, Occupl. and Profl. Licensing Adminstrn., Real Estate Commn.; lic. minister, 1994. Mgr. hardware dept. Gaylord's Dept. Store, New Castle, Pa., 1970-72; sales rep. Gumpert Printing Co., Silver Spring, Md., 1980-82; shipping/receiving mgr. Bradlees, Annandale, VA., 1982-84; warehouse mgr. Juhl Pacific Corp., Landover, Md., 1984-86; resident mgr. William C. Smith Co., Washington, 1989—. Pres. Altar of Ed Ministry, Washington, 1994—. Editor: (newsletter) Breach Repairer News, 1997—; creator: (Web site) Altar of Ed Ministry, 1999; host (radio program) Sta. KYTX, Beeville, Tex., 2001. Bd. dirs. Cmty. Coun. for the Homeless at Friendship Pl., Washington, 1994-96; pres. Student Govt. Assn. Prince George's C.C., 1981-82; advisor Triple C Jaycees, 1979-80; founder, pres. Centennial Slammer Jaycees, 1977-78, advisor, past pres., 1978-79. Specialist 4/E4 U.S. Army, 1966-69, Vietnam. Recipient Keyman award Centennial Slammer Jaycees, 1978-79, Keyman award Triple C Jaycees, 1979-80; named one of 25 Outstanding Jaycees Pres. in U.S., 1977-78. Mem. VFW (life), DAV (life), Internat. Critical Incident Stress Found., Am. Numismatic Assn., Am. Assn. Christian Counselors (charter), Baptist. Avocations: post-prison ministry, eagle collectibles, collecting coins. Office: Altar of Ed Ministry Ste 506 2800 Ontario Rd NW Apt 506 Washington DC 20009-2227 Fax: (202) 319-7704. E-mail: altaredmin@aol.com.

WILDER, JAMES SAMPSON, III, lawyer, judge; b. Knoxville, Tenn., Mar. 15, 1949; s. James Sampson and Florence Louise (Summers) W. BS, Lambuth Coll., Jackson, Tenn., 1971; JD, Memphis State U., 1974. Bar: Tenn. 1974, U.S. Dist. Ct. (we. dist.) Tenn. 1975, U.S. Supreme Ct. 1981, U.S. Ct. Appeals (6th cir.) 1982. Assoc. Lt. Gov. John S. Wilder, Somerville, Tenn., 1974-75, ptnr., 1975-76, Wilder, Wilder & Johnson, Somerville, 1976-83; pvt. practice James S. Wilder III, Somerville, 1983-95; gen. sessions judge Fayette County, Somerville, 1985-90; assoc. Petkoff and Lancaster, Memphis, 1995—2000; pvt. practice Somerville, 2000—02; atty. Law Office of John M. Lannom, Dyersburg, Tenn., 2002—. Scoutmaster troop 95 Boy Scouts Am., Somerville, 1975-77, com. person, 1977—. Paul Harris fellow Rotary, Somerville, 1977. Mem. ABA, Assn. Trial Lawyers Am., Tenn. Bar Assn., Tenn. Trial Lawyers Assn. (dir. 1983-86), Fayette County C. of C. (dir. 1979—), Somerville Rotary (dir. 1976—, charter pres. 1976-78). Methodist. Avocations: hunting, fishing. Home: PO Box 342 Dyersburg TN 38025 Office: 422 McGaughey St PO Box 1729 Dyersburg TN 38024 Office Phone: 731-285-0374.

WILDER, JOHN SHELTON, lieutenant governor; b. Fayette City, Tenn., June 3, 1921; s. John Chamblee and Martha (Shelton) W.; m. Marcelle Morton, Dec. 31, 1941; children: John Shelton Wilder, II, David Morton. Student, U. Tenn.; LLB, U. Memphis, 1957. Bar: Tenn. 1957. Engaged in farming, Longtown, Tenn., 1943—; supr. mgmt. Longtown Supply Co.; judge Fayette County Ct.; mem. Tenn. Senate, 1959—60, 1966—; mem. senate 81st, 85th, 86th through 102nd Gen. Assemblies; lt. gov., spkr. senate State of Tenn. for Dist. 26, Chester, Crockett, Fayette, Hardeman, Hardin, others, 1971—; pres. senate State of Tenn., 1971—. Past pres. Nat. Assn. Soil Conservation Dists., Tenn. Soil Conservation Assn., Tenn. Agrl. Council; exec. com. So. Legis. Conf., Conf. Lt. Govs.; dir. Bank Tenn., Cumberland Bank; chmn. Cumberland BanCorp, Inc. Served with U.S. Army, 1942-43. Mem. Tenn. Cotton Ginners Assn. (past pres.), Shriner, Scottish Rite, Mason, Delta Theta Phi. Clubs: Shriners. Democrat. Methodist. Office: Legislative Plz Ste 1 Nashville TN 37243-0026

WILDER, L(AWRENCE) DOUGLAS, former governor; b. Richmond, Va., Jan. 17, 1931; children: Lynn, Larry, Loren. BS, Va. Union U., 1951; JD, Howard U., 1959. Bar: Va. Mem. Va. Senate, 1969-85; lt. gov. State of Va., 1986-89, gov., 1989-93; Al Douglas Wilder Disting. prof. Va. Commonwealth U., Richmond, 1998—. Del. Democratic Nat. Conv., 1980; agt. NAACP Legal Def. Fund. Bd. dirs. United Givers Fund; chmn. bd. Red Shield Boys' Club. Served with U.S. Army, 1952-53 Decorated Bronze Star. Mem. ABA, Va. Bar Assn., Nat. Bar Assn., Am. Judicature Soc., C. of C., Urban League (bd. dirs. Richmond), Omega Psi Phi. Clubs: Masons; Shriners. Democrat. Office: Virginia Commonwealth Univ 919 W Franklin St PO Box 842028 Richmond VA 23284-2028

WILDER, MICHAEL STEPHEN, former insurance company executive; b. New Haven, Conn., Sept. 8, 1941; BA, Yale U., 1963; JD, Harvard U., 1966. Bar: Conn. 1966. Atty. Hartford (Conn.) Fire Ins. Co., 1967-69, asst. gen. counsel, 1969-71, assoc. gen. counsel, 1971-75, gen. coun., sec., 1975-87, sr. v.p., gen. counsel, sec., 1987-95; sr. v.p., gen. counsel The Hartford Fin. Svcs. Group, Inc., 1995—2001; ret., 2001. Mem. ABA, Conn. Bar Assn. Home: 85 Emily Way West Hartford CT 06107-3136

WILDER, ROLAND PERCIVAL, JR., lawyer; b. Malden, Mass., June 21, 1940; s. Roland Percival and Clarissa (Hunting) W.; m. Susan McAra Randell, Sept. 3, 1965; children: Roland Percival III, William Randell. BA, Washington and Jefferson Coll., 1963; JD, Vanderbilt U., 1966. Bar: D.C. 1967, U.S. Dist. Ct. D.C. 1967, U.S. Dist. Ct. Md. 1994, U.S. Dist. Ct. Colo. 1997, U.S. Dist. Ct. (ea. dist.) Mich. 1999, U.S. Ct. Appeals (D.C. cir.) 1967, U.S. Ct. Appeals (4th, 5th and 6th cirs.) 1976, U.S. Ct. Appeals (8th and 9th cirs.) 1977, U.S. Ct. Appeals (2d cir.) 1978, U.S. Ct. Appeals (11th cir.) 1981, U.S. Ct. Appeals (3d cir.) 1997, U.S. Ct. Appeals (7th cir.) 2002, U.S. Supreme Ct. 1972. Atty. Office of Solicitor U.S. Dept. Labor, Washington, 1967-69; asst. counsel civil rights office of solicitor U.S. Dept. Labor, Washington, 1969-70, counsel civil rights office of solicitor, 1970-71; supr. atty. office gen. counsel NLRB, Washington, 1972-74; assoc. gen. counsel Internat. Brotherhood Teamsters, Washington, 1974-85; sr. mem. Baptiste & Wilder P.C., Washington, 1985—. Lectr. in field. Mng. editor Vanderbilt U. Law Rev., 1965-66; contbr. articles to profl. jours. V.p. Arlington (Va.) Cubs Youth Club, Inc., 1975-81; coach Fairfax (Va.) Hockey Club, 1979-83. Mem. ABA, D.C. Bar Assn., Assn. Trial Lawyers Am., Phi Delta Phi, Pi Sigma Alpha, Phi Alpha Theta, Roosevelt Soc., Joint Council Flight Attendant Unions (hon. flight attendant 1985). Democrat. Avocations: history, tennis, skiing. Office: Baptiste & Wilder PC 1150 Connecticut Ave NW Ste 500 Washington DC 20036-4194 Office Phone: 202-223-0723. Business E-Mail: rpwilderjr@bapwild.com.

WILDER, RONALD PARKER, economics professor; b. Freeport, Tex., Jan. 15, 1941; s. J. Barton and Lois (Parker) W.; m. Charlotte D. Pearson, Sept. 4, 1965; children: Erika, Rachel, David. BA, Rice U., 1963, MA, 1964; PhD, Vanderbilt U., 1969. Asst. prof. econs. U. S.C., Columbia, 1970-75, assoc. prof., 1975-80, prof., 1980—, chmn. dept. econs., 1987—2002. Co-author: Stock Life Insurance Profitability, 1986; mem. editorial bd. So. Econ. J., 1978-80; contbr. articles to profl. jours. Capt. U.S. Army, 1968-70. Fellow Ford Found., Vanderbilt U., 1964-65. Mem. Am. Econ. Assn., So. Econ. Assn., Omicron Delta Epsilon. United Methodist. Avocations: hiking, canoeing. Office: U of SC Dept Of Econs Columbia SC 29208-0001 Office Phone: 803-777-6955.

WILDER, TERRY L. religious studies educator; b. Dayton, Ohio, Nov. 30, 1956; s. Nicodemus and Wilma J. Wilder; m. Denise E. Rodrigues, July 25, 1987; children: Ian N., Aaron A. PhD, U. of Aberdeen, Scotland, 1998. Vis. prof. of N.T. and Greek Midwestern Bapt. Theol. Sem., Kansas City, Mo., 1997—98, asst. prof. of N.T. and Greek, 1998—2001, assoc. prof., 2001—, asst. dir. doctoral studies. Cons. in field. Editor: (journal) Midwestern Journal of Theology, 2002—; author: (book) Pseudonymity, the New Testament, and Deception, 2004; contbr. articles to profl. jours. Recipient Outstanding Young Am. award, Outstanding Young Americans, 1988—91, Am. Bible Soc. award, 1987—88, Religion Dept. award, Dallas Bapt. U., 1985—86; fellow Tyndale Fellowship Small Rsch. grantee, 1992; scholar Pres.'s scholar, Southwestern Bapt. Theol. Sem., 1988—89. Mem.: Inst. for Bibl. Rsch., Evang. Theol. Soc., Soc. of Bibl. Lit. Avocations: sports, travel, reading. Office: Midwestern Baptist Theological Seminary 5001 N Oak Trafficway Kansas City MO 64118 E-mail: twilder@mbts.edu.

WILDER, THOMAS A. county official; b. Ft. Bragg, N.C., Nov. 5, 1943; s. Jack English and Rita Verne Wilder; m. Charlene Marie Rondeau, Oct. 18, 1962; 1 child, Thomas A Jr. B, U. Dallas, 1961—63; M, U. North Tex., 1963—64; student, Tex. A&M, 1995—2002, U. Tex. Law Sch., 1995—2002. Mfr. rep. Self-Employed, Dallas, 1965—75; real estate broker and cons. The Wilder Co., Tarrant County, Tex., 1975—94; elected ofcl. Tarrant County Dist. Clk., Ft. Worth, 1995. Gov. appointee to bd. dirs. Real Estate Ctr., Tex. A&M U., 1987—94; spkr. Mem. Northeast Leadership Forum. Mem.: Real Estate Ctr. at Tex. A&M (chmn. 1991—92), Republican Forum (past pres.), Tarrant County Bar Assn., Tex. Dist. Ct. Alliance (bd. dir. 2002—03), Mid Cities Rotary Club. Republican. Methodist. Avocations: investments, politics. Office: Tarrant County Dist Clk PO Box 20121 Fort Worth TX 76102

WILDER, WALTER LLEWELLYN, allergist, immunologist, pediatrician; b. Ann Arbor, Mich., May 23, 1926; MD, Harvard U., 1950. Diplomate Am. Bd. Allergy and Immunology, Am. Bd. Pediatrics. Rotating intern Cleveland City Hosp., 1950-51; resident in pediatrics U. Hosps. Cleveland, 1951-52, U. Minn. Hosps., Mpls., 1954-55; pvt. practice Edina, Minn.; clin. assoc. prof. U. Minn.; staff Mpls. Children's Hosp., Fairview Southdale, Edina; courtesy staff Meth. Hosp., St. Louis Park, Minn., Abbott Northwestern, Mpls.; ret., 2004. Mem. AMA, Am. Acad. Environ. Medicine, Am. Acad. Pediatrics, Am. Coll. Allergy, Asthma and Immunology. Home: 4905 Payton Ct Edina MN 55435-1544

WILDEROTTER, JAMES ARTHUR, lawyer; b. Newark, July 25, 1944; s. Arthur Walter and Dorothy Theresa (King) W.; children: James, Kristin, Kathryn. BA, Georgetown U., 1966; JD, U. Ill., 1969. Bar: D.C. 1969, U.S. Supreme Ct. 1974. Assoc. Covington & Burling, Washington, 1969-71; spl. asst. to Under Sec. Commerce, Washington, 1971-73; exec. asst. to Sec. HUD, Washington, 1973-74; assoc. dept. atty. gen. U.S. Washington, 1974-75; assoc. counsel to Pres. U.S., 1975-76; gen. counsel U.S. Energy Research and Devel. Adminstrn., Washington, 1976-77; of counsel Morgan, Lewis & Bockius, Washington, 1977-78; ptnr. Jones, Day, Reavis & Pogue, Washington, 1978-91, 95—; v.p., gen. counsel Internat. Paper Co., Purchase, N.Y., 1991-94. Editor in chief: U. Ill. Law Rev., 1968-69. Gen. counsel rules com. Rep. Nat. Conv., 1980; sec. James S. Brady Presdl. Found., 1982-88; gen. counsel Nat. Sudden Infant Death Syndrome Found., 1986-90, sec. Sudden Infant Death Syndrome Alliance, 1990-93. With USN, 1962-68. Mem. ABA Republican. Roman Catholic. Home: 5903 Mount Eagle Dr Alexandria VA 22303 Office: Jones Day Reavis and Pogue 51 Louisiana Ave NW Washington DC 20001-2113 Office Phone: 202-879-3832. Personal E-mail: jawilder@yahoo.com.

WILDEROTTER, MARY AGNES, software company executive, former cable television executive; b. Neptune, N.J., Feb. 9, 1955; d. Denis James and Constance Rosemary (Shields) Sullivan; m. Philip Jay Wilderotter; children: Christopher, Daniel. BA in Econs., Holy Cross Coll., 1977. Accts. receivable supr. CableData, Sacramento, 1979-80, mgr. acctg. svcs., 1980-82, mgr. reg. support, 1982, mktg. mgr., 1982-83, dir. mktg., 1983, dir. nat. accts., 1983-85, v.p., 1985—87, sr. v.p., sales & mktg., 1987—91; sr. v.p. McCaw Cellular Communications, 1991—95; exec. v.p., nat. ops. & CEO, Aviation Communications div. AT&T Wireless Svcs., 1995—97; pres., CEO Wink Communications, 1997—2002; sr. v.p., bus. strategy Microsoft Corp., 2002—. Bd. dirs. Phoenix Cable Ptnrs., San Rafael, Calif., 1988—, Satellite Video Ctr., Rancho Cordova, Calif., 1988—, CAbleData Europe Ltd., Leeds, Eng., 1989—. Outstanding Mentor award, Women in Cable and Telecommunications Found., 1999. Mem. Nat. Cable TV Assn. (bd. dirs. 1987—), Women in Cable (exec. mem.), Cable TV Adminstrn. & Mktg. Soc., Calif. Cable TV Assn., Nat. Acad. Cable Programming. Republican. Roman Catholic. Office: Microsoft Corp 1 Microsoft Way Redmond WA 98052-6399

WILDES, LEON, lawyer, educator; b. Scranton, Pa., Mar. 4, 1933; BA magna cum laude, Yeshiva U., 1954; JD, NYU, 1957, LLM, 1959. Bar: N.Y. 1958, U.S. Dist. Ct. (so. dist.) N.Y. 1960, U.S. Supreme Ct. 1961. Ptnr. Wildes, Weinberg, Grunblatt & Wildes, P.C., N.Y.C., 1960—; adj. prof. law Benjamin N. Cardozo Sch. Law, N.Y.C., 1981—. Contbr. articles to profl. jours. Mem. ABA, Assn. of Bar of City of N.Y. (com. immigration and nationality law 1975-78, 88-91, 95-98), Am. Immigration Lawyers Assn. (nat. pres. 1970-71, bd. govs. 1971—, co-chair ethics com. 1993-96, editor Immigration and Nationality Law Symposium 1983, Elmer Fried Excellence Tchg. award 1998, Edith Lowenstein award Outstanding Contbn. Immigration Practice). Home: 2 E 88th St # 2 New York NY 10128-0555 Office: 515 Madison Ave 8th Fl New York NY 10022-5403 Office Phone: 212-753-3468. E-mail: lwildes@wwgw.com.

WILDHABER, MICHAEL RENE, accountant; b. Jefferson City, Mo., Aug. 4, 1952; s. Rainey A. and Velma W.; m. Paula M. Wildhaber, Sept. 28, 1974; 1 child, Wendy. AA, Florissant Valley Coll., 1972; BS, U. Mo., 1974. CPA, Mo.; cert. info. sys. auditor, cert. internal auditor, cert. tax preparer, assoc. ins. acctg. and fin., enrolled agt. Sr. auditor, enrolled agt. I.T.T. Fin., St. Louis, 1974-79; audit mgr. Navco, St. Louis, 1980-85; contr. Millers mutual, Alton, Ill., 1985-88; pres. R&M Tax and Acctg., St. Louis, 1988—. Tchr. Jr. Achievement, St. Louis, 1993-94; vol. Olympic Festival, St. Louis, 1994, 100 Neediest Cases, St. Louis, 1990-94, Old News Boy, St. Louis, 1992-94. Mem. AICPA, Mo. Soc. CPAs, Inst. Internal Auditors, Habitat for Humanity (pres.). Office: R&M Tax and Acctg 3805 S Kingshighway Blvd Saint Louis MO 63109-1818

WILDHACK, WILLIAM AUGUST, JR., lawyer; b. Takoma Park, Md., Nov. 28, 1935; s. William August and Martha Elizabeth (Parks) W.; m. Martha Moore Allston, Aug. 1, 1959; children: William A. III, Elizabeth L. BS, Miami U., Oxford, Ohio, 1957; JD, George Washington U., 1963. Bar: Va. 1963, D.C. 1965, Md. 1983, U.S. Supreme Ct. 1967. Agt. IRS, No. Va., 1957-65; pvt. prac. Washington, 1965—69; v.p., corp. counsel B.F. Saul Co. and affiliates, Chevy Chase, Md., 1969-87, Chevy Chase Bank, F.S.B. and affiliates, 1987-90; atty. pvt. practice, Arlington, Va., 1990—. Sec. B.F. Saul Real Estate Investment Trust, Chevy Chase, 1972-87. Mem. ABA, Md. Bar Assn., D.C. Bar, Va. Bar, Arlington County Bar Assn., Nat. Acad. Elder Law Attys., Am. Soc. Corp. Secs.

WILDING, DIANE, computer scientist, consultant; b. Chicago Heights, Ill., Nov. 7, 1942; d. Michael Edward and Katherine Surian; m. Manfred Georg Wilding, May 7, 1975 (div. 1980). BSBA in Acctg. magna cum laude, No. Ill. U., 1963; postgrad., U. Chgo., 1972-74; cert. in German lang., Goethe Inst., Rothenburg, Germany, 1984; cert. in internat. bus. German, Goethe Inst., Atlanta, 1994; cert. in Web page design, Kennesaw State U., 2000. Lic. cosmetologist. Sys. engr. IBM, Chgo., 1963-68, SAP cons. Atlanta, 1993—; data processing mgr. Am. Res. Corp., Chgo., 1969-72; system R & D project mgr. Continental Bank, Chgo., 1972-75; fin. industry mktg. rep. IBM Can., Ltd., Toronto, 1976-79; regional telecom. mktg. exec. Control Data Corp., Atlanta, 1980-84; gen. mgr. The Plant Plant, Atlanta, 1985-92. Pioneer installer on-line automatic teller machines Pos Equipment. Author: The Canadian Payment System: An International Perspective, 1977. Mem. Chgo. Coun. Fgn. Rels.; bd. dirs. Easter House Adoption Agy., Chgo., 1974—76. Mem.: Internat. Brass Soc., Mensa, Goethe Inst., Libertyville Racquet Club, Royal Ont. Yacht Club, Ponte Verde Club (Fla.). Avocations: travel, gourmet cooking, languages, antiques. Home: PO Box 723055 Atlanta GA 31139-0055 Office: IBM 1600 Riveredge Pkwy NW Atlanta GA 30328-4697 Personal E-mail: wilding@usa.com.

WILDING, JAMES, music educator, composer; b. Johannesburg, Oct. 31, 1973; MusM, U. of Cape Town, South Africa, 1997, Youngstown State U., Ohio, 2001. Adj. faculty U. Cape Town, South Africa, 1996—97, Youngstown (Ohio) State U., 2001, U. Akron, Ohio, 2002—. Composer: (composition) Etude (Prescribed Piece for the UNISA/Transnet Internat. Piano competition), 1996, String Trio, 1997 (Oude Meester prize for South African Composers, 1997), Poem, 1996 (Prescribed Piece for the Hennie Joubert Nat. Piano Competition, 1998). Grantee Commn. for a New Work for Two Recorders and Piano, South African Music Rights Orgn., 2000; David B. Smith fellow, Kent State U., 2003. Mem.: Phi Beta Delta Honor Soc. for Internat. Scholars. Home: 131 Prestwick Dr Boardman OH 44512 Office: Sch of Music U of Akron 302 Buchtel Hall Akron OH 44325 Office Phone: 330-972-7590. Personal E-mail: jwilding@kent.edu.

WILDING, JAMES ANTHONY, airport administrator; b. Washington, Dec. 22, 1937; s. Anthony Warwick and Dorothy (Lauten) W.; m. Marcella Anne Gibbons, Aug. 5, 1961; children: Matthew, William, Patricia, Marcella. BS in Civil Engring., Catholic U., 1959. With planning dept. Bur. Nat. Capital Airports, Washington, 1959-63, with civil engring. dept., 1963-72, acting dir., 1974; chief engring. staff Met. Washington Airports, 1972-75, dep. dir., 1975-79, dir., 1979-87; pres., CEO Met. Washington Apts. Authority, Alexandria, Va., 1987—. Chmn. Airports Coun. Internat. N.A., 1995. Recipient Sr. Exec. Svc. Performance award Dept. Transp., 1981, Meritorious Exec. award Pres. of U.S., 1982, Outstanding Achievement award Sec. Transp., 1985., Comml. Air Transport award Aviation Week and Space Tech., 1997. Roman Catholic. Office: Metropolitan Washington Airports Authority 44 Canal Center Plz Alexandria VA 22314-1592

WILDMAN, MAX EDWARD, lawyer, director; b. Terre Haute, Ind., Dec. 4, 1919; s. Roscoe Ellsworth and Lena (Shaw) W.; m. Joyce Lenore Smith, Sept. 25, 1948; children: Leslie, William. BS, Butler U., 1941; JD, U. Mich., 1947; MBA, U. Chgo., 1952. Bar: Ill., Ind. Ptnr. Kirkland & Ellis, Chgo., 1947-67; mng. ptnr. Wildman, Harrold, Allen & Dixon, Chgo., 1967-89. Dir. Colt Industries, N.Y., Nat. Blvd. Bank, Ill. Contbr. articles to profl. jours. Trustee Butler U., Indpls., Lake Forest Hosp., Ill., Lake Bluff Library Bd., Ill.; chmn. Lake Bluff Zoning Bd. Served to lt. col. USAF, 1943-46; PTO Fellow Am. Coll. Trial Lawyers; mem. Soc. Trial Lawyers, Law Club, Legal Club, Trial Lawyers Club of Chgo. Clubs: Anglers (Chgo.), Pere Marquette Rod and Gun (Baldwin, Mich.), Shoreacres (Lake Bluff), Univ. of Chgo. Presbyterian. Office: Wildman Harrold Allen & Dixon 225 W Wacker Dr Chicago IL 60606-1224

WILDNAUER, RICHARD HARRY, pharmaceutical executive; b. New Kensington, Pa., Feb. 14, 1940; s. Richard Michael and Rosemary Elizabeth (Moore) Wildnauer; m. Sharon Ann Novick, Jan. 22, 1966; 1 child, Tara Lynne. BS in Chemistry, St. Vincent Coll., 1962; PhD in Biochemistry, W.Va. U., 1966; MBA in Mgmt., Rider Coll., 1974. NIH trainee W.Va. U., 1963—66; sr. rsch. assoc. in skin biology, exploratory rsch. divsn. Johnson & Johnson Domestic Operating Co., New Brunswick, NJ, 1975—77, assoc. mgr. tech. planning, exploratory rsch. divsn., 1975—77; sr. project coord., new products, pharm. divsn. McNeil Labs., Ft. Washington, Pa., 1979—82; dir. new product devel. Janssen Pharmaceutica Inc., New Brunswick, 1979—82, v.p. R&D, 1982—88; v.p. tech. and bus. devel. Johnson & Johnson Corp., New Brunswick, 1988—92; pres. Baker Cummins Dermatologicals, Inc., Lakewood, NJ, 1992—95; pres., CEO NeoStrata Co., Inc., Princeton, NJ, 1995—. Contbr. articles to profl. jours. Trustee, bd. dirs. United Way Ctrl. N.J., 1988—95, pres., 1991—93. Mem.: Soc. Co. Chemists, N.Y. Acad. Scis., Med. Mycology Soc., Soc. Investigative Dermatology, Am. Acad. Dermatology, Am. Mgmt. Assn., Pharm. advt. Club, Sigma Xi. Roman Catholic. Office: NeoStrata Co Inc 4 Research Way Princeton NJ 08540-6618 Office Phone: 609-520-0715 302.

WILDRICK, KENYON JONES, minister; b. Rahway, N.J., June 14, 1933; s. Stanley B. and Adele (Jones) W.; BA, Trinity Coll., Hartford, Conn., 1955, BD, Princeton U., 1958, ThM, 1962, DD, Trinity Coll., Conn., 1985; m. Nancy Ruth Mersfelder, Aug. 23, 1958; children: Catherine Ruth, Margaret Jeanne, Kenyon Douglas. Ordained to ministry Presbyterian Ch., 1958; asst. minister Community Congregational Ch., Short Hills, N.J., 1958-61, assoc. minister, 1961-67, sr. minister, 1967-93, min. emeritus, 1993—; sr. min. Pilgrim Congregational Ch., Warren, N.J., 1993—; campus ministry Middle Atlantic Conf., 1962-65. Bd. dirs. Milburn-Short Hills chpt. ARC, 1963 64; ch. and ministry com. N.J. Assn., 1965—; trustee Ctr. Theol. Inquiry, Princeton, N.J., 1985—; pres. bd. trustees Overlook Protestant Chaplaincy Program, 1973—; trustee investment com. Fellowship Conn. Congregational Chs., 1996—; trustee, vice-chmn. Presbyn. Homes N.J., 1981—. Mem. Millburn Clergy Assn. (chmn. 1987—), Rotary (dir. Milburn Club 1973), Delta Phi. Home: 214 Preston Dr Gillette NJ 07933-1439 Office: 105 Mountainview Rd Warren NJ 07059-5020

WILDS, BONNIE, author, community volunteer; b. Phila. m. Walter Warren Wilds; children: Stephanie Wilds Shea Blackhurst, Eugenia Wilds Ardrey, Vanessa Wilds Cunningham Wassenar, Pamela Wilds Cole. BA, Sarah Lawrence Coll.; MA, PhD, U. Pitts. Desk officer Dept. State, Washington, economist. Author: A Critical Edition of El Animal Profeta by Antonio Mira de Amescua, 1979. Women's com. Carnegie Mus. Art, Pitts.; social svc. bd. Shadyside Hosp., Pitts; pres. women's aux. bd. Magee Women's Hosp., Pitts; v.p. Bethany Lenox Hill Day Care Ctr., N.Y.C.; pres. bd. dirs., v.p. Mary Walton Children's Ctr., N.Y.C.; pres., bd. dirs. Musicians Emergency Fund.; bd. dirs., pres. Hospitality Com. for UN Dels.; resource coordinator Inst. of Internat. Edn.; past v.p. Hospitality Com. for UN Dels. Recipient Pub. Svc. citation, City of Pitts. Fellow: Frick Collection, Pierpont Morgan Libr.; mem.: MLA, The New Eng. Soc., Preservation Soc. Newport County, St. George's Soc., Church Club, Union Club, The Pilgrims, Rolling Rock Club (Ligonier, Pa.), Colony Club (N.Y.). Republican. Episcopalian. Avocations: community service, travel, reading. Home: 20 E 68th St New York NY 10021-5837

WILDS, DANIEL O. health products executive; BA, Calif. State U., L.A.; MBA, Northwestern U., Evanston, Ill. With Baxter Internat., 1968—92, pres. chemotherapy svc. divsn., pres., COO diagnostic joint venture with Genentech, gen. mgr. Mexico City ops., gen. mgr. Container Devel. Bus. Ctr., dir. strategy devel., v.p. corp. alliances; pres., CEO Medisense, Inc., Adeza Biomed. Corp., 1992—96, Shiloov Biotechnologies (USA) Inc., 1997—98; pres., CEO, dir. Northwest Biotherapeutics, Inc., Boethell, Wash., 1998—. Office: Northwest Biotherapeutics Inc 22322 20th Ave SE #150 Bothell WA 98021-8446

WILDSTEIN, EVAN, venture capitalist; BBA, U. Mich., Ann Arbor. Fin. analyst acquisition and pvt. fin. group Dean Witter Reynolds, Inc.; joined Kohlberg & Co., 1994, prin., 1999. Bd. dirs. Allied Aerospace Industries, Inc., Holley Performance Products, Inc., Tinnerman Palnut Engineered Products LLC. Office: Kohlberg & Co LLC 111 Radio Cir Mount Kisco NY 10549 Office Phone: 914-241-7430. Office Fax: 914-241-7476.

WILDT, KATHERINE ANN, literature educator, writer, educator; d. Albert Edward Wildt and Veronica Julia Boesch Wildt. AB in English and Speech, Creighton U., 1970, MA in English, 1975; PhD in English, St. Louis U., 1996. Cert. English and speech tchr. grades 7-12 Mo. Tchr. various grades schs. and locations, 1957—72, St. Elizabeth Acad., St. Louis, 1972—79; instr. St. Mary's Coll., O'Fallon, Mo., 1979—80, 1981—87; tchr. St. Mary's Acad., O'Fallon, 1987—90, St. Mary's H.S., St. Louis, 1992—95; prof. Mo. Valley Coll., Marshall, 1996—. Adj. prof. St. Louis U., St. Louis, 1990—93, St. Louis, 1995—96; mem. Acad. Issues Com., Marshall, 1996—98; co-chair subcom. and steering com. North Ctrl. Com., Marshall, 2002—04; lectr. in field. Author: Elizabeth Gaskell's Use of Color, 1999; co-author: Constitutions of Sisters of the Most Precious Blood, 1981; contbr. articles to jours., poems to jours. Reader Advanced Placement, Daytona Beach, Fla., 2001, 2002. Recipient Govs. award for excellence in tchg., State of Mo., 2001. Mem.: MLA, Victorians Inst., Nat. Coun. Tchrs. English. Roman Catholic. Avocations: reading, drawing, making potpourri. Home: 373 W Jackson Marshall MO 65340 Office: Mo Valley Coll 500 E College Marshall MO 65340

WILE, JOAN, composer, lyricist, singer; b. Rochester, N.Y., July 17, 1931; d. Louis and Janet Louise (Wile) Meltzer; children: Ron Wasserman, Diana Wasserman McCloskey. BA, U. Chgo., 1952. Freelance composer, lyricist, singer, mus. book writer. Rec. artist Vanguard Records, 1954; singer Storyville, 1954, The Crystal Palace, 1957; mem. vocal-revue act The Neighbors performances include The Village Vanguard, Le Ruban Bleu, The Bon Soir and The Living Room; singer, lyricist feature film The Happy Hooker, 1974; singer radio and TV jingles, movie sound tracks, supper clubs, hotels, TV music spls. and variety shows; lyricist, composer mus. Tobacco Road, 1974, Seven Ages of Woman, 1987 (named most promising new musical); writer, producer When They Turned on the Tap at the Watergate, The Truth Come Pourin' Out; lyricist songs for Romper Room, 1983; lyricist, composer, writer People is People, 1983; lyricist, composer script for children's albums for Golden and Peter Pan Records, others; lyricist, composer material in Julius Monk's Upstairs at the Downstairs, 1958; lyricist, composer, performer Nancy's Economic Plan, 1980; lyricist, composer Mothers and Daughters, 1984; lyricist, composer, author The Symposium, 1987; lyricist, composer From There to Here, 1987; writer Rhyme, Women and Song; lyricist, librettist, composer Museum of Natural Sex History, 1992; composer Women Walking, 1997, composer-lyricist What A Woman (Homage to Peggy Lee), 2003. Organizer Women in Def. Eleanor Roosevelt, N.Y.C., 1989—, Grandmothers Against the War, 2003; founder, organizer Revolt Against the Tax Refund, 2001; bd. dirs. Soc. Singers, 2002. Runner-up Am. Song Festival, 1976. Mem.: ASCAP (Popular award 1970—2003), AFTRA, SAG, Theatre Artists Workshop, Dramatists Guild, Soc. of Singers (bd. dirs.). Avocation: political and musical activities. Home and Office: 263 West End Ave Apt 4B New York NY 10023-2613 E-mail: jwile@prodigy.net.

WILE, PHILIP HODGES, law educator; b. Cleve., Dec. 2, 1930; s. Ralph H. and Elizabeth (Mower) W.; m. Nancy D. Wile, Oct. 26, 1952 (dec. Jan. 1992); children: James, Elizabeth Wile Meyerowitz, Janet Wile Melikian; m. JoAnne Steninger, May 29, 1993. AB, Stanford U., 1952, JD, 1957. Bar: Calif. 1957. Assoc. Kimble, Thomas, Snell, Jamison & Russell, Fresno, Calif., 1957-61;

asst. prof. law Stanford (Calif.) Sch. Law, 1961-62; ptnr., shareholder Thomas, Snell, Jamison, Russell & Asperger, Fresno, 1962-87; prof. law, dir. tax programs U. Pacific McGeorge Sch. Law, Sacramento, 1987—. Author: Federal Income Tax—A Case Book on the Basics, 1995; contbr. articles to law jours. Pres. Sacramento Traditional Jazz Soc. Found., 1996-99. Mem. ABA, Order of Coif. Office: U Pacific McGeorge Sch Law 3200 5th Ave Sacramento CA 95817-2705 Office Phone: 916-739-7009. E-mail: pwile@pacific.edu.

WILENSKY, GAIL ROGGIN, economist, researcher; b. Detroit, June 14, 1943; d. Albert Alan and Sophia (Blitz) Roggin; m. Robert Joel Wilensky, Aug. 4, 1963; children: Peter Benjamin, Sara Elizabeth. AB with honors, U. Mich., 1964, MA in Econs., 1965, PhD in Econs., 1968; hon. degree, Hahnemann U., 1993, Rush U., 1997, U. of Scis., Phila., 2002. Economist President's Commn. on Income Maintenance Programs; exec. dir. Md. Coun. of Econ. Advs., 1969-71; sr. rschr. Urban Inst., Washington, 1971-73; assoc. rsch. scientist, pub. policy and pub. health U. Mich., Ann Arbor, 1973-75, vis. asst. prof. econs., 1973-75; sr. rsch. mgr. Nat Ctr. for Health Svcs. Rsch., Hyattsville, Md., 1975-83; assoc. profl. lectr. George Washington U., 1976-78; v.p. div. health affairs Project HOPE, Millwood, Va., 1983-90; adminstr. Health Care Fin. Adminstrn., Washington, 1990-92; dep. asst. to the pres. for policy devel. White House, 1992-93; sr. fellow Project HOPE, Bethesda, Md., 1993—, chair phys. payment rev. com., 1995-97; chmn. Medicare Payment Adv. Commn., 1997—2001; co-chair Pres.'s Task Force to Improve Health-care Delivery for Vets., 2001—03. Contbr. 100 articles in field to profl. jours. Vol. Am. Heart Assn., 1980-85, bd. dirs., 2002—; mem. health adv. com. Compt. Gen. U.S., 1987-90; bd. dirs. United Healthcare Corp., Cephalon, ManorCare, Gentiva Health Svcs., Inc., Quest Diagnostics; mem. vis. com. med. sch. U. Mich., 1993-97; trustee United Mine Workers Am. Retirement Fund, 1993—. Flinn Found. disting. scholar, 1985; recipient Dean Conley award Am. Coll. Healthcare Execs., 1989. Mem. NAS (mem. inst. medicine 1989—), Am. Econ. Assn. (women's com. 1982-84), Fedn. Orgn. of Profl. Women (chmn. econ. task force 1981-83), Am. Statis. Assn., Nat. Tax Assn., Washington Women Economists, Assn. Health Svc. Rsch. (dir. 1984-87), Found. Health Svc. Rsch. (bd. dir. 1987-90), Acad. Health (chair bd. dir. 2000—, Cosmos Club (Washington). Home: 2807 Battery Pl NW Washington DC 20016-3439 Office Phone: 301-656-7401.

WILENSKY, JULIUS M. publishing company executive; b. Stamford, Conn., Oct. 10, 1916; s. Joseph and Mary (Wainstein) W.; m. Dorothy T. Jobrack, July 2, 1939 (dec. 1998); children— Joseph L. (dec.), Nancy L. Jamie, Martha J. Hansen; m. Jennifer Meinert Wilensky, Aug. 13, 2000. Student, Rensselaer Poly. Inst., 1934-36. Methods engr. Yale & Towne Mfg. Co., Stamford, 1939-49, prodn. mgr., 1953-57; dir. purchasing lock and hardware div. Eaton Yale & Towne, Rye, N.Y., 1957-67; mayor of Stamford, 1969-73; dir. materials, arms operations Winchester div. Olin Corp., New Haven, 1973-78; pres. Wescott Cove Pub. Co., 1978—. Lectr. in field. Author guide books on cruising L.I. Sound, Cape Cod, Windward Islands, Bay Islands of Honduras and Abacos; contbr. articles to boating mags. and newspapers; comtbg. editor: Rudder, 1970-77; author cruising columns Ea. and So. edits. Sea mag., 1978-80, Rudder mag., 1981-83; editor cruising guides to Tahiti, French Soc. Islands, Maine (2 vols.), Turkey, Belize, Mexico's Caribbean Coast, I Don't Do Portholes, Lights and Legends, Beachcombing and Beachcrafting, Pacific Wanderer, Irma Quarterdeck Reports, Inside American Paradise, Beachcruising and Coastal Camping, Circumnagivation: Sail the Trade Winds (2 vols.), First Time Around, Chesapeake Bay Cruising Guide-Vol. I, Upper Bay, Florida Keys and Everglades Cruising Guide. Bd. dirs. Stamford Ctr. for Arts, 1981-90; treas. Lifeline, 1983-85; first v.p. Met. Regional Coun., 1973; mem. Tri-State Regional Planning Commn., 1971-73, Stamford Bd. Fin., 1965-69, Stamford Planning Bd., 1963-65; chmn. Coun. Rep. Clubs, Stamford, 1961-62. With USAAF, 1943-46. Named Republican of Yr. Stamford Reps., 1962 Mem. Am. Mgmt. Assn., Stamford Power Squadron, Stamford Good Govt. Assn. (dir., treas. 1949-57), Stamford Chamber Residences (pres. 1953-55) Home: Apt 54 202 Soundview Ave Stamford CT 06902-7046 Fax: (203)383-8143. *To be productive in fields or enterprises which are useful to other people has been my aspiration, and it's a high one. It's important to set goals early in life, then follow a plan to obtain the education and experience required to achieve these goals. Courage, honesty, objectivity, determination, hard work, and consideration for others will enable one to become outstanding in any field.*

WILENSKY, ROBERT J. plastic surgeon, historian; b. N.Y.C., Oct. 2, 1941; s. Thomas and Gertrude Wilensky; m. Gail S. Roggin Aug. 4, 1963; children: Peter, Sara. BA, U. Mich., 1962, MD, 1966; PhD in History, Am. U., 2000. Diplomate Am. Bd. Surgery, Am. Bd. Plastic Surgery. Resident in gen. surgery U. Md., Balt., 1969-73; resident in plastic surgery U. Mich., Ann Arbor, 1973-75; pvt. practice, Washington, 1975-99; historian Am. U., Washington, 2000—, George Mason U., Va., 2000—. Chmn. sect. plastic surgery Columbia Hosp. for Women, Washington, 1983-93. Contbr. articles to med. jours., including Am. Jour. Ob-Gyn., Jour. Plastic and Reconstructive Surgery, Clin. Procs. Children's Hosp., Jour. Mil. Medicine; also chpts. to books. Capt. M.C., U.S. Army, 1967-69, Vietnam. Decorated Bronze Star. Fellow: ACS; mem.: Washington Soc. History Medicine (pres. 2002—03), Nat. Capital Soc. Plastic Surgery (pres. 1992), Am. Soc. Aesthetic Surgery, Am. Soc. Plastic Surgery. Jewish. Avocations: biking, skiing, photography. Home and Office: 2807 Battery Pl NW Washington DC 20016-3439 E-mail: robertjwilensky@erols.com.

WILES, ANDREW J. mathematician, educator; b. England, Apr. 11, 1953; married. BS in Math., Oxford U., England; PhD in Math., Cambridge U., England. Lectr. Inst. Advanced Studies, Princeton, NJ; asst., assoc. prof. math. Harvard U., Cambridge, Mass.; prof. math. Princeton U., 1982—88, 1990—. Recipient Wolf Prize in Math., 1995, NAS award in Math., 1996, Royal medal, Royal Soc., 1996, Frank Nelson Cole prize in algebra, Am. Math. Soc., 1996, Frank Nelson Cole prize in number theory, 1997; fellow John D. and Catherine T. MacArthur Found. fellow, 1997. Achievements include solving (with Richard Taylor) Pierre de Fermat's last theory of 1637. Office: Princeton U Dept Math, 602 Fine Hall Princeton NJ 08544-0001

WILES, CHARLES PRESTON, minister; b. Frederick, Md., Aug. 5, 1918; s. Charles Wesley and Nellie (Burgess) W.; m. Mary McCallum; children: Mary Margaret, Charles Preston, Wade Burgess. AB, Washington Coll., 1939; postgrad., U. Va., 1940; MA, Duke U., 1945, PhD (Univ. fellow 1947-51, Kearns Honor fellow 1949-50), 1951; B.D., Va. Theol. Sem., 1947. Ordained to ministry Episc. Ch., 1947. Priest-in-charge St. Joseph's Ch., Durham, N.C., 1947-51; rector St. Mary's Episcopal Ch., Burlington, N.J., 1951-64; pres., trustee Burlington Coll., 1951-64, faculty cons., 1956-64; mem. faculty Phila. Div. Sch., 1959-62, lectr. ch. history, 1960-62; dean St. Matthew's Episcopal Cathedral, Dallas, 1964-87, dean emeritus, 1989; assoc. priest St. Luke's, Dallas, 1987—. Faculty U.S. Army War Coll., Carlisle, Pa., 1964; dep. gen. Conv. from Diocese Dallas, 1967, 69, 70, 73, 76, 79; del. Provincial Synod from Diocese Dallas, 1966, 69, 72, 75, 78; mem. exec. council Diocese Dallas, 1967-77, 84-86, pres. mem. standing com., 1970-73, pres., 1971-73, mem. bd. missions, 1967-69, chmn. dept. coll. work, 1965-71, mem. bd. examing chaplains, 1965-71; mem. standing liturgical commn.; dean, warden Cathedral Center for Continuing Edn. and Pastoral Concern, 1971-87, Commn. Ministry, 1971-76; dean Dallas Deanery, 1965-69, 84-86, Bicentennial preacher, 1975; pres. convocation and clericus Diocese of N.J., 1961-64; examining chaplain, mem. bd. missions, mem. bd. Christina edn., dean Burlington-Trenton convocation; instr., dean Drew Conf. for Adults in N.J., 1952-56; retreat conductor St. Martin's House, Bernardsville, N.J., St. John Bapt. Convent, Mendhan, N.J.; dean Diocesan Sch. Religion, N.J., 1962-63, Anglican Sch. Theology, 1971-75; parish life lab. and weekend conductor Nat. Dept. Christian Edn., 1962; co-founder, dean Princeton (N.J.) Conf., 1956-64; mem. Goals for Dallas Com.; co-chmn. N.Am. Cathedral Deans' Conf., 1980-81 Author: Sacrament and Sacrifice, 2d edit., 1973, Lancelot Andrews, Caroline Divine, 1951, Lift Up Your Hearts, 1956, A Manual of Prayers, 1975, The Holy Eucharist: Word and Sacrament, 1993, The Gate of Heaven, 1993, A Centennial Narrative History of the Episcopal Diocese of Dallas, 1995, Troubadours of God, 1998, Windows for Faith, 2000. Trustee Gen. Theol. Sem., 1968-80; bd. dirs. Evergreen Home for Aging, St. Philip's Community Center, Overseas Mission Soc. Named Priest of Yr., 1969 Mem. Navy League, Ch. Hist. Soc. (dir. 1960-68), Kiwanian Club (Disting. Svc. award 1951, Disting. Citizen award Brunswick, Md. 1986), Dallas Athletic club, Chaparral, Vesper (Phila.) Club, Burlington County Country Club. Home: 7023 Northwood Rd Dallas TX 75225-2439 Personal E-mail: deanwdallastexas@mymail.com.

WILES, DAVID MCKEEN, chemist; b. Springhill, N.S., Can., Dec. 28, 1932; s. Roy McKeen and Olwen Gertrude (Jones) W.; m. Valerie Joan Rowlands, June 8, 1957; children: Gordon Stuart, Sandra Lorraine. BSc with honors, McMaster U., 1954, MSc, 1955; PhD in Chemistry, McGill U., 1957. Rsch. officer chemistry divsn. NRC Can., Ottawa, 1959-66, head textile chemistry sect. chemistry divsn., 1966-75, dir. chemistry divsn., 1975-90; pres. Plastichem Cons., Victoria, Canada, 1990—. Bd. dirs. MLB Industries; chmn. Can. High Polymer Forum, 1967—69; v.p. N.Am. Chem. Congress, Mexico City, 1975. Contbr. articles to profl. jours.; mem. editl. adv. bd. numerous profl. jours.; patentee in field. Can. Ramsay Meml. fellow, 1957-59. Fellow Chem. Inst. Can. (chmn. bd. dirs. 1972-74, pres. 1975-76, Dunlop Lectr. award 1981), Royal Soc. Chem. London, Royal Soc. Can.; mem. Am. Chem. Soc. (Polymer Chem. divsn.). Home and Office: 3965 Juan Fuca Terr Victoria BC Canada V8N 5W9 Office Phone: 250-721-0732. E-mail: dmwiles@telus.net.

WILES, EDWIN MCKINLEY, education educator, librarian; b. Ponca City, Okla., Sept. 14, 1948; s. William McKinley and Lova Mildred (Rau) Wiles. BA, Ctrl. State U., Edmond, Okla., 1970; MA, Ctrl. State U., 1973; MS, U. Ill., Urbana, 1971. Asst. cataloger, instr. U. Ill., Chgo., 1971—72; catalog libr. Okla. Dept. Libr., Oklahoma City, 1974—75; lectr. libr. sci. Ctrl. State U., Edmond, 1975—76; libr. Southwestern Libr. Assn., Dallas; dir. Edmond Libr., Edmond, 1977—84; info. svcs. coord. Dulaney-Browne Libr. Okla. City U., 1986—. Cons. Maua Meth. Hosp., Maua, Meru, Kenya, 1998, Electric Generating Authority of Thailand, Bangkok, 1999. Recipient Appreciation Cert., Internat. Student Assn., 1995. Mem.: ALA (life), Okla. Libr. Assn. (del. to Internat. Conv. Libr. and Assns. Bangkok 1999), Okla. Bibliographic Instrn. Coun. (pres. 1998—99), Assn. Coll. and Rsch. Libr. Democrat. United Methodist. Avocations: travel, reading, stamp collecting/philately, swimming. Office: Dulaney-Browne Libr Oklahoma City Univ 2501 N Blackwelder Oklahoma City OK 73106 Office Phone: 405-521-5065. Business E-Mail: ewiles@okcu.edu.

WILES, JAMES STEVEN, music educator; b. Tulsa, Okla., Dec. 16, 1963; s. James Merl and Evelyn Wiles; m. Belinda Mizer, Sept. 30, 1965. BA in Edn., Northeastern State U., Tahlequah, Okla., 1987. Cert. tchr. Okla. Band dir. Muskogee (Okla.) Pub. Schs., 1987—. Freelance trumpet player; composer, arranger. Composer: Northeastern State University Alma Mater. Choir dir. Meml. Christian Ch., Disciples of Christ, Muskogee, 1998. Mem.: NEA, Music Educators Nat. Conf., Northeastern State U. Alumni Assn. (life), Kappa Kappa Psi (hon.). Avocations: composing, trumpet performance, fishing. Home: 2914 W Broadway Muskogee OK 74401 Office: Muskogee 7th and 8th Grade Ctr 402 N S St Muskogee OK 74403 Personal E-mail: jswiles@cox.net.

WILES, PAUL MARTIN, hospital administration executive; b. Takoma Park, Md., May 11, 1947; married. BA, St. Michael's Coll., 1969; MHA, Duke U., 1971. Adminstrv. asst. Fanny Allen Hosp., Winooski, Vt., 1968-69; adminstrv. resident Forsyth Meml. Hosp., Winston-Salem, N.C., 1970-71, asst. adminstr., 1971, USAF Hosp., Kincheloe AFB, Mich., 1972-73; med. squad comdr. USAF Regional Hosp., Hampton, Va., 1973-74; asst. to pres. Forsyth County Hosp. Authority, Winston-Salem, 1974-75, v.p., 1975-79, sr. v.p., 1979-84; pres., CEO Carolina Medicorp Inc., Winston-Salem, 1985—; also adminstr. Forsyth Meml. Hosp., Winston-Salem. Contbr. articles to profl. jours. Mem. N.C. Hosp. Assn. (bd. dirs., chmn. regional adv. bd.). Office: Forsyth Meml Hosp 3333 Silas Creek Pkwy Winston Salem NC 27103-3090

WILES, WILLIAM WHARTON, retired federal government official; b. Knoxville, Tenn., June 9, 1931; s. James H. and Sally May (Wharton) W.; m. Lessley K. Decker, Aug., 1961; 1 child, Kenneth W. BA, Murray State U., 1953; MBA, U. Ky., 1959; PhD, U. Wis., 1973. Instr. U. Ky., 1959-61; with Fed. Res. Sys., Washington, 1964-98, sec. of bd., 1981-98. With U.S. Army, 1954-56. Home: 2635 Twin Ln York PA 17402 E-mail: Lessleyva@aol.com.

WILETS, LAWRENCE, physics educator; b. Oconomowoc, Wis., Jan. 4, 1927; s. Edward and Sophia (Finger) W.; m. Dulcy Elaine Margoles, Dec. 21, 1947; children: Ileen Sue, Edward E., James D.; m. Vivian C. Wolf, Feb. 8, 1976. BS, U. Wis., 1948; MA, Princeton U., 1950, PhD, 1952. Rsch. assoc. Project Matterhorn, Princeton, NJ, 1951-53, U. Calif. Radiation Lab., Livermore, 1953; NSF postdoctoral fellow Inst. Theoretical Physics, Copenhagen, 1953-55; staff mem. Los Alamos (N.Mex.) Sci. Lab., 1955-58; mem. Inst. Advanced Study, Princeton, 1957-58; mem. faculty U. Wash., Seattle, 1958—, prof. physics, 1962-95, prof. emeritus, 1995—. Cons. to pvt. and govt. labs.; vis. prof. Princeton U., 1969, Calif. Inst. Tech., 1971. Author: Theories of Nuclear Fission, 1964, Nontopological Solitons, 1989; contbr. over 180 articles to profl. jours. Del. Dem. Nat. Conv., 1968. NSF sr. fellow Weizmann Inst. Sci., Rehovot, Israel, 1961-62; Nordita prof. and Guggenheim fellow Lund (Sweden) U., Weizmann Inst., 1976—; Sir Thomas Lyle rsch. fellow U. Melbourne, Australia, 1989; recipient Alexander von Humboldt sr. U.S. scientist award, 1983. Fellow Am. Phys. Soc., AAAS; mem. Fedn. Am. Scientists, AAUP (pres. chpt. 1969-70, 73-75, pres. state conf. 1975-76), Explorers Club, Phi Beta Kappa (chpt. pres. 1996-97), Sigma Xi. Achievements include research on theory of nuclear structure and reactions, nuclear fission, atomic structure, atomic collisions, many body problems, subnuclear structure and elementary particles. Office: U Wash Dept Physics PO Box 351560 Seattle WA 98195-1560 Business E-Mail: wilets@u.washington.edu.

WILEY, ALBERT LEE, JR., physician, engineer, educator; b. Forest City, N.C., June 9, 1936; s. Albert Lee and Mary Louise (Davis) W.; m. Janet Lee Pratt, June 18, 1960; children: Allison Lee, Susan Caroline, Mary Catherine, Heather Elizabeth. B in Nuclear Engring., N.C. State U., 1958, postgrad., 1958-59; MD, U. Rochester, 1963; PhD, U. Wis., 1972. Diplomate Am. Bd. Nuclear Medicine, Am. Bd. Radiology, Am. Bd. Med. Physics, Am. Bd. Sci. in Nuclear Medicine. Nuclear engr. Lockheed Corp., Marietta, Ga., 1958; intern in surgery-medicine U. Va. Med. Sch., Charlottesville, 1963—64; resident in radiation therapy Sanford U., Palo Alto, Calif., 1964—65; resident, postdoctoral trainee U. Wis. Hosp., Madison, 1965—68; med. dir. USN Radiol. Def. Lab., San Francisco, 1968—69; nuclear safety instr. Navy Nuclear Weapons Training Ctr. North Is. Air Sta., Calif., 1968—70; staff physician Balboa Hosp., USN, San Diego, 1969—70; asst. prof. radiotherapy M.D. Anderson Hosp. U. Tex., Houston, 1972—73; assoc. dir., clin. dir. radiation oncology U. Wis., Madison, prof. radiology, human oncology, med. physics, nuclear safety ctr., 1970—88; vis. prof. U. Helsinki Hosp., Finland, 1979, The Norwegian Radium Hosp., Montebello, Norway, 1979; adj. prof. physics, chmn./prof. radiation, oncology, interim dir. cancer ctr. East Carolina U. Med. Sch., Greenville, NC, 1988—93; clin. prof. Cancer Ctr. East Carolina U., Greenville, NC, 2001—03; prof. emeritus human oncology and radiology U. Wis., Madison, 2000—; cons. radiation medicine Watson Clinic, Lakeland, Fla., 1994—2003; affiliate physician U. So. Fla. Moffit Cancer Ctr., Tampa, 2000—03; dir., sr. physician Radiation Energy Assistance Ctr., 2002—; dir. WHO Collaboratory Ctr. for Radiation Emergency Assistance, Oak Ridge, 2002—. Navy rep. to meetings on radiation accidents Internat. Atomic Energy Agy., U.S. Embassy, Vienna, Austria, 1969; nuclear safety instr. Nuclear Tng. Ctr.; sr. med. officer USN Radiol. Def. Lab. Radiation Accident Team, 1968-70; cons. Los Alamos Meson Therapy Project, 1971-73, U.S. NRC, adv. com. on Nuclear Reactor Safeguards, 1981-82, Nat. Cancer Inst., VA, 1989-2000, Dept. Vet. Affairs, Dept. Homeland Security, 2002—; completed bus. adminstrv. program in med. mgmt. U. N.C.-Chapel Hill, Sch. of Bus., 1999; advisor, cons. numerous univs., govt. agys. and biotech. corps.; gov. apptd. mem. Wis. State Radioactive Waste Bd., Wis. Gov.'s Coun. on Biotech., Gov.'s Com. on UN. Author more than 150 articles and abstracts on med. physics, med. and environ. health physics, neutron radiobiology, nuclear medicine, radiation biology and treatment of pancreatic, prostate, and head/neck cancer; assoc. editor Jour. Med. Physics. Mem. Greenville Mayor's Drug Task Force, 1989—93; bd. dirs. Greenville Salvation Army, 1989—94; Rep. candidate for U.S. Congress for 2d Wis. dist., 1982, 1984; Rep. primary candidate for gov. State of Wis., 1986; Rep. primary candidate N.C. 1st Dist. U.S. Congress, 2000; primary election candidate for U.S. Senate from N.C., 2002, Rep. primary candidate for, 2004. Lt. comdr. USNR, 1959—89, ret. USNR, 1989. Oak Ridge Inst. Nuclear Studies fellow N.C. State U., 1958-59; Phillips Acad. Andover scholar, 1953. Fellow: N.C. Inst. Polit. Leadership, Am. Coll. Nuclear Medicine, Am. Coll. Radiology, Am. Coll. Preventive Medicine; mem.: AMA, AAUP, Fla. Vols. in Medicine, N.C. Med. Soc., Am. Acad. Health Physics, Am. Bd. Sci. Nuc. Medicine (sec.-treas.), Am. Coll. Occupl.-Environ. Medicine, N.C. Assn. Physics Tchrs., Am. Soc. Therapeutic Radiation Oncologists, Am. Assn. Physicists in Medicine, Am. Nuc. Soc., Am. Legion, U.S. Navy Inst., Am. Cancer Soc. (N.C. bd.dirs. 1989—93, pres. Polk County, Fla. 1995), VFW, Vietnam Vets. Am., Scottish Rite, Masons, N.C. Rotary, IEEE (sr.), Tau Beta Pi, Phi Eta Sigma, Sigma Phi Epsilon, Phi Kappa Phi, Sigma Xi. Avocations: fishing, politics, painting, languages, hiking. Home: PO Box 588 Salter Path Rd Salter Path NC 28575-0588 Personal E-mail: aljanwiley@aol.com.

WILEY, CARL ROSS, timber company executive; b. Astoria, Oreg., Apr. 17, 1930; s. Hamilton Ross and Ada Ellen (Smith) W.; m. Dolores Eileen Brice, Dec. 19, 1953; children: Susan, Steven, Kenneth. BS in Indsl. Engring., Oreg. State U., 1958; grad. exec. tng. program, MIT, 1974. Quality control engr. Oreg. Metall. Corp., 1958-59; indsl. engr. Osborne Electronics Corp., Portland, Oreg., 1959-62; v.p. timber and mfg. Boise Cascade Corp., Idaho, 1962-80; exec. v.p. Roseburg (Oreg.) Lumber Co., 1980-85; chief exec. officer Puget Sound Plywood, Tacoma, 1986-93; pres., CEO Lane Plywood, Eugene, Oreg., 1993-96; retired, 1996. Bd. dirs. Boise YMCA, 1975-78. With AUS, 1951-53. Mem. Am. Plywood Assn. (trustee), Western Wood Products Assn. (bd. dirs., chmn. econ. svcs. 1974-80). Lutheran. E-mail: wileycd@juno.com.

WILEY, DAVID COLE, producer; b. Long Beach, Calif., Sept. 12, 1948; s. Norman Cole and Bettigene Rosamond W. Ind. prodr., 1987—. Prodr.: Abduction-the UFO Soap, 1987, Speak-Out, 1988-89, Coal Canyon BMX, 1989, PC 101-Computer Repair, 1989, Young Lives, 1990, A Slice of Life, 1990, 91, Hidden Talents, 1992, Rock Talk, 1992—, History of the Santa Ana Canyon, 1994-2001, Buena Park Journal, 1994-2001, Avenging Angel, 2001; (documentaries) In Search of the Butterfield Trail, 1990, George Key Ranch - Centennial Celebration, 1993, Visitors from Catalan, 1996, History of the Santa Ana River, 1997, The Steam Kalliope, 1998, Plan 10 from Outer Space, 1998, Avenging Angel, 2001, History of Orange County, 2002, The Rocky Road, 2003. Vice-pres. Santa Ana Canyon Hist. Coun., 1995-2001. Recipient Western Access Video Excellence award Nat. Fedn. Local Cable Programmers, 1992, CABY Comcast Cablevision, 1996. Mem. Alliance Cmty. Media. Address: PO Box 6481 Fullerton CA 92834-6481

WILEY, DIANNE, aeronautical engineer; PhD in Applied Mechanics, UCLA; student, Def. Systems Mgmt. Coll., 1996. With Northrop Grumman, mgr. airframe tech., sr. tech. specialist on B-2 program; program mgr. Boeing Phantom Wks., Seal Beach, Calif. Office: Boeing Phantom Works PO Box 2515 Seal Beach CA 90740

WILEY, EDWIN PACKARD, retired lawyer; b. Chgo., Dec. 10, 1929; s. Edwin Garnet and Marjorie Chastina (Packard) W.; m. Barbara Jean Miller, May 21, 1949; children: Edwin Miller, Clayton Alexander, Stephen Packard. BA, U. Chgo., 1949, JD, 1952. Bar: Wis. 1952, Ill. 1952, U.S. Dist. Ct. (ea. dist.) Wis. 1953, U.S. Supreme Ct. 1978. Assoc. Foley & Lardner, Milw., 1952-60, prtnr., 1960-98; ret. Bd. dirs. Genetic Testing Inst., Inc., other corps. and founds. Co-author: Bank Holding Companies: A Practical Guide to Bank Acquisitions and Mergers, 1988, Wisconsin Uniform Commercial Code Handbook, 1971; author: Promotional Arrangements: Discrimination in Advertising and Promotional Allowances, 1976; editor in chief U. Chgo. Law Rev., 1952. Bd. dirs. Blood Ctr. of Southeastern Wis., pres., 1978-82; pres. Blood Ctr. Rsch. Found., Inc., 1983-87; v.p. Friends of Schlitz Audubon Ctr., Inc., 1975-87; active United Performing Arts Fund of Milw.; pres. Wis. Conservatory ofMusic, 1968-73; pres. First Unitarian Soc. Milw., 1961-63; v.p. Mid-Am. Ballet Co., 1971-73, Milw. Ballet Co., 1973-74; pres. Florentine Opera Co., 1983-86; bd. dirs. Milw. Symphony Orch., pres., 1993-95; bd. dirs. Milw. Pub. Mus., Inc., sec., 1992—; bd. dirs. Wis. History Found., v.p., 1998—; bd. dirs. Preserve Our Parks, Inc., 1999—; mem. Wis. Gov.'s Commn. on Historic Sites, 2002--. Mem. ABA, State Bar of Wis., Milw. Bar Assn., Am. Law Inst., Order of Coif, Univ. Club, Phi Beta Kappa (pres. Greater Milw. assn. 1962-63). Home: 929 N Astor St Unit 2101 Milwaukee WI 53202-3488 Office Phone: 414-297-5780. Personal E-mail: epwiley@execpc.com. Business E-Mail: ewiley@foleylaw.com.

WILEY, GREGORY ROBERT, publisher; b. Sept. 21, 1951; s. William Joseph and Terese (Kunz) W.; children: Kathleen, Mary Glennon. BA in Pers. Adminstrn., U. Kans., 1974. Dist. sales mgr. Reader's Digest, St. Loius, 1976-80, regional sales dir. Chgo., 1980-82; nat. sales mgr. retail divsn. Rand McNally & Co., Chgo., 1982-83, nat. sales mgr. premium incentive divsn., 1983-86, nat. sales mgr. bookstore and mass market sales, 1986-88; book pub. The Sporting News, St. Louis, 1988-90; v.p. mktg. Marketmakers Internat., St. Louis, 1990-93, Sofsource Inc., St. Louis, 1993—96; eastern regional v.p. Handleman Co., St. Louis, 1996—2002; dir. sales and marketing, books The Sporting News, St. Louis, 2002—. Mem. Nat. Premium Sales Execs., Promotional Mktg. Assn. Am. Roman Catholic. Avocations: private pilot, historic restoration, golf. Home: Apt 1B 4309 Maryland Ave Saint Louis MO 63108-2748

WILEY, JAMES FRANCIS, emergency medical technician, civilian military employee; b. Lakewood, Calif., Nov. 20, 1963; s. Roy Oliver and Catherine Anne Anderson; m. Susan Lynn Stadtler Barr, Jan. 9, 1988; children: Matthew Ryan Barr, Andrew Joseph Barr, Lauren Michelle. At, Long Beach CC, 1986—87, Monterey Peninsula Coll., 1989—91; cert., Waynesville Tech. Acad., Mo., 2003. Lic. EMT Mo., registered EMT-Basic Nat. Registry of EMT's, 2003. Combat engr. to staff sgt. U.S. Army, 1983—2003; EMT Dixon Ambulance Dist., Dixon, Mo., 2003—; emergency svcs. techniciam U.S. Army Med. Command, Ft. Leonard Wood, Mo., 2004—. Combat lifesaver U.S. Army, 1989—2003. Mem.: Nat. Registry of EMT's.

WILEY, JASON LARUE, JR., neurosurgeon; b. Canandaigua, N.Y., Dec. 2, 1917; s. Jason LaRue and Eva Althea (Moore) W.; m. Alma Williams, Jan. 4, 1944 (div. Feb. 1956); children: Robert W., Richard L.; m. Ann Valentine Gerrish, Apr. 14, 1956 (div. July 1979); children: Martha V., Pamela M., Catherine A. Student, Antioch Coll., 1934-37; MD, Harvard U., 1941. Diplomate Am. Bd. Surgery, Am. Bd. Neurol. Surgery. Intern Kings County Hosp., Bklyn., 1941-42; asst. resident surgery Ellis Hosp., Schenectady, N.Y., 1948-49; from asst. to assoc. resident surgery Rochester (N.Y.) Gen. Hosp., 1949-51; from asst. to assoc. to chief resident neurosurgery Yale U. and Hartford Hosp., New Haven and Hartford, Conn., 1951-54; practice medicine specializing in neurosurgery Kansas City, Mo., 1954—56, Rochester, NY, 1956—89. Chief neurosurgery Rochester Gen. Hosp., 1959-71, emeritus neurosurgeon, 1989—; clin. asst. prof. neurosurgery U. Rochester, 1961-88. Mem. Bd. for Profl. Med. Conduct, N.Y. State Dept. Health, Troy, N.Y., 1985-2004. Served to lt. comdr. USN, 1942-47, PTO. Mem. Med. Soc. County Monroe, Med. Soc. State N.Y., N.Y. State Neurosurg. Soc., Congress Neurol. Surgeons, Am. Assn. Neurol. Surgeons, Canandaigua Yacht Club. Republican. Episcopalian. Avocations: sailing, skiing, fishing, genealogy. Office: 1445 Portland Ave Rochester NY 14621-3036

WILEY, JOHN D. academic administrator; BS in Physics, Ind. U., 1964; MS in Physics, U. Wis., Madison, 1965, PhD in Physics, 1968. Tech. staff Bell Telephone Labs., Murray Hill, NJ, 1968—74; Alexander von Humboldt rsch. and tng. fellow Max Planck Inst., Stuttgart, Germany, 1974—75; mem. elec. and computer engring. faculty U. Wis., Madison, 1975—, co-founder Ctr. for X-Ray Lithography and Engring. Rsch. Ctr. for Plasma-Aided Mfg., chair Materials Sci. program, 1982—86, assoc. dean for rsch., Coll. Engring., 1986—89, dean, Grad. Sch., and sr. rsch. officer, 1989—94, provost and vice chancellor for acad. affairs, 1994—2000, chancellor, 2001—. Office: U Wis 161 Bascom Hall 500 Lincoln Dr Madison WI 53706

WILEY, JOHN EDWIN, cytogeneticist; b. Roanoke, Va., Mar. 2, 1951; s. James Edwin and Marie Rita (Cassell) W. BA, U. N.C., Greensboro, 1973, MA, 1976; PhD, N.C. State U., 1981. Diplomate Am. Bd. Med. Genetics-Clin. Cytogenetics. Biomed. rschr. St. Paul's Coll., Lawrenceville, Va., 1981-82; postdoctoral trainee U. Wis., Madison, 1982-84; mem. faculty East Carolina U. Sch. Medicine, Greenville, NC, 1984—. Contbr. articles to profl. jours. Biomed. rsch. support grantee United Way, Greenville, 1986-87, USPHS, Washington, 1987-90. Mem. AAAS, Am. Soc. Human Genetics, Am. Soc. Zoologists, Am. Soc. Ichthyologists and Herpetologists. Democrat. Achievements include observation that certain genes on frog chromosomes seem to move frequently around, that chromosome constitution in many breast cancer tumors seems normal, that in some patients with ring X chromosomes the ring may not be turned off, that the addition of tumor promoting agents helps white blood cells in many vertebrates to divide, and that DNA sequences on ends of frog chromosomes are the same as those on the ends of human chromosomes. Office: East Carolina U Brody Sch Medicine Moye Blvd Greenville NC 27858-4300 Home: 206 Ravenwood Dr Greenville NC 27834-6737 Office Phone: 252-744-2525. E-mail: wileyj@mail.ecu.edu.

WILEY, MICHAEL E. oil industry executive; BS in Petroleum Engring., U. Tulsa; MBA, U. Dallas. Various engring. and operational positions ARCO Gas and Oil Co., various locations, 1972, sr. and exec. v.p., pres., 1993—2000, COO, 1998—2000; pres. Vastar, 1993—94, CEO, 1994—96, chmn. bd. dirs.; chmn., pres., CEO Baker Hughes Inc., Houston, 2000—. Office: Baker Hughes Inc 3900 Essex Ln Ste 1200 Houston TX 77027-5177

WILEY, MILLICENT YODER, realtor, pianist, accompanist, retired secondary school choir director; b. Mercedes, Tex., June 7, 1923; d. Frank and Grace Yoder; m. William Gregory Wiley, Mar. 25, 1946; children: Sandra Kay Wiley, Patti Gayle Wiley Stickle. BS, Tex. State Coll. Women, 1949; postgrad., U. Houston, 1950-53. Choral dir., music tchr. schs. in Tex. and La., 1945-60; music tchr. Kingsville (Tex.) Ind. Sch. Dist., 1960-80, choral dir., 1960—80, trustee, 1981-87, v.p., 1986-87; choral dir. H.M. King H.S., 1964-80, ret., 1980. Choral adjudication, Tex., 1960—; clinician for area choirs, 1965—86; area admissions advisor, adminstr. Pacific Am. Inst., 1976—80; state dir. South Tex. for Am. Internat. Edn. and Tng., 1980—83; Tex. rep. Internat. Travel Study, Inc., 1983—90; adminstr. Travel Selections, 1990—96, 2000, 04; pianist Tex. State Fedn. Women's Clubs, 1994—96. Ch. organist various Meth. Ch., Tex. and La., 1935-65; bd. dirs. Kingsville chpt. Am. Heart Assn., 1973-78, Cmty. Concerts Assn., 1994-96, Helen Kleberg Cmty. Ctr., 1994-96, Kingsville Action Com.; mem. Tex. All-State Alumni Bd., 1995, 2000; active Mayor's City Com., Mayor's Future Com., 1993-96, Rep. Task Force. Recipient various certs. appreciation. Mem.: NEA, Tex. Assn. Sch. Bds. (trustee 1981—87, Kingsville ISD v.p. 1986—87), Kingsville Ret. Tchrs., Tri-City Ret. Tchrs., Fgn. Study League (counselor 1970—72, adminstr. 1973—76, advisor, prin.), Tex. Music Adjudicators Assn. (charter mem.), Tex. State Tchrs. Assn., Tex. Choral Dirs. Assn. (state clinic condr. 1977, accompanist for vocal and instrumental soloists 1983—85), Tex. Music Educators Assn. (clinician 1973, bd. dirs. 1973—74), Music Educators Nat. Conf., Am. Choral Dirs. Assn., Am. Sch. Bd. Assn. (trustee 1981—87), 36th Infantry Divsn. Assn. (soloist for men's meetings and ceremonies 1980—, 1st v.p. nat. ladies aux. 1989—90, pres. 1990—91, men's bd. dirs. 1990—91, 2nd v.p. 1999—2003, pres. nat. 2003—, men's bd. dirs. 2003—, nat. bd. dirs. 2003—, 1990—91), Kingsville C. of C. Navy League (nat. dir. 1998—2002, nat. dir. emeritus 2003—), Future Homemakers (hon.), Gen. Women's Club Kingsville (parliamentarian 1992—94, pres. 1994—96, chmn. As You Like It dept.), Duplicate Bridge Club, NAS Bridge Club, Kingsville Country Club, Monday Bridge Club, Exxon Bridge Club, Kiwanis (pianist Kingsville Club 1985—98), Rotary (pianist 1966—, first woman mem. 1987, chmn. membership devel. com. 1987—, fellowship chair 1997—98, mem. scholarship com. and social com. 2000—, fellowship chair 2001—03, past social chmn., program chmn. and membership chmn., fellowship chair 2001—04), Exxon Annuitant Club (bd. dirs. 1992—94), Women's Club Kingsville (chmn. "As You Like It" dept. 1990, 1st vice chmn. 1992—94, gen. club parlimentarian 1992—94, pres. 1994—96), Music Club Kingsville (pres. 1982—84, 3d v.p. 1988—89, 1st v.p. 1989—91). Methodist. Home: 229 Helen Marie Ln Kingsville TX 78363-7305

WILEY, PAMELA MICHELLE, science educator, writer; d. R.D. Henson and Betty Joyce Toppen, Henson; m. Doyle Joseph Wiley, May 3, 1956; children: Doyle Joseph Jr., Jeremy Quinn. BS, Tex. So. U., 1980. Cert. computer technologist Electronic Inst., Tex., 1985. Mgr. Gap Inc., Houston, 1979—80; sales sec. All-Pro KYOK-Radio Sta., Houston, 1985—88; owner/operator Daycare Acad., Houston, 1985—91; owner/dir. Miss Jr. Sophisticates, Houston, 1997—2000; tchr./ pvt. tutor North Forest Ind. Sch. Dist., Houston, 1995—; asst. editor The Basketball Report (monthly sport newsletter), Houston, 2000—. Cons. The Glorious Co., Houston, 2001—. Author (illustrator): (self help book) Creative Images, (childrens' book) Who Can, (self help booklet) Teacher's Tool Box, (children's short story) Jeremiah and Smokey #2; author: (comprehensive guide for H.S. grads.) College Bound. Ofcl. mem. Am. Legion, Washington, 2002; v.p. North Forest Alumni Assn., Houston, 1999—2002; vol. Child Advs., Houston, 2000—03. Mem.: Tau Sigma Upslon (assoc.; sec. 1979—80, Miss Tau Sigma Upslon Crown Queen (1980)). Democrat. Roman Catholic. Avocations: clothing design, European travel, drawing/sketching, sewing, writing. Office: Thurgood Marshall Elem Magnet Scho 11421 Suburban Dr Houston TX 77016 Personal E-mail: pampamela2@yahoo.com.

WILEY, RICHARD ARTHUR, lawyer; b. Bklyn., July 18, 1928; s. Arthur Ross and Anna Thorsen (Holder) W.; m. Carole Jean Smith, Aug. 13, 1955; children: Kendra Elizabeth, Stewart Alan, Garett Smith. AB, Bowdoin Coll., Brunswick, Maine, 1948, LLD, 1994; BCL, Oxford (Eng.) U., 1951; LLM, Harvard U., 1959. Bar: Mass. 1954, U.S. Ct. Mil. Appeals 1954, U.S. Dist. Ct. Mass. 1962, U. S. Supreme Ct. 1985. Atty. John Hancock Mut. Life Ins. Co., Boston, 1956-58; from atty. to mng. ptnr. Bingham, Dana & Gould, Boston, 1959-76; gen. counsel, asst. sec. Dept. Def., 1976-77; v.p., counsel First Nat. Bank Boston, 1977-78, exec. v.p., 1978-85, Bank of Boston Corp., 1985; ptnr. Csaplar & Bok, Boston, 1986-90, mem. exec. com., 1987-90, chmn., 1989-90, of counsel, 1990, Gaston & Snow, Boston, 1990-91; dir. Powers and Hall P.C., Boston, 1991-94, of counsel, 1994-95, Hill & Barlow, Boston, 1995—2002, Foley & Hoag LLP, Boston, 2002—. Bd. dirs., chmn. Automated Assemblies Corp., Mass. Higher Edn. Assistance Corp.; bd. dirs. Edn. Rsch. Inst., Microwave Device Tech. Corp., Nomadic Structures, Inc., Nypro, Inc., Carlo Gavazzi Mupac, Inc.; lectr. Boston U. Law Sch., 1961-64; past vice chmn. New Eng. Conf. on Doing Bus. Abroad; trustee New Eng. Legal Found., chmn., 1980-83; adj. prof. govt. and legal studies Bowdoin Coll., 1995-2002; adj. prof. law Boston Coll. Law Sch., 1998—. Author: Cases and Materials on Law of International Trade and Investment, 1961; contbr. articles to profl. jours. Bd. overseers Bowdoin Coll., 1966-81, pres., 1977-80, trustee, 1981-93, trustee emeritus, 1993—; mem. Mass. Edn. Financing Authority, 1986-91, chmn., 1987-91; mem. Wellesley (Mass.) Town Meeting, 1971-75, mem. fin. adv. com., 1973-74; chmn. Mass. Bd. Regents of Higher Edn., 1991; bd. regents Task Force on Student Fin. Aid, 1987; mem. Mass. Higher Edn. Coord. Coun., 1991-95, vice chmn., 1991-93, chmn., 1993-95; chmn. lawyers divsn. United Way Mass. Bay, 1975; mem. devel. com., trustees of donations Episcopal Diocese Mass., 1971-75; trustee, exec. com. North Conway Inst., mem., 1980-92, chmn., 1988-92; bd. trustees Internat. Coun. Trust, Boston; trustee, mem. exec. com., chmn. Mass. Taxpayers Found., 1989-92; chmn. bd. trustees World Peace Found., Boston, 1983-95; corporator Schepens Eye Rsch. Inst., 1991-95; dep. chmn. planning Mass. rep. state com., 1971, vice chmn. fin. com., 1971-72. Officer USAF, 1953-56. Decorated Air Force Commendation medal; recipient Dep. Def. Disting. Pub. Svc. medal, 1977; Rhodes scholar, 1949. Mem.: ABA (vice chmn. fgn. and internat. bus. law com. 1967—69), Boston Bar Assn. (exec. com., antitrust com. 1965—68), Boston Com. on Fgn. Rels. (chmn. 1980—83), Coun. on Fgn. Rels., Phi Beta Kappa.

WILEY, RICHARD EMERSON, lawyer; b. Peoria, Ill., July 20, 1934; s. Joseph Henry and Jean W. (Farrell) W.; m. Elizabeth J. Edwards, Aug. 6, 1960; children: Douglas S., Pamela L. BS with distinction, Northwestern U., 1955, JD, 1958; LLM, Georgetown U., 1962; LLD (hon.), Cath. U. of Am., 1998. Bar: Ill. 1958, D.C. 1972. Pvt. practice, Chgo., 1962-70; gen. counsel FCC, Washington, 1970-72, mem., 1972-74, chmn., 1974-77, chmn. FCC's adv. com. on advanced TV svc., 1987-96; mng. ptnr. Wiley, Rein & Fielding, Washington, 1983—. Prof. law John Marshall Law Sch., U. Chgo., 1963-70. Chmn. bd. Media Inst., 1999—, Inst. for Tele-Info., Columbia U., 1997—. Capt. AUS, 1959-62. Recipient Emmy award Nat. Acad. Arts, 1997, Medal of Honor, Electronic Industries Am., 1996, Disting. Svc. award Nat. Assn. Broadcasters, 2002, Internat. Achievement award N.Am. Broadcasters Assn., 2004. Fellow: Am. Bar Found.; mem.: ABA (chmn. Forum com. on comm. 1969, ho. of dels. 1969—71, 1977—84, chmn. young lawyers sect. 1977—84, chmn. bd. editors ABA Jour. 1984—89, chmn. com. on scope and correlation of work 1989, chmn. adminstrv. law and regulatory practice 1993—94, chmn. nat. law day 2003), Adminstrv. Conf. U.S. (coun., sr. fellow), Chgo. Bar Assn., Ill. Bar Assn., Fed. Comm. Bar Assn. (pres. 1987), Fed. Bar Assn. (pres. 1977), Phi Delta Kappa, Phi Delta Phi. Methodist. Home: 3818 N Woodrow St Arlington VA 22207-4345 Office: Wiley Rein & Fielding 1776 K St NW Ste 1100 Washington DC 20006-2332 Office Phone: 202-719-7010. Business E-Mail: rwiley@wrf.com.

WILEY, S. DONALD, lawyer, food products executive; b. 1926; married. BA, Westminster Coll., 1950; LLB, U. Pa., 1953. Sole practice, 1953—55; asst. dist. atty. Allegheny County, Pa., 1955—56; atty. HJ Heinz Co., Pitts., 1956, asst. to corp. sec., 1962—64, gen. counsel, 1964—70, v.p., gen. counsel, 1970—72, sr. v.p., sec., gen. counsel, 1972—, bd. dir., 1972—. Served USAR, 1945—46. Office: H J Heinz Co 600 Grant St Ste 6000 Pittsburgh PA 15219-2857

WILEY, SHELIA GILBERT, music educator; b. Greenwood, Miss., July 2, 1969; d. Willie and Hallie Gilbert; m. Johnny Wiley Sr., Mar. 21, 1991; children: Johnny Jr., Shannon. MusB in Edn., Miss. State U., 1999; MusM in Edn., U. So. Miss., 2003. Dir., founder Progressive Rural Devel. Assn., Greenwood, Miss., 1995—2003; media specialist Leflare County Sch., 1991—95, tchr., 1999—2000, Greenwood Pub. Sch., 2000—03. Dir., founder PRD/I Can Ctr., Greenwood, 2003; chair jr. high choral Miss. High Sch. Activities, 2002—04. With Army NG, 1988—91. Recipient Cmty. award, Miss. Action Progress Parent Orgn., 1997; scholar, Miss. Valley State U., 1999. Mem.: NEA, Mus. Educator Nat. Conf., Kappa Delta Pi, Miss. Valley State Alumni. Democrat. Baptist. Avocations: music, writing, tennis. Home: 309 Western Cir Greenwood MS 38930 E-mail: jjsswiley@aol.com.

WILEY, SHIRLEY WINONA WALTERS, adult education educator, artist; b. Denver, Colorado, May 20, 1920; d. John and Cressie (Gottschalk) Walters; m. Lee Grandison Wiley, Aug. 20, 1941; 1 child, Lee Walters. BFA, U. Tex., 1938—41; EdM, U. Houston, 1951; attended, C.C., Houston, Tex., 1984—97, Rice U. Continuing Edn., 1982—89, Carnegie Mellon U., Pitts., 1984, The Breadloaf Sch. of English, Santa Fe, N.Mex., 1993. Cert. tchg. Tex. Bilingual tchr. El Paso Elem. Pub. Sch., El Paso, Tex., 1942; English tchr. Reagan H.S., Houston, 1947—54; chmn. English dept. Bellaire Sr. H.S., Houston, 1954—69; master tchr. Rice U., Houston, 1965—92, U. dir. film study for teachers, 1969—75, lectr. in edn. dept., 1970—71; English tchr., curriculum design H.S. for Performing Arts, Houston, 1970—73; chmn. English dept. The Kinkaid Sch., Houston, 1987; citation Nat. Found. for Advancement in the Arts, Miami, Fla., 1991; English tchr. The Kinkaid Sch., Houston, 1974—95; tchr., specialized writing Women's Inst., Houston, 1997—. Guest lectr. Art History The Kinkaid Sch., Houston, 1997; AP cons., lectr. CEEB, So. West Region, 1993—95; leader,advanced composition workshop HISD Area1, Houston, 1977—78; lit. com. CEEB, Princeton, NJ, 1964—70; adv. bd. Rice U., Houston, 1963—64; lectr. Harris County Writing for Tchr., Houston, 1963—64. Author: (book) The English Book Sci. Rsch. Assoc., 1981, The Composition Book 1 and Book 2, 1970, (extra mural studies) The Epic,U. Kans. Press, 1969, (book) Understanding the Novel, Am. Writers, 1962, Understanding the Novel, Brit. Writers, 1962, Team Tchg. HISD, 1960. Lectr. Women's Inst., Houston. Recipient First Film Student Made, KUHT T.V. Sta., 1953, sponsor, Creative Writing Club, Bellaire Sr. H.S., 1956—59, Nat. Honor Soc., Bellaire Sr. H.S., 1958—63, Dist. Judge, S.W. Area Nat. Coun. of English Writing, 1959—63, speaking, So. Tex. Regional Conf. of NEA, 1961, Tex. Joint Com. for Secondary Sch. and Coll., 1962, art dir., Conv. of Nat. Coun. of Teachers of English, 1966, Tchr. of the Yr., Jr. Chamber of Commerce, 1967, Harvard U., 1967, cons., Open U.: The Humanities, U. of Houston, 1975, maj. spkr., Nat. Coun. of Teachers of English, Secondary, 1976, lectr., Advanced Placement Workshops, Houston, 1977—78, Advanced Placement Workshops, Galveston, Tex., 1977, Advanced Placement Workshops, Albuquerque, 1977, Adv. Placement Workshops, Austin,Tex., 1979, Advanced Placement Workshops, El Paso,Tex., 1980, Advanced Placement Workshops, Oklahoma City, 1981, Advanced Placement Workshops, W. Orange Cove, ISD, 1982, Advanced Placement Workshops, Orange Consol. Sch. Dist., 1983, Citation, So. Meth. U., 1985, Spl. Recognition CEEB Award, AP Commn., 1985, Columbianna Award for Outstanding Tchg. at Kinkaid, Kinkaid Sch., 1993, U. Citation, Tufts U., 1994. Mem.: Citywide Creative Writing Anthology, Cum Laude, Houston Soc.division of Phi Beta Kappa. Achievements include Awards to students studying with Shirley Wiley; Five Woodrow Wilson Fellows; Nat. Coun. of Teachers of English Writing Awards, 1961-1965; Atlantic Monthly Crative Writing Awards, 1966-1975. Avocations: painting, sculpting. Home: 263 Chimney Rock Rd Houston TX 77024-5618

WILF, FREDERIC MARSHAL, lawyer; b. Phila., Mar. 3, 1959; s. Leonard R. and Phyllis Hope Wilf; m. Shirley Ann Segal; children: Chelsea Sarah, Robert Ethan. BA, Rutgers U., 1982; JD, Case Western Res. U., 1985. Bar: Pa. 1985, N.J. 1985, U.S. Dist. Ct. N.J. 1985, U.S. Dist. Ct. (ea. dist.) Pa. 1986, U.S. Dist. Ct. (middle dist.) Pa. 1992, U.S. Ct. Appeals (3d cir.) 1986, U.S. Ct. Appeals (Fed. cir.) 1989, U.S. Supreme Ct. 1989. Cons. atty. Bell Tel. Co. of Pa., Phila., 1985-86; assoc. Rapp, White, Janssen & German, Phila., 1986, Elman Assocs., Phila., 1986-88, Lipton, Famiglio & Elman, Media, Pa., 1988-89; ptnr. Elman Wilf & Fried, Media, 1990-95; spl. counsel Saul, Ewing, Remick & Saul LLP, Berwyn, Pa., 1995-99, Morgan, Lewis & Bockius LLP, Phila., 1999—. Mem. ABA, ACLU, Internat. Trademark Assn., Copyright Soc. Am., Licensing Execs. Soc., Phila. Bar Assn. (chmn. cyberspace and ecommerce com.), Computer Law Assn., Phila. Intellectual Property Law Assn., Assn. for Computing Machinery, Electronic Frontier Found. Democrat. Jewish. Avocation: photography. Office: Morgan Lewis & Bockius LLP 1701 Market St Philadelphia PA 19103-2921 Office Phone: 215-963-5453. Business E-Mail: fwilf@morganlewis.com.

WILF, PETER DANIEL, paleobiologist; PhD in Geology, U. Pa., 1998; postgrad., Pushkin Inst., Moscow, 1987; BA cum laude, U. Pa., 1985. Tchr. 7th and 8th grade math Westfield Friends Sch., Cinnaminson, N.J., 1985-88; performing musician, music tchr. Phila. and N.Y.C., 1989-93; Smithsonian Instn. postdoctoral fellow dept. paleobiology Nat. Mus. Natural History, Washington. Contbr. articles to profl. jours. U. Pa. fellow, 1996-97, Smithsonian Instn. fellow, 1997, 98; grantee Sigma Xi, Geol. Soc. Am., Paleontol. Soc., Smithsonian, U. Pa., NSF. Mem. AAAS, Am. Geophys. Union, Bot. Soc. Am., Geol. Soc. Am., Internat. Assn. for Paleobotany, Paleontol. Soc., Paleontol. Soc. Washington (prs.), Soc. for Sedimentary Geology, Sigma Xi. Office: Nat Mus Natural History Dept Paleobiology 10th And Constitution Washington DC 20560-0001

WILFERT, CATHERINE M. medical association administrator, medical educator; Asst. prof. pediatrics Duke U., 1969-80, prof. pediatrics and microbiology, chief pediatric infectious diseases, 1980-98, prof. emeritus; sci. dir. Elizabeth Glaser Pediat. AIDS Found., Santa Monica, Calif., 1997—. Mem. Inst. Medicine. Office: Elizabeth Glaser Pediatric AIDS Found 1917 Wildcat Creek Rd Chapel Hill NC 27516-9786 Office Phone: 919-968-0008. E-mail: wilfert@mindspring.com.

WILFONG, BRENDA ANN, telecommunications executive; b. Ashland, Ohio, Jan. 2, 1963; d. Edward Eugene and Barbara Ann (Butterfield) Bush; m. Duane Hubert Wilfong, Oct. 22, 1984 (dec. Sept. 1994); children: Jessie Leona, Christina Elizabeth. BBA, Kent State U., 1989, postgrad., 1998. Asst. editor Ohio dir. Harris Pub. Co., Twinsburg, Ohio, 1983-84; accounts payable clerk M. O'Neil's Co., Akron, Ohio, 1984-85; network mgmt. asst. Alltel Corp., Hudson, Ohio, 1985-86, treasury asst., 1986-87, assoc. analyst treasury, 1987-92, carrier svcs. coord., 1992-93, sr. staff asst. Twinsburg, 1993-95, adminstr. carrier svcs., 1995—, contracts adminstr. Hudson, Ohio, 1995—. Recipient Brownie Mother Vol. award Girl Scouts Am., Akron, 1994. Mem. Inst. Mgmt. Accts. (editor newsletter 1990-92, dir. ins. 1992-94). Brethren. Avocations: reading medical journals, weightlifting, aerobics, classical music. Office: 50 Executive Pkwy Hudson OH 44236-1605 E-mail: wilfongb@hotmail.com.

WILFORD, DAN SEWELL, hospital administrator; b. Memphis, June 11, 1940; married. BA, U. Miss., 1962; MA, Washington U., 1966. Adminstrv. resident Hillcrest Med. Ctr., Tulsa, 1965-66, asst. adminstr., 1966-69, sr. assoc. adminstr., 1969-74; adminstr. North Miss. Med. Ctr., Tupelo, Miss., 1974-82; pres. North Miss. Health Svcs., Tupelo, Miss., 1982-84, Meml. Healthcare System, Houston, 1984—. With Armed Forces, 1962-64. Home: 730 Chevy Chase Cir Sugar Land TX 77478-3600 Office: Meml Hosp System Meml Hosp SW 7737 Southwest Fwy Ste 200 Houston TX 77074-1800

WILFORD, JOHN NOBLE, JR., science news correspondent; b. Murray, Ky., Oct. 4, 1933; s. John Noble and Pauline (Hendricks) W.; m. Nancy Everett Watts, Dec. 25, 1966; 1 child, Nona. Student, Lambuth Coll., 1951-52; BS, U. Tenn., 1955; MA, Syracuse U., 1956; Internat. Reporting fellow, Columbia, 1961-62; DHL (hon.), R.I. Coll., 1987; DSc (hon.), Middlebury Coll., 1991. Reporter Comml. Appeal, Memphis, summers 1954-55; reporter Wall St. Jour., N.Y.C., 1956, 59-61; contbg. editor Time mag., N.Y.C., 1962-65; sci. reporter N.Y. Times, 1965-73, asst. nat. editor, 1973-75, dir. sci. news, 1975-79, sci. corr., 1979—. Vis. journalist Duke U., 1984; McGraw lectr. Princeton U., 1985; Disting. prof. journalism, U. Tenn., Knoxville, 1989-90; mem. Am. Mus.-Mongolian Gobi Expdn., 1991, Dir.'s Visitor, Inst. for Advanced Study, 1995. Author: We Reach The Moon, 1969, The Mapmakers, 1981, The Riddle of the Dinosaur, 1985, Mars Beckons, 1990, The Mysterious History of Columbus, 1991; co-author: The New York Times Guide to the Return of Halley's Comet, 1985, (with William Stockton) Spaceliner, 1981, Israel: The Historical Atlas, 1997; editor: Scientists at Work, 1979, Cosmic Dispatches, 2000. With CIC AUS, 1957-59. Recipient Book award Aviation/Space Writers, 1970, Writing award Aviation/Space Writers, 1983, G.M. Loeb Achievement award U. Conn, 1972, Press award Nat. Space Club, 1974, AAAS-Westinghouse Sci. Writing award, 1983, Ralph Coats Roe medal ASME, 1995, Pulitzer prize, 1984, N.Y. Times Pulitzer Prize Winning Team, 1987, N.Y.C. Mayor's award, 2001, Am. Geol. Inst. award, 2001, Sagan award Coun. Sci. Soc. Pres., 2001. Mem. Nat. Assn. Sci. Writers, Authors Guild, Soc. Profl. Journalists, Am. Geog. Soc. (councilor 1994—, sec. 2000—), Am. Acad. Arts and Scis., Century Assn., Sigma Chi, Phi Beta Kappa. Home: 232 W 10th St New York NY 10014-2976 Office: 229 W 43rd St New York NY 10036-3913 Business E-Mail: wilford@nytimes.com.

WILHELM, DAVID C. investment company executive; m. Degee Dodds; children: Luke, Logan. BA, Ohio U., 1977; MPP, Harvard U., 1990. Rsch. dir. pub. employee dept. AFL-CIO, 1981-83; campaign mgr. Senator Paul Simon, 1984, Senator Joseph Biden for Pres., Iowa, 1985-87, Richard M. Daley for Mayor, Chgo., 1989, 91, Gov. Bill Clinton for Pres., 1991-92; exec. dir. Citizens for Tax Justice, Washington, 1985-87; pres. The Strategy Group, Chgo., 1988-91; chmn. Nat. Dem. Com., 1993-94; sr. mng. dir. investment banking Kemper Securities, Inc. (now First Union), Chgo., 1995-97; founder, pres. Wilhelm & Conlon, Inc., Chgo., 1998—2004, Woodland Venture Mgmt., Chgo., 2002—; ptnr. Adena Ventures, 2002—, Hopewell Ventures, 2004—. Lectr. Univ. Chgo.; bd. dirs. Christian Century Mag., League of Chgo. Treasures, Children's Meml. Hosp., Chgo. Fellow Inst. of Politics, Harvard U., 1996, recipient hon. Dr. of Public Service, Ohio Univ. Fellow Inst. Politics. Office: Woodland Venture Mgmt 20 N Wacker Dr Ste 2200 Chicago IL 60606 Office Phone: 312-357-4600. E-mail: wilhelm@woodlandve.com.

WILHELM, EDWARD W. corporate financial executive; With PricewaterhouseCoopers, 1981—91; contr., v.p./contr. Kmart Corp., 1991—94; v.p. fin. Borders Group, Ann Arbor, Mich., 1994—97, v.p. planning, reporting and treasury, 1997—2000, sr. v.p., CFO, 2000—. Office: Borders Group 100 Phoenix Dr Ann Arbor MI 48108-2202

WILHELM, FRANK LEO, publisher, writer; b. Kansas City, Mo., Apr. 9, 1926; s. Matilda Theresa Wilhelm; m. Deena L. Levin, Mar. 2, 1950 (div. Sept. 22, 1992); children: David Donne, Anita Sue, Laura Jean. BA in English, U. Ill., 1950, MS in Vocat. Counseling, 1951. Registered social worker, Ill. Tchr. English, Bd. Edn., Windsor and Clifton, Ill., 1951-53; personnel mgr. J.P. Smith Shoes, Chgo., 1953-55; outside sales Ency. Britannica, Chgo., 1955-57; vocat. counselor, supr. tng. Cook County, Ill. and State of Ill., Chgo., 1957-89; owner Books of Am., Evanston, Ill., 1998—. Author: (poetry) Poetry City, USA, 1997, (novels) Orphan's Odyssey, 2002, My Name is Wilson Jones, 2003. Folk dancer Folk Dance Coun. Chgo. With USN, 1944-46. Avocations: bridge, chess, gardening, cooking, ancient mid-east history. Home: 2940 W Sherwin Ave Chicago IL 60645-1210 Office: BOA Pub Co PO Box 6272 Evanston IL 60204-6272 E-mail: BOAPublish@aol.com, xopo@aol.com.

WILHELM, GRETCHEN, retired secondary school educator, volunteer; b. Ames, Iowa, Sept. 30, 1938; d. Harley Almey Wilhelm and Orpha Elizabeth Lutton. BS in Math., Iowa State U., 1960; MS in Math., Oreg. State U., 1969. Permanent profl. endorsement for math. grades 7-12 and gen. sci. Iowa, life endorsement math. grades 7-12 and all scis. grades 7-12 Minn. Math. tchr. Shenandoah (Iowa) H.S., 1960—63, Robbinsdale (Minn.) Sr. H.S., 1963—68; jr. mathematician on faculty Inst. Atomic Rsch. Iowa State U., Ames (Iowa) Lab. U.S. Atomic Energy Commn., 1969; math. tchr. Robbinsdale Cooper Sr. High, New Hope, Minn., 1969—94, math. dept. chmn., 1974—76; ret., 1994. Dist. math. curriculum devel. com. Robbinsdale Sch. Dist., New Hope, 1984—89. Election judge, New Hope, 1994, 1996, 1998, 2000; charter mem. Plymouth (Minn.) Creek Christian Ch., 1978, bd. mem., 1978—79, 1982—84, 1989—91, 1997—2001. Recipient NSF Math. Inst. stipend, Oreg. State U., Corvallis, 1962, 1963, 1964, 1965. Mem.: AAUW (life; Mpls. br. bd. dirs., edn. rep. 1997—98), NEA (life), Minn. Geneal. Soc., Iowa Geneal. Soc., Women Descs. Ancient and Hon. Arty. Co., US Daus. War of 1812, Thomas Stanton Soc., Thomas Minor Soc., New Eng. Women Descs., Dau. Am. Colonists, Colonial Dames the XVII Century, Colonial Dames Am., Nat. Soc. DAR (life; chpt. 2nd vice regent 1987—88, chpt. registrar 1988—94, State constn. week chmn. 1991—95, chpt. 1st vice regent 1994—96, state registrar 1995—97, state officers club v.p., chaplain 1995—97, chpt. chaplain 1996—98, state DAR good citizen chmn. 1997—99, chpt. regent 1998—2000, state regent 2001—03, nat. bd. mgmt. 2001—03, charter mem. State Regents Club 2001—, Nat. Officers Club 2001—, hon. state regent 2003—, state membership chmn. 2003—). Republican. Mem. Christian Ch. (Disciples Of Christ). Avocation: geneaology. Home: 3925 Winnetka Ave N Minneapolis MN 55427

WILHELM, JOHN L. city health department administrator; b. Chgo., 1943; MPH, U. Ill., Chgo., 1979; MD, Loyola U. Stritch Sch. Medicine. Internist Mercy Hosp., Chgo., 1969—71; resident, ob-gyn. Northwestern-Wesley Hosp., Chgo., 1971—73; resident, gyn. endocrinology Michael Reese Hosp., Chgo., 1974—75; chief, bur. pub. health Chgo. Health Dept., 1990; dep. commr. Chgo. Dept. Pub. Health, commr., 2000—.*

WILHELM, JOHN W. labor union administrator; m. Elizabeth B. Gilbertson, 1969; two children. Grad., Yale Coll., 1967. Org. & bus. agent Local 217 Conn./R.I. Hotel and Restaurant Employees Internat. Union, 1969—71, sec., treas., 1971—83, bus. mgr., 1978—86; internat. v.p. Hotel and Restaurant Employees Internat. Union, 1982-1996, gen. sec.-treas., 1996-98, gen. pres., 1998—. Trustee Welfare/Pension Funds Hotel and Restaurant Employees Internat. Union, 1988—; trustee S. Nevada Culinary and Bartenders Pension Fund, 1995—; commr. Nat. Gambling Impact Study Commn., 1997—99. Mem. Phi Beta Kappa. Office: HERE Internat Union 1219 28th St NW Washington DC 20007 Office Phone: 202-393-4373.*

WILHELM, KATE (KATY GERTRUDE), author; b. Toledo, June 8, 1928; d. Jesse Thomas and Ann (McDowell) Meredith; m. Joseph B. Wilhelm, May 24, 1947 (div. 1962); children: Douglas, Richard; m. Damon Knight, Feb. 23,

1963; 1 child, Jonathan. PhD in Humanities (hon.), Mich. State U., 1996. Writer, 1956—. Co-dir. Milford Sci. Fiction Writers Conf., 1963-76; lectr. Clarion Fantasy Workshop Mich. State U., 1968-94. Author: More Bitter Than Death, 1962; (with Theodore L. Thomas) The Clone, 1965, The Nevermore Affair, 1966, The Killer Thing, 1967, Let the Fire Fall, 1969, The Year of the Cloud, 1970, Abyss: Two Novellas, 1971, Margaret and I, 1971, City of Cain, 1971, The Clewiston Test, 1976, Where Late the Sweet Birds Sang, 1976, Fault Lines, 1976, Somerset Dreams and Other Fictions, 1978, Juniper Time, 1979; (with Damon Knight) Better Than One, 1980, A Sense of Shadow, 1981, Listen, Listen, 1981, Oh! Susannah, 1982, Welcome Chaos, 1983, Huysman's Pets, 1986; (with R. Wilhelm) The Hills Are Dancing, 1986, The Hamlet Trap, 1987, Crazy Time, 1988, Dark Door, 1988, Smart House, 1989, Children of the Wind: Five Novellas, 1989, Cambio Bay, 1990, Sweet, Sweet Poison, 1990, Death Qualified, 1991, And the Angels Sing, 1992, Seven Kinds of Death, 1992, Naming the Flowers, 1992, Justice for Some, 1993, The Best Defense, 1994, A Flush of Shadows, 1995, Malice Prepense, 1996, The Good Children, 1998, Defense for the Devil, 1999, No Defense, 2000, The Deepest Water, 2000, Desperate Measures, 2001, Skeletons, 2002, Clear and Convincing Proof, 2003; (multimedia space fantasy) Axoltl, U. Oreg. Art Mus., 1979, (radio play) The Hindenburg Effect, 1985; editor: Nebula Award Stories #9, 1974, Clarion SF, 1976; contbr. articles to popular mags., profl. jours. Mem. Nat. Writers Union, Mystery Writers Am., Authors Guild. Address: 1645 Horn Ln Eugene OR 97404-2957 E-mail: kate@katewilhelm.com.

WILHELM, MORTON, retired surgery educator; b. Roanoke, Va., June 22, 1923; s. Walter LeRoy and Della Mae (Turner) W.; m. Jean Osborne, June 3, 1949; children: Melissa, Christina. BS, Va. Mil. Inst., 1944; MD, U. Va., 1947. Diplomate Am. Bd. Surgery. Intern, resident in surgery VA Mason Hosp., Seattle, 1947-51, 52-53; fellow, instr. surgery Med. Ctr. U. Va., Charlottesville, 53-54, 56-66, assoc. prof. surgery Med. Ctr., 1966-80, prof. surgery Med. Ctr., 1980-93, chief dept. surg. oncology Med. Ctr., 1990-93, Joseph Farrow prof. surg. oncology Med. Ctr., 1990-93. Pres. Va. div. Am. Cancer Soc., Meritorious Svc. award, Horsley award, Nat. Teresa Lasser award. Lt. U.S. Army, 1951-53. Fellow ACS (vice chmn. commn. on cancer 1989-90, pres. Va. chpt.); mem. So. Surg. Assn., So. Soc. Clin. Surgeons, Soc. Surg. Oncology. Avocations: tennis, golf, woodworking.

WILHELM, PHILLIP EUGENE, church administrator, music educator; b. West Palm Beach, Fla., Nov. 17, 1973; MusB, So. Ill. U., 1997, MusM, 2001. Cert. tchr. Ill., 1997, Mo., 1997. Composer: (cd) Simple Gifts. Dir. music O'Fallon U. Ch. Christ, Ill., 2003—04. Mem.: Music Educators Nat. Conf. (assoc.), Am. Orff Schulwerk Assn. (assoc.). Libertarian. Mem. United Church Christ. Home: 224 Brookmont Belleville IL 62221 Office: O'Fallon United Church of Christ 206 W Adams O Fallon IL 62269 Office Phone: 618-632-3496. E-mail: oucc@intertek.net.

WILHELM, ROBERT OSCAR, lawyer, civil engineer, developer; b. Balt., July 7, 1918; s. Clarence Oscar and Agnes Virginia (Grimm) W.; m. Grace Sanborn Luckie, Apr. 4, 1959. BSCE, Ga. Tech. Inst., 1947, MSIM, 1948; JD, Stanford U., 1951. Bar: Calif. 1952, U.S. Supreme Ct. Mem. Wilhelm, Thompson, Redwood City, Calif., 1952—92; gen. cousnel Bay Counties Gen. Contractors; pvt. practice civil engring., Redwood City, 1952—. Pres. Bay Counties Builders Escrow, Inc., 1972-88. Author: The Manual of Procedures for the Construction Industry, 1971, Manual of Procedures and Form Book for Construction Industry, 9th edit., 1995, Construction Law for Contractors, Architects and Engineers; columnist Law and You in Daily Pacific Builder, 1955-2001. With C.E., AUS, 1942-46. Named to Wisdom Hall of Fame, 1999. Mem. Bay Counties Civil Engrs. (pres. 1957), Peninsula Builders Exch. (pres. 1958-71, dir.), Calif. State Builders Exch. (treas. 1971), Del Mesa Carmel Cmty. Assn. (bd. dirs. 1997-99), Masons, Odd Fellows, Eagles, Elks. Home: 134 Del Mesa Carmel Carmel CA 93923-7950 Office: 600 Allerton St Ste 202 Redwood City CA 94083 Office Phone: 650-365-7333.

WILHELM, WILLIAM JEAN, civil engineering educator; b. St. Louis, Oct. 5, 1935; s. Maurice Ferdinand and Winifred Eileen (McClintock) W.; m. Patricia Jane Zietz, Aug. 17, 1957; children: William, Robert, Andrew, Mary, David. BME, Auburn U., 1958, MS, 1963; PhD, N.C. State U., 1968. Lic. profl. engr., Kans. Structural engr. Palmer & Baker Engrs., Mobile, Ala., 1958-60; instr. engring. graphics Auburn U., 1960-64; asst. prof. civil engring. W.Va. U., Morgantown, 1967-72, assoc. prof., 1972-76, prof., 1976-79, chmn., 1974-79; dean engring., prof. Wichita State U., 1979-2000, dean, prof., emeritus, 2000—, dir. Ctr. for Productivity Enhancement, 1984-86, exec. dir. Ctr. for Tech. Application, 1988-91. Bd. dirs. Kans. Tech. Enterprise Corp., Orthopaedic Rsch. Inst. Via Christi Regional Med. Sys.; chair bd. dirs. Envision. Contbr. articles to profl. jours. Officer C.E. U.S. Army, 1959, 62. Recipient Recognition award Wichita State U. Alumni Assn., 1993, Engr. Svc. award Wichita Coun. Engring. Socs., 2000. Fellow NSPE, ASCE, Am. Soc. Engring. Edn. (George K. Wadlin award 1998, MidWest sect. Spl. Appreciation award 2001), Am. Concrete Inst. (Joe W. Kelley award 1986, Henry L. Kennedy award 1994); mem. Soc. Women Engrs. (sr., Rodney D. Chipp Meml. award 2000), Kans. Soc. Profl. Engrs. (pres. 1994-95, Outstanding Engr. of Yr. award 1989, Career Recognition award 2000), Order of the Engr., Sigma Xi, Phi Kappa Phi, Tau Beta Pi, Pi Tau Sigma, Chi Epsilon (chpt. hon. W.Va. U. 1979), Golden Key (hon.). Roman Catholic. Home: 7014 E 25th St N Wichita KS 67226-1734 Office Phone: 316-688-0274. E-mail: wilhelmwj@aol.com.

WILHELM-HASS, ELAINE, operating room nurse; b. San Francisco, Jan. 29, 1955; d. Roger Mathias and Dorothy Jane (Conway) Wilhelm; m. James Hass, Nov. 10, 1978. BSN, U. Wash., 1978; MN, La. State U., New Orleans, 1982; MBA, Averett Coll., Springfield, Va., 1992. RN; cert. profl. in healthcare quality. Maternal child health mgr. Merrimack Valley Region, Mass., 1987-88; dir. oper. rm. and obstetrics Mary Washington Hosp., Fredericksburg, Va., 1989-92; perioperative dir. Bayshore Hosp., Holmdel, N.J., 1992-94; agy. mgr. Slidell Home Health, La., 1994-96; v.p. Health Sphere Cons., Baton Rouge, 1996-97; propr. Wilhelm-Hass Cons., Crownsville, Md., 1997-98; quality improvement dir. Sierra Mil./TRICARE-Region 1, Balt., 1998—2001; oper. rm. mgr. Napa Surgery Ctr., Napa, Calif., 2002—03; with Post St. Surgery, San Francisco, 2003—. Contbr. articles to profl. jours. Mem.: Nat. Assn. Health Care Quality, Sigma Theta Tau. Office: 2299 Post St Ste 108 San Francisco CA 94115

WILHELMI, CYNTHIA JOY, information technology professional, consultant; Student, Iowa State U., 1964—66, BA in Art and Edn., 1966; MA in Comm., U. Nebr., Omaha, 1996. Master Artist-in-Residence Nebr. Arts Coun., Omaha, 1985—91; grad. tchg. asst., tchg. fellow U. Nebr., Omaha, 1993—95; Family Friends of Eastern Nebr. program coord. Vis. Nurse Assn., Omaha, 1996—97; instr. Midland Luth. Coll., Fremont, Nebr., 1997—99; info. tech. cons., project mgr., test engr., bus. analyst Bass & Assocs., Omaha, 1999—2000; info. tech. cons. Robert Half Internat. Cons., 2000, Maxim Group/TEKSystems, 2000—02, Client Resources Inc., 2003; data mgr. TEKsystems, 2003—; govt. bid proposal coord., proposal adminstr. NuGen-Sof cons. co., 2003—04; farmer, 2003—; data mgr. Raytheon, 2003—. Bus. analyst, sr. test engr., project mgmt., third party vendor interface mgmt., CD installation testing, tech. documentation IT data mgr.; govt. info. tech. proposal coord. Editor, pub., contbg. author Salaam mag., 1985-86. Mem. adv. coun. Foster Grandparents, Omaha, 1999—; bd. dirs., pub. rels./publicity chair U. Nebr. Friends of Art, Omaha, 1997-99; bd. dirs. Nebr. SIDS Found., 2002—03. Named Outstanding Grad. Tchg. Asst., U. Nebr., Omaha, 1995, Adm. in the Gt. Navy of Nebr., 1990. Mem. AAUW, Am. Meteor. Soc., Soc. for Tech. Comm. (bd. dirs., chair pub. rels. 1999), Nebr. Adms. Assn., Soc. for Collegiate Journalists (hon.), Phi Delta Gamma, Mensa (Nebr., Western Iowa exec. com. 2003-, SIGHT coord. 2003-, mem. nat. nominating com. 2004). Republican. Address: 13516 Redwood St Omaha NE 68138-6205 Personal E-mail: cwi813@earthlink.net. E-mail: wilhelmi_c@yahoo.com.

WILHELMI, MARY CHARLOTTE, education educator, college official; b. Williamsburg, Iowa, Oct. 2, 1928; d. Charles E. and Loretto (Judge) Harris; m. Sylvester Lee Wilhelmi, May 26, 1951; children: Theresa Ann, Sylvia Marie, Thomas Lee, Kathryn Lyn, Nancy Louise. BS, Iowa State U., 1950; MA in Edn., Va. Poly. Inst. and State U., 1973, cert. advanced grad. studies, 1978. Edn. coord. Nova Ctr. U. Va., Falls Church, 1969-73; asst. adminstr. Consortium for Continuing Higher Edn. George Mason U., Fairfax, Va., 1973-78, adminstr., asst. prof., 1978-83; dir. coll. mktg., pub. affairs, assoc. prof. No. Va. C.C., Annandale, 1983—. Bd. dirs. No. Va. C.C. Ednl. Found., Inc., No. Va. C.C. Real Estate Found.; v.p. audience devel. Fairfax (Va.) Symphony, 1995—; chmn. Health Systems Agy. No. Va., Fairfax; mem. George Mason U. Inst. for Ednl. Transformation. Mem. Editl. bd. Va. Forum, 1990-93; contbr. articles to profl. jours. Bd. dirs. Fairfax County chpt. ARC, 1981-86, Va. Inst. Polit. Leadership, 1995—, Fairfax Com. of 100, 1986-88, 90—, Arts Coun. Fairfax County, 1989—, Fairfax Spotlight on the Arts, Inc., 2002—; bd. dirs. Hospice No. Va., 1983-88, devel. bd., 1997-2000; steering com. Hurrah for Hospice Gala, 1999, Nat. Capital Region Hospices Gala, 2002, 2003, No. Va. Mental Health Inst., Fairfax County, 1978-81, Fairfax Profl. Women's Network, 1981; vice chair Va. Commonwealth U. Ctr. on Aging, Richmond, 1978—; supt.'s adv. coun. Fairfax County Pub. Schs., 1974-86, No. Va. Press Club, 1978—; mktg. chair, exec. com. Internat. Childrens Festival, 1997—; pres. Fairfax Ext. Leadership Coun., 1995; mem. Leadership Fairfax Class of 1992, Commonwealth Va. Combined campaign, State Adv. Coun., 1999-2003. Named Woman of Distinction, Soroptomists, Fairfax, 1988, Bus. Woman of Yr., Falls Church Bus. and Profl. Women's Group, 1993; fellow Va. Inst. Polit. Leadership, 1995. Mem. State Coun. Higher Edn. Va. (pub. affairs adv. com. 1985—), Greater Washington Bd. Trade, Fairfax County C. of C. (legis. affairs com. 1984—, millenium steering com. 1999) Va. Women Lobbyists, 1991—, No. Va. Bus. Roundtable, Internat. Platform Assn., Phi Delta Kappa (20-Yr. Continuous Svc. award 2001), Kappa Delta Alumni No. Va., Psi Chi, Phi Kappa Phi. Roman Catholic. Avocations: piano, organ, reading, hiking. Home: 4902 Ravensworth Rd Annandale VA 22003-5552 Office: NVCC 4001 Wakefield Chapel Rd Annandale VA 22003-3796 Office Phone: 703-323-3753. Business E-Mail: mcwilhelmi@nvcc.edu.

WILHELMSEN, HAROLD JOHN, accountant, operations controller; b. Kansas City, Mo., July 13, 1928; s. Karl John and Cora Irene (Reynolds) W.; m. Audrey Loraine Woodard, Oct. 14, 1950. BBA, U. Wis., 1950. CPA, Wis. With S.C. Johnson & Son Inc., Racine, Wis., 1953-90, dir. fin. South Pacific, 1970-72, mgr. overseas fin. svcs., 1972-76, contr. U.S. ops., 1976-78, v.p., contr. internat. ops., 1978-90, ret., 1990. Pres. Racine Symphony Orch. Assn., 1957-60; trustee Carthage Coll., Kenosha, Wis., 1984-91, dir., sec. Pinnacle Peak Country Club Estates, 1992-95; dir., 1993-97, pres. Pinnacle Peak Country Club, 1996-97; treas. Christ the Lord Luth. Ch. Served with U.S. Army, 1950-52. Mem.: Pinnacle Peak Country (Scottsdale, Ariz.); Am. Nat. (Sydney, Australia). Republican. Lutheran. Avocations: golf, squash, bridge, reading, music. E-mail: hjw-az@att.net.

WILHELMY, ODIN, JR., insurance agent; b. New Kensington, Pa., Oct. 9, 1920; s. Odin and May (Hazeltine) W.; m. Betty M. Rollins, Nov. 23, 1945; children: Ann Leslie, Margaret Linn, Janet Lee. BA with honors, U. Cin., 1941; PhD, Cornell U., 1950. CLU, ChFC. Asst. prof. Cornell U., Ithaca, N.Y., 1949-52; div. chief Battelle Meml. Inst., Columbus, Ohio, 1952-70; sr. agt. Prin. Mut. Life Ins. Co., Columbus, 1970—. Scoutmaster Boy Scouts Am., Ithaca, N.Y., Columbus, Ohio, 1946-74. Sgt. U.S. Army, 1942-46, Aleutian Islands. Recipient Silver Beaver award Boy Scouts Am. Mem. Phi Beta Kappa, Phi Kappa Phi, Pi Kappa Alpha, Omicron Delta Kappa. Presbyterian. Avocations: church work, scouting, gardening. Home: 2942 N Star Rd Columbus OH 43221-2961

WILHIDE, STEPHEN D. medical association administrator; BA in Social Scis., Frostburg (Md.) State U., 1965; MSW, U. Md., 1972; MPH, U. Pitts., 1976. Exec. dir. So. Ohio Health Svcs. Network, 1976—2002, Nat. Rural Health Assn., Alexandria, Va., 2002—. Vol. VISTA, NC. Served with U.S. Army, Vietnam. Named one of Most Powerful People in Healthcare, Modern Healthcare mag., 2003. Office: Nat Rural Health Assn 1307 Duke St Alexandria VA 22314 Office Phone: 703-519-7910. Business E-Mail: wilhide@nrharural.com.

WILHJELM, CHRISTIAN, conductor, artist; b. Long Branch, N.J., Nov. 6, 1949; s. Carl and Alice Wilhjelm; m. Jacqueline Sarracco; children: Carl, Hannah. BA in Music, New Eng. Conservatory, 1972; MA Edn., Coll. of NJ, 1978; EdD, Columbia U., 1998. Musician - french horn Richmond Symphony, Richmond, Va., 1972—76; band dir. North Brunswick Twp. H.S., 1977—79, Ridgewood H.S., Ridgewood, NJ, 1979—82, Rye H.S., Rye, NY, 1982—84; music dir. Ridgewood Concert Band, Ridgewood, NJ, 1983—; band dir. Pascack Hills H.S., Montvale, NJ, 1984—; artist Montclair State U., Montclair, NJ, 1996—; condr./music dir. The Goldman Band, New York, NY, 2000—02. Bd. of directors Classical NJ, Westfield, NJ, 1998, Bergen Youth Orch., Engelwood, NJ, 2001—. Contbr. book Spotlight on Bands. Recipient Sudler Award of Merit, John Philip Sousa Found., 1998; fellow Paul Harris Fellowship, Rotary Internat., 1992. Mem.: Music Educator's Nat. Conf., Coll. Band Dir. Nat. Assn., Am. Fedn. of Musicians. Office: The Goldman Memorial Band 80 Eighth Avenue Suite 1107 New York NY 10011 E-mail: cwilhjelm@msn.com.

WILK, RONALD, physician; b. N.Y.C., Nov. 27, 1944; BA, L.I. U., Bklyn., 1966; MD, U. Bologna, Italy, 1972. Diplomate Am. Acad. Neurology, 1980. Intern, resident Mt. Sinai Hosp., N.Y.C., chief resident, 1977. Fellow Royal Soc. Medicine, Am. Acad. Neurology.

WILK, STUART, publishing executive; Reporter, asst. city editor Milwaukee Sentinel; metro editor The Dallas Morning News, asst. mng. editor, dep. mng. editor, mng. editor, 1996—2004, v.p., assoc. editor, 2004—, Belo Corp. (parent co. of The Dallas Morning News), 2004—. Discussion leader Am. Press Inst.; profl. in residence Marshall U. W. Page Sch. Journalism, 2001; faculty Cross-Media Journalism Pilot Program, Robert C. Maynard Inst. of Journalism Edn. Bd. dir. Freedom of Information Found. Tex. Mem.: Associated Press Mng. Editors (pres., mem. exec. com., chair, Mktg., Ethics and Diversity Com., supervised nationwide survey on diversity in the newsroom 1996). Office: Dallas Morning News 508 Young St. Dallas TX 75202 Office Phone: 214-977-8222. Business E-Mail: swilk@dallasnews.com.*

WILKE, CONSTANCE REGINA, elementary school educator; b. Camden, N.J., Mar. 20, 1944; d. Matthew Stanley Sr. and Regina Rita (Przeradzki) Wojtkowiak; m. Alvin Frank Wilke Jr., Apr. 20, 1968; children: Joseph Alvin, Suzanne Renee. BA in Elem. Edn., Glassboro State U., 1967, MA in Reading and Supervision, 1979. Cert. tchr. and reading speicalist, N.J. Tchr. 5th grade Bellmawr (N.J.) Bd. Edn., 1967-70; tchr. 2d grade Ethel M. Burke Sch., Bellmawr, N.J., 1970-97; tchr. 5th grade Bell Oaks Sch., Bellmawr, 1997—. Author: Wojtkowiak Family History, 1992. Vol. Gloucester (N.J.) City Libr., 1972-75, Vet.'s Standdown, Meals on Wheels, Cathedral Soup Kitchen; contact reassurance vol. Am. Heart Assn. Walk; sec. E.M. Burke Sch. PTA, Bellmawr, 1973-78, publicity person, 1980-85, pres., 1982-85, author and editor publicity book, 1980-83, rec. sec., 1995-97; advisor Cmty. Edn. Bd., Gloucester City, 1973-74; eucharistic minster St. Mary's Ch., Gloucester City, 1990—, 150 yr. Jubilee com., renew com., lector, parish coun.; dir., founder of Literacy Day at E.M. Burke Sch., dir. and founder Vet.'s Day Program, MS Read-a-thon, Jump Rope for Heart, Book It programs, Reading is the Ticket program. Named Citizen of Yr., Polish-Am. Congress, 1983, N.J. VFW Citizenship Tchr. of Yr., 2002. Mem. NEA, N.J. Epilepsy Found., N.J. Edn. Assn., West Jersey Reading Assn., Bellmawr Edn. Assn. (faculty rep.), Asthma Assn. Roman Catholic. Achievements include being instrumental in having Veteran Memorial built honoring Bellmawr veterans. Office: Bell Oaks Sch 256 Anderson Ave Bellmawr NJ 08031-1199

WILKE, LEROY, church administrator; Exec. dir. dist. and congl. svcs. Luth. Ch.-Mo. Synod, St. Louis. Lutheran. Office: 1333 S Kirkwood Rd Saint Louis MO 63122-7226

WILKEN, CLAUDIA, judge; b. Mpls., Aug. 17, 1949; BA with honors, Stanford U., 1971; JD, U. Calif., Berkeley, 1975. Bar: Calif. 1975, U.S. Dist. Ct. (no. dist.) Calif. 1975, U.S. Ct. Appeals (9th cir.) 1976, U.S. Supreme Ct. 1981. Asst. fed. pub. defender U.S. Dist. Ct. (no. dist.) Calif., San Francisco, 1975-78, U.S. magistrate judge, 1983-93, dist. judge, 1993—; ptnr. Wilken & Leverett, Berkeley, Calif., 1978-84. Adj. prof. U. Calif., Berkeley, 1978-84; prof. New Coll. Sch. Law, 1980-85; mem. jud. br. com. Jud. Conf. U.S.; past mem. edn. com. Fed. Jud. Ctr.; chair 9th cir. Magistrates Conf., 1987-88. Mem. ABA (mem. jud. adminstrn. divsn.), Alameda County Bar Assn. (judge's membership), Nat. Assn. Women Judges, Order of Coif, Phi Beta Kappa. Office: US Dist Ct No Dist 1301 Clay St # 2 Oakland CA 94612-5217

WILKENING, LAUREL LYNN, academic administrator, planetary scientist; b. Richland, Wash., Nov. 23, 1944; d. Marvin Hubert and Ruby Alma Wilkening; m. Godfrey Theodore Sill, May 18, 1974 BA, Reed Coll., Portland, Oreg., 1966; PhD, U. Calif., San Diego, 1970; DSc (hon.), U. Ariz., 1996. From asst. prof. to assoc. prof. U. Ariz., Tucson, 1973—80, dir. Lunar and Planetary Lab., head planetary scis., 1981—83, vice provost, prof. planetary scis., 1983—85, v.p. rsch., dean Grad. Coll., 1985—88; divsn. scientist NASA Hdqrs., Washington, 1980; prof. geol scis., adj. prof. astronomy, provost U. Washington, Seattle, 1988—93; prof. earth system sci., chancellor U. Calif., Irvine, 1993—98. Dir. Rsch. Corp., 1991-2003, Seagate Tech., Inc., 1993-2000, Empire Ranch Found., 1998-2003; vice chmn. Nat. Commn. on Space, Washington, 1984-86, Adv. Com. on the Future of U.S. Space Program, 1990-91; chair Space Policy Adv. Bd., Nat. Space Coun., 1991-92; co-chmn. primitive bodies mission study team NASA/European Space Agy., 1984-85; chmn. com. rendezvous sci. working group NASA, 1983-85; mem. panel on internat. cooperation and competition in space Congl. Office Tech. Assessment, 1982-83; trustee NASULGC, 1994-97, UCAR, 1988-89, 97-98, Reed Coll., 1992-2002. Editor: Comets, 1982. U. Calif. Regents fellow, 1966-67; NASA trainee, 1967-70. Fellow Meteoritical Soc. (councilor 1976-80), Am. Assn. Advanced Sci.; mem. Am. Astron. Soc. (chmn. div. planetary scis. 1984-85), Am. Geophys. Union, AAAS, Planetary Soc. (dir. 1994-2000, v.p. 1997-2000), Phi Beta Kappa. Democrat. Avocations: gardening, camping, swimming.

WILKENS, LEONARD RANDOLPH, JR., (LENNY WILKENS), professional basketball coach; b. Bklyn., Oct. 28, 1937; s. Leonard Randolph Sr. and Henrietta (Cross) W.; m. Marilyn J. Reed, July 28, 1962; children: Leesha Marie, Leonard Randolph III, Jamée McGregor. BS in Econs., Providence Coll., 1960, HHD (hon.), 1980. Counselor Jewish Employment Vocat. Services, 1962-63; salesman packaging div. Monsanto Co., 1966; profl. basketball player St. Louis Hawks, 1960-68; player-coach Seattle SuperSonics, 1969-72, head coach, 1977-85, gen. mgr., 1985-86; profl. basketball player Cleve. Cavaliers, 1972-74, player NBA All-Star Game, 1973, head coach, 1986-93; player-coach Portland (Oreg.) Trail Blazers, 1974-76; head coach Atlanta Hawks, 1993-99, Toronto Raptors, 2000—03, N.Y. Knicks, 2004—. Coach 4 NBA All-Star Teams including Ea. Conf. team All-Star game, Mpls., 1994, World Champion basketball team, 1979, IBM NBA Coach of the Year, 1994; winningest coach of all time, 1995, coach 1996 Olympic Basketball Team, asst. coach 1992 Olympic Basketball. Author: The Lenny Wilkens Story, 1974. Bd. regents Gonzaga U., Spokane; bd. dirs. Seattle Ctr., Big Bros. Seattle, Bellevue (Wash.) Boys Club, Seattle Opportunities Industrialization Ctr., Seattle U.; co-chmn. UN Internat. Yr. of Child program, 1979; organizer Lenny Wilkens Celebrity Golf Tournament for Spl. Olympics. 2d lt. U.S. Army, 1961-62. Recipient Whitney Young Jr. award N.Y. Urban League, 1979, Disting. Citizens award Boy Scouts Am., 1980; named MVP in NBA All-Star Game, 1971, Man of Yr., Boys High Alumni chpt. L.A., 1979, Sportsman of Yr., Seattle chpt. City of Hope, 1979, Congl. Black Caucus Coach of Yr., 1979, CBA Coach of Yr., 1979, Coach of Yr., Black Pubs. Assn., 1979, NBA Coach of Yr., 1994; named to NIT-NIKE Hall of Fame, 1988; named to 9 NBA All-Star Teams, elected to Naismith Memorial Basketball Hall of Fame; named One of NBA's 50 Greatest Players; named One of NBA's Top Ten Coaches; most career wins in NBA history. Office: c/o NY Knickerbockers 2 Pennsylvania Plaza New York NY 10121*

WILKERSON, DIANNE, state legislator; BS in public admin., Amer. Intl. Coll.; JD, Boston Coll. Law Sch., 1981. Partner Roche, Carens, & DeGiacomo; mem. Mass. Senate, Boston, 1993—. Mem.: Boston College Law School Alumni Assoc., Delta Sigma Theta. Office: Mass State Senate Rm 312C State House Boston MA 02133

WILKERSON, H. DEAN, JR., association and organization executive; Gen. counsel MADD, Dallas, 1990—93, exec. dir. Irving, Tex., 1993—2004, Amer. Coll. of Emergency Physicians, 2004—. Office: Amer Coll of Emergency Physicians 1125 Executive Cir PO Box 619911 Irving TX 75261-9911

WILKERSON, JAMES NEILL, retired lawyer; b. Tyler, Tex., Dec. 17, 1939; s. Hubert Cecil and Vida (Alexander) W.; m. Cal Cantrell; children: Cody, Ike; stepchildren: Janet, Joseph. AA, Tyler Jr. Coll., 1960; BBA, U. Tex., 1966, JD, 1968. Bar: Tex. 1968, U.S. Supreme Ct. 1973, U.S. Dist. Ct. (we. dist.) Tex. 1974. Pvt. practice, Georgetown and Mason, Tex., 1977-2001; ret., 2001. Instr. Cen. Tex. Coll., Copperaas Cove, Tex., 1973-74; asst prof. law U.S. Mil. Acad., West Point, N.Y., 1971-73; pres. C&N Bus. Developers, 1992-95. Pres. Beautify Georgetown Assn., 1977-80, 81-82; pres. U. Tex. Young Reps., 1964-65; co-chmn. Bush for Pres., 1988, Reagan-Bush campaign, 1988; mem. Williamson County Rep. Com., 1977-81; chmn. Hist. Preservation Com., 1979-85; trustee 1st United Meth. Ch., 1994-95, chmn. bd. trustees, 1996-99; vol. Mason Lions Club, Steady Steps After Sch. Homework Helper; substitute tchr. Mason Schs.; vol. Sage Meml. Hosp., Navajo Health Foundation, Granada, Ariz., 2001-02. Col. USAR, 1968, trial judge JAGC, 1975-91, appellate judge Army Ct. Mil. Rev., 1991-93, ret. 1992. Decorated Legion of Merit, Bronze Star, Air medal. Mem. Tex. State Bar Coll., Williamson County Bar Assn., Sertoma (v.p. 1981-83, 87, sec. 1988-89, pres. 1992-93), Lions (pres. 1982-83), Vietnam War Vets. Address: PO Box 1807 Mason TX 76856-1807

WILKERSON, JANET STAFFORD, publishing executive, educator; d. Laroy W. Stafford and Jeanne F. Bergman; m. David Allen Wilkerson, July 21, 1942; children: Tracy LaVerne, Jordan Thomas, Robert Scott Stillman, Sean David, Kelly Lynn Wikerson, Lani Jeanne'. BS, Ind. State U., 1970; MAT, Ind. U., 1976. Lic. profl. tchr. Ind. Bd. Edn., 1975. C.s. practitioner self-employed, Silver Spring, Md., 1986—2003; owner, pres. Braden River Pub., Sarasota, Fla., 2004. Pub. spkr. C.S. (COP), Silver Spring, Fla., 1978—2004; min. (armed forces & prison) C.S., 1995—2004; tchr. Auburn U., Montgomery, 1976—82, Evelyn Wood Reading Dynamics, Boomington, Ind., 1970—76, Indpls., 1970—76, Muncie, 1970—76, Terre Haute, 1970—76; spkr. in field. Author: Keep Thy Heart; With All Thine Heart; watercolor paintings, Pelicans and Flowers in Window; prodr.(compiler, collector): (children's story books) First Grade Stories. Rep. ofcl. Manatee County Exec. Com., Bradenton, Fla., 2002—04; vol. White Ho., Washington, 2001—02; rep. ofcl. Montgomery County Ctrl. Com., 1990—2002; stop era chair States Ind./ State Ala., Montgomery, 1974—77; cs min. to armed svcs. and prisons C.S., 1995—2002; bd. mem., chair, supt. First Ch. Christ, Scientist, Silver Spring, 1989—2002; officer PTA, Silver Spring, 1989—2001; cmty. vol. Schools, Nursing Homes, 1989—2002. Named Family of Yr., Md. State PTA, 2000. Mem.: Rep. Club (assoc.; media chair 2002—04). Conservative. Christian Science. Avocations: photography, violin, piano, singing, art, animals. Office: Braden River Publishing PO Box 20538 Braden River FL 34204 Personal E-mail: janet@70x7.org. E-mail: brp@70x7.org.

WILKERSON, LUANN, dean, medical educator; BA magna cum laude, Baylor U., 1969; MA in English, U. Tex., 1972; EdD, U. Mass., 1977. Tchg. asst. dept. English U. Tex., Austin, 1970-72; tchr. grade 8 lang. arts Quabbin Regional H.S., Barre, Mass., 1974-75; rsch. asst. Clinic to Improve Univ. Tchg. U. Mass., Amherst, 1974-76, staff assoc., 1976-77; dir. tchg. and media resource ctr., asst. prof. speech and theatre Murray (Ky.) State U., 1977-80; acting dir., coord. faculty devel. office ednl. devel. and resources Coll. Osteopathic Medicine Ohio U., Athens, 1980-81; assoc. dir. office curricular affairs, asst. prof. family medicine Med. Coll. Wis., Milw., 1981-83; ednl. specialist ednl. devel. unit Michael Reese Hosp. and Med. Ctr., Chgo., 1983-84; dir. faculty devel. office ednl. devel. Harvard Med. Sch., Boston, 1984-91, lectr. in med. edn., 1988-91; dir. Ctr. for Ednl. Devel. and Rsch. UCLA Sch. Medicine, 1992-99, asst. dean med. edn., 1992-94, assoc. prof. medicine, 1992-95, prof. medicine, 1996—, assoc. dean med. edn., 1995-97, sr. assoc. dean med. edn., 1998—. Mem. editl. bd. Advances in Health Scis.

Edn., 1995—, Med. Edn., 1995—, Acad. Medicine, 2001—; reviewer: Acad. Medicine, 1989—, Tchg. and Learning in Medicine, 1990—, Jour. Gen. Internal Medicine, 1988—, Am. Ednl. Rsch. Assn., 1987—, Rsch. Med.Edn. Ann. Conf., 1988—; contbr. articles to profl. jours. and chpts. to books; lectr. in field. Recipient Clinician Tchr. award Calif. Regional Soc. Gen. Internal Medicine, 1995, Excellence in Edn. award UCLA Sch. Medicine, 1998. Mem. Am. Assn. Med. Colls. (mem. rsch. med. edn. com. 1990-93, western chair group on ednl. affairs 1995-97, co-dir. fellowship in med. edn. rsch. 1995-97, convenor spl. interest group on faculty devel. 1997-98, chair group on ednl. affairs 1997—), Am. Ednl. Rsch. Assn., Profl. and Orgnl. Devel. Network (mem. nat. core com. 1977-80, 84-86, exec. dir. 1984-85), Phi Beta Kappa. Office: UCLA Sch Medicine Ctr Ednl Devel & Rsch PO Box 951722 Los Angeles CA 90095-1722 E-mail: lwilkerson@mednet.ucla.edu.

WILKERSON, MATHA ANN, oil company executive; b. Mill Creek, Okla., Sept. 1, 1937; d. Frank and Lottie Evelyn (Cordell) Stie; m. Ronald Gene Wilkerson, Dec. 22, 1956; 1 child, Mitchell Linn. BS in Edn., East Cen. U., 1966. Elem. sch. tchr. Moore (Okla.) Pub. Schs., 1966-74; office mgr. S. S. Sanbar, M.D., Oklahoma City, 1974-78; ops. mgr., acct. John A. Taylor Oil Co., Oklahoma City, 1978-84; office mgr., controller Lance Ruffel Oil & Gas Corp., Oklahoma City, 1984—. Mem. Coun. of Petroleum Accounts Soc. (com. mem. 1979—). Baptist. Avocations: handicrafts, reading, theatre, cooking. Office: Lance Ruffel Oil & Gas 210 Park Ave Ste 2150 Oklahoma City OK 73102-5632

WILKERSON, PINKIE CAROLYN, state legislator, lawyer; b. L.A., Feb. 8, 1948; d. Calvin and Dora (Garner) W.; 1 child, John David Barabin Jr. BA cum laude, Grambling (La.) State U., 1968; MA with honors, Ohio U., 1971; JD with honors, So. U., 1979; LLM, Tulane U., 1989. Bar: La., N.Y., U.S. Tax Ct., U.S. Supreme Ct. Asst. dist. counsel IRS, L.A.; asst. prof. law So. U. Sch. Law, Baton Rouge; asst. atty. gen. La. Dept. Justice, Baton Rouge; with Merrill Lynch, Pierce, Fenner & Smith, N.Y.C.; asst. dist. atty. for Lincoln and Union Parishes, 3d Jud. Dist., La.; pvt. practice, Grambling; mem. La. Ho. of Reps., Baton Rouge, 1992—. Mem. So. U. Law Rev., 1978-79. Mem. adv. bd. Grambling State U.; bd. dirs. Phillips Sch. Theology, Atlanta; past pres. United League Voters; past v.p. Ruston-Grambling LWV. Named to Hall of Fame, Grambling State U., 1993; recipient Significant Achievement award Ohio U., 1994. Mem. Nat. Bar Assn. (bd. dirs. 1985-89), La. Bar, N.Y. State Bar Assn., Grambling State U. Alumni Assn. (life), So. U. Alumni Assn. (life), Delta Sigma Theta. Democrat. Methodist. Home: 611 E Grand Ave Grambling LA 71245-2305 Office: 302 College Ave Grambling LA 71245-2626

WILKERSON, WILLIAM HOLTON, banker; b. Greenville, N.C., Feb. 16, 1947; s. Edwin Cisco and Agnes Holton (Gaskins) W.; m. Ellen Logan Tomskey, Oct. 27, 1973; 1 child, William Holton Jr. AB in Econs., U. N.C., 1970. Asst. v.p. 1st Union Nat. Bank, Greensboro, N.C., 1972-77; v.p. Peoples Bank & Trust Co., Rocky Mount, N.C., 1977-79, exec. v.p., 1987-89, pres., 1989-90; sr. v.p. Hibernia Nat. Bank, New Orleans, 1979-86; group exec. officer, vice chmn. bd. dirs. Centura Banks, Inc., Rocky Mount, 1990-97, pres., 1998—2001, Wilkerson Co., Inc., Greenville, NC, 2001—. Bd. visitors U. N.C., Chapel Hill, 1999-2003; mem. Greenville Mus. of Art. Mem. Rocky Mount C. of C. (bd. dirs. 1989-96, vice chmn. 1992-94, chmn.-elect 1994, chmn. 1995), Omicron Delta Epsilon, Chi Beta Phi, Phi Sigma Pi. Republican. Home: 407 Rutledge Rd Greenville NC 27858 Office: PO Box 2095 Greenville NC 27836-0095 E-mail: wwilkerson@ec.rr.com.

WILKES, BRENT AMES, management consultant; b. Melrose, Mass., Sept. 30, 1952; s. Gordon Borthwick and Frances (Ames) W.; 1 child, Erin; m. Linda Dadourian, Oct. 18, 1998. Bachelor, U. Mass., 1974; M of Pub. Affairs, U. Conn., 1977. Cert. assn. exec., 1998, assoc. risk mgmt., 1998. Adminstrv. asst. Town of Tolland, Conn., 1975-76; mgmt. specialist Mass. Dept. Community Affairs, Boston, 1976-79; adminstrv. asst. to mayor City of Gloucester, Mass., 1979-80; assoc. dir., dir. of field svcs. Mass. Mcpl. Assn., Boston, 1980-89; v.p., treas. Mass. Interlocal Ins. Assn., Boston, 1984-89; pres. MMA Consulting Group, Inc., Boston, 1989-94, MMA Mgmt. Svcs. Inc., Boston, 1995-98, N.E. Pub. Risk, Inc., Boston, 1998, Northeast Assn. Mgmt., Inc., Boston, 1999—; v.p., treas. Pub. Employer Risk Mgmt. Assn., Albany, NY, 1989—97, pres., 1997—; bd. dirs. NLC Mut. Ins. Co., 1994—2000. Bd. dirs. Assn. Govt. Risk Pools, 2000—, pres., 2003—; adj. prof. Suffolk U. Grad. Sch. Mgmt., Boston, 1980—82; lectr. numerous regional and nat. trade assns. Author and editor: Managing Small Towns, 1986; contbr. articles to profl. jours. Mem. fin. com. Town of Acton, Mass., 1977-79; mem. town meeting Town of Reading, Mass., 1987-89; pres. Unitarian Universalist Ch. of Reading, 1990-93. Mem. Am. Soc. Assn. Execs., Internat. City Mgmt. Assn. (cert. in mgmt.), Mass. Mcpl. Mgmt. Assn. Democrat. Unitarian Universalist. Avocations: golf, tennis, volleyball, reading, boating. Office: Northeast Assn Mgmt Inc 100 Conifer Hill Dr Ste 307 Danvers MA 01923-1168 E-mail: bwilkes@neami.com.

WILKES, CHRISTOPHER COMAS, judge; b. Annapolis, Md., Apr. 12, 1956; s. Gilbert III and Elizabeth S. (Lewis) W.; m. Patricia Ann Skelly, June 9, 1984; children: Catherine Ann, Lauren Elizabeth. BA, W.Va. U., 1980; JD, Ohio No. U., 1982; postgrad., Nat. Jud. Coll., 1994. Bar: W.Va. 1983, U.S. Dist. Ct. (so. dist.) W.Va. 1983, U.S. Surpeme Ct. 1985, U.S. Dist. Ct. (no. dist.) W.Va. 1986. Ptnr. Wilkes & Wilkes Legal Corp., Martinsburg, W.Va., 1983-93; judge Mcpl. Ct., Martinsburg, 1985-93, Ranson, W.Va., 1985-93, 23rd Jud. Cir., W.Va., 1993—, chief judge, 1995, 1998, 2001—02. Mem. Am. Judges Assn., W.Va. Jud. Assn., Am. Inns of Ct., Phi Kappa Phi. Republican. Office: 23rd Jud Ct 110 W King St Martinsburg WV 25401-3287 Office Phone: 304-264-1992.

WILKES, CLEM CABELL, JR., stockbroker; b. Johnson City, Tenn., Apr. 5, 1953; s. Clem Cabell Sr. and Dorothy Jane (Miller) W.; m. Tonya Jean McCall, July 20, 1974; children: Elizabeth Layne, Clem Cabell III. BS, East Tenn. State U., 1975; postgrad., Med. Coll. Pa., 1978, Owen Sch. Mgmt., Nashville, 1984. Salesman Beecham Labs., Bristol, Tenn., 1975-78, Smith Kline & French Labs., Phila., 1978-81; stockbroker J.C. Bradford & Co., Johnson City, 1981-85; stockbroker, ptnr. Raymond James Fin. Svcs., Inc., Johnson City, 1985-99; dir. Johnson City Med. Ctr. Hosp., 1997—; fin. advisor, v.p. Citizens Investment Svcs. Inc., 1999—, vice chmn., 1999-2000. Bd. dirs. Mountain States Health Alliance, 1999—, vice chmn., 1999-2000, treas., 2000-02, chmn., 2002—. Mem. com. Am. Cancer Soc., Johnson City, 1986—87, 2d v.p., 1989—; treas. Johnson City Ties for the Blind Found., 1998—; mem. Johnson City Parks and Recreation Bd., Johnson City Pub. Bldg. Authority, 2001—02; v.p. Citizens Investment Svcs., 1999—; chmn. Mountain States Health Alliance, 2002—; vestry mem. St. John's Episcopal Ch., 1986—89, treas., 1986—, sr. warden, 1989. Recipient award, Johnson City Ties for the Blind Found., 1989. Mem. Johnson City C. of C. (membership chmn. 1987), Robert Thomas Securities Pres. Club, Raymond James Fin. Svcs. Leaders Coun., Lions (v.p. Johnson City 1986-88, pres. 1989-90, Lion of Yr. award 1985, Lion of Decade award 1992, Melvin Jones fellow 1989), Johnson City Parks and Recreation Bd., Kappa Alpha. Office: Citizens Investment Svcs Inc 901 N Roan St Johnson City TN 37601-4604

WILKES, DELANO ANGUS, architect; b. Panama City, Fla., Jan. 25, 1935; s. Burnice Angus and Flora Mae (Scott) W.; m. Dona Jean Murren, June 25, 1960. BArch, U. Fla., 1958. Cert. Nat. Coun. Archtl.; registration bds. cert. personal trainer, older adult specialty cert. Am. Coun. on Exercise. Designer Perkins & Will Partnership, Chgo., 1960-63; designer, job capt. Harry Weese, Ltd., Chgo., 1963-66; project arch. Fitch Larocca Carrington, Chgo., 1967-69; arch. Mittelbusher & Tourtelot, Chgo., 1970-71; assoc. Bank Bldg. Corp., Chgo., 1972-75; sr. assoc. Charles Edward Stade & Assocs., Park Ridge, Ill., 1975-77; sr. arch. Consoer Morgan Arch., Chgo., 1977-83, mktg. coord., 1980-83; design cons. Chamlin & Assocs., Peru and Morris, Ill., 1969-82, dir. arch., 1983-86, v.p. arch., 1986-2000. Archtl. cons. Sweet's divsn. McGraw Hill, Inc., Chgo., 1984-90; ptnr. Deri Wilkes Assocs., 1990-95; trainer Fitness Barn, 1995-96, Q Sports Club, 1997-98, Alpha Fitness, 1999-2001. Author: Colonel Ebenezer Folsom, 1778-1789, North Carolina Patriot and Tory Scourge, 1975; editor Folsom Bull., 1977-80; prodr. documentary film The Angry Minority, Menninger Found., 1978. Mem. coord. com. Dune Acres Plan Commn. (Ind.), 1983-91; bldg. commr. City of Dune Acres, 1984-89, Arch. Rev. Bd. Marsh Creek Country Club, St. Augustine, Fla., 1988—; chmn. Ind. party Dune Acres, 1987; elected trustee Dune Acres Town Bd., 1988-91, pres., 1988-89; mem. Dune Acres Civic Improvement Found., 1988-91 (leadership recognition for drive to restore Dune Acres Clubhouse); cons. Inst. of Crippled and Disabled, N.Y.C., 1978-83; guest lectr. field trip guide Coll. DuPage, Glen Ellyn, Ill., 1968-76; guest arch. med. adv. com. to Pres.'s Com. for Handicapped, 1977, 78; vice chmn. Westchester County Dem. Precinct, Porter County, Ind., 1986; chmn. selection com. Dem. Hdqrs., Porter County, 1986; treas. Com. to Elect Kovach to Coun., Porter County, 1986; vice chmn. Duneland Dems., 1988-92; pres. Ocean House Condominium Assn., St. Augustine, Fla., 1993-94; mem. architectural Rev. Bd. Marsh Creek, 1998—, chair natural landscape com., 2001—. Mem.: Putnam County Hist. Soc., New Eng. Hist. Geneal. Soc., N.C. Geneal. Soc., Am. Soc. Interior Design (coord. Info. Fair 1979), Chgo. Assn. Commerce and Industry (display dir. 1979 mtg.), Art Inst. Chgo., Chgo. AIA (chmn. design awards display com. 1978-79, prodr. New Mem. Show 1979, chmn. pub. rels. com. 1980), AIA, Folsom Family Assn. Am. (pres. 1978-82, v.p. 1982-, nominating chmn. 1983, host ann. meeting, Chgo. 1981), Businessmen for Pub. Interest, Wilkes Family Rsch. Assn., Marsh Creek Country Club (chmn. Fla. landscape com.), German Shorthaired Pointer Club North Fla., Gargoyle, Soc. Colonial Wars, Cook County Hist. Soc., Chgo. Lyric Opera Guild. Democrat. Unitarian Universalist. Home: 332 Marsh Point Cir Saint Augustine FL 32080-5858 E-mail: dwdw@aug.com.

WILKES, GEORGE GARDNER, JR., landscape architect; b. Baton Rouge, Dec. 5, 1927; s. George Gardner and Irene Ola (Sowar) W.; m. Betty Jay Stokes Partinhimer, July 6, 1949 (div. Nov. 1976); children: George Gardner III, Rebecca Wilkes Yarbrough; m. Royetta Brown, Feb. 19, 1977. BS in Landscape Arch., La. State U., Baton Rouge, 1952, postgrad., 1953. Registered landscape architect, La., Calif., Md., Va., Ga. Landscape architect Lamberts, Shreveport, La., 1953-55, chief landscape architect, 1955-60; owner George G. Wilkes Assocs., Shreveport, 1960-66; land planner U.S. VA, Atlanta, 1966-70, asst. chief appraiser, 1970-72, chief appraiser, 1972-76, land planner Washington, 1976-81; owner George G. Wilkes L.A., Atlanta, 1981—. With USN, 1945-46. Mem. Am. Soc. Landscape Architects (emeritus mem.), Masons, Shriner. Republican. Presbyterian. Avocations: fishing, reading. Home and Office: 112 Foxdale Dr Lagrange GA 30240 E-mail: biggeorge3@juno.com.

WILKES, JEFFREY BLAINE, real estate appraiser; s. William Francis and Betty June Wilkes; m. Cathy G. Wilkes, Apr. 30, 1988; children: Jeffrey Samson, William Scott. Studied, Columbia Coll., Sioux Falls, S.D., 1975—77. Cert. Appraiser Assessor S.D. Dept. Revenue, 1985, S.D. Asssessor S.D. Assn. Assessing Officers, 2001. Supr., residential bldg. permits Minnehaha County, Sioux Falls, SD, 1984—. Nat. chmn. USJC Outstanding Young Farmer Congress, Sioux Falls, SD, 1982—83; internat. dir. Sertoma Internat., Sioux Falls, SD, 1996—98; pres. Sioux Falls Jaycee, SD, 1984—85, S.D. Jaycee Camp for Handicapped, Sioux Falls, 1988—89, S.D. Jaycee Internat. Senator, Sioux Falls, 1990—91, Sioux Falls Noon Sertoma, SD, 1994—95; dist. gov. S.D. Sertoma, Sioux Falls, 1995—96; devel. v.p. S.D. Sch. of the Deaf Found., Sioux Falls, 1997—; chmn., Newton Hills Dist. Boy Scouts of Am., Sioux Falls, SD, 2001—, camp visitation team, Ctrl. Region, 2001—. Photographer's mate first class USN, 1970—74, South Pacific. Mem.: Sioux Falls Noon Sertoma (life; pres. 1994—95, Gold Honor Pres. 1995), Am. Legion (life), DAV (life), VFW (life). Home: 217 W 19th Sioux Falls SD 57105 Personal E-mail: wilkesjb@hotmail.com.

WILKES, JOHN M. sociologist; b. Mineola, N.Y., Sept. 16, 1948; s. Wade Wilkes and Carolyn Williams; m. Kathy Ellen Kuenzel Roseen, Aug. 16, 1969 (div. 1992); children: Carra, Ryan, Kevin, Nathan; m. Sandra Ansaldi, July 2, 2000. BA, Bates Coll., Lewiston, Maine, 1970; MA, Cornell U., 1973, PhD, 1976. Prof. dept. social sci. and policy studies Worcester Poly. Inst., Worcester, Mass., 1975—. Mem. adv. com. on status of women City of Worcester. Recipient Isabel Myers Rsch. award, Assn. for Psychol. Type, 2001; grantee several grants, NSF, NASA, Nat. Cancer Inst. Mem.: AAUP, Nat. Assn. for Sci., Tech. and Soc. (bd. dirs. 1999—2004, exec. dir.), Worcester Poly. Inst. Student Pugwash (chpt. advisor). Office: Worcester Poly Inst 100 Institute Rd Worcester MA 01609

WILKESON, KEVIN M. architect; BArch, Calif. State Polytechnic U., Pomona, Calif. From arch. to prin. HMC Group, Irvine, Calif., 1987—98, prin., 1998—, bd. dirs. Office: HMC Group Irvine 2601 Main St Ste 100 Irvine CA 92614*

WILKEY, ELMIRA SMITH, illustrator, artist, publisher, writer, educator; b. Kankakee, Ill., Dec. 13, 1936; d. Edmond Anthony Dorothy Agnes (Schilling) Smith; m. Lowell Gene Wilkey; children: A. Shelley, Eric, Martin, Barry, Tad, Jeremy. BA cum laude, Loretto Heights Coll. (now Regis U.), 1958. Mgr. Duncan Assocs., Champaign, Ill., 1960-61; English/drama speech tchr. Kankakee Sch. Dist., 1958-60; substitute tchr. Kankakee County, 1965-80; art instr. Kankakee C.C., 1988, 2000; behavior couns. Nutri-Sys., Bourbonnais, Ill., 1987-91; English tchr. Bishop McNamara H.S., Kankakee, 1994-2000; founder, co-owner, printer Studio Sans Serif Divsn., Bronte Press Ltd. Edits., Manteno, Kankakee, Bourbonnais, 1977—. Textbook art cons. DSP, Boston, 1965-74; art adj. Olivet Coll., Bourbonnais, 1993-94; writer, art presenter W.C. Workshops Olivet Coll., Kankakee Art League, 1980-90; lectr. in field. Illustrator: Come Spring, History of Rockville, Hoofbeats, 2001; with Children's Book Program, cable TV, Manteno, Ill., 1996-99, ten books including classic, historical prose, poetry, folklore, herbal subjects, and 2 children's books; columnist Pat's Meanders, 1992—; one woman shows include Galesburg Civic Art Ctr., 1984, Tall Grass Art Assn., ONU Brandenberg Gallery, 1994; exhibited in solo shows at Prairie State Coll., 1980, Western Mich. U.; group shows include Ill. Women in the Arts Invitation, Prairie State Coll., 1980, Copley Soc., Boston, 1986, Tall Grass Art Assn., 2001, Xavier U., 2004, Vanderpol, Chgo., 2004. Cmty. arts. coun. Kankakee; cmty. art adv. bd. Kankakee C.C.; donated artwork Hospice, Catholic Charities, United Way. Recipient numerous awards in art; Straw Series Signature art technique, V.I.P. Mem. Nat. League Am. Penwomen (Ill. state pres, Chgo. br. v.p. 1979—, treas. 2002—), Ill. State Poetry Soc. (charter), Midwest Watercolor Soc., Nat. Mus. Women in Arts, Great Books (charter, pres. 1980-85), Miniature Book Soc., Christians in Visual Arts. Republican. Roman Catholic. Avocations: walking, herb/plant identification, singing, piano, camping. Home and Office: Studio Sans Serif Divsn The Bronte Press 4136 W 6940N Rd Bourbonnais IL 60914-4208 Fax: 815-936-9913. Personal E-mail: miraswilkey@yahoo.com.

WILKEY, MALCOLM RICHARD, retired ambassador, former federal judge; b. Murfreesboro, Tenn., Dec. 6, 1918; s. Malcolm Newton and Elizabeth (Gilbert) W.; m. Emma Secul Depolo, Dec. 21, 1959. AB magna cum laude, Harvard U., 1940, LLB, 1948; LLD (hon.), Rose-Hulman Inst. Tech., 1984. Bar: Tex. 1948, NY 1963, US Supreme Ct. 1952, DC 1970. US atty. So. Dist. Tex., 1954-58; asst. atty. gen. US, 1958-61; ptnr. Butler Binion Rice & Cook, 1961-63; gen. counsel, sec. Kennecott Copper Corp., 1963-70; judge US Ct. Appeals DC Cir., 1970-85; US amb. to Uruguay, 1985-90. Ofcl. in charge fed. forces at Little Rock Sch. Crisis, Dept. Justice, 1958; mem. US-Chile Arbitration Commn., 1991-97; lectr. internat. constl. and adminstrv. law London Poly., 1979, 80; lectr. Tulane U. Law Summer Sch., Grenoble, France, 1981, 83, San Diego Law Summer Sch., Oxford, Eng., 1983, Brigham Young Law Sch., 1984, 93; vis. fellow Wolfson Coll., Cambridge U., 1985; chmn. Pres.'s Commn. on Revision Fed. Ethics Laws, 1989; spl. counsel to Atty. Gen. for inquiry into the House Banking Facility, 1992. Author: Is It Time For A Second Constitutional Convention, 1995, As the Twig is Bent, 2003. Del. Rep. Nat. Conv., 1960. Served from 2d lt. to lt. col. AUS, 1941-45. Named Am. mem., Fulbright Commn., 2002—; hon. fellow, Wolfson Coll., Cambridge. Fellow Am. Bar Found.; mem. Am. Law Inst. (adv. com. restatement fgn. rels. law of US), Jud. Conf. US (com. on standards for admission to fed. cts. 1976-79), Phi Beta Kappa, Delta Sigma Rho, Phi Delta Phi (hon.). Republican. Address: Av El Bosque 379 Providencia Santiago Chile

WILKIE, DONALD WALTER, retired biologist, aquarium museum director; b. Vancouver, B.C., Can., June 20, 1931; s. Otway James Henry and Jessie Margaret (McLeod) W.; m. Patricia Ann Archer, May 18, 1980; children: Linda, Douglas, Susanne. BA, U. B.C., 1960, M.Sc., 1966. Curator Vancouver Pub. Aquarium, 1961-63, Phila. Aquarama, 1963-65; exec. dir. aquarium-mus. Scripps Instn. Oceanography, La Jolla, Calif., 1965-93, exec. dir. emeritus, 1993—. Cons. aquarium design, rschg. exhibit content; sci. writer and editor naturalist-marine edn. programs. coach, Scholastic Clay Targets Prog. Author books on aquaria and marine ednl. materials; contbr. numerous articles to profl. jours. Bd. mem. San Diego Shotgun Sports Assn.; pres. UCSD Retirement Assn. 1999-02. Mem. San Diego (Calif.) Zool. Soc. Home: 4548 Cather Ave San Diego CA 92122-2632 Office: U Calif San Diego Scripps Instn Oceanography Libr 9500 Gilman Dr La Jolla CA 92093-0219 E-mail: dwilkie@ucsd.edu., donaqua27@aol.com. *As a biologist and teacher my major goal has been to increase public interest in learning about our environment and promoting proper use of the earth's resources.*

WILKIE, EDITH B. foundation administrator; BA, Vassar Coll., 1968; degree in french language studies, Monterey Inst. Internat. Study, 1995. Jr. staffer thru adminstrv. asst. Rep. Ogden R. Reid, 1968-75; exec. dir. arms control/foreign policy caucus U.S. Congress, 1978-95; pres./cons. Peace Through Law Edn. Fund, 1995—. Legislative asst. foreign and defense policy/chief of staff, Rep. Fortney Stark, Calif.; bd. dirs. Ploughshares Fund, PEACE-PAC, Coun. for a Livable World, Demilitarization for Democracy. Office: Council for Livable World 322 4th St NE Washington DC 20002-5824

WILKIN, RICHARD EDWIN, clergyman, religious organization executive; b. nr. Paulding, Ohio, Nov. 3, 1930; s. Gaylord D. and Beulah E. (Tarlton) W.; m. Barbara A. Zehender, Aug. 10, 1952; children— Richard Edward, James Lee, Deborah Ann. Student, Giffin Jr. Coll., 1948-49; BS, Findlay Coll., 1952, D.D., 1975; postgrad., Ind. U., 1959-60. Ordained to ministry Churches of God Gen. Conf., 1953; pastor Neptune Ch. of God, Celina, Ohio, 1952-59, Wharton (Ohio) Ch. of God, 1959-64, Anthony Wayne Ch. of God, Ft. Wayne, Ind., 1964-70; adminstr., chief exec. Chs. of God Gen. Conf., Findlay, Ohio, 1970-87; supr. mission work India, Bangladesh, Haiti, 1970-85; dir. field edn. and Inst. for Biblical Studies, faculty mem. Winebrenner Theol. Sem., Findlay, 1987-92, adj. facult O.T., 1993-97; interim sr. pastor Coll. 1st Ch. of God, Findlay, 1992-93. Dir. summer youth camps, sec., mem. exec. com. Ohio Conf., 1952-59, state clk., pres., 1959-64; chmn. Commn. on Edn., mem. exec. com. Ind. Conf., 1964-70; adv. com. Am. Bible Soc.; steering com. U.S. Ch. Leaders, 1979; pres. Ft. Wayne Ministerial Assn.; bd. dirs. Associated Chs. of Ft. Wayne and Allen County, 1966-70; tchr. Center Twp. Jr. High Sch., Celina, Mendon (Ohio) Union High Sch., Van Del High Sch., Van Wert, Ohio, 1954-59; interim pastor Shawnee First Ch. of God, Lima, Ohio, 1987-88, ch. cons., 1987-98. Vice pres. bd. trustees Winebrenner Haven, mem. adv. com. in race rels. regarding sch. reorgn. and busing, Ft. Wayne, 1967-69; trustee Winebrenner Theol. Sem., 1980-87, sec. bd. trustees; trustee U. Findlay, 1985—, chmn. com. trustees; sec. bd. of pensions Gen. Conf., Ch. of God, 1986-99; bd. dirs. Found. Great Lakes Conf. Chs. of God, 1998—, chmn. bd. dirs., chmn. adminstr.'s adv. com., 1997—2003. Recipient Outstanding Tchr. award, 1958; Disting. Alumnus award Findlay Coll., 1973, Outstanding Leadership award Ohio Conf. Chs. of God, 1986, Disting. Assoc. award U. Findlay, 1992; named Hon. Alumnus Winebrenner Theol. Sem., 1978. Home: 1806 Greendale Ave Findlay OH 45840-6918

WILKINS, AMY P. publishing executive; Assoc. pub., advt. dir. Health Mag., 1994—95, pub., 1995—97; pres. Petersen Youth Group1, 1997—98; pub. Biography Mag., 1998—2000, Smithsonian, Smithsonian Air & Space Mag., 2000—. Office: Smithsonian Mag 420 Lexington Ave Ste 2335 New York NY 10170

WILKINS, ARTHUR NORMAN, retired academic administrator; b. Kansas City, Sept. 24, 1925; s. Arthur Miller and Jean (DeWitt) W. AA, Jr. Coll. Kansas City, 1947; MA, U. Chgo., 1950; PhD, Washington U., St. Louis, 1953. Grad. asst. Washington U., St. Louis, 1950-52; instr. English La. State U., Baton Rouge, 1953-56, Jr. Coll. Kansas City, 1956-64, chmn. dept. English, 1961-64; instr. English Met. Jr. Coll., Kansas City, 1964-69, chmn. dept. English, 1964-68, chmn. divsn. humanities, 1968-69; instr. English, chmn. dept. humanities Longview C.C., Lee's Summit, Mo., 1969-70, dean instrn., 1970-84; dir. acad. affairs Met. C.C.s, Kansas City, 1984-90. Author: Mortal Taste, 1965, High Seriusness, 1971, The Lenore Overtures, 1975, Attic Salt, 1984, Dirt Behind Our Ears, 1995; contbr. articles to profl. jours. Mem. Mo. State Libr. Planning com., 1980-83. With U.S. Army, 1943-46. Washington U. fellow, 1952-53. Mem. Bookmark Soc., Phoenix Soc., U. Chgo. Libr. Soc. Home: 210 W 100th Ter Apt 202 Kansas City MO 64114-4431

WILKINS, BARRATT (GEORGE WILKINS), librarian; b. Atlanta, Nov. 6, 1943; s. George Barratt and Mabel Blanche (Brooks) W. BA, Emory U., 1965; MA, Ga. State U., 1968, U. Wis., 1969. Reference libr. SC State Libr., Columbia, 1969-71; instl. libr. cons. Mo. State Libr., Jefferson City, 1971-73; asst. state libr. State Libr. Fla., Tallahassee, 1973-77, state libr., 1977—2003; dir. div. Libr. and Info. Svcs. State Fla., Tallahassee, 1986—2003; acting asst. sec. state Fla. Dept. of State, 1987. Abstractor Hist. Abstracts, 1967—71; dir. survey project Nat. Ctr. Edn. Stats., 1976—77, chmn. state libr. agys. survery steering coun., 2003—; bd. dirs. S.E. Libr. Network, Inc., 1979—82, treas., 1980—81, vice chmn., 1981—82; mem. adv. coun. US Pub. Printer, 1983—86, S.E. Atlantic Regional Med. Libr. Svcs., 1986—89; mem. planning com. Fla. Automated Edn. Commn., 1989—94; del The White House Conf., Libr., Info Svcs., 1991; mem. steering com. pub., state libr. surveys Nat. Ctr. Edn. Stats., 1992—; mem. adv. coun. Fla. State Bd. Ind. Colleges, Universities, 1995—98, Fla. State U. Sch. Info. Studies, 1999—; mem. privacy, tech. task force State Fla., 2000—01; mem. Speakers Legis. Hist. Preservation Com., 2000—03; mem. libr. stats. revision com. Nat. Info. Stds. Orgn., 2001—; del The White House Conf. Sch. Librs., 2002; bd. dirs. First Am. Found., Inc., Fla. Distance Learning Network, Inc.; mem. planning com. Fla. Gov.'s Conf. Libraries, Info. svcs.; cons. in field. Contbr. articles profl. jours. Mem. adv. com. statewide jail project Mo. Assn. Social Welfare, 1971-73, bd. dirs. central div., 1971-73; mem. State Univ. System Interinstl. Library Com., 1977-2003; bd. dirs. Fla. Ctr. Libr. Automation, 1984-2003, Fla. Ctr. for the Book, 1984—, Fla. Coll. Ctr. for Libr. Automation, 1990-2003, Coun. for Fla. Librs., 1981—; v.p. Rose Hollow Homeowners Assn., 2003; patron Atlanta Hist. Soc., Hist. Oakland Found. Recipient Leadership Achievement award Assn. Specialized and Coop. Libr. Agys., 1991, Outstanding Pub. Svc. award Gov. of Fla., 1991, Keppel award and Lorenz award Nat. Ctr. Edn. Stats., 1995—, Profl. Achievement award Assn. Specialized and Coop. Libr. Agencies, 2003, Disting. Alumni award U. Wis. Sch. Libr. and Info. Studies, 2003; U. Wis. fellow, 1969. Mem. ALA (coun. 1981-85, legis. com. 1982-86, com. on orgn. 1988-90, planning com., 1993-95, standards, 1996-98, legis. honor roll 1996), Assn. State Libr. Agys. (pres. 1976-77), Assn. Hosp. Instl. Librs. (bd. dirs. 1973-74), Am. Correctional Assn. (chair instn. libr. com. 1975-80), Southeastern Libr. Assn. (pres. 1982-84), Assn. Specialized and Coop. Libr. Agys. (bd. dirs. 1981-85, 87-89, stds. rev. 1997—), Fla. Libr. Assn. (hon. life mem.), Libr. Adminstrn. and Mgmt. Assn. (chair govt. affair com. 1984-86), Chief Officers of State Libr. Agys. (bd. dirs. 1980-82, pres. 1990-92, chair legis. com. 1992-96, chair rsch. & stats. com. 1998-2003), Univ. Club, Gov.'s Club, Beta Phi Mu, Phi Alpha Theta. Episcopalian. E-mail: barratt.wilkins@mac.com.

WILKINS, BURLEIGH TAYLOR, philosophy educator; b. Bridgetown, Va., July 1, 1932; s. Burleigh and Helen Marie (Taylor) W.; children: Brita Taylor, Carla Cowgill, Burleigh William. BA summa cum laude, Duke U., 1952; MA, Harvard U., 1954, Princeton U., 1963, PhD, 1965. Instr. MIT, Cambridge, 1957-60, Princeton U., 1960-61, 63; asst. prof. Rice U., Houston, 1965-66, assoc. prof., 1966-67, U. Calif., Santa Barbara, 1967-68, prof., 1968—. Author: Carl Becker, 1961, The Problem of Burke's Political Philosophy, 1967, Hegel's Philosophy of History, 1974, Has History Any Meaning?, 1978, Terrorism and Collective Responsibility, 1992. Mem. Phi Beta Kappa. Office: U Calif Dept Philosophy Santa Barbara CA 93106

WILKINS, CAROLINE HANKE, consumer agency administrator, political worker; b. Corpus Christi, Tex., May 12, 1937; d. Louis Allen and Jean Guckian Hanke; m. B. Hughel Wilkins, 1957; 1 child, Brian Hughel. Student, Tex. Coll. Arts and Industries, 1956—57, Tex. Tech. U., 1957—58; BA, U. Tex., 1961; MA magna cum laude, U. Ams., 1964. Instr. history Oreg. State U., 1967-68; adminstr. Consumer Svcs. divsn. State of Oreg., 1977-80, Wilkins Assoc., 1980—. Mem. PFMC Salmon Adv. subpanel, 1982-86. Author: (with B. H. Wilkins) Implications of the U.S.-Mexican Water Treaty for Interregional Water Transfer, 1968. Dem. precinct committeewoman, Benton County, Oreg., 1964-90; publicity chmn. Benton County Gen. Election, 1964; chmn. Get-Out-the-Vote Com., Benton County, 1966; vice chmn. Benton County Dem. Ctrl. Com., 1966-70; vice chmn. 1st Congl. Dist., Oreg., 1966-67, chmn., 1967-68; vice chmn. Dem. Party of Oreg., 1968-69, chmn., 1969-74; mem. exec. com. Western States Dem. Conf., 1970-72; vice chmn. Dem. Nat. Com., 1972-77, mem. arrangements com., 1972, 76, mem. Dem. Charter Commn., 1973-74; mem. Dem. Nat. Com., 1972-77, 85-89, mem. size and composition com., 1987-89, rules com., 1988; mem. Oreg. Govt. Ethics Commn., 1974-76; del., mem. rules com. Dem. Nat. Conv., 1988; 1st v.p. Nat. Fedn. Dem. Women, 1983-85, pres., 1985-87, parliamentarian, 1993-95, 99-2001, chair Pres.'s coun., 2001-2003, chair by-laws com., 2003—; mem. Kerr Libr. bd. Oreg. State U., 1989-95, pres., 1994-95; mem. Corvallis-Benton County Libr. Found., 1991-2001, sec., 1993, v.p., 1994, pres., 1995, mission and goals com. chair 2000-01; bd. dirs. Oreg. chpt. U.S. Lighthouse Soc., pres., 1997-98; bd. dirs. Oreg. State U.-Corvallis Symphony, 1998-2001, v.p. 1999-2000, resources com.; pres. Oreg. Fedn. Dem. Women, 1997-2001, Oreg. State-Corvallis chpt., UNIFEM, 1998-2002; bd. dirs. Oreg. State U. Acad. Lifelong Learning, 2003—; mem. Women and Philanthropy, Oreg. State U. Giving Cir., 2003-. Named Outstanding Mem. Nat. Fedn. Dem. Women, 1992, Woman of Achievement, Oreg. State U. Women's Ctr., 1998. Mem.: Soc. Consumer Affairs Profls., Nat. Assn. Consumer Agy. Adminstrs., Oreg. State U. Folk Club (pres. faculty wives 1989—90, scholarship chair 2000—01, grants com. 2002—03), Zonta Internat. (vice area bd. dirs. dist. 8 1992—94, bd. dist. 8 1994—96, by laws and resolutions chair 1997—98, internat. rels. coord. dist. 8 2000—02, dist. 8 nominating com. 2003—). Office: 3311 NW Roosevelt Dr Corvallis OR 97330-1169

WILKINS, CHRISTOPHER PUTNAM, conductor; b. Boston, May 28, 1957; s. Herbert Putnam and Angela (Middleton) W. BA, Harvard U., 1978; MusM, Yale U., 1981. Condr.-in-residence SUNY, Purchase, 1981-82; asst. condr. Oreg. Symphony, Portland, 1982-83, Cleve. Orch., 1983-86; assoc. condr. Utah Symphony, Salt Lake City, from 1986; condr. Colo. Springs Symphony Orch., 1989-96, artistic advisor, 1998—; music dir. San Antonio Symphony, 1992—. Condr. Exxon Arts Endowment, 1982-86. Home: 168 Nashawtuc Rd Concord MA 01742-1617 Office: San Antonio Symphony Po Box 658 San Antonio TX 78293-0658

WILKINS, DAVID GEORGE, fine arts educator; b. Battle Creek, Mich., Sept. 12, 1939; s. George Henry and Marjorie Ewing (Pierce) Wilkins; m. Ann Thomas, June 25, 1966; children: Rebecca Louise, Katherine May. BA, Oberlin Coll., 1961; MA, U. Mich., 1963, PhD, 1969. Instr. U. N.H., Durham, 1963—64; prof. dept. history of art and arch. U. Pitts., 1967—, chair, 1989—92, 1998—2004, dir. univ. art gallery, 1976—92. Faculty mem summer sessions Sarah Lawrence Col-Univ Mich, Florence, Italy, 1975—81. Author (with Bernard Schultz and Katheryn M Linduff): (book) Art Past/Art Present, 2004; author: (with Bonnie Bennett) Donatello, 1984, Maso di Banco, 1985; author: (with K J Arbitman) The Illustrated Bartsch, Vol 53, Pre-Rembrandt Etchers, 1985, The Art of the Duquesne Club, 2002; author: (with Mark M Brown and Lu Donnelly) The History of the Duquesne Club, 1989, with F. Hartt: History of Italian Renaissance Art, 5th edit., 2002;; editor (with Rebecca L Wilkins): (book) The Search for a Patron in the Middle Ages and the Renaissance, 1996; editor: (with Sheryl Reiss) Beyond Isabella: Secular Women Patrons of Art in the Italian Renaissance, 2001. Mem Humanities Coun, 1984—88; mus adv panel Pa Coun Arts, 1985—87; bd dirs Pittsburgh Ctr Arts, 1979—98; Mendelssohn Choir Pittsburgh, 1979—84. Recipient Chancellor's Distinguishing Teaching Award, Univ Pittsburgh, 1987; fellow William E Suida, Kress Found, Kunsthistorisches Inst, Florence, 1966—67. Mem.: Renaissance Soc Am, Italian Art Soc, Col Art Asn. Democrat. Home: 1217 Shady Ave Pittsburgh PA 15232-2811

WILKINS, DAVID HORTON, state legislator; b. Oct. 12, 1946; m. Susan Clary; children: James, Robert. BA with honors, Clemson U.; JD, U. S.C.; hon. degree, Med. U. S.C., The Citadel. Bar: S.C. Atty. in pvt.practice, 1970s—; mem. S.C. Ho. of Reps., 1980—, chmn. judiciary com., 1986—, speaker pro tem, 1992-95, speaker, 1995—. Recipient Friend of the Taxpayer award S.C. Asn. Taxpayers, others; named Outstanding Legislator of Yr. by S.C. C. of C., Dept. Probation of Parole, S.C. Sch. Bds. Assn., S.C. Troopers Assn., others, Nat. Republican Legislator of Yr. Nat. Rep. Legis. Assn. Republican. Baptist. Office: 508 Blatt Bldg Columbia SC 29201

WILKINS, EARLE WAYNE, JR., surgery educator emeritus; b. Albany, N.Y., Aug. 17, 1919; s. Earle Wayne and Mildred Anna (Dana) W.; m. Suzanne Porter, Aug. 26, 1944; children: Clinton Porter, Wendy Dana Wilkins Hopkins, Wayne Lawrence. AB, Williams Coll., 1941; MD, Harvard U., 1944. Diplomate Am. Bd. Surgery, Am. Bd. Thoracic Surgery. Surg. resident Mass. Gen. Hosp., Boston, 1944-46, 48-51, mem. staff, 1952-59, vis. surgeon, 1968-78; mem. staff Harvard Med. Sch., Boston, 1953—, clin. prof. surgery, 1979-89, prof. emeritus, 1989—. Fulbright vis. prof. Allgemeines Krankenhaus, Vienna, Austria, 1964-65; vis. prof. Nat. Def. Med. Ctr., Taipei, Taiwan, 1989; surgeon Boston Bruins Hockey Club, 1969-85; physician tech. advisor Divsn. Emergency Med. Svcs., Washington, 1977-81, med. dir. Mass. Region IV, Boston, 1980-82; chmn. bd. Boston Med. Flight, 1985-87; Earle W. Wilkins, Jr. vis. prof. MGH, 1998. Editor: Current Therapy in Cardiothoracic Surgery, 1989, Esophageal Cancer, 1988, Emergency Medicine: Scientific Foundations and Current Practice, 1989; contbr. numerous articles to profl. jours. Trustee Williams Coll., Williamstown, Mass., 1971-89, pres. Soc. of Alumni, 1967-69. Lt. (j.g.) USNR, 1946-48. Recipient Sports Illustrated Silver Anniversary All-Am. award Time Inc., N.Y.C., 1965, Commonwealth award Commonwealth of Mass., 1986, Disting. Alumnus award Albany Acad., 1988, Rogerson Cup Williams Coll., 1991, Bicentennial medal Williams Coll., 1993. Fellow ACS, Am. Surg. Assn.; mem. AMA, Mass. Med. Soc., Boston Surg. Soc., Am. Assn. Thoracic Surgery (councillor 1984-88), Soc. Thoracic Surgeons, New England Surg. Soc. (pres. 1980-81), Gen. Thoracic Surg. Club, Taconic Golf Club (pres. 1990-95). Republican. Avocations: golf, tennis, skiing, travel, stamps. Home: 240 South St Williamstown MA 01267-2822

WILKINS, FLOYD, JR., retired lawyer, consultant; b. Fowler, Calif., Sept. 8, 1925; s. Floyd and Kathryn (Springborg) W.; m. Holly Blee, June 18, 1949 (div. Jan. 1964); children: Douglas B., Janet H., Steven B., Kevin D.; m. Sybil Ann Perrault, Feb. 22, 1964. BS, U. Calif., Berkeley, 1946; LLB, Harvard U., 1952. Bar: N.Y. 1953, Calif. 1959. Assoc. Dwight, Royall, Harris, Koegel & Caskey, N.Y.C., 1952-58; v.p., trust officer San Diego Trust & Savs. Bank, 1958-63; assoc., then ptnr., prin. Seltzer Caplan Wilkins & McMahon, P.C. and predecessors, San Diego, 1963-91. Lectr. U. So. Calif. Tax Inst., L.A., 1975, Title Ins. and Trust Co., L.A. and Santa Ana, Calif., 1973, 78, 83, Trust Svcs. of Am. Tax Forum, San Diego, U. Calif. Continuing Edn. of Bar, San Diego, 1977-91. Bd. dirs., pres. San Diego County Citizens Scholarship Found. Served with USNR, 1944-46. Mem. ABA, State Bar Calif., San Diego County Bar Assn. Republican. Avocations: travel, photography, wine, gardening. Home: 2005 Soledad Ave La Jolla CA 92037-3904

WILKINS, GUY (IRA WILKINS), painter, art teacher; b. Seaview, Va., Jan. 7, 1927; s. Ira Guy and Margaret Grace (Nottingham) W.; children: Sarah Gay, Elizabeth, Kate, Johnny. Student, Coll. William and Mary, Norfolk, Va., 1946, U. Va., 1947, 48. Reporter Birmingham (Ala.) News, 1949-51, Greenville (S.C.) Piedmont, 1951-52, Norfolk Virginian Pilot, 1952-54; dir. info. Norfolk Port Authority, 1954-56; press liaison Norfolk Mus. (now Chrysler Mus.), 1963-65; painter, art tchr. Wachapreague, Va., 1975—. Gallery dir. Norfolk Mus.'s Gallery Va. Artists, 1964, 65. Author: (poetry) Day Moon, 1986; one-man shows include Regional Libr., Williamsburg, Va., 1987, Eso Art Ctr., Belle Haven, Va., 1994, Art Ctr., Carrboro, N.C., 2002; exhbns. include Irene Leach Biennial, 1960's; represented by Amsterdam Whitney Gallery, Chelsea, NYC, Smiling Dolphin Gallery, Nassawaddox, Va., Stage Door Gallery, Cape Charles, Va., collections in China, Australia. Recipient Glidden Painting prize Tidewater Artist Assn., 1963, A.B. Jackson award Ghent Arts Festival, 1983, 1st place award for feature writing Va. Press Assn., 1963, Best Oil Tidewater Regional Exhibn., others. Mem. Eastern Shore Art League (bd. dirs. 1980-91). Presbyterian. Office: Seaside Studio Main St Wachapreague VA 23480 Home: 2005 Marions Ford Rd Chapel Hill NC 27516-5499

WILKINS, JEFFREY M. commputer company executive; Co-founder CompuServe, 1969; founder Discovery Sys., 1985-91; pres., CEO Metatec Corp., Dublin, Ohio, 1991—, chmn. bd. dirs. Office: Metatec Internat Inc 7001 Metatec Blvd Dublin OH 43017-3219

WILKINS, JOHN WARREN, physics educator; b. Des Moines, Mar. 11, 1936; s. Carl Daniel and Ruth Elizabeth (Warren) W. BS in Engring, Northwestern U., 1959; MS, U. Ill., 1960, PhD, 1963; DTech (hon.), Chalmers Tekniska Hogskola, Göteborg, 1990. NSF fellow U. Cambridge, Eng., 1963-64; asst. prof. physics Cornell U., 1964-68, assoc. prof., 1968-74, prof., 1974-88; eminent scholar, prof. physics Ohio State U., 1988—. Vis. prof. H.C. Ørsted Inst., Copenhagen, 1968, Nordita, Copenhagen, 1972-73, 75-76, 79-81; cons. Los Alamos Nat. Lab., 1984—, Lawrence Livermore Nat. Lab., 1997—; adv. com. U. Chgo. Sci. and Tech., 1990—. Assoc. editor Physica Scripta, 1977-85, Phys. Rev. Letters, 1982-85, Rev. Modern Physics, 1983-95; mem. editorial bd. Phys. Rev. B, 1991-94; coord. Comments on Condensed Matter Physics, 1985-90. Sloan fellow, 1966; Guggenheim fellow, 1985. Fellow AAAS, Am. Phys. Soc. (publs. oversight com. 1995-97, chmn. 1995-96, councillor divsn. condensed matter physics 1989-93, exec. com. divsn. biol. physics 1973-77, vice-chair through past chair divsn. condensed matter physics 2001—); mem. European Phys. Soc. Office: Ohio State U Dept Physics 174 W 18th Ave Columbus OH 43210-1106

WILKINS, LUCIEN SANDERS, gastroenterologist; b. Sanford, N.C., Mar. 30, 1942; s. Alexander Betts and Olive Elizabeth (Pittman) Wilkins; m. Freda Barry Hartness, July 16, 1966; children: Lucien Sanders Wilkins Jr., Elise Perryman. BA, Duke U., 1963; MD, Med. Coll. Va., 1967. Diplomate Am. Bd. Internal Medicine. Intern Medical Coll. Va., Richmond, 1967-68, resident in internal medicine, 1970-72, gastroenterology fellow, 1972-73; clin. gastroenterologist Wilmington (N.C.) Health Assoc., 1973—99; pres. Lucien Wilkins Cons., 2000—; pres., med. dir. Am. Physician Ptnrs. Assn., 1992—; pres. Strategic Med. Planning and Design, 1992—, DeWitt Healthcare, 2003—, mng. dir., 2003—. Vis. physician Hopital St. Croix, Leogane, Haiti, 1979—84, founder Divsn. Gastrointestinal Endoscopy, 1984; 1st Endoscopic Ambulatory Surgery Facility State of N.C., 1990; chmn. dept. medicine New Hanover Regional Med. Ctr., Wilmington, NC, 1990—92; asst. prof. clin. medicine U. N.C., Chapel Hill, 1974—; bd. dirs. Br. Banking and Trust, Wilmington; physician adv. Nat. Found. Ileitis and Colitis, 1976—78. Author: Progeny, 1994. Bd. dirs. Cape Fear Coun. for Arts, Wilmington, 1976—77, New Hanover Regional Med. Ctr. Found., Wilmington, 1993—95, exec. com., 1994—95; bd. dirs. Com. of 100, Wilmington, 1992—95. Lt. comdr. M.C.1970 USN, 1968. Recipient winner GTP-L Holbert Meml. Race, Sebring, Fla., 1995; fellow D. Williams rsch. fellow, 1965, Paul Harris fellow, Rotary, 1986. Mem.: ACP, New Hanover-Pender County Med. Soc. (pres. 1980), Wrightsville Beach Ocean Racing Assn. (commodore), Figure Eight Island Yacht Club (charter), Surf Club, Cape Fear Country Club. Presbyterian. Avocation: vintage automobile racing. Home: 2215 Lynnwood Dr Wilmington NC 28403-8026 Office: 1135 Military Cutoff Rd Ste 203 Wilmington NC 28405 E-mail: lwilkins@DeWittcorp.com. *Being a true physician means continually learning from your patients, about your patients, and on behalf of your patients.*

WILKINS, MICHAEL JON, state supreme court justice; b. Murray, Utah, May 13, 1948; s. Jack L. and Mary June (Phillips) W.; m. Diane W. Wilkins, Nov. 9, 1967; children: Jennifer, Stephanie, Bradley J. BS, U. Utah, 1975, JD, 1976; LLM, U. Va., 2001. Bar: Utah 1977, U.S. Dist. Ct. Utah 1977, U.S. Ct. Appeals (10th cir.) 1987, U.S. Supreme Ct. 1986. Mng. ptnr. Wilkins, Oritt & Headman, Salt Lake City, 1989-94; judge Utah Ct. Appeals, 1994—2000; justice Utah Supreme Ct, 2000—, mem. jud. coun., 2000—. Mem. Gov.'s Adv. Com. on Corp., Salt Lake City, 1989-94; mem. Utah Supreme Ct. Complex Steering Com., 1993-94; mem. Judiciary Standing Com. on Tech., 1995-2000, chmn., 1995-2000; mem. Legis. Compensation Commn., 1994-95. Trustee Utah Law Related Edn. Project, Inc., Salt Lake City, 1991-95, chmn., 1992-94. 1st lt. U.S. Army, 1968-72. Mem. Lds Ch. Office: Utah Supreme Ct 450 S State St PO Box 140210 Salt Lake City UT 84114-0210

WILKINS, RAY, communications executive; Head bus. comm. svc. group Pacific Bell; pres., CEO Southwestern Bell Tel.; pres. bus. comm. svc. SBC Comm. Inc; group pres. mktg. and sales SBC Comm. Inc., San Antonio, 2000—. Office: SBC Comm Inc 175 E Houston San Antonio TX 78205

WILKINS, ROBERT HENRY, neurosurgeon, educator, editor; b. Pitts., Aug. 18, 1934; s. George H. and Mary M. (Lemon) W.; m. Gloria A. Kohl, Dec. 28, 1957; children: Michael I., Jeffrey K., Elizabeth A. BS, U. Pitts., 1955, MD, 1959. Diplomate Am. Bd. Neurol. Surgery. Intern, resident gen. surgery Duke U. Med. Ctr., Durham, N.C., 1959-61, resident in neurosurgery, 1963-68, asst. prof. neurosurgery, 1968-72, prof. neurosurgery, 1976—, chief divsn. neurosurgery, 1976-96; clin. assoc. surgery br. Nat. Cancer Inst., Bethesda, Md., 1961-63; chmn. dept. neurosurgery Scott and White Clinic, Temple, Tex., 1972-75; assoc. prof. neurosurgery U. Pitts., 1975-76. Lectr. Cook County Grad. Sch. Medicine, Chgo., 1976-96; attending neurosurgeon Durham VA Hosp., 1968-72, 78-98; mem. Nat. Adv. Coun. Nat. Inst. Neurol. Disorders and Stroke, 1989-92. Co-editor: Neurosurgery, 2d edit., 3 vols., 1996, Neurosurgery Updates I and II, 1990, 91, Neurosurgical Operative Atlas, 1991-2000, Principles of Neurosurgery, 1994; editor Clin. Neurosurgery, 1972-75; assoc. editor Surg. Neurology, 1975-76; founding editor Neurosurgery, 1977-82, mem. editl. rev. bd., 1997-2001; mem. editl. bd. Jour. Neurosurgery, 1987-96, chmn., 1996-97, mem. adv. bd., 1997—; neurosurgery editor Key Neurology and Neurosurgery, 1993-96, Yr. Book of Neurology and Neurosurgery, 1994-97. Recipient Travel award Copenhagen, Nat. Inst. Neurol. Diseases and Blindness, 1965, Royal Australasian Coll. Surgeons, Found. lectr. Adelaide 1986. Fellow ACS (gov. 1996); mem. Congress Neurol. Surgeons (pres. 1979-80), Am. Assn. Neurol. Surgeons (treas. 1989-92), So. Neurosurg. Soc. (sec. 1988-91, pres. 1992-93), Soc. Neurol. Surgeons (v.p. 1995-96), Am. Bd. Neurol. Surgery (dir. 1991-97, chmn. 1996-97), Phi Beta Kappa, Alpha Omega Alpha. Democrat. Avocation: medical writing and editing. Office: Duke U Med Ctr PO Box 3807 Durham NC 27710-0001 E-mail: rhwilkins@aol.com.

WILKINS, ROBERT PEARCE, lawyer; b. Jesup, Ga., Sept. 10, 1933; s. Ransom Little and Sarah (Pearce) W.; m. Rose Truesdale, Jan. 7, 1956; children: Robert Pearce, Chisolm Wallace (dec.), Sarah Ruth Weiss, Rose Anne Brooks. BA, U. S.C., 1953, JD, 1954; LL.M., Georgetown U., 1957. Bar: S.C. 1954; cert. mediator and arbitrator, S.C. Atty. Office Gen. Counsel, Sec. Army, Washington, 1956; trust officer First Nat. Bank S.C., Columbia, 1957-60; practice law Columbia, 1960-64; ptnr. McLain, Sherrill & Wilkins, Columbia, 1964-68, McKay, Sherrill, Walker, Townsend & Wilkins, Columbia, 1969-75; sole practice law Columbia and Lexington, S.C., 1975-88; of counsel Nelson, Mullins, Riley & Scarborough, Lexington, 1988—. Pres. Sandlapper Press, Inc., 1967-72, pub. Sandlapper Mag. S.C., 1968-72; editor Sandlapper Mag. S.C., 1968-69, 89—; editor, pub. S.C. History Illustrated, 1970; pres. R.P.W. Pub. Corp.; mem., chmn. S.C. Splty. Adv. Bd. Estate Planning and Probate, 1982-85; lectr. in law U. S.C., 1971-78. Author: Draftin Wills and Trust Agreements in South Carolina, 1971, Drafting Wills and Trust Agreements in Michigan, 1978, Wills and Trust System (Arkansas), 1978, Drafting Wills and Trust Agreements: A Systems Approach, 1998, 3d edit., 1999, software edit.; (with others) Word Processing for a Law Office, 1979, also articles; editor: The Lawyer's Microcomputer, 1982-85, The Lawyer's PC, 1983-97, What a Lawyer Needs to Know to Buy and Use a Computer, 1984, The Perfect Lawyer, 1990-97, The Lawyers' Word, 1991, Shepard's Elder Care/Law Newsletter, 1991-95, Hot docs Toolbox, 1996-97, Drafting Wills and Trust Agreements Newsletter, 1997. Del., Spl. Liaison Tax Com. Southeastern Region, 1967-70; exec. com. Richland County Rep. Com., 1960-64; sec.-treas. Richland County Rep. Club, 1960; bd. dirs. Ctrl. Tb-RD Assn.; trustee Sch. Dist. 1, Lexington County, S.C., 1971-78, sec., 1972-75, chmn., 1975-78; mem. S.C. Commn. on Higher Edn., 1978-80, S.C. Commn. on Lawyer Competence, 1980-82; bd. dirs. Crime Stoppers of the Midlands, 1983-85, RPW Learning Ctr., 1987-94, Mt. Hope Cemetary, 1991—, also v.p., 1992—; v.p. 11th cir. Alumni Coun. U. S.C., 1993-95, mem. awards com., 1995-97; mem. commn. Riverbanks Zoo, 1986—, sec., 1991-95, chmn., 1995-96, 97—, vice-chmn., 1996-97. With AUS, 1954-55. Recipient Compleat Lawyer award Law Sch. U. S.C., 1997, Diamond Circle award U. S.C. Coll. Journalism and Mass Comms., 1998. Fellow Am. Bar Found., Am. Coll. Trust and Estate Counsel (publs. com. 1984-87, bd. regents 1986-87, mem. tech. com. 1989-98), Am. Coll. Tax Counsel, Coll. Law Practice Mgmt. (charter, trustee 1994-98), S.C. Bar (tax coordinating com. 1968-70, chmn. legal econs. com. 1973-75, ho. of dels. 1978-80, editor S.C. Lawyer 1989-91, mem. alternative dispute resolution sect. 1993—), S.C. Bar Found. (life, bd. dirs. 1984-88, v.p. 1986-87, pres. 1987-88); mem. ABA (ho. of dels. 1986-87, chmn. valuation subcom., estate and gift tax com., taxation sect. 1967-73, vice chmn. svc. and assistance to law student div. com. gen. practice sect. 1971-72, vice chmn. corp. counsel com. gen. practice sect. 1972-74, editor econs. of law practice sect. legal econs. 1974-78, sec. 1977-78, vice chmn. 1978-79, chmn. 1980-81, mem. standing com. assn. comm. 1981-84, real property, probate and trust law, mem. publs. com. 1985-89, editor Probate and Property, 1986-89), Richland County Bar Assn. (chmn. probate sect. 1973-74, unauthorized practice of law com. 1976), Lexington County Bar (chmn. mediation com. 1994—), Columbia Jaycees (sec.-treas. 1958-59), Columbia Estate Planning Coun. (pres. 1964-65), Am. Y-Flyer Yacht Racing Assn. (area v.p. 1971, internat. dir. 1972-73), Omicron Delta Kappa, Sigma Chi Clubs: Columbia Sailing (dir. 1968-71), Columbia Tip Off (dir. 1968-73), Columbia (pres. 1971-72). Home: 124 Lake Murray Ct Lexington SC 29072-9104 Office: 955 Old Cherokee Rd Lexington SC 29072-9042

WILKINS, WILLIAM WALTER, federal judge; b. Anderson, S.C., Mar. 29, 1942; s. W. Walter Wilkins and Evelyn Louise (Horton); m. Debra Ann Dill, Aug. 19, 1999; children: Lauren, Lyn, Walt. BA, Davidson Coll., 1964; JD, U. S.C., 1967. Bar: S.C. 1967, U.S. Dist. Ct. S.C. 1967, U.S. Ct. Appeals (4th cir.) 1969, U.S. Supreme Ct. 1970. Law clk. to Hon. Clement F. Haynsworth Jr. U.S. Ct. Appeals (4th cir.), 1969—70; legal asst. to U.S. Senator Strom Thurmond, 1970—71; ptnr. Wilkins & Wilkins, Greenville, SC, 1971—78; solicitor 13th Jud. Cir., 1974—81; judge U.S. Dist. Ct., Greenville, 1981—86, U.S. Ct. Appeals (4th cir.), 1986—, chief judge, 2003—. Lectr. Greenville Tech. Coll., 1973—97, Taft Seminar, Clemson Univ., SC, 1973—97; chmn. U.S. Sentencing Commn., 1985—94; chmn. com. on criminal law Jud. Conf. U.S., 2000—03. Editor-in-chief: S.C. Law Rev., 1967; contbr. articles to profl. jours. With U.S. Army, 1967—69, with USAR, 1969—83, with S.C. Army Nat. Guard, 1983—94. Mem.: S.C. Bar Assn., Wig and Robe. Republican. Baptist. Office: US Cir Ct 4th Ct PO Box 10857 Greenville SC 29603-0857

WILKINSON, ALAN HERBERT, nephrologist, educator; b. Johannesburg, July 11, 1948; came to U.S., 1985; s. Raymond C. and Nonie (Levick) W.; m. Angelika A. E. Adami, Dec. 22, 1973; one child: Rebecca Kate Adami. BS in Physiology, Biochemistry, Philosophy, U. Witwatersrand, South Africa, 1969, BS in Biochemistry with honors, 1970, MB, BCh, 1975; cert. health care mgmt., U. Calif., Irvine, 1998. Fellow Royal Coll. Physicians (U.K.), specialist in clin. hypertension. Vis. assoc. Dept. Internal Medicine U. Iowa, Iowa City, 1987-88; assoc. prof. of medicine UCLA Sch. Med., 1988-95, prof. med., 1995—; dir. clin. nephrology UCLA Dept. Med., 1988-93, dir. kidney and pancreas transplantation, 1993—. Contbr. articles to profl. jours. Mem. steering com. Nat. Kidney Found.; mem. U.S. Transplant Games, L.A., 1992; bd. dirs. So. Calif. Renal Disease Coun., 2002-04, med. adv., 2004—. Recipient Exceptional Svc. award Nat. Kidney Found., 1992; Nat. Kidney Found. fellow. Mem. Am. Soc. Transplantation, Internat. Nephrology Soc., Am. Soc. Nephrology. Avocations: ornithology, gardening. Office: UCLA Dept Med 200 Medical Plz Box 951693 Los Angeles CA 90095-1693

WILKINSON, ALBERT MIMS, JR., lawyer; b. Nashville, June 29, 1925; s. Albert Mims and Mary Nelle (Derryberry) W.; m. Edythe Bush, Mar. 27, 1953 (div.); children: William Terry, Elizabeth Ann, David Bush; m. Dolores Jean Attard, Oct. 22, 1971 (div.); 1 child, Mary Dolores. Student, Emory U., 1942-43; JD, U. Ga., 1949. Bar: Ga. 1948. Pvt. practice law, Atlanta, 1950-85; gen. counsel GEC-Marconi Avionics Inc., Atlanta, 1985-98; hon. legal adviser to Brit. Consul Gen. at Atlanta. Author: The Winning of the Revolutionary War in the South, 1976, The Rights of Unsecured Creditors-The Law in Ga., 1979; editor: Chronicles of the Old Guard of the Gate City Guard of Atlanta, 1858-2001 (3 vols.), 2002. Mem. DeKalb County Bd. Elections, 1966-72; chmn. 4th Congl. Dist. Republican Exec. Com., 1966-70, Ga. State Rep. Exec. Com., 1968-74; 1st vice chmn. Ga. Rep. Party, 1972-74, asst. gen. counsel, 1974-75; vice chmn., trustee Atlanta Counseling Center, Inc., 1960-83. Served with USCGR, 1943-46. Decorated Order Brit. Empire. Fellow Comml. Law Found.; mem. BA, Ga. Bar Assn., Atlanta Bar Assn., Ga. Soc. (pres. 1962-63), SAR, Southeastern Mem.'s Assn. (pres. 1960-61), Comml. Law League Am., Ga. Soc. Colonial Wars, Old Guard of Gate City Guard (comdt. 1986), N.C. Soc. of Cincinnati, Sphinx Club, Gridiron Club, Commerce Club, Civitan, Masons, Blue Key, Omicron Delta Kappa. Baptist. Home and Office: 66 Demorest Ln # 333 Sky Valley GA 30537-2581 E-mail: amims@hemc.net. *By precept and example my parents pointed out the upward way in life, on a foundation of religious faith. "To do justly, to love mercy, to walk humbly with thy God." Later a beloved teacher taught the lines from Ulysses as he prepared to set sail, "To strive, to seek, to find and never yield." Their inspiration has continued throughout my life.*

WILKINSON, CHARLES P. ophthalmologist; b. Syracuse, 1940; MD, Johns Hopkins U. Sch. Medicine, 1966. Intern Johns Hopkins Hosp., 1966—67; resident Wilmer Inst., Balt., 1967—70; fellow U. Miami, 1970—71; chmn. dept., prof. ophthalmology Johns Hopkins U. Sch. Medicine. Co-author: Michels Retinal Detachment, 1996. Mem.: Am. Bd. Ophthalmology (vice chmn. 2003, chmn. 2004). Avocation: golf. Office: Greater Balt Med Ctr 6569 N Charles St #505 Towson MD 21204-5809 Office Phone: 443-849-2196.

WILKINSON, CLAUDE HENRY, writer, artist, English literature educator; b. Memphis, Dec. 17, 1959; s. Henry Bridgforth and Lula (Moncrief) W. BSc, U. Miss., 1981; cert. d'excellence, Alliance Française, Memphis, 1991; MA, U. Memphis, 1992. Instr. English McNeese State U., Lake Charles, La., 1990-91, U. Memphis, 1991-92, Lane Coll., Jackson, Tenn., 1992-94, LeMoyne-Owen Coll., Memphis, 1998-99; owner Claude Wilkinson Fine Art Studio, Nesbit, Miss., 1984—. Editor River City Mag., Memphis, 1991; John and Renée Grisham So. writer in residence U. Miss., 2000. Author: Reading the Earth, 1998 (Naomi Long Madgett Poetry award, 1998), Joy in the Morning, 2004; author poetry; contbr. articles to profl. jours. Recipient New Poets award, Ursus Press, 1984, Grand prize, Miss. Poetry Soc., 1985, W.M. Whittington Jr. Purchase award, Cottonlandia Mus. Juried Exhbn., 1993, 1st prize in painting, Carnegie Ctr. for Arts and History, 1994, Pioneer Br. Poetry award, Ark. Writers' Conf., 1995, Kenneth Beaudoin Meml. award, Mid-South Poetry Festival, 1995, Paul Laurence Dunbar Poetry award, Detroit Black Writers Guild, 1998, Whiting Writer's award, Mrs. Giles Whiting Found., 2000; Walter E. Dakin fellow, Sewanee Writers' Conf., 1999. Avocations: music, mythology, nature study. Office Phone: 662-429-4935.

WILKINSON, DAVID STANLEY, pathologist, consultant, researcher, educator, physician; b. Richmond, Va., Feb. 2, 1945; s. Herbert Carroll and Hattie Mae (Vaughan) Wilkinson; m. Judith Farish Pace, June 16, 1967; children: Jill Marie, Julie Lynne, Virginia Ann. BS in Chemistry, Va. Mil. Inst., Lexington, 1967; PhD in Exptl. Oncology and Pathology, U. Wis.-Madison, 1971; MD, U. Miami, 1978. Diplomate Am. Bd. Pathology. Fellow McArdie Lab. Cancer Rsch. U. Wis., 1967—71; asst. prof. biochemistry U. South Fla., Tampa, 1972—76; resident in pathology Walter Reed Army Med. Ctr., Washington, 1978—82; instr. pathology Uniformed Svc. U. Health Sci., Bethesda, 1979—82; chief clin. pathology Eisenhower Army Med. Ctr., Ft. Gordon, Ga., 1982—84; instr. pathology Med. Coll. Ga., Augusta, 1982—84; assoc. prof. pathology George Washington U. Med. Ctr., 1984—89, dir. clin. pathology div., 1984—92, prof. pathology, 1989—93; med. dir. George Washington U. Hosp., 1992—93; prof. pathology, chmn. dept. pathology Va. Commonwealth

U., 1993—. Lectr. in field. Editor: (other) Clinical Laboratory Management Review, 1989—2004; contbr. articles to profl. jours. Commd. 2nd lt. U.S. Army, 1967, advanced through grades to maj. U.S. Army, 1982. Fellow: Coll. Am. Pathologists, Am. Soc. Clin. Pathology; mem.: Am. Coll. Physician Executives, Am. Med. Assn., Med. Soc. Va. (del.), Richmond Acad. Medicine (trustee), U.S. and Canadian Acad. Pathology, Am. Soc. Investigative Pathology, Am. Assn. Blood Banks, Clin. Lab. Mgmt. Assn., Am. Assn. Clin. Chemistry, Soc. Exptl. Biology and Medicine, Am. Assn. Cancer Rsch., VMI Keydet (Lexington, Va.). Republican. Office: Va Commonwealth Univ Dept Pathology PO Box 980662 Richmond VA 23298-0662

WILKINSON, DORIS, medical sociology educator; b. Lexington, Ky., June 13, 1936; d. Howard Thomas and Regina Wilkinson. BA, U. Ky., 1958; MA, Case Western Res. U., 1960, PhD, 1968; MPH, Johns Hopkins U., 1985; postgrad., Harvard U., summer 1991. Asst. prof. U. Ky., Lexington, 1968-70; assoc. prof., then prof. Macalester Coll., St. Paul, 1970-77; exec. assoc. Am. Sociol. Assn., Washington, 1977-80; prof. med. sociology Howard U., Washington, 1980-84; vis. prof. U. Va., 1984-85; prof. sociology U. Ky., Lexington, 1985—. Chmn. panel women in sci. program NSF, Washington, 1976; rev. panelist Nat. Inst. Drug Abuse, Washington, 1978—79; mem. bd. sci. counselors Nat. Cancer Inst., Bethesda, Md., 1980—84; vis. scholar Harvard U., Cambridge, Mass., 1989—90, vis. prof. (summers), 1992, 93, 94, 97; Rapoport vis. prof. social theory (summers) Smith Coll., 1995, 96; bd. dirs. Nat. Conf. for Cmty. Justice, 1992—96; dir. Heritage Project, 2000—. Author: Workbook for Introductory Sociology, 1968; editor: Black Revolt: Strategies of Protest, 1969; co-editor: The Black Male in America, 1977, Alternative Health Maintenance and Healing Systems, 1987, Race, Gender and the Life Cycle, 1991, Race, Class and Gender, 1996; social history photographic exhbn. "The African American Presence in Medicine" Harvard Med. Libr., 1991, Pearson Mus.- So. Ill. U. Med. Sch., 1992, N.J. Coll. Medicine and Dentistry, 1993, Louisville Mus. History and Sci., 1994, U. Cin. Med. Sch. Libr., 1994, Albert Einstein Coll. of Medicine, 1995, Midway Coll., 1996; contbr. articles to profl. jours. Bd. overseers Case Western Res. U., Cleve., 1982-87; apptd. Ky. Commn. on Women, 1993-96. Recipient Pub. Humanities award U. Ky., 1990, Midway Coll. Women's History Month award, 1991, Gt. Tchr. award Nat. Alumni Assn. U. Ky., 1992, Disting. Scholar award Assn. Black Sociologists, 1993; inducted into Hall of Disting. Alumni, U. Ky., 1989; fellow Woodrow Wilson Found., 1959-61, Ford Found., 1989-90; grantee Social Sci. Rsch. Coun., 1975, Nat. Inst. Edn., 1978-80, Nat. Cancer Inst., 1986-88, Ky. Humanities Coun., 1988, 2001, Am. Coun. Learned Soc., 1989-90, NEH, 1991; Disting. Prof. in Coll. Arts and Scis., U. Ky., 1992-93, Coll. of Social Work Hall of Fame, U. Ky., 1999; Disting. Professorship named in hon., 2000. Mem.: Ea. Sociol. Soc. (v.p. 1983—84, pres. 1992—93, I. Peter Gellman award 1987), Soc. for Study of Social Problems (v.p. 1984—85, pres. 1987—88), D.C. Sociol. Soc. (pres. 1982—83), So. Sociol. Soc. (honors com. 1993—94), Am. Sociol. Assn. (exec. assoc. 1977—80, budget com. 1985—88, v.p. 1991—92, mem. coun. 1994—97, elected History of Sociology sect. 2003, Dubois-Johnson-Frazier award 1988), Phi Beta Kappa.

WILKINSON, EDWARD ANDERSON, JR., retired military officer, manufacturing executive; b. Selma, Ala., Sept. 21, 1933; s. Edward Anderson and Alice Margaret (Moorer) W.; m. Barbara Anne Parker, June 4, 1955 (dec. June 1991); children: Daryl Edward, Daniel Bryan, Edward Anderson III, David Park; m. Sondra Marie Moore, Oct. 2, 1994. BS, U.S. Naval Acad., 1955; MS in Mech. Engring., 1964; grad., Nat. War Coll., 1972. Commd. ensign U.S. Navy, 1955, advanced through grades to rear adm., 1979; dir. Anti-Submarine Warfare Systems Program Office, Washington, 1978-79; dep. dir. Def. Mapping Agy., Washington, 1979-81; cmdr. Patrol Wings, U.S. Atlanta Fleet, Brunswick, Maine, 1981-83; dir. Def. Mapping Agy., Washington, 1983-85; ret., 1985; exec. v.p. Internat. Fed. Systems Intergraph Corp., Reston, Va. Decorated Legion of Merit, D.S.M. (Dept. Def.) Methodist. Home: 1257 Weatherstone Ct Reston VA 20194 Office Phone: 703-264-5644. E-mail: andy.wilkinson@intergraph.com.

WILKINSON, EUGENE PARKS, nuclear engineer, director; b. Long Beach, Calif., Aug. 10, 1918; s. Dennis William and Daisy Amelia (Parks) W.; m. Janice Edith Thuli, Mar. 28, 1942; children: Dennis Eugene, Stephen James, Marian Lynn, Rodney David. AB in Chemistry, San Diego State U., 1938. Instr. chemistry San Diego State U., 1938-39; commd. ensign U.S. Navy, 1940, advanced through grades to vice adm., 1970; served various locations including 1st comdg. officer USS Nautilus (1st nuclear-powered submarine), 1953-57; 1st comdg. officer USS Long Beach, 1959-63, 1st nuclear-powered surface ship; ret., 1974; exec. v.p. Data Design Labs., Cucamonga, Calif., 1977-80; pres., chief exec. officer Inst. Nuclear Power Ops., Atlanta, 1980-84, pres. emeritus, 1984—. Chmn. bd. dirs. MDM Svcs. Corp., Laguna Niguel, Calif. Decorated Legion of Merit, Silver Star, D.S.M. with three oak leaf clusters, others, Second Order Sacred Treasure Japan; recipient George Westinghouse Gold medal ASME, 1983, Oliver Townsend medal Atomic Indsl. Forum, 1984, Gold medal Uranium Inst., 1989. Mem. Am. Soc. Naval Engrs., Am. Nuclear Soc. (Henry DeWolf Smyth Nuclear Statesman medal 1994, Walter Zinn award 1998), Navy League, Submarine League, Nat. Acad. Engring. Avocations: tennis, bridge. Home: 1449 Crest Rd Del Mar CA 92014-2530

WILKINSON, GRANT ROBERT, pharmacology educator; b. Derby, U.K., Aug. 27, 1941; came to U.S., 1966; s. Arthur Henry and Gwendoline Mary (Fox) W.; m. Margaret Kay Fletcher, Aug. 8, 1964 (div. Apr. 1978); children: Grant Russell, Nicole Estelle; m. June Zoe Dass, July 12, 1978 (div. Jan. 1995); children: Tracey Allyson, Erika Lynne; m. Merrily Anne Bossart, Jan. 18, 2000. BSc in Pharmacy, U. Manchester, 1963; PhD, U. London, 1966; DSc, U. Manchester, 2002. Postdoctoral fellow U. Calif., San Francisco, 1966-68; asst. prof. U. Ky., Lexington, 1968-71, Vanderbilt U., Nashville, 1971-73, assoc. prof., 1973-78, prof. of pharmacology, 1978—. Cons. NIH, Bethesda, Md., 1972—, NRC, NAS, Washington, 1986-87, 92-94, also pharm. industry. Author: Drug Metabolism and Disposition: Considerations in Clinical Pharmacology, 1985; assoc. editor: Clin. Pharmacology and Therapeutics; mem. editl. bd. various jours. in field; contbr. over 250 articles and revs. to profl. pubis. Recipient NIH Merit award, 1991. Fellow AAAS (sect. chmn. 1986-87), Am. Assn. Pharm. Sci.; mem. Am. Soc. for Pharmacology and Exptl. Therapeutics, Am. Soc. Clin. Pharmacology and Therapeutics (Rawls-Palmer Progress in Medicine award 1996), Am. Assn. Pharm. Sci. (Rsch. Achievement award 2000), Internat. Soc. Study Xenobiotics (treas. 2001-2003). Achievements include research on drug metabolism in humans, effects of disease-states, pharmacokinetics, clinical pharmacology. Business E-Mail: grant.wilkinson@vanderbilt.edu.

WILKINSON, HARRY EDWARD, management educator, consultant; b. Richmond Heights, Mo., June 30, 1930; s. Harry Edward and Virginia Flo (Shelton) W.; m. Sara Beth Kikendall, Aug. 30, 1958; children: Linda Beth, Cheryl Susan. BA in Physics, Princeton U., 1952; MBA, Washington U., St. Louis, 1957; D Bus. Adminstrn., Harvard U., 1960. Lic. psychologist, Mass. Staff engr. Southwestern Bell Tel. Co., St. Louis, 1954-57; traffic engr. New Eng. Tel. & Telegraph Co., Boston, 1957-60; sr. mgmt. cons. Harbridge House Inc., Boston, 1961-65; dean bus. adminstrn., dir. Mgmt. Inst., Northeastern U., Boston, 1965-67; pres., chmn. bd. Univ. Affiliates Inc., North Port, Fla., 1967-2000; vis. prof. mgmt. Rice U., Houston, 1990-94, 97-2000, dir. office of exec. devel., 1993-97. Cons. to various industries and govt., 1961—. Author: Influencing People in Organizations, 1993; contbr. articles to mgmt. jours. Lt. (j.g.) USNR, 1952-54, Korea. Mem. APA, Acad. Mgmt., N.Am. Case Rsch. Assn., Harvard Bus. Sch. Assn. E-mail: wilkinso@rice.edu.

WILKINSON, JAMES ALLAN, lawyer, healthcare executive; b. Cumberland, Md., Feb. 10, 1945; s. John Robinson and Dorothy Jane (Kelley) W.; m. Elizabeth Susanne Quinlan, Apr. 14, 1973; 1 child, Kathryn Barrett. BS in Fgn. Svc., Georgetown U., 1967; JD, Duquesne U., 1978; MA, U Pitts., 2001. Bar: Pa., U.S. Dist. Ct. (we. dist.) Pa. Legis. analyst Office of Mgmt. and Budget, Washington, 1972-73; dep. exec. sec. Cost of Living Coun., Washington, 1973-74; sr. fin. analyst U.S. Steel Corp., Pitts., 1974-82; ptnr. Buchanan Ingersoll, Pitts., 1982-88; exec. v.p., gen. counsel Meritcare, Pitts., 1988—; sr. v.p. Culwell Health Inc., 1991—2001. Adj. prof. U. Pitts. Sch. Law, 1988-91. Author: Financing and Refinancing Under Prospective Payment, 1985, Family Caregivers' Guide Planning and Decision Making for the Elderly, 1998; contbr. articles to profl. jours. Chmn. Oversight Com. on Organ Transplantation, Pitts., 1986—; sec.-treas. bd. dirs. Pitts. Symphony Soc., 1986-98, exec. com. bd. dirs., 1999-2002, vice-chmn., 2003—; bd. dirs. We. Pa. Com. Prevention of Child Abuse, 1987-90, Comprehensive Safety Compliance, 1988-91, Buchanan Ingersoll Profl. Corp., 1988-90, Parental Stress Ctr., 1990-94; sec. Ross Mountain Club, 1995-98, 1999-2003, v.p., 1999-2001, pres., 2001-03; exec. com. bd. dirs. Carnegie Inst., 1997-2003, Carnegie Mus. Natural History, 1997-2003, Andy Warhol Mus., 1998—, Soc. for Contemporary Craft, 1999—, treas., 2000-01, v.p., 2001-02, pres., 2002-04; bd. dirs. Craft Emergency Relief Fund, 2003—. Mem. Am. Health Lawyers Assn., Audubon Soc. Southwestern Pa. (treas. 1996-2000), Duquesne Club. Republican. Episcopalian. Home: 1005 Elmhurst Rd Pittsburgh PA 15215-1819 Office: Meritcare Inc 2020 Ardmore Blvd Ste 335 Pittsburgh PA 15221 E-mail: wilkinso@bellatlantic.net.

WILKINSON, JAMES HARVIE, III, federal judge; b. N.Y.C., Sept. 29, 1944; s. James Harvie and Letitia (Nelson) W.; m. Lossie Grist Noell, June 30, 1973; children: James Nelson, Porter Noell. BA, Yale U., 1963-67; JD, U. Va., 1972; JD (hon.), U. Richmond, 1997, U. S.C., 1998; LLD (hon.), Christopher Newport U., 2003. Bar: Va. 1972. Law clk. to U.S. Supreme Ct. Justice Lewis F. Powell, Jr., Washington, 1972-73; asst. prof. law U. Va., 1973-75, assoc. prof., 1975-78; editor Norfolk (Va.) Virginian-Pilot, 1978-81; prof. law U. Va., 1981-82, 83-84; dep. asst. atty. gen. Civil Rights div. Dept. Justice, 1982-83; judge U.S. Ct. Appeals (4th cir.), 1984—, chief judge, 1996—2003. Author: Harry Byrd and the Changing Face of Virginia Politics, 1968, Serving Justice: A Supreme Court Clerk's View, 1974, From Brown to Bakke: The Supreme Court and School Integration, 1979, One Nation Indivisible: How Ethnic Separatism Threatens America, 1997. Bd. Visitors U. Va., 1970-73; Republican candidate for Congress from 3d Dist. V a., 1970; bd. dirs. Fed. Jud. Ctr., 1992-96, James Madison Meml. Found, 2003-. Served with U.S. Army, 1968-69. Recipient Thomas Jefferson Found. medal Law, U. Va., 2004. Mem. Va. State Bar, Va. Bar Assn., Am. Law Inst. Episcopalian. Home: 1713 Yorktown Dr Charlottesville VA 22901-3035 Office: US Ct Appeals 255 W Main St Ste 230 Charlottesville VA 22902-5058 Office Phone: 434-296-7063.

WILKINSON, JOAN KRISTINE, nurse, pediatric clinical specialist; b. Rochester, Minn., June 15, 1953; d. A. Ray and Ruth Audrey (Wegwart) Kubly; m. Robert Morris Wilkinson, June 14, 1975; children: Michael Robert, Kathryn Ann. BS in Nursing, U. Wis., 1975; MS, U. Colo., 1986. RN, clin. nurse specialist. Team leader Mendota Mental Health Inst., Madison, Wis., 1975-76; care leader Boulder (Colo.) Psychiat. Inst., 1976-78; pub. health nurse, head nurse Rocky Mountain Poison Ctr., Denver, 1978-83; research teaching asst. U. Colo. Health Scis. Ctr., Denver, 1986-87. Disaster nurse ARC, Boulder, 1976—; participant community service United Way, Denver, 1981-84; vol. nurse Channel 9 Health Fair, Boulder, 1983. Fellow U. Colo. Health Scis. Ctr., 1986; recipient Recognition cert. ARC, Madison, 1978, Gold award United Way, Denver, 1981, Outstanding Citizen award Boulder, 1990, Torch award for outstanding leader Girl Scouts, 1995, Torch award Girl Scouts Am., 1999. Mem. Colo. Nurses Assn. (dist. 12 scholar 1983-86), Am. Nurses Assn., World Health Assn., Sigma Tau Theta, Phi Theta Kappa. Lutheran. Home: 1195 Hancock Dr Boulder CO 80303-1101 Office: Denver Vis Nurse Assn 390 Grant St Denver CO 80203-4022

WILKINSON, JOHN HART, lawyer; b. Newton, Mass., Dec. 31, 1940; s. Roger Melvin and Margaret (Carter) Wilkinson; children: Heather, Carter. BA, Williams Coll., 1962; LLB, Fordham U., 1965. Bar: NY 1965, US Dist. Ct. (so. and ea. dists.) NY 1968, US Ct. Appeals (2d cir.) 1981, US Ct. Appeals (11th cir.) 1982, US Ct. Appeals (3d cir.) 1984, US Ct. Appeals (5th cir.) 1987. Assoc. Donovan, Leisure, Newton & Irvine, NYC, 1965, 67-73, ptnr., 1973-98, editor, contbg. author firm's ADR Practice Book, 1990; law clk. presiding justice US Dist. Ct. (so. dist.) NY, 1967-68; of counsel Fulton, Rowe & Hart, NYC, 1998—. Spkr. field. Contbr. articles to profl. jours. Bd. dirs., pres. Childfind Am., Inc., 1993—94; vol. learning disabled children Chelsea Neighborhood, NYC, 1965—67; v.p. bd. dirs. Pelham (NY) Family Svc., 1982—85; bd. dirs. Catskill Ctr. Conservation Devel., 1993—. Recipient Am. Jurisprudence award, Fordham U. Mem.: ABA (alt. dispute resolution com. 1989—93), Assn. Bar City NY (profl. responsibility com. 1987—89, pub. assistance com. 1991—94), NY State Bar Assn. (alt. dispute resolution com. 1989—93). Avocations: woodworking, fly fishing, bicycling, camping. Office: Fulton Rowe & Hart One Rockefeller Plz New York NY 10020 Office Phone: 212-586-0700.

WILKINSON, LAURA, Olympic athlete; b. Houston, Dec. 17, 1977; d. Ed and Linda Wilkinson; m. Eriek Hulseman. Student, U. Tex.; BS in pub. rels., U. Tex. at Austin. Placed 5th World Championships, 1998; winner platform Gold Medal Goodwill Games, 1998; winner nat. title summer nats., 1999; winner Gold Medal 10 meter platform, 2000. Pub. spkr. Office: US Diving Inc 201 S Capitol Ave Ste 430 Indianapolis IN 46225

WILKINSON, LESTER F., JR., lawyer; b. Mass., Nov. 12, 1956; BA, Bates Coll., 1978; JD, U. San Diego, 1981. Bar: Maine 1981, U.S. Dist. Ct. Maine 1981. Mng. shareholder Bernstein, Shur, Sawyer & Nelson, PA, Augusta, Maine. Instr. real estate law U. Maine, Augusta, 1988—89. Bd. dirs. Children's Ctr., 1990—93, pres., 1994; bd. dirs. Maine Gen. Health Assocs., 1997—2000. Mem.: Kennebec County Bar Assn., Maine State Bar Assn. (bd. govs., treas. 1994—2001, prest.-elect 2002, pres. 2003), Kennebec Valley C. of C. (dir. 1988—, pres. 2001). Office: Bernstein Shur Sawyer and Nelson 146 Capitol St Po Box 5057 Augusta ME 04330-5057

WILKINSON, LOUISE CHERRY, psychology educator, dean; b. Phila., May 15, 1948; BA magna cum laude with honors, Oberlin Coll., 1970; EdM, EdD, Harvard U., 1974. Prof., chmn. dept. ednl. psychology U. Wis., Madison, 1976-85; prof., exec. officer Grad. Sch. PhD Program CUNY, N.Y.C., 1984-86; disting. prof., dean Grad. Sch. Edn. Rutgers U., 1986—2003; dean Sch. Edn., disting. prof. edn., psychology and comm. scis. Syracuse (NY) U., 2003—. Chairperson ednl. strategic planning Rutgers U.; mem. nat. rev. bd. Nat. Inst. Edn., 1977, 85, 87; cons. Nat. Ctr. for Bilingual Rsch., 1982, 84, U.S. Dept. Edn., 1995-96; adv. bd. Nat. Reading Rsch. Ctr., 1992-98. Co-author: Communicating for Learning, 1991; editor: Communicating in Classroom, 1982, Social Context of Instruction, 1984, Gender Influences in the Classroom, 2002; co-editor: Literacy and Language Learning, 2004; mem. editl. bds.:; contbr. articles to profl. jours. Fellow: APA, Am. Assn. for Applied and Preventive Psychology, Am. Psychol. Soc.; mem.: NJ Coun. Acad. Policy Advisors, Am. Ednl. Rsch. Assn. (v.p. 1990—92, program chair 1997). Home: 303 Sedgwick Dr Syracuse NY 13203-1314

WILKINSON, RALPH RUSSELL, biochemistry educator, toxicologist; b. Portland, Oreg., Feb. 20, 1930; s. Tracy Chandler and Lavern (Russell) W.; m. Evelyn Marie Wickman, Aug. 5, 1956. BA, Reed Coll., 1953; PhD, U. Oreg., 1962; MBA, U. Mo., Kansas City, 1974. Rsch. chemist VA Hosp., Kansas City, Mo., 1973-74; sr. rsch. chemist Midwest Rsch. Inst., Kansas City, 1975-84; prof. Rockhurst Coll., Kansas City, 1985-86, Cleve. Chiropractic Coll., Kansas City, 1987-99, prof. emeritus, 1999—. Cons. in biochemistry, toxicology, environ. impact, tech. assessment, Kansas City, 1984—. Author: (book) Neurotoxins and Neurobiological Function, 1987; contbr. articles to profl. jours. Mem. Southtown Coun., Kansas City, Mo., 1989—, Spina Bifida Assn. Am., Kansas City, 1989—. Recipient NSF fellowship, 1959-60. Mem. Am. Chem. Soc., Sigma Xi. Avocations: travel, history, biography, music, antiques. Home: 7911 Charlotte St Kansas City MO 64131-2175

WILKINSON, ROSEMARY REGINA CHALLONER, poet, writer; b. New Orleans, Feb. 21, 1924; d. William Lindsay Challoner Jr. and Julia Regina (Sellen) Challoner/Schillo; m. Henry Bertram Wilkinson, Oct. 15, 1949; children: Denis James, Marian Regina, Paul Francis, Richard Challoner. Lifetime credential to teach poetry, San Francisco State U., 1978; LHD (hon.), Livre U., Pakistan, 1975; DLitt (hon.), World Acad. Arts & Culture, Rep. of China, 1981. Lectr./reader of poetry. Author: (poetry) A Girl's Will, 1973, California Poet, 1976, Earth's Compromise, 1977, It Happened to Me, 1978, I Am Earth Woman, 1979, The Poet and the Painter, 1981, Poetry and Arte, 1982, Gems Within, 1984, Nature's Guest, 1984, In the Pines, 1985, Longing for You, 1986, Purify the Earth, 1988, Sacred in Nature, 1988, Earth's Children, 1990, New Seed, 1991, Angels and Poetry, 1992, Cambrian Zephyr, 1993, Collected Poems, 1994, Poetry: Nature, 1996, Poetry: Spiritual, 1997, Poetry Calendar 2000, 1999, A Song in the Wind with Love, 2001, My Plea, 2001, Selected Verses, 2001, Blessing of Poetry, 2002, others, (epic) An Historical Epic, 1974, Epic of the Ships Captain, 1986. Founder Poetry-Fine Arts Divsn. of San Mateo (Calif.) County Fair, 1977, Dr. Williams Poetry Workshop, Burlingame H.S., 1985; sec.-gen. World Acad. Arts and Culture-USA, San Francisco, 1985—95, pres., 1994—2003. Mem.: Authors League Am., The Authors Guild, Acad. Am. Poets, Poetry Soc. of Am., Nat. League Am. Pen Women Inc. (Washington 4th and 5th v.p. 1986—90, Berkeley, Calif. pres. 1988—90, Lake Tahoe br. 1988—), World Acad. of Arts and Culture/World Congress of Poets, World Congress of Poets (Taipei, Taiwan bd. dirs. 1973—2003, San Francisco pres. 1981, sec.-gen. 1985—95, pres. 1995—2003), Soroptomist Internat. (hon.). Democrat. Roman Catholic. Avocations: reading, research, brush painting, lecturing. Home: 3146 Buckeye Ct Placerville CA 95667-8334

WILKINSON, SHARON P. department of state official, former ambassador; b. Buffalo, Jan. 26, 1947; Grad., Brown U., U. Chgo. Vice consul Dept. State, San Paulo, Brazil, consul Accra, Ghana, program officer for Africa Bur. Cultural Affairs, staff asst. to asst. sec. inter-am. affairs, desk officer for Portugal, mgmt. analyst Office Mgmt. Ops.; dir. Face-to-Face Program Carnegie Endowment for Internat. Peace; dep. prin. officer Tijuana, Mexico; dir. Office of Diplomatic, pub. liaison Bur. Consular Affair Dept. State, consul gen., dep. chief mission Lisbon, Portugal, U.S. amb. to Burkina Faso, 1996—99; dir. Office West African Affairs, 1999—2000; U.S. amb. Mozambique, 2000—03; Dept. State Diplomat in residence Coll. of Liberal Arts & Scis., Ariz. State U., 2003—04. Achievements include career mem. of the Sr. Foreign Service, Class of Minister Counselor; speaks Portuguese, Spanish and French. Office: Dept State Wash DC 2330 Maputo Place Washington DC 20521-2330

WILKINSON, SIGNE, cartoonist; b. Wichita Falls, Tex. married. BA in English, 1972; student, Pa. Acad. Fine Arts. Reporter West Chester (Pa.) Daily Local News, Academy of Natural Scis., Phila.; freelance cartoonist Phila. and N.Y. publs.; cartoonist San Jose (Calif.) Mercury News, 1982-85, Phila. Daily News, 1985—. Illustrator: Abortion Cartoons in Demand, 1992, You Bet Your Tomatoes, 2002, How to Grow the $735 Tomato, 1999; contbr. to Univ. Barge Club News, various mags. Bd. dirs. Fair Hill Burial Ground. Recipient Pulitzer Prize for editl. cartooning, 1992, Overseas Press Club award, 1997, 2001, Robert F. Kennedy award, 2002. Mem. Assn. Am. Editl. Cartoonists (pres. 1994-95). Avocations: gardening, rowing. Office: Phila Daily News PO Box 7788 400 N Broad St Philadelphia PA 19130-4015 Business E-Mail: wilkins@phillynews.com.

WILKINSON, WALTER, soft drink bottling company executive; CFO Honickman Affiliates, Pennsauken, N.J. Office: Honickman Affiliates 8275 Route 130 Pennsauken NJ 08110-1435

WILKINSON, WARREN SCRIPPS, manufacturing executive; b. Detroit, Feb. 2, 1920; s. Almadus DeGrasse and Harriet Gertrude (Whitcomb) W.; m. Joan Todd, June 14, 1941; m. Mireille De Bary, Dec. 17, 1966. Grad., Hotchkiss Sch., Lakeville, Conn., 1937; BS in Math, Harvard U., 1941; student, Calif. Inst. Tech., 1941-42. With U.S. Rubber Co., Detroit, 1942-43, Hanson Van Winkle-Munning Co., Matawan, N.J., 1946-64, pres., 1961-64; v.p., gen. mgr. Hanson-Van Winkle-Munning div. M & Chems. Inc., 1964-66; chmn. RPI Designs, Marlette, Mich., 1966—. Mem. Detroit Hist. Commn., 1994—; mem. overseer's com. on univ. resources Harvard U. With USN, 1943—46. John Harvard fellow, 1996. Home: 2 Woodland Pl Grosse Pointe MI 48230-1920

WILKINSON, WILLIAM SHERWOOD, lawyer; b. Williston, N.D., Sept. 6, 1933; s. John Thomas and Evelyn (Landon) W.; m. Carol Ann Burns, Aug. 20, 1960; children— Leslie Ann, Richard Sherwood, Greta Diann. BS in Bus, U. Idaho, 1955; JD, U. Denver, 1960. Bar: Colo. bar 1960, Mich. bar 1966. Practiced in, Canon City, Colo., 1960-66; asst. dist. atty. 11th Jud. Dist., Colo., 1961-65; gen. counsel, sec. Mich. Farm Bur. Family Cos., Lansing, 1966-96. Lectr. Pre-Parole Release Center, Colo. State Penitentiary, 1961-65; instr. adult edn., Canon City, 1965; counsel Canon City Recreation Dist., 1964-65 Mem. lay adv. bd. St. Thomas More Hosp., Canon City, 1963-66; Del., county, dist. and congl. convs. Republican party, 1964. Served to capt. USAF, 1955-58. Recipient Cmty. Disting. Svc. award Canon City Jr. C. of C., 1964. Mem. ABA, Colo. Bar Assn., Mich. Bar Assn., Am. Judicature Soc., Am. Corp. Counsel Assn., Nat. Coun. Farmer Coops. (legal, tax and acctg. com.), Phi Delta Phi, Tau Kappa Epsilon. Methodist (lay leader, mem. ch. ofcl. bd.). Home: 1707 Foxcroft Rd East Lansing MI 48823-2131 E-mail: wwilca@aol.com.

WILKINSON III, ELWYN NATHANIEL, music educator; b. Baton Rouge, La., Feb. 17, 1965; s. Elwyn Nathaniel and Nancy Wade Wilkinson; m. Jonni Ann Larive, Dec. 22, 1989; children: Hailey Elizabeth Wilkinson, Kathryn Grace Wilkinson. AA, Ms. Gulfcoast Jr. Coll., 1983—85; MusB in edn., U. of Southwestern La., 1985—88; MusM, U. of La. at Lafayette, 1999—2001. Band dir. Patterson H.S., La., 1988—90, Franklin Jr. H.S., La., 1990—97, Patterson Jr. H.S., La., 1997—. Recipient Dist. VII All Youth Honor Band Condr., LMEA Dist. VII, 2001, Avoyelles Parish Honor Band Condr., Avoyelles Parish Band Director's Assoc., 2004. Mem.: Nat. Band Assn., Dist. VII Band Directors Assn. (treas. 1999—2004), La. Music Educators Assn., Music Nat. Educators Conf. R-Consevative. Pentecostal. Avocations: fishing, stamp collecting/philately, coin collecting/numismatics. Home: 118 Becky Dr Patterson LA 70392 Office: Patterson Junior H S 1101 First St Patterson LA 70392 Office Phone: 985-395-6772 4. Personal E-mail: njwilkinson@cox-internet.com. Business E-Mail: nwilkinson@stmary.k12.la.us.

WILKNISS, PETER E. foundation administrator, researcher; b. Berlin, Sept. 28, 1934; U.S. citizen. s. Fritz and Else (Stueber) W.; m. Edith P. Koester, May 25, 1963; children: Peter F., Sandra M. MS in Chemistry, Tech. U., Munich, Ger., 1958, PhD in Radio and Nuclear Chemistry, 1961. Rsch. chemist, radiological protection officer U.S. Naval Ordnance Sta., 1961-64, head nuclear chemistry branch, 1964-66; rsch. oceanographer U.S. Naval Rsch. Lab., 1966-70, head chemical oceanography branch, 1970-75; mgr. Nat. Ctr. Atmospheric Rsch. Program NSF, Washington, 1975-76, mgr. Internat. Phase of Ocean Drilling/Ocean Sediment Coring Program, 1976-80, mgr. Ocean Drilling Project Team, AAEO Directorate, 1980, dir. divsn. Ocean Drilling Programs, 1980-81, sr. sci. assoc. Office of Dir., 1981-82, dep. asst. dir. Sci, Tech., Internat. Affairs Directorate, 1982-84, dir. divsn. Polar Programs, 1984-93, sr. sci. assoc. Geoscis. Directorate, 1993-96; pres. Polar Kybernetes Internat. LLC, Fairbanks, Alaska, 1997—, Transnat. Arctic and Antarctic Inst., Fairbanks, 1997—. Liaison mem. NRC, NAS, Marine Bd., 1978-81, Polar Rsch. Bd., 1984-93; mem. atmospheric chemistry and radioactivity com. Am. Meteorological Soc., 1975-78; mem. interagy. com. atmospheric scis., 1975-76, space station adv. com., NASA, 1988-93. Ontbr. over 60 articles to sci., tech. jours., USN reports; over 100 formal presentations nat., internat. sci. confs., symposia, meetings; participant 16 nat., internat. workshops. Presdl. citation AIA, 1993; Wilkniss mountain Antarctic named in his honor Sec. Interior, U.S. Bd. Geographic Names, 1992. Mem.: AAAS, Antarctican Soc., Am. Polar Soc., Am. Geophys. Union. Episcopalian. Avocations: soccer, swimming, skiing. Office: Polar Kybernetes Internat 1305 W 7th Ave Anchorage AK 99501-3210 Personal E-mail: pwilkniss@aol.com.

WILKS, JACQUELIN HOLSOMBACK, campus ministries director; b. Jan. 18, 1950; d. Jack and Ida Mae (Bass) Holsomback; m. Thomas M. Wilks, Jan. 28, 1972; children: David, Bryan. BS, La. Coll., 1972; MAT., Okla. City U., 1982; postgrad., So. Bapt. Theol. Sem., Louisville, 1974; S.E., Mo. State U., 1977; counseling cert., Cen. State Univ., 1983; PhD, Capella U., 2003. Lic. realtor Mo. Sec. to adminstr. Allen Parish Hosp., Kinder, La., 1968-69; tchr. horseback riding, swimming Triple D Guest Ranche, Warren, Tex., 1969;

singer, speaker Found. Singers, 1970-71; tchr. English Pine Bluff (Ark.) H.S., 1972-74; tchr. kindergarten Doyle Elem. Sch., East Prairie (Mo.) R-2, 1974-75; tchr. 1st grade Bertrand (Mo.) Elem. Sch., 1975-76; tchr. 6th grade sci. A.D. Simpson Sch., Charleston, Mo., 1976-78; dir. admissions and fin. adminstr. Control Data Inst., Control Data Corp., St. Louis, 1980-81; dir. Bapt. collegiate ministry Okla. Bapt. U., Shawnee, 2002—. Bd. dirs. Computer Commn. Svcs. Inc., 1986—, dir. tutorial svcs., instr. tutorial methods Okla. Bapt. U., 1981-83, instr. horsemanship St. Gregory's Jr. Coll., 1981; counselor Gordon Cooper Area Vocat. Tech. Sch., 1982-83, Shawnee Jr. H.S. Okla.), 1983-85, Grove Sch., Shawnee, 1989—; dir. Resource Ctr., instr. English St. Gregory's Coll., Shawnee, Okla., 1985-89; counselor Spanish tchr. North Rock Creek Sch., Shawnee; translator med. grp. missions Dominican Rep. and Guatemala, 1995, 96, Cosecha 2000, Argentina, 1998, El Salvador, 1998, 99, Ecuador, 2000; bd. dirs. Computer Commn. Svcs. Inc., Tulsa; tutor for children under jurisdiction Juvenile Ct., Jefferson County, Ark., 1972-73; leader group counseling/therapy sessions, 1972; dir. devel. Nat. Insts. Devel. Delays, 2000; exec. dir. Narvos & Farms Therapeutic Riding Ctr. Choreographer First Bapt. Ch. Youth Choir, Pine Bluff; v.p. St. Gregory's Coll. Therapeutic Horsemanship Program, 1981-82; Rep. election judge. Recipient Kathryn Carpenter award La. Bapt. Conv., 1971, real Scope award Realty World, St. Louis, 1980, NEH grantee, 1993—. Mem. Univ. Alliance Okla. Bapt. U. Baptist. Home: 18 Woodcrest Shawnee OK 74804-9048 Office: Oklla Bapt U 500 W University Shawnee OK 74804 E-mail: jackie.wilks@okbu.edu.

WILKS, LEWIS O. telecommunications company executive; BS in Pub. Rels. and Computer Sci., Ctrl. Mo. State U. With Wang Labs., MCI Corp.; pres. GET Comms.; pres. bus. markets Qwest Commns. Internat., Denver, pres. Internet and Multimedia Markets. Bd. dirs. Qwest Cyber Solutions, Slinshot Networks, Salus Media Corp. Vice chmn. Spl. Olympics Colo.; co-chmn. Colo. Commn. Sci. and Tech. Office: Internet's Multimedia Markets Quest Comms Internat 1801 California St Denver CO 80202

WILKS, THOMAS MILTON, religious studies educator, minister; b. Mansfield, La., Feb. 14, 1945; s. Milton E. and Bernice (Thompson) W.; m. Jacquelin Holsomback, Jan. 28, 1972; children: T. David, Bryan E. BA, La. Coll., Pineville, 1967; ThM, New Orleans Bapt. Theol. Sem., 1971; DMin, So. Bapt. Theol. Sem., Louisville, 1977. Lic. field traumatologist, in-svc. guidance dir. Youth min. First Bapt. Ch., Bastrop, La., 1968; pastor Magnolia Bapt. Ch., Vancleave, Miss., 1969-71; youth assoc., pastoral intern First Bapt. Ch., Pine Bluff, Ark., 1971-73, pastor Charleston, Mo., 1973-78; min. Bapt. Metro Campus, St. Louis, 1978-80; assoc. dean students for counseling, univ. chaplain Okla. Bapt. U., Shawnee, 1980-84, asst. prof. applied ministry, dir. in-svc. guidance, 1984-87, assoc. prof. applied ministry, dir. in-svc. guidance, 1987-93, prof. applied ministry, dir. in-svc. guidance, 1993-94, dir. off-campus programs and insvc. guidance, prof., 1994-96, prof. applied ministry, dir. in-svc. guidance, 1996-97, Jewell and Joe Huitt prof. religious edn., 1998—, dir. in-svc. guidance, 1998—. Adj. prof. psychology Oklahoma City U. Grad. Sch., 1983-84; adj. prof. pastoral leadership Southwestern Bapt. Theol Sem., 1996, 98; cons. family ministry Bapt. Gen. Conv. Okla., Oklahoma City, 1999—; mem. bd. Summit Youth Camps, Edmond, Okla., 1994—; mem. long-range planning co. So. Bapt. In-Svc. Guidance Conf., 1992-99, pres., 1991, bd. dirs., 1999—, chmn. bd. dirs., 2002-; mem. Youth Matrix Team, Lifeway Christian Resources, Nashville, 1996—; state cons. in family ministry Bapt. Gen. Conv. Okla., 1998—; mem. Nat. Task Force on Bi-Vocat. Ministry, 1992; spkr. various civic clubs and orgns., graduations and faculty devel. workshops for schs. and colls. Author: Blind Faith, 1995; writer youth ministry, local ch. and missions internship, preaching, pastoral care and pastoral ministry study guides. Pres. North Rock Creek Bd. Edn., Shawnee, 1989; treas. Shawnee H.S. Quarterback Club, 1994-95. Mem. Nat. Network Youth Ministries, In-Svc. Guidance Assn. (chmn. exec. com. 1996-99, bd. dirs. 1999—, chmn. bd. dirs. 2002—), Assn. Theol. Field Educators. Republican. Avocations: coach, youth baseball, basketball, soccer, track. Home: 18 Woodcrest Shawnee OK 74804-9048 Office: Okla Bapt U Box 61248 Shawnee OK 74804 E-mail: tom.wilks@okbu.edu.

WILL, ALFRED JOSEPH, lawyer, engineer; b. Jamaica, N.Y., Mar. 11, 1950; s. James George and Catherine Rose (Steinmuller) W.; m. Therese Catherine Buttner, Nov. 23, 1972; children— Peter Simon, Daniel Alfred, Meredith Marie, Eric James. B.S. in Engring., U.S. Merchant Marine Acad., 1972; J.D., St. John's Law Sch., 1975. Bar: N.Y. 1976, U.S. Dist. Cts. (so. and ea. dists.) N.Y. 1976, U.S. Ct. Appeals (2d cir.) 1982, U.S. Supreme Ct. 1982. Assoc. Tabak, Ezratty & Mellusi, N.Y.C., 1975-76; assoc., sr. Vincent, Berg, Russo, Marcigliano & Zawacki, N.Y.C., 1976-81; sr. ptnr. Badiak & Will, N.Y.C., 1981—; past pres., founder Admiralty Law Sch. of St. John's Law Sch., N.Y.C., 1974-75. Served to lt. USNR, 1969-78. Recipient Gov.'s Scholastic award N.Y. State, 1967-68; named Athlete of Yr. (track) U.S. Merchant Marine Acad., 1972. Mem. Maritime Law Assn. of U.S., Average Adjusters Assn. of U.S., N.Y. County Bar Assn. Roman Catholic. E-mail: admiralaw@aol.com. Home: 23 Robbins DrE Williston Williston Park NY 11596-2009 Office: Badiak Will & Ruddy 120 Broadway Ste 1040 New York NY 10271-1040 Also: Badiak Will & Kallen 17071 W Dixie Hwy North Miami Beach FL 33160-3765 Office Phone: 212-376-6767. E-mail: lawbwm@aol.com.

WILL, GEORGE FREDERICK, editor, political columnist, news commentator; b. Champaign, Ill., May 4, 1941; s. Frederick L. and Louise Will. BA, Trinity Coll., 1962, Oxford (Eng.) U., 1964; MA, PhD, Princeton U., 1967; LLD (hon.), U. San Diego, 1977; LittD (hon.), Dickinson Coll. and Georgetown U., 1978; hon. degree, U. Ill., 1988. Prof. polit. philosophy Mich. State U., 1967-68, U. Toronto, 1968-70; mem. staff of Sen. Gordon Allott U.S. Senate, Washington, Can., 1970-72; editor The Nat. Rev., Washington, 1973-76; contbg. editor Newsweek mag., 1976—; syndicated columnist Washington Post, 1974—; TV news analyst ABC-Capitol Cities, 1981—. Bd. dirs. Ctr. for Strategic Internat. Studies, Washington, Balt. Orioles. Author: The Pursuit of Happiness and Other Sobering Thoughts, 1979, The Pursuit of Virtue and Other Tory Notions, 1982, Statecraft as Soulcraft: What Government Does, 1983, The Morning After: American Successes and Excesses, 1986, The New Season: A Spectator's Guide to the 1988 Election, 1987, Men at Work, 1990, Suddenly: The American Idea at Home and Abroad 1988-89, 1990, Restoration: Congress, Term Limits and the Recovery of Deliberate Democracy, 1992, The Leveling Wind: Politics, the Culture and Other News, 1994; participant This Week With David Brinkley, (now This Week) ABC-TV, 1981—; commentator World News Tonight, 1984—. Recipient Pulitzer prize for Commentary, 1977; named Young Leader Am. Time mag., 1974. Avocation: baseball. Address: ABC Pub Rels 77 W 66th St New York NY 10023-6201 Office: The Washington Post 1150 15th St NW Washington DC 20071-0002

WILL, JERRIE ANN, psychologist; b. Hazleton, Pa., Apr. 6, 1950; d. Gordon John and Doris Griffiths (Brown) W.; m. Gene G. Kuehneman, June 26, 1982 (div. Oct. 1984). BA, Bucknell U., 1971; MA, W.Va. U., 1974, PhD, 1977. Lic. psychologist, Maine. Teaching fellow W.Va. U., Morgantown, 1974-76; clin. psychology intern U. Md. Hosp., Balt., 1976-77; sr. child psychologist Michael Reese Hosp., Chgo., 1977-82; cons. psychologist Ridgeway Psychiat. Hosp., Chgo., 1982-83, Sanford Sch. Dept., Maine, 1983—; pvt. practice Sanford and Wells, Maine, 1984—. Team and child psychologist York County Counseling Svcs., Sanford, 1983-85; owner, mgr. Sanford Psychol. Assocs., 1987-95; panelist, reviewer NSF, 1976. Contbr. articles to profl. jours. NIMH Grantee, 1972-75. Mem. APA. Home: 314 Webhannet Dr Wells ME 04090-4225 Office: 828 Main St Sanford ME 04073-3523 Office Phone: 207-490-2100.

WILL, KATHERINE HALEY, academic administrator; m. Oscar Henry Will, III; 4 children. Student, Carleton Coll., 1970-73; BA in English, Tufts U., 1974; MA in English, U. Ill., Urbana, 1975, PhD in English, 1986. Instr. English Augustana Coll., Sioux Falls, S.D., 1977-86, asst. prof. English, 1986-90, faculty dir. new student seminar program, 1987-91, assoc. prof. English, 1990-96, dean grad. study, dir. gen. edn., 1991—96; provost, prof. English Kenyon Coll., Gambier, Ohio, 1996-99; pres. Whittier Coll., Calif., 1999—2004, Gettysburg Coll., Pa., 2004—. Participant Mgmt. Devel. Seminar for Higher Edn. Adminstrs., Harvard U., summer 1992; cons. and presenter in field. Contbr. articles to profl. jours. Bd. dirs. United Way Great L.A. NEH fellow Summer Seminar in Romanticism and Gender, UCLA, 1989. Mem.: Annapolis Group (exec. com.), Coun. Ind. Colls. (bd. dirs.), Nat. Assn. Ind. Colls. and Univs. (bd. dirs.). Office: Gettysburg Coll 300 N Washington St Gettysburg PA 17325*

WILL, TREVOR JONATHAN, lawyer; b. Ashland, Wis., Aug. 11, 1953; s. William Taylor and Geraldine Sue (Trevor) W.; m. Margaret Ann Johnson, Aug. 28, 1976; children: Tyler William, Alexandra Marie, Jennifer Catherine. BA summa cum laude, Augustana Coll., 1975; JD cum laude, Harvard U., 1978. Bar: Wis. 1978, U.S. Dist. Ct. (ea. dist.) Wis. 1978, U.S. DIst. Ct. (we. dist.) Wis. 1980, U.S. Ct. Appeals (7th cir.) 1983, U.S. Supreme Ct. 1984, U.S. Dist. Ct. (ea. dist.) Mich. 1985. Assoc. Foley & Lardner, Milw., 1978-87, ptnr., 1987—. Adj. law prof. Marquette U. Law Sch., 1994-00. Mem. ABA, State Bar Wis., Milw. Bar Assn., Def. Rsch. Inst. Home: 10011 N Waterleaf Dr Mequon WI 53092-6146 Office: Foley & Lardner 777 E Wisconsin Ave Ste 3800 Milwaukee WI 53202-5367 E-mail: twill@foleylaw.com.

WILLADSEN, MICHAEL CHRIS, marketing professional, sales executive; b. Cheboygan, Mich., Sept. 18, 1946; s. Chris Jens and Helen Margaret (Barr) W.; m. Kay Ann Brooks, Dec. 10, 1964, (div. Dec. 10, 1989); children: Michael Jr., Erik; m. Linda Sue Degroff, Apr. 4, 1992; children: Stephanie, Gretchen, Ross. Student, Delta Coll., 1964-66; A in Bus. Mgmt., Northwood Inst., 1968, BA in Bus. Mgmt., 1969. Mktg. rep. Detroit dist. Petemco, Inc., 1970-73, mktg. rep. Indpls. Dist., 1973-74; dist. mgr. Petemco Inc.-Ind. Ohio Mich., Ind., Ohio, Mich., 1974-76, Consolidated Stas. Marathon Oil, Oshkosh, Wis., 1976-79; sales mgr. Champaign (Ill.) Dist. Marathon Oil, 1981-82, supr. Credit Card Ctr., 1982-84; wholesale mktg. profl. Marathon Brand Mktg./Ohio, Mich., Ky., 1982-84; jobber sales Marathon Oil/Ohio, Pa., W.Va., Ohio, Pa., W. Va., 1984-92, Marathon Oil/Ill., Wisc., Chgo., Chgo., 1992-2000, Marathon Ashland Petroleum, Atlanta, Ga., 2000—. Named to Nat. Assn. Intercollegiate Athletes Sml. Coll. All-State Football Team/Dist. 23, 1968; inducted into Mich. Touch Football Hall of Fame/Team Category, 2002. Mem. Cleve. Petroleum Club (v.p. 1988-91), Chgo. Oilmens. Republican. Presbyterian. Avocations: camping, softball, basketball, physical work out. Office: Marathon Ashland Petroleum PO Box 1007 Cumming GA 30028 Office Phone: 678-947-5808. Business E-Mail: mcwilladsen@mapllc.com.

WILLANS, JEAN STONE, bishop, religious organization executive; b. Hillsboro, Ohio, Oct. 3, 1924; d. Homer and Ella (Keys) Hammond; m. Richard James Willans, Mar. 28, 1966; 1 dau., Suzanne Jeanne. Student, San Diego Jr. Coll.; DD (hon.), Am. Coll. Sems., 1996. Ordained archdeacon, 1996, ordained priest 1997, consecrated bishop 1998, Ch. of the East. Asst. to v.p. Family Loan Co., Miami, Fla., 1946-49; civilian supr. USAF, Washington, 1953-55; founder, dir. Blessed Trinity Soc.; editor Trinity mag., L.A., 1960-66; co-founder, exec. v.p., dir. Soc. of Stephen, Altadena, Calif., 1967—; exec. dir. Hong Kong, 1975-81. Lectr. in field. Author: The Acts of the Green Apples, 1974, rev. edit. 1995, Chinese edit., 2003, Taiwan, edit., 2003; co-editor: Charisma in Hong Kong, 1970, Spiritual Songs, 1970, The People Who Walked in Darkness, 1977, The People Who Walked in Darkness II, 1992, 2d edit., 2000; works archived at Fuller Theol. Sem., 2004. Recipient Achievement award Nat. Assn. Pentecostal Women, 1964; monument erected in her honor Kowloon Walled City Park, Hong Kong Govt., 1996. Republican. Office: Soc of Stephen PO Box 6225 Altadena CA 91003-6225 Personal E-mail: rjwillans@att.net.

WILLARD, H(ARRISON) ROBERT, electrical engineer; b. Seattle, May 31, 1933; s. Harrison Eugene and Florence Linea (Chelquist) W. BSEE, U. Wash., 1955, MSEE, 1957, PhD, 1971. Lic. profl. engr., Wash. Staff assoc. Boeing Sci. Rsch. Labs., Seattle, 1959-64; rsch. assoc. U. Wash., 1968-72, sr. engr., rsch. prof. applied physics lab., 1972-81; sr. engr. Boeing Aerospace Co., Seattle, 1981-84; dir. instrumentation and engring. MetriCor Inc. (formerly Tech. Dynamics, Inc.), Redmond, Wash., 1984-92; sr. engr. B.E. Meyers & Co., Inc., Redmond, 1992—. Contbr. articles to profl. jours.; patentee in field. With AUS, 1957-59. Mem. IEEE, Am. Geophys. Union, Phi Beta Kappa, Sigma Xi, Tau Beta Pi. Office: 14540 NE 91st St Redmond WA 98052-4939

WILLARD, HUNTINGTON F. medical association administrator, medical geneticist; PhD, Yale U., 1979. Postdoctoral fellow Johns Hopkins U.; with dept. med. genetics U. Toronto; with dept. genetics Stanford U.; Henry W. Payne prof., chmn. dept. genetics Case Western Res. U., Cleve., 1992, chmn. dept. genetics, 1992—2001, dir. human genetics, 1999—2002; pres., dir. Rsch. Inst. Univ. Hosps. Cleve., 1999—2002; dir. Inst. for Genome Scis. and Policy, Duke U., Durham, NC, 2003—, vice chancellor genome scis., 2003—. Co-author: Genetics in Medicine; co-editor: Human Molecualr Genetics; contbr. articles to profl. jours. Mem.: Am. Soc. Human Genetics (pres.). Office: Inst for Genome Scis and Policy Duke U Box 3382 Durham NC 27710 E-mail: hunt.willard@duke.edu.

WILLARD, JANE, grain company executive; children: Kathy Willard, Brenda Goodell. Founder, pres. Willard Grain & Feed, Inc., Celina, Tex., 1958—. Office: Willard Grain & Feed Inc 104 Ash St Celina TX 75009

WILLARD, JOHN GERARD, consultant, author, lecturer; b. Pitts., Nov. 20, 1952; s. Cornelius Merle and May E. (Hinds) W.; m. Lorraine L. Franze, Sept. 2, 1978; children: Mary Elizabeth, Kristen Anne, Lisa Lorraine, Jessica Kathleen. BA in Journalism, Duquesne U., 1974. Producer, dir. air talent Sta. WDUQ-FM, Pitts., 1971-73; master control tech. dir. Sta. KDKA-TV, Pitts., 1973; cons. comms. Better Bus. Bur., Pitts., 1974; asst. account exec. Marc & Co. Advt., Pitts., 1975; adminstr., employee benefit adminstrn. Rockwell Internat. Corp., Pitts., 1975-80, adminstr. relocation and corp. personnel procedures, 1980-81, mgr. corp. policy, 1981-82; pres. John G. Willard Cons., 1982—. Contbr. articles to profl. jours. Office: 360 Middlegate Dr Bethel Park PA 15102-1438 Office Phone: 412-831-5650. E-mail: jgw7@telerama.com.

WILLARD, LOUIS CHARLES, librarian; b. Tallahassee, Fla., Sept. 28, 1937; s. Bert and Rose (De Milly) W.; m. Nancy Booth, June 22, 1963. BA, U. Fla., 1959; BD, Yale, 1965, MA, 1967, PhD, 1970. Tchr. Tripoli (Lebanon) Boys' Sch., 1959-62; ordained to ministry Presbyn. Ch., 1965; acting librarian Princeton Theol. Sem., 1968-69, librarian, 1969-86; librarian, mem. faculty Harvard Div. Sch., 1986-99; dir. accreditation and instnl. evaluation Assn. Theol. Schs., 1999—. Mem. A.L.A., Theol. Library Assn., Soc. Bibl. Lit., Am. Acad. Religion, Phi Beta Kappa, Chi Phi. Home: PO Box 569 136 Centennial Ave Apt 201 Sewickley PA 15143-1248 Office: Assn Theol Schs 10 Summit Park Dr Pittsburgh PA 15275-1103 Address: PO Box 569 Sewickley PA 15143-0569 Office Phone: 412-788-6505. Business E-Mail: willard@ats.edu.

WILLARD, MATTHEW ASHE, materials scientist, researcher; s. Hubert Ashe and Georda. BS in Materials Sci. and Engring., Carnegie Mellon U., 1995, MS in Materials Sci. and Engring., 1997, PhD in Materials Sci. and Engring., 2000. Rschr. Ames (Iowa) Nat. Lab., 1996—96, Los Alamos (N.Mex.) Nat. Lab., 1997; NRC postdoctoral assoc. U.S. Naval Rsch. Lab., Washington, 2000—03, rsch. metallurgist, 2003—. Session chmn. Magnetism and Magnetic Materials Conf., 2001—04, editor, 2004; session chmn. Intermag Conf., 2001—04. Dir. Sponsored NRC postdoctoral assoc., NRC/Naval Rsch. Lab., 2000—02. Mem.: AAAS, Materials Rsch. Soc. (chmn. rsch. tools symposium 2003—04, Grad. Student Gold medal 1999), Sigma Xi Soc., Phi Kappa Theta (chpt. pres. 1995—95). Achievements include development of HITPERM magnetic alloy. Office: US Naval Rsch Lab 4555 Overlook Ave SW Code 6324 Washington DC 20375 Business E-Mail: willard@anvil.nrl.navy.mil.

WILLARD, NANCY MARGARET, writer, educator; b. Ann Arbor, Mich. d. Hobart Hurd and Margaret (Sheppard) W.; m. Eric Lindbloom, Aug. 15, 1964; 1 child, James Anatole. BA, U. Mich., 1958, PhD, 1963; MA, Stanford U., 1960. Lectr. English Vassar Coll., Poughkeepsie, NY, 1965—. Author: (poems) In His Country: Poems, 1966; Skin of Grace, 1967; A New Herball: Poems, 1968, Testimony of the Invisible Man: William Carlos Williams, Francis Ponge, Rainer Maria Rilke, Pablo Neruda, 1970, Nineteen Masks for the Naked Poet: Poems, 1971, The Carpenter of the Sun: Poems, 1974, A Visit to William Blake's Inn: Poems for Innocent and Experienced Travelers, 1981 (Newbery Medal 1982), Household Tales of Moon and Water, 1983, Water Walker, 1989, The Ballad of Biddy Early, 1989; (short stories) The Lively Anatomy of God, 1968, Childhood of the Magician, 1973; (juveniles) Sailing to Cythera and Other Anatole Stories, 1974, All on a May Morning, 1975, The Snow Rabbit, 1975, Shoes Without Leather, 1976, T0e Well-Mannered Balloon, 1976, Night Story, 1986, Simple Pictures are Best, 1977, Stranger's Bread, 1977, The Highest Hit, 1978, Papa's Panda, 1979, The Island of the Grass King, 1979, The Marzipan Moon 1981, Uncle Terrible, 1982, (adult) Angel in the Parlor: Five Stories and Eight Essays, 1983, The Nightgown of the Sullen Moon, 1983, Night Story, 1986, The Voyage of the Ludgate Hill, 1987, The Mountains of Quilt, 1987, Firebrat, 1988; (novel) Things Invisible To See, 1984, Sister Water, 1993; (play) East of the Sun, West of the Moon, 1989, The High Rise Glorious Skittle Skat Roarious Sky Pie Angel Food Cake, 1991, A Nancy Willard Reader, 1991, Pish Posh said Hieronymus Bosch, 1991, Beauty and the Beast, 1992; illustrator: The Letter of John to James, Another Letter of John to James, 1982, The Octopus Who Wanted to Juggle (Robert Pack), 1990, (novel) Sister Water, 1993, (essays) Telling Time, 1993, (juvenile) A Starlit Somersault Downhill, 1993, (juvenile) The Sorcerer's Apprentice, 1993; author, illustrator: An Alphabet of Angels, 1994; (juvenile) Gutenberg's Gift, 1995, The Good Night Blessing Book, 1996, Cracked Corn and Snow Ice Cream, 1997, The Tortilla Cat, 1998; (poems, with Jane Yolen) Among Angels, 1995, Swimming Lessons, 1996, The Magic Cornfield, 1997; editor: (anthology of poems) Step Lightly: Poems for the Journey, 1998, The Tale I Told Sasha, 1999, (juvenile) Shadow Story, 1999, (juvenile) The Moon and Riddles Diner and the Sunny Side Cafe, 2001, (juvenile) The Mouse, the Cat and Grandmother's Hat, 2003, (scholastic) Cinderella's Dress, 2003, (young adult) Paradise Lost, 2004. Recipient Hopwood award, 1958, Devins Meml. award, 1967, John Newbery award, 1981, Empire State award, 1996; Woodrow Wilson fellow, 1960; NEA grantee, 1987. Mem. The Lewis Carroll Soc. Office: Vassar Coll Dept English Raymond Ave Poughkeepsie NY 12604-0001

WILLARD, RALPH LAWRENCE, surgery educator, physician, former college president; b. Manchester, Iowa, Apr. 6, 1922; s. Hosea B. and Ruth A. (Hazelrigg) W.; m. Norma L. Hattel, Nov. 12, 1943 (div. 1968); children: Laurie, Jane, Ann, H. Thomas; m. Margaret Dyer Dennis, Sept. 26, 1969. Student, Cornell Coll., 1940-42, Coe Coll., 1945; D.O., Kirksville Coll. Osteo. Medicine, 1949; EdD (hon.), U. North Tex., 1985; ScD (hon.), W.Va. Sch. Osteo. Medicine, 1993. Intern Kirksville Osteo. Hosp., 1949-50, resident in surgery, 1954-57; chmn. dept. surgery Davenport Osteo. Hosp., 1957-68; dean, prof. surgery Kirksville Coll. Osteo. Medicine, 1969-73; asso. dean acad. affairs, prof. surgery Mich. State U. Coll. Osteo. Medicine, 1974-75; dean Tex. Coll. Osteopathic Medicine, 1975-76, pres., 1981-85, prof. surgery, 1985-87; v.p. med. affairs North Tex. State U., Denton, 1976-81; assoc. dean W.Va. Sch. Osteo. Medicine, Lewisburg, 1988-91. Mem. Nat. Adv. Council Edn. for Health Professions, 1971-73, Iowa Gov.'s Council Hosps. and Health Related Facilities, 1965-68; chmn. council deans Am. Assn. Colls. Osteo. Medicine, 1970-73, pres., 1979-80 Served with USAAF, 1942-45; Served with USAF, 1952-53; col. USAFR, ret. Decorated D.F.C., Air medal with 4 oak leaf clusters, Meritorious Svc. medal, Legion of Merit; recipient Robert A. Kistner Educator award Am. Assn. Colls. Osteo. Medicine, 1989; named Disting. scholar Acad. Osteo. Medicine Nat. Acads. Practice, 2000. Fellow Am. Coll. Physician Execs., Am. Coll. Osteo. Surgeons; mem. Am. Osteo. Assn. (Disting. Svc. cert. 1992), Tex. Osteo. Assn., W.Va. Soc. Osteo. Medicine, Am. Acad. Osteopathy, Acad. Osteo. Dirs. Med. Edn., Quiet Birdmen, Davis-Monthan Officers Club, Masons, Shriners, Ft. Worth Rotary (Paul Harris fellow), Internat. Comanche Soc., Order of Daedalians. Democrat. Episcopalian. Address: PO Box 79267 Fort Worth TX 76179-0267 Personal E-mail: willardrl@aol.com. *The wise man has faith, the fool is he who betrays that faith.*

WILLARD, RICHARD KENNON, lawyer; b. Houston, Sept. 1, 1948; s. Fair McDaniel Willard and Elsbeth Rowe (Kennon) Willard Armistead; m. Leslie Harral Hopkins, July 10, 1976; children: Stephen Hopkins, Lauren Suzanne. BA, Emory U., 1969; JD, Harvard U., 1975. Bar: D.C. 1988, Tex. 1978, Ga. 1975. Law clk. U.S. Ct. Appeals, San Francisco, 1975-76, U.S. Supreme Ct., Washington, 1976-77; atty. Baker & Botts, Houston, 1977-81; counsel for intelligence policy U.S. Dept. Justice, Washington, 1981-82, dep. asst. atty. gen. civil div., 1982-83, asst. atty. gen., 1983-88; ptnr. Steptoe & Johnson, Washington, 1988-99; sr. v.p., gen. counsel The Gillette Co., 1999—. Adj. prof. Georgetown U. Law Ctr., 1991-96, Boston U. Law Sch., 2002—. Note editor: Harvard U. Law Rev., 1974-75. Gen. counsel Republican Party of Tex., Austin, 1980-81. Served to 1st lt. U.S. Army, 1969-72. Mem. Met. Club. Episcopalian. Office: Prudential Tower Bldg Boston MA 02199-8004*

WILLARD, SHIRLEY ANN OGLE, museum director, editor, historian; b. Morocco, Ind., Sept. 28, 1936; d. Charlie Ernest and Maye Elizabeth (Nicewander) Ogle; m. Willis D. Willard, June 5, 1964; children: Thomas Jefferson, Doyle Allen, William Joseph. BA, Manchester Coll., 1959; MA, Ball State U., 1966. Cert. tchr., Ind. Tchr. Rock Creek Sch., Bluffton, Ind., 1959-60, Kewanna (Ind.) H.S., 1960-67, 76-77, North Miami H.S., Denver, Ind., 1968-73; reporter, page editor Rochester (Ind.) Sentinel, 1975-76; mus. dir. Fulton County Hist. Soc., Rochester, 1978—2001, editor, pres., 1971—2001. Editor, author: Fulton County Folks, Vol. 1, 1974, Vol. 2, 1981; editor Fulton County FolkFinder, 1982—, Indian Awareness newsletter, 1983—. Sec. Indian Awareness Ctr., Rochester, 1982—; founder, dir. Trail of Courage Living History Festival, Rochester, 1976—; organizer, leader Trail of Death Commemorative Caravan, 1988, 93, 98, 2003; founder Trail of Death Regional Hist. Trail, Ind.-Kans., 1994—, editor, 1994—; mem. hist. marker com. Ind. Hist. Soc., 1989-96; rural preservation com. Hist. Landmarks Found. Ind., 1992—; founder Living History Village called Loyal, Rochester, Ind.; County Hist., 1982—. Named Outstanding Young Woman Manchester Coll., 1982, Sagamore of the Wabash, State of Ind., 2001; recipient 20 Yrs. Leadership award Am. Assn. State and Local History, 1989, Cmty. Svc. award Rochester C. of C., 1986, Disting Svc. award Ind. Humanities Coun., 1994, Dorothy Riker award for innovation in field of history Ind. Hist. Soc., 2001. Mem. Nat. Coun. History Edn., Assn. Ind. Mus. Republican. Lutheran. Avocations: reading, writing, historic dancing, living history festivals. Home: 3063 S 425 E Rochester IN 46975-8233 Office: Fulton County Hist Soc 37 E 375 N Rochester IN 46975-8384 E-mail: wwillard@rtcol.com.

WILLARD-JONES, DONNA C. lawyer; b. Calgary, Alberta, Can., Jan. 19, 1944; m. Douglas E. Jones. BA with honors, U. B.C., 1965, student, 1965-66; JD, U. Oreg., 1970. Bar: Ak. 1970, U.S. Dist. Ct. Ak. 1970, U.S. Ct. Appeals (9th cir.) 1971, U.S. Customs Ct. 1972, U.S. Tax Ct. 1975, U.S. Supreme Ct. 1981. Assoc. Boyko & Walton, 1970-71, Walton & Willard, 1971-73; ptnr. Gruenberg & Willard, 1974, Gruenberg, Willard & Smith, 1974-75, Richmond, Willoughby & Willard, 1976-81, Willoughby & Willard, 1981-89; pvt. practice Anchorage, 1990—. Chmn. fed. adv. group Implementation of Civil Justice Reform Act of 1990, 1991-92; lawyer rep. 9th Cir. Jud. Conf., 1979-80; mem. spl. com. on contempt Ak. Supreme Ct., 1991-92; chmn. Bankruptcy Judge Merit Screening com., 1979; mem. Am. Judicature Soc., 1973-92, Am. Trial Lawyers Assn., 1981-92; bd. dirs. Ak. Legal Svcs. Corp., 1979-80; spkr. in field. Mem. U. B.C. Law Rev.; assoc. editor Oreg. Law Rev.; copy editor Ak. Bar Rag, 1979-84, contbg. editor, 1979-92; annual reviser Probate Counsel, 1972-88. Mem. Anchorage Port Commn., 1987-93, chmn., 1990-93; chmn. Ak. State Officers Compensation Commn., 1986-92; mem. Anchorage Transp. Commn., 1983-87, chmn., 1986-87; vice-chmn. Ak. Code Revision Commn., 1976-78; bd. trustees Ak. Indian Arts, Inc., 1970-92; mem. Chilkat Dancer Ak., 1965—. Recipient Rikli Solo Lifetime Achievement. award, ABA Gen. Pract., 1998. Fellow Am. Bar Found. (life); mem. ABA (ho. dels. 1980-84, 86-96, bd. govs. 1992-96, sec. 1995-96), Nat. Conf. Bar Pres. (exec. coun. 1985-88), Nat. Conf. Bar Founds. (bd. trustees 1983-90), Am. Arbitration Assn., We. States Bar Conf. (pres. 1983-84), Ak. Bar Assn. (Bd. Govs. Disting. Svc. award 1991, bd. govs. 1977-80, pres. 1979-80, pres. 1979-80, numerous coms.), Am. Law Inst. Presbyterian. Office: 124 E 7th Ave Anchorage AK 99501-3608 also: Am Bar Assn 750 N Lake Shore Dr Chicago IL 60611-4403 Fax: 907-278-0449.

WILLAUER, GEORGE JACOB, English literature educator; b. Oct. 30, 1935; s. George Jacob and Mary Catherine (Eshleman) W.; m. Cynthia Cameron Thun, June 11, 1966; children: George Jacob III, Elizabeth Christian. BA, Wesleyan U., 1957; MA, U. Pa., 1959, PhD, 1965. Asst. instr. U. Pa., Phila., 1958-62; instr. Conn. Coll., New London, 1962-66, asst. prof., 1966-72, assoc. prof., 1972-78, prof., 1978—2002, chair dept. English, 1972—77, 1991—94, 2000—02. Charles J. MacCurdy prof. of Am. Studies, 1993-2002; coll. marshal, 1989-2002, dean of acad. programs, 1997-2000; instr. Williams Coll.-Mystic Seaport Program in Maritime Studies, 1986-88; vis. prof. lit. U. Dar es Salaam, Tanzania, 1995. Author: A Lyme Miscellany: 1776-1976, 1977; contbr. articles to profl. jours. Trustee Cmty. Found. Southeastern Conn., 1996-2002, pres. 2000-02; trustee Florence Griswold Mus., pres. 1983-88; trustee Lymes Youth Svc. Bur., 1978-83, Lyme Land Conservation Trust, 1996-2002, Lyme Pub. Libr., Inc., Lyman Allyn Art Mus., 1983-88, 1996-2004, Music Masterworks, 2001—, MacCurdy-Salisbury Ednl. Found., Conn. Humanities Coun., 2004—; deacon First Congl. Ch., Old Lyme. English-Speaking Union fellow, 1969, 72. Mem. MLA, Century Assn. Home: 55-1 Beaver Brook Rd Old Lyme CT 06371-3219

WILLAUER, WHITING RUSSELL, retired manufacturing executive, systems engineer; b. Boston, May 24, 1931; s. Whiting Russell and Louise Knapp (Russell) Willauer; m. Julie Mackie McConihe, Mar. 15, 2001; stepchildren: Frances Moran McConihe, Marguerite Isabelle McConihe; m. Julie Matheson Arnold, July 11, 1959 (div.); children: Whiting Russell, Jr., William Arnold. BS, Princeton U., 1955, MS, 1959; PhD, Georgetown U., 1964. Research assoc. joint research com. Dept. Def., 1951-52; ops. mgr. Civil Air Transport Airline Taiwan, 1952-53; scientist Analytic Services, Inc., 1958-61; asst. prof. astronomy Georgetown U., 1965-68; mgr. TRW Systems Group support to chief Naval ops., McLean, Va., 1968-73, TRW support to U.S. Navy Antisubmarine projects, 1973-79, TRW Amphibious Ship Acquisition project, 1979-85; advanced systems mgr. TRW Systems Integration Group, 1985-90, cost estimating mgr., 1990-95, sr. cons., 1995-99; sr. v.p., chief strategist K12Nation.net, 1999-2000. Cons. Nat. Geog. Soc., 1961-65, U. Tex., 1962, NSF, 1963, Booz-Allen & Hamilton, 1966-67 Mng. editor: Jour. Astronautical Scis, 1969-71; Designer: Orrery (planetarium) on permanent exhibit, New Explorers Hall, Nat. Geog. Soc. Asst. chief steward Alpine Venue XIII Olympic Winter Games, Lake Placid, 1980; mem. U.S. Olympic Com., bd. dirs., 1987-94, sec. nat. governing bodies, 1989-92, mem. membership svcs. com., 1988-92, mem. athletic devel. com., 1992-96; chef de mission Winter Pan Am. Games, Las Lenas, Argentina, 1990; asst. chief de mission XVI Winter Olympics, Albertville, France, 1992; U.S. Olympic Com. liaison to VI Paralympic Winter Games, Lillehammer, Norway, 1994. Research fellow Georgetown U., 1961-65 Fellow AAAS (coun.); mem. Am. Astronautical Soc. (v.p. fin.), Blue Ridge Ski Coun. (pres. 1976-78), U.S. Ski Assn. (pres. 1982-87, Julius Blegan award 1988, Mary and Bud Little award 1998), U.S. Ski and Snowboard Assn. (vice chmn. 1994-96, trustee emeritus 1997—), Internat. Ski Fedn. (chmn. U.S. del. 1983, 85, chmn. recreational skiing com. 1987-98, eligibility com. 1988-98), Ea. Ski Assn. (treas. 1980-82), Pan Am Sports Orgn. (winter games adv. com. 1988—), Sigma Xi, Chevy Chase Club (Md.), Nantucket Yacht Club (Mass.) (commodore 1981-83, bd. govs. 1957-59, 68—), Nantucket IOD Fleet Assn. (Fleet Capt. 2002-04), Arthur Knapp Prize 2003 IOD World Championship, USCG Aux. Flotilla 11-7 (Sec. 2003-). E-mail: whitey@willauer.com.

WILLCOX, CHRISTOPHER PATRICK, magazine editor; b. Chgo., Nov. 2, 1946; s. James Christopher and Rita (Donovan) Willcox; m. Emily Turner, July 6, 1976; 1 child, Kathleen. BA, U. Notre Dame, 1968. Editl. writer Detroit News, 1980—82, dep. editl. page editor, 1982—84; program advisor Radio Free Europe/Radio Liberty, Munich, 1984—88; sr. editor Reader's Digest, Pleasantville, NY, 1988—90, sr. staff editor, 1990—91, exec. editor, 1991—96, editor-in-chief worldwide, sr. v.p., 1996—. Adj. prof. journalism Columbia U., N.Y.C., 1993—96. Mem.: Am. Soc. Mag. Editors, Deadline Club. Office: Readers Digest Assn Readers Digest Rd Pleasantville NY 10570-7000

WILLCOX, RODERICK HARRISON, lawyer; b. Columbus, Ohio, Jan. 10, 1934; s. Richard V. and Marcella A. (Rehl) W.; m. Rita Kay Click, July 2, 1955; children: Sharon Marie Willcox Hazlewood, Kathy Lynn, Patricia Ann Willcox Hanna, Roderick Harrison Jr. BA, Williams Coll., 1955; LLB, U. Mich., 1958. Ptnr. Chester, Willcox & Saxbe, Columbus, Ohio, 1971—. Office: Chester Willcox & Saxbe LLP 65 East State St Ste 1000 Columbus OH 43215-3442 E-mail: rwillcox@cwslaw.com.

WILLCOX, ROGER, city planner, consultant; b. N.Y.C., Apr. 10, 1920; s. Henry and Anita Hall (Parkhurst) Willcox; m. Elisabeth Marie Lammerts Van Bueren, Oct. 19, 1947 (dec. Feb. 1974); children: Peter, Michael, Bani; m. Joan Smyth, Jan. 6, 1978. BS in Econ., Harvard U., 1937—41; MS in City Planning, MIT, Cambridge, 1942—47. Rsch. tech. N.Y. Regional Plan Assn., N.Y.C., 1947—49; city planner Harrison, Ballard and Allen, N.Y.C., 1949—51; city planner, asst. to Clarence S. Stein, FAIA N.Y.C., 1951—52; CEO FCH Svcs., Inc., N.Y.C., 1952—72; pres. Cmty. Cooperative Devel. Found., Norwalk, Conn., 1972—86; ind. cons. Norwalk, Conn., 1986—. Sec. Regional Devel. Coun. of U.S.A., N.Y.C., 1947—53; pres., officer Nat. Assn. of Housing Cooperatives, Washington, 1960—2004; bd. mem. Cooperative League of the U.S.A., Washington, 1970—80. Contbr. articles to profl. jours. Bd. mem. Norwalk Pension Fund, Conn., 1980—89; bd. mem., sec. Norwalk Land Trust, Conn., 1980—2004; sec. Conn. Energy Cooperative, Hartford, Conn., 1998—2002. Named to Cooperative Hall of Fame, Cooperative League of the U.S.A., 1986; recipient Jerry Voorhis Meml. award, Nat. Assn. of Housing Cooperatives, 1985, Disting. Svc. award, Cooperative Housing Found., 1999. Mem.: Mamaroneck Frostbite Assn. (safety officer 1957—2004), Nat. Housing Conf. (life; bd. mem. 1958—2004). Avocations: sailing, yachting, boating, offshore racing. Home: 38 Dock Rd Norwalk CT 06854-4717 E-mail: willcoxr@juno.com.

WILLE, LOIS JEAN, retired newspaper editor; b. Chgo., Sept. 19, 1931; d. Walter and Adele S. (Taege) Kroeber; m. Wayne M. Wille, June 6, 1954. BS, Northwestern U., 1953, MS, 1954; Litt.D. (hon.), Columbia Coll., Chgo., 1980, Northwestern U., 1990, Rosary Coll., 1990. Reporter Chgo. Daily News, 1958-74, nat. corr., 1975-76, assoc. editor charge editorial page, 1977; assoc. editor charge editorial and opinion pages Chgo. Sun-Times, 1978-83; assoc. editor editorial page Chgo. Tribune, 1984-87, editor editorial page, 1987-91, ret., 1991. Author: Forever Open, Clear and Free: the Historic Struggle for Chicago's Lakefront, 1972, At Home in the Loop: How Clout and Community Built Chicago's Dearborn Park, 1997. Recipient Pulitzer prize for public svc., 1963, Pulitzer prize for editorial writing, 1989, William Allen White Found. award for excellence in editorial writing, 1978, numerous awards Chgo. Newspaper Guild, numerous awards Chgo. Headline Club, numerous awards Nat. Assn. Edn. Writers, numerous awards Ill. AP, numerous awards Ill. UPI. Home: 1530 S State St Apt 1011 Chicago IL 60605 E-mail: lowille@aol.com.

WILLE, ROSANNE LOUISE, higher education administrator; b. Hackensack, N.J., Aug. 4, 1941; d. Albert Wille and Rose Marie (Rock) Eberhardt; m. George B. Jacobs, Mar. 12, 1980; children: Leigh, Steven, Alexander, Jeffrey. M Pub. Adminstrn., Rutgers U., 1986; PhD, N.Y.U., 1980. Dept. chair Rutgers U., Newark, N.J., 1978-84, Lehman Coll., Bronx, NY, 1984-87, dean, 1987-92, provost, sr. v.p., 1992—2002; cons. for higher edn., 2002—. Contbr. articles to profl. jours. Bd. dirs. Family Support Svcs., Bronx, N.Y., 1994—, bd. dirs. South Bronx Overall Economic Devel., Inc., Bronx, 1991—. Recipient Vision award Family Support Svcs., Bronx, 1996, Thousand Points of Light award Pres. George Bush, Washington, 1991. Mem. N.Y. Acad. Scis., N.Y. Acad. Medicine, Am. Assn. Higher Edn. Avocations: aviation, golf. Address: PO Box 4148 South Hackensack NJ 07606-4148 E-mail: rlwille@earthlink.net.

WILLE, WAYNE MARTIN, retired editor; b. Des Plaines, Ill., Nov. 17, 1930; s. Clarence Louis and Lois Naomi (Martin) W.; m. Lois Jean Kroeber, June 6, 1954. BSJ, Northwestern U., 1952, MSJ, 1953. Reporter Chgo. Sun Times, 1956-57; dir. press info. WBBM-TV and CBS-TV, Chgo., 1957-58; feature editor Sci. and Mechanics mag., 1958-60, mng. editor, 1960-62; news editor Nat. Safety Council, Chgo., 1962-64, asst. dir. pub. info., 1964-67; mng. editor World Book Year Book, Chgo., 1967-69; exec. editor World Book Yr. Book, 1969-83; mng. editor World Book Yr. Book and Sci. Yr. and Health & Med. Ann., 1983-91. Served with AUS, 1953-55. Mem. Chgo. Headline Club (pres. 1967-68), Soc. Profl. Journalists, Art Inst. Chgo., Oriental Inst. Clubs: La Salle Street Rod and Gun.

WILLEFORD, PAMELA P. ambassador; m. George Willeford III; children: Emily Ann, Nancy Kathryn. BA in English and Spanish, U. Tex. Former tchr., Dallas; former dir. devel., coord. Tex. Capitol Rededication Tex. State Preservation Bd.; mem. Tex. Higher Edn. Coordinating Bd., Austin, 1995—, chair, 1998—2003; ptnr., pres. Pico Drilling Ltd., Breckenridge, Tex.; U.S. Amb. to Switzerland, 2003—. Office: Dept of State 5110 Bern Pl Washington DC 20521-5110

WILLEM, KAREN J. business software company financial executive; BA in Biology, Bucknell U.; MBA in Fin., U. Pitts. V.p., corp. contr. Network Gen., v.p. worldwide sales ops.; exec. v.p. fin. and ops., CFO, Brio Tech., Palo Alto, Calif. Office: Brio Tech 3460 W Bayshore Rd Palo Alto CA 94303-4227

WILLEMS, CONSTANCE CHARLES, lawyer; b. Zuilen, Utrecht, The Netherlands, Oct. 31, 1942; came to U.S., 1967, naturalized, 1977; d. Anton Henri and Maria (Van der Meys) Charles; m. Cornelis Franciscus Willems, May 25, 1965; 1 son, Maurice. BA in Sociology magna cum laude, U. New Orleans, 1974; JD with honors, Tulane U., 1977. Bar: La. 1977, U.S. Dist. Ct. (ea. dist.) La. 1977, U.S. Ct. Appeals (5th cir.) 1977, U.S. Dist. Ct. (mid. dist.) La. 1979, U.S. Supreme Ct. 1983, U.S. Dist. Ct. (we. dist.) La. 1997. Assoc. McGlinchey, Stafford, Mintz, Cellini and Lang, New Orleans, 1977-81, ptnr., 1982—, now McGlinchey Stafford, New Orleans. Instr. law office mgmt. Loyola U. Sch. Law, 1986—90; instr. European law Tulane U. Sch. Law, New Orleans, 1994, New Orleans, 96, New Orleans, 98; bd. mem. World Trade Ctr. New Orleans, 2001. Mem. task force on municipalization; hon. consul for The Netherlands, 1989—; sec.-treas. Consular Corps.; bd. visitors Coll. Liberal Arts, U. New Orleans, 1995—, pres., 1999—; bd. dirs. United Way Agy. Rels. Com., 1987—91, Coun. Internat. Visitors, 1992—94, Com. of 21, 1994—, New Orleans Opera Assn., 1995 . Recipient Disting. alumni award U. New Orleans, 1989. Mem. ABA, La. Assn. Women Attys. (pres. 1983-85, 86-87), La. State Bar Assn. (mem. ho. dels. 1984-85, chair internat. law sect. 1994—), Dutch-Am. Bus. Coun. (founder), New Orleans Ballet Assn. (sec. 2000—). Office: McGlinchey Stafford 643 Magazine St New Orleans LA 70130-3477

WILLENBECHER, JOHN, artist; b. Macungie, Pa., May 5, 1936; s. John George and Geneva (Bacon) W. BA, Brown U., 1958; postgrad., N.Y. U., Inst. Fine Arts, 1958-61. Sculptor-mem. N.Y.C. Art Commn., 1980-92; mem. commn. for plaza and pavillion, Mpls. Inst. Arts, 1991. Exhibited in one-person shows including Hamilton Gallery Contemporary Art, N.Y.C., 1977, 80, 82, U. Mass. Art Gallery, Amherst, 1977, Wright State U. Art Gallery, Dayton, Ohio, 1977, Jaffe-Friede Gallery, Dartmouth Coll., Hanover, N.H., 1977, Fine Arts Ctr. U. R.I., Kingston, 1978, Neuberger Mus., SUNY at Purchase, 1979, Allentown (Pa.) Art Mus., 1979, Mpls. Inst. Arts, 1991, U. N.Mex. Art Gallery, Albuquerque, 1996, 5 Myles Gallery, Bklyn., 2003, CUNY Grad. Ctr., N.Y.C, 2003; exhibited in numerous group shows including Albright-Knox Art Gallery, Buffalo, 1963, Whitney Mus. Am. Art, N.Y.C., 1964-68; represented in permanent collections including Solomon R. Guggenheim Mus., N.Y.C., Met. Mus., N.Y.C., Whitney Mus. Am. Art, Albright-Knox Art Gallery, Phila. Mus. Art, Centre d'Art et Culture Georges Pompidou, Paris, Hirshhorn Mus. and Sculpture Garden, Washington, Art Inst. Chgo. Nat. Endowment for Arts grantee, 1977, Esther and Adolph Gottlieb Found. grantee, 1994. Achievements include being subject of profl. articles and catalogues.

WILLENBRINK, ROSE ANN, lawyer; b. Louisville, Ky., Apr. 20, 1950; d. J.L. Jr. and Mary Margaret (Williams) W.; m. William I. Cornett Jr. Student, U. Chgo., 1968-70; BA in Anthropology with highest honors, U. Louisville, 1973, JD, 1975. Bar: Ky. 1976, Ind. 1976, U.S. Dist. Ct. (we. dist.) Ky. 1976, Ohio 1999. Atty. Mapother & Mapother, Louisville, 1976-79; v.p., counsel Nat. City Bank, Louisville, 1980-99, v.p., sr. atty. Cleve., 1999—2004, Louisville, 2004—. Mem. ABA, Ohio Bar Assn., Ky. Bar Assn., Louisville Bar Assn., Conf. on Consumer Fin. Law, Corp. House Counsel Assn., Phi Kappa Phi. Home: 6803 Chadworth Pl Prospect KY 40059 Office: Nat City Bank 101 S 5th St Louisville KY 40202 Office Phone: 502-581-7640. Business E-Mail: rose.ann.willenbrink@nationalcity.com.

WILLENZ, JUNE ADELE, writer, public affairs executive, playwright, screenwriter; BS, U. Mich., 1945, MA, 1947; ABD, New Sch. for Social Rsch., 1951. Instr. English Montgomery Coll., Md. Exec. dir. Am. Vets. Com., 1965—2002; chair standing com. on women World Vet. Fedn., 1983—; conf. organizer Women In and After War, Bellagio, Italy, Rape in Armed Conflicts, Istanbul; lectr. USIA; radio and TV guest appearances; del. White House Conf. on Youth, White House Conf. Aging; planning com. 5th and 6th legis. confs. World Vets. Fedn.; scholar in residence Am. U., 1997—; rep. for U.S. Internat. Seminar on Peace Keeping, Baeria, Norway, 2001; lectr., spkr., presenter in field. Author: Women Veterans: America's Forgotten Heroines, 1983; co-author: Gender Differences, 1991; editor, author: Dialogue on the Draft, 1967, Human Rights of the Man in Uniform, 1969; editor: AVC Bull.; columnist Stars and Stripes; advisor, commentator (film) The GI Bill: The Law That Changed America, 1997; contbr. articles to profl. jours., local newspapers, popular mags. Exec. com. 1st VA Adv. Com. Womens Vets., 1983—86, First Lady's Women's Conf. Cir., 1995; head of working group on refugee women and women in armed conflict UN Decade for Women; accredited non-govtl. orgn. rep. world vets. fedn. UN; organizer Workshops on Refugee Women, Armed Conflict, Gender Justice, and other issues at UN, N.Y.C. and Geneva; pub. mem. 19th Fgn. Officer Selection Bd. USIA; testified before congl. coms., exec. agys., chair Task Force on Vets. and Mil. Affairs for Leadership Com. on Civil Rights; advisor; co-chair Coordinating Com. on Voluntary Nat. Svc.; organizer nat. conf. Dialogue on Nat. Svc., 1989, The Draft, 1966, Human Rights of Man in Uniform, 1968, 1970; chair subcom. on disabled vets. Pres. Com. Employment of People with Disabilities, 1995—96; active Inter-Univ. Seminar Armed Forces & Soc.; adviser Vets. Brain Trust Conf., 1997. Recipient La Médaille de la Ville de Paris, Mayor of Paris, 2000, Human Rights award, UNA Nat. Capital, 2001, honored by Congl. Black Caucus, 1997, honored for outstanding leadership on behalf of disabled vets., U.S. Dept. Labor, 2002. Mem. Non-Govtl. Orgn. Com. on Status of Women (convener task force on women in armed conflict, convener working group on refugee women), Authors Guild. Personal E-mail: willenzj@mindspring.com.

WILLER, EDWARD HERMAN, real estate broker; b. Concord, N.C., June 12, 1941; s. Emil Francis and Mary (McKinley) W.; m. Cornelia Campbell, Nov. 30, 1963; children: Laura Campbell, Edward Groves. AB, Davidson Coll., 1963. V.p., sales mgr. Bacon & Co., Realtors, Raleigh, N.C., 1971-84; pres. residential div. York Properties, Inc., Raleigh, 1984—2001. Treas. N.C. Real Estate Ednl. Found., Greensboro, 1984, pres., 1988; bd. dirs. Rex Hosp. Found., Raleigh, 1988-89, Relo, The Internat. Referral Network, Inc., Chgo., dir., 1988-92, treas., 1992. Author: Real Estate Exam Ready Book, 1984; contbr. articles to profl. jours. Bd. dirs. Ea. N.C. Multiple Sclerosis Soc., Raleigh, 1982-85; campaign chair United Way of Wake County, 1996, bd. dirs., 1994-2000, mem. exec. com., 1996-97, treas., 2001—. 1st lt. U.S. Army, 1963-66, Vietnam. Named Realtor of the Year, 1984. Mem. Nat. Assn. Realtors (cert.), N.C. Assn. Realtors (bd. dirs. 1978-82), N.C. Real Estate Ednl. Found. (pres.), Raleigh Bd. Realtors (pres. 1979), Greater Raleigh C. of C. (bd. dirs. 1991-94), Quite Birdmen Club. Democrat. Presbyterian. Avocations: teaching, flying, woodworking. Home: 1512 Saint Mary's St Raleigh NC 27608-2217 Office: York Simpson Underwood 311 Oberlin Rd Raleigh NC 27605-3125

WILLERSON, JAMES THORNTON, internist, educator; MD, Baylor U., 1965. Prof. medicine U. Tex. Health Sci. Ctr., Houston, 1976—, dir. divsn. cardiology, 1977—; Edward Randall III prof., chair. U. Tex. Med. Sch., Houston, 1989—. Mem. NAS-Inst. Medicine. Office: U Tex Health Sci Ctr Sch Medicine Dept Internal Med 6431 Fannin St Rm 1-150 Houston TX 77030-1501

WILLERT, SISTER ST. JOAN, health care corporation executive; b. Wheeling, W.Va., June 13, 1924; d. Arthur Edgar and Viola (Fitzsimmons) W. BA, Mt. St. Mary's Coll., 1946; human relations cert., Loyola U., L.A., 1951; MS, Mt. St. Mary's Coll., 1953; health care adminstrn., St. Louis U., 1975. Cert. health care adminstrn., elem. sch. adminstrn., secondary sch. adminstrn. Elem. sch. tchr. Diocese of San Francisco, L.A., and Fresno, 1945-54; elem. sch. prin. several cities, 1954-65; secondary sch. prin. Queen of the Valley Acad., Fresno, Calif., 1965-67, Salpointe Catholic High Sch., Tucson, 1967-70; regional superior Sisters of St. Joseph, L.A., 1970-74, Washington, Idaho, 1974-77; with health care adminstrn. Daniel Freeman Hosp., Inglewood, Calif., 1977-79; pres., chief exec. officer Health Care Corp. Ariz., Tucson, 1979—. Bd. dirs. Freeman Health Ventures, St. John of God, L.A.; bd. sec. Downtown Devel. Corp., Tucson, 1986—; bd. pres. Our Lady of Lourdes Health Ctr., Pasco, Wash., 1975-81, 85—; bd. chairperson Health Care Corp., St. Louis, 1986—. Contbr. articles to MSMC, 1966, Health Progress, 1982. Chairperson state campaign Arizonans to Protect Quality Health Svc., Phoenix, Tucson, 1984-85. Named for Outstanding Svc. to Community Una Noche Plateada, Tucson, 1982; honoree Tucson Diocesan Found. Mem. Ariz. Hosp. Assn. (bd. dirs. 1979—, sec. 1988, chairperson-elect 1989-90, Salisbury Leadership award 1985), Cath. Health Assn. (bylaws com. 1985-86, nominating com. 1984-85), Health Care Corp. Sisters of St. Joseph (chairperson 1985—). Democrat. Roman Catholic. Avocations: reading, tennis, writing. Office: Carondelet St Marys Hosp 1601 W Saint Marys Rd Tucson AZ 85745-2623

WILLES, MARK HINCKLEY, media industry executive; b. Salt Lake City, July 16, 1941; s. Joseph Simmons and Ruth (Hinckley) W.; m. Laura Fayone, June 7, 1961; children: Wendy Anne, Susan Kay, Keith Mark, Stephen Joseph, Matthew Bryant. AB, Columbia Coll., 1963, PhD, 1967. Staff banking and currency com. Ho. of Reps., Washington, 1966-67; asst. prof. fin. Wharton Sch. U. Pa., Phila., 1967-69; economist Fed. Res. Bank, Phila., 1967, sr. economist, 1969-70, dir. rsch., 1970-71, v.p., dir. rsch., 1971, 1st v.p., 1971-77; pres. Fed. Res. Bank of Mpls., 1977-80; exec. v.p., chief fin. officer Gen. Mills, Inc., Mpls., 1980-85, pres., COO, 1985-92, vice-chmn., 1992-95; chmn., pres., CEO Times Mirror Co., L.A., 1995-2000; pub. L.A. Times, 1997-99; prof. mgmt. Brigham Young U., Provo, Utah, 2000, 2004—. Pres. Hawaii Honolulu Mission Ch. of LDS, 2001-04. Office: Brigham Young Univ 3651 N 100 E Ste 300 Provo UT 84604 *My success is based on adherence to principles I learned in the home, which is the most basic and important organizational unit in the world. Three of those principles stand out in my mind: Be just, honest and moral—do things not only because they are required, but because they are right. Have mercy—care enough about others to be fair and kind. Be humble—you can get more done effectively with the help of others than you can do on your own.*

WILLET, E. CROSBY (EVERETT CROSBY WILLET), artist; b. Phila., Jan. 8, 1929; s. Henry Lee and Katharine Muriel (Crosby) W.; m. Augusta Winter, Nov. 27, 1954; children: William, Nancy Lee, Katharine Crosby, Henry Lee II. BA, Lafayette Coll., 1950; DFA (hon.), Orthodox Cath. Archdiocese, Phila., 1982. Apprentice Blenko Glass Co., Milton, W.Va., 1950; craftsman Willet Stained Glass Studio Inc., Phila., 1950-54, v.p., 1954-64, pres., 1964—. Works include: Portsmouth Priory, R.I., 1956, Folger Bay Washington Cathedral, 1973, Assocs. Dining Room, Smithsonian Instn., 1976, 2d Bapt. Ch., Houston, 1985-86, Gethsemane Cathedral, Fargo, N.D., 1992-95, Peachtree Road United Methodist Church, Atlanta, 2001, St. Martins Episcopal Ch., Houston, 2004. Recipient George Washington Kidd award Lafayette Coll., 1985, Elbert M. Conover award AIA/IFRAA, 2002. Fellow Stained Glass Assn. Am. (exec. bd. 1958-78, 81, pres. 1964-66); mem. InterFaith Forum, Religion, Art and Architecture (exec. bd. 1979-2001, Conover award, 2002), Am. Soc. Appraisers (sr. mem.), Appraisers Assn. Am., Nantucket Yacht Club, Moorings Club. Republican. Presbyn. Home and Office: Willet Stained Glass Studio 10 E Moreland Ave Philadelphia PA 19118-3539 Office Phone: 215-247-5721. E-mail: crosbyw@earthlink.net.

WILLETT, ANNA HART, composer, painter; b. Bartlesville, Okla., June 18, 1931; d. Thomas Kellogg Willett and Mary Kathryn (Feist) Willett Dalferes; m. Roger Garland Horn, Aug. 1956 (div. June 1962). B in Music Edn., Southwestern La. Inst., 1954; studied with H. Gunderson, 1955—64; MA, La. State U., 1964, postgrad. in piano, voice majors, 1976-87; studied with K. B. Klaus, Jr., studied with D. Constanides, 1976—87. Lifetime tchr. cert. La. Pub. sch. vocal music tchr. Iberville Parish, Plaquemine, La., 1954-55, Orleans Parish, New Orleans, 1966-71; elem. music pedagogy tchr. St. Mary's Dominican Coll., New Orleans, 1972. Post-grad. rsch. history life scholar in late Medieval English Crown changes LSU. Composer: Dances for Solo Violin, 1981, Weaving Song, 1982, Entertainer's Song (from the opera Omar), 1983, Hercules Piano Variations, 1986, En Ivrez Solo Song, 1989, Solo Songson Poems of Alfieri, 1996, 2000, Variations on a Southern Folk Hymn for piano, Memories of New Orleans, variations for piano, voice Recital at Fest for All, (Operas) How to Murder Mother, 1982, Who Murdered Mother, 1982, Omar, 1984, Caught, 1986, Cellini the Opera, 1997, Lines on Wine, 1987, Druid Installation, 1992, Seven Gables, 1998, The Icey Road, 1999; exhibitions include La. State Archives, Baton Rouge, Zeigler Gallery, Jennings, La., Old Bogan Fire Sta., Baton Rouge, Represented in permanent collections David S. Adler, MD; author: The Math. of History, 2000. Mem. ch. choir St. Albans Episc. chapel, 1976—. Scholar, Loyola U. South, New Orleans, 1972—73. Mem.: AAUW, Sigma Alpha Iota, Alpha Sigma Alpha. Avocations: gardening, bridge, local archeology. Home: 2244 Ferndale Ave Baton Rouge LA 70808-2830

WILLETT, LANCE, orchestra executive; Exec. dir. Quad City Symphony Orch., Davenport, Iowa, 1982—. Office: Quad City Symphony Orch Assn PO Box 1144 Davenport IA 52805-1144

WILLETT, LAURA R. internist; MD, U. Calif., San Francisco, 1983. Diplomate Am. Bd. Internal Medicine. Intern Beth Israel Hosp., Boston, 1983—84, resident in internal medicine, 1984—86; physician divsn. gen. internal medicine Robert Wood Johnson U. Med. Group. Office: Robert Wood Johnson Med Grp Clinical Acad Bldg 125 Paterson St Ste 5100 A New Brunswick NJ 08901-1977

WILLETT, ROSLYN LEONORE, public relations executive, food service consultant, writer; d. Edward and Celia (Stickler) Sternberg; m. Edward Willett (div.); 1 child, Jonathan Stanley. BA, Hunter Coll., N.Y.C.; postgrad., Columbia U., CUNY, NYU, New Sch. Dietitian YWCA, N.Y.C.; tech. and patents libr., food technologist in charge tech. svcs. and devel. Stein Hall & Co., N.Y.C.; editor McGraw-Hill, Inc., N.Y.C., Harcourt Brace Jovanovich, Inc., N.Y.C.; pub. rels. writer Farley Manning Assocs., N.Y.C.; cons. pub. rels. and food svc. Roslyn Willett Assocs., Inc., N.Y.C., 1959—. Adj. prof. Hunter Coll., Poly U., Columbia U. Sch. Pub. Health; dir. West End Writers Workshop, 1998—2002; seminar presenter in field. Author: The Woman Executive in Woman in Sexist Society, 1971, also short stories and essays; assoc. editor Timber Creek Rev., Words of Wisdom, 2001—, Bulls Head Creek Rev., 2004—. V.p. North Shore Ams. for Dem. Action; ofcl. rapporteur Post-Assembly Tech. Sessions, WHO; juror Am. Film Festival, Arts and Scis., 1962—88; chmn. Women's Polit. Caucus, Inc. NY, NJ, Conn, 1971—73; v.p. Mid Hudson Arts and Sci. Ctr., Poughkeepsie, NY; apptd. to regional adv. coun. Fed. SBA, 1976—78; bd. dirs. Small Bus. Task Force, Assn. for Small Bus. and Professions, 1981—85, Rhinebeck Chamber Music Soc., 1985—86, Will Inst., New Paltz, 1980—2001, Women Studies Abstracts, 1971—81; pres. Hunns Lake Assn., 1999—2001. Mem. Pub. Rels. Soc. Am. (accredited), Food Svc. Cons. Soc. Internat. (bd. dirs. 1978-80), N.Y. Acad. Scis., Inst. Food

Technologists, Juilliard Assn., Ukiyo-E Soc., Alliance Française, Paris Club, N.Y. Print Club. Avocations: writing, dance, art collecting, hiking, swimming. Home: 97 W Hunns Lake Rd Stanfordville NY 12581-5606 Office: 441 West End Ave New York NY 10024-5328

WILLETT, WALTER CHURCHILL, epidemiologist, educator; b. Hart, Mich., June 20, 1945; s. Elwin Lintin and Lawain (Churchill) W.; m. Gail Valerae Pettiford, June 11, 1973; children: Amani, Kamali. Student, Mich. State U., 1963-66; MD, U. Mich., 1970; MPH, Harvard U., 1973, Dr PH, 1980. Diplomate Am. Bd. Internal Medicine. Lectr. in medicine U. Dar es Salaam, Tanzania, 1974-75, head community health dept., 1975-77; fellow clin. epidemiology Channing Lab. Med. Sch., Harvard U., Boston, 1977-80; asst. prof. epidemiology Sch. Pub. Health, Harvard U., Boston, 1980-84, assoc. prof. epidemiology, 1984-88, prof. epidemiology and nutrition, 1988—, chmn. dept. nutrition, 1991—. Statis. cons. New Eng. Jour. Medicine, Boston, 1987—. Author: Nutritional Epidemiology, 1989, Eat, Drink and Be Healthy: The Harvard Medical School Guide to Healthy Eating; contbr. over 800 articles to sci. publs. Recipient Charles S. Mott prize, GM Cancer Rsch. Found., 2001, Brinker award, Komen Found., 2003. Mem. Am. Epidemiol. Soc., Soc. for Epidemiol. Rsch., Am. Inst. Nutrition, Alpha Omega Alpha. Avocations: gardening, woodworking, skiing, bicycling, kayaking. Office: Harvard Sch Pub Health Dept Nutrition 677 Huntington Ave Dept Boston MA 02115-6096*

WILLETT BIRD, SUSAN, public and motivational speaker; m. John R. Campbell. Law degree, Stanford Law Sch. Practiced law Pillsbury, Madison & Sutro, San Francisco; sr. officer Grubb & Ellis Co.; founder, CEO, chief futurist Wf360, LLC (founded as Women.Future), 1999—. Past. pres. Am. Mediation Coun.; spkr. in field. Co-prodr.: (Broadway plays) Jelly's Last Jam. Mem. Women's Leadership bd. Kennedy Sch. Govt., Harvard U.; mem. internat. coun. Kilby Internat. Awards. Recipient NY Bus. award for success and leadership in bus., Crain, Life of City award, NY Woman mag. Mem.: Internat. Women's Forum, Com. of 200 (founding mem., former chair), Law Review. Achievements include facilitated the MainEvent Middle East Road-Show in Dubai, Cairo, and Amman and the Asia/Pacific RoadShow in Japan, China, Singapore, and Australia. Office: Wf360 1345 Ave Americas 18th Fl New York NY 10105 Office Phone: 917-452-0290.

WILLEY, ANDREA, surgeon, researcher; b. Mountain View, Calif., Nov. 20, 1965; d. Helyn Marie Rozenski and William Arthur Horton. MD, U of CA San Francisco Sch. of Medicine, San Francisco, 1996—2000; BS biochemistry, U of CA Davis, Coll. of Letters and Sci., Davis, Calif., 1994—96; Transfer Curriculum, Am. River Coll., Sacramento, CA, 1990—94; Summer Study Abroad Ethics of Medicine and Comparative Healthcare, Mich. State U., London, Eng., UK, 1995; Animal Health Curriculum, Western Career Coll., Sacramento, CA, 1983—84. Physician and Surgeon Med. Bd. of Calif., 2001, Registered Veterinary Technician State of Calif. Dept. of Consumers Affairs, 1984, Medical Training Certificate Ohio Med. Bd., 2002. Registered vet. technician Rio Linda Vet. Technician, Rio Linda, Calif., 1984—89, Sacramento Cat Hosp., Carmicheal, Calif., 1989—94; internal medicine intern Yale U. / Yale New Haven Hosp., New Haven, 2000—01; clin. hair rsch. fellow U. of Calif. San Francisco Dept. of Dermatology, San Francisco, 2001—02; clin. trials fellow dermatology Case Western Res. U / U Hosp. of Cleve., Cleve., 2002—03; resident dermatology U. Minn., Mpls., 2003—. Vol. Sacramento County Rabies Clinics, Sacramento, 1987—89; tutor english, biology, zoology Am. River Coll., Sacramento, 1991—93; peer instr. chemistry Beacon Coll. Found., Sacramento, 1993—94; primary sch. sci. instr. Sci. and Edn. Partnership, San Francisco, 1996—97; vol. student physician Mission Health Fair, San Francisco, 1997; mem. scientific adv. bd. Cicatrical Alopecia Rsch. Fund, 2003—. Author: (journal) Jour. of the Am. Acad. of Dermatology, (professional newsletter) Psoriasis Forum (Nat. Psoriasis Found.), (poster presentation (exhibition) Yale Univ. Internal Medicine Rsch. Day; speaker (scientific presentation) Cleve. Dermatol. Soc. Meeting; singer: (univ. chorus) Univ. of CA, Davis, (women's acapella choir), (acapella choir) UCSF Vocal Chords. Guest spkr. Calif. state legislature Univ. of Calif. Davis, Sacramento, 1996; organized demonstration for a call to action in support of patients not profits UCSF / Nat. Physician Healthcare, San Francisco, 1997. Recipient Outstanding Biology Student, Am. River Coll., 1993, Outstanding Sr., U of Calif. Davis, Coll. of Letters and Sci., 1996, Sunny Side Up Award, Chief Residents at Yale U., 2001; scholar Scholarship Award, William T. Mooney Scholarhship Found., 1983, William T. Mooney Scholarship Found., 1983, Outstanding Scholastic Enthusiasm, Unusual Ambition, Unique Strength of Character, and Extraordinary Personal Initiative, Frank H & Eva B Buck Found., 1993—2000, Soroptimist Tng. Award, Sorptomist Internat., 1992, Scholarship Award, Widowed Persons Assn. Calif., 1993, Calif. Ret. Teacher's Assn., 1993, Regent's Scholar, U of Calif. Regents, 1994—96, Soroptomist Tng. Award, Soroptomist Internat., 1992—93. Mem.: Am. Acad. of Dermatology, USTA, Alpha Gamma Sigma (life), Phi Sigma (life), Phi Kappa Phi (life). Achievements include first to Founding Member ARC Feline Rescue Club; research in Clinical investigation of new therapies for psoriasis, eczema, and other skin diseases; Clinical research in hair disease and the National Alopecia Areata Registry at UCSF. Avocations: tennis, yoga, reading. Office: U Minn Dept Dermatology 420 Deleware St SE MMC 98 Minneapolis MN 55455 Home: 2900 Thomas Ave S Apt 1604 Minneapolis MN 55416-4474 Office Phone: 612-626-5256. Office Fax: 612-624-6678. E-mail: wille057@umn.edu.

WILLEY, CHARLES WAYNE, lawyer; b. Dillon, Mont., Oct. 7, 1932; s. Asa Charles and Elizabeth Ellen Willey; m. Helene D., July 21, 1962 (div.); children: Stephen Charles, Heather Helene, Brent David, Scott D.; m. Alexis W. Grant, Jan. 26, 1986. BS with honors, Mont. State U., 1954; JD with high honors, U. Mont., 1959. Bar: Mont. 1959, Calif. 1960, U.S. Ct. Claims 1975, U.S. Tax Ct. 1975, U.S. Ct. Appeals (9th cir.) 1959, U.S. Ct. Appeals (Fed. cir.) 1983, U.S. Supreme Ct. 1972. Law clk. to presiding judge U.S. Ct. Appeals (9th cir.), 1959-60; ptnr. Price, Postel & Parma, Santa Barbara, Calif., 1960-77; pvt. practice Santa Barbara, 1977-97; shareholder Hollister & Brace, Santa Barbara, 1998-2001. Prof. law corp.; instr. Santa Barbara City Coll., 1961-63, U. Calif., Santa Barbara, 1963-64; lectr. Mont. Tax Inst., 1990, 92, Am. Agr. Law Assn., 1993, 96. Chief editor Mont. Law Rev., 1958-59. Pres. Legal Aid Found. Santa Barbara, 1970; mem. Laguna Blanca Sch. Bd., pres. 1980-81; v.p. Phoenix of Santa Barbara. Served to capt. USAF, 1954-56. Mem. Santa Barbara County Bar Assn. (pres. 1972-73), State Bar of Calif., State Bar of Montana, Phi Kappa Phi, Phi Eta Sigma, Phi Delta Phi. Lodges: Kiwanis. Republican. Episcopalian. Avocations: reading, writing, travel. Office: 806 Parkview Way Missoula MT 59803

WILLEY, JOHN DOUGLAS, retired newspaper executive; b. Melrose, Mass., June 4, 1917; s. Arthur Peach and Lillian (Holden) W.; m. Marilynn Miller, July 3, 1943; children: Margery Lynn Willey Marshall (dec.), John Douglas, James Campbell, David Spencer, Peter Whitney. LLD (hon.), U. Toledo, 1972. Sec. Boston & Maine R.R., Boston, 1935-40, Jones & Lamson Machine Co., Springfield, Vt., 1940-41; reporter The Blade, Toledo, 1946-49, asst. to pub., 1949-51, city editor, 1952-54, asst. mng. editor, 1954-56, dir. pub. rels., 1956-58, treas., 1962-69, assoc. pub., 1965-81, pres., 1969-81, also bd. dirs. Pres. Clear Water, Inc., 1966-89; bd. dirs. Buckeye Cablevision, Inc., Monterey Peninsula Herald; v.p., dir. Lima Communications Corp., 1971-81, Red Bank Register, 1975-81; mem. Ohio adv. bd. Liberty Mut. Ins. Co., 1976-82. Mem. exec. com. of bd. trustees, treas. Toledo Area Med. Coll. and Edn. Found., 1960-75, hon. trustee, 1975—; mem. adv. bd. St. Vincent Hosp., 1961-75; trustee Maumee Valley Country Day Sch., 1974-77, Med. Coll. Ohio, 1982-91; treas. Amateur Athletic Union Task Force Com., 1976-82, Ohio chmn. U.S. Olympic Commn. 1979-80; mem. Inter-Univ. Coun., Ohio, 1988-91. Capt. A.C., U.S. Army, 1942-46. Recipient Disting. Citizen award Med. Coll. Ohio, 1994. Mem. Belmont Country Club, Med. Coll. Ohio Faculty Club, Sigma Delta Chi. Home: 3534 River Rd Toledo OH 43614-4326

WILLEY, WYTHE, lawyer, cattleman, trade association executive; b. 1942; BS in Agriculture, Iowa State U.; JD U. Iowa. Bar: Iowa 1967. Pvt. practice in law, Cedar Rapids, Iowa; farmer, cattleman Jackson, Cedar and Clayton Counties, Iowa. Mem.: Nat. Cattlemen's Beef Assn. (pres., vice chair Blue Ribbon Commn. and Resolutions Com.), Iowa Cattlemen's Assn. (pres. 1995—96, bd. dirs.), Iowa Bar Assn. Office: Willey Law Firm 101 2nd St SE Ste 502 Cedar Rapids IA 52401-1219

WILLHAM, RICHARD LEWIS, animal science educator; b. Hutchinson, Kans., May 4, 1932; s. Oliver S. and Susan E. (Hurt) W.; m. Esther B. Burkhart, June 1, 1954; children: Karen Nell, Oliver Lee. BS, Okla. State U., 1954; MS, Iowa State U., 1955, PhD, 1960. Asst. prof. Iowa State U., Ames, 1959-63, assoc. prof., 1966-71, prof. dept. animal sci., 1971-78, Disting. prof., 1978—; assoc. prof. Okla. State U., Stillwater, 1963-66. Cons. in field; tchr. livestock history; guest curator exhbn. Art About Livestock, 1990. Author: A Heritage of Leadership - The First 100 Years of Animal Science at Iowa State University, 1996. Recipient Svc. award Beef Improvement Fedn., 1974, Edn. and Rsch. award Am. Polled Herefore Assn., 1979, Rsch. award Nat. Cattlemen's Assn., 1986, 91, Disting. Alumnus award Okla. State U., 1978, Regents Faculty Excellence award Iowa State U., 1993; named to Hall of Fame Am. Hereford Assn., 1982, Am. Angus Assn., 1988. Fellow Am. Soc. Animal Sci. (animal breeding and genetics award 1978, industry service award 1986). Home: 2316 Hamilton Dr Ames IA 50014-8201 Office: Iowa State U Dept Animal Sci Ames IA 50011-0001 E-mail: rwillham@iastate.edu.

WILLI, STEVEN MATTHEW, physician, educator, researcher; b. Amityville, N.Y., Apr. 3, 1959; s. John Edward and Doris Mae (Smith) Willi; children: Matthew, Thomas; m. Maria Szpiech, July 27, 2002. BA cum laude, Johns Hopkins U., 1981, MD, 1985. Diplomate in pediatrics and pediatric endocrinology Am. Bd. Pediatrics. Resident in pediat. Children's Hosp. of Phila., 1985—88; fellow in pediatric endocrinology Children's Hosp. Phila., 1988—91; instr. pediat. U. Pa., Phila., 1991—92; asst. prof. pediat. Med. U. S.C., Charleston, 1992—98, assoc. prof., 1998—. Contbr. chpts. to books, articles to profl. jours. Med. dir. Camp Adam Fisher for Children with Diabetes, Summerton, S.C., 1995—; bd. dirs. Juvenile Diabetes Found., 1995-99; dir. Diabetes Ctr. for Children, Children's Hosp. of Phila., 2004—. Recipient Nat. Rsch. Svc. award NIH, 1990, Clin. Assoc. Physician award NIH, 1996; Healfman scholar, 1985. Fellow Am. Acad. Pediatrics; mem. Endocrine Soc., Lawson Wilkins Pediatric Endocrine Soc., Am. Diabetes Assn. (profl. sect., mem. youth svcs. com. 1993—), So. Med. Assn., Charleston County Med. Soc. Avocations: tennis, bicycling, photography, golf. Office: Childrens Hosp of Phila Divsn Endocrinology/Diabetes 34th St Civic Ctr Bldg Philadelphia PA 19104-0001 E-mail: willis@musc.edu.

WILLIAM, DAVID, director, actor; b. London, Eng., June 24, 1926; arrived in Can., 1986; s. Eric Hugh and Olwen (Roose) W. BA, U. Coll., Oxford, Eng., 1950. Artistic dir. Glasgow Citizen's Theatre, The Nottingham Playhouse, The New Shakespeare Co., London, The National Theatre of Israel, Stratford Festival, Can., 1989-93. Vis. prof. theater dept. De Paul U., Chgo., 1985-88; founder, 1st artistic dir. Ludlow Festival. Prof. debut as Rosencrantz to Richard Burton's Hamlet, Old Vic Theatre, London, 1953; theatre directing credits include: Bacchae, The Importance of Being Earnest, The Tempest, Entertaining Mr. Sloane, Love Letters, Treasure Island, Hamlet, Love for Love, The Shoemaker's Holiday, Murder in the Cathedral, Troilus and Cressida, The Winter's Tale, She Stoops to Conquer, Antigone, Separate Tables, Romeo and Juliet, Othello, King Lear, Volpone, Albert Herring, The Merry Wives of Windsor, Twelfth Night; directing world premièrs of operas include: Therese, Royal Opera House Covent Garden, The Lighthouse, Edinburgh festival, Red Emma; other operas directed include Iphigenie en Tauride, The Fairy Queen, Lisbon, La Traviata, Scottish Opera, Il Re Pastore, Camden Festival, Albert Herring, Aldeburgh Festival, Cosl Fan Tutte, Opera St. Louis, Tosca, Can. Opera Co., Mrs. Mozart, Hartford Symphony Orch., 1999; appeared in Uncle Vanya as Serebryakov, As You Like It as Jaques, Twelfth Night as Malvolio; appeared in numerous TV prodns. most notably as Richard the Second in the BBC series An Age of Kings; compiled, directed and acted in My Shakespeare, Stratford Festival and CBC Radio; played A.E.H. in The Invention of Love, Guthrie Theatre, Mpls., 2000, Studio Theater, Washington, 2001, Under Milk Wood, St. Mary's, Ont., 2004. Home: 194 Langarth St E London ON Canada N6C 1Z5

WILLIAMES, LEE JOHN, university official, history educator; b. Phila., July 4, 1942; m. Frances Gray, Feb. 24, 1968; children: Elizabeth, Lee D., David. BA in Pre-Law and Liberal Arts, LaSalle U., 1964; MA in European History, ACS in Soviet Studies, Niagara U., 1966; PhD in History, SUNY, Binghamton, 1981. Prof., honors dir. Coll. Misericordia, Dallas, Pa., 1966-86; asst. provost, prof. U. Scranton, Pa., 1987-92; v.p. acad. affairs, prof. history U. St. Thomas, 1992—2000, acting pres. summer, 1997, now prof. history and emeritus v.p. acad. affairs, 2000—; vis. prof. Mary Immaculate Coll., U. Limerick, Ireland, 2000. Frequent spkr. Russian univs.; sec. gen. internat. coun. U. St. Thomas, 1995-97. Author: Anton Chekov: Iconoclast, 1989; (curriculum exercises) Odyssey of the Mind, 1988-96, written over 20 articles on history and on teaching, Commr. Northeastern Pa. coun. Boy Scouts Am., 1988-92, v.p., 1984-88; mem. water safety bd. ARC, N.E. Pa., 1988-91; chair steering com. St. Thomas/Shell Oil/Helms Collaboration, 1997—. Recipient Silver Beaver medal Boy Scouts Am., 1984, St. George medal Cath. Com. on Scouting, 1986, Jubalarian medal La Salle U., Phila., Centennial medal U. Scranton. Fellow Am. Coun. on Edn. (exec. com. coun. fellows 1989-92); mem. Mid. Atlantic Hist. Assn. of Cath. Colls. and Univs. (editor jour. 1985-92), Am. Assn. for Advancement of Slavic Studies. Roman Catholic. Avocations: swimming, canoeing, martial arts, stained glass, antique restoration. Office: U St Thomas 3800 Montrose Blvd Houston TX 77006-4626 E-mail: williames@stthom.edu.

WILLIAMS, ALAN HAROLD, economics professor; b. Birmingham, Eng., June 9, 1927; s. Harold George and Gladys May (Clarke) W.; m. June Frances Porter, Nov. 9, 1953; children: Mark Alan, Susan Heather, Paul Robert. B Commerce, U. Birmingham, Eng., 1951; DPhil (hon.), U. Lund, Sweden, 1977. Asst. lectr. Exeter (Eng.) U., 1954-57; vis. lectr. MIT, Cambridge, 1957-58; lectr. in econs. Exeter U., 1958-63; vis. fellow Princeton (N.J.) U., 1963-64; sr. lectr. econs. U. York, Eng., 1964-66, reader in econs., 1968-70, prof. econs., 1970—. Dir. econ. studies, Her Majesty's Treasury: Ctr. Adminstrv. Studies, London, 1966-68. Author: Public Finance and Budgetary Policy, 1963, Efficiency in the Social Services, 1975, Principles of Practical Cost-Benefit Analysis, 1978, Being Reasonable About the Economics of Health, 2002; contbr. articles to econs. publs. Mem. Royal Commn. on Nat. Health Svc., London, 1975-77. Cpl. RAF, 1945-48, Middle East. Sr. fellow, Brit. Acad., 2002. Fellow Brit. Acad. (sr.); mem. Royal Econ. Soc., Am. Econ. Assn., Health Economists Study Group. Avocations: music, walking. Office: U York Heslington York Y01 5DD England

WILLIAMS, ALAN KEISER, management consultant; b. Harrisburg, Pa., Dec. 19, 1928; s. Paul Rupp and Margaret Helen (Keiser) W.; m. Barbara Elaine Hanson, Aug. 7, 1952 (div. Aug. 1975); children: Margaret Vivian Williams Westfall, Bryn Barbara Williams Stuart, Andrew Hanson Williams; m. Peggie Lucille Hall, May 29, 1988. BA, U. No. Colo., 1952. Sr. rsch. mgr. Dow Chem. Co., Golden, 1952-74; v.p. Allied-Gen. Nuclear Svc., Barnwell, S.C., 1974-83; prin. engr., project mgr. Bechtel Nat. Inc., San Francisco, 1983-91; sr. program analyst Sci. Applications Internat. Co., Germantown, Md., 1991-95; pvt. cons. Saddlebrooke, Ariz., 1995—. Contbr. articles to Jour. Electro Chem. Soc. Tech. co-chmn. ENC-3 Brussels, 1982. With U.S. Army, 1946-47. Fellow Am. Nuclear Soc. (chmn. Savannah River sect 1980, bd. dirs. 1982-85); mem. AAAS, Am. Chem. Soc. Achievements include research in processing and handling actinide elements, principally uranium, plutonium and americium. Home and Office: 37966 S Flower Mesa Dr Tucson AZ 85739

WILLIAMS, ALEXANDER HAZARD, III, health care executive, consultant; b. N.Y.C., Sept. 14, 1939; s. Alexander Hazard Jr. and Blanche Mildred (Evans) W.; m. Christine Vanderwaker, June 24, 1961 (div. June 1974); children: Alexander Hazard IV, Ashley, James; m. Caroline Lueloff, Feb. 12, 1977 (div. Jan. 1990); m. Monica Traut Dreuth, Nov. 17, 1990. BA, Williams Coll., 1961; MPA, Cornell U., 1963. Vol. Peace Corps, Monrovia, Liberia, 1963-65; asst. adminstr. Evanston (Ill.) Hosp., 1965-68; dir. planning Am. Hosp. Assn., Chgo., 1968-70, dir. N.Y. office, 1970-72; sr. v.p. Chgo., 1987-91; dir. Univ. Hosp. SUNY Downstate, Bklyn., 1972-76; assoc. dir. Univ. Hosp. U. Mich., Ann Arbor, 1976-77; exec. v.p. St. Lukes-Roosevelt Hosp., N.Y.C., 1977-81; exec. v.p., CEO Ch. Charity Found., Hempstead, N.Y., 1981-87; v.p. Witt Kieffer Ford Hadelman, N.Y.C., 1991—. Contbr. chpts. to books. Bd. dirs. Bklyn. YWCA, 1985-86, Nat. Fire Protection Assn., Quincy, Mass., 1990-96, Medic Alert Found., Turlock, Calif., 1990-96, East End Seaport Mus. Found., Greenport, N.Y., 1996—; chmn. bd. Ednl. Commn. Fgn. Med. Grads., Phila., 1991-2001, Ea. L.I. Hosp., 2000—. Mem. Williams Club N.Y., Cornell Club. Avocation: sailing. Home: 3520 N Lake Shore Dr Chicago IL 60657 Office: Witt/Kieffer Ford Hadelman & Lloyd 2015 Spring Rd Chicago IL 60523

WILLIAMS, ALFRED BLYTHE, retired management consultant; b. Oakland City, Ind., Sept. 17, 1940; s. Ross Merl and Jesse Adell (Helsley) W. BS cum laude, Oakland City U., 1963; MS, Ind. U., 1964; PhD, Ga. State U., 1974. Tchr. Arlington H.S., Indpls., 1964-65, Oakland City (Ind.) U., 1965-69; editor Southwestern Pub. Co., Cin., 1969-72, cons., 1981-93; adj. prof. Ga. State U., Atlanta, 1972-74; prof. mgmt. and bus. comm. U. La., Lafayette, 1975—2002, chmn. dept., 1986-96, prof. emeritus, 2002—; ret., 2002. Cons. John Wiley Pub. Co., N.Y., 1988-89, Irwin Pub., 1989. Author study guides; editor Info. Systems Bus. Comm. Jour., 1983, 93. Patron Lafayette Cmty. Concerts, 1984—; contbr. La. and Nat. Rep. parties, Baton Rouge, Washington, 1983—. Mem. AAUP, Assn. Bus. Communicators (bd. dirs. 1986-90, Francis W. Weeks Merit award 1984), La. Assn. Higher Edn., Sierra Club, Kiwanis, Phi Delta Kappa, Phi Kappa Phi, Delta Pi Epsilon, Beta Gamma Sigma. Methodist.

WILLIAMS, ALUN, artist, curator, art gallery director; b. Manchester, Eng., Apr. 28, 1961; arrived in U.S., 1999; s. Frank and Margaret R. Williams. BA, U. Coll. Wales, Aberystwyth, 1983; MFA, U. London, 1987. Founder, pres. Triangle France Internat. Studio and Exhbn. Program, Marseille, France, 1994—; founder, dir. Parker's Box Gallery, Bklyn., 2000—. Bd. dirs. Triangle Arts Assn., N.Y.C., 1993—; founder, v.p. La Vigie Art Contemporain, Nîmes, France, 1992—. Exhibitions include (Nowhere Better) Metaphysical Effigy of John Adams, Oni Gallery, Boston, 2003, Tour du Roi Rene, Marseille, 1995, residency, exhibition, Gasworks Gallery, London (French Embassy, 2001), 10 year retrospective, Galerie Raph Debarrn, Paris and Nice, 1993. Recipient Artist's award, Welsh Arts Coun., 1983, Exhbn. award, Brit. Coun., 1988, Can. Coun., 1992, Travel award, French Ministry of Fgn. Affairs, 1992, Creativity award, French Ministry of Culture, 1996, Chevalier de l'Ordre des Arts des Lettres, France, 2004. Achievements include marathon runner 2nd masters 9th overall N.J. Marathon, 2003. Office: Parker's Box 193 Grand St Brooklyn NY 11211 E-mail: info@parkersbox.com.

WILLIAMS, ANASTASIA P. state legislator; b. Panama, May 6, 1957; children: Lisa, Dianne, Jonnathon, Eddy. Grad., Bishop Keough Regional H.S., 1976. Mem. R.I. Ho. of Dels. Mem. West Elmhood Devel. Corp., R.I. Housing & Mortgage, Hartford Cmty. Park. Democrat. Office: RI Ho of Reps State Capitol Providence RI 02903

WILLIAMS, ANDREA IRENE, arbitrator, mediator, consultant; d. Jerome Seymour S. and Rosalind Rita Shulman; m. Charles Frank Dewey, July 28, 1978; children: Laura Lynne, Mark Closs. BA, Cornell U., Ithaca, N.Y., 1965; MA, Columbia U., N.Y.C., 1966, JD, 1970. Bar: SD 1970, Colo. 1971, U.S. Dist. Ct., Colo. 1971, 10th Circuit Ct. of Appeals 1971, U.S. Supreme Ct. 1985. Tchr. history Roslyn (N.Y.) High Sch., 1965—67; staff atty. Rosebud Legal Svcs., Rosebud Sioux Indian Reservation, SD, 1970—71; assoc., ptnr., of counsel Davis, Graham & Stubbs, Denver, 1971—93; cons. leadership and collaboration Andrea Williams, Denver, 1993—. Adj. prof. U. Denver, 1992—94. Contbr. articles, chapters to books. Mem. since 1996 President's Coun. of Cornell Women, Ithaca, NY; pres. Lawyers for Colo.'s Women, Inc., Denver, 1975—78; mem., magistrate selection panel U.S. D.C. for the Dist. of Colo., Denver, 1981; co-chair Colo. Women's Leadership Coalition, Denver, 1994—95; bd. mem. Girls Count, Denver, 1997—2001; bd. dirs. Women's Vision Found., Denver, 1995—; v.p. Pres.'s Coun. Cornell Women, Ithaca, 2002—; bd. dirs. Alliance Profl. Women, Denver, 1993—98. Recipient Leader of Excellence, Colo. Women's Leadership Conf., 1996; Harlan Fiske Stone scholar, Columbia U. Sch. of Law, 1970. Mem.: Am. Arbitration Assn. (arbitrator 1993—, mediator 1993—, fact-finder 1993—), Denver Bar Assn. (trustee 1973—76), Colo. Bar Assn. (bd. govs. 1976—78), Alumnae of Columbia Law Sch. Office: Cons Leadership and Collaboration 460 S Marion Parkway Ste 1804C Denver CO 80209 E-mail: anwillia@du.edu.

WILLIAMS, ANDREW W. energy executive; Degree, N.C. State U., 1971; MBA, Loyola Coll., 1984. From v.p. energy and mkt. policy and devel. to sr. v.p., CFO Pepco Holdings, Washington, 1994—2000, sr. v.p., 2000—, CFO, 2000—. Office: Pepco Holdings 701 Ninth St NW Room 4230 Washington DC 20068

WILLIAMS, ANITA MARIE, publishing executive, writer; b. Detroit, Feb. 4, 1963; d. Lawrence Trevone Bartell and Bernadia Hankerson; m. Paul Thomas Williams, Jr., Aug. 25, 1984 (dec. Oct. 16, 1991); children: Ebony Renee, Paul Thomas David III. BA in Africana Studies cum laude, BA in Speech Comm., Wayne State U., 1999, MA in African-Am./African History, 2003. CEO/founder Metro Detroit Intellectual Soc., Detroit, 1997—; CEO AfricanPrincess0204 Photos, Detroit, 1997—; founder, CEO Creating a Legacy for Our Sister and Daughters, Detroit, 1999—; columnist Gazette News, Detroit, 1999—2000, My Life Time Mag., Detroit, 2003. Author, rschr.: historical biography Katherine Dunham: An African-American Cultural Icon; photo exhbn., Eyes of the AfricanPrincess0204; author: (photographic essay) Eyes of the AfricanPrincess0204; prodr.: (multi-media cd) Eyes of the AfricanPrincess0204, Hankerson Family Reunion. Recipient Coleman A. Young scholarship, Africana Studies Dept., Wayne State U., 1998, Dudley Randall scholarship, 1997, Mich. Nat. Bank/Detroit Urban League scholarship, Detroit Urban League, 1999, Dudley Randall scholarship, Africana Studies Dept., Wayne State U., 1998, Coleman Young scholarship, 1999. Achievements include research in Uncovering pertinent data pertaining to the African Diaspora. Personal E-mail: awill27595@aol.com.

WILLIAMS, ANN CLAIRE, federal judge; b. Detroit, Aug. 16, 1949; m. David J. Stewart. BS, Wayne State U., 1970; MA, U. Mich., 1972; JD, U. Notre Dame, 1975; hon. degree, Lake Forest Coll., 1987, U. Portland, 1993, U. Notre Dame, 1997. Law clk. to Hon. Robert A. Sprecher, 1975-76; asst. U.S. atty. U.S. Dist. Ct. (no. dist.) Ill., Chgo., 1976-85; faculty Nat. Inst. for Trial Advocacy, 1979—, also bd. dirs.; adj. prof., lectr. Northwestern U. Law Sch., 1979—, John Marshall Law Sch., 1979—; judge U.S. Dist. Ct. (no. dist.) Ill., 1985-99, U.S. Ct. Appeals (7th cir.), Chgo., 1999—. Chief Organized Crime Drug Enforcement Task Force for North Ctrl. Region, 1983-85; mem. ct. adminstrn. and case mgmt. com. Jud. Conf. U.S., 1990-97, chair, 1993-97. Sec. bd. trustees U. Notre Dame; founder Minority Legal Resources, Inc. Recipient Earl Burns Dickerson award, Chgo. Bar Assn., 1997, Tradition of Excellence award, Minority Legal Resources, Inc., 1997, Thurgood Marshall Jurist of Year, Legal Ministry of Second Baptist Church, 1997, Alumni of Year, Black Law Students Assn, U. Notre Dame, 1997. Mem. FBA, Fed. Judges Assn., Ill. State Bar Assn., Ill. Jud. Coun., Cook County Bar Assn., Women's Bar Assn. Ill., Black Women's Lawyers Assn. Greater Chgo. Office: US Ct Appeals 7th Circuit 219 S Dearborn St Ste 2612 Chicago IL 60604-1803*

WILLIAMS, ANNETTE POLLY, state legislator; b. Belzoni, Miss., Jan. 10, 1937; Student, Milw. Area Tech. Coll.; BS, U. Wis. Mem. Wis. State Assembly, Milw., 1980—. Attendee African-Am. Leadership summit, New Orleans; organizer Com. 21, 1985, Black Ribbon Commn. to study forced busing, Milw., 1989; panelist Nat. Conf. State Legislators, 1989; active parental sch. choice legislation; lectr. numerous colls. and univs. T.V. appearances include 60 Minutes, ABC World News, This Week with David Brinkley, McNeil Lehrer Report, The British Broadcasting Company, Great Lakes Watch on Washington, CBS This Morning, Both Sides with Rev. Jesse Jackson, CNN News; contbr. articles to profl. jours. Dem. adminstrv. and exec. com.; state chairperson Wis. Jesse Jackson for Pres. campaign; del. Nat. Dem. Conv., 1984, 88; mem. Nat. Dem. Platform Com., 1984; bd. dirs. Rainbow Coalition; founder, chmn. bd. dirs. Milw. Parental Assistance Ctr. Recipient

Carrie Chapman Catt award as Nat. Women's Bus. Advocate of Yr., Outstanding Leadership award Dem. party Wis., Harambee Martin Luther King Jr. award for Outstanding Accomplishment and Svc. Am. Legis. Exchange Coun., 1991, Nat. Human Rights award Nat. Cath. Ednl. Assn., 1992, Seton award Career Youth Devel., 1992, Image award for Excellence in Community Svc. and Love of Youth Gamma Phi Delta, 1992, Community Leadership award Libertarian Party Wis., 1992, Liberty award, 1993, Martin Luther King Jr. Community Svc. award Lydell Comm., 1994; named Legislator of Yr. Freedom Mag., 1992; vis. fellow Auckland (New Zealand) Inst. Tech., 1993. Mem. Nat. Black Caucus State Legislators (bd. dirs.). Home: 3927 N 16th St Milwaukee WI 53206-2918 Office: Wis State Assembly State Capitol PO Box 8953 Madison WI 53708-8953

WILLIAMS, ANTHONY A. mayor; b. 1951; s. Lewis and Virginia W.; m. Diana Lynn Simmons; 1 child, Asantewa Foster. BA in Polit. Sci. magna cum laude, Yale U., 1982; JD, M of Pub. Policy, Harvard U., 1987. Law clk. to Hon. David Nelson US Dist. Ct., Boston, 1987-88; asst. dir. Boston Redevel. Authority, 1988-89; exec. dir. Cmty. Devel. Agy., St. Louis, 1989-91; dep. comptr. State of Conn., Boston, 1991-93; exec. dir. Cmty. Devel. Agy., St. Louis, 1989-91; dept. contr. State of Conn., 1991-93; CFO Dept. Agr., Washington, 1995—98; mayor Washington DC, 1999—. Adj. prof. pub. affairs Columbia U., NYC, 1992-93. Pres. pro tempore, chmn. cmty. devel. com. Conn. Bd. Alderman, 1980-83; dir. comm. Conn. Spkr. House and Assembly Dem., 1983; second v.p., Washington, DC-based National League of Cities (NLC), 2002-. Kellogg Found. Nat. fellow, 1991. Democrat. Office: Office of the Mayor 1350 Pennsylvania Ave NW 6th Fl Washington DC 20004

WILLIAMS, ARTHUR BENJAMIN, JR., bishop; b. Providence, June 25, 1935; m. Lynette Rhodes, 1985. AB, Brown U., 1957; MDiv, Gen. Theol. Sem., 1964; MA, U. Mich., 1974; DD, Gen. Theol. Sem., 1986. Clarence Horner fellow Grace Ch., Providence, 1964-65; asst. St. Mark, Riverside, R.I., 1965-67; sub-dean St. John Cathedral, Providence, 1967-68; assoc. & interim rector Grace Ch., Detroit, 1968-70; asst. to bishop Diocese of Mich., 1970-77; archdeacon Ohio Cleve., 1977-85; suffragan bishop Episcopal Diocese of Ohio, Cleve., 1986—; v.p. House of Bishops, 1995—. Chair Com. on Justice, Peace and Integrity of Creation, 1995-97; Epsicopal vis. Order of St. Benedict, 2000—. Chair editl. com. Lift Every Voice and Sing II, 1993. Episcopalian. Office: Diocese of Ohio 2230 Euclid Ave Cleveland OH 44115-2499 E-mail: bishsuff@dohio.org.

WILLIAMS, ARTHUR ROSS, health service and public administrator; b. Dayton, Ohio, June 11, 1946; s. Russell W. Sr. and Violet Ross Williams; m. Phoebe Dauz, Aug. 10, 1972; children: Arthur, Diane, David. BA, Wright State U., 1968; MPA, U. Pitts., 1972; MA in Econ., U. Philippines, 1976; PhD, Cornell U., 1981. Asst. to mgr. City of Dayton, Ohio, 1968-70, Twp. of Mt. Lebanon, Pa., 1970-72; rsch. assoc. Cornell U., Ithaca, N.Y., 1976-80; prof. U. Philippines, Diliman, 1976-81; project dir. Robert Wood Johnson Found., Gainesville, Fla., 1982-84; prof. U. Fla., Gainesville, 1984-90, U. Mo., Kansas City, 1990—2002; chair Health Care Policy and Rsch. Mayo Clinic, Rochester, Minn., 2002—. Cons. U.S. Agy. for Internat. Devel., Manila, 1976-82, Rockefeller Found., Manila, 1974-78; cons., grant dir. Ford Found., Manila, 1976-80; methodology cons. U.S. Dept. of Health and Human Svcs., Washington, 1990-96. Author: Measuring Local Government Performance, 1981, (with others) Path Analysis, 1994, Individual, Family and Community, 2000, Klinische Ökonomik, 2003; contbr. articles to profl. jours. Mem. Friends of Art, Kansas City, Ams. for Dem. Action, Washington; dir. health svcs. rsch. Mo. Assn. for Social Welfare, Jefferson City, Mo. Henry Luce Faculty fellow Luce Found., 1990, Andrew Mellon fellow U. Pitts., 1971-72, Fulbright Rsch. scholar, 2000-01; recipient De la Costa award Philippine-Am. Ednl. Found., 1981. Fellow Philippine Econ. Soc. (life), Am. Pub. Health Assn., Acad. Health, Soc. for Epidemiologic Rsch., Am. Polit. Sci. Assn. (sect. chair), Am. Econ. Assn., Am. Soc. for Pub. Adminstrn. Avocations: chess, stamp collecting/philately, reading, walking, swimming. Home: # 302 600 4th St SW Rochester MN 55902 Office: Divsn Health Care Policy & Rsch Mayo Clin Rochester MN 55905 Business E-Mail: williams.arthur@mayo.edu.

WILLIAMS, B. JOHN, JR., former federal agency administrator, lawyer; b. Lancaster, Pa., Dec. 13, 1949; s. Bernard John and Sarah Elizabeth (Sykes) W.; m. Martha Caroline Roberts, Aug. 6, 1977; children: Robert, Sarah, Anne, Bernard. BA, George Washington U., 1971, JD, 1974. Bar: D.C., Pa., U.S. Tax Ct., U.S. Ct. Appeals (3rd, 9th and fed. cirs.), U.S. Supreme Ct. Law clk. to judge U.S. Tax Ct., Washington, 1974-76; assoc. Ballard, Spahr, Andrews & Ingersoll, Phila., 1976-81; spl. asst. to chief counsel IRS, Washington, 1981-83; dep. asst. atty. gen. Tax Div. Dept. Justice, Washington, 1983-84; ptnr. Morgan, Lewis & Bockius, Washington, 1984-85; judge U.S. Tax Ct., Washington, 1985-90; ptnr. Morgan, Lewis & Bockius, Washington, 1990-2000, Shearman & Sterling, Washington, 2000—02; chief counsel, IRS U.S. Dept. Treasury, Washington, 2002—03. Mem. adv. com. U.S. Ct. Appeals, Fed. Cir. Fellow Am. Coll. Tax Counsel; mem. ABA, Am. Law Inst., Phi Beta Kappa, Omicron Delta Kappa. Republican.

WILLIAMS, BARBARA ANNE, retired academic administrator; b. Camden, N.J., Oct. 14, 1938; d. Frank and Laura Dorothy (Szweda) W. BA cum laude, Georgian Ct. U., 1963; MLS, Rutgers U., 1965; MA, Manhattan Coll., 1973; postgrad., NYU, 1976—81, postgrad., 1993—. Cert. English tchr., N.J.; joined Sisters of Mercy, 1957. Sec. Camden Cath. H.S., 1956-57; registrar Georgian Ct. U., Lakewood, NJ, 1960-66, dir. libr. svcs., 1966-74, dean acad. affairs, 1974-80, pres., 1980-2000, sci. and math. libr., 2000—, pres. emerita, 2000—, archivist, 2003—. Bd. dirs. N.J. Natural Gas Co., 1986-91. Mem. editl. bd. N.J. Woman mag. Bd. dirs., mem. ednl. adv. coun. Diocese of Trenton, N.J., 1983-90; mem. adv. bd. Ocean County Ctr. for Arts, Lakewood, N.J., 1983-91; mem. Ocean County Pvt. Industry Coun., 1983-92; bd. dirs. Monmouth/Ocean Devel. Coun., 1981-84; mem. State of N.J. Student Assistance Bd., 1995-99; mem. Ocean County School-to-Career Com., 1996-2000; mem. art adv. coun. Nat. Mus. Cath. Art and History, 2000—. Named Outstanding Woman N.J. Assn. Women Bus. Owners, 1983; recipient Humanitarian award Monmouth/Ocean Devel. Coun., 1985, Salute to Policymakers award Exec. Women N.J., 1986, Woman in Leadership award Monmouth Coun. Girl Scouts, 1987, Citizen of Yr. Alcoholism & Drug Abuse Coun. Ocean County, 1993, Brotherhood/Sisterhood award Monmouth/Ocean County chpts. NCCJ, 1994, Friend of Scouting award Boy Scouts Am. Jersey Shore Coun., 1999, Leadership award Mercy Higher Edn. Colloquium, 2000. Mem. Assn. of Mercy Colls. (pres. 1981-83, sec. 1996-98), Mercy Higher Edn. Colloquium (mem. exec. com. 1980-87), Ocean County Bus. Assn. (trustee 1982-84), Nat. Assn. Inc. Colls. and Univs. (secretariat 1981-83, 87-91), NAIA (coun. of pres. 1997-2000). Home and Office: Georgian Ct Univ 900 Lakewood Ave Lakewood NJ 08701-2600 Office Phone: 732-987-2441. E-mail: williamssb@georgian.edu.

WILLIAMS, BARBARA IVORY, educational researcher; b. Detroit, Apr. 28, 1936; d. Henry Oliver and Willa Mae (Frazier) I.; m. Alney Elliott Whitener, Jan. 1, 1987. BS, Wayne State U., 1957, MEd, 1960; PhD, U. Washington, 1973. Tchr. Detroit Pub. Schs., 1957-68; program assoc. Mich.-Ohio Regional Lab., Detroit, 1968-70; lectr. predoctoral U. Wash., Seattle, 1970-73; sr. program assoc. Far West Lab. for Ednl. Research and Devel., San Francisco, 1973-76; sr. cons. E.H. White & Co., San Francisco, 1976-77; sr. program assoc. Northwest Regional Lab., Portland, Oreg., 1977-84; area coord. Ednl. Testing Service, Washington, 1984-85; edn. group dir. Research and Evaluation Assocs., Washington, 1985-87; ind. cons. Washington, 1987-89; assoc. dir. edn. studies Westat, Rockville, Md., 1989—. Mem. Am. Ednl. Research Assn., Am. Psychol. Assn., Nat. Assn. Black Sch. Educators, Phi Delta Kappa, Alpha Kappa Alpha (pres. Portland chpt. 1980-84). Democrat. Baptist. Avocations: desk top publishing, needle work. Home: 15320 Pine Orchard Dr Apt 2F Silver Spring MD 20906-8315

WILLIAMS, BARBARA STAMBAUGH, editor; b. Jenkins, Ky., Nov. 22, 1937; d. James Cosby and Jessie Kate (Bise) Stambaugh; m. Manning Williams, Sept. 11, 1963. BS in Journalism, U. Tenn., 1959. Polit. reporter News and Courier, Charleston, S.C., 1961-63, 67-76, asst. mng. editor, 1976-81; city hall reporter Camden (N.J.) Courier Post, 1963-67; editor The Evening Post, Charleston, S.C., 1981-90, The Evening Post and News Courier, Charleston, S.C., 1990-91, The Post and Courier, Charleston, S.C., 1991—. Pres. Nat. Conf. Editl. Writers, Rockville, Md., 1992. Bd. dirs. Charleston Sci. and Cultural Edn. Fund. Named Outstanding Newspaper Woman in S.C., S.C. Press Assn., 1962. Mem. Sigma Delta Chi (ByLiner award 1973). Office: The Post & Courier 134 Columbus St Charleston SC 29403-4800 E-mail: barbara@postandcourier.com.

WILLIAMS, BERNARD, Olympic athlete; b. Balt., Jan. 19, 1978; Student, Barton County C.C., Great Bend, Kans., U. Fla., 2000—. Co-winner Gold Medal 4X100 meter relay U.S.A. Track and Field Team, Sydney, 2000; gold medal 4x100m relay US World Outdoor Champions, 2001. Office: USA Track and Field Team One RCA Dome Ste 140 Indianapolis IN 46225

WILLIAMS, BERNIE (BERNABE FIGUEROA WILLIAMS), professional baseball player; b. San Juan, P.R., Sept. 13, 1968; Outfielder New York Yankees, 1991—. Named ALCS MVP, 1996; named to Am. League All-Star team, 1997—2001; recipient Am. League Gold Glove Award, 1997—2000. Achievements include mem. World Series Champion New York Yankees, 1996, 1998-2000; led Am. League in batting avg. (.339), 1998. Office: New York Yankees Yankee Stadium E 161 St and River Ave Bronx NY 10451*

WILLIAMS, BETTY, peace activist; b. Belfast, Northern Ireland, May 22, 1943; m. Ralph Williams, 1961 (div.); 2 children; m. James T. Perkins, 1983. LL.D. (hon.), Yale U.; L.H.D. (hon.), Coll. Siera Heights, 1977. Co-organizer (with Mairead Corrigan) of movement Women for Peace (now Community of Peace People), Belfast, 1976-80. Co-founder (with Mairead Corrigan) mag. Peace by Peace. Co-recipient Nobel Prize for Peace for 1976 (awarded 1977), Norwegian People's Peace Prize, 1976, Carl von Ossietzky prize German Fed. Republic, 1976. Roman Catholic. Address: 208 Camelia St Gulf Breeze FL 32561-4228 also: PO Box 725 Valparaiso FL 32580-0725

WILLIAMS, BOBBY See EVERHART, ROBERT

WILLIAMS, BRADLEY ROBERT, pharmacy and gerontology educator, consultant; b. LA, Sept. 22, 1953; s. Raymond Ewell and Frances Williams; m. Marilyn D. Williams, July 17, 1976; children: Sean, Shannon. PharmD, U. So. Calif., 1977. Lic. pharmacist, Calif. Pharmacist coord. Beverly Enterprises, Pasadena, Calif., 1978-79; resident in geriatric pharmacy U. So. Calif., L.A., 1977-78, asst. prof. pharmacy and gerontology, 1979-89, assoc. prof., 1989—. Competency com. Calif. Bd. Pharmacy, Sacramento, 1988-99; dir. geriat. pharmacy Rancho Los Amigos Nat. Rehab. Hosp., Downey, Calif., 1991-2003; med. and sci. adv. bd. Alzheimer's Assn., LA, 1992-94; mem. Commn. for Cert. in Geriat. Pharmacy, Alexandria, Va., 1997—, chmn., 2000-01; rsch. subcontractor Archstone Found., LA, 1999-2002. Author: Applied Therapeutics—The Clinical Use of Drugs, 1995, 3rd edit., 2004; editor: Clinical Pharmacology and Nursing, 1996; contbr. articles to profl. jours. Merit badge counselor Boy Scouts Am., Lomita, Calif., 1999—. Rsch. grantee, John A. Hartford Found., 1989, Adminstrn. on Aging, 1989, Health Resources and Svcs. Adminstrn., 2003. Fellow Am. Soc. Cons. Pharmacists (George F. Archambault award 2003); mem. Am. Soc. Health Sys. Pharmacists (geriat. network liaison 1996-98), Am. Geriat. Soc., Gerontol. Soc. Am. Democrat. Roman Catholic. Avocations: photography, hiking. Office: U So Calif 1985 Zonal Ave Los Angeles CA 90089-0121

WILLIAMS, BRIAN, news anchor, correspondent; m. Jane Stoddard; 2 children. Student, George Washington U., Cath. U. Am.; Doctorate (hon.), Elmira Coll. Corr. various stas., Phila., Washington, Pittsburgh, Kans.; anchor, corr. Sta. WCBS-TV, N.Y.C.; anchor, mng. editor NBC Nightly News Sat., N.Y.C., 1993—99; chief White House corr. NBC, Washington, 1994—96; permanent substitute host Nightly News with Tom Brokaw, N.Y.C.; anchor, The News with Brian Williams MSNBC/CNBC, N.Y.C., 1996—. Named Father of Yr., Nat. Father's Day Com., 1996; recipient Emmy award, 1987, 1993, 2001. Office: c/o MSNBC NBC/Microsoft Corp 1 Msnbc Blvd Secaucus NJ 07094-2419

WILLIAMS, BROWN F, media services company executive; b. Evanston, Ill., Dec. 22, 1940; s. Jack Kermit Williams and Virginia Helen (Benjamin) Likar; m. Linda Francee Ludt, Sept. 1961 (div. 1968); 1 child, Eden Carol Williams McCarthy; m. Martha Amidon Powers, Sept. 1970 (div. 1974); m. Sandra Ann Matkowski, Jan. 1984 (dec. May 2000); 1 child, Bronwyn Emily. AB in Math. and Physics, U. Calif., Riverside, 1962, MA in Physics, 1964, PhD in Physics, 1966. Mgr. Electro-Optics Lab., Princeton, N.J., 1969-75; dir. RCA Labs., Princeton, 1976-82, v.p., 1982-87; pres. Williams Cons. Group, Princeton, 1988-90. Chmn. Princeton Video Image, 1990—. Fellow IEEE; mem. AAAS, Am. Phys. Soc., Sigma Xi. Avocations: skiing, ocean sailing, horses. Office: 27 Honey Brook Dr Princeton NJ 08540-7408 E-mail: bfwilliams1@comcast.net.

WILLIAMS, BRYAN, dean, medical educator; b. Longview, Tex., July 28; s. Lewis Bryan and Margaret Louise (Smart) W.; m. Frances Montgomery, Mar. 31, 1950; children: Harrison, Amy, Philip, Nickolas, Margaret, Lincoln. MD, Southwestern Med. Sch., 1947. Diplomate Am. Bd. Internal Medicine. Pvt. practice, Dallas, 1957-70; prof. internal medicine, assoc. dean student affairs Southwestern Med. Sch., 1970-90, prof. internal medicine emeritus, dean student affairs emeritus. Fellow ACP; mem. Inst. Medicine Nat. Acad. Scis. (charter). Home: 1215 Old Bethany Rd Allen TX 75013

WILLIAMS, C. JAMES, III, (JIM WILLIAMS), lawyer; b. Verdun, Alsace, France, Dec. 8, 1960; s. Charles James Jr. and Monique Marielouise (Masure) W.; m. Elizabeth H. (Kessler) W.; 5 children. BS, George Mason U., 1983, JD, 1987. Bar: Va. 1987, U.S. Dist. Ct. Va. 1988, U.S. Ct. Appeals (4th cir.) 1988. Evaluator U.S. Gen. Acctg. Office, Washington, 1980-87; law clk. U.S. Dist. Ct. (we. dist.) Va., Big Stone Gap, 1987-88; assoc. Gentry, Locke, Rakes & Moore, Roanoke, Va., 1988—91, Morris & Morris, PC, 1991—93; house counsel mgr. Progressive Ins. Co., 1993—99; ptnr. Marks & Williams PC, Hopewell, Va., 1999—. Chmn. Roanoke City Rep. Com., 1990-91. Named Chevalier Order of Demolay, 1982. Mem. Masons. Republican. Roman Catholic. Avocations: private piloting, skiing. Office: Marks & Williams PC PO Box 27 Hopewell VA 23860 Office Phone: 703-458-1800. E-mail: cjwilliamsIII@aol.com.

WILLIAMS, CALVIT HERNDON, retired chemist; b. Houston, Dec. 28, 1936; s. Calvit Herndon and Julia Eloise Williams; children: Sabina, Terence, Russel, Damon. BA in Chemistry, U. St. Thomas, Houston, 1958; PhD in Phys. Chemistry, Brown U., 1965. Cert. indsl. hygienist, safety profl.; qualified environ. profl. Postdoctoral fellow Rice U., Houston, 1964-66; rsch. scientist Sandia Labs., Albuquerque, 1966-70; prof. chemistry U. Estadual De Sao Paulo En Campinas, Brazil, 1971-76; lab. dir. Aer-Aqua Labs. Inc., Houston, 1976-77; prin. scientist URS/Radian Corp., Austin, Tex., 1977—2004; ret., 2004. Author: Chlorinated Dioxins and Furans, 1985; contbg. author: Principles of Environmental Sampling, 1996. Fellow Am. Indsl. Hygiene Assn. (com. chair-elect 1994, chmn. 1995, bd. dirs. 1992-93, 94-99, chmn. bd. 1990-92), Am. Inst. Chemists; mem. Am. Chem. Soc. (chmn. ctrl. Tex. chpt. 1980-82), Austin C. of C. (Leadership Austin 1992-93), N.Y. Acad. Sci., Am. Soc. Safety Engrs., Sigma Xi, Delta Epsilon Sigma. Achievements include development of numerous strategies and methods for environmental health monitoring, especially for ambient, indoor and workplace air. Mailing: PO Box 201088 Austin TX 78720-1088

WILLIAMS, CAMILLA, soprano, voice educator; b. Danville, Va. d. Booker and Fannie (Cary) W.; m. Charles T. Beavers, Aug. 28, 1950. BS, Va. State Coll., 1941; postgrad., U. Pa., 1942; studies with, Mme. Marian Szekely-Freschl, 1943-44, 1952, Berkowitz and Cesare Sodero, 1944-46, Rose Dirman, 1948-52, Sergius Kagen, 1958-62; MusD (hon.), Va. State U., 1986, D. (hon.), 1985. Prof. voice Bronx Coll., N.Y.C., 1970, Bklyn. Coll., 1970-73, Queens Coll., N.Y.C., 1974, Ind. U., Bloomington, 1977—, prof. emeritus voice. 1st black prof. voice Cen. Conservatory Music, Beijing, People's Republic China, 1983. Created role of Madame Butterfly as 1st black contract singer, N.Y.C. Ctr., 1946, 1st Aida, 1948; 1st N.Y. performance of Mozart's Idomeneo with Little Orch. Soc., 1950; 1st Viennese performance Menotti's Saint of Bleecker Street, 1955; 1st N.Y. performance of Handel's Orlando, 1971; other roles include Nedda in Pagliacci, Mimi in La Boheme, Marguerite in Faust; major tours include Alaska, 1950, London, 1954, Am. Festival in Belgium, 1955, tour of 14 African countries for U.S. Dept. State, 1958-59, Israel, 1959, concert for Crown Prince of Japan as guest of Gen. Eisenhower, 1960, tour of Formosa, Australia, New Zealand, Korea, Japan, Philippines, Laos, South Vietnam, 1971, Poland, 1974; appearances with orchs. including Royal Philharm., Vienna Symphony, Berlin Philharm., Chgo. Symphony, Phila. Orch., BBC Orch., Stuttgart Orch., many others; contract with RCA Victor as exclusive Victor Red Seal rec. artist, 1944—. Recipient Marian Anderson award (1st winner), 1943, 44, Newspaper Guild award as First Lady of Am. Opera, 1947, Va. State Coll. 75th anniv. cert. of merit, 1957, NYU Presdl. Citation, 1959, Gold medal Emperor of Ethiopia and Key to City of Taiwan during Pres. Johnson's Cultural Exchange Program, 1962, Art, Culture and Civic Guild award, 1962, Negro Musician's Assn. plaque, 1963, Harlem Opera and World Fellowship Soc. award, 1963; named Disting. Virginian Gov. of Va., 1972; inducted Danville (Va.) Mus. Fine Arts and History Hall of Fame, 1974; Camilla Williams Park designated in her honor, Danville, 1974; honored by Ind. U. Sch. Music Black Music Students' Orgn., 1979; named to Hon. Order Ky. Cols., 1979; honored by Phila. Pro Arte Soc., 1982; Disting. award of Ctr. for Leadership and Devel., 1983; Taylor-Williams student residence hall at Va. State U. named in Billy Taylor's and her honor, 1985, hon. by New York Philharmonic, 1998, hon. by Amistad Rsch. Ctr., Tulane Univ., for Outstanding Contbn. to the Arts, 1998. Mem. NAACP (hon. life), Internat. Platform Assn., Alpha Kappa Alpha. Office: Ind U Sch Music Bloomington IN 47401 *Years of travel have given me the chance to meet people of every race, kind, and condition. I have been a witness to the brotherhood and sisterhood of mankind, for we are all children of God. The most important lesson of my life is the value of giving. When you give of yourself you receive the blessings of your talents.*

WILLIAMS, CARL CHANSON, insurance company executive; b. Cin., Oct. 16, 1937; s. Charles J. and Alcie (Brazile) W.; m. Claire Bathé, May 26, 1985; 1 child, Michelle. A.S., U. Cin., 1965; BS, SUNY-Brockport, 1974; MBA, U. Rochester, 1975. Mgr. fin. systems Xerox Corp., Rochester, N.Y., 1972-77; dir. info. mgmt. Am. Can Co., Greenwich, Conn., 1977-79, mng. dir. info. mgmt., 1979-80, mng. dir. ops. control, 1980-82; sr. v.p., dir. mgmt. info. systems DDB Needham Worldwide, N.Y.C., 1982-91; pres. The Intertechnology Group, Inc., N.Y.C., 1990-91; v.p. infosystems and tech. Macmillan Pub. Co., N.Y.C., 1991-93; gen. mgr. info. tech. Amoco Corp., Chgo., 1993-94, v.p. info. tech., 1994-97; sr. v.p., chief info. officer Principal Fin. Group, Des Moines, Iowa, 1997—. Cons. Stamford (Conn.) Bd. Edn., 1981-82; lectr. U. Rochester, N.Y., 1975-77; adj. prof. Fordham U., 1991—. Exec. dir. Concerned Assn. Rochester, N.Y., 1971-75; bd. dirs. Stamford Cmty. Arts Coun., 1983-84; trustee Roosevelt U., 1995-97, U. Rochester, 1999—, Exec. Leadership Found., 2000—; mem. Exec. Leadership Coun. 1993—. Mem. Soc. Info. Mgmr. (exec. coun. 1980-83, pres. 1985, pres. coun. 1986—), Exec. Leadership Coun. (found. bd. trustees). Office: Principal Fin Group 711 High St Des Moines IA 50392-0002 Home: 2420 Vintage Hill Dr Durham NC 27712-9476 E-mail: williams.carl@principal.com.

WILLIAMS, CARL HARWELL, utilities executive; b. Mansfield, Ga., Oct. 22, 1915; s. John Horace and Mary Ruby (Harwell) W.; m. Diane Barnes, June 25, 1967; children: Edward Vincent, Lesa Anne. Student, U. Fla., 1934-35; BS, Ga. Sch. Tech., 1939; postgrad., Harvard Advanced Mgmt. Program, U. Hawaii, 1956. Registered profl. engr., Hawaii. Engr. Fla. Power & Light Co., Miami, 1939-41; with Hawaiian Electric Co., Inc., Honolulu, 1945-80, mgr. engring., 1955-62, v.p., 1962-71, exec. v.p., 1971-72, pres., 1972-80, dir., 1970-85, chmn. exec. com., 1980-85. Chmn. bd., dir. Maui Electric Co. (subsidiary), 1972-80, Hawaii Electric Light Co. (subsidiary), 1972-80; dir. Bank of Hawaii., Hawaiian Electric Industries, Inc., Bancorp Hawaii, Inc. Bd. dirs. Aloha United Way, 1973-79; bd. dirs. Oahu Devel. Conf., 1972-81, chmn., 1979-80; bd. visitors Coll. Bus. Adminstrn., Hawaii, mem. adv. com. advanced mgmt. program, 1969-75, mem. adv. com. Hawaii geothermal project, 1973-78; mem. State Energy Policy Task Force, 1974-78, Hawaii Energy Conservation Council, 1978-80, Gov.'s Com. Alt. Energy Devel., 1978-80; bd. dirs. Am.-Samoa Power Authority, 1981-83. Served to lt. col., Signal Corps AUS, 1941-45. Decorated Legion of Merit. Fellow IEEE; mem. Hawaii C. of C., Engring. Assn. Hawaii, Nat. Soc. Profl. Engrs. (past dir.), Hawaii Soc. Profl. Engrs. (past dir., pres.), Pacific Coast Elec. Assn. (dir. 1972-81, pres. 1979-80), AIEE (past chmn. Hawaii sect.) Clubs: Pacific, Outrigger Canoe. Home: 2969 Kalakaua Ave Apt 501 Honolulu HI 96815-4620

WILLIAMS, CARLISLE M., JR., municipal official; b. Painter, Va., June 27, 1937; s. Carlisle M. and Evelyn Hickman Williams; m. Barbara Belle Schuyler, July 11, 1987; m. Dolly Evans Taylor, June 15, 1958 (div. Mar. 19, 1987); children: Carlisle M. III, Valerie Taylor. AA, Goldey-Beacom Coll., Wilmington, Del., 1958; BA, East Carolina U., 1960; DHL (hon.), Mary Washington Coll., 2003. County adminstr. County of Accomack, Va., 1966—83, County of Stafford, Va., 1984—2003. Adminstrv. officer & sec./treas. George Washington Boyhood Home Found., Stafford, 1992—99; chmn. Fredericksburg Area Met. Planning Orgn., Va., 2001—03, VACO Group Self Ins. Assn., Roanoke, Va., 2001—; pres. Va. Local Govt. Mgmt. Assn., Richmond, Va., 1981—82; sec./treas. Cedar Island Bridge and Beach Authority, Accomac, 1975—83. Pres. Ea. Shore Jaycees, Onancock, Va., 1967—68, Onancock Rotary Club, 1981—82. Recipient Jefferson Cup, Va. Assn. Counties, 2000, James Monroe Medal, Mary Washington Coll., 2003. Methodist. Avocation: sailing. Home: 12 Aiken Rd Fredericksburg VA 22405-3340 Office: County of Stafford 1300 Courthouse Rd PO Box 339 Stafford VA 22555-0339 E-mail: cmwjr@co.stafford.va.us.

WILLIAMS, CARLTON L. communications executive; Pres., CEO Karlkani Infinity Inc., L.A., 1989—. Office: Karlkani Infinity Inc 500 Molino St Ste 215 Los Angeles CA 90013-2268

WILLIAMS, CAROL ANN, state legislator; b. Cambridge, Mass., Feb. 2, 1937; widowed; 4 children. Student, San Jose State U., 1969; grad., N.H. Coll., 1995. Adminstr. Santa Clara County, ret.; mem. N.H. Ho. of Reps. (dist. 39), Concord, 1996—; mem. resources, recreation and devel. coms. N.H. Ho. of Reps., Concord, 1996—. Mem. Gov.'s Commn. on Disabilities, 1994—; bd. dirs. Granite State Ind. Living, 1996—. Roman Catholic. Home: 127 Prout Ave # 1 Manchester NH 03103-2840 Office: NH State Legis State House Concord NH 03301

WILLIAMS, CAROL H. advertising executive; b. Chgo. d. Clarence Earl Williams and Betty Jane Norment-Williams; m. Tipkins Hood; children: Tipkins Hood Jr., Carol Hood. Student, Northwestern U. Creative dir., sr. v.p. Leo Burnett Agy., Chgo., 1969—80, Foote-Cone & Belding, San Francisco, 1980—82; prin. owner Carol H. Williams Advt., Inc., Oakland, Calif., 1986—. Active US Dream Acad. Recipient Outstanding Women in Mktg. and Comms. award, Ebony Mag., 2001, Women to Watch award, Ad Age, 2002, Bus. Achievement award, Nat. Coalition 100 Black Women, Inc., 2003, Ad Agency of Yr., Black Enterprise Mag., 2004. Mem.: NAACP, TEC Internat., Rainbow/PUSH Coalition. Office: Carol H Williams Advertising Inc 555 12th St Ste 1700 Oakland CA 94607-4058

WILLIAMS, CAROLYN, secondary school educator; Resource specialist, tchr. spl. needs students Bernardo Heights Middle Sch., San Diego. Past bd. mem. Internat. Dyslexia Soc. Mem.: Nat. Bd. for Profl. Tchg. Stds. (bd. mem.). Office: Bernardo Heights Middle Sch 12990 Paseo Lucido San Diego CA 92128

WILLIAMS, CAROLYN ANTONIDES, university dean; b. Louisville, Oct. 27, 1939; d. John Dwight and Dorothy Ida Marie (Hoffman) Antonides; m. Frank Canon Williams, Dec. 26, 1961. BS with honors in Nursing, Tex. Woman's U., 1961; MS in Pub. Health Nursing Edn., U. N.C., 1965, PhD in Epidemiology, 1969. Asst. prof. nursing Emory U., Atlanta, 1968, assoc. prof., 1969, prof., dir. grad. programs and rsch., 1969-71; assoc. prof. nursing, asst. prof. epidemiology U. N.C., Chapel Hill, 1971-81, assoc. prof. nursing, rsch.

assoc. Health Svcs. Rsch. Ctr., from 1971, assoc. prof. epidemiology, 1981-84; dean Coll. Nursing, prof. U. Ky., Lexington, 1984—. Mem. Pres.'s Commn. Study of Ethical Problems in Medicine and Biomed. and Behavioral Rsch., 1980-82; chair rsch. adv. com. Am. Nurses Found., 1979-81; mem. planning com. study of nursing and nursing edn. Inst. Medicine of NAS, 1980; cons. WHO in S.Am. Mem. editorial bd. Family and Community Health, 1977-90, Advances in Nursing Sci., 1979-88, Internat. Jour. Nursing Studies, 1981—; also articles, chpts. to books. USPHS fellow U. N.C., 1969. Fellow APHA (publs. bd., Young Practitioner award 1973), Am. Acad. Nursing (pres. 1983-85); mem. ANA (chair commn. nursing rsch. 1980-82), Coun. Nurse Rschrs., Soc. Epidemiol. Rsch., Am. Assn. Colls. Nursing (pres. 2000—), Delta Omega, Sigma Theta Tau (bd. dirs.). Democrat. Baptist. Office: U Ky Coll Nursing 315 Con Hslc Bldg Lexington KY 40536-0001

WILLIAMS, CAROLYN ELIZABETH, manufacturing executive; b. L.A., Jan. 24, 1943; d. George Kissam and Mary Eloise (Chamberlain) W.; m. Richard Terrill White, Apr. 9, 1972; children: Sarah Anne, William Daniel. BS, Ga. Inst. Tech., 1969; MM, Northwestern U., 1988. Saleswoman Ea. Airlines, Atlanta, Montreal (Can.) and Seattle, 1964-69; job analyst Allied Products Corp., Atlanta, 1969-70, mgr. Frankfort, Mich., 1970-71, planning analyst, sr. planning analyst Chgo., 1972-74, dir. planning, 1974-76, staff v.p. planning, 1976-79, v.p. planning and bus. research, 1979-86, v.p. corp. devel., chief planning officer, 1986-93; pres. White, Williams & Daniels, 1993—. Mem. adv. bd. Ga. Inst. Tech.; bd. dirs. United Way. Mem. Winnteka Yacht Club.

WILLIAMS, CECILIA LEE PURSEL, optometrist; b. Lewisburg, Pa., Nov. 15, 1948; d. Lee LaVerne and Geraldine May (Steininger) Pursel; m. Richard Lee Williams, May 17, 1975; 1 son, Kent Lee. Student, Lycoming Coll., 1966-68; BS, Pa. Coll. Optometry, 1970, OD, 1972. Lic. and/or cert. optometrist, D.C., Pa., N.Y., N.J., Va. Rsch. optometrist in soft lens materials Gumpelmayer Optik, Vienna, Austria, 1973; optometrist Sterling Optical Co. Contact Lens Ctr., Washington, 1974-79; pvt. practice optometry Springfield, Va., 1980—. Recipient Clin. Efficiency award Pa. Coll. Optometry, 1972; Women's Aux. of Pa. Optometrists scholar, 1968-70, 70-72; Pa. State grantee, 1968-70, 70-72. Mem. Optometric Ctr. of Nation's Capital (dir. 1977-80), Am. Optometric Assn., Va. Optometric Assn., No. Va. Optometric Soc., Nat. Honor Soc. for Optometry, Omega Delta. Home: 3600 Wilton Hall Ct Alexandria VA 22310-2176 Office: 7241 Commerce St Springfield VA 22150-3411 Office Phone: 703-866-9364.

WILLIAMS, CHARLES EDWARD, engineer; b. Warsaw, N.Y., July 9, 1939; s. Charles Dwight and Oletha (Davenport) W.; m. Grace Norma Robertson, June 30, 1965 (div. 1970); 1 child, Eric Charles; m. Virginia Vee Parker, May 3, 1980. BS in Ceramic Engring., Alfred U., 1961; MS in Phys. Metallurgy, Denver U., 1968. Ceramic engr. Rocky Flats plant Dow Chem., Golden, Colo., 1961-65; ceramic engr. Coors Porcelain Co., Golden, 1965-69; packaging engr. Fairchild Semiconductor, San Diego, 1969-71; sales engr., cons. Otto Jahnke and Assocs., San Diego, 1971-72; plant engr. Tecate (Mex.) Internat., Baja California, 1972-73; prodn. engr. ceramic divsn. Buckbee Mears, San Diego, 1973-75; mem. group tech. staff Tex. Instruments, Dallas, 1975—. Contbr. articles to profl. jours.; 13 patents in field; performer (audiocassette) Up The Trail, 1993. Exec. v.p. Acad. We. Artists, Ft. Worth, 1995-99. Mem. IEEE, Internat. Microelectronic and Packaging Soc. Republican. Presbyterian. Avocations: cowboy poetry, professional storytelling, pottery. Home: 6245 Chesley Ln Dallas TX 75214-2118 Office: Tex Instruments m/s 8719 12500 TI Blvd Dallas TX 75243-4136 E-mail: c-williams7@ti.com.

WILLIAMS, CHARLES JUDSON, lawyer, writer; b. San Mateo, Calif., Nov. 23, 1930; s. John Augustus and Edith (Babcock) W.; children: Patrick, Victoria, Apphia. AB, U. Calif., Berkeley, 1952, LLB, 1955. Bar: Calif. 1955, U.S. Supreme Ct., 1970. Assoc. Kirkbride, Wilson, Harzfeld and Wallace, San Mateo County, Calif., 1956-59; sole practice Solano County, Calif., 1959-64, Martinez, Calif., 1964—2002, Benicia, Calif., 1981-88; city atty. Pleasant Hill, 1962-80, Yountville, Calif., 1965-68, Benicia, 1968-76, 80-82, Lafayette, Calif., 1968—, Moraga, Calif., 1974-92, Danville, Calif., 1982-88, Pittsburg, Calif., 1984-93, Orinda, Calif., 1985-97; of counsel Best, Best and Krieger, 2002—04; atty. pvt. practice, Martinez, Calif., 2004—. Lectr. Calif. Continuing Edn. Bar 1964-65, U. Calif. Extension 1974-76, John F. Kennedy U. Sch. Law 1966-69; spl. counsel to various Calif. cities; legal advisor Alaska Legis. Council 1959-61; advisor Alaska sup. ct. 1960-61; advisor on revision Alaska statues 1960-62; atty. Pleasant Hill Redevel. Agy. 1978-82; sec., bd. dirs. Vintage Savs. & Loan Assn., Napa County, Calif., 1974-82; bd. dirs. 23d Agrl. Dist. Assn., Contra Costa County, 1968-70. Author: California Code Comments to West's Annotated California Codes, 3 vols., 1965, West' California Code Forms, Commercial, 2 vols., 1965, West's California Government Code Forms, 3 vols., 1971, Supplement to California Zoning Practice, 1978, 80, 82, 84, 85, 87, 89, 91, 94, 96, 98, 2000, 01; contbr. articles to legal jours. Mem. ABA, Calif. Bar Assn., Contra Costa County Bar Assn. Office: 1330 Arnold Dr Ste 149 Martinez CA 94553-6538 E-mail: chaslaw@aol.com.

WILLIAMS, C(HARLES) K(ENNETH), poet, literature and writing educator; b. Newark, N.J., Nov. 4, 1936; s. Paul Bernard and Dossie (Kasdin) W.; m. Sarah Dean Jones, June, 1966 (div. 1975); 1 child, Jessica Anne; m. Catherine Justine Mauger, Apr. 15, 1975; 1 child, Jed Mauger. BA, U. Pa., 1958. Vis. prof. lit. Beaver Coll., Jenkintown, Pa., 1975, Drexel U., Phila., 1976, U. Calif., Irvine, 1978, Boston U., 1979-80, Bklyn. Coll., 1982-83; Mellon vis. prof. lit. Franklin and Marshall Coll., Lancaster, Pa., 1977; prof. writing Columbia U., N.Y.C., 1981-85; prof. lit. George Mason U., Fairfax, Va., 1982-95. Halloway lectr. U. Calif., Berkeley, 1986, Princeton U., 1995—. Author: A Day for Anne Frank, 1968, Lies, 1969, I Am the Bitter Name, 1972, With Ignorance, 1977, The Lark, The Thrush, The Starling, 1983, Tar, 1983, Flesh and Blood, 1987, Poems, 1963-1983, 1988, The Bacchae of Euripides, 1990, Helen, 1991, A Dream of Mind: Poems, 1992, Selected Poems, 1994, The Vigil, 1997, Poetry and Consciousness, 1998, Repair, 1999, Misgivings, A Memoir, 2000, The Singing: Poems, 2003; contbg. editor Am. Poetry Rev., 1972—; translator: Women of Trachis (Sophocles), 1978. Sponsor People's Fund, Phila., 1967—. Recipient Nat. Book Critics Circle award in poetry, 1987, Morton Dauwen Zabel prize, Am. Acad. of Arts and Letters, 1989, Lit. prize, 1999, Harriet Monroe prize, 1993, Berlin prize, Am. Acad. in Berlin, 1998, Pulitzer prize, 2000, Book award, L.A. Times, 2000, Weathertop prize, 2000, Pen Marth Albrand Memoir prize, 2001, Nat. Book award, 2003; fellow, Guggenheim Found., 1975, Nat. Endowment for Arts, 1985, 1993; grantee, Lila Wallace-Reader's Digest, 1993—95. Mem. PEN (Voelcker Career Achievement award 1998), Poetry Soc. Am., Am. Acad. Arts and Scis., Am. Acad. Arts and Letters. Avocations: piano, guitar, drawing. Home: 71 Leigh Ave Princeton NJ 08542 Office Phone: 609-258-3176.

WILLIAMS, CHARLES LAVAL, JR., physician, international organization official; b. New Orleans, Jan. 19, 1916; s. Charles Laval and Lewise (McLaurine) W.; m. Ellen Clendenin Ustick, Dec. 14, 1946; children: Ellen Clendenin, Katherine McLaurine. Student, U. Va., 1933-35; MD, Tulane U., 1940; M.P.H., U. Mich., 1945. Diplomate: Am. Bd. Preventive Medicine and Pub. Health. Intern U.S. Marine Hosp., New Orleans, 1941; with USPHS, 1941-67; assigned N.C. State Health Dept., 1941-44, USPHS States Relations div., 1944, U. Mich., 1944-45, Am. Acad. Pediatrics Nat. Study Child Health Services, 1945-47; chief planning unit, asst. chief div. commd. officers, 1947-51; with US/AID Div. Pub. Health, 1951-62; chief pub. health adviser AID Mission to Peru, 1959-62; asso. dir. internat. relations Office Internat. Health, 1962-64; chief Office Internat. Research, NIH, Bethesda, Md., 1965-66; dep. dir., then dir. Office Internat. Health, Office Surgeon General, USPHS, Washington, 1966-67; dep. dir. Pan Am. Health Orgn., 1967-79; ret.; exec. v.p. Am. Assn. World Health, 1980-84. U.S. del./alt. or advisor to eight world health assemblies between 1955 and 1967, and to ten sessions of the Directing Coun. of the Pan Am. Health Orgn. between 1953 and 1966. Fellow Am. Pub. Health Assn.; mem. U.S.-Mexico Border Pub. Health Assn., Phi Kappa Phi, Delta Omega. Home: 5600 Wisconsin Ave Apt 1009 Chevy Chase MD 20815-4411

WILLIAMS, CHARLES WESLEY, technical executive, researcher; b. Palestine, Ark. s. Fredrick Charles and Fannie Rochet (Southall) W.; m. Nancy Sue Rhea, Sept. 5, 1959; children: Brent L., Brian E. BSEE, U. Tenn., 1959, MS, 1963. Registered profl. engr., Ohio. Devel. engr. Mead Rsch. Lab., Chillicothe, Ohio, 1959-60, Oak Ridge (Tenn.) Nat. Lab., 1960-63; tech. mgr. EG & G Ortec, Oak Ridge, 1963-76, tech. dir. phys. and life sci., 1976-81; mgr. Assay Inst. EG & Ortec, Oak Ridge, 1981-85. Contbr. articles to tech. jours., chpt. to book. Fellow IEEE (v.p. Nuc. and Plasma Sci. Soc. 1979); mem. Tau Beta Pi, Eta Kappa Nu Baptist.

WILLIAMS, CHERYL A. secondary school educator; b. Neosho, Mo., July 7, 1957; d. Travestine Williams. BS in Math., Tex A&M U., 1978, postgrad., 1978-79, Rose State Coll., 1980-81, Sheppard Tech. Tng. Ctr., 1980-81; MS in Math., U. Tex., 1997. Computer scientist Tinker AFB, Oklahoma City, 1980-81, Defense Comm. Agy., Washington, 1986; tchr. Parent Child Inc., San Antonio, 1989; asst. sec. Antioch Bapt. Ch., San Antonio, 1989-92; substitute tchr. San Antonio Ind. Sch. Dist., 1990-93; instrnl. asst. Northside Ind. Sch. Dist., San Antonio, 1995-96, asst. tchr., 1994-95, North East Ind. Sch. Dist., San Antonio, 1996—2001; rep. West Telemarketing, 1998-99; math. tutor Alamo C.C. Dist., 1998—99, instr. math., 1998—, St. Philips Coll., 1998—2001; math. tutor Trave and G.G.'s Tutorial Svc., 1999—; instr. math. Guardian Angel Performing Arts Acad., 2002—. Asst. mgr. Fashion Pl., San Antonio, 1994—95; tax preparer H&R Block, 1994—95; distbr. Avon, 1999—2001; indep. beauty cons. Mary Kay Cosmetics, 1999—; scorer Harcourt Brace Corp., 2001, Randstad, 2001; rep. Express Svcs., 2001; cons. Prepaid Legal Svcs., Inc., 2003. Counselor YMCA, San Antonio, 1989-91; active Girl Scouts U.S., 1964-86; mem. choir, asst. sec. area ch., 1972, tutor, 1970—, tchr. Sunday Sch., 1973-86, asst. sec. Sunday Sch., 1973-86, 88—, asst. ch. sec., 1988-91; mem. Dorcas Circle, Lupus Found. Am., Biomed. Rsch. U. Tex., 1995—; mem. Epilepsy Found. Am., Tex. Head Injury Assn., Nat. Head Injury Assn., Smithsonian Instn. Mem. NEA, Tex. Edn. Assn., Mu. Alpha Theta. Avocations: jigsaw puzzles, bowling. Office: 1606 E McKinney #4212 Denton TX 76209

WILLIAMS, CHRISTOPHER, investment company executive; BArch, Howard U.; MBA, Dartmouth Coll. Former sr. v.p. Lehman Brothers, NY; former pres. Williams Finl. Mkts.; CEO Williams Capital Group, L.P., N.Y.C.; chmn. Williams Capital Mgmt., LLC, 2002—, CEO, 2002—. Bd. dirs. Wal-Mart, Harrah's Entertainment. Bd. dirs. NYC Partnership, Nat. Dance Inst., Alvin Ailey Dance Found., WNYC Radio. Mem.: Century Assoc., Young President's Org., Nat. Assoc. Securities Professionals (bd. dirs.), Securities Industry Assn. (bd. dirs. N.Y. dist.), Econ. Club N.Y. (bd. dirs.). Office: Williams Capital Group LP 650 5th Ave 10th Flr New York NY 10019*

WILLIAMS, CLARENCE J, III, photographer; b. Phila., Pa., Jan. 22, 1967; BA Mass Comm., Temple Univ., Phila., Pa., 1992. Staff photographer Los Angeles Times, Los Angeles, Calif., 1996, temp. staff photographer, 1994—95; staff photographer METPRO, 1994, Times Comm. Newspaper, Reston, Va., 1993—94; photography intern Phila. Tribune, Phila., 1992—93. Recipient first Pl., feature photography category, Nat. Headliner, 1996, first Pl. and hon. mention, issues reporting category, Nat. Press Photographers Assoc., 1996, Nat. Monthly Clip Contest, first Pl., 1995, Gold Seal Contest, second Pl., sports feature category, Calif. Press Photographers Assoc., 1995, Winner of one-wk AP Assign., Eddie Adams Workshop, 1995, First Ann. AP, Diverse Visions Photojournalism Workshop, 1994, Photojournalist Award, Kay Kreighbaum, 1992, Fourth Pl., Photographers Forum and Nikon contest, 1991. Mem.: Nat. Press Photographers Assoc., Nat. Assoc. of Black Jour. Office: Los Angeles Times 202 W 1st St Los Angeles CA 90012

WILLIAMS, CLAY RULE, lawyer; b. Milw., Sept. 25, 1935; s. George Laverne and Marguerite Mae (Rule) W.; m. Jeanne Lee Huber, Jan. 18, 1986; children: Gwynne, Amy, Daniel, Sarah. BA, Lawrence U., 1957; LLB, U. Mich., 1960. Bar: Wis. 1960, U.S. Dist. Ct. (ea. and we. dists.) Wis. 1964, U.S. Ct. Appeals (7th cir.) 1965, U.S. Ct. Mil. Appeals 1963, U.S. Supreme Ct. 1963. Assoc. Gibbs, Roper & Fifield, Milw., 1963-67; ptnr., shareholder Von Briesen & Roper, S.C., Milw., 1967-99, of counsel, 1999—. Mem. Gov.'s Task Force Creation Bus. Ct., 1994-99; instr. profl. seminars. Author: Berry, Davis, Deguire and Williams, Wisconsin Business Corporation Law, 1992; contbr. articles to profl. jours. Active Shorewood (Wis.) Sch. Bd., 1976-79. Capt. USAF, Judge Adv. Corps., 1960-63. Fellow Wis. Bar Found.; Fellow, ABA Found., mem. ABA (sect. antitrust law, corp. counseling com.), Wis. Bar Assn. (co-chmn. com. to revise corp. laws 1986-90, chmn. standing com. on bus. corp. law 1990-97, Pres.'s Award of Excellence 1990, 97), Milw. Bar Assn. (probate and real property sect., joint bench-bar com. Ct. Appeals, 1986-88, long-range planning com. 1987), Am. Law Inst., Milw. Club, Univ. Club. Republican. Episcopalian. Avocations: hunting, fishing, skiing, reading. Office: von Briesen & Roper SC 411 E Wisconsin Ave Milwaukee WI 53202 E-mail: cwilliam@vonbriesen.com.

WILLIAMS, COLLEEN, newscaster; b. Winston-Salem, NC; married; 1 child. BS in edn., Creighton U., U. Nebr. Drive-time anchor, gen. assignment reporter WOW Radio, Omaha, 1977; anchor WOWT_TV, Omaha, 1978—81, KPIX-TV, San Francisco, 1981—83, KCBS-TV, Los Angeles, 1983—86; weekend anchor NBC4, Los Angeles, 1986—93, anchor, Channel 4 News at 5pm, 1993—, anchor, Channel 4 News at 11pm, 1997—. Recipient Local Emmy Awards, Los Angeles, Best Daily Newscast (60 min.), 1995, Outstanding contbn. to "OJ Simpson: The Trial" news series, 1995, AP Trophy for best news mini-series, "Kids Who Kill", 1987. Office: NBC4 3000 W Alameda Ave Burbank CA 91523

WILLIAMS, CONSTANCE, state senator; b. June 27, 1944; m. Sankey V. Williams; 2 children. BA, Barnard Coll., 1966; MBA, U. Pa., 1980. Rep. Pa. House of Reps., 1996—2001; Pa. state senator, 2001—. Democrat. Jewish. Office: 352 Capitol Bldg Senate Box 203017 Harrisburg PA 17120-2020 E-mail: cwilliams@pasenate.com.

WILLIAMS, CRAIG FOSTER, osteopathic emergency physician; b. Akron, Ohio, July 23, 1949; s. Robert Daniel and Jeanne Marie (Schulte) W.; m. Carol Giglia, May 6, 1978; children: Joy Caroline, Cara Jeanne, Eric James. BA, Notre Dame U., 1971; DO, U. Health Scis., Coll. Osteo. Medicine, 1977. Diplomate Am. Bd. Emergency Medicine. Intern Doctor's Hosp., Columbus, Ohio, 1977-78; resident in emergency medicine Wright State U., Dayton, Ohio, 1978-80, mem. faculty, 1982—, asst. clin. prof. emergency medicine, 1983—; commd. officer USPHS Indian Health Svc., Phoenix, 1980-82. Staff emergency physician St. Elizabeth Med. Ctr., Dayton, 1982-95, Upper Valley Med. Ctr., Troy, Ohio, 1995-2002, Middletown Regional Hosp., 2003—; dir. Fletcher (Ohio) Emergency Med. Svc., 1995—. Named Clin. Tchr. of Yr., Wright State U., 1985, 88, Miami County Physician of Yr., 1996, Ohio Emergency Physician of Yr., 1999. Fellow Am. Coll. Emergency Physicians; mem. AMA, Am. Osteo. Assn., Notre Dame Alumni Assn. Roman Catholic. Home: 6649 Stamford Pl Dayton OH 45459-3310 Office: 332 Congress Park Drive Dayton OH 45459

WILLIAMS, CRAVEN EDWARD, academic administrator; b. Monroe, NC, Jan. 27, 1940; s. J. Howard and Jessie (Massey) W.; m. Judith C.; children: Jay Howard, Lee Hunley. BA, Wake Forest U., 1962; M of Div., Southeastern U., 1965; D of Ministry, Union Seminary, Richmond, Va., 1973. V.p. devel. Mary Baldwin Coll., Staunton, Va., 1968-73, Davidson Coll., NC, 1973-76; pres. Gardner-Webb Coll., Boiling Springs, NC, 1976-86; pres., chief exec. officer Capitol Dominion Corp., Raleigh, NC, 1986—93; pres. Greensboro Coll., NC, 1993—. Contbr. articles on higher education and real estate development to profl. jours. Bd. trustees Moses Cone Health Sys., Greensboro, NC. Fellow Soc. for Values in Higher Edn. Republican. Baptist. Avocations: running, tennis, bicycle racing. Office: Greensboro Coll 815 W Market St Greensboro NC 27401*

WILLIAMS, DANIEL A. state representative; b. Jefferson City, Mo., Nov. 9, 1970; m. Cheralea Williams; children: Kaitlyn, Rachel, Meagan. BA, MidAm. Nazarene U., 1992; MBA, Keller Sch. Mgmt., 1995; JD, Vanderbilt U., 1998. Owner, operator U. Campus Cafe, Convenience Store, 1996—97; owner TEACH Enterprises, 1996—97; adj. prof. Free Will Bapt. Bible Coll., 1997; intern Kans. State Senator Karin Brownlee, 1998; asst. prof. So. Nazarene U., 1998—99; mem. Kans. Ho. of Reps., 2000—. Adj. prof. MidAm. Nazarene U., 2000—. Columnist: newsletter Polit. Commentary Internet Newsletter, 1999—. Mem. Ctrl. Ch. Nazarene, 1992—. Mem.: Olathe Area C. of C. (govt. affairs task force), Christian Legal Soc. Republican. Office: 427-S State Capitol 300 SW 10th Ave Topeka KS 66612 Address: 1230 N Prince Edward Island Olathe KS 66061

WILLIAMS, DANIEL BRYAN, obstetrician/gynecologist, educator; b. St. Louis, Dec. 13, 1961; MD, U. Mo. Kansas City, 1985. Diplomate Am. Bd. Ob-Gyn, Am. Bd. Reproductive Endocrinology. Intern, resident King-Drew Med. Ctr., L.A., 1985—89; fellow reproduction, endocrinology, infertility UCLA Cedars Sinai Med. Ctr., 1989—91; instr. dept. ob-gyn Washington U., St. Louis, 1991—93, asst. prof., 1993—96, assoc. prof., 1997—2002; assoc. prof. medicine U. Cin., 2002—. Office: Christ Hospital 2123 Auburn Ave A-44 Cincinnati OH 45219

WILLIAMS, DANIEL D. investment company executive; Sr. exec. v.p., CFO Everen Securities Inc., Chgo., until 1999. Office: Everen Securities Inc 77 W Wacker Dr Chicago IL 60601-1651

WILLIAMS, DARRYL MARLOWE, medical educator; b. Denver, Apr. 3, 1938; s. Archie Malvin and Dorothy Merle (Grapes) W.; m. Susan Arlene Moore, June 24, 1966; children: Carol Ruth, Peter Todd, Sarah Elizabeth. Student, U. Colo., 1956—58; BS, Colo. State U., 1963; MD, MS in Anatomy, Baylor U., 1964; MPH, U. Tex., 2001. Diplomate Am. Bd. Internal Medicine, Am. Bd. Hematology. Intern and resident Baylor Affiliated Hosps., Houston, 1964-66, 67-68; resident U. Utah, Salt Lake City, 1966-67, fellow in hematology, 1968-73, asst. prof., 1973-77; assoc. prof. La. State U., Shreveport, 1977-81, prof., 1981-90, chief hematology sect., 1977-85, asst. dean/rsch., 1981-85, dean Sch. Medicine, 1985-90; prof. medicine, dean Sch. Medicine Tex. Tech U. Health Scis. Ctr., Lubbock, 1990-95; prof. medicine, exec. dir. office border health, project dir. Hispanic Ctr. of Excellence Tex. Tech. Health Scis. Ctr., El Paso, 1995—, dir. curriculum planning office, 2002, also bd. dirs., 1995—, dir. med. edn. Cmty. Partnership, 1995—2001. Mem. hemophilia adv. com. La. Legislature, Baton Rouge, 1977-83; vice chair La. Lung and Cancer Bd., New Orleans, 1984-90; pres. N.W. La. AIDS Task Force, Shreveport, 1987. Mem. editl. bd. Tex. Jour. Rural Health, 1990—. Mem. Am. Heart Assn., Lubbock chpt., Shreveport Biracial Commn., 1988, Lubbock Indigent Health Care Coalition Task Force, 1991-92, Health Professions Edn. Adv. Com., Lubbock Friends of Pub. Radio; vice chair health profls. edn. adv. com. Tex. Coord. Bd. Higher Edn., 1992-95; sec. Health Edn. and Tng. Consortium of Tex., 1990-99, vice chmn., 1999-2002, chmn., 2002-04; mem. steering com. Border Vision Fronteriza, 1995-2000; bd. dirs. El Paso Cancer Consortium; project dir. Hispanic Ctr. of Excellence, 2001—; adv. com., Tex. State Dept. Health Cmty. Health Workers, 2003—; exec. dir. Health Edn. Tng. Ctr. Alliance of Tex., 2003-; project dir. Tex. Tech. Regional Ctr. Pub. Health, Medicine Edn., 2003-. Recipient award Nat. Ski Patrol Sys., Salt Lake City, 1975. Fellow ACP, Am. Coll. Nutrition; mem. Am. Soc. Hematology, Am. Inst. Nutrition, Am. Soc. Clin. Nutrition, Tex. Med. Assn. (physicians oncology edn. com.), Am. Cancer Soc. (bd. dirs. El Paso unit 1999—, pres. 2001-03), Alpha Omega Alpha. Office: Tex Tech Health Sci Ctr at El Paso 4800 Alberta Ave El Paso TX 79905-2709 Office Phone: 915-545-6550. Business E-Mail: darryl.williams@ttuhsc.edu.

WILLIAMS, DAVE HARRELL, investment executive; b. Beaumont, Tex., Oct. 5, 1932; s. George Davis and Mary (Hardin) W.; m. Reba White, Mar. 15, 1975. BS in Chem. Engring, U. Tex., 1956; MBA (Baker scholar, Teagle fellow), Harvard U., 1961. Chartered fin. analyst. Chem. engr. Exxon Corp., Baton Rouge, 1959; security analyst deVegh & Co., N.Y.C., 1961—64; dir. research Waddell & Reed, Kansas City, Mo., 1964—67; exec. v.p. Mitchell Hutchins, Inc., N.Y.C., 1967—77; chmn. bd. Alliance Capital Mgmt. Corp., N.Y.C., 1977—2001, chmn. emeritus, 2001—. Contbr.: articles to Fin. Analysts Jour. Trustee Skyscraper Mus.; trustee U.S.S. Intrepid Mus. Found. Served with USNR, 1956-59. Mem. Fin. Analysts Fedn. (past officer, dir.), N.Y. Soc. Security Analysts (past pres.), Bond Club N.Y., Econ. Club N.Y., Knickerbocker Club, Grolier Club. Presbyterian. Office: White Williams Holdings 41 W 57th St New York NY 10019

WILLIAMS, DAVID ALEXANDER, retired chief pilot; b. Helena, Mont., May 29, 1939; s. Daniel samuel and Dorothy (Alexander) W.; m. Jacqouline anders, Feb. 14, 1964 (div. Mar. 1988); children: Daniel Alexander, Darryl Jackson. BA, U. So. Calif., L.A., 1962. Lic. airline transport pilot, FAA. Commd. ensign USNR, 1963, advanced through grades to capt., 1985; tng. and test pilot McDonnel Douglas, Long Beach, Calif., 1980-87, chief pilot flight stds. and safety, 1987-97, Douglas Products divsn. Boeing, Long Beach, 1997-99; ret., 1999. Mem. internat. adv. com. Flight Safety Found., Washington, 1987-99; mem. windshear tng. aid task force FAA/industry, Washington, 1985-87; mem. CFIT tng. com. Flight Safety Found./FAA, 1992-96, joint safety analysis team FAA Industry, 1997-99. Author: Turbulence Education and Training Aid FAA/Industry, 1996-97. Mem.: Mil. Officers Assn. Am., Naval Res. Assn. Avocations: cycling, sailing, scuba diving. Home: 223 Mission Ln San Luis Obispo CA 93405 E-mail: graver@aol.com.

WILLIAMS, DAVID ANTHONY, not-for-profit executive; b. Hazelton, Pa., May 8, 1959; s. John Patrick and Mary (Zeta) W.; m. Martha Ann Carson, July 28, 1957; children: Carson Allen, Kate Barrett. BSBA, Bloomsburg U., 1981; MBA, U. Houston, 1992. Acct. Shell Oil Co., Houston, 1981-83; exec. dir. The Houston Food Bank, 1983-94; sr. v.p. Habitat for Humanity, 1994—. Bd. dirs. Houston Interfaith Hunger Coalition, 1986-90, Second Harvest Nat. Foodbank Network, Chgo., 1988-90, Habitat for Humanity, Houston, 1992-94. Named one of Five Outstanding Young Houstonians, Houston C. of C., 1987. Office: Habitat for Humanity Intl 121 Habitat St Americus GA 31709-3498

WILLIAMS, DAVID C. federal agency administrator; Grad. degrees, U. Ill., 1975. Spl. agent U.S. Secret Svc., 1979; with Office of Inspector Gen. Office of Labor Racketeering U.S. Dept. Labor, spl. agent in charge, N.Y.C., with Pres. Reagan's Commn. on Organized Crime, field dir. Office of Labor Racketeering, dir. Office Spl. Investigations Gen. Acctg. Office; inspector gen. Nuclear Regulatory Commn., 1989—96, Social Security Adminstrn., 1996—98, Dept. of the Treasury, Washington, 1998—99, treasury inspector gen. for tax adminstrn., 1999—. Active mem. Treasury Task Force. Office: US Dept Treasury Tax Adminstrn 1125 15th St NW Washington DC 20005

WILLIAMS, DAVID J. diversified financial services company executive; BA, Yale U., 1965; MBA, Harvard U., 1974. Chartered fin. analyst. Portfolio mgr. T. Rowe Price Assocs., Balt.; chief investment officer Horizon Trust Co., Morristown, NJ; from sr. portfolio mgr. to mng. dir. U.S. Trust Co., N.Y., 1987—92; lead mgr. Excelsior Value & Restructuring Fund, Boston, 1992—. Mem.: Assn. Investment Mgmt. and Rsch. Office: Excelsior Value & Restructuring Fund 73 Tremont St 8th Floor Boston MA 02108*

WILLIAMS, DAVID LEWIS, state senator; b. May 28, 1953; BA, U. Ky., 1975; JD, U. Louisville, 1977. Atty.; mem. Ky. Ho. of Reps., Frankfort, 1985-86; pres. Ky. Senate, 2002—, mem., 1986—, mem. judiciary com. Mem. Ky. Bar Assn., U. Ky. Alumni Assn., U. Louisville Alumni Assn. Republican. Methodist. Office: Ky Senate 16th Dist Rm 204 Capital Annex Frankfort KY 40601-3448 also: PO Box 666 Burkesville KY 42717-0666

WILLIAMS, DAVID PERRY, manufacturing executive; b. Detroit, Nov. 16, 1934; s. M.S. Perry and Virginia (Hayes) W.; m. Jill Schneider, July 27, 1972; children: Tracy, Perry, David, William, Nell. BA, Mich. State U., 1956, MBA, 1964. V.p. sales Automotive div. Kelsey Hayes Co., Romulus, Mich., 1958-71; v.p., mgr. automotive product line ITT, N.Y.C., 1971-76; v.p., dir. Budd Co., Troy, Mich., 1976-79, sr. v.p. ops., dir., 1979-80, sr. v.p., chief ops. officer, 1980-86, pres., chief operating officer, dir., 1986—. Dir. Standard Fed. Bank, Troy, Mich., 1990—, SPX Corp., Muskegon, Mich., 1992—, Budd Canada, Inc., Kitchener, Ont., 1981—, Thyssen Budd Automotive. Served to 1st lt. USAF, 1956-58. Mem. Soc. Automotive Engrs., Bloomfield Hills Country

Club, Country Club of Detroit, Yondotega, PGA Nat. Club (Fla.), Tournament Players Club (Mich.), Question Club, Royal and Ancient Golf Club of St. Andrews (Scotland), Beta Gamma Sigma. Republican. Episcopalian. Home: 333 Lincoln Rd Grosse Pointe MI 48230-1604 Office: Budd Co PO Box 2601 Troy MI 48007 2601

WILLIAMS, DAVID R. sociologist, educator, senior research scientist; BTh hons., Carribean Union Coll.; MDiv cum laude, Andews U., 1979; MPH in Health Edn., Loma Linda U.; PhD; MA in Sociology, U. Mich., 1954, PhD in Sociology, 1986. Prof. sociology U. Mich, Ann Arbor; sr. scientist Survey Rsch. Ctr., U. Mich., Ann Arbor. Faculty assoc. African Am. Mental Health Rsch. Ctr., Ann Arbor, Mich.; mem. editl. bd: Contemporary Sociology, 1990—92, Social Psychology Quarterly, 1996—, Social Problems, 1996—; Mem. Nat. Acad. Scis. Panel on Needle Exchange and Bleach Distrbn. Programs, 1993—95, Nat. Sci. Found. Bd. Overseers for NORC's Gen. Social Survey, 1993—97; mem. rev. panel Nat. Inst. Mental Health Social and Group Processes Grants, 1996—99. Assoc. editor (sociological jour.) Ethnicity and Disease, 1993—; contbr. articles to profl. jours. Recipient Investigator award in Health Policy Rsch., Robert Wood Johnson found., 1995—96; fellow (Jr. faculty) in Social Scis., Yale U., 1990—91, (sr. faculty), 1992—93. Mem.: Internat. Soc. Hypertension in Blacks, Assn. Black Sociologists, Am. Psychol Assn., Am. Pub. Health Assn., Soc. Epedemiological Rsch., Am. Sociological Assn. (sec.-treas. med. sociology sect. 1995—97), Nat. Rsch. Coun., Nat. Acad Scis. Inst. Medicine. Office: Univ Mich Inst Social Rsch 426 Thompson St Rm 2230 Ann Arbor MI 48106-1248 E-mail: wildavid@umich.edu.

WILLIAMS, DAVID R. astronaut; b. Saskatoon, Saskatchewan, Can., May 16, 1954; s. William and Isobel Williams; m. Cathy Fraser; 2 children. BSc in Biology, McGill U., 1976, MSc, MD, CM, McGill U., 1983. Resident in family practice U. Ottawa Faculty Medicine, Canada, 1983—85; resident in emergency medicine U. Toronto, Canada, 1985—88; fellow in emergency medicine Royal Coll. Physicians & Surgeons, Canada, 1988; emergency physician Sunnybrook Health Sci. Ctr., 1988—89, Emergency Assoc. of Kitchener Waterloo, Canada, 1989—90; med. dir. Sunnybrook Health Sci. Ctr., 1990—92; with Can. Space Agy., 1992—95; astronaut NASA, Houston, 1995—. Lectr. dept. surgery U. Toronto, Canada, 1988; course dir. Can. Heart & Stroke Found., Am. Coll. Surgeons; asst. prof. U. Toronto, Canada, 1989—90; asst. prof. surgery McGill U.; mem. staff St. Mary's Hosp., Montreal Gen. Hosp.; mission specialist Neurolab, 1998; dir. space & life sci. directorate NASA, 1998—. Recipient Commonwealth cert. Thanks, 1973, Commonwealth Recognition award, 1975, A.S. Hill bursary, McGill U., 1980, Walter Hoare bursary, 1981, J.W. McConnell award, 1981—83, Psychiatry prize, Wood Gold Medal award. Mem.: Can. Aeronautics & Space Inst., Can. Soc. Aerospace Medicine, Aerospace Med. Assn., Can. Assn. Emergency Physicians, Royal Coll. Physicians & Surgeons Can., Coll. Family Physicians Can., Ontario Med. Assn., Coll. Physicians & Surgeons Ontario. Avocations: flying, scuba diving, hiking, sailing, kayaking. Office: Astronaut Office CB NASA Johnson Space Ctr Houston TX 77058

WILLIAMS, DAVID RUSSELL, retired music educator; b. Indpls., Oct. 21, 1932; s. H. Russell and Mary Dean (Whitmer) W.; m. Elsa Bühlmann, Jan. 30, 1960. AB, Columbia U., 1954, MA, 1956; PhD, U. Rochester, 1965. Dir. music Windham Coll., Putney, Vt., 1959-62; opera coach Eastman Sch. Music, Rochester, N.Y., 1962-65, assoc. prof. theory, adminstr. of MusM program, 1965-80; prof., chmn. dept. music U. Memphis (formerly Memphis State U.), 1980-87, prof. music, 1980-98, prof. emeritus, 1998—. Bd. dirs. Memphis Youth Symphony, Memphis Symphony, 1984-90; mem. exec. bd. Opera Memphis, 1980-87, Salute to Memphis Music, 1980-87. Author: Bibliography of the History of Music Theory, 1971, Conversations with Howard Hanson, 1988, Music Theory from Zarlino to Schenker: A Bibliography and Guide, 1990; producer: Highwater Records album 8201 featuring John Stover, classical guitar, 1983; composer Suite for Oboe, Clarinet and Piano, 1968, Five States of Mind, 1970. Bd. dirs., sec. Rochester Philharm. Orch., 1976-78; v.p., bd. dirs. Rochester Chamber Orch., 1974-78; pres., bd. dirs. Opera Theatre of Rochester, 1973-74; bd. dirs., chmn. Am. Ritual Theatre, 1979-80; bd. sponsors Met. Opera Mid. South Region, Memphis, 1983—. Served as cpl. U.S. Army, 1957-59. Recipient Eastman Sch. Music Pub. award, 1970. Mem. NARAS (treas. Memphis chpt. 1984-86), Coll. Music Soc. (sec. 1973-83), Music Tchrs. Nat. Assn. Sci. (state chmn. 1971-74), Nat. Assn. Schs. of Music (chmn. region 8 1989-92), Tenn. Assn. Music Execs. in Colls. and Univs. (pres. 1986-87), Rochester Club, Univ. Club, Summit Club, Pi Kappa Lambda (pres. U. Memphis chpt. 1988-90), Phi Beta Kappa, Phi Mu Alpha, Sigma Alpha Iota. Avocations: language study, word puzzles. Home: 273 W Central Park St Apt 1 Memphis TN 38111-4570 E-mail: drwillms@memphis.edu. *Having had a family background that was superior in so many ways has helped me to sharpen my purpose in life, in that it has made me realize to what an extent affirmative action is necessary in order to provide a milieu in which truly equal opportunity can exist. Many doors of opportunity have been held open for me; those of disadvantaged access are often not aware that these doors exist. The more individuals I can lead to these portals, the more I will have achieved in my lifetime.*

WILLIAMS, DEBERRAH DEITHRISHA, elementary school educator, researcher; b. Rock Hill, S.C., June 10, 1951; d. Nathan and Thelma (Honeycutt) Williams. BA, Wilberforce U., Ohio, 1973; EdM, U. N.C., 1988; DHL (hon.), New Millennium Bapt. Coll., Charlotte, N.C., 1998. Cert. tchr. N.C. Adminstrv. asst. Henry Ford Hosp., Detroit, 1970; English/cashiering instr. Occupl. Industrialization Inst., Washington, 1971; adminstrv. asst. N.C. Dept. Agr., Raleigh, 1972; substitute tchr. Charlotte-Mecklenburg Schs., Charlotte, 1973—74, K-3 tchr., 1974—91; ret., 1991. Part-time adult h.s. instr. Ctrl. Piedmont C.C., Charlotte. Author: 20 books; contbr. articles to profl. jours. Founder, dir. Temple Twirlettes Baton Corp., Temple Bapt. Ch., 2002—; pastoral care vol. Charlotte Rehab. Hosp., 2002—; literacy vol. Cen. Piedmont C.C., Charlotte. Named Outstanding Young Woman of Am., Outstanding Young Women of Am., 1987, Disting. Woman of N.C., 1988; named to Nat. Honor Soc. of Secondary Schs.; recipient Outstanding Univ. Opportunity Transition Peer Counselor award, U. N.C., 1986, The Choir award, Wilberforce (Ohio) U., Outstanding Peer Counselor award, Wilberforce U., many others. Mem.: Charlotte African-Am. Writers, Internat. Black Writers Conf. (treas., bd. dirs.), Order Ea. Stars (founder, past worthy matron, Outstanding Svc. award 1993—95), Sigma Gamma Rho. Democrat. Baptist. Avocations: reading, writing, crocheting, violin, twirling.

WILLIAMS, DEBORAH LEE, foundation administrator; b. L.A., Feb. 11, 1954; d. Eleazer Deming and Jeanne Sanford Williams; m. Charles (Skip) Robert Roy, Apr. 6, 1985; 1 child, Andrew Roy. BA, Pomona Coll., 1975; JD, Harvard U., 1978. Bar: Alaska 1979. Atty. solicitors honors program Dept. Interior, Washington, 1978—79, atty. Nat. Pk. Svc. and Nat. Fish and Wildlife Svc. Anchorage, 1979—81, spl. asst. to sec. for Alaska, 1994—98; exec. dir. Alaska Consumer Advocacy Program, Anchorage, 1981—82; atty. Hellen, Partnow and Condon, Anchorage, 1983—86, 1989—93; exec. dir. Am. Lung Assn. Alaska, Anchorage, 1986—89, Alaska Conservation Found., Anchorage, 1999—. Pres. bd. dirs. Trustees for Alaska, Anchorage, 1982—85; bd. dirs. TransAlaska Pipeline Liability Fund, Washington, 1994—98; adj. prof. Alaska Pacific U., Anchorage, 1993—94, U. Alaska, Anchorage, 1987—88; commr. Anchorage Mcpl. Health Commn., 1981—85. Founder, editor Harvard Environ. Law Rev., 1976; contbr. law rev. articles to profl. jours. Trustee Exxon Valdez Oil Spill Trustee Coun., Anchorage, 1994—98. Recipient Nat. Performance Rev. award, V.P. of U.S., 1997, 1998. Mem.: Green Star (bd. dirs. 2002—), Planned Parenthood of Alaska (bd. dirs., chair nominating com. 1997—2003), Rotary Internat., Phi Beta Kappa. Achievements include appearances on 60 Minutes, 60 Minutes Australia, BBC, and many Alaskan TV shows; subject of cover stories in Alaska Business Monthly, We Alaskans and other publications. Avocations: backpacking, travel, building. Office: Alaska Conservation Found 441 W 5th Ave Ste 402 Anchorage AK 99501 Business E-Mail: dwilliams@akcf.org.

WILLIAMS, DEBRA ANN, assistant principal; b. San Antonio, May 3, 1958; d. Theodore Roosevelt Thomas and Dorothy Ann Williams; m. Clarence Elbert Williams, Jr., July 29, 1978; 1 child, Clarence Elbert III. BS in Elem. Edn., S.W. Tex. State U., 1980; M in Curriculum Supervision and Instrn., U. Houston, 1990, M in Adminstrn. and Supervision, 1998. Cert. bilingual edn. Tex., mid-mgmt. Tex., tchr. Tex. Tchr. Victoria (Tex.) Ind. Sch. Dist., 1980—98, asst. prin., 1998—. Bd. dirs. Tex. Zoo, Victoria, 2000—02. Mem.: Nat. Assn. Elem. Prins. and Suprs., Tex. Assn. Elem. Prins. and Suprs., Women Partnership for Progress (pres. 2003—), Alpha Delta Kappa (pres., dist. sec. 2001—02), Phi Delta Kappa (pres. 2002—04). Baptist. Avocations: camping, reading, travel, sewing. Office: Hopkin Acad 110 Hopkins Rd Victoria TX 77902 Office Phone: 361-788-9527. Office Fax: 361-788-9635. Business E-Mail: debra.williams@visd.com.

WILLIAMS, DELETA, state legislator; BS, Ctrl. Mo. State U. Mem. Mo. Ho. of Reps. from 121st dist., 1993—. Mem. Citizens for Drug Free Environment, Inc. Mem. Bus. and Profl. Women, C. of C., Women's Dem. Club, Mo. Fedn. Dem. Women's Club. Address: 110 E Hale Lake Rd Warrensburg MO 64093-3015 Office: Mo Ho of Reps State Capitol Building Jefferson City MO 65101-1556

WILLIAMS, DEREK, JR., pharmaceutical professional; b. Ft. Rucker, Ala., June 25, 1958; s. Derek W. Sr. and Carol E. (Kaufman) W.; m. Penny L. Bradly, Apr. 22, 1991 (div.); 1 child, Courtney Elizabeth. AS, U. Nev., 1981; BA, U. Colo., 1984; MA, U. Nev., 1986; postgrad., Pepperdine U. Cert. Inst. Regulatory Affairs, 1997. Rsch. asst. U. Nev., Reno, 1984-86; surgical counselor St. Lukes Hosp., Denver, 1987-89; pub. health advisor Ctrs. for Disease Control, Atlanta, 1989-91; clin. rsch. assoc. Amgen, Inc., Thousand Oaks, Calif., 1991-92, regulatory affairs specialist, 1992-97; mgr. regulatory affairs SangStat Med. Corp., Menlo Park, Calif., 1997-98; assoc. dir. regulator affairs Nexell Therapeutics, Inc., Irvine, Calif., 1998 2000; assoc. dir. U.S. regulatory affairs Purdue Pharma, L.P., Stamford, Conn., 2000—04; dir. worldwide regulatory affairs Pfizer, Inc., New London, 2004—. Named Outstanding Young Men of Am., 1989-90. Mem. Regulatory Affairs Profls. Soc., Brit. Inst. Regulatory Affairs., Drug Info. Assn. Avocations: sports, history, literature. Office: Pfizer Inc 50 Pequot Ave New London CT 06320-5140 Office Phone: 860-732-5296. E-mail: derek.williams@groter.pfizer.com.

WILLIAMS, DEWAYNE ARTHUR, JR., artist; b. San Diego, Aug. 20, 1943; s. DeWayne Arthur Sr. and Mary Elizabeth (Cardell) W.; m. Suelynn Davison, Jan. 18, 1964; children: Regan Lane, Rani Chellane Garcia, DeWayne Arthur III. BA in Biol. Sci., Fla. State U., 1966; MA in Interdisciplinary Studies, Oreg. State U., 1974; postgrad., U. Idaho, 1997-99, Clayton Coll. Natural Health, 2000—. Aquatic biologist Oreg. Game Commn., Corvallis, 1966-72; biol. technician (plants) EPA, Corvallis, 1974-75; crafts shop dir., instr. U.S.Army, Ft. Gulick, Canal Zone, 1975-79; artist/mus. curator U. Mont., Missoula, 1980-88; artist, author, editor, photographer Artistwork, Missoula, 1988-93; biol. technician (fish) Nat. Marine Fisheries Svc., Honolulu, 1994; exhibit specialist Nat. Pk. Svc., Homestead, Fla., 1994-96; environ. protection asst. U.S. Army Corps of Engrs., Boise, Idaho, 1996-2000; fish and wildlife biologist U.S. Fish and Wildlife Svc., Sacramento, 2000-2001; exhibit specialist Nat. Pk. Svc., Mammoth, Wyo., 2001—02; full-time artist, 2002—. Fine arts dir. student union Oreg. State U., Corvallis, 1973; curator, artist Dooby Ave. Art Show. Author, editor, photographer, pub.: Montana Tribute, 1990 (Mont. Offcl. Centennial book); contbg. photographer: Erotic Art by Living Artists, 1988, Am. Photographers, 1989, Living Artists in America, 1989, Photographic Possibilities, 1991, Who's Who in Photography, 1991, Center for Creative Photography, Mont. Hist. Soc., Idaho State U., Oreg. State U.; designed Missoula County seal, 1982; creator of the Correlative Composite Photog., 1976. Boy Scout leader, 1967-93. Democrat. Episcopalian. Avocations: hunting, fishing, camping. Home and Office: 2007 Huron Pkwy Apt 8 Ann Arbor MI 48104-4160 Office Phone: 208-362-4933. E-mail: dewaynearthur@hotmail.com.

WILLIAMS, DIANA, news anchor, reporter, journalist; BA in Econs., Duke U. Gen. assignment reporter WSOC-TV, Charlotte, N.C.; 6 and 11 PM news anchor, reporter WBTV, Charlotte, N.C.; gen. assignment reporter, noon anchor, 5 o'clock news anchor reporter WNEV-TV, Boston; gen. assignment reporter WABC-TV/ABC Inc., N.Y.C., 1991—92, reporter, anchor Eyewitness News, 1992—, host Eyewitness News Up Close. Reporter N.Y.C. Dem. Nat. Conv., 1992, San Diego Rep. Conv., 1996, Phila. Rep. Conv, 2000; trustee Nat. Academy for Television Arts and Sciences. Recipient Headliner award, New York Associated Press award. Mem.: The Duke Library Advisory Bd.

WILLIAMS, DONALD JOHN, physicist, researcher; b. Fitchburg, Mass., Dec. 25, 1933; s. Toivo John and Ina (Kokkinen) W.; m. Priscilla Mary Gagnon, July 4, 1953; children: Steven John, Craig Mitchell, Eino Stenroos. BS, Yale U., 1955, MS, 1958, PhD, 1962. Sr. staff physicist Johns Hopkins U. Applied Physics Lab., 1961-65; head particle physics br. Goddard Space Flight Center, NASA, 1965-70; dir. Space Environ. Lab., NOAA, Boulder, Colo., 1970-82; prin. investigator Energetic Particles expt. NASA Galileo Mission, 1977—2003; prin. staff physicist Johns Hopkins U. Applied Physics Lab., 1982-89, dir. Milton S. Eisenhower Rsch. Ctr., 1990-96, chief scientist rsch. ctr., 1996-99, ret., 1999. Nat. and internat. sci. planning coms.; chmn. NAS com. on solar-terrestrial rsch., 1989-93; sci. adv. bd. USAF, 1993-97. Author: (with L.R. Lyons) Quantitative Aspects of Magnetospheric Physics, 1983; assoc. editor Jour. Geophys. Rsch., 1967-69, Revs. of Geophysics and Space Rsch., 1984-86; editor: (with G.D. Mead) Physics of the Magnetosphere, 1969, Physics of Solar-Planetary Environments, 1976; mem. editl. bd. Space Sci. Revs., 1975-85; contbr. articles to profl. jours. Mem. USAF Sci. Adv. Bd., 1994-98. Lt. USAF, 1955-57. Recipient Sci. Rsch. award NOAA, 1974, Disting. Authorship award NOAA and Johns Hopkins Applied Physics Lab., 1976, 85, 97. Fellow Am. Geophys. Union; mem. Am. Phys. Soc., Internat. Assn. Geomagnetism and Aeronomy (pres. 1991-95), Internat. Acad. Astronautics, Sigma Xi. Home: 14870 Triadelphia Rd Glenelg MD 21737 Office Phone: 240-228-5405. Personal E-mail: donaldwmd@earthlink.net.

WILLIAMS, DONNA LEE H. state agency administrator; b. Wilmington, Del., Nov. 13, 1960; d. Ronald Lee and Loretta M. (Simonson) H.; m. John R. Williams, Oct. 8, 1988. AA, Wesley Coll., 1979; BA in Govt., Coll. William and Mary, 1981; JD, Widener U., 1984. Atty. Prickett, Jones, Elliott, Kristol & Shnee, Dover, Del., 1983-87, Bayard Handelman & Murdock, Dover, 1987-92; ins. commr. State Del., Dover, 1993—. Mem. Nat. Assn. Ins. Commrs., Del. Bar Assn., Kent County Bar Assn. (past pres.), Women Bus. Leaders, Women's Rep. Club Dover (pres. 1985-87). Methodist. Avocations: travel, sewing, english handsmocking, golf. Office: Del Dept Ins 841 Silver Lake Blvd Dover DE 19904-2465

WILLIAMS, DOROTHY STANDRIDGE, soft drink company official, civic worker; b. Powder Springs, Ga. d. Robert Anderson and Bertie Mae (Elsberry) Standridge; m. Harold Thomas Barfield (div.); 1 child, H. Gregory; m. J. Arden Williams (div.). Student, DeKalb Coll., Atlanta, 1982—83, U. Que., 1997, U. Laval, Que., 1998, U. Paris-Sorbonne, 2000. Assoc. promotion mgr., promotion coord. Coca-Cola USA, Atlanta, 1978-83, promotions mgr., 1983-86; mgr. internat. promotion svcs. The Coca-Cola Co., Atlanta, 1986-90, mgr. global promotion svcs., 1990-94. Cons., judge Point-of-Purchase Advt. Inst., 1995. Attaché Atlanta Conv. and Visitors Bur., 1992—; vol. Welcome South Ctr., Atlanta, 1995—; bd. advisors Life Coll. for Knowledge and Tng., 1995—; chmn. cmty. rels. com. Life Coll., 1995-96, vice chmn. bd. adv. Knowledge and Tng. program, 1997-98, chmn. bd. advisors Knowledge and Tng. program, 1998-99. Mem. Ga. Trust for Hist. Preservation, Atlanta High Mus. Art, Atlanta Bot. Garden, Alliance Francaise, Smyrna Hist. Soc. Avocations: travel, french studies, interior design, hiking, bridge.

WILLIAMS, DOYLE Z. university dean, educator; b. Shreveport, La., Dec. 18, 1939; s. Nuell O. and Lurline (Isbell) W.; m. Maynette Derr, Aug. 20, 1967; children: Zane Derr, Elizabeth Marie. BS, Northwestern State U., 1960; MS in Acctg., La. State U., 1962, PhD, 1965. CPA, Tex. Mgr. spl. edn. projects AICPA, N.Y.C., 1967-69; assoc. prof. Tex. Tech. U., Lubbock, 1969-71, prof. acctg., 1972-73, prof. area acctg., coord., 1973-78; prof. acctg. U. So. Calif., L.A., 1978-93, dean Sch. Acctg., 1979-87, interim dean Sch. Bus., 1986-88; dean Walton Coll. Bus. Adminstrn. U. Ark., Fayetteville, 1993—. Vis. prof. U. Hawaii, Honolulu, 1971-72. Author over 40 jour. articles and books. Chmn. Acctg. Edn. Change Commn., 1989-93. Named Mem. of Yr. N.Y. chpt. Nat. Assn. Accts., 1967, Outstanding Acctg. Educator Beta Alpha Psi, 1982; recipient Disting. Faculty award Calif. CPA Found., 1983, Nat. Leadership award Acad. Bus. Adminstrs., 1995, Lifetime Achievement award Ark. Soc. CPAs. Mem.: AICPA (coun. 1983—91, v.p. 1987—88, bd. dirs. 1987—91, Outstanding Educator award 1990, Gold medal 2002), Assn. to Advance Coll. Schs. Bus. Internat. (chair acctg. accreditation com. 1995—97, bus. accreditation com. 1995—97, chair acctg. accreditation com. 1999—2000, bd. dirs. 1999—, vice chair 2003—04, chair 2004—), S.W. Bus. Deans Assn. (pres. 1998—99), Adminstrs. Acctg. Programs (pres. 1977—78), Fedn. Schs. Accountancy (pres. 1982, Faculty Merit award 1993), Am. Acctg. Assn. (dir. edn. 1973—75, pres. 1984—85, Outstanding Educator award 1996). Home: 2447 E Boston Mountain View Fayetteville AR 72701-2802 Office: U Ark Sam M Walton Coll Bus Fayetteville AR 72701

WILLIAMS, DREW DAVIS, surgeon; b. San Augustine, Tex., Jan. 18, 1935; s. Floyd Everett and Villamae (Morehead) W.; m. Marilyn Raus, June 27, 1958; children: Leslie, Cynthia, Matthew, Jennifer, Amelia. BS, Tex. A&M Coll., 1957; MD, U. Tex., 1960; grad., naval flight surgeon, U.S. Naval Sch. Aviation Medicine, 1963. Diplomate Am. Bd. Surgery, Am. Bd. Quality Assurance and Utilization Rev. Physicians. Intern USPHS Hosp., Seattle, 1960-61; resident in gen. surgery U. Tex. Med. Br., Galveston, 1961-62, 64-68; resident in pulmonary svc. M.D. Anderson Hosp., Houston, 1968; pvt. practice Baytown, Tex., 1968—. Active staff San Jacinto (Tex.) Meth. Hosp., 1968-95, chief of surgery, 1972, 73, pres. med. staff, 1976; mem. courtesy staff Bay Coast Hosp., Baytown, 1968-95; cons. staff Baytown Med. Ctr. Hosp., 1972-95; 1st chmn. dept. surgery in devel. of family practice residency program affiliated with Tex. Med. Sch., Houston, 1977; mem. Tex. State Bd. Med. Examiners, 1983-89, sec.-treas., 1984-88, pres., 1988-89; unit med. dir., clin. instr. dept. preventive medicine and cmty. health U. Tex. Med. Br., Galveston, 1995-99. Contbr. chpt. to book and articles to profl. jours. Flight surgeon USN, 1962-64; lt. comdr. USNR, ret., 1967. Am. Cancer Soc. Clin. fellow, 1966-67. Fellow: AMA (Physicians Recognition award), ACS, Tex. Med. Assn. (fed. peer rev. group); mem.: KT, SAR (past pres. local chpt.), Houston Surg. Soc. (past pres.), Baytown Surg. Soc., East Harris County Med. Soc. (pres. 1982), Harris County Med. Soc. (mem. exec. bd. 1994, chmn. coun. med. splty.), Singleton Surg. Soc. (past pres.), Tex. Surg. Soc., Tex. Med. Found., Sovereign Colonial Soc.-Am. of Royal Descent, Magna Carta Barons (Somerset chpt.), Sir William Osler Soc., Sons of Republic of Tex. (life; at large life), Soc. Descendents of Colonial Clergy, Colonial Order of the Crown, Am. Cancer Soc. (pres. Baytown chpt. 1970—71), Shriners, Masons (32 degree), Phi Beta Pi. Democrat. Mem. Ch. of Christ. Avocations: hunting, fishing, genealogy, art, master gardner. Home and Office: 1217 Kilgore Rd Baytown TX 77520-3912

WILLIAMS, DUSTON, electronics company executive; BS in Acctg., Bentley Coll., 1980; MBA, U. So. Calif., 1989. Cert. Mgmt. Acct. With Calcomp; from mgr. corp. planning to v.p. fin. personal storage Western Digital Corp., Irvine, Calif., 1986-94, v.p., treas., 1994-96, sr. v.p. corp. officer, 1996-2000; CFO Enterprise Networking Sys., Inc., Redwood City, Calif., 2000—. Bd. dirs. Orange County chpt. ARC. Office: Enterprise Networking Sys Inc Western Digital Corp 70 Convention Way Redwood City CA 94062

WILLIAMS, EARLE CARTER, retired professional services company executive; b. Selma, Ala., Oct. 15, 1929; s. Henry Earle and Nora Elizabeth (Carter) W.; m. June Esther Anson, Sept. 7, 1951; children: Gayle Marie, Carol Patrice, Sharon Elaine. B.E.E., Auburn U., 1951; postgrad., U. N.Mex., 1959-62; DSc (hon.), Auburn U., 1991. Registered profl. engr., N.Mex. (ret.). Utilities design engr. Standard Oil Co. Ind., Whiting, 1954-56; mem. tech. staff Sandia Corp., Albuquerque, 1956-62; sr. engr. BDM Internat., Inc., El Paso, Tex., 1962-64, spl. projects dir., 1964-66, dir. ops., 1966-68, v.p., gen. mgr. Vienna, Va., 1968-72, pres., CEO, Vienna and McLean, Va., 1972-92, bd. dirs., 1972-97; ret. as CEO, BDM Internat. Inc., Vienna and McLean, Va., 1992. Bd. dirs. JnetDirect, Inc.; chmn. Va. Forward, 1997-2003; mem. Naval Rsch. Adv. Com., 1984-90, chmn., 1986-90; dir. Am. Bus. Conf., 1985-88. Exec. com., steering com. El Paso C.C., 1968-69, trustee, 1969-70; commr. Fairfax County Econ. Devel. Authority, 1976-80, chmn., 1978-80; mem. Va. State Bd. for C.C., 1980-87; bd. dirs. Ctrl. Va. Ednl. TV Corp., 1978-87, Atlantic Coun. U.S., 1987-93; chmn. George Mason Inst. Indsl. Policy Bd., 1982-91; bd. dirs. Wolf Trap Found., 1984-92, 97-2003, vice chmn., 1985-87, chmn., 1988-90, emeritus dir., 1992-97, 2003-; trustee Va. Found. for Ind. Colls., 1984-87, 90-94, Flint Hill Sch., Oakton, Va., 1990-95, George Mason U. Found., 1987-98; trustee Auburn U. Found., 1991—, pres., 2002—; bd. dirs. Potomac KnowledgeWay Project, 1995-99; mem. Va. Bus. Higher Edn. Coun., 1995—; bd. dirs. Spl. Ops. Warrior Found., 1997—. With U.S. Army, 1951—53. Recipient Engr. of Yr. award Va. Soc. Profl. Engrs., 1989, Superior Pub. Svc. award Dept. Navy, 1990; named to Ala. Engring. Hall of Fame, 1994. Mem. NSPE, Profl. Svcs. Coun. (bd. dirs. 1974-92, emeritus bd. dirs. 1992—, pres. 1976-79), Armed Force Comm. and Electronics Assn. (bd. dirs. 1978-82, 86-87, permanent dir. 1990, internat. v.p. 1979-82, 84-85, chmn. 1988-90, Disting. Svc. award 1987), Fairfax County C. of C., City Club (D.C.), Met. Club (D.C.), Tower Club (Vienna, Va.), Bay Colony Club (Naples, Fla.), Eta Kappa Nu. Presbyterian. Home: 1480 Evans Farm Dr #301 Mc Lean VA 22101-5652

WILLIAMS, EDDIE NATHAN, research institution executive; b. Memphis, Aug. 18, 1932; s. Ed and Georgia Lee (Barr) W.; m. Jearline F. Reddick, July 18, 1981; children: Traci Lynne, Edward Lawrence, Terence Reddick. BS, U. Ill., 1954; postgrad., Atlanta U., 1957, Howard U., 1960; LLD, U. D.C., 1986; DHL, Bowie State Coll., 1980, Chgo. State U., 1994, Dillard U., 2001; LLD, Benedict Coll., 2003. Reporter Atlanta Daily World Newspaper, 1957-58; staff asst. U.S. Senate Com. on Fgn. Relations, Washington, 1959-60; fgn. service res. officer U.S. Dept. State, Washington, 1961-68; v.p. U. Chgo., 1968-72; pres. Joint Ctr. for Polit. and Econ. Studies, Washington, 1972—. Vice chmn. Black Leadership Forum, 1996; bd. dirs. The Riggs Nat. Corp. Editorial columnist: Chgo. Sun Times, 1970-72; contbr. articles to profl. jours. Am. Polit. Sci. Assn. fellow, 1958, MacArthur Found. fellow, 1988, Nat. Acad. Pub. Adminstrn. fellow, 1993, Am. Acad. Arts and Scis. fellow, 1998; recipient Adam Clayton Powell Award Congl. Black Caucus, 1981, Washingtonian of Yr. award Washingtonian Mag., 1991, Alumni of Yr. award U. Ill. Alumni Club of Greater Washington, 1994, Outstanding Leadership award Korean Am. Alliance, 1994. Mem. Coun. Fgn. Rels., Kappa Tau Alpha, Omega Psi Phi, Sigma Pi Phi. Office: Joint Ctr Polit & Econ Studies 1090 Vermont Ave NW Ste 1100 Washington DC 20005-4905 E-mail: ewilliams@jointcenter.org.

WILLIAMS, EDSON POE, retired automotive company executive; b. Mpls., July 31, 1923; s. Homer A. and Florence C. Williams; m. Irene Mae Streed, June 16, 1950; children: Thomas, Louise, Steven, Linnea, Elisa. BSM.E. cum laude, U. Minn., 1950. Spl. purpose machinery operator, 1946-50; mfg. mgr., project engr. Crestliner div. Bigelow Sanford Inc., 1950-53, v.p., mgr. mfg. and engring., 1953-58, pres., 1958-63; with Ford Motor Co., 1963-87, mgr. customer svc. div., 1973; gen. mgr. Ford Motor Co. (Ford Mexico), 1973-75; pres. Ford Motor Co. (Ford Mid-East & Africa), 1975-79, Ford Motor Co. (Ford Asia-Pacific Inc.), 1979-87; v.p. Ford Motor Co., 1979-82, v.p.-gen. mgr. N.Am. truck ops., 1982-86, v.p. Ford Diversified Products ops., 1986-87. Served with USAAF, 1942-46. Mem.: The Strand Club. Home: 4795 Aston Gardens Way Unit D-201 Naples FL 34109-7610

WILLIAMS, EDWARD DAVID, consulting executive; b. Scranton, Pa., June 20, 1932; s. David Thomas and Mabel (Sims) W. m. Natalie Imnadze, Oct. 18, 1952; children: Denise, Claudia. BBA, Hofstra U., 1960; postgrad. in Bus. Adminstrn., Fairleigh Dickenson U., 1979. Cons. Cresap, McCormick and Paget, N.Y.C., 1964—65; sr. mgmt. cons. Union Carbide Corp., N.Y.C., 1965—67; asst. contr. data processing We. Union, N.Y.C., 1967—69; v.p. mgmt. info. sys. ABC, Hackensack, NJ, 1970—86; v.p., chief info. officer Blue Cross Blue Shield of N.J., Newark, 1986—88; v.p. Chantico Pub. Co., Carrellton, Tex., 1989—90; pres. SMC-BIS Inc., Basking Ridge, NJ, 1990—93; pres., CEO Strategic Outsourcing Svcs. Inc., Mountain Lakes, NJ, 1993—97; sr. v.p. Computer Horizons Corp., Mountain Lakes, 1997—99; exec. v.p. PRT Group Inc., Windsor, Conn., 1999; pres. Ed. Williams Assoc. Ltd., Franklin Lakes, NJ, 1999—. Spkr. in field. Mem. adv. bd. YMCA. With

U.S. Army, 1948-52. Decorated Silver Star with oak leaf cluster, Bronze Star with V, Purple Heart with 2 oak leaf clusters. Mem. Soc. Mgmt. Info. Systems, N.J. C. of C., Profit Oriented Systems Planning Bd. (bd. dirs.), Masons. Republican. Home and Office: Ed Williams Assoc Ltd 662 Cheyenne Dr Franklin Lakes NJ 07417 Office Phone: 201-847-9148. E-mail: Edward.D.Williams@att.net.

WILLIAMS, EDWARD EARL, JR., entrepreneur, educator; b. Houston, Aug. 21, 1945; s. Edward Earl and Doris Jewel (Jones) W.; m. Susan M. Warren, June 28, 1983; children: Laura Michelle, David Brian. BS, U. Pa., 1966; PhD, U. Tex., 1968. Asst. prof. econs. Rutgers U., New Brunswick, N.J., 1968-70; assoc. prof. fin. McGill U., Montreal, Que., 1970-73; v.p. Svc. Corp. Internat., Houston, 1973-77; prof. adminstrv. sci. Rice U., Houston, 1978-82, Henry Gardiner Symonds prof., 1982—, prof. stats., 1995—. Chmn. bd. dirs. Edward E. Williams & Co., Houston, 1976-92; chmn. bd., pres. Tex. Capital Investment Co., 1979-95; chmn. bd. First Tex. Venture Capital Corp., 1983-92; mng. dir. First Tex. Venture Capital, LLC, 1992-2000, Svc. Corp. Internat, EQUUS II, Inc.; adv. dir. Frost Nat. Bank. Author: Prospects for the Savings and Loan Industry, 1968, An Integrated Analysis for Managerial Finance, 1970, Investment Analysis, 1974, Business Planning for the Entrepreneur, 1983, The Economics of Production and Productivity: A Modeling Approach, 1996, Entrepreneurship and Productivity, 1998, The N.Y. Times Pocket MBA Series: Business Planning, 1999, Models for Investors in Real World Markets, 2003; contbr. articles to profl. jours. Benjamin Franklin scholar, Jesse Jones scholar U. Pa., 1966; fellow Tex. Savs. and Loan League, fellow NDEA U. Tex., 1968. Mem. Am. Statis. Assn., Coll. Innovation and Entrepreneurship, Fin. Mgmt. Assn., So. Pacific Hist. and Tech. Soc., Santa Fe Rlwy. Hist. and Modeling Soc., Soc. on Econs. and Mgmt. in China, Raveneaux Country Club, Jewish Comm. North, Beta Gamma Sigma, Alpha Kappa Psi. Republican. Home: 7602 Wilton Park Dr Spring TX 77379-4672 Office: Rice U Jesse H Jones Grad Sch Mgmt Houston TX 77251 Office Phone: 713-348-5381. E-mail: jmkeynes@rice.edu.

WILLIAMS, EDWARD F(OSTER), III, environmental engineer; b. N.Y.C., Jan. 3, 1935; s. E. Foster Jr. and Ida Frances (Richards) W.; m. Sue Carol Osenbaugh, June 5, 1960; children: Cecile Elizabeth, Alexander Harmon. BS in Engring., Auburn U., 1956; MA in History, U. Memphis, 1974. Registered profl. engr., Tenn. Engr. Buckeye Cellulose Corp. (subs. of Procter & Gamble), Memphis, 1957, process safety engr., 1960, resident constrn. engr. Perry, Fla., 1960-61, staff engr. Memphis, 1961-70; chief engr., v.p. Enviro-trol, Inc., Memphis, 1970-73; from v.p. to pres. Ramcon Environ. Corp., Memphis, 1973-80; pres. E.F. Williams & Assocs., Inc., Memphis, 1980-98; v.p. engring. Environ. Testing & Cons. of the Americas, Inc., 1998—2001, pres., 2001—. Chmn. bd. EFW Comml. Ventures, Inc., 1990—, Spiridon Press, Inc., 1998-99; bd. dirs. Mobile Process Tech. Inc., Memphis; v.p. Environ. Testing and Cons., Inc., Memphis, 1985-94; environ. coord. Shelby County, Tenn., 1995-96. Author: Fustest with the Mostest, 1968, Early Memphis and Its River Rivals, 1969, Great American Civil War Trivia Book, 1998; editor Environ. Control News for So. Industry, 1971—. State rep. Tenn. Gen. Assembly, 1970—78; mem. Shelby County Bd. Commrs., Memphis, 1978-94, chmn., 1987-88, 90-92, Shelby County Records Commn., 1978-, chmn., 1993-, Chickasaw Basin Authority, 1980-94, 98—, vice chmn., 1982-94; historian Shelby County, 1994—; environ. coord. Shelby County Mayor's staff, 1995—96; vice chmn. Shelby County Stormwater Steering Com., 1998—2002; trustee Bolton Coll., 1982-, chmn., 1987-88, 90-92; del. Rep. Nat. Conv., 1988; state chmn. Nat. Conf. Rep. County Ofcls., 1993—96; vice-chmn. Memphis-Shelby local Emergency Planning Com., 1986—2003; bd. dirs. Better Bus. Bur. Memphis, 1995—; chmn. Shelby County Hist. Commn., 1997—98; vice chmn. Shelby County Courthouse Hist. Preservation Commn., 2000—; pres. Christ United Presbyn. Ch. Corp., 1995—98; del. Rep. Nat. Conv., 1992, 1996, state exec. com., 1994—2002; bd. dirs. Southwest Tenn. C.C. Found., 2001—; v.p. Memphis Belle War Meml. Found., 1999—; adv. com. Boy Scouts of Am., Chickasaw Coun., 1980—; vice chmn. Rep. Party of Shelby County, 2003—. Lt. USAF, 1957—60, capt. res. USAF, 1961. Named Tenn. Water Conservationist of Yr., Tenn. Conservation League, 1973, Tenn. Legis. Conservationist of Yr., Nat. Wildlife Fedn., 1974, Memphis Outstanding Engr., Memphis Joint Engrs. Coun., 1980; recipient Shelby County Environ. Improvement award, 1983, Tenn. Lifetime Environ. Stewardship award Tenn. Dept. Environ. and Conservation, 1995. Mem. NSPE, ASME, Am. Acad. Environ. Engrs. (diplomate), Environ. Assesment Assn., TSPE, Water Environ. Fedn., Am. Indsl. Hygiene Assn. (chpt. pres.), Am. Soc. Safety Engrs. (Outstanding Achievement award 1995-96), Air and Waste Mgmt. Assn., Engrs. Club Memphis (bd. dirs. 1979-80, 98-2002, pres. 2000-01), Tenn. Water and Wastewater Assn., Rotary, C. of C. (environ. coun. chmn. 1988-2000, chmn. emeritus 2000—), Tenn. Hist. Soc. (v.p. 1972), Tenn. Hist. Commn. (vice-chmn. 1987-99), West Tenn. Hist. Soc. (pres. 1983-85), Am. Hist. Assn., Memphis-Shelby County Tenn. Bicentennial Commn. (chmn. 1994-96), Davies Manor Assn. (pres. 1999-2000), Miss. Hist. Soc. Republican. Avocation: history. Home: 148 Perkins Ext Memphis TN 38117-3127 Office: ETC of the Americas Inc 751 E Brookhaven Cir Memphis TN 38117-4501 also: PO Box 241813 Memphis TN 38124-1813 also: Shelby Co Office 150 Washington Ave Rm 210 Memphis TN 38103 Office Phone: 901-685-2077. E-mail: efwilliams@etcamemphis.com. *It has been my observation that history does not repeat itself, but human nature does. Knowledge of this principle can be put to use in politics, business, and other endeavors if one knows history.*

WILLIAMS, EDWARD FRANK, poet, entertainment company executive; b. N.Y.C., Oct. 3, 1949; s. Frank and Maggie W.; m. B.L. Williams, 1980 (div. 1985). AAS, Kingsborough C.C., Bklyn., 1970. Instr. bd. edn. Cmty. Sch. Dist. # 13, Bklyn., 1971-99; FCC 3rd class permit FCC, 1980—; performance poet Poet and Writers Inc., N.Y.C., 1980—; CSAC State of N.Y., 1990—; CEO, pres. Libra Prodns./Entertainment Inc., Bklyn., 1998. Author: E.F. Williams, Urban Poet, 1985, (CD version), 1999. Avocations: lyricist, motivational speaker, educational consultant. Home: 1633 Sterling Pl Apt 4H Brooklyn NY 11233-4970

WILLIAMS, EDWARD GILMAN, retired bank executive; b. Ware, Mass., Apr. 11, 1926; s. Carl Emmons and Susan Helen (Gilman) W.; m. Barbara Thompson Russell, June 19, 1959; children: Thomas Clarke, Susan Gilman. BA, Trinity Coll., Conn., 1950. With Union Trust Co., New Haven, 1951-89; asst. trust officer Union & New Haven Trust Co., 1956-59, trust officer, 1959-64, v.p., 1964-65, v.p., sr. adminstrv. officer, 1965-69; sr. v.p. Union Trust Co., 1969-72, exec. v.p., 1972-89; v.p. Northeast Bancorp., Inc., 1972-89. Former treas. Leila Day Nurseries, Inc., New Haven; treas., pres. Ridge Rd. Sch. PTA, Hamden Hall Country Day Sch. Parents Assn.; bd. dirs. Vis. Nurse Assn., New Haven, 1963-86, pres., treas., 1970-75; trustee New Eng. Sch. Banking, 1971-74, 81-88, vice chmn., 1985-86, chmn. 1986-88; trustee Shubert Performing Arts Ctr., New Haven, 1985-90; bd. dirs. New Haven Colony Hist. Soc., 1987-89; trustee, deacon, chmn. music com. Ch. of Redeemer, New Haven; bd. dirs., treas. Edgerton Garden Ctr., 1992-99, asst. treas. 1999-2001; bd. dirs. Friends of Grove St. Cemetery, treas., 1997—, dir. devel., 2003—; bd. dirs. Easter Seals Goodwill Rehab. Ctr., New Haven, 1993-99, Whitney Ctr. Continuing Care Retirement Cmty., Hamden, 1998—2004. Mem. English-Speaking Union (treas. New Haven br. 1994—), New Haven Lawn Club (pres. 1979-82), Masons. Home: 900 Mix Ave Apt 17 Hamden CT 06514-5107 Office: 3074 Whitney Ave # 2-L Hamden CT 06518-2391

WILLIAMS, EDWARD W. information technology executive; BS in Mgmt., Rutgers U.; degree in Bus., Stanford U. Various postions RCA and The Gen. Electric Co., 1959—87; from mem. staff to sr. v.p., CFO ITT Industries, White Plains, NY, 1987—2002, sr. v.p., 2002—, CFO, 2002—. Mem. exec. com. ITT Industries. Office: ITT Industries 4 West Red Oak Lane White Plains NY 10604-3617

WILLIAMS, EDWIN NEEL, newspaper editor; b. Rives, Mo., Jan. 14, 1942; s. Carl Edwin and Vina Marie (Edmonston) W.; m. Marylyn Lentine, 1973; 1 child, Jonathan Lentine. BA in History, U. Miss., 1965. Reporter Clarksdale (Miss) Press-Register, 1965; reporter, editor Delta Dem.-Times, Greenville, Miss., 1967-72; Nieman fellow Harvard U., Cambridge, Mass., 1972-73; writer, researcher Ford Found., N.Y.C., 1973; editorial writer Charlotte (N.C.) Observer, 1973-76, editor of editorial pages, 1976-80, 87—. Chmn. KinderMourn, Charlotte, 1988, N.C. Harvest, 1993-94; bd. dirs. N.C. Ctr. for Pub. Policy Rsch., Raleigh, 1992-95. With U.S. Army, 1965-67. Baptist. Home: 916 Mount Vernon Ave Charlotte NC 28203-4845 Office: Charlotte Observer PO Box 30308 Charlotte NC 28230-0308 E-mail: ewilliams@charlotteobserver.com.

WILLIAMS, ELEANOR CLAFLIN (CLAFFY WILLIAMS), artist; b. Brookline, Mass., Jan. 31, 1916; d. Thomas Mack and Alice Morton (Osborn) Claflin; m. Thomas Blake Williams, Jan. 26, 1940; children: Thomas B. Jr., Susan Williams Dickie, Eleanor Williams Wright, Sandra M. Williams Weiss. Student, Sweet Briar Coll. Art tchr.; lectr. on contemporary art. One woman shows include Pual Platt Libr., Cohasset, Mass., 1998, Cohasset Paul Pratt Meml. Libr., 1999; exhibited in various art shows including Copley Soc., Boston, 1974, 77, 98, 99, 2000, Chinese Cultural Inst., Boston, 1992, 98, 2000, South Shore Art Ctr., Cohasset, 1996, 97, 98, 2000, Modern Art D'unet, Tonniens, 1993, Chinese Cultural Inst., Boston, 1992, 96, Ariel Gallery, Soho, N.Y., 1990, Art Complex, Duxbury, Mass., 1982, 97; 3 paintings in book The Best in Acrylic Painting, 1996, Artexpo in N.Y.C. promoted by ARTREPS, 1998; 3 paintings in Creative Inspirations, 1997. Pres. bd. dirs. South Shore Art Ctr., Cohasset, Mass., 1985-87, mem. adv. bd., 1987—; dir. Prison Art Project, Boston, 1973-76; bd. dirs. Copley Soc., Boston, 1975-79. Recipient 1st prize for graphics North River Art Assn., Marshfield, Mass. Avocations: skiing, tennis, walking, reading, travel.

WILLIAMS, ELEANOR JOYCE, retired government air traffic control specialist; b. College Station, Tex., Dec. 21, 1936; d. Robert Ira and Viola (Ford) Toliver; m. Tollie Williams, Dec. 30, 1955 (div. July 1978); children: Rodrick, Viola Williams Smith, Darryl, Eric, Dana Williams Robinson, Sheila Williams Watkins, Kenneth. Student, Prairie View A&M Coll., 1955-56, Anchorage Community Coll., 1964-65, U. Alaska-Anchorage, 1976. Clk./stenographer FAA, Anchorage, 1965-66, adminstrv. clk., 1966-67, pers. staffing asst., 1967-68, air traffic control specialist, 1968-79, air traffic control supr. San Juan, P.R., 1979-80, Anchorage, 1983-85, airspace specialist Atlanta, 1980-83, with Washington, 1985-87; area mgr. Kansas City Air Rt. Traffic Control Ctr., Olathe, Kans., 1987-89, asst. mgr. Quality Assurance, 1989-91, supr. traffic mgmt., 1991, supr. system effectiveness section, 1991-93, asst. air traffic mgr., 1993-94; air traffic mgr. Cleve. Air Route Traffic Control Ctr., Oberlin, Ohio, 1994-97; acting mgr. sys. mgmt. br. Des Plains, Ill., 1995-96; mem. human resource reform team task force Washington, 1996—; acting regional exec. mgr. Great Lakes Region Des Plaines, Ill., 1996-97. Proprietor Williams Apts., Anchorage. Sec. Fairview Neighborhood Coun., Anchorage, 1967-69; mem. Anchorage Bicentennial Commn., 1975-76; bd. dirs. Mt. Patmos Youth Dept., Decatur, Ga., 1981-82; mem. NAACP; del. to USSR Women in Mgmt., 1990; v.p. A&M Consol. Lincoln H.S. Alumni Assn., 2000—; mem. citizens amb. program People to People Internat.; mem. adv. bd. Lincoln Recreation Ctr. Recipient Mary K. Goddard award Anchorage Fed. Exec. Assn. and Fed. Women's Program, 1985, Sec.'s award Dept. Transp., 1985, Pres. VIP award, 1988, C. Alfred Anderson award, 1991, Disting. Svc. award Nat. Black Coalition of Fed. Aviation Employees, 1991, Paul K. Bohr award FAA, 1994, Nat. Performance Rev. Hammer award from V.P. Al Gore, 1996, Regional Adminstrs. award for meritorious svc. Gt. Lakes Regional Adminstrn., 1997, Top Flight award for outstanding svc. FAA, 1997; A salute to Her Name in the Congl. Record 104th Congress, 1995, Execs. in Profile award for exemplary career performance Region Ten Blacks in Govt., 1998, Pres.'s award for outstanding svc. Lincoln Former Students Assn.; named Disting. Alumnus Lincoln H.S., 2000; named Youth Advocate Cmty. Champion State of Tex., Tex. Commn. Alcohol & Drug Abuse, 2001; inducted into Black Aviation Hall fame, 2001. Mem.: Women in Mgmt. (del. Soviet Union), Internat. Platform Assn., Fed. Mgrs. Assn., Air Traffic Contrs. Assn., Profl. Women Contrs. Orgn., Nat. Black Coalition of Fed. Aviation Employees (pres. cen. region chpt. 1987—92, Over Achievers award 1987, Disting. Svc. award 1988, Sojourner Truth award Great Lakes region 1997), Blacks in Govt., Nat. Assn. Negro Bus. and Profl. Women USA Inc. (North to the Future club, charter pres. 1975—76), Gamma Phi Delta. Democrat. Baptist. Avocations: singing, sewing. Home: 7931 Old Seward Hwy Apt 8 Anchorage AK 99518-3265 E-mail: ejw4atc@aol.com., ejtwmsent@msn.com.

WILLIAMS, ELIZABETH A. financial planner, business consultant; b. San Francisco, Jan. 16, 1948; d. John and Myrtle Mary (Thierry) W.; children: Brian, Jonathan. Cert. in bus., U. Calif., 1979. Cert. computers loan processing. Manpower coord., fed. programs U.S. Govt., San Francisco; patient svc. rep. Health Care Svc., Oakland, Calif.; ins. and real estate cons.; pres. Investments Unlimited, Oakland, EWJ & Assocs. Mktg. Firm; leisure svcs. commr. City of Pitts.; CEO Ultimate Vacations Inc. Mem. NAACP, Contra Costa County Womens Commn.; bd. dirs. Coun. on Child Abuse. Recipient Pub. Speaking award; European Investment fellow. Mem. AAUW, NAFE, Nat. Real Estate Owners Assn., Nat. Notary Assn., Order Ea. Star, Heroines Jericho, Daus. Isis, Soroptimist Inc., Toastmistress Club, Beta Phi Sigma. Home: PO Box 523 Pittsburg CA 94565-0052

WILLIAMS, ELIZABETH A.W. foundation administrator; B, Smith Coll.; M, Northwestern U. City editor, edn. reporter, features writer Phila. Evening Bulletin, 1972-77; various editl. positions Phila. Inquirer, 1977-87, assoc. mng. editor, 1988-92; dir. ops. & spl. projects The Pew Charitable Trusts, Phila., 1998—. Office: Pew Charitable Trusts 2005 Market St Ste 1700 Philadelphia PA 19103-7017

WILLIAMS, ELLEN C. political party official; m. Greg Williams; children: Sam, Joey. Grad., U. Ky. Staff asst. Congressman Larry Hopkins. Cons. Lexington/Bluegrass Bd. of Realtors; active Anderson County United Way Bd., Ch. of Lawrenceburg. Polit. dir. Dole/Kemp Ky.; dep. campaign mgr. Larry Forgy campaign for Gov.; exec. dir. Rep. Party of Ky., 1990-92; regional polit. dir. Nat. Rep. Com.; chmn. Ky. Republican Party, 1999-; exec. asst. Senator Bob Kasten; mem. Regan/Bush '84; exec. dir. Young Rep. Fedn., 1983. Office: Rep Party of Ky PO Box 1068 Frankfort KY 40602 E-mail: chair@rpk.org.

WILLIAMS, EMMA, rail transportation executive; b. Cleveland, Ark., Feb. 8, 1928; d. James and Frazier (Byers) Wallace; m. Augusta Griggs, Mar. 20, 1954 (dec.); children: Judy A., Terri V.; m. John Williams. Grad. H.S., Chgo. Pres., CEO Burlington No. Inc., Inglewood, Calif., 1986—. Republican. Avocations: reading, gardening, housekeeping. Office: Burlington N Santa Fe RR 3300 Manhattan Village Manhattan Beach CA 90266 Office Phone: 323-758-0919. E-mail: judygr7@aol.com.

WILLIAMS, ERIC JOSEPH, transportation executive; b. Havana, Cuba, Nov. 15, 1945; came to U.S., 1961; s. Ereic and Frances (Waterhouse) W.; m. Maria Julia Williams, Mar. 30, 1984; children: Jason, Natasha. BS in Fgn. Svc., Georgetown U., 1968. With Emery Worldwide, Miami, Fla., 1970-88, regional mgr. S.Am., 1977-81, dist. mgr. L.Am.-Caribbean, 1984-86, dir. L.Am.-Caribbean sector, 1986-88; dir. L.Am.-Caribbean region LEP Internat., Miami, 1988-90; mng. dir. sales L.Am. divsn. Fed. Express, 1990-96; sr. mgr. L.Am. sales Fritz Co., 1996-98; v.p. internat. Pilot Air, 1999—2003; v.p. D.F. Young Logistics, 2003—. Adult edn. tchr., Miami, 1973-75; chmn. Air Cargo Ams., 1999. Exec. bd. Hist. Mus. South Fla.; mem. mem. Miami Beacon Coun., 1995-97; pres. G.O.A.L., 2004—. 1st lt. U.S. Army, 1968-70. Mem. Soc. Ams., Coral Gables C. of C., Georgetown U. Alumni Assn. (com.), Coconut Grove Sailing Club (com. 1975-76). Episcopalian. Home: 501 Raven Ave Miami FL 33166-3950 Office Phone: 305-610-0499. E-mail: ejoe04@aol.com.

WILLIAMS, ERIK GEORGE, professional football player; b. Phila., Sept. 7, 1968; Student, Ctrl. State U. Offensive tackle Dallas Cowboys, 1991—2000. Mem. Superbowl Championship team, 1993, 94. Named to Pro Bowl Team, 1993; named offensive tackle on The Sporting News NFL All-Pro Team, 1993; selected to Pro Bowl, 1996.

WILLIAMS, ERVIN EUGENE, religious organization administrator; b. Corning, N.Y., Feb. 25, 1923; s. Douglas Lewis and Mina P. (Barnes) W.; m. Ruth Evelyn Snyder, June 12, 1945; children: Roger Eugene, Virginia Ruth. Student, Toccoa Falls (Ga.) Bible Coll., 1939, Cornell U., 1942; BA, Pa. State U., 1949; MA, Mich. State U., 1961, PhD in Communications, 1971. Ordained to ministry Ind. Bapt. Ch., 1950. Acad. dean Greensburg (Pa.) Bible Inst., 1949-51; min. Bapt. Ch., New Kensington, Pa., 1951-53; instr. Pa. State U., 1953-55; sr. min. East Lansing (Mich.) Trinity Ch., 1955-71; vis. prof. Trinity Evang. Div. Sch., Deerfield, Ill., 1968-71, prof. comm. and practical theology, 1971-77, dir. D Ministry program, 1975-76; gen. dir. Am. Missionary Fellowship, Villanova, Pa., 1977-92; exec. min. Ch. of the Apostles, Atlanta, 1993-95; ch. and instl. cons. Smyrna, Ga., 1995—; sr. pastor New Life Bible Ch., Man-O-War Cay, Abaco, The Bahamas, 1997—98. Chaplain Mich. State U., East Lansing, 1955-71; cons. Haggai Inst. for Advanced Leadership Tng., Atlanta, 1969-95; lectr. Calvary Bapt. Coll., Kansas City, Mo., 1962, Haggai Inst. Third World Leaders, Singapore, 1970-95; Staley lectr. Robert Wesleyan Coll., North Chili, N.Y., 1973, Judson Coll., Elgin, Ill., 1977-79; cons. to mission bds., 1967-76; assoc. dir. Camp of Woods, Speculator, N.Y., 1971-77. Author: 3 books; contbr. numerous articles to religious periodicals, also monographs. Trustee Dorothy H. Theis Meml. Found., Sierra Vista, Ariz., 1987-95, Gospel Vols., Speculator, N.Y., 1963-93; mem. bd. regents Owosso (Mich.) Coll., 1971-73. Pilot USAAF, 1942-45, prisoner of war, ETO, 1945. Decorated DFC, Air medal with two oak leaf clusters, POW medal, ETO Campaign medal with six clusters, Victory medal, Presdl. citation. Mem. Nat. Sunday Sch. Assn., Christian Assn. Psychol. Studies, Mich. Acad. Arts and Scis., Aircraft Owners and Pilots Assn., Phi Beta Kappa, Pi Gamma Mu, Phi Kappa Phi, Alpha Kappa Delta. *It is much more difficult to conceal ignorance and prejudice than it is to acquire knowledge and fairness.*

WILLIAMS, FORMAN ARTHUR, engineering science educator, combustion theorist; b. New Brunswick, N.J., Jan. 12, 1934; s. Forman J. and Alice (Pooley) W.; m. Elsie Vivian Kara, June 15, 1955 (div. 1978); children: F. Gary, Glen A., Nancy L., Susan D., Michael S., Michelle K.; m. Elizabeth Acevedo, Aug. 19, 1978. BSE, Princeton U., 1955; PhD, Calif. Inst. Tech., 1958; Doctorate (hon.), Poly. U. Madrid, 2002. Asst. prof. Harvard U., Cambridge, Mass., 1958-64; prof. U. Calif.-San Diego, 1964-81; Robert H. Goddard prof. Princeton U., N.J., 1981-88; prof. dept. mech. and aerospace engring. U. Calif., San Diego, 1988—, presdidential chair in Energy and Combustion Rsch, 1994—. Adj. prof. Yale U., New Haven, 1997—. Author: Combustion Theory, 1965, 2d edit., 1985; contbr. articles to profl. jours. Fellow NSF, 1962; fellow Guggenheim Found., 1970; recipient U.S. Sr. Scientist award Alexander von Humboldt Found., 1982, Silver medal Combustion Inst., 1978, Bernard Lewis Gold medal Combustion Inst., 1990, Pendray Aerospace Literature award Am. Inst. of Aeronautics and Astronautics, 1993; named Pioneer Rschr. of the 20th Century, Japan Soc. Mech. Engrs., 1995. Fellow AIAA, Am. Phys. Soc.; mem. Combustion Inst., Soc. for Indsl. and Applied Math., Nat. Acad. Engring., Nat. Acad. Engring Mex. (fgn. corr. mem.), Sigma Xi. Home: 8258 Caminito Maritimo La Jolla CA 92037-2204 Office: U Calif San Diego Ctr Energy Rsch 9500 Gilman Dr La Jolla CA 92093-5004 E-mail: faw@ucsd.edu.

WILLIAMS, FRANCINE ANITA, community outreach worker; b. Philadelphia, Pa., Aug. 12, 1963; d. Benjamin Noel and Frances Ann Williams; m. Randy Glen Robinson, June 11, 1993; m. Clyde Edward James, Nov. 9, 1979 (div.); 1 child, Gabrielle Nydera. M of human svc., Lincoln U., 1999—2001; PhD, Walden U., 2003. Audio duplication specialist Recorded Publ. Lab., Camden, NJ, 1988—91; asst. tchr. The Calvary Bapt. Ch. Day Care, Phila., 1991—93; child-care worker Youth Emergency Svc., Youth Svc., Inc., Phila., 1993—, runaway youth program cmty. outreach worker, 1999—. Mem. The Calvary Bapt. Ch., Phila., 1991. FSP Scholarship, Family Svc. of Phila. Tng. Program of YSI, 1999—2001. Mem.: Order of the Ea. Star (apptd. officer 2002), PI Gamma Mu (life). D-Liberal. Bapt. Achievements include research in innovative and positive behavior modification techniques to assist adolescents in short-term care. Avocations: gardening, reading, travel. Office: Youth Emergency Service Youth Service 1526 Fairmount Ave Philadelphia PA 19130 E-mail: fwillams@ysiphila.org.

WILLIAMS, FRANK J. judge, historian, writer; b. Providence, Aug. 24, 1940; s. Frank and Natalie L. (Corelli) W.; m. Virginia E. Miller, Aug. 24, 1966. BA, Boston U., 1962, JD, 1970; MS in Taxation, Bryant Coll., 1986, LHD (hon.), 2004, Lincoln Coll., 1987; LLD (hon.), So. New England Sch. Law, 2001; LHD (hon.), Johnson & Wales U., 2002; diploma (hon.), Lincoln Meml. U., 2002; LLD (hon.), Roger Williams U., 2004, U. Mass., 2004. Bar: R.I. 1970, U.S. Dist. Ct. R.I. 1970, U.S. Supreme Ct. 1976. Assoc. Tillinghast, Collins & Graham, Providence, 1970-75, Leonard Decof Ltd., Providence, 1976-78; law clk. Graham, Reid, Ewing & Stapleton, Providence, 1969; law clk., adminstrv. asst. R.I. Atty. Gen., Providence, 1967-68; pres. Frank J. Williams Ltd., attys.-at-law, Providence, 1978-95; assoc. justice R.I. Superior Ct., 1995-2001; chief justice Supreme Ct. R.I., 2001—. Judge of probate Town of Hopkinton, RI, 1978-82, 84-90, solicitor, 1978-82, 84-87; judge of probate Town of West Greenwich, RI, 1984-86, 92-95, solicitor, 1984-92, asst. solicitor, 1992-95; dep. judge of probate, 1987-92; solicitor Town of Coventry, RI, 1972-74, 76-78, Town of Barrington, RI, 1993-95, Town of Bristol, RI, 1995, Town of South Kingstown, RI, 1995; past spl. counsel Towns of Westerly, Bristol, Hopkinton, South Kingstown, City of Providence; atty. Town of Smithfield Sewer Authority, 1974-90; legis. counsel RI Retail Fedn., 1975-93, Credit Info. Bur., RI Mortgage Bankers Assn., 1992-95; adj. prof. Roger Williams Sch. of Law, 1997—, US Naval War Coll., 2003—; lectr. bus. and legal practice RI Sch. Design, Providence, 1976-80; panel of arbitrators Am. Arbitration Assn., panel of mediators RI Superior Ct., 1993-95; mem. RI Bd. Bar Examiners, 1987-95, chair, 1995; chair RI Housing and Mortgage Fin. Corp., 1995, Lincoln Forum, 1996—; apptd. by pres. to rev. panel for mil. tribunals, Guantanamo Bay, Cuba, 2004—. Pres. Lincoln Group of Boston, 1976—88, Abraham Lincoln Assn., Springfield, Ill., 1986—95, Ulysses S. Grant Assn., 1990—; elected del. R.I. Constnl. Conv., 1986; elected town moderator Richmond, RI, 1992—95; dist. moderator Chariho Regional Sch. Dist., 1994; chmn. Lincoln adv. com. Brown U.; mem. Lincoln prize adv. com. Gettysburg Coll.; bd. dirs. John E. Fogarty Found. for Persons with Mental Retardation, 1975—, South County Hosp., 1995—2004, R.I. Coun. for the Humanities, 2001—, Narragansett Coun. Boy Scouts Am., 1969—80, 1998—2001. Capt. U.S. Army, 1962—67, Germany and Vietnam. Decorated Bronze Star, Combat Infantryman's badge, Army Commendation medal, Air medal with 2 oak leaf clusters, Republic of Vietnam Gallantry Cross with silver star; named Hon. Brigadier Gen., R.I. Militia, 2003; named to RI Heritage Hall of Fame, 2004. Fellow: ATLA (jud.); mem.: RI Bar Assn. (chmn. new lawyers adv. com. 1976—87, ho. of dels. 1986—93, chmn. mcpl. law com. 1993), Conf. Chief Justices (bd. dirs. 2004—), Am. Law Inst., Nat. Assn. for Ct. Mgmt., Am. Judges Assn., Am. Antiquarian Soc., Phi Alpha Delta, Alpha Phi Sigma, Phi Sigma Alpha. Roman Catholic. Office: 250 Benefit St Providence RI 02903 Office Phone: 401-222-3290.

WILLIAMS, FRANKLIN CADMUS, JR., bibliographer; b. Palestine, Tex., July 30, 1941; s. Franklin Cadmus and Cathryn Lucille (Pessoney) W. BA, Baylor U., 1963; MA, Stephen F. Austin State U., 1965; PhD, U. Wis., 1975. Cert. in secondary edn. English and History. Teaching fellow Stephen F. Austin State U., Nacogdoches, Tex., 1964-65, U. Wis., Madison, 1965-68; instr. English Austin Peay State U., Clarksville, Tenn., 1970-71; adj. asst. prof. East Tex. State U., Commerce, 1975; asst. prof. English Jarvis Christian Coll., Hawkins, Tex., 1976-78, 79-81; ind. scholar Palestine, Tex., 1981—; owner, bibliographer Goldsmith Archive, Palestine, 1981—. Cons. Diocese of Galveston-Houston, 1977-84, Tex. State Hist. Assn., Austin, 1988; speaker, editor Jarvis Christian Coll., Hawkins, Tex., 1976-78, 79-81; nat. teaching fellow Office Edn., Washington, 1976-77; del. to Baylor U., U. Wis. System, Madison, 1981. Author: Lone Star Bishops: The Roman Catholic Hierarchy in Texas, 1997; contbr. articles to profl. jours. Mem. Modern Lang. Assn., Tex. State Hist. Assn., Tex. Cath. Hist. Soc., Baylor Alumni Assn. (life), Wis. Alumni Assn. (life), Sigma Tau Delta. Avocations: reading, record collecting, historical genealogy, tennis, swimming. Office: PO Box 96 Palestine TX 75802-0096

WILLIAMS, GARY MURRAY, medical researcher, pathology educator; b. Regina, Sask., Can., May 7, 1940; s. Murray Austin and Selma Ruby (Domstad) W.; m. Julia Christine Lundberg; children: Walter, Jeffrey, Ingrid. BA, Washington and Jefferson Coll., 1963; MD, U. Pitts, 1967. Diplomate Am. Bd. Pathology, Am. Bd. Toxicology. Assoc. prof. pathology Temple U., Phila., 1971-75; mem. Fels Rsch. Inst., Phila., 1971-75; rsch. prof. N.Y. Med. Coll., Valhalla, 1975-98, prof. pathology, environ. pathology and toxicology, dir., 1999—. Mem. toxicology study sect. NIH, Bethesda, Md., 1985-87, metabolic pathol. study sect., 2003; working group Internat. Agy. Rsch. on Cancer, Lyon, France, 1976, 80, 82-83, 85-87, 89, 91, 96-99; subcom. on upper reference levels of nutrients NRC, 1999-2003; advisor joint expert com. on food additives WHO, 2001-04. Founding editor: Cell Biology and Toxicology, 1984—; mem. editl. bd. Archives of Toxicology, 1988—, European Jour. Cancer Prevention, 1991—, Drug and Chem. Toxicology, 1994—, Toxicologic Pathology, 2003—; contbr. over 475 articles to profl. jours.; editor or co-editor 8 books. Lt. comdr. USPHS, 1969-71. Recipient Sheard-Sanford award Am. Soc. Clin. Pathologists U. Pitts., 1967. Fellow Internat. Acad. Toxicol. Pathology (accreditation com.), Royal Coll. Pathologists; mem. Am. Assn. Cancer Rsch., Soc. Toxicology (Mid-Atlantic chpt., amb. in toxicology 2001, Arthur J. Lehman award 1982, Lectr. award 1996, Advancement Animal Welfare award 2002), Soc. Toxicol. Pathology, Phi Beta Kappa, Alpha Omega Alpha. Home: 8 Elm Rd Scarsdale NY 10583-1410 Office: Dept Pathology NY Med Coll Valhalla NY 10595-1549 Office Phone: 914-594-4672. Business E-Mail: gary_williams@nymc.edu.

WILLIAMS, GEORGE CHRISTOPHER, biologist, ecology and evolution educator; b. Charlotte, N.C., May 12, 1926; s. George Felix and Margaret (Steuart) W.; m. Doris Lee Calhoun, Jan. 25, 1951; children: Jacques, Sibyl, Judith, Phoebe. AB, U. Calif., Berkeley, 1949; PhD, UCLA, 1955; ScD (hon.), Queen's U., Kingston, Ont., Can., 1995, SUNY, Stony Brook, 2000. Instr. and asst. prof. Mich. State U., East Lansing, 1955-60; assoc. prof. dept. ecology and evolution SUNY, Stony Brook, 1960-66, prof., 1966-90. Adj. prof. Queens U., Kingston, Ont., Can., 1980—. Author: Adaptation and Natural Selection, 1966, Sex and Evolution, 1975, Natural Selection: Domains, Levels and Challenges, 1992, The Pony Fish's Glow, 1997; co-author: (with R.M. Nesse) Why We Get Sick: The New Science of Darwinian Medicine, 1995; co-editor: (with James Paradis) Evolution and Ethics, 1989; editor Quar. Rev. Biology, SUNY, 1965-98. With U.S. Army, 1944-46. Recipient Eminent Ecologist award Ecol. Soc. Am., 1989, Daniel Giraud Elliot medal Nat. Acad. Sci., 1992, Royal Swedish Acad. Crafoord prize, 1999; fellow Ctr. Adv. Study Behavioral Sci., Stanford, 1981-82, Guggenheim Found., 1988-89. Fellow AAAS, Soc. Study Evolution (v.p. 1973, pres. 1989), Nat. Acad. Sci., Am. Soc. Ichthyologists and Herpetologists, Am. Soc. Naturalists (editor 1974-79), Icelandic Natural History Soc. Office Phone: 631-632-8600.

WILLIAMS, GEORGE EARNEST, engineer, retired business executive; b. Bartow, Fla., Nov. 27, 1923; s. Earnest Roscoe and Ruby Barnett (Mathews) W.; m. Muriel Theodorsen, June 9, 1949. BS in Engring. with honors, USCG Acad., 1944; postgrad., Harvard U., 1945-46; SM in Mgmt., MIT, 1949. Registered profl. engr. 2 states. Project engr., bus. cons. Ebasco, N.Y.C.; design engr., prodn. supr. Minute Maid Corp., Orlando, Fla.; asst. contr., div. contr., group contr., corp. dir. fin. planning and analysis United Technologies Corp., Hartford, 1957-76, v.p., 1977-82; sr. v.p. Kensington Mgmt. Cons., 1982-84; sr. v.p. fin. Otis Elevator Co., N.Y.C., 1976-77. Mem. exec. com. Conn. Commn. Services and Expenditures, 1971, Under then Gov. Meskill. Contbr. articles to fin. jours., chpts. to books. Served with USCG, 1941-47, PTO and Atlantic. Mem. AIAA, Fin. Execs. Inst., Army and Navy Club (Washington), Naples Yacht Club, Port Royal Club. Achievements include originating pricing system purchase of Fla. oranges for concentrate mfg. which is still in use and has made a great change in citrus horticulture to an emphasis on sweeter juice vs. outside appearance. Avocation: yachting. Home: 1325 7th St S Naples FL 34102-7327

WILLIAMS, GEORGE LEO, historian, landmark preservationist, educator; b. N.Y.C., June 29, 1931; s. Leo Dominick and Cathryn Margaret (Schellderfer) W.; m. Adelia Gilda Musa, Feb. 26, 1958; children: Adelia, Marina, Gilda. BA, CUNY, 1953, MA, 1955; PhD, NYU, 1966. Tchr. Port Washington (N.Y.) Pub. Schs., 1953, chairperson integrated studies, 1960-65, coord. Amherst project, 1968-69, chairperson English dept., 1970-90; adminstrv. asst. secondary and higher edn. dept. NYU, N.Y.C., 1965-66. Adj. prof. NYU, 1966-74, Adelphi U., Garden City, N.Y. 1967-69, Hofstra U., Hempstead, N.Y., 1967-74; chmn. profl. growth and devel. com. Port Washington Pub. Schs., 1973-90, chmn. bicentennial com. 1989-90, mem. policy bd. Port Washington Tchr. Ctr., 1987-90; mem. alumni bd. Queens Coll. History Dept., 1996-2000. Co-author: (play) The Triumph of the Constitution, 1988; author: Fascist Thought and Totalitarianism in Italy's Secondary Schools: Theory and Practice, 1922-1943, 1993, Port Washington in the Twentieth Century: Places and People, 1995, Papal Genealogy: The Families and Descendants of the Popes, 1998, (play) Remembrances of the First Colonial Settlement, 1993; contbg. author: Erziehungsstaaten, 1998; editor Port Arrow Community Newsletter, 1973-84, Cow Neck Peninsula Hist. Soc. Newsletter, 1974-77, Cow Neck Peninsula Hist. Soc. Jour., 2001—; contbg. editor L.I. Forum, 1985—; author, prodr. (video) Port Washington into the 21st Century, 1996. Chairperson landmarks com. Cow Neck Peninsula Hist. Soc., Port Warhington, 1980—97, trustee, 1974—77; commr. landmarks com. Village of Port Washington North, 1983—; pres. Hist. Soc. North Hempstead, 2001—04; mem., chairperson Hist. Landmark Preservation Commn., North Hempstead, NY, 1984—, chmn., 1991—; chairperson 1701 Roslyn Grist Mil Com., 1997—; mem. Port Washington Continuing Edn. Adv. Coun., 1988—97; co-chair Roslyn Clock Tower Com., 1994—96; mem. Preservation League of N.Y., Bigelow Soc., N.Y. Pub. Libr., W.A.R. Goodwin Soc.; grant writer Dodge House Restoration Com.; mem. orgnl. com. Landmark on Main St., 1984—90; mem. Cow Neck Peninsula Hist. Soc. Dodge House Restoration Com., 1992—; adv. bd. records Town of North Hempstead, 1994—; mem. 1998 ann. com. L.I.R.R. to Port Washington; trustee Sand Miners Meml., Inc., 2003—. Recipient environ. award Residents for a More Beautiful Port Washington, 1994, numerous Certs. of Appreciation, Civic award for Outstanding Cmty. Svc., Port Washington Rotary, 2001, Cert. of Appreciation, Port Washington Police Dist., 2001, Exec. Citation, Nassau County, 2001, citation N.Y. State Assembly, 2001, Legis. citation Nassau County, 2001, Queens Coll. Dept. History Cert. Appreciation, 2002, Town of North Hempstead's Proclamation, 2002. Mem.: Friends of the Arts, Friends of Planting Fields, Nat. Trust Hist. Preservation, N.Y. State Mus. Assocs., Fulbright Assn., Am. Hist. Assn. (cert. recognition 1988), Port Washington Tchrs. Assn. (v.p. 1963—64, bd. dirs. 1966—74, newsletter editor 1990—92, founder and 1st pres. ret. tchrs. chpt. 1991), Soc. for Preservation L.I. Antiquities, Assn. Pub. Historicans of N.Y. State, Friends for L.I.'s Heritage, N.Y. State Hist. Assn., N.Y. Geneal./Biographical Soc., Residents for a More Beautiful PortWashington (Environ. Quality Recognition award 2003), Roslyn Landmark Soc., Pi Sigma Alpha, Phi Alpha Theta, Phi Beta Kappa. Home: 84 Radcliff Ave Port Washington NY 11050-1600

WILLIAMS, G(EORGE) MELVILLE, surgeon, medical educator; b. Soochow, China, Nov. 16, 1930; came to U.S., 1940; s. Melville Owens and Annie Lee (Young) W.; m. Lee Logan, June 12, 1955 (div. 1985); children: Curtiss John, Steven Hoyt, Lucy Roxanna, Elizabeth Hopkins, Feb. 14, 1986 (div.); m. Linda Parsons, Apr. 14, 1996. BA, Oberlin Coll., 1953; MD, Harvard U., 1957. Diplomate Am. Bd. Surgery. Spl. fellow NIH, Melbourne, Australia, 1963-64; instr. surgery Med. Coll. Va., Richmond, 1964-65, asst. prof. surgery, 1965-66, assoc. prof. surgery, 1966-67, prof. surgery, 1967-69, The Johns Hopkins U. Sch. Medicine, Balt., 1969—. Author: Atlas of Aortic Surgery, Editor: Transplant Rejection. United Network Organ Sharing (pres. 1984 85). Capt. U.S. Army, 1960-62. Grantee NIH, 1969, 82, Am. Heart Assn., 1991. Mem. Am. Surg Assn., The Halsted Soc. (pres. 1983), Am. Soc. Transplant Surgeons (pres. 1982-83), So. Assn. for Vascular Surgery (pres. 1991). Democrat. Methodist. Avocations: carpentry, fishing, boating. Office: Johns Hopkins Hosp 600 N Wolfe St Baltimore MD 21287-8611 Business E-Mail: gwilliam@jhmi.edu.

WILLIAMS, GEORGE WALTON, English educator; b. Charleston, SC, Oct. 10, 1922; s. Ellison Adger and Elizabeth Simonton (Dillingham) W.; m. Harriet Porcher Simons, Nov. 28, 1953; children: George Walton Jr., Ellison Adger II, Harriet Porcher Stoney. BA, Yale U., 1947; MA, U. Va., 1949, PhD, 1957. Asst. cashier Carolina Savs. Bank, Charleston, 1949-54; asst. prof. English, Duke U., 1957-63, asso. prof., 1963-67, prof., 1967, chmn. dept. English, 1982-86, prof. emeritus, 1993—. Dir. summer inst. Commn. on English, Coll. Entrance Exam. Bd., 1962; pres. Durham Savoyards, Ltd., 1966-68, 81-82; sr. fellow Coop. Program in Humanities, Duke-U. N.C., 1969; Historiographer, Diocese of S.C., 1960-78; vis. prof. U.S. Mil. Acad., 1982-83 Author: St. Michael's, Charleston, 1751-1951, 1951, rev. edit., 2001, Image and Symbol in the Sacred Poetry of Richard Crashaw, 1963, The Craft of Printing and the Publication of Shakespeare's Plays, 1985, 4 children's books; editor: Romeo and Juliet, 1964, Complete Poetry of Richard Crashaw, 1970, Jacob Eckhard's Choirmaster's Book, 1971, Shakespeare's Speech-Headings, 1997; contbg. editor Dramatic Works of Beaumont and Fletcher, 1966-96; assoc. gen. editor Arden Shakespeare, 1996—. With U.S. Army, 1943—45, ETO. Decorated Combat Inf. badge; recipient Outstanding Civilian Service medal Dept. Army, 1983; Guggenheim Found. fellow, 1977-78; Huntington Library fellow, 1981 Mem. MLA (com. on new variorum 1980-92, chmn. Shakespeare divsn. 1990), South Atlantic MLA (pres. 1980-81, J.H. Fisher award 2001), Southeastern Renaissance Conf. (editor 1960-70, 91-95, pres. 1973, hon. life 2002), Bibliog. Soc., Royal Soc. Arts London, S.C. Hist. Soc., Carolina Yacht Club (Charleston), St. Cecilia Soc. (Charleston), Elizabethan Club Yale U., Phi Beta Kappa, Phi Kappa Phi. Home: 1 Tradd St Charleston SC 29401 Office: Duke U Dept English PO Box 90015 Durham NC 27708-0015 Office Phone: 919-684-5827.

WILLIAMS, GLEN MORGAN, federal judge; b. Jonesville, Va., Feb. 17, 1920; s. Hughy May and Hattie Mae W.; m. Jane Slemp, Nov. 17, 1962; children: Susan, Judy, Rebecca, Melinda. AB magna cum laude, Milligan Coll., 1940; JD, U. Va., 1948. Bar: Va. 1947. Pvt. practice law, Jonesville, 1948-76; judge U.S. Dist. Ct. (we. dist.) Va., 1976-88, sr. judge, 1988—; commonwealth's atty. Lee County, Va., 1948-51; mem. Va. Senate, 1953-55. Mem. editorial bd.: Va. Law Rev, 1946-47. Mem. Lee County Sch. Bd., 1972-76; trustee, elder First Christian Ch., Pennington Gap, Va.; trustee Milligan Coll., 1990—, Appalachian Sch. of Law, 1995—. Lt. USN, 1942-46, MTO. Recipient Citation of Merit Va. Def. Lawyers Assn., Outstanding Alumnus award Milligan Coll., 1980, Svc. to Region award Emory & Henry Coll., 1996. Mem. ABA, Va. State Bar (citation of merit), Va. Bar Assn. (citation of merit), Fed. Bar Assn., Va. Trial Lawyers Assn. (Meritorious Svc. award 1986, Disting. Svc. award), Am. Legion, 40 and 8. Clubs: Lions, Masons, Shriners. Office: US Dist Ct Fed Bldg PO Box 339 Abingdon VA 24212-0339 E-mail: glenw@vawd.uscourts.gov.

WILLIAMS, GLENN CARL, music educator, secondary school educator; b. Mt. Clemens, Mich., Apr. 11, 1965; s. George Robert and Mary Margaret Williams; m. Teresa Marie Williams, July 15, 1989; children: Josiah, Allison. B in Music Edn., Ind. U., 1988; M in Music Edn., Northwestern U., 1996. Dir. bands Highland Park (Ill.) H.S., 1988—96, Forest Hills Ctrl. H.S., Grand Rapids, Mich., 1996—. Choir dir. Thornapple Cmty. Ch., Grand Rapids, Mich., 2000—. Soccer coach Am. Youth Soccer Orgn., Grand Rapids, 2000—. Mem.: Mich. Sch. Band and Orch. Assn. (v.p. jazz activities 2000—). Avocations: collecting sports memoribilia, cooking, bicycling, running, coaching. Home: 7039 Burger Dr SE Grand Rapids MI 49546 Office: Forest Hills Ctrl HS 5901 Hall St SE Grand Rapids MI 49546

WILLIAMS, GREGG E. professional football coach; b. July 15, 1958; m. Leigh Ann Williams; children: Blake, Chase, Amy. BS, Truman State U.; MEd, Ctrl. Mo. State. Asst. football coach Excelsior Springs High Sch., Mo.; head football coach Belton High Sch., Mo., 1984—87; grad. asst. U. Houston, 1988—89; 1st quality control coach Houston Oilers, 1990, spl. team coach, 1993, linebackers coach, 1994—96; def. coord. Tenn. Oilers (now Titans), Nashville, 1997—2001; head coach Buffalo Bills, 2001—03; def. coord. Washington Redskins, 2004—. Office: Washington Redskins 21300 Redskin Pk Dr Ashburn VA 20147*

WILLIAMS, GREGORY KEITH, accountant; b. Elizabethtown, Ky., Mar. 20, 1958; s. James Marion and Shirley Catherine (Yates) W.; m. Diana Lynn McGuffin, May 26, 1979; 1 child, Kathryn May. BA in Pub. Mgmt., U. Ky., Lexington, 1985; BSBA, U. Louisville, 1987; MPA, Ball State U., 1996. Cert. mgmt. acct., info. sys. auditor, govt. fin. mgr. Supervisory staff acct. Fin. Acctg. Off., Fort Knox, Ky., 1983-85, internal auditor, 1985-89, sys. acct., 1989-93, Def. Fin. and Acctg. Svc. Indpls. Ctr., 1993-95, electronic commerce/data interchange coord., 1995-97; dep. project mgr. corp. database Def. Fin. and Acctg. Svc. Hdqrs., 1997-98, project mgr. corp. database, 1998-2000, program mgr. corp. database/warehouse, 2000—. Mem. Inst. Cert. Mgmt. Acct., Info. Sys. Audit and Control Assn., Am. Soc. Mil. Comptr., Assn. Govt. Acct., Phi Beta Kappa, Beta Gamma Sigma, Phi Kappa Phi. Home: 136 Lake Dr Greenwood IN 46142-9182 Office: Def Fin Acctg Svc 8899 E 56th St Indianapolis IN 46249-0002 Fax: 317-510-7250. E-mail: gkwdlw@msn.com.

WILLIAMS, GRETCHEN MINYARD, food store executive; b. Dallas, Dec. 18, 1956; d. Marvin Tipton and Clarine (Cooper) Minyard; m. Joseph Larry Williams, June 10, 1978. BBA, Tex. Christian U., 1978. Dir. employee rels. Minyard Food Stores, Inc., Coppell, Tex., 1978-80, v.p. employee rels., 1980-83, v.p. corp. rel., 1983-85, vice chmn. of bd. dirs., 1985-88, co-chmn. bd. dirs., 1988-98, co-CEO, co-chmn. bd. dirs., 1998—. Bd. dirs. Cullen/Frost Bank, N.A., Dallas. Adv. bd. mktg. edn. Dallas Ind. Sch. Dist., Dallas, 1981—; campaign mem. Old City Park, Dallas, 1988, Tex. Christian U. Fund Drive, Ft. Worth, 1987-88; adv. bd. Dallas Bapt. U., 1985—. Mem. Dallas/Ft. Worth Retail Grocers Assn. (chmn. bd. 1988—, avt. com.), AGAPE Social Svcs. Inc. (bd. dirs. 1987—), Baylor Health Care System (bd. dirs. 1989—), Zeta Tau Alpha (pres 1986-87). Avocations: reading, travel. Office: Minyard Food Stores Inc PO Box 518 777 Freeport Pky Coppell TX 75019-4411

WILLIAMS, H. THOMAS (TOM), academic administrator, physicist, educator; b. Hampton, Va. BS in Physics, PhD in Physics, U. Va. NSF post-doctoral rsch. fellow Nat. Bur. Stds., 1967—69; rschr. Inst. for Theoretical Physics, U. Erlangen-Nuernberg, Germany, 1970—71; staff scientist Kaman Scis. Corp., Colorado Springs, Colo., 1971—73; mem. faculty Washington and Lee U., Lexington, Va., 1974—, Edwin A. Morris prof. physics, 1994—, chair dept. physics, 1989—2000, assoc. dean, 1986—89, chief acad. officer, provost, 2003—. Cons. Nat. Bur. Stds., 1974—86, Los Alamos Sci. Lab., 1987—93. Office: Washington and Lee Univ Lexington VA 24450*

WILLIAMS, HAROLD MARVIN, foundation official, former government official, former university dean, former corporate executive; b. Phila., Jan. 5, 1928; s. Louis W. and Sophie (Fox) W.; m. Nancy Englander; children: Ralph A., Susan J., Derek M. AB, UCLA, 1946; postgrad. in law, U. So. Calif., 1955-59; DHL (hon.), Johns Hopkins U., 1987, Occidental Coll., 1997, Calif. State U., 1998. Bar: Calif. 1950. Pvt. practice, LA, 1950, 1953—55; with Hunt Food and Industries Inc., 1955-68, v.p., 1958-60, exec. v.p., 1960-68; gen. mgr. Hunt-Wesson Foods, 1964-66, pres., 1966-68, Hunt Food and Industries Inc., 1968; chmn. fin. com. Norton Simon, 1968-70; prof. mgmt. UCLA, 1970-77; chmn. SEC, Washington, 1977-81; pres., CEO J. Paul Getty Trust, 1981-98, pres. emeritus; of counsel Skadden Arps et al, 1998—. Pres., dir. Special Investments Securities, Inc., 1961—66. Pub. mem. Nat. Advt. Review Bd., 1971—75; trustee Nat. Humanities Ctr., 1987—93; mem. Coun. Fgn. Rels Com. Econ. Devel.; mem. Pres.' Com. Arts, Humanities, Commn. Econ. Devel. State Calif., 1973—77; energy coord. City of LA, 1973—74; regent U. Calif., 1983—94; commn. rev. master plan higher edn. State Calif., Calif., 1985—87; co chair Calif. Citizens Commn. Higher Edn.; dir. Ethics Resource Ctr.; mem. Commn. Acad. Presidency; co-chmn. Pub. Comn. LA County Govt. 1st lt. AUS, 1950—53. Mem.: State Bar Calif. Office: J Paul Getty Trust 1200 Getty Center Dr Ste 1100 Los Angeles CA 90049-1668 also: Skadden Arps Slate Meagher Flom LLP 300 S Grand Ave Ste 3400 Los Angeles CA 90071 E-mail: hwilliams@getty.edu.

WILLIAMS, HENRY NEWTON, retired lawyer; b. Dickson, Tenn., May 14, 1917; s. H. Newton and Cora Ethel (Wynns) W.; m. LaVerna Pearl Wharton, July 12, 1944 (dec.); children: John Wharton, George Wynns. BS, Mid. Tenn. State U., 1937; MA, U. Tenn., 1938; PhD, U. Chgo., 1951; JD, Vanderbilt U., 1952; LLM, Columbia U., 1954. Bar: Tenn. 1953, U.S. Ct. Appeals (3d cir.) 1954, U.S. Ct. Appeals (9th and 10th cirs.) 1955, U.S. Supreme Ct. 1956, U.S. Ct. Appeals (D.C. cir.) 1957, D.C. 1960. Asst. prof. polit. sci. Vanderbilt U., Nashville, 1946-53; assoc. prof. law Mercer U., Macon, Ga., 1954-56; atty. U.S. Dept. Justice, 1956-68, FTC, Washington, 1968-70; dep. gen. counsel Selective Svc. Sys., Washington, 1970-76, gen. counsel, 1976-99. Contbr. articles to law and polit. sci. jours. Col. U.S. Army, 1942-46. J.P. Chamberlain fellow Columbia U. Law Sch., 1953-54, Edward Hilman fellow U. Chgo., 1939-40, Univ. fellow, 1938-39. Mem. Am. Law Inst., ABA, Fed. Bar Assn., Tenn. Bar Assn., D.C. Bar Assn., Assn. of Bar of City of N.Y. Episcopalian. Home: 405 Hodencamp Rd Apt 206 Thousand Oaks CA 91360

WILLIAMS, HENRY WARD, JR., lawyer, writer; b. Rochester, N.Y., Jan. 12, 1930; s. Henry Ward and Margaret Elizabeth (Simpson) W.; m. Christina M.; children: Edith Williams Linares, Margaret Williams Warren, Sarah Williams Farrand, Ann Williams Treacy, Elizabeth DeLancey, Victoria Maureen. AB, Dartmouth Coll., 1952; LLB, U.Va., 1958. Bar: N.Y. 1959, U.S. Dist. Ct. (we. dist.) N.Y. 1959, U.S. Dist. Ct. (so. dist.) Mich. 1982, U.S. Ct. Appeals (2d cir.) 1963, U.S. Tax Ct. 1960, U.S. Supreme Ct. 1968, D.C. 1978. Ptnr. Harris, Beach & Wilcox, Rochester, 1958-78, Robinson, Williams, Angeloff & Frank, Rochester, 1978-80, Weidman, Williams, Jordon, Angeloff & Frank, Rochester, 1980-82, The Williams Law Firm, Rochester, 1982—. Exec. editor Va. Law Rev., 1957-58. Chmn. Genesee Finger/Lakes Regional Planning Coun., 1973-89; majority leader Monroe County Legislature, 1967-73; councilman Town of Wheatland, N.Y., 2002--; mem. alumni coun. Dartmouth Coll., 1995-99; mem. no. 8020 Nat. Ski Patrol Sys. Lt. (j.g.) USN, 1952-55. Mem. ABA, N.Y. State Bar Assn., Monroe County Bar Assn. (trustee 1982-85), Rochester Yacht Club, Royal Can. Yacht Club, Lake Yacht Racing Assn. (pres. 1985-87, hon. pres. 1988-90), Royal Ocean Racing Club, Royal Nfld. Yacht Club, Raven Soc., Order of Coif, Omicron Delta Kappa. Office: The Williams Law Firm PO Box 8 Scottsville NY 14546-0008 Office Phone: 585-889-3000.

WILLIAMS, HOWARD RUSSELL, lawyer, educator; b. Evansville, Ind., Sept. 26, 1915; s. Clyde Alfred and Grace (Preston) W.; m. Virginia Merle Thompson, Nov. 3, 1942 (dec. Dec. 2000); 1 son, Frederick S.T. AB, Washington U., St. Louis, 1937; LLB, Columbia U., 1940. Bar: N.Y. 1941. With firm Root, Clark, Buckner & Ballantine, N.Y.C., 1940-41; prof. law, asst. dean U. Tex. Law Sch., Austin, 1946-51; prof. law Columbia U. Law Sch., N.Y.C., 1951-63; Dwight prof. Columbia Law Sch., 1959-63; prof. law Stanford U., 1963-85, Stella W. and Ira S. Lillick prof., 1968-82, prof. emeritus, 1982, Robert E. Paradise prof. natural resources, 1983-85, prof. emeritus, 1985—. Oil and gas cons. President's Materials Policy Commn., 1951; mem. Calif. Law Revision Commn., 1971-79, vice chmn., 1976-77, chmn., 1978-79 Author or co-author: Cases on Property, 1954, Cases on Oil and Gas, 1956, 5th edit., 1987, Decedents' Estates and Trusts, 1968, Future Interests, 1970, Oil and Gas Law, 8 vols., 1959-64 (with ann. supplements/rev. 1964-95), abridged edit., 1973, Manual of Oil and Gas Terms, 1957, 11th edit., 2000. Bd. regents Berkeley Bapt. Divinity Sch., 1966-67; trustee Rocky Mountain Mineral Law Found., 1964-66, 68-85. With U.S. Army,(field arty.) 1941-46. Recipient Clyde O. Martz Tchg. award Rocky Mountain Mineral Law Found., 1994. Mem. Phi Beta Kappa. Democrat. Home: 360 Everett Ave Apt 4B Palo Alto CA 94301-1422 Office: Stanford U Sch Law Nathan Abbott Way Stanford CA 94305

WILLIAMS, HOWARD WALTER, aerospace engineer, engineering executive; b. Evansville, Ind., Oct. 18, 1937; s. Walter Charles and Marie Louise (Bollinger) W.; m. Phyllis Ann Scofield, May 4, 1956 (div. Sept. 1970); m. Marilee Sharon Mulvane, Oct. 30, 1970; children: Deborah, Steven, Kevin, Glenn, Lori, Michele. AA, Pasadena City Coll., 1956; BSME, Calif. State U., Los Angeles, 1967; BSBA, U. San Francisco, 1978; PhD in Comml. Sci. (hon.), London Inst. Applied Rsch., 1992. Turbojet, rocket engr. Aerojet-Gen. Corp., Azusa, Calif., 1956-59, infrared sensor engr., 1959-60, rocket, torpedo engr., 1960-66, power, propulsion mgr. propulsion divsn. Sacramento, 1967-73, high speed ship systems mgr., 1974-78, combustion, power mgr., rocket engine and energy mktg. mgr., 1979-89, dir. strategic planning, 1989-94; strategic analyst, program mgr. Pratt & Whitney Space Propulsion, West Palm Beach, Fla., 1995—2003; cons. bus., 2003—. Mgmt. cons., 2004—. Author: (with others) Heat Exchangers, 1980, Industrial Heat Exchangers, 1985, History of Liquid Rocket Engine Development in the U.S., 1992, Aerojet: The Creative Company, 1997; co-inventor Closed Cycle Power System, 1969. Recipient Energy Innovation award U.S. Dept. Energy, 1985. Mem. AIAA (sr., Best Paper 1966), Am. Soc. Metals (organizing dir. indsl. heat exch. confs. 1985). Avocations: bicycling, grandchildren. *Personal philosophy: I hope to be as good a parent and grandparent as mine have been.*

WILLIAMS, HUGH ALEXANDER, JR., retired mechanical engineer, consultant; b. Spencer, N.C., Aug. 18, 1926; s. Hugh Alexander and Mattie Blanche (Megginson) W.; m. Ruth Ann Gray, Feb. 21, 1950; children: David Gray, Martha Blanche Williams Heidengren. BS in Mech. Engring., N.C. State U., 1948, MS in Diesel Engring., 1950; postgrad., Benedictine U. Inst. Mgmt., 1977. Registered profl. engr., Ill. Jr. engr.-field svc. engr. Baldwin-Lima Hamilton (Ohio) Corp., 1950-52, project engr., 1953-55, Electro-Motive divsn. Gen. Motors Corp., La Grange, Ill., 1955-58, sr. project engr., 1958-63, supr. product devel. engine design sect., 1963-86, staff engr. advanced mech. tech., 1986-87. Editor So. Engr., 1947-48; contbr. articles to profl. jours. Trustee Downers Grove (Ill.) San. Dist., 1965-92, pres., 1974-91, v.p., 1991-92; pres. Ill. Assn. San. Dists., 1976-77, bd. dirs., 1977-89; mem. statewide policy adv. com. Ill. EPA, 1977-79; mem. DuPage County Intergovtl. Task Force Com., 1988-92; elder Presbyn. Ch. Served with USAAC, 1945. Recipient Trustee Svc. award Ill. Assn. San. Dists., 1986, Citizens award Downers Grove Evening chpt. Kiwanis, 1991; Norfolk So. R.R. fellow, 1950. Fellow ASME (chmn. honors and awards com. 1993-96, Diesel and Gas Engine Power Divsn. Spkr. awards 1968, 84, Divsn. citation 1977, 97, Internal Combustion Engine award 1987, exec. com. Internal Combustion Engine divsn. 1981-87, 88-92, chmn. 1985-86, sec. 1988-92); mem. Soc. Automotive Engrs. (life), ASME (chmn. Soichiro Honda medal com. 1987-92, chmn. Internal Combustion Engine Award com. 1993-98), Ill. Assn. Wastewater Agys. (Outstanding Mem. award 1990, hon. mem. 1992), Raleigh Host Lions Club (pres. 1996-97), SAR (pres. Raleigh chpt. 2000-02), St. Andrew's Soc. N.C., Masons (32 degree), Sigma Pi. Republican. Achievements include patentee in field. Home: 2108 Weybridge Dr Raleigh NC 27615-5562 Personal E-mail: Hector26@aol.com.

WILLIAMS, IDA JONES, consumer and home economics educator, writer; b. Coatesville, Pa., Dec. 1, 1911; d. William Oscar and Ida Ella (Ruth) Jones; m. Charles Nathaniel Williams, Mar. 17, 1940 (dec. July 1971). BS, Hampton Inst., 1935; MA, U. Conn., 1965. Cert. high sch. tchr., English, sci., home econs., Va., Pa. Tchr. sci. and home econs. Richmond County H.S., Ivondale, Va., 1935—36; tchr. English and home econs. Northampton County H.S., Chesapeake, Va., 1936—40, tchr. consumer and home econs. Machipongo, Va., 1940—70, Northampton Jr. H.S., Machipongo, 1970—76. Author: Starting Anew After Seventy, 1980 (plaque 1980), News and Views of Northampton County High Principals and Alumni, 1981, Great Grandmother, Leah's Legacy-Remember You're Free, 2000; co-author: The History of Virginia State Federation of Colored Women's Clubs, Inc., 1996; editor: Fifty Year Book 1935-1985 - Hampton Institute Class, 1985, Favorite Recipes of Ruth Family & Friends, 1986. V.p. Ea. Lit. Coun., Melfa, Va., 1987-89; mem. Ea. Shore Coll. Found., Inc., Melfa, 1988-2000; mem. Gov.'s Adv. Bd. on Aging, Richmond, Va., 1992-94; instr. Ladies Community Bible Class, 1976-80 (Plaque 1980); sec., treas., v.p. Hospice Support of Ea. Shore, 1980-94; mem. Northampton/Accomack Adv. Coun., 1992-94; marshall 28th anniv. commencement Ea. Shore C.C., 1996; bd. dirs. Ea. Shore C.C. Found., 1998-2000. Named Home Econs. Tchr. of Yr., Am. Home Econs. Assn. and Family Cir., 1975, Woman of Yr., Prog. Women of E.S., 1997, Ida J. Williams scholarship fund named in her honor, Keller Ch. Christ, 1999; recipient Nat.

Sojourner Truth Meritorious Svc. award, Negro Bus. and Profl. Women's Clubs, Gavel Ea. Shore Ret. Tchrs. Assn., 1994, Jefferson award, Am. Inst. Pub. Svc., Wavy-TV-Bell Atlantic and Mattress Discounters, 1991, Gov.'s award for vol. excellence, 1994, Contribution to Edn. award, Ea. Shore Coll. Found., 1997, Leadership award, 2001, trophy for outstanding and dedicated svc., 2001, plaque, Southeastern Assn. Colored Women's Clubs, Inc., 2001, award for dedicated svc., Nat. Assn. Colored Women's Club, Inc., 1998, E.S. C.C. Found., Inc. Svc. award, 2000, Exemplary Svc. award, Nat. Assn. Colored Women's Club, 2001, Black Achievement award, Ebenezer A.M.E. Ch., 2003, Achievement award, Chester County Hist. Soc. of Pa., 2003, Ednl. Achievement award for commitment to edn., Northampton County H.S. Alumni Assn., 2003, plaque 1st Black Northampton County, Ea. Shore Va. C. of C. outstanding contbns. ea. shore cmty., 2002. Mem. AARP (Citation award 1996, Mem. of Yr. 1997, v.p. Northampton chpt. 1998-2000), Progressive Women of Ea. Shore (pres. 1985-93, Gold Necklace 1993, Woman of Yr. 1997), C. of C., Univ. Women (v.p. Portsmouth br. 1985-87), Ea. Shore Ret. Tchrs. (pres. 1977-84), Dist. L Ret. Tchrs. (pres. 1989-91, chmn. legis. com. 1998, 99, 2001, Dedicated and Outstanding Svc. award 2003), Va. State Fedn. Colored Women's Club (pres. 1990-94, editor history com. 1994-96), Am. Assn. Ret. Persons (Va. state legis. com. 1995-2001). Mem. Ch. of Christ. Avocations: crafts, travel, writing, lecturing. Home and Office: PO Box 236 14213 Lankford Hwy Eastville VA 23347-0236

WILLIAMS, J. LINDA, librarian; b. Bethesda, Md., June 30, 1945; d. Joseph Gordon and Annie Louise (Whitfield) DiMisa; m. Charles Edward Williams, Nov. 2, 1968. BS in Secondary Edn./English and History, Radford U., 1966; MLS, U. Md., 1977; cert. adminstrn., supr., Bowie (Md.) State Coll., 1987. Cert. tchr., librarian. Tchr. English, history Prince William County Pub. Schs., Woodbridge, Va., 1967-73; tchr. English Charles County Pub. Schs., LaPlata, Md., 1973-76; library media specialist St. Mary County Pub. Schs., Leonardtown, Md., 1977-84; staff specialist Md. Dept. Edn., Balt., 1985-94; supr. media and instrnl. materials Prince George's County Pub. Schs., Landover, Md., 1994-99; dir. libr. media and instrnl. technology Anne Arundel County Pub. Schs., Annapolis, Md., 1999—. Named Alumnus of Yr. Coll. Library and Info. Svcs., 1988 U. Md.; profl. devel. grantee 3M, 1981. Mem. ALA (various divs.), Md. Library Assn., Md. Edn. Media Assn. (pres. 1998-99), Beta Phi Mu. Home: 1726 Farmington Ct Crofton MD 21114-2307 Office: 188 Green St Annapolis MD 21401-2502 E-mail: lwilliams@aacps.org., jw177@aol.com.

WILLIAMS, J. MCDONALD, real estate development company executive; With Trammell Crow Co., Dallas, 1973—, pres., CEO, 1991—. Bd. dirs. Mitchell Energy & Devel. Corp. Bd. dirs. numerous civic orgns.; mem. Pres.' Adv. Com. on Trade Policy and Negotiations. Office: Trammell Crow Co 2001 Ross Ave Ste 3400 Dallas TX 75201-2998

WILLIAMS, J. RICHARD, service executive, real estate executive; b. Salt Lake City, Nov. 5, 1924; s. Herbert and May (Wells) W.; m. Lucille T. Timms, Feb., 1946; children: Susan, Steven, Summer, Stacy. Student, Washington Coll., Ellensburg, Wash., 1944, U. Utah, 1946-47. Chmn. bd. Friendship Inns Internat., Salt Lake City, 1960—; chmn., pres. Classic Cars Internat., Salt Lake City, 1970—. Author: World of Friendship, 1972. Served with AC, U.S. Army, 1943-45. Inducted into Hospitality Internat. Hall of Fame, 1972; recipient Disting. Service award Nat. Hotel-Motel Assn., 1974; named Man of Yr., Motel Brokers Am., 1974. Avocations: tennis, skiing, boating. Office: Friendship Inns Internat 355 W 7th S Salt Lake City UT 84101-2609

WILLIAMS, J. VERNON, retired lawyer; b. Honolulu, Apr. 26, 1921; s. Urban and W. Amelia (Olson) W.; m. Malvina H. Hitchcock, Oct. 4, 1947 (dec. May 1970); children— Carl H., Karin, Frances E., Scott S.; m. Mary McLellan, Sept. 6, 1980. Student, Phillips Andover Acad., 1937-39; BA cum laude, Amherst Coll., 1943; LL.B., Yale, 1948. Bar: Wash. 1948. Assoc. Riddell, Riddell & Hemphill, 1948-50, ptnr., 1950-95; sr. prin. emeritus Riddell Williams, P.S., Seattle, 1996—. Sec., dir. Airborne Freight Corp., 1968-79, gen. counsel, 1968-96. Chmn. March of Dimes, Seattle, 1954-55; Mem. Mayor's City Charter Rev. Com., 1968-69; chmn. Seattle Bd. Park Commrs., 1966-68; co-chmn. parks and open space com. Forward Thrust, 1966-69; dir. bd. and commrs. br. Nat. Recreation and Parks Assn., 1968-69; chmn. Gov.'s adv. com. Social and Health Services, 1972-75; Bd. dirs. Seattle Met. YMCA, 1965—, pres., 1976-79; trustee Lakeside Sch., 1971-79; mem. alumni council Phillps Andover Acad., 1970-73, Yale Law Sch., 1969-77; chancellor St. Mark's Cathedral, Seattle, 1964-2000. Served with USAAF, 1943-45. Mem. Univ. Club, Seattle Tennis Club, Birnam Wood Golf Club. Home: 2061 43rd Ave E #201 Seattle WA 98112 Office: 4500 1001 4th Ave Plz Seattle WA 98154-1065

WILLIAMS, JACK JEFF, realtor, retired executive administrator; b. Cushing, Okla., July 28, 1936; s. Jeff Davis and Pauline Vera (Meyers) W.; m. Mary Ann Hill, June 1, 1957; children: Janet Lee Williams Charlin, Jeff Brian. BA in Econs., U. Calif., Dominguez Hills, 1974. Lic. real estate sales, Calif. Exec. adminstr. TRW Space & Electronics, Redondo Beach, Calif.; realtor Moore & Assocs. Hermosa Bch. (Top ten agent). Cons. Delta Airlines, Atlanta, Aerospace Corp., El Segundo, Calif., Amdahl Corp., Santa Clara, Calif., Continental Airlines, L.A. Author, editor: Meyers from Moyers, 1996. Mem. TRW Retirees Assn. (v.p. 1997, pres. 1998), Torrance Rose Float Assn. (bd. dirs. 1996—, v.p., 1997—), South Bay Genealogy Soc., Snow Valley Ski Club, Mason. Republican. Baptist. Avocation: genealogy research. Home: 5216 Emerald St Torrance CA 90503-2724 Office: Moore & Assocs Realtors 2615 Pacific Coast Hwy Ste 100 Hermosa Beach CA 90254-2278

WILLIAMS, JACK RAYMOND, civil engineer; b. Barberton, Ohio, Mar. 14, 1923; s. Charles Baird and Mary Williams; m. Mary Berneice Jones, Mar. 5, 1947 (dec.); children: Jacqueline Rae, Drew Alan; m. Betty Ruth Scholfield, Nov. 9, 1990. Student, Colo. Sch. Mines, 1942043, Purdue U., 1944-45; BS, U. Colo., 1946. Gravity and seismograph engr. Carter Oil Co., Western U.S. and Venezuela, 1946-50; with Rock Island R.R., Chgo., 1950-80, structural designer, asst. to engr. bridges, asst. engr., 1980-82, engr. bridges system, 1963-80; sr. bridge engr. thomas K. Dyer Inc., 1980-82; v.p. Alfred Benesch & Co., 1982-96. Served with USMCR, 1943-45. Fellow ASCE (life); mem. Am. Concrete Inst., Am. Ry. Bridge and Bldg. Assn. (past pres.), Am. Ry. Engrng. Assn. (hon. mem., past chmn. com. 8, Concrete and Foundations, past chmn. com. 10 concrete ties). Home: 293 Minocqua St Park Forest IL 60466-1942

WILLIAMS, JACKIE L. public administrator; b. Madison, Mississippi, June 22, 1964; d. Fillmore and Annie Mae Williams. BS in Computer Sci., Jackson State U., 1986, MS in Ednl. Adminstrn. and Supervision, 1991, PhD Pub. Policy and Adminstrn., 2004; grad., Inst. Cmty. Devel., U. Ctrl. Ark., Econ. Devel. Inst., 1999. Computer sci. instr. Phillips Jr. Coll., Jackson, Miss., 1991—92; cmty. assistance specialist Miss. Dept. of Econ. and Cmty. Devel., Jackson, Miss., 1993—98; dir. Ctr. for Rural and Econ. Devel. Alcorn State U., Miss., 1998—2000; dir. rural housing and econ. devel. U.S. Dept. Housing and Urban Devel., Washington, 2000—. Del. White House Cmty. Empowerment Conf., 1996, 98. Dir. cmty. events The Arts Alliance of Jackson and Hinds County, 1987-93. Grantee Miss. Arts Commn. Jackson, 1992. Mem. ASPA (Miss. state coun. mem. 1995—),Toastmasters. Office: US Dept Housing and Urban Devel Washington DC

WILLIAMS, JACKIE N. law educator, former prosecutor; b. Roosevelt, Okla., Oct. 4, 1943; s. David Coleman and Grace Pearl (Southard) W.; children: Douglas Kennedy, Eric Neil. BBA, Wichita State U., 1967; JD, Washburn U. Law Sch., 1971. Bar: Kans. 1971. Asst. atty. gen. Kans. Atty. Gen.'s Office, Topeka, 1971-73; asst. dist. atty. Wichita, Kans., 1973-77; adminstrv. asst. U.S. Congressman Dan Glickman, Washington, D.C., 1977; asst. U.S. atty. Wichita, 1977-96; U.S. atty. Kans., 1996—2001; sr. fellow, criminal justice prog School of Community Affairs, Wichita State Univ, Kans., 2001—. Office: Wichita State Univ School of Community Affairs 302 Lindquist Hall, Box 135 Wichita KS 67260 E-mail: jackie.williams@wichita.edu.

WILLIAMS, JAMES A. labor union administrator; b. 1951; m. Gerrie Williams; 4 children. Elected pres., bus. mgr. Glaziers, Archtl. Metal and Glass Workers' Local 252, Phila., 1975, former co-chmn. Pension, Annuity, Health & Welfare and Vacation Funds; region gen. v.p. Union of Painters and Allied Trade, 1994—95, sec. and treas., 1995—2002, pres., 2003—. Mem. exec. council AFL-CIO. Contbr. articles to profl. jours. Served in U.S. Army, 1969—71. Recipient Labor Man of the Yr. award, Israeli Bond Assoc., 1990, Vietnam Veterans Labor Leader of the Yr. award, 1992. Office: Internat Union Painters & Allied Trade 1750 New York Ave NW Washington DC 20006*

WILLIAMS, JAMES ARTHUR, retired army officer, information systems company executive; b. Paterson, N.J., Mar. 29, 1932; s. Charles M. and Elsie (Kretszchmar) W.; m. Barbara Widnall, June 26, 1959; children: Steven, Karen. BS, U.S. Mil. Acad.; MA in Latin Am. Studies, U. N.Mex. Commd. 2d lt. U.S. Army, 1954, advanced through grades to lt. gen.; asst. army attache U.S. Def. Attache Office, Caracas, Venezuela, 1966-72; exch. officer State-Def. Exch. Program Office of Sec. Def., Washington, 1972-74; comdr. 650th MI Group, Shape, 1974-76; dep. dir. estimates Def. Intelligence Agy., Washington, 1977-80; dep. chief staff for intelligence U.S. Army, Europe, 1980-81; dir. Def. Intelligence Agy., Washington, 1981-85; ret., 1985; v.p. PSC Corp., 1986; pres. Direct Info. Access Corp., Annandale, Va., 1987—; chmn. bd. dirs. Info. Ops. Inc., 2000—. Sr. fellow Joint Forces Staff Coll., 1998; intelligence advisor Dept. Homeland Security, 2004. Bd. visitors Joint Mil. Intelligence Coll., 1996. Decorated Legion of Merit, Bronze Star with oak leaf cluster, Air medals, D.S.M., Nat. Intelligence D.S.M.; Legion of Honor (France); named Disting. Mem. Mil. Intelligence Hall of Fame. Mem. Assn. U.S. Army, Nat. Mil. Intelligence Assn. (chmn. bd. 1986—). Methodist. Office: Info Ops Inc 1298 Bay Dale Dr Ste 207 Arnold MD 21012-2815 Office Phone: 703-978-9428.

WILLIAMS, JAMES BRYAN, banker; b. Sewanee, Tenn., Mar. 21, 1933; s. Eugene G. and Ellen (Bryan) W.; m. Betty G. Williams, July 11, 1980; children: Ellen, Elizabeth, Bryan. AB, Emory U., 1955. Pres. Peachtree Bank & Trust Co., Chamblee, Ga.; chmn. bd. First Nat. Bank & Trust Co., Augusta, Ga.; pres. Sun Banks, Inc., Orlando, Fla., Trust Co. of Ga., Atlanta; chmn. exec. com. SunTrust Banks, Inc., Atlanta, 1998—. Bd. dirs. The Coca-Cola Co., Atlanta, Genuine Parts Co., Atlanta, Rollins, Inc., Ga.-Pacific Corp., Atlanta, RPC, Inc., Atlanta, Genuine Parts Co., Atlanta. Trustee Emory U.; chmn. bd. trustees Robert W. Woodruff Health Scis. Ctr.; nat. trustee Boys & Girls Clubs Am.; trustee emeritus Westminster Schs., Atlanta. Lt. USAF, 1955-57. Mem.: Bankers Roundtable, Ga. C. of C. (dir. emeritus), Peachtree Golf Club, Augusta Country Club, Commerce Club, Capital City Club, Ocean Forest Golf Club, Piedmont Driving Club, Phi Beta Kappa, Omicron Delta Kappa. Office: SunTrust Banks Inc PO Box 4418 25 Park Pl NE Atlanta GA 30303-2900

WILLIAMS, JAMES CASE, metallurgist; b. Salina, Kans., Dec. 7, 1938; s. Luther Owen and Clarice (Case) W.; m. Joanne Rufener, Sept. 17, 1960; children: Teresa A., Patrick J. BS in Metall. Engring, U. Wash., 1962, MS, 1964, PhD, 1968. Rsch. engr., lead engr. Boeing Co., Seattle, 1961-67; tech. staff N.Am. Rockwell Corp., Thousand Oaks, Calif., 1968-74; mgr. interdivisional tech. program N.Am. Aerospace group, 1974, program devel. mgr. structural materials, 1974-75; prof. metallurgy, co-dir. Ctr. for Joining of Materials, Carnegie-Mellon U., Pitts., 1975-81; pres. Mellon Inst., Pitts., 1981-83; dean Carnegie Inst. Tech., Carnegie-Mellon U., Pitts., 1983-88; gen. mgr. materials dept. GE Aircraft Engines, 1988-99; Honda prof. Ohio State U., Columbus, 1999—, dean engring., 2001—04. Bd. dirs. com. on engring. and tech. systems NRC, 1996-2001; chmn. Nat. Materials Adv. Bd., 1988-95, materials and structures com. NASA Aero. Adv. Com. 1992-97; mem. NASA Propulsion Rsch. and Tech. Com., 1997-99; mem. Materials Sci. and Engring. Study, 1986-88; bd. govs. Inst. for Mechs. and Materials, U. Calif., San Diego, 1989-95; trustee Min. Math. Sci. and Engring., Cin., 1988-99; mem. sci. adv. bd. USAF, 1996-2001; mem. materials rsch. com. Def. Advanced Rsch. Projects Agy., 1981-2000; adv. com. Divsn. Engring. and Phys. Sci., NRC, 2001—. Co-editor: Scientific and Technological Aspects of Titanium and Titanium Alloys, 1976; contbr. numerous articles to tech. jours. Trustee Oreg. Grad. Inst. Sci. and Tech., 1988-94; cons. Cubmaster Boy Scouts Am., 1976-77. Recipient Ladd award Carnegie Inst. Tech.; Adams award Am. Welding Soc.; Boeing doctoral fellow. Fellow: TMS-AIME, Am. Soc. Metals (Disting. lectr. on materials and soc. 1997, Campbell lectr. 1999, Gold medal 1992); mem.: AIME (Leadership award 1993, App to Pract award 2002), NAE, ASM, Internat. Ti Assn. (Achievement award 2003), Alpha Sigma Mu. Republican. Episcopalian. Home: 7711 Charlotte Hull Ct New Albany OH 43054-9680 Office Phone: 614-292-7251. Business E-Mail: williams.1726@osu.edu.

WILLIAMS, JAMES EUGENE, management consultant; b. Macon, Ga., June 23, 1927; s. James Eugene and Margaret Elizabeth (Tinker) W.; m. Linda K. Magnuson, June 23, 1984; children: Paul David, Lisa Jane Williams Robertson, Philip Alan, Gail Ellen Williams Feeney, Amanda Allen Thompson, Jason Douglas Allen, Joel Winston Allen. BS in Aero. Engring., Iowa State Coll., 1950. Engr., Robins AFB, Ga., 1950-54, Hdqrs. USAF, Washington, 1954-61; dep. asst. sec. Office Asst. Sec. Air Force, Washington, 1961-85; dir. govt. bus. policy Northrop Corp., Washington, 1986-88; pvt. practice mgmt. cons. Tempe, Ariz., 1988—. Co-founder The Williams Inst. for Ethics and Mgmt., Tempe, 1993—. Recipient Presdl. Meritorious Exec. award, 1981, Presdl. Disting. Exec. award, 1982. Home: 3223 S College Ave Tempe AZ 85282-3773 E-mail: LJWMS@aol.com.

WILLIAMS, JAMES FRANCIS, JR., religious organization administrator; b. Coffeyville, Kans., June 20, 1938; s. James Francis and Sarah Kathryn (Tavenner) W.; m. Alice Carol Kinney, June 1, 1963; children: James F. III, Todd Alexander, Leslie. BA, So. Meth. U., 1960; ThM, Dallas Theol. Sem., 1964; HHD, U. Tex., 1988. Ordained min. N.W. Presbyn. Ch., 1967. Campus dir. Campus Crusade for Christ, Dallas, 1961-64, area dir. various North Tex. locations, 1964-68; dir. music campus Crusade for Christ, Arrowhead, Calif., 1967-71; regional dir. Campus Crusade for Christ, 1968-71, nat. dir. tng., 1971-72; founder, min. at large Probe Ministries, Internat., Dallas, 1973—, pres., 1973—98. Dir. music Campus Crusade for Christ, Arrowhead, Calif., 1967-71. Soloist, chorus Dallas Opera, 1982-84. Named one of Outstanding Young Men in Am. Dallas Jaycees, 1965. Mem. Evangelical Christian Ch. Office: Probe Ministries 1900 Firman Dr Ste 100 Richardson TX 75081-6796

WILLIAMS, JAMES HENRY, JR., mechanical engineer, educator, consultant; b. Newport News, Va., Apr. 4, 1941; s. James H. Williams and Margaret L. (Holt) Mitchell; children: James Henry III, Mariella Louisa. Student, Newport News Apprentice Sch., 1965; BS, MIT, 1967, MS, 1968; PhD, Cambridge U., 1970. Sr. design engr. Newport News (Va.) Shipyard, 1960-70; asst. prof. mech. engring. MIT, 1970-74, assoc. prof., 1974-81, prof., 1981—2000, duPont prof., 1973, Edgarton prof., 1974-76, prof. writing and humanistic studies, 2000—. Cons. engring. to numerous cos. Contbr. articles on stress analysis, materials and nondestructive testing to profl. jours. Named Prof. of Tchg. Excellence, Sch. Engring., 1991, C.F. Hopewell faculty fellow, 1993; recipient Charles F. Bailey Bronze medal, 1961, Silver medal, 1962, Gold medal, 1963, Baker award, 1976. Mem. ASME, Am. Soc. Nondestructive Testing, Nat. Tech. Assn. Office: MIT Room 3-360 77 Massachusetts Ave Rm 3-360 Cambridge MA 02139-4307 Business E-Mail: jhwill@mit.edu.

WILLIAMS, JAMES LEE, financial industries executive; b. Tampa, Fla., Nov. 5, 1941; s. Donald Clark and Nell (Medlin) W.; m. Linda Taylor, Dec. 28, 1968; children: Donald Clark II, Taylor Lee. AA, St. Petersburg (Fla.) Jr. Coll., 1965; BS, Fla. State U., 1967. Mgmt. Ryder Truck Lines, Jacksonville, Fla., 1967—69; dist. mgr. underwriting divsn. U.S. Leasing Corp., Dallas, 1969—73; area v.p. Mfrs. Hanover Leasing Corp., Houston and London, 1973—79; v.p. corp. fin. Underwood Neuhause & Co. Inc., Houston, 1979—81; chmn., CEO 1st City Leasing Corp., Houston, 1981—85; mng. dir. capital markets 1st City Bancorp., Houston, 1985—89; mng. dir. fin. svcs. M.P.S.I. Sys. Inc., Dallas, 1989—90; pres., CEO Strategic Decisions Holdings Corp., Dallas, 1990—92; sr. mng. dir. Williams and Assocs., 1992; pres. Global Svcs. Capital Corp., Houston, 1993—96; v.p., dist. CFO Ikon Hov Adminstrv. Svc. Ctr., Houston, 1997—98; CFO Insync Internet Svcs., Houston, 1998—99, Walkabout Software, 1999—2001; pres. BancLeasing, Inc., 2001—03; mng. dir. Global Svcs., Houston, 2003—. Served with USN, 1959-62. Mem. Equipment Leasing Assn. (fed. govt. rels. com. 1984-88, 95—), Tex. Assn. Equipment Lessors (bd. dirs. 1985-89), Greater Houston Partnership (vice-chmn. Arabian horse com., announcer Houston Livestock Show and Rodeo), Houston Ctr. Club (bd. dirs. 1985-89), Lakeside Racquet Club (athletic com. 1986-89), Forum Club Houston. Republican. Presbyterian. Avocations: golf, jogging, swimming. Office: Global Svcs 2902 W 12th St Houston TX 77008

WILLIAMS, JAMES ORRIN, university administrator, educator; b. New Orleans, Jan. 8, 1937; married, 1978; 5 children. BS, Auburn U., 1960, MEd, 1963, EdD, 1967; postgrad., Tchrs. Coll., Columbia U., summer 1964. Tchr. social sci., coach Columbus High Sch. Ga., 1960-61; tchr., coach Eufaula High Sch. Ala., 1961-63; prin. Troy Jr. High Sch., 1963-65; grad. asst. Sch. Edn. Auburn U., 1965-66, interim dir. field service, 1966-67; asst. prof. edn. adminstrn. U. Fla., 1967-68; asst. prof. Columbus Coll., 1968-69; assoc. prof., chmn. div. Auburn U., Montgomery, 1969-73, vice chancellor acad. affairs, 1973-80, chancellor, 1980-93; v.p. U. So. Miss.-Gulf Coast campus, Long Beach, 1993—. Contbr. articles to profl. jours. Phi Delta Kappa grantee, 1967. Mem. Am. Assn. State Colls. and Univs., Am. Assn. Coll. Tchr. Edn., Assn. Tchr. Edn., So. Regional Council Edn. Adminstrn., Phi Delta Kappa (v.p. 1965), Phi Kappa Phi. Office: U So Miss 730 E Beach Blvd Long Beach MS 39560-6259

WILLIAMS, JAMES THOMAS, physician, educator; b. Martinsville, Va., Nov. 10, 1933; s. Harry Pemberton and Ruth Ellen (Thomas) W.; m. Jacqueline Cecile Shepard, Apr. 21, 1962; children: Lawrence Dudley, Laurie Cecile. BS, Howard U., 1954, MD, 1958. Diplomate Am. Bd. Internal Medicine, Am. Bd. Endocrinology and Metabolism. Intern Phila. Gen. Hosp., 1958-59; resident in medicine D.C. Gen. Hosp., 1959-60, Freedmen's Hosp., Washington, 1960-62, 64-65; fellow in endocrinology Howard U., Washington, 1965-67, asst. prof. medicine, 1967-74, chief endocrine sect. dept. medicine, 1973-76, assoc. prof. medicine, 1974-85, prof. medicine, 1985—, ret., 2002. Capt. U.S. Army, 1962-64. Fellow ACP, Am. Coll. Endocrinology; mem. Endocrine Soc., Am. Diabetes Assn., Nat. Med. Assn. Democrat. Home: 13414 Tamarack Rd Silver Spring MD 20904-1469 Personal E-mail: james.t.williams@verizon.net.

WILLIAMS, JASON, professional basketball player; b. Nov. 18, 1975; Student, U. Fla. Guard Sacramento Kings NBA, 1999—. Named Schick All-Rookie First Team, 1998—99. Office: Memphis Grizzlies 175 Toyota Plaza, Suite 150 Memphis TN 38103

WILLIAMS, JEFFREY N. astronaut; b. Superior, Wis., Jan. 18, 1958; s. Lloyd D. and Eunice A. Williams; m. Anna-Marie Moore; 2 children. BSc in Applied Sci. & Engring., U.S. Military Acad., 1980; MSc in Aero. Engring., U.S. Naval Postgraduate Sch., 1987; MA in Nat. Security & Strategic Studies, U.S. Naval War Coll., 1996. Commd. 2d lt. USN, 1980, advanced through grades to lt. col., aeroscout platoon leader, 1981—84, various assignments, 1984—92; assigned to Edwards AFB, Calif., 1993—95, Naval War Coll., 1995—96; astronaut NASA, Houston, 1996—. Astronaut Space Shuttle Atlantis, 2000. Decorated Def. Superior Svc. medal USN, Legion of Merit, Meritorious Svc. medal; recipient William Adger Moffett award, Naval Postgraduate Sch., 1988. Mem.: USMA Assn. Graduates, Army Aviation Assn. Am., Am. Helicopter Soc., Soc. Exptl. Test Pilots, Assn. U.S. Army, Officer Christian Fellowship, Order of Daedalians. Avocations: running, fishing, camping, skiing, scuba diving. Office: Astronaut Office CB NASA Johnson Space Center Houston TX 77058

WILLIAMS, JEFFREY P. investment banker; b. July 13, 1951; BArch, U. Cin., 1975; MBA, Harvard U., 1979. Mng. dir. Morgan Stanley, N.Y.C., 1979-96; exec. v.p. McGraw-Hill, N.Y.C., 1996-98; ptnr. Greenhill & Co., LLC, N.Y.C., 1998—. E-mail: jwilliams@greenhill-co.com.

WILLIAMS, JIMY, professional athletics manager; b. Santa Maria, CA, Oct. 4, 1943; m. Peggy Sallee, Feb. 19, 1977; children: Monica, Brady, Shawn, Jenna. BS, Fresno State U. Mgr. Quad Cities affiliate Midwest League Angels, 1974; 3d base coach Blue Jays, 1986—89; mgr. Boston Red Sox, 1996—2001, Houston Astros, 2001—04. Named Mgr. of Yr., Pacific Coast League, 1976, 1979, AL Mgr. of Yr., 1999.*

WILLIAMS, JODY, political organization administrator; b. Rutland, Vt., Oct. 9, 1950; BA, U. Vt.; MA, Sch. Internat. Tng., Johns Hopkins Sch.; PhD (hon.), Briar Cliff Coll., Marlboro Coll., U. of Vermont, Williams Coll. Past English tchr., Washington, Mex.; former coord. Nicaragua-Honduras Edn. Project, Washington; assoc. dir. Children's Project Med. Aid El Salvador, L.A./El Salvador, 1986—92; founder Internat. Campaign to Ban Landmines Vietnam Vet. Found. Am., Washington, 1991—; amb. Internat. Campaign to Ban Landmines, Alexandria, Va., 1997—; founder Sponsor a Mine-Detection Dog program, 1998—. Spkr. in field. Contbr. articles to profl. jours, co-authored After the Guns Fall: The Enduring Legacy of Landmines. Past vol. El Salvadoran rescue group. Recipient Distinguished Peace Leadership award, Nuclear Age Peace Found., Fiat Lux award, Clark U., Nobel Peace Prize, 1997, Hollywood Humanitarian award, 2002. Office: ICBL 110 Maryland Ave NE # 6 Washington DC 20002-5626

WILLIAMS, JOHN ANDREW, physiology educator, consultant; b. Des Moines, Aug. 3, 1941; s. Harold Southall and Marjorie (Larsen) W.; m. Christa A. Smith, Dec. 26, 1965; children: Rachel Jo, Matthew Dallas. BA, Cen. Wash. State Coll., 1963; MD, PhD, U. Wash., Seattle, 1968. Staff fellow NIH, Bethesda, Md., 1969-71; research fellow U. Cambridge, Eng., 1971-72; from asst. to prof. physiology U. Calif., San Francisco, 1973-87; prof. physiology, chair dept. physiology, prof. internal medicine U. Mich., Ann Arbor, 1987—. Mem. gen. medicine study sect. NIH, Bethesda, 1985-88, NIDDK, DDK-C study sect., 1991-95. Contbr. numerous articles to profl. jours.; editor Am. Jour. Physiology: Gastrointestinal Physiology, 1985-91; assoc. editor Jour. Clin. Investigation, 1997-2001. Trustee Friends Sch. in Detroit, 1992—2000. NIH grantee, 1973—. Mem. Am. Physiol. Soc. (Hoffman LaRoche prize 1985, mem. coun. 1996-99, pres. 2003-04), Am. Soc. Cell Biology, Am. Soc. Clin. Investigation, Am. Gastroenterology Assn., Am. Pancreatic Assn. (pres. 1985-86). Democrat. Home: 1115 Woodlawn Ave Ann Arbor MI 48104-3956 Office: Dept Molecular & Intergrative Physiology Univ of Mich Med Sch Ann Arbor MI 48109 E-mail: jawillms@umich.edu.

WILLIAMS, JOHN CHARLES, II, data processing executive; b. Dayton, Ohio, Jan. 29, 1955; s. John Charles and Frances Jerline (McKean) W.; m. Diane Catherine Busch, Feb. 11, 1978 (div. Jan. 1996); 1 child, Tabitha Anne; m. Linda A. Blair, Nov. 24, 2001. BSBA, U. Phoenix, 2001, MBA, 2003. Programmer Kino Starr, Tucson, 1977-78, City of Boise (Idaho), 1978; data processing mgr. Nat. Assn. Ind. Businesses, Inc., Boise, 1978-79; chief exec. officer Williams Rsch. Assoc., Boise, 1979-80, MRW Data Systems, Inc., Tucson, 1981-82, Computer Security, Tucson, 1983-86, Modern Magic, Tucson, 1986-88; tech. support dir. Program Sources, Inc., Tucson, 1988-89; chief exec. officer Cactus Explosives Corp., 1989-90, Systems Cons. Assocs., Tucson, 1990-94; sr. systems analyst Desert Diamond Casino, 1994-97; systems analyst Muscular Dystrophy Assn., Tucson, 1997—. Area coord. Kolbe For Congress Campaign, Tucson, 1984; Ariz. Rep. State Committeeman, 1986—; mem. Ariz. Sonora Desert Mus., Tucson, 1983—. Republican. Avocations: leather crafting, horsemanship, coin collecting/numismatics. Office Phone: 520-529-2000.

WILLIAMS, JOHN EDWARD, lawyer; b. Atlanta, May 21, 1946; s. Edward Carl and Mary E. (Griffin) W.; m. Kristin Forsberg, May 22, 1976; children: Alexandra, Courtney, Charles. BA, Yale U., 1968; JD, U. Va., 1974; LLM in Taxation, Georgetown U., 1977. Bar: Va. 1974, D.C. 1975, U.S. Dist. Ct. D.C. 1975, U.S. Tax Ct. 1975, U.S. Ct. Appeals (D.C. cir.) 1975, U.S. Supreme Ct. 1977. Law clk. to Judge Charles R. Richey U.S. Dist. Ct. (D.C. dist.), 1974-75; assoc. Patton, Boggs & Blow, Washington, 1975-78, Cadwalader, Wickersham & Taft, Washington, 1978-81; asst. to the commr. IRS, Washington, 1981-84;

tax counsel Ropes & Gray, Washington, 1984-86; ptnr. David & Hagner, P.C., Washington, 1986-90, Winston & Strawn, Washington, 1990-2000. Mem. Jud. Conf. of D.C. Cir., 1978, 82, 85, 87, 92. With U.S. Army, 1968-74. Mem. ABA (tax sect., chmn. tech. subcom., adminstrv. practice com. 1986-88), Met. Club, Yale Club N.Y.C., Heritage Hunt Club. Home: 4908A John Ticer Dr Alexandria VA 22304 Office: 3213 Duke St Ste 601 Alexandria VA 22314 Office Phone: 703-838-2939. Business E-Mail: johnedwardwilliams@earthlink.net.

WILLIAMS, JOHN FRANKLIN, anesthesiologist educator and administrator; b. N.Y.C., May 17, 1948; m. Delia DePaola; 1 child, Daniel Stephen. BA, Boston U., 1970; MSc in Health Care Adminstrn., The London Sch. Econs., 1973; MPH in Health Svcs. Adminstrn., Yale U., 1975; MD, The George Washington U., 1979, EdD in Human Resource Devel., 1996. Diplomate Am. Bd. Anesthesiology; MD, D.C., Md. Intern U.S. Office of Edn. Bur. of Higher Edn., Washington, 1970; asst. to dir. admissions Wheelock Coll., Boston, 1970-72, asst. to pres., 1971-72; rsch. coord. The Martin Luther King Jr. Afro-Am. Ctr., Boston, 1972-73; dir. health and employment The Nat. Vets. Frat., Inc., New Haven, 1973-75; intern in ob-gyn. The George Washington Univ. Med. Ctr., Washington, 1979-80, residency in anesthesiology, 1980-82, chief resident in anesthesiology, 1981-82, fellowship in critical care medicine, 1982-83; co-dir. Coronary/ICU The Capitol Hosp., Washington, 1983-84; asst. prof. anesthesiology, co-dir. ICU The George Washington Univ. Med. Ctr., Washington, 1984—; lt. commissioned corps, USPHS, dep. dir. anesthesia Gallup (N.Mex.) Indian Med. Ctr., 1984-85; asst. prof. anesthesiology, co-dir. ICU The George Washington U. Med. Ctr., Washington, 1985-89, assoc. prof. anesthesiology, co-dir. ICU, 1989—; assoc. dean for admissions The George Washington U. Sch. Medicine & Health Scis., Washington, 1993—99; dean, v.p. for health affairs Wash. U. Sch. of Med., Washington, 1999—. Internat. experience on behalf of the George Washington U. Med. Ctr., The Spl. Saudi MD Program, 1991—, Thailand Project for Undergrad. and Grad. Med. Edn., 1995—, Lill Found. Grad. Med. Edn. Program, 1995—, Operation Smile Internat., 1996—. Contbr. numerous articles to profl. jours. Mem. Found. for Critical Care, 1985—, chmn. waiting rm. brochure, 1985-86, chmn. family support program, 1985-90, chmn. profl. edn. com., 1989-90; coord. Disaster Drill for the D.C. Nat. Guard, 1985-87; mem. Mayor's Office of Drug Control Policy, 1989-90, D.C. Drug Control Policy Strategy Team, D.C. Police Chiefs Task Force on Youth Violence, 1991-93, bd. dirs. Superleaders, 1992—, adv. coun. Med. 1995—, Anesthesia, 1992—, bd. dirs. Internat. Med. Data Stds. Found., The George Washington Univ. Health Plan, 1996—; humanitarian med. missions Hosp. Canape Vere, Port Au Prince, Haiti, 1983-86, Kenyatta Gen. Hosp., Nairobi, Kenya, 1987-88, Hangzhous Plastic Surgery Hosp., 1990, Meizou Hosp., Peoples Republic of China, 1991, Shantou Hosp., Peoples Republic of China, 1993, United Arab Emirates, 1993. Recipient Lange Med. Book award, 1977, Mosby Med. Book award for scholastic excellence, 1979, Commendation for Implementation of Pathnet Lab. Info. System, 1987, The Am. Med. Student Assn. Golden Apple award for Outstanding Clin. Tchr. of Yr., 1988, Commendation for Drug Strategy Team Report, Mayor's Office of Drug Control Policy, 1990, The Disting. Alumni award for outstanding contbns. to cmty. and profession, 1990, The People's medal Mayor of Guang Zhou, 1991; grantee Pharmco/Wyeth Ayerst, 1990-93, Robert Wood Johnson, 1995—. Mem. APHA, AMA, N.Y. Acad. Scis., Am. Soc. Anesthesiologists, Soc. Critical Care Medicine. Democrat. Roman Catholic. Home: 5881 Nebraska Ave NW Washington DC 20015-1267 Office: The George Washington U Sch Medicine & Health Scis 2300 Eye St NW # 615 Washington DC 20037-2336

WILLIAMS, JOHN HORTER, civil engineer, oil, gas, telecommunications and allied products distribution company executive; b. Havana, Cuba, Aug. 17, 1918; s. Charles P. and Alice Magruder (Dyer) W.; m. Emily Alice Ijams, June 6, 1942 (dec.); children: John H., Burch I., S. Miller; m. Joanne Harwell Simpson., Feb. 1, 1975. BS, Yale U., 1940. Registered profl. engr., Okla., Minn. With The Williams Cos. Inc., Tulsa, 1940-42, 46-50, pres., dir., 1950-70, chmn., chief exec. officer, 1971-78, now hon. dir. Bd. dirs. Apco Argentina, Inc., Unit Corp., Westwood Corp., Willbros Group, Inc. Served with USNR, 1942-46. Decorated Order of Condor of Andes (Bolivia); named Okla. Hall of Fame, 1977; recipient Outstanding Okla. Oil Man award Okla.-Kans. Oil and Gas Assn., 1982, Disting. Svc. award Nat. Petroleum Hall of Fame, 1985; inducted into Okla. Commerce and Industry Hall of Honor, 1986, Tulsa Hall of Fame, 1993. Mem. ASCE, Yale Engring. Assn. Office: The Williams Cos Inc 10th Fl 1800 S Baltimore Ave Tulsa OK 74119-5210

WILLIAMS, JOHN JAMES, JR., architect; b. Denver, July 13, 1949; s. John James and Virginia Lee (Thompson) W.; m. Mary Serene Morck, July 29, 1972. BArch, U. Colo., 1974. Registered architect, Colo., Calif., Idaho, Va., Utah, N.Mex., Wyo., Ohio, Nebr., Puerto Rico. Project architect Gensler Assoc. Architects, Denver, 1976, Heinzman Assoc. Architects, Boulder, Colo., 1977, EZTH Architects, Boulder, 1978-79; prin. Knudson/Williams PC, Boulder, 1980-82, Faber, Williams & Brown, Boulder, 1982-86, John Williams & Assocs., Denver, 1986-97; John Williams Architecture P.C., 1997—. Panel chmn. U. Colo. World Affairs Conf.; vis. faculty U. Colo. Sch. Architecture and Planning, Coll. Environ. Design, 1986-91; mem. dean's adv. bd. Coll. Arch. and Planning, 2000—. Author (with others) State of Colorado architect licensing law, 1986. Commr. Downtown Boulder Mall Commn., 1985-88; bd. dirs. U. Colo. Fairway Club, 1986-88; mem. Gov.'s Natural Hazard Mitigation Coun., State of Colo., 1990. Recipient Teaching Honorarium, U. Colo. Coll. Architecture and Planning, 1977, 78, 79, 80, 88, Excellence in Design and Planning award City of Boulder, 1981, 82, Citation for Excellenc, WOOD Inc., 1982, 93, Disting. Profl. Svc. award Coll. Environ. Design U. Colo., 1988, James Sudler Svc. award AIA, Denver, 1998. Mem. AIA (sec. 1988, bd. dirs. Colo. North chpt. 1985-86, chair Colo. govtl. affairs com. 1995-98, Design award 1993, 2001, pres. 1990, sec. Colo. chpt. 1988, ednl. fund Fisher I traveling scholar 1988, state design conf. chair 1991, North chpt. Design award 1993, treas. Denver chpt. 1998, v.p. 1999, pres. edn. Colo. chpt. 2001, Disting. Svc. award Colo. chpt. 2001), Architects and Planners of Boulder (v.p. 1982), Nat. Coun. Architect Registration Bd., Nat. Golf Found. (sponsor), Kappa Sigma (chpt. pres. 1970). Avocations: golf, political history, fitness and health. Home: 1031 Turnberry Cir Louisville CO 80027-9594 Office: John Williams Architecture PC 350 Interlocken Blvd Ste 240 Broomfield CO 80021 Office Phone: 303-295-6190.

WILLIAMS, JOHN LEE, lawyer; b. Nashville, Dec. 23, 1942; s. Leslie Elwood and Gladys Mae (Ridings) W.; m. Norma Jean Givens, May 27, 1967; 1 child, Jacob Andrew. BA, Tenn. Technol. U., 1964; JD, U. Tenn., 1967. Bar: Tenn 1967. Ptnr. Porch, Peeler & Williams, Waverly, Tenn., 1967-78, Porch, Peeler, Williams & Thomason, Waverly, 1978—; asst. dist. atty. 23d Jud. Cir. Ct. Tenn., 1972-74; judge Ct. Gen. Sessions of Humphreys County, Tenn., 1978-82. County atty. Humphreys County, 1968—72, 1982—86, 1994—; city atty. City of Waverly, 1978—, City of McEwen, Tenn., 1978—, City of Lobelville, Tenn., 1985—89; gen. counsel Meriwether Lewis Elec. Coop., Centerville, Tenn., 1980—. State legal counsel Tenn. Jaycees, 1970; treas., sec. Humphreys County Dem. Exec. Com., 1978-2001; chmn. Humphreys County Election Commn., 1968-72. Col. U.S. Army ret. Mem.: Humphreys County Bar Assn. (pres. 1978—), Tenn. Bar Assn. (ho. of dels.), Masons (master 1985, 1999). Home: 1739 Ogden Rd Mc Ewen TN 37101 Office Phone: 931-296-7741. E-mail: john.williams@porchpeeler.com.

WILLIAMS, JOHN N. dean, dental educator; DDS Dental-Gen. Practice, U. Louisville, 1980, MBA. Dean U. Louisville Sch. Dentistry, prof. dept. periodontics, endontics and dental hygiene. Mem. editl. bd. Jour. Contemporary Dental Practice. Mem.: Am. Acad. Devel. Medicine and Dentistry. Office: 501 S Preston St #227 Louisville KY 40202*

WILLIAMS, J(OHN) RODMAN, theologian, educator, clergyman; b. Clyde, N.C., Aug. 21, 1918; s. John Rodman and Odessa Lee (Medford) W.; m. Johanna SerVaas, Aug. 6, 1949; children: John, Lucinda Lee, David Bert. AB, Davidson Coll., 1939; BD, Union Theol. Sem., 1943, ThM, 1944; PhD, Columbia U., 1954. Ordained to ministry Presbyn. Ch., 1943. Chaplain USNR, 1944—46; chaplain, assoc. prof. philosophy Beloit Coll., 1949—52; pastor First Presbyn. Ch., Rockford, Ill., 1952—59; prof. systematic theology and philosophy of religion Austin Presbyn. Theol. Sem., 1959—72; prof. Christian doctrine, pres. Melodyland Sch. Theology, Anaheim, Calif., 1972—82; prof. Christian theology Regent U., Virginia Beach, Va., 1982—. Author: Contemporary Existentialism and Christian Faith, 1965, The Era of the Spirit, 1971, The Pentecostal Reality, 1972, Ten Teachings, 1974, The Gift of the Holy Spirit Today, 1980, Renewal Theology, Vol. 1, God, the World, and Redemption, Vol. 2, 1988, Salvation, the Holy Spirit and Christian Living, Vol. 3, 1990, The Church, the Kingdom, and Last Things, 1992, Renewal Theology, 3 vols. in one, 1996. Home: 608 Fleet Dr Virginia Beach VA 23454-7344 Personal E-mail: rodmwil@regent.edu. *There is only one ultimate "Who". Jesus of Nazareth, in whose light all the rest of us are but dimly burning candles.*

WILLIAMS, J(OHN) TILMAN, insurance executive, real estate broker, city official; b. Detroit, Feb. 26, 1925; s. Aubrey and Martha (Lou) W.; m. Sally Jane Robinson, Aug. 22, 1947; children: Leslie Ann, Martha Lou. BS in Agr, Mich. State U., 1951. Pres. Satellite Ins. Brokerage, Garden Grove, Calif., 1959—. Pres. Satellite Real Estate, Satellite Mortgage & Loan Co. Mayor Garden Grove, 1976-78, re-elected, 1987, mem. coun., 1980-92, apptd. vice mayor, 1989—; mem. Ad Hoc Com. on Property Tax to Limit Govt. Spending with Spirit of 13 Initiative; elected to Orange County Dem. Cen. Com., 68th Assembly Dist., 1996; past pres. Garden Grove High Sch. Band Boosters; trustee Garden Grove Unified Sch. Dist., 2000—. With USAAF, World War II, PTO. Mem. Bd. Realtors, Ind. Ins. Agts. Assn., Orange County Esperanto Assn. (pres. 1985—), Am. Legion, VFW. Clubs: Toastmasters (Anaheim, Calif.); Fifty-Plus Sr. Citizens of Garden Grove (pres. 1986—). Lodges: Lions, Elks. Democrat. Home: 11241 Chapman Ave Garden Grove CA 92840-3301 Office: 12311 Harbor Blvd Garden Grove CA 92840-3809 Office Phone: 714-750-4333. *Service to one's fellowman and community is the greatest avocation and pleasure one can follow.*

WILLIAMS, JOHN TOWNER, composer, conductor; b. Flushing, N.Y., Feb. 8, 1932; s. John and Esther Williams; m. Barbara Ruike, 1956 (dec. 1974); children: Jennifer, Mark, Joseph; m. Samantha Winslow, 1980. Student, UCLA; pvt. studies with Mario Castelnuovo-Tedesco, Los Angeles; student, Juilliard Sch.; pvt. studies with, Madame Rosina Lhevinne, N.Y.C.; hon. degree, Berklee Coll. Music, Boston, Northeastern U., Tufts U., U. So. Calif., Boston U., New Eng. Conservatory Music, Providence Coll. Pianist Columbia & Twentieth Century Fox, 1956—; condr. Boston Pops Orch., 1980—93, laureate condr., 1993—; artist-in-residence Tanglewood Music Ctr., Boston, 1993—94. Guest condr. with orchestras including Cleveland Orch., Denver Symphony, Indianapolis Symphony, London Symphony Orch., Los Angeles Philharmonic, Montreal Orch., Philadelphia Orch., and Toronto Orch. Works include: composer (film scores) I Passed for White, 1960, Because They're Young, 1960, The Secret Ways, 1961, Bachelor Flat, 1962, Diamond Head, 1962, Gidget Goes to Rome, 1963, The Killers, 1964, John Goldfarb, Please Come Home, 1964, None But the Brave, 1965, How to Steal a Million, 1966, The Rare Breed, 1966, Not With My Wife, You Don't, 1966, The Plainsman, 1966, Penelope, 1966, A Guide for the Married Man, 1967, Valley of the Dolls, 1967 (Acad. award nominee), Fitzwilly, 1968, Sergeant Ryker, 1968, The Reivers, 1969 (Acad. award nominee), Daddy's Gone A-Hunting, 1969, Goodbye, Mr. Chips, 1969 (Acad. award nominee), The Story of A Woman, 1970, Fiddler on the Roof, 1971 (Acad. award for musical adaptation 1971), The Cowboys, 1972, The Poseidon Adventure, 1972 (Acad. award nominee), Images, 1972 (Acad. award nominee), Pete 'n' Tillie, 1972, The Paper Chase, 1973, The Long Goodbye, 1973, The Man Who Loved Cat Dancing, 1973, Cinderella Liberty, 1973 (Acad. award nominee), Tom Sawyer, 1973 (Acad. award nominee), Sugarland Express, 1974, Earthquake, 1974, The Towering Inferno, 1974 (Acad. award nominee), Conrack, 1974, Jaws, 1975 (Acad. award, Grammy award, Golden Globe award 1976), The Eiger Sanction, 1976, Family Plot, 1976, Midway, 1976, The Missouri Breaks, 1976, Raggedy Ann and Andy, 1977, Black Sunday, 1977, Star Wars, 1977 (Acad. award, 3 Grammy awards, Golden Globe award 1977), Close Encounters of the Third Kind, 1977 (2 Grammy awards, Acad. award nominee 1978), The Fury, 1978, Jaws II, 1978, Superman, 1978 (2 Grammy awards 1979), Meteor, 1979, Quintet, 1979, Dracula, 1979, "1941", 1979, The Empire Strikes Back, 1980 (2 Grammy awards, Acad. award nominee 1980), Raiders of the Lost Ark, 1981 (Grammy award, Acad. award nominee 1981), Heartbeeps, 1981, E.T., 1982 (Acad. award for best original score, 3 Grammy awards, Golden Globe award 1982), Monsignor, 1982, Yes, Giorgio, 1982 (Acad. award nominee), Superman III, 1983, Return of the Jedi, 1983 (Acad. award nominee), Indiana Jones and the Temple of Doom, 1984 (Acad. award nominee), The River, 1984 (Acad. award nominee), Space Camp, 1986, Emma's War, 1986, The Witches of Eastwick, 1987 (Acad. award nominee), Empire of the Sun, 1987 (Acad. award nominee), Jaws: The Revenge, 1987, Superman IV: The Quest for Peace, 1987, The Secret of My Success, 1987, The Accidental Tourist, 1988 (Acad. award nominee, Indiana Jones and the Last Crusade, 1989 (Acad. award nominee), Always, 1989, Born On The Fourth of July, 1989 (Acad. award nominee), Stanley and Iris, 1990, Presumed Innocent, 1990, Home Alone, 1990 (Acad. award nominee), Hook, 1991 (Acad. award nominee), JFK, 1991 (Acad. award nominee), Far and Away, 1992, Home Alone II, 1992, Jurassic Park, 1993, Schindler's List, 1993 (Acad. award 1993, Grammy award 1994), Sabrina, 1995 (Acad. award nominee for best original score 1996), Nixon, 1995 (Acad. award nominee 1996), Sleepers, 1996, Rosewood, 1997, The Lost World: Jurassic Park, 1997, Seven Years In Tibet, 1997 (Acad. award nominee), Amistad, 1997 (Acad. award nominee), Saving Private Ryan, 1998 (Acad. award nominee, Grammy award 1998), Stepmom, 1998, Star Wars Episode I: The Phantom Menace, 1999, Angela's Ashes, 1999 (Acad. award nominee, Grammy award 2000), The Patriot, 2000 (Acad. award nominee), Artificial Intelligence, 2001 (Acad. award nominee), Harry Potter and The Sorcerer's Stone, 2001 (Acad. award nominee), Minority Report, 2002, Star Wars Episode II: Attack Of The Clones, 2002, Harry Potter: The Chamber Of Secrets, 2002, Catch Me If You Can, 2002 (Acad. award nominee), Harry Potter: The Prisoner Of Azkaban, 2004, The Terminal, 2004; composer music for songs including: (from Sabrina, lyrics by Alan and Marilyn Bergman) Moonlight, 1995 (Acad. award nominee 1996); composer: (TV programs) Heidi, 1969 (Emmy award), Jane Eyre, 1971 (Emmy award), others; composer numerous concert pieces and symphonies including Jubilee 350 Fanfare for the Boston Pops, 1980, theme to the 1984 Summer OlympicGames, Liberty Fanfare, 1987; recorded numerous albums with Boston Pops Orch. including Pops in Space, That's Entertainment (Pops on Broadway), Pops on the March, Pops Aroundthe World (Digital Overtures), Aisle Seat, Pops Out of This World, Boston Pops on Stage, America, the Dream Goes On; collaborator: (with Jessye Norman) With A Song in My Heart, Swing, Swing, Swing, Unforgettable; guest condr. major orchs. including London Symphony Orch., Cleve. Orch., Phila. Orch., Toronto Orch., Montreal Orch. Served with USAF, 1952-54. Recipient several gold and platinum records Rec. Industry Assn. Am. Composer of over seventy-five film scores. Office: Gorfaine & Schwartz c/o Michael Gorfaine 13245 Riverside Dr Ste 450 Sherman Oaks CA 91423-2172 also: Boston Symphony Orch 301 Mass Ave Boston MA 02115*

WILLIAMS, JOHN TROY, librarian, educator; b. Oak Park, Ill., Mar. 11, 1924; s. Michael Daniel and Donna Marie (Schaffer) Williams. BA, Ctrl. Mich. U., 1949; MA in Libr. Sci., U. Mich., 1954; PhD, Mich. State U., 1973. Reference libr. U. Mich., Ann Arbor, 1955—59; instr. Bowling Green (Ohio) State U., 1959—60; reference libr. Mich. State U., East Lansing, 1960—62; 1st asst. reference dept. Flint (Mich.) Pub. Libr., 1962—65; head reference svcs. Purdue U., West Lafayette, Ind., 1965—72; head pub. svcs. No. Ill. U., DeKalb, 1972—75; asst. dean, asst. univ. libr. Wright State U., Dayton, Ohio, 1975—80; vis. scholar U. Mich., Ann Arbor, 1980—; cons. in field. Contbr. articles to profl. jours. Served U.S. Army, 1943—46. Mich. State fellow, 1963—64, HEW fellow, 1971—72. Mem.: AAUP, ALA, Coun. Fgn. Rels., Am. Sociol. Assn., Am. Soc. Info. Scis., Spl. Librs. Assn.

WILLIAMS, JOHN ZIGLER, anesthesiologist; b. Washington, 1927; s. Paul Lyle Sr. and Beulah Rebecca (Zigler) Williams; m. Barbara Dorothy Krueger, Oct. 28, 1961; children: Karen Lynn, Lisa Carol. BS, U. Md., 1954, MD, 1956. Intern Harrisburg Hosp., 1956-57; resident St. Joseph Hosp., Joliet, Ill., 1957-59; with Copley Meml. Hosp., Aurora, Ill. Mem. AMA, Am. Soc. Anesthesiology, Am. Bd. Anesthesiology, Kane County Med. Soc. Personal E-mail: jzwill@aol.com.

WILLIAMS, JOSEPH DALTON, pharmaceutical company executive; b. Washington, Pa., Aug. 15, 1926; s. Joseph Dalton and Jane (Day) W.; m. Mildred E. Bellaire, June 28, 1973; children: Terri, Daniel. BS in Pharmacy, U. Nebr., 1950; DSc (hon.), Union U., 1991, U. Nebr., 1989; LHD (hon.), Albany Coll. Pharmacy, Union U., 1980, Rutgers U., 1987, Long Island U., 1988; DSc (hon.), Phila. Coll. Pharmacy and Sci., 1988, Long Island U., 1988, Albany Coll. Pharmacy of Union U., 1991; D Human Svcs. (hon.), Caldwell Coll., 1989; LLD (hon.), Bethune-Cookman Coll., 1990, Coll. St. Elizabeth, 1990, Seton Hall U., 1990, U. Md., 1991, St. Augustine Coll., 1992. Pres. Parke-Davis Co., Detroit, 1973-76; pres. pharm. group Warner-Lambert Co., Morris Plains, N.J., 1976-77; pres. Internat. Group, 1977-79; pres., dir. Warner-Lambert Corp., 1979-80, pres., chief operating officer, 1980-84, chmn., CEO, 1985-91, chmn. exec. com., 1991-97; retired, 1997. Bd. dirs. AT&T, 1984-1997, J.C. Penny & Co., 1985-1998, Exxon Corp., 1985-1997, Rockefeller Fin. Svcs. Inc., Rockefeller and Co., Inc., 1992-1999, Eckerd Corp., 1997-2000. Trustee emeritus Columbia U. With USNR, 1943—46. Mem. Am. Pharm. Assn., Links Club, Pine Valley Golf Club, Baltusrol Golf Club, Mid Ocean Club. Office: Warner-Lambert Co 55 Madison Ave Morristown NJ 07960-7397 Office Phone: 973-285-3277.

WILLIAMS, JOSEPH SCOTT, energy and natural resources company executive, city commissioner; b. Chgo., Nov. 10, 1951; s. Hagle Eugene and Helen Elizabeth (Mellon) W.; m. Tamalou Mitchell, June 10, 1972 (dec. Apr. 2000); children: Troy Scott, Ari Layne. Welding Cert., John A. Logan Coll., Carterville, Ill., 1971; Cert. in Mining Tech., Rend Lake Coll., Ina, Ill., 1975. Dealer S&S Motors, West Frankfort, Ill., 1970-74; coal mine laborer Peabody Coal Co., Freeburg, Ill., 1973; coal mine electrician Old Ben Coal Co., Sesser, Ill., 1973-76; alt. energy cons. Helios Devel. Co., West Frankfort, Ill., 1977-83; instr. Rend Lake Coll., Ina, 1979-82; coal mine repairman Freeman United Coal Co., Pittsburg, Ill., 1979-87; mgr. ops. Royal Talon Co., West Frankfort, 1989—, pres., 2000—, Egyptian Energies, Inc., West Frankfort, 1987—, Horn Dimond Coal Co., West Frankfort, 1991—; commr. pub. health and safety City of West Frankfort, Ill., 1999—2003. Mem. Ill. State Mining Bd., Springfield, 1993-2003, sec., 1996-2003; pres. United Mine Workers Labor Union 9878, West Frankfort, 1990—. Precinct committeeman Rep. Party, Franklin County, 1988-94; reg. coord. Citizens for Sue Suter, 1990, Citizens for Jim Ryan, 1994; transition adv. com. mem. Jim Ryan Ill. Atty. Gen., Chgo., 1995; advisor, dir. Ill. YMCA Youth and Govt., 1992—; chaplain Racers for Christ, 2003—. Mem. Ill. Oil and Gas Assn., West Frankfort C. of C. (dir. 1988-2003), Moose, Masons (32 deg.), Shriner (Krazy Klown unit dir. 1997-99), Lions (pres. 1992-93). Avocations: motorcycling, collecting automobiles and memorabilia. Office: Egyptian Energies Inc 107 S Van Buren St PO Box 127 West Frankfort IL 62896-0127

WILLIAMS, JOUSTON L. service industry executive; Pres., CEO Pacific Network Supply Inc., San Jose, Calif., 1987—. Office: Pacific Network Supply Inc 2320 Kruse Dr San Jose CA 95131-1231

WILLIAMS, JOYCE HALL, secondary school educator; b. Viola, Tenn., Feb. 6, 1926; d. Albert White and Byrde Groom Hall; m. Lewis Blanton Williams, Dec. 14, 1948; children: Susan Joyce Boada, Nancy Hall West, Lewis B.(dec.). BA, U. Tenn., Knoxville, 1947; postgrad., U. Miami, 1967; MA, U. North Ala., 1982. Cert. tchr. Fla., Ala. Tchr. Gulliver Preparatory Sch., Coral Gables, Fla., 1967—70, 1975—79, Am. Internat. Sch., New Delhi, 1970—73, Internat. Inst. Tropical Agr., Ibadan, Nigeria, 1974—79; faculty Faulkner U., Florence, Ala., 1981—88, N.W. C.C., Muscle Shoals, Ala., 1981—88; adj. tchr. U. North Ala., 1994. Owner Off-Ctr. Pub. Co., Ala., 1985. Author: A Volunteer in Romania, 1999, Sunshine and Shadows, 2001, In the Cradle of Mankind, Let's Play Ball and the Taj Mahal!, Roamin Around Romania, 2004. Vol. tchr. Headstart, Handy Ctr., Florence, 2001—03; tchr., vol. Adult Basic Edn., Handy Ctr., 2001—03; vol. ch. libr. Edgemont Meth. Ch., 1987—. Named Tchr. of the Yr., Gulliver Acad.; recipient Diploma of Recognition, Israelite Heritage Instn. for excellence in Bible Study, 1967, winner, Ernest Hemingway Internat. Writing Competition, Key West, Fla. Mem.: AAUW, Assn. Ala. Writers, United Meth. Women. Avocation: golf. Home: PO Box 1842 Florence AL 35631-1842

WILLIAMS, JOYCE MARILYN, artist, business owner; b. Waterbury, Conn., Sept. 12, 1933; d. Carl Vosburgh and Arline Dorothy (Cummings) Miller; m. Ralph Gray, Apr. 8, 1949 (div. 1955); children: Diane Leslie, Jerri Joyce-Gray; m. Charles Edward Williams, July 24, 1958; 1 child, Carol Lea. Grad. h.s., San Mateo, Calif., 1950. Pres., owner JC Enterprises, Phoenix, Ariz., 1993—. Art instr. Sta. KHIZ-TV, Victorville, Calif., 1995; judge fine art San Bernardino County Fair, Victorville, 1995. Author: Painting Portraits, 1994, Painting Horses, 1995; author, artist: (videos) Painting Portraits, 1993, Painting Horses, Wildlife, 1995; numerous commns., U.S. and Can.; commd. cover art for Arabian horse show. Recipient numerous 1st pl. awards various art shows, 1985-95. Mem. High Desert Art League, High Desert GD (editor newsletter 1992-95). Avocations: art, painting, writing. Mailing: 855 Garner St Colorado Springs CO 80905 E-mail: artistinoil@aol.com.

WILLIAMS, JULIE FORD, mutual fund officer; b. Long Beach, Calif., Aug. 7, 1948; d. Julious Hunter and Bessie May (Wood) Ford; m. Walter Edward Williams, Oct. 20, 1984; 1 child, Andrew Ford. BA in Econs., Occidental Coll., 1970. Legal sec. Kadison, Pfaelzer, Woodard, Quinn & Rossi, L.A., 1970-71, 74-77; legal sec. Fried, Frank, Harris, Shriver & Jacobson, N.Y.C., 1971-72, Pallot, Poppell, Goodman & Shapo, Miami, Fla., 1973-74; adminstrv. asst. Capital Research-Mgmt., Los Angeles, 1978-82; corp. officer Cash Mgmt. Trust Am., 1982—, Bond Fund Am., 1982—, Tax-Exempt Bond Fund Am., 1982—, AMCAP Fund, 1984-98, 2000—, Am. Funds Income Series, 1985—, Am. Funds Tax-Exempt Series II, 1986—, Capital World Bond Fund, 1987—, Am. High-Income Trust, 1987—, Intermediate Bond Fund Am., 1987—, Tax-Exempt Money Fund Am., 1989—, U.S. Treasury Money Fund Am., 1991—, Fundamental Investors, 1992-2000, Ltd. Term Tax-Exempt Bond Fund Am., 1993—, Am. High-Income Mcpl. Bond Fund, 1994—; v.p. fund bus. mgmt. group Capital Rsch. Mgmt., 1986—; sec. Growth Fund of Am., 1998-2000; Am. Mutual Fund, 2000—. Pres. Alumni Bd. Govs. Occidental Coll., 1997-98; bd. trustees Occidental Coll., 1999-2003. Democrat. Episcopalian. Office: Capital Rsch & Mgmt Co 333 S Hope St 55th Floor Los Angeles CA 90071-1452

WILLIAMS, JULIE LLOYD, lawyer; b. Washington, May 24, 1950; d. Walter Herbert and Jean (Grabill) W.; m. Don Scroggin, May 9, 1981; 1 child, Patrick Conner. BA, Goddard Coll., 1971; JD, Antioch Sch. Law, 1975. Bar: Va. 1975, D.C. 1976. Assoc. Fried, Frank, Harris, Shriver, Washington, 1975-83; assoc. gen. counsel Fed. Home Loan Bank Bd., Washington, 1983-86, dep. gen. counsel, 1986-89; dep. chief counsel Office of Thrift Supervision, Washington, 1989-91, sr. dep. chief counsel, 1991-93; dep. chief counsel Comptr. of the Currency, Washington, 1993-94, chief counsel, 1994-98, acting comptr., 1998-99, 1st sr. dep. comptr., chief counsel, 1999—. Co-author: (handbook) How to Incorporate: A Handbook for Entrepreneurs & Professionals, 1987; author: Savings Institutions: Mergers, Acquisitions & Conversions, 1988. Mem. ABA (banking law com.), Women in Housing and Fin. Home: 3064 Q St NW Washington DC 20007-3080 Office: Office Comptroller Currency 250 E St SW Washington DC 20024-3208*

WILLIAMS, JULIUS PENSON, composer, conductor; b. Bronx, N.Y., June 22, 1954; BS, CUNY, 1977; MusM, Hartt Sch. Music, 1980; postgrad., Aspen Music Sch., 1984. Music dir. CPTV, 1984-85; asst. condr. Aspen (Colo.) Music Festival, 1985; condr., composer-in-residence Nutmeg Ballet, Bristol, Conn., 1986-88; music dir. Washington Symphony Orch., 1998—2002; Loufente music dir., 2002—. Artist-in-residence U. Vt., 1988-90; choral artistic dir. N.Y. State Summer Sch. of the Arts, Saratoga; music dir., prin. condr. Royal Ethiopian Philharm.; prof. music Berklee Coll. Music; edn. cons. Norwalk Symphony, 1997-98; mem. artistic adv. com. Queens Symphony, 1997—. Composer: A Norman Overture, Tocatinna for Strings, Incommendation of Music, Meditation, Easter Celebration, Cantata for Orch., Chorus, Concerto for Harmonica and Orch., Rise Up Shepherd and Follow; (movie) My Heart Beats Loud; (off-Broadway) The Balm Yard; condr. Symphony Saint Paulia, Carnegie Hall; guest condr. New Haven Symphony, 1987, Savannah Symphony Orch., Dallas Symphony Orch., Norwalk Symphony

Orch., Dubrovnik Symphony Orch., Yugoslavia, Knoxville Symphony, Okla. Symphony, Voldanska Philharm., Yugoslavia, Tulsa Philharm., Brno State Philharm, Czechoslavakia, Sacramento Symphony, 1995-96, Hartford Symphony, 1994, Bohuslau Martinu Philharm., Norfolk Symphony, 1997; appearances on CBS Sunday Morning, CBS Night Watch; recs. include Symphonic Brotherhood, 1994, Shades of Blue; contbr. articles to profl. jours. Named Hon. Disting. Alumnus Langston U., Disting. Alumn Herbert H. Lehman Coll.; recipient Nat. Cultural Through the Arts award, medal of artistic merit Found. Ecuador, Gracie Allen award, 2003; Eminent Dupont scholar, Va. Mem. ASCPA (award 1979—), NARAS, Am. Symphony Orch. League, Am. Choral Dirs. Assn., Music Educators Nat. Conf. Office: Julius Penson Williams Music Ste 293 35-31 Tacottville Rd Vernon Rockville CT 06066 E-mail: jwilliams@berklee.edu.

WILLIAMS, JUSTIN W. government official; b. N.Y.C., Jan. 4, 1942; s. Louis P. and Edith W. Williams. BA, Columbia U., 1963; LLB, U. Va., 1967. Bar: Va. 1967. Atty. Dept. Justice, 1967-68; asst. commonwealth atty. Arlington County, Va., 1968-70; asst. U.S. atty. Ea. Dist. Va., 1970-78, 1st asst. U.S. atty., 1978-79; U.S. atty. Alexandria, Va., 1979-81; asst. U.S. atty., 1981-86; U.S. atty. Ea. dist. Va., 1986, asst. U.S. atty., chief criminal divsn., 1986—. Episcopalian. Office: US Atty's Office 2100 Jamieson Ave Alexandria VA 22314

WILLIAMS, KAREN HASTIE, lawyer; b. Washington, Sept. 30, 1944; d. William Henry and Beryl (Lockhart) Hastie; m. Wesley S. Williams, Jr.; children: Amanda Pedersen, Wesley Hastie, Bailey Lockhart. Cert., U. Neuchatel, Switzerland, 1965; BA, Bates Coll., 1966; MA, Tufts U., 1967; JD, Cath. U. Am., 1973. Bar: D.C. 1973. Staff asst. internat. gov. relations dept. Mobil Oil Corp., N.Y.C., 1967-69; staff asst. com. Dist. Columbia U.S. Senate, 1970, chief counsel com. on the budget, 1977-80; law clk. to judge Spottswood Robinson III U.S. Ct. Appeals (D.C. Cir.), Washington, 1973-74; law clk. to assoc. justice Thurgood Marshall U.S. Supreme Ct., Washington, 1974-75; assoc. Fried, Frank, Harris, Shriver & Kampelman, Washington, 1975-77, 1975-77; adminstr. Office Mgmt. and Budget, Washington, 1980-81; of counsel Crowell & Moring, Washington, 1982, ptnr., 1982—. Bd. dirs. Chubb Corp., Gannett Co., Inc., Sun Trust Bank, Inc., Washington Gas Light Co., Continental Airlines. Trustee, past chair Greater Washington Rsch. Ctr. Mem. ABA (pub. contract law sect., past chair), Nat. Bar Assn., Washington Bar Assn., Nat. Contract Mgmt. Assn., NAACP (legal def. fund, bd. dirs.). Office: Crowell & Moring 1001 Pennsylvania Ave NW Ste 1100 Washington DC 20004-2595 Office Phone: 202-624-2500.

WILLIAMS, KAREN JOHNSON, federal judge; b. Orangeburg, S.C., Aug. 4, 1951; d. James G. Johnson and Marcia Johnson (Reynolds) Dantzler; m. Charles H. Williams, Dec. 27, 1968; children: Marian, Ashley, Charlie, David. BA, Columbia Coll., 1972; postgrad., U. S.C., 1973, JD cum laude, 1980. Bar: S.C. 1980, U.S. Dist. Ct. S.C. 1980, U.S. Ct. Appeals (4th cir.) 1981. Tchr. Irmo (S.C.) Mid. Sch., 1972—74, O-W H.S., Orangeburg, 1974—76; assoc. Charles H. Williams PA, Orangeburg, 1980—92; judge U.S. Ct. Appeals (4th cir.), 1992—. Exec. bd. grievance commn. S.C. Supreme Ct., Columbia, 1983—92. Child devel. bd. First Bapt. Ch., Orangeburg; bd. dirs. Orangeburg County Mental Retardation Bd., 1986—94, Orangeburg-Calhoun Hosp. Found., Columbia Coll., 1988—92, Reg. Med. Ctr. Hosp. Found., 1988—92; adv. bd. Orangeburg-Calhoun Tech. Coll., SC, 1987—92. Mem.: ABA, Nat. Assn. of Women Judges, Bus. and profl. Women Assn., S.C. Trial Lawyers Assn., Orangeburg County Bar Assn. (co-chair Law Day 1981), S.C. Bar Assn., Fed. Judges Assn., Am. Judicature Soc., Rotary, Order of Coif, Order of Wig and Robe. Home: 2503 Five Chop Rd Orangeburg SC 29115-8185 Office: Lewis F Powell Jr US Cthse Annex 1100 E Main St Ste 617 Richmond VA 23219-3517

WILLIAMS, KATHLEEN, advertising executive; Pres., CEO Williams Worldwide, Santa Monica, Calif., 1987—. Office: Williams Worldwide Inc 3130 Wilshire Blvd Fl 4 Santa Monica CA 90403-2358

WILLIAMS, KEITH ROY, museum director; b. Sunnyside, Wash., Sept. 5, 1958; s. Charles N. Williams and Ruth Arlene (Plank) Hicks; m. Nancy Maxson, 1980 (div. 1984); m. Deanna Lynn Murphy, Oct. 26, 1987; children: Steven, Jeremy. AA in Gen. Studies, Columbia Basin C.C., Pasco, Wash., 1979; BA in Anthropology, Wash. State U., 1981, MA in History/Pub. History, 1984, PhD in History, 1991. Interpretive ranger Nez Perce Nat. Hist. Pk. Nat. Pk. Svc., 1984, historian Alaska regional office, 1986; dir. Wenatchee Valley Mus. and Cultural Ctr., Wenatchee, Wash., 1987—. Cons. Office Archaeology and Hist. Preservation, 1985, Batelle N.W. DOSE Reconstruction Project, Hanford, 1987, 88; instr. Wenatchee Valley C.C., 1988, 93—; Wash. state adviser Smithsonian Instn. exhibit Barn Again, 2000-01; field assessor and surveyor Am. Assn. Museums Mus. Assessment program, 1996—; pres., co-owner Spirit Voices Prodns., Inc., 2003—; spkr. in field. Author: (video, booklet) The People and The Plow, 1987, (audio CD) Bullfrogs Amuck: On the Yakima River, 2003; contbr. articles to profl. jours. Active Wash. State Heritage Coun., Olympia, 1988-90, Wash. Centennial Com., Wenatchee, 1989; mem. design com. Wenatchee Downtown Assn., 1993-96; bd. dirs. Wash. Friends Humanities, Seattle, 1990—, Wenatchee Centennial Com., 1992, Wash. Commn. for the Humanities, 2001—. Grantee Assn. Humanities Idaho, Wash. Commn. Humanities, various other founds; nominee Paul Harris Rotary fellow for cmty. leadership, 2004. Mem. Wash. Mus. Assn. (bd. dirs. 1988-90, 94-96), Kiwanis (bd. dirs. 1998-99, past pres.). Avocations: boating, gardening, hunting, camping, reading. Office: Wenatchee Valley Mus and Cultural Ctr 127 S Mission St Wenatchee WA 98801-3039 Office Phone: 509-664-3340. E-mail: k.williams@wenatcheevalleymuseum.com.

WILLIAMS, KEVIN W. automotive executive; b. Lexington Park, Md., Sept. 27, 1961; B in Bus. Mgmt., Tenn. State U., 1983; M in Bus. Adminstrn., Ctrl. Mich. U., 1989. Reliability analyst GM, Flint, Mich., 1983—89; gen. supr. prodn. Lansing Craft Ctr., 1989—91; program readiness mgr. GM EV1 electric vechicle program, 1991—93; reliability engr. N. Am. Truck Group, 1993—95, asst. prodn. supr., 1995—96, area mgr. gen. assembly, 1996; dir., supplier quality GM Europe, 1997—2000; exec. dir., supplier quality GM N. Am., 2000—03, v.p. quality, 2003—. Bd. dirs. Motor Enterprises Inc. Office: GM Corp PO Box 300 300 Renaissance Ctr Detroit MI 48265-3000

WILLIAMS, LARRY BILL, academic administrator; b. Cushing, Okla., June 9, 1945; s. Louis Albert and Morene Ruth (Cox) W.; m. Pam Bryan, May 1, 1993; children: Natalie Michelle, Nicole Diane, Louis Bradley, Sharla Dianne Bryan, Vanessa Joy Bryan. BS, Ctrl. State U., Edmond, Okla., 1967, MBA, 1972; PhD, U. Okla., 1985; grad. Inst. Ednl. Mgmt. program, Harvard U., 1996. Office mgr. Okla. State U., Stillwater, 1967-69; from asst. comptr. to dir. univ. pers. svcs. Ctrl. State U., 1969-80, from asst. v.p. adminstrn. to v.p. adminstrn., 1980-87; interim pres. Southeastern Okla. State U., Durant, 1987, pres., 1987-97, Northeastern State U., Tahlequah, Okla., 1997—. Managerial cons. various municipalities; mktg. cons. State of Okla.; arbitrator Met. Fraternal Order of Police; bd. dirs. Okla. Small Bus. Devel. Ctr., Okla. Acad. State Goals, chmn. S.E. region, 1995. Bd. dirs. Bryan County Econ. Devel. Corp., 1989—, Bryan County United Way, 1988-94; mem. adv. bd. Med. Ctr. Southeastern Okla., 1987-92; bd. dirs. Bryan County Ret. Sr. Vol. Program, 1990-92, Leadership Okla. Class IV, 1991, mem. adv. bd., 1991-95; mem. exec. bd. Boy Scouts Am., 1991; com. mem. Okla. Ctr. for Advancement Sci. and Tech. Long Range Planning Task Force, Most Eminent Scholars and Rsch. Equipment, 1990-91; mem. higher edn. alumni coun. Okla. State Regent for Higher Edn. Tuition Com., mem. budget com., mem. outreach com., mem. quality initiative com., mem. capital com., chmn. legis. affairs com., chmn. acad. affairs com.; mem. adv. coun. Ea. Okla. Schs., 1987—; trustee Southeastern Found., 1990—; past pres. Kickingbird Golf Course Mgmt., Edmond; bd. dirs. Edmond C. of C., 1984; mem. Okla. State Regents for Higher Edn. Coun. of Pres., 1987—, chair, 1994; Chocktaw Nation of Okla. JTPA Adv. Coun., 1987—; mem. Okla. Regional Pres.' Coun., 1987—, chair, 1994; vice chmn. Diamond Jubilee Commn., Edmond; mem. found. bd. trustees Ctrl. State U., Edmond; mem. adv. com. Durant Airport. With USNG, 1962-70. Named One of Outstanding Young Men of Am., Edmond Jaycees, 1971, 74, 79; recipient Presdl. Leadership award Nat. U.S. Jaycee Pres., 1971, Presdl. Leadership, Achievement and Honor awards Nat. Jaycees, 1972, Nat. Presdl. award of Honor Nat. Coll. and Univ. Pers. Assn., 1973, Disting. Svc. award City of Edmond, 1974, Dwight F. Whelan Meml. award for Outstanding Leadership, Edmond, 1972, Disting. Former Student award U. Ctrl. Okla., 1996; named to Cushing Alumni Hall of Fame, 1988, recipient Nat. Order Omega (charter hon. mem), 1991. Mem. Okla. Assn. Coll. and Univ. Pers. Adminstrs. (founder, bd. dirs., chmn.), Nat. Coll. and Univ. Pers. Assn., Nat. Coll. and Univ. Bus. Officers Assn., Okla. Assn. Affirmative Action (co-founder, pres., bd. dirs.), Okla. City Pers. Assn., Am. Assn. State Colls. and Univs., Okla. Assn. Coll. and Univ. Bus. Officers (bd. dirs., pres.), Acad. Cert. Adminstrv. Mgrs., Okla. Small Bus. Devel. Ctr. (bd. dirs. 1987—), Industry Ednl. Coun. McCurtain County, Okla. Acad. for State Goals (bd. dirs. 1992—, vice chair S.E. region 1995), Okla. Advs. for Arts and Humanities (mem. steering com. 1995), Durant C. of C. (past pres., bd. dirs.), Okla. State C. of C. (bd. dirs. 1991—), Blue Key, Rotary. Lodges: Rotary (sec. Edmond club 1986-87). Democrat. Presbyterian. Avocation: golf. Office: Northeastern State Univ Office of the Pres Tahlequah OK 74464

WILLIAMS, LAWRENCE D. surgeon; b. Mocksville, N.C., July 20, 1956; m. Karen Henderson; children: Bryan Dale, Wendy Karen, Megan Janell. BS in Biology, High Point (N.C.) Coll., 1978; MD, Wake Forest U., 1982. Diplomate Nat. Bd. Med. Examiners, Am. Bd. Surgery; registered vascular technologist. Resident in gen. surgery East Carolina U. Sch. Medicine/Pitt County Meml. Hosp., Greenville, N.C., 1982-87; Charles E. Culpepper Transplant fellow East Carolina U. Sch. Medicine, 1983-84; ptnr. Med. Ctr. Surgeons, Inc., 1987-93; employee physician Westwood Surg. Assocs., Inc., 1993-95; shareholder, surgeon Cornerstone Health Care, PA, 1995—; med. dir. Cornerstone Imaging Svcs., 1998—. Active med. staff High Point Regional Hosp., 1987—, chief of surgery, 1991-93; med. dir. Med. Ctr. Diagnostic Imaging, High Point, 1995-98; active med. staff High Point Surg. Ctr., 1989—, Lexington Meml. Hosp., 1999—. Contbr. articles to profl. jours. Mem. fin. com. Covenant United Meth. Ch., 1995-97; vol. physician Cmty. Clinic of High Point, 1993—. Recipient numerous fellowships and honors. Fellow ACS; mem AMA, Am. Soc. Gastrointestinal Endoscopists, Am. Registry Diagnostic Med. Sonographers, N.C. Med. Soc., High Point Med. Soc., Carolina Vascular Soc., Internat. Soc. for Endovascular Surgery, So. Med. Assn., N.C. Vascular Technologists, Old North State Club, High Point Country Club. Office: Cornerstone Health Care PA 611 Lindsay St Ste 100 High Point NC 27262-4305 Office Phone: 336-802-2150. Personal E-mail: ldwbry@aol.com.

WILLIAMS, LAWRENCE (JUDD) MARVIN, artist, education educator; b. Beatrice, Neb., Sept. 1, 1934; s. Henry and Naomi Caroline Williams; m. Julianna Robin Furlong, Oct. 10, 1971; 1 child, Jesse Quinn; m. Nancy Jane Scott, Jan. 7, 1955 (div. Sept. 1970); 1 child, Scott Jeffery. BFA, Kans. City Art Inst., 1958; MFA, U. of Ill., 1960. Artist Self-Employed, Rochester, NY, 1952—; tchg. asst. U. Ill., 1959—60; fine arts instr. Columbus Coll. of Art and Design, Ohio, 1960—63; prof. fine arts Rochester Inst. Tech., 1963—96; ret. Mem. Arts for Greater Rochester, 1995—96; bus. owner and mgr. J & J Art, Spencerport, NY, 1973—; art exhbn. juror and selector George Eastman Sculpture, Rochester, 1988; artist in residence Art Pk., Lewiston, NY, 1984, Hall Walls, Buffalo, 1998. Various exhibitions, Represented in permanent collections Meml. Art Gallery, Rochester, N.Y., Everson Mus., Syracuse, N.Y., Sheldon Meml., Lincoln, Columbus Gallery of Fine Arts, one-man shows include Alan Stone Gallery, N.Y., Meml. Art Gallery, Rochester, Charleston Gallery of Fine Arts, West Va., Gallery 15, Rochester. SP3 U.S. Army, 1955—56, Hawaii. Recipient Lillian Fairchild Meml. award, U. Rochester, 2001. Mem.: Rochester Contemporary (bd. trustees 1987—88), Meml. Art Gallery (art com. 1998—99). Avocations: gardening, building, furniture design.

WILLIAMS, LAWRENCE SOPER, JR., photographer; b. Balt., July 8, 1917; s. Lawrence S. and Ida (Exall) W.; m. Avilda Leyshon Williams, Nov. 21, 1940; children: Jay Stephen, Wendy Lauren. Student, Md. Inst. Wirephoto operator AP, Balt., 1937—38; news photographer Balt. Sun Papers, 1938—40, Harris and Ewing News Photos, Washington, 1940—41; war corr., photographer Bur. Info. U.S. War Dept., Washington, 1941—45; picture editor Holiday mag., Phila., 1945—48; freelance photographer Havertown, Pa., 1949—59; pres. Lawrence S. Williams, Inc., Upper Darby, Pa., 1959—83, chmn., 1983—93. Pres. Archtl. Photographers Assn., N.Y.C., 1968-70, Paoli (Pa.) Woods Homeowner's Assn., 1985-86; chmn. archtl. landscape com. Robynwood Village, Hershey's Mill; vol., TV audio instr. West Chester Sch. Dist. Recipient Gold medal Artist Guild of Phila., 1965, Silver medal Artist Guild of Pa., 1964, George W. Berry trophy Soc. Comml. Photographers Del. Valley, 1961, 66, 78, 79, 82, Best of Show trophy Am. Mus. Photography, Phila., 1966, 71, 77, 79, 82, Best Comml. Print trophy Guild of Profl. Photographers Del. Valley, 1971, 70, Award of Excellence Am. Advtg. Assn. Pa., 1978, Pres.'s Cup Profl. Photographers Assn. Pa., 1971, Silver medal for Sixty Years World in Colour, Internat. Photo competition, Hague, Netherlands, 1973, numerous archtl., comml., indsl., pictorial awards. Fellow Am. Soc. Photographers; mem. Soc. Comml. Photographers Del. Valley (life), Profl. Photographers Assn. Pa. (life), Profl. Photographers Am., Inc. (life, master photography degree 1966, craftsman photography degree 1968), Hershey's Mill Golf Club (West Chester, Pa.), Shriners. Republican. Lutheran. Achievements include assembly of the largest collection of architectural photographs in U.S. consisting of over 250,000 negatives which are now in the archives of the Athenaeum of Philadelphia, Pa. Avocation: travel. Home: 1268 Robynwood Ln West Chester PA 19380-5747 Office: PO Box 694 Kimberton PA 19442-0694 E-mail: larryvil@verizon.com.

WILLIAMS, LEAFORD CLEMETSON, writer, political scientist; b. St. Elizabeth, Jamaica, Oct. 3, 1924; came to U.S., 1948; s. Jeremiah and Alice Williams; m. Bertha M. Bussey, May 19, 1950; children: Valerie, Kharl, Brenda. Student, Georgetown U., 1957-60; BA in Internat. Rels., Am. U., Washington, 1961, MA in Internat. Rels., 1972. Fgn. svc. officer USIA, Washington, 1961-67; pub. affairs officer U.S. Civil Svc. Dept. Transp., Washington, 1968-79; asst. to dir. White House Conf. on Small Bus., Washington, 1979-80. Chief mission, Taegu, Korea; cultural attache, Bombay, India; pub. affairs officer Am. Embassy, Seoul, Korea. Author: Rebirth of a Nation, 1954, Journey Into Diplomacy, 1996, Boys Without Dads: When Dads Abandon Homes, 2000. City Coun. candidate Dem. Party, Washington, 1974; chmn. Disciples Men Christian Ch., Washington, 1990; chmn. UN Assn., Washington, 1980-90; bd. mem. Immigration and Refugees Svcs., Washington, N.Y.C., 1992—. With USAF, 1950-56. Decorated Bronze Star. Mem. Thursday Luncheon Group Dept. State (program officer 1980-84). Avocations: golf, public speaking, writing. Home and Office: 1037 Crittenden St NE Washington DC 20017-2718 E-mail: fort@erols.com.

WILLIAMS, LENA, sportswriter; BA cum laude in English, Howard U.; MS in Journalism, Columbia U. Assoc. editor Black Sports Mag.; from clk. Sports Dept. to sports writer N.Y. Times, N.Y.C., 1974, sports writer. Author: It's the Little Things: The Everyday Interactions That Get Under the Skin of Blacks and Whites, 2000. Named one of Outstanding Women in Mktg. and Comms., Ebony Mag., 2001; recipient Excellence award, Nat. Assn. Black Journalism, 1997, Black Achievers award, Young Men's Christian Assn. Office: New York Times 229 W 43d St New York NY 10036

WILLIAMS, LEOLA WILKERSON, social worker, writer; d. David and Albertha Jones Wilkerson; m. Lafayette H. Williams, Sr., Apr. 30, 1977; children: Byron, Lafayette Jr., Langston, Joseph. BS, Tuskegee (Ala.) U., 1971; MSW, Fla. State U., 1985. Social worker Dept. Health and Rehab. Svcs., Jacksonville, 1971—85; case worker Children's Home Soc., Jacksonville, 1985—93; owner Spl. Occasions Party Shop, Jacksonville, 1993—95; counselor Youth Crisis Ctr., Jacksonville, 1995—98; social worker Fresenius Med. Care-Dialysis Clinic, Jacksonville, 1998—2002, St. Catherine Laboure Manor, Jacksonville, 2002—. Author: How Joseph Met the President, 2001. Mem. Friends of the N.W. Br. Libr., Jacksonville, 2001—02, Open Arms Christian Assembly. Mem.: Tuskegee Alumni Club, Delta Sigma Theta. Democrat. Avocations: reading, walking, real estate investing, writing, serving the Lord. Home: 5012 Princely Ave Jacksonville FL 32208 Office Phone: 904-308-4707.

WILLIAMS, LEWIS T. (RUSTY WILLIAMS), education educator; Pres. Chiron R&D, 1994—, chief scientific officer, 1999; adj. prof. medicine U. Calif., San Francisco. E-mail: rusty_williams@cc.chiron.com.

WILLIAMS, LILLIAN SERECE, historian, social studies educator; BA, U. Buffalo, 1966, MA, 1973, PhD, 1979. Tchr. Buffalo (N.Y.) Bd. Edn., 1966—69; asst. prof. U. Buffalo, 1972—76, vis. asst. prof., 1985—87, assoc. prof., dept. chair, 2002—; asst. prof. Howard U., Washington, 1976—85; from asst. to assoc. prof. U. Albany, NY, 1987—2002. Historian NAACP, Balt., 1992—93, Girl Scouts of the U.S.A., N.Y.C., 1995—97, N.Y. State Mus., Albany, 1997—98; dir. Inst. for Rsch. on Women U. Albany, 1998—2002. Author: Strangers in the Land of Paradise, 1999; editor: (documentary) Records of the National Association of Colored Women, 1993, 1994. Recipient Nuala McGann Drescher award, United Univ. Profls., Lifetime Achievement award, Niagara County Black Achievers, Niagara Falls, N.Y., 2000; State Farm Ins. fellow, Nat. African Am. Women Leadership Inst., 2001. Mem.: Afro-Am. Hist. Assn.the Niagara Frontier, Orgn. Am. Historians, Delta Sigma Theta. Avocations: reading, art, interior decorating. Office: SUNY Buffalo African Amer Studies Dept 732 Clemens Hall Buffalo NY 14260 Office Phone: 716-645-2082.

WILLIAMS, LORI ANNE, foundation administrator, vocalist; b. Bethesda, Md., Jan. 22, 1967; d. Robert and Myrtle Yvonne Washington Williams; 1 child, Lauren Vanessa Highsmith. BA, Hampton Inst. U., 1988. Adminstrv. asst. Dimensions Unlimited Entertainment, Washington, 1989—90; sales coord. CEMA Distbn./Capitol Records, Laurel, Md., 1990—91; tchr./arts and humanities liaison DCPS/DODDS/Thelonious Monk Inst., Japan, 1991—2000; dir. Best Friends Found., Washington, 2000—. Profl. vocalist, dir., Ft. Washington, Md., 1988—. Composer: various compilations. Nat. diamond girls jazz choir dir. Best Friends Found., Washington, 1998—2003. Mem.: Internat. Assn. for Female Exec., Internat. Assn. for Jazz Educators, Delta Sigma Theta. Office: Best Friends Foundation 4455 Connecticut Ave NW Suite 310 Washington DC 20008 Personal E-mail: lorijazz22@aol.com. E-mail: lwilliams@bestfriendsfoundation.org.

WILLIAMS, LOUIS CLAIR, JR., public relations executive; b. Huntington, Ind., Nov. 7, 1940; s. Louis Clair and Marian Eileen (Bowers) W.; children—Terri Lynn, L. Bradley, Lisa C.; m. Mary Clare Moster. B.A., Eastern Mich. U., 1963. Copywriter, Rochester (N.Y.) Gas and Electric Co., 1963-65, editor RG&E News, 1965-66; employee info. specialist Gen. Ry. Signal Co., Rochester, 1966-67, supr. employment and employee rels., 1967-69; supr. pub. rels. Heublein, Inc., Hartford, Conn., 1969-70; dir. corp. communications Jewel Cos., Inc., Chgo., 1970-71; account exec. Ruder & Finn of Mid-Am., Chgo., 1971-73, v.p., 1973-76, sr. v.p., 1976-78; cons. Towers, Perrin, Forster & Crosby, Los Angeles, 1978-79; exec. v.p., gen. mgr. Harshe-Rotman & Druck, Inc., Chgo., 1979, pres. midwest region, 1979-80; v.p. Hill & Knowlton, Inc., Chgo., 1980-81, sr. v.p., 1981-83; pres. Savlin Williams Assocs., Evanston, Ill., 1983-85, L.C. Williams & Assocs., Chgo., 1985—. Recipient Clarion award Women in Communications, 1978, award of Excellence, Internat. Coun. Indsl. Editors, 1969, Bronze Oscar-of-Ind., Fin. World, 1974. Mem. Internat. Assn. Bus. Communicators (pres. 1979-80), Chgo. Assn. Bus. Communicators (pres.), Publicity Club Chgo., Pub. Rels. Soc. Am.

WILLIAMS, LOWELL CRAIG, lawyer, employee relations executive; b. Tehachapi, Calif., Dec. 3, 1947; s. Lyndon Williams and Gertrude (White) Sievert; m. Marsha Mendelssohn; children: John S., Jeffrey A. Bescheinigungeschichte, Georg August U., Germany, 1968; BA, U. Calif., Santa Barbara, 1969; JD, Columbia U., 1972. Bar: N.Y. 1973, U.S. Ct. Appeals (2nd cir.) 1974, U.S. Supreme Ct. 1974. Assoc. Sullivan & Cromwell, N.Y.C., 1972-75; sr. v.p. Elf Aquitaine, Inc., N.Y.C., 1976-95; v.p. Compagnie des Machines Bull, N.Y.C., 1995—, exec. v.p. group human resources, 1998-99; exec. dir. Exult Inc., N.Y.C., 1999—2001; sr. advisor TPI Sourcing Inc., The Woodlands, Tex., 2002—03; v.p. global human resource svcs. EquaTerra, Inc., Houston, 2003—. Past pres. Scarsdale Synagogue. Mem. Internat. Bar Assn., German Law Assn. (dir.). Office: EquaTerra Inc 2919 Mabry Ln Owens Cross Roads AL 35763 Business E-Mail: lowell.williamsl@equaterra.com.

WILLIAMS, LUCINDA, country musician; b. Lake Charles, La., 1953; d. Miller W.; m. Greg Sowders (div.). Albums include: Ramblin' On My Mind, 1979, Happy Woman Blues, 1980, Lucinda Williams, 1988, Passionate Kisses, 1989 (Grammy award Best Country Song 1994), Sweet Old World, 1992, Car Wheels on a Gravel Road, 1998 (Grammy award for best contemp. folk album, 1999), Essence, 2002 (Grammy award for best female rock vocal); contbr. songs to: Sweet Relief, 1993, Born to Choose, 1993. Office: c/o Universal Music Group 1755 Broadway New York NY 10019

WILLIAMS, LUTHER STEWARD, research scientist; b. Sawyerville, Ala., Aug. 19, 1940; s. Roosevelt and Mattie B. (Wallace) W.; m. Constance Marie Marion, Aug. 23, 1963; children: Mark Steward, Monique Marie. BA magna cum laude, Miles Coll., 1961; MS, Atlanta U., 1963; PhD, Purdue U., 1968, DSc (hon.), 1987, U. Louisville, 1992, Capitol Coll., 1996, Bowie State U., 1996, Tuskegee U., 1997, U. D.C., 1999. NSF lab. asst. Spelman Coll., 1961-62, Atlanta U., 1962-63, instr. biology, faculty rsch. grantee, 1963-64, asst. prof. biology, 1969-70, prof. biology, 1984-87, pres., 1984-87; grad. tchg. asst. Purdue U., West Lafayette, Ind., 1964-65, grad. rsch. asst., 1965-66, asst. prof. biology, 1970-73, assoc. prof., 1973-79, prof., 1979-80, NIH Career Devel. awardee, 1971-75, asst. provost, 1976-80; dean Grad. Sch., prof. biology Washington U., St. Louis, 1980-83; v.p. acad. affairs, dean Grad. Sch. U. Colo., Boulder, 1983-84; Am. Cancer Soc. postdoctoral fellow SUNY-Stony Brook, 1968-69; assoc. prof. biology MIT, 1973-74; spl. asst. to dir. Nat. Inst. Gen. Med. Scis., NIH, Bethesda, Md., 1987-88; dep. dir. Nat. Inst. Gen. Med. Scis. NIH, Bethesda, 1988-89; sr. sci. advisor to dir. NSF, Washington, 1989-90, asst. dir. for edn. and human resources, 1990-99; visiting scholar Payson Ctr. Internat. Devel./Tech., Arlington, Va., 1999-2000, edn. cons., 2000—. Educator, cons., 2000—; dir. edn., sr. advisor to dir. Mo. Bot. Garden, St. Louis, 2001—; chmn. rev. com. MARC Program, Nat. Inst. Gen. Med. Scis., NIH, 1972-76; grant reviewer NIH, 1971-73, 76, NSF, 1973, 76-80, Med. Rsch. Coun. of N.Z., 1976; mem. life scis. sreening com. recombinant DNA adv. com. HEW, 1979-81; mem. nat. adv. gen. med. sci. council NIH, 1980-85; mem. adv. com. Office Tech. Assessment, Washington, 1984-87; chmn. fellowship adv. com. NRC Ford Found., 1984-85; mem.-at-large Grad. Record Exam. Bd., 1981-85, chmn. minority grad. edn. com., 1983-85; mem. health, safety and environ. affairs. com. Nat. Labs., U. Calif., 1981-87; mem. adv. panel Office Tech. Assessment, U.S. Congress, 1985-86; mem. fed. task force on women, minorities and the handicapped in sci. and tech., 1987-91; mem. adv. panel to dir. sci. and tech. ctrs. devel. NSF, 1987-88; mem. nat. adv. com. White House Initiative on Historically Black Colls. and Univs. on Sci. and Tech., 1986-89; numerous other adv. bds. and coms. Contbr. sci. articles to profl. jours. Vice chmn. bd. advisors Atlanta Neighborhood Justice Ctr., 1984-87; bd. dirs. Met. Atlanta United Way, 1986-87, Butler St. YMCA, Atlanta, 1985-87; trustee Atlanta Zool. Assn., 1985-87, Miles Coll., 1984-87, Atlanta U., 1984-87, 90-96; mem. nominating com. Dana Found. NIH predoctoral fellow Purdue U., 1966-68, William A. Hinton Rsch. Trng. award, Am. Soc. Microbiology, 1998. Fellow Am. Acad. Microbiology; mem. Am. Soc. Microbiology, Am. Chem. Soc., Am. Soc. Biol. Chemists (mem. ednl. affairs com. 1979-82, com. on equal opportunities for minorities 1972-84). Home and Office: 15286 Brightfield Manor Drive Chesterfield MO 63017 Office Phone: 314-577-5139.

WILLIAMS, MARCUS DOYLE, judge; b. Nashville, Oct. 24, 1952; s. John Freelander and Pansy (Doyle) W.; m. Carmen Myrie, May 21, 1983; children: Aaron Doyle, Adam Myrie. BA with honors, Fisk U., 1973; JD, Cath. U. of Am., 1977. Bar: Va. 1977, D.C. 1978. Asst. commonwealth's atty. County of Fairfax, Fairfax, Va., 1978-80, asst. county atty. Fairfax, Va., 1980-87; dist. ct. judge 19th Jud. Dist., Va., 1987-90; judge 19th Jud. Cir., Va., 1990—. Lectr. bus. legal studies George Mason U., Fairfax, 1980-95; instr. pvt. investigators North Va. Community Coll., Fairfax, 1979; mem. Fairfax Criminal Justice Adv. Bd., 1980-86; faculty advisor Nat. Jud. Coll., 1991, faculty, 1992—; Am. participant lectr. for USIA, 1990; lectr. George Mason U. Law Sch., 1987. Book reviewer for ABA Jour., 1981-84; contbr. articles to legal jours. Bd. visitors Cath. U. Law Sch., 1998—. Recipient cert. of appreciation for

outstanding svc. Burke-Fairfax Jack & Jill, Cert. of Appreciation, Nat. Forum for Black Pub. Adminstrs. and Black Women United for Action, 1995; Thomas J. Watson Found. fellow, 1977, Otis Smith award Black Law Students Assn. of Cath. U. Law Sch.; Outstanding Achievement and Svc. award Black Law Students Assn., 2001. Mem. ABA (chair subcom. Victims of Crimes 1996-2000), Fairfax Bar Assn. (CLE com., vice chmn. 1986-87), Am. Bus. Law Assn., Am. Judges Assn., Phi Alpha Delta, Beta Kappa Chi, Omega Psi Phi. Methodist. Office: Cir Ct 4110 Chain Bridge Rd Fairfax VA 22030-4009

WILLIAMS, MARILYN, state legislator; Mem. Mo. Ho. of Reps. from 159th dist., 1993—. Democrat. Address: RR 1 Box 98 Dudley MO 63936-9719 Office: Mo Ho of Reps State Capitol Building Jefferson City MO 65101-1556

WILLIAMS, MARION LESTER, government official; b. Abilene, Texas, Dec. 1, 1933; s. Martin Lester and Eddie Faye (Wilson) W.; m. Johnnie Dell Ellinger, Dec. 14, 1957; children: Tammy Dawn Cole, Pamela DeAnn Ritterbush. BS, Tex. A&M U., 1956; MS, U. N.Mex., 1967; PhD, Okla. State U., 1971. Test engr. Sandia Nat. Labs., Albuquerque, 1959-61; weapons sys. engr. Naval Weapons Evaluation Facility, Albuquerque, 1961-66; ops. rsch. analyst Joint Chiefs of Staff/Joint Task Force II, Albuquerque, 1966-68; chief reliability div. Field Command DNA, Albuquerque, 1969-71; prin. scientist SHAPE Tech. Ctr., The Hague, Netherlands, 1971-74; chief tech. advisor HQ AF Test & Evaluation Ctr., Albuquerque, 1974-81; chief scientist HQ AF Operational Test & Evaluation Ctr., Albuquerque, 1981-89, tech. dir., 1989—. Vis. adv. com. Okla. State U., Stillwater, 1988—; adv. com. U. N.Mex., Albuquerque, 1985—. Editor T&E Tech. Jour., 1987—; contbr. articles to profl. jour. Sci. advisor N.Mex. Sci. & Tech. Oversigh Com., Albuquerque, 1988; bd. advisors U. N.Mex. Cancer Ctr., 1987—; bd. dirs. Contact Albuquerque, 1986-87. 1st lt. USAF 1956-59. Recipient Presdl. Rank award, 1987, 92. Fellow Mil. Ops. Rsch. Soc. (pres. 1982-83, bd. dir. 1976-81, Wanner award 1991), Internat. Test & Evaluation Ctr. (bd. dirs. 1984-86, 88-90, v.p. 1990, pres. 1992-93), Ops. Rsch. Soc. Am., Tau Beta Pi, Phi Eta Sigma, Alpha Pi Mu, Sigma Tau, Kappa Mu Epsilon. Baptist. Avocations: skiing, computers. Home: 1416 Stagecoach Ln SE Albuquerque NM 87123-4429 Office: HQ AF Operational Test Ctr Kirtland AFB Albuquerque NM 87117-0001 E-mail: mlw505@msn.com.

WILLIAMS, MARK DIDRIK, music educator, composer; b. Harlingen, Tex., Mar. 31, 1959; s. Vincent D. and Verla A. Williams. BA, Luther Coll., Decorah, IA USA, 1977—80; MA, U. of Iowa, Iowa City, IA USA, 1980—82; Mus D musical arts, U. of Ill., Urbana-Champaign, IL USA, 1984—88. Music performance instr. Lake Tahoe C.C., South Lake Tahoe, Calif., 2000—; adj. instr. of music Western Nev. C.C., Carson City, Nev., 1993—99; adj. asst. prof. of music Millikin U., Decatur, Ill., 1987—92. Composer (lyricist): (musical) Beauty; author: (website) Singing Voice, (article) Music Educators Jour.; composer: (musical) Guilty Pleasures. Recipient Who's Who Among Am. Teachers, 2002. Mem.: Nat. Assn. of Teachers of Singing, Am. Soc. of Composers, Authors and Publishers, MENSA. Independent. Christian. Avocations: musicals, reading, movies, skiing, hiking, computers. Office: Lake Tahoe Comty Coll One College Dr South Lake Tahoe CA 96150 Personal E-mail: voxdoc@yahoo.com. E-mail: williams@ltcc.edu.

WILLIAMS, MARSHA C. corporate financial executive; B in Econs., Wellesley Coll.; Masters, U. Chgo. Various positions Amoco Corp., 1989—93, treas., 1993—98, v.p., treas., 1997—98; chief adminstrv. officer Crate & Barrel, 1998—2002; exec. v.p., CFO Equity Office Properties, Chgo., 2002—. Office: Equity Office Properties 2 N Riverside Plz Chicago IL 60606

WILLIAMS, MARSHA RHEA, computer scientist, educator, researcher, consultant; b. Memphis, Aug. 4, 1948; d. James Edward and Velma Lee (Jenkins) W. Cert., Schiller Coll., West Berlin, Germany, 1968; BS in Physics, Beloit Coll., 1969; MS in Physics, U. Mich., 1971; MS in Sys. and Info. Sci., Vanderbilt U., 1976, PhD in Computer Sci., 1982. Cert. data processor. Engring. coop. student Lockheed Missiles & Space Co., Sunnyvale, Calif., 1967-68; asst. transmission engr. Ind. Bell Tel. Co., Indpls., 1971-72; sys. analyst, instr. physics Memphis State U., 1972-74; computer-assisted instrn. project programmer Fisk U., 1974-76; mem. tech. staff Hughes Rsch. Labs., Malibu, Calif., 1976-78; assoc. sys. engr. IBM, Nashville, 1978-80; rsch. and tchg. asst. Vanderbilt U., Nashville, 1980-82, spl. asst. to dean Grad. Sch., spring 1981, minority engr. advisor, 1975-76; cons. computer-assisted instrn. project Meharry Med. Coll., Nashville, summer 1982; assoc. prof. computer sci. Tenn. State U., Nashville, 1982-83, 84-90, full tenured prof., 1990—, univ. marshal, 1992-97. Assoc. prof. U. Miss., Oxford, 1983-84, faculty senator; assoc. program dir. Applications of Advanced Techs. Sci. and Engring. Edn., NSF, 1987-88, apptd. USRA Sci. and Engring. Edn. Coun., Advanced Design Program, 1992-94; cons. on minority scientists and engrs. Univ. Space Rsch. Assn., Washington, 1988; vis. scientist CSNET-Minority Instn. Networking Project Bolt, Beranek & Newman, Cambridge, Mass., 1989; mem. tech. staff Bell Comm. Rsch., Red Bank, N.J., 1990; prin. investigator NSF Computer Sci., Engring. & Math. Scholarships Project, 2002-03; presenter papers profl. meetings. Editor-in-chief newspaper Pilgrim Emanuel Bapt. Ch., 1975-76. Advisr Chi Rho Youth Fellowship, Temple Bapt. Ch., 1975-81, adv. com. Golden Outreach Sr. Citizens Fellowship, 1979-80, 86-87, 89-93, Women's Day spkr., 1979-81, Ebenezer Missionary Bapt. Ch., 1993; adviser Nat. Soc. Black Engring. Students, 1983-84; founder, coord. Tenn. State U. Assn. for Excellence in Computer Sci., Math. and Physics (AE-COMP), 1986-87, coord. Tech. Opportunities Fair, 1986, 87; dir. Tenn. State U. Minorities in Sci., Engring. and Tech. Rsch. Project-MISET, 1989—; child sponsor World Vision, 1981—; mem., newsletter staff Lake Providence Missionary Bapt. Ch. Recipient Disting. Instr. award, 1984, Disting. Svc. citation Beloit Coll. Alumni Assn., 1994; grantee Digital Equipment Corp., 1989-92; rsch. grantee Tenn. State U., 1993, 94, NSF, 2002-03. Mem. AAUP, NAACP (nat. judge ACT-SO sci. olympics 1992), Assn. Computing Machinery, Assn. Info. Tech. Profls. (formerly Data Processing Mgmt. Assn.) (edn. chmn., bd. dirs. 1986), Tenn. Acad. Sci., Am. Assn. of Univ. Profs., Phi Kappa Phi. Achievements include research in developing a formally complete model information/support system (database, network and human-computer interfacing), for minority scientists, especially African American science students, and for providing/locating technical resources for developing countries. Home: PO Box 281946 Nashville TN 37228 Office: PO Box 136 Nashville TN 37203-3401

WILLIAMS, MARTHA, consumer products company executive, entrepreneur; b. 1953; Founder, CEO, pres. StyleMaster, Chgo., 1991—. Office: StyleMaster 1330 W 43rd St Chicago IL 60609

WILLIAMS, MARTHA ETHELYN, information science educator; b. Chgo., Sept. 21, 1934; d. Harold Milton and Alice Rosemond (Fox) W. BA, Barat Coll., 1955; MA, Loyola U., 1957. With IIT Rsch. Inst., Chgo., 1957-72, mgr. info. scis., 1962-72, mgr. computer search ctr., 1968-72; adj. assoc. prof. sci. info. Ill. Inst. Tech., Chgo., 1965-73, lectr. chemistry dept., 1968-70; rsch. prof. info. sci., coordinated sci. lab. Coll. Engring. U. Ill., Urbana, also dir. info. retrieval rsch. lab., 1972—, prof. info. sci. grad. sch. of libr. info. sci., 1974—, affiliate, computer sci. dept., 1979—. Chair large data base conf. Nat. Acad. Sci./NRC, 1974, mem. ad hoc panel on info. storage and retrieval, 1977, numerical data adv. bd., 1979-82, computer sci. and tech. bd., nat. rsch. network rev. com., 1987-88, chair utility subcom., 1987-88, subcom. promoting access to sci. and tech. data for pub. interest; task force on sci. info. activities NSF, 1977; U.S. rep. review com. for project on broad system of ordering, UNESCO, Hague, Netherlands, 1974; vice-chair Gordon Rshc. Conf. on Sci. Info. Problems in Rsch., 1978, chair, 1980; mem. panel on intellectual property rights in age of electronics and info. U.S. Congress, Office of Tech. Assessment; program chmn. Nat. Online Meeting, 1980-2001; founder, pres. Info. Market Indicators, Inc., 1982-; cons. in field; invited lectr. Commn. European Communities, Industrial R&D adv. com., Brussels, 1992. Editor-in-chief: Computer-Readable Databases Directory and Data Sourcebook, 1976—89, founding editor:, 1989—; editor: Ann. Rev. Info. Sci. and Tech., 1976—2001, Online Rev., 1979—92, Online and CD-ROM Rev., 1993—2000; mem. editl. adv. bd.: Database, 1978—88, mem. editl. bd.: Info. Processing and Mgmt., 1982—89, The Reference Libr., founding editor: Online Info. Rev., 2000—; contbr. articles to profl. jours. Trustee Engirng. Info., Inc., 1974-87, bd. dirs., 1976-91, chmn. bd. dirs., 1982-91, v.p., 1978-79, pres., 1980-81; regent Nat. Libr. Medicine, 1978-82, chmn. bd. regents, 1981; mem. task force on sci. info. activities NSF, 1977-78; mem. nat. adv. com. ACCESS ERIC, 1989-91. Recipient best paper of year award H. W. Wilson Co., 1975; Travel grantee NSF, Luxembourg, 1972, Honolulu, 1973, Tokyo, 1973, Mexico City, 1975, Scotland, 1976 Fellow: AAAS (mem. nominating com. 1983, 1985), Nat. Fedn. Abstracting and Info. Svcs. (hon.), Inst. Info. Scis. (hon.); mem.: NAS (mem. joint com. with NRC on chem. info. 1971—73), Internat. Fedn. for Documentation (U.S. nat. com.), Assn. Sci. Info. Dissemination Ctrs. (v.p. 1971—73, pres. 1975—77), Assn. Computing Machinery (pub. bd. 1972—76), Am. Soc. Info. Sci. (councilor 1971—72, mem. publs. com. 1974—, pres. 1987—88, councilor 1987—89, contbg. editor bull. column 1974—78, Award of Merit 1984, Pioneer Info. Sci. award 1987, Watson Davis award 1995), Am. Chem. Soc. Home: 2134 Sandra Ln Monticello IL 61856-8036 Office: U Ill 1308 W Main St Urbana IL 61801-2307 E-mail: m-will13@uiuc.edu.

WILLIAMS, MARTHA GARRISON, lawyer; b. Greenville, S.C., July 3, 1942; d. William Theodore and Edith (Roberts) G.; m. Ray R. Williams Jr.; 1 child, Ray R. III. BA, Randolph-Macon Coll., 1964; JD, U. S.C., 1967. Bar: S.C. 1967, U.S. Dist. Ct. S.C. 1967, U.S. Ct. Appeals 1970. Atty. regulatory div. U.S. Dspt. Agr., Washington, 1967-68; atty. Liberty Corp., Greenville, S.C., 1971-72, asst. v.p., asst. sec., 1972-82, counsel, 1980-82, v.p., gen. counsel, sec., 1982—; atty. investment div. Liberty Life Ins. Co., Greenville, 1968-72, asst. sec., 1972-82, asst. v.p., 1976-79, v.p., 1979—, counsel, 1980-82, gen. counsel, sec., 1982—, also bd. dirs. Bd. dirs. ARC, Greenville, 1981-86, S.C. Dept. Health and Environ. Control, Greenville, 1985—. Mem. ABA, S.C. Bar Assn., Greenville County Bar Assn., Assn. Life Ins. Council, Am. Soc. Life Ins. Council, Am. Soc. Corp. Secs., Fedn. Ins. Counsel, Am. Corp. Counsel Assn., Am. Council Life Ins., Life Insurers Conf. Office: Liberty Corp 2000 Wade Hampton Blvd Greenville SC 29615-1037

WILLIAMS, MARY, state legislator; b. July 8, 1949; m. Al Williams. Grad., U. Wis., Stevens Point, 1974. Former tchr.; restaurant owner; mem. Wis. State Assembly, Madison, 2002—, vice chair agr. com., vice chair rural affairs com., mem. forestry com., mem. natural resources com., mem. small bus. com., mem. tourism com. Republican. Office: State Capitol Bldg Rm 18 W PO Box 8953 Madison WI 53708 Address: 542 Billings Ave Medford WI 54451

WILLIAMS, MARY ALICE BALDWIN, retired home economist, volunteer consultant; b. St. Louis, Mar. 24, 1928; d. Ulysses Grant and Irene (Jenkins) Gray; m. Earl Randolph Baldwin, June 28, 1952 (div. 1973); 1 child, Arlene Denise; m. Robert Williams Jr., Dec. 21, 1985. BS, Lincoln U., 1952; MA, Webster U., 1971; postgrad., Harris Stowe Tchrs. Coll., 1976-78, Cen. Mo. State U., 1979-80, U. Mo., 1981-82. Cert. home economist, Mo. Tchr. home econs. Cen. H.S., Hayti, Mo., 1952-53, Cleve. Pub. Schs., 1953-56; tchr. elem. sch. St. Louis Pub. Schs., 1958-67, tchr. home econs., 1968-83, curriculum supr. home econs., 1984-93, cons. home econs. and character edn., 1993; ret., 1993; vol. cons. Family & Consumer Sci. Fiber Art, 1993—. Presenter in field. Author curriculum materials in home econs. and character edn. Fund raising com. Annie Malone Children's Home, St. Louis, 1987-90; 75th anniversary com. YYWCA Phylliss Wheatley, St. Louis, 1988. Mem. Nat. Assn. Univ. Women (del. 1992, Woman of Yr. 2001, N. Ctrl. sectional lay mem. 1999-2003), Am. Home Econs. Assn. (ethics com. 1990-92, population com. 1990-91), Mo. Home Econs. Assn. (tchr. rep. 1988-90), Am. Vocat. Assn., Mo. Vocat. Assn. (legis. com.), St. Louis Home Econs. Tchrs. Assn. (founder, adviser), Lincoln Univ. Alumni Assn. (chair founders day), Delta Sigma Theta. Avocations: sewing, clothing design, music, reading, tennis, designer and quilter African Am. history and story quilts. Home: 4910 Maffitt Pl Saint Louis MO 63113-1727

WILLIAMS, MARY ELLEN COSTER, judge; b. 1953; married; 2 children. BA in Latin and Greek (summa cum laude), MA in Latin, Cath. U., 1974; JD, Duke U., 1977. Assoc. Fulbright and Jaworski, Washington, 1977—79, Schnader, Harrison, Segal and Lewis, Washington, 1979—83; asst. U.S. atty. civil divsn. Washington, 1983—87; ptnr. Janis, Schuelke and Weschler Law Firm, Washington, 1987—89; adminstrv. judge Gen. Svcs. Adminstrn. Bd. of Contract Appeals, Washington, 1989—2003; judge U.S. Ct. of Fed. Claims, Washington, 2003—. Fellow: Am. Bar Found. (life); mem.: D.C. Bar (sec.), D.C. Young Lawyers Sect. (chair), Bar Assn. of D.C. (found. pres., trustee, bd. dirs.), ABA (section rep. com. of ethics and professionalism 1998—2000, commn. on evaluation of rules of profl. conduct 1998—2000, pres. task force on govt. lawyers 2000—01, chair sect. pub. contract law 2002—, chair elect, vice chair, sec.). Office: US Ct of Fed Claims 717 Madison Pl NW Washington DC 20005

WILLIAMS, MARY PEARL, judge; b. Brownsville, Tex., Jan. 12, 1928; d. Marvin Redman and Theo Mae (Kethley) Hall; m. Jerre Stockton Williams, May 28, 1950; children: Jerre Stockton, Shelley Wiliams Austin, Stephanie Williams Laden. BA, U. Tex., 1948, JD, 1949. Bar: Tex. 1949, U.S. Supreme Ct. 1955, U.S. Dist. Ct. (we. dist.) Tex. 1987. Asst. atty. gen. State of Tex., Austin, 1949-50; relief judge Mcpl. Ct., Austin, 1964; asst. instr. dept. govt. U. Tex., Austin, 1966-67; atty. Office of Emergency Preparedness, Exec. Office of Pres., Washington, 1968-70; labor arbitrator, mem. arbitration panel Am. Arbitration Assn., 1972-73; judge County Ct. Law 2, Travis County, Tex., 1973-80, 53d Jud. Dist. Ct., Austin, 1981-2000, sr. judge, 2000—. Cons. HEW, 1966—67. Mem. adv. com. Juvenile Bd. Travis County, 1964—67; trustee United Way, 1974—78. Named Outstanding Woman, Austin Am.-Statesman, 1974, Austin Citizen, 1978, Woman of the Yr., Austin Dist. Bus. and Profl. Women, 1977; named to Austin HS Hall of Fame, 1996. Fellow: ABA, Am. Bar Found.; mem.: Inst. Jud. Adminstrn., Am. Judicature Soc., Am. Law Inst., Travis County Bar Assn., Coll. State Bar Tex., State Bar Tex., Jr. League Austin, Kappa Alpha Theta, Delta Kappa Gamma (hon.). Democrat. Methodist. Home: 3503 Mt Barker Dr Austin TX 78731-5101 Office: Travis County Courthouse PO Box 1748 Austin TX 78767-1748 E-mail: greatimpy@aol.com.

WILLIAMS, MATT (MATTHEW DERRICK WILLIAMS), former professional baseball player; b. Bishop, Calif., Nov. 28, 1965; Student, U. Nev., Las Vegas. With San Francisco Giants, 1987-96, Cleveland Indians, 1997, Ariz. Diamondbacks, 1998—2003. Player Nat. League All-Star Team, 1990, 94. Recipient Gold Glove award, 1991, 93, 94, Silver Slugger award, 1990, 93-94; named to Sporting News Nat. League All-Star team, 1990, 93-94, Coll. All-Am. team Sporting News, 1986; Nat. League RBI Leader, 1990.

WILLIAMS, MAURICE JACOUTOT, development organization executive; b. New Brunswick, Can., Nov. 13, 1920; s. Alfred Jacoutot and Yvonne (Theberge) W.; m. Betty Jane Bath, Dec. 18, 1943; children: Jon, Peter, Stephen. Student, Northwestern U., 1940-42, U. Manchester, Eng., 1945; MA, U. Chgo., 1949. Research fellow London Sch. Econs., summer 1948; Dir. U.S. student program U. Fribourg, Switzerland, 1946; prin. examiner Chgo. Civil Service Commn., 1949; economist Office Internat. Trade Policy, Dept. State, Washington, 1950-53; econ. officer Am. embassy, London, 1953-55; chief Econ. Def. Coordination, 1955-58; asst. dir. U.S. Operations Mission to Iran, ICA, 1958-60, dep. dir., 1961-63, USAID/Pakistan, 1963-65, dir., 1965-67; chief program div. Near East-South Asia, 1961; asst. adminstr. Nr. East-South Asia AID/W, 1967-70; dep. adminstr. AID, 1970-74; chmn. Devel. Assistance Com. OECD, Paris, 1974-78; exec. dir. UN World Food Council, 1978-86; sec.-gen., pres. emeritus Soc. Internat. Devel., 1986—. Presdl. coordinator Fgn. Disaster Relief, Bangladesh, Peru, Philippines, Managua, Sahel, 1971-74; chief U.S. del. U.S.-N. Vietnam Joint Econ. Commn., 1974— Recipient Nat. Civil Service award, 1971, AID Distinguished Honor award, 1974, Rockefeller Pub. Service award, 1974 Mem.: Cosmos. Address: Overseas Devel Council 1875 Connecticut Ave NW Washington DC 20009-5728 *The principles guiding me have been those of middle-America at mid-century, namely that integrity and concentrated efforts yield their own reward. Implicit are beliefs in democratic values, equity in opportunities for social and economic progress, and the need to build up institutions for their realization. The challenge of our time has been to extend these goals worldwide. They are best pursued in cooperative endeavors through the United Nations. A decent standard of food, health and personal security is possible for all people and nations. Endeavors to these ends have been personally rewarding.*

WILLIAMS, MELVIN DONALD, anthropologist, educator; b. Pitts., Feb. 3, 1933; s. Aaron and Gladys Virginia (Barnes) W.; m. Faye Wanda Strawder, June 20, 1958; children: Aaron Ellsworth, Steven Rodney, Craig Haywood. AB, U. Pitts., 1955, MA, 1969, PhD, 1973. Owner, operator Wholesale Periodical Distbn. Co., Pitts., 1955-66; instr. dept. sociology and anthropology Carlow Coll., 1969-71, asst. prof., 1971-75, chmn. dept. sociology and anthropology, 1973-75; assoc. prof. anthropology U. Pitts., 1976-79, adj. prof., 1979-82; prof. anthropology Purdue U., 1979-83, U. Md., College Park, 1983-88, U. Mich., Ann Arbor, 1988—. Olie B. O'Connor prof. Am. instns. Colgate U., 1976-77 Author: On the Street Where I Lived, Community in a Black Pentecostal Church, The Human Dilemma, The Black Middle Class, An Academic Village, Race for Theory; editor: Selected Readings in Afro-American Anthropology; contbr. articles to profl. publs. Co-chmn. project area com. Urban Redevel. Authority, Pitts., 1972—; co-dir. interdisciplinary family community project Western Psychiat. Inst. and Clinic, 1973-76; bd. dirs. Cath. Social Svc. of Allegheny County, Pa., 1973-76; coll. ombudsman, 1991-93, faculty senate, 1993-96. NSF field tng. fellow in anthropology, 1967; grantee, 1969-72; Community Action Pitts. grantee, 1969-71; Social Sci. Research Council grantee, 1974-75; Lilly Endowment grantee, 1980-83, 85-86; NDEA Title IV fellow, 1969. Fellow Am. Anthrop. Assn.; mem. African Studies Assn., AAAS, AAUP, Am. Sociol. Assn., Assn. Study Afro-Am. Life and History, Soc. for Psychol. Anthropology. Home: 520 W Washington St Ann Arbor MI 48103-4232 Office: University of Michigan Dept Anthropology 101 West Hall 550 E University Ave Ann Arbor MI 48109-1092 Office Phone: 734-764-7274. E-mail: mddoublu@umich.edu. *Personal philosophy: An abiding interest in people has stimulated me to discover more and more about humankind and has been an ever-present motivation to develop, grow and experience.*

WILLIAMS, MICHAEL ANTHONY, lawyer; b. Mandan, N.D., Sept. 14, 1932; s. Melvin Douglas and Lucille Ann (Gavin) Williams; m. Marjorie Ann Harrer, Aug. 25, 1962 (div. 1989); children: Ann Margaret, Douglas Raymond, David Michael; m. Dorothy Ruth Hand, 1989. BA, Coll. of St. Thomas, 1954; LL.B., Harvard U., 1959. Bar: Colo. 1959, N.D. 1959, U.S. Dist. Ct. Colo. 1959, U.S. Ct. Appeals (10th cir.) 1959, U.S. Supreme Ct. 1967. Assoc. Sherman & Howard and predecessor Dawson, Nagel, Sherman & Howard, Denver, 1959—65, ptnr., 1965—91; pres. Williams, Youle & Koenigs, P.C., Denver, 1991—2002; prin. Michael A. Williams LLC, Denver, 2002—. Served as 1st lt. USAF, 1955—57. Mem.: ABA, Arapahoe County Bar Assn., Denver Bar Assn., Colo. Bar Assn., Am. Law Inst., Colo. Bar Found., Am. Bd. Trial Advs., Am. Coll. Trial Lawyers. Office: Michael A Williams LLC 950 17th St Ste 1700 Denver CO 80202-2811 Office Phone: 303-785-7999. E-mail: mwilliams@wyk.com.

WILLIAMS, MICHAEL G. publishing executive; b. NY, Aug. 1956; married. With Aetna Life and Casulaty Co., Emery Air Freight Corp.; chief info. officer Seagram Asia-Pacific; v.p., info. tech., chief tech. officer spirits and wine group Seagram Co., 1992—98; v.p., chief info. officer NY Times, 1998—, NY Times Co., 2000—. Working coun. for chief info. officers Corp. Adv. Bd. Co. Office: New York Times Co 229 W 43rd St New York NY 10036-3959

WILLIAMS, MILDRED JANE, librarian; b. Charlotte, N.C., Nov. 9, 1944; d. Leonard Augustus William and Edith (Long) Frances; m. George E.J. Singleton. BA, Pfeiffer Coll., Misenheimer, N.C., 1966; MS in Libr. Sci., U. N.C., 1968. Reference libr. Pub. Libr. Charlotte and Mecklenburg County, NC, 1967—70, assoc. dir., 1974—77; head dept. documents and serials Libr. Davidson Coll., NC, 1970—73; acting asst. dir. U. N.C.-Charlotte Libr., 1977—78; pub. libr. cons. N.C. State Libr., Raleigh, 1979—80, asst. state libr., 1980—85, state libr., 1986—89; rsch. assoc. U.S. Nat. Commn. on Librs. and Info. Sci., Washington, 1990—98; dir., planning and adminstrv. svcs. U. Md. Librs., College Park, 1998—. Office Phone: 301-405-9124.

WILLIAMS, MILLER, poet, fiction writer, translator; b. Hoxie, Ark., Apr. 8, 1930; s. Ernest Burdette and Ann Jeanette (Miller) W.; m. Lucille Day, Dec. 29, 1951 (div.); m. Rebecca Jordan Hall, Apr. 11, 1969; children: Lucinda, Robert, Karyn. BS, Ark. State Coll., 1951; MS, U. Ark., 1952; postgrad., La. State U., 1951, U. Miss., 1957; HHD (hon.), Lander Coll., 1983; DHL, Hendrix Coll., 1995. Instr. in English La. State U., 1962-63, asst. prof., 1964-66; vis. prof. U. Chile, Santiago, 1963-64; assoc. prof. Loyola U., New Orleans, 1966-70; Fulbright prof. Nat. U. Mex., Mexico City, 1970; co-dir. grad. program in creative writing U. Ark., 1970-84, assoc. prof., 1971-73, prof. English and fgn. langs., dir. program in transl., 1973-87, univ. prof., 1987—2004, dir. poetry-in-the prisons programs div. continuing edn., 1974-79, chmn. program in comparative lit., 1978-80; ret., 2004. Fellow Am. Acad. in Rome, 1976—, mem. adv. coun. Sch. Classical Studies, 1985-91; first U.S. del. Pan Am. Conf. Univ. Artists and Writers, Concepcion, Chile, 1964; invited del. Internat. Assembly Univ. Press Dirs., Guadalajara, Mex., 1991; mem. poetry staff Bread Loaf Writers Conf., 1967-72; founder, exec. dir. Ark. Poetry Cir., 1975; founding dir. U. Ark. Press, 1980-97; participant Assn. Am. Univ. Presses Soviet Mission, 1989. Author: (poems) A Circle of Stone, 1964, Recital, 1965, So Long At the Fair, 1968, The Only World There Is, 1971; (criticism) The Achievement of John Ciardi, 1968, The Poetry of John Crowe Ransom, 1971; (with John Ciardi) (criticism) How Does a Poem Mean?, 1974; (poems) Halfway From Hoxie: New & Selected Poems, 1973, Why God Permits Evil, 1977, Distractions, 1981, The Boys on Their Bony Mules, 1983; translator: (poems) Poems & Antipoems (Nicanor Parra), 1967, Emergency Poems (Nicanor Parra), 1972, Sonnets of Giuseppe Belli, 1981; editor: (poems) 19 Poetas de Hoy en Los Estados Unidos, 1966, (with John William Corrington) Southern Writing in the Sixties: Poetry, 1967, Southern Writing in the Sixties: Fiction, 1966, Chile: An Anthology of New Writing, 1968, Contemporary Poetry in America, 1972, (with James A. McPherson) Railroad: Trains and Train People in American Culture, 1976, A Roman Collection: An Anthology of Writing about Rome and Italy, 1980, Ozark, Ozark: A Hillside Reader, 1981, (criticism) Patterns of Poetry, 1986, (poetry) Imperfect Love, 1986, Living on the Surface: New and Selected Poems, 1989, Adjusting to the Light, 1992, Points of Departure, 1995, The Ways We Touch, 1997, Some Jazz A While: The Collected Poems, 1999, The Lives of Kevin Fletcher: Stories Mostly Short, 2002; poetry editor La. State U. Press, 1966-68; contbr. articles to profl. publs. Named Bread Loaf fellow in poetry, 1963; recipient Henry Bellaman Poetry award, 1957, award in poetry, Arts Fund, 1973, Prix de Rome, Am. Acad. Arts and Letters, 1976, Nat. Poets prize, 1990, Charity Randall citation, Internat. Poetry Forum, 1993, John William Corrington award for excellence in lit., Centenary Coll., Shreveport, La., 1994, Acad. Lit. award, AAAL, 1995, Presdl. Inaugural Poet, 1997. Mem. MLA, PEN, AAUP, South Ctrl. MLA, Am. Lit. Translators Assn. (v.p. 1978-79, pres. 1979-81), Authors' Guild, Soc. Benemerito dell'Assn. Centro Romanesco Trilussa (Rome). Home: 1111 Valley View Dr Fayetteville AR 72701-1603 E-mail: mwms1000@aol.com.

WILLIAMS, MILTON LAWRENCE, judge, educator; b. Nov. 14, 1932; s. Richard and Helen (Riley) W.; m. Rose King, Oct. 22, 1960; children: Milton Lawrence, Darrie T. BS, NYU, 1960; LLB, N.Y. Law Sch., 1963. Bar: N.Y. 1965, U.S. Dist. Ct. (so. and ea. dists.) N.Y. 1967, U.S. Supreme Ct. 1968, U.S. Customs Ct. 1971. Regional counsel SBA, N.Y.C., 1966-68; assoc. gen. counsel Knapp Commn., N.Y.C., 1970-71; exex. dir. Mckay Commn., N.Y.C., 1972; judge N.Y.C. Criminal Ct., 1977-84; acting justice N.Y. State Supreme Ct., 1978-84; adminstrv. judge criminal term N.Y. State Supreme Ct. 1st Jud. Dist., 1983-85, justice, 1985—. Dep. chief adminstrv. judge N.Y.C. Cts., 1985-93; assoc. justice appellate divsn. 1st Dept., 1994-2002, 2003—, presiding justice, 2002. Mem. N.Y. State Commn. on Sentencing Guidelines, N.Y.C., 1983-86; bd. trustees St. Patrick's Cathedral, Inner City Scholarship Fund, St. John's U. With USN, 1951-55. Mem. Assn. of Bar of City of N.Y., Sigma Pi Phi, Zeta Boule, Knight of Malta. Roman Catholic. Office: Assoc Justice Appellate Divsn First Dept 27 Madison Ave New York NY 10010-2201

WILLIAMS, MONTEL, television talk show host; Host The Montel Williams Show. Actor(TV films): Perry Mason: The Case of the Telltale Talk Show Host, 1993, Educating Matt Waters, 1996, (TV series): A Different World, The New Adventures of Robin Hood, JAG; co-author: Bodychange, 2001; author: A Dozen Ways to Sunday, 2001, Mountain Get Out of My Way. Office: 433 W 53rd St New York NY 10019-5603

WILLIAMS, MORGAN LLOYD, retired investment banker; b. N.Y.C., Mar. 30, 1935; s. John Lloyd and Adelaide Veronica (Patchell) W.; m. Margaret Patricia Rooney, May 13, 1961; children: Morgan Lloyd Jr., John Graham, Christine Joyce. BS in Econs., Wharton Sch., U. Pa., 1957; MBA, Columbia U., 1961. V.p., stockholder Kidder, Peabody & Co., N.Y.C., 1970-90, mng. dir., 1985-87. Trustee Inc. Village of Plandome, N.Y., 1982-86, mayor, 1986-87. Lt. USN, 1957-59. Mem. Nassau Country Club (Glen Cove, N.Y.). Republican. Roman Catholic. Home: 79 Long Ridge Rd Plandome NY 11030-1541

WILLIAMS, NATALIE, professional basketball player, restaurant executive; b. Utah, Nov. 30, 1970; d. Nate Williams; 1 adopted child, Sydney 1 child, Turasi. Profl. basketball player Portland Power ABL, 1997—99, Long Beach StringRays, 1998, Utah Starzz, 2000—; mem. U.S. Women's gold-medal winning basketball team, Sydney, Australia, 2000; owner Natalie's, Salt Lake City, 2002—. Named Female Athlete of Yr., USA Basketball, 1999, Winter Championship Team, 2002, Utah's Female Athlete of Century, 2nd Greatest Athlete Utah, Sports Illustrated . Office: 301 W South Temple Salt Lake City UT 84101

WILLIAMS, NEIL, JR., lawyer; b. Charlotte, N.C., Mar. 22, 1936; s. Lyman Neil and Thelma (Peterson) W.; m. Sue Sigmon, Aug. 23, 1958; children: Fred R., Susan S. AB, Duke U., 1958, JD, 1961. Bar: Ga. 1962, U.S. Dist. Ct. (no. dist.) Ga. 1977, U.S. Ct. Appeals (11th cir.) 1977. Assoc. Alston & Bird (and predecessor firm), Atlanta, 1961—65, ptnr., 1966—99, mng. ptnr., 1984-96; gen. counsel, global ptnr. Amvescap PLC, Atlanta, 1999—2002; ret., 2002. Bd. dirs. NDC Health Corp., Atlanta, Printpack, Inc., Atlanta, Acuity Brands, Inc., Atlanta. Chmn. bd. trustees Duke U., 1983—88, trustee, 1980—93; chmn. bd. trustees Vasser Woolley Found., Atlanta, 1975—, Leadership Atlanta, 1976—80; trustee Brevard Music Ctr., 1977—86, 1991—2001, Presbyn. Ch. USA Found., Jeffersonville, Ind., 1983—90, Research Triangle Inst., 1983—88, The Duke Endowment, Charlotte, NC, 1997—; bd. dirs. Atlanta Symphony Orch., 1970—76, 1984—93, 1995—98, pres., 1988—90; bd. dirs. Woodruff Arts Ctr., 1987—98, 1999—, chmn., 2001—; bd. counselors The Carter Ctr., Atlanta, 1987—96, Ctrl. Atlanta Progress, 1984—96; bd. dirs. Am. Symphony Orch. League, Washington, 1990—2000, chmn., 1995—99. Recipient Disting. Alumni award Duke U., 1991, Rhyne award, 1996. Mem. ABA, Am. Bar Found., State Bar Ga., Am. Law Inst., Atlanta C. of C. (bd. dirs. 1992-97, vice chmn. 1994-97), Piedmont Driving Club, Commerce Club (Atlanta), University Club (N.Y.C.), Phi Beta Kappa, Omicron Delta Kappa. Home: 3 Nacoochee Pl NW Atlanta GA 30305-4164 Office: Amvescap PLC 1315 Peachtree St NE Atlanta GA 30309-3503 Office Phone: 404-479-2889. Business E-Mail: neil_williams@amvescap.com.

WILLIAMS, NELLIE JAMES BATT, secondary education educator; b. Nashville; d. Ivan C. and Lottie B. (Phillips) James; A.B., Stowe Coll., 1942; MS, U. Ill., 1945; postgrad. Ill. Inst. Tech., 1959, 64, Oberlin Coll., 1965, St. Louis U., 1962, 63, 67, 68, Rockhurst Coll., 1972, Webster Coll., 1984, 85, U. Mass, 1990; m. Napoleon Williams, July 21, 1973 (dec. 1989); 1 child by previous marriage, Charles W. Batt, Jr. Tchr. Sumner High Sch., St. Louis, 1949-54, Handly High Sch., 1954-63; tchr., head mathematics dept. Northwest High Sch., St. Louis, 1963-76; instr., dept. head, Acad. Math. and Sci., St. Louis, 1976-92; instr., head dept. Harris Teacher Coll., Forest Park C.C. Active NAACP, YWCA. NSF grantee, 1959, 62-65, 67, 72. Mem. Math. Club Greater St. Louis, Top Ladies of Distinction, Math. Assn. Am., Assn. Women in Math., Delta Sigma Theta Sorority (edn. com.). Methodist. Home: 7584 Amherst Ave Saint Louis MO 63130-2803

WILLIAMS, NEVILLE, international solar energy corporation executive; b. Muncie, Ind., Mar. 28, 1943; s. Donald Charles and Rose Eileen (Boughton) W. Student, U. Colo., 1964-66, U. Neuchatel, Switzerland, 1967. Freelance corr., Vietnam, 1968-69; freelance journalist, 1970-71, London, 1971-73; writer, prodr. Sta. WNBC-TV News, N.Y.C., 1973-74; freelance writer Telluride, Colo., 1975-79; media liaison Office of Solar Energy U.S. Dept. Energy, Washington, 1979-80; dir. of mktg. Telluride Ski Resort, Inc., 1981-83; owner, operator Hist. Sheridan Opera Ho., Telluride, 1983-85; nat. media dir. Greenpeace U.S.A., Washington, 1987-89; chmn. exec. dir., founder Solar Electric Light Fund, Washington, 1990—97. Bd. dirs., founder Solar Electric Light Co.; advisor Greenwmpowerment, Engrs. Without Borders, Sustainable Resources, Inc.; chmn. SELCO-India. Author: The New Exiles, 1971, (monograph) Great Telluride Strike, 1977; contbr. articles to N.Y. Times mag., Penthouse, Outside, New Times, The Nation, The New Republic, Nature, Solar Today; others. Apptd. mem. Adv. Com. for Commerce and Devel., State of Colo., 1980-85; apptd. mem. Gov.'s Motion Picture & TV Commn., 1981-85. Recipient Corp. Excellence award, U.S. Dept. of State, 2001. Fellow Internat. Solar Energy Soc. Office: Solar Electric Light Co 50 California St Ste 1500 San Francisco CA 94111 Office Phone: 301-330-8758.

WILLIAMS, NIAMA LESLIE JOANN, writer, educator; b. Los Angeles, Calif., Mar. 25, 1962; d. Lewis Oscar and Lessie Beatrice W., Marian Claudette W. (Stepmother). B in Comparative Lit., Occidental Coll., L.A., 1985; Masters in Profl. Writing, U. So. Calif., L.A., 1991; Masters in African Am. Studies, postgrad., Temple U., Phila., 1994—. Tchg. asst. African-Am. studies Temple U., Philadelphia, Pa., 1993—94; Frederick Douglass tchg. fellow West Chester U., West Chester, Pa., 1998—98. Adj. prof. English Camden County Coll., 1995—96, C.C. of Phila., 1995—97, LaSalle Univ., Phila., 1997; hourly instr. West L.A. Coll., Culver City, Calif., 2000—03, L.A. Trade-Tech. Coll., 2000—02; part-time instr. Loyola Marymount U., L.A., 2000—01. Author: poems (Hon. Mention, Rhyming Poem Category, Writers Digest Competition, 2000), short stories; contbr. articles. Career day presenter, writing and libraries Bret Harte Prep. Mid. Sch., L.A., 1992, 2002; career day guest poet Westwood Elem. Sch., L.A., 2002. Mem.: E-drum, Conpo, Internat. Black Writers and Artists (L.A. chpt.). Democrat.

WILLIAMS, NOEL BROWN, information technology executive; CIO Am. Svc. Group, Tenn.; with Hosp. Corp. of Am.; sr. v.p., CIO HCA Inc., 1997—. Office: HCA Inc 1 Park Pl Nashville TN 37203

WILLIAMS, OLIVER FRANKLIN, priest, educator; b. West Orange, N.J., Dec. 4, 1939; s. Justin James Williams and Ruth Amelda Flammer. BS in Chem. Engring., U. Notre Dame, 1961, MTh, 1969; PhD, Vanderbilt U., 1974. Prof. U. Notre Dame, Ind., 1973—, dir. Master of Divinity program, 1974—77, assoc. provost, 1987—94, dir. Ctr. for Ethics and Religious Values in Bus., 1994—. Chmn. bd. leadership devel. program (USSALEP), U.S. - South Africa, Washington, 1995—; mem. adv. coun. U.S. Cos. in South Africa (Sullivan Principles), N.Y.C., 1987—94; bd. trustees St. Augustine's U., Johannesburg, 1996—; mem. bd. U.N. Global Compact Learning Forum Academic Network, 2002—; vis. prof. U. Cape Town, Stellenbosch U., 2003—. Co-author: (Book) Economic Imperatives and Ethical Values, 2001; author: The Apartheid Crisis, 1986; Editor, contbr.: book Global Codes of Conduct: An Idea Whose Time Has Come; Editor, contbr. (book) Business, Religion and Spirituality: A New Synthesis, 2003. Bd. dirs. Edn. Africa, Johannesburg, 1993, Catholic Charities, Diocese of Fort Wayne, South Bend, 1986—92, King's Coll., Pa., 2004—. Named Recommended by Coun. for Internat. Exch. of Scholars for a Fulbright in South Africa, 2002—03; recipient Charles C. Slater Meml. award, Jour. Macromarketing, 1992. Mem.: Assn. for Practical and Profl. Ethics, Soc. for Bus. Ethics, Acad. Mgmt. (social issues divsn.) (chairperson 1990—91). Roman Catholic. Avocations: hiking, travel, writing. Home: 400 Siegfried Hall Notre Dame IN 46556 Office: U of Notre Dame 255 Mendoza Coll Bus Notre Dame IN 46556 Office Phone: 574-631-5762. Business E-Mail: williams.80@nd.edu.

WILLIAMS, PAT, former congressman; b. Helena, Mont., Oct. 30, 1937; m. Carol Griffith, 1965; children: Griff, Erin, Whitney. Student, U. Mont., 1956-57, William Jewell U.; BA, U. Denver, 1961; postgrad., Western Mont. Coll.; LLD (hon.), Carroll Coll., Montana Coll. of Mineral Sci. and Tech. Mem. Mont. Ho. of Reps., 1967, 69; exec. dir. Hubert Humphrey Presdl. campaign, Mont., 1968; exec. asst. to U.S. Rep. John Melcher, 1969-71; mem. Gov.'s Employment and Tng. Council, 1972-78, Mont. Legis. Reapportionment Commn., 1973; co-chmn. Jimmy Carter Presdl. campaign, Mont., 1976; mem. 96th-102nd Congresses from 1st Mont. dist., 1979-96; sr. fellow W. U. Mont., Missoula, 1996—. Ranking mem. postsecondary edn. subcom. Coordinator Mont. Family Edn. Program, 1971-78. Served with U.S. Army, 1960-61; Served with Army N.G., 1962-69. Mem. Mont. Fedn. Tchrs. Lodges: Elks. Democrat. Home: 3533 Lincoln Hills Pt Missoula MT 59802-3381 Office: U Montana O Connor Ctr Rocky Mtn W Milw Sta 2nd Fl Missoula MT 59812-0001

WILLIAMS, PATRICIA ANNE, philosopher, writer; b. Alexanderia, Va., May 26, 1944; d. Samuel Leonard and Kay Cloaninger Williams. BA, Coll.of William and Mary, Williamsburg, Va., 1966; MA in English, U. Va., 1967, MA Philosophy, 1985; PhD, U. of Guelph, Ont., Can., 1989. Lectr. La Trobe U., Melbourne, Australia, 1968—71; asst. prof. Virginia State U., Petersburg, 1990—95. Del. Citizen Amb. People to People Program, China, 1993. Author: (book) Doing without Adam and Eve: Sociobiology and Original Sin, 2001 (Outstanding Acad. Title award Choice Mag., 2002), Where Christianity Went Wrong, When, and What You Can Do About It, 2001; editor: Evolution and Human Values, 1995; contbr. jours., encys. including Zygon: Jour. of Religion and Sci., Biology and Philosophy, Quar. Rev. of Biology, Ency. Ethics, Friends Jour. Mem. ACLU, 1973—; charter mem. U.S. Holocaust Meml. Mus., Washington, 1993—; mem. So. Poverty Law Ctr. Wall of Toleration, Montgomery. Fellow NEH fellow, 1989. Mem.: Inst. on Religion in an Age of Sci., Internat. Soc. for History, Philosophy, and Social Studies of Biology (program chmn. 1992—93), Philosophy of Sci. Assn., Am. Philos. Assn. Mem. Soc. Of Friends. Avocations: travel, hiking. Home: PO Box 69 Covesville VA 22931 Personal E-mail: theologyauthor@aol.com.

WILLIAMS, PATRICIA C. federal judge; Apptd. bankruptcy judge ea. dist. U.S. Dist. Ct. Wash., 1997. Office: 904 W Riverside Ave Ste 304 Spokane WA 99201-1011 Fax: 509-454-5636.

WILLIAMS, PAUL, retired federal agency administrator; b. Jacksonville, Ill., Aug. 6, 1929; s. Russell and Bernice (Wheeler) W.; m. Ora B. Mosby; 1 child, Reva Williams. BA, Ill. Coll., 1956, LHD, 1980. Dir. fin. City of Chgo., 1956-63; assoc. dir. fin. United Planning Orgn., Washington, 1964-65; internat. adminstrv. officer U.S. Dept. State, Washington, 1965-68; dir. office mgmt. U.S. HUD, Washington, 1968-93, gen. dep. dept. fair housing and equal opportunity, 1993-94, dep. ops. and mgmt., 1994-97, ret., 1997. Cons. S.E. Econ. Devel. Corp., Nat. Exec. Svc. Corp., 1998; Buzan learning instr. for mind mapping, 2000-2002. Author: Questionnaire on Execution of Urban Renewal Programs, 1959. Pres. Bel Pre Civic Assn., Wheaton, Md., 1978, bd. dirs., 1971, 79; pres. Bel Pre PTA, Wheaton, 1973; bd. dirs. Rockville C. of C., African Am. C. of C.; pres. Rossmoor Kiwanis Club, 2002. Sgt. U.S. Army, 1948-52. Recipient letter of recognition for 36 yrs. fed. svc. U.S. Pres., letter of recognition for 36 yrs. govt. svc. Senators of Md., citation for 36 yrs. dedicated govt. svc. Gov. of Md., cert. of recognition Nat. Assn. Black and Minority C. of C., 1987. Baptist. Avocations: reading, jogging, golf, tai chi. Home: Unit 306 2900 N LeisureWorld Blvd Silver Spring MD 20906-2321 E-mail: e-owilli7738@aol.com.

WILLIAMS, PAUL C(HESTER), consultant; b. Ironton, Ohio, Jan. 14, 1926; s. Paul Morton and Elsie Doreta (Venz) W.; m. Jeanne Ellen Potter, Jan. 22, 1955; children: Amber, Mark, Ross. BS in Marine Engring., U.S. Mcht. Marine Acad., Kings Point, N.Y., 1947; BS in Mech. Engring., Ohio State U., 1951; postgrad., Northeastern U., Boston, 1966. Test engr. Babcock and Wilcox Co., Alliance, Ohio, 1951—56, asst. to engring. mgr. Barberton, Ohio, 1957, engring. sect. mgr., 1957—59, gen. prodn. control mgr., 1959—61, purchasing agt., 1962—69; pres. Clifford Industries, Wadsworth, Ohio, 1969—71; gen. mgr., v.p. Stock Equipment Co., Chagrin Falls, Ohio, 1971—86; owner Paul Williams & Assocs., Medina, Ohio, 1986—. Mem., pres. Drug Abuse Commn., Medina County, 1992-98. Lt. USN, 1944-47. Mem. ASME, Am. Nuclear Soc. (local sect. pres. 1962). Achievements include invention of sintering test, superheater slag test, 1954, container filling radioactive waste, 1981. Home and Office: 3364 E Smith Rd Medina OH 44256-8785 Office Phone: 330-723-0915. E-mail: p.williams.pwa@zoominternet.net.

WILLIAMS, PAUL HAMILTON, composer, singer; b. Omaha, Sept. 19, 1940; s. Paul Hamilton and Bertha Mae (Burnside) W.; m. Hilda Keenan Wynn, Apr. 16, 1993. Grad. high sch. Assoc. A & M Records, 1970—; pres. Hobbitron Enterprises, 1973—. Songwriter: (with Roger Nichols) Out in the Country, 1969, Talk it Over in the Morning, 1970, We've Only Just Begun, 1970, (with Craig Doerge) Cried Like A Baby, 1970, (with Jack S. Conrad) Family of Man, 1971, Rainy Days and Mondays, 1971, An Old Fashioned Love Song, 1972, Family of Man, 1972, Let Me Be the One, 1972, (with John Williams) You're So Nice to Be Around, 1973 (Acad. award nomination best song), The Hell of It, 1974, (with Barbara Streisand) Evergreen, 1976 (Acad. award best song, 1976, Golden Globe award 1977, Grammy award 1977), (with Michael Colombier) Wings, 1977, (with Charles Fox) My Fair Share, 1977, (with Kenny Ascher) The Rainbow Connection, 1979; film appearances include The Loved One, 1964, The Chase, 1966, Planet of the Apes, 1967, Watermelon Man, 1970, The Phantom of the Paradise, 1974 (also score 1974, Acad. award nomination best score 1974), Smokey and the Bandit, 1977, The Cheap Detective, 1978, The Muppet Movie, 1979, Stone Cold Dead, 1980, Smokey and the Bandit II, 1980, Smokey and the Bandit III, 1983, The Chill Factor, 1990, The Doors, 1991, A Million to Juan, 1994, Headless Body in Topless Bar, 1995; wrote songs for: The Getaway, 1972, (with John Williams) The Man Who Loved Cat Dancing, 1972, (with Williams) Cinderella Liberty, 1973, (with John Barry) The Day of The Locust, 1975; wrote scores for: (with Ascher) A Star is Born, 1976 (Golden Globe award best score 1976), Bugsy Malone, 1976, One on One, 1977, The End, 1978, (with Ascher) The Muppet Movie, 1979, Agatha, 1979, (with Jerry Goldsmith) The Secret of Nihm, 1982, Ishtar, 1987, The Muppet Christmas Carol, 1992; TV scores include (series) The McLean Stevenson Show, 1976-77, (with Charles Fox) The Love Boat, 1977-86, Sugar Time!, 1977-78, It Takes Two, 1982-83, (movies) No Place to Run, 1972, Emmet Otter's Jug Band Christmas, 1980; numerous TV appearances including 4 NBC Midnight spls; co-host on: numerous TV appearances including Mike Douglas show; actor, voice (TV series) Batman: Gotham Knights, 1997; other TV appearances including, Merv Griffin, Jonathan Winters, others; albums include Simeday Man: Just An Old-Fashioned Love Song, 1971, Life Goes On, 1972, A Little Bit of Love, 1974, Here Comes Inspiration, 1974, Ordinary Fools, 1975, Classics, 1977, A Little on the Windy Side, 1979, Crazy For Loving You, 1981. Co-recipient Best Songwriter Grammy award, 1977. Mem. ASCAP, Nat. Acad. Rec. Arts and Scis. (trustee) Office: 11601 Wilshire Blvd # 2350 Los Angeles CA 90025 also: Tugboat Prodns 4508 Noeline Ave Encino CA 91436-3336 also: Robert Light Agy 6404 Wilshire Blvd Ste 900 Los Angeles CA 90048-5511

WILLIAMS, PAUL STRATTON, lawyer; b. San Francisco, Calif., Oct. 9, 1959; s. Henry Stratton and Frances (Spurlock) W.; m. Laura Dawn Coleman, Sept. 15, 1984; children: Scott Coleman, Ryan Stratton. AB, Harvard Coll., 1981; JD, Yale U., 1984. Bar: Calif. 1984, Ohio 1987. Assoc. Gibson, Dunn & Crutcher, L.A., 1984-87, Vorys, Sater, Seymour & Pease, Columbus, Ohio, 1987-90; gen. counsel Info. Dimensions, Inc., Dublin, Ohio, 1990-95; v.p., asst. gen. counsel Cardinal Health, Inc., 1995—99, sr. v.p., dep. gen. counsel, 2000—01, exec. v.p., chief legal off. and sec., 2001—. Mem. ABA, Ohio Bar Assn., Columbus Bar Assn., Harvard Club Central Ohio, Yale Club Central Ohio. Democrat. Avocations: running, tennis. Home: 204 Springbrook Dr Gahanna OH 43230-6238 Office: Cardinal Health Inc 7000 Cardinal Pl Dublin OH 43017-1092

WILLIAMS, PEARL See GOOD, EDITH

WILLIAMS, PEGGY RYAN, academic administrator; b. Montreal, Que., Can., May 27, 1947; d. Fred Smith and Carol (Kennedy) Ryan; m. David A. Williams, May 30, 1970. BA psychology, U. Toronto, St. Michael's Coll., Can., 1968; MEd, U. Vt., 1976; EdD, Harvard U., 1983. Caseworker, children's svcs. Monroe County Dept. Social Svcs., Rochester, NY, 1968-72; med. social worker Med. Ctr. Hosp. of Vt., Burlington, 1972; coord. instrn, academic advisor CC of Vt., Lamoille County, 1973—75, project dir. Northwestern Vt., 1975—76, regional dir. Montpelier, 1976-82; part-time instr. C.C. Vt., 1978—85; asst. to the pres. Johnson (Vt.) State Coll., summer 1981; tchg. fellow Harvard U., 1981; dir. ednl. and pers. svcs., office of chancellor Vt. State Colleges, Waterbury, 1982-85; assoc. prof. Trinity Coll., Burlington, 1985—89, chair, dept. bus & economics, 1985-88, assoc. acad. dean, 1988-89; pres. Lyndon State Coll., Lyndonville, Vt., 1989-97, Ithaca (N.Y.) Coll., 1997—. Adj. faculty Johnson State Coll., 1984—86; mem. policy adv. group for outcomes and assessment and instnl. effectiveness N.Y. State Edn. Dept., 1998—; external advisor SUNY Adv. Coun. on Tchr. Edn., 2000—. Bd. mem. Tompkins Trust Co., 1999—; active The Ithaca Downtown Partnership Cmty. Adv. Bd.; com. mem. Cornell U. Johnson Mus. Art Cmty. Adv. Coun.; bd. mem. Sacred Heart Sch. Montreal, bd. chair, 1998—2001; mem. adv. bd. Tompkins County Soc. for the Prevention Cruelty to Animals, 1999—; mem. adv. coun. Finger Lakes Land Trust, 2000—. Recipient Jackie M. Gibbons Leadership award, Am. Coun. Edn./Nat. Identification Program, 1984, Margaret R. Williams Emerging Profl. award. Mem. Am. Assn. Higher Edn., 1973-, Am. Coun. on Edn., 1981- (bd. dirs., 2000-), Nat. Assn. Women in Edn., 1985-, Office: Ithaca Coll Job Hall Ithaca NY 14850

WILLIAMS, PENNY, state legislator; b. N.Y.C., May 6, 1937; d. Peter and Polly Sheffield Potter Baldwin; children: Joseph Hill Jr., Peter Baldwin, James Chestnut. Student, Sarah Lawrence Coll., U. Tulsa. Mem. Okla. Ho. of Reps., Okla. City, 1981-89, Okla. Senate from 33rd dist., Okla. City, 1989—. Trustee St. Gregory's Coll.; mem. Tulsa Com. on Fgn. Rels. Mem. LWV, Tulsa C. of C. Democrat. Episcopalian. Home: 1366 E 25th St Tulsa OK 74114-2702

WILLIAMS, PETER MACLELLAN, nuclear engineer; b. N.Y.C., Aug. 30, 1931; s. Gilbert Harris and Evelyn (Buss) W.; m. Lois Crane, Oct. 6, 1956; children: Jane, Gilbert, Katherine, Anne, Louise, Robert. BChemE, Cornell U., 1954; MS in Nuclear Engring., MIT, 1957; PhD in Nuclear Engring., U. Md., 1971. Engr. DuPont Savannah River, Aiken, S.C., 1954-55; task engr. AGN, San Ramon, Calif., 1957-60; project mgr. Am. Machine & Fdry., Greenwich, Conn., 1960-62; research staff Princeton U., N.J., 1962-67; sr. project mgr., specialist in high temperature gas cooled reactors U.S. Nuclear Regulatory Commn., Washington, 1967-91; dir. div. high temperature gas cooled reactors U.S. Dept. of Energy, Washington, 1991-94; cons. Internat. Atomic Energy Agy., Vienna, 1994—; cons. nuclear engr., 1995—. Mem. Chernobyl Tracking Team, 1986; U.S. del. to gas-cooled reactors working group, Internat. Atomic Energy Agy., 1991; steering com. mem. U.S.-Japan Implementing Agreement on gas-cooled reactors, 1991. Contbr. articles to profl. jours.; author various reports. Scoutmaster Boy Scouts Am., Potomac, Md., 1972, cubmaster, 1983-86; pres. PTA Winston Churchill High Sch., Potomac, 1981. Assoc. fellow AIAA; mem. Am. Nuclear Soc., Sigma Xi. Democrat. Unitarian Universalist. Achievements include patent for liquid core nuclear rocket; patent pending for advanced helium turbine reactor. Home and Office: 9418 Thrush Ln Potomac MD 20854-3991 Personal E-mail: peterwill@starpower.net.

WILLIAMS, PHARRELL, music producer, arranger, vocalist; b. Virginia Beach, Va., Apr. 5, 1974; Music prodr., performer (with Chad Hugo) The Neptunes; prodr., performer, group mem. N.E.R.D. Prodr. for artists including Jay-Z, LL Cool J, Britney Spears, Kelis, No Doubt, Bow Wow, Toni Braxton, Snoop Dogg, Busta Rhymes, N'Sync, Mystikal, Ol' Dirty Bastard, Usher, Nelly, and many others, singer, prodr., with the Neptunes (albums) Neptunes Present...Clones, 2003; singer: (albums) (with N.E.R.D.) In Search of..., 2002, Fly or Die, 2004, (songs) Lapdance, 2001, Rock Star, 2002, Live in Paradiso, 2003, She Wants to Move, 2004, (with Jay-Z) Frontin', 2003; background vocals with Justin Timberlake (songs) Rock Your Body, 2002, background vocals with Jay-Z Change Clothes, 2003. Recipient Songwriter of Yr., BMI, 2001, 2002, Prodr. of Yr., Source Awards, 2002, 2003, R&B and Hip Hop Best Prodr. award, Billboard, 2003, Urban Prodr. of Yr., BMI, 2003, Prodr. of Yr. (Neo-Classical), Grammys, 2003. Achievements include selling first song with Chad Hugo, "Rump Shaker," to Wreckx N Effect while still in high school in 1992; signing with Chad Hugo Star Trak Entertainment label to Arista Records in 2002. Office: Star Trak/Rocksoul PO Box 5017 New York NY 10185-5017 Address: Arista Records 888 Seventh Ave New York NY 10106*

WILLIAMS, PHILIP COPELAIN, gynecologist, obstetrician; b. Vicksburg, Miss., Dec. 9, 1917; s. John Oliver and Eva (Copelain) W.; BS magna cum laude, Morehouse Coll., 1937; M.D., U. Ill., 1941; m. Constance Shielda Rhetta, May 29, 1943; children— Philip, Susan Carol, Paul Rhetta. Intern, Cook County Hosp., Chgo., 1942-43, resident in ob-gyn, 1946-48; resident in gynecology U. Ill., 1948-49; practice medicine specializing in ob-gyn, Chgo., 1949—; mem. staff St. Joseph Hosp., Ill. Masonic Hosp., Cook County Hosp., McGaw Hosp.; clin. prof. Med. Sch. Northwestern U., Chgo. Bd. dirs. Am. Cancer Soc. Chgo. unit and Ill. div. Served with U.S. Army, 1943-45. Recipient Civic award Loyola U., 1970; Edwin S. Hamilton Interstate Teaching award, 1984; diplomate Am. Bd. Ob-Gyn, Fellow ACS, Internat. Coll. Surgeons; mem. AMA, Chgo., Ill. med. socs., AMA, Chgo. Gynecol. Soc. (treas. 1975-78, pres. 1980-81), Am. Fertility Soc., Inst. Medicine, N.Y. Acad. Scis., AAAS. Presbyn. Clubs: Barclay, Carlton, Plaza. Contbr. articles to profl. jours. E-mail: pwill2oo@aol.com. Home: 1040 N Lake Shore Dr Chicago IL 60611-1165 E-mail: PWill200@aol.com.

WILLIAMS, PHILLIP WAYNE, former state official and army officer, securities and diversified company executive, consultant; b. Birmingham, Ala., Nov. 1, 1939; s. Louie Alfred and A. Banks (Osborn) Williams; m. Ramsey Waddell, Mar. 19, 1988; children from previous marriage: Phillip Wayne, Christopher N., Charles, Marion, William. BS in Math. and Physics, Florence (Ala.) State Coll., 1961; M in Adminstrv. Sci., U. Ala., Huntsville, 1977; D in Pub. Adminstrn., Nova U., 1978. Dep. sheriff Lauderdale County, Florence, 1960-61; commd. 2d lt. U.S. Army, 1961, advanced through grades to lt. col., 1977; comdr., staff officer, project mgr. laser designators Redstone Arsenal, Ala., 1973-74; ret. U.S. Army, 1982; chmn., pres. COMTEL-South, Inc., Huntsville, 1982-85, Joint Capital Securities, Inc., 1983—90, Joint Capital Svcs., 1983—; cons. def. industry, 1983-95, 96—; dir. fin. State of Ala., 1995-96. Dir. UNA Found., 2001—; Rep. candidate Gov. of Ala., 1998; bd. dirs. BBB No. Ala., 1985; bd. trustees U. No. Ala., 1995—2001. Decorated Legion of Merit, Bronze Star with V and 5 oak leaf clusters, Air medal with V and VII. Mem.: Am. Soc. Pub. Adminstrn. (pres. 1982—84), Am. Def. Preparedness Assn. (bd. dirs. 1982—84, regional v.p. 1985—97), Blackhorse Assn., U.S. Armor Assn., Assn. U.S. Army, Rotary (pres. 1993—94, dist. gov. group rep. 1994—95, dist. gov. 2001—02). Office: PO Box 2319 Huntsville AL 35804-2319

WILLIAMS, PHYLLIS CUTFORTH, retired realtor; b. Moreland, Idaho, June 6, 1917; d. William Claude and Kathleen Jessie (Jenkins) Cutforth; m. Joseph Marsden Williams, Jan. 21, 1938 (dec. 1986); children: Joseph Marlis, Bonnie Lou Williams Thompson, Nancy Kay Williams Stewart, Marjorie Williams Karren, Douglas Claude, Thomas Marsden, Wendy Kathleen Williams Clark, Shannon Irene Williams Ostler. Grad., Ricks Coll., 1935. Tchr. Grace (Idaho) Elem. Sch., 1935-38; realtor Williams Realty, Idaho Falls, Idaho, 1972-77; mem. Idaho Senate, Boise, 1977. Owner, mgr. river property. Compiler: Idaho Legisladies Cookbook, Cookin' Together, 1981. With MicroFilm Ctr., LDS Ch. Mission, Salt Lake City, 1989-90; former block chmn., vol. Cancer Drive; active Idaho State Legisladies Club, 1966-84, v.p., 1982-84; mem. Bonneville County (Idaho) Rep. Women. Avocations: genealogy, music, politics, cooking, attending grandchildren's special events.

WILLIAMS, PRESTON NOAH, theology educator; b. Alcolu, S.C., May 23, 1926; s. Anderson James and Bertha Bell (McRae) W.; m. Constance Marie Willard, June 4, 1956; children— Mark Gordon, David Bruce. AB, Washington and Jefferson Coll., 1947, MA, 1948; B.D., Johnson C. Smith U., 1950; S.T.M., Yale, 1954; PhD, Harvard, 1967. Ordained to ministry Presbyn.

Ch., 1950. Martin Luther King. Jr. prof. social ethics Boston U. Sch. Theology, 1970-71; Houghton prof. theology and contemporary change Harvard U. Div. Sch., Cambridge, Mass., 1971—, acting dean, 1974-75; acting dir. W.E.B. DuBois Inst., 1975-77. Editor-at-large: Christian Century, 1972—; contbr. articles to profl. jours. Mem. Am. Acad. Religion (pres. 1975—), Am. Soc. Christian Ethics (dir., pres. 1974-75), Phi Beta Kappa. Home: 36 Fairmont St Belmont MA 02478-2919 Office: 45 Francis Ave Cambridge MA 02138-1911

WILLIAMS, QUINN PATRICK, lawyer; b. Evergreen Park, Ill., May 6, 1949; s. William Albert and Jeanne Marie (Quinlan) W.; children: Michael Ryan, Mark Reed, Kelly Elizabeth. BBA, U. Wis., 1972; JD, U. Ariz., 1974. Bar: Ariz. 1975, N.Y. 1984, U.S. Dist. Ct. Ariz. 1976. V.p., sec., gen. counsel Combined Comm. Corp., Phoenix, 1975-80; sr. v.p. legal and adminstrn. Swensen's Inc., Phoenix, 1980-86; ptnr. Winston & Strawn, Phoenix, 1985—89, Snell & Wilmer, Phoenix, 1989—2002; shareholder Greenberg Traurig, 2002—; pres. Enterprise network, 2001. Bd. Ariz. Tech. Coun., 2001—, Ariz. Venture Capital Conf., 1993-2000; co-chmn. Gov.'s Small Bus. Advocate Exec. Coun., 1993—; chair, bd. dirs. Greater Phoenix Econ. Coun., 1996-2000, Scottsdale Area Partnership; vice-chair Gov. Regulatory Coun., 1995-97; sec. GSPED High Tech. Cluster, 1993—; mem. Gov.'s Coun. on Innovation and Tech., 2003—; exec. com. A2Tech Coun., 2002—. With USAR, 1967-73. Mem. ABA, State Bar Ariz., Maricopa County Bar Assn., N.Y. Bar Assn., Internat. Franchise Assn., Scottsdale C. of C. (bd. dirs.), Paradise Valley Country Club, Scottsdale Charros. Office: Greenberg Traurig 2375 E Camelback Rd Ste 700 Phoenix AZ 85016-9000 Office Phone: 602-445-8344. E-mail: williamsq@gtlaw.com.

WILLIAMS, RALPH CHESTER, JR., physician, educator; b. Washington, Feb. 17, 1928; s. Ralph Chester and Annie (Perry) W.; m. Mary Elizabeth Adams, June 23, 1951; children: Cathy, Frederick, John (dec.), Michael, Ann. AB with distinction, Cornell U., 1950, MD, 1954, U. Lund, Sweden, 1991. Diplomate Am. Bd. Internal Medicine. Intern Mass. Gen. Hosp., Boston, 1954-55, asst. resident in internal medicine, 1955-56; resident in internal medicine N.Y. Hosp., 1956-57; chief resident Mass. Gen. Hosp., Boston, 1959-60; guest investigator Rockefeller Inst., N.Y.C., 1961-63; physician in internal medicine and rheumatology, 1963—; assoc. prof. U. Minn., Mpls., 1963-68, prof., 1968-69; prof., chmn. dept. medicine U. N.Mex., Albuquerque, 1969-88; Schott prof. rheumatology and medicine U. Fla., Gainesville, 1988-98; with rheumatology dept. U. N.Mex. Sch. Medicine, Albuquerque, 1998, emeritus prof. medicine, 1998—. Assoc. editor: Jour. Lab. and Clin. Medicine, 1966-69; mem. editl. bd.: Arthritis and Rheumatism, 1968—; contbr. articles to profl. jours. Capt. USAF, 1957-59. Recipient Regents' Meritorious Svc. award, U. N.Mex., 2003. Master Am. Coll. Rheumatology (Gold medal award 2004); fellow ACP; mem. Am. Assn. Immunology, Assn. Am. Physicians, Am. Fedn. Clin. Rsch., Am. Soc. Clin. Investigation, Ctrl. Soc. Clin. Rsch., Western Soc. Clin. Investigation, Phi Beta Kappa, Alpha Omega Alpha. Achievements include research in immunologic processes and connective tissue diseases. Home: 624 E Alameda St Apt 13 Santa Fe NM 87501-2293 Personal E-mail: coolypatch22@aol.com.

WILLIAMS, RALPH WATSON, JR., retired securities company executive; b. Atlanta, July 2, 1933; s. Ralph Watson and Minnie Covington (Hicks) W.; m. Nancy Jo Morgan, Mar. 19, 1955 (dec. Dec. 1989); children: Ralph Watson III, Nancy Jane, John Martin Hicks; m. Almonese Brown Clifton, Nov. 24, 1990. Grad., Sewanee Mil. Acad., 1951; BBA, U. Ga., 1955. Trainee banking Trust Co. Ga., Atlanta, 1955; mcpl. sales staff Courts & Co., Atlanta, 1955-57; v.p., salesman securities First Southeastern Corp., Atlanta, 1957-60; br. mgr. Francis I. duPont & Co., 1960-69; spl. partner duPont Glore Forgan Inc., N.Y.C., 1969-70, gen. partner, 1970, exec. v.p., 1971—, sr. v.p., 1972—; also dir.; sr. v.p., dir., mem. exec. com. duPont-Walston Inc., 1973-74; sr. v.p. E.F. Hutton & Co. Inc., 1974-81; exec. v.p., dir. E.F. Hutton & Co., Inc., 1981-88; exec. v.p. Shearson Lehman Hutton Inc., Atlanta, 1988-89; ret., 1989. Former bd. trustees, chmn. fin. com. St. Andrews Sewanee (Tenn.) Sch. Mem. Nat. Assn. Security Dealers (chmn. dist. com. 7), Benedicts Atlanta, Phi Delta Theta. Clubs: Commerce (Atlanta), Capital City (Atlanta), Piedmont Driving (Atlanta). Presbyterian. Home: 3504 Dumbarton Rd NW Atlanta GA 30327-2614 Fax: 404-237-1812.

WILLIAMS, REBECCA LYNN, lawyer, nurse; b. LaGrange, Ill., Jan. 24, 1959; d. Richard Fowler and Anita (Albro) W. BSN magna cum laude, Duke U., 1981; JD, Loyola U., 1986. Bar: Ill. 1986, U.S. Dist. Ct. (no. dist.) Ill. 1986. Nurse Children's Meml. Hosp., Chgo., 1981-84, St. Jude's Hosp., Vieux Fort, St. Lucia, 1983; assoc. McDermott, Will & Emery, Chgo., 1986-88, Winston & Strawn, Chgo., 1988-93; ptnr. Sonnenschein Nath & Rosenthal, Chgo., 1993-98, Davis Wright Tremaine LLP, Seattle, 1998—. Contbr. articles to profl. jours. Patron various civic, environ., charitable and polit. groups. Mem.: ANA, ABA, Workgroup for Electronic Data Interchange (chair preemption subwork group), Am. Health Lawyers Assn. Avocations: scuba diving, reading, hiking, photography. Office: Davis Wright Tremaine LLP 2600 Century Sq 1501 4th Ave Seattle WA 98101-1688

WILLIAMS, REDFORD BROWN, medical educator; b. Raleigh, N.C., Dec. 14, 1940; s. Redford Brown Sr. and Annie Virginia (Betts) W.; m. Virginia Carter Parrott, August 9, 1940; children: Jennifer Betts, Lloyd Carter. AB, Harvard U., 1963; MD, Yale U., 1967. Diplomate Am. Bd. Internal Medicine. Intern, then resident Yale-New Haven Med. Ctr., 1967-70; sr. surgeon USPHS, Bethesda, Md., 1970-72; asst. prof. Duke U. Med. Ctr., Durham, N.C., 1972, prof. psychiatry, 1977—, prof. psychology, 1990—, dir. behavioral medicine rsch. ctr., 1985—; CEO Williams LifeSkills, Inc., 1997—. Cons. NIH rev. coms., Bethesda, 1977—. Author: The Trusting Heart, 1989, Anger Kills, 1993, Lifeskills, 1998; contbr. articles to profl. jours. Dir. N.C. Heart Assn., Chapel Hill, 1980-83. Recipient Rsch. Scientist award NIMH, 1974—; NIH grantee, 1976—. Fellow Soc. Behavioral Medicine (pres. 1984-85, Upjohn Disting. Scientist award 1992), Acad. Behavioral Medicine Rsch. (pres. 1995—); mem. Am. Psychosomatic Soc. (bd. dirs. 1978-81, pres. 1992). Unitarian Universalist. Avocation: tennis. Office: Duke U Med Ctr PO Box 3926 Durham NC 27710-0001 Office Phone: 919-684-3863.

WILLIAMS, RHYS A. surgeon; b. Mexico, Mo., Jan. 2, 1929; MD, Washington U., 1953. Diplomate Am. Bd. Surgery. Intern Brooke Army Hosp., Ft. Sam Houston, Tex., 1953-54; resident surgery St. Louis City Hosp.-Washington U., 1955-59; cons., ret. part time. Cons. Ark. State Med. Bd., 1987-97. Fellow ACS, AMA. Office: 10 Maroon Dr Aspen CO 81611-1059 E-mail: rhysa@msn.com.

WILLIAMS, RICHARD CHARLES, computer programmer, consultant; b. Boston, Dec. 25, 1955; s. Richard Clayton and Nancy Karolyn (Kerr) W. BA, SUNY, New Paltz, 1991. Cert. in software engring. Programmer/cons. Shared Ednl. Computing, Poughkeepsie, N.Y., 1976-78; systems programmer, comms. mgr. Cornell U. Med. Sch., N.Y.C., 1978-79; staff programmer IBM Corp. Hdqrs., White Plains, N.Y., 1979-84; systems programmer IBM Data. Systems Div., Poughkeepsie, 1984-86; adv. programmer IBM Network Systems, White Plains, 1986-89; open systems cons. IBM Large Systems, Kingston, N.Y., 1989-95; sr. R/3 basis architect, cert. SAP cons. IBM-SAP Competency Ctr., Phila., 1996-97, sr. architect, 1997—. Cons. IBM Hudson Valley Fed. Credit Union, Poughkeepsie, 1986—, C-Net, Broomfield, Colo., 1988-89, Toastmasters Bd. Dirs., Santa Ana, Calif., 1987, Landmark Edn., N.Y.C., 1989—. Author: Lasting Legacy, 1987; co-author: Migrating to TSO from VSPC, 1986; inventor, patentee. Bd. dirs. Hudson Valley FCU, 1995-2001, 2d vice chair, 1996-97, 1st vice-chair, 1997—; bd. dirs. SUNY Alumni Bd. Named one of Outstanding Young Men of Am., 1985, Vol. of Yr., NACUSAC, 1995. Mem. IEEE, ACM, SUNY Alumni Assn. (bd. dirs. 1994-99), Poughkeepsie Toastmasters Internat. (chpt. pres. 1982, dist. gov. 1985, Toastmaster of Yr. 1984), Open Online Transactional Programming Users Group (planning bd. 1995-97). Democrat. Methodist. Avocations: skiing, community organizing, travel. also: SAP Neurottstrasse 16 D-69190 Walldorf Germany Home: 160 S Middle Neck Rd Apt 2L Great Neck NY 11021-4604

WILLIAMS, RICHARD CLARENCE, retired librarian; b. Guide Rock, Nebr., Apr. 9, 1923; s. Lyall Wesley and Elsie Marie (Guy) W. Student, Southwestern U., Georgetown, Tex., 1944-45; student, U. Tex., Austin, 1945-46; BA, U. Idaho, Moscow, 1948; BA in Librarianship, U. Wash., Seattle, 1949; MLS, U. Mich., Ann Arbor, 1952. Sec. Schaefer-Hitchcock Co., Sandpoint, Idaho, 1941-42; asst. librarian Willamette U. Library, Salem, Oreg., 1949-51; cataloger U. Mich. Library, Ann Arbor, 1951-59; serials cataloger N.Y.C. Pub. Library, 1959-66, asst. dir. for cataloging, 1967-88, Astor fellow for library research, 1988-89. Mem. subcom. on cataloging standards Research Libraries Group, Palo Alto, Calif., 1978-88. Contbr. poetry to coll. publs., 1944-48; bibliographer for Mexicon, 1986—. Bd. dirs. Eugene James Dance Co., N.Y.C., 1978—. Served with USN, 1943-46 Mem.: ALA, Pre-Columbian Art Rsch. Inst., Coun. on Bot. and Hort. Librs., John Bartram Assn., Am. Assn. Bot. Gardens and Arboreta, Archeol. Inst. Am., Am. Anthrop. Assn., Soc. Am. Archaeology, Phi Beta Kappa (U. Idaho chpt.). Avocations: New World archeology, Black studies, botany.

WILLIAMS, RICHARD DONALD, retired wholesale food company executive; b. Audubon, Iowa, Feb. 19, 1926; s. Walter Edward and Olga M. (Christensen) W.; m. Carol Francis, June 17, 1950; children: Gayle, Todd, Scott. BA, Ohio Wesleyan U., 1948; MBA, Northwestern U., 1949. Dir. indsl. and pub. rels. Gardner div. Diamond Nat. Corp., Middletown, Ohio, 1949-61; with Fleming Cos., Inc., 1961-89, v.p. pers., 1972-76, sr. v.p. human resources, 1976-80, exec. v.p. human resources, 1980-89, ret., 1989. Pres. Jr. Achievement, Topeka, Kans., 1972; pres. adv. bd. St. Francis Hosp., Topeka, 1972' v.p. Last Frontier coun. Boy Scouts Am., Oklahoma City, 1980; campaign chmn. United Way Greater Oklahoma City, 1980, pres., 1985-87, bd. dirs. Cmty. Coun. Ctrl. Okla., Oklahoma City chpt. ARC, Support Ctr. Okla., Better Bus. Bur., Okla. City Beautiful. Served with USN, 1944-46. Mem. Am. Soc. Personnel Adminstrn., Soc. Advancement Mgmt., Am. Mgmt. Assn., Phi Gamma Delta. Clubs: Quail Creek Country (Oklahoma City), Petroleum (Oklahoma City); Baille 'd Oklahoma (hon.), La Chaine des Rotisseurs. Home: 2940 Brush Creek Rd Oklahoma City OK 73120-1858

WILLIAMS, RICHARD DWAYNE, physician, educator, urologist; b. Wichita, Kans., Oct. 7, 1944; s. Errol Wayne and Roseanna Jane (Page) W.; m. Beverly Sue Ferguson, Aug. 29, 1964; 1 child, Wendy Elizabeth. BS, Abilene Christian U., 1966; MD, Kans. U., 1970. Diplomate Am. Bd. Urology, Nat. Bd. Med. Examiners. Intern, then resident in gen. surgery U. Minn., Mpls., 1970-72, resident in urology, 1972-76, asst. prof., 1976-79, U. Calif., San Francisco, 1979-84, assoc. prof., 1984; prof., chmn. dept. urology U. Iowa, Iowa City, 1984—. Chief urology VA Med. Ctr., San Francisco, 1979-84, VA Med. Ctr., Iowa City, 1984-88; mem. task force on bd. exams Am. Bd. Urology, 1981-85, guest examiner Oral exams, 1984-, trustee, 1994-2000; Rubin H. Flocks chair in urology U. Iowa, 1994; mem. nat. adv. coun. NIDDK, NIH. Author: (with others) Advances in Urologic Oncology, 1987, Genitourinary Cancer: Basic and Clinical Aspects, 1987, Adult and Pediatric Urology, 1987, General Urology, 1988, Textbook of Medicine, 1988, also others; editor: Advances in Urologic Oncology, 1987; guest editor Seminars in Urology, 1985, Problems in Urology: Prostate Cancer, 1989; bd. editors Jour. Urology, 1980-88; mem. editorial bd. Urology, Jour. Urology; also articles. Bd. dirs. Iowa chpt. Nat. Kidney Found., bd. sci. advisors 1989-92; pres. Am. Found. for Urologic Diseases, 2003-. Maj. USAR, 1971-77. Bordeau scholar Kans. U. Med. Ctr., 1968-69; NIH, VA, Am. Cancer Soc. grantee. Fellow ACS (chmn. urology sect. No. Calif. chpt. 1980-82, chmn. ann. meeting programs 1988, mem. residency rev. com. urology 1993-99, vice chair 1995, chair 1997); mem. AAAS, Iowa Med. Soc., Iowa Urologic Soc., Am. Urologic Assn. (dir. seminar on residency evaluation 1987, bd. editors alt. 1988-, rep. North Ctrl. sect., prodr. slide presentations 1988, recipient prizes 1982, 87, mem. various coms. 1987-, bd. dirs. 1994, pres.-elect 1997), Am. Assn. for Cancer Rsch., Am. Soc. Clin. Oncology, Am. Assn. GU Surgeons, Clin. Soc. Genitourinary Surgeons (sec.-treas. 1997-2000), Soc. Internat. D'Urologie (pres. U.S. sect. 2003), Soc. Univ. Urologists (chmn. com. on residency evaluation 1986-88, councillor 1987-, pres. 1993), Soc. Surg. Oncology, Soc. Urologic Oncology (chmn. membership com. 1987-90, sec. 1990-91, 91-94, pres.-elect 1995, pres. 1996), Johnson County Med. Soc., Flock's Soc., Western Urologic Forum, Alpha Omega Alpha. Republican. Office: U Iowa Dept Urology 200 Hawkins Dr Iowa City IA 52242-1009 Office Phone: 319-356-0760. Business E-Mail: richard-williams@uiowa.edu.

WILLIAMS, RICHARD LEROY, federal judge; b. Morrisville, Va., Apr. 6, 1923; s. Wilcie Edward and Minnie Mae (Brinkley) W.; m. Eugenia Kellogg, Sept. 11, 1948; children: Nancy Williams Davies, R. Gregory, Walter L., Gwendolyn Mason. LLB, U. Va., 1951. Bar: Va. 1951. Ptnr. McGuire, Woods & Battle and predecessor firms, 1951-72; judge Cir. Ct. City of Richmond, 1972-76; ptnr. McGuire, Woods & Battle, 1976-80; dist. judge U.S. Dist. Ct., Richmond, Va., 1980—, sr. judge, 1992—. 2d lt. Air Corps., U.S. Army, 1940-45. Fellow Am. Coll. Trial Lawyers; mem. Va. State Bar, Va. Bar Assn., Richmond Bar Assn. Office: US Dist Ct/Lewis F Powell Ste 305 1000 E Main St Richmond VA 23219-3525 E-mail: barbarakreuter@uaed.uscourts.gov.

WILLIAMS, RICHARD LUCAS, III, electronics company executive, lawyer; b. Evanston, Ill., Oct. 30, 1940; s. Richard Lucas Jr. and Ellen Gene (Munster) W.; m. Karen Louise Carmody, Nov. 11, 1967 AB, Princeton U., 1962; LLB, U. Va., 1965. Bar: Ill. 1965, D.C. 1968, U.S. Supreme Ct. 1968. Assoc. Winston & Strawn, Chgo., 1968-74, ptnr., 1974-79; sr. v.p., gen. counsel Gould Inc., Rolling Meadows, Ill., 1979-81, sr. v.p., adminstrn., gen. counsel, 1981-90, also bd. dir., 1985-88; ptnr. Smith Williams and Lodge, Chgo., 1990-95, Vedder, Price, Kaufman & Kammholz, Chgo., 1995—. Bd. dirs. GNB Batteries, Inc., 1984-86, ULINE Inc., Waukegan, Ill. Bd. dirs., 1990—, Internat. Tennis Hall of Fame, Newport, R.I., 1993-97; v.p. Chgo. Dist. Tennis Assn., 1968-70; vice chmn. Am. Cancer Soc., Chgo., 1984; bd. dirs., pres. Lake Shore Found. for Animals, Chgo., 1990-94. With JAGC USNR, 1965-68. Mem. ABA, Ill. Bar Assn., Chgo. Bar Assn., Execs. Club Chgo. (co-chmn. Western Europe internat. com. 1990-97, 2003—), The Lawyers Club (Chgo., 1997—), Meadow Club (Rolling Meadows, gov. 1979-90, chmn. 1985-90), Club Internat. Home: 1200 N Lake Shore Dr Chicago IL 60610-2370 Office: Vedder Price 222 N La Salle St Ste 2600 Chicago IL 60601-1104

WILLIAMS, RICHARD THOMAS, lawyer; b. Evergreen Park, Ill., Jan. 14, 1945; s. Raymond Theodore and Elizabeth Dorothy (Williams) W. AB with honors, Stanford U., 1967, MBA, JD, Stanford U., 1972. Bar: Calif. 1972, U.S. Supreme Ct. 1977. Assoc.,then ptnr. Kadison Pfaelzer Woodard Quinn & Rossi, L.A., 1972-87; ptnr. Whitman & Ransom, 1987-93, Whitman, Breed, Abbott & Morgan, L.A., 1993-2000, Holland & Knight, LLP, L.A., 2000—. Contbg. editor Oil and Gas Analyst, 1978-84. Mem. ABA, L.A. County Bar Assn. Office: Holland & Knight LLP 633 W 5th St Los Angeles CA 90071-2005 Office Phone: 213-896-2410. Business E-Mail: richard.williams@hklaw.com.

WILLIAMS, RICHMOND DEAN, library appraiser, consultant; b. Reading, Mass., Dec. 10, 1925; s. Theodore Ryder and Anabel Lee (Hutchison) W.; m. Eleanor Davidson Washbourne, Sept. 26, 1953; children— Richmond Lyttleton, Eleanor Davidson, Anne Ryder. AB cum laude, Williams Coll., 1950; MA, U. Pa., 1952, PhD, 1959. Instr., asst. dean Williams Coll., Williamstown, Mass., 1954-56; dir. Wyo. Hist. and Geol. Soc., Wilkes-Barre, Pa., 1956-60; asst. dir. Am. Assn. State and Local History, Madison, Wis., 1960-61; dir. libraries Eleutherian Mills-Hagley Found., Wilmington, Del., 1962-87. Instr. Acad. Lifelong Learning U. Del., 1996—; cons. archivist M.S. Hershey Found., Pa., 1981—, Md. Dept. Housing and Cmty. Devel., 1993-94; bd. dirs. Rhistoric Inc. Co-author: A Look at Ourselves, 1962, author: They Also Served, 1965; compiler: Directory of Historical Records in Delaware, 1995, (ann. series) Writing Haiku—, 1997—. Sec., U. Del. Library Assocs., Wilmington, 1972-86; mem. adv. bd. Del. Hist. Records, Dover, 1976-2002; mem. Del. Humanities Forum, Wilmington, 1984-91; trustee Conservation Ctr. Phila., 1984-86. Served to 1st lt. AUS, 1943-47. Pennfield fellow U. Pa., 1953 Mem. Econ. History Assn (sec.-treas. 1975-88), Mid-Atlantic Regional Archives Com., Am. Assn. State and Local History (pres. 1974-76), Am. Antiquarian Soc., Libr. Co. Phila., Phi Beta Kappa. Avocations: golf, book collecting. Home and Office: 202 Brecks Ln Wilmington DE 19807-3011 E-mail: rdwms@udel.edu.

WILLIAMS, ROBERT HENRY, oil company executive; b. El Paso, Jan. 12, 1946; s. William Frederick and Mary (Page) W.; m. Joanne Marie Mudd, Oct. 22, 1967; children: Lara, Michael, Suzanne, Jennifer. BS in Physics, U. Tex., El Paso, 1968; PhD in Physics, U. Tex., Austin, 1973; MS in Physics, Va. Poly. Inst., 1971. Dir. Gulf Oil R&D, Houston, 1978-81; tech. mgr. Gulf Oil Internat., Houston, 1981-83; exploration mgr. Gulf Oil Co., Houston, 1983-85; mgr. geophys. rsch. Tenneco Oil Co., Houston, 1985-87, mgr., chief geophysicist, 1987-88; founder, mng. dir. Dover Energy, Houston, 1988—; exec. v.p. Tatham Offshore Inc, Houston, 1989-95, also bd. dirs.; chmn., CEO Dover Tech. Inc., Houston, 1989—. Cons. Tenneco Inc., Houston, 1989—; DeepTech Internat., 1992-95; Ukraine Acad. Sci., 1993; bd. dirs., exec. v.p. DeepTech Inc., 1991-95; founder, pres. Westway tech. Assocs., 1986—; co-founder, chmn. CEO Castaway Graphite Rods, Inc., 1990—; owner, CEO Team Tex. Inc., 1993—; Bulldog Lures, Inc., 1994—; founder, CEO Houston Books Inc., 1994—; founder, CEO, chmn. Dover Energy Exploration, 1995—; pres. Westway Interests; chmn., CEO, bd. dirs. W.B. Oil & Gas Inc., 1997-2001, Dover (Belize), 1996-2002; bd. dirs. Tatham Offshore, Swep, Inc.; CEO Norman Lures, 1997—; founder, bd. dirs., CEO Win Leisure Products, 1997—; dir./founder William Found., 1998—; CEO, chmn. bd. dirs. Airrus Fishing Products, 2003-. Contbr. articles to profl. jours. Coun. mem. Boy Scouts Am., Houston, 1989—. patron Mus. Fine Arts, Houston, 1990—2004, Houston Zool. Soc., 1990—2004; leader Girl Scouts U.S., Houston, 1989—, life mem. Mem. Soc. Exploration Geophysics, Am. Assn. Petroleum Geologists, Am. Geophys. Union. Republican. Avocations: scuba diving, book collecting, fishing. Office: Dover Tech 14420 Westway Ln Houston TX 77077

WILLIAMS, ROBERT JOSEPH, museum director, educator; b. Bennington, Vt., June 21, 1944; s. Joseph and Ruthe Allison (Moody) Williams. BS in Edn., U. Vt., 1970; MA in Interdisciplinary Social Sci., San Francisco State U., 1981. Tchr. adult edn. Mt. Anthony Union H.S., Bennington, Vt., 1972-74; columnist Bennington Banner, 1972-77; tchr. San Francisco State U., 1976-79; founder, dir. NORRAD Drug Rehab. Ctr., San Francisco, 1986 88; mus. curator Shaftsbury (Vt.) Historical Soc., 1989—. Founder, dir. Bennington Tutorial Ctr., 1971-74. Author: Toward Humanness in Education, 1981, Chalice of Leaves: Selected Essays and Poems, 1988, Modern Salvation: Guidelines from Cosmology, 1994, Gravity from Superstring Displacement, 1999; author: (with others) Intimacy, 1985. Recipient Edmunds Essay medal Vt. Historical Soc., Montpelier, 1961, award League Vt. Writers, 1972, Golden Poet award World Poetry, Sacramento, Calif., 1990. Democrat. Avocation: cosmology. Home: 102 Putnam St Bennington VT 05201-2348 Office: Shaftsbury Hist Soc PO Box 401 Shaftsbury VT 05262-0401 *I sought the truth, and sought to live by it.*

WILLIAMS, ROBERT JOSEPH, behavioral health services executive, psychologist; b. Durango, Colo., Feb. 14, 1948; s. Owen C. and Florence K. Williams; m. Kay Lynn Williams, Mar. 24, 1973; children: Robin, Matthew, Nicholas. BA, U. Colo., 1970; MA, U. No. Colo., 1976; PhD, U. Minn., 1979. Diplomate Am. Bd. Forensic Psychol. Specialties. Tchr. math. Jefferson County Schs., Lakewood, Colo., 1970-76; psychologist Pikes Peak Mental Health Ctr., Colorado Springs, Colo., 1979-82, clin. dir., 1982-83; dir. Inst. for Family and Personal Devel., Colorado Springs, 1983-86; mng. ptnr. Marriage and Family Treatment Ctr., Colorado Springs, 1986-90; COO Quinco Behavioral Health Systems, Columbus, Ind., 1990-92, pres., CEO, 1992—. Feedback cons. Ctr. for Creative Leadership, Colorado Springs and San Diego, 1986-96; facilitator Franklin Covey Ctr., Columbus, 1994-99; cons. Trustee Leadership Tng. Program, Indpls., 1991-98; adj. faculty U. Denver, U. Colo., Colorado Springs, 1981-90. Contbr. articles to profl. jours. Trustee Bartholomew Consol. Sch. Corp., Columbus, 1996-2001, pres., 1999-2000; past pres., moderator Leadership Bartholomew County (Healthy Communities Coun. 1995-, co-chair 2004-); bd. dirs. Ind. Philharmonic, 2001- (pres. 2003-). Sgt. USMC, 1970—76. Boettcher Found. scholar, 1966-70; Regents scholar, 1966. Mem. Rotary Club, Masons. Democrat. Presbyn. Avocations: hiking, reading, motorcycling, weight training. Office: Quinco Behavioral Health Sys 720 North Marr Rd Columbus IN 47201 E-mail: rjwilliams@quincoinc.com.

WILLIAMS, ROBERT LEON, psychiatrist, neurologist, educator; b. Buffalo, July 22, 1922; s. Leon R. and L. Paulyne (Ingraham) W.; m. Shirley Glynn Miller, Feb. 5, 1949; Karen, Kevin BA, Alfred U., 1944; MD, Albany Med. Coll., Union U., 1946. Chief neurology and psychiatry Lackland AFB Hosp., USAF, San Antonio, 1952-55; cons. neurology and psychiatry to USAF Surgeon Gen., 1955-58; faculty Coll. Medicine, U. Fla., Gainesville, 1958-72, prof., chmn. dept. psychiatry, 1964-72; prof. psychiatry Baylor Coll. Medicine, Houston, 1972-92, chmn. dept., 1972-90, prof. neurology, 1976-92, acting chmn. dept., 1976-77, prof. emeritus psychiatry and neurology, 1992—. Mem. faculty various univs., part time 1949-58 including Albany Med. Coll. at Union U., Columbia Coll. Physisicans and Surgeons, Boston U., U. Tex., Georgetown U. Author: (with W.B. Webb) Sleep Therapy: A. Bibliography and Commentary, 1966, (with others) EEG of Human Sleep: Clinical Applications, 1974; editor: (with Ismet Karacan and Carolyn J. Hursch) Psychopharmacology of Sleep, 1976, Sleep Disorders: Diagnosis and Treatment, 1978, 2d edit., 1988; (with others) Phenomenology and Treatment of Anxiety, 1979, of Alcoholism, 1980, of Psychophysiological Disorders, 1982, of Psychosexual Disorders, 1983, of Psychiatric Emergencies, 1984 Served from 1st lt. to lt. col. USAF, 1949-58; col. Res., ret. Recipient Cert. Profl. Achievement USAF Surgeon Gen., 1967 Mem. Am. Psychiat. Assn., Am. Electroencephalographic Soc., Am. Coll. Psychiatrists (pres. 1982-83), Am. Acad. Neurology, AMA, Group for Advancement of Psychiatry, Benjamin Rush Soc. (pres. 1986-88), Accreditation Coun. for grad. Med. Edn. (residency rev. com. for psychiatry 1985-93), Alpha Omega Alpha. Achievements include research and publs. on basic psychophysiology of human sleep.

WILLIAMS, ROBERT LEONARD, publishing executive, photographer; b. Hayesville, N.C., June 19, 1932; s. Henry Grady and Ethel Lee Williams; m. Helen Elizabeth Wise, Apr. 24, 1972; 1 child, Robert Williams III. AA, Mitchell Coll.; BA, Lenoir Rhyne Coll.; MA, Appalachian State U. Tchr. English Statesville High Sch., NC, 1959—66; grad. asst. Appalachian State U., Boone, 1966—67; prof. English Gaston Coll., Dallas, 1967—86; freelance writer, 1986—98; editor, author Southeastern Pub., Dallas, 1998—2000; pres. Rusty Gates Books, Lawndale, 2000—. Cons. editor McGraw-Hill, N.Y.C., 1986—88; author-in-residence Gaston Coll., 1973—86. Author: Night of the Damned, 1973, The Thirteenth Juror, 1983, People Worth Meeting and Stories Worth Repeating, 2001; contbr. articles to profl. jours. With U.S. Army, 1953—55. Mem.: N.C. Assn. Educators. Republican. Baptist. Avocations: hiking, gardening, woodworking. Home and Office: 145 Queen Rd Lawndale NC 28090 Office Phone: 704-538-7900. E-mail: wisewms@bellsouth.net.

WILLIAMS, ROBERT LUTHER, city planning consultant; b. Porterville, Calif., June 24, 1923; s. Luther Esco and Mary (Lyon) W.; children: Jeffrey Robert, Derrick Paul, Gail Diane. Student, Utah State Coll., 1944; AB, U. Calif.-Berkeley, 1949, M.C.P., 1951. Asst. planning dir., Stockton, Calif., 1951-54; planning dir. Alameda, Calif., 1954-57, Alameda County, 1957-63; exec. dir. Am. Inst. Planners, Washington, 1963-69; v.p. Hill Devel. Corp., Middletown, Conn., 1969-71; dir. land mgmt. dept. Gulf Oil Corp., Reston, Va., 1971-74; pres. Coleman-Williams, Inc., Greenbrae, Calif., 1975-78, Robert Williams Assocs., Inc., San Rafael, Calif., 1978-87; mem. community affairs panel KQED-TV, San Francisco, 1991-94. Lectr. U. Calif. at Berkeley extension, 1956-59, tech. adviser regional planning Assn. Bay Area Govts., Calif., 1961-63; vis. prof. U. R.I., 1969-71; pres. G.I.F.T. Inst., Inc., 1991-94. Bd. dirs. Planning Found. Am., 1965-70, Communities Found., Inc., 1973-77. Served to 1st lt. AUS, 1943-46, 52, ETO. Named Young Man of Year Alameda, 1956 Mem. Am. Inst. Cert. Planners (pres. Calif. chpt. 1960), Am. Planning Assn., World Future Soc., Lambda Alpha, Lambda Chi Alpha. Presbyterian. Home: 93 N Cobbtown Rd Lincolnville ME 04849

WILLIAMS, ROBERT LYLE, investor, retail executive; b. Nowata, Okla., June 22, 1942; s. Clifford Lyle and Eula Mae (Barnes) W.; m. Lorene Linnet Dillahunty, June 12, 1965; 1 child, Eleanor Lynn BS, Okla. State U., 1964; MBA, Baylor U., 1965. Acctg. supr. Southwestern Bell Telephone Co., Houston, 1965-66; fin. exec. Ford Motor Co., Dearborn, Mich., 1969-80; treas. Ford Brazil, Sao Paulo, 1976-79, Agrico Chem. Co., Tulsa, 1980-82; v.p., chief fin. officer Texas City Refining, Inc., Tex., 1983-88; sr. v.p. Furnishings 2000, Inc., San Diego, 1988-89; pvt. cons. and investor Houston, 1990—. Chmn. Galveston County Taxpayers Research Council, 1987-88. Served to lt. USN, 1966-69 Republican. Presbyterian. Avocation: travel. Office: 2500 E T C Jester Blvd Ste 200 Houston TX 77008-1375 Office Phone: 713-693-1825.

WILLIAMS, ROBERT SANDERS (SANDY WILLIAMS), dean, academic administrator, educator, researcher; b. Athens, Ga. m. Jennifer Williams; children: Molly, Nicholas, Owen. Undergrad. degree, Princeton U., 1970; MD, Duke U., 1974; internship and residency internal medicine, Mass. Gen. Hosp., 1974—76; fellowship in cardiology, Duke U. Med. Ctr., 1977—80. Asst. prof. medicine, physiology, cell biology Duke U. Sch. medicine, 1980—84; assoc. prof. medicine and microbiology Duke U. Sch. Medicine, 1986—90, dean, vice chancellor acad. affairs, 2001—; chief cardiology, prof. internal medicine, biochemistry, and molecular biology, dir. Ryburn Ctr. for Molecular Cardiology U. Tex. Southwestern Med. Ctr., 1990—2001. Rschr. in field; vis. prof. dept. biochemistry Oxford U., 1984—85; vis. scientist Cold Spring Harbor Lab., NY, 1995—96; dir.'s adv. com. NIH; bd. external advisors Nat. Heart, Lung and Blood Inst. Contbr. more than 150 scholarly articles to biomed. jours., Proceedings of the Nat. Acad. Scis. Recipient Disting. Alumnus Award, Duke U. Sch. Medicine, 2000. Fellow: AAAS; mem.: NAS, Inst. of Medicine, Assn. Univ. Cardiologists, Am. Heart Assn. Achievements include being the leader of the Dallas Heart Disease Prevention Project, an innovative program of research in the genetic epidemiology of cardiovascular disease. Office: Duke U Sch Medicine Box 2927 Durham NC 27710*

WILLIAMS, ROBIN, actor, comedian; b. Chgo., July 21, 1952; s. Mr. and Mrs. Robert W.; m. Valerie Velardi, June 4, 1978 (div.); m. Marsha Garces, Apr. 30, 1989 Attended, Claremont Men's Coll., Marin Coll., Juilliard Sch., N.Y.C. Started as stand-up comedian in San Francisco clubs, including Holy City Zoo, The Boardinghouse; later became regular at Comedy Store, Los Angeles; appeared in TV series Laugh-In, The Richard Pryor Show, America 2-Night, Happy Days, Homicide: Life on the Streets, 1993 (Emmy nomination, Guest Actor - Drama Series, 1994); star of TV series Mork and Mindy, 1978-82 (People's Choice award), (cable) Robin Williams: An Evening at the Met, 1986 (Grammy award), host of HBO's Shakespeare: The Animated Tales, 1993 (CableAce Award, Best Entertainment Host); film appearances include: Popeye, 1980, The World According to Garp, 1982, The Survivors, 1983, Moscow on the Hudson, 1984, Club Paradise, 1986, Good Morning Vietnam, 1987 (Golden Globe award 1988, Acad. Award nominee for best actor), The Adventures of Baron Munchausen, 1988, Dead Poets Society, 1989 (Best Actor nomination Golden Globe award, 1994, nominated best actor Acad. award), Cadillac Man, 1990, The Fisher King, 1991 (Golden Globe award, Acad. award nominee for best actor 1991), Dead Again, 1991, Hook, 1991, Aladdin (voice) (Spl. Achievement award Hollywood Fgn. Press, Nat. Bd. Rev. 1992), 1992, Toys, 1992, Mrs. Doubtfire, 1993 (Best Picture, Best Actor in a Musical or Comedy, Golden Globe, 1994, Best Picture, Best Actor, People's Choice award, also prodr.), Nine Months, 1995, Jumanji, 1995, The BirdCage, 1996, Jack, 1996, The Secret Agent, 1996, Hamlet, 1996, Deconstructing Harry, 1997, (tv series, voice) Great Minds Think for Themselves, 1997, Father's Day, 1997, Flubber, 1997, Good Will Hunting, 1997, What Dreams May Come, 1998, Patch Adams, 1998, Bicentennial Man, 1999, Jakob the Liar (also exec. prodr.), 1999, Artificial Intelligence (voice), 2001, One Hour Photo, 2002, Death to Smoochy, 2002, Insomnia, 2002; theatre: Waiting for Godot, 1988; recorded albums: Reality, What a Concept, 1979 (Grammy award), Throbbing Python of Love, A Night at the Met (Grammy award); host Comic Relief, 1986; appeared in TV variety programs, ABC Presents a Royal Gala, 1988 (Emmy award, 1988), Carol, Carl, Whoopi & Robin, 1987 (Emmy award), Robin Williams: Live at the Met, 1986, Robin Williams Live, 1986, Comic Relief, 1986, Young Comedians All Star Reunion, 1988, Robin Williams: Live on Broadway, 2002 (Emmy nomination, Grammy award, 2003) Recipient Golden Apple award Hollywood Women's Press Club; Golden Globe award; ACE award; Am. Comedy award, 1987, 88; Grammy award for best comedy rec., 1987; recipient Man of Yr. award Hasty Pudding Theatricals, 1989, People's Choice award Favorite Comedy Motion Picture Actor, 1994, ShoWest Conv. award Male Star of Yr., 1994.

WILLIAMS, ROGER LAWRENCE, historian, educator; b. Boulder, Colo., June 22, 1923; s. Raymond Ustick and Mabel (Woolf) W. BA, Colo. Coll., 1947; MA, U. Mich., 1948, PhD, 1951. Asst. prof. Minn. State Coll., Mankato, 1950-52, MIT, Cambridge, 1952-55; vis. prof. Mich. State U., East Lansing, 1955-56; assoc. prof. Antioch Coll., Yellow Springs, Ohio, 1956-65; prof. U. Calif., Santa Barbara, 1965-71, U. Wyo., Laramie, 1971-78, Disting. prof., 1978-88. Author: French Revolution of 1870-71, 1969, The Mortal Napoleon III, 1971, The Horror of Life, 1980, Aven Nelson of Wyoming, 1984, Gérard and Jaume: Two Neglected Figures in the History of the Jussiaean Classification, 1988, Napoleon III and the Stoffel Affair, 1993, The Letters of Dominique Chaix, Botanist-Curé, 1997, Botanophilia in 18th Century France: The Spirit of the Enlightenment, 2001; co-author: How Modernity Came to a Provençal Town, 1988, Handbook of Rocky Mountain Plants, 1992, A Guide to Rocky Mountain Plants, 2002, French Botany in the Enlightenment: the Ill-fated Voyages of La Pérouse and His Rescuers, 2003, A Region of Astonishing Beauty, the Botanical Exploration of the Rocky Mountains, 2003; mem. editl. bd. Antioch Rev., 1958-64. Vol. Rocky Mountain Nat. Park, Estes Park, Colo., 1986-87. Mem. French Hist. Studies (life), History Sci. Soc. (life), Hist. Soc., Nat. Coun. for History Edn., N.Y. Bot. Soc., Denver Bot. Soc. Home: 1701 S 17th St Laramie WY 82070-5406

WILLIAMS, RONALD A. insurance company executive; Degree, Roosevelt U.; MS in Mgmt., MIT. Sr. v.p. mktg. and specialty products to exec. v.p. group and network svc. Blue Cross Calif., 1987—95, pres., 1995—99; former sr. v.p. Vista Health Corp.; former group mktg. exec. Control Data Corp.; former pres., co-founder Integrative Sys.; former pres. large group divsn. WellPoint; exec. v.p., chief of health operations Aetna Inc., 2001—02, pres., 2002—. Mem.: bd. dir., Lucent Technologies. Office: Aetna Inc 151 Farmington Ave Hartford CT 06156

WILLIAMS, RONALD DAVID, telecommunications executive; b. Marshall, Ark., Mar. 15, 1944; s. Noble Kentucky and Elizabeth (Karns) W.; m. Beth L. Williams, Nov. 1977; children: Stephanie Noble, Keith Michael. BA, Columbia U., 1966, BS, 1967, MBA, 1973. Process engr. DuPont, Deepwater, N.J., 1966; design engr. Combustion Engring. Co., Hartford, 1971; cons. Arthur Andersen & Co., N.Y.C., 1973-76; corp. planner Amax Inc., Greenwich, Conn., 1976-77, group planning adminstr., 1978-80, mgr. corp. planning and analysis, 1980-94, dir. fin. analysis, 1984-86; project mgr. Olin Corp., Stamford, Conn., 1977-78; mgr. ops. planning and analysis Savin Corp., Stamford, 1986-88; dir. fin. Bandgap Tech. Corp., Broomfield, Colo., 1988-90, v.p. fin. and adminstrn., 1990-93; v.p., gen. mgr. Bandgap Chem. Corp., 1992-94; contr. Heraeus PMR, Inc., Alden, N.Y., 1994-95, v.p. fin. and adminstrn., 1995-96; gen. mgr. Acoustiflo, Boulder, Colo., 1996-97; sr. fin. staff analyst Energy Corp., New Orleans, 1998-99; mgr. fin. planning Energy Tech. Co., 1999—. With USN, 1967-70, Vietnam. NASA trainee, 1971; S.W. Mudd scholar, 1971. Mem. AAAS, Am. Chem. Soc., Am. Mgmt. Assn., Utility Telecom. Coun., Ark. Hist. Assn., Westport Hist. Soc., Colo. Hist. Soc., Appalachian Mountain Club, Boulder Road Runners, Chalmette Track Club, New Orleans Track Club, Gulf Coast Running Club, Pine Belt Pacers, Mesa Monument Striders, West Bank Track Club. Home: 7361 S Meadow Ct Boulder CO 80301-3951 Office: 639 Loyola Ave New Orleans LA 70113-3125

WILLIAMS, RONALD DEAN, minister, religious organization administrator; b. Decatur, Ill, Oct. 23, 1940; s. Henry Lawrence and Ella Loudica Williams; m. Carole Jeanette Lane, June 16, 1962; children: Scott Allan, Mark Lawrence, Derek James. BTh, LIFE Bible Coll., LA, 1965; DD, Internat. Ch. Foursquare Gospel, LA, 1992. Ordained to ministry Internat. Ch. Foursquare Gospel, 1966. Pastor Foursquare Gospel Ch., Surrey, Canada, 1965-69, missionary Hong Kong, China, 1969-85; prof. LIFE Bible Coll., 1985-95; mng. editor Foursquare World ADVANCE, 1993—2002; comm. officer Internat. Ch. of Foursquare Gospel, 1988-2000. Bd. dir. Foursquare Gospel Ch.; pres. exec. bd. Internat. Pentecostal Press Assn., Oklahoma City, 1990-98; comm. officer Pentecostal/Charismatic Ch. North Am., Memphis, 1994—; coord. E. Coun. Foursquare Miss., 1979-82. Editor: The Vine and The Branches, 1992; mng. editor Foursquare World ADVANCE mag., 1985-2002. Coord. 19th Pentecostal World Conf., 2001. With USAF, 1958-61. Mem. Foursquare Gospel Ch. Avocations: writing, golf, reading, music. Office: Internat Ch Foursquare Gospel 1910 W Sunset Blvd Ste 200 Los Angeles CA 90026-3295 Business E-Mail: ron@foursquare.org.

WILLIAMS, RONALD DOHERTY, lawyer; b. New Haven, Conn., Apr. 6, 1927; s. Richard Hugh and Ethel W. (Nelson) w.; m. Laura Costarelli, Aug. 25, 1951; children: Craig F., Ronald D., Ellen A., Jane E. BA, U. Va., 1951; LLB, 1954. Bar: Conn. 1954. Assoc. Pullman, Comley, Bradley & Reeves, Bridgeport, Conn., 1954-60; ptnr., 1960-88, Williams, Cooney & Sheehy, 1989—. Mem. Fed. Jud. Com., 1988-91, com. unauthorized practice law, 1988-94, com. to study rules civil practice & procedure, 1984-86; atty. state trial referee, 1984-90. Selectman Town of Easton (Conn.), 1975-85, justice of the peace, 1977—, town atty., 1985-2000; mem. Bridgeport Area Found., 1971-90, adv. com. U. Bridgeport Law Sch., 1982-92; mem. statewide grievance com., 1985-91, chmn., 1989-91; mem. exec. bd. Sch. Law Quinnipiac Coll., 1994—. Served with U.S. Army, 1945-46. Fellow Am. Coll. Trial Lawyers; mem. ABA, Am. Bd. Trial Advs., Conn. Bar Assn. (bd. govs. 1975-78), Bridgeport Bar Assn. (pres. 1975), Conn. Def. Lawyers Assn. (pres. 1984-85), Trial Attys. Am. Republican. Roman Catholic. Home: 14 Newman Dr Easton CT 06612-1915 Office: 799 Silver Ln Trumbull CT 06611-0753 E-mail: WilCooShee@aol.com.

WILLIAMS, RONALD OSCAR, defense systems engineer; b. Denver, May 10, 1940; s. Oscar H. and Evelyn J. (Johnson) Williams. BS in Applied Math. Coll. Engring., U. Colo., Boulder, 1964; student, Grad Sch. and Coll. Engring., U. Colo., Boulder; student in continuing edn., U. Denver; student Colls. Engring and Arts-Scis., U. Colo., Denver; student in Advanced Tech. Edn. Program, George Washington U. Computer programmer Apollo Sys. dept. Missile and Space div. Gen. Electric Co., Kennedy Space Ctr., Fla., 1965-67, Manned Spacecraft Ctr. (now called Johnson Space Ctr.), Houston, 1967-68; computer programmer Grad. Sch. Computing Ctr. and Lab. Atmospheric and Space Physics U. Colo., Boulder, 1968-73; computer programmer analyst Def. Sys. divsn. Sys. Devel. Corp. for NORAD, Colo. Springs, 1974-75; engr. def. sys. and command-and-info. sys. Martin Marietta Aerospace, Denver, 1976-80; sys. engr., def. info. sys. divsn. space and comm. group Hughes Aircraft Co., Aurora, Colo., 1980-89; rsch. analyst Math. Rsch. Ctr., Littleton, Colo., 1990—, dir., sr. rsch. mathematician, 1996—. Vol. fireman Clear Lake City (Tex.) Fire Dept., 1968; officer Boulder Emergency Squad, 1969-76, rescue squad officer, 1969-76, liaison officer to cadets, 1971, pers. officer, 1971-76, mem. exec. bd., 1971-76, EMT, 1973—; res. dispatcher A-1 Ambulance, Boulder, 1973; spl. police officer Boulder Police Dept., 1970-75; spl. dep. sheriff Boulder County Sheriff's Dept., 1970-71; mem. nat. adv. bd. Am. Security Coun., 1979-91, Coalition of Peace Through Strength, 1979-91. Officer reserves USMC, 1958—66, Marine Corps Recruit Depot (San Diego), Camp Calvin B. Matthews, Camp George F. Elliott, Camp Joseph H. Pendleton (Camp San Onofre), Marine Corps Base Twentynine Palms, Denver Fed. Ctr. Decorated Organized Res. medal; recipient award of merit Boulder Emergency Squad, 1971, 72, Dedicated Svc. award Boulder Emergency Squad, 1976, Cost Improvement Program award, Sys. Performance Improvement award, Top Cost Improvement Program award in Def. Sys. Div., Space and Comm. Group Hughes Aircraft Co., 1982. Mem. AAAS, AIAA (sr.), Math. Assn. Am., Am. Math Soc., Soc. Indsl. and Applied Math., Math. Study Unit of Am. Topical Assn., Armed Forces Comm. and Electronics Assn., Assn. Old Crows, Nat. Def. Indsl. Assn., Assn. Former Intelligence Officers, Nat. Mil. Intelligence Assn., U.S. Naval Cryptologic Vet. Assn., Marine Corps Assn., Air Force Assn., U.S. Naval Inst., Nat. Geog. Soc., Smithsonian Inst., Nat. Space Soc., Soc. Amateur Radio Astronomers, Radio History Soc., Met. Opera Guild, Colo. Hist. Soc., Hist. Denver, Hist. Boulder, Hawaiian Hist. Soc., Denver Bot. Gardens, Denver Mus. Nature and Sci., Denver Zool. Found., Alumni Assn. U. Colo. Boulder, South High Alumni and Friends, Denver Am. Mensa Ltd., Denver Mile-Hi Mensa, Acoustic Neuroma Assn., Nat. Brain Tumor Found. Lutheran.

WILLIAMS, ROY, airport terminal executive; Former dir. Dayton Internat. Airport, Ohio; aviation dir. Louis Armstrong New Orleans Internat. Airport, 2001—. Office: 900 Airline Hwy Kenner LA 70062

WILLIAMS, ROY L. public relations executive, advocate; m. Patricia Ryder Williams, 1961; 2 children. Master of Urban Planning, Wayne State U.; postgrad., U. Manchester, Eng. Exec. asst. to Gov. William G. Milliken; pres. and CEO Detroit Urban League; mgr. cmty. rels. Chrysler Corp., 1984—; chmn. spl. contbn. fund NAACP, mem. nat. bd. dirs. Chmn. Mich. State Housing Devel. Authority; mem. steering com. Detroit Neighborhood Housing Svcs.; past pres. Nat. Coun. State Housing Bds.; exec. v.p. HP Devco; bd. dirs. Detroit City Planning Commn. Named Citizen of Week, WWJ Radio; recipient Human Rights award, Nat. Jewish Labor Com., 1995. Mem.: Highland Pk. C. of C. (v.p.). Office: NAACP 4805 Mt Hope Dr Baltimore MD 21215*

WILLIAMS, RUSS, marketing professional; Grad. summa cum laude, Christian Bros. U.; MBA with honors, U. Va. Pres., prin. Valent USA, Kraft Food Ingredients, Storage USA, CB Richard Ellis, The Conwood Co., Belz Factory Outlet World, Archer Malmo, 2002—. Named featured engr., Memphis Joint Engring. Coun., 1983, Top 40 Under 40, Memphis Bus. Jour., 2000. Office: 65 Union at Front Memphis TN 38103

WILLIAMS, SAM B. engineering executive; Chmn., CEO Williams Internat. Corp. Named to Nat. Aviation Hall of Fame, 1998; recipient Collier trophy, 1979, Wright Bros. Meml. trophy, 1988, Nat. medal of Technology, 1995. Mem.: NAE. Office: Williams Internat Corp PO Box 200 2280 W West Maple Rd Walled Lake MI 48390

WILLIAMS, SAMUEL ROBERT, lawyer; b. Chgo., Feb. 8, 1954; s. Samuel Wesley Williams Jr. and Lilla (Waring) Williams; m. Tracy S. Sherwood, June 8, 1991; children: Lauren Leigh, Haley Anne. BA, Lehigh U., 1976; JD, Syracuse U., 1979. Bar: N.Y. 1982, U.S. Dist. Ct. (no. dist.) N.Y. Assoc. Smiley, Schwartz and Captain, N.Y.C., 1982—84; asst. corp. counsel, sr. trial counsel Torts divsn. N.Y.C. Corp. Counsel, Bklyn., 1984—87; assoc. Sugarman, Wallace, Manheim and Schoenwald, Syracuse, NY, 1988—90; ptnr. Williams and Fleckenstein, Syracuse, 1990—94; pvt. practice Syracuse, 1994—. Mem.: ATLA, N.Y. State Trial Lawyers, Am. Bd. Trial Adv. Avocations: skiing, flying. Office: 250 Harrison St Ste 302 Syracuse NY 13202

WILLIAMS, SANDRA LYNN, management consultant; b. Evanston, Ill., May 11, 1955; d. Robert Chandler and Evelyn Clauson Williams. BS in Fine and Applied Arts, U. Ill., 1977, MBA in Fin. Mgmt., 1980, PhD in Human Resource Devel., 2001. Banking officer Continental Bank N.A., Chgo., 1980, 2nd v.p., 1981—84, v.p., 1984—89, sector credit officer, 1989—93, mng. dir., 1993—94; sr. v.p. Bank of Am., Chgo., 1994—99, human capital cons., 1996—99; pvt. pub. spkr. and cons., 1999—. Tng. mgr. and instr. corp. and instnl. banking tng. dept. Continental Ill. Nat. Bank, N.A., Chgo., 1984—92; guest instr. dept. human resources U. Ill., Coll. Edn., Champaign, Ill., 1999—2001; grad. tchg. asst. dept. human resource edn. U. Ill., 1999—2001; presenter in field. Author: Human Capital Management and Development, 2001, (booklet/guide) Human Capital Planning Guidebook, 1998; contbr. articles to profl. jours. Mem. adv. bd. Ill. Fatherhood Initiative, Chgo., 1997—99; active Rep. Nat. Com., Washington, 1994—2005; judge of elections Maine Twp., Cook County, Ill.; legis. adv. Ill. Connection, Urbana, 1997—; elder, mem. mgmt. session Park Ridge (Ill.) Presbyn. Ch., 1996—99, moderator worship, music and arts com., 1998—99. Recipient Stewart Wesbury award for vol. achievement, Mid-Am. Chpt. ARC, 1992; William Chandler Bagley fellow, 1999, 2000. Mem.: Robert Morris Assocs. (mem. N.Am. pvt. banking steering com. 1992—98), Acad. Human Resource Devel., U. Ill. Alumni Assn. (life; dir./MBA pres., Constituent Leadership award 1993, Disting. Svc. award 1996), Union League Club Chgo. (chair internat. dinners program 1990—92, pub. affairs com., urban affairs sub-com, cultural affairs com. 1992—99, mem. women's initiative network group 1993—, chair mem. activities com., co-chair pub. affairs com. 1996—97, dir. 1996—99, chair com. com. 1997—99, pub. affairs sr. counselor, pers. and adminstrn. com. mem. 2001—04, mem. fin. com. 2002—, mem. admissions com. 2002—, Bd. Recognition award 1999). Avocations: hiking, swimming, singing, piano. Office: 1468 Parkside Dr Park Ridge IL 60068-1559

WILLIAMS, SANDY See WILLIAMS, ROBERT

WILLIAMS, SANKEY VAUGHAN, health services researcher, internist; b. San Antonio, Tex., Apr. 15, 1944; s. James Sankey and Helen (Long) W.; m. Constance Hess, June 27, 1972; children: Elizabeth Helen, Jennifer Lee. AB, Princeton U., 1966; MD, Harvard U., 1970. Diplomate Am. Bd. Internal Medicine. Intern Hosp. of U. Pa., 1970-71, jr. resident, 1971-72, chief med. resident, 1974-75; assoc. dir. clin. rsch. Ctr. for Study of Aging, U. Pa., 1982-86; assoc. dir. for med. affairs Leonard Davis Inst. for Health Econs., U. Pa., 1978-90; dir. clin. scholars program U. Pa., Phila., 1988-96; prof. health care systems Wharton Sch., U. Pa., Phila., 1989—; prof. medicine U. Pa., Phila., 1989—, chief div. gen. internal medicine, 1992—, Sol Katz prof. medicine, 1992—. Commr. Prospective Payment Assessment Commn., U.S. Congress, Washington, 1988-91; chairman health svcs. rsch. devel. grants study sect. Agy. for Health Care Policy and Rsch., 1991-94; counselor for med. affiars to the pres. U. Pa., 1990-92. Co-editor: The Physician's Practice, 1980; author 35 revs, ch. or editorials; contbr. 62 articles to various sci. jour., assoc. editor, annals of Internal Medicine, 2003-. Lt. comdr. USPHS, 1972-74. Recipient Career Devel. award Henry S. Kaiser Family Found., 1981-86. Mem. ACP (master, chmn. clin. privileges com. 1989-93, Soc. for Med. Decision Making (pres. 1985-86), Soc. for Gen. Internal Medicine (coun. 1979-84, editor Jour. Gen. Internal Medicine 1994-99, pres. 2000-01). Office: Hosp Univ of Pa Divsn Gen Internal Medicine 1220 Blockley Hall 423 Guardian Dr Philadelphia PA 19104-6021

WILLIAMS, SERENA, professional tennis player; b. Saginaw, Mich., Sept. 26, 1981; Prof. tennis player WTA Tour, 1995—. Named WTA Most Improved Player, 1999, Player of the Year, TENNIS Mag., 1999, Best Female Athlete in the World, Associated Press, 2002, WTA Tour Player of the Year, 2002, #1 most marketable female athlete, Sports Business Daily, 2003; recipient Espy award for Best Female Athlete, ESPN, 2003, Espy award for Best Female Tennis Player, 2003, 2004. Achievements include winner, 24 Career Singles Titles, 10 Career Doubles Titles, and 2 Mixed Doubles Titles, WTA Tour; Grand Slam Championships: US Open, 1999, 2002, Wimbledon, 2002, 2003, Roland Garros, 2002, Austalian Open, 2003; Doubles Titles (w/ Venus Williams) include Australian Open 2001, 2003, Wimbledon, 2000, 2000, Roland Garros, 1999, US Open, 1999, Mixed Doubles (w/ Max Mirnyi), Wimbledon, 1998; winner, doubles gold medal (w/ Venus Williams), Sydney Olympic games, 2000; won a "Serena Slam" by winning 4 Grand Slam tournaments in a row, 2002-2003; signed largest endorsement deal to date by a female athlete with Nike, 2003. Office: c/o USTA 70 W Red Oak Ln White Plains NY 10604-3602*

WILLIAMS, SIMON, diversified financial services company executive; Degree in Math., Exeter U., Eng.; MBA with distinction, INSEAD Bus. Sch., Fontainebleau, France. Mgmt. cons. Bain & Co.; various sr. mgmt. pos. GE Capital, Europe and the U.S.; in charge Citibank Asia Pacific consumer bus. Citigroup, Inc., 1998—2001, head Citibank L.Am. Consumer Bus., 2001—02, exec. v.p., Global e-Bus., 2002—03, exec. v.p. Internat., Retain Banking, mem. mgmt. com., 2003—. Mem.: Inst. Chartered Accts. in Eng. and Wales. Office: Citigroup Inc 399 Park Ave New York NY 10043

WILLIAMS, SPENCER MORTIMER, federal judge; b. Reading, Mass., Feb. 24, 1922; s. Theodore Ryder and Anabel (Hutchison) W.; m. Kathryn Bramlage, Aug. 20, 1943; children: Carol Marcia (Mrs. James B. Garvey), Peter, Spencer, Clark, Janice, Diane (Mrs. Sean Quinn). AB, UCLA, 1943; postgrad., Hastings Coll. Law, 1946; JD, U. Calif., Berkeley, 1948. Bar: Calif. 1949, U.S. Supreme Ct. 1952. Assoc. Beresford & Adams, San Jose, Calif., 1949, Rankin, O'Neal, Center, Luckhardt, Bonney, Marlais & Lund, San Jose, Evans, Jackson & Kennedy, Sacramento; county counsel Santa Clara County, 1955-67; adminstr. Calif. Health and Welfare Agy., Sacramento, 1967—70; judge U.S. Dist. Ct. (no. dist.) Calif., San Francisco, from 1971, now sr. judge. Chmn. San Jose Christmas Seals Drive, 1953, San Jose Muscular Dystrophy Drive, 1953, 54; team capt. fund raising drive San Jose YMCA, 1960; co-chmn. indsl. sect. fund raising drive Alexian Bros. Hosp., San Jose, 1964; team capt. fund raising drive San Jose Hosp.; mem. com. on youth and govt. YMCA, 1967-68; Candidate for Calif. Assembly, 1954, Calif. Atty. Gen., 1966, 70; Bd. dirs. San Jose Better Bus. Bur., 1955-66, Boys City Boys' Club, San Jose, 1965-67; pres. trustees Santa Clara County Law Library, 1955-66. Served with USNR, 1943-46; to lt. comdr. JAG Corps USNR, 1950-52, PTO. Named San Jose Young Man of Year, 1954 Mem. ABA, Calif. Bar Assn. (vice chmn. com. on publicly employed attys. 1962-63), Santa Clara County Bar Assn., Sacramento Bar Assn., Internat. Assn. Trial Judges (pres. 1995-96), Calif. Dist. Attys. Assn. (pres. 1963-64), Nat. Assn. County Civil Attys. (pres. 1963-64), 9th Cir. Dist. Judges Assn. (pres. 1981-83), Fed. Judges Assn. (pres. 1982-87), Kiwanis, Theta Delta Chi.

WILLIAMS, STEPHEN, anthropologist, educator; b. Mpls., Aug. 28, 1926; s. Clyde Garfield and Lois (Simmons) W.; m. Eunice Ford, Jan. 6, 1962; children: Stephen John, Timothy. BA, Yale U., 1949, PhD, 1954; MA, U. Mich., 1950, Harvard U., 1962. Asst. anthropology dept. Peabody Mus., Yale U., 1950-52; mem. faculty Harvard U., Cambridge, Mass., 1958—, prof. anthropology, 1967-72, Peabody prof., 1972-93, prof. emeritus, 1993—, chmn. dept., 1967-69; rsch. fellow Peabody Mus., Harvard U., Cambridge, 1954-57, mem. staff, 1954—, dir. mus., 1967-77. Curator N.Am. Archaeology, 1962-93, hon. curator 1993—; dir. rsch. of Peabody Mus.'s Lower Miss. Survey, 1958-93. Author books and articles on N.Am. archaeology, "Fantastic" archaeology and the history of Am. archaeology. Home: 1017 Foothills Trail Santa Fe NM 87505-4537 Office: PO Box 22354 Santa Fe NM 87502-2354 Office Phone: 505-983-8836. E-mail: williamsstephen@msn.com.

WILLIAMS, STEPHEN EDWARD, corporate lawyer; b. Clarkesburg, Va., Dec. 8, 1948; AB, Harvard U., 1970; JD, W.Va. U., 1974. Bar: W.Va. 1974. Lawyer Consolidated Gas, 1974-78, sr. lawyer, 1978-82, gen. lawyer, 1982-84, asst. gen. counsel, 1984-87; sec., gen. counsel Consolidated Natural Gas, 1987-92, assoc. gen. counsel, 1992, sr. v.p., gen. counsel, 1992—. Mem. Am. Corp. Counsel Assn., Pa. Bar Assn., Fed. Energy Bar Assn., W.Va. State Bar, Pitts. Symphony Soc. (bd. dirs., exec. com.). Office: Consolidated Natural Gas Co CNG Tower Fl 21 625 Liberty Ave Pittsburgh PA 15222-3110

WILLIAMS, STEPHEN FAIN, federal judge; b. N.Y.C., N.Y., Sept. 23, 1936; s. Charles Dickerman and Virginia (Fain) Williams; m. Faith Morrow, June 11, 1966; children: Susan, Geoffrey Fain, Sarah Margot Nu, Timothy Dwight, Nicholas Morrow. BA, Yale U., 1958; JD, Harvard U., 1961. Bar: N.Y. 1962, Colo. 1977. Assoc. Debevoise, Plimpton, Lyons & Gates, N.Y.C., 1962—66; asst. atty. US Dist. Ct. (so. dist.), NY, 1966—69; asst. prof. law U. Colo., Boulder, 1969—77, prof., 1977—86; judge US Ct. Appeals (D.C. cir.), Washington, 1986—2001, sr. judge, 2001—. Vis. prof. UCLA, 1975—76; vis. prof., fellow in law and econs. U. Chgo., 1979—80; vis. William L. Hutchison prof. energy law So. Meth. U., 1983—84; cons. Adminstrv. Conf. U.S., 1974—76, FTC, 1983—85; mem. Boulder Area Growth Study Commn., 1972—73. Contbr. articles to profl. jours. and mags. With U.S. Army, 1961—62. Mem.: ABA, Fed. Energy Bar Assn., Am. Law Inst. Office: US Courthouse 3rd & Constitution Ave NW Washington DC 20001 E-mail: SFWilliams@cadc.uscourts.gov.

WILLIAMS, STEPHEN LAWRENCE, writer, consultant; b. Birmingham, Ala., Sept. 27, 1944; s. Percy James and Gladys (Harris Moore) Williams. Student, Tuskegee U., 1962—66; BS in Sociology, SUNY, Buffalo, 1971, postgrad., 1973-75. Lectr. SUNY, Buffalo, 1975-77; real estate law clk. City of

Buffalo, 1976-77; investigator Erie County, Buffalo, 1977-78; CEO Starmaker Machinery, Erie County, N.Y., 1988-95. Author: Native Son - Natural Law, 1977—. With U.S. Army, 1967. Home and Office: 140 Niagara St Apt 416 Buffalo NY 14201 Personal E-mail: sw0052@earthlink.net.

WILLIAMS, STERLING L. computer software executive; Salesman RCA, 1969; various positions U. Computing Co.; v.p. Inforex, Inc.; pres. Mfg. Data Sys., Inc.; pres., CEO Sterling Softwared, Inc., 1981—; bd. chmn. Sterling Commerce, chmn., 1981—. Office: 300 Crescent Ct Ste 1200 Dallas TX 75201-1852

WILLIAMS, STEVEN, investment banker, venture capitalist; b. Balt. s. Damon Williams and LaTonya Williams-Shields. Cons. GE Lighting/Collinwood, Cleve., 1999—2000; mng. prin. Internat. Investments, Balt., 2001—; mng. ptnr. Select Capital Group, Balt., 2001—. Investment banker Wright Richardson & Co., Clev., 2003—. Author: International Investment: An Innovative Approach, Raising Capital While Getting Paid For It. Min. Greater Fellowship Assembly Ch. Mem.: Capital Markets Exch. (CEO 2003). Home: 4257 E 119 St Cleveland OH 44105 Office: Internat Investments 4257 E 119 St Cleveland OH 44105 Personal E-mail: swilliams@intlinvest.bizhosting.com. E-mail: swilliams@intlinvest.bizhosting.com.

WILLIAMS, STEVEN A., JR., federal agency administrator; b. Bellows Falls, Vt. m. Beth Williams; 2 children. B in Environ. Resource Mgmt., D in Forest Resources, Pa. State U.; MS, U. N.D. Grad. tchg. asst. U. N.D., 1979—81, Pa. State U., 1981—85; wildlife biologist Mass. Divsn. Fisheries and Wildlife, 1985—89, asst. dir. for wildlife, 1989—92; dep. exec. dir. Pa. Game Commn., 1992—95; sec. Kans. Dept. Wildlife and Parks, 1995—; dir. Fish and Wildlife Svc. U.S. Dept. Interior, Washington, 2002—. Mem.: Wildlife Soc., Internat. Assn. Fish and Wildlife Agys. Office: US Dept Interior Fish and Wildlife Svc 1849 C St NW Washington DC 20240

WILLIAMS, STEVEN MARK, lawyer; b. Guthrie, Okla., Mar. 25, 1954; s. Bob G. and Martha Jane Williams; m. Caron F. Henderson, Dec. 29, 1989 (div.); children: Casey, Blake, Steven Jr. BBA with hons., U. Tex., 1975; JD, Tex. Tech. U., 1979. Bar: Tex. Atty. El Paso Natural Gas Co., 1979-81, Transco Energy Co., Houston, 1981-83, Diamond Shamrock Corp., Dallas, 1983-85; assoc. Troy Douthitt, Wichita Falls, Tex., 1986-87; pvt. practice Wichita Falls, 1988—. Football coach, Boys Clubs Am., Wichita Falls, 1998. Voted Texhoma's Best Atty., Readers of Wichita Falls Times Record Newspaper, 98, 99, 2000, 02; Golden Gloves Boxer. Mem. ATLA, State Bar of Tex., Tex. Trial Lawyers Assn., Wichita County Bar Assn., Phi Delta Phi, Phi Beta Kappa. Office: 901 Lamar St Wichita Falls TX 76301-3414

WILLIAMS, STEVEN ROBERT, lawyer; b. Columbus, Ohio, Oct. 10, 1962; s. Robert O. and Marjorie S. Williams; m. Amy McDaniel, May 26, 1990. BA, Coll. William & Mary, 1985; JD, Cornell Law Sch., 1988. Spl. asst. U.S. atty. So. Dist. Ga., Savannah, 1989-90; capt. U.S. Army, Saudi Arabia, Iraq, 1989-92; from assoc. ptnr. McGuire, Woods, Battle, & Boothe, LLP, Richmond, Va., 1993—. Capt. U.S. Army, 1989-92, Desert Storm. Decorated Meritorious Svc. medals U.S. Army, 1991, 92, S.W. Asian Campaign medal with 2 stars U.S. Army, 1991, Saudi Arabian Def. medal Kingdom of Saudi Arabia, 1991, Kuwait Liberation medal, Kuwait, 1994. Home: 1702 Park Ave Richmond VA 23220-2911 E-mail: srwillia@mwbb.com.

WILLIAMS, STUART W. health facility administrator; b. June 11, 1943; BS, Allegheny Coll., 1954; MBA, U. Chgo., 1967. Adminstrv. resident Evanston (Ill.) Hosp., 1965-67; oper. svc. officer U.S. Naval Hosp., Quantico, Va., 1967-69; asst. dir. U. Mich. Hosp., 1969-74; adminstrv. dir. Children's Hosp., Columbus, Ohio, 1974-76, CEO, 1976—, Children's Hosp. Inc., Columbus, 1982—. Mem. Gov.'s Commn. on Ohio Health Care Costs. Mem. Am. Coll. Healthcare Execs., Am. Hosp. Assn., Assn. Am. Med. Colls., Nat. Assn. Childrens Hosps., Child Health Corp. Am., Ohio Hosp. Assn., Assn. Ohio Childrens Hosps.

WILLIAMS, SUE, artist; b. Chicago Heights, Ill., 1954; Student, Cooper Union, 1973; BFA, Calif. Inst. Arts, 1976. One-woman shows include Laughelton Gallery, N.Y.C., 1989, Amy Lipton Gallery, 1991, Stuart Regen Gallery, L.A., 1992, Gallery 210, St. Louis, 1992, 303 Gallery, 1992, 1994, 1996, 1998, San Francisco Art Inst., 1993, Vera Vitagioia, Naples, 1993, Galerie Rizzo, Paris, 1993, Galerie Walcheturm, Zurich, 1994, Modulo, Lisbon, Portugal, 1994, 1996, Galleria Il Capricorno, Venice, Italy, 1994, 1997, Jack Hanley Gallery, San Francisco, 1995, Galerie Metropol, Vienna, Austria, 1995, Regen Projects, L.A., 1996, Jean Bernier Gallery, Athens, Greece, 1996, 1998, Galerie Ghislaine Hussenot, Paris, 1996, Johnen & Schottle, Cologne, Germany, 1997, Ctr. d'Art Contemporain, Geneva, 1997, Sadie Coles, London, 1998, Neue Galerie un Landesmus. Joanneum, Graz, Austria, 1998, exhibited in group shows at Adam Baumgold Fine Art and Simon Capstick-Dale Fine Art, N.Y.C., 1996, Freidrich Petzel Gallery, 1996, Galerie Andreas Binder, 1996, Spiral Wacoal Art Ctr., Tokyo, 1996, Weatherspoon Art Gallery, Greensboro, N.C., 1997, Elizabeth Harris Gallery, 1997, Fine Arts and Lehmann Maupin, N.Y.C., 1997, Mus. d'Art Contemporani Barcelona, 1997, Whitney Mus. Am. Art, 1997, Emory U., 1998, The Aldrich Mus. Contemporary Art, Ridgefield, Conn., 1998, Pat Hearn and Mattehw Marks Gallery, N.Y.C., 1998, Landesgalerie Oberosterreich, Linz, Austria, 1998, Kunsthalle Krems, Austria, 1998, numerous others, Represented in permanent collections; performer The New Mus., N.Y.C., 1986, contbr. articles to profl. jours., reviewer in field. Office: c/o 303 Gallery 525 West 22d St New York NY 10011

WILLIAMS, SUE DARDEN, library director; b. Miami, Fla., Aug. 13, 1943; d. Archie Yelverton and Bobbie (Jones) Eagles; m. Richard Williams, Sept. 30, 1989. BA, Barton Coll., Wilson, N.C., 1965; M.L.S., U. Tex., Austin, 1970. Cert. librarian, N.C., Va. Instr. Chowan Coll., Murfreesboro, N.C., 1966-68; libr.'s asst. Albemarle Regional Libr., Winston, N.C., 1968-69; br. libr. Multnomah County Pub. Libr., Portland, Oreg., 1971-72; asst. dir. Stanly County Pub. Libr., Albemarle, N.C., 1973-76, dir., 1976-80; asst. dir. Norfolk (Va.) Pub. Libr., 1980-83, dir., 1983-94, Rockingham County Pub. Libr., Eden, NC, 1996—2004, Albemarle Regional Libr., Winton, NC, 2004—. Mem. ALA (coun. 1987-91, orientation com. 1990-92, chair 1991), Libr. Adminstrv. and Mgmt. Assn. (pub. rels. sec. 1985-87bd. dirs. 2004—), Southeastern Libr. Assn. (staff devel. com. 1986-88, Rothrock award com. 1984-86, sec. pub. libr. sect. 1982-84), Va. Libr. Assn. (SELA rep. 1993-96, coun. 1984, 88-91, 93-96, ad hoc conf. guidelines com. 1985-86, chmn. conf. program 1984, awards and recognition com. 1983, mem. SELA outstanding libr. program award com. 2002), Pub. Libr. Assn. (bd. dirs.-at-large Met. area 1986-89), Va. State Libr. (coop edn. com. 88-89), N.C. Libr. Assn. (scholarship com. 1999—, chair 2001—), LAMS. Home: 109 Chowan Rd Murfreesboro NC 27855 Office: Albermarle Regional Libr PO Box 68 303 W Tryon St Winton NC 27986 Office Phone: 252-358-7832. E-mail: swilliams_arl@yahoo.com.

WILLIAMS, SUNITA L. astronaut; b. Euclid, Ohio, Sept. 19, 1965; d. Deepak N. and Ursaline B. Pandya; m. Michael J. Williams. BS in Physical Sci., U.S. Naval Acad., 1987; MS in Engring. Mgmt., Fla. Inst. Tech., 1995. Commn. ensign USN, 1987, advanced through grades to lt. comdr., various assignments, 1987—89, overseas combat, 1989—92; officer in charge Hurrican Andrew Relief Ops. USS Sylvania, 1992—93; various assignments USN, 1993—95; served on USS Saipan, Norfolk, Va., 1995—98; astronaut NASA, Houston, 1998—. Decorated Commendation medal USN, Achievement medal USN & USMC, Humanitarian Svc. medal USN. Mem.: Soc. Flight Test Engrs., Soc. Exptl. Test Pilots, Am. Helicopter Assn. Office: Astronaut Office CB NASA Johnson Space Center Houston TX 77058

WILLIAMS, SUZANNE, state representative; b. Oklahoma City, Feb. 3, 1945; m. Ed Williams; 2 children. BA in Edn., Baylor U.; MA in Spl. Edn., U. Colo. Educator; state rep. dist. 41 Colo. Ho. of Reps., Denver, 1996—, mem. edn. and transp. and energy coms. Recipient Insider award, Aurora Sentinel, 1994, Gov.'s award for curriculum innovation, 1985, Gov.'s Action Plan award, 2000. Mem.: AAUW, Women in Govt., Aurora Sister Cities Internat., Delta Kappa Gamma. Democrat. Avocations: reading, music, exercising. Office: State Capitol # 271 200 E Colfax Ave Denver CO 80203

WILLIAMS, SYLVESTER EMANUAL, III, secondary school educator, consultant; b. Chgo., Feb. 4, 1937; s. Sylvester Emanual and Carita (Brown) W.; children: Sylvia, Sylvester, Sydnee, Steven. BS, No. Ill. U., 1958; MA, Chgo. State U., 1968; PhD, U. S.C., 1992. Cert. tchr., S.C., N.C., Ill. From asst. to supt. Washington D.C. Pub. Schs., 1968-69; tchr. Chgo. Pub. Schs., 1958-68; program officer Dept. Edn., Washington, 1971-86; prof. Lander U., Greenwood, S.C., 1986-89, U. S.C., Akin, 1990-91; tchr., coach Charlotte (N.C.) Mecklenburg Pub. Schs., 1992-93; edn. devel. cons. South Shore Cmty. Ch., Chgo.; rsch. assoc. Houston Ctr., Clemson U., 1999-2000; devel. cons. Rose Garden Cmty. Svcs., Chgo., 1999-2000; cons. DHHS, 1994-2000; demographic rschr., 1992—. Bd. dirs. John de Home Sch., McCormick, S.C. Mem. Phi Delta Kappa. Republican. Baptist. Avocation: motion picture production. Home: 205 Briggs Ave Greenwood SC 29649-1603 E-mail: drsewiii@greenwood.net.

WILLIAMS, TAMBOR, state representative; b. Washington, D.C., Mar. 28, 1941; m. Jim Eckersley; 2 children. BA in English and Philosophy, CUNY; MA in Counseling, Western State U.; JD, U. Colo. Atty.; state rep. dist. 50 Colo. Ho. of Reps., Denver, 1996—, mem. appropriations and edn. coms., and joint com. on legis. audit, chair bus. affairs and labor com. Mem.: Colo. Bar Assn., No. Colo. Latino C. of C., Evans C. of C., Greeley/Weld C. of C. Republican. Congregationalist. Avocations: travel, reading, hiking, cooking. Office: State Capitol # 223 200 E Colfax Ave Denver CO 80203

WILLIAMS, TED VAUGHNELL, physical education educator; b. Bronx, N.Y., Apr. 1, 1952; s. Joseph Alexander and Annie (Canady) W. BS, Springfield Coll., 1977. Cert. tchr., N.Y. Substitute tchr. Valhalla (N.Y.) High Sch., 1977; tchr. aide for handicapped children, tchr. spl. edn. Rye Lake Campus, Valhalla, 1978; supr. recreation activities Springfield (Mass.) Girl's Club Family Ctr., 1979; assoc. dir. boy's and men's phys. edn. dept. Trenton YMCA, 1979—; house supr. Cardinal McCloskey's Group Home, Tappan, N.Y., 1980-81; phys. edn. tchr. Our Lady of Refuge Sch., Bronx, N.Y., 1982-83; tchr. phys. edn. various Cath. elem. schs. Yonkers, N.Y., 1983—. With ops. dept. Hudson Valley Nat. Bank, 1990-92. Active Walk Am. for Healthier Babies, March of Dimes, 1990-93. Recipient Ed Steitz award Basketball Hall of Fame, 1975, Capitol award Nat. Leadership Coun., 1991; named to Wall of Tolerance, Civil Rights Meml. Ctr., Montgomery, Ala. Mem. ASCD, AAHPERD, Am. Assn. Leisure and Recreation, Hudson Valley Leisure Svcs. Assn. Democrat. Baptist. Home: 49 Bradford Ave White Plains NY 10603-2143 Office Phone: 914-965-2356.

WILLIAMS, TEMPLE WEATHERLY, JR., retired internist; b. Wichita Falls, Tex., Apr. 19, 1934; s. Temple Weatherly and Dorothy (Coleman) W.; married; children: Holly Clare, Temple Weatherly III; m. Joan Loos, Apr. 6, 1991. Student, Midwestern U., 1951-53; BS, So. Meth. U., 1955; MD, Baylor U., 1959. Intern, resident in internal medicine Duke U. Hosp., Durham, N.C., 1959-60, 62-63; fellow in infectious disease Baylor U., 1960-62; clin. assoc. infectious disease NIH, Bethesda, Md., 1963—65; mem. faculty Baylor Coll. Medicine, 1965—2004, prof. medicine and microbiology-immunology, 1974—2004, ret., 2004. Contbr. over 100 articles on infectious diseases to profl. jours., chpts. to books. Served with USPHS, 1963-65. Fellow ACP, Infectious Disease Soc. Am.; mem. AMA. Republican. Methodist. Office: 6565 Fannin St # Ms910 Houston TX 77030-2704

WILLIAMS, TERRIE MICHELLE, publicity agency executive; b. Mt. Vernon, N.Y., May 12, 1954; MA, BA cum laude, Brandeis U., 1975; MS, Columbia U., 1977. Exec. dir. World Inst. of Black Community, N.Y.C., 1982; dir. pub. rels. Essence Communications Inc., N.Y.C., 1982-86, v.p., dir., 1986-88; pres. The Terrie Williams Agy., N.Y.C., 1988—. Med. soc. worker N.Y. Hosp., N.Y.C., 1977-80; program adminstr. Black Filmmaker Found., N.Y.C., 1980-81; exec. dir. Black Owned Communications Alliance, N.Y.C., 1981-82. Author: The Personal Touch, 1995. Recipient Entrepeneur of the Yr. award Nat. Assn. Market Developers, 1990, Flo Kennedy Media award, 1990, Matrix award N.Y. Women in Communications, 1991. Mem. Women in Communications, NOW, Brandeis U. Alumni Assn. (bd. dirs.), N.Y. TV Acad. Arts and Scis., Pub. Rels. Soc. Am. (D. Parke Gibson award 1981). Office: The Terrie Williams Agy 1500 Broadway Ste 502 New York NY 10036-4015

WILLIAMS, THEODORE EARLE, retired industrial distribution company executive; b. Cleve., May 9, 1920; s. Stanley S. and Blanche (Albaum) W.; m. Rita Cohen, Aug. 28, 1952; children: Lezlie, Richard Atlas, Shelley, William Atlas, Wayne, Marsha, Patti Blake, Jeff Blake. Student, Wayne U., 1937-38; BS in Engring, postgrad. in bus. adminstrn, U. Mich., 1942. Pres. Wayne Products Co., Detroit, 1942-43, L.A., 1947-49; pres. Williams Metal Products Co., Inglewood, Calif., 1950-69; chmn. bd. Bell Industries, L.A., 1970-2000; ret., 2000. Instr. U. Mich., 1942 Patentee in field. Served to 1st lt. AUS, 1943-46. Recipient Humanitarian award City of L.A., 1977. Democrat. Home: 435 N Layton Way Los Angeles CA 90049-2022 *It seems to me that many of our current problems in this world originate from the drift away from concern for other people to the emphasis on self. We are reluctant to get involved, and as this spaceship gets smaller, we become more interdependent all the time. If we don't learn to live together, I'm afraid we may all perish together.*

WILLIAMS, THEODORE JOSEPH, engineering educator; b. Black Lick, Pa., Sept. 2, 1923; s. Theodore Finley and Mary Ellen (Shields) W.; m. Isabel Annette McAnulty, July 18, 1946; children: Theodore Joseph, Mary Margaret, Charles Augustus, Elizabeth Ann. BSCh.E., Pa. State U., 1949, MSCh.E., 1950, PhD, 1955; MS in Elec. Engring., Ohio State U., 1956. Research fellow Pa. State U., University Park, 1947-51; asst. prof. Air Force Inst. Tech., 1953-56; technologist Monsanto Co., 1956-57, sr. engring. supr., 1957-65; prof. engring. Purdue U., Lafayette, Ind., 1965-94, prof. emeritus, 1995—, dir. control and info. systems lab., 1965-66; dir. Purdue Lab. Applied Indsl. Control, 1966-94, dir. emeritus, 1995—; cons., 1964—. Vis. prof. Washington U., St. Louis, 1962-65. Author: Systems Engineering for the Process Industries, 1961, Automatic Control of Chemical and Petroleum Processes, 1961, Progress in Direct Digital Control, 1969, Interfaces with the Process Control Computer, 1971, Modeling and Control of Kraft Production Systems, 1975, Modelling, Estimation and Control of the Soaking Pit, 1983, The Use of Digital Computers in Process Control, 1983, Analysis and Design of Hierarchical Control Systems - With Special Reference to Steel Plant Operations, 1985, A Reference Model for Computer Integrated Manufacturing (CIM) - A Description from the Viewpoint of Industrial Automation, 1989, The Purdue Enterprise Reference Architecture, 1992; editor: Computer Applications in Shipping and Shipbuilding, 6 vols., 1973-79, Proceedings Advanced Control Confs., 19 vols., 1974-93, Architectures for Enterprise Integration, 1996. Served to 1st lt. USAAF, 1942-45; to capt. USAF, 1951-56. Decorated Air medal with 2 oak leaf clusters. Fellow AAAS, AIChE, Instrument Soc. Am. (hon. mem., pres. 1968-69, Albert F. Sperry gold medal 1990, Lifetime Achievement award 1995), Am. Inst. Chemists, Inst. Measurement and Control (London, Sr. Harold Hartley silver medal 1975), Indsl. Computing Soc.; mem. IEEE (sr.), Internat. Fedn. for Info. Processing (Silver Core award 1978), Soc. for Computer Simulation (hon.), Am. Chem. Soc., Am. Automatic Control Coun. (pres. 1965-67), Am. Fedn. Info. Processing Socs. (pres. 1976-78), Sigma Xi, Tau Beta Pi, Phi Kappa Phi, Phi Lambda Upsilon. Home: 208 Chippewa St West Lafayette IN 47906-2123 Office: Purdue U Potter Rsch Ctr Inst Interdisciplinary Engring Studies West Lafayette IN 47907-1293 Office Phone: 765-494-7434. Business E-Mail: tjwil@ecn.purdue.edu.

WILLIAMS, THOMAS ARTHUR, biomedical computing consultant, psychiatrist; b. Racine, Wis., May 11, 1936; s. Robert Klinkert and Marion Anne (Wisneski) Williams; m. Christine Frances Fannon, July 3, 1970; children: Jennifer, Thomas, Hailey, Renate, Alexa. BA, Harvard Coll., 1958; MD, Columbia U., 1963; postgrad., NIH, 1967-68. Diplomate Nat. Bd. Med. Examiners, Am. Bd. Psychiatry and Neurology. Intern in surgery Columbia Presbyn. Med. Ctr., N.Y.C., 1963-64; resident in psychiatry Columbia Presbyterian Med. Ctr., N.Y. State Psychiat. Inst., N.Y.C., 1964-67; chief depression sect. NIMH, Bethesda, Rockville, Md., 1967-71; asst. prof. U. Pitts., 1969-70; assoc. prof. U. Utah, Salt Lake City, 1971-77; prof., chmn. dept. psychiatry Eastern Va. Med. Sch., Norfolk, Va., 1977-78; clin. dir. Sheppard & Enoch Pratt Hosp., Towson, Md., 1978-80; prof. U. South Fla., Tampa, 1980-83; practitioner psychiat. medicine, med. dir. St. Augustine (Fla.) Psychiat. Ctr., 1983-89, 89-90; prin. Williams & Assocs., Palm Harbor, Fla., 1990—. Treas., pres. Klinkert Realty Co., Inc., Racine, Wis., 1960—85. Chief editor: Psychobiology of Depression, 1972, Mental Health in the 21st Century, 1979; contbr. numerous articles to profl. jours. and chpts. to books. Mem. Gov.'s Adv. Com. on Mental Health, Salt Lake City, 1971-77, Gov.'s Adv. Com. on Penal Code, Richmond, Va., 1978, Dist. Mental Health Bd., Tampa, 1980-83; mem. U.S. Govt. Mission on Psychiatry to USSR, 1974; sponsor, coach Forest Hills Little League Baseball, Tampa, 1980-83. Sr. surgeon USPHS, 1958-67. Recipient Predoctoral fellowship NIMH, 1960-61, Alumni Rsch. award N.Y. State Psychiat. Inst., 1964, Rush Bronze Medal award Am. Psychiat. Assn., 1973, Rsch. grants VA, 1971-77. Mem. AMA, Fla. Med. Assn., Hillsborough County Med. Assn., Columbia U. Alumni Club (dir. 1995—), Harvard Club of the West Coast of Fla. Avocations: computers, classical music, opera, basketball. Home: 3844 Muirfield Ct Palm Harbor FL 34685 Office Phone: 727-787-1913. Personal E-mail: tawmd@earthlink.net.

WILLIAMS, THOMAS EUGENE, pediatric hematologist-oncologist, pharmaceutical executive; b. Texarkana, Ark., May 13, 1936; s. Thomas Earle and Frankie Jo (Garner) W.; m. Peggy Jane O'Neill, May 31, 1958; children: Thomas Eugene, Elizabeth Anne, James David. BA, Yale U., 1958; MD, U. Tex. Southwestern Med. Sch., 1962. Diplomate Am. Bd. Pediat., Am. Bd. Pediat. Hematology and Oncology. Rotating intern Hermann Hosp., Houston, 1962-63; pediat. resident Children's Med. Ctr., Dallas, 1963-65; fellow pediat. hematology U. Va. Sch. Medicine, Charlottesville, 1967-68; rsch. assoc. Cancer Rsch. Lab., U. Va., Charlottesville, 1968-69; asst. prof. pediat. and pathology U. Tex. Health Sci. Ctr., San Antonio, 1969-72, assoc. prof. pediat., asst. prof. pathology, 1972-73, assoc. prof. pediat. and pathology, 1973-79, assoc. prof. pediat., 1985-94. Med. dir. Santa Rosa Children's Hosp. Cancer Rsch. and Treatment Ctr., 1974—79, South Tex. Comprehensive Hemophilia Ctr., 1977—79, dir. pediat. bone marrow transplantation program, 1986—93; sr. clin. rsch. scientist Burroughs Wellcome Co., 1979—85; dir. new drug devel. Orphan Med., Inc., 1994—96; dir. med. affairs Ilex Oncology Svcs., Inc., 1997—98, ILEX Oncology Products, Inc., 1998—2002; clin. assoc. prof. pediat. U. N.C. Sch. Medicine, 1979—85; clin. fellow bone marrow transplantation program Johns Hopkins U. Sch. Medicine, Balt., 1985; sr. dir. Divsn. Oncology ICON Clin. Rsch., Inc., 2002—. Contbr. articles to profl. jours. Exec. dir. Episcopal Med. Missions Found., 1997—. Lt. cmmdr. USNR, 1965—67. Recipient travel award Am. Soc. Pharmacology and Exptl. Therapeutics, 1968; Am. Cancer Soc. advanced clin. fellow, 1968-69, 70-72. Mem. Am. Soc. Clin. Oncology, Am. Soc. Hematology, Am. Assn. for Cancer Rsch. Episcopalian. Office: 11303 Vance Jackson G6 San Antonio TX 78230 Office Phone: 215-616-3250. Business E-Mail: williamst@iconus.com.

WILLIAMS, THOMAS FFRANCON, chemist, educator; b. Colwyn Bay, Wales, Jan. 30, 1928; came to U.S., 1961; s. David and Margaret (Williams) W.; m. Astra Silvia Birins, Jan. 31, 1959; children: Ifor Rainis, Gwyn David. BSc, U. Coll., London, 1949; PhD, U. London, 1960. Sci. officer U.K. Atomic Energy Authority, Harwell, Eng., 1949-55, sr. sci. officer, 1955-61, prin. sci. officer, 1961; rsch. scientist Ill. Inst. Tech. Research Inst., Chgo., 1961; asst. prof. chemistry U. Tenn., Knoxville, 1961-63, assoc. prof., 1963-67, prof., 1967-74, Alumni Distinguished Service prof., 1974—. Tchg. and rsch. assoc. Northwestern U., Evanston, Ill., 1957-58; NSF vis. scientist Kyoto (Japan) U., 1965-66; coord. U.S.-Japan Sci. Sem., Hakone, Japan, 1969; chmn. Gordon Rsch. Conf. on Radiation Chemistry, New Hampton, N.H., 1971, Gordon Rsch. Conf. Radical Ions, Wolfeboro, N.H., 1984; John Simon Guggenheim Meml. Found. fellow, Swedish Rsch. Coun. Lab., Studsvik, Nykoping, 1972-73; vis. scientist Royal Inst. Tech., Stockholm, Sweden, 1972-73; chmn. 10th Southeastern Magnetic Resonance Conf., 1978; mem. chemistry div. rev. com. Argonne (Ill.) Nat. Lab., 1988, 91, 95; cons. Pacific N.W. Nat. Lab., 1996-97. Contbg. author: Fundamental Processes in Radiation Chemistry, 1968, Radiation Chemistry of Macromolecules, 1972; mem. editl. bd. Radiation Rsch., 1993-2000, assoc. editor, 1993-97, cons. editor, 1997-2000; contbr. numerous articles on chem. effects of high energy radiation to profl. jours. AEC, ERDA, Dept. Energy grantee, 1962-99. Mem. Am. Chem. Soc. (program chmn. sect. 1968-69, exec. com. 1986-88), Brit. Chem. Soc., Radiation Rsch. Soc., Phi Beta Kappa (hon.), Sigma Xi (pres. U. Tenn. chpt. 1993-94). Home: 3117 Montlake Dr Knoxville TN 37920-2836 Office: U Tenn Dept Of Chemistry Knoxville TN 37996-1600 Office Phone: 865-974-3468. Business E-Mail: ffwilliams@utk.edu.

WILLIAMS, THOMAS FRANKLIN, physician, educator; b. Belmont, N.C., Nov. 26, 1921; s. T. F. and Mary L. (Deaton) Williams; m. Catharine Carter Catlett, Dec. 15, 1951; children: Mary Wright, Thomas Nelson. BS, U. N.C., 1942; MA, Columbia U., 1943; MD, Harvard U., 1950; DSc (hon.), Med. Coll. Ohio, 1987, U. N.C., 1992; DMS, Thomas Jefferson U., 2003. Intern Johns Hopkins, Balt., 1950—51, asst. resident physician, 1951—53; resident physician Boston VA Hosp., 1953—54; research fellow U. N.C., Chapel Hill, 1954—56, instr. dept. medicine and preventive medicine, 1956—57, asst. prof., 1957—61, assoc. prof., 1961—68, prof., 1968; attending physician Strong Meml. Hosp., Rochester, NY, 1968—; cons. physician Genesee Hosp., Rochester, NY, 1973—; prof. medicine, preventive medicine and cmty. health U. Rochester, 1968—92, prof. radiation biology and biophysics, 1968—91, on leave, 1983—91, prof. emeritus, 1992—; clin. prof. medicine U. Va., 1983—89; lectr. medicine Johns Hopkins U., 1983—89; clin. prof. depts. family medicine and medicine Georgetown U., 1983—89; dir. Nat. Inst. on Aging NIH, 1983—91; asst. surgeon gen. USPHS, 1983—91, ret., 1991; attending physician Monroe Cmty. Hosp., Rochester, 1991—, vice-chmn. cmty. coalition for long term care, 1991—; disting. physician VA Med. Ctr., Canandigua, NY, 1995—98. Adv. bd. U. Rochester Sch. Medicine and Dentistry, 1968—83; med. dir. Monroe Cmty. Hosp., Rochester, 1968—83; mem. rev. coms. Nat. Ctr. for Health Svcs. Rsch.; adv. bd. St. Ann's Home; mem. gov. bd. NRC, 1981—83; sci. dir. Am. Fedn. Aging Rsch., 1992—; cons. in field. Contbr. articles to profl. publs. With USNR, 1943—46. Recipient Civic award for health care, Rochester N.Y. C. of C., 1998; fellow, USPHS, 1966—67; scholar Markle scholar, 1957—61. Fellow: ACP, APHA; mem.: NAS (coun. 1980—83, governing bd. 1981—83, Gustav O. Lienhard award Inst. Medicine 1969), AAAS, Am. Clin. Climatol. Assn., N.C. Coun. for Human Rels. (chmn. 1963—66), Rochester Regional Diabetes Assn. (pres. 1977—79), Am. Gerontol. Soc., Am. Geriatrics Soc., Soc. Exptl. Biology and Medicine, Am. Fedn. Clin. Rsch., Am. Diabetes Assn. (bd. dirs. 1974—80), Monroe County Med. Soc., N.Y. State Med. Soc., Assn. Am. Physicians, Inst. Medicine. Episcopalian. Home: 287 Dartmouth St Rochester NY 14607-3202 Office: Monroe Community Hosp Office Med Dir Rochester NY 14620

WILLIAMS, THOMAS RAYMOND, lawyer; b. Meridian, Miss., Aug. 26, 1940; BS, U. Ala., 1962, LLB, 1964. Bar: Ala. 1964, Tex. 1979, U.S. Supreme Ct. 1980, D.C. 1983. Ptnr. McDermott, Will & Emery, Washington. Mem. D.C. Bar Assn., Ala. State Bar Assn., State Bar Tex. Office: McDermott Will & Emery 600 13th St NW Fl 12 Washington DC 20005-3096 E-mail: rwilliams@mwe.com.

WILLIAMS, THOMAS RHYS, anthropologist, educator; b. Martins Ferry, Ohio, June 13, 1928; m. Margaret Martin, July 12, 1952; children: Rhys M., Ian T., Tom R. BA, Miami U., Oxford, Ohio, 1951; MA, U. Ariz., 1956; PhD, Syracuse U., 1956. Asst. prof., asso. prof. anthropology Calif. State U., Sacramento, 1956-65; vis. asso. prof. anthropology U. Calif. Berkeley, 1962; vis. prof. anthropology Stanford U., 1976; prof. anthropology Ohio State U., Columbus, 1965-78, chmn. dept, 1967-71, mem. grad. council, 1969-72, mem. univ. athletic council, 1968-74, chmn. univ. athletic council, 1973-74, exec. com. Coll. Social and Behavior Scis., 1967-71; dean Grad. Sch. George Mason U., Fairfax, Va., 1978-81, prof. anthropology, 1981—, dir. Ctr. for Rsch. and Advanced Studies, 1978-81, fed. liaison officer, 1978-81, chmn. faculty adv. bd. grad. degree program in conflict resolution, 1980-86. Author: The Dusun: A North Borneo Society, 1965, Field Methods in the Study of Culture, 1967, A Borneo Childhood: Enculturation in Dusun Society, 1969, Introduction to Socialization: Human Culture Transmitted, 1972, Socialization, 1983, Cultural

Anthropology, 1990; editor, contbg. author: Psychological Anthropology, 1975, Socialization and Communication in Primary Groups, 1975; contbr. articles to profl. jours. Mem. United Democrats for Humphrey, 1968, Citizens for Humphrey, 1968. Served with USN, 1946-48. Research grantee NSF, 1958, 62, Am. Council Learned Socs.-Social Sci. Research Council, 1959, 63; Ford Found. S.E. Asia, 1974, 76; recipient Disting. Faculty award Calif. State U., Sacramento, 1961, George Mason U., 1983; Disting. Teaching awards Ohio State U., 1968, 76 Fellow Am. Anthrop. Assn., Royal Anthrop. Inst. Gt. Britain; assoc. mem. Current Anthropology; mem. AAAS, Sigma Xi. Office: George Mason U Robinson Hall B-315 MS 3G5 4400 University Dr Fairfax VA 22030-4444

WILLIAMS, THOMAS W. electrical engineer; b. Rochester, N.Y., Aug. 3, 1943; s. Thomas Alfred and Mary Anne (Boryszewski) W.; m. Suzane Louise Sawyer, Dec. 26, 1964 (div. 1982); children: Megan Ren+245, David Thomas; m. Candace Merrill, Mar. 16, 1985. BSEE, Clarkson U., 1965; MA in Maths., Binghamton U., 1968; PhD in Elec. Engring., Colo. State U., 1971. From staff to sys. designer IBM, Endicott, N.Y., 1968-73, mem. ISI design rules and control group Boulder, Colo., 1973-77, from sr. engr., mgr. to sr. tech. staff, mgr. VLSI Design, 1977-1998; chief scientist Test Technology, Synopsys, Inc. Guest prof., Robert Bosch Fellow, Universitaet Hannover, Hannover, Germany, 1985, 1996-98; adj. prof., U. Colo., Boulder. Contbr. articles to profl. journs. Grantee NSF. Fellow IEEE (W. Wallace McDowell award 1989) mem. Board of Convenors 1987-93, 1995-; mem. Phi Kappa Phi, Eta Kappa Nu.

WILLIAMS, TONDA, entrepreneur, consultant; b. N.Y.C., Nov. 21, 1949; d. William and Juanita (Rainey) W.; 1 child, Tywana. Student, Collegiate Inst., N.Y.C., 1975-78, C.W. Post Coll., 1981-83; BA in Bus. Mgmt., Am. Nat. U., Phoenix, 1983; grad., L.I. Bus. Inst., 1996. Notary pub. N.Y. Asst. controller Acad. Ednl. Devel., N.Y.C., 1971-81; mgr. office Chapman-Apex Constrn. Co., Bayshore, N.Y., 1982-84; specialist computer RGM Liquid Waste Removal, Deerpark, N.Y., 1985-87; contr. LaMar Lighting Co., Freeport, N.Y., 1987—; owner, pres. Omni-Star, Bklyn., 1981—; pres. Omni-Data Tech., Bayshore, N.Y., 1996—. Author: Tonda's Songs in Poetry, 1978, The Magic of Life, 1991; co-author: Computer Management of Liquid Waste Industry, 1986. Recipient Golden Poet award World of Poetry, 1992. Mem. Am. Mus. Natural History, Am. Soc. Notary Pubs. Avocations: bowling, chess, singing. Home: 74 Cedar Dr Bay Shore NY 11706-2419 Fax: 631-968-1016. E-mail: tonda@omnidatatech.com.

WILLIAMS, TREAT (RICHARD TREAT WILLIAMS), actor; b. Stamford, Conn., Dec. 1, 1951; s. Richard Norman and Marian (Andrew) W. BA, Franklin and Marshall Coll., 1973. Appeared in Broadway plays Over There, Grease; (repertory plays) Servant of Two Masters, Ohio, Claptrap, Cambridge, Mass., 1985, Pirates of Penzance at N.Y. Shakespeare Festival, Glass Menagerie, Long Wharf, New Haven, 1986, Bobby Gould in Hell, 1989; (films) Deadly Hero, Eagle Has Landed, Hair, 1941, 1978, Why Would I Lie, 1979, Pursuit, 1980, Prince of the City, 1980, Once Upon a Time in America, 1982, Flashpoint, 1984, Men's Club, 1985, Sweet Lies 1986, Smooth Talk, 1986, The Heart of Dixie, 1989, Russicum, 1989, Where the Rivers Run North, 1994, Parallel Lives, 1994, Handgun, 1994, Things to do When You're Dead, 1995, The Phantom, 1996, Mullholland Falls, 1996, The Devil's Own, 1997, Deep Rising, 1997, The Deep End of the Ocean, 1999, Skeletons in the Closet, 2000, Critical Mass, 2000, Crash Point Zero, 2000, Venemous, 2001, The Circle, 2001, Gale Force, 2002; TV movies Jack Dempsey Story, 1982, Streetcar Named Desire, 1983, Some Men Need Help, 1983, Hoover, Sweet Lies, 1986, Things To Do in Denver When You're Dead, 1995, In the Shadow of Evil, 1995, The Late Shift, 1996, Escape Human Cargo, 1998, Substitute 2: School's Out, 1998, 36 Hours to Die, 1999, The Substitute 3: Winner Takes All, 1999, Journey to the Center of the Earth, 1999, Guilty Hearts, 2002; TV appearances Faerie Tale Theatre, 1984, Men's Club, 1985, Third Degree Burn, 1989, Max and Helen, 1990, Drug Wars: The Enrico Camerena Story, 1990, Bonds of Love, 1993, Eddie Dodd, 1992; (TV series) Good Advice, 1993-94. Mem. AFTRA, SAG, Actors Equity Assn. Episcopalian.

WILLIAMS, TYWANDA MONCEIL, social services administrator; b. Livingston, Tex., May 30, 1964; d. J.W. and Elrine Williams; 1 child, Terrance. AAS, BS, Wayland Bapt. U., 1996; MS, Tex. A&M U., 1998. Correctional officer Tex. Dept. Criminal Justice, Huntsville, 1985—90; detention officer Bexar County Sheriff's Dept., San Antonio, 1990—92; Tex. peace officer San Antonio Ind. Sch. Dist., 1992—99, drug and violence prevention coord., 2002—; prison psychologist Tex. Dept. Criminal Justice, Gatesville, 1999—2002. Mid. sch. coord., life skillw trainer Safe and Drug Free Schs., San Antonio, 2002—. Author: Through My Storms, 2004. Cmty. mem. Youth Alliance of San Antonio, 2002—; foster parent Bapt. Family Svcs., San Antonio, 2004. Named Outstanding Peace Officer, City of San Antonio Eastside, 1995. Mem.: Women in Action. Baptist. Avocation: church singing. Office: Poe Mid Sch 814 Aransas San Antonio TX 78210 E-mail: dalisa2@hotmail.com.

WILLIAMS, UNA JOYCE, psychiatric social worker; b. Youngstown, Ohio, June 24, 1934; d. Samuel Wilfred and Frances Josephine (Woods) Ellis; children: Wendy Louise, Christopher Ellis, Sharon Elizabeth. *Una Williams is descendant of the Ellis family of great-grandparents Thomas and Mary Ellis from Staffordshire, England. Mary came to America with her children after the death and burial of Thomas in Staffordshire. Her grandson, Sam Ellis, was an engineer with Saturn Rockets and her great grandson, Sam Ellis, was a professional baseball player. She is also descended from pioneering families Scott and Woods, who migrated via wagon train into North Georgia from Virginia and the Carolinas in late 1700s and early 1800's. These families were farmers of Scotch-Irish lineage, and both have members who served in the Revolutionary and Civil Wars as well as WWI, WWII and Vietnam.* BA, U. Ala., 1957; MSW, Adelphi U., 1963. Diplomate in profl. counseling Internat. Acad. Behavioral Medicine, Counseling and Psychotherapy. Dir. Huntington Program Sr. Citizens; psychiat. social worker-supr. N.Y. State Dept. Mental Hygiene, Suffolk Psychiat. Hosp., Central Islip; info.-referral counselor Mental Health Assn. Nassau County, Hempstead, NY; therapist Madonna Heights Family Clinic, Dix Hills, NY; med. and psychiat. social worker Northport VA Med. Ctr., NY, psychiat. social worker acute psychiat. treatment svcs., med. social worker dialysis svcs. Cons. on programs for aging Luth. Social Svcs. mem. N.Y., 1959, sr. citizens programs, Bd. Edn. Port Jefferson, N.Y., 1963. Chmn. Huntington Twp. Com. Human Rels., 1970; sec. bd. trustess Unitarian Universalist Fellowship Huntington, 1984. Mem. NASW (diplomate in social work), Am. Assn. Family Counselors and Mediators,Germany Philatelic Soc. (pres. chpt. 30, 1990, Mem. of Yr. 1987). Avocations: painting, stamp collecting/philately, music (voice & piano), family genealogy. Home: 316 Lenox Rd Huntington Station NY 11746-2640 Office Phone: 631-261-4400 2349.

WILLIAMS, VANESSA, recording artist, actress; b. Millwood, N.Y., Mar. 18, 1963; d. Milton and Helen; m. Ramon Hervey II, 1988 (div. 1997); children: Melanie, Jillian, Devin; m. Rick Fox, 1999; 1 child. Recording artist, 1988—. Stage appearances include: (Broadway) Kiss of the Spider Woman, 1994-95; film appearances include Pick-up Artist, 1987, Under the Gun, 1989, Another You, 1991, Harley Davidson and the Marlboro Man, 1991, Eraser, 1996, Hoodlum, 1997, Soul Food, 1997, Dance with Me, 1999, Light It Up, 1999; (TV films) Full Exposure: The Sex Tapes Scandal, 1989, Perry Mason: The Case of the Silenced Singer, 1990, Stompin' at the Savoy, 1992, Jacksons: An American Dream, 1992, Bye Bye Birdie, 1995, Futuresport, 1998, Courage to Love, 2000 (prodr.), Don Quixote, 2000, Keep the Faith, Baby, 2002, A Diva's Christmas Carol, 2000, (TV mini series) Nothing Lasts Forever, 1995, The Odyssey, 1997; (TV guest appearance) The Fresh Prince of Bel-Air, 1990, Vanessa Williams and Friends: Christmas in N.Y., 1996, Star Trek: Deep Space Nine, 1996, The Odyssey, 1997; albums: The Right Stuff, 1988, The Comfort Zone, 1991, The Sweetest Days, 1994, Star Bright, 1996, Next, 1997, Alfie, the Best of Vanessa, 1998, Dance with Me, 1998; # 1 hit single Save the Best for Last; vocalist: (films) Adventures of Priscilla, Queen of the Desert, 1994, Pocahontas, 1995. Recipient 8 Grammy award nominations; named one of 50 Most Beautiful People, People Mag. Achievements include being the first Black to be named Miss America, 1983 (resigned title 1983). Office: Mercury Records care Dawn Bridges 825 8th Ave New York NY 10019-7416 also: Mercury Records 11150 Santa Monica Blvd Los Angeles CA 90025-3380 Address: William Morris Agy 151 El Camino Dr Beverly Hills CA 90212

WILLIAMS, VENUS, professional tennis player; b. Lynwood, Calif., June 17, 1980; d. Richard and Oracene Williams. Profl. debut Bank of West Classic, Oakland, Calif., 1994; owner V Starr Interiors; designer Venus Williams Collection Wilson's Leather Co. Mem. U.S. Fed Cup Team, 1995, 99, 2003, U.S. Olympic Tennis Team, Sydney, 2000, Athens, 04. Recipient ESPY award for outstanding women's tennis player, 2001, Espy award for Best Female Tennis Player, 2001, Espy award for Best Female Athlete, 2002; named Most Impressive Network Newcomer award, 1997, TENNIS Mag. Most Improved Player, WTA Tour, 1998; winner mixed doubles (with Gimelstob) Australian Open, 1998, Roland Garros, 1998, doubles (with Serena Williams) French Open, 1999, U.S. Open, 1999, Australian Open, 2001, 03, Wimbledon, 2002, singles and doubles gold medal winner, Sydney Olympics, 2000, singles U.S. Open, 2000, 01, Wimbledon, 2000, 2001; winner 28 Career Singles Titles and 9 Career Doubles Titles, WTA Tour. Mem.: WTA Tour Players' Coun. Jehovah'S Witness. Avocations: interior decorating, fashion design. Office: US Tennis Assn 70 W Red Oak Ln White Plains NY 10604-3602*

WILLIAMS, VERONICA MYRES, psychotherapist, social worker; b. Shreveport, La., May 11, 1947; d. McEura and Margie Virgina (Reagan) Myres; divorced; children: Nicole Leann, Jennifer Lyn, Erica Maria. BA, La. Tech. U., Ruston, 1969; MSW, U. Mich., Ann Arbor, 1977; PhD, So. Calif. U., 2001. Diplomate Am. Bd. Clin. Social Workers, Am. Psychotherapy Assn.; cert. social worker, Mich. Probation counselor Citizens Probation Authority, Flint, Mich., 1970-72; unit dir., therapist Svcs. to Overcome Drug Abuse Among Teenagers, Flint, 1972-74; psychiat. therapist Psycho-Therapeutic Treatment Clin., P.C., Flint, 1974-77; psychiat. social worker Hurley Med. Ctr., Flint, 1977-79; field instr. Sch. Social Work U. Mich., Ann Arbor, 1978-79, 86—; psychiat. social worker Inst. Mental Health, Flint, 1979-81, Psychotherapeutic Treatment Clinic, 1981-83; clin. social worker Flint Bd. Edn., 1979-83; pupil apprasial spl. edn. Caddo Parish Sch. Bd., Shreveport, La., 1983-85. Developer dropout prevention program Flint Bd. Edn., 1986-98; Beecher Sch. Dist., 1998—; psychiat. therapist Mott Children's Health Ctr., 1986-92, Oakland Psychol. Clinic, P.C., 1991-92; owner, dir. V. Williams, PhD, MSW, ACSW, BCD, PC, 1992—. Bd. dirs. Boys & Girls Club. Mem. NASW, ACSW, NEA, Mich. Edn. Assn. Democrat. Office: 225 E 5th St Ste 110 Flint MI 48502 Office Phone: 810-232-0018. E-mail: vwilliams000@ameritech.net.

WILLIAMS, VIVIAN LEWIE, retired counseling administrator; b. Columbia, SC, Jan. 23, 1923; d. Lemuel Arthur Sr. and Ophelia V. (McDaniel) Lewie; m. Charles Warren Williams, Apr. 4, 1947 (div. 1967); children: Pamela Ann Williams-Coote, Charles Warren Jr. (dec.). BA, Allen U., 1942; MA in Psychology, U. Mich., 1946, postgrad., 1946, 48; MS, U. So. Calif., 1971, postgrad., 1971-72. Cert. marriage and family therapist, Calif.; cert. Calif. C.C. counselor. Asst. prof. psychology Tenn. State Agrl. and Indsl. U., Nashville, 1946-47; asst. prof. edn. Winston-Salem (N.C.) State U., 1947-50; asst. prof. edn., dir. tchr. edn. Allen U., Columbia, SC, 1951-53; specialist reading, coord. lang. arts Charlotte (N.C.) Mecklenburg Schs., 1963-67, cons. comprehensive sch. improvement project, 1967-69; asst. prof. edn., psychology Johnson C. Smith U., Charlotte, 1967-69; counselor, team leader Centennial, U. So. Calif. Tchr. Corps, L.A., 1970-73; counselor Compton (Calif.) C.C., 1973—2003, adv. fgn. student, 1975-85; ret., 2003. Co-developer Hyde Park Estates and The Moors, Charlotte, N.C., 1960-63. Pres. bd. dirs. Charlotte Day Nursery, 1956-59; bd. dirs. Taylor St. USO, Columbia, S.C., 1951-53; sec. southwest region Nat. Alliance Family Life, 1973-74; sec. bd. dirs. NCCJ, Charlotte, 1959-62. Recipient Faculty Audit Program award Ford/Carnegie Found., Harvard U., Cambridge, Mass., 1968, Pub. Svc. Achievement award WSOC Broadcasting Co.; fellow U. Mich., 1946. Mem. NAACP (life, Golden Heritage mem. 1992), AAUW (life), NEA (life), Am. Fedn. Tchrs., Faculty Assn. Calif. C.C., Nat. Acad. Counselors and Family Therapists (life, clin. mem., pres. S.W. region 1989), C.C. Counselors Assn., The Links, Inc. (Harbor area chpt. historian 1985-87, chaplain 1990-94, 96-98), Jack and Jill Am. (charter mem., organizer Charlotte chpt., pres. 1954-56), Women on Target, Calif. Tchrs. Assn., Delta Sigma Theta, Alpha Gamma Sigma (Golden Apple award 1981). Democrat. Methodist. Avocations: sewing, crafts, photography. Home: 6621 Caro St Paramount CA 90723-4755

WILLIAMS, VIVIAN (VINNIE) MARIE, publishing executive, editor, writer; b. Charleston, S.C., July 16, 1920; d. Joseph Harry Ahlsweh and Vivian Estelle Francis; m. Roy Raymond Williams, Mar. 15, 1945 (dec. Dec. 1978); 1 child, Marie DeWitt. BS in Social Work/Sociology, Fla. State Coll. for Women, 1941; LLD, Fla. State U., 1961. Social worker State of Fla., Fla., 1941—44; reporter Sarasota (Fla.) Herald-Tribune, 1944—45; instr. Fla. State Coll. Women, Tallahassee, 1945—46; reporter McDuffie Progress, Thomson, Ga., 1964—71; freelance writer Atlanta Jour. Constn., 1964—71, Augusta (Ga.) Chronicle, 1971—81; owner, pub., editor The Oconee Enterprise, Watkinsville, Ga., 1986—2003. Co-organizer Wrightsboro (Ga.) Quaker Cmty. Found., Ga., 1968—; organizer, individual/sole sponsor Oconee Firefighters/1st Responders; coord. Watkinsville (Ga.) Christmas Parade, 1997—2003, Watkinsville Annual Awards Dinner, 1998—2003. Author: (novels) The Fruit Tramp, 1957 (Best Ga. award, 1957), Walk Egypt, 1960 (Best Ga. award), I Resign You, Stallion, 1965, Greenbones, 1966 (Best Ga. award, 1968). Vol. firefighters Oconee County. Recipient hon. life mem., Bartram Trail Horse Club, 1977. Mem.: Oconee County C. of C. (vol., com. mem., Vol. of the Yr. 2001), Ga. Press Assn. Democrat. Presbyterian/Methodist. Avocation: gardening. Home: 60 Dooley St Watkinsville GA 30677 Address: Box 501 Watkinsville GA 30677 Office: The Oconee Enterprise Box 535 Watkinsville GA 30677 Office Phone: 706-769-5175.

WILLIAMS, W. VAIL, psychologist; b. Denver, Apr. 13, 1940; s. Warren J. and Edna M. (Follen) W.; m. Sandra M. Eisenrich (div. 1972); 1 child, Jason; m. Linda Lou Fain, Dec. 27, 1975; children: Ken, Dan, Davis, Jeremiah. BS, Bradley U., 1963, MA, 1964; PhD, U. Okla., 1968. Lic. psychologist, S.D., Colo., Calif. Owner Social Systems Devel., 1970-78; sr. psychologist Ft. Logan Mental Health Ctr., Denver, 1968-74; sr. rsch. assoc. Mental Rsch. Inst., Palo Alto, Calif., 1974-78; assoc. prof. Med. Sch. U. S. D., Sioux Falls, 1978—; chmn. curriculum and evaluation com. Sch. Medicine U. S.D., Sioux Falls, 1989-92, mem. exec. com. dept. psychiatry Sch. Medicine, 1999—. Bd. dirs. Univ. Physicians, U. S.D. Sch. Medicine, 1997—; cons. Sioux Valley Behavioral Health, Sioux Falls, 1989-94, 99—, Woodfield Home, LSS, 1998—; clin. dir. Psychiatry Assocs., 1989—. Contbr. to books and articles to profl. jours. Bd. dirs. S.D. Jr. Football Assn., Sioux Falls, 1988-92, Citizens Against Rape and Violence, Sioux Falls, 1988-89, Post 15 Baseball Program, 1995-98. Fellow Am. Orthopsychiat. Assn.; mem. APA, AAASS, S.D. Psychol. Assn. (pres. Div. 1 1993-94), Woodlake Athletic Club, El Raid Shrine. Avocation: computers. Office: Psychiatry Assoc 1000 E 21st St Ste 4000 Sioux Falls SD 57105-1015 Home: 3700 S Westport Ave Sioux Falls SD 57106-6344 E-mail: wwilliam@usd.edu.

WILLIAMS, WALKER RICHARD, JR., social services administrator; b. Dayton, Ohio, July 11, 1928; s. Walker Richard Sr. and Addie Mary (Smith) W.; m. Eddora L. Saunders, Aug. 6, 1949 (dec. Sept. 1966); 1 child, Yvette R.; m. Emma Jean Griffin, Sept. 4, 1971; children: Timotny E., Walker R. III. Student, U. Dayton, 1946-48. Commd. 2d lt. U.S. Army, 1952; advanced through grades to capt. USAF, Wright Patterson AFB, Ohio, 1963, supply cataloger, supr., 1963, employee rels. specialist, pers. mgmt. specialist, 1966-71; EEO investigator and grievance examiner, chief EEO and affirmative action programs Army and Air N.G., Wright Patterson AFB, Ohio, 1971-88; retired USAR, 1988; program dir. Youth Svc. U.S.A.-Dayton, 1988-89; pvt. contractor Dayton, 1989—. Mem. Adjutant Gen. Ohio Minority Recruiting Adv. Com., 1988—; bd. dirs. Dayton Opportunities Industrialization Ctr., 1976—, Wright Patterson Domestic Action Programs, Inc., 1984—; pres. Jefferson Twp. Bd. Edn., 1980—; mem. Nat. Black Caucus of Black Sch. Bd. Mems., 1980—, Nat. Black Caucus Local Elected Officials, Gov.'s Com. to Preserve Statue of Liberty, 1987, Citywide Vocat. Ednl. Com., 1986—, adv. com. Dayton Bd. Edn., 1980—, Miami Valley Mil. Affairs Assn., Black Elected Democrats of Ohio. Recipient Air Force Civilian Svc. award, Dayton C. of C., Internat. Personnel Mgmt. Assn. Employee of the Yr., Blacks in Govt. Pres.'s award, Federally Employed Women's Supr. of the Yr. runner up, Hispanic Heritage Wk. Spl. award, NAACP Humanitarian award, Community Svc. award, Dayton Bd. Edn., James W. Cisco award, Vocat. Ednl. award Wilberforce U., Urban League Humanitarian award, Svc. to Youth award Girl Scouts U.S., Spl. award United Negro Coll. Fund, Beautillion Militaire Legacy award, Jack & Jill, 7 Air Force Logistics Command Significant Achievement awards, AG of Ohio award, Ohio State U. award, Black Studies Group award, Russell Lyle award Wright Patterson AFB Quarter Century Club, Student Intervention Program Radcliff Sch., others; a day named in his honor, Dayton, 1987, 88, Svc. award Jefferson Township Bd. Edn. Mem. Miami Valley Pers. Assn., Internat. Pers. Mgmt. Assn., Retired Officers Assn., Air Force Assn., NAACP, Urban League, Blacks in Govt. (Medallion award), Dayton Intergovt. EEO Coun. (chmn., historian 1967—), Miami Valley Mil. Affairs Assn., Wright Patterson Quarter Century Club (past pres.). Democrat. Avocations: reading, photography. Home: 5050 Fortman Dr Dayton OH 45418-2233

WILLIAMS, WALTER JOSEPH, lawyer; b. Detroit, Oct. 5, 1918; s. Joseph Louis and Emma Geraldine (Hewitt) W.; m. Maureen June Kay, Jan. 15, 1944; 1 child, John Bryan. Student, Bowling Green State U., 1935-36; BSBA, Ohio State U., 1940; JD, LL.B., U. Detroit, 1942. Bar: Mich. bar 1942. Title atty. Abstract & Title Guaranty Co., 1946-47; corp. atty. Ford Motor Co., 1947-51, Studebaker-Packard Corp., 1951-56; asst. sec., house counsel Am. Motors Corp., Am. Motors Sales Corp., Am. Motors Pan-Am. Corp., Evart Products Co., Ltd., 1956-65, corp. sec. house counsel, 1965-72; asst. corp. sec., dir. Am. Motors (Can.) Ltd.; dir. Evart Products Co., 1959-72; dir., corporate sec., house counsel Jeep Corp., Jeep Sales Corp., Jeep Internat. Corp., 1968-72; partner Gilman and Williams, Southfield, Mich., 1972-74; atty. Detroit Edison Co., 1974-75; asst. sec., sr. staff atty. Burroughs Corp. (and subsidiaries), 1975-84; pvt. practice, pres. Walter J. Williams P.C., Bloomfield Hills, Mich., 1984—. Charter commr. City of Dearborn Heights, Mich., 1960-63; dir. Detroit Met. Indsl. Devel. Corp., 1962-72, also asst. sec. Served to capt. U.S. Army, 1942-46. Mem. ABA, Detroit Bar Assn. (chmn. corp. gen. counsel com. 1965-68), Fed. Bar Assn., State Bar Mich., Ohio State U. Alumni Assn. (pres. Detroit 1961-63), U. Detroit Law Alumni, Delta Theta Phi. Clubs: Oakland Hills Country. Home and Office: 3644 Darcy Dr Bloomfield Hills MI 48301-2125

WILLIAMS, WAYNE LEROY, lawyer; b. Albany, Oreg., Feb. 21, 1945; s. Verne Delmer and Henrietta Jane (Zeller) W.; m. Kathleen Ann Sharar (div.); children: Brendan Wayne, Brooke Kathleen; m. Melanie Sue Stewart, Dec. 22, 1990; children: Sara Marie Stewart-Gerla, Blaire Starling Stewart-Gerla. BS in Journalism, U. Oreg., 1967, JD, 1970. Bar: Wash. 1970, U.S. Dist. Ct. (we. dist.) Wash. 1970, U.S. Dist. Ct. (ea. dist.) Wash. 1974, U.S. Ct. Appeals (9th cir.) 1972, U.S. Claims Ct. 1992, U.S. Supreme Ct. 1973. Asst. atty. gen. Wash. State Atty. Gen., Olympia, 1970-78; dir., counsel People's Orgn. for Washington Energy Resources, Olympia, 1978-80; pvt. practice Olympia, 1980-85; shareholder Rolland, O'Malley, Williams & Wyckoff, Olympia, 1986. Bar exminer Wash. State Bar, 1978. Coun. mem. City of Tumwater, Wash. Chmn. Parks and Recreation Bd., Tumwater, Wash., 1993-94. Mem.: Wash. State Trial Lawyers Assn. (chmn. workers compensation sect.). Avocations: flyfishing, golf. Office: Rolland O'Malley et al 1405 Harrison Ave NW Olympia WA 98502-5360

WILLIAMS, WAYNE M. music educator; b. Potsdam, N.Y., Mar. 12, 1953; s. Earl Raymond and Jean Marie Williams; m. Diane Elizabeth Williams, July 3, 1976; children: Elaine, Elizabeth, Elyse. B in Music Edn., SUNY, Potsdam, 1975, M in Music Edn., 1980; diploma in piano tuning, Am. Sch. Piano Tuning, 2001; postgrad., Ind. Wesleyan U. Cert. tchr. N.Y. Jr. high instrumental music Sydney (Can.) Bd. Sch. Commr., 1977—84; grades K-8 gen./instrumental music tchr. Cape Breton Dist. Sch. Bd., Sydney, 1984—91; grades 4-12 instrumental music tchr. Schroon Lake (N.Y.) Ctrl. Sch., 1991—. First chair french horn Adirondack C.C. Concert Band, Lake George Chamber Orch., Glens Falls, NY, 1995—; organist, choir dir. Chestertown (N.Y.) Cmty. United Meth. Ch., 2001—; performer various brass and woodwind quintets/ensembles; bell staff Sagamore Resort, Bolten Landing, NY. Mem.: Schroon Lake C. of C. (brass dir. 1991—), Soc. for the Preservation and Encouragement Barbershop Quartet Singing in Am., Inc., Essex County Sch. Music Assn., Ctrl. Adirondack Sch. Music Assn., N.Y. State Sch. Music Assn., Music Educators Nat. Conf., Town of Schroon Lions Club (bd. dirs. 1996—, pres. 1999—2000), Phi Mu Alpha Sinfonia Fraternity Am. Inc. Republican. Methodist. Avocations: hockey, gardening, guitar. Home: 11 Continental Dr Schroon Lake NY 12870 Office: Schroon Lake Ctrl Sch Main St Schroon Lake NY 12870 E-mail: finetuning@nycap.rr.com.

WILLIAMS, WESLEY S., JR., real estate company executive; BA, Harvard U.; JD, HArvard U.; MA, Tufts U.; LLM, Columbia U. Bar: N.Y., Washington. Co-chair bd., co-CEO, mem. exec. com. Lockhart Cos., Inc., St. Thomas, 1987—; co-chair Lockhart Ins. Holding Co., Ltd., Lockhart Fin. Svcs. Corp.; dir. Lockhart Real Estate Corp.; ptnr. Covington & Burling, Washington, 1975—, San Francisco, 1975—, London, 1975—, Brussels, 1975—, Paris, 1975—. Bd. trustees, mem. exec. com. Penn Mut. Lofe Ins. Co.; bd. mgrs. Blackstar LLC; bd. dirs. Blackstar Comm., Inc., Carr/Am. Realty Corp., Fed. Res. Bank, Richmond, Va.; adj. prof. real estate fin. and fin. svcs. law Gerogetown U. Law Ctr. Mem.: N.Y. State Bar Assn., D.C. Bar Assn., Am. Law Inst. Office: PO Box 7020 St Thomas VI 00801

WILLIAMS, WESLEY SAMUEL, JR., lawyer; b. Phila., Nov. 13, 1942; s. Wesley Samuel and Bathrus Amanda (Bailey) W.; m. Karen Roberta Hastie, Aug. 17, 1968; children: Amanda Pedersen, Wesley Hastie, Bailey Lockhart. BA in French Lit. magna cum laude, Harvard U., 1963, JD, 1967; MA (Woodrow Wilson fellow), Fletcher Sch. Law and Diplomacy, 1964; LLM, Columbia U., 1969. Bar: D.C., U.S. Supreme Ct., N.Y. Spl. counsel D.C. City Council, 1967-69; assoc.-in-law Columbia U. Law Sch., 1968-69; legal counsel Com. on D.C. U.S. Senate, 1969-70; assoc. Covington & Burling, Washington, 1970-75, ptnr., 1975—. Trustee Penn Mut. Life Ins. Co., Phila., 1978—; bd. dirs. Broadcast Capital Cos., 1979-92, chmn., 1989-92, Carr Realty, Co., Inc., 1993—; mem. Pres.'s U.S. Circuit Judge Nominating Commn., 1977-80; gen. counsel D.C. Bar, 1979-81; adj. prof. Georgetown U. Law Sch., 1971-73; mem. exec. com. Washington Lawyers Com. Civil Rights Under Law, 1972—; mem. editorial bd. D.C. Real Estate Reporter; vice chmn., bd. dirs. Lockhart Cos., St. Thomas, U.S. Virgin Islands, 1987—, co-chief exec. officer, 1989—; vice chmn., bd. dirs. Blackstar Communications, Cos., 1987—. Author legal articles, texts. Pres. bd. trustee Nat. Child Rsch. Ctr., 1980-82; bd. overseers Harvard U., 1985-91, chmn. vis. com. Harvard U. Div. Sch., 1986-91; bd. dirs. World Affairs Coun. Washington, D.C., Inc., 1980—, Nat. Symphony Orch. Assn., 1977-92; bd. dirs. Family and Child Svcs. Washington, 1970—, pres., 1973-76; exec. com. community adv. com. Jr. League Washington, 1977-86; pres. standing com. Epsic. Diocese of Washington, 1983-88; sec. bd. trustees Protestant Episc. Cathedral Found., 1982-90; bd. regents Smithsonian Inst., 1993—. Fellow Am. Bar Found.; mem. ABA, Am. Law Inst., Nat. Bar Assn., Fed. Bar Assn., D.C. Bar Assn., Washington Bar Assn., Harvard Law Sch. Assn. (pres.), Order Hosp. St. John Jerusalem, Harvard Club, City Tavern Club, Met. Club, Chevy Chase Club, Univ. Club, Alpha Phi Alpha, Sigma Pi Phi. Office: Covington & Burling PO Box 7566 1201 Pennsylvania Ave NW Washington DC 20044

WILLIAMS, WILLIAM COREY, theology educator, consultant; b. Wilkes-Barre, Pa., July 12, 1937; s. Edward Douglas and Elizabeth Irene (Schooley) W.; m. Alma Simmenroth Williams, June 27, 1959; 1 child, Linda. Diploma in Ministerial Studies, NE Bible Inst., 1962; BA in Bibl. Studies, Cen. Bible Coll., 1963, MA in Religion, 1964; MA in Hebrew and Near Ea. Studies, NYU, 1966, PhD in Hebrew Lang. and Lit., 1975; postgrad., Hebrew U., 1977-78, Inst. Holyland Studies, 1986. Ref. libr. Hebraic section Libr. Congress, Washington, 1967-69; prof. Old Testament So. Calif. Coll./Vanguard U., Costa Mesa, 1969—; adj. prof. Old Testament Melodyland Sch. Theology, Anaheim, Calif., 1975-77; vis. prof. Old Testament Fuller Theol. Sem., Pasadena, Calif., 1978-81, 84, Asian Theol. Ctr. Evangelism Missions, Singapore and Sabah, 1985, Continental Bible Coll., Saint Pieters-Leeuw, Belgium, 1985, 2000-01, Mattersey Bible Coll., England, 1985, Inst.

Holy Land Studies, Jerusalem, 1986, Regent U., 1994. Transl. cons. reviser New Am. Std. Bible, 1969-94; transl. cons. New Internat. Version, 1975-76, New Century Version, 1991, The New Living Translation, 1992-95, New Internat. Version, Reader's Version, 1993-94; transl. cons. editor Internat. Children's Version, 1985-86. Author: (books, tapes) Hebrew I: A Study Guide, 1980, Hebrew II: A Study Guide, 1986, They Spoke From God, 2004; contbr. articles to International Standard Bible Encyclopedia, New International Dictionary of Old Testment Theology and Evangelical Dictionary of Biblical Theology; contbr. articles to profl. jours.; contbr. notes to Spirit Filled Life Study Bible; editor: They Spoke From God, 2004. Nat. Def. Fgn. Lang. fellow NYU, 1964-67; Alumni scholar N.E. Bible Inst., 1960-61; NEH fellow, summer 1992; recipient Disting. Educator's award Assemblies God, 1997. Mem. Soc. Bibl. Lit., Evang. Theol. Soc. (exec. office 1974-77), Inst. Bibl. Rsch., Lockman Found. (hon. mem. bd. dirs. 1992-94, mem. editl. bd. 1974-94). Home: 1817 Peninsula Pl Costa Mesa CA 92627-4591 Office: Vanguard U 55 Fair Dr Costa Mesa CA 92626-6520 Office Phone: 714-556-3610. Business E-Mail: wwilliams@vanguard.edu.

WILLIAMS, WILLIAM HARRISON, retired librarian; b. Seattle, Apr. 18, 1924; s. William E. and Letah M. (Hollenback) W.; m. Mary Helen Sims, Apr. 19, 1945; children: Linda Lee, Dee Ann. BS, Brigham Young U., 1969, M.L.S., 1970. Dir. Provo Pub. Library, Utah, 1969-70; Wyo. State Librarian, 1970-78; dir. Wyo. state Archives and Hist. dept., 1971-78; exec. sec. Wyo. Hist. Soc., 1971-78; sr. research analyst Wyo. Taxpayers Assn., 1978-84. Served to lt. col. USAAF, 1943-64. Decorated USAF commendation with oak leaf cluster. Mem. Masonic Order, Order of the Ea. Star, Order of the Amaranth, Beta Phi Mu, Phi Alpha Theta. Home: 21607 N 123rd Dr Sun City West AZ 85375-1950 E-mail: weewilli@juno.com.

WILLIAMS, WILLIAM HENRY, II, publisher; b. Birmingham, Ala., Oct. 21, 1931; s. Calvin Thomas and Lillian Elizabeth (Levey) W.; m. Lewis Mozelle Hensley, Feb. 28, 1959; 1 child, William Henry III. Student, Baylor U., 1952-55. Printer Waco (Tex.) Tribune-Herald, 1950-59; internat. rep. Internat. Typog. Union, Colorado Springs, Colo., 1960-68; editor, gen. mgr. Colorado Springs Free Press, 1969-70; dir. labor relations The Morning Telegraph, N.Y.C., 1970-72; gen. mgr. Daily Racing Form, Hightstown, N.J., 1972-89, nat. gen. mgr. for U.S. and Can., 1990-91, pub., 1991-92; ret., 1992; pub. Kerrville (Tex.) Mountain Sun, 1993-96. Mem. adv. council journalsim dept. Baylor U., Waco, 1970-72. Chmn. CentraState Med. Ctr., Freehold, N.J., 1982-83, CentraState Health Affiliates, Freehold, 1987-94; vice chmn. Ctr. for Aging, Inc., Freehold, 1985-90; dep. mayor Freehold Twp. Com., 1987, mayor, 1989-90, 93, committeeman, 1985-94; county commr. Kerr County, 1999—; chmn. Freehold Mayor's Task Force on Substance Abuse, 1987-91; mem. Upper Guadalupe River Authority, 1995-99, Kerr Econ. Devel. Found.; mem. devel. bd. Alamo River Area Workforce, 1997-99; bd. dirs. Alamo Area Coun. Govts. Named an Hon. Trustee Freehold Area Hosp., 1985—. Mem.: NCCJ (Brotherhood award 1986), Tax Press Assn. (bd. dirs. 1995—96), Lions Club (host, pres. 1998—99), Exec Club (Hightstown) (charter pres.), Optimists (charter mem. Freehold chpt.), Shriners, Masons (32d degree). Republican. Lutheran (congregation pres. 1999-2000). Club: Optimists (charter mem. Freehold chpt.). Avocations: music, golf, football, skiing. Home and Office: 172 Saint Andrews Loop Kerrville TX 78028-6441 E-mail: williams@ktc.com.

WILLIAMS, WILLIAM JOHN, JR., lawyer; b. New Rochelle, N.Y., Feb. 6, 1937; s. William John and Jane (Gormley) W.; m. Barbara Reuter. BA, Holy Cross Coll., Worcester, Mass., 1958; LLB, NYU, 1961. Bar: N.Y. 1961. Practiced in, N.Y.C., 1962—; ptnr. firm Sullivan & Cromwell, 1969—. Trustee NYU Law Sch. Found., 1977—, Holy Cross Coll., 1988-96. Fellow Am. Bar Found.; mem. ABA, Am. Law Inst., N.Y. State Bar Assn., Assn. of Bar of City of N.Y., U.S. Golf Assn. (mem. exec. com. 1978-87, sec. 1980-81, v.p. 1982-85, pres. 1986-87). Democrat. Roman Catholic.

WILLIAMS, WILLIAM JOSEPH, physician, educator; b. Bridgeton, N.J., Dec. 8, 1926; s. Edward Carlaw and Mary Hood (English) W.; m. Margaret Myrick Lyman, Aug. 12, 1950 (dec. Aug., 1985); children: Susan Lyman, William Prescott, Sarah Robb; m. Karen A. Hughes, Feb. 18, 1989. Student, Bucknell U., 1943-45; MD, U. Pa., 1949. Diplomate: Am. Bd. Internal Medicine. (hematology com. 1976-80). From intern to assoc. prof. U. Pa., Phila., 1949—61, assoc. prof. to prof. medicine, chief hematology, 1961—69; sr. instr. microbiology Case We. Res. U., 1952; asst. prof. medicine Washington U., St. Louis, 1959—60; rsch. fellow Oxford U., England, 1960—61; mem. hematology tng. com. Nat. Inst. Arthritis and Metabolic Disease, 1964—68, mem. rsch. career program com., 1968—72; chmn. dept. medicine SUNY Health Sci. Ctr., Syracuse, 1969—92, prof. medicine, 1969—, Disting. Svc. prof., 2002—, interim dean Coll. Medicine, 1991—92, dean coll. medicine and v.p. biomed. scis., 2002—04, disting. svc. prof., 2002—, dean emeritus Coll. Medicine, 2004—. Vis. scientist Walter and Eliza Hall Inst., Melbourne, Australia, 1980; vis. prof. Monash U., Melbourne, 1980; mem. thrombosis adv. com. Nat. Heart and Lung Inst., 1969-73, chmn., 1971-73; adv. coun. Nat. Arthritis, Metabolism and Digestive Diseases, 1975-79; mem. residency rev. com. internal medicine Accreditation Coun. Grad. Med. Edn., 1983-89, mem. bd. appeals panel for internal medicine, 1989-2000; mem. N.Y. State Coun. Grad. Med. Edn., 1987-89. Editor-in-chief: Hematology, 1972, 4th edit., 1989, Williams Hematology Companion Handbook, 1996; co-editor: Williams Manual of Hematology, 2003; contbr. articles to med. lit. Trustee Everson Mus. Art, 1975-81, 83-89. With USNR, 1944-46, 52-54. Recipient Research Career Devel. award Nat. Heart Inst., 1963-68; Daland fellow Am. Philos. Soc., 1955-57; Markle scholar, 1957-62 Mem. ACP (gov. Upstate N.Y. 1976-81), Am. Soc. Biochemistry and Molecular Biologists, Am. Soc. Clin. Investigation, Assn. Am. Physicians, Am. Clin. and Climatol. Assn., Am. Soc. Hematology, Interurban Clin. Club (sec. 1964-70), Alpha Omega Alpha. Mem. Soc. Friends. Home: 5160 Peck Hill Rd Jamesville NY 13078-9724 Office: 750 E Adams St Syracuse NY 13210-2306 Office Phone: 315-464-9788. Business E-Mail: williamw@upstate.edu.

WILLIAMS, WILLIAM MAGAVERN, headmaster; b. Niles, Mich., Dec. 22, 1931; s. Errol Edwin and Mary Elizabeth (Magavern) W.; m. Linda Carol Grush, June 15, 1958; children: Diana, William Jr., Sarah. BA, Williams Coll., 1953, LHD (hon.), 1984; postgrad. in Philosophy, Columbia U., 1954-58, MA in Ednl. Psychology, 1966. Tchr. elem. English, history, phys. edn. McTernan Sch., Waterbury, Conn., 1953-54; head guidance, boarding, and humanities depts., instr. English, coach varsity wrestling Riverdale Country Sch., Bronx, N.Y., 1955-66; headmaster Doane Acad., Burlington, N.J., 1966-70, Poly. Prep. Country Day Sch., Bklyn., 1970-00, headmaster emeritus, 2000—. Trustee Bklyn Inst. Arts and Scis., 1972-79, Bklyn. Ctrl. YMCA, 1974-78, Profl. Children's Sch., 1976-79, Bklyn. Children's Mus., 1979-82, Plymouth Ch. Pilgrims, 1979-86, N.Y. State Assn. Ind. Schs., 1980-86; chmn. bd. dirs. Stafford (Vt.) Sch., 2002-03, United Ch. of Stafford, 2003—; bd. dirs. No. Stage, 2004—. Mem. Headmasters' Assn., Country Day Sch. Headmasters' Assn. (v.p. 1998-99, pres. 1999-2000), Cum Laude Soc. (regent dist. III 1971-87, dep. pres. gen. 1981-87, pres. gen. 1987-96, regent-at-large 1996—), Guild Ind. Schs. N.Y. (pres. 1986-88). Avocations: sailing, skiing, chess, travel, civil war history. Home: PO Box 26 232 Justin Morrill Mem Hwy Strafford VT 05072-9730

WILLIAMS, WILLIE, JR., physicist, researcher; b. Independence, La., Mar. 24, 1947; s. Willie Sr. and Lee Anner (Booker) W.; 1 child, Willie Williams III. BS, So. U., 1970; MS, Iowa State U., 1972, PhD, 1974. Mem. faculty Lincoln U., Lincoln University, Pa., 1974—, assoc. prof. physics, 1979-84, prof. physics, 1984—, chmn. dept., 1976-95, chmn. sci. and math. div., 1978-80, 83-88, founder, dir. Lincoln Advance Sci. and Engring. Reinforcement (LASER) Program, 1980-96, dir. pre-engring., 1976-96, dir., prin. investigator Early Alert-Young Scholars Program, 1992-96. Bd. dirs. women tech. program Lincoln U. Urban Ctr., Phila.; vis. prof. Ctr. for Teaching Innovation, Drexel U., 1975; liaison officer Nat. Assn. for Equal Opportunity in Higher Edn., Dept. Def. Program., 1987—; mem. steering com. NSF Comprehensive Ctr. for Minorities, Phila.; bd. dirs. Prime Inc., Phila. Contbr. articles to profl. jours. Chmn. Cheyney Lincoln Temple Cluster, 1974-78; pres. The Men Fedn., So. U., 1968-69. Recipient Lindback award for Outstanding Teaching, 1976, Outstanding Scientist award White House Initiative, 1988; named one of Outstanding Young Men of Am., 1979; fellow NASA, 1979, Mobil Oil Corp., 1977, Nat. Bur. Standards, 1979, Dept. Def., 1980-81, Navy fellow, 1982 Mem. AAAS, AAUP (pres. Lincoln U. chpt. 2001—), Am. Assn. Physics, N.Y. Acad. Scis., Math. Assn. Am., Am. Phys. Soc., Nat. Soc. Black Physicists, Nat. Geog. Soc., Iowa State Alumna Assn., Sigma Xi, Sigma Pi Sigma. Baptist. Home: 448 W Baltimore Pike West Grove PA 19390-9201 Office: Lincoln U Dept Physics Lincoln University PA 19352 E-mail: wwillie2@aol.com. *Throughout my life I have always striven to achieve the very best and have held on to the belief that wherever possible improve upon today, so that everyone might have a better tomorrow! I have been guided by the the principle of being selective in my endeavors, having specific objectives, followed by detailed analysis, concise actions, and intense work with continous review.*

WILLIAMS, YOLANDA YVETTE, music educator; d. Ernest Thomas Williams and Thelma Christina Williams (Lewis). BA, Hamline U., 1979. Adj. faculty music dept. Mpls. (Minn.) Cmty. and Tech. Coll., 1991—; adj. faculty African-Am. Studies U. of Minn., Minneapolis, Minn., 1998—; dir. of worship and music Redeemer Luth. Ch., Mpls., 2003 . Singer: (opera) La Purpura de la Rose, Porgy and Bess, (musical) Chatouranga, A.My Name Is Alice, (oratorio) Requiem Mass. Mem. steering com. J-Train, St. Paul, 2003. Avocations: reading, composing. Office: University of Minnesota 267 19th Ave S 808 Soc Sci Minneapolis MN 55455-0471 Personal E-mail: williayo@mctc.mnscu.edu. E-mail: willi233@tc.umn.edu.

WILLIAMS, YOTISSE R. music educator; b. Boston, Sept. 15, 1970; s. Ralph Yohuru and Elizabeth Ottie Williams, m. Geraldine Teresa Marie Collins, Aug. 8, 1998; children: Yariah-lynn Kharmyl, Gerressi Lee. A in Criminal Justice, Housatonic C.C., 1991; A in Early Childhood Edn., Housatonic Cmty. Tech. Coll., 1997; B, Charter Oak State Coll., 2003. Asst. tchr. Housatonic C.C., Bridgeport, 1997—2000, head tchr., 2000—. Author: (poem) What Is The Substance Of Which I Am Made? (Golden Poet award, 1987). Youth min. St Pauls Ch., Bridgeport, Conn., 2003—03. Recipient Academic Excellence Early Childhood Edn., Housatonic C.C., 1997; scholar, ASIS, 1992, Gen. Electric, 1994; Joyce Gerber scholar, Housatonic C.C., 1997. Mem.: Conn. Assn. Edn.Young Children (v.p. 2000—01), Nat. Assn. Edn. Young Children (assoc.). Democrat. Avocations: music, writing, movies. Office: Housatonic Community College 900 Lafayette Blvd Bridgeport CT 06604 Office Phone: 332-5029. Personal E-mail: hulk241040@opton.net.

WILLIAMS, YVONNE G. corporate trainer; 1 child, Benjamin. BA in Bus. Mgmt., Eckerd Coll., 1993; MA in Adult Edn., U. South Fla., 1995, PhD, 2000. Mktg. rep. Xerox, Tampa, Fla., 1987—90, account exec., 1990—92, document mgmt. tng. rep., 1992—96, edn. specialist, 1996—97; pres., CEO BYNTER Cons., Inc., St. Petersburg, 1997—. Adv. bd. PIMEG, St. Petersburg, Fla., 1995-97; bd. dirs. Happy Workers Daycare Ctr. Active First Bapt. Instnl. Ch., St. Petersburg; bd. dirs. Happy Workers Childcare Ctr. Mem. NAACP, ASTD, Assn. Voters Edn. Rsch. Com., Nat. Coun. Negro Women, South Ctrl. Rotary, Top Ladies of Distinction, St. Petersburg Urban League Guild, Phi Kappa Phi, Delta Sigma Theta. Home: Apt 210 7300 Sunshine Skyway Ln S Saint Petersburg FL 33711-4957

WILLIAMSEN, DANNYE SUE, personal development educator, health facility administrator; b. Memphis, Mar. 26, 1949; d. Roy Fauntly and Arliss Wyleen Goodroe; m. Jon Charles Beckum, Dec. 23, 1969 (div. Mar. 1972); m. John Dean Williamsen, Dec. 24, 1986. BA cum laude, U. Memphis, 1995. Adminstr. Security Investments, Inc., Memphis, 1972-75; nightclub owner, investor Memphis, 1976-78; internat. tech. analyst ContiCommodity, Inc., Memphis, 1977-80; owner, tech. analyst Commodity Cons., Inc., Memphis, 1981; project mgr. B&P Devel. Co., Austin, Tex., 1982-84; asst. to pres. Memphis C. of C., 1984-86; owner, dental technician Williamsen Dental Lab., Memphis and Prophetstown, Ill., 1986—; ptnr., editor Personal Edn. Network, Prophetstown, Ill., 2001—; owner Networx Pub., Prophetstown, Ill., 2002—. Bd. dirs. Heartland Equine Assisted Therapeutic Ctr., Rock Falls, Ill., 2000—01. Author: Illusions, 1998, IT'S YOUR MOVE! Transform Your Dreams from Wishful Thinking to Reality, 2004; editor: Creative Living-an evolving approach to bus. life, 2001—, (e-newsletter) Metaphysical Minute, 2003—. Mem. AAUW (pres. 1998-99), APA, NOW, NAFE, Am. Bus. Women's Assn., Assn. for Humanistic Psychology, Small Pubs. Assn. N.Am., Pubs. Mktg. Assn., Psi Chi, Chi Beta Phi. Avocations: reading, philosophy. Office: Network Pub PO Box 35 Prophetstown IL 61277 Office Phone: 815-537-2959. Personal E-mail: wmsen@essex1.com. Business E-Mail: dannyew@networxpublishing.com.

WILLIAMS GIFFORD, SUSAN, state legislator; m. Mark Williams Gifford. BA, Western Mich. U. Bd. of selectmen Warcham, 1999—2002; state rep. Mass. House, 2003—. Republican. Office: Rm 540 State House Boston MA 02133

WILLIAMS MADDOX-BROWN, JANICE HELEN, nurse; b. Boston; d. Arthur Hamilton Wade and Edith Josephine (Weekes) Williams; m. Larry Maddox, May 21, 1977 (dec.); m. Richard Brown, Mar. 11, 2000. BS in Nursing, Boston U., 1957; MA, Atlanta U. Sch. Edn., 1971; MPH, Emory U., 1976; PhD, Union Inst., Cin., 1998. Staff nurse Beth Israel Hosp., Boston, 1958, N.Y. Hosp.-Cornell U. Med. Ctr., N.Y.C., 1958-59; ward supr. Jewish Meml. Hosp., Boston, 1959-61; staff and pvt. duty nurse Mass. Gen.Hosp., Boston, 1961-63; pub. health nurse Boston Health Dept., 1963-64; intravenous nurse Hughes Spalding Hosp., Atlanta, 1964-66; pub. health nurse Fulton County (Ga.) Health Dept., 1966-69; sr. tchr. Atlanta Southside Comprehensive Health Ctr., 1970-73, acting dir. edn., 1973-74, assoc. dir. clin. nursing, 1974-76; assoc. dir. mental health planning project So. Region Edn. Bd., Atlanta, 1976-78; nursing cons. Dept. Health and Human Svcs., Atlanta, 1978-81; head nurse VA Med. Ctr., Atlanta, 1982-85; br. mgr. Am. Home Health Care of Ga., Inc., Jonesboro, 1985-86; ind. contractor Med. Emergency Clinic-Grady Meml. Hosp., 1986—91; project dir. Morehouse Sch. Medicine Initiative, W.K. Kellogg Found., 1991-95; assoc. prof. Ctrl. Mich. U., 2000—01. Evening coordinator, instr. for innovative practical nursing program for health para-profl. Atlanta Area Tech Sch., 1971-83; mem. admissions com. M. Pub. Health program Emory U. Sch. Medicine, 1979-91. Mem. coms., including Women's Day com. Ctrl. United Meth. Ch., Atlanta, Beh Hill United Meth. Ch. (mem.). Recipient spl. recognition Am. Cancer Soc., 1975.

WILLIAMSON, ALAN BACHER, English literature educator, poet, writer; b. Chgo., Jan. 24, 1944; s. George and Jehanne (Bacher) W.; m. Anne Winters, Oct. 12, 1968 (div. Feb. 1988); 1 child, Elizabeth Kilner. BA, Haverford Coll., 1964; MA, Harvard U., 1965, PhD, 1969. Asst. prof. U. Va., Charlottesville, 1969-75; Briggs-Copeland lectr. Harvard U., Cambridge, Mass., 1977-80; Fannie Hurst lectr. Brandeis U., Waltham, Mass., 1980-82; prof. English, U. Calif., Davis, 1982—. Poetry panelist Nat. Endowment for Arts, 1989. Author: (criticism) Pity the Monsters, 1974, Introspection and Contemporary Poetry, 1984, Eloquence and Mere Life, 1994, Almost a Girl, 2001, (poetry) Presence, 1983, The Muse of Distance, 1988, Love and the Soul, 1995, Res Publica, 1998, The Pattern More Complicated: New and Selected Poems, 2004. Poetry fellow Nat. Endowment for Arts, 1973; Guggenheim fellow, 1991. Mem. MLA (exec. com. div. on poetry 1987-91). Democrat. Buddhist. Office: U Calif Dept English Davis CA 95616 Business E-Mail: abwilliamson@ucdavis.edu.

WILLIAMSON, BRIAN DAVID, information systems executive, consultant; b. Danbury, Conn., May 14, 1973; s. Robert Garth and Celeste Marie (D'Alessio) W. AA in Specialized Bus., Art Inst. Phila., 1993; BS in Gen. Studies, Teikyo Post U., 1994; postgrad. in Tech. Mgmt., Polytech. U., 1997. Asst. mgr. The New Milford (Conn.) Music Ctr., 1991-93; prodn. asst. Med. Broadcasting Co., Conshohocken, Pa., 1993; CIO Custom Designs, Inc., Danbury, Conn., 1991—; info. systems and telecomms. analyst Datahr Rehab. Inst., Brookfield, Conn., 1996-97; LAN adminstr. Praxair, Inc., Danbury, Conn., 1998—. Video technician Danbury Corp., Bethel, Conn., 1992-97. Author, writer (film script) The Senior, 1994. Republican. Roman Catholic. Avocations: tennis, computer graphics, movies, music, hiking. Home: 34 Lindencrest Dr Danbury CT 06811-4232 Office: Praxair Inc 39 Old Ridgebury Rd Ste 7 Danbury CT 06810-5109

WILLIAMSON, BRUCE A. oil industry executive; b. Great Falls, Mont. B in Fin., U. Mont., 1981; MBA, U. Houston. With Royal Dutch/Shell Group, 1981—95; sr. v.p. fin. bus. develop. and risk mgmt. PanEnergy Corp., v.p. fin., 1995—97; pres., CEO Duke Energy Internat., 1997—2001, Duke Energy Global Markets, 2001—02, Dynegy inc., Houston, 2002—, bd. dirs. 2002—, chmn., 2004—. Chancellor's nat. adv coun. U. Houston, Dean's adv. bd., C.T. Bauer Coll. Bus.; bd. dir. Greater Houston Partnership. Office: 1000 Louisiana Ste 5800 Houston TX 77002 Office Phone: 713-507-6400., 877-439-6349. Office Fax: 713-767-6652., 713-507-3871.*

WILLIAMSON, CARL AUGUSTUS, engineering executive; b. Newport News, Va., Sept. 7, 1950; s. Marvis Harrison Sr. and Annie Lucille (Amos) W.; m. Bonnie Bernel Mitchell, Sept. 21, 1973; 1 child, Carl Michael; 1 stepson, Leon Mitchell. BS, Norfolk State Coll., 1972; MBA, Northeastern U., 1982; DEng, MIT, 1987. Cert. secondary edn. tchr. Electrical estimator Stone & Webster, Boston, 1973-74; instr. D.C. Pub. Schs., Washington, 1974-76; sales engr. Westinghouse, Framingham, Mass., 1976-78; cost engr. Gilbert Commonwealth, Jackson, Mich., 1978-80; instr. Boston Pub. Schs., Boston, 1980-82; cons. Gilbert Commonwealth, Washington, 1983—. Col. U.S. Army, 1968-72. Mem NRA, MBA Assn., Washington Tchrs. Union. Baptist. Avocations: sports, arts, dance. Home and Office: Apt 207 2700 Martin Luther King Jr Ave # A Washington DC 20032-2601

WILLIAMSON, CHARLES R. energy company executive; PhD in Geology, U. Tex., Austin, 1978. Rsch. assoc. Sci. and Tech. Divsn. Unocal Corp., Brea, Calif., 1977-83, chief exploration geologist, 1983-86; exploration mgr., dir. Unocal Netherlands, The Hague, 1986-89; v.p. exploration Unocal Thailand, Bangkok, 1989-92; v.p. Energy Resources Divsn. Unocal, 1992-94, v.p. planning and info. svcs., 1994-95, v.p. corp. planning and econs., 1995-96, group v.p. internat. opers., 1996-97, group v.p. Asia Opers., 1997-99; exec. v.p. internat. energy ops. Unocal Corp., El Segundo, Calif., 1999—2001; CEO Unocal, 2001—, also bd. dirs. Mem. adv. bd. earth scis. dept. Stanford U. Mem. Am. Soc. Petroleum Geologists, Soc. Econ. Paleontologists and Mineralogists, Soc. Petroleum Engrs., Internat. Assn. Sedimentologists. Office: Unocal Corp 2141 Rosecrans Ave Ste 4000 El Segundo CA 90245-4746

WILLIAMSON, CHARLES READY, III, lawyer; b. Boston, Jan. 2, 1944; s. Charles Ready and Anne Margaret (Livingstone) W.; m. Julie Anne Williamson, Nov. 6, 1971; 1 dau., Anne Lucinda. B.A., Colgate U., 1965; LL.B., Suffolk U., 1968. Bar: Mass. 1968, Oreg. 1970, U.S. Supreme Ct. 1977. Law clk. to Judge Joseph B. Silverio, Mass. land ct., Boston 1968-69; VISTA atty., dep. dir. Multnomah County Legal Aid Service, Portland, 1970-74; assoc. Kell, Alterman & Runstein, Portland, 1974-78, 88—; pvt. practice, Portland, 1978-88; pres. Oreg. Legal Service Corp., 1976-77; mem. Oreg. Bd. Psychologist Examiners, 1973-74; chmn. Oreg. Grad. Sch. Profl. Psychology, Pacific U. Pres. Oreg. Consumer League, 1972-74; councilor Met. Service Dist. 1978-84; treas. Democratic Bus. Forum 1982-84. Mem. ABA, Oreg. Bar Assn. (pres.-elect 2002-03, pres. 2003-), Multnomah County Bar Assn. Club: Portland City. Contbr. in field. Home: 5304 SW 34th Pl Portland OR 97201-1125 Office: Kell Alterman & Runstein 520 SW Yamhill Ste 600 Portland OR 97204-1329

WILLIAMSON, DEBORAH DAYWOOD, lawyer; b. Greenville, S.C., Mar. 8, 1954; d. Narcief M. Daywood and Margaret Elizabeth (Guy) Robbins; m. George F. Williamson, Nov. 9, 1974; children: Christal Elizabeth, Victoria Whitney. BA, San Antonio Coll., 1973, S.W. Tex. U., 1974, U. Tex., El Paso, 1977; JD, U. Houston, 1981. Bar: Tex. 1982, U.S. Dist. Ct. (we. dist.) Tex. 1983, U.S. Dist. Ct. (so. dist.) Tex. 1986, U.S. Dist. Ct. (no. dist.) Tex. 1989, U.S. Dist. Ct. Ariz. 1991, U.S. Ct. Appeals (5th cir.) 1983. Atty. Cox & Smith Inc., San Antonio, 1982—. Author: (with others) Single Asset Real Estate Bankruptcies, 1996; columnist Am. Bankruptcy Inst. Jour., 1985—. Fellow Tex. Bar Found., Am. Coll. Bankruptcy, San Antonio Bar Found.; master Am. Inns of Ct., William Session; mem. Am. Bankruptcy Inst. (pres. 1998-99), San Antonio Bankruptcy Bar Assn. Office: Cox & Smith Inc 112 E Pecan St Ste 1800 San Antonio TX 78205-1521 E-mail: ddwillia@coxsmith.com.

WILLIAMSON, DEBORAH MCKIBBEN, social services administrator, educator; b. Cin., May 19, 1958; d. Herbert and Julia Irene McKibben; m. Stephen Ross Williamson, Dec. 5, 1986. BS, No. Ky. U., 1982; MA, U. Cin., 1985; PhD, U. Ky., 2000. Rsch. asst. U. Cin., 1983-86; intake officer juvenile svcs. Adminstrv. Office Cts., Newport, Ky., 1988-90, field supr. juvenile svcs. Frankfort, Ky., 1990-92, dir. law related edn., 1992-98, gen. mgr. juvenile svcs., 1998—. Adj. prof. U. Ky. State U., Lexington and Frankfort, 1997-2001. Editor: Law Related Education and Juvenile Justice, 1997; contbr. articles to profl. jours. Mem. Gov.'s Juvenile Justice Adv. Bd., 1999—. Recipient Outstanding Crime Prevention Practitioner award Ky. Crime Prevention Coun., 2000, Early Intervention Program award Ky. Cert. Bd. Prevention Profls., 2000; Adoptions Opportunities grantee HHS, 1997. Mem. Juvenile Justice Trainer's Assn., Nat. Youth Justice (coord. com. 2000), Civitas (Educator for Democracy com. Bosnia-Herzegovina 1997, Poland 2000). Democrat. Avocation: environmental preservation. Office: Adminstrv Office of Cts 100 Millcrek Pk Frankfort KY 40601 E-mail: deborahw@mail.aoc.state.ky.us.

WILLIAMSON, DONALD ELLIS, state official; b. Louisville, Miss., June 17, 1955; m. Anita Hudspeth; 1 child, Jonathan Stuart. Student, East Miss. Jr. Coll., 1972-73, Miss. State U., 1973-75; MD cum laude, U. Miss., 1979. Diplomate Am. Bd. Internal Medicine. Intern, resident in internal medicine U. Va. Hosp., Charlottesville, 1979-82; with East Miss. State Hosp., Meridian, 1979; state tb control officer Miss. State Dept. Health, 1982-86; dir. divsn. disease control Ala. Dept. Pub. Health, 1986-88, dir. bur. preventive health svcs., 1988-92, state health officer, 1992—. Faculty mem. Injury Control Rsch. Ctr. U. Ala., Birmingham; clin. assoc. prof. dept. internal medicine U. South Ala.; presenter in field. Contbr. articles to profl. jours. Chmn. Ala. Pub. Health Care Authority, Ala. Radiation Adv. Bd. Health; mem. Ala. Commn. Aging, State Bldg. Commn., Statewide Health Coordinating Coun., Ala. Youth Svcs. Bd., Ala. Child Abuse & Neglect Prevention Bd., Ala. Resource Devel. Com., Ala. Anat. Bd., Planning and Adv. Coun. Devel. Disabilities, Ala. Bd. Med. Scholarship Awards, Pesticides Adv. Com., Gov.'s Interagy. Coordinating Coun., Ala. Juvenile Justice Coordinating Coun., Emergency Med. Svcs. Adv. Coun., 1986-92, Legis. Adv. Com. AIDS, 1988-90, Atty. Gen.'s Task Force Med.Waste, 1989, Water Resources Adv. Coun., exec. coun. Ala. Children's Svcs. Facilitation Team, 1993—; mem. med. adv. com. ARC. Recipient Mosby Book award, 1979, Dr. Robert Ramsey award, 1993; Pub. Health Leadership Inst. scholar, 1996. Mem. APHA, Assn. State and Territorial Health Ofcls. (exec. com. 1995-2000, pres. 1997-98), Am. Acad. of Pediatrics (Child Health Advocate of the Yr. award 1999), Pub. Health Found. (Theodore R. Ervin award 1999), Med. Assn. State Ala., Ala. Pub. Health Assn. (bd. dirs. 1991—, chmn. disease control and epidemiology sect. 1991-92, D.G. Gill award 1997), Pub. Health Found. (bd. dirs. 1995-99, treas. 1997—), Phi Theta Kappa, Phi Kappa Phi, Alpha Omega Alpha. Home: 8113 Lichfield Ct Montgomery AL 36117-5124 Office: Ala Dept Pub Health PO Box 303017 201 Monroe St Montgomery AL 36104-3735

WILLIAMSON, DONALD RAY, retired career Army officer; b. Amarillo, Tex., Oct. 13, 1943; s. Floy Edwin and Dorothy Lorene (Orr) W.; m. Beverly Ann Howard, Aug. 31, 1963; children: Rebecca Ann, Catherine Paige. BS in Econs., W. Tex. State U., 1966; MA in Bus., Cen. Mich. U., 1977; degree, Dept. Def. Program Mgrs., 1982, U.S. Army Command and Gen. Staff Coll., 1980. Commd. 2d lt. U.S. Army, 1966, advanced through grades to lt. col., 1982, retired, 1986, comdg. officer combat support co., 1973-74, comdg. officer 2d aviation co., 1974-75, dep. insp. gen. Ft. Leavenworth, Kans., 1975-78, comdg. officer 213th aviation co., 1978-79, asst. program mgr. advanced scout helicopter program, 1981-86; owner Witan Group, Chesterfield, Mo., 1986-88; pres., owner Sys. Test Evaluation Inc., Huntsville, Ala.,

1988-99; gen. mgr. LESCO, Huntsville, Ala., 1999-2000. Contbr. articles to profl. jours. Decorated Bronze Star, 37 Air medals with "V" device, D.F.C. with oak leaf cluster, Legion of Merit. Mem. Army Aviation Assn. Am., Assn. U.S. Army, Lansing Jaycees (past pres.), Mensa. Avocations: flying, reading, tennis. Home: 2110 Greenslope Trl NE Huntsville AL 35811-2608

WILLIAMSON, DONNA C. E. investment company executive; ScB in Applied Math., Brown U.; MS in Mgmt., MIT. Corp. v.p. Baxter Internat.; founding officer, corp. sr. v.p. Caremark Internat., Inc.; mng. dir., sr. v.p. ABN AMRO Pvt. Equity, Chgo., 1999—, also bd. dirs. Bd. dirs. PSS World Med., Inc., A.G. Edwards, Inc., Gulf South Med. Supply, Inc., Haemonetics Corp. Bd. d. Greater Chgo. chpt. ARC. Office: ABN AMRO Pvt Equity 208 S La Salle St Lbby 10 Chicago IL 60604-1004

WILLIAMSON, DOUGLAS FRANKLIN, JR., lawyer; b. Anniston, Ala., Mar. 23, 1930; s. Douglas Franklin and Elizabeth Louise (Connor) W.; m. Barbara Tuerk, Dec. 28, 1957; children: Mary Leyden, Douglas Franklin III, Bruce Reynolds. AB summa cum laude, Amherst Coll., 1952; LLB, Yale U., 1955. Bar: NY 1958, Fla. 1976. Assoc. Breed, Abbott & Morgan, N.Y.C., 1957-63, ptnr., 1963-72, Williamson & Hess and predecessor firm, N.Y.C., 1972-79; of counsel Winthrop, Stimson, Putnam & Roberts, N.Y.C., 1979-81, ptnr., 1982-95, sr. counsel, 1996-2000, Pillbury Winthrop LLP, N.Y.C., 2001—. Bd. dirs. World Wildlife Fund, Washington, 1979-88, treas., 1986-88, mem. nat. coun., 1988—; bd. dirs. Conservation Found., Washington, 1985-88, treas., 1986-88; bd. dirs. Ea. N.Y. chpt. Nature Conservancy, Mt. Kisco, N.Y., 1976-87, 93-97, sec., 1976-87, hon. dir., 1987—, chmn., 1993-94; bd. dirs. Oblong Land Conservancy, Pawling, N.Y., 1990-98, chmn. 1996-98; bd. dirs. Quaker Hill Civic Assn., Pawling, 1974-2000, past pres.; chmn. Pawling Assessment Rev. Bd., 1976-2001. With U.S. Army, 1955-57. Fellow N.Y. State Bar Found.; mem. Assn. Bar City N.Y. (life), English Spkg. Union, Old Guard Soc. Palm Beach Golfers, Everglades Club, Quaker Hill Country Club (pres. 1980-81), Phi Beta Kappa, Phi Beta Kappa Soc. (sec. 1975-77, v.p. 1977-79). Office: Pillsbury Winthrop LLP 1540 Broadway New York NY 10036-4039

WILLIAMSON, EDWARD HENRY, chaplain, army officer; b. Jackson, Miss., Dec. 9, 1957; s. Oliver Frank and Edith Elise (Berch) W.; m. Jeanne Marie Lazio, May 28, 1988. BA in History, Miss. Coll., 1983; MDiv, Golden Gate Sem., 1988; DMin, Trinity Coll. and U., 1999; student in Clin. Pastoral Edn., Penrose St. Francis Hosp., 2003. Ordained to ministry So. Bapt. Ch., 1988. Chaplain Letterman Army Med. Ctr. USAR, San Francisco, 1988-90; post chaplain U.S. Army, Camp Parks, Calif., 1990, chaplain 1-14th AV Ft. Rucker, Ala., 1991, chaplain 46th engr., 1992, chaplain 1-503rd rgt. Camp Casey, South Korea, 1993-94, chaplain 5-29th Field arty. Ft. Carson, Colo., 1994-96, chaplain 1-72 Armor, 1996-97, chaplain 68th corps support, 1997-99; ret. from active duty, 1999; dir. spiritual care Sangre de Cristo Hospice, Pueblo, Colo., 2000. Author: 20 Questions You Should Ask a Potential Spouse. Mem. Army Aviator Assn. Am., VFW (dist. 2 chaplain Colo.), Pi Gamma Mu, Phi Alpha Theta. Republican. Avocations: chess, model aircraft, computer programming, hiking, swimming. Home: 305 Rudd Ave Canon City CO 81212-3255

WILLIAMSON, EDWIN DARGAN, lawyer, former federal official; b. Florence, S.C., Sept. 23, 1939; s. Benjamin F. and Sara (Dargan) W.; m. Kathe Gates, July 12, 1969; children: Samuel Gates, Edwin Dargan Jr., Sara Elizabeth. BA cum laude, U. of the South, 1961, DCL (hon.), 1992; JD, NYU, 1964. Bar: N.Y. 1965, D.C. 1988. Assoc. Sullivan & Cromwell, N.Y.C., 1964-70, ptnr., 1971-76, London, 1976-79, N.Y.C., 1979-88, Washington, 1988-90, 93—; legal adviser U.S. Dept. State, Washington, 1990-93; mem. Permanent Ct. Arbitration, 1991—. Mem. Permanent Ct. of Arbitration, 1991—; mem. U.S. adv. NTT DoCoMo, 2002—04. Regent U. of the South, Sewanee, Tenn., 1981-87, chmn., 1985-87, coun. fgn. rels., 1995—; bd. dirs. Nat. Dance Inst., N.Y.C., 1984-88, Episcopal Ch. Found., N.Y.C., 1986-90; vestryman St. James Episcopal Ch., N.Y.C., 1984-88; bd. mem. S.C. Govs. Sch. for Sci. and Math. Found., 2003—. Mem. U.S. Coun. Internat. Bus., Bus. and Industry Adv. Com. to OECD (vice chmn. com. on multinat. enterprise and investments 1993—, chmn. BIAC expert group on multilat agt. on investment 1996-99, vice-chmn. BIAC 1998—, mem. exec. com. USCIB 1999—), Met. Club. Republican. E-mail: williamsone@sullcrom.com.

WILLIAMSON, EDWIN LEE, wardrobe and costume consultant; b. Downey, Calif., Dec. 2, 1947; s. Cecil Earnest and Edwina Louise (Tedie) W. AA, L.A. City Coll., 1967-70; BA in Theater and Music Edn., 1971, MA in Theater and Music Edn., 1973; student, U. So. Calif., 1971-73. Wardrobe master Ice Capades, 1973-76; mem. wardrobe dept. Paramount Studios, 1976-78, Disney Studios, 1978-81; freelance wardrobe and costume cons., L.A., 1981—. Editor spl. events & theatre presentations Nightlife Mag. Appeared as Michael in original mus. Peter Pan Mem. adv. bd. Halfway House and AIDS Hospsice, Valley Presbyn. Hosp.; founder West Coast Singers L.A., Inner City Athletic Union L.A.; founding mem. Gay Mens Chorus, Gt. Am. Yankee Freedom Band L.A., L.A. Gay and Lesbian Community Ctr.; hon. mem. bd. dirs. U. So. Calif. Idylwild Sch. Music and Arts.; bd. dirs. One Christopher St. West; founding vol. Gay Community Svc. Ctr.; emperor Imperial Ct. of San Fernando Valley. Scholar U. So. Calif., 1971-73; nominee Tony award Best Supporting Actor in musical Happy Time. Mem. SAG, AFTRA, Wardrobe Union, Masons. Lutheran. Address: Nightlife MLagazine 9922 Vicksburg Dr Huntington Beach CA 92646-5338

WILLIAMSON, FLETCHER PHILLIPS, real estate broker; b. Cambridge, Md., Dec. 16, 1923; s. William Fletcher and Florence M. (Phillips) Williamson; m. Betty June Stoker, Apr. 6, 1943 (div. 1972); 1 child, Jeffrey Phillips; m. Helen M. Stumberg, Aug. 28, 1972 (dec. Jan. 2002). Student, U. Md., 1941—42. Test engr. engring. lab. Glen Martin Co., 1942-43; salesman Corkran Ice Cream Co., Cambridge, 1946-50; real estate broker, 1950—. Chmn. bd. Williamson Real Estate, Dorchester Indsl. Devel. Corp., 1963—72; dir. Dorchester indsl. Devel. Corp.; vice-chmn. bd., dir. Nat. Bank Cambridge, 1979—; dir. Cam-Storage, Inc., Delmarva Bank Data Processing Ctr.; co-receiver White & Nelson, Inc.; v.p. Delmarva Bank Shares. Bd. dirs. Delmarva coun. Boy Scouts Am., Dorchester County Pub. Libr.; past pres. Cambridge Hosp., United Fund Dorchester County; bd. dirs., v.p. Game Conservation Internat., Del. Mus. Natural History. Sgt. AUS, 1943—46, ETO. Methodist. Home: 310 E Wilowood Dr San Antonio TX 78212

WILLIAMSON, GLORIA, state legislator; b. Philadelphia, Miss. m. Edward Williamson; children: Sherry Toler, Wendy Sparks. Student, East Ctrl. Jr. Coll. Mem. Miss. Senate from 18th dist., Jackson, 2000—. Vice chair agrl. com. Dem. chair, Miss. Mem. GFWC, MFWC, Futura Club, Jr. Auxiliary, Women's Polit. Network. Methodist. Office: 521 Holland Ave Philadelphia MS 39350

WILLIAMSON, HUGH JACKSON, statistician; b. Dallas, Jan. 12, 1943; s. Hugh and Edna (Mays) W.; m. Sheri Lynn Wooten, Jan. 19, 1980; 1 child, Laura Elizabeth. BA in Math. with Honors, U. Tex., 1965, MA in Math., 1967, PhD in Mech. Engring., 1975. Engr., scientist Tracor, Inc. and subs., Austin, Tex., 1967-73; rsch. engr., scientist assoc. U. Tex., Austin, 1973-77; sr. scientist Radian Internat. LLC, Austin, 1977-85, sr. staff scientist, 1986-91, prin. scientist, 1992-2000, CACI Techs., Inc., Austin, 2000—. Contbr. articles to profl. jours. Mem. Am. Statis. Assn., Sigma Xi, Phi Kappa Phi. Avocations: reading, gourmet cooking, music appreciation, golf. Home: 2401 Indian Trl Austin TX 78703-2337

WILLIAMSON, JACK (JOHN STEWART), writer; b. Bisbee, Ariz., Apr. 29, 1908; s. Asa Lee and Lucy Betty (Hunt) W.; m. Blanche Slaten Harp, Aug. 15, 1947 (dec. Jan. 1985); stepchildren: Keigh Harp (dec.), Adele Harp Lovorn. BA, MA, Eastern N.Mex. U., 1957, LHD (hon.), 1981; PhD, U. Colo., 1964. Prof. English Eastern N.Mex. U., Portales, 1960-77, prof. emeritus, 1977—. Author numerous sci. fiction books including The Legion of Space, 1947, Darker Than You Think, 1948, The Humanoids, 1949, The Green Girl, 1950, The Cometeers, 1950, One Against the Legion, 1950, Seetee Scock, 1950, Seetee Ship, 1950, Dragon's Island, 1951, The Legion of Time, 1952, (with Frederik Phhl) Star Bridge, 1955, Dome Around America, 1955, The Trial of Terra, 1962, Golden Blood, 1964, The Reign of Wizardry, 1965, Bright New Universe, 1967, Trapped in Space, 1968, The Pandora Effect, 1969, People Machines, 1971, The Moon Children, 1972, H.G. Wells: Critic of Progress, 1973, Teaching SF, 1975, The Early Williamson, 1975, The Power of Blackness, 1976, The Best of Jack Williamson, 1978, Brother to Demons, Brother To Gods, 1979, Teaching Science Fiction: Education for Tomorrow, 1980, The Alien Intelligence, 1980, The Humanoid Touch, 1980, Manseed, 1982, The Queen of a Legion, 1983, Wonder's Child: My Life in Science Fiction, 1984 (Hugo award 1985), Lifeburst, 1984, Firechild, 1986, Mazeway, 1990, Undersea Quest, 1954, Undersea Fleet, 1955, Undersea City, 1956, The Reefs of Sapce, 1964, Starchild, 1965, Rogue Star, 1969, The Farthest Star, 1975, Wall Around a Star, 1983, Land's End, 1988, Mazeway, 1990. (with Frederik Phol) The Singers Of Time, 1991, Beachhead, 1992, Demon Moon, 1994, The Black Sun, 1996, The Fortress of Utopia, 1998, The Silicon Dagger, 1999, The Stone from the Green Star, 1999, Terraforming Earth, 2001; (with Miles J. Breuer) The Birth of an New Republic, 1981. Served as staff sgt. USAAF, 1942-45. Mem. Sci. Fiction Writers Am. (pres. 1978-80, Grand Master Nebula award 1976), Sci. Fiction Research Assn. (Pilgrim award 1968), World Sci. Fiction, Planetary Soc. Avocations: travel, astronomy, photography. Home: PO Box 761 Portales NM 88130-0761 Office: Ea NMex U Golden Libr Portales NM 88130 E-mail: Jack.Williamson@enmu.edu.

WILLIAMSON, JOEL RUDOLPH, humanities educator; b. Anderson County, S.C., Oct. 27, 1929; s. James Henry and Carrie Mae (Swaney) W.; m. Marie Ahearn, Nov. 17, 1953 (div. May 1983); children: Joelle, William, Alethea; m. Anna Woodson, Oct. 18, 1986. AB, U. S.C., 1948, MA, 1951; PhD, U. Calif., 1964. Instr. dept. history U. N.C., Chapel Hill, 1960-64, asst. prof., 1964-66, assoc. prof., 1966-69, prof., 1969-85, Lineberger prof. in humanities, 1985—. Resident fellow Rockefeller Ctr., Bellagio, Italy, 1988; Eudora Welty prof. in so. studies Millsaps Coll., 1984; disting. vis. prof. Rhodes Coll., 1984; vis. prof. dept. history, assoc. Lowell House Harvard U., 1981-82. Author: After Slavery: The Negro in South Carolina During Reconstruction, 1861-1877, 1965, The Origins of Segregation, 1968, New People: Miscegenation and Mulattoes in the United States, 1980, The Crucible of Race, 1984 (Francis Parkman prize Soc. Am. Historians, Ralph Waldo Emerson award Phi Beta Kappa, Mayflower Cup, Frank L. and Harriet C. Owsley award 1985, Robert Francis Kennedy Book award, Pulitzer prize in History nomination 1985), A Rage for Order, 1986, William Faulkner and Southern History, 1993 (Pulitzer prize in History nomination 1994, Mayflower Cup), also articles. Lt. USN, 1951-55. Fellow Guggenheim Found., 1970-71, NEH, 1987-88, Ctr. for Advanced Study in Behavioral Scis., Stanford, Calif., 1977-78, summer 1979, 80, 81, So. fellow, 1961-62, Charles Warren Ctr., 1981-82. Mem. Soc. Am. Historians, Orgn. Am. Historians, Am. Hist. Assn., So. Hist. Assn., So. Assn. for Women Historians. Avocation: travel. Home: 211 Hillsborough St Chapel Hill NC 27514-3522 Business E-Mail: william@email.unc.edu.

WILLIAMSON, JOHN, economist; b. Hereford, Eng., June 7, 1937; s. Harry and Eileen (Heap) W.; m. Denise Rausch de Souza, Mar. 30, 1974; children: Andre, Daniel, Theresa. BSc in Econs., London Sch. of Econ., 1958; PhD, Princeton U., 1963. Lectr. U. of York, Eng., 1963-68; cons. UK Treasury, London, 1968-70; prof. U. Warwick, Eng., 1970-77; advisor IMF, Washington, 1972-74; prof. Pontificia Universidade Catolica, Rio de Janeiro, Brazil, 1978-81; sr. fellow Inst. for Internat. Econs., Washington, 1981—. Specialist advisor House of Commons Select Com. on Treasury, London, 1982-83; chief economist South Asia region World Bank, 1996-99; project dir. UN High-Level Panel on Financing for Devel., 2001. Author: Failure of World Monetary Reform, 1977, Political Economy and International Money, 1987; editor: Latin American Adjustment: How Much Has Happened?, 1990; co-editor: After the Washington Consensus: Restarting Growth and Reform in Latin Aamerica, 2003. Pres. U. London Liberal Fedn., London, 1957-58. Mem. Royal Econ. Soc. (coun. 1976-77), Am. Econ. Assn. Avocation: birding. Office: Inst for Internat Econ 1750 Massachusetts Ave NW Washington DC 20036-1903 Office Phone: 202-328-9000. Business E-Mail: jwilliamson@iie.com.

WILLIAMSON, JOHN BUTLER, sociology educator; b. Gloversville, N.Y., Mar. 18, 1943; s. John William and Nancy (Butler) Chambers; m. Nancy Thomas, Mar. 22, 1968; m. Elizabeth Szwarc Johnson, July 7, 1987. BS in Philosophy and Physics, MIT, 1964; PhD in Social Psychology, Harvard U., 1969. Assoc. Inst. Human Scis., Boston Coll., Chestnut Hill, Mass., 1969-72, asst. prof. sociology, 1969-75, assoc. prof., 1975-83, prof., 1983—, asst. chmn. dept., 1977-83, chmn., 1985-88, dir. applied social rsch. sequence, 1979-81. Presenter numerous papers at profl. meetings; manuscript reviewer numerous profl. jours.; reviewer or editorial cons. numerous pub. cos. and univ. presses; cons. project on FCC's funeral rule Nat. Consumer Law Ctr., Boston, 1988; mem. externala rev. team dept. social and cultural scis. Marquette U., Milw., 1987; grant application reviewer NEH, 1980, NSF, 1999, 2001; cons. project on elder and child neglect Mass. Gen. Hosp., Boston, 1987; presider 28th Internat. Congrress Internat. Inst. Sociology, Portugal, 1986. Author: Strategies Against Poverty in America, 1975, (with others) Aging and Society, 1980, Growing Old, 1980, The Research Craft, 1977, 2d edit., 1982, The Politics of Aging: Power and Policy, 1982, Aging and Public Policy: Social Control or Social Justice?, 1985, Poverty and Public Policy, 1986, Poverty in the U.S., 1988, The Senior Movement, 1991, Age, Class, Politics and the Welfare State, 1989, Old-Age Security in Comparative Perspective, 1993, (Chinese Translation, 2002), Death: Current Perspectives, 4th edit., 1995, The Senior Rights Movement, 1996, The Generational Equity Debate, 1999; also more than 100 articles, chpts. in books publ. in foreign langs. Fellow USPHS, 1965-69; grantee NSF, summer 1970, Nat. Inst. on Aging, 1977, 83-86, U.S. Cmty. Svcs. Adminstrn., 1980, Boston Coll. Mellon Found., 1981-82, Am. Coun. Learned Socs., 1994. Mem. Am. Sociol. Assn. (chmn. com. sect. 1996-98, chmn. com. on rsch. groups sect. on aging 1993-96, sec.-treas. sect. on aging and the life course 1995-98), Gerontol. Soc. Am., Nat. Acad. Social Ins., Internat. Sociol. Assn. Home: 50 Paul St Newton MA 02459-2470 Office: Boston Coll Dept Sociology Chestnut Hill MA 02467 E-mail: jbw@bc.edu.

WILLIAMSON, JOHN PRITCHARD, utilities executive; b. Cleve., Feb. 22, 1922; s. John and Jane (Pritchard) W.; m. Helen Morgan, Aug. 3, 1945; children: John Morgan, James Russell, Wayne Arthur. BBA, Kent State U., 1945; postgrad., U. Toledo, 1953-56, U. Mich., 1956. CPA, Ohio, ret. Sr. acct. Arthur Andersen & Co., Detroit and Cleve., 1945-51; dir. methods and procs. Toledo Edison Co., 1951-59, asst. treas., 1959-60, sec., 1960-62, sec.-treas., 1962-65, v.p. finance, 1965-68, sr. v.p., 1968-72, pres., chief exec. officer, 1972-79, chmn., chief exec. officer, 1979-86; chmn. Centerior Energy Corp., 1985-86. Chmn. emeritus Toledo Edison Co., Centerior Energy Corp. (now First Energy Corp.), 1986—; dir. emeritus, chmn. 1st Nat. Bank of Toledo, 1974-75; chmn. N.Am. Electric Reliability Coun., 1984-87; chmn. Nat. Electric Security Com., 1987-88. Pres. Ohio Electric Utility Inst., 1972; chmn. East Cen. Area Power Coordination Pool, 1971-72, mem. exec. com. Edison Electric Inst., 1981-85; trustee Assn. Edison Illuminating Cos., 1982-84; pres. Toledo C. of C., 1970; chmn. Ohio C. of C., 1979-81, life dir.; pres. Toledo Symphony Orch., 1985-86; hon. trustee Toledo Mus. Art, Toledo Hosp., Toledo Symphony; trustee U. Toledo Found., 1980-87; hon. trustee Kent State U. Found.; vice chmn. Greater Toledo Corp., 1984-86; trustee, treas. Rio Verde Cmty. Ch., 1989-92; founding elder Covenant Presbyn. Ch.; pres. Toledo Cmty. Chest, 1972; chmn. Greater Toledo Area United Way, 1971, Epworth Meth. Ch. Found.; dir. Rio Verde Comty. Assn., 1998-2003 Named Toledo Area's Outstanding Citizen, 1976; recipient Kent State U. medallion, 1992; Williamson Alumni Ctr. named in his honor, 1991. Mem. Fin. Analysts Soc. Toledo (pres. 1968-69), Sys. and Procs. Assn. (internat. treas. 1960), Inst. Pub. Utilities (chmn. exec. com. 1969-70), Toledo Boys Club (Echo award 1974), Kent State U. Alumni Assn. (pres. 1971-72, Outstanding Alumnus 1974), Belmont Country Club, Rio Verde Country Club, Inverness Club (gov., treas. 1967-76, chair 1979 U.S. Open, 1986 PGA Championship, winner 1965 Amateur Invitational), Rio Verde Saddle Club (past pres.), Kiwanis (past pres. Toledo chpt., Disting. Svc. award 1977, 2002, past internat. pres. award 2002), Blue Key, Delta Sigma Pi, Beta Alpha Psi, Delta Upsilon. Republican. Home: 10661 Cardiff Rd Perrysburg OH 43551-3404 also: 18524 E Poco Vista Rio Verde AZ 85263-7125 E-mail: williamsonjp@aol.com.

WILLIAMSON, KEITH HARVEY, lawyer; b. St. Louis, May 16, 1952; s. Irving Alexander and Elizabeth Rebecca (Giddings) W.; m. Addie L. Perkins, Oct. 29, 1988.; 1 child. BA, Brown U., 1974; MBA, JD, Harvard U., 1978; LLM in Taxation, NYU, 1986. Bar: DC 1978, NY 1982. Assoc. Covington & Burling, Washington, 1978-81, Reavis & McGrath, NYC, 1981-88; dir. taxes Pitney Bowes Credit Corp., Shelton, Conn., 1988-94, asst. gen. counsel, 1993—94, v.p., sec., gen. counsel, 1994—98; sr. assoc. gen. counsel, mergers and acquisitions Pitney Bowes Inc., 1998—99, pres., capital svcs. divsn., 1999—. Bd. dirs. Stamford (Conn.) Mus. and Nature Ctr., Arts and Entertainment Alliance, NYC, United Way of Stamford, New Canaan Country Sch.; founder Minority Corporate Counsel Assn.; mem. Black Exec. Exchange Program, Urban League. Mem. ABA, Tax Execs. Inst., Harvard U. Bus. Sch. Club. Office: Pitney Bowes Cap Svcs One Elmcroft Rd Stamford CT 06926-0700*

WILLIAMSON, KENNETH LEE, chemistry professor; b. Tarentum, Pa., Apr. 13, 1934; s. James D. and Mary June (Becker) W.; m. Mary Louise Hoerner, Sept. 15, 1956; children: Christopher Lee, Tania Louise, Kevin Keith. BA cum laude (Nat. scholar), Harvard, 1956; PhD (Allied Chem. and Dye Co. fellow), U. Wis., 1960. Mem. faculty Mt. Holyoke Coll., 1961—, prof. chemistry, 1969—, Mary E. Woolley prof. chemistry, 1984-99, Mary E. Woolley prof. chemistry emeritus, 1999—. Mem. Grad. faculty U. Mass., 1965—; vis. prof. Cornell U., 1966, Dartmouth Coll., 1986-87, Harvard U., 1989-90, U. Trondheim, Norway, 1991, U. Louis Pasteur, Strasbourg, France, 1991, U. Amsterdam, Basel U., Switzerland, 1992, U. Canterbury, New Zealand and U. Auckland, New Zealand, 1994; vis. prof. MIT, 1996, 97, Calif. Inst. Tech., 2000. Author papers and books in field; patentee in field. Mem. South Hadley Hist. Commn., 1983—, South Hadley Cultural Coun., 2000—03. NIH postdoctoral fellow Stanford, 1960-61; NSF sci. faculty fellow U. Liverpool, Eng.; also fellow of univ., 1968-69; Guggenheim fellow, 1975-76; Oxford (Eng.) U. fellow of univ., 1976, 1983; research assoc., Calif. Inst. Tech., 1975, 82. Mem. Am. Chem. Soc., AAAS, Sigma Xi. Home: 43 Woodbridge St South Hadley MA 01075-1138 E-mail: williamson98@comcast.net.

WILLIAMSON, KENNETH N. civilian military employee; b. Miss. BS, U. Ala. CEO U.S. Army Res. Command', Fort McPherson, Ga., 1998—; dep. dir. Dep. Chief of Staff Pers., 1996—98, Dep. Chief of Staff Engr. Recipient Meritorious Civilian Svc. award, Superior Civilian Svc. award (3). Mem.: Ret. Officers Assn., Assn. U.S. Army, Res. Officers Assn. (past state sec.), Atlanta Fed. Exec. Bd., Mid. Tenn. Fed. exec. Assn. (past pres./v.p.), Am. Soc. Mil. Comptr. (past pres. Greater Atlanta chpt.). Office: Army Reserve Command Fort Mcpherson GA 30330-1069

WILLIAMSON, KEVIN, writer, producer, director; b. New Bern, N.C., Mar. 14, 1965; Student, East Carolina State U., UCLA. Exec. prodr. (TV series) Wasteland, 1999, Dawson's Creek, 1998, Glory Days, 2002; prodr. Scream 3, 1999, Her Leading Man, 2001; exec. prodr., writer Scream 2, 1997; writer The Faculty, 1998, I Know What You Did Last Summer, 1997, Scream, 1996 (Saturn award Acad. of Sci. Fiction, Horror and Fantasy Films); writer, dir. Teaching Mrs. Tingle, 1999; writer, co-exec. prodr. Halloween H20: Twenty Years Later, 1998; actor Dirty Money, 1994, (TV) Another World, 1990; writer, prodr. Cursed, 2001. Office: Jim Wiatt care Kevin Williamson WMA 151 El Camino Dr Beverly Hills CA 90212

WILLIAMSON, MARILYN, retired secondary school educator; b. St. Louis, Apr. 6, 1930; d. Herschel and Estella (Wolff) W. BA, Roosevelt U., Chgo., 1951; MEd, U. Ill., 1955; life reading spl. cert., Harris-Stowe State Coll., St. Louis, 1968; postgrad., Washington U., St. Louis. Cert. life elem. and secondary tchr., reading specialist, Mo. Elem. tchr. St. Louis Pub. Schs., tchr. verbal skills, head lang. arts dept., reading specialist. Historian met. St. Louis chpt. Coalition 100 Black Women; sec. St. Louis chpt. Top Ladies Distinction; active ch. orgns.; co-chair Lane Tabernacle Scholarship. Recipient Top Ladies Distinction St. Louis chpt. Retirement award, Lane Tabernacle C.M.E. Ch. 50 Yr. Membership Plaque. Mem. Internat. Reading Assn., Mo. Tchrs. Assn., Nat. Coalition of 100 Black Women, (Shero award), NAACP, Phi Delta Kappa (past pres., chair founder's day, v.p. Alpha Nu chpt.), Iota Phi Lambda (Apple for Tchr. award 1984), Delta Sigma Theta. Home: 5236 Vernon Ave Saint Louis MO 63113-1522

WILLIAMSON, MARILYN LAMMERT, English educator, university administrator; b. Chgo., Sept. 6, 1927; d. Raymond Ferdinand and Edith Louise (Eisenbies) Lammert; m. Robert M. Williamson, Oct. 28, 1950 (div. Apr. 1973); 1 child, Timothy L.; m. James H. McKay, Aug. 15, 1974. BA, Vassar Coll., 1949; MA, U. Wis., 1950; PhD, Duke U., 1956. Lectr. Duke U., Durham, N.C., 1955-56, 58-59, N.C. State U., Raleigh, 1957-58, 61-62; asst. prof. Oakland U., Rochester, Mich., 1965-68, assoc. prof., 1968-72; prof. English Wayne State U., Detroit, 1972-90, Disting. prof. English, 1990-97, Disting. prof. emerita, 1997—, chmn. dept. English, 1972-74, 81-83, assoc. dean Coll. Liberal Arts, 1974-79, dir. women's studies, 1976-87, dep. provost, 1987-91, sr. v.p. for acad. affairs, provost, 1991-95, 98-200. Pres. Assn. Depts. English, 1976-77. Author: Infinite Variety, 1974, Patriarchy of Shakespeare's Comedies, 1986, British Women Writers 1650-1750, 1990; editor: Renaissance Studies, 1972, Female Poets of Great Britain, 1981, Shakespeare Studies: Middle Comedies, 2003; contbr. articles to profl. jours. Pres. LWV, Rochester, 1963-65. Recipient Detroit Disting. Svc. award, 1986, Faculty Recognition award Bd. Govs., Wayne State U., 1991; Bunting Inst. fellow, 1969-70, AAUW fellow, 1982-83, J.N. Keal fellow, 1985-86. Mem.: MLA (exec. coun. 1977—80, mem. editl. bd. 1992—94), Fed. State Humanities Coun. (bd. dirs. 1994—2001, chair 1997—99), Mich. Coun. Humanities (bd. dirs. 1988—2001, chair 1991—93), Shakespeare Assn. Am., Mich. Acad. (pres. 1978—79), Coll. English Assn., Renaissance Soc. Am. Democrat. Home: 2275 Oakway Dr West Bloomfield MI 48324-1855

WILLIAMSON, MARVEL, dean, nursing administrator, sexologist, educator, writer; b. Holton, Kans., Nov. 4, 1953; d. Thomas Arthur and Lois M. (Ihrig) Ansley; m. Paul Williamson, May 12, 1973; children: Marcus W., Sean W. BS in Nursing, Wichita State U., 1976; MS in Nursing, U. Ky., 1978; PhD, U. Iowa, 1987. Cert. sex educator. Prof. U. Iowa, Iowa City, 1980-89; dir. patient svcs. Ransom Meml. Hosp., Ottawa, Kans., 1989-91; dir. schs. nursing at Rolla, Sikeston and Kansas City Park Coll., Parkville, Mo., 1991-97; prof. Albany (Ga.) State U., 1997-99; sexologist Silver Spring, Md., 1999—2001; dean Kramer Sch. Nursing, Oklahoma City U., 2001—. Contbr. articles to profl. jours. Mem. ANA, Am. Assn. Sex Educators, Counselors and Therapists, Sigma Theta Tau. Home and Office: 3141 NW 18th St Oklahoma City OK 73107 Office: Oklahoma City U 2501 N Blackwelder Oklahoma City OK 73106 Office Phone: 405-521-5900.

WILLIAMSON, MICHAEL, photographer; b. Washington, dc, 1958; Staff photographer Sacramento Bee, Sacramento, 1978—91; photjournalist-in-residence Western Ky. U., 1991—; staff photographer Washington Post, 1993—. Author: Journey to Nowhere: The Saga of the New Underclass, 1985, (with Dale Maharidge) And Their Children After Them, 1989 (Pulitzer prize for gen. non-fiction 1990), The Last Great American Hobo, 1993; author numerous award winning essays. Special Recognition for the Nikon World Understanding Award, 1983, Photographer of the Year, San Francisco Bay Area Press PHotographer's Assoc., 1989, Kodak Crystal Eagle Award for Impact in Photojournalism, 1994, Newspaper Photographer of the Year & Northern Photogrpaher of the Year, Nat. Press Phographers Assoc., 1995, Pulitzer prize for feature photography, 2000. Office: Washington Post 1150 15th St NW Washington DC 20071-0002

WILLIAMSON, NORMA BETH, adult education educator; b. Hamilton, Tex., Nov. 2, 1939; d. Joseph Lawrence and Gladys (Wilkins) Drake; m. Stuart Williamson, Mar. 14, 1981. BA, Baylor U., 1962; MA, Tex. A&M U., 1969; postgrad., Tex. Tech. U., 1976-80, CIDOC, Cuernavaca, Mex., 1973, 75. Instr. English, Tex. Southmost Coll., Brownsville, 1969-81; sr. English tchr. The Woodlands McCulloch H.S., 1981-83; lectr. in English Sam Houston State U., 1983-85; coll. prep. tchr. Tex. Dept. Corrections, 1985-95; ret., 1995. Lectr. Spanish Sam Houston State U.; faculty advisor Circle K, Sam Houston State.

Vol., reading mentor Houston Elem. Sch.; pres. S.W. Dist. Unitarian Universalist Assn., 1982-86; treas. Huntsville Cmty. Theatre. Mem. AAUW (pres. Huntsville br. 1995-96), Huntsville Kiwanis (pres. 1999-2000), Walker County Geneal. Soc. (editor newsletter), Delta Kappa Gamma, Alpha Mu (pres. 1980-81), Upsilon (pres. 1994-96). Home: 794A Round Prairie Rd Bedias TX 77831-3238 E-mail: betwil@aol.com., fol.nbw@shsu.edu.

WILLIAMSON, OLIVER EATON, economics and law educator; b. Superior, Wis., Sept. 27, 1932; s. Scott Gilbert and Lucille S. (Dunn) W.; m. Dolores Jean (Celeni), Sept. 28, 1957; children: Scott, Tamara, Karen, Oliver, Dean. BS, Mass. Inst. Tech., 1955; MBA, Stanford U., 1960; PhD, Carnegie Mellon U., 1963, Norwegian Sch. Econ. and Bus. Adminstrn., 1986; PhD in Econ. sci. (hon.), Hochschule St. Gallen, Switzerland, 1987, Groningen U., 1989, Turku Sch. Econ. and Bus. Admin, St. Petersburg, Russia, 1996, HEC, Paris, 1997, Copenhagen Bus. Sch., 2000, U. Chile, 2000. Project. engr. U.S. Govt., 1955-58; asst. prof. econ. U. Calif., Berkeley, Calif., 1963-65; assoc. prof. Pa. State U., Phila., 1965-68, prof., 1968-83, Charles and William L. Day prof. econ. and social sci., 1977-83; Gordon B. Tweedy prof. econ. law and orgn. Yale U., 1983-88; Transam. prof. of bus., econ. and law U. Calif., Berkeley, Calif., 1988-94, Edgar F. Kaiser prof. bus. adminstrn., prof. econ. and law, 1994—. Spl. econ. asst. to asst. atty. gen. for antitrust Dept. Justice, 1966—67; dir. Ctr. for Study of Orgnl. Innovation, U. Pa., 1976—83; cons. in field. Author: The Economics of Discretionary Behavior, 1964; Corp. Control and Bus. Behavior, 1970; Markets and Hierarchies, 1975; The Econ. Instn. of Capitalism, 1985; Econ. Orgn., 1986, Antitrust Economics, 1987; The Mechanisms of Governance, 1996; assoc. editor, Bell. Jour. Econ., 1973-74; editor, 1975-82; co-editor Jour. Law, Econ. and Orgn., 1983—2003. Fellow Ctr. for Advanced Study in Behavioral Sci., 1977-78; Guggenheim fellow, 1977 78; Fulbright scholar, 1999; Am. Acad. Arts and Sci. fellow, 1983; recipient Alexander Henderson Award Carnegie-Mellon U., 1962, Alexander von Humboldt Rsch. prize, 1987, Irwin Award Acad. of Mgmt., 1988, John von Newmann lectr., 1999. Fellow Econometric Soc., Am. Acad. Polit. and Social Sci., Acad. Internat. Bus. (eminent scholar); mem. NAS, 1995; Internat. Soc. for New Instnl. Econ. (pres. 1999-2001), Am. Econ. Assn. (v.p. 2000-01), Am. Law and Econ. Assn. (pres. 1997-98), Western Econ. Assn. (pres. 1999-2000). Office: Univ Calif Dept Econ Berkeley CA 94720-0001

WILLIAMSON, PAUL MICHAEL, music educator; b. Kansas City, Mo., Nov. 5, 1971; s. Thomas Wilson and Ruth Colleen Williamson; m. Lorie Beth Williamson, May 19, 2000; children: John Russell Maloy, Miles Kendrick Arndt, Luke Bartel Arndt, Logan Thomas. B of Music Edn., U. of Tulsa, 1996. Lic. tchr. Dept. of Edn., Colo., Dept. of Edn., Okla. Music dir. Edison Prep. Sch., Tulsa, 1997—2003, Wasson H.S., Colorado Springs, 2003—. Worship team bass player First Presbyn. Ch., Tulsa, 2001—03; tournament dir. Tulsa Kids Baseball, 2001—03. Mem.: Internat. Assn. of Jazz Educators (assoc.), NEA, Alpha Chi chpt. Phi Mu Alpha (assoc.; pres. 1994—96). Home: 115 Iveystone Ct Colorado Springs CO 80919 E-mail: willipm@d11.org.

WILLIAMSON, PAUL RICHARD, medical educator, surgeon; b. Asheville, N.C., Aug. 11, 1956; s. William Cooper and Joyce Lee (Sluder) W. BS in Biology, Wake Forest U., 1978, MD, 1982. Asst. clin. prof. surgery U. Ill., Urbana, 1987-88, U. Fla., Gainesville, 1989—; clin. prof. surgery Orlando (Fla.) Regional Med. Ctr., 1988—, co-dir. colon-rectal fellowship program, 1990—, chief of surgery Sand Lake Divsn., 1991-95. Contbr. articles to profl. jours. Recipient medal of Merit, Orange County Sheriff's Dept. Fellow ACS, Am. Soc. Colon and Rectal Surgery, So. Med. Assn. (pres., mem. rectal sect. 1994), Phi Beta Kappa. Baptist. Office: Colon Rectal Clinic 110 W Underwood St Ste A Orlando FL 32806-1132

WILLIAMSON, PETER DAVID, lawyer; b. Houston, Oct. 13, 1944; s. Sam and Sophie Ann (Kaplan) W.; m. Patricia Golemon; children: Heather, Amber, Asia, Ginger. BA, U. Ill., 1966; JD, U. Tex., 1969. Bar: Tex. 1969, U.S. Supreme Ct. 1974, U.S. Ct. Appeals (4th, 5th, 6th, 8th, 9th, 10th, 11th and D.C. cirs.); lic. comml. pilot. Pvt. practice, Houston, 1971—. Founder IMMLAW, The Nat. Consortium of Immigration Law Firms. Mem. Am. Immigration Lawyers Assn. (pres. 1994-95). Home: 2417 Branard St Houston TX 77098-2213 Office: 500 Jefferson Ste 2040 Houston TX 77002 Office Phone: 713-751-0222. E-mail: pwilliamson@pdwlaw.com. *I do not believe in the existence of national boundaries. The philosophy of my practice of the law is to help my clients achieve the ability to pass freely through such artificial political barriers.*

WILLIAMSON, PHILEMONA, artist; b. N.Y.C. BA, Bennington Coll., 1973; MA, NYU, 1979. Various positions Harlem Sch. Arts, 1978—83; vis. artist Norfolk (Va.) State U., 1982; artist Met. Mus. Art, 1983; artist, tchr. workshops Arts Connection, 1986—89; vis. artist Ctr. D'Art, Port-Au-Prince, Haiti, 1987; artist-in-residence Very Spl. Arts, 1987—88; supr. student tchrs. dept. post-baccalaureate edn. Sch. Visual Arts, 1988—89; adj. faculty R.I. Sch. Design, 1989—90; painting faculty Bard Coll. Milton Avery Grad. Sch. Arts, 1991; adj. faculty Parsons Sch. Design, 1991—92, vis. artist MFA program, 1994. Mem. adv. bd. Getty Ctr. Edn. in Arts, 1989—98; panelist in field; artist-in-residence Millay Colony for Arts, Austerlitz, NY, 1983. One-woman shows include The Queens (N.Y.) Mus. Art, 1988, Wenger Gallery, L.A., 1989, Fine Arts Gallery, Southampton (N.Y.) Coll. L.I. U., 1990, June Kelly Gallery, N.Y.C., 1990, 1992, 1995, 1998, African Am. Mus., Hempstead, N.Y., 1991, Powers Art Gallery, East Stroudsburg U., Pa., 1992, Pa. State U., University Park, 1993, Flushing Coun. on Culture and Arts, N.Y.C., 1993, John Michael Kohler Arts Str., Sheboygan, Wis., 1999, exhibited in group shows at The Mint Mus. Art, Charlotte, N.C., 1991, U. Wis. at Milw. Fine Arts Gallery, 1992, Lehman Coll. Art Gallery and Krasdale Foods Arts Gallery, Bronx, 1994, Anderson Gallery, Buffalo, 1994, Kingsborough C.C. Art Gallery of CUNY, Bklyn., 1996, Pratt Manhattan Gallery, N.Y.C., 1996, Rubelle and Norman Schafler Gallery, Pratt Inst., Bklyn., 1996, Spelman Coll. Mus. Fine Art, Atlanta, 1996, numerous others, Represented in permanent collections pub. and corp. collections. Recipient Arts in Transit Poster Commn., Union Sq. Sta., N.Y., 1992, Joan Mitchell Found. award in painting, 1997; fellow Fellow in painting, NEA, 1987—88, fellow in painting, N.Y. Found. Arts, 1991; grantee exhbn. grantee, Artist Space, 1988; Pollock-Krasner Found. grantee, 1989—90, Ludwig Vogelstein grantee, 1993—94. Office: 11 LaSalle Rd Montclair NJ 07043

WILLIAMSON, PHILIP, apparel executive; CEO Williamson-Dickie Mfg. Co., Ft. Worth. Office: Williamson-Dickie Mfg Co PO Box 1779 Fort Worth TX 76101-1779

WILLIAMSON, R. MAX, diversified financial services company executive; married; 4 children. BS, Bowling Green State U. CPCU. With Travelers Ins. Co., 1962—82; pres., CEO Legion Ins. Co., Dallas, 1982—87; sr. vp. Armco Ins. Group, Dallas; chmn., pres., CEO ACCEL Internat. Corp., Ohio; pres., COO Scottsdale Ins. Co., 1995—. Pres., bd. trustees Bowling Green State U. Alumni Orgn.; bd. mem. Griffith Found. for Ins. Edn., Derek Hughes NAPSLO Ednl. Fuond., Nat. Assn. of Profl. Surplus Lines Offices, Scottsdale Cultural Arts Coun. Office: Scottsdale Ins Co 8877 N Gainey Ctr Dr Scottsdale AZ 85258

WILLIAMSON, RAMONA DIANE, special education educator; b. Baton Rouge, Apr. 20, 1962; d. John Thomas and Virginia (Harmeyer) W. BA, Nicholls State U., 1983; MEd, U. New Orleans, 1994, postgrad., 1994, 2000. Mid/moderate spl. edn. tchr. St. Bernard Parish Pub. Schs., Chalmette, La., 1988-96; grad. asst. U. New Orleans, 1996-97. Mem. vis. com. So. Assn. Colls. and Schs., La., 1994-98; new tchr. mentor St. Bernard Parish Pub. Schs., 1997—; presenter internat. profl. confs., U.S., Australia. Contbr. articles to profl. jours. Vol. Algiers Point Assn., New Orleans, 1987—; guide Preservation Resource Ctr./Live in a Landmark Program, New Orleans, 1990-98; vol., neighborhood coord., runner, liaison Christmas in October, New Orleans, 1993—. Recipient Tchr. of Yr. award Wal-Mart Found., 1999; La. State Dept. Edn. grantee, 1991-2001, La. Fedn. Coun. Exceptional Children grantee. Mem. La. Fedn. Coun. for Exceptional Children, St. Bernard Coun. Internat. Reading Assn., Kappa Delta Pi. Republican. Presbyterian. Avocations: travel, gardening, cooking, reading. Office: CF Rowley Elem Sch 49 Madison Ave Chalmette LA 70043-4429 Home: 8408 Prince Dr Chalmette LA 70043-1036 E-mail: ramonaw413@aol.com.

WILLIAMSON, RICHARD CARDINAL, physicist; b. Minocqua, Wis., Sept. 10, 1939; s. Lyman Olaf and Edna (Cardinal) W.; m. Christine Bauer, Sept. 2, 1961; children— Kari, Meagan, Heidi, Ryan BS in Physics, MIT, 1961, PhD in Physics, 1966. Staff physicist NASA Electronics Research Ctr., Cambridge, Mass., 1965-70; staff mem. and assoc. group leader MIT Lincoln Lab., Lexington, Mass., 1970-80, group leader applied physics, electrooptic device rsch., 1980-95, sr. staff electro-optical devices and materials group, 1995—. Contbr. articles to jours., chpts. to books; patentee in field Fellow IEEE (Centennial award 1984, Sonics and Ultrasonics Achievement award 1985); mem. IEEE, Am. Phys. Soc., Optical Soc. Am., Sigma Xi. Methodist. Home: 21 Pendleton Rd Sudbury MA 01776-1612 Office: 244 Wood St Rm C317 Lexington MA 02420-9108 E-mail: williamson@ll.mit.edu.

WILLIAMSON, RICHARD HALL, association executive; b. Canton, N.C., July 29, 1940; s. James Eustace and Gwendolyn (Nevada) H.; m. Julia Draper Brown, Nov. 7, 1965 (div. Jan. 1981); children: Shawn Nicol, Kevin Carson; m. Janie E. Shaheen, Nov. 18, 1998. BS in Physics, N.C. State U., 1962, MS in Nuclear Engring., 1970, postgrad., 1972. Instr. N.C. State U., Raleigh, 1968-72; chief, energy systems analysis AEC, Washington, 1972-75; asst. dir., energy analysis U.S. Energy R & D Adminstrn., Washington, 1975-77; dir., program analysis U.S. Dept. Energy, Washington, 1977-80, dir., policy devel., 1980-84, dep. asst. sec. for internat. affairs, 1984-94; dep. exec. dir. U.S. Energy Assn., Washington, 1995-99. Bd. dirs. Houston World Energy Congress Inc., 1994-99; chmn. Worth Assocs. Inc., Flint Hill, Va., 1998—. Author: A Group Strategy for Energy Research, Development and Demonstration, 1980; contbr. articles to jours. in field. Football ofcl. Atlantic Coast Conf., Greensboro, N.C., 1980-2002, Rose Bowl, Pasadena, Calif., 1995; treas. Sigma Alpha Mu Endowment Fund, 1994—, Sigma Alpha Mu Found., 1989—; treas. St. Simons Island Newcomers Club, 2001—03. 1st lt. U.S. Army, 1962-64; col. USAR, 1964-93. NSF fellow, 1964-65; AEC fellow, 1965-68; recipient Outstanding alumnus award IFC, N.C. State U., 1971, Presdl. Rank award U.S. Dept. Energy, 1990, Atlantic Coast Conf. Svc. to Football Officiating award, 2000. Mem. Sigma Alpha Mu (nat. pres. 1984-86), Tau Beta Pi, Phi Kappa Phi, Omicron Delta Kappa, Sigma Pi Sigma, Pi Mu Epsilon. Republican. Methodist. Avocations: stamp collecting/philately, tennis, golf, skiing. Home: 906 Champney Saint Simons Island GA 31522-5464 Office: Worth Assocs PO Box 456 820 Fodderstack Rd Flint Hill VA 22627 Office Phone: 540-675-1250.

WILLIAMSON, RICHARD SALISBURY, ambassador; b. Evanston, Ill., May 9, 1949; s. Donald G. and Marion (Salisbury) W.; m. Jane Thatcher, Aug. 25, 1973; children: Elizabeth Jean, Craig Salisbury, Richard Middleton. AB with honors, Princeton U., 1971; JD, U. Va., 1974. Bar: Ill. bar 1974, D.C. bar 1975. Legis. counsel, adminstrv. asst. to Congressman Philip M. Crane of Ill., 1974-76; assoc. firm Winston & Strawn, Washington, 1977-80, ptnr., 1980; asst. to Pres. for intergovtl. affairs, Washington, also assoc. dir. President's Task Force on Regulatory Relief, 1981-83; U.S. ambassador Vienna, 1983-85; sr. v.p., corp. and internat. relations Beatrice Cos., Inc., Chgo., 1985-86; ptnr. Mayer, Brown & Platt, Chgo., 1986—2001; asst. sec. of state internat. orgn. affairs U.S. Dept. State, Washington, 1988-89; alt. repr. to the U.N. for special polit. affairs U.S. Dept. State, Washington, 2002—. Rep. UN Orgns., Vienna, 1983-85; dep. ref. with rank of ambassador IAEA. Editor: Trade & Economic Growth, 1993, United States Foreign Policy and the United Nations System, 1996; co-editor: (with Paul Laxalt) A Changing America: Conservatives View the 80's From the United States Senate, 1980; author: Reagan's Federalism: His Efforts to Decentralize Government, 1990, The United Nations: A Place of Promise and of Mischief, 1991, Disorder in the New World, 1997, Seeking Firm Footing: America in the World in the New Centur7, 2001. Chmn. Ill. Rep. Party, 1999-2002. Republican. Office: US Mission UN 799 United Nations Plz New York NY 10017-3505

WILLIAMSON, ROBERT ELMORE, engineering educator; b. York County, S.C., Nov. 8, 1937; s. Charles Edward Jr. and Margaret Gladys (Elmore) W.; m. Eva Evelyn Simpson, June 27, 1964; children: Margaret Edye, Robert Elmore Jr. BS, Clemson U., 1959, MS, 1964; PhD, Miss. State U., 1972. Registered profl. engr., Ga. Rsch. assoc. Miss. State U., Starkville, 1966-71; asst. prof. agrl. engring. U. Ga., Tifton, 1971-78; assoc. prof. Clemson (S.C.) U., 1978-81, prof. biosys. engring., 1981—2003, prof. emeritus, 2003—. Co-inventor bulb, root and leafy vegetable harvester, improved harvesting machinery, multi-purpose horticultural tractor; contbr., co-contbr. numerous articles to scholarly jours.; contbr., co-contbr. numerous articles to sci. jours. Asst. scoutmaster Clemson area Boy Scouts Am., 1972-78, 80—. 1st lt. USAF, 1959-62. Recipient Silver Beaver award Boy Scouts Am., 1999. Mem. Am. Soc. AGrl. Engrs., Phi Kappa Phi (Clemson chpt. pres. 1984-85), Gamma Sigma Delta, Alpha Zeta, Sigma Xi. Presbyterian. Avocations: hunting, camping, backpacking, woodworking, tennis. Home: 303 Princess Grace Ave Clemson SC 29631-1215 Office: Agrl & Biol Engring McAdams Hall Clemson U Clemson SC 29631

WILLIAMSON, ROBERT F. health products executive; BA, Pomona Coll.; MBA, Stanford U. Rsch. asst. Fed. Res. Bd. Govs.; v.p., dir. The Boston Cons. Group; pres., CEO, dir. DoubleTwist, Inc., Oakland, Calif., 1999—.

WILLIAMSON, ROSE ANN, insurance agent; b. Wichita, Kans., Oct. 23, 1946; d. Victor Edward and Barbara Agnes Dewhirst; m. Wilson Wayne Williamson, Nov. 21, 1964; children: Ed Howard Dehning, Lisa Ann Wenger, Michael Wayne, Steven Dean, Annice Cara. BS in Edn., Drake U., 1997. License in life, accident, and health insurance Iowa, 2001. Sr. account specialist Am. Republic Ins. Co., Des Moines, 2003—; marsh affinity group svcs. Third Party Adminstr., West Des Moines, 1998—2003; account mgr. Sears Credit, 1995—99; respiratory therapy technician Greater Cmty. Hosp., Creston, 1976—94; nurse's medication asst. Creston Manor Nursing Home, 1975—76; nursing asst. Crest Haven Nursing Home, 1974—75. Treas. Greater Cmty. Hosp. Assn., Creston, Iowa, 1992—94. Sponsor Compassion Internat., Colo. Springs, Colo., 2003; mem. Care Group, Des Moines, 2001—03; facilitator Home Bible Study, Creston, 2001—02. Recipient Most Conservation Activity, Marsh Affinity Group Svcs., 2002+ 2003, Girls' State, Maryville H.S., 1963, Kappa Delta Pi, Drake U., 1995-1997, Dean's List, 1994-1997, Cum Laude, 1997; scholar Pres. scholarship, 1994-1997, C.C. Transfer scholarship, 1994-1997. Democrat-Npl. Avocations: reading, bible study, politics. Home: 908 W Summit St Creston IA 50801-2005 Office: Am Rep Insurance Co 601 6th Ave Des Moines IA 50306 Personal E-mail: roseann@mchsi.com. E-mail: roseann_williamson@aric.com.

WILLIAMSON, SAMUEL RUTHVEN, JR., historian, emeritus university president; b. Bogalusa, La., Nov. 10, 1935; s. Samuel Ruthven and Frances Mitchell (Page) Williamson; m. Joan Chaffe Andress, Dec. 30, 1961; children: George Samuel, Treeby Andress, Thaddeus Miller. BA, Tulane U., 1958; AM, Harvard U., 1960, PhD, 1966, grad. advanced mgmt. program, 1986; degree (hon.), Furman U., Va. Theol. Sem., Centre Coll. Asst. prof. U.S. Mil. Acad., 1963—66; from instr. history to asst. dean Harvard U., 1966—69, asst. to dean of Harvard Coll., 1969—70; rsch. assoc. Inst. Politics, faculty assoc. Ctr. for Internat. Affairs, 1971—72; mem. faculty J.F. Kennedy Sch. Govt., 1971—72; from assoc. prof. history to provost U. N.C., Chapel Hill, 1972—84, provost univ., 1984—88; pres., vice chancellor U. of South, Sewanee, Tenn., 1988—2000, vice chancellor emeritus, prof. history, 2000—, Robert M. Ayres 1988 distiing. univ. prof., 2001—. Cons. historian's office Office of Sec. Def., 1974—76; vis. fellow Churchill Coll., 1976—77; mem. vis. com. Harvard Coll., 1986—92; dir. Rsch. Triangle Inst., 1984—88; trustee N.C. Sch. Sci. and Coll., 1976—77, Day Found., 1990—93; mem. bd. visitors Air U., 1994—2002. Author: The Politics of Grand Strategy: Britain and France Prepare for War 1904-1914, 1969, 1990; co-author: The Origins of U.S. Nuclear Strategy, 1945-53, 1993, Soldiers, Statesmen and the Coming of the Great War, 2003, July 1914: Soldiers, Statesmen, and the Coming of the Great War, 2003; editor: The Origins of a Tragedy, July 1914, 1981, War and Soc. Newsletter, 1973—88; co-editor: Essays on World War I: Origins and Prisoners of War, 1983, Austria-Hungary and the Origins of the First World War, 1991. Mem. cen. com. Morehead Found., 1978—93; vice chmn. bd. visitors Air U., 1996—98, chmn. bd. visitors, 1998—2000. Capt. U.S. Army, 1963—66. Fellow, NEH, 1976—77, Nat. Humanities Ctr., 1983; grantee, Ford Found., 1976; Fulbright scholar, U. Edinburgh, 1958—59, Woodrow Wilson Ctr. scholar, Washington, 2002, Woodrow Wilson fellow, 1958—63, Danforth fellow, 1958—63. Mem.: Nat. Assn. Colls. and Univs. (vice chmn., chmn. bd. dirs. 1993—95), Internat. Inst. Strategic Studies, Am. Hist. Assn. (George Louis Beer prize 1970). Democrat. Episcopalian. Home: PO Box 837 Sewanee TN 37375-0837 Office: U of South duPont Libr Sewanee TN 37383-1000 E-mail: swilliam@sewanee.edu.

WILLIAMSON, SUSAN, mathematician, educator; b. Boston, Dec. 29, 1936; d. Richard Phillip and Mary Elizabeth Williamson. AB, Radcliffe Coll., Cambridge, Mass., 1958; MA, PhD, Brandeis U., Waltham, Mass., 1963. Instr. Cardinal Cushing Coll., Brookline, Mass., 1962—63; asst. prof. Boston Coll., Chestnut Hill, Mass., 1963—64, Regis Coll., Weston, Mass., 1965—67, assoc. prof., 1967—71, acad. dean, 1973—75, prof., 1971—2002, prof. emerita, 2002—. Reviewer Math. Revs., Ann Arbor, Mich., 1968—. Contbr. articles to profl. jours. Overseer DeCordova Mus., 2004—. Mem.: AAUP, Math. Assn. Am., Am. Math. Soc. Avocation: landscape drawing. Home: 37 Hagen Rd Newton Center MA 02459 Personal E-mail: susanwilliamson@compuserve.com.

WILLIAMSON, THOMAS ARNOLD, publishing executive; b. Sagamore, Pa., Oct. 4, 1939; s. Thomas and Mabel (Kennedy) Williamson; m. Kathryn Steiner White, Mar. 1, 1980, 1 child, Thomas J. Grad., Phillips Exeter Acad., 1957; AB, Harvard U., 1961. From sales person to sr. v.p. Harcourt Brace & Co., N.Y.C., 1962—88, sr. v.p., 1988—95; pres. Psychol. Corp., San Antonio, 1982-88; v.p. Holt Rinehart & Winston Harcourt Brace, 1989-95, pres. sch. publs., 1989-93, pres. ednl. devel. group, 1993-94; pres. Learning Initiative, Austin, Tex., 1994—, T. Williamson Assocs., Inc., Austin, 1995—, Focused Learning, Ltd., Austin, 1998—; assoc. Keller Williams Realty, Austin, 2003—. Bd. dirs. The Austin Project. Co-chmn. vis. com. to psychology dept. U. Tex., Austin, 1986—89, 1995—98; vol., chair chpt. 249 SCORE, 2003—04. Mem.: Hills Country Club, Town and Gown Club, Harvard Club N.Y.C. Home: 5 Cheverly Ct Austin TX 78738-1511 Office: Keller Williams Realty 1927 Lohmans Crossing Ste 102 Austin TX 78734

WILLIAMSON, WAYNE C. preventive medicine physician; b. Hammond, Ind., 1952; MD, U. Cin., 1978. Cert. Am. Bd. Internal Medicine, 1984, in Geriatric Medicine 1992. Intern Rush Presbyn., St. Luke's Med. Ctr., Chgo., 1978—79, resident, internal medicine, 1979—81, physician; asst. prof. Rush Med. Coll. Office: Rush-Presbyn-St Luke's Med Ctr 1653 W Congress Pkwy Chicago IL 60612*

WILLIAMSON, WILLIAM ALLEN, retired optometrist; b. Dossville, Miss., July 29, 1933; s. Donald Wodsworth and Ruth Beatrice (Doss) W.; m. Martha Pearl Taylor, Mar. 28, 1959; children: Lamar Arthur, William Allen, Donna Taylor. AA, Northwest Jr. Coll., Senatobia, Miss., 1952; OD, So. Coll. Optometry, Memphis, 1956. Pvt. practice optometry, Greenville, Miss., 1959-97; ret. Chmn. Adv. Com. to Medicaid, Miss., 1972-75. Mem. Miss. Blind & Deaf Bd. Trustees, 1974-76; charter mem. Optomist Club, Greenville, Miss., 1964; pres. Wash. County Assn. Retarded Citizens, Greenville, 1981-83, S.O.S. Retarded Workshop, Inc., Greenville, 1985-87, Christian Mission Concerns of Miss., Greenville, 1987-89. 1st lt. U.S. Army, 1956-59. Mem. Am. Optometric Assn. (legis. keyman 1971-72), Miss. Optometric Assn. (legis. chmn. 1973-74), Masons (32 degree), Shriners, Elks. Presbyterian. Avocations: the bible, history, genealogy research, politics, fishing.

WILLIAMSON, WILLIAM PAUL, JR., journalist; b. Des Moines, Mar. 30, 1929; s. William Paul and Florence Alice (Dawson) W.; m. Vania Torres Nogueira, Nov. 27, 1959; children: Mary Liz, Jon Thadeus, Margaret Ann (Mrs. Cesar Rocha). Student, Mexico City Coll., 1952, U. Havanna, 1955; BA, U. No. Iowa, 1953; MA, U. Iowa, 1954. Editor Brazilian Bus., Rio de Janeiro, 1958-60; mng. ptnr. Editora Mory Ltd., Rio de Janeiro, 1960-79; editor Brazil Herald, Rio de Janeiro, 1960-80; exec. dir. Inter Am. Press Assn., Miami, Fla., 1981-94, hon. life mem., mem. adv. coun., 1994—, dir., 1966-80, chmn. awards com., 1975-80. Solo navigator 1st passage Madeira Island, Portugal-Madeira Island, Brazil, 1994-95. Editor for Brazil, Fodor's South America, 1970-79; contbr. articles to various newspapers and mags. Pres. Am. Soc., Rio de Janeiro, 1968; bd. dirs. Instituto Brasil-Estados Unidos, Rio de Janeiro, 1977-80, Am. C. of C. for Brazil, Rio de Janeiro, 1964-68; rear commodore Seven Seas Cruising Assn., 2000—. Served with USMC, 1946-48. Decorated Order of Rio Branco (Brazil); recipient Citizen of Rio de Janeiro award State Legislature, 1975; Hon. Carioca award O Globo Newspaper, Rio de Janeiro, 1972; Ralph Greenberg award Am. Soc. Rio de Janeiro, 1977; Outstanding Svc. to Freedom of Expression and Newspapers awards Internat. Fedn. of Newspaper Pubs. and Internat. Assn. of Broadcasting, 1994; Benemeritous Citizen award Mcpl. Legislature, Itaquai, Brazil, 1995. Mem. Am. Soc. Assn. Execs., South Fla. Soc. Assn. Execs. (pres. 1987), Soc. Profl. Journalists, Overseas Press Club Am., Brazil Fgn. Corr. Assn. (founder, mem. honor), Rio Yacht Club, Ilha da Madeira Yacht Club, Kappa Tau Alpha. Home: 3051 NE 47th Ct Apt 204 Fort Lauderdale FL 33308-5304 Office Phone: 954-647-9039. E-mail: billvania@yahoo.com.

WILLIAMS-STEINWENDER, KARIN MAE, artist; b. Santa Monica, Calif., Oct. 14, 1948; d. Marion Glen and Margaret Grace (Long) Williams; m. Helmut Adolf Ludwig Steinwender, Aug. 17, 1985. BA with hons., Calif. State U., Dominguez Hills, Carson, 1983. Cert. tchr. art-dance, Calif.; cert. hypnotist; cert. Shiat-su therapist; cert. Cecchetti Ballet instr. Chmn. bd. South Bay (Calif.) Ballet Co., 1977-78, choreographer, 1976-77; gallery coord. F.O.T.A., Hermosa Beach, Calif., 1978-79; ballet instr. Act III Acad., Redondo Beach, Calif., 1976-83; self-employed ballet instr. South Bay, 1972-93; artist, painter Calif., N.Y., Oreg., 1972—; ballet instr. Banks, Oreg., 1994, Pendleton, Oreg., 1995—; owner, operator, dir. Acad. Classical Ballet, Pendleton, 1996—; owner Body Moves Dancewear, Pendleton, 1998—. Owner Body Moves Dancewear, Pendleton; exhbns. include Art of 80's Gallery, Hermosa Beach, Calif., Barnsdale Mcpl. Gallery, L.A., Community galleries, South Bay, Calif., Ambiente', Redondo Beach, Calif., Everson Mus. exhbn., Syracuse, N.Y., Gallery Syracuse, 1972—, Pendleton Arts Ctr., Oreg., 2000, 01; one-woman show Crackerjack Prodns.; interview and art filming South Bay News, Redondo Beach, Calif.; studio opening/exhbn., 1992. Author: Technique in Balance and Turning, 1985; writer, producer, choreographer (ballets) Woodcutter's Daughter, 1977, Power Plays, 1978; choreographer Midsummer Nights Dream, 1975, Danses for Danses' Sake, 1978, Grand Allegro, 1999, holiday and community programs, 1975-83. Vol. Rep. Party, Syracuse, 1988-89, Park Assn., Syracuse, 1990; mem. Rep. Women, Pendleton, 1996—. Mem. ASPCA, Rodale Inst., Arbor Day Found., Nat. Wildlife Fedn., Greenpeace, Wilderness Soc., Rosicrucians, In Def. of Animals. Avocations: gardening, herbology, reading, dance, hiking. Office: Body Moves Dancewear 423 1/2 Main St Pendleton OR 97801

WILLIAN, CLYDE FRANKLIN, lawyer; b. Indpls., Sept. 20, 1930; s. Clyde W. and Ruth L. (Robinson) Willian; m. Patricia Strong, Aug. 16, 1953; children: James, Jeffrey, John, Mary, Michael. BS, Rose-Hulman Inst. Tech., 1952; postgrad., Ind. U., 1953—54; LLB, George Washington U., 1957; postgrad., Chgo. Kent Coll. Law, 1957. Bar: Ill. 1957, U.S. Dist. Ct. (no. dist.) Ill. 1957, U.S. Ct. Appeals (7th cir.) 1958, U.S. Supreme Ct. 1970. Assoc. Willian Brinks Hofer Gilson & Lione Ltd. and predecessors, Chgo., 1957—96, pres., 1978—95. Bd. dirs. Hadley Sch. for Blind, Rose-Hulman Inst. Tech. Mem.: ABA (chmn.), Chgo. Bar Assn., Ill. Bar Assn., Bar Assn. 7th Fed. Cir., Am. Patent Law Assn., Am. Judicature Soc., Skokie Country Club, Union League Chgo., Phi Alpha Delta. Republican. Episcopalian. Office: Sidley Austin Brown and Wood Bank One Plz Chicago IL 60603-5503 Office Phone: 312-853-6897. E-mail: cwillian@aol.com.

WILLIE, CHARLES VERT, sociology educator; b. Dallas, Oct. 8, 1927; s. Louis James and Carrie (Sykes) W.; m. Mary Susannah Conklin, Mar. 31, 1962; children: Sarah Susannah, Martin Charles, James Theodore. BA,

Morehouse Coll., 1948, DHL (hon.), 1983; MA, Atlanta U., 1949; PhD, Syracuse U., 1957, DHL (hon.), 1992; DD (hon.), Gen. Sem., 1974; DHL (hon.), Berkeley Div. Sch., Yale U., 1972, R.I. Coll., 1983, Johnson C. Smith U., Charlotte N.C., 1991; MA (hon.), Harvard U., 1974; DL (hon.), Framingham (Mass.) State Coll., 1992; DHL (hon.), Franklin Pierce Coll., Rindge, N.H., 1996, Haverford Coll., 2000; D of Engring. Tech. (hon.), Wentworth Inst. Tech., 1996; DD (hon.), Episcopal Div. Sch., Cambridge, Mass., 2004. Instr. to asst. prof. sociology Syracuse (N.Y.) U., 1952-63, assoc. prof., 1964-67, prof., 1968-74, chmn. dept. sociology, 1967-71, v.p., 1972-74; prof. edn. and urban studies Grad. Sch. Edn. Harvard U., Cambridge, Mass., 1974-98, Charles William Eliot prof. edn. Grad. Sch. Edn., 1998-99, prof. emeritus Grad. Sch. Edn., 1999—. Instr. dept. preventive medicine SUNY Upstate Med. Center, Syracuse, 1955-60; rsch. dir. Washington Action for Youth delinquency prevention project, Pres.' Com. on Juvenile Delinquency and Youth Crime, Washington, 1962-64; vis. lectr. Lab. Cmty. Psychiatry, Harvard U. Med. Sch., Boston, Mass., 1966-67; vis. lectr. ch. and soc. Episcopal Div. Sch., Cambridge, Mass., 1966-67; commr. Pres.'s Commn. on Mental Health, 1977-78; mem. tech. adv. bd. Maurice Falk Med. Fund, 1968-99; bd. dirs. Social Sci. Rsch. Coun., 1969-75; master Boston Sch. Desegregation case, Fed. Dist. Ct., 1975; mem. nat. adv. com. Maxwell Sch. Syracuse U., 1992-2000, Hogg Found. for Mental Health, 1998-2002, Morehouse Rsch. Inst., 1997-2002; bd. overseers Boston Sci. Mus., 1997-2001, overseer emeritus, 2002—; corporator Emerson Hosp., Concord, Mass., 1998—; chmn. bd. dirs. Judge Baker Children's Ctr., 2001-2003; mem. nat. adv. com. The History-Makers, 2002—. Author: Church Action in the World, 1969, Black Students at White Colleges, 1972, Race Mixing in the Public Schools, 1973, Oreo, 1975, (with R. Reddick) A New Look at Black Families, 1976, 5th edit., 2003, The Sociology of Urban Education, 1978, The Caste and Class Controversy on Race and Poverty, 1979, 2d edit., 1989, The Ivory and Ebony Towers, 1981, Race, Ethnicity and Socioeconomic Status, 1983, School Desegregation Plans That Work, 1984, Black and White Families, 1985, Five Black Scholars, 1986, (with Michael Grady) Metropolitan School Desegregation, 1986, Effective Education, 1987, (with Michael Grady and Richard Hope) African-Americans and the Doctoral Experience, 1991, Theories of Human Social Action, 1994, (with Michael Alves) Controlled Choice, 1996, (with Ralph Edwards) Black Power/White Power in Public Education, 1998, (with Edwards and Alves) Student Diversity, Choice and School Improvement, 2002, The Family Life of Black People, 1970, (with B. Brown and B. Kramer) Racism and Mental Health, 1973, Black/Brown/White Relations, 1977, (with R. Edmonds) Black Colleges in America, 1978, (with S. Greenblatt) Community Politics and Educational Change, 1981, (with Inabeth Miller) Social Goals and Educational Reforms, 1988, (with A. Garibaldi and W. Reed), The Education of African-Americans, 1991, (with P. Rieker, B. Kramer and B. Brown) Mental Health, Racism and Sexism, 1995. Hon. trustee Episcopal Div. Sch., Cambridge; mem. United Negro Coll. Fund, pres. assembly, 1983-90; mem. nat. exec. coun. Episcopal ch., 1967-74, v.p. gen. conv., 1970-74; host Inner City Beat nat. pub. affairs weekly TV program, monitor channel, 1991-92. Recipient faculty svc. award Nat. Univ. Ext. Assn., 1969, 50th Anniversary Disting. Alumnus award Syracuse U. Maxwell Sch., 1974; Lee-Founders award Soc. for Study Social Problems, 1983, Family Scholar award, 1986; Disting. Career Contbn. award com. on role and status minorities in ednl. R & D, Am. Ednl. Rsch. Assn., 1990, Benjamin E. Mays Svc. award Morehouse Coll., 1994, Father John LaFarge, S.J. award Fairfield U., 1995, Disting. Career award Assn. Black Sociologists, 1996, Outstanding Book award for mental health, racism and sexism Myers Ctr. for Study of Human Rights, 1996, Arents Alumni award Syracuse U., 2000. Mem. Am. Ednl. Rsch. Assn., Am. Sociol. Assn. (coun. 1980-83, 95-98, v.p. 1996-97, DuBois-Johnson-Frazier award 1994), Assn. Black Sociologists, Ea. Sociol. Soc. (past pres.), Phi Beta Kappa, Alpha Phi Alpha. Episcopalian. Home: 41 Hillcrest Rd Concord MA 01742-4615 Office: Harvard U Grad Sch Edn 405 Gutman Libr 6 Appian Way Cambridge MA 02138-3704 Office Phone: 617-495-4678. E-mail: cvmswillie@aol.com.

WILLIFORD, DRURY FISHER, JR., historical researcher, writer, editor; b. Memphis, Nov. 27, 1929; s. Drury Fisher and Irene Frances (Dawson) W.; m. Virginia Lucile Jackson, Dec. 1950 (div. Sept. 1971); children: Peggy Leigh, Virginia Fisher, Alan Lyle, Mark Edward; m. Shirley Ann Hagedorn, Aug. 1981. BA, W.Va. U., 1986. Cert. police firearms instr. Fed. Law Enforcement Tng. Ctr. Audit clk. Nat. Bank of Commerce, Memphis, 1953-54; patrolman Memphis Police Dept., 1954-55; patrol insp. U.S. Border Patrol, El Paso, Tucson and Buffalo, 1955-57; from insp. to ops. officer U.S. Customs Svc., Toronto, 1957-63, Buffalo, 1963-72, Washington, 1972-81; ret., 1981. Freelance photographer. Contbr. articles to profl. jours. Boys hockey coach Amherst (N.Y.) Hockey Assn., 1964-72, Wheaton (Md.) Hockey Club, 1972-73, Morgantown (W.Va.) Hockey Club, 1981-82; literacy vol. tutor, 1985-88. With USN, 1950-52. Named Marion County Tutor of Yr., 1987; elected to Hockey Hall of Fame, Amherst, N.Y., 1984; High Quality Performance award Dept. of Treasury, 1975, 76, 79, Spl. Achievement award, 1981; Judith Herndon fellow W.Va. Legislature, 1984. Democrat. Avocations: animal protection and conservation of natural habitat, ultralight aircraft builder and pilot. Home: PO Box 734 Reedsville WV 26547-0734

WILLIG, KARL VICTOR, computer firm executive; b. Idaho Falls, Idaho, June 4, 1944; s. Louis Victor and Ethel (McCarty) W.; m. Julianne Erickson, June 10, 1972; 1 son, Ray. BA magna cum laude, Coll. of Idaho, 1968; MBA (Dean Donald Kirk David fellow), Harvard U., 1970. Pres. Ariz. Beef, Inc., Phoenix, 1971-73; group v.p. Ariz.-Colo. Land & Cattle Co., Phoenix, 1973-76; v.p. Rufenacht, Bromagen & Hertz, Inc., Chgo., 1976-77; pres. Sambo's Restaurants, Inc., Santa Barbara, Calif., 1977-79; ptnr. Santa Barbara Capital, 1979-85; pres. EURUSA Equities Corp., 1985-86; pres., chief exec. officer InfoGenesis, 1986—. Trustee Am. Bapt. Sem. of West, 1977-85; mem. Chgo. Merc. Exch., 1976-77, mem. audit com. and membership coms., 1976-77. Active Santa Barbara Rescue Mission, 2002—; bd. dirs. Los Padres coun. Boy Scouts Am., 2004—. Named one of Outstanding Young Men of Am., 1972; recipient Assn. of U.S. Army award, 1964.

WILLIG, ROBERT DANIEL, economics professor; b. Bklyn., Jan. 16, 1947; s. Jack David and Meg W.; m. Virginia Mason, July 8, 1973; children: Jared Mason, Scott Mason, Brent Mason, Alexandra Mason. BA, Harvard U., 1967; MS in Ops. Rsch., Stanford U., 1968, PhD in Econs, 1973. Lectr. Stanford U., Palo Alto, Calif., 1971-73; tech. staff Bell Labs., Holmdel, NJ, 1973-77, supr. dept. econs. rsch., 1977-78; prof. econs. and pub. affairs Princeton U., 1978—; task force on future of postal svc. Aspen Inst., 1978-80; dep. asst. atty. gen. U.S. Dept. Justice, Washington, 1989-91. Cons. in field; rsch. fellow U. Warwick, Eng., 1977; organizing com. Telecom Policy Rsch. Conf., 1977-78; rsch. adv. bd. Am. Enterprise Inst., 1980-88; mem. N.J. Gov.'s Task Force on Market-Based Pricing of Electricity, 1987; bd. dirs. Consultants in Industry Econs., Inc., Competition Policy Assocs., Inc.; mem. Def. Sci. Bd. Task Force on Antitrust for the Def. Industry, 1993-94, Transp. Rsch. Bd. Task Force, 1995-96; advisor Inter-Am. Devel. Bank, 1997-00. Author: Welfare Analysis of Policies Affecting Prices and Products, 1973, Contestable Markets and the Theory of Industry Structure, 1982; editor: Handbook of Industrial Organization, 1986, Can Privatization Deliver: Infrastructure for Latin America, 1999, Second Generation Reforms in Infrastructure Services, 2002; contbr. articles to profl. jours.; mem. editl. bd. MIT Press Series on Govt. Regulation, 1978—, Am. Econ. Rev., 1980-83, Jour. Indsl. Econs., 1985-89, Utility Policy, 1989-2001. Adv. bd. B'nai B'rith Hillel Found., Princeton U., 1978-89. Grantee, NSF, 1979—85. Fellow Econometric Soc. (program com. 1978-81); mem. Am. Econ. Assn. (nominating com. 1980-81). Office: Princeton Univ Economics Dept Princeton NJ 08540

WILLIMAN, PAULINE, shorthand reporter, farm foundation administrator; b. Albany County, N.Y., Jan. 11, 1926; d. Harrison and Alta Allen (Hallenbeck) Salisbury; m. Raymond Williman, Jan. 11, 1947 (div. Oct. 1951). Grad., Albany Stenotype Secretarial, 1941-42. Cert. shorthand reporter. Staff reporter Empire Stenographers, Albany, 1942-46; exec. sec. Res. Officers Assn., Dept. of N.Y., Albany, 1947-49; ofcl. reporter N.Y. State Supreme Ct./Third Jud. Dist., Albany, 1958-64; ofcl. stenographer N.Y. State Senate, Albany, 1979-98; profl. shorthand reporter self employed, Albany, N.Y., 1949—. Mem. Cert. Shorthand Reporter Licensure Bd., Albany, 1992-2004; specialized in reporting tech. engring. rev. procs. involving water supply and waste water treatment facilities throughout N.Y. state, 1952-94; mem. edn. and small bus. coms. Bus. Coun. N.Y. State, 1985-2000. Contbr. articles to profl. jours. Mem. RNSC Inner Circle, Washington, 1980-97; mem. Senatorial Bus. Adv. Bd., Washington, 1982-86. Recipient resolution and commendation for svc. N.Y. State Senate, 1998. Mem. Am. Water Works ASsn. (life), Nat. Ct. Reporters Assn., N.Y. State Ct. Reporters Assn., Kiwanis Internat. (club pres. 1997-99, award of excellence 1999). Republican. Mem. Dutch Reformed Ch. Avocations: golf, gardening, exercise, reading, music. Office: 447 Loudonville Rd Albany NY 12211-1499

WILLING, KATHERINE, former state legislator; m. Donald Willing. BS, Purdue U. Formerly tchr.; mem. from 39th dist. Ind. Ho. of Reps., 1992-97, mem. aged and aging, agr., edn., ways and means coms. Mem. Boone County Coun., 1988-92; bd. govs. Boone County Jr. Achievement; v.p. Boone County Leadership; bd. dirs., formerly treas. Witham Meml. Hosp. Found. Recipient Richard G. Lugar Excellence in Svc. award. Mem. Boone County Rep. Women's Club (pres.), Boone County and Carmel Clay County C. of C., Farm Bur., Zonta, Tri Kappa, Alpha Chi Omega. Home: 635 E Vermont St Indianapolis IN 46202-4205

WILLINGHAM, CLARK SUTTLES, lawyer; b. Houston, Nov. 29, 1944; s. Paul Suttles and Elsie Dell (Clark) W.; m. Jane Joyce Hitch, Aug. 16, 1969; children: Meredith Moores, James Barrett. BBA, Tex. Tech U., 1967; JD, So. Meth. U., 1971, LLM, 1984. Bar: Tex. 1971. Ptnr. Kasmir, Willingham & Krage, Dallas, 1972-86, Finley, Kumble et al, Dallas, 1986-87, Brice & Mankoff, Dallas, 1988-98, Moseley Martens, LLP, Dallas, 1999—. Contbr. articles to profl. jours. Bd. dirs. Dallas Summer Musicals, 1971—, exec. com., 1979-93, 97-2003, pres. 1994. Mem. ABA (chmn. agrl. com. tax sect. 1984-86), State Bar Tex. (chmn. agrl. tax com. 1985-87), Dallas Bar Assn., Am. Law Inst., Tex. Rangers Law Enforcement Assn.(bd. dirs. 2000—), Nat. Cattlemen's Beef Assn. (bd. dirs., pres. 1998), U.S. Meat Export Fedn. (exec. com. 1991-93), Beef Industry Coun. (exec. com. 1990-91, promotion chmn. 1992-94), Tex. Cattle Feeders Assn. (bd. dirs., pres. 1988), Tex. Bd. Vet. Med. Examiners (pres. 1994), Tex. Beef Coun. (bd. dirs., pres. 1989), Dallas Country Club. Republican. Episcopalian. Home: 3824 Shenandoah St Dallas TX 75205-1702 Office: Moseley Martens LLP 3878 Oak Lawn Ave Fl 4 Dallas TX 75219-4460 Office Phone: 214-525-3940. E-mail: clarkw@airmail.net.

WILLINGHAM, DEBORAH N. information technology executive; BS in Indsl. and Systems Engring., Ga. Inst. Tech. Various sr. mgmt. pos. IBM Corp.; v.p., support, Enterprise Customer Unit Microsoft, Redmond, Wash., 1993—96, v.p., Enterprise Customer Unit, 1996—99, v.p., bus. and enterprise divsn. mktg., sr. v.p., human resources. Mem. Nat. Bd. Advisors Coll. Bus. and Pub. Adminstrn., U. Ariz.; mem. indsl. and systems engring. alumni adv. bd., pres.'s adv. bd. Ga. Inst. Tech. Office: One Microsoft Way Redmond WA 98052-6399

WILLINGHAM, DOUGLAS BARTON, dentist; b. Mobile, Ala., Feb. 23, 1954; s. Welborn Kiefer and Mary Maxine (McCollum) W.; m. Michele Joy Saunders, Mar. 21, 1981 (div. 1997); 1 child, Sofia. BA, Tex. Tech. U., 1976; DDS, Baylor Coll. Dentistry, Dallas, 1980. Pvt. practice dentistry, Salado, Tex., 1981—. Editor Tex. Dental Jour., Austin, 1986-93. Mem. vestry St Luke's Episcopal Ch., Belton, Tex., 1998-2000, sr. warden, 1999; pres. Salado Hist. Soc., 1983, Railroad & Pioneer Mus., Temple, Tex. 1985-86, Bell County Hist. Commn., 1983-90; Tex. Coun. Advisors, Inst. for Humanities, Salado, 1985-92. Recipient Spirit of Am. award, Salado Ind. Sch. Dist., 2003, Appreciation award for chairmanship, Salado Coll. Preservation Project, 1989. Fellow Internat. Coll. Dentists (co-chair Tex. sect. lit. award com., golden pen award 1988, 89, 91, ann. literary award 1991, golden scroll award 1980, 88), Am. Coll. Dentists, Pierre Fauchard Acad. (Disting. Svc. award 1993); mem. Am. Assn. Dental Editors, Tex. Dental Assn. (historian, editor, Pres.'s award 1993, award of merit 1993, Disting. Svc. award 1992, Svc. Recognition award 2004), Baylor Dental Alumni Assn. (trustee 1989-92), Ctrl. Tex. Dental Soc. (Dentist of Yr. 1988). Republican. Episcopalian. Avocations: maritime history, historic preservation, geneaology, travel. Home: 9 N Church St Salado TX 76571-5690 E-mail: willingham@vvm.com.

WILLINGHAM, EDWARD BACON, JR., ecumenical minister, administrator; b. St. Louis, July 27, 1934; s. Edward and Harriet (Sharon) W.; m. Angeline Walton Pettit, June 14, 1957; children: Katie, Carol. BS in Physics, U. Richmond, 1956; postgrad., U. Rochester, 1958—59; MDiv., Colgate Rochester Div. Sch., 1960. Ordained to ministry Am. Bapt. Ch., 1960. Min. Christian edn. Delaware Ave. Bapt. Ch., Buffalo, N.Y., 1960-62; dir. radio and TV Met. Detroit Coun. Chs., 1962-75; exec. dir. Christian Communication Coun. Met. Detroit Chs., 1976-98. Chmn. N.Am. Broadcast sect. World Assn. for Christian Comm., 1970-71, bus. mgr., 1972-98, archivist, 1999—; broadcast cons. Mich. Coun. Chs., 1965-75; guest cons. religious broadcasting Germany, 1968; mem. coord. com. Mich. Ecumenical Forum, 1986, 90-92, chmn., 1991-92. Bd. mgrs. Broadcasting and Film Commn., Nat. Coun. Chs., 1965-73; mem. Muslim-Christian-Jewish Leadership Forum, 1987—; bd. deacons 1st Bapt. Ch. Birmingham, chmn., 1994-95. Recipient Gabriel award Cath. Broadcasting Assn., 1972, 1st Ann. Ecumenical award Am. Bapt. Chs. of Mich., 1992, Race Rels. award Booker T. Washington Bus. Assn. of Detroit, 1983. Mem. Assn. Regional Religious Communicators (pres. 1969-71), World Assn. Christian Comm. (ctrl. com. 1973-78), Phi Gamma Delta, Sigma Pi Sigma. Office: 21440 Lathrup St Southfield MI 48075-4218

WILLINGHAM, JEANNE MAGGART, dance educator, ballet company executive; b. Fresno, Calif., May 8, 1923; d. Harold F. and Gladys (Ellis) Maggart. Student, Tex. Woman's U., 1942; student profl. dancing schs. worldwide. Tchr. dance Beaux Arts Dance Studio, Pampa, Tex., 1948—; artistic dir. Pampa Civic Ballet, 1972—. Mem. Tex. Arts and Humanities Coun. Mem. Tex. Arts Alliance, Pampa C. of C. (fine arts com.), Pampa Fine Arts Assn. Office: Pampa Civic Ballet Beaux Arts Dance Studio 315 N Nelson St Pampa TX 79065-6013 Office Phone: 806-669-6361.

WILLINGHAM, MARY MAXINE, fashion retailer; b. Childress, Tex., Sept. 12, 1928; d. Charles Bryan and Mary (Bohannon) McCollum; m. Welborn Kiefer Willingham, Aug. 14, 1950; children: Sharon, Douglas, Sheila. BA, Tex. Tech U., 1949. Interviewer Univ. Placement Svc., Tex. Tech U., Lubbock, 1964-69; owner, mgr. buyer Maxine's Accent, Lubbock, 1969—. Speaker in field. Leader Campfire Girls, Lubbock, 1964-65; sec. Cmty. Theatre, Lubbock, 1962-64. Recipient Golden Sun award Dallas Market, 1985, Woman of Excellence award in Bus., YWCA, 2001; named Outstanding Mcht., Fashion Retailer Mag., 1971, also Outstanding Retailer. Mem. Lubbock Symphony Guild, Ranch and Heritage Ctr., Faculty Women's Club. Office: 16 Briercroft Shopping Ctr Lubbock TX 79412-3022

WILLINGHAM, WARREN WILLCOX, psychologist, testing service executive; b. Rome, Ga., Mar. 1, 1930; s. Calder Baynard and Eleanor (Willcox) W.; m. Anna Michal, Mar. 17, 1954; children: Sherry, Judith, Daniel. Student, Ga. Inst. Tech., 1952; PhD, U. Tenn., 1955. Rsch. assoc. World Book Co., N.Y.C., 1959-60; dir. evaluation studies Ga. Inst. Tech., Atlanta, 1960-64; dir. rsch. Coll. Bd., N.Y.C., 1964-68, dir. access rsch. office Palo Alto, Calif., 1968-72; asst. v.p., disting. rsch. scientist Ednl. Testing Svc., Princeton, N.J., 1972—. Vis. prof. U. Minn., 1988; mem. adv. bd. on ednl. requirements on Sec. Navy, 1968; leader Psychometric Seminar, Nat. Inst. Testing and Evaluation, Jerusalem, 1999; cons. to numerous schs., colls. U.S. Office Edn. Author: Free Access Higher Education, 1970, Source Book for Higher Education, 1973, College Placement and Exemption, 1974, Assessing Experimental Learning, 1977, Selective Admissions in Higher Education, 1977, Personal Qualities and College Admissions, 1982, Success in College, 1985, Testing Handicapped People, 1988, Predicting College Grades, 1990; Gender and Fair Assessment, 1997; editor: Measurement in Education, 1969-72; mem. editl. bd. Jour. Ednl. Measurement, 1971-75, Alternate Higher Edn., 1976-80, Am. Ednl. Rsch. Jour., 1968-71; contbr. articles, tech. reports to profl. jours. Served to lt. USNR, 1955-59. Recipient Am. award So. Soc. Philosophy and Psychology, 1958 Fellow Am. Psychol. Assn., AAAS; mem. Nat. Council on Measurement in Edn. (dir.), Am. Ednl. Research Assn., Am. Psychol. Soc., CAEL (hon. life mem.), Sigma Xi. Office: 131 Bertrand Dr Princeton NJ 08540 Mailing: 131 Bertrand Dr Princeton NJ 08540

WILLINGHAM, WELBORN IEFER, psychologist, educator; b. Rotan, Tex., Mar. 12, 1928; s. W.B. and Juanita Madge (Eason) W.; m. Mary Maxine McCollum, Aug. 14, 1950; children: Sharon, Douglas, Sheila. BA, Tex. Tech U., 1949; MEd, U. Tex., 1956; PhD, Tex. Tech U., 1964. Diplomate Am. Bd. Psychol. Specialties. Tchr., prin. elem. sch., Hale Center, Tex., 1951-53; edn. and tng. officer USAF, Brookley Air Force Base, Ala., 1953-55; tchr., coach Hutchinson Jr. High Sch., Lubbock, Tex., 1955-57; counselor Monterey High Sch., Lubbock, 1957-60; asst. dean students Tex. Tech U., Lubbock, 1963-64; clin. psychologist South Plains Guidance Ctr., Lubbock, 1964-66; from asst. prof. to prof. emeritus Tex. Tech U., Lubbock, 1966—; clin. prof. neuropsychiatry and behavioral scis. Tex. Tech. U. Health Scis. Ctr., 1983—. Cons. psychologist Big Spring (Tex.) VA Med. Ctr., 1990—; mem. allied health staff psychology Meth. Hosp., Lubbock, 1990. Cons. editor Individual Psychology, 1989—; tech. reviewer Tex. Dental Jour., 1989—; contbr. articles to profl. jours. Lt. col. USAFR, 1949-77. Paul Harris fellow Rotary Internat., 1985. Fellow Am. Bd. Forensic Examiners (diplomate), Am. Bd. Forensic Medicine (diplomate); mem. N.Am. Soc. Adlerian Psychology (del. assembly 1983-89, chmn. publs. com. 1986-89). Avocations: travel, study, reading. Home: 1605 56th St Lubbock TX 79412-2803 Fax: 806-741-1776.

WILLIS, BEN, writer, artist; b. Racine, Wis., Dec. 4, 1930; s. Ben Sherlock Willis and Beryl Hester (Smith) Young; div. 1971. Attended, Phila. Coll. Art, 1953-54, Pa. Acad. Fine Arts, 1954-55, Academie Julian, Paris, 1955-57. Author: The Tao of Art, 1987, Internet reprint edit., 2001; collaborator: The Art of Oriental Embroidery, 1980; exhibited in group shows Salmagundi Club, N.Y.C., 1971-75, 1980, Am. Watercolor Soc., Nat. Acad. Design, N.Y.C., 1978, Cicchinelli Galleries, N.Y.C., 1980, Nat. Arts Club, N.Y.C., 1980, Manasquan Group Artists, 1981, Pastel Soc., N.Y.C., 1982, Allied Artists Am., N.Y.C., 1982, Am. Artists Profl. League, N.Y.C., 1984; represented in numerous pvt. collections. Seaman 1st class, USN, 1948-52, Korea. Recipient 1st prize N.Y.C. Ctr., 1960, Manasquan Outdoor Art Show, 1981, Best in Show award Manasquan Group Artists, 1981, others. Fellow Alumni Fellowship Pa. Acad. Fine Art, Author's Guild. Episcopalian. Avocations: languages, music, reading, Judo. Home: 10 C Bennington Ln Whiting NJ 08759-1621

WILLIS, BEVERLY ANN, architect; b. Tulsa, Feb. 17, 1928; d. Ralph William and Margaret Amanda (Porter) W. BFA, U. Hawaii, 1954; PhD in Fine Arts (hon.), Mt. Holyoke Coll., 1983. Registered architect, Calif. Prin. Willis Atelier, Honolulu, 1954-58, Willis & Assocs., Inc., San Francisco, 1958-88, Beverly Willis Architects, N.Y.C., 1988—. Pres., dir. Architecture Rsch. Inst., Inc., N.Y.C., 1993—; co-chair Rebuild Downtown Our Town Coalition, 2002; prof. Internat. Women's U., Kassel, Germany, 2000. Author: Invisible Images: The Silent Language of Architecture, 1997; contbg. author: Creating Sustainable Urban Environments: Future Forms and Design for Sustainable Cities, 2004; prin. works include Union St. Stores (merit award San Francisco AIA, award of distinction State of Calif.), Nob Hill Cts. (merit award AIA), 1970, Margaret Hayward Park (grand and merit awards Pacific Coast Bldg. Con., Honor award Design Internat.), 1983, San Francisco Ballet Bldg., 1984, Manhattan Village Acad. H.S., N.Y.C., 1995; contbr. articles to profl. jours., chpts. to books. Founding trustee Nat. Bldg. Mus., Washington, 1976—; bldng. rsch. adv. bd. Nat. Acad. Sci., 1971-79, chair Fed. Construction Coun., 1976-79. Recipient Phoebe Hearst Gold Medal award, 1969. Fellow AIA (v.p. Calif. coun. 1979, pres. 1980); mem. Achievement Rewards for Coll. Scientists, Internat. Women's Forum, Villa Taverna Club, Lambda Alpha (pres. San Francisco chpt. 1981-82). Clubs: Villa Taverna (San Francisco). Avocations: poetry, sketching, tennis, walking. Office: Ste 1100 29 Broadway New York NY 10006-3255 Business E-Mail: bevwillis@architect.org.

WILLIS, BRUCE See WILLIS, WALTER BRUCE

WILLIS, BRUCE DONALD, judge; b. Mpls., Jan. 29, 1941; s. Donald Robert and Marie Evelyn (Edwards) W.; m. Elizabeth Ann Runsvold, July 17, 1971; children: Andrew John, Ellen Elizabeth. BA in English, Yale U., 1962; LLB, Harvard U., 1965. Bar: Minn., 1965, U.S. Dist. Ct. Minn. 1965, U.S. Ct. Fed. Claims 1989, U.S. Ct. Appeals (8th cir.) 1991, U.S. Supreme Ct. 1992. Assoc. Popham, Haik, Schnobrich & Kaufman, Ltd., Mpls., 1965-71, ptnr., 1971-95; judge Minn. Ct. Appeals, 1995—. Mem. jud. adv. bd. Law and Orgnl. Econs. Ctr., U. Kans., 1997—2001; adv. bd. Minn. Inst. Legal Edn., 1986—2003. Contbr. articles to profl. jours. Del. Rep. Nat. convs., 1976, 88; vice chmn. Ind.-Rep. Party Minn., 1979-81; mem. State Ethical Practices Bd., 1990-95, sec. 1990-91, vice chmn. 1991-92, chmn., 1992-93; mem. Minn. Commn. on Jud. Selection, 1991-94; mem. Minn. Bd. Jud. Stds., 1997—; mem. adv. com. on rules of civil appellate procedure Minn. Supreme Ct., 1997—. Named one of 1990's Lawyers of Yr., Minn. Jour. Law and Politics, 1991, one of Minn.'s Best Trial Lawyers, Minn. Lawyer, 1991. Mem.: ABA, Minn. Bar Assn. (professionalism com. 1998—). Mem. United Ch. of Christ. Home: 2940 Walnut Grove Ln N Plymouth MN 55447-1567 Office: Minn Jud Ctr 25 Rev Dr Martin Luther King Jr Blvd Saint Paul MN 55155-1500 E-mail: bruce.willis@courts.state.mn.us.

WILLIS, CAROL, museum director; b. 1949; m. Mark Willis. BA in Art History, Boston U. Founder, dir., curator Skyscraper Mus., N.Y.C., 1996—. Arch. historian, prof. urban studies Columbia U. Author: Form Follows Finance: Skyscrapers and Skylines in New York and Chicago, 1995 (AIA book award), The Lower Manhattan Plan: Visions for Downtown New York. Office: The Skyscraper Mus 55 Broad St #13F New York NY 10004*

WILLIS, CLAYTON, broadcaster, author, former government offical, educator, arts consultant; b. Washington, Aug. 11, 1933; s. William H. and Elizabeth Carl (Keferstein) W. Student, The Sorbonne, Paris, 1953-54; BA, George Washington U., 1957; student, U. Oslo, 1953; grad., N.Y. Inst. Fin., 1966, Assn. Commodities Exch. Firms Inc., 1966. Spl. assignment Am. Embassy, London, 1957; writer NBC Network radio show Tex and Jinx, 1958; spl. corr. NBC News, La Paz, Bolivia, 1959; spl. Washington corr. Fin. News TV Network (now CNBC), N.Y.C., 1988; contbr., anchor, TV prodr., corr. Saudi Arabian TV, Newsweek mag., Philips News Svc. The Hope (Ark.) Star; contbr., corr. Christian Sci. Monitor, L.A. Times-Mirror Syndicate, The Palm Beach (Fla.) Post, The Greenwich (Conn.) Time, The Bar Harbor (Maine) Times, Info-Explo Mining Jour., Rouyn-Noranda, Que., Can., Fin. News TV Network, New York, The Mainichi, Tokyo, The China Post, Taipei, Taiwan, Chattanooga Times, The Nashville Tennesseean, the Daily Nation of Kenya, The Khartoum Echo, Sudan, The Washington Daily News, Washington Post, Cape Argus of Capetown, South Africa, Bangkok Post, Irish Times, Dublin; reporter, movie, art critic Albuquerque Tribune, 1959-61; asst. editor Newsweek Mag., N.Y.C., 1961-62; TV broadcaster-writer UPI Newsfilm, N.Y.C., 1962; White House corr., chief bur., anchor World Radio News, Houston; White House, Washington corr. WAVA Radio Sta., Washington, 1963-65; editorial writer, corr. Hearst Newspapers, N.Y.C., 1965; press officer UN, N.Y.C., 1965-66; spl. assignment Am. Embassy, Reykjavik, Iceland, 1967; editorial writer, critic, reporter N.Y. Amsterdam News, N.Y.C., 1967-68; cons. govt., law, and ethics programs Ford Found., N.Y.C., 1968-69; dir. pub. affairs U.S. EEOC, Washington, 1969-70; cons. OEO, Washington, 1970, Pres.'s Nat. Coun. on Indian Opportunity, Washington, 1970-71, Community Rels. Svc., U.S. Dept. Justice, Washington, 1970-73, Cabinet Com. on Opportunities for Spanish-Speaking People, 1971-72, Fed. Energy Adminstrn., Washington, 1973-74; dir. pub. affairs Office of Petroleum Allocation, U.S. Dept. Interior, 1973-74; dir. Congl. rels., dir. pub. affairs Pres.'s Nat. Commn. on Fire Prevention and Control, 1971-73; pub., editor, owner Four Corners Chieftain, Ignacio and Durango, Colo., 1972-73; lectr. Sch. of Bus., U. D.C., Washington, 1973-74; owner, White House corr., photojournalist Willis News Svc., Washington, 1974—; pub. affairs dir. Inaugural Vets. Com., 1976-77; White House corr., photojournalist Washington Life mag., 1993—; anchor Channel 33, Arlington, Va., 1991—. Adviser to Fernando E.C. de Baca, spl. asst. to the Pres., White House, 1974-76; lectr. nat., internat. affairs, Haiti, art, communications, strategic and precious metals, nickel, copper, and mining, energy; corr.-broadcaster Sta. KTEN-TV, Ada, Okla., 1985; mem. staff presdl. transition office U.S. Pres. Bush, 1988-89, 90; dir. and curator L. Clayton Willis Art

Collection, Palm Beach, Fla.; anchor, corr. Channel 33 Arlington, Va., 1991—; pres., White House corr., congressional corr., photojournalist, Evening News Broadcasting Co., Collector Watch TV Show Ltd. with Clayton Willis, Alexandria, 1991—, 30 Mins. with Clayton Willis, and Willis News Service; prodr., anchor documentary programs Saudi Arabian TV, 1992—; exec. prodr., anchor Glimpses of the World documentaries, 1993; White House corr., photojournalist Hope (Ark.) Star, 1994—; dir., curator L. Clayton Willis Art Collection, Palm Beach; host, commentator The Clayton Willis Talk Show, WPBR, Palm Beach, Fla. Co-author: Capital Fare, 1977, Lott-Willis Pictorial Digest of U.S. Presidential Elections and Inaugurations, 1997; host/exec. prodr. The Clayton Willis Talk Shoe, WPBR, 2000; pres.'s White House corr. Fun Evening News Broadcasting Co., Washington, 2000; contbr. articles to Daily Mail, London, London Sunday Express, Umtali Post, Zimbabwe, Gwelo (Zimbabwe) Times, To the Point news mag., Johannesburg, The Citizen, Johannesburg, Hartford Courant, Sacramento Union, Chattanooga Times, UPI Radio Networks, Washington Post, The Hope (Ark.) Star, Phillips News Svc., also other mags. and newspapers. Broadcaster with Bush/Quayle Nat. Campaign Hdqrs., Washington, 1988; adviser Presdl. Transition Office of Pres. George Bush, 1988-89; loaned Haitian paintings for spl. exhbn. to Haitian Embassy, Washington, 1991, Milw. Art Mus., 1992. Recipient Outstanding Svc. award Harlem Prep. Sch., Johannes Gutenberg medal (Mainz, Germany), 1984, Letters of Cert. Appreciation Pres. of U.S., 1989. Mem. Overseas Press Club Am. Covered Vietnam, Congo, Mid. East, Rhodesian and South African wars; visited 150 countries; specialist gold, diamond, energy, silver, platinum, nickel, copper, and cobalt mining and strategic minerals; covered Clarence Thomas and Robert Gates U.S. Senate confirmation hearings, 1991; covered 2000 presdl. election and re-count, Palm Beach, Fla.; covered Haitian rebellion and fall of Pres. Aristide, Haiti, 2004. Home and Office: PO Box 2233 Palm Beach FL 33480-7877

WILLIS, CLIFFORD LEON, geologist; b. Chanute, Kans., Feb. 20, 1913, s. Arthur Edward and Flossie Duckworth (Fouts) W.; m. Serreta Margaret Thiel, Aug. 21, 1947 (dec.); 1 child, David Gerard. BS in Mining Engring., U. Kans., 1939; PhD, U. Wash., 1950. Geophysicist The Carter Oil Co. (Exxon), Tulsa, 1939-42; instr. U. Wash., Seattle, 1946-50, asst. prof., 1950-54; cons. geologist Harza Engring. Co., Chgo., 1952-54, 80-82, chief geologist, 1954-57, assoc. and chief geologist, 1957-67, v.p., chief geologist, 1967-80; pvt. practice cons. geologist Tucson, Ariz., 1982—. Cons. on major dam projects in Iran, Iraq, Pakistan, Greece, Turkey, Ethiopia, Argentina, Venezuela, Colombia, Honduras, El Salvador, Iceland, U.S. Lt. USCG, 1942-46. Recipient Haworth Disting. Alumnus award U. Kans., 1963. Fellow Geol. Soc. Am., Geol. Soc. London; mem. Am. Assn. Petroleum Geologists, Soc. Mining, Metallurgy and Exploration Inc., Assn. Engring. Geologists, Sigma Xi, Tau Beta Pi, Sigma Tau, Theta Tau. Republican. Roman Catholic. Avocations: travel, reading. Home: 1402 Middlebury Dr Alexandria VA 22307-1720

WILLIS, CONNIE (CONSTANCE E. WILLIS), author; b. 1945; Tchr. elem. and jr. H.S., Branford, Conn., 1967-69. Author: (novels) Letter from the Clearys (Nebula award, 1982, Hugo award, 1983), Lincoln's Dreams, 1987, Doomsday Book (Nebula award, 1992, Hugo award, 1993), Impossible Things, 1993, Unchartered Territory, 1994, Even the Queen (Nebula award, 1992, Hugo award, 1993), Fire Watch (Nebula award, 1982, Hugo award, 1983), The Last of the Winnebagos (Nebula award, 1988, Hugo award, 1989), Death on the Nile (Hugo award, 1994), The Soul Selects (Hugo award, 1997), Uncharted Territory, 1994, Remake, 1995, Bellwether, 1996, To Say Nothing of the Dog (Hugo award, 1999), Miracle, 1999, Water Witch, 1982, Light Raid, 1989, Promised Land, 1997, Miracle and other Christmas Stories, 1999, The Winds of Marble Arch (Hugo award, 2000), Passage, 2001 (Locus award). Named Best Sci. Fiction/Fantasy Author of Nineties Locus Mag. Address: 1716 13th Ave Greeley CO 80631-5418 E-mail: conniewillis@juno.com.

WILLIS, CRAIG DEAN, academic administrator; b. Cambridge, Ohio, Mar. 21, 1935; s. John Russell and Glenna (Stevens) W.; m. Marilyn Elaine Foster, June 9, 1956; Mark Craig, Bruce Dean, Todd Laine, Garth John. BA, Ohio Wesleyan U, 1957; MA, Ohio State U., 1960, PhD, 1969. Registrar Ohio Wesleyan U., 1964-69; dir. admissions Wright State U., 1970-72, dean, 1971-77; v.p. acad. affairs Concord Coll., 1977-82; pres. Lock Haven U. Pa., 1982—. Chmn. internat. affairs com. Am. Assn. State Colls. and Univs.; A.C.E. pres.'s commn. on internat. edn.; vice chmn. Clinton region Mellon Bank Ctr., 1987, chmn., 88, also bd. dirs.; bd. dirs. Lock Haven U.; cons. Ellis Assocs., Princeton, W.Va., 1980—82. Chmn. bd. Kirkmont Preschool, Beavercreek, Ohio, 1974-77, Beavercreek Library, 1976-77, Regional Edn. Service Agy., Beckley, W.Va., 1978-82; mem. N.E.-Midwest leadership Coun., 1989—. Recipient Disting. Alumnus award dept. edn. Ohio Wesleyan U., 1991; scholar Sohio Oil, 1953, Govt. of France, Paris, 1964, Shell Oil Co, 1967. Mem. Commn. State Coll. and Univ. Pres., Assn. State Colls. annd Univs., Clinton County C. of C. (pres.), Rotary (v.p., pres. elect, Citizen of Yr. award Lock Haven 1989), Ohio Wesleyan U. Alumni Assn. (Disting. Sesquicentennial Alumnus of the Edn. 1992), Phi Kappa Phi, Kappa Kappa Psi, Phi Delta Kappa, Kappa Delta Pi. Presbyterian. Office: Lock Haven U North Fairview St Lock Haven PA 17745

WILLIS, DONTRELLE, professional baseball player; b. Oakland, Calif., Jan. 12, 1982; Pitcher Fla. Marlins, Miami, 2003—. Named Nat. League Rookie of the Yr., 2003; named to, Nat. League All-Star Team, 2004. Achievements include member of World Series Champion Florida Marlins, 2003. Office: c/o Florida Marlines Pro Player Stadium 2267 Dan Marino Blvd Miami FL 33056*

WILLIS, EDWARD OLIVER, management consultant, state official; b. St. Louis, Apr. 6, 1948; s. George Washington and Mary (Fantroy) W.; m. Jennifer Linnea Johnson, June 17, 1972 (div. Dec. 1991); children: Linnea, Eric; m. Linda Diane Clark, Aug. 8, 1992. AA, Am. River Coll., Sacramento, 1972; BS in BA, Calif. State U., Sacramento, 1974; MBA in Mgmt., Golden Gate U., San Francisco, 1978. Divsn. ops. supr., casualty claims investigator Allstate Ins. Co., Menlo Park, Sacramento, 1974-75; budget analyst Dept. Fin., State of Calif., Sacramento, 1975-77; assoc. govtl. program analyst Dept. Health, Medi-Cal Procurement Project, State of Calif., Sacramento, 1977-78; chief fiscal br. solid waste mgmt. bd. State of Calif., Sacramento, 1978-79, mgr. adminstrv. svcs. state lands commn., 1979-80, asst. to assoc. supt. pub. instrn. dept. edn., 1980-82, dep. dir. adminstrn. dept. fish and game, 1982-90, acting adminstr. office of oil spill prevention and response, 1990-92, dep. dir. adminstrn. dept. developmental svcs., 1992-93, dep. dir. adminstrv. svcs. program dept. toxic substances, 1993-94, asst. sec. policy devel. Calif. Environ. Protection Agy., 1994-95, chief dep. dir. Calif. Conservation Corps, 1995—; owner, prin. cons. WW Assocs., 1994—. Part-time instr. Cosumnes River Coll., Sacramento, 1980-83 Author: Business Employment Equity Plan, 1994. Vol. United Way Campaign, United Negro Coll. Fund, Sacramento Children's Home, YMCA; 1st v.p. Nat. Black Child Devel. Inst., Sacramento, 1981-82; chmn. Black Adv. Com. to State Pers. Bd., 1984-85; mem. St. Francis of Assisi Sch. Bd., Sacrammento, 1996—, pres., 1991-93; bd. trustees Black Advocates in State Svc., 1992; bd. dirs. Nat. Forum for Black Pub. Adminstrs., Washington, 1993—, pres., 1991-93, 1st v.p. 1990-91); Little League coach, 1996—. With USAF, 1966-70. Decorated Air medals (4). Mem. Nat. Forum for Black Pub. Adminstrs. (Sacramento chpt. bd. dirs. 1993—, 1st v.p. 1990-91, pres. 1991-93), Am. Soc. Pub. Adminstrn. (Pub. Adminstr. of the Yr.). Avocations: golf, softball. Home: 1065 Almaden Village Ln San Jose CA 95120-3361 Office: Conservation Corps State of California 1719 24th St Sacramento CA 95816-7114

WILLIS, FRANK EDWARD, retired air force officer; b. Clinton, Ill., June 19, 1939; s. William Edward and Bernardine (Saveley) W.; m. Clarice Marie Hull, June 7, 1961; children: Michael, Steven, William. BS in Engring., USAF Acad., Colorado Springs, Colo., 1961; MA in Bus. Mgmt., U. Nebr., 1973. Commd. 2d lt. USAF, 1961, advanced through grades to maj. gen., 1989; dep. comdr. 314th Tactical Airlift Group, Little Rock AFB, 1978-79, comdr., 1979-80; vice comdr. 374th Tactical Airlift Wing, Clark Air Base, The Philippines, 1980-81, comdr., 1981-83, 317th Tactical Airlift Wing, Pope AFB, N.C., 1983-84; vice comdr. Air Force Manpower and Pers. Ctr., Randolph AFB, Tex., 1984-85; comdt. Air Command and Staff Coll., Maxwell AFB, Ala., 1985-88; vice comdr. 22d Air Force, Travis AFB, Calif., 1988-89; dir. and dep. chief of staff for requirements Air Mobility and Mil. Airlift Command, Scott AFB, Ill., 1989-93; ret., 1993; co-owner retail hobby shop Tinker Town, Inc., St. Louis, 1994—. Decorated D.S.M. (2), Legion of Merit (2), Air medal (7), Meritorious Svc. medal (2). Presbyterian. Avocations: electronics, computers, model railroading. Home: 1901 Mistflower Glen Ct Chesterfield MO 63005-4713 E-mail: frank@willis.net.

WILLIS, FRANK ROY, history educator; b. Prescot, Lancashire, Eng., July 25, 1930; s. Harry and Gladys Reid (Birchall) W.; children from previous marriage, Jane, Clare, Geoffrey. BA, Cambridge (Eng.) U., 1952, cert. in edn., 1955, diploma in devel. econs., 1974; PhD, Stanford (Calif.) U., 1959. Instr. Stanford U., 1959-60; from instr. to assoc. prof. history U. Wash., Seattle, 1960-64; assoc. prof. then prof. U. Calif., Davis, 1964—. Author: The French in Germany, 1962, France, Germany and the New Europe, 1945-1967, 1968, Europe in the Global Age, 1968, Italy Chooses Europe, 1971, Western Civilization: An Urban Perspective, 1973, World Civilizations, 1982, The French Paradox, 1982, Western Civilization: A Brief Introduction, 1987. Fellow Rockefeller Found., Paris, 1962-63, Guggenheim Found., Rome, 1966-67, Social Scis. Rsch. Coun., Cambridge, 1973-74. Avocation: travel. Office: U Calif Dept History Davis CA 95616

WILLIS, GERRI, news correspondent; Knight-Bagehot fellow, Columbia Bus. Sch., 1991—92. Sr. fin. corr. Smart Money mag.; personal fin. editor CNN Bus. News, 2003—; co-host CNNfn's The Flipside. Author: The SmartMoney Guide to Real Estate Investing, 2003. Recipient Excellence in Retirement Savings Reporting award, Am. U. Sch. Comm. and Investment Co. Inst. Edn. Found., 2001. Office: CNN 5 Penn Plz Fl 20 New York NY 10001-1810 Office Phone: 212-714-7800.

WILLIS, GLADDEN WILLIAMS, pathologist, scientific photographer, tree farmer; b. Minden, La., Mar. 26, 1939; s. John Stillmon and Virgie Williams Willis; m. Lydia Hall, May 14, 1966; children: Charles Austin, Loye Stillmon. BS, Centenary Coll., 1960; MD, Tulane U., 1964. Intern La. State U. Med. Ctr., Shreveport, 1964-65, resident, 1965-69; fellow Meml. Sloan-Kettering Med. Ctr., NYC, 1969-71; pathologist St. Luke's Hosp., Houston, 1971-72, St. Mary's Hosp., Roswell, N.Mex., 1972-73, Ochsner Clinic Found., New Orleans, 1973—, dir. anatomic pathology, 1976—2003, vice chmn. lab. medicine, 1996—2003. Contbr. articles to profl. jours., over 1242 sci. photographs to encys. and books. Past pres. Jefferson Performing Arts Soc., Metarie, La. Capt. USAF, 1966—72. Recipient George Washington Honor medal, Valley Forge Found., 1996. Fellow Arthur Purdy Stout Soc., Royal Microscopical Soc.; mem. Assn. Dirs. of Anatomic Pathology, Internat. Acad. Pathology, Am. Soc. Media Photographers, NY Acad. Scis. Republican. Methodist. Avocation: photography. Home and Office: 4th Fl New Rsch Bldg 1516 Jefferson Hwy New Orleans LA 70121-2429 Office Phone: 504-842-3330. Personal E-mail: gladdenwillis@cox.net. Business E-Mail: gwillis@ochsner.org.

WILLIS, GORDON, construction executive; m. Jean Willis; 3 children. Chmn. Rockydale Quarries Corp., Roanoke, Va.; pres. Old Heritage Corp. Bd. dirs. Jefferson Ctr. Found.; mem. capital campaign com. Art Mus. Western Va. Recipient NCCJ Brotherhood award, 1991. Avocation: golf. Office: Rockydale Quarries Corp 4754 Old Rocky Mount Rd Roanoke VA 24014

WILLIS, HAROLD WENDT, SR., real estate developer; b. Marion, Ala., Mar. 7, 1927; s. Robert James and Della (Wendt) W.; m. Patsy Gay Bacon, Aug. 2, 1947 (div. Jan. 1975); children: Harold Wendt II, Timothy Gay, April Ann, Brian Tad, Suzanne Gail; m. Vernette Jacobson Osborne, Mar. 30, 1980 (div. 1984); m. Ofelia Alvarez, Sept. 23, 1984; children: Ryan Robert, Samantha Ofelia. Student, Loma Linda U., 1950, San Bernardino Valley Coll. Ptnr. Victoria Guernsey, San Bernardino, Calif., 1950-63, co-pres., 1963-74, pres., 1974—. Pres. Energy Delivery Sys., Food and Fuel, Inc. San Bernardino City water commr., 1964-98, pres. bd. water commrs., 1964-98; bd. councillors Loma Linda (Calif.) U., 1968-85, pres., 1971-74; active So. Calif. Strider's Relay Team (set indoor Am. and World record in 4x800 1992, sec distance medley relay U.S. and world record for 60 yr. old 1992); pres. So. Calif. Striders Track and Field Club, 2001-02. With U.S. Mcht. Marine, 1945-46. Mem. Calif. Dairy Industries Assn. (pres. 1963, 64), Liga Internat. (2d v.p. 1978, pres. 1982, 83), Socal Striders Masters Track & Field Club (pres. 2001-02). Seventh-day Adventist (deacon 1950-67). Avocation: pvt. pilot. Office: PO Box 5607 San Bernardino CA 92412-5607

WILLIS, ISAAC, dermatologist, educator; b. Albany, Ga., July 13, 1940; s. R.L. and Susie M. (Miller) W.; m. Alliene Horne, June 12, 1965; children: Isaac Horne, Alliric Isaac. BS, Morehouse Coll., 1961, DSc (hon.), 1989; MD, Howard U., 1965. Diplomate Am. Bd. Dermatology. Intern Phila. Gen. Hosp., 1965-66; fellow Howard U., Washington, 1966-67; resident, fellow U. Pa., Phila., 1967-69, assoc. in dermatology, 1969-70; mem. staff Phila. Gen. Hosp., 1969-70; instr. dept. dermatology U. Pa., Phila., 1970-72; mem. staff Moffit Hosp. U. Calif., San Francisco, 1970-72; asst. prof. Johns Hopkins U., Johns Hopkins Hosp., Balt., 1972-73; mem. staff Johns Hopkins Hosp., Balt. City Hosp., Good Samaritan Hosp., Balt., 1972-72; asst. prof. Emory U., Atlanta, 1973-77; mem. staff Crawford W. Long Meml. Hosp., Atlanta, 1974—, West Paces Ferry Hosp., Atlanta, 1974-2000; assoc. prof. Emory U., Atlanta, 1977-82; prof. Morehouse Sch. Medicine, Atlanta, 1982—, chief dermatology, 1991—; mem. staff Piedmont Hosp., Atlanta, 2000—. Dep. commdr. of 3297th USA Hosp. (1000B), 1990-; mem. gen. medicine group IA study sect., NIH, 1985-; mem. grants review panel EPA, 1986—; adv. bd. Arthritis and Musculoskeletal and Skin Diseases, 1991-, U. Pa. Sch. Medicine, 1995-, adv. bd. U. of Calif. Sch. of Engring. LaJolla, 2000-, Emory U., 1994-; chmn. inst. review bd., mem. pharmacy and therapeutic com.; bd. dirs. Comml. Bank Gwinnett, Comml. Bank of Ga., Heritage Bank, Landmark Bank Fla., Learning Framework, West Paces Med. Ctr., Lupus Specialists, Inc., InterVu, Inc., Lupus Erythematosus Found., Jacquelyn McClure Lupus Erythematosus Clinic, Skin Cancer Found., World Network Solutions; bd. dirs., chmn. audit com. Comml. Bank of Ga., 2000-, Landmark Bank of Fla., 1999-; mem. med. staff Piedmont Hosp., 2000-; adv. bd. Enable, Inc.; mem. adv. coun. U. Calif. Jacobs Sch. Engring., San Diego, 2001-; vice coun. Internat. Biographical Ctr., 2002; cons. in field. Author: Textbook of Dermatology, 1971; contbr. articles to profl. jours. Trustee Friendship Bapt. Ch., Atlanta, 1980-82; mem. gov.'s commn. on effectiveness and economy in govt. State of Ga. Human Resources Task Force, 1991—, Ga. State Bd. of worker's Compensation Med. subcom., 1997—; mem. nat. alumni coun. U. Pa., 1995—; mem. coun. of advisors U. Calif. San Diego Jacobs Sch. Engring., 2001-. Col. USAR, 1983-95. Named Internat. Scientist of Yr. Internat. Biog. Inst. of Cambridge, Eng., 2002, Internat. Biographical Ctr., 2002, 500 Founders of the 21st century, Internat. Biographical Ctr., 2003, dedicatee Am. Biographical Inst., 2002; EPA grantee, 1980—. Fellow Am. Acad. Dermatology, Am. Dermtol. Assn., Am. Soc. Laser Medicine and Surgery, Inc.; mem. AAAS, AMA, Nat. Cancer Inst., Soc. Investigative Dermatology, Nat. Med. Assn., Internat. Soc. Tropical Dermatology, Pan Am. Med. Assn., Am. Fedn. Clin. Rsch., Am. Soc. Photobiology, U. Pa. Nat. Alumni Adv. Coun., State of Ga. Dermatology Found., Frontiers Internat., Sportsman Internat., Phi Beta Kappa, Omicron Delta Kappa. Achievements include a patent for the development of a shaving composition and method for preventing Pseudofollientitis Barbae, 1999; subspecialties in the areas of dermatology and cancer research (medicine). Home: 1141 Regency Rd NW Atlanta GA 30327-2719 Office: NW Med Ctr 3280 Howell Mill Rd NW Ste 342 Atlanta GA 30327-4109 Office Phone: 404-351-8306. Personal E-mail: iwmd@bellsouth.net.

WILLIS, JERRY WELDON, computer systems educator, writer; b. Tuscumbia, Ala., Jan. 27, 1943; s. Elbert Cartr and Lavice Mae (McAlpin) W.; m. Dee Anna Smith, Mar. 28, 1987 (div. 1997); 1 child, Amy Elizabeth. BA, Union U., 1966; MA, PhD, U. Ala., 1970. Asst prof. U. Guelph, Ont., Can., 1972-74, U. Westrn Ont., London, 1974-76, U. B.C., Vancouver, 1976-78; prof. edn. Tex. Tech. U., Lubbock, 1978-87; dean Edn. and Home Econs. Miss. U. for Women, 1987-88; prof., program coord. Instrnl. Tech.-Ednl. Computing, E. Carolina U. Sch. Edn., 1988-91; prof., dir. ctr. for info. tech. and tchr. edn. Coll. of Edn., U. Houston, 1991-98; prof. curriculum and tech. Iowa State U., 1998—, dir., Ctr. for Tech., Learning and Tchg., 1999—. Pres. Willis Pub. Group; adv. Pres's Panel on Tech. in Edn., 1995. Author: Peanut Butter and Jelly Guide to Computers, 1978 (Outstandig Computer Book, Am. Libr. Jour.); Nailing Jelly to a Tree, 1981, Computers for Everybody, 1981 (Outstanding Computer Book, Am. Libr. Jour.), Computers for People, 1982, Computers, Teaching and Learning, 1983, The Essential Commodore 128 User's Guide, 1986, The Essential Atari ST User's Guide, 1986, Super Calc 3: Learning, Mastering and Using, 1986, Using Super Calc 4, 1987, Desktop Publishing with your IBM PC and Compatible, 1987, Educational Computing: An Introduction, 1986, 96, Computer Simulations: A Guide to Educational Applications, 1986, Teaching with Artificial Reality, 1990, Works Tutorial and Applications, 1990, Computers, Reading and Language Arts, 1996; assoc. editor: Computers in the Schools; contbg. editor Educational Technology; also 34 other books and transls. in 9 langs.; contbr. chpt. to book. Mem. Internat. Soc. for Tech. in Edn., Assn. for Computing Machinery, Assn. for Tchr. Educators, Soc. for Info. Tech. and Tchr. Edn. (founder, pres. 1991-95, jour. co-editor 1991—, Outstanding Contbns. award 1996). Office: Iowa State U CTLT Coll of Edn Ames IA 50010 Home: 4949 Tulane Dr Baton Rouge LA 70808-4764

WILLIS, JOHN ALVIN, editor; b. Morristown, Tenn., Oct. 16, 1916; s. John Bradford and George Ann (Myers) W.; m. Claire Olivier, Sept. 25, 1960 (div.); m. Marina Sarda, Jan. 26, 1978 (div.) BA cum laude, Milligan Coll., 1938; MA, U. Tenn., 1941; postgrad., Ind U., Harvard U. Asst. editor Theatre World, N.Y.C., 1945-65, editor, 1965—; asst. editor Screen World, N.Y.C., 1948-65, editor, 1965—; tchr. pub. high schs., N.Y.C., 1950-76; editor Dance World, 1966-80; asst. editor Opera World, 1952-54, Great Stars of Am. Stage, 1952, Pictorial History of Silent Screen, 1953, Pictorial History of Opera in America, 1959, Pictorial History of the American Theatre, 1950, 60, 70, 80, 85. Mem. Tony Theatre Awards Com. Nat. bd. dirs. U. Tenn. Theatre; mem. com. to select recipients for Mus. Theatre Hall of Fame, NYU. Lt. USNR, 1943-45. Recipient Lucille Lortel Lifetime Achievement award, 1993, Drama Desk Lifetime Achievement award, 1994, Nat. Bd. Rev. Lifetime Achievement Film History award, 1999, Profl. Excellence award Milligan Coll., 1999, Tony award for excellence in theater, 2001; high sch. auditorium renamed John Willis Performing Arts Ctr. in his honor, Morristown, 1993. Mem. Actors Equity Assn., Broadway Theatre Insts (Lifetime Achievement award 2003), Nat. Bd. Rev. Motion Pictures (past bd. dirs.). Home and Office: 190 Riverside Dr New York NY 10024-1008

WILLIS, JOHN PATRICK, chemist; b. Albany, N.Y., Mar. 10, 1947; s. John James and Mary Catherine (Varden) W.; m. Tientje Jane Dirzuweit, July 22, 1972. BS, Iona Coll., 1969; MS, SUNY, Oswego, 1974; PhD, U. Conn., 1977. Assoc. prodn. chemist Winthrop Labs., Rensselaer, N.Y., 1970-72; rsch. chemist Uniroyal, Inc., Middlebury, Conn., 1977-79; postdoctoral rschr. U. Minn., Mpls., 1979-80; mgr. chem. rsch. Nova Biomed Corp., Newton, Mass., 1980-83; founder, chmn. Ilex Corp., Marlboro, Mass., 1983-87; med. cons., 1987-88; founder T.J. Assocs., Biomed. Cons., 1987-89; v.p., chief oper. officer Sharon Drive Corp., Westlake, Ohio, 1988-93; dir. rsch. Medisense, Inc., Waltham, Mass., 1993-97; v.p. R&D Marathon Med. Techs., Inc., Worcester, Mass., 1997-98; exec. v.p., chief tech. officer BioValve Techs., Inc., North Grafton, Mass., 1999-2000; pres., CEO Teknow Source Inc., Shirley, Mass., 2000—02; chmn., CEO North Country Naturals, Inc., Shirley, Mass., 2000—; tech. dir. biotech. Mohawk Innovative Tech, Inc., Albany, NY, 2001—04; rsch. prof. Dept. of Chemistry & Chem. Biology, Rensselaer Polytechnic Inst., Troy, NY, 2004—. Mem. adv. bd. Clin. Lab. Practice, Mass. Dept. Pub. Health, 1986-87, 128 Entrepreneurs' Ctr., Waltham, Mass., 1986-88; mem. tech. adv. coun. Edison Biotech. Ctr., Cleve., 1988-90. U. Conn. Rsch. Found. fellow, 1976. Fellow Am. Inst. Chemists; mem. Am. Chem. Soc., Electrochem. Soc., Am. Assn. Clin. Chemistry, N.Y. Acad. Scis., Sigma Xi, Phi Kappa Phi, Phi Lambda Upsilon. Achievements include research in bioelectrochemistry, organic electrochemistry and biosensors; patents in field. Office: Dept Chemistry & Chem Biology Rensselaer Poly Inst 110 8th St Troy NY 12180 Personal E-mail: jwillis@tiac.net.

WILLIS, JOHN T. former secretary of state; b. Nov. 1, 1946; m. Kathy S. Mangan; children: Karen M., James T. BA in Econs. cum laude, Bucknell U., 1968; JD, Harvard Law Sch., 1971. Clk. Army Ct. of Mil. Rev., 1971-74; legal assistance officer Aberdeen Proving Grounds, 1974-75; pvt. practice atty. Westminster, Balt. City, Md., 1975-90; chief of staff County Exec. of Prince George's County, 1990-94; apptd. sec. of state State of Md., 1995—2003. Adj. prof. McDaniel Coll.(formerly Western Md. Coll.), 1979—; chmn. Gov.'s Commn. on Md. Mil. Monuments; adv. bd. U. Balt.'s Schaefer Ctr. for Pub. Policy; adj. prof., gov. & public admin, U. Balt. Author: Presidential Elections in Maryland, 1984; contbg. author: Western Maryland: A Profile, 1980, Justice and the Military, 1972; contbr. articles to profl. jours.; editor: The Advocate, 1973-74. Vice-chmn. Md. Dem. Party, 1987-89, mem. various coms. and del. to Dem. Nat. Convs., 1976-96; former chair Dem. Secs. of State. Judge advocate gen. corps U.S. Army, 1968-75. Mem. Md. Bar Assn., Carroll County Bar Assn., Md. Hist. Soc., Carroll County Arts Coun. (past pres.). Democrat. Office: U Balt 1420 N Charles St Baltimore MD 21201 E-mail: mdsos@sos.state.md.us.

WILLIS, JUDY ANN, lawyer; b. Hartford, Conn., July 7, 1949; d. Durward Joseph and Angeline Raphael (Riccardo) Willis. BA, Ctrl. Conn. State U., 1971; postgrad., U. Conn. Law Sch., 1976—77; JD, Boston Coll., 1979. Bar: Mass. 1979, U.S. Dist. Ct. Mass. 1980, Calif. 1990. Sr. atty. H.P. Hood Inc., Charleston, Mass., 1979-83; v.p. law Parker Bros., Beverly, Mass., 1983-89; sr. v.p. bus. affairs Mattel, Inc., El Segundo, Calif., 1989—. Office: Mattel Inc M1-0920 333 Continental Blvd El Segundo CA 90245-5012 E-mail: judy.willis@Mattel.com.

WILLIS, KEVIN, airport administrator; Mgr. Atlantic City Internat. Airport, until 1996, FAA, Washington, 1996—. Office: FAA Airport Compliance Div AAS-400 Fed Aviation Adm 800 Independence Ave SW Washington DC 20591-0001

WILLIS, KEVIN ALVIN, professional basketball player; b. L.A., Sept. 6, 1962; Student, Jackson C.C., Mich., Mich. State U. Basketball player Atlanta Hawks, 1984—94; with Miami Heat, 1994—95, Golden State Warriors, 1995—96, Houston Rockets, 1996—98, Toronto Raptors, 1998—. Named to NBA All-Star team, 1992. Office: Toronto Raptures 20 Bay St Ste 1702 Toronto ON Canada M5J 2N8

WILLIS, MARK, real estate company executive; b. Apr. 20, 1961; BBA, U. Tex., 1983. Prin., owner Carriage House Realty; br. mgr. Coldwell Banker; from team leader S.W. Mkt. Ctr. to pres. Keller Williams Realty Internat., Austin, Tex., 1991—2002, pres., 2002—. Home: 1921 Cypress Point W Austin TX 78746 Office: Keller Williams Realty Inc 807 Las Cimas Pkwy Ste 200 Austin TX 78746 E-mail: willis@kw.com.

WILLIS, NORMAN HUNT, author, writer, director, producer; b. Ft. Worth, Feb. 11, 1934; s. Ray Logan and Ima H. Willis; m. Andrea Marie Laurent, June 11, 1934 (div. Aug. 1981); children: Christi, Michelle, Leslie; m. Mary Theresa Ciociola, Feb. 19, 1945. Student, Tex. Christian U., 1951-52, San Diego State Coll., 1953, George Washington U., 1955-56. Audio-visual specialist The Asphalt Inst., College Park, Md., 1956-58; film specialist GE, Evendale, Ohio, 1958-60; scriptwriter Scripts by Oeveste Granducci, Washington, 1960-61; supr. med. films Wyeth Labs., Radnor, Pa., 1961-66; exec. prodr. H.G. Peters & Co., Primose, Pa., 1966-68; pres. Intermedica, Inc., Wayne, Pa., 1968-80, Intermedia Comms., Inc., Paoli, Pa., 1980-91; media cons. Paoli, 1991-96; sr. med. writer Otsuka Am., 1997-2000; mgr. Quintiles Inc., 1997-2000; dir. clin. comm. Pfizer La Jolla, 2000—03; dir. med. writing Ligand Pharms., Inc., 2003—. Author: (book) Basic Infant Nutrition, 1964; dir. (film) Drivin' and Drugs, 1968 (CINE Golden Eagle award); writer, dir., prodr. (video) Quinolones: Mechanisms of Action, 1986 (Silver medal N.Y. Internat. Film and TV Festival), (film) Sterilization Procedures for the Medical Office, 1963 (Golden Eagle award), Tracy, 1978 (Silver medal); dir. prodr. (film) Your Life and the Pill, 1975 (Silver medal, CINE Golden Eagle award). With USN, 1952-56, Korea. Mem. Internat. Interactive Comms. Soc., Am.

Med. Writers Assn., Am. Mensa, Drug Info. Assn., Regulatory Affairs Profl. Soc. Avocations: tennis, noncommercial photography. Home: 11301 E San Raphael Dr San Diego CA 92130 E-mail: NormaHW@AOL.Com.

WILLIS, PAUL ALLEN, librarian; b. Floyd County, Ind., Oct. 1, 1941; s. Clarence Charles and Dorothy Jane (Harritt) W.; m. Barbara Marcum, June 15, 1963; children: Mark, Sally. AB, U. Ky., 1963, JD, 1969; MLS, U. Md., 1966. Cataloger Libr. of Congress, Washington, 1963; head descriptive cataloging br. Sci. and Tech. Info. Facility NASA, College Park, Md., 1963-66; law libr., prof. law U. Ky., Lexington, 1966-73, dir. librs., 1973—2002, acting dean Coll. Libr. Sci., 1975-76, 88; dean of libr. U. SC, Columbia, 2002—. Exec. sec. Ky. Jud. Retirement and Removal Commn., 1977-81; mem. adv. com. Ctr. for Jud. Conduct Orgns., Am. Judicature Soc., Chgo., 1979-81; bd. dirs. Southea. Libr. Network, Atlanta, 1980-83, 96-2000, chair, 1998-99; mem. exec. com. Ky. Hist. Soc., 1984-88; mem. Ky. Adv. Coun. on Librs., 1985-2002, adv. com. Online Computer Libr. Ctr., 1986-90; cons. S.E. Consortium for Internat. Devel., U. Sriwijaya, Palembang, Sumatera, Indonesia, 1987-88, Hanoi U. Tech., 1999, 2001, Vietnam Nat. U., Ho Chi Minh City, 1999. Sr. fellow UCLA, summer 1982 Mem. Assn. Southeastern Rsch. Librs. (chair 1986-88, bd. dirs. 2002-), Assn. of Rsch. Librs. (bd. dirs. 2002—). Home: 111 Dene Ct Georgetown SC 29440-1095 Office: U SC Thomas Cooper Library 1322 Green St Columbia SC 29208-0001 Office Phone: 803-777-6212.

WILLIS, RALPH HOUSTON, mathematics professor; b. McMinnville, Tenn., Dec. 26, 1942; s. Carl Houston and Carrie Lee (Hill) W.; m. Gayle Catherine Celestin, June 29, 1973 (div. Apr. 1985); m. Velma Inez Church, Aug. 10, 1985; 1 stepchild, Bobbie Lynn White Buckner. BS in Math., Mid. Tenn. State U., 1964, MA in Math., 1966. Cert. secondary edn. tchr. Instr. depts. math. & computer sci. Western Carolina U., Cullowhee, NC, 1968-73, asst. prof., 1973-83, assoc. prof., 1983—. Co-founder NC State Math. Contest & Contest Network, 1977-78, state maths. contest com., 1977-78, western regional rep. exec. steering com., 1978—, recording sec., 1978—; co-founder NC Math. League, 1981-82, mem. problem writing com., 1981-84. Editor: (newsletters) Abelian Grapevine-Secondary Math, 1970-88, The Child of Mathematics-Elementary-Middle Grade Math., 1972-78; mem. editl. bd. The Centroid, 1995-2000; contbr. articles to profl. jours. Founder, dir., coord. H.S. Math. Contest, Western Carolina U., 1970—, solicitor-coord. Math. Contest Scholarship Program, 1971-82, founder, coord. math dept. student awards program, 1970—, initiator-coord. math. dept.'s Vis. Spkr. Program, 1974-77; founder, faculty sponsor NC Coun. Tchrs. Math. Student Affiliate, Cullowhee, 1988—; coord. state road paving project Univ. Heights Cmty. Devel. Orgn., 1974-76, chmn., founder cmty. watch., 1978-79, coord. pub. water sys. upgrade project, 1980-84; founder, coord., bd. dirs., trustee Hunerwadle Cmty. Cemetery Assn., Beersheba, Tenn., 1983—; co-founder NC State Math. Contest and Contest Network, 1977-78. Recipient hon. mention NC Gov.'s award for Excellence, 1991, Exemplary Site award State Math. Contest Com., 1990. Mem. Nat. Coun. Tchrs. Math., NC Coun. Tchrs. Math. (state bd. dirs. 1993-98, historian 1993-98, Innovator award 1994, editl. bd. Centroid 1995-2000, W.W. Rankin award 2001), Phi Kappa Phi, Kappa Mu Epsilon. Avocations: genealogy, gardening, military history, model building, die cast model collector. Office: Western Carolina U Math Dept Stillwell Bldg Cullowhee NC 28723

WILLIS, RALPH WALKER, retired firefighter; b. Redondo Beach, Calif., Nov. 21, 1921; s. Achatius Walker and Elizabeth Margaret (Dehm) W.; m. Helen Elizabeth Willis, May 18, 1946; 1 child, Ron Lee. Grad. h.s., San Diego. Firefighter Richmond (Calif.) Fire Dept., 1946-67; pres. Firefighters Union IAFF AFL CIO, 1964—67. Author: Sansei Banzai, 1986, War and Remembrance Revisted, 1988, The Eternal Regiment, 1995, My Life as a Jarhead, 1999 (The Ernie Pyle WWII Roundtable award). Sgt. USMC, 1941-45. Mem.: VFW (life), Iwo Jima Survivors Assn. American Independent Party. Avocations: travel, painting, writing. Home: 866 Camino De Oro San Jacinto CA 92583-6807 E-mail: jarheadhandr@aol.com.

WILLIS, RUSSELL EDWARD, academic administrator; b. Ft. Stockton, Tex., Mar. 29, 1955; s. Ben Edward and Billie Jo W.; m. Dawn Orlean Olmstead, July 18, 1981; children: Katherine, Benjamin. BS in Mgmt. Systems, So. Meth. U., 1976, BSEE, 1977, MS in Engring. Mgmt., 1979, M of Theology cum laude, 1982; PhD in Ethics and Soc., Emory U., 1990. Product mktg. engr. Tex. Instruments, Inc., Dallas, 1977-79; pastor Decker United Meth. Ch., Austin, Tex., 1984-86; faculty assoc. Ariz. State U., Tempe, 1987—88; instr. Iowa State U., Ames, 1988-90; asst. prof., instr. sociology Iowa Wesleyan U., Mt. Pleasant, 1990-95; asst. prof., assoc. prof. religion and sociology, dir. instnl. rsch. and planning McMurry U., Abilene, Tex., 1995-2000; acting dir. info. systems & instructional tech. Dakota Wesleyan U., Mitchell, SD, 2000—01, v.p. acad. affairs, dean, 2000—03, prof. religion and philosophy, 2000—03; provost Champlain Coll., Burlington, Vt., 2003—. Acting dir. George and Eleanor McGovern Ctr. Pub. Svc., 2001—03. Co-author: Cosmic Witness: Commentaries on Science-Technology Themes, 1996; contbg. author: Living Responsibility in Community, 1997, George McGovern: A Political Life, A Political Legacy, 2004. Bd. dirs. Friends of Mid. Border Mus., Mitchell, 2000-03. Mem. Am. Acad. Religion, Soc. Christian Ethics, Ctr. Theology and the Natural Scis. Office: Champlain Coll PO Box 670 Freeman Hall 302 Burlington VT 05402-0670 Business E-Mail: willis@champlain.edu.

WILLIS, SELENE LOWE, electrical engineer, software consultant, project manager; b. Birmingham, Alabama, Mar. 4, 1958; d. Lewis Russell and Bernice (Wilson) Lowe; m. André Maurice Willis, June 12, 1987. BS EE, Tuskegee U., 1980; postgrad., U. Calif. at Los Angeles, 1993—94, U. So. Calif., 1996, U. Calif. at Los Angeles, 1999—. Component engr. Hughes Aircraft Corp., El Segundo, Calif., 1980—82; reliability and lead engr. Aero Jet Electro Sys. Corp., Azusa, Calif., 1982—84; sr. component engr. Rockwell Internat. Corp., Anaheim, Calif., 1984, Gen. Data Comm. Corp., Danbury, Conn., 1984—85; design engr. Lockheed Missile and Space Co., Sunnyvale, Calif., 1985—86; property mgr. Penmar Mgmt. Co., L.A., 1987—88; aircraft mechanic McDonnell Douglas Corp., Long Beach, Calif., 1989—93; unix sys. adminstrn. Santa Cruz Ops., Calif., 1994; bus. ops. mgr., cons. New Start, Santa Monica, Calif., 1995; software developer Nat. Advancement Corp., Calif., 1996; entrepreneur Datatronics, Calif., 1996—; exec. v.p., owner L.A. Network Engr. Jet Propulsion Lab., 1996—2000; software engr., network engr., application engr., lead engr. Jet Propulsion Lab, Pasadena, Calif., 1996—2000, project mgr., 1999—2000, lead UNIX engr. L.A., 1998—2000; mgmt. sys. engr. Tech. Jet Propulsion Lab., Pasadena, Calif., 1998—2000, project element mgr., 1999—; cons., sr. project mgr. Amgen, Thousand Oaks, Calif., 1999—2000, sr. sys. engr., 2000—; project mgr. So. Calif. Edison, 2002—03, mgr., settlements, 2003—, mgr. energy supply and mgmt., 2003. Cons., software designer Kern and Wooley, atty., Westwood, Calif., 1995; software developer Nat. Advancement Corp., Santa Ana, Calif., 1995—. Vol. Mercy Hosp. and Children's Hosp., Birmingham, Ala. 1972-74; mrm. L.A. Gospel Messengers, 1982-84, West Angeles Ch. of God and Christ, L.A., 1990; cons., mgr. bus. ops. New Start, Santa Monica (Calif.) Bay Area Drug Abuse Coun., 1995; vol. Pres. Clinton's Going-To-Coll. Program through Univ. Calif. at Los Angeles, 1997—; chair Univ. Calif. at Los Angles Transfer Coll. Scholarship Program, 1998-99. Scholar Bell Lab., 1976-80, Univ. Calif. at Los Angeles, 1994, Gem Award, UTA, 1999, Outstanding Group Award, JPL, 1999. Mem. IEEE, ASME, Aerospace and Aircraft Engr., So. Calif. Profl. Engring. Assn., Tuskegee U. Alumni Assn., UCLA Alumni Assn. (scholarship and adv. com.), Eta Kappa Nu, Christian Ch. Avocations: piano, computers, softball, real estate.

WILLIS, THORNTON WILSON, painter; b. Pensacola, Fla., May 25, 1936; s. Willard Wilson and Edna Mae (Hall) W.; m. Peggy Jean Whisenhant, June, 1960; 1 son, David Shaw.; m. Vered Lieb, 1983; 1 dau., Rachel Elizabeth. BS, U. So. Miss., 1962; MA, U. Ala., 1966. Vis. artist-in-residence La. State U., New Orleans, 1971-72 Represented in U.S. by Todd Selbert, N.Y.C., and André Zarre Gallery, N.Y.C., in Europe by Galerie Nordenhake, Stockholm.; assoc. editor: Re-View, 1978—; one-man exhbns. include: Henri Gallery, Washington, 1968, Paley and Lowe, N.Y.C., 1970, New Orleans Mus. Art, 1972, 55 Mercer St. Gallery, 1979, Galerie Nordenhake, Sweden, 1980, Oscarsson Hood Gallery, N.Y.C., 1980-84, Gloria Luria Gallery, Miami, 1985, Pensacola Mus. retrospective, 1988, Galerie Nordenhake retrospective, Stockholm, 1988, 89, Twining Gallery retrospective, 1990, André Zarre Gallery, N.Y.C., 1993; group exhbns. include: Phila. Civic Center, 1970, Whitney Mus., 1971, Contemporary Art Mus., Houston, 1980, 81, Sidney Janis Gallery, N.Y.C., 1980, 81, Johnson Mus., Ithaca, N.Y., 1981, Mus. Modern Art, N.Y.C., 1981, 84, 85-86, Galerie Arnesen, Copenhagen, 1981, ARS '83, Helsinki, André Emmerich Gallery, N.Y.C., 1992, Anita Shapolsky Gallery, N.Y.C., 1993, The Mobile Mus. of Art, 1995, Rider U., Lawrenceville, N.J, 1997; represented in permanent collections, Whitney Mus., N.Y.C., Mus. Modern Art, N.Y.C., New Orleans Mus. Art, Denver Mus. Fine Art, Rochester Meml. Gallery, Albright-Knox Mus., Phillips Collection, Washington, Herbert F. Johnson Mus., Cornell U., Chase Manhattan Collection, William Paley Collection, CBS, Power Collection, Sidney, Australia, Solomon R. Guggenheim Mus., N.Y.C., pvt. collections, museums Europe, Scandanavia. With USMC, 1954-57. Recipient award, Adolph and Esther Gottlieb Found., 1991; grantee John Simon Guggenheim Found., 1978—79, Nat. Endowment Arts, 1980—81, The Pollock-Krasner Found., 2001—02. Mem. U.S. Golf Assn., Profl. Golf Tchrs. and Coaches of Am. (cert.). Avocation: golf. Home: 85 Mercer St New York NY 10012-4438 Office: 87 Mercer St New York NY 10012-4402 Office Phone: 212-334-3518.

WILLIS, TRICIA LEE, special education educator; d. Harold Lee and Belinda Lee Gibb; m. Don Edward Willis, Dec. 29, 2001; 1 child, Brandon Gibb. BA in History, Calif. State U., San Marcos, 1996; MBS, Southeastern U., 1999. Tchr. Atoka (Okla.)-Coal Alternative Sch., 1997—98, Coalgate (Okla.) Pub. Schs., 1998—. Grantee, Rural Okla. Cmty. Found., 2000, 2001. Mem.: Coun. for Exceptional Children. Achievements include development of program for emotionally disturbed students. Avocations: reading, travel, sports. Office: Coalgate Pub Schs 2 West Cedar Coalgate OK 74538 Office Phone: 580-927-2338.

WILLIS, WALTER BRUCE (BRUCE WILLIS), actor, singer, writer; b. Fed. Republic Germany, Mar. 19, 1955; came to U.S., 1957; s. David and Marlene Willis; m. Demi Moore; children: Rumer Glenn, Scout Larue, Tallulah Belle. Student, Montclair State Coll.; studied with Stella Adler. Mem. First Amendment Comedy Theatre. Actor: (off-Broadway prodns.) Heaven and Earth, 1977, Fool for Love, 1984, The Bullpen, The Bayside Boys, The Ballad of Railroad William, (TV film) Trackdown, (feature films) Prince of the City, 1981, The Verdict, 1982, Blind Date, 1987, Sunset, 1988, Die Hard, 1988, In Country, 1989 (Golden Globe nomination 1990), Look Who's Talking (voice), 1989, Die Hard 2: Die Harder, 1990, Bonfire of the Vanities, 1990, Mortal Thoughts, 1991, Hudson Hawk, 1991, Billy Bathgate, 1991, The Last Boy Scout, 1991, Death Becomes Her, 1992, Striking Distance, 1993, Color of Night, 1994, North, 1994, Pulp Fiction, 1994, Nobody's Fool, 1994, Die Hard With a Vengeance, 1995, 12 Monkeys, 1995, Four Rooms, 1995, Last Man Standing, 1996, The Jackal, 1997, The Fifth Element, 1997, Mercury Rising, 1998, Armageddon, 1998, The Siege, 1998, Breakfast of Champions, 1999, The Sixth Sense, 1999, The Story of Us, 1999, The Whole Nine Yards (also prodr.), 2000, The Kid, 2000, Unbreakable, 2000, Bandits, 2001, Harts War, 2002, Grand Champion, 2002, True West, 2002, Tears of the Sun, 2003, Rugrats Go Wild! (voice), 2003, Charlie's Angels: Full Throttle, 2003, The Whole Ten Yards, 2003; exec. prodr.: Crocodile Hunter: The Collision Course, 2002, (TV) True West, 2002, guest star (TV series) Miami Vice, The Twilight Zone; regular (TV series) Moonlighting, 1985-89 (People's Choice award 1986, Emmy award 1987, Golden Globe award 1987), musician (TV spl.) The Return of Bruno, 1986; rec. artist (album) The Return of Bruno, 1987, If It Don't Kill You, It Just Makes You Stronger, 1989; appeared in numerous commls. Named Internat. Broadcasting Man of Yr. Hollywood Radio and TV Soc.; recipient Star on Walk of Fame, 1998, People Choice award, 2000. Office: Creative Artists Agency c/o Arnold Rifkin 9830 Wilshire Blvd Beverly Hills CA 90212

WILLIS, WILLIAM DARRELL, JR., neurophysiologist, educator; b. Dallas, July 19, 1934; s. William Darrell and Dorcas (Chamberlain) W.; m. Jean Colette Schini, May 28, 1960; 1 child, Thomas Darrell. BS, BA, Tex. A&M U., 1956; MD, U. Tex. Southwestern Med. Sch., 1960; PhD, Australian Nat. U., 1963. Postdoctoral research fellow Nat. Inst. Neurol. Diseases and Blindness, Australian Nat. U., 1960-62, Istituto di Fisiologia, U. Pisa, Italy, 1962-63; from asst. prof. to prof. anatomy, chmn. dept. U. Tex. Southwestern Med. Sch., Dallas, 1963-70; chief lab. comparative neurobiology Marine Biomed. Inst., prof. anatomy and physiology U. Tex. Med. Br., Galveston, 1970—, dir. Marine Biomed. Inst., 1978—2004, chmn. dept. anatomy and neurosci., 1986—2004, Ashbel Smith prof., 1986-95, Cecil and Ida Green prof., 1995—. Mem. neurology B study sect. NIH, 1968-72, chmn., 1970-72, mem. neurol. disorders Program Project rev. com., 1972-76, Nat. Adv. Neurol. and Communicative Disorders and Stroke Coun., 1987-90; tng. grant com. Nat. Inst. of Neurol. Disorders and Stroke, 1994-98. Mem. editl. bd. Neurosci., Exptl. Neurology, 1970-90, Archives Italienne Biologie, Neurosci. Letters, 1976-92; chief editor Jour. Neurophysiology, 1978-83, Pain, 1986-89; assoc. editor Jour. Neurosci., 1986-89, editor-in-chief, 1993-94; sect. editor Exptl. Brain Rsch., 1990-92, 1995-2004. Mem. AAAS, Am. Assn. Anatomists (exec. com. 1980-86), Am. Pain Soc. (pres. 1982-83), Internat. Assn. Study Pain (coun. 1984-90), Am. Physiol. Soc., Soc. Exptl. Biol. Medicine, Soc. Neurosci. (pres. 1984-85), Internat. Brain Rsch. Orgn., Cajal Club, Sigma Xi, Alpha Omega Alpha. Home: 2925 Beluche Dr Galveston TX 77551-1511 Office: U Tex Med Br 301 University Blvd Galveston TX 77555-1069 Business E-Mail: wdwillis@utmb.edu.

WILLIS, WILLIAM ERVIN, lawyer; b. Huntington, W.Va., Oct. 11, 1926; s. Asa Hannon and Mae (Davis) W.; m. Joyce Litteral, Sept. 1, 1949; children: Kathryn Cunningham, Anne Dresser, William. Student, Ind. U., 1944, NYU, 1945; AB, Marshall U., 1948; JD, Harvard, 1951; LHD (hon.), Marshall U., 1997. Bar: N.Y. 1952. Pvt. practice, N.Y.C., 1951—; ptnr. Sullivan & Cromwell, 1960-94, sr. counsel, 1994—. Lectr. Practising Law Inst., 1963—; trustee Fed. Bar Council, 1968-72; mem. 2d Circuit Commn. on Reduction Burdens and Costs Civil Litigation, 1977-82. Co-author Doing Business in America; contbr. Edn. Civil Practice Law Rev. Forms and Guidance for Lawyers, also articles to legal jours. Mem. panel arbitrators Pub. Resources; trustee Tenafly (N.J.) Nature Ctr., 1994—2001, pres., 1997—2001; dir. Soc. Yeager Scholars Marshall U., Huntington, 1995—, v.p., 2001—. With AUS, 1944—46. Fellow Am. Coll. Trial Lawyers, Am. Bar Found.; mem. ABA (standing com. on fed. judiciary 1987-95, chair 1992-93, 94-95), N.Y. Bar Assn. (chmn. antitrust sect. 1976-77, exec. com. 1976-83), Assn. Bar City of N.Y. (chmn. profl. discipline com. 1983-86, chmn. ethics 2000 com. 1999—, judicial conduct 2000—), Fed. Bar Coun. (trustee 1969-72), Am. Judicature Soc., Am. Arbitration Assn. (panel arbitrators), N.Y. Law Inst., N.Y. County Lawyers, Ins. Jud. Adminstrn., India House. Home: 190 Tekening Dr Tenafly NJ 07670-1219 Also: Otterhole Rd West Milford NJ 07480 Office: Sullivan & Cromwell 125 Broad St 28th Fl New York NY 10004-2498 E-mail: willisw@sullcrom.com.

WILLISCROFT-BARCUS, BEVERLY RUTH, lawyer; b. Conrad, Mont., Feb. 24, 1945; d. Paul A. and Gladys L. (Buck) W.; m. Kent J. Barcus, Oct. 1984. BA in Music, So. Calif. Coll., 1967; JD, John F. Kennedy U., 1977. Bar: Calif. 1977. Elem. tchr., Sunnyvale, Calif., 1968-72; legal sec., legal asst. various law firms, 1972-77; assoc. Neil D. Reid, Inc., San Francisco, 1977-79; sole practice Concord, Calif., 1979—. Exam. grader Calif. Bar, 1979—; real estate broker, 1980-88; tchr. real estate King Coll., Concord, 1979-80; judge pro-tem Mcpl. Ct., 1981-93; mem. Stage Right Drama Group, Concord, Calif., 1999—; lectr. in adoption law. Co-author: Adoption Law in California, Adoption Practice, Procedure and Pitfalls in California; lectr. in field. Bd. dirs. Contra Costa Musical Theatre, Inc., 1978-82, v.p. adminstrn., 1980-81, v.p. prodn., 1981-82; mem. community devel. adv. com. City of Concord, 1981-83, vice chmn., 1982-83, mem. status of women com., 1980-81, mem. redevel. adv. com., 1984-86, planning commnr. 1986-92, chmn., 1990; mem. exec. bd. Mt. Diablo coun. Boy Scouts Am., 1981-85; bd. dirs. Pregnancy Ctrs. Contra Costa County, 1991-2001, chmn., 1993-2000 Mem. Concord C. of C. (bd. dirs., chmn. govt. affairs com. 1981-83, v.p. 1985-87, pres. 1988-89, Bus. Person of Yr. 1986), Calif. State Bar (chmn. adoptions subcom. north, 1994), Contra Costa County Bar Assn., Christian Legal Soc., Todos Santos Bus. and Profl. Women (co-founder, pres. 1983-84, pub. rels. chmn. 1982-83, Woman of Achievement 1980, 81), Soroptimists (fin. sec. 1980-81). Office: PO Box 981 Pittsburg CA 94565-0098

WILLISON, BRUCE GRAY, dean; b. Riverside, Calif., Oct. 16, 1948; s. Walter G. and Dorothy (Phillips) W.; m. Gretchen A. Illig; children: Patrick, Bruce G., Kristen, Jeffery, Geoffrey, Lea. BA in econs., UCLA, 1970; MBA, U. So. Calif., 1973. With Bank of Am., LA, 1973-79; joined First Interstate Bancorp, LA, 1979, dir. mktg., 1981, sr. v.p., mem. mng. com., 1981—82; sr. v.p. trust divsn. First Interstate Bank of Calif., LA, 1982—83, exec. v.p. world banking group, 1983-85; pres., CEO First Interstate Bank Ltd., LA, 1985-86; chmn., CEO First Interstate Bank Oreg., Portland, 1986-91; chmn., pres., CEO First Interstate Bank of Calif., LA, 1991—96; vice chmn. First Interstate Bancorp, LA, 1995—96; pres., COO H.F. Ahmanson and Co., Irwandale, Calif., 1996—99; dean Anderson Sch. Mgmt., UCLA, 1999—. Bd. dirs. Homestore Inc., Sun America Inc.'s fund complex, Health Net Inc., 2000—. Bd. dirs. United Way of LA, Operation Hope Inc. Served to lt. USN, 1970—72. Office: PO Box 951481 Los Angeles CA 90095-1481*

WILLKE, THEODORE LAWRENCE, research facility director; b. Indpls., Dec. 27, 1944; s. Myron Gustav and Freda (Payne) W.; m. Sue Ellen Koenig, Aug. 1, 1976; children: Theodore II, Chad, Bradford. BS in Astronautical Engring. & Engring. Sci., U.S. Air Force Acad., 1967; MS in Nuclear Engring., MIT, 1968; MBA, U. Dayton, 1971; PhD in Indsl. and Sys. Engring., Ohio State U., 1974. Registered profl. engr., Ohio, Wash. Sys. engr. Battelle, Columbus, Ohio, 1974-77; sect. mgr. Pacific N.W. Labs., Richland, Wash., 1977-82; dir. tech. assessment Gas Rsch. Inst., Chgo., 1982-84, divsn. dir. adminstrn., 1984-86, v.p., 1987-97; dir., CEO Carnegie Mellon Rsch. Inst., Pitts., 1997—2001; pres. TLW Solutions Inc., Pitts., 2002—. Mem. PRC Internat., Arlington, Va., 1994-97; chmn. Internat. Gas Union Com., Chgo., 1994-97; adj. prof. mech. engring. U. Wash., 1979; vis. disting. svc. prof. Carnegie Mellon U., 2001-02. Contbr. articles to profl. jours. including Pub. Utilities Fortnightly, Internat. Jour. Sys. Sci. Mem. tech. adv. com. pipeline safety U.S. Dept. Transp., 1996—; mem. Leadership Pitts. XVI, 1999-2000. Capt. USAF, 1967-71. Recipient award NSPE, 1975. Mem. ASME (mem. bd. on rsch. and tech. devel. 1988-90), AAAS. Achievements include patent in field. Office: TLW Solutions Inc One Oxford Ctr 37th Fl Pittsburgh PA 15219

WILLKE, THOMAS ALOYS, university official, statistics educator; b. Rome City, Ind., Apr. 22, 1932; s. Gerard Thomas and Marie Margaret (Wuennemann) W.; m. Geraldine Ann Page, Dec. 28, 1954; children: Richard, Susan, Donald, Jeanne, Mary, Kathleen. AB, Xavier U., 1954; MS, Ohio State U., 1956, PhD, 1960. Sr. engr. N.Am. Aviation, Columbus, Ohio, 1959-60; instr. math. Ohio State U., Columbus, 1960-61, assoc. prof., 1966-70, assoc. prof. statistics, 1970-72, prof., 1972-73, dir. stats. lab., 1971-73, vice provost Arts and Scis., 1973-86, acting dean Univ. Coll., 1983-86, dean undergrad. studies Arts and Scis., 1986-87; prof. math. scis. Otterbein coll., Westerville, Ohio, 1987-97, chmn. dept. math. scis., 1988-96; rsch. mathematician U.S. Nat. Bur. Standards, Washington, 1961-66; asst. prof. math. U. Md., College Park, 1963-66; prof. statistics, undergrad. dean Ohio State U., 1987—; prof. math. scis. emeritus Otterbein Coll., 1997—. Contbr. articles on statis. non parametric methods and robustness to profl. jours. Mem. Am. Statis. Assn., Math. Assn. Am. Roman Catholic. Home: 4375 Mumford Dr Columbus OH 43220-4438

WILLKIE, WENDELL LEWIS, II, lawyer; b. Indpls., Oct. 29, 1951; s. Philip Herman Willkie and Rosalie (Heffelfinger) Hall; m. Carlotta Fendig; children: Alexandra Elizabeth, Diana Fendig, Caroline Heffelfinger. AB, Harvard U., 1973; BA, Oxford (Eng.) U., 1975, MA, 1983; JD, U. Chgo., 1978. Bar: N.Y. 1979. Assoc. Simpson Thacher and Bartlett, N.Y.C., 1978-82; gen. counsel NEH, Washington, 1982-84; assoc. counsel to Pres. The White House, Washington, 1984-85; chief of staff, counselor to Sec. U.S. Dept. Edn., Washington, 1985, gen. counsel, 1985-88; counsel Office of the Pres.-elect, Washington, 1988-89; gen. counsel Dept. of Commerce, Washington, 1989-93; v.p. Westvaco Corp., N.Y.C., 1995-96, sr. v.p., gen. counsel, 1996—. Vis. fellow Am. Enterprise Inst., Washington, 1993-94. Co-author, editor: (with J.R. Lilley) Beyond MFN: Trade with China and American Interests, 1994. Harvard U. scholar, 1969-73, Rhodes scholar, 1973-75. Republican. Episcopalian. Office: Westvaco Corp 1 High Ridge Park Stamford CT 06905

WILLMAN, VALLEE LOUIS, physician, surgery educator; b. Greenville, Ill., May 4, 1925; s. Philip L. and Marie A. (Dall) W.; m. Melba L. Carr, Feb. 2, 1952; children: Philip, Elizabeth, Susan, Stephen, Mark, Timothy, Jane, Vallee, Sarah. Student, U. Ill., 1942-43, 45-47; MD, St. Louis U., 1951. Diplomate Am. Bd. Surgery (sr. examiner 1976—), Am. Bd. Thoracic Surgery. Intern Phila. Gen. Hosp., 1951-52; intern, resident St. Louis U. Group Hosps., 1952-56; Ellen McBride fellow in surgery St. Louis U., 1956-57, sr. instr. surgery, 1957-58, asst. prof. surgery, 1958-61, assoc. prof., 1961-63, prof., 1963—, C. Rollins Hanlon prof. surgery, chmn. dept., 1969—, vice chmn. dept., 1967-69; attending physician St. Louis U. Hosp., 1969—; chief of surgery, 1969—; mem. staff Cardinal Glennon Children's Hosp., 1969—. Cons. St. Louis VA Hosp., 1969—. Mem. editorial bd. Jour. Thoracic and Cardiovascular Surgery, 1976-86, Archives of Surgery, 1977-87, Jour. Cardiovascular Surgery, 1982-87, N.Am. editor, 1987—; contbr. over 250 articles to profl. jours. With USN, 1943-45. Recipient Merit award St. Louis Med. Soc., 1973, Health Care Leadership award Hosp. Assn. Met. St. Louis, 1988. Fellow Am. Surg. Assn., Am. Assn. Thoracic Surgery, Cen. Surg. Assn. (pres., mem. ad hoc com. on coronary artery surgery 1971-72); mem. ACS (Disting. Svc. award 1987), Soc. for Vascular Surgery, Internat. Soc. for Cardiovascular Surgery (pres. N.Am. chpt. 1985-87), Phi Beta Kappa, Phi Eta Sigma, Alpha Omega Alpha. Roman Catholic. Office: St Louis U Hosp 3635 Vista Ave Saint Louis MO 63110-2539 Office Phone: 314-977-8751. Business E-Mail: willmavl@slu.edu.

WILLMORE, LUTHER JAMES, JR., neurologist, academic administrator, educator; b. Fredericktown, Mo., Dec. 2, 1941; s. Luther James and Eunice Marie (Burkett) W.; m. Carolyn Lois Gilda, Dec. 10, 1961; children: John Andrew, Sydney Rebecca, Theodore Martin, Charles Caleb. BS, St. Louis U., 1964, MD cum laude, 1968. Diploma Am. Bd. Psychiatry and Neurology and Clin. Neurophysiology. Intern in surgery St. Louis U. Hosps., 1968-69; med. officer Naval Acad. Hosp. USS Austin (LPD-4) USN, Norfolk, Va., Annapolis, Md., 1969-72; resident in neurology U. Va., Charlottesville, 1972-75; from asst. to assoc. prof. neurology and neurobiology U. Fla. Coll. Medicine, Gainesville, 1975-82; faculty U. Tex., Houston, 1982-99, prof. neurology, dir. Tex. Comprehensive Epilepsy program; assoc. dean admissions and student affairs Sch. Medicine St. Louis U., 1999—, prof. neurology and pharmacology and physiology, 1999—. Contbr. numerous articles to profl. jours., book chpts.; editor numerous monographs. Profl. adv. bd. Epilepsy Found. Am., 1979-87; chair profl. adv. bd. Epilepsy Found. SE Tex., 1996-98; pres. Fla. Epilepsy Found., 1978-80; gov.'s commn. advocacy for persons with devel. disabilities State Fla., 1980-82. Named Physician of Yr. Tex. Rehab. Commn., 1984-85. Fellow Am. Acad. Neurology; mem. Am. Epilepsy Soc., Am. Neurol. Assn., Soc. Neurosci., Jesuit Men's Hon. Soc. (John Horsley Meml. prize 1980). Achievements include creation of a model of epilepsy in animals, research contribution in neurochemistry and molecular biology of epilepsy, and clinical drug development. Office: St Louis U Sch Medicine Office of Admissions 1402 S Grand Blvd Saint Louis MO 63104-1004

WILLMOTT, PETER SHERMAN, retail executive; b. Glens Falls, N.Y., June 1, 1937; BA, Williams Coll., 1959; MBA, Harvard U., 1961. Sr. fin. analyst Am. Airlines, N.Y.C., 1961-63; mgr. cons. Booz, Allen & Hamilton, N.Y.C., 1964-66; treas. Continental Baking Co., Rye, N.Y., 1966-69, v.p., 1969-74; sr. v.p. fin. Fed. Express Corp., Memphis, 1974-77, exec. v.p. fin. and adminstrn., 1977-80, pres., chief operating officer, 1980-83; pres., CEO Carson Pirie Scott & Co., Chgo., 1983-89, chmn., 1984-89, also bd. dirs.; chmn., CEO Willmott Svcs., 1989—; CEO Zenith, 1996—97; interim pres., CEO Fleming Cos. Inc., 2003—. Bd. dirs. Fed. Express, Fleming Cos. Office: Fleming PO Box 299013 Lewisville TX 75029

WILLNER, ALAN ELI, electrical engineer, educator; b. Bklyn, Nov. 16, 1962; s. Gerald and Sondra (Bernstein) W.; m. Michelle Frida Green, June 25, 1991. BA, Yeshiva U., 1982; MS, Columbia U., 1984, PhD, 1988. Summer tech. staff David Sarnoff Rsch. Ctr., Princeton, NJ, 1983, 84; grad. rsch. asst. dept. elec. engring. Columbia U., NYC, 1984-88; postdoctoral mem. tech. staff AT&T Bell Labs., Holmdel, NJ, 1988-90; mem. tech. staff Bell Comm. Rsch., Red Bank, NJ, 1990-91; prof. U. So. Calif., LA, 1992—, assoc. dir. Ctr. Photonic Tech., 1994— . Head del. Harvard Model UN Yeshiva U., 1982; instr. Columbia U., 1987; rev. panel mem. NSF, Washington, 1992, Washington, 93, Washington, 94, invited optical comm. workshop, 94; chair panel on optical info. and comm., 94; co-chair Conf. on Lasers and Electro-Optics; steering com. and tech. com. mem. Conf. Optical Fiber Comm. Author 1 book; contbr. articles to profl. jours.; editor-in-chief Jour. Lighwave Tech., IEEE Jour. Selected Topics in Quantum Electronics; assoc. editor Jour. Selected Areas in Comm. Mem. faculty adv. bd. U. So. Calif. Hillel Orgn., 1992. Recipient Disting. Lectr. award, IEEE Lasers and Electro-Optics Soc., Armstrong Found. prize, Columbia U., 1984, Best Engring. Tchr. award, USC/TRW, young investigator award, NSF, 1992, Eddy Paper Award, 2001, USL Assoc. Award for Univ. Wide Excellence in Tchg.; fellow, Semiconductor Rsch. Corp., 1986, Sci. and Engring., David and Lucile Packard Found., 1993, presdl. faculty, NSF, 1994, sr. scholar, Fulbright Found., 1997; grantee NSF, Advanced Rsch. Projects Agy., Packard Found., Powell Found., Ballistic Missile Def. Orgn. Fellow: Optical Soc. Am. (symposium organizer ann. mtg. 1992, panel organizer ann. mtg. 1993, symposium organizer ann. mtg. 1995, panel organizer ann. mtg. 1995, program com. for conf. on optical fiber commn. 1996, 1997, program co-chair ann. mtg. 2001, vice chair optical comm. group, tech. council chair-photonics divsn., co-chair sci. and engring. coun., bd. dirs., program co-chair of OSA Annual Mtg., tech. coun. chair photonics divsn.); mem.: IEEE (sr.; editor-in-chief IEEE/OSA Jour. Lightwave Tech.), Soc. Photo-Instrumentation Engring. (program chair telecomm, engring photonics west 1995, chmn. conf. on emerging techs for all-optical networks photonics west 1995, program com. for Conf. on Optical Fiber Comm. 1996, conf. program com. components for WDM), IEEE Lasers and Electro-Optics Soc. (chmn. optical comm. subcom. ann. mtg. 1994, v.p. tech. affairs, mem. optical comm. tech. com., bd. govs., mem. optical networks tech. com., chmn. optical comm. tech. com., various awards coms., bd. govs. 1998—2001, awards com. mem. Quantum Electronics, IEEE Fellow, Disting. Lectr. award), Sigma Xi. Achievements include patents for localized photochemical etching of multilayered semiconductor body, optical star coupler utilizing fiber amplifier tech., and one-to-many simultaneous optical WDM 2-dim. plane interconnections. Home: 9326 Sawyer St Los Angeles CA 90035-4102 Office: U So Calif Dept Elec Engring Eeb 538 Los Angeles CA 90089-0001

WILLNER, ANN RUTH, political scientist, educator; b. N.Y.C., Sept. 2, 1924; d. Norbert and Bella (Richman) W. BA cum laude, Hunter Coll., 1945; MA, Yale U., 1946; PhD, U. Chgo., 1961. Lectr. U. Chgo., 1946-47, rsch. assoc. Ctr. for Econ. Devel. and Cultural Change, 1954-56, 61-62; advisor on orgn. and tng. Indonesian Ministry for Fgn. Affairs, Jakarta, 1952-53; expert for small scale indsl. planning Indonesian Nat. Planning Bur., Jakarta, 1953-54; fgn. affairs analyst Congl. Reference Svc., Libr. of Congress, 1960; asst. prof. polit. sci. Harpur Coll., Binghamton, NY, 1962-63; postdoctoral fellow polit. sci. and Southeast Asian studies Yale U., New Haven, 1963-64; rsch. assoc. Ctr. Internat. Studies, Princeton U., 1964-69; assoc. prof. polit. sci. U. Kans., Lawrence, 1969-70, prof., 1970-98. Vis. prof. polit. sci. CUNY, 1975; cons. govt. agys. and pvt. industry Polit. sci. editor: Ency. of the Social Scis., 1961; mem. editl. bd. Econ. Devel. and Cultural Change, 1954-57, Jour. Comparative Adminstrn., 1969-74, Comparative Politics, 1977—; author: The Neotraditional Accomodation to Political Independence, 1966, Charismatic Political Leadership: A Theory, 1968, The Spellbinders, 1984; also monographs, jour. articles, book chpts., newspaper columns. Grantee Rockefeller Found., 1965, Social Sci. Rsch. and Am. Coun. Learned Socs., 1966. Mem. Am. Polit. Sci. Assn. (gov. coun. 1979-81), Nat. Press Club. Home: 560 N St SW # N405 Washington DC 20024-4605 Office Phone: 202-484-2092.

WILLNER, DOROTHY, anthropologist, educator; b. N.Y.C., Aug. 26, 1927; d. Norbert and Bella (Richman) W. Ph.B., U. Chgo., 1947, MA, 1953, PhD, 1961; postgrad., Ecole Pratique des Hautes Etudes, U. Paris, France, 1953-54. Anthropologist Jewish Agy., Israel, 1955-58; tech. asst., adminstrn. expert in community devel. UN, Mexico, 1958; asst. prof. dept. sociology and anthropology U. Iowa, Iowa City, 1959-60; research assoc. U. Chgo., 1961-62; asst. prof. dept. sociology and anthropology U. N.C., Chapel Hill, 1962-63, Hunter Coll., N.Y.C., 1964-65; assoc. prof. dept. anthropology U. Kans., Lawrence, 1967-70, prof., 1970-90; professorial lectr. Johns Hopkins U. Sch. Advanced Internat. Studies, 1992. Author: Community Leadership, 1960, Nation-Building and Community in Israel, 1969. Contbr. numerous articles to profl. publs. Fellow Am. Anthrop. Assn., Soc. Applied Anthropology, Royal Anthrop. Inst.; mem. Cen. States Anthrop. Soc. (past pres.), Assn. Polit. and Legal Anthropology (past pres.). Home: # N 407 560 N St SW Washington DC 20024-4605

WILLNER, EUGENE BURTON, food and liquor company executive; b. Chgo., July 27, 1934; s. Fred and Mae (Goodhartz) W.; m. Karen Nell Kaye, Feb. 22, 1962; children: Tracy Fran, Kelly Kaye. BA, Northwestern U., 1956. Pres. World Wide Fisheries Inc., Chgo., 1956-60; merchandiser Edison Bros. Stores Inc., St. Louis, 1960-66; v.p. Mo. Supreme Life Ins. Co., St. Louis, 1966-67; exec. v.p. Exec. Agys., Inc., St. Louis, 1966-67; pres. Bluff Creek Industries, Inc., Ocean Springs, Miss., 1967-69, Purse String Stores, Inc., Miami, Fla., 1969-73, World Wide Fisheries, Miami, 1969-73, Renwill Seafoods, Inc., 1979—. Chmn. bd. Astral Liquors, Inc., Foxy Laidy Lounges, Prime Universal Seafood Corp., Miami, also Key West, Fla., Caracas, Venezuela, San Juan del Sur, Nicaragua, Quito, Ecuador; pres., chmn. bd. Common Markets, Inc., Miami, London and Moscow, 1980—. Mem. Deering Bay Country Club, Turnberry Club, Grove Isle Club, Fisher Island Club, Palm Beach Country Club. Office: 29000 S Dixie Hwy Homestead FL 33033-2302 Address: PO Box 561944 Pinecrest FL 33256-1944 E-mail: asiamoon@att.net.

WILLNER, JOSEPH H. neurologist; b. Newark, Oct. 27, 1944; MD, NYU, 1970. Diplomate Am. Bd. Neurology. Intern Boston City Hosp., 1970—71; resident in neurology Columbia-Prebyn. Neurol. Inst., N.Y.C., 1974—77, clin. fellow in neuromuscular disorders, 1977—79; assoc. clin. prof. Columbia U., N.Y.C.; neurologist Englewood (N.J.) Hosp. and Med. Ctr., 1984—, N.Y. Presbyn. Hosp. Co-dir. Muscular Dystrophy Assn.-sponsored Myasthenia Gravis Clini Englewood Med. Ctr.; mem. adv. bd. The Neuropathy Assn. Named one of Top Drs. in N.Y. Metro Area, Castle Connolly, Top Drs. 2003, N.J. Monthly Mag. Office: Englewood Hosp and Med Ctr 200 Grand Ave Ste 101 Englewood NJ 07631-4363

WILLOCKS, ROBERT MAX, retired librarian; b. Maryville, Tenn., Oct. 1, 1924; s. Willis Lemuel and Hannah (Emert) W.; m. Neysa Nerene Ferguson, May 23, 1947; children— Margret Sharon, Samuel David, Mark Timothy, Robert Daniel, Kent Max. BA, Maryville Coll., 1949; B.D., Golden Gate Bapt. Theol. Sem., 1951, Th.M., 1962; MA in Library Sci, Peabody Coll., 1962. Ordained to ministry Bapt. Ch., 1950; pastor in Calif., 1950-56; missionary to Korea So. Bapt. Fgn. Mission Bd., Taejon, 1956- 65; asso. dir. library Heidelberg Coll., Tiffin, Ohio, 1965-67; dir. library Columbia (S.C.) Coll., 1967-70; asst. dir. libraries Syracuse (N.Y.) U., 1970-76; assoc. dir. libraries U. Fla., Gainesville, 1976-83, acting dir. libraries, 1983-84, dep. dir. libraries, 1984-89, ret., 1989; pastor Northwood Bapt. Ch., Gainesville, 1981-92; libr. Bapt. Theol. Sem., Lusaka, Zambia, 1994-97, Ghana Bapt. Sem., Kumasi, 1998—2004. Acting dir. Fla. Ctr. for Libr. Automation, 1984; cons. Choong Chung Nam Province Library Assn., Republic of Korea, 1962—65; dir. Korea Bapt. Press, 1959—61; prof. ch. history Korea Bapt. Sem., 1957—65, acting pres., 1958—59, librarian, 1959—65; vice chmn. Korea Bapt. Mission, 1962—64; del. Fla. Gov.'s Conf. on Libraries, 1978. Editor: Korean translations Thus it is Written, 1963, The Progress of Worldwide Missions, 1965. Chmn. trustees Wallace Meml. Bapt. Hosp., Pusan, Korea, 1963-65; pres. bd. dirs. Phoenix Homeowners Assn., 1980-88. With USNR, 1943-46. Mem. ALA (chmn. telefacsimile com. 1976-78, tech. com. 1980-84, chmn. standards com. 1985-88), Fla. Libr. Assn., Southeastern Library Assn., AAUP, Peabody Coll. Alumni Assn. (pres. S.C. 1968-69) Home: 1930 NW 12th Rd Gainesville FL 32605-5338

WILLOTT, ELIZABETH, biochemist, educator, ecologist, researcher; m. David Schmidtz. BSc, U. Calgary, 1982; PhD Biochemistry, U.Ariz., Tucson, 1989. Post-doctoral rsch. assoc. Yale U., New Haven, Conn., 1989—90, Duke U., Durham, NC, 1990—92; post-doctoral rsch. assoc./rsch. scientist Kans. State U., Manhattan, Kans., 1992—95; asst. prof. The U. of Ariz., Tucson, Ariz., 1996—. Editor: (book) Environmental Ethics: What really matters; what really works, 2002; contbr. articles to profl. jours. Avocations: philosophy, hiking, running, yoga. Office: Univ Ariz Entomology Dept Forbes 410 Tucson AZ 85721-0036 Business E-Mail: willott@u.arizona.edu.

WILLOUGHBY, ANNE, health facility administrator, researcher, educator; Rschr. NICHD, 1984, leader pediat., adolescent, and maternal AIDS, educator HIV/AIDS in mothers and children; dir. Rsch. Mothers and Children's Ctr., 2002—. Office: 6100 Executive Bldg Rm 4B11 Bethesda MD 20892

WILLOUGHBY, SARAH-MARGARET C. chemist, educator, chemical engineer, consultant; b. Bowling Green, KY, Oct. 15, 1917; d. Austin Burrell Claypool and Minerva Dallas Renfrow-Claypool; m. John Richard Evans, II, Aug. 30, 1938 (dec. Dec. 1942); 1 child, Richard Claypool Evans; m. Olief Glenn Willoughby, June 18, 1948 (dec.); children: Sarah, Stephen(dec.). BS, Western Ky. U., 1938; PhD, Purdue U., 1950. Registered profl. engr., Ind., Tex. Chemist Devoe-Reynolds, Inc., Louisville, 1941—42; jr. engr. chem. lab. div. Curtiss-Wright Corp., Louisville, 1942—44; tech. asst. Purdue U., West Lafayette, Ind., 1944—46, fellow, 1946—50; rsch. chemist, coatings divsn. Monsanto Chem. Co., Boston, 1950—52; assoc. prof. of chemistry U. Tex., Arlington, 1954—84, co-dir. Ctr. for Microcrystalline Polymer Rsch. Studies, 1978—82, prof. emeritus chemistry, 1984. Cons. Albert H. Halff Assocs., Dallas, 1980—86. Nominee Dallas-Ft. Worth Trailblazer award, 1996; named to Hall of Disting. Alumni, Western Ky. U., 1994; recipient Outstanding Chem. Engr. award, Purdue U., 1996. Fellow: Am. Inst. Chemists; mem.: N.Y. Acad. Sci., Soc. Women Engrs. (sr.), Am. Chem. Soc. (emeritus mem.), Nat. Soc. Daughters of Founders and Patriots (v.p. N.E. Tex. chpt. 1997—), Friends of St. George, Plantagenet Soc., Colonial Dames Am., Nat. Soc. Colonial Dames of XVII Century (chpt. regent 1980—82), Nat. Soc. DAR (chpt. regent 1967—69, nat. bicentennial com. mem. 1975—76), Nat. Soc. Children of Am. Revolution (Tex. sr. state pres. 1968—70), Nat. Soc. Magna Carta Dames (Tex. state pres. 1986—88), Colonial Order of the Crown, Soc. Descendants of Knights of the Most Noble Order of the Garter, Sovereign Colonial Soc. Ams. of Royal Descent, Order Ky. Cols., Sigma Xi (emeritus mem.), Alpha Chi Omega (Lambda Epsilon chapt.). Home: 1630 Pecan Park Dr Arlington TX 76012

WILLOUGHBY, STEPHEN SCHUYLER, mathematics professor; b. Madison, Wis., Sept. 27, 1932; s. Alfred and Elizabeth Frances (Cassell) W.; m. Helen Sali Shapiro, Aug. 29, 1954; children: Wendy Valentine (Mrs. Peter Gallen), Todd Alan. AB (scholar), Harvard U., 1953, AM in Teaching, 1955; EdD (Clifford Brewster Upton fellow), Columbia U., 1961. Tchr. Newton (Mass.) Pub. Schs., 1954-57, Greenwich (Conn.) Pub. Schs., 1957-59; instr. U. Wis., Madison, 1960-61, asst. prof. math. edn. and math., 1961-65; prof. math. edn. and math. NYU, 1965-87, dir. math. edn. dept., 1967-83, chmn. math., sci. and stats. edn. dept., 1970-80, 86-87, chmn. U. Faculty Coun., 1981-82; prof. math. U. Ariz., Tucson, 1987—2002; prof. emeritus math. and math. edn. NYU, 1982—; prof. emeritus math. U. Ariz., Tucson, 2002—. Mem. nat. bd. advisor Sq. One TV, 1983-94, U.S. Commn. on Math. Instrn., 1984-95, chmn., 1991-95; math. adv. com. Nat. Tchr. Exam. Successor (Praxis), 1989-94; edn. panel New Am. Schs. Devel. Corp., 1991-97; U.S. Nat. rep. Internat. Commn. on Math. Instrn., 1991-95. Author: Contemporary Teaching of Secondary School Mathematics, 1967, Probability and Statistics, 1968, Teaching Mathematics: What Is Basic, 1981, Mathematics Education for a Changing World, 1990, Real Math, 1981, 85, 87, 91, Math: Explorations and Applications, 1998, College Mathematics Through Applications, 1999, The Other End of the Log: Memoirs of an Education Rebel, 2002; contbr. articles to profl. jours. and encys., chpts. to yearbooks and anthologies. Recipient Leadership in Math. Edn. Lifetime Achievement medal, 1995. Mem. Nat. Coun. Tchrs. Math. (dir. 1968-71, pres. 1982-84), Coun. Sci. Soc. Pres. (chmn. 1988). Home: 5435 E Gleneagles Dr Tucson AZ 85718-1805 Office: U Ariz Dept Math Tucson AZ 85721-0001

WILLOUGHBY, WILLIAM FRANKLIN, II, physician, researcher; b. Washington, Feb. 4, 1936; s. William Westel and Patricia (DeZychlinska) W.; m. Mary Scott Fishburne, 1963 (div. 1974); children: Westel Woodbury, William Franklin III, Laura Fishburne, Mary Scott; m. Judith Eleanor Barbaras, Oct. 25, 1975; 1 child, Robert Alexander Willoughby. AB, Johns Hopkins U., 1957, MD, PhD in Microbiology, Johns Hopkins U., 1965; grad. with distinction, USAF War Coll., 1985. Diplomate Am. Bd. Pathology. Intern then resident in pathology Johns Hopkins Hosp., 1965-67; asst. prof. depts. pathology and microbiology Case Western Res. U., Cleve.; dir. Virginia Mason Rsch. Ctr., Seattle, 1972-75; assoc. prof. dept. pathology Sch. Medicine, Johns Hopkins U., Balt., 1975-87; prof., chmn. dept. pathology Sch. Medicine, U. S.C., Columbia, 1987-92; dir. labs. Cook County Hosp., Chgo., 1992-98, interim med. dir., 1994-96. Cons. NIH, Bethesda, Md., 1979-98, mem. pathology A study sect., 1982-86; cons. NRC, Washington, 1981-84; mem. res. component med. coun., Dept. Def., Pentagon, 1991-93; dep. surgeon gen. for res. affairs USAF, Bolling AFB, D.C., 1993-95; asst. surg. gen. USAF, Operation Desert Storm/Desert Shield, 1990-91. Mem. editorial bd. Am. Rev. Respiratory Disease, 1978-84; contbr. articles to profl. jours., reviewer numerous sci. manuscripts. Vestryman Trinity Episcopal Ch., Long Green, Md., 1984-87; bd. dirs. Ctrl. S.C. chpt. ARC, Columbia, 1989-92; bd. fellow Norwich U., 1992-95. Maj. USAFR, 1975-95, advanced through grades to maj. gen., 1992-95. Decorated D.S.M., Legion of Merit; recipient Edwin E. Osgood prize Va. Mason Rsch. Ctr., 1973; Arthritis Found. fellow Scripps Clinic and Rsch. Found., 1967-69; Poncine scholar Poncine Found., 1972-74; NIH rsch. grantee, 1976-91. Fellow Coll. Am. Pathologists; mem. AAAS, Am. Lung Assn. (nat. rsch. grant rev. com. 1978-82, chmn., 1981-82), Am. Soc. Investigative Pathology, Am. Assn. Immunologists, Am. Soc. Cell Biologists, Chgo. Coun. Fgn. Rels., Internat. Acad. Pathology, Assn. Pathology Chmns., Aerospace Med. Assn., Soc. USAF Flight Surgeons (bd. govs. 1993-96), Soc. Cons. to Armed Forces, Am. Thoracic Soc., Assn. Mil. Surgeons U.S., Army Navy Club (Washington), Air Force Assn., Midtown Tennis Club (Chgo.). Avocations: music, genealogy, antiques, automobiles. Home: 1416A S Federal St Chicago IL 60605-2739 E-mail: wwilloughb@aol.com.

WILLS, CHARLES FRANCIS, former church executive, retired career officer; b. Avalon, N.J., July 26, 1914; s. Charles H. and Anna Margaret (Diemand) W.; m. Charlotte Emily Robson, Aug. 22, 1936; children: C. Frederic, Emily, Sally and Larry (twins). BS, Wheaton (Ill.) Coll., 1935; B.D., Eastern Bapt. Theol. Sem., 1938, Th.M., 1941; grad., Air War Coll., 1961. Commd. 1st lt. U.S. Army, 1941; advanced through grades to col. U.S. Air Force, 1963; chaplain AUS, 1941-49, U.S. Air Force, 1949-67; ret., 1967; exec. dir. chaplaincy services Am. Bapt. Chs., Valley Forge, Pa., 1969-75, exec. dir. profl. services, 1975-78; assoc. sec. Bapt. World Alliance, Washington, 1978-80, treas., 1980-81. Mem. Commn. on Doctrine and Interchurch Cooperation, 1980-90. Decorated Legion of Merit, Bronze Star, Purple Heart. Mem. Mil. Chaplains Assn., Mil. Order of Purple Heart.

WILLS, DAVID WOOD, minister, educator; b. Portland, Ind., Jan. 25, 1942; s. Theodore Oscar Mitchell and Elizabeth Lochore (Wood) W.; m. Carolyn Reynolds Montgomery, Aug. 22, 1964; children: John Brookings, Theodore Worcester, Thomas Churchill. BA, Yale U., 1962; BD, Princeton Theol. Sem., 1966; PhD, Harvard U., 1975. Ordained to ministry Presbyn. Ch., 1970. Asst. prof. Sch. of Religion, U. So. Calif., 1970-72; asst. prof. dept. of religion Amherst Coll., Mass., 1972-78, assoc. prof., 1978-83, prof., 1983-90, prof. religion and Black studies, 1990-94, Winthrop H. Smith '16 prof. Am. history and Am. studies, dept. religion and Black studies, 1994—, also dir. Luce Program in Comparative Religious Ethics 1978-88. Editor (with Richard Newman) Black Apostles at Home and Abroad, 1982, (with Albert Raboteau) Afro-American Religion: A Documentary History Project, 1987—. Kent fellow Danforth Found., 1966-70, 75, Ford Found. fellow, 1972, Inst. for Ecumenical and Cultural Rsch. fellow, 1972, Nat. Humanities Ctr. fellow, 1980-81, 94, NEH fellow for Coll. Tchrs., 1988-89, W. E. B. DuBois Inst. for Afro-Am. Rsch. fellow, 1989-91. Mem. Am. Acad. Religion (chair Afro-Am. religious history group 1975-78), Am. Hist. Assn., Am. Soc. Ch. History, Am. Studies Assn., Orgn. Am. Historians, Phi Beta Kappa. Home: 47 Stagecoach Rd Amherst MA 01002-3527 Office: Amherst Coll Dept Religion Amherst MA 01002 E-mail: dwwills@amherst.edu.

WILLS, E. ASHLEY, ambassador; b. Tenn., 1945; m. Gina Mancuri; 2 children. Grad. with honors, U. Va., 1971; MA in Econs., Johns HOpkins U. Dep. chief of mission and chargé d'affaires Am. Embassy in New Delhi Dept. of State, U.S. amb. to Sri Lanka and Maldives, 2000—. Office: DOS Amb 6100 Colombo Pl Washington DC 20521

WILLS, GARRY, historian; b. Atlanta, May 22, 1934; s. John and Mayno (Collins) Wills; m. Natalie Cavallo, May 30, 1959; children: John, Garry, Lydia. BA, St. Louis U., 1957; MA, Xavier U., Cin., 1958, Yale U., 1959, PhD, 1961; LittD (hon.), Coll. Holy Cross, 1982, Columbia Coll., 1982, Beloit Coll., 1988, Xavier U., 1993, St. Xavier U., 1993, Union Coll., 1993, Macalester Coll., 1995, Bates Coll., 1995, St. Ambrose, 1997, George Washington U., 1999, Spring Hill Coll., 2000, Siena Heights U., 2001, Gettysburg Coll., 2002, Am. U., 2003, Muhlenberg Coll., 2004. Fellow Ctr. Hellenic Studies, 1961—62; assoc. prof. classics Johns Hopkins U., 1962—67, adj. prof., 1968-80; Henry R. Luce prof. Am. culture and public policy Northwestern U., 1980—88, adj. prof., 1988— . Author: (book) Chesterton, 1961, Politics and Catholic Freedom, 1964, Roman Culture, 1966, Jack Ruby, 1967, Second Civil War, 1968, Nixon Agonistes, 1970, Bare Ruined Choirs, 1972, Inventing America, 1978, At Button's, 1979, Confessions of a Conservative, 1979, Explaining America, 1980, The Kennedy Imprisonment, 1982, Lead Time, 1983, Cincinnatus, 1984, Reagan's America, 1987, Under God, 1990, Lincoln at Gettysburg, 1992 (Pulitzer Prize for gen. non-fiction, 1993), Certain Trumpets: The Call of Leaders, 1994, Witches and Jesuits: Shakespeare's Macbeth, 1994, John Wayne's America, 1997, St. Augustine, 1999, A Necessary Evil, 1999, Papal Sin, 2000, Venice, Lion City, 2001, St. Augustine's Childhood, 2001, James Madison, 2002, Why Am I a Catholic, 2002, St. Augustine's Memory, 2002, Mr. Jefferson's University, 2002, St. Augustine's Sin, 2003, Negro President, 2003, St. Augustine's Conversion, 2004. Recipient Merle Curti award, Orgn. Am. Historians, Nat. Book Critics Cir. award (2), Wilbur Cross medal, Yale U., Peabody award, NEH Presdl. medal, 1998, John Hope Franklin award, First Freedom award, Coun. for the First Freedom. Mem.: AAAL, Am. Philos. Soc., Am. Antiquarian Soc., Am. Acad. Arts and Scis., Mass. Hist. Soc. Roman Catholic. Office: Northwestern U Dept History Evanston IL 60208 Business E-Mail: g-wills@northwestern.edu.

WILLS, J. ROBERT, academic administrator, drama educator, writer; b. Akron, Ohio, May 5, 1940; s. J. Robert and Helen Elizabeth (Lapham) W.; m. Barbara T. Salisbury, Aug. 4, 1984 (dec. 1998); m. Jeanne Hokin, June 2002. BA, Coll. of Wooster, 1962; MA, U. Ill., 1963; PhD, Case-Western Res. U., 1971; cert. in arts adminstrn, Harvard U., 1976. Instr. to asst. prof., dir. theatre Wittenberg U., Springfield, Ohio, 1963-72; assoc. prof., dir. grad. studies, chmn. dept. theatre U. Ky., Lexington, 1972-77, prof. theatre, dean Coll. Fine Arts, 1977-81; prof. drama, dean Coll. Fine Arts U. Tex., Austin, 1981-89, Effie Marie Cain Regents chair in Fine Arts, 1986-89; provost, prof. theatre Pacific Luth. U., Tacoma, Wash., 1989-94; prof. theatre, dean coll. fine arts Ariz. State U., Tempe, 1994—. Cons. colls., univs., arts orgns., govt. agencies Author: The Director in a Changing Theatre, 1976, Directing in the Theatre: A Casebook, 1980, rev. edit., 1994; dir. 92 plays; contbr. articles to profl. jours. Bd. dirs. various art orgns., Ky., Tex., Wash., Ariz. Recipient grants public and pvt. agencies. Mem. Nat. Assn. State Univs. and Land-Grant Colls.(chmn. commn. on arts 1981-83), Coun. Fine Arts Deans (exec. com. 1984-89, sec./treas. 1986-89), Univ. and Coll. Theatre Assn. (pres. 1981-82), Assn. for Communication Adminstrn. (pres. 1986-87), Ky. Theatre Assn. (pres. 1976). Office: Ariz State U PO Box 872102 Tempe AZ 85287-2102 Business E-Mail: bob.wills@asu.edu.

WILLS, JOHN ARTHUR, computer programmer, analyst; b. Newport, Wales, Sept. 18, 1946; came to U.S., 1977; s. Gordon Henry and Jean Fances (Maley) W.; m. Sharlene Kuhnheim, May 18, 1972 (div. 1990). Student, St. Mary's Sch., Nairobi, 1957—63, Glasgow U., 1965—67, St. Joseph Coll., Netherlands, 1967—69; BA, Open U., Milton Keynes, Eng., 1974; BA with honors, Open U., 1995. File card sorter East African Posts and Telecomms., Nairobi, Kenya, 1962; posting clk. K. Watson Shipping, London, 1962; messenger G. Ellison & Co., London, 1968, Sterling & Co., London, 1969; libr., programmer Tylin Mgmt., Pangbourne, Eng., 1970-71; programmer Teknotalk, Ltd., London, 1971, City of Berlin, Fed. Republic of Germany, 1972-77; sr. systems programmer Burroughs Corp., Pasadena, Calif., 1977-79; programmer analyst Stationers Corp., L.A., 1979-80; programmer/analyst Pasadena City Coll., 1980-91, Prudential Ins., Florham Park, NJ, 1996, PMSC, Columbia, SC, 1996—98, Sterling Commerce, Columbus, Ohio, 1998, Pacific Bell, San Ramon, Calif., 1999, U.S. Census, 2000, Deloitte & Touche, Norwalk, Calif., 2001, City and County of San Francisco, 2001—. Author: Albatross, 2001. Mem. Assn. Computing Machinery. Roman Catholic. Home: 2335 Market St Apt 3 Oakland CA 94607-3455

WILLS, JOHN ELLIOT, JR., history educator, writer; b. Urbana, Ill., Aug. 8, 1936; s. John Elliot and George Anne (Hicks) W.; m. Carolin Connell, July 19, 1958; children: Catherine, Christopher John, Jeffrey David, Joanne, Lucinda. BA in Philosophy, U. Ill., 1956; MA in East Asian Studies, Harvard U., 1960, PhD in History and Far Ea. Langs., 1967. History instr. Stanford (Calif.) U., 1964-65, U. So. Calif., L.A., 1965-67, asst. prof., 1967-72, assoc. prof., 1972-84, prof., 1984—2004, prof. emeritus, 2004—, acting chair East Asian Langs. and Cultures, 1987-89; dir. East Asian Studies Ctr. USC-UCLA Joint East Asian Studies Ctr., L.A., 1990-94. Rsch. abroad in The Netherlands, Taiwan, China, Japan, Macao, Philippines, Indonesia, India, Italy, Spain, Portugal, Eng. Author: Pepper, Guns, and Parleys: The Dutch East India Company and China, 1662-1681, 1974, Embassies and Illusions: Dutch and Portuguese Envoys to K'ang-hsi, 1666-1687, 1984, Mountain of Fame: Portraits in Chinese History, 1994, 1688: A Global History, 2001; co-editor: (with Jonathan D. Spence) From Ming to Ch'ing: Conquest, Region, and Continuity in Seventeenth-Century China, 1979; editor: Eclipsed Entrepots of the Western Pacific: Taiwan and Central Vietnam, 1500-1800, 2002; contbr. articles to profl. jours. Grantee Nat. Acad. Scis., 1985, Am. Coun. Learned Soc., 1979-80; Younger Humanist fellow NEH, 1972-73. Mem. Assn. for Asian Studies, Am. Hist. Assn., Phi Beta Kappa, Phi Kappa Phi (recognition award 1986, 95). Avocation: travel. Business E-Mail: jwills@usc.edu.

WILLS, KATHERINE V. TSIOPOS, English language educator; b. St. Louis, Sept. 30, 1957; d. Vasilios and Kalliope (Stratos) Tsiopos. BA, Washington U., 1979; MA, Ind. U., 1990; PhD. composition and rhetoric, U of Louisville, 2004. Pres. Port of Nashville (Ind.) Inc., retailer of nautical items and antiques, 1986—. Asst. vis. lectr. English dept. Ind. U. Purdue U., Indpls., 1991—; vol. Women's Writers' Conf. Contbr. over 60 articles to profl. jours, poetry to jours, 60 nat. and internat. conf. presentations. Recipient essay award Scholastic Mag., Inc., 1973, award for acad. excellence and community svc. Am. Hellenic Progessvie and Ednl. Assn., A poetry award Wednesday Club of St. Louis, Mo., 1977, Roger Conant Hatch hon. mention for writing, Washington U., 1977. Greek Orthodox. Home: 7772 Bellsville Pike Nashville IN 47448-8995 Office Phone: 812-348-7215.

WILLS, RICHARD H. electronics manufacturing executive; B in Computer Sys., Linfield Coll.; MBA, U. Oreg. Various positions Tektronix, Inc., Beaverton, Oreg., 1979-91, head TDS line, 1991-93, worldwide dir. mktg., 1993-94, v.p., gen. mgr. design svc. and test bus. unit, 1995-97, pres. European ops., 1997-99, pres. measurement bus., 1999-2000, pres., CEO, 2000—, also bd. dirs. With USAF. Office: Tektronix Inc 14200 SW Karl Braun Dr Beaverton OR 97077

WILLS, RITCHIE JEAN, hospital administrator; b. Belleville, Ill., July 28, 1928; d. Richard and Viola L. (Davis) Grossner; m. Richard R. Wills, Jan. 23, 1948; children: Valann M. Kampf, Sheila L.; m. Lawrence G. Wetherwax, June 29, 1974 (div. Oct. 1988). AA, Crafton Hills Coll., 1977; BA, Redlands U., 1977. Lic. nursing home adminstr., residential care facility for elderly adminstr. Patient svcs. rep. Loma Linda Univ. Hosp., Calif., 1968—72; office mgr. Canyon Crest Convalescent Hosp., Colton, Calif., 1972-74, Highland House Healthcare (Calif.), 1974-76; adminstr. Beverly Manor Convalescent Hosp., Riverside, Calif., 1977-79, Terracina Healthcare Ctr., Redlands, Calif., 1979-94; dir. cmty. rels., adminstr. ARDAN Residential Care, Inc., Irvine, Calif., 1995—98; mktg. profl. HomeCare USA (divsn. of Accent Care), Palm Desert, Calif., 1999-2000; adminstr. Braswell's Yucaipa Valley Convalescent Hosp., Yucaipa, Calif., 2000—02; asst. adminstr. Braswell's Ivy Retreat, Mentone, Calif., 2002—03. Dir. For Your Network Loma Linda/Redlands Connection; pres. bd. San Jacinto Day Care Ctr.; bd. mem. Inland Resources Ctr.; mktg. cons. Crestview Convalescent Hosp., Rialto, Calif., 2004—. Fellow Am. Coll. Health Care Adminstrs.; mem. NAFE, Calif. Assn. Health Facilities (v.p. region V), Redlands C. of C. (amb.), Order Ea. Star, Redlands Noon Soroptimists. Republican.

WILLS, ROBERT HAMILTON, retired newspaper executive; b. Colfax, Ill., June 21, 1926; s. Robert Orson and Ressie Mae (Hamilton) W.; m. Sherilyn Lou Nierstheimer, Jan. 16, 1949; children: Robert L., Michael H., Kendall J. BS, MS, Northwestern U., 1950. Reporter Duluth (Minn.) Herald & News-Tribune, 1950-51; reporter Milw. Jour., 1951-59, asst. city editor, 1959-62; city editor Milw. Sentinel, 1962-75, editor, 1975-91; exec. v.p. Jour./Sentinel, Inc., Milw., 1991-92, pres., 1992-93; vice-chmn., 1993; also bd. dirs. Jour./Sentinel, Inc., Milw.; pub. Milw. Jour. Sr. v.p., bd. dirs. Jour. Communications; pres. Wis. Freedom of Info. Council, 1979-86, charter mem., 1979; Pulitzer Prize juror, 1982, 83, 90. Mem. media-law rels. com. State Bar Wis., 1969-99; vice chmn. privacy coun. Wis. Pub. Svc. Commn., 1996-97; mem. Wis. Privacy Coun., 1994-95. Recipient Leadership award Women's Ct. and Civic Conf. Greater Milw., 1987; inducted into Journalism Hall of Achievement Medill Sch. Northwestern U., 1997, Wis. Newspaper Assn. Found. Hall of Fame, 2001. Mem. Wis. Newspaper Assn. (pres. 1985-86, Disting. Svc. award 1992), Wis. AP (pres. 1975-76, Dion Henderson award Svc. 1993), Am. Soc. Newspaper Editors, Internat. Press Inst., Milw. Press Club (Media Hall Fame 1993), Soc. Profl. Journalists (prs. Milw. chpt. 1979-80, nat. pres. 1986-87), Sigma Delta Chi Found. (bd. dirs. 1993-96, Wis. Newsman of Yr. 1973, Freedom of Info. award Milw. chpt. 1988). Home: 2064 Tiger Links Dr Henderson NV 89012-6111 E-mail: wills2064@juno.com.

WILLS, WILLIAM RIDLEY, II, former insurance company executive, historian; b. Nashville, June 19, 1934; s. Jesse Ely and Ellen (Buckner) W.; m. Irene Weaver Jackson, July 21, 1962; children: William Ridley III, Morgan Jackson, Thomas Weaver. BA, Vanderbilt U., 1956. Agt., staff mgr. Nat. Life & Accident Ins. Co., Nashville, 1958-62, supr., 1962-64, asst. sec., 1964-67, asst. v.p., 1967-70, 2d v.p., 1970-75, v.p., 1975-81, sr. v.p., 1981-83, Am. General Services Co., 1982-83; dir. Nat. Life & Accident Ins. Co., Nashville, 1976-83; pres. Tenn. Hist. Soc., 1985-87; bd. dirs. Nat. Trust for Hist. Preservation, 1988-91. Author: History of Belle Meade: Mansion, Plantation and Stud, 1991, Old Enough to Die, 1996, Touring Tennessee: A Post Card Panorama, 1989-1955, 1996, Tennessee Governors at Home, 1999, Belle Meade Country Club: The First One Hundred Years, 2001. Nat. chmn. Living Endowment Drive Vanderbilt U., 1974; pres. Cumberland Mus. and Sci. Ctr., Nashville, 1977; gen. chmn. campaign United Way, Nashville and Mid. Tenn., 1978; pres. YMCA of Met. Nashville, 1984; trustee Ladies Hermitage Assn., 1981—90; mem. Tenn. Hist. Commn.; chmn. YMCA Found. Mid. Tenn., 1998—99; chmn. bd. Montgomery Bell Acad., 1988—97, gen. chmn. $43 million capital campaign, 1999—2000; mem. adv. bd. Pub. Libr. of Nashville and Davidson County, 2002—; pres. Monteagle Sundy Sch. Assembly, 2002—04; bd. dirs. Vanderbilt U., 1988—. Lt. USN, 1956—58. Recipient awards YMCA, 1977, 1983, United Way De Tocqueville award, 1989, Tenn. History Book award Tenn. Libr. Assn. and Tenn. Hist. Commn., 1991, Disting. Alumnus award Montgomery Bell Acad., 1996, H.G. Hill award YMCA of Mid. Tenn., 2003. Fellow Life Office Mgmt. Assn.; mem. Assn. Preservation Tenn. Antiquities (pres. Nashville chpt. 1987-89), Belle Meade Country Club, Coffee House Club, Round Table Literary Club. Presbyterian.

WILLSE, JAMES PATRICK, newspaper editor; b. N.Y.C., Mar. 17, 1944; s. Sherman Stokes and Katherine (Mackey) W.; m. Sharon Margaret Stack, Sept. 15, 1973; 1 child, Elizabeth Ruth. BA, Hamilton Coll., 1967; MS, Columbia U., 1968. Nat. editor AP, N.Y.C., 1969-74, news editor San Francisco, 1975-78; city editor San Francisco Examiner, 1978-82, mng. editor, 1982-84, N.Y. Daily News, 1984-89, editor, pub., 1989-95; editor Star Ledger, Newark, 1995—. Fellow Stanford U., 1975. Mem. Am. Soc. Newspaper Editors, AP Mng. Editors. Office: Star Ledger 1 Star Ledger Plz Newark NJ 07102-1291 E-mail: jwillse@starledger.com.

WILLSIE, SANDRA K. dean, internist, educator; BS in Med. Tech., Pittsburg (Kans.) State U., 1975; DO, U. Health Sci.-Coll. Osteo., Kansas City, Mo., 1983. Diplomate in internal medicine, pulmonary disease and critical care medicine Am. Bd. Internal Medicine. Rotating intern Univ. Hosp., Kansas City, Mo., 1983-84; resident in internal medicine U. Mo.-Kansas City Affiliated Hosps., 1984-87; fellow in pulmonary diseases Truman Med. Ctr.-West, Kansas City, Mo., 1987-89; instr. medicine U. Mo.-Kansas City Sch. Medicine, 1984-89; med. dir. pulmonary clinic Truman Med. Ctr., 1991-2000; asst. prof. medicine U. Mo. Kansas City Sch. Medicine, 1989-94, assoc. prof. medicine, 1994-99, dep. asst. dean, 1994—97, asst. dean, 1997-2000, prof. medicine, 1999-2000, U. Health Scis., Kansas City, Mo., 2000—, vice dean acad. affairs, adminstrn., med. affairs, 2000—02, v.p. acad. affairs, dean, 2002—. Contbr. articles to profl. jours. Fellow ACP, Am. Coll. Chest Physicians; mem. Am. Thoracic Soc., Mo. Thoracic Soc., Soc. Critical Care Medicine, Met. Med. Soc., Am. Osteo. Assn. Office: Kans City Univ Medicine and Bioscis 1750 Independence Ave Kansas City MO 64106-1453

WILLSON, C. GRANT, chemistry educator, engineering educator; b. Vallejo, Calif., Mar. 30, 1939; s. Carlton P. and Margaret Ann (Cosner) W.; m. Deborah Jeanne Merritt, Dec. 13, 1975; children: William, Andrew. BS in Chemistry, U. Calif., Berkeley, 1962, PhD in Organic Chemistry, 1973; MS in Organic Chemistry, San Diego State U., 1969. With propellent rsch. Aerojet Gen. Corp., Sacramento, 1962-64; tchr., coach Fairfax H.S., L.A., 1964-67; prof. Calif. State U., Long Beach, 1973-74, U. Calif., San Diego, 1974-78; mgr. polymer sci. and tech. IBM Almaden Rsch. Ctr., San Jose, Calif., 1978-93; prof. chemistry, chem. engring. U. Tex., Austin, 1993—. Contbr. articles to profl. jours.; patentee in field. Recipient Kosar award Soc. Imaging Sci. and Tech., 1998, Aristotle award Semicondr. Rsch. Corp., Photopolymer Sci. award, Japan, 2003. Mem. NAE, AAAS, Soc. Photog. and Instrumentation Engrs., Am. Phys. Soc., Am. Chem. Soc. (Arthur K. Doolittle award 1986, award Chemistry of Materials 1991, Carouthers award 1992, Coop. Rsch. award in Polymer Sci. 1993, Applied Polymer Sci. Award, 2004), NAS (award for chem. in svc. to soc. 1999), Coun. for Chem. Rsch. (Malcom Pruitt award 1997), St. Francis Yacht Club, Sigma Xi. Avocations: sailing, skiing. Office: U Tex Dept Chem and Chem Engring Austin TX 78712

WILLSON, CLYDE D. biologist, educator; b. Omaha, May 7, 1935; s. Paul Gallup and Elise Willson; m. Greta Jean Olsen, July 17, 1954; children: Ian, Bjorn, Scott, Gillian. BA in Biochemistry, U. Calif., Berkeley, 1956, PhD in Chemistry, 1960. Postdoctoral fellow Pasteur Inst. (NIH), Paris, 1960—62; asst. prof. biology U. Calif., Berkeley, 1962—67, Miller fellow, 1967—69; prof. biology and chemistry Laney Coll., Oakland, Calif., 1969—. Chair biology dept. Laney Coll., 1975—77, 1995—2002, rep. Acad. Senate, 1990—2002. Contbr. articles to profl. jours. Natural scis. docent Oakland Mus., 1969—72. Mem.: AAUP (sec.-treas., U. Calif. at Berkeley 1963—64), No. Calif. Parasitologists, West Coast Bacterial Physiologists. Avocation: keyboard performance. Home: 136 International Blvd Oakland CA 94606 Office: Laney College 900 Fallon St Oakland CA 94607

WILLSON, DAVID ALLEN, retired reference librarian, writer; b. Seattle, June 30, 1942; s. Robert Richard and Alice Hansine (Aspen) W.; m. Penelope Poeschl, Dec. 13, 1972 (div. Mar. 1986); children: Mungo Park, Darcy Monroe; m. Michele Geraldine DeBruyne, Mar. 8, 1986; children: Joaquin Sandoval, Alice Maria. BA, U. Wash., 1964, MLS, 1970. Reference libr. Green River C.C., Auburn, Wash., 1970—2000. Author: REMF Diary, 1988, The REMF Returns, 1992, In the Army Now, 1995; co-editor: Vietnam War Literature, 1996, Viet Nam War Jour., 2000—. With U.S. Army, 1966—67. Recipient Disting. Faculty award Puget Power, 1996, Vietnam Vets. Am. Contbn. to Am. Culture award, 1997. Mem. Popular Culture Assn., Vietnam Vets. Am. Democrat. Lutheran. Avocations: movies, listening to the blues, especially fred mcdowell. Home: 23630 201st Ave SE Maple Valley WA 98038-8633 E-mail: dawillson@earthlink.net.

WILLSON, JAMES DOUGLAS, aerospace executive; b. Edinburgh, Scotland, May 24, 1915; came to U.S., 1921; s. George William and Margaret (Douglas) W.; m. Genevieve Best, Nov. 11, 1939; children: James Douglas, Stephen J., Wendy. BS with honors, Ohio State U., 1937, MBA, 1938. C.P.A., N.Y. Sr. auditor Arthur Andersen & Co. (C.P.A.'s), N.Y.C., 1938-42; controller Stinson div. Consol. Vultee Aircraft Corp., 1946-48, Plaskon div. Libbey-Owens-Ford Glass Co., 1948-53; treas. Affiliated Gas Equipment Co., Cleve., 1953; v.p. finance, treas. Norris-Thermador Corp., Los Angeles, 1957-59; controller, mgr. finance Tidewater Oil Co., Los Angeles, 1959-60, v.p. finance, 1960-66, Northrop Corp., Los Angeles, 1966-70, sr. v.p. finance, treas., 1970-80, also dir. Author: Controllership, 1952, 63, 81, 90, 95, Business Budgeting and Control, 1956, 57, Internal Auditing Manual, 1983, 89, Budgeting and Profit Planning, 1983, 89, 92, Financial Information Systems, 1986. Served to lt. comdr. USNR, 1942-46. Mem. Nat. Assn. Accts. (Lybrand Gold medal 1960), Am. Inst. C.P.A.s, Controllers Inst. Am. Home: 1715 Chevy Chase Dr Beverly Hills CA 90210-2709

WILLSON, MARY FRANCES, ecology researcher, educator; b. Madison, Wis., July 28, 1938; d. Gordon L. and Sarah (Loomans) W.; m. R.A. von Neumann, May 29, 1972 (dec.). BA with honors, Grinnell Coll., 1960; PhD, U. Wash., 1964. Asst. prof. U. Ill., Urbana, 1965-71, assoc. prof., 1971-76, prof. ecology, 1976-90; rsch. ecologist Forestry Scis. Lab., Juneau, Alaska, 1989-99; sci. dir. Great Lakes program Nature Conservancy, 1999-2000. Prin. rsch. scientist, affiliate prof. biology, Inst. Arctic Biology and Sch. Fisheries and Ocean Scis., U. Alaska, Fairbanks-Juneau. Author: Plant Reproductive Ecology, 1983, Vertebrate Natural History, 1984; co-author: Mate Choice in Plants, 1983. Fellow Am. Ornithologists Union; mem. Brit. Ornithologists Union, Soc. for Study Evolution, Am. Soc. Naturalists (hon. mem.), Ecol. Soc. Am., Brit. Ecol. Soc. E-mail: mwillson@gci.net.

WILLSON, PARKER O. non-profit organization administrator; b. Dallas, Oct. 14, 1945; s. Parker Otwell and Lovie Viola (Orren) W.; m. Sarah Chase Conklin, Apr. 16, 2002 (div. 1989); 1 child, Nikkoli Robin Chase Willson; life ptnr., John Cameron Orr. BFA, U. Okla., 1967, MFA, 1969; cert. in non-profit mgmt., Baylor U., 2000. Lic. neuro linguistic programming practitioner Marzalek & Assocs. Box office mgr. Fox Theatre, Atlanta, 1984-85; spl. project dir. City Rep. Office, Phila., 1985-86; cons. Enterainment Consultants, Inc., Phila., 1986-88; exec. dir. Teen Aid of Tex., Inc., Richardson, 1987-92; dir. support svcs. Life Ptnrs., Inc., Waco, Tex., 1993-94; interim exec. dir. Nat. Viatical Assn., Waco, Tex., 1994; exec. dir. Keep McLennan County Beautiful, Waco, Tex., 1996—. Dir. plays, Waco Civic Theatre, 2000, Tin Bldg. Theater, Clifton. Bd. dirs., McLennan County HIV/AIDS Resources and Edn. Svcs., Waco, 1992—; co-chair, Names Project Waco, 1993-95, Names Project AIDS Meml. Quilt Display, Waco, 1993-94. Mem. Royal, Sovereign and Imperial Ct. of Ctrl. Tex. Empiare (pres. 1998—, sec.-treas. 1996-98, Emperor VII 2000-01. Emperor VIII 2001-02). Avocations: directing, singing, environmental concerns, human rights.

WILLSON, PRENTISS, JR., lawyer; b. Durham, NC, Sept. 20, 1943; s. Prentiss and Lucille (Giles) W. AB, Occidental Coll., 1965; JD, Harvard U., 1968. Bar: Calif. 1969, U.S. Dist. Ct. (no. dist.) Calif. 1971, U.S. Ct. Appeals (9th cir.) 1971, U.S. Tax Ct. 1971, U.S. Supreme Ct. 1975. Instr. law Miles Coll., Birmingham, Ala., 1968-70; ptnr. Morrison & Foerster, San Francisco, 1970-98, Ernst & Young, Walnut Creek, Calif., 1998—. Prof. Golden Gate U., 1971-84; lectr. Stanford U. Sch. Law, 1985-88. Contbr. articles to profl. jours. Mem. ABA, Calif. Bar Assn. Democrat. Office: Ernst & Young 1331 N California Blvd Walnut Creek CA 94596 Home: 66 Ardmore RD Larkspur CA 94939-2124 E-mail: prentiss.willson@ey.com.

WILLS-TORO, LUIS ALBERTO, physicist, mathematician; b. Medellin, Colombia, Aug. 10, 1961; s. Gustavo Wills and Elvira Toro; m. Amalia Bentancur, June 8, 2002. BCE, Escuela de Ingenieria de A., Medellin,Colombia, 1979—83; MS in Physics, Universidad de Antioquia, Medellin,Colombia, 1983—86; MSc in Math, Universidad Nacional, Medellin,Colombia, 1997—99; PhD in Physics, Tech. U Munich, Munich, Germany, 1987—91. Postdoc CBPF/CLAF, Rio, Brazil, 1992—93; post doc Universidad de Granada, Ganada, Spain, 1993—94; prof. Universidad de Antioquia, Medellin, Colombia, 1995—99; PhD student, tchg. asst. U Hawaii, Honolulu, 2000; staff, sr. scientist Optical Network Testing Inc., Honolulu, 2001—03; PhD Student/ Tchg. Asst. U Hawaii, Honolulu, 2003. Author (articles): Internat. Jour. of Theoretical Physics, 2003, Jour of Math. Physics, 2001. Grantee Marie Curie Fellowship, European Cmty., 1993—94. Mem.: Soc. for Indsl. and Applied Math., Am Math. Soc. Achievements include patents pending for "Method and Apparatus for Testing Signal Integrity" authors J.M. Fala and L.A. Wills. Home: 3029 Lowrey Ave F 1123 Honolulu HI 96822 Office: U of Hawaii Math Dept 2565 The Mall Keller 404 G Honolulu HI 96822

WILLUMSON, GLENN GARDNER, curator, art historian; b. Glendale, Calif., June 22, 1949; s. Donald Herbert and Aileen Ann (Gardner) W.; m. Margaret Julia Moore, June 20, 1970; children: Erik Ryan, Ashley Aileen. BA, St. Mary's Coll., 1971; MA, U. Calif., Davis, 1984; PhD in Art History, U. Calif., Santa Barbara, 1988. Asst. curator Nelson Art Gallery, Davis, Calif., 1982-83; curator Getty Rsch. Inst., L.A., 1988-92; sr. curator Palmer Mus. of Art Pa. State U., University Park, Pa., 1992-2001; assoc. prof. art history, dir. mus. studies U. Fla., 2001—. Fellow Nat. Writing Project, 1987; vis. prof. U. Calif., Irvine, 1990; affiliate prof. art history Pa. State U., University Park, 1994-2001. Author: W. Eugene Smith and the Photo-Essay, 1992 (grantee J. Paul Getty Trust 1991), Collecting With a Passion, 1993; mem. editl. bd. History of Photography mag., London, 1991-94, Cambridge Univ. Press., N.Y.C., 1993-97. Haynes fellow Huntington Libr., 1995-96, Univ. Tchr.'s fellow NEH, 1997-98. Mem. Am. Studies Assn. (Annette K. Baxter prize 1987), Coll. Art Assn., Soc. Photog. Edn. (mem. governing bd. Mid-Atlantic region 1993-97), Assn. Historians Am. Art, Am. Assn. Mus. Office: Coll Fine Arts U Fla PO Box 115801 Gainesville FL 32611

WILLUMSTAD, ROBERT B. bank executive; b. Bklyn., Aug. 22, 1945; Various ops., retail banking and computer systems positions Chemical Bank, 1967—87; chmn., CEO consumer finance svcs. Travelers Group; chmn., CEO global consumer group Global Consumer Group, Citigroup, 2000—03; pres. Citigroup, 2002—, COO, 2003—, also pres., CEO Citibank. Vice chmn. bd. dirs. MasterCard Internat. Bd. dirs., vol. Habitat for Humanity Internat.; trustee Am. Scandinavian Found. Mem.: Financial Services Roundtable (bd. dirs.). Office: Citigroup 399 Park Ave New York NY 10043

WILLY, THOMAS RALPH, lawyer; b. Phila., Sept. 30, 1943; s. Albert Ralph and Dorothy Rose (Driver) W.; m. Kay Harris, Jan. 12, 1968; children: Elyn Alexandria, Jon Charles. BA in History, U. Mo.-Kansas City, 1966, JD with distinction, 1974. Bar: Mo. 1974, U.S. Tax Ct. 1982. Assoc. Deacy & Deacy, Kansas City, 1974-75, Logan, Hentzen, Haitbrink & Moore, Kansas City, 1975; ptnr. Hentzen, Haitbrink & Moore, Kansas City, 1976-78, Hentzen, Moore & Willy, Kansas City, 1978-80, Moore & Willy Profl. Corp., Kansas City, 1980-87, pres., dir., 1987-94; shareholder, dir., v.p. Van Osdol, Magruder, Erickson & Redmond, P.C., Kansas City, 1994—. Cons. Ctr. for Mgmt. Assistance, Kansas City, 1990-2000; presenter living will project, Midwest Bioethics Ctr., 1990-2000. Pres. Kansas City Swiss Soc., 1989-91, bd. dirs. 1993-96, 2004—; bd. dirs. Greater Kansas City People to People, 1995-98, 2000-03. Com. on Planned Giving, Friends of Art, Kansas City, Kansas City Consensus, Hist. Kansas City Found. Capt. USAF, 1966-70. Mem. ABA (sect. intellectual property law, sect. bus. law), Mo. Bar Assn., Lions (bd. dirs. Leawood 1986-88, 90-92, sec. 1988-90, v.p. 1996-97). Home: 10314 Lee Blvd Shawnee Mission KS 66206-2629 Office: 2400 Commerce Tower 911 Main St Kansas City MO 64105-2009 Office Phone: 816-421-0644. E-mail: twilly@vomer.com.

WILMER, CHARLES MARK, lawyer; b. Phoenix, Dec. 31, 1938; s. Mark Bernard and Genevieve (Tibshraeny) W.; m. Sandra Jean Provo; children: Charles M. Jr., Thomas C., Jeffrey A., Brian N. LLB, U. Ariz., 1964. Bar: Ariz. 1964, U.S. Dist. Ct. Ariz. 1964. Pvt. practice, Phoenix, 1964—. Judge pro tem Ariz. Ct. Appeals, 1985, 93. Contbr. numerous articles to law jours. Recipient Disting. Svcs. award Ariz. Ct. Appeals, 1985. Fellow Ariz. Bar Found. (founding); mem. Ariz. State Bar (bd. legal specialization 1979), Maricopa County Bar Assn. Avocation: all outdoor activities. Office: 2504 N 3d St Phoenix AZ 85004

WILMER, HARRY ARON, psychiatrist, educator; b. New Orleans, Mar. 5, 1917; s. Harry Aron and Leona (Schlenker) W.; m. Jane Harris, Oct. 31, 1944; children: Harry, John, Thomas, James, Mary. BS, U. Minn., 1938, MB, MS, U. Minn., 1940, MD, 1941, PhD, 1944. Intern Gorgas Hosp., Ancon, C.Z., 1940-41; resident in neurology and psychiatry Mayo Clin., Rochester, Minn., 1945-49, cons. in psychiatry, 1957-58; physician Palo Alto (Calif.) Clinic, 1949-51; pvt. practice medicine, Palo Alto, 1951-55, 58-64; prof. psychiatry U. Calif. Med. Sch., San Francisco, 1964-69; sr. psychiatrist Scott & White Clin., Temple, Tex., 1969-74; emeritus prof. psychiatry U. Tex. Health Sci. Ctr., San Antonio, 1974-87; staff mem.(part-time) Audie Murphy VA Hosp., San Antonio, 1974-82; founder, dir. Internat. Film Festivals on Culture and Psychiatry, U. Tex. Health and Sci. Ctr., 1972-80; founder, emeritus pres., dir. Inst. Humanities, Salado, TX, 1980—; pvt. practice, Salado, 1980—. Author: Huber the Tuber, 1942, Corky the Killer, 1945, This is Your World, 1952, Social Psychiatry in Action, 1958, First Book for the Mind, 1963, Vietnam in remission, 1985, Practical Jung, 1987, Closeness: A Dictionary of Ideas, Vol. I, 1989, Father Mother, 1989; (film) People Need People, 1961, Facing Evil, 1988, Evil, 1989, Creativity, 1990, Creativity Paradoxes and Reflections, 1991, Closeness: Personal and Professional Relations, 1992, Understandable Jung, 1994, How Dreams Help, 1999, Quest for Silence, 2000. Served to capt. M.C., USNR, 1955-57; Guggenheim fell., Zurich, 1969-70; NRC fell., Johns Hopkins Hosp., 1944-45. Fell. Am. Pscyhiatry Assn. (life, emeritus), Am. Coll. Psychiatrists, Am. Acad. Psychoanalysis; mem. AAAS, Internat. Assn. Analytical Pscyhology. Home: 1202 S Ridge Rd Mill Creek PO Box 528 Salado TX 76571-0528 E-mail: hawilmer@aol.com.

WILMERDING, JOHN, art history educator, museum curator; b. Boston, Apr. 28, 1938; s. John Currie and Lila Vanderbilt (Webb) W. AB, Harvard U., 1960, AM, 1961, PhD, 1965. Asst. prof. art Dartmouth Coll., 1965-68, asso. prof., 1968-73, Leon E. Williams prof., 1973-77, chmn. dept. art, 1968-72, chmn. humanities divsn., 1971-72; sr. curator Am. art Nat. Gallery of Art, 1977-83, dep. dir., 1983-88; Sarofim prof. Am. art Princeton (N.J.) U., 1988—, chmn. dept. art and archeology, 1992-99. Vis. lectr. history of art Yale U., 1972; vis. prof. fine arts Harvard U., 1976; vis. prof. art U. Md., 1979; vis. prof. art history U. Del., 1982; hon. curator painting Peabody Mus., Salem, Mass.; vis. curator Met. Mus., 1988—. Author: Fitz Hugh Lane, American Marine Painter, 1964, A History of American Marine Painting, 1968, Pittura Americana dell' Ottocento, 1969, Robert Salmon, Painter of Ship and Shore, 1971, Fitz Hugh Lane, 1971, Winslow Homer, 1972, Audubon, Homer, Whistler and 19th Century America, 1972, The Genius of American Painting, 1973, American Art, 1976, American Light, The Luminist Movement, 1980, American Masterpieces from the National Gallery of Art, 1980, An American Perspective, 1981, Important Information Inside, 1982, Andrew Wyeth, The Helga Pictures, 1987, American Marine Paintings, 2d edit., 1987, Paintings by Fitz Hugh Lane, 1988; American Views: Essays on American Art, 1991, The Artist's Mount Desert: American Painters on the Maine Coast, 1994, Compass and Clock: Defining Moments in American Culture, 1999, Signs of the Artist: Signatures and Self-Expression in American Paintings, 2003. Trustee Coll. of the Atlantic, Bar Harbor, Maine, Guggenheim Mus., N.Y.C., N.E. Harbor Libr., Maine, Wendell Gilley Mus., S.W. Harbor, Maine, Wyeth Endowment for Am. Art, Wilmington, Del.; trustee emeritus Shelburne Mus., Vt.; mem. trustees' coun. Nat. Gallery Art, Washington. Guggenheim fellow, 1973-74. Fellow Phila. Atheneum (hon.); Mem. Coll. Art Assn., Am. Studies Assn. Office: Princeton U Dept Art and Archaeology 105 Mccormick Hl Princeton NJ 08544-1018

WILMERS, ROBERT GEORGE, banker; b. N.Y.C., Apr. 20, 1934; s. Charles K. and Cecilia (Eitingon) W.; m. Elisabeth Roche de la Rigodiere; children: Robert George, Christopher C. BA, Harvard U., 1956; postgrad., Harvard Bus. Sch., 1958-59. Dep. fin. adminstr. City of N.Y., 1966-70; v.p. Morgan Guaranty Trust Co., N.Y.C. and Belgium, 1970-80; chmn., chief exec. officer, dir. M&T Bank Corp., Buffalo, 1982—, chmn. bd., chief exec. officer, dir., 1983—; mem. Coun. Fgn. Rels. Vis. com. John F. Kennedy Sch. Govt., Harvard U.; bd. dirs. Lincoln Ctr., The Bus. Coun. N.Y. State, Buffalo Niagara Partnership, Fin. Svcs. Roundtable. Decorated officer de l'Ordre de la Couronne (Belgium). Mem.: NY State Bankers Assn. Home: 800 W Ferry St Buffalo NY 14222-1660 also: 1 W 64th St New York NY 10023-6734 Office: M&T Bank 1 M&T Plz Buffalo NY 14203 Office Phone: 716-842-5425. Business E-Mail: rwilmers@mandtbank.com.

WILMINGTON, W. PHILLIP, software company executive; BA in Mktg. and Bus. Adminstrn., Bradley U. V.p. sales and ops. Tesseract Corp., 1986—89; exec. v.p. field ops. Trinet, Inc., 1989—92; from gen. mgr. Midwest Region to exec. v.p. Americas PeopleSoft Inc., Pleasonton, Calif., 1992—2000, exec. v.p. Americas, 2000—. Office: PeopleSoft Inc 4460 Hacienda Dr Pleasanton CA 94588*

WILMORE, DOUGLAS WAYNE, surgeon, educator; b. Newton, Kans., July 22, 1938; s. Waldo Wayne and Hilda Gard (Adrian) W.; m. Judith Kay Shabert; 1 child, Carol Kristann. BA, Washburn U., 1960; MD, Kans. U., 1964; MS (hon.), Harvard U., 1979; PhD (hon.), Washburn U., 1995. Diplomate Am. Bd. Surgery. Intern Hosp. U. Pa., Phila., 1964-65, resident, fellow, 1965-71; chief clin. rsch. and staff surgeon U.S. Army Inst. Surg. Rsch., Ft. Sam Houston, 1971-79; staff surgeon Brigham and Women's Hosp., Boston, 1979—; Frank Sawyer prof. surgery Harvard Med. Sch., Boston, 1989—. Editor Scientific American Surgery, 1988, ACS Surgery, 2001—. Mem. Inst. Medicine, 1999. Lt. Col. U.S. Army, 1971-74. Achievements include development of safe modern techniques for providing parenteral nutrition to critically-ill patients, use of the amino acid L-glutamine in clinical nutrition; rehabilitation program for individuals with severe gastrointestinal disease; use of growth factors and specialized nutrition to rehabilitate patients with the short bowel syndrome.

WILMOT, IRVIN GORSAGE, former hospital administrator, educator, consultant; b. Nanking, China, June 30, 1922; s. Frank Alonzo and Ethel (Ranney) W.; m. Dorothy Agnes Mohlfeld, Feb. 6, 1943; children: Marcia Beth, David Michael. BS, Northwestern U., 1955; MBA, U. Chgo., 1957. With Internat. Register Co., Chgo., 1946-47; buyer U. Chgo., 1947-49; adminstrv. asst., then asst. supt. U. Chgo. Clinics, 1949-61; adminstr. NYU Med. Ctr.-Univ. Hosp., 1961-68, exec. v.p., 1968-81, Blue Cross-Blue Shield Greater N.Y., 1981-83, dir., 1977-81; exec. v.p., COO Montefiore Hosp. and Med. Ctr., N.Y.C., 1984-85; healthcare cons., 1985—. Instr. then asst. prof. U. Chgo., 1957-61; assoc. prof. NYU, 1961-68; prof., 1968—; assoc. dir. U. Chgo. Grad. Program Hosp. Adminstrn., 1959-61; mem. hosp. rev. and planning coun. State of N.Y., 1979-87. Bd. dirs. N.Y. Blood Ctr., 1978-81. With USN, 1940-46. Fellow Am. Coll. Hosp. Adminstrs. (life, chmn. ctrl. com. insts. 1959-65, regent N.Y. State and P.R. 1974—); mem. Assn. U. Programs Hosp. Adminstrs. (exec. sec. 1959-61), Am. Hosp. Assn. (mem. coun. rsch. and planning 1965-68, coun. on mgmt. 1979-80, coun. on fin. 1981-84, trustee 1979-81), Assn. Am. Med. Colls. (chmn. coun. tchg. hosps. 1970-71), Greater N.Y. Hosp. Assn. (bd. govs., pres. 1973-74), Hosp. Assn. N.Y. State (trustee, chmn. 1976-77). Home: 34 Helen Ave Rye NY 10580-2447

WILMOT, LOUISE C. charitable organization executive, retired career officer; b. Wayne, N.J., Dec. 31, 1942; d. W.J. Currie and Dorothy Murphy; m. James E. Wilmot. BA in History, Coll. St. Elizabeth, Convent Sta., N.J., 1964; student, Naval War Coll., Newport, R.I., 1977; M in Legis. Affairs, George Washington U., 1978. Commd. ensign USN, 1964; advanced through grades to rear adm., 1991; comm. watch officer, registered publs. custodian, women's barracks officer Naval Air Sta., Pensacola, Fla., with NATO staff Allied Forces, So. Europe, 1966-68; officer recruiter Recruiting Area Seven, Dallas; Naval Senate liaison officer Office Legis. Affairs, Washington; head women's equal opportunity br. Bur. Naval Pers., 1974-76; exec. officer Navy Recruiting Dist., Montgomery, Ala., 1977-79, command of Omaha, 1979-82; dep. dir accession policy Asst. Sec. Def. for Manpower, Installations, and Logistics, Washington, 1982-85; comdr. Navy Recruiting Area Five, Gt. Lakes, Ill., 1985-87; exec. asst., Naval aide Asst. Sec. Navy for Manpower and Reserve Affairs, Washington, 1987-89; comdr. Naval Tng. Ctr., Orlando, Fla., 1989-91; vice chief Naval Edn. and Tng., Pensacola, 1991-93; comdr. Naval Base, Phila., 1993-94; ret. U.S. Navy, 1994; dep. exec. dir. Cath. Relief Svcs., Balt., 1994—. Decorated DSM, Def. Superior Svc. medal, Legion of Merit with 3 gold stars. Office: Cath Relief Svcs 209 W Fayette St Baltimore MD 21201-3403

WILMOTT, TIMOTHY J. recreational facility executive; m. Nancy Wilmott; 1 child, Meghan. BS magna cum laude in Indsl. Engring., MS magna cum laude in Indsl. Engring., Lehigh U.; MBA in Corp. Fin., U. Pa. From mem. staff to COO Harrah's Entertainment Inc., Las Vegas, 1987—2003, COO, 2003—. Office: Harrahs Entertainment Inc One Harrahs Ct Las Vegas NV 89119

WILMOUTH, ROBERT K. commodities executive; b. Worcester, Mass., Nov. 9, 1928; s. Alfred F. and Aileen F. (Kearney) W.; m. Ellen M. Boyle, Sept. 10, 1955; children: Robert J., John J., James P., Thomas G., Anne Marie. BA, Holy Cross Coll., 1949; MA, U. Notre Dame, 1950, LLD, 1984. Exec. v.p., dir. 1st Nat. Bank Chgo., 1972-75; pres., chief adminstrv. officer Crocker Nat. Bank, San Francisco, 1975-77; pres., chief exec. officer Chgo. Bd. Trade, 1977-82; chmn. LaSalle Nat. Bank, 1982-99. Pres., chief exec. officer Nat. Futures Assn., 1982-2002, Spl. Policy Adv. Nat. Futures Assn., 2003-. Life trustee U. Notre Dame; mem. adv. coun. Kellogg Grad. Sch. Mgmt., Northwestern U. Mem. Chgo. Club, Barrington Hill Country Club, Econ. Club. Office: Nat Futures Assn 200 W Madison St Ste 1600 Chicago IL 60606-3415

WILMS, ANNE M. information technology executive; Grad., Trinity Coll., Dublin, Ireland, 1979, U. Chgo., 1993. Dir. info. sys. Wis. Power and Light, Madison; with Oracle Corp., Redwood City, Calif.; mgr. info. tech. So. Nat. Gas Co. Sonat, Inc., 1995, v.p. info. tech. Sonat Svcs., 1996, v.p., CIO Sonat Svcs., 1998; v.p., CIO Rohm and Haas Co., Phila., 1999—. Bd. dirs. Elemica, CIDX. Mem. bd. councillors Hist. Soc. Pa.; bd. mem. Red Cross S.E. Pa.; mem. CIO adv. coun. Villanova U. Office: Rohm and Haas Co 100 Independence Hall West Philadelphia PA 19106-2399

WILNER, ALAN M. judge; b. Balt., Jan. 26, 1937; AB, Johns Hopkins U., 1958, MLA, 1966; JD, U. Md., 1962. Assoc. Sherbow, Shea & Doyle, Balt., 1962-65; asst. atty. gen. State of Md., 1965-68; assoc. Venable, Baetjer & Howard, Balt., 1968-71; asst., then chief legis. officer, govs. staff, 1971-77; assoc. judge Ct. of Spl. Appeals, 1977-90, chief judge, 1990-96; judge Ct. of Appeals, Md., 1996—. Adj. faculty U. Md. Sch. of Law, U. Balt. Sch. of Law; with Judicial Inst. Md., 1997—, chmn. bd. dirs., 1999—; mem. Md. Alternative Dispute Resolution Commn., 1998—. Mem. ABA, Md. Bar. Found., Md. State Bar Assn., Balt. County Bar Assn. Office: Md Ct of Appeals County Courts Bldg 401 Bosley Ave Towson MD 21204

WILNER, THOMAS BERNARD, lawyer; b. Toronto, Ont., Can., July 7, 1944; came to U.S., 1944; s. Morton H. and Zelda (Dunkelman) W.; m. Jane Ten Broeck; children: Amanda, Adam, David. BA, Yale U., 1966; LLB, U. Pa., 1969. Clk. to Chief Judge William Hastie U.S. Ct. Appeals, Phila., 1969-70; assoc. Debevoise Plimpton, N.Y.C., 1970-72; counsel Amtrak, Washington, 1972-73; ptnr. Arnold & Porter, Washington, 1973-89, Shearman & Sterling, Washington and Tokyo, 1989—. Office: 801 Pennsylvania Ave NW Washington DC 20004-2604 Office Phone: 202-508-8050. Business E-Mail: twilner@shearman.com.

WILOCH, THOMAS, writer, editor; b. Detroit, Feb. 3, 1953; s. Joseph and Jane W.; m. Denise Gottis, Oct. 10, 1981. BA, Wayne State U., 1978. Rsch. asst. Wayne State U., Detroit, 1976; editl. asst. The Gale Group, Farmington Hills, Mich., 1977-78, asst. editor, 1978-81, sr. asst. editor, 1981-85, sr. writer, 1985-89, assoc. editor, 1989—; freelance writer, 2004—. Prose poem collections include: Stigmata Junction, 1985, Paper Mask, 1988, The Mannikin Cypher, 1989, Tales of Lord Shantih, 1989, Mr. Templeton's Toyshop, 1995, e-book, 2003; cut-up haiku: Night Rain, 1991, Decoded Factories of the Heart, 1991, Narcotic Signature, 1992, Lyrical Brandy, 1993, Neon Trance, 1997; editor: (with Leonard Kniffel) Directory of Michigan Literary Publishers, 1982, Contemporary Authors, New Revision Series (asst. editor) Vols 1-5, 1981-85, (sr. asst. editor) Vols. 6-15, 1982-85, (sr. writer) Vols. 16-27, 1986-89, (assoc. editor) Vols. 28-117, 1989-2003; editor Grimoire mag., 1982-85, Best of Grimoire, 2003; author Crime: A Serious American Problem, 2004, Authors & Artists For Young Adults, contbr. to over 200 periodicals including Publishers' Weekly, Bloomsbury Rev., Fiction Rev., Small Press Rev., Factsheet 5, Kayak, Asylum, Wormwood Rev. and others. Mem. Assn. Literary Scholars and Critics. Office: The Gale Group Ste 226 42015 Ford Rd Canton MI 48187 E-mail: mssunltd@postmark.net.

WILPON, FRED, professional baseball team executive, real estate developer; b. Bklyn., Nov. 22, 1936; s. Nathan and Frances (Altman) W.; m. Judith Anne Kessler, Sept. 27, 1958; children: Jeffrey Scott, Robin Lynn, Bruce Nathan. BA, U. Mich., 1958. Vice pres. Hanover Equities Corp., N.Y.C., 1959-69, Peter Sharp & Co., N.Y.C., 1969-71; chmn. bd. Sterling Equities, Inc., Manhasset, NY, 1971—; pres. N.Y. Mets Profl. Baseball Team, 1980—, now also chief exec. officer, 1980—; owner Brooklyn Cyclones, 2000—. Mem. Vol. Urban Cons. Group, Mayor N.Y.C. Housing Task Force; trustee Jewish Inst. Geriatric Care, New Hyde Park, N.Y., 1976—, Green Vale Sch., Glen Head, N.Y., 1977— . Served with USAF, 1959. Mem. Young Pres. Orgn. Clubs: KP.

WILS, MADELYN, film company executive; b. Queens, NY, 1955; Owner, prodr. Bread and Butter TV; pres., CEO Tribeca Film Inst., NYC, 2004—. Trustee Alliance Downtown NY, Inc., Conservancy Hist. Battery Pk., Gateway Sch. NY; dir. Hudson River Park Trust; bd. mem. Lower Manhattan Devel. Corp., NYC, 2001—. Office: Tribeca Film Inst 375 Greenwich St New York NY 10013

WILSON, ADDISON GRAVES (JOE WILSON), congressman, former senator, lawyer; b. Charleston, S.C., July 31, 1947; s. Hugh deVeaux And Wray Smart (Graves) W.; m. Roxanne Dusenbury McCrory, Dec. 30, 1977; children: Michael Alan, Addison Graves, Julian Dusenbury, Hunter Taylor. BA, Washington and Lee U., 1969; JD, U. S.C., Columbia, 1972. Bar: S.C. 1972. Staff mem. Sen. Strom Thurmond, Washington, 1967, Congressman Floyd Spence, Columbia, S.C., 1970-72; ptnr. Wilson, Moore, Taylor & Thomas, West Columbia, 1972—2001; US Repr. S.C., 2nd dist., 2002—. Dep. gen. counsel U.S. Energy Sec. Jim Edwards, Washington, 1981-82; bd. dirs. Bank Am., Lexington, S.C.; senator State of S.C., Columbia, 1984-2001; presdl. appointee to Intergovtl. Adv. Coun. on Edn., 1990-91; mem. Internat. Observation Del. for 1990 Bulgarian parliamentary election; mem. House Armed Svcs. Com., House Policy Com., House Education and Workforce Com. Campaign mgr. Congressman Floyd Spence, Columbia, 1974, 78, 80, 82, 98; dist. campaign mgr. Gov. Carroll Campbell, 1986; vice chmn. S.C. Rep. Party, 1972-74. Col. USNG, 1975—. Mem. Rotary, Masons, Shriners. Republican. Presbyterian. also: PO Box 7168 Columbia SC 29201 Home: Apt 202 10401 Montrose Ave Bethesda MD 20814-4159 Office: 212 Cannon House Office Bldg Washington DC 20515

WILSON, ALEXANDRA M. communications executive; B in Comm. summa cum laude, M in Comm., JD, U. Pa. Bar: D.C. 1984. Assoc. Crowell & Moring, Wiley, Rein & Fielding; chief cable svcs. bur. FCC, 1990—94; v.p. pub. policy Cox Enterprises, Atlanta, 1994—. Faculty mem. ann. conf. on cable TV law Practising Law Inst.; co-chair conf. on local cable and tel. competition Strategic Rsch. Inst.; spkr. in field. Mem.: Fed. Comm. Bar Assn. (pres.-elect 2002—03, sec., asst. sec., co-chair various coms., mem. exec. com.). Office: Cox Enterprises Inc 1400 Lake Hearn Dr Atlanta GA 30319

WILSON, ALICE MCATEER, secondary school educator; b. S.I., N.Y., July 28, 1947; d. Charles Francis Jr. and Clorinda)Mardus) McAteer; m. Van Ray Wilson, 1979; 1 child, Clorinda Ann. BA in Math., Wells Coll., 1969; MS in Secondary Math. Edn. with honor, CUNY, 1971. Pemanent tchr. cert., N.Y. State; cert. tchr., N.Y.C. Tchr. math. Tottenville H.S., S.I., 1970—. Mem. alumnae coun. Wells Coll., Aurora, N.Y., 1992—. Mem. Phi Beta Kappa. Avocations: piano, sewing, swimming, sailing. Home: 599 Oakland Ave Staten Island NY 10310

WILSON, ANNE GAWTHROP, artist, educator; b. Detroit, Apr. 16, 1949; d. Gerald Shepard and Nancy Craighead (Gawthrop) Wilson; m. Michael Andreas Nagelbach. Student, U. Mich. Sch. of Art, 1967-69; BFA, Cranbrook Acad. Art, Bloomfield Hills, Mich., 1972; MFA, Calif. Coll. Arts and Crafts, 1976. Prof. Dept. Fiber & Materials Studies Sch. of the Art Inst., Chgo., 1979—. Panelist Nat. Endowment for Arts, Washington, 1986, Western States Arts Fedn./Nat. Endowment for Arts Regional Fellowships for Visual Artists, Santa Fe, 1995; co-curator Artemisia Gallery, Chgo., 1988; co-moderator Women's Caucus for Art, Chgo., 1992; panelist, workshop instr. Internat. Symposium '92, Toyama, Japan, 1992; panelist The Textile Mus., Washington, 1994, bd. trustees Haystack Sch., Deer Isle, Maine, 1990-95; lectr. Kansas City Art Inst., 1996, Australian Nat. U. Canberra Sch. Art, 1996, Textile Conservation Ctr./Courtauld Inst. Art, London, 1995, others; represented by Roy Boyd Gallery, Chgo., Revolution, Detroit and N.Y. One person shows include Chgo. Cultural Ctr., 1988, Halsey Gallery, Sch. Arts, Coll. Charleston, S.C., 1992, Madison (Wis.) Art Ctr., 1993-94, Roy Boyd Gallery, Chgo., 1994, 96, Ill. Wesleyan U., Sch. Art, Bloomington, 1995, Revolution, Detroit, 1998, Revolution, N.Y.C., 1998, Mus. for Textiles Contemporary Gallery, Toronto, Can., 1999, Mus. Contemporary Art, Chgo., 2000; exhibited in group shows Netherlands Textile Mus., 1989, Musee Cantonal des Beaux-Arts, Palais de Rumine, Lausanne, Switzerland, 1989, John Michael Kohler Arts Ctr., Sheboygan, Wis., 1992-93, 95, Mus. Contemporary Art, Chgo., 1996, 97, Ariz. State U. Art Mus., Tempe, 1997-98, Bowdoin Coll. Mus. Art, Brunswick, Maine, 1998, TBA Exhbn. Space, Chgo., 1999, Angel Row Gallery, Halifax, 1999-2000, Boulder (Colo.) Mus. Contemporary Art, 2000, Gallery 400 Sch. Art and Design Coll. Arch. and the Arts, U. Ill., Chgo., 2000, Asheville (N.C.) Mus. Art, 2000, Chgo. Cultural Ctr., 2000, Memphis Coll. Art, 2001, U. Calif. San Diego, La Jolla, 2001; represented in permanent collections Art Inst. Chgo., Met. Mus. Art, N.Y., Mus. of Contemporary Art, Chgo., Calif. Poly. State U., San Luis Obispo, Calif., M. H. De Young Meml. Mus., San Francisco, Art Inst. Chgo., Cranbrook Acad. Art Mus., Bloomfield Hills; contbr. articles and revs. to profl. jours. Recipient Louis Comfort Tiffany Found. award, 1989; Nat. Endowment for Arts curatorial fellow in decorative arts and mus. edn. Fine Arts Mus. San Francisco, 1978; Nat. Endowment for Arts Visual Artists Fellowship grantee, 1982, 88, Chgo. Artists Abroad grantee, 1988, 89, Ill. Arts Coun. Individual Artist grantee, 1983, 84, 87, 93, 99, Chgo. Artists Internat. Program grantee, 1996. Mem. Coll. Art Assn. (regional co-chair annual conf. 2001). Office: Sch of the Art Inst Fiber Dept 37 S Wabash Ave Chicago IL 60603-3002

WILSON, ANNE JUDITH, writer, educator; b. Berkeley, Calif., Jan. 8, 1943; d. Griffith Conrad Evans Jr. and Arlene Callahan Evans; m. Lawrence Felton Wilson, Oct. 4, 1978 (div. Sept. 12, 1990). BA, Calif. State U., 1978; MA, U. N.Mex., 1992. Part-time adj. prof. Grossmont C.C., El Cajon, Calif., 1998—2000, Southwestern C.C., Chula Vista, Calif., 1999, Nazarene U., San Diego, 2001; workshop instr. Whidbey Island (Wash.) Poetry Retreat, So. Calif. Writers' Conf., 2003; instr. extended studies U. Calif., La Jolla, 1999—; part-time lectr. U. San Diego, 2000—; preliminary judge poetry contest San Diego Writers Co-op, 2001; guest dir. Vortex Theatre, Albuquerque, 1992; artist-in-residence Millett's Farm Womens Art Colony, Poughkeepsie, NY, 1997. Author: (book of poetry) Soleá, 2004, poetry, essays, articles to numerous publications including The Bitter Oleander, South Dakota Rev., Rattle Oxford Mag., Hiram Poetry Rev., Weber Studies, New Millenium Writings, Owen Wister Rev., Comstock Rev., Evansville Rev. Proposal writer for youth theater Santa Barbara-Cabrillo Arts Ctr., 1993. Finalist Frances Locke Meml. award, 2001, 2002; recipient Internat. Tanka Splendor award (2), 1997, 2d pl. award, Redwoods Fair Internat. Poetry Competition, 1997, 3d prize in poetry, Nat. Libr. Poetry Open, 1997, Editor's Choice award for poetry, Nat. Libr. Assn., 1997, Poem of Spl. Merit award, Denver Poetry Soc.'s Mile High Poetry Contest, 1997, 2d prize, Phoenix Press's Poetry Contest, 1998, Hon. Mention in Explorations, 2000, Muriel Craft Bailey award, 2000. Democrat. Avocations: photography, gardening, music appreciation, literature, flamenco. Office Phone: 619-260-4783. Personal E-mail: annewilson@eudoramail.com.

WILSON, ARCHIE FREDRIC, medical educator; b. L.A., May 7, 1931; s. Louis H. and Ruth (Kert) W.; m. Tamar Braverman, Feb. 11, 1937; children: Lee A., Daniel B. BA, UCLA, 1953, PhD, 1967; MD, U. Calif., San Francisco, 1957. Intern L.A. County Gen. Hosp., 1957-58; resident U. Calif., San Francisco, 1958-61; fellow in chest disease dept. medicine UCLA, 1966-67, asst. prof., 1967-70, U. Calif., Irvine, 1970-73, assoc. prof., 1973-79, prof., 1979—. Editor: Pulmonary Function Test: Interpretation, 1986; contbr. articles to profl. jours. Bd. mem. Am. Lung Assn., Orange County, 1970-90, Am. Heart Assn., Calif., 1990—. Capt. USMC, 1961-63. Mem. Am. Fedn. Clin. Rsch., Western Soc. Clin. Investigation, best Dr.'s in U.S. 1991—, top Dr.'s in U.S. 2001—. Office: U Calif 101 The City Dr S Orange CA 92868-3201

WILSON, ARTHUR HENRY, charitable institution executive; b. Lynn, Mass., Feb. 25, 1943; s. Norman L. and Gertrude E. (Green) W.; m. Mary E. Robinson, May 25, 1968; children: Patricia, Melissa, David, Jonathan. Student, Budette Coll., 1961-62. Nat. svc. officer DAV, various locations, 1966-74, supr. nat. appeals office Washington, 1974-76, nat. svc. dir., 1976-93, exec. dir. Washington hdqrs., 1993-94, nat. adjutant Cin., 1994—. Founder DAV Nat. Svc. Officer Tng. Acad., U. Colo., Denver; presenter in field. V.p. Nat. Guild Attys. In Fact, Washington, 1972-73, pres., 1973-74; officer PTA, Md., 1980-86. Sgt. USAF, 1962-66, Vietnam. Decorated Vietnam Svc. medal, Nat. Def. Svc. medal, Outstanding Hdqrs. Group award, Small Arms Marksman award, Air Force Outstanding Unit award. Democrat. Roman Catholic. Avocations: golf, reading. Office: DAV Nat Hdqrs PO Box 14301 Cincinnati OH 45250-0301

WILSON, ARTHUR THEODORE, education consultant; b. Newark, July 2, 1945; s. Elmer and Dorothy May (Outlaw-Sloan) W. BA in Humanities, New Sch., 1971, MA in Philosophy, 1974; PhD in Program History, NYU, 1980. Cert. tchr., N.Y., N.J. Rschr. African Studies, N.Y.C., 1972; tchr. Teaneck Alternative High Sch., N.J., 1979-80, Hunter Coll., N.Y.C., 1980-81; gifted and talented program curriculum cons. Bd. Cooperative Ednl. Svcs., SUNY, Farmingdale, 1983—. Apptd. arts & edn. acad. artist N.J. Performing Arts Ctr., Newark, 1996—; advisor, tutor Master's Degree Program in Acting, New Actors Workshop, Antioch U., N.Y., 1995—; workshop leader Young Playwright's Festival, N.Y.C., 1981—; adj. prof. drama Drew U., Madison, N.J.; co-founder, workshop leader N.J. Young Playwrights Festival, 1983; project dir., playwright Am. Folk Theater Young Co.'s exch. program, London, 1984-85; theater workshop cons. Milneck Sch. for Deaf, L.I., 1984; literature workshop cons. Orion Gifted and Talented Program, Lindenhurst, N.Y., 1984—; artistic dir. exch. program Manhattan Empire and Tukak Theater, Denmark; dir. playwriting in sch. project N.Y. Shakespeare Festival, 1986—; instr. N.Y. Lit. Assn., N.Y.C., 1984—; poetry reading and workshop with Poet Laureate Gwendolyn Brooks, Union Coll., 1985, guest poet for Mother Hale of Hale House, 1987; dir. playwriting in edn. dept. schs. N.Y. Shakespeare Festival, dir./prodr. Live! (radio edn. program), cons. arts edn. New Dance Group Ctr., N.Y., 1987—. Editor, writer, publisher Dance Giant Steps, Inc., Bklyn., 1981—; author: (play) The Extended Family, 1987; dir. Daddy Say, 1987, Children of Dahomey and Spirit Ensemble, 1986; dance editor; Feet Mag., 1969-72, Black Creations Mag., 1970-72; editor, pub.: Attitude: The Dancers' Monthly, 1982; contbr. poetry to Open Mag., Other Countries, New Rain, A Taste of Salt; producer: (plays) Life Sea Treasures, 1989-90, Guns Like Candy, 1991, Red High Heels Snap Back, 1995. Workshop leader N.J. Teen Program, 1983-84; advisor, workshop leader, founder N.J. Young Playwrights Festival, 1964-68; rsch. asst. Weeksville Project, Bjlyn., 1969-70; theater dir. local orgns. Recipient numerous scholars, 1970-79; grantee Bklyn. Art and Cultural Assn., 1983, N.Y. Dept. Cultural Affairs, 1983-84, N.Y. State Coun. on Arts, 1982-84, BECA Capezio Found., Heart grant Union County Bd. Freeholders, 1998-2003, N.J. Writers Project, N.J. State Coun. on the Arts, 1999-2004; N.J. State Coun. Arts fellow, 1985-86. Mem. Black Writers Union, Dramatists Guild, Inc., ASSITEJ, Internat. Assn. Children's Theater Professionals. Home: 919 Oak St Roselle NJ 07203-2001 Office: Dance Giant Steps Inc 1040 Park Place Ste 5C Brooklyn NY 11213 Office Phone: 908-245-4060. Personal E-mail: adaddyblack@aol.com.

WILSON, AUGUST, playwright; b. Pitts., 1945; s. David Bedford (Stepfather) and Daisy Wilson; 1 child, Sakina Ansari. Founder Black Horizons Theatre Co., Pitts., 1968; script writer Sci. Mus. of Minn., 1979. Author: (playwright) The Homecoming, The Coldest Day of the Year, 1979, Fullerton Street, 1980, Black Bart and the Sacred Hills, 1981, Jitney, 1982, Ma Rainey's Black Bottom, 1984 (N.Y. Drama Critics Circle award for best play, 1985, Tony award nomination for best play, 1985, Whiting Writers' award, 1986), Fences, 1985 (Theatre Critics Outstanding Play award, 1986, Drama Desk award for outstanding new play, 1986, N.Y. Drama Critics' Circle award for best play, 1986, Pulitzer Prize for drama, 1987, Tony award for best play, 1987, Outer Critics' Circle award for best play, 1987), Joe Turner's Come and Gone, 1986 (N.Y. Drama Critics Circle award for best play, 1988, Tony award nomination for best play, 1988), The Piano Lesson, 1987 (Drama Desk award for outstanding new play, 1990, N.Y. Drama Critics' Circle award for best play, 1990, Pulitzer Prize for drama, 1990, Tony award nomination for best play, 1990, Am. Theatre Critics Outstanding Play award, 1990), Two Trains Running, 1990 (Am. Theatre Critics Assn. award, 1992, N.Y. Drama Critics Circle award for best play, 1992, Tony award nomination for best play, 1992), Seven Guitars, 1995 (N.Y. Drama Critics Cir. award, 1996, Tony nomination Best Play, 1996). Named Artist of Yr., Chgo. Tribune, 1987; recipient John Gassner Best Am. Playwright award, Outer Critics Circle, 1987, Literary Lion award, N.Y. Pub. Libr., 1988. Mem.: AAAL. Office: care John Breglio Paul Weiss Rifkind Wharton & Garrison 1285 Avenue Of The Americas New York NY 10019-6028

WILSON, AVON W. state representative; b. Wichita Falls, Tex., Sept. 24, 1929; m. Bill Wilson. BA, N. Tex. State U., 1949; MED, Ea. N.Mex. U., 1996. Tchr. Fort Stockton and Big Spring Schs., Tex., 1949—55, Roswell Ind. Sch. Dist., N.Mex., 1955—80; owner Gift Shop, Roswell, 1976—86; dir. Adult Basic Edn. Ea. N.Mex. U., Roswell, 1986—; state rep. dist. 59 N.Mex. State Legis., Santa Fe, 2001—. Mem. Edn. com. N.Mex. State Legis., Santa Fe, mem. Human Resources/Labor com. Mem.: Altrusa Internat. Roswell (v.p./pres. 1992—). Republican. Methodist. Home: PO Box 381 Roswell NM 88202-0381 Office: New Mexico State Capitol Rm 202A Santa Fe NM 87501

WILSON, BETH A. college official; BA, Calif. State Coll., Sonoma; MBA, Nat. U. Asst. dir. Am. Bus. Coll., 1976-81; scholarship adminstr. Nat. U., 1982-84; v.p. br. ops. Nat. Coll., 1990-91; from exec. dir. bus. sch., group mgr. to v.p. adminstrn. United Edn. and Sofware, 1984-90; exec. dir. Capital Hill campus, then area ops. mgr. Nat. Edn. Ctrs., Inc., 1991-95; ops. dir., regional ops. dir. Corinthian Schs., Inc., Santa Ana, Calif., 1995-97, regional ops. dir. coll. region of Rhodes Colls. divsn., 1997-98, v.p. ops. parent co., 1998—. Office: Corinthian Colls Inc 6 Hutton Centre Dr Ste 400 Santa Ana CA 92707-5764

WILSON, BLENDA JACQUELINE, foundation administrator; b. Woodbridge, N.J., Jan. 28, 1941; d. Horace and Margaret (Brogsdale) Wilson; m. Louis Fair Jr. AB, Cedar Crest Coll., 1962; AM, Seton Hall U., 1965; PhD, Boston Coll., 1979; DHL (hon.), Cedar Crest Coll., 1987, Loretto Heights Coll., 1988, Colo. Tech. Coll., 1988, U. Detroit, 1989; LLD (hon.), Rutgers U., 1989, Ea. Mich. U., 1990, Cambridge Coll., 1991, Schoolcraft Coll., 1992; DHL (hon.), Marysville U., 1994, Mt. St. Mary's Coll., 1996, Antioch U., 1999, Cambridge Coll., 2001, Salve Regina U., 2002, Merrimack Coll., 2001; D Pub. Svc. (hon.), U. Mass., 2002, Mass. Coll. Liberal Arts, 2003. Tchr. Woodbridge Twp. Pub. Schs., 1962-66; exec. dir. Middlesex County Econ. Opportunity Corp., New Brunswick, N.J., 1966-69; exec. asst. to pres. Rutgers U., New Brunswick, N.J., 1969-72; sr. assoc. dean Grad. Sch. Edn. Harvard U., Cambridge, Mass., 1972-82; v.p. effective sector mgmt. Ind. Sector, Washington, 1982-84; exec. dir. Colo. Commn. Higher Edn., Denver, 1984-88; chancellor and prof. pub. adminstrn. & edn. U. Mich., Dearborn, 1988-92; pres. Calif. State U., Northridge, 1992-99, Nellie Mae Found., Quincy, Mass., 1999—. Am. del. U.S./U.K. Dialogue About Quality Judgments in Higher Edn.; adv. bd. Mich. Consol. Gas Co., Stanford Inst. Higher Edn. Rsch., U. So. Colo. Dist. 60 Nat. Alliance, Nat. Ctr. for Rsch. to Improve Postsecondary Tchg. and Learning, 1988-90; bd. dirs. Alpha Capital Mgmt.; mem. higher edn. colloquium Am. Coun. Edn., vis. com. Divsn. Continuing Edn. in Faculty of Arts and Scis., Harvard Coll., Pew Forum on K-12 Edn. Reform in U.S., The Coll. Bd., Federated Dorchester Neighborhood House, Fed. Res. Bank of Boston; bd. dirs. Ptnrs. Healthcare Sys., Medco Health Solutions, Inc. Dir. U. Detroit Jesuit High Sch., Northridge Hosp. Med. Ctr., 1993-99, Arab Cmty. Ctr. for Econ. and Social Svcs., Union Bank, J. Paul Getty Trust, James Irvine Found., 1996-99, Internat. Found. Edn. and Self-Help, Achievement Coun., L.A.; dir., vice chair Met. Affairs Corp.; exec. bd. Detroit area coun. Boy Scouts Am.; bd. dirs. Commonwealth Fund, Henry Ford Hosp.-Fairlane Ctr., Henry Ford Health System, Met. Ctr. for High Tech., United Way Southeastern Mich.; mem. Nat. Coalition 100 Black Women, Detroit, Race Rels. Coun. Met. Detroit, Women & Founds., Greater Detroit Interfaith Round Table NCCJ, Adv. Bd. Valley Cultural Ctr., Woodland Hills; trustee assoc. Boston Coll.; trustee emeritus Cambridge Coll.; trustee emeritus, bd. dirs. Found. Ctr.; trustee Henry Ford Mus. & Greenfield Village, Sammy Davis Jr. Nat. Liver Inst. Mem. AAUW, Assn. Governing Bds. (adv. coun. of pres.'s), Edn. Commn. of the States (student minority task force), Am. Assn. Higher Edn. (chair-elect), Am. Assn. State Colls. & Univs. (com. on policies & purposes, acad. leadership fellows selection com.), Assn. Black Profls. and Adminstrs., Assn. Black Women in Higher Edn., Women Execs. State Govt., Internat. Women's Forum, Mich. Women's Forum, Women's Econ. Club Detroit, Econ. Club, Rotary. Office: Nellie Mae Edn Found 1250 Hancock St 205N Quincy MA 02169-4331 Business E-Mail: bwilson@nmfedn.org.

WILSON, BONNIE JEAN, lawyer, educator, investor; b. Alameda County, Calif. d. August and Violet Adeline (Lockard) Ritzenthaler; m. Allan Nicholas Wilson (dec.); children: Albert Clyde, Bruce Allan. BA, cert. in elem. tchg., U. Calif., Berkeley; JD, Thomas Jefferson SOL, 1981. Bar: Calif.; cert. tchr., Calif. Elem. sch. tchr. Contra Costa and San Diego Counties; intern San Diego County Dist. Atty. Office, 1981; pvt. practice La Jolla, Calif., 1982—. Mem. La Jolla Presbyn. Ch., San Diego Symphony Assn., Friends of the La Jolla Libr.; adv. dir. San Diego Opera Assn.; edn. activist, 1972-76. Mem. Calif. State Bar Assn., San Diego County Bar Assn., La Jolla Newcomer's Club (bd. dirs. 1968-69), U. Calif. Berkeley Alumni Club (bd. dirs. San Diego chpt. 1961-62), Am. Assn. Ind. Investors (bd. dirs. 1991-97), Pi Lambda Theta Lambda, La Jolla Beach and Tennis Club. Presbyterian. Home: 2235 Bahia Dr La Jolla CA 92037-7007

WILSON, BRUCE BRIGHTON, lawyer, retired transportation executive; b. Boston, Feb. 6, 1936; s. Robert Lee and Jane (Schlotterer) W.; m. Elizabeth Ann MacFarland, Dec. 31, 1958; children: Mabeth, Mary, Bruce Robert, Caroline Daly. AB, Princeton U., 1958; LLB, U. Pa., 1961. Bar: Pa. 1962. Assoc. Montgomery, McCracken, Walker & Rhoads, Phila., 1962-69; atty. U.S. Dept. Justice, Washington, 1969-79, dep. asst. atty. gen. antitrust div., 1971-76; spl. counsel Consol. Rail Corp., Phila., 1979-81, gen. counsel litigation and antitrust, 1981-82, v.p., gen. counsel, 1982-84, v.p. law, 1984-87, sr. v.p. law, 1987-97, sr. v.p. merger, 1997. Bd. dirs. Carload Express, Inc., 2004-, Phila. Indsl. Devel. Corp., Wayne Sr. Ctr., 2001-; mem. mgmt. com. Concord Resources Group, 1989-91. Chmn. Radnor Twp. Cable Commn.

Coun., 1993—2000, mem., 2002—, Radnor Twp. Ethics Commn., 2000—01. Fellow Salzburg Seminar in Am. Studies (Austria), 1965; fellow Felz Inst. State and Local Govt., 1967. Mem. ABA, Phila. Bar Assn., Corinthian Yacht Club, Beach Club Cape May. Home: 224 Chamounix Rd Wayne PA 19087-3606 Personal E-mail: brucewilson224@comcast.net.

WILSON, BRUCE DUXBURY, lawyer; b. Charleston, S.C., Feb. 12, 1948; BA, U. Vt., 1970; JD, Albany Law Sch., 1973. Bar: N.Y. 1974, U.S. Dist. Ct. (no. and we. dists.) N.Y. 1974, U.S. Supreme Ct. 1978. Clk. N.Y. State Atty. Gen., Albany, 1970; pvt. practice Ithaca, N.Y., 1974—; city prosecutor City of Ithaca, 1975-80; town atty. Town of Ulysses, Trumansburg, N.Y., 1993—; dep. county atty. Tompkins County, Ithaca, 1996—. Examining counsel Ticor Title Ins. Corp.; mem. faculty Tompkins-Cortland C.C., Ithaca, 1996. Bd. dirs. Greater Ithaca Activites Ctr., Inc., Alpha House, Inc. drug rehab. ctr., Ctr. for Arts at Ithaca, Inc., McGraw House, Hospicare; dir. Ithaca Theatre Guild; mem. Cmty. Arts Task Force; chmn. Lansing Village Bd. Zoning Appeals. Capt. U.S. Army. Mem. N.Y. State Bar Assn., Tompkins County Bar Assn. (v.p., pres.-elect, pres. 1996-97), U.S. Supreme Ct. Bar Assn., Sertoma (bd. dirs. local club). E-mail: brucedwilson@aol.com.

WILSON, BRUCE KEITH, men's health nurse; b. Alton, Ill., Aug. 18, 1946; s. Lewis Philip and Ruth Caroline Wilson; m. Karen Loughrey, Aug. 14, 1977; children: Sarah Ann, Andrew James. BSN, U. Tex., San Antonio, 1975, MSN, 1977; PhD, North Tex. State U., Denton, 1987. Coord. Pan Am. U., Edinburg, Tex., 1982-83; house supr. HCA Rio Grande Regional Hosp., McAllen, Tex., 1986-87; program dir. Tex. Southmost Coll., Brownsville, 1983-86; prof. U. Tex.-Pan Am., Edinburg, 1986—. Author: Logical Nursing Math., 1987; contbr. chpts. to books, numerous articles to profl. jours. With U.S. Army, 1966-68. Mem. Am. Assembly for Men in Nursing (bd. dirs. 1997-2001), Tex. League for Nursing (bd. dirs. 1993-97). Avocations: photography, computer. Home: 1702 Ivy Ln Edinburg TX 78539-5367 Office: U Tex-Pan Am Dept Nursing Edinburg TX 78539 Office Phone: 956-381-3494. Personal E-mail: wilson@hiline.net.

WILSON, C. DANIEL, JR., library director; b. Middletown, Conn., Nov. 8, 1941; s. Clyde D. and Dorothy M. (Neal) W.; m. M. April Jackson, Apr. 1986; children: Christine, Cindy, Clyde, Ben. BA, Elmhurst Coll., 1967; MA, Dominican U., 1968; MPA, U. New Orleans, 1995. Trainee Chgo. Pub. Libr., 1967-68; instr. U. Ill., 1968-70; asst. dir. Perrot Meml. Libr., Greenwich, Conn., 1970-76; dir. Wilton Pub. Libr., Wilton, Conn., 1976-79; assoc. dir. Birmingham Pub. Libr., Birmingham, Ala., 1979-83; dir. Davenport (Iowa) Pub. Libr., 1983-85, New Orleans Pub. Libr., 1985-97, St. Louis County Libr., 1997—. With USMC, 1962-65. Mem. ALA, Internat. Assn. Met. Librs. (pres. 1998-2002), Mo. Libr. Assn., Am. Soc. Pub. Adminstrs., Rotary, Pi Gamma Mu. Episcopalian. E-mail: dwilson@slcl.lib.mo.us.

WILSON, C. NICK, health educator, consultant, researcher, lecturer; b. Balt., Feb. 18, 1942; s. Anna May (Gallion) W.; m. Nancy Ann King, Sept. 17, 1966 (div. Apr. 1976); children: Eve Anna Nicole, Tara Stacia; m. Linda Persons, Feb. 25, 1984; children: Melissa Anne, Kristin Marie. BS, U. Hartford, 1966; MHA, George Washington U., 1972; PhD, U. Miss., 1983. Dir. ops. Health Am., Louisville, 1976-79, So. Health Svcs., Marks, Miss., 1979-81; rsch. and teaching asst. U. Miss., Oxford, 1981-83; asst. prof. U. Tex., Galveston, 1983-85, U. Okla., Oklahoma City, 1987-91; pres. Shriners Burn Hosp., Galveston, 1985-87; assoc. prof. health, cons., sr. lectr. U. North Fla., Jacksonville, 1991—. Cons., Jacksonville, 1991—. Author: Health Care Management, 1983; contbr. chpts. to books and over 200 articles to profl. jours. Bd. dirs. First Coast Healthcare Execs., Jacksonville, 1991—, past pres. Lt. USAF, 1966-69. Fellow Am. Coll. Healthcare Execs. (various offices, faculty advisor student chpt. Jacksonville 1991—), Royal Soc. Health; mem. APHA (various offices), Am. Hosp. Assn. (various offices). Republican. Episcopalian. Avocations: golf, tennis, hunting, fishing, sailing. Office: U North Fla Coll Health 4567 Saint Johns Bluff Rd S Jacksonville FL 32224-2646

WILSON, CARL WELDON, JR., construction company executive, civil engineer; b. Norfolk, Va., Sept. 4, 1933; s. Carl Weldon and Janie Marie (Ludford) W.; m. Jean Roberts, Feb. 13, 1960; children: Lisa Ann, Carl Weldon III. BCE, Tex. A&M U., 1954. Registered profl. engr., Tex. Engr. Magnolia Petroleum Co., Morgan City, La., 1954-55, Brown & Root, Houston, 1957-60; project mgr. Claude Everett Constrn. Co., Houston, 1960-62; pres. Falcon Constrn. Co., Houston, 1962-63; pres., owner Wilson Engring. and Constrn. Co., Houston, 1963-68; v.p. Divcon, Inc., Houston, 1968-71, Wilson Industries, Inc., Houston, 1971-81; pres., prin. owner BS&B Engring. Co., Inc., Houston, 1981-86; chmn., majority shareholder Task Internat., Inc., Houston, 1986—. Served to 1st lt. U.S. Army, 1955-57. Republican. Episcopalian. Avocations: tennis, running, painting. Home: 750 Bison Dr Houston TX 77079-4401 Office: Task Internat Inc PO Box 940121 Houston TX 77094-7121 E-mail: cwilson@silverfox.org.

WILSON, CAROLYN ROSS, retired school system administrator; b. Lake Charles, La., June 25, 1941; d. Charles Wesley and Lucille Gertrude (Payne) Ross; m. James David Wilson, Apr. 10, 1971; 1 child, Charlise. BS in Music Edn. cum laude, Xavier U., 1962; MMus in Music Edn., Cath. U., Washington, 1968; postgrad., U. D.C., 1985-86, George Washington U., 1987-88, Harvard U., 1989. Tchr. Xavier U. Jr. Sch. Music, New Orleans, 1960-61, Orleans Parish Schs., New Orleans, 1962-63, D.C. Pub. Schs., Washington, 1964-87, curriculum writer, summer 1984, 85, adminstrv. intern Ea. High Sch., 1987-88, asst. prin. Cardozo High Sch., 1988-89, asst. prin. Duke Ellington Sch. of Arts, 1989-93; prin. Duke Ellington Sch. Arts, Washington, 1993-97—; proposal reader U.S. Dept. Edn., 1998, 98, 99. Curriculum writer music dept. D.C. Pub. Schs., Washington, 1984-85, dir. All City High Sch. Chorus, 1973. Composer: A Dedication to Federal City Alumnae Chapter of Delta, Sigma Theta Sorority, Inc., 1973. Lector Immaculate Conception Ch., Washington, 1986—; named D.C. Tchr. of Yr., 1987. Recipient Cert. of Merit-Outstanding Tchr. and Prin. award D.C. Govt., 1994; U.S. Dept. Edn. Effective Schs. grantee, Washington, 1992. Mem. ASCD, Instn. for Devel. Ednl. Activities (6th yr. fellow, session chair 1988, seminar leader 1991, 92, 93, 94), Delta Sigma Theta (Federal City Alumnae chpt.). Roman Catholic. Avocations: reading, travel, bowling, musical arranging, playing the piano.

WILSON, CASSANDRA, singer; b. Jackson, Miss., 1955; Albums include Point of View, 1986, Blue Skies, 1988, Days Aweigh, 1987, Jumpworld, 1990, She Who Weeps, 1991, Cassandra Wilson Live, 1992, Blue Light 'Till Dawn, 1993, Dance to the Drums Again, 1993, After the Beginning Again, 1994, New Moon Daughter, 1996, Travelling Miles, 1999, Belly of the Sun, 2002, Glamoured, 2003. Office: Blue Note Records 150 5th Ave New York NY 10011-4311

WILSON, CATHERINE COOPER (KITTY WILSON), communications executive, writer; b. Dallas, Sept. 17, 1955; d. William Edward and Suzanne (Blessington) Cooper; m. James Alan Wilson, Oct.17, 1981; children: Nicholas James, Gregory Cooper. BA in Journalism, Tex. Tech U., 1977. Pub. rels. asst. Dallas Market Ctr., 1972-75, 77; pub. rels. coord. Herman Blum Engrs., Dallas, 1977-80, coord. new bus. devel., 1980; acct. exec. Helen Holmes & Assoc., Dallas, 1980; mktg. and pub. rels. coord. EDI Architects, Dallas, 1980-82; pres. Catherine Wilson Comm., Dallas, 1982—; owner, v.p. Wilson Creative, Inc., Dallas, 1988—. Craft of Writing conf. chair U. North Tex. and Greater Dallas Writers' Assn., 1997-99. Contbr. articles to trade mags. Mem. membership com. North Tex. Commn., Dallas, 1979-81; mem. pub. rels. com., bldg. com. St. Rita Cath. Ch., Dallas, 1984-87. Mem. Greater Dallas Writers Assn. Roman Catholic. Avocations: travel, reading, music, walking, book collecting. Home and Office: 6435 Sudbury Dr Dallas TX 75214-2435

WILSON, CECIL BRUCE, internist; b. Columbus, Ga., 1935; m. Betty Jane Wilson; 3 children. BA in history, MD, Emory U. Bd. cert. in internal medicine. Intern US Naval Hosp., Portsmouth, Va., 1961—62, resident in internal medicine San Diego, 1966—69; pvt. practice in internal medicine Fla. Past pres. med. staffs Winter Park Meml. Hosp., Fla. Hosp. Med. Ctr., Orlando; past pres. Fla. Statewide Health Coun.; chair Local Health Coun. of East Cent. Fla. Flight surgeon USN, comdr. USN. Master: Am. Coll. Physicians (past chair bd. regents); mem.: AMA (mem. bd. trustees 2002—, mem. ho. del. 1992—), Orange County Med. Soc. (past pres.), Fla. Med. Assn. (FMA) (pres., chair bd. gov. and exec. com.). Office: 1341 Orange Ave Winter Park FL 32789-4911 Office Phone: 407-647-2122. Office Fax: 407-647-6701.

WILSON, CHARLES, former congressman; b. Trinity, Tex., June 1, 1933; Student, Sam Houston State U., Huntsville, Tex., 1951-52; BS, U.S. Naval Acad., 1956. Commd. ensign U.S. Navy, 1956, advanced through grades to lt.; ret., 1960; mem. Tex. Ho. of Reps., 1960-66, Tex. Senate, 1966-72, 93nd-104th Congresses from 2nd Tex. dist., Washington, D.C., 1973-96; ranking minority mem. appropriations subcom. on fgn. ops., export financing & related programs; partner Hooper, Owen, Gould & Winburn, 1996—. Mgr. lumber yard, 1962-72 Democrat. Office: Hooper Owen Gould & Winburn Ste 730 801 Pennsylvania Ave NW Washington DC 20004-2687

WILSON, CHARLES BANKS, artist; b. Springdale, Ark., Aug. 6, 1918; s. Charles Bertram and Bertha Juanita (Banks) W.; children: Geoffrey Banks, Carrie Vee. Student, Art Inst. Chgo., 1936—41. Mag. and book illustrator, 1943-60; head art dept. N.E. Okla. A. & M. Coll., Miami, Okla., 1947-61; painter, printmaker. Executed murals, Okla. State Capitol, 1975; represented in permanent collections Met. Mus., N.Y.C., Libr. of Congress, Washington, U.S. Capitol Bldg., D.C. Corcoran Gallery, Smithsonian Inst., Will Rogers Meml. Mus., Philbrook Art Ctr., Tulsa, Nat. Cowbow Hall of Fame, Oklahoma City. illustrator numerous books. Bd. dirs. Thomas Gilcrease Mus. History and Art, Tulsa, 1957-61; chmn. Pub. Libr. Bd., Miami, Okla., 1954-59. Named to Okla. Hall of Fame, Okla. Historians Hall of Fame, 2001, named an Okla. Treasure, State of Okla. Arts Commn., 2001; recipient Western Heritage award Cowboy Hall of Fame, Disting. Svc. citation U. Okla.; subject of books The Lithographs of Charles Banks Wilson, 1989, Search for the North American Purebloods, 2000, An Oklahoma Portrait, 1989. Mem. Internat. Inst. Arts and Letters (Geneva). Office: 1611 E Mission Blvd Fayetteville AR 72703-3043 E-mail: cvwilson@mail.uark.edu.

WILSON, CHARLES H. (CHARLES HARRISON WILSON), retired air force officer, financial planner, human resource development professional; b. Chgo., Sept. 6, 1941; s. Charles W. and Lorraine F. (Parker) W.; m. Mona Dickerson, July 2, 1988; children: Audrey M., Angela M., Andrew M., Aaron M. BS, So. Ill. U., 1964; BA, U. Md., 1976; MA, Webster U., 1979. Commd. 2d lt. USAF, 1964, advanced through grades to lt. col., 1986, def. logistics agy. Washington personnel dir., 1980-83, ret., 1984; exec. dir. exec. leadership program Dept. Def. (Pentagon), Washington, 1976-88. Mil. liaison Republic of China, 1977-80; adj. prof. Park Univ., St. Louis, 1977-80; mcpl. cons. City of Dayton, Ohio, 1980; pres. Advanced Ethonomics. Sch. bd. Alexandria Pub. Sch., Alexandria, Va., 2003—; bd. dir. Credit Union No. Va. Fellow D.C. Life Under Writers Tng. Coun.; mem. Classification and Compensation Soc., Am. Soc. Tng. and Devel., Internat. Pers. Mgmt. Assn. (human rights commn.), Omega Psi Phi, Toastmasters; elected to Alexandria City Sch. Bd. Democrat. Methodist. Achievements include invention of microwave oven carousel. Avocation: flying. Home: 6101 Edsall Rd Apt 703 Alexandria VA 22304-6004 Office Phone: 202-429-9393. E-mail: chaswill@juno.com.

WILSON, CHARLES REGINALD, federal judge; b. Pensacola, FL, 1954; BS, U. Notre Dame, 1976, JD, 1979. Bar: Fla. 1979. Law clk. to Hon. Joseph W. Hatchett U.S. Ct. Appeal for 11th Cir., 1979—80; asst. county atty. Hillsborough county, Fla., 1980—81; county judge 13th Jud. Cir. of Fla., 1986—90; pvt. practice Fla., 1981—86; U.S. magistrate judge U.S. Dist. Ct. (mid. dist.) Fla., 1990—94, U.S. atty., 1994—99; U.S. cir. judge U.S. Ct. Appeals 11th Cir., Tampa, Fla., 1999—. Mem.: Ferguson-White Inn of Am. Inn of Ct., Fed. Bar Assn., Am. Law Inst. Office: 11th Cir Ct Appeals 801 N Florida Ave Ste 14B Tampa FL 33602-3849

WILSON, CHARLES ROBERT, port captain, harbor master; b. Biloxi, Miss., Aug. 28, 1947; s. William Clayborne, Sr. and Lyna Lowe Wilson; m. Bonnie Atwater, June 12, 1990 (div. Feb. 1995); 1 child, Michael Robert. PhB, State U. West Ga., 1975. Electronic engr. Rockwell, San Francisco, Atlanta, 1975-79; Alaskan bush pilot Anchorage, 1990-95; port capt., harbor master Midway Phoenix Corp., Midway Atoll, Hawaii, 1995—. Cons. Rockwell and subs. cos., Atlanta, 1969-79; ocean sailboat racer, 1979-90. Mem. U.S. Parachute Assn. (pres. 1969, Star Crest 187 award 1971, Night Star Crest 187 award 1973). Avocations: skydiving, sport flying, whitewater activities, sailing. Office: US Fish and WildLife 1082 Makepono St Honolulu HI 96819 E-mail: bwilson@midwayisland.net.

WILSON, CHARLES STEPHEN, cardiologist, educator; b. Geneva, Nebr., June 14, 1938; s. Robert Butler and Naoma Luella (Norgren) Wilson; m. Linda Stern Walt, Aug. 21, 1960; children: Michael Scott, Amy Lynn, Cynthia Lee. BA cum laude, U. Nebr., 1960; MD, Northwestern U., 1964. Diplomate Am. Bd. Internal Medicine subsplty. bd. cardiovascular disease, Nat. Bd. Med. Examiners. Intern Fitzsimons Gen. Hosp., Denver, 1964-65; fellow in internal medicine and cardiology Mayo Grad. Sch. Medicine, Rochester, Minn., 1968-72; practice medicine specializing in cardiology Lincoln, Nebr., 1972—; attending staff Bryan Meml. Hosp., 1972—, chmn. cardiology, 1976-79; clin. prof. medicine and cardiology U. Nebr. Med. Ctr., Omaha; med. dir. Bryan LGH Med. Ctr. Ultrafast CT Scanner, Lincoln, 2001—, Sch. Allied Health, Bryan LGH Coll. of Health Scis., 2002—. Mem. Mayor's Coun. on Emergency Med. Svcs., Lincoln, 1974-78; founder, chmn. Nebr. State Hypertension Screening Program; med. dir. Lincoln Mobile Heart Team, 1977-80, Lincoln Cardiac Rehab. Program, 1978-79; co-founder, pres. Nebr. Heart Inst., 1987; co-founder Lincoln Cardiac Transplant Program, 1987. Contbr. articles to profl. jours.; editorl. cons. Chest, 1975-76; assoc. editor Nebr. Med. Jour., 1981-88. Trustee U. Nebr. Found., 1983—, chmn. Nebr. Coordinating Commn. for Postsecondary Edn., 1984-88; mem. bd. regents U. Nebr., 1991—, chmn. 1994, 2001. Served as maj., M.C., USAR, 1963-68. Gen. Motors Nat. scholar, 1956-60, Nat. Found. Med. scholar, 1960-64, Mead Johnson scholar ACP, 1968-71. Fellow ACP, Am. Coll. Cardiology (bd. govs. 1990-93, pres. Nebr. affiliate 1992-93), Am. Coll. Chest Physicans, Am. Heart Assn. (dir. Nebr. affilate 1973-80, pres. 1976-77); mem. Mayo Cardiovascular Soc., Nebr. Cardiovascular Soc. (pres. 1989-90), Nebr. Coun. on Pub. Higher Edn. (steering com. 1991—), Lincoln Heart Assn. (dir. 1972-75, pres. 1974-75), AMA, Nebr. Med. Assn. Lancaster County Med. Soc., Am. Soc. Internal Medicine, Lincoln Found., U. Nebr. Chancellor's Club, Lincoln U. Club (dir. 1981-84), U. Nebr. Pres. Club, Phi Beta Kappa, Sigma Xi, Alpha Omega Alpha, Phi Delta Theta (pres. Nebr. Alpha chpt. 1959-60). Home: 7430 N Hampton Rd Lincoln NE 68506-1624 Office: Bryan LGH Ultrafast CT Scanner 1500 S 48th St Lincoln NE 68506

WILSON, CHARLES ZACHARY, JR., newspaper publisher; b. Greenwood, Miss., Apr. 21, 1929; s. Charles Zachary and Ora Lee (Means) W.; m. Doris J. Wilson, Aug. 18, 1951 (dec. Nov. 1974); children: Charles III, Joyce Lynne, Joanne Catherine, Gary Thomas, Jonathan Keith; m. Kelly Freeman, Apr. 21, 1986; children: Amanda Fox, Walter Bremond. BS in Econs., U. Ill., 1952, PhD in Econs. and Stats., 1956. Asst. to v.p. Commonwealth Edison Co., Chgo., 1956-59; asst. prof. econs. De Paul U., Chgo., 1959-61; assoc. prof. bus. SUNY, Binghamton, 1961-67, prof. econs. and bus., 1967-68; prof. mgmt. and edn. UCLA, 1968-84, vice chancellor acad. programs, 1985-87; CEO, pub., pres. Cen. News-Wave Publs., L.A., 1987-93; pres. Czand Assocs., Pacific Palisades, Calif., 1994—; CEO Wave Cmty. Newspapers, L.A., 1997—. Mem. adv. council Fed. Res. Bank, San Francisco, 1986-88, 2001 com. Office of Mayor of Los Angeles, 1986-89. Author: Organizational Decision-Making, 1967; contbr. articles on bus. to jours. Bd. dirs. Los Angeles County Mus. Art, 1972-84; mem. Com. on L.A. City Revenue, 1975-76, UN Assn. Panel for Advancement of U.S. and Japan Rels., N.Y.C. 1972-74; chmn. L.A. Mayor's task force on Africa, 1979-82; mem. L.A. Charter Reform Commn. Fellow John Hay Whitney, U. Ill., 1955-56, Ford Found., 1960-61, 81-82, 84, Am. Council of Edn., UCLA, 1967-68, Aspen Inst. for Human Studies; named one of Young Men of Yr., Jaycees, 1965. Mem. AAAS, Am. Econ. Assn., Nat. Newspaper Pub. Assn., Am. Mgmt. Assn., Alpha Phi Alpha (pres., pledgemaster 1952-54), Phi Kappa Phi. Order of Artus (pres.). Avocations: tennis, jogging, collecting old bus. texts. Home: 1053 Tellem Dr Pacific Palisades CA 90272-2243 Office: Cen Newspaper Publs 2621 W 54th St Los Angeles CA 90043-2614

WILSON, CHERYL YVONNE, elementary school educator, secondary school educator; b. Dayton, Ohio, Sept. 25, 1958; d. Samuel Wesley Wilson Sr. and Hazel Oneida Wilson; m. Henry Heard Cofield Jr., July 27, 1985. Student, Ohio State U., 1976—81; AA, Miami U., 1987. Legal sec. Raymond W. O'Neal, Sr. Atty. at Law, Middletown, Ohio, 1982—83; reorder buyer Dason's Hardware Ctr., 1984—85; Writer's Digest Novel Writing Workship Middletown City Sch. Dist., 1986—87; deputy clk. Butler County Clk. Cts., Hamilton, 1990—91; mail room clk. Butler County Printing Co., 1992—95; mail courier, security officer Johnson Controls Svcs., Inc., 1998—2000. Pres., CEO Ohio Writer's Pub. Co., Middletown, 1987—, 1991—. *The USBC, OWPC volunteer institute endowed by the sole-proprietorship of the commission "gives" "altruistically," sympathetically, compassionately, unselfishly, and "selflessly," "advocating" a "peaceful" "affirmation" for "...time-honored..." in the community officially and build-up its establishment in the societal world for the "Innovative Pioneer Calendar-Days" for the "pilot program" since 1966 with "evolution" of H.R. 40 idea logy as the elite "Defense of a policy" to illustrate; facilitate and implement manufacturing "bestseller" book proposals in an editorial column for living an "independent lifestyle" with appropriate H.R. 40 legislative federal funds approval by the 43rd president George W. Bush and the 108th U.S. Congress.* Mem. U.S. Bicentennial Commn., 2003—, curator, exec. dir., 2003. Nominee 87th Spingarn medal award, NAACP, 1998, 2001, Coretta Scott King book award, 2002, Oprah Winfrey Angel Network Use Your Life award, 2003. Mem.: NAACP (life Bronze Plaque award 2002), Internat. African Am. Genealogy Rsch. Pub. Assn. (curator 2003—, exec. dir. 2003—), Middletown Hist. Soc. (life). Republican. Mem. Lds Ch. Avocations: writing, reading, photography. Office Phone: 513-424-7749.

WILSON, CLAUDE RAYMOND, JR., lawyer; b. Dallas, Feb. 22, 1933; s. Claude Raymond and Lottie (Watts) W.; m. Emilynn Wilson; children: Deidra Wilson Graves, Melissa Woodard Utley, Michele Woodard Dunn. BBA, So. Meth. U., 1954, JD, 1956. Bar: Tex. 1956; CPA, Calif., Tex. Assoc. firm Cervin & Melton, Dallas, 1956-58; atty. Tex. & Pacific R.R. Co., Dallas, 1958-60; atty. office regional counsel IRS, San Francisco, 1960-63, sr. trial atty. office chief counsel Washington, 1963-65; ptnr. Wilson & White, Dallas, 1965-98, Vial, Hamilton, Koch & Knox LLP, Dallas, 1998—. Chmn., Dallas dist. dir. IRS Adv. Commn., 1990-91. Chmn. Dallas Hist. Soc., 2000-01; mem. fin. com. Dallas Arboretum and Bot. Gardens, 2003—, City of University Park, 2004—; bd. govs. Dallas Symphony Orch., 2004—. Mem.: AICPA (coun. 1989—93, tax exec. com. 1998—2001), ABA, Tex. Soc. CPAs (pres. 1989—90, pres. Dallas chpt. 1983—84), Dallas Bar Assn. (pres. sect. taxation 1969—70), State Bar Tex., Greater Dallas C. of C. (chmn. appropriations and tax com. 1990—91), Dallas Petroleum Club, Montaigne Club, Masons, Delta Theta Phi., Delta Sigma Phi. Republican. Episcopalian. Office: Vial Hamilton Koch & Knox 1700 Pacific Ave Ste 2800 Dallas TX 75201-7388 Office Phone: 214-712-4418. E-mail: cwilson@vialaw.com.

WILSON, COLIN HENRY, writer; b. Leicester, Eng., June 26, 1931; s. Arthur and Anetta W.; m. Joy Stewart; children: Sally, Damon, Rowan; 1 child from previous marriage, Roderick. Writer in residence Hollins (Va.) Coll., 1966-67; vis. prof. U. Wash., Seattle, 1967, Rutgers U., New Brunswick, NJ, 1974. Author (numerous books including novels): The Outsider, 1956, The Glass Cage, 1967, The Occult, 1971, The Black Room, 1971, The Space Vampires, 1975, Mysteries, 1978; 6 critical studies in the Outsider series; non-fiction: Access to Inner Worlds, 1982, A Criminal History of Mankind, 1983, (with Donald Seaman) Modern Encyclopedia of Murder, 1983, The Essential Colin Wilson, 1984, The Personality Surgeon, 1986, (with Damon Wilson) Encyclopedia of Unsolved Mysteries, 1987, Spider World, 1987, The Misfits, 1988, Beyond The Occult, 1988, Written in Blood, 1989, (with Donald Seaman) The Serial Killers, 1990; (play) Mozart's Journey to Prague, 1991, Spider World: The Magician, 1992, The Strange Life of P.D. Ouspensky, 1993, Unsolved Mysteries Past and Present (with Damon Wilson), 1993, From Atlantis To The Sphinx, 1996, Atlas of Holy Places and Sacred Sites, 1996, Alien Dawn, 1998, The Books in My Life, 1998, The Devil's Party, 2000; (with Rand Fle'math) Atlantis Blueprint, 2000, Spider World: The Magician, 2002, Spiderworld: Shadowland, 2003, autobiography, 2004. Mem.: Savage. E-mail: cdin@chwilson.demon.co.uk.

WILSON, CONSTANCE KRAMER, banker; b. Dayton, Ohio, Aug. 9, 1959; d. Michael Carl and Mona Louise (Miller) Kramer; m. Thomas Singleton Wilson, July 27, 1985; stepchildren: Thomas Douglas, Kirsten Lea, Heather Elizabeth, Ashley Paige. BS in Finance, Ind. U., 1981. Sr. credit analyst NCNB Nat. Bank, Charlotte, 1982-83, commercial loan officer, 1983-86, stockbroker, 1987-88, trust officer, 1988—; investment advisor Planned Mgmt. Co., Charlotte, 1986-87; mem. N.C. State Senate, 1989-90. Mem. Gov.'s Infant Mortality Commn., N.C. State House, 1992—, emerging polit. leader program U. Va., 1993, Gov.'s Commn. on Literacy; del. Rep. Party County Dist. State, 1988-89; vice chmn. Mecklenburg Young Reps., Charlotte, 1989; mem. exec. com. Rep. County and State, 1989. N.C. Inst. fellow, Wilmington, 1989. Republican. Home: 726 Lansdowne Rd Charlotte NC 28270-5902 Office: NCNB Nat Bank 1 Ncnb Pla To9 1 Charlotte NC 28255-0001

WILSON, DARLENE ANDERSON, elementary school educator; b. L.A., 1935; d. Alfred and Alyce Anderson; m. Charles Cecil Wilson, Apr. 18, 1958; 1 child, Scott Wilson. BA, Occidental U., Eagle Rock, Calif., 1957; MA, Calif. State U., 1978. Gen. Elem., Kindergarten Primary, Adminstrv. Svcs., Calif. Kindergarten tchr. Buchanan St. Sch., Highland Park, Calif., 1957-58, Valley View Elem. Sch., Hollywood, Calif., 1959-60; 2nd and 3rd grade tchr. Fair Ave. Sch., N. Hollywood, Calif., 1960-61; kindergarten tchr. Napa St. Sch., Northridge, Calif., 1962-84. 5th grade tchr., acting prin., tng. tchr. Chatsworth Park Elem. Sch., Calif., 1984-95; grad. student advisor Milken Educator Awards, Beverly Hills, Calif., 1991. Author: Strategies for Classroom Management K-6: Making Magic Happen. Tchr., chair Local Sch. Leadership Coun., Chatsworth, 1989-91. Recipient Hon. Svc. award Napa St. PTA, Northridge, Calif., 1983. Mem.: CRTA. Democrat. Avocations: tennis, hiking, dance, reading, theater. Home: 8419 Jason Ave Canoga Park CA 91304-3114 Office: Chatsworth Park Elem Sch 22005 Devonshire St Chatsworth CA 91311-2841

WILSON, DAVID, artist; BA, Kalamazoo Coll., 1969; student, Calif. Inst. Arts. With L.A. Film Oasis collective; artist, designer, curator, founder Mus. Jurassic Tech., Culver City, Calif., 1984—. Office: Mus Jurassic Tech 9341 Venice Blvd Culver City CA 90232

WILSON, DAVID JAMES, chemistry researcher, educator; b. Ames, Ia., June 25, 1930; s. James Calmar and Alice Winona (Olmsted) W.; m. Martha Carolyn Mayers, Sept. 6, 1952; children: John Wesley, Charles Steven, William David, Andrew Lyman, Joyce Ballin. BS in Chemistry, Stanford U., 1952; postgrad., 1952-53, 55-57; PhD, Calif. Inst. Tech., 1958. Mem. faculty U. Rochester, N.Y., 1957-69, assoc. prof., 1963-67, prof. phys. chemistry, 1967-69; prof. Vanderbilt U., Nashville, 1969-95, prof. chemistry and environ. engring., 1977-95, prof. emeritus, 1995—, Alexander Heard disting. service prof., 1983-84; sr. rsch. assoc. Eckenfelder/Brown and Caldwell, Nashville, 1988-95, sr. rsch. fellow, 1995—. Vis. sr. lectr. chemistry U. Ife, Nigeria, 1964-65; vis. prof. U. Málaga, Spain, 1993-94; mem. Rochester Com. for Sci. Info., 1960-69, v.p., 1966-69; chmn. Nashville Com. for Sci. Info., 1971-74. Author: (book) Foam Flotation: Theory and Applications, Hazardous Waste Site Soil Remediation, Modeling of In Situ Techniques for Treatment of Contaminated Soils. Pres. Tenn. Environ. Coun., 1985-87. With AUS, 1953-55. Sp-3 U.S. Army, 1953—55, Army Chemical Center, Maryland. Recipient award Monroe County Conservation Coun., 1967, Tenn. Conservation League, 1971; Alfred P. Sloan Found. fellow, 1964-66. Mem. AAAS, Am. Chem. Soc., Tenn. Acad. Sci., Sigma Xi, Phi Beta Kappa. Avocations: ornithology, music, travel, hiking. Home: 11544 Quirk Rd Belleville MI 48111

WILSON, DAVID VANDIVER, II, lawyer; b. Houston, Jan. 9, 1968; s. David Vandiver and Emma Lee (Binion) W.; m. Susan Graham, Dec. 18, 1988; children: Katherine Elizabeth, Sarah Margaret. BS, Tex. A&M U., 1989; JD, South Tex. Coll. Law, Houston, 1993. Bar: Tex. 1993. Asst. dist. atty. Harris County, Houston, 1993-95; adj. prof. law South Tex. Coll. Law, 1994-95, 98—; asst. dist. atty. Angelina County, Lufkin, Tex., 1995-98; instr. Angelina Coll. Police Acad., Lufkin, 1995-98; shareholder Hays, McConn, Rice & Pickering, Houston, 1998—. Mem. editl. bd. Houston Lawyer, 2002—. Mem. exec. bd. Habitat for Humanity Angelina County, 1996-98; trustee First United Meth. Ch., Lufkin, 1996-98; mem. bd. stewards Meml. Dr. United Meth. Ch., 2001—. Named Child Advocate of Yr. Black Adoption Coun. S.E. Tex., Beaumont, 1997; awarded 1st prize Bruno Bitker Essay Contest, 1992. Mem. ABA (mem. ho. of dels. 1997-2000), Tex. Dist. and County Atty.'s Assn., Angelina County Bar Assn. (bd. dirs. 1996-98), Houston Bar Assn. Methodist. Avocations: hunting, fishing. Office: Hays McConn Rice & Pickering 1200 Smith St Ste 400 Houston TX 77002-4501 Office Phone: 713-654-1111. Business E-Mail: dvw@haysmcconn.com.

WILSON, DEBORA J. broadcast executive; m. Larry Wilson; 1 stepchild, Kevin; 1 child, Christine. BS in Fin. and Bus. Adminstrn., George Mason U. With Bell Atlantic Network Svcs.; joined The Weather Channel, 1994, sr. v.p. new bus. devel., exec. v.p., gen. mgr. online svcs.; pres., CEO The Weather Channel Interactive, 1999—2003; COO The Weather Channel Network and The Weather Channel Interactive, 2003—04; pres. The Weather Channel Cos., 2004—. Recipient Tami Award, 2000. Mem.: Interactive Adv. Bureau, Cable & Telecom. Assoc., National Cable Television Assoc., bd. of dir. Lightbridge, Inc. Office: 300 Interstate North Pkwy SE Atlanta GA 30339-2403*

WILSON, DEBORRAH, physical education educator; b. Tachikowa, Japan, Aug. 18, 1950; BS in Phys. Edn. and Health, U. Del., 1972; MEd, Wilmington Coll., 2000. Elem. phys. edn. tchr. Downes Elem. Sch.; instr. of programs, teen dir. YWCA, 1972—78; phys. edn. specialist Christina Sch. Dist., 1978—. Recipient Outstanding Alumni award U. Del., 1993, Disting. Svc. award Maclary PTA, 1993, Del. Congress Parents and Tchrs. Inc.; named Ea. Region Elem. Sch. Phys. Edn. Tchr. of Yr., Nat. Assn. Sport and Phys. Edn., 1993, Elem. Phys. Edn. Tchr. of Yr., State of Del., 1993, Tchr. of Yr. Elem. Sch., 2000. Home: 731 Art Ln Newark DE 19713-1208

WILSON, DELANO DEE, consultant; b. Great Falls, Mont., Apr. 15, 1934; s. William McKinley and Alvina Henrietta (Beck) W.; m. Marilyn Ann Harant, Nov. 14, 1959; children: Robin David, Leslie Ann Wilson, Christian William. BSEE, Mont. State U., 1959. Analytical engr. GE, Schenectady, N.Y., 1960-69, sr. engr., 1964-69, mgr. alternating current studies, 1969-72, mgr. engring. projects Phila., 1972-74; prin. engr. Power Techs., Inc., Schenectady, 1974-82; v.p., prin. engr. Power Techs., Inc.-Tech. Assessment Group, Schenectady, 1980-85; pres., CEO Power Techs. Inc., Schenectady, 1986-95, chmn. bd. dirs., 1989-95. Expert witness, cons. Internat. Conf. on High Voltage Systems, Paris, 1974-90. U.S. rep., 1986-92. Author, co-author 6 books; contbr. numerous tech. papers to profl. jours.; patentee in field. Bd. dirs. Ellis Hosp., Schenectady, 1987—; trustee Capital Dist. YMCA, 1989-98. With U.S. Army, 1954-56. Fellow IEEE (life, mem. transp. and dist. com., exec. bd. Power Engring. Soc. 1988-94, Disting. Svc. award 1988, Third Millennium medal 2000). Avocations: fishing, amateur auto rebuilding.

WILSON, DENISE See EARLY, TERI WILSON

WILSON, DON WHITMAN, retired archivist, historian; b. Clay Center, Kans., Dec. 17, 1942; s. Donald J. Wilson and Lois M. (Sutton) Walker; m. Patricia Ann Sherrod, July 9, 1983; children— Todd, Jeffrey, Michael, Denise. AB, Washburn U., Topeka, 1964; MA, U. Cin., 1965, PhD, 1972, LittD (hon.), 1988. Archivist Kans. State Hist. Soc., Topeka, 1967-69; instr. history Washburn U., 1967-69; historian, dept. dir. Dwight D. Eisenhower Library, Abilene, Kans., 1969-78; assoc. dir. State Hist. Soc. Wis., Madison, 1978-81; dir. Gerald R. Ford Library and Mus., Ann Arbor, Mich., 1981-87; lectr. history U. Mich., 1982-87; Archivist of the U.S. Washington, 1987-93; rsch. prof. Tex. A&M U., College Station, 1993-98, exec. dir. George Bush libr. found., 1993-98. Author: Governor Charles Robinson of Kansas, 1975; editor: D-Day: The Normandy Invasion, 1971. Mem. Abilene Library Bd., 1973-76; mem. Abilene City Commn., 1976-78; pres. Dickinson County Hist. Soc., Abilene, 1976-77. NDEA fellow, 1964-67; recipient Pub. Service award Gen. Services Adminstrn., 1973 Mem. Am. Hist. Assn. (mem. Beveridge Book Prize com. 1979-82), Am. Assn. State and Local History, Kans. Hist. Soc. (bd. dirs. 1987—), Am. Antiquarian Soc. Republican. Baptist. Office: Tex A&M U PO Box 1145 George Bush Libr Found College Station TX 77843-1145

WILSON, DONALD EDWARD, internist, educator, dean; b. Worcester, Mass., Aug. 28, 1936; s. Rivers Rivo and Licine (Bradshaw) Wilson; m. Patricia C. Littell, Aug. 27, 1977; children: Jeffrey D.E., Sean D., Monique, Sheila L. AB, Harvard U., 1958; MD, Tufts U., 1962. Diplomate Am. Bd. Internal Medicine. Intern St. Elizabeth Hosp., Boston, 1962—63; resident in medicine, research fellow in gastroenterology VA Hosp. and Lemuel Shattuck Hosp., Boston, 1963—66; assoc. chief gastroenterology Bklyn. Hosp., 1968—71; instr. medicine SUNY Downstate Med. Center, Bklyn., 1968—71; asst. prof. medicine U. Ill., Chgo., 1971—73, asso. prof., 1973—75, prof., 1975—80, acting head dept. medicine, 1976—77; dir. divsn. gastroenterology U. Ill. Hosp., Chgo., 1971—78, chief of gastroenterology, 1973—80, physician-in-chief, 1976—77; prof., chmn. dept. medicine SUNY Downstate Med. Center, Bklyn., 1980—91; physician-in-chief State U. and Kings County Hosp., 1980—91; dean U. Md.Sch. Medicine, Balt., 1991—; v.p. of med. affairs U. Md. Sch. Medicine, Balt., 1999—. Vis. prof. medicine U. London, Kings Coll. Med. Sch., 1977—78; mem. gastrointestingal drugs adv. bd. FDA, 1985—87, chmn., 1986—87; mem. Part II test com. Nat. Bd. Med. Examiners, 1985—88; mem. nat. digestive adv. bd. NIH, 1985—87, chmn., 1986—87, mem. gen. clin. rsch. ctrs. com., 1987—; mem. nat. adv. com. Agy. for Health CAre Policy and Rsch., Dept. HHS, 1991—94; chmn. Agy. for Health Care Policy and Rsch., Dept. HHS, 1992—94; mem. residency rev. com. for internal medicine Acque, 1993—; mem. nat. com. fgn. med. edn. and accreditation U.S. Dept. Edn., 1994—; mem. nat. adv. rsch. resources com. NIH, 1997—2000. Contbr. articles to med. jours. Bd. vis. Harvard Sch. Pub. Health, 1992—94. Capt. M.C. USAF, 1966—68. Recipient Rsch. award, HEW, 1971, 1974, John A. Hartford Found., Inc., 1972—79, Distilled Spirits Coun. U.S., 1972—74, VA, 1974. Master: ACP; mem.: AAAS, NAS, Inst. of Medicine, Assn. Profs. Medicine (sec.-treas. 1990—91), Am. Clin. and Climatol. Assn., Nat. Med. Assn., Assn. for Acad. Minority Physicians (sec./treas. 1986—), Assn. Am. Physicians, Chgo. Soc. Gastrointestinal Endoscopy (pres. 1979—80), N.Y. Soc. Gastroenterology, N.Y. Acad. Medicine, N.Y. Acad. Scis., Soc. Exptl. Biology and Medicine, Midwest Gut Club, Digestive Disease Found., Chgo. Soc. Gastroenterology (pres. 1978—79), Ctrl. Rsch. Club, Ctrl. Soc. Clin. Rsch., Accreditation Coun. Grad. Med. Edn. (rev. com. internal medicine), Am. Assn. Study Liver Disease, Am. Fedn. Clin. Rsch., Am. Gastroent. Assn., The Ctr. Club (Balt.), Med. Club Bklyn., 14 West Hamilton St. Club (Balt.), Harvard Club (Chgo., N.Y.C.), Sigma Pi Phi (grand boule). Office: U Md Sch Medicine 655 W Baltimore St Rm 14029 Baltimore MD 21201-1509

WILSON, DONALD GREY, management consultant; b. Bridgeport, Conn., Sept. 20, 1917; s. William Gray and Jeannetta McAvoy (Kerr) W.; m. Elizabeth Jean Lanning, Apr. 24, 1943 (div. Mar. 1971, dec. Mar. 2002); children: Kirk Lanning, Craig Gardner, William Grey. BSEE, Rensselaer Poly. Inst., 1938; SM, Harvard U., 1939, MES, 1947, PhD, 1948. Mgr. automatic fire alarm divsn. Sealand Corp., Bridgeport, Conn., 1939-40; instr. elec. engring. Rensselaer Poly. Inst., 1940-42; staff mem. Radiation Lab. MIT, 1942-45; prof. elec. engring. U. Kan., Lawrence, 1947-55, chmn. dept., 1948-55; dir. Phila. Brass & Bronze, 1962-64, Mallory-Xerox Corp., 1964-65. Cons. U.S. Naval Ordance Test Sta., China Lake, Calif., 1953-54; assoc. dir. rsch. dept. Stromberg-Carlson Co., San Diego, 1955-59, gen. mgr., 1959, asst. v.p., 1959-60; v.p. rsch. P.R. Mallory & Co., Indpls., 1960, v.p. rsch. and engring., 1961-71, v.p. rsch., engring. and environ. affairs, 1971-75; alt. dir. Mallory Metal. Products, Eng., 1967; pres. Contemporary Custom Cabinets, San Diego, 1975-76; v.p. Continental Resources and Minerals Corp., Dayton, Ohio, 1978-79; sr. v.p. Tanzi Mergers/Acquisitions, San Diego, 1983-86; mgmt. cons., 1976—; sr. lectr. U. Rochester, 1956-57; lectr. dept. elec. engring. San Diego State U., 1981-92, asst. dean coll. engring., 1987, prof. emeritus, 1992—; mng. dir., exec. bd. Nat. Bur. Cert. Cons., 1988-94, sr. adv. counsel, 1994-2001. Contbr. articles to profl. jours. Bd. dirs. Speech and Hearing Clinic, Indpls., 1960-66, Washington Twp. Sch. Dist., 1964-68, pres., 1966-67. Recipient Outstanding Acad. Advisor award San Diego State U., 1992. Fellow AAAS; mem. IEEE (sr. life, exec. com. San Diego sect. 1986-2003, chmn. S.W. area region 6 1999-2000, sec. region 6 2001-02, ethics and mem. conduct com. 2002—, Third Millennium medal, Internat. IEEE Outstanding Br. Counselor award 1992), Affiliation Profl. Cons. Orgns. (chmn. bd. govs. 1991-93 San Diego Engring. Coun. Outstanding Svc. award 2000), Intertel, Sigma Xi, Sigma Phi Epsilon, Tau Beta Pi, Eta Kappa Nu. Home: 1950 Silverleaf Cir 310 Carlsbad CA 92009 Personal E-mail: don.wilson@ieee.org.

WILSON, DONALD HURST, III, mediator, biopharmaceutical industry executive; b. Balt., Mar. 1, 1946; s. Donald H. and Winifred W.; m. Catharine A. MacKinnon, June 21, 1968 (div. 1972); m. Beverly Lee Wright, Oct. 3, 1975 (div. 1998); m. Constance Fisher Neely, Sept. 23, 2000; children: Beverly Callaway, Sarah Elizabeth. AB, Yale U., 1968; MBA, JD, Harvard U., 1976. Bar: Mass. 1977, N.C. 2003. Cons. Boston Cons. Group, 1976-78; dir. mktg. I/C divsn. Black & Decker, Hampstead, Md., 1978-83; pres. MWI Tng. Svcs., Inc., Hunt Valley, Md., 1983-96; v.p. Innoversity Edn. Ctrs., Global Knowledge Network, Inc., Hunt Valley, Md., 1996-97; pres., COO Endacea, Inc. (formerly Link Tech., Inc.), Raleigh, 1997-98, pres., CEO, 1998-2000, also bd. dirs., v.p., COO, 2001—02, v.p., gen. counsel, bd. dirs., 2003—, pres., CEO, gen. counsel, 2004—; cert. mediator Superior Ct. N.C. Dispute Resolution Commn., 2004—. Mem. vestry St. John's Episcopal Ch., 1993-96, lay eucharistic min., 1995-98; dir. The Bishop Claggett Ctr., 1995-97. Mem. Assn. Microcomputer Distbrs (bd. dirs. 1988-90), Archaeol. Soc. Md. (trustee 1994-98) Republican. Avocations: archaeology, golf. Home: 1112 Baslow Brook Ct Raleigh NC 27614-8866

WILSON, DONALD KENNETH, JR., lawyer, publisher; b. Lancaster, Pa., Mar. 5, 1954; s. Donald Kenneth and Gloria (Payne) W.; m. Lauren Elaine O'Connor, Sept. 3, 1977; children: Donald, Tameka, Veronica, Matthew. BA, U. So. Calif., 1976; JD, N.Y. Law Sch., 1979. Bar: Calif. 1979, U.S. Ct. Appeals (9th cir.) 1979, U.S. Ct. Appeals (ea. dist.) Mich., 1996, U.S. Ct. Appeals, Colo. 1997. Ptnr. Law Office, L.A., 1987-92; pres., chief operating officer Quincy Jones Productions, L.A., 1983-86; assoc. Garey, Mason & Sloane, L.A., 1979-82, pres., CEO 4 Kids Music, L.A., 1989—, Dotevema Music, L.A., 1989—; of counsel Law Offices Johnnie L. Cochran Jr., L.A., 1992—2000; pvt. practice Law Offices of Donald K. Wilson, L.A., 2000—. Producer: (video documentary) Frank Sinatra, 1984 (Vira award 1985, Grammy nomination 1985); contb. articles to newspapers. Trustee First African Meth. Episc. Ch., 1989-97; mem. NAACP, L.A., 1990. Recipient Citizenship award, Am. Legion, 1972; named Outstanding Young Men of Am., 1982, 83, Outstanding Contbr. to Community, Entertainment Civic Orgn., 1986. Avocations: tennis, reading, walking, fishing. Office: Law Offices Donald K Wilson Jr 4322 Wilshire Blvd Ste 300 Los Angeles CA 90010-3825

WILSON, DONALD MALCOLM, publishing executive; b. Glen Ridge, N.J., June 27, 1925; s. Robert and Adelaide (Streubel) Wilson; m. Susan M Neuberger, Apr. 6, 1957; children: Dwight Malcolm, Katherine Loudon, Penelope. Grad., Deerfield (Mass.) Acad., 1943; BA, Yale U., 1948. Reporter Life mag., 1949-53, chief Far Ea. corr., 1953-56, chief Washington corr., 1956-60, asso. pub., 1968-69; gen. mgr. Time- Life Internat., 1965-68; v.p. corporate and pub. affairs Time, Inc., 1969-81, corp. v.p. pub. affairs, 1981-89; pu. Business News N.J., New Brunswick, 1989—; dep. dir. USIA, 1961-65. Mem adv coun Edward R Murrow Ctr. Tufts Univ, Nat Coun La Raza, 1985—89; mem Pub Broadcasting Authority NJ, 1969—73, 1976—79. Trustee Vassar Col, 1971—79, Brearley Sch, 1977—86; bd dirs Solomon R Guggenheim Mus, 1985—95, Schumann Fund NJ, 1990—95. Decorated Air Medal. Mem.: Coun Foreign Relations, Century Asn (New York City). Home: 4574 Province Line Rd Princeton NJ 08540-2212 Office: Business News NJ 104 Church St New Brunswick NJ 08901-2002 E-mail: donaldmwilson@cs.com.

WILSON, DONNA RAE, music educator; b. High Point, NC, Feb. 4, 1952; d. David Thomas and Blanche Gallion Wilson; children: Kenny Perkins, Jay Beverly, David Perkins. MusB, Appalachian State U., Boone, NC, 1970—74; MusM, U. NC, Greensboro, NC, 1986—88; student, Guilford Tech. C.C., High Point, NC, 2001—. Pvt. music instr. Perkins Music Studio, Wallburg, NC, 1975—90; organist/choir dir. Montlieu United Meth., High Point, NC, 1990—2000; music prof. Guilford Tech. C.C., High Point, NC, 2000—. Music tchr. Ledford Mid. Sch., Thomasville, NC, 1988—2000. Prodr.: (musical productions) Let Freedom Sing, Change Your World, Gotta Be Free. Music dir., heart and soul singers ARC-Adult Retarded Citizens of Guilford County, High Point, NC, 2004. Recipient Tchr. Yr. award, 1994. Home: PO Box 6726 High Point NC 27262 Office: Guilford Tech Cmty Coll 901 South Main St High Point NC 27260 Office Phone: 336-454-1126 3030. E-mail: rayolife@yahoo.com.

WILSON, DORIS H. volunteer; b. Akron, Ohio, Jan. 26, 1921; d. Charles Peter and Emma Clara (Howald) Huff; m. Angus Francis Wilson, June 14, 1952; children: Ann Wilson Lambertus, Lea Wilson MacInnis. BS, U. Akron, 1945; postgrad., Framingham State Coll., 1965, Salem State Coll., 1968. Adminstrv. asst. divsn. comml. engr. Ohio Bell Tel. Co., Akron, 1941-52; adminstr. Framingham Ctr. Kindergarten and Nursery Sch., 1965-68. Author: (book) A History of Great Neck, Ipswich, 1984, 1996. Vol. nurse's aide ARC, Akron, 1940; mem. Gov.'s Coun. Civilian Def., Boston, 1960—66; co-founder, charter mem. Hospice at Home, Wayland, Weston, Natick, Sudbury, Mass., 1978; chmn. W. Suburban Area Boston Symphony Orch., 1978—81; docent Gt. Ho. at Castle Hill, Ipswich, Mass., 1984—, Whipple Ho., Ipswich, 1985—2002; treas. Nuc. Freeze Coun., Ipswich, 1986—87; charter mem., bd. dirs. Aplastic Anemia Found. Am. New Eng. region, Brookline, Mass., 1987—92; vol. office asst. Habitat for Humanity, St. Petersburg, Fla., 1988. Recipient Election Poll Officer citation, Gov. of Mass., 1980, 1st pl. Ann. Short Story Contest, Gen. Fedn. Women's Club, 2002. Mem.: AAUW (charter, pres. Framingham-Wellesley br., pres. North Shore br., Mass. state parliamentarian 1966—76, grantee 1974), Friends Glen Magna (Danvers, Mass. dir. 1991—93), Peace Action, Ipswich Hist. Soc., Boston Symphony Assn. Vols., Ipswich Bay Yacht Club (dir. 1981—82), Ipswich Women's Club, Wayland Women's Club (hon.; pres.). Democrat. Roman Catholic. Home: 8 Bowdoin Rd Ipswich MA 01938-2807

WILSON, DOUGLAS, genetics company executive; COO 21st Century Genetics Cooperative, 1994—. Office: 21st Century Genetics Coop 100 Mbc Dr Shawano WI 54166-6095

WILSON, E. B. business executive, consultant, writer; b. Albany, N.Y., May 13, 1931; s. Harold Edgar and Marie Elizabeth (Brush) W.; m. Mary Beth Weilbacher, Aug. 2, 1956. BA, St. Lawrence U., 1953, PhD (hon.), 2002; MBA, Harvard U., 1955. Mkt. dir. Richardson-Vicks, Inc., N.Y.C., Paris, Manila, 1957-64; CEO Japan Kimberly-Clark Corp., Neenah, Wis., 1964-68, 1968-71; pres., CEO French ops. Kimberly-Clark, Corp., Neenah, Wis., 1968—73; v.p. internat. div., gen. mgr. Pillsbury Co., Mpls., 1971-76; exec. v.p. Shaklee Corp., San Francisco, 1976-79; pres., CEO Almay Cosmetics, Inc., N.Y.C., 1979-84, Hathaway Group of Warnaco, N.Y.C., 1984—89; chmn. Global Brands, Inc., N.Y.C., 1989—; found., pres. EBI, Inc., Chatham, Mass., 1995—. Chmn., chief exec. officer Sero Co., Branford, Conn., Mortin Jonap, Ltd., Hauppauge, N.Y.; bd. dirs. William Schneider, Inc., Miami, HMI, Inc., Norwood, Mass. Author: The Committee on Trustees, 2001; contbr. to columns Trusteeship jour. Trustee St. Lawrence U., Canton, N.Y., 1986-2001, chmn. bd. trustees, 1995-2001, Boston Conservatory, 2000-, San Francisco Ballet, 1978, New Horizons Project, Cambridge, Mass., 2001-; devel. dir. Cen. Park Conservancy, N.Y.C., 1983-89. With USAR, 1955-57. Mem. Eastward Ho Club (v.p., gov., 1985-91), Harvard Club N.Y., Harvard Club Boston, Eagle Scout. Republican. Avocations: cooking, running, golf, reading, international travel. Home and Office: 1114 Orleans Rd North Chatham MA 02650 E-mail: ebi@cape.com.

WILSON, E. DAVID, toy company executive; Sr. v.p., sales Hasbro, Inc., Parker Brothers; pres. Milton Bradley, 1990—95, Hasbro Games Group, 1995—97, Hasbro Americas, 1997—99; sr. v.p. & sector head, games Hasbro, Inc., 1999—2001, pres., games, 2001—. Office: Hasbro Inc 1027 Newport Ave Pawtucket RI 02862*

WILSON, E. DOTSON, legislative staff member; b. Jan. 2, 1954; s. Edward James and Sheila Frances Wilson; m. Jacqueline R. Wilson, Apr. 3, 1993; 1 child, Nicole. BA, UCLA, 1976; JD, U. Calif., San Francisco, 1979. Floor mgr. Calif. Assembly, 1984-88, dep. chief of staff, Speaker Willie L. Brown, Jr., 1988-91, chief clk., parliamentarian, 1992—. Acitve Assembly Fellowship Bd.; former bd. dirs. Women's Civic Improvement Club. Mem.: 100 Black Men of Sacramento. Address: State Capitol Bldg Rm 3196 Sacramento CA 95814

WILSON, EDWARD CONVERSE, JR., oil and natural gas production company executive; b. Cambridge, Mass., Jan. 1, 1928; s. Edward Converse and Jean (McLean) W.; m. Patricia Ann Cairns, Sept. 10, 1953; children— Amy Cairns, Sarah Converse. AB, Harvard U., 1949. Brokerage trainee Estabrook & Co., Boston, 1951; Midwest Stock Exch. clk. Paul H. Davis & Co., Chgo., 1951-52; mem. Chgo. Bd. Trade, 1952-78, dir., 1966-67, chmn., 1970-71; ptnr. Nolan & Wilson Co. (specialists on Midwest Stock Exchange), 1965-72; sr. ptnr. Wilson Prodn. Co., Ft. Smith, Ark., 1972-74. Mem. devel. com. Chgo. chpt. Nat. Multiple Sclerosis Soc., 1970; mem. vis. com. on univ. resources Harvard, 1971-74, 76-81; Bd. dirs. Franklin Blvd. Community Hosp., 1970-74. Served with USAAF, 1946-47. Mem. Racquet Club (Chgo.). Home: 11114 Wickwood Dr Houston TX 77024-7523

WILSON, EDWARD LAWRENCE, civil engineering educator, structural engineering consultant; b. Ferndale, Calif., Sept. 5, 1931; s. James Charles and Josephine (Christen) W.; m. Barbara Diane Farrington, July 24, 1960; children— Michael Edward, Teresa Diane AA, Sacramento City Coll., 1952; BS, U. Calif.-Berkeley, 1954, MS, 1958, D.Eng., 1962. Bridge engr. State of Calif., Sacramento, 1953-64; research engr. Aerojet Gen. Corp., Sacramento, 1963-65; from asst. prof. to assoc. prof. U. Calif.-Berkeley, 1965-72, prof. computational methods for structural analysis, 1972-99, prof. emeritus, 1999—; pres. Structural Analysis Programs, Inc., El Cerrito, Calif., 1980—. Dir. BCDC, San Francisco Author numerous papers, reports. Served with U.S. Army, 1955-56; Korea Recipient E.E. Howard award ASCE, 1995. Mem. ASCE, Structural Engring. Assn. No. Calif., Nat. Acad. Engring. Home: 1050 Leneve Pl El Cerrito CA 94530-2750

WILSON, EDWARD NATHAN, mathematician, educator; b. Warsaw, N.Y., Dec. 2, 1941; s. Hugh Monroe and Margaret Jane (Northrup) W.; m. Mary Katherine Schooling, Aug. 19, 1976; children: Nathan Edward, Emily Katherine. BA, Cornell U., 1963; MS, Stanford U., 1965; PhD, Washington U., St. Louis, 1971. Instr. Ft. Valley (Ga.) State Coll., 1965-67, Washington U., St. Louis, 1968-69, U. Calif., Irvine, 1970-71, Brandeis U., Waltham, Mass., 1971-73; asst. prof. Washington U., St. Louis, 1973-77, assoc. prof., 1977-87, dean grad. sch., 1983-93, dean univ. coll., 1986-88, prof., 1987—, chair dept. math., 1995-99. Mem. Grad. Record Exams. Bd., Princeton, N.J., 1986-90; sec.-treas. Assn. Grad. Schs. Contbr. articles to profl. jours. Mem. Brentwood Sch. Bd., Mo., 1984. Woodrow Wilson fellow, 1963; NSF fellow, 1963-65; NDEA fellow, 1967-70. Mem. Am. Math. Soc., Math. Assn. of Am. Democrat. Office: Washington U Campus Box 1146 1 Brookings Dr Saint Louis MO 63130-4899 Office Phone: 314-935-6729. E-mail: enwilson@math.wustl.edu.

WILSON, EDWARD OSBORNE, biologist, educator, writer; b. Birmingham, Ala., June 10, 1929; s. Edward Osborne and Inez (Freeman) W.; m. Irene Kelley, Oct. 30, 1955; 1 child, Catherine Irene. BS, U. Ala., 1949, MS, 1950, LHD (hon.), 1980; PhD, Harvard U., 1955; DPhil, Uppsala (Sweden) U.; DSc (hon.), Duke U., 1978, Grinnell Coll., 1978, U. West Fla., 1979, Lawrence U., 1979, Fitchburg State Coll., 1989, Macalester Coll., 1990, U. Mass., 1990, Oxford U., 1993, Ripon Coll., 1994, U. Conn., 1995, Ohio U., 1996, Bates Coll., 1996, Coll. Wooster, 1997, U. Guelph, 1997, U. Portland, 1997; LHD (hon.), Hofstra U., 1986, Muhlenburg Coll., 1998, Yale U., 1998, Pa. State U., Bradford Coll., 1997, Conn. Coll., 2000, U. S. Ala., 2003; DHC, U. Madrid Complutense, 1995, Conn. Coll., 2000; LLD, Simon Fraser U.; DrRerNat, U. Würzburg, 2000; DSc (hon.), Kenyon Coll., 2002, U. of the South, 2002, U. South Ala., 2003, Harvard U., 2004. Jr. fellow Soc. Fellows, Harvard U., 1953—56, mem. faculty, 1956—, Baird prof. sci., 1976—94, Pellegrino U. prof., 1994—97, univ. rsch. prof., 1997—2002, curator entomology, 1971—97, hon. curator entomology, 1997—. Mem. selection com. Guggenheim Found., 1982—89; bd. dirs. World Wildlife Fund, 1983—94, Orgn. Tropical Studies, 1984—91, N.Y. Bot. Garden, 1991—95, Am. Mus. Natural History, 1992—2002, Am. Acad. Liberal Edn., 1993—, Nature Conservancy, 1994—2002, Conservation Internat., 1997—. Author: The Insect Societies, 1971, Sociobiology: The New Synthesis, 1975, On Human Nature, 1978 (Pulitzer prize for non-fiction, 1979), Promethean Fire, 1983, Biophilia, 1984, Success and Dominance in Ecosystems, 1990, The Diversity of Life, 1992 (Nat. Wildlife Assn. award, Deutsche Umweltstiftung Book award, Sir Peter Kent Conservation prize), Naturalist, 1994 (L.A. Times Book prize sci., 1995), In Search of Nature, 1996, Consilience: The Unity of Knowledge, 1998 (Forkosch award Internat. Acad. Humanism, 2000), Biological Diversity: The Oldest Human Heritage, 1999, The Future of Life, 2002 (Natural World Book prize, U.K., 2002), Pheidole in the New World: A Dominant, Hyperdiverse Ant Genus, 2003 (Julia Ward Howe prize, 2003); author: (with R.H. MacArthur) The Theory of Island Biogeography, 1967; author: (with C.J. Lumsden) Genes, Mind and Culture, 1981; author: (with Bert Holldobler) The Ants, 1990 (Pulitzer prize for non-fiction, 1991), Journey to the Ants, 1994 (Phi Beta Kappa prize sci., 1995); others. Recipient Cleve.-AAAS rsch. prize, 1967, Nat. Medal Sci., 1976, Leidy medal, Acad. Natural Sci., Phila., 1979, Disting. Svc. award, Am. Inst. Biol. Scis., 1976, Mercer award, Ecol. Soc. Am., 1971, Archie Carr medal, U. Fla., 1978, Tyler Ecology prize, 1984, Silver medal, Nat. Zool. Park, German Ecol. Inst. prize, 1987, Weaver award scholarly letters, Ingersoll Found., 1989, Crafoord prize, Royal Swedish Acad. Scis., 1990, Prix d'Inst. de la Vie, Paris, 1990, Revelle medal, 1990, Gold medal, Worldwide Fund for Nature, 1990, Achievement award, Nat. Wildlife Fedn., 1992, Shaw medal, Mo. Bot. Garden, 1993, Internat. prize biology, Govt. of Japan, 1993, Eminent Ecologist award, 1994, Audubon award, Audubon Soc., 1995, Pub. Understanding Sci. award, AAAS, 1995, John Hay award, Orion Soc., 1995, Schubert prize, Germany, 1996, Washburn award, Mus. Sci., 1996, Hutchinson medal, Garden Club Am., 1997, Stone award, New Eng. Aquarium, 1999, Nonino prize, Letters and Sci., Italy, 2000, King Faisal Internat. prize for sci., 2000, Kistler prize, Found. for the Future, 2000, Phillips Meml. medal, World Conservation Union, 2000, Lewis Thomas prize, Rockefeller U., 2001, Nierenberg prize, Scripps Oceanographic Inst., 2001, Thoreau medal, Thoreau Soc., 2001, Lifetime Achievement award, Time, 2001, Global Environment Citizens award, Harvard U., 2001, Busk medal, Royal Geog. Soc., 2002, Presdl. medal, Republic of Italy, 2002, Silver Cross of Christopher Columbus, Dominican Republic, 2003, others; fellow Guggenheim Found., 1978. Fellow: Deutsche Akad. Naturforsch, Am. Philos. Soc. (Franklin medal 1998), Am. Acad. Arts and Scis.; mem.: NAS, others, Royal Soc. Sci. Uppsala (Sweden), Russian Acad. Nat. Sci., Royal Entomol. Soc. (hon. life), Finnish Acad. Sci. and Letters, Royal Soc. London, Netherlands Entomol. Soc. (hon. life), Royal Soc. Edinburgh (life), Assn. Tropical Biology (hon. life), Acad. Humanism (hon. life), Am. Humanist Assn. (Disting. Svc. award 1982, hon. life, Humanist of Yr.), Zool. Soc. London (hon. life), Entomol. Soc. Am. (Founders Meml. award 1972, L.O. Howard award 1985, hon. life), Brit. Ecol. Soc. (hon. life), Am. Genetics Assn. (hon. life). Home: Apt A-208 1010 Waltham St Lexington MA 02421 Office: Harvard U Mus Comparative Zoology Cambridge MA 02138 Office Phone: 617-495-2315. Business E-Mail: ewilson@oeb.harvard.edu.

WILSON, EDWIN, theater critic, educator; b. Nashville, Tenn., Nov. 10, 1927; s. E. Edwin and Catherine (Jones) Wilson; m. Catherine Stuart, July 8, 1967. BA cum laude, Vanderbilt U., 1950; Grad. diploma in English, U. Edinburgh, Scotland, 1951; MFA, Yale U., 1957, DFA, 1958. Prof. Yale U. Drama Sch., New Haven, 1957—58, 1961—62, Hofstra U., 1958—60, Vanderbilt U., Nashville, 1959; prof. Grad. Ctr. Hunter Coll. CUNY, N.Y.C., 1966—91; theater critic Wall St. Jour., N.Y.C., 1972—94, sr. cultural writer,

1994—96; moderator TV interviews CUNY-TV, PBS, N.Y.C., 1989—93; chair dept. theater and film CUNY Hunter Coll., 1980—83; v.p. faculty Hunter Coll., N.Y.C., 1973—75; exec. dir. Martin E. Segal Theater Ctr. Hunter Coll., 1987—2003. Mem. N.Y. Drama Critics Cir., 1972—94, pres., 1982—84; mem. Pulitzer Prize Drama Jury, 1977—78, 1979—80, 2000—03; mem. nominating com. Tony awards, N.Y.C., 1975—77, N.Y.C., 1988—99; rep USIA to Romania and German Dem. Republic, 1984. Author: The Theater Experience, 1976, 9th edit., 2004; co-author (with Alvin Goldfarb): Lively Art 4th edit., 2002, Lving Theater 4th edit., 2004; editor (and introduction author): Shaw on Shakespeare, 1961; dir.: (plays, for profl companies as well as student performers.); prodr.(numerous off-Broadway plays and one Broadway Play): Agatha Sue I Love You; playwright: plays Waterfall, The Bettinger Prize, Musical Great Expectations. Pres. Theater Devel. Fund, 1982—84; mem. playwright's com. Rockefeller Found., 1983—86; bd. dir. Theater Devel. Fund, 1981—2003, 1981—, John Golden Fund, 1980—. Grantee grant to report on contemporary Japanese theatre, Milwaukee Rep and Japanese-Am. Friendship Commn., 1978—79. Mem.: Am. Theater Critics Assn., Century Assn., Coffee House Club, Phi Beta Kappa. Home: 55 Central Park W New York NY 10023-5003

WILSON, ELDON RAY, minister; b. Tieton, Wash., Apr. 16, 1931; s. Frank Madison and Beatrice Jane (Snider) W.; m. LouCelle Charlotte Seward, Aug. 3, 1957; children: Randall Wayne, Gary Ray. BTh, Internat. Bible Coll., San Antonio, 1967; PhD, Sussex Coll., Hayward's Heath, Eng., 1972. Ordained to ministry Emmanuel Ch., 1956. Founder, pastor Emmanuel Tabernacle, Port Arthur, Tex., 1958-63; evangelist U.S., Can., 1963-65; founder, pastor Gospel Tabernacle, Ilion, N.Y., 1965-70; pastor Full Gospel Ch., Halifax, N.S., Can., 1970-72; missionary Europe, Africa, 1972-77; founder, pastor New Covenant Ch., Columbus, Ohio, 1977-84; missionary New Covenant Ministries, Columbus, 1984-97; acad. dean City Bible Coll., Utica, N.Y., 1998-2001. Bd. dirs. Good News Mission, Bogota, Colombia, 1985—; trustee Mission Teams Internat., Elkton, Md., 1989—. Author: The New Creation, 1975. Bd. dirs. Kuyahoora Valley Libr., Newport, N.Y., 1985—; overseer Shekinah Ministries, Amsterdam, The Netherlands, Bread of Life Ministries, Bastogne, Belgium. With USN, 1951-55. Republican. Home: 7417 West St Newport NY 13416 Office: PO Box 317 Newport NY 13416 E-mail: loucelle.wilson@juno.com.

WILSON, EMERY ALLEN, university dean, obstetrician-gynecologist, educator; b. Frankfort, Ky., Apr. 8, 1942; s. Emery Lee and Mary Catheryne (Cooper) W.; m. Clara Bullock, June 18, 1966; children: Emily, Bryan. BA, Emory U., 1964; MD, U. Ky., 1968. Diplomate Am. Bd. Ob-Gyn (examiner 1979-89), Am. Bd. Reproductive Endocrinology. Intern, resident U. Ky., 1968-72; instr. Harvard U. Med. Sch., Boston, 1974-76; asst. prof. ob-gyn U. Ky. Coll. Medicine, Lexington, 1976-79, assoc. prof., 1979-81, prof., 1981—, dir. Ctr. for Reproductive Medicine, 1983-87; vice chancellor for clin. svcs., dean Coll. Medicine U. Ky., 1987—. Cons. Nat. Inst. Occupational Safety and Health, Cin., 1980-82; dir. Florence Crittendon House, Lexington, 1986-89. Editor: Nutrition in Pregnancy, 1980, Endometriosis, 1987, Professional Management and Practice Management, 1989; author over 100 articles, book chpts., abstracts; reviewer several profl. jours. Maj. USAF, 1972-74. Recipient Acad. Tng. award Ortho Pharms., 1972. Fellow Am. Coll. Obstetricians and Gynecologists; mem. Am. Fertility Soc., Soc. Gynecologic Investigation, Alpha Omega Alpha, Omicron Delta Kappa. Mem. Christian Ch. (Disciples Of Christ). Home: 967 Edgewater Dr Lexington KY 40502-3011 Office: U Ky Coll Medicine 800 Rose St Lexington KY 40536-0001

WILSON, ERIC F.G. information technology executive; BSc with honors, Guelph U. Sr. v.p., chief info. officer Philip Svcs. Corp., Houston, 1997—2000; sr. v.p. operations, chief tech. officer Fusionstorm, San Francisco, 2000—03; chief info. officer Raley's, West Sacramento, Calif., 2003—. Office: Raleys 500 W Capitol Ave West Sacramento CA 95605

WILSON, EVELYN M. literature educator; b. Minco, Okla., Mar. 17, 1939; d. Elvis L. Funderburk and Josephine Ash-Funderburk; m. Elzie Joseph Wilson, Nov. 27, 1957; children: Gregory Joseph, Michael Dean, Terri Lynne. AA, Tarrant County Coll.; BA, Tex. Wesleyan Coll.; MA, M in Edn. Adminstrn., PhD, Tex. Christian U. Cert. ESOL, remedial, gifted and talented, elem. and secondary edn. Tex., writing cons. Tex., adminstrn. Tex. Bookkeeper, office mgr., Ft. Worth, 1957—59; with billing and bookkeeping staff Calif. Almond Orchards, Passo Robles, Calif., 1959—60; tchr. Rabyor Schs., Inc., Ft. Worth, 1971—73, Hill Elem. Sch. for Gifted and Spl. Edn., Ft. Worth, 1971—78; AP English tchr. Ft. Worth Ind. Sch. Dist., 1978—91; writing cons. FWISD, Ft. Worth, 1984—; editor Hayeman Psychol. Assn., Ft. Worth; assoc. prof. English Tarrant County Coll., 1984—85. Author poetry, essays and revs. Mem.: NEA, AAUW, South Ctrl. MLA, Tchg. English in the Two Yr. Coll., Nat. Coun. Tchrs. English, Two Year Coll. English Assn., Tex. C.C. Tchrs. Assn., Tex. State Tchrs. Assn., Ft. Worth Coun. English Tchrs., Tex. State Coun. English Tchrs., Nat. Coun. English Tchrs., Tex. Jr. Coll. Assn. (senator, mem. ways and means com., acad. stds. com., discipline com., rec. sec. for faculty senate), Delta Kappa Gamma Soc., Internat. (Iota Pi chpt., various positions including rec. sec., v.p., pres., Iota Pi Chpt. Achievement award), Kappa Delta Pi (TCU chpt.). Avocations: tennis, writing, softball, dance, reading. Home: 2308 Fifth Ave Fort Worth TX 76110 Office: Tarrant County Coll 5301 Campus Dr Fort Worth TX 76119

WILSON, EWEN MACLELLAN, economist; b. Nairobi, Kenya, July 29, 1944; came to U.S., 1969; m. Kay Stephens, May 31, 1969; children: Libby, Cindy, Riara. BS, U. London, 1965; MS, W.Va. U., 1970; PhD, N.C. State U., 1973. With conservation and extension dept. Ministry of Agrl., Banket, Rhodesia, 1965-68; research fellow U. Rhodesia, Salisbury, 1973-74; asst. prof. Va. Tech., Blacksburg, 1975-77; dir. econs. and stats. Am. Meat Inst., Arlington, Va., 1977-83, v.p., 1983-85; apptd. dep. asst. sec. U.S. Dept. Agrl., Washington, 1985-87, asst. sec., 1987-89; pres. Wilson Agribus. Analysis, 1989-90; exec. dir. Commodity Futures Trading Commn., Washington, 1990-94; chief agriculture and fin. statistics div. U.S. Census Bur., Washington, 1994-98, chief co. stats. divsn., 1998—. Bd. dirs. Nat. Cooperative Bank, 1988-90, Commodity Credit Corp, 1987-89. Mem.: Nat. Assn. Bus. Econ. Republican. Episcopalian. Office: US Census Bur Csd Rm 1182 Fb 3 Washington DC 20233-6400 E-mail: ewen.m.wilson@census.gov.

WILSON, FAYE, retail executive; Exec. v.p. Bank Am. Corp., San Diego; sr. v.p. value initiatives Home Depot, Atlanta. Office: Home Depot Inc 2455 Paces Ferry Rd SE Atlanta GA 30339-4024

WILSON, FRANCES C. career military officer; BS, Mich. State U.; MEd, Pepperdine U.; MA in Psychology, U. No. Colo.; MS in Bus. Mgmt., Salve Regina Coll.; PhD in Edn., U. So. Calif. Commd. 2d lt. USMC, 1972, advanced through grades to maj. gen.; air traffic control officer Marine Corps Air Sta., Yuma, Ariz., Kaneohe, Hawaii, 1975; tchr. instrnl. mgmt. Marine Corps Devel. & Edn. Ctr., Quantico, Va.; staff sec. 3d Marine Divsn., Okinawa, Japan, 1980-81; asst. prof., co. officer brigade of midshipmen U.S. Naval Acad., Annapolis, Md.; mgmt. analyst HQ USMC, Washington; spl. asst. for gen. and flag officer matters Joint Staff, Pentagon, exec. asst. to vice dir., 1987; comdr. 4th Recruit Tng. Battalion, Parris Island, S.C., 1988-90, Camp H.M. Smith, Svc. Battalion Marine Corps Pacific; sec. Joint Staff, until 1997; commanding gen. Marine Corps Base, Quantico, 1997-99, Third Force Svc. Support Group, Okinawa, Japan, 1999—2001; dir. pers. mgmt. divsn. M&RA Hdqrs. Marine Corps, 2001; comdt. Indsl. Coll. Armed Forces, Nat. Def. U., Ft. McNair, DC. Decorated Def. Superior Svc. medal, Def. Meritorious Svc. medal, Meritorious Svc. medal, Navy Commendation medal, Navy Achievement medal.

WILSON, FRANKLIN D. sociology educator; b. Birmingham, Ala., Sept. 3, 1942; s. Ernest and Ollie Lee (Carter) W.; m. Marion F. Brown; children: Rachel, Chareese BA, Miles Coll., 1964; postgrad., Atlanta U., 1964-65; MA, Wash. State U., 1971, PhD, 1973. Instr. Grambling U., La., 1965-66; William H. Sewell-Bascom prof. sociology U. Wis.-Madison, 1973—, chmn. dept. Afro-Am. studies, 1984-87, chmn. dept. sociology, 1988-91, dir. Ctr. for Demography and Ecology, 1994-99. Author: Residential Consumption, Economic Opportunities and Race, 1979; deputy editor Demography, 1995-98; co-editor Am. Sociol. Rev. Bd. of Census adv. com. Profl. Assns., 1993-99. Served with U.S. Army, 1966-69; Vietnam Decorated Purple Heart, Silver Star, Vietnam medal of Valor; Census fellow Am. Statis. Assn., NSF, 1991-92, Population Coun. fellow, 1971-72. Mem. Population Assn. Am., Sociol. Rsch. Assn., Assn. Black Sociologists. Unitarian Universalist. Avocations: swimming, reading. Office: U Wis Ctr for Demography and Ecology Social Sci Bldg Madison WI 53713 E-mail: wilson@ssc.wisc.edu.

WILSON, FRED, retail executive; Grad., Wabash Coll., 1969. With Federated Dept. Stores, 1969—76, Associated Dry Goods, 1976—79, Duty Free Stores, 1979; pres., CEO splty. store retail divsn. LVMH, 1999—2002; chmn., pres., CEO Donna Karan Internat., 2002—03; pres., CEO, chmn. Saks Fifth Ave. Enterprises, N.Y.C., 2003—. Trustee Wabash Coll., 2001. Office: Saks Fifth Ave 12 E 49th St New York NY 10017*

WILSON, FRED M., II, ophthalmologist, educator; b. Indpls., Dec. 10, 1940; s. Fred Madison and Elizabeth (Fredrick) W.; m. Karen Joy Lyman, Sept. 10, 1959 (div. June 1962); 1 child, Teresa Wilson Kulick; m. Claytonia Leigh Pemberton, Aug. 28, 1964; children: Yvonne Wilson Hacker, Jennifer Wilson DeLong, Benjamin James. AB in Med. Scis., Ind. U., 1962, MD, 1965. Diplomate Am. Bd. Ophthalmology. Intern Sacred Heart Hosp., Spokane, Wash., 1965-66; resident in ophthalmology Ind. U., Indpls., 1968-71, fellow in ophthalmology, 1971-72, F.I. Proctor Found., San Francisco, 1972-73; from asst. prof. to assoc. prof. ophthalmology Ind. U., Indpls., 1972-76, prof. ophthalmology, 1981—. Med. dir. Ind. Lions Eye Bank, Inc., Indpls., 1973-99; cons. surgeon Ind. U., Indpls., 1973—. Contbr. articles to profl. jours., chapters to books. Lt. comdr. USNR, 1966-68, PTO. Mem. Am. Acad. Ophthalmology (assoc. sec. 1988-93, Sr. Teaching award 1989), Assn. Proctor Fellows, Soc. Heed Fellows, Am. Ophthalmol. Soc., Am. Bd. Ophthalmology (bd. dirs. 1993-2000), Ill. Soc. Ophthalmology (hon.), Mont. Acad. Ophthalmology (hon.), Pacific-Coast Ophthalmol. Soc. (hon.). Republican. Avocations: photography, guitar, history, language, natural history. Home: 12262 Crestwood Dr Carmel IN 46033-4323 Office: Ind U Sch Medicine Dept Ophthalmolgy 702 Rotary Cir Indianapolis IN 46202-5133

WILSON, FREDERIC SANDFORD, pharmaceutical company executive; b. Schenectady, NY, Mar. 28, 1944; s. Robert Omer and Isabel May (Sandford) W.; children: Amy Kathleen, Adrienne Ann; m. Judith Ann Goettsche, Feb. 7, 1973; children: Marla Ann, Brian Bennett, Jessica Lea, Jennifer Lynn. BS, Syracuse U., 1968. Acct. exec. Mastropaul Design Inc., Syracuse, N.Y., 1969-70; copy editor Norwich Eaton Pharms., Norwich, N.Y., 1970-72, sales rep. Gary, Ind., 1972-73, asst. product mgr. Norwich, 1974-75, mktg. svcs. mgr., 1975-76, product mgr., 1977-81, bus. devel. mgr., 1981-83, sr. product mgr., 1983-85, mgr. med. foods, 1986-89; assoc. mktg. mgr. P&G Pharms., Norwich, 1989-92; dir. profl. rels. P & G Pharms., Cin., 1993-96; mgr. mktg. svcs. P&G, Cin., 1997-98; category mgr. CME P&G, Cin., 1998—. Cons. Sandoz Nutrition Corp., Mpls., 1992., bd. dir. Nat. Bd. of Osteopathic Med. Examiners. Inventor Jejunostomy Kit, 1981, Vivonex T.E.N. med. food, 1983, Tolerex med. food, 1987. Bd. dirs. Syracuse U. Minority Access Program, 1989-91; mem. Nat. Task Force on CME Provider/Industry Collaboration. Mem.: Global Alliance Med. Edn. (bd. dirs., v.p.). Office: Procter & Gamble Box 2075 8700 Mason-Montgomery Rd Mason OH 45040-9462 Office Phone: 513-622-5456. E-mail: wilson.fs@pg.com.

WILSON, FREDERICK ALLEN, medical educator, medical center administrator, gastroenterologist; b. Winchester, Mass., Aug. 22, 1937; s. Warren Archibald and Alice Jane (Springall) W.; m. Lynne Stewart Cantley, Feb. 24, 1962; children: Douglas, Victoria. AB, Colgate U., 1959; MD, Albany Med. Coll., 1963. Intern Hartford (Conn.) Hosp., 1963-64, resident in medicine, 1964-66; fellow in gastroenterology Albany (NY) Med. Coll., 1966-67; USPHS postdoctoral fellow in gastroenterology U. Tex. Southwestern Med. Sch., Dallas, 1969-72; asst. prof. medicine Vanderbilt U. Sch. Medicine, Nashville, 1972-76, assoc. prof., 1976-82, mem. adv. com. clin. rsch. ctr., 1978-81; prof. medicine, chief div. gastroenterology Milton S. Hershey Med. Ctr., Pa. State U., Hershey, 1982-90; prof. medicine, dir. divsn. gastroenterology Med. U. S.C., Charleston, 1990-94, dir. fellowship tng. program in gastroenterology and hepatology, 1990—2003, now prof. medicine divsn. gastroenterology and hepatology, dept. medicine. Mem. ACP Med. Knowledge Self-Assessment Program VI, 1980-81; mem. gastroenterology and clin. nutrition rev. group Nat. Inst. Arthritis, Diabetes, Digestive and Kidney Disease, NIH, Bethesda, Md., 1985-89; pre-reviewer Am. Coun. Grad. Med. Edn., 1994-95. Contbr. numerous articles, abstracts, chpts. to profl. publs.; reviewer for sci. jours. Served to maj. M.C., U.S. Army, 1967-69. Recipient Clin. Investigator award VA Med. Ctr., Nashville, 1972-75; recipient Investigator award Howard Hughes Med. Inst., Vanderbilt U., 1975-78; NIH Fogarty Internat. Ctr. sr. internat. fellow Max Planck Inst. for Biophysics, Frankfurt, Germany, 1979-80. Mem. Am. Fedn. Clin. Rsch., Ctrl. Soc. Clin. Rsch., Am. Gastroenterology Assn., Am. Assn. Study Liver Diseases, Am. Soc. Clin. Investigation, N.Y. Acad. Scis., SC Med. Assn., Ea. Gut Club, Pa. Soc. Gastroenterology. Office: Med U SC Div Gastroenterology 96 Jonathan Lucas St #210 Charleston SC 29425-0001 Office Phone: 843-792-2301. Business E-Mail: wilsonfa@musc.edu.

WILSON, GAHAN, cartoonist, author; b. Evanston, Ill., Feb. 18, 1930; s. Allen Barnum and Marion (Gahan) W.; m. Nancy Dee Midyette ((Nancy Winters)), Dec. 30, 1966; stepchildren— Randy Winters, Paul Winters. Graduate, Art Inst. Chgo., 1952. Commentator, Nat. Public Radio. Collections include Gahan Wilson's Graveyard Manner, 1965, The Man In the Cannibal Pot, 1967, I Paint What I See, 1971, Weird World of Gahan Wilson, 1975, Gahan Wilson's Cracked Cosmos, 1975, First World Fantasy Collection Anthology, 1977, Gahan Wilson's Favorite Tales of Horror, 1977, And Then We'll Get Him, 1978, Nuts, 1979, Chog: A Gothic Fable, 1980, Is Nothing Sacred, 1982, Wilson's America, 1985, Eddy Deco's First Case, 1987, Playboy's Gahan Wilson, 1980, Eddy Deco's Last Caper, 1989, Still Weird, 1994; juvenile works: Harry, The Fat Bear Spy, 1973, The Bang Bang Family, 1974, Harry and the Sea Serpent, 1976, Harry and the Snow Melting Ray, 1980; editor: First World Fantasy Awards, 1977, The Raven & Other Poems, 1990; illustrator: Matthew Looney & the Space Pirates, 1972, Catch Your Breath: A Book of Shivery Poems, 1973, Granny's Fish Story, 1975, Maria Looney & The Cosmic Circus, 1978, Maria Looney & The Remarkable Robot, 1979, Bob Fulton's Amazing Soda-Pop Stretcher, 1982, Plots & Pans, 1989, How To Be A Guilty Parent, Murder For Christmas, Passport to World Band Radio, 1992, The Keep of Two Moons, 1992, The Keep of Two Moons, 1992, A Night in the Lonesome October, 1993, Credo!: The Game of Dueling Dogmas, 1993, A Night in the Lonesome October, 1993, Spooky Stories For A Dark & Stormy Night, 1994; co-editor: Animals, Animals, Animals, 1979; co-author: The Upside-Down Man, 1977, Hairticklers, 1989, The Devil's Dictionary & Other Works; author: Everybody's Favorite Duck, 1989; animator (movie): Gahan Wilson's Diner, 1993; contbr. to Nat. Lampoon, New Yorker, Collier's, Look, Playboy, Punch, Esquire, Fantasy and Sci. Fiction, Paris Match, Pardon. Mem. Mystery Writers Am., Sci. Fiction Writers Am., Soc. Illustrators, Wolfe Pack, Cartoonists Assn. Commentator, Horror Writers Am. (Life Achievement award 1992), Writers Guild East, Authors Guild, Nat. Public Radio. Office: HMH Pubs care Readers Svc 919 N Michigan Ave Chicago IL 60611-1681

WILSON, GAYLE ANN, civic worker; b. Phoenix, Nov. 24, 1942; d. Clarence Arthur and Charlotte Evelyn (Davison) Edlund; m. Theodore William Graham, Sept. 14, 1963 (div. May 1983); children: Todd Chandler, Philip Edlund; m. Pete Wilson, May 29, 1983. BA, Stanford U., 1965; postgrad., U. San Diego, 1982. First lady State of Calif., Sacramento, 1991-99; bd. directors ARCO, Los Angeles, CA, 1999—. Adv. for early childhood health and improved math. and sci. edn.; bd. dirs. Ctr. for Excellence in Edn., McLean, Va., 1985—, also former chmn.; mem. Jr. League San Diego, 1968—, also past pres.; bd. dirs. Calif. Inst. Tech., Pasadena, 1995—, Children's Inst. Internat., Phoenix House; former spokesperson Access for Infants and Mothers (AIM), Calif. Breast Cancer Initiative, Never Shake a Baby Campaign, Partnership for Responsible Parenting; mem. Calif. Sesquicentennial Commn.; hon. chmn. Calif. Sci. Fair, Calif. 4-H Found., Calif. Perinatal Outreach-BabyCal, Calif. Commn. on Improving Life Through Svc., Keep Calif. Beautiful; hon. co-chmn. Calif. Mentor Initiative; mem. adv. coun. Ct. Apptd. Spl. Advs.; mem. adv. coun. computers in schs. program Detweiler Found.; hon. chmn. bd. dirs. Leland Stanford Mansion Restoration Found.; founding mem. Achievement Rewards for Coll. Scientists; mem. San Diego Park and Recreation Commn., 1980-83; regent Children's Hosp. L.A. Found., 1998—; bd. dirs. Center Theatre Group, L.A., 1998—, ARCO. Recipient Guardian Angel award L.A. ChildShare, 1995, lifetime achievemecnt award Jr. League L.A., 1996. Mem. Phi Beta Kappa. Republican. Avocations: lyric writing, singing, performing, watercolors. Office: 2132 Century Park Ln Apt 301 Los Angeles CA 90067-3320

WILSON, GEORGE PETER, international organization executive; b. Perth, Scotland, July 6, 1935; came to U.S., 1985; s. Alan Johnson and Doris L. (Allan) W.; m. Sandra Graham, Feb. 6, 1960 (div. 1984); 1 child, Iain; m. Robbyn Dee LaCroix, Nov. 17, 1984; 1 stepchild, Orion. Diploma in Hotel Mgmt., Scottish Coll. Commerce, Glasgow, 1954. Chartered acct., 1965, cert. internal auditor, 1985. Hotel mgr., auditor Can. Nat. Rys., Ottawa and Montreal, 1956-65; fin. officer Treasury Bd. Can., asst. sec. to Cabinet, dir. Pub. Service Commn., counsellor external affairs Govt. of Can., Ottawa, Geneva, 1965-78; dir. gen. audit UN, N.Y.C., 1978-80; dep. auditor gen. of Can. Govt. of Can., Ottawa, 1980-85; pres. Inst. Internal Auditors, Orlando, Fla., 1985-92; dir. audit FAO UN, Rome, 1992-97, insp. gen., 1997—2003; pres. The Orion Group, Orlando, Fla., 2003—. Contbr. articles to profl. jours. Mem. Can. Inst. Chartered Accts. (com. mem.), Inst. Internal Auditors (com. mem.), Can. Comprehensive Audit Found. (gov. 1985-88), Internat. Consortium on Govt. Fin. Mgmt. (bd. dirs. 1983-92), Inst. for Fin. Crime Prevention. Home: 312 Charleston Pl Celebration FL 34747 E-mail: gpwilsonfl@aol.com.

WILSON, GERALD EVERETTE, financial executive; b. Houston, Nov. 2, 1953; s. Clifford Dennis and Naomi Betty (Falls) W.; m. Marsherria Ervin, Aug. 14, 1974; 1 child, Gerrad Everette. BA in Econs., MA in Econs., Stanford U., 1976; MS in Acctg., U. Houston, 1978. CPA, Tex.; cert. fin. planner. Mem. staff Arthur Young & Co., Houston, 1976-80, mgr., 1980-84, prin., 1984-86; founder, pres., chmn. bd. dirs. Wilson Fin. Group, Inc., Houston, 1986—. Bd. dirs. Cedar Crest Funeral Home Inc., Dallas, Thompson Funeral Home Inc., Sacramento, So. Funeral Home Inc., Memphis, Whitehaven Chapel Inc., Memphis, Mainland Funeral Home, LaMarque, Tex., Morris-Bates Funeral Home, Ft. Worth, Paradise Funeral Home, Houston, Carl Barnes Funeral Home, Inc., Houston. Bd. dirs. Stanford U. Athletic Bd., Palo Alto, Calif., 1985—, Leadership Houston, 1985-87, Houston Proud, 1988; chmn. sec. Steering Com. Harris County Parks, Tex., 1986—; mem. adv. bd. Houston Ind. Sch. Dist., 1986—. Named Outstanding Young Houstonian Houston Jaycees, 1985, Outstanding Young Texan Tex. Jaycees, 1985, Outstanding Black Houstonian Riverside Hosp., 1986. Mem. Am. Inst. CPA's, Tex. Soc. CPA's, Inst. Fin. Planning, Houston C. of C., Katy C. of C. Democrat. Baptist. Avocations: golf, jogging. Office: 15415 Katy Fwy Ste 611 Houston TX 77094-1816

WILSON, GLEN PARTEN, professional society administrator; b. Waco, Tex., Dec. 10, 1922; s. Glen P. and Hazel (Parnell) W. BS in Aero. Engring., U. Tex., Austin, 1943, MA in Psychology, 1948, PhD in Psychology, 1952. Engr. Lockheed Aircraft Co., Burbank, Calif., 1943-44; teaching fellow, rsch. asst., instr. U. Tex., Austin, 1946-52; rsch. psychologist USAF, Lackland AFB, Tex., 1952-53; gen. mgr. Tex. Ednl. Devices Co., Austin, 1953-54; asst. to Senator Lyndon B. Johnson Washington, 1955-57; staff Senate Preparedness Investigating Subcom. and Senate Spl. Com. on Space and Astronautics, Washington, 1957-59; chief clk., profl. staff mem. Senate Com. on Aero. and Space Scis., Washington, 1959-77; cons. Washington, 1977-79; spl. asst. for student activities NASA, Washington, 1979-80, acting dir. acad. affairs div., 1980-82; pres. Marie D. and Glen P. Wilson Found., Washington, 1982-87; exec. dir. Nat. Space Soc., Washington, 1984-88, exec. dir. emeritus, 1988—. Lectr. on aero. and space programs, Senate orgn., sci. policy, tech. assessment, student activities, space activism. Participant as staff passage of Nat. Aeros. and Space Act, 1958, Communications Satellite Act, 1962, NASA Authorization Acts, 1958-77; editor Policy Planning for Aeronautical Rsch. and Devel., Senate Document 90, 89th Congress, 1966; developer NASA shuttle student involvement program, 1980, space edn. orgn., 1984—. With USN, 1944-46. Recipient Exceptional Svc. medal NASA, 1981; named Disting. Engring. Grad., U. Tex. Coll. Engring., Austin, 2000; Nat. Space Soc. Hdqrs. renamed The Glen P. Wilson Internat. Space Ctr., 1988. Mem. AIAA (spl. presdl. citation 1976), AAAS, Nat. Space Soc., Internat. Acad. of Astronautics, Sigma Xi, Nat. Space Club, Cosmos Club.

WILSON, GLENN, economist, educator; b. East St. Louis, Ill., Feb. 4, 1929; s. Herschel and Regina (Hayes) W.; m. Helen Janice O'Dell, Jan. 28, 1951; children— David, Thomas, Ann. BA, U. Okla., 1951; MA, 1952. Adminstr., Welfare and Retirement Fund United Mine Workers, Pitts., Knoxville, Tenn., 1952-58; dir. med. care research Nationwide Ins. Co., Columbus, 1958-62; exec. dir. Community Health Found., Cleve., 1962-68; exec. v.p. Kaiser Community Health Found., Cleve., 1968-69; assoc. dean U. N.C. Med. Sch., Chapel Hill, 1970-88, prof. dept. social medicine, 1977—, chmn. dept., 1977-89. Cons. Sault Ste. Marie and Dist. Group Health Assn.; health adv. Mayor Stokes, Cleve., 1967-69 Contbr. articles to profl. jours. Home: 214 Glandon Dr Chapel Hill NC 27514-3816 Office: U NC Med Sc Dept Social Medicine Chapel Hill NC 27514

WILSON, H. DAVID, dean; b. West Frankfort, Ill., Sept. 13, 1939; m. Jeannette Wilson; children: Jennifer, Jacqueline, Mary Jeanne. AB in Zoology, Wabash Coll., 1961; MD, St. Louis Sch. Medicine, 1966. Diplomate Nat. Bd. Med. Examiners, Am. Bd. Pediatrics. Intern pediatrics Cardinal Glennon Meml. Hosp. for Children, St. Louis U., 1966—67; resident dept. pediatrics U. Ky. Med. Ctr., Lexington, 1967—68, chief resident, 1968—69; NIH rsch. fellow U. Tex. Health Scis. Ctr., Dallas, 1971—73; fellowship Am. Coun. on Edn., 1988—89; dir. admissions Coll. of Medicine, U. Ky., 1986—88; assoc. dean for acad. affairs, prof. Coll. Medicine, U. Ky., 1989—95; dean, prof. U. N.D. Sch. of Medicine, Grand Forks, 1995—, v.p. for health affairs, 2001—. Author: (TV series) For Kids Sake, 1987-88; dir. pediatric infectious diseases U. Ky. Med. Ctr., Lexington, 1973-95, dir. cystic fibrosis care and tchg. ctr., 1975-80, med. dir., clin. virology lab., 1982-95; staff United Hosp., Grand Forks, 1995—; elected univ. senate U. Ky., 1993-96, bd. trustees Gluck Equine Rsch. Found., 1991-95, rules and elections univ. senate standing com., 1991-92, steering com. for U.K. self-study, 1990-95, co-chmn. steering com., 1990-95, chmn. review and search com. for chmn. dept. obstetrics and gynecology, 1990, chmn. curriculum com. Coll. of Medicine, 1989-95; elected acad. coun. of med. ctr. U. Ky. Med. Ctr., 1989-92; lectr. in field. Contbr. numerous articles to profl. jours. Fellow Pediatric Infectious Dieseases Soc.; mem. AMA, Am. Soc. of Microbiology, Am. Thoracic Soc., Am. Acad. Pediatrics, Pan Am. Group for Rapid Viral Diagnosis. Home: 10 Shadyridge Estates Grand Forks ND 58201 Office: U ND Sch Medicine & Health Scis 501 North Columbia Rd Grand Forks ND 58202-9037

WILSON, HAROLD BATTING, treasurer; b. NYC, June 24, 1910; s. William Johnson and May LaForest Wilson; m. Edna Anita Helmling, Jan. 9, 1937 (dec. Apr. 1996). Cert. profiency in acct. and bus. law, Fordham U., 1930—32. Registered pub. acct., N.Y., 1974; cert. data processor Data Processing Mgmt. Assn., 1963, computer technology Inst. Advanced Technology, 1967. Office boy Arthur Andersen & Co., NYC, 1929—32, acct./auditor, 1933—38; acct. Office of Comptr., NYC, 1938—40; prin. systems analyst Divsn. of Employment, NY State, Albany, 1941—70; investment adv. Registered with S.E.C., Naples, Fla., 1975—90; treas. Theatre '90 Inc., Syracuse, NY, 1990—. Corp. dir. Theatre '90 Inc., Syracuse, 1990—. Author: (book) How to Beat Wall St., 1991. Sgt. USAF, 1943—45, US. Recipient NY State cert. of merit, Gov. Nelson A. Rockefeller, 1971. Mem.: SAR Nat. Soc. Avocations: writing, sports. Home: 7235 Canton St Rd Baldwinsville NY 13027

WILSON, H(AROLD) FRED(ERICK), chemist, research scientist; b. Columbiana, Ohio, Aug. 15, 1922; s. Lloyd Ralph and Erma Rebecca (Frederick) W.; m. Alice Marjorie Steer, Aug. 20, 1949; children: Janice, Deborah, James, Kathleen. BA, Oberlin Coll., 1947; PhD, U. Rochester, 1950. With Rohm & Haas Co., Phila., 1950-83, beginning as rsch. scientist,

successively lab. head, rsch. supr., asst. dir., assoc. dir., dir. rsch., 1950-74, v.p., 1974-83, chief sci. officer, from 1981; now with Wilson Assocs., Cape May, N.J. Mem. U.S. nat. com. IUPAC, 1977-84, vice chmn., 1980-82, chmn., 1982-84, fin. com., 1979-89, chmn., 1981-89; chmn. I.R.I. Research Corp., 1980-82, dir., 1979-82 Patentee in field. Served to 1st lt. USAAF, 1942-46. Decorated Air Medal. Mem. Am. Chem. Soc., AAAS, Soc. Chem. Industry, Dirs. Indsl. Research. Home: 5203 Twin Silo Dr Blue Bell PA 19422 E-mail: hfwilson44@comcast.net.

WILSON, HEATHER ANN, congresswoman; b. Keene, N.H., Dec. 30, 1960; d. George Douglas Wilson and Martha Lou Wilson-Kernozicky. m. Jay Hone; 3 children. BS, USAF Acad., 1982; M. Philosophy, Oxford U., 1984, PhD, 1985. U.S. mission NATO, Brussels, 1987-89, Nat. Security Coun., Washington, 1989-91; pres. Keystone Internat., Inc., Albuquerque, 1991-95; cabinet sec. N.Mex. Dept. Children, Youth and Families, Santa Fe, 1995-98; mem. U.S. Congress from 1st N.Mex. Dist., Washington, 1998—; mem. armes svcs. com., energy and commerce com. Adj. prof. U. N.Mex.; mem. Def. Adv. Com. on Women in the Svcs. Contbr. articles to profl. jours. Capt. USAF, 1982-89. Rhodes scholar, 1982. Republican. Avocations: parenting, hiking, skiing. Office: 318 Cannon House Office Blg Washington DC 20515-3101 E-mail: ask.heather@mail.house.gov.

WILSON, HENRY ARTHUR, JR., management consultant; b. Detroit, June 12, 1939; s. Henry Arthur and Ruth (Scott) W.; m. Mildred Rendell, June 17, 1961; 1 child, Suzanne. BS, Mich. Luth. Coll., 1968; MA, U. Detroit, 1976. Police officer Grosse Pointe Park Police Dept., Mich., 1960-68; v.p. Uniflight, Inc., St. Clare Shore, Mich., 1968-73; coord. Criminal Justice Inst., Detroit, 1973-76; ptnr. Grant Thorton (formerly Alexander Grant & Co.), Detroit, 1976-92; pres., owner Thunderboat Racing, Inc., 1998. Grand sec., CEO Grand Lodge F & A.M., Mich., CEO Mich. Masonic Home; pres., CEO, Mich. Masonic Home Charitably Found., 1996-97, Author Masonic Etiquette and Protocol, 1985. Sr. warden St. Columba Episcopal Ch., Detroit, 1976—; bd. dirs. Grosse Pointe Yacht Club, 1997-99. Served with USAF, 1957-60. Mem. Cert. Data Processing Auditors Assn., Masons (grand master Mich. 1984-85). Republican. Avocation: boating. Office: 3516 Cadleux Rd Detroit MI 48226

WILSON, HUGH STEVEN, lawyer; b. Paducah, Ky., Nov. 27, 1947; s. Hugh Gipson and Rebekah (Dunn) W.; m. Clare Maloney, Apr. 28, 1973; children: Zachary Hunter, Samuel Gipson. BS, Ind. U., 1968; JD, U. Chgo., 1971; LLM, Harvard U., 1972. Bar: Calif. 1972, U.S. Dist. Ct. (ctrl. dist.) Calif. 1972, U.S. Dist. Ct. (so. dist.) Calif. 1973, U.S. Ct. Appeals (9th cir.) 1975, U.S. Dist. Ct. (no. dist.) Calif. 1977, U.S. Supreme Ct. 1978, U.S. Dist. Ct. (ea. dist.) 1980. Assoc. Latham & Watkins, L.A., 1972-78, ptnr. San Diego, 1978—. Recipient Jerome N. Frank prize U. Chgo. Law Sch., 1971. Mem. Calif. Club, Coronado Yacht Club, Order of Coif. Republican. Avocations: literature, zoology. Office: Latham & Watkins 600 W Broadway Ste 1800 San Diego CA 92101 E-mail: steve.wilson@lw.com.

WILSON, I. DODD, dean; b. St. Peter, Minn., July 10, 1936; m. Ginger Wilson; 2 children. AB summa cum laude, Dartmouth Coll., 1958; MD, Harvard U., 1961. Diplomate Am. Bd. Internal Medicine. Intern dept. medicine U. Minn. Hosps., Mpls., 1961—62; med. fellow Dept. of Medicine, 1962-63, 65-66; instr. dept. of medicine U. Minn. Med. Sch., Mpls., 1967—68, asst. prof., 1968—71, assoc. prof., 1971—76, dir. sect. of gastroenterology, 1972—83, vice chmn. dept. of medicine, 1983—86, prof. medicine, 1976—86; dean, prof. medicine U. Ark. Coll. of Medicine, Little Rock, 1986—; exec. vice chancellor U. Ark. Med. Scis., 1994—2000, chancellor, 2000—. Mem. Univ. Hosp. Consortium Rsch. Task Force, 1994; adv. bd. UALR Donaghey Project, 1994—; mem. State Crime Lab. Bd., 1992—, chmn. 1991-92; bd. dirs. First Comml. Nat. Bank, Ark. Children's Hosp. Rsch. Inst., Inc.; mem. Ark. Rice Depot Bd., 1988-94; mem. State Med. Examiner's Commn., 1986-90; med. bd. Univ. Hosp., 1986—; mem. chancellor's cabinet U. Ark. for Med. Scis., 1986-2000; chmn. U. Minn. Clin. Assocs., ad hoc com. for fin matters, 1986; vice chmn. U. Minn. Clin. Assocs., 1986, clin. assoc. exec. com., 1985; mem. univ. com. Univ. Press, 1985-86; clin. assoc. planning and mktg. com. U. Minn., 1985; mem. Hosp. Quality Assurance Steering com., 1984-96, chmn. hosp. utilization mgmt. com., 1985; mem. Univ. Bookstore com., 1985; mem. Univ. Senate, 1985-86; chmn. dept. medicine search com. for Dir. of Gen. Internal Medicine, 1985; chmn. med. sch. search com. head of dept. dermatology U. Minn., 1984, chmn. dept. medicine search com. for dir. pulmonary sect. 1984, mem. hosp. bd. govs. com. on planning and devel., 1983-86, med.-surg. hosp. facilities com., 1982-83, mem. steering com. of self-study task force U. of Minn. Med. Sch., 1982-83, many more coms. Contbr. numerous articles to profl. jours. Lt. USNR, 1963-65. Lt. USNR, 1963—65. Fellow ACP; mem. AMA, Am. Fedn. for Clin. Rsch., Am. Gastroenterol. Assn., Ctrl. Soc. for Clin. Rsch., Am. Assn. for the Study of Liver Disease, Ark. Med. Soc. (editl. bd. 1988-93, ex-officio mem., coun. 1987—), Pulaski County Med. Soc., Assn. of Am. Med. Colls. (coun. of deans, chair 1995-96, mgmt. edn. program planning com. 1993—, adv. panel on strategic positioning for health care reform 1992-95, exec. coun. 1992-97, adminstrv. bd. 1992-97, DEANS-VA coordinating com. 1990-94, ad hoc com. on nursing svcs. and the tchg. hosp. 1989, adv. com. on medicare regulations for payment of physicians in tchg. hosps. 1989), So. Med. Phi Beta Kappa, Alpha Omega Alpha. Office: Univ Ark for Med Scis Mail Slot #541 4301 W Markham St Little Rock AR 72205-7101

WILSON, IAN ANDREW, molecular biology educator; b. Perth, Scotland, Mar. 22, 1949; BS in Biochemistry, U. Edinburgh, Scotland, 1971; DPhil in Molecular Biology, Oxford U., Eng., 1976. Tutor and tchg. asst. in biochemistry Harvard U., 1978-82, rsch. assoc. biochemistry and molecular biology, 1980-82; asst. mem. dept. immunology Scripps Rsch. Inst., LaJolla, Calif., 1982-83, asst. mem. dept. molecular biology, 1983-84, assoc. mem. dept. molecular biology, 1984-90, chmn. structure and chem. affinity group, 1987—, prof., lectr. molecular & cell biology/structure and chem., 1988—, prof. molecular biology, 1991—, prof. Skaggs Inst. Chem. Biology, 1996—. Contbr. articles to profl. jours. Recipient Newcomv-Cleve. prize, 1996-97. Mem. Brit. Biophys. Soc., Am. Soc. Virologists, Am. Assn. Pathologists, Am. Crystallographic Assn., Brit. Soc. Immunologists, Protein Soc., Am. Chem. Soc. Office: Scripps Rsch Inst BCC206 Dept Molecular Biol 10550 N Torrey Pines Rd La Jolla CA 92037-1000

WILSON, IAN EDWIN, cultural organization administrator, archivist; b. Montreal, Que., Can., Apr. 2, 1943; s. Andrew and Marion (Mundy) W.; m. Ruth Dyck, Mar. 24, 1979. BA, Queen's U., Kingston, Ont., 1968, MA History, 1974; DLitt York U. (hon.), 2001. Archivist Queen's U., Kingston, Ont., Can., 1966-76; provincial archivist Sask. (Can.) Archives, 1976-86; archivist of Ont. Ont. Govt., Toronto, 1986-99; dir. gen. info. resource mgmt. divsn. Ministry Culture, Tourism and Recreation, Toronto, 1990-93; nat. archivist Canada, 1999—2004; v.p. Internat. Coun. on Archives, 2000—04; libr., archivist Canada, 2004—. Sec. Kingston Hist. Soc., 1967-72, v.p., 1972-76; chair cons. group Social Sci. and Humanities Rsch. Coun. Can., Ottawa, 1979-80; adj. prof. Faculty Info. Studies U. Toronto, 1993-2002; spkr. in field. Author: (with J. Douglas Stewart) Heritage Kingston, 1973; editor: Kingston City Hall, 1975; producer: (with J. William Brennan) Regina Before Yesterday, 1978; contbr. articles to profl. jours. Chmn. congregation Mennonite Ch., Regina, 1981-84; mem. Sask. award merit selection com., 1985-86; chair Sask. Heritage adv. bd., 1978-83; Ont. dir. Forum for Young Canadians, 1995-99. Recipient Queen Elizabeth II silver and gold jubilee medal, 1977, 2002, W.G. Leland cert. commendation Soc. Am. Archivists, 1981, W. Kaye Lamb prize Assn. Can. Archivists, 1983; Woodrow Wilson hon. fellow, 1967; apptd. mem. Order of Can., 2002; apptd. comdr. l'ordre des arts et des lettres, France, 2003. Fellow Soc. Am. Archivists; mem. Ont. Hist. Soc. (exec. coun. 1970-73, v.p. 1973-75, pres. 1975-76), Can. Hist. Assn. (past chmn., vice chmn., pres. archives sect. 1972-74), Champlain Soc. (bd. dirs., v.p. 1989-95, pres. 1995-2003). Home: 10 Bayport Priv Ottawa ON Canada K1V 0Z3 Office: Libr and Archives Canada 395 Wellington St Ottawa ON Canada K1A 0N4 Office Phone: 613-992-2473. E-mail: ian.wilson@lac-bac.gc.ca.

WILSON, IAN HOLROYDE, management consultant, futurist; b. Harrow, Eng., June 16, 1923; came to U.S., 1954; s. William Brash and Dorothy (Holroyde) W.; m. Page Tuttle Hedden, Mar. 17, 1951 (div. Dec. 1983); children: Rebecca, Dorothy, Ellen, Holly, Alexandra; m. Adrianne Marcus, July 12, 1992. MA, Oxford U., 1948. Orgn. cons. Imperial Chem. Industries, London, 1948-54; various staff exec. positions in strategic planning, mgmt. devel. Gen. Electric Co., Fairfield, Conn., 1954—80; sr. cons. to maj. U.S. and internat. cos. SRI Internat., Menlo Park, Calif., 1980-93; prin. Wolf Enterprises, San Rafael, Calif., 1993 . Exec. in residence Va. Commonwealth U., Richmond, 1976; fellow Va. Ctr. for Creative Arts, 1994, 98, 2000. Author: Planning for Major Change, 1976, The Power of Strategic Vision, 1991, Rewriting the Corporate Social Charter, 1992, Managing Strategically in the 1990s, 1993, Executive Leadership, 1995, The New Rules of Corporate Conduct, 2000, The Subtle Art of Strategy, 2003; contbg. editor: Learning from the Future, 1998; mem. editl. bd. Planning Rev., 1973—81; Am. editor: Long Range Planning Jour., 1981—89; sr. editor, mem. editl. bd. Strategy and Leadership, 1993—. Mem. adv. bd. Technol. Forecasting and Social Change, 1989—99; chmn. Citizen's Long Range Ednl. Goals Com., Westport, Conn., 1967—70; mem. strategic process com. United Way of Am., Alexandria, Va., 1985—94. Capt. Brit. Army, 1943—45, ETO. Mem. AAAS, Assn. for Strategic Planning, World Future Soc. Unitarian Universalist. Avocations: travel, writing, photography. Home and Office: 79 Twin Oaks Ave San Rafael CA 94901-1915 Office Phone: 415-454-6062. Personal E-mail: jason415xx@aol.com.

WILSON, IMOGENE R. counselor; b. Atlanta, Feb. 29, 1944; d. Henry and Edna Pope; m. June 9, 1979 (dec. Mar. 1980); 1 child, Bejide. BS in Elem. Edn., W.Va. State Coll., 1968; MA in Tchg., Trinity Coll., 1973; cert. advanced studies, Howard U., 1983, PhD, 1995. Cert. counseling, elem. edn., D.C. Elem. tchr. D.C. Schs., Washington, 1968-95, counselor, 1995—. Counselor Washington Mental Health Counseling Ctr., 1987-89. Home: 11005 Willow Bottom Dr Columbia MD 21044-1065

WILSON, ISABEL GOMEZ, elementary school educator, consultant; b. Bogota, Colombia, Dec. 19, 1939; arrived in U.S., 1951; BS, Fla. Internat. U., 1983; MEd, U. Miami, 1984; PhD, So. Ill. U., 1993. ESL instr. BiNat. Ctr., Bogota, 1970-71; chpt. 1 tchr. Dade County Pub. Sch., Miami, Fla., 1983-84, Oceanside Unified Sch. Dist., Oceanside, Calif., 1990—. Mem. Coalition for Peace, Carlsbad, 1990—. Recipient Bilingual Edn. Promotion award Yeshiva U., 1982. Mem. Nat. Assn. for Bilingual Edn., Coun. for Exceptional Children. Office: St Thomas U 16400 NW 32nd Ave Opa Locka FL 33054

WILSON, JACK, aeronautical engineer; b. Sheffield, Yorkshire, Eng., Jan. 5, 1933; arrived in U.S., 1956; s. George and Nellie (Place) W.; m. Marjorie Reynolds, June 3, 1961 (div. Jan. 1991); children: Tanya Ruth, Cara; m. Carol Blixen, Jan. 3, 1997. BS in Engring., Imperial Coll., London, 1954; MS in Aero. Engring., Cornell U., 1958, PhD in Aero. Engring., 1962. Sr. scientific officer Royal Aircraft Establishment, Farnborough, Eng., 1962-63; prin. rsch. sci. Avco-Everett Rsch. Lab., Everett, Mass., 1963-72; vis. prof. Inst. Mecanique des Fluides, Marseille, France, 1972-73; sr. scientist U. Rochester, N.Y., 1973-80; sr. rsch. assoc. Sohio/BP Am., Cleve., 1980-90; sr. engring. specialist Sverdrup Tech. Inc., Cleve., 1990-93, NYMA, Brook Park, 1994-98, DYNACS Engring. Co., Inc., Brook Park, 1998-2001, QSS Group Inc., Fairview Park, Ohio, 2001—. Author: (chpt.) "Gas Lasers" of Applied Optics in Engineering VI, 1980, "Laser Sources" of Techniques in Chemistry XVII, 1982; contbr. articles to profl. jours. Co-recipient Manly award, Soc. Automotive Engrs., 1995; recipient Soaring Gold Badge award, Fedn. Aero. Internat., Paris, 1998. Fellow AIAA (assoc.; tech. com. 1991-92). Achievements include first to demonstrate gas-dynamic laser, measurement of air ionization rate at high speeds; patents in application of high speed flow to gas laser media, devel. of antimony dopant sources. Office: QSS Group Inc 21000 Brookpark Rd Cleveland OH 44135-3127 Office Phone: 216-977-1204. Business E-Mail: jack.wilson@grc.nasa.gov. E-mail: wilson.blixen@juno.com.

WILSON, JACK FREDRICK, retired federal government official; b. Salt Lake City, Apr. 2, 1920; s. John Lorimer and Mayme J. (James) W.; m. Gwendolyn Gwynn, Nov. 20, 1947; children— Wendy, Elaine, Barbara Ann, Laurel, John F. Jr., James C. BS, Brigham Young U., 1942; postgrad., Mont. State U., 1962, Pa. State U., 1965. Range conservationist Bur. Land Mgmt., Rawlins, Wyo., 1949-57, dist. mgr. Burley, Idaho, 1957-67, dist. and land office mgr. Riverside, Calif., 1967-72; dir. Boise Interagy. Fire Ctr., Idaho, 1972-81; dir. Office Aircraft Services U.S. Dept. Interior, Boise, 1981-87; dir. Boise Interagy. Fire Ctr., 1987-92; ret., 1992. Contbr. articles to profl. jours. Dir. county disaster com. ARC, 1982-88. Maj. USAF, 1942-47 Recipient Meritorious award U.S. Dept. Interior, 1976, Disting. Service award, 1981, EEO Performance award, 1985; Outstanding Contbn. to Fire Mgmt. award U.S. Dept. Agr. Forest Service, 1976, Pub. Lands Found. Life Time Svc. Award 2002. Mem. Soc. Am. Foresters (chmn. fire com. 1980-82), Am. Soc. Range Mgmt. (sec. pres. 1967), So. Calif. Assn. Foresters and Fire Wardens, Lions (sec. 1954-57), Rotary. Mem. Ch. of Jesus Christ of Latter-day Saints. Avocations: long range weather forecasting, genealogy, reading, golf. Home: 1820 Sunrise Rim Rd Boise ID 83705-5138

WILSON, JACKMAN LEE, editor; b. Berkeley, Calif., May 29, 1954; s. Oscar Lee and Sarah Jackman Wilson; m. Heather Leigh McClenaghan, Sept. 21, 1982; children: Seabrook Leigh, Jackman Lee Wilson Jr. BS, U. Oreg., 1977. Editl. writer The Bull, Bend, Oreg., 1977—80; polit. reporter The Gazette-Times, Corvallis, Oreg., 1980—82, editl. page editor, 1982—; assoc. editor The Register-Guard, Eugene, Oreg., 1985—99, editl. page editor, 2000—. Sr. warden St. Mary's Episcopal Ch., Eugene, Oreg., 2004—. Recipient Various editl. writing and reporting awards, various years. Independent. Episcopalian. Avocations: travel, outdoor activities. Office: The Register-Guard 3500 Chad Dr Eugene OR 97440 Office Phone: 541-338-2316. Office Fax: 541-338-2828.

WILSON, JAMES CHARLES, JR., lawyer; b. Birmingham, Ala., Sept. 13, 1947; s. James C. and Angelina (Serio) W.; m. Ann Bullock, Mar. 1, 1975; children: Brent Trammell, Lucy Bullock. BA, Tulane U., 1969, JD, 1972; MBA, Samford U., 1995. Ptnr. Bradley, Arant, Rose & White, Birmingham, 1972-90, Lange, Simpson, Robinson & Somerville, Birmingham, 1990-93, Sirote & Permutt, P.C., Birmingham, 1993-96; v.p. and gen. counsel Shop-A-Snak Food Mart, Inc., Birmingham, 1996; pres. Lucent Holdings, Inc., Golden, Miss., 1997-98; ptnr. Baker, Johnston & Wilson LLP, Birmingham, Ala., 1999—2002; shareholder Baker Donelson, Bearman, Caldwell & Berkowitz, PC, Birmingham, 2003—. Adj. prof. internat. bus. transactions and internat. law U. Ala., Tuscaloosa, 1983-85, 89-96; internat. bus. transactions Cumberland Sch. Law, 1990-95, adj. prof. corp. fin., 2001—, adj. prof. securities regulation, 2003—. Author: Alabama Business Corporation Law, 1980; co-author: Corporate Law for the Healthcare Provider: Organization, Operation, Merger and Bankruptcy, 1993, Alabama Business Corporation Law Guide, 1995. Adv. bd. Jr. League of Birmingham, 1984; bd. dirs. Ala. chpt. Am. Liver Found., 1993-97, sec., 1994-95; trustee The Altamont Sch., 1995-2001, v.p., 1996-98, pres., 1998-2000. With U.S. Army, 1972-76. Mem. ABA (sect. internat. law, tax and corp., banking and bus. law), Am. Law Inst., Ala. Bar Assn., Ala. Law Inst., Birmingham Bar Assn. (chmn. pub. rels. com. 1990, chmn. spl. projects com. 2002, chmn. membership benefits com. 2003), Birmingham Golf Assn. (pres., v.p., treas. 1982-84), Rotary (pres. Birmingham-Sunrise club 1986-87). Office: 1600 South Trust Town 420 North 20th St Birmingham AL 35203 Office Phone: 205-244-3829.

WILSON, JAMES HARGROVE, JR., lawyer; b. Oliver, Ga., Nov. 26, 1920; s. James Hargrove and Louise (Sealy) W.; m. Frances Audra Schaffer, Dec. 24, 1942 (dec. Nov. 1990); children: Susan Frances, James Hargrove. AB with honors, Emory U., 1940; LL.B. summa cum laude, Harvard U., 1947. Bar: Ga. 1947, D.C. 1951. Assoc. firm Sutherland, Tuttle & Brennan (now Sutherland, Asbill & Brennan LLP), Atlanta and Washington, 1947-53, ptnr., 1953—. Lectr. Emory U., 1959, chmn. bd. visitors, 1967-68; trustee The Northwestern Mut. Life Ins. Co., Milw., 1972-91; mem. advisory group Commr. of Internal Revenue, 1963-64 Pres.: Harvard Law Review, 1946-47. Chmn. bd. trustees Met. Atlanta Crime Commn., 1970-71; mem. Harvard U. Overseers Com. to Visit Law Sch., 1959-65; trustee Emory U., 1983-90, trustee emeritus, 1990—. Served to lt. comdr. USNR, 1942-46. Fellow Am. Bar Found., Am. Coll. Tax Counsel; mem. ABA, State Bar Ga., D.C. Bar, Atlanta Bar Assn., Am. Law Inst. (coun. 1974—), Lawyers Club Atlanta (pres. 1960-61), Am. Judicature Soc., Harvard Law Sch. Assn. (coun. 1981-85), Emory U. Alumni Assn. (pres. 1966-67), Capital City Club, Piedmont Driving Club, Peachtree Club, Phi Beta Kappa, Omicron Delta Kappa, Kappa Alpha. Methodist. Home: 3171 Marne Dr NW Atlanta GA 30305-1931 Office: Sutherland Asbill & Brennan LLP 999 Peachtree St NE Ste 2300 Atlanta GA 30309-3996

WILSON, JAMES J. public administration consultant; b. Rahway, N.J., Jan. 29, 1962; s. James William and Sonia Eleanor (Hutchinson) W.; m. Pamela Ann Wilson, June 21, 1989; children: Kandace, Nicole. BA in Computer Sci., The Citadel, 1984; MS in Mgmt., Troy State U., 1992; MA in Econs., U. Ctrl. Fla., 1995; PhD in pub. policy, Fla. State U., 2000. Munitions specialist USAF, Eglin AFB, Fla., 1984-88; systems engr. Sverdrup Tech., Inc., Eglin AFB, Fla., 1988-94; exec. dir. Ctr. for Internat. Pub. Mgmt., Tallahassee, 1995-98. Discussant World Bank, Ohrid, Macedonia, 1996; project dir. Fla. Dept. Environ. Protection, Tallahassee, 1996-98. Contbr. articles to profl. jours.; pres. Fla. State Polich and Social Sci. Rev., 1997. Head coach Pee Wee Tackle Football, Tallahassee, 1997, mem. Big Bros./Big Sisters, Tallahassee, 1995; mentor One-on-One Program, Tallahassee, 1996, mentor/tutor Nims Mid. Sch., Tallahassee, 1996; dir. facilities/transp. Hugh O'Brien Youth Leadership. McKnight doctoral fellow, Fla. Edn. Fund, 1995, grad. rsch. fellow U. Ctrl. Fla., DeVoe L. Moore Dissertation fellow; rsch. grantee Fla. Dept. Cmty. Affairs, 1996. Mem. ASPA, Cmty. Devel. Soc., Omicron Delta Epsilon. Avocations: old movies, bowling, travel, parlor games, nutrition. Home: 640 Elmcroft Blvd Apt 1412 Rockville MD 20850-5641

WILSON, JAMES LAWRENCE, retired chemical company executive; b. Rosedale, Miss., Mar. 2, 1936; s. James Lawrence and Mary Margaret (Klingman) W.; m. Barbara Louise Burroughs, Aug. 30, 1958; children: Lawrence Burroughs, Alexander Elliott. B.Mech. Engring., Vanderbilt U., 1958; MBA, Harvard, 1963. Vice pres. Nyala Properties, Inc., Phila., 1963-65; staff assoc. Rohm & Haas Co., Phila., 1965-67, exec. asst. to pres., 1971-72, treas., 1972-74, regional dir., 1974-77, group v.p., 1977-86, vice-chmn., 1986-88, chmn., CEO, 1988-99; ret., 1999. Treas. Warren-Teed Pharms., Inc., Columbus, Ohio, 1967-68, v.p., 1969; pres. Consol. Biomed. Labs., Inc., Dublin, Ohio, 1970-71; bd. dirs. Vanguard Group Investment Cos., Cummins Inc., MeadWestvaco Corp., AmeriSourceBergen Corp. Trustee Vanderbilt U., 1987—, Culver Ednl. Found., 1988—; chmn. Phila. High Sch. Acads., 1989-99. Mem. Chem. Mfrs. Assn. (bd. dirs. 1988-99, chmn. 1996). Office: 175 Strafford Ave Ste 1 Wayne PA 19087-3331

WILSON, JAMES LEE, retired geology educator, consultant; b. Waxahachie, Tex., Dec. 1, 1920; s. James Burney and Hallie Christine (Hawkins) W.; m. Della I. Moore, May 8, 1944; children: James Lee Jr., Burney Grant, Dale Ross (dec.). Student, Rice U., 1938-40; BA, U. Tex., 1942, MA, 1944; PhD, Yale U., 1949. Geologist Carter Oil Co., Tulsa, 1943-44; asst. and assoc. prof. U. Tex., Austin, 1949-52; rsch. geologist Shell Devel. Co., Houston, 1952-66; prof. Rice U., Houston, 1966-79, U. Mich., Ann Arbor, 1979-86; geol. cons. New Braunfels, Tex., 1986—. Cons. Erico Corp., London, 1985-88, Masera Corp., Tulsa, 1988—, Coyote Geol. Svcs., Boulder, Col., 1990—; adj. prof. Rice U., 1986—. Author: Carbonate Facies in Geologic History, 1975; contbr. articles to tech. jours. With C.E., U.S. Army, 1944-46, Italy. Grantee NSF. Fellow: Geol. Soc. Am. (Sloss award); mem.: Con. Soc. Petroleum Geologists, South Tex. Geol. Soc., West Tex. Geol. Soc., Am. Assn. Petroleum Geologists (hon. Disting. Educator award), Paleontological Soc., Soc. Econ. Paleontology and Minerology (pres. 1972—73, field trip guide books 1989, Sidney Powers Meml. award 2002, Twenhofel award, Hedberg award), Internat. Sedimentological Soc. Avocations: piano, languages. Home and Office: 1316 Patio Dr New Braunfels TX 78130-8505 Office Phone: 830-625-6612. Personal E-mail: strata@nbtx.com.

WILSON, JAMES MILLER, IV, cardiovascular surgeon, educator; b. Atlanta, Mar. 11, 1946; s. James Miller Wilson III and Sara Sharp; m. Lisa VanLandingham; children: James Miller V, Robert Paul, Michael Simpson, Sara Ann. Student, Emory U.; MD, Duke U., 1971. Diplomate Am. Bd. Surgery, Am. Bd. Thoracic Surgery. Intern N.Y. Hosp., 1971-72; resident N.Y. Hosp.-Cornell Med. Ctr., 1972-73, U. Calif., San Francisco, 1975-80; attending staff Christ Hosp., Cin., 1980—, Bethesda Hosp., Cin., 1980—, Jewish Hosp., Cin., 1980—, Univ. Hosp., Cin., 1982—, Deaconess Hosp, Cin., 1982—, VA Med Ctr., Cin., 1983—, Children's Hosp., Cin., 1984—, Good Samaritan Hosp., Cin., 1994—; assoc. prof. clin. surgery U. Cin. Coll. Med., 1985—; dir. cardiac surgery Mercy Hosp., chmn. dept. cardiovasc. surgery, 2001. Open heart surgery adv. com., Ohio, 1995—; tech. adv. panel on cardiac surgery Nat. Quality Forum; dir. cardiac surgery Mercy Hosp., 2001; mem. Thoracic Surgery Found.; lectr. in field. Contbr. articles to profl. jours. Lt. Comdr. submarine svc. USN, 1973-75. Fellow ACS, Am. Coll. Cardiology, Am. Heart Assn. (cardiovasc. coun.), Am. Coll. Chest Physicians; mem. AMA, U.S. Naval Submarine League, UDT/SEAL Assn., U.S. Submarine Vets., Inc., Am. Assn. Thoracic Surgery, Thoracic Surgery Found., Assn. Acad. Surgery, Soc. Thoracic Surgeons, Ohio State Med. Assn., Cin. Acad. Medicine, Howard C. Nafziger Soc. Avocations: music, diving, hiking, skiing, horses. Office: 3050 Mack Rd #33S Fairfield OH 45014 Office Phone: 513-603-8600.

WILSON, JAMES N. health products executive; BA, MBA, U. Ariz. CEO LifeScan, Inc., 1982—88, Neurex Corp., 1989—90; COO Syntex Corp., 1994—95; chmn. bd. dirs. Amira Med., 1996—2001, 2001, Corcept Therapeutics Inc., Menlo Park, Calif., 1999—. Office: Corcept Therapeutics Inc 275 Middlefield Rd Ste A Menlo Park CA 94025

WILSON, JAMES RAY, international business educator; b. Mar. 7, 1930; s. Ray Crawford and Ruth Lee (Walthers) W.; m. Carolyn Dempsey, Feb. 1, 1952; children: Robin E., Victoria, Mark, Jamie. BA (U.S. Navy Coll. Tng. Program scholar), Miami U., Oxford, Ohio, 1952; postgrad., Miami U., 1967-68; MA, Ohio State U., 1956; PhD, U. Minn., 1984. Grad. asst. Ohio State U., 1955-56; grain mcht. Cargill Inc., Balt., 1956-58; pres. Granexport Corp., Manilla, Philipinnes, 1959-66; mng. dir. Tradax Graanhandel B.V., Amsterdam, 1966-67; instr. dept. geography Miami U., 1967-68; pres. Cargill Agricola S.A., Sao Paulo, Brazil, 1968-78; dir. indsl. div. Tradax Geneve S.A., Geneva, 1978-80; corp. v.p. Cargill Inc., Mpls., 1980-83; pres. Cargill S.E. Asia, Ltd., Singapore, 1984-88; internat. bus. prof. Miami U. of Ohio, Oxford, Ohio, 1988-92, prof. mgmt., 1994-98; chmn. Cargill Tech. Svcs., Ltd., Thame, Eng., 1992-94; proprietor Antiquarian Bookstore, 1998—. Served with USN, 1952-55. Fellow Royal Geog. Soc. Congregationalist. Home: 6533 Buckley Rd Oxford OH 45056-9727 Office: Books in Shandon 4795 Cincinnati-Brookville PO Box 8 Shandon OH 45063 Office Phone: 513-738-2962.

WILSON, JAMES REID, JR., publishing executive; b. Phila., Aug. 5, 1934; s. James Reid Wilson and Florence Dunn; m. Eve-Ann Jones; children: Suzanne Witters, Diantha Curtis. BS in Econs., U. Pa., 1956. Assoc. dir. western hemisphere promotion The NY Times, NYC, 1966-69, mgr. indsl. advt., 1969-74; mgr. corp. advt. US News & World Report, NYC, 1974-79, advt. mgr., 1979-85, mktg. mgr., 1985-86; sr. v.p. Newspaper Advt. Bur., NYC, 1986-93; dir. Izvestia/Hearst, WeMbl, NYC and Moscow, 1993-94; pres. Media Ptnr., NYC, 1995-97; ad sales dir. Forbes SIP, NYC, 1997-2000, v.p., 2000—03. Pres. Pa. Assn. Retarded Citizens, 1969-71; sr. v.p. Assn. Retarded Citizens US, Arlington, Tex., 1975-77, pres. 1977-79; bd. mem. Walker Ctr. Mem. St. Nicholas Soc., Union League, Scarsdale Golf Club, Penn Club, NY Sons of the Revolution, Walker Ctr.(bd.). Republican. Presbyterian.

WILSON, JAMES ROSS, communications educator, broadcasting executive; b. Petaluma, Calif., Nov. 25, 1939; s. Stanley Thomas and Billie (Ross) W.; m. Elizabeth Ann Buckleman, Dec. 29, 1964 (div. 1982); children: Greg, Tom. BA, Fresno State Coll., 1961; MA, Calif State U., Fresno, 1976. Radio and TV instr. Dept. Def. Info. Sch., Ft. Slocum, N.Y., 1962-65; news dir. Sta. KVON, Napa, Calif., 1965, Sta. KTIM, San Rafael, Calif., 1966; news reporter Sta. KMJ, Fresno, 1966-67, news dir., 1967-71; program dir. Sta. KMJ/KNAX-FM, Fresno, 1971-78, v.p., gen. mgr., 1978-82; news assignment editor Sta. KFSN-TV, Fresno, 1982-83; prof. mass comm., gen. mgr., faculty advisor KFSR-FM Calif. State U., Fresno, 1983—; jazz disk jockey Sta.

KVPR, Valley Pub. Radio, Fresno, 1984-90; weekend news anchor KMPH-FM News Radio, 1994-96. Co-author: Mass Media/Mass Culture, 4th edit., 1997, 5th edit., 2000. Recipient Best Newscast award Calif. AP-TV-Radio Assn., 1971, Best News Documentary award Calif. AP-TV-Radio Assn., 1973-74, Broadcast Excellence award Billboard mag., 1976; Calif. State U. grantee, 1987. Mem. Broadcast Edn. Assn., Cen. Calif. Broadcasters Assn. (treas., bd. dirs. 1980-83), Assn. for Edn. in Journalism and Mass Communication, Soc. Profl. Journalists, Alpha Epsilon Rho, Phi Kappa Phi. Home: 4747 E Holland Ave Fresno CA 93726-2914 Office: Calif State U Dept Mass Comm Journalism Fresno CA 93740-0001 E-mail: james_wilson@csufresno.edu.

WILSON, JANE, artist; b. Seymour, Iowa, Apr. 29, 1924; d. Wayne and Cleone (Marquis) W.; m. John Gruen, Mar. 28, 1948; 1 child, Julia. BA, U. Iowa, 1945, MA, 1947. Mem. fine arts faculty Parsons Sch. Design, 1973-83, 89-90. Vis. artist U. Iowa, 1974; adj. assoc. prof. painting and drawing Columbia U., 1975-85, assoc. prof., 1985-86, prof., 1986-88, acting chair, 1986-88; Andrew Mellon vis. prof. painting Cooper Union, 1977-78. One-woman shows include Hansa Gallery, N.Y.C., 1953, 55, 57, Stuttman Gallery, N.Y.C., 1958, 59, Tibor de Nagy Gallery, N.Y.C., annually, 1960-66, Graham Gallery, N.Y.C., 1968, 69, 71, 73, 75, Fischbach Gallery, N.Y.C., 1978, 81, 84, 88, 90, 91, 93, 95, 97, D.C. Moore Gallery, N.Y.C., 1999, 2001, 03, Munson-Williams-Proctor Inst., Utica, N.Y., 1980, Cornell U., Ithaca, N.Y., 1982, Compass Rose Gallery, Chgo, 1988, Am. U., Washington, 1989, U. Richmond, Va., 1990, Earl McGrath Gallery, L.A., 1990-91, 93, Dartmouth Coll., Hanover, N.H., 1991, Arnot Mus., Elmira, N.Y., 1993-94, Parrish Mus., Southampton, N.Y., 1996, Glenn Horowitz Gallery, East Hampton, N.Y., 1996, Heckscher Mus., Huntington, N.Y., 2001, McKinney Ave. Contemporary, Dallas, 2003; represented in permanent collections Met. Mus., Mus. Modern Art, Whitney Mus., Wadsworth Athenaeum, Heron Art Mus., NYU Rockefeller Inst., Vassar Coll., Pa. Acad. Fine Arts, Hirsch Horn Mus., Washington, Nelson-Atkins Mus., Kansas City, Mo., San Francisco Mus. Modern Art, Heckscher Mus., L.I. Mus., Stony Brook, others. Recipient Purchase prize Childe Hassam Fund, 1971, 73, 81, Ranger Fund Purchase prize 1977; Ingram-Merrill grantee, 1963, Louis Comfort Tiffany grantee, 1967, Eloise Spaeth award The Guild Hall, East Hampton, N.Y., 1988. Lifetime Achievement award The Guild Hall, 2001. Mem. Am. Acad. Arts and Letters (Award in Art 1985), Nat. Acad. Design (pres. 1992-94), Phi Beta Kappa.

WILSON, JANIE MENCHACA, nursing educator, researcher; b. Lytle, Tex., Mar. 15, 1936; 1 child, Kathryn Lynn Kohlleppel. BSN, Incarnate Word Coll., San Antonio, 1958; MSN, U. Tex., San Antonio, 1973; PhD in Nursing, U. Tex., Austin, 1978. RN. Oper. rm. nurse Santa Rosa Hosp., San Antonio, 1958-59; instr. Brackenridge Hosp. Sch. Nursing, Austin, 1963-66; staff nurse Med. Coll. Ga., Augusta, 1967-68; instr. dept. nursing San Antonio Coll., 1968-72, prof. dept. nursing edn., 1976—; counselor Project GAIN Tex. Nurses Assn., Austin, 1973-76. Rsch. assoc. Ctr. for Health Care Rsch. and Evaluation, U. Tex. System, Austin, 1974-75; cons. Nurse Aide Competency Evaluation Program, San Antonio, 1989—; mem. manuscript rev. panel Nursing Rsch., N.Y.C., 1989-91. Contbr. chpts. to books, articles to profl. jours. Bd. dirs. Ctr. for Health Policy Devel., San Antonio, 1988-92; mem. Nat. Adv. Coun. on Nurse Edn. and Practice, 1995—. 1st lt. USAF, 1960-63. Mem. AAUP, ANA (coun. nurse rschrs., coun. cultural diversity, fellow program for ethnic minorities 1975-77), Am. Acad. Nursing, Nat. League Nursing, Nat. Assn. Hispanic Nurses, Sigma Theta Tau. Roman Catholic. Avocations: music, reading, fishing, dance, sewing. Office: San Antonio Coll 1300 San Pedro Ave San Antonio TX 78212-4201 Home: 78 Gleneden Avenue Oakland CA 94611 E-mail: jwilson@accd.edu.

WILSON, JEAN DONALD, endocrinologist, educator; b. Wellington, Tex., Aug. 26, 1932; s. J. D. and Maggie E. (Hill) Wilson. BA in Chemistry, U. Tex., 1951, MD, 1955. Diplomate Am. Bd. Internal Medicine. Intern, then resident in internal medicine Parkland Meml. Hosp., Dallas, 1955—58; clin. assoc. Nat. Heart Inst., Bethesda, Md., 1958—60; instr. internal medicine U. Tex. Southwestern Med. Sch., Dallas, 1960—61, prof., 1968—. Editor: Jour. Clin. Investigation, 1972—77. Sr. asst. surgeon USPHS, 1958—60. Recipient Amory prize, Am. Acad. Arts and Scis., 1977, Fuller prize, Am. Urol. Assn., 1983, Lita Annenberg Hazen award, 1986, Dale medal, Soc. for Endocrinology, 1991, Pincus medal, Worchester Found., 1992. Fellow: Royal Coll. Physicians; mem.: NAS, Endocrine Soc. (Oppenheimer award 1972, Koch award 1993), Am. Soc. Biochemistry and Molecular Biology, Soc. Exptl. Biology and Medicine, Am. Philos. Soc., Assn. Am. Physicians (Kober medal 1999), Am. Soc. Clin. Investigation, Inst. Medicine, Am. Acad. Arts and Scis. (Amory prize 1977). Office: U Tex Southwestern Med Ctr Dept Internal Medicine 5323 Harry Hines Blvd Dallas TX 75390-8857 Fax: 214-648-8917. Office Phone: 214-648-3685. E-mail: jwils1@mednet.swmed.edu.

WILSON, JEAN L. retired state legislator; b. Phila., June 13, 1928; d. Horace and Catherine (Lennox) Terry; m. Benjamin H. Wilson (dec.); children: Sheryl J. Gordon, Denise T. Munn. BS in Edn., Pa. State U., 1949. Tchr. Columbia Inst., Phila., 1949-50, Wilkes Coll., Wilkes Barre, Pa., 1950-51; office mgr., exec. sec. Camden Fibre Mills, Warminster, Pa., 1969-82; mem. Pa. Ho. of Reps., 1988-92. Legis. chmn. Doylestown V.I.A.; active Benj. H. Wilson Sr. Ctr., Ctr. for Learning in Retirement, Del. Valley Coll.; former mem. bd. Bucks County Opportunity Coun.; treas. Bucks County chpt. Fox Chase Cancer Ctr. Avocations: duplicate bridge, golf. Home: 12 Far View Rd Chalfont PA 18914-2511

WILSON, JERRY CLARK, language educator; b. Boise, Idaho, Jan. 1, 1940; s. Gerald Vern and Betty Lou Wilson; m. Brenda Jean Urvin, June 3, 1960; children: Angela Sue Wilson Newburg, Stephen Jerry. BA in Religion, N.W. Nazarene Coll., Nampa, Idaho, 1963; Cert. of Spanish, Inst. Mexicano Am., Mexico City, 1967; MA in Missiology, Fuller Theol. Sem., Pasadena, 1987; MA in Spanish, U. Calif., Santa Barbara, 1998. Dir. sem. Ch. of the Nazarene, Chiclayo, Peru, 1967—72, dir. bilingual sem. Boca Cuseo Alto Morano Jungle, Peru, 1973—75, sem. Panama City, Panama, 1976—78, dir. study/work program Santo Domingo, Dominican Republic, 1979—83; Spanish prof. Point Loma Nazarene U., San Diego, 1987—. Avocations: reading, repairing old cars, sports. Office: Point Loma Nazarene Univ 3900 Lomaland Dr San Diego CA 92106

WILSON, JERRY MONTY, writer, educator; s. James Lee Wilson and Ann Ophelia Golden; m. Cathy Ann Wilson. BA in Speech Comm., U. Minn, Mpls., 1989; MBC, U. St. Thomas, St. Paul, Minn., 1998. Ops. mgr. Servant Alpha, Mpls., 1988—93; tax rschr. Wilson Cons., Edina, Minn., 1993—; freelance writer, 1999—. Motivational spkr., Mpls. and Neenah, Wis., 2000—01; pt. time instr. writing Cardinal Stritch Coll., Edina, Minn., 2003. Author: Breathless: the Adventure of a Gymnast, Treasure Hunt 2000, 2000, Blue, 2004. Avocations: tennis, chess, acting. E-mail: wilsonjerry@yahoo.com.

WILSON, JOANNE, federal agency administrator; BA, MA, Iowa State U. Tchr. grades 2 and 4, Ames, Iowa; continuing edn. instr. Braille and mobility for blind students La. Tech. U.; founder, dir. La. Ctr. Blind; commr. rehab. svcs. adminstrn. Dept. Edn., Washington, 2001—. Cons. Conn. Bd. Edn. and Svcs. for the Blind, N.J. Orientation and Adjustment Ctr. for the Blind, N.Y. Commn. for the Blind; founder, chair La. Rehab. Svcs. Coun. Office: Dept Edn Rehab Svcs Adminstrn 300 C St SW Washington DC 20202-2531

WILSON, JOHN PASLEY, law educator; b. Newark, Apr. 7, 1933; s. Richard Henry and Susan Agnes (Pasley) Wilson; m. Elizabeth Ann Reed, Sept. 10, 1955 (div.); children: David Cables, John Pasley, Cicely Reed. AB, Princeton U., 1955; LLB, Harvard U., 1962. Bar: N.J. 1962, U.S. Dist. Ct. N.J. 1962, Mass. 1963, U.S. Dist. Ct. Mass. 1963. Budget examiner Exec. Office of Pres., Bur. of Budget, Washington, 1955-56; assoc. Riker, Danzig, Scherer & Brown, Newark, 1962-63; asst. dean Harvard U. Law Sch., Cambridge, Mass., 1963-67; assoc. dean Boston U. Law Sch., 1968-82; dean Golden Gate U. Sch. Law, San Francisco, 1982-88, prof., 1988—2003, prof. emeritus, dean emeritus, 2003—. Vis. prof. dept. health policy and mgmt. Harvard U., 1988; cons. Nat. Commn. Protection Human Subjects Biomedical and Behavioral Rsch.; mem. Mass. Gov.'s Commn. Civil and Legal Rights Developmentally disabled; former chmn. adv. com. Ctr. Cmty. Legal Edn., San Francisco. Author: (book) The Rights of Adolescents in the Mental Health System; contbr. chapters to books, articles to profl. jours. Bd. dirs. Greater Boston Legal Svcs., Chewonki Found.; mem. Health Facilities Appeals Bd., Mass.; assoc. mem. Dem. Town Com., Concord; chmn. Bd. Assessors, Concord; bd. overseers Boston Hosp. Women, past chmn. med. affairs com.; past mem. instl. rev. bd. Calif. Pacific Hosp., San Francisco. Served to lt. (j.g.) USNR, 1956—59. NIMH grantee, 1973. Mem.: Nat. Assn. Securities Dealers (arbitrator). Office: Golden Gate U Sch Law 536 Mission St San Francisco CA 94105-2967 Office Phone: 415-442-6651. Personal E-mail: jwlsn@earthlink.net. Business E-Mail: jwilson@ggu.edu.

WILSON, JOHN ROBERT, JR., pharmaceutical and chemical company executive; b. Key West, Fla., Mar. 16, 1951; s. John R. and Norma Ruth Wilson; m. Betty Elaine Whitten, Oct. 2, 1982; children: Gregory L., Jason L. BS, Centenary Coll. La., 1974; MA, Rice U., 1990, PhD, 1992; MPH, Columbia U., 2000. Sales rep. Reed & Carnrick Pharms. Inc., Little Rock, 1975-78, Boehringer Ingelheim Pharms. Inc., Little Rock, 1978-82, clin. rsch. assoc. Houston, 1982-89, mgr. Ridgefield, Conn., 1989-91, assoc. dir., 1991-94, dir., 1994-98, Boehringer Ingelheim Chems. Inc., Petersburg, Va., 1998-99, v.p., 1999—. Lectr. N.Y. Med. Coll., Valhalla, 1995-98. Mem. Am. Soc. Quality, Drug Info. Assn., Regulatory Affairs Profl. Soc. Avocations: baseball, philosophy. Home: 12121 Ashton Park Dr Glen Allen VA 23059-7126 Office: Boehringer Ingelheim Chems Inc 2820 Normandy Dr Petersburg VA 23805-9372 Fax: 804-504-8869. Office Phone: 804-504-8809. E-mail: jwilson@bichemicals.com.

WILSON, JOSEPH CHARLES, IV, former ambassador; b. Bridgeport, Conn., Nov. 6, 1949; s. Joseph Charles III and Phyllis (Finnell) W.; m. Susan Dale Otchis, Apr. 27, 1973 (div. 1986); m. Valerie Elise Plame, Apr. 3, 1998; children: Sabrina Cecile, Joseph Charles, Trevor Rolph, Samantha Finnell Diana. BA in History, U. Calif., Santa Barbara, 1972. Fgn. svc. officer Dept. of State, Washington, 1976-98; congl. fellow Am. Polit. Sci. Assn., Washington, 1985-86; dep. chief of mission Am. Embassy, Bujumbura, Burundi, 1982-85, Brazzaville, Congo, 1986-88, Baghdad, Iraq, 1988-91; amb. Gabon, Sao Tome and Principe, 1992-95; polit. adv. to Commdr. in Chief U.S. Armed Forces Europe, 1995-97; spl. asst. to pres., sr. dir. for African affairs Nat. Security Coun., Washington, 1997-98; pres. JC Wilson Internat. Ventures, Washington, 1998—. Adj. scholar Mid. East Inst., 2002—. Author: The Politics of Truth, 2004 (N.Y. Times Bestseller). Decorated comdr. Order of Equatorial Star (Gabon); recipient Disting. Alumni award U. Calif. Santa Barbara, 1991, 1995, Disting. Def. Dept. Civilian award, 1997; recipient Ron Ridenhour prize, 2003, Am. Patriot award Ams. for Informed Democracy, 2003. Mem. Am. Polit. Sci. Assn., Am. Fgn. Svc. Assn. (William R. Rivkin award 1987), U. Calif. Santa Barbara Alumni Assn., San Onofre Surfing Club. Avocations: golf, bicycling, exercise. Office: Ste #300 1717 Pennsylvania Ave NW Washington DC 20006-4619 Business E-Mail: joewilson@rockcreekcorp.com.

WILSON, JOSEPH MORRIS, III, lawyer; b. Milw., July 26, 1945; s. Joseph Morris Jr. and Phyllis Elizabeth (Cresson) W.; children: Elizabeth J., Eric M.; m. Dixie Lee Brock, Mar. 23, 1984. BA, Calif. State U., Chico, 1967; MA, U. Washington, 1968; JD summa cum laude, Ohio State U., 1976. Bar: Alaska 1976, U.S. Dist. Ct. Alaska 1976, U.S. Ct. Appeals (9th cir.) 1986. Recruiter and vol. U.S. Peace Corps, Republic of Benin, 1969-73; legal intern U.S. Ho. of Reps., Washington, 1975; ptnr. Guess & Rudd P.C., Anchorage, 1976-88, chmn. comml. dept., 1981-82, ptnr. compensation com., 1982-84; mgr. Alaska taxes, sr. tax atty. BP Exploration Inc., Alaska, 1990-99. Bus. law instr. U. Alaska, Anchorage, 1977-78. Mem. Alaska Bar Assn., World Affairs Coun. Democrat. Avocations: music, sports, travel. Home and Office: 2556 Palmera Cir Las Vegas NV 89121-4016 Office Phone: 702-369-7105. E-mail: jsphwlsn@aol.com.

WILSON, KAREN LEE, researcher; b. Somerville, N.J., Apr. 2, 1949; d. Jon Milton and Laura Virginia (Van Dyke) W.; m. Paul Ernest Walker, 1980; 1 child, Jeremy Nathaniel. AB, Harvard U., 1971; MA, NYU, 1973, PhD, 1985. Rsch. assoc., dir. excavation at Mendes, Egypt Inst. Fine Arts, NYU, 1979-81; coord. exhbn. The Jewish Mus., N.Y.C., 1981-82, adminstrv. cataloguer, 1982-83, coord. curatorial affairs, 1984-86; curator Oriental Inst. Mus. U. Chgo., 1988-96, mus. dir., 1996—2003, rsch. assoc., 1988—. Author, editor: Mendes, 1982; contbr. articles to profl. jours. Mem.: Coll. Art Assn., Am. Oriental Soc. Office Phone: 773-702-9514. E-mail: k-wilson@uchicago.edu.

WILSON, KEITH B. rehabilitation educator; b. Spartanburg, S.C., Feb. 19, 1962; s. George and Helen Annette Wilson; m. Beverly Jean Gaither, June 13, 1992; 1 child, Aliya Imani. BA, Wilberforce U.; MEd, Kent State U., 1985; PhD, Ohio State U., 1997. Cert. rehab. counselor. Case mgr. Ohio Bur. Vocat. Rehab., Canton, 1985; counseling coord. Savannah (Ga.) State U., 1986—89; dir. counseling svc. Brewton-Parker Coll., Mt. Vernon, Ga., 1989—94; grad. program asst. Ohio State U., Columbus, 1994—95, tchg. asst., 1995—97; asst. prof. Pa. State U., State College, 1997—. Cons. Brewton-Parker Coll., Mt. Vernon, 1993; mem. adv. bd. Pa. Office Vocat. Rehab., Harrisburg, 1998—; cons. Indiana U. Pa., 2000. Author: (newsletter) Mosaic, 2001; co-editor: Rehab. Counseling Bull., 2002. Judge Pa. State Grad. Exhbn., State College, 2001; chairperson Multicultural Ad. Com., Harrisburg, 2002—; bd. dirs. Inst. Sci. Advancement, Harrisburg, 2001. Recipient Bobbie Atkins Rsch. award, Nat. Assn. Multicultural, 2001. Mem.: Pa. Counseling Assn. (Named Outstanding Rschr. 2000), Pa. Rehab. Assn., Phi Beta Kappa. Home: 109 Berwick Dr Boalsburg PA 16827 Office: Pa State U Counselor Edn 308 Cedar Bldg State College PA 16802-3110 Office Phone: 814-863-2413. Business E-Mail: kbw4@psu.edu.

WILSON, KEITH DUDLEY, media and music educator, consultant, dean; b. Windermere, July 13, 1936; s. Charles Alexander and Fanny (Shaw) Wilson; 1 child, Nicholas. BA with honors, Kings Coll., Cambridge, 1957, MA, 1960; LittD (hon.), U. Salford, 2000. Lectr. Brit. Coun./Zagreb Univ., Croatia, 1957-58; assoc. prof., dir. TV Brit. Coun. Tehran U., Iran, 1958-64; reader Brit. Coun. Osmania U., Hyderabad, India, 1964-66; head of liberal edn. Salford (Eng.) Coll. Tech., 1967-72, head of humanities, 1972-85; head of performing arts and media U. Coll. Salford, 1985-90; dir. Ctr. Media Performance and Comm. U. Salford, 1990-96, founding chief exec. Internat. Media Ctr., 1993-99, dean faculty of media, music and performance, 1996-99. Tutor, counsellor Open U., 1972—90; dir. TVUK, Adelphi Prodns., Salford, 1988—99, Channel M, 1997—2000; chair PRS John Lennon awards, 1990—93; co-chair NYNEX Cable TV, Manchester, 1993—95; vis. acad. Brit. Coun., Republic of Korea, 1992; founder over 30 higher edn. courses in music, media, drama, rec., entertainment orgns., media and sci., new media; European edn. advisor, cons. media, music and rec. industries, 2000—; resident broadcasts and recs. Edinburgh Internat. Festival, 1986—97. Contbr. articles to profl. jours. and nat. papers;, musician concert tours,, . Mem. City of Salford LS Lowry Centenary, 1988, The Lowry, Nat. Landmark Millennium Project for Arts, Digital World Ctr.; founder Salford U. Brass Band, Wind Band, Big Band, Soundworks, Jazz Ensembles, Groove Machine, Aspects Theatre; mem. City Pride Initiative, Manchester, 1993—97, Fellowship Gt. Britain Sasakawa Found., Japan, 1991; mem. centenary com. U. Salford, 1994—96. Fellow: Royal Soc. Arts (chmn. N.W.); mem.: Prodrs. Assn. Cinema and TV, Brit. Acad. Film and TV, Brit. Film Inst., Royal TV Soc. Avocations: nordic lands and culture, wines of the world, walking. Home and Office: 60 Central Rd Didsbury Manchester M204 ZA England

WILSON, KENNETH GEDDES, physics research administrator; b. Waltham, Mass., June 8, 1936; s. E. Bright and Emily Fisher (Buckingham) Wilson; m. Alison Brown, 1982. AB, Harvard U., 1956, DSc (hon.), 1981; PhD, Calif. Tech. Inst., 1961, U. Chgo., 1976. From asst. prof. to prof. physics Cornell U., Ithaca, NY, 1963—88, James A. Weeks prof. in phys. sci., 1974—87; Hazel C. Youngberg Trustees Disting prof. The Ohio State U., Columbus, 1988—. Co-author: Redesigning Education, 1974. Recipient Nobel prize in Physics, 1982, Dannie Heinemann prize, 1973, Boltzmann medal, 1975, Wolf prize, 1980, A.C. Eringen medal, 1984, Franklin medal, 1982, Aneesur Rahman prize, 1993. Mem.: NAS, Am. Acad. Arts and Scis., Am. Phys. Soc., Am. Philos. Soc.

WILSON, KENNETH JAY, writer; b. Oklahoma City, Aug. 25, 1944; s. Kenneth J. and Betty Wallace (Bleakmore) W. BA magna cum laude, Yale U., 1966, M.Phil., 1969; postgrad. Queen's Coll., Oxford U., Eng., 1969-70; PhD, Yale U., 1973. From instr. to assoc. prof. English U. Rochester, N.Y., 1970-83; assoc. Clare Hall, Cambridge U., Eng., 1977; vis. assoc. prof. English Coll. William and Mary, Williamsburg, Va., 1983; editor in chief Peter Lang Pub., N.Y.C., 1983-87; dir. of rights and permissions Princeton U. Press, 1987-88; commissioning editor polit. sci. and psychology Routledge, N.Y.C., 1988-90; adminstrv. dir. HIV Clin. Rsch. Ctr. Mt. Zion Med. Ctr./U. Calif., San Francisco, 1994-95. Cons. USIA, 1985 Editor: Letters of Sir Thomas Elyot, 1976, English Works of Thomas More, 1978; author: Incomplete Fictions, 1985, Pope John Paul II, 1992; contbr. essays, book revs. and short fiction to mags. and profl. jours. Woodrow Wilson fellow, 1966, 83; sr. fellow Folger Shakespeare Library, Washington, 1976; Am. Philos. Soc. grantee, 1976; Am. Council Learned Soc. fellow, 1977 Mem. Mory's Club, Elizabethan Club (New Haven), Yale Club (N.Y.C.), Palm-Aire Country Club, Phi Beta Kappa. Democrat. Roman Catholic. Home: 5570 Country Club Way Sarasota FL 34243-3759 E-mail: nuboy@comcast.net.

WILSON, L. MICHELLE, lawyer; b. Boise, Idaho, Jan. 20, 1963; d. Tom Martin and George Ann Wilson. BA, U. Wash., Seattle, 1985; JD, U. Chgo., 1988. Ptnr. Perkins Coie, Seattle, 1988—. Recipient Dow Jones award Wall St. Jour., 1985. Mem. ABA, Washington State Bar Assn., Order of Coif, Phi Beta Kappa, Beta Gamma Sigma. Office: Perkins Coie 1201 3rd Ave Fl 40 Seattle WA 98101-3029

WILSON, LANFORD, playwright; b. Lebanon, Mo., Apr. 13, 1937; s. Ralph E(ugene) and Violetta (Tate) W. Student, San Diego State Coll., 1955-56; PhD in Humanities (hon.), U. Mo., 1985, Grinnell Coll., 1994; PhD in Lit. (hon.), Southampton Coll., 1995. Playwright, 1962—; resident playwright, dir., co-founder Cir. Repertory Co., NYC, 1969-95. Author: (plays) So Long at the Fair, 1963, Home Free!, 1964, No Trespassing, 1964, The Sandcastle, 1964, The Madness of Lady Bright, 1964, Ludlow Fair, 1965, Balm in Gilead, 1965, This is the Rill Speaking, 1965, Days Ahead, 1965, Sex is Between Two People, 1965, The Gingham Dog, 1966, The Rimers of Eldritch, 1966, Wandering, 1966, Lemon Sky, 1969, Serenading Louie, 1970, The Great Nebula in Orion, 1970, The Hot L Baltimore, 1972, The Family Continues, 1972, The Mound Builders, 1975, Fifth of July, 1978, Brontasaurus, 1978, Talley's Folly, 1979, A Tale Told, 1981, Angels Fall, 1983, A Betrothal, 1984, Talley & Son, 1985, Burn This, 1987, A Poster of the Cosmos, 1987, The Moonshot Tape, 1990, Redwood Curtain, 1991, Trinity, 1993, I'm Not the Ocean, 1995, Sympathetic Magic, 1996, A Sense of Place (or Virgil is Still the Frogboy), 1997, Your Everyday Ghost Story, 1997, Book of Days, 1998, Rain Dance, 2003; translator Three Sisters, 1984, Ghosts, 2002; author: (books) Balm in Gilead and Other Plays, 1966, The Rimers of Eldritch and Other Plays, 1968, The Gingham Dog, 1969, Lemon Sky, 1970, The Hot L Baltimore, 1973, The Mound Builders, 1976, Fifth of July, 1979, Talley's Folly, 1980, Angels Fall, 1983, Serenading Louie, 1985, Talley & Son, 1986, Burn This, 1988, Redwood Curtain, 1992, 21 Short Plays, 1994, By the Sea, 1996, Collected Plays, Vol. I, 1997, Vol. II, 1999, Vol. III, 1999, A Sense of Place, 1999, Sympathetic Magic, 1999, Book of Days, 2001. ABC Yale fellow, 1969; Rockefeller grantee, 1967, 73, Guggenheim grantee, 1970, NEA grantee, 1990; recipient Vernon Rice award, 1966-67, Inst. Arts and Letters award, 1970, Obie award, 1972, 75, 84, 97, Outer Critics Circle award, 1973, Drama Critics Circle award, 1973, 80, Pulitzer prize, 1980, Brandeis award, 1981, John Steinbeck award, 1990, Edward Albee Last Frontier award, 1994, Am. Acad. of Achievement award, 1995, Am. Assn. Theatre Critics Best Play award, 1998, Guild Hall Lifetime Achievement award, 2000, William Inge Lifetime Achievement award, 2001; inducted into Theater Hall of Fame, 1996, Mo. Writers Hall of Fame, 1998; recipient Lucille Lortel's Edith Oliver award for Sustained Excellence, 2001. Mem. Dramatists Guild Am. Council.

WILSON, LAVERNE, nursing administrator; b. Fontaine, Ark., July 27, 1931; d. James Gordon and Sophronia (Scott) Nutt; m. John Bruce Wilson, June 30, 1950 (div. 1971); children: Deborah French, Emily Wilson-Godinet, Valerie Keating, John B. Jr., B.G. Scott Wilson. AA, Ark. State U., 1974. Cert. health facility surveyor. Charge nurse Ark. Methodist Hosp., Paragould, 1975-78; instr. Delta Vo-Tech, Marked Tree, Ark., 1978-81; clin. nurse educator VA Hosp., North Little Rock, 1981-83; adminstrv. coordi. Ark. Methodist Hosp., Paragould, 1983—, in-svc. coord., 1983-88; coord. inspection of care rev. Ark. Found. for Med. Care, Ft. Smith, 1988-90; nursing home insp. and utilization rev. nurse Office of Long Term Care, Dept. Human Svcs., State of Ark., 1990—; pres. J.G.N., Inc. Mem. Ark. Bus. and Profl. Women's Orgn., Alpha Gamma Delta. Democrat. Baptist. Avocations: travel, boating. Home: 4905 Burrow Dr North Little Rock AR 72116-7019

WILSON, LAWRENCE ALEXANDER, construction company executive; b. Nashville, 1935; Grad., Vanderbilt U., 1957. With H.C. Beck Co., Inc., Dallas, 1959-80, pres., COO, 1976-80; chmn., CEO Beck Co., Inc., Dallas, 1980—; pres., CEO HCB Contractors, Dallas, 1980—. Office: The Beck Group 1807 Ross Ave Ste 500 Dallas TX 75201-8006

WILSON, LELAND EARL, petroleum engineering consultant; b. Ft. Recovery, Ohio, Oct. 28, 1925; s. John Huffman and Matilda Caroline (Sunderhaus) W.; m. Marian Ruthetta Trygstad, Nov. 27, 1948; children: Kathleen Ann, Linda Kay, Mary Lee, John Russell. BS in Petroleum Engring., Tulsa U., 1950. Registered profl. engr., Alaska, Tex. Drilling engr. Atlantic Refining Co., Tex., Ark., and La., 1950-56, drilling supr., 1956-65; drilling supt. Atlantic Richfield, Anchorage, 1965-67, prodn. and drilling supt., 1967-72; ops. mgr. ARCO Oil Prodn. Co., London, 1972-75; resident mgr. ARCO Greenland, Copenhagen, 1975-78; pres. ARCO Indonesia, Inc., Jakarta, 1978-82; v.p. ARCO China, Hong Kong, 1982-85; petroleum cons. Lindale, Tex., 1985—. Author family history Dear John, 1989; contbr. articles to profl. jours.; inventor in field. Aviation cadet AAF, 1943-45. Recipient Pioneer award, East Tex. Soc. Petroleum Engrs., 2004. Mem. NSPE, Tex. Soc. Profl. Engrs., Soc. Petroleum Engrs., Petroleum Club (pres. Anchorage 1971-72), Indonesian Petroleum Assn. (pres. 1981-82). Republican. Roman Catholic. Avocations: geneaology, golf, travel. Home: PO Box 893 428 Lone Star Ln Lindale TX 75771-5230 Office: PO Box 893 2715 S Main St Lindale TX 75771-7724

WILSON, LEONARD GILCHRIST, medical history educator; b. Orillia, Ont., Can., June 11, 1928; s. George Edward and Mary Agnes (MacPhee) W.; m. Adelia Katherine Hans, June 7, 1969; 1 child, George Edward Hans. BA, U. Toronto, Can., 1949; M.Sc., U. London, 1955; PhD, U. Wis., Madison, 1958. Lectr. Mount Allison U., Sackville, N.B., Can., 1950-53; vis. instr. U. Calif., Berkeley, 1958-59; asst. prof. Cornell U., Ithaca, N.Y., 1959-60, Yale U., New Haven, 1960-65, assoc. prof., 1965-67; prof., head dept. history of medicine U. Minn., Mpls., 1967-98, prof. emeritus, 1998—. Author: Charles Lyell: The Years to 1841: The Revolution in Geology, 1972, Medical Revolution in Minnesota, 1989, Lyell in America: The Trans Atlantic Years, 1841-1853, 1998; editor: Benjamin Silliman and His Circle, 1979, Sir Charles Lyell's Scientific Journals on the Species Question, 1971; editor Jour. History Medicine and Allied Scis., 1973-82; co-editor: Readings in History of Physiology, 1966; mem. bd. mgrs. Jour. Hist. Medicine, 1962— . Fellow AAAS; mem. Am. Assn. History of Medicine, Am. Hist. Assn., History of Sci. Soc., Minn. Acad. Medicine (pres. 1984-85, sec.-treas. 1989-98), Brit. Soc. for the History of Sci., Soc. for the History of natural History. Home: 797 Goodrich Ave Saint Paul MN 55105-3344 E-mail: wilso004@umn.edu.

WILSON, LERRY, public relations executive; Pres. Wilson McHenry Co, San Mateo, Calif., 1989—. Office: Wilson McHenry Co 393 Vintage Park Dr Ste 140 Foster City CA 94404-1172

WILSON, LEVON EDWARD, law educator, lawyer; b. Charlotte, N.C., Apr. 2, 1954; s. James A. and Thomasina Wilson. BSBA, Western Carolina U., 1976; JD, N.C. Ctrl. U., 1979; Ed D, 2001. Bar: N.C. 1981, U.S. Dist. Ct. (mid. dist.) N.C. 1981, U.S. Tax Ct. 1981, U.S. Ct. Appeals (4th cir.) 1982, U.S. Supreme Ct. 1984; lic. real estate broker, N.C.; cert. mediator N.C. Alternative Dispute Resolution Commn., arbitrator BBB. Pvt. practice, Greensboro, N.C., 1981-85; asst. county atty. Guilford County, Greensboro,

1985-88; asst. prof. N.C. Agrl. & Tech. State U., Greensboro, 1988-91, Western Carolina U., Cullowhee, NC, 1991-96, prof., 1996—, prof., head dept. bus. adminstrn., law and mktg., 1996—2002; pres. Integrated Mgmt. Resources, Inc., 2000—. Pres. Trade Brokers Cons.; legal counsel, bd. dirs. Rhodes Assocs., Inc., Greensboro, 1982—; legal counsel Guilford County Sheriff's Dept., Greensboro, 1985-88; bd. dirs. Webster Enterprises, Inc. Contbr. articles to profl. jours. Bd. dirs. Post Advocacy Detention Program; active mem. Prison Litigation Study Task Force, Adminstrn. Justice Study Com. Recipient Svc. award Blacks in Mgmt., 1980, Excellence in Tchg. award Jay I. Kneedler Found. of Western Carolina U., 1994-95; Student in Free Enterprise fellow. Mem. ABA, N.C. Bar Assn., Acad. Legal Studies in Bus., Southeastern Acad. Legal Studies in Bus. (former editor-in-chief Jour. of Legal Studies in Bus., mng. editor), N.C. Assn. Police Attys., N.C. Real Estate Educators Assn., So. Acad. Legal Studies in Bus., Phi Delta Phi, Beta Gamma Sigma. Democrat. Methodist. Home: PO Box 620 Cullowhee NC 28723-0620 Office: Western Carolina U Coll of Bus Cullowhee NC 28723 Personal E-mail: levonwilson@msn.com. Business E-Mail: lwilson@wcu.edu.

WILSON, LINDA, librarian; b. Rochester, Minn., Nov. 17, 1945; d. Eunice Gloria Irene Wilson. BA, U. Minn., Morris, 1967; MA, U. Minn., 1968. Libr. rsch. svcs. U. Calif., Riverside, 1968-69, head dept. phys. scis. catalog, 1969-71; city libr. Belle Glade (Fla). Mcpl. Libr., 1972-74; instr. part-time Palm Beach Jr. Coll., Belle Glade, 1973; head adult-young adult ext. Kern County Libr. Sys., Bakersfield, Calif., 1974-80; dir. dist. libr. Lake Agassiz Regional Libr. System, Crookston, Minn., 1980-85; supervising libr. San Diego County Libr., 1985-87; county libr. Merced (Calif.) County Libr., 1987-93; learning network mgr. Merced Coll., 1994-95; city libr. Monterey Park (Calif.) Bruggemeyer Meml. Libr., 1995—. Mem. Leadership Merced, 1987-88, East Site Based Coordinating Coun., Merced, 1990-92, Merced Gen. Plan Citizens Adv. Com., 1992-95, Sister City Com., Merced, 1992-95. Recipient Libr. award Eagles Aux., 1984, Woman of Achievement award Commn. on the Status of Women, 1990, Libr. award Calif. Libr. Trustees and Commrs., 1990, Woman of Yr. award Merced Bus. and Profl. Women, 1990, People Who Make a Difference award Monterey Pk. United Dems., 2003, Woman of Yr. award 29th Congl. Dist., 2004. Mem. ALA (sec. pub. libr. sys. sect. 1988-89), Met. Coop. Library Sys. (pres. 1999-2000), Calif. Libr. Assn. (sec. govt. rels. com. 1991-92, continuing edn. com. 1993-96, pub. rels. 1997-2000, nominations com. 2000-01), Minn. Libr. Assn. (pres. pub. libr. divsn. 1985), Merced County Mgmt. Coun. (pres. 1989), Merced Bus. and Profl. Women (Woman of Yr. 1987, pres. 1988-89), East L.A.-Montebello Bus. and Profl. Women (v.p. 1998-2002, pres. 2002-), Rotary (pres. Monterey Park chpt. 1999-2000). Democrat. Lutheran. Avocations: travel, walking, reading, swimming, stamp collecting/philately. Home: 1000 E Newmark Ave Apt 22 Monterey Park CA 91755-3129 Office Phone: 626-307-1418. Business E-Mail: lwilson@montereypark.ca.gov. E-mail: lindalwilson@juno.com.

WILSON, LINDA SMITH, academic administrator; b. Washington, Nov. 10, 1936; d. Fred M. and Virginia D. (Thompson) Smith; m. Malcolm C. Whatley, June 29, 1957 (div. 1969); 1 child, Helen K. Whatley; m. Paul A. Wilson, Jan. 22, 1970; 1 stepchild, Beth A. BA, Tulane U., 1957, HLD (hon.), 1993; PhD, U. Wis., 1962; DLitt (hon.), U. Md., 1993. Rsch. assoc. U. Md., College Park, 1962—64, rsch. asst. prof., 1964—67; vis. asst. prof. U. Mo., St. Louis, 1967—68; asst. to vice chancellor for rsch., asst. vice chancellor for rsch., assoc. vice chancellor for rsch. Washington U., St. Louis, 1968—75; assoc. vice chancellor for rsch. U. Ill., Urbana, 1975—85; assoc. dean U. Ill. Grad. Coll., Urbana, 1978—85; v.p. for rsch. U. Mich., Ann Arbor, 1985—89; pres. Radcliffe Coll., Cambridge, Mass., 1989—99, pres. emeritus, 1999; sr. lectr. Harvard Grad. Sch. Edn., 1989—2003; bd. dirs. Myriad Genetics, Tulane U., Tulane Murphy Found., Friends of DaPonte String Quartet, 2003—. Rsch. resources adv. coun. NIH, Bethesda, Mass., 1978—82; mem. Nat. Commn. on Rsch., Washington, 1978—80; dir.'s adv. coun. NSF, Washington, 1980—89; com. on govt.-univ. relationships NAS, 1981—83, govt.-univ.-industry rsch. roundtable, 1984—89, coord. coun. for edn., 1991—93; energy rsch. adv. bd. Dept. of Energy, 1987—90; chmn. adv. com. office sci. and engring. pers. NRC, 1990—96; adv. com. edn. and human resources NSF, Washington, 1990—95; sci., tech. and states task force Carnegie Commn. on Sci., Tech. and Govt., 1991—92; overser Mus. Sci., Boston, 1992—2001; trustee Mass. Gen. Hosp., 1992—99, hon. trustee, 1999—2002; trustee Com. on Econ. Devel., 1995—; bd. dirs. Inacom, Inc., 1997—2003, Citizens Fin. Group, Inc., 1997—2000, Value Line, Inc., 1998—2000; bd. vis. Coll. Letters and Sci. U. Wis., 1999—; dean's adv. coun. Newcomb Coll., 1999—. Contbr. articles to profl. jours. and book chpts. Adv. bd. Nat. Coalition for Sci. and Tech., Washington, 1983—87; bd. govs. YMCA, Champaign, Ill., 1980—83. Named One of 100 Emerging Leaders, Am. Coun. Edn. and Change, 1978; recipient Centennial award, Newcomb Coll., 1986, Disting. Alumni award, U. Wis., 1997, Radcliffe medal, 1999. Fellow: AAAS (bd. dirs. 1984—88); mem.: Am. Coun. Edn. (commn. on women in higher edn. 1991—93, chair 1993), Inst. Medicine (coun. mem. 1986—89, com. on setting NIH priorities, com. on govt.-industry collaboration in biomed. edn. and rsch.), Assn. for Biomed. Rsch. (bd. dirs. 1983—86), Nat. Coun. Univ. Rsch. Adminstrs., Soc. Rsch. Adminstrs. (Disting. Contbn. to Rsch. Adminstrn. award 1984), Am. Chem. Soc. (bd. coun. com. on chemistry and pub. affairs 1978—80), Phi Kappa Phi, Phi Delta Kappa, Alpha Lambda Delta, Sigma Xi, Phi Beta Kappa. Home: 47 Keene Neck Rd Bremen ME 04551

WILSON, LIZABETH ANNE, library director; b. Waterloo, Iowa, May 21, 1954; d. Martin Lucien and Joanne Hausser Wilson; m. Dean August Pollack, Sept. 1, 1983. BA, Northwestern U., 1972—77; MLS, U. of Ill., 1977—78. Asst. architecture and art libr. U. of Ill., 1979—80, asst. undergraduate libr., 1980—86, asst. dir. of libraries for undergraduate and instrnl. services, 1986—92; assoc. dir. of libraries for rsch. and instrnl. services U. of Wash., Seattle, 1992—2000, dir. of u. libraries, 2001—. Chair of bd. of trustees OCLC, Inc., Dublin, 2003—; exec. dir. Leopoldo Cicognara Program+, Urbana-Champaign, Ill., 1987—; co-founder UWired collaboration at the University of Washington. Author (co-author): (journal article) The Bottom Line; contbr. chapters to books, articles. Recipient Margaret E. Monroe Libr. Adult Services award, RUSA/Am. Libr. Assn., 1995, Miriam Dudley Instrn. Libr. award, Assn. of Coll. and Rsch. Libraries, 1995, EDUCAUSE Award for Systemic Progress in Tchg. and Learning, EDUCAUSE, 2000. Mem.: OCLC Members Coun. (pres. 1999—2000), Assn. of Rsch. Libraries (bd. of directors 2003—), Instrn. Sect. of ACRL (chair 1990—91), Assn. of Coll. and Rsch. Libraries (pres. 2000—01). Achievements include development of. Office: University of Washington Box 352900 Seattle WA 98195-2900 E-mail: betsyw@u.washington.edu.

WILSON, LLOYD LEE, organization administrator; b. Elkton, Md., Sept. 14, 1947; s. Clifton Laws and Betty Raye (Bare) W.; m. Susan Sieg Wilson, 1992; children: Asa, Ryan, Morgan, Daniel. BS in Mgmt., MIT, 1969, MS in Mgmt., 1977. Bus. mgr. med. clinics Mass. Gen. Hosp., Boston, 1970-73; ptnr. Willow Co., mgmt. cons., Cambridge, Mass., 1974-77; dir. community relations Wilson Neuropsychiat. Hosp., Charlottesville, Va., 1977-78; exec. dir. Jefferson Area United Transp. Inc., Charlottesville, Va., 1978-80, Va. Mountain Housing Inc., Blacksburg, 1980-82; gen. sec. Friends Gen. Conf. Religious Soc. Friends, Phila., 1982-85; dir. rsch. and devel. Va. Mountain Housing, Inc., Christiansburg, 1985-88, dir. multifamily housing, 1989-91, regional dir., 1991-92; pres. Friendly Mgmt. Svcs. Corp., Norfolk, Va., 1992-95, Not-for-Profit Mgmt., Inc., Norfolk, Va., 1995—; registrar Chowan Coll., 2002—. Dir. instnl. rsch. Chowan Coll., Murfreesboro, N.C., 2000—, registrar, 2002—; Asst. prof. of acctg., 2001—; pres., dir. Va. Housing Coalition, Inc., 1981-82; treas., bd. dirs. Fiddle Hill Farm, Inc., Barboursville, Va., 1982-89; bd. mgrs. Bible Assn. Friends in Am., Phila., 1983-85; mem. com. rec. ministers Balt. Yearly Meeting Friends, Sandy Spring, Md., 1984-86; asst. sec.-treas. Friends Meeting House Fund, Inc., Phila., 1984-85; asst. presiding clk. Comm. Commn. of Friends United Meeting, Richmond, Ind., 1987-88; recorded min. of gospel, Soc. of Friends, 1989— (presiding clk. Va. Beach monthly meeting 1990-92); dir. coordinating cabinet Va. Coun. Chs., 1988; presiding clk. N.C. Yearly Meeting of Friends, 1991-92. Author: Essays on the Quaker Vision of Gospel Order, 1993; contbr. articles to profl. jours. Treas., bd. dirs. Norfolk (Va.) Quaker House, Inc., 1995-2000; bd. dirs. New Dominion Housing, Inc., Norfolk, 1992-94; vice chmn. Montgomery County Cmty. Svc. Commn., Christianburg, Va., 1980-82; mem. ednl. coun. MIT, 19777-89; bd. dirs. Am. Friends Svc. Com., Inc., Phila., 1980-83; bd. dirs. Interfaith Housing Corp. Cambridge, Inc., 1975-77, treas., 1976-77, also numerous others. Home: PO Box 647 Woodland NC 27897-0647 Office Phone: 252-398-6246. E-mail: llwilson@alum.mit.edu.

WILSON, LOIS M. minister; b. Winnipeg, Man., Can., Apr. 8, 1927; d. Edwin Gardiner Dunn and Ada Minnie (Davis) Freeman; m. Roy F. Wilson, June 9, 1950; children: Ruth, Jean, Neil, Bruce BA, United Coll., Winnipeg, 1947, BDiv, 1969; Diploma in TV prodn., Ryerson Tech. Inst., 1974; DDiv (hon.), Victoria U., Toronto, 1978, United Theol. Coll., Montreal, 1978, Wycliff Coll., 1983, Queens U., Kingston, 1984, U. Winnipeg, 1986, Mt. Allison U., 1988; LLD (hon.), LLD (hon.), Dalhousie U., 1989, Ripon Coll., Wis., 1992; DCL (hon.), Acadia U., 1984; DHuml (hon.), Mt. St. Vincent, Halifax, 1984. Ordained to ministry United Church of Can., 1965. Minister, Thunder Bay, 1965-69, Hamilton, 1969-78, Kingston, 1978-80; moderator United Church of Can., Kingston, 1980-82, McGeachy sr. scholar, 1989-91; pres. Can. Council of Chs., Toronto, Ont., 1976-79; co-dir. Ecumenical Forum Can., Toronto, Ont., 1983-89; pres. World Council of Chs., Geneva, 1983-91; chancellor Lakehead U., Thurder Bay, Ont., 1990-2000; chmn. contemporary theology Lafayette-Orinda (Calif.) Presbyn. Ch., 1995; ind. senator Senate of Can., 1998—2002. Mem. adv. coun. internt. devel. studies U. Toronto, 1987-93, Fair Oto Can., Across Boundries Multifaith Inst., Mining Watch Can.; spokesperson Project Ploughshares, 1st and 2d UN Conf. on Disarmament, N.Y.C., 1978-82; officer Human Rights Commn., Ont., 1973; mem. bd. regents Victoria U., 1990—; chief Can. Fact finding Mission to Sri Lanka, 1992; team mem. Ctrl. Am. Monitoring Group to El Salvador and Guatemala, 1993; spl. envoy of Can. to The Sudan, 1999—; lectr. in field. Author: Like a Mighty River, 1980, Turning the World Upside Down, 1989, Miriam, Mary and Me, 1992, Telling Her Story, 1992, Stories Seldom Told, 1997, Nuclear Waste, 2000, mem. adv. bd.: Can. Woman Studies Jour., York U., 1993—2004; contbr. articles to profl. publs.; author: Transforming the Faith of Our Fathers. Apptd. Can. Senator, 1998; pres. Social Planning Coun., Thunder Bay, 1967—68, Can. Com. for Scientists and Scholars, Toronto, 1982; mem. Refugee Status Adv. Com., 1985—89; chmn. Urban Rural Mission, Can., 1990—96; mem. environ. assessment panel Can. Nuclear Fuel Waste Mgmt. and Disposal Concept, 1989—96; bd. dirs. Elizabeth Fry Soc., Hamilton, 1976—79, Amnesty Internat., 1978—90, Can. Inst. for Internat. Peace and Security, 1984—88, Energy Probe, 1981—86, Internat. Ctr. Human Rights and Dem. Devel., 1997—98, Can. Univ. Svc. Overseas, 1983—85; trustee Nelson Mandela Fund, 1990—92. Decorated Order of Can., Order of Ont., Companion of Order of Can.; recipient Queens Jubilee medal, Commemorative medal for 125th Anniversary of Confederation of Can., 1992, World Federalist Peace award, 1985, Pearson Peace medal UN Assn. of Can., 1985; named hon. pres. Student Christian Movement of Can., Toronto, 1976. Mem. DPR Korea Assoc., Canada (chmn. 2002-), Women, Peace and Security (co-chair 2001-), CAW (pub. rev. bd. 1986—), Can. Assn. Adult Edn. (bd. dirs. 1986-90), Friends Can. Broadcasting (bd. dirs. 1986-94, v.p.), Civil Liberties Assn. (v.p. 1986—), UNIFEM (nat. v.p. 1993-95, mem. CCIC team to monitor El Salvador election 1994), World Federalists (pres. Can. chpt. 1996-2000, v.p. World Federalist Movement intern, 1998-, acting pres., 2004-), Parliament of World's Religions (del. 1993), Christian-Jewish Dialogue Jerusalem (keynote speaker 1994). Mem. United Ch. Of Can. E-mail: royandlois.wilson@sympatico.ca.

WILSON, LUKE, actor; b. Dallas, Sept. 21, 1971; Actor: (TV series) The X Files, 1993, That '70s Show, 1998; (films) Bottle Rocket, 1996, Telling Lies in America, 1997, Best Men, 1997, Scream 2, 1997, Bongwater, 1998, Dog Park, 1998, Home Fries, 1998, Rushmore, 1998, Kill the Man, 1999, Blue Streak, 1999, My Dog Skip, 2000, Committed, 2000, Preston Tylk, 2000, Charlie's Angels, 2000, Legally Blonde, 2001, Soul Survivors, 2001, The Royal Tenenbaums, 2001, The Third Wheel, 2002, Masked & Anonymous, 2003, Old School, 2003, Alex and Emma, 2003, Legally Blonde 2: Red, White & Blonde, 2003, Charlie's Angels: Full Throttle, 2003. Office: c/o ICM 8942 Wilshire Blvd Beverly Hills CA 90211

WILSON, LYNTON RONALD, retired telecommunications company executive; b. Port Colborne, Ontario, Canada, Apr. 3, 1940; s. Ronald Alfred and Blanche Evelyn (Matthews) W.; m. Brenda Jean (Black), Dec. 23, 1968; children: Edward Ronald, Margot Jean, Jennifer Lyn. BA, McMaster U., 1962, LLD, 1995; MA, Cornell U., 1967; D (hon.), U. Montreal, 1995; D in Civil Law, Bishop's U., Lennoxville, Que., Can., 1997; LLD, U. Cape Breton, 1998, Mount Allison U., 2000, Brock U., 2003. Dep. minister Ministry Industry and Tourism, Ont., Canada, 1978-81; pres., CEO Redpath Industries, Ltd., Toronto, Canada, 1981-88; mng. dir. N.Am. Tate and Lyle, PLC, 1986-89; chmn. bd. Redpath Industries, Ltd., Toronto, Canada, 1988-89; vice chmn. Bank of N.S., Toronto, Canada, 1989-90; pres., COO BCE, Inc., Montreal, Canada, 1990-92, pres., CEO, 1992-93, chmn., pres., CEO, 1993-96, chmn., CEO, 1996-98, chmn. bd. dir., 1998-2000. Chmn. bd. dir. CAE, Inc., Nortel Networks Corp.; bd. dir. Daimler Chrysler Can., Inc.; mem. supervisory bd. and chmn.'s coun. Daimler Chrysler AG. Founding co-chmn. HISTORICA Found., Canada. Decorated officer, Order of Can. Mem. The Mount Royal Club of Montreal, York Club, Toronto Golf Club, Rideau Club, Mount Bruno Country Club. Home: 2038 Lakeshore Rd E L6J 1M3 Oakville ON Canada Office: 483 Bay Ste 7th Fl N Tower M5G 2C9 Toronto ON Canada Office Phone: 416-364-4612.

WILSON, M. ROY, medical educator; b. Yokohama, Japan, Nov. 28, 1953; BS, Allegheny Coll., 1976; MD, Harvard Med. Sch., 1980; MS in Epidemiology, UCLA, 1990. Diplomate Nat. Bd. Medicine, Am. Bd. Ophthalmology. Intern Harlem Hosp. Ctr., N.Y.C., 1980-81; resident in ophthalmology Mass. Eye & Ear Infirmary/Harvard Med. Sch., Boston, 1981-84, glaucoma, 1984-85; clin. fellow in ophthalmology Harvard Med. Sch., 1980-85, clin. asst. ophthalmology, 1985-86; clin. instr. dept. surgery, Divsn. Ophthalmology Howard U. Sch. Medicine, Washington, 1985-86; asst. prof. ophthalmology UCLA, 1986-91; asst. prof., chief Divsn. Ophthalmology Charles R. Drew U. of Medicine and Sci., L.A., 1986-90, assoc. prof., chief Divsn. Ophthalmology, 1991-94, acad. dean, 1993-95, dean, 1995-98, prof., 1994-98, UCLA, 1994-98; dean sch. medicine Creihton U., Omaha, 1998—, interim v.p., 1999-2000, vice pres. health scis., 2001—; pres. Tex. Tech. U. Health Sci. Ctr., Lubbock, 2003—. Asst. in ophthalmology Mass. Eye and Ear Infirmary, 1985-86; cons. ophthalmologist, Victoria Hosp., Castries, St. Lucia, 1985-86; hosp. appointment, UCLA; chief physician Martin Luther King, Jr. Hosp., L.A., 1986—; project dir. Internat. Eye Found., Ministry of Health, 1985-86; biology lab instr., Allegheny coll., 1975; instr. in biochemistry Harvard U. Summer Sch., 1977-78; instr. Harvard Med. Sch., 1980-85, others; cons. and presenter in field; participant coms. in field. Mem. AMA, APHA, Assn. Rsch. in Vision and Ophthalmology, Chandler-Grant Glaucoma Soc., Nat. Med. Assn., Am. Acad. Ophthalmology, Inst. Medicine (elected 2004), Soc. Eye Surgeons Internat. Eye Found., Mass. Eye and Ear Infirmary Alumni Assn., So. Calif. Glaucoma Soc., West Coast Glaucoma Study Club, Assn. Univ. Profs. in Ophthalmology, L.A. Eye Soc., Calif. Med. Assn., Am. Glaucoma Soc., Soc. Epidemiol. Rsch. Office: Tex Tech Univ Health Scis Ctr MS 6258 3601 4th St Lubbock TX 79430*

WILSON, MALCOLM CAMPBELL, bank executive; b. Phila., Dec. 9, 1942; s. James Murray and Janet (Haines) Wilson; m. Barbara Ann Bahmermann, June 10, 1989; children from previous marriage: Jennifer Marie, David Campbell, Andrew Russel. BS in Bus. Adminstrn., Drexel U., 1966, MBA in Fin., 1968. Chartered fin. analyst. Rsch. analyst Provident Nat. Bank, Phila., 1971—77, co-mgr. rsch. dept., 1977—78, dir. equity rsch., 1978—84, dir. econ. and investment rsch., 1984—88, chief investment officer PNC Fin. div., 1986—88, sr. v.p., mgr. personal svcs. group, 1989—92; exec. v.p., mgr. investment mgmt. and trust Phila. market PNC Bank, N.A., 1993—95; sr. v.p., mgr. Personal Svcs. Group, Mercantile-Safe Deposit and Trust Co., Balt., 1996—98, exec. v.p., mgr. investment mgmt. and trust, 1998—2003; exec. v.p., mng. dir. Davidson Capital Mgmt., Devon, Pa., 2003—. Served with USN, 1968—71. Fellow: Fin. Analysts Fedn.; mem.: N.Y. Soc. Security Analysts, Mayflower Soc., Pa. Soc. SAR. Republican. Episcopalian. Avocations: hunting, fishing, golf. Home: 2449 Dixie Ln Forest Hill MD 21050 Office: Davidson Capital Mgmt 20 N Waterloo Rd Devon PA 19333 Office Phone: 610-254-2045. Business E-Mail: swilson@davidsoncapmgt.com.

WILSON, MARGARET BUSH, lawyer; b. St. Louis, Jan. 30, 1919; married; 1 child, Robert Edmund. BA cum laude, Talladega Coll., 1940; LL.B., Lincoln U., 1943. Ptnr. Wilson & Wilson, St. Louis, 1947-65; now with firm Wilson & Assocs. Asst. dir. St. Louis Lawyers for Housing, 1969-72; asst. atty. gen. Mo., 1961-62; atty. Rural Electrification Adminstrn., Dept. Agr., St. Louis, 1943-45; instr. civil procedure St. Louis U. Sch. Law, 1971; chmn. St. Louis Land Reutilization Authority, 1975-76; mem. Mo. Coun. Criminal Justice, 1972—; chmn. Intergroup Corp., 1985-87; bd. dirs. Mut. of N.Y. Mem. gen. adv. com. ACDA, 1978-81; trustee emeritus Washington U., St. Louis; chmn. bd. trustees Talladega Coll., Ala., 1988-92; nat. bd. dirs. ARC, 1975-81, United Way, 1978-84, Police Found., 1976-93; treas. NAACP Nat. Housing Corp., 1971-84, chmn. nat. bd., 1975-84; dep. dir./acting dir. St. Louis Model City Agy., 1968-69; adminstr. Mo. Commn. Svc. and Continuing Edn., 1967-68. Recipient Bishop's award Episcopal Diocese Mo., 1962; Juliette Derricotte fellow, 1939-40, Disting. Lawyer award Bar Assn. Metro St. Louis, 1997. Mem. ABA (chmn. youth edn. for citizenship 1991-94, chmn. Nat. Law Day 1998-2000), Nat. Bar Assn., Mo. Bar Assn., Mound City Bar Assn., St. Louis Bar Assn., Alpha Kappa Alpha. Office: Wilson & Assocs 4054 Lindell Blvd Saint Louis MO 63108-3202 Office Phone: 314-534-4400.

WILSON, MARGARET EILEEN, retired physical education educator; b. Kansas City, Mo., Aug. 4, 1925; d. Edward Leslie and Bertha Mae (Coe) W. BS in Edn., U. Ark., 1944, MS, 1949; PhD, U. Iowa, 1960. Cert. secondary tchr., Ark. Recreation dir. Pine Bluff (Ark.) Arsenal, 1944-45; instr. Ctrl. High Sch., Muskogee, Okla., 1945-48; grad. asst. U. Ark., Fayetteville, 1948-49; instr. Fayetteville High Sch., 1949-52; from instr. to asst. prof. Ark. Poly. Coll., Russellville, 1952-57, assoc. prof., 1959-65; grad. asst. U. Iowa, Iowa City, 1957-59; prof. Tex. Tech. U., Lubbock, 1965-90, dept. chair health, phys. edn. and recreation for women, 1967-76, prof. emerita, 1990—. Mem. Tex. Tech. Faculty Senate, 1978-90, pres., 1978-79, 85-86. Active Lubbock County Dem. Com., 1993, 94, 96. Recipient AMOCO Found. Disting. Tchg. award, 1978, Disting. Faculty award in Tex. Tech. Moms and Dads Assn., 1987. Mem. AAHPERD (life), Tex. Assn. for Health, Phys. Edn., Recreation and Dance (Honor award 1979, David K. Bruce award 1992), Tex. Tech. Faculty Legal Action Assn. (pres. 1990-96), Lubbock Ret. Tchrs. Assn. (cmty. svc. chair 1994-96, co-treas. 1996-99), Double T Connection (chair membership 1991-94), Delta Gamma (house corp. treas. 1982-91, Cable award 1978), Delta Kappa Gamma (chpt. pres. 1972-74, Chpt. Achievement award 1976, state corr. sec. 1979-81, state conv. chair 1979-80, state nominations com. 1985-87, state pers. com. 1987-89, State Achievement award 1987, state necrology com. 1993-95, state fin. com. 1995-96). Presbyterian. Avocations: gardening, needlepoint, reading. Home: 5411 46th St Lubbock TX 79414-1513 Office: Tex Tech U Womens Gymnasium Lubbock TX 79409

WILSON, MARGARET MARY GEORGIANA, geriatrician, researcher, physician; d. Victoria Arit and Andrew Iyere Wilson. BS, U. Ibadan, Nigeria, 1977, MB, 1983. Diplomate Am. Bd. of Internal Medicine, 2000. Sr. registrar U. of Ibadan, Oyo, Nigeria, 1988—90; clin. rsch. fellow Hammersmith Hosp., London, 1990—91, St. Louis U., 1994—97; asst. prof. St Louis U., 2000—; med. dir. Tower Village NH, 2000—, Integrated Health Svcs., Big Bend Woods, Mo., 2003—; dir. clin. svcs. St. Louis U., 2004—. Mem. Nat. Coun. Nutrition, 2001—; editl. bd. mem. Jour. Gerontology: Med. Scis., St. Louis, 2000—; guest editor Clinics in Geriatric Medicine, Phila. Mem. MCC, St Louis, Mo., 2002—04. Recipient Chevening Medicine award, Brit. Fgn. and Commonwealth Office, 1990, Vincent Uzodike; Internal Medicine, Nat. Postgraduate Coll. of Physicians, Nigeria, 1991, Sunderland DGH Excellence in Clin. Presentation, Sunderland DGH, Eng., 1993. Fellow: Nat. Postgrad. Coll. Physicians Nigeria, Acad. Minority Physicians (assoc.); mem.: Royal Coll. Physicians, Am. Geriatric Soc., Brit. Coun. Study Fellows, Am. Med. Dirs. Assn. Christianity. Achievements include development of Geriatric Appetite Evaluation Instrument. Avocation: non-fiction works. Office: Geriatric Div St Louis U 1402 S Grand Blvd Rm M238 Saint Louis MO 63104 E-mail: wilsonmg@slu.edu.

WILSON, MARGARET SCARBROUGH, retail executive; b. Aug. 7, 1930; Student, Smith Coll., 1948-50; BA, U. Tex., 1952. Mem. staff Bayway Refinery Exxon Corp., N.J., 1960-61; mem. staff psychiat. ward VA Hosp., Houston, 1962; from mem. staff to chmn. Scarbroughs, Austin, Tex., 1952—74, chmn. bd., CEO, 1974—. Mem., bd. dirs. audit and contbns. coms. R.J. Reynolds Industries, 1978-85; hon. bd. dirs. Internat. Longevity Ctr., N.Y.C.; bd. dirs. Scarbrough Devel. Corp., Nat. Retail Fedn., 1991-2002, Am. Productivity & Quality Ctr., 1991-2002; chmn. San Antonio br. Fed. Res. Bank Dallas, 1975-76; trustee Nat. Policy Assn., 1997-98; pres., treas. Scarbrough Ventures LLC, 2001-, MSW-NSG Mgmt. LLC, 2000-, MSW-NSG Enterprises Ltd., 2000-, MSW-NSG Real Estate Ventures Ltd., 2001-. Trustee Com. Econ. Devel., 1973—, Cooper Inst. for Aerobics Rsch., Dallas, 1980-93, St. Stephen's Sch., Austin, 1979-83; mem. Nat. Com. U.S.-China Rels., 1976—, dir. 1980-94; mem. U.S. Coun. Internat. Bus., 1977—, mem. exec. com., 1978—, trustee, 1978—; bd. vistors Babcock Grad. Sch. Mgmt.-Wake Forest U., Winston-Salem, N.C., 1983-86; mem. bus. adv. coun. S.W. Tex. State U., 1983-86; mem. deptl. vis. com. dept. home econs. U. Tex.-Austin, 1983-84, pres.'s assocs., 1992—; mem. univ. coun. Rockefeller U., N.Y.C., 1982-86; mem. chancellor's coun. U. Tex. Sys., 1994—; mem. Tex. Rsch. League, 1977—, dir. audit com. 1986—, Friends of L.B.J. Libr., 1980—; assoc. mem. George Bush Presdl. Libr., 1995—; bd. dirs. World Bus. Coun., 1980-89; mem. adv. coun. Coll. Bus. Adminstrn., U. Tex.-Austin, 1964-68, Dean's Assocs. Coll. Fine Arts, 1985-87, Friends of Free Enterprise com. Coll. Engring., 1985-87; mem. India-U.S. Bus. Coun., 1976-82, dir., 1978-82; mem. Pres.'s Commn. on Pers. Interchange, 1972-73, UN Day Com., 1971-74; mem. Mayor's Bus. Roundtable, Austin, 1985-87; mem. Houston Com. Fgn. Rels., 1994—, Dallas Com. Fgn. Rels., 1997—, SRI Internat. Assocs. Program, 1998-99; mem. Conf. Bd. Mem. Alliance Francaise, Asia Soc. (adv. bd. Houston chpt., 1991-94, mem. N.Y. chpt.), Houston World Affairs Coun., Austin World Affairs Coun., English Speaking Union, Tex. Assn. Taxpayers, Retail Industry Trade Action Coalition (trustee 1984), Nat. Planning Assn. (trustee 1985-97), Am. Enterprise Inst. Am. Mgmt. Assn. (dir. 1969-72), Internat. C. of C., British Am. Bus. Inc., U.S. C. of C. (bd. dirs. 1980-82), Tex. Asian C. of C. (mem. adv. coun. 1997—), Tex. State Soc. Wash., World Econ. Devel. Congress (mem. adv. bd. 1993), Internat. Indsl. Conf. (mem. adv. coun. 1996-97), Coun. Fgn. Rels., World Econ. Forum, Bus. Coun. Internat. Understanding, Ctr. Strategic and Internat. Studies (Washington Round Table 1998—), Am. Enterprise Inst., Pacific Coun. on Internat. Policy, World Pres.'s Orgn. (internat. chpt., met. chpt., Dallas chpt., Houston chpt., Cen. Tex. chpt.), Pres.'s Cir. Nat. Acad. Scis., Inst. of Medicine and Inst. Engrs., Houston Forum, Brookings Instn., Bretton Woods Com., Brit.-N.A. Com., Tarry House, The University Club N.Y., Met. Club (Washington), Headliners Club, Tex. Breakfast Club of Washington, Kappa Kappa Gamma, numerous other local and nat. orgns. Office: 517 W 39th St Austin TX 78751-4904 E-mail: Margaret.Wilson@Scarbroughs.com.

WILSON, MARGARET SULLIVAN, retired executive dean, consultant; b. Norwich, Conn., Mar. 21, 1924; d. John Joseph and Margaret Ellen (Connelly) Sullivan; BS, Eastern Conn. State U., 1944; MA, U. Conn., 1949; m. William Robert Wilson, July 20, 1950 (dec.); children: Margaret Ellen, William Robert. Reading cons. Greenwich (Conn.) Pub. Schs., 1948-50; asst. prof. early childhood, chmn. dept. early childhood Eastern Conn. State U., Willimantic, 1967-77, exec. asst. to pres., 1977-78, v.p. adminstrv. affairs, 1978-80, exec. dean, 1980-89, emeritus dean, 1989—; commr. Nat. Commn. Prevention Infant Mortality, 1986-93, chair Norwich Econ. Devel. Commn., 1988-91, Southeastern Connecticut regional Planning Comm., 1999-2001(mem. 1993—); dir. Rose City Community Land Trust Housing, Com. on City Plan, 1992—; del. White House Conf. on Children, 1970, 80, White House Conf. on Travel and Tourism, 1995; corporator Chelsea Groton Savs. Bank, Norwich, Conn. Mem. Conn. Mental Health Bd., 1979-83; mem. adv. bd. Norwich Hosp.; chmn. rev. com. Conn. Health Coordinating Council; mem. Eastern Regional Mental Health Bd., 1976-83, chmn., 1979-81; mem. Norwich Bd. Edn., 1954-69, 80-83, adv. coun. head start and day care programs, 1986-91; mem. Conn. Dem. Cen. Com., 1964-82, Dem. Town Com., 1964-82, 86-90; chmn. Blue Ribbon Commn. To Establish Goals for U. Conn. Health Ctr., 1975-76; sr. warden Ch. of Resurrection, Norwich., 1988-91, Dio Com on Ministry Higher Edn. Named Citizen of Yr., C. of C., 1970; recipient Disting.

Alumni award Eastern Conn. State U., 1972, Mental Health Bell award Conn. Mental Health Assn., 1972, Valiant Women award Council Ch. Women, 1976, Woman of Yr. award Bus. and Profl. Women, 1978, Jefferson award Inst. Pub. Service, 1982, pres. Norwich Mus. Trust, Inc., 1992—; mem., vice chair Southeastern Conn. Regional Planning Commn., 1993—; dir. Family Svc. Southeastern Conn., 1995—, Southeastern Conn. Enterprise Region, Norwich Comm. and Tech. Learning Ctr.; past-pres. Eastern Conn. Cmty. Found.; del. White House Conf. on Aging, 1995. Mem. Norwich Area C. of C. (dir. 1979-81), Greater Willimantic C. of C. (edn. com. 1980-88), United Ch. Women Conn. (bd. dirs.). Democrat. Office: 83 Windham St Willimantic CT 06226-2211 Home: 206 Washington St Apt 65 Norwich CT 06360-3553

WILSON, MARIE C. foundation administrator; b. Ga. 5 children. D in Cmty. Svc.(hon.), Drake U. Dir. women's programs Drake U.; mem. DesMoines City Coun.; pres. Ms. Found. for Women, N.Y.C., 1984—. Co-creator Take Our Daus. To Work Day, 1993—; U.S. govt. del. UN Fourth World Conf. on Women, Beijing, 1995; co-founder, pres. The White House Project, 1998—. Co-author: Mother Daughter Revolution, 1993; author: Closing the Leadership Gap: Why Women Can and Must Help Run the World, 2004. Recipient Robert W. Scrivner award for creative grantmaking, Leadership for Equity and Diversity award, Women & Philanthropy. Office: Ms Found for Women 120 Wall St 33rd fl New York NY 10005

WILSON, MARK, corporate financial executive; BS in Agrl. Econs.; MBA in Fin. and Acctg., Cornell U. V.p. Thomas Learning MacAndrews & Forbes; chief fin. officer Towers Perrin, 2001—. Office: Towers Perrin 1 Stanford Plz Stamford CT 06901

WILSON, MARON LOY, nurse midwife; b. Westmoreland, Jamaica, Feb. 24, 1949; d. Johnaton and Annette Myrtle Wilson; 1 child, Elizabeth Wilson Strudwick. RN, U. Hospital of West Indies, 1968—71. Cert. state cert.nurse, Good Hope Maternity Hosp., 1978, midwifery tutor diploma, Royal Coll. Midwives, 1980, cert. nurse midwife, N.Y., 1995. Nurse midwife Downtown Bronx Med., 1996—; registered nurse Lincoln Hosp., Bronx, Met. Hosp.; life underwriter Mutual Life, Kingston, Jamaica; lectr. Excelsior Cmty. Coll., Kingston, Jamaica; registered nurse U. Hosp. of W.I., Kingston, Jamaica; tchr. Bethel Town Primary Sch., Westmoreland, Jamaica. Curriculum develop. com. Excelsior Coll. Cmty., Kingston, Jamaica, 1983—85. Contbr. articles. Disaster preparedness com. Excelsior Cmty. Coll., 1983—85. Avocations: reading, dance, writing, music, aerobics.

WILSON, MARTIN D. pharmaceutical executive; Pres., COO D & K Healthcare Resources, Inc., St. Louis. Office: D&K Healthcare Resources Inc PO Box 16989 Saint Louis MO 63105-1389

WILSON, MARY ALICE, violinist, music teacher; b. Nov. 2, 1939; MusB, Northwestern U., 1961. Orch. band dir., pvt. tchr. Luth. Schs., Deerfield Pub. Schs., 1961-64; pvt. tchr. violin and piano Cleve., 1964-77; dir. Suzuki Program, violin tchr. W.Va. U., 1977—; founder, leader Seneca String Quartet, Morgantown, W.Va., 1986—. Accompanist. Ch. vol. Tchg. and Music, Cleve., Chgo., Morgantown, 1960—. Mem.: Am. String Tchrs. Assn. (co-developer, chmn. 5th yr. state solo competition), W.Va. Music Tchrs. Assn. (dist. chmn. of strings 1977—, state officer pub. 1989—, State Outstanding Tchr. Yr. 1996), Music Tchrs. Nat. Assn. (state office of composition contest 1989—). Home: 237 Poplar Dr Morgantown WV 26505-2519 E-mail: cbwilson@mail.wvu.edu.

WILSON, MARY ELIZABETH, epidemiologist, physician, educator; b. Indpls., Nov. 19, 1942; d. Ralph Richard and Catheryn Rebecca (Kurtz) Lausch; m. Harvey Vernon Fineberg, May 16, 1975. AB, Ind. U., 1963; MD, U. Wis., 1971. Diplomate Am. Bd. Internal Medicine, Am. Bd. Infectious Diseases. Tchr. of French and English Marquette Sch., Madison, Wis., 1963-66; intern in medicine Beth Israel Hosp., Boston, 1971-72, resident in medicine, 1972-73, fellow in infectious diseases, 1973-75; physician Albert Schweitzer Hosp., Deschapelles, Haiti, 1974-75, Harvard Health Svcs., Cambridge, Mass., 1974-75; asst. physician Cambridge Hosp., 1975-78; hosp. epidemiologist Mt. Auburn Hosp., Cambridge, 1975-79, chief of infectious diseases, 1978—2002, dir. Travel Resource Ctr., 1996—2002, mem. consulting staff, 2003—. Adv. com. immunization practices CDC, Atlanta, 1988-92; acad. adv. com. Nat. Inst. Pub. Health, Mex., 1989-91; cons. Ford Found., 1988; site dir. GeoSentinel network, 1999-2002, spl. cons., 2002--; instr. in medicine Harvard Med. Sch., Boston, 1975-93, asst. clin. prof., 1994-99, assoc. prof. medicine, 1999—, assoc. Ctr. Health & Global Environment, 1996-2000; asst. prof. depts. epidemiology and population and internat. health Harvard Sch. Pub. Health, 1994-99, assoc. prof. population and internat. health, 1999—; lectr. Sultan Qaboos U., Oman, 1991; chair Woods Hole Workshop, Emerging Infectious Diseases, 1993. Author: A World Guide to Infections: Diseases, Distribution, Diagnosis, 1991; co-editor: (with Richard Levins and Andrew Spielman) Disease in Evolution: Global Changes and Emergence of Infectious Diseases, 1994; mem. editl. bd. Current Issues in Pub. Health, 1999-2003, Emerging Infectious Diseases, Global Change and Human Health, 1999-2003; sect. editor, travel medicine and tropical diseases, editl. bd. Infectious Diseases in Clin. Practice; assoc. editor Jour. Watch Infectious Diseases; editl. adv. bd. Clinical Infectious Diseases. Mem. Cambridge Task Force on AIDS, 1987-90, Earthwatch, Watertown, Mass., Cultural Survival, Inc., Cambridge; bd. dirs. Horizon Comm., West Cornwall, Conn., 1990-97. Recipient Lewis E. and Edith Phillips award U. Wis. Med. Sch., 1969, Cora M. and Edward Van Liere award, 1971, Mosby Scholarship Book award, 1971, Leo Blacklow tchg. award, 1999; scholar-in-residence Bellagio (Italy) Study Ctr., Rockefeller Found., 1996; fellow Ctr. for Advanced Study in the Behavioral Scis., Stanford, Calif., 2002. Fellow: ACP, Royal Soc. Tropical Medicine and Hygiene, Infectious Diseases Soc. Am.; mem.: Soc. for Epidemiol. Rsch., Internat. Union Against Tuberculosis and Lung Disease, Soc. for Vector Ecology, Wilderness Med. Soc., Internat. Soc. Travel Medicine, Peabody Soc., Mass. Infectious Diseases Soc., Am. Soc. Tropical Medicine and Hygiene, N.Y. Acad. Scis., Am. Soc. Microbiology, Aesculapian Club, Alpha Omega Alpha, Phi Sigma Iota, Sigma Sigma. Avocations: playing the flute, hiking, reading, travel. Business E-Mail: mary_wilson@harvard.edu.

WILSON, MELVIN EDMOND, retired civil engineer; b. Bremerton, Wash., Aug. 3, 1935; s. Edmond Curt and Madeline Rose (Deal) W.; m. Deanna May Stevens, Nov. 22, 1957 (div. Mar. 1971); children: Kathleen, Debra Wilson Frank. BSCE, U. Wash., 1957, MSCE, 1958. Registered profl. engr., Wash. Asst. civil engr. City of Seattle, 1958-60, assoc. civil engr., 1960-64, sr. civil engr., 1964-66, supervising civil engr., 1966-75, sr. civil engr., 1975-77, mgr. X, 1977-88; owner Wilson Cons. Svcs., Seattle, 1988-89; transp. sys. dir. City of Renton, Wash., 1989-96, ret., 1996. Owner Mel Wilson Photographer, Seattle, 1975-84. Contbr. reports to profl. jours. Rep. Renton transp. work group King County (Wash.) Growth Mgmt. Policy Com.; rep. Renton tech. adv. com. South County Area Transp. Bd., King County, 1992-96, developer svc. policy (adopted by Puget Sound Govtl. Conf.) to encourage travel by transit. successfuly led effort to make Renton first suburban city to receive direct transit svc. under Met. King County Plan, 1994; vol. personal trainer, 1988—; vol. trainer for medical patients, 1988—. Mem. ASCE, Am. Pub. Works Assn., Inst. Transp. Engrs., Tau Beta Pi, Sigma Xi. Avocations: photography, weightlifting, hiking, art.

WILSON, MICHAEL HOLCOMBE, investment banker, former Canadian government official; b. Toronto, Ont., Can., Nov. 4, 1937; s. Harry Holcombe and Constance L. (Davies) W.; m. Margaret Catherine Smellie, Oct. 17, 1964; children: Cameron (dec.), Geoffrey, Lara. Student, Upper Can. Coll.; B in Comm., U. Toronto, 1959. With Harris & Partners Ltd., Toronto, 1961-63, 65-73, v.p., 1972; exec. v.p. following merger with Dominion Securities Ltd., 1973-79; mem. Can. Ho. of Commons, Ottawa, 1979-93; min. of state for internat. trade Govt. Can., Ottawa, 1979-80, min. of fin., 1984-91, min. of industry, sci. & tech., min. internat. trade, 1991-93; bus. advisor Michael Wilson Internat., Toronto, 1993—2000; vice chmn. RBC Dominion Securities Inc., 1995-2000; chmn. UBS Global Asset Mgmt. Co. (formerly Brinson Can. Co.), Canada, 2000—04, UBS Can., 2004—. Mem. bd. Ctr. for Addiction and Mental Health Found., 2000; chmn. Mental Health Implementation Task Force; bd. mem. Cmty. Found. for Greater Toronto; bd. dirs. BP PLC, Manulife Fin.; chmn. Neurosci. Can. Partnership, Can. Coun. Pub.-Pvt. Partnerships, Can. Coalition for Good Governance; chancellor Trinity Coll. Mem. Toronto Club, Toronto Golf, Badminton and Racquet Club, Osler Bluff Ski Club, Mad River Golf Club, Kappa Alpha. Progressive Conservative. Anglican. Office: UBS Can 161 Bay St Ste 4100 PO Box 617 Toronto ON Canada M5J 2S1

WILSON, MICHAEL JOHN, biologist, educator; b. Iowa City, June 3, 1942; s. James H. and Doris E. (Lackender) W.; m. Martha J. Swartzwelter, June 7, 1969; 1 child, Matthew. AA, Divine Word Coll., 1962; BA, St. Ambrose Coll., 1964; MS, U. Iowa, 1967, PhD, 1971. Rsch. fellow Harvard Med. Sch. Boston, 1971-73; scientist VA Med. Ctr., Mpls., 1975—2000, Career Rsch. scientist, 2000—; rsch. assoc. U. Minn., Mpls., 1973-75, asst. prof., 1975—82, assoc. prof., 1982-2000, prof., 2000—. Mem. regional adv. bd. Inst. Disability Studies, 1989-93. Mem. editl. bd. Jour. of Andrology, 1998—; contbr. articles to profl. jours. Chmn. spl. edn. coun. St. Paul Pub. Schs., Minn., 1982-85; bd. dirs. United Cerebral Palsy Minn., 1985-96; mem. devel. disabilities com. Ramsey County Citizens Adv. Coun., 1997-2003; mem. assistive tech. bd. Courage Ctr., 2001-2003. Mem. Am. Soc. Study Cell Biology, Soc. for Study Reprodn., Am. Soc. Andrology, Internat. Soc. Proteolysis, Soc. Basic Urologic Rsch. Democrat. Roman Catholic. Home: 2053 Dayton Ave Saint Paul MN 55104-5732 Office Phone: 612-467-2810. E-mail: wilso042@umn.edu.

WILSON, MICHAEL MOUREAU, lawyer, physician; b. Cheverly, Md., Dec. 30, 1952; s. Kenneth Moureau and Helen (Rice) Smith. BS, MIT, 1974; JD, Georgetown U., 1977, MD, 1986. Bar: D.C. 1977, N.Y. 1980, U.S. Dist. Ct. D.C. 1980, U.S. Dist. Ct. Md. 1992, U.S. Ct. Appeals (D.C. cir.) 1980, U.S. Supreme Ct. 1981. Law clk. Hon. John B. Hannum U.S. Dist. Ct., Phila., 1977—78; assoc. Cravath Swaine & Moore, N.Y.C., 1978—79; asst. to gen. counsel NSF, Washington, 1979—82; resident in psychiatry St. Elizabeth Hosp., 1986—89; pvt. practice med. malpractice litigation, 1989—. Notes editor Am. Criminal Law Rev., 1976-77. Mem. ABA, Assn. Trial Lawyers Am., D.C. Trial Lawyers Assn., Phi Beta Kappa. Office: 1120 19th St NW Ste LL-11 Washington DC 20036 Office Phone: 202-223-4488. Business E-Mail: wilson@wilsonlaw.com.

WILSON, MICHAEL PAUL, pharmacist; b. Houma, La., Mar. 13, 1964; s. Gene Tunny Wilson, Doris Moras Wilson. BS in Pharmacy, U. La., 1996; PharmD. Registered pharmacist Ark. . Intern pharmacist K&B Drugs, Shreveport, La., 1994—96; staff pharmacist K&B Drugs/Rite Aid Corp., Shreveport, 1996—98; pharmacy mgr. Rite Aid Corp., 1998—2000, pharmacy dist. mgr. Baton Rouge, 2000—01, pharmacy dist. trainer Shreveport, 2001—01; pharmacist in charge mgr. Walgreens Pharmacy, Marshall, Tex., 2001—. Corp. adv. bd. Rite Aid Corp., Harrisburg, 2000—01. Bd dir. Northwest La. Interfaith Pharmacy, Shreveport, 2000—01. Recipient McKessan Leadership award, Acad. Students Pharmacy, APHA, 1995—96. Mem.: Red River Pharmacist Assn., Am. Pharm. Assn., Phi Lambda Sigma (life), Phi Delta Chi (life). Avocations: boating, fishing, camping, music. Home: 14423 Garden St Brownsboro TX 75756 Office: Brookshires Grocery Co 703 Hwy 31 E Chandler TX 75758

WILSON, MIRIAM GEISENDORFER, retired physician, educator; b. Yakima, Wash., Dec. 3, 1922; d. Emil and Frances Geisendorfer; m. Howard G. Wilson, June 21, 1947; children— Claire, Paula, Geoffrey, Nicola, Marla. BS, U. Wash., Seattle, 1944, MS, 1945; MD, U. Calif., San Francisco, 1950. Mem. faculty U. So. Calif. Sch. Medicine, L.A., 1965—, prof. pediatrics, 1969—2004, emeritus prof. pediatrics, 2004—. Office: U So Calif Med Ctr 1129 N State St Rm 1g24 Los Angeles CA 90033-1044

WILSON, MIRIAM JANET WILLIAMS, publishing executive; b. London, Ont., Can., July 13, 1939; d. Ralph George and Lillian Conn Williams; m. Carson Winnette, Nov. 20, 1960 (div. 1971); children: Barrie Carson Winnette, Rebecca Lynn Winnette; m. Charles Lindsay Wilson, Dec. 14, 1973; 1 child, Charles William Wilson; stepchildren: Kenneth M., Carol Ann, Catherine S., Nancy L., Patrick L. Diploma in nursing, Glendale (Calif.) Sanitarium & Hosp., 1960. RN, Calif., Va., Ohio, Md., W.Va. Head nurse emergency and med. fls. Glendale Sanitarium and Hosp., 1960-65; psychometrist Harding Hosp., Worthington, Ohio, 1969-73; biofeedback specialist in assn. Dr. Randolph P. Johnston, Winchester, Va., 1980-84; dir. Stress Ctr. for Children and Adults, Shepherdstown, W.Va., 1985-87; pres. Rocky River Pubs. LLC, Shepherdstown, 1987—. Lectr. ednl., profl. and civic groups, 1984—. Author: Help For Children, 7 edits., 1987-2004, Stress Stoppers, 2 edits., 1987-89; contbr. articles to profl. publs. Active Shepherdstown Women's Club, 1986-2004. Mem. NAFE, Internat. Platform Assn., Am. Booksellers Assn., N.Y. Acad. Scis. Avocations: gardening, music, reading. Office: Rocky River Pubs LLC PO Box 1679 Shepherdstown WV 25443-1679 E-mail: rockyriverpublishers@citlink.net.

WILSON, MITCHELL B. fraternal organization administrator; b. Berea, Ky., Jan. 27, 1956; s. William Paul and Shirley Ann (Rose) W.; m. Joan Gentry, May 25, 1985; 1 child, Theodore Mitchell. BA, U. Ky., Lexington, 1980. Chpt. cons. Kappa Sigma Frat., Charlottesville, Va., 1980-82, exec. asst., 1982-83, dir. chpt. ops., 1983-85, dir. pub. rels., 1985-87, exec. dir., 1987—. Editor: The Caducens Mag., 1987—. Mem. Am. Soc. Assoc. Execs., Frat. Execs. Assn. Home: 506 Nottingham Rd Charlottesville VA 22901-1239 Office: Kappa Sigma PO Box 5066 Charlottesville VA 22905-5066

WILSON, MYRON ROBERT, JR., retired psychiatrist; b. Helena, Mont., Sept. 21, 1932; s. Myron Robert, Sr. and Constance Ernestine (Bultman) Wilson. BA, Stanford U., 1954, MD, 1957. Diplomate Am. Bd. Psychiatry and Neurology. Dir. adolescent psychiatry Mayo Clinic, Rochester, Minn., 1965-71; pres., psychiatrist in chief Wilson Ctr., Faribault, Minn., 1971-86, chmn., 1986-90; ret., 1990. Assoc. clin. prof. UCLA, 1985—99. Contbr. articles to profl. jours. Chmn., CEO C. B. Wilson Found., LA, 1972—; bd. dirs. Pasadena (Calif.) Symphony Orch. Assn., 1987; vestryman, treas. St. Thomas' Parish, LA, 1993—96. Lt. comdr. USN, 1958—60. Fellow, Mayo Grad. Sch. Medicine, Rochester, 1960—65. Fellow: Internat. Soc. Adolescent Psychiatry (founder, treas. 1985—88, sec. 1985—88, treas. 1988—92), Am. Soc. Adolescent Psychiatry, Am. Psychiat. Assn.; mem.: Sigma Xi (Mayo Found. chpt.). Episcopalian. Home and Office: Wilson Found 443 W Santa Elena Rd Palm Springs CA 92262 Office Phone: 760-325-4956. Personal E-mail: mrobertwilson@aol.com.

WILSON, NANCY LINDA, religious organization administrator; b. Mineola, N.Y., July 13, 1950; Grad., Allegheny Coll.; student, Boston U.; MDiv, SS, Cyril and Methodius Sem. Ordained to ministry Universal Fellowship of Met. Cmty. Chs. Dist. coord. N.E. dist. Universal Fellowship of Met. Cmty. Chs., clk. bd. of elders Fellowship hdqrs., 1979-86, sr. pastor Met. Cmty. Ch., 1986—; vice-moderator UFMCC, L.A., 1993—. Bd. trustees Samaritan Inst. Religious Studies; founder, chief ecumenical officer Ecumenical Witness and Ministry; vice chair Progressive Religious Alliance. Author: Our Tribe: Queer Folks, God, Jesus and the Bible, 1995; co-author: Amazing Grace; prodr.: (brochure) Our Story Too. Rockefeller scholar. Office: Met Cmty Ch 8714 Santa Monica Blvd West Hollywood CA 90069-4508

WILSON, NORMAN GLENN, church administrator, writer; b. Rensselaer, N.Y., Nov. 3, 1936; s. Lawrence Wilbur and Wilhelmena Augusta (Knapp) W.; m. Nancy Ann Deyo, Nov. 17, 1956; children: Beth, Lawrence, Jonathan. BRE in Religious Edn., United Wesleyan Coll., 1958, DD (hon.), 1986; MA in Biblical Studies, Winona Lake Sch. Theology, 1968. Pastor The Wesleyan Ch., 1958-76, 1963-66, North Lakeport, Mich., 1966-70, Owosso, Mich., 1970-76, dir. comm. Indpls., 1992—. Program prodr., speaker The Wesleyan Hour, Indpls., 1975—; mem. gen. adminstrn. coun. The Wesleyan Ch., Indpls., 1992—; disting. lectr. Staley Found., 1986. Author: How to Have a Happy Home, 1976, Christianity in Shoe Leather, 1978, The Constitution of the Kingdom, 1989, People Just Like Us, 1994, Follow the Leader, A Daily Spiritual Journey, 1996; editor, contbr.: Journey Into Holiness, 2000; The Call to Contentment, 2002; editor The Wesleyan Advocate, 1992-2004, Wesleyan Life, 2004-. Mem. Nat. Religious Broadcasters (bd. dirs. 1984—, Merit award 1984). Mem. Wesleyan Ch. Avocations: painting, antique cars. Home: 304 Scarborough Way Noblesville IN 46060-3881 E-mail: wilsonn@wesleyan.org.

WILSON, OWEN, actor; b. Dallas, Nov. 18, 1968; s. Robert and Laura Wilson. BA in English, U. Tex., Austin, 1991. Actor: (TV films) Heat Vision and Jack, 1999; (TV series) King of the Hill, 1997; assoc. prodr. (films) As Good as It Gets, 1997; exec. prodr.(actor): (films) The Royal Tenenbaums, 2001; writer, actor: films Bottle Rocket, 1996; actor: (films) The Cable Guy, 1996, Anaconda, 1997, Armageddon, 1998, Permanent Midnight, 1998, Rushmore, 1998, The Minus Man, 1999, Breakfast of Champions, 1999, The Haunting, 1999, Shanghai Noon, 2000, Meet the Parents, 2000, Zoolander, 2001, Behind Enemy Lines, 2001, I Spy, 2002, Shanghai Knights, 2003, The Big Bounce, 2004, Starsky & Hutch, 2004. Office: ICM 8942 Wilshire Blvd Beverly Hills CA 90211*

WILSON, OWEN MEREDITH, JR., lawyer; b. Oakland, Calif., Dec. 22, 1939; s. O. Meredith and Marian Wilson; m. Sandra A. Wilson (div.); children: Ann, Melissa, Jennifer; m. Teddi Anne Wilson; children: Amanda, Lisa. Student, U. Utah, 1957-59; AB, Harvard U., 1961; LLB, U. Minn., 1965. Bar: Oreg. 1965, Wash. 1985. Ptnr. Lane Powell Spears Lubersky, Portland, Oreg., 1969—. Mem. mediation panel U.S. Dist. Ct., 1986—. Mem. bd. visitors Law Sch. U. Minn., 1990-96. Mem. ABA, Oreg. State Bar Assn., Wash. State Bar, Multnomah Bar Assn. Office: 601 SW 2nd Ave Ste 2100 Portland OR 97204-3158 Office Phone: 503-778-2131. E-mail: wilsonm@lanepowell.com.

WILSON, PAMELA AIRD, physician; b. Milw., May 13, 1947; d. Rushen Arnold and Marianna (Dickie) W.; m. Paul Quin, June 20, 1981. BS in Zoology, U. Md., 1969; MS in Physiology, U. Wis., 1971; MD, U. Md., Balt., 1976. Diplomate Am. Bd. Internal Medicine. Asst. prof. U. Wis., Madison, 1984-91, assoc. prof., 1991—. Bd. dirs. Wis. chpt. Am. Lung Assn. past pres.; exec. com. Wis. Thoracic Soc., past pres.; mem. Gov.'s Coun. on Phys. Disabilities, 1990—. Office: U Wis Hosps & Clinics 600 Highland Ave # H6380 Madison WI 53792-0001

WILSON, PAMELA K. corporate financial executive; BS, U. Ill.; MBA, NYU. With J.P. Morgan, 1980—2000; sr. v.p. WL Ross & Co. LLC, N.Y., 2000—. Office: WL Ross & Co LLC Manhattan Tower 19th Fl 101 East 52nd St New York NY 10022

WILSON, PATRICIA POTTER, library science and reading educator, educational and library consultant; b. Jennings, La., May 3, 1946; d. Ralph Harold and Wilda Ruth (Smith) Potter; m. Wendell Merlin Wilson, Aug. 24, 1968. BS, La. State U., 1967; MS, U. Houston-Clear Lake, 1979; EdD, U. Houston, 1985. Cert. tchr., learning resources specialist (libr.), Tex. Tchr. England AFB (La.) Elem. Sch., 1967-68, Edward White Elem. Sch./Clear Creek Ind. Schs., Seabrook, Tex., 1972-77; libr. C.D. Landolt Elem. Sch., Friendswood, Tex., 1979-81; instr./lectr. children's lit. U. Houston, 1983-86; with U. Houston/Clear Lake, 1984-87, asst. prof. libr. sci. and reading, 1988-94, assoc. prof. learning resources and reading edn., 1994—2001, assoc. prof. emeritus, 2001—, faculty devel. com. chair, 1995-97, mem faculty senate, 1992-93, reading search com. chair, tchg. task force, 1997-98, reading and libr. sci. program chair, 1997-98, mem. Piper award com., 1996—98, U. Faculty award com., 1997, U. learning assessment task force, 1997-98, promotion and tenure com. chair, 1999. Cons. Hermann Hosp., Baywood Hosp., 1986-87, Bedford Meadows Hosp., 1989-90, Wetcher Clinic, 1989; co-owner, v.p. Potter Farms, Inc., 1994—. Editor: A Review Sampler, 1985—86, 1989—90; author: Happenings: Developing Successful Programs for School Libraries, 1987, The Professional Collection for Elementary Educators, 1996, Premiere Events: Library Programs That Inspire Elementary Patrons, 2001, Leadership for Today's School Library, 2001, Igniting the Spark: Library Programs that Inspire High School Patrons, 2001, Center Stage: Library Programs That Inspire Middle School Patrons, 2002; contbg. editor: Tex. Libr. Jour., 1988—94; contbr. articles to profl. jours. Trustee Freeman Meml. Libr., Houston, 1982—87, v.p., 1985—86, pres., 1986—87; trustee Evelyn Meador Libr., 1993—94, adv. bd., 1994—; mem. Bay Area Houston Symphony League Bd., 2004, Clear Lake Area Panhellic Assn., 2002—, Bay Area Houston Econ. Partnership, 2002—, Banquet Com.; founder Friends of Neumann Libr., 1998; chmn. hospitality com. Lunar Rendevous Festival, 1998—2001; gen. chmn. Lunar Rendezvous Festival, 2002, mem. adv. bd., 2002—; co-chmn. Kickoff Reception, 2003; mem. Assistance League of the Bay Area, 1997—; vol. Houston: A Visit from St. Nicholas Com., 2004—; mem. adv. bd. Bay Area Soc. Prevention Cruelty Animals, 1994—98, Bay Area Turning Point, 1998—; bd. dirs. Sta. KUHT-TV, 1984—87, Friends of Neumann Libr., 1998—99, Bay Area Houston Ballet & Theatre, 2001—04; vice chair bd. dirs. Bay Area Houston Ballet and Theatre, 2003—04; dir. Learning Resources Book Rev. Ctr., 1989—90; bd. dirs. UHCL Alumni Assn., 1988—2001, v.p. adminstrn., 2000, anniversary hon. com., 1999—2000, mem. 25th anniversary com., 1999, alumni ball com., 1999; mem. Armand Bayou Nature Ctr., Houston, 1980, bd. dirs., 1989—94; corp. sponsor Lunar Rendezvous Festival, 1998—. Named Outstanding Vol. of Yr., Houston's Nat. Philanthropy Day, 1999; named one of 10 Men and Women of Heart, Bay Area Turning Point, 2001; recipient Rsch. award, Tex. State Reading Assn., 1993, Pres. award, Tex. Coun. Tchrs. English, Disting. Tchg. award, Enron Corp., 1996, Disting. Alumni award, U. Houston-Clear Lake, 1998, Disting. Alumna award, U. Houston-Ctrl. Campus, Coll. Edn., 2002; grantee, Tex. Libr. Assn., 1993. Mem. ALA, Am. Assn. Sch. Librs., Internat. Reading Assn., Nat. Coun. Tchrs. English (Books for You rev. com. 1985-88, 97-98, Your Reading rev. com. 1993-96), Tex. Coun. Tchrs. English, Antarctican Soc., Alumni Assn. U. Houston-Clear Lake (bd. dirs. 1998-2001, v.p. adminstrn. 2000, anniversary hon. com. 1999-2000, 25th anniversary com. 1999, alumni ball com. 1999), Bay Oaks Country Club, Clear Lake Panhellenic, Phi Delta Kappa, Phi Kappa Phi (sec. 1997-98, pres. 1998-99), Lakewood Yacht Club. Methodist.

WILSON, PAUL, professional baseball player; b. Orlando, Fla., Mar. 28, 1973; Baseball player Tampa Bay Devil Rays, 2000—. Office: Tampa Bay Devil Rays One Tropicana Dr Saint Petersburg FL 33705

WILSON, PAUL HOLLIDAY, JR., lawyer; b. Schenectady, N.Y., Sept. 4, 1942; s. Paul H. and Sarah Elizabeth (MacLean) W.; m. Elaine Hawley Griffin, May 30, 1964; children: Hollace, Paul, Kirsten, Katherine. AB, Brown U., 1964; LLB, MBA, Columbia U., 1967. Bar: N.Y. 1967, U.S. Dist. Ct. (so. dist.) 1968. Law clk. U.S. Dist. Ct. (so. dist.) N.Y., N.Y.C., 1967-68; assoc. Debevoise & Plimpton, N.Y.C., 1968-75, ptnr., 1976—, fin. ptnr., 1980-88, 91-93, 2001—, dep. presiding ptnr., 1993-98. Vice-chmn., trustee St. Michael's Montessori Sch., N.Y.C., 1977-79, chmn. bd. trustees, 1979-81. Mem. ABA, Assn. Bar City N.Y. (mem. commn. on securities regulations 1985-88). Clubs: Vineyard Haven Yacht (Mass.) (vice-commodore 1985, commodore 1986-87). Avocations: sailing, reading, music. Office: Debevoise & Plimpton 919 Third Ave 46th Fl New York NY 10022-6225 Office Phone: 212-909-6000. Business E-Mail: phwilson@debevoise.com.

WILSON, PAUL LOWELL, mortgage company executive, lawyer; b. May 12, 1951; s. James Joseph and Edna Vivian (Halterman) W.; children: Meredith Elaine, Taylor Halterman. AB, W.Va. U., 1973; JD, Coll. of William of Mary, 1976. Bar: W.Va., 1976, U.S. Dist. Ct. (so. dist.) W.Va. 1976, U.S. Dist. Ct. (ea. dist.) Va. 1991. Assoc. Brown & Peyton, Charleston, W.Va., 1976-78; title atty. Lawyers Title Ins. Corp., Williamsburg, Va., 1978-80; assoc. S.J. Baker, Williamsburg, 1981-83; counsel edn. com. W.Va. Legislature, Charleston, 1977-78; gen. counsel A J & L Corp., Williamsburg, 1983-85, v.p., gen. counsel, 1985-91; prin. First Capital Comml. Funding, Inc., 1997—. Bd. dirs. 503 Cert. Devel. Co., Richmond, Sta. WHRO-TV. Mem. York County Sch. Bd., 1986-94, chmn., 1992-94; pres. Nat. Housing Corp., 1986-93, The Preservation Group, Inc., 1991-97. Mem. W.Va. State Bar, Sigma Phi Epsilon. Methodist. Office: 8410 Falls of Neuse Rd Raleigh NC 27615 Home: 4609 Colony Rd Apt J Charlotte NC 28226-3877 E-mail: plwfirstcap@aol.com.

WILSON, PEGGY, state representative, registered nurse; b. Anamosa, Iowa, Sept. 18, 1945; m. Woody Wilson; 3 children. A in Registered Nursing, Kirkwood C.C., 1970; cert. in EMT tng., U. Alaska. Past gen. mgr. life ins. co.; past dairy farmer; past state rep. N.C. House of Rep.; state rep. State of Alaska, 2001—. EMT Tok Area Emergency Mgmt. Svc. Mem.: Rotary, Pilot Internat. (past v.p.). Avocations: reading, travel, hunting, boating, shooting. Office: State Capitol Rm 104 Juneau AK 99801-1182

WILSON, PETE, former governor; b. Lake Forest, Ill., Aug. 23, 1933; s. James Boone and Margaret (Callaghan) W.; m. Betty Robertson (div.); m. Gayle Edlund, May 29, 1983 BA in English Lit., Yale U., 1955; JD, U. Calif., Berkeley, 1962; LL.D., Grove City Coll., 1983, U. Calif., San Diego, 1983, U. San Diego, 1984. Bar: Calif. 1962. Mem. Calif. Legislature, Sacramento, 1966-71; mayor City of San Diego, 1971-83; U.S. Senator from Calif., 1983-91; gov. State of Calif., 1991-98; mng. dir. Pacific Capital Group, Beverly Hills, Calif., 1999—2002. Trustee Conservation Found.; mem. exec. bd. San Diego County council Boy Scouts Am.; hon. trustee So. Calif. Council Soviet Jews; adv. mem. Urban Land Inst., 1985-86; founding dir. Retinitis Pigmentosa Internat.; hon. dir. Alzheimer's Family Ctr., Inc., 1985; hon. bd. dirs. Shakespeare-San Francisco, 1985 Recipient Golden Bulldog award, 1984, 85, 86, Guardian of Small Bus. award, 1984, Cuauhtemoc plaque for disting. svc. to farm workers in Calif., 1991, Julius award for outstanding pub. leadership U. So. Calif., 1992, award of appreciation Nat. Head Start, 1992; named Legislator of Yr., League Calif. Cities, 1985, Man of Yr. N.G. Assn. Calif., 1986, Man of Yr. citation U. Calif. Boalt Hall, 1986; ROTC scholar Yale U., 1951-55. Mem. Nat. Mil. Family Assn. (adv. bd.), Phi Delta Phi, Zeta Psi Republican. Episcopalian.

WILSON, R. DALE, marketing educator, consultant; b. Ironton, Ohio, July 16, 1949; s. Robert J. and Treva L. (Shively) W.; m. Emily J. Ray, June 19, 1971; 1 child, Travis Ray. BBA cum laude, Ohio U., 1971; MBA, U. Toledo, 1972; PhD, U. Iowa, 1977. Asst. prof. mktg. Pa. State U., University Park, 1976-80; v.p., dir. mktg. scis. Batten, Barton, Durstine & Osborn, Inc., N.Y.C., 1980-83; vis. prof. Cornell U., Ithaca, N.Y., 1983-84; assoc. prof. Mich. State U., East Lansing, 1984-87, prof., 1987—. Cons. in field. Contbr. articles to profl. jours. Youth baseball and basketball coach, East Lansing, 1989-98. Faculty Rsch. grantee Pa. State U., Mich. State U. Mem. Am. Acad. Advt., Am. Mktg. Assn., Inst. Ops. Rsch. and Mgmt. Scis. (assoc. editor Interfaces, cert. recognition 1983), Am. Soc. for Competitiveness, Beta Gamma Sigma. Home: 859 Audubon Rd East Lansing MI 48823-3003 Office: Mich State U Eli Broad Grad Sch Mgmt Dept Mktg/Supply Chain Mgmt N322 N Business Complex East Lansing MI 48824-1122 Office Phone: 517-353-6381 239. Business E-Mail: wilsonrr@msu.edu.

WILSON, R. J. state representative; b. Fort Scott, Kans., July 16, 1971; m. Julie Wilson; 1 child, Jameson. BA, Pitts. State U., 1994. Spl. legis. asst. Kans. Ho. Minority Leader, 1994, 1996; exec. dir. Kans. Dem. Party, 1999; mem. Kans. Ho. of Reps., 2000—. Precinct committeeman Crawford County, Kans., 1989—96; co-chair Hough O'Brian Youth Leadership Kans.; bd. dirs. Big Bros. Pitts. Mem.: Pitts. Area C. of C. (bd. dirs.), Kiwanis, Elks. Democrat. Roman Catholic. Office: 372-S State Capitol 300 SW 10th Ave Topeka KS 66612 Address: 608 Oakcrest Pittsburg KS 66762

WILSON, RALPH COOKERLY, JR., professional football team executive; b. Columbus, Ohio, Oct. 17, 1918; s. Ralph Cookerly and Edith (Cole) W.; children: Christy Cole, Linda Brown, Edith Denise. AB, U. Va., 1940; postgrad., U. Mich., 1940-41. Pres. Ralph C. Wilson Jr. Enterprises (privately owned family bus.); engaged in profl. football, roadbuilding 1946—; pres., owner Buffalo Bills Profl. Football Club, 1959—. With USNR, 1941-46. Decorated Commendation medal. Mem. Ocean Club of Fla., Country Club of Detroit, Grosse Pointe (Mich.) Club, Buffalo Country Club, Shriners. Presbyterian.

WILSON, RALPH EDWIN, lawyer, justice; b. Osceola, Ark., Sept. 28, 1921; s. Emmett A. and Lillie (Simmons) W.; m. Mary Ann Murray, Apr. 23, 1949; children: Ralph Edwin, Teresa Ann, Don Alan. Student, U.S. Naval Acad., 1943; AB, Union U., 1946; JD, Vanderbilt U., 1949. Bar: Tenn. 1948, Ark. 1948. Practice in Osceola, 1949—; city atty. Osceola, 1949; dep. pros. atty. 2d Jud. Dist. Ark., 1950-53; spl. asst. to atty. gen. Ark., 1956-60; spl. assoc. justice Supreme Ct. Ark., 1984. Pres. Liberal State Bank, Ct. Eastern Assurance Co., North Little Rock; sec. Farmers Agri Export, Inc.; dir. Allied Cos., Inc., Does-More Products Corp., Allied Real Estate Investment Trust, Osceola Land Devel. Co.; Mem. adv. council Nat. Pub. Works Week, 1964 Alderman Osceola City Council, 1958-61. Served as lt. U.S. Mcht. Marines USNR, 1943-45. Recipient Ark. House and Senate Concurrent Resolutions Commendation, 1971 Mem. Ark. Bar Assn. (past mem. exec. com.), Osceola Bar Assn. (pres.), Am. Trial Lawyers Assn., U.S. Bar (Supreme Ct.), Am. Legion, Phi Alpha Delta, Alpha Tau Omega, Tau Kappa Alpha. Clubs: Kiwanian (internat. v.p. 1970-71, trustee 1966-70, life fellow internat. found.). Democrat. Methodist. Home: 903 W Hale Ave Osceola AR 72370-2428 Office: 109 N Maple St Osceola AR 72370-2537 E-mail: ralphew@arkansas.net. *I believe it is man's highest achievement to reach far and find truth. The adversary system in law is this searching and finding truth. The drama of the courtroom involves all that is precious— life, liberty, property, dominion over children. These interacting forces play against each other, but if all facts are before the court, truth invariably prevails.*

WILSON, RAMON B. retired economics professor; b. Ogden, Utah, Sept. 22, 1922; s. Benjamin Andrew and Hannah Josephine (Browning) W.; m. Ruth G. Worlton, July 27, 1945; children: Lynn, William Scott, Bruce Ramon, JoAnne, Kathleen. BS, Utah State U., 1947; MS, Purdue U., 1948, PhD, 1950. Extension economist Utah State U., Logan, 1950-53; mktg. economist Calif. Dept. Agr., Sacramento, 1953-55; asst. prof. Purdue U., West Lafayette, Ind., 1955-57, assoc. prof., 1957-63, prof. agrl. econs., 1963-78, prof. emeritus, 1978—, market service dir., 1960-68; asst. dir. Ind. Coop. Extension Service, 1963-74; assoc. dir. agrl. expt. sta., asst. to dean agr. Purdue U., 1968-74; from asst. to assoc. dir. Benson Agrl. Food Inst. Brigham Young U., Provo, Utah, 1979-82. Asst. to sec. U.S. Dept. Agr., Washington, 1974-76; cons., lectr. in field. Served with U.S. Army, 1942-46. Home: 435 E 2200 N Provo UT 84604-1725

WILSON, RHONDA HILL, lawyer; b. Phila., Aug. 20, 1955; d. Fleming and Emma (Woodson) Hill; m. Robert A. Wilson (div.); children: Mica, Christian. BA cum laude, C.W. Post Coll., 1976; JD, Am. U., 1979. Bar: Pa., Ohio, N.J. Asst. atty. gen. Office of Atty. Gen. Ohio, Columbus, 1979-81; pvt. practice law Phila., 1981-84; claims mgr. Allstate Ins., Horsham, Pa., 1984-86; atty. Am. Internat. Group, Phila., 1986-88, Crum & Forster Co., Phila., 1988-93; pvt. practice law Phila., 1993—. Host legal and current affairs WURD Radio, Phila., 1992-2002. Active Mt. Carmel Bapt. Ch., Phila.; past bd. dirs. Walden Sch., Swarthmore, Pa. Mem. Nat. Bar Assn. (pres. women lawyers divsn. Phila. 1993-94, presdl. award 1994), ATLA, Phila. Bar Assn., Barristers Assn. Phila. (bd. dirs. 1992-93), Pa. Trial Lawyers Assn., Phila. Trial Lawyers Assn., Phila. Assn. Def. Counsel (past bd. dirs.). Office: Law Office Rhonda Hill Wilson PC 1500 John F Kennedy Blvd Ste 1050 Philadelphia PA 19102 E-mail: rhillwilso.@aol.com.

WILSON, RHYS THADDEUS, lawyer; b. Albany, Ga., May 9, 1955; s. Joseph Farr Jr. and Betty Ann (Wilkins) W.; m. Carolyn Reid Saffold, June 2, 1984. AB, Duke U., 1976; JD, U. Ga., 1979; LLM, Emory U., 1985. Bar: Ga. 1979. Pvt. practice law, Atlanta, 1979-89; sr. v.p., gen. counsel Monarch Capital Group, Inc., Atlanta, 1989-92, Jackson & Coker, Inc., Atlanta, 1992-93; pres. Jackson & Coker Locum Tenens, Inc., Atlanta, 1993-95; ptnr. Robins, Kaplan, Miller & Ciresi, Atlanta, 1995—. Spkr. continuing legal edn. seminars. Contbr. articles to profl. jours. Mem. ABA, Ga. Bar Assn. (chmn. internat. law sect. 1987-88, exec. com. corp. and banking law sect. 1987-89, editl. bd. Ga. State Bar Jour. 1986-89), Atlanta Bar Assn. (editor newsletter 1984-86, Outstanding Svc. award 1986), Assn. for Corp. Growth, Atlanta Network Alliance, Atlanta Tech. Angels, The Exec. Com. TEC, Atlanta Venture Forum, Capital City Club. Episcopalian.

WILSON, RICHARD A. oil/gas industry support services executive; b. 1938; BS in Petroleum Engring., U. Wyo. Pres. Energy Svc. Co. Inc., Dallas, 1988-89, sr. v.p.- ops., 1989—. Formerly with ESSO Exploration; past v.p. Global Marine Drilling Co.; various positions, then exec. v.p. Schlumberger Tech. Corp. Office: ENSCO 500 N Akard St Ste 4300 Dallas TX 75201-3331

WILSON, RICHARD CHRISTIAN, engineering firm executive; b. Bethlehem, Pa., July 17, 1921; s. Christian and Laura Barrows (Langham) W.; m. Jean M. Avis, July 16, 1949; children— Richard A., Christy. BS, Carnegie-Mellon U., 1943; MS, Lehigh U., 1947; PhD, U. Mich., 1961. Mfg. engr. Westinghouse Electric Corp., East Pittsburgh, 1943; instr. mech. engring. Carnegie-Mellon U., Pitts., 1943-44; vacuum test engr. Kellex Corp., N.Y.C., 1944; area supr. Carbide & Carbon Chem. Co., Oak Ridge, 1945-46; apparatus engr. Westinghouse Electric Corp., Jackson, Mich., 1947-55; instr. indsl. and operation engring. U. Mich., 1955-61, asst. prof., 1961-63, assoc. prof., 1963-66, prof., 1966-85, chmn. dept., 1973-77, assoc. dean Coll. Engring., 1968-72; pres. Techware, Inc., 1985-86, ret., 1986. Dir. Cascade Data Corp., 1969-72 Contbr. articles to profl. jours. Bd. dirs. Ecumenical Assn. Internat. Understanding, 1970-87, pres., 1975-76, 86-87; dir. Washtenaw Trombones and Jazzbones, 1995—. Mem. IEEE, Inst. Mgmt. Sci., Am. Inst. Indsl. Engrs., Ops. Research Soc. Am., Sigma Xi, Beta Theta Pi, Phi Kappa Phi. Clubs: Rotary. Home: 805 Mount Pleasant Ave Ann Arbor MI 48103-4776 Office: U Mich Dept Indsl Engring Ann Arbor MI 48109

WILSON, RICHARD EDWARD, composer, pianist, music educator; b. Cleve., May 15, 1941; s. James F. and Edith Ann (Zingler) Wilson; m. Adene Stevenson Green, May 15, 1971; children: Katherine Blanca, James Graham. AB magna cum laude, Harvard U., 1963; MA, Rutgers U., 1966. Asst. prof. music Vassar Coll., Poughkeepsie, N.Y., 1966-70, assoc. prof. music, 1970-76, prof. music, 1976—, chmn. dept. music, 1979-82, 85-88, 95-98, Mary Conover Mellon Chair, 1988—. Composer-in-residence Am. Symphony Orch., 1992—. Composer: Music for Violin and Violoncello, 1969; composer: (four string quartets); composer: Eclogue for Piano Solo, 1974 (Burge prize, 1979), Figuration, 1980, Two Symphonies, 1984, 1987, Agitations, 1994, Pamietam, 1995, Five Love Songs, 1995, Transfigured Goat, 1996, A Child's London, 1997, Triple concerto for horn, bass clarinet, marimba and orch., 1998 (Koussevitzky commn.), Intimations for Piano and Orch., 2000, Revelry for Full Orchestra, 2002, Peregrinations for Viola and Orchestra, 2002, others; composer: (opera) Aethelred the Unready, 1994. Recipient Walter Hinrichsen award, Am. Acad. Inst. Arts and Letters, 1986, Cleve. Arts prize, 1988, Exec.'s award Dutchess County, 1989, Stoeger prize, Chamber Music Soc. Lincoln Ctr., 1994, Acad. award in music, Am. Acad. Arts and Letters, 2004; Guggenheim fellow, 1992. Mem.: Am. Acad. Arts and Letters (Acad. award 2004), ASCAP, Am. Music Ctr., Century Assn., Harvard Club, Phi Beta Kappa. Home: 27 Vassar Lake Dr Poughkeepsie NY 12603-3120 Office: Vassar Coll Dept Music PO Box 18 Poughkeepsie NY 12604-0001

WILSON, RICHARD F. academic administrator; b. Point Pleasant, W.Va. m. Pat Wilson; children: Adam, Rachel. B in Math., Alderson-Broaddus Coll., 1968; MA in Higher Edn., U. Mich., 1970, PhD in Higher Edn., 1978. Math. tchr. Spencerville (Ohio) H.S., 1968—69; dir. admissions Alderson Broaddus Coll., Philippi, W.Va., 1970—74; project asst. to Dr. William Haberl, spl. asst. to the exec. officers U. Mich., Ann Arbor, 1974—75, grad. student rsch. asst. Office Acad. Planning and Analysis, 1975—76, rsch. assoc. Office Acad. Planning Analysis, 1976—78; asst. dir. Office Planning and Evaluation U. Ill., Urbana-Champaign, 1978—80, adj. asst. prof. higher edn., 1981—84, asst. vice chancellor for acad. affairs, 1981—86, assoc. chancellor, 1986—94, interim dir. corp. and found. rels., 1991, adj. prof. higher edn., 1994—2004, assoc. chancellor for devel., 1994—2004; dep. dir. U. Ill. Found., 1994—96, v.p., 1996—2004; pres. Ill. Wesleyan U., 2004—. Mem. Applie Higher Edn. Adv. Group, 1992—. Office: Ill Wesleyan Univ Pres Office Holmes Hall 204 PO Box 2900 Bloomington IL 61702*

WILSON, RICHARD LEE, political science educator; b. Worthington, Minn., Dec. 20, 1944; s. G. Roy and Dorothy Eileen (Johnson) W.; m. Carolyn Ann Dirks, Aug. 24, 1968 (div.); 1 child, Kevin Richard. BA, U. Chgo., 1966, postgrad., 1966-67; PhD, Johns Hopkins U., 1971; postgrad., Columbia U., 1988, Stanford U., 1992. Congl. aide 4th Congl. Dist. Md., 1971; asst. prof. polit. sci. U. Tenn., Chattanooga, 1971-76, assoc. prof., 1976-87, prof., 1988—. Registrar-at-large Hamilton County Election Commn., 1977-84; lectr. Robert A. Taft Inst. Govt., U. Tenn., Nashville, 1978, 79, 81; supr. state legis. and met. internship program U. Chattanooga, 1972-86; vis. prof. Govt. Fgn. Affairs Coll., Beijing, 1986-87; Fulbright prof. govt. Beijing U., 1988-89, Samford U., Birmingham, Ala., 1991-93. Author: Tennessee Politics, 1976, American Government, 1993, 2d edit., 1995, American Political Leaders, 2002 (Choice award 2003); editor: Encyclopedia of American Government, 2001; co-editor: Ready Reference: Censorship, 1997 (named Outstanding Ref. Source 1998 ALA), Encyclopedia of the Supreme Court, 2000 (named OUtstanding Ref. Scouce 2002 ALA); contbr. chpts. to books. Chmn. Hamilton County Health Planning Adv. Council, 1975-79; bd. dirs. Ga.-Tenn. Regional Health Commn., 1978-82; active Tenn. State Health Coordinating Council, 1977-81; exec. com. State Health Coordinating Council, 1979-81. Named Outstanding Educator of Yr., Signal Mountain (Tenn.) Jaycees, 1973, Outstanding Prof. of Yr., SGA, 1985-86, Oustanding Reference Source ALA, 2002; recipient Polit. Edn. award NAACP, 1980, Excellent Prof. award Fgn. Affairs Coll., Beijing, 1987, UTC Exceptional Merit award, 1990, 94; NEH grantee, 1988, 92. Mem. So. Polit. Sci. Assn., Midwest Polit. Sci. Assn., Am. Polit. Sci. Assn. (nat. rsch. grant 1995), Nat. Soc. Internships and Exptl. Edn., SAR, China People's Friendship Assn., Aircraft Owners and Pilots Assn. Methodist. Office: Univ of Tenn Dept Political Sci Fletcher Hall 414 Chattanooga TN 37403

WILSON, RICHARD RANDOLPH, lawyer; b. Pasadena, Calif., Apr. 14, 1950; s. Robert James and Phyllis Jean (Blackman) W.; m. Catherine Goodhugh Stevens, Oct. 11, 1980; children: Thomas Randolph, Charles Stevens. BA cum laude, Yale U., 1971; JD, U. Wash., 1976. Bar: Wash. 1976, U.S. Dist. Ct. (we. dist.) Wash. 1976, U.S. Ct. Appeals (9th cir.) 1977. Assoc. Hillis, Phillips, Cairncross, Clark & Martin, Seattle, 1976-81, ptnr., 1981-84, Hillis, Cairncross, Clark & Martin, Seattle, 1984-87, Hillis Clark Martin & Peterson, Seattle, 1987—, mem. mgmt. com., 1991—. Pres. Plymouth Housing Group, Seattle, 1998—2000, trustee, 1994—2001; bd. dirs. Plymouth Housing Properties, Seattle, 2001—, Quality Child Care Svcs., Inc., Seattle; lectr. various bar assns., 1980—. Contbr. articles to profl. jours. Chmn. class agts. Yale U. Alumni Fund, New Haven, 1985—87, class agt., 1971—2001, mem. class coun., 1991—96, mem. Western Wash. exec. com. Yale capital campaign, 1992—97, vice chmn. leadership gifts com. Yale 25th reunion, 1995—96, 30th reunion, 2000—01; mem., vice chmn. Medina (Wash.) Planning Commn., 1990—92; trustee, performer Gilbert & Sullivan Soc., 1984—91; chmn. capital campaign Plymouth Congl. Ch., 1995, moderator, pres. ch. coun., 1998—2000, pres. ch. corp., 2004—. Mem. ABA, Wash. State Bar Assn. (dir. environ. and land use law sect. 1985-88), Seattle-King County Bar Assn., Kingsley Trust Assn. (trustee 2003—, pres. 1996-98), Yale Assn. We. Wash. Congregationalist. Avocations: acting, singing, rare book collecting. Home: 2305 86th Ave NE Bellevue WA 98004-2416 Office: Hillis Clark Martin & Peterson 1221 2nd Ave Ste 500 Seattle WA 98101-2925 Office Phone: 206-623-1745. *Notable cases include: Barrie vs. Kitsap County, 1980; Sore vs. Snohomish County, 1983; Conv. Ctr. Coalition vs. City of Seattle, 1986; Orion Corp. vs. State, 1987, Cougar Mountain Assocs. vs. King County, 1988; King County vs. Central Puget Sound Growth Management Hearings Board, 1998, 1999.*

WILSON, RITA, actress; b. LA, Oct. 26, 1958; m. Tom Hanks; 2 children. Actor: (films) The Day It Came to Earth, 1979, Cheech & Chong's Next Movie, 1980, Volunteers, 1985, The Bonfire of the Vanities, 1990, Sleepless in Seattle, 1993, Mixed Nuts, 1994, Now and Then, 1995, That Thing You Do!, 1996, Jingle All the Way, 1996, No Dogs Allowed, 1996, Psycho, 1998, Runaway Bride, 1999, The Story of Us, 1999, Perfume, 2001, Auto Focus, 2002; (TV films) Barbarians at the Gate, 1993, If These Walls Could Talk, 1996, From the Earth to the Moon, 1998, Invisible Child, 1999; prodr.: (films) My Big Fat Greek Wedding, 2002, Connie and Carla, 2004; (TV series) My Big Fat Greek Life, 2003. Mailing: 2600 Malibu Rd Malibu CA 90265

WILSON, RITA P. insurance company executive; Sr. v.p. corp. rels. Allstate Ins. Co., Northbrook, Ill., 1990-94, 96—, pres. Allstate Indemnity, 1994-96; sr. v.p. corp. rels. Ameritech, Chgo., 1994-96. Office: Allstate Ins Co 2775 Sanders Rd Ste F8 Northbrook IL 60062-6127

WILSON, ROBERT ALLEN, religion educator; b. Geff, Ill., Oct. 7, 1936; s. Perry Arthur and Eva Mae (Dye) W.; m. Patsy Ann Jarrett, June 1, 1957; children: Elizabeth Ann, Angela Dawn, Christine Joy. AB, Lincoln (Ill.) Christian Coll., 1958, Hanover Coll., 1961; MRE, So. Bapt. Seminary, 1965, EdD, 1972. Ordained to ministry Ch. of Christ, 1958. Minister Fowler (Ind.) Christian Ch., 1955—59, Zoah Christian Ch., Scottsburg, Ind., 1959—64; minister of edn. and youth Shively Christian Ch., Louisville, 1964—69; prof. Christian edn. and family life Lincoln Christian Seminary, 1969—2004. Pres. Christian Marriage and Family Enrichment Services, Lincoln, 1980—. Contbr. articles to profl. jours. Mem. Nat. Assn. Profs. Christian Edn. (editor newsletter 1975-79, pres. 1979-80), Religious Edn. Assn. Lodges: Rotary (bd. dirs. Lincoln chpt. 1988—, pres. 1993-94). Home: 330 Campus View Dr Lincoln IL 62656-2106 Office: Christian Marriage & Family Enrichment Svcs 330 Campus View Dr Lincoln IL 62656 Office Phone: 217-732-1629.

WILSON, ROBERT FOSTER, lawyer; b. Windsor, Colo., Apr. 6, 1926; s. Foster W. and Anne Lucille (Svedman) W.; m. Mary Elizabeth Clark, Mar. 4, 1951 (div. Feb. 1972); children: Robert F., Katharine A.; m. Sally Anne Nemec, June 8, 1982. BA in Econs., U. Iowa, 1950, JD, 1951. Bar: Iowa 1951, U.S. Dist. Ct. (no. and so. dists.) Iowa 1956, U.S. Ct. Appeals (8th cir.) 1967. Atty. FTC, Chgo., 1951-55; pvt. practice, Cedar Rapids, Iowa, 1955—. Pres. Lawyer Forms, Inc.; dir. Lawyers Forms, Inc., mem. Iowa Reapportionment Com., 1968; del. to U.S. and Japan Bilateral Session on Legal and Econ. Rels. Conf., Tokyo, 1988, Moscow Conf. on Law and Bilateral Rels., Moscow, 1990; U.S. del. to Moscow Conf. on Legal and Econ. Rels., 1990. Mem. Iowa Ho. of Reps., 1959-60; pres. Linn County Day Care, Cedar Rapids, 1968-70. Sgt. U.S. Army, 1944-46. Mem. ATLA, Am. Arbitration Assn. (panel arbitrators), Iowa Bar Assn., Iowa Trial Lawyers Assn., Linn County Bar Assn., Am. Legion (judge adv. 1970-75, 87-93), Cedar View Country Club, Elks, Eagles, Delta Theta Phi. Democrat. Home: 2179 Blake Blvd SE Cedar Rapids IA 52403-1128 Office: 810 Dows Bldg Cedar Rapids IA 52403-7010 Office Phone: 319-364-1538. E-mail: rwilsonlaw@aol.com.

WILSON, ROBERT FRANK, graphics designer, property manager; b. Oxford, Pa., Aug. 26, 1949; s. Robert Thomas and Claudine Wilson; m. Barbara Wise. BA, U. Del., 1973; real estate cert., NYU, 2001. Prin. Blue Hen Graphics, N.Y.C., 1980—98; property mgmt. dir. Tier II Mgmt./Andrews Bldg. Corp., N.Y.C., 1998—. Bd. pres. Housing Coop., N.Y.C., 1988—, N.Y.C. Bus. Improvement Dist., 2003. Recipient Achievement award, Cooperator Mag., 2001. Democrat. Avocations: collecting poster stamps, Kitsch, watercolor painting, travel. Home: 3 Great Jones St New York NY 10012

WILSON, ROBERT GODFREY, radiologist; b. Montgomery, Ala., Mar. 18, 1937; s. Robert Woodridge and Lucille (Godfrey) W.; m. Dorothy June Waters, Aug. 31, 1957; children: Amy Lucille, Robert Darwin, Robert Woodridge II, Lucy Elizabeth. BA, Huntingdon Coll., 1957; MD, Med. Coll. Ala., 1961. Diplomate Nat. Bd. Med. Examiners, Am. Bd. Radiology, Am. Bd. Nuclear Medicine. Intern Letterman Gen. Hosp., San Francisco, 1961-62; resident in radiology U. Okla. Med. Center, Oklahoma City, 1965-68, clin. instr. in radiology, 1968—; practice medicine specializing in diagnostic and therapeutic radiology, nuclear medicine Shawnee, Okla., 1968—; mem. med. staff Shawnee Med. Center, Mission Hill Meml. Hosp., Shawnee, 1968—. Served to capt. M.C., USAF, 1960-65. Mem. AMA, Okla., Pottawatomie County med. socs., Okla., Greater Oklahoma City radiol. socs., Am. Coll. Radiology, Soc. Nuclear Medicine, Radiol. Soc. N.Am. Methodist. Home: 26 Sequoyah Blvd Shawnee OK 74801-5570 Office: 5606 Aquarius Shawnee OK 74804-9387

WILSON, ROBERT GORDON, investment banker; b. Mt. Vernon, N.Y., Dec. 16, 1933; s. Gerald and Ella Baxter (Close) W.; m. Valerie Ann Wilson, Apr. 25, 1966 (div. 1986); children: Jennifer Lynn, Kimberly Ann; m. Anne Marie Henriquez, Sept. 27, 1986; 1 child, Anthony H. Crotti. BA, Haverford Coll., 1955; MBA, Columbia U., 1957. Gen. ptnr. Goldman Sachs & Co., N.Y.C., 1967-80, ltd. ptnr., 1981-89; pres. Goldman Sachs Internat., London, 1977-80; chmn., pres. Ecologic Waste Svcs., Inc., Miami, Fla., 1990-94; vice chmn. Carter Kaplan & Co., Richmond, Va., 1993-94; chmn., pres. Ziani Internat. Capital, Inc., Miami, 1995—; dir., founder LendingTree, Inc., Charlotte, NC, 1997—99. Bd. dirs. The Phoenix Cos., Inc. Former chmn. bd. trustees YMCA Greater N.Y., N.Y.C., 1985. Republican. Avocations: golf, wines, travel. Home and Office: Ziani Internat Capital Inc 151 Crandon Blvd Apt 1127 Key Biscayne FL 33149-1596 E-mail: rgw.55@hotmail.com.

WILSON, ROBERT JAMES MONTGOMERY, investment company executive; b. Millbrook, N.Y., Feb. 8, 1920; s. Albert James Montgomery and Charlotte (Kaye) W.; m. Yvette Laneres, May 10, 1952; children— Robert James Montgomery, Olivia Laneres Wilson Welbourn, Geoffrey Laneres. Grad., Choate Sch., 1938; AB, Yale U., 1942. Securities analyst buying dept. Union Securities Corp., N.Y.C., 1946-49; securities analyst Union Service Corp., N.Y.C., 1949-59, v.p., 1959-62; pres., dir. Surveyor Fund, Inc. (formerly Gen. Public Service Corp.), N.Y.C., 1962-71; with Rockefeller Family and Assos., 1972-75; pres. Adams Express Co., N.Y.C., 1975-86, also bd. dirs., 1975—; pres. Petroleum & Resources Corp. (formerly Petroleum Corp. Am.), N.Y.C., 1975-86, also bd. dirs., 1975—. Mem. adv. investment com. Md. State Retirement Systems, 1979-82; bd. dirs. Assn. Publicly Traded Investment Cos., 1968-71, chmn., 1969-71. Mem. 1940 Fahnestock Expdn. of Am. Mus. Natural History to South Seas. Served to capt. AUS, World War II. Mem. Md. Club.

WILSON, ROBERT M. business executive; b. St. Louis, Aug. 10, 1952; s. William H. and Mary E. (Sacksteder) W.; m. Joli S. Schneeberger, Oct. 7, 1978; 1 child, William Wilcox. BS, Miami U., Oxford, Ohio, 1974; JD, Cleve. State U., 1977. Bar: Ohio; CPA, Ohio. Ptnr. Touche Ross & Co., Dayton, Ohio, 1972-88, Roberds, Inc., Dayton, 1988-2000, pres., 1998—2000; exec. v.p. Wealthport, Inc., 2000—01; COO CCA Global Ptnrs. Inc., 2001—. Chmn. Dayton Ballet Assn., 1979-91; trustee Carillon Park, 1988-94, City-Wide Devel. Corp., 1991-2000, Cath. Social Svcs., 1995-2000; assoc. bd. Dayton Art Inst., 1989-95. Mem. ABA (com. chmn. 1990-92), Ohio Soc. CPAs (pres. 1985-86). Republican. Roman Catholic.

WILSON, ROBERT NATHAN, health care company executive; b. Covington, Ky., Aug. 7, 1940; s. Robert Thomas and Ruth (Pearce) W.; m. Anne Wright, Mar. 29, 1969; children: Julie Anne, Jonathan Robert. BA in Bus., Georgetown (Ky.) Coll., 1962; grad. exec. program Grad. Sch. Bus. Adminstrn., Columbia U., 1975; LLD (hon.), Phila. Coll. Pharmacy and Sci., 1991; DHL Georgetown Coll. (hon.), 1998. Sales rep. Ortho Pharm. Corp., Raritan, N.J., 1964; various exec. and mgr. positions, 1964-77; pres. Johnson & Johnson Dental Products Co., East Windsor, N.J., 1977-79; co. group chmn. Johnson & Johnson, New Brunswick, N.J., 1981-83, mem. exec. com., 1983—2002, apptd. vice chmn. exec. com., 1994—2002, vice chmn., bd. dirs., 1989—, sr. vice chmn., bd. dirs., 2001—. Pres. Ortho Pharm. Corp., Raritan, N.J., 1979-83; chmn. Ortho Pharm. Ltd. Can., 1979-83; bd. dirs. U.S. Trust Corp. 1991—, James Black Found., London, Amerada Hess Corp. Nat. coun. World Wildlife Fund, 1995—; trutsee Mus. Am. Folk Art, N.Y.C., 1981—95; mem. Georgetown Coll. Found., World Bus. Coun. for Sustainable Devel., Pharm. Rsch. and Mfrs. Am. Found., 1994—, Trilateral Commn., 1993—99; chmn., bd. dirs. Healthcare Inst. N.J., 1966—99. Recipient Alumni Achievement award Georgetown Coll., 1987. Mem. Pharm. Rsch. and Mfrs. Am. (bd. dirs. 1984-2002, exec. com. 1988-2002, chmn. 2000-01). Presbyterian. Office: Johnson & Johnson 1 Johnson And Johnson Plz New Brunswick NJ 08933-0002

WILSON, ROBERT RUTHERFORD, religious studies educator; b. Louisville, Mar. 29, 1942; s. Ralph Elmer and Dorothy May (Rutherford) W.; m. Sharyn Elaine Beck, July 28, 1967. AB, Transylvania U., 1964; BD, Yale U., 1967, MA, 1969, PhD, 1972. Ordained to ministry Disciples of Christ, 1967. Instr. old testament Union Theol. Sem., N.Y.C., 1971-72; asst. prof. old

testament Yale Univ., New Haven, Conn., 1972-76, assoc. prof. old testament, 1976-83, prof. old testament, 1983—, Hoober prof. religious studies, 1991—, chair dept. religious studies, 1986-92, 95-96. Author: Genealogy and History in the Biblical World, 1977, Prophecy and Society in Ancient Israel, 1980, Sociological Approaches to the Old Testament, 1984; editor (book): Canon, Theology, and Old Testament Interpretation, 1988. Mem. Civic Orch. of New Haven, 1975—. Dir. summer seminar for coll. tchrs. NEH, Washington, 1981; Danforth Grad. fellow Danforth Found., St. Louis, 1964; fellow Am. Coun. Learned Socs., Wash., 1975. Mem. Soc. Bibl. Lit. (coun. mem. 1977-79), Columbia Univ. Seminar Study Hebrew Bible (chair 1978-81), Am. Acad. Religion, Am. Oriental Soc., Am. Soc. for Study Religion, Am. Schs. Oriental Rsch. Avocation: music. Office: Yale Univ 409 Prospect St New Haven CT 06511-2167 E-mail: robert.wilson@yale.edu.

WILSON, ROBERT WARNE, philanthropist, investor; b. Detroit, Nov. 3, 1926; s. Clarence Warne Wilson and Margaret Ballantyne; m. Marillyn Buelow Wilson, Apr. 1957 (div. 1977). BA in Econs. magna cum laude, Amherst (Mass.) Coll., 1946; MA in Econs., U. Mich., 1947; postgrad., Mich. Law Sch., 1948-49. Trainee First Boston Corp., N.Y.C., 1949-50, 52-53; securities analyst Nat. Bank of Detroit, 1953-58; securities analyst to v.p. Gen. Am. Inv., N.Y.C., 1958-62; securities analyst A.G. Becker & Co., N.Y.C., 1962-68; investor, 1968—. Bd. dirs. Bklyn. Mus., 1974-88, Bklyn. Botanic Garden, 1974-88, N.Y.C. Opera, 1977-98, chmn. 1981-93; adv. bd. Met. Opera, 1979-81; trustee Environtl. Def., 1986—, Lyric Opera of Chgo. Nat. Bd., 1995-2001, Manhattan Inst., 1986-2002, Whitney Mus. of Am. Art, 1978—, World Monuments Fund, 1990—, Deafness Rsch. Found., 1998-2001. With U.S. Army, 1951-52. Mem. Phi Beta Kappa. Republican. Avocations: opera, museums, theater, movies, sightseeing. Office: 520 83rd St Brooklyn NY 11209-4520

WILSON, ROBERT WOODROW, radio astronomer; b. Houston, Tex., Jan. 10, 1936; s. Ralph Woodrow and Fannie May (Willis) W.; m. Elizabeth Rhaods Sawin, Sept. 4, 1958; children: Philip Garrett, Suzanne Katherine, Randal Woodrow. BA with honors in Physics, Rice U., 1957; PhD, Calif. Inst. Tech., 1962. Research fellow Calif. Inst. Tech., Pasadena, 1962-63; mem. tech. staff AT&T Bell Labs., Holmdel, N.J., 1963-76, head wireless tech. rsch. dept., 1976-94; sr. sci. Harvard-Smithsonian Ctr. for Astrophysics, Cambridge, Mass., 1994—. Discoverer 3 deg. k microwave background radiation, 1965, CO and other molecules in interstellar space using their millimeter wavelength radiation;. Named Fairchild Disting. scholar, Caltech., 1987; recipient Henry Draper medal, Royal Astron. Soc., London, 1977, Nobel prize in physics, 1978; fellow NSF fellow, 1958—61, Cole fellow, 1957—58. Mem.: NAS (Herschel medal 1977), Internat. Sci. Radio Union, Am. Phys. Soc., Internat. Astron. Union, Am. Astron. Soc., Sigma Xi, Phi Beta Kappa. Office: Harvard-Smithsonian Ctr Astrophysics 60 Garden St Cambridge MA 02138-2306

WILSON, ROBIN SCOTT, retired academic administrator, writer; b. Columbus, Ohio, Sept. 19, 1928; s. John Harold and Helen Louise (Walker) W.; m. Patricia Ann Van Kirk, Jan. 20, 1951; children: Kelpie, Leslie, Kari, Andrew. BA, Ohio State U., 1950; MA, U. Ill., 1951, PhD, 1959. Fgn. intelligence officer CIA, Washington, 1959-67; prof. English Clarion State Coll., (Pa.), 1967-70; assoc. dir. Com. Instnl. Cooperation, Evanston, Ill., 1970-77; assoc. provost instrn. Ohio State U., Columbus, 1977-80; univ. pres. Calif. State U., Chico, 1980-93, pres. emeritus, 1993—. Author: Those Who Can, 1973, Death By Degrees, 1995, Paragons, 1996; short stories, criticism, articles on edn. Lt. USN, 1953-57. Mem. AAAS, Phi Kappa Phi E-mail: wilsonrobin@earthlink.net.

WILSON, ROBLEY CONANT, JR., English educator, editor, author; b. Brunswick, Maine, June 15, 1930; s. Robley Conant and Dorothy May (Stimpson) W.; m. Charlotte A. Lehon, Aug. 20, 1955 (div. 1991); children: Stephen, Philip; m. Susan Hubbard, Jan 17, 1995. BA, Bowdoin Coll., 1957, D.Litt (hon.), 1987; M.F.A., U. Iowa, 1968. Reporter Raymondville Chronicle, Tex., 1950-1951; asst. publicity dir. N.Y. State Fair Syracuse, 1956; instr. Valparaiso U., Ind., 1958-63; asst. prof. English U. No. Iowa, Cedar Falls, 1963-69, assoc. prof., 1969-75, prof., 1975-2000, prof. emeritus, 2000—, editor N.Am. Rev., 1969-2000. Author: The Pleasures of Manhood, 1977, Living Alone, 1978, Dancing for Men, 1983 (Drue Heinz Lit. prize, 1982), Kingdoms of the Ordinary (Agnes Lynch Starrett award, 1986), Terrible Kisses, 1989, A Pleasure Tree, 1990 (Soc. Midland Authors Poetry award, 1990), The Victim's Daughter, 1991, A Walk Through the Human Heart, 1996, Everything Paid For, 1999, The Book of Lost Fathers, 2001, Splendid Omens, 2004; co-editor: 100% Pure Florida Fiction, 2000. Bd. dirs. Associated Writing Programs, Norfolk, Va., 1983-86; pres. Iowa Woman Endeavors, Inc., 1986-90. With USAF, 1951-55. Guggenheim fellow, 1983-84, Nicholl Screenwriting fellow, 1996. Mem.: PEN, Authors' Guild. Home: PO Box 4009 Winter Park FL 32793-4009

WILSON, ROGER GOODWIN, lawyer; b. Evanston, Ill., Sept. 3, 1950; s. G. Turner Jr. and Lois (Shay) W.; m. Giovinella Gonthier, Mar. 7, 1975. AB, Dartmouth Coll., 1972; JD, Harvard U., 1975. Bar: Ill. 1975, U.S. Dist. Ct. (no. dist.) Ill. 1976, U.S. Ct. Appeals (7th cir.) 1977, U.S. Dist. Ct. (no. dist.) Ind. 1985. Assoc. Kirkland & Ellis, Chgo., 1975-81, ptnr., 1981-86; sr. v.p., gen. counsel, corp. sec. Blue Cross/Blue Shield, 1986—. Speaker Nat. Healthcare Inst., U. Mich., 1987-93, Am. Law Inst.-ABA Conf. on Mng. and Resolving Domestic and Internat. Bus. Disputes, N.Y.C., 1988, Washington, 1990; cert. health cons. program Purdue U., 1993-94, Inst. for Bus. Strategy Devel., Northwestern U., 1993-94, The Health Care Antitrust Forum, Chgo., 1995, Am. Health Lawyers Assn Managed Care Law Inst., 1995, Am. Health Lawyers Assn. Conf. on Tax Issues in Healthcare Orgns., 1996. Contbg. editor Health Care Fraud and Abuse Newsletter, 1998-2002. Advisor Constl. Rights Found., Chgo., 1982-87; mem. So. Poverty Law Ctr., Montgomery, Ala., 1981—. Mem. ABA, Am. Health Lawyers Assn. (spkr. 1984, 96), Legal Assistance Found. of Chgo. (bd. dirs.), Chgo. Coun. Lawyers (bd. govs. 1988-92), Coun. Chief Legal Officers (conf. bd. 1995—), Coun. Corp. Governance (conf. bd. 1998-00), Dartmouth Lawyers Assn., Sinfonietta (bd. dirs.), Univ. Club, Mid-Am. Club, Phi Beta Kappa. Home: 330 N Jefferson Ct Unit2004 Chicago IL 60661 Office: Blue Cross/Blue Shield 225 N Michigan Ave Ste 200 Chicago IL 60601-7601 Office Phone: 312-297-6439. E-mail: roger.wilson@bcbsa.com.

WILSON, RONALD LAWRENCE, professional hockey coach; b. Windsor, Ont., Can., May 28, 1955; BA in Econs., Providence Coll. Profl. hockey player Toronto Maple Leafs, 1975-85, Minn. North Stars, 1986-88; asst. coach Milw., Vancouver Canucks, 1989-90, Vancouver Canucks, 1990-93; interim coach Milw. Admirals, 1990; head coach Anaheim (Calif.) Mighty Ducks, 1993-97, Team USA, 1996, Washington Capitals, Landover, Md., 1997—2002, San Jose Sharks, 2002—. Coach Team U.S.A., World Cup of Hockey, 1996, 2004, U.S. Olympic Hockey Team, Nagano, Japan, 1998. Named to NCAA All-Am. East 1st team, 1974-76; Team USA World Cup Champaions, 1996. Office: San Jose Sharks 525 W Santa Clara St San Jose CA 95113*

WILSON, RUBY LEILA, nursing educator; b. Punxsutawney, Pa., May 29, 1931; d. Clark H. and Alda E. (Armstrong) Wilson. BS in Nursing Edn., U. Pitts., 1954; MSN, Case Western Res. U., 1959; EdD, Duke U., 1969. Staff nurse, asst. head nurse Allegheny Gen. Hosp., Pitts., 1951—52, night clin. instr., adminstrv. supr., 1951—55; staff nurse, asst. head nurse Fort Miley VA Hosp., San Francisco, 1957—58; instr. nursing Duke U. Sch. Nursing, Durham, NC, 1955—57, asst. prof. med. surg. nursing, 1959—66, assoc. in medicine, 1963—66, prof. nursing, 1971—, dean sch. nursing, 1971—84, asst. to chancellor for health affairs, 1984—; asst. prof. dept. community and family medicine Duke U. Sch. Medicine, 1971—; cons., vis. prof. Rockefeller Found., Thailand, 1968—71; vis. prof. Case Western Res. U., 1982—84. Mem. Gov.'s Commn. on Health Care Reform in N.C., 1994—96. Contbr. articles to profl. jours. Active N.C. Med. Care Commn., N.C. Ctr. for Nursing, 1990—; adv. bd. Duke U. Cancer Ctr., 1986—. Fellow: Inst. Medicine, Am. Acad. Nursing; mem.: N.C. Found. for Nursing (pres. 1990—94), Women's Forum N.C. (bd. dirs. 1984—88, 1995—), Assn. for Acad. Health Ctrs. (mem. inst. planning com.), Nat. League Nursing, Am. Assn. Higher Edn., Am. Assn. Colls. Nursing, ANA, Sigma Theta Tau. Office: Duke U Med Ctr PO Box 3243 Durham NC 27715-3243

WILSON, S. LIANE, bank executive; Sr. v.p. info. systems Wash. Mut. Inc., Seattle, exec. v.p. corp. comm., 1995-2000, vice-chmn., 2000—01, cons., 2001—02; bd. dirs. Network Assoc., 2002—.

WILSON, SAMUEL MAYHEW, surgeon; b. Phila., June 26, 1950; m. Dorothy Hay Barrus, June 9, 1990; children: Elisabeth, Mary. BA, Swarthmore Coll., 1972; MS, Drexel U., 1975; MD, Temple U., 1979. Diplomate Am. Bd. Surgery. Resident in surgery Temple U. Hosp., Phila., 1979-84; fellow in vascular surgery Presbyn.-U. Pa. Med. Ctr., 1984-86; attending surgeon Evang. Cmty. Hosp., Lewisburg, 1986-88, Albert Einstein Med. Ctr., Phila., 1988-95. Attending surgeon Elkins Park (Pa.) Hosp., 1988-95, Frankford Hosp., Phila., 1988-95, JFK Meml. Hosp., Phila., 1988-95; staff surgeon Bayhealth Med. Ctr.-Kent Gen. Hosp., Dover, 1996—; asst. clin. instr. surgery U. Pa. Med. Sch., Phila., 1984-85, assoc. clin. instr., 1985-86; clin. instr. surgery Temple U. Sch. Medicine, Phila., 1988-95. Contbr. articles to profl. jours. Active Christ Episcopal Ch., Dover, 1996—. Corp. USMCR, 1972-78. Fellow ACS, Southeastern Surg. Congress; mem. AMA (Physician Recognition award), Med. Soc. Del., Kent County Med. Soc., Delaware Valley Vascular Soc., Ea. Vascular Soc. Avocations: sailing, skiing, hiking, photography, reading. Office: 540 S Governors Ave Ste 100A Dover DE 19904-3523

WILSON, SAMUEL V. academic administrator; Pres. Hampden-Sydney Coll., Va., 1992—2000, James C. Wheat Chair in Leadership, 2000—.

WILSON, SLOAN, writer, educator; b. Norwalk, Conn., May 8, 1920; s. Albert F. and Ruth (Danenhower) Wilson; m. Elise Pickhardt, Feb. 4, 1941 (div.); children: Lisa, Rebecca, David Sloan; m. Betty Stephens; 1 child, Jessica. Grad., Fla. Adirondack Sch., 1938; AB, Harvard, 1942; LHD (hon.), Rollins Coll., 1982. Writer, contbr. New Yorker and other mags.; with Providence Jour., 1946-47, Time, Inc., 1947-49, Nat. Citizens Commn. for Pub. Schs., 1949-53; dir. info. svcs., asst. prof. English Buffalo U., 1953-55; asst. dir. White House Conf. on Edn., 1955-56; lectr. creative writing NYU, 1961—62; Disting. writer-in-residence Rollins Coll., Winter Park, Fla., 1981-82; dir. Winter Park Artists Workshop, 1983-85; cons. Philip Crosby Assocs., Winter Park, 1984-87. Lectr. Va. Commonwealth U., 1990. Author: (novels) Voyage To Somewhere, 1946, The Man in the Gray Flannel Suit, 1955, A Summer Place, 1958, A Sense of Values, 1960, Georgie Winthrop, 1962, Janus Island, 1966, Away From It All, 1969, All The Best People, 1970, What Shall We Wear to This Party?, 1976, Small Town, 1978, Ice Brothers, 1979, Greatest Crime, 1980, Pacific Interlude, 1982, The Man in the Gray Flannel Suit II, 1983. Served to lt. USCGR, World War II. *Although some of my books have been widely read, I of course am not as successful a writer as I would like to be. Almost all writers, after all, must (if they are honest) suspect that their triumphs are temporary. This is no cause for lament, for the same happens to almost everybody in all walks of life. I am lucky to have a wife who makes my private life a joy and three daughters and a son who with my ten grandchildren (Ben, Eli, Joseph, Anna, Abigail, David, Katie, Tamar, Rachel, and Joshua) and two great grandchildren (Jacob and Nora), give me a kind of immortality. Much like the characters in most of my books, I find my family the only part of my life which does not disappoint. My children and my wife always give me excellent reviews, which never yellow in a scrapbook. I sometimes lecture on the topic of "Success." Nowadays that word seems to be much more complex than it did when I was young. As I grow old, I love life more and more.* Died May 25, 2003.

WILSON, STEPHEN EDWARD, academic administrator; b. Ellensburg, Wash., May 12, 1945; s. Edward and Marjorie Louise (Tucker) W.; m. Mary Lynne Halwas, Aug. 28, 1966; children: Troy, Aubree-Anna. BA in English, Cen. Wash. State Coll., 1967; MA in Guidance Counseling, Wayne State U., 1973; PhD in Counselor Edn. and Supr., St. Mary's U., 2001. Commd. USAF, 1967, advanced through grades to lt. col., 1983, chief intelligence career mgmt. USAF Mil. Pers. Ctr., 1976-80, br. chief Intelligence Ctr. Pacific Camp Smith, Hawaii, 1980-81, Commdr. in Chief Pacific Staff, 1981-83, dir. Alert Ctr. Hdqrs. Electronic Security Command Kelly AFB, Tex., 1983-84, dir. tng., 1984-85, commdr. 6981 Electronic Security Squadron Elmendorf AFB, Alaska, 1985-88; ret., 1989—99; v.p. logistics and tech. svcs. Operational Tech. Corp., San Antonio, 1989—, mgr. quality assurance, 1989—; free lance writer Psychol. Corp., San Antonio, 1989—; CIO, dir. instl. rsch. U. Incarnate Word, San Antonio, 1999—. Mem. USAF Intelligence Career Field Study Group, Washington, 1978-84, Dept. Def. Intelligence Career Devel. Panel, Washington, 1976-80; chmn. Computer Intelligence Officer Study Group, Washington, 1979-80, Pacific Target Actions Group, Honolulu, 1981-83 Author: North Vietnamese Use of Inland Waterways, 1970, Petroleum Pipelines in the Laotian Panhandle, 1971; contbr. editor: DOD Armed Services Vocational Aptitude Battery (ASVAB) Manual, 1990. Founding mem. San Antonio Council of Adoptable Children, 1976-80; charter mem. Hosanna! Luth. Ch., San Antonio, 1983-85; mem. Friends of Luth. Social Services Tex., San Antonio, 1976-80. Decorated Bronze Star. Mem. Air Force Assn., Am. Soc. Quality Control, Am. Soc. Safety Engrs., Nat. Contract Mgmt. Assn., Am. Def. Preparedness Assn., Assn. Old Crows. Home: 19506 Wittenburg San Antonio TX 78256-2026 Office: 4301 Broadway San Antonio TX 78209

WILSON, STEPHEN R. financial infromation executive; Exec. v.p., CFO Readers Digest Assn., Pleasantville, N.Y.; CFO, exec. v.p. Bridge Information, 2000—. Office: Bridge Information Three World Financial Center 27TH FL New York NY 10281

WILSON, SUE, newspaper editor; Bur. chief AP, Raleigh, N.C., 1999—. Address: 4020 Westchase Blvd Ste 300 Raleigh NC 27607-3960

WILSON, SUE, state legislator; b. Albuquerque; BA, So. Meth. U. Mem. N.Mex. Senate, Dist. 19, Santa Fe, 1996—; mem. fin. com. N.Mex. Senate, mem. Indian and cultural affairs com. Republican. Home: 1516 Gray Rock Pl NE Albuquerque NM 87112-6639

WILSON, SYLVIA ALYCE, musician, educator; b. Mpls., June 19, 1950; d. Robert Leighton and Doris Mae (Seim) Butts; m. Dennis Charles Wilson, Sept. 12, 1970; children: Ryan Bradley, Virginia Anne Cooper. BS in Music Edn. with high distinction, U. Minn., 1972, MA in Music Edn., 1987. Orch. tchr. Anoka-Hennepin Sch. Dist. No. 11, Coon Rapids, Minn., 1972—77, music tchr., 1986—89, 1992—; substitute music tchr. St. Louis Park (Minn.) Sch. Dist. No. 283, 1978—85; orch. tchr. Wayzata (Minn.) Sch. Dist. #284, 1985—86; orch./choir tchr. Roseville (Minn.) Area Pub. Schs. #623, 1989—90. Musician Lake String Quartet, Mpls., 1982—85; piano tuner, pvt. music tchr., 1982—86; preschool music tchr. West Bank Sch. Music, Mpls., 1983—85; judge Minn. State HS League, St. Paul, 2003—; presenter in field. Contbr. articles to profl. jours. Violinist, violist Mpls. Civic Orch., 1970—, Cantati Evangelica, Mpls., 1995—2001; VBS tchr. First Bapt. Ch. Mpls., 1990—94, choir dir., bell choir dir., 1992—2000. Named Outstanding Sr., Am. Legion, 1968; recipient Meritorious Orch. Program award, Minn. String Tchrs. Assn., 1987, 2002; grantee, Anoka-Hennepin Ednl. Found., 1999—2001; scholar, U. Minn., 1968. Mem.: NEA, Anoka-Hennepin Edn. Minn. (bldg. rep. 2000—), Am. String Tchrs. Assn., Music Educators Nat. Conf., Pi Kappa Lambda, Sigma Alpha Iota (pres., vice-president, treas., corr. sec. 1970—, co-chair benefit music scholarships, Music scholar 1970, Sword of Honor 1971). Home: 2700 Joppa Ave S Saint Louis Park MN 55416 Office: Northdale Mid Sch 11301 Dogwood St Coon Rapids MN 55448

WILSON, THEODORE HENRY, retired electronics company executive, aerospace engineer; b. Eufaula, Okla., Apr. 23, 1940; s. Theodore V. and Maggie E. (Buie) W.; m. Barbara Ann Tassara, May 16, 1958 (div. 1982); children: Debbie Marie, Nita Leigh, Wilson Axten, Pamela Ann, Brenda Louise, Theodore Henry II, Thomas John, Margaret Mariana; m. Colleen Fagan, Jan. 1, 1983 (div. 1987); m. Karen L. Lerohl, Sept. 26, 1987 (div. 1997); m. Sandra Rivadeneira, Mar. 27, 1997. BSME, U. Calif., Berkeley, 1962; MSME, U. So. Calif., 1964, MBA, 1970, MSBA, 1971. Sr. rsch. engr. N.Am. Aviation Co. div. Rockwell Internat., Downey, Calif., 1962-65; propulsion analyst, supr. div. applied tech. TRW, Redondo Beach, Calif., 1965-67, mem. devel. staff systems group, 1967-71, sr. fin. analyst worldwide automotive dept. Cleve., 1971-72, contr. systems and energy group Redondo Beach, 1972-79, dir. fin. control equipment group Cleve., 1979-82, v.p. fin. control indsl. and energy group, 1982-85, mem. space and def. group Redondo Beach, 1985-93, ret., 1993. Lectr., mem. com. acctg. curriculum UCLA Extension, 1974-79. Mem. Fin. Execs. Inst. (com. govt. bus.), Machinery and Allied Products Inst. (govt. contracts coun.), Nat. Contract Mgmt. Assn. (bd. advisors), Aerospace Industries Assn. (procurement and fin. coun.), UCLA Chancellors Assocs., Tau Beta Pi, Beta Gamma Sigma, Pi Tau Sigma. Republican. Avocations: golf, bridge. Home: 3617 Via La Selva Palos Verdes Peninsula CA 90274-1115

WILSON, THOMAS, museum director; Dir. Mus. of N.Mex, Santa Fe. Office: Mus of NMex 107 W Palace Ave Santa Fe NM 87501-2014

WILSON, THOMAS DALE, philanthropic fundraising consultant; b. Lincoln, Nebr., June 2, 1952; s. Richard Barr and Charlotte Adele (Brown) Wilson; m. Susette Adele Eddinger, Mar. 9, 1973; children: Christine, Richard, Charles, Kathryn. B in Music Edn., U. Nebr., Lincoln, 1974; MusM, Northwestern U., Evanston, Ill., 1976. Dir. corp. found. rels. Field Mus. Natural History, Chgo., 1984—85; dir. devel. Phoenix Symphony, 1985—86; sr. campaign dir. Devel. Mgmt. Assn., L.A., 1986—89; v.p. devel. Oreg. Grad. Inst. Sci. & Tech., Portland, 1989—93; pres. Wilson and Assocs., Portland, Oreg., 1993—. Co-pres. Assn. Fundraising Profls. Oreg., Portland, 2002—03. Author: Great Grantsmanship, 1997, The Win Win Ask, 1999, Endowment Fundraising, 2000. Music dir. English Handbell Choir, 1989—94; trustee Valley Cmty. Presbyn. Ch. Found., 1989—94. Mem.: Nat. Soc. Fund Raising Execs. (Oreg. pres. 1990). Avocations: biking, reading, jazz saxophone. Office: Wilson & Assocs 4495 NW Malhuer Ave Portland OR 97229

WILSON, THOMAS DOUGLAS, JR., lawyer; b. Winston-Salem, N.C., Aug. 26, 1946; s. Thomas Douglas Wilson and Beatrice Burcham Chapman; m. Betsey Page Bent, Aug. 22, 1984; 1 child, Elizabeth. BA in Econs., U. N.C., Chapel Hill, 1968, JD, 1973. Bar: N.C. 1973, Ga. 1974; cert. arbitrator, mediator Ga., arbitrator N.C. Trial atty. FTC, Atlanta, 1973-78; pvt. practice Atlanta, 1978-81; atty. Ga. Legal Svcs. Corp., Gainesville, 1981-84; mng. ptnr. Wilson, Cobb, Lichstenstein & Lao, Atlanta, 1984-93; pres. Ga. Emission Testing Co., Inc., Atlanta, 1993-95; assoc. McGuire, Wood & Bissette PA, Asheville, N.C., 1995-98, mng. ptnr., 1999—. Vol. atty. Pisgah Legal Svcs., Asheville, 1996—, also bd. dirs. Author: (manual) Social Security Disability Claims, 1984; co-author: (manual) North Carolina Construction Law: Rights and Remedies, 1998. Chmn. bd. dirs. RiverLink, Asheville, 1997-99; vice chmn. bd. dirs. Regional Waterh Authority Task Force, Asheville, 1996-99; mem. Asheville Econ. Devel. Task Force, 1999-2000; mem. Asheville Econ. Devel. Commn., 1997-99; youth basketball coach YMCA, Asheville Recreation League, 1997-2001. Mem. ABA, ATLA, Ga. Bar Assn., N.C. Bar Assn. (bd. dirs., constrn. law coun 2000—), N.C. Acad. Trial Lawyers. Home: 172 Marlborough Rd Asheville NC 28804 Office: 48 Patton Ave Asheville NC 28801-3321 Fax: (828) 252-2437. E-mail: t.d.wilson@home.com., tdwilson@mwbavl.com.

WILSON, THOMAS JOSEPH, insurance company executive; m. Jill Garling; 3 children. BSBA, U. Mich., 1979; M of Mgmt., Northwestern U., 1980. Various fin. positions Amoco Corp., Chgo., 1980-86; mng. dir. mergers and acquisitions Dean Witter Reynolds, Chgo., 1986-93; v.p. strategy and analysis Sears, Roebuck and Co., Chgo., 1993-95; sr. v.p., CFO Allstate Ins. Co., Northbrook, Ill., 1995-98; chmn., pres. Allstate Fin., 1999—2002; pres. Allstate Protection, 2003—. Bd. dirs. Rush-Presbyn.-St. Luke's Med. Ctr. and Francis W. Parker Sch. Office: Allstate Protection 2775 Sanders Rd Northbrook IL 60062-6110

WILSON, THOMAS LEON, physicist, researcher; b. Alpine, Tex., May 21, 1942; s. Homer Marvin and Ogarita Maude (Bailey) W.; m. Joyce Ann Krevosky, May 7, 1978; children: Kenneth Edward Byron, Bailey Elizabeth Victoria. BA, Rice U., 1964, BS, 1965, MA, 1974, PhD, 1976. With NASA, Houston, 1965—, astronaut instr., 1965-74, high-energy theoretical physicist, 1969—. Author: 2 books; contbr. articles to profl. jours. Recipient Hugo Gernsback award, IEEE, 1964; fellow, NASA, 1969—76. Mem. AAAS, Am. Phys. Soc., N.Y. Acad. Scis., Am. Assn. Physicists in Medicine. Achievements include research on grand unified field theory, relativistic quantum field theory, quantum chromodynamics, quantum probability theory, supergravity, quantum cosmology, astrophysics, deep inelastic scattering, neutrino astronomy, neutrino tomography; discoverer classical uncertainity principle; subspeciality: relativity and gravitation; patentee in field; contributor to design of NASA's proposed lunar base; originator olive branch as symbol of man's 1st landing on moon (on Susan B. Anthony and Eisenhower dollars); and manual Saturn takeover for Apollo moon program. Home: 206 Woodcombe Dr Houston TX 77062-2538 Office: NASA Johnson Space Ctr Houston TX 77058 Office Phone: 281-483-2147. Business E-Mail: twilson@ems.jsc.nasa.gov.

WILSON, THOMAS MATTHEW, III, lawyer; b. Ware, Mass., Feb. 22, 1936; s. Thomas Matthew Jr. and Ann Veronica (Shea) W.; m. Deborah Ord Lockhart, Feb. 10, 1962; children: Deborah Veronica, Leslie Lockhart, Thomas Matthew IV. BA, Brown U., 1958; JD, U. Md., 1971. Bar: Md. 1972, U.S. Ct. Appeals (4th cir.) 1976, U.S. Supreme Ct. 1977. Sales mgr. Mid-Ea. Box Mfg. Co., Balt., 1966-74; asst. atty. gen., chief antitrust divsn. State of Md., Balt., 1974-79; ptnr. Tydings & Rosenberg, LLP, Balt., 1979—. Author: Defending an Antitrust Action Brought by a State, 1987, The Spectre of Double Recovery in Antitrust Federalism, 1989; co-author: Reciprocity and the Private Plaintiff, 1972; mem. editl. adv. bd.: Bur. of Nat. Affairs Antitrust and Trade Regulation Report, 1979—. Mem. ABA (sect. on antitrust law 1974—, chmn. state antitrust enforcement com. 1986-89, antitrust sect. coun. 1990-93, coord. com. on legal edn. 1993—), Md. Bar Assn. (antitrust subcom. 1975-78), Internat. Bar Assn. (sect. on bus. law, antitrust law and monopolies com. 1983—), Churchwarden's Chess Club, Annapolis Yacht Club. Republican. Achievements include patents for nail cartons. Home: Baobab Farm Hampstead MD 21074 Office: Tydings & Rosenberg LLP 100 E Pratt St Baltimore MD 21202-1009 Office Phone: 410-752-9708.

WILSON, THOMAS STRONG, JR., (TAM WILSON), judge; b. Portland, Oreg., Aug. 13, 1944; s. Thomas Strong and Ruth (Isherwood) W. BA, Dickinson Coll., 1967; JD, U. Miami, 1971. Bar: Fla. 1971, D.C. 1972, U.S. Dist. Ct. (so. dist.) Fla., U.S. Ct. Appeals (5th cir.). Rsch. aide to Justice James Adkins Fla. Supreme Ct., Tallahassee, 1971-72; assoc. Preddy, Haddad, Kutner & Hardy, 1973, John R. Farrell, PA., 1973; asst. pub. defender Pub. Defender's Office, Dade County, Fla., 1974-77; sole practice Dade County, 1978-84; asst. state's atty. State's Atty.'s Office, Dade County, 1984-87, gen. master Family Divsn., 1987-90; judge Circuit Ct., Dade County, 1990. Served to ensign USNR, 1968-69. Named Judge of Yr., Am. Bd. Trial Advocates, Miami chpt., 1999, Dade County Trial Lawyers, 2003. Mem. Iron Arrow, Skull and Key. Roman Catholic. Office: Dade County Courthouse 175 NW 1st Ave # 2314 Miami FL 33128

WILSON, THOMAS WOODROW, III, research scientist, consultant; b. Greensboro, N.C., Mar. 29, 1956; s. Thomas Woodrow Jr. and Ruth Hanes (Friddle) W. BS in Textile Chemistry with honors, N.C. State U., 1978, MS in Textile Chemistry, 1981, PhD in Fiber and Polymer Sci., 1986. Registered patent agent. Polymer scientist Rsch. Triangle Inst., Research Triangle Park, N.C., 1989-91; rsch. scientist Family Health Internat., Research Triangle Park, N.C., 1991-93, sr. rsch. scientist, 1993-94, assoc. dir., 1994-95; mgr. intellectual property and regulatory affairs Mayer Labs., Oakland, Calif., 1996-97; materials rschr. Nike, Beaverton, Oreg., 1997-99, advanced chemistry rsch. mgr. Taichung, Taiwan, 1999—2003, sr. chemical R & D engr., 2003—. Cons. IPAS, Carrboro, N.C., 1991-94. Patentee med. devices; contbr. articles to profl. jours. Grantee USDA, NASA, NIH/Nat. Inst. Dental Rsch., 1986. Mem. AAAS, Am. Chem. Soc. (polymeric materials sci. and engrng. divsn., polymer divsn., rubber divsn., chemistry and law divsn.), Toastmasters

(Taichang, Taiwan chpt., First Runner Up Nat. Tall Tale contest, 2001, Nat. Speech contest, 2002), Sigma Xi. Avocations: leatherworking, woodworking, writing fiction. Office: Nike 447 Wen Hsin Rd 28th Fl Taichung ROC Taiwan Business E-Mail: Tom.Wilson@Nike.com.

WILSON, TRISHA, interior architectural designer; b. Augusta, Ga. d. Lemuel Edward Wilson and Doris (Howard) Gray. BS in Interior Archtl. Design, U. Tex., 1969. Interior designer Titche-Goettinger Allied Stores, Dallas, 1969-72; ptnr. Merrill/Wilson and Assocs., Dallas, 1972-75; chmn., chief exec. officer Wilson and Assocs., Dallas, N.Y.C., L.A., Singapore and Johannesburg, South Africa, 1975—. Bd. dirs. Shelby Williams Industries, Exec. Travel Svc., SPCA of Tex.; mem. found. adv. coun. U. Tex. Sch. Architecture; devel. bd. U. Tex. Adv. dir. Susan G. Komen Found.; bd. dirs. State Fair of Tex., Dallas; mem. Rep. Nat. Com., Friend of Kennedy Ctr. Found. Dallas Assembly; past chmn. bd. dirs. Tex. bus. Hall Fame Found., corp. com. Dallas Mus. Art; trustee Dallas Mus. Art; past adv. bd. dept. home econs. U. Tex., Austin; founder, chmn. Wilson Edn. Found. Named to Design Hall of Fame, Interior Design Mag., 1993. Mem. Am. Soc. Interior Designers (state chpt. bd. dirs. 1978-80), Ins. bus. Designers, Tex. Women's Forum, Dallas Women's Found., Internat. Women's Forum, Soc. Partially Sighted, U. Tex. Ex-Students' Assn. (adv. bd., at-large rep. exec. council), Young Pres. Orgn. Avocations: travel, fine art and antiques. Office: Wilson and Assocs 3811 Turtle Creek Blvd Fl 15 Dallas TX 75219-4461 also: Wilson and Assocs 415 E 54th St Ste 15D New York NY 10022-5101 also: 8342 1/2 Melrose Ave Los Angeles CA 90069-5420

WILSON, VICKI LYNN, executive secretary, administrative assistant; b. El Paso, Tex., Jan. 16, 1962; d. Theodore Elliott and Pamela Ann Wilson. AA, 2003—. Adminstrv. asst. Rsch. Analysis & Maintenance, Inc. (RAM), El Paso, Tex., 1990—2001; sec. Clint Ind. Sch. Dist., El Paso, Tex., 2001—02; exec. sec. San Marcos Consol. Ind. Sch. Dist., San Marcos, Tex., 2003—. Office: San Marcos CISD 500 West Hutchison San Marcos TX 78666 Home: 1923 Ramona Cir San Marcos TX 78666 E-mail: vwilson62@hotmail.com.

WILSON, W. DAVID, corporate financial executive; b. 1954; At, DePauw U., 1975, Thunderbird Grad. Sch. of Intl. Mgmt., 1977. V.p. and CFO PolyOne Corp., Cleve., 2000—. Office: 33587 Walker RD Avon Lake OH 44012-1145

WILSON, WALTER CLINTON, retired gas industry executive; b. Brownwood, Tex., Sept. 21, 1942, s. Henry Eliga and Lottie Mae (Palmore) Wilson; m. Debra M. Thompson, Aug. 26, 1965; children: Walter Scott, Aimée Renee. BS cum laude, Howard Payne U., 1965. CPA Tex. Fin. mgmt. Exxon Co. USA, Kingsville, Corpus Christi, Houston, Tex., 1965-81; asst. contr. Superior Oil Co., Houston, 1982-85, fin. cons., 1985-87; contr. EOG Resources, Inc. (formerly Enron Oil and Gas Co.), Houston, 1987-88, sr. v.p., CFO, 1988-2000; ret., 2000. Mem. adv. bd. H. S. Grace & Co., Houston, 2001—. Trustee Fin. Exec. Rsch. Found., 1998—2001; chmn. pers. com. 1st Bapt. Ch., Houston, 1985—87, chmn. deacons, 1994—96; trustee Howard Payne U., Brownwood, 1999—, chmn., 2002—; bd. dirs. Lyric Performing Arts Co., Brownwood, 2004—. Lt. USNR, 1966—69, Vietnam. Mem.: AICPA, Tex. Soc. CPAs (Houston chpt.), Fin. Execs. Internat., Kingwood Country Club, Club Corp. Am.-Houston Soc. Republican. E-mail: wwilson2@earthlink.net.

WILSON, WANDA LEE DAVIS, casting director; b. Pitts., May 15, 1950; d. James A. Davis, Jr. and Dorothy (Love) Davis Anselmi; m. Kirby L. Wilson Sr., Apr. 23, 1976 (div. July 1984); children: Le Chon Kirb, Lia Shawnyea. Student, Connelly Tech. Sch., Pitts., 1968-71, Allegheny Community Coll., 1968-71, U. Pitts., 1984, 86. Stand-in co-host The Together Show Sta. KDKA-TV, CBS, Pitts., 1971; adminstrv. sec. GE, Pitts., 1971-78; sec., notary public Sta. WPCB-TV, Wall, Pa., 1979-80; producer, host The Wanda Wilson Show Am. Cablevision Co., Monroeville, Pa., 1981-84, Warner Cable Co. and Pitts. Telecommunications, Inc., 1984-87; mktg. mgr. The Informer newspaper Homewood Brushton Revitalization and Devel., Pitts., 1984-87; pres. local, nat. internat. pub. rels. W-W Prodns./Wanda Wilson Enterprises, Pitts., 1984—; sr. clk./chemical monitor Gencorp Aerojet Tech. Systems, Rancho Cordova, Calif., 1987-90; publicist, cons. Easy Internat., Pitts., 1990—; studio camera operator Sta. WPXI-TV, Pitts., 1990-92; casting dir. for commls., film, print media-theatre Wanda Wilson Enterprises, Pitts., 1992—. Scout Modelsearch Am.; occasional writer, copywriter, announcer local radio shows, Pitts., 1972-85; radio show co-host, announcer Internat. People's Radio and TV, Sacramento, 1987; promoter concerts, screenplays, sound tracke Wan Mar Prodns., 1991—. Author (poetry) Love Traces on My Mind, 1972, (songs lyrics) The First Time I Saw You, 1982; performer poetry recitals, Pitts., 1973, (TV movies) $10,000,000 Getaway, 1990, Bump in the Night, 1990, Dead and Alive, 1991, (feature film) Lorenzo's Oil, 1991, Roommates, 1993; producer, hostess WanMar Info. and Talent Showcase Cable TV, Pitts., 1991—; line prodr., casting dir. With Abandon, 1999; casting dir. The Family Tree, 1999, The Matador, 2000, Recollection Rags, 2000. Active Citizen Action for Reduction of Toxic Chems. in Product Packaging, 1990; organizer civic and cmty. events, energy conservation, 1984-87; mem. Pitts. History and Landmarks Found., Smithsonian Assocs., 1991. Mem. AFTRA, NAFE, Pitts. Film Workers Assn. (bd. dirs.), Pitts. Models Assn., Pitts. Media Fedn. (bd. dirs.), Smithsonian Assocs. Democrat. Avocations: swimming, photography, art, interior decorating. Office: PO Box 100061 Pittsburgh PA 15202

WILSON, WARREN SAMUEL, clergyman, bishop; b. New Orleans, May 15, 1927; s. Charlie Price and Warnie (Hart) W.; m. Lillie Pearl Harvey, Apr. 10, 1947; 1 child, Barbara LaJoyce. BA, So. U., Baton Rouge, 1950; DDiv, Moody Coll., Chgo., 1952; DDiv (hon.), Trinity Hall Coll. and Sem., Springfield, Ill., 1975. Ordained to ministry Ch. of God in Christ, 1952, crowned bishop, apptd. state bishop, Calif., 1970, chmn. internat. fin. and budget com. Min. St. Bernard St. Church of God in Christ, New Orleans, 1952—60, Fresno (Calif.) Temple Ch. of God in Christ, 1963—; jurisdictional biship Central Valley Ch. of God in Christ, 1970—; internat. fin. chmn. bd. of biships Ch. of God in Christ, 1974—. Served with USN, 1942-46, PTO. Mem. NAACP (life). Avocations: bass fishing, boating.

WILSON, WILLIAM ALEXANDER, manufacturing engineer, consultant; b. Cleve., Sept. 8, 1959; s. Raymond and Lydia (Lima) W. Student, Cuyahoga C.C.; BME, Cleve. State U., 1986. Mfg. engr. Physics Internat., Wadsworth, Ohio, 1986-88; sr. mfg. engr. Lucas Aerospace, Broadview Heights, Ohio, 1988-89; mfg. engr. Siemens Energy and Automation, Inc., Norwood, Ohio, 1989—; prin. Wilson Engring., Cin., 1994—. Cons. in field. Mem. SME (5 Yr. award 1992). Avocation: competitive swimming. Office: Wilson Engring 8605 Constitution Dr Cincinnati OH 45215-5301 also: Lemforder Corp 1100 Aviation Blvd Hebron KY 41048-9332

WILSON, WILLIAM CAMPBELL MCFARLAND, gastroenterologist; b. Pitts., Pa., June 8, 1953; s. George Lincoln and Nancy Adair (Lytle) W.; m. Marlis Howland, June 25, 1977; children: Sarah, Stephen, Corrie. BS in Biology, Va. Tech, 1975; MD, Hahnemann U., 1979. Intern, residency R.I. Hosp., Providence, 1978-82; staff internist USAF Med. Ctr., Wright-Patterson AFB, Ohio, 1982-86; fellowship Hahnemann U., Phila., 1986-88; with Digestive Care, Dayton, Ohio, 1988—. Chmn. planning com. Dayton Gastroenterology Symposium, 1990—; com. patient edn. Miami Valley Hosp., Dayton, 1990—94, quality assurance com., 1992—, vice chmn. dept. medicine, 1994—96, chmn. dept. medicine, 1996—98, chief of staff-elect, 2002—04, chief of staff, 2004—. Bd. dirs. Fairhaven Ch., Dayton, 1990—94, 2001—, Dayton Christian Schs., Inc., 1995—, physician, 1993—2003; bd. dirs., physician In His Name Ministries, 2000—02. Physician USAF, 1979—86. Fellow ACP; Mem. AMA, Am. Gastroenterological Assn., Am. Coll. Gastroenterology, Am. Soc. Gastrointestinal Endoscopy, Montgomory County Med. Assn., Alpha Omega Alpha. Avocations: tennis, computer, woodworking, bicycling, photography. Office: 75 Sylvania Dr Dayton OH 45440-3237 Office Phone: 937-320-5050. E-mail: wcmw@aol.com.

WILSON, W(ILLIAM) DANIEL, language professional, educator; b. Sedalia, Mo., Dec. 3, 1950; m. Christina von Hodenberg; children: Adrian, Marguerite, Martin. AB, Shimer Coll., 1973; MA, Cornell U., 1976, PhD, 1978. Asst. prof. U. Toronto, Can., 1978-79; asst. prof., postdoctoral rschr. McGill U., Montreal, Que., Can., 1979-83; asst. prof., assoc. prof. dept. German U. Calif. Berkeley, 1983-93, prof., 1993—, chair, 1997-2001. Author: Narrative Strategy of Wieland's Don Sylvio, 1981, Humanitaet und Kreuzzugsideologie, 1983, Geheimraete gegen Geheimbuende, 1991, Interirdische Gaenge, 1999, Das Goethe-Tabu, 1999, Goethes Weimar und die Franzorsische Revolution, 2004; co-editor: Impure Reason: Dialectic of Enlightenment, 1993; mem. editl. bd. German Quar., 1998—. Mem. MLA (exec. com. divsn. 18th century German lit. 1993-98), Am. Assn. Tchrs. German, Am. Soc. 18th Century Studies, Goethe Soc. Weimar, Goethe Soc. N.Am. (mem. editl. bd. 2001—, v.p. 2004—), German Soc. 18th Century Studies, German Studies Assn., Lessing Soc. (Biberach prize 1979, mem. editl. bd. 1986—). Office: Dept German Univ Calif Berkeley CA 94720-3243 Office Phone: 510-642-2973.

WILSON, WILLIAM J. English language educator; b. Oxford, Ind., Sept. 18, 1932; s. William Woodward Wilson and Esta Ella (Burton) Dilley; m. Edith Lucille McElhaney, June 1, 1955 (dec. Mar. 1969); children: Susan Wilson Siener, Maura A., Kyle A. BS summa cum laude, Ill. State U., 1959; MA, Peabody-Vanderbilt U., Nashville, 1968; EdD, Nova U., Ft. Lauderdale, Fla., 1983. Tchr. Manteno (Ill.) High Sch., 1959-60; teaching asst. U. Ill., Urbana, 1960-61; tchr. Wheaton (Ill.) Central High Sch., 1961-67; editor Laidlaw Pubs., Chgo., 1968-69; asst. prof. Ball State U., Muncie, Ind., 1969-70; assoc. prof. English Palm Beach C.C., Lake Worth, Fla., 1970—. Test reader Ednl. Testing Svc., Princeton, N.J., 1965-96; pres. Am. Lang. Rsch. Found., Lake Worth, 1976—. Editor: New Approaches to Language and Composition, 1969; author children's mus. Winter Comes to Florida, 1974, children's mus. play A Cruise on the S.S. Eternal, 1975, Arnold's Answering Apparatus, 1976. Bd. dirs. Village Green Condominiums, Palm Springs, 1985-86. With USN, 1951-55. No. Ill. U. fellow in linguistics, DeKalb, 1965-66, humanities fellow Peabody-Vanderbilt U., Nashville, 1967. Mem. VFW, NEA, Am. Legion, Nat. Assn. Tchrs. English., Kappa Delta Pi, Sigma Tau Delta. Democrat. Episcopalian. Avocations: kairos prison ministry, sports, square dancing, travel, collecting timepieces. Home: 2100 Springdale Blvd Apt 216Y Palm Springs FL 33461-6366 Office: Palm Beach C C 4200 Congress Ave Lake Worth FL 33461-4705 E-mail: barktree@bellsouth.net., wilsonw@pbcc.edu.

WILSON, WILLIAM JAMES, healthcare executive; b. Racine, Wis., Oct. 9, 1948; s. William Henry and Eileen (Tate) W.; m. Deborah Ann Leon, Nov. 14, 1987; children: Jacob Leon, James Tate. Degree in adminstrn. of justice summa cum laude, Am. U., 1972. Asst. dir. promotions Jerry Lewis Telthon, Richmond, Va., 1975; dir. mktg. Mile High Publs., N.Y.C., 1975-76; dir. bur. Travel Communicatiions, Honolulu, 1976-78; founder Hawaii 800, 1979—; v.p. mktg. Video Vacations, N.Y.C., 1982-84; founder Infovision, Los Angeles, 1984-87; chmn. bd. Visitor Cable Network, Honolulu, 1978—; pres. Comcor, Honolulu, 1976—; pres. bus. devel. 3HO Superhealth Hollistic Treatment Ctr., Tucson, 1990-93; pres. Educational Discovery, 1993-94; CEO Advanced Learning Inst., 1994—; mng. dir. Vet. Inst. Integrated Medicine, 1996—; founder, CEO Inst. Labs., 2001—. Founder Japan Am. News Network. Avocations: skiing, rugby. Home: 1109 Quince Ave Boulder CO 80304-0785 Office: PO Box 88377 Honolulu HI 96830-8377

WILSON, WILLIAM JAMES, marketing professional; b. Mpls., May 8, 1936; s. Elmo C. Wilson and Harriett (Ellis) Russo; m. Julie Steers, Sept. 24, 1960 (div. 1983); children: Amanda Jane, Heather May; m. Gabi Coatsworth, May 7, 1983. AB, Yale U., 1958; MA, Cambridge U., Eng., 1964; postgrad., U. Vienna, summer 1964. Internat. advt. devel. mgr. Reader's Digest, London, 1964-67; exec. v.p., dir. Internat. Rsch. Assn., N.Y.C., 1968-71; chair, CEO Roper Starch Worldwide, Harrison, NY, 1971—2001; exec. chmn. NOP World Roper ASW Inc., Harrison, 2001—. Bd. dirs. Roper Ctr. Storrs Ct.; U.S. rep. ESOMAR, The Netherlands 1982-88; chmn. Coun. of Am. Survey Rsch. Orgn., 1994, Coun. for Mktg. and Opinion Rsch., 1996—; past dir. Market Rsch. Coun; mem. bd. advisors MSMR program U. Tex., Arlington, A.C. Nielsen Ctr. for Market Rsch. U. Wis., Madison; mem. bd. dirs. Intersections Inc. Contbr. articles to profl. jours. Mem. Am. Mktg. Assn., Internat. Advt. Assn., Am. Assn. Pub. Opinion Rsch., World Assn. Pub. Opinion Rsch., European Soc. Opinion & Mktg. Rsch. Avocations: gardening, golf, reading, walking. Office: Roper ASW Inc 500 Mamaroneck Ave #103 Harrison NY 10528-1608

WILSON, WILLIAM JULIUS, sociology educator; b. Derry Twp., Pa., Dec. 20, 1935; s. Esco and Pauline (Bracy) W.; m. Mildred Marie Hood, Aug. 31, 1957; children: Colleen, Lisa; m. Beverly Ann Huebner, Aug. 30, 1970; children: Carter, Paula. BA, Wilberforce U., 1958; MA, Bowling Green State U., 1961; PhD, Wash. State U., 1966; LHD (hon.), U. Mass., 1982, L.I. U., 1982, Columbia Coll., Santa Clara U., Loyola Coll., 1988, De Paul U., 1989; LLD (hon.), Marquette U., Mt. Holyoke Coll., 1989; LHD (hon.), New Sch. for Social Rsch., 1991, Bard Coll., 1992, John Jay Sch. Criminal Justice, 1992, U. Pa., 1993, So. Ill. U., 1993, Northwestern U., 1993, Bowling Green State U., 1994, SUNY, Binghamton, 1994, Princeton U., 1995, Columbia U., Rutgers U., Haverford Coll., 1996, Johns Hopkins U., Morehouse Coll., Niagara U., 1997, Dartmouth Coll., 1997, U. Amsterdam, 1998, Clarion U., 1999, Colgate U., 1999, Clark U., 1999, Bates Coll., 1999; D (hon.), Northeastern U., 1999, Macalester Coll. Ohio State U., 2001; DHL (hon.), Occidental Coll., 2001, Rensselaer Poly. Inst., 2001, Lawrence U., 2001, U Miami, 2002, others. Asst. prof. U. Mass., Amherst, 1965-69, assoc. prof., 1969-71; vis. asso. prof. U. Chgo., 1971-72, assoc. prof. dept. sociology, 1972-75, prof., 1975—, chmn. dept. sociology, 1978—, Lucy Flower prof. urban sociology, 1980-84, Lucy Flower disting. service prof., 1984—; Lucy Flower Univ. prof., 1990-96; Malcolm Wiener Prof. of social policy Harvard U., 1996-98, Lewis P. and Linda L. Geyser Univ. Prof., 1998—. Mem. bd. univ. publs. U. Chgo. Press, 1975-79; bd. dirs. Ctr. for Nat. Policy, 1987-92, Ctr. Budget and Policy Priorities, 1987—, Ctr. for Advanced Study of Behavioral Scis., 1988-2002, Twentieth Century Fund (now called Century Found., 1992—, Jerome Levy Inst., 1992-2002, Manpower Demonstration Rsch. Corp., 1993—; bd. dirs. Pub./Private Ventures, Phila., 1994-2002. Author: Power, Racism and Privilege, 1973, Through Different Eyes, 1973, The Declining Significance of Race, 1978, The Truly Disadvantaged, 1987, The Ghetto Underclass, 1993, Sociology and the Public Agenda, 1993, When Work Disappears, 1996 (award Sidney Hillman Found. 1997), The Bridge Over the Racial Divide, 1999. Bd. dirs. Social Sci. Rsch. Coun., 1979-84, Chgo. Urban League, 1983-97, Spencer Found., 1987-97, George M. Pullman Found., 1986-93, Russell Sage Found., 1989-98, Nat. Humanities Ctr., 1990-95, PolicyLink, 2000-; mem. Com. on Sci., Engring. and Pub. Policy, NAS, 1995-2001; nat. bd. dirs. A. Philip Randolph Inst., 1981-, Inst. Rsch. on Poverty, 1983-87; trustee Spelman Coll., 1989-98, Bard Coll., 2001-;bd. govs. Levy Econs. Inst., 2001-; mem. Pres. Commn. on White House Fellowships, 1994-2001; mem. Pres. Com. Nat. Medal Sci., 1994-98; trustee Wilberforce U.; bd. advisors Frederick D. Patterson Rsch. Inst., 1995-, United Negro Coll. Fund, 1996—; mem. scholars' coun. Libr. of Congress, 2002—. With U.S. Army, 1958-60. Recipient Disting. Tchr. of Year award U. Mass., Amherst, 1970, Regents Disting. Alumnus award Wash. State U., 1988, Burton Gordon Feldman award Brandeis U., 1991, Frank E. Seidman Disting. award in polit. econ., 1994, Martin Luther King Jr. Nat. award, 1998, Nat. Medal of Sci. 1998; MacArthur Prize fellow, 1987. Fellow AAAS, Am. Acad. Polit. and Social Sci., Am. Acad. Arts and Scis.; mem. NAS, Nat. Acad. Edn., Am. Philos. Soc., Inst. of Medicine, Am. Sociol. Assn. (pres. 1989-90, com. for pub. understanding of sociology award 1998, Sydney M. Spivack award 1977, DuBois, Johnson, Frazier award 1990, Lester F. Ward Disting. Contbns. to Applied Sociology award 1998), Soc. for Study Social Problems (C. Wright Mills award 1988), Sociol. Rsch. Assn. (pres. 1987-88), Consortium of Social Sci. Assn. (pres. 1993-94), Internat. Sociol. Assn., Chgo. Urban League (Beautiful People award 1979) Democrat. Home: 75 Cambridge Pkwy Unit E406 Cambridge MA 02142-1229 Office: John F Kennedy Sch Govt Harvard Univ 79 John F Kennedy St Cambridge MA 02138-5801

WILSON, WILLIAM PRESTON, psychiatrist, educator; b. Fayetteville, N.C., Nov. 6, 1922; s. Preston Puckett and Rosa Mae (VanHook) W.; m. Dorothy Elizabeth Taylor, Aug. 21, 1950; children: William Preston, Benjamin V., Karen E., Tammy E., Robert E. BS, Duke U., 1943, MD, 1947. Diplomate Am. Bd. Psychiatry and Neurology (examiner). Intern Gorgas Hosp., Ancon, Panama; resident psychiatry Duke U. Med. Ctr., resident neurology, 1949-54; asst. prof. psychiatry Duke U. Med. Sch., 1955-58; assoc. prof. psychiatry Duke U. Med. Ctr., 1961-64, head divsn. clin. neurophysiology, 1961-83, prof. psychiatry, head divsn. biol. psychiatry, 1964-84, emeritus prof. psychiatry, 1985—; assoc. prof. psychiatry, dir. psychiat. rsch. U. Tex. Med. Br., Galveston, 1958-60; dir. Inst. Christian Growth, Burlington, NC, 1985—; disting. prof. pastoral counseling Houston Grad Sch. Theology, High Point, NC, 1996—. Chief neurophysiol. labs. VA Hosp., Durham, N.C., 1961-76; sec. Am. Bd. Qualification in Electroencephalography, 1971-77; mem. N.C. Gov.'s Task force on Diagnosis and Treatment; mem. med. adv. com. N.C. Found. Mental Health Rsch.; bd. dirs. nat. divsn. Contact Teleminstry USA, also mem. internat. commn. healing; cons. numerous area hosps.; Finch lectr. Fuller Theol. Sem., Pasadena, Calif., 1974; vis. prof. psychiatry Marshall U. Sch. Medicine, Huntington, W.Va., 1985-89. Co-author: The Grace to Grow; editor: Applications of Electroencephalography in Psychiatry; co-editor: EEG and Evoked Potentials in Psychiatry and Behavioral Neurology; contbr. articles to med. jours. Mem. ofcl. bd. Asbury United Meth. Ch., Durham; mem. program and curriculum com. United Meth. Ch., 1973-81; trustee Meth. Retirement Home, Durham; pres. United Meth. Renewal Svcs., Inc., 1978-82. Served with AUS, 1943-46. Recipient Ephraim McDowell award Christian Med. Found., 1982, Pioneer in Christian Psychiatry award Congress on Christian Counseling, 1988; named Educator of Yr., Christian Med. and Dental Soc., 1996; EEG Montreal Neurol. Inst. fellow, 1954-55, postdoctoral fellow NIMH. Mem. Am. Psychiat. Assn., So. Psychiat. Assn. (pres. 1977-78), AMA, So. Med. Assn. (chmn. sect. neurology and psychiatry 1970), Med. Soc. N.C., Durham-Orange County Med. Soc. (chmn. student recruitment com. 1965), Soc. Biol. Psychiatry, Am. EEG Soc. (councillor), So. EEG Soc. (pres. 1964), Assn. Rsch. Nervous and Mental Diseases, Am. Epilepsy Soc., AAAS, Am. Acad. Neurology, Sigma Xi, Alpha Omega Alpha, U.S. Power Squadron Club (comdr. Durham 1971). Republican. Home: 1209 Virginia Ave Durham NC 27705-3263 Office: PO Box 2347 Burlington NC 27216-2347 Office Phone: 336-229-6049. Personal E-mail: williamwilson@verizon.net.

WILSON, WILLIAM R., JR., judge; b. 1939; Student, U. Ark., 1957-58; BA, Hendrix Coll., 1962; LLB, Vanderbilt U., 1965. Atty. Autrey & Goodson, Texarkana, Ark., 1965-66, Wright, Lindsey & Jennings, Little Rock, 1969-72, Wilson & Hodge, Little Rock, 1972-74; prin. William R. Wilson Jr., P.A., Little Rock, 1974-80, Wilson & Engstrom, Little Rock, 1980-83, Wilson, Engstrom & Vowell, Little Rock, 1984, Wilson, Engstrom, Corum & Dudley, Little Rock, 1984-93; judge U.S. Dist. Ct. (ea. dist.) Ark., Little Rock, 1993—. Chair Ark. Supreme Ct. Com. on Model Criminal Jury Instrns., 1978—; active Ark. Supreme Ct. Com. on Civil Practice, 1982—. Lt. USN, 1966-69. Named Disting. Alumnus, Hendrix Coll., 1993, Outstanding Lawyer, Pulaski County Bar Assn., 1993. Mem. ABA, ATLA, Am. Bd. Trial Advocates (Nat. Civil Justice award 1992), Am. Coll. Trial Lawyers, Internat. Acad. Trial Lawyers, Internat. Soc. Barristers, Ark. Bar Assn. (Outstanding Lawyer 1991), S.W. Ark. Bar Assn., Ark. Trial Lawyers Assn. (pres. 1982, Outstanding Trial Lawyer 1988-89), Pulaski County Bar Assn. (Outstanding Lawyer 1993). Office: US Dist Ct Ea Dist 600 W Capitol Ave Ste 423 Little Rock AR 72201-3320

WILSON, WILLIAM ROBERTS, JR., (BOB WILSON), lawyer, apparel executive; b. Rosedale, Miss., July 6, 1941; s. William Roberts Wilson Sr. and Mary Elizabeth (Boatner) W.; m. Elizabeth Ann Smith; children: William Roberts Wilson III, Elizabeth Ann, Augusta Elliott. Student, Vanderbilt U., Tenn., 1964; JD, U. Miss., 1969. Pvt. practice, Jackson, Miss.; chmn. bd., owner Dunn's Mid.-South Sporting Goods Co. Chmn. founder The Charitable Food Bank, Miss. Sportsman Against Hunger; active mem. Rep. Nat. Com. Team 100, Newcomen Soc. of U.S., Am. Intertrade Group, Presdl. Round Table, Rep. Senatorial Inner Circle. Mem. NRA (life mem.), Ala. State Bar Assn., Miss. Bar Assn., Miss. Trial Lawyers Assn. (life mem.), Assn. Trial Lawyers of Am. (sustaining mem.), Roscoe Pound Found. (fellow), Miss. State Bar Assn. (former commr.), Nat. Col. Advocacy, United Conservation Alliance (founding bd. mem.), Congressional Sportsmen Found. (bd. dirs.), Quail Unlimited (life mem., life sponsor), Miss. Wildlife Fedn. (life mem.), Ducks Unlimited (sponsoring mem.), Waterfowl, U.S.A., Delta Wildlife Found. (sponsoring founder), British Field Sport Soc. (life mem.), Catfish Point Hunting Club (gen. ptnr.), Athelstan Club, Country Club of Jackson Miss., Delta Kappa Epsilon (bd. dirs. R.O.A.R.), Delta Theta Phi. Office: PO Box 321444 Flowood MS 39232-1444

WILSON, WILLIAM STANLEY, oceanographer; b. Alexander City, Ala., June 5, 1938; s. Norman W. and Helen C. (Hackemack) W.; m. Anne M. Stout; children: Lauren, Jonathan (dec.). BS, William & Mary Coll., 1959, MA, 1965; PhD, Johns Hopkins U., 1972. Marine biol. collector Va. Inst. Marine Sci., Gloucester Point, 1959-62, computer systems analyst, 1964-65, Chesapeake Bay Inst., Balt., 1965-66; phys. oceanography program mgr. Office of Naval Rsch., Washington, 1972-78; chief oceanic processes program NASA, Washington, 1979-89, program scientist earth observing sys., 1989-92; asst. adminstr. for ocean svcs. and coastal zone mgmt. NOAA, Washington, 1992-97, dep. chief scientist, 1997—2002; sr. scientist Nat. Environ. Satellite Data and Info. Svc., 2002—. U.S. rep. intergovtl. oceanographic commn. UNESCO, 1993—2003. Recipient Antarctica Svc. medal NSF, 1961, Superior Civilian Svc. award USN, 1979, Exceptional Sci. Achievement medal NASA, 1981, Disting. Achievement award MTS and Compass Publs., 1989, award Remote Sensing Soc., 1992, medal French Space Agy., 1994, Portuguese Naval Cross, 1997, Australian Antarctic Divsn. medal, 1998, Group Achievement award NASA, 2000. Mem. Am. Meteorol. Soc., Am. Geophys. Union (Ocean Scis. award 1984), Oceanography Soc. (com. chmn. 1989-92), Sigma Xi, Omicron Delta Kappa. Avocations: bicycling, scuba diving. Home: 219 Tunbridge Rd Baltimore MD 21212-3423 Office: NOAA/NESDIS 1325 E-W Hwy Silver Spring MD 20910 E-mail: stan.wilson@noaa.gov.

WILSON-DAWES, JUDY ANN, music educator; b. Cortez, Colo., Sept. 24, 1957; d. Kenneth Rand and Shirley McDonald Wilson; m. Randel Bruce Dawes, Apr. 2, 1999; 1 child, Jennifer Dawn Stockhausen; m. Gregg Melvin Detton, Dec. 1, 1995 (div. Nov. 1996); children: Derek Detton, Jared Detton, Matthew Detton. BS, Brigham Young U., 1982, MEd, 1983; BA, Ft. Lewis Coll., 1994. Instr. DreamQuest, Huntingtown, Md., Music Mart/Washoe City Sch. Dist., Reno, Grand Junction Sch. Dist., Colo., Mesa State Coll., Plateau Valley Sch. Dist., Collbran; instr., psychologist Katzin Music, Ft. Lewis Coll., Durrango, Page Sch./Judy's Jazz, Ariz. Vocal soloist Morman Choir of Washington, DC, Western Colo. Chorale, Grand Junction, United States; vocalist Mormon Youth Chorus & Symphony, Salt Lake City. V.p. Friend of Libr., Page, Ariz., 1987—90; precinct co-chair Calvert City GOP, Prince Frederick, Md., 1999—2002, hdqrs. chair, 2002—04. Mem. Lds Ch. Home and Office: 4232 Birch Dr Huntingtown MD 20639 Office Fax: 410-474-1284.

WILSON-MCKEE, MARIE, museum director; Dir. Wyo. State Mus., Cheyenne. Office: Wyo State Mus Barrett Bldg 2301 Central Ave Cheyenne WY 82001-3173

WILSON-WEBB, NANCY LOU, education administration consultant, director; b. Maypearl, Tex, Jan. 20, 1932; d. Madison Grady Wise and Mary Nancy Pearson-Bedford (Haney) Wilson; m. John Crawford Webb, July 29, 1972. BS magna cum laude, Abilene Christian U., Tex., 1953; EdM (hon.), Tex. Christian U., 1985. Cert. tchr., mid-mgmt., sch. adminstr., Tex. Tchr. elem. grades Ft. Worth Ind. Sch. Dist., 1953-67, adult edn. tchr., 1967-73; dir. adult edn. consortium for 38 sch. dists. Tex. Edn. Agy., 1973-2000. Pres. Nat. Commn. on Adult Basic Edn., "Most Outstanding adult ed. Admin. in US" by AAAC; 1994-95; pres. Tex. Adult Edn. Adminstrn., 1994; apptd. mem. Tex. State Literacy Coun., 1987-94, Tex. State Sch. Bd. Commn., 1994-99; exec. bd. Tex. Coun. Co-op Dir., 1989-2001, Bd. Nat. Assn. of AAACE, 1988; pres., 1994—; apptd. to Gov. Ann Richard's Task Force for Edn.; ranch owner, mgr., 1998-2003. Cons. to textbooks, 1994-98; editor textbooks, 1999. Pres. Jr. Womans Club, Ft. Worth, 1969, Fine Arts Guild, Tex. Christian U., Ft. Worth, 1970-72, Ft. Worth Womens Civic Club Coun., 1970, pres. Aquarius Women's Club; active Exec. Libr. Bd., Ft. Worth, 1990-2003, Jewel Charity Ball, 1988-2003; bd. dirs. Literacy Plus in North Tex., 1988-99, pres., 2001—; bd. dirs. Greater Ft. Worth Literacy Coun., 1976-88, 2002—, pres., 2001-03; commr. Ed-16 Task Forces Tex. Edn. Agy., 1985-94; literacy bd. dir. Friends

of Libr., 1967-2002, Opera Guild Bd. Ft. Worth, 1965-85, Ft. Worth Ballet Guild, Johnson County (Tex.) Corr. Bd., 1990-2000; bd. dirs. Salvation Army, Ft. Worth, 1996-2003, Ft. Worth Libr.; active Tarrant County Bd. on Aging, 1997-98, Commn. Status of Women, Ft. Worth, 1973-99, Southside Ch. of Christ. Recipient Bevy award Jr. Womans Club, 1968, Proclamation Commr. Ct. Outstanding 43 Yr. Literacy Svc. to Tarrant County Com. Ctr., 1994, Tarrant County Woman of Yr. award, Fort Worth Star Telegram, 1995, Outstanding Leadership award Ft. Worth ISD Sch. Bd., 1985, 95, Mayor's Proclamation of Nancy Webb Week, 1996; named one of Most Outstanding Educators in U.S. Nat. Assn. Adult Edn., 1983, Most Outstanding Woman Edn., City of Ft. Worth, 1991, others; nominated to Tex. Hall of Fame for Women, 1991; named to Ft. Worth Hall of Fame, 1992; scholar Germany, 1983. Mem. NEA, DAR (Mary Isham Keith chpt. 1985-2002, Nat. Literacy award 1992, Leadership Literacy award 1985-87, 89, 94, Nat. Educators award 2003), AAUW, Am. Assn. Adult and Continuing Edn. (v.p. 1987-89, chair 1993 internat. conv. 1992, Nat. Adminstr. of Yr. in Adult Edn. 1998, Most Outstanding Adminstr. Adult Edn. in US 1999), Tex. Assn. Adult and Cont. Edn. (pres. 1985-86, Most Outstanding Adult Adminstr. in Tex. 1984), Tex. Coun. Adult Edn. Dirs. (pres. nat. com. on edn., Nat. Dept. Labor award 1992), Coun. World Affairs (bd. dir. 1980-2002), Am. Bus. Women's Assn., Ft. Worth C. of C., Lecture Found., Internat. Reading Assn. (Literacy Challenge award 1991), Ft. Worth Adminstrv. Assn., Southwest Cattle Raisers Assn., Ligon Assn., Zonta, Tanglewood Garden Club, Ft. Worth Garden Club (exec. bd. dirs. 2000-03), Woman's Club, Ft. Worth Petroleum Club, Carousel Dance Club, Met. Dinner Dance Club, Ridglea Country Club, Girls Svc. League, Aquarius (pres. 2001-02), Crescent Club (Dallas), Alpha Delta Kappa (Nat. Literacy award 1992), Greater Ft. Worth Literacy Coun. (pres. 2000-03), Phi Delta Kappa, Mary Isham Keith DAR (Nat. award 1993, Nat. Found. award 2003). Democrat. Mem. Lds Ch. Home: 3716 Fox Hollow St Fort Worth TX 76109-2616

WILT, JEFFREY LYNN, pulmonary and critical care physician, educator; b. Fairmont, W.Va., Nov. 15, 1963; s. Paul Lynn and Linda (Amos) W. BA, U. Mich., 1986, MD, 1988. Diplomate Am. Bd. Internal Medicine, Am. Bd. Pulmonary Diseases, Am. Bd. Critical Care Medicine, Am. Bd. Med. Examiners, Am. Bd. Nutrition Support; cert. ACLS instr. Fellow sect. pulmonary and critical care medicine W.Va. U., Morgantown, 1992-95; resident in internal medicine Blodgett-St. Mary's Hosp., Grand Rapids, Mich., 1988-91, chief med. resident in internal medicine, 1990-91; asst. dir. internal medicine residency St. Mary's Hosp., Grand Rapids, 1991-92; pvt. practice, Grand Rapids, 1995—. Asst. dir. med. ICU, Blodgett Meml. Med. Ctr., co-dir. transitional residency, 1997-98, COO internal medicine residency, 1998, program dir., 1998-99; assoc. program dir. internal medicine residency Mich. State U., Grand Rapids, 1999—, asst. prof. medicine, 1999-2003, assoc. prof., 2003—. Fellow ACP (Nat. Clin. Vignette winner 1991), Am. Coll. Chest Physicians (Young Investigators award 1993); mem. AMA, Am. Thoracic Soc., Soc. Crit. Care Medicine. Republican. Avocations: bicycling, Tae Kwon Do, magic, reading, chess. Home: 4995 Sequoia Dr SE Grand Rapids MI 49512-9622 Office: 1900 Wealthy St SE Ste 150 Grand Rapids MI 49506-2969

WILTENBURG, ROBERT EDWARD, university dean; b. Evanston, Ill., Aug. 31, 1947; s. Robert Edward and Florence (Fellows) W.; m. Candace O'Connor, Sept. 6, 1970; children: Mary Norton, Katherine Welch. BA in English, Cornell U., 1968; MA in English, U. Rochester, 1974, PhD in English, 1982. Dir. expository writing Washington U., St. Louis, 1982-94, dir. summer sch., 1994-96, dean, 1996—. Trustee Jewish Hosp. Nursing, 1998—. Author: Ben Jonson & Self-Love, 1990; co-editor: Collective Wisdom, 1990. Mem.: Univ. Cont. Edn. Assn., Assn. Cont. Higher Edn., John Donne Soc., Milton Soc. Avocations: music, bicycling, stamps. Home: 6157 Kingsbury Ave Saint Louis MO 63112 Office: Washington U Lindell and Skinker Blvds Saint Louis MO 63130 E-mail: rewilten@wustl.edu.

WILTON, DONALD ROBERT, engineering educator; b. Lawton, Okla., Oct. 25, 1942; m. Joanne Jegen, Aug. 21, 1965; children: Sandra Carol, David Robert, John Cooper. BSEE, U. Ill., Champaign, 1960—64, MSEE, 1964—65, PhD, 1967—70. Mem. of tech. staff Hughes Aircraft Co., Fullerton, Calif., 1965—68; prof., elec. engring. U. Miss., Oxford, 1970—83; prof., elec. and computer engring. U. Houston, 1983—. Recipient Disting. Alumni, U. Ill., 2002. Fellow: IEEE (mem. adm. com. 1992—94, Third Millennium Medal 2000); mem.: U S. Commn. Internat. Union Radio Sci. (chair 1997—99). Office: Univ Houston Dept Elec and Computer Engring Houston TX 77204-4005

WILTON, PETER CAMPBELL, marketing educator; b. Adelaide, S.A., Australia, Jan. 28, 1951; came to U.S., 1975; s. Murray and Kathleen (Ratcliffe) W. B in Commerce with hons., U. New South Wales, Sydney, 1972; PhD in Mgmt., Purdue U., 1979. Product mgr. Colgate Palmolive, Sydney, 1973-75; mktg. prof., Hass Sch. of Bus. U. Calif., Berkeley, 1979-87, 92—; COO Myer Pacific Corp., Melbourne, Australia, 1987-90; sr. assoc. Melbourne U., 1990, Sir Donald Hibberd lectr., 1991. Vis. fellow Griffith U., Brisbane, Australia, 1982; vis. assoc. prof. Duke U., Durham, N.C., 1985-86; pres., dir. Applied Mktg. Analysis, Inc., Wilmington, Del., 1987—, Orbis Assocs., San Francisco, 1992—. Contbr. articles to profl. jours. Recipient Mktg. Rsch. Soc. Australia prize, 1973; Australian Govt. fellow, 1975-79; grantee NSF, 1981, 84. Mem. Assn. Pub. Opinion Rsch. (officer 1985), Am. Mktg. Assn. (officer 1982-84), Australian-Am. C. of C. (dir. 1993-95). Avocations: flying, sailing, music, travel. Office: Haas Sch of Bus UCAL Berkeley S 545 Haas Berkeley CA 94720-1900

WILTROUT, ANN ELIZABETH, foreign language educator; b. Elkhart, Ind., Aug. 3, 1939; d. F. LeRoy and Margaret Elizabeth (Williams) W. BA, Hanover Coll., 1961; MA, Ind. U., 1964, PhD, 1968. Vis. asst. prof. Ind. U., Bloomington, 1968-69; asst. prof. Miss. State U., Mississippi State, 1969-71, assoc. prof., 1971-87, prof., 1987—2002, prof. emerita fgn. lang., 2002—. NEH fellow in residence Duke U., 1977-78. Author: A Patron and a Playwright in Renaissance Spain, 1987; contbr. articles to profl. publs. Recipient Disting. Svc. cert. Inst. Internat. Edn., 1986; named Humanities Tchr. of Yr., 1998. Mem. MLA (life; del. to assembly 1975-78), Am. Assn. Tchrs. of Spanish and Portuguese (life), Starkville Cmty. Theater, Soc. Mayflower Descs. (life), Golden Triangle Civil War Roundtable. Avocations: Shakespeare, travel, reading, roses, antiques. E-mail: wiltrout@ra.msstate.edu.

WILTSE, JAMES CLARK, civil engineer; b. Dearborn, Mich., Apr. 14, 1927; s. Cecil C. and Mary G. (Brashear) W.; m. Marlyn R. Glatus, Feb. 14, 1953; children: Richard, Mary, Michael. BSCE, U. Mich., 1953. Registered profl. engr., Mass. Civil engr. U.S. Army C.E., Detroit, 1954-67; project engr. USAF Civil Engring., London, 1968-72; civil engr. USN Facilities Engring. Command, Norfolk, Va., 1973-75; chief engr. USN Resident Office, Keflavik, Iceland, 1976-81; staff civil engr. USAF Electronic Systems Div., Kaiserslautern, Germany, 1982-91; spl. asst. ROICC Norfolk, Lantnavfac Eng Com, Norfolk, Va., 1992-93; quality assurance engr. HQ Lantnavfac, 1993-94; ret., 1994. Sgt. U.S. Army, 1946-47, Japan. Fellow ASCE (life); mem. Soc. Am. Mil. Engrs. Home: 8555 Lawson Ave Norfolk VA 23503-5220 Personal E-mail: JCWILTSE@aol.com.

WILTSE, MARK EDWARD, academic administrator, director; s. Kenneth E. and June M. Wiltse; m. Nicole C. Medawar, June 28, 1997; 1 child, Kenneth. AA in Criminal Justice, Ill. Valley C.C., 1989; BS Legal Studies, U. Ill., 1991, MPA, 1993. Cert.: Ill. (paralegal) 1991. Intern Bur. County, Princeton, Ill., 1989; legal intern Bur. County States Atty., 1991; exec. field agt. BBB, Rockford, 1995—96; part-time instr. Midstate Coll., Peoria, 1995—96, dir. paralegal services, 1996—. Active Red Ribbon Campaign, Springfield, Ill., 1990—91. Mem.: Am. Soc. Pub. Adminstrs. (hon.), KC. Office: Midstate College 411 West Northmoor Road Peoria IL 61614-3558 Business E-Mail: mwiltse@midstate.edu.

WILTSE, PETER CHRISTIAN, lawyer; b. Buffalo, N.Y., Jan. 13, 1936; s. Harry Hersey and Sally K. (Lutzhoff) W. (div. 1988); m. Christine Wiltse, 1999; children: Lise Rene, Wende, Heather, Jessica. Student, Colgate U., 1953-56; JD, SUNY, Buffalo, 1960. Bar: N.Y., U.S. Dist. Ct. N.Y., U.S. Supreme Ct. Assoc. Saperston, Wiltse & Day, Buffalo, 1960-63; asst. trial atty. Erie County Dist. Atty., Buffalo, 1963; ptnr. Gross, Shuman & Wiltse, Buffalo, 1964-74; pvt. practice Hamburg, N.Y., 1974—. Avocations: marine aquaria, golf, boating. Office: 202 Main St Hamburg NY 14075-4917 Office Phone: 716-649-4423. E-mail: peteski@localnet.com.

WIMBERLY, BEADIE RENEAU (LEIGH WIMBERLY), financial services executive; b. Fouke, Ark., Apr. 18, 1937; d. Woodrow Wilson and Grace B. (Winkley) Reneau; m. Benjamin Leon Price, 1954 (div. 1955); m. Elbert William Wimberly, Dec. 16, 1956; children: Stephanie Elaine Wimberly Davis, Jeffrey Scott, Lael Wimberly Carter Alston. Student, Coll. William and Mary, 1964-65, U. Md., Ludwigsburg/Stuttgart, 1966-68, Northwestern State U. La., 1973-75, Cornell U., 1979, Leonard Sch., 1983. Cert. ins. agt.; registered gen. securities rep. and registered investment advisor SEC. Internat. trainer of trainers North Atlantic coun. Girl Scouts U.S., Germany, 1965—69, internat. trainer North Atlantic coun., 1976—78; inventory master The Myers Co., Inc., El Paso, Tex., 1970; abstract asst. Vernon Abstract Co., Inc., Leesville, La., 1970—71; sec. to chief utilities and pollution control Dept. Army U.S. Civil Svc., Ft. Polk, La., 1971—72, asst. to post safety officer Dept. Army, 1972—73, adminstr. tech. Adj. Gen.'s Office Dept. Army, 1973—75, sr. libr. technician post librs. Dept. Army, 1975, pers. staffing specialist Dept. Army Stuttgart, Germany, 1976—79, voucher examiner Fin. and Acct. Office Dept. Army Ft. Polk, 1980—81; CEO Fin. Strategies, Inc., Leesville, 1981—91, stockbroker, 1984—93, ins. agt., 1983—94, corp. exec., 1983—, mktg exec., 1983—, investment advisor, 1984—93; tax assoc. H&R Block, 2001—. Investment advisor, 1984-93; fashion cons., 1993—; master gardener, 1995—; labor cons. AFL/CIO, Ft. Polk, 1981—; br. office mgr. Anchor Nat. Fin. Svcs. Inc., 1981-91; dir., treas. Wimberly Enterprises, Inc.; charter mem. Sundown Vol. Fire Dept. Bd. dirs. Calcasieu Parish coun. Boy Scouts Am., 1982-83; treas. Vernon Parish Hist./Geneal. Soc., 1986—; pres. Vernon Parish Helpline/Lifeline, 1985; charter mem. Nat. Mus. Women in the Arts; mem. Vernon Parish Arts Coun.; mem. La. Supreme Ct. Task Force on Women in the Cts. of La.; tax vol. Vita, 2002—. Mem. Pilot Internat., Nat. Assn. Govt. Employees (v.p. chpt. 1980-81), C. of C., Assn. U.S. Army, Am. Assn. Fin. Profls., Nat. Women's Polit. Caucus, Am. Soc. Mil. Comptrs., LWV (state bd. dirs. 1986-87, treas. Leesville chpt. 1982-87, La. chpt.), NOW, Toastmasters Club (Competent Toastmaster 1979), Rotary (bd. mem.-at-large Leesville club 1988—, treas. 1991—, v.p.), Leesville Pilot Club. Office: Cable Loop Ste 142 Leesville LA 71446

WIMBERLY, LINDA ROBERTS, music educator, artist; b. Lincoln, Nebr., Sept. 26, 1945; d. Arthur Thomas Roberts and Dorothy Mae Moore; m. Charles Augustus Wimberly, July 2, 1966 (div. Aug. 1985); children: Susan Lynn, Sheri Beth. Student, North Ga. Coll., 1963—64, Shorter Coll., 1964—67; BA, U. Ala., 1995. Pvt. music instr., Marietta, 1965—; entertainer, vocalist The Fireside Restaurant, Marietta, 1973—76; vocalist, contralto soloist N.W. Presbyn. Ch., Atlanta, 1988—96, dir. music, 1991—96; composer vocal, piano, choral works, 1995—; guitar instr. continuing edn. Kennesaw (Ga.) State U., 1996—2003; pres., owner Artist L'Inc Corp., Marietta, 2000—. Edn. ptnr. Ga. Wildlife Fedn., Atlanta, 2000—. One-woman shows include South Trust Bank, Mableton, 2001, Imagine Sta., Lehigh Valley, Pa., 2003, exhibitions include Period Gallery, Omaha, 2001, 2002, Upstream People Gallery, 2002, exhibited in group shows at N.W. Presbyn. Ch., Atlanta, 1995, Mable House Artfest, Mableton, Ga., 2000, Mon-Dak Heritage Ctr., Sidney, Mont., 2000, 2001, Marietta/Cobb Mus. Art, 2002, 2004, many others, Represented in permanent collections;, author articles, poetry and essays. Recipient Writing residency, Vt. Studio Ctr., 1997. Mem.: ASCAP, Acad. Am. Poets, Music Tchrs. Nat. Assn., Golden Key (life). Avocations: environment, nutrition, organic lifestyle, exercise. Office: Artist L Inc Corp PO Box 4833 Marietta GA 30060

WIMER, MARK G. healthcare management company executive; BS in Bacteriology, U. Idaho; M of Health Adminstrn., St. Louis (Mo.) U. Pres. skilled nursing facility subs. Sun Healthcare Group, Albuquerque, 1993-97, sr. v.p. inpatient svcs., pres. COO, 1997—. Office: Sun Healthcare Group Inc 101 Sun Ave NE Albuquerque NM 87109-4373

WIMMER, KATHRYN, retired elementary school educator; b. St. Louis, May 8, 1929; d. Arthur Jordan and Louise Clara Sykes; m. Harry William Wimmer, Aug. 4, 1951; children: Robert William, Richard Jordan. BS in Edn., U. Mo., 1951; postgrad., U. South Fla., 1971—72. Cert. tchr. Mo., Fla. Tchr. Affton (Mo.) Sch., 1951—52, Heege Sch., Affton, 1965—67, Gulf Gate Sch., Sarasota, Fla., 1967—72; piano tchr. Crestwood, Mo., 1963—65. Artist, musician. V.p. Southgate Cmty., Sarasota, 1989—90; pres. bd. dirs. Assoc. Women's Club, Sarasota, 1990—91, bd. dirs., 1986—93; vol. Gulf Gate Libr., Sarasota, 1993—. Recipient tennis trophy, Bath and Racquet Tennis Club, Sarasota, 1979, swimming trophy, Southgate Cmty. Assn., 1987, 1988, Wall of Honor cert., Roosevelt H.S., St. Louis, 2003. Mem.: Mysterium High IQ Soc., Delta Gamma (scholarship chmn., treas., rush chmn., social chmn.). Democrat. Presbyterian. Avocations: sewing, literature, cards, dance, travel.

WIMMER, SCOTT, race car driver; Race car drive ASA ACDelco Challenge Series, Busch Series. Office: c/o Bill Davis Racing 302 Old Thomasville Rd High Point NC 27260

WIMPRESS, GORDON DUNCAN, JR., corporate consultant, foundation executive; b. Riverside, Calif., Apr. 10, 1922; s. Gordon Duncan and Maude A. (Waldo) W.; m. Jean Margaret Skerry, Nov. 30, 1946; children: Wendy Jo, Victoria Jean, Gordon Duncan III. BA, U. Oreg., 1946, MA, 1951; PhD, U. Denver, 1958; LLD (hon.), Monmouth Coll., Ill., 1970; LHD (hon.), Tusculum Coll., Greenville, Tenn., 1971. Lic. comml. pilot. Dir. pub. rels., instr. journalism Whittier (Calif.) Coll., 1946-51; asst. to pres. Colo. Sch. Mines, Golden, 1951-59; pres. Monticello Coll., Alton, Ill., 1959-64, Monmouth Coll., Ill., 1964-70, Trinity U., San Antonio, 1970-77; vice chmn. S.W. Found. for Biomed. Rsch., San Antonio, 1977-82, pres., 1982-92, also bd. govs.; pres. Duncan Wimpress & Assocs., Inc., San Antonio, 1992—. Chmn. scholarship commn. Valero Energy Corp.; bd. dirs. SW Rsch. Inst. Author: American Journalism Comes of Age, 1950. Mem. adv. bd. Alamo Area chpt. Am. Diabetes Assn.; ruling elder United Presbyn. Ch., U.S.A.; bd. dirs. ARC, Am. Heart Assn.; trustee San Antonio Med. Found. 1st lt. AUS, 1942—45, ETO. Decorated Bronze Star. Mem. Aircraft Owners and Pilots Assn., Am. Acad. Polit. and Social Sci., Am. Assn. Higher Edn., MENSA, Nat. Pilots Assn., Pilots Internat. Assn., Inc., Quiet Birdmen, Greater San Antonio C. of C., North San Antonio C. of C., Assn. Former Intelligence Officers, Confederate Air Force, Pi Gamma Mu, Sigma Delta Chi, Sigma Delta Pi, Sigma Phi Epsilon (trustee found.), Sigma Upsilon, Newcomen Soc. N.Am., Argyle Club, San Antonio Country Club, Plz. Club, San Antonio Golf Assn., Rotary (dist. gov. San Antonio club 1983-84). Avocations: golf, skiing, flying. Office Phone: 210-492-8173. E-mail: duncan.w@sbcglobal.net.

WINAWER, SIDNEY J. physician, clinical investigator, educator; b. N.Y.C. s. Nathan and Sally Winawer; children: Daniel, Jonathan, Joanna. BA, NYU, 1952; MD, SUNY, N.Y.C., 1956. Asst. in medicine Harvard Med. Sch., Boston, 1962-66; asst. physician Harvard Med. Svc. Boston City Hosp., 1964-66; with Meml. Sloan-Kettering Cancer Ctr., N.Y.C., 1968—, chief gastroent. and nutrition svc., 1978-98, mem. with tenure of title, 1988—, Paul Sherlock chair, 1991—; prof. medicine Cornell U. Coll. Medicine, N.Y.C., 1980—, dir. integrative oncology program, 1997-98. Head Ctr Prevention Cancer WHO, Geneva, 1985—2000; liaison rep Nat Cancer Adv Bd, Washington, 1984—89; mem adv comt cancer prevention Am Cancer Soc, 1988—90; mem sci adv bd ICRF; consult varios rev comts Nat Cancer Inst, Washington. Editor: (book) Prevention Colorectal Cancer, 1980, Basic and Clinical Perspectives of Colorectal Polyps and Cancer, 1988, Lar Bowel Cancers: Policy, Prevention, Research and Treatment, 1991, Management of Gastrointestinal Disease, 1992, Gastrointestinal Cancer, 1992, Cancer of the Colon, Rectum and Anus, 1994, Cancer Free, 1995, Healing Lessons, 1998; contbr. chapters to books, articles to profl jours. Capt USAF, 1959—61. Recipient Constantine Medal, Italian Govt., 2002, John Wayne Clin. Rsch. award, Soc. Surg. Oncology, 2004, Internat. Laurel award, Cancer Rsch. and Prevention Found., 2004; grantee Nat. Cancer Inst., 1974, 1977, 1980, 1985, 1988, 1990, 1993, 1999, 2003. Master: Am Col Gastroenterology (pres 1979—80, Bker Predl lectr 1992, Distinguished Sci Achiement Award 1982, Clin Achievement Award 1997); fellow: ACP; mem.: Soc. Surg. Oncology (John Wayne Clin. Rsch. award 2004), NY Soc Gastrointestinal Endoscopy (founder, pres 1978—79, ann lectr 1985), Am Asn Cancer Research, Am Soc Clin Oncology (Am Cancer Soc Award 2001), Am Gastroentrological Asn (nat chmn cancer sect 1989—91, Joseph B Kirsner Award 1999), Am Soc Gastrointestinal Endoscopy (bd dirs 1974—78, distinguished lectr 1985, co-chair guidelines com. 2000—03, co-chair internat. digestive cancer alliance 2000—, Schindler award 1994, Laurel award 2004). Jewish. Avocations: opera, chorale, cross country skiing, sailing, dance. Office: Meml Sloan-Kettering Cancer Ctr 1275 York Ave New York NY 10021-6094 Office Phone: 212-639-7678. Business E-Mail: winawers@mskcc.org.

WINBLAD, ANN, investment company executive; BA in Math. and Bus. Adminstrn., MA in Internat. Econs. and Edn., U. St. Thomas, St. Paul, Minn. Programmer; co-founder Open Sys, Inc., 1976-83; strategic planning cons., IBM, Microsoft, Price Waterhouse, and many start-ups; ptnr. Hummer Winblad Venture Ptnrs., San Francisco, 1989—. Bd. dirs. Dean & Deluca, Intacct, Market Wire, The Knot, Voltage Security. Co-author: Object-Oriented Software, 1990. Trustee U. St. Thomas, St. Paul, Mich. Office: Hummer Winblad Venture Ptnrs 2 S Park St 2d Fl San Francisco CA 94107-1807

WINBORNE, SHEILA FAYE, academic administrator; d. Hattie Privott and Starkie Ronnie Winborne. BA, U.N.C, Greensboro, 1980; MA, Old Dominion U., 1990; MTS, Harvard Div. Sch., 1993; MA, Harvard U., 1999, postgrad., 1994—. Tchg. fellow Harvard Div. Sch., Cambridge, 2001; program adminstr. Harvard Med. Sch., Boston, 2002—. Art tchr. Fairview Cmty. Ctr., Greensboro, NC, 1980; calligraphy instr. Roanoke-Chowan Tech. Coll., Ahoskie, NC, 1981; mktg. prodn. artist The Virginian-Pilot Daily Newspaper, Norfolk, Va., 1986—91; videocamera operator, office asst. for Derek Bok Ctr. for Tchg. and Learning Harvard U., 1991—93; textbook cover design, prodn. artist Ginn Press, Needham, Mass., 1992; intern for weekly program In Good Faith WCVB-TV/Channel 5 Boston, Needham, Mass., 1993—94, intern for series Your Baby and Child with Penelope Leach, 1993; tchg. asst. Harvard Div. Sch., 1993; staff asst. for office of recruitment/multicultural affairs Harvard Med. Sch., 1994—2001; rsch. asst. Harvard Div. Sch., 1999—2000; tchg. fellow Harvard U., 2000; asst. to dir., Dance by Designs Dudley Ho. Grad. Ctr., Harvard U., 2001; presenter in field. Participant Hampton Roads Black Achievers' YMCA Program, Norfolk, Va., 1991; founding bd. dirs. Gallery 7-3-7, Norfolk, Va., 1988; co-presenter, interdisciplinary media edn. project Assn. for Professors and Researchers in Religious Edn. (APRRE), Mpls., 2001; keynote spkr. Conf. N.C. Fedn. Negro Women, Ahoskie, NC, 1991; co-presenter, forum on media literacy, representations of race and race rels. Cambridge Ctr. for Adult Edn., 1994; co-moderator for discussion on images of Asian and black women in films Radcliffe Office Edn. for Action, Cambridge, 1994. Recipient First Pl. Merit Award, Direct Mail Brochure Category, Va. Press Assn., 1986, First Pl. Merit Award, Market Rsch./Data Folders Category, 1991; Prize Grad. Fellowship, Harvard U., 1994, Dissertation Fellowship, The Fund for Theol. Edn., 2002—03. Mem.: Soc. Arts in Religious and Theol. Studies, Am. Hist. Assn., Coll. Arts Assn., Am. Acad. Religion.

WINCHELL, GEORGE WILLIAM, curriculum and technology educator; b. Coldwater, Mich., Nov. 12, 1948; s. Elwood F. and Ethel L. (DeBray) W.; m. Marcia A. Hersh, June 7, 1969 (dec.); 1 child, Paul Michael. BA, Mich. State U., 1969; diploma, Leningrad (USSR) State U., 1967; MA, Mich. State U., 1973; EdS, Cen. Mich. U., 1982. Cert. elem., secondary, Russian, lang. arts and social sci. tchr.; cert. adminstr., supt., elem. prin. Elem. tchr. Silverton (Colo.) Pub. Schs.; tech. edn. cons. Stanton, Mich.; off-campus instr. Cen. Mich. U., Mt. Pleasant; profl. devel. coord., facilitator strategic planning, dir. instrnl. tech. Montcalm Area Intermediate Sch. Dist., Stanton, 1997-99; dir. tech. edn. Cen. Montcalm Pub. Sch., Stanton, 1969—99; grants coord., v.p. Crystal Automation Sys., Inc.; master online instr. Mich. Virtual HS, 1999—, regional ambassador. Regional amb. Mich. Virtual HS. Mem. ASCD, Internat. Soc. Tech. Edn., Am. Soc. Distance Learning, Am. Soc. Quality, Mich. Assn. Computer Users in Learning, Nat. Staff Devel. Coun. Office: Crystal Automation Sys Inc 617 E Lake St Stanton MI 48888-8902

WINCHELL, MICHAEL GEORGE, lawyer; b. Ardmore, Okla., Oct. 30, 1949; s. George Stockwell and Willis Marion (Woolery) W.; m. Donna Jean Winchell; children: Merridith Elaine, Candace Michelle. BBA, Cen. State U., 1974; JD, U. Okla., 1976. Bar: Okla. 1977. Assoc. Sokolsky & Becker, Oklahoma City, 1977; asst. regional counsel GSA, Ft. Worth, Tex., 1977-87; adminstrv. judge EEOC Commn., Dallas, 1987-88; counsel S.E. bases USMC, 1988-89; chief counsel John F. Kennedy Space Ctr., 1993-97, Johnson Space Ctr., 1997—. Pres. GSA employee's assn., 1982-84; chief KSC Inter-Tribal Coun., 1993-97. Named Meritorious Exec. of the Federal Sr. Exec. Svc., Pres. Clinton, 2000; recipient Meritorious Civilan Svc. medal, USN, 1993, Exceptional Svc. medal, NASA, 2001. Mem. Fed. Bus. Assn. (pres. 1984-85), FBA (pres. Ft. Worth chpt. 1981-82, bd. dirs. younger lawyers' div. 1981-85, 2d v.p. 5th cir. 1982-83, v.p. 1983-84, sec. cir. officers 1983-84, dep. chmn. cir. officers 1984-85, chmn. rules com. 1985-86), Southeastern Cherokee Confederacy (chief Eagle Clan 1992-93). Office: 728 Night Hawk DR Norman OK 73072-8188

WINCHESTER, JAMES R. state supreme court justice; m. Susan Winchester; 1 child, Davis. BA U. Okla, JD Oklahoma City U. Pvt. practice, Weatherford, Okla., Hinton, Okla.; assoc. dist. judge Caddo County, Okla., 1983; dist. judge 6th Judicial Dist. Okla., 1983—97; U.S. adminstrv. law judge, 1997—2000; justice Supreme Ct. Okla., 2000—. Mem.: Exec. Bd., Ok. Judicial Conf. (pres., 1995 1992—96). Office: Oklahoma Supreme Ct Admin Office 1915 N Stiles Ste 305 Oklahoma City OK 73104-2861

WINCHESTER, RICHARD LEE, JR., lawyer; b. Memphis, May 21, 1924; s. Cassius Lee and Harriet Haywood (Bond) W.; m. Bette Anne Thompson, July 15, 1944; children— Robin Ann, Richard Lee Jr., John Thompson. LL.B., U. Tenn., 1949, J.D., 1965. Bar: Tenn. 1949. Sr. ptnr. Winchester Law Firm, Memphis, 1972—; Shelby County atty., 1961-64; city atty., Arlington, Tenn., 1966—; gen. counsel, bd. chmn. Community Bancshares, Inc.; sec. Beachfront Condos, Inc., N.Fla. Chmn. Germantown Planning Commn., 1958-61; mem. Gov.'s Commn. on Human Relations, 1962-68; vice chmn., treas. Memphis and Shelby County Democratic Exec. Com., 1958-72; state exec. com., pres. Tenn. Young Democrats, 1960-61; del. state and nat. Dem. Convs., 1964-68; nat. elector from Tenn., 1960-72; pres., bd. dirs. Mid-South Fair Assn., ARC.; trustee U. Tenn., 1975-84, Episcopal Girls Home, Bowld Hosp.; pres. Episcopal Planning Commn. Served to capt. inf. AUS, 1942-46, PTO. Fellow Tenn. Bar Found.; mem. ABA (past del.), Tenn. Bar Assn. (past pres. jr. sect.), Memphis Bar Assn. (past pres.), Shelby County Bar Assn. (past pres. jr. sect.), Am. Judicature Soc., Nat. Assn. Legal Aid and Pub. Defenders, Am. Legion (past post comdr., past state vice comdr.), 40 and 8, VFW (past post vice comdr.), U. Tenn. Alumni Assn. (past bd. govs., 9th dist. rep.), Sigma Alpha Epsilon, Phi Eta Sigma, Phi Kappa Phi, Omicron Delta Kappa. Episcopalian. Club: Tennessee. Lodges: Masons, Shriners, Jesters, Kiwanis. Office: Winchester Law Firm 6060 Poplar Ave Ste 38119 Memphis TN 38119 Office Phone: 901-685-9222. Business E-Mail: bmabie@winchesterlawfirm.com.

WINCHESTER, SUSAN, human resources specialist, state representative; b. Chickasha, Okla., Mar. 24, 1950; m. James R. Winchester; 1 child, Davis. BS, U. Okla., Norman, 1972; MHR in Human Resource Devel., U. Okla., 1994. Co-owner Am. Dusting Co., 1974—89; adult tng. and devel. coord. Canadian Valley Vo-Tech., 1987—92; owner Winchester Group, Chickasha, Okla., 1992—; rep. Ho. of Reps. State of Okla., Okla. City, 1999—. Vice chair ins. com. Okla. Ho. of Reps., Okla. City, 1999—, mem. appropriations and budget com. (subcom. on edn.), banking and fin., pub. health coms., 1999—. Mem. Leadership Chickasha; selection com. Okla. Found. for Excellence; bd. dirs. Leadership Okla., Okla. 4H Found. Mem.: Am. Legislative Exchange Coun., Mustang C. of C., Tuttle C. of C., Chickasha C. of C., Am. Soc. Tng. and Devel. Republican. Office: 2300 N Lincoln Blvd Rm 539 Oklahoma City OK 73105 Home and Office: PO Box 2162 Chickasha OK 73023

WINCKLER, CINDY, state representative; b. DesMoines, May 27, 1950; Educator Davenport Cmty. Sch. Dist., Pleasant Valley Sch. Dist., Calamus Sch. Dist., Davis County Sch. Dist.; mem. Iowa Ho. Reps., DesMoines, 2001—, mem. econ. devel. com., mem. appropriations com., mem. edn. com., mem. labor and indsl. rels. com., mem. ways and means com. Past nat. pres. Bus. and Profl. Women USA. Democrat. Office: State Capitol East 12th and Grand Des Moines IA 50319 also: 6 Thode Ct Davenport IA 52802

WINCOR, MICHAEL Z. psychopharmacology educator, clinician, researcher; b. Chgo., Feb. 9, 1946; s. Emanuel and Rose (Kershner) W.; m. Emily E.M. Smythe; children: Meghan Heather, Katherine Rose. SB in Zoology, U. Chgo., 1966; PharmD, U. So. Calif., 1978. Rsch. project specialist U. Chgo. Sleep Lab., 1968-75; psychiat. pharmacist Brotman Med. Ctr., Culver City, Calif., 1979-83; asst. prof. U. So. Calif., L.A., 1983-97, assoc. prof., 1997—, interim chair dept. pharmacy, 2001—02, assoc. dean external programs, 2003—. Cons. Fed. Bur. Prisons Drug Abuse Program, Terminal Island, Calif., 1978—81, Nat. Inst. Drug Abuse, Bethesda, Md., 1981, The Upjohn Co., Kalamazoo, 1982—87, 1991—92, Area XXIV Profl. Stds. Rev. Orgn., L.A., 1983, Brotman Med. Ctr., Culver City, Calif., 1983—88, SmithKline Beecham Pharms., Phila., 1990—93, Tokyo Coll. of Pharmacy, 1991, G.D. Searle & Co., Chgo., 1992—97, 1999—2001, Pfizer, NY, 1998—2004, Wyeth-Ayerst, Phila., 1999—2001, Novartis, East Hanover, NJ, 2002—04, AstraZeneca, Wilmington, Del., 2002—. Contbr. more than 75 articles to profl. jours., chpts. to books, papers presented at nat. and internat. meetings and reviewer. Mem. adv. coun. Franklin Avenue Sch., 1986-89; bd. dirs. K.I. Children's Ctr., 1988-89; trustee Sequoyah Sch., 1992-93; mem. tech. com. Ivanhoe Sch., 1993-96; U. So. Calif. Amb., 2000—. Recipient Cert. Appreciation, Mayor of L.A., 1981, Bristol Labs Award, 1978, DuPont Pharma Innovative Pharmacy Practice award, 1995, Pharmacy Coun. Mental Health award, 1996, Outstanding Chpt. Advisor award Am. Pharm. Assn.-Acad. of Students of Pharmacy, 2003; Faculty scholar U. So. Calif. Sch. Pharmacy, 1978. Mem. Am. Coll. Clin. Pharmacy (chmn. constn. and bylaws com. 1983-84, mem. credentials com. 1991-93, 95-97, ednl. affairs com. 1994, constn. and bylaws com. 1999-00), Am. Assn. Colls. Pharmacy (focus group on liberalization profl. curriculum 1990-92, mem. pharmacy practice planning commn. 1996-97, chmn. pharmacy practice awards com. 1998-2000, mem. bylaws and policy devel. com. 2001-03, mem. computer tech. in edn. task force 2001-02, chmn. coun. of faculties strategic planning and resolutions com. 2001-03), Am. Soc. Health-Sys. Pharmacists (chmn. edn. and tng. adv. working group 1985-88, chmn. com. on academia 1996-97), Am. Pharm. Assn. (del. ann. meeting ho. of dels. 1989, 1998, Acad. Students of Pharmacy Outstanding Chpt. Advisor 2003), Sleep Rsch. Soc., Am. Acad. Sleep Medicine, Calif. Pharmacists Assn. (trustee 1997-2001, chmn. editl. rev. com. 1998-2003), U. So. Calif. Sch. Pharmacy Alumni Assn. (bd. dirs. 1979—, pres. 1998—), Rho Chi. Avocation: photography. Office: 1985 Zonal Ave Los Angeles CA 90089-9121

WINDEBANK, ANTHONY J. dean; b. Bournemouth, Eng., Aug. 14, 1948; BA in biochemistry, Oxford U., 1970, MA in biochemistry, 1973, BMBCh in medicine, 1974. Cert. Am. Bd. Psychiatry and Neurology. Intern Radcliffe Infirmary, Oxford University, England, 1975, resident in internal medicine, 1975—76; resident in neurology Mayo Grad. Sch. Medicine, Mayo Clinic, Rochester, Minn., 1977—81, fellow in neurology, 1981—82; dean Mayo Clinic Coll. Medicine, Rochester, Minn., 1998—, also prof. of neurology and cellular neurobiology, dir., molecular neurosci. program. Named Mayo Grad. Sch. Tchr. of Yr., 1997; recipient Henry Woltman Award for Excellence in Clin.Neurology, Mayo Clinic, 1980, Tchr.-Investigator Devel. Award, NIH, 1982. Fellow: Am. Acad. Neurology, Royal Coll. Physicians. Office: Mayo Med Sch 200 1st St SW Rochester MN 55905-0001

WINDELS, PAUL, JR., lawyer; b. Bklyn., Nov. 13, 1921; s. Paul and Louise E. (Gross) W.; m. Patricia Ripley, Sept. 10, 1955 (dec. 1995); children: Paul III, Mary H., James H.R., Patrick D. AB, Princeton U., 1943; LLB, Harvard U., 1948. Bar: N.Y. 1949. Spl. asst. counsel N.Y. State Crime Commn., 1951; asst. U.S. atty. Ea. Dist. N.Y., 1953-56; N.Y. regional adminstr. SEC, 1956-61, also spl. asst. U.S. atty. for prosecution securities frauds, 1956-58; lectr. law Am. Inst. Banking, 1950-57; mem. Windels, Marx, Lane & Mittendorf and predecessor firms, 1961—98, of counsel, 1998—. Author: Our Securities Markets-Some SEC Problems and Techniques, 1962. Trustee, chmn. Bklyn. Law Sch.; trustee Knox Sch., Lexington Sch. for the Deaf, Gerta Charitable Trust; past pres. Fed. Bar Coun. Capt. F.A., AUS, 1943-46, ETO; maj. USAR, ret. Recipient Flemming award for fed. svc.; decorated chevalier Order French Acad. Palms; officer Nat. Order Merit France. Fellow Am. Bar Found.; mem. ABA, N.Y. State Bar Assn., Assn. of Bar of City of N.Y. Republican. Presbyterian. Office: Windels Marx Lane & Mittendorf 156 W 56th St Fl 23 New York NY 10019-3867

WINDELS, SUE, state senator; b. Nampa, Idaho, July 11, 1946; m. Carl Windels; children: Derek, Daniel. BA, Ea. Wash. U., 1967, MA, 1973. Vol. Peace Corps, 1967-69; tchr., 1969—; Dem. rep. dist. 27 Colo. Ho. of Reps., 1998-2000; Dem. senator dist. 19 Colo. State Senate, 2000—. Mem. edn., state, vets. and mil. affairs and stat audit com. Colo. Ho. of Reps.; mem. edn., judiciary and capitol devel. coms. Colo. State Senate. Founder (legis. newsletter) Voter's Voice, 1996-98. Mem. Interfaith Alliance; legis. dir. Jefferson County PTA, 1996-98; dir. pub. policy Colo. PTA, 1997. Mem. AAUW. LWV, Kiwanis. Office: Colo State Senate State Capitol 200 E Colfax Rm 307 Denver CO 80203 also: 13925 W 73d Ave Arvada CO 80005 E-mail: windels@sni.net., suewindels@aol.com.

WINDER, CLARENCE LELAND, psychologist, educator; b. Osborne County, Kans., June 16, 1921; s. Clarence McKinley and Edna (Ikenberry) W.; m. Elizabeth Jane Jacobs, Aug. 14, 1943; children: David William, Christina Louise. Student, Santa Barbara State Coll., 1941; AB with honors, U. Calif. at Los Angeles, 1943; MA, Stanford U., 1946, PhD, 1949. From instr. to assoc. prof. Stanford U., 1949-61; dir. Psychol. Clinic, 1953-61; prof., dir. Psychol. Clinic, Mich. State U., 1961-62, prof. psychology, 1961-91, prof. emeritus, 1991—, chmn. dept., 1963-67; dean Coll. Social Sci. Mich. State U., 1967-74, assoc. provost, 1974-77, provost, 1977-86, provost emeritus, 1991—; prof., dir. Psychol. Svcs. Ctr., U. So. Calif., 1962-63. Spl. rsch. psychol. aspects schizophrenia, parent-child rels., personality devel., and higher edn. adminstrn. 1st lt. USAAF, 1943-45. Decorated Air medal with 7 clusters, D.F.C. Fellow APA, AAAS; mem. Sigma Xi. Home: 1776 Hitching Post Rd East Lansing MI 48823-2144

WINDER, ROBERT OWEN, mathematician, computer engineer, geophysicist; b. Boston, Oct. 9, 1934; s. Claude V. and Harriet O. W.; m. Kathleen C. Winder; children by previous marriage: Katherine, Amy. AB, U. Chgo., 1954; BS, U. Mich., 1956; MS, Princeton U., 1958, PhD, 1962; MS, Ariz. State U., 2000. With RCA, 1957-78, group head, 1969-75, dir. microprocessors, 1975-77, dir. systems, 1977-78; mgr. workstation devel. Exxon Enterprises, Inc., Princeton, 1978-85; v.p. Syntex Computer Systems Inc., Bordentown, N.J., 1985-88; mgr. product engring., Princeton Operation, Intel Corp., 1988-93; mgr. engring. ops. video products div., Intel, Chandler, Ariz., 1993-95. Vis. scholar dept. geol. scis., Ariz. State U., Tempe, 2001—. Contbr. articles to profl. jours.; patentee in field. NSF fellow, 1956-57; Recipient David Sarnoff award RCA, 1975. Fellow IEEE.

WINDERS, GLENDA, publishing executive; Editl. dir. Copley News Svc., San Diego, 1997—. Office: Copley News Svc PO Box 120190 San Diego CA 92112-0190

WINDHAGER, ERICH ERNST, physiologist, educator; b. Vienna, Nov. 4, 1928; came to U.S., 1954; s. Maximilian and Bertha (Feitzinger) W.; m. Helga A. Rapant, June 18, 1956; children: Evelyn Ann, Karen Alice. MD, U. Vienna, 1954. Rsch. fellow in biophysics Harvard Med. Sch., Boston, 1956—58; instr. in physiology Cornell U. Med. Coll., N.Y.C., 1958—61; vis. scientist U. Copenhagen, 1961—63; asst. to prof. physiology Cornell U. Med. Coll., N.Y.C., 1963—, Maxwell M. Upson prof. physiology and biophysics, 1978—2002, chmn. dept. physiology, 1973—2002, acting chmn. dept. cell biology, 1998—2002. Recipient Homer W. Smith award N.Y. Heart Assn., 1978, Berliner-Abbott award Am. Physiol. Soc., 1999. Office: Weill Med Coll Cornell U Dept Physiology 1300 York Ave New York NY 10021-4805 Office Phone: 212-746-6386. E-mail: ewindhag@med.cornell.edu.

WINDHAM, JOHN FRANKLIN, lawyer, educator; b. Fayette, Ala., Jan. 21, 1948; s. Grover B. Windham Jr. and Nancy Katherine (McAdams) Haynie; 1 child, John Franklin Jr.; m. Denise Roche McNair, Apr. 6, 1999; 1 stepchild, Brittany Danielle McNair. BA, U. West Fla., 1970; JD, U. N.C., 1975. Bar: Fla. 1975, U.S. Dist. Ct. (no. dist.) Fla. 1976, U.S. Ct. Appeals (11th cir.) 1983, U.S. Supreme Ct. 1984. Acctg. supr. Monsanto Co., Research Triangle Park, N.C., 1970-72; law clk. to U.S. Atty Pensacola, Fla., 1974; assoc. Beggs & Lane, Pensacola, 1975-79, ptnr., 1979—. Adj. asst. prof. bus. law Troy State U., Pensacola, 1983-90. Mem. exec. com. Fla. divsn. Am. Cancer Soc., 1982-93, 95-2000, chmn. bd. 1998-99, chmn. elect bd. 1997-98; chmn. legis. and planned giving, 1986-88, chmn. inc. devel., 1989-91, chmn. ad hoc adv. com., 1991—, legal advisor, 1992—, bd. dirs., 1982—, mem. scholarship com., 1995-98, mem. Winn Dixie adv. com., 1996-99, chmn. dist. VII steering com., 1995-96. v.p, 1996-97, chmn. field ops. com., 1996-98; mem. Nat. Assembly, 2002—, mem. budget and fin. com. evaluation adv. com., nom. ad hoc com., bd. governance task force, 1990—, chmn. bylaws com., 2002—; chmn. bd. Escambia Christian Sch., Pensacola, 1976-86; deacon Ch. of Christ, 1985-95, 1999-2002; adminstrv. team First City Ch., 2002-2004, mem. adv. bd.; elder First City Ch., 2004—; mem. adv. bd. Interim Healthcare, 1993-96, Panhandle Rehab. Injury Mgmt. and Evaluation, 1993-96; mem. found. bd. East Hill Christian Sch., 1995-97; bd. govs. Pensacola chpt. Order Granaderos e Dames de Galvez, 1990-98, pres. 1995-98; mem. U. West Fla. Found., 1983-85. Mem. Fla. Bar (workers compensation rules com., 1995-2001, drafting subcom. 2000-01), Fla. Def. Lawyers Assn., Fla. Workers Compensation Inst., Southeastern Admiralty Law Inst. (bd. dirs. 1986-89), Northwest Fla. Blood Ctr. Found. (treas. 2002-), U. West Fla. Nat. Alumni Assn. (bd. dirs.), Kiwanis (pres. Pensacola 1978-79, 88-89). Republican. Avocation: church activities. Office: Beggs & Lane PO Box 12950 Pensacola FL 32591-2950

WINDHAM, REVISH, poet; b. Panola, Ala., May 31, 1940; s. Ike, Sr. and Lillie (Queen) Windham; m. Janice L. Bowman, Sept. 22, 1985; 1 child, Veronice Wiggins-Windham. BA, Morris Brown Coll., 1962; MPA, NYU, 1989. Cert. mediator N.Y. Case worker N.Y.C. Dept. Social Svcs., 1968—70; youth counselor, group and family counselor, job developer N.Y. State Divsn. Youth, N.Y.C., 1970—90; investigator, unit supr. N.Y. State Divsn. Human Rights, N.Y.C., 1990—99; writer, poet NY, 1999—. Author: Shades of Black, 1970, Shade of Anger, 1972, I Wouldn't Take Nothing for My Journey, 2001; co-founder Black Forum; poetry editor: Black Forum, editor-in-chief:. Bd. dirs. S.E. Bronx (N.Y.) Neighborhood Ctr., Inc., 2000—, Philipsburg Manor (N.Y.) African Am. Adv. Bd., 2001—. With USN, 1964—68. Mem.: Morris Brown Coll. Alumni Assn., 369th Vets. Assn. (life), Shriners, Pentecost Consistory, Masons, Am. Legion (life), Corinthian, Phi Beta Sigma (life). Democrat. Baptist. Avocations: fishing, travel, reading, gardening. Home: 24 Hickory Rd Briarcliff Manor NY 10510

WINDHORST, JOHN WILLIAM, JR., lawyer; b. Mpls., July 6, 1940; s. John William and Ardus Ruth (Bottge) W.; divorced; 1 child, Diana Elizabeth. AB, Harvard U., 1962; LLB, U. Minn., 1965. Bar: Minn. 1965, U.S. Tax Ct., U.S. Ct. Appeals (8th cir.) 1965, U.S. Dist. Ct. Minn. 1967, U.S. Supreme Ct. 1975. Law clk. to Hon. H.A. Blackmun U.S. Cir. Ct., Rochester, Minn., 1965-66; assoc. Dorsey & Whitney, Mpls., 1966-70; with office of Revisor of Statutes State of Minn., 1967, 69; ptnr. Dorsey & Whitney, 1971-96, of counsel, 1997—. Bd. dirs. St. Paul Chamber Orch., 1980-86, Harry A. Blackmun Scholarship Found., 1996—, Minn. Taxpayers Assn., 1999—. Mem. ABA (com. on state and local taxes), Minn. Bar Assn., Hennepin County Bar Assn., Harvard Club of Minn. (pres. 1977-78). Home: 1235 Yale Pl Apt 1102 Minneapolis MN 55403-1946 Office: 50 S 6th St Ste 1500 Minneapolis MN 55402 Office Phone: 612-340-2645. E-mail: windhorst.john@dorsey.com.

WINDMAN, ARNOLD LEWIS, retired mechanical engineer; b. N.Y.C., Oct. 17, 1926; s. Raphael and Anna (Wexler) W.; m. Patricia Foley, Dec. 13, 1967; children— Richard, Marjorie, Kevin, Colleen, Sean, JoAnn, Brian, William. B.M.E., Coll. City N.Y., 1947. Bar: registered profl. engr., N.Y., 13 other states. Project engr. F.E. Sutton, N.Y.C., 1947-50; with Syska & Hennessy, Inc., N.Y.C., 1950-90, pres., 1976-86, vice chmn., 1986-90, also bd. dirs. Pres. Am. Cons. Engrs. Coun., 1985-86; chmn. N.Y. State Bd. Engring. and Land Surveying, 1982-84; bd. dirs., v.p. Sea Pines Plantation, 1997-2000. Bd. dirs. Phelps Meml. Hosp., Tarrytown, N.Y., 1974-82; chmn. planning commn. Hilton Head Island, 2000. Mem. Am. Soc. Heating, Refrigerating and Air Conditioning Engrs., chpt. pres. (1965), N.Y. Assn. Cons. Engrs. (pres. 1981-82, dir. 1977), ASME, Tau Beta Pi, Pi Tau Sigma. Democrat. Jewish. Home: 1919 S Beach Club VI Hilton Head Island SC 29928-4068 *Professional integrity, enthusiasm, and a continuing effort to train younger people for advancement are three key ingredients of a successful career.*

WINDOM, HERBERT LYNN, oceanographer, environmental scientist; b. Macon, Ga., Apr. 23, 1941; m. Patricia Woodruff, 1963; children: Kevin, Elizabeth. BS, Fla. State U., 1963; MS, U. Calif., San Diego, 1965, PhD in Earth Sci., 1968. Prof. oceanography Skidaway Inst. Oceanography, Savannah, Ga., 1968—94, acting dir., 1994-2001, prof. emeritus, 2001—. Mem. Am. Soc. Limnol. and Oceanography, Am. Geophys. Union, Oceanography Soc. Office: Skidaway Inst of Oceanography 10 Ocean Science Cir Savannah GA 31411-1011 E-mail: herb@skio.peachnet.edu.

WINDOM, STEPHEN RALPH, former lieutenant governor, lawyer; b. Florence, South Carolina, Nov. 6, 1949; s. Ralph and Connie (Hinds) W.; m. Mary (Becker); children: Robert Stephen, Thomas Patrick. BS, U. Ala., 1971, JD, 1974. Bar: Ala., 1974; U.S. Supreme Ct., 1980. Assoc. McDermott, Slepian, Kittrell, and Fleming, Mobile, Ala., 1974-77; ptnr. McDermott, Slepian, Windom, and Reed, Mobile, Ala., 1974-86, Sirote and Permutt, P.C., Ala., 1984—; mem. Ala. State Senate, 1989-99; lt. gov. State of Ala., 1999—2003. Lectr. in field, 1985—. Pres. Greater Gulf State Fair, Mobile, 1981; Cystic Fibrosis Found., Mobile, 1981. Capt. USAFR, 1971-82. Mem. Ala. State Bar Assn.; Mobile Bar Assn.; Am. Bankruptcy Inst.; Comml. Law League; Jaycees; Shriners; Masons; Phi Delta Phi. Republican. Avocations: hunting, water sports.

WINDOM, WILLIAM, actor; b. N.Y.C., Sept. 28, 1923; s. Paul and Isobel Wells (Peckham) W.; m. Patricia Veronica Tunder, Dec. 31, 1975; children: Rachel, Heather Juliet, Hope, Rebel Russell. Student, Williams Coll., 1942, The Citadel, 1943, Antioch Coll., 1943, U. Ky., 1943, Biarritz Am. U., 1945, Fordham U., 1946. Actor: (Army) Richard III, 1945—46, (Broadway appearances) Mlle. Colombe, 1954, Fallen Angels, 1956, USA, 1958, Androdes and the Lion, Alice in Wonderland, Time Remembered, Viva Madison Avenue, The World of Suzie Wong, Double in Hearts, Come Blow Your Horn; (films) To Kill a Mockingbird, 1962, For Love or Money, 1963, Cattle King, 1963, One Man's Way, 1964, The Americanization of Emily, 1964, Hour of the Gun, 1967, The Detective, 1968, The Angry Breed, 1969, The Gypsy Moths, 1969, Brewster McCloud, 1970, Echoes of a Summer, 1974, Sommersby, 1993, Attack of the 50 ft. Woman, 1993, Children of the Corn: The Gatherine, 1996; (TV series, leading role) The Farmer's Daughter, 1962—65, My World and Welcome to It, 1969—70 (Emmy award, 1970), (one-man theatrical presentation) Thurber I, 1972, Thurber II, 1975, Ernie Pyle I, 1976, Ernie Pyle II, 1979; (TV series) Murder She Wrote, Parenthood, 1990, (appearances in numerous TV movies including) A Great American Tragedy, The Day the Earth Moved, Guilty or Innocent: The Sam Sheppard Murder Case, Seventh Avenue, Blind Ambition, Portrait of a Rebel: Margaret Sanger, Desperate Lives, The Rules of Marriage, Miracle on 34th St., 1994, Fugitive X: Innocent Target, 1996, The Thundering 8th, 1998, Early Bird Special, 1998, True Crime, 1999; actor, actor: others; mem.: Am. Repertory Theatre, 1946—47. Served with 508th parachute inf. AUS, 1943-46. Mem. Catboat Assn., Actors Equity Assn.

WINDSOR, HARRIET SMITH, state official; children: James A. Smith Jr., Julia A. Smith-O'Hanlon. BA, Juniata Coll.; PhD, MA, U. Del. Cert. lay spkr. Peninsula Conf. Former English tchr. Seaford Sr. HS; dean instrn., dept. English Chmn. Del. Tech. and Cmty. Coll. Owens Campus; mem., dir. State Personnel Gov. Thomas R. Carper's Cabinet, 1993—2001; Sec. of State State of Del., 2001—. Writer, spkr. numerous local, state and nat. bds. Serves Dist. Com. Ordained Ministry; mem., choir dir., organist, ch. sch. tchr., supt., adminstrv. bd. chmn., chmn. Pastor Parish Rels. Com. Millsboro Grace United Meth. Ch., lay leader, 2002—. Named Del. Mother of Yr., 1999, Woman of Yr., Sussex Ctrl. Jr. HS students; named to Del.'s Hall of Fame, 1997. Office: Townsend Bldg 401 Federal St Ste 3 Dover DE 19901 E-mail: harriet.windsor@state.de.us.

WINDSOR, PATRICIA (KATONAH SUMMERTREE, PERRIN WINTERS, ANNA SEELING), author, educator, lecturer; b. NYC, Sept. 21, 1938; d. Bernhard Edward and Antoinette (Gaus) Seelinger; m. Laurence Charles Windsor, Jr., Apr. 3, 1959 (div. 1978); children: Patience Wells, Laurence Edward; m. Stephen E. Altman, Sept. 21, 1986 (div. 1989). Student, Bennington Coll., 1956—58, Westchester C.C.; AA, NYU. V.p. Windsor-Morehead Assoc., NYC, 1960—63; info. mgr. Family Planning Assn., London, 1974-76; faculty mem. Inst. Children's Lit., Redding Ridge, Conn., 1976-94, 99—; editor-in-chief AT&T, Washington, 1978-80; instr. U. Md. Writers Inst., Open Univ., Washington, 1980-82; creative developer, faculty mem. Long Ridge Writer's Group, Danbury, Conn., 1988-2000; dir. Summertree Studios, Savannah, Ga., 1992—. Dir. Wordspring Lit. Cons., 1999—, Wordworks Writing Cons., 1999—, Born Author Lit. Cons., 2003-; dir. Devel. Writing Workshops, Katonah, NY, 1976-78; judge Internat. Assn. Bus. Communicators, Washington, 1979, 89; lectr. LI U., Jersey City State Coll., Skidmore Coll., others, 1987—; instr. Coastal Ga. Ctr. for Continuing Edn., 1996—, Armstrong Atlantic U. Continuing Edn., 1997-2000, Anne Arundel (Md.) C.C., 2000—, workshop coord., 2000—; dir., founder Born Author.com, 2002—; dir. Windsomethings Art & Crafts, 2004—. Author: The Summer Before, 1973 (ALA Best Book award 1973, transl. 1980 Austrian State prize 1980, also Brit., Norwegian, German edits.), Something's Waiting for You, Baker D, 1974 (starred selection Libr. Jour., Brit., Japanese edits.), Home Is Where Your Feet Are Standing, 1975, Diving for Roses, 1976 (NY Times Outstanding Book for Young Adults award, starred selection Libr. Jour.), Mad Martin, 1976, Killing Time, 1980, Demon Tree, 1983 (pen name Colin Daniel), The Sandman's Eyes, 1985 (Edgar Allan Poe Best Juvenile Mystery award Mystery Writers Am.), How a Weirdo and a Ghost Can Change Your Life, 1986, The Hero, 1988 (highest rating Voice of Youth Advocate), Just Like the Movies, 1990, The Christmas Killer, 1991 (Edgar nominee, Brit., Danish, French edits.), Two Weirdos and a Ghost, 1991, A Weird and Moogly Christmas, 1991, The Blooding, 1996 (YALSA pick for reluctant readers), The House of Death, 1996; columnist The Blood Rev., 1990-92, Savannah Parent, 1990-92; columnist Coastal Senior, 1997-99; also short stories in anthologies and mags.; actress: The Haunting of Hill House, City Lights Theatre Co., 1991. Mem. City Lights Theatre Co., Savannah, Ga., 1991. Mem. Horror Writers Am., Internat. Women's Writing Guild, Children's Book Guild, Authors Guild, Poetry Soc. Ga., Savannah Storytellers. Avocations: skiing, painting, modern dance. Office: Born Author Dot Com PO Box 799 Severna Park MD 21146 E-mail: info@bornauthor.com.

WINDSOR, WILLIAM EARL, consulting engineer, sales representative; b. Evansville, Ind., Jan. 24, 1927; s. Charles H. and Lora E. (Archey) W.; divorced; children: Kim, William, Robert. Student, Purdue U., 1946-50. Field engr. Philco Corp., Phila., 1950-53; studio ops. engr. Sta. WFBM, Indpls., 1953-55; field engr. RCA Svc. Co., Cherry Hill, N.J., 1955-56; audio facilities engr. ABC, N.Y.C., 1956-62; rsch. engr. Fine Recording, Inc., N.Y.C., 1962-66; chief engr. A & R Recording, Inc., N.Y.C., 1966-68; chief engr., corp. sec. DB Audio Corp., N.Y.C., 1968-70; pres. Studio Cons., Inc., N.Y.C., 1970-72; sr. v.p., v.p., gen. mgr. Quad Eight Electronics-Quad Eight/Westrex, San Fernando, Calif., 1972-85; sr. mktg. exec. Mitsubishi Pro Audio Group, San Fernando, Calif., 1985-89. Pres., CEO Quad Eight Electronics, Inc., Valencia, Calif., 1989-90; ind. cons., Valencia, 1991—. Inventor monitor mixer for multitrack audio consoles, 1967, update function for audio console automation, 1973; designer of new architecture for film scoring and film re-recording sound mixing consoles, 1974 (Acad. award 1974). Served with USNR, 1945-50. Fellow: Audio Engring. Soc. (chmn. NY sect. 1970). Avocations: photography, foreign travel, art collecting. Home and Office: 23112 Yvette Ln Valencia CA 91355-3060 Office Phone: 661-255-3265.

WINE, L. MARK, lawyer; b. Norfolk, Va., Apr. 16, 1945; s. Melvin Leon and Mildred Sylvia (Weiss) W.; m. Blanche Weintraub, June 8, 1969; children: Kim, Lara, Dana. BA with high honors, U. Va., 1967; JD, U. Chgo., 1970. Bar: D.C. 1970, U.S. Supreme Ct. 1977. Assoc. Kirkland & Ellis, Washington, 1970-72, ptnr., 1978—; trial atty. land and natural resources divsn. Dept. of Justice, Washington, 1972-78. Mem. ABA. Office: Kirkland & Ellis LLP 655 15th St NW Ste 1200 Washington DC 20005-5793 Business E-Mail: mwine@kirkland.com.

WINE, MARK PHILIP, lawyer; b. Iowa City, Jan. 6, 1949; s. Donald Arthur and Mary Lepha Schneider; children: Nicholas Cox, Meredith Kathryn. AB, Princeton U., 1971; JD, U. Iowa, 1974. Bar: Iowa 1974, Minn. 1976, Calif. 1997, U.S. Dist. Ct. Minn. 1976, U.S. Ct. Appeals (8th cir.) 1976, U.S. Supreme Ct. 1984, U.S. Ct. Appeals (4th cir.) 1985, U.S. Ct. Appeals (7th and Fed. cirs.) 1992, U.S. Ct. Appeals (9th cir.) 1997, U.S. Dist. Ct. (so., no. and ctrl. dists.) Calif. 1997. Law clk. to judge U.S. Ct. Appeals (8th cir.), St. Louis, 1974-76; ptnr. Oppenheimer Wolff & Donnelly, 1976—2002, McDermott, Will & Emery, LA, 2002—. Mem. ABA, Internat. Assn. Def. Counsel, Calif. Bar Assn., L.A. Bar Assn., L.A. Intellectual Property Law Assn., Princeton Club So. Calif. Democrat. Avocations: cooking, reading, biking, golf. Home: 6220 E Fox Glen Dr Anaheim Hills CA 92087 Office: McDermott Will & Emery 2049 Century Park E Fl 34 Los Angeles CA 90067-3208 Office Phone: 310-551-9322. Personal E-mail: mpwineca@sbcglobal.net. Business E-Mail: mwine@mwe.com.

WINE, SHERWIN THEODORE, rabbi; b. Detroit, Jan. 25, 1928; s. William Harry and Tillie (Israel) W. BA, U. Mich., 1950, A.M., 1952; B.H.L., Hebrew Union Coll., Cin., M.H.L., rabbi, Hebrew Union Coll., Cin., 1956. Rabbi Temple Beth El, Detroit, 1956-60, Windsor, Ont., Can., 1960-64, Birmingham (Mich.) Temple, 1964—. Cons. editor Humanistic Judaism, 1966— Author: A Philosophy of Humanistic Judaism, 1965, Meditation Services for Humanistic Judaism, 1977, Humanistic Judaism-What Is It?, 1977, Humanist Haggadah, 1980, High Holidays for Humanists, 1980, Judaism Beyond God, 1985, Celebration, 1988, Staying Sane in a Crazy World, 1996. Founder Ctr. for New Thinking, Birmingham, 1977—; founder Soc. Humanistic Judaism, 1969; pres. N.Am. Com. for Humanism, 1982-93. Chaplain U.S. Army, 1956-58. Mem. Conf. Liberal Religion (chmn. 1985-96), Leadership Conf. Secular and Humanistic Jews (chmn. 1983-93), Internat. Inst. Secular Humanistic Judaism (co-chmn. 1986—), Internat. Assn. Humanist Educators, Counselors and Leaders (pres. 1988-93), Internat. Fedn. Secular Humanistic Jews (co-chmn. 1993—). Home: 362 Southfield Rd Birmingham MI 48009-3739 Office: 28611 W 12 Mile Rd Farmington MI 48334-4225 E-mail: bhamtmpl@speedlink.net.

WINEBRENNER, WILLIAM PATRICK, writer; b. West Columbia, W.Va., Sept. 26, 1933; s. Richard Arthur Winebrenner and Lucy Ethel Riley; children: Rita Jean Hreha, William Patrick II, Tonya Michelle Noel. Grad. h.s., Mason, W.Va. Journeyman Internat. Brotherhood Elec. Workers, Toledo, 1968-95; ret. Mem. adv. bd. Muskingum Area Tech. Coll., Zanesville, Ohio, 1998; owner Valley Enterprises Pub., Stockport, Ohio, 1993-98. Author: (books) The Woodwalkers, 1993, Smoke in the Valley, 1995, Narrowbackin', 1997, From Out of the Forest, 1998, A Place of Evil, 1999. Mem. Elec. Workers Retirement. Democrat. Avocations: hunting, fishing, writing and promoting books. Home: 2300 State Route 376 Stockport OH 43787-9570

WINEGAR, ALBERT LEE, computer systems company executive; b. Beloit, Wis., Apr. 23, 1931; s. Albert Richard and Theo Rayneta (Hubbell) W.; m. Phyllis M. Everill, June 21, 1953; children: Bradford, Steven, Kristine, Kathleen. BBA, U. Wis., 1954; Stanford Sloan Exec. fellow, Stanford U.,

1970. With IBM Corp., 1956-79, div. dir. mgmt. services, 1977-79; v.p. corp. planning, then group v.p. field ops. Olivetti Corp., Tarrytown, N.Y., 1979-80, pres., 1980-81; v.p. field ops. NBI Inc., Boulder, Colo., 1981-84; pres., chief exec. officer Sensory, Inc., Santa Clara, Calif., 1984-85, VICOM Systems, Inc., Fremont, Calif., 1985-91, ret., 1991. Bd. dirs. JRL Sys., Inc., Advanced Sys. Integration Group, Acad. Software Inc., Adams Globalization, Inc.; pres. Barton Creek Water Supply Corp. V.p. bd. trustees Valley Hosp., Ridgewood, N.J., 1978-81; pres. NJ Bus. Arts Found., 1977-78, Estates of Barton Creek Homeowners Assn., 1992-94; elder Westlake Hills Presbyn. Ch., stewardship chmn., 2002, fin. chmn., 2003 Capt. AUS, 1954-56. Mem. Computer and Bus. Equipment Mfrs. Assn. (dir. 1980-81), Barton Creek Country Club, Beta Theta Pi. Republican. Home: 8401 Hickory Creek Dr Austin TX 78735-1530 E-mail: alwinegar@aol.com.

WINEGAR, ANTHONY C. health care worker; b. Jefferson City, Mo., Oct. 22, 1961; s. Alvon C. and Betty A. Winegar. Vocat. cert., Columbia, Mo., 1983. Data entry operator I Mo. Dept. Revenue, Jefferson City, 1985; data entry clk. Jefferson City Credit Bur., 1985, 87; automation clk. Lincoln U., Jefferson City, 1987-95; clk. St. Marys Health Ctr., Jefferson City, 1996—. Author (poetry book) A Walk Through History, 1998, Inspirational Figures in Song, 2000. Recipient Editors Choice award Nat. Libr. Poetry, 1996. Republican. Roman Catholic. Home: 3108 W Truman Blvd Apt 100 Jefferson City MO 65109-4916

WINEMAN, JEAN D. architecture educator; BA in Psychology and Sociology, Wellesley Coll., 1971; M in Urban Planning, U. Mich., 1973, DArch, 1977. Asst. prof. arch. Ga. Inst. Tech., Coll. Arch., 1977—82, assoc. prof. arch., 1982—99, prof. arch., 1999—2000, acting dir. doctoral program, 1992—94, dir. doctoral program, 1994—2000; prof. arch. U. Mich., Taubman Coll. Arch. and Urban Planning, Ann Arbor, 2000—, assoc. dean for rsch., 2000—, chair doctoral program in arch., 2000—. Editor: Behavioral Issues in Office Design, 1986; contbr. chapters to books, articles to profl. jours. Office: U Mich Taubman Coll Arch and Urban Planning 2000 Bonisteel Blvd Ann Arbor MI 48109-2069*

WINER, WARD OTIS, mechanical engineer, educator; b. Grand Rapids, Mich., June 27, 1936; s. Mervin Augustus and Ina Katherine (Wood) W.; m. Mary Jo Wielinga, June 15, 1957; children: Mathew Owen, James Edward, Paul Andrew, Mary Margaret. Assoc., Grand Rapids Jr. Coll., 1956; BS, U. Mich., 1958, MS, 1959, PhD, 1962; PhD (Cavendish Lab. fellow), Cambridge (Eng.) U., 1964. Asst. prof. dept. mech. engring. U. Mich., Ann Arbor, 1963-66, assoc. prof., 1966-69; assoc. prof. mech. engring. Ga. Inst. Tech., 1969-71, prof., 1971-84, Regents' prof., 1984—, mem. exec. bd., 1983-88, chmn., 1984-86, dir. and chmn. Sch. Mech. Engring., 1988—, Eugene C. Gwaltney Jr. chair George W. Woodruff Sch. Mech. Engring., 2001—. Chmn. Gordon Research Conf. on Friction, Lubrication and Wear, 1980; mem. NRC, 1980-88; chmn. Com. on Recommendations for U.S. Army Basic Sci. Research, 1985-87; mem. div. mech., structural, materials engring. adv. bd. NSF Engring. Directorate, 1984-89. Co-editor: Wear Control Handbook, 1980; tech. editor: Jour. Lubrication Tech., 1980-84, Jour. of Tribology, 1984-87; contbr. articles to profl. jours. Democratic precinct chmn., 1967-68; Mem. exec. bd. Horace H. Rackham Sch. Grad. Studies, U. Mich., 1968. Recipient Disting. Faculty Svc. award Coll. Engring. U. Mich., 1967, Alumni Merit award, 1998, Cert. Recognition, NASA, 1977, Clarence E. Earle Meml. award Nat. Grease Lubricating Inst., 1979, Disting. Prof. award Ga. Inst. Tech., 1987; named Hon. Alumni, Ga. Tech., 2003. Fellow AAAS, ASME (bd. comms. 1987-91, v.p. rsch. 1989-93, Melville medal 1975, Centennial medallion 1980, Mayor D. Hersey award 1986, Charles Russ Richards Meml. award 1988), Soc. Tribologists and Lubrication Engrs. (bd. dirs. 1983-86, Internat. award 1997), Brit. Tribology Trust (gold medal 1987), Am. Soc. Engring. Educators (Benjamin Garver Lamme award 1995, Donald Marlowe award 1996); mem. NAE, Metro Atlanta Engring. Soc. (Engr. of Yr. 1989), Am. Acad. Mechanics, Soc. Rheology, Soc. Engring. Sci. (dir. 1980-84), AAUP (pres. Ga. Tech. chpt. 1972-74, v.p. state conf. 1973-75), Sigma Xi (chpt. pres. 1982-83, Sustained Rsch. in Engring. award 1975), Tau Beta Pi, Pi Tau Sigma, Phi Kappa Phi. Home: 1025 Mountain Creek Trl NW Atlanta GA 30328-3535 Office Phone: 404-894-3200. E-mail: ward.winer@me.gatech.edu.

WINER, WARREN JAMES, insurance executive; b. Wichita, Kans., June 16, 1946; s. Henry Charles and Isabel (Ginsburg) W.; m. Mary Jean Kovacs, June 23, 1968 (div. Feb. 1973); m. Jo Lynn Sondag, May 3, 1975; children: Adam, Lauren. BS in Math., Stanford U., 1968. With Gen. Am. Life Ins. Co., St. Louis, 1968-73, dir. retirement plans, 1973-76, 2d v.p., 1976-80; v.p., sr. actuary Powers, Carpenter & Hall, St. Louis, 1980-84, sr. v.p., dir. pension div., 1984-85, pres., chief operating officer, 1985-86, lobbyist, commentator, 1985—, pres., chief exec. officer, 1986—; pres. W F Corroon, 1988-93; prin. William M. Mercer, 1993-94, mng. dir., 1994-95; exec. v.p. Gen. Am. Life Ins. Co., St. Louis, 1995—. Mem. Actuarial Exam. Com., Chgo., 1973-74. Contbr. articles to profl. jours. Bd. dirs. Lucky Lane Nursery Sch. Assn., St. Louis, 1978-93, pilot divsn. United Way, 1986-87; co-pres. Conway Sch. Parent Assn., 1986-87; bd. dirs. Paraquad, 1991—, chmn., 1994-99; bd. dirs. ATD, 1992—; chair triumph divsn. Unitd Way, 1996—. Fellow Soc. Actuaries; mem. Am. Acad. Actuaries, Enrollment of Actuaries (joint bd.), Am. Life Ins. Assn. (small case task force 1979-80), Life Office Mgmt. Assn. (ICPAC com. 1975-80), St. Louis Actuaries Club. Clubs: St. Louis, Clayton (St. Louis). Jewish. Avocations: bridge, wine tasting, swimming, weight training, biking. Office: Gen Am Benefits 13045 Tesson Ferry Rd Saint Louis MO 63128-3407

WINET, HOWARD, research scientist, medical educator; b. Chgo., Sept. 13, 1937; s. Maurice Winet and Lillian Silver; m. Carol Katherine Kasper; children: Evan Darwin, Wendy Lynn. BS in Zoology, U. Ill., 1959; MA in Zoology, UCLA, 1962, PhD in Zoology, 1969. Cert. tchr. secondary edn., Calif. Tchr. secondary sch. sci. L.A. City Schs., 1962—66; postdoctoral fellow engring. sci. Calif. Inst. Tech., Pasadena, 1970—74, rsch. engr., 1974—77; assoc. prof. physiology So. Ill. U., Carbondale, 1977—80; assoc. prof. rsch. orthopaedics U. So. Calif., L.A., 1980—98, assoc. prof. rsch. biomed. engring., 1996—98; lectr. biomed. engring. UCLA, 1998—, adj. prof. orthop., 1998—. Cons. Commonwealth Sci. & Indsl. Rsch. Orgn., Canberra, Australia, 1979; vis. assoc. prof. math. U. Wis., Madison, 1982; Fogarty internat. fellow orthopaedics Gothenburg U., Sweden, 1984; sr. assoc. U.S. Army M.C., Walter Reed Hosp., Washington, 1990—92. Contbr. (book chpts.) Engineering Science, Fluid Dynamics, 1990, Encyclopaedic Handbook of Biomaterials and Bioengineering, 1995, Clinically Applied Microcirculation Research, 1995, Bone Mechanics Handbook, 2001; mem. sci. editl. bd.: European Cells and Materials Jour. Grantee Rsch. grant, NIH, 1978—81, 1986—89, 1994—97. Mem.: Assn. Rsch. Circulation Osseous (v.p.), Soc. Biomaterials (vice chair spl. interest groups 2002). Avocation: fly fishing. Office: Orthopaedic Hosp UCLA 2400 Flower St Los Angeles CA 90007 Office Phone: 213-742-1007. Business E-Mail: hwinet@ucla.edu.

WINFIELD, JOHN BUCKNER, rheumatologist, educator; b. Kentfield, Calif., Mar. 19, 1942; s. R. Buckner and Margaret G. (Katterfelt) W.; m. Patricia Nichols (div. 1968); 1 child, Ann Gibson; m. Teresa Lee McGrath, 1969 (div. 2000); children: John Buckner III, Virginia Lee; m. Leigh Fleming Callahan, 2001. BA, Williams Coll., 1964; MD, Cornell U., 1968. Diplomate Am. Bd. Internal Medicine. Intern in medicine N.Y. Hosp., N.Y.C., 1968-69; staff assoc. LI/Nat. Inst. Allergy and Infectious Diseases NIH, Bethesda, Md., 1969-71; resident in medicine, fellow in rheumatology U. Va. Sch. Medicine, Charlottesville, 1971-73; fellow in immunology Rockefeller U., N.Y.C., 1973-75; asst. prof. medicine U. Va. Sch. Medicine, Charlottesville, 1975-76, assoc. prof. medicine, 1976-78, U. N.C., Chapel Hill, 1978-81, prof. medicine, 1981—, chief div. rheumatology and immunology, 1978-99; dir. Thurston Arthritis Rsch. Ctr. U. N.C. Sch. Medicine, Chapel Hill, 1982—2001; Smith prof. medicine U. N.C. Sch. Med., Chapel Hill, 1987—, adj. prof. exercise sports physiology, 2003—. Adv. coun. Nat. Inst. Arthritis and Musculoskeletal and Skin Diseases, NIH, 1988-92; chmn. edn. com. Am. Rheumatism Assn., Atlanta, 1980-84; immunol. scis. study sect. NIH, 1979-83, Arthritis Musculoskeletal and Skin study sect., 1992-96; vice-chair fellowship com. Arthritis Found., 1982; med. coun. Lupus Found. Am., 1987-96. Author more than 130 med. and sci. articles in peer reviewer rheumatology and immunology jours.; mem. editl. bd. Arthritis and Rheumatism, Bull. Rheumatic Diseases, Rheumatology Internat., Clin. Exptl. Rheumatology, Am. Jour. Medicine. Sr. asst. surgeon with USPHS, NIH, Bethesda, Md., 1968-71. Recipient Borden prize Cornell U. Med. Coll., 1964, numerous rsch. grants NIH and Arthritis Found., 1975—, Sr. Investigator award Arthritis Found., 1976-79, Kenan award U. N.C., 1985, NIH merit award, 1992. Fellow ACP; mem. Am. Assn. Immunologists, Am. Coll. Rheumatology, Am. Fedn. Clin. Rsch., Am. Soc. Clin. Investigation, Assn. Am. Physicians, Am. Clin. Climatol. Assn., Nat. Soc. Clin. Rheumatologists (treas. 1997-2002), Henry Kunkel Soc. (councilor 2000—), Chapel Hill Country Club. Republican. Episcopalian. Avocations: golf, off-road motorcycling, scuba diving instructor, skiing. Home: 102 Greenwood Ln Chapel Hill NC 27514-5957 Business E-Mail: john_winfield@med.unc.edu.

WINFIELD, MICHAEL D. engineering company executive; b. 1939; BSChemE, Ohio State U.; MBA, U. Chgo. Chem. engr. UOP, Des Plaines, Ill., 1962-74, mgr. refinery projects, 1974-76, asst. dir. tech. svcs., 1976-81, dir. bus. devel., 1981-83, v.p. tech. svcs., 1983-84, v.p. process svcs., 1984-92, pres., CEO, 1992—. Office: UOP 25 E Algonquin Rd Des Plaines IL 60016-6100

WINFIELD, RICHARD NEILL, lawyer; b. Chgo., Jan. 20, 1933; s. Richard Paul and Mary B. (Monaghan) Winfield; m. Deobrah Mary Trainer, June 13, 1959; children: Richard Neill Jr., Pamela, Nicole. AB, Villanova U., 1955; LLB, Georgetown U., 1961. Bar: Va. 1961, N.Y. 1962, U.S. Dist. Ct. (so. dist.) N.Y. 1963. Assoc. Donovan, Leisure, Newton & Irvine, N.Y.C., 1961-65; asst. counsel to Gov. Nelson A. Rockefeller Gov.'s Office, Albany, NY, 1965-67; assoc. Royall, Koegel, Rogers & Wells, N.Y.C., 1967-69; ptnr. Clifford Chance US LLP (formerly known as Rogers & Wells), N.Y.C., 1969—2002. Chmn. bd. consultors Sch. Law Villanova U., Pa., 1980—2004; faculty comm. law confs. Practising Law Inst., N.Y.C., 1977—2001, chmn. libel litig. confs., 1979—2000; prof. Columbia Law Sch., Fordham Law Sch., 2002—. Editor: Libel Litigation, PLI, 1979, 1981, 1984, 1986, 1988, 1990, 1992, 1994, 1996, 1998, 2000; contbr. articles to profl. jours. Chmn. bd. trustees Convent Sacred Heart Sch., N.Y.C., 1987—90; co-chmn. bd. dirs. Fund for Peace, 2000—; mem. bd. visitors Sch. Langs. and Linguistics, Georgetown U., Washington, 1987—93. Lt. USN, 1955—59. Recipient Alumni medallion, Coll. Liberal Arts & Scis. Villanova U., 1984, Loyalty award, Villanova U., 1986, First Amendment award, Deadline Club, 2002. Mem.: ABA (chmn. media law reform working group 1996—, Ctrl. Europe and Eurasian Law Initiative), Internat. Sr. Lawyers Project (co-founder, bd. dirs., treas.), Assn. Bar City of N.Y., N.Y. State Bar Assn., Century Assn. Republican. Roman Catholic. Avocations: travel, history. Home: 40 5th Ave New York NY 10011-8843 Office: Clifford Chance US LLP 31 West 52nd St New York NY 10019 Office Phone: 212-878-8233.

WINFIELD, ROY A. pharmaceutical company executive; CEO Incyte Pharms., Palo Alto, Calif. Office: Incyte Pharms 3160 Porter Dr Palo Alto CA 94304-1212

WINFREE, CHARLES VAN, management consultant; b. Hopkinsville, Ky., June 4, 1917; s. Arthur Alexander and Susan Irene (Thompson) Winfree; m. Dorothy Rosemary Scheb, Sept. 16, 1940 (dec. Dec. 1996); children: Arthur T.(dec.), Phyllis Diane Winfree Laidre, Robert A., Charlie V. CLU. With Metropolitan Life, N.Y.C., v.p., ret., 1974; cons. Internat. Exec. Svc. Corp., Stamford, Conn., 1975. Active Ronald Reagan campaign Rep. Party. With U.S. Army, 1943—46. Republican. Avocation: raising orchids, bananas, bromeliads. Home: 554 Jessmyth Dr Longboat Key FL 34228-2608

WINFREE, LATHAM THOMAS, law educator; b. Wytheville, Va., Dec. 2, 1946; s. Latham Thomas, Sr. and Adelaide (Cole) Winfree; m. Eileen Jeffery, July 12, 1969; 1 child, Matthew Ryan. BA, U. Richmond, 1968; MS, Va. Commonwealth U., 1974; PhD, U. Mont., 1976. Asst. prof. E. Tex. State U., Commerce, 1976-79; from asst. to assoc. prof. La. State U., Baton Rouge, 1979-87; from assoc. prof. to prof. N.Mex State U., Las Cruces, 1987—. Vis. instr. U. N.Mex, Albuquerque, 1975—76; cons. in field. Co-author: Expert Witness, 1987, Crime and Justice, 1992, Understanding Crime, 1996, 2d edit., 2003, Contemporary Corrections, 1998, 3d edit., 2005, Juvenile Justice, 2000; contbr. chapters to books, articles to profl. jours. Sgt. U.S. Army, 1968—70. Grantee, Office Juvenile Justice and Delinquency Prevention, 1988, Nat. Inst. Justice, 1996. Fellow: NIMH; mem.: Acad. Criminal Justice Scis., Am. Soc. Criminology. Democrat. Roman Catholic. Avocations: sailing, carpentry, reading. Home: 4939 Chippewa Trail Las Cruces NM 88011 Office: New Mexico State Univ Dept Criminal Justice Las Cruces NM 88003 Office Phone: 505-646-1592.

WINFREY, CAREY WELLS, journalist, magazine editor; b. N.Y.C., Aug. 1, 1941; s. William Colin and Mary (Robinson) W.; m. Jane Elizabeth Keeney, Feb. 13, 1982; children: Graham William, Wells Millar. AB, Columbia U., 1963, MS in Journalism, 1967. Assoc. editor Time Inc., N.Y.C., 1968-71; exec. producer Ednl. Broadcast Corp., N.Y.C., 1971-77; reporter, fgn. corr. for Africa N.Y. Times, N.Y.C., 1977-80; mag. editor CBS Mags., N.Y.C., 1981-90, editor Cuisine mag., 1983-84, v.p., editorial dir., 1985-87; founding editor-in-chief Memories mag. Diamandis Comm., Inc. (formerly mag. divsn. CBS), N.Y.C., 1987-90; editor-in-chief Am. Health mag. Reader's Digest Publs., N.Y.C., 1990-96; dir. Delacorte Ctr. for Mag. Journalism, Columbia U., N.Y.C., 1996-98; asst. mng. editor People Mag., 1996—2001; editor-in-chief Smithsonian Mag., 2001—. Author: Starts and Finishes, 1975; exec. producer: (TV) Behind the Lines, 1971-75 (Emmy award 1973-74, NYU Don Hollenback award 1974), Assignment America, 1975, WNET Reports, 1976-77; columnist: "Eye on Books" for Book of the Month Club News, 1980, Parenting mag., 1986-89; producer Mixed Bag, video arts mag. for CBS Cable; contbr. articles to publs. including The N.Y. Times Mag., Harpers, N.Y. Mag. Lt. USMC, 1963-66. Pulitzer Travelling fellow, 1967; recipient Meyer Berger award for Disting. Reporting Columbia U., 1978. Home: 3808 Reno Rd NW Washington DC 20008 Office: Smithsonian Mag MRC 951, PO Box 37012 Washington DC 20013-7012 E-mail: cwinfrey@simag.si.edu.

WINFREY, JOHN CRAWFORD, economist, educator; b. Somerville, Tenn., July 2, 1935; s. Arthur Peter and Frances (Crawford) W.; m. Barbara Ann Strickland, July 20, 1957; 1 child, Mae Millicent. AB, Davidson Coll., 1957; PhD, Duke U., 1965. Asst. dir. data processing Hanes Hosiery, Winston Salem, NC, 1959-62; rsch. asst. in econs. Duke U., Durham, NC, 1963-64; asst. prof. econs. Washington and Lee U., Lexington, Va., 1965-68, assoc. prof., 1969-73, prof., 1974—. Vis. prof. Vanderbilt U., Nashville, 1966, Tufts U., Boston, 1975, UCLA, 1978, U. Ill., 1982, U. Va., 1986, Duke U., 1989, 95, U. Calif., Berkeley, 1993, U. Utrecht, Netherlands, 1995. Co-author: The Motion Commotion, 1972; author: Public Finance, Public Choice and the Public Sector, 1973, Social Issues, The Ethics and Economics of Taxes and Public Programs, 1997. Bd. dirs. Lexington Tennis Clinic, 1968-72, Rockbridge Area Conservation Coun., 1982-84, Rockbridge Area Social Svc., 2002—, Lexington Family Mentoring Program; mem. Rockbridge Area Behavioral Health Adv. Bd., 2001—; pres. Rockbridge Arts Guild, 1986-88, 2001-02. Recipient Cmty. Svc. award Lexington Jaycees, 1971; NEH fellow, 1975, 78, 82, 86, 89, 93; vis. fellow U. Coll. Oxford U., Eng., 1979, 95. Fellow Soc. for Values in Higher Edn.; mem. Am. Econ. Assn., So. Econ. Assn., History of Econs. Soc., Eastern Econ. Assn., High Wheelers Club (Lexington), Sunrise Rotary Club. Democrat. Presbyterian. Home: 628 Stonewall St Lexington VA 24450-1933 Office: Washington and Lee U Dept Econs Lexington VA 24450 Business E-Mail: winfreyj@wlu.edu.

WINFREY, MARION LEE, retired television critic; b. Knoxville, Tenn., July 7, 1932; s. Charles Houston and Norma Elsa (Wesenberg) W.; m. Mary Anne Hight, Sept. 5, 1958 (div. 1977); 1 son, David Dylan; m. Kiki Olson, Aug. 24, 1978 (div. 1982). BS, U. Tenn., 1966; M.F.A., U. Iowa, 1968. Reporter Nashville Tennessean, 1957-58, Knoxville News-Sentinel, 1958-60, Miami bur. UPI, 1960-62, Miami Herald, 1962-63, Washington bur. Knight Newspapers, 1963-66, Detroit Free Press, 1968-71; reporter Phila. Inquirer, 1972-74, TV critic, 1974-2001; ret., 2001. Instr. journalism U. Iowa, 1966-68; Bernard Kilgore journalism counselor DePauw U., 1971 Author: Kent State Report, The President's Commission on Campus Unrest, 1970; included in Best Sports Stories (edited by Marsh and Ehre), 1963. Served with U.S. Army, 1954-56. Nieman fellow Harvard U., 1971-72 Mem. TV Critics Assn. (founding pres. 1978-79), Sigma Delta Chi, Phi Gamma Delta. Clubs: Harvard (Phila.); Pen and Pencil; Nat. Press (Washington). Baptist. Home: Ste 1017 121 S Independence Mall E Philadelphia PA 19106-2410

WINFREY, OPRAH, television talk show host, actress, producer; b. Kosciusko, Miss., Jan. 29, 1954; d. Vernon Winfrey and Vernita Lee. BA in Speech and Drama, Tenn. State U. News reporter Sta. WVOL Radio, Nashville, 1971-72; reporter, news anchorperson Sta. WTVF-TV, Nashville, 1973-76; news anchorperson Sta. WJZ-TV, Balt., 1976-77, host morning talk show People Are Talking, 1977-83; host talk show A.M. Chgo. Sta. WLS-TV, 1984; host The Oprah Winfrey Show, Chgo., 1985—; nationally syndicated, 1986—; host series of celebrity interview spls. Oprah: Behind the Scenes, 1992—; owner, prodr., chmn., CEO Harpo Prodns., 1986—. Ptnr. in Oxygen Media, an Internet and cable TV co., 2000—; founder, editl. dir. O. The Oprah Magazine in conjunction with Hearst Mags., 2000—. Appeared in films The Color Purple, 1985 (nominated Acad. award and Golden Globe award), Native Son, 1986, Beloved, 1998 (exec. prodr.); About Us: The Dignity of Children, 1997 (TV), Before Women Had Wings, 1997 (TV; also exec. prodr. ABC series Oprah Winfrey presents); prodr. Dr. Phil (TV series), 2002—; Listen Up: The Lives of Quincy Jones (TV spl.), 1990, prodr., actress ABC-TV mini-series The Women of Brewster Place, 1989, also series Brewster Place, 1990, movie There Are No Children Here, 1993; exec. prodr. (ABC Movie of the Week) Overexposed, 1992; host, supervising prodr. celebrity interview series Oprah: Behind the Scenes, 1992, ABC Aftersch. Spls., 1991-93; host, exec. prodr. Michael Jackson Talks...to Oprah-90 Prime-Time Minutes with the King of Pop, 1993; exec. prodr. miniseries: Oprah Winfrey Presents: The Wedding, 1998, Oprah Winfrey Presents: David and Lisa, 1998, Oprah Winfrey Presents: Tuesdays with Morrie, 1999 (TV), Oprah Winfrey Presents: Amy and Isabelle, 2001 Recipient Woman of Achievement award NOW, 1986, Emmy award for Best Daytime Talk Show Host, 1987, 91, 92, 94, 95, 97, Nat. Book Found's 50th Anniversary gold medal, 1999, America's Hope award, 1990, Industry Achievement award Broadcast Promotion Mktg. Execs./Broadcast Design Assn., 1991, Image awards NAACP, 1989, 91, 92, 94, Entertainer of the Yr. award NAACP, 1989, CEBA awards, 1989, 90, 91, George Foster Peabody's Individual Achievement award, 1996, Gold Medal award IRTS, 1996, Lifetime Achievement award NATAS, 1998, People's Choice award, 1997, 98, Horatio Alger award, 1993; named Broadcaster of Yr. Internat. Radio and TV Soc., 1988; recognized as one of America's 25 Most Influential People, Time mag.; inducted to Television Hall of Fame, 1994, Bob Hope Humanitarian Award, 2002. Office: Harpo Prodns 110 N Carpenter St Chicago IL 60607-2145*

WING, ADRIEN KATHERINE, law educator; b. Aug. 7, 1956; d. John Ellison and Katherine (Pruitt) Wing; children: Che-Cabral, Nolan Felipe. AB magna cum laude, Princeton U., 1978; MA, UCLA, 1979; JD, Stanford, 1982. Bar: N.Y. 1983, U.S. Dist. Ct. (so. and ea. dists.) N.Y. 1983, U.S. Ct. Appeals (5th and 9th cirs.). Assoc. Curtis, Mallet-Prevost, Colt & Mosle, N.Y.C., 1982-86, Rabinowitz, Boudin, Standard, Krinsky & Lieberman, 1986-87; assoc. prof. law U. Iowa, Iowa City, 1987-93, prof., 1993—, disting. prof. law, 2001—. Mem. alumni council Princeton U., 1983-85, 96-2000, mem. exec. com., 2002—, trustee Class of '78 Alumni Found., 1984-87, 93—, v.p. Princeton Class of 1978 Alumni, 1993-98, trustee Princeton U. 1995; mem. bd. visitors Stanford Law Sch., 1993-96; vis. prof. U. Mich., 2002. Mem. bd. editors Am. J. Comp. Law, 1993—. Mem. Iowa Commn. on African Ams. in Prisons, 1999—. Mem.: ABA (exec. com. young lawyers sect. 1985—87, law sch. site inspector 2002—), U.S. Assn. Constl. Law (bd. dir.), Am. Assn. of Law Schs. (minority sect. bd. 1996—, chair 2002), Am. Friends Svc. Com. (bd. dirs. Mid. East 1998—), Am. Soc. Internat. Law (exec. coun. 1986—89, exec. com. 1988—99, nominating com. 1991, 1993, group chair S. Africa 1993—95, membership com. 1994—95, exec. coun. 1996—99), Internat. Assn. Dem. Lawyers (UN rep. 1984—87), Nat. Conf. Black Lawyers (chmn. internat. affairs sect. 1982—95, UN rep.), Internat. Third World Legal Studies Assn. (bd. dirs. 1996—, nominating trustee Princeton com. 1997—2000), Coun. on Fgn. Rels., Iowa Peace Inst. (bd. dirs. 1993—95), Iowa City Fgn. Rels. Coun. (bd. dirs. 1989—94), Transafrica Scholars Forum Coun. (bd. dirs. 1993—95), Black Alumni of Princeton U. (bd. dirs. 1982—87). Democrat. Avocations: photography, writing, poetry. Office: U Iowa Sch Law Boyd Law Bldg Iowa City IA 52242 E-mail: adrien-wing@uiowa.edu.

WING, ELIZABETH SCHWARZ, museum curator, educator; b. Cambridge, Mass., Mar. 5, 1932; d. Henry F. and Maria Lisa Schwarz; m. James E. Wing, Apr. 18, 1957; children: Mary Elizabeth Wing-Berman, Stephen R. BA, Mt. Holyoke Coll., 1955; MS, U. Fla., 1957, PhD, 1962. Interim asst. curator Fla. Mus. Natural History, U. Fla., Gainesville, 1961-69, asst. curator, 1969-73, assoc. curator, 1973-78, curator, 1978—; U. Fla., Fla. Mus. Natural History, Gainesville, 1990-92. U.S. rep. Internat. Congress Archaeozoology, 1981—. Author: (with A.B. Brown) Paleonutrition, 1979, (with E.J. Reitz) Zooarcheology, 1999; editor (with J.C. Wheeler) Economic Prehistory of the Central Andes, 1988; contbr. articles to profl. jours. Recipient Fryxell award Soc. Am. Archaeology, 1996; NSF grantee, 1961-64, 68-73, 79-80, 84-85, 89-91, 95-96. Mem. Soc. Ethnobiology (pres. 1989-91). Office: U Fla Dickenson HALL/Fla Mus Natural History PO Box 117800 Gainesville FL 32611-7800

WING, JAMES DAVID, lawyer; b. Milw., May 4, 1943; s. William H. and Elaine E. (Koehler) W.; children: Benjamin, Tracy, Nathaniel, John. BA, Beloit (Wis.) Coll., 1965; MA, U. Chgo., 1966, JD, 1969. Bar: Wis. 1969, Fla. 1975, U.S. Ct. Appeals (7th cir.) 1973, U.S. Dist. Ct. (mid. dist.) Fla. 1975, U.S. Ct. Appeals (5th cir.) 1978, U.S. Dist. Ct. (so. dist.) Fla. 1981, U.S. Ct. Appeals (11th cir.) 1981, U.S. Supreme Ct. 1979. Assoc. Whyte, Hirschboeck, Minahan, Harding & Harland, Milw., 1969-75, Carlton, Fields, Ward, Emmanuel, Smith & Cutler, Tampa, Fla., 1975-85, Myers, Kenin, Levinson & Richards/Shea & Gould, Miami, Fla., 1985-88, Fine, Jacobson, Schwartz, Nash, Block & England, Miami, 1988-94, Holland & Knight, Miami, 1994—. Fellow Ctr. for Internat. Legal Studies, Salzbury, Austria. Mem. Phi Beta Kappa, Phi Eta Sigma, Omicron Delta Kappa. Avocations: germanistics, tennis. Office: Holland & KnightLLP 701 Brickell Ave Ste 3000 Miami FL 33131 Fax: 305 789 7799. Office Phone: 305-374-8500. E-mail: jwing@hklaw.com.

WING, JOHN RUSSELL, lawyer; b. Mt. Vernon, N.Y., Jan. 20, 1937; s. John R. and Elinore (Smith) W.; m. Mary Zeller, Aug. 24, 1963 (div. June 1975); children: Ethan Lincoln, Catherine Dorothy; m. Audrey Strauss, Aug. 12, 1979; children: Carlin Elinore, Matthew Lawrence. BA, Yale U., 1960; JD, U. Chgo., 1963. Bar: N.Y. 1964. Assoc. Sherman & Sterling, N.Y.C., 1963-66; asst. U.S. atty. So. Dist. N.Y., N.Y.C., 1966-78; chief fraud unit U.S. Dist. Atty. So. Dist. N.Y., 1971-78; ptnr. Weil, Gotshal & Manges, N.Y.C., 1978—. Contbr. articles to profl. jours. Fellow Am. Coll. Trial Lawyers; mem. ABA (white collar crime com. criminal justice sect. 1978—, environ. task force com. 1983-85), Assn. Bar of City of N.Y. (criminal advocacy com. 1985-88), Fed. Bar Coun. (2d cir. cts. com. 1982-84), N.Y. Coun. Def. Lawyers (bd. dirs. 1986-90). Republican. Episcopalian. Avocation: sailing. Home: 52 Livingston St Brooklyn NY 11201-4813 Office: Weil Gotshal & Manges 767 5th Ave Fl Concl New York NY 10153-0119

WING, KENNARD THOMPSON, educational organization official; b. Mobile, Ala., May 27, 1956; s. Kennard Loren and Phyllis Ellen (Thompson) W.; m. Cara Maureen McMenamin, Dec. 27, 1986; children: Thomas, Sara, James. BS, Brown U., 1978; MS, U. Pa., 1989. Cert. mgmt. acct. Statis. mgr. Gimbels, Phila., 1978-80; programmer, analyst Chase Econometrics, Bala Cynwyd, Pa., 1980-82; product mgr. Wharton Econometrics, Phila., 1982-84, acct. mgr., 1985-87; v.p. Thompson-Mayer, Phila., 1984-85; project dir. Interact, Bala Cynwyd, 1987-93; lectr. U. Pa., Phila., 1990-95; owner Kennard T. Wing & Co., Havertown, Pa., 1993-98; project dir. OMG Ctr. for Collaborative Learning, Phila., 1998—. Adv. bd. Weston Inst., West Chester, Pa., 1988—89; adj. prof. Immaculata Coll., 2000. Contbr. articles to profl. jours. Co-founder Township Green, Haverford, Pa., 1990; vol. West Chester

Small Bus. Devel. Ctr., Exton, Pa., 1991; pres. Haverford Twp. Adult Sch., 1994-95. Recipient Silver award, Soc. of Nat. Assn. Publs., 2003. Mem. Inst. Mgmt. Accts. Office: Kennard T Wing & Co 224 Kathmere Rd Havertown PA 19083

WING, MICHAEL JAMES, telecommunications executive; b. Tucson, Ariz., July 1, 1959; s. James and Bess (Acton) W.; m. Pamela Constantz Wing, May 18, 1980; children: Lindsay Leann, Jacqueline McKenna, Broderick James. BA in Internat. Affairs/Internat. Bus., U. Colo., 1981; MBA in Mktg./Fin., Denver U., 1986; M Pub. Policy, Georgetown U., 1988; M in Political Sci., U. Houston, PhD, 2000; JD, S. Tex. U., 1999. Head baseball coach U. Colo., Boulder, 1980-81; area rep. Kansas City Fellowship Christian Athletes, Denver, 1982; divsn. mgr., ops. mgr. Boyd Distbn. Co., Inc., Denver, 1982-84; pres. U.S. ops. Soft Am., Inc., Denver, 1984-88; pres. Lundby of Sweden U.S.A., Inc., N.Y.C. and Tucson, Ariz., 1985-90, InfoPlan, Inc./Info Plan Internat. Inc., Houston, 1987-96; spl. asst. to sec. Dept. Interior, 1993; spl. asst. to chmn. FCC, 1992-93; pres., CEO U.S. Space and Rocket Ctr., 1998-99; pres. Opencon Comm. Sys., Inc., Piscataway, N.J., 1999—. Pub. speaker to profl. sports teams, collegiate teams, luncheons, banquets, others. Author: Talking With Your Customers, 1993, 96. Bd. dirs. Young Life and Fellowship Christian Athletes; mem. Leadership Fairfax, Va., Leadership Tucson. White House fellow, Washington, 1992-93. Mem. C. of C. (legis. affairs com.). Republican. Baptist. Avocations: racquetball, tennis, hiking, bicycling, fishing. Office: 377 Hoes Ln Piscataway NJ 08854-4138 also: 17317 State Hwy 31 E Tyler TX 75705-4116

WING, VANETTE, sales executive, consultant; b. L.A., Feb. 21, 1947; d. Bennett Germaine and Anna Mae W.; children: John Hunt, Valorie Brinker. BA in Philosophy, Calif. State U., Fullerton, 1977. Account exec. Knoll Pharm. Co., Mount Olive, N.J., 1993-99; managed care account mgr. Biovail Pharms. Inc., Morriville, N.C., 2000—. Lobbyist HDS Med., Honolulu, 1994. Health care lobbyist, activist Coalition Health Care Prov., Honolulu, 1994. Recipient fellowship U. Calif., Riverside, 1978, 79. Republican. Presbyterian. Avocations: archery, gardening, reading, cooking. Office: Biovail Pharms Inc 808 Aviation Pkwy Morrisville NC 27560 Home: 3223 N Silverberry Dr Rialto CA 92377-4818 Fax: 926-630-5493. E-mail: wingitv@pacbell.net.

WINGATE, BETTYE FAYE, librarian, educator; b. Hillsboro, Tex., Oct. 31, 1950; d. Warren Randolph and Faye (Gilmore) W. BA summa cum laude, Baylor U., 1971, MA, 1975; MLS, Tex. Womans U., 1985. Cert. prov. sec., learning resources endorsement. English tchr. Mexia HS, Tex.; reading tchr. Connally Ind. Sch. Dist., Waco, Tex.; reading tchr., libr. Grapevine-Colleyville Ind. Sch. Dist., Grapevine, Tex.; libr., ret., May 02 Crockett Mid. Sch., Irving, Tex. Mem. librs. coms., Campus Action Planning Com., 1989-93, Irving Ind. Sch. Dist. Site Based Decision-Making Com., 1992-94, mem. staff devel. coun., 1994-96, chair media fair com., 1996-2001; rev. Linworth Pub.; spkr., presenter in field. Founding sponsor Challenger Ctr., Air Force Meml. Found. Recipient Tex. Media awards, 1988, 89, 94. Mem. ALA, NEA, Am. Assn. Sch. Libr. (vol. libr. Kids Connect), Tex. State Tchr. Assn. (assn. rep.), Tex. Libr. Assn. (chmn. state media awards com. 1989-91), Tex. Assn. Edn. Tech., Tex. Computer Edn. and Tech., Assn. Ednl. Comm. and Tech., Planetary Soc., Nat. Space Soc., Nat. Parks & Conservation Assn., Baylor Alumni Assn. (life), Wilderness Soc., Sierra Club, Beta Phi Mu, Delta Kappa Gamma (scholar 1985). E-mail: bettye.winate@yahoo.com.

WINGATE, C. KEITH, law educator; b. Darlington, S.C., May 12, 1953; s. Clarence L. and Lilly W.; m. Gloria Farley; stepchildren: Brenda, Marvin, Terry and Oliver Champion. BA in Polit. Sci., U. Ill., 1974, JD cum laude, 1978. Bar: Calif., 1978. Assoc. litigation dept. Morrison & Foerster, San Francisco, 1978-80; from asst. to assoc. prof. law U. Calif.-Hastings, San Francisco, 1980-86, prof., 1986—. Dir. Coun. Legal Edn. Opportunity Region I Inst., 1989; vis. prof. law Stanford Law Sch., fall 1990, 94, spring 1998; chair Minority Law Tchrs.' Conf. Com., 1990; mem. acad. assistance work group, 1991; trustee Law Sch. Admission Coun., 1997-2001. Author: (with David I. Levine and William R. Slomanson) Cases and Materials on California Civil Procedure, 1991, (with William R. Slomanson) California Civil Procedure in a Nutshell, 1992, (with Donald L. Doernberg) Federal Courts, Federalism and Separation of Powers, 1994, 2nd edit., 2000. Bd. dirs. Cmty. Housing Devel. Corp., North Richmond, 1990-99. Recipient 10 Outstanding Persons award U. Ill. Black Alumni Assn., 1980; Harno fellow U. Ill., Coll. of Law, 1976. Mem. Assn. Am. Law Schs. (chair sect. minority groups 1990, exec. com. mem. sect. civil proceedure 1991), Charles Houston Bar Assn., Phi Sigma Alpha. Office: U Calif Hastings Coll Law 200 Mcallister St San Francisco CA 94102-4707

WINGATE, CONSTANCE BLANDY, librarian; b. Woodbury, N.J., Mar. 7, 1935; d. John Chase and Josephine Spond (Black) Blandy; m. Len B. Cooke Jr., 1978 (div. 1987); m. John B. Wingate, Mar. 12, 1999. BA, U. Pa., 1956; MA, U. Denver, 1957. Adult cons. Onondaga Library System, Syracuse, N.Y., 1965-66; asst. dir. Mt. Vernon (N.Y.) Public Library, 1966-75; dep. dir. Queens Borough Public Library, Jamaica, N.Y., 1975-79, dir., 1980-94. Founder pres. Literacy Vols. Mt. Vernon, 1972-74. Trustee METRO, 1980-91, v.p., 1985-88, pres., 1988-91; mem. N.Y. State Libr. Svcs. and Constrn. Act Adv. Coun., 1982-88, chmn., 1986-87; bd. dirs. Queens Coun. on the Arts, 1988-94, v.p., 1989-93; bd. dirs. Queens Mus. of Art, 1988-98, v.p., 1994-96, pres. 1996-98; bd. dirs. Queens Libr. Found., 1996-2003. Mem.: ALA, Circumnavigators Club (internat. sec. 2002—). Republican. Episcopalian. Home: 166-25 Powells Cove Blvd Beechhurst NY 11357

WINGATE, ROBERT LEE, JR., internist; b. Columbia, S.C., May 28, 1936; s. Robert Lee and Helen (Owen) W.; m. Ritanne Cooper, Apr. 19, 1962 (div. 1965); 1 child, Elizabeth Anne Butterfield-Wingate; m. Jeannette DeLatte, Mar. 27, 1968 (div. 1980); children: Laura Owen Wingate, Charlotte Cramer; m. Ann Phyfer, Apr. 1, 1999; 1 child, Jeff Stamm. BS, U. S.C., 1957; MD, Med. Coll. S.C., 1961. Intern Cin. Gen. Hosp., 1961-62, jr. resident internal medicine, 1964-65; asst. resident in internal medicine Med. Coll. of Va., Richmond, 1965-66; resident in internal medicine Charity Hosp. of La., New Orleans, 1966-67, resident in neurology, 1967-68; pvt. practice Columbia, 1968-78; PruCare physician Memphis, 1983-85; med. dir. M. Lowennstein and Celanese Corps., Rock Hill, S.C., 1978-80; med. dir. nursing home care unit Dorn VA Hosp., Columbia, 1980-82; med. cons. disability determination div. Vocat. Rehab. S.C., Columbia, 1982-83; cons. Student Health Ctr. U. S.C., Columbia, 1985-86; cons. Urgent Care Ctrs. S.C., 1986-87; pvt. practice Pelion, S.C., 1987-92; staff internist, chief of staff, cons. internal medicine Western Mental Health Inst., Western Institute, Tenn., 1992-2000; with Memphis Mental Health Inst., 2000—. Med. dir. Forest Hills Nursing Ctr., Columbia, 1968-78; med. cons. S.C. Commn. for Blind, Columbia, 1970-78, Mid-Carolina Coun. on Alcoholism, Columbia, 1970-74; instr. internal medicine U. S.C. Sch. Medicine, 1980-82; cons. internal medicine and urgent care Pelion Cmty. Care Ctr., 1989-92; instr. Sch. Nursing, Med. Coll. S.C., Winthrop divsn., 1978-80; lectr. in field; mem. adv. bd. Vector Med. Techs. and Nutrition Superstores; cardiology cons. Western Mental Health Inst., 2000—. Contbr. articles to newspapers; reviewer Annal of Internal Medicine. Ofcl. physician Peanut Party S.C., 1990-92. Lt. comdr. M.C., USNR, 1958-66. Grantee Burroughs-Wellcome Co., 1958, Med. Coll. S.C., 1960, Congress of U.S. 1987. Fellow ACP; mem. AMA (holder Physician's Recognition award 1969, 74, 79, 85, 86, 94-96, 96-99, 99-2002), Am. Soc. Internal Medicine, Am. Occupational Med. Assn., So. Med. Assn., West Tenn. Consolidated Med. Assembly, Soc. of 1824, State of Tenn. Med. Assn.Consol. Med. Assembly of West Tenn. Avocations: chess, hunting, fishing, gardening, billiards. Office: Memphis Mental Health Inst Memphis TN 38174-0966

WINGATE, WILLIAM PETER, theater executive; b. N.Y.C., Mar. 2, 1944; s. Henry Smith and Ardis (Swenson) W.; m. Anne Homstad, July 1, 1965; 1 child, William John. BA, Carleton Coll., 1965; MBA, Harvard U., 1968. Ford Found. adminstrv. intern, Ctr. Theatre Group of L.A./Mark Taper Forum, 1968-69, subscription mgr., 1970-72, mgr. New Theatre for Now, 1972-75, mng. dir., 1975-85, exec. mng. dir. Ctr. Theatre Group, 1985-88, v.p. Taper Media Enterprises, 1983-87; bus. mgr. Tyrone Guthrie Theatre, Mpls., 1969-70; dir. Am. Arts Alliance, Washington, 1981-87, Theatre Communications Group, 1985-89, chmn. long-range planning com., 1987-89; exec. dir. New Musicals, Inc., 1988-89, N.Y.C. Ballet, 1989—; mem. Lincoln Ctr. Coun., 1989—; cons. NEH, Alaska State Arts Coun., Anchorage, Denver Ctr. for Performing Arts, Bush Found., Mpls.; mem. theatre panel Nat. Endowment for Arts, 1984-86, chmn. 1986; mem. theatre panel Calif. Arts Coun., 1987. Co-producer: (feature film) Zoot Suit, 1980; assoc. producer (broadway play) Children of a Lesser God, 1981 (Tony award 1981). Recipient Alumni Disting. Achievement award Carleton Coll., 1985. Mem. League of Resident Theatres (v.p. 1979-83), Music Ctr. Operating Com. (chmn. 1982-87), Calif. Confedn. Arts (chmn. prominent orgns. com. 1982-83), Calif. Theatre Council (v.p. 1975-77). Democrat. Club: Harvard (N.Y.C.).

WINGER, DEBRA, actress; b. Cleve., May 16, 1955; d. Robert and Ruth W.; m. Timothy Hutton, March 16, 1986 (div.); 1 child, Emanuel Noah; m. Arliss Howard, Nov. 28, 1996; 1 child, Gideon Babe. Student, Calif. State U., Northridge. Made 1st profl. appearance in Wonder Woman TV series, 1976-77; appeared TV film Spl. Olympics, 1977; appeared in films Thank God It's Friday, 1978, French Postcards, 1979, Urban Cowboy, 1980, Cannery Row, 1982, An Officer and a Gentleman, 1982, Terms of Endearment, 1983, Mike's Murder, 1984, Legal Eagles, 1986, Black Widow, 1987, Made in Heaven, 1987, Betrayed, 1988, Everybody Wins, 1990, The Sheltering Sky, 1990, Leap of Faith, 1992, Wilder Napalm, 1992, Shadowlands, 1993 (Academy award nominee, Best Actress, 1993), A Dangerous Woman, 1993, Forget Paris, 1995, In the Wild: Pandas, 1995, Big Bad Love, 2001, Radio, 2003, Eulogy, 2004, (TV films) The Wizard of Oz in Concert: Dreams Come True, 1995; voice: Rumi: Poet of the Heart, 1998. Active Israel Def. Forces, 1972—73. Recipient Female Star of Yr. award, NATO, 1984. Office: care Creative Artists Agency 9830 Wilshire Blvd Beverly Hills CA 90212-1804*

WINGER, DENNIS L., health products executive; BS, Siena Coll.; MBA in Fin. and Mktg., Columbia U. Sr. v.p. fin. and adminstrn., CFO Chiron Corp., 1989-97; sr. v.p., CFO PE Corp., Norwalk, Conn., 1997—. Bd. dirs. Cytomedix, Inc. Office: 50 Danbury Rd Wilton CT 06897-4406

WINGER, ROGER ELSON, retired church administrator; b. Fisherville, Ont., Can., Dec. 25, 1933; s. Elson Clare and Bertha Caroline (Schweyer) W.; m. Della Bertha Lebien, June 7, 1958; children: Jeffrey, Karen Mohr, David, Thomas, Susan. AA, Concordia Jr. Coll., Ft. Wayne, Ind., 1953; BA, Concordia Sem., St. Louis, 1955, theol. diploma, 1958; DD (hon.), Concordia Luth. Sem., Edmonton, Alta., Can., 1991. Ordained to ministry, Luth. Ch., 1958. Pastor Holy Trinity Luth. Ch., London, 1958-64, Good Shepherd Luth. Ch., Coventry, Eng., 1964-69, Luth. Mission, Liverpool, Eng., 1969-72, Faith Luth. Ch., Dunnville, Ont., 1972-78, St. Matthew Luth. Ch., Smithville, Ont., 1972-78, St. Paul's Luth. Ch., Kitchener, Ont., 1978-91; pres. ea. dist. Luth. Ch.-Can., Kitchener, 1991-2000; ret., 2000. V.p. Ont. dist. Luth. Ch.-Can., 1982-88; sec. Luth. Ch.-Can., Winnipeg, Man., 1988-91; mem. bd. regents Concordia Luth. Sem., Edmonton, Alta., 1984-88, Concordia Luth. Sem., St. Catharines Ont., 1991-2000. Lutheran. Avocations: photography, golf, woodworking. Home: 76 Deerwood Crescent Kitchener ON Canada N2N 1R3 E-mail: rogerdella@aol.com.

WINGERT, HANNELORE CHRISTIANE, real estate agent, chemical company executive; b. Karlsbad, Czechoslavakia; came to U.S., 1962, naturalized, 1967; d. Andreas and Gisela Maria (Ciharz) Zwickel; m. Rudolf Wingert, Feb. 9, 1963; children: Angela Helene, Christopher Rudolf. I.BA, Stadt. Berufsschule, Germany, 1961; postgrad. in mgmt., Bergen Community Coll., 1983. Lic. real estate, N.J., Calif. Clk. various cos., N.J., 1963, bilingual sec., 1963-78; exec. sec., adminstrv. asst. Lurgi Corp., Hasbrouck Heights, N.J., 1978-81; sr. exec. sec. Degussa Corp., Teterboro, N.J., 1981-83, asst. product mgr. silica, 1983-85, asst. product mgr. H202, 1985-87, sales promotion coord., 1987; sales assoc. Schlott Realtors, Kinnelon, N.J., 1987-90, Coldwell Banker, 1990—2001, Hanson/McMillin Realty, Escondido, Calif., 2002—. Author real estate newsletter, 1992—, community newsletter, 1977-79. Mem. Garden State Multiple Listing Svc.; chmn. master planning com. High Crest Lake, West Milford, N.J., 1974-75; advisor Jr. Woman's Club Kinnelon-Butler (N.J.), 1973-74; techr. computer classes Bd. Realtors, Passaic County, 1989-92. Mem. Nat. Assn. Realtors, Calif. Assn. Realtors, No. San Diego County Assn. Realtors, NJ, 2002-, Fed. of Woman's Clubs (past pres.), High Crest Lake Woman's Club (pres. 1972-73) (West Milford, NJ). Republican. Roman Catholic. Home: 743 Atwood Pl San Marcos CA 92069 Office Phone: 760-233-5320. E-mail: HCWingert@cox.net.

WINGERTER, JOHN PARKER, artist, photographer; b. N.Y.C., July 27, 1940; s. William and Catherine (Parker) W. Student, Columbia U., 1958-61; LLB, LaSalle U., 1968; postgrad., Arts Student League, 1970-72. Dir. Noho Gallery, N.Y.C., 1982-84. One man shows include Nomo Gallery, 1978-88; exhibitions in group shows at Adelphi U., 1983, LeSalon Des Nations Centre for Contemporary Arts, 1984, Smithtownship Arts Coun. Artist Forum-Mill Pond House, 1996-97, North Shore of L.I. Black Ch., 2000, Town Hall and Huntington Enrichment Ctr., N.Y. Grantee Suffolk County Decentralization, 1999, Spl. Opportunity Stipend grant East End Arts coun., 2000; recipient Proclamation for quality of work Huntington Town Hall. Home: 58 Meadow Glen Rd Northport NY 11768-2711 Studio: Main St Huntington NY 11743-6903

WINGET, LARRY J., SR., automotive industry executive; Chmn., CEO, pres. Venture Global Engring. Industries, Fraser, Mich.; chmn. only, 2003—. Office: Venture Industries 33662 James J Pompo Dr Fraser MI 48026

WINGHAM, ERMA DORIS, secondary school educator; b. Hanover, Ind., Oct. 11, 1913; d. Raymond and Mable Irene (Driggs) Kyle; m. Raymond Wingham, Jan. 9, 1933 (dec. Dec. 1996); children: Barbara, Janet, Kenneth. AB, Hanover Coll., 1959; MA, Ind. U., 1964, cert. lang. arts tchr., 1976. Educator lang. arts, Madison, Ind., 1959-76; instr. fgn. studies, 1966-76; dir., writer h.s., 1959-76. Author: Harvest of a Hundred Years, 1990; (poetry booklets) Theme Songs, 1985, 86, 87; writer, dir. 11 plays including Purple Palace, 2001; author numerous poems. Active voter enrollment Dem. Party, Ind., 1960; mentor Old Town Elem. Sch., 2000-01; chair coun. ministries Meth. Ch., Seminole, Fla. Poetry featured in Best Poetry of 20th Century, Internat. Libr. Poetry. Mem. PEO (v.p. 1996-97), Order of Ea. Star (Worthy Matron lodge 525 1936), Delta Kappa Gamma (pres. 1967-69). Democrat. United Methodist. Avocations: painting, singing, teaching sunday school, gymnastics.

WINGO, ROBERT MATTHEW, chemist, chemical engineer; b. Davis-Monthan AFB, Ariz., Nov. 27, 1967; s. Gerald Vern and Jeanette Marion Wingo; m. Suzette Lene Williams, Apr. 24, 1999; 1 child, Logan Gerald. BA in Chemistry, N.Mex State U., 1996, MS in Chemistry, 1999, PhD in Chemistry, 2003. Undergraduate rsch. asst. dept. chemistry and biochemistry N.Mex State U., Las Cruces, 1992—96, grad. rsch. asst., 1996—99; environ. specialist N.Mex Environment Dept., Dept. of Energy Oversight Bur., Los Alamos, 1999—2000; staff rsch. asst. dngring. scis. divsn., applied engring. technolgies group Los Alamos (N.Mex.) Nat. Lab., 2000—03, postdoctoral rsch. assoc. C divsn., 2003—. Contbr. articles to profl. jours. Coach Las Cruces Youth Baseball League, 1994—95; sci. fair judge Pojaque Sch. Sys., Pojaque, N.Mex. With U.S. Army, 1986—90. Rio Grande Environ. Excellence fellow, Waste Edn., Mgmt. and Rsch. Consortium, 1994—96. Mem.: Internat. Union of Pure and Applied Chemistry, Am. Chem. Soc., Phi Beta Gamma. Republican. Achievements include patents for magnetic process for removing heavy metals from water employing magnetites; potassium ferrate synthesis; development of high gradient magnetic field split flow fractionation; research in low temperature ferrite synthesis; patents pending for magnetophoresis (magnetic chromatography technique for separation of paragmagnetic oxides). Avocations: reading, gardening, canine training and canine rescue corp, orienteering, backpacking. Home: 3293A Walnut St Los Alamos NM 87544 Office: Los Alamos Nat Lab C-ACT Ta-46 Los Alamos NM 87545 Personal E-mail: rowingo@excite.com. E-mail: wingo@lanl.gov.

WINICK, BERNYCE ALPERT, artist, photographer; b. N.Y.C. Student, Bklyn. Mus. Art Sch., 1938—41; BA in Fine Arts and Music, NYU; pvt. studies with, Mario Cooper, N.Y.C., 1969—86; student, Traphagen Sch. Fashion, 1958—61, Art Students League N.Y., 1961—64, Nat. Acad. Design Sch. Fine Arts, 1968—72. Artist, Woodmere, L.I., N.Y., 1969—. Designer, fashion artist, fashion con. in field. One-woman shows include Hewlett-Woodmere Pub. Libr., L.I., 1969, Galerie Internat., N.Y., 1977, Salmagundi Club, Thomas Moran (First prize Nat. Acad. Sch., 1972, Salmagundi Club 1981, 87, 90, Nat. Arts Club, 1985, Nat. Acad. Sch., 1972, First Prize Meml. award 2002), Gallery Internat. 57, N.Y., 1989, Discovery Art Gallery, Sea Cliff, L.I., 1989, 96, 98, Glen Cove, N.Y., 1993-94, Chelsea Ctr., East Norwich, N.Y., 1993, 96, 98, 2000, 2002, Z Gallery, SoHo, N.Y., 1994, County Exec. Bldg., 1997, Fine Arts Mus. L.I., 1997, Town Hall, Hempstead, N.Y., 2000, Winners Exhibn. Nat. Arts Club., N.Y. 2002; exhibited in group shows at Discovery Art Gallery, Glen Cove, N.Y., 1988, 91-93, Nat. Acad. Sch. Fine Arts, N.Y., 1972, Long Beach Mus., L.I., 1979, 81-85, 89 (2d prize 1989), Chen Chung Gallery of St. John's U., N.Y., 1980, Salmagundi Club, N.Y., 1980-81, Am. Watercolor Soc., N.Y., 1982, 85, 88, 92, Fine Arts Mus. L.I., N.Y., 1983, 88-89, 91-92, 96 (2d prize), The Nat. Arts Club, N.Y., 1985-86, 88-89, 2002, Nassau County Mus., L.I., 1985-86, 88, Nat. Assn. Women Artists, N.Y., 1986, 88, 91-93, C.W. Post Coll., L.I., N.Y., (Hon. mention 1985), L.I. Arts Coun. Freeport, 1995-96 (Hon. mention), Chelsea Cultural Ctr., N.Y., 1995, 2001, (Suburban Art League award), Rockville Ctr. Guild for the Arts, N.Y., 1995 (Hon. mention), 97 (Best in Show for photography), Chelsea Ctr. (Peacock Showcase award, First prize 2000), (Merit award 2001), East Norwich, N.Y., Discovery Art Gallery, Glen Cove, N.Y., 1996, 2000, 2002, Fine Arts Mus. L.I., N.Y., 1997, Discovery Art Gallery, Sea Cliff, N.Y., 1998, L.I. Arts Coun. Freeport, N.Y. (Hon. mention 1996, First prize in black and white photography 99), Canton Art Inst. Ohio, Galerie Internat., Gallery Internat. 57, Z Gallery, Salle Augustin-Chenier, Quebec, Can., Town Hall, Town of Hempstead, N.Y., 2000, N.Y. Inst. Tech., Wisser Meml. Libr., 2001, Nat. Arts Club (First photography prize 2002), Heckscher Mus., Huntington, N.Y., 2003 (hon. mention), Salmagundi Club, N.Y., 2002 (Thomas Moran Meml. award, First prize), Mills Pond House, St. James, N.Y., 2002 (hon. mention), Nat. Arts Club, N.Y., 2001 (First prize), others; work included in U.S. Dept. State Art in Embassies program, many pvt. and corp. collections; invitationals include Chelsea Cultural Ctr., L.I.; photographs in numerous publications including South Shore Record, 1995, The Encyclopedia of Watercolour Landscape Techniques, 1996, Popular Photography, 1996, 97, 99, 2000, 04, Photography on America Online, 1997, 99, 2000, New York: Sterling Publishing Co., Inc., 1998, Watercolor Planning and Painting, 1998, Abstracts in Watercolor, 1996, New York Times, 1999, 2001; photography in (books) Capturing the Seen and Unseen in Photographs, 2001, Thirty Nine Musical Photographs, 2003, Town and Country Mag.; photographs exhibited in Mill Pond House, Salmagundi Club, NYU, Nat. Assn. Women Artists, and Artists Unlimited, Tampa, Fla. (various photography awards). Fellow Royal Soc. Encouragment Arts Manufactures and Commerce (London); mem. Am. Watercolor Soc., Nat. Assn. Women Artists, Discovery Gallery, Tri County Artists, Long Beach Art League, Nat. Arts Club. Avocation: pianist. Home and Office: 923 Beth Ln Woodmere NY 11598-1507

WINICK, MYRON, educator, physician; b. N.Y.C., May 4, 1929; s. Charles B. and Ruth E. (Gesser) W.; m. Elaine L. Lasky, Sept. 19, 1964; children: Jonathan, Stephen. AB, Columbia U., 1951; MS, U. Ill., 1952; MD, SUNY, 1956. Intern U. Pa., Phila., 1956-57; asst. resident pediatrics Cornell U. Med. Coll., N.Y.C., 1957-59, chief resident, 1959-60; attending pediatrician Stanford U. Hosp., 1963-64; asst. prof. pediatrics Cornell U. Med. Coll., N.Y.C., 1964-68, assoc. prof. pediatrics and nutrition, 1968-70, prof., 1970-71; dir. Inst. Human Nutrition Columbia U. Inst. Human Nutrition, 1972-87, prof. pediatrics, 1972-89, R.R. Williams prof. nutrition, 1973-89, R.R. Williams prof. emeritus, 1990—; pres. U. Health Scis./Chgo. Med. Sch., North Chgo., Ill., 1990-93; dir. Ctr. for Nutrition, Genetics and Human Devel., 1975-87. Vis. prof. pediatrics U. Chile, Santiago, 1967; asst. attending pediatrician N.Y. Hosp., N.Y.C., 1964-68, assoc. attending pediatrician, 1968-70, attending pediatrician, 1970-71; attending pediatrician Presbyn. Hosp., N.Y.C., 1972-89; cons. Pan Am. Health Orgn., 1966—; med. dir. Weight Watchers Internat., 1997—; sr. scientist Am. Health Found., 1999—. Author: Malnutrition and Brain Development, 1976; textbook Nutrition in Health and Disease, 1980; Growing Up Healthy; A Parent's Guide to Good Nutrition, 1982; For Mothers and Daughters: A Guide to Good Nutrition for Women, 1983; Your Personalized Health Profile: Choosing the Diet That's Right for You, 1985; Nutrition, Pregnancy and Early Infancy, 1989; The Fiber Prescription, 1992; editor: textbook Current Concepts in Nutrition, 1972—, Nutrition: Pre- and Postnatal Development, Vol. I, Human Nutrition: A Comprehensive Treatise, 1979, Columbia Ency. of Nutrition, 1988; contbg. editor Nutrition Revs., 1969-76; mem. editorial bd. Jour. Nutrition, 1972-76, 82-86, The Year in Metabolism (now Contemporary Metabolism), 1975—; assoc. editor Growth, 1984—; nutrition editor Cancer Prevention, 1994—. Trustee Found. for Internat. Child Health; mem. nutrition interdisciplinary cluster Pres.' Biomed. Research Panel, 1975; mem. panel on infants and children Pres.' Commn. on Mental Health, 1977; cons. Office of Tech. Assessment, U.S. Congress, 1976-78; mem. Food and Nutrition Bd. NRC, 1982-88. With USNR, 1960-62. Bank of Am.-Gianini Found. fellow Stanford, 1962; NIH Spl. fellow, 1963; recipient NIH Career Devel. award, 1968-71; E. Mead Johnson award pediatric research, 1970; Osborne and Mendel award Am. Inst. Nutrition, 1976; Agnes Higgins award March of Dimes Found., 1983 Fellow Royal Soc. Health, Am. Soc. Nutritional Scis., Am. Acad. Pediatrics; mem. AAAS, Am. Soc. Cell Biology, Soc. Developmental Biology, Harvey Soc., Soc. Pediatric Research, Royal Soc. Medicine, Brit. Nutrition Soc., Am. Inst. Nutrition, Am. Soc. Clin. Nutrition, N.Y. Acad. Scis., N.Y. Acad. Medicine, (cons.), Soc. for Exptl. Biology and Medicine, Soc. for Neurosci., Internat. Soc. for Devel. Neurosci., Cosmos Club. Home: 165 West End Ave Apt 10K New York NY 10023 Office: Inst for Cancer Prevention 390 Fifth Ave New York NY 10018

WINICOV, ILGA BUTELIS, biochemist, educator; b. Riga, Latvia, May 16, 1935; d. Arturs and Zenta (Gutmanis) Butelis; m. Herbert B. Winicov, Aug. 30, 1958 (div. 1979); children: Eric, Mark; m. Rodney E. Harrington, Jan. 26, 1979. AB, U. Pa., 1956, PhD, 1971; MS, U. Wis., 1958. Postdoctoral fellow Inst. Cancer Rsch., Phila., 1972-74, rsch. assoc., 1974-76; rsch. asst. prof. biochemistry Fels Rsch. Inst., Temple U., Phila., 1976-78; asst. prof. U. Nev. Sch. Medicine, Reno, 1979-85, assoc. prof., 1985-95, assoc. prof. microbiology, 1987-95, prof. biochemistry and microbiology, 1995-99; rsch. prof. plant biology Ariz. State U., Tempe, 1999—. Cons. biochemistry nucleic acids and molecular biology and plant biotechnology. Contbr. articles to profl. jours. Fellow: AAAS; mem.: Am. Soc. Plant Biologists, Internat. Soc. Plant Molecular Biology, Am. Assn. Cancer Rsch., Am. Soc. Microbiology, Am. Soc. Biol. Chemists. Office: Ariz Sate U Plant Biology Tempe AZ 85257-1601 Business E-Mail: winicov@asu.edu.

WINIK, JAY B. writer, political scientist, consultant; b. New Haven, Feb. 8, 1957; s. Herbert Edward Winik and Marilyn Joan (Fishman) Abrams; m. Lyric Wallwork, Nov. 17, 1991. BA in Psychology cum laude, Yale U., 1980, PhD in Polit. Sci., 1993; MS in Internat. Rels. with distinction, London Sch. Econs., 1981. Arms control cons. Rand Corp., Santa Monica, Calif., 1983; chief speechwriter Ambassador Benjamin Netanyahu, N.Y.C., 1984; sr. profl. staff mem. House Com. on Armed Svcs., Washington, 1985-88; vis. fellow Ctr. for Strategic and Internat. Studies, Washington, 1988; dep. exec. dir. Def. Sec.'s Commn. on Base Realignment and Closure, Washington, 1988; legis. asst. for def. and fgn. policy Office of Sen. Charls S. Robb & Senate Com. on Fgn. Rels., Washington, 1989-91; sr. fellow Sch. Pub. Affairs U. Md., College Park, 1991—; sr. fellow Hudson Inst., 2000—. Advisor to Sec. Defense, 1993; prin. advisor for def. and fgn. policy, 1986 policy commn. Dem. Nat. Com.; assoc. staff mem. select com to investigate covert arms transactions with Iran, 1987. Author: On the Brink, 1996, April 1865: The Month That Saved America, 2001 (New York Times bestseller); editl. contbr. Wall Street Jour., N.Y. Times, Washington Post, The Washingtonian, others pubs., 1981—. Grantee U.S. Inst. Peace, 1987; fellow Bradley Found. Fellow Ctr. for Strategic and Internat. Studies (adj.); mem. Coun. on Fgn. Rels. Jewish. Avocation: tennis. Home: 30 Grafton St Chevy Chase MD 20815-3428 Office: U Md CISSM Sch Pub Affairs College Park MD 20740

WINIK, JOANNE, broadcast executive; BA, Racine Coll. Pres., gen. mgr. KLRN-TV, San Antonio, 1988—. Board of directors PBS, 1999—. Office: KLRN-TV PO Box 9 San Antonio TX 78291-0009

WINJUM, STEPHEN J. medical association administrator; b. Long Beach, Calif., 1963; BSBA cum laude in Acctg., Creighton U., 1985; JD cum laude, U. Notre Dame, 1988. Atty. Latham & Watkins, Katten Muchin Zavis Rosenman; prin., owner Chgo., 1990—94; founder NovaMed Eyecare Inc., Chgo., 1995—, pres., 1995—, CEO, 1995—, chmn. bd. Office: Novamed Eyecare Inc 3034 West Peterson Ave Chicago IL 60659*

WINKEL, R. DENNIS, family practice physician; b. Des Moines, Aug. 10, 1948; s. Don and Evelyn W.; m. M. Patricia Stewart, Sept. 1, 1973; children: Todd, Kevin. BA, U. Colo., 1970; MD, Creighton U. Sch. Medicine, 1974. Diplomate Am. Bd. Family Practice. Resident Creighton U. Dept. Family Practice, Omaha, 1974-77; pvt. practice Kalispell, Mont., 1977—; chief staff Kalispell Regional Hosp., 1993. Named Physician of Yr., Consumers Rsch. Coun. Am., 2003. Mem. Mont. Med. Soc., Flathead Med. Soc. (pres. 1991-93), Kalispell Daybreak Rotary (bd. dirs. 2001—). Avocations: white-water rafting, downhill skiing, golf, tennis. Office: 1250 Burns Way Ste 1 Kalispell MT 59901-3140

WINKEL, RAYMOND NORMAN, aerospace industry consultant, avionics manufacturing executive, retired naval officer; b. Flint, Mich., Dec. 8, 1928; s. Norman Martin and Evelyn Matilda (Hylen) W.; m. Ellen Stefula, Dec. 29, 1955; children: Raymond Norman, Ann, Maryellen. BS, U.S. Naval Postgrad. Sch., Monterey, Calif., 1964; MS, Villanova (Pa.) U., 1967; grad. advanced mgmt. program, Harvard U., 1973. Enlisted in USN, 1948, commd. ensign, designated naval aviator, 1951, advanced through grades to rear adm., 1979; service in Far East; comdg. officer Naval Electronics Systems Test and Evaluation Facility, 1969-71; dir. avionics U.S. Navy, 1973-76; project mgr. Navy/Marine Corps heavy lift helicopter, 1976-78; gen. mgr. Navy/industry team to develop new ship/aircraft weapon system for anti-submarine warfare LAMPS Mark III, 1978-81; ret. USN, 1981; v.p. Washington ops. Telephonics Corp., Huntington, N.Y., 1981-82; v.p. programs and contracts Astronautics Corp. Am., Milw., 1982-94; aerospace industry cons. Heathsville, Va., 1994-95. Decorated Legion of Merit, Air medal, Navy Achievement medal. Mem. Exptl. Aircraft Assn., U.S. Naval Inst., Assn. Naval Aviation, Mil. Officers Assn. Am., Kiwanis, Indian Creek Yacht and Country Club, U.S. Power Squadron. Republican. Roman Catholic. Home: 1860 Island Point Rd Heathsville VA 22473-3729 E-mail: rwinkel@crosslink.net.

WINKELNKEMPER, HORST ELMAR, mathematician, educator; b. Cologne, Germany, Sept. 20, 1940; s. Anton Winkelnkemper and Anna-Margot Vera Loewenberg. PhD, Princeton U., N.J., 1971. Vis. mem. Inst. for Advanced Study, Princeton, NJ, 1971—73; prof. U. Md., Coll. Pk., 1973—. Contbr. scientific papers to profl. jours. Mem. senate U. Md., Coll. Pk., 1995—2003. Grantee, NSF, 1972—82. Mem.: Am. Math. Soc.

WINKELSTEIN, WARREN, JR., physician, educator; b. Syracuse, N.Y., July 1, 1922; s. Warren and Evelyn (Neiman) W.; children: Rebecca Winkelstein Yamin, Joshua, Shoshana; m. Veva Kerrigan, Feb. 14, 1976. BA, U. N.C., 1942; MD cum laude, Syracuse U., 1947; MPH, Columbia U., 1950. Diplomate Am. Bd. Preventive Medicine. Intern Charity Hosp., New Orleans, 1947-48; with ICA (Vietnam), 1951-53; from dir. div. communicable disease control to 1st dep. comdr. local, environ. health svcs. Erie County Health Dept., 1953-62; from assoc. prof. to prof. SUNY, Buffalo, 1962-68; prof. epidemiology, dean pub. health U. Calif., Berkeley, 1972-96, prof. emeritus, 1996. Dir. Internat. Environ. Epidemiology Inst., 1997. Author: Basic Readings in Epidemiology, 1972; contbr. articles profl. jours. With AUS, 1944-46. Mem. APHA, AAAS, Internat. Am. Epidemiol. Socs., Am. Heart Assn. Address: Dept Epidemiol Univ Calif Sch Pub Health Berkeley CA 94720-7360

WINKENWERDER, WILLIAM, JR., federal agency administrator; b. Apr. 27, 1954; BS, Davidson Coll., 1976; MD, U. N.C., 1981; MBA, U. Pa., 1986; postgrad., Stanford U., 1991. Resident internal medicine N.C. Meml. Hosp. U. N.C., 1981-84; instr. dept. medicine Sch. Medicine U. Pa., 1984-87; spl. asst. to adminstr. Health Care Financing Adminstrn. U.S. Dept. Health and Human Svcs., 1987-88; dir. quality assurance and utilization mgmt. Southeast Permanente Med. Group, Kaiser Permanente, Atlanta, 1988-90, assoc. med. dir., 1990-92; v.p. CMO so. ops. Prudential Health Care, Atlanta, 1992-95; v.p. primary care svcs. Emory Health Care, Atlanta, 1996-98; assoc. v.p. health affairs Robert Woodruff Health Scis. Ctr. Emory U., 1996-98; exec. v.p. health care svcs., vice chmn. Blue Cross Blue Shield Mass., Boston, 1998—; asst. secy. hlth. affairs U.S. Dept. Defense, Washington, 2001—. Mem. exec. com. Emory Healthcare, Emory Clinic, 1996-98; chmn. CMO com. Prudential Healthcare, 1992-95; bd. dirs. Care Sci. Corp., Wharton Sch. Bus. Health Care Alumni, Fed. Employees Program-Blue Cross Blue Shield Assn., The Reed and Barton Co.; founder HCFA Effectiveness Initiative, U.S. Dept. Health and Human Svcs., participant Task Forces on Health and Human Svcs. AIDS and Minority Health, 1987-88, U.S. Pub. Health Risk Assessment and Quality Assurance, Sec.'s Minority Health, Sec.'s Catastophic Illness; rep. Prudential on Med. Dirs. Com. on Group Health Assn. Am.; spkr. in field. Contbr. articles to profl. pubs. Kaiser Family Found. fellow, 1984-86, 87-88, Kellogg Pub. Health Policy fellow U. Pa., 1986, Wharton Washington fellow U. Pa., 1986. Mem. AMA, Am. Coll. Physicians, Am. Coll. Physician Execs., Am. Assn. Health Plans (bd. dirs.), Health Care Forum's Physican Leader Network, Davidson Coll. Alumni Assn. Office: US Dept Defense Hlth Affairs 1200 Defense Pentagon Washington DC 20301-1200

WINKER, MARGARET A. editor; MD, U. Ill. Resident in internal medicine U. Chgo., fellowship in geriatric medicine; clin. asst. prof. geriatrics sect. U. Ill. Med. Ctr.; sr. editor Jour. of AMA. Contbr. articles to profl. jours. Mem. Am. Geriatrics Soc. (chair pub. edn. com. 1997). Office: U Chgo Graham Sch Gen Studies 5835 S Kimbark Ave Chicago IL 60637-1635 Fax: 773-702-6814.

WINKLE, C. CHRISTIAN, health facility administrator; Various positions Integrated Health Svcs., 1991-99; exec. v.p. Mariner Post-Acute Network, Inc., Atlanta, 1999-2000, CEO, 2000—. Office: 1 Ravinia Dr Atlanta GA 30346

WINKLEBACK, ARTHUR, food products executive; BA in Bus. and Econs., UCLA; MBA, U. Pa. Exec. v.p., CFO C. Dean Metropoulos & Co., 1998—99; acting COO Perform.com, 1999—2001; CEO Freeride.com at Indigo Capital, 1999—2001; exec. v.p., CFO H.J. Heinz Co., Pitts., 2002—. Office: HJ Heinz Co 600 Grant St Pittsburgh PA 15219

WINKLEBY, MARILYN A. medical researcher; BA in Social Sci., Calif. State U., Sacramento, 1968, MA in. Clin. Psychology, 1974; MPH in Epidemiology/Biostat, U. Calif., Berkeley, 1983, PhD in Epidemiology, 1986. Project dir. cervical cancer screening study UCLA Sch. Pub. Health, 1974-77; co-prin. investigator Calif. Ctr. Sudden Infant Death Syndrome Risk Factor Study, Sch. Medicine, Dept. Cmty. Health U. Calif., Davis, 1977-81, co-investigator cmty. cardiovascular surveillance program, adj. lectr. Sch. Medicine, Dept. Cmty. Health, 1981-82, project coord. epidemiology unit, stress and hypertension study Dept. Epidemiology Berkeley, 1983-87, rsch. epidemiologist Dept. Behavioral and Devel. Pediat. San Francisco, 1986-91; sr. rsch. scientist/prin. investigator Stanford Ctr. Rsch. in Disease Prevention, Stanford U. Sch. of Medicine, Palo Alto, Calif., 1987—. Epidemiology cons. SIDS Info. and Counseling Project, Dept. Health, State of Calif., Berkeley, 1980-83; founder, dir. Stanford Med. Youth Sci. Program, 1988—; lectr. divsn. health rsch. and policy, dept. medicine Stanford U., 1989—. Contbr. articles to profl. jours. Bd. dirs. Loaves and Fishes Family Kitchen, San Jose, Calif., 1988-92, Mountain View Cmty. Health Clinic, 1992-95. Fellow Am. Heart Assn. (coun. epidemiology 1989, Established Investigator award 1996). Office: Stanford Ctr Rsch in Disease Prevention 1000 Welch Rd Ste 302 Palo Alto CA 94304-1808

WINKLER, AGNIESZKA M. marketing and software executive; b. Rome, Feb. 22, 1946; came to U.S., 1953; naturalized, 1959; d. Wojciech A. and Halina Z. (Owsiany) W.; children from previous marriage: Renata G. Ritcheson, Dana C Sworakowski; m. Arthur K. Lund. BA, Coll. Holy Name, 1967; MA, San Jose State U., 1971; MBA, U. Santa Clara, 1981. Tchg. asst. San Jose State U., 1968-70; cons. to Ea. European bus. Palo Alto, Calif., 1970-72; pres./founder Commart Communications, Palo Alto, 1973-84; pres./founder, chmn. bd. Winkler Advt., Santa Clara, Calif., 1984—; chmn. bd. SuperCuts, Inc.; chmn., founder TeamToolz, 2000—04, The Winkler Group, 2004—. Bd. dirs. Reno Air, Lifeguard, Lifeguard Life Ins., IP Locks, C200; exec. com. C200. Author: Warp Speed Branding, 1999. Trustee Santa Clara U., 1991—; trustee O'Connor Found., 1987-93, mem. exec. com., 1988—, mem. Capital Campaign steering com., 1989; mem. nat. adv. bd. Comprehensive Health Enhancement Support System, 1991—; mem. mgmt. west com. A.A.A.A. Agy., 1991—, vice chair no. Calif. coun., 1996—; project dir. Poland Free Enterprise Plan, 1989-92; mem. adv. bd. Normandy France Bus. Devel., 1989-92; mem. bd. regents Holy Names Coll., 1987—; bd. dirs. San Jose Mus. Art, 1987; mem. San Jose Symphony, Gold Baton, 1986; mem. nat. adv. com. Chess, 1991—; dir. Bay Area Coun., 1994—. Recipient CLIO award in Advt., Addy award and numerous others; named to 100 Best Women in Advt., Ad Age, 1988, Best Woman in Advt., AdWeek and McCall's Mag., 1993, one of 100 Best and Brightest Women in Mktg. & Advt., Nat. Assn. Women Bus. Owners, 1996. Mem. Family Svc. Assn. (trustee 1980-82), Am. Assn. Advt. Agys. (agy. mgmt. west com. 1991), Bus. Profl. Advt. Assn., Polish Am. Congress, San Jose Advt. Club, San Francisco Ad Club, Beta Gamma Sigma (hon.), Pi Gamma Mu, Pi Delta Phi (Lester-Tinneman award 1966, Bill Raskob Found. grantee 1965). Office: The Winkler Group 633 Post # 515 San Francisco CA 94109

WINKLER, CHARLES HOWARD, investment company executive; b. NYC, Aug. 4, 1954; s. Joseph Conrad and Geraldine Miriam (Borok) W.; m. Joni S. Taylor, Aug. 28, 1993. BBA with highest distinction, Emory U., 1976; JD, Northwestern U., 1979. Bar: Ill. 1979, U.S. Dist. Ct (no. dist.) Ill. 1979. Assoc. Levenfeld & Kanter, Chgo., 1979-80, Kanter & Eisenberg, Chgo., 1980-84, ptnr., 1985-86, Neal Gerber & Eisenberg, Chgo., 1986-96; sr. mng. dir., COO Citadel Investment Group, LLC, Chgo., 1996—2001; sr. mng. dir. Citadel Trading Group, Chgo., 1996—2000, Aragon Investments Ltd., Chgo., 1996—2000. Bd. dirs. Kensington Global Strategies Fund, Ltd., Antaeus Internat. Investments, Ltd., Jackson Investment Fund Ltd., Citadel Investment Group (Europe) Ltd., chief oper. officer, and sr. mng. dir. Amaranth Advisors, LLC, 2001—.; hedge fund mgr. Author: (with others) Basic Tax Shelters, 1982, Limited Liability Companies: The Entity of Choice, 1995; mng. editor Northwestern Jour. Internat. Law and Bus., 1979. Mem. ABA (mem. sect. on taxation), Beta Gamma Sigma. Home: 10 Taconic Rd Greenwich CT 06830-3428 Office: Amaranth Advisors LLC One American Ln Greenwich CT 06831 Business E-Mail: cwinkler@amaranthllc.com.

WINKLER, CHERYL J. state legislator; m. Ralph Winkler; children: Robert C., Ralph E. Student, U. Cin. Clk. Green Twp., 1984-85, trustee, 1986-90; former rep. Ohio State Ho. Reps. Dist. 20; rep. Ohio State Ho. Reps. Dist. 34, 1993—, mem. interstate coop. com., children and youth com., mem. reference, edn. and state govt. com., mem. select com. on tech., mem. joint com. on juvenile corrections & overcrowding. Mem. Cin. Bar Assn. Aux., Green Twp. and Bridgetown Civic Clubs, Western Hamilton County Econ. Coun. Home: 5355 Boomer Rd Cincinnati OH 45247-7926 Office: Ohio Ho of Reps State House Columbus OH 43215

WINKLER, DANA JOHN, lawyer; b. Wichita, Kans., Jan. 2, 1944; s. Donald Emil and Hazel Claire (Schmitter) W.; m. Mary Ann Seiwert, Oct. 14, 1967; 1 child, Jonathan. BA, Wichita State U., 1967; JD, Washburn Law Sch., 1971. Staff writer Wichita (Kans.) Eagle & Beacon, 1961-67; ptnr. Davis, Bruce, Davis & Winkler, Wichita, 1972-77; asst. city atty. City of Wichita, 1977-99; dir. Wichita Mcpl. Fed. Credit Union, 1980—, pres., 1982, 99-2000, sec.-treas., 1994-98, v.p., 1998-99. Dir. Deaf and Hard of Hearing Counseling Svc., 1979-80. Vol. Sedgwick County United Way, Wichita, 1973-74; vice-chmn. Wichita Pub. Schs. Spl. Edn. Adv. Coun., 1987-89. 1st lt. U.S. Army, 1967-69. Mem. Kans. Bar Assn., Wichita Bar Assn. Republican. Roman Catholic. Home and Office: 1621 Harlan St Wichita KS 67212-1842 Office Phone: 316-619-3395. E-mail: djwinkler@aol.com.

WINKLER, DOLORES EUGENIA, retired health facility administrator; b. Milw., Aug. 10, 1929; d. Charles Peter and Eugenia Anne (Zamka) Kowalski; m. Donald James Winkler, Aug. 18, 1951; 1 child, David John. Grad., Milw. Bus. Inst., 1949. Acct. Curative Rehab. Ctr., Milw., 1949-60; staff acct. West Allis (Wis.) Meml. Hosp., 1968-70, chief acct., 1970-78, reimbursement analyst, 1978-85, dir. budgets and reimbursement, 1985-95; ret., 1995. Mem. adv. coun., fin. com. Tau Home Health Care Agy., Milw., 1981—83. Mem.: Inst. Mgmt. Accts. (pres. 1983—84, nat. dir. 1986—88, pres. Mid Am. Regional Coun. 1988—89, award of excellence 1989), Healthcare Fin. Mgmt. Assn. (pres. 1989—90, Follmer Bronze award 1980, Reeves Silver award 1986, Muncie Gold award 1989, medal of honor 1993), Beta Chi Rho (pres. 1948). Avocations: travel, photography, golf. Home: 12805 W Honey Ln New Berlin WI 53151-2652

WINKLER, GAIL CASKEY, design historian, writer, educator; b. Chgo., Aug. 5, 1942; d. Robert E. and Ethel (Barquist) Caskey; m. Robert H. Winkler, Jan. 22, 1964 (div. 1976); m. Roger W. Moss, July 19, 1981. BA, Beloit (Wis.) Coll., 1964; MA, U. Wis., 1971, MS, 1977, PhD, 1988. Instr. U. Wis., Madison, 1976-81; sr. ptnr. LCA Assocs., Phila., 1982—; adj. faculty U. Pa., Phila., 1986—; asst. prof. U. Del., 1991-93. Author: Victorian Interior Decoration, 1986, Victorian Exterior Decoration, 1987, Floor Coverings for Historic Buildings, 1988, The Well-Appointed Bath, 1989, An Analysis of Drapery, 1993; (museum installations include), William Conner House, Conner Prairie, Fishers, Ind., Lanier Mansion, Madison, Ind., Tudor Hall in Pamplin Park, Petersburg, Va., Fairlawn Mansion, Superior, Wis., Adams House Mus., Deadwood, S.D., Villa Louis, Prairie du Chien, Wis., Hixon House, LaCrosse, Wis., Campbell House Mus., St. Louis, Dr. Richard Eells House, Quincy, Ill., (projects include) studies of the historic finishes and furnishings of the U.S. Senate and House, Chambers, Va. State Capitol, Richmond, City Hall, Phila., Capitol of the Commonwealth Pa., Rutherford B. Hayes house, Fremont, Ohio, Buchanan house, U.S. Naval Acad., Anderson Cottage (summer White House Abraham Lincoln), Washington, D.C., Wright Bros.' Printing Shop, Dayton, Ohio, Capitol of State of Va. Fellow Am. Soc. Interior Designers (bd. dirs. Pa. East chap. 1983-88, 2001—, Athena award 1989, Medallist award 1995), Found. Interior Design Edn. and Rsch. (rsch. com. 1986-96). Office: 604 S Washington Sq Philadelphia PA 19106-4118 Office Phone: 215-925-8367.

WINKLER, HENRY FRANKLIN, actor; b. N.Y.C., Oct. 30, 1945; s. Harry Irving and Ilse Anna Maria (Hadra) W.; m. Stacey Weitzman, May 5, 1978; children: Zoe Emily, Max Daniel. BA, Emerson Coll., 1967, PhD, 1978; MA, Yale Sch. Drama, 1970. With Yale Repertory Theatre, 1970-71. Founder New Haven Free Theatre, 1968, Off The Wall N.Y., improvisation co., 1972; tchr. drama UCLA Adult Extension. Off-Broadway shows, 1972-73, Cin. Playhouse, 1973; films include The Lords of Flatbush, 1972, Crazy Joe, 1974, Heroes, 1977, The One and Only, 1977, Night Shift, 1983, Wes Craven's Scream, 1996, P.U.N.K.S., 1998, Ground Control, 1998, The Water Boy, 1998, Ugly Naked People, 1999, Dill Scallion, 1999, Down to You, 2000, I Shaved My Legs for This, 2001, Holes, 2003; starred in TV series Happy Days, 1973-84, Monty, 1994, Mr. Sunshine, (voice) Clifford's Puppy Days, 2003; appeared in TV movie An American Christmas Carol, 1979 (ABC), Absolute Strangers, 1991 (CBS), The Only Way Out, 1994 (ABC), Truman Capote's One Christmas, 1994 (NBC), A Child is Missing, 1995 (CBS), Dad's Week Off, 1996 (Showtime), National Lampoon's Dad's Week Off, 1997, Detention: The Siege at Johnson High, 1997; TV guest appearances include (voice) South Park, 1998, The Practice, 1999, 2000, (voice) The Simpsons, 1999, The Drew Carey Show, 2001, Law & Order: Special Victims Unit, 2002, Arrested Development, 2003, 04, Third Watch, 2004; prodr. Sightings; exec. producer TV program Who Are the Debolts and Where Did They Get Nineteen Kids, TV series for ABC Ryan's Four, 1983, TV movie Scandal Sheet, 1984, MacGyver, 1985, producer, host home video Strong Kids, Safe Kids, 1985, PBS animated spl. Happy Ever After, 1985, Two Daddies to Love Me, 1988; producer ABC After Sch. Spl. Losing a Sister, 1988; pres. Fair Dinkum Prodns., Hollywood, Calif., 1979—, Winkler-Daniels Prodns., Hollywood, 1987-91; producer TV program Run, Don't Walk for own co. JZM Prodns., 1981; dir. TV movie A Smokey Mountain Christmas, 1986, feature film Memories of Me, 1988, Cop and a Half, 1992; dir., prodr. Dead Man's Gun, 1999; prodr. So Weird, 1999; dir. Sabrina, the Teenage Witch, 1996. Named Best Actor in Comedy Series, Photoplay mag. 1976-77, recipient Golden Globe award 1976, 77, 78; named King of Baccus, Mardi Gras, New Orleans 1977, Emmy nominee 1975, 76, 77; recipient Golden Plate award Am. Acad. Achievement 1980, Daytime Emmy nomination best dir. All The Kids Do It, produced for JZM Prodns., 1985; Sorrisi e Canzoni Telegatto award (Italian TV award) 1980; nat. spokesperson United Friends of the Children, 1982—. Recipient Humanitarian award Women in Film, 1988; named hon. youth chmn. Epilepsy Found.; chmn. Toys for Tots, 1977. Mem. AFTRA, Screen Actors Guild, Actors Equity. Office: c/o Metro-Goldwyn-Mayer Ste E5018 2500 Broadway Santa Monica CA 90404 Address: Evan Tripoli Internat Creative Mgmt 8942 Wilshire Blvd Beverly Hills CA 90211*

WINKLER, HENRY RALPH, retired academic administrator, historian; b. Waterbury, Conn., Oct. 27, 1916; s. Jacob and Ethel (Rieger) W.; m. Clare Sapadin, Aug. 18, 1940; children— Allan Michael, Karen Jean; m. Beatrice Ross, Jan. 28, 1973. AB, U. Cin., 1938, MA, 1940; PhD, U. Chgo., 1947; hon. degrees, Lehigh U., 1974, Rutgers U., 1977, No. Ky. U., 1978, St. Thomas Inst., 1979, Hebrew Union Coll., 1980, Xavier U., 1981, U. Akron, 1984, U. Cin., 1987, Thomas More Coll., 1989. Instr. U. Cin., 1939-40; asst. prof. Roosevelt Coll., 1946-47; mem. faculty Rutgers U., 1947-77, prof. history, 1958-77, chmn. dept., 1960-64; dean Faculty Liberal Arts, 1967, vice provost, 1968-70, acting provost, 1970, v.p. for acad. affairs, 1970-72, sr. v.p. for acad. affairs, 1972-76, exec. v.p., 1976-77, U. Cin., 1977, pres., 1977-84, pres. emeritus, 1984—, Univ. prof. history, 1977-86, prof. emeritus, 1986—. Mng. editor Am. Hist. Rev., 1964-68; vis. prof. Bryn Mawr Coll., 1959-60, Harvard, summer 1964, Columbia, summer 1967; faculty John Hay Fellows Inst. Humanities, 1960-65; bd. overseers Hebrew Union Coll., 1984—. Author: The League of Nations Movement in Great Britain, 1914-19, 1952, Great Britain in the Twentieth Century, 1960, 2d edit., 1966; editor: (with K.M. Setton) Great Problems in European Civilization, 1954, 2d edit., 1966, Twentieth-Century Britain, 1977, Paths Not Taken: British Labour and International Policy in the Nineteen Twenties, 1994, British Labour Seeks a Foreign Policy, 2004; mem. editorial bd. Historian, 1958-64, Liberal Edn., 1986—; mem. adv. bd. Partisan Rev., 1972-79; contbr. articles to jours., revs. Nat. chmn. European history advanced placement com. Coll. Entrance Exam. Bd., 1960-64; mem. Nat. Commn. on Humanities in Schs., 1967-68, Am. specialist Eastern Asia, 1968; exec. com. Conf. on Brit. Studies, 1968-75; chmn. bd. Nat. Humanities Faculty, 1970-73; chmn. adv. com. on history Coll. Entrance Exam. Bd., 1977-80; mem. council on acad. affairs, mem. bd. trustees, chmn., 1982-84; pres. Highland Park (N.J.) Bd. Edn., 1962-63; mem. exec. com. Nat. Assn. State Univs. and Land-Grant Colls., 1978-81, mem. Cin. Lit. Club, 1978—, pres., 1993—; bd. dirs. Am. Council on Edn., 1979-81; trustee Seasongood Good Govt. Found., 1979—, pres., 1991-93; trustee Thomas More Coll., 1986-93; mem. Ohio Indsl. Tech. and Enterprise Bd., 1983-89; bd. dirs. Nat. Civic League, 1986—, Planning Accreditation Bd., 1988—; mem. adv coun. U. Va.'s Coll at Wise, Ohio Humanities Coun., 1994— With USNR, 1943-46. Recipient Lifetime Achievement award N.Am. Conf. on Brit. Studies, 1995, Bishop William Hughes award for disting. svc. to Cath. higher edn. Thomas More Coll., 1997, Leadership Medallion, Xavier U., 2003. Mem. Am. Hist. Assn., Phi Beta Kappa, Tau Kappa Alpha, Phi Alpha Theta. Clubs: Comml., Bankers, Cin., Lit. Office: U Cin 571 Langsam Library Cincinnati OH 45221-0001 E-mail: Henry.Winkler@uc.edu.

WINKLER, HOWARD LESLIE, business, finance, government relations consultant; b. N.Y.C., Aug. 16, 1950; s. Martin and Magda (Stark) W.; m. Robin Lynn Richards, Sept. 12, 1976; 1 child, David Menachem. AA in Mktg., Los Angeles City Coll., 1973, AA in Bus. Data Processing, 1977, AA in Bus. Mgmt., 1981. Sr. cons. Fin. Cons. Inc., Los Angeles, 1972-81; asst. v.p. Merrill Lynch, Inc., Los Angeles, 1981-83; v.p. Drexel, Burnham, Lambert, Inc., Beverly Hills, Calif., 1983-84; pres. Howard Winkler Investments, Beverly Hills, Calif., 1984-90, Landmark Fin. Group, L.A., 1990-96. Ptnr. N.W.B. Assocs., L.A., 1988-91; chm. bd. United Cmty. and Housing Devel. Corp., L.A., 1986-96; bd. mem./sec. United Housing & Cmty. Svcs. Corp., 1995-97; bd. dirs. Earth Products Internat., Inc., Kansas City, Kans., 1992, Fed. Home Loan Bank of San Francisco, 1991-93. Nat. polit. editor B'nai B'rith Messenger, 1986-95. Mem. Calif. Rep. Cent. Com., 1985-93; mem. L.A. County Rep. Cent. Com., 1985-92, chmn. 45th Assembly Dist., 1985-90; mem. Rep. Senatorial Inner Circle, 1986—, Rep. Presdl. Task Force, 1985— (Legion of Merit award 1992); mem. Rep. Eagles, 1988-92; Nat. Rep. Senatorial Com., 1986—, Golden Circle Calif., 1986-92, GOP Platform Planning Com. at Large del., 1992, 96; del. to GOP nat conv., Houston, 1992, San Diego, 1996; Calif. chmn. Jack Kemp for Pres., 1988, mem. nat. steering com. Bush-Quayle '88, 1987, nat. exec. com. Bush-Quayle '92, 1991; mil. adminstrv. supr. CID US Army, 1969-72, SE Asia; legis. and civic action Agudath Israel Calif., 1985—; mem. L.A. County Narcotics and Dangerous Drugs Commn., 1988—, L.A. County Drug Ct. Planning Com., 1996—; trustee, sec.-treas. Minority Health Professions Edn. Found., 1989-94; program chmn. Calif. Lincoln Clubs Polit. Action Com., 1987-88; state co-chmn. Pete Wilson for Gov. Campaign, 1989, John Seymour for Lt. Gov. Campaign, 1989-90; chpt. pres. Calif. Congress of Reps., 1989-93; chmn. Claude Parrish for Bd. of Equalization, 1989-90; founder, dir. Community Rsch. & Info. Ctr., 1986—; mem. fin. com. John Seymour for Senate '92, 1991. Decorated Legion of Merit; recipient Cmty. Svc. award Agudath Israel Calif., 1986, Pres.'s Cmty. Leadership award, 1986, Disting. Cmty. Svc. U.S. Senator Pete Wilson, 1986, Calif. Gov.'s Leadership award, 1986, Cmty. Svc. award U.S. Congresswoman Bobbi Fiedler, 1986, Resolution of Commendation Calif. State Assembly, 1986, Outstanding Cmty. Svc. Commendation Los Angeles County Bd. Suprs., 1986, 90, Outstanding Citizenship award City of Los Angeles, 1986, 90, 94, Cmty. Leadership award Iranian-Jewish Community L.A., 1990, 95, Resolution of Commendation, State of Calif., 1992, Cmty. Svc. Commendation, 1993, Rep. Senatorial Medal of Freedom award, Senatorial Inner Circle, 1994, Commendation L.A. County Bd. Suprs., 1994, 25 Yrs. of Excellent Svc. to the Cmty. award, 1996, Rep. Senatorial Medal of Freedom, 1999. Mem. Calif. Young Reps., Calif. Rep. Assembly, VFW, Jewish War Veterans. Jewish. Avocations: philanthropy, family time. Office: PO Box 480454 Los Angeles CA 90048-1454

WINKLER, IRWIN, motion picture producer; b. N.Y.C., May 28, 1934; s. Sol and Anna Winkler. BA, NYU, 1955. Mailroom messenger William Morris Agy., N.Y.C., 1955-62; motion picture producer, owner Winkler Films, Culver City, Calif., 1962—. Pres., Chartoff-Winkler Prodns., 1966—. Producer: Rocky, 1976 (10 Acad. award nominations, winner 3 including Best Picture, Los Angeles Film Critics award for best picture), They Shoot Horses Don't They, 1969 (9 Acad. award nominations), Nickelodeon, 1976, The Gambler, 1974, Up the Sandbox, 1972, The New Centurions, 1972, Point Blank, 1967, Double Trouble, 1967, Leo the Last, 1970 (Best Dir. award Cannes Film Festival, Belgrade Film Festival), The Strawberry Statement, 1970 (Jury prize Cannes Film Festival), The Split, 1968, Breakout, 1975, Believe in Me, 1971, The Gang That Couldn't Shoot Straight, 1971, The Mechanic, 1972, Busting, 1974, S.P.Y.S, 1974, Peeper, 1975, New York, New York, 1977, Valentino, 1977, Uncle Joe Shannon, 1978, Comes a Horseman, 1978, Rocky II, 1979, Raging Bull, 1980 (8 Acad. award nominations, winner 2, Los Angeles Film Critics award for best picture), Rocky III, 1981, True Confessions, 1981, Author, Author, 1982, The Right Stuff, 1983 (8 Acad. award nominations), Rocky IV, 1984, Revolution, 1985, 'Round Midnight, 1986 (2 Acad. award nomiations, Acad. award Best Original Score), Betrayed, 1988 (Chgo. Film Festival Lifetime Irwin Achievement award 1987), Goodfellas, 1990 (6 Acad. award nominationThe Net, 1995, The Juror, 1996, Life as a House, 2001, The Shipping News, 2001, Enough, 2002; dir, writer: The Net, 1995, Guilty by Suspicion,1991.s, winner 1, Brit. Acad. award Best Picture, N.Y. Film Critics Best Picture, L.A. Film Critics Best Picture), Rocky V, 1990, Music Box, 1990 (Golden Bear award for best film Berlin Film Festival); writer/dir.: Guilty by Suspicion, 1991 (U.S. selection Cannes Film Festival); producer/dir.: Night and the City, 1992 (N.Y. Film Festival, London Film Festival), The Net, 1995, The Juror, 1997, First Sight, 1998; retrospectives Brit. Film Inst., 1989, Chgo. Film Festival, 1989, Mus. Modern Art, N.Y.C., 1990, L.A. County Mus. Art, 1992. Served with U.S. Army, 1951-53. Named Commander d'Artes et de Lettres, French Govt. Minister of Culture, 1985. Mem. Am. Film Inst. (bd. govs.), Prodrs. Guild Am. (bd. dirs.). Office: Winkler Films 211 S Beverly Dr Ste 200 Beverly Hills CA 90212-3882

WINKLER, JOSEPH CONRAD, former recreational products manufacturing executive; b. Newark, May 20, 1916; s. Charles and Mollie (Abrams) W.; m. Geraldine M. Borok, Sept. 20, 1953; children: Charles H., David J. BS, NYU, 1941. Gen. mgr. Indsl. Washing Machine Corp., New Brunswick, N.J., 1941-48; controller Mojud Corp., N.Y.C., 1948-52; controller, asst. treas. Barbizon Corp., N.Y.C., 1952-57; controller Ideal Toy Corp., N.Y.C., 1957-58, McGregor-Doniger, Inc., N.Y.C., 1958-59; dir. fin. and adminstrn. Ideal Toy Corp., N.Y.C., 1960-62, v.p. fin., 1962-68, sr. v.p. fin., 1968-78, exec. v.p., COO, dir., 1978-81, pres., dir., 1981-83; exec. in residence, bus. adv. coun. Sch. Bus. Adminstrn., Montclair (N.J.) State U., 1983-90. Dir. Ideal of Australia Ltd., Melbourne, 1963-82, Ideal of Canada Ltd., Toronto, 1963-82, Ideal of Japan Ltd., Tokyo and Kiowa, 1963-80, Ideal Toy Co. Ltd., High Wycombe and Wokingham, Eng., 1966-82, Arxon Spiel & Freizeit GmBH, Rotgau, Germany, 1968-82, Perfekta Ltd. and Hollis Industries Ltd., Hong Kong, 1970-74, Ideal Loisirs S.A., Paris, 1972-82. Mem. editl. bd. Issues in Internat. Bus., 1985-92. Committeeman, troop treas. Boy Scouts Am., Tenafly, N.J., 1965-71; bd. dirs. N.Y. League Hard of Hearing, 1982-88; active Nat. Roster Sci. and Splized. Pers., War Manpower Commn., 1941-46. Served with Office Statis. Control USAAF, 1945. Mem. Fin. Execs. Inst. E-mail: chada@worldnet.att.net.

WINKLER, LEE B. business consultant; b. Buffalo; s. Jack W. and Caroline (Marienthal) W., 1 child, James; m. Maria Mal Verde. BS cum laude, NYU, 1945, MS cum laude, 1947. Pres. LBW, Inc. (formerly Winkler Assocs. Ltd.), N.Y.C., Beverly Hills, Calif., 1948—, Winkler Assocs. Ltd., Beverly Hills, Calif., and N.Y.C., 1958—; exec. dir. Global Bus. Mgmt. Inc., Beverly Hills, 1967—. V.p. Bayly Martin & Fay Inc., N.Y.C., 1965-68, John C. Paige & Co., N.Y.C., 1968-71; cons. Albert G. Ruben Co., Beverly Hills, 1971— Served with AUS, 1943-45. Decorated chevalier comdr. Order Holy Cross Jerusalem, also spl. exec. asst., charge d'affaires, 1970; chevalier comdr. Sovereign Order Cyprus, 1970 Mem. Nat. Acad. TV Arts and Scis., Nat. Acad. Recording Arts and Scis., Beverly Hills C. of C., Phi Beta Kappa, Beta Gamma Sigma, Mu Gamma Tau, Psi Chi Omega. Office: 15250 Ventura Blvd Sherman Oaks CA 91403-3201 *In the final analysis, the bottom line, if you will— the only thing that truly matters in life are those friends and family that hold you dear to them. Success, and its attendant monies, rise and fall like the tides, and even vanish at times, but earned love is as constant as the earth's rotation is independent of the tides.*

WINKLER, MATTHEW ADAM, editor-in-chief, reporter, editor; b. June 1, 1955; m. Lisa Winkler; 3 children. AB in History, Kenyon Coll., 1977, LLD. Reporter Mount Vernon News, Ohio, 1976—77; pub. rels. specialist Gehrung Assocs., Keene, NH, 1977—78; reporter, asst. editor Bond Buyer, 1978—80; with Dow Jones Capital Markets Reports, 1980; reporter Wall Street Jour., 1980—90; European Fin. corr. Wall Street Jour. Europe, Jour. London, 1982—87; with Bloomberg L.P.; editor-in-chief Bloomberg News, N.Y.C., 1990—. Chmn. bd. trustees Kenyon Rev. Co-author: Bloomberg by Bloomberg, 1997. Trustee N.J. Symphony Orch., Overseas Press Club, 1998, Knight-Bagehot Fellowship Columbia U. Office: Bloomberg News 499 Park Ave New York NY 10022-1240

WINKLER, MICHAEL, computer company executive; BS in Electrical Engring., Lehigh U.; MBA, Harvard Bus. Sch. Various mgmt. positions Xerox Corp.; v.p., gen. mgr. comp. systems Toshiba Am. Info. Systems, Inc., 1992—95; sr. v.p., group gen. mgr. Compaq Computer Corp. (later acquired by Hewlett-Packard Co.), Houston, 1996—2000, exec. v.p. global bus. units, 2000—01; exec. v.p. global ops. Hewlett-Packard Co., 2001—02, exec. v.p., chief mktg. officer, 2002—. Office: Hewlett-Packard Co 3000 Hanover St Palo Alto CA 94304-1185 Office Phone: 650-857-1501.

WINKLER, PAUL FRANK, JR., astrophysicist, educator; b. Nashville, Nov. 10, 1942; s. Paul Frank and Estelle (Pye) W.; m. Geraldine Huck, Aug. 20, 1966 (div. 1979); children: Katharine Estelle, Johanna Pye; m. Janet Pippitt Beers, June 25, 1983; stepchildren: Sarah Creighton Beers, Nathan Pippitt Beers. BS, Calif. Inst. Tech., 1964; A.M., Harvard U., 1965, PhD, 1970. From instr. to prof. physics Middlebury Coll., Vt., 1969—, chmn. dept., 1980-88, William R. Kenan Jr. prof. physics, 1984-87, chmn. nat. scis. div., 1988-93, asst. to pres. for sci. planning, 1993-96, Gamaliel Painter Bicentennial prof. physics, 1997—. Vis. scientist MIT, Cambridge, 1973-74, 78-80; sr. vis. fellow Inst. Astronomy, U. Cambridge, 1985-86; vis. resident astronomer Cerro Tololo InterAm. Observatory, La Serena, Chile, 1990-91, 96-97; vis. fellow Joint Inst. for Laboratory Astrophysics, U. Colo., Boulder, 1991. Contbr. articles to profl. jours. NSF fellow, 1965-69, Alfred P. Sloan Found. fellow, 1976-80 Mem. Am. Phys. Soc., Am. Astron. Soc., Internat. Astron. Union, Coun. on Undergrad. Rsch., Sigma Xi. Office: Middlebury Coll Dept Physics Middlebury VT 05753

WINKLER, SCOTT ALBER, literature educator; b. Sheboygan, Wis., Nov. 3, 1970; s. Albert Oscar and JoAnn Winkler; m. Brenda Ann Malzahn, July 3, 1994. MA in English, U. of Wisconsin-Milw., 2004. English tchr. Green Bay Pub. Schs., Wis., 1994—. Author: (fiction) Lezcano; contbr. articles to profl. jours. Fellow Univ. fellow, U. Wis.-Milw., 2003—04. E-mail: swinkler@greenbay.k12.wi.us.

WINKLER, SHELDON, dentist, educator; b. N.Y.C., Jan. 25, 1932; s. Ben and Lillian (Barsh) W.; m. Sandra M. Cohen, Aug. 13, 1961; children: Mitchell, Lori. BA, Washington Sq. Coll., 1953; DDS, NYU, 1956. Asst. prof. denture prosthesis NYU Coll. Dentistry, N.Y.C., 1958-61, 66-68, rsch. asst. prof., 1962-63; dir. materials rsch. Consol. Metal Products Industries Inc., Albany, N.Y., 1963-65, cons. materials rsch., 1966-68; asst. prof. removable prosthodontics sch. dentistry SUNY, Buffalo, 1968-70, assoc. prof., 1970-79; prof., chmn. dept. prosthodontics Temple U. Sch. Dentistry, Phila., 1979-86, 94-96, asst. dean for advanced studies, continuing edn./rsch., 1987-89, acting asst. dean, 1993-95, prof. restorative dentistry, 1996—. Asst. dir. dental dept. NYU Med. Ctr. Goldwater Meml. Hosp., NYC, 1966—68, vis. dentist dental dept., 1966—68; attending in prosthodontics E.J. Meyer Meml. Hosp., Buffalo, 1975—79; postgrad instr. First Dist. Dental Soc. NY, NYC, 1963—; cons. Coe Labs., Chgo., 1967—87, Harkness Ctr., Buffalo, Rosa Coplon Home & Infirmary, Buffalo, 1970—79, Erie C.C., Buffalo, 1979—. Lever Bros. Co., NYC, 1981—, VA Hosp., Phila., 1989—, Ivoclar N. Am., Amherst, NY, 2000—; lectr. dept. dental hygiene NYC C.C., 1967—68; hon. prof. Pierre Fauchard Sch. Dentistry, Asuncion, Paraguay, 1999—. Author: (with A. Davidoff and M.H.M. Lee) Dentistry for the Special Patient: The Aged, Chronically Ill and Handicapped, 1972, Essentials of Complete Denture Prosthodontics, 1979, 2d edit., 1988; editor: Resins in Dentistry, 1975, Complete Dentures, 1977, Removable Prosthodontics, 1984, (with B.R. Lang, F.R. Lauciello and G.P. McGivney) Contemporary Complete Denture Occlusion, 2001; editor Jour. Implant Dentistry, 1990-97; sr. editor Jour. Oral Implantology, 2000—; contbr. articles to profl. lit.; co-designer McGowan-Winkler complete denture trays. Served as capt. AUS, 1956-58, 61-62. Recipient Outstanding Layman award Vocat. Tech. Alumni and Student Assn., SUNY, Buffalo, 1974, Internat. Edn. award Internat. Congress Oral Implantologists, 1992, journalism award Internat. Coll. Dentists, 1993, Academic Devotion award Chulalongkorn U., Bangkok, 1995. Fellow Am. Coll. Dentists, Greater N.Y. Acad. Prosthodontics; mem. ADA, Internat. Assn. Dental Rsch., Am. Assn. Dental Schs., Am. Acad. Implant Prosthodontics (Outstanding Personality Implant Prosthodontics award, 2002), Sci. Rsch. Soc. Am., Acad. Plastics Rsch., Am. Prosthodontic Soc., Am. Soc. Geriatric Dentistry, Internat. Congress of Oral Implantologists, Sigma Xi, Sigma Epsilon Delta, Omicron Kappa Upsilon. Home: 1224 Liberty Bell Dr Cherry Hill NJ 08003-2759 Office: Sch Dentistry Temple U Philadelphia PA 19140 Office Phone: 215-707-0115. Personal E-mail: swinkdent@aol.com.

WINMILL, B. LYNN, judge; m. Judy Jones; 4 children. BA, Idaho State U., 1974; JD, Harvard U., 1977. Atty. Holland and Hart, Denver, 1977-79, Hawley, Troxell, Ennis and Hawley, Pocatello, Idaho, 1984-87; judge Idaho Sixth Jud. Dist. Ct., Pocatello, 1987-95; chief judge U.S. Dist. Ct. Idaho, Boise, 1995—. Office: US Dist Ct Idaho US Courthouse 550 W Fort St 6th Fl Boise ID 83724-0001 Fax: 208-334-9209. Office Phone: 208-334-9145.

WINN, ALBERT CURRY, clergyman; b. Ocala, Fla., Aug. 16, 1921; s. James Anderson and Elizabeth (Curry) W.; m. Grace Neely Walker, Aug. 29, 1944; children: Grace Walker (Mrs. Stewart E. Ellis), James Anderson, Albert Bruce Curry, Randolph Axson. AB, Davidson Coll., 1942, LLD, 1968; BD, Union Theol. Sem., Va., 1945, ThD, 1956; ThM, Princeton Theol. Sem., 1949; LLD, Stillman Coll., 1975. Ordained min. Presbyn. Ch., 1945. Asst. prof. Davidson Coll., 1946-47; pastor Potomac Rural Parish, Va., 1948-53; prof. Bible Stillman Coll., 1953-60; prof. theology Louisville Presbyn. Theol. Sem., 1960-73, pres., 1966-73; pastor 2d Presbyn. Ch., Richmond, Va., 1974-81, N. Decatur Presbyn. Ch., Decatur, Ga., 1981-86. Moderator Presbyn. Synod Ala., 1958, Presbyn. Synod Ky., 1969, Gen. Assembly, Presbyn. Ch. in U.S., 1979; vis. prof. Union Theol. Sem. in Va., 1987, Columbia Theol. Sem., 1987, Louisville Presbyn. Theol. Sem., 1988; interim pastor Cen. Presbyn. Ch., Atlanta, 1989-90, St. Andrews Presbyn. Ch., Tucker, Ga., 1993-94; parish assoc. Trinity Prebyn. Ch., Winston-Salem, NC, 1999—. Author: Layman's Bible Commentary on Acts, 1960, The Worry and Wonder of Being Human, 1966, Where Do I Go From Here, 1972, Proclamation Two: Epiphany, 1980, A Sense of Mission, 1981, Christ the Peacemaker, 1982, Plain Talk about the Apostles' Creed, 1985, The Christian Primer, 1990, Ain't Gonna Study War No More, 1993. Chmn. trustees Stillman Coll., 1965-70. Served as chaplain USNR, 1945-46. Mem. Phi Beta Kappa, Beta Theta Pi, Omicron Delta Kappa. Office: 212 Oakwood Ct Winston Salem NC 27103-1952 Office Phone: 336-727-1907. E-mail: al.winn@juno.com.

WINN, FRANCIS JOHN, JR., medical educator; b. Detroit, Aug. 12, 1946; s. Francis John and Margaret (Aubuchon) Winn; m. Cathy Mannion, Aug. 24, 1974 (div. Dec. 1980); m. Gloria Elizabeth Morrow, Feb. 6, 1981; children: Francis John III, Paige Whitney. BS in Psychology, Mich. State U., 1968; MA in Physiol. Psychology, Ctrl. Mich. U., 1974; PhD in Psychology and Stats., Tex. Tech U., 1977. Commd. USPHS, 1978, advanced through grades to comdr., 1984, ret., 1997; chief mental health svcs. and Atlantic area psychiat. screening unit USCG Outpatient Clinic, Governor's Island, NY, 1978-83; staff rsch. psychologist, cons. to chief psychiatry br. USCG Tng. Ctr., Cape May, NJ, 1983-86; sr. scientist psychophysiology & biomechanics sect. Nat. Inst. Occupl. Safety and Health, Cin., 1986-91; sr. rsch. support scientist officer Nat. Inst. Drug Abuse, 1991-92, Substance Abuse and Mental Health Svc. Adminstrn., 1992-95, sr. health statistician Ctr. Substance Abuse Prevention, 1995-97; clin. asst. prof. E. Carolina U., Greenville, NC, 1997—. Cons. assoc. Duke U. Sch. Nursing, 1998—; program evaluation cons. New Bold Assocs., 1998—2001; asst. adj. prof. Med. Coll. Ga., 1995—; bd. collaborators N.C. Agro-Med. Inst., 1998—, exec. com., 2000—01; vis. asst. prof. dept. psychology U. Tex., El Paso, 1977—78; adj. assoc. prof. dept. human svcs., counseling St. John's U., Jamaica, NY, 1980—82; lectr. Stockton State Coll., Pomona, NJ, 1985—86; adj. asst. prof. U. Cin., 1989—91; mem. adv. bd. Conf. Engring. and Aging, Stein Gerontol. Inst., Drexel U., 1990—91; mem. sci. program com. 2d Internat. Conf. Aging and Work, Danish Working Environ. Fund, 1998; program chair tech. group aging Triennial Congress Internat. Ergonomics Assn., 2000; spkr. in field. Assoc. editor: Exptl. Aging Rsch.; contbr. articles to profl. jours. Mem.: DAV, Internat. Soc. Occupl. Ergonomics and Safety (mem. at large to exec. com.), Internat. Commn. Occupl. Health (mem. sci. com. aging and work 2002—), Soc. Air Force Psychologists, Gerontol. Soc. Am., Soc. Exptl. Biology and Medicine, Am. Psychol. Soc., Assn. Physician Assist Programs, Res. Officers Assn., Sigma Xi. Office: E Carolina U W Rsch Campus 1157 V Site 'C' Rd Greenville NC 27834 Home: 216 Bent Creek Dr Greenville NC 27834-7617 E-mail: winnf@mail.ecu.edu.

WINN, H. RICHARD, surgeon; b. Chester, Pa., 1942; MD, U. Pa., 1968; BA, Princeton U., 1964. Diplomate Am Bd. Neurol. Surgeons. Intern U. Hosp., Cleve., 1968-69, resident surgery, 1969-70; resident neurolog. surgery U. Hosp. Va., Charlottesville, 1970-74; neurol. surgeon U. Wash. Hosp., Seattle, 1983—2002; prof., chmn. neurol. surgery U. Wash., Seattle, 1983—2002; prof. neurosurgery and neurosci. Mt. Sinai Med. Sch., N.Y.C., 2003—. Bd. dirs. Am. Bd. Neurol. Surgery, 1995-2001, vice chmn., 2000-01. Founding editor Neurosurgical Clinics of North America; mem. editl. bd. Jour. Neurosurgery, 1995-2001, chair, 2001-2002; mem. editl. bd. Am. Jour. Physiology, 1995-2000, Am. Jour. Surgery. Fellow AAAS, Soc. Brit. Neurol. Surgeons (hon.); mem. AMA, Am. Assn. Neurol. Surgeons, Soc. Neurol. Surgeons, Congress of Neurol. Surgeons. Office: Dept Neurosurgery Mount Sinai Sch Medicine One Gustave L Levy PO Box 1136 New York NY 10029 Office Phone: 212-241-9128.

WINN, HERSCHEL C. retired retail electronics company executive; b. Hill County, Tex., Dec. 14, 1931; s. Herschel C. and Alta Fay; m. Dorothy Carolyn Martin, June 24, 1961; children— Celia Carol, Macey Sheryl. BA, U. Tex., Austin, 1958, LL.B., 1960. Bar: Tex. bar 1960. Atty. Tex. Hwy. Dept., 1960-61; trial atty. Internat. Service Ins. Co., 1961-63; judge Johnson County, Tex., 1963-68; with Tandy Corp., 1968-97, v.p., 1976-79, sec., 1975-97, sr. v.p., 1979-97. Bd. dirs. Ft. Worth Crime Control and Prevention Dist. Bd. dirs. Better Bus. Bur. Tarrant County, 1971-87; dir. Van Cliburn Piano Competition, 1984—; bd. dirs. Downtown Ft. Worth, Inc., 1985-97, Youth Orch. Greater Ft. Worth, 1984-87, Family Svc. Inc., 1984-89; bd. dirs., exec. com. Ft. Worth Conv. and Visitors Bur., 1986-94. With AUS, 1953-55. Mem. ABA, State Bar Tex., Tarrant County Bar Assn. (pres. corp. counsel sect. 1980-81), Fort Worth C. of C. Methodist.

WINN, JAMES JULIUS, JR., lawyer; b. Colon, Panama, Nov. 7, 1941; came to U.S., 1941; s. James Julius and Molly (Brown) W.; m. Elizabeth Kokernot Lacy, Aug. 15, 1970; children: Mary Ann W. Burns, Elizabeth Lacy, James Julius VI. AB, Princeton U., 1964; JD cum laude, Washington and Lee U., 1970. Bar: Md. 1970, U.S. Dist. Ct. Md. 1971, U.S. Dist. Ct. D.C. 1982. Assoc. Piper & Marbury, Balt., 1970-78; ptnr. Piper Rudnick LLP, Balt., 1978—2004. Assoc. editor, contbr. author Washington & Lee U. Law Rev., 1968-70. Counselor St. John's Ch., Western Run Parish, Glyndon, Md., 1974—; mem. com. on canons and other bus., investment com. Episc. Diocese Md., 1986—; dir. Ctr. for Ethics and Corp. Policy, 1988-95, chmn., 1991-95; dir. Ctr. Stage, 1986—; dir. Oldfields Sch., 1991-96; v.p., dir. Ruxton Country Sch., 1988-91; vice chmn., dir. The Jemicy Sch., 1999—. Mem. ABA (chmn. subcoms. on publs. and govt. acctg. standards of com. on law and acctg. of sect. of bus. law), Md. State Bar Assn. (com. on corp. law of sect. of bus. law). Office: Piper Rudnick LLP 6225 Smith Ave Baltimore MD 21209-3600

WINN, JOSEPH LAMPHER, financial officer; b. Cambridge, Mass., Aug. 12, 1951; s. Joseph L. and Alicia M. (Muir) W.; m. Gail A. Cadogan, June 19, 1976; children: Kelly, Caroline, Joseph. BS in Fin., Boston Coll., 1973; MBA, Babson Coll., 1974. Fin. mgr. program Sanders Assocs. Inc., Nashua, N.H., 1974-78; fin. mgr. Digital Equipment Corp., Maynard, Mass., 1978-83; sr. v.p., controller Am. Cablesystems Corp., Beverly, Mass., 1983-88; exec. v.p., chief fin. officer Atlantic Radio Corp., Manchester, Mass., 1988—93; CFO & dir. Am. Radiosystems Corp., 1993—98; CFO Am. Tower Corp., Boston, 1998—2002, vice chmn., 2002—. Roman Catholic. Office: American Tower Corp 116 Huntington Ave Boston MA 02116-5749 E-mail: joe.winn@americantower.com.

WINN, MORRIS X. federal agency administrator; Grad., Prairie View A&M U. Divsn. dir. support svcs. Tex. Atty. Gen.'s Office, 1984—92, dir. employee rels., 1992—94; deputy commr. human resources Tex. Dept. Ins., 1994—99; divsn. mgr. human resources Tex. Comptroller Pub. Accts., 1999—2002; asst. adminstr. adminstrn. and resources mgmt. EPA, Washington, 2002—. Office: EPA 1200 Pennsylvanis Ave NW MC 301A Washington DC 20460

WINN, PAUL T. electronics executive; b. 1944; With IBM, Stamford, Conn.; pres., CEO, dir. Genicom Corp., Chantilly, Va., 1990—2000; pres. and CEO Powerquest, 2000—03; CEO Princeton Softech, Inc., Princeton, NJ, 2003—. Office: Princeton Softech Inc 111 Campus Dr Princeton NJ 08540-6400 Office Phone: 609-627-5500. Office Fax: 609-627-7799.*

WINN, STEVEN JAY, critic; b. Phila., Apr. 25, 1951; s. Willis Jay and Lois (Gengelbach) W.; m. Katharine Weber, Sept. 15, 1979 (div. Dec. 1985); m. Sally Ann Noble, July 22, 1989; 1 child, Phoebe Ann. BA, U. Pa., 1973; MA, U. Wash., 1975. Staff writer, editor Seattle Weekly, 1975-79; theater critic San Francisco Chronicle, 1980—2002, arts and culture critic, 2002—. Co-author: Ted Bundy: The Killer Next Door, 1980, Great Performances: A Celebration, 1997; contbr. articles to various publs. Wallace Stegner fellow Stanford U., 1979-80; recipient first prize Excellence in Writing award Am. Assn. of Sunday and Feature Editors, 2002, 2003. Office: San Francisco Chronicle 901 Mission St San Francisco CA 94103-2905 Office Phone: 415-777-8869. E-mail: swinn@sfchronide.com.

WINN, VALDENIA C. state representative; b. Kansas City, Kans., Dec. 7, 1950; BS, U. Kans., 1972, MA, 1975, PhD, 1993. Prof. Kansas City C.C., 1972—; mem. Kans. Ho. of Reps., 2000—, mem. Com. on Edn., Com. on Higher Edn., Com. on Transp., Com. on Econ. Devel., Joint Com. on Econ. Devel., Joint Select Com. on Sch. Fin. Treas. N.E. Coop. Coun., 1987—; project dir. Fulbright-Hayes Groups Projects Abroad to Senegal, 1999, Title III Planning Grant Adminstr., 2000. Chair Kans. Territorial Sesquicentennial Dinner, Kans. Hist. Mus., 2004—; active BILLD Legis. Leadership Program. Democrat. Office: 284-W State Capitol 300 SW 10th Ave Topeka KS 66612 Address: 1044 Washington Blvd Kansas City KS 66102

WINN, WALTER GARNETT, JR., marketing strategist, advertising executive; b. Wilmington, N.C., Dec. 1, 1941; s. Walter Garnett and Pamela Weber (Bradham) W.; m. Linda Ann Irvin, July 1, 1964; children: Walter Welborn, Katie Hillary. BFA, U. Ga., 1966, MS with honors, 1968. Account exec. Sudler & Hennessey Advt., N.Y.C., 1968-69, Dean Burdick & Assocs. Inc., N.Y.C., 1969-70; v.p., creative dir. Buntin & Assocs. Inc., Nashville, 1970-72; pres. Smith & Winn Advt. Inc., Jacksonville, Fla., 1972-77; mktg. mgr. Standard Telephone Co., Cornelia, Ga., 1977-79; mktg., sales mgr. Commonwealth Telephone Co., Dallas, Pa., 1979-83; advt. dir. CTE Corp., Wilkes Barre, Pa., 1983-84; dir. mktg. North State Telephone Inc., High Point, N.C., 1984—. Creator, designer bus. strategy game Merchants and Movers, 1990, Air Mogul, 2000. Bd. dirs., chair com. High Point Area Arts Coun., 1989—96; bd. dirs. Back Mountain Arts Guild, Dallas, 1980, Misericordia Coll. Arts Endowment, 1982—84; apptd. mem. Gov. Hunt's N.C. Info. Hwy. Com., 1994—96; advisor Market Authority Bd., 2001—; pres. Civitan Found., 1998—2000. Named Advt. Person of Yr. Am. Advt. Fedn., Northeastern Pa., 1983. Mem. N.C. Tel. Assn. (chmn. mktg. 1989-91, 95-97), Civitan (pres. High Point 1994-95, Civitan of Yr. 1996). Libertarian. Avocations: strategy games, model railroading, woodworking. Home: 381 Hunters Pointe Lexington NC 27295-0203 Office: North State Com 111 N Main St High Point NC 27260-5007 E-mail: wwinn@nscom.com.

WINNE, ELIZABETH (LISE), lyricist; d. Mary (Williams) Eliot and Robert Frank Winne, Patricia Holland (Stepmother) and Henrik Hagerup(Stepfather). BS in Studio Art, Skidmore Coll., Saratoga Springs, NY, 1988; M in Art Edn. (hon.), Coll.St. Rose, Albany, NY, 1995. Mem. of co-operative gallery Valley Artisans Market, Cambridge, NY, 1988—. Musician (singer/songwriter, producer): (cd recording) Come To Me In Dreams; musician: (interpreter/composer, producer) Wing'd With Hopes, New Interpretations of Renaissance Songs; musician: (singer/songwriter, composer, producer) The Goldenrod (Grant, 1999); mainline center of the arts exhibit, Springtime (Poole Award for Art Pottery, 1992), 54th cooperstown national art exhibit, Wedding Vase, invitational nat. exhibit (Vt.), Ceramic Pieces, the northeast fine crafts exhibit, Many Juried Works; author: (fiction) Family Tie (1st Pl.: Crandall Libr. Writer's Conf., 1980), (poetry) The News: For Leslie Cook (1st Pl.: Crandall Libr. Writers Conf., 1980). Scholar Fran Simches Art Scholarship Award, Skidmore Coll., 1987. Mem.: Albany/Schenectady League of Arts. Office: Lilac/Goldenrod Records PO Box 145 Saratoga Springs NY 12866 E-mail: sales@lisewinne.com.

WINNECKE, JOYCELYN, editor; m. Bill Adee. Degree, U. So. Ind. Writer obituaries Evansville (Ind.) Courier and Press, 1977; reporter Wash. bur. Scripps Howard; city editor Indpls. Star; dep. metro editor, then metro news editor Chgo. Sun-Times, 1994—99; mng. editor Chgo. Sun Times, 1999—2002, Chgo. Tribune, 2002—. Office: Chgo Tribune 435 N Michigan Ave Chicago IL 60611*

WINNER, DAVID DARIO, humanities educator, writer; b. N.Y.C., Oct. 1, 1964; s. Winner Anthony and Viola Hopkins Winner; m. Angela Laura Starita, Nov. 25, 1964. MFA, U. Ariz., Tucson, 1992; PhD, N.Y. U., N.Y.C., 1994. Prof. Hudson County CC, Jersey City, 1998—. Author: (short stories) A Traveler (First prize The Ledge Fiction Contest, 2003), A Traveler's Tale (Pushcart nomination, 2003), The Rites of Pozzalo (Pushcart nomination, 2000). Home: 275 President Brooklyn NY 11231 Office: Hudson County CC 25 Pathside Jersey City NJ 11231 Personal E-mail: dqw1639@hotmail.com. E-mail: dwinner@hccc.edu.

WINNER, KARIN E. editor; b. White Plains, N.Y., Dec. 27, 1945; BA in Journalism, U. So. Calif. Editor San Diego Union-Tribune, 1995—. Office: San Diego Union-Tribune Pub Co 350 Camino De La Reina San Diego CA 92112-0191 E-mail: Karin.winner@uniontrib.com.

WINNER, MICHAEL ROBERT, film director, writer, producer; b. London, Oct. 30, 1935; s. George Joseph and Helen (Zloty) W. Degree in law and econs. with honors, Cambridge (Eng.) U., 1956. Writer Fleet St. (newspapers), London, 1956-58. Columnist London Sunday Times, 1990, London News of the World, 1995. Engaged in film prodn., 1956; dir. films Play it Cool, 1962, West 11, 1963, The Mechanic, 1972, Death Wish II, 1981; dir., writer The Cool Mikado, 1962, You Must be Joking, 1965, The Wicked Lady, 1982; producer, dir. The System, 1963, I'll Never Forget What's 'isname, 1967, The Games, 1969, Lawman, 1970, The Nightcomers, 1971, Chato's Land, 1971, Scorpio, 1972, The Stone Killer, 1973, Death Wish, 1974, Won Ton Ton The Dog Who Saved Hollywood, 1975, Firepower, 1978, Scream for Help, 1983, Death Wish III, 1985; producer, writer, dir. films The Jokers, 1966, Hannibal Brooks, 1968, The Sentinel, 1976, The Big Sleep, 1977, Appointment With Death, 1987, A Chorus of Disapproval, 1988, Bullseye!, 1989, Dirty Weekend, 1992, Parting Shots, 1997; producer plays Nights at the Comedy, Comedy Theatre, London, 1960, The Silence of St. Just, Gardner Centre, Brighton, 1971, The Tempest, Wyndhams Theatre, London, 1974, A Day in Hollywood, A Night in the Ukraine, Mayfair Theatre, London, 1978, (TV series London Weekend TV) Michael Winner's True Crimes, 1990, 91, 92, 93, 94; author: Winner's Dinners, 1999, rev. edit., 2000, Winner Guide, 2002, Winner Takes All, 2004; actor: (BBC film) For the Greater Good, 1990, Decadence, 1993, The Flump, 2000; actor and/or dir. commls. including Esure Ins., Kenco, Doritos, Books for Schs. Founder, chmn. Police Meml. Trust, 1984. Mem. Dirs. Guild Gt. Britain (coun., trustee, chief censorship officer 1983). Office: Scimitar Films Ltd 219 Kensington High St London W8 6BD England

WINNIE, GLENNA BARBARA, pediatric pulmonologist; b. Lansing, Mich., Oct. 14; d. Robert John and Irene (Fetchik) W.; m. Jeffrey Alan Cooper, Mar. 17, 1990; children: Robert Jefferson Cooper, David Jamison Cooper. BS, Mich. State U., 1973; MD, Vanderbilt U., 1977. Diplomate Am. Bd. Pediatrics, Am. Bd. Pediatric Pumonology. Resident in pediatrics Case Western Res. U./Babies and Childrens Hosp., Cleve., 1977-79, fellow in pediatric pulmonology, 1979-82; asst. prof. pediatrics Albany (N.Y.) Med. Coll., 1982-90, assoc. prof. pediatrcis, 1990-95, head pediatric pulmonology sect., 1982-95; adminstrv. dir. pulmonary divsn., co-dir. cystic fibrosis U. Pitts., 1995—. Dir. Albany Pediat. Pulmonary and Cystic Fibrosis Ctr., 1982—95; adminstrv. dir. pulmonary divsn. Children's Hosp. of Pitts., 1995—99; co-dir. Cystic Fibrosis Ctr., 1995—, dir. pulmonary divsn., 1999—, dir. pediatric sleep lab., 2001—, Children's Hosp. of Pitts., 2001—. Contbr. articles to profl. jours. Bd. dirs. Albany Ronald McDonald Ho., 1986-88, Cystic Fibrosis Found.-Western Pa. chpt., 1996—. Rsch. grantee Nat. Cystic Fibrosis Found., 1984-86, 88-90, 99-01, NIH, 1987-93. Mem.: Soc. Pediat. Rsch., Am. Acad. Sleep Medicine, Capital Dist. Pediatric Soc. (treas. 1985—90, pres. 1990—91), Am. Coll. Physician Execs., Am. Thoracic Soc. (rsch. fellowship review com. 1989—92), Am. Acad. Pediatrics (exec. com. chest sect. 1996—2001). Episcopalian. Achievements include description of role of Epstein Barr virus in pulmonary exacerbations in cystic fibrosis. Office: Childrens Nat Med Ctr 111 Michigan Ave NW Washington DC 20010-2970

WINNING, JOHN PATRICK, lawyer; b. Murphysboro, Ill., Oct. 29, 1952; s. William T. Jr. and Lillian (Albers) W.; m. Jessica Anne Yoder, June 17, 1978 (div. July 1999); children: Erika Anne, Brian Patrick, Derek Matthew. AB with distinction, Mo. Bapt. Coll., 1974; JD, St. Louis U., 1979. Bar: Mo. 1979, U.S. Dist. Ct. (ea. dist.) Mo. 1979, U.S. Ct. Appeals (8th cir.) 1979, U.S. Dist. Ct. (so. dist.) Tex. 1985, U.S. Ct. Appeals (5th cir.) 1987, U.S. Dist. Ct. (we. dist.) Tex. 1988, Tex. 1989. Assoc. Chused, Strauss, Chorlins, Goldfarb, Bini & Kohn, St. Louis, 1979-81; assoc. counsel Mfrs. Hanover Fin. Services, Phila., 1981-83; corp. counsel Cessna Fin. Corp., Wichita, Kans., 1983-85; atty. Southwestern Bell Publs., Inc., St. Louis, 1985-90; pvt. practice, 1990—2000, 2001—; pres. Butler Hill Investments, Inc., St. Louis, 1990-91; prin. Success Mgmt. Group, 1991-96, DPPC Mgmt. Group, St. Louis, 1996-97; v.p., gen. counsel Winning Equipment Co., Herculaneum, Mo., 2000-01; assoc. Vogler Law Firm, St. Louis, 2000—01; with Elco Chevrolet, Ballwin, Mo., 2002—03. Sec., bd. dirs. Winning Equipment Co.; asst. prof. bus. adminstn. Mo. Bapt. Coll., 1986-91. Treas. Concerned Citizens of Chesterfield, 1989-91; deacon, mem. fin. com. 1st Bapt. Ch., Ellisville, Mo., 1992-93, vice chmn. fin. com., 1993-94, chmn. fin. com., 1994-95, vice chmn. deacons, 1993-95, chmn. deacons, 1997-98, dir. Sunday sch., 1993-94; trustee, chmn. athletic com., 1992-97, 98-2000, chmn. by-laws com. Mo. Bapt. Coll., 1992-96, sec. presdl. search com., 1994, mem., exec. com. bd. trustees, 1994-97, 98-2000; mgr. St. Louis Flames Youth Baseball, 1992-95; mgr. St. Louis Thunder Youth Baseball, 1995-97; coach St. Clare Bulls Basketball Team, 1994-97, St. Louis Wolfpack Youth Baseball, 1997-98; asst. scoutmaster troop 313, merit badge counselor Boy Scouts Am., 1997—; Camporee staff New Horizons dist. Boy Scouts Am., 1998-2000, adult leader tng. staff, 1998—, camping com., 1998-2000, dist. roundtable staff, 1999—, chmn. membership com. New Horizons dist., 1999—. Named one of Outstanding Young Men of Am., 1987, Outstanding Alumnus, Mo. Bapt. Coll., 1987-88; named to Athletic Hall of Fame, Mo. Bapt. Coll., 1989; recipient Wood Badge Adult Leadership Tng. award Boy Scouts Am., 1998. Mem. Nat. Lawyers Assn., Eagle Scouts Assn., Met. St. Louis Bar Assn., Christian Legal Soc., Acad. Family Mediators, Assn. Family and Conciliation Cts., Mo. Bapt. Coll. Alumni Assn. (pres. 1980-81, 88-90), St. Louis Assn., Christian Attys., West County C. of C., Chesterfield C. of C. Republican. Southern Baptist. Avocations: coaching baseball and basketball, reading, camping. Home: 868 Gardenway Ballwin MO 63011 Office: 868 Gardenway Ballwin MO 63011 Office Phone: 633-391-1183.

WINNINGHAM, MARE, actress; b. Phoenix, May 16, 1959; m. A Martinez (div. 1981); m. William Maple, 1983; children: Riley, Paddy, Jack, Calla. Appeared in (TV movies and miniseries): The Thorn Birds, 1983, Special Olympics/A Special Kind of Love, 1978, Amber Waves, 1980 (Emmy award 1980), The Women's Room, 1980, Off the Minnesota Strip, 1980, A Few Days in Weasel Creek, 1981, Freedom, 1981, Missing Children: A Mother's Story, 1982, Helen Keller: The Miracle Continues, 1984, Single Bars, Single Women, 1984, Love is Never Silent, 1985 (Emmy award nomination 1986), Who Is Julia?, 1986, A Winner Never Quits, 1986, Eye on the Sparrow, 1991, God Bless the Child, 1988, Turner & Hooch, 1989, Love and Lies, Crossing to Freedom, Fatal Exposure, 1991, She Stood Alone, Those Secrets, Intruders, 1992, Better Off Dead, 1994, The Boys Next Door, 1996, Betrayed by Love, 1994, Letter to My Killer, 1995, George Wallace, 1997, Little Girl Fly Away, 1998, Everything That Rises, 1998, Too Rich: The Secret Life of Doris Duke, 1999, (miniseries) Sally Hemings: An American Scandal, 2000, (TV appearances) Six Feed Under, 2002, Touched by a Angel, 2002; appeared in (films): One Trick Pony, 1980, Threshold, 1983, St. Elmo's Fire, 1985, Nobody's Fool, 1986, Shy People, 1987, Made in Heaven, 1987, Miracle Mile, 1988, Turner and Hooch, 1989, Hard Promises, 1992, Teresa's Tattoo, Wyatt Earp, 1994, Georgia, 1995 (Acad. award nomination best supporting actress 1995), Bad Day On The Block, 1997, The Adventures of Ociee Nash, 2003, Dandelion, 2003; sang title song in (film) Freedom, 1981; singer (solo album) What Might Be, 1992, Red and Brown, 1996. Office: care William Morris Agy 151 El Camino Dr Beverly Hills CA 90212-2704 also: IFA Talent Agy 8730 W Sunset Blvd Ste 490 Los Angeles CA 90069

WINOGRAD, AUDREY LESSER, retired advertising executive; b. N.Y.C., Oct. 6, 1933; d. Jack J. and Theresa Lorraine (Elkind) Lesser; m. Melvin H. Winograd, Apr. 29, 1956; 1 child, Hope Elise. BA, U. Conn., 1953. Asst. advt. mgr. T. Baumritter Co., Inc., N.Y.C., 1953-54; asst. dir. pub. rels. and creative merchandising Kirby, Block & Co., N.Y.C., 1954-56; divsn. mdse. mgr., dir. advt. and sales promotion Winograd's Dept. Store, Inc., Point Pleasant, N.J., 1956-73, v.p., 1960-73, exec. v.p., 1973-86; pres., CEO AMW Assocs., Atlanta, 1976—2002, ret., 2002—. Editor bus. newsletters. Bd. dirs. Temple Beth Am, Lakewood, N.J., 1970-72, Temple Emanuel, Atlanta, 1999-2001. Mem. NAFE, Jersey Pub. Rels. and Advt. Assn. (pres. 1982-83, bd. dirs.), Retail Advt. and Mktg. Assn. Internat., Monmouth Ocean Devel. Coun., Monmouth County Bus. Assn. (bd. dirs. 1985-97, pres. 1988-90, Woman of Yr. 1992-93, Person of Yr. 1995), N.J. Assn. Women Bus. Owners, Am. Soc. Advt. and Promotion, Ocean C. of C. (bd. dirs. 1994-97, award 1993, 94), Retail Advt. Conf. (Career Achievements and Contbns. to Soc. award 1993), Soc. Prevention Cruelty to Animals, Animal Protection Inst. Am., Human Soc., Internat. Fund Animal Welfare, World Wildlife Fund, Friends of Animals, Defenders of Wildlife, Nat. Humane Edn. Soc., In Defense of Animals, Atlanta Humane Soc., Sierra Club, Peta, Natural Resources Def. Coun. Avocations: collecting animal collectibles, gourmet cooking, environmental protection, exercise. Office: AMW Assocs 5304 Vernon Lake Dr Atlanta GA 30338-3527

WINOGRAD, BERNARD, real estate and financial adviser; b. Detroit, Dec. 31, 1950; s. Daniel and Lillian (Walder) W.; m. Carol Leslie Snodgrass, Mar. 8, 1974; children: Simon James Bartholomew, Christina Lynn. BA, U. Chgo., 1970. Pub. affairs mgr. Bendix Corp., Southfield, Mich., 1975; exec. asst. to W.M. Blumenthal, 1975-77, dir. corp. communications, 1977-79, treas., 1979-83; exec. v.p. Taubman Investments, 1983-84; pres. Taubman Investment Co., 1984-96; exec. v.p., CFO Taubman Ctrs., Inc., 1996; exec. asst. to W. Michael Blumenthal, U.S. Sec. Treasury, Washington, 1977; pres., chief exec. Prudential Real Estate Investors. Mem. Urban Land Inst. (bd. dir.), Pension Real Estate Assn. (bd. dirs.). Office: Prudential Real Estate Investors 8 Campus Dr Parsippany NJ 07054-4409 Home: # 9fe 103 E 75th St New York NY 10021-2848

WINOGRAD, NICHOLAS, chemist; b. New London, Conn., Dec. 27, 1945; s. Arthur Selig Winograd and Winifred (Schaefer) Winograd Mayes; m. Barbara J. Garrison. BS, Rensselaer Poly. Inst., 1967; PhD, Case We. Res. U., 1970. Asst. prof. chemistry Purdue U., West Lafayette, Ind., 1970-75, assoc. prof. chemistry, 1975-79; prof. chemistry Pa. State U., University Park, 1979-85, Evan Pugh prof. chemistry, 1985—. Cons. Lawrence Livermore Lab., 1997-2003; mem. chemistry adv. bd. NSF, Washington, 1987-90, analytical chemistry adv. bd., 1986-89. Contbr. articles to profl. jours. A.P. Sloan Found. fellow, 1974; Guggenheim Found. fellow, 1977; recipient Founder's prize Tex. Instruments Found., 1984, Faculty Scholar's Pa. State U., 1985, Bennedetti Pichler award Am. Microchem. Soc., 1991, Outstanding Alumnus award Case We. Res. U., 1991. Fellow AAAS (Sect. award); mem. Am. Chem. Soc. Home: 138 Chemistry Ln Spring Mills PA 16875-9703 Office: Pa State U Dept of Chemistry 152 Davey Lab University Park PA 16802-6300 Office Phone: 814-863-0001. Business E-Mail: nxw@psu.edu.

WINOKUR, MARISSA JARET, actress; b. NYC, Feb. 2, 1973; Studied at, Am. Musical and Dramatic Acad. Actor: (plays, Broadway) Grease, 1995, Hairspray, 2002 (Tony award for best actress, 2003); (plays) Guys and Dolls, Peter Pan, Little Shop of Horrors, Romeo and Juliet, Nunsense II, Grandma Sylvia's Funeral, Hair, Happy Days; (films) Demo Real, 1998, Why Love Doesn't Work, 1999, Never Been Kissed, 1999, American Beauty, 1999, Sleep Easy, Hutch Rimes, 2000, Scary Movie, 2000, Amy's Orgasm, 2001, On Edge, 2001, Now You Know, 2002; (TV films) Beautiful Girl, 2003; co-exec. prodr. (TV films) Beautiful Girl, 2003; actor(guest appearances): (TV series) The Steve Harvey Show, 1998, Felicity, 1999, Dharma & Greg, 1999, 2000, Moesha, 2000, Curb Your Enthusiasm, 2000, Just Shoot Me, 2000, The Ellen Show, 2001, Boston Public, 2001. Office: McKeon-Valeo Mgmt 9107 Wilshire Blvd Ste 321 Beverly Hills CA 90210 Office Phone: 310-288-5888. Office Fax: 310-288-5868.

WINSHIP, DANIEL HOLCOMB, medical educator, dean; b. Houston, July 4, 1933; m. Winnifred Jeneanne Rowold; children: Charles Dwayne, Nancy Ellen, David Rhoads, Rebecca Susan, Molly Beth. BA, Rice U., 1954; MD, U. Tex., Galveston, 1958. Diplomate Am. Bd. Internal Medicine. Intern in internal medicine Ochsner Found. Hosp., New Orleans, 1958-59; asst. resident U. Utah Coll. Medicine, Salt Lake City, 1959-61; fellow in gastroenterology Yale U. Sch. Medicine, New Haven, 1961-63; rsch. fellow med. ethics, fellow law, sci.-medicine program Yale U. Divinity Sch., Yale U. Law Sch., New Haven, 1977; asst. prof., then assoc. prof. medicine Marquette U. Sch. Medicine, Milw., 1963-69; assoc. prof., then prof. U. Mo. Sch. Medicine, Columbia, 1969-84, assoc. dean for VA affairs, 1982-84; prof. U. Kans. Sch. Medicine, Kansas City, 1984-87; assoc. dep. chief med. dir. dept. medicine and surgery VA Ctrl. Office, Washington, 1987-90; prof. medicine, dean Loyola U. Stritch Sch. Medicine, Maywood, Ill., 1990-99; vice chancellor health affairs U. Missouri Columbia Health Scis. Ctr., 1999—. Gastroenterologist Harry S. Truman Meml. Vets. Hosp., Columbia, 1974-79, chief med. svc., 1979-82, chief staff, 1982-84; chief staff VA Med. Ctr., Kansas City, 1984-86, dir., 1986-87; attending physician Loyola U. Med. Ctr., 1990—, Edward Hines (Ill.) Med. Ctr., 1990—; mem. adv. bd. Greater Chgo. Alliance for Mentally Ill, 1991; pres., bd. dirs. gastroenterology adv. com. VA, 1982-85, chmn. clin. and programs adv. coun., 1988-90; mem. rev. com. Mo. Dept. Mental Health, 1981-82; numerous others. Mem. editl. bd. Clin. Rsch., 1970-73, Annals Clin. Gastroenterology, 1978-83, Gastroenterology: A Weekly Update, 1978-81; assoc. editor Jour. Lab. and Clin. Medicine, 1980-83; contbr. numerous articles and abstracts to med. jours. Bd. dirs. John H. Walters Hospice Ctrl. Mo., 1982-84, chmn., 1983-84. Recipient Outstanding Clin. Tchr. in Medicine award Milwaukee County Hosp. Housestaff, 1964, Golden Apple award Student AMA, 1972, Disting. Svc. medal and award VA, 1990, Ashbel Smith Disting. Alumnus award U. Tex. Med. Br., 1992. Mem. Am. Gastroent. Assn. (com. on rsch. 1975-78, com. on tng. and edn. 1978-81, dir. clin. tchg. project 1990-82, program chmn. motility sect. 1987), Gastroenterology Rsch. Group, Ctrl. Soc. for Clin. Rsch., So. Soc. for Clin. Investigation, Am. Fedn. for Clin. Rsch., Midwest Gut Club (presiding pres. 1980-83), Soc. for Health and Human Values, Inst. Society, Ethics and Life Scis., Sigma Xi, Alpha Omega Alpha (vis. prof. U. Mo. Sch. Medicine 1991, Med. Coll. Wis. 1993). Office: U Mo Columbia Health Scis Ctr 1 Hosp Dr Columbia MO 65212-0001

WINSHIP, FREDERICK MOERY, journalist; b. Franklin, Ohio, Sept. 24, 1924; s. Wilbur William and Edna B. (Moery) W.; m. Joanne Tree Thompson, Aug. 29, 1967. AB, DePauw U., 1945; MS, Columbia, 1946. Corr. UPI, 1946—; assigned UN, 1947-49; editorial staff N.Y.C., 1950-60, cultural affairs editor, 1960-72, sr. editor, 1972-75, asst. mng. editor, 1975-80; sr. editor arts/theater N.Y.C., 1980-98; Broadway critic, 1985-98; arts critic at large, 2000—. Contbr. articles mags. Pres. Letters Abroad, Inc., 1962-83; chmn. Easter Seal Soc., N.Y.C., 1964-73, Oratorio Soc. N.Y., 1965-75, N.Y. Conf. Patriotic Socs., 1967-72; Bd. dirs. Odell House-Rochambeau Hdgrs., 1965-75, N.Y. State Easter Seal Soc., 1969-72, Mus. of City of N.Y., 1974—, Am. Philharm. Orch., 1981-82, Friends of the Am. Theater Wing, 1990—. Recipient Am. Legion Journalism award, 1955; Whitelaw Reid Journalism fellow India, 1958; Creative Club Journalism award, 1962 Mem. S.A.R. (sec. N.Y. chpt. 1963-68), St. Nicholas, Founders and Patriots, Mayflower Descs., Soc. Colonial Wars (bd. dirs.), S.R., Soc. Cincinnati, Sigma Delta Chi. Republican. Episcopalian. Home: 419 E 57th St New York NY 10022-3060

WINSLADE, THOMAS EDWIN, lawyer; b. Omaha, May 30, 1952; s. George Edwin and H.I. (Lockhart) W. BA, Claremont Men's Coll., 1974; JD, Columbia U., 1976. Bar: N.Y. 1977, Pa. 1985. Assoc. Shearman & Sterling, N.Y.C., 1976-83; assoc. counsel Mellon Bank, Pitts., 1984-87; v.p., asst. resident counsel Morgan Guaranty Trust Co., N.Y.C., 1987-92; exec. dir. Emerging Markets Traders Assn., N.Y.C., 1992-94; v.p., asst. gen. counsel J.P. Morgan Co., Singapore, 1994—. Office: care JP Morgan Co 60 Wall St New York NY 10260

WINSLET, KATE, actress; b. Reading, Berkshire, Eng., Oct. 5, 1975; m. James Threapleton, Nov. 22, 1998 (div. 2001); children: Mia, Joe; m. Sam Mendes, May 2003. Appeared in plays including Peter Pan, What the Butler Saw (Manchester Evening News award for Best Supporting Actress), A Game of Soldiers, (musical) Adrian Mole; appeared in TV shows including Anglo-Saxon Attitudes, Shrinks, Dark Season, Casualty, Get Back; appeared in films including Heavenly Creatures, 1994 (Best Fgn. Actress award New Zealand Film and TV Awards), Sense and Sensibility, 1995 (SAG award, Brit. Acad. Film and TV award for Best Supporting Actress, Golden Globe nominee, Am. Acad. Motion Picture Arts and Scis. nominee), A Kid in King Arthur's Court, 1995, Jude, 1996, Hamlet, 1996, Titanic, 1997 (nominee for Acad. award for Best Actress), Hideous Kinky, 1998, Plunge, 1999, Holy Smoke, 1999, Quills, 2000 (nominee Best Supporting Actress SAG award 2000), Faeries (voice), 2000, Iris: A Memoir of Iris Murdoch, 2001 (nominee Best Supporting Actress SAG award 2001, Brit. Acad. award 2001), Enigma, 2002 (Best Brit. Actress award), Iris, 2001, Neverland, 2003, The Life of David Gale, 2003, Eternal Sunshine of the Spotless Mind, 2004. Recipient Grammy award for best spoken word album for children, 2000, Best Actress, London Evening Std. Brit. Film Awards, Eternal Sunshine of the Spotless Mind, 2004.*

WINSLETT, STONER, artistic director; b. Jacksonville, Fla., Aug. 17, 1958; m. Donald Paulding Irwin; children: Louise Gray Irwin, Elizabeth Irwin, Alexander Pankoff, Caroline Irwin. Student, Am. Ballet Theatre Sch., N.C. Sch. of the Arts; grad. summa cum laude, Smith Coll., 1980. Artistic dir. Richmond Ballet. Pres. John Butler Found. Mem.: Phi Beta Kappa. Office: Richmond Ballet 407 E Canal St Richmond VA 23219-3811

WINSLEY, SHIRLEY J. state legislator, insurance agent; b. Fosston, Minn., June 9, 1934; d. Nordin Marvel Miller and Helga Christine Sorby; m. Gordon Perry Winsley, July 19, 1952; children: Alan, Nancy. ABS, Tacoma C.C., 1970; BA, Pacific Luth., 1971. Mem. legis. staff Wash. Senate, Olympia, 1971-75; appraiser Pierce County Assessor, Tacoma, 1971-75; mem. Wash. Ho. of Reps., Olympia, 1974, 77-92; exec. dir. Lakewood (Wash.) Chamber, 1975-76; mem. Wash. Senate, Dist. 28, Olympia, 1993—; ins. agent, family counselor New Tacoma Cemetary & Funeral Home, 1996—; pres. Wash. Senate, Dist. 28, 2003—. Mem., Wash. St. Advisory Council Accrditation of Vocational-Technical Institutes, Wash. St. Historical Soc., Lakewood Sr. Ctr., LEAP. Republican. Lutheran. Home: 1109 Garden Cir Tacoma WA 98466-6218 Office: PO Box 40428 Olympia WA 98504-0428

WINSLEY, WILLIAM T. pharmacist, executive director; BS in Pharmacy, Ohio State U., 1974, MS in Hosp. Pharmacy, 1978. Lic. pharmacist, Ohio, W.Va. Supr. drug distbn. Riverside Meth. Hosp., Columbus, Ohio, 1975-78, adminstrv. and clin. resident, 1978; asst. dir. pharmacy, instr. Coll. of Pharmacy W.Va. U. Med. Ctr., Morgantown, 1978-80; asst. dir. pharmacy Akron (Ohio) City Hosp., 1980-88; compliance specialist Ohio State Bd. of Pharmacy, Columbus, 1988-91, asst. exec. dir., dir. internship, 1991-98, exec. dir., 1998—. Mem. Nat. Assn. of Bds. of Pharmacy, Am. Soc. of Hosp. Pharmacists, Ohio Soc. of Hosp. Pharmacists (bd. dirs. 1983, 85-88, others), Akron Area Soc. of Hosp. Pharmacists (pres. 1983-84, v.p. 1982-83).

WINSLOW, DAVID ALLEN, chaplain, retired naval officer; b. Dexter, Iowa, July 12, 1944; s. Franklin E. and Inez Maude (McPherson) W.; children: Frances, David. BA, So. Nazarene U., 1968; MDiv, Drew U., 1971, STM, 1973; cert. of achievement, Emergency Mgmt. Inst., FEMA, 1997. Ordained to ministry United Meth. Ch. Detroit Annual Conf., 1969; cert. FEMA instr. Clergyman, 1969—; assoc. min. All Sts. Episcopal. Ch., Millington, NJ, 1969-70; asst. min. Marble Collegiate Ch., N.Y.C., 1970-71; min. No. N.J. Conf. United Meth. Ch., 1971-75; joined chaplain corps USN, 1974, advanced through grades to lt. comdr., 1980, ret., 1995; chaplain Oak Knoll Naval Med. Ctr., Oakland, Calif., 1993-95; command chaplain USNS Mercy T-AH19, Oakland, 1993—95; disaster cons. Ch. World Svc., Cupertino, Calif., 1997—2001. NDMS/DMAT, CA-6 Contra/Costa County, Calif., 1997—; founding mem. Dept. Homeland SEcurity, 2003; salesperson Dept. real estate State of Calif., 2000—. Author: The Utmost for the Highest, 1993, Epiphany: God Still Speaks, 1994, Be Thou My Vision, 1994, Evening Prayers At Sea, 1995, Wiseman Still Adore Him, 1995, God's Power At Work, 1996; (with Walsh) A Year of Promise: Meditations, 1995, editor: The Road to Bethlehem: Advent, 1993, Preparation for Resurrecton: Lent, 1994, God's Promise: Advent, 1994, The Way of the Cross: Lent, 1995; contbr. articles to profl. jours. Bd. dirs. disaster svcs. and family svcs. ARC, Santa Ana, Calif., 1988-91, Child Abuse Prevention Ctr., Orange, Calif., 1990-91; bd. dirs. Santa Clara County Coun. Chs., 1993-94, del., 1995-98; bd. dirs. Salvation Army Adult Rehab. Ctr. Adv. Coun., San Jose, Calif., 1995-2002; bd. dirs. emergency svcs. Santa Clara Valley chpt. ARC, San Jose, 1995-98; bd. dirs. disaster svcs. Interfaith Svc., Inc., San Jose Internat. Airport. Recipient Navy Achievement medal, Navy Commendation medal with Gold Star in lieu of 2nd award, Navy Expeditionary medal, Humanitarian Svc. medal, Battle "E" award, Nat. Def. Svc. medal, sea svc. deployment ribbon with silver star. Fellow Am. Acad. Experts in Traumatic Stress (cert. expert), USN League (hon.), Sunrise Exch. Club (chaplain 1989-91), Dick Richards Breakfast Club (chaplain 1988-91), Kiwanis, Masons (charter), Shriners, Scottish Rite. Avocations: golf, skiing, sailing.

WINSLOW, F. DANA (FRANCIS DANA WINSLOW), judge, former record company owner; b. N.Y.C., N.Y., Feb. 20, 1939; s. Francis Dana and Flora Brady (Garvan) W.; children: Francis Dana III, Michael, Jennifer. BA, Am. U., 1966; JD, Cath. U. Am., 1969. Bar: N.Y. 1970, U.S. Ct. Appeals (2d cir.) 1972, U.S. Supreme Ct. 1975. Assoc. Beekman & Bogue (now Gaston & Snow), N.Y.C., 1969-73; spl. counsel Sutter, Moffatt, Vannelli & Zevin, Mineola, 1973-78; pvt. law practice, 1978-89; pres., owner Winslow Prodns. Ltd., 1983-96; ptnr. Schiavetti, Geiser, Corgan et al, 1989-96; assoc. justice Village of Old Westbury, 1991-96; village atty. Village of Centre Island, 1988-96; justice N.Y. State Supreme Ct., 1996—; commr. N.Y.State Commn. on The Jury, 2003—. Chair adv. commn. N.Y. State Jud. Inst., 2000—; counsel World Tae Kwan Do championships, 1993; adj. prof. law sect. Grad. Bus. Law, St. John's U., 1998—2000. Judo instr. various univs. Washington met. area; instr. 2d Dan (Black Belt) Judo, 1963—, 5th Dan Tae Kwan Do, 1997; founding pres., chair Winslow Therapeutic Riding, Inc., 1974, bd. dir., 1974—; founder, chmn. Helping Hand Horse Show, 1979-86; mem. N.Y. State Supreme Ct. Justice Task Force on N.Y. Ct. Reform, 1997—, chair, 2003; bd. dir. N.Am. Riding for Handicapped Assn., 1983-87; chmn. publicity and pub. rels. Nat. Equestrian Sports Day; atty., legal counsel, advisor U.S. Tae Kwan Do Union, U.S. Olympic Com. for 1988 Olympics, 1984-89; co-organizer spl. song presentation for benefit Gift of Life program honoring Nancy Reagan, N.Y.C., 1984; appeared off-Broadway and cmty. prodns. musicals; pres. Glen Players, Glen Cove, N.Y., 1985-87, bd. dir., 1986-90; trustee, police commr. Village of Old Wstbury, 1976-81, environ. commr., 19790-81. Spl. agt. M.I., U.S. Army, 1962-65, Korea. Recipient Outstanding Svc. award D.C. Bar Assn., 1968, citation of merit Uniformed Firefighters Assn., N.Y.C., 1983. Mem. Nassau County Bar Assn., Assn. N.Y. State Suprme Ct. Justices, Nassau County Magistrates Assn. (bd. dirs. 1995-96), The Creek Club (Locust Valley, N.Y.), Sigma Nu. Democrat. Office Phone: 516-571-2480.

WINSLOW, JOHN FRANKLIN, lawyer; b. Houston, Nov. 15, 1933; s. Franklin Jarnigan and Jane (Shipley) W. BA, U. Tex., 1957, LLB, 1960. Bar: Tex. 1959, D.C. 1961. Atty., Hispanic law div. Library Congress, Washington, 1965-68; counsel, com. on the judiciary Ho. of Reps., Washington, 1968-71; atty., editor Matthew Bender & Co., Washington, 1973-79; atty. FERC, Washington, 1979-84; sole practice Washington, 1984—. Researcher Hispanic Law Research, Washington, 1979—. Author: Conglomerates Unlimited: The Failure of Regulation, 1974; editor: Fed. Power Service, 1974-79; contbr. articles to Washington Monthly, Nation, 1975—. Mem. Tex. Bar Assn., D.C. Bar Assn. Personal E-mail: jfwinslow@aol.com.

WINSLOW, JULIAN DALLAS, retired lawyer, historian, writer; b. Elizabeth City, N.C., Oct. 10, 1914; s. Joseph D. and Mary Anne (Cooper) W.; m. Jean Littell, Dec. 27, 1941; children: Julian Dallas, Mary P. Winslow Reddick, Helen L. BS in Commerce, U. N.C., 1935, JD, 1941; MA in History, U. Del., 1988. Bar: N.C. 1941, Del. 1949, U.S. Dist. Ct. Del. 1952, U.S. Ct. Appeals (3d cir.) 1982. Assoc. J.H. LeRoy Jr., Elizabeth City, 1941-42; pvt. practice Elizabeth City, 1945-48, Wilmington, Del., 1949-89; ret., 1989; ptnr. Winslow Realty Co., 1974—. Solicitor Currituck County (N.C.) Ct. 1946-47; chief of enforcement heavy machinery and indsl. materials sect. Office Price Stablzn., Del. dist. 1952; arbitrator Am. Arbitration Assn. Author: Samuel Maxwell Harrington, A Pioneer Judge, 1994, Sussex Awakens to the Toot, 1999. Lt. USCG, 1942-45. Decorated Philippine Liberation medal. Mem. ABA (real estate, probate and trust, labor sects.), Del. State Bar Assn. (com. labor and employment law). Republican. Episcopalian.

WINSLOW, NORMA MAE, elementary school educator; b. Pawling, N.Y., Oct. 18, 1942; d. Franklin Norman and Florence (Chandler) Timpson; m. Donald Arthur Winslow, Aug. 5, 1961; children: Gregory Donald (dec.), Kevin Craig. AA in Liberal Arts, Adirondack Coll., 1970; BS in Edn. summa cum laude, Castleton State U., 1973; MS in Adminstrn. and Supervision, SUNY, Plattsburg, 1990; CAS, Plattsburgh State U., 1993. Cert. elem. and secondary tchr., N.Y., SAS and SDA in Adminstrn. Tchr. Ft. Ann Ctrl. Sch., NY, 1973-77, Corinth Ctrl. Sch., 1977—, grade chair, 1984-89, dir. student svcs. adminstrn., 2002—03. Dir. music Corinth Theatre Guild, 1980—. Named Outstanding Tchr. of English, N.Y. State English Coun., 1981, One of 2000 Notable Women, 1995. Mem. Corinth Tchrs. Assn. (pres. 1980-86, 94-95), Rotary (pres. Corinth chpt. 1992, Paul Harris fellow), Delta Kappa Gamma (officer Beta Omega chpt. 1980—). Avocation: music. Office: Corinth Cen Sch 105 Oak St Corinth NY 12822-1203

WINSLOW, NORMAN ELDON, business executive; b. Oakland, Calif., Apr. 4, 1938; s. Merton Conrad and Roberta Eilene (Drennen) W.; m. Betty June Cady, Jan. 14, 1962 (div. Aug. 1971); 1 child, Todd Kenelm; m. Ilene Ruth Jackson, Feb. 3, 1979. BS, Fresno (Calif.) State U., 1959. Asst. mgr. Proctors Jewelers, Fresno, 1959-62; from agt. to dist. mgr. Allstate Ins. Co., Fresno, 1962-69; ins. agt. Fidelity Union Life Ins., Dallas, 1969-71; dist. and zone mgr. 7-Eleven, Inc., Dallas, 1971-78; owner Ser-Vis-Etc. LLC, Goleta, Calif., 1978—. Expert witness, cons. Am. Arbitration/Calif. Superior Cts. *Ser-Vis-Etc. LLC provides a variety of consulting services for 7-Eleven Franchisees, with emphasis on controlling inventory losses, store operations, goodwill sales and serving as an Expert Witness in a variety of legal matters involving 7-Eleven Franchise owners. In that capacity, Mr. Winslow has served as an advocate for Franchisees throughout the United States and has been a guest speaker at five national 7-Eleven Franchise conventions sponsored by the National Coalition of 7-Eleven Franchisees. He reorganized the company from a sole proprietorship to an LLC in July, 2003.* Pub./editor FranchiserviceNews; author: Hands in Your Pockets, 1992; contbr. numerous articles to profl. jours. With USAFNG, 1961-67. Mem. Nat. Coalition of Assn. of 7-11 Franchises (affiliate, mem. adv. bd. 1984-90). Republican. Methodist. Avocations: gardening, photography, travel, model railroading. Home: 1293 N Fancher Ave Fresno CA 93727 Office: Ser-Vis-Etc LLC PO Box 8444 Fresno CA 93747-8444 Personal E-mail: ser-vis-etc@aol.com.

WINSLOW, PAUL DAVID, architect; b. Phoenix, June 12, 1941; s. Fred D. and Thelma E. (Ward) W.; 1 child, Kirk David. BArch, Ariz. State U., 1964. Lic. architect, Ariz., Calif., Nev. Ptnr. The Orcutt/Winslow Partnership, Phoenix, 1972—. Speaker solar energy workshops, Phoenix, 1986-89; adj. prof. Ariz. State U., 1991; mem. profl. adv. coun. Ariz. State U. Coll. Architecture, Tempe, 1970—, bd. dirs. Architecture Found., 1972-76; mem. adv. com. City of Phoenix Bldg. Safety Bd., 1981; mem. adv. bd. Herberger Ctr.; pres. Ariz. State U. Coll. Architecture, Coun. for Design Excellence; bd. dirs. Ctrl. Ariz. Project Assn., Phoenix, 1971-74, Ariz. Ctr. for Law in the Pub. Interest, Phoenix, 1979-86, Phoenix Cmty. Alliance; chmn. Encanto Village Planning Com., Phoenix, 1981-86; chmn. Indian Sch. Citizens adv. com. Ind. Sch. Land Use Planning Team; lectr. on planning Ariz. State U., 1989, city of Presott, Phoenix and Tempe, 1988-89; active Coun. Ednl. Facilities Planners Internat. Mem. Steering Com. on Re-inventing Neighborhoods Project; chmn. Central and Roosevelt Coalition, 1998-99; chmn. City of Phoenix Neighborhood Initiative Area Steering Com., 1998-99; pres. bd. dirs. Harrington House Internat. Ctr. for Universal Design, 1998-99; pres. bd. dirs. Maryvale Edn. Mall, 1998-99; exec. com. Phoenix Cmty. Alliance. Fellow AIA (bd. dirs. ctrl. Ariz. chpt., also sec., treas., pres.); mem. Ariz. Soc. Architects (bd. dirs. 1970-71, 78-82), Bldg. Owners and Mgrs. Assn. Greater Phoenix (pres.

1989-90, 90-91), Boar Valley Forward Assn. (exec. com. 1994-99), Ariz. Club (Phoenix). Methodist. Home: 5941 E Edgemont Ave Scottsdale AZ 85257 Office: The Orcutt/Winslow Partnership 1130 N 2nd St Phoenix AZ 85004-1896 E-mail: winslow.p@owp.com.

WINSLOW, ROBERT A. real estate company executive; With IDC Real Estate (now JonesLangLaSalle), Tex., 1971; mktg. exec. IBM Corp.; co-founder, chmn., CEO US Equities Realty, Chgo., 1978—. Former co-chmn. Chgo. Devel. Coun.; mem. Mayor's Fellows Program, Fin. Rsch. and Adv. Com.; bd. mem. Metra, MB Fin. Inc. Founding chmn. Sculpture Chgo.; former bd. mem. Mus. Contemporary Art; mem. bd. overseers Rush Med. Coll.; trustee Rush-Presbyn.-St. Luke's Med. Ctr., North Ctrl. Coll., Ill. Masonic Med. Ctr., Columbia Coll., Chgo.; active Boy Scouts Am./Chgo. Area Coun., Bright New City, 1989—97; dir. Arts Club Chgo., The Marwen Found.; bd. mem. The Graham Found., Chgo. Pub. Libr. Found. Mem.: Chicagoland C. of C. (v.p. bd. dirs. 1982—91, bd. mem. 1990—, pres. adv. bd. 1991). Office: US Equities Realty Ste 400 20 N Michigan Ave Chicago IL 60602*

WINSLOW, WALTER WILLIAM, psychiatrist, educator; b. Lacombe, Alta., Can., Nov. 23, 1925; came to U.S., 1959, naturalized, 1964; s. Floyd Raymond and Lily Evangeline (Palmer) W.; m. Barbara Ann Spiker; children: Colleen Denise, Dwight Walter, Barbara Jean, Wendi Jae. BS, La Sierra Coll., 1949; MD, Loma Linda U., 1952. Diplomate: Am. Bd. Psychiatry and Neurology. Intern Vancouver Gen. Hosp., 1952; psychiat. resident Provincial Mental Hosp., Essondale, B.C., 1957-59, Harding Hosp., Worthington, Ohio, 1959-60; instr. dept. psychiatry and indsl. medicine U. Cin., 1960-66, dept. preventive medicine, 1964-66; asst. prof. psychiatry U. N.Mex., Albuquerque, 1966-68, assoc. prof. psychiatry, 1969-74, prof., chmn. dept. psychiatry, 1974-91, dir. mental health programs, 1976-91; med. dir. Charter Hosp. of Albuquerque, 1991-95, Charter-Heights BHS, Albuquerque, 1995—99. Assoc. prof. psychiatry Georgetown U., Washington, 1968-69; dir. bernalillo County Mental Health/Mental Retardation Ctr., 1970-78, 81-91. Contbr. articles to profl. jours. Recipient N.Mex. Gov.'s Commendation for 10 yrs. service in mental health, 1979 Fellow Am. Psychiat. Assn. (life, area VII rep. 1981-85, Assembly Speaker's award 1984), Am. Coll. of Psychiatrists (life), Am. Assn. Community Psychiatrists (hon.); mem. AMA, Am. Assn. Psychiatry and the Law, N.Mex. Psychiat. Assn. (pres. 1974-75) Republican. Office: 1625 Catron SE Albuquerque NM 87123-4255

WINSTEAD, DANIEL KEITH, psychiatrist; b. Cin., Dec. 30, 1944; s. Daniel Sebastian and Betty Jane (Kirsch) W.; m. Jennifer Reiner, June 15, 1968; children: Laura Suzanne, Nathaniel Scott. BA, U. Cin., 1966; MD, Vanderbilt U., 1970. Diplomate Am. Bd. Psychiatry and Neurology. Resident U. Cin., 1970-72, fellow, 1972-73; chief VA Med. Ctr. psychiat. svc. Tulane U., New Orleans, 1976-79, dir., consultation/liaison psychiat. tng., 1979-83, dir. psychiatric edn. and residency tng., 1983-87, assoc. prof., 1979-84, prof., 1984—, chmn. dept. psychiatry and neurology, 1987—; chief psychiat. svc. VA Med. Ctr., New Orleans, 1976-80; assoc. chief staff for edn. VA Med Ctr., New Orleans, 1979-87; staff psychiatrist VA Med. Ctr., New Orleans, 1987—. Med. dir. Jefferson Parish Substance Abuse Clinic, 1980-81; cons. E.R. Squibb and Sons, 1985-86; vis. physician psychiatry Charity Hosp., New Orleans, 1979-90. Contbr. articles to profl. jours. Maj. U.S. Army, 1973-76. Mem. AMA, Am. Coll. Psychiatrists, Am. Acad. Psychiatry and Law, Am. Psychiat. Assn., La. State Med. Soc., So. Assn. for Rsch. in Psychiatry, Acad. Psychosomatic Medicine (pres.), Am. Assn. Chairmen Depts. Psychiatry (pres.-elect), Am. Assn. Dirs. Psychiat. Residency Tng., Assn. Acad. Psychiatry, La. Psychiat. Assn. (pres. 1991-92), Soc. Biol. Psychiatry, New Orleans Area Psychiat. Assn., New Orleans Neurol. Soc., Orleans Parish Med. Soc. Republican. Presbyterian. Avocations: oenology, travel. Home: 5348 Bellaire Dr New Orleans LA 70124-1033 Office: Tulane Med Sch 1440 Canal St Ste 1000 New Orleans LA 70112-2703 E-mail: winstead@tulane.edu.

WINSTEAD, ELISABETH WEAVER, poet, writer, English language educator; b. Nashville, July 31, 1926; d. Charles Preston and Carrie Lawrence (Hadley) Weaver; m. George Alvis Winstead, July 18, 1942. BA, Vanderbilt U., 1946; MA, Peabody Coll. Vanderbilt U., 1947; postgrad., Vanderbilt U., 1980-83, Trevecca Nazarene, 1975-79. Cert. tchr. of lang. arts, bus. edn., social sci., English, Tenn., Va., Ind., Idaho, Ariz. Head bus. edn. dept. La Crosse (Ind.) High Sch., 1947-48, Franklin (Tenn.) High Sch., 1952-54, Belmont Coll., Nashville, 1954-56; with English dept. Boise (Idaho) High Sch., 1948-49; critical analyst Dept. Commerce, Washington, 1949-50; with bus. edn. dept. Averitt Coll., Danville, Va., 1950-52; elem. and high sch. tchr. Met. Nashville Schs., 1956-85. Cons. Model Tchr. Program, Nashville Met. Sch., 1958-68, mem. faculty adv. coun., 1970-79, mem. profl. devel. coun., 1980-84. Author: Social Studies Curriculum Guide, 1970, Metro Beautiful Programs, 1976, Metro PTA School History, 1980; contbr. poetry to anthologies and popular mags., including Ideals, New Hope Books, The Vanderbilt Review. Chmn. TB Seal Drive, Franklin, 1956-60, March of Dimes Fund Drive, Nashville, 1982-84, Red Cross Blood Drive, Nashville, 1984-86; capt. Heart Fund Drive, Nashville, 1979-81. Recipient Tchr. Appreciation awrd Sta. WKDA, 1970, Galaxy of Stars award Nashville Met. Schs., 1982, Ednl. Appreciation award City of Nashville, 1983, Commendation for pub. svc. Tenn. Legislature, 1994; named to Honorable Order of Ky. Cols., 1988. Mem. NEA, Am. Childhood Edn. Internat., Tenn. Hist. Soc., Wisdom Soc., Kappa Delta Pi (hon.), Pi Omega Pi (hon.), Pi Gamma Mu (hon.). Baptist. Avocations: camping, boating, gardening, reading, creative writing. Home: 3819 Gallatin Rd Nashville TN 37216-2609

WINSTEAD, GEORGE ALVIS, law librarian, biochemist, educator, consultant; b. Owensboro, Ky., Jan. 14, 1916; s. Robert Lee and Mary Oma (Dempsey) Winstead; m. Elisabeth Donelson Weaver, July 18, 1942. BS, We. Ky. U., 1938; MA, George Peabody Coll., 1940, MLS, 1957, MEd, 1958. Head chemistry and biology dept. Belmont Coll., Nashville, 1952-56; head chemistry dept. George Peabody Coll., Vanderbilt U., Nashville, 1956-58; assoc. law librarian Vanderbilt U., Nashville, 1958-76; dir. Tenn. State Supreme Ct. Law Libraries, Nashville, 1976—. Law cons. Tenn. Youth Legis., Nashville, 1976—; cons. civic clubs, local colls., 1976—, Tenn. State Govt. Depts. Archives, Nashville, 1976—. Author: Tenn. State Law Library Progress Reports, 1975, Supreme Court Library Personnel Guide, 1981, Designing Future Law Libraries' Growth and Expansion, 1982, Problem Identification and Solutions in Law Libraries, Tenn. Supreme Courts, 1985; mem. editl. bd. A Dictionary of Chemical Equations, 1952—. Mem. Col. Tenn. Gov.'s staff, Nashville, 1978. With USAAF, 1943-46. Named to Gov.'s Staff of Ky. Cols., Lexington, 1988. Fellow Am. Inst. Chemists, SAR. Baptist. Avocations: camping, hiking, travel, crafts, antique cars. Home: 3819 Gallatin Pike Nashville TN 37216-2609 Office: Tenn Supreme Ct Libr Nashville TN 37219

WINSTEAD, NASH NICKS, university administrator, phytopathologist; b. Durham County, N.C., June 12, 1925; s. Nash L. and Lizzy (Featherston) W.; m. Geraldine Larkin Kelly, Sept. 17, 1949; 1 dau., Karen Jewell. BS, N.C. State U., 1948, MS, 1951; PhD, U. Wis., 1953. Asst. prof. plant pathology, Raleigh, 1953-58; assoc. prof. N.C. State U., Raleigh, 1958-61, prof., 1961-90, prof. emeritus, 1991—, dir. inst. biol. scis., 1965-67, asst. dir. agrl. exptl. sta., 1965-67, asst. provost, 1967-73, assoc. provost, 1973-74, provost and vice chancellor, 1974-90, acting chancellor, 1981-82. Phillip Found. intern acad. adminstrn. Ind. U., 1965-66; bd. trustees N.C. Sch. Sci. and Math., 1985-90. Author: Home grown and Homemade, 1997, Mama's Book, 1998, The Provost's Office N.C. State U., An Informal History, 1955-93, 1999, The Civil War Campaigns Involving Corporal James Fletcher Winstead, 1999, Featherston Memories, 2002; contbr. articles profl. jours. Mem. N.C. Council on Higher Edn. for Adults, 1967-75; inst. rep. So. Assn. for Colls. and Schs., 1967-74; mem. Cooperating Raleigh Colls., 1968-90, pres., 1971-73, 83-85; chmn. interaction between protoplasm and toxicants com. So. Regional Edn. Bd., 1964-65; Bd. dirs. N.C. State U. YMCA, 1963-65; trustee Meth. Home for Children, 1980-88, pres., 1983-84, N.C. Wesleyan Coll., 1987-97. Served with USAAF, 1943-46. Recipient Sigma Xi research award, 1960 Fellow AAAS; Mem. Am. Phytopath. Soc. (chmn. disease, pathogen physiology com.), Am. Inst. Biol. Scis., N.C. Assn. Colls. and Univs. (exec. com. 1974-80, pres. 1978-79), Nat. Assn. State Univs. and Land Grant Colls. (edn. telecommunications com. 1980-85, equal opportunity com. 1985-88), Acad. Deans for So. States, N.C. Assn. of Acad. Officers (exec. com. 1986-89, v.p., pres. 1987-88), Sigma Xi, Phi Kappa Phi, Omicron Delta Kappa. Clubs: Torch Internat. (sec.). Home: 1109 Glendale Dr Raleigh NC 27612-4709

WINSTEN, SAUL NATHAN, lawyer; b. Providence, Feb. 23, 1953; s. Harold H. and Anita E. Winsten; m. Patricia J. Miller, Aug. 7, 1977; children: David A., J. Benjamin, Jennifer M. BA, Beloit Coll., 1976; JD, Drake U., 1980. Shareholder Whyte Hirschboeck, Milw.; chmn. corp. counsel com. Wis. Mfrs. Commn., 2004—. Contbr. articles to profl. jours. Mem. Wis. Gov.'s Adv. Coun. on Internat. Trade, 1996-2003, co-chmn., 1996-2002; mem. Wis. Gov.'s Internat. Edn. Task Force, 1997-98; chmn. corp. counsel com. Wis. Mfrs. and Commerce, 2004—. Mem. ABA (chmn. com. young lawyers divsn. 1989-90, governing coun., antitrust, bus. and internat. law sects.), Wis. Bar Assn., Internat. Bar Assn., Japan-Am. Soc. Wis. (pres. 1993-94, co-founder 1990, sec. 1990-92), Nat. Assn. Japan-Am. Socs. (bd. dirs. 1991-97, exec. com. 1993-97), Order of Barristers, Hessen-Wisconsin, Inc. (bd. dirs.). Office: Whyte Hirschboeck 555 E Wells St Milwaukee WI 53202-4108 Office Phone: 414-273-2100.

WINSTON, FLAURA K. engineering researcher; Ph. D., Univ. of Penn. School of Medicine. Asst. physician Children's Hosp. of Phila., 1994—; founder, dir. TraumaLink. Recipient Melville medal ASME, 1995. Fellow: Bloomberg School of Public Health, John's Hopkins Univ. Office: The Children's Hosp of Phila 3535 TraumaLink 10th Fl 34th St and Civic Ctr Blvd Philadelphia PA 19104

WINSTON, GEORGE, solo pianist, guitarist, harmonica player; b. Hart, Mich., 1949; Ind. musician, 1967—; founder Dancing Cat Productions, Santa Cruz, Calif., 1983—. Nine solo piano albums, Including Ballads and Blues, 1972, Autumn, 1980, Winter Into Spring, 1982, December, 1982, Summer, 1991, Forest, 1994, Linus & Lucy: The Music of Vince Guaraldi, 1996, Plains, 1999, Night Divides the Day--The music of the Doors, 2002; audiobook soundtracks: (with Meryl Streep) The Velveteen Rabbit, 1984, This is America Charlie Brown--Birth of the Constitution, 1988, (with Liv Ullmann) Sadako and the Thousand Paper Cranes, 1995; prodr. 36 albums of the masters of traditional Hawaiian slack key (finger style) guitar. Office: c/o Dancing Cat Prodns PO Box 639 Santa Cruz CA 95061-0639 E-mail: ml@dancingcat.com.

WINSTON, HAROLD RONALD, lawyer; b. Atlantic, Iowa, Feb. 7, 1932; s. Louis D. and Leta B. (Carter) W.; m. Carol J. Sundeen, June 11, 1955; children: Leslie Winston Yannetti, Lisa Winston Shaw, Laura Winston Moritz. BA, U. Iowa, 1954, JD, 1958. Bar: Iowa 1958, U.S. Dist. Ct. (no. and so. dists.) Iowa 1962, U.S. Tax Ct. 1962, U.S. Ct. Appeals (8th cir.) 1970, U.S. Supreme Ct. 1969. Trust officer United Home Bank & Trust Co., Mason City, Iowa, 1958-59; mem. Breese & Cornwell, Mason City, 1960-62, Breese, Cornwell, Winston & Reuber, Mason City, 1963-73, Winston, Schroeder & Reuber, Mason City, 1974-79, Winston, Reuber, Swanson & Byrne, P.C., Mason City, 1980-92, Winston, Reuber & Byrne, Mason City, 1992-96, Winston & Byrne, P.C., Mason City, 1996—. Police judge, Mason City, 1961-73. Contbr. articles to profl. jours. Past pres. Family YMCA, Mason City, Cerro Gordo County Estate Planning Coun.; active local charitable orgns. Capt. USAF, 1955-57. Fellow Am. Coll. Trust and Estate Counsel, Am. Bar Found. (life), Iowa Bar Found. (life); mem. ABA, ATLA, Iowa Bar Assn. (gov., lectr. ann. meeting 1977-79), 2d Jud. Dist. Bar Assn. (lectr. meeting 1981-82), Cerro Gordo County Bar Assn. (past pres.), Am. Judicature Soc., Mason City Country Club, Kiwanis, Masons. Republican. Presbyterian. Office: Winston & Byrne 119 2d St NW Mason City IA 50401-3105 E-mail: hwinston@netins.net.

WINSTON, JUDITH ANN, lawyer; b. Atlantic City, Nov. 23, 1943; d. Edward Carlton and Margaret Ann (Goodman) Marianno; m. Michael Russell Winston, Aug. 10, 1963; children: Lisa Marie, Cynthia Eileen. BA magna cum laude, Howard U., Washington, 1966; JD, Georgetown U., 1977. Bar: DC 1977, US Supreme Ct. Dir. EEO project Coun. Great City Schs., Washington, 1971-74; legal asst. Lawyers Com. for Civil Rights Under Law, Washington, 1975-77; spl. asst. to dir. Office for Civil Rights, HEW, Washington, 1977-79; exec. asst., legal counsel to chair U.S. EEO Commn., Washington, 1979-80; asst. gen. counsel U.S. Dept. Edn., 1980-86; dep. dir. Lawyers Com. for Civil Rights Under Law, 1986-88; dep. dir. pub. policy Women's Legal Def. Fund, Washington, 1988-90, chair employment discrimination com., 1979-88, ednl. cons., 1974-77; asst. prof. law Washington Coll. Law of Am. U., 1990-93, assoc. prof. law, 1993-95; gen. counsel U.S. Dept. Edn., Washington, 1993-2001; exec. dir. Pres.'s Initiative on Race, 1997-98; undersec. U.S. Dept. Edn., 2000-01; rsch. prof law Washington Coll. Law Am. U., Washington, 2001—02; prin. Winston Withers & Assocs., LLC, Washington, 2002—. Author: (book) Desegregating Schools in the Great Cities: Philadelphia, 1970, Chronicle of a Decade 1961-70, 1970, Desegregating Urban Schools: Educational Equality/Quality, 1970; contbr. articles to profl. jours. Pres. bd. dirs. Higher Achievement Program; bd. dirs. Ptnrs. for Dem. Change, Nat. Pub. Radio, So. Edn. Found.; Nat. Law Ctr. on Poverty and Homelessness. Named Woman Lawyer of the Yr, Women's Bar Asn, 1997; recipient Margaret Brent, Am Bar Asn Comn Women in the Profession, 1998, Thurgood Marshall award, DC Bar, 1999. Fellow: ABA Found; mem.: ACLU, Lawyers Comt Civil Rights Under Law, Nat Bar Asn, Washington Bar Asn, Washington Coun Lawyers, DC Bar Asn, Fed Bar Asn, Links Inc, Phi Beta Kappa, Delta Theta Phi, Alpha Kappa Alpha. Democrat. Episcopalian. Home: 1371 Kalmia Rd NW Washington DC 20012-1444 Office: Winston Withers & Assocs 2120 L St NW # 510 Washington DC 20037 Office Phone: 202-478-6135. Business E-Mail: jwinston@winwithassocs.com.

WINSTON, KRISHNA, foreign language professional; b. Greenfield, Mass., June 7, 1944; d. Richard and Clara (Brussel) W.; 1 child, Danielle Billingsley. BA, Smith Coll., 1965; MPhil, Yale U., 1969, PhD, 1974. Instr. Wesleyan U., Middletown, Conn., 1970-74, asst. prof., 1974-77, assoc. prof., 1977-84, prof., 1984—, acting dean, 1993-94. Coord. Mellon Mays Undergrad. Fellowship, 1993—. Author: O v. Horváth: Close Readings of Six Plays, 1975; translator: O. Schlemmer, Letters and Diaries, 1972, S. Lenz, The Heritage, 1981, G. Grass, Two States, One Nation, 1990, C. Hein, The Distant Lover, 1989, G. Mann, Reminiscences and Reflections, 1990, J. W. V. Goethe, Wilhelm Meister's Journeyman Years, 1989, C. v. Krockow, The Hour of the Women, 1991, E. Heller, With the Next Man Everything Will be Different, 1992, R. W. Fassbinder, The Anarchy of the Imagination, 1992, G. Reuth, Goebbels, 1994, E. Lappin; editor: Jewish Voices, German Words, 1994, P. Handke, Essay on the Jukebox, 1994, P. Handke, My Year in the No-Man's-Bay, 1998, G. Grass, Too Far Afield, 2000, P. Handke, On a Dark Night I Left My Silent House, 2000, G. Grass, Crabwalk, 2003. Vol. Planned Parenthood, Middletown, 1972-77; mem. Recycling Task Force, Middletown, 1986-87; chmn. Resource Recycling Adv. Coun., Middletown, 1989—; trustee Ind. Day Sch., Middlefield, Conn., 1989—. Recipient Schlegel-Tieck prize for translation, 1994, 2001, Helen and Kurt Wolff prize for transl., 2001; German Acad. Exch. Svc. fellow, Kahn fellow Smith Coll., 2000-01. Mem. MLA, ALTA, Soc. for Exile Studies, Am. Assn. Tchrs. German, PEN, Phi Beta Kappa (pres. Wesleyan chpt. 1987-90). Home: 655 Bow Ln Middletown CT 06457-4808 Office: Wesleyan Univ German Studies Dept Middletown CT 06459-0040 Office Phone: 860-685-3378. E-mail: kwinston@wesleyan.edu.

WINSTON, MARY A. publishing executive; BS in Acctg. and Info. Sys., U. Wis.; MBA, Northwestern U. Sr. auditor Arthur Andersen & Co., 1983—87; various positions Ameritech, 1987—91; dir. bus. devel. and strategy Biotech Divsn. Baxter Internat., 1991—95; sr. mgmt. positions Warner-Lambert, 1995—2002; v.p. Visteon Corp., 2002—04, treas., 2002—03, controller, 2003—04; exec. v.p. Scholastic Corp., N.Y., 2004—, CFO, 2004—. Office: Scholastic Corp 557 Broadway New York NY 10012*

WINSTON, MICHAEL RUSSELL, foundation executive, historian; b. NYC, May 26, 1941; s. Charles Russell and Jocelyn Anita Prem Das Winston; m. Judith Ann Marianno, Aug. 10, 1963; children: Lisa Marie, Cynthia Eileen. BA magna cum laude, Howard U., 1962; MA, U. Calif.-Berkeley, 1964, PhD, 1974. Instr. dept. history Howard U., Washington, 1964-66, asst. dean Coll. Liberal Arts, 1968-69, asst. prof. dept. history, 1970-73, v.p. acad. affairs, 1983-90, prof. emeritus, 1990—; assoc. dir. Inst. Svc. to Edn., Washington, 1966; fellow Haus. Hof-und Staatsarchiv, Vienna, 1969; dir. Moorland Spingarn Rsch. Ctr., 1973-83; v.p., bd. dirs. Alfred Harcourt Found., Silver Spring, Md., 1992-93, pres., 1993—. Cons. Smithsonian Instn., 1979—, nat. Inst. Edn., 1978-85, NSF, 1985—. Author: (with R.W. Logan) The Negro in the United States, 1970, The Howard Univ.Dept. of History, 1913-73, 1973; editor: (with R.W. Logan) Dictionary of Am. Negro Biography, 1982, (with G.R. McNeil) Hist. Judgements Reconsidered, 1988; mem. editl. bd. Washington History, 1993-97. Mem. exec. bd. Nat. Capital Area coun. Boy Scouts Am., 1988—90; trustee spl. contbn. fund NAACP, 1980—82; trustee D.C. Pub. Defender Svc., 1985—88; bd. trustees Woodrow Wilson Nat. Fellowship Found., 1997—; bd. mgrs. Hist. Soc. Washington; bd. dirs. Harcourt Brace Jovanovich, 1980—91, D.C. Pub. Libr. Found., 1994—2002, pres., 1995—99, Nat. Coun. for History Standards; mem. bd. overseers' com. to visit dept. history Harvard U., 1996—; mem. nat. adv. com. and coun. of scholars Libr. of Congress; nat. adv. bd. Protect Historic Am.; mem. Commn. on Coll. and Univ. Nonprofl. Studies ABA; mem. Nat. Ctr. for History in the Schs. UCLA/NEH. Moten fellow U. Edinburgh, 1962, Wilson fellow U. Calif., 1962, Ford fellow, 1969-70, Woodrow Wilson Internat. Ctr. Scholars fellow, 1979-80; sr. scholar, 2001 -. Mem.: Nat. Coun. for History Standards, Coun. on Foreign Relations, Atlantic Coun. of U.S., Hist. Soc. Washington, Am. Antiquarian Soc., Orgn. Am. Historians, Am. Hist. Assn., Grolier Club, Century Assn., Cosmos Club (Washington), Phi Beta Kappa (Ralph Waldo Emerson prize com. 2000). Democrat. Episcopalian. Home: 1371 Kalmia Rd NW Washington DC 20012-1444 Office: Alfred Harcourt Found 8401 Colesville Rd Silver Spring MD 20910-3352 Office Phone: 301-589-1551. E-mail: mwinston@erols.com.

WINT, DENNIS MICHAEL, museum director; b. Macon, Ga., Mar. 17, 1943; s. Paul Kenneth and Mary (McClure) W.; m. Patricia McLaughlin, Dec. 27, 1970; 1 child, Laurel Julia BS, U. Mich., 1965; tchr.'s cert., Lake Erie Coll., 1970; PhD, Case Western Res. U., 1977. Dir. environ. edn. Wiloughby Eastlake City Schs., 1968-70; dir. Ctr. Devel. Environment Curiculum, 1970-75; cons. Ohio Dept. Edn., 1975-77; dir. mus. and edn. Acad. Natural Scis., Phila., 1977-79, v.p., dir. natural history mus., 1979-82; dir. Cranbrook Inst. Sci., Bloomfield Hills, Mich., 1982-86; pres. St. Louis Sci. Ctr., 1986-95; pres., CEO The Franklin Inst., Phila., 1995—. Adj. asst. prof. Temple U.; past chmn. edn. and human resources adv. com. NSF, 1991-92; past pres. St. Louis Area Mus. Collaborative, 1991-92, mem. exec. com. Bd. govs. Greater Phila. 1st Partnership for Reform, 1995—98, mem. leadership com., 1995—98. Mem. Am. Assn. Mus. (bd. dirs. 2003-), Assn. Sci.-Tech. Ctrs. (mem. nominating com., v.p. 1993-95, pres. 1995-97, chmn. internat. com. 2000-, strategic planning com. 2002-), Greater Phila. Cultural Alliance (bd. dirs. 1996—, chmn. startegic planning com. 2000-), Benjamin Franklin Fed. Tchg. Commn. (co-chair). Home: 7128 Sheaff Ln Fort Washington PA 19034-2018 E-mail: dwint@fi.edu.*

WINTER, ARCH REESE, retired architect; b. Mobile, Ala., Sept. 13, 1913; s. Augustus Reese and Winona (Battson). BArch, Auburn U., 1935; MArch, Cath. U. Am., 1937; postgrad., Cranbrook Acad. Art, Bloomfield Hills, Mich., 1939-41. Cons. Nat. Resources Planning Bd., Washington, 1941-43; prin. Arch R. Winter, Mobile, 1945-84; ret., 1984. Prin. works include city plans for Natchez and Gulfport, Miss., Shreveport and Monroe, La., Old Louisville, Ky.; restorations include YWCA Youth Center and Residence, Isle Dauphine Country Club, Dauphin Island (Gulf States region AIA Honor award, 1957). Cons. Mobile Planning Commn. Recipient Merit medal Tenn. Soc. Architects, 1971, Thomas Jefferson medal selection com U. Va. Sch. Architecture, 1976-79, cert. of commendation Mobile Historic Devel. Commn., 1981; named Ala. Disting. Arch. Ala. Archtl. Found., 1996. Fellow AIA (pres. Ala. chpt. 1955, nat. AIA engrs. joint coun. 1957-59, urban design com. 1959-64, chmn., del to commn. d'Urbanisme, 1962, design com. 1972-78, bd. dirs. 1968-71, chmn. Honor award, 1969, chmn. environ. commn. 1970-71, Citation for Excellence in Community Architecture 1965), Am. Inst. Cert. Planners; mem. Am. Planning Assn. (Disting Svc. Plaque Ala. chpt. 1984, Lifetime Achievement award 1998).

WINTER, CHESTER CALDWELL, physician, surgery educator, historian, writer; b. Cazenovia, N.Y., June 2, 1922; s. Chester Caldwell and Cora Evelyn (Martin) W.; m. Mary Antonia Merullo, Oct. 22, 1983; children by previous marriage: Paul, Ann, Jane. BA, U. Iowa, 1943, MD, 1946. Diplomate: Am. Bd. Urology. Intern Meth. Hosp., Indpls., 1946-47; med. resident St. Luke's Hosp., Cedar Rapids, Iowa, 1947; resident gen. surgery VA Hosp., Los Angeles, 1952-53; resident urology VA Hosp.-UCLA Med. Ctr., 1953-57; physician Calif., 1950-51; clin. asst. surgery UCLA, 1954-57, instr. surgery and urology, 1957-58, asst. prof. surgery and urology, 1958-59, asst. prof. Step II, 1959-60; prof. surgery and urology Ohio State U., 1960-88, prof. emeritus surgery and urology, 1988—, Louis Levy prof. urology, 1980-88. Dir. urology Ohio State U. Hosp., Columbus, 1960-78; cons. urology VA, Air Force hosps., Dayton, 1960-80. Author: Radioisotope Renography, 1963, Correctable Renal Hypertension, 1964, Nursing Care of Patients with Urologic Diseases, 4th edit, 1977, Practical Urology, 1969, Vesicoureteral Reflux, 1969, A Concise History of the U.S. and the State of Ohio, 2002, A Bicentennial History of the State of Ohio, 2003, Ohio Cities: Historical Descriptions, 2004 editl. cons. Exerpta Medica: Nuclear Medicine, Jour. AMA; mem. editl. bd. Andrology, Jour. Urology; contbr. articles to profl. jours. Served to capt. M.C. U.S. Army, 1943-46, 48-49. Fellow Am. Acad. Pediatricians, Am. Coll. Surgeons; mem. Am. Assn. Genitourinary Surgeons, Am. Urol. Assn., Soc. Univ. Surgeons, Soc. Pediatric Urology, Soc. Univ. Urologists, Internat. Soc. Urology, Urol. Investigators Forum, Ohio State Med. Assn., Columbus Surg. Soc., Central Ohio Urology Soc., Columbus Acad. Medicine, Ohio State U. Med. Soc. Home: 6425 Evening St Worthington OH 43085-3054 E-mail: cwinter3@ameritech.net.

WINTER, DARIUS GERJON, internist; b. Bucarest, Romania, Mar. 30, 1929; came to US, 1973; s. Alex Elek and Dora Winter; m. Jeanette Winter, Mar. 21, 1959; 1 child, Jacqueline. Bachelor's degree, Aurel Vlaicu, Bucarest, 1947; MD, Inst. Medicine and Pharmacy, Bucarest, 1953, PhD in Pharmacology, 1966. Bd. cert. diplomate in internal medicine. Pvt. practice, rschr., Romania, 1953-72; intern, resident in internal medicine Booth Meml. Med. Ctr., 1973-76; pvt. practice Rego Park, N.Y., 1976-98; group practice Mt. Sinai Med. Assoc., Rego Park, 1998—2002; pvt. practice Rego Park, 2002—. Attending physician Parkway Hosp., Forest Hills., 1976—, N.Y. Hosp. Queens, 1976—, Mt. Sinai Hosp., N.Y.C., 1999, N. Shore U. Hosp. at Forest Hills, N.Y., 1999—. Contbr. numerous papers to profl. jours. Fellow ACP; mem. AMA, Am. Soc. Internal Medicine, N.Y. State Med. Soc. Avocations: travel, swimming. Office: 97-85 Queens Blvd Rego Park NY 11374

WINTER, DAVID FERDINAND, electrical engineering educator, consultant; b. St. Louis, Nov. 9, 1920; s. Ferdinand Conrad and Annie (Schaffer) W.; m. Bettie Jeanne Turner; children: Suzanne, Sharie Winter Chappeau. BSEE, Washington U., St.Louis, 1942; MSEE, MIT, 1948. Registered profl. engr., Mo. Staff mem. radiation lab. MIT, Cambridge, 1942-45, rsch. assoc. electronics lab., 1945-48; prof. elec. engring. Washington U., 1948-55, affiliate prof. elec. engring., 1955-67; v.p. engring. and rsch. Moloney Elec. Co., St. Louis, 1955-74; v.p. rsch. and engring. Blackburn div. IT&T, St. Louis, 1974-82, dir. advanced tech. devel., 1982-86; pvt. practice cons. St. Louis, 1986—. Ct. recognized tech. expert on sources, mitigation, and effects of stray voltage on dairy cattle cons. Wis. Pub. Svc. Commn.; cons. Naval Ordanance Lab. of Ind., Indpls., 1950-53, other industries, St. Louis, 1979—. Contbr. articles to profl. jours.; holder 28 patents. Elder, pastor Maplewood Bible Chapel, St. Louis. Recipient Alumni Achievement award, Wash. U., Sch. Engring. & Applied Sci., St. Louis. Mo., 2003, Washington U., 2003. Fellow IEEE (life), Inst. Radio Engrs.; mem. NSPE, Am. Soc. Agrl. Engrs., Mo. Soc. Profl. Engrs., Sigma Xi, Tau Beta Pi, Eta Kappa Nu. Avocations: cabinet maker, photography, music instruments. Home and Office: 735 Harvard Ave Saint Louis MO 63130-3135 Office Phone: 314-727-4532. E-mail: dfwinter@hotmail.com.

WINTER, DAVID LOUIS, systems engineer, human factors scientist, retired; b. Pitts., July 30, 1930; s. Louis A. and Gladys M. (Quinn) W.; m. Nancy L. Tear, July 1, 1952; children: Leeson, Blaise, Gregory, Lauren. BA, U. Pitts., 1952; MA, Columbia U., 1960; cert. computer sci., Northeastern U.,

1971. Assoc. rsch. scientist Am. Insts. Rsch., Washington, 1961-66, sr. rsch. scientist Bedford, Mass., 1966-71, prin. rsch. scientist, 1976-94, retired, 1995; sr. systems analyst RCA Corp.-Sarnoff Labs., Princeton, N.J., 1971-73; mgr. systems engring. Codon Corp., Bedford, 1973-76. Computer systems cons. Mass. Dept. Mental Health, 1971-73. Pres. Mayo Peninsula Civic Assn., Edgewater, Md., 1964-65; v.p. Bedford Human Rels. Coun., 1992-94. Capt. USAF, 1952-64. Mem. Am. Acad. Polit. Sci., Human Factors Soc., Soc. Ednl. Tech. Democrat. Roman Catholic. Achievements include design and human factors test for 8 USAF electronic, intelligence and backscatter radar systems; design of 4 computer-assisted training systems for USAF E3 AWACS radar, computer displays, communications and navigation subsystems; cons. engr. for design and test of E6 Joint Stars battlefield surveillance system. Office: MicroVentures Ltd 27 Gould Rd Bedford MA 01730-1250

WINTER, DONALD C. science administrator; BS in Physics with high distinction, U. Rochester, 1969; MS, U. Mich., 1970, PhD, 1972; grad., U. SC Mgmt. Policy Inst., 1979; grad. exec. program, UCLA, 1987; grad. program for sr. execs. in nat. and internat. security, Harvard U., 1991. Dir. rsch. devel. staff TRW Sys., 1972—80, from sr. sys. engring. and program mgmt. to pres., CEO, 1982—2000; program mgr. for space acquisition, tracking and pointing programs Def. Advanced Rsch. Projects Agy., 1980—82; corp. v.p., pres. mission sys. Northrop Grumman Corp., LA, 2000—. Bd. dirs. Wolf Trap Found., Electronic Industries Alliance, USO Met. Washington. Mem.: Nat. Acad. Engring. Office: Northrop Grumman Corp 1840 Century Park E Los Angeles CA 90067-2199

WINTER, DOUGLAS E. lawyer, writer; b. St. Louis, Oct. 30, 1950; s. William E. and Dorothy E. (Schuster) W.; m. Lynne G. Turner, July 9, 1977; step-children: Carl, John, Stephen. BS, U. Ill., 1971, MS, 1972; JD, Harvard U., 1975; postgrad., Judge Advocate Gen.'s Sch., 1977. Bar: Mo. 1975, Ill. 1976, D.C. 1976. Clk. to Hon. William H. Webster U.S. Ct. Appeals (8th cir.), St. Louis, 1975-76; assoc. Covington & Burling, Washington, 1976-84; ptnr. Bryan Cave LLP, Washington, 1985—. Vis. prof. U. Iowa, Iowa City, 1980-81. Author: Stephen King, 1982, Shadowings: The Reader's Guide to Horror Fiction, 1983, Stephen King: The Art of Darkness, 1984, Faces of Fear, 1985, Black Wine, 1986, Splatter: A Cautionary Tale, 1987, Prime Evil, 1988, Darkness Absolute, 1991, Black Sun, 1994, Millennium, 1997, Revelations, 1997, Run, 2000, Clive Barker: The Dark Fantastic, 2001, American Zombie, 2004, Introduction to Legal Writing, 2004; contbr. articles to popular mags. and nat. newspapers. Capt. U.S. Army, 1973-77. Recipient world fantasy award World Fantasy Conv., 1986, award Internat. Horror Guild, 1995, 96, 98. Mem. Nat. Book Critics Circle, Horror Writers Assn. (chmn. grievance com. 1989—, trustee 1997—). Office: Bryan Cave LLP 700 13th St NW Fl 6 Washington DC 20005-3960 Office Phone: 202-508-6000. E-mail: dewinter@bryancave.com.

WINTER, FREDERICK ELLIOT, fine arts educator; b. Barbados, WI, June 19, 1922; s. Edward Elliot and Constance Mabel (Gill) W.; m. Joan Elizabeth Hay, June 9, 1951; children: Elizabeth, Penelope, Mary, Michael. BA, McGill U., 1945; PhD, U. Toronto, 1957. Instr. U. Toronto, 1947-49, 50-51, lectr., 1951-57, asst. prof., 1957-61, asso. prof., 1961-68, prof., 1968-90, prof. emeritus, 1990—, chmn. dept. fine art, 1971-77, grad. coord. history of art, 1978-81, spl. lectr. history of art, 1990-98; chmn. U. Toronto Assn. Teaching Staff, 1968-69. Mem. mng. com. Am. Sch. Classical Studies, Athens, Greece, 1968-90, chair pers. com., 1975-77; mem. programme com. Can. Archaeol. Inst. at Athens, 1990-94; bd. dirs. Can. Acad. Inst., Athens. Author: (with G.S. Vickers, P.H. Brieger) Art and Man, Vol. I, 1963, Greek Fortifications, 1971; contbr. articles Jour. Classical Assn. Can., Am. Jour. of Archaeology, Echos du Monde Classique/Classical Views. Recipient Gold medal in classics McGill U., 1945; Flavelle fellow U. Toronto, 1947-48; White fellow Am. Sch., Athens, 1949-50; spl. research fellow, 1977-78, 87-88; sr. assoc. fellow, 1982, 83-84, 86, 91; Am. Philos. Soc. grantee, 1957; grantee Soc. Sci. Humanities Rsch. Coun. Can., 1962, 68, 71, 75, 77-78, 82, 83-84, 86, 87-88, 91; grantee U. Toronto Humanities and Social Scis. Rsch. Com., 1993. Mem. Classical Assn. Can., Archeol. Inst. Am. (editorial adv. bd. Am. Jour. Archaeology 1981-85) Home: 164 Highgate Ave Willowdale ON Canada M2N 5G8 Office: Dept Fine Art U Toronto Toronto ON Canada

WINTER, HARVEY JOHN, retired government official; b. New Albion, NY, Apr. 6, 1915; s. George J. and Irene (Harvey) W.; m. Virginia M. Shaw, Sept. 2, 1939; 1 child, Jeffrey S. BA magna cum laude, U. Buffalo, 1938, MA, 1939; teaching fellow, George Washington U., 1939-40. Historian U.S. Nat. Park Service, 1940-42; archivist U.S. Nat. Archives, 1942-43; with U.S. Office Alien Property Custodian, 1943-51, chief reports and stats. sect., 1948- 51; with State Dept., 1951—, chief internat. bus. practices div., 1959- 61, asst. chief, 1961-70, chief bus. practices div., 1970-71, dir. office bus. protection, 1971-73, dir. office bus. practices, 1973-90; dir. office intellectual property and competition, 1991-92; U.S. del. European Productivity Agy. cartel meetings, Paris, 1958-60; mem. U.S. del. diplomatic confs. Internat. Design Agreement, The Hague, 1960, 17th session GATT, Geneva, 1960; U.S. alt. rep. 5th session Intergovtl. Copyright Com., London, 1960, 6th session, Madrid, 1961, 7th session, New Delhi, 1963; U.S. alt. rep. Interunion Coordinating Com., Geneva, 1963-69; U.S. observer African Seminar on Indsl. Property, Brazzaville, Congo, 1963; U.S. alt. observer Latin Am. Indsl. Property Seminar, Bogota, Colombia, 1964, Asian Indsl. Property Seminar, Colombo, Ceylon, 1966, Com. of Experts on Inventors' Certificates, Geneva, 1965, Com. of Experts on Adminstrv. Agreement, Geneva, 1965, Intellectual Property Diplomatic Conf., Stockholm, 1967, Diplomatic Conf. on Agreement for Classification of Indsl. Designs, Locarno, Switzerland, 1968, Diplomatic Conf. on Patent Cooperation Treaty, Washington, 1970, Diplomatic Conf. on Agreement for Internat. Patent Classification, Strasbourg, France, 1971, Diplomatic Conf. on Universal Copyright Conv., Paris, 1971; U.S. alt. rep. Diplomatic Conf. on Phonogram Conv., Geneva, 1971, Diplomatic Conf. on Indsl. Property, Vienna, 1973; U.S. rep. Com. Experts on Type Face Agreement, Geneva, 1972, Com. Experts on Communications Satellites Problems, Nairobi, Kenya, 1973; U.S. del. Diplomatic Conf. on Communications Satellites Conv., Brussels, 1974, Diplomatic Conf. on Treaty for Deposit Microorganisms, Budapest, Hungary, 1977, Diplomatic Conf. on Plant Protection Conv., Geneva, 1978, World Intellectual Property Orgn. Governing Bodies, Geneva, 1979-82, alt. del., 1983-91; alt. U.S. del. Diplomatic Conf. on Revision of Paris Conv., Geneva, 1980, 82, 83, 84 Nairobi, 1981; ret., 1992. U.S. del. UNESCO Experts on Rental of Videograms, Paris, 1984, Com. Govtl. Experts on Audiovisual Works and Phonograms, Paris, 1986, Com. Govtl. Experts on Internat. Register of Audiovisual Works, Geneva, 1988, Diplomatic Conf. on Treaty for Internat. Registration of Audiovisual Works, Geneva, 1989, Com. Experts on Disputes Steelement Treaty on Intellectual Property, 1990; chmn. Internat. Patent Classification Assembly, 1992. Recipient Superior Honor award Dept. State, 1971, 75, 89, 92, 50-Yr. Svc. award, 1990, Jefferson medal, N.J. Patent Law Assn., 1982; honoree Copyright Soc. U.S.A., 1989. Mem. Phi Beta Kappa. Episcopalian (vestry). Home: 1401 S Jruce St Apt 502 Arlington VA 22202-2137

WINTER, HORST HENNING, chemical engineer, educator; b. Stuttgart, Sept. 9, 1941; s. Simon Wilhelm and Hanna (Schwenn) W.; m. Karin Eckert, Aug. 29, 1969; children: Dirk Christopher, Lisa Susanne, Caroline Elke, Peter Benjamin. D of Engring., U. Stuttgart, 1973. Privatdozent U. Stuttgart, 1976-79; prof. U. Mass., Amherst, 1979—. Editor Rheologica Acta, 1989—; mem. edit. bd. Jour. Rheology, 1989—, Jour. Non-Newtonian Fluid Mechanics, 1989—; contbr. articles to sci. and profl. jours., 1977—. Recipient Bingham medal, 1996, NSF Creativity award, 1997, Alexander von Humboldt prize, 1999. Mem. Am. Soc. Rheology (exec. com. 1990-91), Am. Inst. Chem. Engrs., N.Y. Acad. Sci. Achievements include development of novel rheological techniques; discovery of self-similar relaxation of polymers at the gel point; universal time spectrum of linear flexible polymers of uniform length; invention of CSX process for making ultra-clean porous polymers. Office: U Mass Dept Chem Engring Amherst MA 01003 E-mail: winter@ecs.umass.edu.

WINTER, JANE, medical educator; b. N.Y.C., 1952; MD, U. Pa., 1977; intern, U. Chgo., 1977-78, resident int. medicine, 1978-80. Fellow in hematology and oncology Columbia P&S, N.Y.C., 1980-81, Northwestern U., 1981-83, prof., 1983—. Mem.: Ea. Coop. Oncology Group, Am. Soc. for Blood and Marrow Transplantation, Am. Assn. Cancer Rsch., Am. Fedn. for Clin. Rsch., Am. Soc. Clin. Oncology, Am. Soc. Hematology. Office: Divsn Hematology/Oncology 676 N St Clair St Ste 850 Chicago IL 60611-2978 Office Phone: 312-695-4538. E-mail: j-winter@northwestern.edu.

WINTER, JERRY ALAN, sociology educator; b. Bronx, July 23, 1937; s. Herman and Rose (Kavkewitz) Winter; m. Gail Doreen Cameron, June 13, 1964; children: Wendy, Miriam. BA, NYU, 1958; MA, U. Mich., 1960, PhD, 1964. Asst. prof. Rutgers U., New Brunswick, N.J., 1965-68; dir. Rsch. on Tng. for Met. Ministry, Washington, 1967-69; asst. prof. sociology Temple U., Phila., 1968-70; assoc. prof. Conn. Coll., New London, 1970-77, prof. sociology, 1977-2000, Lucretia Allyn prof., 2000—02, prof. emeritus, 2002—. Author, editor: Vital Problems for American Society, 1968, Clergy in Action Training, 1971, The Poor, 1971, Continuities in the Sociology of Religion: Creed, Congregation and Community, 1977, Jewish Choices, 1998. Mem. Ethics Com., Waterford, Conn., 1999—2002; chmn. United Way Campaign Com., Conn. Coll., 1987—88. Mem. Assn. for Sociol. Study of Jewry (editor Contemporary Jewry Jour. 1992-97), Phi Beta Kappa, Psi Chi, Alpha Kappa Delta. Democrat. Jewish. Home: 43 Beacon Hill Dr Waterford CT 06385-4107 Office: Conn Coll Box 5302 270 Mohegan Ave New London CT 06320-4125 E-mail: jawin@conncoll.edu.

WINTER, JOAN ELIZABETH, psychotherapist; b. Aiken, S.C., Feb. 24, 1947; d. John S. and Mary Elizabeth (Caldwell) Winter. BS, Ariz. State U., 1970; MSW, Va. Commonwealth U., 1977; EdS, Coll. William and Mary, 1989, EdD, 1993. Lic. marriage and family therapist; lic. clin. social worker, Va.; diplomate Nat. Assn. Social Workers. Counselor Child Psychiatry Hosp., Phoenix, 1969-70, Ariz. Job Coll., Casa Grande, 1970-71; dir. Halfway House, Richmond, Va., 1971-73; state supr. resdl. treatment Richmond, 1973-75; psychotherapist Med. Coll. Va., Richmond, 1975-76, Va. Commonwealth U., 1976-77; adj. prof., exec. dir. Family Rsch. Project Coll. William and Mary, Richmond, Va., 1979—; dir. Family Inst. Va., Richmond, 1980—. Examiner, approved supr. Bd. Behavioral Scis., Commonwealth of Va., 1982—; faculty dept. psychiatry Med. Coll. Va., Commonwealth U.; mem. adj. faculty dept. counseling Coll. William & Mary, Med. Coll. Va.; mem. Avanta Network, Exec. Coun. and Faculty, Nat. Inst. of Drug Abuse, Rsch. Adv. Com. Author: The Phenomenon of Incest, 1977, The Use of Self in Therapy: The Person and Practice of the Therapist, 1987, Family Life of Psychotherapists, 1987, Enhancing the Marital Relationship: Virginia Satir's Parts Party, 1990, Enhancing the Marital Relationship: Virginia Satir's Parts Party, Satir Theory, 1991, Family Therapy Research Outcomes: Bowen, Haley and Satir; editor Jour. Couple Therapy; contbr. articles to profl. jours. Mem. Am. Soc. Cert. Social Workers, Am. Family Therapy Assn., Am. Assn. Marriage and Family Therapy (approved supr.), Avanta Network Faculty. Address: 2910 Monument Ave Richmond VA 23221-1404 E-mail: fiv1@erols.com.

WINTER, JOHN ALEXANDER, realtor, real estate appraiser; b. Cin., July 2, 1935; s. George Edward and Mary Alma (McAuliffe) W. BS, Georgetown U., 1957; grad., Annapolis Sailing Sch. Ptnr. Winter & Winter, Cleve., 1957-76; residential salesman Moreland Hills Co., Chagrin Falls, Ohio, 1976-77; residential appraiser Kiebler, Smith & Co., Chardon, Ohio, 1977-91; founder, pres., CEO Cert. Appraisal Svc. Co., Shaker Heights, Ohio, 1985—; v.p., dir. The Gas Pipe Co., Chagrin Falls, 1973—; part owner Cleve. Indians, 1998-2000. Contbr. articles to profl. jours. Rep. precinct committeeman Shaker Heights, 1996—2004; pres. New Engl. Soc. of Cleve. and Western Res., 1976—77, 1983—84, 2002—, treas., 1987—2002; pres. Shaker Heights Rep. Club, 1977—84; v.p., trustee Shaker Hist. Soc., 1985—91; trustee Dunham Tavern Mus., 2000—, Early Settlers Assn., 2003; docent Dunham Tavern Mus., 1998—; mem. exec. com. Cuyahoga County Rep. Orgn., 1994—. Recipient Svc. award Pres. Ronald Reagan, 1984, New Eng. Heritage award New Eng. Soc., 1984. Mem. Cleve. Independence Day Assn. (v.p., trustee 1957—, Treharne award 1984), Am. Assn. Cert. Appraisers (v.p. No. Ohio chpt.), Nat. Assn. Ind. Fee Appraisers (cert. mem.), Ohio Assn. Realtors, Nat. Assn. Realtors (Ben Franklin award 1983), Grad. Realtors Inst., Cleve. Bar Assn. (grievance com. 1997—), Cathedral Latin Alumni Assn. (trustee 1965-2002, exec. com. 1988-2002, v.p. 1988-92, pres. 1992-94, Golden Alumni award 1996), Georgetown Club (pres. 1966-67), Cleve. of Washington Club (trustee 1984—), The Wahoo Club (bd. dirs. 2003—). Roman Catholic. Avocations: tennis, sailing, sports collectibles. Home and Office: Cert Appraisal Svc Co 19271 Shaker Blvd Shaker Heights OH 44122-2547 Office Phone: 216-991-1133.

WINTER, JOHN DAWSON, III, blues guitarist, singer; b. Beaumont, Tex., Feb. 23, 1944; s. John Dawson II and Edwina (Holland) W. Grad. high sch. Organizer, performer numerous rock and blues bands, rec. artist, CBS Records, Inc., 1969—, TV and concert appearances through, U.S. and Europe, 1969—; albums include Johnny Winter, 1969, Second Winter, 1969, Johnny Winter-And, 1970, Live, 1971 (Gold Record award 1974), Still Alive and Well, 1973, Saints and Sinners, 1974, John Dawson Winter III, 1974, Captured Live, 1976, Nothin' But the Blues, 1977, White Hot and Blue, 1978, The Johnny Winter Story, 1980, Raisin' Cain, Serious Business, 1985 (Grammy nominee), 3rd Degree, 1986, The Winter of '88, 1988, Winter Scene, 1990, Let Me In, 1991, Hey Where's Your Brother, 1992, Scorchin' Blues, 1992, A Rock n' Roll Collection, 1994, Johnny Winter Live in New York City 1997, 1997; producer recs. by Muddy Waters: albums include Still Hard (Artist of Yr., Rolling Stone mag. 1969), Hard Again, 1977 (Grammy award), I'm Ready, 1978 (Grammy award), Muddy Mississippi Waters Live, 1979 (Grammy award), King Bee, 1980. Mem. Broadcast Music Inc., Musicians Union. Office: Slatus Mgmt 35 Hayward Ave Colchester CT 06415-1221 E-mail: cpwrecds@aol.com.

WINTER, KENNETH MICHAEL, editor, publishing executive, educator; b. Lansing, Mich., Aug. 7, 1950; s. Richard G. and Beverly (Radcliff) W.; 1 child, Michael. Student, Adrian Coll., 1968-69, Am. U., 1970; BA, Mich. State U., 1972; fellow in journalism, U. Mich., 1979. Youth beat writer Lansing State Jour., 1964-72, reporter, 1972-73, pub. svc. dir., 1973; editor Charlevoix (Mich.) Courier, 1974-76; reporter Petoskey (Mich.) News-Rev., 1973-74, asst. gen. mgr., spl. projects editor, 1976-79, editor, gen. mgr., 1979-2001, editor, publisher, 2001—. Adj. faculty North Ctrl. Mich. Coll., Petoskey, 2004—; sec., bd. dirs. Otsego Herald Times Inc., Gaylor, Mich., Rev. Dirs. Inc., Petoskey; v.p. No. Mich. Rev. Inc., Petoskey, 1994—. Author: (chpt. in book) Historical Glimpses - Petoskey, 1986; editor: Million Dollar Memories-A 125 Year Pictorial Recollection of Little Traverse Bay, 2000.; contbr. articles to profl. jours. Pres. Little Traverse Hist. Soc., Petoskey, 1977-82, United Way Emmet County, Petoskey, 1982; trustee Hist. Soc. Mich., 1979-85; trustee, chair Little Traverse Conservancy, Harbor Springs, Mich., 1982-98; v.p. Crooked Tree Arts Coun., Petoskey, 1979-86; bd. dirs. North Ctrl. Mich. Coll. Found., 1999—. No. Cmty. Mediation, 2000-. Nat. journalism fellow U. Mich., 1978-79; journalism awards Nat. Newspaper Assn. Mem. Mich. Press Assn. (bd. dirs. 1992—, pres.-elect 2000, pres. 2001-02, journalism awards), Mich.AP Edit. Assn. (bd. dirs. 1992-98, pres. 1995-96), Am. Soc. Newspaper Editors, Kiwanis (pres. Petoskey chpt. 1983-84). Home: 1004 Lockwood Ave Petoskey MI 49770-3156 Office: Petoskey News-Rev PO Box 528 319 State St Petoskey MI 49770-0528 Office Phone: 231-347-2544. E-mail: kwint@freeway.net.

WINTER, LARRY EUGENE, accountant; b. Williamsport, Pa., Jan. 17, 1950; s. Robert Schrader and Betty Irene (Foresman) W.; m. Constance Dianne Snyder, June 2, 1973; children: John, Matthew, Noël, James. A in Bus. Adminstrn., Palm Beach Jr. Coll., 1969; BSBA, U. Fla., 1971; cert. bus., U. Pa., 1977. Cert. valuation analyst, cert. fraud examiner, CPA, Fla., Ga.; accredited fin. planning specialist. Audit supr. Touche Ross & Co., Atlanta, 1971-74; chief. fin. officer Hawthorne Industries, Dalton, Ga., 1974-79; pvt. practice acctg. Dalton, 1979-89; mng. ptnr. Winter & Harris, CPAs, Dalton, 1990—. Mem. White House Conf. Small Bus., Atlanta, 1979; instr. West Ga. Coll., Carollton, 1985, Ea. European Bus. Coll., Budapest, Hungary, 1995; acct. in residence Ga. Coll., Milledgeville, Ga., 1989; cons. Christian Businessman's Com. Internat., 1986-2003. Author: The American Free Enterprise System and the Ethics that Make it Work, 1991. Trustee Dalton Jr. Coll. Found., 1974—77; chair Whitfield County/Dalton Day Care Ctrs., 1987—92; mem. N.W. Ga. Healthcare Partnership, 1994—2004, chair, 2002—03; mem. Downtown Dalton Devel. Authority, 2001—04; mem. adv. coun. Ga. State Bd. Workers Compensation, 1991—2003; mem. fee arbitration panel State Bar Ga., 1987—; mem. Dalton-Whitfield Planning Commn., 2004—; elder Fellowship Bible Ch., 1985—. Hixson fellow Kiwanis, 2000. Mem. AICPA, Assn. Cert. Fraud Examiners, Nat. Assn. Cert. Valuation Analysts, Ga. Soc. CPAs (pres. 1983-84), Ga. Sheriff's Assn. (Disting. Humanitarian award), Dalton-Whitfield C. of C. (Leadership 1990-91, treas. 1992-94), Walden Club, Kiwanis (life, pres. 1978-79, lt. gov. 1981-84, George Hixon fellow 2000), SAR. Avocations: cooking, credit and financial counseling. Office: PO Box 2644 Dalton GA 30722-2644 Office Phone: 706-278-2834.

WINTER, LEIGH ELLEN, artist, educator; b. St. Louis, Mo., Mar. 31, 1969; d. Richard Lawrence and Vicki Hunt Winter, Kathryn Ann Winter (Stepmother); m. Gabriel Paul Katz, Sept. 29, 2001. BFA Metalsmithing, U. Kans., Lawrence, Kans.; MFA Sculpture, Pratt Inst., Bklyn. Asst. to art critic Robert C. Morgan, N.Y., 1996—98; artist's asst. Artist - Angiola Churchill, N.Y., 1997; curatorial asst./registrar Ian Woodner Family Collection, N.Y., 1998—99; asst. to the chair, art & design edn. Pratt Inst., Bklyn., instr. sch. visual arts, 2000—04, internship coord., 2004—. Artist's lecture Villa Duchesne, St. Louis, 1996; mem. grad. admissions com., art and design edn. Pratt Inst., Bklyn., 2000—04, mem. internship coun., 2001—04, mem. faculty search com., art and design edn., 2001—02, mem. peer rev. com., art and design edn., 2001—02, mem. sen. academic initiatives com., 2002—04. Exhibitions include Convergence, Pratt Inst., Bklyn., U. Kans., Lawrence, Kans., Wash. U., St. Louis, Mo., Olivette Cmty. Ctr. (Second Pl., 1984, Hon. Mention, 1984), St. Louis Artists Guild, Williamsburg Art and Hist. Soc., Bklyn., Caitlyn Gallery, St. Louis, Mo., The Bronx Mus. for the Arts, Bronx, N.Y., Monk Gallery, Williamsburg, Bklyn., N.Y., Mercer SS Gallery, 2004, prin. works include Point Lookout, East Windham, N.Y. Recipient Drawing and Painting, Villa Duchesne, Sculpture, Visual Arts; Artist's Residency, Vt. Studio Ctr., 2003, Artists in the Marketplace Program, Bronx Mus. of the Arts, 1997. Mem.: Coll. Art Assn., Soc. for Ethical Culture. Personal E-mail: winterkatz@earthlink.net. E-mail: winterkatz@optonline.net.

WINTER, MICHAEL ALEX, federal agency administrator; b. Chgo. m. Atsuko Kuwana; 1 child. BA in Philosophy, So. Ill. U., 1974; postgrad. studies in Bus. Adminstrn., U. San Francisco, 1986. Dep. dir. Ctr. for Ind. Living, Berkeley, Calif., 1977-81; exec. dir. Hawaii Ctr. for Ind. Living, Honolulu, 1981-82; CEO Ctr. for Ind. Living, Berkeley, 1982-94; spl. asst. to assoc. dep. sec. U.S. Dept. Transportation, Washington, 1994-98, assoc. adminstr. for budget and policy, 1998—2001; dir. Office of Civil Rights, Washington, 2001—. Chair disability caucus Calif. Dem. Orgn., 1984-93; bd. dirs. Alameda-Contra Costa County Transit Dist., 1988-94, chair fin. com., govt. rels. com.; pres., exec. dir. Nat. Coun. on Ind. Living, 1989-91; chair disability com. Dianne Feinstein for Gov., Calif., 1990. Democrat. Office: Dept Transp 400 7th St SW Washington DC 20590-0003

WINTER, MILDRED M. educational administrator; BA summa cum laude, Harris Tchrs. Coll.; MEd, U. Mo.; postgrad., Harvard U., U. Cin. Exec. dir. Parents As Tchrs. Nat. Ctr. Inc., St. Louis. Tchr., cons., Mo., 1962-68; developer, dir. Ferguson-Florissant Parent-Child Early Edn. Program, Mo., 1969-72; first dir. early childhood edn. Mo. Dept. Elem. and Secondary Edn., 1972-84; sr. lectr. dept. elem. and early childhood edn. U. Mo., St. Louis; cons. in field. Contbr. articles to profl. jours. Named Outstanding Leader in Field of Edn., Mo. House of Reps., 1982, Outstanding Educator and Adv. for Young Children, Mo. Gov. Christopher S. Bond, 1984, Pioneer in Edn., State Bd. Edn., Mo. Dept. Edn., 1991, St. Louis Woman of Achievement in Edn., 1992; cited for Pioneering Leadership in Edn. Resolution, Mo. Senate, 1995; recipient Outstanding Svc. award Assn. Edn. of Young Children, 1984, Vol. Accreditation Leadership award, 1993, Spl. award Nat. Soc. Behavioral Pediat., 1992, Charles A. Dana Pioneering Achievements Health and Edn. Inst. Medicine award NAS, 1995. Office: Parents as Teachers Patnc 2228 Ball Dr Saint Louis MO 63146-8602

WINTER, MIRIAM THERESE (GLORIA FRANCES WINTER), nun, religious education educator; b. Passaic, N.J., June 14, 1938; d. Mathias William and Irene Theresa (Marton) W. BMus, Cath. U. Am., 1964; M in Religious Edn., McMaster Divinity Coll., Hamilton, Ont., Can., 1976; PhD in Liturgical Studies, Princeton Theol. Sem., 1983; LHD (hon.), Albertus Magnus Coll., 1991, St. Joseph Coll., 1993; lhd (hon.), Mount Sait Vincent U., 2004. Joined Med. Mission Sisters, Roman Cath. Ch., 1955. Dir. liturgy and liturgical music Med. Mission Sisters, Phila., 1960-76, pub. rels. dir., coord., 1963-72; assoc. prof. liturgy, worship and spirituality Hartford (Conn.) Sem., 1980-85, prof., 1985—, prof. liturgy, worship, spirituality, and feminist studies, 1994—. Mem. faculty St. Therese's Inst., Phila., 1964-68, acad. dir., 1968-72, Immaculate Conception Sem. Summer Program, Mo., 1969, Cath. U. Summer Grad. Program, Washington, 1970, Hope Ecumenical Inst., Jerusalem, summer 1974, 75, 76, McMaster Divinity Coll. Grad. Program, 1976, Continuing Edn. Program, 1976, N.Y. Archdiocesan Sch. Liturgical Music, summer 1980, 82, Vancouver Sch. Theology, summer 1982, USN Chaplains through Auburn Theol. Sem., 1990; mem. adj. faculty Union Inst., Cin., 1992-94; with emergency relief work Internat. Rescue Com., Cambodia, 1979-80, Malteser-Hilfsdienst Auslandsdienst, Germany, 1984, Med. Mission Sisters, Ethiopia, 1985; lectr., instr., performer, worship leader, song leader for various groups by invitation, nat. and internat., 1967—. Author: Preparing the Way of the Lord, 1978, God-With-Us: Resources for Prayer and Praise, 1979, An Anthology of Scripture Songs, 1982, Why Sing? Toward a Theology of Catholic Church Music, 1984, WomanPrayer, Woman Song: Resources for Ritual, 1987, WomanWord: A Feminist Lectionary and Psalter, 1990, WomanWisdom: A Feminist Lectionary and Psalter, Women of the Hebrew Scriptures, Part I, 1992 (1st pl. award for books on liturgy Cath. Press Assn., 1992), WomanWitness: A Feminist Lectionary and Psalter, Women of the Hebrew Scriptures, Part II, 1992 (1st pl. award for books on liturgy Cath. Press Assn., 1993), The Gospel According to Mary: A New Testament for Women, 1993; co-author: Defecting in Place: Women Claiming Responsibility for Their Own Spiritual Lives, 1994 (2d pl. award for books on gender studies Cath. Press Assn., 1995), The Chronicles of Noah and Her Sisters: Genesis and Exodus According to Women, 1995 (2d pl. award for books on gender studies Cath. Press Assn., 1996), Songlines: Hymns, Songs, Rounds and Refrains, 1996, The Singer and the Song: An Autobiography of the Spirit, 1999, Out of the Depths, The Story of Ludmila Javorova, Ordained Roman Catholic Priest, 2001 (1st pl. award for books on popular presentation of the Cath. faith Cath. Press Assn., 2002); author: numerous songs included in albums Keepsake, Hymns Re-Imagined, SpiritSong, EarthSong, WomanSong, Remember Me, Sandstone, Songs of Promise, RSVP: Let Us Pray, Gold, Incense and Myrrh, In Love, Seasons (Christian Oscar award Nat. Evang. Film Found., 1971), Knock, Knock, Praise the Lord in Many Voices (live rec. of Mass of a Pilgrim People premiered at Carnegie Hall), 1967, I Know the Secret, Joy is Like the Rain (Gold album in USA and Australia); contbr. articles to profl. jours. Bd. dirs. Capitol Region Conf. Chs., 1984-91, v.p., 1986-88. pres. bd. dirs., 1988-90, past pres., 1990-91, Archdiocesan Office Urban Affairs, 1986-95; mem. Christian Conf. ann. event WINFEST, 1986, 87; mem. small christian communities design team Archdiocese of Hartford, 1987-91; mem. major events design team RENEW, 1986; subcommn. chair Archdiocesan Office of Synod, 1991; mem. New Eng. team Ministry of Money, 1984-90, 93; mem. The New Century Hymnal editl. com. United Ch. of Christ, 1993-95; active Ho. of Bread, Pediats. AIDS Unit Yale-New Haven Hosp., Covenant to Care, Voices of Joy Gospel Choir women imprisioned at Niantic. Grantee Lilly Endowment, 1989-90, 91-93; recipient Ho. of Reps. citation Commonwealth of Pa., 1968, Women in Leadership Edn. award YWCA Conn., 1989, Convenant to Care award for ministry to children, 1993; named to McMaster U. Alumni Gallery, 1982, Celebration of 120 Women in Leadership, 1987, Bayley-Ellard H.S. Hall of Fame, 1993, Conn. Women's Hall of Fame, 2002. Mem. ASCAP (Popular Awards list 1968—), AAUW (Excellence in Equity award Conn. chpt. 1995), Nat. Assn. Pastoral Musicians, N.Am. Acad. of Liturgy, Societas Liturgica. Avocations: photography, calligraphy. Office: Hartford Sem 77 Sherman St Hartford CT 06105-2260 Office Phone: 860-509-9558. E-mail: mtwinter@hartsem.edu.

WINTER, PETER MICHAEL, anesthesiologist, educator; b. Sverdlovsk, Russia, Aug. 5, 1934; arrived in U.S., 1938, naturalized, 1944; s. George and Anne Winter; m. Michelle Yakopec, Dec. 28, 1991; children: Karin Anne, Christopher George, Lia Lynn, Tori Anne. BA, Cornell U., 1958; MD, U. Rochester, 1962. Diplomate Am. Bd. Anesthesiology. Intern U. Utah, Salt Lake City, 1962-63; resident in anesthesiology, pharmacology and respiratory physiology Mass. Gen. Hosp., Boston, 1963 65; USPHS fellow Harvard U. Med. Sch., Mass., 1964-66; Buswell fellow dept. physiology, asst. prof. SUNY, Buffalo, 1966-69; assoc. prof. dept. anesthesiology Sch. Medicine, U. Wash., Seattle, 1969-74, prof., 1974-79; prof., chmn. dept. anesthesiology and critical care medicine U. Pitts. Sch. Medicine, 1979-96, Peter and Eva Safar prof. anesthesiology/critical care med., 1987—96, prof. emeritus, dir. faculty devel., 1996—. Anesthesiologist in chief Univ. Health Ctr. Hosps., Pitts., 1979—96. Editl. cons.: Anesthesiology CCMJ; contbr. chapters to books, papers and abstracts to publs. With U.S. Army, 1953—56. Recipient Career Devel. award, NIH, 1971. Mem.: AMA, Assn. univ. Anesthetists, Internat. Anesthesia Rsch. Soc., Undersea Med. Soc., Soc. Critical Care Medicine, N.Y. Acad. Scis., Royal Soc. Medicine, Am. Soc. Anesthesiologists, Am. Coll. Chest Physicians, Morton Soc., Am. Alpine Club. Office: 3471 5th Ave Ste 910 Pittsburgh PA 15213-3221

WINTER, RALPH KARL, JR., federal judge; b. Waterbury, Conn., July 30, 1935; married. BA, Yale U., 1957, JD, 1960; JD (hon.), Bklyn. Law Sch., N.Y. Law Sch. Bar: Conn. 1973. Rsch. assoc., lectr. Yale U., 1962—64, from asst. prof. assoc. prof. law, 1967—78, William K. Townsend prof. law, 1978—82, adj. prof. law, 1982—; spl. cons. subcom. on separation of powers U.S. Senate Com. on Judiciary, 1968—72; sr. fellow Brookings Inst., 1968—70; adj. scholar Am. Enterprise Inst., 1972—82; judge U.S. Ct. Appeals (2d cir.), New Haven, 1982—97, chief judge, 1997—2000, sr judge, 2000—. Vis. prof. law U. Chgo., 1966; adv. com. civil rules Jud. Conf. U.S., 1987 92, chmn. adv, com. rules evidence, 1993—96, exec com., 1998—2000, chmn. exec. com., 1999—2000. Contbr. articles to profl. jours. Recipient Conn. Law Rev. award, Learned Hand award, Fed. Bar Coun. Office: Second Circuit US Courthouse 141 Church St New Haven CT 06510-2030

WINTER, RICHARD LAWRENCE, financial and health care company executive; b. St. Louis, Dec. 17, 1945; s. Melvin Lawrence and Kathleen Jane (O'Leary) W.; children from previous marriage: Leigh Ellen, Jessica Marie, George Bradford; m. Kathryn Ann Geppert, Dec. 4, 1993. BS in Math., St. Louis U., 1967, MS in Math. (fellow), 1969; MBA, U. Mo., St. Louis, 1976 Rsch. analyst Mo. Pacific R.R., St. Louis, 1971-73; dir. fin. rels. Linclay Corp., St. Louis, 1973-74; asst. v.p. 1st Nat. Bank in St. Louis (now Centerre Bank, NA) subs. Boatmen's Nat. Bank, 1974-79; v.p. fin. UDE Corp., St. Louis, 1979-81; pres. Health Care Investments, Ltd., St. Louis, 1981—, Larus Corp., St. Louis, 1981—, Garden View Care Ctr., Inc., O'Fallon, Mo., 1987—. Exec. bd. Duchesne Bank, St. Peters, Mo., 1989-97; lectr. math. U. Mo., St. Louis, 1972-74, St. Louis U., 1982-90. Exec. adv. bd. St. Louis U. Coll. Arts and Scis., 2000—; bd. dirs. Dance St. Louis, 1998—2004; cmty. adv. bd. Coll. Fine Arts and Comm. U. Mo., St. Louis, 2003—; fundraising staff St. Louis Symphony, Jr. Achievement, United Way St. Louis, Arts and Edn. Fund, St. Louis, 1974—79. With U.S. Army, 1969—71. Mem. Nat. Health Lawyers Assn., Mo. Athletic Club (St. Louis), Pi Mu Epsilon. Roman Catholic. Home: 725 S Skinker Blvd Unit 9N Saint Louis MO 63105 Office: Ste 170 12444 Powerscourt Dr Saint Louis MO 63131-3659 Office Phone: 314-965-1991.

WINTER, RICHARD SAMUEL, JR., computer training company owner, writer; b. Denver, Mar. 17, 1958; s. Richard Samuel and Jerryl Dene (Gano) W.; m. Karen Annette Hansen, May 27, 1989. Student, Griffith U., Brisbane, Australia, 1979; BA in Internat. Environment, Colo. Coll., 1981; MA in Pub. Adminstrn., U. Colo., Denver, 1989. Range aide U.S. Forest Svc., Desert Exptl. Station, Utah, 1976-77; pub. health investigator, lab. technician Denver Health Dept., 1982-84; projects mgr. Colo. Statesman, Denver, 1984-85; editor Mile Hi Prep, Denver, 1985; fin. analyst Pan Am. World Airways, N.Y.C., 1985-88; sr. ptnr., owner PRW, Denver, 1988—; tng. mgr. Qwest, 2000-01; tchr. Denver Pub. Schs., 2001—03. Pres. info. systems Trainers, Denver, 1994. Co-author, revisor: MicroRef Quick Reference Bd. Lotus 1-2-3 Rel. 3.0, 1990, MicroRef Quick Reference Gd. Lotus 1-2-3 Rel. 2.2, 1990, Que Q&A QueCards, 1991, Que 123 Release 2.3 QuickStart, 1991, Que 123 Release 2.4 QuickStart, 1992, Que Look Your Best with Excel, 1992, Que Excel for Windows Sure Steps, 1993, Que Using Lotus 123 Release 4, 1994, Que Using Excel 5, 1994, Que Using Microsoft Office, 1994, Que Using Microsoft Office 95, 1995, Que Special Edition Using Microsoft Office Professional for Windows 95, 1996, Que Special Edition Using Microsoft Office 97 Professional, 1997, Que Microsoft Access 97 Quick Reference Guide, 1997, Que Using Microsoft Office 95, 1998, Que Microsoft Office 97 User Manual, 1998, Que Microsoft Excel 2000, Cheat Sheet, 1999, DDC Learning Office 2000, 1999, DDC Learning Access 2000, 1999, DDC One Day Office, Excel, Access, Word, Power Point (1999-00), Rising Moon, Dirty Birdy Feet, 2000. Chmn. N.Y. Victims for Victims, N.Y.C., 1986-87; bd. dirs. Colo. Common Cause, Denver, 1984-85; steering com. Voter Registration "Motor Voter" Amendment, Denver, 1983-84; pres. Broadway Commons Homeowners Assn., Denver, 1982-84; pres. Info. Systems Trainers, 1994, bd. dirs. 1990-96; Dist. Accountability Adv. Com. budget chair Clear Creek Sch. Dist., 1996-98; chair Clear Creek Imagine Ednl. Excellence, 1997-98, Citizens for Improved Edn., 1999-2000, Clear Creek Sch. Bd., 2000—. Recipient Vigil Honor, Order of the Arrow, 1976, Disting. Svc. award Info. Sys. Trainers, 1996. Mem. Phi Beta Kappa, Alpha Lambda Delta.

WINTER, ROGER PAUL, federal agency administrator; b. Hartford, Conn., July 13, 1942; s. Raymond Gustav and Marion Nellie (Stafford) W.; m. Delorise Allen, Aug. 22, 1966; children: Jonathan, Raymond Todd, Nicole. BA in Psychology, Wheaton Coll., 1964; LLD (hon.), Holy Family Coll., 1993. Asst. sec. Md. Dept. Human Resources, Balt., 1970-79, Md. Dept. Budget and Fiscal Planning, Annapolis, 1979-80; dir. Office of Refugee Resettlement, HHS, Washington, 1980-81, U.S. Com. for Refugees, Washington, 1981-2001; exec. dir. Immigration and Refugee Svcs. Am., Washington, 1994-2001; dir. Office U.S. Fgn. Disaster Assistance, Washington, 2001—02; asst. adminr. USAID, Washington, 2002—. Cons. on refugee affairs Women's Refugee Project, Washington, 1981-84; adv. bd. Refugee Policy Group, 1981-86; mem. bd. Refugee Voices, 1988-96; mem. exec. com. Coun. Washington Reps. on UN, 1989-91. Recipient Disting. Service Cambodian Assn. Am., 1982, Disting. Service award Indochina Resource Action Ctr., 1988. Mem. Nat. Ry. Hist. Soc.-Balt., Sudan Relief and Rehab. Assn. (bd. dirs., sec. 1991-93). Lodges: Eagles. Office: USAID Bur Democracy/ Humanitarian Assistanc RRB 1300 Pennsylvania Ave NW Washington DC 20523 E-mail: rwinter@usaid.gov.

WINTER, RUTH GROSMAN (MRS. ARTHUR WINTER), journalist; b. Newark, May 29, 1930; d. Robert Delmas and Rose (Rich) Grosman; m. Arthur Winter, June 16, 1955; children: Robin, Craig, Grant. BA, Upsala Coll., 1951; MS, Pace U., 1989. With Houston Press, 1955-56; gen. assignment Newark Star Ledger, 1951-55, sci. editor, 1956-69; columnist L.A. Times Syndicate, 1973-78, Register and Tribune, syndicate, 1981-85, isyndicate-.com, 1999-2001. Columnist myskinMD.com, 2000-01; contbr. to consumer mags.; instr. St. Peters Coll., Jersey City.; vis. lectr. mag. writing Rutgers U. Author: Poisons in Your Food, rev. edits., 1971, 91, 99, 2004, How to Reduce Your Medical Bills, 1970, A Consumer's Dictionary of Food Additives, 1972, rev. edit., 2004, Vitamin E, The Miracle Worker, 1972, So You Have Sinus Trouble, 1973, Ageless Aging, 1973, So You Have a Pain in the Neck, 1974, rev. edit., 2000, A Consumer's Dictionary of Cosmetic Ingredients, 1974, 4th rev. edit., 1994, 5th rev. edit., 1999, Don't Panic, 1975, The Fragile Bond: Marriage in the 70's, 1976, Triumph Over Tension, 1976 (N.J. Press Women's Book award), Scent Talks Among Animals, 1977, Cancer Causing Agents: A Preventive Guide, 1979, The Great Self-Improvement Sourcebook, 1980, The Scientific Case Against Smoking, 1980, People's Guide to Allergies and Allergens, 1984, A Consumer's Guide to Medicines in Food, 1995; co-author: The Lean Line One Month Lighter Program, 1985, Thin Kids Program, 1985, Build Your Brain Power, 1986, Eat Right: Be Bright, 1988, A Consumer's Dictionary of Medicines: Prescription, Over-the-Counter and Herbal, 1994, 97, Super Soy,: The Miracle Bean, 1996, rev. edit., 2000, Pain in the Neck, 1997, rev. edit., 2000, Anti Aging Hormones, 1997, Brain Workout, 1997, 2003, Vitamin E: Your Protection Against Exercise Fatigue, Weakened Immunity, Heart Disease, Cancer, Aging, Diabetic Damage, Environmental Toxins, 1998, Smart Food, 1999, The Female Athlete's Body Book: Preventing and Treating Sports Injuries in Women and Girls, 2003. Recipient award of merit ADA, 1966, Cecil award Arthritis Found., 1967, Am. Soc. Anesthesiologists award, 1969, Arthritis Found. award, 1978; named Alumnus of Year Upsala Coll., 1971, Woman of Year N.J. Daily Newspaper Women, 1971, Woman of Achievement Millburn Short Hills Profl. and Bus. Women's Assn., 1991, Golden Triangle award Am. Dermatol. Assn., 1998. Mem. Soc. Mag. Writers, Authors League, Nat. Assn. Sci. Writers, Am. Med. Writers Assn. (Eric Martin Meml. award), N.J. Daily Newspaper Women (awards news series 1958, 70, named Woman of Achievement 1971, 83), Am. Soc. Journalists and Authors (pres. 1977-78, spl. service award 1983, Lifetime Achievement award 2004), N.J. Press Women (pres. 1982-84) Home and Office: 44 Holly Dr Short Hills NJ 07078-1318

WINTER, STEVEN, internist, cardiologist; b. Bklyn., July 25, 1950; s. Nathan Harold and Magda (Markowitz) W.; m. Florence Stein, Aug. 20, 1972; children: Amy R., Daniel. BA, Yeshiva U., 1972; MD, U. Med./Dentistry of N.J., 1976. Diplomate Am. Bd. Internal Medicine with subspecialty in cardiovascular disease. Intern North Shore Univ. Hosp., Manhasset, N.Y., 1976-77; resident in medicine North Shore Univ. Hosp, Manhasset, N.Y., 1976-79, Meml. Sloan Kettering Cancer Ctr., Cornell Cooper Tng. Hosp., 1977-79; fellow in cardiology R.I. Hosp.-Brown U., Providence, 1979-81; pvt. practice S.I., N.Y.; attending in medicine and cardiology S.I. U. Hosp., 1981—, St. Vincent's Med. Ctr., Richmond, 1985—; asst. clin. prof. SUNY, Bklyn., 1985—. Fellow ACP, Am. Coll. Cardiology; mem. AMA, Am. Heart Assn. Office: 2627B Hylan Blvd Staten Island NY 10306-4353

WINTER, THOMAS SWANSON, editor, newspaper executive; b. Teaneck, N.J., Dec. 28, 1937; s. Frank J. and Beulah (Swanson) W.; m. Dawne Cina, Mar. 28, 1978; children: Victoria Ruth, Abigail Swanson. AB, Harvard U., 1959, MBA, 1961. Asst. editor Human Events newspaper Human Events, Inc., Washington, 1961-64, editor, 1964—, co-owner, pres., 1966-99, pres., editor-in-chief, 1999—; pres. Fund for Objective News Reporting. Treas. Conservative Victory Fund, Washington, 1975—; 1st vice-chmn. Am. Conservative Union, 1972—. Mem.: Nat. Press, Capitol Hill. Lutheran. Home: 16 4th St SE Washington DC 20003-3804 Office: Human Events 1 Massachusetts Ave NW Washington DC 20001-1401 Office Phone: 202-216-0600. E-mail: twinter@eaglepub.com.

WINTER, WILLIAM EARL, retired beverage company executive; b. Granite City, Ill., Sept. 21, 1920; s. William M. and Ada M. (Compton) W.; m. Dorothy E. Schuster, Feb. 20, 1944 (dec. 1976); children: William C., Douglas E.; m. Mildred E. Stiebel, Mar. 18, 1977. AB, U. Ill., 1942. With Seven-Up Co., St. Louis, 1946-81, v.p., dir. mktg., 1969-71, exec. v.p., 1971-74, pres., chief operating officer, 1974-76, pres., chief exec. officer, 1976-79, chmn. bd., 1979-81, also former dir., cons.; chmn. emeritus, 1996—; cons. Cadbury Beverages/Seven-Up, chmn. emeritus, 1996. Bd. dirs. YMCA Greater St. Louis, U. Ill. Found.; mem. exec. bd. St. Louis Area coun. Boy Scouts Am. Capt. U.S. Army, 1942-46. Named to Promotion Mktg. Hall of Fame, 1979, Beverage World Hall of Fame, 1986 Mem. Am. Mktg. Assn., Sales and Mktg. Execs. St. Louis, Promotion Mktg. Assn. Am. (chmn. bd. 1971-72), Phi Beta Kappa, Phi Eta Sigma, Omicron Delta Gamma. Home: 14112 Baywood Villages Dr Chesterfield MO 63017-3421 Office: Dr Pepper/Seven Up Cos Inc 8900 Page Ave Saint Louis MO 63114-6108 Office Phone: 314-426-8296.

WINTER, WILLIAM FORREST, former governor, lawyer; b. Grenada, Miss., Feb. 21, 1923; s. William Aylmer and Inez (Parker) W.; m. Elise Varner, Oct. 10, 1950; children: Anne, Elise, Eleanor. BA, U. Miss., 1943, LLB, 1949; LLD, William Carey Coll., 1980, Millsaps Coll., 1983, Troy State U., 1988, Davidson Coll., 1996, Miss. U. for Women, 2000, U. N.C., 2004. Bar: Miss. 1949. Practice in Grenada, 1949-58; practice in, 1968—; ptnr. Watkins, Pyle, Ludlam, Winter and Stennis, 1968-80; sr. ptnr. Watkins Ludlam Winter & Stennis, 1985—; mem. Miss. Ho. of Reps., 1948-56; state tax collector, 1956-64; state treas., 1964-68; lt. gov., 1972-76; gov., 1980-84. Eudora Welty prof. So. studies Millsaps Coll., 1989; Jamie Whitten prof. law U. Miss., 1989; prof. pub. policy Miss. Valley State U., 2001—02; chmn. So. Growth Policies Bd., 1981, So. Regional Edn. Bd., 1982, MDC, Inc.; mem. Pres.'s Adv. Bd. on Race, 1997—99; chmn. Adv. Commn. on Intergovtl. Rels., 1993—97. Pres. bd. trustees Miss. Dept. Archives and History; chmn. Kettering Found., 1990-93, Appalachian Regional Commn., 1983, Commn. on Future of South, 1986, Nat. Civic League, 1987-88, Nat. Commn. on State and Local Pub. Svc., Stennis Ctr. for Pub. Svc., Found. for the Mid South. With AUS, 1943-46, 51. Harvard U. Inst. Politics fellow, 1985. Mem. Am., Miss., Hinds County bar assns., U. Miss. Alumni Assn. (pres. 1979), Phi Delta Phi, Omicron Delta Kappa, Phi Delta Theta. Clubs: Univ. (Jackson). Democrat. Presbyterian. Office: 633 N State St Jackson MS 39202-3306 Office Phone: 601-949-4800.

WINTER, WILLIAM PAUL, JR., ministry director; b. Arkansas City, Kans., Apr. 27, 1942; s. Paul William and Dessie Marie (Francis) W.; m. Sharon Ruth Fells, Dec. 26, 1964; children: Todd William, Heidi Reneé. BA, Ashland (Ohio) Coll., 1965; Cert. Electronics Cirs. and Systems Program, RCA Inst., N.Y.C., 1970; MDiv, Ashland Theol. Sem., 1986. Chief engr. radio/TV dept. Ashland Coll., 1967-72; electronic technician CAVEA Studio, Buenos Aires, 1972-74, tech. dir., 1974-93; exec. dir. Open Arms Ministry, Denver, 1998—. Exec. bd. dirs. Evang. Found. of Argentina, Buenos Aires, 1979-93; tech. cons. various evang. orgns. in Argentina, Paraguay, Uruguay; bd. dirs. Trans World Radio, Buenos Aires, Interdenominational Theol. Sem., Buenos Aires. Contbr. articles to profl. jours. Baptist. Avocations: travel, camping, car restoration, amateur radio, photography. Home: 10817 Livingston Dr Northglenn CO 80234

WINTER, WINTON ALLEN, JR., lawyer, state senator; b. Ft. Knox, Ky., Apr. 19, 1953; s. Winton A. and Nancy (Morsbach) W.; m. Mary Boyd, July 28, 1978; children: Katie, Molly, Elizabeth. BA, U. Kans., 1975, JD, 1978. Bar: Kans. 1978. Ptnr. law firm Stevens & Brand, LLP, Lawrence, Kans., 1978—; v.p., gen. counsel Peoples, Inc., 2000-02; pres., CEO Peoples Bank, 2002—; pres. Corp. for Change; mem. Kans. Senate, 1982-92. Bd. dirs. Lawrence United Fund, Boys Club of Lawrence. Mem. ABA, Kans. Bar Assn., Douglas County Bar Assn. Kans. U. Law Soc., Rotary. Republican. Roman Catholic. Note and comment editor Kans. Law Rev., 1977-78. Office: PO Box 1795 4831 W 6th St Lawrence KS 66049 Office Phone: 785-842-4004. E-mail: wwinter@epeoples.com.

WINTERBOTTOM, GODDARD WILLIAMS, retired editor; b. Providence, Dec. 15, 1929; s. Ralph Goddard and Phoebe Wilmarth (Williams) Winterbottom; m. Ann Hutton Burwell, Dec. 17, 1955; children: Ian, Colin. BA, Harvard U., 1951; MA in Theater, Cath. U. Am., 1957. Editl. asst. NAS, Washington, 1951—57; dir. theater Briarcliff Coll., Briarcliff Manor, NY, 1957—59; assoc. editor Grolier, Inc., N.Y.C., 1961—63; editor-in-chief dept. coll. Sci. Rsch. Assocs., Chgo., 1964—67; assoc. editor Ency. Britannica, Chgo., 1967—73; editl. assoc. The Brookings Instn., Washington, 1974—75; editor-in-chief dept. editl. and prodn. World Bank, Washington, 1975—91; ret., 1991. Performer: Swan Song (Mary Goldwater award, 1991). Democrat. Avocation: theater.

WINTEREGG, STEVEN LEE, composer, musician, educator; b. Dayton, Ohio, July 13, 1952; s. Leland Floyd and Shirley Mae Winteregg; m. Candy Sue Cheek, June 26, 1976; children: Joseph Daniel, Carrie Amber. MusB, U. of Cin., 1970—74; MusM, Wright State U., 1977—79; MusD, Ohio State U., 1984—87. Prof. music, chair music and art dept. Cedarville (Ohio) U., 1981—2004; prin. tuba Dayton Philharm. Orch., Dayton, Ohio, 1987—. Composer: (ballet) Robin Hood, Christmas Carol, An American Cinderella, (horn concerto) Visions and Revelations, (marimba concerto) Javarella, (orchestra) Breathless, Fanfare for a City, (chorus and orch.) To Fly Unbound. Recipient First Prize in Composition, Internat. Trumpet Guild, 2002, Music Citation, Ohioana Libr. Assn., 1998, First Prize in Composition, Internat. Horn Soc., 1986, New Louisville Brass Quintet, 1978, The Joy of Life Composition Competition, 1975; Artist Fellowship in Composition, Ohio Arts Coun., Montgomery County Arts Dist. Mem.: ASCAP (ASCAP Plus Award 1988—2004), Coll. Music Soc., AAUP, Am. Music Ctr. Grace Brethren. Home: 419 Westview Place Englewood OH 45322-1148 Office: Cedarville U 251 N Main St Cedarville OH 45314 Office Phone: 937-766-7728. Personal E-mail: swint@erinet.com.

WINTERER, PHILIP STEELE, lawyer; b. San Francisco, July 8, 1931; s. Steele Leland and Esther (Hardy) W.; m. Patricia Dowling, June 15, 1955; children: Edward J., Amey W. Marrella. BA, Amherst Coll., 1953; LLB, Harvard U., 1956. Bar: N.Y. 1957, Republic of Korea 1958. Assoc., then ptnr. Debevoise & Plimpton, N.Y.C., 1956-93, ret. ptnr., 1994, of counsel, 1994—96. Dir. Am. Savs. Bank, 1972-92. Contbr. articles to profl. publs. Past pres. Am. Italy Soc.; trustee Amherst Coll.; chmn. emeritus Sch. of Am. Ballet; chmn. exec. com. Phipps Houses; trustee emeritus N.Y. State Bd. Nature Conservancy; past chmn. Austen Riggs Ctr.; past vice chmn. Adelphi U.; bd. govs. Emily Dickinson Mus.; mem. Com. on the Folger Shakespeare Libr.; mem. adv. coun., past v.p. Adirondack Trail Improvement Soc. Recipient Amherst Coll. medal for Eminent Svc., 1980, Pres medal Adelphi U., 2004. Mem.: Am. Coll. Tax Counsel, Tax Forum, Citizens Housing and Planning Coun. N.Y., Am. Law Inst., Coun. on Fgn. Rels., Ausable Club (trustee, pres.), Fellows of Phi Beta Kappa Soc. (bd. dirs.). Home: 57 Gulf Brook Way Keene NY 12942 also: 1165 5th Ave New York NY 10029-6931 Office: Debevoise & Plimpton 919 3rd Ave New York NY 10022 Personal E-mail: winterhill95@aol.com.

WINTERER, VICTORIA THOMPSON, hospitality executive; b. Chgo., May 4, 1943; d. Henry Lawrence and Charlotte (Mather) Thompson; m. William George Winterer, Sept. 2, 1967; children: William G. Jr., Andrew H., Britton T., Mark L. Cert., Emma Willard Sch., Troy, N.Y., 1961; BA, Vassar Coll., 1965. Picture rschr. Time, Inc., N.Y.C., 1965-72; pres. bd. trustees Conn. River Mus., Essex, 1983-86; dir. Rockfall Found., Middletown, Conn., 1986-92; chairwoman Campaign for Emma Willard, Troy, 1992-97; v.p., trustee Emma Willard Sch., 1986-2000; owner, exec. Griswold Inn, Inc., Essex, 1972-96. Bd. dirs. Conn. River Valley and Shoreline Visitors' Coun., Middletown, 1994-96; sec. Essex Twp. Bd. Trade, Essex, 1990-96; mem. Essex Rep. Town Com., 1976-84; trustee (life) Conn. River Mus. Recipient Disting. Alumnae award for Svc. to Emma Willard Sch., 1996, Tangeman medal, 1997; named Disting. Citizen of Yr., Middlesex County C. of C., 1996. Home: Snail's Pace PO Box 1009 Boca Grande FL 33921-0640 also: Turtle Bay 93 River Rd Essex CT 06426-1307

WINTERLING, ANN, artist; BA, Chatham Coll., 1954. Tchr. numerous classes and workshops; demonstrator in field. Exhbns. include N.H. Farm Mus., Milton, 1988, Found. Gallery of League of N.H. Craftsmen, 1988, 93, 2000, 2001, Thorne Sagendorph Gallery, 1992, Hopkinton (N.H.) Antiquarian Soc., 1992, 95, Newport (R.I.) Arts Ctr. Show, 1993, Cahoon Mus. Am. Art, Cotuit, Mass., 1993-94, 2001, N.H. Hist. Soc., 1994, Worcester (Mass.) Ctr. Crafts, 1994, Currier Gallery Art, Manchester, N.H., 1995, Wenham (Mass.) Mus., 1998; contbr. articles to profl. jours. Mem. League of N.H. Craftsmen, Nat. Assn. Traditional Rug Hooking Artists, Woolen Magic - Hooked Fiber Art Guild, Green Mountain Hooking Craft Guild (Vt.), The Internat. Guild of Handhooking Rug Makers (sec. 1997-2000). Studio: 61 Mountain Rd Concord NH 03301

WINTER-NEIGHBORS, GWEN CAROLE, special education educator, art educator, consultant; b. Greenville, SC, July 14, 1938; d. James Edward (dec. 2002) and Evelyn (Lee) Walters (dec. 1998); m. David M. Winter Jr., Aug., 1963 (dec. Feb. 1980); children: Robin Carole Winter, Charles G. McCuen, Dustin Winter TeBrugge; m. Thomas Frederick Neighbors, Mar. 24, 1989. BA in Edn. and Art, Furman U., 1960, MA in Psychology, 1967; cert. in guidance/pers., Clemson U., 1981; EdD in Youth and Mid. Childhood Edn., Nova Southeastern U., 1988; postgrad., U. S.C., Spartanburg, 1981-89; cert. clear specialist instrn. with honors, Calif. State U., Northridge, 1991; art edn. cert., Calif. State U., L.A., 1991; JD, Glendale U., 1999. Cert. tchr. art, elem. edn., psychology, secondary guidance, S.C. Tchr. 7th grade Greenville Jr. H.S., 1960-63; art tchr. Wade Hampton H.S., Greenville, 1963-67; prin. adult edn. Woodmont H.S., Piedmont, S.C., 1983-85, Mauldin H.S., Greenville and Mauldin, S.C., 1981; tchr. ednl. psychology edn. dept. Allen U., Columbia, S.C., 1969; activity therapist edn. dept. S.C. Dept. of Corrections, Columbia, 1973-76; art specialist gifted edn. Westcliffe Elem. Sch., Greenville, 1976-89; tchr. self-contained spl. day class Elysian Heights Elem. Sch., Echo Park and L.A., Calif., 1989-91; art tchr. medh. drawing Sch. Dist. Greenville County Blue Ridge Mid. Sch., Greer, 1991-95; tchr./asst. head edn. dept. N. Creenville Coll., 2001—02. Participant nat. conf. U.S. Dept. Edn./So. Bell, Columbia, 1989; com. mem. nat. exec. com. Nova Southeastern U., 1988—89; asst. chmn., tchr. edn. dept. North Greenville coll., 2001; adm., staff North Greenville Coll., 2001, U. S.C., Spartanburg; adj., student tchr., supr. U. SC, 2002; adv. bd. S.C. Gov. Sch. for Arts & Humanities; parent/tchr. adv. bd. Spl. Edn.; adj. prof U. SC Univ. Ctr., Greenville, 2002—03; ind. rep. Primerica Fin. Svs., 2003—04. Mozart Book, 1988; author: (drama) Let's Sing a Song About America, 1988 (1st pl. Nat. Music award, 1990); contbr. The International Library of Poetry Ode to Stardust', 2002. Life mem. Rep. Presdl. Task Force, 1970—; mem. voter registration com. Lexington County Rep. Party, 1970—80; grand jury participant 13th Jud. Ct. Sys., Greenville, 1986—88, guardian ad litem, 1988—2004; mem. arts educators adv. task force S.C. Gov. Sch. Arts and Humanities, 2002—; mem. spl. edn. parent adv. bd. representing Sue Cleveland Elem. Sch. Greenville Co. Sch. Dist., Spl. Edn. Topics and Trends, 2001—02; poll manager Greenville Co. Tchr. Incentive grantee Sch. Dist. Greenville County, 1986-88, Project Earth grantee Bell South, 1988-89, 94-95, Edn. Improvement Act/Nat. Dissimination Network grantee S.C. State Dept. Edn., 1987-88, Targett 2,000 Arts in Curricular grantee S.C. Dept. Edn., 1994-95, Alliance grantee Bus. Cmty. Greenville, 1992-95, Greer Art Rsch. grantee, 1993-94, S.C. Govs. Sch. Study grantee, 1994, Edn. Improvement Act Competitive Tchr. grantee S.C. Dept. Edn., 1994-95, Alliance Grand grant, 1995-96; recipient Am. Jurisprudence Bancroft-Whitney award Glendale U. Sch. Law, 1997, 98, Excellence Recognition in Real Property award Glendale Law Faculty, 1997, Excellence in Art of Appellate Advocacy, Glendale U. Sch. Law, 1998, Am. Jurisprudence Bancroft-Whitney award Constl. Law I, 1998. Mem.: ABA, Palmetto State Tchr. Assn., S.C. Art Edn. Assn., S.C. Arts Alliance, Nat. Mus. Women in Arts, Nat. Art Edn. Assn., Phi Delta Kappa. Baptist Avocations: computers, art, writing, music composition, law. Home: 26 Charterhouse Ave Piedmont SC 29673-9139 Office Phone: 864-787-5208. E-mail: gwenneighborslaw@wmconnect.com.

WINTEROWD, WALTER ROSS, English educator; b. Salt Lake City, Jan. 24, 1930; s. Harold Ross and Henrietta Ethel (Fike) W.; m. Norma Graham, Aug. 2, 1952; children: Geoffrey Ross, Anthony Gordon. BS, Utah State U., 1952; PhD, U. Utah, 1962. Asst. prof. U. Mont., Missoula, 1962-66; assoc. prof. U. So. Calif., Los Angeles, 1966-71, prof. English, 1971-79, McElderry prof. English, 1979-97, prof. emeritus, 1997—. Author: Rhetoric: A Synthesis, 1967, Contemporary Rhetoric, 1975, The Contemporary Writer, 1975, Composition/Rhetoric: A Synthesis, 1986, The Culture and Politics of Literacy, 1989, The Rhetoric of the "Other" Literature, 1990, (with Geoffrey Winterowd) The Critical Reader, Thinker, and Writer, 1992, The English Department: A Personal and Institutional History, 1998. Served with U.S. Army, 1953-55. Mem. Nat. Council Tchrs. English, AAUP Democrat. Home: 17551 San Roque Ln Huntington Beach CA 92647-6641

WINTERS, ANNE, poet, educator; b. St. Paul, Minn., Oct. 13, 1939; d. Warrington Woodruff and Helen Winters; 1 child, Elizabeth. BA, NYU, 1961; MA, Columbia U., 1963; Phd, U. Calif., Berkeley, 1993. Lectr. MIT, Cambridge, Mass., 1981—82, U. Calif., Davis, Calif., 1983—85; instr. St. Marys, Calif., 1985—87; asst. prof. Northwestern U., Evanston, Ill., 1991—94; mem. lit. faculty Bennington (Vt.) Coll., 1994—97; assoc. prof. U. Ill., Chgo., 1997—. Lectr. Harvard U., Cambridge, 1995, 96; vis. assoc. prof. U. Chgo., 1997—98. Translator: Salamander: sel Poems of Robert Marteau, 1979 (Poetry prize, 1979); author: The Key to the City, 1986 (nominated Nat. Book Critics Circle prize, 1986), The Displaced of Capital, 2004. Recipient

Poetry award, Wellesley Coll., 1997, Lit. award, Am. Acad. Arts & Letters, 2003; grantee, NEA, 1985. Mem.: Writers Programs Am., Modern Lang. Assn. Democrat. Office: English Dept Univ Ill 601 S Morgan St Dept Mc162 Chicago IL 60607-7100

WINTERS, BARBARA JO, musician; b. Salt Lake City; d. Louis McClain and Gwendolyn (Bradley) W. AB cum laude, UCLA, 1960, postgrad., 1961, Yale, 1960. Mem. oboe sect. L.A. Philharm., 1961-94, prin. oboist, 1972-94; ret. Clinician oboe, English horn, Oboe d'amore. Recs. movie, TV sound tracks. Avocation: painting in oils and mixed media. Home: 3529 Coldwater Canyon Ave Studio City CA 91604-4060 Office: 135 N Grand Ave Los Angeles CA 90012-3013

WINTERS, DARCY LAFOUNTAIN, medical management company executive; b. Middletown, N.J., Aug. 27, 1955; d. Donald Mark LaFountain and Suzanne (Gilman) LaFountain Westergard; m. Leland Monte McNabb, July 4, 1981 (div. Feb. 1989); 1 child, Leland Monte Jr.; m. Stephen H. Winters, May 30, 1997. BBA in Internat. Fin. cum laude, U. Miami, 1977. Real estate agent, Grad. Realtor's Inst. Market rsch. asst. Burger King Corp., Miami, Fla., 1975-77, regional mktg. supr. Huntington Beach, Calif., 1977-78; mgr., restaurant planning Holiday Inns, Inc., Memphis, 1978-79, mgr., nat. promotions, 1979-83; dir., lodging and travel planning Holiday Corp., Memphis, 1983-86; affiliate broker The Hobson Co., Realtors, Memphis, 1986-88, Crye Leike, Memphis, 1988-92; sr. v.p. comm. and planning Medshares Mgmt. Group, Inc., Memphis, 1991-2000. Founder, Lunch for Two, LLC, 2001—. Active Friends Pink Palace Mus., Memphis, 1987-91, Family Link/Runaway, Memphis, 1980-88; chmn. Foster Care Rev. Bd., Memphis, 1988-98; bd. dirs. Bethany Home, Memphis, 1989—, pres., 1995, treas., 1998; bd. dirs. Am. Cancer Soc., 1994—, v.p. 2000, Univ. Club of Memphis, 2000—; mktg. com. Health Industry Coun., 1994-95. Named Profl. Vol. of Yr., Friends of Pink Palace Mus., Memphis, 1989, 93, U.S. Masters Swimming All-Am., 1993, 94; grad. Leadership Memphis, 1995; named Cmty. Hero for Olympic Torch Relay, 1996, named One of Fifty Women Who Make a Differnce in 1998, Women's News, Mertie Buckman Empowerment award, 1999. Mem. Le Bonheur Club, Memphis Runners Track Club, Univ. Club (bd. dirs. 2000—). Republican. Episcopalian. Avocations: competitive long distance running, tennis, swimming. Home: 1004 Murray Hill Ln Memphis TN 38120-2674 Office: Lunch for Two LLC 4745 Poplar Ave #303 Memphis TN 38117

WINTERS, DEAN, actor; b. NYC, July 20, 1964; Grad. with honors, Colo. Coll. Actor: (TV films) The Playroom, 1996, Firehouse, 1997, Strip Search, 2004; (films) Conspiracy Theory, 1997, Lifebreath, 1997, Undercover Angel, 1999, Snipes, 2001, Bullet in the Brain, 2001, Hellraiser:Hellseeker, 2002, Love Rome, 2002, Brooklyn Bound, 2004; (TV series) Homicide: Life on the Street, 1993, NYPD Blue, 1993, New York Undercover, 1994, Millennium, 1996, Oz, 1997—2003, Sex and the City, 1998, Third Watch, 1999, Deadline, 2000, The Twilight Zone, 2002, Rescue Me, 2004—; (TV miniseries) Law & Order: Special Victims Unit, 1999—2000, (guest appearance) I Love the '70s, 2003. Avocations: boxing, tai chi. Mailing: FX Networks LLC 10000 Santa Monica Blvd Los Angeles CA 90067*

WINTERS, HAROLD FRANKLIN, physicist; b. Renton, Wash., May 19, 1932; s. Walter Wade and Ruth Elizabeth (Meyer) W.; m. Marjorie Ann Neiswender, June 9, 1956; children: Kathie Moe, David Winters, John Winters, Janice Assadi, Judy Ahlquist. Attended, Biola Coll., 1950-51; BS, Whitworth Coll., 1958; PhD, Washington State U., 1963. Rsch. staff mem. IBM Almaden Rsch. Ctr., San Jose, Calif., 1963-93, emeritus, 1993—. Vis. prof. Odense U., Denmark, 1979-80; past N.Am. rep. Subcom. on Plasma Chemistry, Internat. Union Pure and Applied Chemistry; past trustee Am. Vacuum Soc.; past lectr. numerous major nat. and internat. confs. throughout the world. Past mem. editl. bd. Plasma Materials Interactions, Jour. Nuc. Instruments and Methods; contbr. numerous articles to sci. jours. Corp. U.S. Army, 1952-54. Recipient (with John Coburn) Thinkers award Tegal Corp., 1983, Disting. Alumni Achievement award Wash. State U., 1992. Fellow Am. Vacuum Soc. (John A. Thornton Meml. award and lectr. 1993, plasma sci. divsn. named grad. student award in honor of John Coburn and Harold Winters 1994); mem. AAAS, Am. Sci. Affiliation. Achievements include patents for plasma processing, ion sources and ion pumps; scientific contributions in the fields of plasma science, surface science, thin films, ion bombardment of solids, dissociation of gases by electron impact. Home: 632 Lanfair Dr San Jose CA 95136-1947 E-mail: hfmwinters@aol.com. *My conversion to evangelical Christianity in high school led to a change in my attitude, lifestyle, behavior, and study habits. I changed from a poor student with a bad attitude to an excellent student with a great love for science. These changes led to a successful and enjoyable scientific career. I find no contradiction or conflict between science and my Christian faith; on the contrary science has increased my respect for God.*

WINTERS, JACKIE F. small business owner, foundation administrator; b. Topeka, Apr. 19, 1937; m. Marc Winters; 4 children. Student, Oreg. State U. Cert. Policy Alternatives Flemming Fellow. Clk. typist Oreg. Health Sci. Ctr., 1959—69; supr. Econ. Opportunity Office Oreg. Gov. Tom McCall, 1969—79; asst. Oreg. Gov. Vic Atiyeh, 1979—85; owner Jackie's Ribs, 1985—; ombudsman Oreg.; mem. Oreg. Ho. of Reps., 1998—2002, Oreg. Senate, 2003—. Pres., campaign chmn. United Way Marion/Polk Counties; creator Oreg. Food Share Program; supporter local activities Scouts, YMCA, battered women's shelters; chair cmty. partnership task force Oreg. State Fair; co-chair Emergency Bd. subcom. Human Svcs.; mem. emergency bd. Gov.'s Task Force on Mental Health, Oreg., joint audit com.; candidate Oreg. Ho. of Reps., 1996. Recipient Disting. Svc. award, City of Salem. Republican. Office: 900 Court St NE H212 Salem OR 97301 Office Phone: 503-986-1710.

WINTERS, J(OHN) OTIS, retired oil industry consultant; b. Tulsa, Nov. 6, 1932; s. John McAfee, Jr. and Marian Dunn (McClintock) W.; m. Ann Allene Varnadow, Oct. 18, 1958; children: John, Richard, David, Paul. MS in Petroleum Engring., Stanford U., 1955; MBA, Harvard U., 1962. Registered profl. engr., Okla. V.p. Warren Am. Oil Co., Tulsa, 1962-65; pres. Ednl. Devel. Corp., Tulsa, 1965-73; exec. v.p., dir. Williams Cos., Tulsa, 1973-77, First Nat. Bank of Tulsa, 1978-79; pres. Avanti Energy Corp., Tulsa, 1980-87, Zephyr Corp., Tulsa, 1980-90; chmn. PWS Group, Inc., 1990—2002; ret., 2003. Chmn. bd. First United Meth. Ch., 1977-79; pres. Downtown Tulsa Unltd., 1977; former vice chmn. bd. Oral Roberts U.; bd. dirs. Jr. Achievement; commr. Tulsa Urban Renewal Authority; 1st v.p. Ark. Basin Devel. Assn. Served as 1st lt., C.E. U.S. Army, 1955-57. Recipient various pub. service awards. Mem. Tulsa C. of C. (bd. dirs.), So. Hills Country Club (Tulsa), Pine Valley Golf Club, Augusta Nat. Golf Club, Cypress Point Club, Royal and Ancient Club, St. Andrews. Home: 8350 N Central Expy #1150 Dallas TX 75206-1600

WINTERS, PETER LEE, dermatologist; b. Lockport, N.Y., Dec. 19, 1938; s. Earl Lloyd and Ruby Josephine (Gilmer) W.; m. Judith Barbara Amenta, June 17, 1965 (div. June 1974); children: Christopher Lee, Jonathan Bright; m. Diana Louise bucher, Nov. 27, 1993. BS, Allegheny Coll., Meadville, Pa., 1960; MD, Temple U., 1965. Diplomate Am. Bd. Dermatology, Nat. Bd. Med. Examiners. Intern Meth. Hosp., Indpls., 1965-66, resident in family medicine, 1966-68; fellow in dermatology Skin and Cancer Hosp./Temple U., Phila., 1968-71; mem. med. staff St. Vincent Hosp., Indpls., Meth. Hosp., Indpls.; pvt. practice dermatology Indpls., 1971—. Lt. USNR, 1966-68. Fellow Am. Soc. Dermatology (pres. 1992-93), Am. Acad. Dermatology (mem. adv. bd.); mem. AMA (alt. del. 1998—), Ind. State Med. Soc. (chmn. bd. 1991-92, spkr. ho. of dels. 1993-96, pres. 1997-98), Indpls. Med. Soc. (pres. 1989-90), Meth. Hosp. Alumni (pres. 1992-94), Ind. Dermatol. Soc. (pres. 1989-90), Highland Country Club, Columbia Club. Republican. Methodist. Avocations: tennis, wine collecting, reading mystery novels. Home: 1591 Preston Trl Carmel IN 46032-8970 Office: 8402 Harcourt Rd Ste 620 Indianapolis IN 46260-2055 Office Phone: 317-872-5295. Personal E-mail: poredoc@concentric.net.

WINTERS, RICHARD ALLEN, mineral economist; b. Butte, Mont., Feb. 19, 1963; s. Allen S. and Doris Ellen (Taylor) W. BS in Fin. and Econs., U. Mont., 1986; MS in Mineral Econs., Colo. Sch. Mines, 1990, postgrad., 1991-93. Office engr. Morrison Knudsen Engrs., Richland, Wash., 1986-88, project acct., 1987-88; ops. analyst Echo Bay Mines, Denver, 1989; instr. Colo. Sch. Mines, Golden, Colo., 1991-92; cons. Coors Brewing Co., Golden, 1991-92; sr. rsch. engr. Phelps Dodge Mining Co., Morenci, Ariz., 1992-94; gold analyst Robertson, Stephens and Co., San Francisco, 1994-95; v.p. corp. devel. Golden Star Resources Ltd., Denver, 1995-99; v.p. RMB Resources, 2000—. Pres. Mineral Econ. Grad. Student Assn., 1989-90. Mem. Soc. Mining, Metallurgy and Exploration, Assn. Environ. Resource Economists, Mineral, Econs. and Mgmt. Soc. Avocations: outdoors, jewelry craft. Office: 303 E 17th Ave Ste 700 Denver CO 80203-1260

WINTERS, ROBERT CUSHING, insurance company executive; b. Hartford, Conn., Dec. 8, 1931; s. George Warren and Hazel Keith (Cushing) W.; m. Patricia Ann Martini, Feb. 10, 1962; children: Sally, Beth. BA, Yale U., 1953; MBA, Boston U., 1963; LHD, Montclair State Coll., 1991, St. Peter's Coll., 1993. With Prudential Ins. Co. Am., 1953—, v.p. actuary, 1969-75, sr. v.p. Cen. Atlantic home office, 1975-78, exec. v.p., Newark, 1978-84, vice chmn., 1984-86, chmn., CEO, 1987-94, chmn. emeritus, 1995—. Trustee, Episcopal Divinity Sch., Boston Symphony Orch. With U.S. Army, 1954-56. Fellow Soc. Actuaries; mem. Am. Acad. Actuaries (past pres.), Am. Coun. Life Ins. (chmn. bd. dirs. 1990-91), Sigma Xi. Office: Prudential Ins Co Am 751 Broad St 10th Fl Newark NJ 07102-3714 E-mail: robert.c.winters@prudential.com.

WINTERS, ROBERT WAYNE, medical educator, pediatrician, healthcare executive; b. Evansville, Ind., May 23, 1926; s. Frank and Clara (Flentke) W.; m. Madoris Seiler, Sept. 5, 1948 (div. Feb. 1972); children: Henry N., R. George; m. Agnete Thomsen, Feb. 11, 1976; children: Charlotte, Anne. AB summa cum laude, Indiana U., 1948; MD cum laude, Yale U., 1952. Diplomate Am. Bd. Pediat. Intern, resident, and fellow U. N.C., Chapel Hill, 1954-58; asst. prof. U. Pa., Phila., 1959-61; prof. Columbia U., N.Y.C., 1962-81; CEO HNS-Healthdyne, Parsippany, NJ, 1985-89; chmn. Nat. Alliance Infusion Therapy, Washington, 1990-92; pres. Winters Assocs., Inc., Jersey City, 1989—. Contbr. to profl. jours.; author 5 books. 2nd lt. cav. U.S. Army, 1944-46. Recipient Mead Johnson award Am. Acad. Pediat., 1966, Borden award, 1972. Address: 11 E 87th St Apt 5C New York NY 10128 E-mail: bobwinters@aol.com.

WINTERS, SAM, lawyer; b. Tex. BA, U. Tex., 1944, JD, 1948. Bar: Tex. 1948. Ptnr. Clark, Thomas & Winters, Austin, Tex.; bd. govs. U.S. Postal Svc., Washington, 1991—99, vice chair, 1996-97, chmn. bd. govs., 1994-95, 98. Chmn. Tex. Rsch. League, 1990, 91; past mem. Nat. Hwy. Safety Adv. Com.; mem. devel. bd. U. Tex., Austin. With USN, World War II. Mem. ABA (past chair sect. pub. utilities, comm. and transp.), Am. Law Inst. (life), State Bar Tex. Office: Clark, Thomas & Winters PO Box 1148 Austin TX 78767

WINTERS, SHELLEY (SHIRLEY SCHRIFT), actress; b. St. Louis, Aug. 18, 1922; m. Vittorio Gassman (div.); 1 child, Vittoria; m. Anthony Franciosa, 1957 (div. Nov. 1960). Student, Wayne U. Began acting career in vaudeville, later played roles on legitimate stage; motion pictures include The Diary of Anne Frank, 1958 (Acad. award best supporting actress), Odds Against Tomorrow, Let No Man Write My Epitaph, Matter of Convictions, Lolita, 1962, Wives and Lovers, 1963, The Balcony, 1964, A House Is Not a Home, 1964, Patch of Blue, 1966 (Acad. award best supporting actress), Time of Indifference, 1965, Alfie, 1965, The Moving Target, 1965, Harper, 1966, Enter Laughing, 1967, The Scalp Hunters, 1968, Buona Sera Mrs. Campbell, 1968, Wild in the Streets, 1968, The Mad Room, 1969, How Do I Love Thee, 1971, What's the Matter with Helen, 1971, The Poseidon Adventure, 1972, Blume in Love, 1973, Cleopatra Jones, 1973, Something to Hide, 1973, Diamonds, 1975, Next Stop Greenwich Village, 1976, The Tenant, 1976, An Average Man, 1977, Tentacles, 1977, Pete's Dragon, 1977, King of the Gypsies, 1978, The Visitor, 1980, Looping, 1981, S.O.B., 1981, My Mother, My Daughter, 1981, Over the Brooklyn Bridge, Ellie, Deja Vu, 1985, The Delta Force, 1986, Marilyn Monroe: Beyond the Legend, 1987, Purple People Eater, 1988, An Unremarkable Life, 1989, Touch of a Stranger, 1990, Stepping Out, 1991, The Pickle, 1993, Raging Angels, 1995, Mrs. Munck, 1995, Jury Duty, 1995, Heavy, 1995, Backfire, 1995, The Portrait of a Lady, 1996; Gideon's Webb, 1998, La Bamba, 1999; appeared in: TV films Revenge!, 1971, The Devil's Daughter, 1973, Double Indemnity, 1974, The Sex Symbol, 1974, Elvis, 1978, Alice in Wonderland; plays A Hatfull of Rain, 1955, Girls of Summer, 1957, Night of the Iguana, Cages, Who's Afraid of Virginia Wolf?, Minnie's Boys, Marlon Brando: The Wild One, 1996; TV miniseries The French Atlantic Affair, 1979; Author: play One Night Stands of a Noisy Passenger, 1971; autobiography Shelley: Also Known As Shirley, 1980, Shelley II: The Middle of My Century, 1989. Recipient Emmy award Best Actress, 1964, Monte Carlo Golden Nymph award, 1964, Internat. TV award as best actress Cannes Festival, 1965 Address: ICM care Jack Gilliardi 8942 Wilshire Blvd Beverly Hills CA 90211-1934

WINTERS, STANLEY B. history educator, writer, civic activist; b. N.Y.C., N.Y., June 5, 1924; m. Helen Plavner, Sept. 12, 1948 (div. Dec. 1969); children: Jenifer O'Neill, Neal Winters; m. Zdenka Müllerová, Jan. 9, 1970. AB, NYU, 1948; AM, Columbia U., 1950; PhD, Rutgers U., 1966. Cert. secondary social studies educator, N.J. Artist, draftsman Art Glass Co., N.Y.C., 1942-43; instr. history NYU, 1949-50; dir., co-propr. Clinton Hill Day Sch., Newark, 1950-56; tchr. social studies Livingston (N.J.) H.S., 1956-57; disting. prof. history Newark Coll. Engring./N.J. Inst. Tech., 1957-91; disting. prof. emeritus history N.J. Inst. Tech., Newark, 1991—. Adj. prof. history Rutgers U., Newark, 1980-91, rsch. assoc. Urban Studies Ctr., New Brunswick, 1961-62; cons., columnist Office of Info., Newark, 1972-80. Author: Karel Kramář's Early Political Career, 1966, From Riot to Recovery: Newark After Ten Years, 1979, T.G. Masaryk, 1850-1937: Thinker and Politician, 1990; co-author, editor: Intellectual and Social Developments in the Habsburg Empire, 1975, Great Britain, the USA and the Bohemian Lands 1848-1938 1991; editor: Dynasty, Politics and Culture, 1991, East Ctrl. Europe jour., 1975-91; mem. editl. bd. Bohemia-Zeitschrift, Munich, 1985-2003; columnist (pseudonymous weekly) N.J. Afro-Am. newspaper, 1958-64; contbr. more than 200 articles to profl. jours. and publs. Pres., co-founder Clinton Hill Neighborhood Coun., Newark, 1955-61; chmn. edn. com. br. office NAACP, Newark, 1960-64; candidate city coun., Newark, 1962; Essex County Freeholder; trustee Preservation and Landmarks Com., Newark, 1980-93; pres. Czechoslovak History Conf., Chapel Hill, N.C., 1988-90. Staff sgt. U.S. Army, 1943-46, ETO. Recipient Szendzimir award Polish Inst. Arts and Scis., N.Y.C., 1971, N.J. Inst. Tech. Pub. Svc. award, 1982, Josef Hlávka Meml. medal Czechoslovak Acad. Scis., Prague, 1991, Disting. Svc. award Czechoslovak History Conf., 1995, Frantisek Palacky Hon. medal Acad. of Scis. of Czech Republic, 2003; grantee NEH, 1967, N.J. Com. for Humanities, Trenton, 1976-77, 85. Mem. Am. Hist. Assn. (life, nominated first Czech historian as hon. fgn. mem.), Organization Am. Historians, Am. Assn. Advancement Slavic Studies, Collegium Carolinum, Josef Pekař Hist. Soc. (hon.), Hist. Assn. of Czech Republic (hon.), Phi Beta Kappa. Avocations: chess, travel, walking, correspondence, pre-contemporary music. Home: 22365 Queens Ave Port Charlotte FL 33952 Home Fax: 941-624-3247.

WINTERS, TERRY, artist; b. Bklyn., 1949; BFA, Pratt Inst., 1971. One-woman shows include Galleria Massimo Valsecchi, Milan, 1993, Morgan Gallery, Kansas City, Mo., 1994, Bobbie Greenfield Gallery, Venice, Calif., 1994, Galerie Lehmann, Lausanne, Switzerland, 1994, Galerie Max Hetzler, Berlin, 1994, 1996, Johnson County C.C., Overland Park, Kans., 1994, Sonnabend Gallery, N.Y.C., 1994, 1995, Galerie Fred Jahn, Munich, 1995, Galerie Lawrence Rubin, Zurich, 1996, Akira Ikeda Gallery, Tokyo, 1997, Galerie Samia Saouma, Paris, 1997, Sch. Mus. Fine Arts, Boston, 1997, Matthew Parks Gallery, N.Y.C., 1997, IVAM Ctr. Julio Gonzalez, Valencia, Spain, 1998, others, exhibited in group shows at Marlborough Gallery, N.Y., 1996, Tribeca 148 Gallery, 1996, Williams Ctr. for the Arts Lafayette Coll., Easton, Pa., 1996, Deichtorhallen, Hamburg, Germany, 1996, Mus. d'Art Contemporary, Barcelona, 1996, Susan Sheehan Gallery, N.Y., 1996, Nat. Gallery Art, Washington, 1996, Marlborough Chelsea, N.Y., 1997, 1998, Barbara Krakow Gallery, Boston, 1997, Pace Prints, N.Y., 1997, Mus. Moderner Kunst Stiftung Ludwig Wien, Vienna, 1997, Whitney Mus. Am. Art, N.Y., 1997, Corcoran Gallery Art, Washington, 1997, Luhring Augusting Gallery, N.Y., 1997, Matthew Marks Gallery and Pat Hearn Gallery, 1998, Drake Hotel, Chgo., 1998, Mus. Modern Art, N.Y., 1998, Galerie Tony Wuethrich, Basel, 1998, Mitchell-Innes & Nash, N.Y., 1998, Gallery at Dieu Donné Papermill, 1998, Mukai Gallery, Tokyo, 1998, Am. Acad. Arts and Letters, N.Y., 1998, Sezon Mus. Art, 1998, Saatchi Gallery, London, 1998, many others. Office: c/o Matthew Marks 523 W 24th St New York NY 10011-1104

WINTERSHEIMER, DONALD CARL, state supreme court justice; b. Covington, Ky., Apr. 21, 1932; s. Carl E. and Marie A. (Kohl) W.; m. Alice T. Rabe, June 24, 1961; children: Mark D., Lisa Ann, Craig P., Amy T., Blaise Q. BA, Thomas More Coll., 1953; MA, Xavier U., 1956; JD, U. Cin., 1959; LHD (hon.), No. Ky. U., 1999. Pvt. practice, Covington, 1960-76; city solicitor City of Covington, 1962-76; judge Ky. Ct. Appeals, Frankfort, 1976-83; justice Ky. Supreme Ct., Frankfort, 1983—, chmn. criminal rules com., 1988-94, chmn. continuing jud. edn. com., 1983—, chmn. rules com., 1994—. Del. Foster Parent Rev. Bd., 1985-2002; mem. adv. bd. Sta. WNKU-FM, 1984-94, Am. Soc. Writers on Legal Subjects. Trustee Sta. WNKU-FM. Recipient Cmty. Svc. award Thomas More Coll., 1968; recipient Disting. Alumnus award Thomas More Coll., 1982, Disting. Alumni award Coll. Law/U.Cin., 1998; named Disting. Jurist Chase Coll. Law, 1983, Outstanding Jurist Phi Alpha Delta Law Frat., 1990. Mem. ABA, Am. Judicature Soc., Ky. Bar Assn., Ohio Bar Assn., Cin. Bar Assn., Inst. Jud. Adminstrn., Am. Inns of Ct. (founder Chase chpt.). Democrat. Roman Catholic. Home: 224 Adams Ave Covington KY 41014-1712 Office: Ky Supreme Ct Capitol Building Room 235 700 Capitol Ave Frankfort KY 40601-3410 Office Phone: 859-292-6300.

WINTERSTEIN, JAMES FREDRICK, academic administrator; b. Copperas Cove, Tex., Apr. 8, 1943; s. Arno Fredrick Herman and Ada Amanda Johanna (Wagnr) W.; m. Diane Marie Bochmann, July 13, 1963; children: Russell, Lisa, Steven, Amy. Student, U. N.M., 1962; D of Chiropractic cum laude, Nat. Coll. Chiropractic, 1968; cert., Harvard Inst. for Ednl. Mgmt., 1988. Diplomate Am. Chiropractic Bd. Radiology; lic. chiropractic, Ill., Fla., S.D., Md. Night supr. x-ray dept. DuPage Meml. Hosp., Elmhurst, Ill., 1964-66; x-ray technologist Lombard (Ill.) Chiropractic Clinic, 1966-68, asst. dir., 1968-71; chmn. dept. diagnostic imaging Nat. Coll. Chiropractic, Lombard, Ill., 1971-73, chief of staff, 1985-86; pres. Nat. U. Health Scis., Lombard, Ill., 1986—; pvt. practice West Chicago, Ill., 1968-73, 1973-85. Faculty Nat. Lincoln Coll. Post-Profl., Grad. and Continuing Edn., 1967—; chmn. x-ray test com. Nat. Bd. Chiropractic Examiners, 1971-73; govs. adv. panel on coal worker's pneumoconiosis and chiropractic State of Pa., 1979; v.p. Am. Chiropractic Coll. Radiology, 1981-83; mem. adv. coun. on radiation protection Dept. Health and Rehabilitative Svcs. State of Fla., 1984-85; cons. to bd. examiners State of S.C., 1983-84, State of Fla., 1980-85; cons. to peer review bd. State of Fla., 1980-84; trustee Chiropractic Centennial Found., 1989-90; mem. adv. coun. Aids Alternative Health Ptnrs., 1996-2000, Consortial Ctr. for Chiropractic Rsch., 1998—; bd. dirs. Fedn. Ill. Ind. Colls. and Univs., 1995—; bd. dirs. Alternative Medicine, Inc., 1999—; spkr. in field. Pub. Outreach (Nat. Univ. Health Scis. monthly); author numerous monographs on chiropractic edn. and practice; co-inventor composite shielding and mounting means for x-ray machines; contbr. articles to profl. jours. Chmn., bd. dirs. Trinity Luth. Ch., West Chgo., 1970-72, Luth. High Sch., Pinellas County, Fla., 1979-82, St. John Luth. Ch., Lombard, 1988; chmn. bd. edn. First Luth. Sch., 1975-79; chmn. First Luth. Congregation, Clearwater, Fla., 1979-82; chmn. bldg. planning com. Grace Luth. Ch. and Sch., St. Petersburg, Fla., 1984-85; bldg. planning com. ch. expansion, new elem. sch., First Luth. Sch., 1975-79; stewardship adv. coun. Fla./Ga. dist. Luth. Ch. Mo. Synod, 1983-85; trustee West Suburban Regional Acad. Consortium, 1993-99. With U.S. Army, 1961-64. Recipient Cert. Meritorious Svc. Am. Chiropractic Registry of Radiologic Technologists, Cert. Recognition for Inspiration, Guidance, and Support Delta Tau Alpha, 1989, Cert. Appreciation Chiropractic Assn. South Africa, 1988, 1st pl. Fund Raiser Ride for Kids award Pediat. Brain Tumor Found. U.S., 1997, Cert. Appreciation Ill. Chiropractic Soc., 1997, Hope and Support award Alternative Health Ptnrs., 1998, Chiropractor of Yr., Ill. Chiropractic Soc., 2000, Person of the Yr., Alternative Medicine, Inc., 2001, NUHS Bd. Trustees Disting. Svc. award, 2002, President's citation award Maryland Chiropractic Assn., 2003. Mem. APHA, Am. Chiropractic Assn., Am. Chiropractic Coll. Radiology (pres. 1983-85, exec. com. 1985-86), Am. Chiropractic Coun. on Diagnostic Imaging, Am. Chiropractic Coun. on Diagnosis and Internal Disorders, Am. Chiropractic Coun. on Nutrition, Nat. Univ. Alumni Assn., Am. Acad. Chiropractic Physicians (sec.), Assn. Chiropractic Colls. (sec.-treas. 1986-91), Coun. Chiropractic Edn. (sec.-treas. 1988-90, v.p. 1990-92, pres. 1992-94, immediate past pres. 1994-96), Fla. Chiropractic Assn. (chmn. radiol. health com. 1977-85, Disting. Svc. award 1999). Republican. Lutheran. Avocations: reading, automobile rehabilitation, harley-davidson motorcycles, fishing.

WINTERTON, JOSEPH HENRY, computer software executive; b. Oneida, N.Y., July 22, 1948; s. Stewart Grant and Margaret (Durant) W.; m. Susan Marie Briggs, May 29, 1971; children: Tamara Leigh, Danielle Marie, Derek James. AAS, Canton (N.Y.) Coll., 1968; BA, SUNY, Potsdam, 1970. Adv. programmer IBM Corp., Poughkeepsie, N.Y., 1970-81; mgr. R & D Candle Corp., L.A., 1981-83, dir. R & D White Plains, N.Y., 1983-96, sr. dir. R&D, 1996—2003; v.p., sr I&O mgr. Bank One, Columbus, Ohio, 2003—. Coach Yorktown (N.Y.) Athletic Club, 1988—2001; treas. Hudson Valley Christian Acad., Mahopac, NY, 1986—87, Yorktown Theatre Workshop, Yorktown Heights, NY, 1989—92; trustee Calvary Bapt. Ch., Ossining, NY, 1986, midnight run vol., 1993—; bd. dirs. Yorktown Theatre Co. Served with U.S. Army, 1970—76, N.G. Republican. Mem. Christian Ch. Avocations: photography, teaching Sunday sch., coaching youth sports, golf. Home: 1521 Hanover St Yorktown Heights NY 10598-4709 E-mail: joe_winterton@candle.com., jowintertn@aol.com.

WINTHROP, EMILIE See CUTHBERT, EMILIE

WINTHROP, JOHN, wines and spirits company executive; b. Salt Lake City, Apr. 20, 1947; children: Grant Gordon, Clayton Hanford. AB cum laude, Yale U., 1969; JD magna cum laude, U. Tex., 1972. Bar: Calif. 1972. Law clk. 9th cir. U.S. Ct. Appeals, L.A., 1972-73; conseil juridique Coudert Freres, Paris, 1973-75; v.p. gen. counsel MacDonald Group, Ltd., L.A., 1976-82; pres., CEO MacDonald Mgmt. Corp. and MacDonald Group Ltd., L.A., 1982-86; pres., chief exec. officer MacDonald Corp. (gen. contractors), L.A., 1982-86; chmn., CEO Comstock Mgmt. Co., L.A., 1986—; pres., CEO Winthrop Investment Properties, Los Angeles, 1986—; CEO Veritas Imports, L.A., 1995—. Bd. dirs. Plus Prods., Tiger's Milk Prods., Irvine, Calif., 1977-80. Contbr. articles to profl. jours. Bd. dirs., sec. L.A. Sheriff's Dept. Found.; bd. dirs. L.A. Opera. Mem. Nat. Eagle Scout Assn. (life), French-Am. C. of C. (bd. dirs. 1982-87), Urban Land Inst., Yale Club N.Y., Calif. Club, The Beach Club, Elizabethan Club, Order of the Coif, Beta Theta Pi. Office: Veritas Imports Penthouse 9460 Wilshire Blvd Beverly Hills CA 90212-2720 E-mail: jwinthrop@veritaswine.com.

WINTHROP, LAWRENCE FREDRICK, judge; b. Apr. 18, 1952; s. Murray and Vauneta (Cardwell) W. BA with honors, Whittier Coll., 1974; JD magna cum laude, Calif. Western Sch., 1977. Bar: Ariz. 1977, Calif. 1977, U.S. Dist. Ct. Ariz. 1977, U.S. Dist. Ct. (so. dist.) Calif. 1981, U.S. Ct. Appeals (9th cir.) 1981, U.S. Dist. Ct. (cen. dist.) Calif. 1983, U.S. Supreme Ct. 1983. Assoc. Snell and Wilmer, Phoenix, 1977—83, ptnr., 1984—93, Doyle, Winthrop, P.C., Phoenix, 1993—2002; judge divsn. one Ariz. Ct. Appeals, Phoenix, 2002—. Judge pro tem Maricopa County Superior Ct., 1987-97; lectr. Ariz. personal injury law and practice and state and local tax law Tax Exec. Inst., Nat. Bus. Inst., Profl. Edn. Systems, Inc., Ariz. Trial Lawyers Assn., Maricopa County Bar Assn.; bd. dirs. Valley of the Sun Sch., 1989-97, chmn., 1994-96; mem. Vol. Lawyers Program, Phoenix, 1980-2002. Editor-in-chief: Calif. Western Law Rev., 1976-77. Fellow Ariz. Bar Found., Maricopa Bar Found.; mem. ABA, Calif. Bar Assn., Ariz. Bar Assn. (mem. com. on exam. 1995-2002), Ariz. Tax Rsch. Assn. (bd. dirs. 1989-93), Maricopa County Bar Assn., Ariz. Assn. Def. Counsel (bd. dirs., pres. 1988-89, chmn. med. malpractice com. 1993-95), Am. Bd. Trial Advs., Aspen Valley Club, Forest Highlands Club. Republican. Methodist. Avocations:

music, golf, tennis. Home: 83 W Cypress St Phoenix AZ 85003 Office: 1501 W Washington St Phoenix AZ 85007 Office Phone: 602-542-1430. Business E-Mail: lwinthro@courts.sp.state.az.us.

WINTHROP, SHERMAN, lawyer; b. Duluth, Minn., Feb. 3, 1931; s. George E. and Mary (Tesler) W.; m. Barbara Cowan, Dec. 16, 1956; children: Susan Winthrop Crist, Bradley T., Douglas A. BBA, U. Minn., 1952; JD, Harvard U., 1955. Bar: Minn. 1955, U.S. Dist. Ct. Minn. 1955, U.S. Tax Ct. Law clk. to chief justice Minn. Supreme Ct., St. Paul, 1955-56; ptnr. Oppenheimer, Wolff & Donnelly, St. Paul, 1956-79; shareholder Winthrop & Weinstine P.A., St. Paul, 1979—. Bd. dirs. Bremer Fin. Corp., St. Paul, Minn., Capital City Partnership; bd. dirs., sec. St. Paul Progress Corp. Mem. ABA, Minn. Bar Assn. (chair exec. coun., bus. law sect. 1992-93), Ramsey County Bar Assn. Avocations: tennis, travel. E-mail: swinthrop@winthrop.com.

WINTLE, ROSEMARIE, biomedical electronics engineer; b. Brigham City, Utah, Sept. 13, 1951; d. DeVere and Kathleen (Layton) W. Student, Weber State U., 1972-76, Brigham Young U., 1978-79, U. Utah, 1980-87, ITT Electronic Tech. Inst., 1986-88, Utah State U., 1991-92. Engr. Morton Internat., Brigham City, Utah; computer technician Salt Lake City; engr. Nuclear Med., Mesa, Ariz., 1976-77, U. Utah Hosp. Lab., Salt Lake City, 1980-87; electronic engr. Varian Assocs., Inc., Salt Lake City, 1987-88; electronic bio-med. experiment and rsch. engr. Clin. Rsch. Assocs., Provo, Utah, 1988-89. Contbr. articles to profl. jours. Engr., builder Honeyville (Utah) town playground equipment; designer, mgr. Honeyville town water system. Recipient grant Brigham City. Mem. IEEE (pres.), NSPE, Inst. for Sci. Info., Am. Statis. Assn., Sci. Am. Libr., Computer Club, Amnesty Internat., Libr. of Science, Newbridge Book Club. Mem. Lds Ch. Avocations: chess, sports, computers.

WINTON, CALHOUN, literature educator; b. Ft. Benning, Ga., Jan. 21, 1927; s. George Peterson and Dorothy (Calhoun) W.; m. Elizabeth Jefferys Myers, June 30, 1948; children: Jefferys Hobart, William Calhoun. Student, Ga. Inst. Tech., 1944-46; BA, U. of the South, 1948; MA, Vanderbilt U., 1950, Princeton U., 1954, PhD, 1955. Instr. Dartmouth Coll., Hanover, N.H., 1954-57; asst. prof. U. Va., Charlottesville, 1957-60; asst. prof. then assoc. prof., asst. dean Grad. Sch. U. Del., 1960-67; prof. dept. English U. S.C., Columbia, 1967-75, chmn. dept., 1970-73; prof. U. Md., College Park, 1975-97, dir. Rsch. Ctr. for Humanities, 1988-90, prof. emeritus, 1997—. Del. Jt. Nat. Com. on Langs., Washington, 1986-90, 95-99. Author: (biography) Captain Steele, 1964, Sir Richard Steele, 1970; editor: Plays of Aaron Hill, 1981, John Gay and the London Theatre, 1993; author (with others) Colonial Book in the Atlantic World, 2000; contbr. entries Oxford Dictionary of National Biography. Pres. faculty guild U. Md., 1986-89; bd. dirs. Md. Fedn. Tchrs., Balt., 1986-89. Capt. USN, 1944-47, 50-52. Am. Philos. Soc. grantee, 1960; Guggenheim Found. fellow, 1965-66, Folger Shakespeare Libr. fellow, Washington, 1970, John Carter Brown Libr. fellow, Providence, 1995, 2003 Fulbright Commn. lectureship, Ankara, Turkey, 1979-80. Mem. MLA (exec. com. South Atlantic chpt. 1977-80), Am. Soc. 18th-Century Studies (founder 1970—), East Cen. Soc. 18th Century Studies (pres. 1987), Assn. Princeton Grad. Alumni (exec. bd. 1986-90), Cosmos Club Washington, Princeton Club (N.Y. and Washington), Am. Antiquarian Soc., Literary Soc. Washington. Democrat. Episcopalian. Avocations: swimming, book collecting. Office: The University of the South PO Box 3133 Sewanee TN 37375-3133 E-mail: cw41@umail.umd.edu.

WINTON, LINDA, international trainer and consultant; b. Phila. BA in Secondary Edn. and Spanish, La Salle Coll., Phila., 1971—75; MA in Spanish Lang. and Lit., NYU, Madrid, 1978—79; MS in Adult Edn. and Human Resource Tng. and Devel., U. So. Maine, Gorham, 1990—91. Cert. Tchr. Spanish Pa. Dept. Edn., 1975, NJ Dept. Edn., 1975, Tchr. French NJ Dept. Edn., 1977, Exhbn. Mgr. Internat. Assn. Exhbn. Mgmt., 2003. Spanish and French tchr. Willingboro HS, NJ, 1975—77; ESL instr. Camden Learning Ctr., NJ, 1975—77, Shell Oil Co., Madrid, 1977—79, Inst. Internat. Madrid, 1977—79, Aldeasa, Madrid, 1977—79; export sales Wheatland Tube Co., EMSI, Pa., 1979—81; Spanish and French tchr. Haddonfield HS, 1981—82; Spanish instr. U. Ky., 1982—84; dir. Gorham Adult and Cmty. Edn., Maine, 1989—93; prin. Tng. Assocs. Maine, 1990—91; sales rep., account exec. Diversified Expn., Maine, 1994—97; pres., CEO New Markets Internat. LLC, Falmouth, Maine, 1997—. Programmer Tampa Bay Coun. Internat. Visitors, Fla., 1986—87; sr. programmer Maine Coun. Internat. Visitors, 2000—. Recipient Ofines Award for Study Linguistics, 1978; fellow, Nat. Endowment Humanities, 1984. Mem.: Meeting Profls. Internat. (internat. devel. com. 2000—01, global issues adv. group 2001—02, New Eng. chpt. fin. com. 2001—02, New Eng. chpt. internat. membership com. 2002—03, New Eng. chpt. mem. com. 2002—, New Eng. chpt. liaison to multicultural initiative 2003—), Internat. Assn. Exhbn. Mgmt. (dept. commerce liaison com. 2001—03, CEM commn. 2003—). Office: New Markets Internat LLC 12 Arbor Rd Falmouth ME 04105 Office Phone: 207-781-2019. E-mail: nmi@maine.rr.com.

WINTOUR, ANNA, editor; b. London, Nov. 3, 1949; arrived in U.S., 1976; d. Charles and Elinor Wintour; m. David Shaffer, Sept. 1984; children: Charles, Kate. Student, Queens Coll., 1963—67. Deputy fashion editor Harper's and Queen Mag., London, 1970—76; fashion editor Harper's Bazaar, NY, 1976—77; fashion and beauty editor Viva Mag., NY, 1977—78; contbg. editor fashion and style Savvy Mag., NY, 1980—81; sr. editor N.Y. Mag., 1981—83; creative dir. U.S. Vogue, NY, 1983—86; editor-in-chief British Vogue, London, 1986—87, House and Garden, NY, 1987—88, Vogue, NY, 1988—. Office: Vogue 4 Times Sq New York NY 10036*

WINTROB, JAY S. insurance company executive; Grad. summa cum laude, U. Calif., Berkeley, 1979; JD, U. Calif., 1982. With O'Melveny & Myers, L.A.; asst. to chmn. AIG Sun Am., 1987, corp. v.p., 1987—89, sr. v.p., 1989—91, exec. v.p., 1991—95, vice chmn., 1995—98, CEO, 1998—2000, pres., 2000—, CEO, 2001—; exec. v.p. Am. Internat. Group, 2002—. Bd. dirs. AIG Sun Am., AIG. Recipient Ecumenical Coun. Leadership award, Archdiocese L.A., 2001, Luis Lainer Founder's award, Bet Tzedel Legal Svcs., 2002. Mem.: Order of Coif. Office: Am Internat Group 70 Pine St New York NY 10270

WINTRODE, RALPH CHARLES, lawyer; b. Hollywood, Calif., Dec. 21, 1942; s. Ralph Osborne and Maureen (Kavanagh) W.; m. Leslie Ann O'Rourke, July 2, 1966 (div. Feb. 1994); children: R. Christopher, Patrick L., Ryan B.; m. Denise A. Beetham, Aug. 24, 1999. BS in Acctg., U. So. Calif., 1966, JD, 1967. Bar: Calif. 1967, N.Y. 1984, Japan 1989, Washington 1990. From assoc. to ptnr. to of counsel Gibson, Dunn & Crutcher, Tokyo, L.A., Newport Beach and Irvine, Calif., 1967—. Sec. Music Ctr. Los Angeles County, 1986-88; bd. dirs. Coro Found., L.A. County, 1986-87. Mem. Newport Harbor Club, Am. Club Tokyo. Avocations: sailboat racing, car racing, flying. Office: Gibson Dunn & Crutcher 4 Park Plz Ste 1400 Irvine CA 92614-8557 also: 333 S Grand Ave Ste 4400 Los Angeles CA 90071-1548

WINTROL, JOHN PATRICK, lawyer; b. Wichita, Kans., Feb. 13, 1941; s. Clarence Joseph and Margaret (Gill) W.; m. Janet Lee Mitchell; children: John Howard, Joanna Lee. BA cum laude, Rockhurst Coll., 1963; JD, Georgetown U., 1969. Bar: DC 1969, U.S. Ct. Appeals (4th, 5th, 11th and DC cirs.) 1981, U.S. Dist. Ct. Md. 1984. Law clk. to Hon. Howard Corcoran U.S. Dist. Ct., Washington, 1969-71; assoc. Howrey & Simon, Washington, 1971-77; mng. ptnr. Perito, Duerk & Pinco, Washington, 1978-85; ptnr. Finley Kumble, Washington, 1985-87, Laxalt, Washington, Perito & Dubuc, Washington, 1988-91, McDermott, Will & Emery, Washington, 1991—2002; atty. John P. Wintrol L.L.C., Washington, 2003—. Mem. jud. conf. U.S. Ct. Appeals (D.C. cir.). Vol. Peace Corps, Turkey, 1963-65; pres. bd. trustees Holton Arms Sch. Mem.: ABA. Roman Catholic. Office: 2000 M St NW Ste 700 Washington DC 20036 Office Phone: 202-261-1056. Business E-Mail: jwintrol@jpwlaw.net.

WINTROUB, BRUCE URICH, dermatologist, educator, researcher; b. Milw., Nov. 8, 1943; s. Ernest Bernard and Janet (Zien) W.; m. Marya Kraus, Jan. 20, 1973; children: Annie, Ben, Molly. BA, Amherst Coll., 1965; MD, Washington U., St. Louis, 1969. Diplomate Am. Bd. Internal Medicine, Am. Bd. Dermatology. Intern in medicine Peter Bent Brigham Hosp., Boston, 1969-70, jr. asst. resident in medicine, 1970-71, jr. assoc. in medicine, 1976-80, asst. then attending physician, 1976-81; resident in dermatology Harvard Med. Sch., Boston, 1974-76, instr., 1976-78, asst. prof., 1978-82; assoc. prof. dermatology Sch. Medicine, U. Calif., San Francisco, 1982-85, attending physician med. ctr., 1982—, prof., mem. exec. com. dept. dermatology, 1985-95, 2000—, mem. dean's adv. com., governing bd. continuing med. edn., other coms., 1986-95; chmn. exec. com. dept. dermatology U. Calif., San Francisco, 1985-95, 2000—, exec. vice dean Sch. Medicine, 1995-97, assoc. dean sch. medicine, 1990-95, 2000—; chief med. officer U. Calif.-San Francisco Stanford Health Care, San Francisco, 1997-99; assoc. dean Sch. Medicine Stanford (Calif.) U., 1997—99; dir. Dermatology Assocs., San Francisco, 1982-85; prof. & chair, dept. dermatology U. Calif.-San Francisco, 1986—95, 1999. Cons. in dermatology Mass. Gen. Hosp., Boston, 1976-82, Beth Israel Hosp. and Children's Hosp. Med. Ctr., Boston, 1978-82, Parker Hill Med. Ctr., Boston, 1980-82; attending physician Robert B. Brigham Hosp. div. Brigham and Women's Hosp., Boston, 1980-81, assoc., 1980-82; chief dermatology svc. Brockton (Mass.) VA Med. Ctr., 1980-82; asst. chief dermatology VA Med. Ctr., San Francisco, 1982-85, mem. space com., 1984-85, dean's adv. com., 1985—, chmn. budget com., 1987—; clin. investigator Nat. Inst. Allergy, Metabolism and Digestive Disease, NIH, 1978; assoc. dean Sch. Medicine Stanford U., 1997—. Author: (with others) Biochemistry of the Acute Allergic Reactions, Fifth International Symposium, 1988; contbr. numerous articles, abstracts to profl. jours. NIH clin. fellow and grantee, 1967-69. Fellow Am. Acad. Dermatology (com. evaluations 1985—, coun. govt. liaison 1987—, congress on tech. planning commn. 1988—, assoc. editor Dialogues in Dermatology jour. 1982 85, Stellwagon prize 1976); mem. Soc. Investigative Dermatology (chmn. pub. rels. com. 1987-88), Assn. Profs. Dermatology (chmn. program com. 1987—, bd. dirs.), Pacific Dermatol. Assn. (chmn. program com. 1987—), San Francisco Dermatol. Soc., Am. Fedn. Clin. Rsch. (chmn. dermatology program 1988-89), Am. Assn. Immunology, Dystrophic Epidermolysis Bullosa Rsch. Am. (bd. dirs. 1981), Internat. Soc. Dermatology, Internat. Soc. Cutaneous Pharmacology (founding mem.), Am. Soc. Clin. Investigation, Skin Pharmacology Soc., Calif. Med. Soc., San Francisco Med. Soc., Clin. Immunology Soc., Dermatology Found., (bd. dirs., exec. com.), AAAS, Am. Assn. Physicians, Calif. Acad. Medicine, Am. Dermatol. Assn., Sigma Xi, Alpha Omega Alpha. Avocation: golf. Office: Dept Dermatology U Calif San Francisco 1701 Divisadero St Rm 342 San Francisco CA 94143-0316 Office Phone: 415-353-7597. E-mail: wintroub@medsch.ucsf.edu.

WINWOOD, STEPHEN LAWRENCE, musician, composer; b. Birmingham, Eng., May 12, 1948; s. Lawrence Samuel and Lillian Mary (Saunders) W.; m. Eugenia Crafton, Jan. 17, 1987; children: Mary Clare, Elizabeth Dawn, Stephen Calhoun, Lillian Eugenia. Rec. artist Spencer Davis Group, 1964-67, Blind Faith, 1970, Traffic, 1967-74; solo artist N.Y.C. and in England, 1974—. Dir. F.S. Ltd. Albums include: Arc of a Diver, 1980, Talking Back to the Night, 1982, Back in the High Life, 1986, Roll With It, 1988 (Grammy 1989), Chronicles, Refugees of the Heart, 1991, Traffic: Far From Home, 1994, Junction 7, 1997, About Time, 2003. Recipient 14 Gold Record awards, 4 Platinum Record awards, 2 Grammy awards, Lifetime Achievement award Ivor Novello's, 2002; Rock 'N Roll Hall of Fame nominee, 2003.

WINZENREID, JAMES ERNEST, lawyer, entrepreneur; b. Wheeling, W.Va., June 9, 1951; s. Ernest Christian and Dorothy Emma (Wolf) W.; m. Rebecca Lee Rice, Aug. 11, 1979; children: Diana Lee, Lauren Rice. AB, W. Liberty State Coll., 1973; MBA, W.Va. U., 1979; JD, Duquesne U., 1987; LLM, Wayne State U., 1989. Bar: Pa. 1987, U.S. Dist. Ct. (we. dist.) Pa. 1987. Staff asst. Wheeling Pitts. Steel Corp., Wheeling, 1974—78, supr. indsl. rels., 1978; mgr. profl. planning and devel. Copperweld Corp., Pitts., 1978—79, mgr. human resources Glassport, Pa., 1979—81, plant mgr., 1981—83, group mgr. human resources Pitts., 1984—85, market program mgr., 1986—87; with lab. and employment dept. Eckert, Seamans, Cherin & Mellott, Pitts., 1986—87; corp. staff rep. Tecumseh (Mich.) Products Co., 1987—89; v.p. human resources Lafarge (Va.) Corp., 1989—94; v.p. human resources western region Lafarge Constrn. Materials, Calgary, Canada, 1994—96, Lafarge Can. Inc., Calgary, Canada, 1996—99; mgr. union rels. GE, Bloomington, Ind., 2000—02; dir. labor rels. and compliance Metaldyne Corp., Plymouth, Mich., 2002—04; dir. employee rels. Lear Corp, Southfield, 2004—. Mng. editor Juris mag., 1986. Bd. dirs. Wheeling Symphony Soc., 1977-86, Wheeling Jaycees, 1976-78; mem. adv. bd. Jr. Achievement Southwestern Pa., 1981-83. Named Outstanding Young Men Am. U.S. Jaycees, 1979. Mem. ABA, Pa. Bar Assn., Allegheny Bar Assn., Am. Soc. Human Resources Mgmt., Human Resource Planning Soc., Indsl. Rels. Rsch. Assn., Phi Alpha Delta. Republican. Lutheran. Avocations: golf, reading. Home: 924 Mill Pond Ct Northville MI 46143 Office: Lear Corp 21557 Telegraph Rd Southfield MI 48034 E-mail: jimwinzenreid@aol.com.

WIORKOWSKI, GABRIELLE KAY, database consultant; b. Tulsa, Nov. 10, 1943; d. Marshall Frank and Iva Ann (Johnson) Patterson; m. John J. Wiorskowski, June 4, 1966; 1 child, Fleur. BA summa cum laude, St. Mary's U., 1971; MS, U. Tex., Dallas, 1979. Adminstrv. asst. Stritch Sch. Med. Loyola U., Chgo., 1963-67; sr. programmer Corn Products Co., Chgo., 1967-68; mgr. data comm. Jewel Co., Chgo., 1971-74; ind. data processing cons. Dallas, 1975—. Lectr. U. Tex., Dallas, 1980—; mgr. data base mgmt. systems Sun Co. Inc., Dallas, 1981-83; DBA systems supr. Tex. Instruments, Inc., Dallas, 1983-85; sr. DB2 cons., founder Gabrielle & Assocs. (subs. Codd & Date Internat.), Dallas, 1985—, pres. DB2 Forum, 1988—. Author: (books) DBS: Design Development Guide, 1988, 3d edit., 1992, DB2 for z/OS and OS/390 Development for Performance, 4th edit., 2002; contbr. chapters to books, articles to profl. jours. Mem. Richardson Assn. Gifted and Talented (treas. 1979-80), Assn. Computing Machinery, Nat. Computer Conf. (publs. chmn., steering com., 1977), Delta Epsilon Sigman, Pi Gamma Mu. Home and Office: 9922 Lincolnshire Ct Rockwall TX 75087-4509 Fax: 972-412-8867. Office Phone: 972-412-8866. E-mail: gabrielle@gabrielledb2.com.

WIOT, JEROME FRANCIS, radiologist; b. Cin., Aug. 24, 1927; s. Daniel and Elvera (Weisgerber) W.; m. Andrea Kockritz, July 29, 1972; children— J. Geoffrey, Jason. MD, U. Cin., 1953. Diplomate: Am. Bd. Radiology (trustee, pres.). Intern Cin. Gen. Hosp., 1953-54, resident, 1954-55, 58-59; gen. practice medicine Wyoming, Ohio, 1955-57; mem. faculty U. Cin., 1959-67, 68—, prof., chmn. radiology, 1973-93, acting sr. v.p., provost for med. affairs, 1985-86, prof. emeritus, 1998—; practice medicine specializing in radiology Tampa, Fla., 1967-68. Contbr. articles to med. jours. Bd. dirs. Ruth Lyons Fund, U. Cin. Found., 1997—. Served with USN, 1945-46. Fellow Am. Coll. Radiology (pres. 1983-84, chmn. commn. on diagnostic radiology); mem. Radiol. Soc. N.Am., Am. Roentgen Ray Soc. (pres. 1986-87), Am. Bd. Radiology (pres. 1982-84), Ohio Med. Assn., Cin. Acad. Medicine, Radiol. Soc. Greater Cin., Ohio Radiol. Soc. Office: U Cin Med Ctr Dept Radiology 234 Goodman St Cincinnati OH 45267-1000

WIPKE, W. TODD, chemistry professor; b. Dec. 16, 1940; BS, U. Mo., Columbia, 1962; PhD, U. Calif., Berkeley, 1965. Rsch. chemist Esso Rsch. and Engring. Co., Baton Rouge, 1962; postdoctoral rsch. fellow Harvard U., 1967-69; asst. prof. Princeton U., 1969-75; assoc. prof. chemistry U. Calif., Santa Cruz, 1975-81, prof. chemistry, 1981—. Founder, sr. v.p. Molecular Design Ltd., San Leandro, Calif., 1978-91; founder, chmn. bd. GluMetrics LLC, 2002-; cons. Ciba-Geigy, Basle, Switzerland, 1978-82, BASF, Ludwigshafen, Fed. Republic Germany, 1974-78, Squibb, Princeton, N.J., 1976-81; adv. EPA, 1984—; mem. sci. adv. bd. Pharmix, Scitegic Tosk, TOSK. Editor: Computer Representation and Manipulation of Chemical Information, 1973, Computer-Assisted Organic Synthesis, 1977; editor-in-chief: (jour.) Tetrahedron Computer Methodology, 1987-92; editor: Tetrahedron and Tetrahedron Letters, 1987-92; contbr. articles to profl. jours. Capt. U.S. Army, 1966-67. Recipient Eastman Kodak Rsch. award, 1964, Texaco Outstanding Rsch. award, 1962, Alexander von Humboldt Sr. Scientist award, 1987; Merck Career Devel. grantee, 1970; NIH fellow, 1964-65. Mem. NAS, Am. Chem. Soc. (assoc., Computers in Chemistry award 1987, St. Charles Found. Alumni award 1996), Assn. Computing Machinery, Chem. Soc., Am. Assn. Artificial Intelligence (charter), Chem. Structure Assn. (charter), Internat. Soc. Study Xenobiotics. Office: U Calif Dept Chemistry Santa Cruz CA 95064

WIPPEL, JOHN FRANCIS, philosophy educator; b. Pomeroy, Ohio, Aug. 21, 1933; s. Joseph Edward and Mary Josephine (Andrews) W. BA in Philosophy, Cath. U. Am., 1955, MA in Philosophy, 1956, STL in Theology, 1960; PhD in Philosophy, Louvain, Belgium, 1965; Maitre agrégé in Philosophy, Louvain, 1981. Ordained priest Roman Cath. Ch., 1960. Instr. philosophy Cath. U., Washington, 1960-61, 63-65, asst. prof. philosophy, 1965-67, assoc. prof. philosophy, 1967-72, ord. prof. philosophy, 1972—, acad. v.p., 1989-96, provost, 1996-97, Theodore Basselin prof. philosophy, 2001—. Vis. assoc. prof. U. Calif., San Diego, 1969 Assoc. editor Yale Libr. of Medieval Philosophy; author: Metaphysical Thought of Godfrey of Fontaines, 1981 (Mercier prize 1981), Metaphysical Themes in Thomas Aquinas, 1984, Boethius of Dacia, 1987, Mediaeval Reactions to the Encounter between Faith and Reason, 1995, The Metaphysical Thought of Thomas Aquinas: From Finite Being to Uncreated Being, 2000; co-author: Medieval Philosophy, 1969, Les questions disputées et les questions quodlibétiques dans les facultés de théologie, de droit et de médécine, 1985; editor: Studies in Medieval Philosophy, 1987; contbr. numerous articles to profl. jours., chpts. to books. Recipient Distinguished Alumni award for Scholarship Cath. U. Am., 2001, John Findlay award Metaphysicial Soc. Am., 2002; Basselin scholar, 1953-56, Penfield fellow, 1961-63; NEH fellow, 1970-71, 84-85. Mem. Am. Philos. Assn.; Medieval Acad. Am., Metaphys., Poutificial Acad. of St. Thomas Aquinas, Soc. Am., Am. Cath. Philos. Assn (pres. 1986-87, Aquinas Medalist 1999), Soc. Medieval and Renaissance Philosophy (pres. 1982-84), Soc. internat. pour l'étude de la philosophie médiévale. Office: Cath Univ of Am 620 Michigan Ave NE Washington DC 20064-0001 E-mail: wippel@cua.edu.

WIRE, WILLIAM SHIDAKER, II, retired apparel and footwear manufacturing company executive; b. Cin., Jan. 5, 1932; s. William Shidaker and Gladys (Buckmaster) W.; m. Alice Dumas Jones, Aug. 31, 1957 (dec.); children: Alice Wire Freeman (dec.), Deborah Wire Suber. Student, U. of South, 1950; AB, U. Ala., 1954, JD, 1956; LLM, NYU, 1957. Bar: Ala. 1956. Atty. Hamilton, Denniston, Butler & Riddick, Mobile, 1959-60; with Talladega Ins. Agy., Ala., 1961-62, Genesco, Inc., Nashville, 1962-94, former chmn. and CEO. Bd. dirs. Genesco Inc., Dollar Gen. Corp., Am. Endoscopy Svcs., Inc., Nashville Bank & Trust Co. Mem.: Burnt Pine Golf Club (Destin, Fla.), Golf Club Tenn., Univ. Club (NY), Belle Meade Country Club (Nashville), Kappa Alpha. Presbyterian. Home: 6119 Stonehaven Dr Nashville TN 37215-5613

WIRKEN, JAMES CHARLES, lawyer; b. Lansing, Mich., July 3, 1944; s. Frank and Mary (Brosnahan) W.; m. Mary Morse, June 12, 1971; children: Christopher, Erika, Kurt, Gretchen, Jeffrey, Matthew. BA in English, Rockhurst Coll., 1967; JD, St. Louis U., 1970. Bar: Mo. 1970, U.S. Dist. Ct. (we. dist.) Mo. 1970. Asst. prosecuter Jackson County, Kansas City, Mo., 1970-72; assoc. Morris, Larson, King, Stamper & Bold, Kansas City, 1972-75; dir. Spradley, Wirken, Reismeyer & King, Kansas City, 1976-88, Wirken & King, Kansas City, 1988-93; CEO The Wirken Law Group, Kansas City, 1993—. Adj. prof. law U. Mo., Kansas City, 1984-89, 2001—. Author: (books) Managing a Practice and Avoiding Malpractice, 1983, Wirken Tips: Law Office Marketing, Management and Economics, The Daily Record, 2003; co-author: Missouri Civil Procedure Form Book, 1984—; mem. editl. bd.: jours. Missouri Law Weekly, 1989—, Lender Liability News, 1990—, Emerging Trends and Theories of Lender Liability, 1991, host: radio show Wirken on the Law, Sta. KMBZ, 1998—, contbr.: columns in newspapers The Daily Record. Mem. ABA (exec. coun.), Nat. Conf. Bar Pres. (coun. 1992-96), Nat. Caucus of Met. Bar Leaders (exec. coun., pres. 1988-94), Am. Trial Lawyers Assn., L.P. Gas Group (founder, chair 1986-90, founder, chair lender liability group 1987-96), Mo. Bar Assn. (bd. govs. 1977-78, chmn. econs. and methods practice com. 1982-84, quality and methods of practice com. 1989-91, vice chmn. young lawyers sect. 1976-78), Mo. Assn. Trial Attys. (bd. govs. 1983-85), Kansas City Met. Bar Assn. (pres. young lawyers sect. 1975, chair legal assistance com. 1977-78, chair tort law com. 1982, pres. 1990). Home: 47 W 53rd Kansas City MO 64112 Office: The Wirken Law Group PC 4740 Grand Blvd Ste 200 Kansas City MO 64112 Office Phone: 816-471-0330. E-mail: jwirken@wirkenlaw.com.

WIRKLER, NORMAN EDWARD, retired architectural, engineering, construction management firm executive; b. Garnavillo, Iowa, Apr. 1, 1937; s. Herbert J. and Irene (Kregel) W.; m. Margaret Anne Gift, Oct. 16, 1959; children: Chris Edward, Scott Norman, Elizabeth Anne. BArch, Iowa State U., 1959. Designer The Durrant Group Inc., Dubuque, Iowa, 1959-64, assoc., 1964-67, prin., 1967-82, pres. Denver, 1982-98; bd. dirs. The Durrant Group, Denver, 1998—, Durant Capital Resources, Denver County, 1995—. Commr., mem. exec. com. Commn. on Accreditation on Corrections, 1985-91; archtl. cons. to Am. Correctional Assn. Standards Program; mem. Am. Correctional Assn. Standards Com., 1992-98; v.p. Garnavillo (Iowa) Bank Corp. Co-author: Design Guide for Secure Adult Correctional Facilities, 1983 Bd. dirs. United Way, Dubuque, 1984. Fellow AIA (pres. Iowa chpt. 1977; mem. nat. com. on arch. for justice 1974—, chmn. 1979; chmn. AIA Ins. Trust 1985-87, mem. Colo. chpt. 1987—); mem. ASTM (detention component standards com. 1982-84), Dubuque C. of C. (legis. com. 1978-83, chmn. 1979; v.p. 1984, exec. com. 1982-85), Iowa State U. Devel. Coun. Club. Republican. Avocations: flying, skiing, jogging, golf, hunting. Office: 3773 Cherry Creek North Dr Ste 1000 Denver CO 80209-3804 E-mail: nwirkler@durrant.com.

WIRSCHING, CHARLES PHILIPP, JR., retired brokerage house executive, private investor; b. Chgo., Oct. 26, 1935; s. Charles Philipp and Mamie Ethel (York) W.; m. Beverly Ann Bryan, May 28, 1966. BA, U. N.C., 1957. Sales rep. Adams-Millis Corp., Chgo., 1963-67; ptnr. Schwartz-Wirsching, Chgo., 1968-70; sec., dir. Edwin H. Mann, Inc., Chgo., 1971-74; stockbroker Paine Webber, Inc., Chgo., 1975-85, account v.p., 1986-95; ret., 1995. Cons. Paine Webber, Inc. Chgo., 1996-99. Adv. coun. John Nuveen & Co., Inc., 1993-95; trustee Wirsching Charitable Trust, 1987—. Mem.: Organ Hist. Soc., Salem (Ohio) Hist. Soc. Republican. Episcopalian. Avocation: foreign travel. Home and Office: 434 Clinton Pl River Forest IL 60305-2249

WIRSIG, WOODROW, magazine editor, trade association administrator; b. Spokane, Wash., June 28, 1916; s. Otto Alan and Beulah Juliet (Marohn) W.; m. Jane Barbara Dealy, Dec. 11, 1942; children: Alan Robert, Guy Rodney, Paul Harold. Student, Kearney (Nebr.) State Tchrs. Coll., Los Angeles City Coll., UCLA, 1933-39; BA, Occidental Coll., 1941; MS, Columbia Grad. Sch. Journalism, 1942. Dir. Occidental Coll. News Bur., 1939-41; radio newswriter WQXR, N.Y.C., 1941-42; news writer, propaganda analyst CBS, 1942-43; rewrite man Los Angeles Times, 1943-44; asst. editor This Week mag., 1944-45; staff writer Look mag., 1946, asst. mng. editor, 1946-49, exec. editor, 1950-52; mng. editor Quick mag., 1949-50; assoc. editor Newsweek mag., Ladies' Home Jour., 1952; editor Woman's Home Companion, 1952-56; editorial cons. Ednl. Testing Service, Princeton, 1957-67; TV cons. NBC-TV, ABC-TV; creator Nat. Daytime Radio Programs, 1957-60; radio documentary Companion; pres. communications firm Wirsig, Gordon and O'Connor, Inc., 1956-58; editor Printers' Ink mag., N.Y.C., 1958-65, Salesweek mag., 1959-60; editorial dir. Overseas Press Club ann. mag. Dateline, 1961, 62; creator, editorial dir. Calif. Life mag.; pres. Better Bus. Bur. Met. N.Y., Inc., 1966-77; also pres. Edn. Research Found.; pres. Bus. Advocacy Center, Inc., 1977—. Creator Corp. Social Accountability Audit and Customer Services/Consumer Affairs Audit.; Cons. to Office Sec. HEW, 1965-66 Author: I Love You, Too., 1990; editor, contbr.: Your Diabetes (Dr. Herbert Pollack), 1951; editor: Advertising: Today-Yesterday-Tomorrow; New Products Marketing; cons. editor: Principles of Advertising; contbr. nat. mags.; lectr.; syndicated columnist: other newspapers L.A. Times, 1964-65. Recipient gold medal Benjamin Franklin Mag. Awards, 1956 Mem. Soc. Consumer Affairs Profls. (pres. 1983), Newcomen Soc., Archons, Players Club, Overseas Press Club, Nat. Press Club, N.Y. Advt. Club, N.Y.C. Club, Springdale Country Club, Evergreen Country Club (v.p.), Nassau Club, Century Assn., Families for Alzheimers Rights Assn. (pres. 1994—), Univ. Club, Sigma Delta Chi, Phi Gamma Delta, Gamma Delta Upsilon. Democrat. Presbyterian. Home and Office: Mount San Antonio Gardens 900 East Harrison Ave E7 Pomona CA 91767

WIRSZUP, IZAAK, mathematician, educator; b. Wilno, Poland, Jan. 5, 1915; came to U.S., 1949, naturalized, 1955; s. Samuel and Pera (Golomb) W.; m. Pola Ofman, July 19, 1940 (dec. 1943); 1 son, Vladimir (dec. 1943); m. Pera Poswianska, Apr. 23, 1949; 1 dau., Marina (Mrs. Arnold M. Tatar). *Izaak Wirszup and his wife Pera (Poswianska Deull) are both survivors of the Nazi-Holocaust. Izaak's entire family, including: his (first) wife Pola (Ofman), their 2 year old son Vladimir, both of Izaak's parents Samuel and Pera (Golomb) Wirszup, Izaak's brother Naum and sister Golda, and their families, all were killed by the Nazis. From September 1941 Izaak Wirszup was imprisoned first in the Ghetto Wilno, then in several Nazi concentration camps in Estonia and in Germany. He was liberated by the American Army on April 30, 1945 from camp Allach-Dachau (near Munich, Germany).* Magister of Philosophy in Math, U. Wilno, 1939; PhD in Math, U. Chgo., 1955. Lectr. math. Tech. Inst. Wilno, 1939-41; dir. Bur. d'Études et de Statistiques Spéciales, Société Centrale d'Achat-Société Anonyme des Monoprix, Paris, 1946-49; mem. faculty U. Chgo., 1949—, prof. math., 1965-85, prof. math. emeritus, 1985—, prin. investigator U. Chgo. Sch. Math. Project (sponsored by Amoco Found., also dir. resource devel. component), 1983—, dir. Internat. Math. Edn. Resource Ctr., 1988—. Dir. NSF Survey Applied Soviet Rsch. in Math. Edn., 1985-91; cons. Ford Found., Colombia, Peru, 1965-66, Sch. Math Study Group, 1960, 61, 66-68; participant, writer tchr. tng. material African Math. Program, Entebbe, Uganda, summer 1964, Mombasa, Kenya, summers 1965-66; assoc. dir. Survey Recent Ea. European Math. Lit., 1956-68, dir., 1968-84; dir. NSF program application computers to mgmt., 1976-83; cons. NSF-AID Sci. Edn. Program, India, 1969; mem. U.S. Commn. on Math. Instn., 1969-73; co-prin. investigator U. Chgo.-Polk Bros. Found. Program for the Devel. of Math. Tchrs. in Chgo. Pub. Schs., 1999—. *A December 1979 comparative studies report by Izaak Wirszup to the National Science Foundation which revealed a crisis in mathematics and science education in the U.S., came to the attention of President Jimmy Carter. The President ordered a review of U.S. science and engineering education policies. Wirszup was subsequently invited to testify six times before the U.S. Senate. With an 8.4 million dollar grant from the Amoco Foundation, Wirszup founded the University of Chicago School Mathematics Project in 1983. More than three million students and teachers are now using UCSMP texts.* Contbr. articles to profl. jours.; Editor Math. books, transls., adaptions from Russian.; Adviser math.: Ency. Brit., 1971—. Recipient Lewellyn John and Harriet Manchester Quantrell award U. Chgo., 1958, Univ. Alumni Svc. medal, U. Chgo., 1994; resident master Woodward Ct., U. Chgo., 1971-85; endowed Wirszup Lecture Series, U. Chgo., 1986. Mem. N.Y. Acad. Scis., Am. Math. Soc., Math. Assn. Am., AAAS, Nat. Council Tchrs. Math. (chmn. com. internat. math. edn. 1967-69, Lifetime Achievement medal for Leadership, Tchg., and Svc. in Math. Edn. 1996) Home: 5750 S Kenwood Ave Chicago IL 60637-1744 Office: U Chgo Dept Math 5734 S University Ave Chicago IL 60637-1514 Office Phone: 773-667-1967.

WIRT, MICHAEL JAMES, library director; b. Sault Sainte Marie, Mich., Mar. 21, 1947; s. Arthur James and Blanche Marian (Carruth) W.; m. Barbara Ann Hallesy, Aug. 12, 1972; 1 child, Brendan. BA, Mich. State U., 1969; MLS, U. Mich., 1971; postgrad., U. Wash., 1990. Cert. libr., Wash. Acting libr. U. Mich. Ctr. for Rsch. on Econ. Devel., Ann Arbor, 1971-72; instnl. svcs. libr. Spokane County (Wash.) Libr. Dist., 1972-76, asst. dir., 1976-79, acting dir., 1979, dir., 1980—. Mem. adv. com. Partnership for Rural Improvement, Spokane, 1982-85, Wash. State Libr. Planning and Devel. Com., 1984-85, Ea. Wash. U. Young Writers Project Adv. Bd., 1988-89; mem. issues selection com. Citizens League of Greater Spokane, 1991-93, City of Spokane Indian Trail Specific Plan Task force, 1992-95; mem. comm. com. United Way Spokane County, 1994, campaign chair local govt. divsn., 1996. Mem. Wash. Libr. Assn. (2d v.p. 1984-86, dir. 1989-91, pub. rels. com. 1993-2001, chair legis. planning com. 2003—, Merit award 1984, Pres. award 1998), Wash. Libr. Network (rep. Computer Svc. Coun. 1983-86, v.p., treas. State Users Group 1986-87), Am. Libr. Assn. (Pub. Libr. Affiliates Network 1990-93, PLA Bus. Coun. 1990-94, chmn. 1991-94), Spokane Valley C. of C. (local govt. affairs com. 1987-2000, co-chair 1996-98, pub. policy com. 2000—, mem. local governance com. 2003—), Spokane Regional C. of C. (inland N.W. legis. coalition 2002, local govt. com. 1990-94, human svcs. com. 1990-92, chmn. 1991-92, govt. reorgn. task force 1995), Spokane Civic Theatre (bd. dirs. 1996—2001, v.p. 1997-98, 2000, sec. 1998-2000), Inland N.W. Legis. Coalition, Momentum (local govt. strategy com. 1992-94), New Century (govt. collaboration com. 1997-98), Inland N.W. Coun. Librs. (bd. dirs. 1979—, chmn. 1997-98). Office: Spokane County Libr Dist 4322 N Argonne Rd Spokane WA 99212-1853 E-mail: mwirt@scld.org.

WIRT, SHERWOOD ELIOT, minister, writer; b. Oakland, Calif., Mar. 12, 1911; s. Loyal Lincoln and Harriet Eliot (Benton) W.; m. Helen Winola Wells, July 2, 1940 (dec. Sept. 1986); 1 child, Alexander Wells; m. Ruth Evelyn Love, Aug. 29, 1987. BA, U. Calif., Berkeley, 1932; BD, Pacific Sch. Religion, Berkeley, 1943; PhD, Edinburgh (Scotland) U., 1951. Ordained to ministry, 1943. Pastor 1st Congl. Ch., Collinsville, Conn., 1943-44, Knox Presbyn Ch., Berkeley, 1951-55, Hillside Presbyn. Ch., Oakland, Calif., 1955-59; editor Decision mag. Billy Graham Evangelistic Assn., 1959-76; min. to students U. Wash., 1946-49. Chmn. San Diego Jesus 2000. Author 28 books including Crusade at the Golden Gate, 1959, Not Me, God, 1966, Social Conscience of the Evangelical, 1968, Translation, Confessions of Augustine, 1971, Jesus Power, 1972, Topical Encyclopedia of Living Quotations, 1974, Afterglow, 1975, A Thirst for God, 1980, The Doomsday Connection, 1986, The Making of a Writer, 1987, The Book of Joy, 1994, Billy, 1997, Spiritual Awakening, 1987 (Gold Medallion Book award Evang. Christian Pub. Assn.), Jesus, Man of Joy, 1999, The God Who Smiles, 2001; editor 7 books. Pres. San Diego Gilbert and Sullivan Soc., 1980-81; scoutmaster Boy Scouts Am., 1936. Capt. USAAF, 1944-46. Recipient Freedom of Valley Forge Found. award, 1968; named Hon. Col., State of Tenn.; Sherwood Eliot Wirt day named in his honor, San Diego, 2001. Mem. Associated Ch. Press (life), Evang. Press Assn. (life, pres. 1969-71), San Diego County Christian Writers Guild (founder/convener 1977-96), Theta Chi, Sigma Delta Chi. Republican. Avocations: hiking, swimming, golf. Home: 813 226th St SE Bothell WA 98021

WIRTA, RAYMOND E. real estate company executive; b. 1944; Grad., Calif. State U.; M in Internat. Mgmt., Golden Gate U. With Golden West Fin. Corp., Bank of Am., The Irvine Co.; CEO Koll Real Estate Svcs., 1994-97, CB Richard Ellis, El Segundo, Calif., 1999—. Office: CB Richard Ellis Svcs Inc 200 N Sepulveda Blvd El Segundo CA 90245-4380*

WIRTH, DAVID EUGENE, software designer, consultant; b. Norfolk, Va., Oct. 20, 1951; s. Eugene Ross and Darlene (Worley) W. BA, Luther Coll., 1975. Systems analyst ASI Computer Systems, Cedar Falls, Iowa, 1974-87, v.p. ops., 1987-2001, pres., COO, 2001—. Avocations: basketball, softball, fishing, hunting. Office: ASI Computer Systems Inc PO Box 338 Cedar Falls IA 50613-0338

WIRTH, FREMONT PHILIP, JR., neurosurgeon, educator; b. Nashville, July 23, 1940; s. Fremont P. and Willa (Dean) W.; children: Fremont Philip III, Andrew Simpson, Carolyn Howe. BA with honors in History, Williams Coll., 1962; MD, Vanderbilt U., 1966. Diplomate Am. Bd. Neurol. Surgery (guest examiner 1989, bd. dirs. 1992-98, vice chmn. 1997-98), Nat. Bd. Med. Examiners; cert. advanced trauma life support ACS. Surg. intern Johns Hopkins Hosp., Balt., 1966-67, resident and fellow in surgery, 1967-68; asst. resident in neurosurgery Barnes Hosp., Washington U., St. Louis, 1970-72, fellow in neurosurgery, 1972-74; pvt. practice, Savannah, Ga., 1974—. Asst. clin. prof. neurosurgery Med. Coll. Ga., Augusta, 1991—, vis. prof., 1978, 79, 86, 87; mem. staff, neurosurg. ICU, St. Joseph's Hosp., 1974—, dir. neurosurg. ICU, 1978—; mem. staff Meml. Med. Ctr., 1974-75, dir. rehab., 1983; mem. staff Candler Gen. Hosp., 1974—; med. dir. Head and Spinal Cord Injury Prevention Project for Ga., 1984—; presenter in field, 1970—; vis. prof. U. Md., Balt., 1981, Tufts New Eng. Med. Ctr., Boston, 1982. Series editor (with R.A. Ratcheson) Concepts in Neurosurgery, 1986-93; editor: (with Ratcheson) Neurosurgical Critical Care, Concepts in Neurological Surgery, Vol. 1, 1987, Ruptured Cerebral Aneurysms, Concepts in Neurological Surgery, Vol. 6, 1994; contbr. articles and book revs. to med. jours., chpts. to books. Elder Skidaway Island Presbyn. Ch., 1981-83; mem. pack 57 com. Cub Scouts Am., Savannah, 1979-84; mem. troop 57 com. Boy Scouts Am., Savannah, 1980-85, mem. fin. com. Coastal Empire coun., 1987-90, mem. adv. bd., 1990-96; chmn. physicians' solicitation United Way Coastal Empire, 1987; bd. dirs. Think First Found., 1990-95. With USPHS, 1968-70. Fellow ACS (bd. govs. 1984-90, sr. mem. trauma com. 1991-93); mem. AMA (physician's recognition award 1973-76, 77-79, 80-82, 83-85, 88-91, 91-94, 95-98, 98—), Congress Neurol. Surgeons (profl. conduct com. 1989-93, v.p. 1985-86, Disting. Svc. award 1989), Am. Acad. Neurol. Surgeons, Neurosurg. Soc. Am., Am. Assn. Neurologic Surgeons (nominating com. 1994-96, bd. dirs. 1998-2001, v.p. 2002-03, pres.elect 2004—), Brain Surgery Soc., Ga. Med. Soc. (pres. 1995, bd. trustees 1996-2001, chmn. 2000-2001), Med. Assn. Ga. (editl. bd. 1987-93), pres. 1995, Ga. Neurosurg. Soc. (exec. com. 1981-88, pres. 1988-89), So. Neurosurg. Soc. (exec. com. 1982-91, pres. 1988-89, Semmes lectr. 1997), N.Am. Skull Base Soc., Am. Heart Assn. (fellow stroke coun.). Avocations: golf, fly fishing, hunting. Office: Neurol Inst Savannah 4 E Jackson Blvd Savannah GA 31405-5810

WIRTH, KELLEY K. state representative; b. Panorama City, Calif., Aug. 2, 1965; m. Thomas Wirth; children: Kennedy, Meghan. BS, Oreg. State U., 1989; MS, U. So. Calif., 1992. State rep., dist. 16 Oreg. House Rep., Salem, 2001—; sys. analyst, planning commr. City of Corvallis, Oreg., 1996—; sys. analyst Asst. to 3d Infantry Divsn. Chief of Staff, 1993—99. Adj. computer tech. faculty City Colls. Chgo.-Europe, 1992; bd. mem. Land Devel. Hearings Bd. City of Corvallis, 1998—, mem. Neighborhood Tech. Rev. Group, 1997—. Mem.: Corvallis LWV. Democrat. Episcopalian. Office: 900 Court St NE H-479 Salem OR 97301

WIRTH, MARY L. GIBSON, writer; b. Clayton, Ill., July 14, 1925; d. Everett Dunreath Gibson and Ethel Emily Coffman; m. Lloyd W. Wirth (dec.); children: Claire Wirth Ford, Stephen Allen, Paul Gibson. Student, U. Ill. Soc. editor Garfieldian Pub., Chgo., 1945; asst. Harry Coleman and Co., Chgo., 1947—48; copy writer Ayres Advt., Lincoln, Nebr., 1948—49; corr. Ill. Jour. Register, Springfield, 1964—72; editor Jargon, Bloomington, Ill., 1985—93; freelance editor Shelbyville, Ill., 1974—79; freelancer writer, 1980—. Methodist.

WIRTH, RUSSELL D. L., JR., investment and merchant banker; b. Milw., June 30, 1930; s. Russell and Mary (McMahon) W.; m. Alice Guion Ardrey, Jan. 4, 1958 (div. Jan. 1971); children: Mary Elizabeth, Russell III. BA summa cum laude, Yale U., 1951; MA honors with distinction, Sch. Advanced Internat. Studies, Johns Hopkins U., 1954; postgrad., NYU, 1957-59; grad. with honors, Airborne Sch. and Spl. Forces Officers Sch., 1980. Mem. staff U.S. Senate Fgn. Relations Com., Washington; personal aide to chmn. Senate Fgn. Rels. Com. Alexander Wiley, coord. with Pres. Eisenhower The White House, Washington, 1954-55; personal asst. to mng. ptnr. corp. underwriting dept. Blyth & Co., Inc., Wall Street, 1957-59; U.S. loan officer for Latin Am., U.S. Devel. Loan Fund, Washington, 1960-61; co-founder, pres. Saint-Phalle, Spalding & Wirth, Inc., Buenos Aires, 1962-63; exec. v.p. Internat. Investment Co., Washington, 1963-64; investment officer Chase Internat. Investment Co., 1965-67; asst. to pres. David Rockefeller, Chase Manhattan Bank, 1965-67; co-founder, pres. Puerto Rican Fin. Group (PRFG), San Juan, 1968-92; co-founder, dir., stockholder jointly with Sun Oil Co. in Hemisphere Oil Co., San Juan, 1978-93, also bd. exec. com., 1978-93; founder and ltd. ptnr. in devel. with Tishman Realty and Constrn. Co., Concord Centre Complex, Concord, Calif., 1980-84; founder, mng. dir. Wirth and Co. Internat. Investment Bankers, 1989—; asst. to chmn. Chase Internat. Investment Corp. Rep. candidate Congress 5th dist. Milw., 1956. 2d lt.-capt. USMCR, Korea, 1951-53; maj. U.S. Army Spl. Forces (Airborne), Res. and N.G., 1977-84. Decorated Silver Star, Bronze Star, Purple Heart, UN Korean War medal with 3 battle stars, Disting. Svc. medal Gov. U.S. V.I., U.S. and Korean presdl. unit citations; named Scholar of the House, Yale U. Mem. Phi Beta Kappa. Episcopalian. Achievements include World and U.S. ranked amateur athlete, 1985-95: U.S. Nat. champion, sprint triathlon; 2x U.S. All-Am. in U.S. Triathlon; 4x Fla. State champion, sprint triathlon; Fla. State half-marathon champion; 4th in world in Iron Man World Triathlon Championship; qualified and completed Boston, N.Y.C., San Francisco, Miami marathons; mem. U.S. Nat. Triathlon Team USA which won World Triathlon Championship, Cancun, Mex., 1995.

WIRTH, SANDRA LEE, real estate company owner; b. Buffalo, June 8, 1945; d. Dominic A. and Santina (Lopez) Liberatore; 1 child, H. William III. Prin. Metro Sandra Lee Wirth Robshaw Gallery of Homes, Tonawanda, N.Y.; regional mgr. Paul Robshaw Galler of Homes, Tonawanda, N.Y., mgr. line Cheektowaga, N.Y.; broker assoc. B.W. Morris and Son Realtors, Buffalo; owner Metro Sandra Lee Wirth, Real Estate; mem. N.Y. Assembly, Dist. 148, Albany, 1994—. Chmn., past pres. West Seneca Druga Abuse Prevention Coun.; sponsor Call Home Free Program, Nat. Crime Prevention Coun.'s Nat. Night Out. Named Realtor of the Yr., Elma Bus. Person of the Yr. Mem. Nat. Assn. Realtors (cert.), N.Y. Assn. Realtors (state dir.), Greater Buffalo Bd. Realtors (1st v.p. 1988, treas. 1989, pres. elect 1990), Greater Buffalo Assn. Realtors (pres.), Buffalo and West Seneca C. of C. Office: 5763 Seneca St Elma NY 14059-9615

WIRTHLIN, JOSEPH B. religious organization administrator; b. Salt Lake City, June 11, 1917; s. Joseph L. and Madeline (Bitner) W.; m. Elisa Young Rogers, May 26, 1941; 8 children. Degree in Bus. Adminstrn., U. Utah. Ordained apostle LDS Ch., 1986. Served a mission to Germany, Austria and Switzerland LDS Ch., 1930s, served in stake and ward aux. positions, counselor, bishop to mem. stake presidency, until 1971, 1st counselor Sunday Sch. Gen. Presidency, 1971-75, asst. to coun. of 12 apostles, 1975-76, gen. authority area supr. Europe area, 1975-78, mem. 1st Quorum of Seventy, 1976-86, exec. adminstr. to S.E. area U.S. and Caribbean Islands, 1978-82, mng. dir. Melchizedek Priesthood Com., Relief Soc. and Mil. Rels. Com., 1978-84, exec. adminstr., 1982-84, pres. Europe area of ch., 1984-86, mem. presidency of 1st Quorum of Seventy, exec. dir. curriculum dept., editor ch. mags., 1986, apostle, 1986—, mem. missionary exec. coun., gen. welfare svcs. coms., 1986—. Office: LDS Ch Joseph Smith Meml Bldg 47 E North Temple Salt Lake City UT 84150-9704

WIRTHLIN, RICHARD BITNER, research strategist; b. Salt Lake City, Mar. 15, 1931; s. Joseph L. and Madeline (Bitner) W.; m. Jeralie Chandler, Nov. 23, 1956; children: Richard L., Mary Ann, J. Mark, Carolyn, Michael, Jill, Susan, John BS, U. Utah, 1956, MA, 1957; PhD, U. Calif.-Berkeley, 1964. Lectr. U. Calif. Med. Ctr., San Francisco, 1960-61; chmn. dept. econs. Brigham Young U., Provo, Utah, 1964-69; ptnr. Merill-Wirthlin Assocs., Provo, 1964-69; pres., chmn. bd. dirs. Decision/Making/Info., McLean, Va., 1969-84; chmn. bd. dirs., CEO The Wirthlin Group, Salt Lake City, 1987—. Dir. planning and strategy Reagan/Bush Campaign, 1980, campaign dir. research, planning and policy, 1980-81; dir. planning and evaluation Pres.-Elect Transition Com., 1980-81; cons. to Prime Minister Margaret Thatcher and Brit. Conservative Party, 1989—. Recipient Disting. Alumni award U. Utah, 1986, Disting. Alumni Service award Brigham Young U., 1987; named Advt. Man of Yr., Advt. Age, 1981, Pollster of Yr. Polit. Cons., 1981. Mem. Acad. Polit. Sci., Am. Econ. Assn., Am. Mktg. Assn., Am. Assn. Pub. Opinion/Research, Council Survey Research Orgns., Sigma Chi, Omicron Delta Epsilon Republican. Office: Ste 550 406 W South Jordan Pkwy South Jordan UT 84095-3940

WIRTSCHAFTER, DAVID, agent; Agent William Morris Motion Picture Divsn., Beverly Hills, CA. Office: William Morris Agy Inc 151 S El Camino Dr Beverly Hills CA 90212-2775

WIRTSCHAFTER, IRENE NEROVE, tax specialist, consultant; b. Elgin, Ill., Aug. 05; d. David A. and Ethel G. Nerove; m. Burton Wirtschafter, June 2, 1945 (dec. 1966). BCS, Columbus U., 1942. Cert. tax profl., enrolled agt., IRS. Commd. ensign Supply Corps, USN, 1944, advanced through grades to capt., 1975; comdg. officer Res. Supply Unit, 1974-75; ret., 1976; agt. Office Internat. Ops. IRS, 1967-75; internat. banking specialist; real estate profl., appraiser, 1976-80; pvt. practice tax cons. Sr. intern program U.S. Senate, 1981; mem. Sec. Navy's Adv. Com. Ret. Pers., 1984—86, VA Adv. Com. Women Vets., 1987—90. Past troop leader Girl Scouts U.S.A.; lt. col. and mission pilot CAP, 21 air races; comml. instrument pilot land and sea; Navy liaison officer Commd.'s Retiree Coun., Patrick AFB, 1985—89; mem. Nat. Com. Internat. Forest of Friendship, Atchison, Kans., 1976—; elected silver rep. Nat. Silver Haired Congress, 1977—2001; elected rep. Silver Haired Legis., 1984, Silver Haired Senate, 1988—; trustee Internat. Women's Air and Space Mus., 1993—, bd. dirs., 1999—; state rep. Nat. Soc. to Preserve Social Security and Medicare, 1999; bd. dirs., treas. Honor Am., 2001—04; sec. Navy League, 2000; cons. Jr. Achievement, 1989—94; founder sr. action com. Brevard County, 1981; chmn. College Park Airport Johnny Horizon Day, 1975; elected dir. Fla. Space Coast Philharm., 1985—, treas., 1986—92; bd. dirs., adv. mgr. Cocoa Beach Citizen's League, 1990—92; co-chmn. Internat. Women's Yr. Take Off Dinner, Washington, 1976; 1st v.p. Friends of Cocoa Beach Libr., 1988—90, pres., 1990—92, bd. dirs., 1993—; apptd. to Cocoa Beach Libr. Br., 1996—; mem. Cocoa Beach Bus. Improvement Coun.; elected senator Silver Haired Legislature, Fla., 1985—; vol., founding mem. Brevard Zoo; chmn. Cocoa Beach Code Enforcement Bd., 1989—96; co-chmn. sr. adv. com. Cape Canaveral Hosp., 1994—; trustee Assn. Naval Aviation, 1988—. Named Hon. Citizen, Winnipeg, Man., Can., 1966, Atchison, 1989, New Orleans, 1988, Hon. Dep. State Fire Marshal, Fla., 1987, Ky. Col., La. Col.; recipient cert. of appreciation, Cocoa Beach Women's Club, 2000, Svc. Above Self award, Rotary, 1998. Mem.: RMGS, TROA, AAUW, Navy League (sec. 2001), WAVES Nat. (bd. dirs. chpt. 75 1989—, founder), Cocoa Beach Area C. of C., Assn. Enrolled Agts., Banana River Squadron (founder, comptr. 1984—), Assn. Naval Aviation (nat. trustee 1988—), Naval Order U.S. (treas. nat. capitol commandry), Naval Res. Assn. (nat. treas. 1975—77, nat. adv. com. 1985—, Nat. award of Merit 1992), Internat. Platform Assn. (life), Ninety Nines (past chpt. sect. and nat. officer, 99 achievement awards), Jazz Soc. Brevard, Patrick Women's Golf Assn. (treas. 1996—97), Silver Wings (nat. sec. 1986, bd. dirs. 1990—, nat. v.p. 2000—, Woman of Yr. award 1985), Tailhook Assn. (life), Rotary. Avocations: aviation, golf, music. Home: 1825 Minutemen Cswy Apt 301 Cocoa Beach FL 32931-2033 Personal E-mail: irenwirt@juno.com.

WIRTSCHAFTER, JONATHAN DINE, neuro-ophthalmology educator, scientist; b. Cleve., Apr. 4, 1935; s. Zolton Tilson and Reitza (Dine) W.; m. Carol Lavenstein, Sept. 13, 1959; children: Jacob Daniel, Benjamin Zolton, Joshua Schon, Sara Louise, David Dine, Brooke Ann. Student, UCLA, 1953; BA, Reed Coll., 1956; MD, Harvard U., 1960; MS in Physiology, Linfield Coll., 1963. Diplomate Am. Bd. Ophthalmology (assoc. examiner 1975—), Am. Bd. Neurology. Intern Phila. Gen. Hosp., 1960-61; resident in neurology Good Samaritan Hosp., Portland, Oreg., 1961-63; resident in ophthalmology Johns Hopkins Hosp., Balt., 1963-66; fellow in neurology Columbia-Presbyn. Hosp., N.Y.C., 1966-67; asst. prof. ophthalmology, neurology and neurosurgery U. Ky., Lexington, 1967-70, assoc. prof., 1970-74, prof., chmn. dept., 1974-77, dir. div. ophthalmology, 1967-74; prof. ophthalmology, neurology, neurosurgery U. Minn. Med. Sch., Mpls., 1977—, Frank E. Burch endowed chair in ophthalmology, 1990-2001. Vis. prof. Hadassah-Hebrew U. Med. Ctr., Jerusalem, 1973-74; Earl G. Padfield, Jr., M.D. Meml. lectr. U. Kans., 1986; vis. prof., lectr. numerous other univs.; cons. VA Hosps., Lexington, 1967-77, Mpls., 1977-99; spl. cons. Nat. Eye Inst., 1981. Co-author: Ophthalmic Anatomy: A Manual with Some Clinical Applications, 1970, rev. edit., 1981, A Decision-Oriented Manual of Retinoscopy, 1976, Computed Tomography: An Atlas for Ophthalmologists, 1982, Magnetic Resonance Imaging and Computed Tomography: Clinical Neuro-orbital Anatomy, 1992; contbr. numerous articles to profl. jours.; patentee in field. Bd. mem. Temple Israel, Lexington, 1970-73, McPhail Suzuki Music Assn., 1979-81, Mpls. Talmud Torah, 1979-85; founder, bd. mem. Jewish Community Assn. of Lexington, 1969-77; alumni interviewer Reed Coll., 1968—. Grantee Nat. Eye Inst., 1968-71, 78-81, 89—, Fight for Sight, 1974, Benign Essential Belpharospasm Found., 1988. Fellow ACS, N.Am. Neuro-Ophthalmology Soc. (pres., 1996-98), Am. Acad. Ophthalmology (Sr. honor award 1994); mem. AAAS, AMA (Hon. Mention award-sci. exhibit 1970), Am. Acad. Neurology, Am. Ophthal. Soc., Assn. for Rsch. in Vision and Ophthalmology, Internat. Soc. Neuro-Ophthalmology, Am. Israeli Ophthal. Soc. (bd. mem. 1984-90), Boylston Med. Soc. Harvard Med. Sch., Alpha Omega Alpha. Democrat. Office: Med Sch 420 Delaware St SE MMC 493 Minneapolis MN 55455-0501 E-mail: Wirtsch@umn.edu.

WIRTZ, ELI J. convenience stores executive; b. West Bend, Iowa, Apr. 28, 1943; BBA, U. Iowa, 1966, JD, 1969. Corp. counsel Casey's Gen. Stores, Ankeny, Iowa, 1989—. Office: Caseys Gen Stores One Convenience Blvd Ankeny IA 50021*

WIRTZ, GREGG LEE, lawyer; b. Pitts., Jan. 30, 1953; s. James Henry and Betty Lee (Pelissier) W.; m. Martha McMahon, Oct. 29, 1977. BA in Econs., Denison U., 1974; JD, Stetson U., 1977. Bar: Fla. 1977, U.S. Dist. Ct. (mid. dist.) Fla. 1977; cert. cir. civil mediator, civil trial specialist. Asst. staff judge adv. USAF, Shaw AFB, SC, 1978-80, area def. counsel, 1980-81, staff judge adv., 1981-82; ptnr. Boyd, Jenerette, Staas, Joos, Williams, Felton & Wirtz, Jacksonville, Fla., 1982—2002, Gregg L. Wintz, P.A., Jacksonville, 2002—. Speaker seminar on civil trial practice Fla. CLE, med. malpractice U. Hosp. Served to capt. (judge adv.) USAF, 1977-82. Mem. Fla. Bar Assn., Jacksonville Bar Assn., Am. Bd. Trial Advocates, Fla. Trial Lawyers Assn., Jacksonville Trial Lawyers Assn. (mediation rules and strategies), Omicron Delta Kappa, Omicron Delta Epsilon. Republican. Methodist. Avocation: sports. Office: 231 E Adams St Jacksonville FL 32202-3305 Office Phone: 904-493-5001. E-mail: gwirtz@bendinc.com.

WIRTZ, WILLEM KINDLER, garden and lighting designer, public relations consultant; b. N.Y.C., Jan. 8, 1910; s. Carel Augustus Marie and Wilhelmina Johanetta (Kindler) W. Ed., Ethical Culture Sch., N.Y.C., also Inst. Musical Art. Dir. exhibits svc. Pa. Art Program, 1937-42, pub. rels. dir., 1937-42; ptnr. Campbell-Wirtz Assos., Phila., 1942-51; pres. Willem Wirtz Assos., Phila., 1952—. Founder, 1961, since pres. Willem Wirtz Garden Assos., Inc., and Willem Wirtz Assocs., mfrs. of Ribbonlite; design assoc. Am. Soc. Interior Decorators; dir. Am. Jour. Nursing Co.; also chmn. Pa. bull. award com., 1964; guest lectr. Charles Morris Price Sch., Phila.; pres. Phila. chpt. Am. Pub. Relations Assn., 1954-56, nat. sec., 1955-57, Eastern v.p., 1960 Inventor (with Isaiah Roossine): Ribbonlite. Mem. Nat. Assn. Pub. Rels. Counsel (dir.), Pub. Rels. Soc. Am. (v.p. 1961, assembly del. 1961-63), Pa. Hort. Soc., Phila. Art Alliance, Zool. Soc. Palm Beaches (sec. 1971), Netherlands-Am. Soc. Office: 228 Phipps Plz Palm Beach FL 33480-4241 Home (Summer): 44 Jesse Halsey Ln Sag Harbor NY 11963 E-mail: wim2004@aol.com.

WIRTZ, WILLIAM WADSWORTH, real estate executive, professional sports team executive; b. Chgo., Oct. 5, 1929; s. Arthur Michael and Virginia (Wadsworth) Wirtz; m. Joan Roney, Dec. 15, 1950 (dec. May 1983); children: William R., Gail W., Karen K., Peter R., Alison M.; m. Alice Pirie Hargrave, Dec. 1, 1987. AB, Brown U., 1950. Pres. Chgo. Blackhawk Hockey Team, Inc., 1966—, Chgo. Stadium Corp., 1966—, Consol. Enterprises, Inc., Chgo., 1966—, Forman Realty Corp., Chgo., 1965—, 333 Bldg. Corp., Chgo., 1966—, Wirtz Corp., Chgo., 1964—. Chmn. bd. govs. Nat. Hockey League. Named to NHL Hall of Fame, 1976; recipient Lester Patrick trophy, 1978. Mem.: Sunset Ridge Country Club (Northbrook, Ill.), Fin and Feather Club (Elgin, Ill.), Mid-America Club (Chgo.), Racquet Club (Chgo.), Saddle and Cycle Club (Chgo.). Office: Wirtz 680 N Lake Shore Dr Fl 19 Chicago IL 60611-3495 also: United Ctr 1901 W Madison St Chicago IL 60612-2459 also: Nat Hockey Leage 1155 Metcalfe St Ste 960 Montreal QC Canada H3B 2W2

WIRTZ, WILLIAM WILLARD, lawyer; b. DeKalb, Ill., Mar. 14, 1912; s. William Wilbur and Alfa Belle (White) W.; m. Mary Jane Quisenberry, Sept. 8, 1936; children— Richard, Philip. Ed., No. Ill. State Teachers Coll., DeKalb, Ill., 1928-30, U. Calif. at Berkeley, 1930-31; AB, Beloit Coll., 1933; LL.B., Harvard, 1937. Instr. Kewanee (Ill.) High Sch., 1933-34; asst. prof. U. Iowa Sch. Law, 1937-39, Northwestern U. Sch. Law, 1939-42; asst. gen. counsel Bd. Econ. Warfare, 1942-43; with War Labor Bd., 1943-45, gen. counsel and pub. mem., 1945; chmn. Nat. Wage Stblzn. Bd., 1946; prof. law Northwestern

U., 1946-54; engaged law practice, 1955-61; sec. of labor Dept. Labor, 1962-69. Prof. law U. San Diego, 0986-98. Mem. Ill. Liquor Control Commn., 1949-53. Mem. Am., D.C., Ill. bar assns., Phi Beta Kappa, Beta Theta Pi, Delta Sigma Rho.

WISBAUM, WAYNE DAVID, lawyer; b. Niagara Falls, N.Y., May 29, 1935; s. Franklin C. and Elizabeth (Boff) W.; m. Janet Katz, July 3, 1960; children: Karen, Wendy, Deborah. BA, Cornell U., 1956; LL.B., Harvard U., 1959. Bar: N.Y. 1960. Assoc. Kavinoky & Cook, Buffalo, 1960-66, sr. ptnr., 1966—. Mem. adv. com. Ticor Title Co.; pres., chmn. bd. dirs. Kleinhans Music Hall Mgmt. Inc., 1990-2000, life emeritus, 2003-. Pres. Buffalo Coun. on World Affairs, 1968-70; mem. Young Leadership Cabinet Nat. United Jewish Appeal, 1967-73; mem. com. on leadership devel. Nat. Coun. Jewish Fedn. and Welfare Funds, 1967-; mem. Mayor's Com. on Youth Opportunity; bd. dirs. Anti-Defamation League; mem. Coun. Internat. Studies, SUNY, Buffalo; chmn. Buffalo chpt. Am. Jewish Com.; pres., chmn. bd. dirs. Buffalo Found. Jewish Philanthropies, 2001-; bd. govs. United Jewish Fedn., Buffalo; chmn. bd. dirs. Buffalo Philharm. Orch. Soc.; bd. dirs., mem. exec. com. Burchfield Art Ctr.; bd. dirs., pres. Jewish Family Service of Erie County; vice chmn., bd. dirs. Artpark, Irish Classical Theatre; trustee Buffalo and Erie County Park Libr., Daeman Coll., 2004-. Served to capt. U.S. Army, 1964. Recipient United Jewish Fedn. Buffalo Leadership award, 1967, Cmty. Rels. award Am. Jewish Com., 1985, Abram Pugash award Jewish Family Service, 1985, Cmty. Leadership award Israel Bonds, 2001, honoree Citation banquet Nat. Conf. for Cmty. and Justice, 2004, Citizen of Yr. award Buffalo News, 2003; named Harvard Alumnus of Yr., 1990. Mem. ABA, N.Y. State Bar Assn. (chmn. com. lawyers title guaranty funds, Root/Stimson award 2003), Erie County Bar Assn., Am. Law Inst., Harvard Law Sch. Assn. Western N.Y. (sec.), Zool. Soc. Buffalo (dir., mem. exec. com.), Harvard Club (pres. Buffalo chpt., mem. N.Y.C. chpt.), Buffalo Club, Cornell Club (N.Y.C. chpt.), Zeta Beta Tau. Home: 180 Greenaway Rd Buffalo NY 14226-4166 Office: Kavinoky & Cook 120 Delaware Ave Rm 600 Buffalo NY 14202-2793 Office Phone: 716-845-6000.

WISCH, DAVID JOHN, structural engineer; b. Jefferson City, Mo., Dec. 6, 1953; s. Theodore A. and Josephine (Lauf) W.; m. Leslie Babin, Oct. 24, 1981; 1 child, Christine. BSCE, U. Mo., Rolla, 1975, MSCE, 1977. Registered profl. engr., La., Calif. Civil engr. Texaco-Ctrl. Offshore Engring., New Orleans, 1977-81, advanced civil engr., 1981-86, sr. project engr., 1986-92, specialist Bellaire, Tex., 1992-96, sr. specialist, 1997, fellow, 1997—, chair fellows, 1999—, tech. leader, 1998-99, chmn. Tex. fellows, 1999—; tech. leader Texaco Upstream Tech., 1999—. Chmn. fixed systems subcom. Am. Petroleum Inst., Dallas, Washington, 1991-93, mem. adv. bd. offshore standardization com., 1991-94, chmn., 1993-94, mem. exec. com. on standardization, 1994-98, chmn. offshore and subsea com., 1994-98, head U.S. Delegation Internat. Orgn. Stds. Tech. Com. 1967/Subcom 7, 1993—, mem. Tech. Com. 67/Subcom. 7/AG1, 1993—, convener Tech. Com. 67/Subcom 7/WG3-Fixed Steel Structures, 1993—; mem. structure subcom. Oil Soc. Internat. Exploration and Prodn. Forum, London, 1993-93; mem. spl. com. on offshore facilities Am. Bur. Shipping, 1996—, mem. marine bd., 1999—. Author numerous papers/presentations, 1984—. Mem. Am. Bur. Shipping (spl. com. on offshore structures), ASCE (program. subcom. for Offshore Tech. Conf. 1993—), Sigma Xi, Phi Kappa Phi, Tau Beta Pi, Chi Epsilon (chpt. pres. 1975-76). Office: Texaco Offshore Engring Dept 4800 Fournace Pl Bellaire TX 77401-2389 E-mail: wischdj@texaco.com.

WISDOM, PEGGY JEAN, neurologist; b. OKeene, Okla., Nov. 4, 1947; d. Clarence W. and Grace V. Wisdom. BS in Biology/Chemistry, Northwestern State Coll., 1968; MD, U. Okla., 1972. Diplomate Am. Bd. Psychiatry and Neurology. Resident in neurology U. Fla., 1972-76; asst. prof. neurology U. Okla., Oklahoma City, 1976-90, assoc. prof. neurology, 1990—2002, prof. neurology, 2002—, vice chair dept. neurology, 1981—; med. dir. neurologic rehab. O'Donoghue Rehab. Inst., Oklahoma City, 1981-89, chief of staff, 1986-90; chief neurology VA Med. Ctr., Oklahoma City, 1994-97, chief neurology/rehab., 1997—. Cons. Commn. on Accreditation of Rehab. Facilities, Tuscon, 1990—, Okla. Dept. Rehab. Svcs., Oklahoma City, 1993-96. Sci. adv. bd. Omniplex Mus., Oklahoma City, 1994—. Mem. Am. Acad. Neurology, Am. Acad. Neurology (chmn. women issues in neurology sect. 1999-2001), Assn. of VA Neurologists, Am. Epilepsy Soc. Republican. Presbyterian. Office: U Okla Health Scis Ctr # 215 711 Stanton L Young Blvd Oklahoma City OK 73104-5021 Office Phone: 405-271-4113. E-mail: peggy-wisdom@ouhsc.edu.

WISE, AARON NOAH, lawyer; b. Hartford, Conn., Feb. 14, 1940; s. Joseph J. and Ethel (Sklar) W.; m. Genevieve Ehrlich, Dec. 17. 1966; children: Haywood Martin, Paul Russell, Renee Alicia. AB, Boston U., 1962; JD, Boston Coll., 1965; LLM in Comparative/Internat. Law, NYU, 1971; certificat de Doctorat, d' Université en Droit U. Paris, 1970. Bar: NY, U.S. Dist. Ct. (so. dist.) NY. Internat. atty. Schering-Plough, Kenilworth, NJ, 1969-74; ptnr. Conboy Hewitt O'Brien & Boardman, NYC, 1974-80, Wise Lerman & Katz P.C. (formerly Rosenbaum Wise Lerman & Katz), NYC, 1981-95, Klepner & Cayea, NYC, 1995-98, Brand, Cayea & Brand, LLC, 1998-2000, Siller Wilk LLP, NYC, 2000—02, Gallet Dreyer & Berkey, LLP, NYC, 2002—. Lectr. bus. and legal groups U.S., Europe, L.Am. Author: International Sports Law and Business (Kluwer Law Internat., 1997, 3 vols.), Foreign Businessman's Guide to U.S. Law-Practice-Taxation; contbr. articles to pubs. in U.S. and Europe. Mem. ABA, NY State Bar Assn. Avocations: multi-lingual including French, Spanish, Portuguese, Italian, Russian, Japanese and German. Home: 38 Cummings Cir West Orange NJ 07052-2264 Office: Gallet Dreyer & Berkey LLP 845 Third Ave New York NY 10022-6601 Office Phone: 212-935-3131. E-mail: anw@gdblaw.com.

WISE, ALLEN F. health care administrator; b. Wichita, Kans., Aug. 20, 1942; BS, Wichita State U. Exec. v.p. of operations Health Care Systems Inc., 1985—90; pres., CEO Keystone Health Plan, 1991-94; COO Independence Blue Cross, Phila., 1991—94; exec. v.p. Metra Health Co., 1994—95; pres., CEO Wise Health System, 1994; exec. v.p. United HealthCare Corp., 1995—96; dir. Coventry Health Care, Inc., Bethesda, Md., 1996-98, pres., CEO, 1996—. Office: 6705 Rockledge Dr Ste 900 Bethesda MD 20817-1814*

WISE, CARL STAMPS, accounting educator; b. Brunswick, Ga., Sept. 2, 1955; s. George Lewis Jr. and Alice (Andrews) W. AA, SUNY, Albany, 1983; BS in Occupl. Edn., So. Ill. U., 1984; MPA, Ga. So. U., 1997, postgrad. in Edn., 1998—. Lic. mobile comm. technician. Enlisted USN, 1975, electronics technician, 1975-85; adj. prof. electronics tech. Fla. Jr. Coll., Jacksonville, 1983-84; comm. electronics technician Hasty's Comm. East, Brunswick, Ga., 1985-94; primary care give maternal grandmother Brunswick, Ga., 1994-95; electronics technician/purchase mgr./accounts receivable Thompson Comm., Savannah, Ga., 1996-97; adj. prof. acctg. Savannah Tech. Inst., Hinesville, Ga., 1997—; adj. prof. gen. studies Ctrl. Tex. Coll., Ft. Stewart and Hunter Army Airbase, Ga., 1998—. Computer upgrade/maintenance Ctrl. Tex. Coll. and Savannah Tech. Inst., Hinesville, 1998—. Recipient Sea Svc. Deployment ribbon, 1978, 79, 80. Mem. ASPA (East Ga. chpt. sec. 1998—), Personal Comm. Industry Assn. Republican. Episcopalian. Avocations: landscape painting, swimming, fishing, cooking. Office: Savannah Tech Inst 501 W General Screven Way Hinesville GA 31313-3059 Home: 88 Margaret Dr Midway GA 31320-7222 E-mail: jandrews@infoave.net.

WISE, CHARLES CONRAD, JR., educator, past government official, author; b. Washington, Apr. 1, 1913; s. Charles Conrad and Lorena May (Sweeney) W.; m. Ruth Miles Baxter, Nov. 19, 1938; children: Gregory Baxter, Charles Conrad III, Jenifer; m. Norma Lee Clasbey, Apr. 28, 1984. AB, George Washington U., 1938, JD, 1936; M. Fiscal Adminstrn., Columbus U., 1943. Bar: D.C. 1935. Clk. U.S. Dept. Agr., 1933-36; adminstrv. asst. Bur. Accounts, Treasury Dept., 1936-39; atty. R.R. Retirement Bd., 1939-41; claims atty. Q.M.C., C.E., U.S. War Dept., 1941-43; asst. counsel Office Gen. Counsel, U.S. Navy Dept., 1946-47; gen. counsel War Contracts Price Adjustment Bd., 1948-51, mem., 1950-51; legislative counsel R.F.C., 1951-53; exec. sec. Subversive Activities Control Bd., 1953-61; dept. counsel indsl. plant security Dept. Def., 1962-71, chief dept. counsel, 1971-73; instr. thanatology, religion and philosophy Blue Ridge C.C., 1973-89. Assoc. English dept. George Washington U., 1960, Am. U., 1961. Author: Windows on the Passion, 1967, Windows on the Master, 1968, Ruth and Naomi, 1971, Mind Is It: Meditation, Prayer, Healing and the Psychic, 1978, Picture Windows on the Christ, 1979, The Magian Gospel, 1979, Thus Saith the Lord: The Autobiography of God, 1984, The Holy Families, 1990, Beyond Love, 2000; various articles for mags. Bd. dirs. Acad. Religion and Psychical Rsch. Served as lt. USNR, 1943-46. Mem. Fed. Bar Assn., Delta Theta Phi, Phi Beta Kappa. Home: PO Box 117 Penn Laird VA 22846-0117

WISE, CHARLES DAVIDSON, science educator; b. Huntington, W. Va., June 13, 1926; s. Fred Eugene Wise and Maggie M. Harshbarger; m. Juanita Irene Meadows, Mar. 22, 1947; 1 child, Sandra. AB, MS, W. Va. U., 1950; PhD, U. N.Mex., 1962. Cert. tchr. N.Mex., W. Va., Tex. Tchr. St. Albans (W. Va.) High Sch., 1951-53; lab. assst. Marshall U., 1950-51; grad. fellow U. N.Mex., Albuquerque, 1953-55, grad. asst., 1960-61; rsch. scientist U. Tex., Port Aransas, Tex., 1958-60; prof. Ball State U., Muncie, Ind., 1961-91; rep. Ind. State Legislature, Indpls., 1967-69; senator Ind. State Senate, Indpls., 1969-73. Contbr. articles to profl. jours., 1958—. Bd. dirs. Mental Health Svc. East Cen. Ind., 1974-77; pres. Muncie Bicentennial Festival Com., 1975-77. With U.S. Army, 1944-46. Recipient fellowship U. Ind., 1957, U. Tex., 1957-58, Marshall U. Alumni Community Achievement award, 1993; named Alumnus of Yr., East Bank High Sch., W.Va., 1977. Fellow Ind. Acad. Sci.; mem. Nat. Assn. State Legislators (life mem.), Nat. Audubon Soc., Ind. Audubon Soc. (past pres., conservation award 1977), E. Cen. Ind. Audubon Soc. (pres. 1988-90, conservation award 1984), Sigma Xi Rsch. Soc. (pres. Ball State U. chpt., bd. dir. Hoosier Environ. coun. 1990-93), Republican. Presbyterian. Avocations: birding, travel, languages, genealogy, history. Home: 1032 Brickyard Ave Milton WV 25541 Office: Ball State Univ Muncie IN 47306-0001

WISE, EVAN M. management consultant; b. Cleve., May 15, 1952; m. Diane R. Weinberg; children: Ryan, Tara. BS in Applied Sci., Miami U., 1974; MBA in Mgmt., U. No. Fla., 1979. Prodn. mgr. St. Regis Paper Co., Jacksonville, Fla., 1974—83, Jacksonville Kraft, 1983—85; world rsch. mgr. Jefferson Smurfit Corp., Carol Stream, Ill., 1985—98; owner., mng. dir., founder Mgmt. One Ltd., Chgo., 1990—2001, Tucson, 2001—. Mem.: No. Pima City C. of C., Pi Mu Epsilon, Gamma Theta, Beta Gamma Sigma, Phi Kappa Phi. Avocations: hiking, bicycling, golf. Office: Mgmt One 7925 A North Oracle Ste 114 Tucson AZ 85704 Office Phone: 520-878-0300. E-mail: evan@management-one.com.

WISE, GEORGE EDWARD, lawyer; b. Chgo., Feb. 26, 1924; s. George E. and Helen L. (Gray) W.; m. Patricia E. Finn, Aug. 3, 1945; children: Erich, Peter, Abbe, Raoul, John. JD, U. Chgo. Bar: Calif. 1949, U.S. Dist. Ct. (no. dist.) Calif. 1948, U.S. Ct. Appeals (9th cir.) 1948, U.S. Dist. Ct. (cen. dist.) 1950, U.S. Supreme CT. 1955. Law clk. Calif. Supreme Ct., 1948-49; sr. ptnr. Wise, Wiezorek, Timmons & Wise, Long Beach, 1949—; of counsel Wise Pearce Yocis & Smith, Long Beach. With USNR, 1943-45. Fellow Am. Coll. Trial Lawyers; mem. ABA, Los Angeles County Bar Assn., Long Beach Bar Assn. (pres. 1970, Atty. of Yr. 1990), Calif. State Bar. Home: 5401 E El Cedral St Long Beach CA 90815-4112 Office: Wise Pearce Yocis & Smith 249 E Ocean Blvd Ste 440 Long Beach CA 90802-4806

WISE, HELENA SUNNY, lawyer; b. Ridgecrest, Calif., Dec. 3, 1954; d. Strother Eldon and Mary Helen (Harinek) W.; children: Marie Evelyn, Shawnie Helene. BA with honors, UCLA, 1976; JD with highest honors, Loyola Marymount U., 1979. Bar: Calif. 1979, Nev. 1992, U.S. Dist. Ct. (ctrl. dist.) Calif. 1980, U.S. Dist. Ct. (ea. dist.) Calif. 2001, U.S. Dist. Ct. Ariz. 1992, U.S. Ct. Appeals (9th cir.) 1980, U.S. Supreme Ct. 2000. Ptnr. Geffner & Satzman, Los Angeles, 1980-87; pvt. practice Burbank, Calif., 1987—. Arbitrator talent agy. disputes SAG. Columnist Los Angeles Lawyer mag., 1985-86. Chmn., founder Barristers Child Abuse Com., L.A., 1982-86; mem. exec. bd. Vols. in Parole, L.A., 1983-90; mem. Dem. Chair's Circle, L.A., 1985; mem. adv. bd. Over Easy Found., 1987—; vol. Love is Feeding Everyone. Fellow ABA (exec. coun. labor and employment law 1986-89, liaison young lawyers sect., bd. dirs. young lawyers divsn. 1986-88, mem. MSN team Nat. Com. on Child Abuse, del., teller Ho. of Dels. 1978-79), L.A. County Bar Assn. (v.p. sr. bar 1984-86, pres. young lawyers sect.), State Bar Calif. (bd. dirs. Calif. Young Lawyers Assn., labor law ad hoc com. on wrongful discharge, mem. juv. law com., UCLA alumni rep., USAC 1992-94, student rels. com. 1992-94), Am. Legion Women's Auz. Avocations: photography, skiing, playing organ. Office: 3111 W Burbank Blvd Ste 101 Burbank CA 91505-2350 Fax: 818 843-7958.

WISE, JOHN AUGUSTUS, lawyer, director; b. Detroit, Mar. 30, 1938; s. John Augustus and Mary Blanche (Parent) W.; m. Helga M. Bessin, Nov. 27, 1965; children: Monique Elizabeth, John Eric. Student, U. Vienna, 1957—58; AB honors cum laude, Coll. Holy Cross, 1959; JD, U. Mich., 1962; postgrad., U. Munich Law Faculty, 1962—63. Bar: Mich. 1963, D.C. 1966. Assoc. Dykema, Gossett, Detroit, 1962-64; asst. to pres. Internat. Econ. Policy Assn., Washington, 1964-66; assoc. Parsons, Tennent, Hammond, Hardig & Ziegelman, Detroit, 1967-70; pres. Wise & Marsac P.C., Detroit, 1970-2001; sr. ptnr. Williams, Mullen, Clark & Dobbins, PLLC, Detroit, 2001—04, Howard & Howard, P.C., Detroit, 2004—. Dir. Peltzer & Ehlers Am. Corp., 1975-80, Colombian Am. Friends Inc., 1974-89. Bd. dirs. Hyde Park Coop., 1974-77; trustee Friends Sch., Detroit, 1977-81, Brighton Health Svcs. Corp., 1991-94, Providence Hosp., 2001—; chmn. bd. dirs. Brighton Hosp., 1995—; mem. Detroit Com. on Fgn. Rels. Ford Found. grantee U. Munich, 1962-63. Mem. ABA, Mich. Bar Assn., Detroit Bar Assn., Internat. Bar Assn., Detroit Athletic Club, Detroit Econ. Club. Roman Catholic. Home: 1221 Yorkshire Rd Grosse Pointe Park MI 48230-1105 Office: Buhl Bldg 11th Fl 535 Griswold St Detroit MI 48226-3604 Office Phone: 313-962-5500. E-mail: jwise@howardandhoward.com.

WISE, JOHN JAMES, retired oil company executive; b. Cambridge, Mass., Feb. 28, 1932; s. Daniel and Alice E. (Donlon) W.; m. Rosemary S. Bishop, Mar. 4, 1967; children: Susannah, Jean. BS, Tufts U., 1953; PhD, MIT, 1966. Rsch. scientist Mobil R & D Corp., Paulsboro, N.J., 1953-76, mgr. process R & D, 1976-77, sect. mgr., 1976-77, v.p. planning N.Y.C., 1977-81, mgr. exploration and producing rsch. Dallas, 1981-82, v.p. planning N.Y.C., 1982-84, mgr. process and products R & D Paulsboro, N.J., 1984-87, v.p. rsch., 1987-97. Cons., 1997—. Patentee in field (25); contbr. articles to profl. jours. Mem. NAE, Am. Inst. Chem. Engrs., Indsl. Rsch. Inst. (Achievement award 1995). Sigma Xi. Office: Mobil R & D Corp PO Box 480 Paulsboro NJ 08066-0480

WISE, MARK B. education educator; b. Montreal, Canada, Nov. 9, 1953; BSc, U. of Toronto, 1976, MSc, 1977; PhD, Stanford U., 1980. Asst. prof. Calif. Inst. of Tech., 1983—85, John A. McCone prof. of high energy physics, 1992—; prof. Calif. Inst. of Tech., Divsn. of Physics, Math. and Astronomy, 1985—. Recipient Loeb lectr., Harvard U., 1998, Sakurai prize, Am. Physical Soc., 2001; Alfred P. Sloan fellowship, Alfred P. Sloan Found., 1984—86. Fellow: Am. Acad. Arts and Scis.; mem.: Harvard Soc. of Fellows (jr. fellow 1980—83). Office: Divsn of Physics Math and Astronomy Calif Inst of Tech M/C 452-48 Pasadena CA 91125

WISE, MIGUEL DAVID, lawyer; b. Mercedes, Tex., Feb. 11, 1960; s. Miguel and Barbara Cecilia (Barbosa) W.; m. Erin Adrienne Duffy, Aug. 4, 1984; children: Miguel David III, Mark Riborg, Zachary August. BA magna cum laude, St. Mary's U., San Antonio, 1981, JD, 1984. Bar: Tex. 1984, U.S. Dist. Ct. (so. dist.) Tex. 1986, U.S. Ct. Appeals (5th cir.) 1986, U.S. Dist. Ct. (no. and we. dists.) Tex. 1988, U.S. Supreme Ct. 1988, U.S. Dist. Ct. (ea. dist.) Tex. 1990, U.S. Ct. Appeals (D.C. cir.) 1993. Law clk. Office Atty. Gen. Tex., San Antonio, 1983-84; assoc. Richard S. Talbert, Weslaco, Tex., 1985-86, Allison, Chavez & Sweetman, Brownsville, Tex, 1986-89; ptnr. Dunn & Wise, P.C., Harlingen, Tex., 1990-92, Sweetman & Wise, LLP, Edinburg, Tex., 1992—. Contbr. articles to profl. jours. Immediate past pres. Rio Grande coun., past dist. chmn. Llano Grande dist. Boy Scouts Am., 1985-90, bd. dirs. Rio Grande coun., post advisor, 1989-90; mem. state com. presdl. campaign Al Gore Jr., 1988; del. Tex. Dem. Conv., 1988, Cameron County Dem. Conv., 1988; adv. bd. mem. Adam Walsh Found., 1992—; mem. Tex. Ho. of Reps., 75th and 76th Regular Sessions. Recipient Big Pine Tree III award City of Donna, 1985, Dist. award of merit, Silver Beaver award, Woodbadge Beads Boy Scouts Am.; Airborne qualified U.S. Army, 1993. Mem. ABA, Mexican Am. Bar Assn., Hispanic Nat. Bar Assn., Tex. Bar Assn., State Bar of Tex. (chair standing com. on legal assts. 1995—, adv. chair Tex. State Bd. Legal Specialization), D.C. Bar Assn., Hidalgo County Bar Assn., Cameron County Bar Assn. (com. 1987—, dir. 1992—), Assn. Trial Lawyers Am. (com. 1987—), Tex. Assn. Defense Coun., Coll. State Bar Tex., Supreme Ct. Hist. Soc., Jaycees, Rotary, Lambda Chi Alpha, Delta Epsilon Sigma, Delta Theta Phi. Roman Catholic. Avocations: antique collecting, hunting, fishing, scuba diving, wine collecting. Home: PO Box 812 711 S Georgia Ave Weslaco TX 78596-6843 Office: State Capitol Rm E2 820 PO Box 2910 Austin TX 78768-2910 also: Bldg W4 800 W Railroad St Ste G3 Weslaco TX 78596-5802

WISE, PATRICIA, opera singer and educator; b. Wichita, Kans. d. Melvin R. and Genevieve F. (Dotson) W.; 1 child, Jennifer. B. Music Edn., U. Kans., Lawrence, 1966. Prof. voice Ind. U. Sch. Music, Bloomington, 1995—; tchr. master classes San Francisco, Vienna Conservatory, Salzburg (Austria) Mozarteum; voice tchr. Domingo Young Artist program Washington Opera. Debut as Susanna in Marriage of Figaro, Kansas City, 1966; prin. roles include Lucia, Gilda, Micaela, Juliette, Zerbinetta, Pamina, Musetta, Lulu, Violetta, Nedda, others; appeared with leading Am. opera cos. including, Chgo., Santa Fe, N.Y.C., San Francisco, Houston, San Diego, Miami, Balt., Phila., Pitts.; European appearances, 1971-76, London Royal Opera, Glyndebourne Festival, Vienna Volksoper, Geneva Opera; guest artist with Vienna, Hamburg, Munich, Cologne, Frankfurt, and Berlin State Operas; guest appearances in Madrid, Barcelona, Rome, La Scala Milan, Nice, Paris Chatelet, Zurich, Dresden, Salzburg Festival, Theatro Colon, Buenos Aires; appeared with orchs. including, Chgo. Symphony Orch., Los Angeles Symphony Orch., N.Y. Handel Soc., Israel Philharm. Orch., Vienna Philharm. Orch., N.Y. Philharm., Cleve. Orch., Berlin Symphonic Orch., BBC Orch., Nat. Orch. France; Angel Recordings; internat. TV, film appearances. Recipient Morton Baum award N.Y.C. Ctr., 1971, Dealey Meml. award Dallas Symphony, 1966, Naftzger young Artist award Wichita Symphony, 1966, Midland Young Artist award Midland (Tex.) Symphony Orch., 1966; M.B. Rockefeller Fund grantee, 1967-70; Sullivan Found. grantee, 1967-68; named Kammersänger Vienna Staatsoper, 1989. E-mail: patwise@indiana.edu.

WISE, RICHARD EVANS, corporate executive; b. Lancaster, Pa., Sept. 24, 1947; s. William Edmund and Dorothy Christelle (Evans) W.; m. Kathrine Suzanne Keller, Jan. 2, 1971; 1 child, Thomas Edmund. BS, West Chester (Pa.) U., 1970; MEd, Pa. State U., 1976, PhD, 1980. Project adminstrn. mgr. Hartford Ins. Group, 1977-80; v.p., tng. mgr. Conn. Nat. Bank, 1980-83; corp. tng. and devel. dir. Travelers Corp., Hartford, 1983-89, dir. corp. strategy and rsch., 1989-93; pres. ValueNet Internat., Inc., Hartford, 1993—. Adj. prof. Hartford Grad. Ctr.; pres. Am. Inst. Banking; bd. dirs. Admiral Farragut Corp., Human Tech. Partnership, Greenfield, Mass. Mem. editl. bd. Internat. Jour. Instrnl. Media; contbr. articles to profl. jours.; designer Travelers Mgmt. Devel. Continuum, 1984-86. Mem. Hartford mgmt. devel. adv. bd. Greater Hartford Arts Coun.; vice chmn. Windsor Govt. Study Commn., 1992-93; bd. dirs., v.p. Better Bus. Bur., Inc. Hartford; chmn. Grand Destiny capital campaign Pa. State U. Coll. Edn., 1997—; bd. dirs. Summer Wind Performing Arts Ctr., 2002—. Named Outstanding Alumnus Pa. State U., 1987; Chapter of Excellence Am. Inst. of Banking, 1983. Mem. Assn. for Ednl. Communications and Tech. (cert. of Merit, 1986, 88, Outstanding Practice award, 1983, div. coun. pres. 1990—), Am. Soc. for Tng. and Devel., Phi Delta Kappa. Independent. Methodist. Lodge: Masons. Avocations: sailing, skiing, music, golf, photography. Home: 8 Cobblestone Way Windsor CT 06095-2224 Office: ValueNet Internat Inc 100 Pearl St Hartford CT 06103 Office Phone: 860-559-5600. Business E-Mail: rwise@valuenet-intl.com.

WISE, RITA J. writer; b. Indpls., June 8, 1954; d. Arlessie T. Byrd; children: Chajuana Marita, Russell Aaron. BGS, Purdue U., Indpls., 1995. Cert. beauty/image cons. Office mgr. State Atty. Gen.'s Office, Indpls., 1973-81; adminstrv. sec. student affairs Ind. U., Indpls., 1980-90; part-time bus. instr. Ind. U.-Purdue U., Indpls., 1993-95; loaned assoc. United Way Ctrl. Ind., Indpls., 1995; adminstrv. sec. materials engring. dept. Kelly Svcs./Allison Gas Turbine, 1996-98; account exec. Indpls. Recorder newspaper, 1996—. Author: (poetry) Relief, 1995, Windows of the World, 1991, What Shall I Tell My Children, 1994, A Mothers' Pay Message, 1989, (poetry) Wise Poetry Celebrating Life. Telefundraiser local charities, 1996-97. Recipient scholarship and Diamond Homer award Soc. Famous Poets, Anaheim, Calif., 1996. Mem. Ind. U.-Purdue U. Sch. of Bus. Alumni. Avocations: poetry, aerobics, dance. Home: 3319 Manor Ct Indianapolis IN 46218-2310 Office: Indpls Recorder Newspaper Advt/Sales Indianapolis IN 46218 E-mail: rjoycew2000@hotmail.com.

WISE, ROBERT, film producer, director; b. Winchester, Ind., Sept. 10, 1914; Student, Franklin Coll., D.F.A. (hon.), 1968. Staff cutting dept. R.K.O., 1933, became sound cutter, asst. editor, film editor, 1939-43, dir., 1943-49; with 20th Century-Fox, 1949-52, M.G.M., 1954-57; free-lance, 1958—; ptnr. ind. film co., 1970-2000. Past mem. Nat. Council of Arts, chmn., spl. project com., 1976-. Ind. producer/dir. various studios; motion pictures include The Curse of the Cat People, 1944, Mademoiselle Fifi, 1944, The Body Snatcher, 1945, A Game of Death, 1945, Criminal Court, 1946, Born to Kill, 1947, Mystery in Mexico, 1948, Blood on the Moon, 1948, The Set-Up, 1949, Two Flags West, 1950, Three Secrets, 1950, The House on Telegraph Hill, 1951, The Day the Earth Stood Still, 1951, The Captive City, 1952, Something For the Birds, 1952, The Desert Rats, 1953, Destination Gobi, 1953, So Big, 1953, Return to Paradise, 1953, Executive Suite, 1954, Helen of Troy, 1955, Tribute to a Bad Man, 1956, Somebody Up There Likes Me, 1957, This Could Be the Night, 1957, Until They Sail, 1957, Run Silent, Run Deep, 1958, I Want to Live, 1958, Odds Against Tomorrow, 1959, West Side Story (Acad. awards best dir. with Jerome Robbins, and best picture, Dir. Guild of Am. award), 1961, Two For the Seasaw, 1962, The Haunting, 1963, The Sound of Music, 1965 (Acad. award best dir., best picture, Dir. Guild of Am. award), The Sand Pebbles, 1966, Star!, 1968, The Baby Maker (exec. prodr.), 1970, The Andromeda Strain, 1971, Two People, 1973, The Hindenburg, 1975, Audrey Rose, 1977, Star Trek-The Motion Picture, 1979, The Baby Maker, 1970, Rooftops, 1989; supervising prodr. At Night the Sun Shines, 1992; dir., TV movies: A Storm in Summer, 2000, prodr. 43rd Ann.Acad. awards, 1971, 57th Ann. Acad. awards, 1985; appeared in The Stupids (acting debut), 1996; editor: Bachelor Mother, 1939, 5th Ave Girl, 1939, The Hunchback of Notre Dame, 1939, My Favorite Wife, 1940, Dance, Girl, Dance, 1940, Citizen Kane, 1941, The Devil and Daniel Webster, 1941, The Magnificent Ambersons, 1942, Seven Days Leave, 1942, Bombardier, 1943, The Fallen Sparrow, 1943, The Iron Major, 1943 Recipient Nat. Medal of Arts award, 1992,Life Achievement award Am. Film Inst., 1998, D.W. Griffith award, 1988, Robert B. Aldrich award, 1984, Dir. Guild of Am. names libr. Robert E. Wise Libr., 1998 Hon mem. Dirs. Guild (pres. 1971-74); mem. Acad. Motion Picture Arts and Scis. (pres. 1985-87) Office: Robert Wise Prodns 222 Ave of Stars Ste 105E Los Angeles CA 90067

WISE, ROBERT ELLSWORTH, JR., (BOB ELLSWORTH), governor, former congressman; b. Washington, Jan. 6, 1948; m. Sandy Casber; children: Robert, Alexandra. BA, Duke U., 1970; JD, Tulane U., 1975. Bar: W.Va. 1985. Sole practice, Charleston, W.Va., 1975—80; atty., legis. coun. for judiciary com. W.Va. Ho. of Dels., 1977—78; mem. W.Va. Senate, 1980—82, 97th-106th Congresses from 2d W.Va. dist., Washington, 1983—2001; whip at large, 1986—2001; mem. govt. reform and oversight com., transp. and infrastructure com.; gov. State of W.Va., 2001—. Dir. West Virginians for Fair and Equitable Assessment of Taxes, Inc. Mem.: ABA, W.Va. State Bar Assn. Democrat. Avocations: physical fitness, bluegrass music. Office: Gov's Office WVa State Capitol Charleston WV 25305-0370 Business E-Mail: gov@wvgov.org.

WISE, ROLAND, retired art educator, artist; b. San Francisco, June 19, 1923; s. Max and Mirian Wise; m. Josephine Deloras Corsello, Dec. 18, 1949; children: Margaret Wise Tenenbaum, David. Student, Art Students League N.Y., 1947—49; BFA, U. Manitoba, 1955; MA, NYU, 1958. Asst. prof. art U.

Manitoba, Winnipeg, Canada, 1951—55; prof. fine arts State U. Coll., Buffalo, 1955—92, chmn. dept. fine arts, 1968—70. Mem. planning com. Prospective H.S. of the Arts. One-man shows include Albright-Knox Art Gallery, Mems. Gallery, Buffalo, 1968, Jewish Ctr., Buffalo-Amherst, 1974, Calif. State Coll., Stanislaus, Turlock, Calif., 1977, More-Rubin Gallery, Buffalo, 1977, Butler Libr., SUNY Coll. Buffalo, 1984, Burchfield-Penney Art Ctr., Buffalo, 1994, exhibited in group shows at Can. Art Mus., Toronto, Montreal, Winnipeg, St. Catherines, and Vancouver, Vangarde Gallery, New London, Conn., Burchfield Ctr., Buffalo, Albright Knox Art Gallery, Columbus Mus., Ohio, Silvermine Gallery, Conn., Represented in permanent collections. With USAF, 1943—46. Recipient Creative Artists Pub. Svc. award for painting, N.Y. State Coun. on the Arts, 1976, Burchfield Ctr. 2d award, Painted Box Exhbn., 1982, numerous exhbn. awards; SUNY Grants-in-Aid, 1971, 1972, 1973. Home: 45 Fordham Dr Buffalo NY 14216

WISE, SANDRA CASBER, lawyer; BA, Macalester Coll., 1969; JD, U. Minn., 1972. Bar: Minn. 1972, D.C., 1986, W.Va., 1987. Legis asst. to Rep. Martha Keys, Washington, 1977-78; asst. to asst. to the pres. for women's issues Sara Weddington, The White Ho., Washington, 1979; staff sub-com. on pub. assistance Ho. Com. on Ways and Means, Washington, 1980, staff sub-com. on health, 1981-85; atty. White, Fine and Verville, 1986; staff dir. sub-com. on social security Ho. Com. on Ways and Means, Washington, 1987-94, minority counsel subcom. on social security, 1995-2000; first lady State of W.Va., 2001—.

WISE, THOMAS NATHAN, psychiatrist; b. Reno, Nev., Dec. 10, 1943; s. Charles Samuel and Irene Ruth (Bernstein) W.; m. Karen Dalinsky, Feb. 10, 1979; children: Catherine Sara, Elizabeth Anne. BA, Dartmouth Coll., 1965; MD, Duke U., 1969. Diplomate Am. Bd. Psychiatry and Neurology. Dir. psychiatry cons. svc. Johns Hopkins Hosp., Balt., 1974-76, assoc. prof. psychiatry, 1990-99, prof. psychiatry, 1999—; chmn. dept. psychiatry Fairfax Hosp., Falls Church, Va., 1976—; pvt. practice psychiatry Falls church, 1976—; prof. psychiatry Georgetown U., Washington, 1984—, vice chmn. dept. psychiatry, 1992—; med. dir. behavioral svcs. Inova Health Systems, Falls Church, 1996—. Author: Anxiety and Depression in Medical Diseases, 1980; editor: Psychiatry for Primary Care Physicians, 1998, Diagnosis and Management of Sexual Disorders, 1992; editor-in-chief Advances in Psychosomatic Medicine, 1984—; editor Psychosomatics, 1986; cons. editor Gen. Hosp. Psychiatry, 1984-98. Bd. dirs. Krasnow Inst., Fairfax, 1997; med. advisor Com. to Combat Huntington's Disease, Fairfax, 1995—. Recipient Disting. Svc. award Soc. for Liaison Psychiatry, 1996; Am. Psychiat. Assn. Rsch. awardee, 1989. Fellow Am. Coll. Psychiatrists; mem. Am. Psychosomatic Soc. (pres. 1994-96), Acad. Psychosomatic Medicine (pres. 1995-96, Disting. Svc. award 1993), Am. Assn. Gen. Hosp. Psychiatrists, Cosmos Club, Hidden Creek Country Club, Yale Club of N.Y.C. Avocations: history of medicine, social history of U.S., golf. Office: Inova Fairfax Hospital 3300 Gallows Rd Falls Church VA 22042-3300

WISE, TIMOTHY LEE, music educator; b. Campbellsville, Ky., Oct. 4, 1968; s. Ernest Lee Jr. and Paula Wise; m. Fritzie Lynn Smathers, June 27, 2002. BME, Morehead (Ky.) State U., 1991; MEd, Western Carolina U., N.C., 2002. Asst. dir. bands Riverdale (Ga.) HS, 1991—93; band dir. Tuscola HS, Waynesville, NC, 1993—. Named one of Top 50 Band Dirs., Sch. Band and Orch. Mag., 2003. Mem.: N.C. Educators Assn., Western N.C. Bandmasters (Mem. of Yr. 1998), Music Educators Conf. Avocations: music, reading, tennis, genealogy. Home: 497 Utah Mt Rd Waynesville NC 28786 Office: Tuscola HS 564 Tuscola Sch Rd Waynesville NC 28786 Office Phone: 828-456-3783. E-mail: twise68@hotmail.com.

WISE, VERNON L., JR., publishing executive; b. Pitts., June 28, 1929; m. Sarah C. Wise; 1 child, Vernon L. III; 1 child, Jamie W. Lanier. BA, Princeton. Publisher Eagle Printing Co., Butler, Pa., 1951—. With U.S. Army, 1952—54. Mem.: Syria Shrine, Masonic Lodge. Avocation: saddle bred show horses. Home: 119 Larchwood Drive Butler PA 16001 Office: Eagle Printing Co 114 W Diamond St Butler PA 16001-5796

WISE, WILLIAM ALLEN, energy company executive; b. Davenport, Iowa, July 10, 1945; s. A. Walter and Mary Virginia (Kuhl) Wise; m. Marie Figge, Sept. 27, 1969; children: Vivian Marie, Genevieve Marie, Mary Elizabeth. BA, Vanderbilt U.; JD, U. Colo. Cert. Colo., 1970. Prin. counsel El Paso Natural Gas, Tex., 1970—80, sr. v.p. mktg., 1985—87, exec. v.p. mktg., 1987—89, pres., chief oper. officer, 1989—90, pres., chief exec. officer, 1990—93, chmn, pres. & CEO, 1994—96; asst. gen. counsel in Houston The El Paso Co., 1980—82, v.p., gen. counsel, 1983, sr. v.p., gen. counsel and sec., 1983—85; chmn., pres. & CEO El Paso Natural Gas Co. dba El Paso Energy Corp., 1996—2003; also bd. dirs. El Paso Energy Corp. Bd. dirs. Tex. Commerce Bank, El Paso, Commerce Bancshares, Inc., Houston, Interstate Natural Gas Assn. Am., Washington; mem. N.Y. Merc. Exch. Tri-Regional Com. Contbr. articles to profl. jours. Bd. dirs. Battle Mt. Gold Co., U. Colo. Found., Boulder, Gas Industry Stds., Natural Gas Coun., Tex., Govs. Bus. Coun.; mem. bus. adv. coun. and devel. bd. U. Tex., El Paso; bd. visitors M.D. Anderson Cancer Ctr. Mem.: Colo. Bar Assn., Nat. Petroleum Coun. (bd. dirs.), Old Baldy Club (Wyo.), River Oaks Country Club (Houston), George Town Club (Washington), El Paso Country Club. Republican. Roman Catholic. Avocations: golf, running.

WISE, WILLIAM HARVEY, IV, human service executive; b. Alexandria, Va., Apr. 28, 1948; s. William Harvey III and Emily Virginia (Miller) W.; m. Susana Andrea Joublanc, July 28, 1973; children: Adam J., Andrea Susana, Virginia Elizabeth. BS, Washington & Lee U., 1970; postgrad, George Washington U., 1972. Acct. Arthur Andersen & Co., Washington, 1970-71; contr. Joint Action in Community Svc., Inc., Washington, 1971-79, dep. dir., 1979-87, exec. dir., 1987—. Mem. Ind. Sector, Washington, 1987—, Nat. Assembly of Nat. Voluntary Health and Social Welfare Orgns., Washington, 1989—. V.p. Whittier Woods Civic Assn., Bethesda, Md., 1983-86; cubmaster Boy Scouts Am., Bethesda, 1984-85; fin. com. chmn. Concord-St.-Andrew's United Meth. Ch., Bethesda, 1983-86, chmn. adminstrv. bd., 1995-2000, trustee, 2000-02; bd. dirs. Ridgeleigh Homes Assn., Potomac, Md., 1988-99, Pax World Svc., 1995-2001, treas., 1996-2000, chmn., 2000-2001; del. Balt. Ann. Conf. United Meth. Ch., 1996-99; bd. ambs. Mercy Corps, 2000—. Mem. Mensa, Kenwood Golf and Country Club. Avocations: tennis, gardening, genealogy. Home: 8229 Gainsborough Ct W Potomac MD 20854-4273 Office: Joint Action Community Svc 5225 Wisconsin Ave NW Washington DC 20015-2014

WISE, WILLIAM JERRARD, lawyer; b. Chgo., May 27, 1934; s. Gerald Paul and Harriet Muriel (Rosenblum) Wise; m. Peggy Spero, Sept. 3, 1959; children: Deborah, Stephen, Betsy, Lynne. BBA, U. Mich., 1955, MBA, JD with distinction, U. Mich., 1958. Bar: Ill. 1959. Spl. atty. Office Regional Counsel, IRS, Milw., 1959-63; with McDermott, Will & Emery, Chgo., 1963-70, Coles & Wise, Ltd., Chgo., 1971—80, Wise & Stracks, Ltd., Chgo., 1980—2000, Querrey & Harrow Ltd., Chgo., 2000—. Lectr., contbr. Ill. Inst. Continuing Legal Edn.; arbitrator Cir. Ct. Cook County Ill., 1990—. Bd. dirs. Blind Svc. Assn., Chgo., 1964—74; mem. Village of Winnetka, Ill., 1974—75; dir., treas. Suzuki Orff Sch. Young Musicians, Chgo., 1981—91. With U.S. Army, 1958—59. Mem.: Chgo. Bar Assn. Home: 1401 Tower Rd Winnetka IL 60093-1628 Office: Querrey & Harrow Ltd 175 W Jackson Blvd Ste 1600 Chicago IL 60604-2827 Office Phone: 312-540-7104. E-mail: dididoe@yahoo.com. *I believe that one succeeds best in our society if one gives as little thought as possible to one's personal well being.*

WISEHART, MARY RUTH, retired religious organization administrator; b. Myrtle, Mo., Nov. 2, 1932; d. William Henry and Ora (Harbison) W. BA, Free Will Bapt. Bible Coll., 1955, George Peabody Coll. Tchrs., 1959, MA, 1960, PhD, 1976. Tchr. Free Will Bapt. Bible Coll., Nashville, 1956-60, chmn. English dept., 1961-85; exec. sec.-treas. Free Will Bapt. Women Nat. Active for Christ, 1985-98. Author: Sparks Into Flame, 1985, Beyond the Gate, 1998; contbr. poetry to jours. Mem. Nat. Coun. Tchrs. English, Scribbler's Club. Free Will Baptist. Avocations: photography, music, drama. Personal E-mail: wisemrw@aol.com.

WISEHEART, MALCOLM BOYD, JR., lawyer; b. Miami, Fla., Sept. 18, 1942; s. Malcolm B. and Dorothy E. (Allen) Wiseheart; m. Michele I. Romanens, Dec. 11, 1976. BA, Yale U., 1965; MA in English Jurisprudence, Cambridge U., 1973; JD with honors, U. Fla., 1970. Bar: Fla. 1970, Eng. 1970, Wales 1970, Jamaica 1970, Trinidad and Tobago 1971, DC 1980. Assoc. Helliwell, Melrose & DeWolf, Miami, 1970-72; pvt. practice Miami, 1973—86, 1987—; sr. ptnr. Wiseheart & Joyce, P.A., Miami, 1986—87. Sec., gen. counsel Wiseheart Found., pres., 1985—2004; spl. master Dade County Property Appraisal Adjustment Bd., 1977—90; pres. Fla. Law Inst., 1980—2004; bd. dirs. Sta. WLRN Pub. Radio, 1982; dir. Yale Alumni Schs. Com. S. Fla., 2001—04; bd. dirs. Coun. Internat. Visitors. Bd. trustees Ransom Everglades Sch., 1995—97; bd. trustees, mem. exec. com. Players State Theater, 1982—84. Named Most Outstanding, U. Fla. Law Rev. Alumnus, 1981. Mem.: Gray's Inn of Ct., London (barrister), Order of Coif, Dade County Bar Assn. (dir. 1971—74, treas. 1974—75, sec. 1975—77, dir. 1986—89), Fla. Bar (chmn. grievance com. 1978—81), United Oxford and Cambridge Univs. Club (London), Yale Club (Miami pres. 1976—77). Office: Wiseheart Bldg 2840 SW 3rd Ave Miami FL 33129-2317 Office Phone: 305-285-1222. E-mail: mbwjr@bellsouth.net.

WISEMAN, ALAN M(ITCHELL), lawyer; b. Long Branch, NJ, July 6, 1944; s. Lincoln B. and Gertrude (Gorcey) W.; m. Paula Wiseman, July 8, 1965; children: Steven, David, Julie. BA, Johns Hopkins U., 1965; JD, Georgetown U., 1968. Bar: Md. 1968, Ill. 1970, DC 1973. Law clk. Hon. William J. McWilliams, Md. Ct. Appeals, 1968-69; assoc. Schiff, Hardin & Waite, Chgo., 1970-74; ptnr. Howrey Simon Arnold White, LLP, Washington, 1976—. Editor Georgetown Law Jour., 1967-68. Mem. US C. of C. (coun. antitrust policy 1983-2001). Office: 1299 Pennsylvania Ave NW Washington DC 20004-2400 Office Phone: 202-383-6638. E-mail: wisemana@howrey.com.

WISEMAN, CARTER STERLING, writer, educator; b. NYC, Oct. 8, 1945; s. Mark Huntington Wiseman and Eleanor (Carter) Wood; m. Eileen Condon, Oct. 19, 1985; children: Emma, Owen, Damian. BA, Yale U., 1968; MA, Columbia U., 1972. Newsman AP, N.Y.C., 1972-74; assoc. editor Newsweek Mag., N.Y.C., 1974-77; sr. editor Horizon Mag., N.Y.C., 1977-79; mng. editor Portfolio Mag., N.Y.C., 1979-80; archtl. critic N.Y. Mag., N.Y.C., 1980-96; editor Yale Alumni Mag., New Haven, 1986—2002; lectr. Yale Sch. Architecture, New Haven, 2002—. Bd. dirs. MacDowell Colony, Peterborough, NH, pres., 1999—; tchr. The Reading Co., Westport, Conn. Author: Twentieth Century American Architecture, 2000, I.M. Pei, 2001; contbg. editor: ARTnews, 1996—. Chair Loeb Fellowship Assn. Harvard U., 1986—95. With U.S. Army, 1968—71. Recipient Spl. Citation award, Am. Inst. Arch., 1984, Inst. Honor award, Am. Inst. Archs., 1987, Interpretative Writing award, Soc. Silurians, 1985, Roger Starr award, Citizens Housing and Planning Coun., 1987, 1990; Loeb fellow, Harvard U., 1985. Mem.: Century Assn., Yale Club N.Y. Office: 16 W Branch Rd Weston CT 06883-2917 Personal E-mail: writertime@aol.com.

WISEMAN, DOUGLAS CARL, education educator, department chairman, dean; b. Nashua, NH, Feb. 28, 1935; s. Howard W. and Ruth D. (Aiken) W.; m. Donna Wiseman; children: Mark, Cynthia, Lori, Alan, Kathleen, Steve. BEd, Plymouth (N.H.) State Coll., 1961; MS, Ind. U., 1962, PED, 1970. Cert. tchr. health, math., phys. edn., sci. Tchr., track coach Nashua (N.H.) Pub. Schs., 1960-61, tchr., baseball coach, 1962-63; tchg. asst. Ind. U., Bloomington, 1961-62; tchr. high sch., wrestling coach Portage (Mich.) High Sch., 1963-64; instr., asst. prof., soccer, wrestling and tennis coach Plymouth (N.H.) State Coll., 1964-69; asst. prof. Northeastern U., Boston, 1969-71; dir. athletics, chmn. phys. edn. dept. Plymouth State Coll., 1971-80, assoc. dean, dir. undergrad. studies, 1993-96, prof., accreditation coord., 1996-98, ret., 1998, prof. emeritus, 1998—; prof., chair dept. edn. Univ. Sys. of N.H., 1980—. Aquatics cons. Am./Nat. Red Cross, Laconia, N.H., 1971-98, State Dept. Edn., Concord, 1980-98. Author, contbg. editor: Adapted Physical Education, 1982, Practical Research, 1989, Quantitative Research, 1992, Physical Education for Exceptional Students, 1994, Introduction to Educational Research, 1995, Educational Research, 1996, Research Strategies for Education, 1999; contbr. more than 50 articles to profl. jours. Cert. police officer Ashland, N.H., 1992-98; chair sch. bd. Plymouth Regional Sch. Dist., 1989-91; divsn. staff officer-pub. edn., flotilla career counseling officer USCG Aux., 2001-2002. AAHPERD Ea. Dist. scholar, 1990-91. Republican. Avocations: reading, hiking, boating. E-mail: douglas.wiseman@att.net.

WISEMAN, JAMES RICHARD, classicist, archaeologist, educator; b. North Little Rock, Ark., Aug. 29, 1934; s. James Morgan and Bertie Lou (Sullivan) W.; m. Margaret Lucille Mayhue, Aug. 20, 1954; children: James Alexander, Stephen Michael. BA, U. Mo., Columbia, 1957; MA, U. Chgo., 1960, PhD, 1966; postgrad., Am. Sch. Classical Studies, Athens, Greece, 1959-60. Instr. U. Tex., Austin, 1960-64, asst. prof. classics, 1964-66, asso. prof., 1966-70, prof., 1970-73; dir. archaeol. excavations at Ancient Corinth, Greece, 1965-72; chmn. archaeol. studies program, 1969-73; prof. classics Boston U., 1973—, prof. art history, 1975—, prof. archaeology, 1980—, chmn. dept. classical studies, 1974-82, chmn. dept. archaeology, 1982-96, dir. archaeol. studies program, 1975-76, 79-82, dir. Ctr. Archeol. Studies, 1980—; dir. summer program Greece, 1976-77, 81, 91-94. Vis. assoc. prof. classics U. Colo., Boulder, 1970; Am. prin. investigator, co-dir. Am.-Yugoslav Archaeol. Excavations at Stobi, Yugoslavia, 1970-81; project supr. Boston U. Archaeol. Excavations in Temple, N.H., 1975-76; vis. rsch. prof. Am. Sch. Classical Studies, Athens, 1978-79; cons. archaeology; chmn. exec. com. Ctr. Remote Sensing; dir. Boston U. Nikopolis Project in N.W. Greece, 1991-; vis. fellow Clare Hall and McDonald Inst. for Archaeol. Rsch., Cambridge, 1997; life mem. Clare Hall, Cambridge, 1997—; co-dir. Boston U. Archaeol. Project, Menorca, Spain, 2001-04. Author: Stobi, A Guide to the Excavations, 1973, The Land of the Ancient Corinthians, 1978, (with Thomas Sever) Remote Sensing and Archaeology: Potential for the Future, 1985; contbr. numerous articles on ancient history, epigraphy, classical studies, archaeology to profl. jours.; editor, contbg. author: Studies in the Antiquities of Stobi I, 1973, II, 1975, III, 1981; co-editor (with K. Zachos), contbg. author: Landscape Archaeology in Southern Epirus Greece 1, 2003; founding editor: Jour. Field Archaeology, 1974—; contbg. editor Archaeology Mag., 1995-2002. Trustee Am. Ctr. Oriental Rsch., 1996—, Am. Schs. Oriental Rsch., 1985-89. Served with USN, 1952-55. Recipient Bromberg award U. Tex., 1964, Bronze Plaque award City of Titov Veles, SR Makedonija, Yugoslavia; disting. alumnus award Coll. Arts and Sci. U. Mo. Columbia, 1989; Am. Council Learned Socs. fellow, 1967-68, 78-79, 90-91; Guggenheim fellow, 1971-72; U. Tex. Research Inst. grantee, summers 1961, 66, 67, and 1967-68, 71-72; NEH grantee, 1968, 69, 76-80; Ford Found. grantee, 1968-72; Smithsonian Instn. grantee, 1970-75, 79-81; Dumbarton Oaks fellow, 1983-84; NGS grantee, 1984, 92; NASA grantee, 1984, 91; W.M. Keck Found. grantee, 1985, 86, 88, 92; J.M. Kaplan Fund grantee, 1997-99; NEH fellow, 1990; Mellon fellow Inst. Advanced Study, Princeton U., 1990-91, Alexander S. Onassis Found. fellow, 2003. Fellow Soc. Antiquaries of London, Explorers Club; mem. Archaeol. Inst. Am. (nat. pres. 1985-88, exec. com. 1973-77, 81-92, trustee 1993-98, hon. pres. 1993—, pres. Ctrl. Tex. Soc. 1962-64, pres. Boston Soc. 1979-81, Gold Seal award 1989, Charles Eliot Norton lectr., Joukowsky Disting. Svc. award 1999), Am. Philol. Assn., Am. Sch. Classical Studies at Athens (exec. com. 1973-76), Am. Acad. at Rome, Assn. Ancient Historians, Assn. Field Archaeology (exec. com. 1970-85), Am. Inst. Nautical Archaeology, Internat. Assn. Archaeology, Ctr. Materials Rsch. in Archaeology and Ethnology (exec. com. 1975-78, 79-83), Soc. Am. Archaeology, Am. Coun. Learned Soc. (del. 1985-89), German Archeol. Inst. (corr.), Macedonian Acad. Sci. Arts (fgn.). Democrat. Office: Boston U Dept Archaeology 675 Commonwealth Ave Boston MA 02215-1406 Office Phone: 617-358-1670. E-mail: jimw@bu.edu.

WISEMAN, JAY DONALD DONALD, photographer, inventor, mechanical designer and contractor, land developer, writer; b. Salt Lake City, Dec. 23, 1952; s. Donald Thomas and Reva (Stewart) W.; m. Barbara Helen Taylor, June 25, 1977; children: Jill Reva, Steve Jay. Ed, Utah State U., Logan, U. Utah, Salt Lake City. Cert. profl. photographer. Pvt. practice; owner, pres. JB&W. Judge Utah State Fair. Represented in (permanent collections) Salt Lake City Internat. Airport, traveling loans collections, U.S. and Europe, loan collection Epcot Ctr., photographs published in profl. jours. Named Photographic Hall Fame, 1989, among World's Best, Walt Disney World and Profl. Photographers Assn., 1988; named one of World's Greatest, Kodak, 1987—88; recipient Grand prize, Utah State Fair, 1986, Kodak Crystal for Photographic Excellence, 1986—87, Master of Photography degree, 1989, Best of Show award, 1991—92, 2 prints tied for Masters Best of Show award, RMPA Regional contest, 1991—92, Master Photographer of Yr., Gold Medallion award Best in Show. Mem. Profl. Photographers Assn. Am. (Best of Best award, one of top 10 scores internat. photo contest), Rocky Mountain Profl. Photographers (Best of Show 1987, Master Photographer of Yr. 1991, Ct. of Honour 1981-91), Inter-Mountain Profl. Photographers Assn. (Master's Trophy Best of Show 1982, 86, 88, Photographer of Yr. award 1986, Ct. of Honour 1981-91), Photographers Soc. Am. (Best of Show award Utah chpt. 1986). Latter Day Saints. Achievements include invention of traffic signal lights for the color blind; development of indsl. subdivsn. Pinnacle Park. E-mail: fotowise@hotmail.com.

WISEMAN, LAURENCE DONALD, foundation executive; b. Washington, Feb. 24, 1947; s. Leon Robert and Marion (Wiseman; m. Robin Lynn Jeweler, May 29, 1978; children: Justin J., David B. AB with highest distinction, Dartmouth Coll., 1969; M in Pub. Affairs, Princeton U., 1971. Exec. producer Sta. WQED-TV (pub. broadcasting), Pitts., 1971-75; prin. Moses, Epstein and Wiseman, Washington, 1975-78; v.p. Yankelovich, Skelly and White, N.Y.C., 1978-81, Am. Forest Council, Washington, 1981-84, pres., 1984—. Pres. Am. Forest Coun., 1984-92, Am. Forest Found., 1993—. Author: Coalition Building, 1977. Bd. dirs. Cystic Fibrosis Found., N.Y.C., 1979-80, Urban Philharm., Washington, 1980-83, Sasha Bruce House, Washington, 1980-82; adv. com. Soc. for Profl. Journalists, Washington, 1984; trustee Nat. Ctr. for Housing and the Environment, 2001—; hon. trustee Nat. Arbor Day Found., Nebraska City, Nebr., 1984—; chair Nat. Coun. on Pvt. Forests, 1997-98, Inst. for Journalism and Natural Resources, 1998—. Mem. Am. Forestry Assn., Soc. Am. Foresters, Pub. Rels. Soc. Am. Home: 10621 Democracy Ln Potomac MD 20854-4016 Office: Am Forest Found 1111 19th St NW Washington DC 20036-3603 E-mail: lwiseman@affoundation.org.

WISEMAN, THOMAS ANDERTON, JR., federal judge; b. Tullahoma, Tenn., Nov. 3, 1930; s. Thomas Anderton and Vera Seleta (Poe) W.; m. Emily Barbara Matlack, Mar. 30, 1957; children: Thomas Anderton III, Mary Alice, Sarah Emily. BA, Vanderbilt U., 1952, LL.B., 1954; LLM, U. Va., 1990. Bar: Tenn. Pvt. practice, Tullahoma, 1956-63; ptnr. Haynes, Wiseman & Hull, Tullahoma and Winchester, Tenn., 1963-71; treas. State of Tenn., 1971-74; ptnr. Chambers & Wiseman, 1974-78; judge U.S. Dist. Ct. (mid. dist.) Tenn., Nashville, 1978—, chief judge, 1984-91, sr. judge, 1995—; 6th cir. rep. Jud. Conf. of the U.S., 1996—2001, chair dist. judges conf., 1998-99. Mem. Tenn. Ho. of Reps., 1964-68; adj. prof. law Vanderbilt U. Sch. Law; cons. to judiciary of Brcko, Bosnia, 2002; mem. pattern jury instrn. com. 6th cir., 1988—. Asso. editor: Vanderbilt Law Rev, 1953-54. Democratic candidate for gov., Tenn., 1974; Chmn. Tenn. Heart Fund, 1973, Middle Tenn. Heart Fund, 1972. Served with U.S. Army, 1954-56. Fellow Tenn. Bar Found.; mem. Fed. Judges Assn. (bd. dirs. 1982-87, v.p. 1982-91, 87-91), Masons (33 deg.), Shriners, Amateur Chefs Soc. Presbyterian. Office: US Dist Ct 777 US Courthouse 801 Broadway Nashville TN 37203-3816

WISER, JAMES LOUIS, political science educator; b. Detroit, Mar. 4, 1945; s. Louis Bernard and Nita Pauline (Neff) W.; m. Bethany Marie Goodall, Dec. 27, 1967; children: Steven Louis, Michael James. BA, U. Notre Dame, 1967; MA, Duke U., 1968, PhD, 1971. Asst. prof. Loyola U., Chgo., 1971-74, assoc. prof., 1974-81, prof., 1981—, chmn. dept. polit. sci., 1980-84, dean Coll. Arts and Scis., 1987-89, sr. v.p., dean of faculties, 1989—. Author: Political Philosophy: A History of the Search for Order, 1983; Political Theory: A Thematic Inquiry, 1986 Bd. dirs. Am. Cancer Soc., Chgo., 1982-84. Recipient dissertation award Woodrow Wilson Found., 1970; Fulbright-Hayes grantee, 1969; NEH grantee, 1979 Mem. Am. Polit. Sci. Assn., Conf. for Study of Polit. Thought (chmn. 1975-77), Internat. Seminar for Philosophy and Polit. Theory Democrat. Roman Catholic. Home: 52 Chabot Ter San Francisco CA 94118-4311 Office: Loyola U 820 N Michigan Ave Ste 613 Chicago IL 60611-2147

WISH, JAY BARRY, nephrologist, specialist; b. Hartford, Mar. 30, 1950; s. Martin and Evelyn Lillian (Lassman) W.; m. Linda Kristina Hansen, June 29, 1971; (div. 1980); children: Allen Jeremy, Robin Lindsey; m. Diane Elizabeth Perkins, June 5, 1983; children: Jeffrey Bryan, David Phillip. BA, Wesleyan U., 1970; MD, Tufts U., 1974. Diplomate Am. Bd. Internal Medicine, Am. Bd. Nephrology. Resident in medicine New England Med. Ctr., Boston, 1974-79; instr. in medicine Tufts U., Boston, 1978-79; lectr. in health sci. Northeastern U., Boston, 1978-79; asst. prof. of medicine Case Western Res. U., Cleve., 1979-85, assoc. prof. of medicine, 1985-96, prof. medicine, 1996—; dir. hemodialysis U. Hosps. of Cleve., 1980—, dir. continuing edn., 1987-95. Chmn. Med. Adv. Bd. Kidney Found. of Ohio, Cleve., 1985-88. Author: Renal Disease and Hypertension, 1982, Disorders of Potassium, 1984, Metabolic Diseases, 1986, Rheumatic Diseases of the Kidney, 1993, Acid-Base and Electrolyte Disorders in the Critically Ill Patient, 1993, Assuring Quality of Care in Dialysis Patients, 1994, Algorithms and Care Paths for Quality Improvement, 2000, Adequacy of Hemodialysis, 2002, Quality, Safety and Accountability in Dialysis, 2004; contbr. articles to med. jours. Chmn. med. rev. bd. End-Stage Renal Disease Network #22, Pitts., 1982-87, End-State Renal Disease Network #9, Indpls., 1992-2000, pres., 2001—; mem. exec. com. Forum of End-Stage Renal Disease Networks, 1992—, v.p., 1996-98, pres., 1998-2001; bd. dirs. Renal Phys. Assn., 1993-99, sec. 1996-97, treas., 1997-98; mem. Nat. Kidney Found. Fellow Am. Coll. of Physicians; mem. Cleve. Restoration Soc., Am. Soc. of Nephrology, Internat. Soc. of Nephrology, Alpha Omega Alpha. Democrat. Jewish. Avocation: performing arts. Office: U Hosps Cleve 11100 Euclid Ave Cleveland OH 44106-1736 Office Phone: 216-844-3163. E-mail: jaywish@earthlink.net.

WISHARD, DELLA MAE, former newspaper editor; b. Bison, S.D., Oct. 21, 1934; d. Ervin E. and Alma J. (Albertson) Preszler; m. Glenn L. Wishard, Oct. 18, 1953; children: Glenda Lee, Pamela A., Glen Ervin. Grad. high sch., Bison. Mem. S.D. Ho. of Reps., Pierre, 1984-96; pub., editor Bison (S.D.) Courier, 1996-2000. Columnist County Farm Bur., 1970-96. Committeewoman state Rep. Cen. Com., Perkins County, S.D., 1980-84, 98-01. Mem. Am. Legis. Exch. Coun. (state coord. 1985-91, state chmn. 1991-96), Fed. Rep. Women (chmn. Perkins County chpt. 1978-84), S.D. Farm Bur. (state officer 1982), Perkins County Rep. (chmn. 2000-03). Lutheran. Avocations: writing, gardening. Home: 1510 Canyon St Spearfish SD 57783

WISHARD, GORDON DAVIS, lawyer; b. Indpls., Jan. 7, 1945; s. William Niles Jr. and Caroline (Davis) W.; m. Anne Emison; children: Claire Wishard Hoppenworth, Gordon Davis Jr. BA, Williams Coll., 1966; JD, Ind. U., 1969. Bar: Ind. 1969, U.S. Dist. Ct. (so. dist.) Ind. 1969, U.S. Ct. Appeals (7th cir.) 1976, U.S. Supreme Ct. 1980, U.S. Tax Ct. 1983. Ptnr. Ice Miller, Indpls. Mem. Am. Coll. Trust and Estate Coun. (Ind. chmn. 1990-95). Avocations: hunting, fishing. Office: Ice Miller 1 American Sq Indianapolis IN 46282-0020 Office Phone: 317-236-2476.

WISHART, RONALD SINCLAIR, retired chemical company executive; b. Bklyn., Mar. 1, 1925; s. Ronald Sinclair and Elizabeth Lathrop (Phillips) W.; m. Betty B. Burnup, Sept. 14, 1951 (dec. Dec. 1973); children: Michael Sinclair, James Ronald; m. Eleanor Dorothy Parrish Dooley, Jan. 11, 1975; stepchildren: Donna Dooley Willix, Arthur D. Dooley. BChemE, Rensselaer Poly. Inst., 1948. Engr., chemist Linde air divsn. Union Carbide Corp., Tonawanda, NY, 1948-51; sales rep. Chgo., Cleve., 1951-56; region mgr. Chgo., 1956-57; product mgr., mktg. mgr. Silicones divsn. N.Y.C., 1957-64; gen. mgr., pres., 1964-66; pres. devel. and coating materials divsns., 1966-71; corp. dir. energy and transp. policy, 1972-82; v.p. fed. govt. rels., 1983-85; v.p. pub. affairs Danbury, Conn., 1985-90; chief of staff to chmn. of corp. Union Carbide, N.Y.C., 1984-85. Mem. adv. coun. Gas Rsch. Inst., Energy Modeling Ctr., Stanford U., 1979-83, Environ. and Energy Policy Ctr., John F. Kennedy Sch. Pub. Policy, Harvard U., 1980-87; energy com. Aspen Inst., 1976-88; chmn., exec. dir. Electricity Consumers Resource Coun., Washington, 1976-79. Author: The Marketing Factor, 1966; contbr. chpts. to books and articles to profl. jours.; patentee silicone formulas. Vol. Am. Field Svc., Burma,

1944-45; pres., trustee, elder White Plains (N.Y.) Presbyn. Ch., 1987-90; elder Palm City Presbyn. Ch., 1996-2002; treas., bd. dirs. St. Christopher's Jenni Clarkson Home, 1968-91; mem. exec. bd. Westchester Putnam coun. Boy Scouts Am., White Plains, 1985-91; v.p. Carbide Retiree Corps.; v.p. Hospice Martin and St. Lucie, Inc., 1994-99, pres. 2000-02; pres. Lancewood Assn., 1997. Mem. NAM (mem. energy com.), Am. Mgmt. Assn. (v.p. 1966-69), Chem. Mfrs. Assn. (chmn. energy com. 1974-78), Nat. Petroleum Refiners Assn. (v.p. 1972-76, chmn. issues com. 1985-89), Internat. Fedn. Ind. Energy Users (chmn. 1978), Am. Chem. Soc., Soc. Chem. Industry, U.S. C. of C. (mem. energy com.), Met. Club Washington, Harbor Ridge Yacht and Country Club. Republican. Presbyterian. Avocations: golf, reading, bridge. Home: 1329 Lancewood Ter Palm City FL 34990

WISHERT, MARTINA, nursing home administrator; b. Phila., Nov. 20, 1942; d. Martin Rulon and Mallette Mary (Holden) Sembach; children: Andrew, Christopher, Roberta, John. AA, Daytona Beach Community Coll., 1978. LPN; lic. nursing home adminstr., Tex. Adminstr. Purple Hills Manor/Gray Enterprises, Bandera, Tex., 1985-86, Comanche View-Nat. Heritage, Ft. Stockton, Tex., 1986-87, Louis Pasteur Care Ctr./Camlu Care Ctrs., San Antonio, 1987-88, Castle Hills Manor/Campbell-White Assocs., San Antonio, 1988-89, Briarcliff Health Care Ctr., Greenville, Tex., 1989-91; mgr. physician orders dept. Cullum Industries Page Drug Nursing Home Svcs., 1992-96; prin. Samples & Assocs., San Antonio, 1992—; adminstr. Our Lady of the Lake Retirement Ctr., McCullough Hail Nursing Ctr., San Antonio, 1996—; lic. adminstr., exec. dir. Meadow Park Care Ctr., Peppertree Sq., Prescott, Ariz., Regency Nursing Ctrs. Inc. Tex.-Cuero Nursing & Rehab. Ctr., Diversecare-Advocat Corp., Goliad Manor, Goliad, 1999—; adminstr. Linwood Pl., Victoria. Sr. long term care cons. Medicare/Medicaid reimbursement, tchr. seminars to long-term care adminstrs.; adj. faculty St. Phillips Coll., San Antonio, 1992—. Mem. NAFE, Tex. Health Care Assn., Tex. Assn. for Homes Svcs. for Aging, Am. Legion, Order Eastern Star, VFW, Nat. Assn. of Miniature Enthusiasts. Republican. Methodist. Avocations: crochet, reading, miniaturist and collector. Office Phone: 361-573-2467.

WISHNER, MAYNARD IRA, retired finance company executive, lawyer; b. Chgo., Sept. 17, 1923; s. Hyman L. and Frances (Fisher) W.; m. Elaine Loewenberg, July 4, 1954; children: Ellen Kenemore, Jane Wishner, Miriam Segel. BA, U. Chgo., 1944, JD, 1947; LHD honoris causa, Spertus Inst., 1998; LHD (hon.), Hebrew Union Coll., 2001; LHD honoris causa, Spertus Coll. Judaica, 2001. Bar: Ill. 1947. Exec. dir. Chgo. Commn. on Human Relations, 1947-52; chief ordinance enforcement div. Law Dept., City of Chgo., 1952-55; mem. law firm Cole, Wishner, Epstein & Manilow, Chgo., 1955-63; with Walter E. Heller & Co., Chgo., 1963-86, pres., 1974-86; of counsel Rosenthal and Schanfield, Chgo., 1986-95; ret. Dir. Walter E. Heller Internat. Corp., Am. Nat. Bank & Trust Co., and br. cos., Chgo. Pres. Jewish Fedn. Met. Chgo., 1987-89; chair Nat. Jewish Community Rels., 1992-94, pres. Coun. Jewish Fedn., 1993-96; chmn. bd. govs. Am. Jewish Com., 1977-80, nat. pres. 1980-83, hon. pres., recipient Human Rights medallion, 1975; bd. dirs. Nat. Found. for Jewish Culture; chmn. Ill. Humanities Coun.; commr. Hillel Found.; mem. vis. com. U. Chgo. Sch. Social Svc. Adminstrn. and Divsn. of the Humanities; chair Ill. Humanities Coun., 1991-93; bd. govs. Jewish Agy. for Israel. Recipient Rosenwald award Jewish Fedn. Met. Chgo., Officers Merit medal Republic of Poland, United Hellenic Leadership Coun. Frisis award, Civic Achievement award U. Chgo. Home: 1410 Sheridan Rd Wilmette IL 60091-1895 E-mail: maynwish@aol.com.

WISHNICK, MARCIA MARGOLIS, pediatrician, geneticist, educator; b. N.Y.C., Oct. 10, 1938; d. Hyman and Tillie (Stoller) Margolis; m. Stanley Wishnick, June 12, 1960; 1 child, Elizabeth Anne. BA, Barnard Coll., 1960; PhD, NYU, 1970, MD, 1974. Diplomate Am. Bd. Pediatrics, Nat. Bd. Med. Examiners. Rsch. technician Lederle Labs./Am. Cyanamid, Pearl River, N.Y., 1960-66; postdoctoral fellow N.Y. Pub. Health Lab., N.Y.C., 1970-71; resident in pediatrics NYU-Bellevue Med. Ctr., N.Y.C., 1974-77, asst. prof. pediatrics, 1977-82; clin. assoc. prof. pediatrics Bellevue Med. Ctr. NYU Med. Ctr., N.Y.C., 1982-87; clin. prof. pediatrics NYU-Bellevue Med. Ctr., N.Y.C., 1987—; pvt. practice, N.Y.C., 1977—2003. Contbr. articles to profl. jours. Fellow Am. Acad. Pediatrics; mem. AMA, N.Y. Pediatric Soc., N.Y. Med. Soc. Office Phone: 808-937-0312. Personal E-mail: docwishnick@earthlink.net.

WISLER, DAVID CHARLES, aerospace engineer; b. Pottstown, Pa., Apr. 21, 1941; s. Lloyd William and Ruth Georgiana (Enos) W.; m. Judith Ann Caleen, Aug. 22, 1964 (dec. Mar. 1979); children: Scott David, Cheryl Lynn; m. Beth Ellen Howard, Jan. 5, 1980; 1 child, Daniel James. BS in Aero Engring., Pa. State U., 1963; MS in Aero. Engring., Cornell U., 1965; PhD in Aero. Engring., U. Colo., 1970. Rsch. engr. GE R & D Ctr., Schenectady, 1965-67; mgr. aero tech. labs. GE Aircraft Engines, Evendale, Ohio, 1985—. Mgr. univ. programs and aero tech. labs.; adj. prof. Ohio State U., U. Cin., Tsinghua U., Beijing. Contbr. articles to profl. jours.; patentee in sloped trenches in compressors. Recipient Gas Turbine award ASME, 1990, 92. Fellow ASME (chmn. turbomachinery com. 1993-, bd. dirs. Internat. Gas Turbine Inst. 1997-, v.p. 2003—, Melville medal for best tech. paper 1989, 98, 2003, editor Jour. Turbomachinery, 2003—); mem. AIAA (assoc.), Nat. Acad. Engring. Avocation: photography. Home: 40 Trappist Walk Fairfield OH 45014-4465 Office: GE Aircraft Engines 1 Neumann Way # A-411 Cincinnati OH 45215-1915 Office Phone: 513-243-2905. E-mail: dave.wisler@ae.ge.com.

WISNE, LAWRENCE A. metal products executive; b. 1947; s. Anthony E. Wisne. With Prog. Tool and Industries Co., Southfield, Mich., v.p., 1977—79, pres., 1979—. Office: Prog Tool & Inds Co 21000 Telegraph Rd Southfield MI 48034-4280

WISNER, DAVID HAMILTON, surgeon, educator; b. San Francisco, May 23, 1955; s. Francis Hamilton Wisner and Marjorie Marlene (Cross) Cross-Wisner; m. Carin Wisner; 1 child, Peter. BA, U. Calif., Davis, 1977; MD, U. Calif., 1981. Diplomate Am. Bd. Surgery. Resident in surgery U. Calif., Sacremento, 1982—87, from asst. prof. to assoc. prof. surgery, 1987—95, prof. surgery, 1995—, chief trauma and critical care, 1991—. Contbr. articles to profl. jours. Fellow: ACS (trauma com. 1999—); mem.: Sacramento Surg. Soc. (pres. 1999—2000), Am. Assn. for Surgery Trauma (bd. dirs. 1999—), Alpha Omega Alpha, Phi Beta Kappa, Phi Kappa Phi. Avocations: travel, history. Office: Univ Calif Davis Med Ctr 2315 Stockton Blvd Rm 4209 Sacramento CA 95817

WISNER, FRANK GEORGE, insurance company executive, former ambassador; b. N.Y.C., July 2, 1938; s. Frank Gardiner W. and Mary Knowles (Fritchey) W.; m. Genevieve de Virel, July, 1969 (dec. 1974); 1 dau., Sabrina; m. Christine de Ganay, June, 1976; 1 son, David; stepchildren: Caroline Sarkozy, Olivier Sarkozy. BA, Princeton U., 1961. With Fgn. Svc. Dept. U.S. Dept. State, Algiers, Morocco, 1962-64; from dep. amabassador's staff aide to sr. advisor Vietnamese province Tuyen Duc Agy. Internat. Devel., Vietnam, 1964-68; officer-in-charge Tunisian affairs U.S. Dept. State, Washington, 1968-71; chief econ.-comml. sect. Am. Embassy, Tunis, Tunisia, 1971-73, chief polit. sect. Dacca, Bangladesh, 1973-74; dir. plans and mgmt. Bur. Pub. Affairs, Washington, 1974-75; spl. asst. to dir., then dep. dir. Pres.' Interagy. Task Force Refugee Resettlement, Washington, 1975; spl. asst. to undersec. polit. affairs, 1975-76; dir. office So. African affairs U.S. Dept. State, Washington, 1976-77, dep. exec. sec., 1977-79; U.S. amb. to Zambia Lusaka, 1977-82; dep. asst. sec. African affairs U.S. Dept. State, Washington, 1982-86; U.S. amb. to Egypt Cairo, 1986-91; U.S. amb. to Philippines Manila, 1991-92; under sec. of state for internat. security affairs Washington, 1992-93; under sec. of def. for policy Dept. Def., Washington, 1993-94; U.S. amb. to India U.S. Dept. State, 1994-97; vice chmn. external affairs Am. Internat. Group Inc., N.Y.C., 1997—. Bd. dirs. EOG Resources; trustee Am. U. of Beirut, Am. U. Cairo; mem. bd. bus. Coun. Internat. Understanding; bd. U.S.-India Bus. Coun.; bd. refugees Internat., United Svcs. Orgn. Decorated Legion of Honor (Romania); recipient meritorious honor award Dept. State, 1973, superior honor award, 1992, disting. svc. award, 1997; recipient Mil. Medal of Honor Govt. Vietnam, 1968, Social Welfare medal of honor, 1968. Mem. Coun. on Fgn. Relations, Metropolitan Club (Washington), Ivy Club (Princeton, N.J.), Knickerbocker Club (N.Y.), Brook Club (N.Y.). Episcopalian. Office: Am Internat Group Inc 18th Fl 70 Pine St New York NY 10270-0002*

WISNICKI, JEFFREY LEONARD, plastic surgeon; b. N.Y.C., May 15, 1957; s. Joseph and Lorraine (Justman) Wisnicki; m. Rebecca Lynn O'Shields, Feb. 2, 1997; children: Justin Robert, Brandon Lawrence. BS summa cum laude, Rensselaer Poly. Inst., 1976; MD cum laude with honors, Union U., 1980. Diplomate Am. Bd. Plastic Surgery. Intern in surgery Stanford (Calif.) U. Med. Ctr., 1980-81, resident in gen., plastic and reconstructive surgery, 1981-84, chief resident in plastic and reconstructive surgery, 1985-86; fellow in plastic and reconstructive surgery Dartmouth-Hitchcock Med. Ctr., Hanover, N.H., 1984; active staff Good Samaritan Hosp., West Palm Beach, Fla., 1986—, Wellington Regional Hosp., West Palm Beach, 1986—; chief divsn. plastic surgery John F. Kennedy Meml. Hosp., West Palm Beach, 1990-93; chmn. dept. surgery Palms West Hosp., West Palm Beach, 1991-93, chief med. staff, 1994-97, chmn. bd. trustees, 1997—2002, trustee, 2002—03; chief divsn. plastic surgery Good Samaritan and St. Mary's Hosp., West Palm Beach, 1997—2001, Good Samaritan Hosp., 2004—. Clin. instr. surgery U. Calif., San Francisco, 1983; bd. dirs. Interplast, 1985-86, clin. faculty, 1986—90; presenter in field. Contbr. chpts. to books and articles to profl. jours. Fellow ACS; mem. Am. Soc. Plastic & Reconstructive Surgeons, Alpha Omega Alpha. Office: 2047 Palm Beach Lakes Blvd West Palm Beach FL 33409-6501 Office Phone: 561-798-1400.

WISNIEWSKI, THOMAS JOSEPH, music educator; b. Chgo., Sept. 17, 1926; s. George Wisniewski and Rose (Jelewski) W.; children: Dieter, Lisa Ann, Ericka (dec.). B.Mus., Am. Conservatory of Music, Chgo., 1948; M.Mus., No. Ill. U., 1964. Instr. string instrument Sch. Dist. 89, Maywood, Ill., 1950-55; orch. dir. Sch. Dist. 44, Lombard, Ill., 1955-67; dir. orchs. Glenbard East High Sch., Lombard, 1959-67; prof. music U. Ill., Urbana, 1967-94, emeritus prof., 1994—, chair music edn. div., 1988-92. Clinician and guest condr. internationally; music cons. Webster Internat. Illustrated Dictionary, 1993; ednl. cons. Wm. Lewis and Son, Chgo., 1965-70, Hal Leonard Pubs., Milw., 1975-84., Glaesel divsn. Selmer Corp., Elkhart, Ind., 1975-90. Prodr. films Playing the String Bass, 1967, Playing the Cello, 1968; developer (with Rodney Mueller) computer software program Visualized Vibrato, 1995, version 2.0, 1998. Author: Learning Unlimited String Program, Vol. 1, 1975, Vol. 2, 1976; editor Orch. Publs., 1990; music editor Webster International Illustrated Dictionary, 1994. Mem. Am. String Tchrs. Assn. Assn. (Disting. Svc. award Ill. unit 1991, Disting. Svc. award Tenn. unit 1993), Ill. Music Educators Assn. (Pres.'s award 1996), Music Educators Nat. Conf., Ill. String Tchrs. Assn. (editor 1967, 87, pres. 1970), Nat. Jazz Educators Assn. (nat. orch. chmn. 1976), Pi Kappa Lambda, Phi Mu Alpha.

WISOTSKY, SERGE SIDOROVICH, engineering executive; b. Chelsea, Mass., Oct. 19, 1919; s. Sidor Radionovich and Anna Epatiovna (Fariba) W.; m. Marion Ellen Ramsdell, Aug. 10, 1952; children: Serge S. Jr. (dec.), Tanya Lloyd, Stephan, John and Alexander (twins), Phillip. Student, Boston Trade Sch., 1933—37, Lowell Inst. Sch., 1937—43; BS in Physics, MIT, 1950; MS in Physics, Brown U., 1952. Registered profl. mech. engr., Mass., Okla.; lic. electrician, Mass. Elec. motor mechanic/armature winder United Motors Corp., Boston, 1937-40; machinist apprentice, mfg. methods, steam turbine test GE River Works, Lynn, Mass., 1940-44; engr. R & D Ultrasonics Corp., Cambridge, Mass., 1952-53; instrument engr. Control Engring. Corp., Canton and Norwood, Mass., 1953-57; staff engr. MIT/Draper Lab., Cambridge, 1957-59; hydroacoustic transducer sect. head Raytheon/Submarine Signal Divsn., Portsmouth, RI, 1959-70; MSR engr. Raytheon Equipment Divsn. North Dighton, Mass. and Kwajalein Atoll, 1958, 1970—; v.p. engring. ORB Inc., Sharon, Mass. and Tulsa, 1970—. Chief engr. Indsl. Vehicles, Internat., (geophys. prospecting vehicles using VIBROSEIS, worldwide), Tulsa, 1974-84; cons. Amoco Prodn. Rsch. Ctr. (geophys. prospecting sound sources), Tulsa, 1985-86, 93. Contbr. articles to profl. jours. including Jour. Underwater Acoustics, Jour. Geophys. Rsch., Jour. Inst. Navigation, ONR, Jour. Acoustical Soc. Am., Offshore Tech. Conf., Soc. Exptl. Geophys., Sea Tech.; displayed high-intensity sonic-siren phenomena on Dave Garroway's morning TV show, 1953. Brass band clarinetist Stoughton VFW, 1937-42, Bklyn. Armed Guard Ctr., 1945, Brockton Cosmopolitan, 1951-65, Shedad Grotto, 1955-74, Shedad and Taleb Grottoes, 1955—, Aleppo Shrine, 1965—, Lawrence Colonial, 1989-99, Canton/Am. Legion, 1992—. With USNR, 1944-46. Mem. ASME, Acoustical Soc. Am., Am. Soc. Materials, Soc. Exploration Geophysicists (life), Masons (Rising Star AFEAM, Stoughton 1954, Mt. Zion RAC, Stoughton, 1960, treas. 1999, Bay State comdr., Brockton 1966, 92, warder 1990-), Am. Legion (Sharon). Russian Orthodox, Congregationalist and Baptist. Achievements include patents for Electro/Syn Pressure Gauge, Electro-HydroSonic Transducer, 6 Water Hammer Piledrivers, and HLR WastePile, also numerous related patents. Home and Office: PO Box 422 89 Bullard St Sharon MA 02067-1007 Office Phone: 781-784-5113.

WISS, MARCIA A. lawyer; b. Columbus, Ohio, May 15, 1947; d. John William and Margaret Ann (Cook) W.; children: Christopher C. Wiss, Joan Merle. BS in Fgn. Svc., Georgetown U., 1969, JD, 1972. Bar: D.C. 1972. Econ. analyst World Bank, Washington, 1969; atty. U.S. Dept. Justice, Washington, 1972-73; atty. office gen. counsel Overseas Pvt. Investment Corp., Washington, 1973-78; gen counsel-designate Inst. for Sci. and Tech. Cooperation, Washington, 1979; ptnr. Kaplan Russin & Vecchi, Washington, 1987-92, Whitman & Ransom, 1992-93, Whitman, Breed, Abbott & Morgan, Washington, 1993-96, Wilmer, Cutler & Pickering, Washington, 1996-2000, Hogan & Hartson, Washington, 2000—. Gen. counsel Washington chpt., Soc. Internat. Devel., 1980-2001; gen. counsel, Assn. for Women in Devel., 1982—; bd. advisers, Procedural Aspects of Internat. Law Inst., 1985—; gen. counsel internat. policy coun. agr., adj. prof. of law Georgetown U. Law Ctr., 1984—, Johns Hopkins Sch. of Advanced Internat. Studies, 2001—. Editor Georgetown Law Ctr. Jour. Law and Policy in Internat. Bus., 1971-72. Chair Holy Trinity Parish Coun., Washington, 1976. Mem. Am. Fedn. Govt. Employees (chmn. 1975-76), D.C. Bar (steering com. divsn. 12, 1985-88, co-chmn. fin. and banking com. 1985), Am. Soc. Internat. Law (v.p. 1991-94, coun. 1987-90), Washington Fgn. Law Soc. (pres. 1983-84). Roman Catholic. Office: Hogan & Hartson 555 13th St NW Washington DC 20004 Office Phone: 202-637-5429.

WISS, MARVIN J. public relations executive, consultant; b. Rock Island, Ill., Feb. 26, 1926; s. Max A. Wiss and Anna B. Cohn; m. Patricia Joy Armstrong; m. Harriet Harris (div.); children: Michael J., Teri F., Pamela S. Karpel, Amie J. Herbert. BA, U. Ill., 1947. Reporter, editor WHBF, Rock Island, Ill., 1947—48; pub. rels. dir. Dem. State Ctrl. Com., Springfield, Ill., 1948—49; pub. rels. cons. Quad City P.R. Consulting, Rock Island, Ill., 1949—50, Marvin J. Wiss, P.R./Polit. Consulting, Dallas, 1950—2000; owner/operator Marbud Ptnrs., Garland, Tex., 1960—99; former elected mem. State of Tex., Democratic Exec. Com. Pub. rels. cons. numerous businesses, including Fortune 500, charitable, trade, profl., labor orgns., polit. campaigns. Author: The Presidential Parade, 2003, The U.S. Constitution, Alive and Well!, 2003. Past pres. Young Dems., Rock Island and Dallas, past Ill. and Tex. state sec.; past precinct chmn. Ill. and Tex. 2d lt., inf. U.S. Army, 1944—46, PTO. Democrat. Jewish. Home: 12009 Coit Rd 3234M Dallas TX 75251

WISSBAUM, DONNA CACIC, lawyer; b. Portage, Wis., Dec. 3, 1956; d. Donald Richard and Rita Margaret (Polcyn) Cacic; m. David Michael Wissbaum, Dec. 29, 1984; children: Nicholas David, Heather Noelle. BA in Am. Instns., U. Wis., 1979; JD, Gonzaga U., 1982. Bar: Wis. 1982, U.S. Dist. Ct. (ea. and we. dists.) Wis. 1983. Assoc. Bennett & Bennett Law Offices, Montello, Wis., 1983-85, Gregory R. Wright Law Offices, Montello, 1985-89; prin. Donna Cacic Wissbaum, Atty. at Law, Montello, 1989—. Lt. col. USAR. Mem. ABA, Wis. Bar Assn., Tri-County Bar Assn. (sec.-treas. 1986-88, v.p. 1988-90, pres. 1990-92), Marquette County Crimestoppers, Inc. (vice chmn. 1994-96), Croatian Fraternal Union, Pardeville Youth Wrestling Club (pres. 2001-2002). Roman Catholic. Home: W5436 County Road P Pardeeville WI 53954-9434 Office: 5 E Park St Montello WI 53949-9366

WISSBRUN, KURT FALKE, chemist, consultant; b. Brackwede, Westphalia, Germany, Mar. 19, 1930; came to the U.S., 1939; s. Hermann and Bertha (Falke) W. BS, U. Pa., 1952; PhD, Yale U., 1956. Rsch. chemist Hoechst-Celanese (formerly Celanese Corp.), Summit, N.J., 1957-60; group leader Hoechst-Celanese, Summit, N.J., 1960-62; rsch. assoc. Hoerst-Celanese (formerly Celanese Corp.), Summit, N.J., 1966-70, sr. rsch. assoc., 1970-90; polymer cons. Summit, 1990—. Author: Melt Rheology and Plastics Processing, 1989, (with others) Blow Molding Handbook, 1988; contbr. articles to profl. jours.; patentee, inventor in field. Mem. Am. Chem. Soc., Soc. Rheology (pres. 1995-97, Bingham medal 1992), British Soc. Rheology, Sigma Xi. Jewish. Avocations: golf, opera, travel. Home: 1 Euclid Ave Apt 4E Summit NJ 07901-2164

WISSEL-LITTMANN, JEFFREY G. health facility executive; b. May 1968; Pres., trustee TIRR Rehab. Ctr., Houston, 2003—. Office: TIRR Rehabilitation Ctr 4200 Montrose Ste 200 Houston TX 77006 Office Phone: 713-521-0020.

WISSLER, ROBERT WILLIAM, physician, cardiovascular pathologist, educator; b. Richmond, Ind., Mar. 1, 1917; s. William Oscar and Muriel (Thomas) W.; m. Elizabeth Anne Polk, Jan. 9, 1940; children: Barbara Anne Wissler-Mayers, Mary Linda Wissler Graham, David William, John Polk. AB, Earlham Coll., Richmond, 1939, DSc (hon.), 1959; MS, U. Chgo., 1943, PhD, 1946, MD with honors, 1948; MD (hon.), Heidelberg (Germany) U., 1973, U. Siena, Italy, 1982; DSc (hon.), UMDNJ, Newark, 1982, Ohio State U., 1990. From instr. to assoc. prof. U. Chgo., 1943-57, prof. McLean Inst., 1953-80, prof. dept. pathology, 1957-82, prof. in the Coll., 1965-80, chmn. dept. pathology, 1957-72, Donald N. Pritzker prof. pathology, 1972-87, Disting. Svc. prof. pathology, 1977-87, emeritus prof., 1987—. Vis. scientist Theodor Kocher Inst., U. Berne, Switzerland, 1963, Baker Inst. for Med. Rsch., Melbourne, Australia, 1985; vis. prof. pathology Nihon U. Sch. Medicine, Tokyo, 1974; mem. faculty Given Inst. Pathology, Aspen, Colo., 1964, 71-73, 78-81; dir. U. Chgo. Spl. Ctr. Rsch. Atherosclerosis, 1972-82., program dir. Pathobiol. Determinates Atherosclerosis Youth, 1985-96. Editor, co-editor monographs; contbr. chpts. to books, more than 300 articles to profl. jours. Scout leader Boy Scouts Am., Chgo., 1951-56, 61-67; trustee First Unitarian Ch., Chgo., 1960-64, chmn. bd., 1962-64; trustee Earlham Coll., 1968-71, 75-85, chmn. edn. com., 1977-85; mem. Hyde Park-Kenwood Cmty. Conf., Chgo., 1960—. Recipient award of merit Am. Heart Assn., Dallas, 1971, Disting. Achievement award Modern Medicine, 1977, Joseph B. Goldberger award AMA, 1979, Coeur d'Or award Chgo. Heart Assn., 1982, Gold Headed Cane award, Am. Assn. Pathologists, 1983, U. Chgo. Gold Key award, 1984, Career Achievement award Internat. Atherosclerosis So., 1994, Rising Sun award Emperor of Japan, 1995. Mem. Am. Soc. Exptl. Pathology (pres. 1961-62), Am. Heart Assn. (chmn. coun. on arteriosclerosis 1965-66), Assn. Pathology Chairmen (pres. 1967-68), Coll. Am. Pathologists (chmn. edn. com. 1985-95), Univ. Assocs. for Rsch. and Edn. in Pathology (bd. dirs., pres. 1969-71), Am. Assn. Pathologists and Bacteriologists, 1952-90 (pres. 1968), others. Avocations: gardening, photography, playing clarinet. Home: 5550 S South Shore Dr Apt 515 Chicago IL 60637-5053 Office: U Chgo Med Ctr MC 3083 5841 S Maryland Ave Chicago IL 60637-1463

WISWALL, DOROTHY ROLLER, language educator; b. Alpirsbach, Germany, Aug. 6, 1947; d. Albert and Else Roller; m. Thomas S. Wiswall, June 5, 1976; children: James, Karen. AB, Cornell Univ., 1971; AM, Univ. Mich., 1972, PhD, 1979. Instr. Sch. for Internat. Tng., Brattleboro, Vt., 1971; tchg. fellow Univ. Mich., Ann Arbor, 1971—75; adj. prof. Niagara Univ., 1981—91, Canisius Coll., Buffalo, 1991—2003, Buffalo State Coll., Buffalo, 2001—. Workshop presenter BOCES, Buffalo, 1998—99; vice pres. Am. Assn. of Teachers of German, Buffalo, 1998—2002; docent Buffalo Mus. Sci., 2004—; tutor Lit. Vols. Buffalo, 2004—. Author: A Comparison of Selected Poetic and Scientific Works of Albrecht von Haller. Mem. coun. St. Timothy Luth. Ch., Grand Island, NY, 1999—, deacon, 2004—; pres. bd. dirs. STLCC Child Care Ctr., Grand Island, NY, 1995—99. Recipient 2d prize, Faculty divsn. Martin Luther King Poetry Contest at Canisius Coll., 2003; Travel grantee, U., Bern, Switzerland, 1977. Mem.: Am. Assn. Tchrs. German (v.p. 1998—2002), Zonta Internat. Club Buffalo (bd. dirs. 2004—), Phi Sigma Iota. Lutheran. Avocations: swimming, playing violin, sewing, history of science.

WISWALL, FRANK LAWRENCE, JR., lawyer, educator; b. Albany, NY, Sept. 21, 1939; s. Frank Lawrence and Clara Elizabeth (Chapman) W.; m. Elizabeth Curtiss Nelson, Aug. 9, 1975; children by previous marriage: Anne W. Kowalski, Frank Lawrence III. BA, Colby Coll., 1962; JD, Cornell U., 1965; PhD in Law, Cambridge U., 1967. Bar: Maine 1965, N.Y. 1968, U.S. Supreme Ct. 1968, D.C. 1975; lic. master near coastal steam and motor vessels, 1960—. Assoc. Burlingham, Underwood, Barron, Wright & White, N.Y.C., 1967-73; maritime legal adviser Rep. of Liberia, 1968-88; prof. (ad honorem) internat. maritime law Internat. Maritime Law Inst., 1999; comdr. U.S. Coast Guard Aux., 2003—; cons. in field internat. maritime law Castine, Maine, 1988—. Legal com. Internat. Maritime Orgn., London, 1972-74, vice-chmn. 1974-79, chmn., 1980-84; tutorial supr. internat. law Clare Coll., Cambridge, Eng., 1966-67; vis. lectr. Cornell Law Sch., 1969-76, 82; lectr. U. Va. Law Sch. and Ctr. for Oceans Law and Policy, 1978-82; prof. law Cornell U., 1984; Johnsen prof. maritime law Tulane U., 1985; vis. prof. law World Maritime U., Malmo, Sweden, 1986-2003; tchg. fellow Internat. Maritime Law Inst., Malta, 1991—, governing bd., 1992—; del. Internat. Conf. Marine Pollution, London, 1973; del., chmn. drafting com. Internat. Conf. Carriage of Passengers and Luggage by Sea, Athens, 1974; del. Internat. Conf. on Safety of Life at Sea, London, 1974, UN Conf. on Law of Sea, Caracas, Venezuela, 1974; del., chmn. com. final clauses Internat. Conf. on Limitation of Liability for Maritime Claims, London, 1976; del. UN Conf. Carriage of Goods by Sea, Hamburg, 1978, XIII Diplomatic Conf. on Maritime Law, Brussels, 1979; chmn. com. of the whole Internat. Conf. Carriage of Hazardous Substances by Sea, 1984; del. internat. conf. on Maritime Terrorism, Rome, 1988; counsel various marine casualty bds. of investigation, 1970-90, harbormaster, Port of Castine, 1960-62; chmn. joint internat. working group acts of piracy and maritime violence, 1998-2001, joint internat. working group criminal offenses on high seas Interpol, UN, ICC-IMB, ICS, CMI, ITF, 2004—; hon. prof. internat. maritime law, IMLI, 1999. Author: The Development of Admiralty Jurisdiction and Practice Since 1800, 1970; editor-in-chief Benedict on Admiralty, Vols. 6, 6A-6F (Internat. Maritime Law), 1992—, Com. Maritime Internat. Handbook of Maritime COnvs., 1997, 2001, 04; mem. editl. bd. Jour. Maritime Law and Commerce, 1993—, Benedict's Maritime Law Bull., 2002—; contbr. articles to profl. jours. Ofcl. prin. Diocese of Mid-Atlantic States, 1988—, Diocese of UK, 1997—, Anglican Cath. Ch.; chancellor Missionary Diocese of N.E., 1993—, Diocese Australia, 1998—; spkr. assembly laity Anglican Cath. Ch., 1995—. Recipient Yorke prize U. Cambridge, 1968-69. Fellow Royal Hist. Soc.; mem. Nat. Lawyers Assn., Comité Maritime Internat. (titulary mem., exec. councillor 1989-96, v.p. 1997—), Maritime Law Assn. U.S. (chmn. com. on intergovtl. orgns. 1983-87, chmn. com. on CMI 1987-95), Ecclesiastical Law Soc., Selden Soc., Am. Soc. Legal History, UK Assn. Average Adjusters, U.S. Assn. Average Adjusters, Maine Bar Assn., US Navy League (pres. Penobscot coun. 1997), Oxford and Cambridge Club (London), Century Assn., Alpha Delta Phi, Phi Delta Phi. Office: PO Box 201 Castine ME 04421-0201

WISZNIA, WALTER, architectural firm executive; CEO, mgr., designer Wisznia and Assocs., New Orleans. Office: Wisznia and Assocs 812 Perdido St New Orleans LA 70112-1075

WIT, DAVID EDMUND, software company executive; b. N.Y.C., Feb. 25, 1962; s. Harold Maurice W. and Joan Leta (Rosenthal) Sovern; m. Kathleen Mary Bentley, Sept. 9, 1989. BA summa cum laude, Hamilton Coll., 1985. Rsch. assoc. E.M. Warburg Pincus and Co., N.Y.C., 1985-86; CEO Logicat Inc., N.Y.C., 1986—2002; co-CEO Micron Sys. Inc., Washington Crossing, Pa., 2003—; CEO Oakdale Capital, LLC, Larchmont, NY, 2003—. Mem. Phi Beta Kappa. Avocation: exercise. Home: 3 Stratford Rd Larchmont NY 10538-1341 Office Phone: 914-834-1343.

WIT, HAROLD MAURICE, investment banker, lawyer, investor; b. Boston, Sept. 6, 1928; s. Maurice and Martha (Bassist) W.; children from previous marriage: David Edmund, Hannah Edna; 1 stepchild, Simon; m. Susan King, Sept. 16, 1999. AB magna cum laude, Harvard, 1949; JD (editor law jour.), Yale, 1954. Bar: N.Y. 1954. Assoc. Cravath, Swaine & Moore, N.Y.C., 1954-58; asst. sec. One William St. Fund, Inc., N.Y.C., 1958-59, v.p., sec., 1959-60; assoc. Allen & Co., 1960-70; assoc Allen & Co., Inc., 1965—, v.p., 1965-70, exec. v.p., 1970-98, mng. dir., mem. exec. com.; ret. Mgr. Allen Investments II LLC. Former trustee South Folk-Shelter Island chpt. Nature Conservancy, 1993-2000; co-founder Group for South Fork; pres. South Fork Watchdogs, Inc.; mem. Panel on Future of Govt. in N.Y., 1979-80; mem. vis. com. Harvard U. Div. Sch., 1990-97. With Mass. N.G., 1947-50; lt. (j.g.) USNR, 1951-53, Korea. Mem. VFW, Am. Legion, Korean War Vets. Assn., University Club (N.Y.C.), Harvard Club (N.Y.C.), Phi Beta Kappa, Phi Delta Phi. Home: 150 E 69th St New York NY 10021-5704 also: 57 Cross Hwy PO Box 348 East Hampton NY 11937-0348 Office: Allen & Co Inc 711 5th Ave New York NY 10022-3111 Office Phone: 212-832-8000.

WITCHER, DANIEL DOUGHERTY, retired pharmaceutical company executive; b. Atlanta, May 17, 1924; s. Julius Gordon and Myrtice Eleanor (Daniel) W.; divorced; children: Beth S., Daniel Dougherty Jr., J. Wright, Benjamin G.; m. Betty Lou Middaugh, Oct. 30, 1982. Student, Mercer U., 1946-47, Am. Grad. Sch. Internat. Mgmt., 1949-50. Regional dir. Sterling Drug Co., Rio de Janeiro and Sao Paulo, Brazil, 1951-56; gen. mgr. Mead Johnson & Co., Sao Paulo, 1956-60; area mgr. Upjohn Internat., Inc., Sao Paulo, 1960-64, v.p. Kalamazoo, 1964-70, group v.p., 1970-73; pres., gen. mgr. Upjohn Internat., 1973-86; v.p. Upjohn Co., 1973-86, sr. v.p., 1986-89, asst. to pres., 1988-89; chmn. Upjohn Healthcare Svcs., 1982-87; ret., 1989. Bd. dirs. Upjohn Co.; trustee Am. Grad. Sch. Internat. Mgmt., 1981—. With USNR, 1943-46. Mem. Pharm. Mfrs. Assn. (chmn. internat. sect. 1981-82, 85-86), Am. Grad. Sch. Internat. Mgmt. Alumni Assn. (pres. 1989-91). Republican. Episcopalian. Avocations: tennis, golf.

WITCHER, ROBERT CAMPBELL, SR., bishop; b. New Orleans, Oct. 5, 1926; s. Charles Swanson and Lily Sebastian (Campbell) W.; m. Elisabeth Alice Cole, June 4, 1957; 2 children. BA, Tulane U., 1949; MDiv, Seabury-Western Theol. Sem., 1952, DD, 1974; MA, La. State U., 1960, PhD, 1968; DCL (hon.), Nashotah House, 1989. Ordained priest Episcopal Ch., 1953; consecrated bishop, 1975. Priest-in-charge St. Andrew Ch., Linton, La. and St. Patrick Ch., Zachary, La., 1953-56, St. Augustine Ch., Baton Rouge, La., 1953-54, rector, 1954-61; canon pastor Christ Ch. Cathedral, New Orleans, 1961-62; rector St. James Ch., Baton Rouge, 1962-75; coadjutor bishop L.I., 1975-77; bishop, 1977-91; prof. ch. history Mercer Sch. Theology, 1975-91; interim bishop of Armed Forces, 1989-90; bishop in residence Baton Rouge, New Orleans, 1991-92. Pres. Mercer Scholarship Fund; trustee Ch. Pension Fund, 1991-92; pres. bd. trustees estate belonging to Diocese of L.I., 1975-91; pres. Anglican Soc. N.Am., 1980-83; chmn. pastoral com. House of Bishops, 1980-90, Com. to Revise Title III, 1980-90; chmn. Com. on Developing Guidelines for Theol. Edn.; cons. Episc. Health Fund L.I.; historiographer Diocese of La. Author: The Episcopal Church in Louisiana, 1801-1861. Trustee U. of South, 1963-69, Seabury-Western Theol. Sem., 1963-82, Gen. Theol. Sem., 1979-88, Ch. Pension Fund, 1985-91, Bch. Reins. Corp., Killough Charitable Trust, Gen. Health Med. Ctr., Gen. Health Found.; pres. Episc. Health Svcs.; bd. dirs. Nat. Coun. Alcoholism, L.I. Coun. Alcoholism, Alcohol and Drug Abuse Coun., Baton Rouge, St. Mary's Hosp. for Children, Baton Rouge Green, La. Urban Forestry Coun., United Way, Gen. Health Sys., GHS Found.; bd. dirs., trustee St. James Place; active NCCJ (Baton Rouge chpt.). Capt. USNR, ret. Mem. N.Y. State Coun. Chs., L.I. Coun. Chs. (com. social justice), Am. Legion, Mil. Order of World Wars, Naval Res. Assn., Res. Officers Assn., Mil. and Hospitaller Order of St. Lazarus, Soc. Colonial Wars. Episcopalian. Address: 1934 Steele Blvd Baton Rouge LA 70808-1673

WITCOFF, SHELDON WILLIAM, lawyer; b. Washington, July 10, 1925; s. Joseph and Zina (Ceppos) W.; m. Margot Gail Hoffner, Sept. 6, 1953; children: Lauren Jill, David Lawrence, Lisa Ann, Julie Beth. BS in Elec. Engring. U. Md., 1949; JD, George Washington U., 1953. Bar: D.C. 1953, N.Y. 1955, Ill. 1956. Patent examiner Patent Office, Dept. Commerce, 1949-53; patent lawyer Bell Telephone Labs., Murray Hill, N.J., 1953-55; ptnr. Bair, Freeman & Molinare, Chgo., 1955-69, Allegretti, Newitt, Witcoff & McAndrews, Chgo., 1970-88, Allegretti & Witcoff, LTD, Chgo., 1988-95, Banner & Witcoff Ltd., Chgo., 1995—. V.p. Art Splty. Co., Chgo., 1967-84; v.p. Caspian Fur Trading Co., N.Y.C.; co-founder Child Abuse Unit for Studies, Edn. and Svcs., Chgo. Fire and police commr., Skokie, Ill., 1960-63. Served with USNR, 1943-46. Mem. Am. Bar Assn., Intellectual Property Assn. of Chgo., Order of Coif, Tau Epsilon Phi, Phi Delta Phi., B'nai B'rith. Home: 2180 Kipling Ln Highland Park IL 60035- Office: 10 S Wacker Dr Chicago IL 60606-7407 Office Phone: 312-463-5000. Business E-Mail: switcoff@bannerwitcoff.com. E-mail: witcoff@hotmail.com.

WITCOVER, JULES JOSEPH, newspaper columnist, author; b. Union City, N.J., July 16, 1927; s. Samuel and Sarah (Carpenter) W.; m. Marian Laverty, June 14, 1952 (div. Oct. 1990); children: Paul, Amy, Julie, Peter; m. Marion Elizabeth Rodgers, June 21, 1997. AB, Columbia Coll., 1949; MS, Columbia Grad Sch. Journalism, 1951. Reporter Hackensack (N.J.) Star-Telegram, 1949-50, Providence Jour., 1951-52, Newark Star-Ledger, 1953, Washington br. Newhouse Newspapers, 1954-69, L.A. Times, Washington, 1970-72, Washington Post, 1973-76; columnist Washington Star, 1977—81, Balt. Sun, Washington, 1981—, Tribune Media Svcs., 1977—. Author: 85 Days: The Last Campaign of Robert Kennedy, 1969, The Resurrection of Richard Nixon, 1970, White Knight: The Rise of Spiro Agnew, 1972, (with Richard M. Cohen) A Heartbeat Away: The Investigation and Resignation of Vice President Spiro T. Agnew, 1974, Marathon: The Pursuit of the Presidency, 1972-76, 1977, (novel) The Main Chance, 1978, (with Jack W. Germond) Blue Smoke and Mirrors: How Reagan Won and Why Carter Lost the Election of 1980, 1981, (with Germond) Wake Us When It's Over: Presidential Politics of 1984, 1985, (with Germond) Whose Broad Stripes and Bright Stars?: The Trivial Pursuit of the Presidency 1988, 1989, Sabotage at Black Tom: Imperial Germany's Secret War in America, 1914-1917, 1989, Crapshoot: Rolling the Dice on the Vice Presidency, 1992, (with Germond) Mad as Hell: Revolt at the Ballot Box 1992, 1993, The Year the Dream Died: Revisiting 1968 in America, 1997, No Way to Pick a President: How Money and Hired Guns Have Debased American Elections, 1999, Party of the People: A History of the Democrats, 2003. With USN, 1945-46. Recipient Washington Corr. award Sigma Delta Chi, 1963, Alumni award Columbia Grad. Sch. Journalism, 1972; Reid Found. fellow, Europe, 1958. Roman Catholic. Home: 3042 Q St NW Washington DC 20007-3080 Office: Washington Bur Balt Sun 1627 K St NW Washington DC 20006-1702

WITEK, JAMES EUGENE, retired public relations executive; b. LaPorte, Ind., Sept. 14, 1932; s. Stanley and Victoria (Peret) W.; m. Mary Carolyn Hood, June 18, 1955; children: James Jay, Janet Marie, Jeffrey Patrick, Jean Theresa. AB, Ind. U., 1954; MA, U. Mo., 1970. Joined U.S. Army, 1954, commd. 2d lt., 1954, advanced through grades to lt. col., 1968; editor, pub. Infantry Mag., Fort Benning, Ga., 1968-70; advisor to Vietnamese Mil. Region IV Ranger Comdr., 1970-71; plans officer CINCPAC, Hawaii, 1971-75; exec. editor Soldiers, Washington, 1975-77, editor in chief, 1977-79; dir. public affairs Nat. Com. for Employer Support Guard and Res., Arlington, Va., 1979-82, ret., 1982; dep. dir. pub. relations Am. Legion, Washington, 1982-86; mgr. pub. rels. Dowty Aerospace, Sterling, Va., 1986-99; ret. Decorated Legion of Merit, Bronze Star, Air Medal, Purple Heart, Vietnamese Cross of Gallantry with Silver Star. Mem. Am. Legion, Ret. Officers Assn., Disabled Am. Vets., Phi Beta Kappa, Tau Kappa Alpha, Pi Kappa Phi. Roman Catholic. Home: 3240 Atlanta St Fairfax VA 22030-2128

WITEK, JOHN W. history professor; b. Chgo., Sept. 13, 1933; s. John Andrew and Antoniette Witek. BA, Loyola U., 1957; Ph. L., West Baden Coll., 1959; MA, Loyola U., 1964; S.T.L., Bellarmine Sch. Theology, 1966; PhD, Georgetown U., 1973. Asst. prof. East Asian history Xavier U., Cin., 1973—75, Georgetown U., Wash., 1975—81, assoc. prof. East Asian history, 1981—2003, prof. East Asian, 2003—. Chmn. scholars' coun. Ricci Inst., U. San Francisco, 1999—. Author: Controversial Ideas in China and in Europe, 1982; editor: Dicionario Portugues-Chines, 2001, Monumenta Sinica, vol. 1, 2002. Mem. bd. dirs. Asian divsn. Libr. Congress Friends Soc., 2004—. Mem.: Am. Asian Studies, Am. Hist. Assn., Am. Cath. Hist. Assn. (2nd v.p. 1999—2001), Assn. Asian Studies (pres., Mid-Atlantic region 1989—90), Phi Beta Kappa (editor Ferdinand Verbiest 1623-1688). Roman Catholic. Home: Jesuit residence Georgetown U Washington DC 20057 Office: Dept History Georgetown U Washington DC 20057 Fax: 202-687-7245.

WITEK, KATE, state senator, trucking company executive; b. Detroit, Oct. 22, 1954; m. Charles Wite, 1974; children: Thomas Charles, Kimberly Rose. Student, Ea. Mich. U. Owner, mgr. Witek Trucking Co.; mem. Nebr. Senate, Lincoln, 1992-98; Auditor of Pub. Accounts NE, Lincoln, 1999—. Mem. commerce and ins. com., govt., mil. and vet. affairs com. Mem. Nat. Small Bus. United, Nebr. Motor Carriers, Millard Jaycees. Republican. Home: 5179 S 147th St Omaha NE 68137-1439 Office: Auditor of Public Accounts State Capitol Suite 2303 PO Box 98917 Lincoln NE 68509-8917

WITHEM, RONALD E. state senator, trade association executive; b. Logan, Iowa, June 9, 1946; m. Diane Weinstein, 1973; children: Susanne, Justin. BA, Wayne State Coll., 1968; MS, U. Nebr., Omaha, 1975. Tchr. Papillion (Nebr.) H.S.; exec. v.p. Mech. Constructors Assn. Omaha; mem. Nebr. Senate, Lincoln, 1983—; assoc. v.p. external affairs & govtl. rels. U. Nebr., Lincoln. Chmn. edn. com., mem. rules com., revenue com., former mem. govt., mil. and vet. affairs coms. Former chmn. Edn. Commn. of States; former office mgr. U.S. Rep. John J. Cavanaugh. Mem. Papillion C. of C., LaVista C. of C., Omaha C. of C. Democrat. Home: 1104 Shady Tree Ln Papillion NE 68046-6194 Office: U Nebr Office External Affairs 3835 Holdege Lincoln NE 68583-0745

WITHERELL, DENNIS PATRICK, lawyer; b. Dec. 15, 1951; s. Thomas William and Kathryn Marie (Savage) Witherell; m. Suzanne Witherell; children: Natalie, Jay stepchildren: Jodi Brouilette, Shelby Watson, Shane Allen. AB with highest honors, U. Mich., 1973; JD summa cum laude, Ohio State U., 1977. Bar: Ohio, U.S. Dist. Ct. (no. dist.) Ohio, U.S. Ct. Appeals (6th cir.). Law clk. U.S. Ct. Appeals (6th cir.), Cin., 1977—78; assoc. Shumaker, Loop & Kendrick LLP, Toledo, 1978—83, ptnr., 1983—. Mem. exec. bd. March of Dimes Birth Defects Found., N.W. Ohio chpt., Toledo, 1978—91, chmn., 1982—84; bd. trustees Kidney Found. of Northwest Ohio, 1988—94, pres., 1992—93; bd. trustee Life Connection of Ohio, 1991—, Vis. Nurse-Extra Care, 1994—99. Mem.: Nat. Multiple Sclerosis Soc. (bd. trustees Northwest Ohio chpt. 1999—), Soc. of Ohio Hosp. Attys., Toledo Bar Assn, Ohio State Bar Assn. (chmn. health care law com. 1988—92), Am. Health Lawyers Assn., ABA. Roman Catholic. Home: 2256 Densmore Dr Toledo OH 43606-3167 Office: Shumaker Loop & Kendrick LLP 1000 Jackson St Toledo OH 43624-1573 E-mail: dwitherell@slk-law.com.

WITHERELL, MARY, editor; Degree, Barnard Coll., 1983. Former acting mng. editor Cosmo Girl; mng. editor Ladies' Home Jour., N.Y.C., 2002—. Office: Ladies' Home Jour 125 Park Ave 20th Fl New York NY 10017-5516

WITHERELL, MICHAEL S. physicist, educator; b. Toledo, Sept. 22, 1949; s. Thomas W. and Marie (Savage) W.; m. Elizabeth Hall. BS, U. Mich., 1968; MS, U. Wis., 1970, PhD, 1973. Instr. Princeton (N.J.) U., 1973-75, asst. prof., 1975-81, U. Calif., Santa Barbara, 1981-83, assoc. prof., 1983-86, prof., 1986-99; dir. Fermi Nat. Accelerator Lab., Batavia, Ill., 1999—. Chmn. physics adv. com. Fermi Nat. Accelerator Lab., Batavia, Ill., 1987-89; mem. high energy physics adv. panel U.S. Dept. Energy, Washington, 1990-93, chair high energy physics adv. panel, 1996-99; chmn. sci. policy com. Stanford Linear Accelerator Ctr., 1995—. Guggenheim fellow John S. Guggenheim Found., 1988; recipient W. K. H. Panofsky prize Am. Phys. Soc., 1990. Fellow AAAS; mem. NAS. Office: Fermi Lab MS 105 PO Box 500 Batavia IL 60510-0500

WITHERS, CARL RAYMOND, lawyer; b. Reading, Pa., Jan. 26, 1924; s. Stuart Snable Withers and Edith Garman; m. Jenny Constance Cory, Sept. 2, 1950; children: Wren, Jill, Bradford. AB, Wittenberg U., 1950; JD, U. Mich., 1953. Bar: Ohio 1954. Pvt. practice, Cleve., 1954—. Former pres. mus. Shaker Hist. Soc., Shaker Heights, Ohio, 1970—; former trustee, treas. N.E. Inter Mus. Coun., Cleve., 1980—; exec. com. Cuyahoga County Rep. Party, Cleve., 1984-94, Fairmount Presbyn. Ch. (former deacon and trustee), Cleve. Soldiers' and Sailors' Monument bd. trustees and sec. Mem. Ohio State Bar Assn. (former coun. of dels. 1955), Cleve. Bar Assn., Am. Legion (Army-Navy Shaker post 54, former comdr., adjutant), Gt. Lakes Curling Assn. (treas., pres. 1985-96), Cleve. Grays, Estate Planning Coun. of Cleve., Cleve. Rotary Club (trustee), Cleve. City Club, Cleve. Skating Club (former trustee), Shaker Heights Rep. Club, Beta Theta Pi (former pres.), Delta Theta Phi. Republican. Presbyterian. Avocations: curling, genealogy, american lithographs. Home: 3419 Courtland Rd Pepper Pike OH 44122-4280 Office: Van Aken Withers & Webster 629 Euclid Ave Cleveland OH 44114-3077

WITHERS, HUBERT RODNEY, radiotherapist, radiobiologist, educator; b. Queensland, Australia, Sept. 21, 1932; arrived in U.S., 1966; s. Hubert and Gertrude Ethel (Tremayne) W.; m. Janet Macfie, Oct. 9, 1959; 1 child, Genevieve. MB BS, U. Queensland, Brisbane, Australia, 1956; PhD, U. London, 1965, DSc, 1982. Bd. cert. Ednl. Coun. for Fgn. Med. Grads. Intern Royal Brisbane and Associated Hosps., 1968; resident in radiotherapy and pathology Queensland Radium Inst. and Royal Brisbane Hosp., 1958-63; U. Queensland Gaggin fellow Gray Lab., Mt. Vernon Hosp., Northwood, England, 1963—65, Royal Brisbane Hosp., 1966; radiotherapist Prince of Wales Hosp., Randwick, Sydney, Australia, 1966; vis. rsch. scientist lab. physiology Nat. Cancer Inst., Bethesda, Md., 1966-68; assoc. prof. radiotherapy sect. exptl. radiotherapy U. Tex. Sys. Cancer Ctr. M.D. Anderson Hosp. & Tumor Inst., Houston, 1968-71, prof. radiotherapy, chief sect. sect. exptl. radiotherapy, 1971-80; prof. dir. exptl. radiation oncology dept. radiation oncology UCLA, 1980-89, prof., dir. exptl. radiation oncology dept. radiation oncology, 1991—94, prof., vice-chair dir. exptl. radiation oncology dept. radiation oncology, 1991-94, Am. Cancer Soc. Clin. Rsch. prof. dept. radiation oncology, 1992—, interim dir. Jonsson Comprehensive Cancer Ctr., 1994-95, chmn. radiation oncology, 1994—. Assoc. grad. faculty U. Tex., Grad. Sch. Biomed. Scis, Houston, 1969-73, mem. grad. faculty, 1973-80; prof. dept. radiotherapy Med. Sch., U. Tex. Health Sci. Ctr., Houston, U. Tex. Med. Sch., Houston, 1975-80; prof., dir. Inst. Oncology, The Prince of Wales Hosp., U. NSW, Sydney, Australia, 1989-91; mem. com. mortality mil. pers. present-at-atmosphere tests of nuc. weapons Inst. Medicine, 1993-94; mem. radiation effects rsch. bd. NRC, 1993-99; mem. com. neutron dose reporting Internat. Commn. Radiation Units and Measurements, 1982-93, mem. report com. clin. dosimetry for neutrons, 1993-98; mem. task force non-stochastic effects radiation Internat. Com. Radiation Protection, 1980-84, mem. com. 1, 1992-2000; mem. radiobiology com. Radiation Therapy Oncology Group, 1979-89, mem. dose-time com., 1980-89, mem. gastroenterology com., 1982-89; fellow Royal Australian Coll. Radiologists Edn. Bd., 1989-91; trustee Am. Bd. Radiology, 1994-2004; mem. cancer rsch. coord. com. U. Calif., 1991-97, mem. standing curriculum com. UCLA biomed. physics grad. program, 1993—; cons. exptl. radiotherapy U. Tex. Sys. Cancer Ctr., 1980—. Mem. Am. editl. bd.: Internat. Jour. Radiat. Oncol. Biol. Phys., 1982-89, 91—, internat. editl. bd., 1989-91; cons. editor: The European Jour. Cancer, 1990-95; editl. bd. dirs.: Endocurietherapy/Hyperthermia Oncology, 1991—2001, Radiation Oncology Investigations, 1992-2002; assoc. editor: Cancer Rsch., 1993-94, editl. bd. 1995-97. Mem. Kettering selection com. Gen. Motors Cancer Rsch. Found., 1988-89, chmn., 2002-03, awards assembly, 1990-94, adv. coun., 1994-95. Decorated officer Order of Australia; recipient Medicine prize Polish Acad. Sci., 1989, Second H.S. Kaplan Disting. Scientist award Internat. Assn. for Radiation Rsch., 1991, Gray medal Internat. Commn. Radiation Units, 1995, U.S. Dept. Energy Fermi award 1997, Radiation Rsch. Soc. Failla award, 1988, Gold medal Australasia Coll. Radiologists, 1997, Charles F. Kettering prize GM Cancer Rsch. Found., 1998; named Gilbert H. Fletcher lectr. U. Tex. Sys. Cancer Ctr., 1989, Clifford Ash lectr. Ont. Cancer Inst., Princess Margaret Hosp., 1987, Erskine lectr. Radiol. Soc. N.Am., 1988, Ruvelson lectr. U. Minn., 1988, Milford Schultz lectr. Mass. Gen. Hosp., 1989, Del Regato Found. lectr. Hahnemann U., 1990, Bruce Cain Meml. lectr. New Zealand Soc. Oncology, 2000, others. Fellow Royal Australasian Coll. Radiologists (bd. cert., Gold medal 1997), Am. Coll. Radiology (bd. cert. therapeutic radiology, adv. com. patterns of care study 1988-93, radiation oncology adv. group 1993-98, ethics com. surgeons oncology group 2002-, others, Gold medal 2004), Am. Radium Soc. (credential com. 1986-89, 93-94, treas. 1993-94, pres. 1996-97, others, Janeway medal 1994), Am. Soc. Therapeutic Radiology and Oncology (Gold Medal awards com. 1993, 2000, publs. com. 1993-97, vice-chair publs. com., 1996-98, keynote address 1990, Gold medal 1991); mem. ACS, Nat. Cancer Inst. (ad-hoc rev. coms. 1970—, radiation sudy sect. 1971-75, cons. U.S.-Japan Coop. Study high LET Radiotherapy 1975-77, cancer rsch. emphasis grant rev. com. 1976, clin. cancer ctr. rev. com. 1976-79, toxicology working group 1977-78, reviewer outstanding investigator grants 1984-93, bd. sci. counselors, 1986-88), Nat. Cancer Inst. Can. (adv. com. rsch. 1992-95), Pacific N.W. Radiol. Soc. (hon.), Tex. Radiol. Soc. (hon.), So. Calif. Radiation Oncology Soc. (sec., treas., 1992-94, pres. 1997-98), European Soc. Therapeutic Radiology and Oncology (hon.; Regaud lectr. 2000), Polish Oncology Soc. (hon., Gold medal 2002), Austrian Radiation Oncology Soc. (hon.), Phila. Roentgen Ray Soc. (hon.), Radiation Rsch. Soc. (pres. 1982-83, honors and awards com. 1984-88, ad hoc com. funds utilization 1987-89, adv. com. Radiation Rsch. Jour. 1988-96). Office: UCLA Med Ctr 10833 Le Conte Ave Los Angeles CA 90095-1714 E-mail: hwithers@mednet.ucla.edu.

WITHERS, RAMSEY MUIR, retired federal agency administrator; s. William Muir and Alice Smith Hope Withers; m. Jean Alison Saunders, May 8, 1954; children— James Scott, Leslie Susan, Deidre Ann BSc, Royal Mil. Coll. Can., Kingston, Ont., 1952, DEng (hon.), 1994; BSc in Elec. Engring., Queen's U., Kingston, 1954; D Mil. Sci. honoris causa, Royal Roads Mil. Coll., Victoria, B.C., 1992. Registered profl. engr., Ont. Commd. officer Can. Army, 1948, advanced through grades to gen., 1980; sta. in Can., Republic of Korea, Fed. Republic of Germany and U.K., 1952-76; comdr. Can. Forces Europe, Fed. Republic of Germany, 1976-77; vice chief def. staff Can. Forces, 1977-80, chief def. staff, 1980-83, ret., 1983; dep. minister transport Dept. of Transp., Ottawa, Ont., 1983-88; pres., chief oper. officer Govt. Cons. Internat., Ottawa, 1988-93; dir. Can. Inst. Strategic Studies, 1990-96, ATS Aerospace Inc., 1993-97; chmn. Industry Govt. Rels. Group Inc. (IGRG Inc.), Ottawa, 1993-98—. V.p., sec. nat. coun. Boy Scouts Can., 1977-84, internat. commr., 1985-90, hon. v.p., 1990-2000; chmn. Can. War Mus. Com., 1988-95; trustee Can. Mus. Civilization, 1990-95; elected mem. Queen's U. Coun., Kingston, 1997-03. Decorated comdr. Order of Mil. Merit, comdr. Order of St. John, Can. Forces Decoration with two bars; Georgian Coll. fellow, 1987; recipient Outstanding Achievement Pub. Svc. award, 1986, Silver Wolf award Boy Scouts Can., 1990, Alumni Achievement award Queen's U., Kingston, 1995, Queen Elizabeth II Golden Jubilee medal, 2003. Mem. Assn. Profl. Engrs. Ont., Royal Mil. Colls. Club Can. (hon. pres. 1997—). Avocation: boating. Home: 150 Waverly St Apt 2C Ottawa ON Canada K2P OV4 E-mail: withers1809@rogers.com.

WITHERS, W. RUSSELL, JR., broadcast executive; b. Cape Girardeau, Mo., Dec. 10, 1936; s. Waldo Russell Sr. and Dorothy Ruth (Harrelson) W.; 1 child, Dana Ruth. BA, S.E. Mo. State U., 1958. Disc jockey Sta. KGMO Radio, Cape Girardeau, 1955-58; account exec. Sta. WGGH Radio, Marion, Ill., 1961-62; v.p. LIN Broadcasting Corp., Nashville, 1962-69; exec. v.p., dir. Laser Link Corp., Woodbury, N.Y., 1970-72; owner Withers Broadcasting of Hawaii, 1975-79, Withers Broadcasting of Minn., 1974-79, Withers Broadcasting Cos., Iowa, 1981—, Mood Music Ill., Mt. Vernon, 1973—, Mood Music, Inc., Cape Girardeau, 1972—, Royal Hawaiian Radio Co., Inc., others. Owner various radio and TV stas. including KREX-TV, Grand Junction, Colo., KREY-TV, Montrose, Colo., KREG-TV, Glenwood Springs, Colo., Page Ins. and Real Estate, Mt. Vernon, Ill.; chmn. bd., CEO Withers Beverage Corp., Mobile, Ala., 1973—79; chmn. adv. bd. Mut. Network; bd. dirs. Theatrevision, Inc., Turneffe Island Lodge, Ltd., Belize, Sta. WDTV, Clarksburg, W.Va., WMIX-AM-TV, Mt. Vernon, KGMO-KAPE, Cape Girardeau, KOKX AM-FM, Keokuk, Iowa, KTRC, Santa Fe, KRHW and KBXB, Sikeston, Mo., WKIB Anna, Cape Girardeau, WMOK, WREZ and WZZL, Paducah, Ky., WSDR-WSSQ, WZZL, Sterling Rock Falls, Ill., WILY, WRXX (FM), Centralia, Ill., WEBQ and WEBQ-FM, Harrisburg, Ill.; pres. Ill. Pub. Airports Assn.; co-chmn. TARPAC. Bd. dirs., chmn. bd. Mt. Vernon Tourism and Conv. Bur.; chmn. Mt. Vernon Airport Authority; bd. regents Lincoln Acad.; past pres. IPAA; past chmn. Conv. & Visitors, Airport Authority; bd. dirs. No. Colo. C.C., Libr. of Am. Broadcasters, Radio Bd., AP. With U.S. Army, 1957-58. Mem. Mt. Vernon C. of C. (bd. dirs.), Nat. Assn. Broadcasters (bd. dirs., exec. com.), Ill. Broadcasters Assn., Stadium Club, Mo. Athletic Club, Elks, Moose, AmVets, Masons, Shriners, Sigma Chi. Christian Scientist. Home: 16074 Hawthorne Rd Mount Vernon IL 62864-2852 Office: PO Box 1508 Mount Vernon IL 62864-0030 Office Phone: 618-242-3500.

WITHERS, W. WAYNE, lawyer; b. Enid, Okla., Nov. 4, 1940; s. Walter O. and Ruby (Mackey) W.; m. Patricia Ann Peppers, Dec. 12, 1974; children: Jennifer Lynn, Whitney Lee. BA, U. Okla., 1962; JD, Northwestern U., 1965. Bar: Okla. 1965, Mo. 1970, U.S. Ct. Appeals (8th cir.), 1972, U.S. Supreme Ct. 1972, U.S. Ct. Appeals (fed. cir.) 1984, U.S. Ct. Appeals (D.C. cir.) 1985, U.S. Ct. Claims, 1984. Staff atty. FTC, Washington, 1965-68; co. atty. Monsanto Co., St. Louis, 1968-78, asst. gen. counsel, 1978—82; gen. counsel Monsanto Agrl. Co., St. Louis, 1978—89, v.p., gen. counsel; sr. v.p., sec., gen. counsel Emerson Electric Co., St. Louis, 1989—. V.p. Internat. Food Biotech. Coun., Washington, 1989-90; bd. dirs. Internat. Life Scis. Inst., Washington, 1988-89. Contbr. articles to profl. jours. Chmn. bd. Mo. Hist. Soc., 2002—; trustee MHS, 1995—; bd. dirs. World Agrl. Forum, 1999—. Mem. ABA (sect. bus. law, com. gen. counsel, antitrust, litigation), Am. Law Inst., Bar Assn. Met. St. Louis, Am. Corp. Counsel Assn., Am. Soc. Corp. Secs., Supreme Ct. Historic Soc., Warren E. Burger Soc., Nat. Ctr. for State Cts., Washington Legal Found., Indsl. Biotech. Assn. (chmn. law com. 1985-88), Environ. Law Inst. (assoc.), Nat. Agrl. Chem. Assn. (chmn. law com. 1983-85), The Conf. Bd. Coun. for Gen. Counsel (vice chmn. 1992-98), MAPI Law Coun. Office: Emerson Electric Co 8100 W Florissant Ave Saint Louis MO 63136-1494

WITHERSPOON, CAROLYN BRACK, lawyer; b. Little Rock, Mar. 29, 1950; d. Gordon Paisley and Mildred Louise (Lemon) Brack; m. Joseph Roger Armbrust, July 25, 1970 (div. 1976); 1 child, Catherine Paisley Armbrust; m. John Leslie Witherspoon, June 15, 1979. Student, U. Ark., 1968-70, So. Meth. U., 1970; BA, U. Ark., 1974, JD with honors, 1978. Bar: Ark. 1978, U.S. Dist. Ct. (ea. and we. dists.) Ark. 1978, U.S. Ct. Appeals (8th cir.) 1979, U.S. Supreme Ct. 1981. Asst. atty. City of Little Rock, 1978, chief dep. atty., acting city atty., 1984-85; assoc. House, Wallace & Jewell, Little Rock, 1985-87, ptnr., 1987-90; dir. McGlinchey Stafford Lang, Little Rock, 1990-97, Cross, Gunter, Witherspoon & Galchus, Little Rock, 1997—. Mem. com. Fed. Ct. Practice, 1988—91; mem. civil practice com. Ark. Supreme Ct., 1989—97, mem. continuing legal edn. bd., 1998—2001; chair adv. com. Civil Justice Reform Act, 1993—95; mem. State Bd. Bar Examiners, 2001—. Contbr. articles to profl. jours. Commr. Ark. Real Estate Commn., 1978—81; past chmn. Little Rock Housing Authority Bd. Commn.; past pres., bd. dirs. Advs. Battered Women; past. bd. dirs., pub. rels. chmn. LWV; past pres. Ark. Women's History Inst. Recipient Labor Law award, Am. Jurisprudence, 1977. Fellow: Coll. Labor and Employment Lawyers, Am. Bar Found. (Ark. Fellows chair); mem.: ABA (TIPS, EEO com., ho. dels. 1997—), William R. Overton Inn of Ct. (pres. 1992—93), Nat. Inst. Mcpl. Law Officers (state chmn. 1985—87, v.p. 1987—89), Pulaski County Bar Assn. (pres. 1989—90), Ark. Assn. Women Lawyers (pres. 1982—83), Ark. Bar Assn. (pres. 1995—96, Golden Gavel award 1989, 1993, Ark. Inst. Cont. Legal Edn. award 1991), Transp. Lawyers Assn. (mem. exec. com. 1997—99), Nat. Conf. Bar Pres. (mem. exec. coun. 1996—99), Am. Jur Soc., Am. Law Inst. Avocations: hunting, fishing, reading, travel. Office: Cross Gunter Witherspoon and Galchus 500 President Clinton Ave Ste 200 Little Rock AR 72201-1747 Office Phone: 501-371-9999. Business E-Mail: cspoon@cgwg.com.

WITHERSPOON, JOHN THOMAS, water resources consultant; b. Springfield, Mo., June 25, 1947; s. Warren Thomas and Kathryn (Corbus) w.; m. C. Frances Teter, June 12, 1971. BS, S.W. Mo. State U., 1969, MA, 1971; PhD, U. Mont., 1975. Water control inspector City of Springfield, Mo., 1976-78; dir. labs. City Utilities, Springfield, 1978-91, mgr. water treatment and supply, 1991—2001. Mem. safe drinking water commn. Mo. State Dept. Natural

Resources, Jefferson City, 1992—, now chair; bd. dirs. James River Basin Partnership, Nixa, Mo., 1996; tech. advisor Watershed Com. of the Ozarks, Springfield, 1983—. Pres. Univ. Club Springfield, 1989. Mem. Am. Water Works Assn. (chair, Boyd Utility Mgr. award 1996, Fuller award 1999), Kiwanis. Avocations: golf, reading, guitar, travel. Home and Office: 1927 E Lark St Springfield MO 65804-4345 Office Phone: 417-861-6025. Personal E-mail: jtwithersp@aol.com.

WITHERSPOON, MARIA BERNARDA PENA, bilingual educator; b. San Cristobal, Dominican Republic, Dec. 20, 1955; came to U.S., 1969; d. Benjamin de Jesus and Belen Pena; m. James Howard Witherspoon, Aug. 6, 1977 (div. Feb. 1991). AA in Social Svcs., Pima (Ariz.) CC, 1980; BS in Child Devel. and Family, U. Ariz., 1981, MEd in Bilingual Edn., 1986, ednl. adminstrn. cert., 1989. Cert. basic elem. tchr. with bilingual endorsement Ariz., prin. Ariz., bilingual elem. edn. NY, sch. adminstr., supr. NY. Family counselor El Rio Neighborhood Ctr., Tucson, 1979; pre-sch. tchr. Project Head Start, Tucson, 1980; data collector U. Ariz., Tucson, 1982; bilingual educator Tucson Unified Sch. Dist., 1984-88; bilingual curriculum specialist Stafford Engring. and Tech. Magnet Sch., Tucson, 1988—; asst. prin. Leonardo da Vinci Intermediate Sch., 1999—2002; prin. Roberto Clemente Pub. Sch., 2002—. Mem. Spanish Lang. Arts Adoption com. Tucson Unified Sch. Dist. Mem. Task Force on Native Am. Studies, Tucson, 1986. Mem. AAUW, NEA, Tucson Edn. Assn. (alt. state del., assembly rep.), Nat. Assn. Bilingual Edn., Assn. for Supervision and Curriculum Devel., Am. Home Econs. Assn., Nat. Assn. Female Execs, N.Y.C. Elem. Sch. Prin.'s Assn., Assn. Family and Consumer Svc. Republican. Roman Catholic. Home: 9550 113th St South Richmond Hill NY 11419-1111 Office: Roberto Clemente Primary Sch PS19K 325 S 3d St Brooklyn NY 11211

WITHERSPOON, REESE (LAURA JEAN WITHERSPOON), actress; b. Nashville, Tenn., Mar. 22, 1976; m. Ryan Phillippe, 1999; 2 children. Motion picture and T.V. actress. Film appearances include The Man in the Moon, 1991, A Far Off Place, 1993, Jack the Bear, 1993, Freeway, 1996, Fear, 1996, Twilight, 1998, Overnight Delivery, 1998, Pleasantville, 1998, Cruel Intentions, 1999, Election, 1999, Best Laid Plans, 1999, Am. Psycho, 2000, Little Nicky, 2000, Legally Blonde, 2001, The Importance of Being Earnest, 2002, Sweet Home Alabama, 2002, Legally Blonde 2: Red, White & Blonde, 2003 (also exec. prodr.), Vanity Fair, 2004, others; appeared in TV series Return to Lonesome Dove, 1993, Friends, 2000; voice (TV) King of the Hill, 2000, The Simpsons, 2002, (TV films) Wildflower, 1991, Desperate Choices: To Save My Child, 1992. Named 25 Most Intriguing People, People, 2001, 50 Most Beautiful People, 2002, Favorite Female Film Star, 2004; recipient Catalan Internat. Film Festival Award Best Actress, 1997, Movieline Young Hollywood Award for Breakthrough Performance (Female), 1999, Online Film Critics Soc. Award for Best Actress, 1999, National Soc. of Film Critics Award for Best Actress, 1999. Office: c/o Steve Dontanville William Morris 151 El Camino Dr Beverly Hills CA 90212-2412 also: c/o Blymel O'Neill 8912 Burton Way Beverly Hills CA 90211-1707*

WITHERSPOON, SOPHIA, professional basketball player; b. July 6, 1969; BA in Recreation, U. Fla., 1991 Guard Nyon, Switzerland, 1991-92, Rouen, France, 1994-95, Ferencvarosi, Hungary, 1995-96, Alcamo, Italy, 1996-97, N.Y. Liberty, N.Y.C., 1997-99, Portland Fire, 1999—. Named Italian All-Star, 1996-97, WNBA Player of the Wk., 1997. Office: Portland Fire 1 Center Ct Ste 150 Portland OR 97227-2104

WITHERSPOON, WALTER PENNINGTON, JR., orthodontist, philanthropist; b. Sept. 3, 1938; s. Walter P. and Florence Evelyn (Jones) W.; m. Joyce Ann Smith, Sept. 6, 1970; 1 child, Annie Melissa. BS, U. S.C., 1960; DDS, U. N.C., 1964, MSO, 1969. Pvt. practice, Columbia, 1969—. Med. staff Bapt. Med. Ctr., Columbia, 1970—, Lexington County Hosp., West Columbia, 1974—. Host Nite Line Broadcasting Co. Adv. bd. 1st Palmetto Bank and Trust, West Columbia, 1982; mem. adv. bd. 1st Citizens Bank; candidate S.C. Ho. of Reps., 1994; del. S.C. Rep. Com., 1989—; mem. platform com. S.C. Rep. Party Conv., poll com., 1992; del. Rep. Nat. Conv., Houston, 1992, rules com., task force on edn.; Rep. nat. committeeman, 1996—, rules com., rep. nat. com.; pres. Rep. Electoral Coll., 1996, 2000; bd. dirs. Southeastern Coll. Assemblies of God, Lakeland, Fla., 1984, Brookland Plantation Home for Boys, Orangeburg, S.C.; pres. Friends of Irmo Libr.; chmn. Lexington County Rep. Party; commr. Richland/Lexington Counties Commn. for Tech. Edn., S.C. Commn. on Alcohol and Drug Abuse; bd. dirs. Centerplace for Homeless; mem. Presdl. Visit-Ticket Com.; amb. Irmo C. of C.; vol. lockup telethon Muscular Dystrophy Assn. Lt. USN, 1964-66. Recipient Century Mem. award Boy Scouts Am., 1984. Mem. ADA, Greater Columbia Dental Assn. (pres. 1975-76), U. NC Dental Alumni Assn. (bd. dirs.), SC Dental Assn. (ho. of dels. 1971-73, 91-96, legis. com. 1993), SC Orthodontic Assn. (ctrl. dist. dir., state rep.), Am. Assn. Orthodontists, (polit. action com.), Sertoma (pres. 1975-76), Am. Legion (mem. baseball com.), So. Assn. Orthodontists (SC rep. Am. Assn. Orthodontists polit. action com.), Cen. Dist. Dental Soc. Home: 250 Lancer Dr Columbia SC 29212-1216 Office: 205 Med Cir W West Columbia SC 29169-3653 Office Phone: 803-796-5300.

WITHERSPOON, WILLIAM, investment economist; b. St. Louis, Nov. 21, 1909; s. William Conner and Mary Louise (Houston) W.; m. Margaret Telford Johanson, June 25, 1938; children: James Tomlin, Jane Telford, Elizabeth Witherspoon McElroy. Student, Washington U. Evening Sch., 1928-47. Chartered fin. analyst; registered investment advisor. Rsch. dept. A. G. Edwards & Sons, 1928-31; pres. Witherspoon Investment Co., 1931-34; head rsch. dept. Newhard Cook & Co., 1934-43, 45-53; ltd. ptnr. St. Louis Ordnance Dist., 1943-45; economist, investment analyst Newhard Cook & Co., 1965-68; chief price analysis St. Louis Ordnance Dist., 1943-45; owner Witherspoon Investment Counsel, 1953-64; v.p. rsch. Stifel, Nicolaus & Co., 1968-81; registered investment advisor St. Louis, 1981—. Lectr. on investments Washington U., 1948-67. Contbr. articles to profl. jours. Mem. Clayton Bd. Edn., 1955-68, treas., 1956-68, pres., 1966-67; mem. Clayton Park and Recreation Commn., 1959-60; trustee Ednl. TV, KETC, 1963-64; mem. investment com. Gen. Assembly Mission Bd. Presbyn. Ch. (USA), Atlanta, 1976-79, mem. permanent com. ordination exams, 1979-85; cons. to investment com. Ctr. Theol. Inquiry, Princeton, N.J., 1995-97. Served as civilian Ordnance Dept., AUS, 1943-45. Mem. St. Louis soc. Fin. Analysts (pres. 1949-50), Mo. Athletic Club (St. Louis). Home: 6401 Ellenwood Ave Saint Louis MO 63105-2228 E-mail: wwspoon@swbell.net. *Many of the current social and ethical problems of today might be partially resolved if theology would be influenced by the 4th dimension of spacetime plus the 5th dimension of the mind, the 6th dimension of the spirit and the 7th dimension of God the Father.*

WITHROW, LUCILLE MONNOT, nursing home administrator; b. Alliance, Ohio, July 28, 1923; d. Charles Edward Monnot and Freda Aldine (Guy) Monnot Cameron; m. Alvin Robert Withrow, June 6, 1945 (dec. 1984); children: Cindi Withrow Johnson, Nancy Withrow Townley, Sharon Withrow Hodgkins (dec.), Wendel Alvin. AA in Health Adminstrn., Eastfield Coll., 1976. Lic. nursing home adminstr., Tex.; cert. nursing home ombudsman. Held various clerical positions, Dallas, 1950-72; office mgr., asst. adminstr. Christian Care Ctr. Nursing Home, Mesquite, Tex., 1972-76; head adminstr. Christian Care Ctr. Nursing Home and Retirement Complex, Mesquite, 1976-91; nursing home ombudsman Tex. Dept. Aging and Tex. Dept. Health, Dallas, 1991-93; legal asst. Law Offices of Wendel A. Withrow, Carrollton, Tex., 1993—. Mem. con. on geriatric curriculum devel. Eastfield Coll., Mesquite, 1979, 87; mem. ombudsman adv. com. Sr. Citizens Greater Dallas; nursing home cons.; notary pub., 1995—. Vol. Dallas Arboretum and Bot. Soc.; mem. Ombudsman adv. com. Sr. Citizens of Greater Dallas; charter mem. Stage Show Prodns. Recipient Volunteerism award, Tex. Atty. Gen., 1987, Tex. Gov., 1992. Mem. Tex. Assn. Homes for Aging, Am. Assn. Homes for Aging, Health Svcs. Speakers Bur., White Rock Kiwanis. Mem. Ch. of Christ. Avocations: reading, travel, theater. Home: 11344 Lippitt Ave Dallas TX 75218-1922 Office: Law Office of W A Withrow 1120 Metrocrest Dr Ste 200 Carrollton TX 75006-5872

WITHROW, MARY ELLEN, federal agency administrator; b. Marion, Ohio, Oct. 2, 1930; d. Clyde Welsh and Mildred (Stump) Hinamon; m. Norman David Withrow, Sept. 4, 1948; children: Linda Rizzo, Leslie Legge, Norma, Rebecca Gooding. Mem. Elgin Local Bd. Edn., Marion, Ohio, 1969-73, pres., 1972; safety programs dir. ARC, Marion, 1968-72; dep. registrar State of Ohio, Marion, 1972-75; dep. county auditor Marion County, Ohio, 1975-77, county treas., 1977-83; treas. State of Ohio, Columbus, 1983-94; treas. of the U.S. Dept. Treasury, Washington, 1994—. Chmn. Ohio Bd. Deposits, 1983—. Mem. exec. com. Ohio Dem. Com., mem. exec. com. women's caucus; mem. Dem. Nat. Com.; mem. Met. Women's Ctr.; pres. Marion County Dem. Club, 1976; participant Harvard U. Strategic Leadership Conf., 1990.; mem. Dem. Leadership Coun. Recipient Donald L. Scantlebury Meml. award, 1991, Women of Achievement award YWCA of Met. Columbus, 1993, Outstanding Govt. Svc. award Am. Numis. Assn., 1995; inducted Ohio Women's Hall of Fame, 1986; named Outstanding Elected Dem. Woman Holding Pub. Office, Nat. Fedn. Dem. Women, 1987, Advocate of Yr., SBA, 1988, Most Valuable State Pub. Ofcl., City and State newspaper, 1990; Women Execs. in State Govt. fellow Harvard U., 1987. Mem. LWV (dem. leadership coun.), State Assn. County Treas. (legis. com. 1979-83, treas. 1982), Nat. Assn. State Treas. (pres. 1992, Jesse Unruh award 1993, chair long range planning com., mem. exec. com.), Nat. Assn. State Auditors Comptrs. and Treas. (pres. 1990, strategic planning com., intergov. rels. com., chair state and mcpl. bonds com.), Coun. State Govts. (exec. com., internat. affairs com., orgnl. planning and coord. com., strategic planning task force), Women Execs. in State Govt. (chair fund devel. com.), Altrusa Bus. and Profl. Women's Club (hon.), Delta Kappa Gamma (hon.), Delta Sigma Pi (hon.). Clubs: Bus. and Profl. Women's. Office: Dept Treasury 1500 Pennsylvania Ave NW Washington DC 20220-0002

WITHROW, SHERRIE ANNE (JIMIE JEAN PEARL), financial specialist; b. Sacramento, Mar. 10, 1960; d. Jim and Ilene (James) Withrow. Student, Diablo Valley C.C., Pleasant Hill, Calif., 1977-81, Tarrant County Jr. Coll., Ft. Worth, 1982-83, Coll. of Marin, Kentfield, Calif., 1988, Merritt Coll., Oakland, Calif., 1990; AA in Bus. Adminstrn. and Mgmt., St. Louis C.C., Florissant, Mo., 1981. Internal cashier AAA Automobile Club Mo., St. Louis, 1977-79; receiving clk. Dayton-Hudson Target Stores, Florissant and Ft. Worth, 1979-81; supr. credit and collection World Svc. Life Ins. Co., Ft. Worth, 1982-83; bank br. balancer, data processing divsn. Tex. Am. Bank Svcs., Inc., Ft. Worth, 1984-85, asst. to contr. Positive Video-Post Prodn., Orinda, Calif., 1985-87; with contractor's desk adminstrn. dept. Shell Oil Co., Martinez, Calif., 1987-88; asst. to CFO J.T. Thorpe & Son, Inc., Richmond, Calif., 1988-89; founder, gen. ptnr. HomeVisions Constrn. Svcs., El Sobrante, Calif., 1989-99, AudioVisions Sound and Lighting Co., El Sobrante, 1990-2000; corp. acctg. and investments Liquidity Fund Mgmt., Inc., 1990-92; founder, gen. ptnr. AV Electric, El Sobrante, 1994-2000; tax and payroll benefits specialist, founder Roll'em!, Martinez, Calif., 2001—. Audio engr., cons. and project fin. cons. Contbr. (poetry) The Brilliance of Night, Internat. Libr. of Poetry Compilation, 2000, The Best Poems and Poets of 2001, 2001, The Silence Within, 2001, Nature's Echoes, 2001, Internat. Libr. Poetry, 2003; contbr.: poetry Expressions Anthology, 2004, Theatre of the Mind, 2004, audio recs.: The Sound of Poetry, 2001; audio recs. The Best Poems and Poets of 2002, Eternal Portraits, 2004, Theatre of the Mind, 2004, Expressions, 2004. Fundraiser Sr. Citizen Subsidized Housing Complex, Martinez, 1987-88. David L. Underwood scholar Florissant Valley (St. Louis) C.C., 1980-81. Mem.: Internat. Platform Assn., Phi Theta Kappa. Democrat. Office: Roll 'em! PO Box 2919 Martinez CA 94553-2919 also: 3776 Raap Ave Martinez CA 94553-3817

WITHUHN, WILLIAM LAWRENCE, museum director, railroad economics and management consultant; b. Portland, Oreg., Aug. 12, 1941; s. Vernon Lawrence and Ruth Eleanor (Ferguson) W.; m. Gail Joy Hartman, Nov. 22, 1964; children: James, Thomas, Harold. BA, U. Calif.-Berkeley, 1963; MBA with distinction, Cornell U., 1977, MA, 1980. Commd. regular 2d lt. USAF, 1963, advanced through grades to capt., 1967; indsl. engr., asst. dir. manpower and orgn. USAF at Western Transport Air Force, 1964-65; global, polar, tactical, and instr. navigator worldwide USAF, 1965-72, spl. ops. navigator, 1968—70, select lead navigator Mil. Airlift Command, 1970-72; ret., 1972; intern, then staff asst. U.S. Ho. of Reps., 1973-74; v.p. Va. & Md. R.R. Co., Cape Charles, Va., 1977-81, Md. & Del. R.R., Federalsburg, Md., 1977-81; sr. v.p. Ont. Midland R.R., Ont. Cent. R.R., Sodus, N.Y., 1979-83; v.p. Rail Mgmt. Svcs., Inc., Syracuse, N.Y., 1979-83, RSA Leasing Co., Syracuse, 1980-83; exec. v.p. Am. Coal Enterprises, Inc., Akron, Ohio, 1980-82; v.p., gen. mgr. Allegheny So. Ry., Martinsburg, Pa., 1982-83; acting dir. R.R. Mus. of Pa., 1982-83; curator transp. Nat. Mus. Am. History Smithsonian Inst., Washington, 1983—, dep. chmn. dept. sci. and tech., 1984-91, spl. asst. to mus. dir., 1990-94. Bd. dirs., chmn. The Waring Group Inc., Transp. Cons., Salisbury, Md., 1983-89; cons. Nat. Pk. Svc., Pa. Hist. & Mus. Commn., UNESCO (India), Expo 2000 (Germany), Fed. Railroad Admnstrn., Nat. Transp. Safety Bd.; apptd. Garrett Morgan Transp. Futures Program steering com. U.S. Dept. Transp.; apptd. founding mem., history com., Transp. Rsch. Bd. Nat. Rsch. Coun.; apptd. mem., task force on transp. Nat. Parks and Pub. Lands, Transp. Rsch. Bd. Nat. Rsch. Coun. Author: Spirit of Steam, 1995; editor, co-author: Rails Across America, 1993; contbr. articles to profl. jours. Decorated D.F.C. with oak leaf cluster, Bronze Star, Air Medal with 12 clusters, Air Force Commendation Medal with cluster, Pres. Unit Citation, Antarctic Svc. Medal; De Karman fellow, 1979-80, Smithsonian fellow, 1980-81; recipient Gold Apple award Nat. Ednl. Film Festival, 1995. Mem. Am. Inst. Indsl. Engrs., Lexington Group in Transp. History, Nat. Parks Conservation Assn., Air Commando Assn., Disting. Flying Cross Soc., Internat. Assn. Ry. Operating Officers, Brotherhood of Locomotive Engrs.,Cornell Club Washington, Theta Chi. mem. Nat. Press Club Washington. Office: Nat Mus Am History Smithsonian Inst Rm 5210 Washington DC 20560-0628

WITKE, DAVID RODNEY, retired newspaper editor, consultant; b. Council Bluffs, Iowa, Mar. 24, 1937; s. Arnold and Rosamond Louise (Storer) W.; m. Priscilla Bill Smith, Oct. 8, 1960; 1 son, Carl. BS in Journalism, Northwestern U., 1959. Reporter, editor The Courier, Champaign-Urbana, Ill., 1962-66; copy editor The Register, Des Moines, 1966-70, city editor, 1970-73, asst. mng. editor adminstrn., 1973-74, asst. mng. editor electronics, 1974-75, mng. editor, 1975-83, dir. ops., 1983-85, dep. editor, omsbudsman, 1985-87, exec. sports editor, 1987-98, sr. editor, 1998—2002, ret., 2002; freelance cons., 2002—. Rep. Iowa Freedom of Info. Coun., Des Moines, 1973—, pres., 1986-88; vis. lectr. Drake U., 1986—, Iowa State U., 1990—; adj. faculty Simpson Coll., 2003—; juror Pulitzer Prize, 1989-91; tng. cons. The Register, Des Moines, 2003—. Served to lt. (j.g.) USN, 1959-62, PTO. Mem. Assoc. Press Mng. Editors Assn., Mid-Am. Newspaper Assn., AP Sports Editors Assn., Iowa Newspaper Found., The Prairie Club, Sigma Delta Chi. Unitarian Universalist. Achievements include early lectures on electronic applications to large newspaper production. Home and Office: 2521 48th Pl Des Moines IA 50310-2506 Office Phone: 515-274-0578.

WITKIN, ERIC DOUGLAS, lawyer; b. Trenton, N.J., May 14, 1948; s. Nathan and Norma Shirley (Stein) W.; m. Regina Ann Bilotta, June 8, 1980; children: Daniel Robert, Sarah Ann. AB magna cum laude, Columbia U., 1969; JD, Harvard U., 1972. Bar: N.Y. 1973, D.C. 1989, U.S. Dist. Ct. (so. and ea. dists.) N.Y. 1974, U.S. Dist. Ct. (we. dist.) N.Y. 2001, U.S. Ct. Appeals (2d and D.C. cirs.) 1974, U.S. Supreme Ct. 1977, U.S. Dist. Ct. D.C. 1989. Assoc. Poletti, Freidin, Prashker & Gartner, N.Y.C., 1972-80, ptnr., 1980-85; sr. atty. labor Kaye, Scholer, Fierman, Hays & Handler, N.Y.C., 1985-88; of counsel Akin, Gump, Strauss, Hauer & Feld, Washington, 1988-90; counsel Benetar, Bernstein, Schair & Stein, N.Y.C., 1990-99; ptnr. Roberts & Finger, LLP, N.Y.C., 1999-2001, Greble & Finger, LLP, N.Y.C., 2001; counsel Brown, Raysman, Millstein, Felder, & Steiner LLP, N.Y.C., 2001—. Treas., founder Property Owners Against Unfair Taxation, N.Y.C., 1983-90; trustee Congregation Emanu-El of Westchester, 1996—, pres., 2002--. Lawrence Chamberlain scholar Columbia U., N.Y.C., 1968; recipient Alumni medal Alumni Fedn. Columbia U., 1982. Mem. ABA (labor and employment law sect.), N.Y. State Bar Assn. (labor and employment law sect., com. on equal employment opportunity law), Assn. of Bar of City of N.Y. (spl. com. on sex and law 1975-82, com. on labor and employment law 1982-85, 92-94), Westchester County Bar Assn., Columbia Coll. Alumni Assn. (pres. 1988-90, bd. dirs. 1974—, Robert Lincoln Carey prize, Alumni prize 1969, Lions award 1990), Alumni Fedn. Columbia U. (alumni trustee nominating com. 1990-97, pres. 1997-99), Am. Soc. Pers. Adminstrn. (contbr. monthly newsletter 1986 88), Soc. Human Resource Mgmt., Soc. Columbia Grads. (bd. dirs. 1994-97), Human Resources Assn. N.Y., Phi Beta Kappa. Clubs: Harvard (N.Y.C.). Avocations: piano, sailing. Home: 103 Wendover Rd Rye NY 10580-1939 Office: Brown Raysman Millstein Felder & Steiner 900 3rd Ave Fl 23 New York NY 10022 E-mail: ewitkin@brownraysman.com., ericwitkin@aol.com.

WITKIN, EVELYN MAISEL, retired geneticist; b. N.Y.C., Mar. 9, 1921; d. Joseph and Mary (Levin) Maisel; m. Herman A. Witkin, July 9, 1943 (dec. July 1979); children— Joseph, Andrew. AB, NYU, 1941; MA, Columbia U., 1943, PhD, 1947; DSc honoris causa, N.Y. Med. Coll., 1978, Rutgers U., 1995. Mem. staff genetics dept. Carnegie Inst., Washington, 1950-55; mem. faculty State U. N.Y. Downstate Med. Center, Bklyn., 1955-71, prof. medicine, 1968-71; prof. biol. scis. Douglass Coll., Rutgers U., 1971-79, Barbara McClintock prof. genetics, 1979-83, Waksman Inst. Microbiology, 1983-91; Barbara McClintock prof. emerita Waksman Inst. Microbiology, Rutgers U., 1991—. Author articles; mem. editorial bds. profl. jours. Postdoctoral fellow Am. Cancer Soc., 1947-49; fellow Carnegie Instn., 1957; Selman A. Waksman lectr., 1960; Phi Beta Kappa vis. scholar, 1980-81; grantee NIH, 1956-89; recipient Prix Charles Leopold Mayer French Acad. Scis., 1977, Lindback award, 1979, Nat. Medal of Science award, 2002. Fellow AAAS, Am. Acad. Microbiology; mem. NAS, Am. Acad. Arts and Scis., Environ. Mutagen Soc., Am. Genetics Soc. (Thomas Hunt Morgan medal, 2000), Am. Soc. Microbiology. Home: 1 Firestone Ct Princeton NJ 08540-5220 E-mail: ewitkin@aol.com.

WITKIN, JEROME, education educator, painter; b. Bklyn., Sept. 13, 1939; s. Max and Mary (Pellegrino) Witkin; m. Lisa Pennela, June 1987; children: Christian, Gwen, Andrew. Cert., Cooper Union for Advancement of Sci. and Art, 1957—60; MFA, U. Pa., 1968—71; spl. student, Berlin Acad., 1961. Prof. Md. Inst. Coll. of Art, Balt., 1965—67, Am. Coll. in Switzerland, 1968, The Moore Coll. of Art., Phila., 1968—71, Syracuse U., Coll. of Visual and Performing Arts, 1971—. Author: (book) Life Lessons: The Art of Jerome Witkin, 1994. Recipient Chancellor's citation for excellence in tchg., lifetime achievement award, 1996; Guggenheim fellowship in painting, Guggenheim Found., NYC, 1962, Ford Found. grants, Syracuse U., 1975, 1976. Mem.: Nat. Acad. Design, U. Pa. Alumni Club. Avocations: reading, history, theology. Home: 201 Whitestone Dr Syracuse NY 13215 Office: Syracuse U Syracuse NY 13210

WITKIN, JOEL-PETER, photographer, poet; b. Bklyn., Sept. 13, 1939; s. Max and Mary (Pellegrino) W.; 1 child, Kersen Ahanu. B.F.A., Cooper Union, 1974; M.F.A., U. N.Mex., 1986; student (fellow), Columbia U., 1973-74. Artist in residence Zerybthia Rome, Italy, summer 1996; represented by Ricco/Maresca Gallery, NYC, Fraenkel Gallery, San Francisco, Galerie Baudoin Lebon, Paris; artist in residence Berlin, fall 1998, Paris, winter 1998. Lectr. Am. Acad. Rome, 1996, Camera Work, Berlin, El Escorial, Spain, 1998, Yale U., 2001, Soc. Photographic Edn., 1999. Exhibited in Projects Studio One, N.Y.C., 1980, Galerie Texbraun, Paris, 1982, Baudoin Lebon, Paris, 1982, 86, 90, 97, 2000, 02, Kansas Ctiy Art Inst., 1983, Stedelijk Mus., Amsterdam, 1983, Fraenkel Gallery, 1983-84, 87, 91, 93, 95, 97, Pace WildenStein MacGill Gallery, N.Y.C., 1983, 84, 87, 89, 91, 93, 95, 97, Pace Wildenstein, L.A., 1998, Ricco.Moresca Gallery, 2002, 04, San Francisco Mus. Modern Art, 1985, Bklyn. Mus., 1986, Galerie Baudoin Lebon, Paris, 1987, 89, 91, 95, 97, 2000, 02, 04, Centro de Arte Reina Sofia Mus., Madrid, 1988, Palais de Tokyo, Paris, 1989, Fahey/Klein Gallery, L.A., 1987, 89, 91, 97, 98, Mus. Modern Art, Haifa, Israel, 1991, Photo Picture Space Gallery, Osaka, Japan, 1993, 95, 2001, Guggenheim Mus., N.Y.C., 1995, Interkamera, Prague, 1995, Il Castello de Rivoli Mus., Turin, 1995, Encontros de Fotografia, Colombia, Portugal, 1996, 98, Rencontres de la Photographie, Arles, France, 1996, Taipei Photo Gallery, Taiwan, 1994, 96, 98, Mus. of Fine Arts, Santa Fe, 1998, Wildenstein Gallery, Tokyo, 1998, Sternburg Mus., Prague, 1999, Sternburg Mus., Prauge, 1999, Mesiac Fotographie, Slovakia, 1999, Hotel De Sully, Paris, 2000, Catherine Edelman Gallery, Chgo., 2000, Athens Sch. Fine Art, 2000, Ctr. Contemporary Art, Honolulu, 2000, Etherton Gallery, Tuscon, 2001, Stadt Mus., Jena, 2002, Picture Photo Space, Osaka, 2002, Infinito Gallery, Turin, 2002, Ricco Maresca Gallery, N.Y.C., 2002, Galeria Juana de Aizpuru, Madrid, 2003, Photoes Pana, Madrid, 2003, Le Garage Galerie, Toulouse, 2003, ARCO, Madrid, 2004; group shows: Mus. Modern Art, N.Y.C., 1959, San Francisco Mus. Moder Art, 1981, Whitney Biennial, 1985, Palais de Tokyo, Paris, 1986, La Photographie Contemporaine en France, 1996, Foto Masson, Goteberg, Sweden, 1997, Hanlin Museum, So. Korea, 1997, Bogardenkapel, Bruges, 1998, Hayward Gallery, London, 1997, Strasborg Mus. d'Art Moderne et Contemporaine, 1998, The Ansel Adams Ctr., San Francisco, 1999, Camera Work, San Francisco, 1999, The Louvre, Paris, 2000, Museé Bourdelle, Paris, 2000, John Gibson Gallery, N.Y.C., 2000, The High Mus. Art, Ga., 2000, The Fotografie Forum, Frankfort, 2001, The Nat. Gallery of Can., 2002, Hotel de Sully, Paris, 2002, The Israel Mus., Jerusalem, 2002, The Whitney Mus., N.Y.C., 2002, H. Lunn Collection, Lille, 2003, Photology, Milan, 2003, Akira Ikeda Gallery, Berlin, 2003, Nat. Gallery of Can., Ottawa, 2004, Yancey Richardson Gallery, N.Y.C., 2004; represented in permanent collections, Mus. Modern Art, N.Y.C., San Francisco Mus. Modern Art, 1980, Nat. Gallery Art, Washington, Victoria and Albert Mus., London, George Eastman House, N.Y., The Getty Collection, Moder Museet, Stockholm, Sweden, Whitney Mus., N.Y.C., The Guggenheim Mus., N.Y.C., Met. Mus., N.Y.C., Tokyo Met. Mus. Photography, Nat. Gallery Can., The Metropolitan Mus. Art, N.Y.C., Phila. Mus. Art; subject of monographs: Joel-Peter Witkin, 1985, 88-89, 91, 93, 95-96, 98, 99, 2000, 01, 02, 03; editor: Masterpieces of Medical Photography, 1987, Harms Way, 1994; visual editor: Songs of Experience, 2002, Songs of Innocence, 2003, Songs of Experience and Songs of Innocence, 2004; artist residency, Paris, 1994, 98, 2000, Rome, 1996, Berlin, 1998, Buenos Aires, 2003. Served with U.S. Army, 1961-64. Decorated commandeur des Arts et de Lettres (France); recipient The Augustus Saint Gaudens medal The Cooper Union, 1996, Disting. Alumni award The Cooper Union, 1986, Internat. Ctr. Photography award, 1988, award for N.Y. Times "The Plague Yr.," Soc. Publ. Designers, 2000; Ford Found. grantee, 1977, 78, Nat. Endowment in Photography grantee, 1980, 81, 86, 92. Address: 1707 Five Points Rd SW Albuquerque NM 87105-3017 *My need is to understand existence. That need becomes art when it reaches into the extreme limit of the possible but with grace and truth.*

WITKOP, BERNHARD, chemist; b. Freiburg, Baden, Germany, May 9, 1917; came to U.S., 1947, naturalized, 1953; s. Philipp W. and Hedwig M. (Hirschhorn) W.; m. Marlene Prinz, Aug. 8, 1945; children: Cornelia Johanna, Phyllis, Thomas. Diploma, U. Munich, 1938, PhD, 1940, Golden Dr. Diploma, 1990; ScD, Privat-Dozent, 1947. Matthew T. Mellon research fellow Harvard U., 1947-48, mem. faculty, 1948-50; spl. USPHS fellow Nat. Heart Inst., NIH, 1950-52; vis. scientist Nat. Inst. Arthritis and Metabolic Diseases, 1953, chemist, 1954-55, chief sect. metabolites, 1956-87, chief lab. chemistry, 1957-87, scholar, 1987-92, hon. scholar emeritus, 1993; vis. prof. U. Kyoto, Japan, 1961, U. Freiburg, Fed. Repubic Germany, 1962; adj. prof. U. Md. Med. Sch., Balt.; Nobel symposium lectr. Stockholm-Karlskoga, 1981. Mem. bd. Internat. Sci. Exchange, 1974; mem. exec. com. NRC, 1975; mem. Com. Internat. Exchange, 1977, Paul Ehrlich Award Com., Frankfurt, 1980-97. Editor: Fedn. European Biochem. Soc. Letters, 1979-90. Bd. dirs. Leo Baeck Inst., N.Y., 1996—. Recipient Superior Service award USPHS, 1967; Paul Karrer gold medal U. Zurich, 1971; Kun-ni-to (medal of sci. and culture 2d class) Emperor of Japan, 1975; Alexander von Humboldt award for sr. U.S. scientists, 1978 Mem. NAS, Am. Chem. Soc. (Hillebrand award 1958, Golden Membership 1997), Am. Acad. Arts and Sci., Am. Philos. Soc., Acad. Leopoldina (fgn.), Pharm. Soc. Japan (hon.), Chem. Soc. Japan (hon.), Japanese Biochem. Soc. (hon.), Acad. Scientiarium et Artium Europaea, Rheinisch-Westfälische Akademie der Wissenschaften. Office: NIH-Dept Health Edn & Welfare 2A 04 Bldg 8 Bethesda MD 20892-0001 Office Phone: 301-496-4181. *A career between two worlds and two wars, spanning 50 years of research aims changing from structural to dynamic aspects, may be considered epigonal in the sense that my teacher H. Wieland (Nobel Prize*

1928) always considered biochemistry as a neglected area of organic chemistry. In a small way I tried to follow his example and interests, such as oxidation mechanisms, natural products and highly active toxins.

WITMAN, EDWARD PAUL, philosophy educator; b. Baldwin, N.Y., Jan. 27, 1945; m. Arlene Marie Rustmann, June 7, 1969; children: Christopher Paul, Michael Harrison. AB, Georgetown U., 1967; MA, PhD, Fordham U., 1978. Cert. in bioethics and medical humanities Columbia U., Coll. of Physicians and Surgeons, 1996. Prof. Georgian Court Coll., Lakewood, NJ, 1972—, chmn. philosophy, history and geography, 2000—03. Vis. lectr. Cathedral Coll., Dougleston, NY, 1971—72; ethics cons. Shoreline Behavioral Health, Toms River, NJ, 1994—96, Cmty. Med. Ctr., Toms River, 1992—. Trustee Citizens Com. Biomed. Ethics N.J., 1988—93, Cath. Charities Ocean County N.J., 1983—93. Mem.: AAUP (chpt. pres. 1996—97), Assn. Practical and Profl. Ethics, Am. Soc. Bioethics and Humanities. Republican. Roman Catholic. Avocations: woodworking, rowing/sculling. Home: 108 Ridge Dr Toms River NJ 08753 Office: Georgian Court Coll 900 Lakewood Ave Lakewood NJ 08701 E-mail: witman@georgian.edu.

WITMAN, LEONARD JOEL, lawyer; b. N.Y.C., Nov. 7, 1950; s. Seymour and Ruth W.; m. Mona Soled, Aug. 25, 1950; children: Rachel, Leah. BA, Rutgers Coll., 1972; JD, N.Y. Law Sch., 1975. Bar: N.J. 1975, U.S. Dist. Ct. N.J. 1975, U.S. Ct. Appeals (2d cir.) 1975, U.S. Dist. Ct. (so. and ea. dists.) N.Y., 1976, U.S. Tax Ct. 1976. Tax law specialist IRS, Newark, 1975-78; assoc. Lampf, Lipkind, West Orange, N.J, 1978-81; ptnr. Brach, Eichler, Rosenberg, Silver, Bernstein, Hammer & Gladstone, Roseland, N.J., 1981-89, Witman, Stadmauer & Michaels, P.A., Florham Park, N.J., 1990—. Adj. law prof. Seton Hall U., N.J., Rutgers U. Grad. Sch. Bus., 1996—. Author: Top Heavy Pension Plans, 1985; contbr. articles to profl. jours. Mem. ABA, N.J. Bar Assn., (chmn. employee benefit com. 1984-86, chmn. taxation sect. 1987-88), Essex County Bar Assn., Morris County Bar Assn. Jewish. Home: 31 Conkling Rd Flanders NJ 07836-9106 Office: Witman Stadtmauer & Michaels 26 Columbia Tpke Florham Park NJ 07932-2213

WITMER, G. ROBERT, retired state supreme court justice; b. Webster, N.Y., Dec. 26, 1904; s. George H. and Lillian (Woodhull) W.; m. Marian P. Costello, June 27, 1936; children: George Robert, John R., Thomas W., Sylvia Witmer Bissell. AB, U. Rochester, N.Y., 1926; LL.B., Harvard U., 1929. Bar: N.Y. 1929. Pvt. practice, Rochester, 1929-45; ptnr. Easton & Witmer, 1931-45; surrogate Monroe County, 1946-53; justice N.Y. State Supreme Ct., 1954-81, assoc. justice appellate div. 1st dept., 1963-67, appellate div. 4th dept., 1968-81; jud. adminstrv. officer, appellate div. N.Y. State Supreme Ct. (4th dept.), 1981-94; adminstrv. judge N.Y. State Supreme Ct. (7th Jud. Dist.), 1962-68; ret., 1994. Town atty., Webster, 1934-35; served on N.Y. State Ct. Appeals, 1974. Co-author: N.Y. Pattern Jury Instructions-Civil, Vol. 1, 1965, rev. edit., 1974, Vol. 11, 1968; co-chmn. pub. com. Practitioner's Handbook for Appeals Appellate Divs. N.Y., 1979, Practitioner's Handbook for Appeals to the Court of Appeals of New York, 1981. Supr. Town of Webster and County of Monroe, 1936-45; chmn. Webster Republican Com., 1933-45, mem. exec. com. of Monroe County Republican Com., 1933-45. Mem. Am., N.Y. State, Monroe County Bar Assns., Am. Law Inst., Webster Grange, Univ. Club (Rochester), Masons, Theta Chi. Home: Apt 612 1570 East Ave Rochester NY 14610-1640

WITMER, GEORGE ROBERT, JR., lawyer; b. Rochester, NY, Mar. 23, 1937; s. George Robert and Marian Pauline (Costello) W.; m. Nancy Rosetta Wenner, Dec. 28, 1968; children: Wendy Lynn, Heidi Dawn, George Robert, III, Frank David. AB, U. Rochester, 1959; LL.B., Harvard U., 1962. Bar: N.Y. 1962, U.S. Dist. Ct. (we. dist.) N.Y. 1963, U.S. Supreme Ct. 1967, U.S. Dist. Ct. (no. dist.) N.Y. 1977, U.S. Ct. Appeals (2d cir.) 1998. Assoc. Nixon, Hargrave, Devans & Doyle, Rochester, 1962-70, ptnr., 1970-99, Nixon Peabody, Rochester, 1999—. Instr. in bus. law U. Rochester, 1965-66; mem. com. to advise and cons. Jud. Conf. State N.Y. on Civil Practice Law and Rules, 1970-77; mem. N.Y. State Jud. Inst. on Professionalism in the Law, 1999—; mem. Adv. Group to N.Y. State and Fed. Jud. Coun., 1999—. Mem. N.Y. State Rep. Com., 1976—93; trustee Eastman Dental Ctr. Rochester, 1977—97, pres. bd. trustees, 1989—90; trustee U. Rochester, 1979—, chmn., 2003—. Fellow: ABA, N.Y. Bar Found. (dir. 1991—96); mem.: N.Y. State Bar Assn. (ho. dels. 1978—, v.p. 1984—88, sec. 1989—90, pres.-elect 1993—94, pres. 1994—95, exec. com. environ. law sect. 1981—96, Disting. Svc. award environ. law sect.), Monroe County (N.Y.) Bar Assn., Am. Law Inst. (life), ABA, Rotary (dir. Rochester club 1977—79, pres. 2001—02), Masons (master local lodge 1971), Phi Beta Kappa. Republican. Lutheran. Home: 892 Lake Rd Webster NY 14580-9008 Office: Nixon Peabody LLP PO Box 31051 Clinton Sq Rochester NY 14604-1729 Office Phone: 585-263-1609. Business E-Mail: grwitmer@nixonpeabody.com.

WITMER, JOHN RICHARD, librarian; b. Dallas, Dec. 26, 1949; s. John Albert and Doris May (Ferry) W.; m. Joyce Ann Pelzl, Nov. 25, 1972; l child, Katherine Anne. Student, Wheaton (Ill.) Coll., 1967-70; BS, West Tex. State U., 1971; MSLS, East Tex. State U., 1974; postgrad., Dallas Theol. Sem., 1978-81. Cert. secondary tchr., driving instr., learning resources specialist, Tex. Learning resources specialist Sherman (Tex.) Ind. Sch. Dist., 1974-76, Ector County Ind. Sch. Dist., Odessa, Tex., 1978-80; acting head libr. Calvary Bible Coll., Kansas City, Mo., 1976-77; head libr. Am. Christian Coll., Tulsa, 1977-78; tech. svcs. libr. Odessa Coll., 1980-82; tchr. county youth ctr. Ector County Ind. Sch. Dist., Odessa, Tex., 1985; reader svcs. libr. Wayland Bapt. U., Plainview, Tex., 1986-87; vis. tchr. Lubbock (Tex.) Ind. Sch. Dist., 1987-88; learning resources specialist Dallas Ind. Sch. Dist., 1988-90, 94-99; head libr. San Elizario Ind. Sch. Dist., El Paso, Tex., 1991-94; audio visual libr. Klein Ind. Sch. Dist., Houston, 1999—. Deacon Scofield Meml. Ch., Dallas, 1971-74, Odessa Bible Ch., 1981-86; mem. cast, crew Permian Playhouse, Odessa, 1979-82. Capt. U.S. Army, 1972-85. Mem. Tex. Libr. Assn. (life), Classroom Tchrs. Dallas (bldg. rep. 1989-90), Odessa Profl. Educators (sec., v.p., pres. state dist. rep. 1978-81), Odessa Univ. Kiwanis (v.p., pres. 1984-85). Republican. Avocations: collecting books and trivia, church work, contests, travel. Home: 15114 Runbell Pl Houston TX 77095-3228

WITMER, MICHAEL DOUGLAS, education educator; b. Everett, Wash., Oct. 4, 1947; s. Robert Lincoln and Lois Caroline Witmer; m. Andrea Lynn Spencer-Witmer, July 5, 1969; children: Allison Estelle, Amanda Leigh. BA, U. Wash., 1969; MS, Western Wash. U., 1974. Caseworker Wash. Dept. Pub. Assistance, Seattle, 1970—71; instr. Skagit Valley Coll., Mount Vernon, Wash., 1972—, dept. chair, 1979—, coord. Title III, 1999—2001, assessment liaison, 1992—. Instr. Chapman Coll., Oak Harbor, Wash., 1983—86, Western Wash. U., Bellingham, 1988—91; stats. cons., Mount Vernon, 1980—. Vol. firefighter Lake Samish Fire Dept., Lake Samish, Wash., 1990—99; mem. Wash. Ctr. Steering Com., 1995—2004. Named Asst. Soccer Coach of the Yr., NWACC, 1978; named to NWAACC Hall of Fame, 2004; recipient Master Tchr. award, NISOD. Mem.: Skagit Racing Assn., APA. Democrat. Avocations: fly fishing, sprint car racing, blues guitar, boating. Home: 4013 Creek Pl Mount Vernon WA 98273 Office: Skagit Valley College 2405 College Way Mount Vernon WA 98273

WITMER, RICHARD H. investment company executive; Gen. ptnr. Brown Bros. Harriman & Co., N.Y.C. Office: Brown Bros Harriman & Co 59 Wall St New York NY 10005-2808

WITMEYER, JOHN JACOB, III, lawyer; b. New Orleans, Dec. 18, 1946; s. John J. and Thais Audrey (Dolese) W. BS, Tulane U., 1968; JD with distinction, Duke U., 1971. Bar: N.Y. Assoc. Mudge Rose Guthrie & Alexander, N.Y.C., 1971-76; ptnr. Ford Marrin Esposito & Witmeyer (now Ford, Marrin, Esposito, Witmeyer & Gleser LLP), N.Y.C., 1976—. Bd. trustees Gregorian U. Found., 1999—; adv. coun. Paul Tulane Coll., Tulane U., 1998—; former bd. dirs. Tulane Assocs., Tulane U., 2001—. Col. U.S. Army. Mem.: Order of the Holy Sepulchre (knight commander). Office: Ford Marrin Esposito Witmeyer & Gleser LLP Wall St Plz New York NY 10005-1875 E-mail: jjwitmeyer@fmew.com.

WITORSCH, PHILIP, internist, educator; b. New York City, July 11, 1937; s. Benjamin and Sarah (Etkin) W.; m. Joan Linda (Pellman), June 7, 1959; children: Beth Joy, Jeffrey Lee. BA, N.Y. Univ., 1958, MD, 1962. Diplomate Am. Bd. Internal Medicine, sub-splty. pulmonary disease. Intern, resident internal medicine Yale U., New Haven Hosp., 1962—64; clin. assoc., clin. investigator Nat. Inst. Allergy and Infectious Diseases NIH, Bethesda, Md., 1964—67; resident, chief resident in internal medicine, fellow pulmonary diseases VA. Hosp., Washington, 1967—69; chmn. pulmonary and critical care medicine, dir. med. intensive care unit, med. dir. respiratory therapy Washington Hosp. Ctr., 1962—82, sr. attending in medicine, 1969—; prof. medicine and physiology, dir. sect. environ. medicine and toxicology, divsn. pulmonary diseases and allergy, med. dir. for respiratory care George Washington U., 1983—95; prof. medicine and pharmacology, clin. dir. toxicology and applied pharmacokinetics program, dir. environ. occupl. toxicology assessment program Georgetown U., 1995—. Adj. prof. pharmacology Georgetown U., 1986-95; cons. pulmonary diseases, Va. Hosp. NIH, Dept. State, Andrews AFB, Dept. Justice, Dept. Labor. Contbr. articles to profl. med. journals. Served in USPHS, 1964-67. Fellow ACP, Am. Coll. Chest Physicians (gov. Washington chpt. 1995-97); Am. Geriatric Soc., Royal Soc. Medicine; mem. AMA (physicians recognition awards 1972, 75, 78, 81, 84, 87, 90, 93, 96, 99); Soc. Critical Care Medicine, Am. Thoracic Soc., D.C. Thoracic Soc., Med. Soc. D.C., Med. Chirurgical Faculty Md., Am. Fedn. Clin. Rsch., Am. Assn. Respiratory Therapy, Am. Heart Assn., Am. Soc. Internal Medicine, Am. Coll. Toxicology, Am. Coll. Occupl. and Environ. Medicine, Montgomery County Med. Soc., Phi Beta Kappa, Alpha Omega Alpha. Office: Dept Pharmacology Georgetown Univ Med Ctr MED-DENT SE 402 Box 571443 3900 Reservoir Rd NW Washington DC 20057-1443 Office Phone: 202-687-0398. Business E-Mail: Witorscp@georgetown.edu.

WITORT, JANET LEE, lawyer; b. Cedar Rapids, Iowa, Mar. 10, 1950; d. Charles Francis Svoboda and Phyllis Harriet (Wilber) Miller; m. Stephen Francis Witort, Oct. 27, 1979. Student, U. Colo., 1968-69, U. Iowa, 1971; BA, U. No. Colo., 1972; JD, Loyola U., 1979. Bar: Ill. 1979, U.S. Dist. Ct. (no. dist.) Ill. 1979, U.S. Dist. Ct. (no. dist.) Ill. 1979, U.S. Supreme Ct. 1987. Paralegal Fed. Nat. Mortgage Assn., Chgo., 1973-75, Sidley & Austin, Chgo., 1975-76; assoc. Frankel, McKay & Orlikoff, Chgo., 1979-81; atty. Mut. Trust Life Ins. Co., Oak Brook, Ill., 1981-86; assoc. counsel, asst. sec. N.Am. Co. for Life and Health Ins., Chgo., 1986-88; sr. atty. AMA, Chgo., 1988-89; gen. coun., sec. AMA Ins., Chgo., 1989-91, v.p. gen. counsel, sec., 1991-93; asst. gen. counsel Prudential Ins. and Fin. Svcs., Chgo., 1994—98; sr. counsel Allianz Life Ins. Co. of N.Am., 1998—99, v.p., dep. gen. counsel, 1999—. Author: (with others) The Legal Assistant-A Self Statement, 1974, (with others) Requirements and Limitations Imposed by Corporate Law, 1989, updated, 1992. Vol. Rep. Campaign, Chgo., 1974-76, 90-93, Children's Hosp. Guild, North Oaks, Minn., 1993—, v.p. 1994-95, pres. 1996; vol. Sci. Mus. Minn., St. Paul, 1994-2001; trustee Hindsdale Ill. Pub. Libr., 1987-93, v.p., 1991-93; bd. dirs. Suburban Libr. Sys., Burr Ridge, Ill., 1988-91, sec. 1990-91; bd. dirs. Children's Hosp. Assn., St. Paul, 1995-96; active Jr. League, St. Paul, 1997-2002, bd. dirs., 2000-01, sustainer, 2002—; active North Oaks (Minn.) Planning Commn., 2000—; del. Mo. State Rep. Conv., 2000. Mem. ABA, Am. Soc. Med. Assn. Coun., Ill. Bar Assn., Chgo. Assn. Paralegal Assts. (sec. 1973-74), Chgo. Bar Assn. (chair life & health ins. subcom. 1992-93), Womans Bar Assn. of Ill. (mem. ins. com. 1987-93), Ill. Paralegal Assn. (v.p. 1975-76), Nat. Fed. Paralegal Assns. (midwest reg. dir. 1975-76), Am. Corp. Counsel Assn. (membership com. 1988-90), Phi Alpha Delta, Student Bar Assn. (class rep. 1976-77). Republican. Avocations: golf, travel, skiing. Office: 1750 Hennepin Ave Minneapolis MN 55403-2115

WITOSKY, GARY J. manufacturing company executive; BA in Acctg. and Bus. Adminstrn., Thiel Coll. Audit mgr. Ernst & Whinney, Cleve.; treas., corp. contr. Park Corp., Cleve., until 1994; tras. Am. Axle & Mfg., Detroit, 1994-97, v.p., 1996-97, v.p. fin., CFO, 1997-99; pres., CEO Colfor Mfg. Inc., Malvern, Ohio, 1999—. Office: Colfor Mfg Inc 3255 Alliance Rd NW PO Box 485 Malvern OH 44644-0485

WITT, ALICIA, actress; b. Aug. 21, 1975; d. Robert and Diane W. Home edn. Actress Internat. Creative Mgmt., Beverly Hills, Calif. TV appearances: Cybill, 1995-98, The Disappearance of Vonnie, 1994, Blackout, 1993, Twin Peaks, 1991, Hotel Room, Ally McBeal, 2000, The Sopranos, 2000; film appearances: Dune, 1984, Liebestraum, 1991, Bodies, Rest and Motion, 1993, Fun, 1994 (Spl. Jury Recognition award Sundance Film Festival 1994), Four Rooms, 1995, Mr. Holland's Opus, 1995, Citizen Ruth, 1996, The Reef, 1997, Bongwater, 1998, Urban Legend, 1998, (voice) Gen 13, 1998, Cecil B. DeMented, 2000, Playing with Mona Lisa, 2000 (Best Actress award U.S. Comedy Arts Festival 2000), Vanilla Sky, 2001, Ten Tiny Love Stories, 2001, American Girl, 2002, Two Weeks Notice, 2002, The Upside of Anger, 2004; TV guest appearances The Sopranos, 2000, Ally McBeal, 2000, The Twilight Zone, 2003, (mus. theater) The Gift, 2000. Recipient Spl. Jury Recognition for acting, Sundance Film Festival, 1994, Ind. Spirit Award nomination, 1995. Avocations: listening to big-band recordings, chess, backgammon, bowling. Office: Internat Creative Mgmt 8942 Wilshire Blvd Beverly Hills CA 90211-1934*

WITT, CATHERINE LEWIS, neonatal nurse practitioner, writer; b. Burlington, Iowa, Nov. 21, 1957; d. Rodney Darrell and Neola Ann (Wharton) Lewis; m. John Robert Witt, Mar. 31, 1984; children: Jeffrey Lewis, Jennifer Diane. BSN, U. No. Colo., 1980; MSN, U. Colo., 1987. Cert. neonatal nurse practitioner. Staff nurse St. Joseph's Hosp., Denver, 1980-85; neonatal nurse practitioner Denver Children's Hosp., 1986-88; coord. neonatal nurse practitioner and neonatal transport Presbyn.-St. Luke's Med. Ctr., Denver, 1988—2002; neotal nurse practitioner NNP Svcs. of Colo., 2003—. Mem clin faculty neonatal nurse practitioner program Regis U. Contbr. chapters to books, articles to profl. jours. Troop leader Girl Scouts US; children's Bible tchr., altar guild Episcopal Ch. Mem. Nat. Assn. Neonatal Nurses (co-chair program com. 1992-94, bd. dir., dir.-at-large 1997-99, sec. 1999-2000, pres. 2003--), Nat. Cert. Corp. (test. com. 1994-96, nominations com. 2004). Democrat. Episcopalian. Avocations: altar guild, reading, sewing, dance. Home: 17586 E Dickenson Pl Aurora CO 80013-4180 Office: Presbyn-St Luke's Med Ctr 1719 E 19th Ave Denver CO 80218-1235 Office Phone: 303-839-7390. E-mail: clwitt@comcast.net.

WITT, DAVID L. curator, writer; b. Kansas City, Mo., Nov. 3, 1951; s. Lloyd Vernon and Dean Witt. BS in Polit. Sci., Kans. State U., 1974; M Liberal Studies, U. Okla., 2000. Naturalist Naish Nature Ctr., Edwardsville, Kans., summers 1967-70; asst. curator Seton Mus., Cimarron, N.Mex., summers 1972-74; curatorial asst. Riley County Hist. Mus., Manhattan, Kans., 1973-74; mus. asst. Millicent Rogers Mus., Taos, N.Mex., 1976-77; curator The Gaspard House Mus., Taos, N.Mex., 1978-79, The Harwood Found., Taos, N.Mex., 1979—. Author: The Taos Artists, 1984, Taos Moderns: Art of the New, 1992 (Southwest Book award Border Regional Libr. Assn. 1993), Modernists in Taos from Martin to Dasburg, 2002 (S.W. Book award Border Regional Libr. Assn. 2003, Ralph Emerson Twitchell award N.Mex. Hist. Soc. 2003); co-author: Spirit Ascendant: The Art and Life of Patrociño Barela, 1996 (S.W. Book award Border Regional Libr. Assn. 1997); contbr. Taos Artists and Their Patrons, 1898-1950; contbr. articles to profl. jour. Organizer first N.Mex. Art History Conf., 1986; founder S.W. Art Hist. Coun., 1990. Mem. PEN, Am. Assn. Mus., N.Mex. Assn. Mus. (pres. 1986-88). Home: PO Box 317 Taos NM 87571-0317 E-mail: davidlwitt@cybermesa.com.

WITT, HUGH ERNEST, technology consultant; b. Winchester, Ky., Nov. 18, 1921; s. Hugh E. and Louella (Milliken) W.; m. Janie Bryan (dec. Oct. 1990); m. Evelyn Chapman, Apr. 22, 1993. Student, Transylvania U., 1941-43; BS, U. Ky., 1945; MS, MIT, 1957. Asst. to dep. asst. sec. Dept. of Air Force, Washington, 1954-61, dep. asst. sec., 1961-70, Dept. of Navy, Washington, 1970-73; prin. dep. asst. sec. of Def., Washington, 1973-74; fed. procurement policy adminstr. Office Mgmt. and Budget, Washington, 1974-77; dir., govt. liaison United Techs. Corp., Washington, 1977-81, v.p., govt. liaison, 1981-87, cons. to United Techs. Corp., 1987—. Pres. Old Town Civic Assn., Alexandria, Va., 1961-63; bd. dirs. Alexandria Hist. Found.; mem. Alexandria Bd. Archtl. Rev., 1964-77; trustee Alexandria Hosp. Found., 1992-94. Alfred P. Sloan fellow MIT, Cambridge, Mass., 1956-57. Fellow Nat. Contract Mgmt. Assn.; mem. Aerospace Industries Assn., Nat. Security Indsl. Assn., MIT Alumni Assn., Soc. Sloan Fellows, Kappa Alpha.

WITT, JAMES LEE, business executive, former Cabinet member; b. Dardanelle, Ark., 1944; m. Lea; children: Jimmy, Michael. Founder Witt Constrn. Co.; county judge Yell County, Ark.; state dir. Office Emergency Svcs., Ark.; dir. Fed. Emergency Mgmt. Agy., Washington, 1993—2001; pres. James Lee Witt Assoc., LLC, 2002—; CEO Internat. Code Coun., 2003—. Chmn. bd. Child Devel., Inc., charter; Gov.'s rep. state disasters, Presdl. disasters; bd. govs. ARC. Recognized for reinvention efforts Nat. Assn. Counties.

WITT, JIM, editor; Asst. mng. editor, news Star-Telegram Arlington, 1986—92, editor, 1992—95; publ. Star Telegram Northeast Tarrant County Ed., 1995—95; editor Ft. Worth Star-Telegram Knight-Ridder, Inc., Ft. Worth, 1996—. Office: Knight-Ridder Inc 400 W 7th St Fort Worth TX 76102-4701

WITT, JOHN J. artist; b. Wilmington, Del., Jan. 30, 1940; s. Alex J. and Josephine G. Witt; m. Constance Giumarro Witt, July 30, 1935. BFA, U. of the Arts, Phila., 1962. Documentary artist USAF, M.C., USN, and USCG, various locations, 1968—; v.p., art dir. Robert Becker, Inc., N.Y.C., 1983—90; exec. v.p., ptnr. Leverte Assocs., Westport, Conn., 1990—2000. Civilian combat artist USMC, Vietnam, 1968, Vietnam, 69, Iraq, 2003; courtroom artist ABC News, N.Y.C., 1974. Contbr. artwork and illustrations to mags. and monographs; Represented in permanent collections New Britain Mus. Am. Art, Soc. Illustrators Mus. of Am. Illustration. Mem. Low illustration com. New Britain (Conn.) Mus. of Am. Art, 1985—. With U.S. Army, 1963—66. Recipient Naval Gold Medal for oil painting, USN/Salmagundi Club, 1978, Graphics Gold medal, Hudson Valley Art Assn., 1972, Best of Show award, Nat. Arts Clu, 1973, Dean Cornwell award for establishing Mus. Am. Illustration. Mem.: Soc. Illustrators (pres. 1980—83, govt. svcs. chair 2002—). Roman Catholic. Home: 1450 Baptist Church Rd Yorktown Heights NY 10598 E-mail: johnwitt@bestweb.net.

WITT, MICHAEL JOHN, history educator, priest; b. St. Louis, July 2, 1948; s. Michael Joseph Witt and Ethel Florence Lang. BA, Christian Bros. Coll., Memphis, 1970; PhD summa cum laude, St. Louis U., 1980; MDiv summa cum laude, Kenrick-Glennon Sem., Shrewsbury, Mo., 1991. Ordained June 16, 1990. History instr. Bishop Kelley H.S., Tulsa, Okla., 1970-75, CBC Mil. Inst., Clayton, Mo., 1975-79; assoc. prof. Christian Bros. Coll., Memphis, 1981-87; assoc. pastor St. Monica Ch., Creve Coeur, Mo., 1990-92, Ste. Genevieve (Mo.) Ch., 1992-94; pastor Most Blessed Sacrament, St. Louis, 1994-2000; assoc. prof. Kenrick Sem., Shrewsbury, Mo., 1999—. V.p. student svcs. Christian Bros. Coll., 1985-86; mem. Continuing Formation, St. Louis, 1992—, Campaign for Human Devel., St. Louis, 1998-2000; retreat master Cenacle Retreat Ctrs., St. Louis, Memphis, New Orleans, 1996—. Author: Devolution of CBC, 1981, I Phil, 1987. Active City Coun. Task Force, Memphis, 1986, Build-up Ste. Genevieve Flood Relief, 1993-94, Kings Area Neighborhood Assn., St. Louis, 1994-2000; founder USA Youth Wrestling Club, Ste. Genevieve, 1992-94. Mem. KC, Pi Kapa Phi (chpt. founder 1986—), Alpha Sigma Nu. Roman Catholic. Avocations: sailing, gardening, coach wrestling, cooking, foreign travel. Home: 11917 Sioux Point Dr Sainte Genevieve MO 63670-7114 Office: Kenrich-Glennon Sem 6500 Glennon Dr Saint Louis MO 63119 Office Phone: 314-792-6392. Business E-Mail: witt@kenrick.edu.

WITT, NANCY ANN, secondary school educator; b. Camp Cook, Calif., Oct. 7, 1951; d. Carl Harry Taft and Nida Zanotto; m. George Joseph Witt, Feb. 16, 1974; children: Kyle, Kevin. AA, Diablo Valley Coll., 1971; BA, Calif. State U., Chico, 1973. Cert. tchr. Calif. Tchr. Griffins Mid. Sch., Downey, Calif., 1974—81, Downey Adult Sch., 1984—87, Wilson Mid. Sch., Glendale, Calif., 1990—91, Glendale HS, 1992, v.p., rec. sec. Cons. tchr. Glendale Unified, 1997—; AP reader Coll. Bd., NJ, 2002—. Bd. dirs. Glenoaks Wilson PTA, Glendale, 1983—92. Named Outstanding History Tchr., State of Calif., 2004; recipient PTA Hon. Svc. award, Glenoaks Elem., 1988. Mem.: Calif. Coun. Social Studies, Nat. Coun. History Educators, Orgn. Am. Historians. Avocations: reading, travel, cooking, needlecrafts. Home: 2123 Lenore Dr Glendale CA 91206 Office: Glendale HS 1440 E Broadway Glendale CA 91205 Personal E-mail: wittnancy@hotmail.com.

WITT, ROBERT E. academic administrator; b. Sept. 16, 1940; m. Anne Witt; children: Peter, Karen. BA in Econs., Bates Coll., 1962; MBA, Dartmouth Coll., 1964; PhD in Bus. Adminstrn., Pa. State U., 1968. Rsch. asst. Amos Tuck Sch., Dartmouth Coll., Hanover, N.H., 1964-65; instr. mktg. Pa. State U., 1967-68; asst. prof. Coll. and Grad. Sch. Bus., U. Tex., Austin, 1968-71, assoc. prof., 1971-75, chmn. dept. mktg., 1973-83, prof., 1975-83, Zale Corp. centennial prof. bus., 1983-85, Betty and Glenn Mortimer centennial prof. bus., 1985-95, centennial chairperson bus. edn. leadership, 1986-95, acting dean, then dean, 1985—; interim pres. U. Tex., Arlington, 1995-96, pres., 1996—. Mem. budget coun. dept. mktg. adminstrn. U. Tex., Austin, 1969-85, mem. faculty exec. devel. program 1969—, mem. dean's coun., 1986—; mem. athletes adv. com. NCAA, 1986—; mem. acad. adv. bd. World Mgmt. Coun., 1988; mem. future directions coun. U. Tex. Ex-Students Assn., 1978-88, mem. exec. coun., 1981-83, 87-89; mem. adv. bd. dirs. Post Oak Bank, 1993—, Frost Nat. Bank, 1993—; mem. Acctg. Edn. Change Commn., 1992—; bd. dirs. Life Ptnrs. Group. Assoc. editor Social Sci. Quar., 1970-72; mem. editl. rev. bd. Jour. Mktg., 1971-73, 82-85; contbr. articles to profl. jours. Bd. dirs. Austin Symphony, 1991—, Univ. Coop. Soc., 1978-82. Recipient Top Hand award U. Tex. Ex-Students Assn., 1988. Mem. Am. Mktg. Assn. (fellow doctoral consortium 1967, program chmn. doctoral consortium 1972, reviewer, presenter), Assn. for Consumer Rsch. (treas. 1976, mem. exec. com. 1975-76, reviewer, conf. session chmn.), Am. Assembly Collegiate Schs. of Bus. (bd. dirs. 1991—, mem. visitation com. 1991, mem. govtl. rels. com. 1986-89, chmn. govtl. rels. com. 1987-89), So. Mktg. Assn. (conf. trach chmn., presenter), Beta Gamma Sigma (v.p. U. Tex. chpt. 1973-74, pres. chpt. 1974-75), Phi Kappa Phi. Office: U Tex Arlington PO Box 19125 Arlington TX 76019-0001

WITT, THOMAS ROY, surgeon; b. Bryn Mawr, Pa., Jan. 7, 1950; BA in Psychology, Duke U., 1971; MD, Northwestern U., 1975. Intern Rush-Presbyn.-St. Lukes Hosp., Chgo., 1975-76, resident surgery, 1976-80; fellow surg. oncology Sloan-Kettering Cancer Ctr., N.Y.C., 1980-82; assoc. attending dept. gen. surgery Rush-Presbyn. St. Luke's Hosp., Chgo., 1986; assoc. prof. surgery Rush Med. Coll., 1988. Mem. ACS, AMA, Am. Soc. Clin. Oncology, Soc. Surg. Oncology, Soc. Head and Neck Surgeons. Office: 1725 W Harrison St Ste 409 Chicago IL 60612-3836 E-mail: trwitt50@aol.com.

WITT, TOM, economics researcher, educator; b. Borger, Tex., Apr. 22, 1944; s. Eugene Thomason and Helen C. (Hathaway) W.; m. Grethe A. Myles, Mar. 4, 1976. BA, Okla. State U., 1966; MA, Washington U., St. Louis, 1968, PhD, 1974. Asst. prof. dept. econs. W.Va. U., Morgantown, 1970-75, assoc. prof. dept. econs., 1975-80, acting asst. dean Grad. Sch., 1977-78, exec. dir. Bur. Bus. Rsch., 1985—, dir. Ctr. Econs. Rsch., 1985—, acting assoc. dean Coll. Bus. and Econs., 1985-86, assoc. dean rsch. and outreach Coll. Bus. and Econs., 1994—. Cons. Nat. Regulatory Rsch. Inst., Columbia, Ohio, 1980-81, Am. Electric Power, 1995—, Allegheny Power, 1997—, exec. legis. br. Govt. W.Va., 1985—; cons., expert witness W.Va. Human Rights Commn., Charleston, 1984; expert witness W.Va. Atty. Gen., 1987-88, Ashland Oil, 1992-93. Author: Power from the Appalachians, 1989, also monographs; co-editor: West Virginia in the Nineties: Policies for Econ. Progress; econs. columnist The State Jour., Charleston; contbr. articles to profl. jours. Pres. Cheat Canyon Park Homeowners, Morgantown, 1979-87, Monongalia Arts Ctr., 1980-81; bd. dirs., treas. Friends of W.Va. Pub. Radio, Charleston, 1985-93, chmn., 1989-91; sec.-treas. Cheat Neck Pub. Svc. Dist., 1989-95, Main Street Morgantown, 1994—; mem. Monongalia County Econ. Devel. Authority, 1994—. Mem. Am. Econ. Assn., Am. Statis. Assn., Regional Sci. Assn., So.

Econ. Assn., Assn. for Univ. Bus. and Econ. Rsch. (pres. 2000-2001). Home: 3202 Deerfield Ct Morgantown WV 26508-8612 Office: Bureau of Bus & Econ Rsch WV U PO Box 6025 Morgantown WV 26506-6025 E-mail: twitt@wvu.edu.

WITT, WALTER FRANCIS, JR., lawyer; b. Richmond, Va., Feb. 18, 1933; s. Walter Francis and Evelyn Virginia (Riggleman) W.; m. Rosemary Winter, Sept. 5, 1964; children: Leslie Anne Millman, Walter Francis III. BS, U. Richmond, 1954, JD, 1966. Bar: Va. 1966, D.C. 1974. Assoc. Hunton and Williams, Richmond, 1966-74, ptnr., 1974—. Contbr. articles to profl. jours. 1st lt. U.S. Army, 1955-57. Mem. ABA (chmn. real property com. sect. gen. practice 1995-2000, Va. Bar Assn., Richmond Bar Assn., D.C. Bar Assn., Phi Beta Kappa, Phi Delta Phi. Home: 8901 Tresco Rd Richmond VA 23229-7725 Office: Riverfront Plaza East Twr 451 E Byrd St Richmond VA 23219-3833

WITTBRODT, EDWIN STANLEY, consultant, former bank executive, former air force officer; b. Flint, Mich., Aug. 13, 1918; s. Stanley Frank and Marie (Ross) W.; m. Joan Helen Miller, Apr. 22, 1950; children: Stephanie Rita, Candace Lee, Edwin Stanley. Student, Gen. Motors Inst. Tech., 1936-38, Grad. Sch. Dept. Agr., 1950-51, Indsl. Coll. Armed Forces, 1961-62, George Washington U., 1962, U. So. Calif., 1963-64. Joined U.S. Army, 1941, commd. 2d lt., 1942; advanced through grades to brig. gen. USAF, 1968, various assignments U.S., 1941-49; budget officer Hdqrs. USAF, 1949-53, 56-61; dir. budget and acctg. Hdqrs. N.E. Air Command, Nfld., 1953-56; comptroller space systems div. Los Angeles, 1962-64; comptroller aero., systems div. Wright-Patterson AFB, 1964-66; asst. comptroller USAF, 1966-67; dir. acctg. and fin. Hdqrs. USAF, 1967-68; asst. comptroller air force for acctg. and fin., comdr. Air Force Acctg. and Fin. Ctr., Denver, 1968-71; v.p. systems Cen. Bank Denver, 1971-81, v.p. info. resources mgmt., 1981-84. Dir. Computer Congenerics Corp. Colo., Hasa Corp. Co-chmn. Combined Fed. Campaign, Denver, 1968-87; Hon. dir. USO, Denver, 1968-71, mem. council, 1971-87. Decorated D.S.M., Legion of Merit, Soldier's medal, Commendation medal with oak leaf cluster; recipient Gen. Jimmy Doolittle Disting. Fellow award, Flint No. Alumni Assn. Disting. Fellow award, 1990, Treas. Dept. Pioneer in Elec. Commerce award, 1995. Mem. Am. Soc. Mil. Comptrollers (past pres. Washington chpt., nat. v.p. 1968-70, pres. Denver chpt. 1971-72), Assn. Govt. Accountants, Assn. Mil. Banks (dir. 1974-84), Am. Inst. Banking, Denver C. of C. (chmn. mil. affairs com. 1979-82), Aurora C. of C. (def. coun. 1987—), Air Force Assn. (v.p. N. Colo. 1971-72, pres. Silver and Gold chpt. 1972-73, state treas. 1976-83, pres. Mile High chpt. 1987-88) Clubs: Columbine Country. Home: 10 Niblick Ln Columbine Valley CO 80123 *I have adopted two attitudes that I believe assisted me in all of my undertakings: (1)— that of being what I call a "responsible non-conformist" and (2)— "no problems— just opportunities."*.

WITTCOFF, HAROLD AARON, chemist; b. Marion, Ind., July 3, 1918; s. Morris and Bessie (Pruss) W.; m. Dorothy Brochin, 1946; 2 sons AB magna cum laude, DePauw U., 1940; PhD, Northwestern U., 1943; grad., Advanced Mgmt. Program, Harvard U., 1964. From mem. staff to v.p., dir. chem. R&D Gen. Mills, Inc., Mpls., 1943—69, v.p., dir. corp. rsch., 1969—79; dir. R & D Koor Chems., Beer Sheva, Israel, 1979-82; dir. process evaluation and rsch. planning Chem Systems, Tarrytown, N.Y., 1982-85; sci. adviser NEXANT/Chem Systems, White Plains, NY, 1985—; adj. prof. chemistry U. Minn., 1973-82. Vis. prof. Chulalongkorn U., Thailand, 1995—; adj. prof. chemistry Weizmann Inst., Israel, 1979—. Author: The Phosphatides, 1951, Industrial Organic Chemistry: A Perspective 2 vols. 1980; Pharmaceutical Chemicals in Perspective, 1989, Industrial Organic Chemicals, 1996, 2nd edit., 2004, Organic Chemistry Principles and Industrial Practice; patentee in field. Recipient Minn. award Am. Chem. Soc., 1976 Mem. Phi Beta Kappa, Sigma Xi, Phi Eta Sigma. Home: Box 307 Apt 4G-I Scarborough Manor Scarborough NY 10510 Office Phone: 914-609-0330. E-mail: hwittcoff@nexant.com.

WITTE, MARLYS HEARST, internist, educator; b. N.Y.C., 1934; MD, NYU Sch. Medicine, 1960. Intern N.C. Meml. Hosp., Chapel Hill, 1960-61; resident Bellevue Hosp. Ctr., N.Y.C., 1961-63; fellow NYU Hosp., St. Louis, 1965-69; instr. Washington U., St. Louis, 1965-69; prof. surgery U. Ariz., 1969—; attending internist Ariz. Health Sci. Ctr., Tucson, 1965-69, 69—. Mem. AAAS, AMA, Alpha Omega Alpha. Office: U Ariz Coll Medicine PO Box 245063 1501 N Campbell Ave Tucson AZ 85724-0001

WITTE, MERLIN MICHAEL, oil company executive; b. Los Angeles, Mar. 28, 1926; s. Anthony A. and Julia (Macke) W.; m. Donna Patricia Hurth, Jan. 22, 1949; children: James Anthony, Daniel Michael, Catherine Ann, Michael Leon, Robert Joseph, Joseph William, Anne Marie, William Benson, Janet Mary. BA, Loyola U., Los Angeles, 1949. With IRS, U.S. Treasury Dept., 1949-51; investment, tax mgr. McCulloch Motors Corp., also Robert P. McCulloch, 1951-55; pres., gen. mgr., dir. McCulloch Oil Corp., Los Angeles, 1956-80; pres., dir. Merlin Assocs., Inc., Los Angeles, 1980—, M.M. Witte & Assocs., Inc., Los Angeles, 1980—; mgr., chief exec. United Oil Producers, Los Angeles, 1984-86. Bd. dirs. Kent Fin. Svcs., Inc., Search Exploration, Inc.; bd. dirs., chmn. McCulloch Energy, Inc., 1991-95; co-chmn. The Am. Drilling Co., L.L.C., 1995-98; dir., CEO South Coast Oil Corp., 1996—. Mem. bd. regents Loyola Marymount U., L.A., 1991-97. Served with USAAF, 1944-45. Mem. Ind. Oil and Gas Producers Assn., Ind. Petroleum Assn., Western, West Cen. Tex. oil and gas assns., Town Hall, Bel-Air Country Club (pres. 1990-91), PGA West Golf Club.

WITTE, OWEN NEIL, microbiologist, molecular biologist, educator; b. Bklyn., May 17, 1949; BS, Cornell U., 1971; MD, Stanford U., 1976. Predoctoral fellow Stanford U. Med. Sch., Palo Alto, Calif., 1971-76, MIT Ctr. Cancer Rsch., Cambridge, Mass., 1976-80; asst. prof. UCLA Dept. Microbiology, Molecular Genetics, 1980-82, assoc. prof., 1982-86, prof., 1986—, pres.'s chair in devel. immunology, 1989—; investigator UCLA Howard Hughes Med. Inst., 1986—; prof., microbiology & immunology UCLA Sch. Medicine, 1996—. Am. Cancer Soc. faculty scholar, 1982-87; recipient Faculty award UCLA, 1990, award in basic cancer rsch. Milken Family Med. Found., 1990, Richard and Hinda Rosenthal Found. award Am. Assn. Cancer Rsch., 1991, William Dameshek prize ASH, 1993; Outstanding Investigator grantee Nat. Cancer Inst., 50th Anniversary Commemorative award, Leukemia Soc. of Amer., 1999. Fellow Am. Acad. Arts and Scis., 1996, Am. Acad. Microbiology, 1997; mem. NAS, 1997, Inst. Medicine, 2004. E-mail: owenw@microbio.ucla.edu.

WITTE, PEGGY, metal products executive; m. Bill Witte. Chair, CEO, pres. Royal Oak Mines, Inc., Kirkland, Wash. Office: Royal Oak Mines Inc 501 Lakeview Dr Kirkland WA 98033

WITTEBOLS, JAMES HENRY, communications educator; b. Mt. Clemens, Mich., Aug. 22, 1955; s. Henry and Agatha (Jarczynski) Wittebols. BA, Ctrl. Mich. U., 1977; MA, Wash. State U., 1979, PhD, 1983. Sr. rsch. assoc. Coun. of Chief State Sch. Officers, Washington, 1986—87; prof. of communication studies Niagara U., Niagara University, NY, 1987—. Mem. Symposium on Democracy Kent State U. Author: (book) Watching M*A*S*H, Watching America: A Social History of the 1972-1983 Television Series, 1998; contbr. articles to profl. jours. Mem. Western NY Peace Ctr., Buffalo, 1991—94. Mem.: Union For Dem. Comms. (coord. steering com.), Internat. Comm. Assn., Assn. for Edn. in Journalism and Mass Comm.

WITTELS, BARNABY CAESAR, lawyer, writer; b. Phila., Mar. 28, 1948; s. David G. and Beatrice Tanya (Graitor) Wittels; m. Heidi Jo Linsk, Sept. 8, 1974 (div. Aug. 1997); children: Kate Sophie, William David; m. Mary M. Labaree, Sept. 20, 1998. BA cum laude, Temple U., 1970; MA in Pol. Sci., Boston U., 1972, JD, 1975. Bar: Pa. 1975, U.S. Dist. Ct. (ea. dist.) Pa. 1985, U.S. Dist. Ct. Appeals (2d, 3d and 4th cirs.) 1986. Asst. defender Defender Assn. Phila., 1975-80; law clk. to Hon. Stanley Kubacki Ct. Common Pleas Phila. County, 1980-84; ptnr. Wittels, Newman & Bomstein, Phila., 1980-82; assoc. LaCheen & Alva, Phila., 1982-86; ptnr. LaCheen & Assoc., Phila., 1986—2003, LeCheen, Dixon, Wittels & Greenburg, Phila., 2003—. Advisor Temple U. Parliamentary Debate Team, 2004—. Contbr. columns in newspapers. Chair N.W. Victim Svcs., Phila., 1981—84, mem. counsel, 1984—90, bd. dirs., 1983—90, chair, 1997—2003, founding mem., mem. bd. dirs. counsel, 2003—; baseball coach Chestnut Hill Fathers Club, 1985—98, commr., 1991—93, 1992—98; vol. Lawyers Concerned for Lawyers, 2003—; committeeman 21st divsn. Dems., Phila., 1985—90; active various polit. and jud. campaigns, 1980—; mem. exec. com. N.W. Interfaith Movement, 1985—86. Mem.: NACDL, Phila. Bar Found. (Apothaker award 1983), Pa. Bar Assn., Phila. Bar Assn. (mem. fee dispute com. 1996—, mem. com. to elect good judges 1987—88, mem. lawyers assistance com. 2003—), Pa. Assn. Criminal Def. Lawyers. Jewish. Avocations: writing, baseball, football, reading, woodworking. Office: LaCheen Dixon Wittels & Greenberg Ste 200 2525 Locust St Philadelphia PA 19102 Fax: 215-735-4649. E-mail: barnabyw@aol.com.

WITTEMYER, JOHN, lawyer; b. Boulder, Colo., Dec. 19, 1939; s. Leonard and Beatrice Augusta (Dickhut) W.; m. Nancy Jean Vincent, June 6, 1964; children— Jon Vincent, Christopher Glen, Luke Leonard. B.S.C.E., U. Colo., 1962, B.S. in Bus., 1962, LL.B., 1965. Bar: Colo. 1965, Alaska 1965. Law clk. U.S. Supreme Ct. Alaska, 1965; dist. atty. 1st Jud. Dist. Alaska, Juneau, 1966-67; sole practice, Boulder, 1967-73; ptnr. Moses, Wittemyer, Harrison & Woodruff, P.C., Boulder, 1973—; gen. counsel Platte River Power Authority, 1973—2002; chmn. bd., chief exec. officer Crowley land and Devel. Co., subs. Aetna Casualty and Surety Co., Ordway, Colo., 1970-75. Mem. ABA, Colo. Bar Assn., Boulder Bar Assn., Colo. Cattlemen's Assn. Republican. Methodist. Club: Country. Home: Sunshine Canyon PO Box 4575 Boulder CO 80306-4575 Office: PO Box PO Box 1440 Boulder CO 80306-1440

WITTEN, ANITA, artist, editor; b. N.Y., May 22, 1930, d. Victor G. Reis and Gertrude C. Mattlage; m. Eugene Witten, Nov. 18, 1953, children: Timothy, Matthew. BA, Columbia Univ., N.Y.C., 1954; artist tng., Art Student League, N.Y.C., 1953; MA, SUNY, Albany, N.Y., 1987. Freelance artist self employed, NY, 1960—2003. Co-found. Coop. Gallery, Cambridge, NY, 1981—93. Contbr. columns in newspapers; exhibitions include collages, watercolors Gallery 668, Boston, Albany Ctr. Gallery, Weeden Gallery, So. Vt. Coll., Rice Gallery-Albany Inst., Libr Galleries, and group shows, Represented in permanent collections. Co-found. Village Food Co-op, Cambridge, NY, 1976—; pres. bd. Literacy Vol., Washington County, 2001—02; sec. Friends of Libr., Salem, NY, 1997—; bd. mem. Planned Parenthood, So. Adirondacks, 1992—96. Home: 131 Hickory Hill Rd Shushan NY 12873

WITTEN, DAVID MELVIN, radiology educator; b. Trenton, Mo., Aug. 16, 1926; s. Buford Isom and Mary Louise (Melvin) W.; m. Netta Lee Watkins, Dec. 23, 1950; children— David Melvin, II, Michael Lee. Student, Trenton Jr. Coll., 1943-44, 46-47; AB, Washington U., St. Louis, 1950, MD, 1954; MS in Radiology, U. Minn., 1960. Diplomate: Am. Bd. Radiology. Intern Virginia Mason Hosp., Seattle, 1954-55; practice medicine specializing in family medicine Trenton, Mo., 1955-57; fellow in radiology Mayo Clinic/Mayo Found., Rochester, Minn., 1957-60; cons. in diagnostic roentgenology Mayo Clinic, 1960-70; instr. Mayo Grad. Sch. Medicine, Rochester, 1960-66, asst. prof. radiology, 1966-70; pvt. practice medicine specializing in radiology Aberdeen, Wash., 1970-71; clin. assoc. prof. U. Wash., 1970-71; prof. diagnostic radiology, chmn. dept. diagnostic radiology U. Ala., Birmingham, 1971-82; diagnostic radiologist in chief Univ. Hosp., Birmingham, 1971-82; prof., chmn. dept. radiology U. Mo., Columbia, 1982-87, prof. emeritus, 1987—, interim chmn. dept. radiology, 1998-99. Pres. U. Ala. Health Services Found., 1973-75 Author: Atlas of Tumor Radiology-The Breast, 1969, Clinical Urography, 1970, 77; contbr. articles on radiology of breast cancer, urologic and gastrointestinal disease to profl. jours.; mem. editorial bd. Am. Jour. Roentgenology, 1976-87, Applied Radiology, 1978-87, Urologic Radiology, 1979-87, Radiographics, 1983-87. Served with USNR, 1944-46. Fellow Am. Coll. Radiology; mem. AAAS, AMA, Radiol. Soc. N.Am., Am. Roentgen Ray Soc., Soc. Genitourinary Radiology (pres. 1981-82), Soc. Uroradiology (gold medal 2003), Assn. Univ. Radiologists, Mo. Radiol. Soc. (pres. 1988-89), Mo. State Med. Assn., Can. Assn. Radiologists (hon.), Audubon Soc. (editor The Bluebird (Mo.) chpt. 1990-98). Home: 601 W Covered Bridge Rd Columbia MO 65203-9562 Office: Univ Mo Health Scis Ctr 1 Hospital Dr Columbia MO 65201-5276 Personal E-mail: dmw8161926@tranquility.net.

WITTEN, EDWARD, mathematical physicist; b. Balt., Aug. 26, 1951; s. Louis Witten; m. Chiara Nappi; 3 children. BA in history, Brandeis U., 1971; MA, Princeton U., 1974, PhD, 1976, Brandeis U., 1988, Hebrew U. of Jerusalem, 1993, Columbia U., 1996, U. Southern Calif., 2004. Postdoctoral fellow Harvard U., 1976—77, jr. fellow, 1977—80; prof. physics Princeton U., NJ, 1980—87; prof. Sch. Natural Scis, Inst. for Advanced Study, Princeton, NJ, 1987—; Charles Simonyi prof. Princeton U., NJ, 1997—. Vis. prof. Calif. Inst. Tech., 1999—2001. Contbr. articles to mags. and profl. jours.; co-author (with M.B. Green and J.H. Schwarz): Superstring Theory, Vol. 1 and 2, Cambridge Univ. Press. Bd. dirs. Americans for Peace Now, 1992—. MacArthur Fellow, 1982; recipient Einstein medal Einstein Soc. Berne, Switzerland, 1985, Phys. and Math. Sci. award N.Y. Acad. Sci., 1985, Dirac medal Internat. Ctr. Theoretical Physics, 1985, Alan Waterman award NSF 1986, Fields Medal, Internat. Union of Mathematicians, 1990, Madison medal, Princeton Univ., 1992, NJ Pride award, 1996, Award of the Golden Plate, Am. Acad. of Achievement, 1997, Klein medal, Stockholm U., 1998, Dannie Heineman prize, Am. Inst. of Physics, 1998, Nemmers prize in Math., Northwestern U., 2000, Clay Rsch. award, Clay Math. Inst., 2001, Shalom award, Americans for Peace Now, 2002, Nat. Medal of Science, 2003. Fellow: Am. Philosophical Soc., Am. Phys. Soc., Am. Acad. Arts & Scis., NAS; mem.: Acad. of Sciences of Paris (assoc.). Office: Inst for Advanced Study Sch Natural Scis Einstein Dr Princeton NJ 08540-4920

WITTEN, LOUIS, physics educator; b. Balt., Apr. 13, 1921; s. Abraham and Bessie (Perman) W.; m. Lorraine Wollach, Mar. 27, 1949 (dec. 1987); children: Edward, Celia, Matthew, Jesse; m. Francis L. White, Jan. 2, 1992. B.E., Johns Hopkins U., 1941, PhD, 1951; BS, NYU, 1944. Research assoc. Princeton U., N.J., 1951-53; research assoc. U. Md., College Park, 1953-54; staff scientist Lincoln Lab., MIT, 1954-55; assoc. dir. Martin Marietta Research Lab., Balt., 1955-68; prof. physics U. Cin., 1968-91, prof. emeritus, 1991—. Trustee Gravity Research Found. Editor: Gravitation: An Introduction to Current Research, 1962, Relativity: Procs. of Relative Conf. in Midwest of 1969, Symposium on Asymptotic Structure of Space-Time, 1976; patentee in field; contbr. numerous articles to sci. jours. Served to 1st lt. USAF, 1942-46 Fulbright lectr. Weitzmann Inst. Scis., Rehovot, Israel, 1963-64 Fellow Am. Phys. Soc.; mem. Am. Math. Soc., Internat. Astron. Union, AAAS. Office: Univ Cincinnati Dept Physics Cincinnati OH 45221-0011 Business E-Mail: witten@physics.uc.edu.

WITTENBERG, JON ALBERT, accountant; b. Valparaiso, Ind., Mar. 22, 1939; s. Fred E. and Elizabeth (DeWaal) W.; m. Joann S. Zachwieja, May 13, 1967; children: Brad, Glen, Pam. BS, Ind. U., 1961. CPA, Ill. Auditor Ernst & Young, Chgo., 1961-66; fin. analyst Amoco Chems., Chgo., 1966-69; contr. Nat. Van Lines, Broadview, Ill., 1969-76, Consol. Millinerey, Chgo., 1976—. Mem. Am. Inst. CPA's, Ill. Soc. CPA's, Inst. Mgmt. Accts. Home: 1297 W New Britton Dr Hoffman Estates IL 60195-1764 Office: Consol Millinerey Co 18 S Michigan Ave Ste 605 Chicago IL 60603-3283

WITTENBORN, DALE, advertising executive; BA, St. Ambrose Coll. Mgr. creative svcs. Hallmark Cards; co-CEO Kuhn & Wittenborn, Kansas City, Mo., 1978—. Pres. Friends of the Zoo, Kansas City; chmn. Kansas City Coun. Bd. of Govs. Am. Assn. Advt. Agys.; bd. dirs. St. Luke's Hosp. Stroke Com. Named Advt. Exec. of Yr., Kansas City Ad Club, 1997; recipient Up and Comers award, 2000. Office: 2405 Grand Blvd Kansas City MO 64108-2519

WITTENBRINK, BONIFACE LEO, priest; b. Evansville, Ill., June 30, 1914; s. Max C. and Catherine Rose (Pautler) W. PhL, Gregorian U., Rome, 1939; STL, Ottawa (Can.) U., 1943; MA, Cath. U. Am., 1947. Ordained priest Oblates of Mary Immaculate, Roman Cath. Ch., 1941. Instr. Latin, logic, history and religion St. Henry's Coll., Belleville, Ill., 1943-48; instr., registrar, prin. high sch. dept. Coll. of Our Lady of the Ozarks, Carthage, Mo., 1948-52; founding dir. King's House of Retreats, Buffalo, Minn., 1952-53; mission procurator Roman Cath. Ch., St. Paul, 1955-56, 59-62; prin. Alemany High Sch. for Boys, Oblate Western Province, San Fernando, Calif., 1956-59; permanent sec. Conf. Maj. Superiors of Men, Washington, 1963-69; exec. dir., sec. Found. for Community Creativity, Washington, 1970-71; founder, dir., then dir. devel. Radio Info. Svc. for Blind and Handicapped, Belleville, 1972-84; pres., then local dir. Friends of Eye Rsch., Boston, 1983-87; exec. v.p. Citizens for Eye Rsch., Belleville, 1987—. Pres. Oblate Ednl. Assn., St. Paul, 1961-62; sci. adv. bd. Nat. Acad. Child Devel., 1984-86; mem. com. Eye Experience St. Louis, 1984; adv. bd. Welfare of the Blind, Inc., 1984—; adv. coun. svcs. for print-handicapped Nat. Pub. Radio, 1976-77; active Internat. Christian Leadership, 1968-72; bd. dirs. LOGOS Translators; ptnr. CBMI. Bd. dirs. Technoserve, 1968-72, Internat. Book Svc., 1969-72; vol. Ill. Literacy Project, 1989-90; founding charter mem., bd. dirs. Washington Workshops Found.; mem. Vision Awards Dinner Com., 1998—. Recipient RPI Internat. Vision award, 27th Annual Vision Awards, Agrama Harmony Gold and Light award, 2000, Beverly Hills, Calif. Mem. Madison County Assn. Blind, Mo. Coun. Blind, Am. Coun. of Blind (ednl. radio com. 1974-76), Am. Found. for Blind (radio talking book com. 1973-76), Inst. for Study of Econ. Systems (bd. dirs. 1971-72), Ednl. Communications Assn., Coun. for Dept. of Peace, Wycliffe Bible Translators Assn., Vols. for Internat. Tech. Assistance, Ill. Radio Info. Svc., Soc. Internat. Devel., UN Assn., Rotary Internat. (Paul Harris fellow), Belleville Econ. Progress, Eagles, KC, Press Club St. Louis, Am. Assn. Ret. Persons. Avocations: reading, travel. Home: 200 N 60th St Belleville IL 62223-3951

WITTENBRINK, JEFFREY SCOTT, lawyer; b. Cairo, Ill., May 24, 1960; s. Howard Samuel and Cherie Ellen (Martin) W.; m. Tamara Inez Parker, Aug. 5, 1989; children: Charlotte Jane, Jeffrey Scott Jr. BA, La. State U., 1984, JD, 1987. Bar: La. 1988, US Dist. Ct. (ea. and mid. dists.) La. 1988, US Dist. Ct. (we. dist.) La. 1989, US Ct. Appeals (5th cir.) 1989, US Supreme Ct. 1996. Law clk. to Judge William H. Brown, 19th Jud. Dist. Ct., Baton Rouge, 1987-88; assoc. Roy, Kiesel, Aaron & Tucker, Baton Rouge, 1988-91, Winston G. DeCuir & Assocs., Baton Rouge, 1991-93; pvt. practice Wittenbrink Law Firm, Baton Rouge, 1993—. Arbitrator Baton Rouge City Ct., 1993—; instr. CPCU's, Baton Rouge, 1991, Office Emergency Planning State of La., 1993; bd. dir. Capital Area Legal Svc., 2000—. Contbr. articles to Around the Bar legal newsletter, 1987—. Coach debate team Cath. HS, Baton Rouge, 1987-91, mock trial team Baton Rouge HS, 1989-93; treas. Ingleside United Meth. Ch., Baton Rouge, 1991-92, trustee, bd. dir., 1991-2001, chair pastor-parish com., 1992-2000, lay leader, 2001; mem., lectr. La. Vol. Lawyers for Arts, Baton Rouge, 1988-89; bd. dir. La. Crafts Coun., Baton Rouge, 1990. Mem. ABA, La. Bar Assn., Baton Rouge Bar Assn. (mem. newsletter com. 1987—, vol. indigent panel 1992, chair CLE 1992—, chmn. membership com. 1993, chair Law Expo com. 1998, chair family law sect. 2002, ex officio bd. dir. 2002, Pres.'s award 1993, Triple Century award 2001), Dean Henry George McMahon Am. Inn of Ct. (barrister, reporter 1993-95), Cortana Kiwanis (bd. dir. 1994-97, pres. 1998-99, Lt. Gov. 2001-2002, Kiwanis Internat., La.-Miss.-W.Tenn. Dist. Divn. 8-B). Avocations: photography, fencing, writing. Office: 533 Europe St Baton Rouge LA 70802-6408 E-mail: jwbrink@aol.com.

WITTES, ROBERT E. physician, science foundation director; b. N.Y.C., Mar. 20, 1943; married; 3 children. AB magna cum laude, Harvard U., 1964, MD cum laude, 1968. Intern in medicine Beth Israel Hosp., Boston, 1968-69, resident, 1969-70; rsch. assoc. lab. biochemistry Nat. Cancer Inst., NIH, Bethesda, Md., 1970-72; fellow in med. oncology Meml. Hosp., 1972-73, clin. asst. physician med. oncology svc., 1973-74, 74-75; physician to outpatients N.Y. Hosp., N.Y.C., 1974-76; asst., then assoc. attending physician solid tumor svc. Meml. Hosp., 1975-83, asst. chief, 1979-83; assoc. dir. cancer therapy evaluation program Nat. Cancer Inst., NIH, Bethesda, 1983-88, chief medicine br. clin. oncology program, 1990-95, dir. divsn. cancer treatment, diagnosis and ctrs., 1995—2002, dep. dir. extramural sci., 1997—2002; Physician in Chief Memorial Sloan-Kettering Cancer Center, 2002—. Asst. in medicine, Harvard U. Sch. Medicne, 1969-70; instr. medicine Georgetown U. Sch. Medicine, Washington, 1970-72; fellow in medicine, Cornell U. Med. Coll., 1972-74, instr. 1974-75, asst. prof., 1975-79, assoc. prof., 1980-83; rsch. assoc. Sloan-Kettering Inst., 1975-83; vis. physician Walter Reed Army Med. Ctr., Washington, 1987-88. Mem. editorial bd. Jour. clin. Oncology, 1983-86, Internat. Jour. Radiation Oncology, Biology and physis, 1987—, Am. Jour. clin. Oncology, 1985—, Cancer Investigation, 1983—, Current Opinion in Oncology, 1988—; editor-in-chief Cancer Treatment Reports, 1983-87, Primry Care and Cancer, 1982—, NCI Monographs, 1986-88, Jour. Nat. Cancer Inst., 1988, Oncology, 1987—. With USPHS. Fellow ACP; mem. AAAS, Am. Assn. Cancer Rsch., Am. Fedn. for Clin. Rsch., Am. Soc. Clin. Oncology, Internat. Assn. for Study of Lung Cancer, Soc. Head and Neck Surgeons (cons.). Office: Meml Sloan-Kettering Cancer Ctr 1275 York Ave New York NY 10021-0001

WITTHUHN, BURTON ORRIN, retired university official; b. Allentown, Pa., Aug. 22, 1934; s. Ray Arthur and Mae Marcella (Kline) W.; m. Patricia King, June 24, 1961; children: Jonathan, Andrew. BS, Kutztown (Pa.) U., 1956; MEd, Pa. State U., 1962, PhD, 1968. Tchr. Allentown (Pa.) Pub. Schs., 1956-63; teaching asst., assoc. Pa. State U., University Park, 1963-66, rsch. asst., 1965-66; asst. prof. Ohio State U., Columbus, 1967-70; prof., chmn. dept. geography Edinboro (Pa.) State Coll., 1970-79, assoc. v.p. acad. affairs, 1980-83; provost, v.p. acad. affairs Edinboro Univ. of Pa., 1984-88, Western Ill. U., Macomb, 1988-93, acting pres., 1993, provost, v.p. acad. affairs, prof. geography, 1994—2002, ret., 2002. Vis. rsch. prof. Nat. Taiwan Normal U., 1978; cons. Project Africa/Carnegie-Mellon U., Pitts., 1967-70, 92, 87, 95; mem. mid. states periodic rev. team, Phila., 1986—; mem. mid. states evaluation team in conjunction with Am. Optometric Assn., 1987; mem. evaluation team Pa. Dept. Edn., 1988; mem. accreditation team Am. Optometric, 1990—; evaluator Higher Learning Commn. North Cen. Assn., 1994—; examiner Lincoln Found. for Bus. Excellence, 1996-2000; vice-chmn. Quad Cities Grad. Ctr., 1991-2000; mem. nat. screening com. for Africa, Inst. of Internat. Edn., 1994-96. Co-author: Discovery in Geography, 1976; co-author: So You Want to Go to College: 50 Questions to Ponder, Strategies for Timely Degree Completion: Connecting the Parts, Strategies for Timely Degree Completion: Myths and Realities, Technology: Bridge or Barrier To More Timely Degree Completion?, 1998;; mem. editl. bd. Pa. Geographer, Chronicle of CQI; contbr. chpts. to books. Mem. Edinboro Planning & Zoning Commn., 1973-77, McDonough County Tuberculosis Sanitorium Bd., 2003-; vol. Habitat Humanity, Loaves and Fishes, McDonough Dist. Hosp. Recipient Disting. Alumnus award Kutztown U., 1990; Fulbright Hays fellow, Ethiopia, Kenya, Uganda, 1965. Mem. Nat. Coun. Geog. Edn. (exec. bd. 1977-80, mem. award com. for region IV 1981), Pa. Coun. Geog. Edn. (exec. sec. 1976-79, pres. 1975-76, Outstanding Prof. award 1978), Rotary (pres. Macomb club 1998-99, Edinboro club 1972-73), State Univ. Annutants Assn. (pres. Macomb Chptr. 2003—). Methodist. Avocations: reading, golf, photography, volunteering. Home: 1106 Bayberry Ln Macomb IL 61455-3518

WITTICH, JOHN JACOB, retired academic administrator, business executive; b. Huntley, Ill., Nov. 13, 1921; s. John and Eva (Karl) W.; m. Leah Elliott, Apr. 2, 1944; children: Karen Ann Zvonar, Jane Ellen Tock, John Elliott. BA, DePauw U., 1943, LLD (hon.), 1971; MA, U. N.Mex., 1949; PhD, Stanford U., 1952; LHD (hon.), Ill. Coll., 1979; DPS (hon.), MacMurray Coll., 1980. Tchr. Albuquerque H.S., 1948-49; tchg. asst. Stanford, 1949-51; asst. prof. psychology Coll. of Pacific, Stockton, Calif., 1951-52; dean of admissions and fin. aid, assoc. prof. DePauw U., Greencastle, Ind., 1952-61; exec. dir. Coll. Center of Finger Lakes, Corning, N.Y., 1961-63, Coll. Student Personnel Inst., Claremont, Calif., 1963-68; adj. prof., dir. grad. studies in student pers. Claremont Grad. Sch., 1963-68; pres. MacMurray Coll., Jacksonville, Ill., 1968-80; dir. Fla. Assn. Colls. and Univs., 1980-84; dir. higher edn. program Stetson U., 1981-88; v.p. Capital Formation Counselors, Inc., Belleaire Bluffs, Fla., 1983—. Contbr. articles to profl. jours. Exec. com. Divsn. Higher Edn., Ctrl. Ill. Conf. of United Meth. Ch., 1968-80; exec. com. Fedn. Independent Ill. Colls. and Univs. and Assoc. Colls. Ill.; mem. non-pub. adv. com. Ill. Bd. Higher Edn., 1972-78; mem. Nat. Merit Scholarship Selection Com., 1956, 61; cons. Calif. Gov.'s Conf. on Edn., 1965, on Youth, 1966; trustee Fla. Endowment for Humanities, 1982-85; presdl. counsellor Stetson U., 1987—; bd. dirs. DeLand House Next Door, 1990-94; citizens adv. com. West Volusia

Hosp. Authority, 1992-2002, vice-chmn., 2001-02; rsch. project evaluator for human subjects regional office U.S. FDA, 2003—. With USMC, 1943-46, PTO. Recipient De Pauw Achievement award, 1969, Alumni citation DePauw U., 1994; Rockefeller fellow Aspen Inst. for Humanistic Studies, 1979. Mem. APA, Am. Coll. Pers. Assn. (commn. chmn.), Nat. Assn. Coll. Admissions Counselors (exec. bd. 1955-58), Cen. States Coll. Assn. (exec. com. 1969-77, sec.-treas. 1970-77), 4th Marine Divsn. Assn., Sigma Chi. Home: 918 Torchwood Dr Deland FL 32724-9407 E-mail: jwittich@totcom.com.

WITTIG, DAVID C. energy executive; BS in Bus. Adminstrn. & Econs., U. Kans., 1977. Analyst rsch. dept. H. O. Peet & Co., Inc., 1977-78, assoc. nat. individual sales, 1978-79, assoc. mergers and acquisitions, 1979-81, asst. v.p. mergers and acquisitions, 1981-83, v.p. mergers and acquisitions, 1983-86, mng. dir., head mergers and acquisitions, 1986-89; mng. dir., co-head investment banking Kidder Peabody & Co., Inc., 1989, mng. dir. mergers and acquisitions, 1989-91; mng. dir., co-head mergers and acquisitions Salomon Bros., Inc., 1991-95; exec. v.p. corp. strategy Western Resources, Topeka, 1995-96, pres., 1996-98, pres., CEO, 1998—, chmn., 1999—. Bd. dirs. Boys Harbor. Office: Western Resources Inc 818 S Kansas Ave Topeka KS 66612-1203 Fax: 785-575-6399.

WITTIG, RAYMOND SHAFFER, lawyer, intellectual property technology manager; b. Allentown, Pa., Dec. 13, 1944; s. Raymond Battie and Alice (Shaffer) Wittig; m. Beth Glover, June 21, 1975; children: Meaghan G., Allison G. BA, Pa. State U., 1966, MEd, 1968; JD, Dickinson Sch. Law, 1974. Bar: Pa. 1974, U.S. Ct. Appeals (DC cir.) 1978. Rsch. psychologist Intext Corp., Scranton, Pa., 1968; minority counsel Small Bus. Com., U.S. Ho. of Reps., Washington, 1975-84; pvt. practice Washington, 1984-92; tech. mgmt. group leader Geo-Ctrs., Inc., Newton Ctr., Mass., 1992—. Capt. U.S. Army, 1969—71. Mem.: ABA, AAAS, Assn. Univ. Tech. Mgrs., Am. Intellectual Property Law Assn., Fed. Lab. Consortium, Nat. Order Barristers, Licensing Execs. Soc. E-mail: wittigsall@verizon.net.

WITTLIFF, DANNY JOE, environmental engineer; b. Corpus Christi, Tex., Nov. 24, 1949; s. Joe Charles and Sarah Mary (Mitchell) W.; m. Donna Kay Covington, June 23, 1973 (div. 1991); children: Matthew Daniel, Juliana Prell; m. Manda Lee Rash, Jan. 24, 1998. BSME, So. Meth. U., 1972; MBA, U. Okla., 1975. Lic. profl. engr., Tex.; registered environ. mgr., environ. profl. Results engr. West Tex. Utilities, Abilene, 1981-85, plant engring. supr. Oklaunion Power Sta., 1985-90, environ. svcs. mgr. Abilene, 1991-95; chief engr. Tex. Natural Resource Conservation Commn., Austin, 1995—99; cons. engr. Naismith Engring. Inc., Austin, 1999—2001; v.p. and COO Hydro Processing LLC, Austin, 2001—02; pvt. practice Dan Wittliff Cons., PLLC, Austin, 2002—. Chair WTU United Way Campaign, Abilene, 1994-95. Col. USAFR, 1981—2002, with USAF, 1972-81. Mem. Tex. Soc. Profl. Engrs. (state water com. 1995—, Chpt. Young Engr. of Yr. 1985, past chpt. pres. 1994-95, state pres. 2002-03, vice chmn. Tex. engrs. task force on homeland security 2001—, Travis County Engr. of Yr. 1998), Soc. Am. Mil. Engrs., Armed Forces Com. Elec. Assn., Electric Reliability Coun. Tex. (chair waste task force 1992-95), Tex. Alliance for Minorities in Engring. (bd. dirs. 1996—2002). Methodist. Avocations: poetry, golf, basketball, fishing. Home and Office: 12410 Deer Trak Austin TX 78727-5744

WITTLINGER, TIMOTHY DAVID, lawyer; b. Dayton, Ohio, Oct. 12, 1940; s. Charles Frederick and Dorothy Elizabeth (Golden) W.; m. Diane Cleo Dominy, May 20, 1967; children: Kristine Elizabeth, David Matthew. BS in Math., Purdue U., 1962; JD with distinction, U. Mich., 1965. Bar: Mich. 1966, U.S. Dist. Ct. (ea. dist.) Mich. 1966, U.S. Ct. Appeals (6th cir.) 1968, U.S. Supreme Ct. 1971. Assoc. Clark Hill (formerly Hill Lewis), Detroit, 1965-72, ptnr., 1973—, head litigation dept., 1976-91, gen. counsel, 1997—, chief litigation officer, 1997—. Mem. profl. assistance com. U.S. Dist. Ct. (ea. dist.) Mich., 1981-82; mem. Mich. Supreme Ct. Com. to Evaluate Mediation Ct. Rule, 1997-98; author, lectr. Ctr. for Internat. Legal Studies, 1999—; mem. coll. fellows Ctr. Internat. Legal Studies, Salzburg, Austria. Mem. ho. of deps. Episc. Ch., N.Y.C., 1979—; vice chmn. Robert Whitaker Sch. Theology, 1983-87; sec. bd. trustees Episc. Ch., Diocese of Mich., Detroit, 1983—, sec. conv. Episc. Diocese of Mich., 1990—, ch. atty., 1997—, mem., sec. Episc. nat. econ. justice implementation com., 1988-95, mem. Episc. nat. exec. coun., 1991-97, mem. nat. audit com.; mem. Nat. Standing Commn. on Ministry Devel., 2000—; active Nat. Episc. Jubilee Ministry Com., Nat. Episc. Coalition for Social Witness and Justice, Fifth Province Episc. Ecclesiastical Ct. Appeal; mem. nat. audit com. Episcopal Ch.; bd. dirs. Episc. Student Found., U. Mich., 1990-93, 2000-2002; chair Grubb Inst. Behavioral Studies Ltd., Washington, 1986—; bd. dirs. Birmingham Village Playhouse, 2000—. Mem. ABA, State Bar Mich., Nat. Bd. Trial Advocacy (cert.), Engring. Soc. Detroit, Coll. of Fellows. Home: 736 N Glenhurst Dr Birmingham MI 48009-1143 Office: Clark Hill 500 Woodward Ave Ste 3500 Detroit MI 48226-3435 Office Phone: 313-965-8526.

WITTMAN, RANDY, professional basketball coach; m. Kathy Wittman; children: Ryan, Lauren. BS, Ind. U., 1983. With Wash. Bullets, 1983, Atlanta Hawks, from 1983; also with Sacramento Kings and Ind. Pacers; head coach Cleve. Cavaliers, 1999—. Office: Minnesota Timberwolves Target Center 600 1st Ave N Minneapolis MN 55403-1416

WITTMANN, DIETMAR H. surgery educator; b. Duisburg, Rhine, Germany, June 16, 1940; s. Harry E. Wittmann and Elisabeth (Moik) Le Danois; m. Heide-Marie Heitmann, 1967; children: Mark-Matthias, Annemarei. MD, Hamburg (Germany) U., 1970; PhD, Dusseldorf (Germany) U., 1972. Asst. prof. Hamburg (Germany) U., 1975-82, assoc. prof. surgery, 1982-88, Med. Coll. Wis., Milw., 1988-92, prof. surgery, 1992—2000; prof., dir. Colonna Inst. for Surg. Rsch., 2001—. Contbr. articles to profl. jours., chpts. to books. Mem. ACS, Am. Assn. Surgery of Trauma, Internat. Surg. Soc., German Surg. Assn., Surg. Infection Soc. Europe (founder, Disting. Svc. award 1994), Columbian Surg. Assn. (hon.), Brazilian Coll. Diestin Surgery (hon.). Roman Catholic. Personal E-mail: dhwittmann@yahoo.com.

WITTMER, JAMES FREDERICK, preventive medicine physician, educator; b. Carlinville, Ill., Dec. 30, 1932; s. Franklin Benjamin and Eva Caroline (Zihlman) W.; m. Juanita Lou Wilkey, June 29, 1962; children: Ellen, Carol, Nancy. MD, Washington U., St. Louis, 1957; MPH, Harvard U., 1961. Diplomate Am. Bd. Preventive Medicine. Intern U. Va. Hosp., Charlottesville, 1857-58; commd. capt. USAF, 1958, advanced through grades to col., 1971; ret., 1979; dean allied health U. Tex. Health Sci. Ctr., San Antonio, 1979-80; asst. med. dir. Conoco Oil Co., Ponca City, Okla., 1980-81; assoc. med. dir. Mobil Oil Corp., N.Y.C., 1981-83; dir. health, environ. and safety ITT, N.Y.C., 1983-95, corp. v.p., 1990-95. Clin. prof. medicine Cornell U. Med. Coll., N.Y.C., 1984—; lectr. environ. medicine NYU, N.Y.C., 1984—; adj. prof. U. Tex. Sch. Pub. Health, Houston, 1987—, prof. occupl. health, 1996-97; nat. coord. com. on clin. preventive svcs. USPHS, 1994-97; cons. office hearings and appeals U.S. Social Security Adminstrn., 1997-2003; cons. Met. Health Dist., San Antonio, Tex., 2002—. Mem. Pres.'s Com. on Employment People with Disabilities, Washington, 1986-2000, chmn. med. and ins. com., 1986-90. Fellow ACP, Am. Coll. Occupational and Environ. Medicine (bd. dirs. 1990-97, sec. 1992-94), Am. Coll. Preventive Medicine, Aerospace Med. Assn., N.Y. Acad. Medicine; mem. AMA, Tex. Occupational Med. Assn. Home and Office: 159 Sabine Rd Boerne TX 78006-6217 Office Phone: 830-537-4782. Business E-Mail: wittmer@gvtc.com.

WITTMEYER, RICHARD ARTHUR, management consulting company executive; b. Trenton, N.J., Oct. 23, 1947; s. Arthur A. and Martha (Rhoads) W.; children: Megan Elizabeth, Richard Arthur, Jr. BA in Psychology and Philosophy, Norwich U., 1969; postgrad., Assumption Coll., 1969-70; MBA in Human Resources Mgmt., Century U., 1986, PhD in Orgnl. Behavior and Mgmt., 1988. Dir. orgnl. devel. and human resources Gen. Tire & Rubber Co., Akron, Ohio, 1972-75; chmn. Wittmeyer & Assocs. Internat. Cons., 1975—; pres. Ctr. for Strategic Mgmt., 1998—. Lectr. Am. Mgmt. Assn., Advanced Mgmt. Rsch. Internat., N.Y.C., 1971-87, Dow Leadership Ctr., Mich., 1976-78; cons. Wittmeyer & Assoc., Mt. Vernon, Ill., 1975—, Ctr. for Strategic Mgmt., 1998—; spl. appearances on TV/60 Minutes, 1972, PBS TV, 1973, others. Author: The Supervisor as a Conference Leader, 1974, Effective Supervision, 1974, Management Effectiveness in the Corporate Structure, 1975, (audiotape series) Assert Yourself, Develop Your Winning Edge, 1984; co-author: Facts Concerning Drug Use and Abuse, 1972. Active Rep. Presdl. Inner Circle, Washington, 1988-90, Rep. Presdl. Task Force, 1991-95; v.p. Prince of Peace Luth. Ch., Mt. Vernon, 1976; bd. dirs. Jefferson Meml. Hosp., Mt. Vernon, 1973-74, Jefferson County Regional Mental Health Ctr., Mt. Vernon, 1974. Recipient Gov. Legion of Merit award Vt. State Legis., 1969; named Internat. Man of Yr., Cambridge, Eng., 1993, Presdl. Legion of Merit award Washington, 1993, others; fellow Heidelburg U. Sch. Behavioral Sci., Germany, 1971. Mem. ASTD, AMA Presidents Assn., Am. Soc. Personnel Adminstrs., Am. Legion, Elks, Hon. Order Ky. Cols. Avocations: boating, swimming, tennis, sailing. Office: 17 Eagle Cove Ln Saint Charles MO 63303-3738

WITTNER-NEIMAN, SLOANE PHYLLIS ANN, realtor, writer, artist; b. Chattanooga, Tenn., May 7, 1944; d. Sterling Wittner and Blanche Kornfeld-Wittner; m. Howard Franklin Wittner, Apr. 12, 1964; children: Miles Keith Neiman, Jordan Gregory Neiman. Student, U. Ga., 1962. Lic. realtor 1978. Realtor Harry Norman Realtors hold Lic., Atlanta, 1980—; writer Sterling Stories, LLC, Atlanta, 2002—. Artist/writer freelance, Atlanta, 1952—; casa Ct. Apptd. Adv. for Abused and Neglected Children, Marietta/Cobb County, Ga., 2000—. Author (artist): (children's book) How Does God Grow?; author: (composer) (musical play) Shiva/Respectfully, The Family. Mem. Riverside Homeowners Assn., Atlanta, 2004. Mem.: SEBA (assoc.). Avocations: gardening, painting, working out, rescue animals. Office: Sterling Stories LLC PO Box 720192 Atlanta GA 30358 E-mail: calvin@howdoesgodgrow.com.

WITTREICH, WARREN JAMES, psychologist, consultant; b. Weehawken, N.J., Aug. 18, 1929; s. Andrew Otto and Muriel Viola (Wilson) Wittreich; m. Mary Shirley Wells, Sept. 10, 1951 (div. Sept. 1959); children: Michael(dec.), Peter; m. Lois Vivian Llewellyn, Sept. 8, 1959 (div. July 1996); children: Benjamin, Debra, Susie(dec.), Andrea; m. Eileen Burke, Aug. 20, 1996 (div. Sept. 1998); m. Diane L. Altif-Meyer, Jan. 8, 2000. AB in Psychology summa cum laude, Princeton U., 1951, MA in Psychology, 1953, PhD in Psychology, 1954; PhD in Clin. Psychology, Cath. U., Washington, 1958. Lic. psychologist, Pa. Guest scientist Naval Med. Rsch. Inst., Bethesda, Md., 1953-54; postdoctoral trainee VA, East Orange, N.J., 1954-55; clin. psychologist Lancaster and Phila., Pa., 1955—; exec. v.p. Nat. Analysts, Inc., Phila., 1959-64; pres. Daniel Yankelovich of Pa., Phila., 1964-67; pres., CEO Crossroads Career Planning Corp., Phila., 1967-85; adj. prof., rsch. cons. U. Pa., Phila., 1968-73; CEO Focus Group Assocs. Ltd., Bethlehem, Pa., 1995—. Advisor to Sec. of Transp., U.S. Dept. Transp., Washington, 1968-72; expert witness FTC, Washington, 1957, U.S. Congress, Washington, 1959, N.Y. State Supreme Ct., N.Y.C., 1963. Exhibited in 4 one-man shows; 2 commd. paintings; contbr. articles to profl. jours. Worker Robert F. Kennedy Campaign Com., Washington, 1967; mem. Citizens Adv. Com. on Transp. Quality, U.S. Dept. Transp., Washington, 1968-74. Recipient fellowship NSF, 1952-53. Fellow: Pa. Psychol. Assn.; mem.: APA, Sigma Xi, Phi Beta Kappa. Episcopalian. Avocation: painting. Home and Office: 18 W Broad St Apt 2 Bethlehem PA 18018

WITTROCK, MERLIN CARL, educational psychologist; b. Twin Falls, Idaho, Jan. 3, 1931; s. Herman C. and Mary Ellen W.; m. Nancy McNulty, Apr. 3, 1953; children: Steven, Catherine, Rebecca. BS in Edn., Biology, U. Mo., Columbia, 1953, MEd in Ednl. Psychology, 1956; PhD in Ednl. Psychology, U. Ill., Urbana, 1960. Prof. grad. sch. edn. UCLA, 1960—, founder Ctr. Study Evaluation, chmn. divsn. ednl. psychology, chmn. faculty, exec. com., univ. com. on outstanding teaching, supr. UNEX Intern Tchr. Preparation Program, 1996—2004. Dir. math. and humanities program, co-founder Urban Tchr. Edn. Program; fellow Ctr. for Advanced Study in Behavioral Scis., 1967—68; vis. prof. U. Wis., U. Ill., Ind. U., Monash U., Australia; co-prin. investigator Calif. Reading Tchr's Insts.; chmn. com. on evaluation and assessment L.A. Unified Sch. Dist.; nat. adv. panel for math. scis. NRC of NAS; chmn. nat. bd. Nat. Ctr. for Rsch. in Math. Scis. Edn.; chmn. charges com. UCLA; adv. bd. Kauffman Found.; dir. evaluation Calif. Reading Tchrs. Profl. Devel. Program; steering com. tchr. cert. program L.A. Unified Sch. Dist. Author, editor: The Evaluation of Instruction, 1970, Changing Education, 1973, Learning and Instruction, 1977, The Human Brain, 1977, Danish transl., 1980, Spanish transl., 1982, The Brain and Psychology, 1980, Instructional Psychology: Education and Cognitive Processes of the Brain, Neuropsychological and Cognitive Processes of Reading, 1981, Handbook of Research on Teaching, 3d edit., 1986, The Future of Educational Psychology, 1989, Research in Learning and Teaching, 1990, Testing and Cognition, 1991, Generative Science Teaching, 1994, Problem-Solving Transfer, 1996, Taxonomy for Learning, Teaching and Assessing, 2001. Mentor Edn. Leadership Program; bd. dirs. Wested R & D Ctr., 1989—2001. Capt. USAF, 1953—55. Grantee, Ford Found. Fellow: APA (pres. divsn. ednl. psychology 1984—85, assn. coun. 1988—91, award for Outstanding Svc. to Ednl. Psychology 1991, 1993, Disting. Svc. award for svc. to sci. adv. coun., Thorndike award for outstanding psychol. rsch. 1987), AAAS, Am. Psychol. Soc. (charter fellow); mem.: Am. Ednl. Rsch. Assn. (chmn. ann. conv., chmn. publs. 1980—83, assn. coun. 1986—89, bd. dirs. 1987—89, chmn. com. on ednl. TV, Outstanding Contbns. award 1986, Outstanding Svc. award 1989), Phi Delta Kappa. Office: UCLA 3339 Moore Hl Los Angeles CA 90095-1521 Office Phone: 310-825-8329.

WITTSTEIN, EDWIN FRANK, stage and film production designer; b. Mt. Vernon, N.Y., Apr. 7, 1929; s. Nathan Harry and Miriam (Goldman) W. Student, Parsons Sch. Design, 1946-50; BS, NYU, 1950; postgrad., Cooper Union, 1950-52. Stage designer Dramatic Workshop prodn. The Inspector General, 1947; set designer Gertrude Stein's Yes Is for a Very Young Man; set and costume designer Ounga Opera, Phila., 1950, (opera) The Celebrated Jumping Frog of Calaveras County, Venice, Italy, 1953, The Transposed Heads, 1958, The Fantasticks, 1960-2002; designer Broadway prodn. Kean, 1961; set and costume designer The Gondoliers, N.Y.C. Opera, 1963, The Knack (directed by Mike Nichols), 1964, The Marriage of Figaro, N.Y.C. Opera, 1965, The Amen Corner, 1965, Happy Birthday Wanda June, Enter Laughing, 1965, The Room, A Slight Ache, 1965, The Yearling, 1965, Serjeant Musgrave's Dance, 1966 (Obie award 1966), You Know I Can't Hear You When the Water's Running, 1967, set designer Merchant of Venice, Shakespeare Festival Conn., 1967, As You Like It, Richard II, Shakespeare Festival Conn., 1968, The Man in the Glass Booth, 1968, The Basement, The Tea Party, Celebration, 1969, (for Cin. Playhouse) The Miser, Volpone, The Good Woman of Setzuan, Angel Street, He Who Gets Slapped, 1968-70, The Country Wife, Shakespeare Theatre, Conn., 1973, Ulysses in Nightown, 1974 (Tony award nomination 1974, Maharam award 1974), The Torchbearers, 1978, The Aspern Papers, 1978, Love's Labors Lost, 1983, Berkshire Theatre Festival, 1988, Tusitala, 1988, Tete a Tete, 1989, The Hasty Heart, 1990, Trains, 1991, (sets, costumes 30th anniversary tour) The Fantasticks, 1990, Sarah, Plain and Tall, 1991 (Emmy nomination 1991), Colette Collage, 1991, March of the Falsettos, 1991, Falsettoland, 1991, (prodn. designer Hallmark Hall of Fame TV) An American Story, 1992, (prodn. designer Hallmark Hall of Fame TV) Skylark, 1993, (prodn. designer Hallmark Hall of Fame TV) A Place for Annie, 1993, (set designer off-Broadway) I Do! I Do!, 1996; designer TV shows Armstrong Circle Theatre, The Tonight Show with Steve Allen, NBC operas Cosi Fan Tutte, La Traviata, La Boheme, Boris Godounov, Cavalleria Rusticana, Blithe Spirit, The Diary of Anne Frank, Camino Real, The Royal Family, The Prince of Homburg; prodn. designer TV series The Adams Chronicles (Emmy nomination 1975); designer TV films A Memory of Two Mondays, 1971, For Ladies Only, 1982, Legs, 1982, Samson and Delilah, 1983, Heartsounds, 1984; designer TV spl. Echoes in the Darkness, 1987; designer films Bananas, 1971, Play It Again Sam, 1971, The Seven-Ups, 1972; art dir. films Smile, 1975, Fame, 1979; prodn. designer film Endless Love, 1981; set and costume designer (ballet) Coppelia, 1992; one-man show (painting) Hammond Museum, N. Salem, N.Y., 1999; drawer, writer Positano Sketch Book, 2000. Home: 339 E 87th St New York NY 10128-4801

WITTY, CHRISTINE (CHRIS WITTY), speed skater; b. West Allis, Wis., June 23, 1975; Student, Carroll Coll. Speed skater, 1985—. Mem. U.S. nat. team, 1988—. Recipient 1000 meter Silver medal Olympic Games, Nagano, Japan, 1998, 1500 meter Bronze medal, 1998; finished 2d U.S. Olympic Team Trials, 2000. Avocations: cycling, movies, mountain biking. Home: PO Box 564 Park City UT 84060-0564

WITTY, THOMAS EZEKIEL, III, psychologist, researcher; b. Greensboro, NC, Oct. 11, 1955; s. Thomas Ezekiel Jr. and Peggy (Coggins) Witty; m. Ginger Lynell Kissee, June 28, 1997; children: Ezekiel Thomas, Zoe Anne. BA in English, U. N.C., Greensboro, 1980; MS, Va. Commonwealth U., 1989; PhD, U. Mo., 1995. Lic. psychologist Miss. Tchr. secondary English, debate and cross-country coach Henry County Pub. Schs., Collinsville, Va., 1981-87; fin. aid. counselor asst. Va. Commonwealth U., Richmond, 1987-89; substance abuse counselor Dist. 19 Alcoholism Svcs., Petersburg, Va., 1990; grad. rsch. asst. U. Mo., Columbia, 1990-94, grad. instr., 1992-94; postdoctoral fellow Rusk Rehab. Ctr., Columbia, 1995-98; chief psychology Mo. Rehab. Ctr., Mt. Vernon, 1998-2001; psychologist North Miss. Med. Ctr., Tupelo, 2001—. Rsch. cons. Coun. on Rehab. Edn., Inc., Champaign, Ill., 1991; ad hoc reviewer Jour. Rehab. Psychology, 1995—98; internship selection com. U. Mo. Health Svcs. Consortium, Columbia, 1996—98; adj. faculty Family Medicine Residency Ctr., Tupelo, Miss., 2001—; alt. mem. instl. rev. bd. North Miss. Med. Ctr., Miss., 2002—. Contbr. articles to profl. jours. NIH postdoctoral fellow in rehab. rsch., 1995-98, Walter Scott Monroe rsch. fellow U. Mo., 1992-95; rsch. grantee U. Mo. Rsch. Bd., 1997. Mem.: Nat. Rehab. Counseling Assn., Am. Pain Soc., Miss. Psychol. Assn., APA (divsn. 17, 22, 38, 50, program rev. com. divsn. 22 1996—), Sierra Club, KC, Kappa Delta Pi. Democrat. Roman Catholic. Avocations: running, swimming, bicycling, hiking, camping. Office: North Miss Med Ctr Dept Behavioral Health 830 S Gloster St Tupelo MS 38801 Office Phone: 662-377-3813. E-mail: twitty@nmhs.net.

WITWER, BRUCE, former newspaper editor; b. St. Petersburg, Fla., Nov. 4, 1940; Mng. editor Tampa Tribune, 1996-99, ret., 1999. Office: Tampa Tribune 202 S Parker St Tampa FL 33606-2395

WITWER, SAMUEL WEILER, JR., lawyer; b. Chgo., Aug. 5, 1941; s. Samuel Weiler and Ethyl Loraine (Wilkins) W.; m. Susan P. Stewart, Sept. 18, 1971; children: Samuel Stewart, Michael Douglas. AB with honors, Dickinson Coll., 1963; JD, U. Mich., 1966. Bar: Ill. 1967, U.S. Dist. Ct. (no. dist.) Ill. 1967, U.S. Ct. Appeals (7th cir.) 1972, U.S. Supreme Ct. 1973, U.S. Ct. Appeals (6th cir.) 1985, U.S. Dist. Ct. (ea. dist.) Mich., 1987. Assoc. Witwer, Moran, Burlage & Atkinson, Chgo., 1967-74; ptnr. Witwer, Poltrock & Giampietro, 1974-2003, mem. Witwer and Waldron, LLC, 2003-; mem. Fed. Trial Bar Admissions Com. No. Dist. Ill., 1982-97. Governing mem. Chgo. Zool. Soc., 1986-90; trustee United Meth. Homes and Services, Chgo., 1974—, Dickinson Coll., Carlisle, Pa., 1976-97; mem. Cook County Home Rule Commn., Chgo., 1974-75; chmn. Agy. Appeals Com. Chgo., 1975-78; atty. Glenview Park Dist., 1982—; spl. asst. atty. gen. Auditor Gen. Ill., 1984-92. Mem. ABA, Meth. Bar Assn. (pres. 1972-73), Chgo. Bar Assn., Ill. Bar Assn., Law Club of Chgo., Sigma Chi, Phi Delta Phi. Republican. Methodist. Club: Union League. Home: 1330 Overlook Dr Glenview IL 60025-5166 Office: Waldron LLC 1603 Orrington Ave Ste 2080 Evanston IL 60201 E-mail: witwer@wqglawyers.com.

WITWORTH, CLARK L. sports team executive; CFO Larry H. Miller Group, Murray, Utah. Office: Larry H Miller Group 5650 S State St Murray UT 84107-6131

WITYK, JOSEPH JOHN, radiologist; b. Krewecia, Ukraine, Oct. 21, 1931; BS, Ohio U., 1955; MD, Case Western Res. U., 1959. Diplomate Am. Bd. Radiology. Intern Pitts. Mercy Hosp., 1959-60; resident in surgery Cleve. Metro. Gen. Hosp., 1960-61, resident in radiology, 1961-64; radiologist Sinai Hosp., Balt., 1964-83; instr. Johns Hopkins Hosp. and Med. Sch., Balt., 1965-74, asst. prof. radiology, 1974-98; chief dept. radiology Homewood Hosp., Balt., 1983-91. Mem. Am. Coll. Radiology, Radiol. Soc. N.Am., Md. Radiol. Soc. Office: Oakwood Profl Bldg 7845 Oakwood Rd Glen Burnie MD 21061-4280

WITZEL, STEVEN M. lawyer; b. Chgo., Feb. 11, 1958; s. Howard B. and Sedelle K. Witzel; married. AB, Dartmouth Coll., 1978; JD, Fordham U., 1983. Law clk. to Judge John M. Cannella U.S. Dist. Ct. (so. dist.) N.Y., N.Y.C., 1983—85; assoc. Cravath, Swaine & Moore, N.Y.C., 1985—89; asst. U.S. atty. So. Dist. N.Y., N.Y.C., 1989—95; ptnr., assoc. gen. counsel PricewaterhouseCoopers LLP, N.Y.C., 1995—. Home: 164 Bank St PH A New York NY 10014 Office: PricewaterhouseCoopers LLP 1177 Ave of the Americas New York NY 10036

WITZIG, WARREN FRANK, nuclear engineer, educator; b. Detroit, Mar. 26, 1921; s. Arthur Judson and Mary (Bender) W.; m. Bernadette Sullivan, Mar. 31, 1942; children: Eric, Leah, Marc, Lisa Witzig Davidson. BEE, Rensselaer Poly. Inst., 1942; MS, U. Pitts., 1944, PhD, 1952. Registered profl. engr., Pa., Wash. Rsch. engr. Westinghouse Research, Pitts., 1942-48; mgr. reactor physics, engr. Bettis Atomic, Pitts., 1948-60; co-founder, sr. v.p., dir. NUS Corp., Washington, 1960-67; head dept. nuclear engring. Pa. State U., 1967-87, emeritus, 1987—. Cons. nuclear engr. utilities industry; chmn. Pa. Gov.'s Com. on Atomic Energy Devel., 1970-80; mem. Saxton safety com., 1970-72; mem. waste com. Atomic Indsl. Forum, 1971-73; adv. com. Dept. Energy, 1980-82; mem. ops. rev. com. Tex. Utility; nuclear safety and compliance com., bd. dirs. GPU, 1983-92; mem. nuclear oversight com. PSE&G, 1983-91; mem. accrediting bd. Inst. Nuclear Power Ops., 1992-96; safety rev. bd. TVA, 1986-91; chmn. Westinghouse Nuclear Safety and Environ. Commn., 1988-93; chmn. safety audit bd. Centichem., 1989; safeguards com. Pa. State U., 1993—, interim dir. nuclear reactor, 1996-97. Designer S5W submarine reactor, 1956-60. Mem. bd. mgmt. YMCA, 1955-64. Fellow AAAS, Am. Nuc. Soc. (exec. com. edn. divsn., past chmn. nat. com. on public info., chmn. nuc. engring. dept. head com. 1980); mem. Am. Phys. Soc., IEEE (past chmn. nuc. engring. and plasma divsn.), Sigma Xi, Eta Kappa Nu, Pi Kappa Alpha, Sigma Pi Sigma (Power Engring. Educator spl. citation) Presbyterian (elder). Achievements include design of S5W submarine reactor; criticality engineer on Nautilus maiden voyage; developed continuing and long distance education in nuclear engineering. Home: 1330 E Park Hills Ave State College PA 16803-3244 Office: Pa State U Breazeale Nuclear Reactor University Park PA 16802-1408 E-mail: wfw1@psu.edu.

WIVAGG, DANIEL EDWIN, biology educator, editor; b. Shrewsbury, Mass., Nov. 14, 1943; s. Edwin Nathaniel Wivagg and Hazel Viola Hokans; children: Jonathan, Jennie, Peter, Eric; m. Becky Cassell, Jan. 3, 2003. BA in Zoology, U. Mass., 1965; PhD in Botany, U. Tex., 1975. Secondary sci. tchr. North Reading (Mass.) H.S., 1966-69; asst. prof. Loyola U., Chgo., 1974-79; from lectr. to instr. to assoc. prof. Baylor U., Waco, Tex., 1979-95, prof., 1995—. Grant reviewer NSF, Arlington, Va., 1994, 99; dir. edn. reform Tapestry, The Inst. for Philosophy, Religion, and Life Scis., Inc., Waco, 1998-2000, chmn. bd. dirs., 2000—; cons. editor Saunders Coll. Pub., Phila., 1996-98; mem. Advanced Placement Biology Test Devel. Com., 2002-04. Editor (assoc.): Am. Biology Tchr., Nat. Assn. Biology Tchrs., 1985—95; contbr.: Test Bank, 1993; editor, 1996, 1999, Test Item File, 2002; contbr. articles to profl. jours. Recipient Disting. Achievement award for editl. Ednl. Press Assn. of Am., 1986, Excellence in Print award for writing/editl. Washington Edn. Press Assn., 1986, 91; course improvement grantee NSF, 1993-95. Fellow Tex. Acad. Scis.; mem. Am. Inst. Biology Scis., Nat. Assn. Biology Tchrs. (publs. com. 1998-2001, assessment task force 1997-2001, chair occasional publs. subcom. 1996-2001), Sci. Tchrs. Assn. Tex., Tex. Assn. Biology Tchrs. (pres.-elect 2003, pres. 2004), Sigma Xi, Phi Kappa Phi. Avocations: timber frame construction, carpentry, cattle ranching. Office: Baylor U 1311 S Fifth St One Bear Pl 97388 Waco TX 76798 Office Phone: 254-710-2128. Office Fax: 254-710-2969. E-mail: dan_wivagg@baylor.edu.

WIVEL, NELSON AUBURN, physician, medical researcher, educator; b. Denver, Sept. 4, 1935; s. Claude Burns and Aubrey (Angus) W.; m. Carol Henderson, June 16, 1963 (dec. 1999); children: Mark Auburn, Ashley Elizabeth. BS, Ea. N.Mex. U., 1957; MD, Stanford U., 1961. Diplomate Am. Bd. Pathology. Intern Cornell U., N.Y.C., 1961-62, asst. resident in medicine, 1962-63; asst. resident in pathology Stanford U., Calif., 1963-65; rsch. trainee in pathology Washington U., St. Louis, 1965-66; head ultrastructural studies sect. Nat. Cancer Inst., Bethesda, Md., 1966-70, head ultrastructural biology sect., 1970-86; med. officer for AIDS rsch. Gen. Clin. Rsch. Ctrs., NIH, Bethesda, 1986-89, dir. Office of Recombinant DNA Activities, 1989-96; dep. dir. Inst. Human Gene Therapy Sch. Medicine U. Pa., Phila., 1996—. Adj. prof. molecular and cellular engring., program chair ethics and pub. policy rsch. program U. Pa. Med. Ctr., Phila., 1996—; exec. dir. recombinant DNA adv. com. NIH. Assoc. editor Jour. Nat. Cancer Inst., 1968-70, Human Gene Therapy, 1993—, Jour. Biolaw and Bus., 1996—, Transplant Video Jour., 2002—, Pre Clinica 2003—; contbr. more than 80 articles to profl. jours. including Sci., Nature, Jour. of Virology, Virology. Recipient Commendation medal USPHS, 1990. Mem. Am. Soc. Cell Biology, Am. Soc. Virology, Am. Soc. Gene Therapy. Achievements include research on murine retroviruses that can function as moveable genetic elements (transposons). Office: U Pa Sch Med Inst Human Gene Therapy Maloney Bldg Rm M630 B 36th and Spruce Sts Philadelphia PA 19104-4283 Office Phone: 215-614-0090. E-mail: naw@mail.med.upenn.edu.

WIXOM, MAX VALENTINE, artist; b. Honolulu, Hawaii, Feb. 6, 1978; s. Gary Lee and Elsa Francis Louise Wixom. BFA, NYU - Tisch Sch. of the Arts, New York, 1996—2000. Creative dir. Acqua Beauty Bar, New York, NY, 2000—04; owner M Industries, New York, NY. Wardrobe supr. Naked Boys Singing!, New York, NY, 2003; wardrobe Michael Mao Dance, New York, NY; art dir. Eva Sins Film, New York, NY, PSM Nat. Tour NBS!, 2003—; window trimmer Bloomingdale's, 2004. Exhibition, Signs, BFA Thesis Exhbn., photographic exhbn., David I - III, exhbn., A Night Out. Recipient Silver Key, Scholastic, 1996; grantee Fin., MAC Cosmetics, 2000. Mem.: Media Bistro Avant Guild, IRBA. Office: M Industries 81 Orchard St #30 New York NY 10002 E-mail: max@m-industries.net.

WIXOM, ROBERT LLEWELLYN, biochemistry educator; b. Phila., July 6, 1924; s. Clinton W. and Beatrice R. (Hunt) W.; m. Edith Ann Smith, Aug. 21, 1949 (dec. Feb. 1967); children: David G., Richard L.; m. Patricia McMillin, Aug. 2, 1986. BA, Earlham Coll., 1947; PhD, U. Ill., 1952. Instr. U. Ark. Sch. Medicine, Little Rock, 1952-54, asst. prof., 1954-60, assoc. prof., 1960-64, U. Mo., Columbia, 1964-72, prof., 1972-92, prof. emeritus, 1992—. Chmn. biol. scis. sector U. Mo., 1989-92, chair environ. affairs coun., 1991-94. Author: Environmental Challenges for Higher Education, 1996; co-editor, author: Chromatography--A Century of Discovery (1900-2000) The Bridge to the Sciences/Technology, 2001; contbr. articles to sci. jours. NIH rsch. fellow, 1970, recipient NIH Rsch. svc. award, 1978. Mem. AAAS, Am. Chem. Soc. (chmn. U. Mo. sect. 1984-85), Am. Soc. Biochemistry and Molecular Biology, Am. Inst. Nutrition, Protein Soc., Sigma Xi. Achievements include research in identification of essential amino acid requirements and metabolism in adult men, in biosynthesis of valine and isoleucine in microorganisms and plants, on the role of histidine in adult men, and in ferritin/hemosiderin/iron metabolism Office: U Mo Sch Medicine Med Sci Bldg Dc008 00 Columbia MO 65212-0001

WIXOM, WILLIAM DAVID, art historian, museum administrator, educator; b. Phila., July 17, 1929; s. Clinton Wood and Beatrice Rachel (Hunt) W.; m. Nancy Coe, Aug. 8, 1959; 3 children. BA, Haverford (Pa.) Coll., 1951; MA, Inst. Fine Arts NYU, 1963. Lecturer The Barnes Foundation, Merion, Pa., 1951—52; asst. curator to curator medieval and renaissance decorative arts Cleve. Mus. Art, 1958-78, chief curator early western art, 1979; chmn. dept. medieval art and The Cloisters Met. Mus. Art, N.Y.C., 1979-98, curator emeritus. Lectr. Barnes Found., Merion, Pa., 1951—52, curatorial cons. for medieval art, mem. curatorial adv. com., 2002—; adj. assoc. prof. history of art Case Western Res. U., Cleve., 1967—78, adj. prof., 1978, N.Y.U., 1981—82; mem. adv. coun. Snite Mus. Art Notre Dame U., 1974—95. Author: Treasures from Medieval France, 1967; Renaissance Bronzes from Ohio Collections, 1975; contbg. author The Royal Abbey of Saint Denis in the Time of Abbot suger, 1981, The Treasury of San Marco, 1985; Gothic and Renaissance Art in Nuremberg, 1986, Festschrift Gerhard Bott, 1987, Hommage a Hubert Landais, 1987, The Cloisters, Studies in Honor of the Fiftieth Anniversary, 1992, Festschrift Gerhard Schmidt, 1994, Enamels of Limoges 1100-1350, 1996, Studies in Honor of Kurt Weitzmann, 1995, The Dictionary of Art, 1996, The Glory of Byzantium, Art and Culture of the Middle Byzantine Era, AD-843-1261, 1997, Sculptures hors contexte, Louvre conférences et colloques, 1997, Mirror of the Medieval World, 1999, Romanesque Sculpture in American Collections, 1999, Tilman Riemenschneider, Master Sculptor of the Late Middle Ages, 1999, Picturing the Apocalypse: Illustrated Leaves from a Medieval Spanish Manuscript, 2002, A Glimpse at the Fountains of the Middle Ages, 2003; contbr. articles to profl. jours. Bd. dirs. Internat. Ctr. Medieval Art, N.Y.C., 1971-82, pres., 1971-74. Belgium-Am. Ednl. Found. fellow, 1962; Nat. Endowment Arts grantee, 1973; fellow Pierpont Morgan Libr., 1979-2001; J. Paul Getty Mus. Guest Scholar, 1996. Fellow Soc. of Antiquaries of London; mem. Coll. Art Assn. (dir. 1979-83), Medieval Acad. Am., Internat. Ctr. Medieval Art. Mem. Soc. Of Friends. Office: Dept Medieval Art Met Mus Art New York NY 10028

WIXTROM, DONALD JOSEPH, translator; b. Republic, Mich., Oct. 14, 1928; s. Joseph Albert and Edith (Johnson) W.; m. Marilynn Jean Sjoquist, Oct. 14, 1961; children: Joe Alan, Lorna Jean, Aaron Matthew. Free lance translator, Republic, 1966—. Mem. Am. Translators Assn. Baptist. Home and Office: RR 1 Box 98 Republic MI 49879-9726

WIZARD, BRIAN, publisher, author; b. Newburyport, Mass., June 24, 1949; s. Russell and Ruth (Hidden) Willard. BA, Sonoma (Calif.) State U., 1976; D of Metaphysics, Universal Life Ch., 1997. Ordained to ministry Universal Life Ch., 1997. Pvt. practice as jeweler, sculptor and craftsman, Calif., 1974-79;, 1991—; prin. The Starquill Pub., Port Douglas, Queensland, Australia, 1981-86; owner Starquill Internat., Wallowa, Oreg. Author: (trilogy) The Will He Make it Saga (contender 1998 Pulitzer prize), Permission to Kill, 1985, Permission to Live, 1992 (Nobel Prize for lit. nominee 2000), Back in the World, 1995; (novels) Shindara, 1990, Heaven on Earth, 1998, Coming of Age, 1990, Pollution IV, 1993, Nigerian 419 Scam "Game Over!", 2000, (audio book on CD), 2003; (short stories) Tropical Pair, 1986, Metempsychosis, 1988 (In Search of) The Silver Lining, 1994, The Moon Whistling By on a Cloud, 1994, (The Princess of the) Wildflowers, 1995, Mushroom Magic, 1996, Vietnam 1999! Make Friends Not War, (novella) Beware of the Reload, 2003, Beware of Classified Ad Fraud, 2004, Psychology of Financial Terrorism, 2004; contbr. to Smithsonian Inst.'s The Vietnam War Generation, (audio version) Game Over!, 2002; contbr. to SpaceArc; prodr. (video documentary) Thunderhawks, 1987, Swift Action Newsteam, Tope Creek Lookout, 1995, Make Friends Not War: Return to Vietnam, 1999 (Aorence Vietnam Short Story winner); songwriter, prodr. (cassette) Brian Wizard Sings for His Supper, 1989 (cert. of achievement Billboard 1993); songwriter, singer, prodr. (I Don't Want) Permission to Kill, 1989, Busker's Theme Song, Living in North Queensland, Circus Act, Hitch Hiking Man, Self-Portrait, The Love We Share Will Never End, 1994, Never Met a Girl Like You, Folk-Rock Opera: A Cover Story: After That Ugly Saloon Incident; contbr. to America's Finest Songwriter and Lyricists CD, 1997, (novels, video and music) Brian Wizard's 20th Century Anthology, 1998 (nominee Nobel Prize in Lit. 2000), (video) Vietnam '99, (audio book) Nigerian 419 Scam Game Over, 2003, The Rocky Raccoon Folk Rock, 2004, Roadkill Sew, 2004; contbr. to TV documentaries History of the Machine Gun, 2000, Vietnam, The Personal Experience, 2001. Renovator hist. landmark The Tope Creek Lookout (Skyship); mem. Nat. Hist. Lookout Register; sponsor Adopt A Hwy., 1995; min. Universal Life Ch.; amb. at large Africa Anti Fraud Alliance. With U.S. Army, 1967-70. Decorated Air medals (26), Aviator Flight Wings; recipient Cert. of Appreciation, Pres. Richard M. Nixon. Mem. 145th Combat Aviation Bn. Assn., Vietnam Combat Vets. Assn., Vietnam Vets. Am., Vietnam Vets. Australia Assn., NRA (cert. handgun instr., 2002). Office: PO Box 42 Wallowa OR 97885-0042

WLADAWSKY-BERGER, IRVING, communications executive; M in Physics, D in Physics, U. Chgo. With IBM, Armonk, N.Y., gen. mgr. RISC Sys./6000 divsn., gen. mgr. internet divsn. Somers, N.Y., 1995-99, v.p. tech., 2000—. Office: IBM Rte 100 Somers NY 10589

WLASCHIN, KEN, cultural organization administrator, writer; b. Bradish, Nebr., July 12, 1934; s. Bernard A. and Lucy M. (Stevens) W.; m. Maureen N. Kennedy Martin, Mar. 22, 1961; 1 child, Scott Martin. BA, Dartmouth Coll., 1956; MA, U. Coll., Dublin, Ireland, 1957; postgrad., U. Poitiers, France, 1960. Program dir. Nat. Film Theater, London, 1969-83, London Film Festival, 1970-83; artistic dir. LA Film Expn., 1984-86; dir. exhbn. Am. Film Inst., LA, 1986-97, dir. creative affairs and preservation, 1998—. Theater critic Rome Daily Am. & Daily Sketch, Rome and London, 1962-67; art critic Art Voices Mag., Rome, 1962-68; film critic Films and Filming Mag., London, 1973-82; story editor London Weekend TV, 1968. Author: (TV play) Ticket to Trieste, 1961, (novel), The Italian Job, 1964, Rome A City, 1964, Guide to Cinema, 1970, Encyclopedia of Movie Stars, 1979, Faber Book of Movie Verse, 1994, Opera on Screen, 1997, Gian Carlo Menotti on Screen, 1999, Encyclopedia of Opera on screen, 2004. With US Army, 1958-61, ETO. Mem. Brit. Film Inst., Brit. Film Acad. Avocation: opera. Home: 2597 Dearborn Dr Los Angeles CA 90068-2239 Office: Am Film Inst 2021 N Western Ave Los Angeles CA 90027-1625 Office Phone: 323-856-7708. Business E-Mail: kwlaschin@afi.com.

WLEUGEL, JOHN PETER, manufacturing executive; b. Hoyanger, Sogn, Norway, July 1, 1929; s. Johan and Helga (Faye) W.; m. Leonor Abaroa, Dec. 1959; children— Jan Andrew, Cecilia Maria. BA, U. Copenhagen, 1953; MBA, U. Toronto, 1957 With Belgium Machine Tool Assn., 1953-54, Massey-Ferguson Ltd., Toronto, 1954-71, treas., 1968-71; sr. v.p. Bata Ltd., Toronto; dir., officer several subsidiaries (Bata Shoe Orgn.), Don Mills, Ont., Can., 1972-89; exec.-in-residence, internat. adv. bd. Schulich Sch. Bus., York U., North York, Canada, 1990—. Bd. dirs. AMR Techs., Inc., Bloomen Networld Inc. Mem. Financial Execs. Inst., Univ. Club (Toronto). Home: 5 Campbell Crescent Toronto ON Canada M2P 1P1 Office: Schulich Sch Bus York U 4700 Keele St Toronto ON Canada M3J 1P3

WNUK, WADE JOSEPH, manufacturing and service company executive; b. St. Louis, Sept. 2, 1944; s. Edward Joseph and Helen Evelyn (Millick) W.; m. Judith Kay Yohe, May 3, 1969; children: Russell Nicholas, Wade Gregory. BS in Math. magna cum laude, St. Louis U., 1966; MS in Engring. Sci., Calif. Inst. Tech., 1967; MBA, Harvard U., 1974. Govt. research analyst, Washington, 1967-69; planner FMC Corp., Chgo., 1974-75, mgr. bus. devel. petroleum equipment divsn. Houston, 1975-77, group planning mgr. petroleum equipment group, 1977-78; ops. mgr. FMC Petroleum Equipment, Singapore, 1978-80; subsea mgr. FMC Wellhead Equipment div., Houston, 1980-81; dir. corp. devel. Marathon Mfg. Corp., Houston, 1981-82, v.p. corp. devel., 1982-84; exec. v.p. Marathon Power Tech., Houston and Waco, 1984-86; v.p., regional gen. mgr. TDW, Inc., Tulsa, 1986-90, sr. v.p. Tulsa and Singapore, 1990-94; pres. Norriseal, Houston, 1995-98, cons., 1999-2000; e. v.p. Echo Environ., N.Y.C., 2000—01; pres. ICO Polymers N.Am., 2001—. Served with U.S. Army, 1969-72. Mem. Internat. Bus. Club (past v.p.), St. Louis U. Alumni Assn., Calif. Inst. Tech. Assn., Harvard Alumni Assns., Harvard Club (Houston). Office: 5333 Westheimer Rd Houston TX 77056 E-mail: wwnuk@icopolymers.com.

WOBUS, REINHARD ARTHUR, geologist, educator; b. Norfolk, Va., Jan. 11, 1941; s. Reinhard Schaffer and Oral (Phares) W.; m. Sheridan Whitcher, Mar. 18, 1967; children: Erik Reinhard, Cameron Wright. BA, Washington U., St. Louis, 1962; MA, Harvard U., 1963; PhD, Stanford U., 1966. Asst. prof. geology Williams Coll., Williamstown, Mass., 1966-72, assoc. prof., 1972-78, prof., 1978-85, Edna McConnell Clark prof. geology, 1985—, dept. chmn., 1988-96. Geologist U.S. Geol. Survey, Denver, 1967-86; vis. prof. Colo. Coll., Colorado Springs, 1976, 82-83, Colo. State U., Ft. Collins, summers 1977-84; bd. dirs. Colo. Outdoor Edn. Ct., Florissant, Williamstown Rural Lands Found.; co-founder Keck Twelve-Coll. Geol. Consortium, mem. governing bd., 1986—. Contbr. maps and articles on Precambrian geology of So. Rocky Mountains to profl. jours. Danforth fellow, 1962, Woodrow Wilson fellow, 1962, NSF fellow, 1962-66. Fellow Geol. Soc. Am.; mem. Am. Geophys. Union, Nat. Assn. Geosci. Tchrs., Coun. on Undergrad. Rsch., Colo. Sci. Soc., Mineral Soc. Am., Phi Beta Kappa, Sigma Xi. Achievements include current work: Petrology and geochronology of Precambrian igneous and metamorphic rocks and mid-Tertiary volcanic rocks, so. Rocky Mountains. Subspecialties: Petrology, Geology. Home: 20 Grandview Dr Williamstown MA 01267-2528 Office: Williams Coll Dept Geoscis Williamstown MA 01267 E-mail: rwobus@williams.edu.

WODARCZYK, FRANCIS JOHN, chemist; b. Chgo., Dec. 11, 1944; s. Sigmund Frank and Josephine Aurelia (Boblak) W. BS, Ill. Inst. Tech., 1966; AM, Harvard U., 1967, PhD, 1971. Postdoctoral U. Calif., Berkeley, 1971-73; rsch. chemist Cambridge Rsch. Labs., Hanscom AFB, Mass., 1973-77; program mgr. Office of Sci. Rsch., Bolling AFB, D.C., 1977-78; mem. tech. staff Rockwell Internat. Sci. Ctr., Thousand Oaks, Calif., 1978-85; program mgr. Office of Sci. Rsch., Bolling AFB, 1985-90; program dir. NSF, Washington, 1990—. Recipient scholarship, George M. Pullman Found., 1962, Ill. Inst. Tech., 1962-66, Ill. State scholarship, 1962-66, NSF fellowship, 1966-71, 71-72. Mem. AAAS, Am. Chem. Soc., Sigma Xi, Alpha Chi Sigma (chpt. v.p. 1965-66, chpt. award 1964). Achievements include development of radio frequency-microwave double resonance spectroscopy; first demonstration of optically pumped molecular laser; laser-excited electronic to vibrational energy transfer studies. Office: NSF 4201 Wilson Blvd Arlington VA 22230-0001

WODICZKO, KRZYSZTOF, artist, architect, educator; MFA, Acad. Fine Arts, Warsaw, Poland, 1968. Adj. prof. Warsaw Poly. Inst., 1970—75; vis. prof. design and mixed media Nova Scotia Coll. Art and Design, 1977—79, asst. prof. intermedia and photography, 1980—81; adj. prof. indsl. design Ont. Coll. Art, 1979; vis. prof. photography and studio art Calif. Inst. Arts, 1988; guest prof. sculpture Cooper Union Sch. Art, 1987, 89; asst. prof. photography U. Hartford, 1988—89, Calif. Inst. Tech., 1991; prof. sculpture Ecole Nat. Superieure Beaux Arts, 1991—95; dir. Ctr. Advanced Visual Studies MIT, 1994—96; dir. interrogative design work group, 1994—. One-man shows include Foksal Gallery, Warsaw, 1973, 1974, 1975, 1976, 1977, Hal Broom Gallery, N.Y.C., 1977, 1978, 1980, 1984, 49th Paralle, 1986, Clocktower, 1988, Hirschhorn Mus., Washington, 1988, Galerie Gabrielle Maubrie, Paris, 1989, 1992, 1996, Exit Art, N.Y.C., 1989—90, Josh Baer Gallery, 1991, Galerie Lelong, 1996, exhibited in group shows at Edinburgh Festival, 1988, Wiener Festwochen, 1988, Whitney Mus., 1989, Ctr. Georges Pompidou, Paris, 1989, 1996—97, The Israel Mus., Jerusalem, 1990, Mus. Modern Art, San Francisco, 1991, Mus. d'Art Contemporain, Montreal, 1992, Mus. Fine Arts, Boston, 1993—94, Kunstmus., Bonn, Germany, 1994, Setagaya Mus. Art, Tokyo, 1995, Sonje Mus. Contemporary Art, Seoul, 1996, Louisiana Mus., Denmark, 1996, Nat. Mus. Modern Art, Kyoto, Japan, 1996, others. Office: MIT 77 Massachusetts Ave Cambridge MA 02139-4307

WOEBER, KENNETH ALOIS, physician; b. Feb. 2, 1935; MB, BChir, MD, U. Witwatersrand, Johannesburg, South Africa, 1957. Intern Johannesburg Hosp., 1958-59; resident Jackson Meml. Hosp., Miami, Fla., 1959-62; rsch. fellow Harvard Med. Sch., 1962-64, instr. medicine, 1965-68, asst. prof. medicine, 1968-70, assoc. prof. medicine, 1970-72, U. Calif., San Francisco, 1972-75, prof. clin. medicine, 1975—, vice-chmn. medicine, 1981-2000, chief clin. endocrinology, 2000—. Chmn. subsplty. bd. endocrinology and metabolism Am. Bd. Internal Medicine, 1985-87. Contbr. articles to profl. jours. Recipient Van Meter prize Am. Thyroid Assn. Fellow Royal Coll. Physicians of Edinburgh. Home: 6 Bartel Ct Belvedere Tiburon CA 94920-1656 Office: U Calif San Francisco at Mt Zion PO Box 1640 San Francisco CA 94143-1640 Office Phone: 415-885-7574. Business E-Mail: woeber@itsa.ucsf.edu.

WOELFEL, JAMES WARREN, philosophy and humanities educator; b. Galveston, Tex., Aug. 16, 1937; s. Warren Charles and Mary Frances (Washinka) W.; m. Sarah Chappell Trulove, Nov. 24, 1982; children by previous marriages: Skye Caitlin, Allegra Eve, Sarah Judith; stepchildren: Ann Marie and Paul Trulove. BA, U. Okla., 1959; MDiv, Episcopal Div. Sch., Cambridge, Mass., 1962; MA, Yale U., 1964; PhD, U. St. Andrews, Scotland, 1967. Asst. prof. philosophy and religion U. Kans., Lawrence, 1966-70, asst. prof. philosophy, 1970-71, assoc. prof. philosophy and religion, 1971-75, prof. philosophy and religious studies, 1975-88, prof. philosophy, 1988—, acting chmn. dept. religious studies, 1983-84, dir. Humanities and Western civilization program, 1985—. Manuscript reader for various presses, jours. Author: Bonhoeffer's Theology, 1970, Borderland Christianity, 1973, Camus: A Theological Perspective (republished as Albert Camus on the Sacred and the Secular, 1987), 1975, Augustinian Humanism, 1979, The Agnostic Spirit as a Common Motif in Liberal Theology and Liberal Scepticism, 1990, Portraits in Victorian Religious Thought, 1997; co-editor (with Sarah Chappell Trulove): Patterns in Western Civilization, 1991, 3rd edit., 2002; contbr. essays, revs. to profl. jours.; contbr. articles to profl. jours. Danforth grad. fellow Episcopal Div. Sch., Cambridge, Mass., 1959-62, U. St. Andrews, 1962-63, 65-66, Yale U., New Haven, 1963-65; Fulbright scholar U. St. Andrews, 1962-63, Pub. Scholar award Kans. Humanities Coun., 1997; grantee NEH, Exxon Found., Mellon Found., Menninger Found., Inst. for Ecumenical and Cultural Rsch. Mem. Am. Philos. Assn., Highlands Inst. for Am. Religious Thought, Assn. for Core Texts and Courses, Phi Beta Kappa. Democrat. Avocations: piano; walking. Home: 808 Alabama St Lawrence KS 66044-3942 Office: U Kans Humanities & Western Civilization Program Bailey Hall 1440 Jayhawk Blvd Rm 308 Lawrence KS 66045-7574 Office Phone: 785-864-3011. E-mail: woelfel@ku.edu.

WOELFEL, ROBERT WILLIAM, broadcast executive, mayor; b. L.A., Nov. 5, 1944; s. William Herman and Mary Jane (Hiatt) W. AA, Mt. San Antonio Coll., 1965; BS in Bus., Calif. State U., L.A., 1969; MBA, U. So. Calif., 1972. Salesman Burroughs Corp., El Monte, Calif., 1969-71; sales mgr., announcer Sta. KMFB/KPMO, Mendocino, Calif., 1973-81; gen. mgr. Sta. KOZT, Ft. Bragg, 1981-85, Sta. KBLC, Lakeport, Calif., 1984-85; v.p., sales mgr. Sta. KZOZ/KKAL, San Luis Obispo, Calif., 1985-86; corp. gen. mgr. Visionary Radio Euphonics, Santa Rosa, Calif., 1986-87; dir. mktg., gen. sales mgr. Sta. KUBA/KXEX, Yuba City, Calif., 1987-88; gen. mgr. Sta. KMRJ, Ukiah, Calif., 1988-91; prin. ptnr. Electoral Target Advt., 1988-91; broadcast cons. Lahaina, Hawaii, Hamilton, New Zealand, Hobart, Tasmania, 1991-93; gen. mgr. radio divsn. Mendocino Broadcasting Co., 1993-2001; gen. mgr. Four Rivers Broadcasting, 2001—. Instr. advt. and mktg. c.c.; bd. dirs. Mendocino Soda Pop Co. Appeared in film Racing with the Moon, 1984. Advt. cons., vice-mayor City of Ft. Bragg, 1982-84, mayor, 1984-85; mem. City Coun., 1979-85; v.p. bd. dirs. Mendocino Coast Ednl. TV Assn., 1983-85; Ft. Bragg planning commr., 1996-2000; active Coll. of the Redwoods Endowment Bd., 1996-2000. With USN, 1966-68. Mem. Ukiah C. of C. (bd. dirs. 1990-91). Home: PO Box 2538 Mendocino CA 95460-2538 E-mail: bobkmfb@email.com.

WOERNER, FREDERICK FRANK, international relations educator; b. Phila., Aug. 12, 1933; s. Frederick Frank and Mary Ann (McCabe) W.; m. Gennie Ehrhorn, Jan. 21, 1956; children: Frederick Frank III, Charles Anthony, Robert John, Michael Scott. BS, U.S. Mil. Acad., West Point, N.Y., 1955; MA, U. Ariz., 1965. Advanced through grades to gen. U.S. Army, 1955-89, ret., 1989; prof. Boston U., 1990—. Chmn. Battle Monuments Commn., Washington, 1994-2001. Mem. Assn. Grads. of Mil. Acad., Assn. U.S. Army, Coun. Fgn. Rels. Lutheran. Avocations: reading, jogging, fishing. Office: Dept Internat Rels Boston U 152 Bay State Rd Boston MA 02215-1501 Home: 154 Heron LN Gilbert SC 29054-9749

WOERNER, LOUISE, management consultant; b. Jackson, Tenn., June 2, 1942; d. Victor I. and Leland (Horner) W. m. Don Kollmorgen, July 2, 1987. BS cum laude, Trinity U., San Antonio, 1964; MBA, U. Chgo., 1965. Pres. Wheels, Inc., Key West, Fla., 1975-87, L. Woerner, Inc. dba HCR, Rochester, N.Y., and Washington, 1978—, L. Woerner Co., Inc., Washington, 1978—; exec. v.p. J.A. Reyes Assocs., Inc., Washington, 1971-79; mem. trade mission U.S. Dept. Commerce, Japan, 1986; dir. communications Memphis Area C. of C., 1968-69; mgr. new bus., dir. pub. relations Allied Stores, Inc., Dallas, 1967-68; sr. assoc. D.R. Fagin & Assocs., Inc., Dallas, 1965-67; exec. dir. Home Care Research Rochester, 1978—; mem. panel of community leaders Buffalo dist. FRS, 1984-87, econ. analyst mem. small bus. and agrl. adv. council Fed. Res. Bank, N.Y.C., 1985-86; econ. analyst exec. office of Pres. U.S., 1970-71; mem. adv. council SBA, 1984; mem. N.Y. State Tax Council, 1984; mem. Chase/Lincoln First Bank Met. Adv. Bd., 1985—, Chase/Lincoln First Bank Health Adv. Bd., 1986—, Pvt. Industry Council of Rochester/Monroe County, 1983-86, N.Y. State Assembly Speaker's Small Bus. Adv. Group, 1984, mem. com., 1987—; mem. long-term health care planning program Monroe Community Coll. Author: Scheduling Home Health Care Personnel, 1988; contbr. numerous articles to profl. jours. Small Bus. Innovation Research award, phase I and phase II grantee; Gannett Found. grantee; recipient citation of appreciation Am. Bus. Women's Assn., 1983, Presdl. award for Entrepreneurial Excellence, White House Conf. Small Bus., 1986, Small Bus. award Office Systems '88, 1988, achievement award Wall St. Jour.; named Outstanding Young Career Woman of Tex., 1968, Small Bus. Person of Yr., SBA, 1983, Bus. Adv. of Yr. Small Bus. Adminstrn. for Upstate N.Y., 1983. Mem. Bus. and Profl. Women's Club Dallas (Dist. 15 Woman of Yr. 1980, cert. of appreciation 1974), Rochester C. of C., Rochester Women's Network, Univ. Chgo. Grad. Sch. Bus. Alumni Cabinet (bd. dirs. 1984-87, award)., Am. Mgmt. Assn., Washington Forum (treas. 1987). Club: Zonta (dir. 1983-85) (Washington).

WOERNER, ROBERT EUGENE, federal agency administrator, editor; b. Cadillac, Mich., Sept. 23, 1947; s. William Reginald and Ellen Hazel (Van Zoeren) W. BA in English summa cum laude, Grand Valley State U., 1969. Logistics coord. Colo. Outward Bound, 1979-80; writer, editor Bur. of Land Mgmt., U.S. Dept. Interior, Grand Junction, Colo., 1977-78, Elko, Nev., 1980-82, Craig, Colo., 1982-84, Denver, 1984—. Free-lance writer, Buena Vista, Colo., 1976-77; mem. computer tech. adv. bd. Warren Tech, Golden, Colo., 1994-97. Newsletter editor Urban Peak, Denver, 1989-95; author book rev.; contbr. articles to profl. jours. including Jour. of Forestry, Govt. Exec. Vol. Craig Hosp., Englewood, Colo., 1994. Capt. USAF, 1970-76. Honors scholar Grand Valley State U., 1966-69; recipient 4 STAR awards Bur. of Land Mgmt., 1999-2002, cert. Excellence in Accountability Reporting Assn. Govt. Accts. U.S. Dept of Interior, 2001. Mem. Denver Astron. Soc., Inst. Noetic Scis., The Nature Conservancy, Grand Canyon Trust. Avocations: hiking, astronomy, travel, reading, Reiki (master/tchr.). Office: Bur Land Mgmt PO Box 25047 Denver CO 80225-0047

WOERTH, DUANE E. labor union administrator; b. Scribner, Nebr. BS, U. Nebr.; MA, U. Okla. First v.p. Air Line Pilots Assn., Herndon, Va., 1990—98, pres., 1998—. Former dir. Internat. Fedn. Air Line Pilots Assn., chmn. indsl. com.; former mem. bd. dirs. N.W. Airlines, 1993—98. Lt. col. USAF. Office: ALPA PO Box 1169 Herndon VA 20172*

WOERTZ, PATRICIA A. petroleum industry executive; b. Pitts., Mar. 1953; B in Acctg., Pa. State U., 1974; grad. Internat. Exec. Devel. Program, Columbia U., 1994. Acct. Ernst & Young, Pitts., 1974; with Gulf Oil Corp., Pitts., 1977-81, Houston, 1981-85; with debt. reduction process, merger of Gulf and Chevron, 1985-87; fin. mgr. Chevron Info. Tech. Co., 1989-91, strategic planning mgr., 1991-93; pres. Chevron Can. Ltd., Vancouver, B.C., 1993-96, Chevron Internat. Oil Co., 1996-98; v.p. logistics and trading Chevron Products Co., Chevron Corp., 1996-98; pres. Chevron Products Co., 1998—2001; v.p. Chevron Corp., 1998—2001; exec. v.p. Global Downstream Chevron Texaco Corp., San Francisco, 2001—, mem. exec. com. Mem.: Calif. C. of C. (bd. mem. 1999—), Am. Petroleum Inst. (bd. dirs.). Office: 6001 Bollinger Canyon Rd San Ramon CA 94583-2324

WOESTENDIEK, JOHN, JR., (WILLIAM JOHN WOESTENDIEK), newspaper reporter; b. Winston-Salem, N.C., Sept. 5, 1953; s. William John Sr. and Josephine (Pugh) W.; 1 child, Joseph Yoon Tae. BJ, U. N.C., 1975. Reporter Ariz. Daily Star, Tucson, 1975-78; reporter, asst. city editor, city editor Lexington (Ky.) Herald-Leader, 1978-81; reporter Phila. Inquirer, 1981-90, nat. corr. West Coast bur., 1990-93, reporter, 1994-96, columnist,

1996-2000; enterprise editor Charlotte (N.C.) Observer, 2000-01; reporter Baltimore Sun, 2001—. Recipient Paul Tobenkin Meml. award Columbia U., 1984, Nat. Headliners award Press Club Atlantic City, 1987, Pulitzer Prize for Investigative Reporting Columbia U., 1987, Ernie Pyle award, 1994, Best Feature Story award Ky. Press. Assn., 1978, Best Investigative Story award Ky. Press Assn., 1979, Nat. Arc of Excellence Nat. Assn. Retarded Citizens, 1984, Best News Reporting First Place award AP Mng. Editors Pa., 1985, Sigma Delta Chi award for Feature Writing, 1994; John S. Knight fellow Stanford U., 1988-89; named to N.C. Journalism Hall of Fame, 2003.

WOFFORD, HARRIS, former senator, national service executive; b. N.Y.C., Apr. 9, 1926; s. Harris Llewellyn and Estelle (Gardner) W.; m. Emmy Lou Clare Lindgren, Aug. 14, 1948 (dec. Jan. 1996); children: Susanne, Daniel, David. BA, U. Chgo., 1948; study fellow, India, 1949, Israel, 1950; LLB, Yale U., 1954, Howard U., 1954. Bar: D.C. 1954, U.S. Supreme Ct. 1958, Pa. 1978. Asst. to Chester Bowles, 1953-54; law assoc. Covington & Burling, Washington, 1954-58; legal asst. to Rev. Theodore Hesburgh, Commn. on Civil Rights, 1958-59; assoc. prof. Notre Dame Law Sch., 1959-60, on leave, 1961-66; asst. to Senator Kennedy, 1960; spl. asst. to Pres. Kennedy, 1961-62; spl. rep. for Africa, dir. Ethiopian program U.S. Peace Corps, 1962-64; assoc. dir. Peace Corps, Washington, 1964-66; pres. Coll. at Old Westbury, SUNY, 1966-70, Bryn Mawr (Pa.) Coll., 1970-78; counsel firm Schnader, Harrison, Segal and Lewis, Phila., 1979-86; chmn. Pa. Dem. State Com., 1986; sec. labor and industry Commonwealth of Pa., 1987-91; U.S. senator from Pa., 1991-95; CEO Corp. Nat. Svc., Washington, 1995—2001; co-chair America's Promise: The Alliance for Youth, Alexandria, Va., 2001—04. Vis. lectr. Howard Law Sch., 1956. Author: It's Up to Us, 1946, (with Clare Wofford) India Afire, 1951, Of Kennedys and Kings, 1980; editor: Embers of the World, 1970; co-editor: Report of the U.S. Commission on Civil Rights, 1959. Mem. Coun. Fgn. Rels., 1968—; co-chmn. Com. for Study of Nat. Svc., 1977-80; mem. U.S. Adv. Com. on Nat. Growth Policy Processes, 1975-76; trustee The Am. Coll., Bryn Mawr, 1975-83; mem. coun. U.S.-South Africa Leader Exch. Program, 1971-87; bd. dirs. Internat. League for Human Rights, 1979-87, pres., 1980-81; bd. dirs. After-Sch. All-Stars, Campus Compact, Points of Light Found., Youth Svc. Am.; trustee Martin Luther King Ctr. for Nonviolent Social Change, 1983-87; governing coun. Wilderness Soc., 1983-87. With USAF, 1944-45. Mem.: ABA. Democrat. Roman Catholic. Home: 955 26th St NW Apt 501 Washington DC 20037-2040 E-mail: hlwofford@aol.com.

WOGAMAN, GEORGE ELSWORTH, insurance company executive, financial consultant; b. Mikado, Mich., May 29, 1937; s. Edgar R. and Leah Katherine (McGuire) W.; m. Sandra Lee Jensen, Apr. 10, 1965; children: Jennifer, Christopher. Grad. various ins. courses. CLU, registered rep.; cert. ChFc. With Blair Transit Co., Dun & Bradstreet, Chrysler Engring. Co., 1955-61; exec. chef Westward Ho!, 1961-68; owner, mgr. George Wogaman Ins. Agy., Grand Forks, N.D., 1969—. Mem. pres. coun. Farmers Ins. Group, 1988—98, 1999—2003; alderman East Grand Forks (Minn.) City Coun., 1979—2000, v.p., 1982—2000. Corp. mem. Altru Health Sys., Grand Forks, 1982—; mem. Nat. Rep. Congl. Com., Rep. Presdl. Task Force; mem. Red River Valley Estate Planning Coun.; mem. Wesley United Meth. Ch., Grand Forks. Recipient Pub. Svc. award East Grand Forks City Coun., 1979. Mem. Am. Soc. CLU's, North Valley Life Underwriters Assn. (Life Underwriter of Yr. 1988), Farmers Ins. Group Pres.'s Coun., Famers Financial Solutions, 2001-. Home: 1818 19 h St NW East Grand Forks MN 56721-1013 Office: 2612 Gateway Dr Grand Forks ND 58203-1406 Office Phone: 701-772-7108. Business E-Mail: gwogaman@farmersagent.com.

WOGAMAN, JOHN PHILIP, retired minister and educator; b. Toledo, Mar. 18, 1932; s. Donald Ford and Ella Louise (Kilbury) W.; m. Carolyn Jane Gattis, Aug. 4, 1956; children: Stephen Neil, Donald George, Paul Joseph, Jean Ann. BA, U. Pacific, 1954; STB, Boston U., 1957, PhD, 1960. Ordained to ministry United Meth. Ch., 1957. Pastor First Meth. Ch., Marlborough, Mass., 1956-58; staff asst. divsn. world missions United Meth. Ch., 1960-61; asst. prof., then assoc. prof. U. Pacific, 1961-66; prof. Christian social ethics Wesley Theol. Sem., Washington, 1966—2002, dean, 1972-83, prof. emeritus, 2002. Sr. pastor Foundry United Meth. Ch., Washington, 1992-2002; mem. com. religious and civil liberties Nat. Coun. Chs., 1966-2003; chairperson United Meth. Infant Formula Task Force, 1980-84, Muskie Com., 1982-91, World Meth. Coun., 1986-91, United Meth. Gen. Conf., 1988, 92, 96, 2000; pres. Interfaith Alliance, 1997-99; chmn. bd. dirs. Interfaith Conf. of Met. Washington, 2002-03. Author: Methodism's Challenge in Race Relations, 1960, Protestant Faith and Religious Liberty, 1967; Guaranteed Annual Income: The Moral Issues, 1968, A Christian Method of Moral Judgement, 1976, Christians and the Great Economic Debate, 1977, Faith and Fragmentation, 1985, Economics and Ethics, 1986, Christian Perspectives on Politics, 1988, rev. edit., 2000, Christian Moral Judgement, 1989, Making Moral Decisions, 1990, Christian Ethics, 1993, To Serve the Present Age, 1995, Speaking the Truth in Love, 1999, From the Eye of the Storm: A Pastor to the President Speaks Out, 1999, An Unexpected Journey: Reflections on Pastoral Ministry, 2004; editor: The Population Crisis and Moral Responsibility, 1973, Readings in Christian Ethics, 1996. Pres. Stockton (Calif.) Fair Housing Com., 1963-64, Suburban Md. Fair Housing, 1970; mem. Calif. Dem. Ctrl. Com., 1964-66. Lilly fellow, 1959-60; recipient Rsch. award Assn. Theol. Schs., 1975. Mem.: Am. Theol. Soc. (pres. 2004—), Soc. Christian Ethics (pres. 1976—77), Cosmos Club (Washington). Home: 4620 45th St NW Washington DC 20016-4479

WOGAN, ROBERT, broadcasting company executive; b. N.Y.C., Oct. 13, 1925; s. Robert and Johanna (Hilderbrandt) W.; m. Phyllis Jayn Volz, Nov. 21, 1965 (div. 1991); children— Robert, Stephen. Grad. pub. schs. Page NBC, 1943, asst. mgr. guest relations, 1945-46, night announcer, sec., 1946, asst. supr. announcing, 1946-47, NBC (prodn. div.), 1947-48, night adminstrv. asst., 1948-50, supr. network program operations, 1950-55, Eastern radio program and prodn. mgr., 1955-63, exec. producer "Monitor" program, 1963-65, v.p. radio network programs, 1965-73; exec. producer spl. programs NBC Radio Network, 1973-75, regional mgr. affiliate relations, 1975-81, regional dir. affiliate relations, 1981-89; regional mgr. Westwood One Cos., 1989—, Mut. Broadcasting System, 1989—, NBC Radio Network, 1989—, Talknet Programs, 1989—; exec. producer conv. entertainment, coordinator NBC/Mus. of Broadcasting to preserve history radio data. Exec. producer X Minus One radio program, 1974-75. Mem. Nat. council Boy Scouts Am., 1970—; chmn. Radio com. United Hosp. Fund, 1972. Served with AUS, 1944-45. Recipient Radio-TV All-Am. of Year award for Experiment in Drama, 1963, Gabriel award for pub. service programming, 1967, Freedoms Found. award, 1972, Peabody awards for "Monitor", 1972, for "Project I Experiment", 1973. Mem. Broadcast Pioneers, Internat. Radio and TV Soc. Home: 360 W 22nd St New York NY 10011-2600 Office: 30 Rockefeller Plz New York NY 10112-0002 also: 1700 Broadway New York NY 10019-5905 also: 1775 S Jefferson Davis Hwy Arlington VA 22202

WOGEN, CATHY LYNN, academic director; b. Farmington, Minn., Aug. 5, 1957; d. Normand Ernest and Betty Ann (Cline) deVaudreuil; m. David Lee Wogen, June 13, 1981; children: Carlene, Elizabeth, Glen. BS in Computer Sci., St. Cloud State U., 1980; student, Alnwick (Eng.) Tchrs. Acad., 1976-77. Cons. MCOS, St. Cloud, Minn., 1985-89; evening computer instr. St. Cloud Bus. Coll., 1983-90, evening dir., 1990-92, acad. dir., 1992—. Post/secondary rep. Bus./Edn. Partnership, St. Cloud, 1993; mem. at large Parochial Sch. Bd., 2000-2002, sec., 2002-03, chmn. diversity enhancement com., 1998-2003. Mem. St. Cloud C. of C. Democratic. Lutheran.

WOGSLAND, JAMES WILLARD, retired heavy machinery manufacturing executive; b. Devils Lake, N.D., Apr. 17, 1931; s. Melvin LeRoy and Mable Bertina (Paulson) W.; m. Marlene Claudia Clark, June 1957; children: Karen Lynn, Steven James. BA in Econs., U. Minn., 1957. Various positions fin. dept. Caterpillar Tractor Co., Peoria, Ill., 1957-64, treas., 1976-81; mgr. fin. Caterpillar Overseas S.A., Geneva, 1965-70, sec.-treas., 1970-76; dir.-pres. Caterpillar Brasil S.A., São Paulo, 1981-87; exec. v.p. Caterpillar, Inc., Peoria, 1989-90, also bd. dirs., vice-chmn., 1990-95; bd. dirs. Ameren Corp., St. Louis, 1997—. Bd. dirs. Ameren Corp., St. Louis. Mem. adv. bd. St. Francis Hosp., Peoria, 1987-95; bd. dirs. Peoria Area Cmty. Found., 1986-92; trustee Eureka Coll., 1987-95; commr. Kootenai County Planning and Zoning Commn., 1997—. Sgt. USAF, 1951-55. Mem. Hayden Lake Golf and Country Club. Republican. Presbyterian. Home: 9675 Easy St Hayden Lake ID 83835-9526

WOHL, FRANK HAROLD, lawyer; b. Richmond, Va., June 5, 1942; AB, Dartmouth Coll., 1963; JD, U. Chgo. Law, 1966. Bar: NY 1967. Asst. U.S. atty. So. Dist. NY, NYC, 1971—79; ptnr. Rosenman & Colin, NYC, 1979—84, Lankler Siffert & Wohl, LLP, NYC, 1984—. Chair NYC Civilian Complaint Rev. Bd., 1999—2002. Fed. RICO adminstr. Fulton Fish Market, NYC, 1988—92; dir. Broodwood Child Care, Bklyn., 1992—99. Lt. comdr. JAGC USNR, 1967—71. Fellow: Am. Coll. Trial Lawyers (Access to Justice award 2000—); mem.: Fed. Bar Coun. (trustee 1999—2001), NY Coun. Def. Lawyers (bd. mem. 1998—2002), Fed. Bar Found. (dir. 1996—2002), Bar Assn. City of NY. Office: Lankler Siffert & Wohl LLP 500 Fifth Ave New York NY 10110-3398 Office Phone: 212-921-8399.

WOHL, ROBERT, historian, educator; b. Butte, Mont., Feb. 13, 1936; s. Albert and Lani Wohl; m. Marisol Jacas-Santoll, Aug. 5, 1987; children: Robert, Alexander. BA, UCLA, 1957; MA, Princeton U., 1959, PhD, 1963. Instr. U. So. Calif., L.A., 1961—64; asst. prof. UCLA, 1964—66, assoc. prof., 1966—69, prof., 1969—, chmn. history dept., 1970—73. Author: French Communism in the Making, 1966, The Generation of 1914, 1979 (Amer Book award, 1982), A Passion For Wings, 1997. Fellow, Guggenheim, 1981—82, Getty, 1993—94, Nat. Air and Space Mus., 1994—95. Democrat. Roman Catholic. Avocation: tennis. Office: Dept History UCLA Los Angeles CA 90095-1473

WOHL, RONALD H. management consultant, writing and editorial expert; b. Washington, Sept. 3, 1942; s. Bernard Carl and Martha (Aberbach) W.; m. Myrna Zelda Chevelier, June 27, 1965; children: Jennifer Lynn Lombard, Amy Beth. Student, Fla. State U., 1960-62; BA in Anthropology, George Washington U., 1965; postgrad., George Washington U. Law Sch., 1965-67, Am. U., Washington, 1969-74. Cert. mgmt. cons. Asst. to regional credit mgr. Sears, Roebuck & Co., Bethesda, Md., 1966-67; supr. payroll & ins. Montgomery Coll., Rockville, Md., 1967-71; supr. program info. & analysis Nat. Rural Elec. Coop. Assn., Washington, 1971-74; employee benefits comms. cons. Wyatt Co., Washington, 1974-77; pres. R.H. Wohl & Assocs./In Plain English, Gaithersburg, Md., 1977—; v.p. Wohl Comm.Svcs., Inc., 2001—. Columnist Gazette Newspapers, Gaithersburg, 1987, Montgomery Jour., Rockville, 1989-90; bd. dirs. Braille Tech., LLC, 1995, BookmarkSystems.com; prin. Future Solutions, 1997; mng. prin. Capital Human Resources Group, 1998; exec. dir. Libr. Connection.org., 2000; v.p. Wohl Comm. Svc., 2002—. Co-author: The Employee Benefits Communication Tool Kit, 2000, Benefits Communication: A Guide, 2002, Benefit Communication Update, 2002; mem. editl. bd., author Employers Guide to Managed Health Care, 1994—, Civic Action Handbook, 1994—, In Plain English Guide to Preparing Summary Plan Descriptions, 1998, Enwisen Guidebook to the Electronic Summary Plan Description, 1998; co-author: Benefit Communication Edge, 1999. Precinct chair Montgomery County Dems., 1978—; Dem. candidate for Md. Ho. of Dels., Annapolis, 1986; chmn. Commn. on Humanities, Montgomery County Md., 1987-96; dir. North Potomac (Md.) Citizens Assn., 1988-95; citizen mem. Comty. Policing Steering Com., Montgomery County, Md., 1992-96; tchr. Am. Jewish history and comparative religion; bd. dirs. Temple Beth Ami Congregation, Temple Beth Ami Brotherhood, Rockville, 1991-95, pres. 1990-92. Mem. Am. Assn. Home Based Bus. (nat. bd. dirs.), Inst. for Mgmt. Cons. (pres. Washington D.C. chpt. 1998-2000, nat. bd. dirs. and chair profl. knowledge 2000), Plain Lang.Internat. Assn. (nat. bd. dir., 2002—), Internat. Assn. Bus. Communicators, Soc. for Human Resource Mgmt. Home: 14501 Antigone Dr North Potomac MD 20878-2484 Office: R H Wohl & Assocs Inc In Plain English PO Box 3300 Gaithersburg MD 20885-3300 E-mail: rwohl@inplainenglish.com.

WOHLEBER, ROBERT MICHAEL, oil industry executive; b. Pitts., Feb. 15, 1951; s. Richard James Jr. and Mary (Gremer) W.; m. Jean Linda Joseph, Nov. 9, 1974; children: Taylor, Robin, Joseph, Charles. BBA, U. Notre Dame, 1973; MBA, U. Pitts., 1978. Investment officer Mellon Bank, Pitts., 1974-78; treasury rep. Copperweld Corp., Pitts., 1978-80, mgr. treasury svcs., 1980-82, asst. treas., 1982-86; dir. corp. fin. Freeport-McMoRan, Inc., New Orleans, 1986-87, asst. treas., 1987-89, treas., 1989-92, v.p., treas., 1992—94, v.p., exec. project mgr., 1994—96, sr. v.p., CFO, 1996, exec. v.p., CFO, dir., McMoRan Exploration Co., pres., CEO, Freeport-McMoRan Sulphur, 1997—99; sr. v.p., CFO Kerr-McGee Corp., 1999—. Guest lectr. Stetson U., Deland, Fla., 1983. Mem. Nat. Investment Sponsor Fedn. (membership chmn. 1985-86), Nat. Cash Mgmt. Assn., Pitts. Pension Fund Assn. (pres. 1984-85), Pitts. Cash Mgmt. Assn. (founder, pres. 1980-81). Republican. Reformed Presbyterian. Avocations: golf, skiing. Office: Kerr-McGee 123 Robert S Kerr Ave Oklahoma City OK 73125*

WOHLEEN, DAVID B. electronics executive; b. Mpls. BS in Engring., U.S. Mil. Acad., West Point, N.Y., 1972; grad. Sch. Mgmt. Exec. Tng. Program, Yale U. Various pos., including project engr., Pontiac Motor Divsn. GM, 1978—85; engring. mgr. Chevrolet-Pontiac-GM of Can. Group, Pontiac, Mich., 1985—90, dir. elec. and chassis systems, 1990—91, dir. advanced vehicle engring., 1991—93; dir. elec., interior, and heater, ventilation, and air conditioning GM Midsize Car Divsn., Warren, Mich., 1994—95, GM MidLux Car Divsn., Warren, Mich., 1995—97; GM v.p., gen. mgr. Delphi Delco Electronics, 1997—98; v.p. Delphi Corp., Troy, Mich., 1998—2000; pres. Delphi Delco Electronics, Troy, Mich., 1998—2000; exec. v.p. Delphi Corp., Troy, Mich., 2000—03, pres. Electronics & Mobile Comm. sector, 2000—03, pres. elec., electronics, safety and interior, 2003—. Bd. trustees Lawrence Technol. U., Southfield, Mich., 2003—. Office: Delphi Safety & Interior Systems 101 Crooks Rd m/c 480-009-130 Troy MI 48084 also: World Hdqrs Adelphi Corp 5725 Delphi Dr Troy MI 48098-2815

WOHLER, RUTH, humanities educator; b. Manhattan, Kans., Aug. 9, 1947; d. L. Joseph and Wanda Marie Wedel; children: Dwayne, Bryan. BS, North West Mo. State U., 1969; EdM, Kans. State U, 1988. Elem. tchr. Unified Sch. Dist. 320, Wamego, Kans., 1969—73, Unified Sch. Dist. 329, Alma, Kans., 1977—79, Unified Sch. Dist. 320, Wamego, Kans., 1979—84; grad. tchr. asst. Kans. State U, Manhattan, Kans., 1987; instr. basic skills Barton County CC, Ft. Riley, Kans., 1985—87; instr. English and edn. Mid Plains CC, North Platte, Nebr., 1987—, humanities divsn. chair. Instrnl. svc. Mid Plains Cmty. Coll., 1991—2003, chair Humanities div., 2002—; presenter Coll. Reading and Learning Assn., 1998. Recipient NISOD Excellence Award, Internat. Conf. on Tchg. and Leadership Excellence, 1997. Mem.: Nat. Edn. Assn. (assoc.; former pres.), Coll., Heartland Reading & Learning Assn. (assoc.; pres. elect), Bus. and Profl. Women, Delta Kappa Gamma, Phi Delta Kappa. Avocations: reading, writing, gardening. Home: PO Box 562 North Platte NE 69103 Office: North Platte Community Coll 601 West State Farm Rd North Platte NE 69101 Office Phone: 308-535-3747.

WOHLGELERNTER, BETH, organization executive; b. N.Y.C., Jan. 30, 1956; d. Maurice Nathaniel and Esther Rachel (Feinerman) W. BA, Barnard Coll., 1977. Exec. aide to pres. Barnard Coll., N.Y.C., 1977-80; spl. asst. to pres. The Commonwealth Fund, N.Y.C., 1980-81; asst. to chief exec. officer/pres. Mary McFadden, Inc., N.Y.C., 1981-84; exec. adminstr. The Donna Karan Co., N.Y.C., 1984-90; nat. exec. dir. Hadassah, The Women's Zionist Orgn. Am., Inc., N.Y.C., 1990-97; v.p. trade svcs. Trade Finance Svcs., N.Y.C., 1998—. Comm. adv. coun. AT&T, 1992—. Bd. dirs., v.p. N.Am. Conf. on Ethiopian Jewry, N.Y.C., 1981-85, 98—, bd. advisors, 1985-98; bd. govs. Lincoln Sq. Synagogue, N.Y.C., 1988-94, bd. trustees, 1994—; bd. trustees United Israel Appeal, 1991—.

WOHLGENANT, RICHARD GLEN, lawyer, director; b. Porterville, Calif., Dec. 2, 1930; s. Carl Ferdinand and Sara Alice (Moore) W.; m. Teresa Joan Bristow, Dec. 27, 1959; children: Mark Thomas, Tracy Patrice, Timothy James. BA, U. Mont., Missoula, 1952; LL.B., Harvard U., Cambridge, Mass., 1957. Bar: Colo. 1957, U.S. Dist. Ct. Colo. 1957. Assoc. Holme Roberts & Owen LLP, Denver, 1957-62; ptnr./mem. Holme Roberts & Owen, Denver, 1962-99, of counsel, 2000—. Bd. dirs. Adopt-A-Sch., Denver, 1976-80, St. Joseph Found., Denver, 1990-93, Denver Com. Coun. Fgn. Rels., 1988-98, Japanese-Am. Soc. Colo., 1993-98, Rocky Mountain chpt. U.S. Mex. C. of C., 1993-00; bi-nat. bd. U.S./Mex. C. of C., 2000—01; chmn. Chamber of the Americas, 2001—03; adv. bd. Human Med. Genetics Prgm., U. Colo. H.S.C., 2000—03; trustee Helen K.and Arthur E. Johnson Found., 2003—. Mem. ABA, Colo. Bar Assn., Denver Bar Assn., Am. Coll. Real Estate Lawyers, Univ. Club, Law Club, City Club, Cactus Club. Republican. Roman Catholic. Home: 300 Ivy St Denver CO 80220-5855 Office: Holme Roberts & Owen LLP 1700 Lincoln St Denver CO 80203-4500

WOHLTMANN, HULDA JUSTINE, pediatric endocrinologist, diabetologist; b. Charleston, S.C., Apr. 10, 1923; d. John Diedrich and Emma Lucia (Mohrmann) W. BS, Coll. Charleston, 1944; MD, Med. U. S.C., 1949. Diplomate Am. Bd. Pediatrics. Intern Louisville Gen. Hosp., 1949-50; resident in pediatrics St. Louis Children's Hosp., 1950-53, 1953-65, instr., 1953-58, asst. prof., 1958-65, postdoctoral fellow biochemistry, 1961-63; assoc. prof. pediatrics, head pediatric endocrinology Med. U. S.C., Charleston, 1965-70, prof., 1970-90, prof. emeritus, 1999—. Bd. dirs. Franke Home, Charleston, 1975-97, treas., 1989-91; mem. adv. bd. for ethics ctr. Newberry (S.C.) Coll., 1989—; trustee Luth. Theol. So. Sem., 1991-97. Contbr. articles to sci. jours. Mem. Am. Pediatric Soc., Ambulatory Pediatric Assn., Endocrine Soc., Am. Diabetes Assn., Am. Acad. Pediatrics, Midwest Soc. Pediatric Rsch., So. Soc. Pediatric Rsch., S.C. Diabetes Assn. (bd. dirs. 1970-86, pres. 1970-73, 84-85, v.p. 1982-83, Profl. Svc. award 1977), Lawson Wilkins Endocrine Soc., Sugar Club; fell. Am. Acad. Pediatrics. Lutheran. Home: 3 46th Ave Isle Of Palms SC 29451-2607

WOICKE, PETER, corporate financial executive; b. Germany; With J.P. Morgan, sr. exec. in Asia; chmn. J.P. Morgan Securities Asia; exec. v.p. Internat. Fin. Corp., 1999—; mng. dir. World Bank Group, Washington, 1999—. Office: The World Bank Group 1818 H St NW Washington DC 20433

WOITACH, PAUL, health products executive; BA in Econs., MBA, U. Rochester. Various positions in distbn., sales, corp. accts., mktg. Eastman Kodak, Rochester, N.Y., 1980-95, v.p. nat. accts. and mktg. channels Health Imaging Divsn., 1995-96; v.p. mktg. and sales Lab. Products divsn. Mettler Toledo, 1996-97; gen. mgr. N.Am. Lab. divsn., 1997-98; pres., COO IGI, Inc., Buena, N.J., 1998—. Office: IGI Inc Wheat Rd & Lincoln Ave PO Box 687 Buena NJ 08310

WOJAHN, R. LORRAINE, retired state senator; b. Tacoma, Washington, Sept. 17, 1920; m. Gilbert M. Wojahn (dec.); children: Mark C., Gilbert M. Jr. (dec.). Student, U. Washington, 1938—39. Mem. Wash. State Ho. of Reps., Olympia, 1969-76, Wash. State Senate, Olympia, 1977—2001, ret., 2001. Pres. pro tempore; vice chmn. rules, health and human svcs. com.; mem. labor and commerce, ways and means coms. Bd. dirs. Allenmore Hosp.; trustee Consumer Credit Counseling Svcs., Inc., Tacoma-Pierce County; active, past pres. Eastside Boys and Girls Club, Tacoma-Pierce County; active Wash. State Hist. Soc. Democrat.

WOJCICKI, ANDREW ADALBERT, chemist, educator; b. Warsaw, May 5, 1935; s. Franciszek Wojcicki and Janina (Kozlowa) Hoskins; m. Marba L. Hart, Dec. 21, 1968; children: Katherine, Christina. BS, Brown U., 1956; PhD, Northwestern U., 1960; postdoctoral fellow, U. Nottingham, Eng., 1960-61. Asst. prof. chemistry Ohio State U., Columbus, 1961-66, assoc. prof., 1966-69, prof., 1969-2000, prof. emeritus, 2001—, acting chmn., 1981-82, assoc. chmn., 1982-83, 84-86. Vis. prof. Academia Sinica, Taipei, Taiwan, 2002-03, Case Western Res. U., 1967, U. Bologna, Italy, 1988, Nat. Sci. Council Chemistry Rsch. Promotion Ctr., Taiwan, 1994, U. Sydney, Australia, 1998; vis. researcher U. Coll. London, 1969; sr. U.S. scientist Alexander von Humboldt Found., Mulheim/Ruhr, Germany, 1975-76; vis. scholar U. Calif.-Berkeley, 1984; assoc. dean Coll. of Math. and Phys. Scis., Ohio State U., 1996-98. Contbr. articles to profl. jours. Guggenheim fellow U. Cambridge (Eng.), 1976; recipient Disting. Teaching award Ohio State U., 1968, Humboldt Sr. award Humboldt Found., 1975-76, Casimir Funk Natural Sci. award, Polish Inst. of Arts and Scis. in Am., 2001. Mem.: Am. Chem. Soc. (Columbus sect. award 1992), Phi Lambda Upsilon, Sigma Xi. Home: 825 Greenridge Rd Columbus OH 43235-3411 Office: Ohio State U 100 W 18th Ave Columbus OH 43210-1185 Office Phone: 614-292-4750.

WOJCICKI, STANLEY GEORGE, physicist, researcher; b. Warsaw, Mar. 30, 1937; came to U.S., 1950; s. Franciszek and Janina (Kozlow) W.; m. Esther Denise Hochman, Nov. 17, 1961; children: Susan Diane, Janet Maia, Anne Elizabeth. AB, Harvard U., 1957; PhD, U. Calif., Berkeley, 1962. Physicist Lawrence Radiation Lab., Berkeley, 1961-66; asst. prof. physics Stanford U., 1966-68, assoc. prof., 1968-74, prof., 1974—, chmn. dept., 1982-85, dep. dir. Superconducting Supercollider Central Design Group, 1984-89; chmn. Stanford Linear Accelerator Center Exptl. Program Adv. Com., 1979-81. Chmn. High Energy Physics Adv. Panel, 1990-96. Assoc. editor Phys. Rev. Letters for Exptl. High Energy Physics, 1978-80. Recipient Alexander von Humboldt Sr. Am. Scientist award, 1981; NSF fellow, 1964-65; Sloan Found. fellow, 1968-72; Guggenheim fellow, 1973-74 Fellow Am. Phys. Soc. Office: Stanford U Dept Physics Stanford CA 94305-4060

WOJCIK, CASS, decorative supply company executive, former city official; b. Rochester, N.Y., Dec. 3, 1920; s. Emil M. and Casimira C. (Krawiecz) W.; student Lawrence Inst. Tech., 1941-43, Yale U., 1943-44, U.S. Sch. for European Personnel, Czechoslovakia, 1945; m. Lilliam Leocadia Lendzion, Sept. 25, 1948; 1 child, Robert Cass. Owner, Nat. Florists Supply Co., Detroit, 1948-88, Nat. Decorative, Detroit, 1950-89; co-owner Creation Ctr., Detroit, 1955-60, Wojcik Family Collection Collectables Mktg., 1995—; cons.-contractor hort.-bot. design auto show displays, TV prodrs., designers and decorators. Mem. Regional Planning and Evaluation Coun., 1969-75; city-wide mem. Detroit Bd. Edn., 1970-75; commr. Detroit Public Schs. Employees Retirement Commn., until 1975; mem. Area Occupl. Ednl. Commn., Ednl. Task Force; chmn., grand marshal Ann. Gen. Pulaski Day Parade, Detroit, 1970, 71; mem. Friends of Belle Isle; mem. Nat. Arboretum Adv. Coun., U.S. Dept. Agr., 1982-83; mem. pastoral coun. Archidiocese of Detroit, 1983-86, 88-92; v.p. rsch. Barna Coll., Ft. Lauderdale, Fla., 1989-94; vice chmn. 13th Congl. Dist. Rep. Party Mich., 1987-91; elected to 1988 electoral coll. With U.S. Army, 1944-46. Decorated Bronze Star; recipient citation Polish-Am. Congress, 1971, Art in Park 3d prize City of Oakland Park, Fla. Mem. S.E. Mich. Coun. Govts., Mich., Nat. sch. bd. assns., Big Cities Sch. Bd. Com., Nat. Coun. Great Cities Schs., Mcpl. Fin. Officers Assn. U.S., Nat. Coun. Tchr. Retirement, Ctrl. Citizens Com. Detroit, Internat. Platform Assn., Mich. Heritage Coun., Nat. Geog. Soc., Polish Century Club. Home: 1729 SW 14th Ct Fort Lauderdale FL 33312-4109 Office Phone: 561-750-9033.

WOJCIK, JOHN CASIMIR, music educator, director; b. South Haven, Mich., Aug. 19, 1952; s. Casimir Joseph and Mary Josephine Wojcik; m. Kimberly Kristine Allison, Mar. 25, 2000; 1 child, Jacob Casimir. MusB in Edn., Mich. State U., 1978; MusM in Trumpet Performance, U. of Okla., 1981; Mus D in Instrumental Conducting, U. of Kans., 1989. Asst. dir. of bands Enid (Okla.) HS, 1980—84; dir. of bands Phillips U., Enid, 1984—87, Graceland U., Lamoni, Iowa, 1989—2001, Tex. A & M U., Corpus Christi, Tex., 2001—. Contbr. articles to profl. jours. Mem.: Internat. Trumpet Guild, Nat. Band Assn., Affiliated Fedn. of Musicians, Music Educators Nat. Conf., Tex. Bandmasters Assn., Tex. Music Educators Assn., Coll. Band Dirs. Nat. Assn., Tau Beta Sigma, Kappa Kappa Psi, Pi Kappa Lambda, Phi Kappa Phi, Phi Mu Alpha Sinfonia (rec. sec. 1976—77, pres. 1977—78). Democrat. Roman Catholic. Avocations: golf, jogging, history. Home: 2810 Quebec Corpus Christi TX 78414 Office: Texas A & M University Corpus Christi Dept of Music 6300 Ocean Drive Corpus Christi TX 78412 Office Phone: 361-825-2375. Personal E-mail: jkwojcik@sbcglobal.net. E-mail: john.wojcik@mail.tamucc.edu.

WOJCIK, MARTIN HENRY, not-for-profit executive; b. Chgo., May 10, 1948; s. Henry Martin and Mary Lorraine (Naughton) W. BS, Ill. Inst. Tech., 1970; M. in Humanities, Bonn U., W. Ger., 1975. Price adminstr. R.R.

Donnelley & Sons., Chgo., 1970-72; dir. devel. Citizens for a Better Environment, Milw., 1976-79, pres. Chgo., 1979-85; dir. found. rels. Northwestern U., Evanston, Ill., 1987-89; dir. corp. and found. rels. Mayo Found., Rochester, Minn., 1989—2002; sr. v.p., COO, Scripps Health Found., La Jolla, Calif., 2002—. Bd. dirs. Citizens for Better Environment, Chgo., 1979—85, 1999—2003, chmn. bd. dirs., 1990—91, 1999—2001; mem. policy adv. com. Ill. EPA, Springfield, Ill., 1980—82. Bd. dirs. Rochester Civic Theatre, 1991-97, pres. bd. dirs. 1994-95; bd. dirs. Wasie Found., 2003—; mem. adv. panel Minn. State Arts Bd., 1995, 97, 99, 2001; adv. coun. KSDS Pub. Radio, San Diego, 2003-. Mem. Ill. Inst. Tech. Alumni Assn. Roman Catholic. Home: 3289 Caminito Eastbluff #191 La Jolla CA 92037 Office: Scripps Health Found 4275 Campus Point Ct San Diego CA 92121 E-mail: wojcik.martin@scrippshealth.org.

WOJDAKOWSKI, WALTER, career military officer; BS, U.S. Mil. Acad., 1972; MBA, M Mil. Arts and Scis., U. Alaska; postgrad., Command/Gen. Staff Coll., Sch. Advanced Mil. Studies, Army War Coll. Commd. 2d lt. U.S. Army, 1972, advanced through ranks to major gen., 2002; various to sr. inf. task frce combat trainer Nat. Tng. Ctr., Ft. Irwin, Calif., 1991-92; comdr. 11th Inf. Regiment, 1993-95; dir. of tng. 7th Army Tng. Command/USAREUR, Grafenwoehr, Germany, 1995-96; comdr. opers. group Combat Maneuver Tng. Ctr., Hohenfels, Germany, 1996 97; asst. commandant Inf. Sch. and Dep. Commanding Gen., Ft. Benning, 1997—98; chief, office of military occupation US Embassy, Kuwait City, Kuwait, 1998—2000; asst. div. comdr. 24th Infantry div. (Mechanized), Ft. Jackson, SC, 2000—02; dep. commanding gen. (South) 1st US Army, 2000—02; dep. commanding gen. V Corps, Heidelburg, Germany, 2002—; acting commanding gen. V Corps., 2004; dep. commanding gen. Multi-Nat. Force-Iraq, 2004—. Decorated Silver Star, Legion of Merit, Bronze Star, Meritorious Svc. medal, Army and Navy Commendation medals, Army Achievement medals, others. Mem. Phi Kappa Phi. Office: USAREUR V Corps 09111 Heidelburg Germany*

WOJTYLA, KAROL JOZEF See JOHN PAUL, HIS HOLINESS POPE II

WOLAK, EDMUND L. engineering program manager; b. Calif. m. Hozumi Miyamchi, Apr. 26, 1992; children: Anton, Owen, Theo. BS in Math. and Physics, U. Wash., 1983; PhD in Applied Physics, Stanford U., 1989. Rsch. asst. Stanford U., Palo Alto, Calif., 1983-89, rsch. assoc., 1989; product devel. engr. SDL, Inc., San Jose, Calif., 1991-94, engr., sect. mgr., 1995 97, sr. sect. mgr., 1997— . Vis. scientist Matsushita, Osaka, Japan, 1989-91. Co-patentee in field; contbr. articles to profl. publs. Mem. IEEE. Avocations: piano, travel, exercise, jogging. Office: JDS Uniphase Inc 80 Rose Orchard Way San Jose CA 95134-1356 E-mail: ed.wolak@jdsu.com.

WOLANDE, CHARLES SANFORD, former computer company executive; b. Chgo., July 25, 1954; s. Sam C. and Marie Helene (Riccio) W.; children: Eric, Jill, Patrick, Ryan, Haley. B, St. Mary's Coll., Winona, Minn., 1976. Lab. tech. Jefferson Electric, Bellwood, Ill., 1976-73; pres. Comark, Inc., Glendale Heights, Ill., 1978—2002, also CFO Bloomingdale, Ill., 1978—2002. Named High Tech. Enterpreneur of the yr., Peat, Marwick, Mitchell, Chgo., 1987; named to CRN Industry Hall of Fame, 2003. Mem. C. of C. Glendale Heights. Republican. Roman Catholic. Avocations: golf, skiing. Office: 444 Scott Dr Bloomingdale IL 60108-3111

WOLANER, ROBIN PEGGY, internet and magazine publisher; b. Queens, N.Y., May 6, 1954; d. David H. and Harriet (Radlow) W.; children: Terry David, Bonnie Lee. BS in Indsl. and Labor Rels., Cornell U., 1975. Sr. editor Viva Mag., N.Y.C., 1975-76; editor Impact Mag., N.Y.C., 1976-77; circulation mgr. Runner's World Mag., Mountain View, Calif., 1977-79; cons. Ladd Assocs., San Francisco, 1979-80; gen. mgr. Mother Jones Mag., San Francisco, 1980-81, pub., 1981-85; founder, pub. Parenting Mag., San Francisco, 1985-91, pres., 1991-92; v.p. Time Pub. Ventures, 1990-96; pres., CEO Sunset Pub. Corp., 1992-95; exec. v.p. CNET, 1997—2002. Bd. dirs. Working Assets, Tides Found. Jewish. E-mail: robinw@cnet.com.

WOLANIN, BARBARA ANN BOESE, art curator, art historian; b. Dayton, Ohio, Dec. 12, 1943; d. William Carl and Elisabeth Cassell (Barnard) Boese; m. Thomas R. Wolanin, 1966 (div. 1980); children: Peter, Andrew; m. Phillip F. Brown, 2001. AB, Oberlin Coll., 1966, AM, 1969; MAT, Harvard U., 1967; PhD, U. Wis., 1981. Art tchr. Newton (Mass.) Pub. Schs., 1969-71; asst. prof. art history Trinity Coll., Washington, 1978-83, James Madison U., Harrisonburg, Va., 1983-85; curator U.S. Capitol, Architect of the Capitol, Washington, 1985—. Author: (exhbn. catalog) Arthur B. Carles, 1983, 2000, Constantino Brumidi, 1998; contbr. articles to profl. jours. Woodrow Wilson fellow, 1967, Kress fellow U. Wis., 1974, Smithsonian fellow, 1976; recipient Faculty Devel. award James Madison U., 1985. Mem. Women's Caucus for Art (pres. D.C. chpt. 1998-2001, nat. bd. 2002-), Art Table (bd. D.C. chpt. 2003-), Coll. Art Assn., Am. Inst. Conservation, Phi Beta Kappa (pres. Trinity Coll. 1982-83). Home: 7807 Hamilton Spring Rd Bethesda MD 20817 Office: US Capitol Office Architect Washington DC 20515-0001 E-mail: bwolanin@earthlink.net.

WOLANIN, THOMAS RICHARD, educator, researcher; b. Detroit, Dec. 1, 1942; s. Chester Richard and Helen Theresa (Luszki) W.; m. Donna M. Christian; children: Peter, Andrew. BA magna cum laude, Oberlin Coll., 1965; MA, Harvard U., 1970, PhD, 1972. Staff dir. subcom. on labor-mgmt. rels. House Edn. and Labor Com., 1975-77, dep. staff dir. subcom. on select edn., 1977-78; exec. asst. to pres. NYU, 1981-82; analyst Senate Budget Com., 1982-83; staff dir. subcom. on investigations House P.O. and Civil Svc. Com., 1983-85, 87-91; staff dir. subcom. on postsecondary edn. House Edn. and Labor Com., 1978-81, 85-87;, 91-93; dep. asst. sec. legis. and congl. affairs U.S. Dept. Edn., Washington, 1993-96; sr. assoc. The Inst. for Higher Edn. Policy, Washington, 1996—. Instr. govt. Oberlin Coll., 1967-69; asst. prof. polit. sci. U. Wis., Madison, 1971-78; rsch. prof. edn. policy and polit. sci. George Washington U., Washington, 1997-00. Author: Presidential Advisory Commissions: Truman to Nixon, 1975; co-author: Congress and the Colleges: Higher Education in National Politics, 1976; contbr. articles to profl. jours. Bd. dirs. Am. Youth Policy Forum. Woodrow Wilson fellow, 1965-66, Harvard Grad. prize fellow, 1965-67, 69-71; guest scholar The Brookings Instn., 1970, Congl. fellow, 1971-72, Ford Found. travel and student grantee, 1972-73, 73-74, Spencer fellow Nat. Acad. Edn., 1975-81, acad. specialist grantee USIA, 1990. Mem. Am. Polit. Sci. Assn., Polish Am. Arts Assn. Washington, Congl. Fellowship Alumni Assn., Phi Beta Kappa. Democrat. Avocations: military history, polish history, literature. Office: Inst Higher Edn Policy 1320 19th St NW Ste 400 Washington DC 20036-1635 Office Phone: 202-861-8223. E-mail: tom@ihep.com.

WOLAVER, STEPHEN ARTHUR, judge; b. Springfield, Ill., Sept. 4, 1950; s. Lynn Ellsworth and Arah Dean Phyllis (Scheele) W.; m. Gayla Sue Howard, Feb. 28, 1987; children: Lindy Allison, Scott. BS, Miami U., Oxford, Ohio, 1972; JD, Valparaiso U., 1975. Bar: Ohio 1975, U.S. Dist. Ct. (so. dist.) Ohio 1976, U.S. Ct. Appeals (6th cir.) 1997, U.S. Tax Ct. 1990, U.S. Supreme Ct. 1979. Ptnr. Gill, Wolaver & Welch, Fairborn, Ohio, 1975-81; asst. pros. atty. Greene County (Ohio), Xenia, 1976—, chief trial counsel, 1989—2003, elected Common Pleas judge, 2003—; ptnr. Wolaver, Sheets & Lewis, Fairborn, 1981—2001, Wolaver, Mayer & Cusack, 2002. Instr. Fairborn Bd. Edn., 1978—; adj. prof. Clark Tech. Coll., 1979-85; instr. Greene County Law Enforcement Police Acad., 1988—, Greene County Career Ctr. Police Acad., 2004; faculty Nat. Advocacy Ctr. U. So. Carolina, 2001; lectr., 1982—, law enforcement adv. com., 1983-86; advisor Fairborn (Ohio) H.S. Mock Trial Team, 1987-96. Greene County campaign chmn. Gov. Rhodes re-election com., 1978, 86, Voinovich for U.S. Senate; active Greene County Rep. Ctrl. Com., 1978-2002; youth counselor Bethlehem Luth. Ch., Fairborn, 1980-96, head usher com. pres. Rona Village Homeowners Assn., 1981; pres. Greene County Rep. Club, 1999-2000. Named one of Outstanding Young Men Am., Jaycees, 1981, Greene County Legal Secs. Boss of Yr. award, 1985; named to Fairborn H.S. Hall of Honor, 2003; recipient Outstanding Asst. Prosecutor of Yr. award Ohio Pros. Attys. Assn., 1998, Outstanding Trial award Nat. Assn. Govt. Attys. in Capital Litigation, 2002, Meritorious Achievement award Ohio Pros. Attys. Assn., 2002. Mem. Greene County Bar Assn. (sec.-treas. 1997, v.p. 1998, pres. 2000), Ohio Bar Assn., Assn. Trial Lawyers Am., Nat. Dist. Attys. Assn., Sertoma (pres. 1982-83), Delta Tau Delta. Home: 3792 Westwind Dr Dayton OH 45440-3500 Office: Courthouse 45 N Detroit Ave Xenia OH 45385

WOLBRINK, JAMES FRANCIS, real estate investor; b. Charles City, Iowa, Sept. 8, 1942; s. Richard William and Anna (Bult) W.; m. Karen Ann Dunkerly, June 18, 1966. BS in Indsl. Engring., Iowa State U., 1966, postgrad., 1968-72. Cert. assn. exec. Tech. writer/editor Lawrence Radiation Lab., Livermore, Calif., 1966-67; editor, head engring. publs. Engring. Research Inst., Iowa State U., Ames, 1967-70; mng. dir., edn. and publs. Am. Inst. Indsl. Engrs., Norcross, Ga., 1971-83; commodities broker Clayton Brokerage, 1983-85; now pres. Wolbrink Properties, 1983—. Named Outstanding Young Alumnus Iowa State U., 1977. Mem. Sandy Springs Optimist Club (pres. 1989-90), Optimist Internat. (gov. Ga. dist. 1994-95), Delta Chi. Home and Office: 4520 Northside Dr NW Atlanta GA 30327-4548 E-mail: wolbrink@mindspring.com.

WOLCOTT, HUGH DIXON, obstetrics and gynecology educator; b. NYC, Jan. 12, 1946; s. Charles Edmund and Joan Degrau (Loveland) W.; m. Jane Jarrell Smith; children: Allison, James. BS, U.S. Naval Acad., 1967; MSE, Princeton U., 1969; MD, Northwestern U., Chgo., 1979. Diplomate Am. Bd. Ob-Gyn, Am. Bd. Med. Examiners. Commd. ensign USN, 1967, advanced through grades to capt., 1990; aviator, Fighter Squadron 14 Naval Air Station, Oceana, Va., 1971-74; test pilot Naval Air Test Ctr., Patuxent River, Md., 1974-76; staff physician Naval Hosp., Portsmouth, Va., 1984, Jacksonville, Fla., 1984-86, dir. colposcopy and laser clins. Portsmouth, Va., 1986-89, dir. ob-gyn. residency program, 1989-91, acting chmn. dept. ob-gyn., 1990-91; ret., 1991, asst. prof. Med. Coll. Hampton Roads, Norfolk, Va., 1991—. Chmn. dept. ob-gyn. Sentara Hosps, Norfolk, 1996—2001; ob-gyn. splty. advisor Sentara Health Mgmt. Corp., 2000—; mem. Maternal Care Futurists Adv. Bd., Hill-Rom Corp., 1998—; pres.-elect, bd. mgrs. Mid-Atlantic Women's Care, LLC, 1999—. Contbr. articles profl. jours. Awarded 1st prize scientific paper by resident physician Am. Coll. Obstetricans and Gynecologists; recipient Guggenheim fellowship Princeton U., 1967-68; Trident scholar U.S. Naval Acad., 1966-67. Fellow Am. Coll. Ob.-Gyns. (chmn. Navy sect. armed forces dist. 1989-91), Assn. Profs. Ob.-Gyns. (assoc.); mem. Am. Assn. Gynecol. Laparoscopists. Episcopalian. Home: 835 Botetourt Gdns Norfolk VA 23507-1814 Office: Woman Care Ctrs 811 Med Tower 400 Gresham Dr Norfolk VA 23507-1901 Office Phone: 757-623-3845. Personal E-mail: hdwolcott@aol.com.

WOLCOTT, JOHN WINTHROP, III, retired corporate executive; b. Balt., Dec. 3, 1924; s. John Winthrop, Jr. and Dorothy C. (Fraser) W.; m. Elizabeth Thelin Hooper, Apr. 24, 1948 (div. 1985); children: John Winthrop IV (dec.), Elizabeth T., Katherine C.; m. Karen E. Jones, Oct. 1, 1985; 1 child, Oliver Lund. B.Indsl. Engring., Gen. Motors Inst., 1951. Registered profl. engr., Ohio. With Gen. Motors Corp., 1946-53, Weatherhead Co., Cleve., 1957-60; v.p. H.K. Porter Co., Inc., Pitts., 1960-64; pres., dir., CEO Ametek, Inc., N.Y.C., 1964-66; v.p. Am. Machine & Foundry Co., 1966-77, group exec. process equipment group, 1967-70; exec. v.p. ops., dir. AMF, Inc., 1970-77; pres., chief exec. officer, dir. Transway Internat. Corp., N.Y.C., 1978-86, chmn. bd., 1982-86. Served with USCGR, 1943-46. Mem. Soc. Colonial Wars, Md. Club (Balt.) Episcopalian. Home: 210 Carrsbrook Dr Charlottesville VA 22901-1004 Personal E-mail: wolcott@cstone.net.

WOLCOTT, NANCY BOOKOUT, music director; b. Rochester, N.Y., Sept. 20, 1932; d. Raymond and Esther Anna (Mohr) Bookout; m. Vernon Wolcott, July 6, 1956; children: Deborah Nan, David Miles. MusB, U. Rochester, 1954; Sacred Music Master, Union Theol. Sem., 1956. Music dir., organist St. Mark's Luth. Ch., Balt., 1957-58; soprano soloist Franklin St. Presbyn. Ch., Balt., 1959-62; youth choir dir. First United Meth. Ch., Bowling Green, Ohio, 1963-70; music dir. Ashland Ave. Bapt. Ch., Toledo, 1971-85, First Presbyn. Ch., Bowling Green, 1986—. Festival coord. Adult Choir Festival, Toledo, 1974, 85, Chorister's Guild Youth Choirs, Toledo, 1976, 84; staff tchr. creative arts Bowling Green State U., 1977-94; workshop leader Am. Guild Organists, Toledo, 1981, Choristers Guild, Toledo, 1981, 83, 85, 87. Editor (Renaissance Madrigal show) Music and Drama of Elizabethan England, 1969, (children's day pageant) An American Heritage, 1972. Mem. Am. Guild Organists (sec. 1983-84), N.W. Ohio Sigma Alpha Iota (pres. 1985-87, Sword of Honor Alumnae chpt. 1983). Democrat. Presbyterian. Avocations: reading, theater, travel. Home: 1056 Fort Dr Bowling Green OH 43402-1205

WOLD, JOHN SCHILLER, geologist, former congressman; b. East Orange, N.J., Aug. 31, 1916; s. Peter Irving and Mary (Helff) W.; m. Jane Adele Pearson, Sept. 28, 1946; children: Peter Irving, Priscilla Adele, John Pearson. AB, St. Andrews U., Scotland and Union Coll., Schenectady, 1938; MS, Cornell U., 1939; LLD (hon.), U. Wyo., 1991. Dir. Fedn. Rocky Mountain States, 1966-68; v.p. Rocky Mountain Oil and Gas Assn., 1967, 68; mem. Wyo. Ho. of Reps., 1957-59; Wyo. Republican candidate for U.S. Senate, 1964, 70; mem. 91st Congress at large from, Wyo.; chmn., CEO Wold Trona Co., Inc.; pres., chmn. Wold Talc Co.; ret. Wold Nuclear Co., Wold Mineral Exploration Co., Casper, Wyo.; founding pres. Wyo. Heritage Soc.; founder Central Wyo. Ski Corp. Chmn. Wyo. Natural Gas Pipeline Authority, 1987-91; chmn. bd. Nuclear Exploration and Devel. Corp., Mineral Engring. Co. Contbr. articles to profl. jours. Chmn. Wyo. Rep. Com., 1960-64, Western State Rep. Chmns. Assn., 1963-64; mem. exec. com. Rep. Nat. Com., 1962-64; chmn. Wyo. Rep. State Fin. Com.; Active Little League Baseball, Boy Scouts Am., United Fund, YMCA, Boys Clubs Am.; former pres. bd. trustees Casper Coll.; trustee Union Coll. Served to lt. USNR, World War II. Named Wyo. Man of Yr. AP-UPI, 1968; Wyo. Mineral Man of Yr., 1979, Wyo. Heritage award, 1992, Wyo. Oil/Gas and Mineral Man of 20th Century, Am. Heritage Ctr. of U. Wyo., 1999; named Benefactor of Yr., Nat. Coun. for Resource Devel., 1993. Mem. Wyo. Geol. Assn. (hon. life, pres. 1956), Am. Assn. Petroleum Geologists, Ind. Petroleum Assn. Am., AAAS, Wyo. Mining Assn., Sigma Xi, Alpha Delta Phi. Episcopalian (past vestryman, warden). Home: 1231 W 30th St Casper WY 82601-5372 Office: Mineral Resource Ctr 139 W 2nd St Casper WY 82601-2473 Personal E-mail: jwold@woldoil.com. Business E-Mail: WOPI@Trib.com.

WOLD, KIMBERLY G. legislative staff member; Grad., Brigham Young U. Pub. affairs program mgr. Phoenix Met. C. of C., 1982-86; asst. dist. dir. U.S. Congressman Jon Kyl, 1987-93, dist. dir., 1993-95; dep. campaign mgr. John Kyl Campaign for U.S. Senate, 1994; dep. state dir. U.S. Sen. John Kyl, 1995-98, state dir., 1998—. Bd. dirs. Drugs Don't Work in Ariz., Maricopa County Victim Compensation Bd.; mem. Gov.'s Commn. on Violence Against Women. Home: 2560 N Lindsay Rd Apt 46 Mesa AZ 85213-1521 Office: Office of Sen Jon Kyl 2200 E Camelback Rd Ste 120 Phoenix AZ 85016-3455

WOLD, MARGARET BARTH, religion educator, author; b. Chgo., Mar. 6, 1919; d. Frank Philip and Esther Sophie (Pedersen) Barth; m. Erling Henry Wold, Oct. 4, 1942 (dec. Dec. 1999); children: John, Michael, Kristi Wold de Merlier, Stephen Ganzkow-Wold, Erling Jr. BA, Luther Coll., 1941; MA, Luth. Sch. Theology, Chgo., 1950; LittD (hon.), Calif. Luth. U., 1973; DD (hon.), Wartburg Sem., 1985, Luther Coll., 1986. Exec. bd. Am. Luth. Ch. Women, Mpls., 1966-73, exec. dir., 1973-74; dir. for ministry in changing communities So. Pacific dist., Am. Luth. Ch., 1977-84; assoc. prof. N.T. Calif. Luth. U., Thousand Oaks, 1985-89, coord. sr. mentor program, 1986-99. Organizer, dir. preschs., Calif. and N.D., 1960-72; cons. Pub. Welfare Bd., Bismarck, N.D., 1967-68; v.p. So. Calif. West Synod, Evang. Luth. Ch. in Am., 1987-90; keynote speaker Luth. World Fedn. Assembly, Budapest, Hungary, 1984; C.C. Hein Meml. lectr., 1985; study leader student conf. Sun-Moon Lake Edn. Ctr., U. Taiwan, 1977; spkr. in field. Author: The Shalom Woman, 1975, The Critical Moment, 1978, Women of Faith and Spirit, 1987, The Power of Ordinary Christians, 1988; also 5 books co-authored with Erling H. Wold. Bd. dirs. Grand Forks (N.D.) Unified Sch. Dist., 1968-70, Pacific Luth. Theol. Sem., Berkeley, Calif., 1974-86, pres. bd. dirs., 1978-84, bd. dirs., Calif. Lutheran Homes, 1996-2000, adv. bd., Ctr. for Spirituality and Ethics, Walnut Manor, Anaheim, 1999-2002. Recipient Martin Luther 450th Anniversary award Luth. Brotherhood, 1967, Disting. Svc. award Luther Coll., 1968, 125th Anniversary award Augustana Coll., S.D., 1968, Hon. Alumna award Pacific Luth. Theol. Sem., 2000. Mem. AAUW, Am. Acad. Religion, Soc. for Bibl. Lit. Democrat. Avocation: reading and writing poetry. *To live and survive with joy in today's kind of world demands the giving and receiving of hope and humor and love. As we bring these gifts into our daily contacts, they come back to enrich our individual lives and move out to increase the collective positive energies of the human spirit.*

WOLD, WILLIAM SYDNEY, molecular biology educator; b. Pine Falls, Manitoba, Can., Feb. 12, 1944; came to U.S., 1973; s. Roy and Nellie (Yurchison) W.; m. Susan Ann Lees, Dec. 30, 1967; children: Loralee Jane, William Guy, Jessica Ann, Jonathan Evered. BSc, U. Manitoba, 1965, MSc, 1968, PhD, 1973. Postdoctoral fellow St. Louis U., 1973-75, instr., 1975-76, from asst. prof. to prof. molecular virology, 1976-92, prof., chmn. dept. molecular microbiology and immunology, 1992—. Reviewer's res. NIH, Washington, 1990—; cons. Genetic Therapy, Inc., 1994. Contbr. articles to Cell Jour., Jour. Biol. Chemistry, Jour. Immunology, Jour. Virology, Virology, others; assoc. editor jour. Virology, 1990—; mem. editl. bd. Jour. Virology, 1997—. NIH grantee, 1980—. Mem. AAAS, Am. Soc. Microbiology, Am. Soc. Virology, Internat. Soc. Antiviral Rsch. Achievements include discovery and characterization of human adenovirus proteins that counteract host immunosurveillance and that either inhibit or promote cell death. Office: St Louis U Molecular Microbiology & Immunology 1402 S Grand Blvd Saint Louis MO 63104-1004

WOLDEGABRIEL, GIDAY, research geologist; b. Mai Misham/Adwa, Tigray, Ethiopia, Sept. 3, 1955; arrived in U.S., 1982; s. Giday WoldeGabriel and Mislal Mesfin; m. Almaz Berhane Tesfamichael, Jan. 15, 1994. BS in Geology with honors, Addis Ababa (Ethiopia) U., 1978, MS in Geology, 1980; PhD in Geology, Case Western Res. U., 1987. Lectr. geology Addis Ababa U., 1980-82; dir.'s postdoctoral fellow Los Alamos (N.Mex.) Nat. Lab., 1987-90, cons., 1990-92, mem. tech. staff, 1992—. Mem.: Am. Geophys. Union. Avocations: running, camping, skiing, body building, swimming. Home: PO Box 4694 Los Alamos NM 87544-3638 Office: Los Alamos Nat Lab EES-6 1 Ms D462 Los Alamos NM 87545-0001 Business E-Mail: wgiday@lanl.gov.

WOLDMAN, SHERMAN, pediatrician; b. Buffalo, Apr. 1, 1932; s. Joseph Harry and Sadie (Weinstein) W. m. Fern Marlene Weinstein, Dec. 28, 1952; children: Deborah Janine Case, Scott Alan, Sabina Heide Muller. BS in Pharmacy magna cum laude, U. Buffalo, 1953, MD with high honors, 1957. Diplomate Am. Bd. Pediat. Intern Millard Fillmore Hosp., Buffalo, 1957-58; resident in pediat. Children's Hosp., Buffalo, 1958-60, active staff, 1961—; pvt. practice Buffalo, 1961-66, Cheektowaga, NY, 1962—; mem. active staff Millard Fillmore Hosp., Buffalo, 1961—, chmn. dept. pediat., 1985-91. Adj. clin. asst. pediat. SUNY Sch. Medicine, Buffalo, 1962, clin. assoc. 1970, clin. asst. prof., 1973, clin. assoc. prof., 2001, preceptor Sch. Nursing, 1976-82; attending pediatrician Booth Meml. Hosp., Buffalo, 1969-72; sch. physician Williamsville (N.Y.) Ctrl. Schs., 1962-94, chmn. of physicians, 1970-94; courtesy staff St. Joseph Intercmty. Hosp., Cheektowaga, 1963-80, Kenmore (N.Y.) Mercy Hosp., 1963-70, 1974-82, Sisters of Charity Hosp., Buffalo, 1991-2003, Erie County Med. Ctr., Buffalo, 1979-83, Buffalo Gen. Hosp., 1987-95; provisional staff Mercy Hosp., Buffalo, 1982-83, courtesy staff, 2000-03. Vol. Leukemia and Lymphoma Soc., 1975—, bd. trustees Western N.Y. and Finger Lakes chpt. 1975—, pres. 1977-79, v.p. 1979-81, mem. profl. edn. com. 1975—, mem. nat. bd. trustees 1978-87, vice chmn. patient aid com., 1980-87; mem. task force on sch. health Erie County (N.Y.) Health Dept; trustee Temple Beth David Ner-Israel, Buffalo, 1964-65. Recipient (with Mrs. Fern Woldman) Recognition cert. Cheektowaga C. of C., 1982; Myron L. Woldman Vol. of Yr. award Western N.Y. chpt. Leukemia Soc. Am., 1987, nat. chmn.'s citation 1999; Disting. Physician award Millard Fillmore Health Sys., 1995. Mem.: Maimonides Med. Soc. (pres. Buffalo chpt. 1982—83), Med. Soc. County of Erie, N.Y. (chmn. pub. health com. 1978—79), Buffalo Pediat. Soc. (pres. 1969—70), Med. Soc. State of N.Y., Am. Acad. Pediat. (PREP fellow 1979—85, 1992—94, 1994—96, 1997—99, 2000—02), Gibson Anat. Soc. (hon.), Phi Lambda Kappa (alumni pres. 1965, v.p. alumni 1980—81), Rho Chi, Alpha Omega Alpha. Avocations: gardening, computers. Office: 2865 Genesee St Cheektowaga NY 14225

WOLD OLSEN, PER, pharmaceutical executive; MBA in Econs. Adminstrn., Norwegian Sch. Mgmt., 1972; MBA in Mgmt. and Mktg., U. Wis., 1973. Mgmt. trainee Sarpsborg Paper Co., 1968—69; product mgr. trainee MSD Norway Merck & Co., Inc., 1973, European area intern, Rahway, 1974, spl. project mgr. MSD Norway, 1974, fin. and adminstrn. mgr. MSD Norway, 1975, mng. dir. MSD Norway, 1976, regional dir. Scandinavia, 1986, v.p. MSD Europe and regional dir. Scandinavia, 1990, sr. v.p. mktg. human health divsn., 1991—94; pres. Merck Human Health, Europe, Middle East and Africa Merck & Co. Inc., Whitehouse Station, NJ, 1994—. Office: Merck & Co Inc One Merck Dr PO Box 100 Whitehouse Station NJ 08889-0100

WOLDT, HAROLD FREDERICK, JR., newspaper publishing executive; b. Atlanta, July 4, 1947; s. Harold Frederick and Dorothy Rose (Lansdowne) W.; m. Lisa Diane Neves; children: Lauren Rae, Katherine Neves, Caroline Neves. BS in Journalism, So. Ill. U., 1969. Classified advt. rep. Chgo. Tribune, 1969-70, classified automobile staff mgr., 1970-72; nat. advt. sales rep. Chgo. Tribune newspapers, N.Y.C., 1972-74, city circulation mgr., 1974-77; nat. circulation mgr. Chgo. Tribune, 1977-80, circulation mgr., 1980-84; v.p., circulation News & Sun Sentinel Co., Ft. Lauderdale, Fla., 1985; circulation mgr. Newsday, Inc., L.I., N.Y., 1985-86, circulation dir. Melville, N.Y., 1986-88, v.p., circulation Melville and L.I., NY, 1988-94; sr. v.p. circulation Newsday, pres. Distbn. Systems. Am. subs. of Newsday, Inc., 1994-98; v.p. sales circulation mktg. The N.Y. Times, N.Y.C., 1998—2000; dir. circulation Omaha World-Herald; v.p. circulation San Jose (Calif.) Mercury News, 2001—. Speaker, participant Am. Press Inst.; bd. dirs. Abilities Health and Rehab. Svcs. (Nat. Ctr. for Disability Svcs.), Albertson, L.I., N.Y., 1992-94. Bd. dirs. Robert R. McCormick Boys Club, Chgo., 1980-81; chmn. United Way campaign, Chgo. Tribune, 1980, Omaha World-Herald United Way Campaign, 1999-2000, bd. dir. San Jose Children's Discovery Mus. Calif., Ronald McDonald House Charities of the Bay Area, San Francisco, 2002—. Mem. Am. Pubs. Newspaper Assn. (circulation and readership com. 1988-93), Internat. Circulation Mgrs. Assn. (pres. 1991-92), Alpha Delta Sigma, Tau Kappa Epsilon. Office: San Jose Mercury News 750 Ridder Park Dr San Jose CA 95190 E-mail: hwoldt@mercurynews.com.

WOLENSKY, JOAN, occupational therapist, interfaith minister; b. Wilkes Barre, Pa., Mar. 4, 1954; d. Paul and Anna (Havrilla) W.; children: Maurisa Ann Fela, Jennifer Andrea Fela. BS, Coll. Misericordia, Dallas, Pa., 1985; DDiv (hon.), New Theol. Sem., N.Y.C., 1992. Cert. interfaith minister; cert. minister Order of Melchizedek, 1992; ordained minister Order of Holy Spirit, 1998; Reiki master, USUI and Karuna Sys.; cert. nat. and internat. spiritual response therapy counselor/tchr.; cert. master tchr. magnified healing. Founder, adminstr. N.E. Pa. Interfaith Ministries/Celestial Pathways Ctr., Harveys Lake, Pa., 1988; founder, dir., adminstr. Occupational Therapy Cons. Svcs., Harveys Lake, 1989; traveling occupational therapist. Dean, mem. adv. bd. Sage Inst., Shokan, N.Y.; mem. adv. bd. and quality assurance bd. At Home Health Care, Wilkes-Barre; mem. Am. Bd. Disability Analysts, 2003; mem., spkr. Am. Congress Rehab. Medicine, 1995. Contbr. articles to profl. jours. Recipient Supr.'s award City of Richmond Nursing Home, 1989; Mary K. Minglin scholar Am. Occupational Therapy Assn., 1984. Mem. Assn. for Interfaith Mins., Holistic Consortium of N.E. Pa., Inst. for Higher Healing/Wellness, Spiritual Response Assn., Universal Holistic Healers Assn., N.E. Native Am. Assn. Avocations: martial arts, yoga, angels, guitar. Home: PO Box 197 Harveys Lake PA 18618-0197

WOLF, ABE, hotel executive; CFO Helmsley Enterprises Inc., N.Y.C. Office: Helmsley Enterprises Inc 230 Park Ave Rm 333 New York NY 10169-0399

WOLF, ALFRED A. physicist, educator; b. Phila., July 21, 1925; s. Jacob Wolf, Anna Wolf; m. Enid G. Wolf, Nov. 24, 1957 (div. Dec. 1981); children: Marcus M., Laurence J. BSEE, Drexel U., 1948; MSEE, U. Pa., 1954, PhD, 1958; MD, U. Juarez, 1978. Engr.-in-charge Naval Air Devel., Johnsville, Pa.,

1949—56; chief scientist Gen. Dynamics, Rochester, NY, 1957—60; dir. rsch. Litton Industries, Silver Spring, Md., 1960—63; disting. prof. elec. engring. Drexel U., Phila., 1963—65; tech. dir. RCA, Burlington, Mass., 1965—67; assoc. tech. dir. Naval Ship R&D Ctr., Annapolis, Md., 1967—78; pres. Prime Rsch. Found., Annapolis, 1978—. Asst. prof. elec. engring. U. Pa., Phila., 1949—59; Pa. scholar, 1952—54; sr. sci. advisor USN, 1971—76; adj. assoc. prof. U. Rochester, 1960—62; adj. prof. U. Md., Annapolis, 1967—69, George Washington U., Washington, 1969—99. Author (prize winning): Biophysics of Wound Healing, 1989; contbr. 105 articles to profl. jours. (14 awards). Cpl. U.S. Army, 1943—46. Nominee Nobel Prize in Physics, 1972; named Notable Am. of Bicentennial Era, Am. Biog. Inst., 1976; recipient Citation of Honor, Drexel U., 1961, Honor citations (8), USN, 1972—83; grantee, NSF, 1956—59; Pa. scholar, 1952—54. Mem.: IEEE (life), Engring. in Medicine and Biology Soc. (chmn. Balt. sect. 1990—95), Sigma Xi. Democrat. Jewish. Achievements include patents for electronics devices and systems that include 24 in field. Avocation: writing. Home and Office: Prime Rsch Found 562 Ferry Point Rd Annapolis MD 21403-1308

WOLF, ALFRED CLARENCE, retired economist; b. Nov. 5, 1911; s. Louis and Clara (Ost) Wolf; m. Agnes Strauss, June 30, 1945; children: Sally Kathryn, John Alexander, Steven Sidney, Andrew Michael David. AB, Harvard U., 1934, MPA, 1954; postgrad., Grad. Sch. Arts and Scis., 1935—37, Army Indsl. Coll., 1941. Rsch. supr., asst. rsch. economist, assoc. rsch. economist, divsn. rsch. Works Project Adminstrn., Washington, 1938—41; head Navy Indsl. Manpower Program USN, 1941—46; spl. asst. Vet. Emer. Housing Expediter Office of War Mobilization and Reconversion, 1946—47; mem. staff office of sec. of the interior U.S. Dept. Interior, 1947—49, dir., 1949—50, exec. asst. to the sec. for defense prodn. office of the sec. of interior, 1950—53; rsch. dir. Harvard-Pakistan Planning Bd. project Harvard U., 1953—55; asst. dir. overseas devel. program Ford Found., 1955—57, developed program in Africa, 1957—58, dir. program L.Am. and Caribbean, 1959—61; dir. social devel. divsn. Inter-Am. Devel. Bank, Washington, 1961—64, program advisor to pres., 1964—77, ret., 1977. Cons. Inter-Am. Devel. Bank, Devel. & Resources, Inc., Nat. Acad. Pub. Adminstrn., George Washington U., Carnegie Endowment for Internat. Peace, The Policies Sci. Ctr., Inc., Wilcox an dAssocs., others, 1977—. Comdr. USNR, 1938—68, ret. USNR, 1968. Decorated Legion of Merit; recipient Disting. Svc. awsard, Interior Dept., 1953; fellow Conservation fellow, Harvard U., 1953—54. Mem.: Cosmos Club (Washington), Harvard Club (N.Y.C.). Home: 1057 Rocky Run Rd Mc Lean VA 22102 Office: 2011 I St NW Ste 601 Washington DC 20006-1808

WOLF, ALICE K. state legislator, former mayor; b. Vienna, Dec. 24, 1933; d. Frederick Koerner and Renee (Engel) K.; m. Robert A. Wolf, 1955; children: Eric Jeffrey, Adam Nathaniel. BS, Simmons Coll., 1955; MPA, Harvard U., 1978; EdD (hon.), Wheelock Coll., 2001. Residence staff MIT, Lincoln Lab, 1955-62, Computer Corp Am., 1967-71, pers. dir., 1971-76; mem. Cambridge Sch. Com., 1974-81, vicechairwoman, 1976-77, 80-81; chairwoman Ward 7 Dem. Com., 1976-85; committeewoman Mass. State Dem. Com.; former vice mayor City of Cambridge, Mass., mayor, 1990-91; mem. dist. 25 Middlesex Mass. Ho. of Reps., Boston. Del. Dem. Nat. Conv., 1980, 84, 88, 92, State Conv. Mem. NOW, Mass. Women's Polit. Caucas Cambridge Mental Health Assn., Am. for Dem. Action, Nat. Orgn. Women Am. Civil Liberties Union, Nat. Office: Mass Ho of Reps State House Rm 238 Boston MA 02133 Home: 48 Huron Ave Cambridge MA 02138-6706 Office Phone: 617-722-2380. Business E-Mail: rep.alicewolf@hou.state.ma.us.

WOLF, ARTHUR HENRY, museum administrator; b. New Rockford, N.D., June 18, 1953; s. Louis Irwin and Vivian Joyce (Grinde) W.; m. Holly M. Chaffee, Oct. 18, 1984. BA in Anthropology, U. Nebr., 1975; MA, U. Ariz., 1977. Lab. asst., acting curator anthropology U. Nebr. State Mus., Lincoln, 1973-75; rsch. asst. Ariz. State Mus., Tucson, 1975-77; curator of collections Sch. Am. Rsch., Santa Fe, 1977-79; dir. Millcent Rogers Mus., Taos, N.Mex., 1979-87, Nev. State Mus. and Hist. Soc., Las Vegas, 1988-92, Mus. of Rockies, Bozeman, Mont., 1992-96; pres. High Desert Mus., Bend, Oreg., 1996—2000; pres. and CEO Mus. of No. Ariz., Flagstaff, 2000—. Speaker in field; cons. Pueblos of Zuni, Picuris, San Ildefonso and Taos. Contbr. articles and revs. to profl. jours. Trustee Kokopelli Archeol. Rsch. Fund, Bozeman, 1992-96; active Mont. Ambs. Recipient Young Alumnus award U. Nebr. Lincoln, 1990. Mem. Am. Assn. Mus. (bd. dirs. 1994—, vis. com. roster 1989—, vice chair 1996-97), Rotary, Assn. Sci. Mus. Dirs. Avocations: travel, reading, music. Office: Mus No Ariz 3101 N Fort Valley Rd Flagstaff AZ 86001

WOLF, BARRY, genetics, pediatric educator; b. Chgo., June 19, 1947; s. Bert D. and Toby E. (Urkoff) W.; children: Michael Loren, Bryan Phillip. BS, U. Ill., 1969; MD, U. Ill. Coll. Medicine, 1974; PhD, U. Ill., 1974. Diplomate Am. Bd. Pediatrics, Med. and Biochem. Genetics. Intern, resident in pediatrics Childrens Meml. Hosp., Northwestern U., Chgo., 1974-76; fellow Yale U. Sch. Medicine, New Haven, Conn., 1976-78; prof. human genetics Med. Coll. Va., Richmond, 1978-2001, vice chair for rsch. dept. pediatrics, 1996-2000; dir. rsch. Conn. Children's Med. Ctr., 2001—. Assoc. chair, dir. rsch. dept. pediats. U. Conn. Sch. Medicine, 2001—. Author over 175 jour. articles and book chpts. dealing with inherited disorders of metabolism and biochem. genetics, specifically disorders of biotin metabolism. Recipient E. Mead Johnson award for pediatric rsch. Am. Acad. Pediatrics, 1988, Borden award in nutrition Am. Inst. Nutrition, 1987, Outstanding Scientist of Va. award Va. Sci. Mus., 1986, Ounce of Prevention award Action for Prevention of Va., 1985. Mem. Am. Soc. Clin. Investigation, Am. Pediat. Soc., Soc. Pediatric Rsch., Soc. for Inherited Metabolic Diseases, Am. Soc. Clin. Nutrition, Am. Inst. Nutrition, Soc. for the Study of Inborn Errors of Metabolism, Am. Soc. Human Genetics. Avocation: japanese cloisonne. Office: Conn Childrens Med Ctr 282 Washington St Hartford CT 06106 Office Phone: 860-545-9944. Business E-Mail: bwolf@ccmckids.org.

WOLF, CARL F.W. physician, biomedical engineer; b. New Hyde Park, N.Y., Feb. 4, 1933; s. Fritz J.C. and Bertha E. (Heidemann) W. BSChemE, MIT, 1953; MS in Chem. Engring. Practice, MIT, Cambridge, 1954; MD, Hahnemann Med. Coll., Phila., 1968. Diplomate Am. Bd. Pathology in Anatomic & Clin. Pathology. Intern in pathology N.Y. Hosp., N.Y.C., 1968-69, asst. pathologist II, 1969-71, provisional asst. pathologist, 1971-72, asst. dir. blood bank, 1971-76, asst. attending pathologist, 1972-79, assoc. attending pathologist, 1979-87, attending pathologist, 1987—, dir. Blood Bank & Transfusion Svc., 1976—; cons. in clin. pathology N.Y. Hosp.-Westchester Divsn., 1976-94; attending pathologist, dir. clin. lab. Burke Rehab. Ctr., White Plains, N.Y., 1974-96. Fellow in pathology Cornell U. Med. Coll., 1969-72, instr. in pathology, 1972-73, asst. prof. pathology, 1973-79, assoc. clin. prof. pathology, 1979-83, assoc. prof. clin. pathology, 1983-87, prof. clin. pathology, 1987—; vis. fellow dept. pathology Meml. Hosp. for Cancer and Allied Diseases, N.Y., 1970; USPHS trainee in exptl. pathology Cornell U. Med. Coll., 1969-71; rsch. assoc. N.Y. Blood Ctr., 1969-75; assoc. investigator Lindsley F. Kimball Rsch. Inst.-N.Y. Blood Ctr., 1975-83, 84-87. Contbr. numerous articles to profl. jours., chpts. to books; invited lectr. in field. Fellow Am. Soc. Clin. Pathologists, N.Y. Acad. Medicine; mem. AMA, AIChE, Am. Assn. Blood Banks, Coun. Hosp. Blood Bank Dirs. Greater N.Y. Region (bd. dirs., chmn.), Soc. for Study of Blood, Blood Banks Assn. N.Y. State, Am. Chem. Soc., Acad. Clin. Lab. Physicians and Scientists, Alpha Omega Alpha, Phi Lambda Upsilon, Tau Beta Pi. Home: 435 E 70th St Apt 21-j New York NY 10021-5347 Office: NY Presbyn Hosp Weill Cornell Ctr 525 E 68th St New York NY 10021-4870

WOLF, CHADWICK LINWOOD, small business owner, firefighter; s. Charles Louis Wolf and Linda Grace Carew; m. Kelly Ann Zeegers, Apr. 25, 1998. A in Fire Sci., Fox Valley Tech. Coll., Appleton, Wis., 1994—97. Profl. firefighter City of Green Bay, Wis., City of Eau Claire, Wis.; firefighter Grand Chute Fire Dept., Wis.; engineman/firefighter US Navy. Tchr., fire safety and owner Personal Sec. & Awareness, Green Bay. SP,E4 USN, 1991—93, SP, E4 USN, 2002—04. Recipient Black Belt, Tae Kwon Do, Cho's Black Belt Acad./Green Bay, 1991. Mem.: Cho's Black Belt Acad. Republican. Catholic. Achievements include promoting fire safety in local schools in Green Bay and Eau Claire, Wis.; trained as hazardous materials tech., City Hazmat Team; emer. med. tech.; cert. state fire insp. Avocations: guitar, martial arts, poetry, history.

WOLF, CHARLES, JR., economist, educator; b. NYC, Aug. 1, 1924; s. Charles and Rosalie W.; m. Theresa van de Wint, Mar. 1, 1947; children: Charles Theodore, Timothy van de Wint. BS, Harvard U., 1943, M.P.A., 1948, PhD in Econs., 1949. Economist, fgn. service officer U.S. Dept. State, 1945-47, 49-53; mem. faculty Cornell U., 1953-54, U. Calif., Berkeley, 1954-55; sr. economist The Rand Corp., Santa Monica, Calif., 1955-67, head econs. dept., 1967-81; dean The Rand Grad. Sch., 1970-97, sr. econ. advisor, 1981—, corp. fellow in internat. econs., 1996—; sr. fellow Hoover Inst., 1988—. Bd. dirs. Capital Income Builder Fund, Capital World Growth Fund; lectr. econs. UCLA, 1960-72; mem. adv. bd. ctr. internat. bus. and econ. rsch., UCLA Anderson Grad. Sch., 1996—. Author: The Costs and Benefits of the Soviet Empire, 1986, Markets or Governments: Choosing Between Imperfect Alternatives, 1989, 2d edit., 1993, Linking Economic Policy and Foreign Policy, 1991, Long-Term Economic and Military Trends: The United States and Asia, 1994-2015, 1995, The Economic Pivot in a Political Context, 1997; co-author: Economic Openness: Many Facets, Many Metrics, 1999, Asian Economic Trends and Their Security Implications, 2000, European Military Prospects, Economic Constraints and the Rapid Reaction Force, 2001, Straddling Economics and Politics: Cross-Cutting Issues, in Asia, the United States and the Global Economy, 2002, Fault Lines in China's Economic Terrain, 2003; mem. editl. bd.: Korean Jour. Def. Econs., 1995—, Society, 1997—; contbr. articles to profl. jours. Mem. Assn. for Public Policy Analysis and Mgmt. (pres. 1980-81), Am. Econs. Assn., Econometric Soc., Coun. on Fgn. Rels., Internat. Inst. Strategic Studies London. Clubs: Cosmos (Washington); Riviera Tennis (Los Angeles); Harvard (N.Y.). Office: The Rand Corp 1700 Main St Santa Monica CA 90407-2138 Business E-Mail: wolf@rand.org.

WOLF, CHARLES A. retail camera and photographic supplies executive; m. Missi Harnell; children: Alex, Tracey, Madeline. BBA, U. Okla., 1963. Founder Wolf Camera, Atlanta, 1974, now pres., CEO. Bd. dirs. First Union Bank. Bd. advisors Ga. State U. Bus. Sch.; bd. visitors Emory U.; bd. councilors the Carter Ctr., Atlanta; bd. dirs. Buckhead Coalition, Atlanta Symphony Orch., Atlanta C. of C., Paralympic Games, Ga. Ctr. for Children, Genesis Shelter, Jr. Achievement, United Way; chmn. adv. bd. united Way Drug Abuse Action Ctr.; chmn. Good-Touch/Bad-Touch, Atlanta. Named Retailer of Yr., Photographic Trade News mag., Entrepreneur of Yr. Bus. Atlanta mag., marketof of Yr. Atlanta chpt. Am. Mktg. Assn.; named to Ga. State U. Bus. Hall of Fame. Mem. Golf Club of Ga. Office: Wolf Camera 115 Perimeter Ctr Pl NE Ste 1040 Atlanta GA 30346-1281

WOLF, CHRISTINE STRELOW, piano teacher; b. Rochester, Minn., Jan. 27, 1964; d. Donald Eugene and Arlene Audrey Strelow; m. Michael Joseph Wolf, Nov. 02, 1991; children: Elizabeth and Gregory. MusB cum laude, St. Cloud State U., 1986; postgrad. piano performance, Hartt Sch. Music, 1987-89. Nat. cert. tchr. music. Ind. music tchr. Music Tchrs'. Nat. Assn., Rochester, St. Cloud, and Hartford, Minn., Conn., 1982-89, Apple Valley, Minn., 1992—; music link tchr. Nat. Assn. Music Tchrs., 1999—. Chmn. Nat. Guild Auditions, Apple Valley, 1999—; contest judge coord. Minn. Assn. Music Tchrs., 1991-98; accompanist Mayo H.S., Redeemer Lutheran Ch., Rochester, 1979-82, St. Cloud State U. choirs, vocal dept., 1982-86; dir. children's choir Emanuel Lutheran Ch., Hartford, 1988-89; music dir. Lutheran Ch. Our Savior, Rosemount, Minn., 1994—; min. of music All St. Eagen, 2002-. Composer, arranger contemporary Christian songs; TV and radio appearances including Live From Landmark, 1972-82, 86, 88-89; composer (piano duet) Porcupine Polka, 2003. Performer various nursing homes, Dakota county; organizer student performances nursing homes, malls, Dakota County. Recipient Hiawathaland 1st place Rochester Keyboard Club, 1981, Duet Competition 1st place Dorian Music Festival Luther Coll., Decorah, Iowa, 1982; Ruth Gant Meml. scholar, St. Cloud State U., 1984-86. Mem.: Minn. Assn. Music Tchrs. (v.p. conv. 2002—), Minn. Music Tchrs. Assn. (judge 1991—, contest judge coord. 1992—, adjudication com. 2000—, conv. com. 2001—, Young Artist of 1986), Am. Coll. Musicians (adjucator, chmn. 1991, judge 1999, Paderewski Gold medal, Piano diploma 1982), Music Tchrs. Nat. Assn., Nat. Fedn. Music Clubs. E-mail: wolfpiano@Prodigy.net.

WOLF, CHRISTOPHER ROBIN, investment executive; b. Richmond, Va., Apr. 29, 1954; s. Rene Arthur and Charlotte Elizabeth W.; m. Lise Holt Honoré; children: Eleonor Charlotte, Elyssa Harriet. BA summa cum laude, univ. honors, Ohio Wesleyan U., 1978; MBA, Yale U., 1983. Pres. Computer Data Designs Co., San Francisco, 1978-81; v.p. investment banking Kidder, Peabody & Co. Inc., N.Y.C., 1983-88; sr. v.p., ptnr. mergers and acquisitions Oppenheimer & Co., Inc., N.Y.C., 1989-91; mng. ptnr. The Georgica Group, N.Y.C., 1991—96; sr. v.p., group head investment banking Fahnestock & Co., Inc., N.Y.C., 1996; exec. v.p., CFO Hyseq, Inc., Sunnyvale, Calif., 1996-99; pres., CEO Protogene Labs., Inc., Palo Alto, Calif., 1999—2001; CEO, chief investment officer KingsGate Capital Mgmt., LLC, San Francisco, 2001—. Adj. prof. Columbia U. Grad. Sch. Bus. Trustee Arneson Inst., Delaware, Ohio; ptnr. Blue Hill Ptnrs., N.Y.C., 604 Ptnrs., San Francisco, Rock Creek Ptnrs., Boulder, Colo. Mem. Knickerbocker Club, River Club, Yale Club, Phi Beta Kappa. Episcopalian. Avocations: expedition trekking, tennis, collecting antiquities, sailing. Office: KingsGate Capital Mgmt LLC 410 Jessie St Ste 801 San Francisco CA 94103 E-mail: cwolf@kingsgatecapital.com.

WOLF, CYNTHIA TRIBELHORN, librarian, library educator; b. Denver, Dec. 12, 1945; adopted d. John Baltazar and Margaret (Kern) Tribelhorn (dec.); m. H.Y. Rassam, Mar. 2l, 1969 (div. Jan. 1988); children: Najma Christine, Yousuf John; adopted children: Leonard Joseph Lucero, Lakota E. Narsay Rassam-Lucero, McKinley William Osborn, Kevin Trey, Jackson Andrew Lee, Rachel A., Andrew C.A.; m. Walter Larry Peck, June 21, 1965 (div. Feb. 1967). BA, Colo. State U., 1970; MLS, U. Denver, 1985. Cert. permanent profl. librarian, N.Mex. Elem. tchr. Sacred Heart Sch., Farmington, N.Mex., 1973-78; asst. prof. libr. sci. edn. U. N.Mex., Albuquerque, 1985-91, dir. libr. sci. edn. divsn., 1989-91; pres. Info. Acquisitions, Albuquerque, 1990-99; libr. dir. Southwestern Coll., Santa Fe, 1992-94; mem. youth resources Rio Grande Valley Libr. Sys., Albuquerque, 1994-95, adult reference svc., 1995-98; with Albuquerque Pub. Schs., 1998—, coach nat. sch. reform policy, 2000—; instr. U. N.Mex., 1998-99. Fine arts resource person for gifted edn. Farmington Pub. Schs., 1979-83; speaker Unofficial Mentorships and Market Rsch., 1992-98. Mem. Farmington Planning and Zoning Commn., l980-8l; bd. dirs. Farmington Mus. Assn., l983-84; pres. Farmington Symphony League, 1978. Mem. ALA, N.Mex. Library Assn., LWV (bd. dirs. Farmington, 1972-74, 75, pres.). Avocations: mixed media graphics design, market research, creative approaches to personal journals, board game design.

WOLF, DALE B. corporate financial executive, health facility administrator; V.p. specialty ops. The Travelers, 1988—94; sr. v.p. bus. devel. MetraHealth Cos., Inc., 1995; exec. v.p. SpectraScan Health Svcs., Inc., 1995—96; sr. v.p. Coventry Health Care, Bethesda, Md., 1996—98, CFO, 1996—, treas., 1996—, exec. v.p., 1998—. Office: Coventry Health Care 6705 Rockledge Dr Bethesda MD 20817

WOLF, DALE EDWARD, state official; b. Kearney, Nebr., Sept. 6, 1924; m. Clarice Wolf; 4 children. BSc, U. Nebr., 1945; PhD in Agronomy and Weed Control, Rutgers U., 1949. With Dept. Agr., 1946; assoc. prof. agronomy Rutgers U., 1949; with E.I. duPont de Nemours & Co., Inc., from 1950, dir. agrichem. mktg., then gen. mgr. biochem. dept., 1972-79; v.p. biochems., also chmn. bd. subs. Endo Labs., Inc., Wilmington, Del., from 1979; group v.p. Agrl. Products, Wilmington, Del., from 1983; dir. Del. Devel. Office, Dover, 1987-89; lt. gov. of Del. Dover, 1989-93; gov. State of Del., Dover, 1993. Vice chmn. WSFS Bank, 1998, Emerald Bioagr. Corp., 2002—; trustee Christiana Care Health Svcs., 2002—. Co-author: Principles of Weed Control, 1951. Bd. dirs. Del. chpt. ARC, 1975; gen. campaign chmn. United Way Del., 1978, also bd. dirs.; gen. campaign chmn. Girls Club Del., 1987; chmn. Del. Found. for Literacy, 1993-98; mem. adv. bd. U. Del. Hotel, Restaurant Mgmt. Sch., 1993—; chmn. Stand Up for What is Right and Just, 2003--. 1st lt. AUS, 1943-46. Decorated Bronze Star, Purple Heart. Mem. Nat. Agrl. Chem. Assn. (chmn. 1981-83), Pharm. Mfrs. Assn. (dir.), Masons, Farmhouse Fraternity, Sigma Xi, Alpha Zeta. Republican.

WOLF, DALE JOSEPH, utilities company executive; b. Hays, Kans., Aug. 21, 1939; s. Henry and Irene Elizabeth (Basgall) W.; m. Patricia Ann Ceule, May 28, 1966; children: Suzanne, Sara. BS in Bus. Adminstrn., Ft. Hays State U., 1961; MBA in Fin., U. Mo., 1970. Various acctg. and fin. positions Mo. Pub. Service Co., Kansas City, Mo., 1962-77, treas., 1977-84, v.p., treas., 1984-85; v.p. fin. UtiliCorp United, Inc., Kansas City, 1985—. Mem. Fin. Execs. Inst., Corp. Fin. Inst. Lodges: Kiwanis (pres. 1977-78). Republican. Roman Catholic. Office: UtiliCorp United Inc 20 W 9th St Kansas City MO 64105-1704

WOLF, DICK (RICHARD A. WOLF), television producer, film company executive; b. N.Y.C., Dec. 20, 1946; m. Susan Scranton, 1970 (div. 1981); m. Christine Marburg, 1983; 3 children. Student, U. Pa. Exec. producer, pres. Wolf Films, Inc. Copywriter, producer over a dozen campaigns and 100 TV commls., 1969-76; producer, writer (screenplay) Skateboard, 1978, School Ties, 1992; writer, script cons. (TV series) Hill Street Blues, 1985 (Emmy award, Writer's Guild nominations for episode What are Friends For); writer, producer (film) No Man's Land, 1987; writer, producer and actor (film) Masquerade, 1988; writer, exec. producer 4 installments (series TV movies) Gideon Oliver, 1989; writer, creator, exec. producer (series TV movies) Christine Cromwell, 1989-90, (TV series) Nasty Boys, 1990, H.E.L.P., Law & Order, 1990, (Producers Guild Am. shared award Episodic TV 1996, Emmy award Outstanding Drama Series, 1996/97), Mann & Machine, 1992, The Human Factor, 1992, Crime and Punishment, 1993, South Beach, 1993, New York Undercover, 1994, Swift Justice, 1996, Arrest and Trial, 2000, Dragnet, 2003-04; creator, exec. producer (TV series) Feds, 1997, Players; exec. producer (TV series) Law & Order: Special Victims Unit, 1999—, D.C., 2000, Deadline, 2000-01, Law & Order Crime & Punishment, 2002—; exec. prodr., writer Law & Order Criminal Intent, 2001—; prodr. (TV documentary) Twin Towers, 2003. Office: Wolf Films Inc c/o Universal TV 100 Universal City Plz Universal City CA 91608-1002*

WOLF, DONALD JOSEPH, industrial engineer, consultant; b. Waynesboro, Pa., Feb. 28, 1925; s. Joseph Herman and Olive Mae (Kepner) W.; m. Betty Irene Stull, May 26, 1950; children: Darrell Joseph, Robert Lee, David Wayne. BS in Wood Tech., N.C. State U., 1953; MS in Indsl. Engring., LaSalle U., 1995, PhD, 1996. Registered profl. engr., Calif., Md. Foreman, indsl. engr. York County Chair Co., Red Lion, Pa., 1953-57; supt. indsl. engr. Hoke Furniture Co., Thurmont, Md., 1957-60; plant mgr., indsl. engr. Statton Furniture Co., Hagerstown, Md., 1960-70; internat. cons. Ross Assocs., Inc., Asheville, N.C., 1970-78; pres., prin. cons. Wood Arts, Inc., Frederick, Md., 1978—. Staff cons. Samuel Lawrence Furniture Co., Phoenix, 1990-98. Active Citizen Amb. program People to People Internat; forestry bd. vice chmn. Frederick County, Md.; cubmaster, scoutmaster Boy Scouts Am., Red Lion and Thurmont, 1957-60; v.p. Jr. C. of C., Red Lion, 1958-59; v.p. St. John's Luth. Ch., Thurmont, 1986-88, lay asst. min., 1988-93. Sgt. U.S. Army C.E., 1943-47, ETO. Mem. NSPE (life), Md. Soc. Profl. Engrs. (life), Calif. Soc. Profl. Engrs., Inst. Indsl. Engrs. (life, sr.), Order of the Engr., Md. Hist. Soc., Frederick County (Md.) Hist. Soc., Adams County (Pa.) Hist. Soc., York County (Pa.) Hist. Soc., Buckinghamshire (Eng.) Hist. Soc., Kitochtinny Hist. Soc., Libr. of Congress (assoc.), Nat. Trust, Smithsonian Resident Assoc., N.C. State Alumni Assn., Soc. of War of 1812, Elks, Am. Legion (life), VFW (life), SAR (past pres., v.p., newsletter editor, historian, Bronze medal, Cert. of Disting. Svc., War Svc. medal, Silver medal, Silver Disting. Svc. medal), Soc. of Wood Sci. and Tech., Forest Products Rsch. Soc. (divsn. chmn.), Nat. Congress of Patriotic Orgns. (founding fellow), Ho. of Gordon, Clan MacLean Internat. (life), Clan McLaine of Lochbuie, Xi Sigma Pi. Republican. Avocation: genealogy. Home and Office: Wood Arts Inc 6905 Balsam Ct Frederick MD 21703-7146

WOLF, EDITH MALETZ, retired educator; b. Warsaw, Nov. 12, 1922; came to U.S., 1923; d. Michael and Sonia Chai (Ingerov) Maletz; m. Jordan Melvin Wolf, July 7, 1946; 1 child, David Richard (dec.). BS, U. Wis., 1944, MS, 1968. Cert. tchr. Wis. Tchr. Milw. Pub. Schs., 1945-85, acting vice prin., 1980-81, ret., 1985. Author: The Magic Dreydle, 1962, The New Governess, 1970, (play) The Dream. Mem. Saturday Arts, Milw., 1970-80, Wis. Painters and Sculptors, Milw., 1944—. Scholarship Dudley Krafts Watson, 1944. Mem. AAUW, Hadassah (sec. 1980-81, pres. emeritus, donor chair, program chair), Nat. Mus. Women in the Arts, Florentine Opera Club (founding mem.), U. Wisc. Alumni Assn., Cousteau Soc. Avocations: reading, writing fiction, plays, painting, gardening.

WOLF, ELIZABETH ANN, writer, storyteller, visual arts; d. Walter LeRoy and Ruth Estelle Wolf; children: Theresa Marie, Sharon Michelle, Robert Anthony. Comml. artist, freelance Gen. Store Inc., NJ, 1970—79; freelance Britt's Dept. Store, NJ, 1970—79; mktg. promotions, freelance Sear's Dept. Store, Am. appliance, Bamberger's Dept. Store, Kiiack Pools, Krupps, Litton Co., and Silverstone, NJ. Author: (poetry) Flights of Mind, 1996, (children's stories and audio books) Bedtime and Other Time Stories, 2001, Secret Places, 2002, Journey Down Story Book Lane, 2002, Alley Cat and Birdie Blue, 2002, Frogs in a Bogg, 2003; author: (creator) Stories by Lamplight, 2004; music pub. Storytime Music BMI, recording artist StoryBookZone.com. Mem.: Nat. Poet's Soc., Am. Fedn. Astrologers. Achievements include audio books with sound effects and music designed to be entertaining, especially for visually impaired children and adults; several awards for art and poetry. Avocations: art, woodcarving, meditation, walking, swimming. Home and Office: PO Box 7503 Seminole FL 33772 Office Phone: 877-633-1123.

WOLF, ELLEN C. water company executive; BA, Duke U.; MBA in Acctg. and Fin., U. Pa. With Bell Atlantic Corp. and subs. cos.; CFO Bell Atlantic Mobile; exec. dir. strategic planning and bus. devel. Bell Atlantic Enterprises Internat., v.p., treas., officer, 1995-99; CFO Am. Water Works Co., Inc., Voorhees, N.J., 1999—. Office: Am Water Works Co Inc 1025 Laurel Oak Rd Kirkwood Voorhees NJ 08043

WOLF, FRANK R. congressman, lawyer; b. Phila., Jan. 30, 1939; m. Carolyn Stover; children: Frank, Virginia, Anne, Brenda, Rebecca. BA, Pa. State U., 1961; LL.B., Georgetown U., 1965. Bar: Va., D.C. Legis. asst. former Congressman Edward G. Biester, Jr., 1968-71; asst. to Sec. of Interior Rogers B. Morton, 1971-74; dep. asst. sec. for Congl. and Legis. Affairs, Dept. Interior, 1974-75; mem. U.S. Congress from 10th Va. dist., Washington, 1981—. Mem. appropriations com. Served with USAR, 1962—63. Republican. Presbyterian. Office: US Ho of Reps 241 Cannon Bldg Washington DC 20515-4610

WOLF, FREDERICK GEORGE, environmental scientist, administrator; b. Paterson, N.J., Aug. 30, 1952; s. Frederick George and Doris (Miller) W. BS, U. S.C., 1974; postgrad., Clemson U., 1976-77; MS in Environ. Health, East Tenn. State U., 1978; MS in Sys. Mgmt., U. Denver, 1990; DBA in Mgmt., Nova Southeastern U., 2000. Phys. scientist U.S. Army Environ. Hygiene Agy., Edgewood, Md., 1974-75, S.C. Dept. Health and Environ. Control, Columbia, 1977-78; environ. scientist EPA, Atlanta, 1978-79, Boston, 1979—81, Seattle, 1981—86; mgr. hazardous waste sect. Parametrix Inc., Bellevue, Wash., 1986-88; regional mgr. environ. remediation Atofina Chems., Inc., Tacoma, 1988—. Bd. dirs. Acad. of Hazardous Materials Mgmt.; Lt. USNR, 1974-87. Recipient Spl. Svc. award EPA, 1982, Bronze medal, 1983. Mem. Soaring Soc. Am. (Bronze badge number 338), Sigma Xi, Epsilon Nu Eta, Sigma Beta Delta. Office: Atofina Chems Inc 2901 Taylor Way Tacoma WA 98421-4330

WOLF, G. VAN VELSOR, JR., lawyer; b. Balt., Feb. 19, 1944; s. G. Van Velsor and Alice Roberts (Kimberly) W.; m. Ann Holmes Kavanagh, May 19, 1984; children: George Van Velsor III, Timothy Kavanagh (dec.), Christopher Kavanagh, Elisabeth Huxley. BA, Yale U., 1966; JD, Vanderbilt U., 1973. Bar: N.Y. 1974, U.S. Dist. Ct. (so. dist.) N.Y. 1974, U.S. Ct. Appeals (2d cir.) 1974,

Ariz. 1982, U.S. Dist. Ct. Ariz. 1982, U.S. Ct. Appeals (9th cir.) 1982. Agrl. advisor U.S. Peace Corps., Tanzania and Kenya, 1966-70; assoc. Milbank, Tweed, Hadley & McCloy, N.Y.C., 1973-75; vis. lectr. law Airlangga U., Surabaya, Indonesia, 1975-76; editor-in-chief Environ. Law Reporter, Washington, 1976-81; assoc. Lewis & Roca, Phoenix, 1981-84, ptnr., 1984-91, Snell & Wilmer, Phoenix, 1991—. Vis. lectr. law U. Ariz., 1990, Vanderbilt U., 1991, U. Md., 1994, Ariz. State U., 1995; cons. Nat. Trust Hist. Preservation, Washington, 1981. Editor: Toxic Substances Control, 1980; editor in chief Environ. Law Reporter 1976-81; contbr. articles to profl. jours. Bd. dirs. Ariz. divsn. Am. Cancer Soc., 1985—96, sec. Ariz. divsn., 1990—92, vice-chmn. Ariz. divsn., 1992—94, chmn. Ariz. divsn., 1994—96, bd. dirs. S.W. divsn. Ariz. divsn., 1996—2003, chmn. Ariz. divsn., 1996—98, nat. bd. dirs., 1999—, bd. dirs. Gt. West divsn., 2003—, bd. dirs., Cancer Action Network, 2002—, pres. Cancer Action Network, 2003—; bd. dirs. Herberger Theatre Ctr., 1998—, sec., 2001—03, vice chmn., 2003—; bd. dirs. Phoenix Little Theatre, 1983—90, chmn., 1986—88. Recipient St. George medal Am. Cancer Soc., 1998. Mem. ABA (vice-chmn. SONREEL comm. state and regional environ. coop. 1995-98, co-chmn. 1998-2000, vice-chmn. environ. audits task force 1998-99, vice-chmn. SONREEL ann. meeting planning com. 1998-99), Assn. of Bar of City of N.Y., Ariz. State Bar Assn. (coun. environ. & nat. res. law sect. 1988-93, chmn. 1991-92, CLE com. 1992-98, chmn. 1997-98), Maricopa County Bar Assn., Ariz. Acad., Union Club N.Y.C., Univ. Club Phoenix, Phoenix Country Club. Office: Snell & Wilmer 1 Arizona Ctr Phoenix AZ 85004-0001 E-mail: vwolf@swlaw.com.

WOLF, GARY WICKERT, retired lawyer; b. Slinger, Wis., Apr. 19, 1938; s. Leonard A. and Cleo C. (Wickert) W.; m. Jacqueline Weltzin, Dec. 17, 1960; children: Gary, Jonathan. BBA, U. Minn., 1960, JD cum laude, 1963. Bar: N.Y. 1964, U.S. Ct. Appeals (2d cir.) 1969, U.S. Dist. Ct. (so. dist.) N.Y. 1969, U.S. Supreme Ct. 1971. Assoc. Cahill, Gordon & Reindel, NYC, 1963—70, ptnr., 1970—2003, counsel, 2004. Bd. dirs. N.J. Resources Corp., N.J. Natural Gas Co. Mem. N.Y. State Bar Assn. (com. on securities regulation), Anglers Club (N.Y.C.), Downtown Assn. (N.Y.C.), Mashomack Fish and Game Club.

WOLF, GREGORY H. insurance company executive; b. Erie, Pa. married; 2 children. BS, Penn State U.; MS in Hosp. and Health Svcs. Adminstrn., Ctrl. Mich. U.; postgrad., Cornell U., U. Pa. V.p. mktg. and sales, then sr. v.p., exec. v.p., pres. Employers Health, Green Bay, Wis., 1988-95; sr. v.p. sales and mktg. Humana Inc., Louisville, 1995-96, COO, pres., 1996—97, CEO, pres., 1997—99; pres. Cigna Inc., Small Bus. Initiative, 2001—; mem. bd. of dir. Shopko Stores, Inc., Green Bay. Past bd. dirs. Boys and Girls Club of Green Bay, Cystic Fibrosis Found. Green Bay. Office: Cigna Corp 1 Liberty Place Philadelphia PA 19192-1550

WOLF, HANS ABRAHAM, retired pharmaceutical company executive; b. Frankfurt, Fed. Republic Germany, June 27, 1928; came to U.S., 1936, naturalized, 1944; s. Franz Benjamin and Ilse (Nathan) W.; m. Elizabeth J. Bassett, Aug. 2, 1958; children: Heidi Elizabeth, Rebecca Wolf Eckert, Deborah Wolf Streeter, Andrew Robert. AB magna cum laude, Harvard U., 1949, MBA, 1955; PhB, Oxford U., 1951. Math instr. Tutoring Sch., 1946-47; statis. research Nat. Bur. Econ. Research, N.Y.C., 1948-49; researcher Georgetown U., 1951-52; confidential aide Office Dir. Mut. Security, Washington, 1952; analyst Ford Motor div. Ford Motor Co., Dearborn, Mich., summer 1954; foreman prodn. M&C Nuclear Inc., Attleboro, Mass., 1955-57; asst. supt. prodn. Metals & Controls Corp., Attleboro, 1957-59, mgr. product dept., 1959-62, controller, 1962-67; asst. v.p., controller materials and services group Tex. Instruments Inc., Dallas, 1967-69, treas., v.p., 1969-75; v.p. fin., chief fin. officer Syntex Corp., Palo Alto, Calif., 1975-78, exec. v.p., 1978-86, vice chmn., chief adminstrv. officer, 1986-92, vice chmn., 1992-93, also bd. dirs., 1986-93. Bd. dirs. Tab Products Co., San Jose, Calif., chmn., 1995—; bd. dirs. Network Equipment Techs., Fremont, Calif., chmn., 1996—; bd. dirs. Satellite Dialysis Ctrs., Inc., Redwood City, Calif. Author: Motivation Research—A New Aid to Understanding Your Markets, 1955. Mem. Norton (Mass.) Sch. Bd., 1959-62, chmn., 1961-62; pres., bd. dirs. Urban League Greater Dallas, 1971-74; bd. dirs. Dallas Health Planning Coun., mem. community adv. com., 1973-75; bd. dirs., pres. Children's Health Coun. of the Mid Peninsula; cubmaster Boy Scouts Am., 1976-78; elder United Ch. Christ, 1970-73, vice chmn. gen. bd., 1970-71, moderator, 1978-80; trustee Pacific Sch. Religion, 1986-94, chmn., 1990-94; trustee World Affairs Coun. San Francisco, 1986-92, 94-97; dir. Tech Mus. San Jose, 1992-98. With USAF, 1952-53. Mem. Am. Mgmt. Assn. (planning council fin. div. 1970-76), Phi Beta Kappa. Office: Network Equipment Technologies Inc 6500 Paseo Padre Pkwy Fremont CA 94555

WOLF, HAROLD ARTHUR, finance educator; b. Lind, Wash., Feb. 10, 1923; s. Edward and Olga (Limert) W.; March 23, 1961; children: Mark, Suellen. BA, U. Oreg., 1951; MA, U. Mich., 1952, PhD, 1958. Instr. Lehigh U., 1955-56; economist Prudential Life Ins. Co., Newark, 1957-58; asst. prof. fin., money, banking U. Colo., 1958-60, assoc. prof., 1961-64, prof., 1965-68; prof. fin. U. Tex., Austin, 1969—; pvt. practice consulting for fin. instns., 1960—. Author: Personal Finance, 1978, 8th edit., 1989, Managing Your Money, 1977, Personal Financial Planning, 8th edit., 1989, 3d custom edit., 2000. Served with U.S. Navy, 1941-47. Mem. Am. Economic Assn., Am. Fin. Assn., So. Fin. Assn. Home: 7004 Edgefield Dr Austin TX 78731-2926 Office: U Tex Dept Finance Austin TX 78712

WOLF, HAROLD HERBERT, pharmacy educator; b. Quincy, Mass., Dec. 19, 1934; s. John I. and Bertha F. (Sussman) W.; m. Joan Z. Silverman, Aug. 11, 1957; children: Gary Jerome, David Neal. BS, Mass. Coll. Pharmacy, 1956; PhD, U. Utah, 1961; LLD (hon.), U. Md., 1994. Asst. prof. pharmacology Coll. Pharmacy Ohio State U., 1961-64, assoc. prof., 1964-69, prof., 1969-76, Kimberly prof., 1975-76, chmn. divsn. pharmacology, 1973-76; dean Coll. of Pharmacy, U. Utah, Salt Lake City, 1976-89, prof. pharmacology, 1976—, dir. Anticonvulsant Drug Devel. Program, 1989—2002. Vis. prof. U. Sains Malaysia, 1973-74; mem. Nat. Joint Commn. on Prescription Drug Use, 1976-80; mem. NIH rev. com. Biomed. Rsch. Devel. Grant Program, 1978-79; external examiner U. Malaya, 1978, 92, 96, U. Sains Malaysia, 1980. Contbr. articles in field of ctrl. nervous sys. pharmacology and field of pharm. edn. Recipient Alumni Achievement award Mass. Coll. Pharmacy, 1978, Disting. Faculty award U. Utah, 1989, Rosenblatt prize, 1989, Disting. Alumnus award Coll. Pharmacy, U. Utah, 1991, Weaver prize, 2000. Fellow AAAS, Acad. Pharm. Scis.; mem. Am. Soc. Pharmacology and Exptl. Therapeutics, Am. Pharm. Assn. (task force on edn. 1982-84), Am. Assn. Colls. of Pharmacy (pres. 1977, Disting. Pharmacy Educator award 1988, scholar in residence 1989, chmn. commn. on implementing change in pharmacy edn. 1989-92, 95-96), Am. Soc. Hosp. Pharmacists (commn. on goals 1982-84), Am. Coun. on Pharm. Edn. (bd. dirs. 1985-88), Soc. Neurosci. Jewish. Home: 4467 Adonis Dr Salt Lake City UT 84124-3922 Office: Univ Utah Coll Pharmacy Salt Lake City UT 84112

WOLF, J. STEVEN (JOHN STEVEN WOLF), construction executive, land developer; b. Portsmouth, Ohio, Sept. 4, 1947; s. John Andrew and Betty Lee Wolf; m. Pamela Gahm, Mar. 11, 1995. BS in Civil Engring., Ohio U., 1975. Registered profl. engr., Ohio, Ind. Project engr. Columbus & So. Ohio Electric Co., 1974-75; staff project engr. Goodyear Atomic Corp., Piketon, Ohio, 1975-78; constrn. mgr. Am. Electric Power Svc. Corp., Lancaster, Ohio, 1978-83; project mgr. F. and P. Mgrs., Inc., Columbus, Ohio, 1983-85, Target Constrn. Co., Columbus, 1985-91; area mgr. Sherman R. Smoot Co., Indpls., 1991-93; dir. constrn. Pizzuti Devel., Inc., Columbus, 1993-2000; v.p. ops. Renier Constrn. Corp., Columbus, 2000—01; land devel. projects dir. C.V. Perry & Co., Columbus, Ohio, 2001—03; project mgr. Exxcel Project Mgmt., Columbus, 2003—. Panel mem., spkr. at seminars and classes in mgmt. and constrn. related areas. With U.S. Army, 1968-69, Vietnam. Decorated Army Commendation medal (2), Combat Infantryman badge. Mem. NSPE, Ohio Soc. Profl. Engrs., Masons, Scottish Rite, Shriners. Methodist. Home: 13675 Bevelheimer Rd Westerville OH 43081-9651 Office: Exxcel Project Mgmt Two Miranova Pl Ste 250 Columbus OH 43215 E-mail: jstevenwolf@aol.com.

WOLF, JACK KEIL, electrical engineer, educator; b. Newark, Mar. 14, 1935; s. Joseph and Rosaline Miriam (Keil) W.; m. Toby Katz, Sept. 10, 1955; children: Joseph Martin, Jay Steven, Sarah Keil. BS, U. Pa., 1956; MSE., Princeton, 1957, MA, 1958, PhD, 1960. With R.C.A., Princeton, N.J., 1959-60; asso. prof. N.Y. U., 1963-65; from asso. prof. to prof. elec. engring. Poly. Inst. Bklyn., 1965-73; prof. dept. elec. and computer engring. U. Mass., Amherst, 1973-85, chmn. dept., 1973-75; Stephen O. Rice prof. Ctr. Magnetic Rec. Research, dept. elec. engring. and computer sci. U. Calif.-San Diego, La Jolla, 1985—. Mem. tech. staff Bell Telephone Labs., Murray Hill, N.J., 1968-69; prin. engr. Qualcomm Inc., San Diego, 1985. Editor for coding IEEE Transactions on Information Theory, 1969-72. Served with USAF, 1960-63. NSF sr. postdoctoral fellow, 1971-72; Guggenheim fellow, 1979-80 Fellow AAAS, IEEE (pres. info. theory group 1974, co-recipient info. theory group prize paper award 1975, co-recipient Comm. Soc. prize paper award 1993, Koji Kobayashi medal 1998, Claude Shannon lectr. 2001, Richard W. Hamming medal 2004), Nat. Acad. Engring.; mem. Sigma Xi, Sigma Tau, Eta Kappa Nu, Pi Mu Epsilon, Tau Beta Pi. Achievements include research on information theory, communication theory, computer/communication networks, magnetic recording. Home: 8529 Prestwick Dr La Jolla CA 92037-2025 Office: U Calif San Diego 9500 Gilman Dr La Jolla CA 92093-5004

WOLF, JAMES ANTHONY, insurance company executive; b. Washington, May 10, 1945; s. Arthur William and Marie Antoinette (Dalton) Wolf; m. Sheila Marie Regan, June 27, 1968; children: Jayne Ann, Elizabeth. BS in Fin. cum laude, Boston Coll., 1967. Mktg. rep. IBM, Newark, N.J., 1967-68, Boston, 1970-78, mktg. mgr. N.Y.C., 1978-81; 2nd v.p. Tchrs. Ins. & Annuity Assn., N.Y.C., 1981-82, v.p., 1982-85, sr. v.p., 1985-98, exec. v.p., 1998-00; pres. Retirement Svcs., 2000—. Served to sgt. U.S. Army, 1968-70, Vietnam. Mem. Am. Mgmt. Assn. Republican. Roman Catholic. Home: 233 Ridge Common Fairfield CT 06430-7010 Office: Tchrs Ins & Annuity Assn Am 730 3rd Ave New York NY 10017-3206

WOLF, JEFFREY STEPHEN, physician; b. Hartford, Conn., July 30, 1946; s. Abraham and Norma Wolf; m. Nina Loving Lockridge; children: Sarah Loving, Lawren Hiley. BS, McGill U., 1968; MD, Med. Coll. Va., 1972, MS, 1973. Diplomate Am. Bd. Colon and Rectal Surgery. Intern in surgery Mt. Sinai Hosp., N.Y.C., 1972-73, resident, 1973-75, N.Y. Med. Coll.-Met. Hosp., N.Y.C., 1975-77; chief resident in surgery Met. Hosp., N.Y.C., 1977-78; fellow colon-rectal surgery Grtr. Balt. Med. Ctr., 1978-79; colon-rectal surgeon Portsmouth, Va., 1979—. Fellow ACS, Am. Soc. Colon and Rectal Surgery; mem. AMA, Portsmouth Acad. Medicine, Med. Soc. Va., Am. Soc. Colon and Rectal Surgeons, So. Med. Assn., Chesapeake Colon-Rectal Soc., S.E. Va. Soc. Colon-Rectal Surgeons. Office: 3235 Academy Ave Ste 200 Portsmouth VA 23703-3200 Office Phone: 757-484-9653.

WOLF, JEROME THOMAS, lawyer; b. Austin, Minn., June 13, 1937; s. William B. and Charlotte Elaine (Rosenstock) W.; m. Ellen L., Jan. 9, 1965; children: Margo Ann, Gregory Thomas. BA, Yale U., 1959; JD, Harvard U., 1962. Bar: Minn. 1962, Mo. 1966, Kans. 1984. Ptnr. Sonnerschein, Nath & Rosenthal, Kansas City, Mo., 1994—, founding mng. ptnr. Kans. City office, 1994-2000, chmn. firm mktg. com., 1999—. Co-chair Justice for All campaign Legal Aid of Western Mo., 2000—; mem. coun. of fellows Nelson Atkins Mus., Kansas City, Mo., 2001—; chmn. Jewish Cmty. Rels. Bur. Kansas City, 1973—79, 2001—; mem. CPR commn. on future of arbitration Best Lawyers in Am. Capt. JAGC U.S. Army, 1962—66. Mem.: ABA, Mo. Bar, Kansas City Bar Found. (pres. 1979—80, founding), Kansas City Bar Assn. (pres. 1979), Phi Beta Kappa. Democrat. Home: 2411 W 70th Ter Shawnee Mission KS 66208-2741 Office: 4520 Main St Ste 1000 Kansas City MO 64111 Office Phone: 816-460-2420. Business E-Mail: jwolf@sonnerschein.com.

WOLF, JOHN HOWELL, retired publisher; b. Narberth, Pa., Mar. 19, 1918; s. W. Dale and Ruth Coryell (Howell) W.; m. Jane Belmeur, May 18, 1946 (div. Dec. 16, 1969); children: John B., Wendy J.; m. Emily West Asbury, Dec. 21, 1969. Student, DePauw U., Greencastle, Ind., 1935-39, Xavier U., Cin., 1940-41. Pub. Cin. Suburban Newspapers, Inc., 1946-73; pres., pub. Cin. Suburban Newspapers, Inc./Clermont Newspapers, Inc., 1973-82. Chmn. Nat. Better Newspaper Contests, Washington, 1957-58; adv. bd. U.S. Suburban Press, Inc., Chgo., 1970-75. Dir. Suburban Press Found., Chgo., 1972; del. 5th UNESCO Conf., 1956; chmn. Police Media Adv. Com., Cin., 1968; chmn. small media com. United Appeal, Cin., 1965; mem. com. of mgmt. YMCA, Norwood, Ohio, 1947—; pres. Y Men's Club, Norwood, 1952, Carlisle (Ky.) Nicholas County Indsl. Authority, 1984-89, chmn., 1988-89. Maj. U.S. Army, 1942-46. Recipient Silver medal Advertisers Club, Cin., 1973. Mem. Soc. Profl. Journalists, Suburban Newspapers of Am. (pres. 1973, pres. suburban newspapers sect. 1968), Nat. Newspaper Assn. (dir. 1978-83, exec. com. 1980-83, fin. com. 1980-83, Outstanding Dir. 1980), Accredited Home Newspapers of Am. (dir. 1972), Norwood Club (pres. 1950), Masons. Presbyterian. Avocations: reading, travel. Home: 244 Azalea Ct Carlisle KY 40311-9053

WOLF, JOHN MICHAEL, adult education seminar consultant; b. Upper Darby, Pa., Aug. 21, 1946; s. Herbert Michael and Elizabeth (Collins) W.; m. Gloria Ann Pettinati, Feb. 1, 1969 (div. 1978); m. Diane Elaine Batterson, Sept. 10, 1983 (div. 1994); children: John Michael Jr., Jessica Diane. BS, Drexel U., 1969; MBA, Temple U., 1972; PhD, Walden U., 1990. Salesman Lit Bros., Upper Darby, 1961-63, Cousins Shoes, Upper Darby, 1963-69; purchasing agt. Philco-Ford Co., Phila., 1969-70; sales rep. Conn. Gen. Life Ins. Co., Phila., 1970-75, Provident Life & Accident Ins. Co., Cherry Hill, N.J., 1975-78; pres. Associated Cons., Haddonfield, N.J., 1978-96; sr. ptnr. Lifelong Learning Ptnrs., Bradenton, Fla., 1996—. Cons. Chrysler Corp., Detroit, 1987, Maccabbes Mut. Life Corp., Detroit, 1989, Security-Conn. Life, Hartford, 1989, U.S. Air Pitts., 1989, GE, Paris, 1991, Ashland Chem. Co., Columbus, 1992, Campbell Soup Co., 1993, N.J. Prins. Assn., 1994, F.T.D. Aetna Ins., Tex. Instruments, 1995, Starbucks Coffee Co., Fedex, SunAmerica, 1996, Met P&C, HBO, 1997, Time Warner Cable, 1998, AIG, 1999, Comcast Cable 2000, Great West Life, 2001, Danka, John Hancock, 2002, Eli Lilly, 2003, Amway, MetLife, 2004. Chmn. U.S. Jaycees, Haddonfield, 1979; co-chmn. March of Dimes, Haddonfield, 1983. Mem. Am. Mgmt. Assn., Soc. for Accelerative Learning & Tchg., Internat. Alliance Learning Creative Edn. Found., Statue of Liberty Found., Tau Kappa Epsilon. Avocations: soccer, music, travel, skiing. Office: Lifelong Learning Ptnrs 4301 32nd St W Ste C14 Bradenton FL 34205-2796 Office Phone: 941-758-1800. E-mail: wolfman73@aol.com.

WOLF, JOHN S. ambassador, federal agency administrator; b. Sept. 12, 1948; BA, Dartmouth Coll., 1970; postgrad., Princeton U., 1978-79. Fgn. svc. officer, 1970—; prin. dep. asst. sec. for int. orgn. affairs U.S. Dept. State, 1989—92; amb. to Malaysia Kuala Lumpur, 1992—95; coord. APEC, 1996, amb., 1997; spl. advisor to Pres. and Sec. of State, Caspian Basin Energy Diplomacy, 1999—2000; asst. sec. for non-proliferation U.S. Dept State, 2001—, chief U.S. Coordination Monitoring Mission (Middle East), 2003—. Recipient Pres.'s Meritorious Svc. award, 1992, APCAC award, Asia Pacific Coun. Am. C. of C., 1996. Office: US Dept State Non-Proliferation Bureau 2201 C St NW Washington DC 20520

WOLF, JOSEPH ALBERT, mathematician, educator; b. Chgo., Oct. 18, 1936; s. Albert M. and Goldie (Wykoff) W. BS, U. Chgo., 1956, MS, 1957, PhD, 1959. Mem. Inst. for Advanced Study, Princeton, 1960-62, 65-66; asst. prof. U. Calif., Berkeley, 1962-64, assoc. prof., 1964-66, prof., 1966—94, Miller research prof., 1972-73, 83-84, prof. grad. sch., 1994—; prof. honorario Universidad Nacional de Cordoba, Argentina, 1989. Vis. prof. Rutgers U., 1969-70, Hebrew U., Jerusalem, 1974-76, Tel Aviv U., 1974-76, Harvard U., 1979-80, 86 Author: Spaces of Constant Curvature, 1967, 72, 74, 77, 84, Unitary Representations on Partially Holomorphic Cohomology Spaces, 1974, Unitary Representations of Maximal Parabolic Subgroups of the Classical Groups, 1976, Classification and Fourier Inversion for Parabolic Subgroups with Square Integrable Nilradical, 1979; co-editor, author: Harmonic Analysis and Representations of Semisimple Lie Groups, 1980, The Penrose Transform and Analytic Cohomology in Representation Theory, 1993, Geometry and Representation Theory of Real and P-Adic Grps., 1997, Global Differential Geometry: The Mathematical Legacy of Alfred Gray, 2000; editor Letters in Math. Physics, Jour. of Group Theory in Physics; contbr. articles to profl. jours. Alfred P. Sloan rsch. fellow, 1965-67, NSF fellow, 1959-62; recipient Médaille de l'Université de Liège, 1977, Humboldt prize, 1995. Mem. Am., Swiss Math. Socs. Office: U Calif Dept Math Berkeley CA 94720-3840 E-mail: jawolf@math.berkeley.edu.

WOLF, KARL EVERETT, aerospace and communications corporation executive; b. Hartford, Conn., Aug. 19, 1921; s. Carl Fred and Anna (Voss) W.; m. Lola Sue Stoner, Aug. 1, 1948; children: Paula R., Gloria J., Glenn K. BS, U.S. Mil. Acad., 1943; JD, U. Pa., 1953; SJD, George Washington U., 1963. Bar: D.C. 1953, Conn. 1953, U.S. Supreme Ct. 1960, Calif. 1971, Mich. 1975. Commd. 2d lt. U.S. Army, 1943, advanced through grades to lt. col., 1959, ret., 1963; assoc. counsel Philco. Corp., Phila., 1963-73; v.p., gen. counsel Ford Aerospace Corp., Detroit, 1973-88; ret., 1988. Mem. adv. bd. Bur. Nat. Affairs, Fed. Contract Reports, Washington, 1963-73 Author: State Taxation of Government Contractors, 1964. Decorated Silver Star, Bronze Star, Purple Heart; Croix de Guerre (Belgium) Mem. ABA, Calif. Bar Assn. Home: 1633 Castle Cove Cir Corona Del Mar CA 92625 Office Phone: 949-759-8003. E-mail: karlwolf@cox.net.

WOLF, KATIE LOUISE, state legislator; b. Wolcott, Ind., July 9, 1925; d. John H. and Helen Munsterman; m. Charles W. Wolf, 1945; children: Mark, Marcia. Grad., Ind. Bus. Coll., 1944. Registration officer County of White, Ind., 1960, mgr. lic. bur., 1960-68; clk. 39th Jud. Cir. Ct., 1968-78; mem. Ind. Ho. of Reps., 1985-86, Ind. State Senate, 1987—. Mem. Dem. Nat. Com., 1968-90; del. Dem. nat. convs., 1972, 76, 80, 84. Recipient Athens award, 1987; named Woman of Yr. Bus. and Profl. Women's Club, 1984, Outstanding Freshman Legislator, 1985. Lutheran. Office: Ind Senate Dist 7 200 W Washington St Indianapolis IN 46204-2728

WOLF, KENNETH BAXTER, writer, educator; b. Santa Barbara, Calif., June 1, 1957; s. Baxter Keyt and Ruth Elizabeth (Adams) Wolf; m. Friederike Liese-Lotte von Franqué, Aug. 16, 2003; children: Owen Clement, Eleanor Kashmar. BA, Stanford U., Calif., 1979, MA, 1981, PhD, 1985. Lectr., history Stanford U., Calif., 1984—85; prof., history Pomona Coll., Claremont, Calif., 1985—. Author: (book) Christian Martyrs in Muslim Spain, 1988, Making History, 1995, Poverty of Riches: St. Francis of Assisi Reconsidered, 2003. Fellow, Inst. for Advanced Study, Princeton, N.J., 1989—91. Office: History Dept Pomona Coll 551 N College Ave Claremont CA 91711 Business E-Mail: kwolf@pomona.edu.

WOLF, LINDA S. advertising executive; Grad., Ohio Wesleyan U. Asst. account exec. Leo Burnett Group, Chgo., 1978; exec. v.p. new bus., dir. worldwide, group pres. N.Am. Leo Burnett Co., Inc., Chgo., 1978-2000; CEO Leo Burnett USA, Chgo., 2000—. Office: Leo Burnett Co Inc 35 W Wacker Dr Ste 3710 Chicago IL 60601-1648

WOLF, MARK LAWRENCE, federal judge; b. Boston, Nov. 23, 1946; s. Jason Harold and Beatrice (Meltzer) W.; m. Lynne Lichterman, Apr. 4, 1971; children: Jonathan, Matthew. BA cum laude, Yale U., 1968; JD cum laude, Harvard U., 1971; hon. degree, Boston Latin Sch., 1990. Bar: Mass. 1971, D.C. 1972, U.S. Supreme Ct. 1976. Assoc. Surrey, Karasik & Morse, Washington, 1971-74; spl. asst. to dep. atty. gen. U.S. Dept. Justice, Washington, 1974-75, spl. asst. to atty. gen., 1975-76, dep. U.S. atty. Boston, 1981-85; from assoc. to ptnr. Sullivan & Worcester, Boston, 1977-81; judge U.S. Dist. Ct. Mass., Boston, 1985—. Lectr. Harvard U. Law Sch., Cambridge, Mass., 1990—; adj. prof. Boston Coll. Law Sch., 1992. Bd. dirs. Albert Schweitzer Fellowship, Boston, 1974—, pres., 1989-97, chmn., 1997—; chmn. John William Ward Fellowship, Boston, 1986—. Recipient cert. appreciation U.S. Pres., 1975, Disting. Service award U.S. Atty. Gen., 1985. Mem. Boston Bar Assn. (coun. 1982-85, Citation of Jud. Excellence 2002), Am. Law Inst. Office: US Dist Ct 1 Courthouse Way Boston MA 02210-3002

WOLF, MARTIN EUGENE, lawyer, educator; b. Balt., Sept. 9, 1958; s. Eugene Bernard and Mary Anna (O'Neil) W.; m. Nancy Ann Reinsfelder, May 9, 1980; children: Matthew Adam, Allison Maria, Emily Elizabeth. BA, Johns Hopkins U., 1980; JD, U. Md., 1991. Bar: Md. 1991, U.S. Dist. Ct. Md. 1992, U.S. Ct. Appeals (4th cir.) 1992, U.S. Ct. Appeals (2nd cir.) 1993, U.S. Ct. Appeals (3rd cir.) 1998, U.S. Ct. Appeals (11th cir.) 2000, U.S. Ct. Appeals (Fed. cir.) 2003, U.S. Ct. Fed. Claims 2001. Mgmt. trainee Giant Foods, Inc., Landover, Md., 1980-82, dept. mgr., 1982-83, ops. analyst, 1983-86, fin. coord., 1986-89; law clk. Piper & Marbury, LLP, Balt., 1989-91, assoc., 1991-96; prin. Law Office of Martin E. Wolf, Abingdon, Md., 1996-99; ptnr. Quinn, Gordon & Wolf Chartered, Towson, Md., 2000—. Pres. bd. dirs. Chesapeake Search & Rescue Dog Assn., Inc., 2000—02. Mem. ABA, Md. State Bar Assn., Harford County Bar Assn., Harford County Bar Found. (Vol. Svc. award 1992, 94), Am. Trial Lawyers Assn. Democrat. Roman Catholic. Avocations: lacrosse, hockey. Home: 11 Mitchell Dr Abingdon MD 21009-1628 Office Phone: 410-825-2300. E-mail: mwolf@quinnlaw.com.

WOLF, MILTON ALBERT, economist, former ambassador, investor; b. Cleve., May 29, 1924; s. Sam and Sylvia (Davis) W.; m. Roslyn C. Zehman, June 23, 1948 (dec.); children: Leslie Eric, Caryn Sue, Nancy Gail, Sherri Hope. BA in Chemistry and Biology, Ohio State U., 1948, D (hon.) in Diplomacy, 1997; BS in Civil Engring. summa cum laude, Case Inst. Tech., 1954; MA in Econs., Case Western Res. U., 1973, LHD (hon.), 1980, PhD in Econs., 1993; LLD (hon.), Cleve. State U., 1980. Pres. Zehman-Wolf Constrn. Co., Cleve., 1948—76; U.S. amb. to Austria, 1977-80; disting. professorial lectr. in econs. Case Western Res. U., 1981-87; chmn. Milton A. Wolf Investors, 1980—. Bd. dirs. Town and Country Trust; U.S. del. UN conf. on Sci. and Tech. for Devel., 1979; U.S. del. dedication of UN Internat. Ctr., Vienna, 1979; host Salt II Summit, Vienna, 1979; trustee Cleve. Clinic; chmn. Fulbright Commn. for Austria, 1977-80. Trustee emeritus Ohio State U., 1988-96, chair, 1995-96; hon. trustee Case Western Res. U., Cleve. Orch.; co-chmn. Coun. Am. Ambs.; chmn. Am. Austrian Found.; chmn. Am. Jewish Joint Distbn. Com.; mem. econ. adv. task force Carter Presdl. Campaign, 1976; mem. Carter Inauguration Com.; nat. trustee United Israel Appeal, United Jewish Appeal, Coun. Jewish Fedns.; trustee United Way Svcs.; life trustee Park Synagogue, Cleve.; past pres., life trustee Jewish Cmty. Fedn., Cleve.; bd. dirs. Grad. Sch. Internat. Econs. and Fin., Brandeis U. With USAAF 1943-48. Recipient Austrian-Am. medal of honor, 1999, Austrian Cross of Honor for Sci. and Art 1st Class, 1997, Gt. Gold medal of honor with sash Republic of Austria, 1980, Gt. Gold medal of State Province of Salzburg, Republic of Austria, 1979, Eisenman award Jewish Cmty. Fedn. Cleve., 1990, Internat. Humanitarian award Raoul Wallenberg Com., 1995; Hooded a fellow Brandeis U., 2002—. Mem. Am. Econ. Assn., Cleve. Engring. Soc., Cleve. Builders Assn., Coun. Fgn. Rels., Fgn. Policy Assn., Acad. Polit. Sci., Cleve. Com. World Affairs, UN Assn.- U.S. (bd. govs., nat. coun.), Tau Beta Pi. Home: 19200 S Park Blvd Shaker Heights OH 44122-1857 Office: 25700 Science Park Dr Beachwood OH 44122-7319

WOLF, PETER MICHAEL, investment manager, writer; b. New Orleans, Dec. 6, 1935; s. Morris and Ruth (New) W.; m. Alessandra Cantey, July 3, 1967; children: Phelan Godchaux, Alexis Ambler. BA, Yale U., 1957; MA, Tulane U., 1963; PhD, NYU, 1968. Ptnr. Wolf and Co., New Orleans, 1958-62; assoc. Wilbur Smith & Assocs., N.Y.C., 1968-70; faculty mem. NYU, 1966-67, Pratt Inst., N.Y.C., 1968-70; adj. prof. Cooper Union, N.Y.C., 1971-87; chmn. bd. fellows, mem. faculty Inst. Arch. and Urban Studies, N.Y.C., 1972-82; prin. Peter Wolf Assocs., N.Y.C., 1970—. Participant, advisor Investment Policy com. Fiduciary Counsel Inc., 2000—; organizer of exhbns. Mus. Modern Art, N.Y.C., 1969; writer exhbns. Whitney Mus. Art, N.Y.C., 1970; contbr. exhbns. Mus. Modern Art, N.Y.C., 1973, Albany Inst Art, 1975; vis. scholar/artist Am. Acad. in Rome, 2001. Author: Hot Towns: The Future of the Fastest Growing Communities in America, 1999; Land in America: Its Value, Use and Control, 1981; On Streets, 1978; The Future of the City: New Directions in Urban Planning, 1974; The Evolving City, Urban Design Proposals by Ulrich Franzen and Paul Rudolph, 1974, Another Chance for Cities, 1970, Eugene Hénard and the Beginning of Urbanism in France 1900-1914, 1969. Trustee Guild Hall, East Hampton, N.Y., 1981-86, 99—, Van Allen Inst., 1995—, Godchaux Res. Plantation Fund, pres., 1994—; chmn.

bd. trustees Van Allen Inst., N.Y., 1999-2000; adv. bd. Nat. Acad. Design, 1999—. NEA Fellow, 1979; Graham Found. Fellow, 1967-68, 94-95; Fulbright Fellow, 1965-66; Ford Found. grantee, 1971-74. Recipient Nat. Rsch. Ednl. Trust Fund, Charles P. Shattuck award 1983. Mem. Am. Inst. Cert. Planners, Contemporary Arts Coun. Museum of Modern Art, Inst. for Pvt. Investors, The Econ. Club N.Y. Avocation: tennis. Home: 325 W End Ave New York NY 10023-8135 Office: 36 W 44th St New York NY 10036-8102

WOLF, ROBERT B. lawyer; b. Phila., Aug. 18, 1914; s. Morris and Pauline (Binswanger) W.; children— Edwin David, Virginia. BA, Haverford Coll., 1936; LL.B., Harvard, 1939. Bar: Pa. 1939. Ptnr. Wolf, Block, Schorr & Solis-Cohen, 1940-43, 46-56, 57-85, of counsel, 1985—; gen. counsel FHA, Washington, 1956-57. Instr. humanities Haverford Coll., 1948-49, 71-72. Chmn. mayor's coordinated housing improvement program, Phila., 1951, Phila. Youth Svcs. Coordinating Com., 1978-84; past chmn. Pa. Com. Crime and Delinquency; mem. juvenile adv. com. Pa. Commn. on Crime and Delinquency, 1976-86; ct. master Phila. Youth Study Ctr., 1989-91; trustee Benjamin Franklin Found., Berlin, Germany, 1955-56 request Dept. State. Mem. Am., Pa., Phila. bar assns., Phi Beta Kappa. Home: 2101 Harts Ln Conshohocken PA 19428-2416 Office: Wolf Block Schorr & Solis-Cohen 1650 Arch St Fl 20 Philadelphia PA 19103-2029

WOLF, ROBERT EDWARD, physician, educator; b. Houston, Jan. 20, 1942; s. John Eaton and Ruby Lucile (Bukowski) W.; m. Ann Elizabeth Killebrew, Dec. 23, 1967; 1 child, Robert Edward, Jr. BA, Baylor U., 1964; MA, U. Tex. Med. Br., 1968, MD, 1969, PhD, 1973. Diplomate Am. Bd. Internal Medicine. Intern in internal medicine U. Tex. Med. Br., Galveston, 1969-70, resident in internal medicine, 1970-71; fellowship in rheumatology U. Tex. Health Scis. Ctr., Dallas, 1973-75; rsch. assoc. VAMC, Dallas, 1975-77; asst. prof. of medicine U. Tex. Health Scis. Ctr., Dallas, 1975-77; staff physician, chief rheumatology VA Med. Ctr., Shreveport, La., 1977—; chief rheumatology La. State U. Health Scis. Ctr., 1997—2003, assoc. prof. medicine, 1977-89, prof. medicine, 1989—2003, dir. Arthritis Ctr., 1990—2003, prof. emeritus, 2004—. Mem. faculty promotions com. La. State U. Health Scis. Ctr., 1994—98, rsch. adv. coun., 1992—2003, adminstrv. coun., 1994—2003, utilization rev. com., 1983—95. Contbg. author: Selected Topics in Clinical Chemistry, 1972, Serum Protein Abnormalities, 1975; contbr. articles to profl. jours. Mem. undergrad. edn. com. Arthritis Found., Atlanta, 1979-82, pres., 1983-85, exec. com.; mem. Lupus Found., Shreveport. Lt. comdr. USPHS, 1971-73. Recipient Grand (Student) award Nat. Rsch. Forum, Galveston, 1968, 3rd (Resident) award, 1970, Multipurpose Arthritis Ctr. award NIH, Bethesda, Md., 1977, Ctr. of Excellence-Arthritis award State of La., Baton Rouge, 1990-2003. Fellow Am. Coll. Rheumatology; mem. Am. Assn. Immunologists, Clin. Immunology Soc. Office: VA Med Ctr 510 E Stoner Ave Shreveport LA 71101

WOLF, STEPHEN M. airline executive; b. Oakland, Calif., Aug. 7, 1941; BA, San Francisco State U., 1965. Various positions Am. Airlines, Los Angeles, 1965-79, v.p. western div., 1979-81; sr. v.p. mktg. Pan Am. World Airlines, N.Y.C., 1981-82; pres., chief operating officer Continental Airlines, Houston, 1982-83; pres. Republic Airlines, Mpls., 1984-85, pres., chief exec. officer, 1985-86; chmn., pres., chief exec. officer Tiger Internat., Los Angeles, 1986-87, UAL Corp. and United Airlines, Chgo., 1987-92, chmn., CEO, 1992-94, former pres., dir.; adviser Air France, 1994-96; chmn., CEO USAIR Inc, Arlington, Va., 1996-98, chmn., 1998—2001, non exec. chmn., 2002—. Bd. dirs. Air Transport Assn., Bus. Roundtable, Washington, conf. bd. N.Y. Internat. Air Transport Assn., Geneva, World Travel and Tourism Coun., London. Bd. dirs. Alzheimer's Disease and Related Disorders Assn., Chgo., Art Inst., Chgo., Chgo. Symphony Orch., Muscular Dystrophy Assn., Rush-Presbyn.-St. Luke's Med. Ctr., Chgo., J.L. Kellogg Sch. Bus. Adv. Coun., Northwestern U. Trustee Northwestern U., mem. bus. adv. com. Transportation Ctr. Office: USAIR Inc 2345 Crystal Dr Ste 1 Arlington VA 22227-0001

WOLF, STEWART GEORGE, JR., physician, medical educator; b. Balt., Jan. 12, 1914; s. Stewart George and Angeline (Griffing) W.; m. Virginia Danforth, Aug. 1, 1942; children: Stewart George III, Angeline Griffing, Thomas Danforth. Student, Phillips Acad., 1927-31, Yale U., 1931-33; AB, Johns Hopkins U., 1934, MD, 1938; MD (hon.), U. Göteborg, Sweden, 1968. Intern N.Y. Hosp., 1938-39, resident medicine, 1939-42, NRC fellow, 1941-42; rsch. fellow Bellevue Hosp., 1939-42, clin. assoc. vis. neuropsychiatrist, 1946-52; rsch. head injury and motion sickness Harvard neurol. unit Boston City Hosp., 1942-43; asst., then assoc. prof. medicine Cornell U., 1946-52; prof., head dept. medicine U. Okla., 1952-67, Regents prof. medicine, psychiatry and behavioral scis., 1967—, prof. physiology, 1967-69; dir. Marine Biomed. Inst., U. Tex. Med. Br., Galveston, 1969-78, dir. emeritus, 1978—, prof. medicine univ., also prof. internal medicine and physiology med. br., 1970-77; prof. medicine Temple U., Phila., 1977—. V.p. med. affairs St. Luke's Hosp., Bethlehem, Pa., 1977-82; dir. Totts Gap Inst., Bangor, Pa., 1958—; supr. clin. activities Okla. Med. Rsch. Found., 1953-55, head psychosomatic and neuromuscular sect., 1952-67, head neuroscis. sect., 1967-69; adv. com. Space Medicine and Behavioral Scis., NASA, 1960-61; cons. internal medicine VA Hosp., Oklahoma City, 1952-69; cons. (European Office), Paris, Office Internat. Rsch., NIH, 1963-64; mem. edn. and supply panel Nat. Adv. Commn. on Health Manpower, 1966-67; mem. Nat. Adv. Heart Coun., 1961-65, U.S. Phamacopeia Scope Panel on Gastroenterology, Regent Nat. Libr. Medicine, 1965-69; chmn., 1968-69; mem. Nat. Adv. Environ. Health Scis. Coun., 1978-82; exec. v.p. Frontiers Sci. Found., 1967-69; mem. sci. adv. bd. Muscular Dystrophy Assns. Am., Inc., 1974-91, chmn., 1980-89; mem. gastrointestinal drug adv. com. FDA, 1974-77; bd. Internat. Cardiology Fedn.; mem. bd. visitors dept. biology Boston U., 1978-88; mem. vis. com. Ctr. for Social Rsch., Lehigh U., 1980-90; chmn. adv. com. Wood Inst. on History of Medicine, Coll. Physicians, Phila., 1980-90, mem. program com. Coll. Physicians, 1990-91; dir. Inst. for Advanced Studies in Immunology and Aging, 1988—. Author: Human Gastric Function, 1943, The Stomach, 1965, Social Environment and Health, 1981, others; adv. editor Internat. Dictionary Biology and Medicine, 1978—; editor in chief Integrative Physiol & Behavioral Sci.: The Official Jour. of Pavlovian Soc., 1990—. Pres. Okla. City Symphony Soc., 1956-61; mem. Okla. Sch. of Sci. and Math. Found., 1961—. Recipient Disting. Svc. Citation U. Okla., 1968, Dean's award for disting. med. svc., 1992; Horsley Gantt medal Pavlovian Soc., 1987, Hans Selye award Am. Inst. Stress, 1988, Rsch. award Carolinska Inst., Stockholm, 1994, Wilém Laufberger medal Acad. Scis. of Czech Republic, Citation for sci. and humanitarian achievement The J.E. Purkyně Bohemian Med. Assn. Fellow Am. Psychiat. Assn. (disting., trustee 1992—, Hofheimer prize for rsch. 1952); mem. AMA (coun. mental health 1960-64), Am. Soc. Clin. Investigation, Am. Clin. and Climatol. Assn. (pres. 1975-76), Assn. Am. Physicians, Am. Psychosomatic Soc. (pres. 1961-62), Am. Gastroent. Assn. (rsch. award 1943, pres. 1969-70), Am. Heart Assn. (chmn. com. profl. edn., com. internat. program, awards), Romanian Acad. Med. Sci. (hon.), Coll. Physicians Phila., Collegium Internat. Activitas Nervosae Superioris (exec. com. 1992—, pres. 1994), Philos. Soc. Tex., Sigma Xi, Alpha Omega Alpha, Omicron Delta Kappa. Clubs: Cosmos (Washington). Home: 1430 Totts Gap Rd Bangor PA 18013-5632 Office: Totts Med Rsch Labs Bangor PA 18013

WOLF, TIMOTHY VAN DE WINT, food products company executive; b. Apr. 27, 1953; s. Charles and Theresa Wolf; m. Mary Therese Merritt. BA in Econs. cum laude, Harvard U., 1974; MBA, U. Chgo., 1976. Fin. analyst to sr. fin. analyst Tennant Co., Mpls., 1976-79; mgr. mktg. planning and analysis Electrolux div. Consolidated Food Corp., Stamford, Conn., 1979-80; mgr. bus. planning Pepsi USA, Purchase, N.Y., 1980-81, mgr. bus. devel. and competitive analysis, 1981-82, dir. bus. planning fountain beverage div., 1982-84; sr. dir. bus. planning Taco Bell Corp., Irvine, Calif., 1984-86, v.p., controller, 1986—. Bd. dirs. Irvine Med. Ctr. Harvard Coll. scholar, Cambridge, Mass. Mem.: Harvard of So. Calif., U. Calif. Chancellor's (Irvine). Avocations: tennis, skiing, golf, German history, internat. relations. Office: Adolph Coors Co 311 Tenth St Golden CO 80401*

WOLF, WAYNE LOWELL, criminal justice educator, researcher; b. June 2, 1947; s. Joseph John and Vivian Irene (Knuth) Wolf; m. Lynn Benedik, May 10, 1989; children: Bret W., Kristy L., Stacey N. BA, U. South Fla., Tampa, 1967, MA, 1970; MAPA, Governors State U., University Park, Ill., 1976; EdD, No. Ill. U., 1982, EdS, 1986. Sgt. Hazel Crest (Ill.) Police Dept., 1973—76; prof. criminal justice South Suburban Coll., South Holland, Ill., 1976—. Adj. prof. Webster U., St. Louis, 1977—, Columbia Coll., St. Louis, 1978—, Calumet Coll., Whiting, Ind., 1982—. Author: The Gin Bottle Riot of 1968, 1975, From Clergyman to Professional: A History of American Law Enforcement, 1996; editor: Readings in Crime and Delinquency, 1982, Heroes and Rogues of the Civil War (4 vols.), 1991, Given Campbell, Confederate Hero, 1983, Chicago's Old Houses, Lore and Legend, 1998, Rebs, Raids and Rifle Pits of the Civil War, 1999, Dollars & Sense: The Psychology of Money, 2000, Soldiers, Sailors and Scoundrels of the Civil War, 2001. Commr. Blue Island (Ill.) Park Dist., 2003—; precinct capt. Rep. Party, Cook County, Ill., 1976—83. Recipient Palmer award for excellence in current affairs. Mem.: Fraternal Order Police, Kappa Delta Pi. Roman Catholic. Office: South Suburban Coll 15800 State St South Holland IL 60473-1200 Office Phone: 708-596-2000.

WOLF, WILLIAM B., JR., lawyer; b. Washington, Sept. 11, 1927; s. William B. and Ruth (Pack) W.; m. Edna Russell Jacobs, Aug. 8, 1952 (div. Oct. 1976); children: Susan Marcia, William B. III, Victoria Katharine; m. Audrey Ann Riven, Nov. 29, 1980. AB, Princeton, 1948; postgrad., Oxford U., 1950; LLB, Yale U., 1951. Bar: D.C. 1951, U.S. Supreme Ct. 1954, Md. 1963. Ptnr. Wolf & Wolf, Washington, 1951-64, 82—; sole practice Washington, 1964-72, 75-81; ptnr. Wolf & Rosenblatt, Washington, 1972-75, Wolf, Amram & Hahn, P.C., Washington, 1981-82. Vice chmn. Security Nat. Bank, Washington, 1984-85. Author: Lawyers Are a Dime a Dozen, 1999. Pres. Nat. Capital USO, 1966—67, Jewish Hist. Soc. Greater WAshington, Brotherhood Washington Hebrew Congregation, 1967—68. With USN, 1945, sgt. U.S. Army, 1946—48. Mem.: ABA, Bar Assn. D.C., University (Washington), Nassau (Princeton, N.J.), Edgartown (Mass.) Yacht, Woodmont Country. Republican. Jewish. Home: Watergate East Washington DC 20037 Office: Wolf & Wolf 2510 Virginia Ave NW Washington DC 20037

WOLF, WILLIAM MARTIN, computer company executive, consultant; b. Watertown, NY, Aug. 29, 1928; s. John and Rose (Emrich) Wolf; m. Eileen Marie Jolly, Aug. 19, 1952 (div. 1972); children: Rose(dec.), Sylvia, William. BS, St. Lawrence U., 1950; MS, U. N.H., 1951; postgrad., U. Pa., 1951—52, MIT, 1952—55. Programmer digital computer lab. MIT, Cambridge, 1952—54, dir., exec. dir. Tech. Capital Network, 1992—94; pres. Wolf R & D Corp., Boston, 1954—69, Wolf Computer Corp., Boston, 1966—76, Planning Sys. Internat., Boston, 1976—81, Micro Computer Software Inc., Cambridge, 1981—88, Tech. Acquisition Corp., Boston, 1989—91, Planning Internat., Inc., Boston, 1989—94, Wolfsort Corp., Boston, 1989—; chmn. Wolf & McManus, Brookline, Mass., 1995—; founder Year 2000 Software Corp., Brookline, Mass., 1996—2000; co-founder, pres., CEO Eureka.Com, Inc., Rockport, Mass., 1999—2000, FocuSystems, Inc., Rockport, Mass., 2000—; founder, pres., CEO Mass. Med. Agy., 2002—. Co-founder, pres. Assn. Ind. Software Cos., Washington, 1965—67, Design Sci. Inst., Phila., 1969—73, Nat. Coun. Profl. Svc. Firms, Washington, 1970—75; seminar leader MIT Sloan Sch., Cambridge, 1970; co-founder, bd. dirs. Harbor Nat. Bank, Boston. Trustee Addison Gilbert Hosp., Gloucester, Mass., 1963; co-founder X-10 Orgn., Boston, 1962; v.p. Young Pres. Orgn., Boston, 1970; overseer Mus. Sci., Boston, 1989—97. Named Outstanding Young Man in Boston, Jaycees, 1962; recipient Spkr.'s award, Data Processing Mgmt. Assn., 1966. Mem.: World Bus. Coun., MIT Club (Alumni award 1991), Forty-Niners. Achievements include invention of management system; orbit calculator; patents for sorting method; method for solving Year 2000 problem. Office Phone: 978-273-0344.

WOLFBERG, MELVIN DONALD, optometrist, educational administrator, consultant; b. Altoona, Pa., June 24, 1926; s. Max Alex and Claire (Schiffman) Wolfberg; m. Audrey Iris Koch, Apr. 26, 1952; children: Debra Lynn, Michael Alex, Daniel Ben; m. Linda Diane Machesic, Dec. 4, 1979. OD, Pa. Coll. Optometry, Phila., 1951; D of Ocular Sci. (hon.), New England Coll. Optometry, 1989, Ill. Coll. Optometry, 1990; LHD (hon.), Pa. Coll. Optometry, 1998. Lic. optometrist, Pa. Pvt. practice and ptnr. optometric practice, Selinsgrove, Pa., 1951-79; pres. Pa. Coll. Optometry, Phila., 1979-89, chmn. bd., 1976-79; v.p. profl. rels. Bausch and Lomb, Rochester, N.Y., 1991-95; pres. In Vision Inst., Boston, 1991-95; ptnr./dir. Sylvan Learning Ctr., Vero Beach, Fla., 1996—. Cons. to sec. HEW, Washington, 1970-77; dir. Better Vision Inst., N.Y.C., 1960-80. Mem. Selinsgrove City Coun., 1961-62; pres. Selinsgrove Community Chest, 1957; chmn. Optometrists Rep. Nat. Com., 1972, 76; chmn. Nat. Inter-Profl. Health Coun., Washington, 1972-77; dir. Univ. City Sci. Ctr., Phila., 1980-87; adv. com. Coun. Higher Edn., Commonwealth Pa., 1980-89. Served with U.S. Army, 1944-46, ETO. Decorated Purple Heart, Bronze Star, Silver Star; named Man of Yr. Central Pa. Optometric Soc., 1964, Alumnus of Yr. Pa. Coll. Optometry, 1970; recipient Carel C. Koch Meml. medal, 1989. Fellow Am. Acad. Optometry (pres. 1985-86); mem. Pa. Assn. Colls. and Univs. (exec. com. 1982-89, sec.-treas. 1985-88, vice chmn. 1988-89), Pa. Optometric Assn. (pres. 1959-61, Optometrist of Yr., Ewalt Meritorious Svc. award 2003), Am. Optometric Assn. (pres. 1969-70, Disting. Svc. award 1994, named to Nat. Optometry Hall Fame 2004), Pa. Coll. Optometry Alumni Assn. (pres. 1957), Beta Sigma Kappa.

WOLF-DEVINE, CELIA CURTIS, philosophy educator; b. Phila., Sept. 14, 1942; d. Robert Bunsen Wolf and Nancy Anne Brady; m. Philip Edwards Devine, June 28, 1986. BA, Smith Coll., 1964; MA, U. Wis., 1971, PhD in Philosophy, 1984. Instr. Tufts U., Medford, Mass., 1971-72, Simmons Coll., Boston, 1972-73, U. Mass., Boston, 1975, U. San Francisco, 1978-81; asst. prof. Coll. St. Benedict, St. Joseph, Minn., St. Cloud (Minn.) State U., 1986-87; assoc. prof., chair philosophy dept. Stonehill Coll., Easton, Mass., 1987—. Part-time instr. Chapman Coll., St. Marys, Moraga, Calif., Suffolk U., Boston State Coll., 1974-79; invited visitor NEH Summer Seminar on Early Modern Philosophy, Brown U., summer 1988; media dir. Women Experts, 1995-96; presenter in field. Author: Descartes on Seeing: Epistemology and Visual Perception, 1993, Diversity and Community in the Academy: Affirmative Action in Faculty Appointments, 1997, Sex and Gender: a Spectrum of Views, 2002 (co-edited with Philip Devine); (chpts. to books) The New Catholics, 1987, Affirmative Action and the University: A Philosophical Inquiry, 1993, The Affirmative Action Debate, 1995, 2d edit., 2002, Images of the Human, 1995, The Abortion Controversy, 1994, Social and Personal Ethics, 2d edit., 1997, The Problem of Abortion, 1997, The Family, Civil Society and the State, 1999, Contemporary Moral Issues, 2000, Descartes' Natural Philosophy, 2000, Liberalism at the Crossroads, 2d edit., 2003, In the Socratic Tradition: Essays on Teaching Philosophy, 2003; referee Internat. Philos. Quarterly; contbr. articles to profl. jours. and newspapers. Sec. R.I. br. Nat. Assn. Scholars, 1996—; grant proposal evaluator NSF; fellowship evaluation panel NEH; publs.' reader Wadsworth and Prentiss Hall. Grantee Carthage Found., 1995-96, Earhart Found., 1996, 2003. Mem. Am. Philos. Assn., Am. Cath. Philos. Assn., Soc. Christian Philosophers. Roman Catholic. Home: 41 Hilltop Ave Providence RI 02908-2810 Office: Stonehill Coll Philosophy Dept Washington St North Easton MA 02357-0001 Office Phone: 508-565-1263. E-mail: cwolfdevine@stonehill.edu.

WOLFE, AL, marketing and advertising consultant; b. Wyo., May 3, 1932; s. Clyde A. and Margaret V. (Joyce) W.; m. F. Carilouise, 1957 (div. 1994); m. Helen S., 1997; children: Kirk, Kelley, Alison. BA in Psychology, U. Wyo., 1958. Product mgr., merchandising mgr. Gen. Mills, Mpls., 1958-62; asst. mktg. dir., v.p., account supr. Compton Advt., Chgo. and N.Y.C., 1963-66; v.p., account supr., exec. v.p., gen. mgr. Wells Rich Greene, N.Y.C., 1967-76; exec. v.p., dir. N.W. Ayer ABH Internat., N.Y.C., 1976-81; mng. dir., pres., bd. dirs. DDB Needham Worldwide, Chgo., 1981-87, pres. U.S. Div., 1987-88; pres. Al Wolfe Assocs., Inc., Mktg. and Advt. Cons., Sedona, Ariz., 1989—. Bd. dirs. Clorox Co., Oakland, Calif. Bd. dirs. U. Wyo. Found., pres., 1993-94; past pres. bd. dirs. U. Wyo. Art Mus.; chmn. Sedona Med. Ctr. Found.; bd. dirs. Sedona Acad.; bd. dirs. Sedona Cultural Park. Recipient Disting. Alumnus award U. Wyo. 1981 Mem. Econ. Club (Chgo.), Sedona 30 Club. Home: 134 Back O Beyond Cir Sedona AZ 86336-6806 Office: Al Wolfe Assocs Inc PO Box 2367 Sedona AZ 86339-2367

WOLFE, ALAN, political science educator, writer; b. Phila., June 10, 1942; s. Leon L. and Jean (Birnbaum) W.; m. Jytte Klausen, Feb. 28, 1982; children: Rebekka, Jan, Andreas. BS, Temple U., 1963; PhD, U. Pa., 1967. Dean grad. faculty New Sch. Social Rsch., N.Y.C., 1990-93; univ. prof. Boston U., 1993-99; dir. ctr. for religion and am. pub. life Boston Coll., Chestnut Hill, Mass., 1999—. Summer seminar leader NEH, 1994-96; advisor State of the Union Address, President Clinton, Washington, 1995. Author: Whose Keeper?, 1989 (C. Wright Mills award 1989), America At Century's End, 1992, The Human Difference, 1993, Marginalized in the Middle, 1996, One Nation, After All, 1998, Moral Freedom, 2001; contbg. editor The Wilson Quar., 1993—, The New Republic, 1994—. Rsch. grantee Russell Sage Found., 1994—, Lilly Endowment, 1998. Office: Boston Coll 24 Quincy Rd Chestnut Hill MA 02467-3937 E-mail: wolfe@bc.edu.

WOLFE, BARBARA L. economics educator, researcher; b. Phila., Feb. 15, 1943; d. Manfred and Edith (Heimann) Kingshoff; m. Stanley R. Wolfe, Mar. 20, 1965 (div. Mar. 1978); m. Robert H. Haveman, July 29, 1983; children: Jennifer Ann Wolfe, Ari Michael Wolfe. BA, Cornell U., Ithaca, N.Y., 1965; MA, U. Pa., 1971; PhD, U Pa., 1973. Asst. prof. Bryn Mawr (Pa.) Coll., 1973-76; rsch. assoc. Inst. Rsch. on Poverty, Madison, Wis., 1976-77, dir., 1994—2000; from asst. prof. to assoc. prof. U. Wis., Madison, 1977-88, prof., 1988—. Adj. prof. Australian Nat. U., 2002-; resident scholar NIAS, Wassenear, Netherlands, 1984-85, 96-97; vis. scholar Russell Sage Found., N.Y., 1991-92. Co-author: Succeeding Generations, 1994; editor: (book) Role of Budgetary Policy in Demographic Transitions, 1994, contbr. articles to profl. jours. Active Commn. on Children with Disabilities, Washington 1994-95, Tech. Adv. Panel Social Security, Washington, 1994-95. Recipient Best Article of Yr. award Rev. Income and Wealth, 1992, Fulbright award Coun. Internat. Exch. of Scholars, 1984. Mem.: Inst. of Medicine, Assn. Pub. Policy Mgmt. (policy coun. 2001—), Internat. Inst. Pub. Fin. (bd. mgmt. 1994—2000, v.p. 2000—03), Am. Econ. Assn. (bd. com. 1989—92, exec. bd. 1996—99), Office: U Wis Inst Rsch on Poverty 1180 Observatory Dr Madison WI 53706-1320 Office Phone: 608-262-0662. E-mail: wolfe@LaFollette.wisc.edu., bwolfe@wisc.edu.

WOLFE, BRUCE MCLAREN, surgery educator; b. Oakland, Calif., May 22, 1942; s. Cameron Withgot and Jean (Brown) W.; children: John C., Michael B., Catherine B.; m. Marybeth Masters, Sept. 1, 1997; 1 child, Lauren M. AB, Stanford U., 1963; MD, St. Louis U., 11967. Diplomate Am. Bd. Surgery. Intern, resident in surgery St. Louis U., 1967-73; rsch. fellow in surgery Harvard U. Med. Sch.-Peter Bent Brigham Hosp., Boston, 1975-77; asst. prof. surgery U. Calif.-Davis Sch. Medicine, Sacramento, 1977-81, assoc. prof., 1981-88, prof., 1988—, chief gastrointestinal surgery svc., 1986—2003; prof. emeritus of surgery, 2003. Merit rev. bd. for surgery VA, 1986—90; co-chmn. consortium on bariatric surgery NIH. Mem. editl. bd. Jour. Parenteral and Enteral Nutrition, 1978-96, Jour. Metabolism and Nutrition, 1995, Am. Jour. Clin. Nutrition, 1997-2003, Obesity Surgery, 2002—, Sry Endose, 2002—; contbr. over 100 articles and abstracts to med. jours., including Am. Jour. Surgery, Annals Surgery, Surg. Forum, Survery, Gynecology and Obstetrics, Lancet, Surgery, Annals Plastic Surgery, Jour. Parenteral and Enteral Nutrition, Western Jour. Medicine, Surg. Clinics N.Am., Diagnostic Microbiol. and Infectious Diseases, Am. Jour. Clin. Nutrition, Am. Jour. Vet. Rsch., Jour. Lab. and Clin. Medicine, Nutrition in Clin. Practice, Metabolism, Nutrition in Clin. Practice, Jour. AMA, Life Scis., Surg. Endoscopy, World Jour. Surgery, Jour. Royal Coll. Surgeons Edinburgh, Fedn. Procs., also numerous chpts. to books. Physician Nat. Ski Patrol, Homewood, Calif., 1986-2000. Lt. comdr. USN, 1973-75. Rsch. grantee NIH, 1979-82, 1985-95, Abbott Labs., 1981, Mead Johnson Labs., 1982-84, 96-87, Nat. Inst. Gen. Med. Scis., 1993-98, Nat. Inst. Diabetes, Digestive and Kidney Diseases, 1990-94, 2003—, Ethicon Endo-Surgery, 1992-94, Am. Women Surgeons, 1996-97. Mem. ACS, AMA, Am. Coll. Sports Medicine, Am. Inst. Nutrition, Am. Soc. for Cln. Nutrition (com. on subsplty. tng. 1988-91), Am. Soc. for Parenteral and Enteral Nutrition (bd. dirs. 1980-81, 87-96, pres. No. Calif. chpt. 1987-88, mem. exec. com. 1990-95, pres. 1994-95), Am. Soc. Bariatric Surgery, Am. Surg. Assn., Soc. for Surgery Alimentary Tract, Soc. Am. Gastrointestinal Endoscopic Surgeons (ednl. resources com. 1994—, rsch. com. 1994—), Soc. Univ. Surgeons, Western Surg. Assn., Nat. Assn. Vascular Access Networks (bd. dirs. 1990-92), Nat. Found. for Ileitis and Colitis, Pacific Coast Surg. Assn., Pancreas Club, Sacramental Surg. Soc., Sacramento-El Dorado Med. Soc., Sacramento Valley Gut Club, Sigma Xi. Avocations: skiing, bicycling. Address: 131 Clunie Dr Sacramento CA 95864-6965 Office: 2260 Coyle Ave Ste 218 Carmichael CA 95608 Office Phone: 916-965-2401. Office Fax: 916-734-3951. Business E-Mail: bmwolfe@ucdavis.edu.

WOLFE, CHARLES MORGAN, electrical engineering educator; b. Morgantown, W.Va., Dec. 21, 1935; s. Slidell Brown and Mae Louise (Maness) W.; children— David Morgan, Diana Michele BSE.E., W.Va. U., Morgantown, 1961, MSE.E., 1962; PhD, U. Ill., 1965. Research assoc. U. Ill., Urbana, 1965; mem. staff MIT Lincoln Lab., Lexington, Mass., 1965-75; prof. elec. engring Washington U., St. Louis, 1975-97, Samuel C. Sachs prof., 1982-90, dir. semicondr. research lab., sr. prof., 1979-90. Cons. MIT Lincoln Lab., 1975-76, Fairchild Semicondr., Palo Alto, Calif., 1975-76, Air Force Avionics Lab., Dayton, Ohio, 1976-79, U. Ill., 1983-85 Author: Physical Properties of Semiconductors, 1989; editor: Gallium Arsenide and Related Compounds, 1979; contbr. articles to profl. jours., chpts. to books Served as sgt. USMC, 1955-58 Fellow IEEE (field awards com. 1984-87, Jack A. Morton award 1990); mem. NAE, AAAS, Electrochem. Soc. (Electronics divsn. award 1978).

WOLFE, CHRISTOPHER, political science educator; b. Boston, Mar. 11, 1949; s. Walter Brewster and Margaret Mary (Conway) W.; m. Anne, June 17, 1973; children: Julia, Jared, Rebecca, Thomas, Stephen, Trevor, Patrice, Elena, Marisa, Alex. BA, U. Notre Dame, 1971; PhD, Boston Coll., 1978. Instr. Assumption Coll., 1975-78; asst. prof. Marquette U., Milw., 1978-85, assoc. prof., 1985-92, prof., 1992—. Author: The Rise of Modern Judicial Review, 1986 (Benchmark Book of the Year), Essays on Faith and Liberal Democracy, 1987, Judicial Activism Bulwark of Freedom or Precarious Security, 1991, How to Interpret the Constitution, 1996; editor: Liberalism at the Crossroads, 1994, The Family, Civil Society, and the State, 1998, Homosexuality and American Public Life, 1999, Natural Law and Public Reason, 2000, Same-Sex Matters, 2000. Earhart Found. Summer fellow Earhart Found., 1995, Nat. Endowment for the Humanities fellow, 1994, Presdl. grantee Randolph Found., 1994, Bradley Found. grante, 2000; named to Templeton Honor Roll, Templeton Found./Intercollegiate Studies Inst. Mem. Am. Pub. Philosophy Inst. (pres. 1989—), Am. Polit. Sci. Assn., The Federalist Soc., Fellowship of Cath. Scholars. Republican. Roman Catholic. Office: Marquette U, Poli Sci D PO Box 1881 Milwaukee WI 53201-1881 E-mail: christopher.wolfe@marquette.edu.

WOLFE, CLAIRE V. physiatrist; b. Bronx, N.Y., 1943; MD, Ohio State U., 1968. Diplomate Am. Bd. Phys. Medicine and Rehab. Intern L.A. County-U. So. Calif. Med. Ctr., 1968—69; resident Ohio State U. Hosps., Columbus, 1969—72; pvt. practice phys. med. and rehab. Columbus, 1972—. Staff physiatrist Mt. Carmel Med. Ctr., Columbus; clin. asst. prof. Ohio State U. Coll. Medicine. Mem.: AMA, Am. Acad. Phys. Medicine and Rehab. (v.p. 2002—), Ohio State Med. Assn. Office: 793 W State St Columbus OH 43222-1551

WOLFE, DEBORAH ANN, lawyer; b. Detroit, May 4, 1955; d. Adam and Mary A. (Smyth) Wolfe; m. Lester D. McDonald, May 23, 1987; children: Molly, Thomas. Student, Ariz. State U., Tempe, 1973-76; BA in Polit. Sci., Bus., Tex. Christian U., Ft. Worth, 1977; postgrad., So. Meth. U., 1977-78; JD, U. San Diego, 1980; grad., Gerry Spence's Trial Lawyers Coll., 1999. Bar: Calif. 1981, Ariz. 1982. Sole practice, San Diego, 1981-83; ptnr. Kremer & Wolfe, San Diego, 1983-86; assoc. D. Dwight Worden, Solana Beach, Calif., 1986-89; pvt. practice San Diego, 1989-91; owner Wolfe & McDonald, 1991-96; shareholder Nugent & Newnham, San Diego, 1996—2003, Nugent Newnham Abbene Adock & Wolfe, 2004—. Instr. San Diego Inn of Ct. Evidence, 1988-95. Floutist San Diego City Guard Band, 1981-93, Grossmont Sinfonia, La Mesa, 1982-83, Classical/Chamber Music Quartet, San Diego,

1983-87, Foothills United Meth. Ch. band, 1997—; leader Girl Scouts. Named one of Lawyers of the Yr. Calif. Lawyer Mag., 1996, one of top ten plaintiff legal malpractice lawyers in Calif., 2001. Mem. ATLA, Consumer Attys. Calif., Consumer Attys. San Diego (pres. 1996, Outstanding Trial Lawyer award 1996, 2000, 02, Trial Lawyer of Yr. award 1996), Lawyers Club (San Diego), San Diego Trial Lawyers Assn. (Outstanding Trial Lawyers award 1987), Am. Inns of Ct. (master), Nat. Bd. Trial Advocates. Office: Nugent & Newnham 1010 2nd Ave Ste 2200 San Diego CA 92101-4911

WOLFE, DEBORAH CANNON PARTRIDGE, government education consultant, educator, minister; b. Cranford, N.J. d. David Wadsworth and Gertrude (Moody) Cannon; 1 son, H. Roy Partridge. BS, N.J. City U.; MA, EdD, Tchrs. Coll., Columbia U.; postgrad., Vassar Coll., U. Pa., Union Theol. Sem., Jewish Sem. Am.; hon. doctorates, Seton Hall U., 1963, Coll. New Rochelle, 1963, Morris Brown U., 1964, Glassboro/Rowan Coll., 1965, Bloomfield Coll., 1988, Monmouth Coll., 1988, William Paterson Coll., 1988; LLD (hon.), Kean Coll., 1981; LHD (hon.), Stockton State Coll., 1982; LLD (hon.), Jersey City State Coll., 1987, Centenary Coll., William Paterson Coll., 1989, Tuskegee U., 1989, Glassboro State Coll., 1985, Tuskegee U., 1989, St. Peter's Coll., 1989, Rider Coll., 1989, Georgian Court Coll., 1990; DSc (hon.), Stevens Inst. Tech., 1991; LLD (hon.), Rutgers U., 1992, Thomas Edison Coll., 1992; DSc, U. Med. and Dentistry N.J., 1989, CUNY, 2001, LHD (hon.), 2001. Former prin., tchr. pub. schs., Cranford, also Tuskegee, Ala.; faculty Tuskegee Inst., Grambling Coll., NYU, Fordham U., U. Mich., Tex. Coll., Columbia U.; supervision and adminstrn. curriculum devel., social studies U. Ill., summers; prof. edn., affirmative action officer Queens Coll., officer; prof. edn. and children's lit. Wayne State U.; edn. chief U.S. Ho. of Reps. Com. on Edn. and Labor, 1962—. Fulbright prof. Am. lit. NYU; U.S. rep. 1st World Conf. on Women in Politics; chair non-govtl. reps. to UN (NGO/DPI exec. com.), 1983—; editl. cons. Macmillan Pub. Co.; cons. Ency. Brit.; adv. bd. Ednl. Testing Svc.; mem. State Bd. Edn., 1964-94; chairperson N.J. Bd. Higher Edn., 1967-94; mem. nat. adv. panel on vocat. edn. HEW; mem. citizen's adv. com. to Bd. Edn., Cranford; mem. Citizen's Adv. Com. on Youth Fitness, Pres.'s Adv. Com. on Youth Fitness, White House Conf. Edn., 1955, White House Conf. Aging, 1960, White House Conf. Civil Rights, 1966, White House Conf. on Children, 1970, Adv. Coun. for Innovations in Edn.; v.p. Nat. Alliance for Safer Cities; cons. Vista Corps, OEO; vis. scholar Princeton Theol. Sem., 1989—; chairperson Human Rels. Coun., N.J., 1994—; vis. prof. U. Ill., U. N.C., Wayne State U.; theologian-in-residence Duke U.; mem. trustee bd. Sci. Svc.; mem. N.J. Commn. on Holocaust Edn., 1996. Contbr. articles to ednl. publs. Bd. dirs. Cranford Welfare Assn., Cmty. Ctr., 1st Bapt. Ch., Cranford Cmty. Ctr. Migratory Laborers, Hurlock, Md.; trustee Sci. Svc., Seton Hall U., bd. regents; mem. Pub. Broadcasting Authority, N.J. Commn. on Holocaust Edn., 1996—, Tuskegee U. Alumni, 1995; mem. N.J. Conv. of Progressive Baptists, 1995, v.p., 1996—, pres., 1999-2001; parliamentarian Progressive nat. Bapt. Conv.; sec. Kappa Delta Pi Ednl. Found., nat. bd. dirs., 2001—, laureate rep.; mem. adv. com. Elizabeth and Arthur Schlesinger Libr., Radcliffe Coll., trustee Edn. Devel. Ctr., 1965—; assoc. min. 1st Bapt. Ch.; chair Human Rels. Commn., Monroe, 1995; v.p., then pres. N.J. Conv. Progressive Bapt., 1996—; parliamentarian Progressive Nat. Baptist Conv.; mem. exec. com. Nat. Coun. Agrl. Rsch., Ext. and Teaching, 1997—; mem. N.J. Holocaust Commn., 1996— Named N.J. Educator of Yr., 2003; named to, NABSE Hall of Fame; recipient Woman of Yr. award, Delta Beta Zeta, Morgan State Coll., Medal of Honor, DAR, 1990, Disting. Svc. medal, Nat. Top Ladies of Distinction, 1991, Disting. Svc. award, Nat. Assn. State Bds. Edn., 1992, 1994, Disting. Svc. to Edn. award, N.J. Commn. on Status of Women, 1993, Svc. to Children award, N.J. Assn. Sch. Psychologists, 1993, Disting. Medal award, U. Medicine and Dentistry N.J., Union Coll., citation, N.J. State Coun. on Vacat. Edn., 1994, N.J. State Bd. Edn., 1994, Svc. award for 50 Yrs., Cranford Bd. Edn., 1995, Women Who Count award, Zonta Internat., 1996, Minister's Appreciation award, Progressive Nat. Bapt. Conv., 1996, Edn. award, Tuskegee U. Alumni, 1996, Women Who Make a Difference award, Zonta Internat., 1995, Dr. George Washington Carver award, Pa. Acad. Sci., 1998, Lifetime Svc. award, William Patterson U., 1999, Triumph award, N.J. Dept. State, 2001. Mem.: NAACP (Medal of Honor 1994), AAUP, AAUW (nat. edn. chmn.), NCCJ, NEA (life), ASCD (rev. coun.), AAAS (chmn. tchr. edn. com.), LWV, N.J. Conv. of Progressive Bapts. (1st woman elected pres. 1999), Alliance Black Clergywomen (pres.), Nat. Assn. State Univs. and Colls. and Land Grant Colls. (mem. exec. bd. 1996, mem. coun. on agr. ext. and tchg.), Ch. Women United (UN rep., mem. exec. com.), Internat. Platform Assn., Am. Coun. Edn. (mem. commn. fed. rels.), Nat. Soc. Study Edn., Internat. Assn. Childhood Edn., Am. Acad. Polit. and Social Sci., Comparative Edn. Soc., Internat. Reading Assn., Fellowship So. Churchmen, Am. Tchrs. Assn., N.Y. Tchrs. Assn., Nat. Assn. Black Educators (pres.), Nat. Assn. Negro Bus. and Profl. Women (chmn. spkrs. bur., Nat. Achievement award 1958), Nat. Panhellenic Coun. (dir.), Am. Coun. Human Rights (v.p.), Coun. Nat. Orgns. Children and Youth, N.J. Commn. Holocaust Edn., N.J. Holocaust Commn., N.J. Fedn. Colored Women's Clubs, UN Assn.-USA (mem. exec. com.). Home: 4102 Monroe Village Monroe Township NJ 08831 *I feel I am extremely fortunate to have been born into a family where love of God and love of knowledge have been major concerns. The knowledge we have sought has not been 'knowledge for knowledge's sake' but 'knowledge to improve society and the world'. I have always felt that 'God power' linked with 'Brain power' was the greatest force in the world and I knew that in order to achieve such strength one must work diligently and constantly. Because knowledge changes so rapidly this quest for wisdom must be eternal. Hence I hope I'm still learning and growing; for education must be involved from 'the womb to the tomb'.*

WOLFE, DOUGLAS E. science educator, researcher; b. St. Marys, Pa., Jan. 2, 1972; s. David Leroy and Florence Theresa Wolfe. BS, Penn State U. Park, 1994, MS, 1996, PhD, 2001. Rsch. asst. Applied Rsch. Lab. Penn State U., 1998—2001, rsch. assoc., 2001—, asst. prof. of materials sci. and engring. rsch. assoc., 2003—. Cons., State Coll., Pa., 2002—. Avocation: racquetball. Home: Calder Sq PO Box 10548 State College PA 16805 Office: Penn State Univ 119 Materials Rsch Inst University Park PA 16802 Office Phone: 814-865-0316. Fax: 814-863-2986. E-mail: dew125@psu.edu.

WOLFE, ELAINE CLAIRE DAUGHETEE, junior high school educator; b. Indpls., May 29, 1940; d. Arthur and Lois Eleanor (Grieger) D.; m. Steven Roger Allen, June 17, 1962 (dec. Oct. 1969); m. Howard Evans Wolfe, Jan. 30, 1971 (div. Dec. 1981); children: Leah Denise Wolfe-Garcia, Scott Arthur. BS in Biol. Scis., Purdue U., 1962; MA in Vertebrate Zoology, UCLA, 1964; EdS in Curriculum & Instrn./Sch. Admin., Ind. U., 1994, EdD in Sch. Admin./Curriculum & Instrn., 1997. Cert. tchr. Ind., Calif., Pa.; cert. prin., Ind.; cert. supt., Ind. Tchr. biology Canoga Park (Calif.) H.S., 1963-64; instr. biology Purdue U., West Lafayette, Ind., 1964-65; sci. instr. Tex. Christian U., Ft. Worth, 1965-66; sci. tchr. Ft. Worth Pub. Schs., 1966-67; tchr. biology Upper Merion H.S., King of Prussia, Pa., 1967-71, Fulton Jr. H.S., Indpls., 1982; tchr. sci. and chair sci. dept. Guion Creek Mid. Sch., Indpls., 1982—. Free-lance artist, 1971—; evaluator N.Ctrl. Assn. visitation teams, 1986, 90; cons. in field. Contbr. articles and poetry to profl. jours.; exhibitor Ctr. for Creative Arts Gallery, Indpls., Rocky Mills Art Gallery, Indpls. Art Mus. Mem. adv. bd. Pike Outdoor Classroom, Indpls., 1995—; mem. Project 2061 Benchmarks Sci. Com., State of Ind., 1995; piano accompanist Guion Creek Mid. Sch., 1982-90; mem. Guion Creek Mid. Sch. PTA, 1982—; active Am. Bapt. Women, 1981—. Named Tchr. of the Yr., Met. Sch. Dist. of Pike Twp., 1991; recipient Disting. Alumna award for excellence Purdue U. Sch. Sci., 1998, Golden Apple award, 1995, Regional Excellence in Sci. Tchg. award Suburu Mid. Sch. Midwester, 2003; Mt. St. Helens Honors Workshop grantee Nat. Sci. Tchrs. Assn./NSF, 1988, Sigma Xi grantee, 1991, Take Pride in Am. awardee, 1992. Winner Midwestern Region for Mid. Subaru Excellence in Sci. Tchg., 2003 Mem. Nat. Sci. Tchrs. Assn., Hoosier Assn. Sci. Tchrs., Nat. Mid. Sch. Assn., Ind. Mid. Sch. Edn. Assn., Purdue U. Alumni Assn., Purdue Assn. of Indpls., Nat. Wildlife and World Wildlife Assn., Nat. Geog. Soc., Nat. Parks Assn., Smithsonian Inst., Kappa Delta Pi, Phi Lambda Theta. Republican. Avocations: gardening, knitting, travel, photography, sewing. Home: 3541 Windham Lake Trace Indianapolis IN 46214-1400 Office: Guion Creek Middle Sch 4401 W 52d St Indianapolis IN 46254 E-mail: ewolfe@pike.k12.in.us.

WOLFE, ETHYLE RENEE (MRS. COLEMAN HAMILTON BENEDICT), college administrator; b. Burlington, Vt., Mar. 14, 1919; d. Max M. and Rose (Saiger) Wolfe; m. Coleman Hamilton Benedict, Dec. 4, 1954. BA, U. Vt., 1940, MA, 1942; postgrad., Bryn Mawr Coll., 1942—43; PhD, NYU, 1950; LHD (hon.), CUNY, 1989; LittD (hon.), Iona Coll., 1989. Tchg. fellow U. Vt., 1940—42; rsch. fellow Latin Bryn Mawr (Pa.) Coll., 1942—43; instr. classics Bklyn. Coll., 1947—49, instr. classical langs., 1949—54, asst. prof., 1954—59, assoc. prof., 1960—68, prof., 1968—, acting chmn. dept. classics and comparative lit., 1962—63, chmn. dept., 1967—72; dean Bklyn. Coll. Sch. Humanities, 1971—78; exec. officer Bklyn. Coll. Humanities Inst., 1980—89; provost and v.p. for acad. affairs Bklyn. Coll., 1982—88, provost emeritus, 1989. Exec. com., chmn. com. on undergrad. affairs, com. on univ.-wide programs CUNY; study group AAAS, 1987—89, pub., 1987—89; dir. Nat. Core Visitors Programs, 1985—89, Fund for Improvement of Postsecondary Edn.-funded Ctr. for Core Studies, 1987—88; co-chair senate report Chancellor's Coll. Prep. Initiative, 1991; exec. com The Liberal Art of Sci.: Agenda for Action. Mem. editl. bd.: Classical World, 1965—71; co-editor: The Am. Classical Rev., 1971—76; contbr. articles to profl. jours. Named Ethyle R. Wolfe Inst. for the Humanities Bklyn. Coll. in her honor, 1989; named to Hall of Honor, U. Vt., 1991, Disting. U. Faculty Sen. Emeritus, CUNY, 1992; recipient Kirby Flower Smith award, 1939, Goethe prize, U. Vt., 1940, Alumni Achievement award, 1985, Nat. Presdl. medal, NEH, Charles Frankel prize, 1990; grantee, 1971, 1982—84, Mellon Found., 1982—85, 1986—89, Exxon, 1986—89, Josiah Macy, 1986—90. Mem.: Am. Soc. Papyrologists, Classical Assn. Atlantic States (exec. com.), Vergilian Soc. Am., Archeol. Inst. Am., Am. Philol. Assn., N.Y. Classical Club (past pres., exec. com.), Phi Beta Kappa (pres. 1988—90, past pres. Rho of N.Y. chpt., Spl. Citation of Honor on Sesquicentennial U. Vt. 1998). Home: 360 W 22nd St New York NY 10011-2600 Office: care Ethyle R Wolfe Inst Humanities Bklyn Coll Bedford Ave # H Brooklyn NY 11222

WOLFE, GARY DONALD, library commissioner, retired state education official; b. Altoona, Pa., Mar. 19, 1941; s. Donald George and Norma Rosmond (Cooper) W.; m. Mary Susan Olex, Aug. 5, 1967; children: Mark Douglas, Michelle Marie. BS in Elem. Edn., St. Francis Coll., Loretto, Pa., 1970; MLS, U. Pitts., Pa., 1972. Libr. clk. Altoona Pub. Libr., 1959-61; acting children's libr. Coyle Free Libr., Chambersburg, Pa., 1961-63; asst. prof. librarianship St. Francis Coll., 1963-75; adminstr. Centre County Libr., Bellefonte, Pa., 1975-89; dir. libr. devel. State Libr. Pa., Harrisburg, Pa., 1989-95; dep. sec. edn., commr. for libr. State of Pa., Harrisburg, Pa., 1995—. Editor: Automated Circulation: A Study, 1981. Sgt. USAR, 1963-69. Recipient Disting. Alumni award St. Francis Coll., 1997, Cert. of Commendation, Am. Assn. Sch. Librs., 2003. Mem. ALA, Pa. Libr. Assn. (treas. 1983-85, cert. of merit 1986, Disting. Svc. award 1997), Pa. Citizens for Better Librs. Republican. Avocation: reading. Home: 2407 Wicklow Dr Harrisburg PA 17112-9620

WOLFE, GEORGE C. theater director, producer, playwright; b. Frankfurt, Ky., Sept. 23, 1954; s. Costello and Anna Wolfe. BA, Pomona Coll., 1976; MFA, NYU, 1983. With Inner City Cultural Center, Los Angeles, Calif., 1975—78; teacher City Coll. of N.Y. & Richard Allen Ctr. for Cultural Art; resident dir. Public Theatre, N.Y.C., 1990—93; prodr. N.Y. Shakespeare Festival, N.Y.C., 1993—; head prodr. Public Theatre, N.Y.C., 1993—. Works include: writer, lyricist (plays) Paradise!, 1985; writer, dir. The Colored Museum, 1986 (Elizabeth Hull-Kate Warriner award, Dramatists Guild, 1986), Jelly's Last Jam, 1992 (Drama Desk award, 1992, Joe A. Callaway award, Stage Dirs. and Choreographers Found., 1993); writer Queenie Pie, 1987, The Wild Party, 2000; scene contbr. Urban Blight, 1988; curator Festival of New Voices, 1990, 92; adaptor, dir. Spunk, 1990 (Obie award best dir., 1990); dir., prodr. (Broadway shows) Angels in America, 1992, (Tony award best dir., 1993), Perestroika, 1993 (Tony award nominee best dir., 1994), Twilight: Los Angeles, 1994, The Tempest, 1995, On the Town, 1998, Elaine Stritch At Liberty, 2002, Topdog/Underdog, 2002, Caroline, or Change, 2004 (Tony nom. best dir. of a musical, 2004); prodr., lyrics, Bring in Da Noise, Bring in Da Funk, 1996 (Tony award for best dir., 1996); prodr. Golden Child, 1998, Take Me Out, 2003; actor: A Delicate Balance, 1996 (Tony award best leading actor, 1996). Grantee Rockefeller Found., Nat. Endowment for Arts, Nat. Inst. Musical Theatre; recipient Hull-Warriner award, 2 Audleco awards, The George Oppenheimer/Newsday award, CBS-FDG New Play award, NYU Disting. Alumni award, HBO/USA Playwrights award, Person of Yr. award Nat. Theatre Conf., Spl. Achievement award Audleco, Spirit of the City award, LAMBDA award; named A Living Landmark, N.Y. Landmarks Conservancy. Mem. Dramatists Guild (mem. exec. bd.), Dir. Guild of Amer., Writers Guild of Amer., bd. dirs. Young Playwrights Festival, N.Y.C. Office: Joseph Papp Pub Theater 425 Lafayette St New York NY 10003-7087*

WOLFE, GEORGE CROPPER, retired private school educator, artist, writer; b. New Orleans, Sept. 6, 1933; s. Howard Edward and Amaryllis (Brannen) Wolfe; m. Catherine Vasterling, June 2, 1955; children: David, Michael, Philip. BFA, La. State U., 1956; MEd, U. New Orleans, 1972, MS in Urban Planning, 1975; postgrad., Tex. Tech U., Junction, 1986-93, Northwestern State U., La. Cert. tchr. art, social studies La. Elem. tchr. Live Oak Manor Sch., Waggaman, La., 1962-65; tchr. art Isidore Newman Sch., New Orleans, 1965-96; adj. prof. art Northwestern State U., Natchitoches, La., 1997-99; co-owner design studio Wolf Patrol Prodns. Author: (video) Sculpture in Motion, 2000 (Silver Telly award, 2001), 3-D Wizardry (Telly award, 1996), Papier Maché Plaster and Foam; contbr. articles to profl. jours.; one-man shows include Hanchley Gallery, Northwestern U., 1999, exhibited in group shows at New Alexandria (La.) Mus. Art, commn. sculpture, Echo Totem, Alexandria Mus. Art, 1998, Alex the Red, 1998, Hands Supporting Hands, Wesley Found., 1999, commn. life size puppets, Two by Two, Northwestern State U. Summer Theatre, 1999. With USCG, 1956—58. Mem.: La. Art Edn. Assn. (pres. 1978—79), Nat. Art Edn. Assn. (La. Art Educator of the Yr. 1990, Ret. Art Educator of the Yr. 2000—01, Victor Lowenfeld award 2002), Phi Delta Kappa (v.p., Rsch. award 1996), Kappa Delta Pi. Home: 342 Jefferson St Natchitoches LA 71457-4382

WOLFE, GERALDINE, administrator; b. Monticello, Ark., Mar. 29, 1944; d. John Wesley and Hazeline (Daniels) Fisher; 1 child, Arin. BA, Keuka Coll., 1965; MA, Mt. Holyoke Coll., 1967; MSEd, Elmira Coll., 1981; cert. ednl. adminstrn. SUNY-Brockport, 1985; PhD Cornell U., 1988. Tchr. biology and health Corning Sch. Dist., N.Y., 1967-90; asst. prof. SUNY, Plattsburgh, 1990-93; adminstr. Saranac Lake Ctrl. Sch. Dist., 1993-96; asst. supt. Schenectady City Sch. Dist., 1996-99; supt. Catskill (N.Y.) Ctrl. Sch. Dist., 1999—. Mem. Mid. States Evaluation Team, 1985; chmn. bd. trustees Friendship Bapt. Ch., Corning, 1984-90; bd. dirs. Hamilton Hill Arts Ctr., 1996-99, Oslo scholar U. Oslo, 1964, Coop. Ext., Common Ground of Catkill, Workforce Investment Act, Youth Coun., Grene County Collubirative Community Partnership for Youth; Mem. N.Y. State Profl. Health Educators Assn., Women in Ednl. Adminstrn., LWV, Sigma Xi, Sigma Lambda Sigma. Club: Cosmopolitan (officer 1979-81) (Elmira). Mem. allocations com. United Way, 1982-90; mem. edn. com. Planned Parenthood, 1984-90. Mem. NAACP, ASCD, Nat. Assn. Sec. Sch. Prins., Am. Assn. Sch. Adminstrs., Nat. Alliance Black Sch. Educators, N.Y.S. Assn. for Computers and Technologies in Edn., N.Y.S. Assn. Compensatory Educators, N.Y. State Coun. Sch. Supts., Cornell Edn. Soc., Jr. League of Elmira, Rotary Club of Catskill, Capital District Assn. of Women Adminstrs., Delta Kappa Gamma, Phi Delta Kappa. Avocations: tennis; cross countryskiing; travel; piano; reading. Home: 7 Forest Hills Dr Elmira NY 14905-1141 Office: Catskill Ctrl Sch Dist 343 W Main St Catskill NY 12414-1621

WOLFE, GREGORY BAKER, international relations educator; b. L.A., Jan. 27, 1922; s. Harry Norton and Laura May (Baker) W.; m. Mary Ann Nelson, June 15, 1946; children: Gregory Nelson, Laura Ann, Melissa Helene. AB, Reed Coll., 1943; MA, Fletcher Sch. Law and Diplomacy, 1947, PhD, 1961; Dr. honoris causa, U. Autonoma de Guadalajara, Mex., 1984; D.H.L., S.E. Coll. Osteo. Medicine, Miami, Fla., 1985; DHL, U. Tecnologica Equinoccial, Quito, Ecuador, 2000, U. Tecnologica de Santiago, Dominican Republic, 2001. With internat. div. Arthur D. Little, Inc., Cambridge, Mass., 1951-57; dir. Greater Boston Econ. Study Com., 1957-61; dir. Latin Am. program Com. Econ. Devel., 1961-64; dir. intelligence and rsch. for Am. republics State Dept., 1964-68; pres. Portland State U., 1968-74; dean Sch. Internat. Svc. Am. U., Washington, 1975-79; pres. Fla. Internat. U., Miami, 1979-86, prof. internat. rels., 1979—; vis. scholar Cambridge U., Eng., 1986-87; chmn. Ednl. Facility Authority, Dade County, Fla., 1998—. Fed. negotiator Joint Transp. Com. Washington 1962 66 Contbr. articles to profl. jours. Chmn. bd. trustees Internat. Fine Arts Coll., 1993—, U. de Palermo Found., Buenos Aires, 1998—; bd. dirs. Chopin Found. U.S., Inc., 1988-96, Concert Assn. Fla., Inc., 1988—; founding chmn. Brickell Ave. Lit. Soc., 1 988-96. Recipient Fla. Internat. Ctr. award, 1980, Leonard Abess award, 1984, Orden del Merito Civil, King of Spain, 1986, Fulbright lectr., Ecuador, 1989. E-mail: wolfeg@fiu.edu., andes79@hotmail.com.

WOLFE, JAMES MICHAEL, education educator, researcher; s. Dianne Adams and James Ralph Wolfe, Richard L Martin (Stepfather); m. Krista Lynn Gilman, Oct. 31, 2001; children: James Christopher, Joslyn Marie. AA, Daytona Beach C.C., 1990; BS in Mgmt., U. of Ctrl. Fla., 1998, MS in Mgmt., 2001, MS in Info. Sys., 2003. Sr. lab technologist Syncor Internat. Corp., Gainesville, 1990—95; computer assoc. Tandy Corp., Orlando, 1995—98; p.c. lan support analyst Walt Disney World, Orlando, 1998—98; sr. virus rschr. Lockheed Martin Corp., Orlando, 1998—; adj. prof. U. of Ctrl. Fla., Orlando, 2002—. Mem. certification bd. Anti Virus Info. Exch. Network, Toronto, Canada, 2001—; cons. Team Anti-Virus, Harrisburg, Pa., United States, 2002—; mis adv. bd. U. of Ctrl. Fla., 2003—. Co-author: (handbook) Info. Security Mgmt. Handbook; contbr. magazine Virus Bull. Mag., mag. The EICAR Mag. Mem.: The Digital Forensics Info. Exch. Network, Anti Virus Info. Exch. Network (disciplinary com. 2002—03, chmn. disciplinary com. 2002—04), The Wild List Orgn. (reporter 2000—04), The European Inst. of Computer Anti Virus Researchers (rschr. 2000—04). Republican. Methodist. Achievements include research in computer virus and malicious code rsch; nuclear medicine pharmacological rsch. Avocations: paintball, music, golf, travel.

WOLFE, JAMES RONALD, lawyer; b. Pitts., Dec. 10, 1932; s. James Thaddeus and Helen Matilda (Corey) W.; m. Anne Lisbeth Dahle Eriksen, May 28, 1960 (dec. 1996); children: Ronald, Christopher, Geoffrey; m. Patricia D. Yoder, Oct. 30, 1999. BA summa cum laude, Duquesne U., 1954, DHL (hon.), 1997; LLB cum laude, NYU, 1959. Bar: N.Y. 1959. Assoc. Simpson Thacher & Bartlett, N.Y.C., 1959-69, ptnr., 1969-95, counsel, 1996-99. Co-editor: West's McKinney's Forms, Uniform Commercial Code, 1965. Served to 1st lt. U.S. Army, 1955-57. Mem. Assn. Bar City N.Y. Roman Catholic. Home: 500 SE 5th Ave Apt 601 Boca Raton FL 33432-5510 Office: Simpson Thacher & Bartlett 425 Lexington Ave New York NY 10017-3954

WOLFE, JANE, writer; b. Columbus, Ohio, Feb. 26, 1957; d. William Culver and Relna Fay (Kalfs) W.; m. Leon A. Harris, Jr., Sept. 27, 1996; 1 child, Lee Harris III. BA, Denison U., 1980. Soc. editor The Dallas Morning News, 1986-87; pub. The Gold Book of Dallas Soc., 1988-92. Author: The Murchisons: The Rise and Fall of a Texas Dynasty, 1989, Blood Rich: When Oil Billions, High Fashion and Royal Intimacies Are Not Enough, 1993; bus. reporter The N.Y. Times, 1999—. Home: 4300 Saint Johns Dr Dallas TX 75205-4335

WOLFE, JOAN, non-profit organizations consultant; b. Detroit, May 2, 1929; d. William R. and Mary Lucinda (Deane) Luedders; m. Willard Wolfe, June 26, 1953; children; John Roberts, Peter Harper (dec.). BA in Econ., U. Mich., 1951; Dr. Pub. Svc. (hon.), Western Mich. U., 1973. Founder, chmn. West Mich. Environ. Action Coun., exec. dir., 1971-73; 1st woman mem. Mich. Natural Resources Commn., 1973-82, chair, 1977. Author: Making Things Happen: The Guide for Members of Volunteer Organizations, 1981, Making Things Happen: How to Be an Effective Volunteer, 1991. Named Conservationist of Yr. Mich. United Conservation Clubs, 1971, Funep 500 Environ. Achiever Friends of UN Environ. Program, one of Mich. 50 Hist. Women to Know, Mich. History Mag., 2002; inducted Mich. Women's Hall of Fame, 1996; recipient Women of Achievement and Courage award Mich. Women's Found., 1998, Environ. Quality award Mich. Soc. Internal Medicine, 1970, Conservation award Am. Motors Corp., 1973, others. Mem. Nat. Audubon Soc. (nat. bd. dirs. 1982-87).

WOLFE, JOHN LESLIE, lawyer; b. Cuyahoga Falls, Ohio, Dec. 6, 1926; s. Leslie George and Phyllis (Bond) W.; m. Barbara Lou Carle, Dec. 27, 1950 (div.); children: David, Karla. AB, U. Akron, 1950; JD, U. Mich., 1953. Bar: Ohio 1953, U.S. Dist. Ct. (no. dist.) Ohio 1955, U.S. Ct. Appeals (6th cir.) 1966, U.S. Supreme Ct. 1970. Sole practice, Akron, 1953—56; asst. pros. atty. Summit County, Akron, 1956—57; assoc. Hershey & Browne, Akron, 1957—61, ptnr., 1961—85, Wolfe, Williams & Abdenour, Akron, 1986—90; sole practice Akron, 1991—. Asst. atty. gen. State of Ohio, 1971-74; adj. prof. trial practice U. Akron, 1975-80; counsel Tri County Regional Planning Commn. of Portage, Summit and Medina Counties, 1960-74. Trustee Akron Law Libr., 1961—; past pres. Progress Through Preservation. Served with U.S. Army, 1945-47. Recipient Ohio Legal Ctr. Inst. award of merit, 1966. Mem.: ATLA, ABA, Nat. Employment Lawyers Assn., Ohio Acad. Trial Lawyers, Akron Bar Assn., Ohio State Bar Assn. Office: National City Center 1 Cascade Plz Ste 740 Akron OH 44308-1154 Office Phone: 330-535-2441. Personal E-mail: wolfe81@attglobal.net.

WOLFE, KENNETH L. food products manufacturing company executive; b. 1939; married. BA, Yale U., 1961; MBA, U. Pa., 1967. With Bankers Trust Corp., 1961—62; with Hershey Foods Corp., Hershey, Pa., 1968—, asst. treas., 1968—69, budget dir., 1969—74, dir. ops. and finl. analysis, 1974—76, treas., 1976—80; v.p. fin. adminstrn. Hershey Chocolate Co., Hershey, Pa., 1980—81, v.p., CFO, 1981—84, sr. v.p., CFO, 1984—85, pres., COO, 1985—93, chmn., CEO, 1994—, also dir. Office: Hershey Foods Corp 100 Crystal A Dr Unit 8 Hershey PA 17033-9702

WOLFE, LESLIE R. think-tank executive; Exec. dir. Ctr. for Women Policy Studies, Washington, D.C., pres. Office: Ctr Women Policy Studies 1211 Connecticut Ave NW Ste 312 Washington DC 20036-2709

WOLFE, LINDA, writer; b. N.Y.C., Nov. 15, 1932; d. Harry M. Friedman and Mina Romanoff Kaufman; m. Max Pollack; 1 child, Jessica Wolfe Bernstein. MA, NYU, 1958. Editl. asst. Oxford U. Press, N.Y.C., 1955—60, Partisan Rev., N.Y.C., NY, 1958—60; writer, rschr. Time, Inc., N.Y.C., 1960—71; contbg. editor N.Y. Mag., N.Y.C., 1971—96; consulting editor Woman Mag. (Conde Nast), N.Y.C., 1990—90. Author: (book) The Literary Gourmet, 1962, The Cooking of the Caribbean Islands, 1970, Playing Around: Women and Adultery, 1975, The Cosmo Report: Women and Sex in the Nineteen-Eighties, 1981, Private Practices (a novel), 1981, The Professor and the Prostitute and Other True Tales of Murder and Madness, 1986, Wasted: The Preppie Murder, 1989 (Notable Book of Yr., N.Y. Times, 1989), Double Life: The Shattering Affair Between New York's Chief Judge Sol Wachtler & Socialite Joy Silverman, 1994, Love Me To Death: A Journalist's Memoir of the Hunt for her Friend's Killer, 1998, The Murder of Dr. Chapman: The Legendary Trials of Lucretia Chapman and Her Lover, 2004. Recipient Edgar Allan Poe award nominee, Mystery Writers of Am., 1989. Mem.: PEN (exec. bd. dirs. 1994—95), Nat. Book Critics Circle (v.p. 1997—2002). Avocations: 18th-century English dance, travel.

WOLFE, MARGARET RIPLEY, historian, educator, consultant; b. Kingsport, Tenn., Feb. 3, 1947; d. Clarence Estill and Gertrude Blessing Ripley; m. David Earley Wolfe, Dec. 17, 1966; 1 child, Stephanie Ripley. BS magna cum laude, East Tenn. State U., 1967, MA, 1969; PhD, U. Ky., 1974. Instr. history East Tenn. State U., 1969-73, asst. prof., 1973-77, assoc. prof., 1977-80, prof., 1980—, sr. rsch. prof. history, 1999—. Author: Lucius Polk Brown and Progressive Food and Drug Control, Tennessee and New York City, 1908-1920, 1978, An Industrial History of Hawkins County, Tennessee, 1983, Kingsport, Tennessee: A Planned American City, 1987, Daughters of Canaan: A Saga of Southern Women, 1995; gen. editor: Women in Southern Culture Series; contbg. author to books, also introductions to books; contbr. articles to profl. jours. Mem. Tenn. Com. for Humanities, 1985-85, exec. coun. mem., 1984-85; mem. Women's Symphony Com., Kingsport, 1990-95; exec. com. Tenn. Commemorative Woman's Suffrage Commn., 1994-95; mem. state rev.

bd. Tenn. Hist. Commn., 1995—. Haggin fellow U. Ky., 1972-73; recipient Disting. Faculty award East Tenn. State U., 1977, East Tenn. State U. Found. rsch. award, 1979, Alumni cert. merit, 1984. Mem. AAUP, ACLU (exec. com. Tenn. 1991-92), NOW, Tenn. State Employees Assn., Am. Studies Assn. (John Hope Franklin Prize com. 1992), Am. Hist. Assn., Orgn. Am. Historians, So. Assn. Women Historians (pres. 1983-84, exec. com. 1984-86), So. Hist. Assn. (com. on status of women 1987, program com. 1988, interim chair program com. 1988, mem. com. 1993, 94, 95, nominating com. 1994, chair nominating com. 1995, chmn. mem. com. 1997, exec. coun. 1998-2000), Smithsonian Assocs, Tenn. Hist Commn. (state rev. bd. 1995—), Tenn. Hist. Soc. (editl. bd. 1995—), Coordinating Com. for Women in History, East Tenn. Hist. Soc. (mem. editl. bd. Jour. East Tenn. History), St. George Tucker Soc., Phi Kappa Phi. Office: ETSU at Kingsport Kingsport TN 37660 also: East Tenn State U Dept History Johnson City TN 37614

WOLFE, MARY JOAN, physician; b. Pa., May 26, 1949; d. Dermot F. and Jean M. Wolfe; m. Thomas R. Roberts, June 9, 1979; children: Douglas Roberts-Wolfe, Rebecca Roberts-Wolfe. AB in Chemistry, Cornell U., 1971; MD, M.S. Hershey (Pa.) Med. Ctr., 1976. Diplomate Am. Bd. Internal Medicine, Am. Bd. Emergency Medicine. Intern Rochester (N.Y.) Gen. Hosp., 1976-77; resident in internal medicine Westchester County Med. Ctr., Valhalla, N.Y., 1977-79, attending physician emergency dept., 1979-83; practice medicine specializing in internal medicine Ossining, N.Y., 1986—. Attending physician emergency room No. Westchester Hosp., Mt. Kisco, NY, 1986—89. Mem. ethics com. Phelps Meml. Hosp., 1994-97, mem. bylaws com., 1989-96, chmn., 1996-2004. Mem. N.Y. Soc. Internal Medicine, Am. Soc. Internal Medicine. Avocations: gardening, camping, swimming, computers, painting. Home: 6 Cecilia Ln Pleasantville NY 10570-1502 Office: 14 Church St Ossining NY 10562-4831 E-mail: robrtswolf@aol.com.

WOLFE, MAURICE RAYMOND, retired museum director, educator; b. Paris (Neuilly), France, Oct. 13, 1924; s. Guy Ellsworth and Genevieve (Plion) W.; m. Warwick Ellen Griffin, Nov. 4, 1955; 1 child, Shavaun. BA, U. Calif. in Sociology, Berkeley, 1948; MA in Sociology, U. Calif., Berkeley, 1952; postgrad. study, U. Paris Sorbonne, 1951; Cert. of Completion Sch. of Edn., U. Calif., Berkeley, 1954, postgrad., 1955. Rsch. asst. dept. of edn. U. Calif., Berkeley, 1949; tchr. of English and history Castlemont H.S., Oakland, Calif., 1954; lectr. in anthropology, philosophy, sociology and edn. U. Md. Overseas, 1956-59; lectr., instr. in philosophy and sociology U. Md., Munich, 1960-62; faculty mem. Merritt Coll., Oakland, Calif., 1962-88, chmn. dept. behavioral scis., 1967-87; dir. and founder Merritt Coll. Anthropology Mus., Oakland, 1973-88; rsch. assoc. U. Calif. Lowie Mus. of Anthropology, 1985-89. Lectr. Pers. Mgmt. for Execs., U.S. Govt. Sponsored, Berkeley, Calif. 1966-67, San Francisco State U., 1967-68, Calif. State U., Hayward, Dept. Sociology, 1970-71; adj. instr. Monterey Peninsula Coll., 1990, 91, Hartnell Coll., Salinas, Calif., Chapman U., 1992-95, Golden Gate U., 1995-98; adj. prof. Golden Gate U., 1997—. Editor: (jour.) Socioloqus, 1952. Recipient French Govt fellowship, Sorbonne, Paris, 1956; named to list of Great Teachers of Calif., Calif. Assn. Comty. Colls., Santa Barbara, 1984. Home: 33751 E Carmel Valley Rd Carmel Valley CA 93924-9303 E-mail: azal@aol.com.

WOLFE, MELINDA BETH, human resources executive; b. Chgo., July 30, 1956; d. Seymour Louis and Muriel Sharlene (Hyman) W.; m. Kenneth D. Inadomi, Oct. 10, 1987; 1 child, Molly. BA magna cum laude, Wash. U., 1978; MCRP, Harvard U., 1981. Investment banker Merrill Lynch, N.Y., 1981-95, dir. diversity strategy, 1995-96; dir. global recruiting and tng. Credit Suisse First Boston, N.Y., 1996-99; mng. dir. staffing and devel. Goldman Sachs, N.Y.C., 1999—2001, head office of global leadership and diversity, 2001—. Chair corp. cir. Nat. Coun. for Rsch. on Women, 1999—; mem. coun. of advocates Planned Parenthood, 1995—; mem. leadership cir. Women's Campaign Fund; mem. The Dalton Sch. Coun., 1999—, The Dalton Sch. Bd., 2000—; bd. dirs. Art Sweats Inc., 1995—. Mem. Fin. Womens Assn. Home: 607 W End Ave New York NY 10024-1606 Office: Goldman Sachs 85 Broad St New York NY 10004 Office Phone: 212-357-4961. Business E-Mail: melinda.wolfe@gs.com.

WOLFE, RICHARD PEEL, lawyer; b. Brookhaven, Miss., May 31, 1937; s. Hubert Heuck and Nell (Peel) W.; m. Ann Perkins Terrell, Aug. 20, 1960; children: Susan Wolfe Huppman, Emily Wolfe Leigh. AB magna cum laude, Princeton U., 1959; JD, Harvard U., 1962; M in Civil Law, Tulane U., 1965. Bar: La. 1963, U.S. Dist. Ct. (ea. dist.) La. 1963, U.S. Ct. Appeals (5th cir.) 1963; cert. tax law specialist. Assoc. Monroe & Lemann, Attys., New Orleans, 1963—68, ptnr., 1968—96, sect. head, corp. sect., 1974—96, mgmt. com., 1989—93; ptnr. Jones, Walker, Waechter, Poitevent, Carrère & Denègre Attys., New Orleans, 1997—. Mem. IRS-Tax Lawyers S.W. Regional Liaison Com., 1976-77; presenter in field. Bd. deacons St. Charles Ave. Presbyn. Ch., 1967—70, 1972—75, chmn., 1970; mem. planning com. Tulane Corp. Law Inst., Tulane Law Sch., 1988—2000; bd. dirs. Met. Crime Commn. of New Orleans, 1997—2001, Bur. Govtl. Rsch., 1984—90; trustee La. Nature and Sci. Ctr., 1980—84; chmn. Gallier Ho. Mus. Coun., Tulane U., 1986—88, trustee, 1978—86; mem. com. to nominate alumni trustees Princeton U., 1979—81, chmn., 1981; mem. Audobon Pk. Commn., New Orleans, 1971—77; trustee Metairie Pk. Country Day Sch., 1973—77; mem. agy. rels. com. United Way of Greater New Orleans, 1973—75. Mem.: ABA (sect. taxation 1967—77, corp. stockholder relationships com.), La. State Bar Assn. (liaison com. with dist. dir. IRS 1974—80, chmn. sect. on taxation 1975—76, task force on legal practice designation and specialization 1981—83), Soc. of War of 1812, Cap and Gown Club (Princeton U.), Harvard Club (N.Y.C.), New Orleans Country Club, Boston Club, La. Club, New Orleans Lawn Tennis Club, Phi Beta Kappa. Republican. Presbyterian. Home: 7916 Plum St New Orleans LA 70118 Office: Jones Walker 201 St Charles Ave Ste 5100 New Orleans LA 70170

WOLFE, ROBERT A. aerospace executive; BS in Aerospace Engring., MS in Aerospace Engring., Ga. Inst. Tech. With McDonnell Douglas Corp.; sys. integration dir. for the Peacekeeper MIssile Martin Marietta, 1981-84; exec. v.p. govt. and space propulsion bus. Pratt & Whitney, 1990-93, sr. v.p. Ams., exec. v.p. Pratt & Whitney Group, 1994-97; pres. Pratt & Whitney Aircraft divsn. United Techs., 1994-97; pres. Aerojet GenCorp, Inc., Rancho-Cordova, Calif., 1997—, chmn., CEO, 1997—. With USN. Office: PO Box 537012 Sacramento CA 95853-7012

WOLFE, ROSE, former academic administrator; b. Toronto, Ont., Can. m. Ray D. Wolfe, July 5, 1940 (dec.); children: Jonathan, Elizabeth. BA, U. Toronto, 1938, diploma in Social Work, 1939. Chancellor U. Toronto, 1991—97, chancellor emeritus, 1997—. Case worker, supr., bd. dirs., mem. exec. com., life mem. Jewish Family & Child Svcs.; case worker, supr. Protestant Children's Home, Young Men's Hebrew Assn. Trustee Bantine Rsch. Inst., Lester Pearson Coll. of the Pacific, McMichael Can. Art Collection; mem. endowment com. Women's Legal Edn. & Action Fund Found.; v.p. Ont. region Can. Jewish Congress; mem. exec. com. nat. Can. Jewish Congress; dir. Mt. Sinai Hosp.; mem exec com., bd. dirs., mem. advt. com. Can. Jewish News. Decorated Order of Can., Order of Ont. Avocations: tennis, golf, swimming, theater. Home: 89 Bayview Ridge Willowdale ON Canada M2L 1E3

WOLFE, SCOTT W. orthopedic hand surgeon; b. Rye, NY, Aug. 28, 1958; MD, Cornell U., 1984. Intern Roosevelt Hospital, NYC, 1984—86; orthopedics resident Hospital for Special Surgery, NYC, 1986—89; fellowship in hand surgery Columbia U. Coll. of Physicians & Surgeons, NYC, 1989—90; assist. prof. Yale U. Sch. of Medicine, New Haven, dir. hand & upper extremity div.; prof. orthopedic surgery Cornell-Weill Med. Ctr., NYC; chief hand service Hospital for Special Surgery, NYC, clin. dir. orthopedic surgery & attending orthopedic surgeon, dir. hand surgical fellowship; assoc. dir. clinical rsch. Alberto Vilar Ctr. for Hand and Upper Extremity Surgery. Named one of NY Mag. Best Doctors in NY, 2003. Office: Hospital for Special Surgery 535 E 70th St New York NY 10021

WOLFE, SHEILA A. journalist; b. Chgo. d. Leonard M. and Rena (Karn) W. BA, Drake U. Reporter Chgo. Tribune, 1956-73, asst. city editor, 1973-75; day city editor Chgo. Tribune, 1975-79; city editor Chgo. Tribune, 1979-81, met. coordinator, 1981-83, adminstrv. asst. to mng. editor, 1983-2000. Pres. City News Bur. Chgo. 1986-88, 94-96. Recipient Beck award for outstanding profl. performance Chgo. Tribune, 1979; recipient Disting. Service award Drake U., 1982 Mem. Phi Beta Kappa. Home: 71 E Division St Chicago IL 60610-8307 E-mail: chicagoshe@aol.com.

WOLFE, SIDNEY MANUEL, physician; b. June 12, 1937; s. Fred and Sophia Esther (Marks) W.; m. Suzanne M. Goldberg; children: Hannah, Leah, Rachel, Sarah. BS, Western Res. U., 1960, MD, 1965. Intern. Cleve. Met. Gen. Hosp., 1965-66, resident internal medicine, 1969-70; staff assoc. NIH, 1966-72; dir. Pub. Citizens Health Research Group, Washington, 1972—. Contbr. articles to med. jours. Served with USPHS, 1966-69. McArthur fellowship, 1990—. Office: Pub Citizen Health Research Group 2000 P St NW Ste 708 Washington DC 20036-6919

WOLFE, STANLEY, composer, educator; b. N.Y.C., Feb. 7, 1924; s. Bert S. and Dorothy (Sanders) W.; m. Marguerite Wiberg, Aug. 10, 1960; children: Jeffrey, Madeleine. Student, Stetson U., 1946-47, Henry St. Music Sch., 1947-48; BS in Composition, Juilliard Sch. Music, 1952, MS in Composition, 1955. Faculty Juilliard Sch., N.Y.C., 1955—, dir. extension div., 1956-89; adj. prof. music Lincoln Ctr. campus Fordham U., 1969-73; lectr. N.Y. Philharmonic Pre-Concert Series, 1985—. Prin. compositions include King's Heart; dance score, 1956, Canticle for Strings, 1957, Lincoln Square Overture, 1958, Symphony Number 3, 1959, String Quartet, 1961, Symphony Number 4, 1965, Symphony Number 5 (Lincoln Center Commn.), 1970, Symphony Number 6, 1981; Violin Concerto, 1987. Served with AUS, 1943-46. Recipient award Am. Acad. and Inst. Arts and Letters, 1990; Guggenheim fellow in composition, 1957; Nat. Endowment for Arts grantee, 1969, 70, 77 Mem. ASCAP, Am. Music Center, Am. Symphony Orch. League (Alice Ditson award 1961), U.S. Chess Fedn. Home: 32 Ferndale Dr Hastings On Hudson NY 10706 Office Phone: 212-799-5000.

WOLFE, SUZANNE L. artist, art educator; b. Chgo., Feb. 4, 1942; d. John Charles and Rosetta Wolfe; 1 child, Kalu Alexander Wolfe. BA in Anthropology, U. Mich., 1965, BFA, 1968, MFA, 1970. Prof. art U. Hawaii, Honolulu, 1971—. Dir., curator East-West Ceramics Collaboration Exhbn. and Workshop, Honolulu, 1995, 98, 2002. Exhibited in solo shows at Contemporary Mus., Honolulu, 1988; group exhbns. at Pottery Workshop, Hong Kong, 2003, Taipei Yingke County Mus., 2002, Mint Mus., Charlotte, 2001, Honolulu Acad. Arts, 2001, Slusser Gallery U. Mich., Ann Arbor, 2000, Bechtold Gallery, Amsterdam, 1997, Duchamp Gallery, Taipei, 1995, Dinnerworks, Louisville, 1993. Mem. Nat. Coun. Edn. in the Ceramic Arts. Office: U Hawaii Art Dept 2535 McCarthy Mall Honolulu HI 96822-2233 Office Phone: 808-956-5264. E-mail: swolfe@hawaii.edu.

WOLFE, THOMAS KENNERLY, JR., writer, journalist; b. Richmond, Va., Mar. 2, 1931; s. Thomas Kennerly and Helen (Hughes) W.; m. Sheila Berger; children: Alexandra, Thomas AB, Washington and Lee U., 1951, DLitt (hon.), 1974; PhD in Am. Studies, Yale U., 1957; DFA (hon.), Mpls. Coll. Art, 1971, Sch. of Visual Arts, 1987; LHD (hon.), Va. Commonwealth U., 1983, Southampton Coll. (N.Y.), 1984, Randolph-Macon Coll., 1988, Manhattanville Coll., 1988, Longwood Coll., 1989; DLitt (hon.), St. Andrews Presbyn. Coll., 1990, Johns Hopkins U., 1990, U. Richmond, 1993. Reporter Springfield (Mass.) Union, 1956-59; reporter, Latin Am. corr. Washington Post, 1959-62; city reporter N.Y. Herald Tribune, 1962-66; mag. writer N.Y. World Jour. Tribune, 1966-67; contbg. editor New York mag., 1968-76, Esquire Mag., N.Y.C., from 1977. Writer N.Y. Sunday Mag., 1962-66; contbg. artist Harper's Mag., N.Y.C., 1978-81. One-man show of drawings include Maynard Walker Gallery, N.Y.C., 1965, Tunnel Gallery, N.Y.C., 1974; author: The Kandy-Kolored Tangerine-Flake Streamline Baby, 1965, The Electric Kool-Aid Acid Test, 1968, The Pump House Gang, 1968, Radical Chic and Mau-mauing the Flak Catchers, 1970, The Painted Word, 1975, Mauve Gloves and Madmen, Clutter and Vine, 1976, The Right Stuff, 1979 (Am. Book award 1980), In Our Time, 1980, From Bauhaus to Our House, 1981, The Purple Decades: A Reader, 1982, The Bonfire of the Vanities, 1987, A Man in Full, 1998, (audio) Ambush at Fort Bragg, 1997, Hooking Up, 2000; editor, contbr. The New Journalism, 1973; contbr. articles to Esquire Mag., others. Recipient Front Page awards for humor and fgn. news reporting Washington Newspaper Guild, 1961, Soc. Mag. Writers award for excellence, 1970, Frank Luther Mott Rsch. award, 1973, Harold D. Vursell Meml. award Am. Acad. and Inst. Arts and Letters, 1980, Columbia Journalism award, 1980, Nat. Sculpture Soc. citation for art history, 1980, John Dos Passos award, 1984, Gari Melchers medal, 1986, Benjamin Pierce Cheney medal Ea. Wash. U., 1986, Washington Irving medal St. Nicholas Soc., 1986, Theodore Roosevelt medal Theodore Roosevelt Assn., 1990, Wilbur Cross medal Yale Grad. Sch. Alumni Assn., 1990, St. Louis Literary award, 1990, Quinnipiac Coll. Pres. award, 1993; named Va. Laureate for Lit., 1977; Chicago Tribune Literary Prize for lifetime achievement, 2003. Office: Farrar Straus & Giroux Inc 19 Union Sq W 11th Fl New York NY 10003-3304*

WOLFE, TOWNSEND DURANT, III, retired art museum director, curator; b. Hartsville, S.C., Aug. 15, 1935; m. Brooks Gibson Wolfe; children from previous marriage: Juliette Elizabeth, Mary Bryan, Townsend Durant. BFA, Atlanta Art Inst., 1958; MFA, Cranbrook Acad. Art, 1959; postgrad, Harvard Inst. Arts Adminstrn., 1970; DFA (hon.), Memphis Coll. Art, 1996; PhD (hon.), Montserrat Coll. Art, 2001, Ark. State U., 2002. Instr. Atlanta Art Assn., 1956-59, Memphis Acad. Art, 1959-64, Scarsdale Studio Workshop and Seamen Inst., N.Y.C., 1964-65; dir. Ford Found. Fund for Advancement of Edn. Wooster Community Art Ctr., Danbury, Conn., 1965-68; lectr. art U. Ark., Little Rock, 1969—; dir., chief curator The Ark. Arts Ctr., Little Rock, 1968—, ret., 2003—. Sec. Ark. Arts Ctr. Found., 1973—; pres. Ark. Consortium Arts, 1976-80; pres. Ark. Arts in Edn. Adv. Coun., 1977-79; bd. dirs. Mid-Am. Arts Alliance, 1982-89; mem. adv. bd. Ark. Artists Registry, 1986—, Ark. Repertory Theatre, 1976-84; reviewer Inst. Mus. Svcs., 1984-87, examiner mus. assessment program, 1985-87; overview panel Nat. Endowment for Arts, 1986-88, rev. panel utilization of mus. resources, 1986, grant rev. panel conservation and collection maintenance, 1987; curator 20th Century Am. Sculpture Exhbn., First Ladies' Garden, The White House, 1995, Powerful Expressions: Recent American Drawings Nat. Acad. Design, N.Y., 1996. One-man shows include Madison Gallery, N.Y.C., 1961, U. Miss., 1963, Soutwestern U., Memphis, 1964, Ark. State U., Jonesboro, 1964, 70; group shows include Ball State Tchrs. Coll., Muncie, Ind., 1959, 63,65, 67, Ann. New Eng. Exhbn., 1966-67, Wadsworth Atheneum, Hartford, Conn., 1967, Audubon Artists, N.Y.C., 1968; represented in permanent collections Ark. State U., Union Planters Nat. Bank, Memphis, Mint Mus. Art, Charlotte, N.C., East Tenn. State U., others; author: Trustee Handbook, 1978, Appraiser Handbook, 1979, Selections from the Permanent Collection of the Arkansas Arts Center Foundation catalogue, 1983, Twentieth Century American Drawings from the Arkansas Arts Center Foundation Collection, 1984, American Drawings, 1986, National Drawings Invitational, 1986, 87, 88, 91, 92, 93, 94, 96, National Objects Invitational, 1987, 88, 89, 91, National Crafts Invitational, 1987, Picasso: The Classical Years 1917-1925, 1987, Carroll Cloar Arkansas Collections, 1987, Revalations Drawing/America catalogue, 1988, The Face, 1988, 90, American Abstract Drawings, 1989, The Figure, 1990, Will Barnet Drawings: 1930-90, 1991, Silverpoint Etc., 1992, Edward Faiers Retrospective, 1994, exhbn. catalogue Memphis Coll. Art, Paul Zwietnig-Rotterdam, 1995, Hans Burkhardt Drawings: 1932-1989, 1996, Large Drawings and Objects, 1996, various catalog essays. Presdl. appt. Nat. Mus. Svcs. Bd., 1995, Elizabeth Found. for the Arts, 1995, Nat. Coun. on the Arts, 1995. Recipient 20 awards for painting, 1958-68, Winthrop Rockefeller Meml. award, 1973, James R. Short award Southeastern Mus. Conf., 1981, Individual Achievement award Ark. Mus. Assn., 1984, Ark. Art Edn. Advocacy award, 1985, Promethean award for excellence in the arts March of Dimes, 1986, Chevalier dans l'ordre des Arts et Lettres, 1988, Diamond award Ark. chpt. Pub. Rels. Soc. Am., 1996, Dr. Martin Luther King Jr. Cmty. Svc. award, 1996, Disting. Svc. award outside the profession Nat. Art Edn. Assn., 1997, Nat. Humanitarian award NCCJ, 1998, Edwin Hanlon Meml. award Individual Contbrn. to Arts Little Rock Arts & Humanities Promotion Commn., 1998, Creative Spirit award, Black Alumni Pratt Inst., N.Y.C., Bus. and Profl. Leader award, Rotary Club, 1999, Gov.'s Arts Awards Lifetime Achievement award, 2002; 75th Anniversary Paul Harris fellow Rotary Found., 1999. Mem. Assn. Art Mus. Dirs., Assn. Am. Museums (membership com. 1982-88, accreditation com., sr. examiner 1972—). Democrat. Episcopalian.

WOLFE, TRACEY DIANNE, distributing company executive; b. Dallas, June 13, 1951; d. George F. Wolfe and Helen Ruth Cline Lemons; children: Bronson Alan, Travis Aaron. BS in Edn. and Social Sci., Tex. A&M U., Commerce, 1973, MS in Elem. Edn., 1976. Asst. to dir. student devel. East Tex. State U., 1973-74; corp. sec., v.p. Wolfe Distbg. Co. (beer distbrs.), Terrel, Tex., 1974-90, pres., 1990—. Mem. adv. bd. Tex. A&M U. Commerce Coll. Bus. and Tech., 1998—, mem. broadcast adv. bd., 1999—, vice chmn., 2003—; v.p. Wholesale Beer Distributors Tex., 2003—. Vice-chair Chancellor's Century Coun. Tex. A&M U., 2003—; panel mem. grievance com. State Bar Tex., 1994—2000; bd. dirs. CASA Rockwall County, 1995—; active Rockwall Leadership Class, 1996—97, Leadership Tex., 2002, mem., 2002, Rockwall County Child Protective Svcs. Bd.; bd. dir., chmn. Tex. A&M U. Commerce Found.; bd. dir. Friends Terrell Libr., 1995—2001, Crimestoppers, Rockwall, Tex., 2003—. Mem. Tex. A&M U.-Commerce Alumni Assn. (bd. dirs. 1992-96), Wholesale Beer Distributors Tex. (bd. dirs. 1995-, v.p. 2003), Rotary, Kappa Delta (nat. province pres. 1980-82). Republican. Methodist. Home: 3316 Lakeside Dr Rockwall TX 75087-5323 Office: 100 Metro Dr Terrell TX 75160-9104 Personal E-mail: tdwolfe@flash.net.

WOLFE, WILLIAM DOWNING, nuclear energy industry executive; b. Zanesville, Ohio, Nov. 14, 1947; s. William Jr. and Wava Benetta (Downing) Wolfe; m. Laura Olivia Soza, July 29, 1972; children: Lisa Anne, Erin Nicole. BBA, U. Ariz., 1969. Instr. RTV Internat., N.Y.C., 1969-70; mgr. prodn. Sta. KUAT-TV/AM/FM, Tucson, 1969-76; lectr. U. Ariz., Tucson, 1970-78; mgr. prodn. Sta. KGUN-TV, Tucson, 1976-79; exec. producer Sta. KTVK-TV, Phoenix, 1979-82; writer, producer Ariz. Pub. Svc. Co., Phoenix, 1982-83, supr. pub. info., 1983-86; sr. coord. emergency planning Palo Verde Nuclear Generating Sta., Phoenix, 1986—. Cons. Nat. Student Films, Hollywood, Calif., 1975, Warner for Gov., Phoenix, 1986, various advt. agys., 1974—83; chair NRC Region IV Utility Group; mem. NEI Task Force on Emergency Comm.; steering com. Nat. Radiol. Emergency Preparedness Conf. Writer, prodr. TV and multi-media programming and comml. advertisements, 1969—. Mem. budge. adv. com. Deer Valley Sch. Dist., mem. long-range planning com., supt. search profile com., supt. search com., bond election com., curriculum exit outcomes planning com., campus improvement team, strategic planning team; mem. planning com. Deer Valley Village, 2000—; mem. med. assistance team com. Maricopa County Disaster, 2002—; mem. Maricopa Citizen Corps Coun.; bd. dirs. Ariz. chpt. Muscular Dystrophy Assn., 1976—79; advisor Jr. Achievement, Tucson, 1976; chmn. com. Ariz. Citizens for Edn., Phoenix, 1988—. Recipient Golden Sch. Bell award, Ariz. Dept. Edn., 1974—79, Emmy nomination, NATAS, 1979, Bronze Anvil nat. award, Pub. Rels. Soc. Am., 1983, award Excellence, Internat. Assn. Bus. Communicators, award in Pub. Archaeology, Ariz. Archaeology Adv. Commn., 2001; grantee, Ford Found., 1969. Mem.: Nat. Radiol. Emergency Preparedness Conf., Nat. Emergency Mgmt. Assn. Democrat. Roman Catholic. Avocation: music. Office: Palo Verde Nuclear Generating Sta PO Box 52034 MS 6050 Phoenix AZ 85072-2034 Office Phone: 602-393-6096. E-mail: wwolfe@apsc.com.

WOLFE, WILLIAM J. management consultant; With First Washington Mgmt., Inc., Bethesda, Md., 1980—. Office: First Washington Mgmt Inc 4350 E West Hwy Ste 400 Bethesda MD 20814-4426

WOLFE, WILLIAM JEROME, librarian, English language educator; b. Chgo., Feb. 24, 1927; s. Fred Wiley and Helen Dorothea (Lovaas) W.; m. ViviAnn Lundin O'Connell, June 25, 1960 (div. 1962); 1 child, Lund. AB, U. Chgo., 1948; BA, Roosevelt U., Chgo., 1953; MEd, Chgo. State U., 1963; AA with high honors, Pima C.C., 1992; BA in Art magna cum laude, U. Ariz., 1994. Tchr. English John Marshall High Sch., Chgo., 1956-60; libr. Safford Jr. High Sch., Tucson, Ariz., 1961-71, Santa Rita High Sch., Tucson, 1971-75, Tucson High Sch., 1975-87. Tutor Eastside Ctr., Literacy Vols. Tucson, 1988-2001, supr., 1993-2001. Co-founder Tucson Classic Guitar Soc., 1969-72; docent U. Ariz. Mus. Art, Tucson, 1989-2002; mem. adv. bd. U. Ariz. Sch. Music, 1995—; singer U. Ariz. Collegium Musicum, 1981-96, 2002—; mem. U. Ariz. Scholarship Devel. Adv. Coun., 2000—, liaison Coll. Fine Arts. With U.S. Army, 1945-46, ETO. Recipient U. Ariz. Alumni Assn. Slonaker award, 2001. Mem.: Nat. Assn. of Scholars, Assn. Lit. Scholars and Critics, Tucson Guitar Soc. (treas. 2001—), Tucson Post Card Exch. Club, Friends of the Libr. U. Ariz., U. Ariz. Pres. Club, Friends of the Sch. of Music U.Ariz., Phi Kappa Phi. Mem. Ch. of Christ Scientist. Avocations: poetry writing, drawing, singing, piano, classical guitar. Home: 8460 E Rosewood St Tucson AZ 85710-1702 E-mail: wjwolfe@earthlink.net. *Through every turn of events, a pleasing composition of life develops from love of family, wise counsel of teachers, inspiration of friends, and trust in God.*

WOLFEN, WERNER F. lawyer; b. Berlin, May 15, 1930; came to U.S., 1939; s. Martin and Ruth Eva (Hamburger) W.; m. Mary Glasier, July 1, 1956; children: Richard, James, Lawrence (dec.). BS, U. Calif., Berkeley, 1950, JD, 1953. Bar: Calif. 1953. Assoc. Irell & Manella, L.A., 1953-57, ptnr., 1957-98, sr. ptnr. emeritus, 1999—; pres. Capri Investment Co. LLC, 1999—. Bd. dirs. Broadcom Corp., Calhoun Vision, Inc.Rokenbok Toy Co., Pre-Cash Corp.; mem. bd. visitors UCLA Sch. Arts and Arch., 1995—. Bd. dirs. UCLA Found., 1992-2003; bd. dirs. L.A. Goal, 1994-, pres., 1994-99. Mem. ABA. Democrat. Jewish. Office: Capri Investment Co LLC 1800 Avenue of the Stars Los Angeles CA 90067-4212 Business E-Mail: wwolfen@irell.com.

WOLFENDEN, RICHARD VANCE, biochemistry educator; b. Oxford, Eng., May 17, 1935; s. John Hulton and Josephine (Vance) W.; m. Anita Gaunitz, June 25, 1965; children: Peter, John. BA, MA, Exeter Coll., Oxford U., Eng., 1958; PhD, Rockefeller Inst., 1964. Asst. prof. chemistry Princeton U., N.J., 1964-70; assoc. prof. biochemistry U. N.C., Chapel Hill, 1970-73, prof. biochemistry, 1973-83, alumni disting. prof., 1983—. Vis. fellow Exeter Coll., Oxford, 1969; vis. prof. U. Montpellier, France, 1976; mem. molecular biology panel NSF, Washington, 1973-76; mem. bio-organic and natural products study sect. NIH, Washington, 1981-86. Mem. editl. bd. Bioorganic Chemistry, 1983—, Biomed. Chem. Letters, 1993—. Fellow AAAS, Am. Acad. Arts and Scis.; mem. NAS, Am. Chem. Soc. (chair biol. divsn. 2000-02), Am. Soc. Biol. Chemists. Democrat. Home: 104 Jolyn Place Chapel Hill NC 27517 Office: U North Carolina Dept Biochemistry Chapel Hill NC 27514

WOLFENSOHN, JAMES DAVID, government agency administrator; b. Sydney, Australia, Dec. 1, 1933; naturalized, 1980. s. Hyman and Dora (Weinbaum) W.; m. Elaine Ruth Botwinick, Nov. 26, 1961; children: Sara, Naomi, Adam. BA, U. Sydney, 1954, LLB, 1957; MBA, Harvard U., 1959. Bar: Supreme Ct. of Australia 1957. Ptnr. Ord Minnett (brokers), Australia, 1963-65; mng. dir. Darling & Co. (investment bankers), Australia, 1965-67, J. Henry Schroder Wagg, London, 1968-70; pres. J. Henry Schroder Banking Corp., N.Y.C., 1970-76; exec. dep. chmn., dir. Schroders Ltd., London; prin. exec. officer Schroder Group, London, 1974-77; exec. ptnr. Salomon Bros., N.Y.C., 1977-81; chmn. Salomon Bros. Internat., London, 1977-81; pres., CEO James D. Wolfensohn, Inc., 1981-95; pres. World Bank Group, 1995—. Vis. lectr. fin. U. New South Wales, 1963-66. Contbr. articles to profl. jours. Mem. Australian Olympic Team, 1956; chmn. bd. dirs. John F. Kennedy Ctr. for the Performing Arts, Washington, 1990-95, chmn. emeritus, 1995—; bd. dirs. Met. Opera Assn., 1977-93, Joint Ctr. for Polit. Studies, 1978-88, mem. emeritus, 1988—; trustee Rockefeller Found., 1979-85, Population Coun., 1977-84; trustee Inst. for Advanced Study, Princeton, N.J., 1978—, chmn., 1986—; trustee Brookings Inst., 1983-90, hon., 1990—; trustee Rockefeller U., 1985-94, Howard Hughes Med. Inst., 1987-96; steering com. Bilderberg mtgs., treas. Am. Friends of Bilderberg, Inc., 1985—; pres. Internat. Fedn. Multiple Sclerosis Socs., 1977-83, Carnegie Hall, 1972—, bd. dirs., chmn., 1980-91, chmn. emeritus, 1991; bd. dirs. Nat. Multiple Sclerosis Soc., 1977-82. With Royal Australian Air Force, 1952-57. Recipient Business Com. for the Arts Leadership award, 1994; decorated by govts. of Australia,

Germany, France, and Russia; honored by HM Queen Elizabeth of Eng. with KBE and HM, King of Morocco, 1995. Fellow Am. Acad. Arts and Scis.; mem. Coun. on Fgn. Rels., Century Assn., Harvard Club (N.Y.C.), Australian Club (Sydney). Office: The World Bank 1818 H St NW Washington DC 20433-0001 E-mail: ccase@worldbank.org.

WOLFENSON, AZI U. electrical, mechanical and industrial engineer, consultant; b. Rumania, Aug. 1, 1933; arrived in Peru, 1937; s. Samuel G. and Polea S. (Ulanowski) Wolfenson; m. Rebeca Sterental, Jan. 10, 1983; 1 child, Michael Ben; children from previous marriage: Ida, Jeannette, Ruth, Moises, Alex. Mech., Elec. Engr., U. Nacional de Ingenieria, Peru, 1955; Indsl. Engr., U. Nacional de Ingenieria, 1967; MSc in Indsl. Engring., U. Mich., 1966; PhD in Engring. Mgmt., Pacific Western U., 1983; PhD in Engring. Energy, Century U., 1985; D in Philosophy of Engring. (hon.), World U. Roundtable, Ariz., 1987. Power engr. Peruvian Trading Co., 1956-57; gen. mgr. AMSA ingenieros S.A., 1957-60; prof. U. Nacional de Ingenieria, Peru, 1956-72, dean mech. and elec. engring., 1964-66, dean indsl. engring., 1967-72; dir. SWSA Automotive Parts, Peru, 1954-77; project mgr. Nat. Fin. Corp., Cofide, 1971-73; Peruvian dir. Corporacion Andina de Fomento, CAF, 1971-73; rep. in Peru CAF, 1973-74; pres. DESPRO cons. firm, 1973-76; exec. pres. Electroperu, 1976-80. Cons. engr., 1964—; dir. Tech. Transference Studies, 1971—72. Author: (book) Work Communications, 1966, Programmed Learning, 1966, Production Planning and Control, 1968, Transfer of Technology, 1971, National Electrical Development, 1977, Energy and Development, 1979, El Gran Desafio, 1981, Hacia una politica economica alternativa, 1982, The Power of Communications: The Media, 1987; contbr. articles to newspapers and jours. Mem. Nat. Coun. Fgn. Investment and Tech. Transfer, 1972—73, Superior Coun. Electricity, 1964—66; metal mech. expert for andean group, 1970—71; promoter, co-founder, gen. mgr. La Republica Newspaper, Peru, 1981; pres. PROA Project promotion AG, Switzerland, 1982—; chmn. Inst. for the Devel. of the Ams., Inc., Fla., 1993—; co-founder El Popular, 1983, El Nacional, 1985, Todo Sport, 1993, El Chino, 1994, La Reforma, 1997, El Men, 1999, La Razon, 2001; pres. bd. dirs., newspapers; v.p. bd. dirs. Island Way Cmty. Assn., 1995—97; mem. exec. bd. dirs. Miami State Israel Bonds, 1997; mem. consultative coun. Instituto Pervano de Deportes, 1999; mem. consultive coun. Min. Econ. and Fin., 1973—74; councilman at the Concejo Provincial De Lima, 1969—75; pres. Peruvian Jewish Cmty., 1966—70, Peruvian Hebrew Sch., 1976—78. Named Exec., Gente Mag., 1979; recipient Disting. Svc. awards, Order Merit, Peru, 1980, Disting. award, City Coun. Huancayo, 1980, Trujillo, 1978, Huaral, 1979, piura, 1980, Disting. Contbn. award, City of Lima, 1970, 1971, Disting. Contbn. to Elec. Devel. in Peru, 1979, El Sol Radiante, City Hall of Magdalena, Peru, 1995, Recognition award, Israel Govt., 1967, Disting. Comision Integracion Electrica Regional medal, CIER, 1984, Medal of Honor, Electrical Engring. Colegio de Ingenieros del Peru, 2003. Fellow: Brit. Inst. Mgmt., Inst. Prodn. Engrs.; mem.: J.C.C. Fla., FCL, AIIE (sr.), ASME, MTM Assn., AAAS, World Assn. of Newspapers (exec. mem. 2003), Asociacion Periodistas Peru, Circulo Periodistas Peru, Swiss sect. PEN Club INternat., Swiss Soc. Writers, United Writers Assn., Assn. Energy Engrs., Am. Nuc. Soc. (vice chmn. 1988, 1990, chmn. Swiss sect. 1991—93, Significant Contbn. to Advancement of Nuc. Sci. award 1995), Inst. Adminstrv. Mgmt., Asociacion Peruana Avance Ciencia, Assn. Mgmt. Sci. (dir. 1968), Am. Inst. Mgmt. Sci., Am. Soc. Engring. Edn., Asociacion Electrotechnica del Peru, Inst. Peruano Ingenieros Mecanicos (pres. 1965—66, v.p. 1967, dir. 1969, 1970, 1976), Colegio Ingenieros Peru (medal of honor award 2003), Alumni Assn. Mich., Pacific Western and Century U., Hebraica Club, Club dr 2000. Home: 3781 NE 208th Ter Miami FL 33180-3835 Office Phone: 305-682-0456. E-mail: aziwolfenson@aol.com.

WOLFERT, FREDERICK E. (RICK WOLFERT), healthcare financial services company executive; BSBA, La. State U., 1976; grad. degree in banking, U. Del. With U.S. Leasing Corp., San Francisco, 1979—88; chmn., pres., CEO KeyCorp Leasing divsn., pres., CEO KeyBank USA divsn. KeyCorp, 1988—97; pres., CEO, bd. dirs. Heller Fin., 1997—2001; pres., CEO GE Capital Healthcare Fin. Svcs., Chgo., 2001—. Bd. dirs. Jr. Achievement, Chgo., Brookfield Zoo, Chgo., St. Joseph's Carondelete Child Ctr., Chgo., La. State U. Ourso Coll. Bus. Adminstrn. Mem.: Equipment Leasing Assn. (former chmn., chmn. membership com.). Office: GE Healthcare Fin Svcs 500 W Monroe St Chicago IL 60661-3679

WOLFF, BRIAN RICHARD, metal products executive; b. LA, Dec. 11, 1955; s. Arthur Richard and Dorothy Virginia (Johnson) Wolff; children from previous marriage: Ashley Rachael, Taryn Nicole. BSBA, Calif. State U., Chico, 1980; postgrad., U. Phoenix, 1990—. Registered counseling practitioner Calif., cert. emergency response team Huntington Beach Fire Dept., 2003; ordained min. Prog. Universal Life Ch., 1996; registered guidance practitioner Calif. Sales rep. Federated Metals Corp./ASARCO, Long Beach, Calif., 1980-82, dist. sales mgr., 1983-84; sales mgr. Copper Alloys Corp., Beverly Hills, Calif., 1982-83; dir. mktg. Federated-Fry Metals/Cookson, Long Beach, Industry and Paramount, Calif., 1984-87; regional sales mgr. Colonial Metals Co., L.A., 1987-91; nat. sales mgr. Calif. Metal X/Metal Briquetting Co., L.A., 1991-93; sales engr. Ervin Industries, Inc., Ann Arbor, Mich., 1993-95. Tech. sales mgr. GSP Metals & Chems. Co., 1987—91; cons. sales Calif. Metal Exch., L.A., 1987—91, Atlas Pacific, Inc., Bloomington, 1993—. Contbr. poetry to various publs. Mem. citizens adv. com. bus. Calif. Legislature., 1983; mem. Cmty. Emergency Response Team, Huntington Beach Fire Dept., Calif., 2003—; pres. Newport Beach (Calif.) Alano Club, 2003—; bd. dirs. How Hall, Inc., Huntington Beach, Calif., 1998—99; bd. trustees Newport Beach (Calif.) Alano Club, 2002—, pres., 2003—. Mem.: NRA, Soc. Die Cast Engrs., Am. Electroplaters Soc., Steel Structures Painting Coun., Calif. Cast Metals Assn., Am. Foundrymen Soc., Non Ferrous Founders Soc., Newport Beach Alano Club (bd. dirs. 2003—, pres. 2003—). Republican. Presbyterian. Avocations: scuba diving, tennis, freshwater fishing, trap shooting, hunting. Office Phone: 714-378-9871.

WOLFF, CATHERINE ELIZABETH, opera company executive; b. Evanston, Ill., June 11, 1957; AB with honors, Vassar Coll., 1979; MA in Performing Arts Mgmt., Am. U., 1982. Adminstrv. asst. Opera Am., 1982-85; artistic adminstr. Pitts. Opera, 1985-94; exec. dir. Del. Symphony Orch., Wilmington, 1994-95; gen. dir. Syracuse (N.Y.) Opera Co., 1996—. Music panelist N.Y. State Coun. Arts, 2000—02, co-chair music panel, 2003. McGuire fellow Vassar Coll., 1979. Mem. Opera Am., Am. Symphony Orch. League, Phi Beta Kappa. Office: Syracuse Opera Co PO Box 1223 Syracuse NY 13201-1223

WOLFF, CYNTHIA GRIFFIN, humanities educator, author; b. St. Louis, Aug. 20, 1936; d. James Thomas and Eunice (Heyn) Griffin; m. Robert Paul Wolff, June 9, 1962 (div. 1986); children— Patrick Gideon, Tobias Barrington; m. Nicholas J. White, May 21, 1988. BA, Radcliffe Coll., 1958; PhD, Harvard U., 1965. Asst. prof. English Manhattanville Coll., Purchase, N.Y., 1968-70; asst. prof. English U. Mass., Amherst, 1971-74, assoc. prof., 1974-76, prof., 1976-80; prof. humanities MIT, Cambridge, 1980-85, Class of 1922 prof. lit. and writing, 1985—. Exec. com. for Am. lit. MLA, 1979-81; mem. selection bd. Literary Classics Am., 1981—; exec. bd. for fgn. grants Am. Council Learned Socs., 1981-84. Author: (literary criticism) Samuel Richardson, 1972, (literary biography) A Feast of Words: The Triumph of Edith Wharton, 1977, 2d edit., 1995, Emily Dickinson, 1986; bd. editors Am. Quar., 1979-84. Grantee AAUW, 1964-65, NEH, 1975-76, 1983-84, 97-98; Am. Council Learned Socs., 1984-85, Guggenheim, 1998—. Mem. Am. Studies Assn.

WOLFF, DEBORAH H(OROWITZ), lawyer; b. Phila., Apr. 6, 1940; d. Samuel and Anne (Manstein) Horowitz; m. Morris H. Wolff, May 15, 1966 (div.); children: Michelle Lynn, Lesley Anne; m. Walter Allan Levy, June 7, 1987. BS, U. Pa., 1962, MS, 1966; postgrad., Sophia U., Tokyo, 1968; JD, Villanova U., 1979, LLM, 1988. Tchr. Overbrook H.S., Phila., 1962-68; homebound tchr. Lower Merior Twp., Mongomery County, 1968-71; asst. dean U. Pa., Phila., 1975-76; law clk. Stassen, Kostos and Mason, Phila., 1977-78; assoc. Spencer, Sherr, Moses and Zuckerman, Norristown, Pa., 1980-81; ptnr. Wolff Assocs., Phila., 1981—. Lectr. law and estate planning, Phila., 1980—. Founder Take a Brother Program; bd. dirs. Germantown Jewish Ctr.; h.s. sponsor World Affairs Club, Phila., 1962-68; mem. exec. com., sec. bd. Crime Prevention Assn., Phila., treas., bd. dirs., 1965—; v.p. bd. dirs. U. Pa. Alumnae Bd., Phila., 1965—, pres. bd. dirs., 1993—, v.p. organized classes, bd. crime prevention; chmn. urban conf. Boys Club Am., 1987, treas., 1999; active Hahnaman Brain Tumor Rsch. Bd.; v.p., bd. dirs. Crime Prevention; treas. Assn. of Alumnae Bds.; mem. Alumni Class Leadership Counsel bd. U. Pa., 2001—. Recipient 3d Ann. Cmty. Svc. award Phila. Mayor's Com. for Women, 1984; named Pa. Heroine of Month, Ladies Home Jour., 1984. Mem. Lions (pres. Germantown Club 1997—). Home and Office: 422 W Mermaid Ln Philadelphia PA 19118-4204 E-mail: debbyw@comcast.net.

WOLFF, DERISH MICHAEL, economist, company executive; b. Boston, May 14, 1935; s. Nathan and Ruth Mae (Derish) W.; m. Maureen Robinson; children: Jeffrey Scott, Hayley Beth Kissel. BA, U. Pa., 1957; MBA, Harvard U., 1959. Fin. analyst Sigmund Werner, Inc., Belleville, NJ, 1959-61; devel. economist Louis Berger, Inc., East Orange, NJ, 1961-65, chief economist, 1965-67, v.p., 1968-75, exec. v.p., 1976-82, pres., CEO, 1982—2002, chmn., 2002—. Dir. Louis Berger Internat., Bronkonsult, CHELBI, Ammann & Whitney, Va. Maintenance Svcs., Klohn-Crippen; guest lectr. UN, Fgn. Svc. Inst., Newark Inst. Tech., U. Nev., Ga. Inst. Tech., The New Sch., Harvard U., Rutgers U., U. Denver; vis. lectr. MIT, 2001—; mem. industry adv. panel Dept. of State, 2001—; mem. Bretton Woods Com., 1987—. Mem. editl. bd. Modern Engring. Tech, 1978-80, Nat. Devel.-Modern Govt., 1972-79, Constrn. Bus. Review, 1991—. Mem. adv. com. N.J. Inst. Tech.; class chmn. U. Pa. Ann. Giving, 1975-82, class pres., 1982-92, mem. adv. bd. Huntsman Program of Internat. Studies and Bus., U. Pa., 1997—; mem. U.S. Presdl. Trade Del. to Japan, 1986; mem. indsl. sector adv. com. Dept. of Commerce, 1988-92; mem. adv. com. U.S. Trade and Devel. Program, 1989-92. Recipient Pres.'s medal for lifetime achievement, N.J. Inst. Tech., 2003. Mem. Am. Cons. Engrs. Coun. (chair internat. engring. com. 1983-85, vice chair 1986-93), Internat. Engring. and Constrn. Industries Coun. (del. 1986, 87, chmn. 1988-90), Bldg. Futures Coun. (vice chair 1994—), Ctr. for Strategic and Internat. Studies (steering group/GATT negotiations 1989), Phi Beta Kappa. Clubs: Harvard, Penn. Jewish. Office: Berger Group Holdings Inc 100 Halsted St East Orange NJ 07018-2699 Office Phone: 973-678-1960. E-mail: dwolff@louisberger.com.

WOLFF, DIANE PATRICIA, writer, film producer; b. N.Y.C., Oct. 12, 1945; d. Irving Mark and Catherine Halkett (Grossman); m. Wallace Gorell (div.). BS, Columbia U., 1968; postgrad., U. Calif., Berkeley, 1977-78, Stanford U., 1978-79; student, Interuniv. Ctr., Tokyo. Prodr. Sta. KRON-TV, San Francisco, 1983-87; prodr. ind. films, 1990-92; prodr. CD-ROM Exec. Prodrs., 1994-96; contbg. editor New Asia Pacific Review, Westport, Conn., 1996-98. Journalist Nat. Interest, N.Y. Times, San Francisco Chronicle, San Jose Mercury News, Orlando Sentinel Author: Chinese Writing: An Introduction, 1975, Gone with the Gator, 2001; project editor: A Sun-Herald Serial Novel, Sack of Baghdad and Other Stories of Muslims and Mongols, Pitless Measurement of History: China and Tibet. Nat. def. fgn. lang. fellow Columbia U., 1967; recipient Most Notable Book award Am. Libr. Assn., 1975. Mem. Author's Guild, Am. Soc. Journalists & Authors, Assn. For Asian Studies, Asia Soc. Avocations: sailing, swimming, exercise, cooking. Home: 1184 Green Oak Trail Port Charlotte FL 33948 E-mail: wuwolff@msn.com.

WOLFF, EDWARD ALVIN, electronics engineer; b. Chgo., Oct. 31, 1929; s. Samuel S. and Lillian P. Wolff; m. Anna Lee Tishk, June 19, 1951; children: David Steven, Eliot Marvin, Susan Toby. BSEE, U. Ill., 1951, MS, 1953; PhD, U. Md., 1961. Electronic scientist Naval Research Lab., Washington, 1951-54; project engr. Md. Electronic Mfg. Corp., Litton Industries, College Park, Md., 1956-59, Electromagnetic Research Corp., College Park, Md., 1959-61; engring. mgr. Aero Geo Astro-Keltec Industries/Aiken Industries, Alexandria, Va., 1961-67; v.p. Geotronics, Inc., Falls Church, Va., 1967-71; supervisory electronics engr. NASA Goddard Space Flight Ctr., Greenbelt, Md., 1971—; system mgr. Network TDRS System, 1981-89, MRJ, Inc., Oakton, Va., 1989-98; cons. in field, 1998—. Instr. Tex. A&M U., 1962. Author: Spacecraft Technology, 1962, Antenna Analysis, 1966, 2d edit., 1988, Geoscience Instrumentation, 1974, Urban Alternatives, 1975, Microwave Engineering and Systems Applications, 1988. Mem. Md. Gov.'s Sci. Resources Adv. Bd., 1963—67; pres. U.S. Environment and Resources Coun., 1972—75; treas. World Environment and Resources Coun., 1975—81. With U.S. Army, 1954—56. Fellow: IEEE (bd. dirs. 1971—72), Washington Acad. Scis.; mem.: NSPE, AIAA, Phi Eta Sigma, Sigma Tau, Eta Kappa Nu. Home: 16870 Island Cove Dr Apt 130 Jupiter FL 33477-2356 Personal E-mail: ewolff@bigfoot.com. *Everything I have done has been with the help of others. In return, as I have acquired management responsibilities, a primary objective has been to help others achieve their goals.*

WOLFF, EDWARD NATHAN, economist, educator; b. Long Branch, NJ, Apr. 10, 1946; s. Arthur Seymour and Ethel (Kalmenoff) Wolff; m. Jane Zandra Forman, Nov. 27, 1977; children: Spencer, Ashley. BA, Harvard U., 1968; PhD, Yale U., 1974. Rsch. assoc. Nat. Bur. Econ. Rsch., N.Y.C., 1974-77, 2001—; asst. prof. NYU, N.Y.C., 1974-79, assoc. prof., 1979-84, prof., 1984—; mng. editor Rev. Income and Wealth, 1987—2004; sr. scholar Levy Econs. Inst., 1999—. Cons. UN, 1981—82, 1998, 2000—02, Com. Econ. Devel., N.Y.C., 1981—82, Inst. Social Rsch., Ann Arbor, Mich., 1982—85, Inst. Rsch. Poverty, Madison, Wis., 1984—88, Jerome Levy Econs. Inst., 1989—91, 1995—96, Econ. Policy Inst., 1992—95, 2000—02, 20th Century Fund, 1992—93, 1999—2002, Aspen Inst., 1993, World Bank, 1994—97, Math. Policy Rsch., 2002—03; vis. scholar Russell Sage Found., 2003—04. Author: Growth, Accumulation and Unproductive Activity, 1987, Top Heavy: A Study of Increasing Unequality of Wealth in America, 1995, Economics of Poverty, Inequality, and Discrimination, 1997, Retirement Insecurity, 2002; editor: International Comparisons of Household Wealth Distribution, 1987, Research in Economic Inequality, Vol. 4, 1993; co-author: Productivity and American Leadership: The Long View, 1989, Competitiveness, Convergence, and International Specialization, 1993, Downsizing in America, 2003; co-editor: International Perspectives on Profitability and Accumulation, 1992, Poverty and Prosperity in the USA in the Late Twentieth Century, 1993, Convergence of Productivity, 1994, Economics of Productivity, 1997, Assets for the Poor, 2001; contbr. articles to profl. jours. Fellow, Ford Found., 1997—2003, Kaufman Found., 2004—07; grantee, NSF, 1984—90, Exxon Found., 1984—88, Fishman-Davidson Ctr. U. Pa., 1987—89, Sloan Found., 1990—98, Mellon Found., 1991—95, Russells Sage Found., 1997—2001, Ford Found., 1997—, Russell Sage Found., 1997—2003. Mem.: Eastern Econs. Assn. (pres. 2002—03), European Soc. Population Economists, Internat. Input-Output Assn. (coun. 1995—2003), Internat. Inst. Pub. Fin., Internat. Assn. Rsch. Income and Wealth (coun. 1987—2004), Am. Econ. Assn. Avocations: tennis, skiing. Office: NYU Dept Econs 269 Mercer St Rm 700 New York NY 10003-6633 Office Phone: 212-998-8917. E-mail: ew1@nyu.edu.

WOLFF, EDWIN RAY, retired construction engineer, consultant; b. Continental, Ohio, Mar. 24, 1933; s. Ray Simeon and Datha Ruth (Donaldson) W.; m. Elizabeth I. Sutterlin, Feb. 16, 1963; children: Sandra Jean, Donald Scott. BSME, U. Toledo, 1969. Registered profl. engr., Ohio. Mem. design staff City of Ft. Lauderdale, Fla., 1965-67; mem. design/spl. orders staff Devilbliss Co., Toledo, 1967-69; engineer, mem. R & D staff Toledo Scale, 1969-70; design/constrn. engr. Lucas County Engr., Toledo, 1970-98, ret., 1998. Cons. G.A.F., Inc., Oregon, Ohio, 1980—. Vol. Spl. Olympics, Lucas County, 1989—; trustee, bd. elders Fairgreen Ch., Toledo, 1975—; trustee Beneficial Union Pittsburg, 1986—; former bd. dirs. Lucas County ARC; bd. dirs. Cmty. Residential Svcs., Inc. With Combat Engrs. Corps, 1956-58. Mem. Phi Kappa Chi, Pi Kappa Alpha. Democrat. Presbyterian. Home: 4312 Grantley Rd Toledo OH 43613-3738

WOLFF, ELEANOR BLUNK, actress; b. Bklyn., July 10, 1931; d. Sol and Bessie (Schultz) Blunk; m. William Howard Wolff, June 19, 1955; children: Ellen Jill, Rebecca Louise. BA in Edn., Speech and Theatre, Bklyn. Coll., 1972, MS in Spl. Edn., 1975; postgrad., Adelphi U., 1980-81. Cert. tchr., N.Y. Fashion model Garment Ctr., N.Y.C., 1949—50; sec. to v.p. out-of-town/export sales Liebmann Breweries Inc., Bklyn., 1950—58; tchr. N.Y.C. Bd. Edn., Bklyn., 1971-76; sec. to dir. environ. programs, pub. affairs officers, speakers bur. project leader Power Authority State of N.Y., N.Y.C., 1976-85; tchr. Hewlett-Woodmere (N.Y.) Sch. Dist., 1986-89; instr. adult edn. County of Nassau, N.Y., 1986-97. Actress/model, N.Y.C., 1992—; mem. Love Creek Prodns. V.P. program devel. for youth ctr. Wavecrest Gardens Community Assn., Far Rockaway, N.Y., 1959-63; teen leader Far Rockaway Jewish Ctr. Youth Coun., 1965-68; pres. Parents Assn. P.S. 215Q, Far Rockaway, 1966-67; tutor N.Y. C. Bd. Edn. Sch. Vol. Program, Far Rockaway, 1969-71; chair civic affairs Dem. Club, Far Rockaway, 1961-63; vol. program presenter Child Abuse Prevention Svcs., Roslyn, N.Y., 2003-; committeewoman Dem. Ctrl. Com., Queens County, N.Y., 1963-64; v.p. membership, mem. constn. com. Nassau County Dem. Women's Caucus, 1988, 89; awards com. Bklyn. Coll., 1993-97, chair theatre arts affiliate, 1990-94, 2001-; mem. comm. adv. com. Hewlett-Woodmere Sch. Dist. 14, 1996-97; committeewoman Nassau County Dem. Party, 1998—; press/media steward vol. Goodwill Games, 1998. Named Mother of Yr. Congregation Shaaray Tefila, Far Rockaway, 1968; recipient Merit award Wavecrest Gardens Cmty. Assn., 1960, Theater Arts Trophy for disting. svc. Bklyn. Coll. Alumni, 1992. Mem.: SAG (awards nominating com. 2000—01), AFTRA, Actors Equity Assn., Alumni Assn. Bklyn. Coll. (life), Cmty. Garden Club of North Woodmere Park (corr. sec. 2001—03). Avocations: painting, piano, gardening. Office: 1344 Broadway Ste 110 Hewlett NY 11557-1353 Business E-Mail: eleanorwolff@cs.com.

WOLFF, ELROY HARRIS, lawyer; b. N.Y.C., May 20, 1935; s. Samuel and Rose Marian (Katz) W.; children: Ethan, Anna Louise. AB, Columbia U., 1957, LL.B., 1963. Bar: N.Y. 1963, D.C. 1969. Assoc. Kaye, Scholer, Fierman, Hays & Handler, N.Y.C., 1963-65; atty.-adviser to commr. FTC, Washington, 1965-67; sr. trial atty. Dept. Transp., 1967-69; assoc. Leibman, Williams, Bennett, Baird & Minow, Washington, 1969-70, ptnr., 1970-72, Sidley & Austin, Washington, 1972-99; sr. counsel Sidley Austin Brown & Wood, Washington, 2000—. Mem. adv. com. on practice and procedure FTC, 1969-71; chmn. adv. com. on procedural reform CAB, 1975 Served to 1st lt. USAF, 1957-60. Mem. ABA (chmn. spring meeting program 1992-94, coun. 1995-98), Union Internationale des advocats (chmn. competition law com. 1994-98), Army and Navy Club. Office: Sidley Austin Brown & Wood 1501 K St NW Washington DC 20005 Office Phone: 202-736-8666. Business E-Mail: ewolff@sidley.com.

WOLFF, GRACE SUSAN, pediatrician, pediatric cardiologist; b. Rome, N.Y. BS, Le Moyne Coll., 1961; MD, Med. Coll. Wis., 1965. Diplomate Am. Bd. Pediatrics, Pediatric Cardiology. Intern St. Vincents Hosp., N.Y.C., 1965-66; pediat. resident Babies Hosp.-Columbia Presbyn., 1967-69; fellow in pediat. cardiology Childrens Hosp., Boston, 1969-71; pediatrician, pediatric cardiologist U. Miami (Fla.) -Jackson Meml. Hosp., 1977—; chief divsn. pediat. cardiology, 1995—; prof. U. Miami. Mem. Am. Acad. Pediats., Am. Bd. Pediats., NASPE, Am. Acad. Pediat., Am. Coll. Cardiology, Am. Heart Assn. Office: U Miami-Jackson Meml Hosp PO Box 016960-R76 Miami FL 33101 Office Phone: 305-585-6683. Business E-Mail: gwolff@med.miami.edu.

WOLFF, GREGORY STEVEN, insurance company executive; b. Manchester, Conn., Dec. 10, 1951; s. Thomas J. and M. Elizabeth (Grandburg) W.; m. Elizabeth Mae Heppenstall, June 3, 1971; children: Keith J., James T., Kyle M. BA in Edn., U. Conn., 1974. Cert. fin. planner. Insurance salesman Northwestern Mut. Life, Glastonbury, Conn., 1974-76, Wolff-Zackin & Assocs., Inc., Vernon, Conn., 1976—2001; chmn. bd. dirs., mng. mem. Wolff-Zackin Fin. LLC, Vernon, 2001—. Lectr. in field; bd. dirs. Savs. Bank of Manchester Found., bd. dirs., Ea. Conn. Health Network, bd. dirs. Greater Hartford Hosp. Club. Contbr. articles to profl. jours.; co-author: Financial Need Analysis I, cassette prog. Co-founder Manchester Soccer Camp, 1981; bd. overseers Internat. Inst. of Sport. Mem. Nat. Assn. Life Underwriters, Conn. Assn. Life Underwriters, Hartford Assn. Life Underwriters (past pres.), Million Dollar Round Table, Ct. of Table. Methodist. Avocations: tennis, golf, coaching youth sports. Home: 126 Tamarac Dr Glastonbury CT 06033-1941 Office: Wolff-Zackin Fin LLC PO Box H Vernon Rockville CT 06066-1620

WOLFF, HERBERT ERIC, banker, former army officer; b. Cologne, Germany, May 24, 1925; s. Hugo and Juanna Anna (Van Dam) W.; m. Alice (Billy) Rafael, Nov. 13, 1946 (dec. July, 1987); children: Karen (dec. Jan., 1992), Herbert E., Allen R. BA, Rutgers U., 1953; BS, U. Md., 1957; MA, George Washington U., 1962; grad., U.S. Army War Coll., 1962, Harvard U., 1979. Commd. 2nd lt. U.S. Army, 1945, advanced through grades to maj. gen.; served in Fed. Republic of Germany, Greece, Iran, Republic of Korea, Australia, New Guinea, The Phillipines, Japan and Socialist Republic of Vietnam; dep. dir. ops. NSA Chief CSS, Ft. Meade, Md., 1973-75; dep. corps. comdr. V. Corps U.S. Army, Frankfurt, Germany, 1975-77, comdr. gen. U.S. Army Western Command, 1977-81; with First Hawaiian Bank, Honolulu, 1981-2000, sr. v.p., corp. sec., to 2000; hon. consul gen. (Datò) U.S. Pacific region Govt. of Malaysia, Honolulu, 1985—. Author: The Man on Horseback, 1962, The Tenth Principle of War Public Support, 1964, The Military Instructor, 1968. Exec. bd. Aloha coun. Boy Scouts Am.; bd. dirs. USO, Girl Scouts of U.S., Hawaii; v.p. Hawaii Com. Fgn. Rels.; past pres. Pacific Asian Affairs Coun.; pres. Hawaii Army Mus. Soc. Decorated Bronze Star with V and 3 oak leaf clusters, Air medal (24) U.S. Army, Purple Heart, Gallantry Cross with 2 palms, Gallantry Cross with palm and silver star Nat. Order 5th class South Vietnam, Order Nat. Security Merit Choen-Su S. Korea, D.S.M. with oak leaf clusters (2), Silver Star with oak leaf cluster U.S. Army, Legion of Merit with 3 oak leaf clusters, D.F.C., Combat Infantry Badge with two stars, master parachutist, Army aviator; named Citizen of Yr. Fed. Exec. Bd., 1987. Mem. 1st Inf. Divsn. Assn., 1st Cav. Divsn. Assn., Plaza Club (pres., bd. dirs.), Honolulu Country Club, Waialae Country Club, Rotary, Phi Kappa Phi. Office: First Hawaiian Center 999 Bishop St Honolulu HI 96813-0001 Personal E-mail: generalherbwolff@aol.com. *History is a gift we borrow and hope to pass on. Forget the past and be doomed to repeat it. Remember the past and accept the challenge to convince others.*

WOLFF, HUGH LIPMAN, urologist, educator; b. Apr. 24, 1931; m. Sylvia Musin; children: Stephanie, Timothy, Amy, Jane. BA, U. Iowa, 1952, MD, 1955. Diplomate Am. Bd. Urology. Intern King County Hosp., Seattle, 1955-56; resident in urology Univ. Hosps., Iowa City, 1958-62; pvt. practice San Antonio, 1962-94; v.p. med. affairs Santa Rosa Health Care, San Antonio, 1991—2000, ret., 2000. Clin. prof. divsn. urology U. Tex. Health Sci. Ctr., San Antonio, 1971—; chmn. bd. Preferred Choice Health Plan, San Antonio, 1985-91. Capt. USAF, 1956-58. Home: 7510 Forrestglen Dr San Antonio TX 78209-2735 Personal E-mail: hlwolff@swbell.net.

WOLFF, JEAN WALTON, writer; b. San Rafael, Calif., Apr. 12, 1955; d. Warren and Alice Eleanor (Broadbent) W. BA with honors, U. Calif., Santa Cruz, 1978; MPH, U. Calif., Berkeley, 1987. Sr. account rep. Preferred Health Network, Emeryville, Calif., 1989-90; writer U. Calif., Berkeley, 1990-91, Aptos, Calif., 1987—. Editor: Long Baptisms, 1997; author: (play) Love Radio; contbr. articles to San Francisco Chroicle, San Jose Mercurty News-.contbr.; creator In Your Dreams greeting cards. Vol. Janus Recovery Ctr., Santa Cruz, 1979, Santa Cruz County Fair, 1991, In Celebration of Muse, Santa Cruz, 1998, 2001. Recipient Poetry award Santa Cruz County Fair, 1991, 93, 94; Regents fellow, 1986. Mem. Nat. Writers Union, Santa Cruz Art League. Avocations: painting, collages. Office: In Your Dreams Prodns PO Box 851 Capitola CA 95010

WOLFF, JESSE DAVID, lawyer; b. Mpls., Aug. 26, 1913; s. Maurice I. and Annalee (Weiskopf) W.; m. Elizabeth Hess, Nov. 22, 1939; children: Nancy Nicholas, Paula, Daniel Jesse. BA summa cum laude, Dartmouth Coll., 1935; JD, Harvard U., 1938. Bar: N.Y. 1938. Practiced in, N.Y.C., 1938—; assoc., then ptnr., to counsel Weil, Gotshal & Manges, 1938-88, 88—, sr. mng. ptnr., 1966-86. Past dir., dep. chmn. Sotheby Parke Bernet Group (Eng.); past mem. adv. bd. Sotheby's Inc. Hon. trustee Greater N.Y. ARC; past mem. exec. com. Salvation Army, N.Y.C. Served with AUS, 1942-45. Mem. ABA, Judge Adv. Gen. Assn. Office: Weil Gotshal & Manges 767 5th Ave Fl Concl New York NY 10153-0119

WOLFF, KURT JAKOB, lawyer, director; b. Mannheim, Germany, Mar. 7, 1936; s. Ernest and Florence (Marx) W.; m. Sanda Lynn Dobrick, Dec. 28, 1958; children: Tracy Ellin, Brett Harris. AB, NYU, 1955; JD, U. Mich., 1958. Bar: N.Y. 1958, U.S. Supreme Ct. 1974, Hawaii 1985, Calif. 1988. Atty. pvt. practice, N.Y.C., 1958-2000; assoc. Hays, Sklar & HErzberg, N.Y.C., 1958-60; sr. assoc. Nathan, Mannheimer, Asche, Winer & Friedman, N.Y.C., 1960-65, Otterbourg, Steindler, Houston & Rosen, N.Y.C., 1965-68, sr. ptnr., 1968-70, dir., treas., 1970—, CEO, 1982-99, gen. counsel, 1999. Spl. master N.Y. Supreme Ct., 1977-85; vol. master U.S. Dist. Ct. (so. dist.) N.Y., 1978-82. Lectr., U. Mich. Law Sch.; mem. com. of visitors U. Mich. Law Sch., 1993—; spl. mediator Dept. Disciplinary Com. Appellate Divsn. First Judical Dept., 1991-99. Contbr. articles to profl. jours. Mem. ABA (chmn. ins. com. econs. sect. 1980-82, editor arbitration newsletter, arbitration com. sect. litig.), N.Y. State Bar Assn. (lectr.), Am. Arbitration Assn. (arbitrator), N.Y.C. Bar Assn. (arbitration com. 197-83, state cts. of superior jurisdiction com. 1983-86, mem. com. legal edn. & admission to the bar 1991-94), Hawaii State Bar Assn., Calif. State Bar Assn., Gen. Arbitration Coun. Textile Industry N.Y.C., Fed. Bar Coun. Home: 4 Juniper Ct Armonk NY 10504-1356 also: 79-835 Rancho LaQuinta Dr La Quinta CA 92253 also: John Hancock Bldg 175 E Delaware Pl Apt 6504 Chicago IL 60611-7731 Office: 4 Juniper Ct Armonk NY 10504

WOLFF, L. THOMAS, physician, educator; b. Suffern, N.Y., 1942; MD, Albany Med. Coll., 1968. Dir. rural med. edn. program Upstate Med. U., Syracuse, NY; assoc. dir. N.Y. State Area Health Edn. Ctr.; disting. teaching prof. family medicine SUNY Upstate Med. U., NY. Co-investigator IDE-ATEL. Mem.: ABFP (pres. 1998—2003). Office: SUNY Upstate Med U Div Family Medicine 200 Madison Irving Med Ctr Syracuse NY 13210*

WOLFF, MANFRED ERNST, medicinal chemist, pharmaceutical company executive; b. Berlin, Feb. 14, 1930; came to U.S., 1933; s. Adolph Abraham and Kate (Fraenkel) W.; m. Helen S. Scandalis, Aug. 1, 1953 (div. 1971); children: Stephen Andrew, David James, Edward Allen; m. Susan E. Hurbert, Jan. 19, 1973 (div. 1975); m. A. Gloria Johnson, Dec. 25, 1982. BS, U. Calif. at Berkeley, 1951, MS, 1953, PhD, 1955. Registered U.S. patent agt. Rsch. fellow U. Va., 1955-57; sr. medicinal chemist Smith, Kline & French Labs., Phila., 1957-60; mem. faculty U. Calif., San Francisco, 1960-82, prof. medicinal chemistry, 1965-82, chmn. dept. pharm. chemistry, 1970-82; dir. discovery rsch. Allergan Labs, Irvine, Calif., 1982-84; v.p. discovery rsch. Allergan Pharms., Irvine, 1984-89; v.p. R & D Immunopharmaceutics Inc., San Diego, 1989-91, sr. v.p. R & D, 1991-95; pres. Intellepharm., Inc., Laguna Beach, Calif., 1997—. Adj. prof. medicinal chemistry U. So. Calif., 1982—; elected mem. U.S. Pharm. Conv. Com. of Revision, 1990—. Editor: Burger's Medicinal Chemistry and Drug Discovery, Vol. 1-5, 5th edit., 1995-97; asst. editor Jour. Medicinal Chemistry, 1968-71; mem. editl. bd. Medicinal Chemistry Rsch., 1991-95, PharmSci., 1999—; contbr. articles to profl. jours.; patentee in field. Fellow AAAS, Am Assn. Pharm. Scientists; mem. Am. Chem. Soc. Achievements include discovery of Alphagan and Lumigan medicines for glaucoma, Tazorac medicine for psoriasis, and medicine for pulmonary arterial hypertension. E-mail: drwolff@aol.com.

WOLFF, MANFRED PAUL (FRED PAUL WOLFF), geologist, educator, environmental scientist, consultant; b. N.Y.C., Apr. 26, 1938; s. Kurt F. Wolff and Marie M. Muller; m. Suzanne Charlene Mosier, July 2, 1988; children: Brian P., Mark P. BS, Hofstra U., 1961; MS, U. Rochester, 1963; PhD, Cornell U., 1967. Asst. prof. geology Hofstra U., Hempstead, NY, 1967—74, assoc. prof. geology, 1974—81, prof. geology, 1981—2004. Asst. prof. Geology Dept. - Hofstra U., Hempstead, NY, 1967—74. Mem. citizens adv. com. L.I. Rgional Planning Bd.-208 Wastewater Mgmt. Study, Hauppauge, NY, 1981—84; mem. state emergency preparedness commn. Sci. Adv. Com., Albany, 1989—99; exec. sec. NY State Geol. Assn., N.Y.C., 1978—90. With USAR, 1956—60. Grantee, Hofstra U.; scholar, U. Rochester, 1961—62, Cornell U., 1963—67; Wilson P. Foss Sr. fellow, NY State Geologic Survey, 1963—64, Penrose Bequest grantee, Geol. Soc. Am., 1966. Mem.: N.Y. State Coun. Profl. Geologists, Soc. Econ. Geologists & Paleontologists, Geol. Soc. Am., Nassau Sci. Exploration Day Com. (co-chmn. 2002—03), Explorers Club. Independent. Achievements include research in Provided evidence of landward barrier island migration for Long Island's beaches; Provided evidence for lateral offset of barrier island spits at Long Island Inlets; Provided video of inlet breach (Little Pike's Inlet) at Westhampton Beach -Dec. 1992-April 1993. Avocations: travel, hiking, photography, computer scanning & printing. Home: 72 Suffolk Avenue West Babylon NY 11704-3313 Office: Geology Department 114 Hofstra University Hempstead NY 11549-1140

WOLFF, MARGARET LOUISE, lawyer; b. Rochester, N.Y., Jan. 27, 1955; d. Harvey A. and Miriam W. (Weinstein) W. BA cum laude, Mt. Holyoke Coll., 1976; JD, Case Western Res. U., 1979. Bar: N.Y. 1980. Assoc. Skadden, Arps, Slate, Meagher & Flom, N.Y.C., 1979-87, ptnr., 1987—. Editor Case Western Res. U. Law Rev. Home: 114 E 90th St New York NY 10128-1550 Office: Skadden Arps Slate Meagher & Flom 919 3rd Ave New York NY 10022-3902

WOLFF, MICHAEL A. state supreme court judge; Grad., Dartmouth Coll., 1967; JD, U. Minn., 1970. Lawyer Legal Svcs.; mem. faculty St. Louis U. Sch. Law, 1975-98; judge Mo. Supreme Ct., 1998—. Chief counsel to gov., 1993-94, spl. counsel, 1994-98. Co-author: Federal Jury Practice and Instructions, 4th edit. Chief counsel to Gov. St. Louis, 1993-94, spl. counsel, 1994-98. Office: Supreme Ct MO PO Box 150 Jefferson City MO 65102-0150

WOLFF, OTTO, federal agency administrator; Grad., Pa. State U. Profl. staff mem. com. on house adminstrn. U.S. Ho. Reps.; dep. asst. sec. for adminstrn. Dept. Commerce, 1981—93, asst. sec., CFO for adminstrn., CFO, 2001—. Office: Dept Commerce Adminstrn CFO 14th and Constitution Ave NW Washington DC 20230

WOLFF, PAUL D. weight management products executive; married; 2 children. Grad. cum laude, Bowdoin Coll., Maine. U.S. dir. bus, develop., Parade Mag., Inc Am. Health Partners, exec. v.p. Communication Channels, Inc.; corp. v.p., data base media Am. Express Travel Related Services; pres. sports publishing group Times Mirror Magazines, corp. v.p., chief innovation officer; co-owner, ptnr. Basic Media Group, Inc.; Chmn., CEO Atkins Nutritionals, Inc., 2000—. Vice chmn. bd. dirs. Christian Heritage Sch., Conn.; advisor Bowery Mission, NYC. Office: Atkins Nutritionals 2002 Orville Dr N Ste A Ronkonkoma NY 11779 Office Phone: 631-738-7370. Office Fax: 631-738-8710.

WOLFF, PAUL MARTIN, lawyer; b. Kansas City, Mo., July 22, 1941; s. Joseph L. and Eleanor B. Wolff; m. Rhea S. Schwartz, Oct. 9, 1976. BA, U. Wis., 1963; LLB, Harvard U., 1966. Bar: D.C. 1968, U.S. Ct. Appeals (D.C. and 2d cir.) 1968, U.S. Supreme Ct. 1975, U.S. Ct. Appeals (10th and fed. cirs.) 1981, U.S. Ct. Appeals (8th cir.) 1982, U.S. Tax Ct. 1982, U.S. Ct. Claims 1984. Law clk. to Judge James R. Durfee U.S. Ct. Claims, Washington, 1966-67; assoc. Williams & Connolly, Washington, 1967-75, ptnr., 1976—. Adj. prof. Catholic U. Law Sch., 1970-73. Co-author: Forensic Sciences; contbr. articles to legal jours. Bd. dirs. Washington Coun. for Civil Rights Under Law, 1980-90, Renwick Alliance, Washington, 1987-93, Am. Jewish Com., Washington, 1988-92, Washington Legal Clinic for Homeless, 1988-99, Opportunities for Older Ams. Found., 1988-92, Emeritus Found., 1992-99; bd. dirs. Washington Performing Arts Soc., 1990-2002, hon. dir., 2002—; vice chmn. D.C. Pub. Charter Schs. Resource Ctr., 1999—; dir. D.C. Sports Commn., 1994-2000; dir. Com. Pub. Edn., 1994-99; trustee Fed. City Coun., bd. trustees, 1996—; trustee Am. U., 1996—; overseer Corcoran Mus. of Art, 1997—; mem. adv. bd. Woodrow Wilson Ctr. for Internat. Studies, 1999—; mem. acquisitions com. Jewish Mus., 2003—. Mem. Georgetown Club, Econ. Club Washington (dir.), Phi Beta Kappa. Independent. Avocations: photography, gardening, fly fishing, sculpting. Home: 4770 Reservoir Rd NW Washington DC 20007-1905 also: 1602 Ridge Rd Warrenton VA 20186 Office: Williams & Connolly 725 12th St NW Washington DC 20005-5901: 1250 Villager Sun Valley ID 83353 Fax: 202-434-5580. E-mail: pwolff@wc.com., dcpmw@aol.com.

WOLFF, PETER ADALBERT, physicist, researcher; b. Oakland, Calif., Nov. 15, 1923; s. Adalbert and Ruth Margaret W.; m. Catherine C. Carroll, Sept. 11, 1948; children: Catherine Mia, Peter Whitney. AB in Physics, U. Calif., Berkeley, 1945, PhD in Physics, 1951. Rsch. scientist Lawrence Radiation Lab., 1951-52; staff scientist Bell Telephone Lab., Murray Hill, N.J., 1952-63, dept. head, dir. electronic rsch. lab., 1964-70; prof. physics U. Calif., San Diego, 1963-64; prof. physics, head solid state and atomic physics div., assoc. dir. Material Sci. Ctr. MIT, Cambridge, 1970-76, dir. rsch. lab. of electronics, 1976-81, prof. physics, 1976-89, prof. emeritus, 1994—, 1994—; dir. Francis Bitter Nat. Magnet Lab., 1981-87. Dir. Draper Lab. Contbr. articles to profl. jours. Served with C.E. U.S. Army, 1945-46. Fellow Nippon Electric Co. Rsch. Inst., Princeton, 1989-94. Mem. Am. Phys. Soc.

WOLFF, RICHARD CARL, financial planner, insurance agency and pension planning company executive; b. Boston, July 17, 1933; Student, Boston U., 1957-60. CLU. Pres. Richard C. Wolff Ins. Agy., Swampscott, Mass., 1960—, Fiscal Planning Corp., Swanpscott, 1978—, Multi Pension Planning Co., Swanpscott, 1979—. Mem. adv. bd. para-actuary program Bentley Coll., Waltham, Mass., 1979-90; past chmn. adv. bd. Elite Club of Western Life, St. Paul; lectr. on fringe benefits. Author: Measure of Success, 1987. Pres. Temple Israel, Swampscott, 1981-83, pres. Bortherhood, 1987-89. Recipient Legion of Honor, DeMolay, 1978, Man of Yr. award, Temple Israel, 1989. Mem. Top of Table (charter), Million Dollar Round Table (life), Mass. Assn. Accident/Health Underwriters (pres. 1965-66), Essex County Estate Planning Assn. (founder, pres. 1975-76), Boston Life Underwriters Assn. (founder, pres. North Shore br. 1979-80), Swampscott Bus. Council (pres. 1980), Lynn C. of C. (v.p. 1982-85, disting. svc. award 1984, community leader award 1985), Peabody C. of C. (bd. dirs. 1985-86, 96-97), Masons (master 1974), K.P., Rotary (Peabody award, Paul Harris fellow, pres. 1975-76), B'nai B'rith (pres. 1962-63, bd. dirs. 1991, Jewish family svc.), Kernwood Country Club (membership com., house com.). Avocations: golf, boating. Office: Fiscal Planning Corp PO Box 182 Swampscott MA 01907-0382

WOLFF, RICHARD JOSEPH, public relations executive, consultant, historian; b. Hackensack, N.J., Oct. 13, 1952; s. Richard Hamilton and Irene Marie (Ciruzzi) W. AB, Georgetown U., 1974; MA, Columbia U., 1976, PhD, 1979. Asst. dean, prof. St. John's U., Queens, N.Y., 1980-85; ptnr. pub. rels. Kekst & Co., Inc., N.Y.C., 1985-97; mng. dir. Eastern region and L.Am. Golin/Harris Internat., N.Y.C., 1997—2002, worldwide mng. divsn. G/H Fin., 1997—2002; CEO, The Global Cons. Group, N.Y.C., 2002—. Mem. Columbia U. Seminar on Modern Italy, N.Y.C., 1983—; founding mem. St. John's U. Seminar on Vatican Studies, Queens, 1994—; mem. Legatus, 2000—. Author: Between Pope and Duce, 1990, Dorothy Day, 1994; contbr. articles to profl. jours.; editor Catholics, the State and the European Radical Right, 1987. Chmn., commr. North Hudson Sewerage Authority, Hudson County, N.J., 1988—; mem. adv. com. Congressman Robert Menendez, Jersey City, N.J., 1994—. Recipient Howard Marraro prize Am. Cath. Hist. Assn., 1982, Internat. fellow Columbia U., 1977. Mem. Phi Beta Kappa. Roman Catholic. Avocations: golf, reading, travel, politics. Office: The Global Consulting Group 22 Cortlandt St 14th Fl New York NY 10007

WOLFF, ROBERT PAUL, philosophy educator; b. N.Y.C., Dec. 27, 1933; s. Walter Harold and Charlotte (Ornstein) W.; m. Cynthia Griffin, June 9, 1962 (div. 1986); children: Patrick Gideon, Tobias Barrington; m. Susan Gould, Aug. 25, 1987. AB, Harvard U., 1953, MA in Philosophy, 1954, PhD, 1957. Instr. Harvard U., 1958-61; asst. prof. philosophy U. Chgo., 1961-63; vis. lectr. Wellesley Coll., 1963-64; assoc. prof. philosophy Columbia, 1964-69, prof., 1969-71; prof. philosophy U. Mass., Amherst, 1971-92, prof. Afro-Am. studies, 1992—; grad. program dir. doctoral program in Afro-Am.; devel. cons. U. QwaQwa, South Africa, 1998—. Author: Kant's Theory of Mental Activity, 1963, A Critique of Pure Tolerance, 1965, Political Man and Social Man, 1966, Kant: A Collection of Critical Essays, 1967, Poverty of Liberalism, 1968, The Ideal of the University, 1969, In Defense of Anarchism, 1970, 2d edit., 1998, Ten Great Works of Philosophy, 1970, The Rule of Law, 1971, Styles of Political Action in America, 1971, Philosophy: A Modern Encounter, 1971, The Autonomy of Reason, 1973, 1984 Revisited, 1973, About Philosophy, 1975, 8th edit., 2000, Understanding Rawls, 1977, Understanding Marx, 1985, Moneybags Must Be So Lucky, 1988, Autobiography of an Ex-White Man, 2004. Exec. dir. Harvard-Radcliffe Alumni/ae Against Apartheid, 1988-90; pres., exec. dir. Univ. Scholarships for South African Students, 1990—; co-dir. inst. advanced study in humanities U. Mass., 1992-98, grad. program dir. Doctoral Program in Afro-Am. Studies, 1996—. Home: 107 Buffam Rd Amherst MA 01002-9723 also: 17 rue Maître Albert 75005 Paris France Office Phone: 413-545-2751. Business E-Mail: rwolff@afroam.umass.edu.

WOLFF, RONALD KEITH, toxicologist, researcher; b. Brantford, Ont., Can., July 25, 1946; s. Roy Clifford and Agnes Audrey (Stratton) W.; m. Mary Carole Cromien Wolff, Aug. 26, 1972; children: Mark, Sarah, Andrew, Brian. BS, U. Toronto, 1964-68; MS, 1968-69, PhD, 1969-72. Diplomate Am. Bd. Toxicology, 1983. Rsch. assoc. McMaster U., Hamilton, Can., 1973-76; scientist Lovelace Inhalation Toxicology Rsch. Inst., Albuquerque, N.Mex., 1976-88; sr. rsch. scientist Eli Lilly and Co., Greenfield, Ind., 1988—. Author: (book chpt.) Comprehensive Treatise on Pulmonary Toxicology, 1992, Comprehensive Toxicology, 1997; contbr. articles to profl. jours. Recipient Frank Blood award Soc. Toxicology, 1989, Thomas T. Mercer joint prize Am. Assn. for Aerosol Rsch. and Internat. Soc. Aerosols in Medicine, 2002. Mem. Am. Assn. for Aerosol Rsch., Internat. Soc. Aerosols in Medicine, Soc. Toxicology, Am. Indsl. Hygiene Assn. Avocations: camping, hiking, hockey. Office: Lilly Rsch Labs PO Box 708 Greenfield IN 46140-0708

WOLFF, SHELDON, radiobiologist, educator; b. Peabody, Mass., Sept. 22, 1928; s. Henry Herman and Goldie (Lipchitz) W.; m. Frances Faye Farbstein, Oct. 23, 1954; children: Victor Charles, Roger Kenneth, Jessica Raye. BS magna cum laude, Tufts U., 1950; MA, Harvard U., 1951, PhD, 1953. Teaching fellow Harvard U., 1951-52; sr. research staff biology div. Oak Ridge Nat. Lab., 1953-66; prof. cytogenetics and radiology U. Calif., San Francisco, 1966-94; prof. emeritus, 1994—; dir. Lab. Radiobiology and Environ. Health U. Calif., San Francisco, 1983-95; vice chmn., chief rsch. Radiation Effects Rsch. Found., Hiroshima, Japan, 1996-2000. Vis. prof. radiation biology U. Tenn., 1962, lectr., 1953-65; cons. several fed. sci. agys.; mem. health and environ. rsch. adv. com. U.S. Dept. Energy, 1986—, chmn., 1987-95; co-chmn. Joint NIH/Dept. Energy Subcom. on Human Genome, 1989-94. Editor: Chromosoma, 1983-97; assoc. editor: Cancer Research, 1983-97; Editorial bd.: Radiation Research, 1968-72, Photochemistry and Photobiology, 1962-72, Radiation Botany, 1964-86, Mutation Research, 1964-97, Caryologia, 1967-96, Radiation Effects, 1969-81, Genetics, 1972-85; Contbr. articles to sci. jours. Recipient E.O. Lawrence meml. award U.S. AEC, 1973, 1st ann. Belle award, 1998. Mem. Genetics Soc. Am., Radiation Rsch. Soc. (counselor for biology 1968-72, Failla lectr. 1992, medal 1992), Am. Soc. Cell Biology, Environmental Mutagen Soc. (coun. 1972-75, pres. 1980-81, award 1982), Internat. Assn. Environ. Mutagen Socs. (treas. 1978-85), Sigma Xi. Democrat. Home: 41 Eugene St Mill Valley CA 94941-1717 Office: U Calif Dept Radiology San Francisco CA 94143-0628 Business E-Mail: shellyw@itsa.ucsf.edu.

WOLFF, SIDNEY CARNE, astronomer, observatory administrator; b. Sioux City, Iowa, June 6, 1941; d. George Albert and Ethel (Smith) Carne; m. Richard J. Wolff, Aug. 29, 1962 BA, Carleton Coll., 1962, DSc (hon.), 1985; PhD, U. Calif., Berkeley, 1966. Postgrad. research fellow Lick Obs, Santa Cruz, Calif., 1969; asst. astronomer U. Hawaii, Honolulu, 1967-71, assoc. astronomer, 1971-76; astronomer, assoc. dir. Inst. Astronomy, Honolulu, 1976-83, acting dir., 1983-84; dir. Kitt Peak Nat. Obs., Tucson, 1984-87, Nat. Optical Astronomy Observatories, 1987-2001; dir. Gemini Project Gemini 8-Meter Telescopes Project, 1992-94; astronomer, project scientist Large Synoptic Survey Telescope, 2001—04. Pres. SOAR Inc., 1999-2003; project scientist Large Synoptic Survey Telescope, 2002—; bd. mem. LSST Corp. Author: The A-Type Stars--Problems and Perspectives, 1983, (with others) Exploration of the Universe, 1987, Realm of the Universe, 1988, Frontiers of Astronomy, 1990, Voyages Through the Universe, 1996, 2nd edit., 2003, Voyages to the Planets, 1999, 2nd edit., 2003, Voyages to the Stars and Galaxies, 1999, 2nd edit., 2003; founding editor: Astronomy Edn. Rev., 2002; contbr. articles to profl. jours. Trustee Carleton Coll., 1989—, chair acad. affairs com., 1995—. Rsch. fellow Lick Obs. Santa Cruz, Calif., 1967; recipient Nat. Meritorious Svc. award NSF, 1994. Fellow Royal Astronical Soc.; mem. Astron. Soc. Pacific (pres. 1984-86, bd. dirs. 1979-85), Am. Astron. Soc. (coun. 1983-86, pres.-elect 1991, pres. 1992-94). Office: Nat Optical Astronomy Obs PO Box 26732 950 N Cherry Ave Tucson AZ 85719-4933

WOLFF, TOBIAS (JONATHAN ANSELL WOLFF), writer; b. Birmingham, Ala., June 19, 1945; s. Arthur Saunders and Rosemary (Loftus) Wolff; m. Catherine Dolores Spohn, 1975; children: Michael, Patrick, Mary Elizabeth. BA, Oxford Univ., 1972, MA, 1975, Stanford Univ., 1978; LHD (hon.), Santa Clara Univ., 1996. Mem. faculty Stanford (Calif.) U., Goddard Coll., Plainfield, Vt., Ariz. State U., Tempe, Syracuse (N.Y.) U., Stanford (Calif.) U.; reporter Washington Post. Author: In the Garden of the North American Martyrs, 1981 (St. Lawrence award for fiction 1982), The Barracks Thief, 1984 (PEN/Faulkner award for fiction 1985), Back in the World, 1985, This Boy's Life: A Memoir, 1989 (L.A. Times Book prize 1989), In Pharaoh's Army: Memories of the Lost War, 1994 (Esquire-Volvo-Winterstone's award, Eng., 1994), The Night in Question, 1996, Old School, 2003 (PEN/Faulkner Award for Fiction nominee, 2004); editor: Matters of Life and Death: New American Stories, 1983, The Stories of Anton Chekhov, 1987, Best American Short Stories, 1994, The Vintage Book of Contemporary American Stories, 1994. Recipient Wallace Stegner fellowship in creative writing, 1975-76, Mary Roberts Rinehart award, 1979, Rea award, 1989, Whiting Writer's award, 1989, Lila-Wallace-Reader's Digest award, 1993, Lyndhurst Found. award, 1994, award merit Am. Acad. Arts and Letters, 2001, Fairfax prize for lit., 2003; Nat. Endowment for the Arts fellowship in creative writing, 1978, 85, Ariz. Coun. on Arts and Humanities fellowship in creative writing, 1980, Guggenheim fellowship, 1982. Office: Stanford U Dept English Stanford CA 94305-2087

WOLFF, VIRGINIA EUWER, writer; b. Portland, Oreg., Aug. 25, 1937; d. Eugene Courtney and Florence Evelyn (Craven) Euwer; m. Art Wolff, July 19, 1959 (div. July 1976); children: Anthony Richard, Juliet Dianne. AB, Smith Coll., 1959; postgrad., Goddard Coll., Warren Wilson Coll., L.I. U., Portland State U., Lewis & Clark Coll. Cert. tchr., Oreg. Tchr. The Miquon Sch., Phila., 1968-72, The Fiedel Sch., Glen Cove, N.Y., 1972-75, Hood River Valley (Oreg.) H.S., 1976-86, Mt. Hood Acad., Govt. Camp, Oreg., 1986-98. 2d violinist Quartet con brio, Portland, 1989-94, Parnassius Quintet, Portland, 1996—. Author: Probably Still Nick Swansen, 1988, The Mozart Season, 1991, Make Lemonade, 1993, Bat 6, 1998, True Believer (Nat. Book award, Michael L. Printz honor, Pacific N.W. Booksellers Assn. award, Jane Addams Book honor, 2002), 2001, represented US, honor book, Internat. Board on Books for Young People, 2004. Violinist Mid-Columbia Sinfonietta, Hood River, 1976—, Oreg. Sinfonietta, Portland, 1988—, Parnassius Chamber Ensemble, 2000-. Recipient Young Adult Book award Internat. Reading Assn., 1989, PEN U.S.A. Ctr. West, 1989, Best Young Adult Book of Yr. award Mich. Libr. Assn., 1993, Child Study Children's Book award Bank Street Coll., 1994, Oreg. Book award Oreg. Lit. Arts, 1994, 2001, Jane Addams Children's Book award Jane Addams Peace Assn. and the Women's Internat. League for Peace and Freedom, 1999, Nat. Book award, 2001, Printz Honor Book award, 2002, Jane Addams Honor Plaque, 2002; named to Carnegie medal Shortlist, ALA, 2002. Mem. Soc. Children's Book Writers/Illustrators (Golden Kite 1994, 2002), Chamber Music Soc. Oreg. Avocations: chamber music, swimming, hiking, playing violin, gardening. Office: Curtis Brown Ltd care Elizabeth Harding 10 Astor Pl Fl 3 New York NY 10003-6982

WOLFF, WILLIAM F., III, investment banker; b. N.Y.C., Apr. 12, 1945; s. William F., Jr. and Nancy (Wimpfheimer) Wolff; m. Phyllis Fox, June 1, 1969; children: Kenneth, Laura, Jonathan, Gillian. BA, U. Mich., 1967; JD, Columbia U., 1970, MBA, 1971. Bar: N.Y. 1970. V.p. Salomon Bros., Inc., N.Y.C., 1971-78; prin. Morgan Stanley & Co., N.Y.C., 1978-83; mng. dir. Lehman Bros., N.Y.C., 1983-2000, UBS Warburg, N.Y.C., 2000—02, Endurance Capital, N.Y.C., 2002—03, Lykos Capital Mgmt., 2003—. Trustee St. David's Sch., N.Y.C., 1985—2004; dir. City Harvest. Mem.: Ocean Beach Club (Elberon, N.J.) (trustee 1985—89), Univ. Club (N.Y.). Office: 153 E 53d St New York NY 10022 E-mail: rwolff3@yahoo.com.

WOLFF, WILLIAM I. surgeon, educator; b. N.Y.C., Oct. 24, 1916; s. Julius Louis and Matilda (Brick) W.; m. Lillian Myrick, June 30, 1952 (div. 1967); children: Richard, Deborah, David, Alan, Lisa, Mitchell, George, Rebecca, Barbara; m. Rita T. Smith, Feb. 15, 1972. BS, NYU, 1936; MD, U. Md., 1940. Diplomate Am. Bd. Surgery, Am. Bd. Thoracic Surgery. Intern Cornell U. divsn. Bellevue Hosp., 1940-42, resident specializing in chest surgery Columbia U. divsn., 1942-43; resident, chief Bronx Vets. Hosp., 1946-48; chief thoracic surgery Deshon Vets. Hosp., 1949; practice medicine specializing in surgery N.Y.C., 1950—; emeritus dir. surgery Beth Israel Med. Ctr., N.Y.C., 1962-76; prof. surgery Mt. Sinai Sch. Medicine, N.Y.C., 1965—. 1st disting. lectr. soc. Am. Gastrointestinal Surgeons, 1987; vis. prof. or invited guest lectr. over 40 med. schs. univ. ctrs., over 150 tchg. hosps., numerous nat. and internat. cancer confs. in U.S., Eng., South Africa, Kenya, Israel, Mex., Can., USSR, France and P.R. Contbr. over 120 articles to med. jours., chpts. to books. Served to maj. M.C. AUS, 1943-46, ETO. Mem. ACS, Am. Coll. Gastroenterology (bd. govs.), Am. Assn. for Thoracic Surgery, Soc. Thoracic Surgeons (founding), Soc. for Surgery Alimentary Tract, Am. Coll. Chest Physicians, Am. Gastroenterologic Assn., Internat. Soc. Surgery, Internat. Cardiovasc. Surg. Soc., N.Y. Surg. Soc. (pres. 1980-81), N.Y. Acad. Medicine (chmn. sect. on surgery), Assn. Alumni Bellevue Hosp. (pres. 1982), Aspetuck Valley Country Club. Achievements include early contributor to subject of cardiac resuscitation by ccardiac message; originator of scientific procedure of colonoscopy and removal of colonic polyps. Office: 44 Gramercy Park N New York NY 10010-6310 Office Phone: 212-755-4144.

WOLFGANG, BONNIE ARLENE, musician, bassoonist; b. Caribou, Maine, Sept. 29, 1944; d. Ralph Edison and Arlene Alta (Obetz) W.; m. Eugene Alexander Pridonoff, July 3, 1965 (div. Sept. 1977); children: George Randall, Anton Alexander, Stephan Eugene. MusB, Curtis Inst. Music, Phila., 1967. Soloist Phila. Orch., 1966; soloist with various orchs. U.S., Cen. Am., 1966-75; prin. bassoonist Phoenix Symphony, 1976—, with Woodwind Quintet, 1986—. Home: 9448 N 106th St Scottsdale AZ 85258-6056

WOLFHARD, HANS GEORG, research scientist; b. Basel, Switzerland, Apr. 2, 1912; arrived in U.S., 1956, naturalized, 1961; s. Albert Georg and Helen (Buerck) W.; m. Adelheid Rohde, Jan. 18, 1940 (dec. 1995); children: George, John (dec. 2002), Bernie; m. Clara Ralston, Jan. 4, 1997. Student, U. Berlin, 1934-35; Dr.Rer.Nat., U. Goettingen, 1938. Scientist Aero. Rsch. Sta., Brunswick, Germany, 1939—46; rsch. scientist Imperial Coll., London, Royal Aircraft Establishment, England, 1946—56; sr. prin. scientific officer Bur. Mines, Pitts., 1956—59; head dept. physics reaction motors divsn. Thiokol Chem. corp., Denville, NJ, 1959—63; mem. sr. rsch. staff Inst. Def. Analyses, Alexandria, Va., 1963—96. Cons. Sverdrup Tech., AEDC-Arnold AFB, Tenn., 1996—2004. Co-author: Flames, 4th edit., 1979, Chinese transl., 1990. Recipient 1st Gen. Goodpastor award for Excellence in Rsch., 1983. Fellow Am. Optical Soc., Mil. Sensor Symposium (First Jamieson award); mem. AIAA, Combustion Inst. Episcopalian. Home: 711 Bright Ave Fayetteville TN 37334-2255

WOLFINGER, AUDREY JANE, retired librarian; b. Mt. Penn, Pa., June 21, 1933; d. Harry Charles and Eva (Trace-Eckenroth) W. BS in Edn., Kutztown State Tchrs. Coll., 1955; tchrs. cert., Temple U., 19576; MS in Libr. Sci., Fla. State U., 1970. Mem. adminstrv. libr. staff Neshaminy Sch. Dist., Langhorne, Pa., 1955-84; libr., audio visual coord. Neshaminy Jr. High, Langhorne, 1955-76; libr. Neshaminy H.S., Langhorne, 1976-84; ret., 1984. Editor Wolfinger Family Newsletter, 1988—. Bd. dirs. Neshaminy Valley Music Theatre, Langhorne, 1964-65. Mem. Nat. Soc. DAR, Nat. Soc. Daus. of the Am. Colonists, Nat. Geneal. Soc., Geneal. Soc. Pa., Bucks County Geneal. Soc. (v.p. 1990-94, pres. 1994-98; resource ctr. dir. 1998, pres. protem 2001—), Kutztown U. Alumni Assn., Fla. State U. Alumni Assn. Avocations:

piano baroque music, reading british mysteries, researching family history. Home: 14 Brook Dr Furlong PA 18925-1037 Office: Bucks County Geneal Soc PO Box 1092 Doylestown PA 18901-0020 E-mail: a.j.wolfinger@rcn.com.

WOLFMAN, ALAN, medical educator, researcher; b. Bronx, N.Y., Mar. 12, 1956; married. Postdoctoral fellow dept. biophysics U. Rochester Med. Ctr., 1988—90; assoc. staff dept. cell biology Cleve. Clinic Found., 1990—. Adj. prof. dept. biology Cleve. State U., 1994—. Contbr. articles to profl. jours.; periodic reviewer: Molecular Cell Biology, Jour. Biol. Chemistry, Biochemistry, BBA, ad hoc reviewer for program project: Nat. Inst. Diabetes and Digestive Kidney Diseases, 1995, invited reviewer: DRTC Pilot Project Ind. U., 1995—; presenter in field. Recipient Postdoctoral fellowship award, NIH, 1985—88, Established Investigatorship award, Am. Heart Assn., 1996—; grantee Cell Biology Tng., 1979, NIH First, 1988—93. Office: Cleve Clinic Found Rsch Inst Dept Cell Biology NC10 9500 Euclid Ave Cleveland OH 44195-0001

WOLFMAN, BRUNETTA REID, education educator; b. Clarksdale, Miss., Sept. 4, 1931; d. Willie Orlando and Belle Victoria (Allen) Reid Griffin; m. Burton Wolfman, Oct. 4, 1952; children: Andrea, Jeffrey. BA, U. Calif. Berkeley, 1957, MA, 1968, PhD, 1971, DHL (hon.), Boston U., 1983; DP (hon.), Northeastern U., 1983; DL (hon.), Regis Coll., 1984, Stonehill Coll., 1985; DHL, Suffolk U., 1985; DET (hon.), Wentworth Inst., 1987; AA (hon.), Roxbury Community Coll., 1988. Asst. dean faculty Dartmouth Coll., Hanover, N.H., 1972-74; asst. v.p. acad. affairs U. Mass., Boston, 1974-76; acad. dean Wheelock Coll., Boston, 1976-78; cons. Arthur D. Little, Cambridge, Mass., 1978; dir. policy planning Dept. Edn., Boston, 1978-82; pres. Roxbury C.C., Boston, 1983-88, ACE sr. assoc., 1988-94, NAWE sr. assoc., 1994-98; assoc. v.p. acad. affairs George Washington U., Washington, 1989-92, prof. edn., 1992-96, prof. edn. emeritus, 1996—. Mem. Accrediting Commn. on Edn. on Health Svcs. Administrn.; pres. bd. dirs. Literacy Vols. of Capitol Region; mem. comm. com. bd., pub. rels. com. LVA, Inc.; bd. dirs. Am. Coun. Edn., Harvard Cmty. Health Plan. Author: Roles, 1983; contbr. articles to profl. jours. Mem. bd. overseers Wellesley Coll., 1981, Boston Symphony Orch.; trustee Mus. Fine Arts, Boston; mem. Coun. on Edn. for Pub. Health; chair Provincetown bd. Coun. on Aging, 1999—; bd. dirs. Boston-Fenway Program, 1977, Freedom House, Boston, 1983, Boston Pvt. Industry Coun., 1983; bd. dirs., co-chmn. NCCJ, Boston, 1983; bd. dirs. Elder Svcs. Cape Cod and the Islands, 2003. Named Wolfman Courtyard in their honor, Evergreen Ctr., 2000; recipient Freedom award, NAACP No.Calif., 1971, Amelia Earhart award, Women's Edn. and Indsl. Union, Boston, 1983, Provincetown Sr. Citizen of Yr., 2004; scholar Nat. Assn. Women in Edn. Mem. AAUW, Am. Sociol. Assn., Assn. Black Women in Higher Edn., Greater Boston C. of C. (edn. com. 1982), Sierra Club, Mass. Audubon Soc., Cosmos Club (Washington), Provincetown Art Assn. (sec. bd. trustees, mus. sch. com.), Alpha Kappa Alpha (Humanitarian award 1984), Phi Delta Kappa. Home: 657 Commercial St Provincetown MA 02657-1759 E-mail: bruburt2@comcast.net.

WOLFMAN, EARL FRANK, JR., surgeon, educator; b. Buffalo, Sept. 14, 1926; s. Earl Frank and Alfreda (Peterson) W.; m. Lois Jeannette Walker, Dec. 28, 1946; children— Nancy Jeannette, David Earl, Carol Anne. BS cum laude, Harvard U., 1946; MD cum laude, U. Mich., 1950. Diplomate Am. Bd. Surgery. Intern U. Mich., Ann Arbor, 1950-51, asst. resident in surgery, 1951-52, resident in surgery, 1954-55, from jr. clin. instr. surgery to assoc. prof., 1955-66, asst. to dean, 1960-61, asst. dean, 1961-64; practice medicine specializing in surgery, 1957—, 1966—; prof. surgery Sch. Medicine, U. Calif., Davis, 1966—, founding chmn. dept. surgery, 1966-78, founding assoc. dean, 1966-76, mem. staff, chief surg. svcs. Med. Ctr., 1966-78, founding chmn. div. surg. scis., 1966-78. Contbr. articles to profl. jours. Served to lt. M.C. USNR, 1952-54. Fellow ACS; mem. AMA (del. 1987-99), Ctrl. Surg. Soc., Western Surg. Soc., Sacramento Surg. Soc., Pacific Coast Surg. Soc., Frederick A. Coller Surg. Soc., Soc. Surgery Alimentary Tract, Am. Assn. Endocrine Surgeons, Sierra Sacramento Valley Med. Soc., Calif. Med. Assn. (trustee 1991-2000), Am. Soc. Gen. Surgeons. Methodist. Office: U Calif Davis Sch Medicine Dept Surgery 2221 Stockton Blvd Fl 3 Sacramento CA 95817-2214 Business E-Mail: efwolfman@ucdavis.edu.

WOLFMAN, IRA JOEL, editor, writer; b. Oct. 7, 1950; s. Aaron and Beatrice Ruth (Perlo) W.; m. Julia Diamant, June 24, 1979 (dec. 1982); m. Ronda Small, Dec. 20, 1991. BA cum laude, SUNY, Albany, 1971. News editor Washington Park Spirit, Albany, N.Y., 1971-73; sr. editor Smash mag., N.Y.C., 1975-76, Circus mag., N.Y.C., 1976-79; assoc. editor 3-2-1 Contact mag., N.Y.C., 1979-80; editor Sesame St Parents' Newsletter, N.Y.C., 1980-83; editor in chief Enter mag., N.Y.C., 1983-85, Sesame St. mag., Parents Guide, 1990-94; v.p., editor-in-chief Adult Consumer mags. Children's Television Workshop, N.Y.C., 1994-97, v.p., editorial dir. mags. and sch. products, 1997-2000, group v.p., publ. mags. Sesame Workshop, 2000-01; prin. POE Comms., 2001—; sr. v.p. editl. Weekly Reader, 2004. Newsletter editor Found. for Grandparenting, Mt. Kisco, N.Y., 1984-87; editor Am. Writer, 1988-89; freelance writer and editor, contbr. to Travel & Leisure, Reader's Digest, Archtl. Record, Metropolis, N.Y. Daily News, Ms., Spy, 1985—. Author: Do People Grow on Family Trees? Genealogy for Kids and Other Beginners, 1991, My World and Globe, 1991, Climbing Your Family Tree: Online and Offline Genealogy, 2002, Jewish New York: Notable Neighborhoods and Memorable Moments, 2003. N.Y. State Legis. Corrs. scholar, 1970. Jewish.

WOLFORD, KATHRYN FRANCES, religious organization executive; b. Reading, Pa., Dec. 12, 1957; d. Howard Francis Wolford and Katherine Eva (Auker) Carbaugh. BA in History, Gettysburg Coll., 1979; MA in Religious Studies, U. Chgo. Divinity Sch., 1980; MA in Pub. Policy, U. Chgo., 1981; PhD (hon.), Gettysburg Coll., 1995; PhD (hon.), Muhlenberg Coll., 2003. Country program rep. Ch. World Svc., Dominican Republic, 1983-85; regional rep. Nat. Coun. Chs., U.S.A., N.Y.C., 1985-90; program dir. for L.Am., Luth. World Relief, Balt., 1991-93, pres., 1993—. Named Md. Top 100 Women, 2002, 2004. Democrat. Lutheran. Avocation: sailing.

WOLFORD, RICHARD, food products executive; CEO Del Monte Foods, San Francisco, 1997—. Office: Del Monte Foods PO Box 193575 San Francisco CA 94119-3575

WOLFORD, RICHARD HOWARD, lawyer; b. Chgo., Aug. 12, 1922; s. Darwin H. and Lila (Ferguson) W.; m. Helen Moore, Feb. 13, 1943; children: Richard George, Felicia Jane, Peter Arlington. AB, Harvard U., 1944, JD, 1948. Bar: Calif. 1949. Law clk. U.S. Ct. Appeals 9th Cir., San Francisco, 1948-49; sr. ptnr. Gibson, Dunn & Crutcher, L.A., 1963-80, of counsel, 1981—. Mem. Calif. Law Revision Commn., L.A., 1968-70; adj. prof. law (antitrust) U. Hawaii Law Sch., 1983. Pres. L.A. Jr. Bar Assn., 1957-58. Mem. ABA, Hawaii State Bar Assn., L.A. County Bar Assn. (trustee 1957-58), L.A. Country Club. Home: 3101 Old Pecos Trail 661 Santa Fe NM 87505

WOLFOWITZ, PAUL DUNDES, federal official, former ambassador to Indonesia; b. N.Y.C., Dec. 22, 1943; s. Jacob and Lillian (Dundes) W.; m. Clare Selgin, Nov. 25, 1968; children: Sara Elizabeth, David Samuel, Rachel Dahlia. BA in Math. and Chemistry, Cornell U., 1965; MA, U. Chgo., 1967, PhD in Polit. Sci., 1972. Lectr., asst. prof. Yale U., 1970-73; with U.S. Arms Control and Disarmament Agy., 1973-77, spl. asst. to dir., 1974-75, dep. asst. dir., 1976; spl. asst. for SALT, 1976-77; with Dept. Def., Washington, 1977-80; dep. asst. sec. of def., regional programs, program analysis and evaluation Office of Sec. of Def., 1977-80; vis. assoc. prof. Sch. Advanced Internat. Studies, Johns Hopkins U., 1980-81; dir. policy planning staff U.S. Dept. State, 1981-82, asst. sec. of state for East Asian and Pacific affairs, 1982-86; U.S. amb. to Indonesia, 1986-89; undersec. def. for policy Office of Sec. of Def., Washington, 1989—93; dean, prof of intl. relations Paul H. Nitze Sch. of Advanced Intl. Studies, Johns Hopkins U., 1994—2001; deputy sec. of def. US Dept. of Def., Washington, 2001—. Recipient Presdl. Citizens medal. Office: Dep Sec of Def The Pentagon Washington DC 20301-0001

WOLFRAM, CHARLES WILLIAM, law educator; b. Cleve., Feb. 28, 1937; s. Carl P. and Dona M. (Minitch) W.; m. Nancy Russell Bass, Dec. 18, 1965; children: Catherine Dana, Peter Russell. AB, Notre Dame U., 1959; LLB, U. Tex., 1962. Bar: D.C. 1962, Minn. 1974. Assoc. Covington & Burling, Washington, 1962-64; mem. FAA Contract Appeals Panel, Washington, 1964-65; asst. prof. law U. Minn., 1965-67, assoc. prof., 1967-70, prof., 1970-81; prof. law Cornell U., Ithaca, N.Y., 1982-84, Charles Frank Reavis Sr. prof. law, 1984-99, Charles Frank Reavis Sr. prof. emeritus, 1999—. Assoc. dean acad. affairs Cornell U., Ithaca, 1986-90, interim dean, 1998-99; vis. prof. U. So. Calif. Law Center, 1976-77. Author: (with J. Morris Clark) Professional Responsibilty: Issues for Minnesota Attorneys, 1976, Modern Legal Ethics, 1986; contbr. chpts. to books, articles to profl. jours. Mem. Am. Law Inst. (chief reporter Restatement of Law Governing Lawyers, 1986-2000), Order of Coif. Democrat. Office: 2887 College Ave #148 Berkeley CA 94705 E-mail: charles-wolfram@postoffice.law.cornell.edu.

WOLFRAM, DAVID ANTHONY, computer scientist; b. Melbourne, Australia, Sept. 20, 1962; s. Hans Gerhard (dec.) and Bettine Rosalind (Kauffmann) W. BSc with honors, U. Melbourne, 1984, MSc, 1986; PhD, U. Cambridge (Eng.), 1990, U. Oxford (Eng.), 1991; MBA (exec.), Australian Grad. Sch. of Mgmt., 2004. Chartered engr., IT profl.; European engr. Rsch. asst. U. Oxford, 1990; jr. rsch. fellow Christ Ch., Oxford, 1990-94, BT fellow, 1994; lectr. in computer sci. Australian Nat. U., Canberra, 1995-2000, vis. fellow Rsch. Sch. Info. Sci. and Engring., 2000; with Microsoft Corp., USA, Redmond, Wash., 2000—02; project mgr. Expert Info. Svc. (now Infosys Tech. Australia), Melbourne, 2003—. Mem. program com CATS Computing: The Australasian Theory Symposium, 1999, 2000, 03, 04, program chair, 00. Author: The Clausal Theory of Types, 1993; contbr. articles to profl. jours., guest editor: Electronic Notes in Theoretical Computer Science, Vol. 31, 2000; guest editor spl. issue Theoretical Computer Science, 2003. Fellow: Cambridge Philos. Soc.; mem.: Assn. Computing Machinery, IEEE Computer Soc., N.Y. Acad. Sci., London Math. Soc., Brit. Computer Soc., Internat. Soc. for Philos. Enquiry (diplomate), Melbourne Cricket Club, Am. Australian Assn., Ordre du Tastevin (chevalier). Avocations: photography, tennis, chess.

WOLFRAM, STEPHEN, physicist, computer company executive; b. London, Aug. 29, 1959; came to U.S., 1978; Degree, Eton Coll., 1976, Oxford U., 1978; PhD in Theoretical Physics, Calif. Inst. Tech., 1979. With Calif. Inst. Tech., Pasadena, 1979-82, Inst. for Advanced Study, Princeton, N.J., 1983-86; prof. physics, math, computer sci. U. Ill., Champaign, 1986-90; founder, dir. Ctr. for Complex Sys. Rsch., 1996—98; pres., CEO Wolfram Rsch. Inc., Champaign, 1987—. Author: Theory and Applications of Cellular Automata, 1986, Mathematica: A System for Doing Mathematics by Computer, 1998, 2d edit., 1991, Mathematica Reference Guide, 1992, Mathematica: The Student Book, 1994, The Mathematica Book, 3rd edit., 1996, 4th edit., 1999, Cellular Automata and Complexity, 1994, A New Kind of Science, 2002; editor jour. Complex Systems, 1986— Fellow MacArthur Found., 1981; recipient World Leadrers of Tomorrow award, World Economic Forum, 1999; named Scientist of Yr., R&D Mag., 2002. Office: Wolfram Rsch Inc 100 Trade Centre Dr Champaign IL 61820-7237 E-mail: s.wolfram@wolfram.com.

WOLFRAM, THOMAS, physicist, educator; b. St. Louis, July 27, 1936; s. Ferdinand I. and Audrey H. (Calvert) W.; m. Eleanor Elaine Burger, May 22, 1965; children: Michael, Gregory, Melanie, Susan, Steven. BA, U. Calif., Riverside, 1959, PhD in Physics, 1963; MA in Physics, UCLA, 1960. Engr. Atomics Internat., Canoga Park, Calif., 1960-63; mem. tech. staff N.Am. Aviation Corp. Sci. Ctr., Thousand Oaks, Calif., 1963-68; group leader in solid state physics Rockwell Internat. Sci. Ctr., Thousand Oaks, 1968-72, dir. div. physics and chemistry, 1972-74; prof. physics, chmn. dept. physics and astronomy U. Mo., Columbia, 1974-83; dir. phys. tech. divsn. AMOCO Corp., 1983-87; v.p., gen. mgr. AMOCO Laser Co., 1987-95; bus. cons., 1995—. Cons. in field. Author: (novel) The Venture; (novel) The Dragon Tamers; editor: Inelastic Electron Tunneling Spectroscopy, 1978; contbr. rsch. articles to numerous publs. in field. Recipient Disting. Prof. award Argonne Univs. Assn., 1977 Fellow Am. Phys. Soc. Home and Office: 228 Trafalgar Ln San Clemente CA 92672 E-mail: ewolfram@cox.net. *Crisis is the catalyst for constructive change.*

WOLFSCHMIDT, WILLI See FLINT, WILLIS

WOLFSON, AARON HOWARD, radiation oncologist, educator; b. Nashville, May 13, 1955; s. Sorrell Louis and Jacqueline Adele (Falis) W.; m. Adrienne Sue Mates, Dec. 16, 1979; children: Alexis Ellyn, Andrew Lane. BA, U. Fla., 1978, MD, 1982. Diplomate Am. Bd. Radiology. Intern internal medicine Jackson Meml. Hosp., Miami, Fla., 1982-83; staff physician Pub. Health Svc., Miami, 1983-85; pvt. practice Palm Beach Gardens, Fla., 1985-86; resident in radiation oncology Med. Coll. Va., Richmond, 1986-89; from instr. radiation oncology to prof. U. Miami (Fla.) Sch. Medicine, 1989—2003, prof., 2003—. Co-dir. Gynecology Site dis. group, Sylvester Cancer Ctr., 2001—. Contbr. articles to profl. jours. Bd. dirs. Children's Home Soc., Ft. Lauderdale, Fla., 1993—, Temple Beth Israel, Sunrise, Fla., 1994—; mem. spkrs. bur. U. Miami, 1993—; vol. spkr. Broward County Schs., 1990—; exec. v.p. Temple Beth Israel, 1996-98, pres., 1998-99. Sylvester Cancer Ctr. grantee, 1992. Mem. Gynecologic Oncology Group, Radiation Therapy Oncology Group, Am. Soc. Therapeutic Radiology and Oncology. Jewish. Achievements include research on malignant tumors of the female genital tract; patent for radiation implant for gynecologic cancer. Office: Univ Miami 1475 NW 12th Ave # D-31 Miami FL 33136-1002 Office Phone: 305-243-4210. Business E-Mail: awolfson@med.miami.edu.

WOLFSON, IRWIN M. insurance company executive; b. Bronx, NY, May 29, 1937; s. Herman M. and Kate (Greenstein) W.; m. Pauline S. Frechtel, Dec. 25, 1962; children: Fran M., Lisa G. BS in Econs., NYU, 1960; grad., Life Underwriting Tng. Coun., 1975. Owner/CEO Wolfson Agency, Yonkers, N.Y., 1973—. Instr., owner Successful Adult Fin. Seminars, Yonkers, 1990—. Mem. operating bd. Child Abuse Prevention Ctr., White Plains, N.Y. Sgt. U.S. Army, 1960-66. Recipient Achievement award Congressman Elliot Engel, 1992, proclamation From T. Zaleski (Mayor) City of Yonkers, 1992, letter of Recognition from M. Cuomo (Governor) N.Y. 1992; Irwin M. Wolfson Day proclaimed by A. O'Rourk (County Exec.) N.Y. 1992. Mem. Yonkers Exch. Club (pres. 1990-91, NY dist. dir. 1991-95, 99--, NY dist. pres. 1996-97), Million Dollar Round Table. Home: 11 Jackson Ave Unit 4 Scarsdale NY 10583-3134 Office: Wolfson Agy 475 Tuckahoe Rd Yonkers NY 10710-5712 Office Phone: 914-779-1982.

WOLFSON, MARK ALAN, investor, business educator; b. Chgo., Ill., Sept. 25, 1952; s. Jack and Maribelle (Simen) W.; m. Sheila Rae Aronesti, Aug. 3, 1975; children: Laura Rachel, Charles Michael. BS in Acctg. and Fin., U. Ill., 1973, M in Acctg. Sci., 1974; PhD in Acctg., U. Tex., 1977. Asst. prof. acctg. Stanford (Calif.) U., 1977-81, assoc. prof., 1981-85, prof., 1985-87, Joseph McDonald prof., 1987-92, assoc. dean, 1990-93, Dean Witter prof. acctg. and fin., 1992-96, cons. prof., 2001—; mng. ptnr. Oak Hill Capital Mgmt., 1998—; ptnr. Oak Hill Venture Ptnrs., 1999—; prin. Oak Hill Platinum Ptnrs., 2001—. Ford Found. vis. assoc. prof. U. Chgo., 1981-82; Thomas Henry Carroll vis. prof. Harvard U., Boston, 1988-89; cons. Fin. Acctg. Stds. Bd., Norwalk, Conn., 1985, 89-92; rsch. assoc. Nat. Bur. Econ. Rsch., Cambridge, Mass., 1988—; steering com. Stanford Inst. Econ. Policy Rsch., 1990-2000, exec. com. 2001-; task force Fed. Home Loan Bank Bd., 1989; v.p. Keystone Inc., 1995—; bd. dirs. Investment Tech. Group, eGain Comm., Fin. Engines, Inc., 230 Park Investors, Accretive Healthcare; trustee Menlo Sch., 2001-. Contbr. numerous articles to profl. jours. Recipient Pomerance prize Chgo. Bd. Options Exch., 1981, Disting. Tchg. award Stanford U., 1990, Notable Contbn. to Lit. award AICPA-Am. Acctg. Assn., 1990, 92, Wildman award, 1991; named Disting. Accountancy Alumnus, U. Ill., 1989. Jewish. Office: Oak Hill Capital 2775 Sand Hill Rd Ste 220 Menlo Park CA 94025-7019

WOLFSON, MICHAEL GEORGE, lawyer; b. Chgo., Sept. 1, 1938; s. A. Lincoln M. Weingarten and Brina (Nelson) W.; m. Rita Sue Parsont, Sept. 11, 1966; children: Bethany Lynne, Sara Wynne, Deborah Kay. Student, MIT, 1956-58; BA, U. Chgo., 1961, JD, 1964, postdoctoral, 1964-65. Bar: Ill. 1964, N.Y. 1969. Assoc. Cravath, Swaine & Moore, N.Y.C., 1965-71, Brown, Wood, Fuller, Caldwell & Ivey, N.Y.C., 1971-73; ptnr. Sidley Austin Brown & Wood LLP, N.Y.C., 1974—2002, sr. counsel, 2003—. Mediator, specializing in comml. and internat. disputes. Woodrow Wilson fellow, 1961; Ford Found. fellow in internat. trade and devel., 1965. Fellow Am. Bar Found. (life); mem. ABA. Avocations: reading, photography, fly fishing, bicycling. Office Phone: 212-839-5321. Business E-Mail: mwolfson@sidley.com.

WOLGAMOTT, GARY DEAN, medical educator; b. Weatherford, Okla., July 23, 1940; s. Kenneth Blaine and Winona Irene Wolgamott; m. Sandra Jean Wolgamott, Apr. 26, 1962; children: Thad Dean, Dotti D'Lane Wolgamott-Forehand. BS in Biology and Chemistry, Northwestern Okla. State U., 1963; PhD in Microbiology, Okla. State U., 1968. Postdoctoral fellow U. Iowa Coll. Medicine, Iowa City, 1971, NASA, Houston, 1974-75; prof. Southwestern Okla. State U., Weatherford, 1968—, chmn. allied health scis., 1975—, assoc. dean Sch. Health Scis., 1994—, Bernhardt prof., 1996—. Mem. med. tech. rev. com. Nat. Accrediting Agy. of Clin. Lab. Scis., 1980-90. Editor/author Lambda Tau Newsletter, 1976—. Named to Outstanding Profs. Acad., 1999-2000. Fellow: Okla. Acad. Sci. (chmn.collegiate acad. 1968—80, pres. 1980); mem.: Am. Soc. Microbiology (edml. coord. 1971—79), Kiwanis (bd. dirs., pres. 1990—91), Lambda Tau (nat. sec.-treas. 1976—), Beta Beta Beta (nat. pres. 2001—). Methodist. Avocations: bicycling, running, backpacking, guitar, skiing. Office: Southwestern Oklahoma State U 100 Campus Dr Weatherford OK 73096-3001 E-mail: wolgamg@host1.swosu.edu.

WOLIN, ALFRED M. former federal judge; b. Orange, N.J., Sept. 17, 1932, s. George and Juliet (Rosenstock) W.; m. Jane Zapiekov, Mar. 27, 1960; children: Roger, Marc. BA, U. Mich., 1954; LLB, JD, Rutgers U., 1959. Pvt. practice, Elizabeth, N.J., 1960-80; judge Union County Dist. Ct., Elizabeth, N.J., 1980-85, Union County Superior Ct., Elizabeth, N.J., 1985-87, U.S. Dist. Ct., Newark, 1987—2004. Atty. Roselle Bd. Adjustment, 1965-74; legis. aide to Senator Matthew J. Rinaldo, N.J. Senate, 1970-72; spl. asst. prosecutor Union County, 1970; congl. field rep. 12th congl. dist., 1972-79; mcpl. prosecutor Town of Westfield, N.J., 1973-74. Chief staff atty. Union County Legal Aid Soc., 1964-74; mem. Union County Ethics Com., sec., 1970-78, exec. com. Statewide Speedy Trial Com., Conf. Presiding Criminal Judges, Criminal Practice Com.; active Temple Emanuel, Jewish Fedn. Cen. N.J. SPC 2 U.S. Army, 1954-56, Germany. Mem. ABA, Am. Judicature Soc., N.J. Bar Assn. (judicial selection, discipline of the bar, lawyer referral coms.), Union County Bar Assn. (sec. 1970-74, pres. elect 1975, pres. 1976, judicial appointments com.), Fed. Judges Assn. Jewish. *Notable cases include: (as judge) presided over trademark rights suit involving Procter & Gamble vs. Revlon, 1990, which alleged that Revlon's creation of Ivory Coast shampoo infringed on name of Procter & Gamble's Ivory soap. The suit was settled for an undisclosed amount.*

WOLIN, NEAL STEVEN, lawyer; b. Chgo., Dec. 9, 1961; s. Harry S and Doris (Wacker) Wolin. BA summa cum laude, Yale U., 1983; MSc, U. Oxford, Eng., 1985; JD, Yale U., 1988. Bar: Ill 1989, DC 1989, US Supreme Ct 1995. Adj. asst. prof. of law Bklyn. Law Sch., 1989; law clk. U.S. Judge Eugene H. Nickerson, Bklyn., 1988-89; assoc. Wilmer, Cutler & Pickering, Washington, 1989-90; spl. asst. to dirs. ctrl. intelligence Webster Gates & Woolsey, 1990-93; dep. legal adviser Nat. Sec. Coun. The White House, 1993-94; exec. asst. to the nat. sec. adviser The White House, 1994-95; dept. gen. counsel U.S. Dept. Treasury, 1995-99, gen. counsel, 1999-2001; exec. v.p., gen. counsel The Hartford Fin. Svcs. Group, Inc., Hartford, 2001—. Vis. fellow Brookings Inst., Washington, 2001; adj. lectr. in pub. policy JFK Sch. Govt., Harvard U., 2001. Bd. overseers Rand Inst. Civil Justice; mem. bd. regents U. Hartford; mem. Presdl. Adv. Commn.Holocaust Assets in U.S., 1999—2000, 2001—. Fellow Henry, Henry Trust, Oxford Univ, 1983—84, Coker Teaching, Yale Law Sch, 1987—88. Mem.: Coun on Foreign Relations, Phi Beta Kappa. Office: The Hartford Fin Svcs Group Inc Hartford Plz Hartford CT 06115 Business E-Mail: nwolin@thehartford.com.

WOLINSKY, EMANUEL, physician, educator; b. N.Y.C., Sept. 23, 1917; s. Jacob and Bertha (Siegel) W.; m. Marjorie Claster, Nov. 15, 1946; children: Douglas, Peter. BA, Cornell U., 1938, MD, 1941. Diplomate Am. Bd. Med. Microbiology. Intern, resident medicine N.Y. Hosp., 1943-45; bacteriologist Trudeau Lab., Saranac Lake, N.Y., 1947-56; mem. faculty Case Western Res. U. Sch. Medicine, 1956-98, prof. medicine, 1968-88, prof. pathology, 1981-88, prof. emeritus, 1988-98, ret., 1998. Dir. microbiology Cleve. Met. Gen. Hosp., 1959-91, acting dir. dept. pathology, 1980-86, chief div. infectious diseases, 1961-83. Co-editor Textbook of Pulmonary Diseases, 5th edit., 1993; Asso. editor: Am. Rev. Respiratory Diseases, 1973-79; Contbr. articles to profl. jours., textbooks. Mem. Tb panel U.S.-Japan Co-op. Med. Sci. Program, 1969-75. Recipient Crystal Cross award Ohio Thoracic Soc., 1995, Louis Weinstein award Clin. Infectious Diseases, 1995, Maurice Saltzman award Mt. Sinai Healthcare Found., 1999; named to Med. Hall of Fame, Cleve. Mag., 1998. Mem. Am. Soc. Microbiology (Gardner Middlebrook award 1998), Am. Thoracic Soc. (Trudeau medal 1986), Infectious Diseases Soc. Am. (Soc. Citation award, 2004), Phi Beta Kappa, Alpha Omega Alpha. Home: 24761 S Woodland Rd Cleveland OH 44122-3327

WOLINTZ, ARTHUR HARRY, neurologist, ophthalmologist; b. Bklyn., May 30, 1937; s. Louis and Celia (Ragofsky) W.; m. Carol Sue Bergstein, Nov. 28, 1963; children: Robyn Joy, Ellen Sharon. Student, NYU, 1955-58; MD summa cum laude, SUNY, Bklyn., 1962; postgrad., Columbia U., 1967-68. Diplomate Am. Bd. Psychiatry and Neurology, Am. Bd. Ophthalmology; licensee Nat. Bd. Med. Examiners, U. State of N.Y. Intern Maimonides Hosp., Bklyn., 1962-63, jr. resident in medicine, 1963-64; resident Nat. Inst. Neurol. Diseases and Blindness, Bethesda, Md., 1964-66; chief resident Mt. Sinai Hosp., N.Y.C., 1966-67; clin. asst. prof. neurology Downstate Med. Ctr. SUNY, Bklyn., 1968-69, resident in ophthalmology, 1969-71, from asst. prof. to prof., 1971—, prof. clin. ophthalmology and clin. neurology, 1977—, interim chief ophthalmology, 1983, acting regional chmn. dept. ophthalmology, 1984, prof. ophthalmology, 1987—, chmn. dept. ophthalmology, 1987-96; Disting. tchg. prof., chair emeritus dept. ophthalmology SUNY-Health Sci. Ctr. Bklyn., 1995, 96—; asst. neurologist Presbyn. Hosp., N.Y.C., 1967-68; instr. neuropathology Coll. Physicians and Surgeons Columbia U., N.Y.C., 1967-68; instr. neurology Mt. Sinai Sch. Medicine, N.Y.C., 1967-68; assoc. dir. neurology Maimonides Med. Ctr., Bklyn., 1968-69; asst. neurologist Coney Island Hosp., Bklyn., 1968-69. Vis. neurologist Kings County Hosp. Ctr., Bklyn, 1968-69; chief divsn. ophthalmology and neuro-ophthalmology Kingsbrook Jewish Med. Ctr., Bklyn., 1971, sec. med. and dental staff 1976-77, v.p. 1978-79, pres. 1980-81, dir. ophthalmology 1981; attending physician State Univ. Hosp., Bklyn., 1971, Kings County Hosp. Ctr., Bklyn., 1971; cons. Luth. Med. Ctr., Beth Israel Med. Ctr., Brookdale Hosp. Med. Ctr., Bklyn., L.I. Coll. Hosp., Bklyn., Maimonides Med. Ctr., Cath. Med. Ctr. Bklyn. and Queens, Bklyn. VA Hosp. Author: Essentials of Clinical Neuro-Ophthalmology, 1976; contbr. chpts. to sci. textbooks and handbooks, articles to profl. jours. Pres. Flatbush Jewish Ctr., Bklyn. With USPHS 1964-66. Recipient J. Eugene Chalfin Meml. Lectr. award Alumni Assn. State Univ.-Kings County, 1981, Tchr. of Yr. award dept. ophthalmology Interfaith Med. Ctr., 1988. Fellow ACP, ACS, Am. Acad. Ophthalmology and Otolaryngology, Am. Acad. Neurology; mem. AMA, AAAS, Med. Soc. County Kings, Med. Soc. State N.Y., Bklyn. Ophthal. Soc., N.Y. Acad. Medicine, Am. Acad. Neurology, Alumni Assn. SUNY (pres.-elect 1989, pres. 1990-91, Richard C. Troutman M.D. Master Tchr. award in ophthalmology 1987, Disting. Alumni Achievement award 1997, Frank L. Babbott M.D. Meml. award 2002, Clarence and Mary Dennis Dedicated Svc. award 2004, Kingbrook Pres.'s award 2004), Oddfellows, Alpha Omega Alpha. Avocations: Torah reader, cantor. Home and Office: 100 Ocean Pky Brooklyn NY 11218-1755

WOLITARSKY, JAMES WILLIAM, securities industry executive; b. Tarrytown, N.Y., Feb. 19, 1946; s. Edward and Beulah (Kemmet) W.; m. Jean T. Nalle; children: James Jr., Matthew; stepchildren: Timothy, Joan. BA, Franklin and Marshall Coll., 1968; MBA, NYU, 1973. Auditor Hertz, Herson & Co., N.Y.C., 1970-73; comml. loan officer Phila. Nat. Bank, 1973-76; CFO, Almo Electronics Corp., Phila., 1976-80; dir. budget and control Paine Webber Inc., N.Y.C., 1981-82, dir. mktg. adminstrn., 1982-83, sr. v.p., dir. mut. funds

and asset mgmt., 1983-84; sr. v.p., dir. product mgmt. Phila. Nat. Bank, 1984-86; exec. v.p., CFO, Moseley Holding Corp., N.Y.C., 1986-87; pres., CEO Moseley Securities Corp., N.Y.C., 1987-88; exec. v.p. Gruntal Fin. Corp., N.Y.C., 1988-91; CFO, Janney Montgomery Scott Inc., Phila., 1992-99, pres., 2000—, pres., CEO, 2001—, also bd. dirs. Bd. dirs. Independence Sq. Properties, Pa. Trust Co. Bd. dirs. Cliveden of Nat. Hist. Trust, Inc., World Affairs Coun. Phila., Securities Industry Assoc. Sgt. U.S. Army, 1968—70. Decorated Bronze Star, Vietnam Cross of Gallantry. Mem. Securities Industry Assn., Phila. Country Club. Episcopalian. Avocations: fishing, skiing, tennis, golf. Office: Janney Montgomery Scott Inc 1801 Market St Philadelphia PA 19103-1675 Home: 674 Knox Rd Wayne PA 19087-2044 E-mail: jwolitarsky@jmsonline.com.

WOLK, BRUCE ALAN, law educator; b. Bklyn., Mar. 2, 1946; s. Morton and Gertrude W.; m. Lois Gloria Krepliak, June 22, 1968; children: Adam, Daniel. BS, Antioch Coll., 1968; MS, Stanford U., 1972; JD, Harvard U., 1975. Bar: D.C. 1975. Assoc. Hogan & Hartson, Washington, 1975-78; prof. U. Calif. Sch. Law, Davis, 1978—, acting dean, 1990-91, dean, 1993-98. Danforth Found. fellow, 1970-74, NSF fellow, 1970-72, Fulbright sr. research fellow, 1985-86. Mem. ABA, Am. Law Inst. Office: Univ Cal Davis Sch Law King Hall 400 Mrak Hall Dr Davis CA 95616-5201

WOLK, LOIS, state legislator; b. Philadelphia, May 12, 1946; m. Bruce Wolk; children: Adam, Dan. BA, Antioch Coll., 1968; MA, Johns Hopkins U., 1971. Tchr. Edmund Burke Sch., Davis Joint Unified Sch. Dist., 1979—81; mem. Davis Recreation and Parks Commn., 1989; mem. coun., mayor Davis City Coun., 1990—98; bd. suprs., chair Yolo County (Calif.) Bd. Suprs., 1998—2002; mem. dist. 8 Calif. State Assembly, 2002—. Chair Children and Families Commn., proposition 10, 1999—2002; mem. Pub. Adv. Com., 2001—02; CSAC rep. Water Plan Update; chair Health and Human Svcs. Com.; mem. Budget Com., Natural Resources, Utilities and Commerce Com., Water, Parks and Wildlife Com. Founding mem. TREE Davis, Yolo Land Trust; bd. dirs. Davis Sci. Ctr., Univ. Retirement Cmty. Found.; charter mem. Yolo Basin Found. Bd. Mem.: Calif. Elected Women, Soroptimist, Rotary. Democrat. Mailing: PO Box 942849 Rm 6012 Sacramento CA 94249 Office: 555f Mason St Ste 275 Vacaville CA 95688

WOLKEN, JONATHAN, performing company executive; m. JoAnne Wolken; 4 children. Grad., Dartmouth Coll. Co-founder, artistic dir. Pilobolus Dance Theatre, Washington Depot, Conn., 1991, devel. dir., 1991—. Artist-in-residence USIS Arts Am. Program, Kuopio, Finland; tchr. Pilobolus Summer Workshop, Maine. Choreographer (Operas) Where the Wild Things Are, Glyndebourne Festival Opera, creator (television feature) Oneiric, Pilobolus/Danish TV. Office: Pilobolus Dance Theatre Bo 388 Washington Depot CT 06794

WOLKOFF, EUGENE ARNOLD, lawyer; b. N.Y.C., June 9, 1932; s. Oscar and Jean (Zablow) W.; m. Judith Gail Edwards, Oct. 15, 1967; children—Mandy, Elana, Alexa, Justine. AB, Bklyn. Coll., 1953; LLB, St. John's U., 1961. Bar: N.Y. 1962, N.Mex. 1994. Practiced in, N.Y.C and Santa Fe; mem. Callahan & Wolkoff, N.Y.C., 1965—; gen. counsel BGK Group of Cos. Bd. dirs. Babylon Enterprises, Inc., Hist. Newspaper Archives, Inc., Beacon Concessions, Inc.; mem. nat. panel arbitrators Am. Arbitration Assn. Served to lt. col. USAFR, 1953-75. Mem. N.Y. State Bar Assn., N.Mex. Bar Assn., Pi Beta Gamma. Office: 2124 Broadway New York NY 10023-1722 also: 330 Garfield St Santa Fe NM 87501-2640 Office Phone: 505-992-5100. E-mail: gene@bgkgroup.com.

WOLKOV, HARVEY BRIAN, oncologist, researcher; b. Cleve., Feb. 8, 1953; s. Sidney and Norma Wolkov; m. Lauren Cronin, Jan. 9, 1993; 1 child, Nicole. BSc, Purdue U., 1975, MSc, 1977; MD, Medical Coll. Ohio, 1979. Diplomate Am. Bd. Radiology. Intern U. Calif., San Francisco, 1979-80; resident Stanford (Calif.) Med. Ctr., 1980-83; rsch. asst. Stanford U., 1982; from asst. clin. prof. to assoc. clin. prof. U. Calif., Davis, 1983-97, assoc. clin. prof., 1997—; med. dir. Mercy Hosps., Sacramento, 1987-90, Sutter Cancer Ctr. Dept. Radiation Oncology, Sacramento, 1990—. Mem. adv. bd. Nat. Graves Disease Found., Jacksonville, Fla., 1993—; dir. Sutter Gamma Knife Ctr., 1997—; co-prin. investigator radiation oncology Children's Oncology Group, 2001—. Author (with others): (book) Intraoperative Radiation, 1989, Frontiers in Radiation, 1991, Textbook Radiation Oncology, 1998; contbr. articles to profl. jours. Bd. dirs. Sutter Hosps. Found., Sacramento. Mem.: Calif. Radiol. Soc. (exec. com. 2001—), Sutter Inst. Med. Rsch. (chair rsch. com. 1996—, hosp. chair oncology com. 2003—, neuroscience inst. leadership com. 2003—), Calif. Radiation Oncology Soc. (pres.-elect 1999, pres. 2000—01), Am. Soc. Therapeutic Radiology and Oncology (bd. dirs. 2000—03, vice chair outcome rsch., corp. rels., workforce, comm., coronary artery radiation therap coms., fin. com., Travel award 1987), Radiation Therapy Oncology Group (com. chair 1986—90, publ. com. 1990—, mem. com. 1990—, lung and brain com. 1990—), No. Calif. Radiation Oncology Soc. (pres. 1999—2001), Coun. Affiliated Radiation Oncology Soc. (pres. 1999—2001), Assn. Residents Radiation Oncology (exec. com. 1997-2000 1997—2000, advisor emeritus 2000—), Am. Cancer Soc. (reviewer 1990—, fellow 1978, 1983), Am. Coll. Radiology (chmn. stds. accreditation com. 1997—2003, councilor at large 1999, alt. councilor 2000—03, councillor 2003—, mem. expert panels, credentials com., fellow 1997). Avocations: painting, sculpture, travel. Office: Sutter Cancer Ctr 2800 L St Ste 10 Sacramento CA 95816-5616 E-mail: hbwolkov@comcast.net.

WOLKOVICH-VALKAVICIUS, WILLIAM LAWRENCE, priest; b. Hudson, Mass., June 29, 1929; s. Liudvikas Steponas Wolkovich-Valkavičius and Elena Žukauskaite. BA, St. John Sem., 1953; MA, Boston Coll., 1980; PhD (hon.), Vytautas Magnus U., Lithuania, 2004. Ordained priest Roman Cath. Ch., 1953. Parish priest Roman Cath. Archdiocese of Boston, 1953—. Author 13 books, including Lithuanian Religious Life in America, 3 vols., 1986, 92, 98; contbr. articles to profl. jours. Named to Order of Gediminas, Republic of Lithuania, 1997; recipient Amicus Poloniae award Polish Am. Hist. Assn., 2001. Mem. Orgn. Am. Historians, Lithuanian Acad. Arts and Scis., Am. Cath. Hist. Assn. Avocations: performing one-man shows of comedy, violin and voice. Home and Office: 14 Highgate Rd Marlborough MA 01752-1659 E-mail: vincasvalk@aol.com.

WOLL, HARRY J. electrical engineer; b. Farmington, Minn., Aug. 25, 1920; s. Henry L. and Clara M. (Fredrickson) W.; m. Mary V. Cowan, Feb. 15, 1947; children: Daniel, Alice. BSE.E., N.D. State U., 1940; postgrad., Ill. Inst. Tech., 1940-41; PhD, U. Pa., 1953. With RCA Corp., 1941-85, chief engr. aerospace systems div., 1963-69, div. v.p. govt. engring. Moorestown, N.J., 1969-75; div. v.p., gen. mgr. RCA Automated Systems, Burlington, 1975-81; staff v.p., chief engr. RCA Electronic Products and Labs., Princeton, N.J., 1981-85. Patentee in field. Chmn. bd. trustees Moore Sch. Elec. Engring., U. Pa. 1976-90; trustee U. Pa., 1989-91. Recipient 50th Anniversary gold medal Moore Sch. Elec. Engring., U. Pa., 1973 Fellow AAAS, IEEE (past chmn. Phila. sect., past chmn. fellow com.), Aerospace Industries Tech. Council (past chmn.); mem. KC, Sigma Phi Delta, Phi Kappa Phi. Roman Catholic. Home: PO Box 679 Concord MA 01742-0679 E-mail: hjwoll@cs.com.

WOLLAN, CURTIS NOEL, theater producer, theater director; b. Mpls., Nov. 10, 1951; s. Curtis Berdins and Lorraine Alice (Walser) Wollan; m. Jane Ellen Deter, May 17, 1980; children: Alexis Lorraine, Chet Curtis. BA in Speech and Theatre, Luther Coll., Decorah, Iowa, 1973; MFA in Directing, U. Iowa, 1976. Ptnr., artistic dir. Stage Two Prodns., Mpls., 1977-85; artistic dir. Chimera Theatre Co., St. Paul, 1985-87; ptnr., artistic dir. T.C.C. Prodns., Mpls., 1990-92; pres., prodr., dir. Troupe Am., Inc., Mpls., 1987—. Guest dir. Circa 21 Prodns., Rock Island, Ill., 1983—, Big League Theatricals, N.Y.C., 1988—93, Ryman Auditorium, Nashville, 1999, Lucas Theatre for the Arts, Savannah, 2001, Theatre Under the Stars, Houston, 2001, Dollywood Holiday Show, 2003, Foothills Repertory Theatre, Worcester, Mass., 2004; past sec., bd. dirs. Midwest Citizens for Arts, Mpls., 1985—87; dir., asst. prodr. Sheehan Prodns. Medora Mus., Mpls., 1987—91; prodr., dir. Medora Musical, 1992—. Creator, dir. mus. concept revue: (plays) The Lovely Liebowitz Sisters, 1986—; dir.(nat. tour): Pump Boys and Dinettes, 1987—88, 1995, 2000, Big River, 1988—89, Oil City Cymphony, 1989—90, Gifts of the Magi, 1990, Driving Miss Daisy, 1991—92, Steel Magnolias, 1992—93, Steven King's Ghost Stories, 1993, 1994, On Golden Pond, 1994, A Christmas Carol, 1996—2002, The Odd Couple, 1997, Moon Over Buffalo, 1998—99, Hank Williams, Lost Highway, 2000—01, The Sunshine Boys, 2001—, Same Time, Next Year, 2002; co-author, dir. nat. tour: Mr. Pickwick's Christmas, 1987—92; prodr., dir. nat. tour 1940's Radio Hour, 1988, 1990; prodr.(nat. tour): A Child's Christmas in Wales, 1988—89, Forbidden Broadway, 1990—91, 1994, Babes in Toyland, 1992—96, Tap Dance Kid, 1995, Mahalia, 1996, Miracle on 34th St., The Musical, 1997—98, Schoolhouse Rock Live!, 1997—2000, Here's Love, 1999; prodr., dir.: Pump Boys and Dinettes, 1999—; Hank and My Honky Tonk Heroes, 1999—; Forever Plaid, 1999—; actor: (films) Bix, 1990, The Childhood Friend, 1993. Recipient Best Prodn. award, Twin Cities Critics Cir., 1981, Best Direction award, 1981, Patriotism award, Am. Legion, 1995. Mem.: Southeastern Theatre Conf. Lutheran. Avocations: movies, restaurants, travel, history, horseback riding. Office: Troupe Am Inc 528 Hennepin Ave Ste 206 Minneapolis MN 55403-1810 Office Phone: 612-333-3302. E-mail: cwollan@mninter.net.

WOLLAN, EUGENE, lawyer; b. N.Y.C., Nov. 2, 1928; s. Isidor and Mollie (Elterman) W.; m. Jean B. Sack, June 6, 1954 (div. 1974); children— Eric G., Jennifer J.; m. Marjorie Cama, Nov. 25, 1977; stepchildren: Valerie M. Rosenwasser, Jon J. Rosenwasser. BA cum laude, Harvard U., 1948, JD, 1950. Bar: NY, 1950, U.S. Dist. Ct. (so. and ea. dists.) NY 1953. U.S. Ct. Appeals (2d cir.) 1955, U.S. Ct. Mil. Appeals 1951, U.S. Supreme Ct. 1960; cert. arbitrator and umpire. Assoc. Rein Mound & Cotton, NYC, 1953-62, ptnr., 1963-87, Mound, Cotton, Wollan & Greengrass, 1987—. Col. USAR, 1951-81. Mem. Internat. Assn. Ins. Counsel, Def. Rsch. Inst., Internat. Soc. Barristers, Assn. Internationale De Droit Des Assurances, NYC Bar Assn., NY County Lawyers, Judge Advocates Assn., Aida Reins. and Ins. Arbitration Soc., Harvard Club (NYC), Met. Opera Guild (NYC). Home: 430 E 57th St New York NY 10022-3061 Office: Mound Cotton Wollan & Greengrass One Battery Park Plz New York NY 10004 Office Phone: 212-804-4222. Business E-Mail: ewollan@moundcotton.com.

WOLLE, CHARLES ROBERT, judge; b. Sioux City, Iowa, Oct. 16, 1935; s. William Carl and Vivian (Down) W.; m. Kerstin Birgitta Wennerstrom, June 26, 1961; children: Karl Johan Knut, Erik Vernon, Thomas Dag, Aaron Charles. AB, Harvard U., 1959; JD, Iowa Law Sch., 1961. Bar: Iowa 1961. Assoc. Shull, Marshall & Marks, Sioux City, 1961-67, ptnr., 1968-80; judge Dist. Ct. Iowa, Sioux City, 1981-83; justice Iowa Supreme Ct., Sioux City and Des Moines, 1983-87; judge U.S. Dist. Ct. (so. dist.) Iowa, Des Moines, 1987-92, chief judge, 1992-99, sr. U.S. dist. judge, 2001—. Faculty Nat. Jud. Coll., Reno, 1983—. Editor Iowa Law Rev., 1960-61 Vice pres. bd. dirs. Sioux City Symphony, 1972-77; bd. dirs. Morningside Coll., Sioux City, 1977-81 Fellow Am. Coll. Trial Lawyers; mem. ABA, Sioux City C. of C. (bd. dirs. 1977-78) Avocations: sports, art, music, literature. Office: Sr US Dist Judge US Dist Ct SD IA 110 E Ct St Des Moines IA 50309 Office Phone: 515-284-6289. E-mail: wolle@iasd.uscourts.gov.

WOLLE, WILLIAM DOWN, foreign service officer; b. Sioux City, Iowa, Mar. 11, 1928; s. William Carl and Vivian Lucille (Down) W.; m. Zanie L. Donahue, Feb. 7, 1992; children from previous marriage: Laila Jean, William Nicholas. BA, Morningside Coll., 1949; M.Internat. Affairs, Columbia U., 1951. Joined U.S. Fgn. Svc., 1951, consular officer, 1951-52, econ. officer, 1952—53, consular officer, 1954—56, trainee Arab lang. and area Beirut, 1957-58, fgn. service officer gen. Aden, Yemen, 1958—59, econ. officer Jidda, Saudi Arabia, 1959-62, internat. rels. officer, 1962-64; officer in charge Arab-Israeli affairs, 1965-67; detailed Nat. War Coll., 1967-68; counselor polit. affairs Kuwait City, Kuwait, 1968-70; econ. officer, dir. AID, Amman, Jordan, 1970-73; econ. officer Nairobi, 1973-74; ambassador to Oman, Muscat, 1974-78. Dir. Middle Eastern/South Asian Research Office, Dept. State, 1978-79; ambassador to United Arab Emirates, 1979-81; adviser internat. affairs Indsl. Coll. Armed Forces, 1981-84; chief sr. officer assignments, Washington, 1984-86. Served with AUS, 1946-47. Recipient Superior Service award Dept. State, 1974, Outstanding Civilian Service award Dept. Def., 1984. Home: 17141 Shell Cast Loop 204 Dumfries VA 22026

WOLLENBERG, RICHARD PETER, paper manufacturing company executive; b. Juneau, Alaska, Aug. 1, 1915; s. Harry L. and Gertrude (Arnstein) W.; m. Leone Bonney, Dec. 22, 1940; children: Kenneth Roger, David Arthur, Keith Kermit, Richard Harry, Carol Lynne. BSME, U. Calif., Berkeley, 1936; MBA, Harvard U., 1938; grad., Army Indsl. Coll., 1941; D in Pub. Affairs (hon.), U. Puget Sound, 1977. Prodn. control Bethlehem Ship, Quincy, Mass., 1938-39; with Longview (Wash.) Fibre Co., 1939—, safety engr., asst. chief engr., chief engr., mgr. container operations, 1951-57, v.p., 1953-57, v.p. ops., 1957-60, exec. v.p., 1960-69, pres., 1969-78, pres., chief exec. officer, 1978-85, pres., chief exec. officer, chmn. bd., 1985—2001, chmn. bd. dirs., 2001—. Mem. Wash. State Council for Postsecondary Edn., 1969-79, chmn., 1970-73; mem. western adv. bd. Factory Mutual Ins Co. Trustee Reed Coll., Portland, 1962—, chmn. bd. 1982-90. Served to lt. col. USAAF, 1941-45. Recipient Alumni Achievement award Harvard U., 1994. Mem. NAM (bd. dirs. 1981-86), Pacific Coast Assn. Pulp and Paper Mfrs. (pres. 1981-92), Inst. Paper Sci. and Tech. (trustee), Wash. State Roundtable. Home: 1632 Kessler Blvd Longview WA 98632-3633 Office: Longview Fibre Co PO Box 606 Longview WA 98632-7391

WOLLER, BASIL R. gas industry executive, auditor; BS, U. Notre Dame; MBA, U. Tex. CPA, cert. internal auditor. Joined El Paso Corp., 1979, various tax acctg. and audit positions El Paso Natural Gas Co., dir. corp. audit El Paso Natural Gas, v.p., gen. auditor, 1997—2001, sr. v.p., gen. auditor, chief ethics officer, 2001—. Mem.: Inst. Internal Auditors (bd. mem.). Office: El Paso Corp 1001 Louisiana St Houston TX 77002-2511

WOLLER, JAMES ALAN, lawyer; b. Adrian, Mich., Dec. 27, 1946; s. Robert Arthur and Florence Emma (Jacob) W.; m. Jill Ann Samis, Aug. 18, 1968 (div. Aug. 1978); 1 child, Emily Erin; m. Elizabeth Julia Frey, May 22, 1982 (div. Apr. 1999); m. Carol Pierini, Oct. 29, 1999. BA, U. Mich., 1969; JD, Columbia U., 1974. Bar: N.J. 1974, U.S. Dist. Ct. N.J. 1974, U.S. Tax Ct. 1976, U.S. Supreme Ct. 1995. Assoc. McCarter & English, Newark, 1974-79; v.p. Pfaltz & Woller, PA, Summit, N.J., 1979-86, pres., 1987—. Editor Columbia U. Human Rights Law Rev., 1973-74. Mem.: ABA, Summit Bar Assn. (pres. 1987—88), Union County Bar Assn., NJ Bar Assn., Columbia Law Sch. Assn. NJ (trustee 1992—97, v.p. 1997—2001, pres. 2001—03), Raritan Yacht Club (Perth Amboy, NJ) (fin. sec. 1988—89, treas. 1989—92, vice commodore 1993—94, commodore 1994—95), Downtown Club (trustee 1997—99, treas. 1999, v.p. 2000, pres. 2001). Republican. Methodist. Avocation: sailing. Home: 110-52 Shearwater Ct Jersey City NJ 07305 Office: Pfaltz & Woller PA 382 Springfield Ave Ste 217 Summit NJ 07901-2780 E-mail: jimwoller@aol.com.

WOLLERSHEIM, JANET PUCCINELLI, psychology educator; b. Anaconda, Mont., July 24, 1936; d. Nello J. and Inez Marie (Ungaretti) Puccinelli; m. David E. Wollersheim, Aug. 1, 1959 (div. June 1972); children: Danette Marie, Tod Neil; m. Daniel J. Smith, July 17, 1976. AB, Gonzaga U., 1958; MA, St. Louis U., 1960; PhD, U. Ill., 1968. Lic. psychologist, Mont. Asst. prof. psychology, asst. dir. testing/counseling ctr. U. Mo., 1968-71; prof. psychology U. Mont., Missoula, 1971—, dir. chin. psychology, 1980-87; chair Mont. Bd. Psychologists, 1977-78; cons. Mont. State Prison, 1971-85, Trapper Creek Job Corps, 1973—2003; pvt. practice Missoula, 1971—. Author numerous rsch. articles. Bd. dirs. Crisis Ctr., Missoula, 1972-73; mem. profl. adv. bd. Head Start, Missoula, 1972-79. Recipient Disting. scholar award U. Mont., 1991. Fellow Am. Psychol. Assn. (bd. dirs. div. clin. psychology 1990-92); mem. Rocky Mountain Psychol. Assn. (pres. 1983-84), Nat. Coun. Univ. Dirs. Clin. Psychology (bd. dirs. 1982-88). Home and Office: 105 Greenwood Ln Missoula MT 59803-2401 Office Phone: 406-543-6946. E-mail: jpwoller2000@yahoo.com.

WOLLERT, GERALD DALE, retired food company executive, investor; b. LaPorte, Ind., Jan. 21, 1935; s. Delmar Everette and Esther Mae W.; m. Carol Jean Burchby, Jan. 26, 1957; children— Karen Lynn, Edwin Del. BS, Purdue U., 1957. With Gen. Foods Corp., 1959-89, dir. consumer affairs, 1973-74, mng. dir. Cottee Foods div. Sydney, Australia, 1974-76, gen. mgr. Mexico div. Mexico City, 1978-79, pres. Asia/Pacific ops. Honolulu, corp. v.p. worldwide coffee and internat. div., 1979-89; ret., 1989. Dir. Gen. Foods cos., Japan, Peoples Republic China, Korea, India, Taiwan, Singapore, Philippines. Webelos leader Boy Scouts Am., Mexico City, 1978-79; co. gen. chmn. United Fund campaign, Battle Creek, Mich., 1964-65, White Plains, N.Y., 1972-73. Served with U.S. Army, 1958. Mem. Asian-U.S. Bus. Coun., Oahu Country Club (Hawaii), Venice Golf and Country Club (Fla.), Beacon Hills and Beechwood (Ind.) Club.

WOLLMAN, ERIC, lawyer; b. Bklyn., May 26, 1951; s. Harry and Lillian (Levine) W. AA, Kingsborough Community Coll., 1970; BA, Bklyn. Coll., 1973; JD, Bklyn. Law Sch., 1993. Bar: N.J. 1994, N.Y. 1996. Exec. asst. to treas. Dept. Fin., N.Y.C., 1973-76; supervising investment analyst Office of Comptroller, N.Y.C., 1976-85, project mgr., 1985-90, adminstrv. mgr.proxy unit, 1990-92, dir. corp. governance, 1993-94, adminstrv. mgr., 1994-96, assoc. gen. counsel, 1996—2001, dep. dir. contracting, 2001—. Exec. prodr., host Second to None TV program, 1995-2001. Vice pres. Com. to Preserve Brighton Beach, Bklyn., 1989; aux. capt. N.Y.C. Police Dept., 1973—; mem. Pub. Works Forum, 1991-96, commr. of deeds. Recipient award of valor N.Y.C. Police Dept., award of merit United Fund of Greater N.Y., 30 Yr. Svc. award N.Y. Police Dept. Aux. Police. Mem. ABA, NRA, N.Y. County Lawyers Assn., Am. Assn. Jewish Lawyers and Jurists, Bklyn. Coll. Alumni Assn., Bklyn. Law Sch. Alumni Assn., Aux. Police Benevolent Assn., Phi Delta Phi. Democrat. Jewish. Home: 2209 E 28th St Brooklyn NY 11229-5057 Office: NYC Office of Comptroller 1 Centre St Rm 736 New York NY 10007-1602 Office Phone: 212-669-4766. E-mail: stnonradio@yahoo.com.

WOLLMAN, JUNE ROSE, clothing executive; b. Bklyn., June 14, 1929; d. Louis and Ella (Klein) Nierenberg; m. Howard Louis Wollman, Sept. 29, 1922; children: Jodi Ann (dec.), Randi Sue. Interior designer June Rose Decors Ltd., Valley Stream, N.Y., 1951—; with Louella Realty, N.Y.C., 1956-85; designer Lou Nierenberg Corp., N.Y.C., 1956-80; with Lou Nierenberg Internat., N.Y.C., 1974-85, Lou Nierenberg Ltd., N.Y.C., 1985—, real estate pres., 1985—. Cons. fake furs, jackets, coats, N.Y.C., 1985—. Trustee Green Acres Civic Cos., Valley Stream, 1951—; bd. dirs. Mill Brov Civic Assn., 1990—; presenter Meml. Jodi Ann Wollman Scholarship Ann., South High Sch., Valley Stream, 1969—; life mem. Temple Emanu-El, Lynbrook, 1969—, asst. to chair Long Island (N.Y.) inter temple networking caring cmtys., 1989—, bd. dirs. sisterhood, 1990—; founding sponsor Mt. Sinai Med. Ctr., past v.p.; pres. Sam & Rose Klein Family Inc., 1975-85, CEO, 1985—; pres. Jodi Ann Wollman Glioblastomn Rsch. Fund, 1970-90. Recipient L.I.J.H. Med. Ctr. award Ladies Svc. Guild, New Hyde Park, N.Y., 1965-85, Mt. Sinai Med. Ctr. award, N.Y.C., 1969-89. Mem. Am. Jewish Congress (pres. South Shore chpt. 1957-63). Republican. Jewish. Avocations: reading, golf, tennis, swimming, travel. Home and Office: June Rose Decors Ltd 4581 Painted Fern Court Murrells Inlet SC 29576-2421 Office Phone: 843-357-9645. Personal E-mail: washes@sc.rr.com.

WOLLMAN, ROGER LELAND, federal judge; b. Frankfort, S.D., May 29, 1934; s. Edwin and Katherine Wollman; m. Diane Marie Schroeder, June 21, 1959; children: Steven James, John Mark, Thomas Roger. BA, Tabor Coll., Hillsboro, Kans., 1957; JD magna cum laude, U. S.D., 1962; LLM, Harvard U., 1964. Bar: S.D. 1964. Law clerk Hon. George T. Mickleson US Dist. Ct (So. Dist, SC), 1962—63; sole practice Aberdeen, 1964—71; states atty. Brown County, Aberdeen, 1967—71; justice S.D. Supreme Ct., 1971—85, chief justice, 1978—82; judge US Ct. Appeals (8th cir.), 1985—, chief judge, 1999—2002. Mem. Jud. Conference of US, 1999—2002. Served with U.S. Army, 1957—59. Mem.: Am. Jud. Soc. Office: US Ct Appeals US Courthouse & Fed Bldg 400 S Phillips Ave Rm 315 Sioux Falls SD 57104-6851

WOLLMER, RICHARD DIETRICH, statistics and operations research educator; b. LA, July 27, 1938; s. Herman Dietrich and Alice Myrtle (Roberts) W. BA in Math., Pomona Coll., 1960; MA in Applied Math., Columbia U., 1962; MS in Engring. Sci., U. Calif., Berkeley, 1963, PhD Engring. Sci., 1965. Scientist Rand Corp., Santa Monica, Calif., 1965-70; prof. info. systems Calif. State U., Long Beach, 1970—, dept. chair, 2000—03, vis. prof. Northridge, 1981—82. Cons. McDonnell Douglas, Long Beach, Calif., 1978-80, 82, 85-91, Logicon, San Pedro, Calif., 1979-81, Behavioral Tech. Labs., U. So. Calif., 1973-75; vis. assoc. prof. Stanford U., 1976; rsch. scientist Electric Power Rsch. Inst., Palo Alto, Calif., 1977; rsch. engr. Jet Propulsion Lab., Pasadena, Calif., 1971. Contbr. articles to profl. jours. Deacon Bel Air Presbyn. Ch., L.A., 1982-84, treas. 1983; mem. St. Andrews Presbyn. Ch., Newport Beach, Calif., 1999—. Mem.: Internat. Fedn. Ops. Rsch. Mgmt. (So. Calif.), Internat. Fedn. Ops. Rsch. Mgmt. Sci. (sec. 2003, treas. 1999), Ops. Rsch. Soc. Am., So. Calif. Inst. Mgmt. Sci.-Ops. Rsch. Soc. (treas. 1979, vice chmn. 1980, chmn. 1981, vice chmn. 1988, chmn. 1989). Republican. Avocations: classical music, sports, reading, antique cars. Home: 6132 Fernwood Dr Huntington Beach CA 92648-5574 Office: Calif State U 1250 N Bellflower Blvd Long Beach CA 90840-0001

WOLLPERT, SANDRA COX, horse breeder; b. Phila., July 8, 1950; d. Robert Miller and Audrey Olive (Fullam) Cox; m. Worth Alan Wollpert, Sept. 29, 1973; children: Worth Douglas, Shaunna Lee. BA, BS, Pa. State U., 1971. Cert. secondary sch. tchr., Pa. Tchr. Cheltenham (Pa.) High Sch., 1972-73; officer Four Seasons Devel. Inc., Ohio, 1975-86; pres. SW Acquisitions and SW Realty Inc., Chardon, Ohio, Blythswood Farm, Inc., Chardon. Bd. dirs. CW Holding Co., Wilmington, Del., Spruco Investment Co., Wilmington, Diamondtech Inc., Chardon; chmn. Arabian Race Com., Ohio, 1990-95. Author: Cerissa, 1976, Rebel's Honor, 1980, Winter Roses, 1983, Rapture's Fury, 1988; contbg. editor (pedigrees) Arabian, 1996—; contbr. articles to profl. jours. including Finish Line. Contbr. WWF, NRDC. Mem. Nat. Trust for Scotland, Arabian Jockey Club, Deep Springs Trout Club, Concord Country Club, Union League Phila., EARA, The Baronial Order of Magna Carta, Phi Kappa Phi (hon.). Avocations: horseback riding, fishing, horse racing, reading, travel. Office: Blythswood Inc 401 South St Chardon OH 44024-2805

WOLMAN, ERIC, health care consultant; b. N.Y.C., Sept. 25, 1931; s. Leo and Cecil (Clark) W.; m. Sandra Rosman, July 27, 1963; children: Karin, Alastair. AB in Math., Harvard Coll., 1953; PhD in Applied Math., Harvard U., 1957. Mem. tech. staff AT&T Bell Labs., Murray Hill, Holmdel, N.J., 1957-66, dept. head traffic rsch. and network engring. Holmdel, 1966-77, dept. head ops. rsch. and computing syss. West Long Branch, N.J., 1977-82, dept. head human performance engring. Piscataway, Summit, N.J., 1983-87; v.p. cmty. programs and rsch. Mich. Cancer Found., Detroit, 1988-91; asst. leader cancer prevention and control program Prentis Comprehensive Cancer Ctr. Met. Detroit, 1990-94; mem. faculty grad. program in cancer biology Wayne State U. Sch. of Medicine, Detroit, 1992-96; vis. rsch. prof. dept. sys. engring and ops. rsch. George Mason U., Fairfax, Va., 1996—. Mem. evaluation panel for fire programs Nat. Bur. of Standards, Gaithersburg, Md., 1966-74, evaluation panel for nat. engring. lab., 1974-80, working group on info. tech. NSF, Arlington, Va., 1980-81. Contbr. articles to profl. jours. Trustee Rumson (N.J.) Country Day Sch., 1973-81, Sea Edn. Assn., Woods Hole, Mass., 1981—. Fellow AAAS; mem. Inst. Ops. Rsch. and The Mgmt. Scis. (coun. 1979-82), Seabright Beach Club, Harvard Club (N.Y.C.). Avocation: cruising. Home: 7806 Hidden Meadow Ter Potomac MD 20854-1792 E-mail: eric.wolman@erols.com.

WOLMAN, J. MARTIN, retired newspaper publisher; b. Elizabeth, N.J., Mar. 8, 1919; s. Joseph D. and Dora (Baum) W.; m. Anne Paley, Sept. 12, 1943; children: Natalie, Jonathan, Ruth Ellen, Lewis Joel. Student, U. Wis., 1937-40. With Wis. State Jour., Madison, 1936-84, pub., 1968-84; pres., gen. mgr. Madison Newspaper, Inc., 1969-84, ret., 1984, dir., 1969—, Lee Enterprises, Inc., 1971-74; treas. Lee Endowment Trusts, 1988—. Sec.-treas. Madison Improvement Corp., 1958-62 Treas. Wis. State Jour. Empty Stocking Club, 1948, Children and Youth Services Inc., 1962—; mem. Mayor Madison Adv. Com., 1965; bd. dirs. United Givers Fund, 1960-64, trustee, 1980—;

ex-officio Roy L. Matson Scholarship Fund, 1961, Central Madison Com., Madison Art Assn.; trustee Edgewood Coll., Madison, U. Wis. Hosp. and Clinic; chmn. Madison Area Arts Coalition, 1984-85; bd. dirs. Univ. Health Sci. Center, 1975; chmn. U.S. Savs. Bond Met. Wis., 1983; coordinator Barneveld Disaster Fund, Wis., 1985-86; mem. U. Wis. Found., 1968-95; bd. dirs., trustee Wisc. Clin. Cancer Ctr., 1986—; Dir. Wisc. Newspaper Found., 1986-88; v.p., treas. Lee Endowment Found., 1989- . Served with AUS, 1942-46. Named Advt. Man of Year Madison Advt. Club, 1969, Madison Man of Achievement, 1976, Man of Yr. Salvation Army, 1993; recipient Disting. Service award Wis. Newspaper Assn., 1982, Community Service award Inland Daily Press Assn., 1983, Ralph D. Casey Minn. award for Disting. Service in Journalism, 1987, First Ringling Bros. Silver Smile award, 1993, Outstanding Svc. for Youth award Wis. State Jour., 1995, Rounders Youth Lifetime award, 1997. Mem. Madison C. of C. (dir. 1966-70, 74-84), Inland Daily Press Assn. (dir. 1961-65), Wis. Daily Newspaper League (pres. 1961-65), Wis. Newspaper Assn. (dir. 1977-84) Clubs: B'nai B'rith. Office: 1901 Fish Hatchery Rd Madison WI 53713-1248

WOLMAN, JONATHAN PALEY, journalist; b. Madison, Wis., Aug. 1, 1950; s. Joseph Martin and Anne (Paley) W.; m. Deborah Eve Lamm, Sept. 24, 1978; children: Jacob, Emma, Sophia. BA, U. Wis., 1972. Reporter AP, Detroit, 1973-74, Madison, 1973, news editor, 1975, Urban Affairs Team, 1976-77, nat. writer, 1978-80, news editor, 1980-84, asst. bur. chief, 1984-88, bur. chief, 1989-98, mng. editor New York, 1998-2000, exec. editor, 2000—02, sr. v.p., 2002—04; editl. page editor Denver Post, 2004—. Mem. Am. Soc. Newspaper Editors, 1994—. Office: Denver Post 1560 Broadway Denver CO 80202 Office Phone: 303-820-1780. Business E-Mail: jwolman@denverpost.com. E-mail: wolmanjp@fastmail.fm.

WOLMAN, M. GORDON, geography educator; b. Balt., Aug. 16, 1924; s. Abel and Anna (Gordon) W.; m. Elaine Mielke, June 20, 1951; children: Elsa Anne, Abel Gordon, Abby Lucille, Fredericka Jeannette. Student, Haverford Coll.; AB in Geology, Johns Hopkins U., 1949; MA in Geology, Harvard U., 1951, PhD, 1953. Geologist U.S. Geol. Survey, 1951-58, part-time, 1958—; assoc. prof. geography Johns Hopkins U., Balt., 1958-62, prof., 1962—. Prof. Johns Hopkins U., 1962—, chmn. dept. geography and environ. engring., 1958—90, interim provost, 1987—90, prof. environ. health sci., 1998—; adv. com. geography U.S. Office Naval Rsch., Oak Ridge Nat. Lab.; exec. com. divsn. earth sci. NRC; internat. environ. programs com., environ. studies bd., com. water, com. mineral resources and environ., chmn. nat. commn. water quality policy NAS; chmn. NRC Com. Adv. U.S. Geol. Survey; chmn. NAS Commn. Geoscis., Environment and Resources, NRC Bd. Sustainability, 1995—2000; chmn. study land use and populationNRC Tri-Acad., China, India; environ. adv. com. Savannah River Tech. ctr.; chmn. U.S. Com. for IIASA, 1999—2003. Author: Fluvial Processes in Geomorphology, 1964; editl. bd.: Science mag. Pres. bd. trustees Park Sch., Balt.; pres. bd. dirs. Sinai Hosp., Balt., Resources for Future, 1980-87; adv. com. Inst. Nuc. Power Ops., 1982-85; active Balt. City Charter Revision Commn., Cmty. Action Com., Balt. With USNR, 1943-46. Recipient Meritorious Contbn. award Assn. Am. Geographers, 1972, Disting. Career award Geomorphology, 1993, D.L. Linton award Brit. Geomorphological Rsch. Group, 1994, Rachel Carson award Chesapeake Appreciation Inc., Ian Campbell medal Am. Geol. Inst., 1997, Nev. Med. Desert Rsch. Inst., Abel Wolman award Chesapeake sect. AWWA, 2003, Lifetime Achievement award Nat. Coun. for Sci. and the Environment, 2004. Fellow Am. Acad. Arts and Scis.; mem. ASCE, NAS, NAE, Am. Geophys. Union (chmn. subcom. sedimentation, pres. hydrol. sect., Robert Horton medal 2000), Geol. Soc. Am. (v.p. 1983, pres. 1984, Penrose medal 1999), Am. Philos. Soc., Am. Geog. Soc. (councillor 1965-70, Cullum Geog. medal 1989), Washington Geol. Soc., Agrl. Hist. Soc., Md. Acad. Scis. (exec. com. 1970-75), Phi Beta Kappa, Sigma Xi. Home: 2104 W Rogers Ave Baltimore MD 21209-4553 Office: Johns Hopkins U Dept Geography/Environ Engr Baltimore MD 21218 Office Phone: 410-516-7090. Business E-Mail: wolman@jhu.edu.

WOLMAN, MARTIN, lawyer; b. Albany, NY, Feb. 2, 1937; s. Benjamin S. and Sonya (Kogan) W.; children: Koren M. Wolman-Tardy, Barton T., William B., Brandon S. AB, Brown U., 1958; LLB, U. Calif., Berkeley, 1964. Bar: Calif., 1964, Conn., 1965. Atty. Conn. Bank & Trust Co., Hartford, 1964-67; assoc. Day, Berry & Howard, Hartford, 1967-72, ptnr., 1972—. Mem. Conn. Law Revision Commn., 1985-2002. Trustee Russell-Sage Coll., Troy, NY, 1990-96, Wadsworth Atheneum, 1994-2002, Lyme Acad. Coll. Fine Arts, 2003—; trustee Kingswood-Oxford Sch., West Hartford, Conn., 1980-93, chmn., 1986-89; bd. dirs. Hartford Hosp., 1991—, chmn., 2003—; bd. dirs. Inst. Living, 1994, Hartford Health Care Corp., 1996—; bd. govs. Hill-Stead Mus., Farmington, Conn., 1990-94. Lt. (j.g.) USN, 1958-61. Fellow Am. Coll. Trust and Estate Counsel (chmn. Conn. chpt. 1981-86); mem. Conn. Bar Assn. (chmn. exec. com. probate sect. 1979-82). Office: Day Berry & Howard City Place I 25th Fl Hartford CT 06103-3499 Business E-Mail: mwolman@dbh.com.

WOLMAN, SANDRA R. health science association administrator, pathologist, geneticist; b. New York City, NY, Nov. 23, 1933; d. Alexander Jerome and Sophie Raffel Rosman; m. Eric Wolman, July 27, 1963; children: Karin, Alastair. BA cum laude, Radcliffe Coll./Harvard U, Cambridge, MA, 1951—55; MD, NYU Sch. of Medicine, New York, NY, 1955—59. Pathology, anatomic Am. Bd. of Pathology, 1964, cert. Am. Bd. Med. Genetics, 1982. Asst. prof. NYU Sch. of Medicine, New York, NY, 1967—76, assoc. prof., 1976—84, prof. of pathology, 1984—88, Wayne State U. Sch. of Medicine, Detroit, 1988—93; med. dir. Oncor, Inc., Gaithersburg, Md., 1993—96; adminstrv. officer ISBER (Internat. Soc. for Biol. and Environ. Repositories), Bethesda, Md., 1998—. Sci. societies adv. coun. ATCC (Am. Type Culture Collections), Manassas, Va., 1999—; bd. of directors AACR (Am. Assn. for Cancer Rsch.), Phila., 1988—91; chair, Gordon conf. on cancer Gordon Conferences, AAAS, RI, 1988; chair, faculty coun. NYU, N.Y.C., 1985; councilor Am. Soc. for Investigative Pathology, Bethesda, 1993—95, 1997—2001. Author: Human Cytogenetic Cancer Markers, 1997; contbr. articles to sci. publs. Mem. Mon. County Narcotics Coun., Long Br., NJ, 1973—77, chair, 1975; mem. of bd. Mon. County Planned Parenthood, Lincroft, NJ, 1973—77. Recipient AOA membership, NYU Sch. of Med, membership in Sigma Xi, Wayne State U. Mem.: Seabright Beach Club, Detroit Athletic Club, Cosmopolitan Club. Avocations: sailing, cooking, travel. Office: ISBER/ASIP 9650 Rockville Pike Bethesda MD 20814-3993 E-mail: swolman@asip.org.

WOLMAN, WILLIAM, economist, journalist, broadcaster; b. Montreal, Que., Can. s. Nathan and Toba (Wexler) W.; m. Ann Livia Colamosca, Jan. 7, 1982; children: John, Flora. BA, McGill U., 1948; PhD, Stanford U., 1957. Asst. prof. econs. Wash. State U., Pullman, 1954-60; v.p. Citicorp, N.Y.C., 1969-71, Argus Rsch. Corp., N.Y.C., 1971-74; chief economist CNBC, Ft. Lee, N.J., 1989—; econs. editor Bus. Week, N.Y.C., 1960-69, sr. editor, 1974-83, editor, 1984-89, exec. editor, 1983-84, chief economist, 1989—. Author: The Judas Economy: The Triumph of Capital and the Betrayal of Work, 1997, The Great 401K Hoax, 2002. Avocations: skiing, photography. Office: Bus Week 1221 Ave of Americas New York NY 10020-1001

WOLNEK, STEPHEN S. religious organization administrator; Pres. United Synagogue of Conservative Judaism, NYC, 1997—2002, hon. pres., 2002—. V.p. Jewish Nat. Fund. Jewish. Office: United Synagogue of Conservative Judaism 155 5th Ave New York NY 10010-6802

WOLOSHCHUK, CANDACE DIXON, secondary school educator, artist, consultant; b. Joliet, Ill., Jan. 11, 1947; d. Harold Russell and Beatrice Diane (Johnson) Dixon; m. Christopher Ralph Jose, Mar. 1, 1969 (div. Sept. 1982); children: Amy Russell, Jennifer Seavey; m. Thomas Woloshchuk, Dec. 23, 1988; stepchildren: Michael, Debbie, Paul, John. BA in Art, Salem Coll., 1969; postgrad., Merrimac Coll., 1969; MA in Art Edn., U. Hartford, 1977; Cert. Dir. Fine Arts, Fitchburg State Coll., 1994; student, CAGS Mus., 2000. Cert. tchr., Mass., Conn. Art dir. Fred D. Wish Sch., Hartford, Conn., 1969-71; art tchr. Timothy Edwards Jr. H.S., South Windsor, Conn., 1971-72; art coord. Hebron (Conn.) Elem. Sch., Gilead Hill Sch., 1974-78; art tchr. Longmeadow (Mass.) Pub. Schs., 1978-82, Agawan (Mass.) Pub. Schs., 1982-85; visual arts coord. Wilbraham (Mass.) Mid. Sch., 1985—. Coord. medieval festival Wilbraham Mid. Sch., 1986-87, coord. Oriental festival, 1987-88; pres., owner Scholarships Unltd., Monson, Mass., 1992-94; mem. tchr.-trainer program U. Hartford, 1974-78; enrichment, art tchr. Elms Coll., 1988-93; v.p. Pioneer Valley Decorative Painters, 1996-97. One-women show Garrett Gallery, 1981; group shows include Spencer Arts Ctr., 1993, Craft Adventure Expo '93, 1993 (2nd and 3rd pl. awards), Craft Expo '92, 1992 (2nd pl. award), Wilbraham Pub. Libr., 1992, 93, 94. Chairwomen, mem. Wilbraham Arts Lottery Coun., 1987-88; program chairwoman Pioneer Valley Decorative Painters of Mass., 1996—, v.p., 1997—. Recipient Outstanding Visual and Performing Arts Edn. award, Mass. Alliance for Arts Edn., 1988, gold award Am. Sch. Food Svc. Assn., 1987. Mem. ASCD, NAFE, Nat. Art Edn. Assn., Mass. Art Edn. Assn., Mass. Tchrs. Assn., Wilbraham Tchrs. Assn., Am. Craft Coun. Republican. Avocations: sailing, painting, equestrian riding. Office: Wilbraham Mid Sch 466 Stony Hill Rd Wilbraham MA 01095-1574 E-mail: cwoloshchuk@hwrsd.org., cwoloshchuk@samnet.net.

WOLOSONOVICH, STEPHEN, violinist; b. Linden, N.J., Nov. 7, 1934; s. Stephen and Mary Wolosonovich. Student, N.Y. Coll. of Music, 1949-51, Eastman Sch. of Music, 1951-54, Meadowmount Sch. of Music, 1951 55; BS, Juilliard Sch. Music, 1959. Violinist Rochester Philharm., 1952-54, Rudié Syfonietta, 1962-63, Montovani Orch., 1962; violin soloist Ballet Russ de Monte Carlo, 1962; violinist, prodr., dir. Music for Young Listeners, N.Y., N.J., 1962-75; violin solo recital, lectr., tchr. U. Beijing, 1986. Violin solo lectr. Lehigh U., 1980. Violin soloist Svc. Electric Cable T.V., Allentown, Pa., 1978, 79, 81, violin soloist, interview Channel T, Nutley, N.J., 1981-82; arranger (concerto) Butterfly Concerto, 1996, Polonaise, 1995; debut recital Carnegie Recital Hall, 1982.

WOLPER, ALLAN, journalist, educator; b. N.Y.C. s. Sydelle Wolper; m. Joanna Wolper; children: Jill Miller, Richard, Kim Arminen. BS, NYU, 1965. Reporter Providence Jour., 1965-67; polit. writer AP, N.Y.C., 1967-69, N.Y. Post, N.Y.C., 1970-73; writer, producer WABC Eyewitness News, N.Y.C., 1974-75; managing editor, columnist Soho Weekly News, N.Y.C., 1974-82; host, writer, producer of Right to Know Suburban Cablevision and N.J. Network, Sta. WNYC-TV, N.Y.C., Newark and Avenel, N.J., 1982-89; host, producer series on media Right to Know Right to Know syndicated pub. radio series on the media, Newark, 1989-93; assoc. prof. journalism Rutgers U., 1978-92, prof. journalism, 1995—; commentator on media urban issues WBGO-FM, 1993—. Host, prodr., writer documentary The Marielitos, 1984, Hillside: Desegregation, 1985, Impact, 1988, TV spl. The First Amendment, 1989 (Joseph Brechner First Amendment award 1995); columnist Sports Media, Washington Journalism Rev., 1980-82, media N.J. Reporter, Princeton, 1982-85; ethics columnist, contbg. editor Editor and Pub. mag., 1987—. Recipient best pub. affairs program award Internat. TV and Video Festival, 1985, Nat. Cable TV Assn., 1986, award for cable excellence, 1986, 3 Aces award Nat. Cable TV, 1985, 86, Lowell Mellett award Pa. State U., 1985, Alfred I. DuPont award Columbia U., 1985, award in broadcast journalism (1st cable prodr. to win) N.J. Press Assn., 1987, N.J. Bell Enterprise award for best radio documentary, 1992, Best Radio Commentary and Media Nat. Headliner award 1993, Hildy Johnson award North Jersey Press Club, 2000, First Place Best Personal Column, Deadline Club N.Y., 2000, Bart Richards award for media criticism, 2002, second place, tied, Best Personal Column award, Deadline Club, 2003, Paul Mongerson award of distinction for investigative reporting on news coverage Ctr. Media Pub. Affairs, 2003. Mem.: AAUP (Arhtur rowse award for Press Criticism, Hon. Mention Nat. Press Club 2004, Personal Dir. Cert. of Merit, Deadline Club NY 2004), Soc. Profl. Journalists (chmn. freedom of info. com. Deadline Club N.Y.C. br. 1980, Outstanding Broadcast Journalism award 1984, 1987, Disting. Svc. award 1989, 1st pl. Bicentennial Broadcast Competition 1989, spl. award N.J. chpt. media criticism 1991, radio documentary 1992, investigative report 1992, 1st pl. Pub. Svc. award Mag. N.J. chpt. 1994, Brechner 1st Amendment award 1996, Best Column, Deadline Club, N.Y. chpt. 2000, spl. award N.J. chpt.). Office: 327 Central Park W New York NY 10025-7631 also: Rutgers U Journalism Dept Bradley Hall Newark NJ 07102 Office Phone: 212-663-6614. Office Fax: 212-531-0719. E-mail: allanwolper@msn.com.

WOLPER, DAVID LLOYD, motion picture and television executive; b. N.Y.C., Jan. 11, 1928; s. Irving S. and Anna (Fass) W.; m. Margaret Dawn Richard, May 11, 1958 (div.); children: Mark, Michael, Leslie; m. Gloria Diane Hill, July 11, 1974. Student, Drake U., 1946, U. So. Calif., 1948. V.p., treas. Flamingo Films, TV sales co., 1948-50, v.p. West Coast Ops., 1954-58; chmn., pres. Wolper Prodns., L.A., 1958—. Cons., exec. producer Warner Bros., Inc., 1976—. TV prodns. include Race for Space, Making of the President 1960, 64, Biography series, Story of... series, The Yanks are Coming, Berlin: Kaiser to Khrushchev, December 7: Day of Infamy, The American Woman in the 20th Century, Hollywood and The Stars, March of Time Specials, The Rise and Fall of the Third Reich, The Legend of Marilyn Monroe, Four Days in November, Krebiozen and Cancer, National Geographic, Undersea World of Jacques Cousteau, China: Roots of Madness, The Journey of Robert F. Kennedy, Say Goodbye, George Plimpton, Appointment With Destiny, American Heritage, Smithsonian, They've Killed President Lincoln, Sandburg's Lincoln, Primal Man, The First Woman President, Chico and the Man, Get Christie Love, Welcome Back, Kotter!, Collison Course, Roots, Victory at Entebbe, Roots: The Next Generations, Moviola, The Thorn Birds, North and South Books I, II, III, Napoleon and Josephine, Alex Haley's Queen, Men Of The Dragon, Unwed Father, The Morning After; feature films include The Hellstrom Chronicle, Devil's Brigade, The Bridge at Remagen, If It's Tuesday, This Must Be Belgium, Willy Wonka and The Chocolate Factory, Visions of Eight, This is Elvis, Murder in the First, Surviving Picasso, L.A. Confidential; live spl. events include Opening and Closing Ceremonies 1984 Olympic Games, Liberty Weekend July 3-6, 1986. Trustee L.A. County Mus. Art, Am. Film Inst., L.A. Thoracic and Cardiovascular Found., Boys and Girls Clubs Am., U.S. Golf Assn. Found.; bd. dirs. Amateur Athletic Assn. L.A., L.A. Heart Inst., Acad. TV Arts and Scis. Found., So. Calif. Com. for Olympic Games, U. Soc. Calif. Cinema/TV Dept.; bd. govs. Cedars Sinai Med. Ctr.; com. mem. U.S. Olympic Team Benefit; mem. adv. com. Nat. Ctr. Jewish Film. Recipient award for documentaries San Francisco Internat. Film Festival, 1960, 7 Golden Globe awards, 5 George Foster Peabody awards, Disting. Service award U.S. Jr. C. of C.; 40 Emmy awards, 145 Emmy nominations Acad. TV Arts and Scis.; Monte Carlo Internat. Film Festival award, 1964, Cannes Film Festival Grand Prix for TV Programs, 1964; Oscar award, 11 Oscar nominations, Jean Hersholt Humanitarian award Acad. Motion Picture and TV Scis., medal of Chevalier The French Nat. Legion of Honor, 1990; named to TV Hall of Fame, 1988. Mem. Nat. Acad. TV Arts and Scis., Acad. Motion Picture Arts and Scis., Producers Guild Am., Caucus for Producers, Writers and Dirs. Office: The David L Wolper Co Inc 617 N Rodeo Dr Beverly Hills CA 90210

WOLPERT-DEFILIPPES, MARY K. science administrator; BS in Pharmacy cum laude, Creighton U., 1963; MS in Pharmacology, U. Mich., 1966, PhD in Pharmacology, 1969; postdoctoral student, Yale U., 1969—. Rsch. assoc. in pharmacology Yale U., New Haven, 1970-71; staff fellow lab. chem. pharmacology NIH, Bethesda, Md., 1971-75, pharmacologist drug evaluation br., 1976-81, supervisory pharmacologist drug evaluation br., 1981-82, dep. chief drug evaluation br., 1982-85, pharmacologist Office of Assoc. Dir., 1985-88, program dir. Grants and Contracts Ops. Br., 1988-97, chief Grants and Contracts Ops. Br., 1997—. Contbr. articles to profl. jours.; patentee in field. Mem. Gamma Pi Epsilon, Rho Chi. Office: Nat Cancer Inst Divsn Cancer Treatment and Diagnosis Rm 8153 Exec Pla N Bethesda MD 20892 Office Phone: 301-496-8783. Business E-Mail: wolpertm@exchange.nih.gov.

WOLPERT RICHARD, CHAVA, artist; b. Frankfurt, Germany, Feb. 26, 1933; arrived in Palestine, 1934,arrived in U.S., 1958; d. Ludwig Y. and Else (Ahrens) Wolpert; m. Henry A. Richard, 1959 (dec. Jan. 1971). Student, Bezalel Acad. Arts and Crafts, Jerusalem, 1954-56. Artist-in-residence The Jewish Mus., N.Y.C., 1958—88. Painter, designer/creator of contemporary style ceremonial Judaica such as candelabra, Passover sets, Torah ornaments, decorative Judaica in enamel, silver, other metals, glass, porcelain, wood, acrylics, fabrics and oil painting; represented in 10 mus. collections in U.S., Australia, Europe, Israel. Pvt. Israeli Army, 1951—53. Recipient 2 Merit awards Interfaith Forum on Religion, Art and Arch., 1980, 83, Jurors' Choice award Liturgical Art Guild, 1991, Best in Judaica award Liturgical Art Guild, 1997. Mem. Judaic Art Guild, Liturgical Art Guild. Avocation: reflexology.

WOLRAICH, MARK LEE, pediatrician, educator; BA, SUNY, Binghamton, 1966; MD, SUNY, Syracuse, 1970. Diplomate Am. Bd. Pediat. Pediatric intern SUNY, Syracuse, 1970-71; pediatric resident U. Okla. Health Scis. Ctr., Oklahoma City, 1973-74; pediatric fellowship U. Oreg. Health Scis. Ctr., 1974-76; asst. prof. U. Iowa, 1976-81, assoc. prof., 1981-86, prof., 1986-90, Vanderbilt U., 1990-2001, dir. divsn. child devel., dir. child devel. ctr., 1990-99, dir. ctr. for chronic illnesses and disabilities in children, 1990-2000; investigator J.F. Kennedy Ctr. for Rsch. on Edn. and Human Devel., 1990-2001; prof. pediat., dir. Child Study Ctr. Okla. U. Health Scis. Ctr., 2001—. Med. supr. U. Iowa Divsn. of Devel. Disabilities, 1980-90; vis. prof. Great Ormond St. Hosp. for Sick Children, London, 1983, U. Cape Town, Rondebosch Cape, South Africa, 1986, Columbus Children's Hosp., Ohio State U., Dept. Pediat., 1988; mem. Iowa State Foster Care Rev. Bd. Co-editor Advances in Developmental and Behavioral Pediatrics, 1981-92; cons. editor Am. Jour. on Mental Deficiency; editl. adv. bd. A Guide to Parent Counseling, editor The Classification of Child and Adolescent Mental Disorders in Primary Care-Diagnostic and Statistical Manual for Mental Disorders in Primary Care Child and Adolescent Version, 1996; cons. reviewer Developmental Medicine and Child Neurology, Pediatrics, Nutrition and Behavior, Jour. Pediatrics, Jour. of Social and Personal Relationships, Applied Rsch. in Mental Retardation, Jour. of Clin. Psychology, Jour. Developmental and Behavioral Pediatrics, Clin. Pediatrics, others; contbr. numerous articles to profl. publs. Recipient Disting. and Dedicated Svc. award Spina Bifida Assn. Iowa, 1979, Lou Holloway award Health Scis. Edn.; grantee NIMH, 1987-90, 98 2001, Nat. Inst. on Disability and Rehab. Rsch., 1987-89, NIH, 1988-91, Iowa Dept. Human Svcs., 1986-89, U. Iowa, 1979-87, United Cerebral Palsy Rsch. and Endl. Found., Inc., 1978-87, Iowa March of Dimes, 1980, Sugar Assn., Inc., 1983, Internat. Life Scis. Inst., 1988-91, W.T. Grant Found., 1989; MCH Lend grant, 1999—, CDC grant, 2002; named to Children and Adults with Attention-Deficit/Hyperactivity Disorder Hall of Fame, 2003. Fellow Am. Acad. Pediat. (com. 1992-2000, chair com. on psychosocial aspects of child and family health 1997-2000, chair child & adolescent health action group 2000-), Am. Acad. Cerebral Palsy and Devel. Medicine; mem. Soc. for Devel. and Behavioral Pediat. (pres. 1994-95, program dir. 1990-93), Soc. Pediatric Psychology Assn. (assoc., Lee Salk award for disting. svc.), Soc. for Pediatric Rsch. (sr.), Am. Acad. Physician and Patient (charter), Am. Pediatric Soc. Office: Okla U Health Scis Ctr 1100 NE 13th St Oklahoma City OK 73117

WOLSIFFER, PATRICIA RAE, retired insurance company executive; b. Indpls., Aug. 15, 1933; d. Charles L. and Dorothy M. (Smith) Bohlsen; m. Edward C. Wolsiffer, Oct. 5, 1956; children: John M., Anderson, Sherry L. Anderson Cooney, Edward J. Wolsiffer. Student, Ind. Central U., 1974-75. Various secretarial positions, 1964-71; with Blue Cross/Blue Shield Ind. (Associated Ins. Cos., Inc.), Indpls., 1971-88, supr. personnel, 1973-76, exec. asst. to pres., 1976-79, corp. sec., 1979-85, exec. asst. to chmn. bd., chief exec. officer, 1985-88; ret. Vol. Hancock Meml. Hosp. Guild. Mem.: Daus. of the Nile, Order Eastern Star. Republican.

WOLSKI, L.G. heavy manufacturing executive; CFO Heico Cos., St. Charles, Ill. Office: Heico Companies 2075 Foxfield Saint Charles IL 60174 Office Fax: (630) 443-4696.

WOLSON, CRAIG ALAN, lawyer; b. Toledo, Feb. 20, 1949; s. Max A. and Elaine B. (Cohn) W.; m. Ellen Carol Schulgasser, Oct. 26, 1986; children: Lindsey, Michael and Geoffrey (triplets). BA, U. Mich., 1971, JD, 1974. Bar: N.Y. 1975, U.S. Dist. Ct. (so. and ea. dists.) N.Y. 1975, U.S. Ct. Appeals (2d cir.) 1975, U.S. Supreme Ct. 1978. Assoc. Shearman & Sterling, N.Y.C., 1974—81; v.p., asst. gen. counsel Thomson McKinnon Securities Inc., N.Y.C., 1981—85; v.p., sec., gen. counsel J.D. Mattus Co., Inc., Greenwich, Conn., 1985—88; also bd. dirs. J.D. Mattus Co., Inc. and affiliated cos., Greenwich, Conn.; v.p., asst. gen. counsel Chem. Bank, N.Y.C., 1988—95; of counsel Williams & Harris, N.Y.C., 1995-96; ptnr. Williams & Harris LLP, N.Y.C., 1996-97; counsel Brown & Wood L.L.P., N.Y.C., 1997-98, Mayer, Brown & Platt, N.Y.C., 1999-2001; spl. counsel Schulte Roth & Zabel LLP, N.Y.C., 2001—03; ptnr. Duane Morris, LLP, N.Y.C., 2003—. Dep. clk. Lucas County Courthouse, Toledo, 1968-69, 71-72. Articles and adminstrv. editor U. Mich. Law Rev., 1973-74. Mem.: ABA, Assn. of Bar of City of N.Y. (securities regulation com. 1994—97, corp. law com. 1997—2000, project fin. com. 2000—03, corp. law com. 2003—), N.Y. State Bar Assn., Pi Sigma Alpha, Phi Eta Sigma, Phi Beta Kappa. Avocations: reading, playing piano, fine dining, theater. Home: 29 Punch Bowl Dr Westport CT 06880-2130 Office: Duane Morris LLP 380 Lexington Ave New York NY 10168 Office Phone: 212-692-1081. Business E-Mail: cawolson@duanemorris.com.

WOLSTEIN, SCOTT ALAN, real estate company executive; b. Cleve., June 24, 1952; s. Bert L. and Iris (Shur) W. BS in Econs. cum laude, U. Pa., 1974; JD, U. Mich. cum laude, 1977. Assoc. Thompson, Hine & Flory, Cleve., 1977-81; co-owner, exec. v.p. Cleve. Force Soccer Team, 1979—; officer Sasson of Israel, Cleve., 1980—, also bd. dirs.; gen. ptnr. Diversified Equities, Moreland Hills, Ohio, 1981—; v.p. DE Properties Corp., Moreland Hills, 1982—, DE Transp. Co., Moreland Hills, 1983—. Participant Leadership Cleve., 1983-84; bd. trustees Men's ORT, United Cerebral Palsy, Anti-Defamation League; bd. overseers Case Western Reserve U. Athletic Dept.; alumni steering com. Leadership Cleve. Mem. ABA, Ohio Bar Assn., Cleve. Bar Assn., Maj. Indoor Soccer League (competition com., chmn. referee com. 1986—). Clubs: Wharton, U. Mich. (Cleve.). Jewish. Avocations: skiing, running, tennis, golf, bicycling. Home: 32200 Chestnut Ln Cleveland OH 44124-4328 Office: Devels Diversified Realty Corp 3300 Enterprise Pkwy Beachwood OH 44122

WOLTER, JOHN AMADEUS, librarian, government official; b. St. Paul, July 25, 1925; s. Amadeus Frank and Marjorie (Wears) W.; m. Joan Patricia Venard, July 6, 1956; children: Mark, Thomas, Matthew, David. Student, Coll. of St. Thomas, 1950; BA, U. Minn., 1956, MA, 1965, PhD, 1975; postgrad., Georgetown U., 1957. Officer, seaman Isthmian Lines Inc., N.Y.C., 1943-50, 57-60; marine transp. officer Mil. Sea Transp. Ser., Washington, 1956-57; instr., map libr. U. Minn., 1961-64, asst. to dir. univ. librs., 1964-65, research fellow, 1965-66; asst. prof. Wis. State U., River Falls, 1966-68; asst. chief geography and map. div. Libr. of Congress, Washington, 1968-78, chief, 1978-91, acting dir. pub. svc. and collections MGMT I, 1989-90; cons. in geography, 1991-93. Mem. U.S. Bd. Geog. Names, 1969-83, vice chmn., 1980-81, chmn., 1981-83. Editor: Progress of Discovery: Johann Georg Kohl, 1993, Images of the World: The Atlas Through History, 1996, The Napoleonic War in the Dutch East Indies. The Minto Collection: Essay and Bibliography, 1999; rev. editor cartography divsn. Surveying and Mapping, 1971-72; mem. editl. bd. Cartographica, 1971-80, Am. Cartographer, 1974-79, Terrae Incognitae, 1973-75, ACSM Bull., 1974-80, Surveying and Mapping, 1972-80; editl. advisor The Portolan, 1986—; contbg. editor Imago Mundi, 1979-91; contbr. articles to profl. jours. Served with U.S. Army, 1950-52. Libr. of Congress Disting. Svc. award, 1992, Smithsonian Inst. Cert. of award, 1986. Mem. Internat. Geog. Union (U.S. nat. com. 1972-80, 84-88), Internat. Cartographic Assn. (U.S. mem. commn. on history of cartography 1972-76, corr. 1976-92, Assn. Am. Geographers (editorial bd. Annals 1988-92), Spl. Librs. Assn. (sec.-treas. geog.and map div. 1965), Soc. History Discoveries (sec.-treas. 1972-75, coun. 1976-78, v.p. 1983-85, pres. 1985-87), Am. Congress Surveying and Mapping (chmn. publs. com. 1978-80, Presdl. citation 1985), N.Am. Soc. Oceanic History, N.Mex. Geog. Soc. (bd. dirs., governing bd.), Soc. for History of Discoveries, Washington Map Soc., Soc. Nautical Rsch., Ariz. Hist. Soc., U.S. Naval Hist. Found., Philip Lee Phillips Soc. (bd. dirs. ex officio), Soc. Southwestern Authors, DAV, Am. Legion, Am. Mcht. Marine Vets., Theta Delta Chi. Home: 712 Canvasback Court Salisbury MD 21804 E-mail: jaw54jo@earthlink.net.

WOLTERS, RAYMOND, historian, educator; b. Kansas City, Mo., July 25, 1938; s. Raymond M. and Margaret G. (Reilly) W.; m. Mary McCullough, June 23, 1962; children: Jeffrey, Kevin, Thomas. BA, Stanford U., 1960; MA, U. Calif.-Berkeley, 1962, PhD, 1967. Instr. dept. history U. Del., Newark,

1965-67, asst. prof., 1967-70, assoc. prof., 1970-75, prof., 1975-96, Thomas Muncy Keith prof., 1996—. Mem. editl. adv. bd. Acad. Am. Ency.; author: The New Negro on Campus, 1975, The Burden of Brown, 1984, Right Turn, 1996, Du Bois and His Rivals, 2002. Fellow NEH, 1971-72, Am. Coun. Learned Socs., 1978-79, Earhart Found., 1989-90; recipient Silver Gavel award ABA. Mem. Am. Hist. Assn., Orgn. Am. Historians, So. Hist. Assn. Home: 20 Bridlebrook Ln Newark DE 19711-2061 Office: U Del History Dept Newark DE 19716 Office Phone: 302-831-2378.

WOLTIL, ROBERT D. healthcare management company executive; BS in Acctg. and Finance, U. South Fla. CPA, Fla. Various positions including pres., CEO pharmacy subs. Beverly Enterprises Inc., then CFO; CFO, sr. v.p. fin. svcs. Sun Healthcare Group Inc., Albuquerque, 1996—. Office: Sun Healthcare Group Inc 101 Sun Ave NE Albuquerque NM 87109-4373

WOLTZ, HOWARD OSLER, JR., steel and wire products company executive; b. Mt. Airy, N.C., Apr. 2, 1925; s. Howard Osler and Louise (Elliott) W.; m. Joan Elizabeth Moore, Dec. 29, 1949; children: Louise, Joan Woltz Robins, Howard O. III, Edwin Moore. LLB, U. Va., 1948. Bar: N.C., 1948. Ptnr. law firm, Mt. Airy, 1948-54; pres., founder Dixie Concrete Products, Inc., Mt. Airy, 1953-69; founder Dixie Exposaic, Inc., Mt. Airy, 1963; pres., chmn. bd. Insteel Industries (formerly Exposaic Industries, Inc.), Mt. Airy, 1969-89, chmn., CEO, 1989-91. Mem. N.C. Ho. of Reps., 1951-53; chmn. Mt. Airy-Surry County Airport Authority, 1987-93; former pres. Greater Mt. Airy United Fund. Mem. Nat. Concrete Masonry Assn. (pres. 1965), N.C. Concrete Masonry Assn. (pres. 1959), Wire Reinforcement Inst. (chmn. 1982), Am. Wire Producers Assn. (bd. dirs. 1987-91), N.C. State Bar Assn., Mt. Airy C. of C. (Citizen of Yr. 1991). Rotary (past pres. Mt. Airy). Republican. Home: 243 Old Green Hill Rd Mount Airy NC 27030-9240 Office: Insteel Industries Inc 1373 Boggs Dr Mount Airy NC 27030-2145 Office Phone: 336-786-2141 ext 3005. E-mail: howardwoltz@insteel.com.

WOLVERTON, THOMAS FRANK, automotive company supervisor; b. Saginaw, Mich., Dec. 26, 1954; s. Francis Edward and Donna Muriel Wolverton; m. Holly Louise Muller, Dec. 20, 1978 (div. May 1980); 1 child, Brian Thomas; m. Trudy Reneé Surprenant, Oct. 26, 1985; 1 adopted child, Renee Lynn. Cert. Trident submarine test dir., Gen. Dynamics. With USN, 1974-83, missile technician, 1974-80, lead instr., 1980-83; submarine test technician Gen. Dynamics, Groton, 1984, engrng. asst., 1985, program coord., 1986, test dir., 1987-94; skilled trades supr. Kelly Svcs./GM, Flint, Mich., 1995—. V.p. Electric Boat Mgmt. Assn., Groton, 1992-94; vol. Big Bros Am., Norwich, Conn., 1981-83. Mem. Am. Legion. Avocations: stamps, fishing, softball. Home: 9600 East Rd Burt MI 48417

WOLYNES, PETER GUY, chemistry researcher, educator; b. Chgo., Apr. 21, 1953; s. Peter and Evelyn Eleanor (Etter) W.; m. Jane Lee Fox, Nov. 26, 1976 (div. 1980); m. Kathleen Cull Bucher, Dec. 22, 1984; children: Margrethe Cull, Eve Cordelia, Julia Jean. AB with highest distinction, Ind. U., 1971; AM, Harvard U., 1972, PhD in Chem. Physics, 1976; DSc (hon.), Ind. U., 1988. Rsch. assoc. MIT, Cambridge, 1975-76; asst. prof., assoc. prof. Harvard U., Cambridge, 1976-80; vis. scientist Max Planck Inst. für Biophysikalische Chemie, Gottingen, Fed. Republic Germany, 1977; assoc. prof. chemistry U. Ill., Urbana, 1980-83, prof. chemistry, 1983-2000, prof. physics, 1985-2000, prof. physics and biophysics, 1989-2000, mem. Ctr. for Advanced Study, 1989-2000; William H. and Janet LyCan prof. chemistry Ctr. for Advanced Study U. Ill., Urbana, 1993-96, Robert Eiszner prof., 1996-2000; prof. chemistry and biochemistry U. Calif., San Diego, 2000—, Francis H.C. Crick prof., 2001—, prof. physcis, 2003—. Vis. prof. Inst. for Molecular Sci., Okazaki, Japan, 1982, 87; vis. scientist Inst. for Theoretical Physics, Santa Barbara, Calif., 1987, Ecole normale Supérieure, Paris, 1992; Merski lectr. U. Nebr., 1986; Denkewalter lectr. Loyola U., 1986; Hinshelwood lectr. Oxford U., 1997; Harkins lectr. U. Chgo., 1997; FMC lectr. Princeton U., 1998; Matsen lectr. U. Tex., 2002. Contbr. numerous articles to profl. jours. Sloan fellow, 1981-83, J.S. Guggenheim fellow, 1986-87; Beckman assoc. Ctr. for Advanced Study, Urbana, 1984-85; Fogarty scholar NIH, 1994-98. Fellow AAAS, Am. Phys. Soc. (Biol. Physics prize 2004), Am. Acad. Arts and Scis., The Biophys. Soc.; mem. NAS, Am. Chem. Soc. (Pure Chemistry award 1986, Peter Debye award 2000), N.Y. Acad. Scis., Phi Beta Kappa, Sigma Xi, Phi Lambda Upsilon (Fresenius award 1988), Sigma Pi Sigma, Alpha Chi Sigma. Home: 12737 Sandy Crest Ct San Diego CA 92130-2795 Office: U Calif San Diego Dept Chem and Biochemistry 9500 Gilman Dr MC 0371 La Jolla CA 92093-0371 Office Phone: 858-822-4825. Business E-Mail: pwolynes@ucsd.edu.

WOLYNIES, EVELYN See GRADO-WOLYNIES, EVELYN

WOMACK, DAVID ANDREW (ANDY WOMACK), insurance agent, state legislator; m. Cheryle Womack; children: David, Dana. Student, U. Tenn., 1963-66; BS in Psychology, Middle Tenn. State U., 1970. With State Farm Mgmt. Fire Co., 1970; agt. N.Y. Life Ins. Co., 1972, asst. mgr., 1974; agt. State Farm Ins. Co., 1981—; mem. Tenn. Senate 96th-101st Gen. Assemblies; chmn. senate edn. com., vice-chmn. edn. oversight com. Tenn. Senate 96th-100th Gen. Assemblies, mem. senate state and local govt. coms., mem. senate transp. com., mem. senate ethics com., others. Active First Bapt. Ch., Murfreesboro, Tenn.; mem. Middle Tenn. Nat. Alumni Assn., 1982-86, Blue Raider Club, 1983-86; chair ins. Middle Tenn. State U., 1986-90, exec. com. bd. trustees, 1994-96, found. pres., 1996-97; adv. for K-12 schs. Tenn. Orgn. Sch. Supts., 1995; active Friends of Edn., Murfreesboro Edn. Assn., 2000—. Recipient Disting. Alumni award Middle Tenn. State U., 1993, Philander P. Claxton award Am. Assn. U. Profs., 1994, award Tenn. Assn. for Adult and Continuing Edn., 1994, Outstanding Leadership award Tenn. Tech. Ctr., Shelbyville, 2000, William Baird Leadership award Tenn. Ind. Colls. and Univs., 2000; named Outstanding Legislator of Yr., Cmty. Mental Retardation Agys. Tenn., 1991, Supporter of Pub. Edn., Tenn. Sch. Bd. Assn., 1993, Legislator of Yr., County Ofcls. Assn. Tenn., 1994. Mem. Middle Tenn. Assn. Life Underwriters (past pres.), Murfreesboro Optimist Club (past pres.), Retail Devel. for C. of C. (past pres.), Phi Kappa Phi. Democrat. Office: 9A Legislative Plaza Nashville TN 37243-0216 also: 1535 W Northfield Blvd Ste 5 Murfreesboro TN 37129-1474 E-mail: sen.andy.womack@legislature.state.tn.us.

WOMACK, EDGAR ALLEN, JR., energy executive, consultant, nuclear technology consultant; b. Humboldt, Tenn., Oct. 29, 1942; s. Edgar Allen Sr. and Lucy Opal (George) W.; m. Linda Jane Cochran, Dec. 28, 1963; children: Connie Britton, Cynthia Womack. BS, MIT, 1963, MS, 1965, PhD, 1969. With U.S. Atomic Energy Commn., Washington, 1968-73, Babcock and Wilcox Co., 1975-85, v.p. sales and mktg., 1983-85; v.p. R&D, chief tech. officer McDermott Internat., 1985—98; pres., COO BWX Techs., 1998—2002; prin. Cyncon LLC, 2003—. Mem. bd. Naval Submarine League. Patentee in field. Served to lt. USNR, 1968-70. Hon. Woodrow Wilson Found. fellow. Fellow ASME (ind. adv. bd. 1988—, chmn. 1997), AAAS, Indsl. Research Inst. (bd. 1989-96, pres. 1994-95), Sigma Xi. Presbyterian. Avocations: photography, diving, golf. Home: 401 Saint Andrews Cir Lynchburg VA 24503-3750 E-mail: cyncon@adelphia.net.

WOMACK, JAMES ERROL, college president; b. Eugene, Oreg., June 27, 1940; s. John Leon and Dorothy Laverne (Yarbrough) W.; m. Sharron Kay McCullough, June 8, 1963; children: Timothy, Stephen, Joseph, Marilee. BS, N.W. Christian Coll., 1963; M Teaching, Cen. Okla. State U., 1968; postgrad., Pacific Luth. U., 1958-60, U. Oreg., 1960-63, Phillips U., 1966-68, DHum (hon.), 1987. Cert. tchr., Okla., Calif.; cert. fund raising exec.; ordained to ministry Christian Ch. (Disciples of Christ), 1963. Youth min. Lowell (Oreg.) Christian Ch., 1962-63, First Christian Ch., The Dalles, Oreg., 1963-65; youth and edn. min. Putnam City Christian Ch., Oklahoma City, 1965-68; tchr. English and social studies, coach basketball Patterson (Calif.) High Sch., 1968-71; min. youth and edn. Maze Blvd. Christian Ch., Modesto, Calif., 1968-71; dir. devel. Nat. Benevolent Assn. (Colo. Christian Home), Denver, 1976-86; coord. campus activities, coach basketball N.W. Christian Coll., Eugene, 1971-73, dir. planned giving, 1973-76, pres., 1986—. Cons. Luth. Social Svcs. Colo., Denver, 1984-85, Dayton, Ohio, 1986-89, Florence Crittenton Home Svcs., Little Rock, 1985-98; presenter in field. Mem. devel. coun. Woodhaven Learning Ctr.; mem. fin. com. and nurture commn. Cen. Rocky Mountain Region Christian Ch.; chmn. N.W. Oklahoma City Youth Week Activities; trustee N.W. Christian Coll.; active Denver Planned Giving Roundtable; regional bd. dirs. N.W. Regional Ch., Christian Ch. in Kans. Recipient Book Award for Acad. Excellence Christian Bd. of Pub. Mem. Nat. Soc. Fund Raising Execs., Nat. Benevolent Assn. (trustee best of caring fund), Oreg. Ind. Coll. Assn. (mem. exec. com.), Colo. Assn. Fund Raisers (past sec., bd. dirs.), Emerald Empire Fellowship of Christian Athletes (charter mem., sec., bd. dirs.), Ministerial Alliance (chmn. migrant ministries), Rotary (mem. program com. Eugene chpt. 1990), Optimists (bd. dirs. Highland Park chpt.), Civitan, Denver City Club. Avocations: fishing, reading, sports. Home: 1363 Windsor Ct Springfield OR 97477-8107 Office: NW Christian Coll 828 E 11th Ave Eugene OR 97401-3745 E-mail: pres@nwcc.edu.

WOMACK, JOHN W. pharmacist; b. St. Louis, Dec. 6, 1930; s. John Anderson and Della Long Womack; children: Peter Frank, Elin Vera, Brian William, John Anderson, Kimberly Ann. BS in pharmacy, U. Toledo, 1957. Registered Pharmacist Ohio. Chief pharmacist Cunningham Drug Co., Cleve., 1958—73, U. Pharmacy, Cleve., 1973—76, Revco Drug, Cleve., 1976—85, Neon, Cleve., 1985—. Mem. football camp Camp Stonem, Calif., 1953; mem. football team, 1954, AAU Basketball, Cleve., 1959; bd of trustees Free Clinic Greater Cleve., 1968—99; worker Carl Stokes Election, Cleve., 1968. Cpl. U.S. Army, 1952—54, Korea. Mem.: Nat. Pharm. Assn., Ohio State Pharm. Assn., Omega Psi Phi. Episcopal. Avocations: basketball, football. Home: 17707 Fed Rd Cleveland OH 44128

WOMACK, JOSEPH DARRYL, academic administrator; b. Oklahoma City, Okla., May 22, 1968; m. Ruby Kristine Rhee, Dec. 27, 1992; children: James Rhee, Benjamin Joseph. BSc, Tex. Christian U., 1987—91; M in edn., Azusa Pacific U., 1995—98. Admissions counselor NW Christian Coll., Eugene, Oreg., 1991—92; asst. dir. of admissions Calif. Bapt. U., 1992—94, dir. of student leadership & activities, 1994—97; dean of students San Jose Christian Coll., 1997—2000; vp for advancement William Jessup U., Rocklin, Calif., 2000—. Mem.: Coun. for Support and Advancement of Edn., Nat. Assn. of Student Pers. Advisors, Assn. of Christians in Student Devel. Office: William Jessup University 333 Sunset Blvd Rocklin CA 95648 E-mail: jwomack@jessup.edu.

WOMACK, MARY PAULINE, lawyer; b. Chattanooga, Tenn., Dec. 3, 1942; d. Lucille (Thomas) W. BS, U. Chattanooga, 1964; JD, Woodrow Wilson Coll. Law, 1984. Bar: Ga. 1988, U.S. Dist. Ct. (no. dist.) Ga. 1988. Pvt. practice, Atlanta, 1988—. DeKalb County Dems., 6th dist., regional com. State of Ga. Mem. Ga. Bar Assn., Sigma Delta Kappa (past regional v.p.). Office: 100 Peachtree St NW Ste 1950 Atlanta GA 30303-1919 Home: 10170 Big Canoe Jasper GA 30143-5118

WOMACK, STEVEN JAMES, education educator, writer; b. Nashville, Tenn., July 31, 1952; s. Harry Emmett Womack and Katherine Virginia Fudge; m. Lisa Alana Berry, Mar. 25, 2000; children: Carrie Isabel, Ava Denton. BA, Tulane U., New Orleans, 1970—74; MFA, LI U., Southampton, NY, 2000—03. Prof. Watkins Coll. of Art & Design/Watkins Film Sch., Nashville, Tenn., 1995—. Contbr. nonfiction book; author: (novel) The Software Bomb; contbr. textbook; author: (novel) Dead Folks' Blues (Edgar Allan Poe Award, 1994), Smash Cut, Murphy's Fault (NY Times Notable Book, 1990); screenwriter (movie) Volcano: Fire On The Mountain, Proudheart;, author short story in a book-length anthology A Confederacy of Crime, (novel) Dirty Money (Shamus Award Nominee, 2001), (short story in a book-length anthology Canine Crimes) Like Alpo For Chocolate, (novel) Murder Manual (Shamus Award, 1999); contbr. book excerpt; author: (novel) Chain of Fools (Shamus & Anthony Award Nominees, 1997), Way Past Dead (Shamus Award Nominee, 1996), Torch Town Boogie (Shamus Award Nominee, 1994). Mem.: PEN Am. Ctr., Associated Writing Programs, AAUP, Writers Guild of Am., East, Novelists Inc., MENSA. Office: Watkins College of Art & Design 2298 Metrocenter Boulevard Nashville TN 37228 Office Phone: 615-383-4848. Personal E-mail: dfblooz@bellsouth.net. E-mail: swomack@watkins.edu.

WOMACK, THOMAS HOUSTON, manufacturing executive; b. Gallatin, Tenn., June 22, 1940; s. Thomas Houston and Jessie (Eckel) W.; Linda Walker Womack, July 20, 1963 (div. Dec. 1989); children: Britton Ryan, Kelley Elizabeth; m. Pamela Ann Reed, Apr. 20, 1991. BSME, Tenn. Tech. U., Cookeville, 1963. Project engr. U.S. Gypsum Co., Jacksonville, Fla., 1963-65; project mgr. Maxwell House Divsn. Gen. Foods Corp., Jacksonville, 1965-68, mfg. mgr. Hoboken, NJ, 1968-71, divsn. ops. planning mgr., 1971-73; industry sales mgr. J.R. Schneider Co., Tiburon, Calif., 1973-79; pres., CEO Womack Internat., Inc., Mare Island, Calif., 1979—; chmn., CEO Ceramic Microlight Techs., Inc., Mare Island, 1995—; pres., CEO WestAmerica Engrng. and Mfg. Co., 1997—. Holder 5 U.S. patents. Mem. Soc. Tribologists and Lubrication Engrs., Am. Filtration Soc., Soc. Mfg. Engrs., Am. Soc. Chem. Engrs. Avocations: skiing, vintage exotic sports cars. Office: Womack Internat Inc PO Box 2175 Vallejo CA 94592-0175 Office Phone: 707-562-1000. Office Fax: 707-562-1010. Business E-Mail: womack@womack.com.

WOMBLE, WILLIAM FLETCHER, lawyer; b. Winston-Salem, N.C., Oct. 29, 1916; s. Bunyan Snipes and Edith (Willingham) Womble; m. Jane Payne Gilbert, Oct. 11, 1941; children: William Fletcher, Jr., Jane Womble Haver, Russell G., Ann Womble Strader. AB, Duke U., 1937, JD, 1939. Bar: N.C. 1939. Assoc. Womble Carlyle Sandridge & Rice P.L.L.C. and predecessors, Winston-Salem, 1939-47, mem., 1947—. Campaign chmn. Forsyth County Cmty. Chest, 1949; mem. N.C. Gen. Statutes Commn., 1953—55, N.C. Bd. Higher Edn., 1955—57, 1960—63, N.C. Adv. Budget Commn., 1957—58; life trustee, past chmn. High Point U.; trustee Winston-Salem State U., 1953—55; past trustee, past pres. Children's Home; bd. dirs. Triad United Meth. Home (now Arbor Acres United Meth. Retirement Cmty.), 1976—87; treas. Triad United Meth. Home, 1975—79, pres., 1979—85; hon. chair United Way, Forsyth County, 1998; mem. People-to-People Citizen Amb. Program, 1981, 1986, N.C. Ho. of Reps., 1953—58, chmn. com. higher edn., vice chmn. fin. com., 1957; chmn. adminstrv. bd. Centenary United Meth. Ch., 1961—63, chmn. bd. trustees, 1983—85; trustee Sr. Svcs., Inc., 1998—. Served to maj. USAF, 1941—46. Named Trustee of the Yr., Gen. Bd. Global Mins. of United Meth. Ch., Health and Wlfare Minst. Dept., 1989. Fellow: Am. Bar Found. (life; state chmn. 1984—89, Fifty Yr. award 1995); mem.: ABA (ho. dels. 1978—87, bd. govs. 1982—85, exec. coun. Nat. Conf. Bar Pres. 1985—88, ethics com. 1985—91, resource devel. coun. 1986—92, chmn. jud. code subcom. 1988—91, chair affiliate outreach com. 1994—97, coun. mem. sr. lawyers divsn. 1995—97), Forsyth County Bar Assn. (pres. 1962), Am. Judicature Soc., N.C. State Bar (trustee Interest on Lawyers Trust Accounts 1983—91, vice chmn. 1989—91, Chief Justice's Professionalism award 2001), N.C. Bar Assn. (pres. 1966—67, chmn. endowment founders campaign 1986—87, chair sr. lawyers divsn. 1994—95, Judge John J. Parker award 1984), Soc. Cin., Winston-Salem C. of C. (pres. 1960—61), Twin City Club, Old Town Club, Rotary (local pres. 1964). Democrat. Home: 1244 Arbor Rd 441 Winston Salem NC 27104-1139 Office: Womble Carlyle Sandridge & Rice One W 4th St Winston Salem NC 27101 Fax: (336) 733-8369. Office Phone: 336-721-3603. E-mail: wwomble@wcsr.com.

WOMER, CHARLES BERRY, retired hospital executive, management consultant; b. Cleve., Mar. 30, 1926; s. Porter Blake and Margaret (Berry) W.; m. Elizabeth Benson, Oct. 7, 1950; children: Richard B., Carol E., John C. MS in Hosp. Adminstrn., Columbia U., 1953; BS in Mech. Engring., Case Inst. Tech., 1949. Asst. dir. Univ. Hosps., Cleve., 1957-61, assoc. dir., 1961-65, pres., 1976-82; mgmt. cons., 1982-90; ret., 1990. Adminstr. Yale-New Haven Hosp., 1965-67, dir., 1968-76, pres., 1976; lectr. Yale U., 1965-78, 87-91; adj. asst. prof. Case Western Res. U., 1976-83; mem. Conn. Commn. on Hosps. and Health Care, 1973-76; bd. dirs. New Haven Savings Bank, 1969-76. Bd. govs. U. New Haven, 1972-76. Served with AUS, 1944-46. Fellow Am. Coll. Healthcare Execs. (life); mem. Am. Hosp. Assn. (chmn. coun. on mgmt. and planning 1977-79), Conn. Hosp. Assn. (trustee 1970-74, pres. 1972-73, Disting. Svc. award 1976), Assn. Am. Med. Colls. (exec. coun. 1974-77, 78-80, treas. 1975-76, chmn. 1979-80, adminstrv. bd. coun. tchg. hosps. 1972-77, chmn. 1975-76, Disting. Svc. Mem. 1982—). Home: 88 Notch Hill Rd Apt 382 North Branford CT 06471-1861

WON, DELMOND JACK HING, commissioner; b. Honolulu, Nov. 18, 1953; BS in Engring., U. Hawaii, 1975, MBA, 1977. Various positions, including dir. planning affairs Hawaiian Tug & Barge Corp. & Young Bros., Ltd., 1977-90; v.p. Hawaii Pacific Industries, Oahu, Hawaii, 1990-93; cons., 1993-94; commr. Fed. Maritime Commn., Washington, 1994—. Office: Fed Maritime Commn 800 N Capitol St NW Washington DC 20573-0001 E-mail: delmondw@fmc.gov.

WONDER, STEVIE (STEVLAND MORRIS), singer, musician, composer; b. Saginaw, Mich., May 13, 1950; m. Syreeta Wright, 1971 (div. 1972); children: Aisha, Keita, Mumtaz. Student pub. schs. in Detroit until age 12; then transferred to, Mich. Sch. for Blind. Singer (solo): Whitestone Bapt. Ch., 1959; rec. artist Motown Records, Detroit, 1963—70, founder, pres. music pub. co. Black Bull Music, Inc., 1970—, Wondirection Records, Inc., 1982—, rec. Fingertips, 1963, Uptight/Purple Raindrops, 1965, Someday At Christmas/The Miracles of Christmas, I'm Wondering/Everytime I See You I Go Wild, 1966, I Was Made To Love Her/Hold Me, 1967, Shoo-Be-Doo-Be-Doo-Da-Day/Why Don't You Lead Me To Love, You Met Your Match/My Girl, 1968, For Once In My Life, I Don't Know Why, My Cherie Amour, Yester-Me, Yester-You, Yesterday, Never Had a Dream Come True, Signed, Sealed, Delivered I'm Yours, Heaven Help Us All, I Wish (Grammy award, 1977), Don't You Worry 'Bout a Thing, You Haven't Done Nothin', Boogie on Reggae Woman (Grammy award, 1975), Isn't She Lovely, Sir Duke, Another Star, As, You Are the Sunshine of My Life (Grammy award, 1974), Superstition (Grammy award, 1974), Higher Ground, Living For the City (Grammy award 1975, 1975), albums Little Stevie Wonder: The Twelve-Year Old Genius, Tribute to Uncle Ray, Jazz Soul of Little Steve, 1963, At The Beach, 1965, Uptight, Down To Earth, 1966, I Was Made To Love Her, Someday At Christmas, 1967, Stevie Wonder's Greatest Hits, 1968, For Once in My Life, 1969, My Cheric Amour, Talk of The Town, 1970, Music of My Mind, Stevie Wonder Live, Where I'm Coming From, Talking Book, 1972, Portrait, 1976, Innervisions, 1973 (Grammy award, 1974), Fulfillingness' First Finale (Grammy award, 1975), Songs In the Key of Life, 1976 (Grammy award, 1977), Journey Through the Secret Life of Plants, 1979, Hotter than July, 1980, I Just Called to say I Love You, 1984 (Acad. award, Golden Globe award for single, 1984), In Square Circle, 1986 (best soul/R&B album of yr., Down Beat mag. Readers' poll, 1986), Characters, 1987, Jungle Fever, 1991, Inner Peace, Motown Legends, 1995, albums(with others) Natural Wonders, 1995, Conversation Peace, 1996, numerous others, appeared in (films) Bikini Beach, Muscle Beach Party, 1964, frequent appearances (TV series) Mike Douglas Show, guest host Saturday Night Live. Named Musician of Year, Down Beat mag. Rock/Blues Poll, 1973—75, 1977—78; named to Rock and Roll Hall of Fame, 1989, Songwriters Hall of Fame, 1982; recipient Nelson Mandela Courage award, 1991, Best Selling Male Soul Artist of Year, Nat. Assn. Rec. Merchandisers, 1974, numerous Grammy awards, numerous awards for best singer/songwriter, Rock Music award, 1977, Am. Music award, 1978, Am. Video award for best rhythm and blues video for Ebony and Ivory, 1982. Office: 4616 W Magnolia Blvd Burbank CA 91505-2731 also: Motown Records 1755 Broadway New York NY 10019-3743

WONDERS, WILLIAM CLARE, geography educator; b. Toronto, Apr. 22, 1924; s. George Clarence and Ann Mary (Bell) W.; m. Lillian Paradise Johnson, June 2, 1951; children: Karen Elizabeth, Jennifer Anne, Glen William. BA with honors, Victoria Coll., U. Toronto, 1946; MA, Syracuse U., 1948; PhD, U. Toronto, 1951; Fil. Dr. h.c., Uppsala U., 1981. Teaching asst. dept. geography Syracuse U., 1946-48; lectr. dept. geography U. Toronto, 1948-53; asst. prof. geography dept. polit. economy U. Alta., 1953-55, assoc. prof. geography, 1955-57, prof., head dept. geography, 1957-67, prof. dept. geography, 1967-87, Univ. prof., 1983—, prof. emeritus, 1987—. Vis. prof. geography U. B.C., 1954, U. Okla., 1965-66, St. Mary's U., 1977, U. Victoria, 1989, J.F. Kennedy Inst., Free U. Berlin, 1990; guest prof. Inst. Geography, Uppsala (Sweden) U., 1962-63; rsch. fellow in Geography U. Aberdeen, Scotland, 1970-71, 78; vis. fellow in Can. Studies, U. Edinburgh, Scotland, 1987. Author: Looking at Maps, 1960, The Sawdust Fusiliers, 1991, Norden and Canada-A Geographer's Perspective, 1992, Alaska Highway Explorer, 1994; (with T. Drinkwater et al) Atlas of Alberta, 1969, (with J.C. Muller et al) Junior Atlas of Alberta, 1979; contbr., editor: Canada's Changing North, 1971, revised edit., 2003, The North, 1972, The Arctic Circle, 1976, Knowing the North, 1988, Geographica, 1999, Geographica's Pocket World Reference, 2000, Frontiersmen & Settlers, 2002; contbr. articles to jours. and encys., chpts. to books. Active Nat. Adv. Com. on Geog. Rsch., 1965-69; chmn. Boreal Inst. No. Studies (Can. Circumpolar Inst.), 1960-62; mem. Can. Permanent Com. on Geog. Names, 1981-94, Alta. Hist. Sites Bd., 1978-83, vice-chmn., 1982-83; policy bd. Can. Plains Rsch. Centre, U. Regina (Sask.), 1975-86; adv. bd. Royal Tyrrell Mus. Paleontology, 1984-89; bd. dirs. Muttart Found., 1986-93, 95-98, v.p., 1991-93. Decorated Order of Can., Can. Forces Decoration; recipient Queen's Jubilee medal; NSF sr. fgn. scientist fellow, 1965-66; Can. Coun. leave fellow, 1969-70, 77-78; Nuffield Found. fellow, 1970-71. Fellow Arctic Inst. N.Am., Royal Soc. Can., Royal Can. Geog. Soc. (Massey medalist 1998); mem. Can. Assn. Geographers (past pres.), Can. Assn. Scottish Studies (councillor 1974-77), Scottish Soc. No. Studies, Champlain Soc. (councillor 1981-86), Sigma Xi, Gamma Theta Upsilon. E-mail: wwonders@shaw.ca.

WONG, B.D. actor; b. San Francisco, Oct. 24, 1962; s. William D. and Roberta Christine (Leong) W. Grad. high sch., San Francisco. Bd. dirs. Alliance of Resident Theatres, N.Y.C.; lectr. Royce Carlton Inc. Speakers, N.Y.C., 1991—. Appeared (Broadway play) M. Butterfly, 1988-90 (Tony award, N.Y. Drama Desk award, N.Y. Outer Critics Circle award, Theatre World award, Clarence Derwent award, 1988), (films) Family Business, 1990, The Freshman, 1990, Mystery Date, 1991, The Lounge People, 1991, Father of the Bride, 1991, The Lounge People, 1992, Jurassic Park, 1993, Men of War, 1994, The Ref, 1994, Father of the Bride II, 1995, Executive Decision, 1996, Stinkers, 1997, Seven Years in Tibet, 1997, Mulan, 1998, Slappy and the Stinkers, 1998, The Salton Sea, 2002; (TV movies) And the Band Played On, 1993, Judith Krantz's Dazzle, 1995, Dazzle, 1995, The Substitute 2: School's Out, 1998, (voice) Reflections on Ice: Michelle Kwan Skates to the Music of Disney's Mulan, 1998, Miss USA, 2004; (TV series) The X Files, 1996, Oz, 1997, Chicago Hope, 1999, Law & Order: Special Victims Unit, 2001—; TV guest appearances include (voice) Kim Possible, 2002. Recipient Arts in Leadership award, Coro Found., San Francisco, 1991, Jimmie award for Arts Advocacy, Assn. Asian- Pacific Am. Artists, L.A., 1991. Mem. SAG, AFTRA, Asian-Pacific Alliance for Creative Equality (co-founder 1990), Asian Am. Legal Def. and Edn. Fund (Justice in Action award, 1991), Actors' Equity Assn. Office: Innovative Artists Talent & Lit Agy 141 5th Ave 3d Fl New York NY 10010-7105*

WONG, BELLA TOY FUNND, lawyer; b. Boston, Feb. 5, 1961; d. Perry Wai Yee and Joan Hung (Lem) W.; m. Steven M. Brand, Sept. 18, 1993. BA, Harvard U., 1982, EdM, 1991; postgrad., Stanford U., 1982-84; JD, U. Calif., Davis, 1987. Bar: Calif. 1987, Mass., 1990; cert. gen. sci. and biology tchr., Mass. Assoc. LeBoeuf, Lamb, Leiby, MacRae, San Francisco, 1987-90; sci. instr. Lincoln Sudbury (Mass.) Regional H.S., 1991-98, head sci. dept., 1996-98; asst. supt. Wellesley (Mass.) Pub. Schs., 1998—. Mem. ABA, ASCD, Am. Assn. Sch. Personnel Officers, Calif. Bar Assn., Mass. Bar Assn., New Eng. Assn. Chemistry Tchrs., Mass. Assn. Sch. Supts., Mass. Assn. Sch. Personnel Officers. Office: Wellesley Pub Schs 40 Kingsbury St Wellesley MA 02481-4831

WONG, BERT YUAN SHU, internist, cardiologist; b. Shanghai, 1940; MD, Yale U., 1965. Diplomate in internal medicine and cardiovascular diseases Am. Bd. Internal Medicine. Intern Georgetown Hosp., Washington, 1965-66, resident in internal medicine, 1966-67; resident in cardiology VA Hosp., West Haven, Conn., 1969-70; resident in internal medicine Yale-New Haven Hosp., 1970-71, fellow in cardiology, 1971-73. Fellow ACP, Am. Coll. Cardiology, Am. Coll. Chest Physicians. Office: 625 N Cascade Ave Ste 120 Colorado Springs CO 80903

WONG, BRIAN JET-FEI, surgeon; b. L.A., Sept. 23, 1963; s. Richard Toy and Hazel F. (Lue) W. BS, U. So. Calif., 1985; postgrad., Oxford U., 1985-86; MD, Johns Hopkins U., 1990; PhD, U. Amsterdam, 2001. Resident U. Calif., Irvine, 1990-96, clin. instr., 1997-98, asst. prof., 1998—2001, assoc. prof., 2001—. Rsch. assoc. Beckman Laser Inst., Irvine, 1994—. Mem. ACS, Biomed. Optical Soc., SPIE, Am. Acad. Facial Plastic Surgery. Avocation: surfing. Office: U Calif Dept Otolaryngology 101 City Dr S # B25r81 Orange CA 92868-3201 Office Phone: 714-456-5753.

WONG, CARRIE, public relations executive; BS in Cellular & Molecular Biology, U. Wash. Ptnr. Niehaus Ryan Wong, South San Francisco. Avocation: bug collecting. Office: 601 Gateway Blvd Ste 900 South San Francisco CA 94080-7006

WONG, CHING-PING, chemist, materials scientist, engineer, educator; b. Canton, China, Mar. 29, 1947; came to U.S., 1966; s. Kwok-Keung and Yun-Kwan W. BS in Chemistry, Purdue U., 1969; PhD in Organic/Inorganic Chemistry, Pa. State U., 1975. Postdoctoral scholar Stanford (Calif.) U., 1975-77; mem. rsch. staff AT&T Bell Labs., Princeton, N.J., 1977-82, sr. mem. tech. staff, 1982-87, disting. mem. tech. staff, 1987-92; AT&T Bell Labs. fellow, 1992-96; Regents prof. Sch. of Materials Sci. and Engring., Ga. Inst. Tech., Atlanta, 1996—; assembly, reliability and thermal mgmt. rsch. dir. NSF Packaging Rsch. Ctr. Program chmn. 39th Electronic Components Conf., 1989; gen. chmn. 41st Electronic Components and Tech. Conf., 1991; bd. govs. IEEE-Components, Hybrids and Mfg. Tech. Soc., 1987-89, tech. v.p., 1990-91, pres., 1992-93. Author, editor: Polymers for Electronic and Photonic Applications, 1993; contbr. articles to profl. jours. Recipient Outstanding Papers and Contbns. award IEEE-Components, Hybrids and Mfg. Tech. Soc., 1990, 91, 94, 96, 1998, 2001, Ga. Tech. Outstanding Faculty award, London, 1999, award of excellence Univ. Press, 2000, Ga. Tech. Disting. Profl award, 2004, Fellow: Nat. Acad. Engring., IEEE (Outstanding Sustained Tech. Contbns. award 1995, Millenium medal 2000, EAB Exceptional Continuation Edn. award 2001, CPMT Outstanding Exceptional Tech.Contbn. award 2002). Achievements include over 40 U.S. and numerous internat. patents for integrated device passivation and encepsulation area; pioneer in application of gel polymers for device reliability without hermeticity, nano technology, a new application on electronic device packaging. Office: Ga Inst Tech Sch Materials Sci & Engring 771 Ferst Dr Atlanta GA 30332-0001 Business E-Mail: cp.wong@mse.gatech.edu.

WONG, DAVID YUE, academic administrator, physics educator; b. Swatow, China, Apr. 16, 1934; came to U.S., 1953; s. Fan and Wen (Tsang) W.; m. Katherine Young, Sept. 3, 1960 (div. Mar. 1988); children: Amy, Eric; m. Elizabeth Elkins, Mar. 26, 1988 BA, Hardin Simmons U., 1954; PhD, U. Md., 1957. Theoretical physicist Lawrence Radiation Lab., U. Calif., Berkeley, 1958-59; asst. prof. physics U. Calif., San Diego, 1960-63, assoc. prof., 1963-67, prof., 1967—, chair dept. physics, 1977-80, provost Warren Coll., 1985-94. Alfred P. Sloan fellow, 1966-68 Mem. Am. Inst. Physics.

WONG, EDWINA A. LEE, real estate broker; b. Honolulu, Feb. 12, 1947; d. Edwin M.S. and Grace K. (Aipa) Lee; m. Michael Kam Hoong Wong, Feb. 15, 1970; children: Michelle L.M.Y., David M.K. Cet., Stapleton Real Estate Sch., Honolulu. Lic. real estate broker, Hawaii. Real estate broker Fin. Realty, Honolulu, 1976-80, Pacific Real Estate Investments, Honolulu, 1982-89; owner, mgr., broker Edwina A.L. Wong, Honolulu, 1989—. Sec. Bishop Estate, Honolulu, 1985-86; extra Walt Disney Inc., Honolulu, 1989. Alt. Hawaii Dem. Conv., 1988, 90; pres. bd. dirs. Makakilo (Hawaii) Gardens Assn., 1989; mem. planning com. Friends of Mike Wong for Hawaii Ho. of Reps., 1990. Mem. Nat. Assn. Realtors, Honolulu Bd. Realtors. Avocations: swimming, tennis, golf, volleyball, hula dancing. Home: 92-344 Hookili Pl Kapolei HI 96707-2802

WONG, ELAINE DANG, foundation executive; b. Canton, China, June 3, 1936 (parents Am. citizens); d. Robert G. and Fung Heong (Woo) Dang; A.A. (Rotary scholar), Coalinga Coll., 1956; B.S. (AAUW scholar, Grad. Resident scholar), U. Calif., Berkeley, 1958, teaching credential, 1959; m. Philip Wong, Nov. 8, 1959; children— Elizabeth, Russell, Roger, Edith, Valerie. Tchr. acctg. San Mateo (Calif.) High Sch., 1959-60; acct., 1960-75; substitute tchr. Richmond County Schs., Augusta, Ga., 1975-77; comptroller Central Savannah River Area, United Way, Augusta, 1977-82; asst. controller Hammermill Hardwoods div. Hammermill Paper Co., Augusta, 1982-84; controller SFN Communications of Augusta, Inc. (WJBF-TV), 1984-85; acct. Med. Coll. Ga. Found., Inc., 1986-88, Nat. Sci Ctr. Found., Inc., 1988-89; cons. small bus.; pvt. tutor acctg. Mem. adv. bd. Richmond County Bd. Edn., 1985-87; bd. dirs. Cen. Savannah River chpt. Girl Scouts US, 1986-92. Panel judge Jr. Achievement Treas. award, 1980, 81; treas. Chinese Lang. Sch., 1973-75, Merry Neighborhood Sch., 1974-75. Recipient Achievement award Bank of Am., 1954. Mem. Nat. Assn. Accts. (dir. 1978-85, treas. 1982-84), Chinese Assn. Republican. Presbyterian.

WONG, JAMES BOK, economist, engineer, technologist; b. Canton, China, Dec. 9, 1922; came to U.S., 1938, naturalized, 1962; s. Gen Ham and Chen (Yee) W.; m. Wai Ping Lim, Aug. 3, 1946, (dec.); children: John, Jane Doris, Julia Ann; m. Betty K.C. Yeow, May 25, 2002. BS summa cum laude in Agr., U. Md., 1949, BS summa cum laude in Chem. Engring., 1950; MS, U. Ill., 1951, PhD, 1954. Rsch. asst. U. Ill., Champaign-Urbana, 1950-53; chem. engr. Std. Oil of Ind., Whiting, 1953-55; process design engr., rsch. engr. Shell Devel. Co., Emeryville, Calif., 1955-61; sr. planning engr., prin. planning engr. Chem. Plastics Group, Dart Industries, Inc. (formerly Rexall Drug & Chem. Co.), L.A., 1961-66, supr. planning and econs., 1966-67, mgr. long range planning and econs., 1967, chief economist, 1967-72, dir. econs. and ops. analysis, 1972-78, dir. internat. techs., 1978-81; pres. James B. Wong Assocs., L.A., 1981—. Chmn. bd. dirs. United Pacific Bank, 1988—; tech. cons. various corps. Author: Jade Eagle, 2000; contbr. articles to profl. jours. Bd. dirs., pres. Chinese Am. Citizens Alliance Found.; mem. Asian Am. Edn. Commn., 1971-81. Served with USAAF, 1943-46. Recipient L.A. Outstanding Vol. Svc. award, 1977. Mem. Am. Chem. Soc., VFW (vice comdr. 1959), Commodores (named to exec. order 1982), Sigma Xi, Tau Beta Pi, Phi Kappa Phi, Pi Mu Epsilon, Phi Lambda Upsilon, Phi Eta Sigma. Home: 2460 Venus Dr Los Angeles CA 90046-1646 *Personal philisophy: A man's reputation is his most prized possession.*

WONG, JEE K, education educator, music consultant; b. Batu Pahat, Malaysia, July 2, 1972;, US, 1991; s. Yin-Nam Wong and Lye-Hiok Lim. BSc, MusB piano performance musicology, MusM, U. Mont. Cert. Music Tchr. Nat. Assn. Edn. cons. Prosser Piano and Organ; grad. tchg. asst. U. Mont.; performing artist Yamaha Piano; dance accompanist U. Mont.; adjudicator Music Tchr. Nat. Asst. Home: 15410 SE 212d ST #86 Kent WA 98042 Office: 312 Whitworth Ave S Renton WA 98055

WONG, JOE BING, retired architect; b. Clifton, Ariz., Aug. 17, 1921; s. Hing Chong and Mock See Wong; m. Lillian Phyllis Jew, Dec. 19, 1942; children: Jeffrey(dec.), Judy Margaret. Student, U. Calif., Berkeley, 1938—41, Calif. Sch. Fine Arts, 1946—48. Registered arch., Calif., 1952, Ariz., 1954, Nev., 1963, Colo., 1968, Tex., 1990, Nat. Coun. Archtl. Registration, 1964. Ship conversion engr. Gen. Engring.-Drydock, San Francisco, 1941—42; designer, chief draftsman Higgins & Root Archs., San Jose, Calif., 1946—53, Nichols-White Archs., Palo Alto, Calif., 1945—46; arch., owner Wong Assocs., Scottsdale, Ariz., 1954—98; ret., 1998. Pres. Associated Scottsdale Archs., 1968—85. Active Scottsdale Libr. Bd., 1962—68; mem., chmn. Scottsdale Design Rev. Bd., 1968—71, Scottsdale Bldg. Adv. Bd., 1971—83, Scottsdale Adv. Bd. Appeals, 1983—90. With U.S. Army, 1943—46. Fellow: Internat. Inst. Arts and Letters (life); mem.: AIA (emeritus), Nat. Soc. Lit. and the Arts, Scottsdale Charros (life). Avocations: fishing, painting. Home: 7782 Via Sonrisa Scottsdale AZ 85258

WONG, JOHN WING-CHUNG, psychiatrist; b. Canton, China, Aug. 12, 1934; came to U.S., 1962; s. Min Sam and Yee Fern (Lau) W.; m. Lily Jent-Ju Chen, May 4, 1962; children: Diana, John Wing-Chung Jr., Gloria, Angela. MD, Queen's U., Kingston, Ont., Can., 1959. Diplomate Am. Bd. Psychiatry and Neurology. Resident physician in psychiatry Ohio State U. Hosp., Columbus, 1963-65; intern St. Michael's Hosp., Toronto, 1959-60; resident internal medicine univ. med. unit Queen Mary Hosp., Hong Kong, 1960-61; practice medicine specializing in psychiatry L.A., 1969-97; med. dir. inpatient unit Ventura County Health Care Agy., 1994-96, med. dir. behavioral health dept., 1996-2000; med. dir. Behavioral Medicine Ctr., San Gabriel Valley Med. Ctr., San Gabriel, Calif., 1991—; emeritus assoc. clin. prof. U. So. Calif. Sch. Medicine, 1998—. Dir. Pacific Clinic, Pasadena, Calif., 1987-90; med. dir. psychiat. consultation liaison svc. Hosp. of the Good Samaritan, L.A., 1989-90, Behavioral Medicine Ctr., Gabriel (Calif.) Valley Med. Ctr., 1991—; bd. dirs. Ea. Internat. Bank, Alhambra, Calif.; dir. day treatment program Resthaven Cmty. Mental Health Ctr., L.A., 1967-69; dir. area XXIV Profl. Standard Rev. Orgn., L.A., 1980-83; chmn. dept. psychiatry St. Vincent Hosp., 1978-79; dir. The Assocs.-Calif. Inst. Tech., Pasadena, 1990-91. Bd. dirs. San Marino (Calif.) Community Chest, 1986-88, pres., 1987-88; bd. dirs. San Gabriel Region United Way Inc., L.A., 1989-91, systemwide bd. dirs., 1990-91; mem. Los Angeles County Commn. on Aging, 1992-96. Mem. Am. Psychiat. Assn., So. Calif. Psychiat. Soc., Assocs. of Calif. Inst. Tech. Office: San Gabriel Valley Med Ctr Behavioral Medicine Ctr 438 W Las Tunas Dr San Gabriel CA 91776-1216 Home: 1005 Nightingale Pl Oxnard CA 93030-8507

WONG, JOSEPH H. religious organization administrator, theology studies educator; b. Canton, China, Apr. 7, 1942; arrived in U.S., 1992; s. Tin-Kwai Wong and Yin-Fan Cheng. BA in English Lit., U. London, 1969; BTh, Urbanian U., Rome, 1975; MTh, U. London, 1977; STD, Gregorian U., Rome, 1982. Benedictine monk. Lectr. theology Holy Spirit Sem., Hong Kong, 1982—84; assoc. prof. theology Salesian U., Rome, 1984—92; founding dir. Camaldolese Inst. for East-West Dialogue, Big Sur, Calif., 1994—; rsch. assoc. Ricci Inst. for Chinese-Western Cultural History, U. San Francisco, 1995—. Lectr. theology Sheshan Sem., Shanghai, 1996—; bd. dirs. Monastic Interreligious Dialogue, Grove Beach, Mo.; organizer internat. symposium of monastic dialogue between Christian and Asian Traditions, New Camaldoli Hermitage, 2000. Author: (book) Logos-Symbol in the Christology of Karl Rahner, 1984; co-editor: Purity of Heart and Contemplation: A Monastic Dialogue Between Christian and Asian Traditions, 2001. Roman Catholic. Avocations: Chinese gymnastics, sitting meditation, hiking. Home: 62475 Coast Hwy 1 Big Sur CA 93920 Office: New Camaldoli Hermitage 62475 Coast Hwy 1 Big Sur CA 93920 Office Phone: 831-667-2456.

WONG, KUOK-SHOONG DANIEL, research scientist; BSE in Elec. Engring., Princeton U., 1992; MS in Elec. Engring., Stanford U., 1994, PhD in Elec. Engring., 1998. Rsch. scientist Telcordia Techs., Red Bank, NJ, 1998—. Vice-chair IEEE NJ Coast Sect., Comm. Chpt., 2002—03; tech. program com. mem., session organizer, session chair, tutorial tchr. at various tech. confs. IEEE, 2001—; invited external phd examiner Nat. U. of Singapore, Computer Sci. Dept.; bd. mem. Comsoc Sister Societies, 2004—. Author: (book chpt.) Wireless IP and Building the Mobile Internet, (jour.) IEEE Transactions on Vehicular Tech., IEEE Jour. on Selected Areas in Comms., Internat. Jour. on Parallel and Distributed Sys. and Networks, IEEE Comms. Letters, IEEE Personal Comms. Mag.; guest editor IEEE Comms. Mag. Pianist, leader small group bible studies Monmouth Chinese Christian Ch., NJ, 1999—2003. Fellowship, Stanford U. Sch. of Engring., 1992—93. Mem.: IEEE (sr.; vice chair, N.J. coast sect., comm. chpt. 2000—03), Sigma Xi, Phi Beta Kappa, Tau Beta Pi. Achievements include patents for Multicarrier personal access comms. sys. Address: B-09-3A Ken Condo Jalan SS 2/72 Petaling Jaya Selangor 47400 Malaysia

WONG, LILIANE, architect, architecture educator; BA, Vassar Coll., 1981—81; MA, Harvard U.,, 1985. Registered arch. Assoc. Perry Dean Rogers & Ptnrs., Boston, 1985—94; prin. Mahon Wong Assocs., Cambridge, Mass., 1994—; assoc. prof. RISD, Providence, 1998—. Furniture line, Kore libr. furnishings line, 1995. Named Bulfinch Arch Competition winner, Hist. Neighborhood Found., 1987. Mem.: AIA, Boston Soc. Archs. (Women in Architecture award 1994, Women in Design aard 2002).

WONG, MARTIN D.F. computer scientist, educator; b. Canton, Guangdong, China, Oct. 21, 1956; s. Po Shin Wong and Po Ping Cheung-Wong; m. Jing Li, Dec. 9, 1989; children: Michelle Gar-Yee, Patrick Gar-Lok. BS in Math., U. of Toronto, Can., 1979; MS in Math., U of Ill., 1981, PhD in Computer Sci., 1987. Asst. prof. computer sci. U. of Tex., Austin, 1987—93, assoc. prof. computer sci., 1993—99, full prof. computer sci., 1999—2001; David Bruton Centennial prof. U. Tex., Austin, Tex., 2001—02; full prof. elec. and computer engring. U. of Ill., Urbana, 2002—. Cons. Ark. Dept. of Higher Edn., 1995; editor ACM Transactions on Design Automation of Electronic Sys., 1998—; chair ACM Internat. Symposium on Phys. Design, 1999. Editor: (jour.) IEEE Transactions on Computers, 1995—2000, author publ. over 250 books and articles in computer-aided design; editor: (jour.) ACM Transactions on Design Automation of Electronic Sys., 1998—. Recipient NSF Engrng. Rsch. award, NSF, 1989, ACM Recognition of Svc. award, Assn. of Computing Machinery, 1999, Faculty Partnership award, IBM, 2000; grantee Rsch. on Phys. Design of VLSI, NSF, 1999—2002. Mem.: Assn. of Computing Machinery, Inst. of Elec. and Electronic Engrs. Achievements include research in many fundamental algorithms used by industry in their computer-aided design software for silicon chip design. Office: Univ of Ill at Urbana-Champaign Dept of Elec and Computer Engring Urbana IL 61801 Office Phone: 217-244-1729. Business E-Mail: mdfwong@uiuc.edu.

WONG, OTTO, epidemiologist; b. Canton, China, Nov. 14, 1947; came to U.S., 1967, naturalized, 1976; m. Betty Yeung, Feb. 14, 1970; children: Elaine, Jonathan. BS, U. Ariz., 1970; MS, Carnegie Mellon U., 1972, U. Pitts., 1973, ScD, 1975. Cert. epidemiologist Am. Coll. Epidemiology, 1982. USPHS fellow U. Pitts., 1972-75; asst. prof. epidemiology Georgetown U. Med. Sch., 1975-78; mgr. epidemiology Equitable Environ. Health Inc., Rockville, Md., 1977-78; dir. epidemiology Tabershaw Occuopational Med. Assocs., Rockville, 1978-80; dir. occupational rsch. Biometric Rsch. Inst., Washington, 1980-81; exec. v.p., chief epidemiologist ENSR Health Scis., Alameda, Calif., 1981—; chief epidemiologist, pres. Applied Health Scis., San Mateo, Calif., 1991—. Adj. prof. epidemiology and biostats. Tulane U. Med. Ctr., New Orleans; vis. prof. epidemiology and occupl. health Nat. Def. Med. Ctr., Taipei, Taiwan, Shanghai Med. U.; adj. prof. dept. cmty. and family medicine Chinese U. Hong Kong; hon. prof. cmty. medicine U. Hong Kong; cons. WHO, Nat. Cancer Inst., Nat. Inst. Occupl. Safety and Health, Occupl. Safety and Health Adminstrn., Nat. Heart, Lung and Blood Inst., Internat. Agy. for Rsch. on Cancer, U.S. EPA, Ford Motors Co., Gen. Electric, Mobil, Chevron, Union Carbide, Fairfax (Va.) Hosp., Agy. for Toxic Substances and Disease Registry, U. Ariz. scholar, 1967-68; hon. prof. Cmty. Med. Hong Kong U.; assoc. editor The Annals of Epidemiology, Occupl. and Environ. Medicine. Contbr. articles to profl. jours. Fellow Am. Coll. Epidemiology, Human Biology Council; mem. Am. Pub. Health Assn., Biometric Soc., Soc. Epidemiologic Rsch., Phi Beta Kappa, Pi Mu Epsilon. Republican. Office: Applied Health Scis PO Box 2078 181 2nd Ave Ste 628 San Mateo CA 94401-3812

WONG, PANCRAS C. biomedical researcher, educator; b. Hong Kong, Apr. 5, 1953; BA, U. Oreg., 1976; PhD, U. Minn., 1981; MBA, U. Del., 1999. Rsch. asst. dept. pharmacology U. Minn., Mpls., 1976—81, rsch. specialist dept. pharmacology, 1981; sr. rsch. pharmacologist Hoechst-Roussell Pharms., Inc., Somerville, NJ, 1981—82; rsch. pharmacologist med. products dept. E.I. duPont Nemours & Co., Inc., Wilmington, Del., 1983—87, sr. rsch. pharmacologist med. products dept., 1988—89, rsch. assoc. med. products dept., 1990; prin. rschr. DuPont Merck Pharm. Co., Wilmington, 1991—96; rsch. fellow DuPont Pharms. Co., Wilmington, 1996—2001, sr. rsch. fellow, 2001, Bristol-Myers Squibb Co., Wilmington, 2002—. Adj. prof. dept. pharmacology Temple U., Phila., 2000. Recipient Team Innovation award, 1997, Dale Carnegie Award for Highest Achievement, Leadership Inst., Inc., 1996. Fellow: Am. Heart Assn. (coun. for high blood pressure rsch. 1984—); mem.: Heart Failure Soc. Am., Soc. Chinese Bioscientists in Am., Mid-Atlantic Pharmacology Soc., Am. Soc. for Pharmacology and Exptl. Therapeutics (Student Travel award 1979), Internat. Soc. Thrombosis and Haemostasis, Phi Beta Kappa. Office: Bristol-Myers Squibb Co Cardiovasc Biology PO Box 80400 Wilmington DE 19880-0400

WONG, PHILLIP ALLEN, osteopathic physician; b. Oakland, Calif., Dec. 8, 1956; s. Timothy Him and Lillian (Lee) W.; m. Lisa Perreault, Apr. 30, 1983; children: Ashley, Heather. BS in Microbiology and Chemistry, No. Ariz. U., 1979; DO, Kirksville Coll. Osteo. Med., 1983. Intern Kirksville Osteo. Health Ctr., 1983-84; staff family physician USAF, Kirtland AFB, N.Mex., 1984-87; CEO, pvt. practice Albuquerque, 1987—. Capt. USAF, 1984—87. Mem. Am. Acad. Osteopathy (bd. cert. in osteo. manipulative medicine), Am. Osteo. Assn., Am. Coll. Osteo. Family Physicians (bd. cert. family practice), N.Mex. Osteo. Med. Assn. (bd. mem.), Ariz. Acad. Osteopathy (bd. mem.), Cranial Acad. (bd. cert. in cranial in the osteo. field). Office: 10211 Montgomery Blvd NE Ste A Albuquerque NM 87111-3608 Office Phone: 505-296-8968.

WONG, RAYMOND SHIU-LOONG, radiologist; b. Hong Kong, Jan. 25, 1942; came to U.S., 1958; s. Jason Y. and Nancy L. (Tamm) W.; m. Jo-Lien Hsieh; 1 child, Florence W. BS in Chemistry, UCLA, 1962; MD, U. Chgo., 1966. Diplomate Am. Bd. Radiology with subspecialty in nuclear radiology, Am. Bd. Pediats. Diagnostic radiologist Hollywood Presbyn. Med. Ctr., L.A., 1981-94, Huntington Meml. Hosp., Pasadena, Calif., 1994—. Contbr. articles to profl. jours. Mem. Am. Coll. Radiology, Soc. Nuclear Medicine, Calif. Radiol. Soc., L.A. Radiol. Soc., Radiol. Soc. N.Am. Office: Huntington Meml Hosp 100 W California Blvd Pasadena CA 91105-3097

WONG, RICHARD LEE, lawyer; b. Austin, Tex., May 5, 1964; s. Richard and Narcissus Faye (Lee) W.; m. Judy Hyon. BA, Calif. State U., Hayward, 1987; JD, Georgetown U., 1990. Mem. Office of Presdl. Pers. The White House, Washington, 1989-90; with Sedgwick Detert Moran & Arnold, San Francisco, 1990-91, dist. office staff U.S. Senator John Seymour, San Francisco, 1991-92; atty.-advisor U.S. Dept. Transp., Washington, 1992—. Judge Md. State Nat. History Day Competition, 2004; mem. Chinese Christian Ch. of Greater Washington. Recipient Nat. Performance Rev. Reinventing Govt. award, 1997, Govt. Tech. Mag. Leadership award, 1999, Pres.'s Coun. on Y2K Conversion award, 2001. Mem.: Asian Pacific-ABA, Conf. on Asian Pacific Am. Leadership., U.S. Naval Inst. Address: 15621 Gold Ring Way Derwood MD 20855 Office Phone: 202-366-4011.

WONG, STEPHEN T.C. radiology, neurology, computer scientist, and bioengineer educator; b. Hong Kong, Sept. 8, 1959; came to U.S., 1985; s. Cheuk and Sam Kuk (Lam) W.; m. Sandie P.K. Ho, Jan. 26, 1960; children: Solomon, Gabriella. B of Engring., U. Western Australia, Perth, 1983; MSc in Computer Sci., Lehigh U., 1989, PhD in Computer Sci., 1991. Registered profl. engr., Pa. Mech. engr. Mass. Engring. Co., Manila, Philippines, 1977-78; rsch. assoc. Australian Nat. U., Canberra, 1982-83; elec. engr. Hewlett Packard Co., Singapore, 1984-85; tech. staff AT&T Bell Labs., Allentown, Pa., 1985-87; rsch. assoc. NSF Engring. Rsch. Ctr., Lehigh Valley, Pa., 1988-91; rschr. Japan MITI ICOT Lab., Tokyo, 1992-93; asst. prof. U. Calif., San Francisco, 1993—; sr. tech. staff Philips Rsch. Lab., Palo Alto, Calif., 1996-97; chief arch., dir., dir. engring. Philips Med. Sys., Best, The Netherlands, 1999-2000; v.p. info. tech. Charles Schwab & Co., 2000—01; mem. exam. bd. LOMA, 2000—. Grant rev. com. NSF, Washington, 1995—, NIH, Bethesda, 1997—; tech. adv. com. Internat. Conf. Computer Assay Radiology, Berlin, 1996—. Editor: Medical Image Databases, 1997; mem. editl. bd. Jour. Computer Med. Imaging, 1997—; editor Digital Librs. in Medicine, 1998. Australian Nat. U. scholar, 1982, Gleddon Tour scholar, 1983; NSF fellow, 1987-91; Japan Sci. and Tech. grant, 1992-93. Mem. IEEE (chpt. chmn. 1984—), Am. Assn. Med. Physicists. Achievements include patent disclosures and product devel. in biometrics on the World Wide Web; digital trust center of medical imaging; broadcasting model of electronic medical record; personalization of electronic medical record; development of the first working prototype of optical time domain reflectometer and hospital-wide PACS in U.S. Academic Medical Centers, and product development of radiology information systems PACS, computerized patient record and Healthcare systems and on-line global trading systems. Office: UC San Francisco Sch Medicine Dept Radiology 505 Parnassus Ave # 628 San Francisco CA 94122-2722 E-mail: swong@radiology.ucsf.edu.

WONG, SUN YET, engineering consultant; b. Honolulu, Dec. 6, 1932; s. Chip Tong and Shiu Inn (Chang) W.; m. Janet Siu Hung Lau; children: Cathleen, Bryan, Jonathan. BS in Civil Engring. with honors, U. Hawaii, 1954; MS in Civil Engring., Yale U., 1955. Engr. N.Am. Aviation, Downey, Calif., 1955-58; mem. tech. staff Ramo Woolridge Space Tech. Labs., Redondo Beach, Calif., 1958-64; exec. v.p., treas., tech. dir. Mechanics Rsch. Inc., El Segundo, Calif., 1964-77; treas. System Devel. Corp., Santa Monica, Calif., 1977-79; chmn. bd., pres., treas. Applied Rsch. Inc., El Segundo, 1979-81; ind. cons. Rolling Hills Estates, Calif., 1981—. Cons. J.H. Wiggins Co., Redondo Beach, 1982—84, Intercon, Cerritos, Calif., 1982—84, Acurex, Mountain View, Calif., 1983, Applied Tech., Mountain View, Calif., 1983—85, Aston., Mountain View, 1983—85, Electromech. Sys. Inc., Anaheim, Calif., 1984, Measurement Analysis Corp., Torrance, Calif., 1984—96, MRJ, Fairfax, Va., 1984, Tompkins and Assocs., Torrance, 1984—, TRW, Redondo Beach, 1984, E Sys., Garland, 1986—93, Statis. Scis., Inc., Beverly Hills, Calif., 1986, Kodak Datatape, Pasadena, Calif., 1989, Odectics, Anaheim, 1990, Ampex, Redwood City, Calif., 1991, Swales & Assocs., Beltsville, Md., 1992—93, Hughes Space and Comms. Co., El Segundo, 1992, El Segundo, 94, El Segundo, 1996—2000, Lion Engring., Rancho Palos Verdes, Calif., 1994—, NASA Goddard, Greenbelt, Md., 1997, Boeing Space Sys., El Segundo, 2000—, Raytheon, El Segundo, 2000—02, Boeing Space and Intelligence, Seal Beach, 2003—. Recipient Intelligence Cmty. Seal medallion, U.S. Govt., 2001, Nat. Reconnaisance Office Dir.'s award, 2001. Avocation: metal machining. Home and Office: 7 Club View Ln Rolling Hills Estates CA 90274 Office Phone: 310-534-4713. E-mail: sywong@gte.net.

WONG, THOMAS TANG YUM, engineering educator; b. Hong Kong, July 27, 1952; arrived in U.S., 1976; s. Kwai Sun and Yee Yuen (Fung) W.; m. Mini-i Lee, June 9, 1984; children: Clara Joyce, Lillian Denise. BSc in Engring., U. Hong Kong, 1975; MS, Northwestern U., Evanston, Ill., 1978, PhD, 1981. Product engr. Motorola Semiconductor, Inc., Hong Kong, 1975-76; teaching asst. Northwestern U., 1976-78, rsch. asst., 1978-80, postdoctoral fellow, 1980-81; asst. prof. Ill. Inst. Tech., Chgo., 1981-86, assoc. prof., 1986-96, prof., 1996—, dir. grad. program dept. elec. engring., 1987-95, chmn. dept. elec. and computer engring., 2001—; dir. rsch. and devel. Telecomm. Equipment Corp., Chgo., 1994—; chief sci. authority Quintech Electronics & Comms., Inc., Indiana, Pa., 1997-99. Cons. to pvt. industry, 1981—; chmn. Chicagoland Microwave Symposium, 1988. Author: Fundamentals of Distributed Amplification, 1993; contbr. articles to profl. jours.; book reviewer tech. publs.:. Trustee Sch. Dist. 73.5, Ill., 1995—2001. GE fellow, 1983; rsch. grantee NASA, 1989-91, U.S. Dept. Energy, 1992—, pvt. industry, 1993—. Mem. IEEE (chmn. joint Chgo. chpt. Antenna Propagation and Microwave Theory Techniques Soc. 1987-88, mem. steering com. joint symposium Antennas Propagation Soc./Internat. Union of Radio Sci./Nuclear Electromagnetic Pulse 1992), AAUP, Am. Soc. Engring. Edn., Am. Phys. Soc., Tau Beta Pi, Eta Kappa Nu. Achievements include several patents in the areas of microwave electronics and communications. Office: Ill Inst Tech Dept Elec/Computer Engring Chicago IL 60616 Business E-Mail: twong@ece.iit.edu.

WONG, TIMOTHY C. language and literature educator; b. Hong Kong, Jan. 24, 1941; came to U.S., 1951; s. Patrick J. and Rose (Poon) W.; m. Elizabeth Ann Steffens, Dec. 18, 1970; children: Sharon Elizabeth, Rachel Margaret, Laura Katherine. BA, St. Mary's Coll., Moraga, Calif., 1963; MA, U. Hawaii, 1968; PhD, Stanford U., 1975. Vol. U.S. Peace Corps, Thailand, 1963-65; asst. prof. Ariz. State U., Tempe, 1974-79, assoc. prof., 1979-85; resident dir. Coun. on Internat. Ednl. Exchange Peking Univ., China, 1984-85; assoc. prof. Ohio State U., Columbus, 1985-95; prof. Ariz. State U., Tempe, 1995—, dir. Ctr. for Asian Studies, 1995—2002. Author: Wu Ching-tzu, 1978, Stories for Saturday: Twentieth-Century Chinese Popular Fiction, 2003. Mem. Chinese Lang. Tchrs. Assn., Assn. Asian Studies, Am. Oriental Soc. (dir.-at-large 1996-2000, v.p. western br. 2000-02, pres., 2001-03). Democrat. Roman Catholic. Office: Ariz State U Dept Langs and Lits Tempe AZ 85287-0202 E-mail: timothy.wong@asu.edu.

WONG, WALLACE, medical supplies company executive, real estate investor; b. Honolulu, July 13, 1941; s. Jack Yung Hung and Theresa (Goo) W.; m. Amy Ju, June 17, 1963; children: Chris, Bradley, Jeffery. Student, UCLA, 1960-63. Chmn., pres. South Bay Coll., Hawthorne, Calif., 1965-86; chmn. Santa Barbara (Calif.) Bus. Coll., 1975—; gen. ptnr. W B Co., Redondo Beach, Calif., 1982—; CEO Cal Am. Med. Supplies, Rancho Santa Margarita, Calif., 1986-96, Cal Am. Exports, Inc., Rancho Santa Margarita, 1986-96, Pacific Am. Group, Rancho Santa Margarita, 1991-96; chmn., CEO Alpine, Inc., Rancho Santa Margarita, Calif., 1993-96; pres. Bayside Properties, Rancho Santa Margarita, 1993—, San Juan Capistrano, Calif., 1993—. Bd. dirs. Metrobank, L.A. FFF Enterprises; chmn. bd. 1st Ind. Fin. Group., San Juan Capistrano, 1994—; chmn. Affinity Fin. Corp., 1996—; bd. dirs. 2 Advanced Studios, LLC. Acting sec. of state State of Calif., Sacramento, 1982; founding mem. Opera Pacific, Orange County, Calif., 1985; mem. Hist. and Cultural Found., Orange County, 1986; v.p. Orange County Chinese Cultural Club, Orange County, 1985. Named for Spirit of Enterprise Resolution, Hist. & Cultural Found., Orange Country, 1987; recipient resolution City of Hawthorne, 1973. Mem. Westren Accred Schs. & Colls. (v.p. 1978-79), Magic Castle (life), Singapore Club. Avocations: travel, skiing. Office: Bayside Properties 31752 S Coast Hwy Ste 200 Laguna Beach CA 92651 Office Phone: 949-584-8090. Personal E-mail: WWong1025@cox.net.

WONG, WALTER FOO, county official; b. San Francisco, Apr. 11, 1930; s. Harry Yee and Grace (Won) W. AA, Hartnell Coll., 1952; BS, U. Calif., Berkeley, 1955; MPH, U. Hawaii, 1968. Registered sanitarian, Calif. Sanitarian Stanislaus County Health Dept., Modesto, Calif., 1955-56, Monterey County Health Dept., Salinas, Calif., 1956-67, sr. sanitarian, 1968-69, supervising sanitarian, 1969-70, dir. environ. health, 1971—2002. Sec. Monterey County Solid Waste Mgmt. Com., 1976—, Monterey County Hazardous Waste Mgmt. Com., 1987—; coord. Monterey County Genetic Engring. Rev. Com., 1987—; mem. Monterey County Genetic Engring. Experiment Permit Rev. Panel, 1995; mem. Monterey County Hazardous Materials Response Task Force, 1988—; mem. tech. adv. com. Monterey Peninsula Water Mgmt. Dist., 1985—, Monterey Regional Water Pollution Control Agy., 1985—; chmn. task force Monterey Regional Wastewater Reclamation Study for Agr., EPA and State of Calif. Chmn. Salinas Bicentennial Internat. Day Celebration, 1974, Pollution Clean-up Com. of Fort Ord Task Force, 1992; mem. Calif. Bare Closure Environ. adv. com., 1993. Recipient Community Svc. award Monterey County Med. Soc., 1998, Lifetime Achievement award, 2002, Mem. of Yr. award Salinas Valley C. of C., 2002, Lifetime Achievement award Calif. State Assembly and Calif. State Senate, 2002, Calif. Conf. of Dirs. Environ. Health Lifetime Achievement award, 2002, Lifetime Achievement award San Francisco Bay Area Dirs. Environ. Health, 2002, numerous others. Mem. Calif. Conf. Dirs. Environ. Health (pres. 1982-83), Assn. Environ. Health Adminstrs. (pres. 1982-83), Salinas C. of C. (Mem. of Yr. award 1971), U. Calif. Berkeley Alumni Assn., U. Hawaii Alumni Assn. (Disting. Alumni award 1992), Monterey County Hist. Soc. (pres. 1995-96), Ethnic Cultural Coun. (chmn. 1995). Republican. Presbyterian. Avocations: sports, music, outdoor recreation. Home: 234 Cherry Dr Salinas CA 93901-2807 Office: Monterey County Health Dept 1270 Natividad Rd Rm 301 Salinas CA 93906-3198

WONG, WAYNE D. nutritionist; b. San Francisco, May 13, 1950; s. Chaney Noon and La Dean Maryan (Mah) W. m. Betty Lee, Oct. 16, 1977; children: Michael Gabriel, Elizabeth Catherine, Whitney Forbes, Ellesse Florence. BS in Dietetic Adminstrn., U. Calif., Berkeley, 1972; MS in Sch. Bus. Mgmt., Pepperdine U., 1976; student, Nikon Sch. Photography, San Francisco, 1969, Canyon Hills Bible Coll., Bakersfield, Calif., 1998. Cert. food svc. dir.; cert. cmty. coll. tchr., Calif.; registered dietitian, sch. bus. ofcl., benefit specialist. Food svc. worker, lab. asst. U. Calif., Berkeley, 1968-69, 70-71; mgmt. intern Mich. State U., East Lansing, 1970; dietetic intern Milw. Pub. Schs., 1972-73; food svc. cons. Trader Vic's, San Francisco, 1973; dir. food svcs. Bakersfield (Calif.) City Sch. Dist., 1973—. Instr. Bakersfield Coll., 1978—; cons. Wong, R.D., Bakersfield, 1978—; registered Benefit Specialist Investors Retirement Mgmt., Carpinteria, Calif., 1988-99; mem. nat. child nutrition adv. coun. USDA, Washington, 1977-79; 1st v.p. Ptnrs. in Nutrition Coop., Lancaster, Calif., 1988-90; food svc. edn. task force Calif. Dept. Edn., Sacramento, 1979; project coord. nutrition edn. and tng. exemplary program adoption grant Bakersfield City Sch. Dist., 1982, webmaster food svcs. website; project dir. basic skills, basic foods course, curriculum and recipe devel. grant Calif. Dept. Edn., 1985, cons. tchg. course, 1985-88; mem. adv. coun. Calif. State U. Long Beach Child Nutrition Program Mgmt. Tng. Ctr., 1991; mem. Sch. Nutrition Adv. Coun., Bakersfield, 1990—; graphics and tech. writing cons. Cal-Pro-Net Ctr., Fresno City Coll., 1995—; program panelist Ptnrs. Nutrition Coop., Am. Sch. Food Svc. Assn., Ann. Nat. Conf., 1995; curriculum cons. Cal-Pro-Net Ctr., San Jose State U.; USDA field tester, trainer Food Safety Internet Course, 2000; Sch. Breakfast Survey field tester Nat. Food Svc. Mgmt. Inst.; website cons. Three Stranded Cord Ministries, 2001; mem. Kern Region Prayer Watch; guest artist Bakersfield Sch. Dist. Found., East Hills Mall Christmas Program; presenter in field. Author: Food Service Equipment-How Long Should It Last?, 1985, (poetry) The Slaughter of the Innocents, 2003, (songs) Lift Up Your Heads, O Ye Gates, 2001, Psalms 911, 2001, Psalms 126, 2003, El Regalo: Una Cancion para La Libertad, 2003, Tumbleweed Blues, 2004; co-author (videotape) Bettermade Plastics, 1991, Recycle: Save Earth's Resources Now; programmer Food Svc. Pers. Database, 1988, Dishmachine Labor and Energy Matrix, 1991; contbr. articles to profl. jours.; guest soloist classical guitar Highland High Orch., 1996, Glorious Christmas Prodn., 1997-98; classical guitarist Wong Family Trio, A Night to Honor Israel Prodn., 1996—; videographer Assembly of God, Canyon Hills; graphic artist Elizabeth in Recital; guest artist Barnes and Noble, 1999-00, In Jesus Name Ministries, 2003, BCSD Migrant Edn. Program, 2003, Global Harvest Ministries, 2003; mem. choir Bakersfield Centennial Spiritual Heritage Celebration, 1997. BBQ fund-raiser co-chmn. Citizens for Yes on Measure B, Bakersfield, 1989; legis. com. Child Nutrition Facilities Act 1975, Sacramento, 1973-76; expert witness State Senate Select Subcom. on Nutrition and Human Needs, Sacramento, 1973; asst. troop leader Boy Scouts Am., Troop 219, San Francisco, 1965-67; participant Chinese Family Life Study U. Calif., Berkeley; dir. polystyrene recycling project Bakersfield City Sch. Dist., 1990; team leader Healthy Kids, Healthy Calif. program Calif. Dept. Edn., 1985-87; sponsor Christian Broadcasting Network Satellite Comms. Ctr., 1978; world vision sponsor India Cmty. Devel. Program, 1974-92; guitarist Canyon Hills Assembly of God Ch. Orch., 1996—, choir mem., 2001; publicity coord. Bakersfield Youth Symphony, 1996-99; bd. dirs., MIS cons. Young Artists Internat., 1999; mem. nutrition adv. coun. Bakersfield Coll., 1999; mem. Men's Prison Ministry, 2001. Recipient Eastman Kodak Scholastic Photography award Hon. Mention All State, 1968, Leadership award Calif. State Dept. Edn., 1987, Outstanding Sch. Lunch Program award USDA, 1989, Outstanding Summer Food Svc. Program award, 1999,; 1st pl. Calif. Sch. Food Svc. Assn. Country Cook-off, 1983, 84, Order of the Arrow, Boy Scouts Am., 1966; Toto Wizard nominee Sabatasso Foods, 1985, Best Practice award USDA, 1992. Mem. Am. Dietetic Assn. (Young Dietitian of Yr. 1976), Am. Sch. Food Svc. Assn. (child nutrition mktg. bike ride 1991, Cycle Across Am. for Child Nutrition and Fitness 1993), Calif. Assn. Sch. Bus. Ofcls. (photographer 1985, food svc. R&D chmn. 1985-87, recognition 1987, food and nutrition R&D com. 1984), Calif. Sch. Food Svc. Assn. (edn. tng. chmn. 1975-76, wellness awareness bike ride 1990-91, child nutrition bike ride 1991, 1st pl. photo contest 1993, cover photographer assn. jour. Poppyseeds 1992), Sports and Cardiovasc. Nutritionists, Kern County Sch. Food Svc. Assn. (pres. 1987-90, Golden Poppy award 1990), Kern Wheelmen (v.p. 1992), MENSA, 2001-02, Pi Alpha Phi, Omicron Nu. Republican. Mem. Assemblies of God Ch. Avocations: long distance bicycling, tennis, photography, classical guitar, bible study. Office: Bakersfield City Sch Dist 1300 Baker St Bakersfield CA 93305-4326

WONG, WILLIE, former mayor, automotive executive; b. Mesa, Ariz., Oct. 12, 1948; m. Cobina Wong; children: Kevin, Jeremy. Grad., Ariz. State U. Vice mayor City of Mesa (Ariz.), 1988-90; councilmem., 1990-91; mayor City of Mesa (Ariz.), 1992-96; mgr., owner, pres. Wilky's Performance Ctr., Mesa, 1992—. Pres. Wilky's Performance Ctr., Mesa, Ariz.; prev. employment with AT&T. Treas. Regional Pub. Transp. Authority; chmn. Williams Redevel. Ptnrship., Maricopa Assn. Govts. Regional Devel. Policy Com.; vice-chmn. Williams Gateway Airport Authority, Mesa Sister Cities; exec. com. League of Ariz. Cities and Towns; bd. dirs. YMCA (past pres.), Child Crisis Ctr., Southwest Pub. Recycling Assn. Named Outstanding Young Man Mesa Leadership, Tng., & Devel. Assn., 1989. Mem. MAG Regional Coun., Econ. Devel. Adv. Bd., Rotary Club-Mesa West. Avocations: baseball, fishing, travel, reading. Home: 1343 E Mclellan Rd Mesa AZ 85203-3838 also: Wilky's Performance Ctr 402 E Main St Mesa AZ 85203-8739

WONG, Y. S. diversified financial services company executive; Dollar money market trader Citibank Hong Kong, 1975—77, fgn. exch. trader, 1981, treas., 1981—85, North Asia regional treas., 1985—94, head fin. markets Asia Pacific, 1994—98; exec. v.p., global head emerging markets sales and trading Citibank, N.Y.C., 1998—. Office: Citigroup Inc 399 Park Ave New York NY 10043

WONG, Y(ING) WOOD, real estate investment company executive, real estate development company executive, venture capital investment company executive; b. Hong Kong, Apr. 28, 1950; came to U.S., 1969; s. Loyee K.H. and Margaret M.C.L. Wong; m. Leslie K.P. Chan, Dec. 18, 1977; children: Joshua H., Jonathan H. AA in Biology, Menlo Coll., 1971, BS in Bus. Adminstrn., 1974; BA in Zoology, U. Calif., Berkeley, 1972; MBA, Northwestern U., 1976. Auditor Touche Ross & Co., CPAs, San Francisco, 1976-78; founder, mng. dir. Wong Properties, Palo Alto, Calif., 1976—; founder, venture capital ptnr. Wongfratris Investment Co., Palo Alto, 1986—; founder, ptnr. Corona Main Devel., L.L.C., Palo Alto, 2003—. Instr. Golden Gate U., 1977. Trustee Crystal Springs Uplands Sch., Hillsborough, Calif., 1993-98; advisor The Pui Ying Mid. Sch., Guangzhou, China, The Pui Ying Christian Svcs. Soc., Vancouver, Can.; bd. dirs. Peninsula Symphony, Los Altos, Calif., 2002-03. Named Hon. Citizen of Taishan City, China; established Wood Wong Fgn. Students Exch. Grant, Menlo Coll., 1997—. Mem. Internat. Platform Assn., Commonwealth Club Calif., Beta Alpha Psi. Office: 51 Jordan Pl Palo Alto CA 94303-2903 E-mail: wood.wong@wongfratris.com.

WONG-DIAZ, FRANCISCO RAIMUNDO, lawyer, educator; b. Havana, Cuba, Oct. 29, 1944; came to U.S., 1961; s. Juan and Teresa (Diaz de Villegas) Wong; 1 child, Richard Alan. BA with honors, No. Mich. U., 1965; MA with highest honors, U. Detroit, 1967; PhD, MA, U. Mich., 1974; JD, U. Calif., Berkeley, 1976. Bar: Calif. 1980, U.S. Dist. Ct. (no. dist.) Calif. 1990, Fla. 1987. Prof. City Coll. San Francisco, 1975—, dept. chmn., 1978-85; rsch. atty. Marin Superior Ct., 1980-81; ct. arbitrator Marin Mcpl. Ct., 1985; atty. pvt. practice, Kentfield, Calif., 1980—. Adj. asst. prof. San Francisco State U., 1977; assoc. dean Miami-Dade Coll., 1986; dir. Cutcliffe Cons., Inc., Hawthorne, LaFamila Ctr., Inc., San Rafael, Calif., 1980-85, Small Bus. Inst., Kentfield, 1982-86; cons. ICC Internat., San Francisco, 1980-82; polit. commentator Univision KDTV, 1980—; bd. dirs. Pedro Pan Group, Inc. Author: American Politics in a Changing World, 1999, 2d edit., 2004; bd. editors Indsl. Rels. Law Jour., 1975-76; mem. editl. bd. Calif. Lawyer, 1991-93. Lector St. Sebastian's Ch., 1984—, parish coun., 1995; bd. dirs. Am. Cancer Soc., 1999—; mem. devel. rsch. program, fellowship com. U. Calif.-San Francisco, 2002—; mem. adv. bd. Redes en Accion, 2002—. Vis. scholar U. Calif., Berkeley Sch. Bus., 1983-84, U.S. Dept. State scholar, Washington, 1976; Horace C. Rackham fellow U. Mich., 1970, summer fellow U. Calif. Berkeley, 1995, Nat. Security Law Ctr. U. Va., 1996; recipient Patient Courage award, ACS, 2004; named Best New Vol. of Yr., Am. Cancer Soc., 2000, One of One Hundred Most Influential Hispanics in the Nation, Hispanic Bus. Mag., Oct. 2000. Mem. ABA, Am. Polit. Sci. assn., Latino Ednl. Assn. (treas. 1985), Cuban Am. Nat. Coun., World Affairs Coun. (sem. leader San Francisco 1980), U. Calif. San Francisco PC Advocates, U. Calif. San Francisco Cancer Ctr., Commonwealth Club. Roman Catholic. Office Phone: 415-239-3000.

WONG-STAAL, FLOSSIE, geneticist, medical educator; BA, UCLA, 1968, PhD, 1972. Tchg. asst. UCLA, 1969-70, rsch. asst., 1970-72; post-doctoral fellow U. Calif., San Diego, 1972-73; Fogarty fellow Nat. Cancer Inst., Bethesda, Md., 1973-75, vis. assoc., 1975-76, cancer expert, 1976-78, sr. investigator, 1978-81, chief molecular genetics of hematopoietic cells sect., 1982-89; Florence Seeley Riford chair in AIDS rsch., prof. medicine U. Calif. San Diego, La Jolla, 1990—. Vis. prof. Inst. Gen. Pathology, First U. Rome, Italy, 1985. Mem. editl. bd. Gene Analysis Techniques, 1984—, Cancer Letters, 1984-94, Leukemia, 1987—. Cancer Rsch., 1987, AIDS Rsch. and Human Retroviruses (sect. editor), 1987—, DNA and Cell Biology (sect. editor), 1987—, Microbial Pathogenesis, 1987-90, AIDS: An Internat. Jour., 1987—, Internat. Jour. Acquired Immunodeficiency Syndrome, 1988—, Oncogene, 1988—, Jour. Virology, 1990—; contbr. articles to profl. jours. Recipient Outstanding Sci. award Chinese Med. and Health Assn., 1987, The Excellence 2000 award U.S. Pan Asian Am. C. of C. and the Orgn. of Chinese Am. Women, 1991. Mem. Am. Soc. for Virology (charter), Phi Beta Kappa. Office: U Calif San Diego Dept Med 0665 9500 Gilman Dr La Jolla CA 92093-5003

WONHAM, WALTER MURRAY, electrical engineer, educator; b. Montreal, Que., Can., Nov. 1, 1934; m. Vera Anne Hale; children: Marjorie Jane, Cynthia Margaret. B of Engring., McGill U., Montreal, 1956; PhD, U. Cambridge, Eng., 1961. Asst. prof. elec. engring. Purdue U., Lafayette, Ind., 1961-62; rsch. scientist Rsch. Inst. for Advanced Studies, Balt., 1962-64; assoc. prof. Brown U., Providence, 1964-69; rsch. assoc. NASA, Cambridge, Mass., 1967-69, cons., 1969; prof. elec. engring. U. Toronto, Ont., Can., 1970—, J. Roy Cockburn prof., 1991-96, Cockburn chair, 1991, univ. prof., 1996—2000, univ. prof. emeritus, 2000—. Author: Linear Multivariable Control: A Geometric Approach, 1974, 3d edit., 1985 (Russian transl. 1980, Chinese transl. 1984); assoc. editor Soc. for Indsl. and Applied Math., Jour. on Control and Optimization, 1965-79, Sys. Control Letter, 1981-85. Recipient Brouwer medal Netherlands Math Soc., 1990; Athlone fellow, Gt. Britain, 1956-58; spl. scholar Nat. Rsch. Coun. Can., 1958-60; sr. postdoctoral resident rsch. assoc. NAS USA, 1967-69. Fellow IEEE (life, Control Sys. Sci. and Engring. award 1987), Royal Soc. Can. Office: U Toronto Dept Elec Engring 35 St George St Toronto ON Canada M5S 3G4

WONNACOTT, JAMES BRIAN, physician; b. Charlottetown, P.E.I., Can., Feb. 24, 1945; came to U.S., 1978, naturalized, 1984; s. Earl Lepage and Eunice Deborah (Eaton) W. Honors diploma, Prince of Wales Coll., 1964; BSc with honors in biology, Dalhousie U., 1966, MD, 1972. Diplomate Am. Bd. Family Practice, Coll. Family Physicians Can. Intern Victoria Gen. Hosp., Halifax, N.S., Can., 1971-72; gen. practice medicine Summerside, P.E.I., 1975-78; med. dir. alcoholism treatment unit Raleigh Hills Hosp., 1981-83; preceptor tchg. staff U. Tex. Med. Sch., Baylor Coll. Medicine, Houston, 1984-95; exec. med. dir. Oak Forest Med. Ctr., 1990-95, Vis. Nurse Assn., Hospice, Houston, 1991-95; pvt. practice family medicine rural Kans., 1975—2000; med. dir. Rural Health Clinic, Spearman, Tex., 2000—03; pvt. practice Jacksonville, Tex., 2003—. Mem. med. adv. bd. Med. World News, 1983-90. Served as flight surgeon RCAF, 1967-75. Fellow Am. Acad. Family Physicians; mem. AMA. Methodist. Office: 203 Nacogdoches St Ste 265 Jacksonville TX 75766

WONNACOTT, PAUL, retired economics professor; b. London, Ont., Can., Mar. 16, 1933; s. Gordon Elliott and Muriel Johnston Wonnacott; m. Donna Elizabeth Cochrane, July 2, 1960; children: David, Ann, Alan, Bruce. BA, U. Western Ont., 1955; MA, Princeton U., 1957, PhD, 1959. Instr., asst. prof. econs. Columbia U., N.Y.C., 1958-62; assoc. prof. then prof. econs. U. Md., College Park, 1962-91, prof. emeritus, 1992; ret., 2000. Mem. Pres.'s Coun. Econ. Advisers, 1991-93; Alan Holmes prof. econs. Middlebury Coll., 1994-2000; rsch. staff Royal Commn. Banking and Fin., Toronto, 1962; sr. staff economist Coun. Econ. Advisers, Washington, 1968-70; assoc. dir. divsn. internat. fin. Fed. Res. Bd., Washington, 1974-75; vis. scholar Office Internat. Monetary Rsch., U.S. Treasury, 1980; econ. adviser to Under Sec. of State, 1990-91. Author: The Canadian Dollar, 1960, 2d rev. edit., 1965, (with R.J. Wonnacott) Free Trade between the United States and Canada: The Potential Economic Effects, 1967, (with H.G. Johnson and H. Shibata) Harmonization of National Economic Policies under Free Trade, 1968, Macroeconomics, 1974, 3d rev. edit., 1984, (with R.J. Wonnacott) Economics, 1979, 4th rev. edit. 1990, Spanish edit., 1981, 3d rev. edit., 1987, (with Y. and C. Crusius) Portuguese edit., 1982, 2d rev. edit., 1985, (with A. Blomquist) Can. edit., 1983, 4th rev. edit., 1994, Lithuanian edit., 1998, The United States and Canada: The Quest for Free Trade, 1987; contbr. articles to profl. jours. Fellow Brooking Inst., 1957-58, Ford Found., 1963-64; vis. fellow Inst. Internat. Econs., 1986, 93-94. Home: 11511 S Glen Rd Potomac MD 20854 E-mail: paulwon@wam.umd.edu.

WONNACOTT, RONALD JOHNSTON, economics professor; b. London, Ont., Can., Sept. 11, 1930; s. Gordon and and Muriel (Johnston) W.; m. Eloise Howlett, Sept. 11, 1954; children: Douglas, Robert, Cathy Anne. BA, U. Western Ont., 1955; A.M., Harvard U., 1957, PhD, 1959. Mem. faculty U. Western Ont., London, 1958-96, prof. econs., 1964-96, chmn. dept., 1969-72, prof. emeritus, 1996—. Vis. assoc. prof. U. Minn., Mpls., 1961-62; cons. Resources for the Future, Econ. Council Can., Can.-Am. Com., Nat. Planning Assn., C.D. Howe Inst. Author: Canadian-American Dependence: An Interindustry Analysis of Production and Prices, 1961, Canada's Trade Options, 1975, Selected New Developments in International Trade Theory, 1984, The Economics of Overlapping Free Trade Areas and the Mexican Challenge, 1991, (with G.L. Reuber) The Cost of Capital in Canada, 1961, (with Paul Wonnacott) Free Trade Between the U.S. and Canada, 1967, Economics, 1979, 4th edit., 1990, (with Thomas H. Wonnacott) Introductory Statistics, 1969, 5th edit., 1990, Econometrics, 1970, 2d edit., 1979, Regression, 1981 Fellow Royal Soc. Can.; mem. Am. Econ. Assn., Can. Econ. Assn. (pres. 1981), London Hunt Club, Sunningdale Golf Club (Eng.), Hon. Co. Edinburgh Golfers, Craigleith Ski Club. Home: 171 Wychwood Pk London ON Canada N6G 1S1 E-mail: Wonnacot@uwo.ca.

WONSER, MICHAEL DEAN, retired public affairs director, art history educator; b. Long Beach, Calif., Mar. 12, 1940; s. Franklin Henry and Dorothy Mae (Harris) W.; children: Therice Michele, Sherice Michele, Christopher Franklin; m. Mary L. Van Epps, Dec. 22, 1990. BS, U. Oreg., 1963, MFA, 1965; postgrad., U. Colo., 1976. Instr. Cen. Oreg. Coll., Bend, 1966-68; prof. Adams State Coll., Alamosa, Colo., 1969-91, dir. pub. affairs, 1982-90; adj. prof. art history Ctrl. Oreg. C.C., Bend. Pres. Colo. Faculty Com. Trustees, 1980-82. Mem. Chamber Edn. Com., Monte Vista, Colo., 1982-88; pres. Luth. Ch. Alamosa, 1980-85; bd. dirs. Creede Repertory Theatre, 1989-91; mem. Commerce Comm. and Resources Comm., 1995, Cmty. Improvement Commn., Sisters, Oreg., 1996-97. Mem. Higher Edn. Assn. of Rockies (pres. Colo. chpt. 1985-88), C. of C. Ambassador (treas. 1982), Alamosa, C. of C. Tourism Bd., Alamosa (chmn. 1987-89), Sisters C. of C. (v.p. 1995-97, pres. 1996-97, bd. dirs.), Rotary (pres. Alamosa County 1990-91), Lambda Chi Alpha (Hall of Fame 1993). Republican. Avocations: golf, skiing. Home: 24 NW Shasta Pl Bend OR 97701-2633 E-mail: mmwonser@bendcable.com.

WOO, BENSON, financial executive; BSEE, MIT; MBA, Harvard U. Various positions GM, 1979-94; v.p., treas. Case Corp., 1994-98; corp. v.p., CFO, York Internat. Corp., 1998—99; sr. v.p. Metris Cos., Inc., Minnetonka, Minn., 1999—2003; CFO TriMas Corp., Minnetonka, 2003—.

WOO, CAROLYN YAUYAN, dean; b. Hong Kong, Apr. 19, 1954;, US, 1972; m. David Bartkus; children: Ryan, Justin. BS in econ., Purdue U., 1975, MS in indsl. adminstrn., 1976, PhD in strategic mgmt. Krannert scholar, 1979. Asst. prof. mgmt. Purdue U., 1981—85, assoc. to full prof., 1985—93; dir. profl. master's programs Krannert Sch. Mgmt., Purdue U., 1993—95, assoc. exec. v.p. acad. affairs, 1995—97; Martin J. Gillen dean and Ray and Milann Siegfried chair entrepreneurial studies Mendoza Sch. Bus., Notre Dame U., 1997—. Bd. dirs. Bindley Western Industries, 1997—2000, Aon Corp., 1998—, Nisource Industries Inc., 1999—, Circuit City Stores Inc., 2001—. Bd. dirs. Caritas Internationalis, 2004—. Recipient TIEM Found. Disting. Scholar award, Internat. Coun. Small Bus., 1987, Excellence award for edn., Asian Am. Alliance, 2002. Mem.: Com. of 100, Assn. to Advance Collegiate Sch. Bus. (mem. bus. accrediation com. 1998, bd. dirs. 1999—2002, vice chair 2002—03, chair 2003—04). Office: Notre Dame Univ 204 Mendoza Coll Bus Notre Dame IN 46556-5646 Office Phone: 574-631-7992. Business E-Mail: Carolyn.Y.Woo.5@nd.edu.

WOO, JOHN See WU, YUSEN

WOO, JONATHAN C. G. chemist, portfolio manager, management consultant; b. San Francisco, Oct. 22, 1968; s. Gar Lok and Julia Y. P. Woo. AB, U. Calif., Berkeley, 1990; MS, Northwestern U., 1992, PhD, 1994. Rsch. fellow Memorial Sloan Kettering Ctr., N.Y.C., 1994-97, Mitchell Madison Group, 1997-99, Bristol-Myers Squibb, Princeton, NJ, 1999—2002, Johnson and Johnson, Titusville, NJ, 2002—. Contbr. articles to profl. jours. Fellow NIH, 1995. Mem. Am. Chem. Soc.

WOO, S. B. (SHIEN-BIAU WOO), former lieutenant governor, physics educator; b. Shanghai, Aug. 13, 1937; came to U.S., 1955; s. C.K. and Kuo-Ying (Chang) W.; m. Katy K.N. Wu, July 20, 1963; children: Chih-I, Chih-Lan. BS in Physics and Math. summa cum laude, Georgetown Coll., Ky., 1956; MS in Physics, Washington U., St. Louis, 1962, PhD in Physics, 1964. Prof. physics U. Del., Newark, 1966—2002; lt. gov. State of Del., Dover, 1985-89. Pres. Del. State Senate; chmn. Bd. Pardons; cons. E.I. DuPont Co., Wilmington, Del., 1968, Del. State Coll., Dover, 1980—81; steering com. 80-20 initiative, 1998—; pres. 80-20 PAC, 2001—, Com.of100, 1989—. Contbr. articles to profl. jours. Chmn. bd., chief exec. officer Chinese Am. Community Ctr., Hockessin, Del., 1982-83; sec. Asian-Am. caucus Democratic Nat. Conv., 1983-84; pres., co-chmn. Gov.'s Internat. Trade Council, 1985-89; chmn. Gov.'s task force on High Tech., 1985-89. Recipient Highest Achievement award Asian Am. High Tech. Conv., 1985; Army Rsch. grantee, 1972-87, NSF grantee, 1978-81; Inst. fellow Kennedy Sch., Harvard U. Mem. Am. Phys. Soc., AAAS, AAUP (exec. com. nat. council 1974-77), Orgn. Chinese Ams. (bd. dirs. 1977-79, nat. pres. 1990-91), Sigma Xi. Democrat. Home: 5 Farm House Rd Newark DE 19711-7458 E-mail: sbw@udel.edu.

WOO, SAVIO LAU CHING, molecular medical geneticist; b. Shaghai, China, Dec. 20, 1944; came to U.S., 1966; s. Kwok-Cheung and Fun-sin (Yu) W.; m. Emily H. Chang, July 14, 1973; children: Audrey C. C., Brian Y.Y. BSc, Loyola Coll., Montreal, Can., 1966; PhD, U. Wash., 1971. Asst. prof. cell biology Baylor Coll. Medicine, Houston, 1975-78, assoc. prof., 1979-83, dir. ctr. for gene therapy, 1991-96, prof., 1984-96, prof. Inst. Molecular Genetics, 1985-96, dir. grad. tng. program cell and molecular biology, 1987-94; assoc. investigator Howard Hughes Med. Inst., Bethesda, Md., 1977-79, investigator, 1979-96; prof., dir. Inst. for Gene Therapy and Molecular Medicine Mount Sinai Sch. Medicine, N.Y.C., 1996—; organizer, 1st chmn. Gordon Conf. on Molecular Genetics, 1985; co-organizer Searle-UCLA Symposium, 1986; organizer 3d Soc. Chinese Bioscientists in Am. Internat. Symposium, 1990; cons. Cooper Lab., Palo Alto, Calif., 1982-84, Zymos Corp., Seattle, 1982-86; sr. sci. advisor Molecular Therapeutics, Inc., West Haven, 1986-92; spl. advisor Gene Medicine, Inc., Woodlands, Tex., 1992-96. Mem. editorial bd. DNA, 1983—, Am. Jour. Human Genetics, 1986-89, Genomics, 1987-95, Biochemistry, 1988-94; U.S. editor: Gene Therapy, 1995—; contbr. over 200 sci. articles to prof. publs. Mem. bd. dirs. March of Dimes Birth Defects Found., Met. Houston chpt., 1979-87. Mem. NIH (study sect. on molecular biology 1983-85, merit award, 1988—), Nat. Inst. Child Health and Human Devel. (bd. sci. counselors 1988-93). Am. Soc. Biol. Chemists, Am. Soc. Cell Biology, N.Y. Acad. Scis., Soc. Study Inborn Errors of Metabolism (D. Noel Raime meml. award 1983).

WOO, SAVIO LAU-YUEN, bioengineering educator; b. Shanghai, June 3, 1942; s. Kwok Chong and Fung Sing (Yu) Woo; m. Patricia Tak-kit Cheong, Sept. 6, 1969; children: Kirstin Wei-Chi, Jonathan I-Huei. BSME, Chico State U., 1965; MS, U. Wash., 1966, PhD, 1971; DSc (hon.), Calif. State U., 1998. Rsch. assoc. U. Wash., Seattle, 1965—70; asst. research prof. U. Calif.-San Diego, La Jolla, 1970—74, assoc. rsch. prof., 1974—75, assoc. prof., 1975—80, prof. surgery and bioengring., 1980—90; vice chmn. for rsch. and dir. Musculoskeletal Rsch. Ctr., U. Pitts., 1990—; prof. ortho surgery U. Pitts., 1990—93, prof. mech. engring., 1990—, Albert B. Ferguson Jr. prof. orthopaedic surgery, 1993—, prof. civil and environ. engring., 1994—, prof. rehab. sci. and tech., 1994—, prof. bioengring., 1998—. Prin. investigator VA Med. Ctr., San Diego, 1972—90, Pitts., 1990—; cons. bioengr. Children's

Hosp., San Diego, 1973—80; cons. med. implant cos., 1978—85; vis. prof. biomechanics Kobe (Japan) U., 1981—82; dir., CEO M&D Coutts Inst. for Joint Reconstrn. and Rsch., 1984—90; mem. sci. adv. com. Whitaker Found., 1986—95, Steadman-Hawkins Sports Medicine Found., 1990—, Aircast Found., 1998—, OsteoArthritis Scis. Inc., 1992—95; mem. adv. bd. Coll. of Engrng., Computer Sci. and Tech. Calif. State U., Chico, 1994—; mem. adv com. coord. grad. program in biomed. engring. U. Edmunton, U. Calgary, 1997—; mem. bioengring. adv. com. NHRI, 1996—. Assoc. editor Jour. Biomech. Engring., 1979—87, Jour. Biomechanics, 1978—, Jour. Orthopedic Rsch., 1983—, 1983—, Materials Sci. Reports, 1990—97, Proc. Inst. Mech. Engrs. (Part H), 1990—94, mem. internat. adv. bd. Jour. Knee Surgery, Sports Tramuatology, Arthroscopy, 1993—, mem. editl. bd. Jour. of Ortho. Sci., 1995—, Jour. Ortho. Surgery, 1998—, Jour. Musculoskeletal Rsch., 1998—, Am. Acad. Ortho. Surgery, 1995—, Healthcare Eng., 1999—. Recipient Elizabeth Winston Lanier Kappa Delta award, 1983, 1986, awards for excellence in basic sci. rsch., Orthopaedic Rsch. Soc. and Am. Acad. Orthopaedic Surgeons, 1983, 1986, 1990, 1994, O'Donoghue award, Am. Orthopaedic Soc. Sports Medicine, 1990, 1997, Wartenweiler Meml. Lectureship, 1987, Citation award, Am. Coll. Sports Medicine, 1988, Rsch. Career Devel. award, NIH, 1977—82, Muybridge medal, Internat. Soc. Internat. Biomechanics, 1995, GOTS-Beiersdorf AG Res. award, 1996, Internat. Olympic Com. prize for Sp. Sci., 1998, Cabaud Meml. award, AOSSM, 1999, Albert Trillat Young Inventors award, ISAKOS, 1999, Chancellor's Disting. Res. award, U. Pitts., 1999; fellow Japan Soc. Promotion of Sci., 1981. Fellow: ASME (sec., chmn. biomechanics com., chmn. honors com. bioengring. divsn., mem. exec. com. 1984—89, chmn. bioengring. divsn. 1986—87, H.R. Lissner award 1991), Am. Inst. Med. and Biol. Engring. (chmn. coll. fellows 1992—94, bd. dirs. 1992—94, founding); mem.: NAS, NAE, U.S. Nat. Commn. Biomechanics (chmn. 1994—97, exec. com. 1998—), European Orthopedic Rsch. Soc., Chinese Speaking Ortho Soc. (chmn. edn. com. 1997—, bd. dirs. 1997—), Internat. Soc. Fractures Repair (bd. dirs. 1986—94, v.p. 1987—90, pres. 1990—92), Am. Soc. Biomechanics (pres. 1985—86, bd. dirs. 1977—87, Giovanni Borelli award 1993), Orthopaedic Rsch. Soc. (chmn. program com. 1983—84, bd. dirs. 1983—87, pres. 1985—86), Can. Orthopedic Rsch Soc. (hon.), We. Orthopaedic Assn. (hon.), Am. Acad. Orthopedic Surgeons, World Coun. for Biomechanics (chmn. 1998—), Biomed. Engring. Soc. (bd. dirs. 1984—86), Internat. Olympic Com. Olympic Acad. of Scis., Acad. Sinica, Inst. Medicine (chmn. sect. I 1996—98).

WOO, SHARON Y. healthcare organization executive; b. Honolulu; BA in Music and Math., Mills Coll.; secondary tchg. credential, San Francisco State U. Bd. dirs. Sutter Health Inc., Sacramemto. Trustee Gateway H.S., Golden Gate nat. Parks Assn., Multicultural Alliance, San francisco Ballet, numerous others; chmn. adv. coun. San Francisco Sch. Vols. Office: Sutter Health Inc 2200 River Plaza Dr Sacramento CA 95833-4134

WOO, VERNON YING-TSAI, lawyer, real estate developer, judge; b. Honolulu, Aug. 7, 1942; s. William Shu-Bin and Hilda Woo; children: Christopher Shu-Bin, Lia Gay. BA, U. Hawaii, 1964, MA, 1966; JD, Harvard U., 1969. Pres. Woo Kessner Duca & Maki, Honolulu, 1972-87; pvt. practice law Honolulu, 1987—. Judge per diem Honolulu Dist. Family Ct., 1978-84, 1995-2002. Bd. dirs. Boys and Girls Club of Honolulu,. 1985-95, pres., 1990-92. Mem.: ABA, Honolulu Bd. Realtors, Hawaii Bar Assn. Home: 3936 Waokanaka St Honolulu HI 96817 Office: Harbor Ct 55 Merchant St Ste 1900 Honolulu HI 96813 Office Phone: 808-529-8822.

WOOD, ALLEN JOHN, electrical engineer, consultant; b. Milw., Oct. 1, 1925; s. Alfred John and Kathleen Francis (Welch) W.; m. Barbara Ann Cook, Oct. 29, 1949; children: John Scott, Susan Beth Wood Richmond. BEE, Marquette U., 1949; MS in Elec. Engring., Ill. Inst. Tech., 1951; PhD, Rensselaer Poly. Inst., 1959. Registered profl. engr., N.Y. Engr. Allis Chalmers Mfg. Co., West Allis, Wis., 1949-50, GE, Lynn, Mass., 1951-52, Schenectady, N.Y., 1952-59, sr. engr., 1960-69; mem. tech. staff Hughes Aircraft Co., Culver City, Calif., 1959-60; cons., prin., dir. Power Techs., Inc., Schenectady, N.Y., 1969-91, treas., chief fin. officer, 1989-91, also bd. dirs., 1969-91; ind. cons., 1991—. Adj. prof. Rensselaer Poly. Inst., Troy, 1966-2000; cons. in field, 1992—. Author: Power System Reliability Calculations, 1973, Power Generation Operation and Control, 1984, 2d edit. 1996; contbr. numerous articles to profl. jours. With U.S. Army, 1942-46, ETO, PTO. Fellow IEEE (life); mem. AAAS. Republican. Mem. Reformed Ch. in Am. Avocations: amateur radio, photography. E-mail: al2wood@hotmail.com.

WOOD, ALLISON LORRAINE, lawyer; b. N.Y.C., May 30, 1962; d. Walter C. and Joan T. Wood. BA, Pace U., 1984; JD, DePaul U., 1987; postgrad., Northwestern U. Bar: Ill. 1987, U.S. Dist. Ct. (no. dist.) Ill. 1989, Fed. Trial Bar 1990. Judicial extern U.S. Bankruptcy Ct., Chgo., 1987; pub. defender, Office of Pub. Defender Cook County, Ill., 1987-89; counsel Peoples Energy Corp., Chgo., 1989-93; ptnr. Albert, Whitehead, P.C., Chgo., 1993—. Adj. prof. DePaul U. Coll. Law, 1992—; hearing bd. chair Atty. Registration Disciplinary Commn. Chmn. bd. dirs. Ctr. for New Horizons, 2001—; mem. Target Hope-Mentor; spkr. We Care Role Model. Mem. ABA (products sect., columnist trial sect. newsletter), Chgo. Bar Assn. (mem. editl. bd., columnist trial practice), Cook County Bar Assn. (bd. dirs., treas. 1993-98). Office: Albert Whitehead PC Ten N Dearborn Ste 600 Chicago IL 60602

WOOD, ANDRÉE ROBITAILLE, archaeologist, researcher; b. Chgo., Feb. 10, 1929; d. Andrew George and Alice Marie (Fortier) Robitaille; m. Richard Lawrence Wood, Jan. 14, 1956; children: Mary Wood Molo, Matthew William Wood, Melissa Irene Wood, Elizabeth Wood Wesel, John Andrew Wood. BA, No. Ill. Univ., DeKalb, 1977, MA, 1982. Freelance archaeologist, 1981-84; rsch. asst. Prehistoric Project Oriental Inst., Univ. Chgo., Ill., 1984—. Rsch., discovery, removal, analysis and identification of ancient blood residues on lithic material excavated at ten millenium old site, Çayönü in Ergani, Turkey. Contbr. articles to profl. jours. Avocations: poetry, boating, tennis, golf. Home: 356 Old Sutton Rd Barrington Hills IL 60010-9113 also: 8735 Midnight Pass Rd Apt 604B Sarasota FL 34242-2892

WOOD, BERENICE HOWLAND, retired secondary school educator; b. Newport, R.I., Oct. 21, 1910; d. Horatio Gates and Margaret Lorraine (Doyle) W. AB, Vassar Coll., 1934; MA, Columbia U., 1936; postgrad., U. R.I., 1961-65. Clk. 1st Dist. Ct. R.I., Newport, 1942-50; home service dir. ARC, Newport, 1950-61; tchr. Cranston, R.I., 1961-62, Elmhurst Sch., Portsmouth, R.I., 1962-64, Newport, 1964-82. Sec. to mayor City of Newport, 1941. Pres. Coun. Social Agys., Newport, 1955—57; active Hist. Soc. Newport, Art Mus. Newport, Redwood Libr., Newport, Preservation Soc., Newport, Hill Assn., Newport. Mem. Point Assn. Newport, Nat. Trust Hist. Preservation. Roman Catholic. Avocations: maintaining and preserving antiquities, foreign travel. Home: 82 Mill St Newport RI 02840-3146

WOOD, BERNARD ANTHONY, anthropology educator; b. London, Apr. 17, 1945; came to US, 1997; s. Anthony Frederick and Joan Faith (Slocombe) W.; m. Hazel Pamela Francis, Aug. 21, 1965 (div. July 1980); children: Nicholas James, Penelope Clare; m. Alison Margretta Richards (div. Dec. 2003); 1 child, Hannah Elin. BSc, U. London, 1966, MD, 1969, PhD, 1975, DSc, 1996. S.A. Courtauld prof. anatomy U. London, 1982-85; Derby prof. anatomy U. Liverpool, Eng., 1985-97, dean Faculty of Medicine, 1996-97; Henry R. Luce prof. human origins George Washington U., Washington, 1997—. Chair sci.-based archeology com. Natural Environment Rsch. Coun., UK, 1989-96; mem. bioarcheology panel Wellcome Trust, UK, 1994-2000. Author: Koobi Fora Research Project: Vol. 4, 1991; editor: Food Acquisition and Processing in Primates, 1984, Major Topics in Primate and Human Evolution, 1986. Avocations: running, woodchopping, salt glaze stoneware, Verdi. Office: George Washington U 2110 G St NW Washington DC 20052-0001 Home: PO Box 303 Wardensville WV 26851 Office Phone: 202-994-6077. E-mail: bwood@gwu.edu.

WOOD, CHARLES TUTTLE, history educator; b. St. Paul, Oct. 29, 1933; s. Harold Eaton and Margaret (Frisbie) W.; m. Susan Danielson, July 9, 1955; children: Lucy Eaton, Timothy Walker, Martha Augusta, Mary Frisbie. AB, Harvard, 1955, AM, 1957, PhD, 1962. Investment analyst, trader Harold E. Wood & Co., St. Paul, 1955-56; teaching fellow gen. edn. Harvard, 1959-61, instr. history, 1961-64; mem. faculty Dartmouth, 1964-96, prof. history, 1971-80, Daniel Webster prof. history, 1980-91, Daniel Webster prof. history and comparative lit., 1991-96, Daniel Webster prof. emeritus, 1996—, chmn. dept. history, 1976-79, chmn. dept. comparative lit., 1977. Vis. Keeney prof. of history Brown U., 1992-93; vis. prof. U. Coll. London, 1996. Author: The French Apanages and the Capetian Monarchy, 1223-1328, 1966, Philip the Fair and Boniface VIII, 2d edit., 1971, reprint, 1976, Felipe el Hermoso y Bonifacio VIII: Mexico: UTEHA, 1968, The Age of Chivalry: Manners and Morals 1000-1450, 1970, The Quest for Eternity, reprint edit., 1983, Joan of Arc and Richard III, 1988, The Trial of Charles I, 1989, Fresh Verdicts on Joan of Arc, 1996; also articles. Chmn. Dresden Bd. Sch. Dirs., 1972-74. Guggenheim fellow, 1986-87; recipient Disting. Service award N.H. Sch. Bds. Assn., 1975; Am. Council Learned Socs. fellow, 1980-81; Am. Bar Found. fellow, 1981-82 Fellow Medieval Acad. Am. (treas. 1989-2001, fin. com. 1979-2001, council 1985-87); mem. Am. Hist. Assn. (chmn. nominating com. 1977, Adams prize com. 1976-78), Conf. Brit. Studies, Soc. for French Hist. Studies, N.H. Sch. Bds. Assn. (2d v.p. 1974-75), New Eng. Medieval Conf. (pres. 1978-79), Am. Soc. Legal History, Phi Beta Kappa (pres. Alpha of N.H. 1997-99). Clubs: St. Botolph (Boston). Home: 7 N Balch St Hanover NH 03755-1502 E-mail: charles.t.wood@dartmouth.edu.

WOOD, CHRISTOPHER L.J. real estate executive; b. London, Jan. 20, 1947; came to U.S., 1983; s. Sidney John and Lillian Ballantine (Pollock) W.; m. Pamela Wood, Dec. 14, 1978; 1 child, Alexander Wood. BSc, London U., 1969. Ptnr., dir. Debenham, Tewson & Chinnocks, London, 1972—96; COO America's Best, 1996—98; mng. dir. Peracon Inc.; prin. DTZ Debenham Thorpe Internat., 1996—. Mem. St. George's Soc. N.Y., Thames Rowing Club, Union League Club (Phila.). Office: DTZ PO Box 412 Pawling NY 12564

WOOD, CONNIE GARRISON, music educator; d. Maisie Smith and Ira Valdora, Jr. Garrison; m. James Ray Wood, Aug. 31, 1969; children: Allison Anne, Robert Garrison. B in Music Edn., Baylor U., 1970; M in Music Edn., Ind. U., 1982. Piano instr. The Conservatory at UMHB, Belton, Tex., 2000—; adj. piano instr. U. of Mary Hardin-Baylor, Belton, Tex., 2001—. Classroom music instr. NE Ind. Sch. Dist., San Antonio, 1971—76; piano instr. Pvt. Studio, Temple, Tex., 1980—2002; pianist First Bapt. Ch., Del Rio, Tex., 1982—83; profl. accompanist Temple I. S. D., Tex., 1993—, U. of Mary Hardin-Baylor, Belton, Tex., 1995—; pianist Immanuel Bapt. Ch., Temple, Tex., 1996—2002; profl. accompanist Temple Coll., Tex., 1996—2000. Actor: (civic theater production) Sound of Music, 2001; profl. accompanist (undergraduate recitals) Vocal and Instrumental Soloists and solo piano performances, 1998—, soloist (piano performance). Mem. and officer Parent-Teachers Orgn. in Temple I.S.D., Tex., 1983—2001. Mem.: Music Tchrs. Nat. Assn., Tex. Music Tchrs. Assn., Ctrl. Tex. Music Tchrs. Assn. (student affiliate membership chmn. 2000—04, competition chmn. 2000—04), Ctrl. Tex. Med. Alliance (hearing and vision screening com. 1984—93), Jr. League of Temple, Wildflower Guild (performance edn. instr. 1994—97), Mu Phi Epsilon. Avocation: reading. Office: U of Mary Hardin-Baylor & Conservatory Box 8012 Belton TX 76513

WOOD, CORINNE GIESEKE, former lieutenant governor; b. Barrington, Ill., May 28, 1954; m. Paul R. Wood; children: Ashley, Brandon, Courtney. BS, U. Ill.; JD, Loyola U. Bar: Ill. 1979. Pvt. practice; counsel Ill. Savs. and Residential Fin. Bd.; atty. Hopkins & Sutter, Chgo.; gen. counsel Ill. Commr. of Banks and trusts; state rep. 59th dist. 90th Ill. Gen. Assembly, Springfield; rep. State of Ill., 1997—99, former lt. gov., 1999—2003. Appointed spec. asst., Ill. Atty. Gen. Former co-capt. Shields Twp. Rep. Precinct; Lake Forest chmn. John E. Porter for Congress, 1994, 96; adv. mem. Coun. of Women Advisors to U.S. Congress; past 1st v.p., bd. dirs. Women's Rep. Club, past pres., bd. mem. 10th Congl. Dist. of Lake Forest/Lake Bluff chpt.; past pres. (fin. chmn.), mem. bd. govs. Lake County Rep. Fedn.; bd. dirs. Allendale Shelter Club, Allendale Assn.; adv. bd. A Safe Place; transition bd. dirs. Anne M. Kiley Ctr. for the Developmentally Disabled; mem. LWV of Lake Forest/Lake Bluff; mem. Lake Forest Open Lands Assn.; former Lake Forest chmn., sustaining mem. Jr. League of Chgo.; former new mems. chair, membership com., Sunday sch. tchr. First Presbyn. Ch. of Lake Forest; den leader Pack 43, Boy Scouts Am.; plan commr. City of Lake Forest, 1993-97, sr. housing commr., 1993-97, ad hoc com. on sr. housing bd. mem. Recipient City of Lake Forest Spl. Recognition of Pub. Svc. award. Mem. ABA, Ill. Bar Assn., Lake County Bar Assn., Chgo. Bar Assn., House Financial Insts. Comm., Comm. on Aging, Edn. Appropriations Comm., Labor and Commerce Comm., appointed mem., Legislative Rsch. Bureau, bd. mem. Republican.

WOOD, CRAIG BRECKINRIDGE, paleobiologist, natural science educator; b. Washington, Jan. 27, 1943; s. William Ernest Wood and Christina Mae (DeBrito) Phillips; m. Sung He Lee, May 21, 1982; children: William, Violet, Virginia. AB in Geology, U. N.C., 1966; MS in Geology, U. Wyo., 1967; MA in Geology, Harvard U., 1980, PhD in Geology, 1992. Tchg. fellow geology, anthropology, biology depts. Harvard U., Cambridge, Mass., 1968-70, 73-74; rsch. assoc. geology dept. Princeton (N.J.) U., 1970-71; geologist Herbert & Assocs. Ltd., Virginia Beach, Va., 1972-73; instr. natural sci. Providence Coll., 1974-79, asst. prof. natural sci., spl. lectr. geology, 1979—, assoc. prof. natural sci., 1993-2001, prof., 2001—, dir. natural sci. program, 1993-95; lectr. biology and geology Asian divsn. U. Md., Yokota AFB, Japan, 1981-82, Osan AFB, Korea, 1981-82. Harvard U. exch. scholar dept. paleontology U. Calif., Berkeley, 1988-89; rsch. assoc. in mammalogy Mus. Comparative Zoology, Harvard U., 1994—; hon. guest prof. Jilin U., 2002—; expdn. mem. Rift Valley Rsch. Mission in Ethiopia, Addis Ababa, 1976, Blue Nile region, Ethiopia, 1993, 96, 97, 98; Mesozoic fieldwork in Gyeongsangdo, Korea, 1998-2000, 2003; fieldwork in Jilin Province, China, 2000, 2002, 2003. Co-discoverer of "Bodo Man", 1976, first Ethiopian highland Mezozoic vertebrates, 1993, first Ethiopian dinosaurs, 1996, first Triassic vertebrates in Tigray Province, 1997-98, first Ethiopian Mesozoic mammal, 1999, first Mesozoic mammals in Jilin Province, China, 2000; assoc. editor: Jour. Paleontology Soc. Korea, 2001-2003. Mem. Soc. Vertebrate Paleontology, Paleontol. Soc., Soc. for Study of Mammalian Evolution, R.I. Carolina Club (treas. 1994-97), R.I. Harvard Club, Sigma Xi, Phi Mu Alpha Sinfonia. Office: Providence Coll Biology Dept Providence RI 02918-0001 Office Phone: 401-865-2250. E-mail: cbwood@providence.edu.

WOOD, DARRYL SCOTT, criminologist, educator; b. Espanola, N.Mex., July 18, 1965; BA in Criminal Justice, N.Mex State U., 1987, MA in Criminal Justice, 1989; PhD, Simon Fraser U., 1997. Asst. prof. U. of Alaska, Anchorage, 1995—2001, assoc. prof., 2001—. Contbr. articles to profl. jours. Grantee, Can. Social Scis. and Humanities Rsch. Coun., 1991—95, U.S. Dept. of Justice and Nat. Inst. of Justice, 1998—2000; postdoctoral fellow, NIH, 2003—04. Mem.: Am. Soc. of Criminology, Acad. of Criminal Justice Scis. Office: University of Alaska Anchorage 3211 Providence Drive Anchorage AK 99508 Office Phone: 907-786-1126. E-mail: dwood@uaa.alaska.edu.

WOOD, DAVID CLARENCE, lawyer; b. Phila., Mar. 20, 1921; s. Clarence E. and Helen (Boley) W.; B.S. in Econs., U. Pa., 1943, postgrad. Law Sch., 1948; postgrad. Dickinson Law Sch., 1947; J.D., Temple U., 1949; m. Joan Herrold, June 25, 1960. Bar: Pa. 1950. Trial atty. U.S. Dept. Justice, Washington, 1952-55; practice, N.Y.C., 1956—; mem. Hill, Betts & Nash, 1956-78, Burke and Burke, 1978-80, Harlow and Wood, 1980—; mem. Com. Comite Maritime Internat., 1976-81. Deacon, elder Fifth Ave. Presbyterian Ch., 1968-71, trustee, 1972-75, 77-82; trustee Westminster Choir Coll., Princeton, N.J., 1972—, mem. exec. com., 1973—, chmn. bd. affairs com., 1974—; bd. dirs. Vis. Nurse Assn. N.Y., 1971—, chmn. employees benefit and pension com., 1977, mem. fin., audit, and real estate coms.; treas. Vis. Nurse Soc. Home Care; mem. Trustees Acad., Ohio U., 1975—; vice chmn. 1804 Fund Eastern U.S., 1978— . Served with USN, 1942-46, USNR, 1950-52. Recipient hon. alumnus degree, 1980. Mem. Am. Arbitration Assn., Assn. Average Adjusters (London), Assn. Average Adjusters U.S., Am. Soc. Internat. Law, Internat. Law Assn., ABA, Bar Assn. City and State N.Y., Phila. Bar Assn., Maritime Law Assn. U.S. (exec. com. 1973-76, 78-80, v.p. 1978-80), English Speaking Union, Pilgrims, Newcomen Soc. N.Am., Phi Delta Phi. Clubs: University, India House (N.Y.C.); Nassau (Princeton). Home: 201 E 62nd St New York NY 10021-7627 Office: 74 Trinity Pl New York NY 10006-2003

WOOD, DENNIS, communications executive; Mgr. Berkeley Walcoverings Inc.; chmn. bd. dirs., pres., CEO C-MAC Industries, Montreal, Canada. Bd. dirs. Gen. Trust Can., Maax Inc., Groupe Bocenor, Blue Mountain Coverings, Nat. Bank of Can. Bd. dirs. Orchestre Metropolitaine of Montreal. Office: C-MAC Industries 610 Sherbrook St W Ste 1610 Montreal QC Canada H3A 2R7

WOOD, DIANE PAMELA, judge; b. Plainfield, N.J., July 4, 1950; d. Kenneth Reed and Lucille (Padmore) Wood; m. Dennis James Hutchinson, Sept. 2, 1978 (div. May 1998); children: Kathryn Hutchinson, David Hutchinson, Jane Hutchinson. BA, U. Tex., 1971, JD, 1975, Georgetown U., 2003. Bar: Tex. 1975, D.C. 1978, Ill. 1993. Law clk. U.S. Ct. Appeals (5th cir.), 1975—76, U.S. Supreme Ct., 1976—77; atty. advisor U.S. Dept. State, Washington, 1977—78; assoc. Covington & Burling, Washington, 1978—80; asst. prof. law Georgetown U. Law Ctr., Washington, 1980—81, U. Chgo., 1981—88, prof. law, 1988—95, assoc. dean, 1989—92, Harold J. and Marion F. Green prof. internat. legal studies, 1990—95, sr. lectr. law, 1995—; spl. cons. antitrust divsn. internat. guide U.S. Dept. Justice, 1986—87, dep. asst. atty. gen. antitrust divsn., 1993—95; judge U.S. Ct. Appeals (7th cir.), 1995—. Contbr. articles to profl. jours.; bd. editors: Am. Jour. Internat. Law. Bd. dirs. Hyde Park-Kenwood Cmty. Health Ctr., 1983—85. Mem.: Am. Law Inst (elected coun. mem. 2003), Am. Soc. Internat. Law, Phi Alpha Delta. Democrat.

WOOD, DIRK GREGORY, surgeon, physician, forensic consultant; b. Springfield, Ohio, Sept. 19, 1953; s. Carlos Paul and Evelyn Cecelia (Bird) W. BA magna cum laude, Urbana (Ohio) U., 1973; postgrad., Ohio State U., 1973-75; MD, UAG Facultad de Medicina, Guadalajara, Mexico, 1980; mini pupilage, Inns of Court School of Law, London, 1990; JD, Capital Law Sch., Columbus, Ohio, 1991. Diplomate Am. Bd. Ob-Gyn, Am. Bd. Forensic Medicine. Intern Bronx (N.Y.) Lebanon Hosp., 1981-82; resident William Beaumont Hosp., Royal Oak, Mich., 1982-86; physician, surgeon Her Care, Inc., Springfield, 1986—2001. CEO Just What the Doctor Ordered, Springfield, 1992-2001; dir. of obstetrics Mercy Med. Ctr., Springfield, Ohio, 1999-2000; chief collaborative physician Nurse Midwives Ctr., 1999-2000. Coroner Clark County, Ohio, 1991-97; mem. Clark County Rep. Ctrl. Com., Clark County Dist. 14, 1992—. Named Ky. col., Ala. col. Fellow Internat. Coll. Surgeons, Am. Coll. Legal Medicine, Am. Coll. Forensic Examiners, Interam. Coll. Physicians and Surgeons; mem. SAR, Am. Soc. Law and Medicine, Phi Delta Epsilon (past chpt. pres.), Phi Alpha Delta. Republican. Avocations: scuba diving, bibliophilia, travel. Home: 2900 Cleveland Ave Saint Joseph MI 49085 E-mail: drdirk@gcctv.com.

WOOD, DONALD CRAIG, retired marketing professional; b. Wilmington, Del., June 24, 1937; s. Thomas Henry and Madelyn (Brehm) W.; m. Elizabeth Haring, Apr. 28, 1962; children: Craig Standish, Allison Jean. BA, U. Del., 1959; MBA, Northwestern U., 1967. Sales engr. NVF Corp., Broadview, Ill., 1960-62, Synthane Corp., Morton Grove, Ill., 1962-68; account exec., mgr. sales Donnelley Mktg. subs. Dun and Bradstreet Corp., Oakbrook, Ill., 1968-76, from dir. to v.p. market devel. to v.p. mktg. Stamford, Conn., 1977-1980; from v.p., gen. mgr. to pres. Donnelley Mktg. Info. Svcs. subs. Dun and Bradstreet Corp., Stamford, 1980-86; sr. v.p. Donnelley Mktg. Inc. subs. Dun and Bradstreet Corp., Stamford, 1987-90; v.p., gen. mgr. info. svcs. Trinad Systems Corp., Livermore, Calif., 1990-96; ret., 1996. Served to 1st lt. U.S. Army, 1959-60. Home: 6312 Providence CC Dr Charlotte NC 28277

WOOD, DONALD EURIAH, lawyer; b. Guymon, Okla., May 27, 1935; s. Theodore and Lula Elizabeth (Rider) W.; m. Lynda Sharon Harris, Sept. 30, 1960; children: Donald Craig, Tana Dawn, Kristen Lynn. BA, Panhandle A&M Coll., 1958; LLB, Okla. U., 1964, JD, 1970. Bar: Okla. 1964. Asst. county atty., Texas County, 1964; county atty., 1965-67; dist. atty. Okla. 1st Jud. Dist., Guymon, 1967—2002; ret., 2002. Mem. adv. com. Okla. Commn. Criminal and Traffic Enforcement Systems, 1972; mem. Gov.'s Commn. Cmty. Affairs and Planning, 1972-75; mem. faculty Panhandle State Coll., 1974-92; mem. Okla. Dist. Atty. Tng. Coun., 1976—; mem. Okla. Bur. Narcotics and Dangerous Drugs Commn., 1992-98. Served with inf. AUS, 1958-60. Named Okla. Prosecutor of Yr., Assn. Okla. Narcotic Enforcers, 1994-95. Mem. Okla. Bar Assn. (legal ethics com. 1971-72), Texas County Bar Assn. (pres. 1966, 1970-71), Nat. Dist. Attys. Assn., Okla. Dist. Attys. Assn. (pres. 1972, exec. com. 1971-2003), Elks Club, Rotarian Club, Phi Alpha Delta. Presbyterian. Home: 605 Hillcrest Dr Guymon OK 73942-3345 E-mail: done@ptsi.net.

WOOD, ELIJAH, actor; b. Cedar Rapids, Iowa, Jan. 28; Appeared in films Back to the Future Part II, 1989, Internal Affairs, 1990, Avalon, 1990, Paradise, 1991, Radio Flyer, 1992, Forever Young, 1992, The Adventures of Huck Finn, 1993, The Good Son, 1993, North, 1994, The War, 1994, Flipper, 1996, The Ice Storm, 1997, Deep Impact, 1998, Black and White, 1999, The Bumblebee Flies Anyway, 2000, Chain of Fools, 2000, The Lord of the Rings: The Fellowship of the Ring, 2001, The Lord of the Rings: The Two Towers, 2002, The Lord of the Rings: The Return of the King, 2003, Spy Kids 3-D: Game Over, 2003, Eternal Sunshine of a Spotless Mind, 2004; TV movies include Child in the Night, 1990, Day-O, 1992, Oliver Twist, 1997; also appeared in music video Paula Abdul's Forever Your Girl. Office: William Morris Agency c/o Nichole David 151 S El Camino Dr Beverly Hills CA 90212-2775

WOOD, EMILY CHURCHILL, special education educator, social studies educator, consultant; b. Summit, N.J., Apr. 11, 1925; d. Arthur Burdett and Ruth Vail (Pierson) Churchill; m. Philip Warren Wood, June 22, 1946; children: Martha, Arthur, Warren, Benjamin. BA, Smith Coll., 1946; MA in Teaching, Manhattanville Coll., 1971; postgrad., U. Tulsa, 1974-79, Langston U., 1990-92. Cert. tchr. social studies, learning disabilities, elem. edn., econs., Am. history, world history. Tchr. Miss Fines Sch., Princeton, N.J., 1946-47, Hallen Ctr. for Edn., Portchester, N.Y., 1973-74, Town and Country Sch., Tulsa, Okla., 1974-79, Tulsa Pub. Schs., 1979-97, Heritage Acad., Tulsa, 1998—; adj. instr. Tulsa C.C., Tulsa, 1998—. Ednl. cons. Tulsa, 1997—; leader colloquia Bill of Rights Arts and Humanities Coun., Tulsa, 1989; mem. literacy task force Tulsa 2000 Edn. Com., 1990-92; chmn. internat. student exch. Eisenhower Internat. Sch., Tulsa, 1992-97. Author: (with others) Visual Arts in China, 1988, Applauding Our Constitution, 1989, The Bill of Rights: Who Guarantees What, 1993; contbr. articles to profl. jours. Leader, founder Am. Field Svc., Tulsa, 1982—84; pres., v.p. Booker T. Washington H.S. PTA, Tulsa, 1985; campaign mgr. auditors race Dem. Party, Tulsa, 1988, 1992, 1994; bd. dirs. Smith Coll. Alumnae, Northampton, Mass., 1956—59, Sister Cities Internat., Tulsa, 1992—2001, nominations chair, 1999—2001; bd. dirs. Tulsa Global Alliance; trustee Okla. Found. for Excellence, 2000—. Named Tulsa Tchr. of Yr. Tulsa Classroom Tchrs. Assn., 1988, Nat. Elem. Tchr. of Yr., Nat. Bar Aux., 1992, Outstanding Elem. Social Studies Tchr., Nat. Cound. or Social Studies, 1999; recipient Elem. Medal of Excellence, Okla. Found. for Excellence, 1990, Valley Forge Tchrs. medal Freedoms Found., 1992, Paragon award Tulsa Commn. on Status of Women, 1996, Pinnacle award Mayor's Commn. on Status of Women, 1998, Liberty Bell award Tulsa Bar Assn., 1998, Global Vision award Tulsa Global Alliance, 2002. Mem. UN Assn. Ea. Okla. (pres. 2000—), Nat. Coun. Social Studies (religion program com. 1984—, bd. dirs. 1997—), DAR, Okla. Edn. Assn., Okla. Coun. Social Studies (pres. 1995, tchr. of yr. 1984), Okla. Bar Assn. (law related com. 1988—, tchr. of yr. 1990), Okla. Coun. Econ. Edn. (state and nat. awards 1981, 89, 92), Kent Place Alumnae Assn. (disting. alumna award 1992). Avocations: reading, swimming, travel, walking. Home: 3622 S Yorktown Pl Tulsa OK 74105-3452 E-mail: emily_wood46@hotmail.com.

WOOD, EVAN RACHEL, actress; b. Raleigh, NC, Sept. 7, 1987; Actor: (films) Digging to China, 1998, Practical Magic, 1998, Detour, 1999, Little Secrets, 2001, S1m0ne, 2002, Thirteen, 2003, The Missing, 2003; (TV films)

In the Best of Families: Marriage, Pride & Madness, 1994, Search for Grace, 1994, A Father for Charlie, 1995, Death in Small Doses, 1995, Get to the Heart: The Barbara Mandrell Story, 1997, Down Will Come Baby, 1999; (TV series) Profiler, 1998—99, Once and Again, 1999—2002, (guest appearances) American Gothic, 1995—98, Touched by an Angel, 2000, The West Wing, 2002, CSI: Crime Scene Investigation, 2003. Office: Agy for Performing Arts 9000 Sunset Blvd Ste 1200 Sherman Oaks CA 91403

WOOD, FRANK, actor; b. Lincoln, Mass. Grad. acting program, NYU; grad. theater program, Wesleyan U. Broadway debut in Side Man (Tony award, 1999); actor: (plays) Three Sisters, Tomorrowland, King of Rats, Dark Ride, Hollywood Arms, 2002; many roles in Gil Kofman plays at Soho Rep, Adobe Theater and Dallas Theater Ctr., has worked with Fifty Second Street Project; actor: (TV appearances) Ed, 2001, The Sopranos, 2001, Third Watch, 2001, Law and Order, 2002; (films) Down to You, 2000, Small Time Crooks, 2000, Pollock, 2000, Thirteen Days, 2000, The Royal Tenenbaums, 2001. Recipient 1995 Drama-Logue award for best ensemble in Kofman's Entrevista 187, Padua Hills Playwrights Festival. Mem.: East Coast Artists.

WOOD, FRANK MAXWELL, lawyer; b. Forest Park, Ga. m. Suzanne Brunson; children: Frank, Sydney, James. BA, LaGrange Coll., 1981; JD, U. Ga., 1985. Law clk. Floyd County Superior Ct., 1985—87; staff atty. Pros. Attys.' Coun. Ga., 1992—94; asst. dist. atty. Ocmulgee Dist. Atty.'s Office, 1994—97; pvt. practice Macon, Ga.; U.S. atty. Mid. Dist. Ga., 2001—. Mem. Martha Bowman Meml. United Meth. Ch. With USAF, lt. col. Ga. Air Nat. Guard. Office: Mid Dist Ga Thomas Jefferson Bldg 433 Cherry St Macon GA 31201

WOOD, GEORGE AMBOS, city manager; b. Savannah, Ga., Feb. 3, 1952; s. Herbert Lee and Louise (Ambos) W.; m. Pamela Sue Hinson, Dec. 9, 1979; 1 child, Andrew Hinson. BS in Polit. Sci., Ga. So. U., Statesboro, 1974; MPA, U. Kans., 1978. Adminstrv. asst. to city mgr. City of Salina, Kans., 1977-79; city adminstr. City of Lancaster, S.C., 1979-80; town mgr. Town of Kingstree, S.C., 1980-82; village mgr. Village of Pinehurst, N.C., 1982-88; city mgr. City of Kings Mountain, N.C., 1988-94, City of Cleveland, Tenn., 1994-2000, City of Statesboro, Ga., 2000—. Bd. dirs. United Way, Cleveland, 1994—; mem. Econ. Devel. Coun., Cleveland, 1994—. Recipient George C. Franklin award N.C. League of Municipalities, Raleigh, 1988, Excellence in Pub. Svd. award Am. Soc. Pub. Adminstrn., 2000; Ga. Municipal Assn.,"City of Excellence" award, 2002. Former mem. Tenn. City Mgmt. Assn. (award for excellence in mcpl. govt. 1997), mem. Ga. City/County mgmt. Assn., Tenn. Mcpl. League (City Overall Improvement award 1995), Rotary (bd. dir. Kings Mountain chpt. 1992-94), Local Govt. Stewardship award Tenn. Dept. Environment and Conservation, 1997, Disting. Budget Presentation award GFOA, 1999. Baptist. Avocations: golf, reading, travel. Office: City of Statesboro PO Box 348 50 E Main St Statesboro GA 30459

WOOD, GORDON STEWART, historian, educator; b. Concord, Mass., Nov. 27, 1933; s. Herbert G. and Marion (Friberg) W.; m. Louise Goss, Apr. 30, 1956; children: Christopher, Elizabeth, Amy. AB, Tufts U., 1955; AM, Harvard, 1959; PhD, Harvard U., 1964. Fellow Inst. Early Am. History and Culture, Williamsburg, Va., 1964-66; asst. prof. Harvard U., Cambridge, Mass., 1966-67; assoc. prof. U. Mich., Ann Arbor, 1967-69; prof. history Brown U., Providence, 1969—; Pitt. prof. Cambridge U., 1982-83. Bd. trustees Tufts U.; Bancroft lectr. U.S. Naval Acad., 1986; Anson G. Phelps lectr. NYU, 1986; Charles Edmundson lectr. Baylor U., 1987; Samuel Paley lectr. Hebrew U., Jerusalem, 1987; presdl. lecture series on presidency, 1991. Author: The Creation of the American Republic, 1776-1787, 1969, The Rising Glory of America, 1760-1820, 1971; co-author: The Great Republic, 1977, The Radicalism of the American Revolution, 1992 (Pulitzer Prize for history 1993); co-editor: Imagined Histories: American Historians Interpret the Past, 1998, The American Revolution: A History, 2002. Mem. coun. Inst. Early Am. History and Culture, 1980-83; bd. trustees Colonial Williamsburg. With USAF, 1955-58. Recipient Bancroft prize Columbia U., 1970, Disting. Visitor award Australian-Am. Ednl. Found., 1976, Douglass Adair prize, 1984, Emerson prize Phi Beta Kappa, 1992, Kidger award New Eng. Tchrs. Assn., 2001; Sunderland fellow U. Mich. Law Sch., 1990, All Souls Coll. fellow, 1991, Fletcher Jones Found. Disting. fellow The Huntington, 1997-98; Woodrow Wilson Ctr. guest-scholar, 1993-94; named to Rhode Island Heritage Hall of Fame, 2000; Dr. of Letters, La Trobe Univ., Austrailia. Mem. Am. Hist. Assn. (John Dunning prize), Orgn. Am. Historians, Soc. Am. Historians, Nat. Hist. Soc. (chmn. bd. advisors), Soc. Historians of the Early Am. Republic (pres.), Am. Acad. Arts and Scis., Am. Philos. Soc. Office: Brown Univ Dept of History Box N Providence RI 02912-9040

WOOD, HARLINGTON, JR., federal judge; b. Springfield, Ill., Apr. 17, 1920; s. Harlington and Marie (Green) W. AB, U. Ill., 1942, JD, 1948. Bar: Ill. 1948. Practiced in, Springfield, 1948-69; mem. firm Wood & Wood, 1948—58, 1961—69; U.S. atty. So. Dist. Ill., 1958-61; assoc. dep. atty. gen. for U.S. attys. Justice Dept., Washington, 1969-70, assoc. dep. atty. gen., 1970-72, asst. atty. gen. civil div., 1972-73; U.S. dist. judge So. Dist. Ill., Springfield, 1973-76; circuit judge U.S. Ct. Appeals (7th cir.), Springfield, 1976—92, sr. judge, 1992—. Adj. prof. Sch. Law, U. Ill., Champaign, 1993; disting. vis. prof. St. Louis U. Law Sch., 1996-2000. Chmn. Adminstrv. Office Oversight Com., 1988-90; mem. Long Range Planning Com., 1991-96. U.S. Army, 1942—46. Recipient Profl. Lifetime Achievement award, Inns of Ct., 2002. Office: US Ct Appeals PO Box 233 Petersburg IL 62675-0233

WOOD, HEIDI, commissioner; BA with honors, Brown U., 1987. Analyst SG Cowen; fin. cons. Shearson Lehman Hutton, Wedbush Morgan; from v.p., sr. analyst to exec. dir. Morgan Stanley, 1999—; commr. aerospace investment Aerospace Commn., Arlington, Va. Mem.: N.Y. Aerospace Analyst Soc. (treas.). Office: Aerospace Commn Crystal Gateway One Ste 940 1235 Jefferson Davis Hwy Arlington VA 22202-3283

WOOD, JACKIE DALE, physiologist, educator, researcher; b. Picher, Okla., Feb. 16, 1937; s. Aubrey T. Wood and Wilma J. (Coleman) Wood Patterson. BS, Kans. State U., 1964, MS, 1966; PhD, U. Ill., 1969. Asst. prof. physiology Williams Coll., Williamstown, Mass., 1969-71; asst. prof. U. Kans. Med. Ctr., Kansas City, 1971-74, assoc. prof., 1974-78, prof., 1978-79; prof., chmn. dept. physiology Sch. Medicine, U. Nev., Reno, 1979-85; chmn. dept. physiology coll. medicine Ohio State U., Columbus, 1985-97, prof. physiology and internal medicine, 1997—. Cons. NIH, Bethesda, Md., 1982-88. Recipient Rsch. Career Devel. award NIH, 1974; named Hon. Citizen City of Atzugi Japan, 1987; Alexander von Humboldt fellow, W.Ger., 1976, grantee NIH, 1971—. Mem. AAAS, Am. Physiol. Soc. (assoc. editor 1984-96, rsch. award 1986), Soc. Neurosci., Am. Gastroent. Assn. Office: Ohio State U Dept Physiology and Cell Biology 304 Hamilton Hall 1645 Neil Ave Columbus OH 43210-1218 Office Phone: 614-292-5449. Business E-Mail: wood.13@osu.edu.

WOOD, JAMES, supermarket executive; b. Newcastle-upon-Tyne, Eng., Jan. 19, 1930; came to U.S., 1974; s. Edward and Catherine Wilhelmina (Parker) W.; m. Colleen Margaret Taylor, Aug. 14, 1954; children: Julie, Sarah. Grad., Loughborough Coll., Leicestershire, England; hon. LHD, St. Peter's Coll., N.J. Chief food chain Newport Coop. Soc., S. Wales, U.K., 1959-62, Grays Food Coop. Soc., Eng., 1962-66; dir., joint dep. mng. dir. charge retailing Cavenham, Ttd., Hayes, Eng., 1966-80; pres. Grand Union Co., Elmwood Park, N.J., 1973-79, chief exec. officer, dir., from 1973, chmn. bd., 1979-80, Gt. Atlantic & Pacific Tea Co., Inc., 1998-00. Bd. dirs. Asarco, Inc., Irma Fabrikerne A/S, Denmark, Schering-Plough Corp. Active World USO, UNICEF, United Jersey Bank. With Brit. Army, 1948-50. Mem. Food Mktg. Inst. (bd. dirs.) Roman Catholic. Office: Gt Atlantic & Pacific Tea Co 2 Paragon Dr Montvale NJ 07645-1718

WOOD, JAMES ALLEN, retired lawyer; b. McMinnville, Tenn., Jan. 14, 1906; s. Ira and Emma (Calhoun) W.; m. Eva Beth Sellers, Dec. 28, 1941; 1 son, Eben Calhoun. AB, U. Tenn., 1929; LL.B., U. Tex., 1934. Bar: Tex. 1934. Tchr. Bolton H.S., Alexandria, La., 1929-32; since practiced in Corpus Christi, 1971-97; ret., 1998. State dist. judge, Corpus Christi, 1941-43; mem. rules adv. com. Supreme Ct. Tex., 1949-86. Author 7 vols. poetry; contbr. articles to profl. jours.; author: Life on a Warren County Farm (Tenn.) 1906-1923, 1996, Early Bench and Bar of Corpus Christi, 1996, Items: Serious of Not, 1997, Moody Shadows, 1962, Muted Echoes, 1970, For Exiles, 1973, Last Sunset, 1974, Blunt Arrows, 1979, Bottom Lines, 1987, Wandering Lines, 1993. Bd. dirs. Nueces River Authority, 1972-89, pres., 1981-84, life time hon. dir., 1989—. Lt. USNR, 1943-45. Fellow Am. Coll. Trial Lawyers; mem. ABA, Tex. Bar Assn., Nueces County Bar Assn. (pres. 1941) Home and Office: 458 Dolphin Pl Corpus Christi TX 78411-1514

WOOD, JAMES ANDERSON, cardiac surgeon; b. Newton, Mo., Nov. 5, 1926; s. Frank and Lula Wood; m. Joann Wood, 1950; children: Diane, James, Jeff, Carol. BA, Reed Coll., 1953; MD, U. Oreg., 1957. Diplomate Am. Bd. Thoracic Surgey, Am. Bd. Surgery. Co-founder St. Vincent Hosp. Cardiac Surg. Program, Portland, VA Hosp. Cardiac Surg. Program, Portland; founder Bend OR Cardiac Surg. Program, Portland, Corvallis OR Cardiac Surg. Contbr. articles to profl. jours. With Marine Corps. Recipient Young Rschr. award Am. Heart Assn., Meritorious award AMA, 1965. Mem. AMA, Portland Surg. Soc., U.S. Polo Assn., Robert Wise Surg. Soc., El Dorado Polo Club, William Conklin Surg. Soc., Albert Starr Club, Am. Soc. of Thoracic Surgeons, Portland Acad. of Medicine, Dant Found., Wesley Eager Cardiac Surg. Found. (pres.), Pan Pacific Assn., Pacific Coast Surg., North Pacific Surg., Internat. Cardiovascular. Home: PO Box 5 North Plains OR 97133-0005

WOOD, JAMES EDWARD, JR., religion educator, author; b. Portsmouth, Va., July 29, 1922; s. James E. and Elsie Elizabeth (Bryant) W.; m. Alma Leacy McKenzie, Aug. 12, 1943 (dec. Oct. 2000); 1 son, James Edward III BA, Carson-Newman Coll., 1943; BD, So. Bapt. Theol. Sem., 1947, ThM, 1948; MA, Columbia U., 1949; postgrad., U. Tenn., 1943-44; cert. in Chinese, Yale U., 1949-50; Japanese diploma, Naganuma Sch. Japanese Studies, Tokyo, 1950-51; PhD., So. Bapt. Theol. Sem., 1957; LLD, Seinan Gakuin U., Japan, 1983; LLD (hon.), Capital U., 1996; DHC (hon.), Bucharest (Romania) U., 1998. Ordained to ministry So. Bapt. Ch., 1942. Pastor So. Bapt. chs., Tenn. and Ky., 1942-48; Bapt. missionary to Japan, 1950-55; prof. religion and lit. Seinan Gakuin U., Japan, 1951-55; assoc. prof. history of religions Baylor U., Waco, Tex., 1955-58, prof. hist. religions, dir. J. M. Dawson Inst. Ch. State Studies, 1958—73, 1980—99, 1st dir. honors program, 1959-64, founder chmn. interdeptl. grad. degree program in ch.-state studies, 1962-73, 80-95, founder Baylor Univ. Ch. State Rsch. Ctr., 1968, founder, chmn. faculty-student Far Eastern exch. program, 1970-72, Simon and Ethel Bunn Disting. prof. ch.-state studies, 1980-99, Simon and Ethel Bunn Disting. prof. emeritus, 1999—. Exec. dir. Bapt. Joint Com. on Pub. Affairs, Washington, 1972-80; mem. ctrl. panel Bapt. World Alliance Commn. on Religious Liberty and Human Rights, 1965-75, 80-2000, Commn. on Freedom, Justice and Peace, 1975-80; chmn. Bapt. Com. on Bicentennial, 1973-76; mem. So. Bapt. Inter-Agy. Coun., 1972-80, vice chmn., 1975-76, sec. 1976-77; fellow Internat. Acad. for Freedom of Religion and Belief, 1985-, pres. 1990-2000, hon. pres. 2000-; vis. prof. So. Bapt. Theol. Sem., 1974, N.Am. Bapt. Theol. Sem., Sioux Falls, S.D., 1974, 79, Okla. Bapt. U., Shawnee, 1977, vis. scholar, Christ Coll. Oxford U., 1983, Naval Coll. Chaplains, Providence, 1988-95, others; vis. prof. Bulgarian Baptist Theol. Sem., Sofia, 1998, Faculty of Canon Law, Cath. U., Leuven, Belgium, 1999, others; vis. lectr. Tex. A&M U, 1962, 65, 68, Ashland (Ohio) Theol. Sem., 1971; Vernon Richardson lectr. U. Bapt. Ch., Balt., 1975, Ea. Bapt. Theol. Sem., Phila., 1975, Duquesne U., 1976, Wake Forest U., 1978, U. Richmond, 1979; lectr. First World Congress on Religious Liberty, Amsterdam, 1977, Notre Dame Law Sch., 1980, U. Kans., 1982, 2d World Congress on Religious Liberty, Rome, 1984, U. Faculty of Law, Warsaw, Poland, 1984, Loyola U., 1985, U. So. Calif., 1983, Rice U., 1984, U. Oviedo, Spain, 1989, Chinese Inst. Religion, Beijing, 1986, Brigham Young U., 1986, 95, 97, Union Theol. Sem., Va., 1989, U. Kans. Law Sch., 1990, U. Tirana, Albania, 1992, U. Malta, 1994, Austin Coll., 1989, 95, U. Pitts. Law Sch., 1997; chair Internat. Consultation on Relig. Rights and Ethnic Identity, Budapest, 1992; co-chair Internat. Conf. Religious Freedom, Moscow, 1993; mem. internat. adv. bd. World Report on Freedom Conscience Human Rights Ctr., U. Sussex, U.K.; co-chair consultation on Freedom of Conscience and Belief, Moscow, 1993; chair Internat. Consultation Religious Liberty and Social Peace, Malta, 1994; Carver-Barnes lectr. Southeastern Bapt. Theol. Sem., 1981; Asian Found. lectr. Seinan Gakuin U., Japan, 1983; ecumenical consultation on edn. Nat. Coun. Chs., 1974. Co-author: Church and State in Scripture, History and Constitutional Law, 1958; author: A History of American Literature: An Anthology, 1952, The Problem of Nationalism, 1969, Nationhood and the Kingdom, 1977, Secular Humanism and the Public Schools, 1986, Reflections on Church and State, 1995; (edited by Derek H. Davis) The Separation of Church and State Defended: Selected Writings of James E. Wood, Jr., 1995, Church-State Relations in the Modern World, 1999, Church and State In Historical Perspective, vol.1, 2004, Church and State In the Modern World, vol. 2, 2004, and numerous others; editor: Markham Press Fund, Baylor U. Press, 1970-72; editor, contr.: Jewish-Christian Relations in Today's World, 1971, Baptists and the American Experience, 1976, Religion and Politics, 1983, Religion, the State, and Education, 1984, Religion and the State: Essays in Honor of Leo Pfeffer, 1985, Ecumenical Perspectives on Church and State, Protestant, Catholic and Jewish, 1988, Readings on Church and State, 1989, The First Freedom: Religion and the Bill of Rights, 1990, contr. co-editor: The Role of Religion in the Making of Public Policy, 1991, The Role of Government in Monitoring and Regulating Religion in Public Life, 1993, Problems and Conflicts Between Law and Morality in a Free Society, 1994, founding editor Jour. Ch. and State, 1959-73, 80-93, mem. editl. coun., 1973-80; mem. editl. bd. Religion and Public Edn., Religious Freedom Reporter; area editor, contbr. Ency. So. Bapts., 1982, Church and State in Am. History, 1987; contbr. Changing Trends in Education, 1992, Law, Religion and Human Rights in Global Perspective, 1995, Dialogue of Democracy: An American Politics Reader, 1996, United Nations' Contributions to the Prevention and Settlement of Conflicts, 2003, The New Inquisitors, 2004, many others; contbr. over 300 articles to profl. jours. Speaker in field. Sponsor Ams. for Public Schs., 1963-68; bd. dirs. Waco (Tex.) Planned Parenthood, 1966-72, pres., 1971-72; sponsor Christians Concerned for Israel, 1968—, Tex. Conf. Chs. Consultation on Religion and Public Edn., 1971, Nat. Christian Leadership Conf. for Israel, 1978—; pres. Waco area ACLU, bd. dirs. Tex. unit, 1968-72; pres. Nat. Council Religion and Public Edn., 1979-83, exec. com., 1975-90, bd. dirs., 1972-90; chmn. exec. com. Council Washington Reps. on UN, 1977-80, mem. council exec. com., 1973-80; exec. com. Nat. Coalition on Public Edn. and Religious Liberty, 1973-95; mem. religious liberty com. Nat. Council Chs. U.S.A., 1972—, mem. com. internat. concerns on human rights, 1973-80; Am. rep. Chs. Montreux Colloquium on Helsinki Final Act, 1977; v.p. Waco Conf. Christians and Jews, 1983-86, Internat. Acad. for Freedom of Religion and Belief, 1985-90, pres., 1990-2000, hon. pres., 2000—; mem. internat. adv. bd. World Report on Freedom of Conscience, Human Rights Ctr., U. Sussex, Eng.; trustee Internat. Devel. Conf., 1974-80; nat. coun. Am.-Israel Friendship League, 1977—; founder, chmn. Waco Human Rights Week, 1981-86; mem. ch. rels. com., U.S. Holocaust Meml. Coun., 1990-97; adv. com. on religious freedom abroad U.S. State Dept., 1998—. Recipient Disting. Alumnus award Carson-Newman Coll., 1974, Religious Liberty award Alliance for Preservation of Religious Liberty, 1980, Henrietta Szold award Tex. region Hadassah, 1981, Human Rights award Waco Conf. Christians and Jews, 1986, Cir. of Achievement award Baylor U. Mortar Bd., 1991, Religious Freedom Lifetime award Ams. United Ctrl. Tex., 1993, W.R. White Meritorious Svc. award, 1996, Human Rights Leadership award Freedom mag., 1998; hon. Tex. col., 1969; Alma M. and James E. Wood., Jr. endowed scholarship Baylor U., 2004—. Mem. Am. Soc. Ch. History, Am. Acad. Religion, Am. Soc. Internat. Law, Am. Soc. Sci. Study of Religion, N. Am. Soc. Ecumenists, NCCJ (ad. com. on ch. state and taxation 1979-85), Supreme Court Hist. Soc., Soc. for Scholarly Publishing, Va. Hist. Soc., Phi Eta Sigma, Pi Kappa Delta, Alpha Psi Omega. Democrat. Home: 203 Barrington Ln Yorktown VA 23693-5622 E-mail: james_wood@baylor.edu.

WOOD, JAMES JERRY, lawyer; b. Rockford, Ala., Aug. 13, 1940; s. James Ronald and Ada Love Wood; m. Earline Luckie, Aug. 9, 1959; children: James Jerry, William Gregory, Diana Lynn. AB, Samford U., 1964, JD, 1969. Bar: Ala. 1969, U.S. Supreme Ct. 1976. Dir. legal affairs Med. Assn. State of Ala., Montgomery, 1969-70; asst. atty. gen. State of Ala., Montgomery, 1970-72; asst. U.S. atty. Middle Dist. Ala., Montgomery, 1972-76; pvt. practice, 1977-78; pres. Wood & Parnell, P.A., Montgomery, Ala., 1979-89; pvt. practice Montgomery, 1990—. Gen. counsel Ala. Builders Self-Insurers Fund, Home Builders Assn. of Ala.; chmn. character and fitness com. Ala. State Bar, 1981-84, 86-89, chair task force on quality of life, 1990-92, chair task force on mem. svcs., 1994-96. Capt. USAR, 1974-79. Fellow: Ala. Law Found., Am. Bar Found.; mem.: FBA (pres. Montgomery chpt. 1974—75), ABA (ho. of dels. 1990—98), Def. Rsch. Inst., Ala. Coun. Assn. Execs. (pres. 2001), Ala. Bar Assn., Ala. Assn. Workers Compensation Group Self-Insured Funds (chmn.), Am. Soc. Assn. Execs., Am. Nat. Inns of Ct., Rotary (pres. Montgomery Capital chpt. 1986—87, 1996—97). Republican. Baptist. Office: PO Box 241206 Montgomery AL 36124-1206 Office Phone: 334-834-3006. E-mail: jjwood@mindspring.com.

WOOD, JAMES MICHAEL, lawyer; b. Oakland, Calif., Mar. 22, 1948; s. Donald James and Helen Winifred (Reimann) Wood; m. Cynthia Ahart Wood; children from previous marriage: Nathan, Sarah, Ruth 1 stepchild from previous marriage, Alexandra. BA, St. Mary's Coll., 1970; JD, U. San Francisco, 1973. Bar: Calif. 1973, U.S. Dist. Ct. (no., ctrl. and so. dists.) Calif. 1973. Rsch. atty. Alameda County Superior Ct., Oakland, 1973-76; ptnr. Reed Smith LLP, Oakland, 1976—. Presenter profl. confs. Contbr. articles to profl. jours. Mem.: ABA (litig. sect., mem. health litig. com., mem. litig. products liability com.), Food Drug Law Inst. (mem. bd. dirs., adv. com. 1999—), Drug Info. Assn., Nat. Health Lawyers Assn., Am. Acad. Hosp. Attys., Def. Rsch. Inst., Alameda County Bar Assn., No. Calif. Assn. Def. Counsel, State Bar Calif. Office: Reed Smith LLP 1999 Harrison St Ste 2200 Oakland CA 94612-3572 Office Phone: 510-763-2000. E-mail: jmwood@reedsmith.com.

WOOD, JAMES NOWELL, museum director and executive; b. Boston, Mar. 20, 1941; s. Charles H. and Helen N. (Nowell) W.; m. Emese Forizs, Dec. 30, 1966; children: Lenke Hancock, Rebecca Nowell. Diploma, Universita per Stranieri, Perugia, Italy, 1962; BA, Williams Coll., Williamstown, Mass., 1963; MA (Ford Mus. Tng. fellow), NYU, 1966. Asst. to dir. Met. Mus., N.Y.C., 1967-68, asst. curator dept. 20th century art, 1968-70; curator Albright-Knox Art Gallery, Buffalo, 1970-73, assoc. dir., 1973-75; dir. St. Louis Art Mus., 1975-80, Art Inst. Chgo., 1980—. Vis. com. visual arts U. Chgo., 1980-94; head com. Nat. Endowment Arts Mem. Intermuseum Conservation Assn. (past pres.), Assn. Art Mus. Dirs. Office: Art Inst Chgo 111 S Michigan Ave Chicago IL 60603-6492*

WOOD, JANE ROBERTS, writer; m. Dub Wood. Author: The Train to Estelline, 1987, A Place Called Sweet Shrub, 1990, Dance a Little Longer, 1993, Grace, 2001, Roseborough, 2003, Mocha, 2004. Recipient Tex. Inst. Letters award for best short story, 1998; fellow NEA, NEH. Office: c/o U North Texas Press PO Box 311336 Denton TX 76203-1336

WOOD, JEAN CAROL, poet, lyricist; b. Okla. City, Apr. 6, 1940; d. Howard Melvin and Ethel Matillda (Caroll) Sage; m. Harold David Wood; children: Howard David, Troy Don, Kevin Dale, L'lana Cayé. Freelance writer, 1976—. Contbr. poems in collections; lyricist: songs As It Should Be, 2001—02; author: (poem) Rest On His Thumb, 2003, The Transport Of a Winged Being. Recipient trophy, Internat. Soc. Poets, 2003. Avocations: writing, gardening, reading. Home: 1047 W Windsor Way Mustang OK 73064

WOOD, JEANNE CLARKE, charitable organization executive; b. Pitts., Dec. 21, 1916; d. Joseph Calvitt and Helen Caroline (Mattson) Clarke; m. Herman Eugene Wood, Jr., May 6, 1936 (dec.); children: Helen Hamilton (Mrs. John Harry Mortenson), Herman Eugene III. Student, Collegiate Sch. for Girls, Richmond, Va., 1932-33. Asst. to Dr. and Mrs. J. Calvitt Clarke, Christian Children's Fund, Inc., Richmond, 1938-64; founder Children, Inc., Richmond, 1964, pres., internat. dir., 1964—. Author: (with Helen C. Clarke) In Appreciation: A Story in Pictures of the World-Wide Family of Christian Children's Fund, Inc, 1958, Children's Christmastime Around the World, 1962, Children's Games Around the World, 1962, Children-Hope of the World-Their Needs, 1965, Children-Hope of the World-Their Friends, 1966; Editor: CI News, 1964. Recipient citation Eastern Council Navajo Tribe, 1970, citations Mayor of Pusan (Korea), 1971, citations Mayor of Seoul, 1971, citations Gov. of Kanagawa Prefecture (Japan), 1972, commendation Pres. of U.S., 1972, citation Stephen Philibosian Found., 1975, citation Santa Ana (El Salvador) Dept. Edn., 1975, citation Nat. Sch. for Blind, Dominican Republic, 1982, citation Navajo Tribal Council of Navajo Nation, Window Rock, Ariz., 1982 Home and Office: Children Inc PO Box 5381 1000 Westover Rd Richmond VA 23220-6624 Office Phone: 804-359-4562. *While there are many things about which we can make no choice in this volatile world where change is constant and sometimes disastrous, it has seemed to me that one can make the choice between accepting things positively or negatively. I have chosen to accept them positively.*

WOOD, JEREMY SCOTT, architect, urban designer; b. Glen Ridge, N.J., Oct. 23, 1941; s. William Gamble and Alice-Marguerite (Scott) W.; m. Robin Benensohn-Rosefsky, June 14, 1970; children: Alexis, Jonas, Augusta. AB, Yale U., 1964, M in Architecture, 1970. Registered architect, Ma. Sr. assoc. TAC/The Architects Collaborative, Inc., Cambridge, Mass., 1970-94; sr. project mgr. Domenech Hicks & Krockmalnic, Inc., Boston, 1995-97; sr. project architect Elkus/Manfredi Architects, Ltd., Boston, 1997—. Instr. Boston Archtl. Ctr., 1970-76; head tutor dept. art history, history of modern architecture Yale U., 1969-70, Emerson Coll. Performance and Prodn. Ctr./Cutler Majestic Theatre Renovation, Boston, 2001-03. Author: (sect. and chpt. in books) Adaptive Reuse: Issues and Case Studies in Building Preservation, 1988, Office Buildings, 1989, Exposed Structure in Building Design, 1993; prin. works include Emerson Coll. Prodn. and Performance Ctr., Boston, 2001—03, Allen House Restoration & Condominiums, South End, Boston, 1998, MBTA/AMTRAK North-South Rail Link Stations (Boston), MBTA Subway Station Modernization State St. and Govt. Ctr. Stations (Boston), Complejo Medico de las Americas, Guatemala City, Guatemala, Health Care Internat. Hosp. and Hotel, Clydebank, Glasgow, Scotland, Copley, Place, Boston, The Westin Hotel at Copley Place, Boston, Liberty Ctr. and Vista Internat. Hotel, Pitts., Wellington Bus. Ctr. Offices, Medford, Mass., Two Portland (Maine) Sq. Office Bldg., One Mifflin Pl., Cambridge, Groton (Mass.) Sch. Dormitories, Coll. Engrng. and Applied Sci., Shuwaikh Campus, Kuwait U., Kuwait City, Kuwait, Hosp. U. Pa., Phila.; asst. editor Perspecta 11; corr. Architecture and Urbanism, 1976; contbr. articles to profl. jours. Recipient Award of Excellence, Assn. Sch. Bus. Ofcls., Coun. Ednl. Facilities Planners, AIA, 1976, Concrete Industry Bd. Spl. Recognition award The Westin Hotel, Boston, 1983, Prestressed Concrete Inst. award, 1983, Honor award Associated Gen. Contractors of Mass., 1985, Grand award Urban Land Inst., 1988, hon. mention New Eng. Healthcare Design Awards, 1994, 1997 Move Massachusetts 2000 design award for engrng. and arch. of North South Rail Link Project, Boston Preservation Alliance award for renovation of Cutler Majestic Theatre, 2003. Mem. AIA, Boston Soc. Architects, Mass. State Assn. Architects, Am. Planning Assn., Soc. Archtl. Hists. (life, Nat. chpt.), The Archtl. League N.Y. Home: 10 Pigeon Hill Rd Weston MA 02493-1620

WOOD, JERRY, investment company executive; Former sr. mng. dir., fixed income sales Morgan Stanley; co-head, fixed income div. Credit Suisse First Boston, NY, 2003—. Office: Credit Suisse First Boston Eleven Madison Ave New York NY 10010 Office Phone: 212-325-2000.

WOOD, JOAN E. state representative; b. Milo, Idaho, June 3, 1934; m. Thomas D. Wood; 5 children. Grad., Ririe (Idaho) H.S. Ptnr. ranch/farm/trucking corp.; state rep. dist. 35A Idaho Ho. of Reps., Boise, 1996—, vice chair resources and conservation com., chair transp. and def. com., mem. revenue and taxation com.; mem. drug and alcohol rehab. caucus com. Mem.: Multistate Hwy. Transp. Agreement Com., Am. Legis. Exch. Coun., Outdoors Unltd. Multiple Use Resource Orgn., Ctr. Constnl. Studies, Upper Valley Rep. Women, Jefferson County Rep. Women (past pres.). Republican. Lds Ch. Office: State Capitol PO Box 83720 Boise ID 83720-0038

WOOD, JOHN ARMSTEAD, planetary scientist, geological sciences educator; b. Roanoke, Va., July 28, 1932; s. John Armstead and Lillian Cary (Hall) W.; m. Elisabeth Mathilde Heuser, June 12, 1958 (div.); children: Crispin S., Georgia K.; m. Julie Marie Nason, Sept. 9, 1989. BS in Geology, Va. Polytech. Inst., 1954; PhD in Geology, Mass. Inst. Tech., 1958; post-doctoral study, U. Cambridge, Eng., 1959-60. Staff scientist Smithsonian Astrophys. Obs., Cambridge, Mass., 1959, 61-62, 65—; research asso. Enrico Fermi Inst. U. Chgo., 1962-65; prof. dept. geol. scis. Harvard, 1976-95; asso. dir. Harvard-Smithsonian Center for Astrophysics, 1981-98. Vice chmn. Lunar Sample Analysis Planning Team, 1971—72; mem. space studies bd. NRC, 1998—2001; chair Com. on Lunar and Planetary Exploration, 1999—2001. Author: Meteorites and the Origin of Planets, 1968, The Solar System, 1979, 2d edit., 2000. Recipient NASA medal for exceptional sci. achievement, 1973, J.L. Smith medal NAS, 1976, G.K. Gilbert award Geol. Soc. Am., 1992. Fellow AAAS, Am. Geophys. Union, Meteoritical Soc. (pres. 1971-72, Leonard medal 1980); mem. NAS, Am. Acad. Arts and Scis., Cosmos Club. Achievements include having asteroid no. 4736 named in his honor Johnwood. Home: 71 Langdon St Cambridge MA 02138-2501 Office: 60 Garden St Cambridge MA 02138-1516

WOOD, JOHN ARTHUR, nurse; b. Lincoln, Nebr., Mar. 30, 1964; s. Earl Wayne and Lorene Wilma (Kuhn) W.; m. Julie Kristin Gray, June 5, 1993; children: Amy, Will. BSN, U. Nebr., 1988. RN, Nebr. Nurse's asst. Tabitha Nursing Home, Lincoln, Nebr., 1986-88, staff nurse, 1988-89, Truman Med. Ctr. West, Kansas City, Mo., 1989-93, Via Christi-St. Francis, Wichita, Kans., 1993-96. Preceptor Med. ICU, Via Christi-St. Francis, Wichita, Truman Med. Ctr. CPR instr., ARC, Lincoln, 1982-86, mem. Red Cross Youth Leadership Camp Staff, Lincoln, 1978-84, first aid team instr., 1981-84, first aid instr., 1981-84. Recipient awards Adm. Nebr. State Navy, Lincoln, 2000, ARC, Lincoln, 1983. Mem. NRA (life). Republican. Avocations: sportsman, outdoorsman, reading, music. E-mail: jaw1964@sbcglobal.net.

WOOD, JOHN MARTIN, lawyer; b. Detroit, Mar. 29, 1944; s. John Francis and Margaret Kathleen (Lynch) Wood; m. Judith Anne Messer; children: Timothy Peter, Meagan Anne. BA, Boston Coll., 1966; JD, Cath. U. Am., 1969. Bar: D.C. 1970, Va. 2001, U.S. Dist. Ct. D.C. 1970, U.S. Dist. Ct. Va. 2001, U.S. Ct. Appeals (D.C. cir.) 1973, U.S. Ct. Appeals (3d cir.) 1973, U.S. Ct. Appeals (4th cir.) 1973, U.S. Supreme Ct. 1973. Trial atty, tax divsn. Dept. Justice, Washington, 1969-73; assoc. Reed Smith LLP, Washington, 1973-80, ptnr., 1980—, mng. ptnr., 1989-95, dir. legal pers., 1995-98. Dir. adv. bd. Salvation Army, Va. and Met. Washington, Leadership Washington, 1993—. Mem.: Fairfax Bar Assn., The Currituck Club N.C., River Bend Golf and Country Club, Barristers Club Washington, Delta Sigma Pi, Phi Alpha Delta. Home: 9490 Oak Falls Ct Great Falls VA 22066-4143 Office: Reed Smith LLP 3110 Fairview Park Dr Ste 1400 Falls Church VA 22042 Office Phone: 703-641-4248. E-mail: jwood@reedsmith.com.

WOOD, JONATHAN STUART, economist, educator; b. New Orleans, Nov. 14, 1944; s. John Joseph and Linelle Marie (Waguespack) W.; m. Ann M., Apr. 7, 1973; children: Elizabeth, Christopher, Julie, Jonathan. Grad., NASA Summer Inst. in Space and Engrng., 1965; BS in Mech. Engrng., Tulane U., 1966; MS in Aerospace Engrng., Princeton U., 1970; MBA in Econs., NYU, 1975, MPhil in Econs. and Fin., 1978, PhD in Econs. and Fin., 1980. Rschr. on bio-engring study of neck whiplashes Tulane Med. Sch. and Tulane Sch. Engrng. (for US Dept Health, Edn. and Welfare), 1963; materials tester and lab. analyst Svc. Foundry, New Orleans, 1964; ops. rsch. & econ. analyst Grumman Aerospace Corp., Bethpage, N.Y., 1969-74; sr. investment analyst, cons. to common stock dept. Prudential Ins. Co., Newark, 1974-76; instr. fin. & acctg. Sch. Bus. U. Conn., Storrs, 1976-78; Liberty Fund Rsch. fellow Stanford U. Inst. Humane Studies Rsch. Seminar in Econs., Palo Alto, Calif., 1977; asst. prof. econs. & fin. Tulane U., New Orleans, 1978-84; assoc. prof. econs. & fin. Coll. Bus. Adminstrn. Loyola U., New Orleans, 1984—. Prof. econs. and fin. Pace U. Grad. Sch. Bus. Adminstrn., N.Y.C., 1975-76; vis. prof. fin. Grad. Sch. Bus. Adminstrn. NYU, 1980; vis. prof. fin. Grad. Sch. Bus. Tulane U., 1985, 91, lectr., 1990; presenter in field.; cons. economist; expert in bus. valuation; adj. prof. in econ. and fin. Pace U. Grad. Sch. Bus. Adminstrn., N.Y., 1975-76; appeared on WWL-TV discussing current econ. and fin. events focusing on La. econ. matters; rschr., lectr. in field; conducted interviews and seminars in field. Author: Chemical Kinetic Influences, 1968, Chemical Kinetic Influences in Liquid Propellant Rocket Combustion Instability, 1969, 70, Effectiveness Evaluation of Orbital Observatories (with Joseph R. Fragola), 1975, Heterogeneous Expectations and Security Price Distributions, 1978, Entrepreneurship and the Co-Ordination of Expectations in the Stock Market, 1980, 82, Some Refinements in the Austrian Trade-Cycle Theory, 1984, Capital Formation Problems in the United States and the Question of a Capital Shortage, 1984, Methodologies for Valuation of Closely-Held Companies (with Dr. Michael A. Dalton and Robert I. Glover), 1989, Valuation of Closely-Held Companies & Professional Practices by Experts (with Dr. Michael A. Dalton and Dr. Robert I. Glover), 1989, Real Value of Damage Caps for Medical Malpractice in Louisiana (with Michael A. Dalton), 1997; referee Quarterly Rev. Econs. and Bus., 1982, Rev. Austrian Econs., 1989; contbr. chpts., reviews to books. Chmn. fin. com., mem. exec. bd. Short-Fern St. Neighborhood Assn., 1984-85; lectro. Eucharistic min., mem. com. univ. Parish St. Thomas More Tulane U.; dir. Operation New Start, Inc.; softball coach Carrollton Boosters; elected to u. senate, 1986—; U. Senate Parking Com., 1986-87; faculty acad. affairs budget com., 1986-89, 89-92; Blue Ribbon Task Force for libr.'s acad. future, 1986-87; u. senate designatee to Fin. Com. of bd. trustees, 1991-92, 92-93; advisor to Endowment Com. of Bd. Trustees, 1991-93. Recipient MBA Top Gun award as Outstanding Tchr., Loyola U., 1993. Mem. Am. Econ. Assn., Am. Fin. Assn., We. Econ. Assn., We. Fin. Assn., So. Econ. Assn., So. Fin. Assn., Ea. Fin. Assn., Southwestern Social Scis. Assn., Opers. Rsch. Soc. Am./Inst. Mgmt. Sci., Pontchartrain Astronomy Soc., Student Recruitment Team, Grad. Edn. Task Force, Entrepreneurship Task Force, Curriculum Com., Advising Com. (chmn. 1986-87), MBA Curriculum Task Force. Avocations: astronomy, music. Home: 500 Arlington Dr Metairie LA 70001-5516 Business E-Mail: jswood@loyno.edu. E-mail: jsjewood@aol.com.

WOOD, JOSEPH GEORGE, neurobiologist, educator; b. Victoria, Tex., Dec. 8, 1928; s. Harold Robert and Frances Josephine (Marcak) W.; m. Jane L. Andrews; 1 dau., Marian. BS, U. Houston, 1954, MS, 1958; PhD, U. Tex., Galveston, 1962. Teaching asst. biology, U. Houston, 1956-58; instr. anatomy U. Tex. Dental Br., Houston, 1961, Yale U., 1962-63; asst. prof. U. Ark. Med. Sch., Little Rock, 1963-66; assoc. prof. U. Tex., San Antonio, 1966-70, asst. dean acad. devel., 1967-69, prof. and chmn. dept. neurobiology and anatomy, 1970-84, prof. neurobiology and anatomy, 1984—88; prof., chmn. dept. anat. sci. U. Okla. Coll. Medicine, 1988-93; dir. Okla. Ctr. Neurosci., 1990-95. Guest prof. dept. pathobiology, cell biology and neuroanatomy U. Minn., 1993—96; sr. lectr. molecular and cell biology U. Tex., Dallas, 1997—, asst. dean pre-health professions, 1998—2002, assoc. dean pre-health edn., 2002—, clin. prof. human devel., 2002—; vis. prof. Philips U., Marburg, Germany, 1984. Served with AUS, 1954-56. Recipient Basic Sci. Tchg. award U. Ark. Med. Ctr., 1963, U. Tex. Houston, 1972, 75, 86, Disting. Alumnus award U. Tex. Med. Br., 1976 Mem.: Tex. Assn. Advisors for the Health Professions (chair), Tex. Soc. Electron Microscopy (pres. 1970—71, exec. coun. 1971—79), Assn. Anatomy Chmn., Histochem. Soc., Assn. Am. Med. Colls., Soc. Neurosci. (exec. com. Houston chpt. 1971—77, pres. 1973—77, rsch. award 1962), Am. Assn. Anatomists (exec. com. 1974—78), Cajal Club, Alpha Omega Alpha, Sigma Xi, Golden Key, Phi Kappa Phi. Office: U Tex at Dallas MS FN II PO Box 830688 Richardson TX 75083-0688 Office Phone: 972-883-2571. Business E-Mail: woodj@utdallas.edu.

WOOD, JOSHUA WARREN, III, lawyer, alternative dispute resolution executive; b. Portsmouth, Va., Aug. 31, 1941; s. Joshua Warren and Mary Evelyn (Carter) W.; m. Marcia Neal Ramsey, Feb. 29, 1964; children: Lauren Elaine Yeh, Joshua Warren IV. AB, Princeton U., 1963; JD, U. Va., 1971. Bar: Va. 1971, N.J. 1976, U.S. Supreme Ct. 1977, N.Y. 1982. Comml. banking asst. Bankers Trust Co., N.Y.C., 1967-68; assoc. McGuire, Woods & Battle, Richmond, Va., 1971-75; v.p., gen. counsel, sec. Robert Wood Johnson Found., Princeton, NJ, 1975—2003; pres., gen. counsel Global Ctr. for Dispute Resolution Rsch., N.Y.C., 2004—. Mem. AAA/ABA/AMA Commn. on Alternative Dispute Resolution in Health Care; master Marie L. Garbaldi Am. Inn Court for Alternative Dispute Resolution. Mem. editl. bd. Va. Law Rev., 1969-71. Capt. arty. U.S. Army, 1963-67. Decorated Army Commendation medal. Mem. ABA, Princeton Bar Assn., N.Y. Bar Assn., Va. Bar Assn., N.J. Bar Assn., Nat. Health Lawyers Assn., Am. Arbitration Assn. (bd. dirs., mem. panel of arbitrators, task force Mass torts & alternative dispute resolution), Order of Coif, Princeton Club. Office: 335 Madison Ave 10th Fl New York NY 10017 Office Phone: 212-716-3929. E-mail: woodw@adr.org.

WOOD, JULIENNE LOUISE, librarian, historian; d. John Henry Wood and Lilas Naomi Lothen; m. Samuel Claude Shepherd, Jr., Sept. 2, 1978. BA magna cum laude, Gustavus Adolphus Coll., 1970; MA in U.S. History, U. WI-Madison, Madison, 1972; MLS, U. WI-Milwaukee, Milwaukee, 1978; PhD in U.S. History, U. WI-Madison, Madison, 1994. Copyright acquisitions libr. Libr. Congress, Washington, 1979—80, sr. copyright acquisitions libr., 1980—83, supr. libr. copyright office, 1983—85; dir. Barksdale Air Force Base Libr., Bossier City, La., 1985—87; lectr. history Centenary Coll., Shreveport, La., 1995—98; govt. info. libr. LSU, Shreveport, 1999—2000; head rsch. svc. Noel Memorial Libr. LSU Shreveport, 2000—. Mem. nat. comm. Amer. Libr. Assn., Chgo., 2000—; mem. state com. (Membership, Information Literacy) La. Libr. Assn., La., 2001—03. Author: (hist. articles) Dictionary of American History, 2003, (biog. articles) American National Biography, 1999; Book Reviewer (reference book reviews) American Reference Books, Annual, 2001—. Co-chmn. program com. La. Hist. Assn., Forty-second ann. meeting, Lafayette, La., 2000; mem. bd. dir. Ark.-La.-Tex. Genealogical Assn., Shreveport, 1990; mem., treas., show chair. Red River Quilters, Shreveport, 1992—; grants reviewer Alliance Edn., Shreveport, 2001—. Higher Edn. Act Title II-B fellow, U. Wis.-Milw. Sch. Libr. Sci. Mem.: Southern Hist. Assn., Orgn. Amer. Historians, Amer. Libr. Assn., Phi Kappa Phi, Beta Phi Mu, Phi Alpha Theta. Office: Noel Memorial Libr LSU Shreveport One Univ Pl Shreveport LA 71115-2399

WOOD, KENNETH ANDERSON, artist, designer, consultant; b. Cleve., May 11, 1913; s. George Robert and Leonore (Anderson) Wood; m. Ruth Eleanor Diehm, Sept. 14, 1937 (dec. May 1999). Student, Fenn Coll., Cleve., 1932-34, Cleve. Inst. Art, 1935-45. Artist Patterson Displays, Cleve., 1934-35; art dir. Bailey Meter Co., Wickliffe, Ohio, 1936-71; owner Kenwood Designers and Assocs., Chesterland, Ohio, 1971—; designer of stained glass windows, 1979—. Pres. Artist and Craftsman Assocs., Cleve., 1940—44, Geauga Artists Assn., Geauga County, Ohio, 1950—53. Exhibitions include nat., regional and local, 1939—97, Represented in permanent collections Butler Mus. Am., Youngstown, Ohio, Inlander Collection of Gt. Lakes Regional Paintings, Cleve. Mus. Art, numerous pvt. collections; patents for product design. Mem.: Indsl. Designers Soc. Am. (life). Republican. Seventh Day Adventist. Avocation: travel. Office: Kenwood Design and Assocs 11950 Sperry Rd Chesterland OH 44026-2225

WOOD, KENNETH ARTHUR, retired editor, writer; b. Hastings, Sussex, Eng., Feb. 25, 1926; came to U.S., 1965; s. Arthur Charles and Ellen Mary (Cox) W.; m. Hilda Muriel Harloe, Sept. 13, 1952. Editor Stamp Collector newspaper Van Dahl Publs., Albany, Oreg., 1968-80, editor emeritus, 1980—. Author (ency.) This Is Philately, 1982, (atlas) Where in the World, 1983, Basic Philately, 1984, Post Dates, 1985, Modern World, 1987; author several hundred articles and columns published in the U.K. and U.S.A., 1960—. Served with Brit. Army WW II. Recipient Disting. Philatelist award Northwest Fedn. Stamp Clubs, 1974, Phoenix award Ariz. State Philatelic Hall of Fame, 1979, Disting. Philatelist award Am. Topical Assn., 1979. Fellow Royal Philatelic Soc. (London); mem. Am. Philatelic Soc. (hon. life, Luff award 1987, Hall of Fame Writers Unit, 1984). Avocations: stamp collecting/philately, aviation history, modern history, gardening. Office: 2430 Tudor Way SE Albany OR 97322-5661

WOOD, KERRY, professional baseball player; b. Irving, Texas, June 17, 1977; Pitcher Chicago Cubs, 1998—. Named Nat. League Rookie of the Yr., 1998; named to Nat. League All-Star Team, 2003. Achievements include led Nat. League in strikeouts (266), 2003. Office: c/o Chicago Cubs 1060 W Addison Chicago IL 60613*

WOOD, KIMBA M. judge; b. Port Townsend, Wash., Jan. 2, 1944. BA cum laude, Conn. Coll., 1965; MSc, London Sch. Econs., 1966; JD, Harvard U., 1969. Bar: U.S. Dist. Ct. D.C. 1969, U.S. Ct. Appeals D.C. 1969, N.Y. 1972, U.S. Dist. Ct. (ea. and so. dists.) N.Y. 1974, U.S. Ct. Appeals (2d cir.) 1975, U.S. Supreme Ct. 1980, U.S. Dist. Ct. (we. dist.) N.Y. 1981. Assoc. Steptoe & Johnson, Washington, 1969-70; with Office Spl. Counsel, OEO Legal Svcs., Washington, 1970-71; assoc., then ptnr. LeBoeuf, Lamb, Leiby & MacRae, N.Y.C., 1971-88; judge, U.S. Dist. Ct. (so. dist.) N.Y., N.Y.C., 1988—. Mem. ABA (chmn. civil practice, procedure com. 1982-85, mem. coun. 1985-88, jud. rep. 1989-91), N.Y. State Bar Assn. (chmn. antitrust sect. 1983-84), Fed. Bar Coun. (trustee from 1978, v.p., 1984-85), Am. Law Inst. Office: US Dist Ct US Courthouse 500 Pearl St New York NY 10007-1316

WOOD, L. LIN, JR., lawyer; b. Raleigh, N.C., Oct. 19, 1952; s. Lucian Lincoln and Josephine (Currin) W.; m. Deborah Anne Jamison, July 25, 1987; children:, Elizabeth Ashley, Matthew Carlton. BA cum laude Mercer U., 1974, JD cum laude, 1977. Bar: Ga. 1977, U.S. Dist. Ct. (no. and mid. dist.) Ga. 1977, U.S. Ct. Appeals (5th cir.) 1977, U.S. Ct. Appeals (11th cir.) 1981. Assoc. f Jones, Cork, Miller & Benton, Macon, Ga., 1977-80, Freeman & Hawkins, Atlanta, 1980-83; ptnr. Wood & Grant, Atlanta, 1983— . Mem. staff Mercer Law Rev., 1975-77. Recipient Am. Jurisprudence award 1976, 77, U.S. Law Week award, 1977. Mem. ABA, Assn. Trial Lawyers Am., State Bar Ga., Atlanta Bar Assn., Lawyers Club Atlanta, Ga. Trial Lawyers Assn. Republican. Methodist. Club: Atlanta City. Office: The Equitable Bldg Ste 2140 100 Peachtree St Atlanta GA 30303 E-mail: llwood@linwoodlaw.com.

WOOD, LARRY (MARY LAIRD), journalist, writer, public relations executive, educator, environmental consultant; b. Sandpoint, Idaho; d. Edward Hayes and Alice (McNeel) Small; children: Mary, Marcia, Barry. BA summa cum laude, U. Wash., 1939, MA summa cum laude, with highest honors, 1940; postgrad., Stanford U., 1940—43, U. Calif., Berkeley, 1946—47, cert. in photography, 1971; postgrad. in journalism, U. Wis., 1971—72, U. Minn., 1971—72, U. Ga., 1972—73; postgrad. in art, architecture and marine biology, U. Calif., Santa Cruz, 1974—76, Stanford Hopkins Marine Sta., 1977—80. Lifetime secondary and jr. coll. tchg. cert., Wash., Calif. Feature writer and columnist Oakland Tribune and San Francisco Chronicle, Calif., 1939—; archtl. and environ. feature and travel writer and columnist San Jose (Calif.) Mercury News (Knight Ridder), 1972-90; tchg. fellow Stanford U., 1940-43; dir. pub. rels. 2-counties, 65-park 100,000 acre East Bay Regional Park Dist., No. Calif., 1948-68; pres. Larry Wood Pub. Rels., 1946—; pub. rels. dir. Calif. Children's Home Soc., 1947-58. Prof. pub. rels., mag. writing, journalism, investigative reporting San Diego State U., 1974-75; disting. vis. prof. journalism San Jose State U., 1976; assoc. prof. journalism Calif. State U., Hayward, 1978; prof. sci. and environ. journalism U. Calif. Berkeley Ext. grad. divsn., 1979—; press del. nat. convs. Am. Geophys. Union Internat. Conf., 1986—, AAAS, 1989—, Nat. Park Svc. VIP Press Tour, Yellowstone after the fire, 1989—, Nat. Assn. Sci. Writers, 1989—, George Washington U./Am. Assn. Neurol. Surgeons Sci. Writers Conf., 1990, Am. Inst. Biol. Scis. Conf., 1990, Nat. Conf. Sci. Writers, Am. Heart Assn., 1995, Internat. Cardiologists Symposium for Med./Sci. Writers, 1995, Annenberg Program Electronic Media Symposium, Washington, 1995; EPA del. to USSR and Ea. Europe; expert witness on edn., pub. rels., journalism and copyright; cons. sci. writers interne project Stanford U., 1989—; spl. media guest Sigma Xi, 1990—; mem. numerous spl. press corps; selected White House Spl. Media, 1993—; selected mem. Duke U. 14th Ann. Sci. Reporters Conf., 1995; internat. press guest Can. Consulate Gen. Dateline Can., 1995—, French Govt. Tourist Office, 1996—, Ministerio delle Risorse Agricole Alimentari e Forestali and Assocs. Conf., 1995; appeared in TV documentary Larry Wood Covers Visit of Queen Elizabeth II. Contbr. over 5,500 articles to newspapers, nat. mags., nat. and internat. newspapers including L.A. Times-Mirror Syndicate, Knight-Ridder Syndicate, Washington Post, Phila. Inquirer, Chgo. Tribune, Miami Herald, Oakland Tribune, Seattle Times, San Francisco Chronicle, 36 Million Circulation Parage, Parade, San Jose Mercury News (Nat. Headliner award), Christian Sci. Monitor, L.A. Times/Christian Sci. Monitor Worldwide News Syndicate, Washington Post, Phila. Inquirer, Hawaiian Airlines In Paradise and other in-flight mags., MonitoRadio, Donnelly Pubs., Sports Illus., Life, Mechanix Illus., Popular Mechanics, Parents (contbg. editor), House Beautiful, Am. Home (awards 1988-89), Archl. Digest, Better Homes and Gardens, Sunset, Architectural Digest, National Geographic World, Travel & Leisure, Chevron USA/Odyssey (Calif. Pub.'s award 1984), Xerox Edn. Publs., Europe's Linguapress, PSA Mag., Off Duty, Oceans, Sea Frontiers, AAA Westways, AAA Via, Travelin', others; home and garden columnist, editor, 5-part series Pacific Coast Ports, 5-part series Railroads of the West, series Immigration, Youth Gangs, Endangered Species, Calif. Lighthouse Chain, Lighthouses of the World, Pacific Coast Wetlands, Elkhorn Slough Nat. Estuarine Res., Ebey's Landing Nat. Hist. Island Res., Calif. Water Wars, BLM's Adopt a Horse Program, Mt. St. Helen's Eruption, Oreg's Covered Bridges, Loma Prieta Earthquake, Oakland Firestorm, Missing Children, Calif. Prison Reform, Columbia-Alaska's Receding Glacier, Calif. Underwater Parks, and many others; author: Wonderful U.S.A.: A State-by-State Guide to Its Natural Resources, 1989; co-author: McGraw-Hill English for Social Living, 1944, Fawcett Boating Books, 1956-66, Fodor's San Francisco, Fodor's California, 1982-89, Bell and Howell/Charles Merrill Focus on Life Science, Focus on Physical Science, Focus on Earth Science, 1983, 2d edit, 1987, State of California's Golden State Travel Guide, 1998; contbr. Earth Science 1987; 8 works selected for use by Europe's Woltors-Nordoff-Longman English Language Texts, U.K., Netherlands, 1988; author: (with others) anthology West Winds, 1989; reviewer Charles Merrill texts, 1983-84; book reviewer Profl. Communicator, 1987—; selected writings in permanent collections Oakland Pub. Libr., U. Wash. Main Libr.; environ. works included in Dept. Edn. State of Md. textbook; contbr., author Journalism Quar.; author script PBS/AAA America series, 1992; contbg. editor: Parents, Fashion Showcase, Spokane Mag. Nat. chmn. travel writing contest Assn. for Edn. in Journalism and Mass Communication/Soc. Am. Travel Writers, 1979-83; judge writing contest for Nat. Assn. Real Estate Editors, 1982—; cons. S. Carolina Dept. Parks, Recreation and Tourism, 1999—; press del. 1st Internat. Symposium Volcanism and Aviation Safety, 1991, Coun. for Advancement of Sci. Writing, 1977—, Rockefeller Media Seminar Feeding the World-Protecting the Earth, 1992, Global Conf. on Mercury as Pollutant, 1992, Earth Summit Global Forum, Rio de Janeiro, 1992; invited Nat. Park Svc. Nat. Conf. Sci. Writers, 1985, Postmaster Gen.'s 1992 Stamps, 1991, Internat. Geophys. Union Conf., 1982—, The Conf. Bd., 1995—, Corp. Comm. Conf., Calif. Inst. Tech.'s Media and Sci. Seminar, 1995—, Medical Writers Delegation to Russia and Estonia, 1997, N.Y. Times Opinion Rsch. Co. Corp. Image Conf., 1999, EPA and Dept. Energy Tech. Conf., 1992, Am. Soc. Photogrammetry and Remote Sensing Internat. Conv. Mapping Global Change, 1992, U.S. Conf. on Oceans, 1998, N.Y. Mus. Modern Art Matisse Retrospective Press Rev. and all media previews, 1992—, celebration 150th anniversary Oreg. Trail, 1993, Nat. Coun. Advancement Sci. Writing, 1977-2003, Sigma Xi Nat. Conf., 1988-2003, Nat. Sci. Writers Confs., 1977-2003, PRSA Travel and Tourism Conf., 1993—, Internat. Conf. Environment, 1994, 95, Quality Life Europe, Prague, 1994, Calif. Sesquicentennial, 1996, 14th Ann. Sci. Writers Conf., 1996, Picasso Retrospective, 1996, others; mem. Gov.'s Conf. Tourism N.C., 1993 2002, Calif., 1976—, Fla., 1987—, N.C. Govs. conf. on tourism and film, 2000-, U.C. Irvine Calif. Computer Sci. Symposium, 2000, Sea Grant's conf. on sci. in the news, 2000, N.Y. conf. bd. conf. on environ. journalism, 2000, on economics, 2001; press guest 14 U.S. states and 12 fgn. countries' Depts. Tourism, 1986—. Named to Broadway Hall of Fame, U. Wash., 1984; recipient Broadway Disting. Alumnus award, 1995; citations for environ. writing Nat. Park Svc., U.S. Forest Svc., Bur. Land Mgmt., Oakland Mus. Assn., Oakland C. of C., Chevron USA, USN plaque and citation, Best Mag. articles citation Calif. Pubs. Assn., 1984, U.S. Treasury award, 1946; co-recipient award for best Sunday newspaper mag. Nat. Headliners, citation for archtl. features Oakland Mus., 1983; honoree for achievements in journalism Nat. Mortar Bd., 1988, 89; named one of 10 V.I.P. press for Yellowstone Nat. Park field trip on "Let Burn" rsch., 1989, Calif.'s top 40 Contemporary Authors for writings on Calif. underwater parks, 1989, nat. honoree Social Issues Resources Series, 1987, Gov.'s Calif. Women of Achievement award, 1988-90; invited V.I.P. press, spl. press guest. Mem. AAAS, Am. Bd. Forensic Examiners, Calif. Acad. Scis., San Francisco Press Club, Nat. Press Club, Pub. Rels. Soc. Am. (charter mem. travel, tourism, environment and edn. divs.), Nat. Sch. Pub. Rels. Assn., Environ. Cons. N.Am., Am. Assn. Edn. in Journalism and Comm. (exec. bd. nat. mag. divsn. 1978, panel chmn. 1979-80, author Journalism Quar. jour.), Women in Comm. (nat. bd. officer 1975-77, book reviewer Prof. Communicator), Soc. Profl. Journalists (nat. bd. for hist. sites 1980—), Nat. Press Photographers Assn. (hon. life, cons. Bay Area interne project 1989—, honoree 1995), Investigative Reporters and Editors (charter), Bay Area Advt. and Mktg. Assn., Nat. Assn. Sci. Writers, Calif. Writers Club (state bd., Berkeley bd. 1989—, honoree ann. conv. Asilomar, Calif. 1990), Am. Assn. Med. Writers, Internat. Assn. Bus. Communicators, Soc. Environ. Journalists (charter), Am. Film Inst., Am. Heritage Found. (citation 1986, 87, 88), Soc. Am. Travel Writers, Internat. Oceanog. Found., Oceanic Soc., Calif. Acad. Environ. News Writers, Seattle Advt. and Sales Club (former officer), Nature Conservancy, Smithsonian Audubon Soc., Nat. Wildlife Fedn., Nat. Parks and Conservation Assn., Calif. State Parks Found., Calif. Environ. Leadership Roundtable (trustee), Fine Arts Mus., San Francisco, Seattle Jr. Advt. Club (charter), U. Wash. Comm. Alumni (Sch. Comm. alumni, life, charter mem. ocean scis. alumni, Disting. Alumni 1987), U. Calif., Berkeley Alumni (life, v.p., scholarship chmn. 1975-81), Stanford Alumni (life), Mortar Board Alumnae Assn. (life, honoree 1988-89), Am. Mgmt. Assn., Nat. Soc. Environ. Journalists (charter), Calif. Environ. Leadership Roundtable, Phi Beta Kappa (v.p., bd. dirs. Calif. Alumni Assn., statewide chmn. scholarship awards 1975-81), Purple and Gold Soc. (planning com., charter, 1995—), Pi Lambda Theta, Theta Sigma Phi. Home: Piedmont Pines 6161 Castle Dr Oakland CA 94611-2737 Office Phone: 510-531-0977. *A creed I follow is Ralph Waldo Emerson's statement: "Nothing great was ever achieved without enthusiasm.".*

WOOD, LESLIE ANN, retail administrator; b. Chgo., Apr. 9, 1957; d. Howard Arnold and Anita Eleanor (Andler) W. AA, Harper Coll., 1977; BS in Comm. Scis., Ill. State U., 1979; MBA, Olivet Nazarene U., 1998. Advt. asst. Harry Alter Co., Chgo., 1979-80; clk. typist Career Guild, Evanston, Ill., 1980-81; reporter Aparacor, Evanston, 1981-82; sales mgmt. trainee Prudential Ins. Co. Am., Millburn, NJ, 1983-84; fin. cons. Summit Fin. Resources, Livingston, NJ, 1984; mgr. Chgo. area Renault Inc. divsn. AMC/Jeep/Renault, Elk Grove Village, Ill., 1985-87; customer rels. specialist Chrysler Motors, Lisle, Ill., 1987-88; dist. svc. and parts mgr. Chrysler, Lisle; dist. parts mgr. Subaru of Am., Addison, Ill., 1989-91, dist. fixed ops. mgr., 1992-95; univ. rep. Olivet Nazarene U., Schaumburg, Ill., 1996-97; mktg. cons. WZSR STAR 105.5, Crystal Lake, Ill., 1997-99; parts cons. Am. Isuzu Motors, Cerritos, Calif., 1999—2001, Hyundai Motor Am., Aurora, Ill., 2002—, dist. parts svc. mgr., 2002—. Avocations: aerobics, circuit weight training, sewing, stained glass crafts. Home and Office: PO Box 517 O Fallon MO 63366-0517

WOOD, LINCOLN JACKSON, aerospace engineer; b. Lyons, NY, Sept. 30, 1947; s. William Hulbert and Sarah Brock (Strumsky) Wood. BS with distinction, Cornell U., 1968; MS in Aeronautics and Astronautics, Stanford U., 1969, PhD, 1972. Staff engr. Hughes Aircraft Co., El Segundo, Calif., 1974-77; tech. staff Jet Propulsion Lab. Calif. Inst. Tech., Pasadena, 1977-81, tech. group supr. Jet Propulsion Lab., 1981-89, tech. mgr., 1989-91, dep. tech. sect. mgr., 1991-99, dep. leader Ctr. of Excellence for Deep Space Comm./Nav. Sys., 2000—, tracking and nav. svc. sys. mgr., deep space mission sys. engring. and ops. programs, 2003—. Bechtel instr. engring. Calif. Inst. Tech., Pasadena, 1972—74, lectr. in sys. engring., 1975—76, vis. asst. prof., 1976—78, vis. assoc. prof., 1978—84; cons. in field. Contbr. articles to profl. jours. Bd. dirs. Boys Republic, Chino Hills, Calif., 1991, 1997—. Fellow: AIAA (assoc.; assoc. editor Jour. Guidance, Control and Dynamics 1983—89, tech. com. astrodynamics 1985—86, chmn. 1986—88); mem.: AAAS, IEEE (sr.), Am. Astron. Soc. (sr.; assoc. editor Jour. Astron. Scis. 1980—83, gen. chmn. AAS/AIAA Space Flight Mechanics Meeting 1993, space flight mechanics com. 1980—97, chmn. 1993—95), Los Solteros (pres. 1991, 1997—), Sigma Xi. Office: Jet Propulsion Lab 4800 Oak Grove Drive Mail Stop 301-125L Pasadena CA 91109 Business E-Mail: Lincoln.J.Wood@jpl.nasa.gov.

WOOD, LINDA MAY, librarian; b. Ft. Dodge, Iowa, Nov. 6, 1942; d. John Albert and Beth Ida (Riggs) Wiley; m. C. James Wood, Sept. 15, 1964 (div. Oct. 1984). BA, Portland State U., 1964; M in Librarianship, U. Wash., 1965. Reference libr. Multnomah County Libr., Portland, Oreg., 1965-67, br. libr., 1967-72, adminstrv. asst. to libr., 1972-73, asst. libr., asst. dir., 1973-77; asst. city libr. L.A. Pub. Libr., 1977-80; libr. dir. Riverside (Calif.) City and County Pub. Libr., 1980-91; county libr. Alameda County Libr., Fremont, Calif., 1991—. Adminstrv. coun. mem. Bay Area Libr. and Info. Svcs., Oakland, Calif., 1991—. Chair combined charities campaign County of Alameda, Oakland, Calif., 1992; bd. dirs. Inland AIDS project, Riverside, 1990-91; vol. United Way of Inland Valleys, Riverside, 1986-87, Bicentennial Competition on the Constitution, 36th Congl. Dist., Colton, Calif., 1988-90. Mem. ALA (CLA chpt. councilor 1992-95), Calif. Libr. Assn. (pres. 1985, exec. com., ALA chpt. councilor 1992-95), Calif. County Librs. Assn. (pres. 1984), League of Calif. Cities (cmty. svcs. policy com. 1985-90), OCLC Users Coun. (Pacific Network del. 1986-89). Democrat. Avocations: folk dancing, opera, reading. Office: Alameda County Libr 2450 Stevenson Blvd Fremont CA 94538-2326 Office Phone: 510-745-1536. E-mail: lwood@aclibrary.org.

WOOD, MARCUS ANDREW, lawyer; b. Mobile, Ala., Jan. 18, 1947; s. George Franklin and Helen Eugenia (Fletcher) W.; m. Sandra Lee Pellonari, July 25, 1971; children: Edward Alan, Melinda Janel. BA cum laude, Vanderbilt U., 1969; JD, Yale U., 1974. Bar: Oreg. 1974, U.S. Dist. Ct. Oreg. 1974, U.S. Ct. Appeals (9th cir.) 1982. Assoc., then ptnr. Rives, Bonihadi & Smith, Portland, Oreg., 1974-78; ptnr. Stoel Rives LLP and predecessor firms, Portland, 1974—. Pres., bd. dirs. Indochinese Refugee Ctr., Portland, 1980, Pacific Ballet Theatre, Portland, 1986-87; bd. dirs. Outside In, Portland, 1989—. Lt. USNR, 1969-71. Mem. ABA, Phi Beta Kappa. Home: 9300 NW Finzer Ct Portland OR 97229-8035 Office: Stoel Rives 900 SW 5th Ave Ste 2300 Portland OR 97204-1229 Office Phone: 503-294-9434. Business E-Mail: mwood@stoel.com.

WOOD, MARGARET, performing company executive; Entertainment and spl. events dir. Stratton Mountain Resort, Stratton, Va.; gen. mgr. Broward Ctr. for the Performing Arts, Ft. Lauderdale, Fla.; interim gen. dir. Anchorage Opera; gen. dir. Dance Conneticut, 2000—. Co-founder Performing Artservices Inc., NY; founder Dance Umbrella, 1975. Office: Dance Conneticut 224 Farmington Ave Hartford CT 06105

WOOD, MARIAN STARR, publishing company executive; b. N.Y.C., Mar. 30, 1938; d. Edward James and Betty (Starr) Markow; m. Anthony Stuart Wood, Mar. 21, 1963. BA, Barnard Coll., 1959; postgrad., Columbia U., 1959—64. Tchg. asst., lectr. Columbia U., N.Y.C., 1960-64; editor Praeger Pubs., N.Y.C., 1965-71; sr. editor Henry Holt & Co., N.Y.C., 1972-81, exec. editor, 1981-96, assoc. pub. Marian Wood Books, 1996-99; v.p. Marian Wood Books at G.P. Putnam's Sons, N.Y.C., 1999—. Recipient Roger Klein Found. award for career achievement, 2001. E-mail: marian.wood@us.penguingroup.com.

WOOD, MARY LOUISE, humanities educator; b. Gettysburg, Pa., June 9, 1945; d. Margaret Gillelan (Hays) and Albert Jones Wood; m. James Peter Shedel, Apr. 8, 1983; 1 child, James Albert Andrew Shedel. BA, Hood Coll., Frederick, Md., 1969; MA, Syracuse U., 1971; PhD, Johns Hopkins U., 1978. Tchr. Balt. County Pub. Schs., Towson, Md., 1967—69, classroom tchr., 1971—72; tchg. asst. Pietro Verri Tech. Commerical H.S., Milan, 1972—74; sr. staff lectr., docent coord. The Walters Art Gallery, Balt., 1977—81; program specialist, Western Europe, Academic Travel Abroad, Washington, 1981—85; asst. dir., bus. programs, Falls Church Ctr. U. Va., Falls Church, 1985—86; curator of edn. Nat. Mus. Women in the Arts, Washington, 1986—90; dir., internat. programs Am. Assn. Mus., Washington, 1990—97; tchr., history of art & western civilization Sidwell Friends Sch., Washington, 1998—. Cons. Nat. Cathedral, Washington, 1997; tchr. Am. Acad., Rome, 2003. Contbr. articles to profl. jours. Chair arts coun. Met. Meml. United Meth. Ch., Washington, 2001—. Fulbright-Hays Travel grantee, Italian Govt., 1972—74. Office: Sidwell Friends Sch 3825 Wisconsin Ave NW Washington DC 20016 E-mail: woodm@sidwell.edu.

WOOD, MAURICE, medical educator; b. Pelton, Eng., June 28, 1922; came to U.S., 1971; s. Joseph and Eugenie (Lumley) W.; m. Erica Joan Noble, May 1, 1948; children: Roger Lumley, Ashley Michael, Frances Jane. MB BS, U. Durham, Eng., 1945. Diplomate Am. Bd. Family Practice. Sr. ptnr. med. practice South Shields County, Durham, 1950-71; gen. practice teaching group U. Newcastle, Newcastle-on-Tyne, Eng., 1969-71; gen. clin. asst. dept. psychology-medicine South Shields Gen. Hosp., 1966-71; assoc. prof., dir. rsch. in family practice Med. Coll. Va.-Va. Commonwealth U., Richmond, 1971-73, prof., dir. rsch. in family practice, 1973-87, prof. emeritus, 1987—. Cons. advisor WHO, Geneva, 1979-90, chmn. working party to develop a classification for primary care, 1979-90; founding mem. exec. dir. N.Am. Primary Care Rsch. Group, Richmond, 1983-92, past pres., pres. emeritus, 1993—; chmn. com. on cmty. oriented primary care Insts. of Medicine, 1982-84. Assoc. editor Jour. Family Practice, 1976-83. Recipient award for meritorious svc. Va. Acad. Family Physicians, 1976; Maurice Wood award for career achievement in primary care rsch. founded in his honor, 1995. Fellow Royal Coll. Gen. Practitioners, Am. Acad. Family Physicians; mem. Inst. Medicine-Nat. Acad. Sci., Soc. Tchrs. Family Medicine (Curtis Hames Career Research award 1984), Inst. of Medicine, NAS, Ambulatory Sentinel Practice Network, Internat. Primary Care Network (treas., bd. dirs.), N.Am. Primary Care Rsch. Group (treas., bd. dirs., exec. dir., 1982-92). Lodges: Rotary. Episcopalian. Home and Office: PO Box 823 Nellysford VA 22958-0823 E-mail: wood150w@earthlink.net.

WOOD, MICHAEL B. chief executive officer, president; Grad., McGill U. Fellowship microvascular surgery, hand surgery U. Louisville; residency Mayo Grad. Sch. of Medicine; prof. of orthopedics Mayo Med. Sch., orthopedic surgeon; vice-chair bd. of gov. Mayo Regional Health Sys., Rochester, Minn.; CEO, pres. Mayo Found., 1999—2003, Pres. Emeritus, 2003—. Pres. of bd. Malcolm Baldrige Nat. Quality Award Found., 2000. Mem.: bd. dir., Visionshare Inc., Am. Soc. Surgery of the Hand, Soc. of Med. Adminstrn., Minn. Med. Assn., Am. Med. Assn., Am. Soc. Reconstructive Microsurgery (pres. 1990—91). Office: Mayo Clinic 200 First St SW Rochester MN 55905

WOOD, MICHAEL BRUCE, orthopaedic surgeon, researcher, educator; b. Glasgow, Mont., Oct. 7, 1943; s. Benjamin Joseph and LaVaun Adele (Gray) W.; m. Mary Elizabeth Magnotto, June 17, 1967; children: Michael S., Hadley M., Benjamin D., Luke E. BA in Chemistry, Franklin and Marshall Coll., 1965; MD CM, McGill U., 1969; MS in Orthopedic Surgery, U. Minn., 1974. Diplomate Am. Bd. Orthopedic Surgery, Sub-bd. Hand Surgery. Asst. prof. Med. Coll. Ohio, Toledo, 1977-79; from asst. prof. to prof. orthopedic surgery Mayo Med. Sch., Rochester, Minn., 1979—. Cons. orthopedic surgery Mayo Clinic, Rochester, 1979—. Author: Atlas of Microsurgery, 1990, Vascularized Bone, 1996; co-editor: Jour. of Microsurgery, 1986-92; dep. editor Jour. Bone and Joint Surgery, 1996, assoc. editor, 1989-94. Trustee Mayo Found., Rochester, 1995-2003, chair exec. com., 1998-2003, pres., CEO, 1999-2003; bd. govs. Mayo Clinic, 1993-98. Maj. U.S. Army, 1974-76, Germany. NIH grantee, 1987-97; Bunnell fellow, 1986-87. Fellow Am. Assn. Orthopedic Surgery, Am. Orthopedic Assn., Am. Soc. Surgery of Hand, Am. Soc. for Reconstructive Microsurgery, Internat. Soc. for Reconstructive Microsurgery, Sigma Xi. Office: Mayo Clinic 200 1st St SW Rochester MN 55905-0002

WOOD, NANCY ELIZABETH, psychologist, educator; d. Donald Sterret and Orne Louise (Erwin) W. BS, Ohio U., 1943, MA, 1947; PhD, Northwestern U., Evanston, Ill., 1952. Prof. Case Western Res. U., Cleve., 1952-60; specialist, expert HEW, Washington, 1960-62; chief rsch. USPHS, Washington, 1962-64; prof. U. So. Calif., L.A., 1965—. Learning disabilities cons., 1960-70; assoc. dir. Cleve. Hearing and Speech Ctr., 1952-60; dir. licensing program Brit. Nat. Trust, London. Author: Language Disorders, 1964, Language Development, 1970, Verbal Learning, 1975 (monograph) Auditory Disorders, 1978, Levity, 1980, Stoneskipping, 1989, Bird Cage, 1994, Out of Control, 1999. Pres. faculty senate U. So. Calif., 1987-88. Recipient Outstanding Faculty award Trojan Fourth Estate, 1982, Pres.' Svc. award U. So. Calif., 1992. Fellow APA (cert.), AAAS, Am. Speech and Hearing Assn. (legis. coun. 1965-68); mem. Internat. Assn. Scientists. Republican. Methodist. Office: U So Calif University Park Los Angeles CA 90089-0001

WOOD, NEIL RODERICK, real estate development company executive; b. Winnipeg, Man., Can., Aug. 22, 1931; s. Reginald and Pearl (Beake) W.; m. Jean Mitchell Hume, Aug. 10, 1957 (div.); children: Barbara, David, John, Brian. B in Commerce, U. Man., 1952; MBA, Harvard U., 1955. Asst. mgr. Ont. real estate investment office Gt. West Life Assurance Co., Canada, 1955-59; with Cadillac Fairview Corp. Ltd. (and predecessor), Willowdale, Canada, 1959-61, 63-81, exec. v.p., 1968-71, pres., 1971-81, vice chmn., 1980-81; pres. N.R. Wood Devel. Co. Ltd., 1982—; exec. v.p., dir. Campeau Corp., 1985-86; pres., CEO, dir. Markborough Properties Inc., 1986-95. Bd. dirs. Dorsay Devel. Corp.; past pres., trustee Internat. Coun. of Shopping Ctrs. Mem. Toronto Club, Rosedale Golf Club, Craigleith Ski Club, Beaumaris Club, Lost Tree Club, Loxahatchee Golf Club, Beacon Hall Club. Home and Office: RR # 3 Newmarket ON Canada L3Y 4W1

WOOD, OLIVER GILLAN, JR., economist, educator; b. Greer, S.C., Apr. 27, 1937; s. Oliver Gillan and Grace (McBrayer) W.; m. Jean Collier Wood; children: Brian Jay, Joseph Corey, Andrew Oliver. BBA, U. S.C., 1958, MA in Econs., 1963; PhD, U. Fla., 1965. Asst. prof. banking and fin. U. S.C., Columbia, 1965-68, assoc. prof. banking and fin., 1968-73, prof. banking and fin., 1973-94; disting. prof. emeritus, 1994—. Chmn. U. S.C. Press com. 1981-94; cons. in field, 1969—. Author: Commercial Banking, 1978, (with others) Analysis of Bank Financial Statements, 1979, Introduction to Money and Banking, 1980, (with others) How to Borrow Money, 1981. Bd. dirs., founder Republic Nat. Bank, Columbia, 1975-87, Edisto Farm Credit Agrl. Credit Assn., 1990-2000; adv. bd. Lexington State Bank, 1990-94, BB&T Fin. Corp., 1994-2000, First South Bancorp., 2000—; pres. Wood Charolais Ranch, Dandridge, Tenn. Mem. Beta Gamma Sigma (pres. 1972). Avocations: farming, golf. Home: 121 Running Fox Rd Columbia SC 29223-3020 Office: PO Box 24677 Columbia SC 29224-4677

WOOD, PATRICK HENRY, III, federal agency administrator; b. Tex. Grad., Tex. A&M U. With Baker & Botts, Washington; engr. Arco Indonesia; legal counsel to chmn. Tex. Railroad Commn.; staff mem. Fed. Energy Regulatory Commn., 1991—93; chmn. Pub. Utility Commn. Tex.; chmn. Fed. Energy Regulatory Commn. U.S. Dept. Energy, Washington, 2001—. Office: US Dept Energy 888 1st St NE Washington DC 20426-4205

WOOD, PAULA DAVIDSON, lawyer; b. Oklahoma City, Dec. 20, 1952; d. Paul James and Anna Mae (Ferrero) Davidson; m. Andrew E. Wood; children: Michael Paul, John Roland. BS, Okla. State U., 1976; JD, Oklahoma City U., 1982. Bar: Okla. 1983, U.S. Dist. Ct. (we. dist.) Okla. 1983, U.S. Supreme Ct. 1995; cert. pub. mgr. Pvt. practice, Oklahoma City, 1984-85; ptnr. Davidson & Wood, Oklahoma City, 1985-87; child support enforcement counsel Okla. Dept. Human Svcs., Oklahoma City, 1987-92, child support adminstr. (IV-D dir.), 1992-96; pvt. practice Oklahoma City, 1997—2004; counsel Legal Aid Svcs. Okla., Inc., Oklahoma City, 2004—. Adj. instr. Tech. Inst. Okla. State U., Oklahoma City, 1985. Articles editor Oklahoma City U. Law Rev., 1982. Bd. dirs. Okla. Youth Symphony, 2000-01. Mem. Okla. Bar Assn. (sec. family law sect. 1987, Golden Gavel award 1987, Artist of the Yr. 1999), Nat. Child Support Enforcement Assn. (bd. dirs. 1995, sec. 1997), Okla. Child Support Enforcement Assn. (pres. 1992), S.W. Regional Child Assn. (pres. 1996), Western Interstate Child Support Enforcement Coun. (sec. 1995). Republican. Roman Catholic. Home: 3020 Shadybrook Dr Midwest City OK 73110-4133 Office: Legal Aid Svcs Okla Inc 2901 Classen Blvd Ste 112 Oklahoma City OK 73106 E-mail: paula.wood@legalaidok.org.

WOOD, PETER WYATT, education educator, writer; b. Pitts., Oct. 6, 1953; s. Walter Preston and Isabel (Reynolds) W. BA, Haverford Coll., 1975; MLS, Rutgers U., 1977; MA in Anthropology, U. Rochester, 1980, PhD in Anthropology, 1987. Asst. to provost Boston U., 1987—91, asst. provost, 1991—93, assoc. provost, 1993—2002, pres. chief of staff, 1996—2002, assoc. prof. of anthropology, 1996—. Mem. Young Leaders Conf., Am.-Swiss Assn., N.Y.C., 1991—. Author: Diversity: The Invention of a Concept, 2003. Mem. Am. Anthrop. Assn. Office: Boston U 143 Bay State Rd Boston MA 02215 Office Phone: 617-353-2219.

WOOD, PHOEBE A. food products executive; Grad., Smith Coll.; MBA, UCLA. With Atlantic Richfield Co.; v.p. CFO Propel, Inc. divsn. Motorola, Inc.; exec. v.p., CFO Brown-Forman Corp., Louisville, 2002—. Office: Brown-Forman Corp 850 Dixie Hwy Louisville KY 40210*

WOOD, QUENTIN EUGENE, oil company executive; b. Mechanicsburg, Pa., Mar. 5, 1923; s. Lloyd Paul and Greta (Myers) W.; m. Louise Lowe, Apr. 14, 1958. BS, Pa. State U., 1948. Petroleum engr. Quaker State Oil Refining Corp., Parkersburg, W.Va., 1948-52, chief engr. Bradford, Pa., 1952-55, mgr. prodn., 1955-68, v.p. prodn., 1968-70, exec. v.p., 1970-73, pres., chief ops. officer, 1973-75, pres., chief exec. officer, 1975-82, chmn., chief executive officer, 1982-88, chmn. bd., 1988-90, dir., 1990-93. Bd. dirs. Pa. Mfrs. Ins. Co.; chmn. industry tech. adv. com. U.S. Bur. Mines, 1960-70, Penn Grade Tech. Adv. Com., 1955-69, Pa. Oil and Gas Conservation Commn., 1961-71. Trustee Pa. State U., 1976-94, pres., 1979-87. 1st lt. USAAF, 1943-46. Mem. Am. Inst. Metall. Engrs., Pa. Grade Crude Oil Assn. (dir.), Pa. Oil Producers Assn. (past pres., dir. Bradford dist.), Am. Petroleum Inst. (dir.), Nat. Petroleum Refiners Assn. (dir.). Home: 1402 Spinnakers Reach Dr Ponte Vedra Beach FL 32082

WOOD, R. L. (BOB WOOD), chemicals executive; BA in History, U. Mich. With human resources, sales and mktg. depts. Dow Chem. Co., 1977—89; v.p. mktg. household products DowBrands, 1989—90, v.p. sales, 1990—93; group v.p., gen. mgr. household products DowBrands N.Am., 1993—94; v.p. polyolefins and elastomers Dow Plastics, Dow N.Am., 1994—95, bus. v.p. engring. plastics, 1995—97, bus. v.p. polyurethanes, 1997—2000; bus. group pres., mem. corp. operating bd. Thermosets and Dow Automotive, 2000—04; pres., CFO Crompton Corp., Middlebury, Conn., 2004—. Bd. dirs. Jarden Corp. Immediate past chmn. Big Bros./Big Sisters Am. Office: Crompton Corp 199 Benson Rd Middlebury CT 06762*

WOOD, R. STEWART, JR., retired bishop; b. Detroit, June 25, 1934; s. Raymond and Marjorie Wood; m. Kristin Lie Miller, June 25, 1955; children: Lisa, Raymond, Michael. AB, Dartmouth Coll., 1956; MDiv, Va. Theol. Sem., 1959; MA in Counseling and Sociology, Ball State U., 1973; postgrad., Va. Seminary. Ordained to diaconate and priesthood Episc. Ch., 1959. Vicar Episc. Ch., Seymour and Bean Blossom, Ind., 1960—63; assoc. rector Grace Ch., Muncie, Ind., 1963—66, rector, 1966—70; exec. dir. Episc. Cmty. Svcs., Indpls., 1970—76; rector All Saint's Episc. Ch., Indpls., 1973—76, Christ Ch., Glendale, Ohio, 1976—84, St. John's Ch., Memphis, 1984—88; elected Bishop Coadjutor Diocese Mich., Detroit, 1988—89, diocesan bishop, 1990—2000; ret., 2000. Dir. summer camps, conf. ctr.; dep. Gen. Conv. 1970, 73, 76, 82; exec. coun. 1972-76, Coalition for Ordination of Women, bd. dirs. Episcopalian. Avocations: camping, golf, tennis, photography. Office: Box 968 255 Robert Frost Ln Quechee VT 05059-0968 Office Phone: 802-295-8412.

WOOD, REV. DR. BENTON, retired editor, priest; b. Arlington, Mass., Aug. 14, 1927; s. Edward E. Wood, Jr. and Dorothy Benton Wood; m. Joan Spodnyak Wood, Sept. 4, 1954; 1 child, John Benton. BS, Northwestern U., Evanston, IL, 1951; MS, State U. NY, Albany, NY, 1952; Religious Edn. Degree, Geneva Theol. Coll., Byfield, MA, 1974, Dr. (hon.) Humane Letters, 1979. Ordained Anglican Priest Diocese Albany, NY, 1957. Counsellor Camp Pasquaney, E. Hebron, NH, 1944—64; chaplain Northwood Sch., Lake Placid, NY, 1954—57, history dept. head, 1954—57; chaplain Trinity-Pawling Sch., Pawling, NY, 1958—62; dir. of studies, summer sch. St. Andrew's Sch., Boca Raton, Fla., 1962—65; headmaster York Sch., Monterey, Calif., 1965—67; academic dean Trinity Prepatory Sch., Winter Park, Fla., 1967—74; rector Ch. Annunciation, Anna Maria Island, Fla., 1975—88. Dir. St. Alban's Stamp Mission, Parrish, Fla., 1974—2001; editor Northwestern U. Alumni newsletter, Sarasota, Fla., 1990—2001; chaplain Baker St. Irregulars, 1980—. Author: (reference) Philatelic & Numismatic Holmes. Chaplain Anna Maria Fire Dept., Anna Maria Island, Fla., 1978—88. Pvt. U.S. Army, 1945—46. Recipient Two Shilling award, Baker St. Irregulars, 1997. Fellow: Am. Geog. Soc. Avocations: philatelist, sherlockian. Home: 9840 Sucia Circle Parrish FL 34219 Personal E-mail: bwscannu51@aol.com.

WOOD, RICHARD COURTNEY, library director, educator; b. Spartanburg, S.C., Aug. 8, 1943; s. Herman Alva and Mildred Eloise (Porter) W.; m. Amy Louise Black, Aug. 16, 1974. BA, U. Tex., 1966; MLS, U. S.C., 1977. Head cataloging Wofford Coll. Libr., Spartanburg, 1969-78; hosp. libr. John Peter Smith Hosp., Ft. Worth, 1978-80; reference libr. Tex. Coll. Osteo. Medicine, Ft. Worth, 1980-82, assoc. dir. libr., 1982-91; exec. dir. librs., assoc. prof. Sch. Medicine, chair HCOM dept. Tex. Tech U. Health Scis. Ctr., Lubbock, 1991—. Cons. Tarrant County Med. Libr. Assn., Fort Worth, 1978-82, 84, Med. Plaza Hosp., Fort Worth, 1979-82, Grand Prairie (Tex.) Community Hosp., 1980-81, Cook-Fort Worth Children's Hosp., 1988-91. Patron Kimball Art Mus. Fort Worth, 1987—; spokesman Neighborhood Assn., Fort Worth, 1989; vis. exec. United Way, Fort Worth, 1990. Recipient Dean's award Sch. Nursing, Tex. Tech U. Health Sci. Ctr., 1998. Mem. Dallas-Tarrant County Consortium (chmn. 1980-81), Metroplex Consortium Health Scis. (chmn. 1980-81), South Cen. Regional Group, Med. Libr. Assn. (chmn. osteo. librs. sect. 1986-87), South Cen. Acad. Med. Librs. (bd. dirs. 1991—, past chair), Nat. Network Librs. Medicine (bd. dirs. South Cen. region 1991-93), Deutsche Gesellschaft für Heereskunde, LIS Users Group (chair exec. bd.), Sigma Tau Delta. Republican. Presbyterian. Avocations: languages, travel, history, gardening, music. Home: 1805 Bangor Ave Lubbock TX 79416-5518 Office: Preston Smith Libr Health Scis 3601 4th St Lubbock TX 79430-0001 E-mail: richard.wood@ttuhsc.edu.

WOOD, RICHARD D., JR., retail executive; b. 1938; BS in Commerce, U. Va., 1961; LLB, U. Pa., 1964. Law clk. U.S. Dist. Ct., Ea. Dist. Pa., 1964—65; with Montgomery McCracken Walker & Rhoads, 1965—70; v.p., counsel Wawa Inc., Media, Pa., 1970—74, exec. v.p., 1974—77, pres., CEO, 1977—. With USMC, 1964-68. Office: Wawa Inc 260 W Baltimore Pike Media PA 19063

WOOD, RICHARD HARVEY, JR., economics professor; b. Phila., Dec. 12, 1938; s. Richard Harvey and Frances (Manning) Wood; m. Maria Graciela Jave, Aug. 17, 1968; 1 child, Maria Frances. BA in Geography, Antioch Coll., 1963; MA in Agrl. Econs., U. Wis., 1965, PhD in Econs., 1972. Asst. prof. econs. U. Portland, Oreg., 1968—70; from asst. prof. to assoc. prof. econs. Stetson U., DeLand, Fla., 1970—88, prof. econs., 1988—. Fulbright lectr., Monterrey, Mexico, 1978—79. Pres. bd. dirs. Sugar 'N Spice Day Care Ctr., DeLand, 1984—85, Wesley House, DeLand, 1984—85. Land Tenure Ctr. fellow, U. Wis., Madison, 1963—65. Mem.: Latin Am. Studies Assn., Am. Econ. Assn. Democrat. Avocations: tennis, canoeing, hiking, running, camping. Home: 495 Oakridge Ave Deland FL 32724-2463 Office: Stetson U PO Box 8322 Deland FL 32720 Office Phone: 386-822-7572.

WOOD, RICHARD ROBINSON, real estate company executive; b. Salem, Mass., Nov. 8, 1922; s. Reginald and Irene Margaret (Robinson) Wood; m. Pamela Vander Wiele, Mar. 8, 1951 (div. Apr. 1969); children: Christopher Robinson, Bryant Cornelius, Marcella Wood Mackenzie; m. Jane Philbin, Sept. 19, 1970. AB, Harvard Coll., 1944; postgrad., Mass. Inst. Tech., 1947-48. V.p. Hunneman & Co., Boston, 1959-72; trustee, sec. Mass. Real Estate Investment Trust, Boston, 1967-69; trustee Suffolk Franklin Savings Bank, 1967-74; pres., chmn. Continential Real Estate Equity, Boston, 1972-74; exec. v.p. ITEL Real Estate Corp., San Francisco, 1974-75; v.p. Baird & Warner, Chgo., 1976-80; pres., chmn. Renwood Properties, Inc., Cambridge, Mass., 1981—. Founder Real Estate Securities 2d Syndication Inst., 1972, pres., 1976—78; pres., chmn. ILCO Properties, Chgo., 1981—87; v.p., dir. Common Goal Capitol Group, Balt., 1986—; gen. ptnr. Common Goal Mortgage Fund, Balt., 1986—; mem. Coun. Rural Housing and Devel., 1988—; v.p., bd. dirs. St. Katherines Care Ctrs., 1990—; chmn. Inst. Responsible Housing Preservation, 1994—99, 19 Chauncy St. Trust, 1995—. Mem. Mayor's Citizen Adv. Bd., Boston, 1965—67, Coun. Rural Housing and Devel., 1988—; committeeman, treas. Mass. Rep. State Com., Boston, 1964—72; pres. Boston Rep. City Com., 1965—67. With M.C. U.S. Army, 1943—44. Mem.: Nat. Leased Housing Assn., White Mountain Ski Runners, Badminton and Tennis Club, Harvard Club N.Y., Longwood Cricket Club, Harvard Club Boston. Avocations: tennis, skiing. Home: 19 Chauncy St Cambridge MA 02138-2549 Office: Renwood Properties Inc 875 Massachusetts Ave Cambridge MA 02139-3067 Personal E-mail: renwoodprops@aol.com.

WOOD, ROBERT CHARLES, lawyer, real estate developer; b. Chgo., Apr. 8, 1956; s. Roy Edward and Mildred Lucille (Jones) W.; m. Jennifer Jo Briggs, Oct. 1984; children: Jacqueline Jones, Reagan Keith. BA in History, BBA in Real Estate, So. Meth. U., 1979, JD, 1982. Bar: Tex. 1983. Appraiser McClellan-Massey, Dallas, 1977-79; researcher, acquisitions officer Amstar Fin. Corp., Dallas, 1979-80; prin. Robert Wood Cons., Dallas, 1981-98; ptnr. Welch & Wood Attys. and Y2K Cons., Dallas, 1998-2000; pvt. practice, Dallas, 1995—; real estate investor and developer, 1998—. Cons. Plan Mktg. Cos., 1983-84; pvt. practice law, Dallas, 1983-84; gen. counsel Diversified Benefits, Inc., Dallas, 1984-86; nat. accts. mgr. Lomas & Nettleton Real Estate Group, Dallas, 1987-88; sr. pension cons., prin. Eppler, Guerin &Turner, 1988-93; chmn. adv. coun. on devel. Medisend, 1991; nat. consulting coord. fin. advisors coun., v.p. Callan Assocs., San Francisco, 1994-95; atty. at law, 1995—; exec. v.p., gen. counsel, Rushmore Investment Advisors, Plano, Tex., 2002-. Author: Electionomics: How the Money Managers View the Election, 1992, After the Congress Vote: How the Managers See Things Now, 1993, Y2K--The Year 2000 Issue: How Y2K Affects the Markets, 1998; mem. So. Meth. U. Law Rev., 1981-82; contbr. articles to profl. publs. Bd. dirs. Dallas unit Am. Cancer Soc., 1982-87, mem. spl. events com., 1986-87, mem. crusade com., 1987-88, mem. medisend adv. com., 1988-94, chmn. corp. devel. bd., 1989-95. Mem. Tex. Bar Assn., Phila. Bar Assn., Phi Gamma Delta. Avocations: skiing, tennis, bicycling. Office Phone: 214-369-3209. E-mail: rccwood@aol.com.

WOOD, ROBERT COLDWELL, political scientist; b. St. Louis, Sept. 16, 1923; s. Thomas Frank and Mary (Bradshaw) W.; m. Margaret Byers, Mar. 22, 1952; children— Frances, Margaret, Frank Randolph. AB, Princeton U., 1946; MA, Harvard U., 1947, MPA, 1948, PhD, 1950; LLD or DHL (hon.), St. Bonaventure Coll., U. Pitts., 1965, Bklyn. Poly. Inst., 1966, Princeton U., 1969, Rhode Island Coll., U. Mass., 1970, Worcester Poly. Inst., 1971, U. Maine, 1972, Hokkaido U., Japan, 1975, North Adams Coll., 1977, Boston U., 1978, Stonehill Coll., 1979. Assoc. dir. Fla. Legis. Reference Bur., Tallahassee, 1949-51; mgmt. orgn. expert U.S. Bur. Budget, Washington, 1951-54; lectr. govt. Harvard U., 1953-54, asst. prof., 1954-57; asst. prof. polit. sci. MIT, 1957-59, assoc. prof., 1959-62, prof., 1962-66, head dept., 1965-66, 69-70; undersec. HUD, Washington, 1966-68, sec., 1969; chmn. Mass. Bay Transp. Authority, Boston, 1969-70; dir. Harvard U.-MIT Joint Center for Urban Studies, Cambridge, 1969-70; pres. U. Mass., 1970-77; supt. Boston Public Schs., 1978-80; prof. U. Mass., Boston, 1981-83; Henry Luce prof. Dem. Instns. and the Social Order Wesleyan U., Middletown, Conn., 1983-93, John E. Andrus prof. govt., 1993; prof. emeritus U. Mass., Boston, 1994—. Sr. fellow McCormack Inst. Pub. Affairs, U. Mass., Boston, vis. prof. U. Mass., 1998—. Author: Suburbia, Its People and Their Politics, 1958, Metropolis Against Itself, 1959, 1400 Governments, The Political Economy of the New York Region, 1960, The Necessary Majority, Middle America and Urban Crisis, 1972, Whatever Possessed the President? Academic Experts and Presidential Policy, 1960-88, 1993; (with others) Schoolmen and Politics, 1962, Government and Politics of the U.S, 1965; author, editor: Eastward Ho: Options for Metropolitan Boston, 1997, Remedial Law: When Courts Become Administrators, 1990, Turnabout Time: New Choices for U/Mass, 1996. Trustee Coll. Bd., 1979-83, Kettering Found., 1971-76; mem. Commn. on Acad. Health Ctrs. and Economy New Eng.; bd. dirs. Lincoln Inst. Land Policy, 1976-80; chmn. Inst. for Resource Mgmt., 1982-84, 20th Century Task Force Fed. Ednl. Policy, 1983, Conn. Gov.'s Coalition on Adult Literacy, 1986-89; mem. Gov.'s Commn. on Quality and Integrated Edn., 1989-90.

Served with inf. AUS, World War II, ETO. Decorated Bronze Star; recipient Hubert H. Humphrey award, 1985. Fellow Am. Acad. Arts and Scis., Am. Polit. Sci. Assn. (Career Achievment award 1989), Cosmos Club Washington, Phi Beta Kappa.

WOOD, ROBERT EMERSON, pediatrics educator; b. Jacksonville, Fla., Nov. 15, 1942; s. Waldo E. and Verda V. Wood. BS in Chemistry magna cum laude, Stetson U., 1963; PhD in Physiology, Vanderbilt U., 1968, MD, 1970. Bd. cert. pediatrics; bd. cert. pediatric pulmonology. Intern in pediatrics Duke U. Med. Ctr., Durham, 1970-71, resident in pediatrics, 1971-72; fellow pediatric pulmonology Case Western Res. U., Cleve., 1974-76, asst. prof. pediatrics, 1976-82, assoc. prof. pediatrics, 1982-83; assoc. prof. pediatrics, chief divsn. pediatric pulmonary medicine Dept. Pediatrics, U. N.C., Chapel Hill, 1983-88, prof. pediatrics, chief divsn. pediatric pulmonary medicine, 1988-94, dir. pediat. ICU, 1984-86, dir. Ctr. Pediat. Bronchology, 1994-99; prof. pediats. Cin. Children's Hosp. Med. Ctr., U. Cin., 1999—; chief, divsn. pulmonary medicine Children's Hosp. Med. Ctr., U. Cin., 2001—. Mem. editorial bd.: Pediatric Pulmonology, 1992—, Jour. Bronchology, 1993—; contbr. chpts. to books and articles to profl. jours. Lt. comdr. USPHS, 1972-74. Named Grad. fellow Danforth Found., 1963-68, Med. Scientist fellow Life Ins. Med. Rsch. Found., 1965-70, Clin. Rsch. fellow Cystic Fibrosis Found., 1974-76. Mem. Am. Bronchesophagological Assn., Am. Assn. for Bronchology, Soc. for Pediatric Rsch., Am. Thoracic Soc., N.C. Pediatric Soc. Office: Cin Children's Hosp Med Ctr Pediat Pulmonary Medicine 3333 Burnet Ave Cincinnati OH 45229-3039 Fax: 513-636-7734. E-mail: rewood@chmc.org.

WOOD, ROBERT L. chemicals executive; BA, U. Mich. Field seller Dow Chem. Co., Cleveland, Ohio, 1978—80, mktg. recruiting and placement dept. Midland, Mich., 1980—82, product sales mgr., 1982—84, mktg. mgr., 1984—87, dir. mktg., 1987—89, v.p. mktg. Indpls., 1989—90, v.p. sales, household products, 1990—93, group v.p. and gen. mgr. household products, 1993—94, v.p. polyolefins and elastomers, 1994—95, bus. v.p. engring. plastics, 1995—97, bus. v.p. polyurethanes, 1997—2000, bus. group pres. thermosets and Dow automotive, 2000—. Mem. Big Brothers Big Sisters of Am. Mem.: Jarden Corp. (bd. dirs.). Mailing: The Dow Chem Co 47 Building Midland MI 48667

WOOD, ROBERT WARREN, lawyer; b. Des Moines, July 5, 1955; s. Merle Warren and Cecily Ann (Sherk) W.; m. Beatrice Wood, Aug. 4, 1979; 1 child, Bryce Mercedes. Student, U. Sheffield, Eng., 1975-76; AB, Humboldt State U., 1976; JD, U. Chgo., 1979. Bar: Ariz. 1979, Calif. 1980, Wyo. 2000, NY 1989, D.C. 1993, Mont. 1998, US Tax Ct. 1980, Wyo.; Roll of Solicitors of Eng. and Wales, 1998. Assoc. Jennings, Strouss, Phoenix, 1979-80, McCutchen, Doyle, San Francisco, 1980-82, Broad, Khourie, San Francisco, 1982-85, Steefel, Levitt & Weiss, San Francisco, 1985-87, ptnr., 1987-91, Bancroft & McAlister, San Francisco, 1991-93; prin. Robert W. Wood, P.C., San Francisco, 1993—. Instr. in law U. Calif. San Francisco, 1981-82. Author: Taxation of Corporate Liquidations: A Complete Planning Guide, 1987, 2nd edit., 1994, The Executive's Complete Guide to Business Taxes, 1989, Corporate Taxation: Complete Planning and Practice Guide, 1989, S Corporations, 1990, The Ultimate Tax Planning Guide for Growing Companies, 1991, Taxation of Damage Awards and Settlement Payments, 1991, 3d edit., 2004, Office Tax Guide, 1991; co author: (with others) California Closely Held Corporations: Tax Planning and Practice Guide, 1987, Legal Guide to Independent Contractor Status, 3d edit., 2000; editor: California Small Busines Guide, 4 vols., 1998, Home Office Money & Tax Guide, 1992, Tax Aspects of Settlements and Judgements, 1993, 2d edit., 1998, cumulative supplement, 2000; editor-in-chief The M & A Tax Report; editor: Limited Liability Companies: Formation, Operation and Conversion, 1994, 2d edit., 2001, Limited Liability Partnerships: Formation, Operation and Taxation, 1996; mem. editl. bd. Real Estate Tax Digest, The Practical Accountant, Jour. Real Estate Taxation. Fellow Am. Coll. Tax Counsel; mem. Calif. Bd. Legal Specialization (cert. specialist taxation), Can. Bar Assn., Bohemian Club, Law Coun. Australia. Republican. Office: 639 Front St #200 San Francisco CA 94111 Office Phone: 415-834-1800. E-mail: wood@rwwpc.com.

WOOD, ROBERTA SUSAN, retired foreign service officer; b. Clarksdale, Miss., Oct. 4, 1948; d. Robert Larkin and Dorothy Eloise (Shelton) Wood. BA with distinction, Rhodes Coll., Memphis, 1970; postgrad., Nat. U. Cuyo, Mendoza, Argentina, 1970-71; MPA, Harvard U., 1980. Joined U.S. Fgn. Svc., 1972; svc. in Manila, Phillippines, Naples and Turin, Italy, and Port-au-Prince, Haiti; mgmt. analyst Dept. State, Washington, 1980-84; U.S. consul gen. Jakarta, Indonesia, 1984-87, NATO Def. Coll., Rome, 1987-88, Marseilles, France, 1988-91, Montreal, Que., Can., 1991-94; min., dep. chief of mission Am. Embassy, Quito, Ecuador, 1994-95; U.S. consul gen. Moscow, 1997-98; dep. asst. sec. state wstn. hemisphere affairs Washington, 1998—2001.

WOOD, RONALD, musician; b. London, June 1, 1947; Owner Woody's on the Beach (nightclub), Miami, 1987—. Guitarist and bassist with Jeff Beck Group, 1966—69, Faces, 1969—75, Rolling Stones, 1975—, New Barbarians, 1979, solo (albums) Gimme Some Neck, 1979, I've Got My Own Album To Do, Now Look, albums (with Rolling Stones) Black and Blue, 1976, Love You Live, 1977, Some Girls, 1979, Emotional Rescue, 1979, Sucking in the Seventies, 1981, Tattoo You, Still Life, 1982, Undercover, 1983, Between the Sheets, 1985, Dirty Work, Rewind, 1986, Steel Wheel, 1988, Flashpoint, 1991, Voodoo Lounge, 1994 (Grammy award Best Rock Album), Bridges to Babylon, No Security, 1997, (with Faces) Long Player, A Nod's As Good As A Wink... To a Blind Horse, Ooh-La-La, (with Small Faces) First Step, Ogden's Nut Gone Flake, There Are But Four Small Faces, 1991, All or Nothing, 1992, films Let's Spend the Night Together, 1982, Digital Dreams, 1983. Named to Rock and Roll Hall of Fame, 1989. Office: Virgin Records 1540 Broadway New York NY 10036-4039

WOOD, SHELTON EUGENE, education educator, consultant, minister; b. Douglas, Ga, May 20, 1938; s. Shelton and Mae Lillie (Pheil) Wood; m. Edna Louise Wood, Aug. 25, 1961; children: Shelton John, Deirdre Louise. AA, St. John's U., 1958; BA, U. Nebr., 1959; MEd, Coll. William and Mary, 1971; PhD, Sussex U., 1973; EdD, Southeastern U., 1975; MBA, Ctrl. Mich. U., 1977; MA, U. Okla., 1980; D in Ministry, Wesleyan Bible Coll., 1999; Cert. in Internt. Rels., Fgn. Svc. Inst., 1971; Cert. in Mgmt., Indsl. Coll. Armed Forces, 1970. Area mgr. Marshall Fields Corp., Fla., 1957-58; transp. supr. Greyhound Corp., Jacksonville, Fla., 1959-62; officer US Army, 1963, advanced through grades to inf. col., 1996; with Redstone Readiness Group, 1977-80; chief studies and analysis divsn. Korean Inst. for Def. Analysis, 1981-83; faculty St. John River C.C., 1984-90; nat. and internat. bus. and mgmt. cons., 1995—; sr. pastor Fellowship Wesleyan Ch., Spring Hill, Fla., 1998—. Mem. faculty Wesleyan Bible U., 1997—, dean Grad. Sch. Author: Strategic for Implementing A Family Life Ministry Ctr., 1997; contbr. over 120 articles and reports in field of mil. tng., edn., mgmt., pastoral studies, and practical theology. Active Boy Scouts Am., 1977—90; lay leader United Meth. Ch., Falls Ch., Va., 1977—79, St. James United Meth. Ch., 1986—90; mem. dist. bd. ministerial develop. Fla. Dist. of Wesleyan Ch., 1999, chair evangelism and ch. growth com., 1999—; bd. dir. Baby Love. Decorated Bronze Star with 2 oak leaf clusters, Air medal with 3 oak leaf clusters, Purple Heart with 2 oak leaf clusters; Sussex Coll. fellow, 1969-70. Mem. NEA, Am. Soc. Trainers and Developers (pres. S.E. chpt. 1974-75), Am. Def. Preparedness Assn., Putnam County C. of C. (pres. 1990-91), Toastmasters Internat. (Disting. Toastmaster 1989), Kiwanis (pres. 1989-90), Phi Kappa Delta, Phi Delta Kappa. Address: 8485 Chatsworth St Spring Hill FL 34608

WOOD, SUSAN, applied technology center executive; Honours BS in Physics, Victoria U., Manchester, Eng., 1969; MS in Metall. Engring., U. Pitts., 1973, PhD in Materials Engring., 1976. Rsch. mgmt. positions to gen. mgr. materials tech. divsn. Westinghouse Sci. and Tech. Ctr., Pitts.; various positions to mgr. mfg. tech. dept. Westinghouse Electronic Sys., Balt.; v.p., dir. Savannah River Tech. Ctr., Westinghouse Savannah River Co., Aiken, S.C., 1994—. Presenter, spkr. at nat. and internat. confs.; former mem. Def. Sci. Bd.; mem. nuclear materials tech. divsn. rev. com. Los Alamos (N.Mex.) Nat. Lab. Contbr. articles to profl. jours. Bd. Dirs. Women in Engring. Program Advs. Network, United Way Aiken County, 1997; bd. dirs., advisor univs. throughout U.S. Named Disting. Alumnus, U. Pitts. Sch. Engring., 1997. Achievements include patents in materials engineering. Office: Westinghouse Savannah River Savannah River Tech Ctr Aiken SC 29808-0001

WOOD, SUSAN, poet, literature educator; b. Commerce, Tex., 1946; BA, East Tex. State U., 1968; MA, U. Tex., Arlington, 1970; postgrad., Rice U., 1973—76. H.S. tchr., 1970—73; prof. English., chmn. dept. Rice U., Houston, 1981—. Presenter in field; book editor Houston Chronicle, 1975—76; editor, writer Washington Post, 1977—81. Editor: newspaper and mag.; author: Bazaar, 1981, Campo Santo, 1991 (Lamont Poetry Selection, 1991), Asunder, 2001; contbr. poems to jours. Guggenheim fellow, 1998. Office: Rice Univ 6100 Main Houston TX 77005

WOOD, THOMAS E. lawyer; b. L.A., Apr. 20, 1939; s. Louis Earl and Youda (Hays) Wood; m. Sally Ann Wood, June 22, 1963; children: Julia W. DeVuono, Melissa W. Brewster. BA, Amherst Coll., 1961; LLB, U. Pa., 1966. Bar: Pa. 1966. Assoc. Drinker Biddle & Reath LLP, Phila., 1966-72, ptnr., 1972—, ptnr.-in-charge Berwyn office, 2001—. Chmn. Easttown Zoning Hearing Bd., Easttown Twp., Pa., 1976—. Mem. Phila. Club. Office: Drinker Biddle & Reath LLP 1000 Westlakes Dr Ste 300 Berwyn PA 19312-2409 Office Phone: 610-993-2211. E-mail: thomas.wood@dbr.com.

WOOD, THOMAS WESLEY, humanities educator, editor; b. Hugo, Okla., Mar. 16, 1920; s. Thomas Wesley Wood Sr. and Alma Elora (Rogers) Daniel; m. L. Deloris Gray, May 31, 1968; m. Doreen Anderson, June, 1950 (div. 1966); children: John William, Thomas Wakefield. BA in History and Journalism, Tulsa U., 1951, MA in History, 1952, MS in Journalism, Northwestern U., 1953; PhD in European History, U. Okla., 1966. Reporter City News Bur, Chgo., 1952-54; prof. Tulsa (Okla.) U., 1954-73, So. Ill. U., Carbondale, 1973-76; vis. prof. Am. U., Cairo, Egypt, 1976-78, U. Ark., Little Rock, 1978-80; prof. Temple U., Phila., 1980-90, emeritus prof., 1990—. Reporter, corr. Tulsa World, 1954-84; editor, pub., founder Lost Generation Jour., Salem, Mo., 1973—. Author: Tulsa U. Editing Hankbook, 1956, 60, Tulsa U. Reporting Handbook, 1958, 60, 69, Outline History of American Journalism, 1961, Influence of the Paris Herald on the Lost Generation Writers, 1966; sub.-editor Egyptian Gazette, 1977-78. Recipient editing and writing award Mo. Press Women, 1985, writing award Pa. Press Club, 1983, writing award Ark. Press Women, 1979, 80, photography award Soc. Profl. Journalists, 1972. Mem. Overseas Press Club Am., Assn. Edn. Journalism and Mass Comm., Hemingway Soc., Soc. Scholar Editors, Coun. Editors Learned Journals, Pi Alpha Mu (nat. pres. 1956-60). Republican. Baptist. Avocations: fly fishing, travel, interviewing expatriate 20's americans. Home: RR 5 Box 134 Salem MO 65560-9008 Office: Lost Generation Jour RR 3 Box 387 Salem MO 65560-9315

WOOD, THOMAS WILLARD, health care industry executive; b. Logan, Utah, Jan. 21, 1939; s. Elmer Raymond and Leola (Pitkin) W.; m. Blanche Loila Dowdle, Sept. 11, 1959 (div.); children: Dianna Wood Perry, Jeffery Thomas (dec.); m. Charlene Taulbee, Oct. 5, 1974; children: Douglas Winston Remington, Angela Christine Douglas, Thomas Willard II, Michael Joseph, Matthew David. BA, Utah State U., 1962; MS, Cen. Mich. U., 1975; postgrad., Indsl. Coll. Armed Forces, 1975, Armed Forces Staff Coll., 1976. Commd. 2d lt. USAF, 1962, advanced through grades to col., 1983; chief protocol Hdqrs. Air Force Logistics Command, Wright-Patterson AFB, Ohio, 1972-75; chief spl. project div. Hdqrs. 21st Air Force, McGuire AFB, N.J., 1977-78; chief inquiries br. Office Legis. Liaison, The Pentagon, Washington, 1978-82; dep. dir. Directorate Competition Advocacy Ogden Air Logistics Ctr., Hill AFB, Utah, 1982-85; air attache U.S. Def. Attache Office, Am. Embassy, Wellington, New Zealand, 1985-88; chief protocol, dep. dir. pub. and govtl. affairs Hdqrs. U.S. Comdr.-in-Chief Pacific, Camp Smith, Hawaii, 1988-89; ret., 1989; adminstrv. asst. to v.p. mktg. Hawaii Med. Svc. Assn., Honolulu, 1989-91; sr. account exec. client rels. Baxter Internat. Inc., San Antonio, 1991-92; sr. account exec. prescription svc. divsn. Caremark, Inc., San Antonio, 1992-95; with corp. accts. prescription svc. divsn. Caremark Inc., San Antonio, 1996-97; sr. account exec. field ops. Caremark Pharm. Svcs., Medpartners Inc., San Antonio, 1997-99; sr. acct. mgr. field ops. CaremarkRx Inc., San Antonio, 1999-2000. Sr. nat. acct. mgr. SBC Comms., Inc., Caremark, Inc., San Antonio, 2000-02, assoc. nat. acct. exec., 2003—; dean New Zealand Mil. Attache Corps, 1986-88. Elder LDS Ch., also ch. organist, pianist, tchr.; music chmn. San Antonio North Stake, 2000—; mem. groundbreaking and dedication com. San Antonio Temple, 2002—. Decorated DFC, Air medal with nine oak leaf clusters; Gallantry Cross with palm (Vietnam); named hon. Royal New Zealand Air Force Navigator, 1988. Mem. Disting. Flying Cross Soc. (pres. Alamo chpt.). Republican. Avocations: jogging, swimming. Home: 1351 Grey Oak Dr San Antonio TX 78213-1602 Office: CaremarkRx Inc 7034 Alamo Downs Pkwy San Antonio TX 78238-4509

WOOD, VIVIAN POATES, mezzo soprano, educator, writer; b. Washington, Aug. 19, 1923; d. Harold Poates and Mildred Georgette (Patterson) W. Studies with Walter Anderson, Antioch Coll., 1953-55; Denise Restout, Saint-Leu-A-Fôret, France and Lakeville, Conn., 1960-62, 64-70; Paul A. Pisk, 1968-71; Paul Ulanowsky, N.Y.C., 1958-68; Elemer Nagy, 1965-68, Vyautas Marijosius, 1967-68; MusB, Hartt Coll. Music, 1968; postgrad. (fellow), Yale U., 1968; MusM (fellow), Washington U., St. Louis, 1971, PhD (fellow), 1973. Debut in recital series Internat. Jeunesse Musicals Arts Festival, 1953; solo fellowship Boston Symphony Orch., Berkshire Music Ctr., Tanglewood, 1964, St. Louis Symphony Orch., 1969, Washington Orch., 1949, Bach Cantata Series Berkshire Chamber Orch., 1964, Yale Symphony Orch., 1968. Appearances in U.S. and European recitals, oratorios, operas, radio and TV, 1953-68; soloist Landowska Ctr., Lakeville, 1969, Internat. Harpsichord Festival, Westminister Choir Coll., Princeton, N.J., 1973; prof. voice, head voice area Sch. of Music, U. So. Miss., Hattiesburg, 1971-2000, ret. 2000, prof. emerita, 2000—; asst. dean Coll. Fine Arts, 1974-76, acting dean, 1976-77; guest prof. Hochschüle für Musik, Munich, 1978-79; prof. Italian Internat. Studies Program, Rome, 1986; Miss. coord. Alliance for Arts Edn., Kennedy Ctr. Performing Arts, 1974—; mem. Miss. Gov.'s Adv. Panel for Gifted and Talented Children, 1974—, 1st Miss. Gov.'s Conf. on the Arts, 1974—. Author: Polenc's Songs: An Analysis of Style, 1971. Recipient Young Am. Artists Concert award N.Y.C., 1955; Wanda Landowska fellow 1961-68. Mem. Miss. Music Tchrs. Assn., Nat. Assn. Tchrs. of Singing, Music Tchrs. Nat. Assn., Am. Musicology Soc., Golden Key, Mu Phi Epsilon, Delta Kappa Gamma, Tau Beta Kappa (hon.), Pi Kappa Lambda. Democrat. Episcopalian.

WOOD, WENDY DEBORAH, filmmaker; b. N.Y.C., Oct. 4, 1940; d. John Meyer and Marion Emily (Peters) W.; m. William Dismore Chapple, Dec. 7, 1963; 1 child, Samuel Eliot. BA cum laude, Vassar Coll., 1962; MA, Stanford U., 1964. Tchg. asst. Stanford U., 1962-64; photographer, film editor Bristol (Eng.) U., 1964-66, asst. dir. Internat. Conf. Film Schs., 1966; rsch. asst. biology dept. U. Conn., Storrs, 1970-72; sr. media specialist Aetna Life & Casualty Co., Hartford, Conn., 1972-89; media writer, prodr., dir. U. Conn. Ctr. for Media and Tech., Storrs, 1989—. Pres. Chapple Films, Inc., 1972—. Films include: Yankee Craftsman, 1972, Alcoholism, Industry's Costly Hangover, 1974, Draggerman's Haul, 1975, Flight Without Wings, 1977, Auto Insurance Affordability, 1981 (2 awards), Where Rivers Run to the Sea, 1981 (award), Our Town is Burning Down, 1982 (6 awards), Wellness at the Worksite, 1984 (4 awards), Aenhance, 1989 (3 awards), Tiffany: Magician in Glass. Mem. jury N.Y. Internat. Video and Film Festival; bd. dirs. Windham Regional Arts Coun., 1987, 88, 89; mem. peer rev. com. Conn. Commn. Higher Edn., 1992-96. Recipient CINE Golden Eagle award Coun. on Internat. Non-Theatrical Events, 1972, 76, 84, 1st Place award Indls. Photography, 1974, cert. Outstanding Creativity U.S. TV Commls. Festival, 1974, EFLA award Am. Film Festival, 1974, 76, Dir's. Choice award Sinking Creek Film Festival, 1975, award Columbus Film Festival, 1975, award Excellence Life Ins. Advts. Assn., 1975, Silver Screen award U.S. Indsl. Film Festival, 1976, 81, 1st place award Conn. Film Festival, 1977, 1st prize Nat. Outdoor Travel Film Festival, 1978, 1st pl. Houston Film Festival, 1982, CINE Golden Eagle, 1982, 84, award Am. Film Festival, 1982, N.Y. Film Festival, 1982, 83, Silver CINDY award Assn. Visual Communicators, 1985, Conn. Film/Video Festival 1st pl. award, 1997, Gold award Conn. Film Festival, 1997, others. Mem. Info. Film Prodrs. Am. (nat. dir., pres. chpt. 1981-82, Cindy award 1971, 72, 81, 82, 85, 87), Internat. Quorum Motion Picture Prodrs., Audio Visual Communicators (pres. Conn. chpt. 1985, treas. 1988). Democrat. Mem. Soc. Of Friends. Home: 604 Phoenixville Rd Chaplin CT 06235-2211 E-mail: woodwendy@earthlink.com.

WOOD, WILLIAM BARRY, III, biologist, educator; b. Balt., Feb. 19, 1938; s. William Barry, Jr. and Mary Lee (Hutchins) W.; m. Marie-Elisabeth Renate Hartisch, June 30, 1961; children: Oliver Hartisch, Christopher Barry. AB, Harvard U., 1959; PhD, Stanford U., 1963. Asst. prof. biology Calif. Inst. Tech., Pasadena, 1965-68, assoc. prof., 1968-69, prof. biology, 1970-77; prof. molecular, cellular and developmental biology U. Colo., Boulder, 1977—, chmn. dept., 1978-83. Mem. panel for developmental biology NSF, 1970-72; physiol. chemistry study sect. NIH, 1974-78; mem. com. on sci. and public policy Nat. Acad. Scis., 1979-80; mem. NIH Cellular and Molecular Basis of Disease Rev. Com., 1984-88. Author: (with J. H. Wilson, R.M. Benbow, L.E. Hood) Biochemistry: A Problems Approach, 2d edit., 1981, (with L.E. Hood and J.H. Wilson) Molecular Biology of Eucaryotic Cells, 1975, (with L.E. Hood and I.L. Weissman) Immunology, 1978, (with L.E. Hood, I.L. Weissman and J.H. Wilson) Immunology, 2d edit., 1984, (with L.E. Hood and I.L. Weissman) Concepts in Immunology, 1978; editl. rev. bd. Science, 1984-92; mem. editl. bd. Cell, 1984-87, Developmental Biology, 1995-1999; contbr. articles to profl. jours. Recipient U.S. Steel Molecular Biology award, 1969; NIH Rsch. grantee, 1965—, Merit awardee, 1986-96; Guggenheim fellow, 1975-76. Fellow AAAS; mem. Nat. Acad. Scis., Am. Acad. Arts and Scis., Am. Soc. for Cell Biology, Genetics Soc. Am. Soc. for Developmental Biology, Soc. Nematology. Office: U Colorado Dept MCD Biology Box 347 Boulder CO 80309

WOOD, WILLIAM MCBRAYER, lawyer; b. Greenville, S.C., Jan. 27, 1942; s. Oliver Gillan and Grace (McBrayer) W.; m. Nancy Cooper, 1973 (dec. 1993); children: Walter, Lewis; m. Jeanette Dobson Haney, June 25, 1994. BS in Acctg., U. S.C., 1964, JD cum laude, 1972; LLM in Estate Planning (scholar), U. Miami, 1980. Bar: S.C. 1972, Fla. 1979, D.C. 1973, U.S. Tax Ct. 1972, U.S. Ct. Claims 1972, U.S. Supreme Ct. 1977. Intern ct. of claims sect., tax divsn. U.S. Dept. Justice, 1971; law clk. to chief judge U.S. Ct. Claims, Washington, 1972-74; ptnr. firm Edwards Wood, Duggan & Reese, Greer and Greenville, 1974-78; asst. prof. law Cumberland Law Sch., Samford U., Birmingham, Ala., 1978-79; faculty Nat. Inst. Trial Advocacy: N.E. Regional Inst., 1979, 83-90, 95-97, Fla. Regional Inst., 1989; teaching team 5th intensive trial techniques course Hofstra U., 1983; assoc. then capital ptnr. firm Shutts & Bowen, Miami, 1980-85; sole practice Miami, 1985—; also Rock Hill, S.C., 1994—; of counsel Griffin, Smith, Caldwell, Helder & Lee, Monroe, N.C., 2001—. Contbg. editor: The Lawyers PC; Fla. editor: Drafting Wills and Trust Agreements; substantive com. editor ABA: The Tax Lawyer, 1983—. Pres. Piedmont Heritage Found., Inc. 1975-78; del. State Rep. Conv., 1985, 87, 90; exec. committeeman Miami-Dade County Republicans, 1988-94, co-gen. counsel, 1990-91; apptd. Miami-Dade County Indsl. Devel. Authority, 1990-94; mem. vestry Episc. Ch., 1993-94. With USAF, 1965-69, Vietnam. Decorated Air Force Commendation medal; recipient Am. Jurisprudence award in real property and tax I, 1971; winner Grand prize So. Living Mag. travel photo contest, 1969. Mem. ABA (taxation sect., teaching law com., 1994—), Greer C. of C. (pres. 1977, Outstanding leadership award 1976), Greater Greenville C. of C. (dir. 1977), Order Wig and Robe, Estate Planning Council South Fla., Omicron Delta Kappa. Club: Bankers (bd. govs. 1989-94). Lodge: Masons, Scottish Rite, Rotary. Office: 5345 Wilgrove Mint Hill Rd Charlotte NC 28227-3467

WOOD, WILLIAM PRESTON, author, lawyer; b. Bronxville, NY, Apr. 23, 1951; s. Preston and Eleanor Catherine (Auby) W. BA, Middlebury Coll., 1973; JD, U. of the Pacific, 1976. Bar: Calif. 1976, U.S. Dist. Ct. (ea. dist.) Calif. 1976. Dep. dist. atty. Sacramento County District Atty., Sacramento, 1977—82; dir. publs. Calif. Dist. Attys. Assn., Sacramento, 1984—85; chief counsel Office Sec. State, Sacramento, 1999—2003; commr. Calif. Dept. Corps., 2003—; freelance writer, Sacramento, 1985—. Author: (novels) Rampage, 1985, Gangland, 1988, Fugitive City, 1990, Court of Honor, 1991, Stay of Execution, 1994, The Bone Garden, 1994, Quicksand, 1998, (motion picture) Rampage, 1992, Broken Trust, 1995; co-author (TV series) Kaz, 1978; contbr. articles to profl. jours. Pres. Citizens for a Better Sacramento, 1986. Mem. Writers Guild Am.-West. Republican. Episcopalian. Office Phone: 916-324-9011.

WOOD, WILLIS BOWNE, JR., retired utilities executive; b. Kansas City, Mo., Sept. 15, 1934; s. Willis Bowne Sr. and Mina (Henderson) W.; m. Dixie Gravel, Aug. 31, 1955; children: Bradley, William, Josh. BS in Petroleum Engring., U. Tulsa, 1957; grad. advanced mgmt. program, Harvard U., 1983; JD (hon.), Pepperdine U., 1996. With So. Calif. Gas Co., L.A., 1960-74, from v.p. to sr. v.p., 1975-80, exec. v.p., 1983-84; pres., CEO Pacific Lighting Gas Supply Co., L.A., 1981-83; from sr. v.p. to chmn., pres., CEO, Pacific Enterprises, L.A., 1984-93, chmn., CEO, 1993-98; ret., 1998. Bd. dirs. Washington Mut., Seattle; vice chmn. Automobile Club So. Calif.; trustee U. So. Calif. Trustee, past vice-chmn. Harvey Mudd Coll., Claremont, Calif., 1984—; trustee emeritus, past chmn. Calif. Med. Ctr. Found., L.A., 1983-2002; past trustee, past pres. S.W. Mus., L.A.; trustee John and Dora Haynes Found., 1998—; past bd. dirs. L.A. World Affairs Coun.; past dir., past chmn. bus. coun. for Sustainable Energy Future, 1994—; past dir. Pacific Coun. for Internat. Affairs. Recipient Disting. Alumni U. Tulsa, 1995; inductee U. Tulsa Engring. Hall of Fame, 2001. Mem. Soc. Petroleum Engrs., Pacific Energy Assn., Calif. State C. of C. (past bd. dirs.), Am. Automobile Assn. (dir. 1999, chmn. 2002—), NAM (past bd. dirs.), Hacienda Golf Club, Calif. Club. Republican. Office Phone: 213-244-2140.

WOODALL, DAVID MONROE, research engineer, dean; b. Perryville, Ark., Aug. 2, 1945; m. Linda Carol Page, June 6, 1966; 1 child, Zachary Page. BA, Hendrix Coll., 1967; MS, Columbia U., 1968; PhD, Cornell U., 1976. Registered profl. engr., Idaho. Nuc. engr. Westinghouse Corp., Pitts., 1968-70; asst. prof. U. Rochester, N.Y., 1974-77, U. N.Mex., Albuquerque, 1977-79, assoc. prof., 1979-83, chair dept., 1980-83, prof., 1984-86; group physics mgr. Idaho Nat. Engring. Lab., Idaho Falls, 1986-92; assoc. dean, dir. rsch. U. Idaho, Moscow, 1992-99, acting dean, 1999; dean coll. sci., engring., math. U. Alaska, Fairbanks, 1999—2003; dir. Ctr. for Nanosensor Tech., 2001—03. Provost & v.p. for academic affairs, Oregon Inst. of Tech., 2003-, EAC commr. Accreditation Bd. Engring. Tech., 1990-95, bd. dir., 1997-; cons. in field. Contbr. articles to profl. jours. Grantee NSF, DOE, AFOSR, Office Naval Rsch., DMEA, others. Mem. IEEE, Am. Nuc. Soc. (chpt. chair 1982-83), Am. Soc. Engring. Edn. (divsn. chair 1993, 95, bd. dirs. engring. rsch. coun.). Office: Oregon Institute of Technology 3201 Campus Drive Klamath Falls OR 97601 E-mail: woodalld@oit.edu.

WOODALL, GILBERT EARL, JR., medical administrator; b. Oak Ridge, Tenn., Dec. 21, 1954; m. Sarah Lee Blackburn, Sept., 1989; children: John Sage, Anna Alleen. BA, U. Tenn., 1976; MD, U. Tenn., Memphis, 1977; MS in Pub. Health, Western Ky. U., 1986. Med. dir. GM-Corvette Plant, Bowling Green, Ky., 1982-91, Alliant-Health at Work, Louisville, 1992-94, Jackson Madison-County Gen. Hosp.-Occupl. Medicine, Jackson, Tenn., 1995—. Mem. Mayor's Commn. on Employment and Disability Issues, Bowling Green, 1991, Meharry Med. Sch. Occupational Medicine Residency Adv. Bd., Nashville, 1987-88. Lt. comdr. USNR, 1978-82. Fellow Am. Coll. Occupational and Environ. Medicine (bd. dirs. 1987-90), Am. Coll. Preventive Medicine; mem. Tenn. Med. Assn. Avocation: computer science. Office: GW Occmed Clinic PO Box 12256 Jackson TN 38308-0137

WOODALL, HUNTER EARL, physician, educator; b. Richmond, Va., Mar. 4, 1957; s. H. Earl and June A. Woodall; m. Sylvia G. Woodall, May 26, 1980; children: Ruth, Paul, Alan. BS cum laude, Davidson Coll., 1979; MD, Vanderbilt U., 1983. Diplomate Am. Bd. Family Practice. Intern Charlotte Meml. Hosp., 1983—84, resident in family medicine, 1984—86, chief resident in family medicine, 1986—87; med. dir. Allendale County Rural Health Program, 1987—91. Asst. prof. family medicine MUSC, Anderson, SC, 1991—97, assoc. prof. family medicine, 1997—2003, clin. prof. family medicine, 2003—; med. dir. Anderson-Oconee Behavioral Health Svcs., 1992—2002, Hospice of the Upstate, 1998—; chmn. dept. family practice

Anderson Area Med. Ctr., 1999—2000, chmn. utilization mgmt. com., 1995—99; lectr., presenter in field. Contbr. articles to profl. jours. Vol. Anderson Free Clinic; bass singer Greater Anderson Chorale; elder, choir mem. Ctrl. Presbyn. Ch. Named Primary Care Provider of Yr., SC Primary Care Assn., 1989. Fellow: Am. Acad. Family Practice; mem.: Anderson County Med. Soc., SC Acad. Family Practice, SC Med. Assn., Am. Acad. Hospice and Palliative Medicine, Am. Soc. Addiction Medicine (pain com.). Presbyterian. Avocations: motorcycling, singing, chess. Office: Anmed Family Practice 600 N East St Anderson SC 29621

WOODALL, SAMUEL ROY, JR., lawyer; b. July 8, 1936; s. Samuel Roy Woodall; m. Jane Marvin Brock, Aug. 5, 1958; children: Samuel Roy III, Lawrence B., Claiborne A., George G. BA, U. Ky., 1958, LLB, 1962; postgrad., Yale U., 1959. Bar: Ky. 1962. Atty. Ky. Dept. Ins., 1962-64, gen. counsel, 1965-66; commr. ins. Commonwealth Ky., 1966-68; assoc. firm Wyatt, Grafton and Sloss, Louisville, 1968-69, ptnr., 1969-72; pres. Western Pioneer Life Ins. Co. (and predecessors), Louisville, 1972-76; asst. to pres. Am. Life & Accident Ins. Co., Louisville, 1976-80; pres. Nat. Assn. Life Cos., Washington, 1980-93; v.p. and chief counsel state rels. Am. Coun. Life Ins., Washington, 1993-98; with Morris, Manning & Martin (Atlanta-based firm), Washington, 1998—2001; ins. cons. Congl. Rsch. Svc., Libr. of Congress, Washington, 2001—; sr. ins. policy analyst U.S. Treasury Dept., 2002—. Guest instr. ins. law U. Louisville, 1968—69. Note editor: U. Ky. Law Rev., 1961—62. Pres. Citizen's Met. Planning coun., Louisville, 1970—71; chmn. City of Louisville Riverfront Commn., 1970—75, Ky. Heritage Commn., 1964—77; bd. dirs. Bingham Child Guidance Clinic, Louisville, 1969—76, Youth Performing Arts Coun., 1979—80. Named one of Ky.'s 3 Outstanding Young Men, Ky. Jr. C. of C., 1968; recipient Sullivan medallion, U. Ky., 1958; fellow Woodrow Wilson, Yale U., 1959. Mem.: ABA, Fedn. Ins. Counsel, D.C. Bar Assn., Ky. Bar Assn., Phi Beta Kappa, Phi Alpha Delta (pres. chpt. 1961—62). Home: 2851 29th St NW Washington DC 20008-4111 Office: US Dept Treasury 15th and Pennsylvania Ave NW Washington DC 20220

WOODALL, THOMAS A. state supreme court justice; b. Meridian, Miss., July 14, 1950; m. Debbie Bogan, 1972; children: Scott, Matthew, Claire. BA in History, Millsaps Coll., 1972; JD, U. Va., 1975. With Rives and Peterson, Birmingham, Ala., 1975—91; ptnr. Woodall and Maddox, Birmingham, 1991—96; circuit judge Jefferson County, 1996—2001; assoc. justice Ala. Supreme Ct., 2001—. Mem. Ala. Pattern Jury Instrn.-Civil Com., 1985—2001, vice chmn., 1992—2001. Republican. Methodist. Office: 300 Dexter Ave Montgomery AL 36104-3741

WOODARD, ALFRE, actress; b. Tulsa, Nov. 8, 1953; m. Roderick Spencer; 2 children. Student, Boston U. Appeared in (films) Remember My Name, 1976, Health, Cross Creek, 1983 (Acad. award nomination), Extremities, 1986, Scrooged, 1988, Mandela, 1988, Miss Firecracker, 1989, Grand Canyon, 1991, The Gun in Betty Lou's Handbag, 1992, Passion Fish, 1992, Heart and Souls, 1993, Rich in Love, 1993, Bopha!, 1993, Blue Chips, 1994, Crooklyn, 1994, How to Make an American Quilt, 1995, (TV series) Tucker's Witch, 1982-83, Sara, 1985, St. Elsewhere, 1985-87, Hill Street Blues (Emmy award for guest appearance in drama series 1984), L.A. Law (Emmy award for guest appearance in drama series 1987), (TV spls.) For Colored Girls Who Have Considered Suicide/When the Rainbow is Enuf, Trial of the Moke, Words by Heart, (TV films) A Mother's Courage: The Mary Thomas Story, Child Saver, Ambush Murder, Freedom Road, 1979, Sophisticated Gents, 1981, The Killing Floor, Unnatural Causes, 1986, Mandela, 1987, The Child Saver, Sweet Revenge, 1990, Blue Bayou, 1990, Bopho, 1993, Race to Freedom: The Underground Railroad, 1994, Blue Chips, 1994, Crooklyn, 1994, Wizard of Oz in Concert, 1995, Statistically speaking, 1995, The Piano Lesson, 1995, How to Make an American Quilt, 1995, Journey to Mars, 1996, Gulliver's Travels, 1996, Primal Fear, 1996, A Step Toward Tomorrow, 1996, Star Trek: First Contact, 1996, Member of the Wedding, 1997, Miss Evers' Boys, 1997, Follow Me Home, 1997, Cadillac Desert (mini series), 1997, Down in the Delta, 1998, Brown Sugar, 1998, Funny Valentines, (tv) 1999, Mumford, 1999, others,(plays) For Colored Girls Who Have Considered Suicide, When the Rainbow is Enuf, (off-Broadway plays) A Map of the World, 1985, A Winter's Tale 1989, So Nice They Named Twice, Horatio, What's Cookin', 2000, Love and Basketball, 2000, Dinosaur, 2000. Recipient Emmy awards for guest appearance in drama series.

WOODARD, ALVA ABE, business consultant; b. Roy, N.Mex., June 28, 1928; s. Joseph Benjamin and Emma Lurania (Watkins) W.; m. Esther Josepha Kaufmann, Apr. 5, 1947 (div. Sept. 1991); children: Nannette, Gregory, Loreen, Arne, Mark, Kevin, Steven, Curtis, Marlee, Julie, Michelle; m. Margaret Adele Evenson, Oct. 1, 1994. Student, Kinman Bus. U., 1948-49, Whitworth Coll., 1956, Wash. State U., 1953-54. Sec.-treas., dir. Green Top Dairy Farms, Inc., Clarkston, Wash., 1948-52; v.p., treas., sec., dir. ASC Industries, Inc. (subs. Gifford-Hill and Co.), Spokane, Wash., 1952-75; dir. Guenther Irrigation, Inc., Pasco, Wash., 1966-71; mng. dir. Irrigation Rental, Inc., Pasco, 1968-75, Rain Chief Irrigation Co., Grand Island, Nebr., 1968-75; sec., dir. Keeling Supply Co., Little Rock, 1969-72; pres., dir. Renters, Inc., Salt Lake City, 1971-75, Woodard Western Corp., Spokane, 1976-86, Woodard Industries, Inc., Auburn, Wash., 1987-90; cons. Woodard Assocs., Spokane, Wash., 1985—. Pres., dir. TFI Industries, inc., Post Falls, Idaho, 1989-90; v.p., sec., treas., dir. Trans-Force, Inc., Post Falls, 1989-90, TFI Computer Scis., Inc., Post Falls, 1989-90. Newman Lake (Wash.) Rep. precinct committeeman, 1964-80; Spokane County del. Wash. Rep. Conv., 1968-80. Mem. Adminstrv. Mgmt. Soc. (bd. dirs. 1966-68), Optimists. Avocations: fishing, theater, golf, reading, dance. Home and Office: 921 E 39th Ave Spokane WA 99203-3034

WOODARD, BETH STUCKEY, librarian, educator; b. Fairbury, Ill., Oct. 25, 1956; d. James Dale and Helenjean (Lauterbach) Stuckey; m. Billy Dean Woodard, July 14, 1979 (div. June 1993); children: Rebecca Lindsay, Sarah Lauren; m. Gregory Allen Wolfe, Oct. 21, 1995. BA, Ill. Wesleyan U., 1978; MS, U. Ill., 1979. Reference libr. U. S.C., Columbia, 1979-82; reference libr., asst. prof. libr. adminstrn. U. Ill., Urbana, 1983-85, cen. info. svcs. libr., 1985-99, 2001—, assoc. prof., 1990—, acting head of reference, 1993-94, 97, 2002—03, interim commerce librarian, 1999-2001, staff devel. and tng. coord., 2002—. Cons. Oberlin (Ohio) Coll., 1996, Ea. Ill. U., 1999, So. Ill. U., Edwardsville, 1999, U. Toronto, 2001, Lincoln Christian Coll., 2003, U. Chgo., 2004. Contbr. book chpts. to Reference and Information Services, 1991, 95, 2001; editor: (spl. jour. issue) Ill. Librs., 1991; contbr. articles to profl. jours. Chair fund raising com. Oakwood (Ill.) Twp. Pub. Libr., 1997-98, trustee, 2001—, v.p., 2003—. Mem. ALA, Reference and User Svcs. Assn. (evaluation of reference and adult svcs. com. 1990-92, chair 1992-94, bd. dirs. 1994-2001, editor newsletter 1997-2001, Isadore Gilbert Mudge/ R.R. Bowker award 1998), Assn. Coll. and Rsch. Librs. (mem. continuing edn. com. 1988-90, chair 1990-92, chair guidelines for bibliographic instrn. programs 1994-96, sec. instrn. sect. 1992-93, chair comms. com. 1993-94, vice-chair instrn. sect. 2000-01, chair instrn. sect. 2001-2002, chair Dudley awards com. 2002-03, chair nominating com. 2003-04), Phi Kappa Phi, Beta Phi Mu, Alpha Lambda Delta. Office: U of Ill 1408 W Gregory Dr Urbana IL 61801-3607 Office Phone: 217-244-1882. E-mail: bswoodar@uiuc.edu.

WOODARD, CAROL JANE, educational consultant; b. Buffalo, Jan. 19, 1929; d. Harold August and Violet Maybelle (Landsittel) Young; m. Ralph Arthur Woodard, Aug. 19, 1950; children: Camaron Jane, Carsen Jane, Cooper Ralph. BA, Hartwick Coll., 1950; MA, Syracuse U., 1952; PhD, SUNY, Buffalo, 1972; LHD (hon.), Hartwick Coll., 1991; postgrad., Bank St. Coll., Harvard U. Cert. tchr., NY State. Tchr., Orchard Park, NY, 1950-51, Danville, Ind., 1951-52, Akron, NY, 1952-54; dir. Garden Nursery Sch., Williamsville, NY, 1955-65; tchr. Amherst Coop. Nursery Sch., NY, 1967-69; asst. prof. early childhood edn. SUNY, Buffalo, 1969-72, lab. demonstration tchr. and student teaching supr., 1969-76, assoc. prof., 1972-79, prof., 1979-88, prof. emeritus, 1988—; dir. Consultants in Early Childhood, 1988—. Cons. Lutheran Ch. Am., Villa Maria Coll., Buffalo Pub. Sch., Buffalo Mus. Sci., Headstart Tng. Programs, Erie Cmty. Coll., NY State Dept. Edn., numerous workshops.; cons. sch. systems, indsl. firms, pub., civic orgns. in child devel.; vis. prof. The Netherlands and East China Univ., Shanghai, People's Republic of China; sci. trainer The Wright Group, 1995. Author 7 books for young children, 2 textbooks in field; co-author: Physical Science in Early Childhood, 1987; co-author nat. curriculum for ch. sch. for 3-yr.-olds; author: (booklet) You Can Help Your Baby Learn; author/coord. TAKE CARE child protection project, 1987; contbr. chpt. to books, articles to profl. jour. Trustee Hartwick Coll., Oneonta, NY, 1978-87; cons. EPIC Birth to Three Program, 1992; design cons. indoor playground Noah's Ark Jewish Ctr., Buffalo, 1992; Sites Project coord., cons. Let's Talk project Buffalo Pub. Sch., 1994—; student tchg. supr. SUNY, Fredonia, 1994-2004. Mem. Nat. Assn. Edn. Young Children, Early Childhood Edn. Council Western NY, Assn. Childhood Edn. Internat., Phi Delta Kappa, Pi Lambda Theta. Home: 85 Ruskin Road East Aurora NY 14052-3028

WOODARD, CLAUDETTE J. state representative, retired educational association administrator; b. 1945; married; 2 children. MEd in Curriculum and Instr. School improvement facilitator; ret.; rep. Ohio State Ho. Reps., Columbus, 2000—. Mem. edn. com. Ohio State Ho. Reps., mem. fed. grant review and edn. oversight subcom., mem. fin. and appropriations com., mem. primary and secondary edn. subcom., mem. ins. com.; adv. bd. Case Western Res. Mental Devel. Ctr. Chmn. spl. needs com. Boy Scouts Am. Spl. Projects; mem. Nat. Coun. Negro Women; treas. Coun. Exceptional Children; pres. Black Women's Polit. Action Com.; co-chmn. Women in Appt. Office Project; bd. dirs. Heights Cmty. Congress; mem. Cleve. Heights-Univ. Heights Bd. Edn., 1991—99. Mem.: Sch. Union Assn., Alpha Kappa Alpha (Meritorious Svc. award 1996). Democrat. Office: Ohio State House Reps 77 South High Street 10th Floor Columbus OH 43215-6111

WOODARD, DEANA SAFFORD, artist; b. Springfield, Mass., June 18, 1946; d. Dean Wilbur and Merle Watkins (Woodard) Safford; m. Richard Peter Bean, Oct. 17, 1968 (div. Oct. 1999); children: Duane Matthew (dec.) and David Andrew (twins), Dana Robert, Matthew Adams. Student, W.Va. Wesleyan Co., 1964-66. Cert. tax preparer 2002. Co-owner McCarthy Gallery, Rockport, Mass., 1995, Gallery Six, Rocky Neck, Mass., 1996; owner Gallery 43, Rocky Neck Art Colony, Gloucester, Mass., 1997; travel cons. Magic World travel, Springfield, Mass., 1991-94, The Cruise and Vacation Store, East Longmeadow, Mass., 1994-97. Hist. and geneal. rsch.; vol. U.S. Peace Corps, Iran, 1968-69; distbr. Seamless Internat., Inc., 1996-97. Author: East and Me: A Personal Encounter With the Mid East, 1992; editor: Woodard Footprints, 2003. Mem. coun. Springfield Art League, 1992-95; host parent Internat. Exch. Students, 1986, 87, 89, 91. Recipient Watercolor award Longmeadow Shops, 1991, 94, Pastel award, 1989, 93. Mem. N.Am. Marine Arts Soc. (Excellence award 1991), Acad. Artists Assn. (membership chmn. 1993-97, pres. 1997, Watson-Guptill award 1991), Nat. Mus. Women in the arts (charter), Am. Artist Profl. League, Rocky Neck Art Colony, Nat. Safety Assocs. (sales coord. 1995-2004, Bronze medal 1995), Art Mart Sedona, Art Wholesaler, Mingus Mountain Gem and Mineral Club. Avocations: researching Native Am. mythology, rock hounding, history, hiking, camping.

WOODARD, DONALD MARVIN, marketing professional; b. LaPorte, Ind., Jan. 10, 1948; s. Roy Marvin and Josephine Irene Woodard; m. Carol Jean Woodard, Nov. 23, 1973; children: Kelli, Corey. Pres. Image Industries, Boulder, 1973—95, Laarhoven Design, Denver, 1995—2001; mktg. cons. Don Woodard Internat., Broomfield, Colo., 2001—. Author: (book) T.S.K.S. Handbook; co-author: Still More Secrets of Success Exhibiting, 1999; author: (sign business and digital printing magazines) Exhibit Builder Magazine. Mem.: Rocky Mountain Inventors Congress, Nat. Woodcarver's Assn. Achievements include founder, Trade Show Knowledge seminar program; former NASCAR driver, listed in Legends of Colorado Auto Racing; speaking for exhibit companies throughout the US. Avocations: woodcarving, motorcycling, auto racing, skiing, horseback riding. Office: Don Woodard International 2853 West 132nd Avenue Suite A Broomfield CO 80020 Office Phone: 888-520-9910.

WOODARD, DOROTHY MARIE, insurance broker; b. Houston, Feb. 7, 1932; d. Gerald Edgar and Bessie Katherine (Crain) Floeck; student N.Mex. State U., 1950; m. Jack W. Woodard; June 19, 1950 (dec. May 1972); m. Norman W. Libby, July 19, 1982 (dec. Dec. 1991). Ptnr. Western Oil Co., Tucumcari, N.Mex., 1950—; owner, mgr. Woodard & Co., Las Cruces, N.Mex., 1959-67; agt., dist. mgr. United Nations Ins. Co., Denver, 1968-74; agt. Western Nat. Life Ins. Co., Amarillo, Tex., 1976—. Exec. dir. Tucumcari Indsl. Commn., 1979—; dir. Bravo Dome Study Com., 1979—; owner Libby Cattle Co., Libby Ranch Co.; regional bd. dirs. N.Mex., Eastern Plains Council Govts., 1979—. Mem. NAFE, Tucumcari C. of C., Mesa Country Club. Home: PO Box 823 Tucumcari NM 88401-0823 *Personal philosophy: A never ending search and quest for knowledge, through participation and understanding.*

WOODARD, JOSEPH LAMAR, law librarian, law educator; b. Auburndale, Fla., Dec. 28, 1937; s. Wilbur Allen and Florence Virginia (Ladd) W.; m. Eleanor Eugenia Cummings, Aug. 7, 1964; children: Robert Edward, James Frederick. BA, U. Fla., 1959, J.D., 1962; MS in Libr. Sci., Columbia U., 1964. Bar: Fla. 1962, U.S. Dist. Ct. (mid. dist.) Fla. 1970. Asst. reference libr. Columbia U., NYC, 1962-64; asst. libr.Cahill, Gordon, Reindel and Ohl, NYC, 1964-65; law libr. Tulane U., 1965-69; ptnr. Schuh, Schuh and Woodard, St. Petersburg, Fla., 1969-71; law librarian Stetson U., 1971-2001, prof. law, 1979-2001. Law libr. and prof. emeritus, 2001-. Pres. Tampa Bay Library Consortium, 1981, 88-89. Served with USAR, 1957-63. Mem. Fla. Bar, Am. Assn. Law Librs. (sec.-treas. S.E. chpt. 1975-78), Pinellas Pub. Lib. Coop. (sec.-treas. 1993-94, pres. 1994-95). Republican. Presbyterian. Office: 1401 61st St S Saint Petersburg FL 33707-3246 E-mail: jwoodar2@tampabay.rr.com.

WOODARD, NINA ELIZABETH, banker; b. L.A., Apr. 3, 1947; d. Alexander Rhodes and Harriette Jane (Powers) Matthews; divorced; children: Regina M., James. D. Grad., Pacific Coast Banking Sch., 1987; BS in Mgmt., Calif. Coast U., 1993; postgrad., Ctr. for Creative Leadership, 1994. Lifetime cert. sr. profl. in human resources. Dental asst. Donald R. Shire DDS, L.A., 1965-66; with Security Pacific Nat. Bank, Marina Del Rey, Calif., 1968-69, First Interstate Bank, Casper, Wyo., 1971—. adminstr. asst. pers., 1975-78, asst. v.p., asst. mgr. pers., 1978-82, v.p., dir. mktg. and pers., 1982-84, v.p., mgr. human resources, 1984-88; v.p., mgr. employee rels. First Interstate Bank Ltd., L.A., 1988-93; v.p., mgr. employee rels. Ams. region Standard Chartered Bank, 1993-95, sr. v.p. human resources, 1995-99, sr. v.p. advisor cultural integration and employee comm., 1999-2000, sr. v.p. mgmt. cultural integration, 2000—. Instr. mktg. Am. Inst. Banking, 1983, Casper Coll., 1982; mng. dir. Aradhana Human Resources Consulting Pvt. Ltd., India, 2002-2003; dir. Western Region Performance Consulting Internat. India, 2003. Mem. Civil Svc. Commn., City of Casper, 1983-88; bd. dirs. YMCA, 1984-87, Downtown Devel. Assn.; pres. Downtown Casper Assn.; instr. St. Patrick's Parish Religious Edn., 1991-92, mem. parish coun., 1993-94; advisor to the parish coun. Parish of the Resurrection, Jersey City, 1999. Named Bus. Woman of Yr., Bus. and Profl. Women, 198, Young Career Woman, 1975. Mem. Nat. Assn. Bank Women, Bus. and Profl. Women (dist. dir.), Am. Soc. Pers. Adminstrn. (regional v.p., state coun. Wyo. 1987-88), Pers. and Indsl. Rels. Assn. (chmn. govt. affairs com. 1989-90, Fast Track award 1991, Pres.'s Achievement award 1993, conf. chmn. 1991, 92, dist. chair 1993, 2d v.p. 1994), Fin. Women Internat. (Wyo. state chair 1986, regional edn. and tng. chair 1987, dist. coord. L.A. 1993, L.A. group chair 1994, nat. bd. dirs.), Soc. Human Resource Mgmt. (area I v.p. 1996-99, N.Y. chpt., NEHRA chpt.), Am. Alumni Assn. India, Bombay Mgmt. Assn., Bombay Midtown Rotary Club. Republican. Roman Catholic. Office: Standard Chartered Bank 2d Fl 23-25 MG Rd Fort Mumbai Mumbai India

WOODARD, PETER CLARK, music educator, musician; b. Bethesda, Md., May 17, 1950; s. Charles Clark and Catherine Marie Woodard; m. Lisa Anne Baker, Sept. 7, 1989 (div.); children: Clark, Kirk. MusB, U. Hartford, 1973; MusM, U. Conn., 1989. Music adv. Hartford (Conn.) Ballet Co., 1973—80; dance accompaniest Mary Anthony Dance Theatre, NYC, 1980—84; faculty U. Hartford Hartt Sch., 1984—. Vocal accompanist undergrad. Cleve. Inst., 1968—69; vocal accompanist Hartt Sch., Hartford, 1969—73; chmn. jazz studies U. Hartford Hartt Sch., 1995—. Composer, performer (CD) Pictures from Fortaleza, 2001. Jazz performer, faculty Eleazar De Carvalho Festival, Forteleza, Brazil, 2000—03; judge jazz piano competition Music Club Hartford, 1998; panelist Sinatra; Conf. Hofstra U., 1999; organizer, host Iraqi Forum, Hartford, 2002, Dorothy Day Forum, Hartford, 2003; organist St. Mary's Ch., Norwalk, Conn., 1964—68. Mem.: Conn. Composers Orgn., Pi Kappa Lambda. Democrat. Avocations: reading, literature. Home: 25 Loomis Ave Windsor CT 06095 Office Phone: 860-768-4123. Business E-Mail: pwoodard@hartford.edu.

WOODARD,JR. FREDRICK JAMES, music educator, musician; b. Kansas City, Mo., Mar. 2, 1961; s. Fredrick James Woodard,Sr and Sandra Josephine Woodard, Barbara Ann Woodard (Stepmother); m. Rochelle Mareace Breeden, May 4, 1996; children: Kahmal London, Fredrick Woodard,III, Deniece Woodard. MusB, Berklee Coll. of Music, Boston, 1983; MEd, U. of Mass., Boston, 2000. Cert. Tchr. Mass., 1990, Ednl Administr. Mass., 2000. Gen. music tchr. St Joseph and St. Patrick Schs., Roxbury, Mass., 1992—94; guitar tchr. and instrumental ensemble dir. Belmont Hill Sch., Belmont, Mass., 1992—94; guitar,electric bass and strings tchr. Roland Hayes Divsn. of Music, Roxbury, Mass., 1994—; pres./owner Ujam Records, Roxbury, Mass., 1996—; bandleader The Fred Woodard Trio, Roxbury, Mass., 1988—; freelance musician Various bands in the Boston area, Boston, 1983—. Musician (guitarist,producer,composer,arranger): (jazz compact disc) Arrival, 1999, (compact disc) 1715, 2001 (GBOS Image Award Jazz Artist of the Yr., 2002). Mem. Dudley St. Neighborhood Initiative, Roxbury, Mass., 2001—02. Mem.: Mass. Music Educators Assn., Internat. Assn. for Jazz Edn. Avocations: history, photography, travel. Office: Ujam Records PO Box 190586 Boston MA 02119 Office Phone: 617-438-1719. E-mail: fwtrio@hotmail.com.

WOODBRIDGE, JOHN DUNNING, history and church history educator; b. Salisbury, N.C., May 24, 1941; s. Charles Jahleel and Ruth (Dunning) W.; m. Susan Jane Frerichs, June 28, 1970; children: Elisabeth Anne, Joshua, David. BA in History, Wheaton Coll., 1963; MA in History, Mich. State U., 1965; PhD de Troisième Cycle, U. Toulouse, France, 1969; MDiv, Trinity Evang. Div. Sch., Deerfield, Ill., 1971. Vis. prof. history U. Toulouse, 1968-69; asst. prof. history Trinity Coll., Deerfield, 1970-74; prof. ch. history Trinity Evang. Div. Sch., Deerfield, 1970—; vis. prof. history Northwestern U., Evanston, Ill., 1988-95. Vis. prof. religion Hautes Etudes, Sorbonne, U. Paris, 1996, 99. Author: Biblical Authority, 1982, Revolt in Pre-revolutionary France, 1995; editor: Great Leaders of the Christian Church, 1988; co-editor: Historische Kritik und biblischer kanon, 1988; sr. editor Christianity Today, 1997-99. NEH fellow, 1973-74, Herzog August Bibliothek fellow, 1982, ACLS fellow, Paris, 1976-77; NEH summer grant, Chgo., 1995. Mem. Am. Soc. Eighteenth Century Studies, Soc. French History. Mem. Evangelical Free Ch. Avocation: composing music.

WOODBRIDGE, NORMA JEAN, registered nurse, writer; b. Flushing, N.Y., Apr. 21, 1931; d. Charles Jahleel Woodbridge and Ruth Eyman Dunning. BS in Nursing Edn., Temple U., 1958; RN, U. Pa., 1952; LittD, World Congress Poets, Cairo, 1990. RN, Fla. Sr. RN, forensic State of Fla. Dept. Corrections, 1992-95; staff nurse Pines Village, North Ft. Myers, Fla., 1995—97; staff RN Lee Convalescent Ctr., Ft. Myers, Fla., 1997-98; unit mgr. Tandem Health Care, Norht Ft. Myers, 1998-99; nurse Cape Coral (Fla.) Gen. Staff Rehab., 1999—. Author-in-residence Highland Pk. (N.J.) Sch. Sys., 1988-90. Author: African Realities and Dreams, 1987, Resting Places, 1988, Meditations of a Modern Pilgrim, 1990; contbr. Christmas Blessings, 2002; composer (jazz album) Watercolor Dreams, 1982; playwright Switch: Switch, 1998; poetry reading on NPR, 2001. Recipient Poet of the Millenium award, Internat. Poets Acad., 2000; fellow, Yaddo Writing Colony, 1988. Mem.: ASCAP, N.J. Poetry Soc. (v.p. 1987—88), Soc. Am. Poets, Peace River (Fla.) Writers Group. Avocations: travel, fishing, gourmet cooking, hiking, theater. Home: 2606 Zoysia Ln Fort Myers FL 33917-2476

WOODBURN, RALPH ROBERT, JR., lawyer; b. Haverhill, Mass., Nov. 3, 1946; s. Ralph Robert and Josephine Marie (McClure) W.; m. Janet M. Smith, Sept. 15, 1985. BA, Mich. State U., 1967; JD, Harvard U., 1972; LLM, Boston U., 1981. Bar: Mass. 1972, U.S. Tax Ct. 1987. Assoc. Bowers, Fortier & Lakin, Boston, 1972-76; from assoc. to ptnr. Haussermann, Davison & Shattuck, Boston, 1976-83; ptnr. Palmer & Dodge, Boston, 1983—. Tchr. Harvard Ctr. for Lifelong Learning, Cambridge, Mass., 1986-89; chmn. Wellesley Cable Access Bd., 1993-95. Contbr. articles to Boston Bar Jour. and Estate Planning. Treas. Exeter Assn. of New Eng., Boston, 1985-89, v.p., 1989-91, pres., 1991-93. Fellow Am. Coll. Trust and Estate Counsel; mem. ABA, Boston Bar Assn. (chmn. probate legislation 1983-93), Brae Burn Country Club (Newton, Mass.), Harvard Club of Boston, Boston Probate and Estate Planning Forum (program chair 1996-97, moderator 1997-98), Harvard Travellers Club. Home: 25 Cypress Rd Wellesley MA 02481-2918 Office: Palmer & Dodge LLP 111 Huntington Ave Boston MA 02199-7613 E-mail: rwoodburn@palmerdodge.com.

WOODBURN, WILLIAM A. utilities executive; With Union Carbide, McKinsey & Co.; mgr. bus. devel. Gen. Electric Co., 1984—94; v.p., gen. mgr. GE Superabrasives, 1994—2000; exec. v.p., mem. office of the CEO GE Capital, 2000—01; pres., CEO GE Specialty Materials, 2001—. Office: General Electric Co 3135 Easton Turnpike Fairfield CT 06828

WOODBURY, DIXON JOHN, physiologist, educator, research scientist; b. Seattle, Dec. 31, 1956; s. John Walter and Betty (Gunderson) Woodbury; m. Susan Diana Harvey, Mar. 20, 1980; children: James Dixon, Thomas Walter, Emily Susan, Kara Leigh. BS in Physics and Chemistry magna cum laude, U. Utah, 1980; PhD in Physiology and Biophysics, U. Calif., Irvine, 1986. Postdoctoral fellow in biochemistry Brandeis U., Waltham, Mass., 1986-89; rsch. assoc. Howard Hughes Med. Inst., Waltham, 1989-90; asst. prof. Wayne State U., Detroit, 1990-97, assoc. prof., 1997-2001, Brigham Young U., Provo, Utah, 2001—03, prof., 2003—. Unit commr. Boy Scouts Am., 1984—86, 1996—98; bishopric Ch. Jesus Christ LDS, 1997—99. Fellow, U. Calif., 1980, 1981, 1985, Muscular Dystrophy Assn., 1986—88. Mem.: IEEE, Biophysical Soc., Soc. Neuroscience. Office: Brigham Young U 574 Widtsoe Bldg Provo UT 84602-5255 Office Phone: 801-422-7562.

WOODBURY, MARDA LIGGETT, librarian, writer; b. N.Y.C., Sept. 20, 1925; d. Walter W. and Edith E. (Fleischer) Liggett; m. Philip J. Evans, Sept. 1948 (div. 1950); 1 child, Mark W. Evans; m. Mark Lee Woodbury, 1956 (div. 1969); children: Brian, Heather. Student, Bklyn. Coll., 1942-44; BA in Chemistry and Polit. Sci., Bard Coll., 1946; BS in L.S., Columbia U., 1948; postgrad., U. Calif., Berkeley, 1955-56, 60-61, MJ, 1995. Cert. tchr. Libr. various spl., med. and pub. librs., San Francisco, 1946-60, Coll. Pk. High Sch., Mt. Diablo, Calif., 1962-67; elem. sch. libr. Oakland and Berkeley, Calif., 1967-69; libr. dir. Far West Lab. Ednl. Rsch. & Devel., San Francisco, 1969-73; libr., editor Gifted Resource Ctr., San Mateo, Calif., 1973-75; libr. cons. Rsch. Ventures, Berkeley, Calif., 1975—2003; libr. dir. Life Chiropractic Coll., San Lorenzo, Calif., 1980-95. Author: A Guide to Sources of Educational Information, 1976, 2d edit., 1982, Selecting Instructional Materials, 1978, Selecting Materials for Instruction, Vol. I: Issues and Policies, 1979, Vol. II: Media and the Curriculum, 1980, Vol. III: Subject Areas and Implementation, 1980, Childhood Information Resources, 1985 (Outstanding Ref. Work, Assn. Ref. Librs. 1985), Youth Information Resources, 1987, Stopping the Presses: The Murder of Walter W. Liggett, 1998; mem. editorial bd. Ref. Libr., 1980-95. Home: 145 Monte Cresta Ave Apt 402 Oakland CA 94611-4809 Office Phone: 510-653-5876. E-mail: mardawoodbury@msn.com.

WOODBURY, RICHARD BENJAMIN, anthropologist, educator; b. West Lafayette, Ind., May 16, 1917; s. Charles Goodrich and Marion (Benjamin) W.; m. Nathalie Ferris Sampson, Sept. 18, 1948. Student, Oberlin Coll., 1934-36; BS in Anthropology cum laude, Harvard U., 1939, MA, 1942, PhD, 1949; postgrad., Columbia U., 1939-40. Archeol. research, Ariz., 1938, 39, 1940, 1947-49, 1953-56, Tehuacan, Mex., 1964; archaeologist United Fruit Co. Zaculeu Project, Guatemala, 1947-50; assoc. prof. anthropology U. Ky., 1950-52, Columbia U., 1952-58; rsch. assoc. prof. anthropology interdisciplinary arid lands program U. Ariz., 1959-63; curator archeology and anthropology U.S. Nat. Mus., Smithsonian Instn., Washington, 1963-69, acting. head office anthropology, 1965-66, chmn. office anthropology, 1966-67; prof., chmn. dept. anthropology U. Mass., Amherst, 1969-73, prof., 1973-81, prof. emeritus, 1981—, acting assoc. provost, dean grad. sch., 1973-74. Mem.

divsn. anthropology and psychology NRC, 1954-57; bd. dirs. Archaeol. Conservancy, 1979-84, Valley Health Plan, Amherst, 1981-84, Mus. of No. Ariz., 1983-90; liason rep. for Smithsonian Instn., Com. for Recovery of Archeol. Remains, 1965-69; assoc. seminar on ecol. systems and cultural evolution Columbia U., 1964-73; mem. exec. com. bd. dirs. Human Relations Area Files, Inc., New Haven, Conn., 1968-70; cons. Conn. Hist. Commn., 1970-72. Author (with A.S. Trik) The Ruins of Zaculeu, Guatemala, 2 vols., 1953, Prehistoric Stone Implements of Northeastern Arizona, 1954, Alfred V. Kidder, 1973, Sixty Years of Southwestern Archaeology, 1993, (chpt.) (with James A. Neely) The Prehistory of the Tehuacan Valley, Vol. 4, 1972; editor: (with I.A. Sanders) Societies Around the World (2 vols.), 1953, (with others) The Excavation of Hawikuh, 1966, Am. Antiquity, 1954-58, Abstracts of New World Archaeology; editor-in-chief: Am. Anthropologist, 1975-78; mem. editorial bd.: Am. Jour. Archeology, 1957-72. Mem. sch. com., Shutesbury, Mass., 1979-82; chmn. finance com. Friends of Amherst Stray Animals (Dakin Animal Shelter), 1983-85, trustee, 1991—; sec. Shutesbury Hist. Commn., 1999—. With USAF, 1942-45. Fellow Mus. No. Ariz., 1985. Fellow AAAS (coun. rep. Am. Anthrop. Assn. 1961-63, com. on desert and arid zones rsch. Southwest and Rocky Mountains divsn. 1958-64, vice-chair 1962-64, com. arid lands 1969-74, sec. 1970-72), Am. Anthrop. Assn. (exec. bd. 1963-66, A.V. Kidder award 1989), Archeol. Inst. Am. (exec. com. 1965-67); mem. Soc. Am. Archeology (treas. 1953-54, pres. 1958-59, chmn. fin. com. 1987-89, Fiftieth Anniversary award 1985, Disting. Svc. award 1988), Ariz. Archeol. and Hist. Soc., Nature Conservancy, Archeol. Conservancy (life). Office: U Mass Dept Anthropology Machmer Hall Amherst MA 01003

WOODBURY, ROBERT CHARLES, lawyer; b. Sheridan, N.Y., July 7, 1929; s. Wendell F. and Lillian S. (Towne) W.; m. Martha Bayard Page, Jan. 25, 1958. BEE, Rensselaer Poly. Inst., 1950; JD, Cornell U., 1953. Bar: N.Y. 1954, U.S. Dist. Ct. (so. dist.) N.Y. 1965, U.S. Dist. Ct. (we. dist.) N.Y. 1979, U.S. Ct. Appeals (4th cir.) 1964, U.S. Ct. Claims 1961, U.S. Ct. Mil. Appeals 1956, U.S. Patent Office 1961; lic. profl. engr., N.Y. Project engr. Army reactors program U.S. Atomic Energy Commn., 1957-60; assoc. Reid & Priest, N.Y.C., 1962-70; pvt. practice Dunkirk, N.Y., 1971—; ptnr. Aular & Woodbury, Dunkirk, N.Y., 1973-81, Morten & Woodbury, Dunkirk, N.Y., 1982-88. Gen. counsel N.Y. State Temp. Commn. Environ. Impact Major Pub. Utility Facilities, 1970-71; del. N.Y. 8th Jud. Dist. Rep. Jud. Nominating Conv., 1985—; chmn. bd. dirs. Woodbury Farms, Ltd., 1965-98, Woodbury Vineyards, 1968-91. Assoc. trustee Buffalo Gen. Hosp. Found., 1994-96; trustees coun. Buffalo Gen. Healthcare Sys., 1996-98, steering com. 1996-98; mem. trustees coun. Kaleida Health Sys., Buffalo, 1998-2001, Kaleida Health Cmty. Coun., 2001—; founding pres. Chautauqua County Arts Coun., 1971; town atty. Town of Sheridan, 1972-75; dist. counsel city sch. dist. City of Dunkirk, 1973-82; co-founder No. Chautauqua Indsl. Roundtable, 1979; co-chmn. Chmn.'s Club, Chautauqua County Rep. Com. 1988-98; chmn., pres., dir., counsel Historic Harbor Renaissance, Inc., 1999—. Lt. USN, 1954-57. Fellow N.Y. Bar Found.; mem. N.Y. State Bar Assn. (chmn. com. atomic energy law 1967-69, chmn. com. pub. utility law 1969-71, mem. action unit 5 regulatory reform N.Y. 1980-83), Bar Assn. No. Chautauqua (pres. 1979), Cornell Law Assn., Rensselaer Alumni Assn., Dunkirk C. of C. (pres. 1979), Mid-Day Club Buffalo, Chautauqua Yacht Club. Republican. Presbyterian. Avocations: skiing, wine, sailing. Home: 3300 S Roberts Rd Fredonia NY 14063-9418 Office: PO Box 800 87 E 4th St Dunkirk NY 14048-2225 E-mail: bobhere@netsync.net.

WOODBURY, STEPHEN ABBOTT, economics educator; b. Beverly, Mass., Oct. 25, 1952; s. Stephen E. and Barbara (Sandberg) W.; m. Susan Pozo, May 29, 1982 (div. June 1992); 1 child, Ricardo Pozo; m. Virginia Baldwin, Dec. 7, 1996. AB, Middlebury (Vt.) Coll., 1975; MS, U. Wis., 1977, PhD, 1981. Asst. prof. of econs. Pa. State U., University Park, 1979-82, Mich. State U., East Lansing, 1982-88, assoc. prof. econs., 1988-94; prof. econs., 1994—; sr. economist W.E. Upjohn Inst., Kalamazoo, Mich., 1984—. Dep. dir. Fed. Adv. Coun. on Unemployment Compensation, Washington, 1993-94, cons., 1994-96; cons. U. Hawaii/State of Hawaii, Honolulu, 1991-96, State of Mich. Task Force, Lansing, 1989-90, U.S. Dept. Labor, Washington, 1988, 96—, European Communities Commn., Brussels, 1987-88; vis. prof. U. Stirling, Scotland, 1992; vis. scholar Fed. Res. Bd., Washington, 1992. Author: Tax Treatment of Fringe Benefits, 1991; editor: Search Theory and Unemployment, 2002, Employee Benefits and Labor Markets in the U.S. and Canada, 2000, Reform of the Unemployment Insurance System, 1998, Long-Term Unemployment and Reemployment Policies, 2000; contbr. articles to profl. jours. Recipient Rsch. grants William H. Donner Found., 1991, U.S. Dept. Health and Human Svcs., 1985, 99, U.S. Dept. Labor, 1995, 98, 2002, Filene Rsch. Inst., 1996, Ctr. Credit Union Rsch., U. Wis., 1997, AMA, 2001. Mem. Am. Econ. Assn., Am. Statis. Assn., Assn. for Evolutionary Econs., Indsl. Rels. Rsch. Assn., Midwest Econs. Assn. (1st v.p. 1993-94, pres. 1998-99), Nat. Acad. Social Ins., Soc. Labor Economists, Nat. Tax Assn. Office: Dept Econs Marshall Hall Mich State U East Lansing MI 48824 also: WE Upjohn Inst 300 S Westnedge Ave Kalamazoo MI 49007-4630

WOODCOCK, DAVID GEOFFREY, architect, educator; b. Manchester, Eng., May 28, 1937; s. Herbert Edwin and Constance Mary (Bristol) W.; m. Kathleen Mary Bishop, Oct. 1, 1960 (dec. 1964); 1 child, Jonathan Alfred; m. Valerie Frances Gubbins, July 4, 1964; children: Frances Mary, Penelope Jane. BA in Architecture with 1st class honors, U. Manchester, 1960, D in Town Planning, 1966. Registered arch., Tex. Lectr. U. Manchester, 1961; asst. prof. Tex. A&M U., College Station, 1962-66, assoc. prof., 1970-76, prof., 1976—; sr. lectr. Kent. Inst. Art & Design, Canterbury, England, 1966-70. Pvt. practice, College Station, 1980—, Canterbury, 1966-70. Bd. dirs. Opera and Performing Arts Soc. Tex. A&M U., 1980-83, 88-91, pres., 1993-94, adv. bd. Hammons Sch. Architecture Drury Coll., Mo., 1990-93, Savannah (Ga.) Coll. Arts and Design/Architecture, 1987-93; active Episc. Diocese Tex. Archtl. Commn., 1987-95. Recipient Rsch. Excellence award Tex. Hist. Commn., 1991, Romieniec award for archtl. edn. Tex. Soc. Archs., 1995, Truett Latimer Profl. award Preservation Tex., Inc., 1998. Fellow AIA, Soc. Antiquaries London; mem. Assn. for Preservation Tech. Internat. (bd. dirs. 1990—, v.p. 1998-99, pres. 1999-2001, Harley J. McKee award 2003), Nat. Coun. for Preservation Edn., Assn. Collegiate Schs. Architecture (regional dir. 1981-84, Disting. Prof. 1991). Avocations: drawing, creative and gifted education, choral singing. Office: Tex A&M U Dept Architecture College Station TX 77843-3137 Office Phone: 979-845-7850. E-mail: woodcock@archone.tamu.edu.

WOODCOCK, JANET, federal official; b. Washington, Pa., Aug. 29, 1948; d. John and Frances (Crocker) W.; m. Roger Henry Miller, Nov. 16, 1981; children: Kathleen Miller, Susanne Miller. BS cum laude, Bucknell U., 1970; MD, Northwestern U., Chgo., 1977. Diplomate Am. Bd. Internal Medicine. Intern Hershey Med. Ctr./Pa. State U., 1977-78, resident in internal medicine, 1978-80, chief resident in medicine, 1980-81; fellow in rheumatology U. Calif./VA Med. Ctr., San Francisco, 1982-84; instr. medicine divsn. rheumatology and immunology VA Med. Ctr., San Francisco, 1984-85; med. officer divsn. biol. investigational new drugs Ctr. for Biologics Evaluation and Rsch./FDA, Rockville, Md., 1986-87, group leader divsn. biol. investigational new drugs, 1987-88, dep. dir. divsn. biol. investigational new drugs, 1988, dir. divsn. biol. investigational new drugs, 1988-90; dir. office of therapeutics rsch. and rev. Ctr. for Biologics Evaluation and Rsch., FDA, Rockville, Md., 1992-94, acting dep. dir., 1990-92; dir. Ctr. for Drug Evaluation and Rsch., FDA, Rockville, Md., 1994—2003. Instr. medicine, asst. prof. divsn. gen. internal medicine Hershey Med. Ctr./Pa. State U., 1981; analytical chemist rsch. divsn. A.B. Dick Co., Niles, Ill., 1971-73. Nat. Merit scholar Bucknell U., 1966, Pa. State scholar, 1966; Rsch. fellow Am. Rheumatism Assn.; VA Investigator grantee, 1985. Mem. Alpha Omega Alpha, Alpha Lambda Delta. Office: Ctr Drug Evaluation & Rsch US Food & Drug Admin 5600 Fishers Lane Rockville MD 20857*

WOODCOCK, RICHARD WESLEY, educational psychologist; b. Portland, Oreg., Jan. 29, 1928; s. Carol Wesley and Captola Winifred (Catterlin) W.; m. Annie Lee Plant, Aug. 16, 1951; children: Donna, Dianne, Judy, Wayne; m. Ana Felicia Muñoz-Sandoval, June 14, 1991. BS, U. Oreg., 1949, MEd, 1953, EdD, 1956. Diplomate of Am. Bd. of Profl. Psychol. Lt. USN, 1945-46, 50-51; elem. tchr. Arago Schs., Oreg., 1951-52; dir. spl. edn. Coos County Sch., Coquille, Oreg., 1952-54, Corvallis (Oreg.) Pub. Schs., 1955-57; asst. prof. psychology Western Oreg. U., 1957-61; assoc. prof. spl. edn. U. No. Colo., Greeley, 1961-63; prof. spl. edn. Peabody Coll. Vanderbilt U., 1963-68; editor, dir. rsch. Am. Guidance Svc., 1968-72; dir. Measurement Learning Cons., Tenn., Oreg., 1972—; vis. scholar U. Ariz., 1985-88, U. So. Calif., L.A., 1988-91; rsch. prof. psychology U. Va., 1993-97; vis. prof. hearing and speech scis. Vanderbilt U. Sch. Medicine. Cons. NCAA, 1989-94. Author: (battery tests) Mini-Battery of Achievement, 1994, Woodcock Language Proficiency Battery English and Spanish forms, 1991, 95, Woodcock-Muñoz Language Surveys, 1993, W-J Psycho-Edn. Battery, 1977, 89, 2001, Bateria Woodcock Psico-Educativa en Español, 1982, 96, Woodcock Reading Mastery Tests, 1973-87, Scales of Independent Behavior, 1984, 95, G-F-W Auditory Skills Battery, 1976, The Peabody Rebus Reading Program, 1967, The Colorado Braille Battery, 1966, Woodcock Diagnostic Reading Battery, 1997, Mather-Woodcock Group Writing Tests, 1997, Dean-Woodcock Sensory-Motor Battery, 2003; contbr. numerous articles to profl. jours. Scholar vis. scholar, Vanderbilt U., 2002—. Fellow Am. Acad. Sch. Psychology.

WOODEN, JOHN ROBERT, former basketball coach; b. Martinsville, Ind., Oct. 14, 1910; s. Joshua Hugh and Roxie (Rothrock) W.; m. Nellie C. Riley, Aug. 8, 1932; children: Nancy Anne, James Hugh. BS, Purdue U., 1932; MS, Ind. State U., 1947. Athletic dir., basketball and baseball coach Ind. State Tchrs. Coll., 1946-48; head basketball coach UCLA, 1948-75. Lectr. to colls., coaches, business. Author: Practical Modern Basketball, 1966, They Call Me Coach, 1972; co-author: Wooden--a Lifetime of Reflections and Observations On and Off the Court, 1997, Inch and Miles--Pyramid to Success for Kids, 2004, One on One, 2004; contbr. articles to profl. jours. Served to lt. USNR, 1943-46. Named All-Am. basketball player Purdue U., 1930-32, Coll. Basketball Player Yr., 1932, to All-Time All-Am. Team Helms Athletic Found., 1943, Nat. Basketball Hall of Fame, Springfield (Mass.) Coll., as player, 1960, as coach, 1970, Ind. State Basketball Hall of Fame, 1962, Calif. Father of Yr., 1964, 75, Coach of Yr. U.S. Basketball Writers Assn., 1964, 67, 69, 70, 72, 73, Sportsman of Yr. Sports Illustrated, 1973, GTE Acad. All-Am., 1994; recipient Whitney Young award Urban League, 1973, 1st ann. Velvet Covered Brick award Layman's Leadership Inst., 1974, 1st ann. Dr. James Naismith Peachbasket award, 1974, Medal of Excellence Bellarmine Coll., 1985, Sportslike Pathfinder award to Hoosier with extraordinary svc. on behalf of Am. youth, 1993, 40 for the Age award Sports Illustrated, 1994, the 1st Frank G. Wells Disney award for role model to youth, 1995, Disting. Am. award Pres. Reagan, 1995, Svc. to Mankind award Lexington Theol. Sem., 1995, NCAA Theodore Roosevelt Sportsman award, 1995, Vince Lombardi award for excellence, 2000, Ind. Legend award, 2000, Presdl. Medal of Freedom, 2003; named Basketball Coach of Century, 2000. *I have tried to live the philosophy of my personal definition of success which I formulated in the middle thirties shortly after I entered the teaching profession. Not being satisfied that success was merely the accumulation of material possessions or the attainment of a position of power or prestige, I chose to define success as "peace of mind which can be attained only through the self-satisfaction that comes from knowing you did your best to become the best that you are capable of becoming."*

WOODFORD, ARTHUR MACKINNON, library director, historian; b. Detroit, Nov. 23, 1940; s. Frank Bury and Mary-Kirk (MacKinnon) W.; children: Mark, Amy. Student, U. Wis., 1958-60; BA in History, Wayne State U., 1963; AM in LS, U. Mich., 1964. Libr. Detroit Pub. Libr., 1964-74; asst. dir. Grosse Pointe (Mich.) Pub. Libr., 1974-77; dir. St. Clair Shores (Mich.) Pub. Libr., 1977—. Author: All Our Yesterdays, 1969, Detroit and Its Banks, 1974, Detroit: American Urban Renaissance, 1979, Charting The Inland Seas, 1991, Tonnancour, 1994, vol. 2, 1996, This Is Detroit: 1701-2001, 2001. With USNR, 1958-64. Mem. Mich. Libr. Assn. (v.p. 1988-89), Gt. Lakes Maritime Inst., Prismatic Club Detroit (pres. 1982), Algonquin Club of Detroit and Windsor (treas. 1983-93). Avocations: tennis, bridge, reading, model shipbuilding. Office: St Clair Shores Pub Libr 22500 Eleven Mile Rd Saint Clair Shores MI 48081-1399 Home: 3284 S Channel Dr Harsens Island MI 48028 E-mail: woodfora@libcoop.net.

WOODFORD, DUANE HUGH, aerospace equipment manufacturing company executive, electrical engineer; b. Dunseith, N.D., Jan. 1, 1939; s. Harold George and Edna Evelyn (Lagerquist) W.; m. Grace Carol Vandal, July 18, 1962; children: Robert Kent, Kim Ann. BS in Elec. Engring., U. N.D., 1961; student Western Electric grad. engring. tng. program, 1962; Mini MBA, Coll. St. Thomas, 1977, postgrad., 1978. Sr. sales engr. Electric Machinery, Hartford, Conn., 1969-76, product mktg. mgr., Mpls., 1976-79, mgr. parts and svc., 1979-80, commercial ops. mgr., 1980-83, gen. mgr., 1983-87, v.p., gen. mgr., 1987-89; pres. PTC Aerospace, Seating Products Divsn., Litchfield, Conn., 1989-94; pres., CEO Burns Aerospace Corp., 1994-96; group v.p. B/E Aerospace Ops., Winston-Salem, 1996—; power engr. Western Electric, Chgo., 1961-63; application engr. Electric Machinery, Mpls., 1963-65, sales engr., N.Y.C., Pitts., 1965-68. Scoutmaster Boy Scouts U.S., Aurora, Ill., 1962-63; coach, Babe Ruth Baseball, Plymouth, Minn., 1978-80; treas. PTA, Wayzata (Minn.) Sch. Dist. 284, 1978-79; chmn. adv. bd. child guidance Bowman Grey Hosp., Winston-Salem, 1995—. Served with USMC, 1960-66. Mem. ASME (sec. gas turbine div. electric utility com. 1972-74), TAPPI, N.W. Conn. C. of C. (bd. dirs. 1991-95). Republican. Methodist. Home: 3101 Allerton Lake Dr Winston Salem NC 27106-4481 Office: Burns Aerospace Corp 1455 Fairchild Rd Winston Salem NC 27105-4549

WOODHAM, JOSEPH ED, artist, art educator; b. Atlanta, Sept. 23, 1957; s. Billy Joe Woodham and Carrol M. Hedger. BFA in Theatre, Berry Coll., 1979. Founder, dir. 800 East Arts Ctr., Atlanta, 1989—97; tchr. Marquis Studios, N.Y.C., 1998—, Bklyn. Arts Coun., N.Y.C., 1999—, Young Audiences, N.Y.C., 2002—; dir. Earth Sch. Aftersch., N.Y.C., 2002—04. Curator, dir. Art in Odd Places Atlanta Arts Festival, 1995—98; dir. sch. age programs 14th St. Jewish Cmty. Ctr., N.Y.C., 2004. Writer, dir.: plays Create the Opportunity, 1997, Constance Holiday; puppeteer: Symphonie Fantastique, 1999—2000; creator (TV program) The It Factor, 2001; author: (plays) Useful Tables, 2002; writer, dir.: Head, 2003. Founder Margarite Daisy Soc. Garden Party, 2004. Recipient award, Jim Henson Found., N.Y.C., 2003; Village Halloween Parade grantee, Dream Music Puppetry, N.Y.C., 2001. Home: 391 Bond St #3 Brooklyn NY 11231 Office Phone: 212-780-0800 241.

WOODHOUSE, GAY VANDERPOEL, former state attorney general, lawyer; b. Torrington, Wyo., Jan. 8, 1950; d. Wayne Gaylord and Sally (Rouse) Vanderpoel; m. Randy Woodhouse, Nov. 26, 1983; children: Dustin, Houston. BA with honors, U. Wyo., 1972, JD, 1977. Bar: Wyo. 1978, U.S. Dist. Ct. Wyo., U.S. Supreme Ct. Dir. student Legal Svcs., Laramie, Wyo., 1976—77; assoc. Donald Jones Law Offices, Torrington, 1977—78; asst. atty. gen. State of Wyo., Cheyenne, 1978—84, sr. asst. atty. gen., 1984—89, spl. U.S. atty., 1987—89, asst. U.S. atty., 1990—95, chief dept. atty. gen., 1995—98, atty. gen., 1998—2000. Chmn. Wyo. Tel. Consumer Panel, Casper, 1982—86; advisor Cheyenne Halfway House, 1984—93; chmn. Wyo. Silent Witness Initiative Zero Domestic Violence by 2010, 1997, Wyo. Domestic Violence Elimination Coun., 1999—2001; mem. State Bar Commn. First Dist., 2002—05; spl. projects cons. N.Am. Securities Adminstrs. Assn., 1987—89; Chmn. bd. Pathfinder, 1987; S.E. Wyo. Mental Health. Mem.: Federalist Soc. for Law and Pub.Policy Studies (v.p., Wyo. chpt. 2003—04), Prevent Child Abuse Wyo., Laramie County Bar Assn., Cheyenne (Wyo.) C. of C., Toastmasters, Rotary. Republican. Avocations: inline speed skating, stained glass. Address: 211 W 19th St Ste 308 Cheyenne WY 82001 Office: 123 Capitol Bldg Cheyenne WY 82002-0001 Office Phone: 307-432-9399. Personal E-mail: gaywoodhouselaw@aol.com. Business E-Mail: gay@woodhouselawoffice.com.

WOODHOUSE, JOHN FREDERICK, food distribution company executive; b. Wilmington, Del., Nov. 30, 1930; s. John Crawford and Anna (Houth) W.; m. Marilyn Ruth Morrow, June 18, 1955; children: John Crawford II, Marjorie Ann Woodhouse Purdy. BA, Wesleyan U., 1953; DHL, 1997; MBA, Harvard U., 1955. Bus. devel. officer Can. Imperial Bank of Commerce, Toronto, Ont., 1955-59; various fin. positions Ford Motor Co., Dearborn, Mich., 1959-64, Cooper Industries, Inc., Mount Vernon, Ohio, 1964-67; treas. Houston, 1967-69, Crescent-Niagara Corp., Buffalo, 1968-69; exec. v.p., CFO Sysco Corp., Houston, 1969-71, pres., COO, 1972-83, pres., CEO, 1983-85, chmn., CEO, 1985-96, mem. exec. and fin. coms., 1996-98, chmn. bd. dirs., chmn. exec. com., 1998-2000, sr. chmn., 2000—01. Bd. dirs., men. exec. com. Shell Oil Co., 1991-2002; bd. dirs. Harvard Bus. Sch. Assocs., 1995 2001. Chmn. Mich. 16th dist. rep. Club, 1962-64; treas. Cooper Industries Found., 1967-69; trustee Wesleyan U., 1976-92, vice-chmn., 1986-92, chmn. comprehensive capital campaign, 1998—; ruling elder Presbyn. Ch.; trustee, chmn. audit com., mem. exec. com. Mt. Holyoke Coll., South Hadley, Mass., 1996—; bd. dirs. Winrock Internat. Inst. for Agrl. Devel., 1993-2000, mem. fin. com., mem. exec. com., chmn. investment com.; bd. advisors The Retail Food Industry Ctr., U. Minn.; trustee The Am. Inst. Food Distbn., Elmwood Pk., N.J., 2001—, The Food Inst., 2001—, Presbyn. Mo-Ranch Assembly, Hunt, Tex., 2002—. Recipient Herbert Hoover award for disting. svc. to food industry, 2000, Diplomate recognition Nat. Restaurant Assn., 2001, Hall of Fame award Nat. Frozen Foods Assn., 2002. Mem. Nat. Am. Wholesale Grocers Assn. (bd. dirs. 1990-2002, vice chmn. 1992, chmn. 1994-96), Internat. Foodservice Distbrs. Assn. (Herbert Hoover award 2000), Fin. Execs. Inst., Harvard Bus. Sch. Club, Sigma Chi. Avocations: backpacking, canoeing, tennis. Office: Sysco Corp 1390 Enclave Pkwy Houston TX 77077-2099 Office Phone: 281-584-1420. Business E-Mail: woodhouse.john@sysco.com.

WOODHOUSE, MICHAEL A. restaurant holdings company executive; BS in Natural Scis., MS in Natural Scis., Queen's Coll., Cambridge, Eng. Exec. v.p., CFO S&A Restaurant Corp.; pres., internat. divsn. Pearle Health Svcs., Inc.; exec. v.p., CFO T.G.I. Friday's Inc., 1987; CFO Tia's Inc., Dallas; v.p., fin. Daka Internat. Inc., 1993—94, sr. v.p., CFO, 1994—95; sr. v.p., fin., CFO CBRL Group, 1995—99, exec. v.p., COO, 1999—2000, pres., COO, 2000—01, pres., CEO, 2001—. Bd. dirs. CBRL Group, 1999—. Office: CBRL Group 305 Hartmann Dr Lebanon TN 37088*

WOODHOUSE, THOMAS EDWIN, lawyer; b. Cedar Rapids, IA, Apr. 30, 1940; s. Keith Wallace and Elinor Julia (Cherny) W.; m. Kiyoko Fujiie, May 29, 1965; children: Miya, Keith, Leighton. AB cum laude, Amherst Coll., 1962; JD, Harvard U., 1965. Bar: N.Y. 1966, U.S. Supreme Ct. 1969, Calif. 1975. Assoc. Chadbourne, Parke, Whiteside & Wolff, N.Y.C., 1965-68; atty./adviser AID, Washington, 1968-69; counsel Pvt. Investment Co. for Asia S.A., Tokyo, 1969-72; ptnr. Woodhouse Lee & Davis, Singapore, 1972-74; assoc. Graham & James, San Francisco, 1974-75; asst. gen. counsel Natomas Co., San Francisco, 1975-81; mem. Lasky, Haas, Cohler & Munter, San Francisco, 1982-90; trust adminstr. Ronald Family Trust A, 1989—, Gordon P. Getty Family Trust, 1994—; sole practice Berkeley, 1990—2001. Of counsel Wilson, Sonsini, Goodrich & Rosati, Palo Alto, Calif., 1992-95; instr. law faculty U. Singapore, 1972-74; CEO, Vallejo Investments, 1997—. chmn. Police Rev. Com. of Berkeley (Calif.), 1980-84; mem. Berkeley Police Res., 1986—; bd. dirs. Friends Assn. of Svcs. for Elderly, 1979-84; clk. fin. com. Am. Friends Svc. Com. of No. Calif., 1979-83; pres. Zyzzyva Inc., lit. quar., 1985-87. Trustee Freedom from Hunger, 1989-99, Coun. of Friends Bancroft Libr., 1997-2002, chmn. 2002-2003, Mark Twain Luncheon Club, 2002—, Dominican Sch. of Philosophy and Theology, 1998-2003. With U.S. Army, 1958. Fellow Am. Bar Found. (life); mem. Calif. Bar Assn., Assn. Internat. de Bibliophilie, Harvard Club, Univ. Club, Book Club Calif., Roxburghe Club, Travellers Club, Grolier Club, Faculty Club U. Calif.-Berkeley, Mira Vista Golf and Country Club. Republican. Roman Catholic. Home and Office: 1800 San Antonio Ave Berkeley CA 94707-1618 E-mail: robert606@earthlink.net.

WOODHURST, ROBERT STANFORD, JR., architect; b. Abbeville, S.C., July 12, 1921; s. Robert Stanford and Eva (Ferguson) W.; m. Dorothy Ann Carwile, Aug. 4, 1945; 1 son: Robert Stanford III. BS in Architecture, Clemson U., 1942. Registered arch., S.C., Ga., NCARB. Designer Harold Woodward, Arch., Spartanburg, S.C., 1946-47; assoc. arch. F. Arthur Hazard, Arch., Augusta, Ga., 1947-54; ptnr. Woodhurst & O'Brien, Architects, Augusta, Ga., 1954-83, Woodhurst Partnership, Augusta, Ga., 1983—. V.p. Southeastern Architects and Engrs., Inc., Augusta, 1964-83; lectr. history architecture N. Augusta Community Coll.; mem. nat. exam. com. Nat. Council Arch tl. Regis. Bds.; pres. Ga. State Bd. Archs. Chmn. Augusta-richmond County Planning Commn., 1966-68; trustee Hist. Augusta, Inc., active Mayor's Adv. Com., 1965-68; mem. Augusta Bldg. Code Bd. Appeals, 1955-58. Served to capt. U.S. Army, 1942-45. Decorated Air medal with 7 oak leaf clusters; Croix de Guerre avec palms (France); prisoner of war, Germany. Fellow AIA (Bronze medal 1942); mem. Ga. Assn. AIA (pres. 1977, Bronze medal 1977, Rothchild Silver Medal 1987), Soc. Archtl. Historians, Nat. Coun. Archtl. Registration Bds., Augusta Country Club, Pinnacle Club. Democrat. Baptist. Achievements include designed and built: Deacon 1st Bapt. Ch., Augusta, Univ. Hosp. Med Ctr., Augusta, Peabody Apts. and Irvin Towers, Augusta, W. Lake Country Club, Augusta, Med. Libr., Med. Coll. Ga., Libr. Voorhees Coll., Denmark, S.C., Ambulatory Care Ctr. Univ. Hosp. Augusta, Married Students Apts., Med. Coll. Ga., Covenant Presbyn. Ch., Augusta, Student Ctr. Voorhees Coll., Pres.' Home Voorhees Coll., others. Home: 810 Dogwood Ln Augusta GA 30909-2704 Office: Woodhurst Partnership 607 15th St Augusta GA 30901-2601 Office Phone: 706-724-4343. E-mail: twparch@aol.com.

WOODING, WILLIAM MINOR, statistics consultant; b. Waterbury, Conn, Aug. 24, 1917; s. George Lee and Ella Elizabeth (Asher) W.; m. Nina C. Peaslee, May 30, 1940; children: Barbara Lee Wooding Bose, Elizabeth Ann. B Chem. Engring. cum laude, Poly. Inst. Bklyn., 1953. Lab. asst. Am. Cyanamid Co., Stamford, Conn., 1941-44, chemist, 1945-50, rsch. chemist, 1950-56, rsch. adminstrv. svc. coord., 1956-57; asst. chief chemist Revlon Rsch. Ctr., NYC, 1957-60, assoc. rsch. dir., 1960-65, Carter-Wallace, Inc., Cranbury, NJ, 1965-67, dir. tech. svcs., 1967-75; dir. statis. svcs. Carter-Wallace, Inc. and Wallace Labs., Cranbury, NJ, 1975-82; cons. med. statis. and clin. trials BioStatistics, Swanton, Vt., 1982—. Instr. Stat-a-Natrix Inst., Edison, NJ., 1983-86. Author: Planning Pharmaceutical Clinical Trials, 1994; contbr. over 20 articles to profl. jours. Home and Office: BioStatistics 298 Maquam Shore Rd Swanton VT 05488-9639

WOODLAND, IRWIN FRANCIS, lawyer; b. New York, Sept. 2, 1922; s. John James and Mary (Hynes) W.; m. Sally Duffy, Sept. 23, 1954; children: Connie, J. Patrick, Stephen, Joseph, William, David, Duffy. BA, Columbia U., 1948; JD, Ohio State U., 1959. Bar: Calif. 1960, Wash., 1991, U.S. Dist. Ct. (cen. dist.) Calif. 1960, U.S. Dist. Ct. (no. dist.) Calif. 1962, U.S. Dist. Ct. (so. dist.) Calif. From assoc. to ptnr. Gibson, Dunn & Crutcher, L.A., 1959-88. Bd. dirs. Sunlaw Energy Corp., Vernon, Calif. With USAF, 1942-45, ETO. Mem. ABA, Calif. Bar Assn., L.A. Bar Assn., Wash. State Bar Assn., Phi Delta Phi, Jonathan Club. Roman Catholic. Address: Gibson Dunn & Crutcher 333 S Grand Ave Ste 4400 Los Angeles CA 90071-1548

WOODLAND, N. JOSEPH, retired optical engineer, retired mechanical engineer; b. Atlantic City, N.J., Sept. 6, 1921; BSME, Drexel U., 1947, DEng (hon.), 1998; MME, Syracuse U., 1956. Tech. asst. to unit chief, liquid thermal diffusion project for separating uranium isotopes Manhattan Project, Oak Ridge, Tenn., 1943—46; mech. designer Burlington Industries, 1947; lectr. in mech. engring. Drexel U., 1948—49, cons., 1987; cons. in aircraft hydraulics design, 1950; various positions at staff and sr. levels IBM Corp., 1951—87; cons., 1987—88. Named one of Drexel U.'s 100 Most Outstanding Alumni, 1992; recipient Nat. Medal Tech. for invention of bar code, 1992. Mem.: Anthony J. Drexel Soc. Achievements include patents for (with Bernard Silver) Classifying Apparatus and Method, the basic bar code patent.

WOODLEY, DAVID TIMOTHY, dermatology educator; b. Aug. 11, 1948; s. Raoul Ramos-Mimosa and Marian (Schlueter) W.; m. Christina Paschall Prentice, May 4, 1974; children; David Thatcher, Thomas Colgate, Peter paschall. AB, Washington U., St. Louis, 1968; MD, U. Mo., 1973. Diplomate Am. Bd. Internal Medicine, Am. Bd. Dermatology, Nat. Bd. Internal Medicine. Intern Beth Israel Med. Ctr., Mt. Sinai Sch. Medicine, N.Y. Hosp., Cornell U. Sch. Medicine, N.Y.C., 1973-74; resident in internal medicine U. Nebr., Omaha, 1974-76; resident in dermatology U. N.C., Chapel Hill, 1976-78; asst. prof. dermatology U. N.C., Chapel Hill, 1983-85, assoc. prof. dermatology, 1985-88; prof. medicine, co-chief divsn. dermatology Cornell U. Med. Ctr., N.Y.C., 1988-89; prof., vice chair dept. dermatology Stanford (Calif.) U., 1989-93; prof., chair dept. dermatology Northwestern U., Chgo., 1993-99; co-chief dermatology U. So. Calif. Sch. Medicine, L.A., 1999—.

Research fellow U. Paris, 1978-80; expert NIH, Bethesda, Md., 1983-89; prof., assoc. chmn. dermatology Stanford U Sch. Medicine, 1989-93; chmn. dermatology Sch. Medicine Northwestern U., 1993-99; prof., chmn. dermatology U. So. Calif., 1999—; mem. study sect. NIH. Contbr. chpts. to books and articles in field to profl. jours. Mem. Potomac Albicore Fleet, Washington, 1982-83, Friends of the Art Sch., Chapel Hill, 1983—, Jungian Soc. Triangle Area, Chapel Hill, 1983—. Fellow Am. Acad. Dermatology; mem. ACS (assoc.), Dermatology Found., Am. Soc. for Clin. Rsch., Soc. Investigative Dermatology, Assn. Physician Poets, Am. Soc. for Clin. Investigation. Office: U So Calif Divsn Dermatology LAC & USC Med Ctr 8th Fl 1200 N State St Los Angeles CA 90033-1029 Business E-Mail: dwoodley@usc.edu.

WOODLOCK, DOUGLAS PRESTON, judge; b. Hartford, Conn., Feb. 27, 1947; s. Preston and Kathryn (Ropp) W.; m. Patricia Mathilde Powers, Aug. 30, 1969; children: Pamela, Benjamin. BA, Yale U., 1969; JD, Georgetown U., 1975. Bar: Mass. 1975. Reporter Chgo. Sun-Times, 1969-73; staff mem. SEC, Washington, 1973-75; law clk. to Judge F.J. Murray U.S. Dist. Ct. Mass., Boston, 1975-76; assoc. Goodwin, Procter & Hoar, Boston, 1976-79, 83-84, ptnr., 1984-86; asst. U.S. atty. Boston, 1979-83; judge U.S. Dist. Ct., Boston, 1986—. Instr. Harvard U. Law Sch., 1981, 82; mem. U.S. Jud. Conf. Com. on Security Space and Facilities, 1987-95; chmn. New Boston Fed. Courthouse Bldg. Com., 1987-98. Articles editor Georgetown Law Jour., 1973-75; contbr. articles to profl. jours. Chmn. Commonwealth of Mass. Com. for Pub. Counsel Svcs., 1984-86, Town of Hamilton Bd. Appeals, 1978-79. Recipient Dir.'s award U.S. Dept. Justice, 1983, Thomas Jefferson award for Pub. Architecture, AIA, 1996. Mem. ABA, Mass. Bar Assn., Boston Bar Assn., Am. Law Inst., Am. Judicature Soc., Am. Bar Found., Fed. Judges Assn. (bd. dirs. 1996-01), Mass. Hist. Soc. Office: US Courthouse 1 Courthouse Way Ste 4110 Boston MA 02210-3006

WOODMAN, GREY MUSGRAVE, psychiatrist; b. Birmingham, England, Jan. 26, 1922; came to U.S., 1959, naturalized 1963; s. Edward Musgrave and Ida (Cullen) W.; m. Irene Woodman; children: Sheila, Shonagh. BA, Oxford (Eng.) U., 1943, MA, BM, BChir, 1945; grad., Clinton Citizens Police Acad., 2001. Ship's surgeon Brit. Merchant Marines, 1946-48; intern Whipps Cross Hosp., London, 1949-50, med. registrar, 1951-53, Gen. Hosp., Newcastle-on-Tyne, England, 1953-54; gen. practice London, 1954-56; physician USAF Hosp., 1956-59; resident in psychiatry U. Okla. Med. Ctr., 1959-62; staff psychiatrist Western Mo. Mental Health Ctr., Kansas City, 1962-76; med. dir. Mental Health Ctr. Clinton County, Clinton, Iowa, 1976-87; pvt. practice Clinton, 1976—; founder, dir. Lincolnshire Clinic, The London Psychiat. Clinic, 1997—. Mem. staff Jane Lamb Health Ctr., Mercy Hosp., Comphealth; psychiat. cons. Mufon; mem. mental health specialist chpt. ARC. Mem. Prevent Child Abuse Coun. Recipient Internat. Order of Merit, 1999. Fellow Royal Soc. Medicine (London, life); mem. AMA (life), Am. Psychiat. Assn. (life), Am. Acad. Med. Hypoanalysts (clin.), Brit. Med. Assn., World Fedn. Mental Health, Iowa Med. Soc. (past chmn. hospice com.), Internat. Assn. Social Psychiatry, Clinton Co. Prevent Child Abuse Coun., Am. Red Cross (mental health specialist 1996—), Oxford Club (life). Republican. Episcopalian. Home: 515 N 13th St Clinton IA 52732-4816 Office: London Psychiat Clinic 212 Wilson Bldg 5th Ave Clinton IA 52732 Office Phone: 563-243-7721.

WOODMAN, HAROLD DAVID, historian, educator; b. Chgo., Apr. 21, 1928; s. Joseph Benjamin and Helen Ruth (Sollo) W.; m. Leonora Becker; children— Allan James, David Edward. BA, Roosevelt U., 1957; MA, U. Chgo., 1959, PhD, 1964. Lectr. Roosevelt U., 1962-63; asst. prof. history U. Mo., Columbia, 1963-66, assoc. prof., 1966-69, prof., 1969-71, Purdue U., West Lafayette, Ind., 1971-97, Louis Martin Sears disting. prof., 1990-97, prof. emeritus, 1997—; chmn. Com. on Am. Studies, 1981-94. Author: Conflict and Consensus in American History, 1966, 9th rev. edit., 1996, Slavery and the Southern Economy, 1966, King Cotton and His Retainers, 1968, Legacy of the American Civil War, 1973, New South-New Law, 1995; mem. editorial bd. Jour. So. History, 1972-75, Wis. Hist. Soc., 1972-76, Bus. History Rev., 1971-77, Agrl. History, 1976-82, Am. Hist. Rev., 1981-84, Jour. Am. History, 1985-88. Served with U.S. Army, 1950-52. Recipient Otto Wirth award Roosevelt U., 1990; Woodrow Wilson Internat. Center for Scholars fellow, 1977; Social Sci. Rsch. Coun. faculty grantee, 1969-70; Nat. Humanities Ctr. Fellow, 1983-84 Mem. Am. Hist. Assn., Orgn. Am. Historians, Econ. History Assn., Agrl. History Soc. (pres. 1983-84, Everett E. Edwards award 1963), Soc. Am. Historians, Bus. History Conf. (pres. 1981-82), Ind. Assn. Historians (pres. 1983-84), So. Hist. Assn. (exec. coun. 1982-85, Ramsdell award 1965, pres. 1995-96). Home: 1100 N Grant St West Lafayette IN 47906-2460 Office: Purdue U Dept History West Lafayette IN 47907 Business E-Mail: hwoodman@sla.purdue.edu.

WOODMAN, WALTER JAMES, lawyer; b. Talara, Peru, Jan. 21, 1941; s. Walter James and Nora Carmen (Wensjoe) W.; m. Ruth Meyer, Dec. 19, 1970; children: Justin Meyer, Jessica Hilary. BA, U. Miami, 1964; JD, So. Meth. U., 1967. Bar: Tex. 1967, La. 1980, U.S. Dist. Ct. (no. dist.) Tex. 1967, U.S. Ct. Appeals (5th cir.) 1981, U.S. Supreme Ct. 1971, U.S. Dist. Ct. (we. dist.) La. 1980, U.S. Dist. Ct. (ea. dist.) Tex. 1983, U.S. Dist. Ct. (mid. dist.) La. 1988, U.S. Dist. Ct. (ea. dist.) La. 1989. Pvt. practice, Dallas, 1967-72, Waxahachie, Tex., 1972-79, Shreveport, La., 1979—. Bd. dirs. N.W. La. Legal Svcs., Shreveport, 1993-96. Contbr. articles to profl. jours. Candidate Tex. Ho. of Reps., 1972; bd. dirs. Gov.'s Pan Am. Commn., Baton Rouge, 1993-96. Home: Nonesuch Farm 12250 Ellerbe Rd Shreveport LA 71115 Office: 9045 Ellerbe Rd Ste 103 Shreveport LA 71106-6799 Personal E-mail: legalwoody@yahoo.com.

WOODMANSEE, GLENN EDWARD, employee relations executive; b. Feb. 8, 1936; s. Glenn E. and Elaine (Turnquist) W.; m. Sharon E. Horne, Sept. 5, 1959; chidlren: Lynn Ann, Thomas Edward. Student, Coe Coll., 1954-55; BS, Ariz. State U., 1960. Assoc. group mem. Prudential Ins. Co., Seattle, 1960-64; regional mgr. Blue Cross, N.Y.C., 1964-72; mgr. employee benefits McDermott Inc./Babcock & Wilcox, New Orleans, 1972-82; dir. employee relations Tidewater Inc., New Orleans, 1982-95; v.p. S&E Enterprise Co., Carriere, Miss., 1995-96. Bd. dirs. CPC Hosp., New Orleans, 1988-94; pres. Manalapan Rep. Club, Englishtown, N.J., 1977; mem. Twp. Zoning Bd.; county committeeman N.J. Rep. Party, Englishtown, 1970-77. Served to cpl. U.S. Army, 1955-57. Recipient N.Y.C. Marathon medal N.Y.C. Track Club, 1987. Mem. AARP, SAR, Am. Soc. Pers. Assocs., Bus. Coalition Health (treas. 1986-88, pres. 1988-90), Tng. and Devel. Assn. Am., Risk Ins. Mgmt. Soc., Toastmasters, Masons (32 degree), Shriners, Tau Kappa Epsilon. Clubs: New Orleans Athletic, South Shore Yacht. Republican. Presbyterian. Avocations: running, swimming, golf, boating. Home: 104 Pine Burr Rd Carriere MS 39426-7704

WOODRESS, JAMES LESLIE, JR., English language educator; b. Webster Groves, Mo., July 7, 1916; s. James Leslie and Jessie (Smith) W.; m. Roberta Wilson, Sept. 28, 1940. AB, Amherst Coll., 1938; A.M., NYU, 1943; PhD, Duke U., 1950; LittD, U. Nebr., 1995. News editor Sta. KWK, St. Louis, 1939-40; rewriteman, editor UPI, N.Y.C., 1940-43; instr. English, Grinnell (Iowa) Coll., 1949-50; asst. prof. English, Butler U., Indpls., 1950-53, asso. prof., 1953-58; asso. prof. English, San Fernando Valley (Calif.) State Coll., 1958-61, prof., 1961-66, chmn. dept., 1959-63, dean letters and scis., 1963-65; prof. English, U. Calif.-Davis, 1966-87, chmn. dept., 1970-74; vis. prof. Sorbonne, Paris, 1974-75, 83. Author: Howells and Italy, 1952, Booth Tarkington: Gentleman from Indiana, 1955, A Yankee's Odyssey: The Life of Joel Barlow, 1958, Dissertations in American Literature, 1957, 62, 68, Willa Cather: Her Life and Art, 1970, 75, 81, American Fiction 1900-50, 1974, Willa Cather: A Literary Life, 1987; editor: Eight American Authors, 1971, American Literary Scholarship: An Annual, 1965-69, 75-77, 79, 81, 87, Critical Essays on Walt Whitman, 1983, Cather's The Troll Garden, 1983, (with Richard Morris) Voices from America's Past, anthology, 1961-62, 75. Served to lt. AUS, 1943-46. Ford Fund for Advancement Edn. fellow, 1952-53; Guggenheim fellow, 1957-58; Fulbright lectr. France, 1962-63; Fulbright lectr. Italy, 1965-66; recipient Hubbell medal, 1985 Mem. MLA (sec. Am. Lit. group 1962-63), AAUP, Phi Beta Kappa. Address: 892 Harrison Ave Claremont CA 91711-4128

WOODRICK, ROBERT, food products executive; Chmn. D W Food Ctrs., Grand Rapids, Mich. Emeritus trustee, Aquinas Coll.; trustee, Grand Rapids Community Coll. Office: D&W Food Ctrs 3001 Orchard Vista Dr SE Grand Rapids MI 49546-7078*

WOODRING, DEWAYNE STANLEY, religious organization administrator; b. Gary, Ind., Nov. 10, 1931; s. J. Stanley and Vera Luella (Brown) Woodring; m. Donna Jean Wishart, June 15, 1957; children: Judith Lynn Bigelow, Beth Ellen Carey. BS in Speech with distinction, Northwestern U., 1954, postgrad. studies in radio and TV broadcasting, 1954-57; MDiv, Garrett Theol. Sem., 1957; LHD, Mt. Union Coll., Alliance, Ohio, 1967; DD, Salem (W.Va.) Coll., 1970. Ordained to ministry Meth. Ch., 1955. Assoc. youth dir. Gary YMCA, 1950-55; min. edn. Griffith (Ind.) Meth. Ch., 1955-57; min. adminstrn. and program 1st Meth. Ch., Eugene, Oreg., 1957-59; dir. pub. rels. Dakotas area Meth. Ch., 1959-60, dir. pub. rels. Ohio area, 1960-64; adminstrv. exec. to bishop Ohio East area United Meth. Ch., Canton, 1964-77, asst. gen. sec. Gen. Coun. Fin. and Adminstr. Evanston, Ill., 1977-79, assoc. gen. sec., 1979-84; exec. dir., CEO Religious Conf. Mgmt. Assn., Indpls., 1982—. Staff dept. radio svcs. 2d Assembly World Coun. Chs., Evanston, 1954; vice-chmn. commn. entertainment and program North Ctrl. Jurisdictional Conf., 1968—72, chmn., 1972—76; mem. commn. gen. conf. United Meth. Ch., 1972—93, mgr., exec. dir., 1976—93, mem. divsn. interpretation, 1969—72; chmn. commn. Ohio Coun. Chs., 1961—65; exec. com. Nat. Assn. United Meth. Found., 1968—72, World Meth. Coun., 1986—2001; v.p. Ohio East Area United Meth. Found., 1967—76; chmn. bd. mgrs. United Meth. Bldg., Evanston, 1977—84; mem. adv. bd. Nassau/Paradise Island, 1997—99, Red Lion Hotels and Inns, P.R. Conv. Ctr., GMG Solutions; lectr., cons. in field. Creator (radio series) The Word and Music, prodr., dir. (TV series) Parables in Miniature, 1957—59. Bd. dirs. First Internat. Summit Edn., 1989; adviser East Ohio Conf. Comm. Commn., 1968—76; trustee, 1st v.p. Copeland Oaks Retirement Ctr., Sebring, Ohio, 1969—76; pres. Guild Assocs., 1971—. Named to, Ky. Cols., 1989, Hall of Leaders, Conv. Liaison Coun., 1994; recipient Cert. Meeting Profl. award, 1985, Cert. Expt. Mgr. award, 1988. Mem.: Marriot Customer Leadership Forum (mem. customer adv. bd.), Found. Internat. Meetings (bd. dirs.), Internat. Assn. Exhbn. Mgmt., Cert. Meeting Profls. (bd. dirs. 1983—92), Ind. Conv. Visitors Assn. (bd. dirs. 1996—2000), Def. Orientation Conf. Assn. (chaplain), Conv. Industry Coun. (bd. dirs., past chmn.), Meeting Profl. Internat., Ind. Soc. Assn. Execs. (Meeting Planner of the Yr. award 1990), Am. Soc. Assn. Execs. Home: 7224 Chablis Ct Indianapolis IN 46278-1540 Office: 1 RCA Dome Ste 120 Indianapolis IN 46225-1023 Office Phone: 317-632-1888.

WOODRING, JOHN HOWELL, radiologist; b. Louisville, Ky., Sept. 10, 1951; s. Franklyn Howell and Dorothy Moore Woodring; m. Catherine Anne Martin, Aug. 27, 1977; children: Paul Martin, Mark Reynolds. BS, U. of Louisville, 1972; MD, U. of Ky., 1976. Lic. diagnostic radiology Am. Bd. of Radiology. Intern Louisville Gen. Hosp., 1976—77; resident physician U. of Ky. Med. Ctr., Lexington, 1977—80; asst. prof. of diagnostic radiology U. of Ky., Lexington, 1980—84, assoc. prof. of diagnostic radiology, 1984—92, prof. of diagnostic radiology, 1992—98; staff radiologist Lexington VA Med. Ctr., Lexington, 1999—. Chief of radiology svc. Lexington VA Med. Ctr., 2000—02. Contbr. articles to sci. jours. (Cert. of Merit Am. Roentgen Ray Soc., 1994). Asst. scoutmaster Boy Scouts of Am., Louisville, 1968—77; senior-high counselor 1st United Meth. Ch., Lexington, 1984—87, Sunday sch. tchr., 1992—2000. Fellow: Am. Coll. of Chest Physicians (hon.), Am. Coll. of Radiology (hon.); mem.: Soc. of Thoracic Radiology, Radiol. Soc. of N.Am. (life), So. Med. Assn. Liberal. Methodist. Achievements include First to demonstrate role of computed tomography in evaluation of coronary artery disease; First to demonstrate role of computed tomography in the evaluation of cervical spine fractures; First to propose the use of endobronchial stents in the treatment of right pneumonectomy syndrome; First to demonstrate role of computed tomography in the evaluation of congenital lobar emphysema; First to identify risk factors for the development of salicylate-induced pulmonary edema; development of pulmonary artery-bronchus ratio as a means of diagnosing congestive heart failure. Avocations: model trains, antique cars, music, literature. Home: 336 Arcadia Park Lexington KY 40503 Office: Radiology Svc Lexington VA Med Ctr CDD-114 1101 Veterans Dr Lexington KY 40502

WOODRING, MARGARET DALEY, architect, planner; b. N.Y.C., Mar. 29, 1933; d. Joseph Michael and Mary (Barron) Daley; m. Francis Woodring, Oct. 25, 1954 (div. 1962); m. Robert Bell, Dec. 20, 1971 (dec.); children: Ward, Gabrielle, Phaedra. Student, NYU, 1959-60; BArch, Columbia U., 1966; MArch, Princeton U., 1971. Registered architect; cert. planner. Architect, planner various firms, N.Y.C.; environ. design specialist Rutgers U., New Brunswick, N.J., 1966-68; programming cons. Davis & Brody, N.Y.C., 1968-71; planning cons. William H. Liskamm, San Francisco, 1971-74; mgr. planning Met. Transp. Commn., Oakland, Calif., 1974-81; dir. Internat. Program for Housing and Urban Devel. Ofcls. Ctr. for Environ. Design Rsch. U. Calif., Berkeley, 1981-89; prin. Woodring & Assocs., San Rafael, Calif., 1989—. Adj. lectr. dept. architecture U. Calif., Berkeley, 1974-84; mem. faculty Dominican U., San Rafael, 2003; founder New Horizons Savs. Assn., San Rafael, 1977-79; cons. U.S. Agy. for Internat. Devel., Washington, 1981-89; mem. jury Nat. Endowment Arts, others. Chair Bicentennial Com., San Rafael, 1976; bd. dirs. Displaced Homemakers Ctr., Oakland, 1981-84; pres. Environ Design Found., San Francisco, 1984-90. William Kinne Travel fellow Columbia U., 1965-66; Richard King Mellon fellow Princeton U., 1968-71. Mem. AIA (chair urban design com. San Francisco chpt. 1980-81), Am. Inst. Cert. Planners, Urban Land Inst., Soc. for Internat. Devel. (pres. San Francisco chpt. 1980-83), World Affairs Coun., Internat. World Congress on Land Policy. Avocations: hiking, gardening, reading, race walking. E-mail: mdwoodring@aol.com.

WOODROW, KENNTH B. retail company executive; Degree, Yale U., Harvard U. With Dayton Hudson Corp., 1970; pres. Target stores divsn. Target Corp., 1994-99, vice chmn., 1999—. Office: Target Corp 1000 Nicollet Mall Minneapolis MN 55403-2467

WOODROW, NATILE LATREECE, accountant, educator; b. Amherst, Tex., June 26, 1951; d. Glenford Travis and Lulu Marie Marr; m. Jeffrey Wayne Woodrow, Dec. 25, 1979; children: Timothy Travis Bouton, Debra Marie. BS, Wayland Bapt. U., Plainview, TX, 1973; MA, Tex. Tech U., 1975. Cert. secondary sch. tchr. Tex., 1975. Math tchr. Anton Jr. High and H.S., Anton, Tex., 1978—80; math instr. Austin Peay State U., Clarksville, Tenn., 1980—82; math and sci. tchr. Shallowater H.S., Shallowater, 1982—84; math and computer tchr. Littlefield H.S., Littlefield, 1984—86; math instr. Tex. State Tech. Coll. West Tex., Sweetwater, 1986—2002, acct., 2002—. Bible drill: children and youth leader First Bapt. Ch., Sun. sch. tchr., substitute, and care leader, 1988—. Recipient Excellence award, Nat. Inst. for Staff and Orgnl. Excellence, 2001, Chancellor's Award for Excellence, Tex. State Tech. Coll., 2001. Mem.: Am. Math. Assn. of Two-Yr. Colls. (presenter 1996—2000), Tex. Math. Assn. of Two-Yr. Colls. (past. pres. 2004—, v.p. 2000—01, pres. 2001—04), Tex. Math and Sci. Coaches Assoc., Tex. State Tech. Coll. Faculty Senate (sec., exec. bd. mem., campus rep 2002), Tex. C.C. Teachers Assoc. Office: Texas State Technical College West Texas 300 College Dr Sweetwater TX 79556 Office Phone: 325-235-7496. Personal E-mail: natile.woodrow@tstc.edu.

WOODRUFF, BRUCE EMERY, lawyer; b. Mason City, Iowa, June 23, 1930; s. Frederick Bruce and Grace (Emery) W.; m. Carolyn Clark, Aug. 18, 1956; children: David C., Douglas B., Lynn M., Daniel R. BS in Bus., U. Ill., 1952; JD, Washington U., St. Louis, 1959. Bar: Mo. 1959, D.C. Dist. Ct. (ea. dist.) Mo. 1959, U.S. Ct. Appeals (8th cir.) 1960, U.S. Supreme Ct. 1979. Assoc. Armstrong, Teasdale, Schlafly, Davis & Dicus, St. Louis, 1959-65; ptnr. Armstrong Teasdale, Schlafly & Davis (and predecessor firms), St. Louis, 1966-95; sr. counsel Armstrong Teasdale LLP, St. Louis, 1996—. Prin. counsel St. Louis C.C., 1962-89; bd. dirs. Cass Bank & Trust Co., Cass Info. Sys., Inc., Red Lion Beef Corp.; city atty., Kirkwood, Mo., 1986. Named Kirkwood Citizen of Yr., 1983. Mem. ABA (banking law com.), Mo. Bar Assn., Bar Assn. Met. St. Louis, Health Lawyers Assn. Clubs: Algonquin (Glendale, Mo.); Noonday (St. Louis (bd. dirs. 1988-91). Republican. Presbyterian. Avocations: golf, swimming, sailing, photography. Home: 9 Taylor Est Kirkwood MO 63122-2914 Office: Armstrong Teasdale LLP 1 Metropolitan Sq Ste 2600 Saint Louis MO 63102-2740

WOODRUFF, C(HARLES) ROY, consultant, retired professional association executive; b. Anniston, Ala., Sept. 27, 1938; m. Kay Carolyn Jernigan, June 26, 1962; children: Charles R. Jr., Earl David. BA, U. Ala., 1960; BD, So. Bapt. Theol. Sem., 1963, PhD in Psychology of Religion and Pastoral Care, 1966. Diplomate Am. Assn. Pastoral Counselors; lic. profl. counselor, Va. Asst. pastor Ft. Mitchell Bapt. Ch., South Ft. Mitchell, Ky., 1960-63; Protestant chaplain Silvercrest Hosp., New Albany, Ind., 1963-66; dir. dept. pastoral care and edn. Bryce State Hosp., Tuscaloosa, Ala., 1966-71; assoc. prof., chaplain supr. dept. patient counseling Med. Coll. Va., Richmond, 1971-76; assoc. prof., chmn. dept. psychology of religion and pastoral care Midwestern Bapt. Theol. Sem., Kansas City, Mo., 1976-78; exec. dir. Peninsula Pastoral Counseling Ctr., Newport News, Va., 1978-88, Am. Assn. Pastoral Counselors, Washington, 1988—2003. Lecturing fellow Interpreter's House, Lake Junaluska, N.C., 1968-78; pastoral counselor, clin. supr. Psychol. Clinic, U. Ala., Tuscaloosa, 1969-71; adj. staff mem. The Counseling Inst., Kansas City, 1976-78, adj. prof., John Leland Ctr. for Theol. Studies, Fairfax, Va., vis. prof., Korea Profl. Inst. of Psychotherapy and Spirtuality, Seoul, Korea. Author: Alcoholism and Christian Experience, 1968; (with others) Alcohol, In and Out of the Church, 1968, Work Adjustment: The Goal of Rehabilitation, 1973, Pastoral Theology and Ministry, Key Resources, 1983, The Dictionary of Pastoral Care and Counseling, 1990; also articles. Apptd. by Gov. of Va. to Bd. Profl. Counselors, Commonwealth of Va., 1987-95 (chmn. 1993-95); mem. Nat. Mental Health Leadership Forum, 1990-93; pres. Coalition on Ministry in Specialized Settings, 1996-2000. Recipient Disting. Contbns. award Am. Assn. Pastoral Counselors, 2003; United Meth. Ch. Gen. Bd. Christian Social Concerns grantee, 1965; So. Bapt. Theol. Sem. teaching fellow, 1965-66. Fellow Coll. Chaplains of Am. Protestant Hosp. Assn.; mem. Assn. for Clin. Pastoral Edn. (cert. supr.), Assn. Couples for Marriage Enrichment (cert.). Home: 10827 Burr Oak Way Burke VA 22015-2416

WOODRUFF, ELLEN LOUISE, chaplain; b. Bertha, Minn., Jan. 30, 1942; d. Harold Ernest and Ruth Eleanor (Olson) Klebs; m. John S. Woodruff, July 31, 1969; children: Ruth Ellen, Jonathan C. BA, U. Minn., 1969; Assoc. in Ministry, Luther Sem., St. Paul, 2000. Recreation therapist St. Mary's Hosp., Mpls., 1969, Belgrade Nursing Home, Minn., 1971—73; dir. youth camp Elks Assn., Brainerd, Minn., 1976—95; student chaplain Regions Hosp., St. Paul, 1997—98, Good Samaritan Homes, Mpls. & St. Paul, 1998—99; conservator St. Paul, 2000—03; chaplain St. Gertrude's Health and Rehab. Ctr., 2003—. Mem. program com. Mid-States Camping Assn., Chgo., 1992—94; leader/spkr. Ch. Retreats, 1985—. Author (editor): Klebs Family History, 2001, Awesome Angels, 2000. Mem. Shepherd of the Valley Luth. Ch. Recipient J.B. Fritzjerald award, Mpls. Park & Recreation, 1969; grantee, U. Minn., 1966—68. Mem.: Assn. Profl. Chaplains, Am. Camping Assn. (sec. newsletter 1983—95, bd. dirs. 1980—83, 1990—93, Sue Tinker award 1993). Home: 9391 Knighton Woodbury MN 55125-3721

WOODRUFF, FAY, paleoceanographer, geological researcher; b. Boston, Jan. 23, 1944; d. Lorande Mitchell and Anne (Fay) W.; m. Alexander Whitehill Clowes, May 20, 1972 (div. Oct. 1974); m. Robert G. Douglas, Jan. 27, 1980; children: Ellen, Katerina. RN, Mass. Gen. Hosp. Sch. Nursing, Boston, 1966; BA, Boston U., 1971; MS, U. So. Calif., 1979. Rsch. assoc. U. So. Calif., L.A., 1978-81, rsch. faculty, 1981-96. Keynote spkr. 4th Internat. Symposium on Benthic Foraminifera, Sendai, Japan, 1990. Contbg. author: Geological Society of America Memoir, 1985; contbr. articles to profl. jours. Life mem. The Nature Conservancy, Washington, 1992; bd. dirs. Friends of Friendship Park, Inc., 1995-2001; co-founder, v.p. Resources Families Adopted Ea. European Children, Inc., L.A., 1996-2000. NSF grantee, 1986-94. Mem. Am. Geophys. Union, Geol. Soc. Am., Internat. Union Geol. Scis. (internat. commn. on stratigraphy, subcommn. on Neogene stratigraphy 1991-99), Soc. Woman Geographers (sec. So. Calif. chpt. 1990-96), Soc. Econ. Paleontologists and Mineralogists (sec., editor N.Am. Micropaleontology sect. 1988-90), Sigma Xi. Office: U So Calif Earth Scis Los Angeles CA 90089-0001

WOODRUFF, GENE LOWRY, nuclear engineer, university dean; b. Greenbrier, Ark., May 6, 1934; s. Clarence Oliver and Avie Erscilla (Lowry) W.; m. Marylou Munson, Jan. 29, 1961; children— Gregory John, David Reed BS with honors, U.S. Naval Acad., 1956; MS in Nuclear Engring., MIT, 1963, PhD in Nuclear Engring., 1966. Registered profl. engr., Wash. Asst. prof. nuclear engring. U. Wash., Seattle, 1965-70, assoc. prof., 1970-76, prof., 1976-93, chmn. dept., 1981-84, dir. nuclear engring. labs., 1973-76, dean Grad. Sch., 1984-93, prof. chem. engring. environ. studies, 1989-98, dean emeritus, prof. emeritus, 1998—. Vice-chair, chair-elect Grad. Record Exam., 1991-92, chair, 1992-93; cons. to govt. and industry. Contbr. numerous articles to sci. and tech. jours. Served to lt. USN, 1956-60 Mem. Nat. Soc. Profl. Engrs. (Achievement award 1977), Am. Nuclear Soc. (Achievement award 1977, chmn. honors/awards com. 1981-84, nat. program com. 1971-75, exec. com. fusion div. 1976-80, vice chmn. edn. div. 1983-84, Arthur Holly Compton award 1986), Am. Soc. Engring. Edn., Assn. Grad. Schs. (v.p./pres.-elect 1990-91, pres. 1991-92). Democrat. Home: 19081 11th Ave NW Shoreline WA 98177-2610 Office: U Wash Box 351750 Seattle WA 98195-1750 E-mail: woodruff@u.washington.edu.

WOODRUFF, JANE, sales executive; b. Derby, Eng., July 20, 1945; d. George John Schwaegerman and Joyce (Robinson) Turnock; m. Charles Walter Woodruff, Aug. 1, 1964 (div. 1976); 1 child, Jon Bradley. BA, Purdue U., 1967, MS, 1968, MA, 1970. Tchr. Kansas City (Mo.) Schs., 1970-73; asst. dir. communicatons Skyline Corp., Elkart, Ind., 1974-77; market analyst Motor Wheel Corp. subs. Goodyear Tire and Rubber Co., Lansing, Mich., 1977-80, mgr. planning and research, 1980-82, mgr. car and light truck mktg., 1982-84; account exec. Motor Wheel Corp., Farmington Hills, Mich., 1984-96; acct. exec. Enkei Internat., Madison Heights, Mich., 1996-98, asst. dept. mgr., O.E.S., 1998—. Chmn. Motor Wheel Savs. Bond Drive, Lansing, 1980; fundraiser Capital Area United Way, Lansing, 1981; cons. bus. projects Jr. Achievement, Lansing, 1981-82. NDEA scholar U.S. Dept. Edn., 1967-68; teaching fellow Purdue U., 1968-70; recipient Cert. Achievement YWCA, Lansing, 1980. Mem. Indsl. Mktg. Group Am. Mktg. Assn. (treas.), Automotive Market Research Council, Soc. Automotive Engrs. Office: Enkei Internat 32400 Industrial Dr Madison Heights MI 48071-1527

WOODRUFF, JAY NOEL, editor, writer; b. Cooperstown, NY, Oct. 31, 1960; s. Robert Arnold Woodruff, Jr. and Marcia Shick Woodruff; m. Sarah Jean Carew, Oct. 1, 1988; children: Joseph Francis, Samuel Robert, Anne Elizabeth. BA in English, Harvard U., 1983; MFA, U. Iowa, 1987. Rsch., tchg. fellow Harvard U., Cambridge, Mass., 1987—91; mng. editor DoubleTake Mag., Durham, NC, 1993—96; sr. editor Esquire Mag., New York, 1998—2000; asst. mng. editor Entertainment Weekly, New York, 2000—. Editor: (book) A Piece of Work; contbr. essays; author: (short stories) various publications. Mem.: Am. Soc. Mag. Editors. Catholic. Office: Entertainment Weekly 1675 Broadway New York NY 10019 Business E-Mail: jay_woodruff@ew.com.

WOODRUFF, JOAN LESLIE, occupational therapist, counselor; b. Albuquerque, Apr. 4, 1954; d. Charles Wofford and Lila Raye Woodruff. BS, Loma Linda Med. U., 1975; MA, EdM, Calif. State U., San Bernardino, 1983. Registered occupl. therapist Am. Occupl. Therapy Assn. Dir. rehab. Orthop. Surgery Practice, San Bernardino, 1975—91; pvt. practice forensic counselor Mountainair, N.Mex., 1993—. Author: (novels) Neighbors, 1993, The Shiloh Renewal, 1998, Ghost In The Rainbow, 2002, Traditional Stories & Foods, 1991, (novels) Wishes and Windmills, 2003. Sec. Riverside Am. Indian Ctr., Riverside, Calif., 1986—91. Mem.: Am. Occupl. Therapy Assn. (licentiate). Democrat. American Indian. Avocations: writing, consulting, travel. Home: Box 687 Mountainair NM 87036 Office: PO Box 687 Mountainair NM 87036 Personal E-mail: inabobooks@earthlink.net.

WOODRUFF, JUDY CARLINE, broadcast journalist; b. Tulsa, Nov. 20, 1946; d. William Henry and Anna Lee (Payne) W.; m. Albert R. Hunt, Jr., Apr. 5, 1980; children: Jeffrey Woodruff, Benjamin Woodruff, Lauren Ann Lee. Student, Meredith Coll., 1964-66; BA, Duke U., 1968. News announcer, reporter Sta. WAGA-TV, Atlanta, 1970-75; news corr. NBC News, Atlanta, 1975-76, White House corr. Washington, 1977-83; anchor Frontline, PBS documentary series, 1983-90; corr. MacNeil-Lehrer News Hour, PBS, Washington, 1983-93, anchor, sr. corr. CNN, Washington, 1993—, prime anchor, sr. coord.; moderator Vice Presidential Debate, 1998, America Votes, 2003, 2004. Bd. advisors Henry Grady Sch. Journalism, U. Ga., 1979-82, Benton Fellowship in Broadcast Journalism, U. Chgo., 1984-90, Knight Fellowship in Journalism, Stanford U., 1985—; bd. visitors Wake Forest U., 1982-89; trustee Duke U., 1985 (emerita); founding bd. dirs. Internat. Women's Media Found. Author: This is Judy Woodruff at the White House, 1982. Active Commn. on Women's Health, The Commonwealth Fund.; bd. trustee Freedom Forum, Urban Inst. Recipient award Leadership Atlanta, Class of 1974, Atlanta chpt. Women in Comms., 1975, Edward Weintal award for excellence in fgn. policy reporting, 1987, Joan Shorenstein Barone award for series on def. issues, 1987, Helen Bernstein award for excellence in journalism N.Y. Pub. Libr., 1989, Pres.'s 21st Century award Nat. Women's Hall of Fame, 1994, CableAce award for best newscaster, 1995, CableAce Best Anchor Team award, 1996, Allen H. Neuharth award for excellence in journalism, 1995, News and Documentary Emmy award, 1997, Internat. Matrix award, Assn. for Women in Comm., 2003, Leonard Zeidenberg First Amendn=ment award, Radio-Television News Directors Assn. and Found., 2003; named to Ga. Assn. of Broadcasters Hall of Fame, 2003. Mem. NATAS (Atlanta chpt. Emmy award 1975), White House Corrs. Assn. Office: Cable News Network 820 1st St NE Washington DC 20002-4243*

WOODRUFF, KATHRYN ELAINE, English language educator; b. Ft. Stockton, Tex., Oct. 12, 1940; d. James Arthur and Catherine II. (Stevens) Borron; m. Thomas Charles Woodruff, May 18, 1969; children: Robert Borron, David Borron. BA, Our Lady of the Lake U., San Antonio, 1963; MFA, U. Alaska, 1969; PhD, U. Denver, 1987. Cert. tchr., Tex., Colo. English and journalism tchr. Owensboro (Ky.) Cath. High Sch., 1963-64, Grand Junction (Colo.) Dist. 12, 1964-66; English tchr. Monroe High Sch., Fairbanks, Alaska, 1966-67; teaching asst. U. Alaska, Fairbanks, 1967-69, instr., 1969-70, U. Colo., Boulder, 1979, Denver, 1988-89, Regis Coll., Denver, 1987-89; asst. prof. Econs. Inst., Boulder, 1989-92; prof. English Colo. Christian U., Lakewood, 1993—. Tchr. Upward Bound, Fairbanks, 1968; instr. ethnic and women writers course U. Colo., Denver, 1988-93; mem. Assoc. Writing Programs; soprano Boulder Chorale, Cantabile Singers, St. John's Cathedral Choir, Augustana Chamber Choir; mem. Women's Studies Delegation to South Africa, 1998; active in missionary work in Ecuador, 1998, European Singing Tour with Augustana Arts, 1998, 2000. Author: (poetry) Before the Burning, 1994; poetry readings in Colo., Tex. and Paris; contbr. poems to lit. publs. Friend Chautauqua Music Festival, Boulder, 1985—; dir. 12th Annual Arts Festival, Fairbanks, 1969; active Augustana Chamber Chorus, St. John's Cathedral Choir; bd. mem. Denver Bach Soc. Recipient Poet's Choice award Internat. Soc. Poetry, 1997; named one of Outstanding Young Women Am., 1966; nominated for Poet Laureate of Colo., 1996; NEH grantee, 1996. Mem. AAUW, MLA, Am. Assn. Univ. Professors, Assoc. Writing Programs, Soc. Internat. Devel. UN Assn., Nat. Women's Hall of Fame, Acad. of Am. Poets, Denver Bach Soc. (bd. dirs. 2003-04), Internat. Women's Writing Guild. Democrat. Mem. Christian Ch. Avocations: singing, tennis, skiing, volleyball, travel. Office: Colo Christian U 180 S Garrison St Lakewood CO 80226-1053

WOODRUFF, KAY HERRIN, pathologist, educator; b. Charlotte, N.C., Sept. 22, 1942; d. Herman Keith and Helen Thelma (Tucker) Herrin; m. John T. Lyman, May 3, 1980; children: Robert, Geoffry, Carolyn. BA in Chemistry, Duke U., 1964; MD, Emory U., 1968. Diplomate Am. Bd. Pathology (trustee 1993—, sec. 1998-2000, v.p. 2000-2001, pres. 2001—). Medicine and pediat. intern U. N.C., Chapel Hill, 1968-69, resident in anatomic pathology, 1969-70; chief resident in anatomic pathology, instr. U. Okla., Oklahoma City, 1970-71, fellow in electron microscopy-pulmonary pathology, instr., 1971-72; chief resident in clin. pathology U. Calif., San Francisco, 1972-74, asst. clin. prof. dept. anatomic pathology, 1974-91, assoc. clin. prof., 1991—; chief electron microscopy VA Hosp., San Francisco, 1974-75; pvt. practice, San Pablo, Calif., 1981—. Pres. med. staff Brookside Hosp., San Pablo, 1994, med. dir. Regional Cancer Ctr., 1995-98; assoc. pathologist Children's Hosp., San Francisco, 1979-81, St. Joseph's Hosp., San Francisco, 1977-79; cons. pathologist Lawrence Berkeley (Calif.) Lab., 1974-93; med. dir. Bay Area Tumor Inst. Tissue Network, San Pablo, 1989—; asst. clin. prof. pathology health and med. scis. program U. Calif., Berkeley and U. Calif., San Francisco Joint Med. Program, 1985-91, assoc. clin. prof., 1991—, others. Contbr. articles and abstracts to med. jours. Mem. exec. bd. Richmond (Calif.) Quits Smoking, 1986-90, Bay Area Tumor Inst., Oakland, Calif., 1987—; mem. exec. bd. Contra Costa unit Am. Cancer Soc., Walanut Creek, Calif., 1985-87, mem. profl. edn. com., 1985-90, mem. pub. edn. com., 1985-86, mem. task force on breast health Calif. div., 1992-93; mem. transfusion adv. com. Irwin Meml. Blood Bank, San Francisco, 1977-83; chmn. transfusion adv. com. Alameda Contra Costa County Blood Bank, 1989-92; commr. Calif. Bd. Med. Quality Assurance, 1978-80; pres. Brookside Found., San Pablo, Calif., 1998-2000. Recipient young investigator award Am. Lung Assn., 1975-77; Outstanding Svc. awards Am. Cancer Soc., 1986, 87, Disting. Svc. award, 1988; Disting. Clin. Tchg. award U. Calif., San Francisco and Berkeley Joint Med. Program, 1987, Outstanding Tchg. award, 1988, Excellence in Basic Sci. Instrn. award, 1990, Excellence in Tchr. Clin. Scis. award, 1993; cert. of recognition Cmty. Svc. Richmond, 1989. Mem. AMA, Coll. Am. Pathologists (editl. bd. CAP Today 1986-90, bd. govs. 1990-96, chmn. coun. on practice mgmt. 1994, William Kuhn award for outstanding comm. 1996, Presdl. Medal of Honor 1995, 96), Am. Med. Women's Assn. (exec. bd. 1984-87, regional bd. govs. 1984-87), No. Calif. Women's Med. Assn. (pres. 1982-84), Calif. Soc. Pathologists (bd. dirs. 1988-90), No. Calif. Oncology Group, South Bay Pathology Soc. (pres. 1987), Am. Assn. Blood Banks, Calif. Med. Assn., Alameda-Contra Costa County Med. Soc., Am. Soc. Clin. Pathology, Calif. Pathology Soc. Avocation: classical piano. Office: Doctors Med Ctr 2000 Vale Rd San Pablo CA 94806-3808

WOODRUFF, MARK REED, magazine editor; b. Roanoke, Va., Jan. 3, 1957; s. James Moses and Elizabeth (Reed) W. BFA, Va. Commonwealth U., 1981; postgrad., San Francisco State U., 1983-84. Freelance writer, N.Y.C., 1984-88; features editor Taxi Mag., N.Y.C., 1988-90; mng. editor Spin Mag., N.Y.C., 1990-95; sr. editor Rolling Stone, N.Y.C., 1995-97, asst. mng. editor, 1997-98; editor-in-chief Tennis mag., N.Y.C., 1998—. Mem. Am. Soc. Mag. Editors. Democrat. Avocation: tennis. Home: 118 Glendale Rd Ossining NY 10562-1619 Office: Tennis Mag 79 Madison Ave 8th Fl New York NY 10016 E-mail: mwoodruff@tennismagazine.com.

WOODRUFF, MARY BRENNAN, elementary school educator, educator; d. John L. and Josephine (Martino) Brennan; m. Paul R. Woodruff; children: Christopher, Jeffery. BS, SUNY, Brockport; MS, SUNY, Buffalo, 1987. Cert. elem. tchr. N.Y., 1968. Third grade tchr. Middleport (N.Y.) Elem., fifth grade tchr., 1979—2003, math specialist K-6, 2003—. Sch. improvement presenter, mem., dist. curriculum guide, facilitator Social Studies curriculum, Royalton-Hartland Cen. Sch., Middleport, NY, 1989—, co-author mentor program for Royalton-Hartland District, Project "Deep" Elem. Econ. faciliator Contributing author Royalton-Hartland Curriculum Guide 1989; designer of spelling program 5th grade. Campaign mgr. Rep. Legislator, Orleans County, 1979-87. Mem.: ASCD, Royalton-Hartford Tchrs. Assn. (v.p., pres. 1998—, chmn. grievance com.), N.Y State United Tchrs. (v.p. exec. coun., Leadership award 1997, 2004), Delta Kappa Gamma, Delta Xi. Avocations: political action, writing, reading.

WOODRUFF, THOMAS ELLIS, electronics consulting executive; b. Stockton, Calif., Feb. 8, 1921; s. Ennis Casselberry and Gracella (Scotford) W.; m. Doris Elaine Walters, Jan. 14, 1947 (div. Aug. 1962); children: Mary Ann Woodruff Mahaffy, Patricia Lee; m. Ruth Elizabeth Craik, Feb. 25, 1964; 1 child, Robert Peter; stepchildren: Gordon Lee Vickers, Barbara Ann Vickers, Mary Jean Vickers. AA, Stockton Jr. Coll., 1941; BSEE, U. Calif., Berkeley, 1943. Registered profl. engr., Calif. Engr. GE, Syracuse, N.Y., 1944-47; staff engr. Hughes Aircraft Co., Culver City, Calif., 1947-56; mgr. electronics design Sanders Assocs., Nashua, N.H., 1956-58, chief engr. preliminary design, 1958-60, mgr. spl. programs div., 1960-62, corp. dir. systems, 1962-65, v.p., gen. mgr. corp. systems group, 1965-73, v.p. antisubmarine weapons and communications, 1966-72, dir., 1968-70, sr. dir., 1970-76, v.p. gen. mgr. ocean systems group, 1972-76, v.p. sci. and tech., 1976-88, corp. cons., 1989—; v.p. Sanders Nuclear Corp., Nashua, 1966-71. Mem. adv. com. Def. Intelligence Agy., Washington, 1978-83; joint adv. com. MIT Lincoln Lab., Bedford, Mass., 1988-89; cons. Superconductor Tech., Inc., Santa Barbara, Calif., 1988—, Oryx, Inc., Paramus, N.J., 1989—, Sanders/Lockheed, 1988-91, ret. 1992. Patentee, co-patentee 14 inventions in electronics for computers, control systems, video displays, submarine detection devices, others. Mem. IEEE (sr.). Republican. Avocations: skiing, photography, motorcycling, swimming. Home and Office: 8 Berkeley St Nashua NH 03064-2309 Personal E-mail: twuff@ieee.org.

WOODRUFF, TRUMAN O(WEN), physicist, emeritus educator; b. Salt Lake City, May 26, 1925; s. Wilford Owen and Evelyn (Ballif) W.; m. Ambrosina Lydia Solaroli, Sept. 14, 1948 (dec. June 1991); m. Patricia O'Keefe Vincent, Sept. 23, 1995. AB, Harvard U., 1947; BA, Oxford (Eng.) U., 1950; PhD, Calif. Inst. Tech., 1955. Nat. scholar Harvard, 1942-44, 46-47, Sheldon traveling fellow, 1947-48; Rhodes scholar Oxford U., 1948-50; Dow Chem. Co. fellow, Howard Hughes fellow Calif. Inst. Tech., 1950-54; research asso. physics U. Ill., 1954-55; physicist Gen. Elec. Research Lab., 1955-62; prof. physics Mich. State U., 1962-85, prof. emeritus, 1985—, chmn. dept., 1972-75; sr. scientist research labs. Hughes Aircraft Co., Malibu, Calif., 1986-87; cons. in physics Los Angeles, 1987-91. Vis. prof. Scuola Normale Superiore, Pisa, Italy, 1982—. Contbr. articles to sci. jours. Served with USNR, 1944-46. Fulbright fellow U. Pisa, 1968-69 Fellow Am. Phys. Soc.; mem. Assn. Harvard Chemists, Phi Beta Kappa, Sigma Xi.

WOODRUFF, VALERIE, secretary of education; m. Frank Woodruff; 1 child, Scott 1 stepchild, Sheri. BEd in Secondary Edn., Alderson Broaddus Coll., W. Va.; MA in guidance and counseling, U. Del.; postgrad. studies in vocat. edn. and curriculum devel., Temple U., 1999—. From tchr. to prin. New Castle County, Del., Cecil County Md.; assoc. sec. for curriculum and instructional improvement Del. Dept. Edn., Dover, Del., 1992—99, acting sec., 1999—2000, sec, 2000—. Office: Del Dept Edn Townsend Bldg #279 401 Federal St Ste 2 Dover DE 19903-1402

WOODRUFF, VIRGINIA, broadcast journalist, writer; b. Morrisville, Pa. d. Edwin Nichols and Louise (Meredith) W.; m. Raymond F. Beagle Jr. (div.); m. Albert Plaut II (div.); 1 child, Elise Meredith. Student, Rutgers U. News corr. Sta. WNEW-TV Metromedia, N.Y.C., 1967; nat., internat. critic-at-large Mut. Broadcasting System, 1968-75; lectr. Leigh Bur., 1969-71; byline columnist N.Y. Daily Mirror, N.Y.C., 1970-71; first Arts critic Teleprompter and Group W Cable TV, 1977-84; host/producer The First Nighter N.Y. Times primetime cable highlight program, 1977-84; pres., chief exec. officer Starpower, Inc., 1984-91; affiliate news corr. ABC Radio Network, N.Y.C., 1984-86; pres. Promarket People Inc., 1991-93; S.W. contbg. corr. Am. in the Morning, First Light, Mut. Broadcasting System, 1992; S.W freelance corr. Voice of Am., USIA, 1992—. Perennial critic Off-Off Broadway Short Play Festival, N.Y.C., 1984—; was 1st Woman on 10 O'Clock News, WNEW-TV, 1967. Contbg. feature writer Vis a Vis mag., 1988-91. Mem. celebrity panel Arthritis Telethon, N.Y.C., 1976. Selected episodes of First Nighter program in archives N.Y. Pub. Libr., Billy Rose Theatre Collection, Rodgers and Hammerstein Collection, Performing Arts Rsch.Ctr. Mem. Drama Desk. Clubs: National Arts, Dutch Treat. Presbyterian. Personal E-mail: vwoodruff50@yahoo.com.

WOODRUM, CLIFTON A., III, lawyer, former state legislator; b. Washington, July 23, 1938; s. Clifton A. Jr. and Margaret (Lanier) W.; m. Emily Abbitt, Aug. 10, 1963; children: Robert, Meredith W. Snowden, Anne. AB, U. N.C., 1961; LLB, U. Va., 1964. Bar: Va. 1964, U.S. Dist. Ct. (we. dist.) Va. 1964, U.S. Ct. Appeals (4th cir.) 1968, U.S. Supreme Ct. 1970. Assoc. Dodson, Pence & Coulter, Roanoke, Va., 1964-68; ptnr. Dodson, Pence, Viar, Woodrum & Mackey, 1968-95; counsel Dodson, Pence & Viar, 1995-98; mem. Va. Ho. of Dels., 1980—2004; ret., 2004—. Chmn. 6th Dist. Dem. Com., Va., 1972-76; mem. State Water Commn., 1981-2000, State Crime Commn., 1982-2000, chmn., 1995-98; chmn. Med. Malpractice Study, Va., 1984-85, Freedom of Info. Study, 1998-2000; mem. Electric Utility Restructing Com., 1997-2003, Freedom of Info. Adv. Coun., 2000-2002, chmn.; bd. dir. Va. Coalition Open Country, 2004—, We. Va. Land Trust, 2004—. Recipient Freedom of Info. award, Va. Coalition on Govt., 1999, 2003, Outstanding Legislator award, Va. Assn. Chiefs of Police, 1999, Child Advocate award, Am. Acad. Pediats. (Va. chpt.), 1997, Profiles in Courage award, Coalition of Labor Union Women, 2002, Outstanding Svc. award, Va. Firefighters Assn., 2003. Mem. ABA, Va. Bar Assn., Roanoke Bar Assn. Episcopalian. Home: 2641 Cornwallis Ave SE Roanoke VA 24014-3339 Office: Clifton A Woodrum PO Box 990 Roanoke VA 24005-0990 Office Phone: 540-982-5547.

WOODRUM, PATRICIA ANN, librarian; b. Hutchinson, Kans., Oct. 11, 1941; d. Donald Jewell and Ruby Pauline (Shuman) Hoffman; m. Clayton Eugene Woodrum, Mar. 31, 1962; 1 child, Clayton Eugene, II. BA, Kans. State Coll., Pittsburg, 1963; MLS, U. Okla., 1966. Br. libr. Tulsa City-County Libr. System, 1964-65, head brs., 1965-66, head reference dept., 1966-67, chief extension, chief pub. svc., 1967-73, asst. dir., 1973-76, exec. dir., 1976-96; owner Paradigm Mgmt. Cons. Svcs., 1997—. Active Leadership Tulsa Alumni; mem. Ct. Apptd. Spl. Advocates Bd.; interim exec. dir. Bot. Garden/Edn. and Rsch. Ctr.; adv. bd. chair Ctr. for Edn. and Counseling; pres. Tulsa Garden Ctr. Recipient Disting. Libr. award Okla. Libr. Assn., 1982, Leadership Tulsa Paragon award, 1987, Women in Comm. Newsmaker award, 1989, Outstanding Alumnus award U. Okla. Sch. Libr. Info. Studies, 1989, Headliner award Tulsa Press Club, 1996, Disting. Alumnus Coll. Arts and Scis., U. Okla., 2000; inducted into Tulsa City-County Libr. Hall of Fame, 1989, Okla. Womens Hall of Fame, 1993. Mem. ALA, Pub. Libr. Assn. (pres. 1993-94), Okla. Libr. Assn. (pres. 1978-79, Disting. Libr. award 1982, Meritorious Svc. award 1996), Tulsa Press Club. Democrat. Episcopalian. Avocations: swimming, gardening. Office Phone: 918-728-2707. E-mail: pwoodrum@tulsaconnect.com.

WOODRUM, ROBERT LEE, executive search consultant; b. Merkel, Tex., Mar. 3, 1945; s. Bill and Norma (Shea) W.; m. Linda Mary Larkin, July 20, 1968; children: Jennifer, Michael. BA, Calif. State U., Northridge, 1967; postgrad., U. Okla., 1974. Press sec. U.S. Senate, Washington, 1977-78; dir. pub. affairs U.S. Office Personnel Mgmt., Washington, 1979-80; pres. Corp. Communications, Washington, 1980-82; v.p. Norton Simon Inc., N.Y.C., 1982-83; spl. asst. to the commr. NFL, N.Y.C., 1983-84; exec. dir. Ritz Paris Hemingway Award, 1984-87; pres. Ritz Paris Internat., 1984-86; sr. v.p. AmBase Corp., 1986-91; mng. dir. Korn/Ferry Internat., N.Y.C., 1991—; dir. DataBuilt, Inc., 2000—. Advisor USIA, Washington, 1980-93, ARC, 1983, White House Vets. Com., 1979-80. Trustee N.Y.C. Meals on Wheels, Inc. Lt. comdr. USN, 1968-77. Mem.: Ocean Reef Club, N.Y. Sky Club. Office: 117 Harbour PSGE Hilton Head Island SC 29926-1265 Business E-Mail: woodrumr@kornferry.com.

WOODS, CATHI L. human services administrator; b. Chattanooga, Oct. 4, 1961; d. Robert L. and Shirley Phillips Woods; 1 child, Joshua Barbour. Degree in exec. edn., Harvard U., 1999. Exec. dir. Hope Resource Ctr., Knoxville, 1996-97; CEO, pres. Daybreak, Boston, 1998—. Exec. dir. Women's Care Ctr., Dayton, Tenn., 1991-96; mem. Rhea County Health Coun., 1994-96; mem., bd. chair Adolescent Pregnancy Initiative Coun., 1994-96. Mem. NAFE. Avocations: reading, travel. Office: Daybreak Pregnancy Resource 132 Boylston St Fl4 Boston MA 02116-4616 E-mail: ceo@daybreakinc.org.

WOODS, CHERYL, financial analyst; b. Cleve., Nov. 15, 1960; d. Virgle Lee and Mary Grace Woods; m. Danny Thomas Couch, Jan. 18, 1984 (div. Nov. 1988); m. Eddie Lee Grays, Jr., Feb. 2, 1992 (div. Mar. 1997); m. Neil Hollis Moss, July 19, 2003; children: Camille Dana Couch, Eddie Lee Grays, III. BS in Bus. Adminstrn., U. Akron, 1980—87; MBA, Cleve. State U., 1994—95, postgrad., 1997—. Letter carrier US Postal Svc., Cleve., 1979—92, customer svc. supr., 1992—93, fin. systems coord., 1993—2000, budget/fin. analyst, 2000—01, mgr., budget/fin. analyst, 2001—. Deacon Eastside Christian Ref. Ch., Warrensville Hts., Ohio, 1997—2000; lay min. Christ Cmty. Fellowship Ch., Twinsburg, Ohio, 2002, dir. of christian edn., 2002. Recipient Disting. alumni, Aurora H.S., 2001; Nat. Merit scholarship, 1978. Mem.: Acad. of Mgmt., Nat. Honor Soc., Mensa, Beta Gamma Sigma. Democrat. Methodist. Avocations: travel, reading, dance, cooking. Office Phone: 216-443-4104. Personal E-mail: woodsc@alltel.net.

WOODS, DAN, information technology manager, consultant; BA in Computer Sci., U. Mich., 1982; MS in Journalism, Columbia U., 1989. Database editor The News and Observer/Nando.net, 1992—95; info. tech. cons. Time Inc. New Media, 1995—99, TheStreet.com, 1998—99; CTO CapitalThinking, 1999—2002. Mem. CTO adv. coun. InfoWorld; bd. mem. Big Star Entertainment; mem. policy adv. bd. on pub. key infrastructure Am. Bankers Assn. Author: The Education of a CTO, 2003; co-author: Developers Guide to the Java Web Server, 1999; contbr. articles to profl. jours. Home: Apt 3B 890 West End Ave New York NY 10025*

WOODS, DAVID LYNDON, publishing and broadcast executive, former federal agency executive; b. San Jose, Calif. s. Donald Mason and Lynda Rosalia (Mueller) W.; m. Barbara Sue Vacin, June 9, 1956 (div. July 1987); children: Stephanie Lynn Woods Snide, Allison Elizabeth Woods Traba, Roberta Lee, Dana Royce Woods Bunce, Meredith Mason; m. Jeanne-Renee Jones, July 5, 1998. AB, San Jose State Coll., 1957; MA, Stanford U., 1955; postgrad., U. So. Calif., 1962-63; MBA, Rollins Coll., 1965, Oxford (U.K.) U., 1974; PhD, Ohio State U., 1976. Dir. univ. broadcasting Lehigh U., Bethlehem, Pa., 1953-54; project officer NARAD Briefing Reports Navy Chief of Naval Ops., 1956-59; mgr. presentations and advt. Bendix-Pacific divsn. Bendix Corp., North Hollywood, Calif., 1959-60; dir. pub. rels. and advt. Librascope divsn. GPI, Glendale, Calif., 1961-62; sr. writer-editor Martin-Marietta Corp., Orlando, Fla., 1963-65; head program support br. Navy Dept. Speech Bur., Washington, 1965-70; spl. asst. to chief naval material Naval Material Command, Washington, 1970-84; dir. Navy sci. and tech. info. Naval Material Command (later at Office Naval Rsch.), Arlington, Va., 1984-93; pres. DaleWood Enterprises, Inc., Hedgesville, W.Va., 1987—. Adj. prof. bus. and pub. adminstrn. George Washington U., 1975-86; instr. Stanford (Calif.) U., Lehigh U., Ohio State U., U. Md., U. Va., and other colls., 1953-88, 94-97, Marshall U., 1998—; bd. correction naval records Sec. of Navy, Washington, 1980-85; commentator, on-air musical host local radio, 1994-95, 96-97; ptnr. Cap'n Dave's Flotsam and Jetsam, 1996—. Author: A History of Tactical Communication Techniques, 1965, 82, The Development of Visual Signals on Land and Sea, 1976, (four histories): U.S. Naval and Marine Corps Bases (2 vols.), 1986; editor: Signaling and Communicating at Sea (2 vols.), 1984; author, editor numerous fed. publs.; editl. columnist newspaper, 1998-2004; contbr. over 350 articles and revs. to mags. and jours. Chmn. fin. Commn. on Aging, Alexandria, 1993; bd. dirs. Middleway Hist. Conservancy, 1994-2002, The Station at Shepherdstown, W.Va., 1998-2000; vice chmn. Coun. on Aging of Jefferson County, 1995—, Nat. Assn. for Uniformed Svcs., 1986-91; U.S. del. NATO Congress Internat. Res. Officers, 1984-91, U.S. v.p., 1988-89. Capt. USNR, 1949-87. Recipient Navy Superior Pub. Svc. medal, 1986. Mem.: Naval Officers Assn. Can., Nat. Comm. Assn. (emeritus, chair mass comm. divsn. 1970—71), Naval Enlisted Res. Assn. (life assoc., pub. 1987—93), Naval Order of the U.S. (life; recorder-gen. 1996—97), Armed Forces Comm. and Electronics Assn. (life; author), Res. Officers Assn. (life; nat. pres. 1985—86, columnist 2000—01), Naval Res. Assn. (life; dist. pres. 1974—75, 1993—94, nat. pub. affairs officer 1966—72), U.S. Naval Inst. (life; author 1966—), Nat. Def. Indsl. Assn. (life; author 1991—92), Army and Navy Club, Alpine Club of Can., Sons of the Revolution, Mil. Officers Assn. Am., Lambda Chi Alpha. Avocations: american musical comedy, acting and directing theatre, bluegrass and old-time banjo music, military signals, history of technology. Office Phone: 304-754-4818. E-mail: dlwoods70@earthlink.net.

WOODS, DENNIS OLIVER, headmaster, market and political research analyst; b. Spirit Lake, Iowa, Mar. 11, 1947; s. Peter Ashton and Edna Elizabeth Woods; m. Jane Robertson; children: Miranda, Viyaj, Catherine. BS in Agrl. Journalism, Iowa State U., 1970; MEd, Oreg. State U., 1973; postgrad., Multnomah Bible Coll., 1973—74, Computer Career Inst., 1974—75. Polit. rsch. asst., vol. several polit. and social action coms., Portland, 1976—79; market/polit. rsch. analyst Bardsley & Haslacher, Portland, 1980—84; market/statis. rsch. analyst Columbia Info. Sys., Portland, 1985—90; owner Target Market Strategies LLC, Clackamas, 1991—2004; founder, headmaster ClassicalFree Virtual Acad., Clackamas, 2001—. Conducted about 400 mktg. and polit. rsch. studies at mgmt. level; six years helping to pioneer devel. of the perception analyzer sys. for testing print and TV advt.; lead mem. start-up team to deliver classical edn. via internet to remote and low-income populations; one of the first to blend ancient trivium methodology and classical content with internet delivery tech. Author: textbooks on hist., sociol. and religious influences leading to U.S. constnl. settlement; contbr. articles to profl. jours. Issues and strategy cons. Multnomah County Rep. Party, Portland, 1986—90, vice chmn., 1990; bd. mem. Oreg. Mktg. Assn., Portland, 1973—74. First lt. art. U.S. Army, 1971—72. Presbyterian. Avocation: woodworking. Office: ClassicalFree Virtual Acad PO Box 497 Clackamas OR 97015 Office Phone: 503-658-1755.

WOODS, DONALD E. healthcare executive; b. Memphis, Nov. 1, 1946; s. John Thomas and Hazel O. (Perry) W.; m. Shirlene M. Durutta, 1978 (div. 1992); children: Donald E. Jr., Lori Ann, Ryan Christopher; m. Joan M. Turley, 1995 (div. 2000); children: Kathryn Ashley, Lauren Rose. BS in Acctg., U. So. Calif., 1972, MBA, 1976. CPA, Calif. Audit supr. Ernst and Young, L.A., 1972-76; asst. v.p. Am. Med. Internat., Beverly Hills, Calif., 1976-80; corp. contr. Safeco Title Ins. Co., Panorama City, Calif., 1980-82; sr. v.p. fin. Heritage divsn. Beverly Enterprises, Md., 1982-84; co-founder, CFO Hannover Health Care, Inc., Md., 1984-85; founder, pres., CEO Oakwood Living Ctrs., Inc., McLean, Va., 1985-91; owner, pres. HMS of Newport (R.I.), Inc., 1992—; owner, gen. mgr. Lizzie Borden Bed and Breakfast, LLC, Fall River, Mass. Sgt. USMC, 1964-68. Mem. AICPA, Newport C. of C. Avocations: sailing, skiing. Home: 13 Gideon Lawton Ln Portsmouth RI 02871 Office: HMS of Newport Inc PO Box 610 Newport RI 02840-0011

WOODS, EMILY, apparel executive; b. 1961; m. Cary Woods, 1991 (div.); m. Tom Scott; 1 child, Walt Scott. BA, U. Denver, 1982. Co-founder (with Arthur Cinader) J Crew, N.Y.C., 1983—; former chief designer J Crew Group Inc., N.Y.C., chmn. of bd., 1997—2003. Bd. dirs. J. Crew, Inc., Beringer Wine Estates, 1998, Yankee Candle Co., Inc. Office: J Crew Group Inc 770 Broadway New York NY 10003-9522

WOODS, GARY V. professional football team executive, former professional basketball team executive, automotive executive; b. Nov. 9, 1943; BBA, So. West Tex. State; MBA, SMU. Pres. San Antonio Spurs, 1988—93; ceo, pres., chair. McCombs Enterprises, San Antonio, 1979—; pres., ceo Minnesota Vikings, Eden Prairie, 1998—. Office: Minnesota Vikings 9520 Viking Dr Eden Prairie MN 55344-3898 Address: McCombs Enterprises 9000 Tesoro Dr Ste 122 San Antonio TX 78217-6132

WOODS, GEORGE EDWARD, judge; b. 1923; m. Janice Smith. Student, Ohio No. U., 1941-43, 46, Tex. A&M Coll., 1943, Ill. Inst. Tech., 1943; JD, Detroit Coll. Law, 1949. Sole practice, Pontiac, Mich., 1949-51; asst. pros. atty. Oakland County, Mich., 1951-52; chief asst. U.S. atty. Ea. Dist. Mich., 1953-60, U.S. atty., 1960-61; assoc. Honigman, Miller, Schwartz and Cohn, Detroit, 1961-62; sole practice Detroit, 1962-81; judge U.S. Bankruptcy Ct., 1981-83, U.S. Dist. Ct. (ea. dist.) Mich., Detroit, 1983-93, sr. judge, 1993—. Served with AUS, 1943-46. Fellow Internat. Acad. Trial Lawyers, Am. Coll. Trial Lawyers; mem. Fed. Bar Assn., State Bar Mich. Office: US Dist Ct 277 US Courthouse 231 W Lafayette Blvd Detroit MI 48226-2700

WOODS, HARRIETT RUTH, retired political organization president; b. Cleve., June 2, 1927; d. Armin and Ruth (Wise) Friedman; m. James B. Woods, Jan. 2, 1953; children: Christopher, Peter, Andrew. Student, U. Chgo., 1945; BA, U. Mich., 1949; LLD (hon.), Webster U., 1988, U. Missouri, 2003. Reporter Chgo. Herald-Am., 1948, St. Louis Globe-Democrat, 1949-51; prodr. Star, KPLR-TV, St. Louis, 1964-74; moderator, writer Sta. KETC-TC, St. Louis, 1962-64; council mem. University City, Mo., 1967-74; mem. Mo. Hwy. Commn., 1974, Mo. Transp. Commn., 1974-76, Mo. Senate, 1976-84; lt. gov. State of Mo., 1985-89; pres. Inst. for Policy Leadership, U. Mo., St. Louis, 1989-91, lectr., 1995—. Pres. Nat. Women's Polit. Caucus, 1991-95; fellow inst. politics J.F. Kennedy Sch. Govt., Harvard U., 1988; adj. prof. U. Mo., St. Louis, 1995—, Hunter Coll., N.Y.C., 2004—. Author: Stepping Up to Power: The Political Journey of American Women, 2000. Bd. dirs. LWV of Mo., 1963, Nat. League of Cities, 1972-74; Dem. nominee for U.S. Senate, 1982, 86; commr. St. Louis Regional Conf. and Sports Complex Authority, 2000—. Jewish. Office Phone: 314-863-4055.

WOODS, HOWARD JAMES, JR., civil engineer; b. Elizabeth, N.J., Oct. 11, 1955; s. Howard James and Catherine (Hurring) W.; m. Roseann Schmidt, Jan. 30, 1999. BCE cum laude, Villanova U., 1977, MCE, 1985. Registered profl. engr. N.Y., N.J., Pa., Md., N.Mex. Environ. engr. EPA, Phila., 1977-81; project engr. Johnson, Mirmiran & Thompson, Silver Spring, Md., 1981-83; dir. engring. ea. div. Am. Water Works Svc. Co., Haddon Heights, N.J., 1983-85, mgr. ops. ea. div., 1985-86, dir. planning, 1986-88, east regional mgr. ops., 1988-92; v.p. N.J. Am. Water Co., Haddon Heights, 1992-97, Am. Water Works Svc. Co., 1997-98; sr. v.p. Am. Water Svcs., Marlton, NJ, 1998-2000; pres. Howard J. Woods, Jr. & Assocs., LLC, 2000—. Apptd. by gov. to N.J. Water Supply Adv. Coun., 1991-97. Named one of Oustanding Young Men Am., Jaycees, 1984, Outstanding Civil Engring. Alumnus, Grad. Sch. Villanova U., 1986; recipient John J. Gallen award Villanova U. Coll. of Engring. Tech. Achievement award. Mem. ASCE, Nat. Water Well Assn., Am. Mgmt. Assn., Am. Water Works Assn., Amnesty Internat., Water Environ. Fedn., Villanova Club (So. N.J.), Tau Beta Pi. Democrat. Roman Catholic. Avocations: skiing, music, photography. Home: 138 Liberty Dr Newtown PA 18940-1111 Office: Howard J Woods Jr & Assocs LLC 138 Liberty Dr Newtown PA 18940-1111 E-mail: budwoods@earthlink.net.

WOODS, J. P. religious organization administrator; b. Houston, June 22, 1950; s. William Oliver and Lilly Virginia (Hetherington) W. Student, Blinn Coll., Brenham, Tex., 1968—69; BA, Ft. Lewis Coll., Durango, Colo., 1971; PhD in Bus. Adminstrn., Trinity So. U., Dallas, 2003. Ordained to ministry, Life Bible Coll., 1996. V.p. sales Bon Ton, Inc., Dallas, 1977-80; regional sales mgr. John O. Butler Co., Chgo., 1980-81; sales mgr. Fox Meyer, Inc., Oklahoma City, 1981-82; sales cons., trainer Rugby Labs., Inc., N.Y.C., 1982-83; nat. dir. key accounts United Rsch. Labs., Inc., Mut. Pharm., Inc., Phila., 1983-88; v.p. Western div. Barr Labs., Pomona, N.Y., 1988-94; pres., CEO J. P. Woods Ministries, Inc., 1996—. Sr. pastor Aspen Christian World Outreach, Aspen, Colo., 1996—; elected to Tex. State Bd. Pharmacy, 1992. Author, editor: Sales and Marketing Techniques, 1984. Mem. Rep. Presdl. Task Force, Washington, 1982—, life membership honor roll; mem. Presdl. Commn., 1988; sustaining mem. Rep. Nat. Com., Washington, 1983—, cert. recognition, 1991-92; preferred mem. Nat. Conservative Polit. Action Com., Washington, 1983—; elected mem. Rep. Campaign Coun. Com., 1992—; elected del. State Tex. Rep. Party, 1992; founding mem. CBN Founders, Virginia Beach, Va., 1986—; active Christian Coalition, 1992—, Kenneth Copeland Ptnrs. Ministries, 1992. Recipient Medal of Merit, Ronald Reagan, Pres., Washington, 1985, Presdl. Commn. from Ronald Reagan, 1986, Cert. of Recognition Rep. Nat. Com., 1991-92; named to Rep. Presdl. Task Force Life Membership Honor Roll. Mem. Nat. Assn. Chain Druggists, Nat. Wholesale Drug Assn., Nat. Assn. Retail Druggists, Tex. Pharm. Assn. (com. mem. 1991-92), DAV Comdrs., U.S. Senatorial Club (founder). Mem. Full Gospel Ch. Avocations: collecting southwestern art, golf, tennis, skiing, travel. Personal E-mail: TheRevJPW@aol.com.

WOODS, JACQUELINE F. telecommunications industry executive; B.A., Univ. of Calif. (Davis); M.A., Univ. of Southern Calif. Pres. Ameritech Ohio subs. Ameritech Corp., Cleve., Ameritech Ill., Cleve.; v.p. of licensing and pricing Oracle Corp. Office: 500 Oracle Pwky Redwood City CA 94065 Fax: 312-207-1601.

WOODS, JAMES H. research scientist, consultant; b. Louisa, Ky., Sept. 18, 1937; BS, Ohio U., 1959; MA, U. Va., 1962, PhD, 1968. NDEA fellow psychology dept. U. Va., Charlottesville, Va., 1959—62; instr. psychology dept. Randolph-Macon Woman's Coll., Lynchburg, Va., 1963—64; lectr. psychology dept. U. Mich., Ann Arbor, 1965; from rsch. asst. to rsch. assoc. pharmacology dept. U. Mich. Med. Sch., Ann Arbor, 1965—70; from asst. prof. to assoc. prof. psychology dept. U. Mich., Ann Arbor, 1969—80; from asst. prof. to assoc. prof. pharmacology dept. U. Mich. Med. Sch., Ann Arbor, 1970—80; prof. psychology dept. U. Mich., Ann Arbor, 1980—; prof. pharmacology dept. U. Mich. Med. Sch., Ann Arbor, 1980—. Cons. Nat. Inst. Drug Abuse, Bethesda, Md.; cons. divsn. neuropharmacol. drug products FDA, Rockville, Md.; cons. Eli Lilly Co., Indpls., 1976—86; cons. expert adv. panel on drug dependence and alcohol problems WHO, 1983—98; cons. G.D. Searle/Monsanto, 1986—89, Nat. Inst. Drug Abuse/Nat. Adv. Coun. Alcohol, Drug Abuse and Mental Health Adminstrn., Bethesda, 1987—91; Parke Davis Rsch. Unit, Cambridge, England, 1989; cons., mem. adv. bd. Rand Corp., Drug Policy Rsch. Ctr., Santa Monica, Calif., 1990; cons. Burroughs Wellcome Co., Research Triangle Park, NC, 1990—, Eli Lilly Co., Indpls., 1991, Gliatech Corp., Cleve.; cons. expert adv. panel on drug dependence: dependence liability evaluation WHO, 1998; grant reviewer NSF, NIMH, VA, Med. Rsch. Coun. Can., others. Editl. cons.: Jour. Pharmacology and Exptl. Therapeutics, Behavioral Brain Rsch., Jour. AMA, others. Recipient rsch. grants in field. Fellow: APA, Am. Coll. Neuropsychopharmacology (mem. neuropharmacology divsn., pres. divsns. 5, 6, 25, and 28 psychopharmacology 1984); mem.: AAAS, Behavioral Pharmacology Soc. (pres. 1978—80), European Behavioral Pharmacology Soc., Sigma Xi, Soc. for Neurosci., Am. Soc. for Pharmacology and Exptl. Therapeutics (mem. com. on substance abuse 1994), Collegium Internationale Neuro-Psychopharmacologicum, Am. Pain Soc., Assn. for Chemoreception Scis. Office: U Mich Med Sch Dept Pharmacology 1301 Med Sci Rsch Bldg 1150 W Medical Center Dr Ann Arbor MI 48109-0632

WOODS, JAMES HOWARD, actor; b. Vernal, Utah, Apr. 18, 1947; m. Kathryn Morrison-Pahoa, 1980 (div. 1983); m. Sarah Owen, 1989 (div. 1990). Student, MIT, 1965-69. Performances include (Broadway prodns.) Borstal Boy, Trial of the Catonsville 9, Finishing Touches, Moonchildren (Theatre World award), off-Broadway prodn. Saved (Obie award, Clarence Derwent award); (films) The Visitors, 1971, Hickey and Boggs, 1972, The Way We Were, 1973, The Gambler, 1974, Night Moves, 1975, Distance, 1975, Alex & the Gypsy, 1976, The Choirboys, 1977, The Onion Field, 1979 (Golden Globe award nomination), The Black Marble, 1980, Eyewitness, 1981, Split Image, 1982, Fast-Walking, 1982, Videodrome, 1983, Against All Odds, 1984, Once Upon a Time in America, 1984, Cat's Eye, 1985, Joshua Then and Now, 1985, Salvador, 1986 (Acad. award nomination, 1987), Best Seller, 1987, Cop, 1988, The Boost, 1988, True Believer, 1989, Immediate Family, 1989, The Hard Way, 1991, Straight Talk, 1992, Diggstown, 1992, Chaplin, 1992, The Getaway, 1994, The Specialist, 1994, Curse of the Starving Class, 1994, Nixon, 1995, Casino, 1995, Ghosts of Mississippi, 1996 (Acad. award nomination, Golden Globe nomination), For Better or Worse, 1996, Hercules, 1997, Contact, 1997, Vampires, 1998, Kicked in the Head, 1998, Another Day in Paradise, 1998, True Crime, 1998, The General's Daughter, 1998, Any Given Sunday, 1999, The Virgin Suicides, 2000, Race to Space, 2001, Riding in Cars with Boys, 2001, John Q, 2002, (voice) Stuart Little 2, 2002, Northfork, 2003, This Girl's Life, 2003; (TV miniseries) Holocaust, 1978; (TV movies) All the Way Home, 1971, Footsteps, 1972, A Great American Tragedy, 1972, Foster and Laurie, 1975, F. Scott Fitzgerald in Hollywood, 1976, The Disappearance of Aimee, 1976, Raid on Entebbe, 1977, The Gift of Love, 1978, And Your Name is Jonah, 1979, The Incredible Journey of Doctor Meg Laurel, 1979, Badge of the Assassin, 1985, Promise, 1986 (Emmy award, Golden Apple award, Golden Globe award), In Love and War, 1987 (Golden Globe award nomination), (Hallmark TV) My Name Is Bill W. (Emmy award 1989), Women & Men: Stories of Seduction, 1990, The Boys, 1991, Citizen Cohn, HBO, 1992 (Emmy nomination, Lead Actor - Miniseries, 1993), Jane's House, 1994, Indictment: The McMartin Trial, 1995 (Emmy nomination, Cable Ace nomination), The Summer of Ben Tyler, 1996 (Golden Globe nomination), Dirty Pictures, Showtime, 2000 (Best Actor in Mini-Series of Motion Picture Made for TV award Golden Satellite 2000), (voice) Legend of the Lost Tribe, 2002, Rudy: The Rudy Giuliani Story, 2003; guest on The Simpsons, 1994 (voice only). Recipient Daytime Emmy for Outstanding Performer Animated Program for Disney's Hercules, 2000. Mem. Acad. Motion Picture Arts and Scis., Internat. Platform Assn., Players Club, Mountaingate Country Club. Office: Guttman Assocs 118 S Beverly Dr Ste 201 Beverly Hills CA 90212-3016*

WOODS, JAMES MELVIN, writer; b. Weona, Ark. s. Virgil Neff and Ethel Marie (Burns) Woods; m. Sandra Isobel Mitchell, June 15, 1959 (div. July 1969); children: James Gregory, Lauro Jo; m. Jacqueline Ann Summers, May 16, 1970. BSEE, Pierce Coll., Woodland Hills, Calif., 1958; postgrad., Moorpark Coll., Ventura, Calif., 1962. Tech. editor Litton Industries, Canoga Park, Calif., 1960—73; editor various mags. Petersen Pub. Co., L.A., 1973—79; field editor Guns Mag., Pubrs. Devel. Corp., San Diego, 1979—85; ind. author/editor Tucson, 1985—. Motivational spkr. Words are Your Wheels, Literacy Day, Tucson, 2003; pubs. cons. Chris Reeve Knives; tech. editor Honeywell, Inc.; contract author Omega Group; tech. writer/editor Hughes Aircraft; tech. writer RCA Svc. Co. Author: Journeys, 2002, Lessons From an Editor, 2002; co-editor: Away With Murder, 2004; contbr. over 400 mag. articles to jours. With USN, 1953—57. Mem.: Outdoor Writers of Am., Soc. Tech. Writers and Pubs., Soc. Southwestern Authors, Am. Soc. Journalists and Authors. Home: 6213 N Silk Tree Pl Tucson AZ 85704

WOODS, JAMES ROBERT, lawyer; b. San Francisco, Aug. 3, 1947; AB with honors, U. Calif., Berkeley, 1969; JD, U. Calif., Davis, 1972. Bar: Calif. 1972, N.Y. 1973, U.S. Dist. Ct. (so. & ea. dists.) N.Y. 1975, U.S. Ct. Appeals (2d cir.) 1975, U.S. Dist. Ct. (no. dist.) Calif. 1984. Ptnr. LeBoeuf, Lamb, Greene & MacRae L.L.P., San Francisco, 1983—. Co-author: California Insurance Law and Practice; contbr. articles to profl. jours. Office: LeBoeuf Lamb Greene & MacRae LLP 1 Embarcadero Ctr Ste 400 San Francisco CA 94111-3619 Office Phone: 415-951-1100.

WOODS, JAMES STERRETT, toxicologist; b. Lewistown, Pa., Feb. 26, 1940; s. James Sterrett and Jane Smith (Parker) W.; m. Nancy Fugate, Dec. 20, 1969; 1 dau., Erin Elizabeth. AB, Princeton U., 1962; MS, U. Wash., 1968, PhD, 1970; MPH, U. N.C., 1978. Diplomate Am. Bd. Toxicology. Rsch. assoc. dept. pharmacology Yale U. Sch. Medicine, New Haven, 1970-72; staff fellow environ. toxicology. Nat. Inst. Environ. Health Scis. br. NIH, Research Triangle Park, N.C., 1972-75, head biochem. toxicology sect., 1975-77; sr. rsch. leader environ.-occupational health risk evaluation Battelle Ctrs. for Pub. Health Rsch. and Evaluation, Seattle, 1978—; rsch. prof. U. Wash., Seattle, 1979—. Pres. Am. Bd. Toxicology, 1997-98. Contbr. articles to profl. jours. With USN, 1962-66. Scholar USPHS, 1966-70; Fellow Am. Cancer Soc., 1970-72. Mem. AAAS, Am. Assn. Cancer Rsch., Am. Soc. Pharmacology and Exptl. Therapeutics, Pacific NW Assn. Toxicologists (founding pres.), Soc. Epidemiology Rsch., Soc. Toxicology, Am. Coll. of Epidemiology, Am. Bd. Toxicology (pres. 1997-98). Home: 4525 E Laurel Dr NE Seattle WA 98105-3838 Office: Battelle Research Ctr 1100 Dexter Ave N Ste 400 Seattle WA 98109-3598 Office Phone: 206-528-3111. E-mail: woods@battelle.org.

WOODS, JANE HAYCOCK, state legislator; b. Bethesda, Md., Oct. 10, 1946; d. Stephen Pineo and Ruth (Yanovsky) Haycock; m. James Richard Fitzalan Woods, July 14, 1973. BA in Edn., Am. U., 1968. Tchr. Fairfax (Va.) County Pub. Sch., 1968-74, 76-87; co-mgr. Comml. Real Estate, Fairfax, 1982-91; mem. Va. Ho. of Dels., Fairfax, 1988-92, Va. Senate, 1992-2000. Chair City of Fairfax (Va.) Rep. Com., 1983-88, 11th Congl. Rep. Dist. Com., 1992; bd. mem. Va. Fedn. Rep. Women, 1986—. Named Outstanding Woman, City of Fairfax Commn. on Women, 1987. Mem. Nat. Assn. Parliamentarians (Outstanding Tchr. 1990), Va. Girls State (bd. mem.), Annandale C. of C. (Citizen of Yr. 1990), Fairfax C. of C. (Outstanding Woman 1989), Am. Legion Aux., Phi Delta Kappa. Methodist. Avocations: gardening, reading. Office: 3932 Old Lee Hwy # B Fairfax VA 22030-2417

WOODS, JOHN ELMER, plastic surgeon; b. Battle Creek, Mich., July 5, 1929; m. Janet Ruth; children: Sheryl, Mark, Jeffrey, Jennifer, Judson. BA, Asbury Coll., 1949, DHL, 1999; MD, Western Res. U., 1955; PhD, U. Minn., 1966. Intern Gorgas Hosp., Panama Canal Zone, 1955-56, resident in gen. surgery, 1956-57, Mayo Grad. Sch., Rochester, Minn., 1960-65, resident in plastic surgery, 1966-67, Brigham Hosp., Boston, Mass., 1968; fellow, transplant cons. Harvard Med. Sch., Cambridge, Mass., 1969; cons. in gen. and plastic surgery Mayo Clinic, Rochester, 1969-93, vice chmn. Dept. Surgery; asst. prof. Mayo Med. Sch., Rochester, 1973-76, assoc. prof., 1976-80, prof. plastic surgery, 1980-93, Stuart W. Harrington prof. surgery. Vis. prof. Yale Sch. Medicine, New Haven, 1984, Harvard Sch. Medicine, Cambridge, 1984. Contbr. over 200 articles to profl. jours.; also 26 book chpts. and 1 film. Recipient Disting. Mayo Clinician award, 1991, Disting. Mayo Alumnus award, 1999. Mem. AMA (coun. on sci. affairs 1985-87), ACS (grad edn. com. 1985-87), Am. Bd. Med. Specialties, Am. Bd. Plastic Surgery (sec.-treas. 1985-88, chmn. 1988-89), Am. Soc. Plastic Surgeons Ednl. Fedn. (pres. 1984-85). Avocations: skiing, sailing, reading, the arts. Office: Mayo Clinic Plummer N-10 Rochester MN 55905-0001 Business E-Mail: woods.john@mayo.edu.

WOODS, JOHN WILLIAM, electrical, computer and systems engineering educator, consultant; b. Washington, Dec. 5, 1943; s. John Gill and Margaret (McHugh) W.; m. Harriet Hemmerich, June 17, 1972; children: Anne, Christopher. BSEE, MIT, 1965, MSEE, 1967, PhD, 1970. Sr. rsch. engr. Lawrence Livermore (Calif.) Nat. Lab., 1973-76; asst. prof. Rensselaer Poly. Inst., Troy, N.Y., 1976-78, assoc. prof., 1978-84, prof., 1985—. Vis. prof. Delft Tech. U., The Netherlands, 1985, Heinrich-Hertz Inst., Berlin, 2000; program dir. NSF, Washington, 1987-88; assoc. dir. Ctr. for Image Processing Rsch., 1992—; cons. Kodak, Rochester, N.Y., 1985-86, Johns Hopkins Applied Physics Lab., Laurel, Md., 1987, Calian Comms. Ltd., 1990-91; co-founder Focus Interactive Tech., Inc., 1993; assoc. dir. NSF I/U Ctr. for Next Generation Video, 1998-2001, dir. 2002—; mem. compression com. Digital Cinema Initiatives, 2003-04. Co-author: Probability and Random Processes for Engineers, 1986, 3d edit., 2002; editor: Subband Image Coding, 1991; co-editor: Handbook of Visual Communications, 1995; mem. editl. bd. Graphical Models and Image Processing, 1989-93; contbg. author book chpts., articles to profl. jours. Mem. Com. Acad. Excellence, Clifton Park, N.Y., 1984. Capt. USAF, 1969-73. Grantee NSF, Army Rsch. Office, Advanced Rsch. Projects Agy., Ctr. Advanced TV Studies, 1978-2004. Fellow: IEEE (editl. bd. Trans. on Video Tech. 1990—2002, Third Millennium medal 2000); mem.: Nat. Com. for Info. Tech. Stds., Internat. Stds. Orgn., IEEE Signal Processing Soc. (com. chmn. 1983—85, edl. com. chmn. 1987—93, ad. com. 1986—88, assoc. editor jour. 1979—82, co-chmn. tech. program com., 1st IEEE Internat. Conf. on Image Processing 1994, Best Paper awards 1977, 1986, Meritorious Svc. award 1989, Tech. Achievement award 1993). Roman Catholic. Home: 43 Longview Dr Clifton Park NY 12065-2318 Office: Rensselaer Poly Inst ECSE Dept Troy NY 12180-3590 Office Phone: 518-276-6079. E-mail: woods@ecse.rpi.edu.

WOODS, LAWRENCE MILTON, airline company executive; b. Manderson, Wyo., Apr. 14, 1932; s. Ben Ray and Katherine (Youngman) Woods; m. Joan Frances Van Patten, June 10, 1952; 1 child, Laurie. B.Sc. with honors, U. Wyo., 1953; MA, N.Y. U., 1973, PhD, 1975; LL.D., Wagner Coll., 1973. CPA Colo., Mont.; bar: Mont. 1957. Acct. Peat, Marwick, Mitchell & Co. (C.P.A.'s), Billings, Mont., 1953; supervisory auditor Army Audit Agy., Denver, 1954-56; acct. Mobil Producing Co., Billings, Mont., 1956-59; planning analyst Socony Mobil Oil Co., N.Y.C., 1959-63, planning mgr., 1963-65; v.p. N.Am. divsn. Mobil Oil Corp., N.Y.C., 1966-67, gen. mgr. planning and econs. N.Am. divsn., 1967-69, v.p. N.Am. divsn., 1969-77, exec. v.p. N.Am. divsn., 1977-85, also dir. N.Am. divsn.; pres., CEO, dir. Centennial Airlines, Inc., 1985-87; pres., dir. Woshakie Travel Corp., 1988—, High Plains Pub. Co. Inc., 1988—. Bd. dirs. The Aid Assn. for Lutherans Mut. Funds. Author: Accounting for Capital, Construction and Maintenance Expeditures, 1967, The Wyoming Country Before Statehood, 1971, Sometimes the Books Froze, 1985, Moreton Frewen's Western Adventures, 1986, British Gentlemen in the Wild West, 1989; editor: Wyoming Biographies, 1991, Wyoming's Big Horn Basin, 1996, Agent R, 2000, John Clay, Jr., 2001, Asa Shinn Mercer, 2003; co-author: Takeover, 1980; contbr. Accountants' Encyclopedia, 1962. Bd. dirs. U. Wyo. Rsch. Corp. Served with U.S. Army, 1953—55. Mem.: AICPA, ABA, Mont. Bar Assn. Republican. Lutheran. Office: High Plains Pub Co PO Box 1860 Worland WY 82401-1860

WOODS, MAE, minister; b. Orlando, Fla., May 23, 1945; d. Doris Jane Woods. BSN, U. Fla., 1967. Staff nurse State of Fla., Gainesville, 1967—72; pub. health nurse Levy County Health Dept., Breman, Fla., 1973—78; nurse educator maternal infant care Gainesville, 1978—83; cottage rounds nurse Sunland Tng. Ctr. for Mentally Retarded, Gainesville, 1983—88; nurse specialist Children's Med. Svcs., Gainesville, 1988—2000; chaplain, pastoral care minister Oakbrook Life Enrichment Ctr., Ocala, DC, 2000—. Home: Rt 2 Box 751-d Lake Butler FL 32054 Office: Oakbrook Life Enrichment Ctr 2009 NE 28th Ave Ocala FL 34470

WOODS, NANCY FUGATE, dean, women's health nurse, educator; BS, Wis. State U., 1968; MSN, U. Wash., 1969; PhD, U. N.C., 1978. Staff nurse Sacred Heart Hosp., Wis., 1968, Univ. Hosp., Wis., 1969-70, St. Francis Cabrini Hosp., 1970; nurse clinician Yale-New Haven Hosp., 1970-71; instr. nursing Duke U., Durham, N.C., 1971-72, from instr. to assoc. prof., 1972-78; assoc. prof. physiology U. Wash., Seattle, 1978-82, prof. physiology, 1982-84, chairperson dept. parent and child nursing, 1984-90, prof. dept. parent and child nursing, 1990—, dean Sch. Nursing, 1998—; dir. Ctr. Women's Health Rsch., U. Wash., Seattle, 1989—. Pres. scholar U. Calif., San Francisco, 1985-86. Contbr. articles to profl. jours. Fellow ANA, Am. Acad. Nursing, Inst. Medicare, N.A.S.; mem. AAUP, APHA, Am. Coll. Epidemiology, Soc. Menstrual Cycle Rsch. (v.p. 1981-82, pres. 1983-85), Soc. Advancement Women's Health Rsch. Office: U Wash Sch Nursing PO Box 357260 Seattle WA 98195-7260

WOODS, NIKKI, radio personality; Former 5th grade tchr.; morning radio host, entertainment reporter Sta. WGCI-FM, Chgo. Vol. Big Sister, Little Sister Program, Chgo. Rape Crisis Ctr., Walter S. Christopher Sch. for Children. Office: WGCI 332 S Michigan Ave Ste 600 Chicago IL 60604

WOODS, PENDLETON, college director, author; b. Ft. Smith, Ark., Dec. 18, 1923; s. John Powell and Mabel (Hon) W.; m. Lois Robin Freeman, Apr. 3, 1948; children: Margaret, Paul Pendleton, Nancy Cox. BA in Journalism, U. Ark., 1948. Editor, asst. pub. mgr. Okla. Gas & Electric Co., Oklahoma City, 1948-69; dir. Living Legends of Okla., Okla. Christian U., Oklahoma City, 1969-82; project, promotion dir. Enterprise Sq. and Am. Citizenship Ctr., 1982-92, dir. Nat. Edn. Program and Am. Citizenship Ctr., 1992. Arbitrator BBB; leader youth seminars in field; state pub. affairs officer Employer Support Guard and Res. Author: You and Your Company Magazine, 1950, Church of Tomorrow, 1964, Myriad of Sports, 1971, This Was Oklahoma, 1979; recorded Sounds of Scouting, 1969, Born Grown, 1974 (Western Heritage award Nat. Cowboy Hall of Fame), One of a Kind, 1977, Countdown to Statehood, 1982, The Thunderbird Tradition, 1989, A Glimpse at Oklahoma, 1990, Historic Oklahoma County, 2002; editor Libertas. Vol. reader Okla. Libr. for the Blind; past pres. Okla. Assn. Epilepsy, Keep Okla. Beautiful, Okla. City Mental Health Clin.; past pres., hon. lifetime dir. Variety Health Ctr.; pub. rels. chmn. Okla. County chpt. ARC; past chmn. Western Heritage award Nat. Cowboy Hall of Fame; Am. Freedom Coun.; charter dir. Okla. Vets. Med. Rsch. Found.; cons. Exec. Svc. Corps.; ex-state comdr. Am. ex-Prisoners of War; mem. Coun. Pub. Affairs; vol. Okla. City VA Hosp.; state historian Okla. N.G.; chmn. Okla. City Independence Day Parade; exec. com. Okla. City Centennial Commn.; v.p. Okla. City chpt. Freedom Found.; bd. dirs. Campfire Girls Coun., Okla. Jr. Symphony, past pres.; bd. dirs. Zoo Amphitheater of Okla. City, Will Rogers Centennial Commn., Greater Okla. City Tree Bank Found., Boy Scout Am. (life); bd. dirs., co-founder Ctrl. Pk. Neighborhood Assn.; dir. Okla. for Resource Preservation; chmn. State Directional Signage Task Force. With U.S. Army, WWII and Korean War, ret. col. Named Outstanding Young Man of Yr., Oklahoma City Jr. C. of C., 1953; recipient Silver Beaver award Boy Scouts Am., 1963, Wokan award Oklahoma City Coun. Camp Fire girls, 1968, Silver medal Advt. Fedn. Am., Disting. Cmty. Svc. award Neighborhood Devel. and Conservation Ctr., 2 Commendation awards Am. Assn. for State and Local History, 4 honor medals Freedoms Found., Jefferson Davis medal United Daus. of the Confederacy, Okla. Disting. Svc. medal (2), Outstanding Contbn. to Okla. Mus., Okla. Mus. Assn., 1987, Outstanding Contbn. to Okla. Tourism award Okla. Dept. Tourism, 1989, Cmty. Svc. award U. Ark. Alumni Assn., 1992, Citizenship and Patriot award SAR, 1992, 5 Who Care award KOCO-TV, 1993, Jefferson award Am. Inst. for Pub. Svc., 1993, Mayor's award in Beautification, 1994, George Washington award Youth Leadership Found., St. Augustine, Fla., 1993, Golden Rule award J.C. Penney Found., 1999, Lifetime Achievement award Keep Okla. Beautiful; inducted into Okla. Journalism Hall of Fame, 2001, Okla. Mil. Hall of Fame, 2002, U. Ark. Journalism Hall of Fame, 2002. Mem.: VFW, DAV, Okla. Distributive Edn., Okla. Jr. C. of C. (hon. life, past internat. dir.), Ctrl. Okla. Bus. Communicators (past pres., hon. life mem.), Advt. Fedn. Am. (past dist. dir.), Soc. Assoc. Indsl. Editors (past v.p.), Okla. Vets. Coun. (chmn.), Mil. Order World Wars (regional comdr., Oklahoma City comdr., Okla. State comdr., nat. staff, Gold and Silver Patrick Henry Patriotism medals), Okla. Travel Industries Assn., Okla. Heritage Assn., Okla. City Beautiful (publ. editor), Okla. Safety Coun. (publ. editor), Okla. County Hist. Soc. (dir., past pres.), 45th Inf. Divsn. Assn. (past pres.), Korean War Vets. Assn., Am. Legion, Mus. Unassigned Lands (chmn.), Okla. Hist. Soc. (life; publ. editor,), Words of Jesus Found. (pres.), Okla. Zool. Soc. (past pres.), Okla. Geneal. Soc., Okla. County Sr. Nutrition Found. (sec., bd. dirs.), Freedom's Found. (v.p.), Nat. Eagle Scout Assn. (Okla. chmn.), U. Ark. Alumni Assn. (charter pres. Oklahoma City chpt.), Okla. Lung Assn. (pub. rels. com.), Am. Cancer Soc. (dir. Okla. County chpt.), Okla. City Hist. Preservation Commn., Am. Ex-Prisoners of War (state comdr.), Okla. City Clean and Green Coalition, Lincoln Pk. Country Club (pres.), Oklahoma City Advt. Club (past pres., hon. life mem.), Kappa Sigma (nat. commr. publs.), Sigma Delta Chi. Home: 541 NW 31st St Oklahoma City OK 73118-7334 E-mail: penwoods@cox.net.

WOODS, PHYLLIS MICHALIK, librarian; b. New Orleans, Sept. 12, 1937; d. Philip John and Thelma Alice (Carey) Michalik; 1 child, Tara Lynn Woods. BA, Southea. La. U., 1967. Cert. speech and English tchr., libr. sci., La. Tchr. speech, English and drama St. Charles Parish Pub. Schs., Luling, La., elem. tchr., secondary tchr. remedial reading, Chpt. I reading specialist, Wicat tchr. coord., elem. sch. libr.; media specialist Jefferson Parish Pub. Sch. System. Tchr. cons. St. Charles parish writing project La. State U. Writing Project. Author: Egbert, the Egret, Egbert's Picnic, Egbert Visits Sammy, Angel Without Wings, The Necklace and Egbert's Calf, The Hurricane, The Cleanup Day, The Rainbow, The Fair, The Tornado; songwriter; musical compositions include The Fruits of the Spirit, Father's Day Song, Mother's Day Song; contbr. articles and poems to River Parish Guide, St. Charles Herald. Sch. rep. United Fund, St. Charles Parish Reading Assn.; parish com. mem. Young Authors, Tchrs. Who Write; active 4-H leader; bd. trustees Michalik Scholarship Trust. Mem. ASCD, Internat. Platform Assn., Internat. Reading Assn., Am. Fedn. Tchrs., St. Charles Parish Reading Coun., Newspaper in Edn. (chmn., historian), La. Assn. Newspapers in Edn. (state com.), Jefferson Parish Libr. Assn., Jefferson Parish Reading Assn., Jefferson Parish Tchrs. Union.

WOODS, RANDALL E. pharmaceutical executive; With Eli Lilly and Co., 1973—93; v.p. mktg. and sales Boehringer Mannheim Pharms. Corp., 1993—94, pres. U.S. ops., 1994—96; pres., CEO, bd. dirs. Corvas Internat., Inc., San Diego, 1996—. Office: Corvas Internat Inc 3030 Science Park Rd San Diego CA 92121-1102

WOODS, REGINALD FOSTER, management consulting executive; b. Charleston, W.Va., Sept. 25, 1939; s. Reginald Foster and Jean Lee (Hill) W.; m. Katharine Terry Norden, May 11, 1963; children: Eric Arthur, Elizabeth Terry, Tracy Lee. BME, Cornell U., 1961, MME, 1962, MBA, 1963. Mktg.

specialist Gen. Electric Co., N.Y.C., 1963-64; dir. flight equipment and facilities planning Eastern Airlines, N.Y.C., 1964-70; v.p. planning Butler Internat., Inc., Montvale, N.J., 1970, sr. v.p. fin., 1971-80, exec. v.p., 1980-86, pres., 1986-87; chmn. Mgmt. Resources Group, Inc., Saddle River, N.J., 1987-96; pres., ceo The Advantage Ptnrs., Chatham, N.J., 1992-94. Bd. dirs. Benedetto, Gartland & Co., Inc., N.Y.C., DCG Corp., Roseville, Calif., The Greenleaf Co., Cranford, N.J., pres. DCG Corp., 1994—. Mem. Ridgewood Country Club, Glenmore Country Club, Keswick Club, Keswick Hunt Club. Home and Office: Fox Ridge Farm PO Box 490 Keswick VA 22947-0490

WOODS, RICHARD DALE, lawyer; b. Kansas City, Mo., May 20, 1950; s. Willard Dale and Betty Sue (Duncan) W.; m. Cecelia Ann Thompson, Aug. 11, 1973 (div. July 1996); children: Duncan Warren, Shannon Cecelia; m. Mary Linna Lash, June 6, 1999. BA, U. Kans., 1972; JD, U. Mo., 1975. Bar: Mo. 1975, Kans. 2000, U.S. Dist. Ct. (we. dist.) Mo. 1975, U.S. Tax Ct. 1999. Assoc. Shook, Hardy & Bacon L.L.P., Kansas City, Mo., 1975-79, ptnr., 1980-2000; shareholder Kirkland & Woods, P.C., Overland Park, Kans., 2001—. Gen. chmn. Estate Planning Symposium, Kansas City, 1985-86; chair Northland Coalition, 1993. Chmn. fin. com. North Woods Ch., Kansas City, 1986-88, 93-96; mem. sch. bd. N. Kansas City Sch. Dist., 1990-97, treas., 1992-97; mem. North Kansas City Ednl. Found., 1998-2002, pres., 1999-2002; mem. endowment com. Truman Med. Ctr., 1992—, chmn., 1992-98; mem. Clay County Tax Increment Fin. Commn., 1990-99; bd. dirs. Heart of Am. Family Svcs., 1998—, sec., 2000-2001, v.p. 2003-. Fellow Am. Coll. Trust and Estate Counsel; mem. ABA, Mo. Bar Assn., Johnson County Bar Assn., Kansas City Met. Bar Assn., Lawyers Assn. Kans. City (sec., v.p., pres. young lawyers sect. 1981-84), Kans. City Estate Planning Soc. (bd. dirs. 1985-88, 93-95), Ea. Kans. Estate Planning Coun. Democrat. Office: Kirkland & Woods PC 6201 College Blvd Ste 250 Overland Park KS 66211 Office Phone: 913-469-0900. E-mail: rwoods@kcnet.com.

WOODS, ROBERT EVANS, JR., banker; b. Sapporo, Japan, Oct. 15, 1947; s. Robert Evans Sr. and Geraldine (Harrington) W.; m. Saralyn Lankford, June 13, 1970; children: Avery Lankford, Baker Harrington. AB, Conn. Wesleyan U., 1970; MBA, U. Pa., 1972. Agribus. commodities banker Citicorp, N.Y.C. and Paris, 1972-79, adminstrn. officer energy div. N.Y.C., 1980-85, head of syndications, 1985—90, mng. dir. portfolio mgmt., 1991-92, head of real estate investment banking, 1992—97; head of syndications in Am. Societe Generale, NYC, 1997—. Dir. CRIMMI MAE (NYSE), 1998—. Rep. Darien (Conn.) Town Meeting, 1983-86; chmn. Tokeneke Assn., 1997-2000 Avocations: tennis, skiing, golf. Home: 30 Goodwives River Rd Darien CT 06820-5918 Office: Societe Generale 1221 Ave of the Americas New York NY 10020

WOODS, ROSE MARY, former presidential assistant, consultant; b. Sebring, Ohio, Dec. 26, 1917; d. Thomas M. and Mary (Maley) W. Ed. high sch.; L.D.H., Pfeiffer Coll., 1971. With Royal China, Inc., Sebring, 1935-43, Office Censorship, 1943-45, Internat. Tng. Adminstrn., 1945-47, Herter Com. Fgn. Aid, 1947, Fgn. Service Ednl. Found., 1947-51; sec. to senator, then v.p. Nixon, 1951-61; asst. Mr. Nixon with firm Adams, Duque & Hazeltine, Los Angeles, 1961-63, firm Nixon, Mudge, Rose, Guthrie, Alexander & Mitchell, N.Y.C., 1963-68; exec. asst. to former Pres. Nixon, 1969-75. Now consultant. Named 1 of 10 Women of Year Los Angeles Times, 1961, 1 of 75 Most Important Women in Am. Ladies Home Jour., 1971 Home: 3700 S Union Ave Alliance OH 44601-9446

WOODS, SANDRA KAY, real estate executive; b. Loveland, Colo., Oct. 11, 1944; d. Ivan H. and florence L. (Betz) Harris; m. Gary A. Woods, June 11, 1967; children: Stephanie Michelle, Michael Harris. BA, U. Colo., 1966, MA, 1967. Personnel mgmt. specialist CSC, Denver, 1967; asst. to regional dir. HEW, Denver, 1968-69; urban renewal rep. HUD, Denver, 1970-73, dir. program analysis, 1974-75, asst. regional dir. cmty. planning and devel., 1976-77, regional dir. fair housing, 1978-79; mgr. ea. facility project Adolph Coors Co., Golden, Colo., 1980, dir. real estate, 1981, v.p. chief environ. health and safety officer, 1982-96, v.p. strategic selling initiatives, 1996—2000; pres. Woods Properties LLP, Golden, 2000—. Mem. Exec. Exch., The White House, 1980. Bd. dirs. Golden Local Devel. Corp., 1981-82; fundraising dir. Coll. Arts and Scis., U. Colo., boulder, 1982-89, U. Colo. .found.; mem. exec. bd. NCCJ, Denver, 1982-94; v.p. women in bus. Inc., Denver, 1982-83; mem. steering com. 1984 Yr. for All Denver Women, 1983-84; mem. 10th dist. Denver br. Fed. Res. Bd., 1990-96, chmn. bd., 1995-96; bd. dirs. Nat. Jewish Hosp., 1994—; chmn. Greater Denver Corp., 1991—. Named one of Outstanding Young Women Am., U.S. Jaycees, 1974, 78, Fifty Women to Watch, Businessweek, 1987, 92, Woman of Achievement YWCA, 1988. Mem. Indsl. Devel. Resources Coun. (bd. dirs. 1986-89), Am. Mgmt. Assn., Denver C. of C. (bd. dirs. 1988-96, Disting. Young Exec. award 1974, mem. Leadership Denver, 1976-77), Colo. Women's Forum, Nat. Assn. Office and Indsl. Park Developers (sec. 1988, treas. 1989), Committee of 200 (v.p. 1994-95), Phi Beta Kappa, Pi Alpha Alpha, PEO Club (Loveland). Republican. Presbyterian. E-mail: sandrawoods@qwest.net.

WOODS, SHARHONDA MICHELE, military officer; b. Jacksonville, NC, Aug. 22, 1976; d. Richard Cecil and Linda Joyce Berry; m. David Lawrence Woods, Dec. 18, 1998. BA in Criminal Justice, U. Ala., 1998. Dir. Cmty. Svc. Ctr., U. Ala., Tuscaloosa, 1997—98; commd. USAF, 1998, advanced through grades to capt., 1998; chief logistics plans 55th Logistics Support Squadron, Offutt AFB, Nebr., 2000; installation deployment officer 42d Air Base Wing, Maxwell AFB, Ala., 2000—02; exec. officer 42d Logistics Group, Maxwell AFB, 2001—02; chief plans and programs 12AF Davis-Monthan AFB, Ariz., 2002—03; chief transportation 12AF, Davis-Monthan AFB, Ariz., 2003—. Facilitator Dorothy I. Height Leadership Inst., Washington, 1998—2003; trainer Faith Cmtys. Adv. Bd./Ala. Coalition Against Domestic Violence, Montgomery, Ala., 2001—02. Vice chair Nat. Coun. Negro Women, Washington, 1999—2003; judge Shell Oil Excellence in Tchg. Award, 2001; bd. dirs. Brewster Ctr. Domestic Violence Shelter, 2003—; adv. bd. Girls First Inc., 2003—; co-chair Black Youth Vote!, Washington, 2002—; adv. bd. Rap the Vote, 2002. Mem.: Delta Sigma Theta, Inc. Avocations: reading, travel, volunteer work, fencing. Office: 12AF Transportation 2915 S 12th Air Force Dr Davis Monthan AFB AZ 85707 E-mail: ladywoods2003@yahoo.com.

WOODS, STEPHANIE, television producer, reporter; BA in Comm., George Mason U. Prodr. The Insiders with Jack Anderson, Fin. News Network; prodr. CNBC, Ft. Lee, N.J.; sr. prodr., reporter Nightly Bus. Report, Washington. Office: NBR 1325 G St NW Ste 1005 Washington DC 20005-3126

WOODS, SUSANNE, academic administrator, educator; b. Honolulu, Hawaii, May 12, 1943; d. Samuel Ernest and Gertrude (Cullom) W. BA in Polit. Sci., UCLA, 1964, MA in English, 1965; PhD in English and Comparative Lit., Columbia U., 1970; MA (hon.), Brown U., 1978. Institute of Educational Management Harvard U., 1993. Staff Senator Daniel K. Inouye, 1963; asst. editor Rand Corp., Calif., 1963-65; instr. Ventura Coll., Calif., 1965-66; lectr. CUNY, 1967-69; asst. prof. U. Hawaii, 1969-72; asst. prof. English Brown U., Providence, 1972-77, assoc. prof., 1977-83, prof., 1983-93, dir. grad. studies, 1986-88, assoc. dean faculty, 1987-90; v.p., dean Franklin and Marshall Coll., Lancaster, Pa., 1991-95, prof. English, 1991—99; provost, prof. English Wheaton Coll., Norton, Mass., 1999—. Vis. assoc. prof. U. Calif., 1981-82; chair exec. bd. NEH-Brown Women Writers Project, 1988—. Author: Natural Emphasis, 1984; gen. editor: Women Writers in English, 1350-1850, 1992—; editor: The Poetry of Aemilia Lanyer, 1993; contbr. numerous articles to profl. jours. and scholarly books; reviewer for various profl. jours., including Renaissance Quar., Jour. of English and Germanic Philology; reader for PMLA Jour., SEL Jour., also others; editorial bd. Hunting Libr. Quar., 1987-90, Ben Jonson Jour., Duquesne U. Press. Pres. Cultural Coun. of Lancaster County, 1993-95, bd. dirs., 1990-95; bd. dirs. Lancaster Gen. Hosp. Found., 1992-95; active various polit. campaigns, 1960-64, 68-76, 84, 92. Bronson fellow, 1976, Huntington Library, 1979-80, 81, Clark Library, 1981, Huntington-NEH, 1984-85, Woodrow Wilson Found., 1968-70 Mem. Am. Council Edn. (R.I. women's coord. 1988-90), MLA (chmn. div. 17th Century English lit. 1982), N.E. MLA (chmn. English Renaissance sect. 1978, Milton sect. 1983), Am. Assn. Higher Edn., Nat. Women's Studies Assn., Renaissance Soc. Am., Milton Soc. (exec. com. 1987-89), Lyrica Soc. (pres. 1987-90), Alpha Gamma Delta. Democrat. Episcopalian. Episcopalian. Achievements include Founding Director, Brown University Women Writers Project (literary recovery and text encoding). Avocations: music, travel, boating, scuba. Office: Wheaton Coll Office of Provost 26 E Main St Norton MA

WOODS, TIGER (ELDRICK WOODS), professional golfer; b. Cypress, Calif., Dec. 30, 1975; s. Earl and Kultida W. Student, Stanford U. Winner Optimist Internat. Jr. World Championship, 1984, 1985, 1988, 1989, 1990, 1991, Ins. Youth Golf Classic (youngest ever to win), 1990, 1992, second pl., PGA Nat. Jr. Championship, 1990, semi-finalist, U.S. Jr. Amateur Championship, 1990, CIF-So. Calif. H.S. Invitational Championship, 1991, So. Calif. Jr. Championship, 1991, PING/Phoenix Jr. Championship, 1991, 1992, Edgewood Tahoe Jr. Classic, 1991, L.A. City Jr. Championship, 1991, Orange Bowl Jr. Internat. Championship, 1991, U.S. Jr. Amateur Championship (youngest ever to win), 1991, U.S. Jr. Amateur Championship (only golfer to win twice), 1992, U.S. Jr. Amateur Championship, 1993, Nabisco Mission Hills Desert Jr. Championship, 1992, Pro Gear San Antonio Shootout, 1992, So. Calif. Jr. Best Ball Championship, 1993, second pl., Am. Jr. Golf Assn. Taylor Made Woodlands, 1993, U.S. Amateur Championship (youngest ever to win, also largest comeback ever), 1994, U.S. Amateur Championship, 1995, 1996, Western Amateur Championship, 1994, So. Calif. Golf Assn. Amateur Championship, 1994, Pacific Northwest Amateur Championship, 1994, William Tucker Invitational, 1994, Jerry Pate Invitational, 1994, semi-finalist, Calif. State Amateur Championship, 1994, Stanford Invitational, 1995, tied for 41st, Masters Tournament (first profl. maj. championship), 1995, tied for 67th, Brit. Open, 1995, Walt Disney World/Oldsmobile Classic, 1996, Las Vegas Invitational, 1996, NCAA Championship, 1996, John A. Burns Invitational, 1996, Cleve. Golf Championship, 1996, Tri-Match Championship (Stanford U., Ariz. State U., U. Ariz.), 1996, Cougar Classic, 1996, Pac-10 Championship (shot course record 61), 1996, NCAA West Regional, 1996, Masters Tournament, 1997, 2001, 2002, Mercedes Championships, 1997, 2000, Asian Honda Classic, 1997, GTE Byron Nelson Classic, 1997, Motorola Western Open, 1997, 1999, Johnnie Walker Classic, 1998, 2000, BellSouth Classic, 1998, PGA Grand Slam, 1998, 1999, 2000, 2001, 2002, Meml. Tournament, 1999, 2000, 2001, PGA Championship (fifth youngest ever to win), 1999, Buick Invitational, 1999, 2003, Deutsche Bank-SAP Open, 1999, 2001, 2002, WGC NEC Invitational, 1999, 2000, 2001, Nat. Car Rental Classic, 1999, Tour Championship, 1999, WGC Am. Express Championship, 1999, 2002, 2003, World Cup individual and team titles (with Mark O'Meara), 1999, AT&T Pebble Beach Pro-Am, 2000, Bay Hill Invitational, 2000, 2001, 2002, 2003, U.S. Open Championship, 2000, 2002, Brit. Open Championship, 2000, PGA Championship, 2000, Bell Can. Open, 2000, World Cup (with David Duval), 2000, The Players Championship, 2001, Williams World Challenge, 2001, Buick Open, 2002, WGC Accenture Match Play, 2003, Western Open, 2003. Mem. U.S. Team World Amateur Team Championships, Versailles, France, 1994, Walker Cup Match, Porthcawl, Wales, 1995; qualified for U.S. Ryder Cup Team, 97, 99, 2002; qualified for U.S. Presidents Cup Team, 1998, 2000. Named Player of Yr., Am. Jr. Golf Assn., 1991, Golf Digest, 1991, 1992, Golf World, 1993, 1994, L.A. Times, 1994, Orange County, 1994, So. Calif. Player of Yr., 1991, 1992, 1993, Nat. Amateur of Yr., Titleist-Golfweek, 1991, 1992, Orange County League MVP, 1994, Pac-10 Player of Yr., 1995, 1996, First Team All-Am., 1995, 1996, Sportsman of Yr., Sports Illustrated, 1996, 2000, Reuters, 2000, PGA Tour Rookie of Yr., 1996, Fred Haskins Coll. Player of Yr. award, 1996, Jack Nicklaus Coll. Player of Yr., 1996, Male Athlete of Yr., AP, 1997, 1999, Male Athlete of Yr. (with Ken Griffey, Jr.), ESPN, 1997, Male Athlete of Yr., 1999—2001, World Sportsman of Yr., World Sports Acad., 1999, Most Powerful Person in Sports, Sporting News, 2000, World Champion of Champions, L'Equipe, France, 2000; named to First Team Rolex Jr. All Am., 1991, 1992; recipient Dial award, 1993, Jack Nicklaus award, PGA Am., Golf Writers Assn. Am., 1997, 1999—2003, Byron Nelson award, PGA Tour, 1999—2003, Vardon Trophy, PGA of Am., 1999—2003, Mark H. McCormack award as No. 1 player on world ranking, 1999—2003. Achievements include being the youngest player, first African Am., first Asian Am., and having largest margin of victory (12 strokes) to win Masters Tournament, 1997; being first player ever to win U.S. Open, Brit. Open and PGA Championship in same yr. (2000); first player ever to hold all 4 maj. golf championships at the same time, 2001; ranked No. 1 player in world for a record 264 consecutive weeks, 1999-2004. Office: PGA PO Box 109601 100 Avenue Of Champions Palm Beach Gardens FL 33418-3665*

WOODS, WARD WILSON, JR., investment company executive; b. Ann Arbor, Mich., June 27, 1942; m. Priscilla Bacon; children: Katherine, Alexandra. BA, Stanford U., 1964. With constrn. and real estate firm, San Francisco, 1964-66, gen. mgr., 1966-67; with Lehman Bros., N.Y.C., 1967-78, ptnr., 1973-1978; mng. dir. Lehman Bros. Kuhn Loeb Inc., N.Y.C., 1973-78; sr. ptnr. Lazard Freres & Co., N.Y.C., 1978-89; pres., chief exec. officer Bessemer Securities Corp., N.Y.C., 1989-99; mng. ptnr. Bessemer Holdings L.P., N.Y.C., 1989-99. Bd. dirs. Boise Cascade, Contour Energy Co., Bessemer Securities Corp., Stanford Mgmt. Co. Trustee Stanford U. Boys Club of N.Y., Wildlife Conservation Soc.; chmn. Freshwater Initiative; mem. Coun. on Fgn. Rels.; mem. bd. visitors Inst. for Internat. Studies Stanford U. Office: Bessemer Holdings 630 5th Ave New York NY 10111-0100

WOODS, WILLIAM ELLIS, lawyer, pharmacist, association executive; b. Ballinger, Tex., Sept. 25, 1917; s. Cary Dysart and Gertrude Mae (Ellis) W.; m. Martha Brockman, May 28, 1954. BS, U. Tex. Sch. Pharmacy, 1938; JD, Sch. Law, 1953. Bar: Tex. bar 1954, U.S. Supreme Ct 1957. Dir. emergency med. service Tex. State Health Dept., 1942-43, USPHS, 1943-47; asst. dir. Nat. Pharm. Survey Office, 1947-48; with Eli Lilly & Co., 1948-51; first dir. U. Tex. Pharmacy Extension Service, Austin, 1953-54; pvt. practice law Corpus Christi, Tex., 1954-58; asst. to exec. v.p. Nat. Pharm Council, N.Y.C., 1958-64, sec., 1964-65; Washington rep., assoc. gen. counsel Nat. Assn. Retail Druggists, 1965-76, exec. v.p., 1976-84, hon. past pres., 1984. Presenter testimony on health, pharmacy and small bus. before coms. of U.S. Congress and various fed. agys.; mem. Joint Commn. on Pharmacy Practitioners; chmn. Nat. Small Bus. Legis. Coun., 1981; pres. Nat. Drug Trade Conf., 1981; del. U.S. Pharmacopoeial Conv., 1975, 80. Contbr. articles to pharmacy publs. Recipient Achievement Medal award Alpha Zeta Omega, 1975, Lubin Profl. Pharmacy award U. Tenn., 1982; established Wm. E. Woods Endowed Presdl. Scholarship in Elder Law, U. Tex., 1994. Mem. ABA, Tex. Bar Assn., Law Sci. Acad., Phi Delta Phi, U. Tex. Chancellor's Coun., Nat. Assn. Execs., Capitol Hill Club, Can. Club (N.Y.C.). Methodist. Home: 102 Tuxents Branch Ln Fruitland MD 21826-1105

WOODS, WILLIE E. information specialist; CEO, pres. Digital Sys. Internat. Corp., Arlington, Va., 1988—. Office: DSIC 1100 N Glebe Road Arlington VA 22201

WOODSIDE, FRANK C., III, lawyer, educator, physician; b. Glen Ridge, N.J., Apr. 18, 1944; s. Frank C. and Dorothea (Poulin) W.; m. Julia K. Moses, Nov. 15, 1974; children: Patrick Michael, Christopher Ryan. BS, Ohio State U., 1966, JD, 1969; MD, U. Cin., 1973. Diplomate Am. Bd. Legal Medicine, Am. Bd. Forensic Medicine, Am. Bd. Profl. Liability Attys. Mem. Dinsmore & Shohl, Cin.; clin. prof. pediats.emeritus U. Cin., 1992—. Adj. prof. law U. Cin., 1973—. Editor: Drug Product Liability, 1985—. Fellow Am. Coll. Legal Medicine, Am. Coll. Forensic Examiners, Am. Soc. Hosp. Attys., Soc. Ohio Hosp. Attys.; mem. ABA, FBA, Ohio Bar Assn., Internat. Assn. Def. Counsel, Def. Rsch. Inst. (chmn. drug and med. svc. com. 1988-91), Cin. Bar Assn. Office: Dinsmore & Shohl 1900 Chemed Ctr 255 E 5th St Cincinnati OH 45202-4700 Office Phone: 513-977-8266. Business E-Mail: frank.woodside@dinslaw.com.

WOODSIDE, LISA NICOLE, humanities educator; b. Portland, Oreg., Sept. 7, 1944; d. Lee and Emma (Wenstrom) W. Student, Reed Coll., 1962—65; MA, U. Chgo., 1968; PhD, Bryn Mawr Coll., 1972; cert., Harvard U. Inst. Ednl. Mgmt., 1979; MA, West Chester U., 1994. Cert. tchr. ecstatic trance postures Cuyamungue Inst., N.Mex., 2003, wellness counseling, creative energy options. Mem. dean's staff Bryn Mawr Coll., 1970-72; asst. prof. Widener U., Chester, Pa., 1972-77, assoc. prof. humanities, 1978-83, asst. dean student svcs., 1972-76, assoc. dean, 1976-79, dean, 1979-83; acad. dean, prof. humanities Holy Family Coll., Phila., 1983—, v.p., dean acad. affairs, prof. humanities, 1990-98, prof. humanities, 1998—. Cons. State NJ Edn. Dept., 1990, Houghton-Mifflin for English reader, 2000; cons., reader Test of Spoken English Ednl. Testing Svc., 2002—; accreditor Commn. on Higher Edn., Mid. States Assn., 1977—83, 1994. Co-author: New Age Spirituality: An Assessment. City commr. for cmty. rels., Chester, 1980-83; mem. Adult Edn. Coun. Phila. Recipient Crasilneck award for best paper Am. Soc. Clin. Hypnosis; Am. Assn. Papyrology grantee Bryn Mawr Coll., S. Maude Kaemmerling fellow. Mem.: MLA, AAUW (univ. rep. 1975—83), APA, Pa. Coll. Tchrs. Assn., Mid. States Classics Assn., Am. Philol. Assn., Audubon Soc., Psi Chi, Alpha Sigma Lambda, Phi Eta Sigma. Home: 360 Saybrook Ln # A Media PA 19086-6761 Office: Humanities Dept Holy Family Univ Torresdale Philadelphia PA 19114 E-mail: woodside@holyfamily.edu.

WOOD-SMITH, DONALD, plastic surgeon; b. Sydney, Australia, June 30, 1931; s. William Frederick and Vera Mary; children: Christina Margaret, Donald William, Phillip Raynor. MB, BChir, Sydney U., 1954. Diplomate Am. Bd. Plastic Surgery. Surg. resident Lewisham Hosp., Sydney, 1954-56, Royal Marsden Hosp., 1957-58; resident plastic surgery NYU Hosp. Med. Ctr., 1960-64, asst., assoc. and attending surgeon, 1964-92; prof. plastic surgery Columbia Presbyn. Med. Ctr., 1991—. Vis. surgeon Bellevue Hosp., 1964-92, London Ind. Hosp., 1999—; chmn. plastic surgery Manhattan Eye Ear and Throat Hosp., 1975-77; assoc. prof. plastic surgery NYU, 1977-84, prof., 1984-92; surgeon, dir. plastic surgery Manhattan Eye Ear and Throat Hosp., 1977-84; cons. plastic surgeon N.Y. Eye and Ear Infirmary, chmn. dept. plastic and reconstructive surgery, 1984—. Author: Nursing Care of the Plastic Surgery Patient, 1967, Cosmetic Facial Surgery, 1973; contbr. articles to med. jours. Fellow ACS, Royal Coll. Surgeons of Edinburgh; mem. Am. Assn. Plastic Surgeons, Am. Soc. Plastic Surgeons, Am. Soc. Maxillofacial Surgeons, N.Y. Acad. Medicine, Brit. Assn. Plastic Surgeons, N.Y. Athletic Club. Republican. Office: 830 Park Ave New York NY 10021-2757 Office Phone: 212-744-2224. Personal E-mail: dw830@aol.com.

WOODSON, ADRIANNE MARIE, secondary school educator and coordinator; b. Chgo., Sept. 1, 1951; d. Theodore Roosevelt and Adah Mae Hull; m. Rudolph Woodson, June 26, 1976; children: Porsha M., Patrice A., Kellen E., Karley A. BS, Lincoln U., 1973; MS, Ind. U., South Bend, 1981. Lic. sch. adminstr. Spl. edn. tchr. Gary (Ind.) Cmty. Sch. Corp., 1973-76; spl. edn. multi-category tchr. South Bend (Ind.) Cmty. Schs., 1976-77; spl. edn. resource tchr. Sch. City of Hammond, Ind., 1977-86, facilitating tchr., 1986-97, homebound instr., 1997—, spl. edn. coord., 1998—. Student tchr. supr. Purdue U. Calumet, Hammond, summers 1993—, mem. spl. edn. search com.; participant for standardizing nat. diagnostic test W.I.A.T., Westchester, Ind., 1990; presenter at state conf. Coun. for Exceptional Children, Indpls., 1987, 99; spl. edn. dir.'s program Cohort 2000, Bloomington, Ind., 1999-2000. Pres. Jack and Jill Am., Inc.; children's program dir. Delaney United Meth. Ch., pianist. Mem. Ind. Coun. Adminstrs. in Spl. Edn., Lincoln U. Alumni Assn. (sec.-treas.), Sigma Gamma Rho (com. chairperson, Membership award 2000), Delta Kappa Gamma (v.p.). Democrat. Methodist. Avocations: travel, fashion, home and interior decorating, singing, playing the piano. Office: 5727 Sohl Ave Hammond IN 46320-2356 Office Phone: 219-933-1557 336. E-mail: amwoodson@m1.hammond.k12.in.us.

WOODSON, GAYLE ELLEN, otolaryngologist; b. Galveston, Tex., June 9, 1950; d. Clinton Eldon and Nancy Jean (Stephens) W.; m. Kevin Thomas Robbins; children: Nicholas, Gregory, Sarah. BA, Rice U., 1972; MD, Baylor Coll. Medicine, 1975. Diplomate Am. Bd. Otolaryngology (bd. dirs., residency rev. com. for otolaryngology, exam. chair). Fellow Baylor Coll. Medicine, Houston, 1976, Inst. Laryngology & Otology, London, 1981-82; asst. prof. Baylor Coll. Medicine, 1982-87; asst. attending Harris County Hosp. Dist., Houston, 1982-86; with courtesy staff Saint Luke's Episcopal Hosp., Houston, 1982-87; assoc. attending The Methodist Hosp., Houston, 1982-87; asst. prof. U. Calif. Med. Sch., San Diego, 1987-89; chief otolaryngology VA Med. Ctr., San Diego, 1987-92; assoc. prof. U. Calif. Sch. Med., San Diego, 1989-92; prof. otolaryngology U. Tenn., Memphis, 1993—2000, So. Ill. U., 2003—. Numerous presentations and lectures in field. Contbr. numerous articles and abstracts to med. jours., also videotapes. Recipient deRoldes award, Am. Layrngol. Assn., 2003. Fellow ACS (bd. govs.), Royal Coll. Surgeons, Soc. Univ. Otolaryngologists (past pres.), Am. Soc. Head and Neck Surgery, Am. Laryngol. Assn. (historian, de Roaldes award, 2003), Triological Soc.; mem. AMA, Am. Acad. Otolaryngology-Head and Neck Surgery (bd. dirs. 1993-96), Am. Med. Women's Assn. (past pres. Memphis br.), Soc. Head and Neck Oncologists Eng., Am. Physiol. Soc., Assn. Women Surgeons, Am. Soc. Head and Neck Surgeons, Johns Hopkins Soc. Scholars, Collegium OtoRhinolaryngolicum Amicus Sacrum. Office: Southern Illinois Univ PO Box 19662 Springfield IL 62794-9662 Office Phone: 217-545-4777. Business E-Mail: gwoodson@siumed.edu.

WOODSON, HERBERT HORACE, retired electrical engineering educator; b. Stamford, Tex., Apr. 5, 1925; s. Herbert Viven and Floy (Tunnell) W.; m. Blanche Elizabeth Sears, Aug. 17, 1951; children: William Sears, Robert Sears, Bradford Sears. SB, SM, MIT, 1952, ScD in Elec. Engring., 1956. Registered profl. engr., Tex., Mass. Instr. elec. engring., also project leader magnetics divsn. Naval Ordnance Lab., 1952-54; faculty M.I.T., 1956-71, prof. elec. engring., 1965-71, Philip Sporn prof. energy processing, 1967-71; prof. elec. engring., chmn. dept. U. Tex., Austin, 1971-81, Alcoa Found. prof., 1972-75, Tex. Atomic Energy Research Found. prof. engring., 1980-82, Ernest H. Cockrell Centennial prof. engring., 1982-93, dir. Center for Energy Studies, 1973-88, assoc. dean devel. and planning Coll. Engring., 1986-87, acting dean, 1987-88, dean's chair for excellence in engring., 1988—96; ret. Staff engr. elec. engring. div. AEP Service Corp., N.Y.C., 1965-66; cons. in field. Author: (with others) Electromechanical Dynamics, parts I, II, III. With USNR, 1943-46. Recipient Fed. Engr. Yr. award Nat Soc. Profl. Engr., 1990. Fellow IEEE (life, pres. Power Engring. Soc. 1978-80); mem. AAAS, Am. Soc. Engring. Edn., Nat. Acad. Engring. Achievements include patents in field. Home: Apt 144 1034 Liberty Park Dr Austin TX 78746-6876 E-mail: hhwoodson@mail.utexas.edu.

WOODSON, JACQUELINE, writer; b. Columbus, Ohio, Feb. 12, 1964; 1 child. Fellow MacDowell Colony and the Fine Arts Work Ctr., Provincetown, Mass. Author: (book) Last Summer With Maizon, 1990, Martin Luther King Jr., and His Birthday, 1990, The Dear One, 1991, Maizon at Blue Hill, 1992, I Hadn't Meant to Tell You This, 1994, Between Madison and Palmetto, 1995, Autobiography of a Family Photo, 1995, From the Notebooks of Melanin Sun, 1995, A Way Out of No Way, 1996, The House You Pass on the Way, 1997, We Had a Picnic this Past Sunday, 1997, If You Come Softly, 1998, Lena, 1998, Miracle's Boys, 2000, Sweet, Sweet Memory, 2000; (book) The Other Side, 2001; author: (book) Hush, 2002, Our Gracie Aunt, 2002, Visiting Day, 2002, Locomotion, 2003 (Nat. book award nominee, 2003). Recipient Coretta Scott King Honors, 2001, Kenyon Review award for lit. excellence in fiction, 3 Am. Libr. Assn. awards, 2 Jane Adams Peace award honors, 3 Lambda Lit. awards.

WOODSON, LINDA TOWNLEY, English educator, writer; b. Clifton, Tex., Oct. 14, 1943; d. Richmond Alyet and Gena Lee (Wade) Townley; m. James Charles Woodson, Sept. 6, 1963 (div. Dec. 1982); 1 child, Rachel Woodson Garrett; m. Richard Patrick Smith, Mar. 24, 1983. BS in Edn., Tex. Christian U., Fort Worth, 1964, PhD, 1977. Cert. tchr., Tex., Calif. Elem. tchr. Fort Worth Ind. Dist., 1964-65, Austin (Tex.) Ind. Sch. Dist., 1965-67, Fairfield (Calif.)-Suisun Unified Sch., 1969-71; instr. English So. Meth. U., Dallas, 1977-79; asst. prof. English Tex. Tech. U., Lubbock, 1979-81; prof. English U. Tex., San Antonio, 1981—. Author: A Handbook of Modern Rhetorical Terms, 1979, From Cases to Composition, 1982, The Writer's World, 1986; co-author: Writing in Three Dimensions, 1995; co-editor: Modes of Inquiry, 1998. Mem. Nat. Coun. Tchrs. English (commn. on composition 1980-82), Conf. Coll. Composition and Communication (nominating com. 1985, exec. coun. 1995-98), Cormac McCarthy Soc., South Ctrl. MLA. Avocations: reading philosophy, dogs, gardening. Home: 16519 Loma Lndg Helotes TX 78023-3438 Office: U Tex at San Antonio Dept English Classics & Philosophy San Antonio TX 78249 E-mail: lwoodson@utsa.edu.

WOODSON, PORSHA MARIE, speech pathology/audiology services professional; b. Gary, Ind., Apr. 1, 1978; d. Rudolph and Adrianne Marie Woodson. BS, Southern Univ., Baton Rouge, 2001. Ballet dancer Am. Ballet Ctr., Ill., 1993—94, Ballet Legeré, Chgo., 1992—94; ballet instr. Gary Art Wks., Gary, Ind., 2001—, asst. dir., 2003—; speech therapist N.W. Ind. Spl. Edn. Coop., Crown Point, Ind., 2001—. Contbr. articles to profl. jours. Legacy mem. Jack & Jill of Am., Gary, 1979—2001. Scholar Full Dance scholar, State of Mo. Ballet, 1990, Chgo. City Ballet, 1988, Partial Dance scholqr, Munster Acad. Dance, Ind., 1991. Mem.: Sigma Gamma Rho. Methodist. Avocations: painting, music, interior decorating, dance choreography. Home: 4324 Jefferson St Gary IN 46408

WOODSON, STEPHEN WILLIAM, collection agency executive; b. Kansas City, Mo., May 31, 1950; s. William Albert and Patricia Marguerite (May) W. AA, Maple Woods C.C., 1977. Asst. mgr. Pub. Fin., San Pedro, Calif., 1973-74; asst. to v.p. MOAMCO, Mpls., 1974-75; collection cons. Blue Valley Fed. Savs. & Loan, 1975-86; pres. Met. Collection Svcs., Inc., North Kansas City, Mo., 1975-81, Regional Collection Svcs., 1981-84, Transam. Collection Svcs., Kansas City, Mo., 1986—. Collection agency executive; b. Kansas City, Mo., May 31, 1950; s. William Albert and Patricia Marguerite (May) W.; A.A., Maple Woods Community Coll., 1977. Asst. mgr. Pub. Fin., San Pedro, Calif., 1973-74; asst. to v.p. MOAMCO, Mpls., 1974-75; pres. Met. Collection Svcs., Inc., North Kansas City, Mo., 1975-81, Regional Collection Svcs., 1981-84; collection cons. Blue Valley Fed. Savs. & Loan, 1975-86; pres. Transam. Collection Svcs., 1986—; pres. Transam. Credit, 1988—, Trans-Am. Investigations Pvt. Detective Agy., 1996—. Active Big Bros. and Sisters, Kansas City, Mo., 1977—; counselor Mo. Dept. Probation and Parole; pres. Job Readiness, Inc., 1983-86; mem. citizens adv. bd. Kansas City Alliance Bus. Task Force. Served with USN, 1967-70. Recipient Whitehall Found. Scholastic award, 1968. Mem. Internat. Traders Assn., Am. Collectors Assn., Northland C. of C. Republican. Lutheran. Active Big Bros. and Sisters, Kansas City, Mo., 1977—; counselor Mo. Dept. Probation and Parole; pres. Job Readiness, Inc., 1983-86; citizens adv. bd. Kansas City Alliance Bus. Task Force. With USN, 1967-70. Recipient Whitehall Found. Scholastic award, 1968. Mem. Internat. Traders Assn., Am. Collectors Assn., Northland C. of C. Republican. Lutheran. Office: 1920 Swift Ave Ste 203 Kansas City MO 64116-3445 Office Phone: 816-471-2323. Personal E-mail: steve_woodson@yahoo.com.

WOODSON-GLENN, YOLANDA, social worker; b. L.A., July 29, 1958; d. Lewie B. and Clareece Woodson; children: James Glenn, Kimberly Glenn. MA in Counseling Psychology, Bowie State U.; postgrad. Social worker Dept. Children and Family Svcs., Baltimore, MD, 1994-95; victim advocate State's Atty's Office, Annapolis, MD, 1995-96; social worker Children of the Village, Carson, CA, 1997-99, Dept. of Children and Family Svcs., Lakewood, CA, 1999—. Counselor City of Refuge Ch., Compton, Calif., 2000—. Author: Suffering for Righteousness, 2001. Pentecostal. Avocations: cooking, crafts, museums, concerts. Home: 3908 Hathaway Ave # 964 Long Beach CA 90815 Office: 4060 Watson Plaza Dr Lakewood CA 90712

WOODSON-HOWARD, MARLENE ERDLEY, former state legislator; b. Ford City, Pa., Mar. 8, 1937; d. James and Susie (Lettrich) Erdley; m. Francis M. Howard; children: George Woodson, Bert Woodson, Robert Woodson, Daniel Woodson, David Woodson. BS, Ind. U. of Pa., 1958; MA, U. South Fla., 1968; EdD, Nova U., 1981. Prof. math. Manatee Community Coll., 1970-82, dir., Inst. Advancement, 1982-86; exec. dir. Manatee Community Coll. Foundation, 1982-86; pres. Pegasus Enterprises, Inc., 1986—; state senator Fla., 1986-90. Candidate for gov. of Fla., 1990; past pres. New Coll. Libr. Assn.; past pres. Manatee Symphony; bd. dirs. Manatee Red Cross; bd. dirs. Manatee Players, Inc., v.p.; trustee Fla. Kiwanis Found. Mem. Manatee C. of C., Sarasota C. of C., Sarasota Kiwanis (bd. dirs., v.p., pres.). Republican. Roman Catholic. Home: 12 Tidy Island Blvd Bradenton FL 34210-3301 E-mail: marlenewhoward@aol.com.

WOODSWORTH, ANNE, university administrator, librarian; came to U.S., 1983; d. Thorvald Ernst and Roma Yrsa Lindner; 1 child, Yrsa Anne. BFA, U. Man., Can., 1962; BLS, U. Toronto, Ont., Can., 1964, MLS, 1969; PhD, U. Pitts., 1987. Edn. libr. U. Man., 1964—65; reference libr. Winnipeg Pub. Libr., 1965—67; reference libr. sci. and medicine dept. U. Toronto, 1967—68; med. libr. Toronto We. Hosp., 1969—70; rsch. asst. to chief libr. U. Toronto, 1970—71, head reference dept., 1971—74; pers. dir. Toronto Pub. Libr., 1975—78; dir. librs. York U., Toronto, 1978—83; assoc. provost for librs. U. Pitts., 1983—88, assoc. prof., 1988—91; dean Palmer Sch. Libr. and Info. Sci., L.I. U., 1991—98; dean Sch. Edn. Dowling Coll., Oakdale, NY, 1999—2000; dean sch. info. and libr. sci. Pratt Inst., Bklyn., 2000—02, acting provost, 2002—03; provost Katharine Gibbs Sch., Melville, NY, 2003; learning sys. advisor Bklyn. Pub. Libr., 2004, 2004—. Pres. Anne Lindner Ltd., 1974-83; rsch. libraries adv. coun. OCLC, 1984-87. Author: The Alternative Press in Canada, 1972, Leadership and Research Libraries, 1988, Patterns and Options for Managing Information Technology on Campus, 1990, Library Cooperation and Networks, 1991, Managing the Economics of Leasing and Contracting Out Information Services, 1993, Reinvesting in the Information Job Family, 1993, The Future of Education for Librarianship: Looking Forward from the Past, 1994. Sec., mem. bd. trustees Katharine Gibbs Sch., L.I., 2003-; dir. Sr. Fellows Inst., 1995-98; trustee L.I. Librs. Resources Coun., 1993-96; bd. dirs. Population Rsch. Found., Toronto, 1980-83. Grantee Can. Coun., 1974, Ont. Arts Coun., 1974, Coun. on Libr. Resources, 1986, 88, 91, 93; UCLA sr. fellow, 1985. Mem. ALA (com. on accreditation 1990-94, councillor 1993-97), Can. Assn. Rsch. Librs. (pres. 1981-83), Assn. Rsch. Librs. (bd. dirs. 1981-84, v.p. 1984-85, pres. 1985-86), Assn. Coll. and Rsch. Librs. (chair K.G. Saur award com. 1991-93), Assn. for Libr. and Info. Sci. Edn. (chair honors and awards com. 1995, bd. dirs. 1998-99, v.p. 1998-99), Am. Soc. Higher Edn., Internet Soc., Am. Soc. Info. Sci. (convenor 1999-2000), Archons of Colophon. Office Phone: 718-230-2003.

WOODWARD, CLIFFORD EDWARD, chemical engineer; b. Richmond, Va, Jan. 17, 1941; s. Clifford Rawlings and Myrtis (Wilson) W.; m. Katherine Roberts, June 1, 1967; children: Ted, Robert, Christopher, John. BSChemE, Va. Poly. Inst. and State U., 1962, MS in Nuclear Sci. and Engr., 1963; MSChemE, U. Houston, 1975. Registered profl. engr., Tex. Devel. engr. Olin Corp., 1963-65; supervising engr. Monsanto Co., 1965-72; lead engr. Brown & Root Inc., Houston, 1972-74; process mgr. Kvaerner Process Inc., Houston, 1974-77, 1979-81, process dir., 1983-88, process mgr., 1992—2000; prin. engr. Jacobs Engring. Group, Inc., Houston, 1977-79; process mgr. M.W. Kellogg, Amsterdam, N.C., 1981-83, sr. engr. mgr. Houston, 1988-89; process dept. mgr. BE&K, Houston, 1989-92; pres. Protective Environ. Engring. Svcs. Inc., Houston, 2000—. Mem. planning comm. City of Alvin, Tex., 1970-72; founder Cypress Creek Emergency Med. Svc. Assn., 1975; pres. Klein (Tex.) Sch. Bd., 1979-90. Mem. AIChE, Engrs. Coun. of Houston (v.p., sec. 1991). Achievements include electrodeposition of polymers from latex solutions and surface kinetics and direct contact heat transfer. Home: 4114 Oxhill Rd Spring TX 77388-9705 E-mail: cwoodward@peesiengineering.com.

WOODWARD, GRETA CHARMAINE, construction company executive, rental and investment property manager; b. Congress, Ohio, Oct. 28, 1930; d. Richard Thomas and Grace Lucetta (Palmer) Duffey; m. John Jay Woodward, Oct. 29, 1949; children: Kirk Jay, Brad Ewing, Clay William. Bookkeeper Kaufman's Texaco, Wooster, Ohio, 1948-49; office mgr. Holland Furnace Co., Wooster, 1948-49; acctg. clk. Columbus and So. Ohio Electric, 1949-50; interviewer, clk. State Ohio Bur. Employment Services, Columbus, 1950-51; clk. Def. Constrn. Supply Ctr. (U.S. Govt.) (formerly Columbus Gen. Depot), 1951-52; treas. Woodward Co., Inc., Reynoldsburg, Ohio, 1963—. Newspaper columnist Briarcliff News, 1960-63. Active Reynoldsburg PTA, 1960-67; Reynoldsburg United Meth. Ch.; mem. women's service bd. Grant Hosp. Avocations: bike riding, crocheting, writing poetry, water aerobics. Office: Woodward Excavating Co Inc 7340 Tussing Rd Reynoldsburg OH 43068-4111

WOODWARD, JAMES HOYT, academic administrator, engineer; b. Sanford, Fla., Nov. 24, 1939; s. James Hoyt and Edith Pearl (Breeden) W.; m. Martha Ruth Hill, Oct. 13, 1956; children: Connie, Tracey, Wade. BS in Aero. Engring. with honors, Ga. Tech. Inst., 1962, MS in Aero. Engring., 1963, PhD in Engring. Mechanics, 1967; MBA, U. Ala.-Birmingham, 1973. Asst. prof. engring. mechanics USAF Acad., Colo., 1965-67, assoc. prof., 1967-68; asst. prof. engring. mechanics N.C. State U., 1968-69; assoc. prof. engring. U. Ala., Birmingham, 1969-70, assoc. prof., 1973-77, prof. civil engring., 1977-89, asst. v.p., 1973-78, dean engring., 1978-84, acad. v.p., 1984-89; chancellor U. N.C., Charlotte, 1989—. Dir. tech. devel. Rust Engring. Co., Birmingham, 1970-73; cons. in field. Contbr. articles to profl. jours. With USAF, 1965-68. Mem. ASME, Am. Soc. Engring. Edn., Am. Mgmt. Assn., Sigma Xi. Methodist. Office: U NC Charlotte Office of Chancellor 9201 University City Blvd Charlotte NC 28223-0002

WOODWARD, JAMES KENNETH, retired pharmacologist; b. Anderson, Mo., Feb. 5, 1938; s. Audley J. and Doris Evelyn (Fields) W.; m. Kathleen Ruth Winget, June 25, 1960 (div. Nov. 1994); children: Audley J., Kimie Connette; m. Lisa Marie Stuart, Feb. 28, 1996. AB in Chemistry, S.W. Mo. State Coll., BS in Biology, 1960; postgrad., U. Kans. (USPHS fellow), 1960-62; PhD (USPHS fellow), U. Pa. Sch. Medicine, 1967. Pharmacologist Stine Lab., Newark, Del., 1963-65, rsch. pharmacologist, 1967-71; sr. rsch. pharmacologist Merrell-Nat. Labs., Cin., 1972-73, sect. head, 1973-74, head dept. pharmacology, 1974-78; head dept. pre-clin. pharmacology Merrell Rsch. Ctr. Merrell Dow Pharms., Inc., 1978-83; assoc. dir. research adminstrn. Merrell Dow Rsch. Inst., 1983-88, dir. biol. devel., 1988-90, dir. int. reg. affairs, 1990-93; dir. clin. cand. prep. Marion Merrell Dow, 1993; ret., 1993; cons., 1993. Patentee in field. Pres. Golf Manor Recreation Commn., Cin., 1973-75. USPHS post-doctoral fellow U. Pa., 1967. Mem. AAAS, Phila. Physiol. Soc. Democrat. Baptist. Home: 972 Sheridan Dr Lancaster OH 43130-1923 Personal E-mail: lisadocwoodward@aol.com.

WOODWARD, JOANNE GIGNILLIAT, actress; b. Thomasville, Ga., Feb. 27, 1930; d. Wade and Elinor (Trimmier) W.; m. Paul Newman, Jan. 29, 1958; children: Elinor Terese, Melissa Stewart, Clea Olivia. Student, La. State U., 1947-49; grad., Neighborhood Playhouse Dramatic Sch., N.Y.C. First TV appearance in Penny, Robert Montgomery Presents, 1952; understudy broadway play Picnic, 1953; appeared in plays Baby Want a Kiss, 1964, Candida, 1982, The Glass Menagerie, Williamstown Theatré Festival, 1985, Sweet Bird of Youth, Toronto, 1988; motion pictures include Three Faces of Eve, 1957 (Acad. award Best Actress, Nat. Bd. Rev. award, Fgn. Press award), Count Three and Pray, 1955, Long Hot Summer, 1958, No Down Payment, 1957, Sound and the Fury, 1959, A Kiss Before Dying, 1956, Rally Round the Flag Boys, 1958, The Fugitive Kind, 1960, Paris Blues, 1961, The Stripper, 1963, A New Kind of Love, 1963, A Big Hand for the Little Lady, 1965, A Fine Madness, 1965, Rachel, Rachel, 1968, Winning, 1969, WUSA, 1970, They Might Be Giants, 1971, The Effect of Gamma Rays on Man-in-the-Moon Marigolds, 1972 (Cannes Film Festival award), Summer Wishes, Winter Dreams, 1973 (N.Y. Film Critics award), The Drowning Pool, 1975, The End, 1978, Harry and Son, 1984, Glass Menagerie, 1987, Mr. & Mrs. Bridge, 1990, Philadelphia, 1993, The Age of Innocence (voice), 1993, My Knees Were Jumping: Remembering the Kindertransports, (voice) 1998; TV appearances include All the Way Home; TV-film appearances in Sybil, 1976, Come Back, Little Sheba, 1977, See How She Runs, 1978 (Emmy award), Streets of L.A., 1979, The Shadow Box, 1980, Crisis at Central High, 1981, Do You Remember Love?, 1985 (Emmy award), Blind Spot, 1993 (Emmy nomination, Lead Actress - Miniseries, 1993), Breathing Lessons, 1994 (Emmy nomination, Lead Actress - Special, 1994, Golden Globe award, Best Actress), James Dean: A Portrait, 1996; narrator film documentary Angel Dust, TV documentary on Group Theatre, 1989. Co-recipient (with Paul Newman) Kennedy Ctr. Honors for Lifetime Achievement in the Performing Arts. Democrat. Episcopalian. Office: ICM 40 W 57th St Fl 16 New York NY 10019-4098*

WOODWARD, JOHN SIMPSON, JR., orthopedic surgeon; b. San Pedro, Calif. s. John Simpson and Frances Louisa Woodward; m. Kristin T. Woodward, June 8, 1996. BS magna cum laude, UCLA, 1992; MD, Tufts U., 1996. Diplomate Am. Bd. Orthopaedic Surgeons. Intern Maricopa Med. Ctr., Phoenix, 1996—97; resident Phoenix Orthop. Residency, Phoenix, 1996—2001; orthop. surgeon Orthop. Physicians of Colo., Englewood, 2001—. Instr. AO/ASIF, Denver, 2001—02, Denver, 2003. Contbr. articles to profl. jours. Recipient Howard P. Aidem Meml. award, Ariz. Orthop. Soc., 1998. Mem.: AMA, Arapahoe Med. Soc., Colo. Med. Soc., UCLA Alumni Assn. (scholarship 1988), Golden Key Nat. Honor Soc., Phi Beta Kappa. Republican. Avocations: basketball, mountain biking, teaching. Office: Orthopaedic Physicians Colo 799 E Hampden Ste 400 Englewood CO 80110

WOODWARD, JONATHAN MORGAN, mental health specialist; b. Vancouver, Wash., Dec. 18, 1955; s. Jessie Charles and Catherine (Agustus) W.; children: Shane, Joshua, Christopher, Miranda, Jacob. MBA, Oxford (Eng.) U., 1983; D in Naturopathy, LaSalle U., Mandeville, La., 1994. Lic. cert. counselor, Wash. CEO Rivercrest Health Care, Inc., Vancouver, Wash., 1986-94; owner, mgr. N.W. Counseling Ctr., Vancouver, Wash., 1994—. Keynote spkr. Drug Free Am., Washington; counselor Conf. on Excellence in Edn.; legis. chmn. Chem. Dep. Profl. Wash. Author: Instructions Not Included, 1999, 2001. Bd. dirs. Franklin House. Recipient Cert. Appreciation White House Conf. on Drug Free Am.; named Outstanding Vol. Dept. Social and Health Svcs. Mem. U.S. C. of C., Charles F. Menninger Soc., CDP Washington, NAADAC. Republican. Episcopalian. Office: Ste 300 8000 NE Parkway Dr Vancouver WA 98662-6737 E-mail: drjmw98@aol.com.

WOODWARD, KENNETH EMERSON, retired mechanical engineer; b. Washington, Oct. 30, 1927; s. George Washington and Mary Josephine (Compton) W.; m. Mary Margaret Eungard, Mar. 29, 1956; children: Stephen Mark, Kristi Lynn. BME, George Washington U., 1949, M Engring. Adminstrn., 1960; MS, U. Md., 1953; PhD, Am. U., 1973. Mech. engr. Naval Rsch. Lab., Washington, 1950-54; supr. med. engring. program, chief engring. support branch, chief reliability and assessment, value engring. program mgr. Harry Diamond Labs., Washington, 1955-74; sci. adviser U.S. Army Med. Bioengring. R & D Lab., Ft. Detrick, Md., 1974-75; mech. engr. Woolcott & Co., Washington, 1975-90; ret., 1990. Author: Solar Energy Applications for the Home, 1978; contbr. over 40 articles to profl. publs. With U.S. Army, 1946-47. Recipient Dept. of the Army Decoration for Exceptional Civilian Svc., Honors Achievement award Angiology Rsch. Found., Purdue Frederick Co., Engring. Alumni Achievement award George Washington U., Washington, 1987. Mem. ASME, Am. Soc. for Artificial Internal Organs. Republican. Baptist. Achievements include 12 U.S. and 2 foreign patents, development of artifical human heart. Home: 1701 Hunts End Ct Vienna VA 22182-1833

WOODWARD, LESTER RAY, lawyer; b. Lincoln, Nebr., May 24, 1932; s. Wendell Smith and Mary Elizabeth (Theobald) W.; m. Marianne Martinson, Dec. 27, 1958; children: Victoria L. Woodward Eisele, Richard T., David M., Andrew E. BSBA, U. Nebr., 1953; LLB, Harvard U., 1957; LLD (hon.), Bethany Coll., 1974. Bar: Colo., 1957. Assoc. Davis, Graham & Stubbs, Denver, 1957-59, 60-62, ptnr., 1962—. Teaching fellow Sch. Law Harvard U., 1959-60. Bd. dirs. Bethany Coll., Lindsborg, Kans., 1966-74, 87-95, chmn., 1989-92; bd. dirs. Pub. Edn. Coalition, Denver, 1985-92, chmn., 1988-89; mem. Colo. Commn. Higher Edn., Denver, 1977-86, chmn., 1979-81; mem. bd. edn. Denver Pub. Schs., 1999—, pres., 2003—. Mem. ABA, Colo. Bar Assn., Am. Law Inst. Republican. Lutheran. Home: 680 Bellaire St Denver CO 80220-4935 Office: Davis Graham & Stubbs 1150 17th St Ste 500 Denver CO 80202-5682

WOODWARD, RALPH FREDERICK, JR., elementary school educator, consultant, education educator; b. Nouméa, New Caledonia, South Pacific, July 6, 1944; arrived in U.S., 1945; s. Ralph Frederick and Monique Madline Woodward; m. Sandy Ann Wylie, Oct. 24, 1970. BA, San José U., 1970; MS, U. So. Calif., LA, 1983; PhD, Iowa State U., 1994. Elem. tchr. Dept. Def. Dependent's Schs., Milpitas, CA, Germany, 1971—84, sch. counselor, 1984—88, sch. improvement, 1989—91, sch. adminstr., 1991—92; curriculum dir. Gilbert Sch. Dist., Iowa, 1994—96; co-dir. Ackerman Lab Sch., Eastern Oreg. U., La Grande, 1995—96; title I coord. La Grande Sch. Dist., Oreg., 1996—98. Adv. bd. to state superintendent Oreg. State, Salem, 1995—. Sargent Army, Paratroops U.S. Army, 1963—66, Dominican Republic. Mem.: ASCD (recognition svc. 2002), First Book (treas. 1998—, appreciation award 2002), Cmty. Forestry Commn. (civic award 2000), Phi Kappa Phi. Avocations: cooking, skiing, hiking, bicycling, woodworking. Office: Eastern Oreg Univ 1 University Blvd La Grande OR 97850

WOODWARD, RALPH LEE, JR., historian, educator; b. New London, Conn., Dec. 2, 1934; s. Ralph Lee and Beulah Mae (Suter) W.; m. Sue Dawn McGrady, Dec. 30, 1958; children: Mark Lee, Laura Lynn, Matthew McGrady; m. Janice Chatelain, Aug. 8, 1996. AB cum laude, Central Coll., Mo., 1955; MA, Tulane U., 1959, PhD, 1962. Asst. prof. history Wichita (Kans.) U., 1961-62, U. S.W. La., Lafayette, 1962-63; asst. prof. history U. N.C., Chapel Hill, 1963-67, asso. prof., 1967-70; prof. history Tulane U., New Orleans, 1970-99, head dept. history, 1973-75, chmn. dept. history, 1986-88; dir. Tulane Summer in C. Am., 1975-78; prof. in charge Tulane Jr. Year Abroad, Paris, 1975-76; Penrose prof. L.Am. studies Tex. Christian U., Ft. Worth, 1999—2003; ret., 2003. Fulbright lectr. U. Chile, U. Catolica de Valparaiso, Chile, 1965-66, U. del Salvador, Universidad Nacional, Buenos Aires, 1968; vis. prof. U.S. Mil. Acad., West Point, N.Y., 1989; regional liaison officer Emergency Com. to Aid Latin Am. Scholars, 1974. Author: Class Privilege and Economic Development, 1966, Robinson Crusoe's Island, 1969, Positivism in Latin America, 1850-1900, 1971, Central America: A Nation Divided, 1976, 3d edit., 1999, Tribute to Don Bernardo de Galvez, 1979, Belize, 1980, Nicaragua, 1983, 2d edit., 1994, El Salvador, 1988, Guatemala, 1992, Rafael Carrera and the Emergence of the Republic of Guatemala, 1993 (Alfred B. Thomas Book award); editor: Central America: Historical Perspectives on the Contemporary Crises, 1988, Here and There in Mexico: The Travel Writings of Mary Ashley Townsend, 2001; assoc. editor: Revista del Pensamiento Centroamericano, 1975, Research Guide to Central America and the Caribbean, 1985, Encyclopedia of Latin American History and Culture, 1996; contbg. editor: Handbook of Latin American Studies, 1987-90; series editor: World Bibliographical Series, 1987-2000; contbr. articles to profl. jours. Capt. USMC, 1955-58. Recipient Alfred B. Thomas Book award Southeastern Coun. Latin Am. Studies, 1994; Henry L. and Grace Doherty Found. fellow Tulane U., 1962; named La. Humanist of Yr. La. Endowment for Humanities, 1995, Disting. Svc. award, Conf. Latin Am. History, 2002. Mem. Am. Hist. Assn. (mem. Conf. L.Am. History, pres. 1989, mem. gen. com. 1974-76, Disting. Svc. award 2002), Southeastern Conf. L.Am. Studies (program chmn. 1975, pres. 1975-76), L.Am. Studies Assn., Com. on Andean Studies (chmn. 1972-73), Geography and History Acad. Guatemala. Home: 206 Boardman Ave Bay Saint Louis MS 39520 E-mail: clioclio@bellsouth.net.

WOODWARD, ROBERT SIMPSON, IV, economics professor; b. Easton, Pa., May 7, 1943; s. Robert Simpson and Esther Evans (Thomas) W.; m. Mary P. Hutton, Feb. 15, 1969; children: Christopher Thomas, Rebecca Marie. BA, Haverford Coll., 1965; PhD, Washington U., St. Louis, 1972. Econ. policy fellow HEW, Washington, 1975-76; asst. prof. U. Western Ont., London, Can., 1972-77; asst. prof. Sch. Medicine Washington U., St. Louis, 1978-86, assoc. prof., 1986-2001; McKerley prof. health econ. U. N.H., Durham, 2001—. Pres. Writing Assessment Software, Inc., 1987-91. Contbr. articles to profl. jours. Mem. adv. coun. Mo. Kidney Program, 1980-86, vice-chmn., 1983, chmn., 1984-85; coop. mem. Haverford Coll., 1968-90. NDEA fellow, 1968-71, Kellogg Nat. fellow, 1981-84. Mem. Am. Econs. Assn., Am. Statis. Assn. Home: 131 Wednesday Hill Rd Lee NH 03824-6546 Office: U NH Dept Health Mgmt and Policy Hewitt Hall Durham NH 03824-3563 Business E-Mail: rsw@unh.edu.

WOODWARD, ROBERT UPSHUR, newspaper reporter, writer; b. Geneva, Ill., Mar. 26, 1943; s. Alfred E. and Jane (Upshur) W.; m. Elsa Walsh, Nov. 25, 1989; children: Tali, Diana. BA, Yale U., 1965. Reporter Montgomery County (Md.) Sentinel, 1970-71; reporter Washington Post, 1971-78, met. editor, 1979-81, asst. mng. editor, 1981—. Author: (with Carl Bernstein) All the President's Men, 1974, The Final Days, 1976, (with Scott Armstrong) The Brethren, 1979, Wired, 1984, Veil: The Secret Wars of the CIA, 1987, The Commanders, 1991, (with David S. Broder) The Man Who Would Be President, 1991, The Agenda: Inside the Clinton White House, 1994, The Choice, 1996, Shadow: Five Presidents and the Legacy of Watergate, 1999, Maestro, Greenspan's Fed and the American Boom, 2000, Bush At War, 2002, Plan of Attack, 2004. Served with USN, 1965-70. Office: Washington Post Co 1150 15th St NW Washington DC 20071-0002

WOODWARD, STEPHEN RICHARD, newspaper reporter; b. Fukuoka City, Japan, July 27, 1953; came to U.S., 1954; s. Leonard Edwin and Etsuko (Okumura) W.; m. Sandra Elizabeth Richardson, Dec. 31, 1979; children: Daniel Joseph, Elizabeth Etsuko. BA in English, Wright State U., 1975; MA in Journalism, U. Mo., 1979. Advt. coordinator Wright State U., Dayton, Ohio, 1976-77; reporter Kansas City (Mo.) Star, 1979-82; assoc. editor then editor Kansas City Bus. Jour., 1982-83; editor then gen. mgr. Portland (Oreg.) Bus. Jour., 1984-86; exec. bus. editor The Hartford (Conn.) Courant, 1986-87; editor San Francisco Bus. Times, 1987-88; bus. editor The Oregonian, Portland, 1989-93, reporter, 1993—. Recipient 1st Place Investigative Reporting award Assn. Area Bus. Publs., 1983, 1st Place Column Writing award Assn. Area Bus. Publs., 1985. Mem. Investigative Reporters and Editors Inc. Avocations: astronomy, chess, creative writing. Office: The Oregonian 1320 SW Broadway Portland OR 97201-3499

WOODWARD, THEODORE ENGLAR, retired medical educator, internist; b. Westminster, Md., Mar. 22, 1914; s. Lewis Klair and Phoebe Helen (Neidig) Woodward; m. Celeste Constance Lauve Woodward, June 24, 1938; children: William E., R. Craig, Celeste L. Woodward Applefeld, Lewis O.(dec.). BS, Franklin and Marshall Coll., 1934, DSc (hon.), 1954; MD, U. Md., 1938; DSc (hon.), Western Md. Coll., 1950, Hahnemann U., 1993. Diplomate Am. Bd. Internal Medicine. Asst. prof. medicine U. Md. Sch. Medicine, Balt., 1946—48, assoc. prof., also dir. sect. infectious disease, 1948—54, prof., 1954—83, prof. emeritus, 1983—, chmn. dept., 1954—81; attending physician Balt. VA Med Ctr., 1949—. With Armed Forces Epidemiol. Bd., Washington, 1952—92, mem. commns., 1952—72, pres. bd., 1976—78, Washington, 1980—92; mem. U.S./Japan Coop. Med. Sci. Program, Washington, 1965—95, emeritus, 1995—; disting. physician Cen. VA, Washington, 1981—87. Author: Chloramphemicol, 1958, 200 Years of Medicine in Baltimore, 1976, A History of the Department of Medicine, University of Maryland, 1807-1981, 1987, A History of Armed Forces Epidemiological Board, 1940-1990, 1990, Carroll County (Md.) Physicians of the 19th and Early 20th Centuries, 1990, The Armed Forces Epidemiological Board: The History of the Commissions, 1995, Make Room for Sentiment: A Physician's Story, 1998, Research on Infectious Diseases at the University of Maryland School of Medicine and Hospital. A Global Experience: 1807-2000, 2000; contbr. chpts. to textbooks. Life trustee Gilman Sch., Balt., 1955—. Lt. col. Medical Svc. Corp U.S. Army, 1941—46, ETO, PTO. Decorated Order of the Sacred Treasure Gold and Silver Star Govt. of Japan; named Student Coun. Faculty awardee of Yr., U. Md., 1966, 1972, 1974—78, 1981—93, 1985—89, 1991, 1993—96, 1998, 2000; recipient U.S.A. Typhus Commn. medal, Dept. Def., 1945, Exceptionally Disting. Svc. award, 1990, Outstanding Civilian Svc. medal with oak leaf cluster, Dept. Army, 1981, Louis Pasteur medal, Inst. Pasteur, 1961, Disting. Svc. award, AMA, 1995. Master: ACP (gov. Md. regent 1969—70, James D. Bruce Meml. award 1970, Disting. Tchr. award 1992); mem.: Inst. Medicine NAS, Infectious Disease Soc. Am. (pres. 1976—77, Finland award 1972, Bristol award, Kass award 1991), Am. Clin. and Climatol. Assn. (pres. 1969—70), Mayo Fellows Assn. (hon.), Hamilton St. Club, Elkridge Club (Towson, Md.). Republican. Avocations: photography, gardening, raising wild fowl. Home: 1 Merrymount Rd Baltimore MD 21210-1908 Office: Balt VA Med Ctr 10 N Green St Baltimore MD 21210

WOODWARD, THOMAS MORGAN, actor; b. Ft. Worth, Sept. 16, 1925; s. Valin Ridge and Francis Louise (McKinley) W.; m. Enid Anne Loftis, Nov. 18, 1950; 1 child, Enid Anne. AA, Arlington State Coll., 1948; BBA, U. Tex., 1951. Motion picture and TV actor, 1955—; numerous TV appearances include Dallas; motion pictures include The Great Locomotive Chase, 1955, Slaughter on 10th Ave., 1957, The Gun Hawk, 1962, Cool Hand Luke, 1966,

The Wild Country, 1973, Which Way Is Up, 1977, Speed Trap, 1978, Battle Beyond the Stars, 1980, Girls Just Want to Have Fun, 1985, Dark Before Dawn, 1987, Gunsmoke III, 1991. With USAAF, 1944-45; to capt. USAF, 1951-53. Recipient Golden Boot award Motion Picture and TV Fund, 1988, Golden Lariat award Nat. Western Film Festival, 1988, Lifetime Achievement award in the arts Arlington Tex. Arts Coun., 1994, Lifetime Achievement award for western film acting Wild West Film Festival, 1995, Internat. Star award 1997; named Disting. Alumnus of Arts U. Tex., 1969; inducted into the Walk of Western Stars William S. Hart Mus., L.A., 1990. Mem. Acad. Motion Picture Arts and Scis., SAR, Pi Kappa Alpha (Disting. Achievement award 1981, inducted into Order of West Range 1988). Office Phone: 323-876-7877.

WOODWARD, WILLIAM LEE, retired savings bank executive; b. Lexington, Ky., Jan. 12, 1926; s. Joel Henry and Ophelia Martha (Wallace) W.; m. Dorothy J. Dekle, Dec. 31, 1949; children: Pamela, William Lee, Martha. AB, U. Ky., 1950, MA, 1952. Tchr. Lafayette H.S., 1950-52; asst. prin. Ft. Benning (Ga.) Children's Schs., 1952-53; asst. mgr. Lexington Fed. Savs. & Loan Assn., 1953-54, exec. v.p., 1954-73, pres., 1973-96. Pres. Lexington Deaf Oral Sch., 1968; trustee Midway (Ky.) Coll., 1968-80; treas. Bluegrass Found., 1967-95; bd. dirs. Ky. Housing Corp., 1979-80. Served with USN, 1944-46. Mem. Ky. Savs. and Loan League (pres. 1969) Rotary. Mem. Christian Ch.

WOOD-WARREN, MAXINE, artist, art educator; b. Ponca City, Oklahoma, Jan. 14, 1927; d. William Roy and Helen Enrica (Huffer) Wood; m. William Guy Warren, Jr., June 1, 1949; one child, Alison. BFA, Okla. State U., 1948, MS, 1971; student, Santa Fe Inst. Fine Arts, 1986, student, 1992. Art tchr. McKinley Elem. Sch., Ponca City, Okla., 1950, 1956—60; dir., initiator Pk. Bldg. Contemporary Art Gallery Conoco, Inc., Ponca City, Okla., 1962—65; art tchr. Trout Elem., Ponca City, Okla., 1967—70; chmn. art dept. Ponca City Sr. H.S., Okla., 1797—1986; studio artist paintings and monotypes Riverbluff Studio, Ponca City, 1986—. Artist cons. Native Am. Found., Chief Standing Bear, Ponca City, Okla., 1994—; mem. art faculty Arts Adventure, Ponca City, 1993, 94; bd. dir. Okla. Visual Arts Coalition, Oklahoma City, 1992-2001, Arts Place, Ponca City, 2003; initiator artists survival kit, 1998—, Charter bd. dir., Arts Place, Ponca City, 2003, chmn. visual arts Marland Estate Commn., Ponca City, 1976-79, initiator Artists in Residence,1976. Represented in permanent collections Okla. Contemporary Art Mus., Oklahoma City, 1969, Philbrook Art Mus., Tulsa (honorable mention 1948, 66, 68). Recipient 2d prize Internat. Am. Greetings, 5th prize Internat. Ford Times Mag., 1963, 2d prize Internat. Golden Press Book Illustration, 1962. Mem. Individual Artists Okla.(I.O.A.), O.U.A.C., Tulsa Artists Coalition (T.A.C.) Ponca City Art Assn., Okla. Edn. Assn., Okla. Retired Educators Assn., Living Artists Soc., Nat. Mus. Women in Arts, Okla. Art Inst., Ind. Artists Okla., Tulsa Artists Coalition, Zeta Tau Alpha. Republican. Avocations: discussion group, books, dogs. Studio: 7182 River Ridge Dr Ponca City OK 74604-9103

WOODWELL, GEORGE MASTERS, ecology research director, lecturer; b. Cambridge, Mass., Oct. 23, 1928; s. Philip McIntire and Virginia (Sellers) W.; m. Alice Katharine Rondthaler, June 23, 1955; children: Caroline Alice, Marjorie Virginia, Jane Katharine, John Christopher. AB, Dartmouth Coll., 1950; AM, Duke U., 1956, PhD, 1958; DSc (hon.), Williams Coll., 1977, Miami U., 1984, Carleton Coll., 1988, Muhlenberg Coll., 1990, Duke U., 1994, Dartmouth Coll., 1996. Mem. faculty U. Maine, 1957-61, assoc. prof. botany, 1960-61; vis. asst. ecologist, biology dept. Brookhaven Nat. Lab., Upton, N.Y., 1961-62, ecologist, 1965-67, sr. ecologist, 1967-75; founder, dir. Ecosystems Center, 1975-85; dep. and asst. dir. Marine Biol. Lab., Woods Hole, Mass., 1975-76; founder, pres. and dir. Woods Hole Research Ctr., 1985—. Founder, chmn. Conf. on Long Term Biol. Consequences of Nuclear War, 1982-83; bd. trustees Inst. Rsch. on Amazon Bason, Belem, Brazil, 1995—. Editor: Ecological Effects of Nuclear War, 1965, Diversity and Stability in Ecological Systems, 1969, (with E.V. Pecan) Carbon and the Biosphere, 1973, The Role of Terrestrial Vegetation in the Global Carbon Cycle: Measurement by Remote Sensing, 1984, The Earth in Transition: Patterns and Processes of Biotic Impoverishment, 1990, (with K. Ramakrishna) Forests for the Future, 1993, (with F.T. Mackenzie) Biotic Feedbacks in the Warming of the Earth, 1995. Founding trustee Environ. Def. Fund, 1967, Natural Resources Def. Coun., 1970, vice chmn., 1974—, World Resources Inst., 1982-96; bd. dirs. Conservation Found., 1975-77, Ctr. for Marine Conservation, 1990-98, World Wildlife Fund, 1970-84, chmn., 1980-84, Ruth Mott Fund, 1984-91, chmn., 1989-91; bd. trustees Inst. Environ. Rsch. in Amazon, 1996—; adv. com. TMI Pub. Health Fund, 1980-94. Recipient Joseph Priestley award Dickinson Coll., 1993, Hutchinson medal Garden Club of Am., 1993, Disting. Svc. award Am. Inst. Biol. Scis., 1982, Heinz Environ. prize, 1996. Fellow AAAS, Am. Acad. Arts and Scis.; mem. NAS, Brit. Ecol. Soc., Ecol. Soc. Am. (v.p. 1966-67, pres. 1977-78), Sea Edn. Assn. (bd. dirs. 1980-85), World Comm. on Forests and Sustainable Development, 1994-98, Sigma Xi. Achievements include rsch., pub. on structure and function of natural communities, biotic impoverishment, especially ecological effects of ionizing radiation, effects of persistent toxins, world carbon cycle and warming of the earth, sci. and internat. environ. affairs. Office: Woods Hole Research Ctr PO Box 296 Woods Hole MA 02543-0296

WOODWORTH, RAMSEY LLOYD, lawyer; b. Syracuse, N.Y., Dec. 26, 1941; m. Diane Elizabeth McMillion, June 12, 1971; children: Scott, Ashley, Jeffrey. AB, Brown U., 1964; LLM cum laude, Syracuse (N.Y.) U., 1967. Bar: N.Y. 1967, D.C. 1968, U.S. Ct. Appeals (D.C. cir.) 1968. Atty., advisor FCC, Washington, 1967-68; from assoc. to ptnr. Hedrick & Lane, Washington, 1968-82; prin. Wilkes, Artis, Hedrick & Lane, Chartered, Washington, 1982-99; of counsel Shook, Hardy & Bacon LLP, Washington, 1999—2003, Irwin, Campbell & Tannenwald, PC, Washington, 2003—. Convenor Peace Luth. Ch., Alexandria, 1985-86; chair Libr. Am. Broadcasting Found., Inc., 1997—. Mem. Fed. Comm. Bar Assn. (exec. com. 1986-89, chair profl. responsibility com. 1984-86, treas. 1989-90, chmn. Fed. Commn. Bar Assn. Found. 1991-93, trustee 1991-94, Univ. Club Washington, Order of Coif. Avocation: swimming. Office: Irwin Campbell & Tannenwald PC 1730 Rhode Island Ave NW Washington DC 20036 Office Phone: 202-772-0013. E-mail: rwoodworth@ictpc.com.

WOODY, CAROL CLAYMAN, data processing executive; b. Bristol, Va., May 20, 1949; d. George Neal and Ida Mae Clayman; m. Robert William Woody, Aug. 19, 1972. BS in Math., Coll. William and Mary, Williamsburg, Va., 1971; MBA with distinction, Wake Forest U., 1979; PhD in Info. Sys., Nova Southeastern U., 2004. Programmer trainee GSA, 1971-72; systems engr. Citizens Fidelity Bank & Trust Co., Louisville, 1972-75; programmer/analyst-tng. coord. Blue Bell, Inc., Greensboro, N.C., 1975-79; supr. programming and tech. svcs. J.E. Baker Co., York, Pa., 1979-82; fin. design supr. bus. systems Lycoming divsn. AVCO, Stratford, Conn., 1982-83; project mgr. Yale U., New Haven, 1984-97; cons. ImageWork Technologies Corp., 1998-2001; co-owner Sign of the Sycamore, antiques; product developer Software Engring. Inst. Carnegie Mellon U., 2001—. Mem. Data Processing Standards Bd., 1977, CICS/VS Adv. Council, 1975; speaker Nat. Fuse Conf., 1989, Aion expert systems nat. conf., 1990, bus. sch. Coll. William & Mary, 1994. Author various manuals; contbr. articles to profl. jours. IBM Corp. fellow, 1978; Stephen Bufton Meml. Ednl. Found. grantee, 1978-79. Mem. Am. Bus. Woman's Assn. (chpt. v.p. 1978-79, Merit award 1978), NAFE (founder shoreline network 1993), Assn. for System Mgmt., Assn. for Image Info. Mgmt., Project Mgmt. Inst., Network Inc. of Conn. (treas. 1996-97), Delta Omicron (alumni pres. 1973-75, regional chmn. 1979-82). Republican. Presbyterian. Home: PO Box 1450 Guilford CT 06437-0550

WOODY, JOHN FREDERICK, retired secondary education educator; b. Indpls., Apr. 27, 1941; s. Ralph Edwin and Crystal Oleta (Thomas) W.; m. Nancy Ann Henry, July 7, 1963; children: Michael, Laura. BS in Secondary Sch. Teaching, Butler U., 1963, MS in Edn., 1967, adminstrn. lic., 1979, postgrad., 1991—, UCLA, 1980-82, Ind. U., 1990, U. Amsterdam, The Netherlands, 1985, Mont. State U., 1993, Purdue U., 1994. Tchr. Pub. Sch. 90, Indpls., 1963-66, Broad Ripple High Sch., Indpls., 1966-89; tchr., head social studies dept. Arlington H.S., Indpls., 1989—2003; ret., 2003. Author: (resource kits for hist. events) Cram, Inc., 1976-81, (filmstrips) Lowe Sheldrew, 1976-81; contbr. articles to profl. jours. and sch. materials. Sponsor Rep. Nat. Com., 1982—; deacon North Star Bapt. Ch., 1983—; mem. U.S. Congress German Bundestag Select Com. Ind., 1986-93. Fulbright scholar U.S. Info. Agy., 1985. Mem. ASCD, Nat. Coun. Social Studies, Ind. Coun. Social Studies, Arlington Acad. Com. Avocations: reading, writing, swimming, lifting weights. Home: 7362 Woodside Dr Indianapolis IN 46260-3137

WOODY, MARY FLORENCE, nursing educator, university administrator; b. Chambers County, Ala., Mar. 31, 1926; d. Hugh Ernest and May Lillie (Gilliland) W. Diploma, Charity Hosp. Sch. Nursing, 1947; BS, Columbia U., 1953, MA, 1955. Staff nurse Wheeler Hosp., Lafayette, Ala., 1947-48; polio nurse Willard Parker Hosp., N.Y.C., 1949; staff nurse, supr. VA Hosp., Montgomery, Ala., 1950-53; faculty, field supr. nursing dept. Columbia U. Tchrs. Coll., N.Y.C., 1955-56; asst. dir. nursing Emory U. Hosp., Atlanta, assoc. dir., DON, 1984-93; clin. asst. prof. Emory U. Sch. Nursing, Atlanta, 1956-68, interim dean, 1992-93; asst. dir., DON Grady Meml. Hosp., Atlanta, 1968-79; founding dean, prof. Auburn (Ala.) U. Sch. Nursing, 1979-84; disting. emeritus prof. Emory U., 2003—. Chair Ga. Statewide Master Planning Com. for Nursing and Nursing Edn., 1971-75; faculty preceptor patient care adminstrn. Sch. Public Health, U. Minn., 1977-79; bd. dirs. Wesley Woods Found. & Long Term Hosp.; chair bd. dirs. Am. Jour. Nursing Co., 1978-83. Recipent Spl. Recognition award 5th Dist. and Ga. Nurses Assn., 1978, 93, Disting. Achievement in Nursing Svc. award Columbia U. Tchrs. Coll. Alumni Assn., 1992, Jane Van de Vrede Outstanding Svc. to Citizens Ga. award Ga. League Nursing, Cert. Spl. Recognition award Ga. Nurses Assn., 1993, Internat. Founders award Sigma Theta Tau, 1999, The Marie Hippensteel award, 1999, Disting. Emeritus award Emeritus Coll., Emory U., 2003; named Ga. Women Pioneer in Health Care, Ga. Commn. on Women and Ga. Womens History Month Com., 1998. Fellow Am. Acad. Nursing (charter, Living Legend 1997); mem. Am. Nurses Assn., Nat. League Nursing, Am. Heart Assn., Emory U. Nell Hodgson Woodruff Sch. Nursing Alumni Assn. (hon.), Sigma Theta Tau (Marie Hippensteel Lingemald award for excellence in nursing 1999). Democrat. Address: 907 Lenox Hill Ct NE Atlanta GA 30324-2957

WOODY, THOMAS CLIFTON, II, assistant district attorney; b. Portsmouth, Va., Mar. 31, 1962; s. Thomas Clifton Sr. and Jean (Whitehead) W.; m. Sherry Carpenter, Aug. 15, 1981; children: Thomas Clifton III, Seth Chandler, Spencer David. BA, Old Dominion U., 1984; JD, Mercer U., 1987. Bar: Ga. 1987, U.S. Dist. Ct. (mid. dist.) Ga. 1987, U.S. Ct. Appeals (11 cir.) 1987. Assoc. Adams & Hemingway, Macon, Ga., 1987-92; asst. dist. atty. Dist. Atty's. Office-Macon Judicial Cir., Macon, 1992—. Lectr. Ga. Coll., Milledgeville, 1992—. Pres. Bibb County Young Reps., Macon, 1986-90; mem. exec. coun. Bibb County Rep. Party, Macon, 1986-92; chmn. Peach County Rep. party. Mem. Ga. Bar Assn., Macon Bar Assn., Pros. Attys. Coun. Ga., The Federalist Soc. (exec. bd. Ctrl. Ga. Lawyers Divsn.). Republican. Baptist. Avocations: golf, reading, baseball, theological studies, coaching youth sports. Home: 153 Red Oak Rd Byron GA 31008-6311 Office: Macon Judicial Dist Office of Dist Atty 661 Mulberry St Macon GA 31201-2605

WOODY, WILLIAM DOUGLAS, social sciences educator, researcher; b. Dayton, Ohio, Feb. 18, 1970; s. William Ray and Francis Ann Woody. BS, Colo. State U., 1992—92, MS, 1996—96, PhD in Psychology, 1999. Asst. prof., dept. of psychology U. of Wis. - Eau Claire, 1999—2001, U. of No. Colo., Greeley, 2002—. Contbr. 11 jour. articles Jury Decision Making, Revenge, Tchg., History Of Psychology, chapters to books;, author 2 instructor's manual/test banks. Mem.: Coun. of Teachers of Undergraduate Psychology, Rocky Mountain Psychol. Assn., Am. Psychol. Soc., APA (McKeachie Early Career Tchg. Excellence award 1999). Office: Dept of Psychology U of No Colo Greeley CO 80639 E-mail: william.woody@unco.edu.

WOOLAM, GERALD LYNN, surgeon; b. Lubbock, Tex., Apr. 16, 1937; s. Rawson Harp and Christine Leta (Rampy) W.; m. Nan Kelly, Feb. 28, 1959; children— Kelly Ann, Gerald Lynn, Gregory Alan. BA, Tex. Tech. U., 1958; MD, Baylor U., 1962. Diplomate Am. Bd. Surgery. Intern Parkland Meml. Hosp., Dallas, 1962-63; resident in gen. surgery Mayo Clinic and Mayo Grad. Sch. Medicine, U. Minn., Rochester, 1963-67, chief resident assoc. in surgery, 1967-68; surgeon Lubbock, 1968—; assoc. clin. prof. surgery Tex. Tech. U. Sch. Medicine, 1972-74, clin. prof., 1975—, prof., interim chmn. dept. surgery, 1980-81. Contbr. articles to profl. jours. Bd. dirs. Community Concert Assn. of Lubbock, 1968-71, 1st United Meth. Ch., Lubbock, 1970—, South Plains Health Systems, 1976-81; trustee West Tex. Found., 1971-74. With USNR. Recipient Outstanding Clin. Prof. award Tex. Tech. U., 1977; named Disting. Alumnus, Tex. Tech. U., 2000. Fellow ACS; mem. AAAS, Priestley Soc. (dir. 1970-73, pres. 1981-82), Lubbock Surg. Soc. (pres. 1972), AMA, Lubbock-Crosby-Garza County Med. Soc. (treas., exec. com. 1971—, pres. 1986), Osler Soc., Am. Cancer Soc. (del. 1980-88, dir. 1988—, nat. pres. 1999-2000, pres. Lubbock unit 1972-73, pres. Tex. divsn. 1978-79), Am. Heart Assn. (pres. Lubbock County divsn. 1973-74), Tex. Surg. Soc., Soc. Surgery Alimentary Tract, Soc. for Surg. Oncology, Central Assn. Dentists and Physicians, So. Surg. Assn., Sigma Xi, Phi Chi, Alpha Omega Alpha, Phi Kappa Phi, Phi Eta Sigma, Alpha Epsilon Delta. Home: 4007 69th St Lubbock TX 79413-5945 Office: 3611 22d Pl Lubbock TX 79410 E-mail: gwoolam@lubbocksurgical.com.

WOOLARD, CONNIE WARD, artist, retired art gallery manager; b. Wilkes-Barre, Pa., Mar. 25, 1931; d. Harold Walton and Betty Bertha (Mandeville) Ward; m. Maurice Emmett Woolard, Oct. 25, 1952; 1 child, Karin Elise Woolard Snoots. Student, U. Md., 1949—50, Abbott Art Sch., 1951—52. Comml. artist Rex Engraving Co., Silver Spring, Md., 1953-60, art dir., 1959-60; mgr. Town Ctr. Gallery, Rockville, Md., 1978—90, Bethesda, Md., 1990—99, ret., 1999. Freelance artist, fine artist, 1965—. One-woman shows include Town Ctr. Gallery, 1984, 1986, 1989, 1991, 1993, 1996, Art Contemporary, Bethesda, 1982, Sugar & Frichtl Gallery, 1993, exhibited in group shows at Glenview Mansion Gallery, 2004. Recipient Salmagundi Non-Member award Salmagundi Club, NYC, 1983, Judges Choice award Nat. League Am. Penwomen, 1996, Juror's award Miniature Painters Sculptors and Gravers Washington, 1997, Grumbacher award 2d pl. and 3d pl. pencil drawing, 2002, 1st pl. Landscape award Cider Painters Am., 2004, Arthur M. Wagman award Peerless Rockville Hist. Preservaton Ltd., 2003, Mid Atlantic Regional award, Balt. Watercolor Soc., 1985, others. Mem.: Potomac Valley Watercolorists, Miniature Painters, Sculptors & Engravers Soc. Washington, Nat. League Am. Penwomen (past sec., pres., named Women Yr. 1984), So. Watercolor Soc. (signature mem.), Phila. Watercolor Soc. (Cert. of Merit), Washington Watercolor Assn. (past pres.), Rockville Art League (past pres.), Salmagundi Club (Maria Szerti Meml. award 2001, Nat. Soc. Painters in Casein and Acrylic award). Avocations: gardening, reading, photography. Home: 3922 Havard St Silver Spring MD 20906-4311

WOOLARD, WILLIAM LEON, lawyer, electrical distributing company executive; b. Bath, N.C., Aug. 26, 1931; s. Archie Leon and Pearl Irene (Boyd) W.; m. Virginia Harris Stratton, June 17, 1961; children: William Leon Jr., Margaret Anne. AB, Duke U., 1953, LLB, JD, 1955. Bar: N.C. 1955, U.S. Dist. Ct. (we. and mid. dists.) N.C. 1960. Claims analyst Md. Casualty Co., Charlotte, N.C., 1955-56; dist. mgr. Chrysler Corp., Charlotte, 1956-60; ptnr. Jones, Hewson & Woolard, Charlotte, 1960-86, of counsel, 1986—; pres. Armature Winding Co., Inc., Charlotte, 1970—, also bd. dirs.; v.p. Power Products Mfg. Co., Charlotte, 1970—, also bd. dirs. Mem. adminstrv. bd. 1st United Meth. Ch., Charlotte, 1961-78, trustee, 1984-87; trustee Lawyers Ednl. Found., Charlotte, 1970-78, N.C. Sch. Sci. and Math., 1997—; bd. dirs. Christian Rehab. Ctr., Charlotte, 1972-73, N.C. Eye and Human Tissue Bank, Winston-Salem, 1978-79. Recipient Order of Civil Merit Moran award Republic of Korea, 1990, Disting. Svc. medal Republic of China, 1990, Medal of Friendship Pope John Paul II, 1990, Humanitarian Citizen of Merit medal Republic of China, 1990, Humanitarian medal France, 1990, Outstanding Svc. medal Mayor of Paris, 1990, Order of Long Leaf Pine, Gov. of N.C., 1990, numerous others; Angier B. Duke scholar Duke U., 1949-53; Carnegie Found. fellow Duke U., 1951-52, Melvin Jones fellow Lions Found., 1978. Mem. ABA, N.C. Bar Assn., N.C. State Bar Assn., 26th Jud. Dist. Bar Assn., Am. Judicature Soc., Lions (pres. Charlotte Ctrl. club 1972-73, pres., trustee ednl. found. 1973-87, dist. gov., chmn. coun. govs. internat. orgn. 1978-79, internat. bd. dirs. 1981-85, Ambassador of Goodwill award 1983, internat. 3rd v.p. 1986-87, 2nd v.p. 1987-88, 1st v.p. 1988-89, internat. pres. 1989-90, immediate past pres. 1990-91, chmn. bd. trustees 1990-91), Masons, Shriners, Phi Kappa Sigma, Delta Theta Phi. Avocations: collecting antique and rare books, opera, boating, fishing. Home: 638 Hempstead Pl Charlotte NC 28207-2320 Office: PO Box 32277 Charlotte NC 28232-2277 also: 1001 W First St Charlotte NC 28202 Office Phone: 704 333-2158. E-mail: billwoolard@mymailstation.com.

WOOLDREDGE, WILLIAM DUNBAR, health facility administrator; b. Salem, Mass., Oct. 27, 1937; s. John and Louise (Sigourney) W.; m. Johanna Marie; children: John, Rebecca Wistar. BA, Colby Coll., 1961; MBA, Harvard U., 1964. Staff assoc. Sun Oil Co., Phila., 1964-67; treas. Ins. Co. N.Am., Phila., 1967-72, B.F. Goodrich Co., Akron, Ohio, 1972-84, sr. v.p., 1978-79, exec. v.p., chief fin. officer, mem. mgmt. com., 1979-84; chief fin. officer, exec. v.p., dir. Belden & Blake Corp., North Canton, Ohio, 1984-89; sr. v.p., chief fin. officer, dir. Belden & Blake Oil Prodn., Inc., 1984-89; prin. dir. Carleton Group, Cleve., 1989-92; CFO, COO, v.p. King's Med. Co., Hudson, Ohio, 1993—, also bd. dirs. Pres. Hudson Econ. Devel. Corp. Bd. dirs. Salvation Army, North Park Coll. and Seminary; trustee Children's Hosp. Med. Ctr., Akron. With U.S. Army, 1956-58. Mem. Fin. Execs. Inst. Clubs: Country of Hudson. Episcopalian. Home: 100 College St Hudson OH 44236-2925 Office: King's Med Co 1920 Georgetown Rd Hudson OH 44236-4060 E-mail: wdwooldred@aol.com.

WOOLDRIDGE, DEAN EVERETT, engineering executive, scientist; b. Chickasha, Okla., May 30, 1913; s. Auttie Noonan and Irene Amanda (Kerr) W.; m. Helene Detweiler, Sept. 1936; children— Dean Edgar, Anna Lou, James Allan. AB, U. Okla., 1932, MS, 1933; PhD, Calif. Inst. Tech., 1936. Mem. tech. staff Bell Telephone Labs., N.Y.C., 1936-46, co-dir. research and devel. labs Hughes Aircraft Co., Culver City, Calif., 1946-52, v.p. research and devel., 1952-53; pres., dir. Ramo-Wooldridge Corp., Los Angeles, 1953-58, Thompson Ramo Wooldridge, Inc., Los Angeles, also Cleve., 1958-62; research assoc. Calif. Inst. Tech., 1962-79. Author: The Machinery of the Brain, 1963, The Machinery of Life, 1966, Mechanical Man, 1968, Sensory Processing in the Brain, 1979, also articles. Recipient Citation of Honor Air Force Assn., 1950, Raymond E. Hackett award, 1955, Westinghouse Sci. Writing award AAAS, 1963, Disting. Svc. Citation U. Okla, Disting. Alumnus award Calif. Inst. Tech., 1983. Fellow AAAS, Am. Acad. Arts and Sci., Am. Phys. Soc., IEEE, AIAA; mem. Nat. Acad. Scis., Nat. Acad. Engring., Calif. Inst. Assos., Am. Inst. Physics, Phi Beta Kappa, Sigma Xi, Tau Beta Pi, Phi Eta Sigma, Eta Kappa Nu. Address: 4545 Via Esperanza Santa Barbara CA 93110-2319

WOOLDRIDGE, PATRICE MARIE, marketing professional, personal trainer; b. Chgo., June 3, 1954; d. Charles E. and Marlys E. Reardon; m. Patrick Woolridge, June 27, 1981. AS, Moraine Valley Coll., 1974; BA, Govs. State U., 1976, MA, 1977; MBA, Loyola U., Chgo., 1983. Cmty. prof. Govs. State U., University Park, Ill., 1977-78; counselor, social worker Bloom Twp. HS, Chicago Heights, Ill., 1977-78; market analyst Dr. Scholl Footcare, Chgo., 1978-79; supr. consumer rsch. Unocal, Schaumburg, Ill., 1979-84; group rsch. dir. Tatham-Laird & Kudner, Chgo., 1984-87; v.p., assoc. dir. strategic planning & rsch. Bayer Bess Vanderwarker Advt., Chgo., 1987-90; v.p. dir. qualitative svcs. Goldring/MIL Rsch., 1990-91; pres. Wooldridge Assocs., Inc., Chgo., 1991—. Instr. dancing, 1969—89; instr. Arica Inst., N.Y.C., 1978—; instr. T'ai Chi Sch. Q'ai Chi Chuan/T'ai Chi Found., N.Y.C., 1986—. Performer: Anawim Players, 1985—97. Participant White House Conf. Small Bus., 1996; treas. Karma Thegsum Choling, Chgo., 1987—97; bd. dirs. Illustrated Theatre Co., Chgo., 1987, Human Process, Chgo., 1992—, T'ai Chi Found., Inc., 1994—97, pres. bd. dirs., 2003—04; adv. bd. N.W. Suburban Boy Scouts Am., Schaumburg, 1984. Recipient Gold medallion, Ogilvy Awards, 2000. Mem.: Union Concerned Scietists, Qualitative Rsch. Cons. Assn., Am. Mktg. Assn., Planetary Soc. Home and Office: 1717 W Rascher Ave Chicago IL 60640-1117 Business E-Mail: office@wastrategy.com.

WOOLDRIDGE, RAYMOND, former investment company executive; CEO Southwest Securities, Dallas; chmn. capital campaign steering com. U. Dallas, 2000—. Office: U Dallas 1845 E Northgate Dr Irving TX 75062

WOOLDRIDGE, WILLIAM CHARLES, lawyer; b. Miami, Fla., Feb. 24, 1943; s. Clarence Edward and Easter Marguerite (Souders) W.; m. Joyce L. Norton, June 15, 1968; children: William Charles, John Michael. BA, Harvard U., 1965; LLB, U. Va., 1969. Bar: Va. 1969. Atty. Norfolk and Western Ry. Co., 1973-82; with Norfolk So. Corp., 1982-2000, v.p. dept. law, 1996-2000. Pres. John Marshall Found., Richmond, Va., 1992-94; pres. Norfolk Hist. Soc., 1995-96; chair Friends of Chrysler Mus. Hist. Houses, 1997-99; bd. dirs. Sta. WHRO (FM and TV), 1997-2000, WHRO Found., Libr. of Va. Found. Capt. JAGC, U.S. Army, 1969-73. Mem. Va. Bar Assn. Republican.

WOOLEVER, NAOMI LOUISE, retired editor-in-chief; b. Williamsport, Pa., Sept. 17, 1922; d. Samuel Bruce and Kathryn Elizabeth (Schmidt) W. BS, Pa. State U., 1944, MA, 1966, postgrad., 1974-76. Reporter, women's editor Gazette & Bulletin, Williamsport, 1944-53; women's editor Sun-Gazette, Williamsport, 1953-72, assoc. city editor, 1972-74; prof. journalism Williamsport Area Community Coll., 1974-76; nat. editor, mng. editor Grit Pub. Co., Williamsport, 1976-81, editor in chief, 1981-88. Career cons. high sch. and coll. journalism classes, Pa. Contbr. articles to profl. jours. Named Woman of Yr., Williamsport Univ. Women, 1967. Mem. Pa. Women's Press Assn. (pres. 1960-62, Pa. Newswoman of Yr. 1958), Nat. Fedn. Press Women (bd. dirs. 1960-62), Soroptimist Club (pres. Williamsport chpt. 1958-60), Univ. Women's Club (pres. 1961-63), Friends of James V. Brown Libr., Williamsport Country Club, Williamsport Woman's Club, Lycoming County Hist. Soc., Gen. John Burrow's Hist. Soc. (bd. dirs.), Clio Club (pres. 1991-93), Pa. State Alumni Assn. (life mem.), Phi Kappa Phi, Kappa Tau Alpha, Zeta Tau Alpha. Republican. Mem. United Methodist Ch. Avocations: music, duplicate bridge, photography, sports. Home: 326 N Montour St Montoursville PA 17754-1832

WOOLEY, GERALDINE HAMILTON, poet, writer; b. Idlewild, Mich., Feb. 15, 1942; d. Charles Loren and Alice (Smith) Hamilton; m. David Wooley, June 11, 1961 (div. 1983); children: Vickie Wooley Houston, Monica Wooley Roberts, Deborah Wooley Williams. GED, Flint, Mich. Cosmetologist pvt. practice, Flint, Mich., 1967-70; tchr's. aide Flint Comty. Schs., 1969-71; nurse's aide Clara Barton Home, Flint, 1972; factory worker GM AC Plant, Flint, 1973-76; child care worker Beecher Cmty. Schs., Flint, 1987-89; poet, songwriter Flint, 1994—. Songwriter Hilltop Records, Hollywood, Calif., 1996—. Author: (poems) Between The Raindrops, 1995 (Editor's Choice 1995), At Water's Edge, 1995 (Editor's Choice 1995), Tapestry, 1996 (Editor's Choice 1996), Memories of Tomorrow, 1996 (Editor's Choice 1996), (poems) A Treasury of Famous Poets, 1997 (Editor's Choice award 1997). Mem. PTA Flint Sch. Dist., 1969-70. Named to Internat. Poetry Hall of Fame, 1996. Mem. Internat. Soc. Of Poets, Nat. Writers Assn., Internat. Black Writers. Democrat. Avocations: camping, playing organ, exploring old houses, writing. E-mail: LadyKnight77@webtv.net.

WOOLEY, JOHN C. food service executive; b. 1948; BBA, JD, U. Tex. Bar: Tex. 1974. Chmn., pres. Schlotzsky's Inc., Austin, 1981—. Office: Schlotzsky's Inc 203 Colorado St Austin TX 78701-3922

WOOLF, KENNETH HOWARD, architect; b. N.Y.C., Aug. 19, 1938; s. Howard Walter and Elizabeth Ann (Levy) W.; m. Elizabeth Adair Rainwater, July 3, 1965; children: Robert Gregg, Susan Adair, Jennifer Adair. BArch, Cornell U., 1961. Staff arch. Look & Morrison, Archs., Pensacola, Fla., 1965-72; pvt. practice arch. Pensacola, Fla., 1972—. Instr. architecture Pensacola Jr. Coll., part-time 1967-76; chmn. Pensacola Archtl. Rev. Bd., 1970-81; mem. Gulf Breeze Planning Bd., 1976-78; chmn. Pensacola City Bd. Adjustment and Appeals, 1995—. Prin. works include Coca-Cola Bottling Co. Plant, Pensacola, 1974, 3 profl. office bldgs. towers, Pensacola, 1976, 84, 92, Bapt. Hosp. addition, 1977, The Village, Housing for Elderly, 1978, 81, 98, Azalea Trace Ret. Cmty. Complex, 1980, 99, Northview Cmty., 1981, Coca-Cola Bottling Plant, Beaumont, Tex., 1983, Episcopal Day Sch., Pensacola, 1993. With USN, 1961-65. Named Jaycee of Yr., 1970. Mem. AIA (sec. N.W. Fla. chpt. 1976-77, 77-78, pres. 1979-81, Comml. Design Hon.

award 1975), Rotary. Episcopalian. Home: 15 N Sunset Blvd Gulf Breeze FL 32561-4051 Office: 100 W Gadsden St Pensacola FL 32501-3910 Office Phone: 850-438-3653. Business E-Mail: khwarch@networktel.net.

WOOLF, STEVEN H. medical educator, researcher, preventive medicine physician; MD, Emory U., Atlanta; MPH, Johns Hopkins U., Balt. Diplomate Am. Bd. Family Practice. Prof. family practice medicine Med. Sch. Va. Commonwealth U., Richmond; dir. rsch. Dept. Family Practice Va. Commonwealth U. Author two books plus over 60 articles in profl. jours. Mem.: Nat. Acad. Sci. Inst. Medicine. Office: Va Commonwealth U Dept Family Practice Med Sch PO Box 980251 Richmond VA 23298-0251 E-mail: shwdf@aol.com.

WOOLF, STEVEN MICHAEL, artistic director; b. Milw., Dec. 23, 1947; s. Raleigh and Lenore (Shurman) W. BA in Theatre, U. Wis., 1968, MFA, 1971; D of Fine Arts (hon.), U. Mo., 1993. Prodn. stage mgr. The Juilliard Sch. Drama, N.Y.C., 1973-75; project prodr. Musical Theatre Lab., N.Y.C., 1974-75; prodn. stage mgr. Barter Theatre, Abingdon, Va., 1976-79, Stagewest, Springfield, Mass., 1976-79; prodn. mgr. Repertory Theatre of St. Louis, 1980-83, acting artistic dir., mng. dir., 1983-85, mng. dir., 1985-86, artistic dir., 1986—. Adj. faculty Webster U., St. Louis, 1982—; mem. nat. negotiating coms. League of Resident Theatres, N.Y.C., 1986—; on-site evaluator Nat. Endowment for the Arts, 1985. Dir. plays A Life in the Theatre, 1982, the Crucible, 1986, Company, 1987, The Voice of the Prairie, 1988, 90, The Boys Next Door, 1989, Dog Logic, 1990, Born Yesterday, 1990, Terra Nova, 1991, The Diary of Anne Frank, 1991, Other Peoples Money, 1991, Six Degrees of Separation, 1992, Sight Unseen, 1993, Lion in Winter, 1993, Death and the Maiden, 1993, The Living, 1994, Wait Until Dark, 1994, The Caine Mutiny Court Martial, 1994. The Life of Galileo, 1995, Death of a Salesman, 1995, Betrayal, 1996, As Bees in Honey Drown, 1997, Who's Afraid of Virginia Woolf, 1998, Closer, 1998, Dinner With Friends, 2000, The Dresser, 2001, The Shape of Things, 2002, Copenhagen, 2003, Two Rockin' Gents, 2003, The Goat, Or Who is Sylvia, 2003, Blue/Orange, 2004, The Crucible, 2004, The Retreat From Moscow, 2004, others. Mem. ad hoc coms. for funding Mo. Arts Coun., St. Louis, 1988; chair citizen rev. panel Reg. Arts Commn., St. Louis, 1986; bd. dirs. Mo. Citizens for the Arts, 1990—; exec. com. League of Resident Theatres, 1990—. Recipient award Mo. Citizens for the Arts, 1992, Women's Polit. Caucus, 1993, award for Individual Excellence in the Arts, Arts Edn. Coun., 1993. Mem. AFTRA, Soc. of Stage Dirs. and Choreographers, Actors Equity Assn. Office: Repertory Theatre St Louis 130 Edgar Rd Saint Louis MO 63119-3228 Office Phone: 314-968-7340. E-mail: swoolf@repstl.org.

WOOLF, WILLIAM BLAUVELT, retired association executive; b. New Rochelle, N.Y., Sept. 18, 1932; s. Douglas Gordon and Katharine Hutton (Blauvelt) W. AA, John Muir Jr. Coll., 1951; student, U. Calif. at Berkeley, 1951; BA, Pomona Coll., 1953; MA, Claremont (Calif.) Grad. Sch., 1955; PhD, U. Mich., 1960. Instr., asst. prof., asso. prof. U. Wash., Seattle, 1959-68; assoc. sec., dir. adminstrn. AAUP, Washington, 1968-79; mng. editor Math. Revs., Am. Math. Soc., Ann Arbor, Mich., 1979-90, acting exec. editor, 1984-85; assoc. exec. dir. Am. Math. Soc., Providence, 1990-96. Bd. dirs. Nat. Child Rsch. Ctr., Washington, 1975-77; trustee Friends Sch., Detroit, 1985-90, treas., 1986-90; mem. Law and Justice Coun., Jefferson County, Wash., 1998—, chmn., 2001; mem. Wash. State U. Jefferson County Adv. Team, 1999-2003, chmn., 2002-2003, Jefferson County Edn. Com., 1998-2003, chmn., 1999-2001; bd. dirs. Jefferson County Farmers Market Assn., 2002-03. Fulbright Research fellow U. Helsinki, Finland, 1963-64 Fellow AAAS; mem. ACLU (life, treas. Washington 1966-68, bd. dirs. Washtenaw County and Mich. State 1989-90, bd. dirs. R.I. State 1993-95, treas. 1994-95, chmn. Jefferson County chpt. 2003—), Am. Math. Soc., Math. Assn. Am. Mem. Soc. Of Friends. Home: PO Box 235 Port Townsend WA 98368-0235

WOOLFENDEN, JAMES MANNING, nuclear medicine physician, educator; b. L.A., Nov. 8, 1942; BA with distinction, Stanford U., 1964; MD, U. Wash., 1968. Diplomate Am. Bd. Nuclear Medicine (chmn. credentials com. 1993-94, vice chmn. exams. com. 1993-95, chmn. exam. com. 1995-96, sec. 1994-96, chmn. 1996-97, life mem.), Nat. Bd. Med. Examiners. Med. intern L.A. County-U. So. Calif. Med. Ctr., 1968-69; med. resident West L.A. VA Med. Ctr., 1969-70; nuclear medicine resident L.A. County-U. So. Calif. Med. Ctr., 1972-74; from asst. prof. radiology to assoc. prof. radiology U. Ariz., Tucson, 1974-84, prof. radiology, 1984—. Mem. med. staff Univ. Med. Ctr., Tucson, 1974—; cons. VA Med. Ctr., 1974—; cons. med. staff Tucson Med. Ctr., 1975-2004, Carondelet St. Joseph's Hosp., 1974-98, St. Mary's Hosp., Tucson, 1976-90; mem. Nat. Cancer Inst. site visit team NIH, 1976, mem. NHLB Inst. site visit team NIH, 1976, mem. diagnostic radiology study sect., 1993-97, chmn., 1995-97; mem. med. liaison officer network EPA, 1983—; cons.-tchg. med. staff Kino Comty. Hosp., 1984-94; med. officer Clin. Ctr., NIH, Bethesda, 1984-85; mem. Ariz. Cancer Ctr., U. Ariz., 1988—, sr. clin. scientist Univ. Heart Ctr., 1990—; Ariz. bd. regents U. Ariz. Presdl. Search Com., 1990-91; chmn. Ariz. Atomic Energy Commn., 1979-80, Ariz. Radiation Regulatory Hearing Bd., 1981—; bd. dirs. Calif. Radioactive Materials Mgmt. Forum, 1989—, chmn., 1994-95, Western Forum Edn. in Safe Disposal of Low-Level Radioactive Waste, 1990—, vice chmn., 1991-92, chmn., 1992-94. Manuscript reviewer: Noninvasive Med. Imaging, 1983-84, Jour. Nuclear Medicine, 1985—, Investigative Radiology, 1989-94, Archives of Internal Medicine, 1990—; contbr. book chpts.: Diagnostic Nuclear Medicine, 2d edit., 1988, Adjuvant Therapy of Cancer, 1977, Fundamentals of Nuclear Medicine, 1988, others; contbr. articles and book revs. to profl. publs. Mem. Am. Heart Assn. Coun. on Cardiovasc. Radiology. Maj. U.S. Army, 1970-72, Vietnam. Fellow Am. Coll. Nuc. Physicians (long range planning com. 1981-83, govt. affairs com. 1984-94, exec. com. 1987-91, sec. 1989-91, parliamentarian 1991-95, treas. 1996-98, mem. publs. com. 1993-98, chmn. publs. com. 1993-94, pres.-elect 1998-99, pres. 1999-2000, others); mem. AMA (diagnostic and therapeutic tech. assessment reference panel 1982-98), Am. Nuc. Soc., Soc. Nuc. Medicine (com. on audit 1992-99, trustee 1992-96, ho. dels. 1996-2003, fin. com. 1996-99, bd. dirs. 1997-99, bronze medal for sci. exhibit 1984, bd. dirs., sec.-treas. So. Calif. chpt. 1993-95, pres.-elect 1995-96, pres. 1996-99), Assn. Univ. Radiologists, Ariz. Med. Assn., European Assn. Nuc. Medicine, Pima County Med. Soc., Radiol. Soc. N.Am. Office: Ariz Health Scis Ctr Nuc Medicine 1501 N Campbell Ave Tucson AZ 85724-5068

WOOLLAM, JOHN ARTHUR, electrical engineering educator; b. Kalamazoo, Mich., Aug. 10, 1939; s. Arthur Edward and Mildred Edith (Hakes) W.; children: Catherine Jane, Susan June. BA in Physics, Kenyon Coll., 1961; MS in Physics, Mich. State U., 1963, PhD in Solid State Physics, 1967; MSEE, Case Western Res. U., 1978. Rsch. scientist NASA Lewis Rsch. Ctr., Cleve., 1967-80; prof. U. Nebr., Lincoln, 1979—, dir. Ctr. Microelectronic and Optical Materials Rsch., 1988—; pres. J.A. Woollam Co., Inc., Lincoln, 1987—. Editor Jour. Applied Physics Com., 1979-94. Grantee NASA, NSF, USAF, Advanced Rsch. Projects Agy. Fellow Am. Phys. Soc.; mem. Am. Vacuum Soc. (chmn. thin film divsn. 1989-91). Office: U Nebr Dept Elec Engring 209NWSEC Lincoln NE 68588-0511

WOOLLATT, PAUL G. financial company executive; COO Downey Fin. Corp., Newport Beach, Calif., 1998—. Office: Downey Fin Corp 3501 Jamboree Rd Newport Beach CA 92660

WOOLLCOMBE, GRAHAM DOUGLAS, dean; b. Plymouth, Devon, Eng., Apr. 22, 1956; s. Richard Edward De Ambrosis and Phoebe (Morshead) W. MA, Cambridge U., 1982; MS in Creative Intelligence, Maharishi European Rsch. U., Seelisberg, Switzerland, 1982. Cert. Royal Inst. Brit. Archs.; cert. Maharishi Ayurveda cons. EEG asst. Maharishi European Rsch. U., Boppard-am-Rhein, Germany and Eng., 1982-85; rsch. and edn. cons. Ministry of Ayurveda, Sri Lanka, 1985; arch. Maharishi Nagar, Ghazhirbad Up, India, 1986; graphics designer Mentmore Video, Buckinghamshire, Eng., 1986-92; Ayurvedic cons. and bus. cons., The Hague, The Netherlands, 1993-94. Candidate Natural Law Party, Northampton, Eng., 1997. Anglican. Avocations: croquet, painting, computer graphics. Home and Office: 639 Whispering Hills Rd Boone NC 28607-5599

WOOLLEN, EDMUND, electronics executive; b. Rocky Mount, N.C., Nov. 1944; BS, U. Wash., 1967. With Hughes Aircraft, OTI; systems application engr. Raytheon Co., 1979—81; Raytheon Overseas Ltd./Raytheon Co., 1981—90; v.p. govt. mktg. Raytheon Co., 1990—99, mission area exec. integrated info. systems, 1999—2002, v.p., 1990—, v.p. bus. devel. and mktg. for Homland Security, 2002—. With USN, 1967—76. Office: Raytheon Co 1100 Wilson Blvd Arlington VA 22209

WOOLLEN, EVANS, retired architectural firm executive; b. Indpls., Aug. 10, 1927; s. Evans Jr. and Lydia (Jameson) Ritchey; m. Nancy Clarke Sewell, July 16, 1955 (dec. 1992); children: Ian, Malcolm Sewell. BA, MArch, Yale U., 1952. Lic. architect Ind., Ala., Conn., Del., Ill., Ky., La., Maine, Mass., N.C., Ohio, Tenn. Chmn. Woollen, Molzan & Ptnrs., Indpls., 1955—; resident Am. Acad. in Rome, spring 1996. Architect Pilot Ctr., Cin. (Nat. HUD 1975), St. Marys Coll. Libr. (Nat. AIA-ALA 1983), Grainger Libr., U. Ill., Urbana, Asbury Coll. Libr., Wilmore, Ky., Indpls. Cen. Pub. Libr, Mem. bd. Ind. State Welfare Bd., 1956-59, Art Assn., 1956-66, Indpls. Capital Improvement Bd., 1965-69. With Signal Corps U.S. Army, 1946-47. Fellow: AIA. Democrat. Address: 2801 Eagle Ridge Longmont CO 80503 E-mail: ewoollen3@indra.com.

WOOLLEY, ALMA SCHELLE, nursing educator; b. NYC, Oct. 3, 1931; d. Max Carl and Matilda Louise Schelle; m. Arthur E. Woolley Jr., Sept. 11, 1954; children: Mariel Therese, Mark Stephen, Peter James, Jane Frances. Student, CUNY, 1949—51; BSN, Cornell U., 1954; MSN, U. Pa., 1965, EdD, 1980. Instr. sch. nursing U. Pa., Phila., 1965-69; asst. prof. nursing Atlantic Community Coll., Mays Landing, N.J., 1969-74; coord. nursing program Stockton State Coll., Pomona, N.J., 1974-81; dir., Carolyn F. Rupert prof. nursing Sch. of Nursing, Ill. Wesleyan U., Bloomington, 1981-86; dean Sch. Nursing Georgetown U., Washington, 1986-92, prof., 1992-96, prof. emeritus, 1996—. Vis. prof. U. Md., 1996—2000; adj. prof. Uniformed Svcs. U. Health Scis., 1997—. Author: History of Georgetown University School of Nursing, 1903-2000, 2001; mem. editl. bd.: Nurse Educator; editor: Bull. of Am. Assn. for History of Nursing; contbr. articles to profl. jours. Recipient Dist. Alumni award Cornell U. Sch. Nursing, 1989. Mem. ANA, Am. Assn. Colls. of Nursing (bd. dirs. 1988-90), Nat. League for Nursing (bd. of rev.), Am. Assn. for History of Nursing, Cosmos Club, Sigma Theta Tau, Phi Delta Kappa. Episcopalian. Address: 13 Basswood Ct Catonsville MD 21228-5870 Personal E-mail: awooll@aol.com.

WOOLLEY, BRYAN (LOWELL BRYAN WOOLLEY), author, journalist; b. Gorman, Tex., Aug. 22, 1937; s. G.L. Jr. and Beatrice Voleta (Gibson) W.; m. Julianne Nelson, Aug. 31, 1958 (div. 1968); m. Margaret Ray Hilpert, July 13, 1968 (div. 1978); children: Bryan Edward, John Patrick; m. Isabel Catherine Rickert, Apr. 14, 1979. BA, U. Tex., El Paso, 1958; BDiv, Tex. Christian U., 1963; MTh, Harvard U., 1966. Reporter El Paso Times, 1955-58; tchr. Bel Air H.S., El Paso, 1958-59; bank teller Ft. Davis (Tex.) State Bank, 1959-60; corr. AP, Tulsa, 1967-68; city editor The Anniston (Ala.) Star, 1968-69; reporter, editl. writer The Courier-Jour., Louisville, 1969-76; sr. writer, columnist The Dallas Times Herald, 1976-89; sr. writer The Dallas Morning News, 1989—. Author: Some Sweet Day, 1974, We Be Here When the Morning Comes, 1975, Time and Place, 1977, November 22, 1981, Sam Bass, 1983 (Spur award 1984), The Time of My Life, 1984, Where Texas Meets the Sea, 1985, The Edge of the West, 1990, The Bride Wore Crimson, 1993, Generations, 1995, Mythic Texas, 1999. Named Bernard DeVoto fellow, Bread Loaf Writers Conf., 1975; named to Authors of the Pass: El Paso Writers Hall of Fame, 1989; recipient Tex. Headliner award, 1977, 1981, 1983, 1990, Lit. award in journalism, PEN West, 1993, U. Mo. Lifestyle Journalism award in arts and entertainment, 1995, Sweepstakes award, Tex. AP Mng. Editors Assn., 1999. Mem.: Tex. Folklore Soc., West Tex. Hist. Assn., Tex. State Hist. Assn., Tex. Inst. Letters (pres. 1993—94, Stanley Walker Journalism award 1981, 1983, 1999, O. Henry award for mag. journalism 1991). Democrat. Home: 18040 Midway Rd Apt 215 Dallas TX 75287-6503 Office: Dallas Morning News 508 Young St Dallas TX 75202-4828 E-mail: lbwoolley@aol.com.

WOOLLEY, CATHERINE (JANE THAYER), writer; b. Chgo., Aug. 11, 1904; d. Edward Mott and Anna L. (Thayer) W. AB, UCLA, 1927. Advt. copywriter Am. Radiator Co., N.Y.C., 1927-31; freelance writer, 1931-33; copywriter, editor house organ Am. Radiator & Standard San. Corp., N.Y.C., 1933-40; desk editor Archtl. Record, 1940-42; prodn. editor SAE Jour., N.Y.C., 1942-43; pub. relations writer NAM, N.Y.C., 1943-47. Condr. workshop on juvenile writing Truro Ctr. for Arts, 1977, 78, 92, Cape Cod Writers Conf., 1990, 91, 92; instr. writing for juveniles Cape Cod Writers Conf., 1965, 66, 92. Author: juvenile books (under name Catherine Woolley) I Like Trains, 1944, rev., 1965, Two Hundred Pennies, 1947, Ginnie and Geneva, 1948, paperback edit., 1988, David's Railroad, 1949, Schoolroom Zoo, 1950, Railroad Cowboy, 1951, Ginnie Joins In, 1951, David's Hundred Dollars, 1952, Lunch for Lennie, 1952 (pub. as L'Incontentabile Gigi in Italy), The Little Car That Wanted a Garage, 1952, The Animal Train and Other Stories, 1953, Holiday on Wheels, 1953, Ginnie and the New Girl, 1954, Ellie's Problem Dog, 1955, A Room for Cathy, 1956, Ginnie and the Mystery House, 1957, Miss Cathy Leonard, 1958, David's Campaign Buttons, 1959, Ginnie and the Mystery Doll, 1960, Cathy Leonard Calling, 1961, paperback edit., 1988, Look Alive, Libby!, 1962, Ginnie and Her Juniors, 1963, Cathy's Little Sister, 1964, paperback edit., 1988, Libby Looks for a Spy, 1965, The Shiny Red Rubber Boots, 1965, Ginnie and the Cooking Contest, 1966, paperback 1979, Ginnie and the Wedding Bells, 1967, Chris in Trouble, 1968, Ginnie and the Mystery Cat, 1969, Libby's Uninvited Guest, 1970, Cathy and the Beautiful People, 1971, Cathy Uncovers a Secret, 1972, Ginnie and the Mystery Light, 1973, Libby Shadows a Lady, 1974, Ginnie and Geneva Cookbook, 1975, adult book Writing for Children, 1990, paperback, 1990; (under name Jane Thayer) The Horse with the Easter Bonnet, 1953, The Popcorn Dragon, 1953, rev. edit. 1989, Korean edit., 1999, Where's Andy?, 1954, Mrs. Perrywinkle's Pets, 1955, Sandy and the Seventeen Balloons, 1955, The Chicken in the Tunnel, 1956, The Outside Cat, 1957, English edit., 1958, 83, Charley and the New Car, 1957, Funny Stories To Read Aloud, 1958, Andy Wouldn't Talk, 1958, The Puppy Who Wanted a Boy, 1958, rev., 1986, paperback edition, 1988, French translation Le Petit Chien Qui Voulait Un Garcon, 1991, Korean translation, 1998, The Second-Story Giraffe, 1959, Little Monkey, 1959, Andy and His Fine Friends, 1960, The Pussy Who Went To the Moon, 1960, English edit., 1961, A Little Dog Called Kitty, 1961, English edit., 1962, 75, The Blueberry Pie Elf, 1961, English edit., 1962, revised edit., 1994, Spanish edit., 1995, Andy's Square Blue Animal, 1962, Gus Was a Friendly Ghost, 1962, English edit., 1971, Japanese edit., 1982, A Drink for Little Red Diker, 1963, Andy and the Runaway Horse, 1963, A House for Mrs. Hopper; the Cat that Wanted to Go Home, 1963, Quiet on Account of Dinosaur, 1964, English edit., 1965, 74, paperback edit., 1988, Emerald Enjoyed the Moonlight, 1964, English edit., 1965, The Bunny in the Honeysuckle Patch, 1965, English edit., 1966, Part-Time Dog, 1965, English edit. 1966, The Light Hearted Wolf, 1966, What's a Ghost Going to Do?, 1966, English edit. 1972, Japanese edit., 1982, The Cat that Joined the Club, 1967, English edit. 1968, Rockets Don't Go To Chicago, Andy, 1967, A Contrary Little Quail, 1968, Little Mr. Greenthumb, 1968, English edit., 1969, Andy and Mr. Cunningham, 1969, Curious, Furious Chipmunk, 1969, I'm Not a Cat, Said Emerald, 1970, English edit. 1971, Gus Was A Christmas Ghost, 1970, English edit. 1973, Japanese edit., 1982, Mr. Turtle's Magic Glasses, 1971, Timothy And Madam Mouse, 1971, English edit., 1972, Gus And The Baby Ghost, 1972, English edit. 1973, Japanese edit., 1982, The Little House, 1972, Andy and the Wild Worm, 1973, Gus Was a Mexican Ghost, 1974, English edit. 1975, Japanese edit., 1982, I Don't Believe in Elves, 1975, The Mouse on the Fourteenth Floor, 1977, Gus Was a Gorgeous Ghost, 1978, English edit., 1979, Where Is Squirrel?, 1979, Try Your Hand, 1980, Applebaums Have a Robot, 1980, Clever Raccoon, 1981, Gus Was a Real Dumb Ghost, 1982, Gus Loved His Happy Home, 1989; contbr. stories to juvenile anthologies in U.S., Great Britain, France, Germany, and Holland, sch. readers, juvenile mags. Trustee Truro Pub. Libraries, 1974-84; Mem. Passaic (N.J.) Bd. Edn., 1953-56, Passaic Redevel. Agy., 1952-53; pres. Passaic LWV, 1949-52. Named mem. N.J. Literary Hall of Fame, 1987; recipient Phantom Friends Lifetime Achievement award, 1992; dedication of Catherine Woolley Children's Rm. in Truro Pub. Libr., 1999. Mem. Authors League Am., Friends of Truro Libr., Truro Hist. Soc., Amnesty Internat. U.S.A., Kenilworth Soc. Democrat. Home: PO Box 71 Truro MA 02666-0071

WOOLLEY, DONNA PEARL, lumber company executive; b. Drain, Oreg., Jan. 3, 1926; d. Chester A. and Mona B. (Cheever) Rydell; m. Harold Woolley, Dec. 27, 1952 (dec. Sept. 1970); children: Daniel, Debra, Donald. Diploma, Drain High Sch. Sec. No. Life Ins. Co., Eugene, Oreg., 1943-44; sec., bookkeeper D & W Lumber Co., Sutherlin, Oreg., 1944, Woolley Logging Co. & Earl Harris Lumber Co., Drain, 1944-70; pres. Woolley Logging Co., 1970—, Smith River Lumber Co., 1970—, Mt. Baldy Mill, 1970-81, Drain Plywood Co., 1970-81, Woolley Enterprises, Inc., Drain, 1973—, Eagle's View Mgmt. Co., Inc., Eugene, 1981—. Bd. dirs. Wildlife Safari, Winston, 1991, Oreg. Cmty. Found., Portland, 1990-99, chair, 1997-99; bd. trustees Linfield Coll., McMinnville, U. Oreg. Found., Eugene, Oreg. Trl. coun. Boy Scouts Am., 1980—, World Forestry Ctr., Portland, 1990, Umpqua C.C. Fedn., 2001. Recipient Pioneer award, U. Oreg., 1982, Econ. and Social Devel. award, Soroptimist Club, 1991, First Citizen of Eugene award, 2000, Aubrey Watzek award, Lewis & Clark Coll., Howard Vollum award, Associated Fund Raisers in Philanthropy Oreg. chpt., 2001, Pioneer award, Umpqua C.C., 2003, Hart Pioneer award, Wildlife Safari, 2003. Mem. Oreg. Women's Forum, Pacific Internat. Trapshooting Assn., Amateur Trapshooting Assn., Eugene C. of C. (bd. dirs. 1989-92), Arlington Club, Town Club (bd. dirs., pres.), Sunnydale Grange, Cottage Grove/Eugene Rod & Gun Club. Republican. Avocations: golf, travel. Office: Eagle's View Mgmt Co Inc 1399 Franklin Blvd Eugene OR 97403-1979

WOOLLEY, JOHN EDWARD, trade association executive; b. Jersey City, July 17, 1935; s. Ogden Price and Catherine Hildegard (Tanney) W.; m. Sandra Marina Turtzo, Oct. 23, 1984. BA, Rutgers U., 1957; MBA, U. Ala., 1970; grad., U.S. Naval War Coll., 1977. Commd. U.S. Army, 1957-82, advanced through grades to col., co. comdr. 1st Inf. Divsn., 1965-66; ops. staff officer, exec. officer Office of Dep. Chief of Staff, Ops., U.S. Army, Washington, 1967-69; ops. staff officer, White House briefer Orgn. of Joint Chiefs of Staff, Washington, 1970-73; bn. comdr. and chief of staff 1st Inf. div. U.S. Army, Germany, 1973-76; chief ops. officer III US Corps, U.S. Army, Ft. Hood, Tex., 1977-78; comdr. 2nd Brigade, 2nd Armored div. U.S. Army, Ft. Hood, Tex., 1978-79; planner Office of Dep. Chief of Staff Ops., U.S. Army, Washington, 1979-82; v.p. and sr. v.p. United Coal Co., Bristol, Va., 1982-86; dir. Food Mktg. Inst., Washington, 1988-99, v.p. ops., 1999—. Contbr. articles to profl. jours. Bd. dirs. Jr. Achievement, Bristol, Va., 1984-86. Decorated Legion of Merit (3), Bronze Star medals (2), Army Commendation medal. Mem. Ret. Officers Assn., Am. Soc. Assn. Execs., Country Club of Bristol (bd. dirs. 1983-86), Army Navy Country Club, Tau Kappa Epsilon (chpt. pres. 1956-57). Republican. Roman Catholic. Avocation: golf. Home: 214 Skyline Dr Bristol TN 37620-4141 Office: Food Mktg Inst 655 15th St NW Ste 700 Washington DC 20005-5701 E-mail: jwoolley@fmi.org.

WOOLLEY, MARY ELIZABETH, research administrator; b. Chgo., Mar. 16, 1947; John Joseph and Ellen Louise (Bakke) McEnerney; m. John Stuart Woolley, Dec. 6, 1969 (div. 1985); children: George Newsom, Nora Ellen; m. Michael Howland Campbell, Jan. 1, 1989. BS, Stanford U., 1969; MA, San Francisco State U., 1972; postgrad., U. Calif., San Francisco and Berkeley, 1974-75. Assoc. dir. Inst. Epidemiology and Behavioral Medicine, San Francisco, 1979-81; adminstr. Med. Rsch. Inst. of San Francisco, 1981-82, v.p., adminstr., 1982-86, v.p., exec. dir., 1986-90; pres. Research! Am., Alexandria, Va., 1990—. Cons. in fin. and mgmt. NIH, Bethesda, Md., 1984—92; adj. faculty U. Calif. Sch. Pub. Health, Berkeley, 1983—92, mem. Dean's adv. coun., 1995—2002; founding mem. Whitehead Inst. Bd. Assocs., 1995—; bd. dirs. Lovelace Inst., Respiratory Rsch. Inst., vice chmn., 1999—; bd. dirs. Children's Rsch. Inst., Washington, 2003—; lectr. to profl. assns.; mem. bd. visitors Harvard U. Sch. Pub. Health, Cambridge, 2002—; mem. dean's coun. Johns Hopkins Sch. of Nursing, 2002—; mem. bd. advisors IBM Life Scis., 2003—. Editor Jour. of Soc. Rsch. Adminstrs., 1986-89, mem. editl. rev. bd., 1989-95; mem. editl. bd. Jour. Women's Health, 1992—, Sci. Comm., 1994—; contbr. articles and editls. to profl. jours. Bd. dirs. Kensington (Calif.) Edn. Found., 1986-89, Enterprise for H.S. Students, 1990-92; mem. capital campaign com. Calif. Shakespeare Festival, 1989-91, v.p. Med. Rsch. Assns. Am., 1993-95; bd. advisors Friends of Cancer Rsch., 1996—; bd. dirs. Nat. Patient Safety Found., 1998-2000, Friends of Nat. Inst. of Nursing Rsch., 2001—. Recipient Silver Touchstone award Am. Hosp. Assn., 1994, Disting. Svc. award Columbia Coll. Physicians and Surgeons, 1994, Advocacy award Fedn. Am. Socs. Exptl. Biology, 1998, Advocacy award Friends Nat. Inst. Nursing Rsch., 1999, Leadership award Coun. Scientific Soc. Pres.'s, 1999, Advocacy award Friends of Dental Rsch., 2002. Fellow AAAS; mem. Assn. Ind. Rsch. Insts. (pres.-elect 1987-89, pres. 1989-90), Inst. Medicine (elected), Soc. Rsch. Adminstrs. (bd. dirs. 1986-90, bd. advisors 1990-93, Hartford-Nicholson Svc. award 1990, Disting. Contbn. to Rsch. Adminstrn. award, 1993), Calif. Biomed. Rsch. Assn,. (bd. govs. 1986-90), Md. Gov.'s Commn. on Women's Health, 1993-96. Democrat. Office: Research! Am 1101 King St Ste 520 Alexandria VA 22314-3067 Office Phone: 703-739-2577. E-mail: mwoolley@researchamerica.org.

WOOLLEY, ROGER SWIRE, lawyer; b. Chgo., Nov. 18, 1924; s/ Anthony Walter and Agnes Louise (MacMurray) W.; m. Patricia Ann Jundt, 1951 (dec. 1978); children: Elliott Payne, Merrit Ann. BA, Coll. William & Mary, 1947; student, Exeter Coll., London, 1947-48; LLB, Columbia U., 1951. Bar: Calif., U.S. Supreme Ct. Legal counsel Solar Aircraft, San Diego, 1952-54; prin. Law Offices of Roger S. Woolley, Rancho Santa Fe, Calif., 1954—. Active Automobile Club So. Calif., L.A., dir. 1974-98, chmn. 1988-90; active Am. Automobile Assn., Falls Church, Va., Orlando, Fla., dir., 1986-97, chmn., 1991-93; founding dir., sec. Bank La Jolla, 1962-68; founding dir., sec. Rancho Santa Fe Savs. & Loan, 1972-78; founding dir., sec. Torrey Pines Bank, 1979-84; dir. Scripps Meml. Hosp. Found., La Jolla, Calif. 1984—; trustee emeritus The Endowment Assn. of Coll. William & Mary, Williamsburg, Va.; chmn., mem. Calif. State Hwy. Commn., 1958-67. Mem. ABA, State Bar Calif., San Diego County Bar Assn., Rotary Club Rancho Santa Fe. Office: Law Offices of Roger S Woolley PO Box R 16903 Avenida de Acacias Rancho Santa Fe CA 92067

WOOLLING, KENNETH RAU, vascular internist; b. Indpls., Mar. 6, 1918; m. Catherine Margaret McColl, Mar. 20, 1948; 2 children. BA magna cum laude, Butler U., 1939; postgrad., Harvard U., 1939-40; MD, Ind. U., 1943; MS in Medicine, U. Minn., 1951. Diplomate Nat. Bd. Med. Examiners, Am. Bd. Internal Medicine, Am. Bd. Cardiovascular Disease. Intern Indpls. City Hosp. (now Wishard Meml.), Indpls., 1943-44; resident in internal medicine Marion County Gen. Hosp., Indpls., 1947; fellow, first asst. internal medicine Mayo Found., Rochester, Minn., 1948-52; mem. med. staff, mem. tchg. staff postgrad. med. edn. Marion County Gen. Hosp. (name now Wishard Meml. Hosp.), Indpls., 1952—; founder, dir., peripheral vascular diseases clinic Indpls City & Marion County Gen. Hosp. (now Wishard Meml.), Indpls., 1952-68; pvt. practice internal medicine and cardiovascular diseases Indpls, 1952—; founder, dir. peripheral vascular diseases clinic Meth. Hosp., Indpls., 1967-72, founder, dir. vascular lab., 1970-73, mem. med. staff, tchr. staff postgrad. med. edn., 1952—. Mem. med. staff St. Vincent Hosp., St. Francis Hosp. and Winona Meml. Hosp., Indpls., 1952—; charter mem. med. staff Cmty. Hosp., Indpls., 1952—; charter mem. med. adv. com. Butler U., Indpls, 1956—. Contbr. articles to profl. jours., 1950—. Capt. Med. Corps U.S. Army, 1944-46. Fellow ACP, Am. Coll. Chest Physicians, Coun. on Cardiology Am. Heart Assn., Am. Coll. Angiology (gov. state of Ind. 1979-80); mem. AMA (50 Yr. award 1993), SAR, Internat. Union Angiology, Am. Soc. Internal Medicine, Am. Diabetes Assn., Ind. State Med. Soc., Ind. Diabetes Assn., Am. Fedn. for Clin. Rsch., N.Y. Acad. Med. Scis., North Ctrl. Clin. Soc., Mayo Cardiovascular Soc., Ind. Hist. Soc., Res. Officers Assn., Indpls. Med. Soc., Am. Legion, Shriners, Masons (Scottish Rite and Mystic Tie Lodge, 50 yr. award 1989), Contemporary Club of Indpls., Indpls. Athletic Club, Highland Golf and Country Club, Phi Delta Theta (50 yr. award 1985), Phi Kappa Phi, Phi Chi. Presbyterian. Office: PO Box 80192 Indianapolis IN 46280-0192

WOOLLS, ESTHER BLANCHE, library science educator; b. Louisville, Mar. 30, 1935; d. Arthur William and Esther Lennie (Smith) Sutton; m. Donald Paul Woolls, Oct. 21, 1953 (div. Nov. 1982); 1 son, Arthur Paul AB in Fine Arts, Ind. U., 1958, MA in Libr. Sci., 1962, PhD in Libr. Sci., 1973. Elem. libr. Hammond (Ind.) Pub. Schs., 1958-65, libr. coord., 1965-67, Roswell (N.Mex.) Ind. Schs., 1967-70; prof. libr. sci. U. Pitts., 1973-97, prof., dir. Sch. Lib. and Info. Sci. San Jose (Calif.) State U., 1997—. Exec. dir. Beta Phi Mu, 1981-95. Author: The School Library Media Manager, 1995, 3d edit., 2004, So You're Going to Run a Library, 1995, Ideas for School Library Media Centers, 1996, Whole School Library Handbook, 2004; co-author: Information Literacy, 1999; editor: Continuing Professional Education and IFLA: Past, Present, and a Vision for the Future, 1993, Delivering Lifelong Continuing Professional Education Across Space and Time, 2001. Fulbright scholar, 1995-96; recipient Disting. Svc. award Pa. Sch. Librs. Assn., 1993. Mem. ALA (mem. coun. 1985-89, 95—2003), Am. Assn. Sch. Librs. (bd. dirs. 1983-88, pres. 1993-94, Disting. Svc. award 1997), Pa. Learning Resources Assn. (pres. 1984-85), Internat. Assn. Sch. Librs. (pres. 1998-2001), Internat. Fedn. Libr. Assns. (mem. standing com. sch. librs. 1991-99, sec. Continuing Profl. Edn. Round Table 2000—). Home: 144 S 4th St # 637 San Jose CA 95112 Office: San Jose State U Sch Libr and Info Sci 1 Washington Sq San Jose CA 95192-0029

WOOLRIDGE, ORLANDO, former professional basketball coach, Olympic coach; Profl. player Chgo. Bulls, 1981, N.J. Nets, L.A. Lakers, 1988-90, Denver Nuggets, Detroit Pistons, Milw. Bucks, Phila. 76ers, 1993-94; asst. coach L.A. Sparks, 1997-98, head coach, 1998-99; asst. coach USA Women's Basketball, 1999—. Cons. L.A. Sparks. Coach various recreational leagues, asst. girls coach Harvard Westlake H.S., Studio City, Calif. Office: USA Basketball 5465 Mark Dabling Blvd Colorado Springs CO 80918

WOOLSEY, DAVID ARTHUR, leasing and commercial company executive; b. Oakland, Calif., Nov. 27, 1941; BS, U. San Francisco, 1963; MBA, U. Calif., Berkeley, 1965. Mgr. lease and spl. projects fin. Kaiser Aluminum & Chem. Corp., Oakland, Calif., 1965-68; v.p. U.S. Leasing Internat., Inc., San Francisco, 1968-78; exec. v.p. GATX Capital Corp., San Francisco, 1978, 1982-88, also bd. dirs.; COO Orix U.S.A. Corp., San Francisco, 1988-98, also bd. dirs.; group pres. Capital Fin., Heller Fin., Inc., 1998—2002. Republican. Roman Catholic. Home: 308 Village View Ct Orinda CA 94563-2700 E-mail: davidwoolsey@aol.com.

WOOLSEY, JOHN MUNRO, JR., retired lawyer; b. NYC, Apr. 22, 1916; s. John M. and Alice B. (Bacon) W.; m. Ledlie Laughlin, Dec. 27, 1948; children: John, Alice, Henry, Mary. BA, Yale U., 1938, LL.B., 1941. Bar: N.Y. 1941, Mass. 1947. Assoc. Debevoise, Stevenson, Plimpton & Page, N.Y.C., 1941-42; with Bd. Econ. Warfare, Washington, 1942, Herrick & Smith and predecessor firms, Boston, 1946—86; of counsel Palmer & Dodge, Boston, 1986—2001; ret., 2001. With Office of U.S. Chief of Counsel, Nürnberg Trials, Germany, 1945-46 Former pres. Trustees of Reservations, Shady Hill Sch. Served to lt. USNR, 1942-46. Decorated Order of White Lion (Czechoslovakia) Mem. Am. Antiquarian Soc., Am. Law Inst., Century Assn., Tavern Club.

WOOLSEY, LYNN, congresswoman; b. Seattle, Nov. 3, 1937; BS, U. San Francisco, 1981. Mgr. human resources Harris Digital Telephone, 1969—80; owner Woolsey Personnel Svs., 1980—92; mem. U.S. Congress from 6th Calif. dist., 1993—, ranking mem. edn. reform subcom. ho. com. edn. and the workforce. Mem. Petaluma City Coun., 1984-92 Democrat. Office: US Ho Reps 2263 Rayburn Ho Office Bldg Washington DC 20515-0506 Address: 1101 College Ave St 200 Santa Rosa CA 95404 also: 1050 Northgate Dr St 140 San Rafael CA 94903

WOOLSEY, THOMAS ALLEN, neurobiologist; b. Balt., Apr. 17, 1943; s. Clinton Nathan and Harriet (Runion) W.; m. Cynthia Tull Ward, June 8, 1969; children: Alix, Timothy. BS, U. Wis., 1965; MD, Johns Hopkins, 1969. Asst. prof. anatomy Washington U. Sch. Medicine, St. Louis, 1971-75, asst. prof. anatomy, neurobiology, 1975-77, assoc. prof. anatomy, neurobiology, 1977-80, assoc. prof. anatomy, neurobiology, physiology biophysics, 1980-83, coord. neurosci. program, 1980-84, sr. neuroscientist, 1982—, prof. neurology, neurological surgery, 1984—, dir. experimental neurology, neurological surgery, 1984—. Chmn., Washington U. Teaching Space Evaluation, 1989-90. Contbr. articles to profl. jours. NIH Rsch. grantee, 1970—; George H. and Ethel R. Bishop scholar, 1984—; recipient McKnight Neurosci. Devel. award, 1982-85, Jacob Javits award NIH, 1993-2000; fellow John Simon Guggenheim Found., 2004. Fellow AAAS; mem. Am. Assn. Anatomists, Am. Acad. Neurology, St. Louis Acad. Sci., Soc. Neurosci., Johns Hopkins Med. Surgical Assn., Cajal Club. Avocations: hiking, history, woodworking. Office: Washington U Sch Medicine 660 S Euclid Ave # 8057 Saint Louis MO 63110-1010

WOOLSTON-CATLIN, MARIAN, psychiatrist; b. Seattle, Jan. 20, 1931; d. Howard Brown and Katharine Nichols (Dally) Woolston; m. Randolph Catlin Jr., July 5, 1959; children: Laura Louise, Jennifer Woolston, Randolph III. *Now fifteenth generation in America. Paternal Line: Woolston. English. Lost to William the Conqueror in 1066. English Landed Gentry. Quakers who left England circa 1670 to settle in the Harrisburg area before it became Pennsylvania. Maternal Line: Hewlett and Willets. Arrived on Mayflower and later settled in Cold Spring Harbor, Long Island. Father: Howard Brown Woolston (Who's Who 1930-1950). Distinguished scholar, educator and author, who pioneered the field of sociology early in the Twentieth Century. He earned degrees from Yale, Harvard, Chicago, Columbia, Sorbonne and the University of Berlin. His scholarship, brilliant intellect, historical scope and vitality inspired generations. A superb father.* BA cum laude, Vassar Coll., 1951; MD, Harvard U., 1955. Diplomate Nat. Bd. Med. Examiners. Intern in pediatric medicine Children's Hosp., Boston, 1956, asst. resident in pediatric medicine, 1956; resident in psychiatry Mass. Mental Health Ctr., Boston, 1957-59; fellow in child psychiatry Tavistock Clin., London, 1960; Commonwealth fellow in child psychiatry Harvard U. at Gaebler Children's Unit, Waltham, Mass., 1975-78, clin. instr. psychiatry, 1978-79; pvt. practice Wellesley Hills, Mass., 1978-91, Medfield, Mass., 1991—. Clin. instr. psychiatry Harvard U. at Mass. Mental Health Ctr., Boston, 1957-59, 78-82, Tufts U. at Mass. Mental Health Ctr., 1957-59; mem. exec. bd. Parents' and Children's Svcs., Boston, 1983-86. Designer H.H. Hunnewell Meml. Garden for New Eng. Flower Show Mass. Hort. Soc., 1975 (Ames Cup award). Mem. exec. bd. Ext. Divsn. New Eng. Conservatory Music, 1972-75; charter mem. reuse com. Medfield State Hosp., 1992—. Fellow Am. Acad. Child and Adolescent Psychiatry; mem. AMA, Am. Psychiat. Assn. (life), Mass. Psychiat. Assn., Mass. Med. Soc., New Eng. Coun. Child and Adolescent Psychiatry (hon.), Boston Vassar Club (exec. bd. 1963-75), Hills Garden Club Wellesley (exec. bd. and design chief 1973-75). Episcopalian. Avocations: landscape design, sculpting. Home and Office: 314 North St Medfield MA 02052-1204

WOOLWORTH, SUSAN VALK, primary school educator; b. Toledo, Ohio, Apr. 24, 1954; d. Robert Earl and Alice (Melick) Valk; children: Alison Valk, Andrew Baker. BA, Pine Manor Jr. Coll., Chestnut Hill, Mass., 1974; BS, Boston U., 1976. Tchr. kindergarten Lancaster (Pa.) Country Day Sch., 1986—. Bd. dirs. Fulton Opera House; past bd. dirs. Planned Parenthood, Vis. Nurse Assn., Hands-On House. Mem.: Jr. League (sustainer), Sigma Gamma. Republican. Episcopalian. Avocations: walking, gardening, tennis, decorating.

WOOSLEY, RAYMOND, pharmacologist, educator; b. Ky., Oct. 2, 1942; m. Julianne Buchert. BS, Western Ky. U., 1964; PhD, U. Louisville, 1967; MD, U. Miami, 1973. Intern, resident Vanderbilt U. Hosp., Nashville, 1973-76; sr. pharmacologist, dir. rsch. Meyer (GSK) Labs., Ft. Lauderdale, Fla., 1968-71; instr. dept. medicine, pharmacology Vanderbilt U., Nashville, 1976-77, asst. prof., 1977-79, assoc. prof., 1979-84, assoc. dir. clin. rsch. ctr., 1981-88, prof., 1984-88; prof. pharmacology, medicine, chmn. dept. pharmacology Georgetown U. Sch. Medicine, Washington, 1988-2000, assoc. dean clin. rsch., 2000—01, also chief divsn. clin. pharmacology, 1988-94; dir. Inst. Cardiovascular Scis., Washington, 1995-2000, Gen. Clin. Rsch. Ctr., Washington, 1999-2001; v.p. Ariz. Health Scis. Ctr., 2001—; dean Sch. Medicine U. Ariz., 2001—02. Rschr. in field. Contbr. chapters to books, articles to profl. jours. Recipient Career Devel. award in Clin. Pharmacology, Pharm. Mfrs. Assn. Found., 1977—80; fellow, Am. Coll. Clin. Pharmacology, 1974; Predoctoral fellow, NIH, 1964—67, Postdoctoral fellow, U. Louisville, 1967—68, Vanderbilt U., 1976—77, Ogden scholar, Western Ky. U., 1960—64. Fellow: ACP, Am. Coll. Clin. Pharmacology; mem.: Soc. Women's Health Rsch. (bd. dirs. 1999—2001), Assn. Med. Sch. Pharmacology (pres. 1996—98), Am. Bd. Clin. Pharmacology, Am. Soc. Clin. Pharmacology and Therapeutics (v.p. 1998—99, pres. 1999, Rawls-Palmer award 1990), Am. Fedn. Clin. Rsch., Am. Soc. Pharmacology and Exptl. Therapeutics (mem. clin. pharmacology exec. com. 1981—92, Harry Gold award 2001), Am. Heart Assn. (fellow coun. clin. cardiology 1985—). Office: Ariz Health Sci Ctr 1501 N Campbell Ave # 2222 Tucson AZ 85724-5018 Business E-Mail: WoosleyR@u.arizona.edu.

WOOSNAM, IAN HAROLD, professional golfer; b. St. Martins, Shropshire, U.K., Mar. 2, 1958; s. Harold and Joan Woosnam; m. Glendryth Mervyn Pugh, Nov. 12, 1983; children: Daniel Ian, Rebecca Louise, Ami Victoria. Ed., St. Martins Modern Sch. Profl. golfer, 1976—. Tournament winner News of the World under 23 match-play, 1979, Cacharel under 25 Championship, 1982, Swiss Open, 1982, Silk Cut Masters, 1983, Scandinavian Enterprise Open, 1984, Zambian Open, 1985, Lawrence Batley TPC, 1986, 555 Kenya Open, 1986, Hong Kong Open, 1987, Jersey Open, 1987, Cepsa Madrid Open, 1987, Bell's Scottish Open, 1987, 90, Lancome Trophy, 1987, 93, Suntory World Match-Play Championship, 1987, 90, World Cup (Wales) Team and Individual, 1987, Million Dollar Challenge, 1987, Welsh Pro Championship, 1988, Volvo PGA Championship, 1988, Panasonic European Open, 1988, Carrols Irish Open, 1988, 89, AmEx Med Open, 1990, Epson Grand Prix, 1990, Torras Monte Carlo Open, 1990, 91, Fujitsu Mediterranean Open, 1991, U.S. Masters, 1991, USF&G Classic, 1991, PGA Grand Slam of Golf, 1991, World Cup Individual, 1991, European Montecarlo Open, 1992, Murphy's English Open, 1993, Air France Cannes Open, 1994, Brit. Masters, 1994, Johnnie Walker Classic, 1996, Scottish Open, 1996, German Open, 1996, Heineken Classic, 1996, Volvo PGA Championship, 1997, Hyundai Motor Masters, 1997; ranked 1st Sony world rankings, 1991, Ryder Cup Team Mem., 1983, 85 (winners), 87 (winners), 89, 91, 93, 95 (winners), 97 (winners), Cisco World Match Play championship, 2001, vice-capt. Ryder Cup winners, 2001-02. Avocations: snooker, sports, water-skiing.

WOOSNAM, RICHARD EDWARD, venture capitalist, lawyer; b. Anderson, Ind., June 27, 1942; s. Richard Wendell and Ruth (Cleveland) W.; m. Diane Dalto; children: Cynthia S., Elizabeth C. BS, Ind. U., 1964, JD, 1967, MBA, 1968. Bar: Ind. 1967, U.S. Dist. Ct. (so. dist.) Ind. 1967. Instr. bus. law Ind. U., Bloomington, 1966-68; assoc. Ferguson, Ferguson & Lloyd, Bloomington, 1967-68; dep. pros. Monroe County, Bloomington, 1967-68; tax acct. Price Waterhouse, Phila., 1968-69; v.p., treas. Innovest Group, Inc., Phila., 1969-82, chmn., pres., 1983—. Bd. dirs. Capital Mgmt. Corp., N.Y. Achievement, L.L.C., Innovest Talent Svcs., Inc., Command Equity Group, LLC, Bridges Learning Sys., Inc., Ind. U. Found., World Affairs Coun. of Phila., Fairmount Park Conservancy, Phila. Hospitality, Inc., Phila. Zoo, Pa. Acad. Fine Arts. Active Walnut St. Theatre. Mem. ABA, Ind. Bar Assn., Union League of Phila., Sunday Breakfast Club, The Pa Soc. Office: 1528 Walnut St Ste 1701 Philadelphia PA 19102

WOOSTER, ROBERT, history professor; b. Beaumont, Tex., Aug. 27, 1956; s. Ralph Ancil and Edna Lee (Jones) W.; m. Catherine Cox, 1992. BA, Lamar U., 1977, MA, 1979; PhD, U. Tex., 1985. Scholar in residence Tex. State Hist. Assn., Liberty, 1985-86; asst. prof. Tex. A&M U., Corpus Christi, 1986-90, assoc. prof., 1990-95, prof., 1995—, chmn. dept. humanities, 1997—2000, Frantz prof. history, 2001—. Author: Soldiers, Sutlers and Settlers (Bates award 1987), U.S. Military and Indian Policy, 1988, History of Fort Davis, 1990, Nelson A. Miles and The Twilight of the Frontier Army, 1993, The Civil War 100, 1998, The Civil War Bookshelf, 2001; editl. adv. bd. Southwestern Hist. Quar., Austin, Tex., 1989—, Military History of the West, 1995—, Jour. of the West, 1996-2000; editor: Soldier, Surgeon, Scholar: The Memoirs of William Henry Corbusier, 2003. Dep. dir. U.S. Mil. Acad./ROTC fellowship U.S. Mil. Acad., West Point, N.Y., 1990. Mem. Tex. State Hist. Assn., Orgn. Am. Historians. Democrat. Home: 4600 Ocean Dr Apt 708 Corpus Christi TX 78412-2543 Office: Texas A&M Univ 6300 Ocean Dr Corpus Christi TX 78412-5599 Office Phone: 361-825-2402.

WOOTEN, CECIL AARON, retired religious organization administrator; b. Laurel, Miss., June 3, 1924; s. Cecil A. and Alice (Cox) W.; m. Helen Moss, Apr. 4, 1947; children: Michael, Margaret, Martin, Marsha, Mark. BS in Mech. Engring, U. Ala., 1949. With CBI Industries, 1941—, bd. dirs., 1965-83, mng. dir. CBI Constructors Ltd., London, 1957-62, mgr. Houston sales dist., 1962-64, v.p. engring., 1964—68, v.p., mgr. corp. svcs., 1968-69, sr. v.p.-gen. sales mgr., 1969-78; sr. v.p. comml. devel. Chgo. Bridge & Iron Co. (subs. CBI Industries), 1978-79; sr. v.p. corp. adminstrn. CBI Industries, Oak Brook, 1980-83; dir. devel. Christian Family Services, Gainesville, Fla., 1983-86, Denver Ch. of Christ, 1986-88, Boston Ch. of Christ, 1988-92; pres. Internat. Chs. of Christ, Inc., L.A., 1994-99; chair Internat. Chs. Christ, L.A., 1999—2000, retired, 2002. Bd. dirs. Oak Brook (Ill.) Bank. Former trustee Elmhurst (Ill.) Coll.; former bd. sponsors Good Samaritan Hosp., Downers Grove, Ill. Served to 1st lt. AUS, 1943-46. Mem. ASME, NSPE, Rotary. E-mail: cecilwooten@hotmail.com.

WOOTEN, FRANK THOMAS, retired research facility executive; b. Fayetteville, N.C., Sept. 24, 1935; s. Frank Thomas and Katherine (McRae) Wooten; m. Linda Walker, July 14, 1962; children: Laurin Walker, Patrick Thomas, Ashley Tripp. BSEE, Duke U., 1957, PhD, 1964. Engr. Corning Glass Works, Raleigh, NC, 1964—66; from engr. to pres. Rsch. Triangle Inst., Research Triangle Park, NC, 1966—89, pres., 1989—99, ret., 1999. Bd. dirs. N.C. Biotech. Ctr., Troxler Electronics Labs., N.C. Biosci. Investment Fund. Contbr. articles on semiconductors and biomedical engring. to profl. publs.; patentee semiconductors tech. Lt. (j.g.) USN, 1957—59. Recipient Disting. Engring. Alumnus award, Duke U., 1991; fellow, Shell, 1961. Mem.: IEEE, Nat. Inst. Statis. Scis. (corp. 1990—98), Ballistic Missile Def. Orgn. (tech. application rev. panel 1990—94), Assn. for Advancement Med. Instrumentation (chmn. com. on aerospace tech. 1971—77). Baptist.

WOOTEN, GLEN DONOVAN, media consultant; s. Lester Lee Wooten and Veda Diloros Johnson; 1 child, Jennifer Rachel Pitts. BA in Psychology, U. Nev., Las Vegas, 2000. Ops. mgr. Procell, Las Vegas, Nev., 1992—97; technician Network, Las Vegas, Nev., 1998—. Cons., media editor Profitscape, Las Vegas, Nev., 1997—98. Contbr. articles to publs. Mentor, tutor math., stats. Student Devel. Ctr., Las Vegas, Nev., 1997. Mem.: Top One Percent Soc., Triple Nine Soc., Intertel, Prometheus Soc., Mensa, Internat. Soc. for Philos. Enquiry, Omicron Psi, Psi Chi, Omicron Delta Epsilon, Golden Key, Phi Kappa Phi, Nat. Forensic League, Phi Sigma Tau. Achievements include development of novel relational ideas in fields of calculus and graph theory. Avocations: frisbee, working out, reading, mathematics, philosophy. Office: PO Box 70122 Las Vegas NV 89170-0122

WOOTEN, JOAN HEDRICH, minister; b. Washington, Jan. 4, 1953; d. Albert Louis Hedrich and Maxine Keller (Smith) Smith; m. David Randall Wooten, Jan. 11, 1983; children: Michael, Sarah. BA, Coll. William and Mary, 1975; MA, Bryn Mawr Coll., 1978; MDiv, Gordon-Conwell Theol. Sem., 1981; ThM, Duke U. Div. Sch., 1987. Ordained 1982. Chaplain U.S. Navy, Oak Harbor, Wash., 1982—84, Yokosuka, Japan, 1984—86, Norfolk, Va., 1987—90, res. chaplain, 1990—, capt.; pastoral counselor Episcopal Diocese of So. Va., Norfolk, 1990—93; campus min. Presbytery of Ea. Va., Portsmouth, 1993—2001; interim and stated supply pastor Presbytery Fla., 2003—. Doctoral fellow Union Theol. Sem., Richmond, 2001—. Singer Va. Symphony Chorus, Norfolk, 1992—2001. Decorated Commendation medal U.S. Navy. Presbyterian. Avocations: music, languages, cooking. Office Phone: 850-682-2835.

WOOTEN, JOEL ORBA, JR., lawyer; b. Hazlehurst, Ga., June 4, 1950; s. Joel Orba and Mary Eleanor (Whitlock) W.; m. Sybrina G. Franklin; children: Joel III, Katherine, Frank. BBA, U. Ga., 1972, JD, 1975. Bar: Ga. 1975, U.S. Dist. Ct. (mid. dist.) Ga. 1976, U.S. Ct. Appeals (11th cir.) 1981. Ptnr. Kelly, Denney, Pease & Allison, Columbus, Ga., 1975-88, Butler, Wooten, Overby & Cheeley, Columbus, Ga., 1988—. Bd. dirs. Columbus Symphony Orch., Columbus, Ga., 1983-88. With U.S. Army, 1972. Mem. Am. Bar Assn., Fed. Bar Assn., Ga. Trial Lawyers Assn., State Bar Ga. (chmn. gen. practice & trial sect. 1990-91), Columbus Lawyers Club (pres 1988-89), Columbus Younger Lawyers (pres. 1983-84), Assn. Trial Lawyers Am., The Breakfast Club (pres. 1982-83), Roscoe Pound Found., U. Ga. Alumni Coun. (v.p. 1981-82), U. Ga. Alumni Soc. (bd. dirs. 1981-83, 89-91). Office: Butler, Wooten, Fryhofer, Daughtery & Crawford, LLP 105 Thirteenth St PO Box 2766 Columbus GA 31901

WOOTEN, RALPH G. career officer; b. La Grange, N.C. Commd. officer U.S. Army, advanced through grades to maj. gen., 1996; comdg. gen. U.S. Army Chem., Mil. Police Ctrs., and Ft. McClellan, Ft. McClellan, Ala., 1996—. Address: 125 Cross Foxes Dr Fort Washington MD 20744-5566

WOOTEN, ROBERT E. musician, educator; b. Chgo., Feb. 17, 1930; s. John and Flora (Watts) W.; m. Frances Louise Carter, Aug. 26, 1956; children: Robert Jr., Carol Lynne, John D. BMus, Chgo. Conservatory Music, 1956; M in Music Edn., Roosevelt U., 1968; D in Music Edn., Va. Seminary & Coll., 1983. Min. music Beth Eden Bapt. Ch., Chgo., 1941—; founder, dir. Wooten Choral Ensemble, 1949—; dir. music Greater Harvest Bapt. Ch., 1950-86. Music dept. chair Parker H.S., Chgo., 1957-62; staff asst., Chgo. Pub. Schs. 1962-75, dist. adminstr., 1976-95. Mem. Am. Choral Dirs., Music Educators Nat. Conf. Home: 9531 S Union Ave Chicago IL 60628-1031 Personal E-mail: maestrob1@aol.com.

WOOTEN, ROSALIE, automotive company executive; Exec. v.p. O'Reilly Automotive Inc., Springfield, Mo. Office: O'Reilly Automotive Inc 233 S Patterson Ave Springfield MO 65802-2298

WOOTEN-GREEN, RONALD CLARENCE, writer; b. Palermo, NY, Jan. 15, 1939; s. Leo Turner and Gladys Florence (Barnes) Green; m. Dawn Elizabeth O'Brien (dec.); children: Dennis Green, Carl Green, Brian Green, Marcea Green, Valerie Green, Kelly Green; m. Linda Ann Wooten, May 25, 1996. BS in Edn., SUNY, Oswego, 1961; MA in Polit. Sci., SUNY, Albany, 1964, PhD, 1971; MA in Adult Religious Edn., Regis U., 1987. Asst. prof. polit. sci. Millersville (Pa.) State U., 1965—68; prof. polit. sci. Indiana (Pa.) U., 1968—79; dir. adult religious edn. Diocese of Cheyenne, Casper, Wyo., 1979—86, Archdiocese of Omaha, 1986—95; chaplain Hospice Preferred Choice, Inc., Council Bluffs, Iowa, 1995—2003; pvt. practice Crestone, Colo., 1998—. Chmn. bd. N.Am. Forum for Small Christian Communities, 1990—95; resident writer Hambidge Ctr. for Creative Arts, Rabun Gap, Ga., 2001—03; spkr. in field. Editor: Harvest, 1995; author: When the Dying Speak, 2002. State bd. ACLU, Lancaster, Pa., 1966—68; bd. dirs. Indiana County Housing Authority, 1977—79; chmn. bd. Nebraskans for Peace, Lincoln, 1991—92. Staff sgt. N.G. USAF, 1957—62. Mem.: Colo. Hospice Orgn., Nat. Assn. Cath. Chaplains (bd. dirs. region 9 1998—2001, cert., chaplain emeritus). Democrat. Roman Catholic. Avocations: music, reading. Home and Office: PO Box 844 Crestone CO 81131

WOOTTEN, JOHN ROBERT, investor; b. Feb. 5, 1929; s. Henry Hughes and Ella Gayle (Ditzler) W.; m. Mary Lou Schmausser, Mar. 15, 1952 (div.); children: Pamela Jean, Robert Hughes; m. Geraldine Ann Theisen, Aug. 14, 1982. BS, Colo. A&M U., 1953. Sec. S.W. Radio & Equipment Co., Oklahoma City, 1953-55; pres. Belcaro Homes, Inc., 1955-60, Bob Wootten Ford, Yukon, Okla., 1960-68, Bus. Data Sys., 1968-72; chmn., CEO 1st Nat. Bank, Moore, Okla., 1970-72; pres. Commn. Enterprises, Inc., Liberal, Kans., 1967-79, Trebor Leasing Co., 1965-87, Okla. Sch. Book Depository, Inc., Oklahoma City, 1976-80, S.W. Sch. Depository, Inc., Dallas, 1976-86; chmn., CEO Exch. Nat. Bank Del City, Okla., 1976-78; dir. S.W. Bancshares Corp., Oklahoma City. Pres. Okla. chpt. Am. Cancer Soc., 1966-67, Okla. chpt. Arthritis Found., 1973-76, Lyric Theater, Okla., 1976-77; chmn. bd. trustees Bone and Joint Hosp., 1976-81; bd. dirs. Okla. Theater Ctr., Dallas Theater Ctr.; trustee Oklahoma City U.; pres. Last Frontier coun. Boy Scouts Am., 1968-70; Rep. nominee for Lt. Gov. of Okla., 1966. Mem. Ind. Bankers Assn., Am. Bankers Assn., Tex. Bookmen's Assn., Okla. Bookmen's Assn., Tex. Assn. Sch. Adminstrs., Econ. Club Okla., Navy League, Rotary (pres. Oklahoma City 1963-64, dist. gov. 5520 1998-99). Home: 6760 Gato Rd El Paso TX 79932-3210 Personal E-mail: woottens@aol.com.

WOOTTON, JOHN FRANCIS, physiology educator; b. Penn Yan, N.Y., May 31, 1929; s. John Edenden and Margaret Eliza (Smith) W.; m. Joyce Albertine Mac Mullen, Aug. 28, 1959; children: J. Timothy, David M., Barbara H., Bruce C. BS, Cornell U., 1951, MS, 1953, PhD, 1960. Grad. rsch. asst. Cornell U., Ithaca, N.Y., 1956-60, from asst. prof. to prof. emeritus, 1962—2004, prof. emeritus, 2004—, assoc. dean Grad. Sch., 1980-83; post doctoral fellow U. Coll., London, 1960-62. Grad. faculty rep. field of physiology Cornell U., 1990-92, 93-97, chmn. dept. physiology, 1997-98, co-chmn. dept. biomed. scis., 1998-99, chmn. 1999-2000; vis. scientist MRC Molecular Biology, Cambridge, Eng., 1969-70, Nat. Inst. Med. Rsch., London, 1985-86, 92-93, 2002; temporary sr. rsch. assoc. Stanford (Calif.) U., 1977-78. Contbr. articles to profl. jours. 1st lt. USAR, 1954-56. Rsch. and Travel grantee NIH, USDA Burroughs Wellcom Fund, Med. Rsch. Coun., Cornell Biotech. Program. Mem. AAAS, Am. Soc. Biochemistry, Molecular and Cell Biology, Am. Chem. Soc., Biophys. Soc., Protein Soc., Sigma Xi (v.p., pres. Cornell chpt.). Avocations: travel, choral singing, gardening, art, fishing. Office: Cornell U Dept Biomed Scis T8-014 Vet Rsch Tower Ithaca NY 14853-5908

WORBY, RACHAEL BETH, conductor; b. Nyack, N.Y., Apr. 21, 1949; d. Louis Lincoln and Diana (Zacharia) W.; m. David Obst, Sept. 7, 1986. BS in Music, Crane Sch. of Music, 1971; postgrad., Ind. U., 1971-72; ABD, Brandeis U., 1979. Music dir. N.H. Philharmonic, Manchester, 1979-82, New Eng. Conservatory Youth Orch., Boston, 1980-82; Exxon asst. conductor Spokane (Wash.) Symphony, 1982-84; asst. conductor L.A. Philharmonic, 1983-87; music dir. Carnegie Hall, N.Y.C., from 1984, Wheeling (W.Va.) Symphony, 1986—. Instr. New Eng. Conservatory of Music, Boston, 1979-82, MIT, Boston, 1980-82; lectr. N.Y. Philharmonic, N.Y.C., 1978-86. Rockefeller Found. grantee, 1981, Exxon/NEA grantee, 1982. Mailing: 87 N Raymond Ave Ste 500 Pasadena CA 91103

WORBY, RACHEL, conductor; b. Nyack, N.Y. m. David Obst (div.); m. Gaston Caperton (div.); 1 child, Diana. MusB in Piano Performance, SUNY; MA in Musicology, Ind. U.; PhD in Musicology, Brandeis U. Dir., condr. Youth Concerts Carnegie Hall, N.Y.C., 1984; condr. Youth Concerts LA (Calif.) Philharm., 1985—86; music dir. Wheeling (W.Va.) Symphony Orch., 1986—2002, Pasadena (Calif.) POPS Orch., 1999—. Guest condr. Barcelona (Spain) Symphony Orch., Irish Chamber Orch., Transylvania Philharm., London (Eng.) Philharm. Orch., Adelaide Symphony Orch., Queensland Symphony, Ojai Festival; mem. Nat. Coun. Arts, 1994—98. Founder Am. Music Fesitival, Cluj, Romania. Nominee ACE award, 1990; grantee, Martha Baird Rockefeller Fund, 1982. Office: The Pasadena Pops Orchestra 81 North Raymond Ave Ste 500 Pasadena CA 91103

WORCESTER, HOWARD LESTER, internist; b. Kansas City, Mo., Jan. 3, 1945; s. Howard Elmer and Alma Jane (Evans) W. div.; children: Tiffany, Chase. BS, U. Oregon, 1967, MD, 1971. Diplomate Am. Bd. Internal Medicine, Am. Bd. Forensic Pathology. Intern Harbor Gen. Hosp. UCLA, 1971-72; med. officer U.S. Army, West Germany, 1972-75; resident U. Calif., Irvine, 1975-77, chief med. resident, 1977-78; pvt. practice internal medicine Meml. Hosp., Long Beach, Calif., 1978—. Dir. utilization rev. Long Beach Meml. Hosp., 1983—, trustee, 1983—, also bd. dirs.; cons. Sultanate of Oman, Muscat, Oman, 1984—. Patron L.A. County Mus. Major U.S. Army, 1972-75. Recipient Merck scholarship U. Oreg. Med. Sch., 1969 Mem. Long Beach Meml. Hosp. Med. Group (pres. 1983—), Long Beach Meml. Med. Svc. Orgn. (pres. 1993-96), Phi Beta Kappa, Alpha Omega Alpha. Episcopalian. Avoca-

tions: cooking, wine collecting, travel, sports. Home: 11042 Skyline Dr Santa Ana CA 92705-2473 Office: Meml Med Group 2650 Elm Ave Ste 309 Long Beach CA 90806-1600 Office Phone: 562-595-7927. Personal E-mail: hworcester@cox.net.

WORDEN, ELIZABETH ANN, artist, author, comedy writer, singer, musician, playwright, screenwriter; b. Karnes City, Tex., Nov. 8, 1954; d. Alan Walker and Mary Paralee (Long) W. BS in Comms., U. Tex., 1977; MA, Tex. A&M U., Corpus Christi, 2003. Disc jockey, newsperson KMMK Radio, McKinney, Tex., 1978, KPBC Radio, Irving, Tex., 1979-80, KDNT Radio, Denton, Tex., 1980-81, KJIM Radio, Ft. Worth, 1981-82, KPBC Radio, Irving, 1983, KRYS Radio, Corpus Christi, Tex., 1984; owner Worden Art Enterprises, Corpus Christi, Tex. Executed paintings for Am. Embassy, Bogota, Colombia; one-woman shows include Art Ctr., Corpus Christi, 1990; exhibited in group shows at Tex. A&M, Corpus Christi, 1986, 92, Galeria Chapparal, Corpus Christi, 1988, New Eng. Fine Art Inst., Boston, 1993, Am. Embassy, Bogota, Art Ctr. Corpus Christi, 2000; paintings in pvt. collections throughout the country. Mem. Art Ctr. Corpus Christi. Mem. Tex. Fine Arts Assn., Pastel and Colored Pencil Soc. Avocations: writing fiction and poetry, acting, photography, reading. Home and Office: Worden Enterprises 3842 Brookhill Dr Corpus Christi TX 78410-4404 E-mail: elizworden@aol.com.

WORDEN, KATHARINE COLE, sculptor; b. N.Y.C., May 4, 1925; d. Philip Gillette and Katharine (Pyle) Cole; m. Frederic G. Worden, Jan. 8, 1944; children: Fred, Dwight, Philip, Barbara, Katharine. Student, Potters Ch., Tucson, 1940-42, Sarah Lawrence Coll., 1942-44. Exhibited in group shows at Royce Galleries, Galerie Francoise Besnard, Paris, Cooling Gallery, London, Galerie Schumacher, Munich, Selected Artists Gallery, N.Y.C., Art Inst. Boston, Reid Gallery, Nashville, Weiner Gallery, N.Y.C., Boston Athanaeum, House of Humor and Satire, Gabrovo, Bulgaria, 1983, Newport Bay Club, 1984; pvt. collections Grand Palais, Paris, Dakar and Bathurst, Africa. Dir. Stride Rite Corp., 1980-85; occpl. therapist psychopathic ward L.A. County Gen. Hosp., 1953-57; Headstart vol., Watts, Calif., 1965-67; tchr. sculpture Watts Towers Art Ctr., 1967-69; participant White House Women Doers Luncheon meeting, 1968; dir. Cambridgeport Problem Ctr., Cambridge, Mass., 1969-71; mem. Jud. Nominating Commn., 1976-79; bd. overseers Boston Mus. Fine Arts, 1980-83; bd. govs. Newport Seamens Ch. Inst., 1989-91; tustee Comm. Rsch., Miami, Fla., 1960-69, chmn. bd., 1966-69; trustee Newport Art Mus., 1984-86, 92-94, Jamestown Cmty. Theatre, 1994-97, 99—, Newport Health Found., 1986-91, Hawthorne Sea Fund, 1990-93; bd. dirs. Boston Ctr. for Arts, 1976-80, Child and Family Svcs. of Newport County, 1983-97, 99—. Mem. Common Cause (Mass adv. bd. 1971-72, dir. 1974-75), Mass. Civil Liberties Union (exec. bd. 1973-74, dir. 1976-77). Home: 24 Fort Wetherill Rd Jamestown RI 02835-2908 Office Phone: 401-423-1758.

WORDEN, MARNY, artist, musician; b. Williamsport, Pa., Sept. 23, 1926; d. Harold Ernest and Marion Francis (Tillinghast) W.; m. Richard Dean Blair, Sept. 9, 1949 (div. 1957); 1 child, Brian Eric; m. John Riley Olson, Dec. 19, 1957. BA, U. Toledo, 1946; MAT, Ind. U., 1968. English tchr. Tex. Sch. for Deaf, Austin, 1954-62, Ind. Sch. for Deaf, Indpls., 1962-65; French, Spanish tchr. Indpls. City Schs., 1965-70; curriculum projects dir. Ind. Sch. for the Deaf, Indpls., 1970-71, tchr. English, Latin, 1972-79. Symphony musician and pvt. tchr. flute, piccolo, 1942—; dir. Tillinghast Early Music Consort; adjudicator Ind. Sch. Music Competitions. Author: (textbooks) 1,2,3 Language Series, 1970, (adaptations for the deaf) Beowulf, 1973, Song of Roland, 1974. Recipient of craftsman's rating in lapidary work, silversmithing; stone sculptures. Mem. Internat. Porcelain Artists & Tchrs., Inc. Avocations: oil paintings, watercolors, porcelain painting, performing. Address: 5504 Nordic Ln Richmond VA 23237-3807

WORDEN, WILLIAM PATRICK, deacon; b. Chgo., July 23, 1933; s. Shannon Gerard and Florence Marie (Chouinard) W.; m. Shirley Ann Poerio, Apr. 1, 1956; children: Mary Patricia Maloney, Judith Ann Laverdiere, Ellen Jean. BEE, Ill. Inst. Tech., 1955; MA in Pastoral Studies, Loyola U., Chgo., 1986; D Ministry, Grad. Theol. Found., Bristol, Ind., 1991. Deacon St. Peter and Paul Parish, Naperville, Ill., 1980-85, St. Thomas the Apostle Parish, Naperville, 1985—; chaplain DuPage County Jail, Wheaton, Ill., 1991-96; mem. reactor safety rev. com. Argonne Nat. Lab., Darien, Ill., 1989-97; dir. Diaconate for the Diocese of Joliet, 1997—. Del. Region VII Deaconal Orgn., 1981-84. Author: (with others) Decontamination and Decommissioning of Nuclear Facilities, 1980; contbr. articles to religious column in newspaper, jours. in field. Bd. dirs. Interfaith Counseling Svc., Naperville, 1980-85, Just of DuPage Jail Ministry, Wheaton, 1986-90. Office: St Thomas the Apostle Ch 1500 Brookdale Rd Naperville IL 60563-2129

WORDSWORTH, JERRY L. wholesale distribution executive; b. Charlotte, N.C., Sept. 22, 1945; BS, N.C. State U., 1963. With MBM, Rocky Mount, N.C., 1966—, chmn., pres. now. Office: MBM 2641 Meadowbrook Rd Rocky Mount NC 27802

WORELL, JUDITH P. psychologist, educator; b. N.Y.C. d. Moses and Dorothy Goldfarb; m. Leonard Worell, Aug. 11, 1947 (div.); children: Amy, Beth, Wendy; m. H.A. Smith, Mar. 23, 1985 BS magna cum laude, Queens Coll., 1950; MA, Ohio State U., 1952, PhD in Clin. Psychology, 1954; DHL (hon.), Colby-Sawyer Coll., 1993. Research assoc. Iowa Psychopathic Hosp., Iowa City, 1957-59; research assoc. Okla. State U., 1960-66; asst. prof. U. Ky., Lexington, 1969-71, assoc. prof., 1971-75, prof. edn1. and counseling psychology, 1976—, dir. counseling psychology tng. program, 1980-93, chairperson dept. ednl. and counseling psychology, 1993-97, prof. emerita, 1999—. Author: (with C.M. Nelson) Managing Instructional Problems, 1974; (with W.E. Stilwell) Psychology for Teachers and Students, 1981; Psychological Development in the Elementary Years, 1982; (with Fred Danner) The Adolescent as Decision-maker: Applications to Development and Education, 1989; (with Pam Remer) Feminist Perspectives in Therapy: An Empowerment Model for Women, 1992; (with N. Johnson) Shaping the Future of Feminist Psychology: Education, Research, and Practice, 1997, (with Norine Johnson & Michael Roberts) Beyond Appearance: A New Look at Adolescent Girls, 1999, Encyclopedia of Women and Gender: Sex Similarities and Differences and the Impact of Society on Gender, 2001, (with Pam Remer) Feminist Perspectives in Therapy: Empowering Diverse Women, 2002; assoc. editor Jour. Cons. and Clin. Psychology, 1976-79, mem. editl. bd., 1984-89; assoc. editor Psychol. Women Quar., 1984-89, editor, 1989-95; mem. editorial bd. Sex Roles, 1984-2000, Psychol. Assessment, 1991-97, Clin. Psychology Rev., 1991-97, Women and Therapy, 1992-2000; cons., reviewer 10 jours.; contbr. articles to profl. jours. Named U. Ky. Campus Woman of Yr., 1976, Outstanding Univ. Grad. prof., 1991, Disting. Ky. psychologist, 1990; USPHS fellow, 1953; NIMH rsch. grantee, 1962-69. Fellow APA (pres. Clin. Psychology of Women 1986-88, chmn. com. state assn. rels. 1982-83, fellow selection divsn. 35 com. 1983-84, policy and planning bd. 1989-92, publs. and comm. bd. 1992-99, chair 1996-98, chair jours. com., pres. divsn. psychology of women 1997-98, Disting. Leader for Women in Psychology 1990, Carolyn Wood Sherif award, 2001, Psychology of Women Heritage award 2004, coun. rep. 2000-02, chair women's caucus 2002), Ky. Psychol. Assn. (pres. 1981-82, rep. at large 1995-97), Southeastern Psychol. Assn. (exec. coun. mem.-at-large, pres.-elect 1993-94 pres. 1994-95), Am. Women in Psychology, Phi Beta Kappa. Home: 3892 Gloucester Dr Lexington KY 40510-9729 Office: U Ky Dept Ednl and Counseling Psychology 245 Dickey Hl Lexington KY 40506-0017 E-mail: jworell@alltel.net.

WORENKLEIN, JACOB JOSHUA, lawyer; b. N.Y.C., Oct. 1, 1948; s. Abraham and Cela (Zyskind) W.; divorced; children: David, Daniel, Laura; m. Cindy Sternkler, Feb. 26, 1995; 1 child, Sasha Anne. BA, Columbia U., 1969; MBA, JD, NYU, 1973. Bar: N.Y. 1974. From assoc. to ptnr. Milbank, Tweed, Hadley & McCloy, N.Y.C., 1973-93, chmn. firm planning com., 1988-90, exec. com., 1990-93, sr. advisor to exec. com., 1993-94; mng. dir., group head of global project fin. group Lehman Bros., N.Y.C., 1993-96; mng. dir., head project fin, commodity fin., export fin. Soc. Gen., N.Y.C., 1996-98, mng. dir., global head project and sector fin. Paris and N.Y.C., 1998—2003; pres., CEO U.S. Power Generating Co., N.Y.C., 2003—. Mem. investment banking mgmt. com. Lehman Bros., 1993-96; mem. adv. coun. Amoco Power Resources Corp., 1995-97; adj. prof. fin. NYU Stern Sch. of Bus.; bd. dirs., mem. audit com. CDC Globeleq, 2004—. Mem. editl. bd. Jour. Structured and Project Fin., 1996—; contbr. articles to profl. jours. Chmn. bd. Old Broadway Synagogue, N.Y.C., 2001-, pres. 1978-2001; trustee Fedn. Jewish Philanthropies, N.Y.C., 1984-86; bd. overseers United Jewish Appeal-Fedn. Jewish Philanthropies, 1987, chmn. lawyers divsn. major gifts, 1989-91, chmn. lawyers divsn., 1991-93, bd. dirs., 1991-97; trustee Jewish Cmty. Rels. Coun. N.Y., 1995-98, Com. for Econ. Devel., 2001-. Mem. Coun. on Fgn. Rels. Office: US Power Generating Co 499 Park Ave New York NY 10022 Office Phone: 212-652-3757. Business E-Mail: jworenklein@uspowergen.com.

WORK, BRUCE VAN SYOC, business consultant; b. Monmouth, Ill., Mar. 20, 1942; s. Robert M. and Evelyn (Rusken) W.; m. Janet Kay Brown, Nov. 12, 1966; children: Bruce, Terra. BA, Monmouth Coll., 1964; BS, U. Mo.-Rolla, 1966; postgrad., U. Chgo., 1978-79. Registered profl. engr., Ill. Various mgmt. positions Midcon Corp. (and subs.), 1966-79; pres. Indsl. Fuels Corp., Troy, Mich., 1979-85, Costain Coal Inc., Troy, Mich., 1985-89; pvt. practice small bus. cons., 1989-92; bus. cons. Wallis Oil Co., 1992-2000; small bus. cons., 2000—. Mem. various coms. Cuba United Meth. Ch. Mem. Detroit Athletic Club, Blue Key. Office: 2280 Hwy DD Cuba MO 65453-9684 E-mail: jbwork@fidnet.com. *People are the key to our success. Treat each individual as you would like to be treated.*

WORK, CHARLES ROBERT, lawyer; b. Glendale, Calif., June 21, 1940; s. Raymond P. and Minna M. (Fricke) W.; m. Linda S. Smith, Oct. 4, 1965 (div.); children: Matthew Keehn, Mary Lucila Landis, Benjamin Reed; m. Veronica A. Haggart, Apr., 1985, 1 child, Andrew Haggart. BA, Wesleyan U., 1962; JD, U. Chgo., 1965; LLM, Georgetown U., 1966. Bar: D.C. 1965, Utah 1965. Asst. U.S. atty. D.C., 1966-73; dep. adminstr. law enforcement assistance adminstrn., U.S. Dept. Justice, 1973-75; ptnr. Peabody, Lambert & Meyers, Washington, 1975-82, McDermott, Will & Emery, Washington, 1982—. Recipient Rockefeller Pub. Service award 1978. Mem. D.C. Bar (pres. 1976-77). Office: McDermott Will & Emery 600 13th St NW Fl 12-8 Washington DC 20005-3005 E-mail: cwork@mwe.com.

WORK, DAVID R. pharmacist, executive director; b. Clinton, Iowa, June 14, 1939; m. Rebecca Dean Stewart, Oct. 9, 1976; children: Dana, Amy, Susan. BS, U. Iowa, 1961; JD, U. Denver, 1968. Pharmacist, mgr., sec.-treas. Lyons Drug Co. Inc., Clinton, Iowa, 1961-65; asst. house counsel Blue Cross and Blue Shielf of Ill., 1968-69; asst. dean fiscal affairs Sch. of Pharmacy, U. N.C., Chapel Hill, 1970-73, asst. prof., 1969-73; dir. of assn. affairs The Nat. Assn. of Retail Druggist, 1973-76; exec. dir. N.C. Bd. of Pharmacy, 1976—; pres. Nat. Assn. of Bds. of Pharmacy, 1993-94. Contbr. articles to profl. jours. Recipient Meritorious Svc. award N.C. Pharm. Assn., 1972, Commrs. Spl. Citation U.S. FDA, 1988; named Pharmacist of Yr., N.C., 1995. Mem. Nat. Assn. of Bd. of Pharmacy (pres. 1993-94, pres.-elect 1992-93, v.p. 1991-92), Am. Pharm. Assn., Nat. Assn. of Retail Druggists, Am. Soc. for Pharmacy Law, Fedn. of Assn. of Health Regulatory Bds., Assn. of Food and Drug Ofcls., N.C. Pharm. Assn. Avocations: tennis, cooking, photography.

WORK, GEORGE PAUL, cellist; b. Lincoln, Nebr., June 20, 1957; s. George Arthur Work, Carol Puckett Work; m. Dawn Elizabeth Work MaKinne. cert. in performance, B in Music Performance, Eastman Sch. Music, 1979, M in Music Performance, 1981. Founder, dir. Iowa State Summer Chamber Music Workshop, Ames, Iowa, 1993—2000; prof. cello Iowa State U., Ames, 1981—. Cellist Ames Piano Quartet, Ames, 1981—; artist faculty mem. Luth. Music Program, Mpls., 1984—97, Bravo! Summer String Inst., Mpls., 1994; adj. prof. cello Drake U., Des Moines, 1997—98; artist faculty mem. Brevard (N.C.) Music Ctr., 1998—. Musician: (recording) Piano Quartets by Chausson and Saint-Saens, 1989, Dvorak: The Two Piano Quartets, 1990, Faure: The Two Piano Quartets, 1991, Piano Quartets by Strauss and Widor, 1993, Piano Quartets of Schumann and Brahms, 1994, Piano Quartets of Brahms, 1995, The Russian Piano Quartet, 2000, Dorian Sampler, Volume 2, 1989, Gemini, 2001, (chamber music performances) over 300 concerts throughout N.Am., also France, Austria, Taiwan, and Mex. Mem. Amnesty Internat., Ames, Iowa; case coord. Amnesty Internat, Ames, 1986—91. Grantee Grants for Ames Quartet concerts and workshops, Affiliated Arts Agencies of Upper Midwest, 1985—87, 1989—91, Grant for Ames Quartet concerts and workshops, Nat. Endowment for Arts, 1982—83. Mem.: Am. String Tchrs. Assn. (Studio Tchr. of Yr. award, Iowa 1991). Avocations: astronomy, travel. Office: Iowa State Univ Ames IA 50011 Office Phone: 515-294-4013. Business E-Mail: gwork@iastate.edu.

WORK, HENRY HARCUS, psychiatrist, educator; b. Buffalo, Nov. 11, 1911; s. Henry Harcus and Jeannette (Harcus) W.; m. Virginia Codington, Oct. 20, 1945 (dec. Nov. 1991); children: Henry Harcus III, David Codington, William Bruce, Stuart Runyon. AB, Hamilton Coll., Clinton, N.Y., 1933; MD, Harvard, 1937. Intern, resident Boston Children's Hosp., 1937-40, Emma P. Bradley Home Providence, 1940, Buffalo Children's Hosp., 1940-42, N.Y. Hosp., 1945-47; psychiat. services adviser, chief U.S. Children's Bur., Washington, 1948-49; assoc. prof. pediatrics U. Louisville, 1949-55; mem. faculty UCLA, 1955-72, prof. psychiatry and pub. health, 1966-72; chief profl. svcs. Am. Psychiat. Assn., Washington, 1972-83; clin. prof. George Washington U., Georgetown U., Uniformed Svcs. U. of Health Scis., U. Md., 1973—. Author: A Guide to Preventive Child Psychiatry, 1965, Minimal Brain Dysfunction: A Medical Challenge, 1967, Psychiatric Emergencies in Childhood, 1967, Crisis in Child Psychiatry, 1975, also articles. Served to capt. AUS, 1942-45. Recipient Simon Wile Award, Amer. Acad. of Child and Adolescent Psychiatry, 1994. Mem. So. Calif. Psychiat. Assn. (pres. 1966-67), Am. Orthopsychiat. Assn. (v.p. 1968-69), Am. Coll. Psychiatry (sec.-gen. 1979-93), Group for Advancement of Psychiatry (pres. 1982-85) Home: 4986 Sentinel Dr Apt 504 Bethesda MD 20816-3581

WORKING, RUSSELL CRAIG, reporter, writer; b. Long Beach, Calif., Oct. 12, 1959; s. Kenneth Calvin and Marjorie Anne Working; m. Nonna Working, Oct. 20, 2002; children: Sergei, Lev Russell. BA, Whitworth Coll., Spokane, 1978—82. Reporter Grants Pass Daily Courier, Oreg., 1985—92, Mail Tribune, Medford, 1992—96, Tacoma News Tribune, 1996—97; editor The Vladivostok News, Russia, 1997—2001; freelance writer Vladivostok, 1998—2001, Limassol, Cyprus, 2001—03; reporter Chgo. Tribune, 2003—. Author: (novels) Word Parasites, (short stories) Resurrectionists (Iowa Short Fiction award, 1987, H.L.Davis award, 1997), The Irish Martyr (Richard O. Sullivan award, 2003). Mem.: PEN Internat. Office: Chgo Tribune 435 N Michigan Blvd Chicago IL 60611 Office Phone: 312-222-3232. E-mail: rworking@tribune.com.

WORKMAN, GEORGE HENRY, structural engineering consultant; b. Muskegon, Mich., Sept. 18, 1939; s. Harvey Merton and Bettie Jane (Meyers) W.; m. Vicki Sue Hanish, June 17, 1967; children: Mark, Larry. AS, Muskegon C.C., 1960; BS in Engring., MS in Engring., U. Mich., 1966, PhD, 1969. Registered profl. engr., Ohio. Prin. engr. Battelle Meml. Inst., Columbus, Ohio, 1969-76; pres. Applied Mechanics Inc., Longboat Key, Fla., 1976—. Instr. dept. civil engring. Ohio State U., 1973, 82. Contbr. tech. papers to nat. and internat. confs. With USN, 1961-64. Mem. ASME, Am. Acad. Mechanics, Sigma Xi, Chi Epsilon, Phi Kappa Phi, Phi Thea Kappa. Congregationalist. Home and Office: 3431 Bayou Ct Longboat Key FL 34228-3028 Office Phone: 941-383-0721.

WORKMAN, JAMES E. retired school psychologist; b. Hillsboro, Ohio, Mar. 19, 1938; s. Russell Cochran and Stella Mae W.; m. Brenda Lee Staats, Oct. 8, 1960; children: Jennifer Nakayama, Loretta Workman. AB, Cin. Bible Sem., 1961; postgrad., Cin. Bible Grad. Sch., 1961—63; MEd, U. Cin., 1969—72; postgrad., Gestalt Inst. of Cleve., 1975. Cert. sch. psychologist Ohio; motorcycle riding instr. Motorcycle Safety Found. English tchr. Clermont Northeastern Local Schs., Owensville, Ohio, 1964—66; social worker Clermont County Human Svcs., Batavia, Ohio, 1966—69; dir. Regional Spl. Edn. Ctr., Wilmington, Ohio, 1969—71; intern psychologist Hamilton County Office Edn., Ohio, 1971—72; psychologist Zanesville (Ohio) City Schs., 1972—97. Bd. dirs. SCI, Inc., Zanesville, 1975—, chairperson 1992-93; bd. dirs., v.p. Residential Resources, Inc., Zanesville, 1992—; bd. dirs. Southeastern Ohio Symphony, New Concord, Ohio, 1980—, Friends of the Libr., Zanesville, 1995-2004, pres., 2000, sec., 2002-2003. Mem. Ohio Sch. Psychologists assn., East Cen. Ohio Sch. Psychologists Assn. (pres. 1974). Avocations: flying, sailing, reading, writing, motorcycling. Home: 1450 Lectric Ln Zanesville OH 43701-6928

WORKMAN, JEROME JAMES, JR., chemist; b. Northfield, Minn., Aug. 6, 1952; s. Jerome James and Louise Mae (Sladek) W.; m. Rebecca Marie Zittel, Aug. 3, 1974; children: Cristina Louise, Stephannie Michelle, Daniel Jerome, Sara Marie, Michael Timothy. BA with honors, St. Mary's U., Winona, Minn., 1976, MA, 1980; PhD, Columbia Pacific U., San Rafael, Calif., 1984; postgrad., Columbia U., 1990-91, 99-00, MIT, Cambridge, Mass., 2001—; grad., Columbia Sr. Exec. Program, 2004. Prin. Workman & Assocs., Mankato, Minn., 1980-82; pres. Biochem. Cons., Mankato, Minn., 1982-84; sr. chemist Technicon Instruments, Tarrytown, N.Y., 1984-87; supervising scientist Bran & Luebbe/Technicon, Tarrytown, 1987; sr. scientist Hitachi Instruments, Danbury, Conn., 1987-89; mgr. tech. support NIR Systems/Perstorp Analytical, Silver Spring, Md., 1989-90, mgr. mktg., 1990-92, dir. mktg., 1992-93; assoc. advisor Inst. Textile Tech., Charlottesville, Va., 1992—; prin. scientist Perkin Elmer Corp., Norwalk, Conn., 1993-96; sr. rsch. fellow Kimberly-Clark Corp., Analytical and Measurement Tech., Neenah, Wis., 1996—2002; chief tech. officer, v.p. rsch. and engring. Argose, Inc., Waltham, Mass., 2002—. Instr. Fedn. Analytical Chemistry and Spectroscopy Socs.; external examiner U. Guelph, Ont., Can., 1993-94, chair rep. indsl. adv. bd. Ctr. for Process Analytical Chemistry 1993—2002; apptd. mem. subcom. on process analytical techs. U.S. FDA, 2002, vis. prof., 2002; mem. Nat. Acads. nat. rsch. panel on assessment of NIST programs, 2003—; mem. NRC panel U.S. Nat. Acads., 2003—. Author: Handbook of Organic Compounds: NIR, IR, Raman, and UV-Vis Spectra Featuring Polymers and Surfactants, 3 vols., 2000; co-author: Statistics in Spectroscopy, 1991, 2003, (series) Chemometrics in Spectroscopy, UV-Vis Spectroscopy, 1993, Near-Infrared Spectroscopy in Agr., 2003; editor: The Process Pages for NIRnews, Internat. Com. for Near Infrared Spectroscopy, 1993—97; co-editor: Applied Spectroscopy: A Compact Reference for Practitioners, 1998, Near-Infrared Reflectance Spectroscopy in Analysis of Agricultural Products, 2003, Spectroscopy Letters 1996-2002, 2003; contbg. editor: Spectroscopy Mag.; mem. adv. editl. bd. Spectroscopy, 1995—, assoc. editor Wiley-Intersci. Series in Lab. Automation, 1993, Applied Spectroscopy Reviews, 1995—, Lab. Robotics and Automation, 1995—98, process editor Jour. Near Infrared Spectroscopy, 1995—97; contbr. articles. Recipient Heart of Gold award Minn. affiliate Am. Heart Assn., 1984, Ea. Analytical Symposium award, 2002; Am. Heart Assn. H.N. and H.B. Shapira scholar, 1971-72; NSF grantee, 1977-78. Fellow: ASTM (exec. com., chair main com. on molecular spectroscopy, Appreciation awards 2000, award of Merit 2002), Am. Inst. Chemists, Royal Soc. Chemistry U.K. (chartered chemist); mem.: Coblentz Soc. (bd. mgrs. 2002—), Joint Com. Atomic and Molecular Phys. Data (chmn. UV-VIS, exec. coun.), Coun. Near-Infrared Spectroscopy (pres.), Soc. for Applied Spectroscopy, Am. Chem. Soc. (instr. course on Practical Near-IR Analysis), Nat. Honor Soc., Sigma Xi, Delta Epsilon Sigma. Achievements include research in molecular spectroscopy, statistics and chemometrics; development and applications of spectroscopic methods and sensors to consumer products and processes; U.S. and international patents for analytical systems. Office: Argose Inc 299 Cypress St Brookline MA 02445 E-mail: workmans@rcn.com.

WORKMAN, JOHN MITCHELL, chemist; b. Uniontown, Pa., Oct. 25, 1949; s. Hugh Lawrence and Mary Louise (Mitchell) W.; m. Gayle Sue Zappin, Nov. 20, 1987. BA in Psychology, Miami U., Oxford, Ohio, 1971; MS in Edn., Kans. State U., 1976; MS in Chemistry, U. Cin., 1985, PhD in Chemistry, 1987; MBA in Fin., Wright State U., Dayton, Ohio, 1995. Teaching and rsch. asst. dept. chemistry Wright State U., Dayton, Ohio, 1977-81; grad. teaching asst. U. Cin., 1982-83, grad. rsch. asst., 1983-86; sr. scientist Chemsys Inc., Fairborn, Ohio, 1986-89, dir. elemental analysis, 1989—; lab. dir., 1994—. Contbr. articles to jours. Analytical Chemistry, Applied Spectroscopy. With U.S. Army, 1972-75. Mem.: Am. Phys. Soc., Am. Chem. Soc., Sigma Iota Epsilon, Sigma Pi Sigma, Sigma Xi. Episcopalian. Office: Chemsys Inc PO Box 427 Fairborn OH 45324-0427 E-mail: gopackard@aol.com.

WORKMAN, LEATTA ARDYCE, management consultant; b. Murphysboro, Ill., Jan. 8, 1973; d. Larry Dean and June Irene Bergeson; m. Edward Lind Workman, Sept. 26, 1998; children: Grace Leatta, Hannah Kay, Corrine Faith. AA, Mineral Area Coll., Park Hills, Mo., 1992; BS in Psychology, S.W. Mo. State Coll., 1999; MS in Human Resource Devel., Pittsburg (Kans.) State U., 2002, degree in indsl. edn., 2004. Access specialist S.W. Ctr. for Ind. Living, Springfield, Mo., 1994—98; exec. dir. The Ind. Living Ctr., Inc., Joplin, Mo., 1998—2003; pres. Workman & Assocs., Springfield, 2003—. Recipient hon. mention Mo. Governor's Advocate of Yr., 2000. Mem.: Phi Kappa Phi (life), Phi Theta Kappa (life). Home: 1329 Buena Vista Ave Carthage MO 64836 Office: Workman & Associates 508 S Main Carthage MO 64836 Office Phone: 417-693-1103. E-mail: lworkman@workman-associates.com.

WORKMAN, MARGARET LEE, lawyer; b. May 22, 1947; d. Frank Eugene and Mary Emma (Thomas) W.; m. Edward T. Gardner III; children: Lindsay Elizabeth, Christopher Workman, Edward Earnshaw. AB in Polit. Sci., W.Va. U., 1969, JD, 1974. Bar: W.Va. 1974. Asst. counsel to majority, pub. works com. U.S. Senate, Washington, 1974-75; law clk. 13th jud. cir., W.Va. Ct., Charleston, 1975-76, judge, 1981-88; pvt. practice Charleston, 1976-81, 99—; justice W.Va. Supreme Ct. Appeals, Charleston, 1989-99, chief justice, 1993, 97. Advance person for Rosalyn Carter, Carter Presdl. Campaign, Atlanta, 1976. Democrat. Episcopalian.

WORKMAN, NORMAN ALLAN, accountant, graphic arts consultant; b. Boston, Apr. 20, 1918; s. William Horace and Estelle Emily (Hanlon) W.; m. Harriet Patricia Banfield, Aug. 1, 1946; children: Stephen, Mark, Brian, Patricia. Student, Coll. William and Mary, 1938-39; BS in Econs. magna cum laude, Bowdoin Coll., 1941. CPA, Oreg. Staff acct. Lybrand Ross Bros. & Montgomery, Boston, 1941-43, Whitfield Stratford & Co., Portland, Oreg., 1946-51; ptnr. Workman, Shephard & Co., CPAs, Portland, 1951-60; sole practitioner Portland, 1961-96; ret. Newsletter columnist Good Impressions, 1993-98. Chmn. bd. Sylvan Sch., Portland, 1956-57; pres. Doernbecher Children's Hosp. Found., Portland, 1963-85, Bowdoin Club Oreg., Portland, 1963—; trustee Oreg. Episcopal Schs., Portland, 1974-76. Lt. (j.g.) Supply Corps, USNR, 1944-46. Named Mr. Doernbecher, Doernbecher Children's Hosp. Found., 2002. Mem. AICPA, Inst. Mgmt. Accts. (pres. Portland chpt. 1954-55), Oreg. Soc. CPA's, Pacific Printing and Imaging Assn., Arlington Club, Multnomah Athletic Club, Phi Beta Kappa. Avocations: bird hunting, fishing, horticulture. Home: 4381 SW Fairview Blvd Portland OR 97221-2709

WORKMAN, ROBERT PETER, artist, cartoonist; b. Chgo., Jan. 27, 1961; s. Tom Okko and Virginia (Martin) Workman. Doctorate d'Etat, Diplome 3d Cycle, Sch. of Louvre, Paris, 1997; prof. habilite, France, 1997; DEA, French U. Lumiere, Lyon; Doctorate in Hieroglyphics, Nat. Inst. Lang./Civilizations, Egypt, 1997; PhD, Roosevelt U., Belgium; postgrad., Sch. of Art Inst. Chgo.; Ecole Doctorale des Sciences, U. Blaise-Pascal/U. D'Auvergue, 1998; Prof., Mus. Nat. d'histoire Naturelle. Freelance artist, Chgo.; artist Villager Newspaper, Chgo., 1991—; instr. St. Xavier Coll., Chgo., 1985; cartoonist Bridge View News, Oak Lawn, Ill., 1983-89, Village View Pubs., Oak Lawn, 1989; artist Villager News, 1991; creator acrylic sculpture ArtStyle; adj. faculty U. Ariz. TV art dir. Media-In-Action, Oak Lawn; lectr. Oxford U., Eng., U. Ariz., 1996; substitute tchr. Morgan Park Acad., Chgo.; artist-in-residence Chgo. Pub. Libr.; featured voice Am. Radio, 1992; maitre de confs., Paris; creator acrylic sculpture art style; creator 3-D Art Form, Tri-d' Art 21st Century; designer Oak Lawn War Meml., Ill.; prof. Nat. Mus. Natural History, France, 2001. Author: (cartoon strip) Cypher, 1983-89; Sesqui Squirrel Coloring Book, 1982, Sesqui Squirrel History of Chicago, 1983, Book of Thoth, The Great Pyramid A Book in Stone, 1998, Easter Island and Egypt,(artists' books) Sesqui Squirrel History of the Constitution, Sesqui Squirrel Presents How Columbus Discovered America, The Sesqui-Squirrel Chicago Millennium Book, 1999; author: (novel) Angels of Doom, Book of THOTH, The Great Pyramid a Book in Stone, 1998, Easter Island and Egypt; contbr. to books on photography including: Wondrous Worlds, Hidden Silhouettes, Meadows of

Memories, Eternal Moments; artworks and books in collections of over 120 mus. and librs. and pvt. collections, including Mus. du Louvre, Paris, Lincoln Collection, Ill., Smithsonian, Art Inst. Chgo., Daley Br. Libr., Chgo., Ill. Exec. Mansion Mus., Sesquicentennial Archives Chgo. Pub. Libr. (awards and honors), Vatican Libr., Rome, Bodleian Libr. Oxford (Eng.) U., Mt. Greenwood br. Pub. Libr. Chgo., Ill. Collection, Libr. Nat. Mus. Am. Art, Nat. Portrait Gallery, Carter Presdl. Libr., Reagan Presdl. Libr., Expo. U.S. Pavilion Lisbon, Portugal, 1998; exhibited Am. Pavilion, Expo 92, Seville, Spain, Royal Acad. Arts, 1995, Am. Pavilion, Expo 98, Lisbon, Portugal, inaugural exhbn. of the New Millennium/Chgo. Pub. Libr., 2000, online exhibitions at www.artq.net, VisualArtArray.com; featured on Sta. WBBM-TV, Chgo., 1998; contbr. poetry to books: Journey to Infinity, America at the Millennium, Treasured Poems of America; creator of Planetnet Concept; inventor Tri-CAR; inventor millenium star explorer spacecraft, Tri-CAR. Mem. nat. adv. bd. Am. Security Coun., Boston, Va.; founder Kennedy Pk. Libr., Chgo. Featured in Artist's mag., 1990; recipient Resolution City Coun. Chgo., 1992; honored with Ill. House Resolution #443, 2003, Chgo. Pub. Schs. 2003 Prin. for a Day program; nominee Tchr. in Space Program, 1985. Mem. Am. Watercolor Soc., Gen. Med. Coun. (Eng.), No. Ill. Newspaper Assn., Art Inst. Chgo. (freelancer 1991), Artists' Resource Trust Ft. Wayne Mus. Art, Ridge Art Assn., VFW, S.W. Archdiocesan Singles, Friends Oxford U., Alumni Sch. Art Inst. Chgo., Alumni Sch of the Louvre, KC, Mensa. Roman Catholic. Home and Office: 2509 W 111th St Apt 2E Chicago IL 60655-1325

WORKMAN, WILLARD ALLYN, association executive; b. Milford, Del., Oct. 30, 1946; s. Willard Harold and Louise Elizabeth Workman; 1 child, Amanda. BA in Polit. Sci., L.I. U., 1969. Spl. negotiator internat. trade controls Dept. State, Washington, 1987-88; v.p., gen. mgr. internat. U.S. C. of C., Washington, 1988-2001, sr. v.p. Internat. Affairs, 2001—. V.p. Ctr. Internat. Pvt. Enterprise, Washington, 1992; trustee U.S. Coun. for Internat. Bus., N.Y.C., 1993-2001. With USN, 1969-73. Mem. Univ. Club. E-mail: wworkman@uschamber.com.

WORLEY, DAVID, lawyer; b. Stuttgart, Germany, Sept. 30, 1958; AB, Harvard U., 1980; JD, U. Va., 1985. Atty. Arnall, Golden & Gregory, Atlanta, 1985-87; pvt. practice Jonesboro, Ga., 1987-90; atty. Glave, Glave, Fincher and Breakfield, Jonesboro, 1991-94, Jacobs and Slowsky, Atlanta, 1994—. Chmn. Ga. State Dem. Party, 1998-2001; chmn. bd. trustees Clayton County Libr. Bd., 1993—. Mem. Assn. of State Dem. Chairs. Office: Jacobs and Slowsky 100 Peachtree St NW Ste 1950 Atlanta GA 30303-1919 also: 1100 Spring St NW Ste 710 Atlanta GA 30309-2829

WORLEY, JANE LUDWIG, lawyer; b. Reading, Pa., Sept. 4, 1917; d. Walter Schearer and Marion Grace (Johns) L.; m. Floyd Edwin Worley, Oct. 30, 1946 (dec. Jan. 1982); children: Laetitia Anne, Thomas Allen, Christopher Ludwig. AB, Bryn Mawr Coll., 1938; JD, Temple U., 1942. Bar: Pa. 1943, U.S. Dist. Ct. (ea. dist.) Pa. 1980, U.S. Supreme Ct. 1968. Assoc. Richardson Moss & Richardson, Reading, 1943-48; pvt. practice Wernersville, Pa., 1948—. V.p., bd. dirs. Worley Lumber Co. Inc., Wernersville, 1955—. Sec. Friends of Reading Mus., 1986-91; sec. Berks County chpt. ARC, 1986-87, v.p., 1987-91. Mem. ABA, Pa. Bar Assn., Berks County Bar Assn., DAR, Jr. League Reading. Republican. Mem. United Ch. of Christ. Avocations: antique and art collecting, travel. Office: 404 Sheridan Rd Womelsdorf PA 19567

WORLEY, JOE, editor; Editor Tulsa World, Okla., now mng. editor. Office: Tulsa World PO Box 1770 Tulsa OK 74102-1770

WORLEY, LLOYD DOUGLAS, English language educator; b. Lafayette, La., Sept. 11, 1946; s. Albert Stiles and Doris (Christy) W.; m. Maydean Ann Mouton, Apr. 4, 1966; children: Erin Shawn, Albert Stiles II. BA, U. SW La., 1968, MA, 1972; PhD, So. Ill. U., 1979. Ordained priest, Liberal Cath. Ch. Tchr. Lafayette H.S., 1969-74; vis. asst. prof. dept. English So. Ill. U., Carbondale, 1979-80; asst. prof. dept. English Pa. State U., DuBois, 1980-87; assoc. prof., assoc. dir. composition dept. English U. No. Colo., Greeley, 1987-88, prof. dept. English, 1988—. Acting dir. Writing Component Ctr. Basic Skills, So. Ill. U., 1980. Editor: Ruthven Literary Bull., 1988-92; contbr. book chpts., articles. Rector Parish of St. Albertus Magnus The Liberal Cath. Ch., 1987-2001, sec-treas. Am. Province; provost Am. Clerical Synod Chpt. The Liberal Cath. Ch., 1991-2001; Sovereign Grand Master, Order of Holy Sepulchre, 1982-; vicar-gen. The Liberal Cath. Ch. Decorated Knight Bachelor, 1996, Hereditary Knight of San Luigi, 1996, Knight Cmdr. Order of Merit St. Angilbert, 1993, Prelate Comdr. Order of Noble Companions of Swan, 1993, Grand Chamberlain, 1995, Knight Order of Guadalupe, 1995, Knight Comdr. Justice Sovereign Order St. John, Knight Grand Cross of Bear of Alabona, 1995, Knight Grand Cross Order St. Stanislaus, 1998, Knight Comp. Crown of Alabona, 1998, Knight Grand Cross Order St. John, 1998, Knight Grand Cross Order Sts. Constantine the Great and Helen, Grand Cross with Collar of Order of Noble Companion of Swan, 2000; created hereditary Baron, Royal and Serene House of Alabona-Ostrogojsk et de Garama, HRSH Prince William I, created Count Palatine of Maxalla, 1996, created Hereditary Duke of Maxalla, 2000. Fellow Philalethes Soc.; mem. ASCD, Internat. Assn. for Fantastic in Arts (divsn. head Am. Lit. 1987-93), Lord Ruthven Assembly (pres. 1988-94, founding pres. emeritus 1994), Conf. Coll. Composition and Commn., Nat. Coun. Tchrs. English, Am. Conf. Irish Studies, Sigma Tau Delta (bd. dirs. 1990-96, high plains regent various states 1992-96, 10-Yr. Outstanding Advisor award 1997), Masons (century lodge #190), Order of DeMolay (chevalier, cross of honor, legion of honor), Knights Holy Sepulchre (Sov. Grand Master), Rose Croix Martinist Order (pres. premier nat. coun.). Democrat. Office: 3620 W 10th B-150 Greeley CO 80634-9655 Office Phone: 206-350-2268.

WORLEY, NANCY L. secretary of state; b. Madison County, Ala., Nov. 7, 1951; d. Leonard O. and Lillian (Smith) W. BA magna cum laude, U. Montevallo, Ala., 1973; MA, Jacksonville (Ala.) State U., 1974; postgrad., U. Ala., Tuscaloosa and Huntsville, 1974, U. Edinburgh, Scotland, 1975. Cert. English, speech and Latin tchr., Ala. Instr. English, NE State Jr. Coll., Rainsville, Ala., Calhoun Community Coll., Decatur, Ala.; tchr. lang. arts Decatur City Schs.; sec. of state State of Ala., Montgomery, 2003—. Contbr. articles to profl. jours. Named Ala.'s Outstanding Young Educator, Dist. Tchr. of Yr., Decatur City Schs.; grantee grantee UN. Mem. NEA, Ala. Edn. Assn. (pres., 1983-84, 95-97, legis. com.), Ala. Fgn. Lang. Tchrs. Assn. (past pres.), Ala. Classroom Tchrs. Assn. (past pres., bd. dirs.), Sigma Tau Delta, Kappa Delta Pi, Lambda Sigma Chi, Omicron Delta Kappa. Office: Office of the Sec of State PO Box 5616 Montgomery AL 36103-5616*

WORLEY, ROBERT WILLIAM, JR., retired lawyer; b. Anderson, Ind., June 13, 1935; s. Robert William and Dorothy Mayhew (Hayler) W.; m. Diana Lynn Matthews, Aug. 22, 1959; children: Nathanael, Hope Hillegas. BS in Chem. Engring., Lehigh U., 1956; LLB, Harvard U., 1960. Bar: Conn. 1960, U.S. Supreme Ct. 1966, Fla. 1977. Assoc. then ptnr. Cummings & Lockwood, Stamford, Conn., 1960-91; gen. counsel Consol. Asset Recover Corp. sub. Chase Manhattan Corp., Bridgeport, Conn., 1991-94; v.p., asst. gen. counsel The Chase Manhattan Bank, N.Y.C., 1994-2001; ret., 2001. Trustees com. on bequests and trusts Lehigh U., 1979—; mem. Conn. Legis. Task Force on Probate Court Sys., 1991-93; chmn. Greenwich Arts Coun., 1981-82; v.p., bd. dirs. Greenwich Choral Soc., 1962-77, 80; bd. dirs. Greenwich Ctr. for Chamber Music, 1981-85, Greenwich Symphony, 1986-89; commr. Greenwich Housing Authority, 1972-77; bldg. com. for sr. ctr. Greenwich Bd. Selectman, 1980-81. Capt. JAGC, AUS, 1965. Mem. Conn. Bar Assn. (exec. com. probate sect. 1980), Sippican Choral Soc., Harvard Club Boston. Christian Scientist. Home: PO Box 1055 Marion MA 02738-0019

WORMAN, HOWARD JAY, internist, educator; b. Paterson, N.J., May 21, 1959; s. Louis and Dora (Rubin) W. BA, Cornell U., 1981; MD, U. Chgo., 1985. Diplomate Am. Bd. Internal Medicine. Intern N.Y. Hosp., N.Y.C., 1985—86, resident, 1986—87; guest investigator Rockefeller U., N.Y.C., 1987—90; asst. prof. Mt. Sinai Sch. Medicine, N.Y.C., 1990—94; asst. attending physician Mt. Sinai Hosp., N.Y.C., 1990—94; asst. prof. Columbia U. Coll. Physicians and Surgeons, N.Y.C., 1995—98, assoc. prof., 1998—; asst. attending physician N.Y. Presbyn. Hosp., Columbia-Presbyn. Ctr., N.Y.C., 1995—98, assoc. attending physician, 1998—; dir. divsn. digestive and liver diseases Presbyn. Hosp., N.Y.C., 1999—2002. Mem. med. adv. com. Muscular Dystrophy Assn., 2000—. Mem. editl. bd. Hepatology, Frontiers in Biosci., World Jour. Gastroenterology; contbr. articles to profl. jours. Recipient Physician-Scientist award NIH, 1987-92; Charles E. Culpeper scholar in Med. Scis., 1994-95, Irma T. Hirschl scholar, 1997-2002. Mem. AAAS, ACP, Am. Chem. Soc., Am. Fedn. Med. Rsch. (Trainee award in clin. rsch. 1989, Henry Christian award 1990), Am. Soc. Cell Biology, Am. Assn. Study of Liver Diseases, Am. Gastroent. Assn., Am. Soc. Clin. Investigation, N.Y. Acad. Scis. (vice chmn. biol. scis. sect. 1992-93, chmn. 1993-94), Am. Diabetes Assn., Hon. Order Ky. Cols., Phi Beta Kappa. Democrat. Jewish. Avocations: music, reading. Office: Columbia U Coll Physicians-Surgeons 630 W 168th St New York NY 10032-3795 Office Phone: 212-305-8156. Business E-Mail: hjwl4@columbia.edu.

WORMER, THOMAS ANDREW, surgeon; b. Buffalo, Dec. 3, 1956; s. Donald Andrew and Elinor Ann (Bliss) W.; m. Melissa Jane Ertell, Apr. 11, 1988; children: Matthew Thomas, Margaret Elizabeth, Samuel James, Sarah Jane. BS, Allegheny Coll,, 1979; MD, Albany Med. Coll., 1984. Diplomate Am. Bd. Surgery. Intern Millard Fillmore Hosp., Buffalo, 1984-85, resident in gen. surgery, 1985-89; attending surgeon F.F. Thompson Hosp., Canandaigua, N.Y., 1989-95, chief surgery, 1994-99. Fellow ACS; mem. Canandaigua Med. Soc. (pres. 1994), N.Y. State Med. Soc. Presbyterian. Office: Canandaigua Medical Group 335 Parrish St Canandaigua NY 14424-1794 E-mail: twormer@rochester.rr.com.

WORMLEY, DAVID, dean; Assoc. dean engring., head dept. mech. engring. MIT; dean engring. Pa. State U., 1992—. Prin. in devel. of NSF-supported coalition of 7 univs. Engring. Coalition of Schs. for Excellence in Edn. and Leadership; chmn. exec. com. Nat. Rsch. Coun.'s Transp. Rsch. Bd.; chair adv. com. NSF Engring. Directorate; mem. ednl. adv. com. NSPE. Assoc. editor: Jour. Engring. Edn. Fellow: ASME (Lewis Moody award, Dynamic Sys. and Control Divsn. Edn. award 1997). Achievements include research in dynamic systems and control with application to transportation, energy production and conversion and fluid actuation systems. Office: Pa State U 101 Hammond Bldg University Park PA 16802

WORNER, THERESA MARIE, internist, educator; b. Breckenridge, Minn., Feb. 19, 1948; d. William Daniel and Elizabeth (Stelten) W.; m. Martin Herbst, Mar. 24, 1979. AB, St. Theresa Coll., 1970; MD, U. Minn., 1974. Diplomate Am. Bd. Internal Medicine. Rotating intern Kings County Hosp., Bklyn., 1974-75, resident medicine, 1975-77; fellow VA Med. Ctr., Bronx, N.Y., 1977-78, chief med. sect. Alcoholism treatment program, 1978-87; asst. prof. medicine Mt. Sinai Sch. Medicine, N.Y.C., 1984-87; mem. faculty Postgrad. Ctr., 1985-90; physician in charge alcoholism svcs. L.I. Coll. Hosp., Bkyn., 1987-92; assoc. prof. clin. medicine SUNY, Health Sci. Ctr., Bkyn., 1988—; dir. rsch. 32BJ Health Fund, 1992-99; clin. assoc. prof. Pub. Health Cornell U. Med. Coll., 1996—; pres. Menachem Publ., Bethlehem, N.H., 1999—. Pres./founder Alcohol. Info, 1995-97; advisor Patient Care Mag., 1984—; cons. REA, 1996—. Referee Hepatology, 1986, Jour. Study Alcohol, 1984—, Substance Abuse, 1992—, Alcoholism: Clinical and Exptl. Rsch., 1992—, Drug and Alcohol Dependence, 1993—, Drug Therapy, 1994—, Addiction, 1996—; contbr. numerous articles to profl. jours. Active Israel Mus., Israeli Opera, Israel Symphony. Grantee Child Welfare Adminstrn., 1991, 92, 93; recipient Physicians Recognition award AMA, 1984, 89, 91, 96, Cert. of Merit Govt. Employees Ins. Co., 1986, PACT Intern Site award, 1991, 92. Fellow ACP, N.Y. Acad. Medicine; mem. AAAS, Am. Med. Soc. on Alcoholism and Other Drug Dependence, Am. Soc. Internal Medicine, Am. Assn. for Study Liver Diseases (Travel award 1978), N.Y. Acad. Scis., Rsch. Soc. on Alcoholism, Internat. Soc. Biologic Rsch. in Alcoholism.

WORONOFF, ISRAEL, former psychology educator; b. Bklyn., Dec. 30, 1926; s. Samuel and Lena (Silberman) W.; m. Fay Goldberg, Feb. 11, 1950; 1 child, Gary. AB in Psychology, U. Mich., 1949, MA in Sociology, 1952, PhD in Edn., 1954. Lic. psychologist, Mich. Instr. Flint (Mich.) Jr. Coll., 1953-54; asst. prof. St. Cloud (Minn.) State Coll., 1954-56, Ea. Mich. U., Ypsilanti, 1956-59, assoc. prof., 1959-62, prof., 1962-92. Cons. psychologist Midwest Mental Health Clinic, Dearborn, Mich., 1978-83, Orchard Hills Psychiat. Ctr., Novi, Mich., 1983—; mem. Bd. Jewish Fedn. Washtenaw County, 1997-2003; co-chair Bd. Jewish Family Svc. of Ann Arbor, 1997. Author: Educator's Guide to Stress Management, 1986. Mem. bd. Jewish Family Svc. of Ann Arbor, 1996—; mem. cmty. rels. com. Jewish Cmty. Assn., Ann Arbor, Mich., 1990-92; v.p. edn. Beth Israel Congregation, Ann Arbor, 1985-87; mem. adv. bd. Mich. Anti-Defamation League of B'nai B'rith, 1958—. Mem. APA, Mich. Psychol. Assn., Am. Ednl. Rsch. Assn. Democrat. Home: 2519 Londonderry Rd Ann Arbor MI 48104-4017

WORONOV, MARY PETER, actress; b. Bklyn., Dec. 8, 1946; d. Victor D. and Carol W.; m. Ted Gershuny, 1969 (div.); m. Ted Whitehead, 1979. Student, Cornell Univ. Actress (films) The Chelsea Girls, 1967, Death Race 2000, 1975, Rock 'n' Roll High School, 1979, Eating Raoul, 1982, Black Widow, 1987, Warlock, 1989, Good Girls Don't, 1995, The Munster's Scary Little Christmas, 1996, Invisible Mom II, 1999, (TV series) Logan's Run, 1977, Sledge Hammer!, 1987, (TV movie) Challenge of a Lifetime, 1985, (TV special) Cheech and Chong's Get Out of My Room, 1985, (stage prodns.) Kitchenette, 1968, Boom Boom Room, 1974; author: Wake for the Angels: Paintings and Stories, 1994, Swimming Underground: My Years in the Warhol Factory, 1995. Avocation: painting.

WORRALL, JOHN DENNIS, economics educator, consultant, writer; b. Wildwood, N.J., July 29, 1942; s. John and Adele Veronica (McKenna) W.; m. Suzanne Elizabeth Hopkins; children: Heather, John; m. Janet Priscilla Moran; 1 child, Kevin. BA, Rutgers U., 1969, MA, 1972, PhD, 1976. Asst. dir. Rutgers Bur. Econ. Rsch., New Brunswick, NJ, 1974-77; dir. rsch. Nat. Ctr. for Employment Handicapped-Human Resources Ctr., L.I., NY, 1977-78; v.p., dir. econ. rsch. NCCI, N.Y.C., 1979-83; prof. econs. Rutgers U., Camden, NJ, 1983—, asst. dir. Bur. Econ. Rsch. New Brunswick, NJ, 1983—. Advisor Courier Post newspaper, Camden, 1994-97; John R. Commons lectr. U. Wis. Bus. Sch., Madison, 1991. Co-author: An Evaluation of Policy Related Rehabilitation Research, 1975; co-editor: Placement in Rehabilitation, 1979, Benefit Issues in Workers' Compensation, 1985; editor: Safety and the Workforce, 1983; assoc. editor Jour. Ins.: Math. and Econs., 1990-2000, Jour. Risk and Ins., 1992—. Del. White House Conf. on Handicapped, Washington, 1977; pres. South Jersey Irish Am. Unity Conf., Fedn. Irish Am. Socs., Phila., 1996-98; bd. dirs. St. Patrick's Day Observance Com., Phila., 1996-98, Phila. Immigration Resource Ctr., 1999-2001. Sgt. U.S. Army, 1960-66. Named Outstanding Faculty Mem. Rutgers U. Alumni Assn., 1991; honoree Gaelic Ball, Ladies Ancient Order Hibernians, Phila., 1998. Fellow Risk Theory Soc. (sec. 1990, pres. 1991); mem. Nat. Acad. Social Ins., Am. Econs. Assn., Am. Risk and Ins. Assn. (Robert I. Mehr award 2001), Commodore John Barry Soc. (pres. 1996-98). Roman Catholic. Avocations: golf, fishing. Office: Rutgers U Armitage Hall Camden NJ 08102 Office Phone: 856-225-6290. Business E-Mail: jworrall@crab.rutgers.edu.

WORRELL, ANNE EVERETTE ROWELL, newspaper publisher; b. Surry, Va., Mar. 7, 1920; d. Charles Gray and Ethel (Roache) Rowell; m. Thomas Eugene Worrell, Sept. 12, 1941; 1 child, Thomas Eugene. Student, Va. Intermont Coll., 1939, LittD (hon.), 1991; student, U. Richmond, 1965. Founding stockholder Worrell Newspapers Inc., 1949, v.p., dir., 1969-73; v.p., sec. Worrell Investment Co., Charlottesville, Va.; pres. The Genan Co. (formerly Bristol Newspapers). Pres. Bristol Jr. League, 1959; bd. dirs. The Corp. for Thomas Jefferson's Poplar Forest Found., Va. Hist. Soc., Va. Intermont Coll., Antiquities; active Bayly Mus., Monticello Cabinet. Named Outstanding Alumna, Va. Intermont Coll., 1981. Mem.: DAR (Shadwell chpt.), Nat. Trust for Hist. Preservation, Greencroft Club, Farmington Country Club, Contemporary Club. Episcopalian. Home: Seven Sunset Circle Farmington Charlottesville VA 22901 Office: Pantops PO Box 5386 Charlottesville VA 22905-5386

WORRELL, AUDREY MARTINY, geriatric psychiatrist; b. Phila, Aug. 12, 1935; d. Francis Aloysius and Dorothy (Rawley) Martiny; m. Richard Vernon Worrell, June 14, 1958; children: Philip Vernon, Amy Elizabeth. MD, Meharry Med. Coll., 1960. Diplomate Am. Bd. Psychiatry and Neurology. Intern Misericordia Hosp., Phila., 1960-61; resident SUNY-Buffalo Affiliated Hosp., NY, 1961-63, Buffaflo Psychiat. Ctr., NY, 1963-64; dir. capitol region Mental Health Ctr., Hartford, Conn., 1974-77; acting regional dir. Region IV State Dept. Mental Health, 1976-77; asst. chief psychiatry VA Med. Ctr., Newington, Conn., 1977-78, acting chief psychiatry, 1978-79, chief psychiatry, 1978-80; dir. Capitol Regional Mental Health Facilities, Hartford, Conn., 1980-87; clin. prof. psychiatry U. Conn., 1981-87; commr. State Dept. Mental Health, Hartford, 1981-86; CEO, med. dir. Vista Sandia Hosp., Albuquerque, 1986-88; dir. consultation liason Lovelace Med. Ctr., Albuquerque, 1988-89, geriatric psychiatry, 1989-93; dir. geriatric psychiatry Charter Hosp., Albuquerque, 1993-96, St. Joseph Med. Sys., Albuquerque, 1994—; pvt. practice, 1996—2003; part-time cons. Albuquerque VA Hosp., 2003—. Contbr. articles to profl. jour. Bd. dir. Transitional Svc., Buffalo, 1973-74, ARC, Buffalo, 1973-74, Child and Family Svc., Hartford, 1972-73, co-chmn. United Way/Combined Health Appeal, State of Conn., 1983, 84; active Child Welfare Inst. Adv. Bd., Hartford, 1983—, Conn. Prison Bd., Hartford, 1984-85; chmn. Gov. Task Force on Mental Health Policy, 1982-85; mem. Gov.Task Force on Homeless, 1983-85. Recipient Leadership award Conn. Coun. Mental Health Ctr., 1983, Outstanding Contbn. award to Health Svc., YWCA, Hartford, 1983. Mem. AMA, APHA, NASMHPD (sec., bd. dir. 1982-86), New Eng. Mental Health Commr. Assn., Am. Med. Women's Assn., Conn. Assn. Mental Health and Aging, Conn. Coalition for Homeless Inc., Conn. Rehab. Assn., Am. Assn. Psychiat. Adminstr., Am. Hosp. Assn., Am. Orthopsychiat. Assn., Assn. Mental Health Adminstr., Hosp. and Cmty. Psychiatry Svc., Corporators of Inst. of Living of Hartford, Am. Psychiat. Assn., Conn. Psychiat. Soc., Am. Coll. Psychiatrists, Am. Coll. Mental Health Adminstr. Office: Albuquerque VA Hosp Gibson & San Mateo Albuquerque NM 87107

WORRELL, PETER, professional hockey player; b. Pierrefonds, Que., Can., Aug. 18, 1977; Left wing Fla. Panthers, Sunrise, 1997—. Office: Fla Panthers Nat Car Rental Ctr 2555 Panther Pkwy Sunrise FL 33323

WORRELL, RICHARD VERNON, orthopedic surgeon, college dean, dean; b. Bklyn., June 4, 1931; s. John Elmer and Elaine (Callender) Worrell; m. Audrey Frances Martiny, June 14, 1958; children: Philip Vernon, Amy Elizabeth. BA, NYU, 1952; MD, Meharry Med. Coll., 1958. Diplomate Am. Bd. Orthop. Surgery, Nat. Bd. Med. Examiners. Intern Meharry Med. Coll., Nashville, 1958—59; resident in gen. surgery Mercy-Douglass Hosp., Phila., 1960—61; resident in orthop. surgery State U. N.Y. Buffalo Sch. Medicine Affiliated Hosps., 1961—64; resident in orthop. pathology Temple U. Med. Ctr., Phila., 1966—67; pvt. practice orthop. surgery Phila., 1967—68; asst. prof. acting head divsn. orthop. surgery U. Conn. Sch. Medicine, 1968—70; attending orthop. surgeon E.J. Meyer Meml. Hosp., Buffalo, Millard Fillmore Hosp., Buffalo, VA Hosp., Buffalo, Buffalo State Hosp.; clin. instr. orthop. surgery SUNY, Buffalo, 1970—74; chief orthop. surgery VA Hosp., Newington, Conn., 1974—80; asst. prof. surgery (orthop.) U. Conn. Sch. Medicine, 1974—77, assoc. prof., 1977—83, asst. dean student affairs, 1980—83; prof. clin. surgery SUNY Downstate Med. Ctr., Bklyn., 1983—86; dir. orthop. surgery Brookdale Hosp. Med. Ctr., Bklyn., 1983—86; prof. orthop. U. N.Mex. Sch. Medicine, 1986—97, prof., vice chmn. dept. orthop., 1997—99, prof. emeritus, 1999—; dir. orthop. oncology U. N.Mex. Health Scis. Ctr., 1987—99; mem. med. staff U. N.Mex. Cancer Ctr., 1987—99; chief orthop. surgery VA Med. Ctr., Albuquerque, 1987—97. Cons. in orthop. surgery Newington (Conn.) Children's Hosp., 1968—70; mem. sickle cell disease adv. com. NIH, 1982—86. Bd. dirs. Big Bros. Greater Hartford. Served to capt. M.C. USAR, 1962—69. Fellow: ACS, Royal Soc. Medicine, London, Am. Acad. Orthop. Surgeons; mem.: AMA, N.Mex. Soc. Clin. Oncology, Internat. Soc. Orthop. Surgery and Traumatology, Orthop. Rsch. Soc., Internat. Fedn. Surg. Colls. (assoc.), Am. Soc. Clin. Oncology, Am. Soc. Clin. Pathologists, Am. Orthop. Assn., Alpha Omega Alpha. Personal E-mail: rworrellmd@aol.com. Business E-Mail: rworrell@salud.unm.edu.

WORRELL, SHARYN DIANNE, retired flight attendant; b. Lynn, Mass., Feb. 23, 1948; d. Richard Allen Kelley and Norma Lovett (Gregory); m. Blaine Patten Worrell, Feb. 15, 1979 (div. Dec. 20, 1985); 1 child, Ryan Richard. Flight attendant United Airlines, Chgo., 1966—2002. Spkr., co-founder Speakers' Bur. for LA-based Flight Attendants. Author: (book) Ancestral Lines of Joseph Browne of Essex County, Massachusetts and Mary Brown (Joseph's wife) of Kensington, New Hampshire with Related Brown Lines, From Stewardess to Flight Attendant-The Changing Years, When You Were A Boy; co-author: The History of the Auxiliary of Good Shepherd Hospital, Barrington, Illinois; compiler (book) Illinois Court, National Society Women Descendants of the Ancient and Honorable Artillery Company, Celebrating 60 Years, (books) A Few of My Favorite E-Mails. Co-founder Young Women's League for Muscular Dystrophy Assn., LA, 1975; pres's. vol. svc. award chmn. Immanuel Luth. Ch. and Sch., Palatine, Ill., 2000—04, asst. supt. of Sunday sch.; summer Sunday sch. supt.; sch. bd., 1990—93, pub. rels. chair, 1992—2002, bd. of human care ministry com. mem., 1999—2001, bd. of trustees, sec. of congregation, 2001—03; founding mem. Immanuel Luth. Sch. Edn. Found., Palatine, Ill., 1998—2003, reach for the stars event chairperson, 1998—2003; membership chmn. Aux. of Good Shepherd Hosp., Barrington, Ill., 2000—02, historian, 2002—03, mardi gras chef festival bd. mem., 2003; clin. ethics bd. mem. Good Shepherd Hosp., Barrington, Ill., 2003—04. Recipient Vol. Recognition, YMCA, 1988, Servant of Youth award, Boy Scouts Am. Mem.: DAR (presenter good citizenship award 1994—2004, libr., pub. rels. chair, schs. chair, good citizen chair, scholarship chmn.), Huguenot Soc. Ill. (dir.), Presdl. Families Am. (life), Bench and Bar (life), Antelbellam Planters (life), Daughters Union Vets. of Civil War 1861-1865 (life), Clipped Wings (ways and means com. 2002—04), Nat. Soc. New Eng. Women (program spkr., Vol. Cmty. Svc. award 1995, Pres. Vol. Svc. award 2003), The Nat. Soc. Colonial Dames XVII Century (lac des Ill. chpt. charter mem., historian, chaplain), Soc. of the Descendants of Washington's Army at Valley Forge (life), Associated Daughters of Early Am. Witches (life; corr. sec.), Nat. Soc. Women Descendants of the Ancient and Hon. Arty. Co. (life; first v.p., hospitality chmn., program spkr., treas.), Ill. Cameo Soc., Nat. Soc. DAR (life), Piscataqua Pioneers (life), The Soc. of the Descendants of the Colonial Clergy (life), Soc. of Mayflower Descendants in the State of Ill. (life; chmn. jr. membership). Lutheran. Achievements include Lobbied 3 years for exoneration of 6 women executed in 1692 as Salem witches during the Witch Hysteria. Acting Gov. Jane Swift signed the Bill on October 31, 2001 exonerating all 6. Avocations: genealogy, volunteering. Home: 2416 Oak Hill Rd Lake Barrington IL 60010-3898

WORRELL, STEWART PHILLIP, lawyer, trust executive; b. Montreal, Apr. 13, 1956; s. Arthur Agustus and Sybil Agatha (Jones) Worrell. Chmn. The Libr. Trust, Montreal, 1999—. Charter mem. Mbanx, Toronto, 1998—. Author: (poetry) Children Dressed in Black, 1999. Mem. Fed. Bar Assn., InterAm. Bar Assn., Conseil de Roi, U.S. Ski Assn., Beaconsfield Yacht Club, Univ. Club. Avocations: skiing, sailing, chess, golf, photography.

WORSHAM, BERTRAND RAY, psychiatrist; b. Atkins, Ark., Feb. 14, 1926; s. Lewis Henry and Emma Lavada (Burris) W.; m. Margaret Ann Dickson, June 4, 1947 (div. 1960); children: Eric Dickson, Vicki Gayle; m. Lynne Ellen Reynolds, Aug. 27, 1976; children: Mary Ellen Clarice, Richard Andrew (dec.). BA, U. Ark., 1951; MD, U. Ark., Little Rock, 1955. Intern Hillcrest Med. Ctr., Tulsa, 1955-56; resident in psychiatry Menninger Sch. Psychiatry, Topeka, 1956-59; pvt. practice, 1959-78; clin. instr. U. Okla. Sch. Medicine, 1965-78; coord. drug and alcohol treatment unit Washington D.C. VA Med. Ctr., 1978-84; med. dir. Norman divsn. Okla. State Vets. Ctr., 1984-89; psychiat. cons. Cmty. Counselling Ctr., Oklahoma City, 1989—. Cons. Oklahoma City Vets. Hosp., 1959-72, State Dept. Pub. Health, 1960-65, helping to establish cmty. mental health ctrs. throughout Okla.; dir. Cmty. Mental Health Ctr., Shawnee, Okla., 1965-72; mem. staff Coyne Campbell Hosp., 1960-78, Bapt. Med. Ctr., 1960-78, Mercy Health Ctr., 1960-78, Deaconess Hosp., 1963-78, Dr.'s Gen. Hosp., 1963-78, Presbyn. Hosp., 1962-78, U. Health Sci. Ctr., 1962-78, Children's Meml. Hosp., 1968-78, Oklahoma City VA Hosp., 1960-78, Washington D.C. Va. Hosp., 1978-84,

Okla. Vets. Ctr., Norman, 1984-89. Mem. Civil Disaster Com., Oklahoma City, 1966, USN League, Okla., 1972—. With USAF, 1944-46; capt. USNR, 1957-86, ret. Fellow Menninger Found., Charles F. Menninger Found.; mem. AMA, Am. Psychiat. Assn. (Okla. dist. br. 1959-78, 84—), Assn. Mil. Surgeons of U.S., Ret. Officers Assn., World Fedn. for Mental Health, Internat. Platform Assn., Washington Psychiat. Assn., No. Va. Mental Health Assn., Masons (32 degree), VFW, Phi Beta Pi (Beta Theta chpt.). Republican. Episcopalian. Avocations: golf, church activities. Home: 9915 N Kelley Ave Oklahoma City OK 73131-2022 Office: 9915 N Kelley Ave Oklahoma City OK 73131-2022 *Man's ability to do goal-directed work is mans greatest asset. And as results add together we more nearly approach an infinitely profound civilization.*

WORSHAM, HAL GLENN, marketing professional; b. Ypsilanti, Mich., July 12, 1955; s. Francis Glenn and Priscilla June Worsham; m. Pamela Jean Wusthoff, Oct. 8, 1977; children: Aimee Laurel, Kimberly Victoria. BBA, U. Mich., 1977; MBA, Case Western Res. U., 1981. Mktg. and product mgr. BF Goodrich, Akron, Ohio, 1977—84, advt. mgr., 1977—84; product and mktg. mgr. Dunlop Tire Corp., Buffalo, 1984—87; brand mgr. Fisher Price divsn. Quaker Oats, East Aurora, NY, 1987—91; dir. internat. mktg. Hanna-Barbera Studios, Hollywood, Calif., 1991—92; dir. of licensing and pub. rels. Converse Inc., North Andover, Mass., 1992—2000; sr. v.p. of global licensing Everlast Worldwide Inc., N.Y.C., 2000—. Solicitor Cleve. Orch., 1983; chmn. of bd. of deacons Westminster Presbyn. Ch., Akron, 1983; mem. music com. United Ch. of Christ, South Ch., Andover, Mass., 1999; publicity chmn. Am. Mktg. Assoc., Chgo., 1983—84; bd. dirs. WYDACA Sch., Akron, 1983—84. Scholar, U. of Chgo., 1973. Mem.: Mensa (assoc.). Democrat. Home: 260 Summer St North Andover MA 01845-4819 Office: Everlast Worldwide Inc 1350 Broadway 23d Fl New York NY 10018 E-mail: halw@everlast.com.

WORSLEY, JAMES RANDOLPH, JR., lawyer; b. Rocky Mount, N.C., July 28, 1924; s. James Randolph and Helen Marie (Killian) W.; m. Cornelia Cheston, Feb. 11, 1956; children: Cornelia Worsley Newell, Julia Worsley Neilson, Charlotte Cheston Worsley. BS, E. Carolina U., 1944; postgrad., Harvard U., 1944-45, LLB, 1949. Bar: N.C. 1949, D.C. 1949. Assoc. Klagsbrunn, Hanes & Irwin, Washington, 1949-54; ptnr. Ober, Kaler, Grimes & Shriver (and predecessor firm), Washington, 1955-94, coun., 1995—. Chmn. Md. Potomac Water Authority, 1969-71, Montgomery County (Md.) Charter Revision Commn., 1967; mem. pastoral coun. Archdiocese of Washington, 1975-78; bd. dirs. Madeira Sch., McLean, Va., 1975-81. Fellow Am. Bar Found.; mem. Chevy Chase Club, Met. Club, Knights of Malta. Democrat. Roman Catholic. Avocations: sailing, tennis. Home: 11 Quincy St Chevy Chase MD 20815-4226 Office: Ober Kaler Grimes & Shriver 1401 H St NW Ste 500 Washington DC 20005-2175

WORTH, FRED, mathematician, educator; b. Cranford, N.J., Feb. 24, 1958; s. Edward and Stephana Gay Worth; m. Elisabeth Wells, Sept. 21, 1953; 1 child, Mark. BS in Math., Evangel Coll., 1982; MS in Applied Math., U. Mo., Rolla, 1987, PhD in Math., 1991. Math. tchr. St. Anthony H.S., Jersey City, 1984—85; grad. tchg. asst. U. Mo., Rolla, 1985—91; prof. math. Henderson State U., Arkadelphia, Ark., 1991—. Contbr. articles to profl. jours. Bd. dirs. Boys and Girls Club, Arkadelphia, 1992—93; asst. scout master/merit badge coord. Boy Scouts Am., Arkadelphia, 2000—04; min. Ch. of the Nazarene, Arkadelphia, 2002—04. Mem.: S.W. Ark. Coun. Tchrs. Math., Ark. Coun. Tchrs. Math., Assn. Christians in the Math. Scis., Nat. Coun. Tchrs. Math., Math. Assn. Am. (program coord. 2002—04), Soc. for Am. Baseball Rsch. Nazarene. Avocations: baseball research, racquetball, softball, camping. Office: Henderson State Univ 1100 Henderson St Arkadelphia AR 71999-0001 E-mail: worthf@hsu.edu.

WORTH, GARY JAMES, communications executive; b. Berkeley Township, N.J., Dec. 13, 1940; s. Melvin Raymond and Viola Vista (Landis) W. Student, Trenton State Coll., 1964, Palm Beach Jr. Coll., 1958-59. Dir. sta. relations MBS, Inc., N.Y.C., 1972, v.p. sta. relations, 1972, exec. v.p., 1972-79, mem. exec. com., 1978-79; v.p. Mut. Reports, Inc., Washington, 1972-79, dir., 1972-79; v.p., dir. WCFL, Inc., Chgo., 1979, Mut. Radio N.Y., Inc., N.Y.C., 1979; pres., dir. Robert Wold Co. Inc. and subs. Wold Communications, Inc., L.A., 1980-85; pres., chief exec. officer, dir. WesternWorld Inc. and subs. WesternWorld TV, L.A., 1986-93, The Video Tape Co., North Hollywood, Calif., 1987-93; sec. dir. WesternWorld Video Inc., L.A., 1986-87; CEO Starcom Television Svcs., Inc., 1993—96; chmn., CEO Starcom Entertainment, Inc., 1993—; CEO Starcom Mgmt. Svcs. Inc., 1993—, New Age Conversions, Inc., 1996—. Producer, dir.: USAF movie Assignment McGuire. Served to capt. USAF, 1960-66, Vietnam. Decorated Air Force Commendation medal, Armed Forces Expeditionary medal.; recipient Chief Herbert H. Almers Meml. award Bergen County (N.J.) Police Acad., 1972 Mem. Nat. Assn. Broadcasters, Nat. Assn. TV Program Execs., Nat. Informercial Mktg. Assn. Methodist. E-mail: star2874@msn.com.

WORTH, GEORGE JOHN, English literature educator; b. Vienna, June 11, 1929; came to U.S., 1940, naturalized, 1945; s. Adolph and Theresa (Schmerzler) W.; m. Carol Laverne Dinsdale, Mar. 17, 1951; children: Theresa Jean (Wilkinson), Paul Dinsdale. AB, U. Chgo., 1948, MA, 1951; PhD, U. Ill., 1954. Instr. English U. Ill., Urbana, 1954-55; faculty U. Kans., Lawrence, 1955—, assoc. prof., 1962-65, prof. English lit., 1965-95; prof. emeritus English, 1995—; asst. chmn. dept. U. Kans., Lawrence, 1961-62, assoc. chmn., 1962-63, acting chmn., 1963-64, chmn., 1964-79. Author: James Hannay: His Life and Work, 1964, William Harrison Ainsworth, 1972, Dickensian Melodrama, 1978, Thomas Hughes, 1984, Great Expectations: An Annotated Bibliography, 1986, (book) Macmillan's Magazine, 1859-1907, 2003; editor: (with Harold Orel) Six Studies in Nineteenth Century English Literature and Thought, 1962, The Nineteenth Century Writer and His Audience, 1969, (with Edwin Eigner) Victorian Criticism of the Novel, 1985. Mem. AAUP, MLA, Dickens Fellowship, Dickens Soc., Midwest Victorian Studies Assn., Rsch. Soc. for Victorian Periodicals. Office: U Kans Dept English Wescoe Hall Lawrence KS 66045-7590 E-mail: GJWorth@aol.com.

WORTH, MARY PAGE, mayor; b. Balt., Jan. 23, 1924; d. Christian Allen and Margaret Pennington (Holbein) Schwarzwaelder; m. William James Worth, Nov. 4, 1947 (dec. May 1986); children: Margaret Page, William Allen, John David III. Student, Ladycliff Coll., Highland Falls, N.Y., 1941-42, Abbott Sch. Art, Washington, 1942-44; grad., Packer Coll. Inst., Brooklyn. Selectman Town of Searsport, Maine, 1973-75; mayor City of Belfast, Maine, 1986-2000. Recreation chmn. Town of Searsport, 1970-72. Del. Rep. State Conv., Maine, 1970-94; pres. Searsport Reps., 1974-76; active ARC Overseas Assn., 1976—; pres. Searsport C. of C., 1976-79; mem. exec. bd. Waldo County Com. for Social Action, Belfast, 1986—; mem. Abnacki coun. Girl Scouts U.S.; tutor Literacy Vols. Am.; recreation specialist ARC, Camp Haugen, Japan, 1946-47; bd. dirs. RSVP-Waldo County, Heat Start Waldo County; vol. tchr. Sch. for Blind, Cholon, Republic Vietnam, 1959-61, Am. Sch. at Saigon, Republic Vietnam, 1959-61; club dir. USAF Spl. Svcs., Ft. Meyer, Va., 1962-63, U.S. Army Spl. Svcs., Ft. Belvoir, Va., 1963-64; mem. Congresswoman Olympia Snowe's Mpcl. Adv. Bd.; town chair Rep. Party; mem. adv. Belfast History Project. Mem. Gibson Island Club, 1938-73, mem. DAR (officer Maine 1986—), Internat. Platform Assn., Ret. Officers Assn. (life), 11th Airborne Assn./511th Parachute Infantry Regiment Korea War Vets. Assn., Waldo County Humane Soc. (pres. 1990—), Waldo County Law Enforcement (v.p. 1990—), VFW Aux., Am. Legion Aux., Belfast Garden Club (parliamentarian 1984—), Rotary (bd. govs. com. Maine St. '90), ARC Overseas Assoc. Avocations: great dane breeding, antiques. Office: City of Belfast Mayor's Office 71 Church St Belfast ME 04915-6208 Home: 10 Shoreland Dr Apt 306 Belfast ME 04915-6062

WORTH, MELVIN H. surgeon, educator; b. Norwich, Conn., July 14, 1930; s. Melvin H. and Stella E. (Cline) W.; m. Alice Tenzer, May 17, 1953; children: Nancy, David. AB, Clark U., 1950; MD, NYU, 1954. Diplomate Am. Bd. Surgery. Intern Bellevue Hosp., N.Y.C., 1954-55, resident, 1957-61, dir. trauma svc., 1966-79; dir. surgery S.I. U. Hosp., N.Y.C., 1979-96; assoc. prof. NYU, N.Y.C., 1968-69; prof. clin. surgery SUNY, Bklyn., 1979—, Uniformed Svc. U. Health Sci. Ctr., 1996—. Chmn. trauma designation com. N.Y.C. Emergency Med. Svc., 1990; mem. Office of Profl. Med. Conduct of N.Y. State, 1983-98. Vice chmn. N.Y. State Health Rev. and Planning Coun., 1988-94, chair, 1995. Capt. USMC, 1955-57. Scholar-in-residence Inst. Medicine, 1996—. Fellow ACS, Am. Coll. Gastroenterology; mem. Internat. Soc. Surgery, Soc. Am. Gastrointestinal Endoscopic Surgeons, Am. Assn. for Surgery of Trauma, Assn. Acad. Surgery, Soc. Critical Care Medicine, Assn. Surg. Edn., N.Y. Surg. Soc. (pres. 1989), Alpha Omega Alpha. Home: 4914 Jamestown Rd Bethesda MD 20816-1756

WORTHAM, JAMES CALVIN, retired mathematics educator; b. Oconee County, Ga., Sept. 12, 1928; s. James Notley and Effie (Cross) W.; m. Mary Helena Shelley, Dec. 23, 1953; children: Sharon Elaine, Marilyn Kay, Deborah Louise, James Donald. BA, U. Akron, 1957; MA (NSF Scholar), Ohio State U., 1969. Tchr. jr. H.S. Akron Pub. Schs., 1956-62, tchr. sr. H.S., 1962-66; math. curriculum specialist Akron (Ohio) Pub. Schs., 1966-90; instr. math. U. Akron, 1966-90; ret., 1990. Served with USAF, 1951-55. Mem. NEA, Ohio Edn. Assn., Math. Assn. Am., Nat., Ohio couns. tchrs. of Math., Nat. Coun. Suprs. of Math., Greater Akron Math. Educators Soc. (pres. 1984-86), Pi Mu Epsilon. Republican. Mem. Ch. of Nazarene. Home: 229 Sand Run Rd Akron OH 44313-5364

WORTHAM, THOMAS RICHARD, English language educator; b. Liberal, Kans., Dec. 5, 1943; s. Tom and Ruth (Cavanaugh) W. AB, Marquette U., 1965; PhD, Ind. U., 1970. From asst. prof. to assoc. prof. UCLA, 1970-82, prof., 1982—, vice-chmn. and dir. undergrad. studies, 1993-97, chmn. dept., 1997—. Vis. prof. Am. lit. U. Warsaw, Poland, 1976-77; sr. rsch. fellow Am. Coun. of Learned Socs., 1983-84. Editor: James Russell Lowell's The Biglow Papers: A Critical Edition, 1977, Letters of W. D. Howells, vol. 4, 1892-1901, 1983, The Early Prose Writings of William Dean Howells, 1853-1861, 1990, William Dean Howells' My Mark Twain, 1996, Mark Twain's Chapters From My Autobiography, 1999; asst. editor Nineteenth-Century Fiction, 1971-75, mem. adv. bd., 1976-83, co-editor, 1983-86; co-editor Nineteenth-Century Literature, 1986-95, editor, 1995—; mem. editl. bd. The Collected Works of Ralph Waldo Emerson, 1996—, Am. Documentary Heritage Libr., 1999—. Regent's faculty fellow in the humanities U. Calif., 1971; travel grantee Nat. Endowment for the Humanities, 1985-86, 88-89; grants-in-aid of rsch. Am. Philos. Soc., 1976, 81. Mem. MLA Am. (Norman Foerster prize com. of Am. Lit. sect. 1973, chmn. Pacific coast region, com. on manuscript holdings of Am. Lit. sect. 1972-78, mem. Hubbell prize com. of Am. Lit. sect. 1989-91), Am. Studies Assn., Ralph Waldo Emerson Soc. (bd. dirs. 1992-95), Assn. for Document Editing, Internat. Assn. Univ. Profs. English, Soc. Textual Scholarship. Episcopalian. Avocation: breeding and training arabian horses. Office: U Calif Dept English 405 Hilgard Ave Los Angeles CA 90095-1530 Office Phone: 310-825-4459. Business E-Mail: wortham@humnet.ucla.edu.

WORTHEN, JOHN EDWARD, retired academic administrator; b. Carbondale, Ill., July 15, 1933; s. Dewey and Annis Burr (Williams) W.; m. Sandra Damewood, Feb. 27, 1960; children: Samantha Jane, Bradley Edward. BS in Psychology (Univ. Acad. scholar), Northwestern U., 1954; MA in Student Pers. Adminstrn., Columbia U., 1955; EdD in Adminstrn. in Higher Edn. (Coll. Entrance Exam. Bd. fellow), Harvard U., 1964; PhD (hon.), Yeungnam U., Daegu, Korea, 1986; DL (hon.), Ball State U., 2001. Dean of men Am. U., 1959-61; dir. counseling and testing and asst. prof. edn., 1963-66; asst. to provost and asst. prof., 1966-68; acting provost and v.p. acad. affairs, 1968; assoc. provost for instrn., 1969; v.p. student affairs, 1970-75; v.p. student affairs and adminstrn., 1976-79; pres. Ind. U. of Pa., 1979-84, Ball State U., Muncie, Ind., 1984-2000; ret., 2000. Cons. to universities and public schs. Bd. dirs. Ball State U. Found.; mem. adv. bd. Muncie-Delaware County Found.; mem. Cmty. Alliance to Promote Edn. Mem. Am. Assn. State Colls. and Univs. (chair, bd. dirs. 1999), Rotary Internat., Phi Delta Kappa, Kappa Delta Pi. E-mail: johneworthen@aol.com.

WORTHEN, WILLIAM JAMES, architect; b. Syracuse, N.Y., Apr. 30, 1971; s. William Sidney and Anna Marie Worthen. BS in Bldg. Sci., Rensselaer Poly. Inst., Troy, N.Y., 1995. Registered architect, D.C. Archtl. designer The Kearns Group, Troy, 1992-95; architect Bernard Johnson Young, Bethesda, Md., 1995-96, Blackburn Architects, Washington, 1996-97; project architect Hellmuth, Obata & Kassabaum, Washington, San Francisco, 1997—. Vol. coord. Clinton 98 Re-election Campaign, Washington, 1998; mem. Human Rights Campaign. Mem AIA, Lambda Chi Alpha. Avocation: marathon running. Office: Hellmuth,Obata & kassabaum-Hok 1 Bush St Ste 200 San Francisco CA 94104-4404

WORTHINGTON, BRUCE R. lawyer; b. 1949; BA Econ.(hon.), Claremont KcKenna Coll.; JD, King Hall, Univ. of Calif. at Davis, Calif. Bar: State Bar of Calif. 1974. Sr. v.p. and gen. counsel PG&E Corp, San Francisco, 1995—; sr. v.p. and gen. coun. Pacific Gas and Electric Co., 1974; v.p. and gen. coun. PG&E Corp., San Francisco, 1994. Mem.: Section of Pub. Utility, Comm. and Transportation Law of the Am. Bar Assoc., Calif. Bar Assoc., San Francisco Bar Assoc. Worthington has more than 20 years in the energy industry legal sector and is responsible for the corp. legal, internal auditing, business ethics, and compliance functions. He provides oversight of these functions for the Company's bus. including PG&E Nat. Energy Group, Pacific Gas and Electric Co. and Pacific Venture Captial, LLC. Office: PG&E Corp Ste 2400 One Market Spear Tower San Francisco CA 94105 E-mail: Bruce.Worthington@pge-corp.com.

WORTHINGTON, CAROLE YARD LYNCH, lawyer; b. Knoxville, Tenn., Aug. 29, 1951; d. Charles R. and Alma (Allred) Yard; m. Robert F. Worthington Jr., Sept. 14, 1996; 1 child, Cassandra Kathleen. BA, U. Tenn., 1972, JD, 1977. Bar: Tenn. 1977, Ga. 1982. Assoc. Thomas, Leitner, Mann, Warner & Owens, Chattanooga, 1977-78, Thomas, Mann & Gossett, Chattanooga, 1978-81, ptnr., v.p., 1981-86; ptnr. Grant, Konvalinka & Harrison, P.C., Chattanooga, 1987-96, Carole Lynch Worthington, Atty. at Law, Knoxville, 1996—. Sec. Nat. Transp. Rsch. Ctr., Inc. Author: Estate Planning Tennessee Practice, 1992; asst. editor Tenn. Law Rev., 1976-77. Vice chmn. allocations United Way of Chattanooga, 1985, pilot campaign, 1986; active Jr. League of Chattanooga, 1981-92; mem. alumnae adv. coun. U. Tenn. Coll. Law, 1983-92, dean's cir., 1989—; bd. dirs. Mental Health Assn. Chattanooga Inc., 1986-92, 1st v.p., 1988-89, sec., 1989-92; trustee St. Nicholas Sch., 1992-95, East Tenn. Opera Guild, 2001—. Recipient Alumni Leadership award U. Tenn. Coll. Law, 1988, 92. Fellow Am. Bar Found., Tenn. Bar Found., Chattanooga Bar Found.; mem. ABA (del. at large 1991-97, 98-2001), com. on legal aid and indigent defendants 1994-95, select com. of house 1994-96, standing com. on charter and by laws 1999-2000, standing com. on credentials and admissions 1999-2000, standing com. on credentials and admissions 1999-2000, com. on client rels. 2000-2002), Chattanooga Bar Assn. (bd. govs. 1982-89, sec.-treas. 1985-86, pres. 1987-88), Knoxville Bar Assn. (chair pro bono com. 2002), Tenn. Bar Assn. (vice chair comml. law, banking and bankruptcy 1988-90, unified bar study com. 1990-91, chair bar leadership conf. 1990, editl. bd. Tenn. Bar Jour. 1991-94, Tenn. Bar Assn. long range planning com. 1992-95, 97-99, bd. govs. 1994-96, chair long range planning com. 1995-96, future of bar com. 1998-2001), Ga. Bar Assn., Nat. Conf. Lawyers and Realtors (ABA del. 1990-92), Nat. Conf. Bar Pres.'s (exec. coun. 1989-92, treas. 1992-93, sec. 1993-94, pres.-elect 1994-95, pres. 1995-96), Tenn. Bd. Profl. Responsibility, Phi Alpha Delta, East Tenn. Opera Guild Bd., 2001-02. Home: First Tennessee Plaza Ste 1950 800 S Gay St Knoxville TN 37929 Office Phone: 865-540-4400. E-mail: carole@clw-law.com.

WORTHINGTON, DEBORAH ECKHARDT, language educator; b. Anderson, Ind., Jan. 14, 1949; d. Obert Edward and Cecil May (Myers) Eckhardt; m. Arthur Nathaniel Worthington (div.); children: Drew, A. Eric, Jason. BA in Reading, Purdue U., 1971; MA in English, Montclair State U., 1991. Cert. ministry Global U., Mo., 2003, English tchr., spl. edn. tchr., reading tchr. State of N.J. English tchr. Harrison HS, West Lafayette, Ind., 1974, Bloomington (Ill.) HS, 1978—79; spl. edn. English tchr. Dover (N.J.) HS, 1988—. Christian counselor Calvary Temple, Wayne, NJ, 2002—, griefshare ministry mem., 2004—. Author: (Bible study) Standing on the Promise of God, 2002, Picking Up Your Cross, 2004, (book) Breath of the Morning, 2004, Bearing One Another's Burdens, 2004, Trusing God, 2004. Missionary to Peru. Mem. Assemblies Of God.

WORTHINGTON, GEORGE RHODES, retired naval officer; b. Louisville, July 11, 1937; s. William Bowman and Elizabeth (Frost) W.; m. Sydna Anne Alexander, Mar. 28, 1981 (div. Oct. 1990); children: Rhodes Ballard, Graham Rankins, Greer Anne. BS, U.S. Naval Acad., 1961; postgrad., USMC, Quantico, Va., 1975-76, Nat. War Coll., 1978-79. Commd. ensign USN, 1961, advanced through grades to rear adm., 1989, communications officer USS Halsey Powell, 1961-63, flag lt., aide comdr. cruiser-destroyer Flotilla Seven, 1963-65, exec. officer Underwater Demolition Team Eleven Coronado, Calif., 1965-68, ops. officer USS Strong Charleston, S.C., 1969-71, exec. officer Naval Spl. Warfare Group Saigon, Vietnam, 1971-72, comdg. officer SEAL Team One Coronado, 1972-74, naval attache Def. Attache Office Phnom Penh, Cambodia, 1974-75, comdg. officer Undersea Warfare Group One Coronado, 1976-78, program sponsor Office of Chief of Naval Ops. Washington, 1979-85; comdr. Naval Spl. Warfare Group One, Coronado, 1985-87; chief of staff Spl. Ops. Command Europe USN, Stuttgart, Fed. Republic Germany, 1987-88; dep. asst. sec. of def. (spl. ops.) Def. Dept., Washington, 1988-89; comdr. Naval Spl. Warfare Command, Coronado, 1989-92; mktg. agent, cons. PIDEAC Inc., Coronado, 1992-96. Naval adv. IFG Ltd.; with Burdeshaw Assoc., Inc.; former v.p. govt. rels. WarRoom Rsch., Inc.; bd. dirs. ZODIAC N.Am., WESCAM-Sonoma, Inc., Spl. Ops. Warrior Found. Decorated D.S.M., Legion of Merit (2), Def. Superior Svc. medal, Meritorious Svc. medal. Mem. Res. Officers Assn. (past chpt. pres.), U.S. Parachute Assn., Underwater Demolition Team-Seal Assn. (life), Mayflower Soc. D.C. (life), Naval Acad. Alumni Assn., Naval Inst., Navy League San Diego, Nat. Def. Indsl. Assn. (life), Army-Navy Club, Army-Navy Country Club. Republican. Episcopalian. Avocations: masters swimming, skiing, sport parachuting. Address: 1118 Pacifica Ave Chula Vista CA 91913-1550 Fax: 619-216-1712. E-mail: grw7@cox.net.

WORTHINGTON, JANET EVANS, retired academic dean, English language educator; b. Springfield, Ill., Jan. 30, 1942; d. Orville Ray and Helen May (Tuxhorn) Evans; m. Gary H. Worthington; children: Rachael Allene, Evan Edmund, Adam Nicholas Karl. Student, Blackburn Coll., 1960-62; BA in English Lang. and Lit., U. Chgo., 1965; MA in English, U. Iowa, 1969; PhD in English Edn., Fla. State U., 1977; postgrad., W. Va. Inst. Tech., 1981-82, Rensselaer Poly. Inst., 1984. Teaching. fellow Fla. State U., Tallahassee, 1971-72, grad. assistant, 1972-73; coord. lang. arts rsch. Piedmont Schs. Project, Greer, S.C., 1973-76; English instr. Woodrow Wilson High Sch., Beckley, W.Va., 1976-77; Reading specialist, adj. instr. in English W. Va. Inst. Tech., Montgomery, W.Va., 1977-78; asst. prof. W.Va. Inst. Tech., Montgomery, 1979-82, assoc. prof., 1983-87, prof. English, 1987-88, dir. Oak Hill, 1988-90, tech. writing program coord. Community and Tech. Coll. Montgomery, 1983-88; dir. continuing edn. Nicholls State U., Thibodaux, La., 1990-97; dean Ctr. for Lifelong Learning, Plattsburgh (N.Y.) State U., 1997—2003. Tech. writing cons., various bus., 1986—, Dept. of Mines, State of W.Va., 1980-81; reading cons. Dept of Mines, 1980-81, Mt. Hope (W.Va.) High Sch., 1980-81, Reading Tchrs. Study Group, Kanawha County, W.Va., 1981-83; project mgr. Dept. of Mines, State of W.Va., 1981-83, Dept. of Nat. Resources, State of W.Va., 1984-85; involved in curriculum devel. for various depts., W.Va. Inst. Tech., 1973-90, Raleigh County Schs., Beckley, W.Va., Piedmont Schs. Project, Greer, S.C., English and reading instr. Upward Bound Program, W.Va. Inst. Tech., 1980-85; adj. instr. W.Va. Coll. Grad. Studies, 1979, 81, 83. Author (with William Burns): Practical Robotics: Systems, Interfacing, and Applications, 1986, (with A.B. Somers): Candles and Mirrors: Response Guides for Teaching Novels and Plays in Grades Six through Twelve, 1984, Response Guides for Teaching Children's Books, 1979; editorial bd.: W.Va. Community Coll. Jour.; reviewer: Macmillan Pub. Co. texts, 1985; editor: Diamond Shamrock, 1985; co-producer, host (TV series): About the Author; contbr. numerous articles to profl. jours.; participated in numerous presentations. Mem. W.Va. Community Coll. Assn.; bd.dirs., Curtain Callers, 1979-89, Fayette Fine Arts Coun., 1986-87; promotions chair, W.Va. Children's Book award com., 1984-85. Mem. AAUW (recording sec. 1983-85, pres. 1985—), Assn. for Tchrs. of Tech. Writing, Nat. Assn. for Devel. Edn., Soc. for Tech. Comm. Home: 4 Pinewood Dr Peru NY 12972-4638 Office: Plattsburgh State U of NY Ctr for Lifelong Learning 101 Broad St Plattsburgh NY 12901-2637

WORTHINGTON, JOHN M. information technology executive; BS summa cum laude, Ea. Mich. U., 1974, MS summa cum laude, 1978; MBA, U. Mich., 1982. Test engr. Chrysler Corp., 1978—80; various fin. and operating capacities UGI Corp., 1982—85; prin. Synotic Tech., Inc., 1986—94, COO, 1994—96; corp. planning analyst Scott Paper Co.; environ. planner Diaz-Seckinger & Assocs.; pres. TransCore, Inc., 1999, COO, 1996—99, pres., CEO, chmn. Bd. dirs., chmn. audit com. ACAD Weston Holdings, Inc.; bd. dirs. TCA Party Ltd. (Australia), Weston Solutions. Mem.: Internat. Bridge, Tunnel and Turnpike Assn. (com. mem.), Intelligent Transp. Soc. Am. (bd. dirs., com. mem. exec. forum). Office: TransCore Inc Ste 200 Liberty Ctr Bldg 8158 Adams Dr Hummelstown PA 17036

WORTHINGTON, MELVIN LEROY, minister, writer; b. Greenville, N.C., June 17, 1937; s. Wilbur Leroy and Alma Lee (Braxton) W.; m. Anne Katherine Wilson, Sept. 12, 1959; children: Daniel Edward, Lydia Anne. Diploma, Imperial Detective Acad., Cin., 1965; B.Bibl.Edn., Columbia Bible Coll., S.C., 1959; B.Th., Luther Rice Sem., Jacksonville, Fla., 1967, B.Div., 1969, M.Th., 1970, D.Th., 1974; M.Ed., Ga. State U.-Atlanta, 1979; EdD, Vanderbilt U., 1998. Ordained to ministry, Central Conf. Free Will Baptists, 1957. Pastor Union Chapel Free Will Bapt. Ch., Chocowinity, N.C., 1959-62, Palmetto Free Will Bapt. Ch., Vanceboro, N.C., 1959-62, First Free Will Bapt. Ch., Darlington, S.C., 1962-66, Wesconnett Free Will Bapt. Ch., Jacksonville, Fla., 1967, First Free Will Bapt. Ch., Amory, Miss., 1967-72, Albany, Ga., 1972-79; exec. sec. Nat. Assn. Free Will Bapt., Inc., Antioch, 1979—2002, chmn. Sunday Sch. bd., 1975-77, asst. moderator, 1977-79, chmn. grad. study com., 1976-77, exec. sec. emeritus, 2002—; pastor Liberty Free Will Bapt. Ch., Ayden, NC, 2003—. Clk. S.C. State Assn. Free Will Bapt., Florence, 1966-67; asst. moderator Ga. State Assn. Free Will Bapt., Moultrie, 1973-74, moderator, 1975-79; pres. Ga. Bible Inst., Albany, 1978 Editor in chief: Contact mag., 1979—2002, author editorial, 1980—2002; contbr. articles to profl. jours. Adv. bd. Nat. Fedn. Decency, 1985; nat. bd. dirs. Christian Leaders for Responsible TV, 1986 Mem. Evang. Press Assn., Religious Conf. Mgmt. Assn. (dir. 1983, v.p. 1986, pres. 1989-92), Nashville C. of C., Future Farmers Am. (N.C. Farmer degree 1955, Am. Farmer degree 1957). Democrat. Mem. Free Will Baptist Ch. Office: Nat Assn Free Will Bapt Inc 5233 Mount View Rd Antioch TN 37013-2306 Office Phone: 252-746-3132. *The basic principle which has guided, governed and guarded my life has been a burning desire to find, follow and finish the will of God.*

WORTHINGTON, SANDRA BOULTON, lawyer; b. Phila., July 12, 1956; BA with high distinction, U. Va., 1978; JD, Temple U., 1983. Bar: Pa. 1983, U.S. Dist. Ct. (ea. dist.) Pa. 1984. Summer clk. Ct. of Common Pleas Montgomery County, Pa., summer 1981; legal intern Peruto, Ryan & Vitullo, Phila., 1982-83; assoc. Michael D. Fioretti Law Office, Phila., 1983-84; founding ptnr. Stocker & Worthington Law Office, Jenkintown, Pa., 1984—. Legal counsel Phila. Women's Squash Racquets Assn., 1985—. Mem. Pa. Trial Lawyers Assn., Phila. Trial Lawyers Assn., Pa. Bar Assn., Montgomery County Bar Assn. Avocations: small business consulting, squash, tennis. Office: Stocker & Worthington Law Offices The Rectory Ste 2 436 Old York Rd Jenkintown PA 19046-2840

WORTHINGTON, WARD CURTIS, JR., university dean, anatomy educator; b. Savannah, Ga., Aug. 8, 1925; s. Ward Curtis I and Pearl Mabel (Farris) W.; m. Floride Calhoun McDermid, June 21, 1947; children: Ward Curtis III, Amy Lynne Worthington Hauslohner. BS, The Citadel, 1952; MD, Med. U. S.C., 1952. Intern Boston City Hosp., 1952-53; instr. anatomy John Hopkins, 1953-56; asst. prof. anatomy U. Ill., 1956-57; asst. prof., assoc. prof. Med. U. S.C., Charleston, 1957-66; prof. anatomy Med. U. S.C., Charleston, 1966-91; prof. emeritus, 1991—. prof. history med. scis. M. U. S.C., Charleston, 1987—, asst. dean curriculum, 1966-69, chmn. dept. anatomy, 1969-77, acting v.p. acad. affairs, 1975-77, v.p. acad. affairs, 1977-82, assoc. dean acad. affairs, 1982—, dir. Waring Hist. Library, 1982—. Contbr. articles to profl. jours. Bd. dirs. Charleston Symphony Orch. Assn., 1980-84, 2d v.p., 1982. Served with USNR, 1944-46. Research grantee The Commonwealth Fund, 1957-61, NIH, 1962-73; NIH spl. fellow, 1964-65. Mem. Waring Library Soc., S.C. Acad.

Sci., S.C. Med. Assn., Charleston County Med. Soc., Endocrine Soc., Am. Physiol. Soc., Am. Assn. Anatomists, Sigma Xi, Alpha Omega Alpha, Phi Kappa Phi. Episcopalian. Lodge: Rotary (bd. dirs. 1982-83). Home: 17 Morton Ave Charleston SC 29407-7231 Office: 171 Ashley Ave Charleston SC 29425-0001

WORTHINGTON, WILLIAM ALBERT, III, lawyer; b. June 26, 1950; s. William Albert Jr. and Patricia Lou (Reynolds) W.; m. Melanie Ann McDonald, Oct. 30, 1993; children: Elizabeth Clark, Emily Robin, Katherine Anne, William Jackson. BS, U. Utah, 1972; JD, Washington and Lee U., 1976. Bar: Tex. 1976, U.S. Dist. Ct. (so. dist.) Tex. 1977, U.S. Ct. Appeals (5th cir.) 1977, U.S. Ct. Appeals (11th cir.) 1981, U.S. Supreme Ct. 1981, U.S. Dist. Ct. (we. dist.) Tex. 1982, U.S. Dist. Ct. (ea. dist.) Tex. 1986, U.S. Dist. Ct. (no. dist.) Tex. 1993. Assoc. Sewell & Riggs, Houston, 1976-82, ptnr., 1982-89, shareholder, 1990-94; ptnr. Strasburger & Price, LLP, Houston, 1994—. Exec. editor Washington and Lee Law Rev., 1976; contbr. articles to law jours. Active Houston YMCA, Amnesty Internat. U.S.A., ARC; del. state bar of Tex. to Rep. Cuba, 2001. Mem. Am. Law Inst., Def. Rsch. Inst., Product Liability Adv. Coun., Houston Bar Found., Tex. Bd. Legal Specialization (cert. civil trial lawyer, personal injury trial lawyer), U.S. Cycling Fedn., Sierra Club. Office: Strasburger & Price LLP 1401 Mckinney Ste 2200 Houston TX 77010 3033 E-mail: bill.worthington@strasburger.com.

WORTHLEY, HAROLD FIELD, retired minister, educator; b. Brewer, Maine, Nov. 3, 1928; s. Herbert Morrison and Aline May (Field) W.; m. Barbara Louise Bent, June 25, 1955; children: Susan Louise Field, Laura May, David Bruce. AB, Boston U., 1950, MA, 1951; STB, Harvard Div. Sch., 1954, STM, 1956, ThD, 1970. Ordained to ministry United Ch. of Christ, 1954. Min. Congl. chs., Maine, N.H. and Mass., 1952-62; assoc. prof. religion, chaplain Wheaton Coll., Norton, Mass., 1963-77; exec. sec., archivist Congl. Christian Hist. Soc., Boston, 1971—2004; exec. dir. Am. Congl. Assn., 1999—2004; libr. Congl. Libr., Boston, 1977—2004; ret., 2004. Editor Bull. of Congl. Library, 1976—, Hist. Intelligencer, 1980-86. Author: Inventory of the Records of the Particular Churches of Massachusetts, 1620-1805, 1970; contbr. articles to profl. jours. Mem. Hist. Coun. United Ch. of Christ. Fellow Pilgrim Soc., Congl. Christian Hist. Soc. Home: 14 Mansfield Ave Norton MA 02766-2212

WORTHY, K(ENNETH) MARTIN, retired lawyer; b. Dawson, Georgia, Sept. 24, 1920; s. Kenneth Spencer and Jeffrie Pruett (Martin) W.; m. Eleanor Vreeland (Blewett), Feb. 15, 1947 (dec. July 26, 1981); children: Jeffrie Martin, William Blewett; m. Katherine Teasley (Jackson), June 17, 1983. Attended, The Citadel, 1937-39; PhB, Emory U., 1941; MBA cum laude, Harvard Univ., 1943; JD cum laude, Emory U., 1947. Bar: Ga., 1947; D.C., 1948. Assoc. Foley and Lardner (formerly Hopkins, Sutter, Hamel, and Park), Washington, 1948-51, ptnr., 1952-69, 72-90, sr. counsel, 1991—; chief counsel IRS, 1969—72; asst. gen. counsel Treasury Dept., 1969—72. Dir. Beneficial Corp., 1977-96; emeritus, 1996-98; mem. Nat. Coun. Organized Crime, 1970-72; cons. Justice Dept., 1972-74. Co-author: (with John M. Appleman) Basic Estate Planning, 1957; contbg. articles to profl. jour. Del. Montgomery County Civic Fedn., 1951—61, D.C. Area Health and Welfare Coun., 1960—61; chmn. dept. fin., mem. diocesan coun. Episc. Diocese, Washington, 1969—70; trustee Associated Marine Inst. Found., 1999—2002, Ga. Wilderness Inst., 1997—2003, St. Simons Island Libr. Found., 2000—, chmn., 2001—; fellow Aspen Inst., 1982—92; trustee St. John's Coll., Annapolis and Santa Fe, 1987—93, 1995—2001, Sherman Found., Newport Beach, Calif., 1991—; mem. coun. Emory U. Law Sch., 1976—2001; chmn., 1993—95; trustee Chelsea Sch., 1981—2001, trustee emeritus, 2001—. Capt. U.S. Army, 1943—46, 1951—52. Recipient Army Commendation Ribbon, 1945; Treasury Exceptional Svc. Award and medal, 1972; IRS Commr. Award, 1972; Disting. Alumnus Award, Emory U., 1992. Fellow Am. Bar Found., Am. Coll. Tax Counsel (bd. regents 1980-88, chmn. 1985-87), Atlantic Coun. (counselor 1989-99); mem. ABA (coun. taxation sect. 1965-69, 72-75, chmn. 1973-74, del. Nat. Conf. Lawyers and CPAs 1981-87, ho. of dels. 1983-89, chmn. audit com. 1985-90; Disting. Svc. award taxation sect. 2004), Fed. Bar Assn. (nat. coun. 1969-74, 77-79), Ga. Bar Assn., D.C. Bar, Am. Law Inst., Am. Tax Policy Inst. (trustee 1989-98), Rotary, Chevy Chase Club, Met. Club, Sea Island Club, Ivy League Club (pres. 2002-03), Harvard Club N.Y.C., Phi Delta Theta, Phi Delta Phi, Omicron Delta Kappa. Home: PO Box 30264 189 W Gascoigne Sea Island GA 31561 Office: Foley and Lardner 3000 K St NW Ste 500 Washington DC 20007-5143 Personal E-mail: kmartinworthy@aol.com. Business E-Mail: kworthy@foley.com.

WORTIS, AVI See AVI

WORTLEY, GEORGE CORNELIUS, government affairs consultant, investor; b. Syracuse, N.Y., Dec. 8, 1926; s. George C. and Arlene (Hirsh) W.; m. Barbara Jane Hennessy, May 13, 1950; children: George C. IV, Ann Wortley Lavin, Elizabeth Wortley Ring. BS, Syracuse U., 1948. Newspaper pub., pres. Manlius Pub. Corp., Fayetteville, N.Y., 1950-92; pres. Nat. Editorial Found., 1968-73; mem. 97th-100th Congresses from 27th N.Y. Dist., 1981-89, mem. Banking, Fin. and Urban Affairs com., mem. Select Com. on Aging, Select Com. on Children, Youth and Family; pvt. bus. cons., investor Washington, 1989—. Pres. Am. Newspapers Reps., 1966—68; bd. dirs. Dierman, Wortley, Zola & Assocs., Washington Solutions. Pres. Hiawatha coun. Boy Scouts Am., 1972-75; mem. Nat. Commn. on Hist. Publs. and Records, 1977-80, Fayetteville Sr. Citizen Housing Commn., 1977-80; mem. allocations com. United Way of Ctrl. N.Y., 1979-81; mem. pub. rels. com. St. Camillus Health Care Ctr., 1971-78; mem. fed. legis. com. Am. Lung Assn., 1974-77; bd. dirs. Crouse-Irving Meml. Hosp. Found., 1975-87, pres. 1979-81; bd. dirs. Am. Heart Assn., Upstate N.Y., 1960-80, chmn. pub. rels. com., 1970-74, chmn. legis. com. 1977, mem. fund raising adv. com., 1974-79; trustee Cazenovia Coll., 1981-94; bd. dirs. Onondaga Hist. Assn., 1980-90; dir. Global Leadership Inst., 1987-2001. Served with MMR, USNR, WWII. Recipient Silver Beaver award Boy Scouts Am., 1973, Silver Antelope award, 1981 Mem. Nat. Newspaper Assn. (legis. com. 1976-80), Greater Syracuse C. of C. (dir. 1979-81), Upstate Coun. Indsl. Editors, LeMoyne Coll. Pres.'s Assocs., Syracuse U. Alumni Asn. (nat. treas. 1973-77), Former Mems. of U.S. Congress Assn., Navy League of U.S., Cosmos Club, Georgetown Club, Coral Ridge Yacht Club, Lions, KC, Kappa Sigma (pres. 1957-59). Republican. Roman Catholic. Office: 1776 K St NW Ste 400 Washington DC 20006-2326

WORTMAN, RICHARD S. historian, educator; b. N.Y.C., Mar. 24, 1938; s. Joseph R. and Ruth (Nacht) W.; m. Marlene Stein, June 14, 1960; 1 child, Leonie. BA, Cornell U., 1958; MA, U. Chgo., 1960, PhD, 1964. Instr. history U. Chgo., 1963-64, asst. prof., 1964-69, asso. prof., 1969-76, prof., 1976-77; prof. history Princeton U., 1977-88, dir. Russian studies, 1982-88; prof. history Columbia U., 1988—; Bryce prof. history, 2001—. Trustee Nat. Council for Soviet and Eastern European Research, 1983-89; sr. fellow Harriman Inst., 1985-86 Author: The Crisis of Russian Populism, 1967, The Development of a Russian Legal Consciousness, 1976, (with Leopold Haimson and Ziva Gallili) The Making of Three Russian Revolutionaries: Voices from the Menshevik Past, 1987, Scenarios of Power: Myth and Ceremony in Russian Monarchy, vol. I, 1995, vol. II (George L. Mosse prize Am. Hist. Assn.), 2000. Social Sci. Rsch. Coun. grantee, 1975-76; Guggenheim fellow, 1981-82 Mem. Am. Assn. Advancement Slavic Studies (pres. Mid-Atlantic Slavic Conf. 1982-83), AAUP., Am. Hist. Assn. Home: 410 Riverside Dr Apt 91 New York NY 10025-7924 Business E-Mail: rsw3@columbia.edu.

WORTMAN, WILLIAM JEROME, JR., obstetrician-gynecologist; b. Morganton, N.C., Aug. 2, 1934; s. William Jerome and Roberta May (Royster) W.; m. Carolyn Mabel Cane, Mar. 28, 1957 (div. 1974); children— Laura Wortman Solitario, Richard Ashley; m. 2d, Mary Ellen Moore, Jan. 18, 1975 (div.); m. Andrea Denise Edwards, May 20, 1995. A.B., Duke U., 1956; M.D., Wake Forest Coll., 1964. Diplomate Am. Bd. Ob-Gyn. Intern, U.S. Naval Hosp., Charleston, S.C., 1964-65; resident Virginia Mason Med. Center, Seattle, 1965-66, Kings County Hosp., Bklyn., 1966-69; practice medicine specializing in ob-gyn, Charlotte, N.C., 1969—; mem. staff Presbyn. Hosp., Mercy Hosp.; instr. ob-gyn SUNY-Downstate Med. Center, 1968-69; prin. Tryon Distbg., also bd. dirs.; cons. in field. Served to lt. USN, 1957-64; bd. dirs. Opera Carolina; to lt. comdr. M.C., USN, 1964-67. Mem. So. Med. Assn., Am. Coll. Obstetricians and Gynecologists, Am. Fertility Soc., Am. Assn. for Colposcopy and Colpomicroscopy, Am. Assn. Gynecol. Laparoscopists, Am. Assn. Sex Educators, Counsellors and Therapists, Am. Physicians Poetry Assn. (treas.), Royal Soc. Medicine Great Britain, Les Chevaliers du Tastevin. Clubs: Peninsula Club, Chaine Des Rotisseurs Peninsula Yacht Club. Contbr. numerous articles to profl. jours. Home: PO Box 1250 Cornelius NC 28031-1250 Address: PO Box 1250 Cornelius NC 28031-1250

WORTMANN, DOROTHY WOODWARD, physician; b. Easton, Pa., Mar. 14, 1945; d. Robert Simpson III and Esther (Thomas) Woodward; m. Robert Lewis Wortmann, June 14, 1969; children: Jonathan Thomas, William Lewis. BA, Mount Holyoke Coll., 1967; MD, U. Kans. Sch. Medicine, 1971. Diplomate Am. Bd. Pediatrics, subspecialty pediat. rheumatology. Clin. instr. pediatrics Med. Coll. Wis., Milw., 1979-80, instr. pediatrics, 1980-82, asst. prof. pediatrics, 1982-92; assoc. clin. prof. pediatrics East Carolina U. Sch. Medicine, Greenville, N.C., 1993—. Med. dir. rheumatology Children's Hosp. Wis., Milw., 1980-92. Chair for juvenile arthritis and mem. pub. and patient svcs. com. Arthritis Found., Milw., 1981-92, bd. dirs. Carolinas chpt., 1997—; med. adv. bd. Lupus Found., Milw., 1983-92. Recipient Disting. Svc. award Arthritis Found., 1991. Fellow Am. Acad. Pediatrics (mem. exec. coun. for rheumatology 1993-98), Am. Coll. Rheumatology (mem. sect. pediat. rheumatology); mem. N.C. Med. Soc., N.C. Pediat. Soc. Home: 9849 S Winston Ave Tulsa OK 74137-4840

WOSK, JULIE, humanities educator; m. Averill M. Williams. BA, Washington U., St. Louis, 1966; MAT, Harvard U., 1967; PhD, U. Wis., 1974. Prof. SUNY Maritime Coll., Bronx, 1975—. Author: Breaking Frame, 1992, Women and the Machine, 2001; contbr. articles to profl. jours. Grantee Alfred P. Sloan Found., N.Y.C., 2000. Mem. Soc. for History of Tech., Internat. Soc. for History of Tech. Office: SUNY Maritime Coll Dept Humanities 6 Pennyfield Ave Ft Schuyler Bronx NY 10465

WOSNITZER, MOREY, urologist; b. Passaic, N.J., Sept. 4, 1944; s. Morris and Ethel (Saltzman) W.; m. Nancy Joell Coplin, Sept. 18, 1978; children: Matthew, Brian. BS, Rutgers U., 1951, MS, 1952; MD, Columbia U., 1956. Diplomate Am. Bd. Urology, Am. Bd. Sexology. Intern in surgery Mt. Sinai Med. Ctr., N.Y.C., 1956-57, asst. resident in surgery, 1957-58; asst. resident in urology Columbia Presbyn. Med. Ctr., N.Y.C., 1958-59, Mass. Gen. Hosp., Boston, 1959-60; resident in urology Peter Bent Brigham Hosp., Boston, 1962-63; pvt. practice Springfield, N.J., 1964—. Assoc. in Clin. Urology Columbia U., N.Y.C., 1975—; clin. instr. in Urology Cornell U., N.Y.C., 1989—. Lt. Comdr. USN, 1960-62. Fellow ACS, Internat. Coll. Surgeons, Soc. Urology and Engring., Am. Assn. Clin. Sexologists. Avocations: gardening, computer, reading, music, horticulture. Office: 420 Morris Ave Springfield NJ 07081-1149

WÖSSNER, MARK MATTHIAS, retired publishing company executive; b. Berlin, Oct. 14, 1938; DEng, Tech. U. Stuggart, Germany. Asst. to top mgr. Bertelsmann AG, Gütersloh, Germany, 1968-70, prodn. mgr. Mohndruck unit, offset printing operation, 1970-72, tech. mgr. Mohndruck unit, 1972-74, mng. dir. Mohndruck unit, 1974-76, mem. exec. bd. in charge corp. divsn. for printing and mfg., 1976-81, dep chmn. exec. bd., 1981-82, CEO, chmn. exec. bd., 1982-98, chmn. supervisory bd., 1998-99; chmn. bd. Bertelsmann Found., 1999; ret., 1999. Exec. bd. dirs. Bertelsmann Found., 1996-99, chmn., CEO, 1999—. Office: Bertelsmann AG 1540 Broadway New York NY 10036-4039

WOTEKI, CATHERINE ELLEN, nutritionist; b. Fort Leavenworth, Kans., Oct. 7, 1947; d. Joseph Jeremiah and Catherine (Costello) O'Connor; m. Thomas Henry Woteki, June 7, 1969. BS, Mary Washington Coll., 1969; MS, Va. Poly. Inst. and State U., 1971, PhD, 1973. Registered dietitian. Asst. prof. Drexel U., Phila., 1975-77; project dir. Congl. Office of Tech. Assessment, Washington, 1977-80; group leader USDA, Washington, 1980-83; dep. dir. Nat. Ctr. for Health Statis., Washington, 1983-90; dir. Food and Nutrition Bd., Washington, 1990-93; dep. assoc. dir. for sci. Office of Sci. and Tech. Policy, Washington, 1994-95; undersec. food safety USDA Office of Food Safety, Washington, 1996—. Contbr. over 43 articles to profl. jours. Named Outstanding alumna Va. Poly. Inst. and State U., 1987; recipient Elijah White award Nat. Ctr. for Health Statis., 1987, Spl. Recognition award USPHS, 1987, Staff Achievement award Inst. of Medicine, 1991. Mem. Am. Inst. Nutrition, Am. Dietetic Assn. Coun. on Rsch., Inst. Food Technologists, Am. Pub. Health Assn. Office: USDA Office Food Safety 1400 Independence Ave SW Washington DC 20250-0002

WOTIPKA, CHRISTINE MIN, education educator; BA in Internat. Rels. and French with highest honors, U. Minn., Twin Cities, 1993; MA in Sociology, Stanford U., 1999, PhD in Internat. Comparative Edn., 2001. Vol. U.S. Peace Corps, Thailand, 1993—95; econ. rschr., English editor 1st Econ. Rsch. Inst., 1995—96; rsch. asst. Comparative Sociology Workshop, 1996—2001; cons. MentorNet, 2001; asst. prof. edn., dir. master's program in internat. and comparative edn. Stanford (Calif.) U., 2001—. Faculty affiliate Expansion and Impact of World Human Rights Regime project, 2002—; MacArthur Consortium affiliate Ctr. for Internat. Security and Coop., 2000—; mem. adv. bd. sci. and tech. TV Digital Turbulence, 2002—. Office: Stanford U Sch Edn 485 Lasuen Mall Stanford CA 94305-3096

WOTRING, MELANIE JEAN See HASTINGS, MELANIE

WOTT, JOHN ARTHUR, arboretum and botanical garden executive, horticulture educator; b. Fremont, Ohio, Apr. 10, 1939; s. Arthur Otto Louis and Esther Wilhelmina (Werth) W.; children: Christopher, Timothy, Holly. BS, Ohio State U., 1961; MS, Cornell U., 1966, PhD, 1968. Mem. staff Ohio State Coop. Extension Svc., Bowling Green, 1961-64; rsch. asst. Cornell U., Ithaca, N.Y., 1964-68; prof. Purdue U., West Lafayette, Ind., 1968-81; prof. Ctr. Urban Horticulture U. Wash., Seattle, 1981—; assoc. dir. Ctr. Urban Horticulture U. Wash., Seattle, 1990-93; dir. arboreta Washington Park Arboretum, Seattle, 1993—. Acting dir. Ctr. Urban Horticulture U. Wash. Writer columns for Nursery Mgmt. Profession, Balls and Burlap, Am. Nurseryman, The Arboretum Found.; contbr. articles to profl. jours. and papers including Nursery Mgr. Profl., Balls and Burlap, Arboreteum Found. Bull., Am. Nurseryman. Mem. Am. Soc. Hort. Sci. (com. chmn. 1967-82), Am. Assn. Bot. Gardens and Arboreta, Internat. Plant Propagators Soc. (internat. pres. 1984, internat. sec.-treas. 1985—). Avocations: music, antiques. Office: Internat Plant 2300 Arboretum Dr E Seattle WA 98112-2300 Personal E-mail: jwott10623@aol.com. Business E-Mail: jwott@u.washington.edu.

WOUK, HERMAN, writer; b. NYC, May 27, 1915; s. Abraham Isaac and Esther (Levine) W.; m. Betty Sarah Brown, Dec. 9, 1945; children: Abraham Isaac (dec.), Nathaniel, Joseph. AB with gen. honors, Columbia U., 1934; LHD (hon.), Yeshiva U., 1954; LLD (hon.), Clark U., 1960; LittD (hon.), Am. Internat. Coll., 1979; PhD (hon.), Bar-Ilan U., 1990, Hebrew U., 1997; DLitt (hon), George Washington U., 2001, Trinity Coll., 1998. Writer radio programs for various comedians, N.Y.C., 1935; asst. writer weekly radio scripts comedian Fred Allen, 1936-41. Presdl. cons. to U.S. Treasury, 1941; vis. prof. English Yeshiva U., 1952-57; scholar-in-residence Aspen Inst. Humanistic Studies, 1973-74 Author: (novels) Aurora Dawn, 1947, The City Boy, 1948, Slattery's Hurricane, 1949, The Caine Mutiny, 1951 (Pulitzer Prize award for fiction, 1952), Marjorie Morningstar, 1955, Youngblood Hawke, 1962, Don't Stop the Carnival, 1965, The Winds of War, 1971, War and Remembrance, 1978, Inside, Outside, 1985 (Washingtonian Book award, 1986), The Hope, 1993, The Glory, 1994, A Hole in Texas, 2004, (dramas) The Traitor, 1949, The Caine Mutiny Court-Martial, 1953, (comedy) Nature's Way, 1957, (non-fiction) This is My God, 1959, The Will to Live On, 2000, (screenplays for TV serials) The Winds of War, 1983, War and Remembrance, 1986. Trustee Coll. of V.I., 1961-69; bd. dirs. Washington Nat. Symphony, 1969-71, Kennedy Ctr. Prodns., 1974-75. Exec. officer U.S.S. Southard USNR, 1942-46, PTO. Recipient Richard H. Fox prize, 1934, Columbia U. medal for Excellence, 1952, Alexander Hamilton medal, 1980, U. Calif.-Berkeley medal, 1984, Golden Plate award Am. Acad. Achievement, 1986, USN Meml. Found. 'Lone Sailor' award, 1987, Yad Vashem KaZetnik award, 1990, Bar Ilan U. Guardian of Zion award, 1998, USCD medal U. Calif.-San Diego, 1998. Mem. Naval Res. Assn., Dramatists Guild, Authors Guild, Internat. Platform Assn. (Ralph Waldo Emerson award 1981), PEN Clubs: Bohemian (San Francisco); Cosmos, Metropolitan (Washington); Century Assn (N.Y.C.). Jewish. Office: care BSW Literary Agy 3255 N St NW Washington DC 20007-2845

WOVSANIKER, ALAN, lawyer, educator; b. Newark, Mar. 19, 1953; s. Harold and Sally (Gooen) Wovsaniker; m. Susan Orme, Aug. 23, 1987. AB, Brown U., 1974; JD, Harvard U., 1977. Bar: N.J. 1977. Law clk. to presiding judge U.S. Dist. Ct. N.J., Camden, 1977-78; ptnr. Lowenstein Sandler PC, Roseland, NJ, 1978—. Adj. prof. Seton Hall Law Sch., 1988—91, Rutgers U. Law Sch., 1989—95; chmn. dist. ethics com. Supreme Ct. Contbr. articles to profl. jours. Mem. exec. com. N.J. chpt. Anti-Defamation League. Mem.: Essex County Bar Assn. (trustee 1996—99, chmn. banking law com. 1994—97, chmn. corp. law com. 1999—2003). Office: Lowenstein Sandler PC 65 Livingston Ave Roseland NJ 07068-1791 E-mail: awovsaniker@lowenstein.com.

WOYCZYNSKI, WOJBOR ANDRZEJ, mathematician, educator; b. Czestochowa, Poland, Oct. 24, 1943; came to U.S., 1970; s. Eugeniusz and Otylia Sabina (Borkiewicz) W.; m. Elizabeth W. Holbrook; children: Lauren Pike, Gregory Holbrook, Martin Wojbor. MSEE, Wroclaw (Poland) Poly., 1966; PhD in Math., Wroclaw U., 1968. Asst. prof. Inst. Math. Wroclaw U., 1968-72, assoc. prof., 1972-77; prof. dept. math. Cleve. State U., 1977-82; prof., chmn. dept. math. and stats. Case Western Res. U., Cleve., 1982-91, dir. Ctr. for Stochastic and Chaotic Processes in Sci. and Tech., 1989 2001, chmn. dept. stats., 2002—02, Rsch. fellow Inst. Math. Polish Acad. Scis., Warsaw, 1969-76; postdoctoral fellow Carnegie-Mellon U., Pitts., 1970-72; vis. assoc. prof. Northwestern U., Evanston, Ill., 1976-77; vis. prof. Aarhus (Denmark) U., 1972, U. Paris, 1973, U. Wis., Madison, 1976, U. S.C., 1979, U. N.C., Chapel Hill, 1983-84, Gottingen (Germany) U., 1985, 91, 96, U. NSW, Sydney, Australia, 1988, Nagoya (Japan) U., 1992, 93, 94, U. Minn., Mpls., 1994, Tokyo U., 1997, Princeton U., 1998. Dep. editor in chief: Annals of the Polish Math. Soc., 1973-77; assoc. editor Chemometrics Jour., 1987-94, Probability and Math. Stats., 1988—, Annals of Applied Probability, 1989-96, Stochastic Processes and Their Applications, 1993-99; co-editor: Martingale Theory and Harmonic Analysis in Banach Spaces, 1982, Probability Theory and Harmonic Analysis, 1986, Nonlinear Waves and Weak Turbulence, 1993, Nonlinear Stochastic PDE's: Hydrodynamic Limit and Burgers' Turbulence, 1995, In a Reporter's Eye: The Life of Stefan Banach, 1996, Stochastic Models in Geosystems, 1997; author: (monograph) Martingales and Geometry in Banach Spaces I, 1975, part II, 1978, Burgers-KPZ Turbulence: Göttingen Lectures, 1998; co-author: Random Series and Stochastic Integrals: Single and Multiple, 1992, Distributions in the Physical and Engineering Sciences, vol. 1: Distributional and Fractal Calculus, Integral Transforms and Wavelets, 1997, Introductory Statistics and Random Phenomena. Uncertainty, Complexity and Chaotic Behavior in Engineering and Science, 1998. Rsch. grantee NSF, 1970, 71, 76, 77, 81, 87—, Office of Naval Rsch., 1985-96. Fellow Inst. Math. Stats.; mem. Am. Math. Soc., Am. Statis. Assn., Polish Math. Soc. (Gt. prize 1972), Polish Inst. Arts and Scis., Racquet Club East. Roman Catholic. Avocations: tennis, music, skiing, sailing, rare books collecting. Home: 3296 Grenway Rd Cleveland OH 44122-3412 Office: Case Western Res U Dept Statistics Cleveland OH 44106 E-mail: waw@po.cwru.edu.

WOYSKI, MARGARET SKILLMAN, retired geology educator; b. West Chester, Pa., July 26, 1921; d. Willis Rowland and Clara Louise (Howson) Skillman; m. Mark M. Woyski, June 19, 1948; children: Nancy Elizabeth, William Bruno, Ronald David, Wendelin Jane. BA in Chemistry, Wellesley (Mass.) Coll., 1943; MS in Geology, U. Minn., 1945, PhD in Geology, 1946. Geologist Mo. Geol. Survey and Water Resources, Rolla, 1946-48; instr. U. Wis., Madison, 1948-52; lectr. Calif. State U., Long Beach, 1963-67, lectr. to prof. Fullerton, 1966-91, assoc. dean Sch. Natural Sci. and Math., 1981-91, emeritus prof., 1991—. Contbr. articles to profl. jours.; author lab. manuals; editor guidebooks. Fellow Geol. Soc. Am. (program chmn. 1982); mem. South Coast Geol. Soc. (hon. pres. 1974), Mineral Soc. Am. Home: 880 Morningside Dr Apt M-320 Fullerton CA 92835-3577

WOZENCRAFT-ORNELLAS, (BETTY) JEAN, singer, music educator; b. Alamogordo, N.Mex., Oct. 24, 1957; d. John George and Betty Jean Wozencraft; m. Jerry Ornellas, Nov. 1, 1991. MusB in Vocal Performance, Oberlin Coll., 1979; MusM in Vocal Performance, Bowling Green State U., 1981; MusD in Vocal Performance, Fla. State U., 1987. Free lance singer, Portales, N.Mex., 1979—; prof. voice Ea. N.Mex U., Portales, 1984—. Profl. debut: Cleve. Opera, 1979; singer: (songs) various venues internationally. Recipient 2d pl. award, Hemphill-Wells Sorantin Young Artists, 1987, W.Va. Symphony, 1979; regional finalist, winner, Met. Opera Auditions, 1986, 1988. Mem.: Rotary. Office: Eastern New Mexico University Station 16 Portales NM 88130 Personal E-mail: jean.ornellas@enmu.edu. E-mail: jean.ornellas@enmu.edu.

WOZNIAK, CURTIS S. electronics company executive; Various positions in mfg., mktg. and ops. Gen. Motors Corp.; prodn. engring. mgr. Hewlett-Packard Co.; v.p. Desktop Graphics devel. Sun Microsys. Computer Corp., v.p., gen. mgr. Ednl. Products divsn., v.p. engring., v.p. worldwide mktg.; pres., COO Xilinx Inc.; CEO Electroglas Inc., 1996—, also chmn., 1997—. Bd. dirs. SEMI/SEMATECH consortium, Mgmt. Inst. Office: Electroglas 6024 Silver Creek Valley Rd San Jose CA 95138-1011

WOZNIAK, JOHN S. dean; b. Stevens Point, Wis., Sept. 18, 1944; s. John C. and Bernadine C. (Prais) Wozniak. BA in Religious Edn., History and English cum laude, St. Mary's U., Winona, Minn., 1966; MA in History, N.D. State U., 1969; PhD in Anthropology, U. Tex., 1974; postgrad., Carnegie Mellon U., 1991, Harvard U., 1996. Tchr. Shanley H.S., Fargo, ND, 1966—69, 1970—71, LaSalle H.S., Cedar Rapids, Iowa, 1969—70; prof. anthropology St. Mary's U., Winona, Minn., 1974—91; exec. adminstrv. asst. to pres. Christian Bros. U., Memphis, 1991—92; v.p. acad. affairs Clarke Coll., Dubuque, Iowa, 1992—99; dean arts and scis. St. Leo U., Tampa, Fla., 1999—2003; v.p. acad. affairs Divine Word Coll., Epworth, Iowa, 2003—. Sec.-treas. gen. unit Am. Anthropol. Assn., Washington, 1984—86; cons. evaluator North Ctrl. Assn., Chgo., 1995—99. Author: Contact, Negotiation and Conflict, 1978; editor: Historic Lifeways in the Upper Mississippi River Valley, 1983; contbr. articles to profl. jours. Mem. planning com. Tampa Bay Regional Planning Coun., 2001—03; county rep. S.E. Regional Arts Coun., 1975—78; mem. Iowa Humanities Bd., 1993—99. Recipient award of merit for publ., Wis. State Hist. Soc., 1979. Mem.: Am. Anthropol. Assn., AAAS (A/V and book reviewer 1983—), Current Anthropology (assoc.), Phi Kappa Phi. Democrat. Roman Catholic. Avocations: fishing, travel, reading. Home: 2695 Raven Oaks # 4 Dubuque IA 52001 Office: Divine Word Coll 102 Jacoby Dr SW Epworth IA 52045-0380 E-mail: johnswoz442000@yahoo.com.

WOZNIAK, RICHARD ANTHONY, computer engineer; b. Buffalo, Aug. 24, 1959; s. Richard Anthony and Julia Marie (Cefaratti) W. BA, U. Buffalo, 1981, MS, 1983. Software engr. Sierra Rsch., Buffalo, 1983-85; sr. analyst Marine Midland Bank, Buffalo, 1985-91, project mgr., 1991-93, tech. specialist, 1993—2000, IT mgr., 2001—. Pres. South Cheektowaga Baseball Assn., Cheektowaga, N.Y., 1984—. Recipient award Cheektowaga C. of C., 1992. Home: 33 Grand Prix Dr Cheektowaga NY 14227-3613 Office Phone: 716-841-1245.

WOZNIAK, STEPHEN GARY, computer scientist, philanthropist; b. San Jose, Calif., Aug. 11, 1950; married. BS in comp. sci. and EECS, U. Calif., Berkeley. Designer calculator chips Hewlett Packard, 1976; designer, co-founder Apple Computer, Inc., 1979—81; founder U.S. Festivals, 1982—83; re-joined as principal engr. Apple Computer, Inc., 1983—85, consultant, 1985—; co-chmn. Axlon, Inc., Sunnyvale, Calif., 1986—. Founder Elec. Frontier Found.; founding sponsor Tech Museum, Silicon Valley Ballet, Children's Discovery Museum, San Jose, Calif. Named to Inventor's Hall of Fame, 2000; recipient Nat. Medal Tech., presented by Pres. Ronald Reagan, 1985, Grace Murray Hopper award, Assn. Computing Machinery, 1979, Heinz Award for Technology, 2000. Mem.: Charity Lodge (life). Achievements

include invention of the first line of Apple products - the Apple I and II computers; influenced the popular Macintosh computer; supports the Los Gatos School Dist., providing students and teachers with hands-on teaching and donations of state-of-the-art tech. equip.

WOZNY, DAVID, utilities executive; BS in Acctg., Ball State U. CPA. From acct. to sr. mgr. Arthur Andersen LLP, 1981—95; from mgr. spl. projects and acctg. rsch. to controller Cinergy Corp., Cin., 1996—2003, controller, 2003—. Office: Cinergy Corp 139 E 4th St Cincinnati OH 45202

WRAASE, DENNIS RICHARD, utilities company executive, accountant; b. Washington, Mar. 15, 1944; s. Richard Harold and Esther Morelle (Cowan) W.; m. Cecilia Anne Kirby, Dec. 30, 1987; children: Richard Reid, Elisabeth Kirby. BS, U. Md., 1966; MS, George Washington U., 1975. CPA, Md. Acct. Exxon Corp., Balt., 1966-70, fin. analyst Houston, 1970-74; mgr. fin. systems Potomac Electric Power Co., Washington, 1974-78, asst. comptr., 1978-81, dir. computer and gen. svcs., 1981-83, comptr., 1983-92, v.p., 1986-89, sr. v.p., 1989—, CFO, 1996—; exec. v.p. Potomac Capital Investment, Washington, 1999, pres., COO, 2000—; pres., CEO Pepco Holding Inc., 2002—. Pres. Olney Jaycees, Md., 1978; bd. dirs. v.p. Nat. Capital area Boy Scouts Am., Washington, 1987-2002, Better Bus. Bur., Washington Bd. Trade, Federal City Coun., 2001—; bd. dirs. Washington Performing Arts Soc., 2002—, U. Md. Found., 2003, Washington Hosp. Ctr., 2002. With USAR, 1967-73. Mem. Am. Inst. CPAs, Fin. Execs. Inst. Democrat. Lutheran. Office: Potomac Electric Power Co 701 NInth St NW Ste 1000 Washington DC 20068

WRAGA, WILLIAM GERARD, educator; b. Teaneck, N.J., Mar. 21, 1957; s. William Francis and Maryjane M. (Conlon) W.; m. Amy Jeanne Schneider, June 26, 1982; children: William Frederic, Ian Thomas. AB, Rutgers Coll., 1979; MAT, U. Chgo., 1980; EdD, Rutgers U., 1991. Tchr. Hillsborough H.S., Belle Mead, N.J., 1980-81, Green Brook (N.J.) H.S., 1981-84, Mendham (N.J.) H.S., 1984-86; dept. supr. Freehold (N.J.) Twp. H.S., 1986-87; dist. supr. K-12 Bernards Twp. Pub. Schs., Basking Ridge, N.J., 1987-94; adj. asst. prof. Rider U., Lawrenceville, 1994; asst. prof. dept. edn. leadership U. Ga., Athens, 1995-99, assoc. prof., 1999—2004, interim founding head dept. ednl. adminstrn. and policy, 2002—04, prof. dept. ednl. adminstrn. and policy, 2004—. Chmn. civics com. N.J. State Dept. Edn., 1988—90, mem. social studies core course proficiencies panel, 1989—91; bd. dirs. N.J. Coun. for Social Studies, 1988—90, chmn. publ. com., 1988—89; mem. exec. bd. N.J. ASCD, 1992—93; mem. adv. com. N.J. Vietnam Vets. Meml. Ednl. Ctr., 1993—94; cons. La. Bd. Regents, 2004; presenter in field. Author: Democracy's High School, 1994; contbg. author: Readings in Middle School Curriculum, 1993, Curriculum Issues and the New Century, 1995, Handbook on Teaching Social Issues, 1996, Encyclopedia of Education, 2003; exec. editor Focus on Edn. Jour., N.J. ASCD, 1993; co-editor: Rsch. Rev. for Sch. Leaders, 1996, 1998, 2000; guest co-editor Social Edn., 1990, mem. editl. bd. HIstory of Edn. Quar., former mem. editl. bd. Jour. Curriculum and Supervision, The Ednl. Forum; contbr. articles and book revs. to profl. jours. Grad. Merit scholar Rutgers U., 1984-85, 85-86; recipient Excellence in Dissertation award Rutgers Grad. Sch. Edn. Alumni Assn., 1992. Fellow John Dewey Soc. (bd. dirs. 2000-02); mem. Am. Ednl. Rsch. Assn., Profs. of Curriculum (Factotum 1998-99), Soc. Study Curriculum History (pres. 2001—03), Soc. Profs. Edn. (exec. bd. 2003—), Phi Delta Kappa, Pi Lambda Theta, Kappa Delta Pi. Office: U Ga Coll Edn Dept Ednl Adminstrn and Policy 850 College Station Rd Athens GA 30605-4808 E-mail: wwraga@coe.uga.edu.

WRAY, BETTY BEASLEY, allergist, immunologist, pediatrician; b. Ga., 1935; MD, Med Coll. Ga., 1960. Diplomate Am. Bd. Allergy and Immunology, Am. Bd. Clin. Lab. Immunology. Intern Talmadge Meml. Hosp., Augusta, Ga., 1960-61, resident in pediatrics, 1962, 64-65, fellow in pediatric allergy, 1966-68; staff mem. Med. Coll. Ga., Augusta, 1979—, prof. pediat. medicine, interim dean Sch. Medicine, v.p. clin. activities, 2000—02, prof. emeritus, 2002—. Mem.: Am. Coll. Allergy, Asthma and Immunology, Am. Acad. Pediat., Am. Acad. Allergy and Immunology, Am. Pediatric Soc. Office: Med Coll Georgia BG 1009 Augusta GA 30912 Office Phone: 706-721-3531. E-mail: bettyw@mail.mcg.edu.

WRAY, CECIL, JR., lawyer; b. Memphis, Nov. 19, 1934; s. Thomas Cecil and Margaret (Malone) W.; m. Gilda Gates, Sept. 11, 1964; children: Christopher A., Kathleen Wray Baughman. Student, U. Va., 1952-53; BA magna cum laude, Vanderbilt U., 1956; LLB, Yale U., 1959. Bar: Tenn. 1959, N.Y. 1961, U.S. Supreme Ct. 1964. Registered conseil juridique, France, 1978-82. Law clk. to justice Tom C. Clark U.S. Supreme Ct., Washington, 1959-60; assoc. Debevoise & Plimpton, N.Y.C., 1960-67, ptnr., 1968-96, of counsel, 1997-99, resident ptnr. Paris, 1976-79. Adj. prof. N.Y. Law Sch., 1997-2001. Co-author: Innovative Corporate Financing Techniques, 1986. Bd. dirs. Search & Care, Inc., N.Y.C., pres., 1981-87; bd. dirs. Episcopal Charities, N.Y., pres., 1995-2002; vestryman St. James' Ch., N.Y.C., 1982-87, warden, 1988-94; trustee Fondation des Etats-Unis, Paris, 1976-79, Ch. Pension Fund; bd. dirs. East Side Comty. Ctr., Inc.; bd. fgn. parishes Episcopal Ch., 1995—; bd. dirs. Hudson Highlands Land Trust; commr. Adirondack Park Agy.; bd. dirs. Ch. Ins. Co. Fellow Am. Coll. Investment Counsel (trustee 1981-86, pres. 1983-84); mem. Am. Law Inst., Assn. Bar City N.Y., Coun. Fgn. Rels., Ausable Club (St. Huberts, N.Y.), Union Club, Century Club, Order of Coif, Phi Beta Kappa. Episcopalian. Home: 47 E 88th St New York NY 10128-1152 Office: Debevoise & Plimpton 919 3rd Ave New York NY 10022-3902

WRAY, GERALDINE SMITHERMAN (JERRY WRAY), artist; b. Shreveport, La., Dec. 15, 1925; d. David Ewart and Mary Virginia (Hoss) Smitherman; m. George Downing Wray, June 24, 1947; children: Mary Virginia Hill, Deanie Galloway, George D. Wray III, Nancy Armistead. BFA with honors, Newcomb Art Sch., Tulane U., 1946. Tchr. children's art. One woman shows include Don Batman Gallery, Kansas City, Mo., 1982, Gallery II, Baton Rouge, 1985, McNeese Coll., Lake Charles, La., 1987, Dragonfly Gallery, Shreveport, La., 1987, Barnwell Garden and Art Ctr., Shreveport, 1988, 95, Southdown Mus., Houma, La., 1989, La. State U., Shreveport, 1991, WTN Radio Station, Shreveport, 1993, The Cambridge Club, Shreveport, 1993, Centenary Coll., 1993, Northwestern State U., Natchitoches, La., 1995, Goddard Mus., Ardmore, Okla., 1996, Art Buyers Caravan, Atlanta, 1996, Lockhaven (Pa.) U., 1996, Billingsley Gallery, Pensacola, Fla., 1996, Casa D'Arte, Shreveport, La., 1996, N.E. State U., Monroe, La., 1997, Art Expo, N.Y.C., 1997, Palmer Gallery, Hot Springs Ark., 1998, Tower Art Gallery, Shreveport, La., 1999, Meadows Mus. Retrospective, Shreveport, 2003, Schumpert Hosp. Integrated Medicine, Shreveport, 2003, Midwestern Tex. U., 2003, Wichita Falls, Tex., 2003; group shows include Watercolor USA Springfield, Mo., 1988, Waddell's Gallery, Shreveport, 1988, 91, Water Works Gallery, Dallas, 1990, Southwestern Watercolor Show, 1991 (D'Arches award, Creative Artist award 1997), Masur Mus. Exhbn. (honorable mention 91, 92), Bossier Art Ctr., Bossier City, La., 1992, Irving Art Assn. (honorable mention), 1992, Leon Loard Gallery, Montgomery, Ala., 1993, Ward-Nasse Gallery, N.Y.C., 1993, 97, Soc. Experimental Artists Internat. (1st place, honorable mention), 1993, Palmer Gallery, Hot Springs, Ark., 1994, Nat. Watercolor Soc. Ann., 1994-96, 98, 2003, Art Expo, N.Y.C., 1996, Casa D'Arte, Shreveport, 1996, Art Buyers Caravan, Atlanta, 1996, Off The Wall Gallery, Savannah, Ga., 1997, Art Effects Gallery, Merian, Pa., Boulevard Art Gallery, Macon, Ga., 1997, Visual Inspirations, Newton, N.J., 1997, Mossey Brake Gallery, Tex., 1997, Barnwell Ctr. (with children & grandchildren), Shreveport LA, 1998, Manhattan Arts Mag. Showcase Award, Nat. Assn. Women Artist Traveling Show, Meadows Mus., Shreveport, La., 2003, Integrated Medicine, 2003, Northwestern U., La., 2004; permanent collections include NAWA, Zimmerli Mus., Rutgers Univ., N.J.-Meir Mus., Lynchburg, Va., Goddard Mus. Ardmore, Okla., Bibl. Arts Ctr., Dallas, La. State Capitol Bldg., Lockhaven Univ. Penn., LSUS Med. Ctr., Shreveport, LA., Shacknow Mus., Plantation, Fla., Meadows Mus., Shreveport, La., 2003, Integrated Medicine Schompert Wellness Ctr., Shreveport, 2003, Northwestern U., Natchitoches, La., 2004, Midwestern U., Tex., 2003. Art chmn. Jr. League, Shreveport, 1955-60; bd. dirs. Holiday-in-Dixie Cotillion, Shreveport, 1974-76. Inducted into Visual Artists Hall of Fame, Shreveport, La., 1998. Mem. Nat. Assn. Women Artists, Nat. Watercolor Soc. (signature mem. 1994, 96), Southwestern Watercolor Soc. (signature mem. 1991), La. Watercolor Soc. (signature mem. 1990), La. Artists Inc. (elected mem.), Internat. Soc. Exptl. Artists (signature mem.), Western Fedn. Soc. Artists (signature mem.), Watercolor Soc. Houston (signature mem.). Episcopalian. Avocation: tennis. Home: 573 Spring Lake Dr Shreveport LA 71106-4603 Personal E-mail: jerrywray@bellsouth.net.

WRAY, KENT, academic administrator; m. Wanda Wray. BS in Physics, Washburn U.; BS in Civil Engring., Kans. State U.; MS in Civil Engring., Air Force Inst. Tech.; PhD in Civil Engring., Tex. A&M U. Engr. Kans. Hwy. Dept.; chmn. dept. civil engring. Tex. Tech. U.; dean engring. and tech. Ohio U.; provost and sr. v.p. for acad. and student affairs Mich. Technol. U., Houghton, 2000—. Chair Ohio Engring. Deans Coun., 1990. Contbr. articles to profl. jours. Recipient Coll.-level Halliburton Outstanding Rsch. award, Halliburton Outstanding Tchr. award. Fellow: ASCE. Office: Mich Technol Univ Rm 503A Adminstrn Bldg 1500 Townsend Dr Houghton MI 49931-1295*

WRAY, NELDA PARK, medical association administrator; b. San Antonio, Sept. 7, 1947; d. Adrian L. and Arrawannah T, Park. BA with high honors, U. Tex.; MD with honors, Baylor Coll. Medicine; MPH, U. Tex. Sch. Pub. Health. Internal medicine intern Johns Hopkins Hosp., Balt., 1972—73; resident in internal medicine Baylor Coll. Medicine Affiliated Hosp., 1975—77, chief resident in medicine, 1975, fellow in pulmonary diseases, 1975—77; prof. medicine and med. ethics Baylor Coll. Medicine; dir. Houston Ctr. Quality Care and Utilization Studies. Adj. prof. U. Tex. Sch. Pub. Health; chief gen. medicine sect. Houston VA Med. Ctr. Mem. editl. rev. bd. Jour. Gen. Internal Medicine; reviewer New Eng. Jour. Medicine. Apptd. chair Tex. Health Info. Coun., 1995. Robert Wood Johnson Health Policy fellow, Washington. Office: Houston Ctr Quality Care & Utilization Studies VA Med Ctr (152) 2002 Holcombe Blvd Houston TX 77030-4211

WRAY, ROBERT, lawyer; s. George and Ann (Moriarty) W.; m. Lila Keogh (dec.); children: Jennifer, Edward, Hillary. BS, Loyola U., 1957; JD, U. Mich., 1960. Bar: DC, Ill. 1960. Assoc. Hopkins & Sutter, Chgo., 1964—69; gen. counsel Agy. for Internat. Devel., 1969—71; sr. counsel TRW, Inc., 1972—73, Export-Import Bank of the U.S., 1974—79; prin. Robert Wray Assocs., 1979—86; internat. ptnr. Pierson, Ball & Dowd, 1986—87; prin. Robert Wray Assocs., 1988—; spec. counsel Graham & James, 1988—97; ptnr. Holland & Knight, Washington, 1997—2003; mng. mem. Robert Wray PLLC, Washington, 2003—. Recipient medal of superior honor Dept. of State. Mem.: ABA, Internat. Bar Assn., Am. Soc. Internat. Law, Fed. Bar Assn., Chevy Chase Club, Annapolis Yacht Club, Talbot Country Club, Met. Club, Bretton Woods Com. Office: 1150 Connecticut Ave NW Ste 350 Washington DC 20036

WRAY, THOMAS JEFFERSON, lawyer; b. Nashville, July 17, 1949; s. William Esker and Imogene (Cushman) W.; m. Susan Elizabeth Wells, Aug. 19, 1972; children: William Clark, Caroline Kell. BA, Emory U., 1971; JD, U. Va., 1974. Bar: Tex. 1974, U.S. Dist. Ct. (so., no. and ea. dists.) Tex. 1976, U.S. Ct. Appeals (5th and 11th cirs.) 1976, U.S. Supreme Ct. 1987. Assoc. Fulbright & Jaworski, L.L.P., Houston, 1974-82; ptnr. Fulbright & Jaworski, Houston, 1982—. Mem. ABA, Coll. Labor and Employment Lawyers, Houston Bar Assn., Houston Mgmt. Lawyers Forum (chmn. 1981-82), Briar Club, Phi Beta Kappa. Republican. Episcopalian. Home: 3662 Ella Lee Ln Houston TX 77027-4105 Office: Fulbright & Jaworski 1301 Mckinney St Ste 5100 Houston TX 77010-3095 Office Phone: 713-651-5151. Business E-Mail: tjwray@fulbright.com.

WREN, GAYDEN, playwright, theater director; b. N.Y.C., May 24, 1961; s. Gayden and Mary Alice Wren; m. Sara Holliday, July 7, 2001. BA, Oberlin Coll., 1983. Entertainment editor NY Times Syndicate, N.Y.C., 1995—. Author: (book) A Most Ingenious Paradox: The Art of Gilbert & Sullivan, (theater) As If, Baseball, Sex and Other Facts of Life, Ernest, An Evening with Gilbert & Sullivan, A Gilbert & Sullivan Christmas Carol, ID, Moonlight and Midnight, A Night on the Tomb, Swords & Frenchmen, Tales from the Bible, Two for the Show, Very Truly Yours, Gilbert & Sullivan, The World According to Gilbert & Sullivan; dir.: (opera) The Sorcerer, HMS Pinafore, The Pirates of Penzance, Patience, Iolanthe, Princess Ida, Ruddigore, Opera, (opera) The Gondoliers, Utopia, Limited. Dir. The Gilbert & Sullivan Light Opera Co. of LI, Merrick, NY, 1984—; artistic dir. The New Punctuation Army Inc., N.Y.C., 1984—; chmn. Citizens for Classic Movies, N.Y.C., 1992—; artistic dir. Troupers Light Opera, New Canaan, Conn., 2002—03. Home: 19-92 78th St Steinway NY 11370 Office: The New York Times Syndicate 122 E 42nd St New York NY 10168 E-mail: wreng@nytimes.com.

WREN, JOHN D. advertising executive; married; 2 children. BA, MBA, Adelphi U., 1975. Mgmt. cons. Arthur Anderson & Co.; with Norton Simon Inc., Needham Harper Worldwide; joined Diversified Agency Services (subs. Omnicom Group, Inc.), 1986, CFO, pres., 1990—93, chmn., CEO, 1993—95; pres. Omnicom Group, Inc., NYC, 1995—97, pres., CEO, 1997—. Office: Omnicom Group Inc 437 Madison Ave Fl 9 New York NY 10022-7001*

WREN, ROBERT JAMES, aerospace engineering manager; b. Moline, Ill., May 12, 1935; m. Jordis Wren; children: James, Patrick, Kiley. BSCE, U. Tex., 1956; MSCE, So. Meth. U., 1962; doctoral candidate, U. Houston. Registered profl. engr. Tex. Engring. aide Ctrl. Power and Light Co., Corpus Christi, 1954; sta. clk. City of Austin (Tex.) Power Plant, 1954-55; assoc. engr., hydraulic engr. U.S. Bur. of Reclamation, Austin, 1955-57; structural test engr. Gen. Dynamics, Ft. Worth, 1957-62; sr. structural dynamics engr., mgr. vibration and acoustic test facility NASA-Manned Spacecraft Ctr., Houston, 1962-63, 63-66, head exptl. dynamics sect., 1965-70; mgr. Apollo Spacecraft 2TV-1 CSM Test Program, 1966-68, Apollo Lunar Module-2 Drop Test Program, 1968-70; mgr. structural design space sta., space base, lunar base, mars mission NASA-Manned Spacecraft Ctr., Houston, 1970-73; mgr. structural design and devel., space shuttle carrier aircraft-747 NASA Johnson Space Ctr., Houston, 1973-74, mgr. structural divsn. space shuttle payload systems, 1974-84; mgr. engring. directorate for space shuttle payload safety NASA-Johnson Space Ctr., Houston, 1984-94, mem. space shuttle payload safety rev. panel, 1984-2000, alternate chmn. space shuttle payload safety review panel, 1990-2000, mgr. engring. dir. vehicle and payload flight sys. safety, 1994-2000. Mem. NASA Internat. Space Sta. Flight sys. safety panel, 1994-2000; dir. safety and mission assurance Internat. Space Sta. Program Office, United Space Alliance Hdqs., Houston, 2000—. Pres. Friendswood Little League Baseball, 1980-83; bd. dirs. Bay Area YMCA, Houston, 1982—, chmn., 1983-84. Recipient Sustained Superior Performance award NASA, Personal Letter of Commendation, George Low NASA Apollo Program, Outstanding Svc. award NASA, Group Achievement awards NASA; Paul Harris fellow Rotary. Mem. Space Ctr. Rotary (dir., treas., sec., v.p. 1979-85, pres. 1985-86, Rotary dist. 5890/govt. rep. 1986-87, area coord. 1987-89, zone leader 1988-89, gov.'s aide 1989-90, chmn. dist. assembly 1989-90, 93-94, fin. com. 1989-91, Rotary Nat. award for Space Achievement Found./co-founder, bd. dirs. 1984—), Rotary World Health Found. Plastic Surgery for Children (co-founder, bd. dirs. 1985—), Rotary Space Meml. Found. (co-founder, bd. dirs. 1986—, co-founder, bd. dirs. Space Ctr. Rotary Endowment Found., 1987—). Methodist. Avocations: snow and water skiing, running, scuba diving, tennis, sailing. Home: PO Box 1466 Friendswood TX 77549-1466 Office: United Space Alliance Hdqrs 1150 Gemini Houston TX 77058 E-mail: robert.j.wren@usahq.unitedspacealliance.com.

WREN, STEPHEN COREY, mathematician, inventor; b. St. Louis, Sept. 4, 1956; s. Donald W and Jo V (Mask) Wren; 1 child, Corey. BA in Math./Computer Sci., Washington U., St. Louis, 1979. Actuary William Mercer, St. Louis, 1980-83; pres. CIM, St. Louis, 1983—2000; managing mem Variant USA, St Louis, 2000—. Instr St Louis Univ, 1986—87, Webster Univ, 1985—86. Achievements include invention of computerized marketing networks. E-mail: stevewr@synerty.net.

WRENN, CHRISTOPHER JAY, physician; b. Margarita, Panama Canal Zone, July 16, 1947; s. Earl Walton and Maxine Elizabeth (Luther) W.; m. Nancy Margaret Bowie, June 27, 1970; children: Kristina Elizabeth, Courtney Bowie. BS, Baylor U., 1969; MD, U. Nebr., 1973. Diplomate Am. Bd. Pediatrics, Am. Bd. Allergy and Immunology. Intern pediatrics Children's Med. Ctr., Dallas, 1973-74, resident pediatrics, 1974-76, chief resident pediatrics, 1976-77; staff pediatrician Los Barrios Unidos Community Clinic, Dallas, 1977-78; fellow allergy and immunology Med. Br. U. Tex., Galveston, Tex., 1978-80; practice medicine specializing in allergy Graves-Gilbert Clinic, Bowling Green, Ky., 1980-83, Wichita Clinic, 1983-84, Allergy Clinic, Tyler, Tex., 1984—. Staff pediatrician Dallas County Children's Shelter, 1975-78, Dallas County Juvenile Detention Ctr., 1975-78, Buckner Bapt. Children's Home, 1977-78. Author (chpt. of book) Pediatrics by Self Instruction, 1982. Fellow Am. Acad. Pediatrics, Am. Coll. Allergists; mem. Am. Acad. Allergy and Immunology. Presbyterian. Avocation: writing fiction and poetry. Office: Allergy Clinic PA 1128 Medical Dr Tyler TX 75701 Office Phone: 903-593-8273.

WRENN, JAMES JOSEPH, East Asian studies educator; b. New Haven, Conn., July 7, 1926; s. James Joseph and Mariea (Enright) W.; m. Harriet Huddleston Calhoun, July 7, 1953; children: Annemarie Wrenn-Bessmer, James Joseph, Michael Enright, Christopher David. BA, Yale U., 1953, PhD, 1964. Lectr. in Chinese Grad. Sch., Yale U., New Haven, 1961-62, Brown U., Providence, 1962-64, asst. prof., 1964-67, assoc. prof. linguistics, 1967-73, prof., 1974-91, co-chmn. East Asian Studies, 1987-95, dir. Ctr. for Lang. Studies, 1987-90, prof. emeritus, 1996. Contbr. articles to profl. jours. Platoon sgt. USMCR, 1944-46, PTO, 1950-52, Korea. Fgn. area fellow Ford Found., Republic of China, 1958-59 Mem. AAUP, MLA, Am. Council Tchrs. Fgn. Langs., Assn. Asian Studies, Chinese Lang. Tchrs. Assn. Clubs: Faculty. Home: 22 Rhode Island Ave Providence RI 02906-5506 Office: Brown U PO Box 1850 Providence RI 02912-1850

WRENN, WALTER BRUCE, marketing educator, consultant; b. Mobile, Ala., Nov. 9, 1950; s. Walter P. and Winona A. (Jeffrey) W.; m. Jan F. Carmichael, June 12, 1971. BS, Auburn U., 1973; M of Mgmt., Northwestern U., 1974, PhD, 1989. Market analyst The UpJohn Co., Kalamazoo, 1974-78; asst. prof. mktg. Andrews U., Berrien Springs, Mich., 1978-89; assoc. prof. Ind. U., South Bend, 1995—2001, prof., 2002—. Cons. The UpJohn Co., Kalamazoo, 1982, N.Am. Div. SDA, Washington, 1983, Worthington (Ohio) Foods, 1985—, Adventist Health System, Austin, Tex., 1986, Leco, 1991, Bio-Met, 1991, Maple Leaf Farms, 1998. Co-author: Marketing for Congregations, 1994, The Marketing Research Guide, 1997, Marketing Planning Guide, 1997, Marketing Research: Text and Cases, 2002, Marketing Essentials, 2002, Marketing Management: Text and Cases, 2004; contbr. articles to profl. jours. Dir. University Press, Berrien Springs, 1986-89, Sta. WAUS, Berrien Springs, 1987—. Named Outstanding Young Man of Am. Jr. C. of C., 1980; univ. scholar Northwestern U., 1980-83. Mem. Am. Mktg. Assn. (Outstanding Mktg. Student 1973), Acad. Mktg. Sci., Phi Kappa Phi, Alpha Mu Alpha, Omicron Delta Epsilon, Delta Sigma Pi, Delta Mu Delta. Seventh Day Adventist. Avocation: golf. Home: 5027 E Bluffview Dr Berrien Springs MI 49103-1435 Office: Ind Univ 1700 Mishawaka Ave South Bend IN 46615-1400

WRIGHT, ALFRED GEORGE JAMES, band symphony orchestra conductor, educator; b. London, June 23, 1916; arrived in U.S., 1923, naturalized, 1936; s. Alfred Francis and Elizabeth (Chapman) W.; m. Bertha Marie Farmer, Aug. 6, 1938; children: Adele Marie Wright Needham, Cynthia Elaine Wright Williams; m. Gladys Violet Stone, June 28, 1953. BA, U. Miami, 1937, MEd, 1947; LLD (hon.), Troy State U., 1980. Dir. music Miami Sr. HS, 1938-54; prof., head dept. bands Purdue U., Lafayette, Ind., 1954-85; founder, condr. US Coll. Wind Band Tours, 1971—. Pres. Internat. Music Tours, Inc.; v.p., exec. sec. Music Tour Svcs., Inc.; dir. prerace pageantn Indpls. 500 Mile Automobile Race, 1957—82; mem. adv. com. Performing Arts Abroad, 1972—2001; chmn. N.Am. Band Dirs. Coordinating Commn., 1974—75, Nat. H.S. Honors Band, 1975—76, 1977—; mem. jury World Music Contest, The Netherlands; bd. dirs. 500 Festival Assocs., 1961—81; founder, chmn. bd. dirs. Hall of Fame Disting. Band Condrs.; pres. All Am. Hall of Fame Band Found.; chmn. bd. John Philip Sousa Meml. Found., 1979—. Founding condr., Purdue U. Symphony Orch., 1971-81; Author: The Show Band, 1957, Marching Band Fundamentals, 1963, Bands of the World, 1970; marching band editor: Instrumentalist mag, 1953-81; contbr. articles to profl. mag. Mem. bd. advisors Internat. Music Festivals, 1989; bd. dir. World Assn. Wind Bands and Ensembles Found., 1991-94. Decorated Star of the Order John Philip Sousa; recipient Disting. Svc. award Purdue U., 1993. Mem. Nat. Band Assn. (founder, pres. 1960-63, hon. life pres. 1973), Coll. Band Dir. Nat. Assn., Am. Sch. Band Dir. Nat. Assn., Japan Marching Band Assn. (hon. bd. dir. 1971-77), Big Ten Band Dir. Assn. (pres. 1977), Am. Bandmasters Found. (bd. dir. 1987—), Am. Bandmasters Assn. (pres. 1979-80), elected Hon. Life mem., 2003, Nat. Acad. Wind and Percussive Arts (founder, chmn. 1961-81), Phi Mu Alpha, Kappa Kappa Psi (Disting. Svc. award 1981), Phi Beta Mu. Home and Office: 345 Overlook Dr West Lafayette IN 47906-1249 E-mail: agwright@gte.net.

WRIGHT, ANDREW, English literature educator; b. Columbus, Ohio, June 28, 1923; s. Francis Joseph and Katharine (Timberman) W.; m. Virginia Rosemary Banks, June 27, 1952; children: Matthew Leslie Francis, Emma Stanbery. AB, Harvard U., 1947; MA, Ohio State U., 1948, PhD, 1951. Prof. English lit. U. Calif., San Diego, 1963—, chmn. dept. lit., 1971-74; dir. U. Calif. Study Center, U.K. and Ireland, 1980-82. Vis. prof. U. Queensland, Australia, 1984, Colegio de la Frontera Norte, San Antonio del Mar, Baja, Calif., 1991-92. Author: Jane Austen's Novels: A Study In Structure, 1953, Joyce Cary: A Preface to His Novels, 1958, Henry Fielding: Mask and Feast, 1965, Blake's Job: A Commentary, 1972, Anthony Trollope: Dream and Art, 1983; Fictional Discourse and Historical Space, 1987; contbg. author numerous books, articles to profl. jours., numerous short stories to lit. mags.; editorial bd. Nineteenth Century Fiction, 1964-86. Bd. dirs. Calif. Coun. Humanities, 1983-87. Guggenheim fellow, 1960, 70; Fulbright Sr. Research fellow, 1960-61 Fellow Royal Soc. Lit.; mem. MLA, Jane Austen Soc., Athenaeum (London), Trollope Soc., Santayana Soc., Phi Beta Kappa. Home: 7227 Olivetas Ave La Jolla CA 92037-5335 Office: U Calif San Diego Dept Lit La Jolla CA 92093-0410 Business E-Mail: ahwright@ucsd.edu.

WRIGHT, ANTOINETTE D. museum administrator; Dep. dir. Donor's Forum Chgo., 1990—93, dir. fin./adminstrn., asst. treas., 1993—97; pres., CEO DuSable Mus. African Am. History, Chgo., 1997—. Office: DuSable Mus African Am History 740 E 56th Pl Chicago IL 60637*

WRIGHT, BARBARA WINCKLHOFER, nursing educator; b. Cranbury, N.J., Aug. 3, 1933; BS, Boston Coll.; EdD, Rutgers U.; MA, PhD, NYU. RN. Dep. mayor, then mayor Plainsboro Twp., 1977-85; assemblywoman dist. 14 N.J. State Assembly, 1992-2000, dep. spkr., 1998-99; assoc. dean, assoc. prof. Seton Hall U. Coll. Nursing, South Orange, N.J., 2000—. Mem. N.J. Soc. for Assn. Execs. (assn. exec. of yr. 1989). Office: Seton Hall U 400 S Orange Ave South Orange NJ 07079-2697

WRIGHT, BETTY REN, children's book writer; b. Wakefield, Mich., June 15, 1927; d. William and Revena Evelyn (Trezise) W.; m. George Albert Frederiksen, Oct. 9, 1976. BA, Milw.-Downer Coll., 1949. With Western Pub. Co., Inc., 1949-78, mng. editor Racine Editl., 1967-78. Author numerous juv. and jr. novels, including The Doll House Murders, 1983, Christina's Ghost, 1985, The Summer of Mrs. MacGregor, 1986, A Ghost in the Window, 1987, The Pike River Phantom, 1988, Rosie and the Dance of the Dinosaurs, 1989, The Ghost of Ernie P., 1990, A Ghost in the House, 1991, The Scariest Night, 1991, The Ghosts of Mercy Manor, The Ghost of Popcorn Hill, 1993, The Ghost Witch, 1993, A Ghost Comes Calling, 1994, Out of the Dark, 1995, Haunted Summer, 1996, Too Many Secrets, 1997, The Ghost in Room 11, 1998, A Ghost in the Family, 1998, The Moonlight Man, 2000, The Wish Master, 2000, Crandalls' Castle, 2003; also numerous picture and ednl. books including Pet Detectives, 1999, The Blizzard, 2003; contbr. fiction to mags. Recipient Alumni Svc. award Lawrence U., 1973, Lynde and Harry Bradley Maj. Achievement award, 1997, numerous awards for books including Mo. Mark Twain award, 1986, 96, Tex. Bluebonnet award, 1986, 88, Young Readers award Pacific N.W. Libr. Assn., 1986, Reviewer's Choice Booklist, Ala. Young Readers award, 1987, Ga. Children's Choice award, 1988, Ind. Young Hoosier Book award, 1989, 96, Children's Choice Book/Internat. Reading Assn.—CBC, 1984, S.C. Children's Choice award, 1995, Okla.

Sequoyah Children's Choice award, 1988, 95, award Fla. Sunshine State, 2001. Mem.: Coun. Wis. Authors (Juvenile Book award 1985, 1996), Allied Authors, Phi Beta Kappa. Avocations: reading, travel. Home and Office: 6223 Hilltop Dr Racine WI 53406-3479

WRIGHT, BLANDIN JAMES, lawyer; b. Detroit, Nov. 29, 1947; s. Robert Thomas and Jane Ellen (Blandin) Wright; m. Gina Almente; children: Steven Blandin, Martha Kay, Oliver Steffan. BA, U. Mich., 1969; JD, Dickinson Law Sch., 1972; LLM in Taxation, NYU, 1973; MS in Taxation with honors, Am. U., 1992. Bar: Pa. 1973, Fla. 1976, U.S. Tax Ct. 1977, D.C. 1979, U.S. Supreme Ct. 1979, Va. 1984, N.Y. 1991; CPA, Tex., 1978, Va., 1985. Atty. Office Internat. Ops. Nat. Office IRS, Washington, 1973-76; tax dir. Intairdril Ltd., London, 1976-78; tax atty. Allied Chem. Corp., Houston, 1978-79; v.p., gen. counsel Assoc. Oiltools, Inc., London, 1979-82; v.p. taxes, gen. counsel J. Lauritzen (USA), Inc., Charlottesville, Va., 1982-85; sole practice Charlottesville, Va., 1985-88; ptnr. Richmond & Fishburne, Charlottesville, Va., 1988-90, of counsel, 1990-91; tax counsel Mobil Oil Corp., N.Y.C., 1990, Fairfax, Va., 1990-95; vice chmn., gen. counsel Cruise Holdings, Ltd., Miami, 1996-97; pres. Maritime Capital Group, Inc., Miami, 1998—; chmn. Internat. Hospitality, Inc., 1999—. Officer Pamaco Partnership Mgmt. Corp., Va., 1986-91, CRW Energy Corp., 1986-90, Transp. & Tourism Internat., Inc., 1986—, Hotsprings Assocs., Inc., 1989-91, MDM Hotels, Inc., 1992-95, Internat. Shipping & Resorts, Inc., 1992—, United Holdings Ltd., 1993-96, Cruise and Resorts Internat., Inc., 1994—; bd. dirs. Blandin J. Wright, P.C., Internat. Hospitality, Inc., CRS Holdings, Inc. Contbr. articles to profl. jours. Coach Charlottesville Youth Soccer, Baseball and Basketball, 1984-89; coach London Youth Baseball, 1982. Mem. ABA, AICPA, Am. Arbitration Assn. (arbitrator 1985—), Tex. Soc. CPAs, Va. Soc. CPAs, Fairfax County Bar Assn., Farmington Country Club, Deering Bay Yacht and Country Club, Mensa, Beta Gamma Sigma. Roman Catholic. Office: 4770 Biscayne Blvd Ph G Miami FL 33137-3251 E-mail: blandin@earthlink.net.

WRIGHT, BRIAN THEODORE, retired engineering executive; b. Philadelphia, Pa., Dec. 17, 1944; s. Theodore William and Ruth Dorothea Wright; m. Julene Capps, Mar. 16, 1966; children: Christina Grace, Paige Leanne. BS in biochemistry, Auburn U., 1962—66; MS in ops. rsch., US Naval Postgraduate Sch., 1969—71. Cert. Quality Engineer, ASQC, 1988. Comm. engr. Dept. of Def., 1975—77; engrng. dir. ITT, 1977—86; v.p. engring. ITT Acrospace and Comm., Ft. Wayne, Ind., 1986—92, Collins Comm. and Avionics Divsn., Cedar Rapids, Iowa, 1992—97; v.p. engring. and tech. Rockwell Collins, Cedar Rapids, 1997—99, v.p. integrated architectures, 1999—2001, v.p. strategic tech., 2001—03; ret., 2003. Chmn. U. of Ill. Coll. of Engring. Adv. Bd., 1998—2000. Lt. col. USMC, 1966—86. Mem.: World Future Soc., Licensing Exec. Soc., Soc. of Sigma Xi. Episcopal. Achievements include patents for in field of avionics and communications. Avocations: skiing, hiking, dogs.

WRIGHT, BURTON, sociologist; b. Detroit, Jan. 31, 1917; s. Burton and Hazel Marie (Thomas) Wright; m. Marie Fidelis Gallivan, Jan. 26, 1942; children: Burton III(dec.), Catherine Margaret(dec.). AA, C.Z. Coll., 1944; BA, U. Wash., 1947, MA, 1949; PhD, Fla. State U., 1972. Enlisted USN, 1937, commd. and advanced through grades to comdr., 1957; dir. Naval Res. Recruiting, 1960-64; ret., 1964; mem. faculty U. Wash., 1947-49, George Washington U., Washington, 1954-60, Rollins Coll., Winter Park, Fla., 1966-69; prof. dept. sociology U. Ctrl. Fla., Orlando, 1972-82, prof. emeritus, 1982-89; ret., 1989; prof. sociology Troy State U., 1991—. Cons. Ford Found., 1951, Dept. Air Force, 1955, U.S. Army Chem. Corps, 1956; mem. faculty Northwestern U., summers 1956-59; vis. prof. sociology Troy State U., Dothon; dir. Am. Sociol. Assn. Nat. Honors Program, 1981-89; vis. prof. Troy State U., Dothan. Author: (with J.P. Weiss and C.M. Unkovic) Perspective: An Introduction to Sociology, 1975, (with V. Fox) Criminal Justice and the Social Sciences, 1978, (with J.P. Weiss) Social Problems, 1980. Decorated Navy Commendation medal. Fellow Am. Anthrop. Assn.; mem. AAUP, Am. Sociol. Assn. (membership com. 1983-86), Soc. Psychol. Study Social Problems, Am. Acad. Arts and Scis., Soc. Study Social Problems, So. Sociol. Soc., North Ctrl. Sociol. Soc., Univ. Club (Winter Park). Roman Catholic. Home: 502 Dunleith Blvd Dothan AL 36303-2936

WRIGHT, C. T. ENUS, former academic administrator; b. Social Circle, Ga., Oct. 4, 1942; s. George and Carrie Mae (Enus) W.; m. Mary Stephens, Aug. 9, 1974. BS, Fort Valley State U. (Ga.), Ga., 1964; MA, Atlanta U., 1967; PhD, Boston U., 1977; LHD, Mary Holmes Coll., 2000. Tchr. Ga. Pub. Schs., Social Circle, 1965-67; mem. faculty Morris Brown Coll., Atlanta, 1967-73, divsn. chmn., 1973-77; program dir., asst. provost Eastern Wash. U., Cheney, 1977-81; v.p. acad. affairs Talladega Coll. (Ala.), 1981-82; pres. Cheyney U. Pa., Cheyney, 1982-85; v.p. and provost Fla. Meml. Coll., 1985-89; pres. Internat. Found. and Coord. African-African Am. Summit, 1989-2001; pres., CEO IFESH, 2001—. Cons. and lectr. in field; bd. dirs. Internat. Found. for Edn. and Self Help, England, Leow Sullivan Trust, So. Africa, Peoples Investment Fund for Africa. Author: (booklet) The History of Black Historical Mythology, 1980; contbr. articles to profl. jours. Commnr., Wash. Pub. Broadcasting, Olympia, 1980-84; exec. com. Boy Scouts Am., Phila., 1982—; Goodwill Amb. State of Ga., 1997—. Human Rels. scholar, 1969, Nat. Tchg. fellow Boston U., 1971. Mem. Am. Assn. Colls. and Univs. (coms. 1982—), Am. Hist. Assn. (coms. 1970—), Assn. Study Afro-Am. Life & History (coms. 1965—), Nat. Assn. Equal Opportunity in Higher Edn. (coms. 1982—), NEA (coms. 1965—). Am. Baptist. Clubs: Lions (Cheyney, Wash. (v.p. 1979-81), Tuscan, Fountain Hills Times, Atlanta Constitution. Address: 17420 E Dull Knife Dr Fountain Hills AZ 85268 E-mail: wrightjack@aol.com.

WRIGHT, CAROLE DEAN, reading specialist; b. Mt. Clemens, Mich., Aug. 18, 1943; d. Edward Lawrence and Alice Agnes Hundt; m. David John Wright, Dec. 20, 1964 (div. Sept. 1984); 1 child, Amy Elizabeth. BA, Mich. State U., 1964, MA, 1967. Reading specialist Holt (Mich.) Pub. Schs., 1965-70, Ypsilanti (Mich.) Pub. Schs., 1970-71, Aurora (Colo.) Pub. Schs., 1972—; pres. Aurora Edn. Assn., 1978-80, Colo. Edn. Assn., Denver, 1982. Mem. adv. com. Nat. Assessment of Ednl. Progress, Denver, 1975; chair unit accreditation bd. Nat. Coun. Accreditation of Tchr. Edn., Washington, 1990-99; trustee Pub. Employees Retirement Assn. Colo., 1993X. Contbg. author to Idea's for Children's Literature, 1976. Mem. Colo. Commn. on Tchr. Edn. and Accreditation, Denver, 1976-82; vice chair Gov.'s Chpt. 2 Adv. Com., Denver, 1987-93. Named Outstanding Educator, Fed. Programs Adminstr. Coun. U.S. Dept. Edn., 1991. Mem. NEA (bd. dirs. 1984-87), Internat. Reading Assn., Colo. Edn. Assn. (v.p. 1980-81, 83-84, pres. 1982, award 1999), Phi Delta Kappa (Leadership award 1998). Home: 2268 Clermont St Denver CO 80207-3740

WRIGHT, CAROLE YVONNE, chiropractor; b. July 12, 1932; d. Paul Burt and Mary Leoan (Staley) Fickes; 1 child, Morgan Michelle. D. Chiropractic, Palmer Coll., Davenport, Iowa, 1976. Instr. Palmer Coll., Davenport, Iowa, 1975-76; dir., owner Wright Chiropractic Clinic, Rocklin, Calif., 1978-88, Woodland, Calif., 1980-81; co-owner Ft. Sutter Chiropractic Clinic, Sacramento, Calif., 1985-89; owner Wright Chiropractic Health Ctr., Sacramento, 1989-93, Capitol Chiropractic, Sacramento, 1993-95. Cons. in field; lectr., speaker on radio and TV programs, at seminars. Contbr. articles to profl. jours. Co-chmn. Harold Michaels for Congress campaign, Alameda, Calif., 1972; dist. dir. 14th Congle. Dist., 1983-95. Mem. Internat. Chiropractic Assn. Calif. (bd. dir. 1978-83), Rocklin C. of C. (bd. dirs. 1979-81). Republican. Avocations: reading, travel. Home: 425 Cirby Way Ste 70 Roseville CA 95678-4244

WRIGHT, C(ARROLL) LEE, JR., architecture educator; BArch, U. Tex., 1963, MArch, 1969. With Hirsch and Cassetti, Elmira, NY, 1964—65, Claude Pendley, Austin, Brook, Barr, Graeber and White, Austin, Pierce/Lacey Assocs., Dallas, 1965; mem. faculty U. Tex., Arlington, 1968—, assoc. prof. arch., 1972—, assoc. dean, 1975—77, dir. arch. program, 1978—79, undergrad. advisor, 1989—99, interim dean Sch. Arch., 1999—2001, assoc. dean Sch. Arch., 1993—99, dir. arch., 2002—04; pvt. practice Lee Wright Assocs., 1968—. Mem. univ. curriculum com. U. Tex., Arlington; bd. dirs. Dallas Arch. Found., 1999—2002; acad. and career counselor Sch. Arch., 2004—. Named Outstanding Advisor, U. Tex. Arlington, 1993. Office: Univ Tex Arlington Sch Arch Rm 203 Box 19108 701 S Nedderman Dr Arlington TX 76019-0108

WRIGHT, CATHIE, state legislator; b. Old Forge, Pa., May 18, 1929; 1 child, Victoria. AA in Acctg., Lackawanna Jr. Coll.; student, U. Scranton. Former mayor and city councilwoman City of Simi Valley; mem. Calif. State Assembly, 1980-92, Calif. State Senate, 1992—. Chair Simi Valley Cmty. Devel. Com., Simi Valley Drug Abuse Program; former mem. transp., adv. planning, criminal justice planning bd., animal control com. for Ventura County. Named Woman of Yr., Simi Valley C. of C., 1979, Am. Mothers' Legis. Mother of the Yr., 1985, Outstanding Woman of the Yr., Zonta-Santa Clarita Valley, 1986. Mem. VFW, Las Manitas Aux. Republican. Office: State Capitol Rm 5052 Sacramento CA 95814 E-mail: senator.wright@sen.ca.gov.

WRIGHT, CHARLES PENZEL, JR., English language educator; b. Pickwick Dam, Tenn., Aug. 25, 1935; s. Charles Penzel and Mary Castleman (Winter) Wright; m. Holly McIntire, Apr. 6, 1969; 1 child, Luke Savin Herrick. BA, Davidson Coll., 1957; MFA, U. Iowa, 1963; postgrad., U. Rome, 1963—64. Mem. faculty U. Calif., Irvine, Calif., 1966—83, prof. English, 1976—83; mem. faculty U. Va., Charlottesville, Va., 1983—. Vis. prof. N.Am. Lit. U., Padua, Italy, 1968—69; disting. vis. prof. U. Degli Studi, Florence, Italy, 1992. Translator: The Storm and Other Poems (Eugenio Montale), 1978, Orphic Songs (Dino Campana), 1984. With AUS, 1957—61. Recipient Pen Transl. prize, 1979, Nat Book award for Poetry, 1983, citation in poetry, Brandeis U. Creative Arts Awards, 1987, L.A. Times Book prize, 1997, award, Nat. Book Critics Circle, 1997, Pulitzer Prize, 1998, Ambassador Book award, 1998; fellow Guggeheim fellow, 1976, Ingram Merrill fellow, 1980, 1993; scholar, Fulbright Found., 1963—65. Mem.: Acad. Am. Poets (chancellor), Am. Acad. Arts and Sci., Am. Acad. Arts and Letters, Fellowship of So. Writers. Home: 940 Locust Ave Charlottesville VA 22901-4030 Office: English Dept Univ Va Charlottesville VA 22901

WRIGHT, CHATT GRANDISON, academic administrator; b. San Mateo, Calif., Sept. 17, 1941; s. Virgil Tandy and Louise (Jeschien) W.; children from previous marriage: Stephen Brook, Jon David, Shelley Adams; m. Janice Teply, Nov. 28, 1993. Student, U. Calif., Berkeley, 1960-62; BA in Polit. Sci., U. Calif., Davis, 1964; MA in Econs., U. Hawaii, 1968. Instr. econs. U. Hawaii, Honolulu, 1968-70; mgr. corp. planning Telecheck Internat., Inc., Honolulu, 1969—70; economist State of Hawaii, Honolulu, 1970—71; adminstr. manpower City & County of Honolulu, 1971-72; bus. adminstr., dean. Hawaii Pacific U., Honolulu, 1972-74, v.p., 1974-76, pres., 1976—. Mem. City and County of Honolulu Manpower Area Planning Commn., 1976—82; mem. Mayor's Salary Commn. City and County of Honolulu, 1977—80; mem. Honolulu City Ethics Commn., 1978—84, City and County of Honolulu Labor Market Adv. Coun., 1982—84; bd. dirs. Hawaii Econ. Devel. Corp., 1980—84; trustee Queen's Med. Ctr., Honolulu, 1986—92, Honolulu Armed Svcs. YMCA, 1984—86, Hawaii Maritime Ctr., 1990—92; chmn. bd. trustees Hist. Hawaii Found., 1995—96, trustee, 1990—96; mem. adv. bd. Cancer Rsch. Ctr. Hawaii, 1987; trustee St. Andrew's Priory Sch., 1994—98; bd. dirs. Hawaii Visitors Bur., 1995—97; bd. dir. Downtown Improvement Assn., 1988—96; bd. dirs. Outrigger Duke Kahanamoku Found., 1996—98, Hawaii Opera Theatre, 1997—99; bd. govs. Hawaii Coun. on Econ. Edn., 1998—; trustee Oceanic Inst., 1998—, chmn., 2003—; mem. Hawaii Execs. Coun., 1996—, chmn., 2002, Hawaii Exec. Conf., 2002; bd. govs. Hawaii Med. Libr., 1989—92; mem. adv. bd. Aloha coun. Boy Scouts Am., 1991—2002; trustee Molokai Gen. Hosp., 1991—92; mem. Pacific Asian Affairs Coun., 1998—2001; steering com. Asian Devel. Bank, 2000—. With USN, 1968—70. Recipient Pioneer award Pioneer Fed. Savs. Bank, 1982, Stephen J. Jackstadt award, 1998; named Sales Person of Yr., Sales and Mktg. Execs. of Honolulu, 1998; Paul Harris fellow Rotary, 1986. Mem.: Hawaii Assn. Ind. Colls. and Univs. (chmn. 1986), Western Coll. Assn. (exec. com. 1989—92), Hawaii Joint Coun. Econ. Edn. (bd. dirs. 1982—88), Nat. Assn. Intercollegiate Athletics (mem. 1985—98, vice chair NAIA coun. of pres. 1994), Assn. Governing Bds. Univs. and Colls., Am. Assn. Higher Edn., Soc. Sci. Assn. (mem. 1994—99), Japan-Am. Soc. Honolulu, Waialae Country Club, Plaza Club (bd. govs. 1992—97), Pacific Club (Honolulu), Outrigger Canoe Club. Republican. Episcopalian. Avocations: hunting, fishing, reading, travel. Office: Hawaii Pacific U Office of Pres 1166 Fort Street Mall Honolulu HI 96813-2708 E-mail: president@hpu.edu.

WRIGHT, CLARK PHILLIPS, computer systems specialist; b. Orange, Tex., Aug. 30, 1942; s. Madison Brown and Mary Elizabeth (Phillips) W.; m. Stacy Charlotte Klutz, June 5, 1965 (div. Oct. 1979); m. Cora Lou Alexandria Schelling, Oct. 31, 1979; 1 child, Isaac Schelling. BA, U. Tex., 1965. Computer programmer Lockheed Electronics Co., Houston, 1965-67; prin. analyst Control Data Corp., St. Paul, 1967-76; computer scientist DBA Systems, Inc., Lanham, Md., 1976-79; engring. specialist Ford Aerospace Corp., Houston, 1979-90, Loral Aerospace Corp., 1990-97, Lockheed Martin Space Mission, 1997—. Precinct chmn. Rep. Party of Tex., 1982-86. Mem. IEEE, Math. Assn. Am., Assn. Computing Machinery, SAR (chartered, sec., treas.), Sons Republic Tex., Info. Sys. Security Assn., Masons, Rotary. Avocations: travel, photography. Home: 5000 Park Ave Dickinson TX 77539-7013 Office: Lockheed Martin Space Ops PO Box 58487 Houston TX 77258-8487 E-mail: cpwright@ghg.net., Clark.P.Wright@lmco.com.

WRIGHT, CONNIE HOTCHKISS, educational association administrator, researcher; d. Robert Francis Marion Wright and Daughtry. BA, Calif. U. of Dominguez Hills, L.A., 1972; MA in Spl. Edn., UCLA, 1975; PhD, Calif. Grad. Inst., L.A., 1998. Lic. treatment of chemically dependent Calif. Grad. Inst., 1998; bd. cert. ednl. therapist Assn. of Ednl. Therapists, 2002. Post-doctoral psychiat. fellow Cedars-Sinai Mental Health Ctr., 2002—. Mental health intake coord. Open Paths Counseling Ctr., L.A., 1999—2002. Mem.: Marriage & Family Therapist (L.A. chpt.) (licentiate; post doctoral registered intern 1998—2004), Marriage & Family Therapist (Calif. chpt.) (licentiate; post doctoral registered intern 1998—2004). Liberal. Achievements include patents pending for ednl.therapy reading program; Awakenings. Avocations: artist, photographer, poetry. Office: Ctr for Learning 1951 Westwood Blvd Los Angeles CA 90025 Office Phone: 310-234-0774.

WRIGHT, CREIGHTON BOLTER, cardiovascular surgeon, educator; b. Washington, Jan. 29, 1939; s. Benjamin Washington and Catherine Adele (Bolter) W.; m. Carolyn Eleanor Craver, Jan. 29, 1966; children: Creighton Bolter, Benson, Kathryn, Elizabeth. BA, Duke U., 1961, MD, 1965; MBA, Xavier U., Cin., 1995. Diplomate Am. Bd. Surgery, Am. Bd. Thoracic Surgery, Am. Bd. Gen. Vascular Surgery. Intern Duke U., Durham, NC, 1965—66; resident in surgery U. Va., Charlottesville, 1966—71; asst. prof., then assoc. prof. George Washington U., Washington, 1974—76; assoc. prof., then prof. surgery U. Iowa, Iowa City, 1976—81; prof. clin. surgery, assoc. dean U. Cin., 1982—; prof. clin. surgery Uniformed Svcs. U., 1982—; dir. dept. surgery Jewish Hosp., Cin., 1989—2003; med. dir. cardiovasc. svcs. Health Alliance Cin., 1999—2003; chief of staff VA Med. Ctr., Cin., 2003—. Councilor Acad. Medicine, 2003—. Editor: Vascular Grafting, 1983, (with others) Venous Trauma, 1983; contbr. articles to med. jours., chpts. to books. Col. USAR, 1966-93. Decorated Bronze Star; recipient Kindred Resident Tchr. award, 1967, Golden Apple Tchg. award, 1975, Tchg. award Jewish Hosp., 2001. Mem. Assn. Acad. Surgery (pres. 1980), Soc. Univ. Surgeons, Soc. Vascular Surgery, Am. Assn. Thoracic Surgery, Soc. Thoracic Surgery, Ctrl. Surg. Assn., Internat. Soc. Cardiovasc. Surgery, Am. Heart Assn. S.W. Ohio (v.p. 1998—, pres. 2000, Kaplan award 1999, Award of Excellence 2003), Muller Surg. Soc. (pres. 1985-87), So. Thoracic Surgery Assn., Midwestern Vascular Surgery Soc., Cin. Surgery Soc. (pres. 1996), Greater Cin. Vascular Soc. (pres. 1997-98), Comml. Club, Alpha Omega Alpha, Sigma Chi (Significant Sig award 1993). Home: 312 E 2d St Covington KY 41011-1704 Office: Cardiovascular & Thoracic Surgeons 2123 Auburn Ave Cincinnati OH 45219-2906 Office Phone: 513-475-6302. E-mail: cbw@one.net.

WRIGHT, DANIEL A. lawyer; b. Washington, Sept. 30, 1946; s. William L. and Mary J. Wright; m. Deborah J. Wright, Sept. 5, 1981. BA, U. Calif., Davis, 1968; JD, Golden Gate U., 1978; Cert. in Pub. Adminstrn., U. Ala., 1969. Bar: Wash., U.S. Dist. Ct. (we. dist.) Wash. Claims officer Dept. Social and Health Svcs., Olympia, Wash., 1979—85; staff atty. Dept. of Licensing, Olympia, 1985—95; sole practitioner Tumwater, Wash., 1986—96; atty. William B. Pope & Assocs., Olympia, 1996—2001, McConnell, Meyer & Assocs., LLP, Olympia, 2001—. Adjudicator VA, San Francisco, 1979; law examiner Wash. State Bar Assn., Seattle, 1998. Asst. scoutmaster Boy Scouts Am., 1990—2001. Capt. U.S. Army, 1969-71, Vietnam. Regional Tng. Program in Pub. Adminstrn. fellow, 1968-69. Mem.: Wash. State Bar Assn. (fee dispute arbitration com. 1988—90, com. on professionalism 1998—2000, law office mgmt. assistance program com.), Clan Gregor (elections com., fundraising chmn. Pacific N.W. chpt. 1995—, fundraising chmn. 2000—). Avocations: woodworking, auto racing, astronomy, photography. Office: McConnell, Meyer & Assocs 207 West Main St Centralia WA 98531 E-mail: dwright@lewiscountylaw.com.

WRIGHT, DAVID ALLEN, mechanical engineer, councilman; b. Rochester, NY, June 7, 1946; s. David Kelly and Helen May Wright; m. Dorothy Ida DiLella, Sept. 3, 1966; children: David Allen II, Jennifer Teresa McCrone, Jeffrey Patrick. BSME, Rochester Inst. Tech., 1972. Supt. The Gleason Works, Rochester, NY, 1996—98, new product design engr., 1998—2001, chief engr., 2001—. Asst. scoutmaster Boy Scouts of Am., Geneva, NY, 1985—; town councilman Town of Victor, 2000—; chmn. Victor (NY) Hiking Trails, Inc., 1995—; v.p. Genesee River Trails Coalition, Mendon, NY, 2002—; bd. dirs. Boughton Pk., East Bloomfield, NY, 2000—, pres., 2003. Mem.: ASME, Gleason Elder Statesmen's Club (pres. 2000), Genesee Valley Hiking Club. Republican. Baptist. Achievements include patents for Spindle for Machine Tool; Method and Apparatus for Lapping Gears; Method of Determining Backlash; Mechanism for Loading and Unloading Workpices; design of New Bevel Gear Lapping Machine. Avocations: hiking, camping, golf, bicycling, sports.

WRIGHT, DAVID ANDREW, music educator; b. Star Lake, NY, Mar. 18, 1969; s. Michael E and Linda S Wright; m. Jenee Patricia Martinez, May 13, 1995. MusB, SUNY Fredonia, 1989—92; MusM, U. of So. Miss., 1993—97. Asst. prof. of music W.Va. Wesleyan Coll., Buckhannon, W.Va., 2000—. Musician traverser saxophone quartet. Office: West Virginia Wesleyan College 59 College Avenue Buckhannon WV 26201 Personal E-mail: wright@wvwc.edu.

WRIGHT, DAVID BURTON, retired newspaper publishing company executive; b. Fowler, Ind., Aug. 29, 1933; s. Claude Matthew and Rose Ellen (Lavelle) Wright; m. Geraldine F. Gray, May 9, 1964; children: David Andrew, Anne Kathleen. AB, Wabash Coll., 1955. CPA Ind. Audit staff George S. Olive Co. C.P.A.s, Indpls., 1958-63, mgmt. cons., 1963-65; controller Herff Jones Co., 1965-69, corp. controller, asst. sec., 1970-71; asst. bus. mgr. Indpls. Newspapers Inc., 1971-77; asst. sec., treas. Central Newspapers Inc., 1975-79, Muncie Newspapers Inc., 1975-93, Indpls. Newspapers Inc., 1975-93, bus. mgr., 1977-93; sec., treas. Central Newspapers Inc., 1979-89; v.p. Indpls. Newspapers Inc., 1982-93. Mem. St. Francis Hosp. Adv. Bd., Indpls., 1983—99. Sec. St. Francis Hosp. adv. Bd., Indpls., 1986—87, v.p., 1987—91, pres., 1991—93. Served U.S. Army, 1956—58. Mem.: Ind. Assn. CPAs, Knights Columbus, Indpls. Econ. Club. Roman Cath. Home: 6713 Forrest Commons Blvd Indianapolis IN 46227-2396

WRIGHT, DAVID L. food and beverage company executive; b. Wenatchee, Wash., Mar. 12, 1949; s. Franklin Sven and Mary Elizabeth (Collins) W.; m. Karen Sue Rice, Mar. 28, 1981; children: Kara, Erin, Jonathan, Anna Catherine. BA, U. Calif., Davis, 1971. Chief of rsch. dept. of benefit payments State of Calif., Sacramento, 1972-75; profl. staff mem. com. on agr. U.S. Ho. Reps., Washington, 1975-77; adminstrv. asst. Rep. William C. Wampler, Washington, 1977-81; spl. asst. for legis. affairs to Pres. The White House, Washington, 1981-84; dir. govt. affairs Pepsico Inc., Purchase, N.Y., 1984-87; v.p. worldwide govt. affairs Pepsico, Inc., Purchase, NY, 1987—. Mem. exec. com. U.S. Coun. for Internat. Bus., 1997—; bd. dirs. U.S. C. of C. Capt. USAR, 1971-79. Mem Capitol Hill Club. Republican. Office: Pepsico Inc 700 Anderson Hill Rd Purchase NY 10577-1444

WRIGHT, DAVID LAWRENCE, realtor, real estate broker; b. Ft. Belvoir, Va., July 7, 1951; s. John Bacon Wright and Elizabeth Anderson Wright Baird; m. Laury Ann Bershad, June 2, 1990; m. Caroline Newcomb (div. 1989); children: Kevin, Katherine. BS, Denison U., 1973. Realtor Chris Coile Assocs., Annapolis, Md., 1976—80, Merrill Lynch Realty, 1980—89; broker, owner Manis & Wright Realty, 1989—94; assoc. broker O'Conor, Piper & Flynn Pardoe, 1994—2002, Coldwell Banker Residential Brokerage, 2002—. Bd. dir. Anne Arundel County Assn. Realtors. Pres. Annapolis Touchdown Club, 1996; trustee Severn Sch. Bd. Trustees, Severna Park, 1995—96. Mem.: Anne Arundel County Assn. Realtors, So. Lacrosse Ofcl. Assn., Annapolis Rotary Club (Crabfest chmn. 1996), The Annapolitan Club. Avocations: golf, lacrosse, boating. Office: Coldwell Banker Residential Brokerage 4 Church Cir Annapolis MD 21401

WRIGHT, DEBRA DENISE, education educator; BS in Mech. Engring., Mich. Tech. U., Houghton, Mich., 1993; MS in Biomedical Engring., PhD, Northwestern U., Evanston, IL, 1999. Rsch. asst. Northwestern U., Evanston, Ill., 1993—99; asst. prof. Mich. Tech. U., Houghton, Mich., 1999—. Recipient Acad. of Dental Materials Award, Acad. of Dental Materials, 1996, Disting. Undergraduate Award, Mich. Assn. of Governing Boards, 1993; Grad. Rsch. Fellowship, NSF, 1993-1997, Selected Professions Fellowship, AAUW, 1998. Mem.: Am. Soc. for Engring. Edn., Am. Assn. for U. Women, Assn. for Women in Sci., Soc. for Exptl. Mechanics, Soc. for Biomaterials (sec., orthopaedic biomaterials sig 2003—04). Office: Mich Tech 1400 Townsend Dr/309 M&M Bldg Houghton MI 49931 Business E-Mail: wright@mtu.edu.

WRIGHT, DEIL SPENCER, political science educator; b. Three Rivers, Mich., June 18, 1930; s. William Henry and Gertrude Louise (Buck) W.; m. Patricia Mae Jaffke, Aug. 22, 1953; children: David C., Mark W., Matthew D., Lois L. BA, U. Mich., 1952, M in Pub. Adminstrn., 1954, PhD, 1957. Asst. prof. polit. sci. Wayne State U., Detroit, 1956-59; from asst. to assoc. prof. U. Iowa, Iowa City, 1959-67; assoc. prof. U. Calif., Berkeley, 1965-66; prof. U. N.C., Chapel Hill, 1967-83, alumni disting. prof., 1983—; Carl Hatch vis. prof. U. N.Mex., Albuquerque, 1987. Lectr. USIA, Washington, various dates; cons. Office Mgmt. and Budget, Washington, 1979-80. Author: Understanding Intergovernmental Relations, 3d edit., 1988; editor: Federalism and Intergovernmental Relations, 1984, Globalization and Decentralization, 1996; contbr. over 100 articles to various polit. sci. and pub. adminstrn. jours. Mem. dir's. adv. com. NIH, Bethesda, Md., 1970-74, N.C. Coun. on State Goals and Policies, Raleigh, 1973-77, N.C. State Internship Coun., Raleigh, 1985-93. Internat. Inst. Mgmt. research fellow, Berlin, 1977. Fellow Nat. Acad. Pub. Adminstrn.; mem. AAAS, Am. Polit. Sci. Assn., Am. Soc. Pub. Adminstrn. (Waldo Lifetime Career Achievement award), Midwest Polit. Sci. Assn., Policy Studies Orgn., So. Polit. Sci. Assn. (pres. 1981-82). Lodges: Rotary (bd. dirs. Chapel Hill club 1981, 84, 90, v.p. 2000-01, pres. 2001-02). Republican. Methodist. Home: 204 Velma Rd Chapel Hill NC 27514-7641 Office: U North Carolina Dept Polit Sci CB 3265 Chapel Hill NC 27599-3265

WRIGHT, DELL, residential care and treatment facility executive; b. Greenville, S.C., Aug. 29, 1944; s. Thomas C. and Marie (Tate) W.; m. Ines R. Teran, Oct 22, 1977; children: Anthony, Andre, Fionna, Al-Jonn. Diploma in computer tech., Control Data Inst., 1969. Electronic tester RCA, Marlboro, Mass., 1970-71; customer svc. rep. Honeywell Info. Systems, Inc., Waltham, Mass., 1971-75; computer technician Bendix Field Engring., Columbia, Md., 1975-78; sr. field engr. Ford Aerospace and Comm. Corp., Palo Alto, Calif., 1978-79; systems integration engr. Kentron Internat./NASA/JPL, Pasadena, Calif., 1979-83; sr. fabrication technician Rockwell Internat., Anaheim, Calif., 1983-84; computer engr. Al-Johi Internat., Dhahran, Saudi Arabia, 1984-85; sr. test engr. Gen. Dynamics, San Diego, 1985-88; owner Wrights Food Vending Svc., 1988—90; pres., founder Residential Care and Treatment Facility for Youth, 1991—. Author: Inspirational, 1995; inventor mechanical multiple picture frame. Vice chair, utilities commr. City of Colton, Calif., 1996—. With U.S. Army, 1962-65. Democrat. Avocations: rv camping, fishing.

WRIGHT, DIXIE LEE, special needs persons consultant; b. Winslow, Ind. d. Edward Franklin and Ann Berenece Corne; m. Lendon L. Wright; children: Kevin, LeeAnn, Michael. BS in Edn., Ind. U.; postgrad., U. No. Colo., 1980. Self employed workshop developer for schs. and agys.; career coord. postsecondary sch.; ind. contractor Colo. State Rehab. and other govtl. and ind. agys. working with spl. needs persons. Cons., job assessor for special need persons, Colo.; presenter in field. Author: Know How is the Key, 1997, Job Survival: How to Adjust and Keep Your Job, 2000, Stuff You Need to Know to Teach Job Retention, 2000, Job Smarts, 2004. Bd. dirs. Littleton C. of C. Mem.: AARP (state coord. works program), Bus. Profl. Women (adv. bd., pres.). Avocations: art, drawing, public speaking.

WRIGHT, DONALD FRANKLIN, retired newspaper executive; b. St. Paul, July 10, 1934; s. Floyd Franklin and Helen Marie (Hansen) Wright; m. Sharon Kathleen Fisher, Dec. 30, 1960; children: John, Dana, Kara, Patrick. BME, U. Minn., 1957, MBA, 1958. With Mpls. Star & Tribune Co., 1958—77, rsch. planning dir., then ops. dir., 1971—75, exec. editor, 1975—77; exec. v.p., gen. mgr. Newsday, Inc., L.I., 1977—78, pres., COO, 1978—81, L.A. Times, 1981—87, pres., CEO; sr. v.p. Times Mirror Co., L.A., 1988—98, exec. v.p., 1998—99; ret., 1999. Former vice chmn. bd. trustees Claremont Grad. Sch. and Univ. Ctr.; chmn. L.A. Area coun. Boy Scouts Am., 1988, pres. western region, 1998—2000, mem. nat. exec. bd., 1998—2003; dir. emeritus Assocs. Calif. Inst. Tech.; past chmn. bd. dirs. U. Minn. Found.; trustee Mus. N.Mex. Found.; bd. dirs. United Way Long Island, 2000—03. Mem.: Newspapers Pubs. Assn., Am. Newspaper Pubs. Assn. (past chmn. telecom. com. and prodn. mgmt. com.), U. Minn. Alumni Assn., Mpls. Club. Presbyterian.

WRIGHT, DONALD GENE, accountant; b. Grand Junction, Tenn., June 7, 1950; s. Ernest Young and Frances Irene (Reeder) W.; children: Richard Benjamin, Jacqueline; m. Helen "Vicki" Elizabeth Holt Wright, Oct. 1, 1988; step children: Veronica Reynolds Garcia, Mindy Reynolds Barrett. A Engring. (equivalent), U. Tenn., Martin, 1970; BBA in Acctg., Lambeth U., 1995. Cost acctg. clk. Harman Automotive, Inc., Bolivar, Tenn., 1975-79, sr. acct., 1979-85, budget & spl. projects mgr., 1985-92, acctg., estimating mgr., 1992-95; contr. Hutchinson Sealing Sys., Inc., Wytheville, Va., 1995-2000, Hutchinson Rubber Mixing Tech. Ctr., Wytheville, Va., 1995-99, Dura Automotive Sys., Pikeville, Tenn., 2000—. Bd. dirs. West Tenn. Chpt. NAA, Jackson, Tenn., 1987-95. Editor: VP Communications Monthly Newsletter, 1991, Director of Newsletter Monthly Newsletter, 1989. Mem. Nat. Assn. Accts. (pres. West Tenn. chpt.), Gideon's Internat. Methodist. Avocations: martial arts, home improvement, travel. Office: Dura Automotive Sys Inc 132 Ferro Rd Pikeville TN 37367 also: Rubbu Mixing Tech Ctr 455 Industry Rd Wytheville VA 24382-3491 Address: 524 E Main St Union City TN 38261-3409

WRIGHT, DOUGLAS, playwright; b. Dallas, 1962; BA, Yale U., 1985; MFA, Tisch Sch. Arts, NYU, 1987. Author: (plays) The Stonewater Rapture, 1987, Buzzsaw Berkeley, 1989, Watbanaland, 1994, Quills, 1995 (OBIE award for Playwriting, 1996), I Am My Own Wife, 2003 (Pulitzer prize for Drama, 2004, Tony award best play, 2004, Drama Desk award best play, 2004), Interrogating the Nude; author, dir.: Unwrap Your Candy, 2001 (Paul Selvin award, Writers Guild Am., 2001); author: (screenplays) Quills, 2000 (Golden Satellite for Best Motion Picture Screenplay, 2000, Phoenix Film Critics Soc. award for Best Screenplay, 2000). Office: Lyceum Theatre 149 W 45th St New York NY 10036*

WRIGHT, DOUGLAS TYNDALL, business executive, university executive emeritus; b. Toronto, Ont., Can., Oct. 4, 1927; s. George C. and Etta (Tyndall) W. BASc. with honors in Civil Engring, U. Toronto, 1949; MS in Structural Engring, U. Ill., 1952; PhD in Engring, U. Cambridge, 1954; D.Eng. (hon.), Carleton U., 1967; LLD (hon.), Brock U., 1967, Concordia U., 1982; DSc (hon.), Meml. U. Nfld., 1969; DHL (hon.), Northeastern U., 1985, U. Waterloo, 1995; DUniv (hon.), Strathclyde U., Glasgow, 1989; D de L'Université, Compiegne U., France, 1991; D Univ. (hon.), Université de Sherbrooke, 1992; DSc, McMaster U., 1993, Queen's U., 1993; LLD (hon.), U. Waterloo, 1995. Lectr. dept. civil engring. Queen's U., 1954-55, asst. prof., 1955-58, assoc. prof., 1958; prof. civil engring. U. Waterloo, 1958-67, chmn. dept. civil engring., 1958-63, dean engring., 1959-66; chmn. Ont. Com. on Univ. Affairs Govt. of Ont., 1967-72, Ont. Commn. Post-Secondary Edn., Toronto, 1969-72, dep. provincial sec. for social devel., 1972-79; dep. minister culture and recreation, 1979-80; pres. U. Waterloo, Ont., 1981-93, prof. engring., 1981—, pres. emeritus, 1995—. Vis. prof. U. Autónoma Mex., 1964, 66, U. Sherbrooke, 1966—67; cons. engr. Netherlands and Mexican Pavillions Expo, 1967, Olympic Sports Palace, Mexico City, 1968, Ont. Place Dome and Forum, 1971; tech. advisor Toronto Skydome, 1984—92; bd. dirs. Com Dev Ltd., Geometrica Inc., RIM Ltd., Glenmount Corp., Perimeter Inst. for Theoretical Physics, RDM Corp., TST, Inc.; mem. Premier's Coun. on Sci. and Tech., Ont., 1985—91; Can. rep. Coun. Internat. Inst. Applied Sys. Analysis, Laxenburg, Austria, 1986—97; prime min.'s personal rep. to Coun. Misn. of Edn., 1990—91. Contbr. articles to profl. jours. Bd. dirs. African Students Found., Toronto, 1961-66, Ont. Curriculum Inst., 1964-67, Ont. R&D Challenge Fund, 1998—, N.B. Innovatio Found.; bd. govs. Stratford Shakespearian Festival, 1984-86, mem. senate, 1987. Decorated Officer Order of Can., chevalier Ordre National du Mérite (France); recipient Gold medal Ont. Profl. Engrs., 1990, Gold Medal award Can. Coun. Profl. Engrs., 1992, Sir John Kennedy Medal award Engring. Inst. Can., 1995, Can. Entrepreneur of Yr. award, 1997; Athlone fellow, 1952-54. Fellow ASCE, Can. Acad. Engring., Engring. Inst. Can. (del. Engrs. Coun. Profl. Devel., N.Y.C. 1961-70); mem. Assn. Profl. Engrs. Province Ont., Internat. Assn. Bridge and Structural Engring., Internat. Assn. Shell Structures, Royal Can. Yacht Club, Univ. Club (Toronto). Office: U Waterloo Waterloo ON Canada N2L 3G1 E-mail: dtwright@uwaterloo.ca.

WRIGHT, DOUGLASS BROWNELL, retired judge, lawyer; b. Hartford, Conn., May 30, 1912; s. Arthur Brownell and Sylvia (Stephens) W.; m. Jane Hamersley, Sept. 24, 1938 (dec. Feb. 1997); children: Jane C., Douglass B., Hamersley S., Elizabeth B., Arthur W.; m. Ann Hallowell Ferguson, Nov., 1999. AB, Yale U., 1933; LL.B., Hartford Coll. Law, 1937. Bar: Conn. 1937. Legal dept. Aetna Life Ins. Co., 1937-39; partner Davis, Lee, Howard & Wright, Hartford, 1939—; lectr. law U. Conn., 1946—; asst. state's atty. State of Conn., 1952-59; judge Conn. Circuit Court, 1959-65, Conn. Superior Ct., 1965—98; ret., 1998. Leader orch. Judge Wright and the Four Wrongs Author: Connecticut Law of Torts, 1956, Connecticut Legal Forms, 5 vols., 1958, Connecticut Jury Instructions, 3 vols., 1960, 76. Sec., dir. Captioned Films for the Deaf, Inc.; bd. dirs., pres. Am. Sch. for Deaf, 1942—; trustee Hartt Mus. Found., 1949—, Good Will Boys Club Hartford, 1950—; regent U. Hartford; bd. dirs. Vis. Nurse Assn., Newington Home for Crippled Children, Hartford Times Farm, Loomis Sch.; incorporator Conn. Inst. for Blind. Served as lt. USNR, 1942-45. Mem. Phi Beta Kappa, Psi Upsilon. Clubs: University (Hartford), Hartford Golf (Hartford), Hartford Tennis (Hartford), 20th Century (Hartford); Coral Beach and Tennis (Bermuda); Hillsboro (Pompano Beach, Fla.). Congregationalist. Home: 20 Loeffler Rd Apt T519 Bloomfield CT 06002-2273 Office: 95 Washington St Hartford CT 06106-4431

WRIGHT, ELEASE, insurance company executive; B.S. in education, Univ. of Conn. Sr. v.p. human resources Aetna Inc., Hartford, Conn., 1999—. Mem.: advisory bd., Cornell Univ. Center for Advanced Human Resource Studies, bd. of advisors, Univ. Conn. School of Bus., Exec. Leadership Council. Office: 151 Farmington Ave Hartford CT 06156-0001

WRIGHT, ELIZABETH REBECCA, humanities educator; b. Urbana, Ill., Dec. 5, 1963; d. Richard Newport and Teresa Rios Wright. BA, U. Ill., 1985; MA, Northwestern U., 1992; PhD, Johns Hopkins U., 1998. Asst. v.p. Harris Bank, Chgo., 1985—92; asst. prof. U. Ga., Athens, Ga., 1998—. Author: Pilgrimage to Patronage: Lope de Vegn and the Court of Philip III, 2001. Grantee, Fulbright Assn., 1995—96; Audrey Lumsden-Kovnel grant, Newberry Libr., 2001, Andrew W. Mellon grant, John Carter Brown Libr., 2002, grantee, Am. Philos. Soc., 2003, Nat. Endowment Humanities, 2003, grant, Nat. Endowment for Humanities, 2004—. Mem.: Renaissance Soc. Am., Soc. Renaissance and Baroque Hispanic Poetry (sec. 2002—, treas. 2002—).

WRIGHT, ERNEST MARSHALL, physiologist, consultant; b. Belfast, Ireland, June 8, 1940; came to U.S., 1965; BSc, U. London, 1961, DSc, 1978; PhD, U. Sheffield, Eng., 1964. Research fellow Harvard U., Boston, 1965-66; from asst. prof. to full prof. physiology UCLA Med. Sch., 1967—, chmn. dept. physiology, 1987—. Cons. NIH, Bethesda, Md., 1982—, Senator Jacob K. Javits neurosci. investigator, 1985. Office: UCLA Sch Med Dept Physiology 10833 Le Conte Ave Los Angeles CA 90095-3075

WRIGHT, ETHEL, secondary school educator; b. Apr. 5, 1947; m. James A. Wright, Sept. 26, 1969; children: Cassandra, Hannibal, Omari. BS in English, Alcorn State U., Lorman, Miss., 1970; MS in Edn., Butler U., Indpls., 1975. Tchr. Simmons H.S., Arcola, Miss., 1970-71; tchr. English Indpls. Pub. Schs., 1971—. Mem. textbook adoption com. Indpls. Pub. Schs., 1979, liaison for Tchrs. Ctr., mem. film preview com. Clk., Dem. Com., Indpls. Recipient ABCD award Indpls. Pub. Schs., 1985, 92; Gregg and Reed scholar Indpls. Pub. Schs. Mem. NEA, Indpls. Edn. Assn. Avocations: reading, gardening, sewing, growing houseplants, travel.

WRIGHT, EVELYN LOUISE, artist; b. Odessa, Mo., Aug. 2, 1913; d. Elmer Clarence and Anna Bell (Ford) Adams; m. Douglas P. Wright, July 19, 1934 (dec. Dec. 27, 1986); children: Annetta Louise, Judith Elaine, Duane Douglas. Student, Stockton Coll., Calif., 1958—60, U. of Pacific, Stockton, 1960—61, Merced Coll., Calif., 1962—64, Columbia Coll., 1962—64. Graphic artist, Independence, Mo., 1928—34; asst. mgr., bookkeeper Wrights, Stockton, 1945—86; owner, instr. Evelyn's Art Classes and Workshops, Stockton, 1980—; instr. Stockton Sch. Sys., 1945—, Ripona Sch., Calif., 1992—94. Recipient Best of Show award, Richard Yip Art Co., 1980, award, Sonora Nat. Festival, 1982, 1984, Lodi Grape Festival, 1986. Avocation: travel. Home and Studio: 508 W Morada Ln Stockton CA 95210

WRIGHT, FAITH-DORIAN, artist; b. Bklyn., Feb. 9, 1934; d. Abraham and Molly (Janoff) J.; children: Jordan Merritt, Igrid-beth. BS, NYU, 1955, MA, 1958; postgrad., Pratt and Parsons Sch. of Design. Works exhibited in Kathryn Markel Gallery, N.Y.C., 1981, 92, Cumberland Gallery, Nashville, 1981, 92, Barbara Gillman Gallery, Miami, 1982, Hand and Hand Gallery, 1985, 86, Suzanne Gross, Phila., 1986, 87, Gallery Four, Alexandria, Va., 1986, 87, 88, Henri Gallery, Washington, 1986, 87, 88, 89. 90. 91. 92. 93. 94, Benton Gallery, Southampton, 1986, 87, 88, 89, 91, 92, 93, King Stephen Mus., Hungary, 1987, Nat. Gallery Women in the Arts, 1987, 88, 90, 91, 92, Ruth Volid Gallery, Chgo., 1990, James Gallery, Pitts., 1990, Aart Vark Gallery, Phila., 1990, Merrill Chase Gallery, Chgo., 1990, 91, 92, Guild Hall Mus., East Hampton, N.Y., 1991, Joy Berman Gallery, Phila., 1992, Ctr. for Book Arts, N.Y.C., 1992, Barnard-Biederman Fine Arts, N.Y.C., 1994, Arlene Bujese Gallery, East Hampton, 1994, 95, 96, Stoney Brook U., 1994, Harper Collins Exhbn. Space, 1995, Ctr. for Book Arts, 1996, arlene bujese, 1997, Galerie Cargo, Paris, 1997, N.Y. State Mus., Albany, 1997, U. Mont., Missoula, 2002, Nat. Mus. Women in Arts, Washington, 2002, Arlene Bupene, East Hampton, N.Y., 1997-03, Seton Hall U., NJ, 2003, Arlene Bujese Gallery, East Hampton, N.Y. 2003—, Gayle Wilson Gallery, Southampton, N.Y., 2003—; permanent collections Nat. Postal Art Mus., Ottawa, Can., Nat. Inst. Design, Ahmedabad, India, Fine Arts Acad., New Delhi, India, Mus. Modern Art, N.Y.C., Nat. Mus. Women in the Arts, Washington, D.C., Israel Mus., Jerusalem, Brenau Coll., Grainsville, Ga. Blue Cross, Blue Shield, Phila., Mc Donald's, Oakbrook, Ill., The Hyatt Collection, Chgo., Guild Hall Mus., Saul, Ewing, Reineck & Saul, Phila., Shevick, Ravich, Koster, Tobin, Clark, N.J., Sidley & Austin, L.A., Catalano & Sparber, N.Y., Islip (N.Y.) Mus. of Art, NY Pet Rescue Orgn., Larchmont, Islip (NY) Mus.; contbr. critical essays to various periodicals. Mem. Women in Arts, Women's Caucus for Arts, Artists Equity, Visitation Bd. of Met. Mus.-Rockefeller Connection. Address: 300 E 74th St New York NY 10021-3712

WRIGHT, FELIX E. manufacturing executive; b. 1935; married Student, East Tex. State U., 1958. With Leggett & Platt, Inc., Carthage, Mo., 1959—, sr. v.p. from 1976, chief operating officer, exec. v.p., 1979, pres., COO, 1985-2000, pres., CEO, 2000—. Office: Leggett & Platt Inc 1 Leggett Rd Carthage MO 64836-9649

WRIGHT, FRANK, artist, educator; b. Washington, Oct. 10, 1932; s. John Franklin and Margaret (Young) W.; m. Mary Eleanor Dow, May 31, 1957; 1 child, Suzanne Elizabeth. BA, Am. U., 1954; MA in Art History, U. Ill., 1960. Instr. Am. U., Washington, 1958-59; Paul J. Sachs fellow Nat. Gallery of Art, Washington, 1959-60, Harvard U., Cambridge, Mass., 1960-61; printmaking fellow Atelier 17, Paris, 1961—64; instr. Corcoran Sch. Art, Washington, 1966-70; asst. prof. to prof. fine arts George Wash. U., Washington, 1970—. NASA guest artist Columbia Space Launch STS-5, 1982. Exhibited in shows at Corcoran Gallery of Art, Washington, 1981, Kennedy Galleries, N.Y, 1981, Johnson Space Ctr., Houston, 1983, Allentown (Pa.) Art Mus., 1983, Md. Hall, Annapolis, 1998, Strathmore Hall, Bethesda, Md., 1998. Mem. Hist. Soc. D.C. Fellow Leopold Schepp Found., 1956, Print Coun. Am., 1959. Mem. Nat. Soc. Arts and Letters (advisor 1992—), Cosmos Club (art com. 1993), Omicron Delta Kappa (Beta Cir.). Avocations: collecting Washingtoniana material, lecturer on Washington, D.C. Home: 3520 Bradley Ln Chevy Chase MD 20815-3260 Office Phone: 202-822-4989. E-mail: fwright@gwu.edu.

WRIGHT, FRANK GARDNER, retired newspaper editor; b. Moline, Ill., Mar. 21, 1931; s. Paul E. and Goldie (Hicks) W.; m. Barbara Lee Griffiths, Mar. 28, 1953; children: Stephen, Jeffrey, Natalie, Gregory, Sarah. BA, Augustana Coll., Rock Island, Ill., 1953; postgrad., U. Minn., 1953-54. Suburban reporter Mpls. Star, 1954-55; with Mpls. Tribune, 1955-82, N.D. corr., 1955-56, Mpls. City Hall reporter, 1956-58, asst. city editor, 1958-63, Minn. polit. reporter, 1963-68, Washington corr., 1968-72, Washington bur. chief, 1972-77, mng. editor, 1977-82; mng. editor/news Mpls. Star and Tribune, 1982-84, assoc. editor, 1984-98; ret., 1998. Juror for Pulitzer Awards, 1983-84 Chmn. Golden Valley Human Rights Commn., 1965-67; mem. exec. com. Nobel Peace Prize Forum, 2000-04; mem. faculty Augsburg Coll., 3d Age, U. St. Thomas, Ctr. for Sr. Citizens Edn., 2000-04; bd. dirs. Luth. Social Svcs., Washington. Recipient several Page 1 awards Twin Cities Newspaper Guild, 1950's, 60's, Worth Bingham prize Worth Bingham Meml. Fund, 1971; runnerup Raymond Clapper award for Washington correspondence, 1971; Outstanding Achievement award Augustana Alumni Assn., 1977; citation for excellence in internat. reporting Overseas Press Club, 1985; Minn. SPJ/SDX 1st Place Page One award for in-depth reporting, 1988, MWAP award Human Interest Reporting, 1995. Mem. Am. Newspaper Guild (chmn. Mpls. unit 1961-67, editorial v.p. Twin Cities 1963-67), Minn. AP Editors Assn. (pres. 1981), Phi Beta Kappa Home: 4912 Aldrich Ave S Minneapolis MN 55419-2353 E-mail: fgwright@aol.com.

WRIGHT, FRANZ PAUL, poet, writer, translator; b. Vienna, 1953; s. James Wright and Liberty Kardulis. Grad., Oberlin College, 1977; studied postgrad., U. Va. Translator, author of introduction Rainer Maria Rilke, The Unknown Rilke, 1990; translator modern and contemporary French and German poets; author: (poems) Tapping the White Cane of Solitude, 1976, The Earth Without You, 1980, Eight Poems, 1981, The One Whose Eyes Open When You Close Your Eyes, 1982, No Siege Is Absolute, 1983, Going North in Winter, 1986, Entry in an Unknown Hand, 1989, Midnight Postscript, 1990, And Still the Hand Will Sleep in Its Glass Ship, 1990, Rorschach Test, 1995, The Night World and the Word Night, 1993, Knell, 1998, ILL LIT: Selected and New Poems, 1998, The Beforelife, 2001, Walking to Martha's Vineyard, 2003 (Pulitzer Prize for poetry, 2004); represented in anthologies; contbr. articles to profl. publs. Recipient Witter Bynner prize for Poetry, 1995, PEN/Voelcker award, 1996, Pulitzer prize in Poetry, 2004; NEA fellow, 1985, 92, Guggenheim fellow, 1989, Whiting fellow, 1991. Office Phone: 781-788-0540. E-mail: franzwright@earthlink.net.

WRIGHT, FREDERICK LEWIS, II, lawyer; b. Roanoke, Va., Sept. 17, 1951; s. Frederick Lewis and Dorothy Marie (Trent) W.; m. Margaret Suzanne Rey, Oct. 16, 1982; children: Lauren Elizabeth, Emily Trent. BA, Ga. State U., 1978; JD, U. Ga., 1981. Bar: Ga. 1982, U.S. Dist. Ct. (no. dist.) Ga. 1984, U.S. Ct. Appeals (11th, 8th and 4th cirs.) 1984, U.S. Supreme Ct. 1990. Law clk. to presiding justice U.S. Ct. Appeals, Atlanta, 1981-82; ptnr. Smith, Currie and Hancock, Atlanta, 1982-96, Vaughn, Wright and Stearns, Atlanta, 1997—. Articles editor Ga. Law Rev., 1980—81. Mem.: ABA (forum com. constrn. industry), Ga. Def. Lawyers Assn. (chmn. constrn. law com.), Fed. Bar Assn., Def. Rsch. Inst., Order of Coif. Methodist. Office: One Paces West Ste 1740 2727 Paces Ferry Rd Atlanta GA 30339 Office Phone: 770-805-9889. Business E-Mail: fwright@vws-attys.com.

WRIGHT, GLADYS STONE, music educator, composer, writer; b. Wasco, Oreg., Mar. 8, 1925; d. Murvel Stuart and Daisy Violet (Warren) Stone; m. Alfred George Wright, June 28, 1953. BS, U. Oreg., 1948, MS, 1953. Dir. bands Elmira (Oreg.) U-4 H.S., 1948-53, Otterbein (Ind.) H.S., 1954-61, Klondike H.S., West Lafayette, Ind., 1962-70, Harrison H.S., West Lafayette, 1970-84. Organizer, condr. Musical Friendship Tours, Ctrl. Am., 1967-79; v.p., condr. U.S. Collegiate Wind Band, 1975—; bd. dirs. John Philip Sousa Found., 1984—; chmn. Sudler Cup, 1986—, Sudler Flag, 1982; pres. Internat. Music Tours, 1984—, Key to the City, Taxco, Mex., 1975. Editor: Woman Conductor, 1986—; composer: marches Big Bowl and Trumpets and Tabards, 1987; contbg. editor: Informusica (Spain). Recipient Medal of the order John Philip Sousa Found., 1988, Star of Order, 1991, Internat. Contbrn. to Music award Phi Beta Mu, 2000; 1st woman guest condr. U.S. Navy Band, Washington, 1961, Goldman Band, NYC, 1958, Kneller Hall Band, London, 1975, Tri-State Music Festival Massed Orch., Band, Choir, 1985; elected to Women Bd. Dirs. Hall of Fame of Disting. Women Condrs., 1994; inductee Hall of Fame Disting. Condrs., Nat. Band Assn., 1999; named Ind.'s Sagamore of the Wabash, 2004. Mem. Am. Bandmasters Assn. (bd. dirs. 1993, 1st woman mem.), Women Band Dirs. Nat. Assn. (founding pres. 1967, sec. 1985, recipient Silver Baton 1974, Golden Rose 1990, Hall of Fame 1995), Am. Sch. Band Dirs. Assn., Nat. Band Assn. (Citation excellence 1970), Tippecoanoe Arts Fedn. (bd. dirs. 1986-90), Tippecanoe Fife and Drum Corps. (bd. dirs. 1984), DAR, Col. Dames-Pre Quitanen Chpt., New Eng. Women, Tau Beta Sigma (Outstanding Svc. to Music award 1970), Phi Beta Mu (1st hon. woman mem. 1972), N.Am. Wildlife Park (Battleground, Ind., bd dirs. 1985, 1990—). Avocations: historic preservation, environmental activities.

WRIGHT, GORDON BROOKS, musician, conductor, educator; b. Bklyn., Dec. 31, 1934; s. Harry Wesley and Helen Philomena (Brooks) W.; m. Inga-Lisa Myrin Wright, June 13, 1958 (div. 1979); children: Karin-Ellen Sturla, Charles-Eric, Daniel Brooks. MusB, Coll. Wooster, 1957; MA, U. Wis., 1961; postgrad., Salzburg Mozarteum, 1972, Loma Linda U., 1979; studied with, René Leibowitz, Carl Melles, Wilfred Pelletier, Herbert Blomstedt, Hans Swarowsky. Founder, music dir. Wis. Chamber Orch., 1960-69; music dir. Fairbanks (Alaska) Symphony Orch., 1969-89; prof. music Univ. Alaska, Fairbanks, 1969-89, prof. emeritus, 1989—; founder, music dir. Arctic Chamber Orch., Fairbanks, 1970-89; exec. dir. The Reznicek Soc., Indian, Alaska, 1982—. Prin. guest condr. Fla. Keys Chambor Orch., 2003—. Guest condr. Philharmonia Hungarica, Philomusica London, Norwegian Radio Orch., Orch. St. Luke's, Anchorage Symphony Orch., Musashino Orch., Tokyo, Tohoku Orch., Sendai, Japan; prin. guest condr. Fla. Keys Chamber Orch., 2003—; composer: Suite of Netherlands Dances, 1965, Six Alaskan Tone Poems, 1974, Symphony in Ursa Major, 1979 (Legis. award 1979), 1984 Overture, Scott Joplin Suite, 1987, Toccata Festiva, 1992, Meditation for Orchestra, 2000; columnist Alaska Advocate. Founder, bd. dirs. No. Alaska Environ. Ctr., Fairbanks, 1971-78. Served as pvt. AUS, 1957-59. Mem.: Am. Fedn. Musicians, Arturo Toscanini Soc., Condr.'s Guild, Am. Symphony Orch. League, Royal Musical Assn., Am. Musicol. Soc., Ctr. for Alaskan Coastal Studies (bd. dirs. 1982—), Alaska Conservation Soc. (editor Rev. 1971—78), Audubon Soc., Wilderness Soc., Friends of Earth-Alaska (bd. dirs. 1978—), Sierra Club (chmn. Fairbanks Group 1969—71). Avocations: hiking, kayaking, collecting books, photography. Home: HC 52 Box 8899 Indian AK 99540-9604 Office Phone: 907-653-1163. Personal E-mail: turnagain@earthlink.net.

WRIGHT, GWENDOLYN, art center director, writer, educator; b. Chgo., May 14, 1946; d. William Kemp and Mary Ruth (Brown) W.; m. Paul Rabinow, Nov. 18, 1980 (div. 1982); m. Thomas Bender, Jan. 14, 1984; children: David, Sophia. BA, NYU, 1969; MArch, U. Calif., Berkeley, 1974, PhD, 1980. Assoc. prof. Columbia U., N.Y.C., 1983-87, prof., 1988—; dir. Buell Ctr. for Study Am. Architecture, N.Y.C., 1988-92. Cons. Fulbright Scholars, Coun. Internat. Exch. Scholars, Washington, 1988-91, ArchNet, 1999--, Nat. Bldg. Mus., Washington, 2001--. Author: Building the Dream: A Social History of Housing in America, 1980, Moralism and the Model Home, 1981, The History of History in American Schools of Architecture, 1990, The Politics of Design in French Colonial Urbanism, 1991; writer N.Y. Times, 1999; presenter PBS TV series History Detectives, 2003—. Fellow Ford Found., 1979-80, Stanford Inst. for Humanities, 1982-83, Mich. Inst. for Humanities, 1991, Getty Ctr. for History of Art and the Humanities, 1992-93, Guggenheim Found., 2004—. Fellow Soc. Am. Historians, N.Y. Inst. for Humanities; mem. Soc. Archtl. Historians, Coll. Art Assn., Am. Hist. Assn., Orgn. Am. Historians. Democrat. Home: 54 Washington Mews New York NY 10003-6608 Office: Columbia U Avery Hall New York NY 10027 Office Phone: 212-854-1587.

WRIGHT, HARRISON MORRIS, historian, educator; b. Phila., Oct. 6, 1928; s. Sydney L. and Catharine W. (Morris) W.; m. Josephine Stearns Cole, July 20, 1957; children— Rebecca H., J. Rodman, Thomas F., Daniel H., James L. BA, Harvard, 1950, MA, 1953, PhD, 1957. Teaching fellow Harvard, 1955-57; mem. faculty Swarthmore Coll., 1957—, prof. history, 1968-87, Isaac H. Clothier prof. history and internat. relations, 1987-93, chmn. dept., 1968-79, provost, 1979-84, Clothier prof. and provost emeritus, 1993—, acting pres., 1982. Author: New Zealand, 1769-1840: Early Years of Western Contact, 1959, The Burden of the Present: Liberal-Radical Controversy over Southern African History, 1977; Editor: The New Imperialism— Analysis of Late Nineteenth-Century Expansion, 1961, 2d edit., 1976, Sir James Rose Innes: Selected Correspondence (1884-1902), 1972. Mem. Jamestown (R.I.) Harbor Commn., 2000—03. Fulbright scholar New Zealand, 1950-51; Ford Found. fgn. areas fellow Eng. and Ghana, 1961-62; grantee Am. Philos. Soc., S. Africa, 1966-67; grantee Old Dominion Fund, S. Africa, 1971 Mem.: Hist. Soc. Pa. (coun. 1984—91, coun. emeritus 1992—, v.p. 1986—88, chmn. 1989—91), African Studies Assn., Internat. Sailing Inst. (bd. dirs. 1998—), Humanities Forum R.I. (bd. dirs. 1995—2000), R.I. Hist. Soc. (bd. dirs. 1998—), Newport Hist. Soc. (bd. dirs. 1973—88), Phi Beta Kappa. Home: PO Box 209 Jamestown RI 02835-0209 Office Phone: 401-423-2978.

WRIGHT, HARRY HERCULES, psychiatrist; b. Charleston, S.C., Jan. 4, 1948; s. Harry Vernon and Agnes Lucile (Simmons) W. BS, U. S.C., 1970; MD, MBA, U. Pa., 1976. Resident in psychiatry Wm. S. Hall Psychiat. Inst., Columbia, S.C., 1977-79; adminstrv. fellow in psychiatry NIMH, Rockville, Md., 1979; fellow in child psychiatry William S. Hall Psychiat. Inst., 1979-81, teaching child psychiatrist, 1981—; instr. dept. neuropsychiatry and behavioral sci. U. S.C. Sch. Medicine, 1981-82, asst. prof., 1982-86, assoc. prof., 1986-90, prof., 1990—. Contbr. articles to profl. jours. Bd. dirs. Carolina Children's Home, 1992—, Zero to Three, 1997—; bd. trustees, First Steps to Sch. Readiness, 1999-2003; mem. landmarks commn. City of Columbia, 1986-98. Recipient Freed award, Hall Psychiat. Inst., 1978, Outstanding Svc. award, Sickle Cell Found., Clin. Sci. Rsch. award, 1998, America's Top Doctors award, 2001—04, Rsch. Advancement award, 2002; grantee Falk fellow, 1977—79, Laughlin fellow, 1979. Mem.: Am. Soc. Human Genetics, Soc. Study Psychiatry and Culture, Acad. Orgnl. and Occupl. Psychiatry, So. Med. Assn., Am. Soc. Adolescent Psychiatry, World Assn. Infant Mental Health, World Psychiat. Assn., Am. Acad. Child Psychiatry, AAAS, Autism Soc. Am., Riverbank Zool. Soc., Sigma Xi, Omicron Delta Kappa. Methodist. Home: PO Box 12474 Columbia SC 29211-2474 Office: 3555 Harden St Ext Ste 104 Columbia SC 29203-6894 Office Phone: 803-434-4250.

WRIGHT, HASTINGS KEMPER, surgeon, educator; b. Boston, Aug. 28, 1928; s. Donald M. and Lucia (Durand) W.; m. Nancy E. Howell, June 19, 1954; children: Mark, Kenneth, Barbara, Donald. AB, Harvard U., 1950, MD, 1954, MA, 1973. Diplomate: Am. Bd. Surgery. Intern Univ. Hosps. Cleve., 1954, resident, 1957-61; asst. prof. surgery Western Res. U., Cleve., 1961-66; assoc. prof. surgery Med. Sch. Yale U., New Haven, 1967-72, prof. Med. Sch., 1972-95; prof. surgery emeritus, 1995—; chief gen. surgery Yale-New Haven

Hosp., 1968-79, asst. chief surgery, 1979-95. Author: Complications of GI Surgery, 1972; asst. chief editor Archives of Surgery, Chgo., 1977-89. Capt. U.S. Army, 1955-57. Fellow ACS, Am. Surg. Assn.; mem. Soc. Univ. Surgeons (program dir. 1972), Am. Gastroent. Assn., Soc. Surgery Gastrointestinal Tract Clubs: Mory's Assoc. (New Haven); Yale (N.Y.C.). Republican. Episcopalian. Home: 35 Wood Rd Branford CT 06405-4935 Office: Yale U Med Sch Dept Surgery 333 Cedar St New Haven CT 06510-3289

WRIGHT, HELEN KENNEDY, retired professional association administrator, publisher, editor, librarian; b. Indpls., Sept. 23, 1927; d. William Henry and Ida Louise (Crosby) Kennedy; m. Samuel A. Wright, Sept. 5, 1970 (dec. 1998); 1 child, Carl F. Prince II (dec.). BA, Butler U., 1945, MS, 1950; MSLS, Columbia U., 1952. Reference libr. N.Y. Pub. Libr., N.Y.C., 1952-53, Bklyn. Pub. Libr., 1953-54; reference libr., cataloger U. Utah, 1954-57; libr. Chgo. Pub. Libr.; asst. dir. pub. svcs. ALA, Chgo., 1958-62, editor Reference Books Bull., 1962—85, asst. dir. for new product planning, pub. svcs., 1985-89, dir. office for libr. outreach svcs., 1987—88, mng. editor yearbook, 1988-89. Contbr. to Ency. of Careers, Ency. of Libr. and Info. Sci., New Book of Knowledge Ency., Bull. of Bibliography, New Golden Book Ency. Recipient Louis Shores/Oryx award, 1991. Mem. Phi Kappa Phi, Kappa Delta Pi, Sigma Gamma Rho. Roman Catholic. Home: 1138 W 111th St Chicago IL 60643-4508

WRIGHT, HELEN PATTON, professional society administrator; b. Washington, Jan. 15, 1919; d. Raymond Stanton and Virginia (Mitchell) Patton; m. James Skelly Wright, Feb. 1, 1945 (dec. 1988); 1 son, James Skelly; m. John H. Pickering, Feb. 3, 1990. Student, Sweet Briar Coll., 1936-38; grad., Washington Sch. Secretaries, 1939, Am. U., 1989. Tchr. Washington Sch. Secs., N.Y.C., 1939-40; sec. The White House, 1941-43, Am. Embassy, London, 1943-45; asst. to exec. dir. Senate Atomic Energy Com., 1946-47. Bd. dirs. Constitution Project, 2001—. Author: My Journey Recollections of the First Seventy Years, 1995. V.p., mem. budget and admissions com. United Fund New Orleans, 1960-62; chmn. met. divsn., campaign; v.p. Dept. Pub. Welfare, Orleans Parish and City New Orleans, 1960-62, Milne Asylum for Destitute Orphan Boys, New Orleans, 1958-62; mem. bd. New Orleans Social Welfare Planning Coun., 1954-62, New Orleans Cancer Soc., 1958-60; v.p. Juvenile Ct. Adv. Com. New Orleans, 1961; successively sec., v.p., pres. Parents' Assn. Metairie Park Country Day Sch., 1956-59; v.p. La. Assn. Mental Health, 1960-62; del. dir. to Nat. Assn. Mental Health, 1960-62; bd. mem. Washington Health and Welfare Coun., 1962-64, Hillcrest Children's Ctr., Washington, 1963-69, D.C. Mental Health Assn., 1962-72, 73-76; bd. dirs. Hospice Care of D.C., 1981-88, 90-96, pres., 1986-88; mem. adv. bd. civil commitment project Nat. Ctr. for State Cts., 1981; bd. dirs. Nat. Assn. Mental Health, 1960-66, 67-74, sec., 1968-70, pres.-elect, 1970-71, pres., 1972-73, cons. on assn. film, 1972; mem. commn. on mentally disabled ABA, 1973-80, commn. on legal problems of elderly, 1997; mem. adv. bd. Alzheimer's Assn. Greater Washington chpt., 1996, bd. dirs. Constn. Project; chmn. altar guild Christ Ch. Cathedral, New Orleans, 1960, Little Sanctuary of St. Albans Sch., Washington, 1965; pres. Altar Guild, St. Alban's Ch., 1976, 77; chmn. Washington com. Nat. Cathedral Assn., 1976-79, trustee, 1976-90, sec., 1977, v.p., 1980-83, trustee emeritae, 1997; bd. dirs. Nat. Ctr. Voluntary Action; mem. task panel Mental Health Problems, Scope and Boundaries, Pres.'s Commn. Mental Health, 1977; mem. tech. rev. com. Md. Psychiat. Rsch. Ctr., 1979-81. Mem. ABA (commn. on legal problems of the elderly 1997-99). Address: Apt 1007 8100 Connecticut Ave Chevy Chase MD 20815

WRIGHT, HERBERT E(DGAR), JR., geologist; b. Malden, Mass., Sept. 13, 1917; s. Herbert E. and Annie M. (Richardson) W.; m. Rhea Jane Hahn, June 21, 1943; children: Richard, Jonathan, Stephen, Andrew, Jeffrey. AB, Harvard U., 1939, MA, 1941, PhD, 1943; DSc (hon.), Trinity Coll., Dublin, Ireland, 1966, U. Minn., 1996; PhD (hon.), Lund U., Sweden, 1987. Instr. Brown U., 1946-47; asst. prof. geology U. Minn., Mpls., 1947-51, asso. prof., 1951-59, prof., 1959-74, Regents' prof. geology, ecology and botany, 1974-88, Regents' prof. geology, ecology & botany emeritus, 1988—; dir. Limnological Research Center, 1963-90. Served to maj. USAAF, 1942-45. Decorated D.F.C., Air medal with 6 oak leaf clusters; recipient Pomerance award Archeol. Inst. Am., 1985, Ann. award Sci. Mus. Minn., 1990; Guggenheim fellow, 1954-55, Wenner-Gren fellow, 1954-55. Fellow AAAS, Geol. Soc. Am. (Ann. award archeol. divsn. 1989, Disting. Career award geology and geomorphology divsn. 1992), Soc. Am. Archeology (Fryxell award 1993); mem. NAS, Ecol. Soc. Am., Internat. Quaternary Assn. (hon. pres. 16th Congress 2003), Am. Quaternary Assn. (Career award 1996). Achievements include research on Quaternary geology, paleoecology, paleolimnology and environ. archaeology in Minn., Wyo., Sweden, Yukon, Labrador, Peru, eastern Mediterranean. Home: 1426 Hythe St Saint Paul MN 55108-1423 Office: U of Minn 310 Pillsbury Dr SE Minneapolis MN 55455-0219 Business E-Mail: hew@umn.edu.

WRIGHT, I. MELISSA, secondary school educator; d. Orville E. and Edna L. Burton; children: Nyika M., Paul B. BS in Edn., MS in Edn., Ark. State U., Jonesboro, 1987. Diplomas, Am. Inst. Banking, 1977; lic. tchr. Ark. Dept. Edn., 1987. Tchr., libr. Parkin (Ark.) Sch. Dist., 1987—97; tchr. Green Forest (Ark.) Sch. Dist., 1997—2002; H.S. tchr. Rogers (Ark.) Sch. Dist., 2002—. Club sponsor Future Tchrs. Am., Parkin, 1990—97; presenter in field. Bd. mem., cons. Nat. Envirothon, 1990—94; vol., tutor Cross County Literacy Coun., Wynne, 1886—1994; dist. coord., county judge Cross County Spelling Bee, Parkin, 1990—97; mem. Green Forest Sch. Dist. Leadership Coun., 2000—02. Named Educator of the Yr., Ark. Assn. Conservation Dists., 1992, Secondary Tchr. of the Yr., 1993; grantee Books for Literacy, Rogers Earybirds Rotary Club, 2003. Mem.: Ark. Coun. on Econ. Edn. (assoc.; past dist. coord. 1999—2003), Internat. Reading Assn. (assoc.; past presenter), Phi Delta Kappa (assoc.; v.p. 1999—2001), Beta Sigma Phi (assoc.; pres., v.p., treas. 1976—79). Avocations: travel, reading. Office: Rogers High School 2300 Dixieland Rd Rogers AR 72756 E-mail: mwright@rhs.k12.ar.us.

WRIGHT, JACQUELYN DIANNE, special education educator, performing arts educator; b. St. Louis, Dec. 23, 1950; d. William Lambert and Barbara Mae Jones; m. Glenn Papa Wright, July 22, 1974. BA in Edn., Harris Teachers Coll., 1977; MA in Edn., Washington U., St. Louis, 1982. Cert. spl. edn. tchr. Mo., reading specialist Mo., elem. tchr. Mo. Spl. edn. tchr. St. Louis Pub. Schools, 1977—91, Spl. Sch. Dist. of St. Louis County, Mo., 1991—; profl. storyteller Wright Entertainment, University City, Mo., 1995—; distbr. Nat. Safety Associates, Memphis, 2000—. Workshop leader Mt. Vernon (Ill.) Teachers Conf., 1998—. Mem. St. Louis Storytelling Festival Planning Com., St. Louis, 2000—03; advisor Vocat. Indsl. Clubs Am., St. Louis, 1991—98; mem. Harambee Inst., St. Louis, 2003—03. Recipient Chancellors's award for Cmty. Svc., U. Mo., Louis, 2003. Mem.: Nat. Storytelling Network (assoc.), Puppeteers of Am. (assoc.), Puppet Guild of Greater St. Louis (assoc.; treas. and v.p. 1996—2003), St. Louis Gateway Storytellers (assoc.; treas.), Mo. Storytelling (assoc.), NEA (assoc.). Avocations: travel, shopping, reading, theater, puzzles. E-mail: jwright@ssd.k12.mo.us.

WRIGHT, JAMES DAVID, sociology educator, writer; b. Logansport, Ind., Nov. 6, 1947; s. James Farrell and Helen Loretta (Moon) W.; m. Christine Ellen Stewart, July 25, 1987; children: Matthew James, Derek William. BA, Purdue U., 1969; MS, U. Wis., 1970, PhD, 1973. Cert. specialist social policy and evaluation rsch. Asst. prof. sociology U. Mass., Amherst, 1973-76, assoc. prof., 1976-79, prof., 1979-88; Favrot prof. human rels. Tulane U., New Orleans, 1988-2001; prof. sociology U. Ctrl. Fla., Orlando, 2001—. Author/co-author: The Dissent of the Governed, 1976, Under the Gun, 1983, The State of the Masses, 1986, Homelessness and Health, 1987 (commendation Nat. Press Club 1988), Address Unknown: Homeless in America, 1989, The Greatest of Evils: Urban Poverty and the Urban Underclass, 1993, Beside the Golden Door, 1998, Fixin' to Git: One Fan's Love Affair with NASCAR, 2002, others; editor: (book series) Social Institutions and Social Change, 1984—, (jour.) Social Sci. Rsch. Jour., 1978—; contbr. numerous articles, essays, book chpts. to profl. publs. Mem. Am. Sociol. Assn. Democrat. Avocations: cooking, gardening, travel. Office Fax: 407-823-6738. E-mail: jwright@mail.ucf.edu.

WRIGHT, JAMES EDWARD, judge; b. Arlington, Tex., Jan. 15, 1921; s. James Robert and Clairette (Smith) W.; m. Eberta Adelaide Slataper, June 25, 1946; 1 child, Patricia Diane Wright Rogers. JD, U. Tex., 1949. Bar: Tex. 1949. Practice in Ft. Worth, 1949-69; city atty. Arlington, 1951-61; judge 141st Dist. Ct., Ft. Worth, 1970-88, sr. dist. judge, 1988—. Served with USAAF, World War II. Paul Harris fellow, 1981; named Disting. Alumnus U. Tex.-Arlington, 1982; named to Mil. Sci. Dept. Hall of Honor, U. Tex.-Arlington, 1985 Fellow Tex. Bar Found. (life); mem. ABA, Ft. Worth-Tarrant County Bar Assn. (pres. 1958-59), Tex. Bar Assn., Sons of the Rep. of Tex., Rotary (pres. Downtown Ft. Worth club 1966-67), Masons (32 degree), Shriners, Jesters (life), Phi Alpha Delta. Methodist. Home: 717 Briarwood Blvd Arlington TX 76013-1502 Personal E-mail: bewright@sbcglobal.net.

WRIGHT, JAMES EDWARD, academic administrator, historian, educator; b. Madison, Wis., Aug. 16, 1939; s. Donald J. and Myrtle (Hendricks) Wright; m. Joan Bussan, Sept. 3, 1962 (div.); children: James J., Ann Marie, Michael J.; m. Susan DeBevoise, Aug. 18, 1984. BS, Wis. State U., 1964; MS, U. Wis., 1966, PhD, 1969; MA (hon.), Dartmouth Coll., 1980. From asst. prof. to assoc. prof. history Dartmouth Coll., Hanover, NH, 1969—80, prof. history, 1980—, assoc. dean faculty, 1981—85, dean faculty, 1989—97, acting pres., 1995, provost, 1997—98, pres., 1998—. Sr. historian U. Mid Am., Lincoln, Nebr., 1976—77; humanist-in-residence Colo. Humanities Coun., Georgetown, 1975. Author: Galena Lead District, 1966, Politics of Populism, 1974, Progressive Yankees, 1987; author: (co-editor) Great Plains Experience, 1978. Trustee Kimball Union Acad., Meriden, NH, 1990—94; dir. Sherman Fairchild Found., Greenwich, Conn., 1991—; chair Hanover Dem. Town Com., 1970—74; bd. dirs. Divsn. 1 NCAA, 2001—03. Cpl. USMC, 1957—60. Danforth fellow, 1964—69, Guggenheim fellow, 1973—74, Charles Warren fellow, Harvard U., 1980—81. Fellow: Am. Acad. Arts and Scis.; mem.: Western History Assn. (chair Caughey prize 1986—87), The Century Assn., Orgn. Am. Historians (chair film, media com. 1983—85), Phi Beta Kappa. Home: 1 Tuck Dr Hanover NH 03755-3575 Office: Dartmouth Coll Office of the President 207 Parkhurst Hall Hanover NH 03755 E-mail: james.wright@dartmouth.edu.

WRIGHT, J(AMES) LAWRENCE, lawyer; b. Portland, Oreg., Apr. 12, 1943; s. William A. and Esther M. (Nelson) W.; m. Mary Aileene Roche, June 29, 1968; children: Rachel, Jonathan, Christopher. BBA, Gonzaga U., 1966, JD, 1972; LLM, NYU, 1977. Bar: Wash. 1972, U.S. Ct. Mil. Appeals 1974, U.S. Tax Ct. 1976, U.S. Supreme Ct. 1976. Prin. Halverson & Applegate, P.S., Yakima, Wash., 1972-74, 77—, pres., 1998—. Mem. St. Elizabeth Hosp. Found., Yakima, 1986-89, Yakima Meml. Hosp. Found., 1990—; pres. fin. bd. St. Paul's Cathedral, Yakima, 1979—; mem. fin. coun. Diocese of Yakima, 1994—; v.p. Apple Tree Racing Assn., 1986-87; bd. dirs. Capital Theatre, Yakima, 1985-95. Capt. U.S. Army, 1966-68, 74-76. Mem. ABA, Wash. Bar Assn., Yakima County Bar Assn., Rotary. Roman Catholic. Avocations: tennis, golf. Office: Halverson & Applegate PS PO Box 22730 311 N 4th St Yakima WA 98901-2467

WRIGHT, JAMES TIMOTHY, music educator, composer; b. Waterloo, Iowa, July 23, 1959; s. Richard R. Wright, Jr. and Nadine I. Wright; m. Linda S. Armbrest, July 9, 1983; 1 child, Adam James. BA, Luther Coll., 1981. Music educator Mallard (Iowa) Cmty. Sch. Dist., 1981—82; instrumental music educator Ctrl. Webster Cmty. Sch. Dist., Burnside, Iowa, 1982—87, Mormon Trail Cmty. Sch. Dist., Humeston, Iowa, 1988—89, United Cmty. Sch. Dist., Boone, Iowa, 1989—90, St. Edmond HS, Fort Dodge, Iowa, 1990—99, Sumner (Iowa) Cmty. Sch. Dist., 1999—. Mem.: NEA, Sumner Edn. Assn., Iowa State Edn. Assn., Music Educator's Nat. Conf., Iowa Bandmasters Assn. Republican. Presbyterian. Avocations: woodworking, reading, fishing, photography. Office: Sumner Community School District 802 West 6th Street Sumner IA 50674 E-mail: wrightj@sumner.k12.ia.us.

WRIGHT, JANE COOKE, oncologist, educator, consultant; b. N.Y.C., Nov. 30, 1919; d. Louis T. and Corinne (Cooke) W.; m. David D. Jones. AB, Smith Coll., 1942; MD with honors, N.Y. Med. Coll., 1945; D in Med. Scis., Women's Med. Coll. Pa., 1965; ScD, Denison U., 1971. Intern Bellevue Hosp., N.Y.C., 1945-46, resident, 1946, mem. staff, 1955-67; resident Harlem Hosp., 1947, chief resident, 1948; clin. Cancer Rsch. Found., Harlem Hosp., 1949-52; dir., 1952-55; mem. staff Harlem Hosp., 1949-55; practice medicine specializing in clin. cancer chemotherapy N.Y.C.; mem. faculty dept. surgery Med. Ctr., N.Y. U., N.Y.C., 1955-67, adj. assoc. prof., 1961-67, also dir. cancer chemotherapy services research, 1955-67; prof. surgery N.Y. Med. Coll., N.Y.C., 1967-87, prof. surgery emeritus, 1987—, assoc. dean, 1967-75; mem. staff Manhattan VA Hosp., 1955-67, Midtown, Met., Bird S. Color, Flower-Fifth Ave. Hosps., all N.Y.C., 1967-79, Westchester County Med. Center, Valhalla, N.Y., 1971-87, Lincoln Hosp., Bronx, N.Y., 1979-87. Cons. Health Ins. Plan of Greater N.Y., 1962-94; cons. Blvd. Hosp., 1963—, St. Luke's Hosp., Newburgh, N.Y., 1964—; pelvic malignancy rev. com. N.Y. Gynecol. Soc., 1965-66, St. Vincent's Hosp., N.Y.C., 1966—, Dept. Health, Edn. and Welfare, 1968-70, Wyckoff Heights Hosp., N.Y.C., 1969—, NIH, 1971—, others; adv. bd. Skin Cancer Found. Contbr. articles to profl. jours. Mem. Manhattan coun. State Commn. Human Rights, 1949—, Pres.'s Commn. Heart Disease, Cancer and Stroke, 1964-65, Nat. Adv. Cancer Coun. NIH, 1966-70, N.Y. State Women's Coun., 1970-72; bd. dirs. Medico-CARE, Health Svcs. Improvement Fund Inc.; trustee Smith Coll., Northampton, Mass., 1970-80. Recipient numerous awards, including; Mademoiselle mag. award, 1952; Lady Year award Harriet Beecher Stowe Jr. High Sch., 1958; Spirit Achievement award Albert Einstein Sch. Medicine, 1965; certificate Honor award George Gershwin Jr. High Sch., 1967; Myrtle Wreath award Hadassah, 1967; Smith medal Smith Coll., 1968; Outstanding Am. Women award Am. Mothers Com. Inc., 1970; Golden Plate award Am. Acad. Achievement, 1971; Exceptional Black Scientists Poster Ciba Geigy, 1980 Fellow N.Y. Acad. Medicine; mem. Nat. Med. Assn. (edit. bd. jours.), Manhattan Ctrl. Med. Soc., N.Y. County Med. Soc. (nominating com.), AMA, AAAS, Am. Assn. Cancer Rsch. (dir. Rsch. Salute 1971-74), N.Y. Acad. Scis., N.Y. Cancer Soc., Internat. Med. and Rsch. Found. (v.p.), Am. Cancer Soc. (dir. div.), N.Y. Cancer Soc. (pres. 1970-71), Am. Soc. Clin. Oncology (sec. treas. 1964-67), Contin Soc., Sigma Xi, Lambda Kappa Mu, Alpha Omega Alpha. Clubs: The 400 (N.Y. Med. Coll.). Address: 7002 Kennedy Blvd East Apt 9C Guttenberg NJ 07093

WRIGHT, JASON H. communications executive; b. Waterbury, Conn., Nov. 2, 1960; s. Joseph Thomas and Lyda (Hawkins) W. AB, Georgetown U., 1982. With Aetna Life & Casualty Co., Hartford, Conn., 1982—87, mgr. corp. pub. rels., 1987-88, dir. corp. communications, 1988—90; v.p. comm. RJR Nabisco, 1990—93; dir. comm. Nabisco Group Holdings Corp. (formerly RJR Nabisco), 1993—2000; principal Geer Mountain Holdings, LLC, 2000—03; sr. v.p. comm. & public affairs Merrill Lynch & Co. Inc., 2003—. Project mgr. TV, newspaper advt., personal fin. campaign, 1983-84; mgr. mag. advt., instl. investment svcs., 1988. Mem. admissions com., Georgetown U., Washington, 1982—; statechmn. Nat. Jr. Tennis Leagued, Hartford, 1983-88; mentor, Project Concern, Hartford, 1988—. Recipient awards, Ann. Report Conf., Investor Rels. Forum, 1988. Mem. Fin. Communications Soc., Nat. Investor Rels. Inst. Democrat. Methodist. Avocation: tennis. Office: Merrill Lynch & Co Inc 4 World Fin Ctr New York NY 10080 Office Phone: 212-449-1000.

WRIGHT, JEFFREY, actor; b. Wash., D.C., Dec. 7, 1965; Actor: (plays) Les Blancs, 1989, She Stoops to Conquer, 1990—91, Juno and the Paycock, Search and Destroy, 1990—91, Playboy of the West Indies, Daylight in the Exile, Othello (NY Shakespeare Fest.), Angels in America: Millennium Approaches, 1993—94, Angels in America: Perestroika, 1993—94 (Outer Critics Circle award best sup. actor, 1994, Drama Desk award for featured actor, 1994, Tony award for featured actor, 1994), Bring in da Noise, Bring in da Funk, 1996, King Lear, 1996; (films) Presumed Innocent, 1990, Jumpin' at the Boneyard, 1991, Basquiat, 1996, Critical Care, 1997, Celebrity, 1998, Ride With the Devil, 1999, Cement, 1999, Sin's Kitchen, 2000, Crime and Punishment in Suburbia, 2000, Hamlet, 2000, Shaft, 2000 (Toronto Film Critics Assoc. award for best sup. actor, 2000), Boycott, 2001, Ali, 2000, Eye See You, 2001, Intolerable Cruelty, 2002, The Manchurian Candidate, 2004; (TV miniseries) Angels in America (HBO), 2004 (Golden Globe for best supporting actor in a miniseries, 2004). Office: Creative Artists Agency 9830 Wilshire Blvd Beverly Hills CA 90211*

WRIGHT, JESSE HARTZELL, psychiatrist, educator; b. Altoona, Pa., Sept. 21, 1943; s. Jesse H. and Marion (Stone) W.; m. Susanne Judy Wright, July 9, 1967; children: Andrew, Laura. BS, Juniata Coll., 1965; MD, Jefferson Med. Coll., 1969; PhD, U. Louisville, 1976. Diplomate Am. Bd. Psychiatry and Neurology, Am. Bd. Med. Examiners; lic. psychiatrist, Ky. Asst. prof. U. Louisville, 1975-79, assoc. prof., 1979-87, prof., 1987—; clin. dir. Norton Psychiat. Clinic, Louisville, 1975-83, med. dir., 1983—; chief adult psychiatry U. Louisville, 2000—; resident in psychiatry U. Mich., Ann Arbor, 1970-73. Author: first multimedia computer program for psychotherapy, Good Days Ahead, chpts. to books; contbr. articles to prof. jours; author: (self help book for depression) Getting Your Life Back, others. Fellow APA; mem. Ky. Psychiat. Assn. (sec. 1979-80, v.p. 1980-81, pres. 1982-83), Acad. Cognitive Therapy (founding pres.). Avocations: gardening, running, theater, skiing. Home: 15 Indian Hills Trl Louisville KY 40207-1532 Office: Norton Psychiat Clinic 200 E Chestnut St Louisville KY 40202-1822

WRIGHT, JO ANNE, Episcopal priest; b. Wichita, Kans., May 31, 1935; d. Everett Joseph and Agnes Josephine (Ketcham) Steinheimer; m. John Cook Wright, June 25, 1955 (div. June 1976); children: Elizabeth, Jennifer, Melanie, Kennedy Weston. AB, Oberlin Coll., 1955; MDiv, Ch. Divinity Sch. of Pacific, Berkeley, Calif., 1987. Ordained deacon Episcopal Ch., 1987, ordained priest, 1987. Pre-sch. tchr. Children's Hour Headstart, Lawrence, Kans., 1977 79; reference libr. Lawrence (Kans.) Pub. Libr., 1979-84; rector St. Luke's Episcopal Ch., Wamego, Kans., 1987-98, St. John's Episcopal Ch., Vinita, Okla., 1999—; mem. diocesan coun. Diocese of Okla., 2000—01. dean NE region, 2001—. Youth officer Diocese of Kans., Topeka, 1987-92, rural missioner, 1992-98, mem. standing com., mem. diocesan coun., 1997-98; pres. Vinita Minsterial Alliance, 2001, sec., 2003. Writer monthly column Plenteous Harvest, 1987-92. Chair Wamego Coun. Chs., 1998, CROP walk organizer, 1988, 92, 95; tour leader Ednl. Opportunities, Israel, 1998. Roanridge grantee Episcopal Ch. U.S.A., 1995. Mem. Phi Beta Kappa. Democrat. Avocations: reading, travel. Home: 221 S Bell St Vinita OK 74301-3408 Office: St John's Episcopal Ch 522 W Canadian Ave Vinita OK 74301-3612 Office Phone: 918-256-3766. E-mail: jowright@junct.com.

WRIGHT, JOHN, classics educator; b. N.Y.C., Mar. 9, 1941; s. Henry and Dorothy (Chaya) W.; m. Ellen Faber, June 16, 1962; children: Jennifer, Emily. BA, Swarthmore Coll., 1962; MA, Ind. U., 1964, PhD, 1971. Instr. classics U. Rochester, 1968-72, asst. prof., 1972-75; assoc. prof. Northwestern U., Evanston, Ill., 1975-77, prof., 1977-83, John Evans prof. Latin lang. and lit., 1983-2001, chmn. dept., 1978-97, 00-01, prof. emeritus in svc., 2002—. Author: The Play of Antichrist, 1967, Dancing in Chains: The Stylistic Unity of the Comoedia Palliata, 1974, The Life of Cola de Rienzo, 1975, Essays on the Iliad: Selected Modern Criticism, 1978, Plautus: Curculio, Introduction and Notes, 1981, rev. edit., 1993, Ralph Stanley and the Clinch Mountain Boys: A Discography, 1983, The Five-String Banjo Stanley Style, 1984, rev. edit. (Clyde Pharr) Homeric Greek: A Book for Beginners, 1985, It's the Hardest Music in the World to Play: The Ralph Stanley Story in His Own Words, 1987, Traveling the High Way Home: Ralph Stanley and the World of Traditional Bluegrass Music, 1993; albums Everything She Asks For, 1993, Traveling the High Way Home, 1995, Promises, 1996, Ellen and John Wright 1, Ellen and John Wright 2, 1998, I Shook Hands with Eleanor Roosevelt, 2004; contbr. articles to profl. jours. Fellow Am. Acad. Rome, 1966-68; Nat. Endowment Humanities Younger humanist fellow, 1973-74; named to Honorable Order of Ky. Colonels; recipient songwriting prize Santa Fe Bluegrass and Old Time Music Festival, 1996. Mem.: Am. Fedn. of Musicians, Local 1000, BMI, Nat. Acad. Recording Arts and Scis., Am. Acad. in Rome Soc. of Fellows, Internat. Bluegrass Music Assn. (Print Media Personality of Yr. 1994), Chgo. Area Bluegrass Music Assn. Home: 1137 Noyes St Evanston IL 60201-2633 Office: Northwestern U Dept Classics Evanston IL 60208-2200 Office Phone: 847-491-8039. Business E-Mail: jhwright@northwestern.edu.

WRIGHT, JOHN COLLINS, retired chemistry educator; b. Oak Hill, W.Va., Aug. 5, 1927; s. John C. and Irene (Collins) W.; m. Margaret Ann Cyphers, Sept. 11, 1949; children: Jeffrey Cyphers, John Timothy, Curtis Scott, Keith Alexander. BS, W.Va. Wesleyan Coll., 1948, LLD, 1974; PhD, U. Ill., 1951; DSc (hon.), U. Ala., 1979, W.Va. Inst. Tech., 1979. Research chemist Hercules, Inc., 1951-57; mem. faculty W.Va. Wesleyan Coll., 1957-64; asst. program dir. NSF, 1964-65; dean Coll. Arts and Scis., No. Ariz. U., 1966-70, W.Va. U., Morgantown, 1970-74; vice chancellor W.Va. Bd. Regents, Charleston, 1974-78; pres. U. Ala., Huntsville, 1978-88, prof. chemistry, 1988-95, prof. emeritus, 1995—; interim pres. W.Va. Coll. Grad. Studies, Institute, 1975-76. Hon. research assoc. Univ. Coll., London, Eng., 1962-63; cons. NSF, 1965—, Army Sci. Bd., U.S. Army, 1979-82. Served with USNR, 1945-46. Mich. fellow Center Study Higher Edn., U. Mich., 1965-66 Mem. AAAS, NSTA. Office: 2312 Carlton Cove Blvd Huntsville AL 35802

WRIGHT, JOHN F. judge; BS, U. Nebr., 1967, JD, 1970. Atty. Wright & Simmons, 1970-84, Wright, Sorensen & Brower, 1984-91; mem., coord. Commn. on Post Secondary Edn., 1991-92; judge Nebr. Ct. Appeals, 1992-94; assoc. justice Nebr. Supreme Ct., 1994—. Chmn. bd. dirs. Panhandle Legal Svcs., 1970. Mem. Scottsbluff Bd. Edn., 1980-87, pres., 1984, 86. Served with U.S. Army, 1970, Nebr. N.G., 1970-76. Recipient Friend of Edn. award Scottsbluff Edn. Assn., 1992. Office: Nebr Supreme Ct 2207 State Capitol PO Box 98910 Lincoln NE 68509-8910

WRIGHT, JOHN ROBERT, pathologist, educator; b. Winnipeg, Man., Can., Aug. 18, 1935; came to U.S., 1961, naturalized, 1968; s. Ross Grant and Anna Marie (Crispin) W.; m. Deanna Pauline Johnson, June 25, 1960; children—Carolyn Deanna, David John. MD with honors, U. Man., 1959. Diplomate: Am. Bd. Pathology. Intern Winnipeg Gen. Hosp., 1959-60, resident, 1960-61, Balt. City Hosp., 1961-63, Buffalo Gen. Hosp., 1963-64; teaching fellow in medicine U. Man., 1960-61; instr. in pathology, Buswell fellow SUNY-Buffalo, 1965-67, prof. pathology, chmn. dept. pathology, 1974-96, interim dean medicine, v.p. clin. affairs, 1997-98, dean medicine, 1998—2001; asst. chief pathology Balt. City Hosps. and; asst. prof. Johns Hopkins U., 1967-74; cons. Roswell Park Meml. Inst., 1975—, bd. visitors, 1981-97, interim dir., 1985-86, chmn. bd. visitors, 1987-97. Recipient Louis A. and Ruth Siegel Disting. Teaching award SUNY-Buffalo, 1977, 78, 88, Deans award SUNY, 1987. Fellow Assn. Pathology Chairs (sr., pres. 1994-96); mem. AMA, AAAS, Coll. Am. Pathologists, Am. Soc. Investigative Pathologists, Am. Soc. Clin. Pathologists, U.S. and Can. Acad. Pathology, Alpha Omega Alpha. Achievements include research in amyloidosis and aging. Home: 46 Wynngate Ln Williamsville NY 14221-1840 Office: 204 Farber Hall SUNY Buffalo NY 14214 E-mail: jrwright@buffalo.edu.

WRIGHT, JOSEPH ROBERT, JR., corporate executive; b. Tulsa, Sept. 24, 1938; s. Joe Robert and Ann Helen (Cech) W. BS, Colo. Sch. Mines, 1961; M.I.A., Yale U., 1964. Vice pres. Booz, Allen & Hamilton, 1965-71; dep. dir. Bur. Census, Dept. Commerce, 1971-72; dep. adminstr. Social and Econ. Statis. Adminstrn., 1972-73, acting asst. sec. econ. affairs, 1973; asst. sec. adminstr. Dept. Agr., 1973-76; pres. Citicorp Retail Inc. and Retail Consumer Services Inc., N.Y.C.; v.p. Citicorp, Inc., 1976-81; dep. sec. Dept. Commerce, Washington, 1981-82; dep. dir. Office Mgmt. and Budget, Washington, 1982-88; chmn. Pres.'s Council on Integrity and Efficiency, 1982-89; chmn. Pres.'s Coun on Mgmt. Improvement, 1984-89; dir. Office Mgmt. and Budget, 1988-89; exec. v.p., vice chmn. W.R. Grace & Co., N.Y.C., 1989-94; chmn., CEO and Dir. AmTec, Inc., New York, 1994—. Chmn. Grace Environ., Inc., 1989-94, Amtec, Inc., 1995-2000, GRC, Internat., 1997-2000; co-chmn. Baker & Taylor, 1996—; vice-chmn. Jefferson Consulting, 1998—, Tennemark Worldwide, 2000—; bd. dirs. Pan Am. Sat, Inc., AT&T Govt. Mkts., Titan Corp., Real Med, Inc., Fusion Tech., Inc., Terremark Worldwide, Baker & Taylor, Verso Tech., Bion Enviorn. Tech., Travelers, 1990-99, Harcourt Brace Janovich, 1990-92, GRC Internat., 1994-99; fed. co-chmn. Coastal Plains Regional Commn., 1981-82, Four Corners Regional Commn., 1981-82, New Eng. Regional Commn., 1981-82, Old West Regional Commn., 1981-82, Pacific N.W. Regional Commn., 1981-82, S.W. Border Regional Commn.,

1981-82. Mem. Pres. Export Coun., 1989-93, adv. bd. Coun. for Excellence in Govt., 1988-96; trustee Hampton U., 1990-98. 1st lt. AUS, 1963-65. Recipient Pres.'s Citizens award and medal, 1989; named Govt. Exec. of Yr., Govt. Computer News Mag., 1988, medal disting. achievement Colo. Sch. Mines, 1985. Mem. Young Pres. Orgn. (coun. on fgn. rels.), Nat. Acad. Pub. Adminstrn. (com. for responsible fed. budget), Colo. Sch. Mines Alumni Assn., Chief Execs. Orgn., World Bus. coun., Reagan Alumni Assn., Hampton Hills Golf Club (N.Y.), Banyon Country Club (Fla.), Sky Club (N.Y.C.), N.Y. Econ. Club (N.Y.C.). Office: Terremark 36th Fl 405 Lexington Ave New York NY 10174 Address: 10 Gracie Sq # 7G New York NY 10028-8031

WRIGHT, JOSEPHINE ROSA BEATRICE, musicologist; b. Detroit, Sept. 5, 1942; d. Joseph Le Vander and Eva Lee Garrison W.; Mus.B., U. Mo., Columbia, 1963, M.A., 1967; Mus.M., Pius XII Acad., Florence, Italy, 1964; Ph.D., N.Y.U., 1975. Instr. music York Coll., CUNY, 1972-75, asst. prof., 1975; asst. prof. Afro-Am. studies in musicology Harvard U., Cambridge, Mass., 1976-81; assoc. dir. integration of Afro-Am. folk arts with music project, Nat. Endowment Humanities, 1979-82; assoc. prof. music and Black Studies Coll. of Wooster, 1981-90, prof. music and balck studies, 1991-2000, prof. Music and the Josephine Lincoln Morris prof. black studies, 2000; panelist, cons. on music Mass. Coun. of Arts and Humanities, 1978-80; cons. Nat. Endowment Humanities, 1982-83, 87, 89, 90, Ohio Humanities Coun., 1986; apptd. mem. Nat. Artistic Directorate, Am. Classical Music Hall of Fame, Cin. Author: Ignatius Sancho (1729-1780), An Early African Composer in England: The Collected Edition of His Music in Facsimile, 1981; editor: Am. Music, 1993-97, Journal American Music, 1994-1994, Music in African Am. Culture series, 1995—; editor of new music: The Black Perspective in Music, 1979-91, (with Sam Floyd) New Perspectives on Music: Essays in Honor of Eileen Southern, 1992; co-editor: The Bicentennial Issue of The Black Perspective in Music, 1976, (with Eileen Southern) African-American Traditions in Song, Sermon, Tale and Dance, 1991 with Eileen Southern, Images: Iconography of Music in African-American Culture, 2000; mem. editl. bd. Jour. Am. Musicol. Soc., 2003; contbr. articles to profl. jours. Mem. Am. Musicol. Soc. (dir.-at-large 1998-2000), Soc. Am. Music (trustee), Nat. Coun. for black studies, U. Mo. Faculty of Arts and Sci. Alumni Assn. (trustee 1982-85), Pi Kappa Lambda. Democrat. Episcopalian. Business E-Mail: jwright@wooster.edu.

WRIGHT, JUDITH MARGARET, law librarian, educator, dean; b. Jackson, Tenn., Aug. 16, 1944; d. Joseph Clarence and Mary Catherine (Key) Wright; m. Mark A. Johnson, Apr. 17, 1976; children— Paul, Michael BS, U. Memphis, 1966; MA, U. Chgo., 1971; JD, DePaul U., 1980. Bar: Ill. 1980. Librarian Oceanway Sch., Jacksonville, Fla., 1966-67; program dir. ARC, South Vietnam, 1967-68; documents and reference librarian D'Angelo Law Library, U. Chgo., 1970-74, reference librarian, 1974-77, dir., lectr. in law, 1980-99, assoc. dean for libr. and info. svcs., lectr. in law, 1999—. Mem. adv. bd. Legal Reference Svcs. Quar., 1981—. Mem. ABA, Am. Assn. Law Libraries, Chgo. Assn. Law Libraries. Democrat. Methodist. Office: U Chgo Law Sch D'Angelo Law Libr 1121 E 60th St Chicago IL 60637-2745 Fax: 773-702-2889. E-mail: jm-wright@uchicago.edu.

WRIGHT, JUDITH RAE, retired accountant; b. Paoli, Ind., Feb. 16, 1929; d. Samuel Earl and Bernice Louise (Lomax) Hudelson; m. James Edward Walters, July 11, 1947 (div. June 1971); children: Jamie Jo, Jennifer Rae; m. George Ralph Wright, Feb. 20, 1972 (dec. Apr. 1977). Student, Northwood Inst., West Baden, Ind., 1968-69, Ind. U.-Purdue U., Indpls., 1972-77. Acct. Ind. Hwy. Commn., Indpls., 1969—75, Ind. Dept. Correction, Indpls., 1975—76, Ind. Dept. Pub. Welfare, Indpls., 1976-78, Ind. Office Social Svcs., Indpls., 1978-79; acct. supr. Ind. Dept. Pub. Welfare, Indpls., 1979-92, ret., 1992. Mem. First Christian Ch. Recipient Gov.'s Spl. Achievement award, 1992. Mem. Assn. Govt. Accts., Am. Legion Aux., Order of Eastern Star, Kappa Kappa Kappa. Republican.

WRIGHT, KATIE HARPER, educational administrator, journalist; b. Crawfordsville, Ark., Oct. 5, 1923; d. James Hale and Connie Mary (Locke) Harper; m. Marvin Wright, Mar. 21, 1952; 1 child, Virginia K. Jordan. BA, U. Ill., 1944, MEd, 1959; EdD, St. Louis U., 1979. Elem. and spl. edn. tchr. East St. Louis (Ill.) Pub. Schs., 1944-65, dir. Dist. 189 Instrnl. Materials Program, 1965-71, dir. spl. edn. Dists. 188, 189, 1971-77, asst. supt. programs, 1977-79; interim supt. East St. Louis Sch. Dist. 189, 1993-94. Adj. faculty Harris/Stowe State Coll., 1980, adj. prof. edn. emeritus; mem. staff St. Louis U., 1989—; interim supt. Dist. 189 Schs., 1994—; mem. Pres.'s Commn. on Excellence in Spl. Edn. Author: Delta Sigma Theta/East St. Louis Chapter History, 1992; contbr. articles to profl. jours.; feature writer St. Louis Argus Newspaper, 1979—. Mem. Ill. Commn. on Children, 1973-85, East St. Louis Bd. Election Comms., East St. Louis Fin. Adv. Authority, 1999—; pres. bd. dirs. St. Clair County Mental Health Ctr., 1970-72, 87—; bd. dirs. River Bluff coun. Girl Scouts USA, 1979—, nat. bd. dirs., 1981-84; bd. dirs. Jackie Joyner-Kersee Youth Ctr. Found., 1991—, United Way, 1979—, Urban League, 1979—, Provident Counseling Ctr., 1995-98; pres. bd. trustees East St. Louis Pub. Libr., 1972-77; pres., bd. dirs. St. Clair County Mental Health Ctrs., 1987; mem. adv. bd. Magna Bank; charter mem. Coalition of 100 Black Women; mem. coord. coun. ethnic affairs Synod of Mid-Am., Presbyn. Ch. U.S.A.; mem. Ill. Dept. Corrections Sch. Bd., 1995—; charter mem. Metro East Links Group, Gateway chpt. The Links, Inc.; mem. Ill. Minority/Female Bus. Coun., 1991—; mem. Pres.'s Commn. on Excellence in Spl. Edn., 2001--. Recipient of more than 150 awards including Lamp of Learning award East St. Louis Jr. Wednesday Club, 1965, Outstanding Working Woman award Downtown St. Louis, Inc., 1967, Ill. State citation for ednl. document Love is Not Enough, 1974, Delta Sigma Theta citation for document Good Works, 1979, Girl Scout Thanks badge, 1982, award Nat. Coun. Negro Women, 1983, Cmty. Svc. award Met. East Bar Assn., 1983, Journalist award Sigma Gamma Rho, Spelman Coll. Alumni award, 1990, A World of Difference award, 1990, 92, Edn. award St. Louis, YWCA, 1991, SIU-E-Kimmel award, 1991, St. Clair County Mental Health award, 1992, Gateway East Met. Ministry Dr. M.L. King award, 1993, Nat. Coun. Negro Women Black Leader of Yr., 1995, Disting. Alumni award U. Ill., 1996, Pioneer award Mosque 28B, 2000, Tri Del Globe award, 2001, Urban League Merit award, 2002, Ill. Office of Edn. award, 2002, Eugene B. Redmond Writers Club award, 2002, NFPW Quest award, 2004; named Woman of Achievement, St. Louis Globe Democrat, 1974, Outstanding Adminstr. So. region III Office Edn., 1975, Woman of Yr. in Edn. St. Clair County YWCA, 1987, Nat. Top Lady of Yr., 1988, Disting. Alumnus U. Ill., 1996, Vashon H.S. Hall of Fame, 1989, Citizen Amb., South Africa, 1996, Sr. Illinoisan Hall of Fame, 1997. Mem. Am. Librs. Trustees Assn. (regional v.p. 1978-79, 92, nat. sec. 1979-80), Ill. Commn. on Children, Mensa, Coun. for Exceptional Children (mem. pres.'s commn. excellence spl. edn.), Top Ladies of Distinction (pres. 1987-91, nat. editor 1991—, Journalism award 1992, Media award 1992), Delta Sigma Theta (chpt. pres. 1960-62, Letters award 2000), Kappa Delta Pi (pres. So. Ill. U. chpt. 1973-74), Phi Delta Kappa (Svc. Key award 1984, chpt. pres. 1984-85), Iota Phi Lambda, Phi Lambda Theta (chpt. pres. 1985-87), East St. Louis Women's Club (pres. 1973-75). Republican. Home: 733 N 40th St East Saint Louis IL 62205-2138

WRIGHT, KENNETH BROOKS, lawyer; b. Whittier, Calif., June 5, 1934; s. Albert Harold and Marian (Schwey) W.; m. Sandra Beryl Smith, June 20, 1959; children: Margo Teresa, Daniel Brooks, John Waugh. BA cum laude, Pomona Coll., 1956; JD, Stanford U., 1960. Bar: Calif. 1961, U.S. Supreme Ct. 1979. Assoc., then ptnr. Lawler, Felix & Hall, 1961-77; ptnr. Morgan, Lewis & Bockius, LA, 1978—99, counsel, 1999—2003, ret. ptnr., 2004. Teaching team leader Nat. Inst. Trial Advocacy, 1978-80; governing com. Calif. Continuing Edn. of Bar, 1973-77, chmn., 1975-76; nat. panel arbitrators Am. Arbitration Assn., 1970-91; lectr. ABA Sect. Litigation Nat. Inst., 1979-86; bd. dirs. L.A. Internat. Comml. Arbitration Ctr. Chmn. bd. editors: Am. Bar Jour, 1977-81. Pres. Pomona Coll. Alumni Assn., 1970-71; pres. parent tchr. coun. Campbell Hall Sch., 1973-74, bd. dirs., 1976—, vice chmn., 1994—; counsel Vol. League San Fernando Valley, 1979-81; chmn. sect. adminstrn. of justice Town Hall of Calif., 1970-71; sr. warden Episcopal Ch., 1973-74. Served with U.S. Army, 1956-57. Mem. ABA (dir. programs litigation sect. 1977-81, mem. coun. 1982-88, mem. standing com on comm. 1978-88, chmn. 1987-88, chmn. sect. book pub. com. 1986-89, pres. fellows young lawyers 1985-86, bd. dirs. 1980-89), Internat. Bar Assn., Assn. Bus. Trial Lawyers (chair com. alt. dispute resolution 1991-93, bd. dirs. 1993-96), Am. Law Inst., Am. Bar Found., State Bar Calif. (mem. gov. com. continuing edn. of the bar 1972-77, chmn. 1975-76), Conf. Barristers (exec. com. 1966-69, 1st v.p. 1969), L.A. County Bar Assn. (com. on judiciary 1981-83, chmn. continuing legal edn. adv. com. 1989-91, vice-chmn. continuing legal edn. com. 1991-93, bd. dirs. L.A. Lawyers 1989-94), L.A. County Bar Found. (bd. dirs., trustee 1993-99, mem. exec. com. internat. sect. 1996-99), Jonathan Club, Phi Beta Kappa. Republican. Avocations: skiing, tennis. Home: 3610 Longridge Ave Sherman Oaks CA 91423-4918 Office: Morgan Lewis & Bockius 300 S Grand Ave Los Angeles CA 90071-3109

WRIGHT, KIRBY MICHAEL, writer, editor; b. Honolulu, Sept. 1, 1955; s. Harold Stanley and June Gertrude (McCormack) W.; m. Darcy Laureen Mobraaten, Dec. 28, 1991. BA, U. Calif., San Diego, 1983; MFA, San Francisco State U., 1994. Pub. rels. dir. Winners Circle Resorts, Carlsbad, Calif., 1987-90; instr. Palo Alto (Calif.) Adult Sch., 1994-95; writer GT Prodn. Co., Palo Alto, 1995-96, editor, 1997—. Author: The Rainbow Warrior, 1998; (screenplay) Gordon & Al, 1996; (dramatic monologue) Blue Mesa Review, 1994 (1st pl. award Browning Soc. 1993, 94); (play) Houdini, 1999; (novel) Ulua Lines, 2000; (poetry) Before the City, 2003. Rschr. Ctr. for Auto Safety, Washington, 1980; advisor SAT Success, Palo Alto, 1998. Recipient Poetry prize Ann Fields Trust, San Francisco, 1993, 1st pl. Poets award Acad. Am. Poets, San Francisco, 1993, 1st pl. San Diego Book awards, 2002. Fellow Arts Coun. Santa Clara County, Arts Coun. Silicon Valley. Democrat. Roman Catholic. Avocations: boxing, surfing, gourmet cooking. Home: 1604 Marbella Dr Vista CA 92081 Office: GT Prodn Co 3259 Alma St Palo Alto CA 94306-2925 E-mail: kirby33@earthlink.net.

WRIGHT, LAURA KEITH, editor, writer; d. Keith Edward and Deborah St. Clair Robinson; m. Jason Michael Wright, Aug. 29, 1998. Grad., Georgetown U. Inst. on Polit. Journalism, Fund for Am. Studies, 1991; BS in Journalism, U. of Colo., 1992. Fiction editor Inklings Mag., Denver, 1995—2000; account supr. Heinrich Relationship Mktg., Denver, 1996—2000; prodn. editor WaterBrook Press, Colorado Springs, 2000—. Author: (novels) Harbinger. Mem.: The Writers Group (assoc.; organizer 2003—04), Gourmet Club (assoc.; gourmet cook 2001—04), Book Group 2 (assoc.), Bible Study Fellowship (assoc.), Alpha Chi Omega (assoc.; various offices 1990—92), PEO (assoc.; various offices 1994—97). Republican. Avocations: travel, reading, hiking, cooking. Office: WaterBrook Press Ste 160 2375 Telstar Dr Colorado Springs CO 80920 Office Phone: 718-965-1999.

WRIGHT, LINDA ELLEN, nursing educator; b. Elmira, N.Y., Mar. 4, 1943; d. Marcus Alton and Helen Marie (Eaton) Wright. Diploma, Arnot-Ogden Meml. Hosp., 1964; BSN, Alfred U., 1987; MS, Syracuse U., 1990. Staff med.-surg. nurse Arnot-Ogden Meml. Hosp., Elmira, 1964-67, charge nurse, 1967-72, charge nurse NICU, 1972-76, asst. ob.-gyn. coord., 1976-78, asst. instr. Sch. Nursing, 1978-87, instr., 1987—, asst. dir. Sch. Nursing, dir. faculty and student affairs, 2002. Exch. nurse Rainbow Babies and Children's Hosp., Univ. Hosp., Cleve., 1971; vis. nurse Med. Coll. Va., Richmond. Supporter, vol. Children's Miracle Network. Mem.: AAUW, NOW, Am. Cancer Soc. (edn. com.), Oncology Nursing Soc. (cons.), N.Y. State Nurses Assn., Assn. Women's Health, Obstetrics and Neonatal Nurses, World Wildlife Fund, Nat. Parks and Conservation Assn., Ctr. Marine Conservation, Nature Conservancy, Wilderness Soc., Colonial Dames XVII Century, Sigma Theta Tau. Presbyterian. Home: 915 Lincoln St Elmira NY 14901-1806 Office: Arnot Ogden Med Ctr Grove St Elmira NY 14905 E-mail: lwright@aomc.org.

WRIGHT, LINDA JEAN, manufacturing executive; b. Chgo., Dec. 14, 1949; d. Eugene F. and Rosemary Margaret (Kiley) Kemph; m. Kelly W. Wright, Jr., Feb. 1979 (div. 1984); m. Samuel Neuwirth Klewans, Aug. 28, 1986 (div. 1991). Student, Loretto Heights Coll., 1967-69, U. Ill., 1970-71. Asst. to v.p. Busey 1st Nat. Bank, Urbana, Ill., 1969-72; spa mgr., supr. sales tng. Venus and Apollo Health Club, San Antonio, 1973-76; owner Plant Shop, San Antonio, 1976-77; with Enterprise Bank, Falls Church, Va., 1977-84, comml. lending officer, 1978-84, sr. v.p., 1979-84, corp. sec. of bd. dirs., 1980-84; pes., CEO Fairfax Savs. Bank, 1984-87, Bankstar, N.A. (formerly Bank 2000 of Reston, N.A.), 1988-90; v.p. Ryan-McGinn Inc., Arlington, Va., 1991-95, Bethlehem Corp., 1995—. Bd. dirs. INOVA Inst. Rsch. and Edn., 1990-94. Apptd. pub. ofcl., chmn. Va. Small Bus. Fin. Authority, Richmond, 1984-88; trustee Inova Health System, 1992-95; mem. exec. com. Fairfax-Falls Church United Way, United Way Capital Area, Washington, 1984-85; mem. Fairfax County Spl. Task Force, 1986; bd. dirs. Fairfax Com. of 100, 1993095; mem., bd. dirs. Hospice No. Va., Arlington, 1985-86, chmn. No. Va. Local Devel. Corp., 1986; mem. ops. bd. Fairfax Hosp., 1987-94; pres. No. Va. Transp. Alliance, 1987-92; bd. dirs. Va. Found. for Rsch. and Econ. Edn., 1989-91, No. Va. coun. Am. Heart Assn., 1989-94. Mem. Fairfax County C. of C. (dir., v.p., pres. 1987-88), Nat. Assn. Bank Women (chmn. No. Va. group 1980-81), Fairfax Hunt Club, Tower Club (bd. govs. 1989-95). Roman Catholic. Avocations: aviation, fox hunting.

WRIGHT, MALCOLM STURTEVANT, nuclear energy industry executive, retired military officer; b. Orange, NJ, Sept. 2, 1941; s. Malcolm Everett and Margaret Sommer (Kohler) Wright; m. Barbara Jean Larsen, June 5, 1963 (div. Aug. 1988); children: Tracy Ann, Karen Elizabeth; m. Lya Hanfri Baughman, Nov. 5, 1988; children: Zachary Seth, Sara Ann. BS in Engring., U.S. Naval Acad., 1963; MA in Polit. Sci., Villanova U., 1974. Commd. ensign USN, 1963, advanced through grades to capt., 1983, ret., 1993; dir. tactical tng. dept. U.S. Naval Submarine Sch., Groton, Conn., 1982-84; commdg. officer USS Alabama, Silverdale, Wash., 1984-87; planner polit.-mil. strategy Staff of Chmn. Joint Chiefs of Staff, Pentagon, Washington, 1987-90; comdr. Submarine Squadron Seventeen, Silverdale, Wash., 1990-92; chief of staff to comdr. Naval Base Seattle, 1992-93; mgr. waste and decontamination plant Westinghouse Hanford Co., Richland, Wash., 1993-96; mgr. 324/327 facility stblzn. project Babcock and Wilcox Hanford Co., Richland, 1996-99; dir. 324 bldg. deactiviation project Fluor Hanford Co., Richland, 1999—. Tech. advisor Disney Studios, Burbank, Calif., 1994—95. Vol. ARC, East Orange, NJ, 1957—59. Decorated Legion of Merit. Mem.: U.S. Naval Submarine League, U.S. Naval Inst., U.S. Naval Acad. Alumni Assn. Republican. Presbyterian. Avocations: military history, Civil War, Scottish culture, golf. Office: Flour Hanford Inc PO Box 1000 Richland WA 99352-1000 Home: 3111 S Neel Pl Kennewick WA 99337-2538 Office Phone: 509-373-5864.

WRIGHT, MARGARET HAGEN, computer scientist, administrator; b. San Francisco, 1952; m. 1965; 1 child. BS, Stanford U., 1964, MS, 1965, PhD in Computer Sci., 1976. Devel. engr. Sylvania Electronic System, 1965-71; sr. rsch. assoc. Stanford U., Palo Alto, Calif., 1976-88; mem. tech. staff Bell Labs. now Lucent Techs., Murray Hill, N.J., 1988—; head sci. computer rsch. dept. Lucent Techs., Murray Hill, 1999—. Assoc. editor Jour. Sci. Stats. Computer Programming. Mem. NAE, Assn. Computing Machinery (bd. dirs. numerical analysis assn. spl. interest group), Soc. Indsl. and Applied Math., Math. Programming Soc. Achievements include research contributing to enlarged knowledge of methods for nonlinear programming, particularly unconstrained; linearly constrained and nonlinearly constrained optimization; mathematical software, numerical linear algebra; software library development. Office: AT&T Bell Labs Lucent Tech Rm 2C 462 600 Mountain Ave New Providence NJ 07974-2008

WRIGHT, MARGARET TAYLOR, marketing consultant, publisher; b. Wilmington, N.C., Nov. 8, 1949; d. Thomas Henry and Margaret (Taylor) W. BA, U. N.C., 1972; MBA, Wake Forest U., 1978. Child advocacy specialist Child Advocacy Council Dept. Human Resources, Raleigh, N.C., 1973-74; region dir. N.C. Office for Children Dept. Human Resources, Winston-Salem, 1974-76; product mgr. food div. Am. Home Products, N.Y.C., 1978-80; account exec. Ted Bates Advt., N.Y.C., 1981; product mgr. C.F. Mueller div. McKesson, Inc., Jersey City, 1981-83; mgr. new products Popsicle div. Sara Lee Corp., Englewood, N.J., 1983-86; pres. Wright Mktg. Blueprint, Old Chatham, N.Y., 1987—; chmn. Equatorial Group, Ltd., Old Chatham, N.Y., 1994—; pub. Grey Play Round Table Mag. on African Grey Parrots, Old Chatham, N.Y., 1994—. Pub. web pages www.Africangreys.com and www.Africanature.com Author: African Grey Parrots, A Complete Owner's Manual, 2001; co-author: (pamphlets) Children--Helping Them Grow, 1973; pub.: Grey Play Round Table mag., 1994—. Youth coord. Jim Holshouser Gubernatorial Campaign, New Hanover County, N.C., 1972; mem. Jr. League, N.Y. and N.C., 1972-84. Episcopalian. Avocations: tennis, sailing, golf, travel. Office: Wright Mktg Blueprint 400 E 54th St Ste 2D New York NY 10022- E-mail: maggie@africangreys.com.

WRIGHT, MARIE BEULAH BATTEY, retired advertising executive; b. Cordell, Okla., Jan. 12, 1917; d. John William and Mary (Yoder) Battey; m. Joseph Barney Gifford, Sept. 3, 1948 (dec. 1960); m. Harold Arthur Wright, May 18, 1979. BFA, U. Okla., 1937; posTgrad., Oklahoma City Symphony, 1939—40; postgrad., Baylor U., 1943-44. Host 15-minute daily piano show U. Okla. Radio Sta., 1935; supt. music Woodward (Okla.) Pub. Schs., 1937-38; sales and promotion mgr. KOME, Tulsa, 1940-43; instr. Sch. Radio Baylor U., Waco, Tex., 1943-45; asst. program mgr. KWKH, Shreveport, La., 1945-47; salesman KTBS Radio, Shreveport, 1947-55; comml. mgr. KTBS-TV, Shreveport, 1955-57, KEEL Radio, Shreveport, 1957-62, v.p., gen. mgr., 1963-75; v.p. Lin Broadcasting, Shreveport, 1963-75; gen. mgr. KEEL/AM and KMBQ/FM, Shreveport, 1968-80; v.p. Multimedia Broadcasting, Shreveport, 1975-80. Freelance mus. in arrangements Okla. City radio stas., 1938-39; editl. writer radio stas.; author: The Killing of the Presidency, 1974 (RTNDA Best Editl. 1973). Mem. publicity com. United Fund, 1955-62, exec. com. Shreveport Symphony, 1976-82, Strand Theatre of Shreveport Corp., 1977-94; bd. dirs. Downtown Devel. Corp., 1975-81; La. rep. So. Growth Policies Bd., 1985-96; mem. La. State Arts Coun., 1992-96; bd dirs. Caddo-Bossier Cmty. Action, 1969-71; mem. housing com. Caddo Parish, Shreveport, 1969; mem. City Charter Com., Shreveport, 1970; bd. dirs. Amb. Club, Shreveport, 1971-74; bd. dirs. David Raines Assn., Shreveport, 1969; mem. Com. of 500 March of Dimes, Shreveport, 1969; exec. asst. Shreveport Summer Theatre, 1950-60. Named Broadcaster of Yr., La. Assn. Broadcasters, Shreveport, 1970, Women Who Have Made a Differnce, YWCA, Shreveport, 1988; recipient Humanitarian award Shreveport Negro C. of C., 1969, Humanitarian award for outstanding contbn. to the arts, 1995. Mem. Shreveport C. of C. (bd. dirs. 1968-71, 1st woman mem.). Democrat. Avocations: theater, symphony, reading, politics. Home: 701 Livingston Ave Shreveport LA 71107-3914

WRIGHT, MARK G. entomologist; b. Cape Town, South Africa, Mar. 6, 1964; s. Gerald Ep and Helen C. Wright; m. Ania M. Wieczorek, Nov. 1, 1997; children: Caitlin E., Johnathan M., Taryn L. MSc, U. Stellenbosch, 1988—91; PhD, U. Natal, Pietermaritzburg, 1992—97. Rsch. entomologist Agrl. Rsch. Coun., Cape Town, South Africa, 1988—98; rsch. assoc. Cornell U., Ithaca, NY, 1999—2001; asst. prof. U. Hawaii at Manoa, Honolulu, 2001—. Recipient Ka Pouhana award, Outstanding Mentor, Coll. Tropical Agr. and Human Resources, U. Hawaii at Manoa, 2003-2004. Mem.: Hawaiian Entomol. Soc. (chief editor 2004). Achievements include research in Insect ecology. Avocations: running, music. Office: U Hawaii at Manoa 3050 Maile Way Honolulu HI 96822 Business E-Mail: markwrig@hawaii.edu.

WRIGHT, MARSHA JANE, pastor; b. Fort Wayne, Ind., Sept. 17, 1947; d. Morris J and Margaret Jane Ringenberg; m. Stephen Harlan Wright, July 29, 1972; children: Jonathan Alan, Joseph David, Joshua Peter, Jairus Stephen, Jaala Joy. BA in Music Edn., Ft. Wayne Bible Coll., Ind., 1965—70; Masters in Music Edn., Ball State U., Muncie, Ind., 1970—72. Lic. ministerial The Missionary Ch. Jr. high music tchr. Ft. Wayne Cmty. Schools, Ft. Wayne, Ind., 1970—76; min. of music Grabill Missionary Ch., Ind., 1975—. Home: 11107 Grabill Road Leo IN 46765

WRIGHT, MARY JAMES, senior education consultant; b. Charlottesville, Va., Aug. 20, 1946; d. Harry Beech and Virginia Allen (Root) James; m. Paul Sims Wright, July 26, 1969; children: Christopher Brennan, Keith Allen. BA summa cum laude, Mary Washington Coll., 1968; MA, Northwestern U., 1969. Instr. drama and speech Mary Washington Coll., Fredericksburg, Va., 1969-71, Charles County Community Coll., La Plata, Md., 1973-79; arts and media coord. Charles County Arts Coun., La Plata, 1973-82, Gen. Smallwood Mid. Sch., Indian Head, Md., 1980-82, No. Va. Community Coll., Annandale, 1982-84; computer-based learning specialist USDA Grad. Sch., Washington, 1984-85, U.S. Army Engr. Sch., Ft. Belvoir, Va., 1985-87, Battelle Meml. Inst., Columbus, Ohio, 1987-88; videodisc designer Kendrick & Co., Washington, 1988-90; instrnl. design mgr. The Discovery Channel, Bethesda, Md., 1990-93; instnl. design mgr., writer Edunetics Corp., Arlington, Va., 1994-97. Project mgr., instl. designer Toby Levine Comms., Inc., 1990-97; mng. editor Time-Life Edn., Alexandria, Va., 1997-99, sr. edn. cons. ThinkNet, 1999—. Author, dir.: Story-Theatre for Children, 1979; contbr. articles to profl. jours.; pub. children's books, videos, videodiscs, CD-ROMS, Web sites, multimedia kits and classroom guides for Time Life, PBS, Discovery Channel, Nat. Geographic Soc., Edunetics/Steck Vaughn. Pres. Am. Christian Television System of No. Va., Action for Women, Charles County AAUW; sign lang. interpreter Deaf Ministry; ministry vol. Sports and Rec Plus. Nat. Danforth fellow 1969; recipient Achievement award Dept. of Army, 1986, Kendrick & Co., 1989; recipient Outstanding Arts Programming award Md. Dept. Parks and Recreation, 1980, Silver and Bronze Cindy awards (Cinema in Industry and Edn.), 1992, Red Ribbon Am. Film & Video Assn. Festival, Special Gold Jury award Houston Internat. Film Festival, 1992, Gold award Nebr. Interactive Media, 1993, award for Excellence, Time Life, Inc., 1999. Mem. Internat. Interactive Courseware Soc. (Mark of Excellence award 1992), Assn. for Devel. Computer-Based Instrn. Systems (coord. spl. interest groups D.C. chpt. 1989-90), Mortar Bd., Alpha Psi Omega, Alpha Phi Sigma. Home and Office: 4302 Rolling Stone Way Alexandria VA 22306-1225 E-mail: writght1mj@aol.com.

WRIGHT, MICHAEL WILLIAM, wholesale distribution and retail executive; b. Mpls., June 13, 1938; s. Thomas W. and Winifred M. W. BA, U. Minn., 1961, JD with honors, 1963. Ptnr. Dorsey & Whitney, Mpls., 1966-77; sr. v.p. Supervalu Inc., Mpls., 1977-78; pres., COO, Super Valu Stores, Inc., Mpls., 1978-82, CEO, 1981-82; chmn., CEO Supervalu Inc., Mpls., 1982—. Bd. dirs., past chmn. Fed. Res. Bank, Mpls.; bd. dirs. Norwest Corp., Honeywell, Inc., The Musicland Group, Shopko, Inc., S.C. Johnson & Co., Inc., Cargill, Inc., Internat. Ctr. for Cos. of the Food Trade and Industry, Food Mktg. Inst., Nat. Am. Wholesale Grocers Assn., Inc.; vice chmn. Food Mktg. Inst. 1st lt. U.S. Army, 1964-66. Office: Supervalu Inc 11840 Valley View Rd Eden Prairie MN 55344

WRIGHT, MINTURN TATUM, III, retired lawyer; b. Phila., Aug. 7, 1925; s. Minturn T. and Anna (Moss) Wright; m. Nonya R. Stevens, May 11, 1957; children: Minturn T., Richard S., Robert M., Marianne F. BA, Yale U., 1949; LLB, U. Pa., 1952. Bar: Pa. 1953, U.S. Ct. Appeals (3d cir.) 1953, U.S. Supreme Ct. 1962. Law clk. US Ct. Appeals (3d cir.), 1952-53; assoc. Dechert, Price & Rhoads, Phila., 1953-61, ptnr., 1961-95, chmn., 1982-84; ret. Vis. prof. U. Pa. Law Sch., 1965—69, 1993—97; bd. dirs. Cotiga Devel. Co. Contbr. articles to profl. jours. Trustee Acad. Natural Scis., Phila., 1958—, chmn., 1976—81; trustee Rare Ctr., Exec. Svc. Corps., Marshall-Reynolds Found., Hawk Mountain Sanctuary Assn., chmn. bd. dirs., 1992—97. With U.S. Army, 1943—46. Mem.: ABA, Eastern Mineral Law Assn. (trustee), Nat. Coal Lawyers Assn., Phila. Bar Assn., Pa. Bar Assn., Milldam Club, Phila. Club. Episcopalian. Office: Dechert LLP 4000 Bell Atlantic Tower 1717 Arch St Ste 4000 Philadelphia PA 19103-2793

WRIGHT, MURIEL DEASON See WELLS, KITTY

WRIGHT, NANCY HOWELL, interior designer; b. Sept. 6, 1932; d. David Austin and Catherine Howell; m. Hastings Kemper Wright, June 19, 1954; children: Mark, Barbara; children: Kenneth, Donald. BFA, Ohio Wesleyan U.; student, Parsons Sch. Design, 1977. Interior decorator Country Manor of Branford (Conn.), 1971-75; design mgr., 1976-97; pres., owner Nancy Wright Interiors, 1997—. Sec. Branford Art League, 1977; bd. dirs. Harrison House Hist. House, Branford, Conn., 1983-84; mem. Rep Town Com., Branford, 1990-92; recording sec. Branford Garden Club, 1991—. Mem. Am. Soc. Interior Designers (award for best Conn. retail store design, 1980, Conn. Coalition), Branford Garden Club (rec. sec. 1990-94, membership chmn. 1995, v.p. 1997-99, pres. 1999-2000), Delta Phi Delta. Republican. Episcopalian. Home and Office: 35 Wood Rd Branford CT 06405-4935

WRIGHT, NANNIE BELL, retired secondary school educator; b. Laing, W.Va., May 7, 1934; d. Samuel Thomas and Edna (Irving) W. BS in Edn. magna cum laude, W.Va. State Coll., 1956; MA, U. Chgo., 1960; postgrad., NYU, 1966, L.I. U., 1990. Tchr. social studies, math., and English Wiley H. Bates Jr. H.S., Annapolis, Md., 1956-63; English tchr. Copiague (N.Y.) Jr. H.S., 1963—95. Resource tchr. Copiague Jr. High Sch., 1970-75. Chmn. edn. com. AAUW, Annapolis, 1960; pres. women' s aux. Crownsville Hosp., 1960—61. Mem.: NAACP (v.p.Long Island br. 1992—), Nat. Coun. English Tchrs., Inst.Gen. Semantics, Noetic Scis., U. Chgo. Alumni Assn., Copiague Retired Tchrs. Assn., Delta Sigma Theta (v.p. Annapolis alumnae chpt. 1961), Pi Lambda Theta, Alpha Kappa Mu. Republican. Roman Catholic. Avocations: reading, travel, energy healing, poetry, attending plays and concerts. Home: 27 Wellington Pl Amityville NY 11701-3030 E-mail: nanbwlucky@aol.com.

WRIGHT, PAMELA JEAN, academic administrator; b. Flint, Mich., Mar. 7, 1947; d. Richard Dardine and Mary Louise Smith; m. Arnold Freeman Wright, Dec. 11, 1972; 1 child, Jason Freeman. AA in Edn., Harford C.C., 1969; BA in Edn., Augusta Coll., 1972; MEd of Guidance Counseling, U. S.C., 1975. Employment counselor Fla. State Employment Svcs., Miami, 1975-79, area counseling supr., 1979-80; cons. Tradcom Internat., Miami, 1986-87; dir. student employment and career svcs. and One Stop Ctr. Miami-Dade Coll. (formerly Miami-Dade C.C.), 1981—. Bd. dirs. Dade Employ the Handicapped Com., 1978-80; tenor drummer St. Andrews Scottish Pipe and Drum Band, Miami. Mem. Fla. Assn. C.C. (pres., v.p., membership chair, region V dep. dir.), Coral Gables C. of C., South Dade C. of C., Fla. Coll. Placement Assn. (bd. dirs. 1994-97). Roman Catholic. Avocations: sailing, camping, skiing, reading. Office: Miami-Dade Coll 11011 SW 104th St Rm 3105 Miami FL 33176-3393 E-mail: pwright@mdc.edu.

WRIGHT, PETER MELDRIM, lawyer; b. Charlottesville, Va., Apr. 10, 1946; s. David McCord and Caroline Wallace (Jones) W.; m. Astrid Gabriella Mercedes Sandberg, June 4, 1972; children: David Habersham, Christian Langdon. AB, U. Ga., 1967, JD, 1972. Bar: Ga. 1972, U.S. Dist. Ct. (no. dist.) Ga. 1972. Assoc. Jones, Bird & Howell, Atlanta, 1972-77, ptnr., 1977-82, Alston & Bird, Atlanta, 1982-2001; gen. counsel Resource Healthcare of Am., Inc., 2001—. Sec. Atlanta coun. Soc. Colonial Wars in Ga., 1985-88, dep. gov., 1989-91, mem. coun., 2003—; mem. Soc. Cin. Ga., Savannah, historian, 1996—, v.p., 1998-2004, pres., 2004—. Mem. Ga. Bar Assn., Nat. Assn. Bond Lawyers (chmn. blue sky laws and legal investment law coms. 1982-85, bd. dirs. 1985-86), Ga. Hist. Soc. (bd. curators 1993-2000, sec. 1994-98; v.p. Atlanta chpt. 1998-2000), Skidway Health and Living Svs., Inc. (pres., dir. 2003-), Oglethorpe Club (Savannah, Ga.), St. Andrew's Soc. Savannah. Home: 3502 Woodhaven Rd NW Atlanta GA 30305-1011 Office: Resource Healthcare Am One Buckhead Plz Ste 900 3060 Peachtree Rd NW Atlanta GA 30305

WRIGHT, RANDOLPH EARLE, retired petroleum company executive; b. Brownsville, Tex., Dec. 22, 1920; s. William Randolph and Nelle Mae (Earle) W.; m. Elaine Marie Harris, May 9, 1943; 1 son, Randolph Earle. BS, U. Tex., 1942. With Texaco Inc., 1946-82, mgr. gas div., 1968-70, gen. mgr. producing dept., 1970-71, v.p. gas dept., 1971-82, v.p., sr. officer, 1972-80; past pres., dir. Sabine Pipe Line Co.; v.p., asst. to pres. Texaco U.S.A., 1980-82, ret., 1982; past v.p. Texaco Mineral Co. Past chmn. engring. found. adv. council U. Tex., Austin. Past mem. exec. bd. Sam Houston Area coun. Boy Scouts Am.; past bd. dirs., past pres. Jr. Achievement S.E. Tex.; past bd. dirs. Houston Symphony Soc., Tex. Research League, Houston C. of C.; past trustee U. St. Thomas, S.W. Rsch. Inst. Served with USNR, World War II.

WRIGHT, RICHARD KIRK, physicist, materials researcher, physiologist, consultant; b. Portland, Oreg., May 24, 1945; s. Roscoe Kirk and Esther Agnes (Hobbs) W.; m. Judie Kay Patterson, June 9, 1969; children: Kimberlee, Jamie, Ashlee, Lindsay. BS, Ariz. State U., 1975; DSc, Eurotech. Rsch. U., Palo Alto, Calif., 1989. Engr. Motorola Semicondr., Phoenix, 1973-77, Tektronix Inc., Beaverton, Oreg., 1977-83; sr. engr. Amdahl Corp., Sunnyvale, Calif., 1983-90; mfg. engr. TAQ Comms., Santa Clara, Calif., 1990-93; cons. Loral Fairchild, Milpitas, Calif., 1993-94; sr. mem. tech. staff Infineon Techs. Corp. (formerly Siemens Microelectronics), San Jose, Calif., 1994—2001; ret., 2001; cons., 2001—. Cons. Ultra Fine Assembly Co., Fremont, 1990-2001. Author articles and procs. Served with U.S. Army, 1966-68, Germany. Mem. Am. Phys. Soc. Achievements include research in thermal fatigue in semiconductor packaging; room temperature re-crystallization of tin; Brownian motion of tin whiskers; also patents applied for in micro electronic assembly. Home: 2702 E River Rd Livingston MT 59047 E-mail: richard@wrightsstuff.com.

WRIGHT, RICHARD NEWPORT, III, retired engineering executive, engineering educator; b. Syracuse, NY, May 17, 1932; s. Richard Newport and Carolyn (Baker) Wright; m. Teresa Rios, Aug. 23, 1959; children: John Stannard, Carolyn Maria, Maria, Elizabeth Rebecca, Edward Newport. BCE, Syracuse U., 1953, MCE (Parcel fellow), 1955; PhD, U. Ill., 1962. Jr. engr. Pa. R.R., Phila., 1953-55; instr. civil engring. U. Ill., Urbana, 1957-62, asst. prof., 1962-65, assoc. prof., 1965-70, prof., 1970-74, adj. prof., 1974-79; chief structures sect. Bldg. Rsch. divsn. U.S. Bur. Stds., Washington, 1971—72; dep. dir. Ctr. Bldg. Tech., 1972—73, dir., 1974—91; dir. Bldg. and Fire Rsch. Lab. Nat. Inst. Stds. and Tech., 1991—99; chmn. Bd. Infrastructure and Constructed Environment, 1999—2002; ret., 2002. Pres. Internat. Coun. Bldg. Rsch., Studies and Documentation, 1983—86. Contbr. articles to profl. jours. Govt. ofcl., Gaithersburg, Md., 1971—99; pres. Montgomery Village Found., 1989—90, 2001—03, bd. dirs., 1985—. With AUS, 1955—57. Named Fed. Engr. of the Yr., Nat. Soc. Profl. Engrs.; recipient Henry L. Michel award Industry Advancement Rsch., Civil Engring. Rsch. Found., 1999. Fellow: AAAS; mem.: NAE, ASCE (hon.). Home: 20081 Doolittle St Montgomery Village MD 20886-1354 Office: Dept of Commerce Nat Inst Standards & Tech Bldg And Fire Research Labs Gaithersburg MD 20899-0001 E-mail: richard.n.wright@verizon.net.

WRIGHT, RICHARD OSCAR, III, pathologist, educator, clinical ethicist; b. La Junta, Colo., Aug. 9, 1944; s. Richard O. Jr. and Frances R. (Curtiss) W.; m. Bernale Trout, May 31, 1969; children: Lauren Diane, Richard O. IV. BS in Biology, Midwestern State U., 1966; MS in Biology, U. Houston, 1968; DO, U. Health Sci., 1972; MA in Bioethics, Midwestern U., 2001. Cert. anatomic pathology and lab. medicine Am. Osteo. Bd. Pathology. Sr. attending pathologist Normandy Met. Hosps., St. Louis, 1977-81, Phoenix (Ariz.) Gen. Hosps., 1981-97, dir. med. edn., 1989-92, 96—; clin. asst. prof. pathology Coll. Osteo. Medicine, Western U., Pomona, Calif., 1985—; dir. labs., chmn. dept. John C. Lincoln Hosp., Deer Valley, 1997—, dir. med. edn., dir. labs., 1997—; v.p. Osteo. Postdoctoral Tng. Inst., Kirksville, Mo., 1998—. Clin. instr. pathology Ohio U. Coll. Osteo. Medicine, Athens, 1976—77; clin. prof. pathology Kirksville Coll. Osteo. Medicine, 1985—; vis. lectr. pathology New Eng. Coll. Osteo. Medicine, Biddeford, Maine, 1989—92; clin. asst. prof. pathology Midwestern U. Ariz. Coll. Osteo. Medicine, 1997—; cons. pathologist Phoenix Indian Med. Ctr., 1992—94; adv. bd. Inter Soc. Coun. Pathology, Chgo., 1992—; sec. med. staff John C. Lincoln Hosp.-Deer Valley, 1997—99, v.p. med. staff, 2000—03, pres. med. staff, 2004—; dir. John C. Lincoln Health Network Bd., 2001—. Active Ariz. Rep. Party, Phoenix, Rep. Nat. Coun., Washington; precinctman Dist. 18 Maricopa County, Ariz., 1996-98, Madison Heights Precinct, 1996-98; dir. John C. Lincoln Healthcare Network, 2001—; chmn. bd. trustees Phoenix (Ariz.) Gen. Hosp., 1994-95; ex-officio, trustee, 1995-97; dir. John C. Lincoln Health Network Guild, 1997—; dir., v.p. found. adv. coun. Lincoln Health Found.-Phoenix Gen. Hosp. Osteo. Endowment Fund. Recipient Mead-Johnson award, Nat. Osteo. Assn., 1975. Fellow Am. Osteo. Coll. Pathologists (disting., pres. 1989-90, bd. govs. 1984-91), Coll. Pathologists, Coll. Am. Pathologists, Am. Soc. Clin. Pathologists; mem. Ariz. Osteo. Med. Assn. (del. dist. 2 ho. of dels. 1998), Century Club Alumni Assn., AAAS, Alpha Phi Omega, Rho Sigma Chi, Psi Sigma Alpha. Presbyterian. Office: Anatomic Pathology Assoc 19829 N 27th Ave Phoenix AZ 85027-4001 Office Phone: 623-879-5500. E-mail: rwrigh@jcl.com.

WRIGHT, ROBERT C. broadcast executive; b. Rockville Center, N.Y., Apr. 23, 1943; m. Suzanne Werner, Aug. 26, 1967; children: Kate, Christopher, Maggie. AB in History, Coll. Holy Cross, 1965; LLB, U. Va., 1968. Bar: N.Y. 1968, Va. 1968, Mass. 1970, N.J. 1971. With GE Co., 1969—70, 1973—80, gen. mgr. plastics sales dept., 1978—80; law sec. to chief judge U.S. Dist. Ct., NY, 1970—73; pres. Cox Cable Comm., Atlanta, 1980—83; exec. v.p. Cox Comm., 1980—83; v.p., gen. mgr. housewares, audio and cable TV ops. GE, 1983—84; pres., CEO GE Fin. Svcs. Inc., 1984—86; vice chmn., exec. officer GE, 2000—; pres., CEO NBC, N.Y.C., 1986—2001, chmn., CEO, 2001—04, NBC Universal, 2004—. Bd. dirs. GE, 2000—, Motion Picture & Television Fund Corp., Damon Runyon Cancer Res. Found.; bd. trustees Am. Film Inst., Mus. Television & Radio; hon. trustee Found. Am. Women in Radio & Television; bd. governors New York - Presbyterian Hosp.; mem. Soc. N.Y. Hosp. Inc.; trustee Coll. Holy Cross. Office: GE 3135 Easton Tpke Fairfield CT 06431-0001*

WRIGHT, ROBERT G. engineering executive; m. Mary Brent; children: Brent, Rob. BSCE, N.C. State U., 1968; MBA, U. N.C. Acct. Peat Marwick; contr. Kimley-Horn & Assocs. Inc., pres., 1992—2002, chmn., 2002. Dir. N.C. Citizens for Bus. and Industry. Mem.: Profl. Svcs. Mgmt. Assn. of Triangle Area chpt. CPAs, Consulting Engrs. Coun. N.C., N.C. Assn. CPAs, N.C. State Engring. Found. (bd. dirs. 2000—), Profl. Engrs. N.C. Mailing: PO Box 33068 Raleigh NC 27636-3068 Office: 3001 Weston Pkwy Cary NC 27513

WRIGHT, ROBERT JOSEPH, lawyer; b. Rome, Ga., Dec. 13, 1949; s. Arthur Arley and Maude T. (Lacey) W.; m. Donna Ruth Bishop, Feb. 18, 1972; children: Cynthia Ashley, Laura Christine. BA cum laude, Ga. State U., 1979; JD cum laude, U. Ga., 1983. Bar: Ga. 1983, U.S. Dist. Ct. (no. dist.) Ga. 1983, U.S. Dist. Ct. (mid. dist.) Ga. 1985. Assoc. Craig & Gainer, Covington, Ga., 1983-84, Heard, Leverett & Adams, Elberton, Ga., 1984-86; gen. counsel Group Underwriters, Inc., Elberton, 1987—2002. Mem. editl. staff Ga. Jour. Internat. and Comparative Law, 1981-82. Mem. State Bar Ga. (sec. legal econs. sect. 1987-88, chmn. legal econs. sect. 1988-90), Order of Coif, Masons, Phi Alpha Delta. Baptist. Home: 1030 E Canyon Creek Ct Watkinsville GA 30677-1500

WRIGHT, ROBERT PAYTON, lawyer; b. Beaumont, Tex., Feb. 15, 1951; s. Vernon Gerald and Huberta Read (Nunn) W.; m. Sallie Chesnutt Smith, July 16, 1977; children: Payton Cullen, Elizabeth Risher. AB, Princeton U., 1972; JD, Columbia U., 1975. Bar: Tex. 1975. Ptnr. Baker Botts L.L.P., Houston, 1975—. Author: The Texas Homebuyer's Manual, 1986. Mem. Am. Coll. Real Estate Lawyers (bd. govs. 2002—), State Bar Tex. (chmn. coun. real estate, probate, trust law sect. 1994-95), Houston Bar Assn. (chmn. real estate sect. 1989-90), Tex. Coll. Real Estate Lawyers, Houston Real Estate Lawyers Coun., Houston Club. Episcopalian. Office Phone: 713-229-1237.

WRIGHT, ROBERT ROSS, III, law educator; b. Ft. Worth, Nov. 20, 1931; m. Susan Webber; children: Robert Ross IV, John, David, Robin. BA cum laude, U. Ark., 1953, JD, 1956; MA (grad. fellow), Duke U., 1954; SJD (law fellow), U. Wis., 1967. Bar: Ark. 1956, U.S. Supreme Ct. 1968, Okla. 1970. Instr. polit. sci. U. Ark., 1955-56; mem. firm Forrest City, Ark., 1956-58; ptnr. Norton, Norton & Wright, Forrest City, 1959; asst. gen. counsel, asst. sec. Crossett Co., Ark.; atty. Crossett divsn. Ga.-Pacific Corp., 1960-63; asst. sec. Pub. Utilities Co., Crossett, Triangle Bag Co., Covington, Ky., 1960-62; faculty U. Ark. Law Sch., 1963-70; asst. prof., dir. continuing legal edn. and rsch., then asst. dean U. Ark., Little Rock, 1965-66, prof. law, 1967-70; prof. U. Okla., 1970-77; dean U. Okla. Coll. Law; dir. U. Okla. Law Ctr., 1970-76; vis. prof. U. Ark., Little Rock, 1976-77; Donaghey Disting. prof. U. Ark, 1977-99, Donaghey Disting. prof. emeritus, 1999—. Vis. disting. prof. U. Cin., 1983; vis. prof. law U. Iowa, 1969-70; vis. prof. U. Ark., Little Rock, 1976-77; Ark. commr. Nat. Conf. Commrs. Uniform State Laws, 1967-70; past chmn. Com. Uniform Eminent Domain Code; past mem. Com. Uniform Probate Code, Ark. Gov.'s Ins. Study Commn.; chmn. Gov. Commn. on Uniform Probate Code; chmn. task force joint devel. Hwy. Research Bd.; vice chmn. Okla. Jud. Council, 1970-72, chmn., 1972-75; chmn. Okla. Center Criminal Justice, 1971-76 Author: Arkansas Eminent Domain Digest, 1964, Arkansas Probate Practice System, 1965, The Law of Airspace, 1968, Emerging Concepts in the Law of Airspace, 1969, Cases and Materials on Land Use, 3d edit., 1982, supplement, 1987, 6th edit., 2004, Uniform Probate Code Practice Manual, 1972, Model Airspace Code, 1973, Land Use in a Nutshell, 1978, 4th edit., 2000, The Arkansas Form Book, 1979, 2d edit., 1988, Zoning Law in Arkansas: A Comparative Analysis, 1980, Old Seeds in the New Land: A History and Reminiscences of the Bar of Arkansas, 2001; contbr. articles to profl. jours. Mem. Little Rock Planning Commn., 1978-82, chmn., 1982. Named Ark. Man of Year Kappa Sigma, 1958. Fellow: Am. Coll. Trust and Estate Counsel (acad.), Am. Law Inst.; mem.: ABA (past chmn., exec. coun. gen. practice, solo and small firm sect., former chmn. new pubs. editl. bd., sect. officers conf., ho. of dels. 1994—2000, standing com. fed. jud. improvements 1998—), Pulaski County Bar Assn., Ark. Bar Assn. (life; exec. coun. 1985—88, ho. of dels., chmn. eminent domain code com., past mem. com. new bar ctr., past chmn. preceptorship com., exec. com. young laywers sect.), Okla. Bar Assn. (past vice-chmn. legal internship com., former vice-chmn. gen. practice sect.), U. Ark. Alumni Assn., U. Wis. Alumni Assn., Duke U. Alumni Assn., Omicron Delta Kappa, Phi Alpha Delta, Phi Beta Kappa, Order of Coif. Episcopalian. Home: 249 Pleasant Valley Dr Little Rock AR 72212-3170 Office Phone: 501-225-6171.

WRIGHT, RODNEY H. architect; b. Valparaiso, Ind., June 2, 1931; s. George and Lena May (Cahoon) W.; m. Sydney Sullivan Goelitz, Feb. 16, 1966; children by previous marriage: Weston, Julie-An; stepchildren: Louise Goelitz, Ann Marie Goelitz, Thomas Goelitz. Grad. high sch. With various archtl. firms, 1953-60; pvt. practice architecture, 1960—; architect Hawkweed Group Ltd., Chgo., 1978-85; sole propr. Rodney Wright, Architect; lectr Northwestern U., 1971. Keynote speaker First Solar Symposium, Sao Paulo, Brasil, 1976; presenter 1987 European Conf. on Architecture, Munich, 1st/2d conf. How Successful Directors Manage, 1986-93; speaker for various child care mtgs. and workshops. Author: Hawkweed, 1975, Passive Solar House Book, 1980, Urban Brickyard, Saving Energy Serving Children, 1993. Bd. dirs. Lake County Urban League, 1961-69, chmn., 1961-65; bd. dirs. Uptown Devel. Ctr., Chgo., 1969-73. With U.S. Army, 1950-53 Design fellow Nat. Endowment for Arts, 1975; recipient award U. Wis./Early Childhood Edn. Conf. Fellow AIA (chpt. dir. 1971, co-chmn. task force 1 1969-72, mem. nat. com. community devel. ctrs. 1970-72). Achievements include pioneering in design of passive solar and superinsulated bldgs. Research design of child care environments, including use of color, equipment, natural nonpolluting materials. Address: 2722 Woodrum Ridge Rd Liberty KY 42539-7772 Office Phone: 606-787-8699. E-mail: rwarch@alltel.net.

WRIGHT, RON, retail executive; BS in Econs., Lowell Technol. Inst. (now U. Mass.). Grocery buyer C&S, 1983, v.p. grocery procurement, 1987—90, sr. v.p. grocery and frozen procurement, 1990—95, exec.v.p., COO, 1995—98; pres. C&S Holdings, Brattleboro, Vt., 1998—. Mem. adv. bd. C&S, 1995—; bd. dirs. Food Distbn. Inst.; former chmn. New Eng. Wholesale Food Distbrs. Assn. Gen. co-chmn. Deborah Hosp. Found., 2000. Named Conn. Food Stores Man of Yr., 2000. Office: C&S Wholesale 47 Old Ferry Rd PO Box 821 Brattleboro VT 05302

WRIGHT, RUSSELL D. electrical utility executive; m. June Wright; three children. Degree in Acctg., Bentley Coll.; MBA, U. Mass. Fin. v.p., treas. COM/Energy, pres. electric subsidiaries; pres., COO NSTAR, Boston, 1999—. Bd. dirs. Reed & Barton Corp.; mem. BankBoston South Region Bd., Cape Cod Econ. Devel. Coun. Campaign chmn. United Way Greater New Bedford. Office: NSTAR 800 Boylston St Boston MA 02199

WRIGHT, SANDRA, science administrator; B in Acctg., Calif. State U., Long Beach. V.p., contr. Aerojet; with Litton; corp. v.p., contr. Northrop Grumman Corp., LA, 2001—. Office: Northrop Grumman Corp 1840 Century Park E Los Angeles CA 90067-2199

WRIGHT, SARAH ELIZABETH, writer, poet; b. Wetipquin, Md., Dec. 9, 1928; d. Willis Charles and Mary Amelia (Moore) Wright; m. Joseph Gilbert Kaye, June 17, 1960; children: Michael, Shelley. Student, Howard U., 1945—49, Pa. State Tchrs. Coll., 1950—52, New Sch. Social Rsch., L.I. U.; BS, SUNY, Albany. MacDowell Colony fellow MacDowell Colony, Peterborough, NH, 1973; writer-in-residence Finkelstein Meml. Libr., Spring Valley, NY, 1978, 1979, 1980. Pres. Pen & Brush, Inc., N.Y.C., 1992—93, cons., prodr. Black History Month celebration and commemoration; cons. for creative artists pub. svc. program N.Y. State Coun. on the Arts. Co-author (with L. Smith): Give Me A Child, 1955; author: (novels) This Child's Gonna Live, 1969, A. Philip Randolph, 1990 (N.Y. Pub. Libr. award, 1990). Recipient Disting. Writer award, Middle Atlantic Writers Assn., 1988, The Sarah E. Wright Best Grad. Paper award, Salisburg State U., 1997, Outstanding Contbn. to Am. Lit. award, Zora Neale Hurston Assn., U. Md. Ea. Shore, Princess Anne, Md., 1999. Mem.: Pen Am. Ctr. (events com.), Authors Guild, Inc. (coun. mem. 1980—90), Harlem Writers Guild, Inc. (v.p., pres. 1958—65, award enduring commitment 1998), Nat. Assn. for Poetry Therapy (cert. poetry therapist). Home: 780 West End Ave New York NY 10025

WRIGHT, SCOTT OLIN, federal judge; b. Haigler, Nebr., Jan. 15, 1923; s. Jesse H. and Martha I. Wright; m. Shirley Frances Young, Aug. 25, 1972. Student, Central Coll., Fayette, Mo., 1940-42; LLB, U. Mo., Columbia, 1950 Bar: Mo. 1950. City atty., Columbia, 1951-53; pros. atty. Boone County, Mo., 1954-58; practice of law Columbia, 1958-79; U.S. dist. judge Western Dist. Mo., Kansas City, from 1979. Pres. Young Democrats Boone County, 1950, United Fund Columbia, 1965. Served with USN, 1942-43; as aviator USMC, 1943-46. Decorated Air medal. Mem. ABA, Am. Trial Lawyers Assn., Mo. Bar Assn., Mo. Trial Lawyers Assn., Boone County Bar Assn. Clubs: Rockhill Tennis, Woodside Racquet. Lodges: Rotary (pres. Columbia 1965). Unitarian Universalist. Office: Charles E Whitaker Courthouse 400 E 9th St Ste 8662 Kansas City MO 64106-2684 Office Phone: 816-512-5700.

WRIGHT, SHARON, reporter; BA Broadcast Journalism, Mich. State U. Gen. assignment and state capitol reporter, weekend anchor Sta. WBRE-TV, Wilkes Barre, Pa., 1976—79; gen. assignment reporter, investigative reporter Sta. KMGH-TV, Denver, 1979—81; consumer investigative reporter Sta. WBZ-TV, Boston, 1981—86; gen. assignment reporter, consumer investigative reporter NBC 5, Chgo., 1986—. Recipient Outstanding Alumna award, Mich. State U., 1986, 10 Emmys. Office: NBC 5 454 N Colmbus Dr Chicago IL 60611

WRIGHT, STEPHEN NATHAN, religious organization administrator; b. Springfield, Ill., Oct. 18, 1956; s. William Nathan and Judith Elaine Wright; m. Rebecca Lynne Wright, July 9, 1976; children: Daniel, Jonathan, Mary, Benjamin. BA in Bus. Adminstrn., Cornerstone U., 1991; MDiv, Grand Rapids Bapt. Coll., 1995; postgrad., Grand Rapids Bapt. Sem., 1995—. Ordained min. Bapt. Ch., 1995. Various mgmt. positions The ServiceMaster Co., Downers Grove, Ill., 1977—89; pastor Pleasantview Family Ch., Dowling, Mich., 1992-97; v.p. Kent Cmty. Hosp., Grand Rapids, Mich., 1997-99; pres. David's House Ministries, Wyoming, Mich., 1999—2002, Prospects USA, 2003—. Adj. faculty Cornerstone U., Grand Rapids, 1995—. Grad. Leadership Grand Rapids, 2001. Mem. Hastings Area Ministerial Assn. (sec.-treas., 1996-97, pres. 2000-02), Alliance Christian Providers Individuals with Disabilities (chair 2000-02). Achievements include being two-time Boston Marathon finisher. Home and Office: 2551 Center Rd Caro MI 48723 E-mail: pastorstephen@centurytel.net.

WRIGHT, STEVEN, comedian; b. N.Y.C., Dec. 6, 1955; s. Dolly Wright. Bachelor's, Emerson Coll., 1978. Ind. standup comedian, 1979—. First appearance on The Tonight Show with Johnny Carson, 1982, numerous appearances since then, also Late Night with David Letterman, An Evening at the Improv, various HBO comedy spls. including starring role in On Location; film debut in Desperately Seeking Susan, 1985, other films include So I Married an Axe Murderer, 1993, Speechless, 1994, Natural Born Killers, 1994, Mixed Nuts, 1994, Canadian Bacon, 1994, (voice) Reservoir Dogs, 1992, (voice) The Swan Princess, 1994, For Better of Worse, 1996, Half Baked, 1998, (voice) Babe: Pig in the City, 1998, The Muse, 1999, Loser, 2000, Coffee and Cigarettes, 2003; appeared in TV series Mad About You, 1993; TV series The Downer Channel, 2001; rec. artist (album) I Have a Pony, 1985; standup comedian numerous concerts in clubs, colls. and univs. Office: c/o Agy for Performing Arts Inc 888 7th Ave New York NY 10106-0001*

WRIGHT, SUSAN WEBBER, judge; b. Texarkana, Ark., Aug. 22, 1948; d. Thomas Edward and Betty Jane (Gary) Webber; m. Robert Ross Wright, III, May 21, 1983; 1 child, Robin Elizabeth. BA, Randolph-Macon Woman's Coll., 1970; MPA, U. Ark., 1972, JD with high honors, 1975. Bar: Ark. 1975. Law clk. U.S. Ct. Appeals (8th Cir.), 1975-76; from asst. prof. to assoc. prof. law U. Ark., Little Rock, 1976—83, prof., 1983-90, asst. dean, 1976-78; dist. judge U.S. Dist. Ct. (ea. dist.) Ark., Little Rock, 1990—, chief judge, 1998—. Vis. assoc. prof. Ohio State U., Columbus, 1981, La. State U., Baton Rouge, 1982—83; mem. adv. com. U.S. Ct. Appeals (8th cir.), St. Louis, 1983—88. Author (with R. Wright): Land Use in a Nutshell, 1978, Land Use in a Nutshell, 2d edit., 1985; editor-in-chief: Ark. Law Rev., 1975; contbr. articles to profl. jours. Mem.: Ark. Assn. Women Lawyers (v.p. 1977—78), Am. Law Inst., Pulaski County Bar Assn., Ark. Bar Assn., Am. Judicature Soc., Ark. Women's Forum. Episcopalian. Office: US District Court 600 W Capitol Ave Ste 522 Little Rock AR 72201-3329 Office Phone: 501-604-5100. Business E-Mail: susan_wright@ared.uscourts.gov.

WRIGHT, SYLVIA, government agency administrator; b. Balt. BA, Temple U., 1963, MA, 1965. Group leader Sch. Improvement Program Office U.S. Dept. Edn., Washington, dir. Sch. Support and Tech. Programs, 2001—. Office: US Dept Edn FB6 Rm 3E121 400 Maryland Ave SW Washington DC 20202

WRIGHT, THEODORE OTIS, forensic engineer; b. Gillette, Wyo., Jan. 17, 1921; s. James Otis and Gladys Mary (Marquiss) Wright; m. Phyllis Mae Reeves, June 21, 1942 (div. 1968); children: Mary Suzanne, Theodore Otis Jr., Barbara Joan; m. Edith Marjorie Jewett, May 22, 1968; children: Marjorie Jane, Elizabeth Carter. BSEE, U. Ill., 1951, MS in Engring., 1952; postgrad., Air Command and Staff Coll., 1956-57, UCLA, 1958. Registered profl. engr., Wash. Commd. 2d lt. USAF, 1942-65, advanced through grades to lt. col., 1957, ret., 1965; dep. for engring. Titan SPO, USAF Sys. Command, L.A., 1957-65; rsch. engr. Boeing Co., Seattle, 1965-81; pres. Pretzelwich, Inc., Seattle, 1981—2002; cons., forensic engr. in pvt. practice Bellevue, Wash., 1988—. Adj. prof. U. Wash., 1967—68, Greenriver Jr. Coll., 1967—68; presenter in field. Contbr. articles to profl. jours. Decorated Purple Heart, Air medal. Fellow: NSPE (life; v.p. western region 1985—87); mem.: ASTM (mem. com. E-43 metric practice 1988—, chmn. 2004—), Am. Nat. Metric Coun. (bd. dirs. 1978—94), Wash. Soc. Profl. Engrs. (state pres. 1981—82, Disting. Svc. award 1980, Engr. of the Yr. 1996, Columbia award 1996), Nat. Coun. Weights and Measures, U.S. Metric Assn. (life cert. advanced metrication specialist), Air Force Assn. (life; state pres. 1974—76, 1990—91, Jimmy Doolittle fellow 1975), Order of Daedalians (life), Tau Beta Pi, Pi Mu Epsilon, Eta Kappa Nu. Democrat. Presbyterian. Avocations: flying, photography, classical music, archaeology. Home: 22975 SE Black Nugget Rd Apt 453 Issaquah WA 98029 Personal E-mail: towright1969@msn.com.

WRIGHT, THEODORE PAUL, JR., political science educator; b. Pt. Washington, N.Y., Apr. 12, 1926; s. Theodore Paul and Margaret (McCarl) W.; m. Susan Jane Standfast, Feb. 18, 1967; children: Henry Sewall, Margaret Standfast, Catherine Berrian (Mrs. Matthew H. Smith). BA magna cum laude, Swarthmore Coll., 1949; MA, Yale U., 1951, PhD, 1957. Instr. govt. Bates Coll., Lewiston, Maine, 1955-57; asst. prof., 1957-64; assoc. prof., 1964-65; assoc. prof. polit. sci. Grad. Sch. Public Affairs, SUNY, Albany, 1965-71, prof., 1971-95; prof. emeritus SUNY, Albany, 1995—. Author: American Support of Free Elections Abroad, 1964; contbr. chpts. to books, articles to profl. jours. Trustee Am. Inst. Pakistan Studies, 1973-82; bd. dirs. Am. Coun. Study of Islamic Societies, 1998—, European Conf. on Modern South Asian Studies, 1974-. Served with USNR, 1944-46. Carnegie intern Indian civilization U. Chgo., 1961-62; Fulbright rsch. prof. India, 1963-64; Am. Inst. Indian Studies rsch. fellow India, 1969-70; Am. Coun. Learned Socs. grantee on South Asia in London, 1974-75; Am. Inst. Pakistan Studies/Fulbright rsch. fellow, Pakistan, 1983-84, Fulbright lectr., 1990-91. Mem. South Asian

Muslim Studies Assn. (pres. 1988-2000), Assn. Asian Studies (chmn. N.Y. Conf. on Asian Studies 1988-89), Coun. for Study of Islam and Democracy, Dutch Settlers Soc. of Albany (pres. 1988-90, 98-2001, 1st v.p. 2002-), The New Netherland Project (bd. dirs. 2000-), Adirondack Mountain Club, Phi Beta Kappa (chpt. pres. 1992-93), Phi Delta Theta. Unitarian Universalist. Home: 17 Wellington Way Niskayuna NY 12309 Personal E-mail: wright15@juno.com.

WRIGHT, THEODORE ROBERT FAIRBANK, biologist, educator; b. Kodaikanal, Tamil Nadu, India, Apr. 10, 1928; s. Horace Kepler and Adelaide Caskey (Fairbank) Wright; m. Eileen Marie Yongen, Jan. 6, 1951 (dec. Jan. 2002). AB in Biology, Princeton U., 1949; MA in Biology, Wesleyan U., 1954; PhD in Zoology, Yale U., 1959. Asst. professor biology Johns Hopkins U., Balt., 1959-65; assoc. prof. biology U. Va., Charlottesville, 1965-75, prof. biology, 1975-95; prof. emeritus, 1995—. Vis. scientist Max Planck Inst. for Biology, Tubingen, 1975-76, Devel. Biology Ctr., U. Calif., Irvine, 1982. Editor: The Genetics and Biology of Drosophila, vol. 2a-c, 1978, vol. 2d, 1980, Genetic Regulatory Hierarchies in Development, 1990; co-editor: Advances in Genetics, 1988-92. With U.S. Army, 1950-52. NIH postdoctoral fellow Max Planck Inst. for Biology, Tubingen, Fed. Republic Germany, 1958-59; NSF grantee, 1967-72, 90-93; NIH grantee, 1972-93; Am. Cancer Soc. grantee, 1988-90. Fellow AAAS; mem. AAUP, Genetics Soc. Am., Soc. for Devel. Biology, Va. Acad. Sci., Sigma Xi. Office: U Va Dept Biology Gilmer Hall Charlottesville VA 22903-2477

WRIGHT, THOMAS PARKER, application developer; b. Springfield, Mo., July 3, 1924; s. James Lewis and Vesta Marie (Parker) Wright; m. Elizabeth Jane Smith; children from previous marriage: Jeffrey, Kathleen, Thomas, Ramona, Karen. BA in Math., Henderson State U., 1948; MA in Math., La. State U., 1962. Math., sci. tchr. Hondo (N.Mex.) Union H.S., 1950-53; prin. Westridge (Ark.) H.S., 1954-55; math. tchr. Santa Ana (Calif.) Unified Sch. Dist., 1955-63; math., computer instr. Santa Ana Coll., 1963-71; adminstrv. dean Rancho Santiago CC., Santa Ana, 1971-79; art gallery mgr. Lahaina (Hawaii) Galleries, Inc., 1979-80; pres. Maui Fine Arts, Inc., Kihei, 1981—; computer sci. instr. Maui C.C., Kahului, Hawaii, 1983-94. Multi-media and internet software developer NSF projects; dir. Maui Ednl. Tech. R&D Ctr. Internet Website, 1995—. One-man shows include Maui C.C., 1989, exhibited in group shows at Art Maui, 1984, 1986, 1989; contbr. chapters to books. Pres. Santa Ana Tchrs. Assn., 1960, Santa Ana Coll. Faculty Assn., 1965. 2d lt. USMCR, 1944—46, 1st lt. USMCR, 1950—52. Mem.: NEA, U. Hawaii Profl. Assembly. Republican. Presbyterian. Avocations: water color and acrylic painting, computer art, ocean fishing, photography. Home: 811 S Kihei Rd Apt 3L Kihei HI 96753-9086 Office: Univ Hawaii Nat Ctr of Excellence in High Performanc 590 Lipoa Pkwy Kihei HI 96753 Business E-Mail: wrightt@hawaii.edu.

WRIGHT, VERNON HUGH CARROLL, bank executive; b. Bronxville, N.Y., Sept. 24, 1942; s. Dudley Hugh and Helen Margurite (Carroll) W. m. Lucy Hiss Babb, June 7, 1966; children: Dudley Hugh II, Katherine Babb. BS in acctg., U. Balt., 1969. Sr. v.p. Maryland Nat. Bank, Balt., 1969—91, MNC Fin., Balt., 1990—91; chief corp. fin. officer MBNA Am. Bank N.A., Wilmington, Del., 1992—; sr. vice chmn. MBNA Am. Bank, N.A., 2001—; CFO MBNA Corp., Wilmington, Del., 2003—. Bd. dirs. MBNA Am. Bank, Wilmington, Del. Exec. v.p., chief corp. fin. officer MBNA Corp. With USN, 1962-66. Avocations: farming, teaching. Office: MBNA Am Bank 1100 N King St Wilmington DE 19884-0151 Business E-Mail: vernon.wright@mbna.com.

WRIGHT, WAYNE KENNETH, federal agency statistician; b. Chelsea, Mass., Jan. 26, 1944; s. Wayne K. and Louise Annette (Olson) W.; m. Sharon Kay Brown, Aug. 30, 1964 (div. 1974); 1 child, Trent Edward; m. Linda Susan Berkel, Mar. 15, 1975 (div. 1979); 1 child, Stacey Danielle; m. Bonnie Sue Oberhelman, Apr. 3, 1982; 1 child, Forrest Kenneth. BS in Sociology, U. Iowa, 1971; postgrad., U. North Iowa, 1971-72; cert. in marketing, Atlanta U., 1988. Survey asst. Shive-Hall-Hattery Engring., Cedar Rapids, Iowa, 1962-66; chem. lab technician Wilson Packing Plant, Cedar Rapids, 1966-71; grad. rsch. asst. U. No. Iowa, Cedar Falls, 1971-72, grad. tchg. asst., demographic and econ. stats., 1972-73; survey statistician U.S. Bur. Census, Kansas City, Kans., 1973-74, info. specialist, 1974-83, Charlotte, NC, 1983—; data specialist U.S. Bur. of Census, Charlotte, N.C., 1991—. Named Ky. Col., 1987; named Hon. Citizen, City of Beloit (Wis.), 1974. Fellow Alpha Kappa Delta. Lutheran. Avocations: fishing, camping, hiking, alpine skiing and racing. Home: 1417 Morrocroft Trl Gastonia NC 28054-6499 Office: US Bur Census 901 Center Park Dr Ste 106 Charlotte NC 28217-2935 Office Phone: 704-424-6431. Personal E-mail: wrghtgmp@aol.com. Business E-Mail: w.kenneth.wright@census.gov.

WRIGHT, WILEY REED, JR., lawyer, retired judge, mediator; b. Seattle, Jan. 31, 1932; s. Wiley Reed and Gertrude Ellen (Datson) W.; m. Sally Harrison Clarke, 1955 (div. 1963); children: Wiley III, Margaret, Andrew; m. Roberta Hostinsky, Oct. 18, 1963; children: Cathryn, Amy, Susan. BS in Commerce, Washington and Lee U., 1954, LLB, 1956. Bar: Va. 1956, U.S. Dist. Ct. (ea. dist.) Va. 1956, U.S. Ct. Appeals (4th cir.) 1956, U.S. Supreme Ct. 1993. Law clk. to hon. judge U.S. Dist. Ct., Alexandria, Va., 1958-59; ptnr. Clarke, Richard, Moncure & Whitehead, Alexandria, 1959-68; judge corp. and cir. cts. Alexandria, 1968-79; chief judge cir. ct., 1979-84; ptnr. Hazel & Thomas P.C., Alexandria, 1984-96; mediator McCammon Mediation Group Ltd., Richmond, Va., 1996—. Mem. at large Va. State Bar Coun., 1984-90; mem. Jud. Coun. Va., 1982-84, vice chmn. jud. conf. Va., 1980-82. Assoc. editor: Virginia Circuit Judges Benchbook, 1987. Legal counsel to Alexandria C. of C., 1984-88. 1st lt. U.S. Army, 1956-58. Fellow: Va. Law Found., Am. Bar Found.; mem.: Boyd-Graves Conf., Va. Bar Assn., Omicron Delta Kappa, Phi Delta Phi. Avocations: boating, fishing. Home: 579 Lovers Ln Lancaster VA 22503 Office: McCammon Group Bank of Am Ctr 1111 E Main St Ste 1700 Richmond VA 23219 Office Phone: 804-343-0922.

WRIGHT, WILLIAM COOK, archivist, historian, researcher; b. Jersey City, July 11, 1939; s. Harry Cook and Edna Marguerite Tompkins) W. BA, Gettysburg Coll., 1961; MA, U. Del., 1965, PhD, 1971. Tchr. Salem (N.J.) High Sch., 1961-65; adj. instr. U. Del., Newark, 1968-70; assoc. dir. N.J. Hist. Commn., Trenton, 1970-76; head Bur. Archives and History N.J. State Libr., Trenton, 1976-83; dir. Div. Archives and Records Mgmt., N.J. State Dept., Trenton, 1983-85; chief Bur. Records Mgmt., Trenton, 1985-89, ret., 1989. Coord. state hist. records adv. bd. Nat. Hist. Publs. and Records Commn. 1976-87; mem. adv. com. for papers of William Livingston; sec. N.J. State Records Com., 1976-85, chmn., 1985; mem. adv. bd. dirs. N.J. Archives Series, 1971-86; mem. region 2 adv. coun. Nat. Archives and Records Svc., 1976-77; mem. adv. com. N.J. Newspaper Project, 1983-85, state rev. com. for hist. sites, 1976-79; mem. implementation and planning com. N.J. Supreme Ct., 1982 Author monograph: The Secession Movement in the Middle Atlantic States, 1972; compiler Directory of N.J. Newspapers, 1765-1970; contbr. articles and book revs to profl. jours. Mem. Lawrence Twp. Cultural and Heritage Adv. Com., 1989-92, chmn., 1991. Recipient Award of Recognition N.J. Hist. Commn., 1992. Mem. Acad. Cert. Achivists (cert.). Home: 10 Windsor Ct Sewell NJ 08080-2815 Personal E-mail: wcwright@comcast.net.

WRIGHT, WILLIAM EVAN, physician, consultant; b. N.Y.C., Aug. 1, 1946; s. Samuel and Frances Elnora (Perpente) W.; m. Diana Claire Dryer, Aug. 15, 1970; children: Jason William, Elizabeth Garland, Edwin Samuel. BA in Music, U. Rochester, 1968; MD, U. Pa., 1972; MSPH, U. Utah, 1979; MS in Physiology, Harvard U., 1980. Diplomate Am. Bd Internal Medicine, Am. Bd. Preventive Medicine, Occupl. Medicine, Am. Bd. Ind. Med. Examiners; ACOEM cert. med. rev. officer; cert. FAA med. examiner. Intern LDS Hosp., Salt Lake City, 1972-73, resident, 1973-75, U. Utah Med. Ctr., Salt Lake City, 1978-79, Harvard Sch. Pub. Health, Boston, 1979-80; asst. prof. U. So. Calif., L.A., 1980-86; med. dir. U.S. DEA, Arlington, Va., 1986-96; program mgr., site med. dir. DynCorp, Reston, Va., 1991-96; med. dir. Md. Office, CORE, Inc., Irvine, Calif., 1996—2003; cons. Office of Worker Advocacy, U.S. Dept. Energy, Washington, 2003—. Cons. Westwood Group, 2003—. Contbr. articles to profl. jours. Maj. M.C., U.S. Army, 1975-77. Fellow ACP, Am. Coll. Occupl. and Environ. Medicine, mem. Cosmos Club (Washington), Alpha Omega Alpha. Avocation: performing music. Home: 6801 Wemberly Way Mc Lean VA 22101-1532 Office Phone: 703-556-0092. E-mail: ww40hs@cox.net.

WRIGHT, WILLIAM EVERARD, JR., lawyer; b. New Orleans, Dec. 4, 1949; s. William E. and Claire (Carter) W.; m. Alice Marquez, May 26, 1972; children: Matthew, Caroline. BA, Tulane U., 1971, JD, 1974. Bar: La. 1974. Assoc. Little, Schwartz & Dussom, New Orleans, 1974-76; ptnr. Baldwin & Haspel, New Orleans, 1976-91, Deutsch, Kerrigan & Stiles, New Orleans, 1991—. Mem. La. Bd. Examiners, 1981-84. Mem. ABA (chmn. profl., officers' and dirs. liability law com. 1997-98, constrn. forum), Associated Builders and Contractors (bd. dirs.), La. Bar Assn. (bd. dels. 1985-90), New Orleans Bar Assn. (exec. com. 1980-86, officer 1983-86), New Orleans C. of C. Home: 700 Eleonore St New Orleans LA 70115-3249 Office: Deutsch Kerrigan & Stiles 755 Magazine St Ste 100 New Orleans LA 70130-3672 E-mail: wwright@dkslaw.com.

WRIGHT CARRIER, J. T. business owner; b. McKenzie, Tenn., July 31, 1952; d. Gilbert M. and Mildred B. Wright; m. William W. Carrier III, July 28, 1973; 1 child, Morgan Bailey. BA in Psychology cum laude, Memphis State U., 1974, MA in Ednl. Counseling, Pers. Svcs., 1976, PhD, 1992. Sales rep. API Inc., Memphis, 1980—; casting dir. Theatrics Etc., Memphis, 1980—. Profl. model; casting dir., crew svcs. staff for nat. feature and advt. accts. including Warner Bros., Disney, Phillips 66, Exxon, KC Masterpiece BBQ Sauce, Northwest Airlines; scriptwriter for corp. videos, including Fed. Express, Memphis Bus. Jour.; developer Careers 2000 ednl. video series for adolescents. Pub. Crisis Intervention Studies for Memphis Police Dept.; crew svcs. for U.S. Def. Dept. tng. videos. Co-founder Memphis and Shelby County Film, Tape and Music Commn. Named Miss Memphis, 1972, Top Casting Co. Adweek Mag., 1986. Mem. Nat. Career Devel. Assn. Avocations: environmentalism, ballet, modern dance, theater. Office: Theatrics Etc PO Box 11862 Memphis TN 38111-0862 Office Phone: 901-278-7454.

WRIGHTON, MARK STEPHEN, chemistry professor; b. Jacksonville, Fla., June 11, 1949; s. Robert D. and Doris (Cutler) Wrighton; children: James Joseph, Rebecca Ann. BS, Fla. State U., 1969; PhD, Calif. Inst. Tech., 1972; DSc (hon.), U. West Fla., 1983. From asst. prof. chemistry to provost MIT, Cambridge, 1972—90, provost, 1990—95; prof., chancellor Washington U., St. Louis, 1995—. Bd. dirs. A.G. Edwards, Inc., Cabot Corp., Ionics, Inc., Helix Tech. Corp., Danforth Plant Sci. Ctr., Nidus Ctr. for Sci. Enterprise, Barnes Jewish Hosp., BJC HealthCare, Assn. Am. Univs., Nat. Assn. of Independent Colleges and Univs., St. Louis Regional Chamber and Growth Assn.; mem. Nat. Sci. Bd. Author: Organometallic Photochemistry, 1979. Trustee St. Louis Art Mus., Mo. Bot. Garden, St. Louis Symphony, St. Louis Sci. Ctr.; bd. dirs. United Way Greater St. Louis. Recipient Herbert Newby McCoy award, Calif. Inst. Tech., 1972, Disting. Alumni award, 1992, E.O. Lawrence award, Dept. Energy, 1983, Halpern award in photochemistry, N.Y. Acad. Scis., 1983, Fresenius award, Phi Lambda Upsilon, 1984, Dreyfus tchr.-scholar, 1975—80; fellow, Alfred P. Sloan, 1974—76, MacArthur fellow, 1983—88. Fellow: AAAS; mem.: Acad. of Sci. of St. Louis, Electrochem. Soc., Am. Chem. Soc. (award in pure chemistry 1981, award in inorganic chemistry 1988), Am. Philos. Soc., Am. Acad. Arts and Scis. Office: Washington Univ Office of Chancellor One Brookings Dr Campus Box 1192 Saint Louis MO 63130-4899

WRIGHT PENN, ROBIN, actress; b. Dallas, Apr. 8, 1966; d. Fred Wright; m. Sean Penn, Apr. 27, 1996; children: Dylan Frances, Hopper Jack. Television appearances include The Yellow Rose, 1983-84, Santa Barbara, 1984-87 (Emmy awards Best Ingenue in a Daytime Drama series 1985-87); films include Hollywood Vice Squad, 1986, The Princess Bride, 1987, State of Grace, 1990, Denial, 1991, The Playboys, 1992, Toys, 1992, Forrest Gump, 1994, The Crossing Guard, 1995, Moll Flanders, 1995, Loved, 1996, Moll Flanders, 1996, She's so Lovely, 1997, Loved, 1997 (Seattle Film Festival Award for best actress, 1997), Hurly-Burly, 1998, Just to Be Together, 1999, Message in a Bottle, 1999, Unbreakable, 2000, The Pledge, 2001, The Last Castle, 2001, White Oleander, 2002, The Singing Detective, 2003, A Home at the End of the World, 2004; actor, exec. prodr. (films) Virgin, 2003. Office: United Talent Agy 9560 Wilshire Blvd Beverly Hills CA 90212*

WRIGHT-RIGGINS, AIDSAND F., III, religious organization executive; b. Oct. 31; m. Betty Wright-Riggins; 3 children. BA in Comparative Religions, Calif State Univ., Fullerton; MDiv, Am. Bapt. Sem., W. Berkeley, Calif.; postgrad. and doctoral studies, Sch. Theology, Claremont, Calif.; PhD in Ministry, Va. Union Univ., Richmond, Va.; LHD (hon.), Benedict Coll., Columbia, SC. Lic. Gospel Min. 1960, Ordained Bapt. Ch., 1975. Pastor Macedonia Bapt. Ch., LA; dir., Peace with Justice Ministry So. Christian Leadership Conf. of Greater LA, Calif.; pastor Garden of Gethsemane Bapt. Ch., LA; dean Ecumenical Ctr. for Black Ch. Studies, LA; commd. Am. Bapt. home missionary, 1991; exec. dir. ABCUSA Bd. of Nat. Ministries, Valley Forge, Pa., 1991. Adj. prof, philosophy and preaching Univ. La Verne, Calif. Office: ABC Bd of Nat Ministries PO Box 851 Valley Forge PA 19482-0851*

WRIGLEY, DREW H. lawyer; b. Fargo, N.D., Oct. 1965; BA, U. N.D., 1988; JD, Am. U., 1991. Pros. atty. City of Fargo, 1992—93; asst. dist. atty. Phila. Dist. Atty.'s Office, 1993—98; gen. counsel for pub. policy N.D. Workers Compensation Bur., 1998—99; exec. dir., legal counsel ND Rep. Party, 1999—2000; dep. chief of staff Office of Gov. of N.D., 2000—01; U.S. atty. N.D., 2001—. Office: 655 First Ave N Ste 250 Fargo ND 58102

WRIGLEY, WILLIAM, JR., candy company executive; Asst. to pres. William Wrigley Jr. Co., Chgo., 1985—92, dir., 1988—, v.p., 1991—98, sr. v.p., 1999, pres., CEO, 1999—, chmn., 2004—. Recipient Hunt-Scanlon Human Capitol Advantage award, 2003. Office: William Wrigley Jr Inc 410 N Michigan Ave Chicago IL 60611

WRINKLE, JOHN NEWTON, lawyer; b. Chattanooga, July 31, 1929; s. John Stuart and Anne (Ownbey) W.; m. Louise Rucker Agee, Feb. 1, 1958; children: Anne Blair, Margaret Rucker. BA, Vanderbilt U., 1951; LLB, Yale U., 1955. Bar: Ala. 1955, U.S. Dist. Ct. (no. dist.) Ala. 1956, U.S. Ct. Appeals (5th cir.) 1958, U.S. Ct. Appeals (11th cir.) 1981, U.S. Tax Ct. 1957. Assoc. White, Bradley, Arant, All & Rose, Birmingham, Ala., 1955-63; ptnr. Bradley Arant Rose & White LLP, 1963-92, counsel, 1993—. Coord. pre-law students Birmingham So. Coll., 1989—. Trustee Birmingham Symphony Assn., 1970-79, 80-83, Episcopal Found. Jefferson County, 1994-2000; mem. bd. advisors St. Andrew's Sewanee Sch., 1985—. With USAF, 1951-52. Disting. fellow Birmingham-Southern Coll., 1995—. Fellow Am. Coll. Trust and Estate Counsel; mem. ABA, So. Employee Benefits Conf. (steering com. 1970-73), Birmingham Bar Assn., Assn. of Bar of City of N.Y., Birmingham Com. Fgn. Rels., Redstone Club, Mountain Brook Club, Summit Club, Knickerbocker Club (N.Y.C.), Yale Club (N.Y.C.), Phi Beta Kappa, Phi Alpha Delta. Episcopalian. Home: 2 Beechwood Rd Birmingham AL 35213-3914 Office: Bradley Arant Rose & White LLP 1819 5 Ave N Birmingham AL 35203 Office Phone: 205-521-8000. Business E-Mail: jwrinkle@bradleyarant.com.

WRISTEN, EDWARD L. health facility administrator; BA, Kettering U.; MBA, Ohio State U. Cons., 1976; from mem. staff to pres. First Health Group Corp., Downers Grove, Ill., 1990—2001, pres., 2001—, CEO, 2002—. Exec. com. bd. dirs. Coun. Affordable Quality Healthcare, co-chmn. quality care and patient safety com., 2003—. Office: First Health Group Corp 3200 Highland Ave Downers Grove IL 60515*

WRISTON, WALTER BIGELOW, bank executive, director; b. Middletown, Conn., Aug. 3, 1919; s. Henry M. and Ruth (Bigelow) W.; m. Barbara Brengle, Oct. 24, 1942 (dec.); 1 dau., Catherine B.; m. Kathryn Ann Dineen, Mar. 14, 1968. BA with distinction, Wesleyan U., Middletown, Conn., 1941; LL.D., Wesleyan U., 1984; postgrad., Ecole Francaise Middlebury, Vt., 1941, Am. Inst. Banking, 1946; MA, Fletcher Sch. Internat. Law and Diplomacy, 1942; LLD, Lawrence Coll., 1962, Tufts U., 1963, Brown U., 1969, Columbia U., 1972, Morehouse Coll., 1985; D.C.S., Pace U., 1974; DCS, St. John's U., 1974; DHL, Lafayette Coll., 1975; LLD, Fordham U., 1977, Hamilton Coll., 1996; DCS, NYU, 1977. Officer spl. div. Dept. State, Washington, 1941-42; jr. insp. comptrollers div. Citibank (N.A.), 1946-50, asst. cashier, 1950-52, asst. v.p., 1952-54, v.p., 1954-58; sr. v.p., 1958-60; exec. v.p., 1960-67; pres., 1967-70; chmn., 1970-1984; also dir. Bd. dirs. ICOS Corp., Cygnus, Inc., Vion Pharms., Inc.; trustee Rand Corp., 1973-83; mem. Nat. Commn. on Productivity, 1970-74, Nat. Commn. for Indsl. Peace, 1973-74; chmn. Pres.' Econ. Policy Adv. Bd., 1982-89. Author: Risk and Other Four-Letter Words, 1986, The Twilight of Sovereignty, 1992. Trustee, pres. N.Y.Presbyn.Hosp.; trustee Manhattan Inst. for Policy Rsch. Inc. Served with AUS, 1942-46. Recipient U.S. Presdl. Medal of Freedom, 2004. Mem. Bus. Coun., Links Club, River Club, Sky Club, Palm Beach Bath and Tennis Club, Ocean Club Fla. Office: 425 Park Ave Fl 3 New York NY 10022-3506

WRITER, SHARON LISLE, secondary school educator; b. L.A., Aug. 29, 1939; d. Harlan Lawerance and Emma Mae (Cordery) Lisle; m. Robert Vincent Writer, Dec. 30, 1961; children: Martin Carl, Cynthia Louise, Brian Robert, Scott Andrew. BS, Mt. St. Marys Coll., 1961; MS in Sci. Edn., Calif. State U., Fullerton, 1989; postgrad., U. Calif., Irvine, 1987, Colo. Sch. Mines, 1994. Cert. secondary tchr., Calif. Tchr. St. Mary's Acad., L.A., 1961-62, Escambia High Sch., Pensacola, Fla., 1962-63; rsch. asst. U. So. Calif., L.A., 1964-65, U. Calif., Irvine, 1965-66; tchr. aide Cerro Villa Jr. High Sch., Villa Park, Calif., 1975-76, tchr., 1976-88, Villa Park High Sch., 1988—98, mentor tchr., 1990—97; lectr. Calif. State Univ., Long Beach, 1999—; CA Dir. of Sci. Olympiad, Southern Section, 2000—. Tchr. of yr. com. Orange (Calif.) Unified Sch. Dist., 1992, supt. adv. coun., 1990-1998, curriculum sci. com., 1991-1997. Active Villa Park Womens League, 1975—, Assistance League of Orange, 1991—; project leader, county coord. Orange County 4-H Assn., Anaheim, Calif., 1975-84; bd. sec. Orange County Sci. Fair, 1986-91, awards chmn., 1991-94, pres., 1994—; mem. judging policy adv. com. Calif. State Sci. Fair, 1996-2001. Recipient Outstanding Sci. Tchr. award Orange County Sci. Tchrs. Assn., 1993; named Tchr. of Yr. Villa Park High Sch., 1990, 94, Outstanding Coach Orange County Sci. Olympiad, 1990, 92, 94, 96, Calif. State Sci. Olympiad, 1987. Mem. NSTA (conv. hospitality com. 1989, 90, hospitality co-chair 1994 nat. conv.), Am. Chem. Soc., Calif. Sci. Tchr. Assn., Orange County Sci. Educators Assn. (Disting. Sci. Tchr. award 1993). Roman Catholic. Avocations: tennis, swimming, water-skiing, needlepoint. Home: 18082 Rosanne Cir Villa Park CA 92861-6431 Office: CSULB Dept Sci Edn 1250 Bellflower Blvd Long Beach CA 90840-4501

WROBEL, BRUCE J. energy and utilities company executive; Degree in econ. and mgmt. sci., MIT, 1980. Co-founder US power co. (acquried by Sithe Energies Inc., 1986), 1981; exec. v.p. worldwide bus. devel. and fin. Sithe Energies Inc., 1986—99; founder EnCom, Japan, 1999, Guinea Aluminum Products Corp. (GAPCO); CEO, pres. Herakles Capital Corp., NYC; CEO Sithe Energies Inc., NYC, 2003—. Office: Sithe Energies Inc 335 Madison Ave 28th Fl New York NY 10017*

WROBLE, ARTHUR GERARD, judge; b. Taylor, Pa., Jan. 21, 1948; s. Arthur S. and Sophia P. Wroble; m. Mary Ellen Sheehan, Nov. 19, 1977; children: Sophia Ann, Sarah Jean, Stacey Margaret. BSBA with honors, U. Fla., 1970, MBA, 1971, JD, 1973. Bar: Fla. 1973, U.S. Ct. Appeals (5th cir.) 1974, U.S. Dist. Ct. (so. dist.) Fla. 1974, U.S. Supreme Ct. 1976, U.S. Ct. Appeals (11th cir.) 1981, U.S. Dist. Ct. (mid. dist.) 1982, U.S. Dist. Ct. (no. dist.) Fla. 1986, U.S. Army Ct. Mil. Rev. 1989, U.S. Ct. Mil. Appeals 1990. Ptnr. Burns, Middleton, Farrell & Faust (now Steel, Hector, Davis), West Palm Beach, Fla., 1973—82, Wolf, Block, Schorr & Solis-Cohen, Phila. & West Palm Beach, 1982-87, Scott, Royce, Harris & Bryan, P.A., Palm Beach, Fla., 1987-89, Grantham and Wroble, P.A., Lake Worth, Fla., 1989-92; prin. Arthur G. Wroble, P.A., West Palm Beach, 1992-2000; cir. judge 15th Jud. Ct. Fla., Palm Beach, 2001—. Mem. 15th Jud. Cir. Ct. Nominating Commn., 1979-83; mem. U. Fla. Law Ctr. Coun., 1981-84, 99—, U.S. Magistrate Merit Selection Panel, so. dist. Fla., 1987; mem. adv. bd. alternative sentencing program Palm Beach County Pub. Defender's Office; adj. instr. bus. law Coll. of Boca Raton (now Lynn U.), 1988; mem. U.S. Mil. Acad. Screening com., 16th Dist., Fla., 2001-. Contbr. articles to profl. jours. Bd. dirs. Palm Glades Girl Scout Coun., 1996—. Served to lt. col. JAG, USAR. Named Eagle Scout, Boy Scouts Am., 1962. Mem. ABA, Fla. Bar (bd. govs. young lawyers sect. 1979-83, bd. govs. 1985-89), Palm Beach County Bar Assn. (pres. young lawyers sect. 1978-79, bd. dirs. 1979-81, sec.-treas. 1981-83, pres. 1984-85), Fla. Bar Found. (bd. dirs. 1990-93), Fla. Assn. Women Lawyers, Fla. Coun. Bar Assn. Pres. (bd. dirs. 1986-92), Hispanic Bar Assn. of Palm Beach County, F.M. Cunningham Bar Assn., Guild Cath. Lawyers Diocese Palm Beach, Inc. (pres. 1980-81, bd. dirs. 1981-2001, Monsignor Jeremiah P. O'Mahoney Outstanding Lawyer award 1993), Legal Aid Soc. Palm Beach County, Inc. (bd. dirs. 1981-2000), Univ. Fla. Alumni Assn., Palm Beach County Club (pres. 1983-84), Kiwanis (pres. 1980-81, pres. West Palm Beach found. 1989-2000, dir. 1991—, Citizen of Yr. 1994, George F. Hixon fellowship 1999), KC (grand knight 1978-79), Am. Inns of Ct LIV (West Palm Beach chpt. pres. 1999-2000, bd. dirs. 1995-2000). Roman Catholic. Office: Palm Beach County Cthse 205 N Dixie Hwy West Palm Beach FL 33401-4522

WROBLESKI, JEANNE PAULINE, lawyer; b. Phila., Feb. 14, 1942; d. Edward Joseph and Pauline (Popelak) Wrobleski; m. Robert J. Klein, Dec. 3, 1979. BA, Immaculata Coll., 1964; MA, U. Pa., 1966; JD, Temple U., 1975. Bar: Pa. 1975. Pvt. practice law, Phila., 1975—; pres., shareholder Jeanne Wrobleski & Assocs., LLC, Phila., 1999—. Lectr. Bus. Law Wharton Sch., Phila.; mem. Commn. on Women and the Legal Profession, 1986—89; v.p. Ctr. City Residents' Assn.; Eisenhower Citizen Amb. del. Soviet Union; judge Pro Tem Phila. Ct. Common Pleas; chmn. bd. dirs. Charlotte Cushman Found. Bd. dirs., mem. exec. com. Temple Law Alumni; del. Moscow Conf. on Law and Econ. Coop., 1990; del. to jud. conf. 3d Cir. US Ct. Appeals, 1991; mediator US Dist. Ct. (ea. dist.) Pa., 1996; sec. bd. trustees Phila. Prisons; bd. dirs. South St. Dance Co., Women in Transition; bd. dirs., vice chair The Wilma Theater. Rhea Liebman scholar, 1974. Mem.: ABA, AAUW, Jagiellonian Law Soc. (exec. com.), Am. Judicature Soc., Phila. Bar Assn. (chmn. women's rights com. 1986, com. on jud. selection and retention 1986—87, chmn. appellate cts. com. 1992, bus. cts. task force, com. on bus. litig.), Pa. Bar Assn., Phila. Art Alliance, Nat. Mus. Women in the Arts, Pa. Acad. Fine Arts, Penn Club, Lawyers Club, Founders Club, Cosmopolitan Club, Lambda Iota Tau, Alpha Psi Omega. Democrat. Office: Jeanne Wrobleski & Assocs LLC 1845 Walnut St Fl 24 Philadelphia PA 19103-4708 Office Phone: 215-814-9320. E-mail: jwrobleski@wwdlaw.com.

WROBLEY, RALPH GENE, lawyer; b. Denver, Sept. 19, 1935; s. Matthew B. and Hedvig (Lyon) W.; m. Madeline C. Kearney, June 13, 1959; children: Kirk Lyon, Eric Lyon, Ann Lyon. BA, Yale U., 1957; JD, U. Chgo., 1962. Bar: Mo. 1962. With Bell Tel. Co., Phila., 1957-59; asoc. Stinson, Mag & Fizzell, Kansas City, Mo., 1962-65, mem., 1965-88; ptnr. Bryan, Cave, McPheeters & McRoberts, Kansas City, 1988-92, Blackwell, Sanders, Peper, Martin LLP, Kansas City, 1002—, mem. exec. com., 1992—2000. Bd. dirs. Human Resources Corp., 1971; mem. Civic Coun. Kansas City, 1986-2001; chmn. Pub. Housing Authority of Kansas City, 1971-74; vice chmn. Mayor's Adv. Commn. on Housing, Kansas City, 1971-74; bd. govs. Citizens Assn., 1965—, vice chmn., 1971-75, chmn., 1978-79; bd. dirs. Coun. on Edn., 1975-81, v.p., 1977-79; bd. dirs., pres. Sam E. and Mary F. Roberts Found., 1974-96; trustee Clearinghouse for Mid Continent Founds., 1977-96, chmn. 1987-89; bd. dirs. Bus. Innovation Ctr., 1984-91, vice-chmn. 1987-91, adv. bd. dirs., 1993-99, Midwest Regional Adv. Bd. Inst. Internat. Edn., 1989-93, Internat. Trade Assn., 1989-92, v.p., 1990; vice chmn., bd. dirs. Mid-Am. Coalition on Healthcare, 1991-2003. Mem. Mo. Bar Assn., Yale Club (pres. 1969-71, outstanding mem. award 1967). Republican. Presbyn. (elder) Home: 1015 W 67th Ter Kansas City MO 64113-1942 Office: 2300 Main St Kansas City MO 64108-2416 E-mail: rwrobley@blackwellsanders.com.

WROBLOWA, HALINA STEFANIA, electrochemist; b. Gdansk, Poland, July 5, 1925; came to U.S., 1958, naturalized, 1970; 1 child: Krystyna Wrobel-Knight, grandson Christopher E. Knight. MSc, U. Lodz, Poland, 1949; PhD, Warsaw Inst. Tech., 1958. Chmn. dept. prep. studies U. Lodz, 1950-53; adj. Inst. for Phys., Chemistry Acad. Scis., Warsaw, Poland, 1958-60; dept. dir. electrochemistry lab. energy inst. U. Pa., Phila., 1960-67; dir. electrochemistry lab., 1968-75; prin. research scientist Ford Motor Co., Dearborn, Mich.,

1976-91; pvt. practice cons., 1991. Chmn. Gordon Rsch. Conf. on Electrochemistry, 1983. Contbr. chpts. to books, articles to profl. jours., patent lit. Served with Polish Undeground Army, 1943-45, decorated Mil. Silver Cross of Merit with Swords. Mem. Electrochem. Soc., Internat. Electrochem. Soc., Mensa, Sigma Xi. Personal E-mail: chris777@voicenet.com.

WRONG, DENNIS HUME, sociologist, educator; b. Toronto, Nov. 22, 1923; s. Humphrey Hume and Mary Joyce (Hutton) W.; m. Elaine L. Gale, Nov. 24, 1949 (div. Oct. 1965); 1 child, Terence Hume; m. Jacqueline Conrath, Mar. 26, 1966. BA, U. Toronto, 1945; PhD, Columbia U., 1956. Tchr. Princeton U., 1949-50, Rutgers U., 1950-51, U. Toronto, 1954-56, Brown U., 1956-61; mem. grad. faculty New Sch. Social Research, 1961-63; prof. sociology, chmn. dept. Univ. Coll., NYU, 1963-65; prof. sociology NYU, 1966-94, prof. emeritus, 1994—; retired. Vis. prof. U. Nev., 1965-66; vis. fellow Oxford (Eng.) U., 1978, European U. Inst., 1996-97; Simon vis. prof. U. Manchester, Eng., 1978. Author: American and Canadian Viewpoints, 1955, Population, 1956, 59, Population and Society, 1961, 67, 77, Skeptical Sociology, 1976, Power: Its Forms, Bases and Uses, 1979, 88, 95, Class Fertility Trends in Western Nations, 1980, The Problem of Order: What Unites and Divides Society, 1994, 95, The Modern Condition: Essays at Century's End, 1998, The Oversocialized Conception of Man (reissue of Skeptical Sociology), 1999; editor: Social Research, 1961-64, (with Harry L Gracy)Readings in Introductory Sociology, 1967, 72, 77, Contemporary Sociology: A Journal of Reviews, 1972-74, Max Weber, 1970; mem. editl. bd. Dissent, 1966—; contbg. editor Partisan Rev., 1981-87. Guggenheim fellow, 1984-85, Woodrow Wilson Internat. Ctr. for Scholars fellow, 1991-92. Mem.: Soc. for Advancement of Socio-Econs., Eastern Sociol. Soc., Am. Sociol. Assn. E-mail: dhwrong@voicenet.com.

WROTH, JAMES MELVIN, retired military officer; b. Lincoln, Nebr., Feb. 2, 1929; s. Charles M. and Reba (Sharp) Wroth; m. Donna Mae Benson, June 4, 1951 (dec.); children: Mark, David S., Mary E. Bannon; m. Molly B. Mullan, June 15, 1975; stepchildren: Edward H. Mullan(dec.), Philip C. Mullan. BS, U. Nebr., 1951; MBA, Syracuse U., 1963; postgrad., F.A. Sch., 1957, Command and Gen. Staff Coll., 1962, Armed Forces Staff Coll., 1967, Army War Coll., 1968, Harvard U., 1972. Commd. 2d lt. U.S. Army, 1951, advanced through grades to brig. gen., 1973, 40th inf. divsn., 1952-53; instr. A.A.A. Sch., Ft. Bliss, Tex., 1954-56; with 3d Inf. Div., Ft. Benning, Ga., 1957-61; with Office Chief of Staff U.S. Army, 1963-66; comdg. officer 1st Bn. 31st Arty., Republic of Korea, 1967; exec. asst. to asst. sec. Army U.S. Army, 1968-70; exec. officer I Field Force Vietnam Arty., 1970; comdg. officer 52d Arty. Group, Vietnam, 1971; with Office Dep. Chief Staff for Personnel, Dept. Army, 1972-75; comdg. gen. VII Corps Arty. and Augsburg Germany Mil. Community, 1975-77; comdr. 2d ROTC region, Ft. Knox, Ky., 1977-79; ret., 1979; v.p., dir. mgmt. scis. ops. Gen. Research Corp., McLean, Va., 1979-82; group v.p Info. Systems & Network Corp., Bethesda, Md., 1982-93. Trustee Washington Adventist Hosp. Found., 1989—93. Decorated D.S.M., Legion of Merit, Bronze Star, Air Medal with V device, Army Commendation medal, Vietnamese Gallantry Cross with palm; recipient F. A. Assn. award, 1950, John J. Pershing award, 1951, 40 and 8 award, 1951. Mem.: U.S. Coast Guard Aux. (past flotilla comdr.), Ret. Officers Assn. (past chpt. pres.), Nat Soc. Pershing Rifles (past nat. comdr.), Indian Creek Yacht and Country Club (dir. 2000—03), Indian Creek Yachting Assn. (past commodore), Beta Gamma Sigma, Alpha Kappa Psi. Home: 286 Breezy Pt White Stone VA 22578-2400 E-mail: jim@j-tech.biz.

WROTH, L(AWRENCE) KINVIN, lawyer, educator; b. Providence, July 9, 1932; s. Lawrence Counselman and Barbara (Pease) W.; m. Susan Collins, May 2, 1958 (div. 1972); children: Ann K., Caroline D., Eliza H.; m. Deborah Bethell, Aug. 10, 1972; 1 dau., Katharine L.; stepchildren— John H., David H., Elizabeth T. and Sarah B. Zobel. BA, Yale U., 1954; LLB, Harvard U., 1960. Bar: Mass. 1960, Maine 1974. Teaching fellow, asst. prof. law Dickinson Sch. Law, 1960-62; rsch. assoc. Harvard U., 1962-64; assoc. prof. law U. Maine Sch. Law, Portland, 1964-66, prof., 1966-96; assoc. dean Sch. Law U. Maine, 1977-78, acting dean, 1978-80, dean, 1980-90; prof. Vt. Law Sch., 1996—, dean, 1996—2004, pres., 2003—04. Rsch. fellow Charles Warren Center Studies in Am. History, Harvard U., 1968-74; cons. civil and probate procedure, profl. and jud. responsibility, and ct.-bar rels. Maine Supreme Jud. Ct., 1967-96; cons. civil, probate, family ct. and criminal procedure and evidence Vt. Supreme Ct., 1969— Author (with R.H. Field and V.L. McKusick) Maine Civil Practice, 2d edit., 1970; editor-in-chief: Province in Rebellion, 1975; editor: (with H.B. Zobel) Legal papers of John Adams, 1965; reporter: Vermont Rules of Civil Procedure, 1971, Vermont Rules of Criminal Procedure, 1974, Maine Rules of Probate Procedure, 1980, (with J. Dooley) Vermont Rules of Evidence, 1982, Maine Code of Judicial Conduct, 1993, Vermont Code of Judicial Conduct, 1994. Pres. Greater Portland Landmarks, Inc., 1966—69, adv. trustee, 1969—85; adv. coun. Nat. Trust Hist. Preservation, 1967—70; mem. Maine Commn. on Legal Needs, 1989—90, Commn. to Study Future of Maine's Cts., 1991—93, Commn. on Future of Vt.'s Judiciary, 1998—99, Vt. Bus. Roundtable, 1998—2004; bd. dirs. Maine Bar Found., 1983—89, sec., 1983—86, v.p., 1987, pres., 1988, fellow, 1991; bd. dirs. Pine Tree Legal Assistance Inc., 1985—96, Nat. Assn. IOLTA Programs, Inc., 1988—90, Portland Symphony Orch., 1990—98, v.p. ops. and resources, 1991—95, pres., 1995—96. Recipient Littleton-Griswold prize Am. Hist. Assn., 1966, Howard H. Dana award Maine Bar Found., 1991, Justice Louis Scolnik award Maine Civil Liberties Union, 1992, Herbert Harley award Am. Judicature Soc., 1994. Fellow Am. Bar Found.; mem. ABA, Maine Bar Assn. (Disting. Svc. award 1990), Am. Law Inst., Vermont Bar Assn., Colonial Soc. Mass., Mass. Hist. Soc. Office: Vt Law Sch PO Box 96 South Royalton VT 05068-0096 Office Phone: 802-831-1268. E-mail: kwroth@vermontlaw.edu.

WROTTEN, MARYLEAN, medical coordinator, counselor; d. Evelyn Saxton and Perry Elmore; 1 child, Evelyn DeShawn Wroten. Grad., Audrey Cohn Coll., 1984. Approved medical authorize personnel Fedn. Puerto Rican Org, 1991; Strategist crisis Intervention Personnel Fedn. Puerto Rican Org, 1991, cert. CPR-First Aid Fedn. Puerto Rican Org, 2004. Med. coord. Fedn. Multicultural Orgn., NY, 1999—. Author: (poetry) I Love God (Editor's Choice award, 2004). Youth coord. Jackson Dem. Club, Bronx, 1995—99; Sunday sch. tchr. Praying Band Of Faith, Bronx, 1985—89; proposal rev. com. Neighborhood Adv. Bd., Bronx, 1995—96; del. 1199 Nat. Health&Human Employees Union, NYC, 1996—2004. Democrat-Npl. Pentecostal. Avocations: hiking, reading, volunteering, singing. Home: 1195 Fulton Ave Bronx NY 10456 Office: Federation Multicultural Organization 2 VanSinderen Ave Brooklyn NY 11207

WRUBEL, BARBARA, lawyer, educator, former editor; b. N.Y.C., Aug. 16, 1942; d. Harold and Rose (Friedberg) Kolsky; m. Peter Stefan Wrubel, July 30, 1966; 1 dau., Dana. B.A. cum laude, Queens Coll., N.Y.C., 1964; postgrad. U. Calif.-Berkeley, 1964-65; J.D., Fordham U., 1981. Bar: N.Y. 1982, U.S. Dist. Ct. (so. dist.) N.Y. 1982, U.S. Dist. Ct. (ea. dist.) N.Y. 1983. Atty., Skadden, Arps, Slate, Meagher & Flom, N.Y.C., 1981; adj. assoc. prof. law NYU, N.Y.C., 1982—, Fordham U. Sch. Law, N.Y.C., 1981—; lectr. Am. Law Inst., Practising Law Inst., ABA, 1982—; editor edn. books, N.Y.C., 1965-78; freelance photographer. Author: (with Leon J. Saul) Psychodynamics of Hostility, 1976; columnist (with Sheila L. Birnbaum) on products liability Nat. Law Jour., 1981—; contbr. articles to law publs.; editor Law Rev. Fordham U., 1980-81. Mem. Assn. Bar City N.Y., ABA, N.Y. Bar Assn., Fed. Bar Council, Women's Bar Assn. State N.Y. Home: 351 E 84th St New York NY 10028-4423 Office: Skadden Arps Slate Meagher & Flom 4 Times Sq Fl 24 New York NY 10036-6595

WRUBLE, BERNHARDT KARP, lawyer; b. Wilkes-Barre, Pennsylvania, Mar. 21, 1942; s. Maurice and Ruth Yvonne (Karp) W.; m. Judith Marilyn (Eyges), Nov. 16, 1968 (div. 1987); children: Justine, Vanessa, Alexis; m. Jill (Diamond), Nov. 24, 1990; children: Mattia, Austin. BA in Polit. Sci., Williams Coll., Williamstown, Mass., 1963; JD, U. Pa., 1966; postgrad., N.Y. Univ., 1972—74, Harvard U., 1978. Bar: Conn.; 2003, U.S. Dist. Ct. (so. dist.) N.Y., 1969, U.S. Dist. Ct. (ea. dist.) N.Y., 1972, U.S. Ct. Appeals (2d cir.), 1972, U.S. Supreme Ct., 1972, U.S. Ct. Appeals (7th cir.), 1974, U.S. Ct. Appeals (D.C. and 4th cir.), 1984, U.S. Ct. Appeals (5th cir.), 1985, U.S. Ct. Appeals (11th cir.) 1986. Law clk. to presiding judge U.S. Ct. Appeals (3d cir.), 1966—67; assoc. Simpson, Thacher, and Bartlet, N.Y.C., 1968—73, ptnr., 1974—77; prin. dep. gen. counsel U.S. Dept. Army, Washington, 1977—79; dir. Office Govt. Ethics, Washington, 1979; exec. asst. to sec. and dep. sec. U.S. Dept. Energy, Washington, 1979—81; dir. President's Interagy. Coal Export Task Force, Washington, 1980—81; ptnr. Verner, Liipfert, Bernhard, McPherson, and Hand, Washington, 1981—99; sr. v.p. legal affairs N.W. Airlines, St. Paul, 1999—2001. Bd. dir. Epilepsy Found. Am., 1983, chmn., 1991. Hartford County Pro Bono Award, 2004. Mem. ABA, D.C. Bar Assn., N.Y. State Bar Assn., Williams Coll. Alumni Assn. (pres. Washington chpt. 1986-91), Williams Coll. Soc. Alumni Assn. (exec. com. 1988-91). Democrat. Personal E-mail: bkwruble@yahoo.com.

WRUBLE, BRIAN FREDERICK, private investor; b. Kalamazoo, Apr. 18, 1943; s. Milton and Rose Muriel (Nathanson) W.; m. Susan Roberta Shifrin, June 23, 1968 (div. Oct. 1984); children: Amy Carolyn, Jordan Todd; m. Kathleen Wilson Bratton, Apr. 20, 1985; 1 child, Henrietta Zane Bratton. BEE, Cornell U., 1965, MEE, 1966; MBA with distinction, NYU, 1976. Field engr. Sperry Gyroscope Corp., Lake Success, NY, 1966—70; v.p. Alliance One Instl. Svcs., Inc., N.Y.C., 1970-76, H. C. Wainwright and Co., Inc., N.Y.C., 1976-77, Wainwright Securities, Inc., N.Y.C., 1977; v.p., co-mgr. fundamental equities rsch. Smith Barney, Harris Upham & Co., N.Y.C., 1977-79; exec. v.p. chief fin. ops. Equitable Life Assurance Soc. U.S., N.Y.C., 1979-92; chmn., pres., CEO Equitable Capital Mgmt. Corp., N.Y.C., 1985-92; chief investment officer Equitable Life Assurance Soc. U.S., N.Y.C., 1991-92; pres., COO, dir. Delaware Mgmt. Holdings, Inc., 1992-95; pres., CEO The Delaware Group, 1992-95; pres., COO Delaware Mgmt. Co., 1992-95; chmn. Delaware Distributors, Inc., 1992-95; chmn., CEO Delaware Svc. Co., Inc., 1992—95; gen. ptnr. Odyssey Ptnrs., L.P., N.Y.C., 1995—; mng. prin. Odyssey Investment Ptnrs., LLC, NYC, 1997—98, spl. ltd. ptnr., 1999—2004. Chmn., pres. Equitable Realty Assets Corp., Atlanta, 1983—92; v.p., dir. TELMARI, Inc., N.Y.C., 1982—83, Equitable Variable Life Ins. Co., 1987—92; chmn. Equico Capital Corp., N.Y.C., 1984—92; CEO Equitable Gen. of Okla., Oklahoma City, 1985—86; trustee Equitable Retirement Plans, N.Y.C., 1980—86, Oppenheimer Funds, 2001—; pres. Hudson River Trust, 1991—92, Equitable Funds, 1991—92; investment adv. bd. Zurich Fin. Svc. Group. Vice-chmn. Boys Choir of Harlem, N.Y.C., 1984—92; vice chmn. Corp. Ptnrs. Phila. Art Mus., 1993—95; bd. govs. Jerome Levy Econ. Inst., 1990—2001; bd. dirs. Harlem Youth Devel. Found., 1989—92, Corp. Ptnrs. Phila. Art Mus., 1992—95, The Jackson Lab., Inc., 1990—, Inst. for Advanced Study, 1992—. Recipient Heroes award Boys Choir Harlem, 1990, Founders award, 1993. Mem.: IEEE, Phila. C. of C. (bd. dirs. 1992—95, mem. exec. com. 1993—95), Inst. CFAs (CFA, bd. trustees 1992—98, vice chmn. 1993—94, chmn. 1994—95, bd. trustees rsch. found. 1994—95, 2000—02, assoc. editor CFA Digest 1983—), N.Y. Soc. Security Analysts, Assn. Investment Mgmt. and Rsch. (gov. 1992—98, C. Steward Sheppard award 2000). Republican. Jewish. Avocations: skiing, amateur radio. Personal E-mail: bwruble@ix.netcom.com.

WRUCK, ERICH-OSKAR, retired foreign language educator, administrator; b. Gross-Kroessin/Pomerania, Germany, Oct. 29, 1928; came to U.S., 1952, naturalized, 1954; s. Erich Albert and Erna (Kroening) W.; m. Esther Emmy Schmidt, Oct. 3, 1953; children: Eric Gordon, Karin Esther, Krista Elisabeth. BA magna cum laude, Rutgers U., 1959; MA, 1961, PhD, 1969. Asst. instr. Rutgers U., New Brunswick, N.J., 1959-62; asst. prof. Davidson (N.C.) Coll., 1962-69, assoc. prof., 1969-73, prof., chmn. dept. German, 1983-87; established exch. program Marburg (Germany) U., 1963; with U. Würzburg, Germany, 1985; dir. Davidson abroad program Marburg, 1966-67, 71-72; jr. yr. abroad program Würzburg, 1986-87, 89-92; ret., 1994. Cons. faculty U.S. Army Command and Gen. Staff Coll., 1974-85. 1st lt. U.S. Army, 1953-57, to col. USAR, 1988. Recipient Julius Maximilians medal U. Wuerzburg, 1987; named to Arty. OCS Hall of Fame, 1996; Henry Rutgers scholar. Mem. Goethe Assn., Freies Deutsches Hochstift, Schiller Assn., Goethe Soc. of N. Am. (charter), Soc. German Am. Studies. Lutheran. Avocations: painting, photography, soaring, skiing, running.

WRUCKE-NELSON, ANN C. elementary school educator; b. Mankato, Minn., Nov. 5, 1939; d. G.F. and Dorothy (Thomas) Wrucke; children: Chris, Dor-Ella. BS, Mankato State U., 1961; MLA, So. Meth. U., 1974; postgrad., U. Minn., 1963, Tex. Woman's U., EdD in Early Childhood Edn., 1992. Cert. elem., kindergarten, ESL, history tchr., Tex. Tchr. Rochester (Minn.) Pub. Schs., Christ the King Sch., Dallas; dir., tchr. Norway Christian Presch., Dallas; Every Student Learns Lang. program kindergarten tchr. Dallas Ind. Sch. Dist., 1971—. Tchr. summer session Tex. Woman's U., 1991; presenter in field. Prodr.: (video) A Year of Language Learning, 1990. Sunday sch. tchr. Holy Trinity Ch. Recipient Tchr. of Yr. award, 1989, Tex. TESOL scholarship, 1994; Bill Martin Literacy Conf. scholar; named ESL Tchr. of Yr., 1991. Mem. Internat. Reading Assn., Assn. for Childhood Edn. Internat., So. Assn. on Children Under Six, TESOL, Kindergarten Tchrs. Tex., Tex. TESOL, Dallas Assn. for Edn. of Young Child, Phi Delta Kappa. Office: 201 N Adams Ave Dallas TX 75208-4624

WSANDOVAL, BRIAN, state attorney general; m. Kathleen Sandoval; 3 children. Grad., U. Nev.; law degree, Ohio State U., 1989. Mem. Assembly, 1995—97; chmn. Nev. State Gaming Commn.; atty. gen. Nev., 2002—. Named Public Lawyer of the Yr., Nevada St. Bar Assoc., 2004; recipient Torch of Liberty, Anti-Defamation League, 2003. Republican. Office: Old Supreme Ct Bldg 100 N Carson St Carson City NV 89701

WU, ALBERT W. medical educator; b. N.Y.C., July 27, 1957; s. Ray J. and Christina (Chan) W. BA, Cornell U., 1980, MD, 1984; MPH, U. Calif. Berkeley, 1990. Resident in medicine Mt. Sinai Hosp., N.Y.C., 1984-86, U. Calif. San Diego, 1986-87, clin. instr., 1987-88; Robert Wood Johnson scholar U. Calif. San Francisco, 1988-90; asst. prof. Johns Hopkins U., Balt., 1990-96, assoc. prof., 1996—. Pres. Internat. Soc. for Quality of Life Rsch., 2003—. Office: Johns Hopkins U 624 N Broadway Baltimore MD 21205-1900 E-mail: awu@jhsph.edu.

WU, BIN, industrial engineering, professor; b. Han Dan, He Bei, China, Dec. 17, 1957; s. BingZe and Jing Yi Wu; children: Daniel, Christopher, Anthony. BSc, Brunel U., London, 1984, PhD, 1988. Mfg. sys. analyst Dowty Indsl. Group, Cheltenham, Gt. Britain, 1984-89; assoc. prof. Brunel U., London, 1988-95; prof. Cranfield (Eng.) U., 1995-2001, U. Mo., 2001—. Author: Manufacturing Systems Design and Analysis, 1992, Manufacturing and Supply Systems Management, 2000, Handbook of Manufacturing and Supply Systems Design, 2001; editor-in-chief Internat. Jour. Mfg. Sys. Design, 1993. Recipient Univ. prize Brunel U., 1992, Spl. Acad. prize Dowty Indsl. Group, 1994. Achievements include devel. of unified conceptual framework of mfg. and supply sys. mgmt. Office: Dept Indsl and Mfg Sys Engring 3437 Engring Bldg East Columbia MO 65211 Office Phone: 573-882-5540. Office Fax: 573-882-2693. Business E-Mail: wubi@missouri.edu.

WU, CHAI WAH, research scientist; b. Hong Kong, China; BS in Computer Engring., BA in Cognitive Sci., Lehigh U., 1990; MSEE, U. Calif., Berkeley, 1991, MA in Math., 1994, PhD in Elec. Engring., 1995. Rschr. U. Calif., Berkeley, 1996; postdoc IBM, Yorktown Heights, NY, 1996—97, rsch. staff mem., 1997—. Author: (book) Synchronization in Coupled Chaotic Circuits and Systems, 2002. Fellow: IEEE (assoc. editor 1997—99, 2002—, Fellow 2001); mem.: Am. Math. Soc. Achievements include invention of several inventions in field. Office: IBM T J Watson Rsch Ctr PO Box 218 Yorktown Heights NY 10598

WU, DAVID, congressman; b. Taiwan, Apr. 8, 1955; came to U.S., 1961; m. Michelle Wu; children: Matthew, Sarah. BS, Stanford U., 1977; student, Harvard Med. Sch.; JD, Yale U., 1982. Ptnr. Cohen & Wu, 1988-98; mem. edn. and workforce com., sci. com. 106th-108th Congress from 1st Oreg. dist., 1999—; mem. edu. workforce com., science com. Mem. Congl. Asian Pacific Caucus (chair), New Democrat Coalition Democrat. also: 620 NW Main Ste 606 Portland OR 97205 Office: 1023 Longworth House Office Building Washington DC 20515

WU, FRANK H. law educator, journalist; b. Cleve., Aug. 20, 1967; s. Hai and Grace (Ma) Wu. BA, Johns Hopkins U., 1988; JD, U. Mich., 1991. Bar: Calif. 1992, DC 1995. Law clerk to Honorable Frank Battisti, Cleve., 1991—92, assoc. Morrison & Foerster, San Francisco, 1992-94; fellow Stanford U. Law Sch., Palo Alto, Calif., 1994-95; asst. prof. Howard U. Law Sch., Washington, 1995—98, assoc. prof., 1998—2002, prof., 2001—04, clinic dir., 2000—02; dean Wayne State U., Detroit, 2004—. Scholar-in-residence Deep Springs Coll., 2001—03; vis. prof. U. Mich., 2002—03; adj. prof. Columbia U., 2002—04. Co-author: (book) Beyond Self Interest, 1996, Race, Rights and Reparation: Law and the Japanese American Internment, 2001; contbg. author: book The Affirmative Action Debate, 1996, Illegal Immigration Viewpoints, 1996; author: Yellow: Race in Amercia Beyond Black and White, 2001. Chmn. DC Human Rights Commn., 2001—03, DC Ct. Appeals Bd. Profl. Responsibility, 2003—04; bd. dirs. Leadership Conf. on Civil Rights Edn. Fund, 2004—; trustee Gallaudet U., 2000—. Fellow: ABA Found.; mem.: Com. of 100, Am. Law Inst., Asian Pacific ABA (dir. ednl. fund 1995—98). Home: 5160 Linnean Ter NW Washington DC 20008 Office: Wayne State Univ Law Sch 471 W Palmer St Detroit MI 48202 Office Phone: 313-577-3933.

WU, GUOFA FELIX, computer company executive; b. Nanchang, Jiangxi, China, Oct. 19, 1945; s. Luxing Wu and Guande Xiong; m. Juan Liu, Jan. 1987; 1 child, Libby; m. Youming Zhong, June 1971 (div. Nov. 1985); 1 child, Zhehui. M in Engring., Tsinghua U., Beijing, China, 1984; M in Sci., U. Toledo, 1993; PhD, Harrington, Eng., 1995. Pres. Global Internet Corp., Boston, 1999—. Tech. specialist Nat. Transp. Systems Ctr. of U.S. Dept. Transp., Cambridge, Mass., guest prof. Xi'an Jiaotong U., 2001—, Harbin Inst. Tech., China, 2002—. Fellow. North Am. Soc.Experts and Entrepreneurs (pres. 2001—); mem.: Pres. Bus. Commn. Home: 36 Parsons St Boston MA 02135

WU, H. DENIS, communications educator; b. Kaohsiung, Taiwan, Aug. 21, 1967; m. Jenny Chen. BA, Nat. Taiwan U., Taipei, 1989; MA, U. Pa., 1993; PhD, U. N.C., 1998. Assoc. prof. La. State U., Baton Rouge. Mem.: World Assn. Pub. Opinion Rsch., Internat. Communication Assn., Assn. Edn. Journalism and Mass. Communication. Office: La State U Sch Mass Communication Baton Rouge LA 70803 Office Phone: 225-578-2095. Business E-Mail: hdeniswu@lsu.edu.

WU, HARRY PAO-TUNG, retired librarian; b. Jinan, Shandong, China, May 1, 1932; arrived in U.S., 1960; s. James Ching-Mei and Elizabeth Hsiao (Lu) Wu; m. Irene I-Len Sun, June 23, 1961; children: Eva Pei-Chen, Walter Pei-Liang. BA, Nat. Taiwan U., Taipei, 1959; student, Ohio State U., 1962; MLS, Kent State U., 1966. Archive and libr. asst. Taiwan Handicraft Promotion Ctr., Taipei, 1959-60; student asst. Kent State U. Libr., 1960-61; reference libr. Massillon (Ohio) Pub. Libr., 1964-65, acting asst. dir., 1965, asst. dir., head adult svcs., 1966; dir. Flesh Pub. Libr., Piqua, Ohio, 1966-68, St. Clair County Libr. Sys., Port Huron, Mich., 1968-96; founder, dir. Blue Water Libr. Fedn., Port Huron, 1974-96; ret., 1996. Pres. Mich. Libr. Film Cir., Lansing, 1977—79; mem. St. Clair County Literacy Project Com., 1986—96. Cmty. mem. editl. bd. Times Herald, 1998—99. Bd. dirs. Mich. Waterways Coun. Girl Scouts U.S., Port Huron, 1985—86, Blue Water Reading Coun., 1987—88, United Way St. Clair County, Mich., 1990—91; trustee Libr. Mich., 1992—95; mem. sister city com. City of Port Huron, 2002—04. Mem.: ALA, Chinese-Am. Librs. Assn., Detroit Suburban Librs. Roundtable, Assn. Ednl. Comm. and Tech., Am. Mgmt. Assn., Mich. Libr. Assn., Port Huron Internat. Club (pres. 1988), Rotary (dir. 1972—74, 1988—90, Paul Harris fellow 1988). Home: 1518 Holland Ave Port Huron MI 48060-1511

WU, HSIU KWANG, economist, educator; b. Hankow, China, Dec. 14, 1935; came to U.S., 1952, naturalized, 1963; s. Kao Cheng and Edith (Huang) W.; m. Kathleen Gibbs Johnson, Aug. 17, 1968. Grad., Lawrenceville Sch., 1954; AB, Princeton U., 1958; MBA, U. Pa., 1960, PhD, 1963. Prof., group coordinator fin., econs. and internat. bus. Boston U., 1968-72; prof., chmn. fin., econs. and legal studies faculty U. Ala., 1972-81, Lee Bidgood prof. fin. and econs., 1978-97, Ala. Banker Edn. Found. Banking Chair prof., 1973-78, prof. emeritus fin., 1997—; econ. adviser Office of Comptroller of Currency, U.S. Treasury, 1966-69, 75-80; dir. Ala. Fed., 1984-88, SECOR Bank FSB, 1988-93, chmn. bd., 1992-93. Cons. instl. investor study SEC, 1969-70; mem. com. examiners undergrad. program for counseling and evaluation test in bus. Ednl. Testing Service, 1971, 77 Co-editor: Elements of Investments, 2d rev. edit, 1972; Contbr. articles to law and econ. jours. Sloan Faculty fellow Sloan Sch. Mgmt., Mass. Inst. Tech., 1965-66 Mem. Am. Fin. Assn., Fin. Mgmt. Assn. Home: 3201 Old Barn Ct Ponte Vedra Beach FL 32082-3713

WU, HUAN-TER, statistician; arrived in USA, 1971, naturalized, 1978; s. Chin-mu and Lin-lun Wu; m. Ling-Ling Wu, July 18, 1976; 1 child, Joy. BS(hon.), Nat. Chung Hsing U, Taichung, Taiwan, 1964; MS, Va. Poly. Inst. & State U, Blacksburg, Va., 1975, PhD, 1979. Cons. Stats. Cons. Lab., Va. Poly. Inst. & State U, Blacksburg, Va., 1973—79; asst. prof. statis. State U of NY, Oneonta, NY, 1980—82; prin. Biostatis. R.W. Johnson Pharm. Rsch. Inst., Raritan, NJ, 1982—95; statis. cons. Bristol-Myers Squibb Pharm. Rsch. Inst., Princeton, NJ, 1995—96; asst. dir. of Biometrics Ohmeda Inc./Baxter Healthcare Corp., Liberty Corner, NJ, 1996—98; VP Sinney Assoc., Princeton Jct., NJ, 1998—. Cons. Bristol-Myers Squibb Pharm. Rsch. Inst., Princeton, NJ, 1995—96, Baxter Healthcare Corp., New Providence, NJ, 1999—2004. Mem.: Am. Statis. Assoc. (assoc.). Avocations: movies, music, fishing, picnics. Home: 6 Baylor Place Princeton Junction NJ 08550 Office: Sinney Associates Inc 6 Baylor Place Princeton Junction NJ 08550 E-mail: htwu03@yahoo.com.

WU, JAMES CHEN-YUAN, aerospace engineering educator; b. Nanking, China, Oct. 5, 1931; came to U.S., 1953, naturalized, 1963; s. Chien Lieh and Cheng-Ling Wu; m. Mei-Ying Chang, Sept. 7, 1957; children— Alberta Yee-Hwa, Norbert Mao-Hwa. Student. Nat. Taiwan (Formosa) U., 1949-52; BS, Gonzaga U., 1954; postgrad., Columbia U., 1954; MS (univ. fellow), U. Ill., 1955, PhD, 1957. Engr. Wah Chang Corp., N.Y.C., 1954; researcher Mass. Inst. Tech. at Cambridge, 1957; asst. prof. Gonzaga U., Spokane, Wash., 1957-59; research specialist Douglas Aircraft Co., 1959-65, group leader, 1960-61, supr., 1961-62, br. chief, 1963-65; prof. aerospace engring. Ga. Inst. Tech., 1965-96; pres. Applied Aero, LLC, 1996—. Cons. N.Am. Aviation Co., Geophys. Tech. Corp., European Atomic Energy Commn., Ispra, Italy, European Atomic Energy Commn. (research center), U.S. Army Research Office, Durham, S.C. Contbr. articles to profl. jours. Chmn. bd. dirs. Chinese-Am. Inst. Recipient profl. achievement award Douglas Aricraft Co., 1963, Outstanding Tchrs. award Gonzaga U., 1959; Assoc. fellow Am. Inst. Aeros. and Astronautics Mem. Am. Soc. Engring. Sci. (founding), Soc. Indsl. and Applied Math. (vice-chmn. Pacific N.W. 1958-59), Am. Astron. Soc. (sr.), Am. Phys. Soc., Nat. Assn. Chinese Ams. (pres. Atlanta chpt.), Sigma Xi, Tau Beta Pi, Sigma Alpha Nu. Office: Sch Aerospace Engring Georgia Inst Tech 48365 Avalon Heights Ter Fremont CA 94539-8005

WU, JIA HAO, transportation executive, researcher, consultant; PhD, U of Montreal, Montreal, Que., Can., 1988—91; MS engring., Shanghai U of Sci. and Tech., Shanghai, 1982—88, BS engring., 1978—82. Pres. Traffic Moves, Pleasanton, Calif., 2002—; dir. of its TJKM Transp. Consultants, Pleasanton, Calif., 2000—. Mng. dir. INRO Solutions, Montreal, Que., Canada, 1999—2000; project mgr. INRO Consultants, Montreal, Montreal, Canada, 1991—99; invited rschr. U of Montreal CRT, Montreal, Que., Canada, 1994—2000, rsch. assoc., 1988—91; asst. prof. Shanghai U of Sci. and Tech., Shanghai, 1983—91. Contbr. transportation system modeling Transport. Modeling and Math. Programming (Natural Sciences and Engring. Rsch. Coun. of Can., 1994), transportation system modeling Transport. Modeling and GIS (Natural Sciences and Engring. Rsch. Coun. of Can., 1997); author: (book transportation and network analysis) A multi-class multi-mode variable demand network equilibrium model with hierarchical logitimate structures, (transportation research b) Two improved numerical algorithms for continuous dynamic network loading problem, On the equivalence between stationary link flow patterns and traffic network equilibria, (transportation science) Advances in the dynamic network loading problem, (transportation research b) A continuous dynamic network loading problem and its math. formulations, (mathematical programming) A gen. descent framework for the monotone variational inequality, (transportation science) Transit equilibrium assignment

study: model and algorithm. Recipient Third Prize, Shanghai City, 1988, Machine Bldg. Commn. of China, 1988, Adv. Prof., Shanghai U. of Sci. and Tech. of China, 2000, Invited Prof., The Gan Su U of Tech. of China, 1999; scholar PhD Study, 10. Can. Internat. Devel. Agy. Fellowship, 1990, U of Montreal, 1988. Mem.: Math. Programming Soc. (Internat.), Inst. of Ops. Rsch. and the Mgmt. Sci. (INFORMS, Internat.), Transp. Rsch. Bd. (TRB, Internat.), Inst. of Transp. Engineers (ITE, Internat.) (assoc.). Achievements include first to Transit Network Optimization in Shanghai. Office: TJKM Transport Cons 5960 Inglewood Dr Suite 100 Pleasanton CA 94588 Office Phone: 925-463-0611. Personal E-mail: wu_jia_hao@hotmail.com. E-mail: jhwu@tjkm.com.

WU, KENNETH KUN-YU, physician, scientist; b. Kaohsiung, Taiwan, Taiwan, July 6, 1941; came to U.S., 1967; m. Lung-Chin Wu, Mar. 29, 1969; children: Stanley, David. MD, Nat. Taiwan U., 1966; MS, Yale U., 1968; PhD, The Univ. London, 1997. Diplomate in internal medicine and hematology Am. Bd. Internal Medicine, 1973. Assoc. in medicine U. Iowa, Iowa City, 1973-74, asst. prof. medicine, 1974-76; assoc. prof. medicine, dir. coagulation and thrombosis unit Rush Med. Coll., Chgo., 1976-81, prof. medicine, dir. coagulation and thrombosis unit, 1981-83; prof. medicine, dir. divsn. hematology and oncology U. Tex. Med. Sch., Houston, 1983—, prof. pathology and lab. medicine, 1984—, dir. Gen. Clin. Rsch. Ctr., 1985-91, dir. Vacular Biology Rsch. Ctr., 1988—, vice chmn. dept. medicine, 1990—; adj. prof. Biomed. Rsch. Lab. Rice U., Houston, 1984—; vis. prof. The William Harvey Rsch. Inst. St. Bartholomew's Hosp. Med. Coll., London, 1991-92; Royl M. and Phyllis Gough Huffington prof. in gerontology U. Tex. Health Sci. Ctr. Mem. hematology study sect. NIH, Bethesda, Md.; mem. rev. com. Nat. Heart Lung and Blood Inst., Nat. Neurologic and Stroke Inst. Contbr. over 300 articles to profl. jours. Mem. Assn. Am. Physicians, Am Soc. Clin. Investigation, Academia Sinica (Taiwan). Office: U Tex Health Sci Ctr 6431 Fannin St Houston TX 77030-1501 E-mail: Kenneth.K.Wu@uth.tmc.edu.

WU, LAWRENCE MG HLA MYIN, physician; b. Rangoon, Burma, May 12, 1937; arrived in U.S., 1964; s. John and Maria (Wong) W.; m. Margaret Perez, June 1968. MBBS, U. Rangoon, Burma, 1961. Internship Knickerbocker Hosp., N.Y.C., residency, chief residency; house phys. (fell.) St. Mary's Hosp., Bklyn.; surgeon Harrison Cmty. Hosp., Cadiz, Ohio, Harris Walker Clin., S. Williamsoms, Ky.; priv. prac. Boenger Clin., Edgerton, Ohio. Med. dir., Boenger Clin., Edgerton, Ohio, 1991—; bd. govs., Community Meml. Hosp., Hicksville, Ohio, 1996—. Mem. C. of C., Edgerton, Ohio. Fellow Am. Coll. Emergency Medicine (life, charter); mem. AMA, Am. Coll. Gen. Practice (life, charter), Ohio St. Med. Assn., Williams Co. Med. Assn., Am. Coll. Internal Phys., Midwest Burma Med. Assn. Republican. Roman Catholic. Home: 3804 Lake Rd Edgerton OH 43517-9536 Office: 104 N West St Edgerton OH 43517-9697

WU, LI-PEI, banker; b. Changhwa, Taiwan, Sept. 9, 1934; came to U.S., 1968; m. Jenny S. Lai, Mar. 24, 1963; children: George T., Eugene Y. BA, Nat. Taiwan U., 1957; MBA, Kans. State U., Ft. Hays, 1969; Comml. Banking Exec. Program, Columbia U., 1974. Staff acct., asst. controller, asst. v.p., v.p. Nat. Bank Alaska, Anchorage, 1969-73, v.p. controller, 1973-76, sr. v.p. chief fin. officer, 1976-78; chmn. exec. com. Alaska Nat. Bank of the North, Anchorage, 1978-79, chief adminstrv. officer, 1979-80, pres., 1980-81; pres., chief exec. officer Gen. Bank & GBC Bancorp, Los Angeles, 1982-84, chmn., pres, chief exec. officer, 1984-98, chmn., CEO, 1998-2000, chmn., 2001—. Sr. adv. to pres. of Taiwan, 2000—; dir. Pacific Coast Banking Sch., 1995—99; bd. advisors Asia Soc., 1998—; mem. Pacific Coun. on Internat. Policy, 1999; chmn. United Taiwanese Found. of So. Calif., 1998—2001; founder and chmn. Formosa Found., 2001—; benefactor Pacific Coun. Internat. Policy, 2000—01. Founder, pres. Taiwanese Am. Polit. Action Com., 1992-93; pres. Taiwanese United Fund, 1990-92; founder, 1st pres. Nat. Taiwanese Am. Citizens League, 1989-91; mem. White House Pacific Rim Econ. Conf., 1995. Recipient Alumni Achievement award Fort Hays U., 1995, Entrepreneur of Yr. award Greater L.A. Ernst & Young, 1998. Office: Gen Bank 800 W 6th St Los Angeles CA 90017-2704 E-mail: lpw@generalbank.com.

WU, MARGARET ANNE, computer scientist, educator; b. Chgo., Apr. 11, 1935; d. Aloys Joseph and Beatrice Rose (Kubal) Schlosser; m. Shih-Yen Wu, June 24, 1967; children: Jennifer, Gregory. BS in Math., Ill. Inst. Tech., 1956; MS in Math., Northwestern U., 1958; PhD in Computer Sci., U. Iowa, 1980. Rsch. computer scientist IIT Rsch. Inst., Chgo., 1958—67; rsch. assoc. U. Iowa, 1967—71, vis. asst. prof. mgmt. info. sys., 1979—93. Author: Computers and Programming: An Introduction, 1973, Introduction to Computer Data Processing, 1975, 2d edit., 1979, Introduction to Computer Data Processing with Basic, 1980; author: (with Shih-Yen Wu) Systems Analysis and Design, 1994. Mem.: Ariz. Sr. Acad.

WU, MIN, cell biologist, researcher, educator; b. Qixian, China, Oct. 4, 1958; s. Han Zhang Wu and Su Bi Cheng; m. Yun Zeng, July 12, 1985; 1 child, Lu-shen. BSc in Medicine, Luzhou (China) Med. U., 1983; MD, Shanghai Second Med. U., 1988; PhD, Leeds (Eng.) U., 1997. Lectr. Luzhou (China) Med. Sch., 1988-91, assoc. prof., 1992—, rsch. asst., 1993-94; rsch. officer Leeds (Eng.) U., 1994-97; rsch. assoc. pulmonary divsn. Ind. U./Purdue U., Indpls., 1998-2001, asst. scientist, 2001—. Sr. scientist Synvirion, Ltd., Leeds, 1988—; hon. prof. Tsinghua U., Beijing, 1988—; vis. scientist Peking U., Beijing, 1994-95, Tohoku U., Sendai, Japan, 1991-92; mem adv. coun., GM Cancer Rsch. Found. Author: Medical Microbiology, 1990; contbr. articles to profl. jours. Mem. Life Sci. Soc. for Chinese Bioscientists in U.K. (v.p. 1995-96, pres. 1996-97), Drug Delivery System Soc., chinese Immunology Soc., Biochem. Soc., Chinese Scholars Assn. (exec. mem. 1993-94), Leeds Chinese Scholars Assn. (pres. 1994-95). Avocations: football, painting, singing. Office: Res Asso Pulmonary Divsn IUPU 1 1001 W 10th St #425 Indianapolis IN 46202-2859

WU, NAN FAION, pediatrician; b. Malaysia, July 13, 1943; came to U.S., 1969; m. Chia F. Wu, June 22, 1969; children: Edwin, Karen. MD, Nat. Taiwan U., 1969. Diplomate Am. Bd. Pediatrics. Intern Atlantic City Med. Ctr., 1969-70; resident in pediatrics Martland Hosp. U. Medicine and Dentistry of N.J., N.J. Med. Sch., Newark, 1970-73; pvt. practice pediatrics West Orange, N.J. Fellow Am. Acad. Pediatrics. Office: 35 Park Ave West Orange NJ 07052-5526

WU, ROBIN CHI CHING, lawyer; b. Guangxi, People's Republic of China, Jan. 6, 1941; came to U.S., 1955; s. Paul S.C. and Janny S.F. (Wong) W. BA, Fordham U., 1964; MA, Columbia U., 1967; LLD, N.Y. Law Sch., 1983. Bar: N.Y. 1983, N.J. 1984. Asst. libr. Fed. Res. Bank N.Y., N.Y.C., 1967-68; asst. dir. rsch. Nat. Rev. mag., N.Y.C., 1968-72, dir. rsch., 1972-79; dir. rsch. TV program Firing Line, N.Y.C., 1972-79; pvt. practice N.Y.C., 1983—. Editor Bridge, 1972, Asian-Am. jour. Mem. N.Y. State Bar Assn., N.Y. County Lawyers Assn., N.J. State Bar Assn. Avocations: reading, writing, movies. Office: 8 Chatham Sq New York NY 10038-1000

WU, RU-SHAN, geophysicist; b. XingYang, Henan, China, Dec. 9, 1938; came to U.S., 1990; s. Yue Ren Wu and Song Zhen Zhang; children: Xili, Hui-han. BSc in Physics, North-western Univ., Sian, China, 1962; PhD in Geophysics, MIT, 1984. Rsch. asst. Inst. Geophysical Prospecting, Min. Geology, Peking, China, 1962-65, rsch. scientist, 1966-77, sr. rsch. scientist, 1977-78; asst. rsch. physicist Univ. Calif., Santa Cruz, 1986, assoc. rsch. geophysicist, 1987-88, 90-95; rsch. geophysicist Inst. Geophys. and Planet Phys., Univ. Calif., Santa Cruz, 1995—; dir. modeling and imaging lab. Inst. Tectonics, Univ. Calif., Santa Cruz, 1997—; assoc. rsch. geophysicist Inst. Geophysics, Chinese Acad. Scis., Beijing, 1988-89, rsch. geophysicist, 1989-90. Vis. sci. MIT, Cambridge, 1978-80, postdoc. assoc., 1984-85; vis. sci. Nat. Rsch. Ctr. Disaster Prevention, Tsukuba, Japan, 1988-89; vis. prof. Fed. Univ. Bahia, Salvador, Brazil, 1990-91; Karlsruhe (Germany) Univ., 1992. Guest editor Jour. Pure Applied Geophysics, 1987-88; mem. editl. bd. Acta Geophysica Sinica; contbr. over 100 articles to profl. publs. Recipient Cert. of Merit, Nat. Conf. Sci. Tech. China, 1977. Fellow Chinese Geophys. Assn.; mem. Am. Geophy. Union, Soc. Exploration Geophys., Seismol. Soc. Am., Internat. Assn. Seismology Physics Earth Interior (mem. com. heterogeneity, chair subcom. heterogeneity, com. wave propagation). Avocations: music, arts, poetry, languages. Office: Inst Geophys and Phys/Earth Scis Univ Calif Santa Cruz 1156 High St Santa Cruz CA 95064-1077

WU, SARAH ZHENG, investment banker; b. Shanghai, Dec. 2, 1963; came to U.S., 1987; d. Chunzhuo Wu and Zhifen Chen; m. Sagun Raj Tuladhar, Jan. 28, 1995. Student, Tongji U., Shanghai, 1979-82; BA in Town and County Planning, Manchester (Eng.) U., 1987; MS in Urban and Regional Planning, Columbia U., 1989. Rsch. asst. Manchester U. Sch. Town and Country Planning, 1987-89, Columbia U. Grad. Sch. Arch., Planning & Hist. Preservation, N.Y.C., 1987-89; urban and transp. planner Parsons Brinckerhoff, N.Y.C., 1989-92, sr. environ. planner Honolulu, 1992-95; fin. analyst, privatization and project fin. Parson Brinckerhoof Infrastructure Devel. Co., N.Y.C., 1995-97; portfolio mgr. Global Project Fin. Credit Suisse First Boston, N.Y.C., 1997—. Editor Jour. Chinese Student Assn. Manchester U., 1987; rsch. asst.: Parks and Gardens of Cheshire Park and Plains, U.K., 1987, The Global City: New York, London and Tokyo, 1991. Recipient William Kennie fellowship Columbia U., N.Y.C., 1988. Mem. Internat. Chinese Transp. Profls. Assn. (treas., bd. dirs.), Am. Planning Assn. (Robert C. Weinberg award for acad. excellence in urban planning 1989), Chinese Am. Assn. Engrs. Avocations: asian art, chinese antique furniture and porcelain, stamp collecting/philately, travel, opera. Office: Credit Suisse First Boston Global Project Fin 11 Madison Ave New York NY 10010-3698 Home: 1708 Tower Dr Edgewater NJ 07020-2207

WU, SUSAN YING CHU LIN (YING-CHU LIN), engineering company executive, engineer; b. Beijing, June 23, 1932; came to U.S., 1957; d. Chi-yu and K.C. (Kung) Lin; m. Jain-Ming Wu, June 13, 1959; children: Ernest H., Albert H., Karen H. BSME, Nat. Taiwan U., 1955; MS in Aero. Engring., Ohio State U., 1959; PhD in Aeros., Calif. Inst. Tech., 1963. Sr. engr. Elecro-Optical Systems, Inc., Pasadena, Calif., 1963-65; asst. prof. aero. engring. U. Tenn. Space Inst., Tullahoma, 1965-67, assoc. prof., 1967-73, prof., 1973-88; adminstr. Energy Conversion R&D Programs, Tullahoma, 1981-88; pres., chief exec. officer ERC, Inc., Huntsville, Ala., 1987-2000, chmn., 2000—. Presdl. appointee adv. bd. Nat. Air and Space Mus., Smithsonian Inst., 1993-2000. Contbr. over 90 articles to profl. jours. Mem. Better Sch. Task Force, Tullahoma, 1985-86; founding mem. Tullahoma Edn. Found. for Excellence; trustee Rochester Inst. Tech., 1992-94; mem. adv. com. NASA Aeronautics and Space Transp. Tech., 1994-2000. Recipient Chancellor's Rsch. award U. Tenn., 1978, Outstanding Educator of Am. award, 1973, 75; Amelia Earhart fellow, 1958, 59, 62, Plasmadynamics and Lasers award AIAA, 1994, Faraday Meml. medal Internat. Liaison Group for MHD Pow Generation, 1999. Fellow ASME, AIAA (assoc.); mem. Soc. Women Engrs. (hon., life; achievement award 1985), Sigma Xi. Office: ERC Inc 555 Sparkman Dr NW Ste 1622 Huntsville AL 35816-3431 E-mail: swu@erc-incorporated.com., susanwu@comcast.net.

WU, TAI TE, biological sciences and engineering educator; b. Shanghai, Aug. 2, 1935; m. Anna Fang, Apr. 16, 1966; 1 son, Richard. MB, BS, U. Hong Kong, 1956; BS in Mech. Engring, U. Ill., Urbana, 1958; SM in Applied Physics, Harvard U., 1959, PhD in Engring. (Gordon McKay fellow), 1961. Rsch. fellow in structural mechanics Harvard U., 1961-63; rsch. fellow in biol. chemistry Harvard U. (Med. Sch.), 1964, rsch. assoc., 1965-66; rsch. scientist Hydronautics, Inc., Rockville, Md., 1962; asst. prof. engring. Brown U., Providence, 1963-65; asst. prof. biomath. Grad. Sch. Med. Scis., Cornell U. Med. Coll., N.Y.C., 1967-68, assoc. prof., 1968-70; assoc. prof. physics and engring. scis. Northwestern U., Evanston, Ill., 1970-73, prof., 1973-74, prof. biochemistry and molecular biology and engring. scis., 1973-85, acting chmn. dept. engring. scis., 1974, prof. biochem., molecular biology, cell biology and biomed. engring., engring. scis., applied math., 1985-94, prof. biochemistry, molecular biology, cell biology, biomed. engring., 1994—. Author (with E.A. Kabat and others): Variable Regions of Immunoglobulin Chains, 1976, Sequences of Immunoglobulin Chains, 1979, Sequences of Proteins of Immunological Importance, 1983, Sequences of Proteins of Immunological Interest, 1987, 5th edit., 1991; editor: New Methodologies in Studies of Protein Configuration, 1985, Analytical Molecular Biology, 2001; contbr. articles to profl. jours. Recipient progress award Chinese Engrs. and Scientists Assn. So. Calif., Los Angeles, 1971; C.T. Loo Scholar, 1959-60; NIH Research Career Devel. awardee, 1974-79 Mem. Am. Soc. Biochem. and Molecular Biology, Biophys. Soc., Sigma Xi, Tau Beta Pi, Pi Mu Epsilon. Office: Northwestern U Dept Biochem Molecular and Cell Biology Evanston IL 60208-3500 E-mail: t-wu@northwestern.edu.

WU, THOMAS XINZHANG, engineering educator; b. Urumuqi, Xinjiang, China, Nov. 21, 1968; came to U.S., 1995; m. Nadine Xiufang Guo, June 15, 1992; children: Lucy, John. BS in Engring., U. Sci. and Tech., Hefei, Anhui, China, 1988, MS in Engring., 1991, U. Pa., 1997, PhD, 1999. Asst. U. Sci. and Tech., Hefei, 1991-93, lectr., 1993-95; asst. prof. Sch. Elec. Engring./Computer Sci. U. Ctrl. Fla., Orlando, 2000. Presenter in field. Contbr. articles to profl. jours. Head evangelism of the core group of mandarin svc. Chinese Christian Ch. and Ctr., Phila., 1998, worship leader mandarin svc., 1997—. Rsch. fellow U. Pa., 1995-99; recipient Pres. award Chinese Acad. Scis., 1991, Excellent Papers award China Microwave Soc., 1993, Young Scientist Found. award U. Sci. and Tech., 1994-95. Mem. IEEE (reviewer 1996—), Optical Soc. Am. (reviewer 1999—). Achievements include research in liquid crystal devices, RF ICS, packaging, chaotic electromagnetics, liquid crystal device electromagnetic metamaterials, China C-band satellite beam forming network design using rectangular coaxial waveguide technology; invention of omni-directional leaky wave antenna. Office: U Central Fla EE Program Sch Elec Engring Orlando FL 32817 Fax: 407-823-5835. Office Phone: 407-823-5957. Business E-Mail: tomwu@mail.ucf.edu.

WU, TIEN HSING, civil engineering educator, consulting engineer; b. Shanghai, Mar. 2, 1923; arrived in U.S., 1947, naturalized, 1957; s. Chong-Yung and Ying Mei (Pih) Woo; m. Pei-Hsing Lin, Aug. 14, 1952; children: Mei, Anne. BS, St. John's U., Shanghai, 1947; MS, U. Ill., 1948, PhD, 1951. Registered profl. engr., Ohio, Ill. Civil engr. DeLeuw Cather & Co., Chgo., 1951—52, Ill. Divsn. Hwys., Springfield, 1952—53; from asst. prof. to prof. Mich. State U., East Lansing, 1953—65; prof. civil engring. Ohio State U., Columbus, 1965—. Vis. prof. Norwegian Geotech. Inst., Oslo, 1959, 70, 76, Nat. U. Mex., Mexico City, 1964, Royal Inst. Tech., Stockholm, 1980, S.W. Jiaotung U., Chengdu, China, 1986; UN cons. Punjab Agrl. U., Ludhiana, India, 1981. Author: Soil Dynamics, 1970, Soil Mechanics, 2d. rev. edit., 1976; contbr. articles to profl. jours. Recipient Antarctica Svc. medal, 1967, Lichtenstein award, Ohio State U., 1973, rsch. award, 1984. Mem.: ASCE (hon. State of the Art award 1990, Ernest award 2000), Transp. Rsch. Bd., Sigma Xi. Home: 160 Brookside Oval Worthington OH 43085-3638 Office Phone: 614-292-1071. Business E-Mail: wu.26@osu.edu.

WU, TSE CHENG, research chemist; b. Hong Kong, Aug. 21, 1923; came to U.S., 1947, naturalized, 1962; s. Shau Chuan and Shui (Chan) W.; m. Janet Ling, June 14, 1963; children: Alan, Anna, Bernard. BS, Yenching U., 1946; MS, U. Ill., 1948; PhD, Iowa State U., 1952. Prodn. chemist Yungli Industries, Tangku, China, 1946-47; rsch. assoc. Iowa State U., Ames, 1952-53; rsch. chemist duPont Co., Waynesboro, Va., 1953-60, GE, Waterford, N.Y., 1960-71; sr. rsch. chemist Abcor, Inc., Wilmington, Mass., 1971-77; rsch. assoc. Allied-Signal, Inc., Morristown, N.J., 1977-88; cons., 1989—. Contbr. articles to profl. jours; patentee in polymer chemistry and organosilicon chemistry. Mem. Troy Arts Guild, 1968-71, Morris County Art Assn., 1981, Rossmoor Art Assn., 1999. Recipient Gold medallion award for inventions GE, 1967; Allied Corp. patent award, 1983; Eastman Kodak Rsch. fellow, 1951-52. Mem. Am. Chem. Soc., Sigma Xi, Phi Kappa Phi, Phi Lambda Upsilon, Alpha Chi Sigma. Home: 601 Red Wing Ct Walnut Creek CA 94595-3927

WU, TUNG, curator, art historian, art educator, artist; b. Fuzhou, Fukien, China, Dec. 10, 1940; came to U.S., 1965; s. Chin-Wen and Jingrong (Chen) W.; m. Ying Chin, July 16, 1974. BA, Normal U., Taipei, Taiwan, 1962; postgrad., U. Mich., 1967-70, Harvard U., 1979—. Rsch. asst. Nat. Palace Mus., Taichung, Taiwan, 1962-65; with visual art archive U. Mich., 1966-68; rsch. asst. Cleve. Mus. Art, 1968; Ford Found. curatorial intern Nelson-Atkins Mus. Art, Kansas City, Mo., 1969; rsch. fellow Mus. Fine Arts, Boston, 1971-79, asst. curator, 1980-84, assoc. curator, 1984—85, curator Asian art, 1985—91, Matsutaro Shoriki curator Asian art, 1992—, head dept. art of Asia, Oceania and Africa, 1999—2004. Tchg. asst. U. Kans., Lawrence, 1969, Harvard U., 1978; vis. lectr. Harvard U., Cambridge, Mass., 1975, Emmanuel Coll., Boston, 1992; assoc. prof. Simmons Coll., Boston, 1993; advisor Chinese Inst. Am., N.Y.C., 1985—, Chinese Cultural Found., San Francisco, 1985-87, Nat. Mus. History, Taipei, 1984—; cons. Project Emperor-One, Boston, 1983-86; panelist mus. program NEA, 1995; panelist Korea Found. Workshop on Korean painting, Seoul, South Korea, 2000, Workshop on Korean Buddhist art, Gyoengju Korea, 2002, Workshop of Korean crafts, 2003. Mem. Nat. Com. on U.S.-China Rels., Washington, 1985—, Nat. Devel. Seminar Taipei, 1989, 92, Nat. Edn. Reform, Taipei, 1994; The Ink Soc. of Hong Kong (advisor 2003), dept. Asian trade art Peabody Mus., Salem. Mass., 191—; trustee W.A. Compton Found. Oriental Arts. Grantee Freer Found. U. Mich., 1968, Ford Found., Kansas City, 1969, Smithsonian Instn., Washington, 1978; recipient Outstanding Alumnus award Taiwan Normal U., 1997. Mem. Taoist Soc. Japan, Soc. Chinese Kunqu Opera, Soc. Chinese Calligraphy. Office: Mus Fine Arts Asiatic Dept 465 Huntington Ave Boston MA 02115-5597 E-mail: wutung@hotmail.com.

WU, WAYNE WEN-YAU, artist; b. Tachia, Taiwan, Republic of China, Oct. 5, 1935; s. K. C. Kau and Chin-Fong (Chen) Wu; m. Amy Hsueh, Dec. 25, 1961; children: Ingrid, Judy, David. BA in Fine Arts, Taiwan Normal U., 1959. Supr. art edn. ctr. Taichung (Taiwan) Libr., 1970-74; instr. fine arts dept. Taiwan Normal U., Taipei, 1973-74; instr. paintings Hunter Mus. of Art, Chatanooga, Tenn., 1980-92; artist, painting instr. Wayne Wu's Art Studio, Atlanta, 1994-2000, San Jose, Calif., 2000, Salinas, Calif., 2000—. One-man shows include Taiwan Mus. Art, 1995, Hunter Mus. Am. Art, 1980, 1998, Taipei Internat. Art Fair, 2001, 2004, Korea Internat. Art Fair, 2004, others, over 100 group shows. Mem.: Am. Watercolor Soc. Home: 815 Cactus Ct Salinas CA 93905-4606

WU, XIAOGANG, social sciences educator, researcher; b. Zhenjiang, Jiangsu, China, Sept. 27, 1969; s. Yongxiang Wu and Qiaoying Ni; m. Ye Li, Dec. 29, 1999. LLB, Renmin U. of China, Beijing, 1991; ML, Peking U., Beijing, China, 1994; PhD, UCLA, 2001. Policy rsch. officer Shanghai Mcpl. Govt., Shanghai, 1994—96; Mellon post doc. fellow U. Mich., Ann Arbor, 2001—03; asst. prof. Hong Kong Univ of Sci & Tech., Kowloon, 2003—. Contbr. research to profl. jours. Co-organizer Workers for Human Rights, Shenzhen, China, 1998—2001. Recipient Ann. Excellence award, China for Future. Determination Party. Home: U Sci and Tech Tower D Flat 5C HK Kowloon Hong Kong Office: Hong Kong U Sci and Tech Clear Wanter Bay Kowloon 12345 Hong Kong Office Phone: (852)23587827. Home Fax: (852)23350014. Office Fax: (852)23350014. Personal E-mail: sowu@ust.hk. E-mail: sowu@ust.hk.

WU, XINGLU, writer; b. Shanghai, Feb. 25, 1937; m. Beili Cheng, Mar. 22, 1981; 1 child, Linda W. Author: TOEFL Testing Skills, 1984, A New Journey To West, 2002, Swordswoman of Absurdity, 2002; author: (as X.L. Woo) Useful Strategies in Everyday Life, 2001, Empress Dowager Cixi, 2002, Kungfu Masters, 2004; contbr. articles to jours. Mem.: Famous Poets Soc., N.Y. Worldwide Chinese Poetry Soc., Wenxin Literary Soc., Mystery Writers Am., N.J. Book Club.

WU, YIDER, semiconductor scientist, researcher; b. Taipei, Taiwan, Jan. 11, 1968; arrived in U.S., 1992; s. Jui-han and Hsiu-yu Wu. BS, Nat. Tsing-Hua U., Taiwan, 1990; MS, U. Mass., Lowell, 1994; PhD, N.C. State, Raleigh, 1999. Rsch. asst. N.C. State, Raleigh, 1994—99; mem. of tech. staff Advanced Micro Devices, Sunnyvale, Calif., 1999—; dept. mgr. Macronix, 2004—. Patent adv. Advanced Micro Devices, Sunnyvale, Calif., 2000—; presenter at profl. confs. Contbr. scientific papers, articles to profl. jours. (introductory invited paper, 2000). Mem. Taiwanese Assn. of N.C., Raleigh, 1995—98; v.p. Taiwanese Student Assn., N.C. State, Raleigh, 1995—96. Scholar Outstanding Rschr., Semiconductor Rsch. Corp., 1998. Mem.: IEEE, Semiconductor Rsch. Corp. Achievements include patents in field. Avocations: jogging, swimming, travel, hiking. Office: Advanced Micro Devices One AMD Pl PO BOX 3453 M/S 177 Sunnyvale CA 94088 Personal E-mail: yider_wu@yahoo.com.

WU, YING, economics educator, researcher; b. Beijing, Sept. 22, 1955; s. Dazhi and Chengying (Mao) W.; m. Hong Yao, Jan. 20, 1987; children: Danke, Danlei. BA in Econs., Peking (China) U., 1984, MA in Econs., 1987; PhD in Econs., U. Oreg., 1992. Instr. Peking U., 1986-87; grad. tchg. fellow U. Oreg., 1987-92; asst. prof. U. Portland, 1992-93; instr. Lane C.C., 1993-94; lectr. Nanyang Technol. U., Singapore, 1994-98; asst. prof. Salisbury U., 1998—2002, assoc. prof., 2002—. Guest prof. Peking U., 1995, 2003; guest commentator Asia Bus. News, Singapore, 1996-97, Brit. Broadcasting Corp., 1997. Author: An Analysis of Credit and Equilibrium Credit Rationing, 1994; jour. referee Journ. Macroecons., 1996; contbr. articles to profl. jours. Libr. svc. coord. Nanyang Technol. U., 1997-98. Recipient 20th Century Achievement award Internat. Biog. Ctr., U.K., 1998, 2000 Millennium medal, Am. Biog. Inst., 1999. Mem. Am. Econ. Assn., Western Econ. Assn., Pi Gamma Mu. Avocations: ping pong/table tennis, jogging, swimming, hiking, movies. Office: Salisbury U Franklin P Perdue Sch Bus 1101 Camden Ave Salisbury MD 21801-6860 E-mail: yxwu@salisbury.edu.

WU, YUSEN (JOHN WOO), film director; b. Guangzhou, Canton, China, May 1, 1946; Asst. dir. Shaw Bros. Studios, 1969. Dir. (films) A Better Tomorrow, 1986, The Killer, 1989, Bullet in the Head, Hard Boiled, Hard Target, 1993, Broken Arrow, 1996, Face/Off, 1997 (Acad. Sci. Fiction, Horror and Fantasy Films Saturn award Best Dir.), Black Jack, 1998, Kings Ransom, 1998, Hong Kong Face-Off, 1998, Mission Impossible 2, 1999, Windtalkers, 2002, Hire: The Hostage, 2002, Paycheck, 2003; writer, prodr., dir. (TV) Once a Thief: Brother Against Brother, 1996; exec. prodr. The Replacement Killers, 1998. Recipient CineAsia Lifetime Achievement award, 1996. Office: William Morris Agency c/o Mike Simpson 151 S El Camino Dr Beverly Hills CA 90212-2775*

WU, ZHENG Y. hydroinformatics engineer, hydrologist, consultant; b. Tongzi, Guizhou, China, Aug. 21, 1963; arrived in U.S., 2000; s. Xian C. Wu and Yue Q. Yang; m. Feng Hua Zhang, Aug. 22, 1963; children: Shelley X., Annie X. BSc in Civil Engring.(hon.), Guizhou Inst. Tech., 1983; MSc in Hydroinformatics, Internat. Inst. for Infrastructural, Hydraulic and Environ. Engring., Delft, Netherlands, 1994; PhD in CIvil and Environ. Engring., U. Adelaide, South Australia, 1998. Sr. lectr. Guizhou Inst. Tech., Guiyang, 1986—92; hydroinformatics rsch. scholar Danish Hydraulics Inst., Horsholm, 1993—94; sr. project engr. Sembawang Project Engring., Singapore, 1994—95; sr. engr. Sinclair Knight Merz Pty. Ltd., Sydney, Australia, 1996—97; hydroinformatics specialist Montgomery Watson Australia, Melbourne, 1998—2000; supervising profl. software engr. Montgomery Watson Am., Pasadena, Calif., 2000—01; chief hydroinformatics engr. Haestad Methods, Inc, Waterbury, Conn., 2001—. Contbr. scientific papers to profl. jours. Netherlands fellow, 1992, Rsch. fellow, Danish Hydraulics Inst., 1993, Overseas Rsch. fellow, Australia, 1995, Frank Perry scholar, U. Adelaide, South Australia, 1995. Mem.: ASCE, Am. Water Works Assn. (Best Paper award 2002), Am. Assn. Artificial Intelligence. Achievements include patents pending for Method and System for Automatic Water Distribution Model Calibration; first to Competent Genetic Algorithm Optimization of water distribution System; development of Rehabilitation of water distribution system using genetic algorithm; research in Evaluation of Critical Transient Loading for Optimal Design of Water Distribution Systems; Verification of Hydrological and Hydrodynamic Models Calibrated by Genetic Algorithms; first to Optimal operation of urban sewer system by using genetic algorithm and expert system; patents pending for Method and System for Optimal Design and Rehabilitation of Water Distribution System; Method and System for Reduction of a Network Topology-based System Having Automated Optimization Features; first to Automatic Model Calibration by Simulating Evolution; research in Messy Genetic Algorithm for Optimization of water Distribution System Including Water Hammer; Self-adaptive boundary search of genetic algorithms and application to water distribution systems; development of An Efficient Genetic Algorithms Approach to an Intelligent Decision Support System for Water Distribution Networks; Calibrating Water Distribu-

tion Model Via Genetic Algorithms; research in Optimal Capacity of Water Distribution Systems; development of Mining Water consumtion and GIS Data for Loading Water Distribution Model, rsch. in Integrating Water Quality Analysis and GIS Spatial Sys. for Water Security Modeling. Avocations: swimming, travel, reading. Office: Haestad Methods Inc 37 Brookside Rd Waterbury CT 60708 Office Phone: 203-805-0562. E-mail: zwu@haestad.com.

WUBBELS, GENE GERALD, chemistry professor; b. Preston, Minn., Sept. 21, 1942; s. Victor and Genevieve M. (Sikkink) W.; m. Joyce Ruth Honebrink, Aug. 26, 1967; children: Kristen, Benjamin, John. BS, Hamline U., 1964; PhD, Northwestern U., 1968. Asst. prof. Grinnell Coll., Iowa, 1968-73, assoc. prof., 1973-79, prof. chemistry, 1979-92, Dack prof., 1986-92; provost, dean of coll. and prof. chemistry Washington Coll., Chestertown, Md., 1992-95, sr. vice chancellor acad. affairs, 1995-97; prof. chemistry U. Nebr., Kearney, 1995—. Editor: Survey of Progress in Chemistry, vol. 10, 1983. Program dir. NSF, Washington, 1990-92; moderator United Ch. of Christ Congl., Grinnell, 1980-82, 83-84; bd. dirs. Edgerton Explorit Ctr., Aurora, Nebr., 1996—. Grantee NSF, 1971-95; recipient Sci. Faculty Prof. Devel. award NSF, 1981-82, Catalyst award for excellence in tchg. Chem. Mfrs. Assn., 1989. Fellow Iowa Acad. Sci.; mem. ACS (rsch. grantee 1970-86, mem. editl. adv. bd. Accounts Chme. Rsch. 1977-83, adv. bd. Petroleum Rsch. Fund 1986-89, pres. Chem. Coun. Undergrad. Rsch. 1986-87). Republican. Avocation: music. Office: U Nebr Kearney 905 W 25th St Kearney NE 68849-0002 E-mail: wubbelsg@unk.edu.

WU-CHU, STELLA CHWENYEA, nutritionist, consultant; b. Kaohsiung, Taiwan, Sept. 22, 1952; came to U.S., 1976; d. Jin-Shoui and Sue-Tuan (Ling) Wu; children: Christine, Whitney. BS, Fu-Jen Cath. U., Taiwan, 1974; MA, San Francisco State U., 1979. Registered dietitian. Intership U. Calif., Berkeley, 1978; food svc. supr. Calif. Surgery Hosp., Oakland, 1979—80; nutritionist, cons. Solano Napa Agy. on Aging, Vallejo, Calif., 1980—; nutrition cons. Marin County Div. of Aging, San Rafael, Calif., 1981—; nutritionist San Francisco Commn. on Aging, 1990—; nutrition cons. Contra Costa Office on Aging, 1995—. Mem. adv. bd. Staying Health project Am. Soc. on Aging, 1999—2000; nutritional advisor Veggie Life Mag., Walnut Creek, Calif., 1993, Salt Free Cooking Made Easy. Chief editor quar. publ. Taiwanese Assn. publ., 1991-94. Cmty. liaison East Bay Taiwanese Assn., Walnut Creek, 1992-93; v.p. No. Calif. Formosan Fedn., 1993; dist. supportive com. chair United Meth. Women, 1995-97, Bayview dist. social actions mission coord., 1997-98; adv. bd. Overseas Chinese Inst. on Aging, 2000—, Am. Soc. Aging, 2000. Mem. Am. Dietetic Assn., Am. Pub. Health Assn., Jacob Inst. of Women's Health, Nat. Assn. Nutrition and Aging Svcs., Formosan Assn. for Pub. Affairs, Am. Assn. of Meals on Wheels. Avocations: reading, concerts, dance, creative writing (in chinese). Home: 70 Seabreeze Dr Richmond CA 94804-7410 Office: San Francisco Commn Aging 25 Van Ness Ave Ste 650 San Francisco CA 94102-6057 E-mail: stellawc@aol.com.

WUDL, FRED, chemistry professor; b. Cochabamba, Bolivia, Jan. 8, 1941; came to U.S., 1958; s. Robert and Bertha (Schorr) W.; m. Linda Raimondo, Sept. 2, 1967. BS, UCLA, 1964, PhD, 1967. Postdoctoral rsch. fellow Harvard U., 1967-68; asst. prof. dept. chemistry SUNY, Buffalo, 1968-72; mem. tech. staff AT&T Bell Labs., Murray Hill, N.J., 1972-82; prof. chemistry and materials U. Calif., Santa Barbara, 1982-97; Courtaulds prof. UCLA, 1997—. Recipient Arthur C. Cope scholar award Am. Chem. Soc., 1993, Arthur D. Little award Boston U., 1993, Stouffer award U. So. Calif., 1993, Award for Chemistry of Materials, 1996, Natta medal Italian Chem. Soc., 1994, Wheland medal U. Chgo., 1994, Herbert Newby McCoy award UCLA, 2001. Fellow AAAS, Am. Acad. Arts and Scis. Office: UCLA Dept Chemistry Los Angeles CA 90095-1569 E-mail: wudl@chem.ucla.edu.

WUDUNN, SHERYL, journalist, correspondent; b. N.Y.C., Nov. 16, 1959; d. David and Alice (Mark) WuDunn; m. Nicholas D. Kristof, Oct. 8, 1988. BA, Cornell U., Ithaca, N.Y., 1981; MBA, Harvard U., 1986; MPA, Princeton U., 1988. Lending officer Bankers Trust Co., N.Y.C., 1981—84; intern reporter Wall St. Jour., L.A., 1986; bus. reporter South China Morning Post, Hong Kong, 1987; corr. N.Y. Times, Beijing, 1989—93, Tokyo, 1995—99, exec. dir. Nexgen group N.Y.C., 1999—. Co-author: China Wakes, 1994, Thunder From the East, 2000. Recipient Pulitzer Prize for fgn. reporting, 1990, George Polk award, L.I. U., N.Y., 1990, Hal Boyle award, Overseas Press Club, 1990. Avocations: aerobics, singing. Office: Nexgen Group The New York Times 229 W 43rd St New York NY 10036

WUEBKER, COLLEEN MARIE, retired librarian; b. LaCrosse, Wis., June 22, 1943; d. Harris M. and Mary Frances (Collins) Gruber; m. William Joseph Wuebker, Aug. 14, 1965; children: Jon Paul, Timothy William, Maree Jean. BA, Mt. Mercy Coll., 1965; MS, Mankato State U., 1975. Cert. permanent profl. media specialist, tchr. Iowa. Secondary tchr. Luverne Cmty. Sch., Minn., 1965-66; tchr. St. Mary's Sch., Larchwood, Iowa, 1966; secondary tchr. SEMCO Community Sch., Gilman, Iowa, 1966-67; substitute tchr. West Bend-Mallard (Iowa) Cmty. Schs., 1968-74, sch. media specialist, 1974—2002, 1975—2002; ret., 2002. Mem. selection com. Lakeland Area Edn. Agy., Cylinder, Iowa, 1977—; mem. Gov.'s Sch. Efficiency Task Force, West Bend, 1987; mem. sch. evaluation team Dept. Pub. Instrn., Des Moines, 1986. Spkr. Marriage Encounter Movement, Sioux City Diocese, 1985—, Pre-Cana Workshops, Emmetsburg, 1985—; mem., liturgy and music coord., song leader Sts. Peter and Paul Parish Coun., West Bend, 1987—; chmn. Parish Liturgy Com., West Bend, 1987—. Mem.: Iowa Ednl. Media Assn., Cath. Daus. Am. (past v.p. West Bend). Roman Catholic. Avocations: genealogy, music. Home: Box 426 11 1st Ave NE West Bend IA 50597-0426

WUENSCH, BERNHARDT JOHN, ceramic engineering educator; b. Paterson, NJ, Sept. 17, 1933; s. Bernhardt and Ruth Hannah (Slack) W.; m. Mary Jane Harriman, June 4, 1960; children: Stefan Raymond, Katrina Ruth. SB in Physics, MIT, 1955, SM in Physics, 1957, PhD in Crystallography, 1963; DEng (hon.), Hanyang U., Seoul, 2003. Rsch. fellow U. Bern, Switzerland, 1963-64; asst. prof. ceramics MIT, Cambridge, 1964-69, assoc. prof. ceramics, 1969-74, prof., 1974—, TDK chair materials sci. and engring., 1985-90, dir. Ctr. Materials Sci. and Engring., 1988-93, acting dept. head dept. materials sci. and engring., 1980. Vis. prof. Crystallographic Inst., U. Saarland, Fed. Republic Germany, 1973; physicist Max Planck Institut für Festkorperforschung, Stuttgart, Fed. Republic Germany, 1981; mem. U.S. nat. com. for crystallography NRC, NAS, 1980-82, 89-94; mem. N.E. regional com. for selection of Marshall Scholars, 1970-73, chmn., 1974-80. Co-editor: Modulated Structures, 1979, Neutron Scattering in Materials Science, 1995; adv. editor: Physics and Chemistry of Minerals, 1976—85; assoc. editor Can. Mineralogist, 1978—80; editor: Zeitschrift fuer Kristallographie, 1981—88, Jour. Ceramic Processing Rsch., 2000—. Ford Found. postdoctoral fellow, 1964-66. Fellow Am. Ceramic Soc. (Outstanding Educator award 1987), Mineral. Soc. Am.; mem. AAAS, Am. Crystallographic Assn., Mineral. Assn. Can., Materials Rsch. Soc. Episcopalian. Home: 190 Southfield Rd Concord MA 01742-3432 Office: MIT 77 Massachusetts Ave Rm 13-4037 Cambridge MA 02139-4307 Business E-Mail: wuensch@mit.edu.

WUENSCHE, VERNON EDGAR, construction company executive; b. Elgin, Tex., Nov. 25, 1945; s. Harry Edwin Jacob and Emma Martha (Dube) W. BBA, U. Tex., 1967, MBA, 1968. CPA, Tex. Audit asst. Arthur Andersen & Co., Houston, 1968-70; tax cons. Peat Marwick Mitchell & Co., Houston, 1970; cost acct. Bemis Bros. Bag Co., Houston, 1970-71; asst. controller Prodn. Systems Internat., Inc., Houston, 1971-72; controller Am. Housing Guild, Inc., Houston, 1972-73, Wood Bros. Homes, Inc., Houston, Dallas, 1973-74, Oklahoma City, 1975; pres., founder, custom home builder Woodmark Homes, Inc., Houston, Dallas, Austin, Tex., 1975—; founder, kitchen and bath renovator Woodmark Kitchen & Bath, Inc., 1994—. Election judge Harris County, Houston, 1978, Rep. state del., Tex., 1978, 80, 94, 96, 98, 2000, 02; elder Meml. Luth. Ch., Houston, 1982—2002, elder emeritus, 2003; finisher marathon, Galveston, Tex., 1970, 71; founder Texans for Efficiency in Govt., 1991, Bus. Consensus, 1999; dir. Houston Entrepreneurs Forum. With USAR, 1968-74. Recipient Builder of Tex. Design award Tex. Arch. Mag., 1994. Mem. Alley Theater Guild, Tex. Wendish Heritage Soc., U. Tex. Ex-Students Assn., Rice Design Alliance, Mus. of Fine Arts, Arts Symposium of Houston, Phi Kappa Phi, Beta Gamma Sigma. Avocation: distance running. Home: 14211 Swiss Hill Dr Houston TX 77077-1029 Office Phone: 713-468-3300. Business E-Mail: vern@woodmarkkitchens.com.

WUGHALTER, EMILY HOPE, physical education educator; b. Bklyn., Nov. 24, 1954; d. Milton and Leah (Isaacs) W. BA in Phys. Edn. and Teaching, CUNY, 1977; MS in Phys. Edn. and Motor Learning, Univ. Colo., 1978; EdD, U. Ga., 1981. Tchr. math. COMPASS House, N.Y.C.; tchr. phys. edn. St. Pius High Sch., Bronx, Hebrew Acad. of West Queens, 1976-77; instr. Boulder City Parks and Recreation, 1977; grad. asst. Univ. Ga., 1978-81; assoc. prof. NYU, 1981-91; prof. San Jose Univ., 1991—. Measurement, design, and evaluation cons. N.Y. Alliance for the Pub. Schs.; phys. fitness evaluator N.Y.C. Affiliate Am. Heart Assn.; exercise science trainer Young Women's Christian Assn. Author: (with A.L. Rothstein) Basic Stuff Series I- Motor Learning, 1987; contbr. articles to profl. jours. Recipient Recognition award N.Y.C., 1989 and 1990, Mable Lee award, 1992; Curricular Change grantee N.Y.U., 1987, 91, Spencer Found. Young Scholars Rsch. award grantee, 1982-83, and numerous others. Mem. Am. Alliance of Health, Phys. Edn., Recreation, and Dance, Am. Coll. of Sports Medicine, Am. Edn. Rsch. Assn., Nat. Assn. for Phys. Edn. in Higher Edn., Nat. Women's Studies Assn., Western Soc. for Phys. Edn. Coll. Women, No. Am. Soc. for the Study of Psychol. of Sport and Phys. Activity, Calif. Assn. of Health, Phys. Edn. Recreation and Dance. Home: 358 Hihn St Felton CA 95018-9201 Address: San Jose Univ Dept of Human Performance 1 Washington Sq San Jose CA 95192-0001

WUHL, CHARLES MICHAEL, psychiatrist; b. N.Y.C., Sept. 24, 1943; s. Isadore and Sali (Ackner) W.; m. Gail; children— Elise, Amy. M.D., U. Bologna, 1973. Diplomate Am. Bd. Psychiatry and Neurology. Intern, N.Y. Med. Coll., 1975-76, resident in psychiatry, 1976-77; fellow in child psychiatry Columbia Presbyn. Med. Center, 1977-78; practice medicine specializing in psychiatry and child psychiatry, Englewood, N.J., 1978—; attending staff, mem. faculty N.Y. Med. Coll.; psychiatrist NYU, also asst. clin. prof. psychiatry NYU Sch. Medicine. Contbr. to Psychosocial Aspects of Pediatric Care, 1978, World Book Ency., 1980—. Mem. Am. Psychiat Assn., AMA, Am. Acad. Child Psychiatry. Office: 163 Engle St Englewood NJ 07631-2530 Office Phone: 201-569-2228. E-mail: cw3@nyu.edu.

WUHL, ROBERT, actor; b. Union, N.J., Oct. 9, 1951; Student, U. Houston. Actor: (films) The Hollywood Knights, 1980, Flashdance, 1983, Good Morning, Vietnam, 1987, Ray's Male Heterosexual Dance Hall, 1987, Bull Durham, 1988, Batman, 1989, Blaze, 1989, Wedding Band, 1990, Missing Pieces, 1991, Mistress, 1992, The Bodyguard, 1992, Sandman, 1993, Blue Chips, 1994, Cobb, 1994, Dr. Jekyll and Ms. Hyde, 1995, Good Burger, 1997; actor, writer: Open Season, 1996; actor: (TV films) Percy and Thunder, 1993, A Kiss Goodnight, 1994; (TV miniseries) The Last Don, 1997, The Last Don II, 1998; writer, actor, exec. prodr., dir. (TV series) Arliss, 1996—2002.

WUKOVITS, JOHN FRANCIS, secondary school educator, writer; b. Akron, Ohio, Nov. 3, 1944; s. Thomas William and Grace Annette Wukovits; children: Amy Dickerman, Julie, Karen. BA in History, U. Notre Dame, 1967; M in Am. History, Mich. State U., 1968. Cert. secondary tchr. Mich. Tchr. St. Timothy Sch., Trenton, Mich., 1968—71, Trenton Pub. Schools, 1971—73, St. Joseph Sch., Trenton, 1981—91, Trenton Pub. Schools, 1991—. Author: (book) Devotion to Duty: A Biography of Admiral Clifton A. F. Sprague, 1995, Barry Sanders, 1995; contbg. author: book Men of War: Great Naval Leaders of World War II, 1992, Reference Guide to United States Military History, 1995, Quarterdeck & Bridge: Two Centuries of American Naval Leaders, 1997,: book The Great Admirals: Command at Sea, 1587-1945, 1997; author: Jesse James, 1997, The Gunslingers, 1997, Vince Lombardi, 1997, Wyatt Earp, 1997, Annie Oakley, 1997, The Black Cowboys, 1997, Butch Cassidy, 1997; Scientists & Inventors, 1998; author: John Stockton, 1998, Jack Nicklaus, 1998, Tim Allen, 1998, The Composite Guide to Auto Racing, 1998, The Composite Guide to Soccer, 1998, Anne Frank, 1998, Martin Luther King, Jr., 1998, Stephen King, 1999, Jim Carrey, 1999, Life of an American Soldier in Europe, 2000, Life As A POW, 2000, Colin Powell, 2000, The 1910s, 2000, The 1920s, 2000, George Bush, 2000 (NY Pub. Library's "Books for the Teen Age List", 2001), Bill Gates, 2000, The Encyclopedia of World Sports, 2001, The Persian Gulf War: Leaders and Generals, 2001, History of Sports: Hockey, 2001, The Spanish-American War, 2001, Strategic Battles of World War I, 2001, World War I Flying Aces, 2002, The Encyclopedia of The Winter Olympics, 2002, Michael J. Fox, 2002, Oskar Schindler, 2003, Pacific Alamo: The Battle for Wake Island, 2003; contbg. author: book Book of Days, 1988, Best Little Stories from World War II, 1989, Best of the Wild West, 1996. Mem.: Orgn. Am. Historians, The Golf Writers Assn. Am., Soc. for Mil. History. Roman Catholic. Avocations: golf, reading. Home: 1235 Harbour # 22 Trenton MI 48183 Office: Trenton Pub Schs 4000 Marian Dr Trenton MI 48183 Personal E-mail: johnwukovits@comcast.net.

WULBERT, DANIEL ELIOT, mathematician, educator; b. Chgo., Dec. 17, 1941; s. Morris and Anna (Greenberg) W.; children: Kera, Noah. BA, Knox Coll., 1963; MA, U. Tex., Austin, 1964, PhD, 1966. Rsch. assoc. U. Lund, Sweden, 1966-67; asst. prof. U. Wash., Seattle, 1967-73; prof. U. Calif.-San Diego, La Jolla, 1973—, provost Revelle Coll., 2003—. Vis. prof. Northwestern U., Evanston, Ill., 1977. Contbr. articles in field. Office: Provost Bldg Revelle Coll 0321 U Calif San Diego La Jolla CA 92093-0321 Business E-Mail: dwulbert@ucsd.edu.

WULF, GENE C. manufacturing executive; b. Arlington, Nebr., 1950; BS in Acctg., Dana Coll., 1972; MBA, U. Utah, 1975. CPA. With Bemis Co., Inc., Mpls., 1975—, v.p., asst. contr., 1997—98, v.p., contr., 1998—2002, v.p., CFO, treas., 2002—. Office: Bemis Co Inc 222 S 9th St Ste 2300 Minneapolis MN 55402-4099*

WULF, MELVIN LAWRENCE, lawyer; b. N.Y.C., Nov. 1, 1927; s. Jacob and Vivian (Hurwitz) W.; m. Deirdre Howard, Dec. 18, 1962; children: Laura Melissa, Jane Miranda. BS, Columbia U., 1952, LL.B., 1955. Bar: N.Y. 1957. Asst. legal dir. ACLU, 1958-62, legal dir., 1962-77; Distinguished vis. prof. Hofstra Law Sch., 1975, spl. prof. law, 1976-77; mem. firm Clark Wulf & Levine, 1978-83, Beldock, Levine & Hoffman, 1983—2001; of counsel, 2002—. Author articles. Served to lt. (j.g.) USNR, 1955-57. Ford Found. fellow, 1967 Home: 340 Riverside Dr New York NY 10025-3423 Office: 99 Park Ave New York NY 10016-1601 E-mail: mwulf@blhny.com.

WULF, NORMAN, federal official; b.; married; two children. BA, Iowa Wesleyan Coll.; JD, U. Iowa; LLM, U. Miami. Office dir. State Dept.; dep. gen. counsel ACDA; acting asst. dir. for Nonproliferation/Regional Arms Control U.S. Arms Control and Disarmament Agy., Washington, 1985—. Leader efforts to strengthen the internat. inspections regime underpinning the Nuclear Non-Proliferation Treaty in sixty countries, Internat. Atomic Energy Agy., Vienna; active North Korean issues. Office: Office Pub Affairs Us Arms Control Disarm Agy Washington DC 20451-0001

WULF, SHARON ANN, management consultant; b. New Bedford, Mass., Aug. 23, 1954; d. Daniel Thomas and Norma Dorothy (McCabe) Vieira; m. Stanley A. Wulf, 1983. BS in Acctg. cum laude, Providence Coll., 1976; MBA, Northeastern U., 1977; PhD, Columbia Pacific U., 1984. Staff acct., intern Laventhol & Horwath, Providence, 1977; jr. fin. analyst Polaroid Corp., Waltham, Mass., 1977-78, fin. analyst Freetown, Mass., 1978-79, Cambridge, Mass., 1979-81; sr. fin. cons., mktg. strategic planner Digital Equipment Corp., Stow, Mass., 1981-82, Maynard, Mass., 1982-83, mgr. fin. devel. program, 1983-84, strategic fin. cons. engring. divsn., 1984-86, group mgr. planning & strategic ops. Hudson, Mass., 1986-87, group mgr. strategic bus. planning, 1987-89; mktg. planning mgr. Digital Equipment Corp., Marlboro, Mass., 1989-90, new ventures bus. devel. mgr., 1990-92; pres. Enterprise Sytems, Framingham, Mass., 1993—; sr. instr. Cambridge Coll., 1997—, prof., 1998—. Lectr. fin. acctg. Southeastern Mass. U., 1979—81; adj. prof. acctg., mgmt. & fin., knowledge mgmt. strategies Northeastern U., Boston, 1980—; instr. Nat. Tech. U., 1991—95; instr., vis. asst. prof. mgmt. Framingham State Coll., 1999—; instr. Curry Coll., 2004—; exec. com. enterprise forum MIT, 1987—92, lectr. network leadership workshop, 2003; prin. Work Sys. Assocs., Inc., Marlborough, Mass., 1992—93; bd. advisors Spaceball Tech., Inc., Lowell, Mass., Terasys., Inc.; sr. faculty advisor healthcare master's degree program Mass. Gen. Hosp., 2000—02; frequent keynote spkr.; cons. in field. Author: Building Performance Values, 1996, Customer Service Action Plans, 1997, Leadership in Action: The Way It Is Census The Way It Should Be, 1997. Chair pub. support and fund raising ARC, New Bedford, 1974-84; bd. dirs. Vets. Outreach Ctr., Metrowest, Framingham, 1989-93; v.p. MIT Leadership Found., Cambridge, 1991-93; mem. exec. com. MIT Enterprise Forum, also co-chair stant up clinics, 1986-92. Mem. Black Alumni of MIT (bd. advisors 1989-92), Univ. Coll. Faculty Soc., Phi Sigma Tau. Home: 902 Salem End Rd Framingham MA 01702-5532 Office: Enterprise Systems 1257 Worcester Rd Ste 301 Framingham MA 01701-5217 Fax: 508-626-9038. Office Phone: 508-626-2233. E-mail: sharonw@enters.com.

WULF, WILLIAM ALLAN, computer information scientist, educator, federal agency administrator; b. Chgo., Dec. 8, 1939; s. Otto H. and Helen W. (Westermeier) Wulf; m. Anita K. Jones, July 1, 1977; children: Karin, Ellen. BS, U. Ill., 1961, MSEE, 1963; PhD in Computer Sci., U. Va., 1968. Prof. computer sci. Carnegie-Mellon Univ., Pitts., 1968—81; chmn., CEO Tartan Labs., Pitts., 1981—87; AT&T prof. computer sci. U. Va., Charlottesville, Va., 1988—; asst. dir. Nat. Sci. Found., Washington, 1988—90; pres. Nat. Acad. of Engring., Washington, 1996—. Bd. dir. Charles Strak Draper Labs., Cambridge, Mass., Nat. Action Coun. Minorities Engring., Inst. Women and Tech. Biblioteque Alexandrina; cons. various computer mfr. Author: Fundamental Structures of Computer Science, 1981. Bd. dirs. Pitts. High Tech. Coun., 1982—88. Fellow: AAAS, IEEE, Assoc. Women in Sci., Assoc. Computing Machinery; mem.: Russian Acad. Sci., Spanish Acad. Engring., Am. Acad. Arts and Sci., Nat. Acad. Engring. Avocations: woodworking, photography. Office: Nat Acad Engring 2101 Constitution Ave NW Washington DC 20418-0007

WULKAN, MARK LEWIS, pediatrician, surgeon; b. Pitts., Nov. 27, 1963; m. Kristi LeCole Miller. BS, Emory U., 1985; MD, Emory U. Sch. of Medicine, 1985. Diplomate Am. Bd. Surgery, Am. Bd. Surg. Critical Care, Am. Bd. Pediat. Surgery. Asst. prof. surgery and pediat. Sch. Medicine Emory U., Atlanta, 1998—. Dir. of minimally invasive surgery ctr. of excellence Children's Healthcare of Atlanta, 1989—94; fellowship, critical care Children's Hosp. of Pittsburgh, 1994—95; pediatric surg. residency Children's Hosp. Alabama, 1995—98; surg. dir. of picu Children's Healthcare of Atlanta. Mem. editl. bd. Pediat.Endosurgery and Innovative Tecniques. Fellow: ACS, Internat. Pediat. Endoscopy Group (program com. 2000—02), Am. Acad. of Pediat.; mem.: Am. Pediatric Surg. Assn. Achievements include first to Established One Of The Busiest Pediatric Minimally Invasive Surgery Centers In The Country; research in Establishment of Safety Of Laparoscopy In Children With Congenital Heart Disease. Office: Emory Children's Center 2040 Ridgewood Rd NE Atlanta GA 30329 Office Phone: 404-982-9938. Business E-Mail: mark.wulkan@oz.ped.emory.edu.

WULKER, LAURENCE JOSEPH, portfolio manager, educator, financial planner; b. Cin., Apr. 6, 1945; s. Joseph Laurence and Dorothea Clare (Link) W. BS, Xavier U., Cin., 1967, MA, 1971; cert. fin. planner, Coll. Fin. Planner, 1985. Instr. Lloyd High Sch., Erlanger, Ky., 1967-68, Elder High Sch., Cin., 1968-73, Peoples High Sch., Cin., 1973-74, Regina High Sch., Cin. Tech. U., Cin., 1974-75; stockbroker Harrison-Bache, Cin., 1976-78; portfolio mgr., fin. planner, v.p. investments UBS, Cin., 1978—; formed Wulker/Cummins Group Paine Webber, Cin., 1997; instr. U. Cin., 1981-98, Nat. Inst. Fin., South Plainfield, N.J., 1986-88; systems operator, Fin. Planning Forum Tristate Online, Cin., 1991—93. Speaker at numerous seminars 1984—; systems operator Investor Forum, Compuserve, 1985-86. Author column Japanese-Am. League Newsletter, 1985-96; contbr. articles to Cin. Enquirer, Cin. Post, Cin. Bus. Courier. Bd. dirs., v.p., pres. No. Ky. Symphony, 1993-99; treas. Friends of Findlay Market, Findlay Market Assn., 1999—; bd. dirs. Riverwinds Condo Assn., Behringer- Crawford Mus., 2003—. Fulbright scholar Dept. Health, Edn. and Welfare, 1972; named one of best 200 Stockbrokers, Country-Money mag., 1987. Mem. Fulbright Soc., Order Ky. Cols. Roman Catholic. Avocations: computers, tennis, golf, volleyball, reading. Home: Riverwinds Condos 558 Davenport Ave No 11 Cincinnati OH 45204-1362 Fax: 513-369-4020. Office Phone: 513-369-4181. E-mail: laurence.wulker@ubs.com.

WUNDER, CHARLES C(OOPER), physiology and biophysics educator, gravitational biologist; b. Pitts., Oct. 2, 1928; s. Edgar Douglas and Annabel (Cooper) W.; m. Marcia Lynn Barnes, Apr. 4, 1962; children: E(dgar) Douglas, David Barnes, Donald Charles. AB in Biology, Washington and Jefferson Coll., 1949; MS in Biophysics, U. Pitts., 1952, PhD in Biophysics, 1954. Assoc. U. Iowa, Iowa City, 1954-56, asst. prof. physiology and biophysics, 1956-63, assoc. prof. physiology and biophysics, 1963-71, prof. physiology and biophysics, 1971-98, prof. emeritus, 1998—. Cons. for biol. simulation of weightlessness U.S. Air Force, 1964; vis. scientist Mayo Found., Rochester, Minn., 1966-67. Author: Life into Space: An Introduction to Space Biology, 1966; also chpts., numerous articles, abstracts Recipient Research Career Devel. award NIH, 1961-66; AEC predoctoral fellow U. Pitts., 1951-53; NIH spl. fellow, 1966-67; grantee NIH, NASA Mem. Am. Physiol. Soc., The Biophys. Soc. (charter), Aerospace Med. Assn., Iowa Acad. Sci. (chmn. physiology sect. 1971-72, 83-84, 96-97), Am. Soc. Biomechanics (founding), Aerospace Physiologist Soc., Iowa Physiol. Soc. (pres. 1996-97), Am. Soc. for Gravitational and Space Biology (Founders award 2000). Presbyterian. Achievements include the establishment of chronic centrifugation as an approach for investigating gravity's role as a biological determinant. Home: 702 W Park Rd Iowa City IA 52246-2425 Office: U Iowa BSB Iowa City IA 52242 Personal E-mail: charles-wunder@uiowa.edu.

WUNDERLICH, BERNHARD, physical chemistry educator; b. Brandenburg, Germany, May 28, 1931; came to U.S., 1954, naturalized, 1960; s. Richard O. and Johanne (Wohlgefahrt) W.; m. Adelheid Felix, Dec. 28, 1953; children: Caryn Cornelia, Brent Bernhard. Student, Humboldt U., Berlin, Germany, 1949-53, Goethe U., Frankfurt, Germany, 1953-54, Hastings Coll., 1954-55; PhD, Northwestern U., 1957. Instr. chemistry Northwestern U., Evanston, Ill., 1957-58, Cornell U., Ithaca, N.Y., 1958-60, asst. prof., 1960-63; assoc. prof. phys. chemistry Rensselaer Poly. Inst., Troy, N.Y., 1963-65, prof. phys. chemistry, 1965-88, prof. emeritus, 1988—; prof. chemistry U. Tenn., Knoxville, 1988-2001, prof. emeritus, 2001—; Disting. scientist div. chemistry Oak Ridge Nat. Lab., 1988-2001. Cons. E.I. duPont de Nemours Co., 1963-88; dir. Lab. for Advanced Thermal Analysis; rsch. in solid state of linear high polymers and thermal analysis, 1980-2001. Author: Macromolecular Physics, Vol. 1, 1973, Vol. 2, 1976, Vol. 3, 1980, Thermal Analysis, 1990; author computer and audio courses on Crystals of Linear Macromolecules, and Thermal Analysis of Materials; contbr. over 500 articles to profl. jours.; mem. editl. bd. Chemistry, 1965-68, Makromolekulare Chemie, 1966-96; mem. editl. bd. Jour. Thermal Analysis and Calorimetry, 1963-2001, mem. hon. bd., 2004—; mem. adv. bd. Jour. Polymer Sci., 1963-2001, Macromolecules, 1984-88, Polymers for Advanced Tech., 1988-2001, Macromolecular Sci. and Physics, 1995-2001, Thermochim. Acta, 1996-2001. Recipient Humboldt award, 1987-88, award for applied chem. thermodynamics Swiss Soc. for Thermal Analysis and Calorimetry, 1993, TA Instruments award Internat. Conf. Thermal Analysis and Calorimetry, 1996. Fellow Am. Phys. Soc., N.Am., Thermal Analysis Soc. (Mettler award in thermal analysis 1971, Disting. Svc. award 2002); mem. Am. Chem. Soc. Home: 200 Baltusrol Dr Knoxville TN 37922-3707

WUNDERMAN, JAN DARCOURT, artist; b. Winnipeg, Man., Can., Jan. 22, 1921; d. Rene Paul and Georgette Marie (Guionet) Darcourt; m. Frank Joseph Malina, 1938 (div. 1945); m. Lester Wunderman (div. 1967); children: Marc, Geroge, Karen Renee. BFA, Otis Art Inst., L.A., 1942. One man shows include Easthampton Guild Hall, L.I., 1977, Denise Bibro Fine Art Gallery, N.Y.C., 1996-98, 2002, Roko Gallery, 1963, 66, 68, 71, 73, 76; represented in numerous permanent pub., corp. and pvt. collections including Zimmerli Mus., NYU Loeb Collection, Norfolk Mus., Alfred Kouri Collection, Skidmore Coll. Print Collection, Nat. Assn. of Women Artists, Rutgers U., 1994, Albright Knox Mus., 1998-99, Daimler Chrysler Coll., Germany, 2002, Northwest Airlines, Detroit, 2003, abstract-nonrepresentational. Recipient Ohashi award

Pan Pacific Exhbn., Tokyo and Osaka, 1962, Emily Lowe award 1965, J.J. Akston Found. prize, 1965, Canaday Meml. prize, 1979, Marian De Solo Mendes prize, 1981, Charles Horman Meml. prize, 1983, Amelia Peabody award Nat. Assn. Women, 1991, Grumbacher Gold medal of honor, 1992, Doris Kreindler award 1992. Mem. Nat. Assn. Women Artists (medal of honor 1966, Marcia Brady Tucker award 1965, E. Holzinger prize 1966, Jane C. Stanley prize 1977, Marge Greenblatt award 1990, Amelia Peabody award 1991, Solveig Stomsoe Palmer prize 1997), Am. Soc. Contemporary Artists (corr. sec. 1977-78, Bocour award 1980, Elizabeth Erlanger Meml. award 1990, Kreindler award 1992, N. Ransom award 2002), Contemporary Artists Guild (Irwin Zlowe Meml. award 1998). Avocations: history, travel. Studio: 41 Union Sq W Rm 516 New York NY 10003-3208 Office Phone: 212-989-9197.

WUNNICKE, BROOKE, lawyer; b. Dallas, May 9, 1918; d. Rudolph von Falkenstein and Lulu Lenore Brooke; m. James M. Wunnicke, Apr. 11, 1940; (dec. 1977); 1 child, Diane B. BA, Stanford U., 1939; JD, U. Colo., 1945. Bar: Wyo. 1946, Colo. 1969, U.S. Dist. Ct. Wyo. 1947, U.S. Dist. Ct. Colo. 1970, U.S. Supreme Ct. 1958, U.S. Ct. Appeals (10th cir.) 1958. Pvt. practice law, 1946-56; ptnr. Williams & Wunnicke, Cheyenne, Wyo., 1956-69; of counsel Calkins, Kramer, Grimshaw & Harring, Denver, 1969-73; chief appellate dep. atty. Dist. Atty's Office, Denver, 1973-86; of counsel Hall & Evans L.L.C., Denver, 1986—. Adj. prof. law U. Denver Coll. of Law, 1978-97; lectr. Internat. Practicum Inst. Denver, 1978-2003. Author: (book) Ethics Compliance for Business Lawyers, 1987; co-author: Standby Letters of Credit, 1989, Corporate Financial Risk Management, 1992, Legal Opinion Letters Formbook, 2002, 2004, UCP 500 and Standby Letters of Credit-Special Report, 1994, Standby and Commercial Letters of Credit, 1996, 2000, 2004; contbr. articles. Pres. Laramie County Bar Assn., Cheyenne, Wy., 1967-68; Dir. Cheyenne C. of C., Cheyenne, Wy., 1965-68. Named 1st Frank H. Ricketson Jr. Adj. Prof., U. Denver Coll. Law, 1997; recipient awards for outstanding svc., Colo. Dist. Attys. Coun., 1979, 1982, 1986, Disting. Alumni award, U. Colo. Sch. of Law, 1986, 1993, Lathrop Trailblazer award, Colo. Women's Bar Assn., 1992, William Lee Knous award, U. Colo. Sch. Law, 1997, Eleanor P. Williams award for disting. svc. to legal profession, 1997, Potter Lifetime Profl. Svc. award, 1999, Def. Rsch. Inst. Nat. award, 1999, Law Star award, U. Denver Coll. Law, 2003, Excellence in Tchg. award, Denver Coll. Law, 2003. Fellow Colo. Bar Found. (hon.); mem. ABA, Wyo. State Bar, Denver Bar Assn. (hon. life; trustee 1977-80, award of merit 2004), Colo. Bar Assn. (hon., life, Award of Merit 1999), Am. Arbitration Assn. (nat. panel, regional panel), William E. Doyle Inn of Ct. (hon.), Order of Coif, Phi Beta Kappa. Republican. Avocations: reading, writing, teaching, lecturing. Office: Hall & Evans LLC 1125 17th St Ste 600 Denver CO 80202-2052 Office Phone: 303-628-3363.

WUNSCH, BONNIE RUBENSTEIN, fraternal organization executive; b. Shreveport, La., Feb. 7, 1961; d. David Ochs and Marilyn Sue (Goldstein) Rubenstein; m. Alan V. Wunsch. BBA, Emory U., Atlanta, 1983. Office adminstr. Sanger-Harris, Dallas, 1983-85, asst. buyer, 1985-87, Foley's, Houston, 1987-88; exec. dir. Alpha Epsilon Phi Sorority, Stamford, Conn., 1988—, province dir., pledge programming chmn., 1985-87, nat. v.p. collegiate chpts., 1987-88, now exec. dir. Dir. devel. Alpha Epsilon Phi Found., 1992—; mem. Fraternity Ins. Purchasing Group, 1991—, bd. dirs., 1994—. Contbr. articles to profl. jours. Tchr. religious sch. Temple Israel, Columbus, 1989-95, pres. young adults congregation, 1991-93, bd. dirs., 1990-93, bd. dirs. sisterhood, 1991-95, also mem. dues revision com. and recruitment com., search com., ritual com. Mem. Assn. Frat. Advisors, Ctrl. Office Execs. Assn. (sec. 1993-94), Frat. Execs. Assn. (bus. mgr. 1993-94), Nat. Coun. Jewish Women (exec. bd. 1996—), Order of Omega, Women's Am. ORT (activities chmn. 1986-87). Republican. Jewish. Avocations: needlecrafts, reading, cooking, travel. Home: 1403 Pinnacle Way Danbury CT 06811-2669 Office: Alpha Epsilon Phi 111 Prospect St 2d Fl Stamford CT 06901-1208

WUNSCH, KATHRYN SUTHERLAND, retired lawyer; b. Tipton, Mo., Jan. 30, 1935; d. Lewis Benjamin and Norene Marie (Wolf) Sutherland; m. Charles Martin Wunsch, Dec. 22, 1956 (div. May 1988); children: Debra Kay Wolff, Laura Ellen Stubberud, AB, Ind. U., 1958, JD summa cum laude, 1977; postgrad., Stanford (Calif.) U., 1977. Founder Wunsch and George, San Francisco, 1989-93, Kathryn Wunsch and Assoc. Counsel, San Francisco, 1993-99; ret., 1999. Articles editor Ind. U. Law Rev., 1975-76. Trustee Minuteman Found., 2002—03; founder, pres. Sun City Anthem Lifelong Learning Ctr., 2004—. Mem. Sun City Anthem Garden Club (founder, pres. 2001—), Phi Beta Kappa. Republican. Avocations: collecting fine art and antiques, theater, opera, gardening, hiking.

WUORINEN, CHARLES PETER, composer; b. NYC, June 9, 1938; s. John Henry and Alfhild (Kalijarvi) W. BA, Columbia U., 1961, MA, 1963; DMus (hon.), Jersey City State Coll., 1971. Lectr. Columbia U., 1964-65, instr., 1965-69, asst. prof., 1969-71, co-dir. Group Contemporary Music, 1962—; prof. music Rutgers U., 1984—. Vis. lectr. Princeton U., 1967-68, New England Conservatory, 1968-71, Yale U., 1983; adj. lectr. U. South Fla., 1971-72; faculty Manhattan Sch. Music, 1972-79, U. So. Calif., 1981; artistic dir., chmn. Am. Composers Orch., 1973-87; composer-in-residence Ojai Festival, 1975, Santa Fe Chamber Music Festival, 1993, 2001, Tanglewood Music Festival, 2001; San Francisco Symphony, 1984-89; condr. Cleve. Orch., 1976, Finnish Radio Orch., 1979, Helsinki Philharm., 1979; disting. prof. Rutgers U., 1984—; vis. prof. SUNY, Buffalo, 1989-94, NYU, 1990 Author: Simple Composition; mem. editorial bd. Perspectives of New Music; bd. mem. Composers Recs. Inc., 1962-89; composer numerous works including Music for Orchestra, 1956, Be Mery All That Be Present, mixed chorus, 1957, Concert for Four Trombones, 1960, Madrigale Spirituale, 1960, Turetzky Pieces, 1960, Evolutio: organ, 1961, Evolution Transcripta for chamber orch., 1961, Tiento Sobre Cabezon, 1961, Concert for Double Bass Alone, 1961, Trio No. 1 for flute, cello and piano, 1961, Invention for percussion quintet, 1962, Octet, 1962, Duuiensela for cello and piano, 1962, Bearbeitungen über das Glogauer Liederbuch, 1962, The Prayer of Jonah, 1962, 2d Flute Trio: Piece for Stefan Wolpe, 1962, Chamber Concerto for cello and 10 players, 1963, Piano Variations, 1963, Flute Variations, 1963, Composition for violin and 10 instruments, 1964, Chamber Concerto for flute and 10 players, 1964, Orchestral and Electronic Exchanges, 1965, Composition for oboe and piano, 1965, Chamber Concerto for oboe and 10 players, 1965, Super Salutem for male voices and instruments, 1964, Piano Concerto, 1966, The Bells for carillon, 1966 (revised 1997), Bicinium, 2 oboes, 1966, Janissary Music for 1 percussionist, 1966, Harpsichord Divisions, 1966, Making Ends Meet for piano four-hands, 1966, John Bull: Salve Regina Versus Septem, 1966, Duo for violin and piano, 1967, The Politics of Harmony: A Masque, 1967, String Trio, 1968, Flute Variations II, 1968, Time's Encomium (electronic), 1969, Adapting to the Times for cello and piano, 1969, The Long and the Short for violin, 1969, Nature's Concord trumpet and piano, 1969, Piano Sonata, 1969, Ringing Changes for percussion, 1970, A Song, 1970, Tuba Concerto, 1970, A Message to Denmark Hill, 1970, Cello Variations, 1970, String Quartet, 1971, Canzona for 12 instruments, 1971, Grand Bamboula for string orch., 1971, Amplified Violin Concerto, 1972, Harp Variations, 1972, Bassoon Variations, 1972, Violin Variations, 1972, On Alligators for 8 instruments, 1972, Speculum Speculi for 6 players, 1972, Third Trio for flute, cello and piano, 1973, 12 Short Pieces for piano, 1973, Grand Union for cello and drums, 1973, Arabia Felix for 6 Instruments, 1973, Second Piano Concerto, 1974, Fantasia for violin and piano, 1974, The W. of Babylon (opera), 1975, TASHI, 1975, Hyperion for 12 instruments, 1975, Cello Variations 2, 1975, 2d Piano Sonata, 1976, Percussion Symphony, 1976, The Winds, 1977, Fast Fantasy for cello and piano, 1977, Archangel for trombone and string quartet, 1977, Six Pieces for violin and piano, 1977, Six Songs for two voices, Wind Quintet, Self Similar Waltz for piano, Ancestors for chamber ensemble, 1978, Two-Part Symphony, 1978, Archaeopteryx for bass trombone and chamber ensemble, 1978, The Magic Art, A Masque for chamber orch, 1979, Fortune for 4 instruments, 1979, 2d String Quartet, 1979, The Celestial Sphere for chorus and orch., 1979, Psalm 39 for baritone and guitar, 1979, Percussion Duo, 1979, Joan's for 5 instruments, 1979, Blue Bamboula for piano, 1980, Capriccio for piano, 1981, Horn Trio, 1981, Trio for bass instruments, 1981, New York Notes for 6 players, 1982, Mass, 1982, Divertimento, 1982 (string quartet), Divertimento for alto sax and piano, 1982, Spinoff for violin, double bass and congas, 1983, Trio for violin, cello and piano, 1983, Third Piano Concerto, 1983, Rhapsody for violin and orch., 1984, Concertino, 1984, Natural Fantasy for organ, 1985, Horn Trio Continued, 1985, Trombone Trio, 1985, Prelude to Kullervo for tuba and orch., 1985, Double Solo for Horn Trio, 1985, Fanfare for the Houston Symphony, 1986, The Golden Dance for orch., 1986, Third Piano Sonata, 1986, Third String Quartet, 1987, Galliard for chamber orch., 1987, Bamboula Beach for orch., 1987, FIVE: Concerto for amplified cello and orch., 1987, Sonata for violin and piano, 1988; (piano) Bagatelle, 1988, Ave Christe, 1988; Contrafactum, 1969 (orch.), Reliquary for Igor Stravinsky, 1975, Short Suite, 1981, Crossfire, 1984, Movers and Shakers, 1984, Bamboula Squared, 1984, Another Happy Birthday, 1988, Machault Mon Chou, 1988, String Sextet, 1989, A Solis Ortu, 1989, Astra, 1990, Delight of the Muses, 1991, Missa Brevis, 1991, The Mission of Virgil, 1993; (soprano and piano) Twang, 1989; Genesis, 1989 (chorus and orch.), A Winter's Tale for Soprano and Six Instruments, 1992, Microsymphony, 1992, Missa Renovata, 1992, Saxophone Quartet, 1992, Concerto for Saxophone Quartet and Orch., 1993, Percussion Quartet, 1994, Piano Quintet, 1994, Christes Crosse, 1994, Lightenings VIII, 1994, Guitar Variations, 1994, Sonata for Guitar and Piano, 1995, The Great Procession, 1995, Katz Fugue for piano, 1995, Windfall for band, 1994, Schoenberg Op. 31 Variations, 1996 (remade for two pianos), The River of Light, 1996 (string orch. and percussion), Epithalamium, 1997 (two instruments), Symphony Seven, 1997, Fenton Songs, 1997, Cello Variations III, 1997, Lepton trio for celeste, piano and harp, 1998; An Orbicle of Jasp, 1999 (cello and piano); Brass Quintet, 2000, Fourth String Quartet, 2000; Cyclops 2000 (chamber orch.); Haroun and the Sea of Stories, 1997-2001 (opera); Stanzas Before Time, 2001 (tenor and harp); Buttons and Bows, 2001 (cello and accordion); Alap, 2001, Josquiniana, 2001; Two Machine Portraits, September 11, 2001, 2001 (tenor and piano); Fifty Fifty, 2001 (two pianos); The Haroun Songbook, 2002 (4 vocal soloists and piano); Hexadactyl, 2002 (guitar); Pentecost, 2002 (tenor and harp), 4th Piano Concerto, 2003, Fenton Songs II (soprano and piano trio), 2002, The Long Boat (mezzo, English horn), 2003, The Haroun Piano Book (solo piano), 2003, Dodecadactyl (two guitars), 2003, Visible (mezzo and violin), 2004, Ashberyana (baritone and ensemble), 2004. Recipient Philharmonic Young Composers award, 1954; Bennington Composers Conf. scholar, 1956-60; Bearns prize, 1958-59, 61; MacDowell Colony fellow, 1958; Alice M. Ditson fellow, 1959; Arthur Rose teaching fellow, 1960; Broadcast Music-Student Composers award, 1959, 61, 62, 63; Lili Boulanger Meml. award, 1963; Festival fellow Santa Fe Opera, 1962; Festival fellow World's Fair Music and Sound, 1962; commd. by Koussevitzky Found., 1964, Berkshire Music Center, 1963, Fromm Found., 1963-71, Ford Found., 1962, Orch. of Am., 1958, Columbia U., 1956, Washington and Lee U., 1964, Fine Arts Quartet, 1969, Naumberg Found., 1971, U. South Fla., 1972, Nat. Opera Inst., 1973, Light Fantastic Players, 1973, N.Y. State Council on the Arts, 1974, N.Y. Philharm., 1974, Balt. Chamber Music Soc., 1974, Buffalo Philharm., 1974, Ojai Festival, 1974, Contemporary Chamber Ensemble, 1974, TASHI, 1974, Beethoven Festival, Bonn, 1978, Albany Symphony, 1981, San Francisco Symphony, 1984, 86, 88, 89, Cleve. Orch., 1984, Balt. Symphony, 1984, Houston Symphony, 1986, N.Y.C. Ballet, 1987, 90, Libr. of Congress, 1988, New World Symphony, 1987, Chamber Music Soc. Lincoln Ctr., 1989, 92, Am./ Soviet Youth Orch., 1990, Phila. Orch., 1992, Beethorenhalle Orch., Bonn Mönchengladbach and Ludwig Forum, Germany; grantee Nat. Inst. Arts and Letters, 1967, Nat. Endowment Arts, 1974, 76; Guggenheim fellow, 1968, 72; Ingraham Merrill fellow, 1972, Rockefeller Found. fellow, 1979, 80, 81, John D. and Catherine T. MacArthur fellow, 1986-91; recipient Pulitzer prize, 1970, Brandeis U. creative arts award, 1970, Creative Artists Pub. Svc. award, 1976; Arts and Letters award Finlandia Found., 1976, Koussevitzky Internat. Rec. award, 1970, 72. Mem. AAAS, AAAL, Am. Soc. Univ. Composers, Am. Composers Alliance (former bd. dirs.), Am. Music Ctr. (bd. dirs.), Internat. Soc. Contemporary Music (bd. dirs.), Am. Acad. Arts and Scis., Phi Beta Kappa. Office: care Howard Stokar Mgmt 870 W End Ave New York NY 10025-4918 Office Phone: 212-866-5798. E-mail: hstukar@stokar.com.

WURDEMAN, LEW EDWARD, Internet company executive, consultant; b. Colorado Springs, Colo., Oct. 31, 1949; s. Robert Martin and Shirley Gladys (Reetz) W. Student, U. Tex., 1967-69, U. Minn., 1969-72. Adminstr. Control Data Corp., Bloomington, Minn., 1969-81; product splst., 1981-83; sys. mgr., 1983-84; cons., 1984-89; mgr. The Roach Orgn., Inc., Mpls., 1989-90; computer cons. Wurdeman Enterprises, Inc., Farmington, Minn., 1991-93; sr. cons. Norstan Consulting, Minnetonka, Minn., 1993-2001; photographer Vividere Glamour Photography, 1996—; tree farm owner Golden Pond Farm, 2003—. Freelance photographer; virtual tour photographer 360 Minn., 2003—. Commr. Parks and Recreation Dept., City of Farmington, Minn., 2001-03. Mem. Internat. Freelance Photographers Orgn., Internat. Glamour Photographers Assn., Photog. Soc. Am. Profl. Photographers Am., German Shepherd Dog Club Mpls., German Shepherd Dog Club Am. Republican. Lutheran. Avocations: dog breeding and training, computers, photography. Office: Vividere Photography PO Box 332 Farmington MN 55024-0332 Office Phone: 612-327-6178. E-mail: lew@vividere.com.

WURLITZER, FRED PABST, surgeon; b. San Francisco, Dec. 26, 1937; s. Raimund Billings and Pauline (Pabst) W.; m. Lee Jones Wurlitzer (div. Jan. 1991); children: Ricky, Arnisha, Susan, Elena; m. Ann Marie Allan, June 2, 1992; children: Melanie, Heather, Gregory. BA, Stanford U., 1960; MD, U. Cin., 1965; MBA, Golden Gate U., 1985. Diplomate Am. Bd. Gen. Surgery. Intern, resident Highland-Almeda County Hosp., 1965-67; resident in surgery UCLA Sch. Medicine/VA Hosp., 1967-60; fellow in surg. oncology U. Tex./M.D. Anderson Hosp., Houston, 1970-71; instr. surgery U. So. Calif., Los Angeles, 1971-73; physician Pasadena (Calif.) Tumor Inst., 1971-73, San Mateo (Calif.) Med. Clinic, 1973-77; pvt. practice, Burlingame, Calif., 1977-84; vol. surgeon various hosps., 1989-93; pres. Wurlitzer Properties, Burlingame, 1976—. Contbr. articles to profl. jours. Comdr. USPHS, 1992—. Recipient Acknowledgement of Outstanding Svc. award Am. Cancer Soc., 1974, Disting. Svc. award Health Vols. Overseas, 1994. Fellow ACS; mem. AMA, Soc. Head and Neck Surgeons, Southwestern Surg. Congress, So. Med. Assn. Unitarian Universalist. Avocations: skiing, tennis. Home: 8129 Regents Ct University Park FL 34201-2234

WURMAN, RICHARD SAUL, architect; b. Phila., Mar. 26, 1935; s. Morris Louis and Fannie (Pelson) W.; m. Gloria Nagy; children: Joshua, Reven, Vanessa, Anthony. BArch (T.P. Chandler fellow), MArch with highest honors, U. Pa.; DFA (hon.), U. of the Arts, 1994; LHD (hon.), Art Ctr College of Design, 1995. Mem. faculty N.C. State U., Raleigh, 1962-64, 77, Washington U., St. Louis, 1965, Princeton U., 1965-67, Cambridge (Eng.) U., 1967-68, N.Y.C. program Cornell U., 1968-70, CCNY, 1968-70, UCLA, 1976, U. So. Calif., 1976; prof. architecture, dean Sch. Environ. Design, Calif. State Poly. U., Pomona; chmn. dept. Otis/Parsons, Los Angeles; with Archtl. Office Louis I. Kahn, London, 1960-62; chmn. dept. environ. design Otis Parsons Calif. Founding dir. Group Environ. Edn., 1968; bd. dirs. Internat. Design Conf., Aspen, Colo., 1970-2002, chmn., 1972; co-chmn. 1st Fed. Design Assembly, 1973; trustee Center Bldg. Edn. Programs, 1976—; dep. dir. Phila. Office Housing and Community Devel., 1977; bd. dirs., chmn., creative dir. TED Confs.-Tech. Entertainment Design Conf., 1984-2002, Kobe, Japan, 1992, Monterey, Calif., 1994—, Tedmed Conf., Phila., 2003; pres. Access Press Ltd., The Understanding Bus., 1981-91; designer exhbns., cons. in field; vis. scholar MIT, 1993—, RISD, 1995—; found. bd. eBook. Author 85 books including The Notebooks and Drawings of Louis I. Kahn, The Nature of Recreation, Urban Atlas, Man Made Philadelphia, Aspen Visible, Our Man Made Environment; also author 27 vols. ACCESS travel and info. guidebook series; editor: What Will Be Has Alway Been: The Words of Louis I. Kahn, Information Anxiety 2, Follow the Yellow Brick Road, The Wall Street Journal Guide to Understanding Money and Markets, Fortune Guide to Understanding Personal finance, 1992, USAtlas, 1990, N, The Newport Guide, 1995, Information Architects, 1996, C, Understanding USA, 1996, The Charleston Guide, 1997, Wills, Trusts and Estate Planning, 2001, Diagnostic Tests for Men, 2001, Diagnostic Tests for Women, 2001, Heart Disease and Cardiovascular Health, 2001, Drugs Prescription, non-prescription and Herbal, 2001, Can I Afford to Retire?, 2001, Information Anxiety, 2001, Understanding Children, 2002, Understanding Healthcare, 2003; DE contbr. articles to profl. jours.; retrospective exhbn. AXIS Design Gallery, Tokyo, 1991. Recipient Thornton Oakley medal, 1954, Arthur Spayd Brookes Gold medal, 1958, Kevin Lynch award MIT, 1991, Stars of Design award and Chrysler award for innovation in design Pacific Design Ctr., 1996, Chrysler award for Innovation in Design, 1996; Graham fellow, 1966, 76; T.P. Chandler fellow, 1968; fellow Guggenheim Found., 1969; fellow Rockefeller Bros. Fund, 1972; fellow Nat. Endowment Arts, 1970, 73, 74, 76, 79-80; fellow World Econ. Forum, Davos, Switzerland, 1994—; grantee Fels Found., 1970; grantee Ednl. Facilities Lab., 1972, 74; grantee Rohm & Haas Co., 1976 Fellow AIA (medal 1958); mem. Am. Inst. Graphic Artists (v.p., bd. dirs. 1985), Alliance Graphique Internat. Address: The Orchard 180 Narragansett Ave Newport RI 02840-6929

WURMFELD, SANFORD, artist, educator; b. N.Y.C., Dec. 6, 1942; s. Charles Jacob and Esther (Witzling) W.; m. Rella Stuart-Hunt, Dec. 11, 1971; children: Jeremy Philip, Treva. BA in Art with honors, Dartmouth Coll., 1964; ind. study, Rome, 1964-65. Lectr. Hunter Coll., N.Y.C., 1967-72, asst. prof., 1972-77, assoc. prof., 1977-80, chmn. dept. art, 1978—, prof. art, 1980—, Caroff prof., 2000—. Vis. artist lectr. Calif. State Coll., Hayward, Cooper Union, NY, Bar Coll., Arondale-on-Hudson, NY, Drexel U., Phila., 1970, SUNY, Fredonia, 1971, Livingston Coll., New Brunswick, NJ, 1973, Whitney Mus., 1982, Met. Mus. Art, 1987, 87, Princeton U., 1990, The Slade Sch. U. Coll., London, 1991, Chelsea Coll. Art, London, 1991, Whitney Mus., 1992, Hochschule der Kurst, Berlin, 1995, Simon Fraser U., Vancouver, 1996, U. Victoria, B.C., 1996, Acad. Minerva, The Netherlands, Glasgow Sch. of Art, Scotland, 1997, external examiner, 1999—2003. One-man shows include Talbot Rice Gallery, Edinburgh, 2004, Altötting, Germany, 2003, Karl Ernst Osthaus Mus., Hagen, Germany, 2000, Susan Caldwell Gallery, Inc., NY, 1978, Bard Coll. Invitational Exhibit, 1977, Susan Caldwell Gallery, 1976-77, Galarie Denise Rene, 1974, Rockefeller Meml. Gallery, Fredonia, NY, 1971, Tibor de Nagy Gallery, 1968, Bryant Park, NY, Fischbach Gallery, 1969; group shows include Mus. Modern Art, NY, 1968, Grank Palais, Paris, 1968, Kunsthaus, Zurich, 1968, Tate Gallery, London, 1968, Ft. Worth Art Ctr., 1969, Galerie de Gestlo, Kunstfair, Basel Switzerland, 1970, 72, Columbia Film Festival, 1973, Galerie Denise Rene, 1974, Hopkins Ctr. Galleries, 1974, Lehigh U., 1976, Susan Caldwell Gallery, 1977-79, Toni Birckhard Gallery, Cin., 1980, Carnegie Internat., 1983, Shanghai Exhbn. Hall Shanghai, China, 1986, Long Beach Mus. of Art, Calif., 1989, William Paterson Coll. of NJ, 1990, Hallwells Contemporary Arts Ctr., Buffalo, 1991, Louis Stern Fine Arts, LA, 1995, Andre Zarre Gallery, NY, 1996, Karl Ost Haus-Mus., Hagen, Germany, Mucsarnok, Budapest, 2002, others; represented in permanent collections at Espace de l'Art Conret, Mouans-Sartoux, France, Karl Ernst Osthaus Mus., Hagen, Germany, Met. Mus. Art, NY, Guggenheim Mus., NY, Espace de l'Art Concrete, Mouans-Saroux, France, SUNY, Fredonia, Cen. Trust Co., Cin., Am. Telephone and Telegraph, NY, Baxter Travenol Labs., Deerfield, Ill., Gen. Electric Corp., Fairfield, Conn., Sprengler Mus., Hanover, Fed. Republic of Germany, City of Hannover, Fed. Republic of Germany, Shreve, Lamb & Harmon Corp., NY, Silkscreeners Guild, W. Ger., Warner Nat. Corp., Cin., U. NC, William Hayes Ackland Meml. Art Ctr., Chapel Hill, others; contbr. articles to profl. jour. Recipient Ames award Dartmouth Coll., 1964; fellow Guggenheim Found., 1974, Nat. Endowments for the Arts Individual Artist's, 1987-88; CUNY faculty rsch. grantee. Home: 18 Warren St New York NY 10007-1066 Office: Hunter Coll Dept Art 695 Park Ave New York NY 10021-5024 Office Phone: 212-772-5051. Business E-Mail: sanford.wurmfeld@hunter.cuny.edu.

WÜRSIG, BERND GERHARD, marine biology educator; b. Barsinghausen, Germany, Nov. 9, 1948; s. Gerhard Paul and Charlotte Annemarie (Yorkowski) W.; m. Melany Anne Carballeira, Nov. 19, 1969; children: Kim, Paul. BS, Ohio State U., 1971; PhD, SUNY, Stony Brook, 1978. Postdoctoral researcher U. Calif., Santa Cruz, 1978-81; prof. Moss Landing (Calif.) Marine Labs., 1981-89; prof. marine biology, dir. Marine Mammal Lab. Tex. A&M U., Galveston, 1989—, dir. The Inst. of Marine Life Scis., 1996—. Govt. cons. Minerals Mgmt. Service, Washington, 1980—. Contbr. articles to profl. jours., 7-part miniseries to TV on lives of dolphins, dolphin problems induced by humans, also Discovery Channel show on Life of B Würsig; co-author: The Hawaiian Spinner Dolphin, 1994, Whales, Dolphins and Porpoises, 1995; sr. advisor (IMAX film) Dolphins, 2000 (nominee Acad. award best spl. category nature movie), sr. author The Marine Mammals of the Gulf of Mexico, 2000; co-editor: The Encyclopedia of Marine Mammals, 2002. Recipient Chmn.'s award for rsch. and exploration, Nat. Geog. Soc., 1998, Alban-Heiser award for excellence in Tex. conservation rsch., Zool. Soc. Houston, 1991; Fulbright Found. scholar, 2001—03. Mem. Marine Mammal Soc. (pres. 1991-93), N.Y. Acad. Scis., Soc. Cryptozoology, Am. Behavior Soc., Am. Mus. Natural History, Soc. Archimedes. Clubs: Explorers (N.Y.C.) (fellow of research). Avocations: photography, diving, airplane piloting, skiing, hiking. Home: 2402 Creekridge Pearland TX 77581- Office: Tex A&M U Marine Mammal Rsch Program 4700 Avenue U Ste 303 Galveston TX 77551-6900

WURSTER, CHARLES FREDERICK, environmental scientist, educator; b. Phila., Aug. 1, 1930; s. Charles Frederick and Helen B. Wurster; children: Steven Hadley, Nina F., Erik Frederick. SB, Haverford Coll., 1952; MS, U. Del., 1954; PhD, Stanford U., 1957. Tchg. asst. U. Del., 1952-54; rsch. asst. Stanford U., 1954-57; Fulbright fellow Innsbruck, Austria, 1957-58; rsch. chemist Monsanto Rsch. Corp., 1959-62; rsch. assoc. biol. scis. Dartmouth Coll., 1962-65; asst. prof. biol. scis. SUNY, Stony Brook, 1965-70; assoc. prof. environ. scis. Marine Scis. Rsch. Ctr., 1970-94, prof. emeritus, 1994—. Vis. prof. Macquarie U., Sydney, Australia, 1988; founding trustee, sec., mem. exec. com. Environ. Def., 1967—; mem. adminstr.'s pesticide policy adv. com. EPA, 1975—78; leader ecol. tours worldwide. Contbr. articles to profl. publs. Fellow: AAAS; mem.: Nat. Pks. Conservation Assn. (trustee 1970—79), Defenders Wildlife (dir. 1975—84, 1987—96). Achievements include research on DDT, PCBs, other chlorinated hydrocarbon effects on phytoplankton, birds; relationship between environmental sciences and public policy; seabird protection; instrumental in banning several insecticides, including DDT, Dieldrin and Aldrin. Office: SUNY Marine Scis Research Ctr Stony Brook NY 11794-5000 E-mail: cfwurster@yahoo.com.

WURSTER, DALE ERIC, pharmacy educator; b. Madison, Wis., Jan. 19, 1951; s. Dale Erwin and June M. (Peterson) W.; m. Pamela Ann Marvin, May 31, 1975; children: Elizabeth Ann, Kristin Gail, Dale Edward. BS in Chemistry, U. Wis., 1974; PhD in Phys. Pharmacy, Purdue U., 1979. Asst. prof. Sch. Pharmacy U. N.C., Chapel Hill, NC, 1979—82; asst. to assoc. prof. Coll. Pharmacy U. Iowa, Iowa City, 1982—95, prof. Coll. Pharmacy, 1996—, divsn. head pharmaceutics, 2000—01, assoc. dean Grad. Coll., 2002—. Cons. Nat. Assn. Bds. of Pharmacy, Park Ridge, Ill., 1982—; apptd. to U.S. Pharmacopeial Conv. Com. of Revision, 1995—; cons. in field. Contbr. articles to profl. jours. Fed. and indsl. grantee. Fellow Am. Assn. Pharm. Scientists; mem. Am. Chem. Soc., Am. Assn. Colls. Pharmacy, Materials Rsch. Soc., Sigma Xi. Achievements include research in tablet coatings for controlled release, surface phenomena, solution and differential scanning calorimetry, chemical kinetics; dissolution kinetics and testing, physics of tablet compression, analytical applications of Fourier transform infrared spectroscopy. Home: 3808 County Down Ln NE North Liberty IA 52317-9388 Office: Coll Pharmacy S215 Iowa City IA 52242 Also: Grad Coll 205G Gilmore Hall Iowa City IA 52242 Address: Univ Iowa Grad Coll 205G Gilmore Hall Iowa City IA 52242 E-mail: dale-e-wurster@uiowa.edu.

WURSTER, DALE ERWIN, pharmacist, educator, retired dean; b. Sparta, Wis., Apr. 10, 1918; s. Edward Emil and Emma Sophia (Steingraeber) W.; m. June Margaret Peterson, June 16, 1944; children: Dale Eric, Susan Gay. BS, U. Wis., 1942, PhD, 1947. U. Wis. Sch. Pharmacy, Madison, 1958-71, mem. faculty, 1947-71; prof., dean N.D. State U. Coll. Pharmacy, 1971-72; prof. Dale E. Wurster Ctr. Pharm. Tech., Iowa City, 2003, dean, 1972-84, dean emeritus, 1984—. George B. Kaufman Meml. lectr. Ohio State U., 1968; Hancher Finkbine Medallion prof. U. Iowa, 1984; Joseph V. Swintosky disting. lectr. U. Ky., 2000; cons. in field; phys. sci. adminstr. USN, 1960-63; sci. advisor U. Wis. Alumni Rsch. Found., 1968-72; mem. revision com. U.S. Pharmacopoeia, 1961-70; mem. pharmacy rev. com. USPHS, 1966-72; mem. tech. adv. com. contraceptive R&D program Ea. Va. Med. Sch., 1987-2002, rsch., U. Wis. Contbr. articles to profl. jours., chpts. to books; patentee in field. With USNR, 1944-46. Recipient Superior Achievement citation Navy Dept., 1964, merit citation U. Wis., 1976, Disting. Alumni award U. Wis. Sch. Pharmacy, 1984; Dale E. Wurster Ctr. Pharm. Tech. at U. Iowa named in his honor. Fellow Am. Assn. Pharm. Scientists (founder, sponsor Dale E. Wurster rsch. award 1990—, Disting. Pharm. Scientist award 1991); mem. Am. Assn.

Colls. Pharmacy (exec. com. 1964-66, chmn. conf. tchrs. 1960-61, vis. scientist 1963-70, Disting. Educator award 1983), Acad. Pharm. Scis. (exec. com. 1967-70, chmn. basic pharmaceutics sect. 1965-67, pres. 1975, Indsl. Pharm. Tech. award 1980), Am. Pharm. Assn. (chmn. sci. sect. 1964-65, rsch. achievement award 1965, Wis. Disting. Svc. award 1971), Iowa Pharmacists Assn. (Robert G. Gibbs award 1983), Wis. Acad. Scis., Arts and Letters, Soc. Investigative Dermatology, Rumanian Soc. Med. Sci. (hon.), Am. Found. Pharm. Edn. (bd. grants 1987-92), Sigma Xi, Kappa Psi (past officer), Rho Chi, Phi Lambda Upsilon, Phi Sigma. Home: 16 Brickwood Cir NE Iowa City IA 52240-9129 Office Phone: 319-335-8799.

WURTELE, CHRISTOPHER ANGUS, paint and coatings company executive; b. Mpls., Aug. 25, 1934; Valentine and Charlotte (Lindley) W.; m. Heather Campbell (div. Feb. 1977); children: Christopher, Andrew, Heidi; m. Margaret Von Blon, Aug. 21, 1977. BA, Yale U., 1956; MBA, Stanford U., 1961. V.p. Minn. Paints, Inc. (merged with Valspar Corp. 1970), Mpls., 1962-65, exec. v.p., 1965, pres., CEO, 1973-96, chmn., 1973-98. Bd. dirs. Walker Art Ctr. With USN, 1956-59. Mem. Mpls. Club. Episcopalian. Home: 2970 Gale Rd Wayzata MN 55391 Office: 4900 IDS Ctr 80 S 8th St Minneapolis MN 55402

WURTMAN, RICHARD JAY, physician, educator, inventor; b. Phila., Mar. 9, 1938; s. Samuel Richard and Hilda (Schreiber) W.; m. Judith Joy Hirschhorn, Nov. 15, 1959; children: Rachael Elisabeth, David Franklin. AB, U. Pa., 1956; MD, Harvard U., 1960. Intern Mass. Gen. Hosp., 1960-61, resident, 1961-62, fellow medicine, 1965-66, clin. assoc. in medicine, 1985—; research assoc., med. research officer NIMH, 1962-67; mem. faculty MIT, Cambridge, 1967—, prof. endocrinology and metabolism, 1970-80, prof. neuroendocrine regulation, 1980-94, Cecil H. Green disting. prof., 1994—; dir. Clin. Rsch. Ctr., MIT, Cambridge, 1985—; prof. neuroscience MIT, 1984-94. Lectr. medicine Harvard Med. Sch., 1969—; prof. Harvard-MIT Divsn. Health Scis. and Tech., 1978—; Smithies lectr. Oxford U., 2002; sci. dir. Ctr. for Brain Scis. and Metabolism Charitable Trust, 1981—; invited prof. U. Geneva, 1981; Sterling vis. prof. Boston U., 1981; vis. fellow Balliol Coll., Oxford U., 1997; mem. small grants study sect. NIMH, 1967-69, preclin. psychopharmacology study sect., 1971-75; behavioral biology adv. panel NASA, 1969-72; coun. basic sci. Am. Heart Assn., 1969-74; rsch. adv. bd. Parkinson's Disease Found., 1972-80, Am. Parkinson's Disease Assn., 1978—; com. phototherapy in newborns NRC-Nat. Acad. Scis., 1972-74, com. nutrition, brain devel. and behavior, 1976, mem. space applications bd., 1976-82; mem. task force on drug devel. Muscular Dystrophy Assn., 1980-87; chmn. life scis. adv. com. NASA, 1979-82; chmn. adv. bd. Alzheimer's Disease Assn., 1981-84; assoc. neuroscis. rsch. program MIT, 1974-82; chmn. life scis. adv. bd. USAF, 1985—; Bennett lectr. Am. Neurol. Assn., 1974; Flexner lectr. U. Pa., 1975; founder, chmn. sci. adv. bd. Interneuron Pharms., Inc., 1989-99; co-founder Wurtco, 1999, Back Bay Sci., 1999. Author: Catecholamines, 1966; (with others) The Pineal, 1968; editor: (with Judith Wurtman) Nutrition and the Brain, Vols. I and II, 1977, Vols. III, IV, V., 1979, Vol. VI, 1983, Vol. VII, 1986, Vol. VIII, 1990, also some 1000 other articles and books; mem. editl. bd. Endocrinology, 1967-73, Jour. Pharmacology and Exptl. Therapeutics, 1968-75, Jour. Neural Transmission, 1969-88, Neuroendocrinology, 1969-72, Metabolism, 1970-80, Circulation Research, 1972-77, Jour. Neurochemistry, 1973-82, Life Scis., 1973-81, Brain Rsch., 1977—. Mem. bd. overseers Boston Symphony Orch., 1997—; bd. dirs. Fenway Cmty. Health Ctr., Boston, 1998—, Provincetown Art Assn. and Mus., 2000—. Recipient Alvarenga prize and lectureship Phila. Coll. Physicians, 1970, CIBA-Geigy Drew award in Biomed. Rsch., 1982, Roger Williams award in Preventive Nutrition, 1987, NIMH Merit award, 1989—, Internat. Prize for Modern Nutrition, 1989, Hall of Fame Disting. Alumni award Ctrl. H.S. Phila., 1992; Disting. lectr. Purdue U., 1984; Rufus Cole lectr., Rockefeller U., 1985; Pfizer lectr. NYU Med. Sch., 1985; Grass Fedn. lectr. U. Ga., 1985, Alan Rothballer Meml. lectr., N.Y. Med. Coll., Valhalla, N.Y., 1989, Gretchen Kerr Green lectr in the neuroscis., 1989; Wellcome Vis. Prof. Washington State U., Pullman, 1989; Julius Axelrod Disting. lectr. in neurosci., CUNY, 1990, Sigma Tau Found. lectr. on aging, Rome, 1990, Disting. lectr. in neurosci. La. State U., 1991, McEwen lectr. Queen's U., Ont., 1991; Plenary lectr. 3d Internat. Symposium on Microdialysis, 1993; Hans Lindner Meml. lectr. Weizmann Inst., 1993, Waldo E. Nelson Meml. lectr. St. Christopher's Hosp., Phila., 1997, Sidney Kibrick M.D. lectr. Boston U. Med. Sch., 1998. Mem. Am. Soc. Clin. Investigation, Endocrine Soc. (Ernst Oppenheim award 1972), Am. Physiol. Soc., Am. Soc. Biol. Chemists, Am. Soc. Pharmacology and Exptl. Therapeutics (John Jacob Abel award 1968), Am. Soc. Neurochemistry, Soc. Neuroscis., Am. Soc. Clin. Nutrition, Am. Inst. Nutrition (Osborne & Mendel award 1982), Harvard Club (Boston). Achievements include some 60 U.S. patents on new treatments for diseases and conditions; invention of melatonin for promoting sleep, of dexfenfluramine for treating obesity, of citicoline for treating stroke and of Sarafem for the treatment of premenstrual syndrome. Home: 300 Boylston St Boston MA 02116-3923 Office: Mass Inst Tech 45 Carleton St # E25-604 Cambridge MA 02142-1323 Office Phone: 617-253-6731. Business E-Mail: dick@mit.edu.

WURTZ, GEORGE W., III, paper company executive; b. L.I., N.Y., June 19, 1956; BS in Edn. and Indsl. Engring., SUNY, Oswego, 1978. Various mfg. positions Miller Brewing Co. divsn. Phillip Morris, Milw., 1978—87; dir. logistics James River Corp., Norwalk, Conn., 1987—90, dir. mfg. planning, 1990—91, plant mgr. Berlin Gorham, NH, 1991—94; v.p. procurement Fort James, Norwalk, 1994—97, sr. v.p. logistics and procurement Deerfield, Ill., 1997—98, sr. v.p. mfg., 1998—2001; sr. v.p. consumer products mfg. ctrl. Ga.-Pacific Corp., Green Bay, Wis., 2001, pres. paper, bleached board and kraft Atlanta, 2001—03, exec. v.p., pres. pulp and paper, 2003—. Mem.: Am. Prodn. Inventory Control Soc., Coun. Logistics Mgmt., Paper Distbn. Coun., Nat. Paper Trade Assn., Am. Forest & Paper Assn., Brotherhood Eagles. Office: Georgia Pacific Corp 133 Peachtree St NE Atlanta GA 30303

WURTZ, MARGARET JOHNSTON, artist, calligrapher; b. Yonkers, N.Y., Feb. 19, 1930; d. James and Leontine (Orbanes) Johnston; m. Elmer S. Wurtz, May 5, 1951; children: Marguerite, Raymond, Eileen, James, Jeanette. BA, Molloy U., 1973; MA/L.S., SUNY, Stonybrook, 1985. Art tchr. St. Joseph, Babylon, N.Y., 1963-80; freelance artist and calligrapher Babylon, 1980—; propr. Marline Designer Shirts, Bolton Landing, NY, 1986-90. Student workshops Soc. of Scribes, N.Y.C., 1984—; active artist/exhibitor Wet Paints, Sayville, N.Y., 1994—. Artist fabric collage, 1985, pastel painting, 1998-2003. Vol. L.I. Maritime Mus., 1998—, St. Lawrence Soup Kitchen, Sayville, N.Y., 1998—, St. Patrick Soup Kitchen, Bay Shore, N.Y., 1995-2002, Cabinet for Sick, Sayville, 2003—. Mem. Sumpwams Garden Club (various awards 1985-2003). Roman Catholic. Avocations: gardening, piano, golf, bicycling, boating. Home: 15 Poplar St Sayville NY 11782-3116

WURTZ, ROBERT HENRY, neuroscientist; b. St. Louis, Mar. 28, 1936; s. Robert Henry and Alice Edith (Popplwell) Wurtz; m. Sally Smith, Dec. 20, 1958 (div.); children: William, Erica; m. Emily Otis, Apr. 23, 1983. AB, Oberlin Coll., 1958; PhD, U. Mich., 1962. Rsch. assoc. Com. for Nuclear Info., St. Louis, 1962-63; fellow Sch. Medicine, Washington U., 1962-65; rsch. psychologist NIH, Bethesda, Md., 1965-66, physiologist, 1966-78, sr. scientist Lab. Sensorimotor Rsch., 1978—. Vis. scientist Cambridge U., England, 1975—76. Editor: Neurobiology of Saccadic Eye Movement, 1989. Recipient Karl Spencer Lashley award, Am. Philos. Soc., 1995, Dan David prize for brain sci., 2004. Fellow: AAAS; mem.: NAS, APA (Disting. Sci. Contbn. award 1997), Soc. Exptl. Psychologists, Assn. for Rsch. in Vision and Opthalmology, Am. Physiol. Soc., Soc. Neurosci. (pres. 1991), Am. Acad. Arts and Scis., Inst. Medicine (Dan DAvid prize for brain scis. 2004). Office: NIH Nat Eye Inst Bldg 49 Rm 2A50 Bethesda MD 20892-4435

WURTZEL, ALAN LEON, retail company executive; b. Mount Vernon, N.Y., Sept. 23, 1933; s. Samuel S. and Ruth (Mann) W.; m. Irene C. Rosenberg, Oct. 9, 1988; children from previous marriage: Judith Halle, Daniel Henry, Sharon Lee. AB, Oberlin Coll., 1955; postgrad., London Sch. Econ., 1955-56; LLB cum laude, Yale, 1959. Bar: Conn. 1959, D.C. 1960, Va. 1968. Law clk. Chief Judge David L. Bazelon, U.S. Ct. Appeals, D.C., 1959-60; assoc. Fried, Frank, Harris, Shriver & Kampelman, Washington, 1960-65; legisl. asst. to Senator Joseph Tydings, 1965-66; with Cir. City Stores, Inc. (formerly Wards Co., Inc.), Richmond, 1966-2001, v.p., 1968-70, pres., 1970-83, chief exec. officer, 1973-86, chmn., 1983-94, vice chmn., 1994-2001; chmn. emeritus, 2002—. Pres. NATM Buying Corp., 1978-86; pres. Operation Independence, 1987-88; bd. dirs. Office Depot, Inc., Boca Raton, Fla., 1989-96, Dollar Tree Stores, Norfolk, Va., Nat. Alliance of Bus., Washington, 1992-1999, SchoolNet, Bethesda, MD, Metametrics, Inc., Durham, NC, Storetrax, Inc., Bethesda, MD; mem. Nat. Skills Stds. Bd. Bd. visitors Va. Commonwealth Ednl. U., 1985-92; trustee Oberlin Coll., 1989-96; dir. Washington Ednl. Television Assn., 1989-95; pres. Jewish Community Fedn., Richmond, 1983-85. Mem. Va. State Bd. Edn., 1992-1996, Gov.'s Econ. Adv. Coun. 1990-1991. Office: 2134 R St NW Washington DC 20008-1907 E-mail: alwurtzel@aol.com.

WURZBACH, LINDA, educational consultant; b. San Antonio, Jan. 21, 1954; d. Delmar Earl Wurzbach, Dorothy Lang Wurzbach; m. Mark Allison Tatom. BS, U. Tex., 1975, MEd, 1978. Lic. tchr. Tex. Tchr. Austin Indep. Sch. Dist., Austin, Tex., 1976—81; project mgr. Tex. Sch. for the Blind and Visually Impaired, Austin, 1981—82, tchr., 1982—89; project dir. The Psychol. Corp., San Antonio, 1989—90; planner Tex. Edn. Agy., Austin, 1990—96; sr. project assoc. Coun. Chief State Sch. Officers, Washington, 1996—98; pres. Resources for Learning, LLC, Austin, 1998—. Cons. Tex. Edn. Agy., Austin, 1998—, Region 20 Edn. Svc. Ctr., San Antonio, 1998—, State Bd. Educator Cert., Austin, 1998—, Calif. Comm. Tchr. Credentialing, Sacramento, 1998—2000, Alain Locke Charter Acad., Chgo., 1998—99, Ill. State Bd. Edn., Springfield, Ill., 1998—99, Ky. Profl. Standards Bd., Frankfort, 1999—2000, Region 13 Edn. Svc. Ctr., Austin, 2000—, Region 18 Edn. Svc. Ctr., Midland, 2002—03, Chgo. Children's Choir, 2000—00, Parks and Recreation Dept., Austin, 2001—02, Charles A. Dana Ctr., U. Tex., Austin, 2001, Inner-City Tchg. Corps, Chgo., S.W. Ednl. Devel. Lab., 2002—, Okla. Commn. Tchr. Preparation, 2003—, La. State Dept. Edn., 2003—, N.Mex. State Dept. Edn. and U. Mex., 2003—. Editor: TxBESS Activity Profile, 2001, Fine Arts Curriculum Frameworks, 2000; author: Works in Progress, 1997, Portfolio Assessment for Beginning Teachers, 1999, Performance Assessment System, 2000; prodr.: (video) If You Love It, Teach It., 2000, Express Yourself, 2001, Fine Arts for All Students, 2003, Beginning Teacher Induction Toolkit: A Systems Approach, 2004; contbr. articles to profl. jous. Mem.: U.S. Women's C. of C., Internat. Game Developers Assn., Nat. Coun. Measurement in Edn., Am. Ednl. Rsch. Assn., Nat. Staff Devel. Coun., Assn. Supervision and Curriculum Develop. Home: 4504 Moose Dr Austin TX 78749 Office: Resources for Learning Bldg A Ste 103 206 Wild Basin Rd Austin TX 78746 Office Phone: 512-327-8576. Office Fax: 512-327-8577. Business E-Mail: lindaw@resourcesforlearning.net.

WURZEL, LEONARD, retired candy manufacturing company executive; b. Phila., Feb. 4, 1918; s. Maurice L. and Dora (Goldberg) W.; m. Elaine Cohen, Aug. 18, 1949; children— Mark L., Lawrence J. BS, Washington and Jefferson Coll., 1939; MBA, Harvard, 1941. With Loft Candy Corp., Long Island City, N.Y., 1946-64, v.p., 1949-56, exec. v.p., 1956-57, pres., 1957-64, dir., 1949-64; chmn., dir. Calico Cottage Candies, Inc., 1964-94; ret., 1994; mayor Village of Sands Point, N.Y., 1989—. Capt. U.S. Army, 1941—46. Decorated Bronze Star. Mem. Assn. Mfrs. Confectionery and Chocolate (bd. dirs., past pres., chmn.), Candy Chocolate and Confectionery Inst. (bd. dirs., treas.), Retail Confectioners Internat. (bd. dirs., past pres.) Home: 25 Woodland Dr Sands Point NY 11050-1136 Office: 26 Tibbits Ln Sands Point NY 11050-1135 Office Phone: 516-883-3044.

WUSSLER, ROBERT JOSEPH, broadcasting executive, media consultant; b. Newark, Sept. 8, 1936; s. William and Anna (MacDonald) W.; children: Robert Joseph, Rosemary, Sally, Stefanie, Christopher, Jeanne. BA in Communication Arts, Seton Hall U., 1957, LLD (hon.), 1976, Emerson Coll., 1976. With CBS News, N.Y.C., 1957-72; v.p., gen. mgr. Sta. WBBM-TV, Chgo., 1972-74; v.p. CBS Sports, N.Y.C., 1974-76, pres., 1977-78, Sta. CBS-TV, N.Y.C., 1976-77, Pyramid Enterprises Ltd., N.Y.C., 1978-80; exec. v.p. Turner Broadcasting System Inc., Atlanta, 1980-87, sr. exec. v.p., from 1987, bd. dirs.; pres. Atlanta Sports Teams, Inc., 1981-87; pres., chief exec. officer COMSAT Video Enterprises, Inc., Washington, 1989-92; pres. Wussler Group, 1992—. Chmn. bd. dirs. Nat. Acad. TV Arts and Scis., 1986-90; bd. dirs. Atlanta Hawks Ltd., Atlanta Braves Nat. League Baseball Club, Inc.; co-owner Denver Nuggets, NBA, 1989-92. Bd. regents Seton Hall U., 1978-84; trustee Marymount Manhattan Coll., 1977-81. Recipient Emmy awards, numerous other nat. and internat. news and sports awards. Mem. Dirs. Guild Am., Internat. Radio and TV Soc., Ariz. Heart Inst., Cable Advt. Bur., Nat. Cable TV Assn. (satellite network com.), European Broadcasting Union. Roman Catholic. Home and Office: Unit 4630 75 Fourteenth St Atlanta GA 30309 Office Phone: 404-522-5070. Personal E-mail: rjwtv@aol.com.

WUTHNOW, SARA MARGERY, retired nursing educator; b. Kansas City, Kans., Mar. 9, 1946; d. D. Ray and L. Elizabeth (Edgar) Wilcox; m. Robert Wuthnow, June 15, 1968; children: Robyn, Brooke, Joel. BSN, U. No. Colo., 1969; MSN, U. Calif., San Francisco, 1971; EdD, Rutgers U., 1982. Staff nurse Herrick Hosp., Berkeley, Calif., 1969-70; clin. supr. Samuel Merritt Hosp., Oakland, Calif., 1971-74; faculty U. Ariz., Tucson, 1975-76, Helene Fuld Sch. Nursing, Trenton, N.J., 1976-77, Trenton State Coll., 1977-78, 83-84, Holy Family Coll., Phila., 1984-93; chair dept. Nursing Eastern Coll., St. David's, Pa., 1993-99; acting MSN chair Holy Family Coll., Phila., 1999—2002; ret. Contbr. articles to profl. jours. Mem. Sigma Theta Tau.

WÜTHRICH, KURT, molecular biologist, biophysical chemist, educator; b. Oct. 4, 1938; MS in Chemistry, Physics and Maths., U. Bern, Switzerland, 1962; Eidenössisches Turn-und Sportlehrerdiplom, U. Basel, Switzerland, 1964; D Chem (hon.), U. Siena, Italy, 1997; PhD in Chemistry, U. Basel, Switzerland, 1964; PhD (hon.), U. Zürich, Switzerland, 1997, Ecole Poly. Lausanne, 2001, U. Valencia, Spain, 2004, U. Sheffield, 2004. Postdoctoral tng. U. Basel, U. Calif., Berkeley, Bell Telephone Labs., Murray Hill, N.J., 1964-69; prof. biophysics Swiss Fed. Inst. Tech., Zürich, 1972—, chmn. dept. biology, 1995-2000; prof. structural biology The Scripps Rsch. . Inst., 2001. Mem. coun. Internat. Union Pure and Applied Biophysics, 1975-78, 87-90, sec. gen., 1978-84, v.p., 1984-87; mem. gen. com. Internat. Coun. Sci. Unions, 1980-86, standing com. on free circulation of scientists, 1982-90. Editor Jour. Biomolecular NMR, Quar. Rev. Biophysics, Macromolecular Structures; contbr. articles to profl. jours. Recipient Friedrich Miescher prize Schweizerische Biochemische Gesellschaft, 1974, shield of faculty of medicine Tokyo U., 1983, P. Bruylants medal Cath. U. Louvain, 1986, Stein and Moore award Protein Soc., U.S., 1990, Louisa Gross Horwitz prize Columbia U., 1991, Gilbert N. Lewis medal U. Calif., Berkeley, 1991, Marcel Benoist prize Swiss Confederation, 1992, Disting. Svc. award Miami Winter Symposia, 1993, Prix Louis Jeantet de Médecine, Geneva, 1993, Kaj Linderstrøm-Lang prize Kaj Linderstrøm-Lang Found., Copenhagen, 1996, Eminent Scientist of RIKEN (Tokyo), 1997, Kyoto prize in Advanced Tech., 1998, Guenther Laukien prize Exptl. Nuclear Magnetic Resonance Conf., 1999, Otto Warburg medal Soc. for Biochemistry and Molecular Biology, Germany, 1999, World Future award M. Gorbatschow Found., 2002, Nobel Prize in Chemistry, 2002; Swiss Soc. award, 2002; Fgn. fellow Indian Nat. Sci. Acad.; hon. fellow NAS India. Fellow: AAAS; mem.: Schweizerische Akademie der Medizinischen Wissenschaften, Schweizerische Akademie der Technischen Wissenschaften, Academia Europea, European Molecular Biology Orgn., Deutsche Akad. der Naturforscher Leopoldina, Hungarian Acad. Sci. (hon.), Internat. Soc. Magnetic Resonance in Med. (hon.), Royal Soc. Edinburgh (hon.), Royal Soc. Chemistry (hon.), World Innovation Found. (hon.), Swiss Chem. Soc. (hon.), World Innovation Found. (hon.), Nat. Magnetic Resonance Soc. India (hon.), Japanese Biochem. Soc. (hon.), Am. Acad. Arts and Scis (hon.), Acad. Scis., Inst. France (assoc.), U.S. Nat. Acad (assoc.). Office: Inst Molecular Biology & Biophysics ETH Hönggerberg 8093 Zurich Switzerland also: Dept Molec Biology TSRI 10550 N Torrey Pines Rd La Jolla CA 92037

WYAND, MARTIN JUDD, economics educator, retired military officer; b. Greenwich, Conn., May 28, 1931; s. Charles Samuel and Marian (Winter) W.; m. Margaret Alison Knox, May 26, 1974. BA in Social Sci., Pa. State U., 1953, MA in Econs., 1954; JD in Law, U. Denver, 1969; PhD Econs., U. Ill., 1964. Graduate teaching asst. Pa. State U., Univ. Park., 1953-54; grad. teaching asst. U. Ill., Urbana, 1960-64; from asst. prof. to prof. U. Denver, 1964-82; adj. prof. econs. Metro State Coll., Denver, 1982-84. Adj. prof. Coll. Bus. Adminstrn., U. Colo. Denver, 1984-90; lectr. Coll. Bus. Adminstrn., Pa. State U., 1990—99, ret.; instr. Armed Forces Intelligence Tng. Ctr., 1974-76. Contbr. articles to profl. jours. Adminstrv. bd. dirs. Washington Park Meth. Ch., Denver, 1977-85. Served to col. USAFR, 1953-83, ret. 1991. Grantee Shell Oil Co., 1966, U. Denver, 1976. Mem. Am. Econ. Assn., Am. Collegiate Sch. Bus., Rocky Mountain Social Sci. Assn., Res. Officers Assn. (pres. Geddes chpt. 1978-82, ret.), Ret. Officers Assn., Air Force Assn., Alpha Kappa Psi, Pi Gamma Mu, Alpha Phi Omega. Avocations: reading, chess, classical music, swimming. Home: 1066 Crabapple Dr State College PA 16801-4252

WYANT, CAROL SHUMAKER, not for profit management consultant; b. Alameda, Calif., May 26, 1939; d. Paul Russell and Helen Carolyn (Overstreet) Shumaker; m. Clyde William Wyant, Jr., Sept. 4, 1960 (div. Apr. 1984); children: John Russell, James William. BA, Stanford U., 1961; MA, Tulsa U., 1980. Fin. feasibility analyst Williams Realty Corp., Tulsa and San Antonio, 1980, real estate developer, 1981-84, leasing and bldg. mgr., 1984-85, cmty. affairs, 1985-87; exec. dir. Landmarks Preservation Coun. Ill., Chgo., 1987-94; dir. statewide partnerships Nat. Trust for Hist. Preservation, Washington, 1995-99; founder, pres. Pathfinder Cons., Chgo., 1999—. Vice chmn. Sales Tax Overview Com., Tulsa, 1983; v.p. Univ. Roundtable, San Antonio, 1982. V.p. Jr. League Tulsa, 1976; chmn. Citizens Coalition for Cmty. Devel., Tulsa, 1980; chmn. com. Downtown Owners Assn., San Antonio, 1982; advisor Isle La Motte Reef Preservation Trust. Named one of Outstanding Young Women of Am., 1968; recipient Pres.'s award, Nat. Trust for Hist. Preservation, 1999, Cert. of Merit Ill. Hist. Preservation Agy, 1990. Mem.: AIA (Chgo. br. hon.), The Chgo. Network (issues com. chair), Internat. Women's Forum, Mensa, Lambda Alpha Internat. Avocations: hiking, bicycling, singing, travel. Home: 161 W Harrison St Unit 407 Chicago IL 60605-1019 Office: Pathfinder Cons 203 N Wabash Ave Ste 1800 Chicago IL 60601 also: PO Box 4224 Sedona AZ 86340-4224 Office Phone: 312-346-5942. E-mail: carolwyant@mindspring.com.

WYANT, CLYDE W., JR., manufacturing executive; b. Ada, Okla., Sept. 20, 1938; s. Clyde W. and Geneva Pauline (George) W.; m. Anne L. Edgerton, Nov. 23, 1984; children: Lynn, John, James, Markham, Carolyn BA in History, Stanford U., 1960; MBA, Harvard U., 1965. Asst. to pres. Helmerich & Payne, Inc., Tulsa, 1965-68, fin. v.p., 1968-85; exec. v.p., chief fin. officer Purolator Products Co. (formerly Facet Enterprises, Inc.), Tulsa, 1985-90; exec. v.p., CFO, treas. Lennox Internat., Inc., 1990-2001. Dir. Am. Nursery Products, Tahlequah, Okla., Hawkins Energy Co., Tulsa. Vice pres., trustee Holland Hall Sch., Tulsa, 1978-86; trustee Hillcrest Med. Ctr., Tulsa; vice chmn. admissions com. Tulsa Area United Way, 1979-86, chmn. allocations com., 1987, pres.-elect 1989, pres., 1990; fin. com. chmn. Community Network for Public Edn., Tulsa, 1983-85, Okla. Profl. Affairs Tribunal, 1989—; pres., treas., dir. Jr. Achievement of Greater Tulsa, 1978-86; community advisor Jr. League of Tulsa, 1979-82. Served to lt. U.S. Army, 1960-62 Recipient Bronze Leadership award Jr. Achievement, 1983 Mem. Fin. Execs. Inst. (pres. 1979-80), Am. Petroleum Inst., Mid-Continent Harvard Bus. Sch. Assn. (pres. 1980-82) Clubs: Tulsa Tennis (pres. 1985). Avocations: tennis; fishing; cooking. Office: Lennox Internat Inc PO Box 799900 Dallas TX 75379-9900 also: Two Warren Pl E 61st St Ste 1100 Tulsa OK 74136-0523 Home: 2140 Lake Park Blvd Richardson TX 75080-2252

WYANT, CORBIN A. newspaper publisher; m. Donna Lee Humphrey, Oct. 5, 1963; children: Mrs. Blair Milliken, Corbin W., Beth Ashley. BA, Bucknell U., 1958; student, Pa. State U., 1973-74. Reporter, photographer Daily Leader-Times, Kittanning, Pa., 1958-69, advt. sales rep., circulation mgr., 1960-61, co-pub., gen. mgr., 1961-73; pres. Daily Dispatch, Douglas, Ariz., 1965-73; pub. Daily Herald News, Punta Gorda, Fla., 1974-76; v.p., gen. mgr. Naples (Fla.) Daily News, 1977-85, pub., 1985—, pres., 1986—. Host Byline, WGCU pub. TV. Past treas., founder Mental Health Clinic Armstrong County, Pa.; past bd. dirs. Mental Health and Mental Retardation Assn. Armstrong and Ind. Counties, Med. Ctr. Hosp., Punta Gorda, Fla.; past chmn. Armstrong County Airport Authority; past v.p., bldg. chmn. YMCA Charlotte County; elder First Presbyn. Ch., Naples; asst. coach Babe Ruth Baseball, Naples, 1983; coach Little League, Naples, 1979; bd. dirs. Naples Philharm., Inc., 1987—, Cmty. Concert Assn., 1978-84; mem. adv. bd. Salvation Army, Naples, 1987—; v.p. Collier Cultural Ctr., Inc., 1978-82, YMCA Collier County, 1977-87. Recipient Nat. Journalism award for literacy Scripps Howard Found., 2000. Mem. Fla. Press Assn. (bd. dirs. 1986-92, pres. 1993-94, chmn. 1994-95), Fla. Newspaper Advt. Network (founder, bd. dirs. 1987—), Econ. Devel. Coun. Collier County (bd. dris. 1995—), Edison C.C. Endowment Corp. (bd. dirs. 1994-98), Gulf Coast Sailing Assn., Collier Athletic Club, Forum Club Collier County (pres. 1988-89), Rotary (pres. Naples 1982-83). Office: Naples Daily News PO Box 7009 Naples FL 34101-7009

WYANT, JAMES CLAIR, engineering company executive, educator; b. Morenci, Mich., July 31, 1943; s. Clair William and Idah May (Burroughs) W.; m. Louise Doherty, Nov. 20, 1971; 1 child, Clair Frederick. BS, Case Western Reserve, 1965; MS, U. Rochester, 1967, PhD, 1968. Engr. Itek Corp., Lexington, Mass., 1968-74; instr. Lowell (Mass.) Tech. Inst., 1969-74; prof. U. Ariz., Tucson, 1974—; pres. WYKO Corp., Tucson, 1984-97; dir. optical sci. ctr. U. Ariz., 1999—. Chmn. Gordon Conf. on Holography Plymouth (N.H.) State Coll., 1984; vis. prof. U. Rochester, N.Y., 1983. Editor: Applied Optics and Optical Engineering, vols. VII-X, 1979-80, 83, 87. Recipient of Joseph Fraunhofer-Robert M. Burley Prize, 1992, Optical Soc. Am. Mem. Optical Soc. Am. (bd. dirs. 1979-81, Tech. Achievement award 1988, Joseph Fraunhofer award 1992, R&D 100 award 1993, Gold medal 2003), Soc. Photo-Optical Instrumentation Engring. (pres. 1986, Gold medal 2003). Home: 1881 N King St Tucson AZ 85749-9367 Office: U Ariz Optical Scis Ctr Tucson AZ 85721-0001 E-mail: jcwyant@optics.arizona.edu.

WYATT, BILL, airport executive; b. Astoria, Oreg. Student, Willamette U., U. Oreg. Mem. Oreg. Legislature, 1975; dir. employee benefits and govt. rels. Oreg. State Employees Assn.; dir. intergovtl. affairs City of Portland; exec. dir. Assn. for Portland Progress; pres. Oreg. Bus. Coun.; chief of staff Gov. of Oreg., Salem, 1995—2001; airport exec. PDX, Portland, Oreg., 2001—. Bd.dirs. Crabbe-Huson family mut. funds. Past chmn. bd. Urban League of Portland; bd. dirs. Oreg. Pub. Broadcasting. Mem. City Club of Portland (past bd. govs.). Office: PDX 7000 NE Airport Way Portland OR 97218 Mailing: US Hdqs Port Portland PO Box 3529 Portland OR 97208

WYATT, BRETT MICHAEL, secondary school educator; b. Toledo, Dec. 31, 1958; s. Warren Dale and Jacqueline Elizabeth (Angelides) W.; 1 child, Adrian. BA in Geography, Calif. State U., San Bernardino, 1981; MA in Geography, U. Calif., Davis, 1985. Elem. tchr. Sacramento City Unified Sch. Dist., 1987-89, tech. resource tchr., 1989-91; ednl. cons. IBM, Sacramento, 1989-92; asst. editor Computers in the Schs., Reno, Nev., 1991-93; media specialist L.A. Unified Sch. Dist., 1998—. Author: Jewish Settlement in Sacramento, A Pictorial History, 1987; prodr.: (video) Sacramento Educational Cable Consortium, 1991, 92; contbg. poet: Nevada High Desert Rev., 1997, 98; contbr. articles to profl. jours. Advisor Tech. Preparation Com., Sacramento, 1991; founding dir. Nev. Schs. Network, Reno, 1992; advisor WCSD Internet Task Force, Reno, 1994—; archivist Temple B'hai Israel, Sacramento, 1986-87; computer technician vol. Ptnrs. in Edn., Sparks, Nev., 1994—. Named Vol. of the Yr., Ptnrs. in Edn., Sparks, 1995; recipient award for outstanding ednl. video Sacramento Ednl. Cable Consortium, 1991, 92. Democrat.

WYATT, BRYANT NELSON, education educator, writer; b. Waverly, Va., Sept. 6, 1937; s. Merlin DeWitt and Hazel Lelease Wyatt. BA in English, Va. State U., 1959; MA in English, Boston U., 1960; PhD in English, U. Va., 1970. English tchr. Ctrl. HS, Sussex, Va., 1962—63; prof. English Va. State U., Petersburg, Va., 1963—92, disting. prof. emeritus, 1992—. Vis. prof. English U. Va., 1970, Va. Commonwealth U., 1973. Contbr. articles various profl. jours. Reading tutor Tri-City Reading Coun., Petersburg, Va., 1983—88. Capt. USAR, 1959—68. Decorated Commendation medal U.S. Army; recipient Woodrow Wilson Tchg. Internship, 1965; Wemyss Found. Am. Studies

Fellowship, 1964, Ford Found. Advanced Study Grant, 1969. Mem.: Scabbard & Blade, Sigma Tau Delta, Kappa Delta Pi. Avocations: reading, guitar, songwriting, writing. Home: 416 Clinton St Petersburg VA 23803-5136

WYATT, DEBORAH CHASEN, lawyer; b. Atlanta, Apr. 19, 1949; d. S.H. and Catherine Jane (Hudlow) Chasen; m. Richard Haste Wyatt, Jr., Feb. 19, 1972; children: Thomas Clayton, William Tyler. Student, Sweet Briar Col., 1968-70; BA, Tufts U., 1971; JD, U. Va., 1978. Bar: Va. 1978, U.S. Dist. Ct. (we. and ea. dists.) Va. 1978, U.S. Ct. Appeals (4th cir.) 1980, U.S. Ct. Appeals (D.C. cir.) 1984, U.S. Supreme Ct. 1983. Assoc. Lowe & Gordon, Charlottesville, Va., 1978-80; ptnr. Wyatt & Rosenfield, Charlottesville, Va., 1980-83, Gordon & Wyatt, Charlottesville, Va., 1984-92, Wyatt & Carter, Charlottesville, Va., 1993-2000, Wyatt & Assocs., PLC, Charlottesville, Va., 2000—02, Wyatt & Assocs., PLC, 2004—, Wyatt & Armstrong PLC, Charlottesville, 2002—04. Mem. ATLA, Va. Coll. Criminal Def. Attys. (bd. dirs. 1997—), Charlottesville-Albemarle Criminal Bar Assn., Charlottesville Bar Assn. Avocations: writing, painting. Office: Wyatt & Assocs PLC 300 Court Sq Charlottesville VA 22902-5160

WYATT, EDWARD AVERY, V, city manager; b. Petersburg, Va, Nov. 1, 1941; s. Edward Avery IV and Martha Vaughan (Seabury) W.; m. Regina Helen Stec, Aug. 23, 1969; children: Edward Avery VI, Stephen Alexander, Kent Seabury. AS in Bus., Bluefield Coll.; BS in Bus., Pub. Adminstrn., Va. Poly. Inst. and State U., 1964; M.Commerce, U. Richmond, 1969; MA in Polit. Sci., Appalachian State U., 1977. Chief gen. svc. City of Petersburg, Va., 1966-67, asst. to city mgr., 1967-70; city mgr. City of Washington, NC, 1970-73, City of Morganton, NC, 1973-78, City of Greenville, NC, 1978-82, City of Fairfax, Va., 1982-91; ncity mgr. City of Wilson, NC, 1991—2004. Adj. lectr. George E. Mason U. Bus. Sch., 1985-86, 1995-2003; bd. dir. Electricities of NC, sec. 2000; commr. NC Ea. Mcpl. Power Agy. Contbr. numerous articles to profl. jour. and newsletters. Chmn. NC Code Ofcl. Qualification Bd., 1980-82; mem. adv. bd. Wilson Salvation Army, 1992—; vice-chair adv. coun. Wilson Boys and Girls Club.Flynn Home Bd. of Dir.; bd. dirs. Diversified Opportunites, Wilson United Way; Served with USNG and USAR, 1964-70. Paul Harris fellow Rotary Internat.; Dennis Duffey Meml. award Fairfax Police Youth Club. Internat. City Mgmt. Assn. (endowment com. 1985-2000, chair 1991-92, city mgr. plan task force 1993-94), Va. Local Govt. Mgmt. Assn. (pres. 1989-90), NC City/County Mgmt. Assn. (pres.2000-2001), Soc. Cincinnati in Va., Descendants of Francis Epes of Va., 2000-2003 (pres.), Rotary (#7720 asst. dist. gov. 2003-2004). Home: 1307 Waverly Rd NW Wilson NC 27896-1483

WYATT, GERARD ROBERT, biology professor, researcher; b. Palo Alto, Calif., Sept. 3, 1925; came to Can., 1935; s. Horace Graham and Mary Aimee (Strickland) W.; m. Sarah Silver Morton, Dec. 19, 1951 (dec. Mar. 1981); children— Eve Morton, Graham Strickland, Diana Silver; m. Mary Evelyn Rogers, Mar. 16, 1985 BA, U. B.C., Can., 1945; postgrad., U. Calif.-Berkeley, 1946-47; PhD, Cambridge U., 1950. Research scientist Can. Dept. Agr., Sault Ste. Marie, Ont., 1950-54; asst. prof. biochemistry Yale U., New Haven, 1954-60, assoc. prof., prof. biology, 1960-73; prof. biology Queen's U., Kingston, Ont., 1973-94, prof. emeritus, 1994—; sci. dir. Insect Biotech Can., 1990-93. Contbr. articles to profl. jours. Guggenheim fellow, 1956; Killam Research fellow, 1985 Fellow Royal Soc. Can. Avocation: natural history. Home: 114 Earl St Kingston ON Canada K7L 2H1 Office: Queen's Univ Dept Biology Kingston ON Canada K7L 3N6 E-mail: wyattg@biology.queensu.ca.

WYATT, JAMES FRANK, JR., lawyer; b. Talladega, Ala., Dec. 1, 1922; s. James Frank and Nannie Lee (Heaslett) W.; m. Rosemary Barbara Slone, Dec. 21, 1951; children: Martha Lee, James Frank III. BS, Auburn U., 1943; JD, Georgetown U., 1949, postgrad., 1950. Bar: D.C. 1949, Ala. 1950, Ill. 1953, U.S. Supreme Ct 1953. Atty. Office Chief Counsel, IRS, 1949-51; tax counsel Universal Oil Products Co., Des Plaines, Ill., 1951-63, asst. treas., 1963-66, v.p. fin., treas., 1966-75; treas. CF Industries, Inc., Long Grove, Ill., 1976-78, v.p. fin., treas., 1978-82; assoc. Tenney & Bentley, 1983-85, Arnstein, Gluck, Lehr, Barron & Milligan, 1985-88; pvt. practice, 1989—. Dir. 1st Nat. Bank, Des Plaines. Village trustee, Barrington, Ill., 1963-75; bd. dirs. Buehler YMCA, Barrington Twp. Republican Orgn., 1963—; pres. Barrington Area Rep. Workshops, 1962-63. Served to capt., Judge Adv. Gen. Corps AUS, 1944-47. Mem. Tax Execs. Inst. (v.p. 1965-66, chpt. pres. 1961-62), Fed., Am., Chgo. bar assns., Barrington Home Owners Assn. (pres. 1960-61), Newcomen Sco., Assn. U.S. Army, Scabbard and Blade, Phi Delta Phi, Sigma Chi. Clubs: Barrington Hills Country; Economics, University (Chgo.). Episcopalian. Home: 625 Concord Pl Barrington IL 60010-4508 Office: 200 Applebee St Barrington IL 60010-3063

WYATT, JAMES LUTHER, drapery hardware company executive; b. Williamsburg, Ky., May 13, 1924; s. Jesse Luther and Grace Edwina (Little) W.; m. Barbara Christman, Aug. 28, 1946; children— Linda Lou, William Charles Christman (dec.). BS, U. Ky., 1947, MS, 1948; Sc.D., Mass. Inst. Tech., 1952. Registered profl. engr., Ohio, Pa. Devel. engr. titanium div. Nat. Lead Co., Sayreville, N.J., 1948-50; tech. mgr., head, dept. metall. engring., mgr. new products Horizons, Inc., Cleve., 1953-57; cons., asso. Booz, Allen & Hamilton, N.Y.C., 1957-61; v.p. program devel. Armour Research Found., Chgo., 1961-63; v.p. new product devel. Joy Mfg. Co., Pitts., 1963-67; v.p. corp. devel. Nat. Gypsum Co., Buffalo, 1967-69, Max Factor & Co., Hollywood, Calif., 1969-71; pres. Wyatt & Co., 1971—, Jimbabs, Inc., 1983—, Ambassador Industries, Inc., Los Angeles, 1988—. U.S. del. 1st World Metall. Congress. Contbr. tech., mgmt. papers to profl. lit.; patentee in field. Mem. Pompano Beach Power Squadron, adminstr. officer, 1991, exec. officer, 1992, comdr., 1993; chmn. bd. trustees Meth. Ch., 1992, mem. fin. com., 1993, mem. adminstrv. bd.; chmn. bd. trustees 1st United Meth. Ch., Boca Raton; bd. dirs., v.p. Golden Harbour Homeowners Assn., 1997—. Lt. col. USAAF, 1942-46. Elected to U. Ky. Hall of Distinction, 2001. Mem. AIME, Am. Soc. Metals, Econ. Club (Chgo.), Execs. Club (Chgo.), Univ. Club (N.Y.C.), Calif. Yacht Club, Pompano Beach Power Squadron (comdr.), Sigma Phi Epsilon, Alpha Chi Sigma. Clubs: Econs. (Chgo.), Execs. (Chgo.); Univ. (N.Y.C.); Calif. Yacht. Home: 510 Golden Harbour Dr Boca Raton FL 33432-2942 Office: 510 Golden Harbour Dr Boca Raton FL 33432-2942 Personal E-mail: jim_wyatt@juno.com.

WYATT, JOE BILLY, academic administrator; b. Tyler, Tex., July 21, 1935; s. Joe and Fay (Pinkerton) Wyatt; m. Faye Hocutt, July 21, 1956; children: Joseph, Sandra Faye. BA, U. Tex., 1956; MA, Tex. Christian U., 1960. Systems engr. Gen. Dynamics Corp., 1956—65; mgr. Digital Computer Lab., 1961—65; dir. computer ctr., assoc. prof. computer sci. U. Houston, 1965—72; dir. Office Info. Tech. Harvard U., 1972—76, sr. lectr. computer sci., 1972—82, v.p. adminstrn., 1976—82; chancellor Vanderbilt U., Nashville, 1982—2000, chancellor emeritus, 2000. Faculty Harvard U. Kennedy Sch., 1976—82; bd. dirs., chmn. com. on math/sci. Am. Coun. of Edn.; bd. dirs. El Paso Energy, Inc., Ingram Micro., Inc., Advanced Networking and Sys. Corp., Hercules Corp., Aerostructures Corp.; prin. Washington Adv. Group. Author (with others): Financial Planning Models for Colleges and Universities, 1979; editor-in-chief: Jour. Applied Mgmt. Sys., 1983; contbr. articles to profl. jours.; patentee in field. Trustee EDUCOM, Princeton, NJ, 1973—81, Harvard U. Press, 1976—83, pres., 1975—76, chmn. bd., 1976—79; trustee Leadership Nashville, 1983—93; active Coun. Competitiveness; bd. dirs. Nashville Inst. Arts, 1982—83, Ingram Industries, 1990—96; chmn. adv. com. IST, NSF, 1978—85; vice-chmn. bd. Mass. Tech. Devel. Corp., Boston, 1977—83; alumni bd. dirs. Harvard Bus. Sch., 1982—92; chmn. New Am. Schs., 2002—, Edn. Quality Inst., 2002—. Named Outstanding Tennessean, Gov. of Tenn., 1986; recipient award for exemplary leadership, CAUSE, 1982, Nat. Tree of Life award, Jewish Nat. Fund, 1988; fellow, Gallaudet Coll., 1981—83. Fellow: AAAS; mem.: IEEE, Bus. Higher Edn. Forum (exec. com. 1990—93), So. U. Rsch. Assn., Inc. (chmn. coun. pres. 1988—89), U. Rsch. Assn. (bd. trustees 1988—, chmn. 1997—), Assn. Computing Machinery (pres. Dallas and Ft. Worth chpt. 1963—65), Am. Coun. Edn. (chmn. adv. com. on tech. edn. 1980—81, bd. dirs. 1990—92), Nat. Assn. Ind. Colls. and Univs. (policy bd. 1980—82), Hosp. Corp. Am. (bd. dirs. 1984—89), Assn. Am. Univs. (chmn. exec. com. 1990—91), Govt. Univ. Industry Rsch. Roundtable (chmn. 1998—), Nashville C. of C. (bd. dirs. 1983—86, pres. 1996—97), Experimental Aircraft Assn. (pres. adv. com., found. bd. 1997—), Aircraft Owners and Pilots Assn., Harvard Club, Beta Gamma Sigma, Sigma Xi, Phi Beta Kappa (hon.). Methodist. Office: Vanderbilt U 2525 West End Ave Ste 1430 Nashville TN 37203 E-mail: joe.b.wyatt@vanderbilt.edu.

WYATT, JOSEPH LUCIAN, JR., lawyer, writer; b. Chgo., Feb. 21, 1924; s. Joseph Lucian and Cecile Gertrude (Zadico) W.; m. Marjorie Kathryn Simmons, Apr. 9, 1954; children: Daniel, Linn, Jonathan. AB in English Lit. with honors, Northwestern U., 1947; LLB, Harvard U., 1949. Bar: Calif. 1950, U.S. Dist. Ct. (cen. dist.) Calif. 1950, U.S. Ct. Appeals (9th cir.) 1950, U.S. Tax Ct., U.S. Supreme Ct. 1965. Assoc. firm Brady, Nossaman & Walker, Los Angeles, 1950-58, ptnr. L.A., 1958-61; pvt. practice L.A., 1961-71; sr. mem. Cooper, Wyatt, Tepper & Plant, P.C., L.A., 1971-79; of counsel Beardsley, Hufstedler & Kemble, L.A., 1979-81; ptnr. Hufstedler & Kaus, L.A., 1981-95; sr. of counsel Morrison & Foerster, L.A., 1995—. Mem. faculty Pacific Coast Banking Sch., Seattle, 1963-92, Southwestern Grad. Sch. Banking, 1988-89; advisor Restatement, Trusts 3d, 1988—. Author: Trust Administration and Taxation, 4 vols., 1964—; editor: Trusts and Estates, 1962-74. Lectr. continuing legal edn. programs, Calif. and Tex.; trustee Pacific Oaks Coll. and Children's Sch., 1969-97; counsel, parliamentarian Calif. Democratic party and presdl. conv. dels., 1971—; mem. Calif. State Personnel Bd., 1961-71, v.p., 1963-65, pres., 1965-67; bd trustees Calif. Pub. Employees Retirement System, 1963-71. Served with USAAF, 1943-45. Fellow Am. Coll. of Trust and Estate Counsel; mem. ABA, Internat. Acad. Estate and Trust Law (treas. 1990-96), Am. Law Inst., Calif. State Bar Assn. (del. state conf. 1956, 62-67), L.A. Bar Assn. (trustee 1956). Democrat. Christian Scientist. Avocations: fishing, composing doggerel. Home: 1119 Armada Dr Pasadena CA 91103-2805 Office Phone: 213-892-5200. E-mail: jwyatt@mofo.com., jwyatt3@charter.net.

WYATT, LANCE B. pharmaceutical executive; married. BChemE, U. Ala. Registered profl. engr. Mgr. process/project engring. Abbott Labs., Rocky Mount, NC, 1976—81, various positions hosp. products divsn., 1981—84, plant quality assurance mgr., 1984—90, dir., divisional v.p. quality assurance hosp. products divsn. Abbott Park, Ill., 1990—91, divisional v.p. quality assurance and regulatory affairs pharm. products divsn., 1991—95, corp. officer, v.p. corp. engring. divsn., 1995—2000, sr. v.p., pres. specialty products divsn., 2000—02, sr. v.p. specialty products, 2002—. Lt. U.S. Army C.E. Office: Abbott Labs 100 Abbott Park Rd Abbott Park IL 60064-6400

WYATT, LENORE, civic worker; b. N.Y.C., June 12, 1929; d. Benedict S. Rosenfeld and Ora (Copel) Kanner; m. Bernard D. Copeland, May 17, 1953 (dec. March 1968); children: Harry (dec.), Robert (dec.); m. C. Wyatt Unger, Mar. 26, 1969 (dec. Feb. 1992); 1 child, Amy Unger; m. F. Lowry Wyatt, Sept. 12, 1992 (dec. Nov. 1996). Student, Mills Coll., 1946-48; BA, Stanford U., 1950, MA, 1952; postgrad., NYU, 1952-53. Instr. Stanford U., Palo Alto, Calif., 1952, Hunter Coll., N.Y.C., 1952-53, Calif. State U., Sacramento, 1956-60, U. Calif., Davis, 1965-69; property mgr. Unger, Demas & Markakis, Sacramento, 1974-83. Former actress and model; fin. com. Charles Wright Acad.; fin. mgr. several trusts. Pres. Sacramento Opera Assn., 1972—73; treas. Sacramento Children's Home, 1990—92, v.p., 1992—; former mem. bd. dirs. Sutter Hosp. Aux., Sutter Hosp. Med. Rsch. Found., Sacramento Symphony League, Temple B'nai Israel Sisterhood, Sacramento chpt. Hadassah, Sacramento Children's Home Guild; formerly active Sacramento Opera Assn., Crocker Soc. of Crocker Art Gallery, Sacramento Symphony Assn., Sacramento Reportory Theater Assn.; founding mem. Tacoma Cmtys. Art Sch.; past mem. bd. dirs. Charles Wright Acad.; past mem., bd. dirs. Tacoma Art Mus. Mem.: Pathfinders of Palm Springs, Stanford U. Alumni Assn. (past bd. dirs. Sacramento), Sacramento Pioneer Assn., Am. Contract Bridge League, Pathfinders Palm Springs, Del Paso Country Club (past capt. women's golf group, Sacramento), Thunderbird Country Club, Tacoma Club, Wash. Athletic Club, Maui Country Club, Tacoma Country and Golf Club, Sutter Club. Republican. Jewish. Avocations: golf, duplicate bridge. Home: 70551 Placerville Rd Rancho Mirage CA 92270

WYATT, LESLIE, III, academic administrator; b. Tex., Aug. 24, 1945; m. Jeanne Cogburn, 1968; children: Cathey and Will (twins), Betsy. BA, Abilene Christian U.; BFA in Studio Graphic Arts, MFA in Mus. Edn., PhD in Edn., U. Tex. Assoc. dean Coll. Fine Arts U. Tex., 1977—83; vice chancellor univ. advancement, dean Coll. Fine Arts U. Ark., Little Rock; vice chancellor exec. affairs U. Miss.; pres. Ark. State U., 1995—. Speaker and presenter in field. Exhibited art work in solo shows at Gardner Galley, Abilene, Tex., 1969, Huntington Gallery, U. Tex., 1970, The Clean Well-Lighted Place Gallery, Austin, 1971; group shows include DuBose Gallery, Houston, Contemporary Gallery, Dallas, U. Ark. Little Rock; contbr. articles to profl. jours. Bd. dirs. Jonesboro Indsl. Devel. Corp., United Way, Jonesboro; chmn. St. Vernards Regional Med. Ctr. Heart Walk. Recipient awards, fellowships and grants. Mem.: Greater Jonesboro C. of C. (bd. dirs.). Office: Office of Pres PO Box 10 State University AR 72467-0010

WYATT, OSCAR SHERMAN, JR., energy company executive; b. Beaumont, Tex., July 11, 1924; s. Oscar Sherman Sr. and Eva (Coday) Wyatt; m. Lynn Sakowitz; children: Steven, Douglas, Oscar Sherman III, Brad. BS in Mech. Engring., Tex. A&M U., 1949. With Kerr-McGee Co., 1949, Reed Roller Bit Co., 1949—51; ptnr. Wymore Oil Co., 1951—55; founder Coastal Corp., Corpus Christi, Tex., 1955—2001, chmn. exec. com. Houston. Trustee DeBakey Med. Found., 1987—; founding mem., bd. stewards Tex. Aviation Hall of Fame, 1997—. With USAF, WWII. Office: 9 Greenway Plz Houston TX 77046-0892

WYATT, ROBERT LEE, IV, lawyer; b. Robert Lee III and Louise Carole (Bard) W.; m. Vicki Harris Wyatt. BS, Southeastern Okla. State U., 1986; JD, U. Okla., 1989. Bar: Okla. 1989, U.S. Dist. Ct. (we. dist.) Okla. 1990, U.S. Ct. Appeals (10th cir.) 1990, U.S. Dist. Ct. (no. dist.) Okla. 1991, U.S. Ct. Appeals (8th cir.) 1991, U.S. Supreme Ct. 1993, U.S. Dist. Ct. (Ea. Dist.) 2004. Intern Okla. State Bur. Investigation, Oklahoma City, 1988-89, guest lectr., 1989; dep. spl. counsel Gov. of Okla., 1995; atty. Jones & Wyatt, Enid, Okla., 1989-2000. Criminal justice panel atty. We. Dist. Okla. Contbr. Vernon's Forms Oklahoma, Criminal Law and Procedure, 1999. Counsel to Fire Civil Svc. Commn. City of Enid, 1998-2000. Mem. ABA (mem. criminal and litigation sects.), Okla. Bar Assn. (mem. ins., mem. criminal law com., guest lectr. 2003), Oklahoma County Bar Assn., Okla. Criminal Def. Lawyers Assn., Nat. Inst. for Trial Advocacy, Nat. Assn. Criminal Defense Lawyers, Luther Bohanon Am. Inn of Ct. (barrister), Phi Delta Phi, Alpha Chi. Democrat. Baptist. E-mail: bobwyatt@wyattlaw.com.

WYATT, ROLAND GRATTS, music educator, voice educator, consultant; b. Ft. Worth, Tex., June 23, 1932; s. Charles Henry Robinson and Marguerite Collins Pennybacker; m. Deborah Kay West, Nov. 28, 1987 (div. Dec. 22, 2001). MusB in edn., Lincoln U., Jefferson, Mo., 1954; MA, San Jose State U., Calif., 1968. Instr. Yankton Coll., SD, 1967—68; asst. prof. Seattle U., 1968—70, U. Wis., Eau Claire, 1970—71; vis. prof. Humboldt State U., Arcata, Calif., 1971—72; prof. Mannes Sch. of Music, NYC, 1972—74; lectr. San Francisco State U., 1974—76; voice coach Manhattan Transfer, LA, 1974—95; vis. prof. SUNY, 1986—87; cons., therapist, tchr. Roland Wyatt Voice Studio, LA, San Francisco and San Diego, 1987—. Dir. Inst. of Self Directed Learning, Pitts. and San Diego, 1991—. Performer: (recording) Voice Lessons with Manhattan Transfer, 1989; co-author with Dr. Hans von Leden (book) A Handbook for Correcting Vocal Problems, 2003. Recipient Robert Shaw award, 1958, Mack Harrel scholarship at Aspen Music Sch., Am. Choral Soc. Conducting award, 1969, 1972. Studio: PO Box 1102 Cortaro AZ 85652-1102 E-mail: wyatt-voice-studio@sbcglobal.com.

WYATT, ROSE MARIE, clinical social worker; b. San Angelo, Tex., Feb. 16, 1937; d. James Odis and Annie LaVernia (Lott) W. BA, Fisk U., 1957; MS, U. So. Calif., 1963; MA, MSW, U. Chgo., 1972; postgrad., Ill. Inst. Tech., 1976—. Tchr. Chgo. Bd. Edn., 1959-63, clin. social worker, 1979—; adult program dir. Chgo. YWCA, 1963-64; youth counselor Chgo. Commn. on Youth Welfare, 1964-66; supervising social worker for Head Start, Chgo. Com. on Urban Opportunity, 1966; social worker Chgo. Commn. on Youth Welfare, 1966-68, Jewish Vocat. Svc., 1968; social worker sch. cmty. rels. Detroit Pub. Schs., 1968-70; social worker Rosman-Wyatt and Assocs., Chgo., 1980—, pres., 1981—; instr. dept. corrections Chgo. State U., 1972—. Adj. instr. Chgo. State U. Mem. adv. bd., chmn. program com. Calumet area United Chritities, 1974-80; vol. Assn. Cmty. Agts., 1968-70, Southside Sr. Citizens Coalition, Chgo., 1963-66, Roseland Health Planning Com., 1974-76, Teen Pregnancy Caucus, 1978-82; mem. social work adv. coun. Chgo. Bd. Edn., 1976. Recipient Outstanding Employee award for med.-social work svcs. Maternal dn Child Health Scis. divsn. HEW, 1971; Ford Found. scholar Fisk U., 1953-57, U. Chgo. scholar, 1970-72, United Charities scholar, 1970-72. Mem. NASW, NEA, Acad. Cert. Social Workers, Ill. Cert Social Workers, Chgo. Psychol. Club. Ill. Acad. Criminology, Ill. Assn. Sch. Social Workers, Am. Assn. Mental Deviciency, Qualified Mental Retardation Profls., Fisk U. Alumni Assn., Am. Bridge Assn., Alpha Kappa Alpha.

WYATT, THOMAS CSABA, lawyer; b. Toronto, Ont., Can., Mar. 19, 1952; arrived in U.S., 1979; s. Charles Wojatsek and Marietta Marcinkova; m. Helen A. Johnson, Dec. 24, 1979; children: J.P. Max, Stephen M. BCL, McGill U., 1974; BA, Bishop's U., 1975; LLM, U. Montréal, 1980; JD, U. San Francisco, 1981. Bar: Que. 1975, Calif. 1982, U.S. Dist. Ct. (no. dist.) Calif. 1982, U.S. Ct. Appeals (9th cir.) 1982. Assoc. counsel Can. Gen. Electric, Montreal, 1975—77; solicitor Du Pont Can., Inc., Montreal, 1977—79; internat. counsel Computerland Corp., Oakland, Calif., 1982—85; sr. counsel Bank of Am., San Francisco, 1985—87, Intel Corp., Santa Clara, Calif., 1987—90; gen. counsel Philips Semiconductors, Sunnyvale, Calif., 1990—2001; founder, dir. Actineon, Inc., Sunnyvale, Calif., 2001—. Arbitrator Am. Arbitration Assn., San Francisco, 1985—. Bd. dirs. Silicon Valley Law Found., 2000—02. Mem. Silicon Valley Assn. of Gen. Counsel (chmn. 1998-2000), Santa Clara County Bar Assn. (bd. trustees 2001-02), Knightly Order of Vitez, Knights of Malta. Roman Catholic. Office: Actineon Inc 236 West Portal Ave San Francisco CA 94127 E-mail: tcwyatt236@aol.com.

WYATT, WILSON WATKINS, JR., management and public affairs executive, writer; b. Louisville, Dec. 3, 1943; s. Wilson Watkins Sr. and Anne (Duncan) W.; m. Jane Clay, Aug. 15, 1964 (dec. 1975); children: Carol, Wilson III, Sarah Wyatt; m. Kathleen Valonis, June 14, 1998. Student, U. of the South, 1961-65. Reporter The Courier-Jour., Louisville, 1965-67; pub. rels. account exec. Doe-Anderson Advt., Louisville, 1967-68; account exec. Zimmer-McClaskey-Lewis (McCann-Ericksn Advtsg.), Louisville, 1968-70; ptnr. Bennett & Wyatt Pub. Rels., Louisville, 1970-71; state rep., vice chair appropriations and revenue com. Ky. Gen. Assembly, Frankfort, 1969-71; exec. dir. Louisville Cen. Area Inc., 1971-77; dir. corp. affairs and communications Brown & Williamson Tobacco Corp., Louisville, 1977-82; v.p. pub. policy BATUS Inc., Washington, 1982-86, v.p. corp. affairs Louisville, 1986-90; sr. v.p. corp. affairs PNC Fin. Corp., Pitts., 1990-92; sr. v.p. corp. comm. and govt. rels. The Travelers Cos., Hartford, 1992-94; exec. dir., CEO Am. Acad. of Actuaries, Washington, 1995-98; CEO Wyatt Comm. Cons., 1998—. Lead U.S. def. pub. rels. activities against hostile takeover for B.A.T. Industries, U.K., 1989-90; chmn. Travelers Found., 1991-94, Travelers Good Govt. Com., 1992-94. Mem. youth adv. com. Atlantic Inst., 1967-68; del. North Atlantic Treaty Assn. Young Leaders Conf., 1967; chmn. Leadership Effort for All Dems., Ky., 1967-68; regional campaign coord. for Robert F. Kennedy, Ky.-Ind., 1968; mem. Pres.'s Forum, Washington, 1988-91; trustee Conn. Policy Econ. Commn., 1992-95; mem. exec. com. Hartford Downtown Coun., 1992-94; mem. adv. bd. Dem. Leadership Coun., Washington; mem. Am. Savings Edn. Campaign U.S. Dept. Labor, 1996. Named one of Outstanding Young Men in Am., Ky. Jaycees, 1973. Mem. The Pres.'s Forum, Pub. Affairs Rsch. Coun. (conf. bd. 1986-95), Forum I, Assn. Chief Execs. Coun., Pub. Affairs Coun. (bd. dirs. 1982—, exec. com. 1982-86), Speakers Club (Washington), Greater Hartford C. of C. (exec. com. 1992-94), Hartford Stage (bd. dirs. 1993-95), University Club (Washington), Md. Writers Assn., Am. Soc. of Assn. Execs. Avocations: boating, photography, writing. Home and Office: PO Box 298 7291 Bozman-Neavitt Rd Bozman MD 21612 Office Phone: 410-745-2616. Personal E-mail: wwwtwo@earthlink.ney.

WYCHE, CYRIL THOMAS, lawyer; b. Greenville, S.C., Jan. 28, 1926; C. Granville and Mary (Wheeler) W.; m. Harriet Smith, June 19, 1948; children: Sara McCall, Bradford Wheeler, Mary Frances. BE, Yale U., 1946; LLB, U. Va., 1949; LLD (hon.), Clemson U., 1997, Furman U., 1997; HLD (hon.), Wafford Coll. Bar: S.C. 1948, U.S. Dist. Ct. S.C. 1950, U.S. Ct. Appeals (4th cir.) 1952, U.S. Ct. Claims 1964, U.S. Supreme Ct. 1970. Ptnr. Wyche, Burgess, Freeman & Parham, P.A., Greenville, S.C., 1948—. Pres., bd. dirs. YMCA, Greenville, 1960; pres. Greenville Little Theatre, 1965, Arts Festival Assn., Greenville, 1970, Greenville Community Corp., 1976—; bd. dirs. Greater Greenville C. of C., 1980. Served with USN, 1943-46. Named Environmentalist of Yr., State of S.C., 1979; recipient Conservation award Gulf Oil Corp., 1983, Alexander Calder award, 1996, Garden Clubs Am., 1999, Oak Leaf award The Nature Conservancy, 1996, Order of the Palmetto award S.C. Gov., 1996. Mem. ABA (Environ. award 2002), S.C. Bar Assn., Greenville County Bar Assn., Am. Judicature Soc., Nat. Wildlife Fedn. (Spl. Conservation Achievement award 2003). Presbyterian. Avocations: skiing, scuba diving, piano, tennis, white water canoeing. Office: Wyche Burgess Freeman & Parham 44 E Camperdown Way PO Box 728 Greenville SC 29602-0728 Office Phone: 864-242-8213. E-mail: twyche@wyche.com.

WYCHE, RUTH SKYLER, rehabilitation contractor, researcher; b. Houston, Aug. 10, 1955; d. Malcolm Joseph and Dorothy Earlene (King) LeGrande; 1 child: Patricia Ann. BS, Sam Houston State U., 1977, lic. min., 1996; cert., Inst. Child Lit., 1988; postgrad., San Jacinto Coll., 1993, Sam Houston State U., 1996-2000. Cert.elem. tchr., Tex., 1977. Med. records Green Acres Convalescent Home, Huntsville, Tex., 1979-80, 81-82; tchr. Magnolia (Tex.) High Sch., 1980-81; sec. Harris Engring., Huntsville, 1982-83; artist M&M Design, Huntsville, 1983-84; fin. sec. First United Meth. Ch., Huntsville, 1984-87, nursery sch. coord., 1986-87; contractor Tex. Rehabilation Commn., Huntsville, 1986-87, Pasadena, Tex., 1990-92; counselor Houston Substance Abuse Clinic, Pasadena and Houston, 1992-93, Lake Charles Substance Abuse Clinic, 1992-93; adminstr. Johnson Glass & Mirror, Pasadena, 1993-96; contractor Tex. Rehab. Commn., Pasadena, 1996-97. Author poetry, 1985. Ballot counter Voting Polling places, Huntsville, 1977, 78, 79. Recipient Lady Kentiggerma Soc. Creative Anachronism, 1986, Sable Comet, 1986. Mem. NAFE, Tex. Acad. Sci., Phi Beta Chi. Republican. Avocations: biology, mathematics, writing, crochet, driving.

WYCHE, SAMUEL D(AVID), professional football coach, retired professional football player; b. Atlanta, Jan. 5, 1945; m. Jane Wyche; children: Zak, Kerry BA, Furman U., 1966; M, U. S.C., 1969. Profl. football player Continental Football League, Wheeling Ironmen, 1966; profl. football player Cin. Bengals, 1968-70, Washington Redskins, 1971-73, Detroit Lions, 1974-75, St. Louis Cardinals, 1976, Buffalo Bills, 1976; owner sporting goods store, Greenville, S.C., 1974-92; asst. coach San Francisco 49ers, 1979-82; head coach Ind. U., Bloomington, 1983, Cin. Bengals, 1984-91, Tampa Bay (Fla.) Buccaneers, 1992-95; quarterbacks coach Buffalo Bills, 2004—; sports analyst NBC Sports, 1996-97, former co-host NFL on NBC Pre-Game Show, 1998—99; sports analyst NFL on CBS, N.Y.C., 1999—2000. Named Coach of Yr. NFL, 1988, 2004. Office: c/o Buffalo Bills One Bills Dr Orchard Park NY 14187

WYCKOFF, E. LISK, JR., lawyer; b. Middletown, N.J., Jan. 29, 1934; m. Elizabeth Ann Kuphal; children: Jenny Adele, Edward Lisk III, Elizabeth Hannah Longstreet. BA, Duke U., 1955; JD, U. Mich., 1960. Bar: N.Y. 1961, U.S. Dist. Ct. (so. and ea. dists.) N.Y. 1962, U.S. Ct. Appeals (2d cir. 1963), U.S. Tax Ct. 1974. Ptnr. Trubin Sillcocks, 1975—79, Kelley Drye & Warren, 1979—93, Kramer, Levin, N.Y.C., NY, 1993—2001. Lectr. Practising Law Inst., 1970—, various profl. and bus. orgns. in U.S. and abroad; spl. counsel N.Y. Bankers Assn., 1974-98; counsel N.Y. State Senate Com. Housing and Urban Renewal, 1969-71, N.Y. State Senate Com. Judiciary, 1963-64, Com. Affairs of the City of N.Y., 1962; mem. N.Y.C. Mayor's Taxi Study Commn., 1967 Directing editor, author West's McKinney's Forms on Estates and Trusts, 1974—; commentator McKinney's Not-For-Profit Corp. law, 1995—; contbr. articles to profl. jours. Trustee Inner-City Scholarship Fund., Inc., 1993—; chmn., bd. dirs. 1652 Wyckoff House and Assn., Inc., 1982—; trustee Goodspeed Opera Co., 1996—, Florence Griswold Mus., 1997—, Wildlife

Conservation Soc., 1993—; elector Wadsworth Atheneum; trustee, pres. Homeland Found., 1988—; mem. Concilium Socalium to Vatican Mus., 1991—; dir., treas. NY Geneal. and Biographic Soc., 2002—. Named papal hon. Knight Commdr., Order of St. Gregory the Great, 1998; recipient Star, 2002. Fellow: Am. Bar Found., Am. Coll. Trust and Estate Counsel; mem.: ABA, St. Nicholas Soc., Holland Soc., Assn. of Bar of City of N.Y., N.Y. State Bar Assn., Internat. Bar Assn., Internat. Fiscal Assn., N.Y. Yacht Club, Essex Yacht Club (Conn.), Mashomack Fish and Game Preserve Club (Pine Plains, N.Y.), Racquet and Tennis Club (N.Y.C.), Knickerbocker Club. Avocations: tennis, sailing. Office: 20th Fl 505 Park Ave New York NY 10022 E-mail: eliskwyckoff@aol.com.

WYCOFF, CHARLES COLEMAN, writer, retired anesthesiologist; b. Glazier, Tex., Sept. 2, 1918; s. James Garfield and Ada Sharpe (Braden) W.; m. Gene Marie Henry, May 16, 1942 (dec.); children: Michelle, Geoffrey, Brian, Roger, Daniel, Norman, Irene, Teresa. AB, U. Calif., Berkeley, 1941; MD, U. Calif., San Francisco, 1943; postgrad., U. London, 1954-55. Diplomate Am. Bd. Anesthesiology. Intern San Francisco County Hosp., 1943-44; resident in anesthesiology U. Calif. Hosp., San Francisco, 1944-45; tng. in anesthesiology Walter Reed Gen. Hosp., 1945; founder The Wycoff Group of Anesthesiology, San Francisco, 1947-53; chief of anesthesia St. Joseph's Hosp., San Francisco, 1947-52, organizer residency tng. program in anesthesiology, 1950, San Francisco County Hosp., 1954, chief anesthesia, 1953-54; tchr. practice anesthesiology Presbyn. Med. Ctr., N.Y.C., 1955-63; asst. prof. anesthesiology Columbia U., N.Y.C., 1955-63; clin. practice anesthesiology St. Francis Meml. Hosp., San Francisco, 1963-84. Prodr., dir. films on regional anesthesia; contbr. articles to sci. jours. Scoutmaster Boy Scouts Am., San Francisco, 1953-55. Capt. M.C., U.S. Army, 1945-47. Mem. Alumni Faculty Assn. Sch. Medicine U. Calif.-San Francisco (councilor at large 1979-80). Democrat. Avocations: researching origins of human behavior, writing, gardening. Home: 1400 Carpenter St Unit 133 San Leandro CA 94577-3655 E-mail: ccwycoff@pacbell.net.

WYDEN, RON, senator; b. Wichita, Kans., May 3, 1949; s. Peter and Edith W.; m. Laurie Oseran, Sept. 5, 1978; 1 child, Adam David Student, U. Santa Barbara, 1967-69; AB with distinction, Stanford U., 1971; JD, U. Oreg., 1974. Campaign aide Senator Wayne Morse, 1972, 74; co-founder, co-dir. Oreg. Gray Panthers, 1974-80; dir. Oreg. Legal Services for Elderly, 1977-79; instr. gerontology U. Oreg., 1976, U. Portland, 1980, Portland State U., 1979; mem. 97th-104th Congresses from 3d Oreg. dist., Washington, D.C., 1981-96; senator from Oreg. U.S. Senate, 1996—, mem. aging com., mem. budget com., mem. commerce sci. and transp. com., mem. energy and natural resources com., mem. environ. and pub. works com. Recipient Service to Oreg. Consumers award Oreg. Consumers League, 1978, Citizen of Yr. award Oreg. Assn. Social Workers, 1979, Significant Service award Multnomah County Area Agy. on Aging, 1980; named Young Man of Yr. Oreg. Jr. C. of C., 1980 Mem. Am. Bar Assn., Iowa Bar Assn. Democrat. Jewish. Office: US Senate 516 Hart Senate Office Bldg Washington DC 20510-0001

WYDERSKI, RICHARD JOSEPH, internist; b. Dayton, Ohio, Apr. 1, 1960; d. Josef and Gertrude Vera Wyderski; m. Karen Louise Wyderski, May 2, 2002; m. Mary Teresa Wyderski, June 12, 1982 (div. Sept. 1995). BS, U. Dayton, 1982; MD, U. Cin., 1986; M in Med. Mgmt., U. So. Calif., 2002. Diplomate Am. Bd. Internal Medicine, Nat. Bd. Med. Examiners. Resident U. Cin. Dept. Medicine, 1986—89, gen. medicine fellow, 1989—90, chief med. resident, 1990—91; pvt. practice Assoc. Specialists of Internal Medicine, Dayton, 1991—97; med. dir., Bethany Luth. Village Luth. Social Svcs., Centerville, Ohio, 1991—96; med. dir., Ambulatory clinics Miami Valley Hosp., Dayton, 1996—; assoc. residency program dir. Wright State U. Dept. Medicine, Dayton, 1997—. Mem. ethics com. Luth. Social Svcs. of the Miami Valley, Dayton, 1997—; mem. quality improvement/utilization mgmt. com. United HealthCare of Ohio, Inc., Dayton/Cin., 1996—2002. Vol.; bd. trustees Alzheimer's Assn. of the Miami Valley, Dayton, 1991—; treas., mem. bd. trustees Med. Vols. of Cin., 1990—91; founder, chair adv. com. Domestic Abuse and Violence Inst. of Dayton, 1999—; trustee Epilepsy Found. We. Ohio, 2002—, v.p., 2004. Recipient Leadership award, AMA, Chgo., 1989. Fellow: ACP; mem.: Dayton Soc. Internal Medicine (pres. 2000—01), Am. Med. Dirs. Assn. (ho. of dels. 1993—96, pres.-elect Ohio chpt. 1994—96), ACP-Am. Soc. Internal Medicine (assocs. com., Ohio chpt. 2001—, program com. 2002—, awards com. 2002—), Am. Coll. Physician Execs., Am. Geriat. Soc. (Geriat. Recognition award 1998, 2002). Democrat. Roman Catholic. Avocation: automobile racing (amateur, Sports Car Club of Am.). Home: 164 Earlsgate Rd Dayton OH 45440 Office: Miami Valley Hosp 1 Wyoming St Dayton OH 45409 Office Phone: 937-208-3955. Business E-Mail: rjwyderski@mvh.org.

WYDEVEN, JOSEPH JUDE, university dean, educator; b. Appleton, Wis., Aug. 31, 1940; s. Joseph Henry and Anna Wydeven; m. Alice Camille Laoang, May 7, 1983; children: Rachel, John Eric. PhD, Purdue U., 1979. Prof. English, humanities Bellevue (Nebr.) U., 1979—, dean Coll. Arts and Scis., 1995—. Author: Wright Morris Revisited, 1998. Vol. Joslyn Art Mus., Omaha, 2000—, ARC, 1999—. Staff sgt. USAF, 1966-70. Recipient Tchg. and Campus Leadership award Sears Roebuck Found., 1990. Mem. Am. Assn. Higher Edn., Am. Studies Assn., Western Lit. Assn., Soc. for the Study of Midwestern Lit., Nebr. Humanities Coun. Spkrs. Bur. Avocations: writing, photography, travel, research. Home: 807 Waterford Cir Papillion NE 68046 Office: Bellevue Univ 1000 Galvin Rd S Bellevue NE 68005 Fax: 402-293-2023. E-mail: aliceandjoe@cox.net., jjw@bellevue.edu.

WYDICK, RICHARD CREWS, lawyer, educator; b. Pueblo, Colo., Nov. 1, 1937; s. Charles Richard and Alice Wydick; m. Judith Brandli James, 1961; children: William Bruce, Derrick Cameron. BA, Williams Coll., 1959; LL.B., Stanford U., 1962. Bar: Calif. bar 1962. Asso. firm Brobeck, Phleger & Harrison, San Francisco, 1966-71; mem. faculty U. Calif. Law Sch., Davis, 1971—, prof. law, 1975—; dean, 1978-80. Author: Plain English for Lawyers, 4th edit., 1998. Served to capt. USAR, 1962-66. Office: Sch Law U Calif Davis CA 95616

WYDRA, FRANK THOMAS, healthcare executive; b. Republic, Pa., May 11, 1939; s. Frank T. and Anne M. (Kois) W.; m. Karen Branch, June 24, 1961; children: Denise Lee, Sheryl Lynn, Frank Thomas III. BS in Mgmt., U. Ill., 1961. V.p. Allied Supermarkets, Inc., Detroit, 1967-75; sr. v.p. HGH Health System, Detroit, 1975-85; pres. Radius Health Care Sysytems, Inc., Detroit, 1983-85; cons. Birmingham, Mich., 1985-88; exec. v.p. The Chi Group, Ann Arbor, Mich., 1988-91; mng. ptnr., CEO, owner IRI, Mgmt. Cons., Detroit, 1991—. Lectr. various profl. groups; bd. dirs. Mich. Health Systems Inc., Saber-Salisbury Assocs. Inc., Midwestern Health Ctr., MultiCare Med. Inc., RHS Inc. Author: Learner Controlled Instruction, 1980, (with others) Hospital Survival Guide, 1984, The Cure, 1992; creator 2 mgmt. games Performulations, 1978, The Dynamics of Power and Authority, 1981; contbr. articles to profl. jours. Personnel program advisor Mich. State U. Sch. Labor Relations, 1979-83; chmn. new programs Wayne County Community Coll., Detroit, 1979-80; bd. dirs. Detroit Metro Youth Found., 1980-83, State Mich. Health Occupations Council, Lansing, 1982-85. Capt. U.S. Army, 1961-63. Recipient numerous awards ASTD, Nat. Soc. Performance and Instrn., Mich. SOc. Instructional Tech., Supermarket Inst. Mem. Am. Hosp. Assn., Planning Soc. of Am. Hosp. Assn., Hosp. Personnel Adminstrs. Assn. (pres. 1981-82, numerous awards), Am. Mgmt. Assn., Am. Soc. Hosp. Pers.Adminstrs. (bd. dirs. 1981-83), Mich. Soc. Instrnl. Tech. (life, pres. 1973-74), Mich. Hosp. Assn., Employers Assn. Detroit (bd. dirs. 1982-85), Detroit Athletic Club. Avocations: writing, sailing. Home: 8945 Reese Rd Clarkston MI 48348

WYER, JAMES INGERSOLL, lawyer; b. Denver, June 9, 1923; s. William and Katherine (Rolfe) W.; m. Joan Best Connelly, Aug. 13, 1960; children: Joan Connelly Tatnall, Peter Ford, June Wyer Nugent. BA, Yale U., 1945, LL.B., 1949. Bar: N.Y. 1950, N.J. 1987. Assoc. Dewey, Ballantine, Bushby, Palmer & Wood, N.Y.C., 1949-56, Am. Cyanamid Co., Wayne, N.J., 1956, v.p., gen. counsel, 1973-86; of counsel St. John & Wayne, Newark, 1987—. Bd. dirs. TherMold, Inc., William Penn Life Ins. Co. N.Y. Bd. dirs. Nat. Legal Ctr. for the Pub. Interest. Served with USNR, 1943-46. Mem. Assn. Gen. Counsel (1st v.p. 1982-84, pres. 1985-86), ABA, Assn. of Bar of City of N.Y., Atlantic Legal Found. (chmn. 1986-97). Clubs: Jupiter Island (Hobe Sound, Fla.); Seabright (N.J.) Beach, Seabright Lawn, Tennis and Cricket (Rumson, N.J.); Coral Beach and Tennis (Bermuda), Rumson (N.J.) Country. Republican. Office: St John & Wayne 2 Penn Plz E Ste 1 Newark NJ 07105-2249 Office Phone: 973-491-3322.

WYETH, ANDREW, artist; b. Chadds Ford, Pa., July 12, 1917; s. Newell Converse and Carolyn (Bockius) W.; m. Betsy Merle James, May 15, 1940; children: Nicholas, James Browning. Educated pvt. tutors; DFA (hon.), Colby Coll., Maine, 1954, Harvard U., 1955, Dickinson Coll., 1958, Swarthmore Coll., 1958, Nasson Coll., 1963, U. Md., U. Del., Northeastern U., Temple U., 1964; LHD (hon.), Tufts U., 1963; DFA (hon.), Princeton U., 1965; LHD (hon.), Franklin and Marshall Coll., 1965, Lincoln U., 1966, Amherst Coll., 1967; DFA (hon.), Bowdoin Coll., 1970; LHD (hon.), Ursinus Coll., 1971; DFA (hon.), U. Pa., 1972; LHD (hon.), West Chester U., 1984; DFA (hon.), Dartmouth Coll., 1984, Bates Coll., 1987; LHD (hon.), U. Vt., 1988. Artist, landscape painter, 1936—; first one-man show William Macbeth Gallery, N.Y.C., 1937, first solo exhbn. ever held in White House, 1970, first exhbn. by living Am. artist Royal Acad. Arts, London, 1980; exhibited Doll & Richards, Boston, 1938, 40, 42, 44, Cornell U., 1938, Macbeth Gallery, 1938, 41, first tempera show, 1943, 45, Currier Gallery, Manchester, N.H., 1939, room of watercolors, Art Inst. Chgo., 1941; room at Realist and Magic Realist show, Mus. Modern Art, N.Y.C., 1943; one-man exhbn., M. Knoedler & Co., N.Y.C., 1953, 58, Mass. Inst. Tech., Cambridge, 1960, Fogg Art Mus., William Farnsworth Library and Mus., 1963, Helga Pictures at numerous art museums, other univs. and museums; also exhbns. Arnot Mus., Elmira, N.Y., 1986, Seibu-Pisa, Tokyo, 1986, Kenesaw (Ga.) Mus. Art, 1986, Thomasville (Ga.) Art Ctr., 1987, Acad. of the Arts of USSR, Leningrad, 1987, Acad. of the Arts USSR, Moscow, 1987, Nat. Gallery of Art, Washington, 1987, Corcoran Gallery Art, Washington, 1987, An American Vision: Three Generations of Wyeth Art, various mus., 1987, Dallas Mus. Art, 1987, Mus. Fine Arts, Boston, 1988, Terra Mus. Am. Art, Chgo., 1988, Mus. Fine Arts, Houston, 1988, Setagaya Art Mus., Tokyo, 1988, L.A. County Mus. Art, L.A., 1988, Palazzo Reale, Milan, Italy, 1988, Fitzwilliam Mus., Cambridge, Eng., 1988, Fine Arts Mus. San Francisco, 1988, Brandywine River Mus., Chadds Ford, Pa., 1988, Detroit Inst. Arts, k1989, Sezon Mus. Art, Tokyo, 1991, Heckscher Mus., Huntington, N.Y., 1989, Gilcrease Mus., Tulsa, 1989, Portland (Maine) Mus. Art, 1989, Nukaga Gallery, Japan, 1990, Marcelle Fine Art Inc., N.Y.C., 1990, Takuji Kato Modern Art Mus., Tokyo, 1991, Takuji Kato Modern Art Mus., Chichibu City, Japan, 1991, Jacksonville (Fla.) Art Mus., 1992, Portland (Maine) Mus. Art, 1993, Farnsworth Art Mus., Rockland, Maine, 1994, San Francisco Mus. Modern Art, 1995, Charles and Emma Frye Art Mus., 1995; represented in permanent collections Met. Mus. Art, Nat. Gallery Art. Awarded 1st prize Wilmington Soc. Fine Arts, 1939, Obrig prize Am. Watercolor Soc., 1945, award of Merit, Am. Acad. Arts and Letters and Nat. Inst. Arts and Letters, 1947, 1st prize in watercolor Nat. Acad., 1946, Gold medal Nat. Inst. Arts and Letters, 1965, George Walter Dawson Meml. medal Phila. Watercolor Club, 1957, Mellon Gold medal of Achievement Pa. Artists Exhibit, Ligonier Valley, Pa., 1958, Arts Festival award and Citation for bringing dignity to Am. art Phila. Mus. Art, 1959, Percy M. Owens Meml. award Fellowship of Pa. Acad. Fine Arts, Phila., 1960, Presdl. Medal of Freedom, 1963, citation LaSalle Coll., Phila., 1965, Gold medal of honor Pa. Acad. Fine Arts, 1966, Carnegie Inst. award, award for excellence 1st award recognize outstanding performance in arts, Washington Coll., Chestertown, Md., 1976; Gold medal Nat. Arts Club, 1978, first Am. artist awarded Presdl. award Gold Congl. medal, 1988. Mem. Am. Watercolor Soc. (certificate of merit 1962), Nat. Inst. Arts and Letters, Soviet Acad. Arts (hon.), Academie des Beaux-Arts, Chester County Art Assn. (dir.), Audubon Soc. (dir.), N.Y. Watercolor Soc., Wilmington Soc. Fine Arts, Phila. Watercolor Club (dir.), Washington Watercolor Club (dir.), Balt. Watercolor Club (dir.), Am. Acad. Arts and Letters. (Nat. Academician elect May 1945, Gold medal preeminence in painting 1965), Am. Acad. Arts and Scis., Royal Soc. Painters and Watercolours (London). Office: care Frank E Fowler PO Box 247 Lookout Mountain TN 37350-0247

WYETH, JAMES BROWNING, artist; b. Wilmington, Del., July 6, 1946; s. Andrew and Betsy (James) W.; m. Phyllis Overton Mills, Dec. 12, 1968. Privately tutored. One-man shows include M. Knoedler & Co., N.Y.C., 1966, William A. Farnsworth Mus., Rockland, Maine, 1969, 1992, 1995, Coe Kerr Gallery, N.Y.C., 1974, 1990, Brandywine River Mus., Chadds Ford, Pa., 1974, 1994, 1995, 1999, Joslyn Art Mus., Omaha, 1976, Pa. Acad. Fine Arts, 1980, Greenville County Art Mus., Greenville, N.C., 1981, Amon Carter Mus., Ft. Worth, 1981, Anchorage Fine Arts Mus., 1983, James Graham and Sons, N.Y.C., 1993, 1995, 1999, 2000, Decatur House, 1995, Double Door Gallery, Isleboro, Maine, 1996, Butler Art Inst., Youngstown, Ohio, 1999, Russell Rotunda, Washington, 2000, Ringling Mus. Art, Sarasota, Fla., New Britain (Conn.) Mus. Am. Art, one-man shows include touring exhbn. An American Vision: Three Generations of Wyeth Art, various mus. worldwide, 1987—, Farnsworth Art Mus., 1988—2000, Terra Mus. Am. Art, Chgo., 1997—. Mem. NEA, 1972; mem. stamp adv. com. U.S. Postal Svc., 1969; bd. govs. Nat. Space Inst., 1975. Served with Del. Air N.G., 1966—71. Office: care Priscilla Vail Caldwell James Graham & Sons 1014 Madison Ave New York NY 10021-0103 Fax: (212) 794-2454. E-mail: jgsgal@aol.com.

WYGANT, FOSTER LAURANCE, art educator, educator; b. Dayton, Ohio, Oct. 30, 1920; s. Harold F. and M. Esther (Weber) W.; m. Rae E. Hoyt, 1 child, Nancy Laura Profl. diploma, Juilliard Sch. Music, 1942; BA, Columbia U., 1949, MA, 1956, Ed.D., 1959; postgrad., Am. Art Sch., Art Students League, 1951-53. Clarinetist Dallas Symphony and free-lance clarinetist, N.Y.C., 1945-47; publicity, fund-raising positions, and free-lance artist, 1952-56; tchr. art, pub. schs., 1956-59; asst. prof. Montclair State Coll., N.J., 1959-63, assoc. prof., 1963-68; prof. art edn. U. Cin., 1968-87, chmn. dept., 1968-84, dir. Sch. Art Edn. and Art History, 1984-86, emeritus prof., 1987—. Pub., owner Interwood Press, 1987—; vis. sr. lectr. Leeds Coll. Art, Eng., 1966; regional chmn. Scholastic Awards Program, 1968-84; chmn. Action for Arts in Ohio Schs., 1974-75. Author: Art in American Schools in the Nineteenth Century, 1983, School Art in American Culture 1820-1970, 1993, School Art in American Culture Supplement: 1900-1915, 1997; editor, prin. author: Standards for Art Teacher Preparation Programs, 1979, Principles, Purposes and Standards for School Art Programs, 1982; contbr. numerous articles to profl. jours. Exec. dir. Tri-State Chamber Players, Inc., 2002—. Served with U.S. Army, 1941—45. N.Y. State and Juilliard Sch. Music scholar, 1939-41; Kellogg Found. fellow Columbia U., 1955-56 Nat. Art Edn. Assn. (V. Pres., nat. dir. higher edn. divsn. 1975-79, Recognition award 1980, Disting. Svc. award 1982, Disting. fellow 1995), Ohio Art Edn. Assn. (pres. 1972-74, Disting. fellow 2000), Seminar for Rsch. in Art Edn., Coun. for Policy Studies in Art Edn., Am. Fedn. Musicians, Phi Beta Kappa. Home: 3562 Interwood Ave Cincinnati OH 45220-1824 E-mail: wygantfl@ucmail.uc.edu.

WYGOD, MARTIN J. pharmaceuticals executive; b. N.Y.C. BS, N.Y.U., 1961. Chmn., pres., chief exec. officer Medco Containment Inc., Montvale, N.J., 1983-94; chmn. Synetic, Inc., Elmwood Park, N.J., 1994—. Office: Medica Mgr Corp 669 River Dr Ctr 2 Elmwood Park NJ 07407-1361

WYGZA, MICHAEL S. health care products and services executive; b. 1955; BS, Suffolk U.; MBA, Providence Coll. V.p. fin. Lotus Devel. Corp.; CFO Sovereign Hill Software; joined Genzyme Corp., Cambridge, Mass., 1998, sr. v.p., corp. contr., chief acctg. officer, CFO, 1999—. Office: 500 Kendall St Cambridge MA 02142-1108 Fax: 617-252-7600.

WYKLE, MAY L. dean, educator, researcher; BSN, Case Western Res. U., 1956, MSN Psychiat. Nursing, PhD Edn., Case Western Res. U. Dean, Cellar prof. gerontological nursing Frances Payne Bolton Sch. Nursing, Ohio, 1988—; dean, dir. u. ctr. aging and health Case Western Res. U. Established ednl. programs, Europe, Africa, Asia; vis. prof. U. Mich., U. Tex.-Houston, U. Zimbabwe-Africa; del., served on planning com. White Ho. Conf. on Aging, 1993. Contbr. articles, chapters to books; author: Decision Making in Long-Term Care, Practicing Rehabilitation with Geriatric Clients, Stress and Health Among the Elderly, Family Caregiving Across the Lifespan, Service Minority Elders in the 21st Century (AJN Book of Yr. award, 2000). Dir. Robert Wood Johnson Tchg. Nursing Home Project; project dir. several tng. grants; cons. nursing homes, psychiat. hosps.; mem. bd. dirs. numerous cmty. orgns., nursing homes, profl. assns. Named first Pope Eminent scholar, Rosalynn Carter Inst. Human Devel. Southwestern State U., Americus, Ga., Outstanding Rschr. in State of Ohio, Ohio Rsch. Coun. on Aging, Ohio Network Edn. Cons. in field of Aging, 1992; recipient Humanitarian award, Outstanding Contbns. to Nursing Profession, 1999, Acad. award, NIMH Geriatric Mental Health, Merit award, Cleve. Coun. Black Nurses, Gerontological Doris Schwartz Nursing Rsch. award, Gerontological Soc. Am., Belle Sherwin award, Cleve. Vis. Nurse Assn., Leadership award excellence in geriatric care, Midwest Alliance in Nursing, Disting. nurse-scholar lectr. award, Nat. Coun. Nursing Rsch., Nursing Educator award, New Cleve. Woman mag. . Fellow: Gerontological Soc. Am., Am. Acad. Nursing; mem.: NIA, NIMH, NINR, Vets Adminstrn. (geriatric/gerontology adv. com.), Sigma Theta Tau Internat. (pres.-elect 1999). Office: 10900 Euclid Ave Cleveland OH 44106*

WYLAN, BARBARA, artist; b. Providence, 1933; divorced; children: Andrea, Brock. BFA, R.I. Sch. of Design, Providence, 1955; studied with Donald Stoltenberg, Claude Croney, Murray Wentworth, Ruth Wynn, Charles Movalli, Dong Kingman. Tchr. watercolor workshops; juror various exhbns. One-woman shows include Sturgis Libr., Mass., 1974, 77, 83, Falmouth Artists' Guild, Mass., 1977, Skylight Gallery, Colo., 1979, Market Barn Gallery, Falmouth, Mass., 1981, 89, 91, Dom's Restaurant, Mass., 1981, Spectrum Am. Artists and Craftsmen, Brewster, Mass., 1983-84, 86-87, 88, 90, 92-93, 95, 2000, 03, Two Islands: Nantucket and New Zealand, 1985, Cape Cod Conservatory, Mass., 1984, 86, Cape Cod Mus. Nat. History, Brewster, Mass., 1987, Old Selectmens' Gallery, West Barnstable, Mass., 1995, Cahoon Mus. Am. Art, Cotuit, Mass., 1998; exhibited in group shows at Watercolor USA (Springfield award 1982), Nat. Soc. Painters in Casein and Acrylic 38th Ann., Nat. Arts club, NYC (Dr. David Soloway award 1991); represented in permanent and pvt. collections Mobile (Ala.) Mus. Art, Cahoon Mus. Am. Art, Cotuit, Mass., Cape Mus. Fine Arts, Dennis, Mass.; represented by Spectrum of Am. Artists and Craftsmen, Brewster, Hyannis, Nantucket, Mass., Palm Beach Gardens, Fla., North Conway, NH, Woods Hole (Mass.) Art Gallery, Field Gallery, West Tisbury, Mass. Mem. Nat. Soc. Painters in Casein and Acrylic, Watercolor USA Honor Soc., New Eng. Watercolor Soc., Copley Soc. Art, and Twenty-one in Truro.

WYLAND, MARK, state official; b. Escondido, Calif. 1 child, Nicole. BA in Internat. Rels., Pomona Coll.; MA in Polit. Sci., Columbia U. Co-owner family bus.; state assembly mem. Dist. 74 Calif. State Assembly, 2000—. Mem. bus. and professions com.; mem. edn. com.; mem. govtl. orgn. com.; vice-chair revenue and taxation com.; mem. VA com.; mem. Escondido Union Sch. Bd.; trustee Pomona Coll. Mem.: YMCA, Encinitis. Republican. Mailing: Rm 4130 PO Box 942849 Sacramento CA 94249 Office: Ste 205 221 E Main St Vista CA 92084

WYLDE, KATHRYN S. business organization executive; BA, St. Olaf Coll., 1968. Pres., CEO, N.Y.C. Housing Partnership, 1982—96; founding pres., CEO, N.Y.C. Investment Fund, 1996- ; pres., CEO. Partnership for N.Y.C., 2000—. Chair Luth. Med. Ctr., Bklyn.; mem. bus. adv. bd. CUNY; bd. dirs. N.Y.C. Econ. Devel. Corp., Biomed. Rsch. Alliance N.Y., Manhattan Inst. Recipient HBSCNY Bus. Statesman award. Office: Partnership for NYC One Battery Pk Plz 5th Fl New York NY 10004 Business E-Mail: kwylde@nycp.org.

WYLE, FREDERICK S. lawyer; b. Berlin, May 9, 1928; came to U.S., 1939, naturalized, 1944; s. Norbert and Malwina (Mauer) W.; m. Katinka Franz, June 29, 1969; children: Susan Kim, Christopher Anthony, Katherine Anne. BA magna cum laude, Harvard U., 1951, LL.B., 1954. Bar: Mass. 1954, Calif. 1955, N.Y. 1958. Teaching fellow Harvard Law Sch., 1954-55; law clk. U.S. Dist. Ct., No. Dist. Calif., 1955-57; assoc. firm Paul, Weiss, Rifkind, Wharton & Garrison, NYC, 1957-58; pvt. practice San Francisco, 1958-62; spl. asst. def. rep. U.S. del. to NATO, Paris, 1962-63; mem. Policy Planning Council, Dept. State, Washington, 1963-65; dep. asst. sec. def. for European and NATO affairs Dept. Def., Washington, 1966-69; v.p. devel., gen. counsel Schroders, Inc., NYC, 1969-71, atty., cons., 1971-72; chief exec. officer Saturday Rev. Industries, Inc., San Francisco, 1972-76; individual practice law San Francisco, 1976—82. Internat. counsel to Fed. States Micronesia, 1974-82; cons. Rand Corp., Dept. Def., Nuclear Regulatory Commn. Contbr. to: Ency. Brit, 1972, also articles in profl. publs., newspapers. Trustee US Interest Bicycle Club Casino, 1996-99; trustee in bankruptcy Garden City, Inc., 2000-; liquidating trustee Synthetic Industries, 2000—, Biosurg. Industries, 2000—; negotiator for Gov. of Calif. with Indian tribes re gambling, 2003. Served with AUS, 1946-47. Mem. Internat. Inst. Strategic Studies, Phi Beta Kappa. Office: 3 Embarcadero Ctr Fl 7 San Francisco CA 94111-4065

WYLE, NOAH, actor; b. Hollywood, Calif., June 4, 1971; Represented by IFA Talent Agy., L.A. Artistic prodr. The Blank Theatre Co., Los Angeles. Actor: Crooked Hearts, 1991, A Few Good Men, 1992, Swing Kids, 1993, There Goes My Baby, 1994, The Myth of Fingerprints, 1997, Can't Stop Dancing, 1999, Pirates of Silicon Valley, 1999, Scenes of the Crime, 2001, Enough, 2002, White Oleander, 2002; (TV films) Blind Faith, 1990, Fail Safe, 2000; TV appearances include ER, 1994—, Guinevere, 1994, assoc. prodr. Myth of Fingerprints, 1997; actor: (TV films) Pirates of Silicon Valley, 1999. Recipient SAG awards, 1998, 1999.

WYLIE, JAMES MALCOLM, adult education educator; b. N.Y.C., Mar. 16, 1938; s. James M. and Nancy Beatrice (Worthy) Wylie. BS, Boston U., 1960. Columnist Mexico City Times, 1964; prof. Cooper Union Coll., N.Y.C., 1986. Author: The Lost Rebellion, 1971, The Homestead Grays, 1977, The Sign of Dawn, 1981; participant Spoleto Festival U.S.A., 2001. Office: 51 Astor Pl New York NY 10003-7132

WYLIE, PAMELA JANE, writer, producer, consultant, small business owner; BA in English, U. So. Calif., 1967, MFA in Profl. Writing, 1983, postgrad., 1979-83. Sys. programmer IBM, Poughkeepsie, N.Y., 1967-68; cons. CS/SD, Fountain Valley, Calif., 1968-69, Price Waterhouse, L.A., 1969-72; ind. cons., L.A., 1973-77; pres. PJW Enterprises, Inc., Fullerton, Calif., 1977—; dir. info. sys. NorthWest Quadrant, Newport Beach, Calif., 1985-86; sr. cons. Richard J. Yost & Assocs., San Gabriel, Calif., 1986-87; pres. Thorn Tree Prodns., L.A., 1998-99. Bd. dirs. Valdy Corp., L.A. Author: Power Your Way Through Y2K, 1999, (play) Doctor Franklin and Madam President, 1998, (internet) Harambee! Year 2000 Action Pack, 1998, (play) Heather on the Battlefield, 2001. Home: 1429 N Genesee Ave Los Angeles CA 90046-3905

WYLIE, PAUL RICHTER, JR., lawyer; b. Dec. 25, 1936; s. Paul Richter and Alice (Dredge) W.; m. Arlene Marie Klem, Mar. 6, 1982; children: Lynne Catherine, John Michael, Thomas Robert. BSChemE, Mont. State U., 1959; JD, Am. U., 1965. Bar: Utah 1978, Calif. 1970, U.S. Supreme Ct. 1971, Mont. 1990. Patent examiner U.S. Patent and Trademark Office, Washington, 1962-64; asst. gen. patent counsel Dart Industries Inc., L.A., 1967-81; pvt. practice L.A., 1981-86, Pacific Palisades, Calif., 1986-90, Bozeman, Mont., 1990—. Mem. ABA, AIChE, Am. Intellectual Property Law Assn., L.a. Intellectual Property Law Assn., Am. Chem. Soc., Licensing Execs. Soc., Tech. Transfer Soc. Home: 106 Silverwood Dr Bozeman MT 59715-9255 Office: 1805 W Dickerson St Ste 3 Bozeman MT 59715-4131

WYLIE, QUINETA G. BEAGLE, state political party executive; b. Higgins, Tex., July 5, 1948; d. Quinten Howare and Gerri Stimson Beagle; m. Allan George Wylie, 1969; children: Trevor McClean, Allan Stimson. BS, Okla. State U., 1973; MBA, U. No. Colo., 1978. Vice chmn. Okla. State Rep. Party, 1993-95, chmn., 1995—. Former adminstrn. Alaska Flying Club. Rep. chmn. Logan County, Okla., 1988; former Rep. chmn. Okla. County; mem. exec. com. Rep. Nat. Com. Mem. Freedoms Found. at Valley Forge, Okla. Hist. Soc., Okla. Fedn. Rep. Women (bd. dirs. 1990-93, chmn. 1st Ladies 1990-92), Oklahomans for Integrity in Govt. (adv. bd. 1992-93). Home: 5701 Parkhurst Rd Edmond OK 73034-9233

WYLLIE, STANLEY CLARKE, retired librarian; b. Clearwater, Fla., Nov. 19, 1935; s. Stanley Clarke and Euginia Lee (Tison) W.; m. Martha Ann Thomason, June 14, 1963; children: Stanley Clarke Jr., Susan Lynne DeHerder, Patricia Anne. BS in History and Social Scis., Fla. So. Coll., 1958; MS in Libr. Sci., Fla. State U., 1963. Tchr. civics and English Lakeland (Fla.) Jr. H.S., 1960-61; libr. I Tampa (Fla.) Pub. Libr., 1962; dir. Chestatee Reg. Libr. Sys., Gainesville, Ga., 1963-64; ind. and sci. ref. libr. Dayton and Montgomery County Pub. Libr., Dayton, Ohio, 1964-66, collection libr., 1967-73, social scis. and genealogy ref. libr., 1973-90; ret. Editor Mad River Currents newsletter, 1996-97, Bits, 1964-66. Corr. sec. Montgomery County Geneal. Soc., 1990-91, rec. sec., 1997-98; pres. Men's Rep. Club, Lakeland, 1960-61; mem. TV cable commn. City of Riverside, Ohio, 1997-98; presiding judge Riverside, Montgomery County Bd. Elections, 1992—; mem. exec. com. Montgomery County Rep. Party, 2004—, ctrl. com., 2004—. Recipient Edward M. Selby award Ohio Chpt. of Rsch., 1991-92, Alumnus Disting. svc. award Fla. So. Coll., 1991; Knight York Cross of Honor, Ohio Priory #18, KYCH, 1983; named Ky. Col. Mem.: AARP (dist. coord. 1997—99), Dayton and Montgomery County Pub. Libr. Staff Assn. (pres. retiree chpt. 2004—), Mensa, Pub. Employee Retirees Inc. (chpt. pres. 1998, dist. 3 rep. 1999—2002), Am. Fedn. State, County, Mcpl. Employees, United Ancient Order of Druids (noble arch Franklin Grove #2), Fla. State Geneal. Soc., SAR (pres. Richard Montgomery chpt. 1990—91, Silver Good Citizenship medal 1997), Dayton High Twelve (pres. 1994), Odd Fellows (Noble Grand Steuben Rebekah Lodge 1997, chief patriarch Mad River Encampment # 16 1998—99, grand lodge rep. 1998—2000, Noble grand 1998—2001, Noble Grand Steuben Rebekah Lodge 2000, pres. S.W. Boosters Assn. 2001—, pres. S.W. Promotional Assn. 2001—, grand lodge rep. 2002—, maj. occidental Canton patriarchs militant 2003—, Marion lodge #18 Noble Grand 2003—04, grand patriarch Grand Encampment Ohio 2003—), Grand Monarch, El Aliman Sanctorum, Ancient Mystic Order of Samaritans, Toastmasters (area 3 gov. 1995, v.p. edn. 1997), Audubon Soc., Order of DeMolay (adv. bd. 3d dist. 1996—2002, Cross of Honor, Legion of Honor), Order Rainbow for Girls (Grand Cross of Color), Far Hills High Twelve Club, Fla. Geneal. Soc., Pres.'s Club of Dayton (pres. 2000—01), Knights of Khorassan (royal vizier 2004—), Grand Herald, Grand Grove of the Midwest of the United Ancient Order of Druids, Lions (pres. 1996—97, zone chmn. 1996—98, Pres. Excellence award 1997), Jr. Order Mechanics, Grange, Marion Lodge, Orange Order (worthy master Gideons Hope 802 2002—), Improved Order of Redmen (Sachem Lone Eagle Lodge 2004—), Elks (leading knight Dayton Lodge), KP (chancellor comdr. Red Star Lodge 2000—01, Grand Lodge rep. 2002—), Shriners, Masons. Anglican Catholic. Avocations: reading, stamp collecting/philately. Home: 4960 Franlou Ave Dayton OH 45432-3120

WYLLY, BARBARA BENTLEY, performing arts association administrator; b. Bala-Cynwyd, Pa., June 10, 1924; d. William Henry and Virginia (Barclay) Bentley; m. William Beck Wylly, Apr. 26, 1947; children: Virginia Wylly Johnson, Barbara Wylly Klausman, Thomas C. II. A, Briarcliff Jr. Coll., 1943. Pres. bd. dirs. Hillside Hosp. Inc., Atlanta, 1982, mem. adv. coun., 1982—; pres. Atlanta Symphony Assocs., 1975-76, mem. adv. bd., 1976—; chmn. bd. dirs. Ctr. for Puppetry Arts, Atlanta, 1988-. Bd. dirs. Mountain Conservation Trust, Atlanta Opera Guild, 1999—, bd. sponsors Georgian Chamber Players Bd., 2000-. Republican. Episcopalian. Avocations: walking, reading, music. Home: 940 Foxcroft Rd NW Atlanta GA 30327-2622 Office: Ctr Puppetry Arts 1404 Spring St NW Atlanta GA 30309-2820

WYLY, CHARLES JOSEPH, JR., corporate executive; b. Lake Providence, La., Oct. 13, 1933; s. Charles Joseph and Flora (Evans) W.; m. Caroline Denmon; children: Martha, Charles Joseph III, Emily, Jennifer. BS, La. Tech. U., 1956. Sales rep. IBM Service Bur. Corp., 1956-64; v.p. Wyly Corp., Dallas, 1964-65, exec. v.p., 1965-69, pres., 1969-73, chmn. exec. com., 1973-76, dir., 1964-76; chmn. bd. Earth Resources Co., 1968-80. Vice chmn. bd. dirs. USACafes, Inc. (Bonanza Internat., Inc.), 1968-89, Sterling Software, Inc., Michaels Stores, Inc.; chmn. Tex. High-Speed Rail Authority, 1990-91, Maverick Capital, 1990-96. Mem. Pres.'s Advisory Council on Mgmt. Improvement, 1970-73; vice-chmn. Devel. Council So. Methodist U. Found. Sci. and Engring., 1970-71; Mem. Republican Nat. Fin. Com., 1970—; Bd. dirs. Dallas County United Way Fund; pres. Dallas Theater Center., 1972-79. Mem. Am. Mgmt. Assn., Pi Kappa Alpha, Omicron Delta Kappa, Delta Sigma Pi, Beta Gamma Sigma. Clubs: City, Crescent, Park City, Brookhollow (Dallas). Office: Ste 1000 300 Crescent Ct Dallas TX 75201-7852

WYLY, SAM, retail executive; Founder Univ. Computing Co., 1963-79; co-owner, chmn. Bonanza Steakhouse, 1967-89; founder Datran, Inc., 1968; co-founder, mem. exec. com. Earth Resources Co., 1968-80; co-founder, chmn. Sterling Software, Inc., 1981—; chmn. Michaels Stores Inc., Irving, Tex., 1984—. Office: Michaels Stores Inc 8000 Bent Branch Dr Irving TX 75063

WYMAN, DAVID SWORD, historian, educator; b. Weymouth, Mass., Mar. 6, 1929; s. Hollis Judson and Ruth (Sword) W.; m. Mildred Louise Smith, Sept. 13, 1950; children: James Nayler, Teresa Carol. AB, Boston U., 1951; EdM, Plymouth State Coll., 1961; AM, Harvard U., 1962, PhD, 1966; DHL (hon.), Hebrew Union Coll. Jewish Inst. Religion, 1986, Yeshiva U., 1988. Various positions, 1951-57; tchr. pub. schs., 1957-60; tchr. pub. high sch. Penacook, N.H., 1960-61; prof. history U. Mass., Amherst, 1966-91, Josiah DuBois prof. history, 1986-91, Josiah DuBois prof. emeritus, 1991—, chmn. Judaic Studies Program, 1977-78, 82-84, chmn. David S. Wyman Inst. for Holocaust Studies, 2003—. Acad. advisor Simon Wiesenthal Ctr., L.A., 1983—; nat. coun. Nat. Christian Leadership Conf. for Israel, 1986, numerous radio and TV appearances; historian advisor to films. Author: Paper Walls: America and the Refugee Crisis, l938-4l, l968, The Abandonment of the Jews: America and the Holocaust, l94l-45, l984 (Anisfield-Wolf award l984, Stuart Bernath award l984, Theodore Saloutos book award l984, Present Tense Lit. award l984, Boston Hadassah Myrtle Wreath award l985, Nat. Jewish Book award l985), new edit., 1998; co-author: A Race Against Death: Peter Bergson, America, and the Holocaust, 2002; editor: America and the Holocaust, l3 vols. documents, l989-90, The World Reacts to the Holocaust, 1996; contbr. articles to profl. jours., chpts. to books. Recipient Chancellor's medal, U. Mass., 1986, Achievement award Isaac M. Wise Temple, Cin. 1986, Humanitarian award Bklyn. Holocaust Meml. Com., 1986, Herbert Katzki award Am. Jewish Joint Distbn. Com., 1999; elected to Boston U. Collegium Disting. Alumni, 1986; Woodrow Wilson fellow, 1961-62, 65-66; grantee Social Sci. Rsch. Coun., 1969-70, Am. Coun. Learned Socs., 1969-70, Charles Warren Ctr. at Harvard U., 1969-70. Mem. Soc. for Am. Baseball Rsch., N.H. Hist. Soc., Friends Hist. Assn., Phi Beta Kappa. Avocations: baseball, greyhounds as pets, local N.H. history. Home: 61 Columbia Dr Amherst MA 01002-3105

WYMAN, JAMES VERNON, newspaper executive; b. Brockton, Mass., Nov. 17, 1923; s. George Dewey and Christine Laverne (Skinner) W.; m. Viola Marie Bousquet, June 24, 1950; children: J. Vernon, Douglas Phillip, Carolyn Anne. Student, Northeastern U., Boston, 1946-48; BS in Journalism, Boston U., 1951. From staff to dep. exec. editor Providence Jour.-Bull., 1951-88, v.p., exec. editor, 1989-95, ret., 1995. Served with AUS, 1942-46, PTO. Recipient Yankee Quill award, 1989, Disting. Alumni award Boston U. Coll. of Comm. Alumni Bd., 1996; named to R.I. Journalism Hall of Fame, 1999. Mem. New Eng. AP News Execs. Assn. (past pres.), AP Mng. Editors Assn., New Eng. Soc. Newspaper Editors, Acad. New Eng. Journalists (past dir.), New Eng. Newspaper Assn., Sigma Delta Chi (past pres. New Eng. chpt.). Roman Catholic. Home: 44 Starflower Ct Wakefield RI 02879-5475

WYMAN, NANCY S. state legislator; b. Bklyn., Apr. 21, 1946; d. Arthur and Ann (Rosenzweig) Schmukler; m. Ronald Michael Wyman, Sept. 11, 1966; children: Stacey, Meryl. Student, L.I. Coll. Hosp., 1966. X-ray technician Bapt. Hosp., Miami, Fla., 1966-67, Baird Orthopedics, Miami, 1967-70, Rockville (Conn.) Orthopedics, 1975-83; legis. aide State of Conn., Hartford, 1983-87, state rep., 1987-94; state comptroller, 1995—. Named Legislator of Yr., Nat. Abortion Rights Reproductive Rights Action League, 1990, Arts Commn., 1992, Coun. Small Towns, 1992; recipient Friend of Edn. award Conn. Edn. Assn., 1990. Democrat. Jewish. Home: 18 Pilgrim Dr Tolland CT 06084-2906

WYMAN, RALPH MARK, finance company executive; b. Usti, Czechoslovakia, Feb. 7, 1926; arrived in U.S., 1941, naturalized, 1946; s. Hans and Stella (Parnas) Wyman; m. Lotte Ann Novak, Oct. 25, 1947; 1 child, Leslie Andrea Wyman Cooper. Student, Upper Can. Coll., 1942, Bucknell U., 1942-43; BSBA, NYU, 1945; postgrad., Columbia U., 1945-46. Asst. mgr. export dept. Liebermann Waelchi & Co., Inc., N.Y.C., 1946-47; trainee White Weld Co., 1947-48; v.p. H. O. Canfield Co., 1948-65, vice chmn. bd. dirs., 1965-79, bd. dirs., 1953-79, Pantasote Inc., 1960-89, vice chmn. bd. dirs., 1967-89; mng. partner United Eagle Mgmt. Co., Eagle Mgmt. Co., 1960-95; pres. Veritas Co., 1960—; bd. dirs., chmn. Eagle Capital Internat. LLC, 1985—; bd. dirs., vice chmn. Affiliate Artists, Inc., 1971-88; chmn. AMA Eagle LLC, 2003—. Pres. Panwy Found.; bd. dirs. United Way Greenwich, Conn., 1980—86, Kids in Crisis, Greenwich, 1993—2001, sec., 1995—2001; trustee Greenwich Acad., 1963—71, chmn., 1968—70; elder, trustee Synod New Eng., 1974—76; trustee Princeton Theol. Sem., 1976—2001, vice chmn., 1997—2001, trustee emeritus, 2001—; trustee Ctr. Theol. Inquiry, 1997—. Mem.: Indian Harbor Yacht Club, Greenwich Country Club, Lambda Chi Alpha. Home: 34 Baldwin Farms N Greenwich CT 06831-3307 Office: # 4 Greenwich Office Park IV Greenwich CT 06831-5246 Business E-Mail: ralph.wyman@amaglobal.com.

WYMAN, RICHARD THOMAS, information services consultant; b. Wilmington, Del., June 4, 1951; s. William Harper and Marian Kathryn (Bode) W.. Pa. State U., 1969-71, Def. Language Inst., 1974-75, Control Data Inst., Dallas, 1979. Enlisted U.S. Army, 1971, served to staff sgt., 1979; data ctr. mgr. thrift svcs. divsn. ADP Inc., Dallas, 1979-80; support mgr. Electronic Data Sys., Inc., Dallas, 1980-85, info. modeling analyst, 1985-90; pres. Strategic InfoSource, Plano, Tex., 1991-93; sr. cons. The SABRE Group, Ft. Worth, 1993-97; assoc. Perot Sys. Corp., Richardson, Tex., 1997-98; info. architect The Technical Resource Connection, Inc., Tampa, Fla., 1998—. Rep. 101st Airborne Divsn. Nat. Conf. Skill Maintenance, Ft. Meade, Md., 1977. Author: (spl. course) U.S. Army Intelligence, 1978-79. Co-chmn. sub-com. City Bond Referendum Com., Plano, 1990; mem. City of Plano Historic Landmark Com., 1993-97, vice chmn. 1996, chmn. 1996-97. Recipient Army Commendation medal, 1978, 79, Vol. Svc. award, Office of Mayor, Plano, 1990. Home: 3608 Trailview Dr Plano TX 75074 Office: Technical Resource Connection Inc 12320 Race Track Rd Tampa FL 33626-3115 E-mail: rwyman@trcinc.com.

WYMAN, RICHARD VAUGHN, engineering educator, exploration company executive; b. Painesville, Ohio, Feb. 22, 1927; s. Vaughn Ely and Melinda (Ward) W.; m. Anne Fenton, Dec. 27, 1947; 1 son, William Fenton. BS, Case Western Res. U., 1948; MS, U. Mich., 1949; PhD, U. Ariz., 1974. Registered profl. engr., Nev., Ariz.; registered geologist, Ariz., Calif.; lic. water right surveyor, Nev. Geologist N.J. Zinc Co., 1949, 52-53, Cerro de Pasco Corp., 1950-52; chief geologist Western Gold & Uranium, Inc., St. George, Utah, 1953-55, gen. supt., 1955-57, v.p., 1957-59; pres. Intermountain Exploration Co., Boulder City, Nev., 1959-93; tunnel supt. Reynolds Electric & Engring. Co., 1961-63, mining engr., 1965-67; asst. mgr. ops. Reynolds Electric and & Engring. Co., 1967-69; constrn. supt. engr. Sunshine Mining Co., 1963-65; lectr. U. Nev., Las Vegas, 1969-73, assoc. prof., 1973-80, dept. chmn., 1976-80, prof., 1980-92, prof. emeritus, 1992—, chmn. dept. civil and mech. engring., 1984-90, chmn. dept. civil and environ. engring., 1990-91. Mineral rep. Ariz. Strip Adv. Bd., 1976-80, U.S.B.L.M.; mem. peer rev. com. Nuclear Waste Site, Dept. Energy, Las Vegas, 1978-82; pres. Ariz. Juno Resources, Boulder City, 1980-87, v.p., 1990-97; pres. Wyman Engring. Cons., 1987—; cons. Corp. Andina de Fomento, Caracas, Venezuela, 1977-78; v.p. Comstock Gold, Inc., 1984-93; program evaluator Accreditation Bd. for Engring. and Tech., 1995-2001. Contbr. articles to profl. jours. Sec. Washington County Republican Party, Utah, 1958-60; del. Utah Rep. Conv., 1958-60; scoutmaster Boy Scouts Am., 1959-69; mem. citizens adv. com., tech. adv. com. Clark County Regional Flood Control Dist., 1998—. Served with USN, 1944-46. Recipient Order of Engr. award, 2000. Fellow ASCE (life; edn. divsn. 1990, local rep. nat. conv. Las Vegas), Soc. Econ. Geologists (life); mem. AIME/SME (life, chmn. So. Nev. sect. 1971-72, dir. 1968-2002, sec.-treas. 1974-92, chmn. Pacific S.W. Minerals Conf. 1972, gen. chmn. nat. conv. 1980, Disting. Mem. award 1989, Legion of Honor 1999), Assn. Engring. Geologists (dir. S.W. sect. 1989-91), Am. Inst. Minerals Appraisers, Am. Water Works Assn., Nev. Mining Assn. (assoc.), Northwest Mining Assn., Geological Soc. Nev., Assn. Ground Water Scientists and Engrs., Arctic Inst. N.Am. (life), Am. Soc. Engring. Edn., Soc. for History of Discoveries, Am. Philatelic Soc., SAR, Am. Legion, Sigma Xi (pres. Las Vegas sect. 1986-91), Phi Kappa Phi (pres. U. Nev. Las Vegas chpt. 100 1982-83), Sigma Gamma Epsilon, Tau Beta Pi (hon.). Congregationalist. Home: 610 Bryant Ct Boulder City NV 89005-3017 Office: Wyman Engring PO Box 60473 Boulder City NV 89006-0473 Office Phone: 702-293-1098.

WYNAR, BOHDAN STEPHEN, librarian, writer, editor; b. Lviv, Ukraine, Sept. 7, 1926; came to U.S., 1950, naturalized, 1957; s. John I. and Euphrosina (Doryk) W.; children: Taras, Michael, Roxolana. Diplom-Volkswirt Econs., U. Munich, Germany, 1949, PhD, 1950; MA, U. Denver, 1958. Methods analyst, statistician Tramco Corp., Cleve., 1951-53; freelance journalist Soviet Econs., Cleve., 1954-56; adminstrv. asst. U. Denver Librs., 1958-59, head tech. svcs. div., 1959-62; assoc. prof. Sch. Librarianship, U. Denver, 1962-66; dir. div. libr. edn. State U. Coll., Geneseo, N.Y., 1966-67, dean Sch. Libr. Sci., prof., 1967-69; pres. Libraries Unlimited Inc., 1969—2002. Author: Soviet Light Industry, 1956, Economic Colonialism, 1958, Ukrainian Industry, 1964, Introduction to Bibliography and Reference Work, 4th edit, 1967, Introduction to Cataloging and Classification, 8th edit, 1992, Major Writings on Soviet Economy, 1966, Library Acquisitions, 2d edit, 1971, Research Methods in Library Science, 1971, Economic Thought in Kievan Rus', 1974; co-author: Comprehensive Bibliography of Cataloging and Classification, 2 vols., 1973, Ukraine: A Bibliographic Guide to English Language Publications, 1990, Independent Ukraine: A Bibliographic Guide to English Language Publications, 1989-99, 2000, Wynar's Introduction to Cataloging and Classification, 2000; editor Ukrainian Quar., 1953-58, Preliminary Checklist of Colorado Bibliography, 1963, Studies in Librarianship, 1963-66, Research Studies in Library Science, 1970—, Best Reference Books, 3d edit., 1985, 4th edit., 1992, Colorado Bibliography, 1980; gen. editor: American Reference Books Ann., 1969-2001; editor: ARBA Guide to Subject Encyclopedias and Dictionaries, 1985, ARBA Guide To Biographical Dictionaries, Reference Books in Paperback, An Annotated Guide, 2d edit., 1976, 3rd edit., 1991, Dictionary of Am. Library Biography, 1978, Ukraine-A Bibliographic Guide to English-Language Publications, 1990, 99, International Writings of Bohdan S. Wynar 1949-1992, 1993, Independent Ukraine, Bibliographic Guide, 2000, My Life-Memoirs-, 2003, Recommended Reference Books for Medium-Sized and Small Libraries, 1981-2001; co-editor, contbr. Ency. Ukraine, 1955—; editor Library Sci. Ann., 1984-90, 98, Libr. Info. Sci. Annual 1984-90, 98—. Bd. dirs., mem. exec. bd. ZAREVO, Inc. Mem. ALA (pres. Ukrainian Congress com. br., Denver 1976), Colo. Library Assn., N.Y. Library Assn., Am. Assn. Advancement Slavic Studies (pres. Ukrainian Research Found. 1976-90), AAUP, Ukranian Hist. Assn. (exec. bd.), Sevčenko Societe Scientifique (Paris), Ukrainian Acad. Arts and Scis. (N.Y.C.).

WYNDRUM, RALPH WILLIAM, JR., communications executive consultant; b. N.Y.C., Apr. 20, 1937; s. Ralph W. and Virginia M. (Woolley) W.; m. Meta Schmidt, Apr. 23, 1960; children: Dorothy, Jeanne, Ralph, Joan. BS, Columbia U., 1959, MS in Elec. Engring., 1960, MS in Bus. Adminstrn., 1978; Sc.D., NYU, 1963. Mem. tech. staff Bell Labs., Murray Hill, N.J., 1963-65, supr. exploratory circuit design, 1965-69, head loop transmission tech. dept., 1969-79, head advanced loop transmission systems dept. Whippany, 1979-87, head internat. loop systems dept., 1987, dir. systems analysis ctr., 1987-90, dir. quality process ctr., 1990-92, dir. quality, engring., software and techs., 1993-94; v.p. AT&T World Svcs., 1994—, dir. process engr. ctr., 1995-96; tech. v.p. AT&T Labs., 1996-99, v.p. program mgmt., 1999-2000, exec. cons., 2000—; staff exec. SmartOrg, Inc., Menlo Park, Calif., 2001—; CEO, Wyndrum Assocs., 2000—. Adj. prof. N.J. Inst. Tech., 1965, Rutgers U., 2004; adj. prof. Stevens Inst. Tech., 1980-88, mem. industry adv. bd., 2000—. Contbr. articles to profl. jours.; patentee in field. Fellow: IEEE (bd. dirs. 1988—90, v.p. publs. 1990—91, bd. dirs. 2000—01, v.p. tech. activities 2003—04, bd. dirs., exec. com. 2004, Pres.'s Leadership award 1991); mem.: IEEE-USA (v.p. tech. policy 2002—03, bd. dirs. 2002—04), IEEE Components, Packaging and Mfg. Tech. Soc., IEEE Comm. Soc. (chmn. conf. bd. 1981—87), Shrewsbury River Yacht Club, Sigma Xi, Beta Gamma Sigma, Eta Kappa Nu. Republican. Roman Catholic. Home: 35 Cooney Ter Fair Haven NJ 07704-3001 Office: 35 Cooney Ter Fair Haven NJ 07704-3001 Office Phone: 732-219-0005. E-mail: rww@monmouth.com., r.wyndrum@ieee.org., rww@wyndrum.com.

WYNER, YEHUDI, composer, pianist, conductor, educator; b. Calgary, Alta., Can., June 1, 1929; s. Lazar and Sarah Naomi (Shumiatcher) Weiner; m. Nancy Joan Braverman, Sept. 16, 1951 (div. 1967); children: Isaiah, Adam, Cassia; m. Susan M. Davenny, June 15, 1967. Diploma, Juilliard Sch. Music, 1946; AB, Yale U., 1950, B.Mus., 1951, M.Mus., 1953; MA, Harvard U., 1952. Vis. assoc. prof. Hofstra Coll., 1959; lectr. Queens Coll., N.Y.C., 1959-60; instr. Hebrew Union Coll., N.Y.C., 1957-59; music dir. Westchester Reform Temple, N.Y.C., 1959-68; asst. prof. theory Yale U., 1963-69, assoc. prof. theory, 1969-77, chmn. composition dept., 1969-73; prof. music SUNY, Purchase, 1978-89, dean music, 1978-82. Faculty Tanglewood Music Ctr. (formerly Berkshire Music Ctr.), 1975-97; vis. prof. composition Cornell U., 1987, Ziskind vis. prof. composition Brandeis U., 1987-88, Walter Naumburg prof. composition, dir. contemporary ensemble, 1989—; vis. prof. Harvard U., 1991-93, 96-98, 2003-04; Mary Duke Biddle Disting. composer Duke U., 1995. Mus. dir. Turnau Opera Assn., 1961—64, New Haven Opera Soc., 1968—77, mem. Bach Aria group, 1968—, composer, condr. Tanglewood, 1961, composer-in-residence Santa Fe Chamber Music Festival, 1982, Am. Acad. Rome, 1991; composer: Easy Suite for Piano, 1949, Songs, 1950—2004, Two Chorale Preludes for Organ, 1951, Partita for piano, 1952, Dance Variations for wind octet, 1953, rev., 1959, Psalm 143, chorus, 1952, Sonata for piano, 1954, Concert Duo for violin and piano, 1955—57, Dedication Anthem, 1957, Serenade for Seven Instruments, 1958, Passover Offering for Flute, Clarinet, Cello and Trombone, 1959, Three Informal Pieces for violin and piano, 1961, Friday Evening Service for Cantor, Chorus, Organ, 1963, orchestrated, 1992, (incidental music for play) The Old Glory, 1964, Torah Service with Instruments, 1966, Da Camera for piano and orch., 1967, Cadenza! for clarinet and harpsichord (or piano), 1969, De Novo for cello and small ensemble, 1971, Liturgical Fragments for the High Holidays, 1971, Three Short Fantasies for piano, 1963—71, Canto Cantabile for soprano and concert band, 1972, (music for play) The Mirror, 1972—73, Memorial Music for soprano and 3 flutes, 1971—73, Intermedio for soprano and string orchestra, 1974, Wedding Music, 1976, Dances of Atonement for violin and piano, 1976, Fragments from Antiquity: 5 songs for soprano and symphony orch., 1978, Romances for Piano Quartet, 1980, All the Rage for flute and piano, 1980, Processionals and Marches, 1979, 1980, Tanz and Maissele for clarinet, violin, cello, piano, 1981, On This Most Voluptuous Night for soprano and 7 instruments, 1982, Wind Quintet, 1984, String Quartet, 1985, Composition for Viola and piano, 1987, Toward the Center for piano, 1988, Sweet Consort for flute and piano, 1988, Leonardo Vincitore for 2 sopranos, string bass and piano, 1988, O To Be a Dragon, four songs for women's chorus and piano, 1989, Trapunto Junction for brass trio and percussion, 1991, Changing Time for small ensemble, 1991, New Fantasies for piano, 1991, Amadeus' Billiard for small ensemble, 1991, Il Cane Minore for 2 clarinets and bassoon, 1992, Wedding Dances: From the Notebook of Suzanne de Venné, 1993, Post Fantasies for piano, 1993, Prologue and Narrative for cello and orch., 1994, Song Cycle for soprano, baritone and piano: Restaurants, Wines-Bistros, Shrines, 1994, More Fantasies for piano, 1994—2002, Lyric Harmony for orch., 1995, Praise Ye the Lord for soprano and ensemble, 1996, Brandeis Sunday for string quartet, 1996, A Mad Tea Party for soprano, 2 baritones, flute, violin, cello and piano, 1996, Epilogue for orch., 1996, Horntrio, 1997, Madrigal for string quartet, 1999, The Second Madrigal: Voices of Women for soprano and eleven players, 1999, Quartet for oboe and string trio, 1999, Commedia for clarinet and piano, 2002, Tuscan Triptych: Echoes of Hannibal (string orch. version of String Quartet 1985), 2002, (commns.) Yale U., 1958, Mich. U., 1959, Fromm Found., 1960, Koussevitzky Found. at Lib. Congress, 1960, 1991, Ford Found., 1971, Yale Band, Yale Repertory Theater, Cantilena Chamber Players, Aeolian Chamber Players, Santa Fe Chamber Music Festival, Collage of Boston, N.Y. Woodwind Quintet, Frank Taplin project, NEA Consortium, Boston Symphony Chamber Players, Atlantic Symphonietta, Carnegie Hall Am. Composers Orch., RNCM Mancester Internat. Cello Festival, Boston Symphony; pub. Associated Music Pub., Inc.; recs.: Bridge, New World, Albany, Pro Arte & Columbia Records. Recipient Elise Stoeger prize, Lincoln Ctr. Chamber Music Soc., 1998; Rome Prize fellow, 1953—56, Alfred E. Hertz fellow, U. Calif., 1953—54, Guggenheim fellow, 1960, Rockefeller Found. fellow, Bellagio, 1998, Inst. Arts and Letters grant, 1961, grantee, NEA, 1976. Mem. Am. Composers Alliance, Am. Music Center, Am. Acad. Arts and Letters (elected). Office: Music Dept Brandeis U Waltham MA 02454

WYNESS, STEVEN CHARLES, illustrator; b. Carmel, N.Y., Sept. 25, 1967; s. Tom and Marion J. (Sewell) W.; m. Lorraine E. Disanza, June 20, 1992; children: Erin Skylar, Logan Scott. AAS, Dutchess C.C., Poughkeepsie, N.Y., 1987; BA, We. Conn. State U., 1990. Mgr. photography, illustrator Cannondale Corp., Georgetown, Conn., 1987-92; illustrator, designer Steven C. Wyness Designs, Middletown, N.Y., 1991-98; print prodn. specialist Seiko Corp., Mahwah, N.J., 1995-96; art dir. The Orton Group, Salt Lake City, 1998-99, HGM Med. Lasers, Salt Lake City, 1999—2002; graphic designer IHC Health Plans, 2002—. Sculptor, painter Aesthetic Concerns Inc., Middletown, N.Y., 1997. Executed woodstock mural Peace Now, 1994; designed Seiko trademark Windward, 1995, Freedom, 1988; photographer nat. and internat. photos for pubs. including Forbes, VeloVert, L.L. Bean. Home: 6329 S Fairwind Dr West Jordan UT 84084-6211 E-mail: sclwyness@earthlink.net.

WYNGAARDEN, JAMES BARNES, physician; b. East Grand Rapids, Mich., Oct. 19, 1924; s. Martin Jacob and Johanna (Kempers) W.; m. Ethel Vredevoogd, June 20, 1946 (div. 1977); children: Patricia Wyngaarden Fitzpatrick, Joanna Wyngaarden Gandy, Martha Wyngaarden Krauss, Lisa Wyngaarden, James Barnes Jr. Student, Calvin Coll., 1942-43, Western Mich. U., 1943-44; MD, U. Mich., 1948; DSc (hon.), U. Mich. and Med. Coll. of Ohio, 1984, U. Ill., 1985, George Washington U., 1986; PhD (hon.), Tel Aviv U., 1987; DSc. (hon.), U. S.C., West Mich. U., 1989. Diplomate: Am. Bd. Internal Medicine. Intern Mass. Gen. Hosp., Boston, 1948-49, resident, 1949-51; vis. investigator Pub. Health Rsch. Inst., N.Y.C., 1952-53; investigator NIH, USPHS, Bethesda, Md., 1953-56; asso. prof. medicine and biochemistry Duke U. Med. Sch., 1956-61, prof., 1961-65; vis. scientist Inst. Biologie-Physiochemique, Paris, 1963-64; prof., chmn. U. Pa. Med. Sch., 1965-67; physician-in-chief Med. Svc. Hosp. U. PA., Phila., 1965-67; Frederic M. Hanes prof., chmn. dept. medicine Duke U. Sch. of Medicine, Durham, N.C., 1967-82; physician-in-chief Med. Svc. Duke U. Hosp., Durham, 1967-82; chief of staff Duke U. Hosp., Durham, 1981-82; dir. NIH, Bethesda, MD, 1982-89; assoc. dir. life scis. Office of Sci. and Tech. Policy, Exec. Office of Pres., The White House, 1989-90; dir. Human Genome Orgn., 1990-91; fgn. sec. NAS, 1990-94; prof. medicine, assoc. vice chancellor for health affairs Duke U., Durham, N.C., 1990-94, ret., 1994; mem. staff VA, Durham County Hosps.; sr. assoc. dean internat. med. programs U. Pa., Phila., 1995-97. Cons. Office Sci. and Tech. Exec. Office of Pres., 1966-72; Mem. Pres.'s Sci. Adv. Com., 1972-73; mem. Pres.'s Com. for Nat. Medal of Sci., 1977-80; mem. adv. com. biology and medicine AEC, 1966-68; mem. bd. sci. counselors NIH, 1971-74; mem. adv. bd. Howard Hughes Med. Inst., 1969-82; mem. adv. council Life Ins. Med. Research Fund, 1967-70; adv. bd. Sci. Yr., 1977-81; vice chmn. Com. on Study Nat. Needs for Biomed. and Behavioral Research Personnel, NRC, 1977-81; bd. dirs. Hybridon Corp., Human Genome Scis., Genaera Pharm., Van Andel Rsch. Inst.; prin. Washington Adv. Group, 1995-2002. Author: (with W.N. Kelley) Gout and Hyperuricemia, 1976; mem. editorial bd. Jour. Biol. Chemistry, 1971-74, Arthritis and Rheumatism, 1959-66, Jour. Clin. Investigation, 1962-66, Ann. Internal Medicine, 1964-74, Medicine, 1963-90; editor: (with J.B. Stanbury, D.S. Fredrickson) The Metabolic Basis of Inherited Disease, 1960, 66, 72, 78, 83, (with O. Sperling and A. DeVries) Purine Metabolism in Man, 1974, (with L.H. Smith, Jr.) Cecil Textbook of Medicine, 16th edit., 1982, 19th edit., 1992. Bd. dirs. Royal Soc. Medicine Found., 1971-76, The Robert Wood Johnson Found. Clin. Scholar Program, 1973-78. Ensign USNR, 1943-46; sr. surgeon USPHS, 1951-56, rear adm. USPHS, 1982-90. Recipient Borden Undergrad. Research award, U. Mich., 1948, N.C. Gov.'s award for sci., 1974, Disting. Alumnus award We.

Mich. U., 1984, Robert Williams award Assn. Profs. Medicine, 1985, Dalton scholar in medicine, Mass. Gen. Hosp., 1950, Richard Schweiker Excellence in Govt. award, 1985, Fedn. of Am. Socs. of Exptl. Biology Pub. Svc. award, 1989, Humanitarian award Nat. Orgn. for Rare Diseases, 1990; Royal Coll. Physicians fellow, 1984. Mem. Am. Rheumatism Assn., Am. Fedn. Clin. Research, So. Soc. Clin. Investigation (pres. 1974, founder's medal 1978), ACP (John Phillips Meml. award 1980), Am. Soc. Clin. Investigation, AAAS, Am. Soc. Biol. Chemists, Assn. Am. Physicians (councillor 1973-77, pres. 1978, Kober medal 1991), Endocrine Soc., Nat. Acad. Scis., Royal Acad. Scis. Sweden, Am. Acad. Arts and Sci., Inst. Medicine, Sigma Xi. Clubs: Interurban Clinical (Balt.). Democrat. Presbyterian. Avocations: tennis, skiing, painting.

WYN-JONES, ALUN (WILLIAM WYN-JONES), software developer, mathematician; b. Tremadoc, Gwynedd, Great Britain, Aug. 15, 1946; came to U.S., 1976; s. Goronwy Wyn and Mai Jones; m. Jocelyn Ripley, July 29, 1977; 1 stepchild, Electra Truman. BSc with honors, U. Manchester, U.K., 1968; MSc, Univ. Coll. London, 1970. Rsch. engr. Marconi-Elliott Computer Labs., Borehamwood, U.K., 1970-71; asst. tutor math. Poly. North London, 1971-72; programmer CRC Info. Sys., Ltd., London, 1972-76; mgr. devel. Warner Computer (now Warner Ins.), N.Y.C., 1976-80; pres., owner, developer Wallsoft Sys., Inc., N.Y.C., 1982-92, Integrity Sys. Corp., N.Y.C., 1980-94. Cons. investment banking divsn. Goldman, Sachs & Co., N.Y.C., 1994-2000, FirstRain, Inc., N.Y.C., 2000-02, Thomson Fin., 2002-; invited spkr. at profl. confs. Author, co-author computer software. Recipient Byte Award Distinction Byte Editors and Columnists, 1988, Readers Choice award Data Based Advisor Readers, 1990, 91. Mem. AAAS, Am. Math. Soc., Math. Assn. Am. Achievements include development of template programming in automatic code generation. Home: 609 Columbus Ave Apt 14D New York NY 10024-1436 E-mail: awynjones@att.net.

WYNN, ALBERT RUSSELL, congressman; b. Phila., Sept. 10, 1951; m. Jessie Jackson, Jan. 14, 1994 (sep.); 1 child, Gabrielle. BS, U. Pitts., 1973; student, Howard U.; JD, Georgetown U., 1977. Intern African Regional Affairs, U.S. State Dept., 1972-73; exec. dir. consumer protection divsn. Prince George's County, 1977-81; mem. Md. Ho. of Dels., 1983-86; lawyer Albert R. Wynn & Assocs., 1982-86; mem. Md. State Senate from Dist. 25, 1987-92, U.S. Congress from 4th Md. Dist., Washington, 1993—; dep. Dem. whip; mem. commerce com. Mem. banking & fin. svcs com., internat. rels. com., Patuxent Inst. reform task force, 1988-92, joint com. econ. devel. strategy, 1989-92; del. Dem. Nat. Conv. 1984, 88,96; pres. Metro. Washington coun. consumer agenices. Mem. NAACP legal assistance program, coalition on black affairs, voter registration, edn. coalition, gov.'s task force drunk & drugged driving; 1st vice chmn. legis. black caucus; chmn. Prince George's County black elected officials alliance. Mem. J. Franklin Bourne Bar Assn., Kappa Alpha Psi (past pres.). Democrat. Baptist. Office: US Ho of Reps 434 Cannon House Ofc Bldg Washington DC 20515-0001

WYNN, BRENDA RENEAU, trade association executive; b. Ft. Hood, Tex. d. Norman L. and Marjorie L. (Shaffer) Fallen; 1 child from previous marriage, Jennifer G. Houghton. Student, U. Okla. Dir. edn. Associated Builders and Contractors Western Okla., Oklahoma City, exec. dir.; commr. of labor OK, Okla. City, 1995—. Contbr. articles to trade publs. Mem. Okla. Soc. Execs., Okla. State C. of C., Oklahoma City C. of C. Achievements include 1st female exec. dir. of Assoc. Builders and Contractors Western Okla. Address: 200 W Wilshire Blvd Ste A-12 Oklahoma City OK 73116-7756 Office: Dept of Labor 4001 N Lincoln Blvd Oklahoma City OK 73105-5298 Office Phone: 405-528-1500. Business E-Mail: reneau_wynn@oklaosf.state.ok.us.

WYNN, JOHN CHARLES, clergyman, retired religion educator; b. Akron, Ohio, Apr. 11, 1920; s. John Francis and Martha Esther (Griffith) W.; m. Rachel Linnell, Aug. 27, 1943; children: Mark Edward, Martha Lois Borland, Maryan Kay Ainsworth. BA, Coll. Wooster, 1941; BD, Yale U., 1944; MA, Columbia U., 1963, EdD, 1965; DD, Davis and Elkins Coll., 1958. Ordained to ministry Presbyn. Ch. (U.S.A.), 1944. Student asst. pastor Trinity Luth. Ch., New Haven, 1943-44; assoc. minister First Presbyn. Ch., Evanston, Ill., 1944-47; pastor El Dorado, Kans., 1947-50; dir. family edn. and research United Presbyn. Bd. Christian Edn., Phila., 1950-59; prof. Colgate Rochester/Bexley Hall/Crozer Divinity Sch., 1959-85; prof. emeritus Colgate Rochester/Bexley Hall/Crozer Theol. Sem., 1985—; pvt. practice family therapy; adj. prof. U. Rochester, San Francisco Theol. Sem., St. Bernard's Sem., Wesley Theol. Sem., Hartford Theol. Found.; postdoctoral fellow Cornell U., 1973-74, St. John's U., 1980; lectr. Sch. Continuing Edn. Johns Hopkins U. Mem. summer faculty Union Theol. Sem., N.Y.C., San Francisco Theol. Sem.; del. study conf. World Coun. Chs., 1953, 57, 64, 65, 67, 75, 80; lectr. 5 univs., Republic of South Africa, 1968; chmn. com. on sexuality in human cmty. U.P. Ch.; vol. mem. chaplaincy staff Charlestown Care Ctr., Balt. Author: How Christian Parents Face Family Problems, 1955, Pastoral Ministry to Families, 1957, Families in the Church, A Protestant Survey, 1961, Christian Education for Liberation and Other Upsetting Ideas, 1977, Family Therapy in Pastoral Ministry, 1982 (rev. and expanded as Family Therapy in Pastoral Ministry: Counseling for the Nineties, 1991), The Family Therapist, 1987; Editor: Sermons on Marriage and Family Life, 1956, Sex, Family and Society in Theological Focus, 1966, Sexual Ethics and Christian Responsibility, 1970; Contbr. articles to mags. and religious jours. Bd. dirs. Presbyn. Life, Planned Parenthood League Rochester and Monroe County, Family Service Rochester, Samaritan Pastoral Counseling Ctr. Fellow Am. Assn. Marriage and Family Therapy (approved supr.); mem. Religious Edn. Assn., Nat. Coun. Chs. of Christ in U.S.A. (chmn. com. family life 1957-60), Nat. Coun. Family Rels., Family Svc. Assn. Am., Rochester Coun. Chs. (dir.) Address: 717 Maiden Choice Ln Apt 523 Catonsville MD 21228-6173 E-mail: RLWynn@erols.com.

WYNN, JOHN THOMAS, retired academic administrator, farming executive, economic consultant, oil and gas producer; b. Corsicana, Tex., May 4, 1938; s. Sam Grady and Marjorie (Reese) W.; m. Sally Ruth Adams, Mar. 19, 1958 (div. 1975); children: Martha Maria, Catherine Clarissa, Lorraine Lemae; m. Myra Louise Alexander, Oct. 30, 1976; l child, John Thomas. AA, Wharton County Jr. Coll., 1960; BBA in Gen. Bus., Agrl. and Mech. Coll. Tex., 1962; MBA, Tex. A&M U., 1965; PhD in Higher Edn. Mgmt., U. So. Miss., 1973. Asst. registrar, then. instr. Tex. A&M U., College Station, 1962-67; exec. dean Delgado Community Coll., New Orleans, 1967-74, program dir., 1977-78; asst. exec. sec. So. Assn. Colls and Schs., Atlanta, 1974-77; pres. emeritus Williamsburg Tech. Coll., Kingstree, S.C., 1978-94; pres., CEO econ. cons. M&W Farm & Ranch, Egypt, Tex., 1994—. Cons. AID, Dominican Republic, 1966; bd. govs. Coastal Edn. Consortium, Conway, S.C., 1982-90; mem. exec. com. pres.'s coun. S.C. Tech. Edn. Coll., Columbia, 1985-86. Vestryman St. Thomas Episc. Ch., College Station, 1962-67, St. George Episc. Ch., New Orleans, 1969-72; vestryman St. Thomas' Episc. Ch., Wharton, Tex., 1998-2001, sr. warden, 1999-2000; Rep. precinct 2 chmn., Wharton County, Tex., 1998-2000. Served as sgt. USAR, 1955-62. Recipient Order of the Palmetto S.C. Gen. Assembly, 1994; named Hon. Order of Ky. Cols.; col. Aide-de-Camp, La., col. Aide-de-Camp, col. Aide-de-Camp, N.Mex. Mem. Future Farmers Assn. (hon.), S.C. Tech. Edn. Assn. (bd. dirs. 1985-88), Kingstree C. of C. (bd. dirs. 1981-84), Kiwanis, Masons (32 degree), Shriners (hon.), Phi Delta Kappa, Kappa Delta Pi. Avocations: chess, camping, music composition, reading. Home and Office: PO Box 307 Egypt TX 77436 Personal E-mail: egypt@intertex.net.

WYNN, NAN L. historic site administrator; b. Rock Island, Ill., Dec. 4, 1953; BA, Western Ill. U., 1975. Spl. events coord. Ill. Dept. Conservation, Springfield, 1975-77; mus. dir. Blackhawk State Hist. Site, Rock Island, 1977-81; site dir. Old State Capital Hist. Site, Vandalia, Ill., 1981-87; site mgr. Lincoln Tomb State Hist. Site, Springfield, 1986—. Office: Lincoln Tomb State Hist Site Oak Ridge Cemetery 1500 Monument Ave Springfield IL 62702-2500

WYNN, ROBERT E. electronics executive, retired career officer; b. Dallas, Jan. 31, 1942; s. Wendell W. and Thelma (Smart) W.; m. Lavenia K. Davis, Mar. 25, 1972; children: Leslie, Lauren. Bachelors degree, West Point, 1964; MEE, U. Tenn., 1971. Commd. 2d lt. U.S. Army, 1964, advanced through grades to commdg. gen., 1990; chief comm. Ops. Divsn. 5th Signal Command, Heidelberg, Germany, 1979-81, chief of staff Worms, Germany, 1984-85; chief plans and programs, dep. chief staff Ops. and Plans DCS for OPS and PLANS, Washington, 1981-84; comdr. 2d Signal Brigade, Mannheim, Germany, 1986-88, U.S. Army Info. Systems Command/Tng. Doctrine Command, Ft. Monroe, Va., 1988-90; commdg. gen. 7th Signal Command, Ft. Ritchie, Md., 1990-92, U.S. Army Info. Systems Engring. Command, Ft. Huachuca, Ariz., 1992-95; ret., 1995; mgr. C3 sys. Raytheon E-Systems Inc., Richardson, Tex., 1995-97; v.p. Harris Corp., Alexandria, Va., 1997—. Decorated Bronze Star, Legion of Merit, Silver Order of Mercury. Mem. Assn. U.S. Army Assn. Grads. (life), Armed Forces Comm. and Electronics Assn. (life, bd. dirs.), Sky Soldier (life, 173d airborne brigade), Signal Corps Regiment (life). Avocations: golf, tennis. Office: Harris Corp 1201 E Abingdon Dr Ste 300 Alexandria VA 22314-1487 Home: PO Box 411158 Melbourne FL 32941-1158

WYNN, STEPHEN A. hotel, entertainment facility executive; b. 1942; m. Elaine Paschal, 1963; children: Kevin, Gillian. BA, U. Pa, 1963. Pres., chief exec. officer Best Brands, Inc., 1969-72; chmn. bd. dirs., pres., CEO Mirage Resorts Inc. (formerly Golden Nugget Inc.), 1973—2000; mng. mem. Valvino Lamore, LLC, 2000—02; chmn., CEO Wynn Resorts Ltd., 2002—. Office: Wynn Resorts Ltd 3145 Las Vegas Blvd S Las Vegas NV 89109*

WYNN, THOMAS JOSEPH, judge, educator; b. Chgo., Aug. 30, 1918; s. Phillip H. and Delia B (Madden) W.; m. Bernadette L. Lavelle, Apr. 17, 1948; children: Thomas Joseph, John P. AB, DePaul U., 1941, JD, 1942. Bar: Ill. 1942. Spl. investigator Phoenix & Murphy, Chgo., 1942; pvt. practice law Chgo., 1946-59; ptnr. Wynn & Ryan, Chgo., 1959-79; assoc. judge Cir. Ct. Cook County, Ill., 1979-83, judge chancery div. mechanic's lien sect., 1983-96, retired, 1996. Lectr. bus. law Latin Am. Inst., Chgo., 1946-47; mem. faculty Coll. Commerce, DePaul U., Chgo., 1947-98, assoc. dean Evening div., 1957-73, prof., 1972-79, part-time faculty, 1979-83, adj. prof. bus. law, 1983-98; asst. atty. gen. Ill., 1957-58; bd. dirs., gen. counsel Suburbanite Bowl, Inc., 1958-79; gen. legal counsel Chgo. Consortium Colls. and Univs., GM Tool Corp.; pres., bd. dirs. Metroplex Leasing and Financing, Inc. Candidate for alderman Chgo. City Coun., 1951; candidate for judge Mcpl. Ct. Chgo., 1956; exec. sec., bd. dirs. Ill. Good Govt. Inst., 1958-79; mem. adv. bd. to dean Coll Law DePaul U., 1992—. Ensign-lt. (S.G.) USNR, 1942-46. Mem. Ill. Bar Assn., Chgo. Bar Assn. (mem. arbitration and alternative dispute resolution com., civil practice coms., mem. internat. law com., mem. judiciary com., mem. cir. ct. com.), Ill. Judges Assn. (com. mandatory arbitration alt. dispute resolution, com. pubs.), Assn. Univ. Evening Colls. (past chmn.), Am. Bus. Law Assn. (pres. 1972-73), Am. Real Estate and Urban Econs. Assn., Chgo. Area Evening Deans and Dirs. Assn., U.S. Adult Edn. Assn., Ill. Adult Edn. Assn., Am. Right-of-Way Assn. (advisor chmn., nat. ednl. com., 1963-64), St. Vincent DePaul Soc., DePaul Law Alumni Assn. (past pres.), Smithsonian Inst., Pres.'s Club, (DePaul U. 1996—), Blue Key, Gamma Eta Gamma, Beta Gamma Sigma, Delta Mu Delta. Home: 27592 W Cuba Rd Barrington IL 60010-2770

WYNN, WILL, mayor; b. Beaumont, Tex. m. Anne Elizabeth Wynn, 1992; 2 children. B in Environ. Design cum laude, Tex. A&M U., 1984. Founder CIVITAS Investments, Inc., 1997; mayor City of Austin, Tex., 2003—. With Hill Country Conservancy, St. David's Found., Women and their Work, KLRU, Blanton Mus., Austin Poetry Slam, Austin Film Soc.; chmn. Downtown Austin Alliance; dir. Children's Mus. and Heritage Soc. Named Austinite of Yr., Austin Under Forty; recipient Scenic Hero award, Scenic Austin. Mem.: Urban Land Inst. Avocations: listening to music, canoeing, bicycling. Mailing: PO Box 1088 Austin TX 78767 Office: Mcpl Bldg 124 West 8th St #103 Austin TX 78701

WYNNE, BRIAN JAMES, former association executive, consultant; b. N.Y.C., Dec. 2, 1950; s. Bernard and Dolores (Doyle) W. Student, Institute des Sciences Politiques, Paris, 1970-71; BA, Coll. Holy Cross, 1972; MA, U. So. Calif., 1974. Staff Exec. Cons., Inc., McLean, Va., 1974-76; prin., 1976-78; exec. dir. Indsl. Designers Soc. Am., Washington, 1978-88. Cons. to various non-profit orgns.; dir. Worldesign 85, founder Worldesign Found. Mem. Am. Soc. Assn. Execs., Indsl. Designers Soc. Am. (hon.), Phi Sigma Iota. Home: 5200 N Ocean Blvd Apt 1004 Lauderdale By The Sea FL 33308-3019

WYNNE, JAMES, research scientist; B Physics, M Physics, PhD Physics, Harvard U. Mgr. Laser Physics and Chemistry Group IBM T.J. Watson Rsch. Ctr.; rsch. scientist IBM Watson Rsch. Ctr., 1971—. Contbr. articles, scientific papers. Named to National Inventors Hall of Fame, 2002. Achievements include patents in field; development of Lasik eye surgery. Office: Watson Rsch Ctr 1101 Kithawan Rd Ste 134 Yorktown Heights NY 10598*

WYNNE, KENNETH J. chemical engineer, educator; b. Providence, R.I. m. Anne Wynne; children: Jamie, Brian. BS, Providence Coll., 1961; MS, PhD, U. Mass., 1965. Postdoctoral fellow U. Calif., Berkeley, 1965—67; asst. prof. chemistry U. Ga., Athens, 1967—73; program scientist/chemistry Office of Naval Rsch., Arlington, Va., 1973—85, scientific officer, 1985—2000; vis. scholar Stanford U., Palo Alto, Calif., 1983—84; vis. scientist IBM-San Jose (Calif.) Rsch. Lab., 1983—84; prof. chem. engring. Va. Commonwealth U., Richmond, 2000—. Mem. adv. bd. Chemistry of Materials, Jour. Applied Polymer Sci., Macromolecules, Jour. Inorganic and Organometal Polymers. Contbr. articles to profl. jours. Recipient Biennial Marvel Symposium honor, 2001. Mem.: Am. Chem. Soc. (budget com. 1996—99, membership com. 1999—2003, program com. 1986—88, chmn. polymer divsn. 2003). Achievements include patents in field of methods for fabricating a low dimensionality electroconductor; multilayer second-order nonlinear optical films of head-to-head mainchain chromophoric polymers. Office: Va Commonwealth U 601 W Main St Richmond VA 23284

WYNNE, LOUIS, psychologist; b. Leeds, Yorkshire, Eng., Mar. 29, 1938; came to U.S., 1951; s. Philip and Rachel (McLinsky) W.; m. Rochelle L. Harris, Nov. 26, 1959 (div. Aug. 1968); children: Mark R., Ronald J., Roberta E.; stepchildren: Heather L. Edison, Cheryl A. Edison, James A. Edison; m. Sema Edison, Dec. 28, 1968. BS, Mass. State Tchrs. Coll., 1959, MEd, 1961; PhD, Ohio State U., 1967. Cert. clin. psychologist, N.Mex. Chief Combat Intelligence br. 494th Bombardment Wing Strategic Air Command, Sheppard AFB, Tex., 1963-65; dep. dir. Comparative Psychology divsn. 6571st Aeromedical Rsch. Lab., Holloman AFB, N.Mex., 1969—73; assoc. prof. psychiatry and psychology U. N.Mex., 1973-81; clin. dir. N.Mex. State Hosp., Las Vegas, 1983-85; pvt. practice psychology Albuquerque, 1988—. Cons. Blue Cross/Blue Shield of N.Mex., 1992—, Albuquerque Job Corps Ctr., 1996—. Author: Deliver Us From Evil, 2002; co-author: Warm Logic: The Art of the Intuitive Lifestyle, 1990; editl. bd. mem. Jour. Analysis of Verbal Behavior; contbr. articles to profl. jours. Mem. Internat. Ctr. for Study of Psychiatry and Psychology (adv. coun.), Assn. For Behavior Analysis. Avocations: trap shooting, skeet shooting, cross country skiing, films of the 40s, soccer. Office: 1420 Carlisle NE Albuquerque NM 87110 E-mail: landswy@aol.com.

WYNNE, WILLIAM JOSEPH, lawyer; b. Little Rock, July 17, 1927; Student, Little Rock U., 1946-48; JD, U. Ark., 1951. Bar: Ark. 1951, U.S. Dist. Ct. Ark. 1951, U.S. Supreme Ct. 1958; ordained to ministry Presbyn. Ch. Pres. Diversified Drilling Svcs., Inc., Elco Equipment Leasing Co., Inc.; v.p., gen. counsel El Dorado Paper Bag Mfg. Co., Inc.; sr. counsel Murphy Oil Corp., El Dorado, 1951-68; atty. Crumpler, O'Connor & Wynne, El Dorado, 1963—. Adj. prof. law U. Ark., Little Rock; gen. counsel and hearing officer Ark. Oil and Gas Commn., 1975—. Mem. ABA, Ark. Bar Assn., Union County Bar Assn., Assn. Trial Lawyers Am., Ark. Trial Lawyers Assn., El Dorado C. of C. (Outstanding Young Man 1961-62). Home: 1501 W Block St El Dorado AR 71730-5300 Office: NBC Pla Ste 308 El Dorado AR 71730 Office Phone: 870-863-8118. E-mail: wynne2@ipa.net.

WYNNE-EDWARDS, HUGH ROBERT, geologist, educator, entrepreneur; b. Montreal, Que., Can., Jan. 19, 1934; s. Vero Copner and Jeannie Campbell (Morris) W.-E.; married; children from previous marriages: Robin Alexander, Katherine Elizabeth, Renée Elizabeth Lortie, Krista Smyth, Jeannie Elizabeth, Alexander Vernon. BSc with 1st class honors, U. Aberdeen, Scotland, 1955; MA, Queen's U., Kingston, Ont., Can., 1957, PhD, 1959; DSc (hon.), Meml. U., 1975. Registered profl. engr., B.C., 1995. With Geol. Survey Can., 1958-59; lectr. Queen's U., 1968-72, asst. prof., then assoc. prof., 1961-68, prof., head dept. geol. scis., 1968-72; prof., then Cominco prof., head dept. geol. scis. U. B.C., Vancouver, Canada, 1972-77; asst. sec. univ. br. Ministry of State for Sci. and Tech., Ottawa, Canada, 1977-79; sci. dir. Alcan Internat. Ltd., Montreal, 1979-80, v.p. R & D, chief sci. officer, 1980-89; CEO Moli Energy Ltd., Vancouver, 1989-90; pres. Terracy Inc., Vancouver, 1989—; sci. advisor Teck Corp., Vancouver, 1989-91; pres., CEO B.C. Rsch. Inc., Vancouver, 1993-97, exec. chmn., pres., 1997-2000. Chmn. Silvagen Inc., 1996-99; advisor Directorate Mining and Geology, Uttar Pradesh, India, 1964, Grenville project Que. Dept. Natural Resources, 1968-72; vis. prof. U. Aberdeen, 1965-66, U. Witwatersrand, Johannesburg, South Africa, 1972; UN cons., India, 1974; pres. SCITEC, 1977-78; mem. sci. adv. com. CBC, 1980-84; mem. Sci. Coun. Can., 1983-89, Nat. Adv. Bd. on Sci. and Tech., 1987-90 indsl. liaison com. UN Ctr. for Sci. and Tech. in Devel., 1982-84; vice chmn. tech. adv. group Bus. Coun. for Sustainable Devel., Geneva, 1991; mem. Nat. Biotech. Adv. Coun., 1995-98; chmn. Neurosci. Can. Partnership, 1999-2003, Azure Dynamics Inc., 2000-01; pres. Silvagen Holdings Inc., 1999-2000; bd. dirs. Welichem Biotech Inc., chmn., 2000-; bd. dirs. Photon Control Inc. Bd. dirs. Royal Victoria Hosp., Montreal, 1984-89. Decorated officer Order of Can., 1991; recipient Spendiarov prize 24th Internat. Geol. Congress, Montreal, 1972. Fellow Can. Acad. Engring., Royal Soc. Can., World Acad. Arts and Scis.; mem. Can. Rsch. Mgmt. Assn. (vice chmn. 1982-84, chmn. 1984-85, Assn. medal 1987), Univ. Club (Montreal). Mem. United Ch. Canada. Avocations: tennis, skiing, carpentry. Office: Terracy Inc 2030 27th St West Vancouver BC Canada V7V 4L4 E-mail: hughwynn@terracy.com.

WYRICK, CHARLES LLOYD, JR., publisher, writer, editor; b. Greensboro, N.C., May 5, 1939; s. Charles Lloyd and Edythe Ellen (Ellis) W.; m. Constance Michelle Hooper, Aug. 22, 1964; 1 child, Charles Lloyd, III; m. Katherine Harrison, Apr. 26, 1997; 1 child, Christopher Conrad. BA, Davidson (N.C.) Coll., 1961; M.F.A., U. N.C., 1967. Instr. Stephens Coll., Columbia, Mo., 1964-66; asst. head programs div. Va. Museum, Richmond, 1966-68; exec. dir. Assn. Preservation Va. Antiquities, Richmond, 1968-70; pres. Research & Restoration, Inc., Richmond, 1970-73; dir. Del. Art Mus., Wilmington, 1973-79, Gibbes Mus. Art, Charleston, S.C., 1980-86; pres. Wyrick & Co., Charleston, 1986—, Dixie Media, Inc., Charleston, 1989—; editor, pub. "Omnibus", 1989-94. Mem. Richmond Commn. Archt. Rev., 1969-72, New Castle County (Del.) Hist. Rev. Bd., 1975-88, also vice chmn.; mem. bd. Archtl. Rev. City of Charleston, 1988-94, chmn., 1992-94; mem. Charleston Consortium on Higher Edn.; cons. in field. Author: "The 17th Street Market", 1972; contbr. articles to profl. jours. Bd. visitors Davison Coll., 1974-77; chmn. Econs. of Amenities City of Charleston, 1978; chmn bd. dirs. S.C. Coastal Conservation League, 1989-94, Charleston Area Arts Coun., 1989-91, Friends of Charleston County Courthouse, 1989-94, Pub. Art Trust, 1988-90; adv. com. S.C. Dept. Natural Resources, 1992—. 1st lt. U.S. Army, 1961—63. Recipient 1st award spl. column writing Va. Press Assn., 1973 Mem. Assn. Am. Pubs., Pubs. Assn. of South (bd. dirs. 1990-92, pres. 1991-92), S.C. Acad. Authors (bd. dirs. 1990-92), Carolina Yacht Club, Yeamans Hall Club. Office: 284 A Meeting St Charleston SC 29401 Home: 3 Chisolm St Unit 201 Charleston SC 29401-1838

WYRICK, JERMAINE ALBERT, lawyer; b. Detroit, Oct. 19, 1971; s. Albert and Loretta Wyrick. BA in Polit. Sci., U. Mich., 1993; JD, Wayne State U., 1996. Mich., U.S. Dist. Ct. (ea. dist.) Mich., U.S. Ct. Appeals (6th cir.),-1997, U.S. Supreme Ct. Pvt. practice, Detroit, 1997—. Bd. dirs. Coalition Affirmative Action Preservation NAACP, 1997—, Legal Redress, Detroit, 1997—, NAACP lectr. Crockett Comty. Law Sch., 1998-2001. Bd. dirs. N.W. Youth Orgn., Coleman A. Young Scholarship Found.; with Angels Night Wayne County Juvenile Ct., 1998, Safe Night Lincoln Br. Libr., 1998, adult reading ptnr. CLEO fellow, Ohio, 1993, Coun. on Legal Edu. Opportunity Fellowship; recipient Achievement award Coleman A. Young Found., 1989, 90, 91, 92, Disting. Grad. award, 1993, Pro Bono Project award FBA ea. dist. Mich., 1997, Fed Bar Assn. award, 1997, 2001. Mem. ABA, ATLA, Nat. Bar Assn., Mich. Trial Lawyers Assn., Detroit Met. Bar Assn., Wolverine Bar Assn.(bd. dirs., 2003-2004), Booker T. Washington Bus. Assn., Econ. Club Detroit, Met. Detroit Optimist Club. Democrat. Mem. Hartford Meml. Bapt. Ch. Avocations: basketball, golf, weightlifting. Home: PO Box 44646 Detroit MI 48244 Office: Law Offices Jermaine A Wyrick P L C Ste 1610 615 Griswold Detroit MI 48226-3319

WYRSCH, JAMES ROBERT, lawyer, educator, writer; b. Springfield, Mo., Feb. 23, 1942; s. Louis Joseph and Jane Elizabeth (Welsh) W.; m. B. Darlene Wyrsch, Oct. 18, 1975; children: Scott, Keith, Mark, Brian, Marcia. BA, U. Notre Dame, 1963; JD, Georgetown U., 1966; LLM, U. Mo., Kansas City, 1972. Bar: Mo. 1966, U.S. Ct. Appeals (8th cir.) 1971, U.S. Ct. Appeals (10th cir.) 1974, U.S. Ct. Appeals (5th cir.) 1974, U.S. Ct. Appeals (6th cir.) 1982, U.S. Ct. Appeals (11th cir.) 1984, U.S. Ct. Appeals (7th cir.) 1986, U.S. Ct. Appeals (4th cir.) 1990, U.S. Ct. Appeals (9th cir.) 1998, U.S. Ct. Mil. Appeals 1978, U.S. Tax Ct. 1983, U.S. Supreme Ct. 1972. Assoc. Wyrsch, Hobbs & Mirakian P.C., Kansas City, 1970-71, of counsel, 1972-77, ptnr., 1978—, pres., shareholder, 1988—; adj. prof. U. Mo., 1981—. Mem. Mo. Supreme Ct. Procedures Com., 1983—; mem. adv. coun. legal assts. program U. Mo. at Kansas City, 1985-88; mem. cir. ct. adv. com. Jackson County, Mo., 1998—; mem. jud. selection com. U.S. Magistrate U.S. Dist. Ct. Mo., 1985; mem. fed. practice com. U.S. Dist. Ct. Mo., 1985-88; mem. subcom. to draft model criminal instrns.for dist. cts. of 8th cir., 1986—; bd. dirs. Kansas City Bar Found.; Mo. membership co-chmn. U.S. Supreme Ct. Hist. Soc., 2002—. Co-author: Missouri Criminal Trial Practice, 1994; contbr. articles to profl. jours. Capt. U.S. Army, 1966—69. Recipient Joint Svcs. Commendation medal, 1969, U. Mo. Kansas City Svc. award Law Found., 1991-92, Lawyer of Yr. award Mo. Lawyers Weekly, 2001, Dean of Trial Bar award Kansas City Met. Bar Assn., 2002, Practitioner of the Yr. award U. Mo. Kans. City Law Sch. Alumni Assn., 2002; named Best of the Bar, Kansas City Bus. Jour., 2002-03. Fellow: Mo. Bar Found., Am. Coll. Trial Lawyers (access to justice com., Mo. State chair 2002—04), Am. Bar Found. (life); mem.: ATLA, ABA, Nat. Lawyers Assn. (chmn. criminal law com. 2003), Coll. Master Advs. and Barristers (sr. counsel), Mo. Assn. Criminal Def. Attys. (dir. 1978, sec. 1982, Chas. Shaw Trial Adv. award 2004), Nat. Assn. Criminal Def. Attys., Am. Bd. Trial Advs. (adv.), Kansas City Bar Assn. (chmn. anti-trust com. 1981, chmn. bus. tort, anti-trust, franchise com. 1998), Mo. Bar Assn. (vice chmn. criminal law com. 1978—79), Am. Arbitration Assn. (panel arbitrators 1976—2000), Country Club of Blue Springs, Kansas City Club, Phi Delta Phi. Democrat. Roman Catholic. Home: 1501 NE Sunny Creek Ln Blue Springs MO 64014-2044 Office: Wyrsch Hobbs & Mirakian PC 1101 Walnut St Fl 13 Kansas City MO 64106-2134

WYRSCH, MARTHA B. lawyer; b. Laramie, Wyo., 1958; m. Gerry Wyrsch; 2 children. BA in Lit. with honors, U. Wyo., 1980; JD, George Washington U., 1986; graduate, Harvard Bus. Sch. Advanced Mgmt. Program, 2002. Legis. asst. to Sen. Alan K. Simpson of Wyo., 1980—83; assoc. Davis, Graham & Stubbs, 1986—91; v.p., gen. counsel and sec. KN Energy Inc. (now Kinder Morgan, Inc.), 1991—99; sr. v.p., gen. counsel, sec., Duke Energy Field Svcs. Duke Energy Corp., Charlotte, NC, 1999—2001, sr. v.p., gen. counsel, energy transmission and distbn., 2001—03, sr. v.p., legal affairs, 2003—04, group v.p., gen. counsel, sec., 2004—. Bd. advisors George Washington Law Sch.; bd. dirs. Inst. and Sch. for Environ. and Natural Resources, U. Wyo. Mem.: ABA (vice chair, pub. utility, comm. and transp. law sect.), Interstate Natural Gas Assn. Am., Edison Elec. Inst., Am. Gas Assn., Am. Corp. Counsel Assn., Colo. Bar Assn. Office: Duke Energy Corp 526 S Church St Charlotte NC 28202-1904*

WYRTKI, KLAUS, oceanography educator; b. Tarnowitz, Germany, Feb. 7, 1925; came to U.S., 1961; s. Wilhelm and Margarete (Pacharzina) W.; m. Helga Kocher, June 6, 1954 (div. 1970); children: Undine, Oliver; m. Erika Maassen. PhD magna cum laude, U. Kiel, Germany, 1950. With German Hydrographic Inst., Hamburg, 1950-51; German Rsch. Coun. postdoctoral rsch. fellow U. Kiel, 1951-54; head Inst. Marine Rsch., Djakarta, Indonesia, 1954-57; sr. rsch. officer, then prin. rsch. officer div. fisheries and oceanogra-

phy Commonwealth Sci. and Indsl. Rsch. Orgn., Sydney, Australia, 1958-61; assoc. rsch. oceanographer, then rsch. oceanographer Scripps Instn. Oceanography, U. Calif., 1961-64; prof. oceanography U. Hawaii, Honolulu, 1964—, prof. emeritus, 1993. Chmn. North Pacific Expt., 1974-80, com. on climate changes and ocean Internat. Assn. Phys. Scis. of the Oceans; mem. Spl. Com. on Ocean Rsch. Working Group on Prediction of El Nino, Sci. Working Group on Topography Expt., panel on climate and global change NOAA. Author: El Nino—The Dynamic Response of the Equatorial Pacific Ocean to Atmospheric Forcing, 1975; editor: Oceanographic Atlas of the International Indian Ocean Expedition, 1971; mem. editl. bd. Jour. Phys. Oceanography, 1971-79. Recipient Excellence in Rsch. award U. Hawaii, 1980, Rosenstiel award U. Miami, 1981, Prince Albert I medal Internat. Assn. of the Phys. Scis. of the Ocean, 2003, Alexander Agassiz medal NAS, 2004. Fellow Am. Geophys. Union (Maurice Ewing medal 1989), Am. Meteorol. Soc. (Harald Ulrick Sverdrup Gold medal 1991), Deutsche Meteorologische Gesellschaft (Albert Defant medal 1992). E-mail: wyrtki@aloha.net.

WYSCHOGROD, EDITH, philosophy educator; b. N.Y.C. d. Morris and Selma Shurer; m. Michael Wyschogrod, Mar. 6, 1955; children: Daniel, Tamar. AB, Hunter Coll., 1957; PhD, Columbia U., 1970. Prof. philosophy Queens Coll., Flushing, N.Y., 1967-92; J. Newton Rayzor prof. philosophy and religious thought Rice U., Houston, 1992—2003, emerita, 2003—. Author: Emmanuel Levinas: The Problem of Ethical Metaphysics, 1974, 2d edit., 2000, Spirit in Ashes, 1985, Saints and Postmodernism, 1990, An Ethics of Remembering: History, Heterology and the Nameless Others; co-editor: Lacan and Theological Discourse, 1989, The Enigma of Gift and Sacrifice, 2002, The Ethical, 2003. Nat. Humanities Ctr. fellow, 1981, Woodrow Wilson Ctr. fellow, 1987-88, Guggenheim fellow, 1995-96. Fellow Am. Acad. Arts and Scis.; mem. Am. Acad. Religion (pres. 1992-93). Home: Apt 9C 522 West End Ave New York NY 10024 E-mail: stedith@rice.edu.

WYSE, LOIS, advertising executive; b. Cleve. d. Roy B. Wohlgemuth and Rose (Schwartz) Weisman; m. Marc Wyse (div. 1980); m. Lee Guber (dec. 1988). Pres. Wyse Advt. Inc., 1951—, Media and Mktg./Health Expo, 2004—. Author: 60 books; syndicated columnist: Wyse Words; contbg. editor: (mag.) Good Housekeeping, 1983—98. Mem. bd. overseers Beth Israel Med. Ctr. Ctr. for Communications, N.Y.C. Mem. Woman's Forum, PEN, Author's Guild, League of Profl. Theater Women. Office: 18 E 41st St New York NY 10017 Office Phone: 212-689-8787. E-mail: lolowy@fastmail.fm.

WYSE, MATTHEW F. small business owner; b. Fullerton, Calif., May 16, 1938; s. Richard F. and Lillian Wise; m. Karen Ann Miller; 1 child, Sean P. Moton. BA, U. Calif., Berkeley, 1960. Owner Pendragon Fine Books, Oakland, Calif., 1972—95, Orinda, Calif., 1998—, Western Book Distbrs., Berkeley, 1978—93, Pegasus Fine Books, Berkeley, 1980—93. Libertarian. Home and Office: Pendragon Fine Books 125 Canon Dr Orinda CA 94563 Office: 7 37th Pl Long Beach CA 90803

WYSE, ROGER EARL, physiologist, department chairman; b. Wauseon, Ohio, Apr. 22, 1943; BS in Agr., Ohio State U., 1965; MS, Mich. State U., 1967, PhD in Crop Sci., 1969. Fellow Mich. State U., 1969-70; plant physiologist Agr. Rsch. Svc. USDA, 1970-86; dean of rsch. Cook Coll. Rutgers U., 1986-92; dean, dir. Coll. Agr. and Life Sci. U. Wis., Madison, 1992-98; mng. dir. Burrill & Co., San Francisco, 1998—. Recipient Arthur Flemming award, 1982. Fellow Am. Soc. Agronomy, Crop Sci. Soc. Am.; mem. AAAS, Am. Soc. Plant Physiol. Office: Burrill & Co 1 Embarcadero Ctr Ste 2700 San Francisco CA 94111-3744

WYSE, WILLIAM WALKER, lawyer, real estate executive; b. Spokane, Wash., July 20, 1919; s. James and Hattie (Walker) W.; m. Janet E. Oswalt, Jan. 30, 1944; children: Wendy L., Scott C., Duncan E. AB, U. Wash., 1941; JD, Harvard U., 1948. Bar: Oreg. 1948. Pvt. practice, Portland; ptnr. Stoel, Rives, Boley, Jones & Gray, 1953-88; chmn Wyse Investment Svcs., 1988—. Past trustee, sec. Pacific Realty Trust; past trustee Holladay Park Plaza. Chmn. ctrl. budget com. United Fund, 1958—60; 1st v.p. United Good Neighbors; chmn. bd. dirs. Portland Sch. Bd., 1959—66; pres. Tri-County Cmty. Coun., 1970—71; bd. dirs., sec. Oreg. Parks Found.; bd. dirs. Cmty. Child Guidance Clinic, 1950—57, pres., 1956—57; bd. dirs. Oreg. Symphony Soc., 1965—74, 1993—99, pres., 1968; bd. dirs. Loaves and Fishes Ctrs., Inc., 1997—2003. Mem. ABA, Oreg. Bar Assn., Multnomah County Bar Assn., Am. Coll. Real Estate Lawyers, Univ. Club, Arlington Club, Portland City Club (past gov.), Wauna Lake Club, Delta Upsilon. Republican. Presbyterian. Home: 3332 SW Fairmount Ln Portland OR 97201-1446 Office: 111 SW Fifth Ave Ste 1100 Portland OR 97204-5753 Office Phone: 503-294-0400.

WYSHAK, LILLIAN WORTHING, lawyer; b. N.Y.C., July 19, 1928; d. Emil Michael and Stefanie (Dvorak) Worthing; m. Robert H. Wyshak, 1961 (div. 1986); children: Robin, Susan, Jeanne, Patricia. BS in Acctg., UCLA, 1948, MA in Anthropology, 1971; JD, U. So. Calif., L.A., 1956. Bar: Calif. 1956, U.S. Dist. Ct. (ctrl. dist.) Calif. 1956, U.S. Ct. Appeals (9th cir.) 1967, U.S. Supreme Ct. 1967; cert. specialist in taxation law Calif. Bd. Legal Specialization; lic. real estate broker, Calif. Assoc. Boyle, Bissell & Atwill, Pasadena, Calif., 1956-57, Parker, Milliken, Kohlmeier, L.A., 1957-58; asst. U.S. atty. Tax Div., Office of U.S. Atty., L.A., 1958-62; ptnr. Wyshak & Wyshak, Beverly Hills, Calif., 1963-86; pvt. practice Beverly Hills, Calif., 1986—. Former referee State Bar Ct., L.A.; arbitrator La. County Bar Dispute Resolution Svcs. Contbr. articles to profl. jours. Trustee U. Redlands, 1972-81. Mem. ABA (civil and criminal tax penalties com. tax sect.), Assn. Tax Counsel, Beta Gamma Sigma, Phi Alpha Delta. Presbyterian. E-mail: lillin@pacbell.net.

WYSK, RICHARD A. engineering educator, researcher; b. Holyoke, Mass., Sept. 22, 1948; s. Stanley and Sophia Dorothy (Mazurowski) W.; m. Caryl Lynne Ray, Jan. 18, 1969; children: Richard Patrick, Rebecca Jeanne, Robyn Caryl. BS in Indsl. Engring. & Ops. Rsch., U. Mass., 1972, MS in Indsl. Engring. & Ops. Rsch., 1973; PhD in Indsl. Engring., Purdue U., 1977. Prodn. control mgr. Gen. Electric, Erie, Pa., 1973-75; rsch. analyst Caterpillar Tractor, Inc., Peoria, Ill., 1975-76; assoc. prof. Va. Polytechnic Inst., Blacksburg, 1977-83; prof. Pa. State U., State College, 1983-90, William Lionhard chair in engring., 1995—; dir. Inst. Mfg. Systems, College Station, 1990-94; Royce Wisenbaker chair Tex. A&M U., College Station, 1990-94; William Lionhard chair in engring. William Leonhard chair in engring., State College, 1995—. Co-author: A Study Guide for the P.E. in I.E., 1982, An Intro to Automated Proc. Plan., 1985, Modern Manufacturing Process Engineering, 1989, Computer-aided Manufacturing, 1991 (Book-of-the-Yr. award Inst. Indsl. Engrs. 1992, E. Eugene Merchant Mfg. Textbook award Soc. Mfg. Engrs. 1992). Pks. commr. Montgomery County Pks. & Recreation, Blacksburg, 1982-83; adv. mem. Inst. Systems Rsch. U. Md., 1991-95. With U.S. Army, 1969-71, Vietnam. Decorated Army Commendation medal with 2 oak leaf clusters. Fellow Inst. Indsl. Engrs. (chpt. pres. 1990—, Region III Award of Excellence 1982, D. Baker award 1993), Soc. Mfg. Engrs. (sr., Outstanding Young Mfg. Engr. 1981), Engring. Accreditation Commn. (commr. 1990-92), Sigma Xi. Avocations: racquetball, basketball. Office: Pa State U 310 Leonard Bldg University Park PA 16802 Office Phone: 814-863-1001. Business E-Mail: rwysk@psu.edu.

WYSLOTSKY, IHOR, engineering company executive; b. Kralovane, Czech Republic, Dec. 22, 1930; arrived in U.S., 1958; s. Ivan and Nadia (Alexiew) Wyslotsky; m. Marta Farion, 1983; children: Katria, Bodhan, Roman, Alexander. ME, Sch. Aeros., Buenos Aires, 1955. Design engr. Kaiser Industries, Buenos Aires, 1955-58; cons. design engr. Newark, 1959-64; dir. engring. Universal Tool Co., Chgo., 1964-69; pres. CBC Devel. Co., Inc., Chgo., 1969-74, TEC, Inc., Chgo., 1972-83, REDEX Corp., Chgo., 1983-89, chmn., 1993—; engring. advisor to bd. dirs. Biosystems Insts., Inc., La Jolla, Calif. Mem. mgmt. adv. bd. Modern Plastics Publs. Co-founder, pres. Am. Ukrainian Bus. Coun., 1991—93; mem. Ukrainian working com. Ctr. Strategic Internat. Studies, Washington; pres. Kyiv Mohyla Found. Am.; mem. vis. com. Harvard U.; co-founder Ukrainian Studies, U. Ill. Mem.: Brit. Engring. Assn. River Plate, Packaging Inst. U.S., Am.-Israeli C. of C. (v.p.), Chgo. Econ. Club. Achievements include patents in field. Home: 6133 N Forest Glen Ave Chicago IL 60646-5015 Personal E-mail: ihorchicago@aol.com.

WYSONG, EARL EDWARD, sociologist, educator; b. Kokomo, Ind., June 25, 1944; s. Earl Wysong and June Maxine Talbert; m. Janet Sue Myers, Aug. 30, 1966; children: Kristi Lynn, Heather Sue. BS in Edn., Ind. U., 1968; MA in Sociology, Ball State U., 1971; PhD in Sociology, Purdue U., 1990. Cert. secondary edn. Ind. Dept. Pub. Instrn., 1968. Asst. prof. sociology Ind. U., Kokomo, 1991—95, assoc. prof. sociology, 1995—98, prof. sociology, 1998—. Author: (book) High Risk and High Stakes: Health Professionals, Politics, and Policy, 1992; co-author: The New Class Society, 1999, The New Class Society, 2d edit., Goodbye American Dream?, 2003; mem. editl. bd.: Jour. Contemporary Sociology, 2001—; contbr. chapters to books, articles to profl. jours. Doctoral Dissertation Improvement grantee, NSF, 1990, Faculty Fellowship Rsch. grantee, Ind. U. Kokomo, 1992. Mem.: Am. Fedn. Tchrs., Am. Sociol. Assn., Ind. Acad. Social Scis. (dir. sociology and anthropology 1993—96, exec. v.p. 1997—98, pres. 1998—99), North Ctrl. Sociol. Assn., Midwest Sociol. Soc., Soc. for the Study Social Problems (program co-chair 1999—2000). Home: 2850 East Southway Blvd Kokomo IN 46902 Office: Ind Univ Kokomo 2300 South Washington St Kokomo IN 46904-9003 Office Phone: 765-455-9394. E-mail: ewysong@iuk.edu.

WYSS, DAVID ALEN, financial service executive; b. Ft. Wayne, Ind., Nov. 14, 1944; s. Alen G. and Anne W. (Winicker) W.; m. Grace H. Hawes, June 11, 1966; children: Sarah J., Alen D. BS, MIT, 1966; PhD, Harvard U., 1971. Economist Fed. Res., Washington, 1970-74, sr. economist, 1975-77; advisor Bank Eng., London, 1974-75; sr. staff economist Council Econ. Advisers, Washington, 1977-79; v.p. DRI Ltd., London, 1979-83; rsch. dir. DRI/McGraw Hill, Lexington, Mass., 1983-97; chief economist Std. & Poor's/DRI, Lexington, 1997-99, Std. & Poor's, N.Y.C., 1999—. Dir. Nat. Assn. for Bus. Econ., N.Y. Collegium. Contbr. numerous articles to profl. jours. Mem. Am. Econ. Assn., Nat. Assn. Bus. Office: Standard & Poors 55 Water St Ste 44th Fl New York NY 10041-0003 Office Phone: 212-438-4952. Business E-Mail: david_wyss@sandp.com.

WYSS, JOHN BENEDICT, lawyer; b. Evanston, Ill., Nov. 23, 1947; s. Walther Erwin and Caroline Nettie (Benedict) W.; m. Joanne P. Comstock, Oct. 22, 1994; children: John Christian, Kirsten Dunlop. BS in Physics summa cum laude, Stanford U., 1969; JD, Yale U., 1972. Bar: Calif. 1972, D.C. 1974, U.S. Supreme Ct. 1976. Trial atty. antitrust div. U.S. Dept. Justice, Washington, 1972-74; assoc. Kirkland & Ellis, Washington, 1974-78, ptnr., 1978-83, Wiley, Rein & Fielding, Washington, 1983—. Mem. ABA, Phi Beta Kappa. Office: Wiley Rein & Fielding 1776 K St NW Washington DC 20006-2304 Office Phone: 202-719-7038. E-mail: jwyss@wrf.com.

WYSZOMIERSKI, JACK L. pharmaceutical executive; CFO, exec. v.p. Shering-Plough Corp., Kenilworth, N.J. Office: Shering Plough Corp 2000 Galloping Hill Rd Kenilworth NJ 07033

WYSZYNSKI, DIEGO FEDERICO, epidemiologist, educator; b. Buenos Aires, May 19, 1967; m. Caroline Panhuysen, Sept. 7, 1963; children: Shoshana Basia, Sara Yentl, Daniel Yehoshua. MD, U. Buenos Aires Sch. of Medicine, Argentina, 1991; MHS, Johns Hopkins Sch. of Pub. Health, 1994, PhD, 1996. MD Min. of Health, Argentina, 1991. Asst. prof. of medicine and epidemiology Boston U. Sch. of Medicine, Boston, Mass., 1999—. Editor: (reference book) Cleft Lip and Palate: From Origin to Treatment. Pres. Congregation Etz Chaim, Sharon, Mass., 2001. Recipient NIH FARE fellow, NIH, 2000, Rsch. award, Cleft Palate Found., 2002. Achievements include research in the etiology of birth defects; patents pending for Use of genetic markers for the identification of metabolic syndrome. Office: Boston Univ Sch of Medicine 715 Albany Str L-320 Boston MA 02118 E-mail: dfw@bu.edu.

WYTKO, JOSEPH RUDOLPH, music educator; b. Morgantown, W.Va., May 19, 1949; s. Joseph Rudolph and Anna P Wytko; m. Mary Susan Teter, July 29, 1972; 1 child, Anna Marie. MusB, W.Va. U., 1967—71; MusM, Mus D, Northwestern U., 1975—77. Prof. of music Ariz. State U., Tempe, Ariz., 1975—; artist-clinician The Selmer Co., Elkhart, Ind., 1976—; orchestral saxophonist Phoenix Symphony Orch., Phoenix, Ariz., 1975—; concert performing artist Ind., Tempe, Ariz., 1975—. Musician: (albums) Recital Music for Saxophone (LP), Joseph Wytko, Saxophones, Waterworks and Firemusic, EnTangoment, Macedonia: Solo Concert Artist, Concert by Invitation: East Room of the White House. Bd. mem. Streams in the Desert Adult Care Home, Tempe, Ariz., 2002—03. Avocation: gardening. Office: Arizona State University - Music School Post Office Box 870405 Tempe AZ 85287-0405 E-mail: joseph.wytko@asu.edu.

WYZNER, EUGENIUSZ, diplomat; s. Henryk and Janina Wyzner; m. Elzbieta Laudanska, June 27, 1961; 1 child, Jaroslaw. Student, U. Warsaw, Poland, 1952; LLM, U. Warsaw, 1954; postgrad., Hague (The Netherlands) Acad. of Internat. Law, 1958. Mem. staff Ministry Fgn. Affairs, 1956—71, dir. legal dept., 1971—73; ambassador to Geneva, 1973-78; dir. dept. internat. orgns. Ministry Fgn. Affairs, Warsaw, 1978-81; chmn. UN Disarmament Commn., 1982; undersec. gen. conf. services and spl. assignments UN, N.Y.C., 1982-92, undersec. gen. pub. info., 1992-94; dep. min. for fgn. affairs Republic of Poland, Warsaw, 1994-95, 1st dep. min. for fgn. affairs, sec. of state, 1996-97; permanent rep. amb. to UN N.Y.C., 1998-99; vice-chmn. Internat. Civil Svc. Commn., N.Y.C., 1999—. Vice-chmn. preparatory com. Internat. Conf. on Human Rights, chmn. com. on periodic reports on human rights, 1965-68; chmn. sub-com. of UN Com. on Peaceful Uses of Outer Space, 1967-82; pres. Rev. Conf. of Parties to Treaty on Prohibition of Nuclear Weapons, 1977; mem. Polish del. of UN Gen. Assembly, UN Programme Planing and Budgeting Bd., 1984-93; chmn. UN Publs. Bd., 1982-93; chmn. com. for 2000 review conf. of the parties to the treaty on the non-proliferation of nuclear weapons, 1998-99. Decorated Cross of Polonia Restituta Polish Council of State, 1969, 77, Golden Cross of Merit, 1964, Comdr.'s Cross with a star Order of Polonia Restituta, 1996, Comdr. of the Legion d'Honneur, Pres. of France and Grand Comdr.'s Cross of the Order of the Phoenix, Pres. of Greece, 1996. Mem. Internat. Inst. Outer Space Law (bd. dirs. 1974—, Citation 1977), Internat. Peace Acad. (bd. dirs. 1983-91), Internat. Congress Inst. (bd. dirs. 1987-90), Internat. Congress Acad. (mem. senate 1990-95). Office: Internat Civil Svc Commn Rm 1050 2 United Nations Plz New York NY 10017-4403 E-mail: wyzner@un.org.

XAGAS, STEVEN GEORGE JAMES, diversified employment services firm executive; b. St. Charles, Ill., May 9, 1951; s. Gus and Carolyn Ann (Schneider) X.; m. Yvonne Schafer, Oct. 19, 1985; 1 child, Jacob Steven. BS in Psychology, Guilford Coll., 1973; postgrad., George Williams Coll., 1975. Cert. pers. cons.; black belt in Isshinryu karate, 1990-. Homebound detention supr., sr. counselor 16th Judicial Ct. Dist., Geneva, Ill., 1974-77; project coord., psychotherapist Tri City Family Project and Kane County Sch. Office, Geneva, 1977-80; exec. recruiter Search Dynamics, Chgo., 1980-82, CPS, Inc., Westchester, 1982-83; founder, pres. Xagas & Assocs., Geneva, 1983—; founder, chmn., CEO Universal All Stars, Inc., Geneva, 2004—. Columnist-:CareerLine" Chronicle Newspaper, St.Charles, Il., 1987-91, "From the Files..." Am. Soc. Quality-Chgo. Newsletter, 1987-90; condr. job search seminars., employment cons., met. area Chgo., 1980—; spkr. in field; voice over projects for pvt. sector cos., 2000—; self-def. instr., pub. demonstrations, 1990-. Columnist Y2K Line, Kane County Chronicle, 1999-2000; moderator, exec. prodr. video Face The People: Roundtable 2000, 1999-2000. Fundraiser Cancer Soc., Kane County, Ill., 1975—, Heart Assn., Kane County, 1982—; moderator city govt. and utilities reps. Year 2000 Panel Forum, Kane County, 1998; chmn. St. Mark's Year 2000 Task Force, Kane County, 1998-99; ad hoc mem. State of Ill. Yr. 2000 Tech. Task Force, 1998-99; cmty. vol. numerous social and human svc. orgns., Kane County, 1974—. Recipient Community Svc. Recognition, Tri City Family Project, Geneva, 1980, Honorable Mention award, Nat. Communicator Awards, 2001, Svc. recognition award Am. Soc. Quality, 1986, Editor's Choice award for poem Internat. Libr. Poetry, 2003; named to Exemplary Status Law Enforcement Assistance Adminstrn., 1980. Mem. Am. Soc. Quality (sr.), 1983. Lutheran. Avocations: martial arts, sports cards, softball, gardening, poker. Office: Xagas & Assocs 1127 Fargo Blvd Ste 1 Geneva IL 60134-2949 Office Phone: 630-232-7044. Fax: 630-232-7154. E-mail: sxagas@sbcglobal.net.

XENAKIS, STEPHEN NICHOLAS, psychiatrist, army officer; b. Washington, July 5, 1948; s. Stanley Steve and Mary Alexandria (Poulos) X.; m. Mary Elizabeth Boddie, Jan. 19, 1974 (dec.); children: Nicholas John, Lea Elizabeth. AB, Princeton U., 1970; MD, U. Md., Balt., 1974; postgrad., Balt.-D.C. Psychoanalytic Inst., 1972-75, Armed Forces Staff Coll., 1984-85, U.S. Army War Coll., 1989-90. Diplomate Am. Bd. Psychiatry and Neurology. Commd. U.S. Army, 1972, advanced through grades to brig. gen., 1994; resident U. Md., Balt., 1974; intern Letterman Army Med. Ctr., Presidio of San Francisco, 1974-75, resident in psychiatry, 1975-78; fellow in child and adolescent psychiatry Letterman Army Med. Ctr., U. Calif., San Francisco, 1978-80; chief dept. psychiatry Darnell Army Cmty. Hosp., Ft. Hood, Tex., 1980-82; divsn. surgeon 1st Cav. Divsn., Ft. Hood, Tex., 1982-84; chief child, adolescent, family psychiatry Eisenhower Army Med. Ctr., Ft. Gordon, Ga., 1985-86, dep. comdr. clin. svcs., dir. med. edn., 1986-89; comdr. Blanchfield Army Cmty. Hosp., 1990-93; project mgr. AMEDD Vanguard, Fairfax, Va., 1993, TRICARE S.E., Augusta, Ga., 1994-95; cmdg. gen. Southeast Regional Command Eisenhower Army Med. Ctr., Ft. Gordon, Ga., 1995-97, asst. surgeon gen., 1997-98. Pres., CEO XenaLex, 1998—; clin. prof. Uniformed Svcs. of Health Scis., Bethesda, Md., 1985—, Med. Coll. of Ga., Augusta, 1985—; lectr., author Porter Lecture, 1989. Contbr. articles to profl. jours. Bd. dirs. Univ. Health Found., 1998. Fellow Am. Acad. and Adolescent Psychiatry, Am. Psychiat. Assn., Am. Coll. Physician Execs., Assn. Mil. Surgeon U.S. Greek Orthodox. Office: Xana Lex 730 Somerset Way Augusta GA 30909 E-mail: sxenakis@alltel.net.

XEPAPAS, ANARGYROS, architect; b. Sparta, Greece, Apr. 10, 1932; came to U.S., 1951. s. Nicholaos and Penelope N. X.; m. Aliki A. B in Architecture, Catholic U. Am., 1956, M in Architecture, 1957, PhD in Architecture, 1958. lic. Nat. Coun. Architects. Architect Murphy and Locraft, Washington, U.S. Dept. Edn. and Welfare, Washington, U.S. Dept. Defense, Washington, Vets. Adminstrn., Washington. Bd. trustees Riddle Aeronautical U., Daytona Beach, Fla., 1984, Bethune Cookman, U., Daytona Beach, 1983; bd. commn. Halifax Hosp., 1983; delegate (Fla.) Nat. Democratic Convention, San Francisco, 1984. Recipient Architect of Yr., Catholic U. Am., 1977, Key to the City award, Daytona Beach, Fla., 1977, St. Paul's award, Greek Orthodox Ch., 1992, Superior Performance award U.S. Govt., 1961. Mem. Am. Hellenic Progressive Assn. (Aristotelian award 1996, Ahepan of Yr. 1999), Nat. Democratic Com. Greek Orthodox. Avocations: design, soccer. Home: 2612 N Halifax Ave Daytona Beach FL 32118-3244

XI, HONGWEI, computer scientist, educator; b. Ningbo, Zhejiang, China, June 23, 1967; arrived in U.S., 1992; s. Shaolun Xi and Xingying Dai. BS, Nanjing U., China, 1985; PhD, Carnegie Mellon U., 1998. Asst. prof. U. Cin., 1999—2001, Boston U., 2001—. Recipient Career award, NSF, 2001. Achievements include research in implementation and design of programming languages. Home: 10 Athena Cir Andover MA 01810 Office: Boston U Computer Sci Dept 111 Cummington St Boston MA 02215 Office Phone: +1 (617) 358-2511. Office Fax: +1 (617) 353-6457. E-mail: hwxi@bu.edu.

XI, XUEMEI, electrical engineer, researcher; d. Yunlong Xi and Meifen Lu; m. Yan Luo, Jan. 16, 1992; 1 child, Jiajie Luo. PhD, Peking U., China, 1995. Rsch. assoc. Peking U., Beijing, 1997—99; sr. engr. Motorola, Beijing, 1999—2000; asst. rsch. engr. U. Calif., Berkeley, 2000—. Recipient Best Student Paper award, IEEE ICSICT com., 1992. Mem.: IEEE, Compact Model Coun. Achievements include development of BSIM4 that is now the new compact model standard for CMOS circuit simulation; SALICIDE CMOS/SOI process technology and CMOS/SOI MOSFET models and IC simulations at Peking University; technology synthesis tool that allows top-down device design to match user specified requirements at Motorola; research in next generation compact MOSFET model for mix-signal applications. Avocations: swimming, travel. Office: U Calif Berkeley Dept EECS 373 Cory Hall Berkeley CA 94720 Personal E-mail: xi_x_m@hotmail.com. E-mail: janexi@eecs.berkeley.edu.

XIA, JIDING, chemical engineering educator; b. Jiangyin, Jiangsu, China, Mar. 23, 1921; s. Baogen Xia; m. Ming Yu, Oct. 1, 1958; children: Wei, Men. BS, Zhejiang U., Hangzhou, China, 1945, MS, 1948. Assoc. prof. Haijiang U., Fujian, China, 1949-50, Nanjing (China) Normal U., 1953-54; dir. teaching and rsch. divsn. Southeast U. (China), 1954-58; assoc. prof. and dir. teaching/rsch. divsn. Wuxi (China) U. Light Industry, 1958-85; prof. chem. engring. Wuxi U. of Light Industry, 1985-92; rsch. chemist U. Wis., Madison, 1995-96. Vis. prof. Wayne State U., Detroit, 1993-95; mem. expert group synthetic detergents and fatty acids, Ministry of Light Industry China, 1979-86; vis. prof. The VI Univ. of Paris, 1986;, evaluation com. acad. degree Authorized U., 1980-84, Jiangsu Light Industry Sr. Engrs., 1982-92; project evaluator China Nat. Natural Sci. Found. Surface Chemistry, 1985—; cons. Chemithon Co., Seattle, 1990-93, Aging Toilet Soap Factory, China, 1991—, Tianjin Rsch. Inst. Interface and Colloid Scis., 1993, Stepan Co., Chgo., 1994, Proctor & Gamble Co., Cin., 1994-95, Vista Chem. Co., Houston, 1994—;mem. adv. com. Internat. Symposium on Surfactants in Solution, 1993. Author: Synthetic Detergents, 1976, Chemistry and Technology of Surfactants and Detergents, 1997; author and editor: Protein-Based Surfactants, 2001, Gemini Surfactants-Synthesis Interface Behavior and Applications, 2004; editor: Composite Soaps, 1987; translator: Comprehensive Refining of Sunflower Seed Oil, 1956, Chemistry of Oil and Fats, 1958, Manufacture of Detergents, 1986; mem. editl. bd. Jour. Surfactant Industry, 1982-90, Jour. Petro-Finechemicals, 1982, Chinese Ency. LIght Industry, 1987-91; contbr. more than 120 articles to acad. jours. Recipient award Ministry of Petroleum Industry for EOR Project, 1992, Outstanding Contbn. to Chinese Higher Edn. award State Coun., 1992, Ministry of Light Industry for rsch. on composite soaps, 1983, Remarkable Achievement in Sci. and Tech. Invention and Innovation, UN, 1994; Excellent Advanced Sci. Rsch. fellow Wuxi, 1990, 93. Mem. China Assn. Surfactants and Detergent Industry (hon. dir. 1992, standing dir. 1983-92), Jiangsu Soc. of Daily Chem. Industry (chmn. 1978-85), Am. Chem. Soc. Home: 500 E Irving Ave Apt 620 Madison Heights MI 48071-1957 Office Phone: 248-577-1453. E-mail: xiajiding@aol.com.

XIA, LULIN, private equity investor; BA summa cum laude, Mount Holyoke Coll., 1997. Rsch. fellow Rockefeller U., N.Y.C., 1996; fin. analyst Credit Suisse First Boston, N.Y.C., 1997—; investment profl. Forstmann Little & Co., N.Y.C. Recipient Achievement award Chemistry Rubber Co., 1994, Abby Howe Turner Found. award, 1996; Sarah Williston scholar Mount Holyoke Coll., 1995, 96, 97. Mem. Sigma Xi, Phi Beta Kappa. Avocations: travel, photography, cooking. Office: Forstmann Little and Co 767 Fifth Ave New York NY 10153 Fax: 212-759-9059. E-mail: lxia@forstmannlittle.com.

XIA, YANG, physicist, educator; b. Shanghai, China; s. Zhen-Ao and Yue Xia; children: Aimee, Derek. PhD, Massey U., New Zealand, 1989—92. Rsch. officer Massey U., New Zealand, 1991—92; post-doctoral assoc. Cornell U., Ithaca, NY, 1992—94; asst. prof. Oakland U., Rochester, Mich., 1994—99, assoc. prof., 1999—. Recipient New Investigator Rsch. Excellence award, Oakland U., 2000, Disting. Scientist Lecture, Hosp. for Spl. Surgery, N.Y., 2002; grantee R01, NIH, 1998—2004; Guest Scholar, Ctr. for Atomic and Molecular Nanosciences and Dept. of Physics, Tsinghua U., Beijing, China, 2001. Mem.: AAUP, OsteoArthritis Rsch. Soc. Internat., Am. Phys. Soc., Orthopaedic Rsch. Soc., Internat. Soc. Magnetic Resonance in Medicine, Divsn. of Spatially Resolved Magnetic Resonance of AMPERE Soc. (mem. divsn. com. 2003—), Internat. Soc. Magnetic Resonance, Sigma Xi (chpt. treas. 2002—). Office: Oakland Univ Dept of Physics 276 Hannah Hall Rochester MI 48309 Office Phone: 248-370-3420. E-mail: xia@oakland.edu.

XIANG, HUI, biochemist, researcher; b. Wanxian, Sichuan, China, Sept. 6, 1968; arrived in U.S., 2001; s. Jun Xiang and Yuhua Wen; m. Yu Zhu, Dec. 25, 1995; 1 child, Angela. BSc, Sichuan U., Chengdu, China, 1989; MSc, Dalhousie U., Halifax, Can., 1993. Cert. regulatory affairs. Quality insp.

Shuyang Pharm. Co., Chengdu, 1989—92; tech. officer Biotech. Rsch. Inst. Nat. Rsch. Coun., Montreal, Canada, 1995—99; assoc. scientist DSM Biologics, Montreal, 1999—2001; staff scientist DuPont Pharm., Wilmington, Del., 2001, Bristol-Myers Squibb, Wilmington, 2001—02; scientist Allergan, Inc., Irvine, Calif., 2002—. Contbr. articles to profl. jours. F.C. Harrison fellow, McGill U., Montreal, 1994—95, grad. fellow, Dalhousie U., 1992—93. Mem.: Am. Soc. Quality, Regulatory Affairs Profl. Soc., Am. Chem. Soc., European Fedn. Biotechnology. Office Phone: 714-246-5330. E-mail: hxgmtlqc@yahoo.com.

XIAO, JIARUN, mechanical engineer; b. Shangrao, JiangXi, China, Jan. 3, 1968; arrived in US, 2002; s. DingYu Xiao and XiuYing Wang. PhD, Nanyang Technol. U., Singapore, 1999. Sr. rsch. officer U. Limerick, Ireland, 2001—02; rsch. assoc. U. Del., Newark, 2002—. Contbr. articles to profl. jours. Recipient Science and Tech. award, Ministry Water Resource of China, 1997. Mem.: ASME.

XIAO, JIZHONG, engineering educator, researcher; b. Nanjing, China, Jan. 13, 1969; s. Heming Xiao and Yuye Xi; m. Jing Ye; 1 child, Bowen. BS, East China Inst. Tech., Nanjing, 1990; MS, East China Inst. Tech., 1993; M in Engring., Nanyang Technol. U., Singapore, 1999; PhD, Mich. State U., 2002. Rsch. engr. Robotics Rsch. Ctr. Nanyang Technol. U., 1998—99; rsch. asst. Mich. State U., East Lansing, 1999—2002; asst. prof. CCNY, N.Y.C., 2002—. Contbr. articles to profl. jours. Mem.: IEEE, N.Y. Acad. of Sci.s, Sigma Xi. E-mail: jxiao@ccny.cuny.edu.

XIAO, SHUYI, finance company executive; b. Aug. 1, 1966; 1 child, eMing. MBA, Pace U., 1996—98. Prin. Option123, Purchase, NY, 1999—. Author: (accounting software) Option123, (reference book) Black-Scholes Option Valuation Factor Table @ $1, (software) E-Model of Stock Historical Volatility Calculation. Mem.: The Nat. Assn. of Cert. Valuation Analysts, NY Soc. of Security Analysts. Achievements include patents pending for. Office: Option123 PO Box 603 Purchase NY 10577 E-mail: sxiao@option123.com.

XIE, BIN, epidemiologist, research scientist; s. Shide Xie and Huifen Yang; m. Jing Fan. MS in Biostatistics, U. So. Calif., 2001; M.D., Beijing Med. U., 1993; MS in Nutritional Sci., U. Utah, 1999; PhD, U. So. Calif., 2004. Rsch. assoc. Inst. Nutrition, Food Hygiene, Chinese Acad. of Preventive Medicine, Beijing, 1993—97; rsch. asst. U. Utah, Salt Lake City, 1997—99, U. of So. Calif., LA, 1999—2003, rsch. assoc., 2004—. Rschr. Adolescent Health Behavior Rsch., China, 1996. Contbr. articles to profl. jours. Recipient Nat. Sci. Achievement Award, issued by the Nat. Sci. and Tech. Com. of the People's Republic of China, 1996, Poster Session Award, Ann. Meeting of Utah Dietetic Assn., 1999, Academic Achievement Award, Office of Internat. Svc., U. of So. Calif., 2001; scholar Soc. for Prevention Rsch. Early Career Scholarship, Soc. for Prevention Rsch., 2003. Mem.: Soc. Epidemiol. Rsch., Am. Soc. of Nutritional Scis., Internat. Soc. Behavioral Nutrition and Phys. Activity, Soc. Prevention Rsch. (Early Career scholarship 2003). Achievements include research in National Codex standards for nitrite and lead tolerance limits, P.R.China. Office: U So Calif 1000 South Fremont Ave Alhambra CA 91803 E-mail: bxie@hsc.usc.edu.

XIE, HUIKAI, electrical engineer, educator; s. Chengmei and Fuqing (Du) Xie; m. Yuxiao Tong, Sept. 19, 1968; children: Yutong, Brian Yucheng. MS, Tufts U., Medford, Mass., 1998; PhD, Carnegie Mellon U., Pitts., 2002. Lectr. Tsinghua U., Beijing, 1992—96; dir. of engring. Akustica, Inc., Pitts., 2002; asst. prof. U. Fla., Gainesville, 2002—. Tech. cons. Robert Bosch Corp., Palo Alto, Calif., 2000—02; presenter and com. mem. tech. confs. Author: (journal article) Chinese Jour. Semiconductors (Best paper of the yr., 1996); contbr. scientific papers to many confs. and meetings. Recipient Motorola Edn. Award, Tsinghua U./Motorola Inc., 1996; grantee UCF-UF Space Rsch. Initiative, NASA, 2002-2003. Mem.: IEEE (assoc.), Am. Soc. Engring. Edn. (assoc.), Optical Soc. Am. (assoc.). Achievements include patents pending for Five in the areas of MEMS, sensors and biomedical imaging. Home: 7904 Sw 51st Blvd Gainesville FL 32608 Office: Univ Florida 221 Benton Hall Gainesville FL 32611 Office Phone: 352-846-0441. Office Fax: 352-846-1416. Personal E-mail: hkx@ufl.edu. E-mail: hkx@ufl.edu.

XIE, SONG, musician, music educator; b. Nanning, China, Oct. 25, 1963; arrived in U.S., 1991; s. Shun-Feng Xie and Shu-Nan Yang; m. Renee Chen, July 25, 1991; 1 child, David. BA, Guangxi Inst. Art, 1987; MusM, La. State U., 1995. Mem. violin faculty Guangxi Inst. Arts, Nanning, China, 1987—91; prin. 2d violin Miss. Symphony Orch., Jackson, 1997—; string dir. Belhaven Coll., 1998—. Concertmaster Met. Chamber Orch., 1999—; asst. concert master Lyric Mountain Festival, Pitts., 1998; adj. prof. Millsaps Coll., Jackson State U., 1998—, Miss. Coll. Named winner, La. State U. Symphony Concerto Competition, 1991, 1994; recipient Excellent Performance award, Chinese Arts/Culture Ministry, 1984. Mem.: Nat. Sch. Orch. Assn., Am. String Tchr. Assn. (pres. elect Miss. chpt.), Music Tchrs. Nat. Assn., Miss. Music Tchrs. Assn., Coll. Music Soc., Am. Fedn. Musicians. Office Phone: 601-974-6149. Personal E-mail: songxie66@hotmail.com.

XIE, XIAOLIANG SUNNEY, chemist, educator; arrived in U.S., 1985; PhD in Chemistry, U. Calif., 1990. Postdoctoral fellow U. Chgo., 1990—92; sr. rsch. scientist Environ. Molecular Scis. Lab. Pacific N.W. Nat. Lab., Richland, Wash., 1992—95, chief scientist Environ. Molecular Scis. Lab., 1995—98; prof. chemistry Harvard U., Cambridge, Mass., 1999—. Recipient Coblentz award, Coblentz Soc., 1996, Raymond and Beverly Sackler Prize in Phys. Scis., Israel, 2003. Mem.: Biophysical Soc., Optical Soc. Am., Am. Chem. Soc. Achievements include research in single molecule spectroscopy at room temperature, single molecule enzymology, conformational dynamics of proteins, and near-field optical microscopy; patents for Coherent Anti-Stokes Raman Scattering Microscopy, a noninvasive method for imaging live cells and tissues. Office: Harvard Univ Chemistry & Chem Biology Dept 12 Oxford St M026 Cambridge MA 02138

XIE, YU, adult education educator; b. Zhenjiang, Jiangsu, China, Oct. 12, 1959; s. Liangyao Xie and Huazhen Zhao; m. Yijun Helen Gu, Dec. 1985; children: Raissa, Kevin. BA in Metallurgical Engring., Shanghai U. of Tech., China, 1982; MA in History of Sci., MS in Sociology, U. Wis., Madison, 1984, PhD in Sociology, 1989. From asst. to assoc. prof. U. Mich., Ann Arbor, 1989-96, John Stephenson Perrin prof. sociology, 1996—. Mem. adv. panel sociology program NSF, 1995-97; bd. dirs. Bd. Overseers of Gen. Social Survey. Dep. editor Am. Sociol. Review, 1996—; mem. editl. bd. Sociol. Methods and Rsch., 1989—, Am. Jour. Sociology, 1994-96, Sociol. Methodology, 1994-97; presenter in field; contbr. articles to profl. jours. Spencer fellow Nat. Acad. Edn., 1991-92; recipient Young Investigator award NSF, 1992-97, Faculty Scholar award William T. Grant Found., 1994-99. Mem. Am. Stat. Assn., Am. Sociol. Assn., Sociol. Rsch. Assn. (elected mem.), Population Assn. of Am. Office: U Mich Population Studies Ctr 426 Thompson St Ann Arbor MI 48104-2321 Fax: 734-998-7415. E-mail: yuxie@umich.edu.

XING, BAOSHAN, science educator; b. Harbin, Heilongjinang, China, Jan. 1, 1964; s. Shulan Xing and Yunxiang Zhou; m. Ting J. Song, Dec. 16, 1988; 1 child, Monica. BSc, HALR U., China, 1984; MSc, U. Alta., Can., 1990; PhD, U. Alta., 1994. Profl. Soil Scientist 1996. Post-doctoral scientsit Ct. Agrl. Expt. Sta., New Haven, 1994—95; asst. prof. U. Mass., Amherst, 1996—99; adj. prof. Chem. Dept, U. of Mass., 1998—; assoc. prof. U. Mass., 1999—2003, full prof., 2004—. Sci. adv. bd. Ann. Internat. Conf. of Contaminated Soils, Sediments, and Water, Amherst, Mass., 1996—; sci. com. Humic Substances Seminar Series, Boston, 1997—; assoc. editor Jour. of Environ. Quality, SSSA/ASA, 2001—; editl. bd. Internat. Jour. of Phytoremediation, Amherst, Mass., 2002—, Pedosphere, Beijing, 2004—. Contbr. articles varius profl. jours. Deacon bd. Ch., Amherst, Mass. Fellow The Queen Elizabeth II Doctoral fellowship in Environ. Studies, Province of Alta., 1992-94; Rsch., USDA, 1997, 1998, 1998, 2002, BARD, 2003, USGS, 2003. Mem.: ACS, Internat. Humic Substance Soc., Soli Sci. Soc. of Am., Agronomy Soc. of Am. Achievements include research in dual-mode sorption in natural organic matter; crystalline and amorphous aliphatics in natural organic matter; mineral effect on conformation of humic molecules; preferential sorption of aliphatic fractions of humics by clay minerals; one of the most cited papers pub. Environ. Sci. Technol. Office: U Mass Rm 12 Stockbridge Hall Amherst MA 01003

XING, GUANG-QIAN, aerospace scientist; b. Nai Ling, Ah Hui Province, China, Nov. 19, 1938; m. Ming Zhu, Feb. 5, 1978; children: Lei Zhu, Neil, Meng Chen. Equivalent Master, Peking U., Beijing, China, 1957—63. Graduated Certification, Peking U., China, 1963. Engr. Beijing Inst. of Control Engring., Chinese Acad. of Space Tech., 1963—86; sr. rsch. assoc. Howard U., Inst. of Large Flexible Space Structure, Howard U, NASA, 1986—95; prin. scientist Space Products and Applications, Inc., Fairfax, Va., 1996—. Author: (profl. jours.) Jour. Guidance, Control, and Dynamics; Acta Astronautica; The Jour. of the Astronautical Sciences; ASME Tranction: Journal of Dynamic System, Measurement and Control;Book Chapter:Control and Dynamics System Advance, Volum 79. Recipient The first class Citation of Merit due to successfully Design and implementation of the Chinese First Communication satellite, Chinese Ministry of Astronautics, 1984, The Nat. Prize(Super Class) for Promoting Progress of Sciences and Technologies., The State Sci. and Tech. Commn. of China, 1985. Achievements include patents for The first patent is used for Autonomous Spacecraft Constellation Control Using GPS; The second patent is used for the Autonomous Orbit/Attitude Unified Control for Spacecraft Formation Flying Usng GPS. Home: 8515 Pelham Rd Bethesda MD 20817 Office: Space Products and Applications(SPA)Inc 3900 Jermantown Rd Ste 300 Fairfax VA 22030 Personal E-mail: xingspa@erols.com.

XIONG, TOUSU SAYDANGNMVANG, minister; b. Hmong Long Chieng, Laos, June 23, 1966; arrived in U.S., 1976; s. Nhialue Saydang and May (Vang) X.; m. Zoua Pahoua Moua, Sept. 14, 1993; children: Chivkeeb Genesis Toupa, Naamonunas Ruth, Nujsimloob Hebrews. BA in Bibl. Studies, Simpson Coll., San Francisco, 1989; MA in Theology, Mennonite Brethren Bibl. Sem., Fresno, Calif., 1991; AS in Computerized Acctg., Phillips Jr. Coll., Fresno, Calif., 1993. Ordained to ministry Christian and Missionary Alliance, 1991. Assoc. min. Hmong San Raphael (Calif.) Bapt. Ch., 1986-88; youth min. Hmong Alliance Ch. of Santa Barbara, Goleta, Calif., 1984-85, Hmong Alliance Ch. of Fresno, 1989—. Scoutmaster Boy Scouts Am., 1984—85, Eagle Scout, 1983. Office: Hmong Alliance Ch Fresno 8234 E Belmont Ave Fresno CA 93727-9725 Home: PO Box 37032 Tallahassee FL 32315-7032 E-mail: xteagle76@wmconnect.com. *In my life as I have experienced both the world of the Hmong Animistic Religion in the East and the Christian faith from the West, I have come to realize that Jesus Christ is superior, for Jesus is the way, the truth and the life pointing us towards the Supreme and Creator Being.*

XIONG, XIAOPING, statistician, researcher; s. Zhengzhong Xiong and Xianlie Li; m. Ying Fu, Feb. 24, 1983; 1 child, Lingyun. PhD in Statis., Purdue U., W. Lafayette, Ind., 1991—95. Asst. lectr., dept. math. Southwestern Jiaotong U., Chengdu, China, 1982—85; postdoctoral rschr., dept. statis. Purdue U., West Lafayette, Ind., 1991—94; rsch. fellow, dept. biostatistics and epidemiology The Cleve. Clin. Found., 1994—96; assoc. mem., dept. biostatistics St. Jude Children's Rsch. Hosp., Memphis, 1996—. Adj. grad. prof., dept. math. scis. U. Memphis, 1998—. V.p. Greater Memphis United Chinese Assn., 2003. Grantee, NIH, 1998, 1999, 2000. Mem.: AAAS, Chinese Statis. Assn., Internat. Biometrics Soc., Am. Statis. Assn. Office: St Jude Children's Rsch Hosp 332 N Lauderdale St Memphis TN 38105

XU, BIQIANG, engineer, researcher; s. Zhiming Xu and Qinyu Luo; m. Shuang Qi, Sept. 20, 1996. PhD, S.W. Jiaotong U., Chengdu, Sichuan, China, 1992—97. Postdoctoral fellow S.W. Jiaotong U., Chengdu, China, 1997—98; rsch. engr. U. Nev., Reno, 1998—. Contbr. articles to profl. jours. Grantee, Nat. Key Lab. Found. of China, 1998, Nat. Ctr. for Super-computing Applications, 1999. Mem.: ASME, Soc. of Automotive Engrs., Materials Rsch. Soc. Achievements include Achievements include self-loosening of bolted joints; mechanical characterization of multifunctional woven materials; elastic-plastic stick-slip rolling contact fatigue; rate-independent crystal cyclic plasticity model; computational mechanics; fretting fatigue, micro-mechanics; multiscale materials modeling; multiaxial fatigue.

XU, PING, chemist; b. Shanghai, Apr. 29, 1957; came to U.S., 1985; s. Yuan Xu and Changfu Zhu; m. Shuhong Wang, Feb. 17, 1987; children: Helen W., Olivia W. BS, East China U. Chem. Tech., Shanghai, 1982, MS, 1984, U. Cin., 1987, PhD, 1991. Asst. prof. East China U. Chem. Tech., 1984-85; Paul J. Flory meml. fellow U. Cin., 1990-92; sr. rsch. chemist Quantum Chem. Corp., Cin., 1991-94; polymer scientist W.L. Gore & Assocs., Inc., Elkton, Md., 1994—. Vis. scientist Oak Ridge (Tenn.) Nat. Lab., 1998—; vis. scientist Nat. Inst. Stds. and Tech., Gaithersburg, Md., 1999—. Contbr. numerous articles to sci. jours. Mem. AAAS, Am. Chem. Soc., Material Rsch. Soc. Achievements include research in engineering, rubber elasticity, polymer morphology and polymer physics. Home: 22 Piersons Rdg Hockessin DE 19707-9291 Office: WL Gore & Assocs Inc 2401 Singerly Rd Elkton MD 21921-2733 E-mail: pxu@aol.com.

XU, SHUCHENG, chemistry educator, research scientist; arrived in U.S., 2000; s. Rong Xu and Guiqin Fan; m. Wensheng Li; 1 child, Muzi. PhD, Dalian Inst. Chem. Physics, China, 1998. Postdoctoral fellow Free U., Amsterdam, Netherlands, 1999; rsch. assoc. dept. chemistry U. Akron, Ohio, 2000—03; rsch. assoc., Emerson vis. fellow U. Atlanta, 2004—. Contbr. articles pub. to profl. jour. Mem.: ACS (assoc.), Sigma Xi (assoc.). Achievements include research in Cavity Ringdown Spectroscopy, Theo Calculations of chem. reacation kinetics and nano materials. Home: 2205 Briarcliff Rd NE Apt 19 Atlanta GA 30329-3436 Office: Emory Univ Dept Chem Atlanta GA 30322 E-mail: scxu@uakron.edu., sxu@emory.edu.

XU, TAO, electrical engineer, biomedical researcher; b. Luzhou, Sichuan, China, Oct. 26, 1966; s. Ziqiang Xu and Huiyuan Deng; m. Mei Zuo; 1 child, Haotian. BS, Chongqing U., China, 1989, MS, 1994, PhD, 1997. Cert. Nat. Com. for Engr. Evaluation, 1991. Mgr. Lu Tian Hua, Inc., Luzhou, China, 1989—91; rsch. assoc. Chongqing U., Chongqing, China, 1991—97; postdoctoral rschr. Peking U., Beijing, 1998—2000, U. Calif., Irvine, 2000—; vis. scholar Hong Kong U. Sci. and Tech., Hong Kong, China, 2000. Investigator (proposal) MEMS Hearing Aid and Cochlear Implant Based on Polymeric Micro-cantilever Filters (UCI Whitaker Fellowship, 2002), Next Generation Hearing Aid and Cochlear Implant Based on MEMS Technology (Faculty Career Devel. Award, 2003); author: Polymeric Micro-mechanical Filter Array for Auditory Prostheses (The Best Poster Award, 2003); contbr. articles various profl. jours. Recipient The Best Life Sci. Poster award, 2003; Nat. Key Lab. Found. grant, Nat. Key Lab. Micro Nano Tech., China, 2000. Mem.: IEEE (sr.), Optical Soc. of Am. Achievements include patents pending for vibration detectors, sound detectors, hearing aids, cochlear implants and related methods. Home: 6103 Palo Verde Rd Irvine CA 92617 Office: U Calif Irvine 3312 Engring Gateway Irvine CA 92697 Office Phone: 949-824-4019. Office Fax: 949-824-3732. Personal E-mail: xutao1966@hotmail.com. E-mail: taox@uci.edu.

XU, XIAO-BANG, engineering educator; b. Huize, Yunnan, China, Feb. 15, 1945; came to U.S., 1981; s. Bailing Xiong and Lan Xu; m. Yi Hong Wu, Sept. 30, 1973; 1 child, Jack J. Xiong. BSc, Tsinghua U., Beijing, China, 1968; PhD, U. Miss., 1985. Lectr. U. Houston, 1985; vis. instr. Clemson (S.C.) U., 1985, vis. asst. prof., 1986-88, asst. prof., 1988-94, assoc. prof., 1994—. Contbr. articles to profl. jours. Rsch. grant Elec. Power Rsch. Inst., 1992, NSF, 1996, Duke Power Co., 1992, 99, S.C. Elec. and Gas Co., 1992. Mem. IEEE, Electromagnetics Acad., Profl. Soc. of Antennas and Prop., Prof. Soc. of Microwave T&T, Phi Kappa Phi. Avocations: music, tennis, gardening, walking, reading. Office: ECE Dept Clemson U Clemson SC 29634-0001 Office Phone: ecexu@ces.clemson.edu., 864-656-5923.

XU, XIAOCHUN, biologist, researcher; b. Qianshan, Anhui, China, Aug. 13, 1958; came to U.S., 1992; s. Daren Xu and Shuping Wang; m. Gouqing Ge, July 1, 1983; 1 child, Jany. MD, Anhui Med. Coll., Hefei, 1982, MS, 1985; PhD, U. Göttingen, Germany, 1991. Rsch. asst. Anhui Med. U., 1985-86, asst. prof., 1987-88; rsch. assoc. U. Göttingen, 1988-91; postdoctoral fellow U. Tex., M.D. Anderson Cancer Ctr., Houston, 1992-95, asst. prof., 1995—. Author: (books) Meth. Mol. Biol. Retinoids, 1998, Handbook Exp. Pharm. Retinoids, 1999; contbr. rsch. papers to profl. jours. Grantee NIH, Nat. Cancer Inst., 1998. Mem. AAAS, Am. Assn. for Cancer Rsch., Am. Assn. for Preventive Oncology, M.D. Anderson Assn. Avocations: jogging, travel, movies, playing chess. Office: U Tex M D Anderson Cancer Ctr 1515 Holcombe Blvd Houston TX 77030-4009 E-mail: xxu@mdanderson.org.

XU, XIE GEORGE, engineering educator; s. Zhiyang and Chunlan (Qui) Xu; m. Crystal Xiong, Dec. 30, 1988; children: Wendy M., Jeffrey X. PhD, Tex. A & M U., Coll. Sta., Tex., 1994. Engr. Wuhan Inst. Engring. Sciences, Wuhan, China, 1983—88; assoc. prof. Rensselaer Poly. Inst., Troy, NY, 1995—. Grantee, NSF, 1997—99, Dept. Of Energy, 1998—2001, NSF, 1998—2003, Nat. Inst. Of Health, 2003—05, Electric Power Rsch. Inst., 2003—05. Mem.: IEEE Engring. in Medicine and Biology Soc., Am. Assn. of Physicists in Medicine, Am. Nuc. Soc., Coun. on Ionizing Radiation Measurements and Standards (pres. 1999—2000), Health Physics Soc. (several committees). Achievements include patents for U.S. Patent for non destructive in-situ method and apparatus for determining radionuclide depth in media; U.S. Patent for Terahertz imaging with dynamic apertureChen, Z. Jiang, and provisional application 1/25/2001 and non-provisional 1/25/2002; first to world's most detailed 3d whole body radiation dosimetry simulation model with a voxel size Of 0.33 mm X 0.33 mm X 1 mm; research in NSF Faculty Early Career Award. Office: Rensselaer Poly Inst 110 8th St Troy NY 12180 Office Phone: 518-276-4014. Office Fax: 518-276-4832. Business E-Mail: xug2@rpi.edu.

XU, XIPING, adult education educator, director; b. Anhui, China, Aug. 1, 1956; m. Xiaobin Wang; children: Benjamin, Richard. MS, HSPH, 1982; PhD, U. Tsukuba, Japan, 1988; MD, Anhui Med. U., 1996. Dir., program for population genetics Harvard Sch. of Pub. Health, Harvard U., Boston, 1994—. Instr., guest lectr. on modern genetic epidemiology and gene mapping Harvard U., Boston, 1998—. Author over 130 articles regarding genetic rsch. Pres. Chinese Prof. in Biomedicine, Boston, 1998—2002. Home: 15 Sycamore Rd Newton MA 02459 Office: Harvard Sch Pub Health 665 Huntington Ave Boston MA 02115 E-mail: xu@hsph.harvard.edu.

XU, YING, computational biologist; b. Changchun, Jilin, People's Republic of China, Dec. 21, 1960; came to U.S., 1985; s. Ruran and Wengin (Pang) X.; m. Cindy Chenxin Zeng, Aug. 1, 1988; 1 child, Tony DongYi. BS in Computer Sci., Jilin U., Changchun, 1982, MS in Computer Sci., 1985; PhD in Computer Sci., U. Colo., 1991. Rsch. assoc. Oak Ridge (Tenn.) Nat. Lab., 1993-95; staff scientist Oak Ridge Nat. Lab., 1995-97, group leader, 1997—. Vis. asst. prof. Colo. Sch. Mines, Golden, 1991-93. Guest editor Jour. Combinational Optimization; contbr. more than 40 articles to profl. jours. including Jour. Computer and Sys. Scis., Jour. Computational Biology. Mem. AAAS, N.Y. Acad. Scis. Avocations: reading, popular science books, photography, chinese chess. Office: Oak Ridge Nat Lab MS 6480 1060 Commerce Park Dr Oak Ridge TN 37830-8043

XU, YING-PEI, artist; b. Ningbo, Zheijiang, China, Jan. 31, 1941; came to U.S., 1992; s. Tong-Da and Yu-Mei(Ding) X.; m. Man-Li Bao, Jan. 1968; 1 child, Bing-Li; m. Jun Bi, Feb. 4, 1974; 1 child, Jing. BA, China Acad. Art, 1965, MA, 1980. Editor Fedn. Jiangxi Province, Nan Chang, China, 1965-68; artist Mus. Jiangxi Province, Nan Chang, 1968-78; prof. China Acad. Art, Hangzhou, 1980-92; freelance artist Two World Arts Inc., N.Y.C., 1993-94; artist Julia Gray Ltd., N.Y.C., 1994—. Exch. scholar Acad. Bildenden Kust, Hamburg, Germany, 1992. Author: Canadian Eskimos Art (translated), 1987, The World of Print, 1988; lectr. Hammand Mus., North Salem, N.Y., 1997; exhibited in group shows at Salmagundi Club, N.Y., 1997, Heckscher Mus. Art, L.I., N.Y., 1997, Internat. Graphic Art Exhbn., Stockholm, 1997, Oriental and Western Arts Auction, L.A., 1995, N.Y. State Mus., 1998, Cmty. Arts Assn., 1999; one man shows include Interchurch Ctr., N.Y., 1996, Gallery of Amerasia Bank, N.Y., 1994. Mem. Am. Artists Profl. League, All-China Artist Assn., All-China Printmaking Artist Assn. Avocation: dance. Home: 18524 Dunlop Ave Saint Albans NY 11412-1514

XU, YONGLI, research scientist; arrived in U.S., 1999; s. F.H. and H.R. Xu; m. Ling Cheng Xu, Oct. 10, 1990; 1 child, Sunny. BS, Beijing U., 1987, MEng, 1990; PhD, U. Cin., 2003. Asst. prof. Beijing U., 1990—95, assoc. prof., 1995—99; rsch. asst. U. Cin., 1999—2001; rsch. assoc. Oak Ridge Nat. Lab., Tenn., 2001—03; scientist UES Inc., Dayton, Ohio, 2003—. Cons. Xihang Tech. Ceramics Inc., Jingdezhen, China, 1995—99; adv. bd. mem. Beijing K.X. New Materials Inc., 1996—99. Contbr. chapters to books, articles to profl. jours. Mem.: Materials Rsch. Soc. Office: Oak Ridge Nat Lab Bethel Valley Rd #1 Oak Ridge TN 37831

XU, YU, nursing educator; s. Philip Hsu Xu and Shuqin Zhang; m. Jianhui Zhang, Oct. 15, 1957; children: Claude You, Leon Apollo. BA in English, Henan U., Kaifeng, China, 1982; MEd, Xiamen (China) U., 1987; PhD, SUNY, Buffalo, 1995; MSN, U. S. Ala., 1999. RN Ala. Bd. Nursing, cert. transcultural nurse, Transcultural Nursing Soc. Lectr. Henan U., Kaifeng, 1982—85; asst. prof. Xiamen U. Inst. Higher Edn. Sci., 1987—90, U. S. Ala., Mobile, 1999—2004, U. Conn., Storrs, 2004—. Vis. prof. Henan U. Sch. Nursing, Kaifeng, 2002—; coun. mem. State of Ala. Minority Health Adv. Coun., Montgomery, 2001; cons. Hangzhou (China) Med. Coll. Dept. Nursing, 2002—. Translator: (book chapters) Supervision in Education: Problems and Practices, 1987, (book) Educational Adminstration: Theory, Research, and Practice, 1988, (book chapter) Economic & Management Education in Japan: History and Current Scene, 1990. Mem. minority recruitment com. ARC Gulf Coast chpt., Mobile, 2002. Recipient Graduation Spkr., U. South Ala. Coll. Nursing, 2002, Excellent Paper award, Chinese Higher Edn. Assn., Beijing, 1988, Excellent Paper to Young Scholars in Philosophy & Social Sci., Xiamen U., China, 1987, Disting. Higher Edn. Rsch. award, 1988, Inaugural Faculty Excellence in Scholarship award, U. S. Ala. Coll. Nursing, 2001, Dean's Grant award, 2001, Disting. Svc. award, Alba Elem. Sch., Bayou La Batre, Ala., 2001; grantee, State Edn. Commn., Beijing, China, 1988; Mark Diamond Dissertation grantee, SUNY, Buffalo, 1993, Profl. Nurse Traineeship grantee, U. S. Ala. Coll. Nursing, 1998, Rsch. grantee, 2001, Helene Fuld Health Trust, N.Y.C., 2000, U. S. Ala. Rsch. Coun., 2002, Sigma Theta Tau Internat., 2002, Rsch. scholar, Zeta Gamma chpt. Sigma Theta Tau Internat., 2000. Mem.: Soc. Rsch. Nicotine and Tobacco, So. Nursing Rsch. Soc., Transcultural Nursing Soc., Nat. League Nursing, Sigma Theta Tau. Office: U Conn Sch Nursing 231 Glenbrook Rd U 2026 Storrs Mansfield CT 06269-2026 Office Phone: 860-486-0593. E-mail: yu.xu@uconn.edu.

XUE, RUI-DE, entomologist; s. Youcai Xue and Qingye Shao; m. Minjin Hao; 1 child, Hui. PhD, Chinese Acad. of Med. Sciences, Beijing, 1986—89. Asst. prof. Shanxi Med. U., Taiyuan, China, 1981—85; assoc. prof. Beijing Inst. of Microbiology and Epidemiology, Beijing, 1989—91; vis. scientist U. of Mass., Ahmerst; rsch. assoc. U. of Fla., IFAS, Mid. Fla. Rsch. and Edn. Ctr., Apopka, Fla., 1992—93; rsch. entomologist USDA, ARS, Ctr. for Med., Agrl. and Vet. Entomology, Gainesville, Fla., 1993—2003, Anastasia Mosquito Control Dist., St. Augustine, Fla., 2003—. Author (reviewers) co-editor, Chinese jour. of pest control. Worldwide com. mem. Am. Mosquito Control Assn., Eatontown, NJ, 1995—98. Mem.: Fla. Mosquito Control Assn., Soc. for Vector Ecologists, Am. Mosquito Control Assn., Entomol. Soc. of Am. Achievements include discovery of new oviposition repellents, mosquito larvicides. Home: 1820 SW 78th St Gainesville FL 32607 Office: Anastasia Mosquito Control Dist 500 Old Beach Rd Saint Augustine FL 32085 Office Phone: 904-471-3107. Home Fax: 352-332-4088; Office Fax: 904-471-3189. Business E-Mail: xueamcd@bellsouth.net.

XUE, YONGKANG, science educator; m. Su Q. Liu, Jan. 10, 1973; children: Fransis, Cathleen. PhD, U. Utah, 1987. Rsch. scientist Ctr. for Ocean-Land-Atmosphre Studies, Bletsville, Md., 1993—97, U. Md., College Park, 1997—99; assoc. prof. UCLA, 1999—2003, prof., 2003—. Mem.: Am. Assn. Geography, Am. Geophys. Union, Am. Meteorol. Soc. Office: UCLA 1255 Bunche Hall Los Angeles CA 90094-1524 Personal E-mail: yxue@geog.ucla.edu. Business E-Mail: yxue@geog.ucla.edu.

YABLON, JEFFERY LEE, lawyer; b. Chgo., June 28, 1948; s. Robert R. and Faye I. (Goldberg) Y.; m. Jean C. LaPrade, Apr. 17, 1983. BA with honors, U. Wis., 1970; JD, Stanford U., 1973. Bar: Calif. 1974, D.C. 1975. Law clk. to Judge Cynthia Holcomb Hall U.S. Tax Ct., Washington, 1973-75; Fulbright scholar U. Florence, Italy, 1975-76; assoc. Covington & Burling, Washington, 1976-80, Lee, Toomey & Kent, Washington, 1980-82, Shaw Pittman, Washington, 1982-84, ptnr., 1984—. Mem. bd. advisors Taxation of Exempts Jour., 1998—. Contbr. articles to legal jours.; editl. adv. bd. Moment Mag., 2000—. Mem. ABA, State Bar Calif., D.C. Bar. Jewish. Office: Shaw Pittman 2300 N St NW Washington DC 20037-1172 Office Phone: 202-663-8441. Business E-Mail: jeffery.yablon@sharwpittman.com.

YABLON, LEONARD HAROLD, publishing company executive; b. N.Y.C., June 3, 1929; s. Philip A. and Sarah (Herman) Y.; m. Carolyn Sydney Torgan (dec. Aug. 1995); children: Scott Richard, Bonnie Michelle; m. Pamela Gallin; children: Laura, Abigail, Hilary, Peter. BS, L.I. U., 1950; MBA, CCNY, 1969. CPA, N.Y. Acct., 1950-63; emeritus dir. Forbes Inc., N.Y.C.; chmn. emeritus Forbes Family Holdings Inc.; pres. Sangre de Cristo Ranches, Fiji Forbes; v.p. Forbes Investors Adv. Inst.; pres. Forbes Trinchera, Forbes Europe, pres. emeritus, 2004—. Sec.-treas. Forbes Found.; bd. dirs. Yablon Found., Mack Goldner Found. Home and Office: 2 Fargo Ln Irvington NY 10533-1202 Office Phone: 914-591-8387. Business E-Mail: lyablon@forbes.com.

YABLONOVITCH, ELI, electrical engineering educator; b. Puch, Austria, Dec. 15, 1946; BSc, McGill U., 1967; AM, Harvard U., 1969, PhD in Applied Physics, 1972. Tchg. fellow Harvard U., 1971—72, asst. prof. applied physics, 1974-76, assoc. prof., 1976-79; mem. tech. staff Bell Labs., 1972-74; rsch. assoc., group head Exxon Rsch. Ctr., 1979-84; mem. tech. staff Bellcore, 1984-90, disting. mem. staff, 1990-93, dir. solid state physics, 1991-93; prof. elec. engring. UCLA, 1993—. Chmn. Gordon Conf. on Nonlinear Optics and Lasers, 1979; Clifford Paterson lectr. Royal Soc. London, 2000. A.P. Sloan fellow, 1978-79; recipient Julius Springer prize in applied physics, 2001. Fellow: IEEE (W. Streifer Sci. Achievement award 1993), Optical Soc. Am. (Adolph Lomb medal 1978, R.W. Wood prize 1996), Am. Physics Soc.; mem.: NAS, NAE. Achievements include research solar cells, strained-semiconductor lasers, photonic band structure. Office: UCLA Dept Elec Engring 56 125B Engring Bldg IV Los Angeles CA 90095-1594 Business E-Mail: eliy@ee.ucla.edu.

YABLONSKI, MICHAEL EDWARD, application developer; b. Gardner, Mass., Dec. 1, 1971; s. Edward Stanley Yablonski and Barbara Ann Borkowski. BS in Computer Sci., Fitchburg State Coll., 1993, MS in Computer Sci., 1995. Elec. asst. Raburne Elec. Corp., Gardner, Mass., 1992—95; sr. programmer, analyst Meditech, Westwood, Mass., 1995—. Acolyte St. Joseph's Ch., Gardner, 1979—. Mem.: Gardner Mus., Polish Am. Vets. Greater Gardner (hon.; transcriber 1991—). Roman Catholic. Avocations: writing, organ, piano, music box collecting, softball. Home: 164 Sherman ST Gardner MA 01440

YABUKI, JEFFREY W. diversified financial services company executive; BBA, Calif. State U. Cert. CPA Calif., Minn., lic. Nat. Assn. Securities Dealers. V.p., mergers & acquisitions Am. Express Tax Bus. Svcs., Mpls., 1996—98, pres., CEO N.Y.C., NY, 1998—99; pres. H&R Block Internat., 1999; exec. v.p., COO H&R Block Inc., Kans. City, Mo. Former mem. Minn. Bd. Accountancy. Office: H&R Block 4400 Main St Kansas City MO 64111

YACANTE, MARIA LUCY, music educator, researcher; b. San Juan, Argentina, July 4, 1941; arrived in U.S., 1978; d. Carlos Alberto Yacante and Maria Elena Cuello. Maestra Normal Nacional, Sarmiento Normal Sch., San Juan, Argentina, 1966; MusB in piano, Tex. Wesleyan U., Ft. Worth, 1982; MusM in piano pedagogy, Tex. Christian U., Ft. Worth, 1984; post grad., Tex. Christian U., 1989. Prof. of music Sarmiento Normal Sch., Argentina, 1975—76, Nat. U. of San Juan, Argentina, 1975—78; piano accompanist Tex. Wesleyan U., 1978—82; piano instr. piano prep. divsn. Tex. Christian U., 1983—88; piano tchr. Our Lady of Victory, Ft. Worth, 1985—86, Ft. Worth Music and Arts Sch., 1986—87, piano studio, Ft. Worth, 1983—. Piano tchr. Inst. Superior de Artes, San Juan, Argentina, 1963—64; spkr. Reflections on Learning and Tchng., 2001—; adjudicator piano festivals, 1989, 92, 2000. Performer solo recitals. Mem.: Tex. Fedn. of Music Clubs, Tex. Music Tchrs. Assn., Music Teachers Nat. Assn., Ft. Worth Piano Tchrs. Forum (first v.p., piano recitals 2004—), Ft. Worth Music Tchrs. Forum (chair 2002—04), Ft. Worth Music Tchrs. Assn. (bd. mem. 2001—, chmn. Sunday piano rcitals 2001—, chair 2002—04, ind. piano tchrs. forum chair 2001—), Pi Kappa Lambda. Avocations: reading, writing, drawing. Home: PO Box 100912 Fort Worth TX 76185-0912

YACAVONE, DAVID WILLIAM, military officer, consultant, researcher; b. Newark, Feb. 5, 1945; s. William Michael and Rose Marie (Cerrato) Y.; m. Nancy Weissman; children: Nancy Christine, Rebecca Noel, Jason David, Briana Lynn. BA in Non-Western History, Seton Hall U., 1966, MA in Chinese History, 1968; DO, Chgo. Coll. Osteo. Medicine, 1974; MPH, Harvard U., 1986. Diplomate Am. Bd. Gen. and Preventive Medicine, Am. Bd. Aerospace Medicine. Rotating intern Chgo. Osteo. Med. Ctr., 1975; asst. prof. community medicine Mich. State U., East Lansing, 1975-76; bn. surgeon USN, Lansing, Mich., 1975-77; flight surgeon U.S. Naval Aerospace Med. Inst., Pensacola, Fla., 1977, USN, Jacksonville, Fla., 1977-79, sr. med. officer USS Saratoga, 1979; resident aerospace medicine U.S. Naval Aerospace Med. Inst., Pensacola, Fla., 1986-88; capt. med. corps USN USN, USS Dwight D. Eisenhower, 1988-90, 93-96; head aeromed. div. Naval Safety Ctr., Norfolk, Va., 1990-93; capt. med. corps USN USS Harry S. Truman, 1996-98, USS Nimitz, 1998—2001; comdr. carrier Airborne Early Warning Wing, 2001—. Staff mem. Lansing (Mich.) Gen. Hosp., 1975-76, Jackson (Much.) Gen. Hosp., 1976-77, Jacksonville (Fla.) Gen. Hosp., 1977-81, Daytona Beach (Fla.) Gen. Hosp., 1979-81, Naval Hosp., Corpus Christi, Tex., 1982-85, dir. mil. medicine, 1982-84; adj. instr. W.Va. Coll. Osteo. Medicine, 1977-79; tng. instr. Flight Instr.'s Tng., 1982-85, flight surgeon's sch. Naval Aerospace Med. Inst., 1986-88, 90-93, aircraft accident investigation technique, Armed Forces Inst. Pathology, 1990—; presenter in field. Author: (with others) Aviation, Space and Environmental Medicine, 1987, edit., 1992; editor: Aeromedical News, 1990-93. ACLS instr. Tex. Heart Assn., 1983-85. Recipient Steinbaum Meml. award, Kirksville Coll. Osteo. Medicine, 1971. Fellow Aerospace Med. Assn.; mem Soc. U.S. Naval Flight Surgeons (past officer), Assn. Mil. Surgeons of U.S., numerous coms.

YACK, PATRICK ASHLEY, editor; b. Little Rock, Oct. 25, 1951; s. Leo Patrick and Sarah Ann (Dew) Y.; m. Suzanne Burnett; children: Alexander Ryan, Kendall Elizabeth. BFA, So. Meth. U., 1974. Staff asst. U.S. Rep. Alan Steelman, Washington, 1975-76; press aide U.S. Senator Charles Percy, Chgo., 1977-78; reporter Fla. Times-Union, Jacksonville, 1979-80, regional reporter Atlanta, 1981-82; reporter The Denver Post, 1983-85, Washington bur. chief, 1985-87; nat. editor Atlanta Constitution, 1987-89; mng. editor The Register-Guard, Eugene, Oreg., 1989-94; editor News & Record, Greensboro, NC, 1994-98, Fla. Times-Union, Jacksonville, 1998—. Mem. univ. coun. Jacksonville U. Mem. journalism adv. coun. U. Fla., Gainesville, 2003—; mem. news/editl. adv. bd. Am. Press Inst.; bd. dirs. Fresh Ministries. Mem.: Am. Soc. Newspaper Editors (past membership com. chair), Fla. Soc. Newspaper Editors (former pres., bd. dirs.).

YACKEL, JAMES WILLIAM, mathematician, academic administrator; b. Sanborn, Minn., Mar. 6, 1936; s. Ewald W. and Marie E. (Heydlauff) Y.; m. Erna Beth Seecamp, Aug. 20, 1960; children: Jonathan, Juliet, Carolyn. BA, U. Minn., 1958, MA, 1960, PhD, 1964. Rsch. instr. dept. math. Dartmouth Coll., Hanover, N.H., 1964-66; asst. prof. dept. stats. Purdue U., West Lafayette, Ind., 1966-69, from assoc. prof. to prof., 1969-76, assoc. dean sci., 1976-87; vice chancellor acad. affairs Purdue U. Calumet, Hammond, Ind., 1987-90, chancellor, 1990-2001, chancellor emeritus, 2001—. Rsch. mathematician Inst. Def. Analysis, Washington, 1969. Author: Applicable Finite Mathematics, 1974; editor Statistical Decision Theory, 1971; contbr. articles to profl. jours. Fellow AAAS; mem. Am. Math. Soc., Math. Assn. Am., Inst. Math. Stats. Achievements include research on Ramsey's theorem and finite graphs. E-mail: yackelj@calumet.Purdue.edu.

YACKIRA, MICHAEL WILLIAM, power company executive; b. N.Y.C., Aug. 14, 1951; s. Alan Israel and Lillian (Landau) Y.; m. Roberta Guido, July 24, 1977; children: Steven, Andrew. BS in Acctg., Herbert H. Lehman Coll., CUNY, 1972. Sr. acct. Arthur Andersen, N.Y.C., 1972-75; v.p. St. Joe Petroleum, Houston, 1975-83; mgr. fin. analysis U.S. Industries, Stamford, Conn., 1983-84; dir. bus. analysis and research GTE Svc. Corp., Stamford, 1984-85, dir. bus. devel. and analysis, 1985-86, asst. controller budget planning and analysis, 1986-87; v.p. fin. and revenues GTE Fla., Tampa, 1987-88; v.p. fin. and info. mgmt. GTE Info. Svcs., Tampa, 1988-89; v.p. corp. devel. and planning FPL Group, Inc., Juno Beach, Fla., 1989-91; chief planning officer Fla. Power and Light Co., 1990-91; sr. v.p. market and regulatory svcs. Fla. Power & Light Co., Juno Beach, 1991—. Bd. dirs. Ctr. for Family Svcs., West Palm Beach, Fla. Home: 1028 Diamond Head Way Palm Beach Gardens FL 33418-5815*

YACKTMAN, DONALD ARTHUR, financial executive, investment counselor; b. Chgo., Sept. 12, 1941; s. Victor and Matilda (Chamberlain) Y.; m. Carolyn I. Zuppann, June 15, 1965; children: Donald, Stephen, Jennifer, Melissa, Brian, Robert, Michael. BS magna cum laude in Econs., U. Utah, 1965; MBA with hons., Harvard U., 1967. Chartered investment counselor. Trainee Continental Bank, Chgo., 1967-68; assoc. Stein Roe & Farnham, Chgo., 1968-74, ptnr., 1974-82; pres. Selected Am. Shares, 1982—92; sr. v.p. Prescott Asset Mgmt., 1982-92; pres. Yacktman Asset Mgmt. Co., Buffalo Grove, Ill., 1992—, CIO, 1992—. Past pres. N.W. Suburban coun. Boy Scouts Am. Named Portfolio Mgr. of Yr., Morningstar Mag., 1991. Mem. Investment Analysis Soc. Chgo. Office: Yacktman Asset Mgmt Co 1110 Lake Cook Rd Ste 385 Buffalo Grove IL 60089

YACKTMAN, STEPHEN, investment company executive; BS in Econs., Brigham Young U.; MBA in Fin., Brigham Young Y., 1993. Co-mgr. funds Yacktman Asset Mgmt. Co., Buffalo Grove, Ill., 1993—. Bd. dir. 1-800 CONTACTS. Office: Yacktman Asset Management Co 1110 Lake Cook Rd Ste 385 Buffalo Grove IL 60089*

YACOUB, IGNATIUS I. university dean; b. Dwar Taha, Syria, Jan. 5, 1937; came to U.S. 1978; s. Immanuel and Martha (Kharma) Y.; m. Mary Haddad, Sept. 14, 1961; children: Hilda, Lena, Emile. AB, Mid. East Coll., Beirut, Lebanon, 1960; MA, Pacific Union Coll., Angwin, Calif., 1964; PhD, Claremont Grad. Sch., Calif., 1976. Dean studies Mid. East Coll., Beirut, 1967-73, 75-78; dir. dept. edn. Afro-Mideast divsn. Seventh-Day Adventist Ch., 1970-73, dir. dept. pub. affairs, 1975-78; prof., chmn. dept. bus. econs. Southwestern Union Coll., Keene, Tex., 1978-80; prof., chmn. dept. bus. and econs. Loma Linda U., Riverside, Calif., 1980-86, founding dean Sch. of Bus. and Mgmt., 1986-90, prof. mgmt., 1995—; founding dean Sch. Bus. and Mgmt., La Sierra U., Riverside, 1990—95; prof. adminstrn. and mgmt. Loma Linda U., Loma Linda, Calif., 1995—. Bd. dirs. Riverside Nat. Bank; bd. advisors City Nat. Bank, 1997—2003. Mem. Exec. 2000 Coun. Riverside Cmty. Hosp. Found., 1991-95. Recipient Gov.'s Appreciation award, Lions Club, Lions Club award, Beirut, cert. Appreciation Exec. 2000 Coun., 1994, 95, Cert. of Appreciation Claremont Grad. Sch. Alumni Coun., 1996, Mentemoreles Univ. Mex., 1992, 94. Mem. Am. Mgmt. Assn., Acad. Mgmt., Soc. for Advancement Mgmt., Greater Riverside C. of C. (Svc. award 1995), Corona C. of C. Seventh-Day Adventist. Home: 2722 Litchfield Dr Riverside CA 92503-6213 Office Phone: 909-558-7148. E-mail: iyacoub@charter.net.

YACOUB, JEAN, cardiologist; s. Adeeb Yacoub and Werjine Saliba; m. Rima Baho, Jan. 31, 1993. MD, Aleppo U., Syria, 1985. Diplomate Am. Bd. of Internal Medicine with subspecialty in nuclear cardiology, 1994, Nat. Bd. of Echocardiography, 2001. Chief of med. staff Commonwealth Health Ctr., Saipan, 1999—2001; dir. of cardiac catheterization lab. Heart and Vascular Inst. of Guam, Tamuning, 2002—03; dir. of cardiology svc. Guam meml. Hosp., Tamuning, 2003—. Contbr. articles to profl. jours. Mem. St. Matthews Ch., West Roxbury, Mass., 1996—97. Recipient Recognition Award for Dedication and Commitment in Profl. Med. Edn., Guam Acad. of Family Physicians, 2002, Recognition and Memorialization for outstanding med. svcs., Mcpl. Coun. of Saipan and No. Islands, 2000. Fellow: Mass. Med. Soc., Am. Coll. of Cardiology; mem.: Guam Med. Soc., Am. Soc. of Nuc. Cardiology, Am. Soc. of Echocardiography. Syrian Orthodox. Avocations: swimming, classical music, travel. Office Phone: 671-647-6652.

YACOWITZ, HAROLD, biochemist, nutritionist; b. N.Y.C., Feb. 17, 1922; s. Louis and Clara (Kurtzberg) Y.; m. Ann Ruth Barnett, Dec. 31, 1941; children: Caryn R., Richard S., Suzanne Yacowitz Dragan. BS, M in Nutritional Sci., Cornell U., 1948, PhD, 1950. Rsch. biochemist Parke-Davis Inc., Detroit, 1950-51; assoc. prof. Ohio State U., Columbus, 1951-55; head nutrition rsch. dept. Squibb Inst. for Med. Rsch., New Brunswick, N.J., 1955-59; dir. rsch. Nopco Chem. Co. Inc., Harrison, N.J., 1959-61, Amburgo Co. Inc., Phila., 1961-80; rsch. assoc. Fairleigh Dickinson U., Madison, N.J., 1961-80; pres., dir. rsch. Dr. H. Yacowitz & Co., Piscataway, N.J., 1961—, Animal Identification & Marking Systems Inc., Piscataway, 1982-97. Pres. Peninsula Investment & Devel. Inc., Cambridge, Md., 1961—; pres., bd. dirs. rsch. Drug Delivery Devices Inc., Piscataway, 1991—. Contbr. articles to profl. jours.; patentee in field. Leader Boy Scouts Am., Ithaca, N.Y., 1946-50, Piscataway, 1955-59. With U.S. Army, 1943-46, ETO, PTO. Grange League Fedn. fellow Cornell U., 1947-48, Robert Gould rsch. fellow, Cornell U., 1949-50, Coun. on Arteriosclerosis fellow Am. Heart Assn., 1970. Fellow N.Y. Acad. Scis. (chmn. sect. biology and medicine 1972-76); mem. Am. Chem. Soc., Am. Inst. Nutrition, Am. Assn. Lab. Animal Scientists, Exptl. Investors Club (New Brunswick, pres. 1955-59). Jewish. Avocations: gardening, sailing, fishing, swimming. Office: Drug Delivery Devices Inc 221 2nd Ave Piscataway NJ 08854-3519 Office Phone: 732-356-9366. E-mail: halyacowitz@webtv.net.

YADEKA, THEOPHILUS ADENIYI, hospital administrator; b. Ibadan, Nigeria, Apr. 16, 1939; came to U.S., 1971; s. Joshua A. and Alice (Opawole) Y.; m. Julianah M., Aug. 23, 1965; children: Olatunde, Mofoluke, Ayoola, Mobolaji, Adedoja. Diploma, S.D.A. Nursing Sch., 1965, SUNY, 1972; BS in Healthcare Adminstrn., St. Francis Coll., 1976; MS in Healthcare & Hosp. Adminstrn., L.I. U., 1977. Lic. pvt. sch. tchr. clin. instr. Charge and staff nurse Met. City Hosp., N.Y.C., 1971—74, Barnabas Hosps., N.Y.C., 1974—77; prin. hosp. adminstr. Ministry of Health/State Hosp. Mgmt. Bd., Ibadan, Nigeria, 1978-85; asst. chief hosp. adminstr. State Hosps. Mgmt. Bd., Ibadan, Nigeria, 1985-89; asst. DON Lincoln Hosp., Bronx, NY, 1977—78, 1989-90; asst. dir. Bronx Lebanon Hosp. Ctr., 1990—95; clin. instr., healthcare cons., 1999—. Fellow Internat. Biog. Ctr. Eng.; mem. Am. Coll. Hosp. Adminstrs., Am. Coll. Nursing Home Adminstrs., Inst. Health Svc. Adminstrs. Nigeria. Home: Bronx GPO 496 Bronx NY 10451 Office: Bronx Lebanon Hosp Ctr Bronx NY 10457

YADRICK, ROBERT MARTIN, occupational analyst; b. Kansas City, Mo., Oct. 24, 1949; s. John George and Joanne Jean Yadrick; m. Patricia Eileen (Koelzer), May 30, 1986 (div. 2004); children: Lauren Nicole, John Nicholas. BA, Rockhurst Coll., 1971; MA, U. Mo., 1973, PhD, 1975. Cert. profl. ergonomist Bd. Certification in Profl. Ergonomics, Inc. Asst. prof. psychology Columbia (Mo.) Coll., 1975-78; rsch. assoc. U. Mo., Columbia, 1978-79; sr. rsch. assoc. Ctrl.-N.E. Colo. Health Sys. Agy., Inc., Denver, 1979-82; sr. human factors engr. McDonnell Douglas Corp., St. Louis, 1982-90; rsch. scientist Metrica, Inc., San Antonio, 1991; pers. rsch. psychologist USAF Rsch. Lab., Brooks AFB, Tex., 1991-99; occupl. analyst USAF, Randolph AFB, Tex., 1999—, quality assurance mgr., 2001—03. Adj. lectr. U. Tex. San Antonio, Our Lady of the Lake U., St. Mary's U., Wayland Bapt. Univ.; editor newsletter Insight, Human Factors and Ergonomics Soc., Santa Monica, Calif., 1994-96, reviewer visual performance tech. group, 1995-97; reviewer jour. Behavior Rsch. Methods, Instruments and Computers, 1996. Contbr. articles to profl. jours. Mentor, tutor Judson Sch. Dist., San Antonio, 1999—. Recipient Lab. Dir.'s award Armstrong Lab., 1996. Mem.: Sigma Xi. Avocations: flying, hiking, water sports. Personal E-mail: sloper52@aol.com. Business E-Mail: robert.yadrick@randolph.af.mil.

YAFFA, JACK BER, healthcare administrator, educator, surgeon; b. Camden, N.J., Apr. 28, 1941; s. Harry and Rose (Plotkin) Y.; m. Phyllis A. Pollack, June 21, 1964; children: Andrew, Samuel, Jodi, Gregory. BA, U. Richmond, 1963; MD, Med. Coll. of Va., 1968. Cert. Am. Bd. Surgery; cert. Fla. Bd. Med. Examiners, Va. Bd. Med. Examiners. Surg. intern U. Miami (Fla.) Med. Ctr., 1968-69, surg. resident, 1969-73, chief resident in surgery, 1972-73; pvt. practice in gen.-vascular surgery Miami, 1973-95; assoc. chief of staff ambulatory care Miami VA Med. Ctr., 1995—2001, chief emergency svc.; asst. prof. clin. surgery U. Miami Med. Sch., 1995—2001, asst. prof. clin. medicine, 1998—; med. dir. Baptist Hosp. Miami, 2001—, dir. hospitalist program, 2004—. Chief med. officer Oakland Park Outpatient Clinic, Dept. VA Med. Ctr.; asst. chief of surgery Bapt. Hosp. Miami, 1978-79, chief of surgery, 1980-81, 91-93, chief of cardiac surgery, 1982-84, chief of trauma surgery, 1983, chmn. peripheral vascular lab., 1982-83, chief of staff, 1984-88, adminstrv. dir. critical care, 1988-92; active staff South Miami Hosp.; mem. governing bd. emergency med. svcs. tng. U. Miami Sch. Medicine, 1989-95. Fellow ACS (gov.-at-large 1990, bd. govs. 1991-96, instr. advanced trauma life support 1981-93, mem. state com. trauma 1985-93, sec.-treas. Miami chpt. 1983-85, pres. Miami chpt. 1985-87, councilor Miami chpt. 1990-92); mem. AMA, Fla. Med. Assn. (com. on emergency med. svcs., coun. on hosp. med. staffs), Fla. Surg. Soc. (bd. dirs. 1990—), South Fla. Noninvasive Vascular Soc., Miami Surg. Soc., Jackson Surg. Soc., Dade County Med. Assn., Soc. Laparendoscopic Surgeons, Southeastern Surg. Congress, So. Med. Congress (assoc. councilor 1989), Surg. Hist. Soc. Jewish. Avocations: boating, fishing. Office: Miami VA Med Ctr 1201 NW 16th St Miami FL 33125-1624

YAFFE, BARBARA MARLENE, journalist; b. Montreal, Que., Can., Mar. 4, 1953; d. Allan and Anne (Freedman) Y.; m. Wilson E. Russell, Aug. 30, 1985. Student, McGill U., 1970-73; BA, U. Toronto, 1974; B in Journalism, Carleton U., 1975. Reporter Montreal Gazette, 1975-76, Toronto Globe and Mail, 1976-79, reporter, columnist, 1979-81; chief nat. TV news bur. CBC, St. Johns, Canada, 1981-84, Edmonton, Canada, 1983; reporter Toronto Globe and Mail, St. John's, 1984-86; editor Sunday Express, St. John's, 1987-88, Vancouver Sun, 1988-93, columnist, edit. bd. adv., 1993—. Recipient Gov. Gen.'s award Roland Michener Found., 1977. Office: c/o Vancouver Sun Ste 1 200 Granville St Vancouver BC Canada V6C 3N3 Office Phone: 604-605-2189. E-mail: byaffe@png.canwest.com.

YAFFE, JAMES, writer; b. Chgo., Mar. 31, 1927; s. Samuel and Florence (Scheinman) Y.; m. Elaine Gordon, Mar. 1, 1964; children: Deborah Ann, Rebecca Elizabeth, Gideon Daniel. Grad., Fieldston Sch., 1944; BA summa cum laude, Yale U., 1948. Prof. Colo. Coll., Colo. Springs, 1968—2002, prof. emeritus, 2002—. Author: Poor Cousin Evelyn, 1951, The Good-for-Nothing, 1953, What's the Big Hurry?, 1954, Nothing But the Night, 1959, Mister Margolies, 1962, Nobody Does You Any Favors, 1966, The American Jews, 1968, The Voyage of the Franz Joseph, 1970, So Sue Me!, 1972, Saul and Morris, Worlds Apart, 1982, A Nice Murder for Mom, 1988, Mom Meets Her Maker, 1990, Mom Doth Murder Sleep, 1991, Mom Among the Liars, 1992, My Mother the Detective, 1997; play The Deadly Game, 1960, (with Jerome Weidman) Ivory Tower, 1967, Cliffhanger, 1985; also TV plays, stories, essays, revs. Served with USNR, 1945-46. Recipient Nat. Arts Found award, 1968 Mem. P.E.N., Authors League, Writers Guild of Am., Dramatists Guild, A.A.U.P., Mystery Writers of Am., Phi Beta Kappa. Clubs: Elizabethan (Yale). Jewish. Avocations: music, bridge, movies. Home: 12 W 72 St New York NY 10023

YAFFE, STUART ALLEN, physician; b. Springfield, Ill., July 6, 1927; m. Natalie, 1952; children: Scott, Kim Yaffe Schoenburg. BS cum laude, U. Alaska, 1951; MD, St. Louis U., 1956. Diplomate Am. Bd. Family Practice. Intern St. Louis CIty Hosp., 1956-57, resident, 1957-58; physician pvt. practice, 1958—; clin. assoc. prof. So. Ill. U. Sch. Medicine., Springfield, 1971—; ptnr. Springfield Clinic, 1989—. With U.S. Army, 1945-47. Mem. AMA, Am. Acad. Family Physicians, Ill. Acad. Family Physicians, Ill. State Med. Soc., Sangamon County Med. Soc. Office: 1100 Centre West Dr Springfield IL 62704-2100

YAFFE, SUMNER JASON, pediatrician, educator, science administrator; b. Boston, May 9, 1923; s. Henry H. and Ida E. (Fisher) Yaffe; children: Steven, Kris, Jason, Noah, Ian, Zachary. AB, Harvard U., 1945, MA, 1950; MD, U. Vt., 1954. Diplomate Am. Bd. Pediatrics. Rsch. fellow in pharmacology U. Vt. Coll. Medicine, Burlington, 1950—52; intern in pediat. Children's Hosp., Boston, 1954—55, resident, 1955-56; resident in pediatrics St. Mary's Hosp., London, 1956-57; instr. pediatrics Stanford U., Palo Alto, Calif., 1959-60, asst. prof., 1960-63; assoc. prof. pediatrics SUNY-Buffalo, 1963-66, prof., 1966-75, adj. prof. biochem. pharmacology, 1968-75, acting chmn. dept. pediatrics, 1974-75; prof. pediatrics and pharmacology U. Pa., Phila., 1975-81; clin. prof. pediat. Johns Hopkins Hosp., 1986—2001; vis. prof. pediat. UCLA Sch. Medicine, 2001—. Vis. prof. pharmacology Karolinska Inst., Stockholm, 1969—70; dir. Pediat. Renal Clinic, Stanford Med. Ctr., 1960—63; dir. newborn nursery svc. Palo Alto-Stanford Hosp., 1960—63, program dir. Clin. Rsch. Ctr. for Premature Infants, 1962—63; dir. Clin. Rsch. Ctr. for Children Children's Hosp., Buffalo, 1963—70, dir. Poison Control Ctr., 1967—75, dir. divsn. clin. pharmacology, Phila., 1975—81; dir. Ctr. for Rsch. for Mothers and Children Nat. Inst. Child Health and Human Devel., NIH, 1981—2001, program cons., 1963—71, mem. tng. grant com., 1963—65, mem. reproductive biology com., 1965—67; mem. adv. panel on maternal and child health WHO, Geneva, 1970—; liaison rep. drug rsch. bd. NRC, 1971—75, com. on drug dependence, 1972—75, mem. com. on problems of drug safety, 1972—75; mem. adv. panel in pediat. U.S. Pharmacopeia, 1970—, mem. adv. panel in toxicology, 1974—75; cons. Am. Found. for Maternal and Child Health, Inc., 1973—; pres. Maternal and Child Health Rsch. Found., Children's Hosp., 1974—75; Wall Meml. lectr. Children's Hosp., Washington, 1968—; Dr. W.E. Upjohn lectr. Can. Med. Assn., 1974; Louisville pediat. lectr. Sch. Medicine U. Louisville, 1974; William N. Creasy vis. prof. clin. pharmacology SUNY, 1976; advisor Internat. Childbirth Assn. Greater Phila., 1979—83; guest lectr. dept. pediat. Georgetown U. Hosp., Washington, 1988—2001; lectr. in pediat. Johns Hopkins Sch. Medicine, Balt., 1988—2001; mem. Roundtable on Drug Devel., Inst. of Medicine. Author: (book) Clinics in Perinatology, 1974, Drug Assessment: Criteria and Methods, 1979, Pediatric Pharmacology, 1980, Pediatric Pharmacology, 2d edit., 1992; author: (with R. Galinsky) Clinical Therapeutics, 1978; editor (with R. H. Schwartz): Drug and Chemical Risks to the Fetus and Newborn, 1980; editor: (with G. G. Briggs, T. w. Bodendorfer, R. K. Freeman) Drugs in Pregnancy and Lactatin, A Reference Guide to Fetal and Neonatal Risk, 1983, Drugs in Pregnancy and Lactatin, A Reference Guide to Fetal and Neonatal Risk, 2d, edit., 1986, Drugs in Pregnancy and Lactatin, A Reference Guide to Fetal and Neonatal Risk, 4th edit., 1994, Drugs in Pregnancy and Lactatin, A Reference Guide to Fetal and Neonatal Risk, 5th edit., 1998; editor: (with J. V. Aranda) Pediatric Phyarmacology, 2d edit., 1993, Neonatal and Pediatric Pharmacology, 3d edit., 2004; mem. editl. bd.: Pediatric Alert, 1977—, Pharmacology, 1977—, Devel. Pharmacology and Therapeutics, 1979—95, mem. editl. adv. bd.: Drug Therapy, 1979—, cons. editor: Clin. Pharacokinetics, 1977; co-editor: Developmental Pharmacology, 1979—94; contbr. articles to profl. jours. With U.S. Army, 1943—44. Recipient Oscar Hunter award, ASCPT, 2002, Sumner J. Yaffe award, PPAG, 2002; scholar Fulbright, 1956—57. Fellow: Acad. Pharm. Scis.; mem.: AAUP, AMA (com. on drugs 1963—68), Soc. Pediat. Rsch., Perinatal Rsch. Soc., Fedn. Am. Socs. Exptl. Biology, Am. Soc. Pharmacology and Exptl. Therapeutics, Am. Soc. Clin. Pharmacology and Therapeutics (chmn. sect. pediatric pharmacology 1977—83), Am. Pub. Health Assn., Soc. Maternal Fetal Medicine (hon.), Am. Pharmaceutics Assn., Am. Pediat. Soc., Am. Fedn. for Clin. Rsch., Am. Coll. Clin. Pharmacology and Chemotherapy, Am. Acad. Pediat. (chmn. com. drugs 1967—76), Alpha Omega Alpha, Sigma Xi. Home: 416 Comstock Ave Los Angeles CA 90024 Office: UCLA Sch Medicine Dept Pediats 10833 Le Conte Ave Los Angeles CA 90095-3075 Office Phone: 310-825-2575. Personal E-mail: sjyla@aol.com.

YAGAHASHI, TAKASHI, chef; C. chef Tribute, Farmington Hills, Mich., 1996—. Named Best Restaurant in Detroit, NY Times; named one of America's Best Restaurants, Gourmet mag.; recipient award, James Beard Found., 2001. Office: Tribute 31425 W 12 Mile Rd Farmington Hills MI 48334

YAGER, JOSEPH ARTHUR, JR., economist; b. Owensville, Ind., Apr. 14, 1916; s. Joseph Arthur and Edna (Pratt) Y.; m. Virginia Estella Beroset, Sept. 2, 1938; children: Thomas, Martha. AB, U. Mich., 1937, JD, 1939, MA, 1940; grad., Nat. War Coll., 1955. Economist OPA, 1942-44; economist State Dept., 1946-47, chief China research br., 1949-50, chief div. rsch. for Far East, 1952—57; attaché U.S. consulate gen., Canton, China, 1947-48, consul Hong Kong, 1950-51; econ. counselor Taipei, 1957-59; dep. chief of mission, 1959-61; dir. Office Chinese Affairs, 1961, Office East Asian Affairs, 1961-63; mem. Policy Planning Council, 1963-66, vice chmn., 1966-68; dep. dir. internat. and social studies div. Inst. Def. Analyses, 1968-72; sr. fellow Brookings Instn., 1972-83, guest scholar, 1983-86; resident cons. Sci. Applications Internat. Corp., 1986-89, sr. fellow, 1989-96; cons., 1996—. Author: Transforming Agriculture in Taiwan, 1988, Prospects for Nuclear Weapons Proliferation in a Changing Europe, 1992; co-author: Energy and U.S. Foreign Policy, 1974, New Means of Financing International Needs, 1978, Military Equation in Northeast Asia, 1979, Nonproliferation and U.S. Foreign Policy, 1980, International Cooperation in Nuclear Energy, 1981, Energy Balance in Northeast Asia, 1984, Energy Policy Experience of Asian Countries, 1987. Served in AUS, 1944-45. Mem. Phi Delta Phi, Delta Tau Delta. Home: 10450 Lottsford Rd #5109 Bowie MD 20721 Office Phone: 301-541-5094.

YAGER, THOMAS C. retired judge; b. L.A., Feb. 16, 1918; s. Thomas C. and May M. (McGowan) Yager; m. Antonia M. Gussenhoven, Nov. 2, 2000. AB in pol. sci., UCLA, 1939, gen. secondary lifetime tchg. credential, 1940; JD, USC, 1948; LLD, Western State U., Calif., 1972. Reader UCLA Philosophy Dept., 1940; atty. L.A., 1949-57; legal advisor Gov. Calif., 1957, 58; superior ct. sr. judge, 1959-78; founder Cmty. Betterment Svc., L.A. Author: numerous legal and religious books; contbr. articles to profl. jours. Founder Judge Thomas C. Yager Found., L.A., Cmty. Betterment Svc., L.A. Maj. U.S. Army, 1942—46. Office: The Cmty Betterment Svc 108 N Gower St Los Angeles CA 90004-3828 E-mail: pvtsecty@aol.com.

YAGER, VINCENT COOK, bank executive; b. Chgo., June 15, 1928; s. James Vincent and Juanita (Cook) Yager; m. Dorothy Marie Gallagher, Sept. 28, 1957; children: Susan Marie, Sheila Ann. BA, Grinnell Coll., 1951. Asst. cashier Chgo. Nat. Bank, 1954-60, Harris Trust & Savs. Bank, Chgo., 1960-63; v.p. comml. loan dept. Madison Bank & Trust, Chgo., 1963-68; v.p. fin. Cor-Plex Internat. Corp., Chgo., 1968-70; pres., CEO, dir. First Nat. Bank Blue Island, Ill., 1970-89; pres., CEO Great Lakes Fin. Resources, Inc., Matteson, Ill., 1982-96, also bd. dirs. With U.S. Army, 1951—53, ETO. Mem.: Econ. Club Chgo., Bankers Club Chgo., Robert Morris Assocs. (pres. chpt. 1981—82), Midlothian Country Club, Rotary. Home: 1032 S Rand Rd Villa Park IL 60181-3145 Office: Great Lakes Bank Blue Island 13057 S Western Ave Blue Island IL 60406-2418

YAGLE, ANDREW EMIL, engineering educator; b. Ann Arbor, Mich., Sept. 17, 1956; s. Raymond Arthur and Anne Joan Yagle. BSEE, U. Mich., 1978; PhD, MS in Engring., MIT, 1985. Exxon tchg. fellow MIT, Cambridge, Mass., 1982—85; prof. elec. engring. U. Mich., Ann Arbor, 1985—. Chief program advisor Elec. Engring. U. Mich., 2001—04. Contbr. numerous tech. papers to profl. jours. Recipient Presdl. Young Investigator award, NSF, 1988—93, Young Investigator award, Office of Naval Rsch., 1990—93. Mem.: IEEE (mem.-at-large, bd. govs. Signal Processing Soc. 1998—2000). Office: U Mich 1301 Beal Ave Ann Arbor MI 48109-2122 Office Fax: 734-763-1503. Business E-Mail: aey@eecs.umich.edu.

YAGODA, HARRY NATHAN, system engineering executive; b. Bklyn., May 19, 1936; s. Hyman and Sylvia (Yoskowitz) Y.; m. Myrna Rita Hirschel; children: Michelle Robin, Randi Noelle. BSEE, CUNY, 1958; MSEE, NYU, 1960; PhDEE, Poly. U. N.Y., 1963. Registered profl. engr. 19 states including N.Y., N.J., Calif. Mem. tech. staff AT&T Bell Labs., Whippany, N.J., 1958-62; assoc. prof. engring. Poly. U. N.Y., Bklyn., 1962-70; pres. Computran Systems Corp., Hackensack, N.J., 1970—. Named Disting. Alumnus, Poly. U. N.Y., 1980. Fellow Inst. Transp. Engring. (bd. dirs. 1982-84). Home: 2077 Center Ave Fort Lee NJ 07024-4901 Office: Computran Systems Corp 100 1st St Hackensack NJ 07601-2124

YAHALOM, JOACHIM, radiologist, educator, oncologist, researcher; b. Tel Aviv, Dec. 21, 1949; came to U.S., 1985; s. Lipa and Lea Yahalom; m. Judith Yahalom; children: Shira, Roni, Tali, Orlee. MD, Hebrew U., Jerusalem, 1976. Diplomate Am. Bd. Radiation Oncology. Lectr. Hebrew U., 1982-86; asst. attending physician Meml. Sloan-Kettering, N.Y.C., 1985-92, assoc. attending physician, 1992-97, attending physician, 1997—; asst. prof. Cornell U., N.Y.C., 1987-93, assoc. prof., 1993-98, prof., 1998—. Tenured mem. Meml. Sloan-Kettering Cancer Ctr., N.Y.C., 1997—, co-leader Lymphoma Disease Mgmt. Team, 1998. Contbr. articles to profl. jours.; mem. editl. bd. Leukemia & Lymphoma, 1991—. Served with Israel Def. Forces, 1980-85. Recipient clin. rsch. prize Astro/Varian, 1990; named one of Best Drs. in Am., Woodward/White, 1994-95, Castle Connoly, 1996-2004. Mem. Am. Assn. Cancer Rsch., Am. Soc. Clin. Oncology, Am. Soc. Therapeutic Radiology and Oncology, Am. Soc. Hematology, Am. Coll. Radiology, Am. Radium Soc. Office: Meml Sloan Kettering Cancer Ctr 1275 York Ave New York NY 10021 Home: 351 E 51st St #14c New York NY 10022-6702 E-mail: yahalomj@mskcc.org.

YAHN, MIMI, writer; b. NYC, June 16, 1954; d. Erle Brierly Yahn and Annette Norma Nagin; m. Vernon Marquez Cope, Jan. 27, 1993. Project coord. Agt. Orange Veterans Adv. Com., Berkeley, Calif., 1979—80; dir. Agt. Orange Info. Ctr., San Francisco, 1980—81; editor, pub. The Feminist Broadcast Quar. of Oreg., Portland, Oreg., 1992—94, The Swiftian Report, West Mifflin, Pa., 2003—. Writer, prodr. KBOO-FM, Portland, 1986—87; musical dir. Raging Grannnies, Pitts., 2003—; spkr., panelist, lectr. in field. Editor (graphic designer): The Feminist Broadcast Quarterly of Oregon; composer (singer): numerous political and satirical songs; prodr.(writer): (radio series) The American Chronicles: The Rise and Fall of Hollywood D.C.; author: Chloracne, Guide to Agent Orange, Annotated Bibliography of 2, 4-D, The Swiftian Report; columnist: Gulf War Revue. Steering com. mem. Nat. Veterans Task Force Agt. Orange, St. Louis, 1980—81; master gardener LSU Ext. Svc., New Orleans, 1998—2000, Pa., 2004—; brigade mem. Ben Linder Constrn. Brigade, Portland, 1989—91; steering com. mem. Californians Against Proposition 41, San Francisco, 1984—84; organizer, moderator town hall meetings The Feminist Broadcast Quar. Oreg., Portland, 1992—94; moderator at town halls meetings on the Balkans New Orleans, 1999—99; bd. dirs. Veterans Career Svcs., San Francisco, 1982—82, Portland Corinto Sister City Assn., Portland, 1991—91; legis. com. mem. Assn. Retarded Citizens, San Francisco, 1984—86. Achievements include development of objective methodology for determining and quantifying hate speech and bias language in the popular media; feminist theory of the Gender Minstrel Show; research in methodology for measuring gender statistics in Hollywood films; chloracne. Avocations: singing, gardening, cooking, photography, dance.

YAHYA, MUHAMMAD JAVAID, financial consultant, economist; b. Lahore, Panjab, Pakistan, Mar. 21, 1945; came to U.S., 1971; s. Mohammed Raza Shamsi and Syeda Zamina Khatoon; m. Ansa S. Yahya, June 19, 1971; children: Sofia, Sadia, Daniel. MS in Chem. Tech., U. Panjab, Lahore, 1967, MA in Econs., 1970; MBA, Pace U., 1978; advanced studies in banking, Am. Inst. of Banking, 1979; diploma in bank mktg., U. Colo., 1980. Sr. officer Muslim Comml. Bank, Lahore, 1967-71; asst. mgr. Habib Bank Ltd., n.Y.C., 1971-73; asst. treas. Bankers Trust Co., N.Y.C., 1973-79, asst. v.p., 1979-82, v.p., 1982-91; asst. v.p. Merrill Lynch, East Brunswick, N.J., 1991—. Advisor DHL Internat. Ltd., N.Y.C., 1983-85. Gen. sec. Am. Muslim Assn., N.J., 1995-97. Republican. Moslem. Avocations: stamps, coins, poetry, travel, economics. Home: 857 Inman Ave Edison NJ 08820-1236 Office: Merrill Lynch 197 Route 18 Ste 301 East Brunswick NJ 08816-1400

YAKE, SARAH LOUISE, poet; b. Bryn Mawr, Pa., Mar. 15, 1968; d. George Robert Yake and Doris Helen Kouba; m. Timothy Alan Seasholtz, Sept. 11, 1999; 1 child, Evelyn Jane Seasholtz. BA, Ea. U., 1990; MA, West Chester U., 2001. Mgr. Encore Books, Wayne, Pa., 1994—96; corp. account exec. Random Ho., Inc., Boston, 1996—98, sales rep. Westminster, Md., 1998—99. Poet: published in print anthologies & online. Home: 23 Moreland Rd Paoli PA 19301 Personal E-mail: slyyake@comcast.net.

YAKES, PENNY ANNE, advocate, writer; b. Westport, Conn., Jan. 2, 1948; d. Emmett Patrick and Agnes Anne Toal; m. David Craig Yakes, Aug. 16, 1969; children: Tyler Craig, Kasey Anne, Nealy Corcoran. Student, Mary Mount U., 1966—67. Author: (journal) Anorexia Nervosa, A Mother's Story, (short stories) Beyond The Silent Cry Of Anorexia. Recipient hon. mention, Writer's Digest, 2003. Mem.: Families And Parents Action Com. Eating Disorders, Anorexia Nervosa And Associated Disorders (state rep. and resouce person), Coalition Fairness Mental Illness and Substance Abuse (steering com., lobbyist). Non-Partisan. Catholic. Achievements include Advocate for families seeking treatment and funding for eating disorders. Avocations: prevention, awareness and the education of eating disorders, the proper and necessary treatment of eating disorders, to establish a national foundation for the funding of residential treatment of eating disorders, to end the stigma and discrimination of mental illness and substance abuse. Home: 10223 N Pearson Rd Hayward WI 54843 Personal E-mail: pyakes@pressenter.com.

YAKLIN, LORI STILLWAGON, government agency administrator; BBA, U. Mich.; M in Adminstrn., Ctrl. Mich. U. Founding exec. dir. Mich. Sch. Bd. Leaders Assn.; dir. Sch. Choice Office of the Under Sec. U.S. Dept. Edn., sr. advisor on family ednl. rights Office of Innovation and Improvement. Spkr. in field. Office: US Dept Edn FOB-6 Rm 7E306 400 Maryland Ave Washington DC 20202

YAKSH, TONY L. pharmacologist, educator, health facility administrator; b. San Angelo, Tex., June 14, 1944; BS, Ga. Inst. Tech., 1966; MS, U. Ga., 1968; PhD, Purdue U., 1971. NDEA Title IV fellow U. Gal., Athens, 1966—67; rsch. asst. in neuropsychology Purdue U., Lafayette, Ind., 1967—68, tchg. asst. in physiol. psychology, 1968—69, NIH predoctoral fellow in neurobiology, 1969—70, Nat. Inst. Mental Health predoctoral rsch. fellow, head rsch. fellow lab. neuropsychology, 1970—71; rsch. psychologist biomed. lab. U.S. Army, Edgewood Arsenal, Md., 1971—73; rsch. assoc. U. Wis. Sch. Pharmacy, Madison, 1973—74; pharmacologist, GS-11 cons. biomed. lab. U.S. Army, Edgewood Arsenal, Md., 1973—74; asst. scientist U. Wis. Sch. Pharmacy, Madison, 1974—76; rsch. assoc. neurol. surgery dept. Mayo Clinic, Rochester, Minn., 1977—78, assoc. cons. neurol. surgery and pharmacology depts., 1978—80; assoc. prof. pharmacology Mayo Med. Sch., Rochester, 1981—83, prof. pharmacology, 1984—88; vice chmn. for rsch. in anesthesiology U. Calif.-San Diego, La Jolla, 1988—, prof. anesthesiology, 1988—. Cons. neurol. surgery dept. Mayo Clinic, Rochester, 1980—88; dir. Mayo Clinic, Lab. Neurosurg. Rsch., neurosci. study sect. NIH, Bethesda, Md., 1984—88; interim dir. Mayo Clinic, GI Hormone Rsch. Lab., Rochester, Minn., 1985—88; adj. prof. pharmacology U. Calif.-San Diego Sch. Medicine, La Jolla, 1988—2000; group mem. dept. neuroscis. U. Calif.-San Diego, La Jolla, 1991—; mem., co-leader Symptom Control Cancer Ctr. Program, La Jolla, 1997—; prof. pharmacology U. Calif.-San Diego Sch. Medicine, La Jolla, 2000; chmn. Anesthesiology Rsch. Adv. Group. Assoc. editor: Pain, 1989—93, Anesthesiology, 1990—95, mem. editl. bd.: Regional Anesthesiology, 1992—, mem. editl. adv. bd.: APS Jour., 1993—94, Pain Forum, 1995—99, mem. editl. bd.: Pain Revs., 1999—, mem. editl. adv. bd.: Jour. of Pain, 2000—. Recipient rsch. grants in field, Hehre lectr., Soc. Ob. Anesthesiology and Perinatology, 1988, Bristol-Myers Unrestricted Grant award, 1988, Janssen Rsch. award, Mt. Sinai Med. Ctr., 1988, Javitz award in neurosci., Nat. Inst. Neurol., Communicative Diseases and Stroke, 1988, John J. Bonica award/lectr., Ea. Pain Assn., 1993, Benjamin J. Covino Meml. lectr., Brigham and Womens Hosp., 1996, Award for Outstanding Contbns. to Pain Medicine, Am. Acad. Pain Medicine, 1998, John Liebeskind award for pain rsch., Am. Acad. Pain Mgmt., 1999. Mem.: AAAS, Soc. for Neurosci., Am. Pain Soc., Internat. Assn. for Study of Pain, Am. Soc. Anesthesiology, Calif. Soc. Anesthesiologists, Inc., Assn. Univ. Anesthesiologists, Am. Soc. Pharmacology and Exptl. Therapeutics, Soc. Toxicology, Am. Soc. Regional Anesthesia (hon.), Am. Soc. Regional Anesthesia (assoc.). Office: U Calif San Diego Sch Medicine Dept Anesthesiology 9500 Gilman Dr La Jolla CA 92093

YAKUBOVICH, LIDIA, physician; b. Russia, Dec. 17, 1936; arrived in U.S., 1981; d. Alexander and Na Schulimovich; widowed; 1 child. Physician USSR Hosp., Russia, 1959—73, Israel Med. Office, 1973—81, Raritan Bay Med. Ctr., 1990—. Author: Lily, The Story of a Woman. Home: 56 Oakland Rd Old Bridge NJ 08857-2785

YALAM, ARNOLD ROBERT, allergist, immunologist, consultant; b. N.Y.C., Apr. 1, 1940; s. Herman and Sylvia (Taber) Y.; m. Carol Ann Strocker, June 16, 1964; children: John, Matthew. AB, Johns Hopkins U., 1960; MD, U. Md., Balt., 1964. Diplomate Am. Bd. Internal Medicine, Am. Bd. Allergy and Immunology. Intern Jackson Meml. Hosp., Miami, Fla., 1964-65; resident in internal medicine SUNY Downstate Med. Ctr., Bklyn., 1965-67; fellow Scripps Clinic and Rsch. Found., La Jolla, Calif., 1967-68; cons. allergist and immunologist San Diego, 1970—. Maj. U.S. Army, 1968—70. Fellow Am. Acad. Allergy and Immunoloy; mem. Am. Soc. Addiction Medicine (cert.), San Diego Allergy Soc.

YALDEN, MAXWELL FREEMAN, Canadian diplomat; b. Toronto, Ont., Can., Apr. 12, 1930; s. Frederick and Marie (Smith) Y.; m. Janice Shaw, Jan. 28, 1952; children: Robert, Cicely (dec.). BA, Victoria Coll., U. Toronto, 1952; MA, U. Mich., 1954, PhD, 1956; D.U. (hon.), U. Ottawa; LLD (hon.), Carleton U. With Can. Dept. External Affairs, 1956-69, asst. undersec. state, 1969-73, dep. minister communications, 1973-77, commr. ofcl. langs., 1977-84; Can. amb. to Belgium and Luxembourg, 1984-87; chief commr. Can. Human Rights Comms., Ottawa, 1987—96; elected UN Human Rights Com., 1996—. Decorated companion Order of Can. Office: 52 Crichton St Ottawa ON Canada K1M 1V7

YALE, JOHN PAUL, computer systems developer; b. Uhrichsville, Ohio, Sept. 4, 1945; s. Vernon Elna and Joan (Papworth) Y.; m. Mary Anne Hinkley, Feb. 9, 1966; children: John Vernon, Eric Kendall. AAS, Orange County C.C., 1968; BS, Ohio U., 1971. Dir. Pub. Broadcasting, Athens, Ohio, 1969-71; freelance prodr./dir. GGT, Niantic, Conn., 1971-79; dir. media svcs. L & M Hosps., New London, Conn., 1979-96; dir. sys. devel. C&E group MPTN, Ledyard, Conn., 1996—. Mem. Internat. TV Assn., Internat. Teleconf. Assn., Assn. fo Multimedia Internat., Toastmasters Internat., Project Mgmt. Inst. Home: 38 Sea Spray Ave Niantic CT 06357-3336 Office: 110 Pequot Trail PO Box 3180 Mashantucket CT 06339-3180 E-mail: john@jpyale.com.

YALE (YELEYENIDE-YALE), MELPOMENE FOTINE, anthropologist, archaeologist, art historian, conservator, researcher; b. N.Y.C., Mar. 31, 1963; d. John P. and Serina Yale (Yeleyenide-Yale). *Father John, businessman, was one of the first to aid in the rebuilding of Europe after WWII sending medical relief to Greece without economic recompense. Mother Serina, born 1924 in Moudros Lemnos Greece to Adam Chiros, is a philanthropist who served as president on various charity organizations and as NGO representative to the UN in 1992. She was awarded the highest title of Archon of the Knights of St. Andrew from Patriarch Athenagoras for decades of selfless, important humanitarian work. Her name is inscribed in the rolls of the Knights of St. Andrew at the Patriarchate in Constantinople. She was awarded the Archdiocesan Medal of Saint Paul by Archbishop Iakovos.* BA in Art History, Columbia U., 1985, MA in Art History and Arch., 1998, MA in Anthropology, 2001; studied lithics and flint knapping with Prof. William Parry, Hunter Coll., 2001. Sci. asst. dept. anthropology The Am. Mus. Natural History, N.Y.C., 1987—89, collections mgmt. asst. dept. anthropology, 1989—90; fieldwork archeologist (excavations) Brit. Sch. Arch., Palaikastro, Crete, 1990, 1991; fieldwork archeologist Fordham U., Rose Hill Excavations, NY, 2000; conservator The Benaki Mus., Athens, Greece, 1991, 1992, The Monastery of St. John the Theologian, Patmos, Greece, 1992, The Hispanic Soc. Am., N.Y.C., 1989—93, Brit. Sch. Archeol. Excavations, Palaikastro, Crete, 1990, 1991, Nat. Acad., 1997, Lilly Hollander Conservation Studio, NY, 1998—99, N.Y. Acad. Medicine, NY, 1999, Sherman Faichild Ctr. Objects Conservation, Met. Mus. Art, NY, 2000; pvt. conservator, 1993—; rsch. asst. Ani project Columbia U.-World Monuments Found., NY, 1997; curatorial asst. Nat. Acad. N.Y., 1997; rsch. asst. to prof. emeritus Ralph Solecki and Dr. Rose Solecki Shanidar project Columbia U., 2001—03, coord. Ralph Holloway Endocast collection preservation and rsch. project, 2002—04, ind. rschr. prehistoric collection, 2003—. Mem.: Archeol. Inst. Am., Registered Profl. Archaeologists, Am. Inst. Conservation (profl.), Am. Anthrop. Assn., The Prehistoric Soc. Achievements include research in emergence of human cognition in the Palaeolithic as indicated by stone tools and art; research on brain casting techniques; research towards a PhD on emergence of human cognition in the Palaeolithic Period of Greece and Aegean based on Palaeontological-Palaeonanthropological data, stone tools and art, and their relation; to and their influence throughout the Palaeonanthropogeographic region of Europe and the World. Avocations: flintknapping, mosaics, painting, collecting art, archel. material, and stone tools for study. E-mail: mfy2@columbia.edu.

YALE, SEYMOUR HERSHEL, dental radiologist, educator, university dean, gerontologist; b. Chgo., Nov. 27, 1920; s. Henry and Dorothy (Kulwin) Y.; m. Muriel Jane Cohen, Nov. 6, 1943; children: Russell Steven, Patricia Ruth. BS, U. Ill., 1944, D.D.S., 1945, postgrad., 1947-48, Spertus Inst. Jewish Studies, 1995—. Pvt. practice of dentistry, 1945-54, 56—; asst. clin. dentistry U. Ill., 1948-49, instr. clin. dentistry, 1949-53, asst. prof. clin. dentistry 1953-54, assoc. prof. dept. radiology Coll. Dentistry, 1956, prof., head dept. Coll. Dentistry, 1957-65, adminstrv. asst. to dean Coll. Dentistry, 1961-63, asst. dean Coll. Dentistry, 1963-64, acting dean Coll. Dentistry, 1964-65, dean, 1965-87, dean emeritus, 1987—, also mem. grad. faculty dept. radiology Coll. Medicine, prof. dentistry and health resources mgmt. Sch. Pub. Health, 1987—. Sr. dental dir. Dental Care Plus Mgmt. Corp., Chgo.; pres., dir. dental edn. Dental Care Plus Mgmt. Ednl. Svcs., Ltd.; health care facilities planner; dir. tng. Dental Technicians Sch., U.S. Naval Tng. Ctr., Bainbridge, md., 1954-56; mem. subcom. 16 Nat. Com. on Radiation Protection; mem. Radiation Protection Adv. Bd., State of Ill., 1971, City of Chgo. Health Sys. Agy.; founder Ctr. for Rsch. in Periodontal Disease and Oral Molecular Biology, 1977; organizer, chmn. Nat. Conf. on Hepatitis-B in Dentistry, 1982; organizer, dir. Univ. Taskforce Primary Health Care Project, U. Ill., Chgo.; chmn. U. Ill.-U. Stockholm-U. Gothenberg Conf. on Geriatrics, 1985; dir. planning AMVETS/UIC Tchg. Nursing Home Project, 1987-91; co-sponsor 1st Egyptian Dental Congress, 1984; adj. prof. Ctr. for Exercise Sci. and Cardiovasc. Rsch., Northeastern Ill. U., Chgo., 1991, Northwestern U. Sch. Dentistry Divsn. Behavioural Scis., Evanston, Ill., 1996—. Editor-in-chief Dental Care Plus Mgmt. Digest, 1995—. Bd. dirs., co-benefactor (with wife) World Heritage Mus., U. Ill., Urbana, 1985; mem. Hillel Bd., U. Ill.-Chgo.; life mem. (with wife) Bronze Circle of Coll. Liberal Arts, U. Ill., Urbana; mem. (with wife) Pres.' Council, U. Ill. Recipient centennial research award Chgo. Dental Soc., 1959; Distinguished Alumnus award U. Ill., 1973; Harry Sicher Meml. Lecture award Am. Coll. Stomologic Surgeons, 1983 Fellow Acad. Gen. Dentistry (hon.), Am. Coll. Dentists; mem. Ill. Dental Soc. (mem. com. on radiology), Chgo. Dental Soc., Internat. Assn. Dental Rsch., Am. Acad. Oral Roentgenology, Am. Dental Assn., Odontographic Soc. Chgo. (Award of Merit 1982), Council Dental Deans State Ill. (chmn.), N.Y. Acad. Scis., Gerontol. Soc. Am., Pierre Fauchard Acad. (Man of Yr. award Ill. sect. 1988), Am. Pub. Health Assn., Gerontol. Soc. Am., Omicron Kappa Upsilon, Sigma Xi, Alpha Omega (hon.) Achievements include established (with wife) collection of Coins of Ottoman Empire and Related Mohammedan States and supplemental antique map collection at World Heritage Mus., U of Ill.; established Muriel C. Yale Collection, antique maps of Holy Land collection at Spertus Inst. Jewish Studies. Home: 155 N Harbor Dr Chicago IL 60601-7364 Office: 30 N Michigan Ave Chicago IL 60602-3402 E-mail: ddssy@uic.edu.

YALE, STEVEN HOWARD, internist; b. Chgo., Jan. 11, 1962; s. Eugene Alan and Irene Yale; m. Eileen Scott, Apr. 24, 1994; children: Ryan Conner, Allison Jessica. BS, Cornell Coll., 1988; MD, Cornell U., 1994. Cert. Am. Bd. of Internal Medicine. Intern, resident Mayo Grad. Sch. Medicine, Rochester, Minn., fellow, advanced gen. medicine; asst. prof. internal medicine U. Fla., Jacksonville, 1995—97; asst. staff Cleve. Clinic, Ft. Lauderdale, Fla., 1998—99; assoc. program dir. internal medicine residency program Marshfield (Wis.) Clinic, 1999—, assoc. staff, 2001—; assoc. dir. clin. rsch. Marshfield Rsch. Found., 2002—; clin. assoc. prof. U. of Wis., Madison, 2002—. Trustee Marshfield Rsch. Found., 2002—, mem. rsch. com., 2001—; assoc. editor Rsch. and Medicine Jour., Marshfield, 2001—. Vol. provider for primary health care svcs. for indigent and homeless We Care Jacksonville, Fla. Recipient Duval County Recognition award, Duval County Med. Soc., 1996. Mem.: AMA, ACP (assoc. Young Internist of the Yr. Wis. chpt. 2002), Soc. of Gen. Internal Medicine (assoc.). Office: Marshfield Clinic 1000 North Oak Av Marshfield WI 54449 E-mail: yale.steven@marshfieldclinic.org.

YALE-LOEHR, STEPHEN WILLIAM, lawyer, editor; b. Newport News, Va., June 10, 1954; s. Raymond Charles and Joan Mary (Briggs) Loehr; m. Amy Janet Yale, July 16, 1977; children: Elizabeth, Jonathan, Alexander. BA, Cornell U., 1977, JD cum laude, 1981. Bar: D.C. 1981, U.S. Dist. Ct. D.C. 1982, U.S. Ct. Appeals (D.C. cir.) 1983, U.S. Supreme Ct. 1990, N.Y. 1993. Co-founder, editor Imagework mag., 1977; law clk. to chief judge U.S. Dist. Ct. (no. dist.) N.Y., Syracuse, 1981-82; assoc. Sutherland, Asbill & Brennan, Washington, 1982-86; co-editor Interpreter Releases, Washington, 1986-94; exec. editor Immigration Briefings, Washington, 1988-94; of counsel True, Walsh & Miller, Ithaca, N.Y., 1990—. Adj. prof. Georgetown U. Law Sch., 1988-90, Cornell Law Sch., 1991—; cons. Ford Found., 1997-99. Author: (with others) Understanding the 1986 Immigration Law, 1987, Understanding the Immigration Act of 1990, 1991, Immigration Law and Procedure, 1994— (20 vols.), Carnegie Endowment for Internat. Peace, 1994-96, Balancing Interests: Rethinking U.S. Selection of Skilled Immigrants, 1996, America's Challenge: Domestic Security, Civil Liberties and National Unity After September 11, 2003; immigration law columnist N.Y. Law Jour., 1997—; contbr. articles to profl. jours. Mem.: ABA (immigration coord. com. 1998—2001), Am. Immigration Lawyers Assn. (chmn. bus. immigration com., investors com., Elmer Fried award for excellence in tchg. 2001, Edith Lowenstein award for excellence in immigration law 2004), D.C. Bar Assn., N.Y. Bar Assn., Amnesty Internat. (chmn. refugee steering com.), Phi Beta Kappa. Democrat. Avocations: photography, hockey. Home: 301 Highgate Rd Ithaca NY 14850-1437 Office: True Walsh & Miller 202 E State St Ithaca NY 14850-5551 Office Phone: 607-273-4200. Business E-Mail: syl@twmlaw.com.

YALEN, GARY N. retired insurance company executive; b. NYC, May 17, 1942; s. Sidney Leo and Mildred (Epstein) Y.; m. Rena Lynn Gear, Nov. 3, 1968; children— Robert, Lesley BEE, Rensselaer Poly. Inst., 1964; MBA, U. Mich., 1965. Chartered fin. analyst. Mktg. engr. N.Y. Telephone Co., N.Y.C., 1965-69; security analyst Merrill Lynch, N.Y.C., 1969-74; from security analyst to exec. v.p. Irving Trust Co., NYC, 1974—89; exec. v.p. Bank of N.Y., 1989-90; chief investment officer, exec. v.p. Fortis Asset Mgmt. (formerly Amev), 1990-95; pres., chief investment officer Fortis Advisers, 1995-2001, Fortis Asset Mgmt., 2001—02; ret., 2002. Served with U.S. Army, 1966-68, Vietnam Mem. N.Y. Soc. Security Analysts, Beta Gamma Sigma Avocations: chess, golf. Home: 360 E 88th St Apt 36B New York NY 10128

YALMAN, ANN, judge, lawyer; b. Boston, June 9, 1948; d. Richard George and Joan (Osterman) Y. BA, Antioch Coll., 1970; JD, NYU, 1973. Trial atty. Fla. Rural Legal Svcs., Immokalee, Fla., 1973-74; staff atty. EEO, Atlanta, 1974-76; pvt. practice Santa Fe, N.Mex., 1976—; probate judge Santa Fe County, 1999—. Part time U.S. magistrate, N. Mex., 1988-96. Commr. Met. Water Bd., Santa Fe, 1986-88. Mem. N.Mex. Bar Assn. (commr. Santa Fe chpt. 1983-86). Home: 441 Calle La Paz Santa Fe NM 87505-2821 Office: 304 Catron St Santa Fe NM 87501-1806 Office Phone: 505-988-8838.

YALOW, ROSALYN SUSSMAN, nobel laureate, biophysicist; b. N.Y.C., N.Y., July 19, 1921; d. Simon and Clara (Zipper) Sussman; m. Aaron Yalow, June 6, 1943; children: Benjamin, Elanna. AB, Hunter Coll., 1941; MS, U. Ill.,

Urbana, 1942, PhD, 1945; DSc (hon.), U. Ill., Chgo., 1974, Phila. Coll. Pharmacy and Sci., 1976, N.Y. Med. Coll., 1976, Med. Coll. Wis., Milw., 1977, Yeshiva U., 1977, Southampton (N.Y.) Coll., 1978, Bucknell U., 1978, Princeton U., 1978, Jersey City State Coll., 1979, Med. Coll. Pa., 1979, Manhattan Coll., 1979, U. Vt., 1980, U. Hartford, 1980, Rutgers U., 1980, Rensselaer Poly. Inst., 1980, Colgate U., 1981, U. So. Calif., 1981, Clarkson Coll., 1982, U. Miami, 1983, Washington U., St. Louis, 1983, Adelphi U., 1983, U. Alta. (Can.), 1983, SUNY, 1984, Tel Aviv U., 1985, Claremont (Calif.) U., 1986, Mills Coll., Oakland, Calif., 1986, Cedar Crest Coll., Allentown, Pa., 1988, Drew U., Madison, N.J., 1988, Lehigh U., 1988; LHD (hon.), Hunter Coll., 1978; DSc (hon.), San Francisco State U., 1989, Technion-Israel Inst. Tech., Haifa, 1989, Med. Coll. Ohio Toledo, 1991; LHD (hon.), Sacred Heart U., Conn., 1978, St. Michael's Coll., Winooski Park, Vt., 1979, Johns Hopkins U., 1979, Coll. St. Rose, 1988, Spertus Coll. Judaica, Chgo., 1988; DHC (hon.), U. Rosario, Argentina, 1980, U. Ghent, Belgium, 1984; D. Humanities and Letters (hon.), Columbia U., 1984; DSc (hon.), Fairleigh Dickinson U., 1992, Conn. Coll., 1992, Smith Coll., Northampton, Mass., 1994, Union Coll., Schenectady, 1994. Diplomate Am. Bd. Scis. Lectr., asst. prof. physics Hunter Coll., 1946-50; physicist, asst. chief radioisotope service VA Medical Ctr., Bronx, NY, 1950-70, chief nuclear medicine, 1970-80, acting chief radioisotope service, 1968-70, sr. med. investigator emeritus; research prof. Mt. Sinai Sch. Medicine, CUNY, 1968-74, Disting. Service prof., 1974-79, Solomon A. Berson Disting. prof.-at-large, 1986—; Disting. prof.-at-large Albert Einstein Coll. Medicine, Yeshiva U., 1979-85, prof. emeritus, 1986; chmn. dept. clin. scis. Montefiore Med. Ctr., Bronx, 1980-85. Cons. Lenox Hill Hosp., N.Y.C., 1956—62, WHO, Bombay, 1978; sec. U.S. Nat. Com. on Med. Physics, 1963—67; mem. nat. com. Radiation Protection, subcom. 13, 1957, Pres.'s Study Group on Careers for Women, 1966—72; sr. med. investigator VA, 1972—92, sr. med. investigator emeritus, 1992—. Co-editor: Hormone and Metabolic Research, 1973—79; editl. adv. coun. Acta Diabetologica Latina, 1975—77, Ency. Universalis, 1978—, editl. bd. Mt. Sinai Jour. Medicine, 1976—79, Diabetes, 1976, Endocrinology, 1967—72, contbr. numerous articles to profl. jours. Bd. dirs. N.Y. Diabetes Assn., 1974. Recipient VA William S. Middleton Med. Rsch. award, 1960, Eli Lilly award, Am. Diabetes Assn., 1961, Van Slyke award, N.Y. met. sect. Am. Assn. Clin. Chemists, 1968, ACP award, 1971, Dickson prize, U. Pitts., 1971, Howard Taylor Ricketts award, U. Chgo., 1971, Gairdner Found. Internat. award, 1971, Commemorative medallion, Am. Diabetes Assn., 1972, Bernstein award, Med. Soc. State N.Y., 1974, Boehringer-Mannheim Corp. award, Am. Assn. Clin. Chemists, 1975, Sci. achievement award, AMA, 1975, Exceptional Svc. award, VA, 1975, A. Cressy Morrison award, N.Y. Acad. Scis., 1975, sustaining membership award, Assn. Mil. Surgeons, 1975, Disting. Achievement award, Modern Medicine, 1976, Albert Lasker Basic Med. Rsch. award, 1976, La Madonnina Internat. prize, Milan, 1977, Golden Plate award, Am. Acad. Achievement, 1977, Nobel prize in physiology or medicine, 1977, citation of esteem, St. John's U., 1979, G. von Hevesy medal, 1978, Rosalyn S. Yalow R&D award established, Am. Diabetes Assn., 1978, Banting medal, 1978, Torch of Learning award, Am. Friends Hebrew U., 1978, Virchow Gold medal, Virchow-Pirquet Med. Soc., 1978, Gratum Genus Humanum Gold medal, World Fedn. Nuc. Medicine or Biology, 1978, Jacobi medallion, Assoc. Alumni Mt. Sinai Sch. Medicine, 1978, Jubilee medal, Coll. of New Rochelle, 1978, VA Exceptional Svc. award, 1978, Fed. Woman's award, 1961, Harvey lectr., 1966, Am. Gastroenterol. Assn. Meml. lectr., 1972, Joslin lectr., New Eng. Diabetes Assn., 1972, 1st Hagedorn Meml. lectr., Acta Endocrinologica Congress, 1973, Franklin I. Harris Meml. lectr., 1973, Sarasota Med. award for achievement and excellence, 1979, Gold medal, Phi Lambda Kappa, 1980, Achievement in Life award, Ency. Britannica, 1980, Theobald Smith award, 1982, Pres.'s Cabinet award, U. Detroit, 1982, John and Samuel Bard award in medicine and sci., Bard Coll., 1982, Disting. Rsch. award, Dallas Assn. Retarded Citizens, 1982, Nat. medal of Sci., 1988, Abram L. Sachar Silver medallion, Brandeis U., 1989, Disting. Scientist of Yr. award, ARCS, N.Y.C., 1989, Golden Scroll award, The Jewish Advocate, Boston, 1989, spl. award, Clin. Ligand Assay Soc., Washington, 1988, numerous others. Fellow: Clin. Soc. N.Y. Diabetes Assn., Am. Coll. Radiology (assoc. in physics), N.Y. Acad. Scis. (chmn. biophysics divsn. 1964—65); mem.: NAS, Am. Physiol. Soc., Endocrine Soc. (pres. 1978, Kocn award 1972), Soc. Nuc. Medicine, Soc. Nuc. Medicine (hon.), Am. Gastroenterol. Assn. (hon.), Am. Coll. Nuc. Physicians (hon.), Harvey soc. (hon.), Med. Assn. Argentina (hon.), Diabetes Soc. Argentina (hon.), The N.Y. Acad. Medicine (hon.), N.Y. Roentgen Soc. (hon.), Biophys. Soc., Am. Assn. Physicists in Medicine, Radiation Rsch. Soc., Am. Phys. Soc., Am. Acad. Arts and Scis., Tau Beta Pi, Sigma Delta Epsilon, Pi Mu Epsilon, Sigma Pi Sigma, Sigma Xi, Phi Beta Kappa. Office: Vet Affairs Med Ctr 130 W Kingsbridge Rd Bronx NY 10468-3904*

YAMADA, KENNETH MANAO, cell biologist; b. Mpls., Sept. 18, 1944; s. Paul Manao and Masaye (Uriu) Yamada; m. Susan Jane Sleeper, July 1, 1973. BA in Biol. Scis., Stanford U., 1966, PhD in Biol. Scis., 1971, MD, 1972. Intern Mary's Help Hosp./Seton Med. Ctr., Daly City, Calif., 1972-73; commd. lt. USPHS, 1974, advanced through grades to capt., 1982—2003, ret., 2003; sect. chief Nat. Cancer Inst., Bethesda, Md., 1980-90; lab. chief Nat. Inst. Dental and Craniofacial Rsch., NIH, Bethesda, 1990-96, br. chief, 1996—. Mem. Cell Biology Study sect. NIH, 1979—83; mem. external adv. com. Cancer Rsch. Ctr. Howard U., 1979—88; co-chmn. Gordon Conf. on Fibronectin, 1982; Stadtler lectr. U. Tex. Sys. Cancer Ctr. M.D. Anderson Hosp., 1988; Swerling lectr. Dana-Farber Cancer Inst. Harvard Med. Sch., 1988. Editor: Jour. Cell Biology, 1999—; contbr. more than 350 publs. to biomed. lit. Recipient Eli Luke and Jacob David Rsch. award, 1972; Biology Dept. fellow, U. Oreg., 1973—74. Fellow: AAAS; mem.: Soc. Devel. Biology, Southeastern Cancer Rsch. Assn. (bd. dirs. 1980—83), Am. Soc. Matrix Biology (coun. 2003—), Internat. Soc. Matrix Biology (coun. 1994—), Am. Soc. Biochemistry and Molecular Biology, Am. Soc. Cell Biology (coun. 1992—95), Sigma Xi, Phi Beta Kappa (Undergrad. rsch. award). Office: Nat Inst of Dental and Craniofacial Rsch Rm 426 30 Convent Dr Bldg 30 Bethesda MD 20892-4370 Office Phone: 301-496-9124. Business E-Mail: kenneth.yamada@nih.gov.

YAMADA, TADATAKA, internist; b. Tokyo, June 5, 1945; MD, NYU, 1971. Intern Med. Coll. Va. Hosps., Richmond, 1971-72, resident in internal medicine, 1972-74; gastrointestinal fellow UCLA, 1977-79; prof. medicine U. Mich., Ann Arbor, 1996, adj. prof. internal medicine and physiology, 1996—; mem. staff U. Mich. Hosp., Ann Arbor, 1996. Adj. prof. medicine U. Mich. Hosp., Ann Arbor. Mem. AAAS, ACP, AAP, AGA, ASCI, IOM. Office: U Mich Gastroenterology Divsn U Mich Med Ctr 1550 E Med Ctr Dr Ann Arbor MI 48109

YAMADA, TETSUJI, health economist, educator; M of Internat. Affairs, Columbia U., 1978; MPhil, Grad. Ctr. of CUNY, 1983; PhD in Econs., CUNY, 1987. Instr. CUNY, NYC, 1982—86; postdoctoral fellow Grad. Ctr. of CUNY, NYC, 1987; asst. prof. dept. econs. Rutgers U., Camden, NJ, 1987—91; assoc. prof. Ritsumeikan U., Kyoto, 1991-92; rsch. fellow NBER, 1987-90, rsch. assoc., 1991-94; health economist Internat. Leadership Ctr. Longevity and Soc., 1993-94; rsch. assoc. Ctr. Pacific Basin Fed. Res. Bank, San Francisco, 1990—; assoc. prof. Rutgers U., 1993—2004, prof., 2003—, chair dept. econs., 1996-99, assoc. Inst. Health, Health Care Policy and Aging Rsch., 2004—; exec. bd. China East Inst. Soc. Ins., China, 1998—2004. Rep. Japan Econ. Fedn., Ditchley, Oxford, England, 1994; vis. rsch. scholar Inst. Policy and Planning Scis., Tsukuba U., Japan, 1997—2004; temp. advisor WHO, 1999; faculty assoc. The Walter Rand Inst., 1999—; ctr. assoc. The Ctr. for Children and Childhood Studies, 2000—; cons. Japan Found., 2001; reviewer and referee profl. jours., books and rsch. grants. Contbr. articles to profl. jours. Grantee, Ministry Edn., Japan, 1991, Iryo Kagaku Kenkyu Jo, Japan, 1991—92, Pfizer Health Rsch. Found., 1992—93, 21st Century Cultural Rsch. Found., 1993, Ministry Health and Welfare, Japan, 1993—94, Nomura Found., Japan, 1995—96, Iryo Kagaku Kenkyu Jo, Japan, 1996—97, Iryo Keizai Kenkyu Kiko, Japan, 1997—98, Ctr. for Children and Childhood Studies, 2000—01, Ministry of Edn., Sci., Sports and Culture of Japan, 2002—04, Pfizer Health Rsch. Found., 2003—04, Inst. Statis. Rsch., Labor Market Rsch. Com., 2003—04; ORSP grantee, Rutgers U., 1992—, Dialogues grantee, 2002—03. Mem. Am. Econ. Assn., So. Econs. Assn., We. Econ. Assn., Internat. Health Econ. Assn., Japan Econ. Sem., Inst. Statis. Rsch. (labor market rsch. com. 2003-04), Omicron Delta Epsilon (award). Home: 300 East 40th St #4M New York NY 10016 Office: Dept Econs-CCAS Rutgers Univ State Univ NJ Camden NJ 08102 Office Phone: 856-225-6136. Home Fax: 212-297-0192. Personal E-mail: ytetsuji@aol.com. Business E-Mail: tyamada@crab.rutgers.edu.

YAMAGUCHI, COLLEEN S. lawyer; BBA, U. Hawaii, 1982, MBA, 1985; JD, Georgetown U., 1986. Bar: Wash. 1986. Law firm, Seattle, from 1986; ptnr. Sidley & Austin, L.A., 1998—. Assoc. editor Tax Lawyer, 1995-86. Former mem. steering com. Women in Leadership, Wash. Mem. Exec. Devel. Inst., Japanese Am. C. of C. Office: Sidley & Austin 555 W 5th St Los Angeles CA 90013-1010 Fax: 213-896-6600. E-mail: cyamaguc@sidley.com.

YAMAGUCHI, KRISTI TSUYA, ice skater; b. Hayward, Calif., July 12, 1971; d. Jim and Carole (Doi) Y.; m. Bret Hedican, July 8, 2000. Gold medalist, Figure Skating Albertville Olympic Games, 1992; U.S. Skating champion, 1992; World Skating champion, 1991, 1992; World Junior champion, 1988; world profl. figure skating champion, 1994. Founder Always Dream Found., 1996—; goodwill amb. Winter Olympics, Salt Lake City, 2002. Named Skater of the Yr., 1996, Favorite Female Athlete, Nickelodeon's Kid's Choice Awards, 1996—98, Athlete of the Yr. for figure skating, US Olympic Com., 1989; named to World Figure Skating Hall of Fame, 1999, US Figure Skating Hall of Fame, 1998; recipient Women First award, YWCA, 1993, Make a Wish grantor recognition for the yr. award, 1999. Avocations: tennis, rollerblading, reading, dance.

YAMAGUCHI, MASAYA, musician, educator; b. Japan, July 18, 1970; s. Shigenori and Mieko Yamaguchi. BA in English, Meikai U., Chiba, Japan, 1994; MA in Jazz Performance, CCNY, 1999. *Masaya Yamaguchi is not only a musician but also a conceptualist who established his own system to explore the imaginative formation of musical scales by "The Complete Thesaurus of Musical Scales," which is a meta-contribution to music pedagogy of a high standard. Jazz Education Journal wrote, "It's worth mentioning that this book comprrehensively covers all theoretical possibilities in constructing scales (July-August 2002)." The concept is revealed in many of his writings and compositions. He remains active as an author, guitarist, transcriber, translator, and educator in and around New York City. www.masayayamaguchi.com.* Author: The Complete Thesaurus of Musical Scales, 2000, Symmetrical Scales for Jazz Improvisation, 2001, Pentatonicism in Jazz: Creative Aspects & Practice, 2002, John Coltrane Plays Coltrane Changes, 2003, A Creative Approach to Multi-Tonic Changes: Beyond Coltrane's Harmonic Formula, 2004; contbr. articles to profl. jours. Home: 321 W 54th St Apt 305 New York NY 10019 E-mail: masayayamaguchi@hotmail.com.

YAMAGUCHI, YURIKO FUJITA, artist; b. Japan, Jan. 25, 1948; came to the U.S., 1971; d. Alexander and Michi (Hirose) Fujita; m. Hiroyuki Yamaguchi, Mar. 25, 1975; children: Seiji, Mariko. BA, U. Calif., Berkeley, 1975; MFA, U. Md., 1979. Instr. U. Md., College Park, 1988—97; adj. faculty Corcoran Sch. Art, Washington, 1988-97, George Washington U., 2003—. Vis. artist Md. Inst. Art, Balt., 1991, Balt., 95, Mass. Coll. Art, Boston, 1994; adj. faculty George Washington U., 2002—; artist in residence Oberpfälzer Kunstllerhaus. Exhibited in group shows at Hirshhorn Mus., 1984, L.A. County Mus., 1987, Koplin Gallery, L.A., 1991, 1994, 1996, 1999, 2002, Gallery Emon, Japan, 1997, 2000, Numark Gallery, 1999, 2003, Hand Workshop Art Ctr., 2000, Howard Scott Gallery, Columbia U., 2003, Del. Ctr. for Contemporary Arts, 2001, Suyama Space, Seattle, 2002, one-woman shows include Penine Hart Gallery, N.Y., 1989, 1994, Columbia U., NY, commd. wall mural, Atlanta Internat. Airport, 1998, Represented in permanent collections Hirshhorn Mus., Nat. Mus. Women in Arts, Nat. Mus. Am. Art, Smith Coll. Art Mus., exhibited in group shows at Kanagawa Modern Art Mus., Japan, 2004, Represented in permanent collections Corcoran Gallery of Art. Va. Mus. Fine Arts fellow, 1988, 85, 2001; Mid-Atlantic Found. fellow, 1995; Va. Commn. Arts grantee, 1994, 2000, Salzburg Kunstlerhaus Residency grantee, 1993. E-mail: yuriko414@aol.com. Home: 1517 Snughill Ct Vienna VA 22182-1724

YAMAKAWA, ALLAN HITOSHI, academic administrator; b. San Francisco, Oct. 18, 1938; s. Victor Tadashi and Alice Tsugie (Sato) Y.; m. Nancy Ann Habel, Apr.17, 1977 (div. Mar 1987); children: Bryan Allan, David Scott. BS, Roosevelt U., 1962, MEd, 1970. Tech. svcs. dir. audio visual libr. Roosevelt U., Chgo., 1958-60; dean, exec. dir. Ency. Britannica Schs., Inc., Chgo., 1960-67; curriculum svcs. dir. Field Enterprises Newspaper Div., Chgo., 1967-70; edn. svcs. dir. Chgo. Tribune Co., 1970-76; tng. svcs. dir. Dialogue Systems Inc., N.Y.C., 1976-79; orgn. devel. dir. U. Ill., Chgo., 1979-99. Cons., trainer Can. Daily Newspaper Pub. Assn., Toronto, 1973-84, Am. Newspaper Pub. Found., Reston, Va., 1972-80, Gifted Students Found. Dallas, 1974-75; cons. Cedars Sinai Med. Ctr., Beverly Hills, Calif., 1983-98, W. K. Kellogg Found., 1987-2000; developer Nat. Leadership Program; faculty Internat. Ctr. for Health Leadership Devel., 1996-2000. Author: Handbooks of Teaching Methods, 1974, Communicate, 1975, Catalysts For Change, 1976, Evaluation of Senior Administrators, 1994; patentee experiential learning method. Instr. ARC, Chgo., 1954-85; bd. dirs. Edison Regional Gifted Ctr. Sch., Chgo., pres., 1989-93; dist. program chmn. Boy Scouts Am., 1985—. Recipient Founders award Boy Scouts Am., 1997. Mem. ASTD, ASCD, Soc. Programmed and Automated Learning, Toastmasters (pres. 1974-76), Order of Arrow. Avocations: photography, computer programming, electronics, pyrotechnics, film production. Office: 1524 W Pratt Blvd Unit G Chicago IL 60626-4297 E-mail: allanyamakawa@sprintpcs.com.

YAMAKOV, VESSELIN IVANOV, aerospace scientist, researcher; b. Sofia, Bulgaria, Sept. 1, 1965; arrived in U.S., 1999; s. Ivan Yakov and Anna Borisova Yamakov; m. Milena Momcheva Marinova, Dec. 20, 2002; children: Ioan Vesselinov, Miroslava Marinova Marinova. PhD, Inst. Phys. Chemistry, Sofia, 1999. Rsch. scientist Argonne Nat. Lab., Ill. Rsch. scientist Inst. of Applied Mineralogy, Bulgarian Acad. of Scis., Sofia, 1991—95, Inst. for Phys. Chemistry, Bulgarian Acad. of Scis., Sofia, 1995—99, Argonne Nat. Lab., 1999—2003; staff scientist Nat. Inst. of Aerospace, Hampton, Va., 2003—. Office: Nat Inst of Aerospace 144 Research Dr Hampton VA 23666 Office Phone: 757-864-2850. Personal E-mail: vyamakov@mail.com. Business E-Mail: yamakov@nianet.org.

YAMAMOTO, AKIMASA, transportation executive; m. Kyoko Yamamoto; children: Maki, Ayami. Degree in Law, Keio U., 1972. Lawyer Toyota Motor Corp., Toyota Aichi, Japan, 1972—74; treas. Toyota Deutschland, Germany, 1994—97; from gen. mgr. Dept. Fin. Reporting to sr. v.p. and treas. Toyota Motor Corp., Toyota Aichi, Japan, 1998—2001; sr. v.p. and treas. Toyota Motor Sales, USA, Inc, Torrance, Calif., 2001—. Office: Toyota Motor Sales USA Inc 19001 South Western Ave Torrance CA 90509

YAMAMOTO, ALICE M. educator; b. Phoenix, Ariz., Sept. 8, 1958; d. Frank and Kumiko Yamamoto. BA in Journalism, U Ariz., 1981; MEd in curiculum and instrn., Ariz. State U, 1997. Cert. Cmty. Coll. Tchg. Cert. Ariz., 1999. English tchr. Mountain Pointe HS, Phoenix, 1993—96, Desert Vista HS, Phoenix, 1996—99, 1999—; tchr. Rio Salado Coll., Tempe, 1999—. Academic decathalon coach Desert Vista HS, Phoenix, 1996—2001, asian student union co-sponsor, 1999—. Recipient Most Improved Coach Award, Ariz. Acad. Decathalon, 1999. Mem.: Modern Lang. Assn. (assoc.), Nat. Edn. Assn. (assoc.). Home: 779 E Park Ave Chandler AZ 85225-1757 Office: Desert Vista HS 16440 S 32nd St Phoenix AZ 85048-7807

YAMAMOTO, IRWIN TORAKI, editor, publishing executive; b. Wailuku, Maui, Hawaii, Apr. 5, 1955; s. Torao and Yukie (Urata) Y. B in Bus. Adminstrn., Mktg., Chaminade U., 1977. Pres., editor, publisher The Yamamoto Forecast, Kahului, Hawaii, 1977—. Author: (book) Profit Making in the Stock Market, 1983; columnist The Hawaii Herald, 1978—. Named Top Market Timer, Top Gold Timer, Top Bond Timer, and to Timer Digest Honor Roll by Timer Digest, also honored by Select Info. Exchange and Rating the Stock Selectors. Avocations: exercise, music, reading, philosophy. Home and Office: PO Box 573 Kahului HI 96733-7073 Office Phone: 808-877-2690.

YAMAMOTO, JANET KAZUKO, science educator; d. Shunta and Chizuko Catherine Yamamoto. BA, U. Calif., Davis, 1976; PhD, U. Tex. Med. Br., 1981. Rsch. assoc. scientist Okla. Med. Rsch. Found., Oklahoma City, 1982—83; rschr. U. Calif., Davis, 1983—85; asst. rsch. immunologist U. Calif. Sch. Vet. Medicine, 1985—91, adj. assoc. prof., 1991—93; assoc. prof. U. Fla. Coll. Vet. Medicine, Gainesville, 1993—2001, prof., 2001—. Cons. Ft. Dodge Animal Health, Iowa, 2000—. Bd. dirs. Creating Hope Internat. (Afghanistan Projects), Mich., 1996—. Recipient Pfizer Animal Health award, U. Fla., 1996; fellow, U. Tex. Med. Br., Galveston, 1979—81, U. Calif., San Diego, 1981—82. Mem.: Clin. Immunology Soc., Internat. AIDS Soc., Am. Assn. Immunologists, Phi Zeta Upsilon. Achievements include discovery of FIV (feline immunodeficiency virus) and vaccine. Avocation: music. Office: U Fla Coll Vet Medicine PO Box 110880 Gainesville FL 32611 E-mail: yamamotoj@mail.vetmed.ufl.edu.

YAMAMOTO, JOE, psychiatrist, educator; b. Los Angeles, Apr. 18, 1924; s. Zenzaburo and Tomie (Yamada) Y.; m. Maria Fujitomi, Sept. 5, 1947; children: Eric Robert, Andrew Jolyon. Student, Los Angeles City Coll., 1941-42, Hamline U., 1943-45; BS, U. Minn., 1946, M.B., 1948, MD, 1949. Asst. prof. dept. psychiatry, neurology, behavioral sci. U. Okla. Med. Center, 1955-58, asst. prof., 1958-60; assoc. prof. dept. psychiatry U. So. Calif. Sch. Medicine, Los Angeles, 1961-69, prof., 1969-77, co-dir. grad. edn. psychiatry, 1963-70; prof. UCLA, 1977-94, emeritus prof., 1994—; dir. Psychiat. Outpatient Clinic, Los Angeles County-U. So. Calif. Med. Center, 1958-77; dir. adult ambulatory care services UCLA Neuropsychiat. Inst., 1977-88, chief Lab. for Cross Cultural Studies. Contbr. articles in field to profl. jours. Served to capt., M.C. U.S. Army, 1953-55. Fellow Am. Psychiat. Assn. (life), Pacific Rim Coll. Psychiatrists, Am. Acad. Psychoanalysis (trustee, mem. exec. com., pres. 1978-79), Am. Coll. Psychiatrists, Am. Orthopsychiat. Assn. (pres.-elect 1993-94, pres. 1994-95, past pres.), Am. Assn. for Social Psychiatry (trustee 1981-84, v.p. 1984-86); mem. So. Calif. Psychoanalytic Inst. and Soc. (pres. 1972-73), Soc. for Study of Culture and Psychiatry, Group for Advancement Psychiatry (bd. dirs. 1992-94), Kappa Phi, Alpha Omega Alpha. *Learning about the diverse peoples of America, I have been fascinated with how we can be Asian, Hispanic, Black, European, and Native American and still identify with our national values. We value our freedom, individual rights and our ability to be someone different but equal. In mental health also there is a need for recognition of cultural differences and the need of treatment response to the individual.*

YAMAMOTO, KAORU, retired psychology and education educator; b. Tokyo, Mar. 28, 1932; arrived in U.S., 1959; s. Saburo and Hideko (Watanabe) Y.; m. Etsuko Hamazaki, Apr. 6, 1959 (div. 1986); m. Carol-Lynne Moore, Oct. 4, 1986; children: Keita Carey Moore, Kiyomi Lynne Moore. BS in Engring., U. Tokyo, 1953; MA, U. Minn., 1960, PhD, 1962. Engr. Toppan Printing Co., Tokyo, 1953; engr., rsch. chemist Japan Oxygen Co., Tokyo, 1954-57, 58-59; asst. prof. Kent (Ohio) State U., 1962-65; from asst. to assoc. prof. U. Iowa, Iowa City, 1965-68; prof. Pa. State U., University Park, 1968-72, Ariz. State U., Tempe, 1972-87, U. Colo., Denver, 1987-99, prof. emeritus, 1999—. Vis. prof. U. Minn., Mpls., 1974, Simon Fraser U., Burnaby, B.C., Can., 1984, U.Victoria, B.C., 1986, U. Wash., Seattle, 1987, Zhejiang Normal U., Jinhua, China, 1991; Fulbright lectr. U. Iceland, 1985. Author: The Child and His Image, 1972, Their World, Our World, 1993; author, editor 7 books, including Children and Stress, 2001; co-author: Beyond Words, 1988; editor Am. Ednl. Rsch. Jour., 1972-75, Ednl. Forum, 1984-92; contbr. chpts. to books and articles to profl. jours. Recipient Disting. Tchr. award Ariz. State U., 1980; Landsdowne scholar U. Victoria, 1985, Ctr. scholar Ctr. for Rsch. on Ethics and Values Azusa Pacific U., 1998-2000. Fellow: APA; mem.: Motus Humanus. Avocations: winter sports, travel, classical music, reading. Office: 13651 W 54th Ave Arvada CO 80002

YAMAMOTO, KEITH ROBERT, molecular biologist, educator; b. Des Moines, Feb. 4, 1946; BS, Iowa State U., 1968; PhD, Princeton U., 1973. Asst. prof. biochemistry U. Calif., San Francisco, 1976-79, assoc. prof., 1979-83, prof. biochemistry, 1983—, dir. biochemistry and molecular biology program, 1988—2001, prof., chmn. cellular and molecular pharmacology, 1994—; vice dean for rsch. UCSF Sch. Medicine, 2002—. Co-author: Gene Wars: Military Control Over the New Genetic Technologies, 1988; co-editor: Transcriptional Regulation, 1992; assoc. editor: Jour. Molecular Biology, 1988—2001; editor: Molecular Biology of the Cell, 1991—2001; editor-in-chief:, 2002—. Testifier hearings on biol. warfare com. on govtl. affairs U.S. Senate, Washington, 1989. Recipient Gregory Pincus medal Worchester Found. for Exptl. Biology, 1990; Dreyfus tchr.-scholar, 1982-86. Fellow: AAAS; mem.: IOM (elected 2004), NAS. Office: U Calif San Francisco Dept Cellular Molecular Phm 600 16th St GH-S572D San Francisco CA 94143-2280

YAMAMOTO, YOSHIRO, former diversified financial services company executive; b. Mar. 8, 1936; Grad., U. Tokyo, 1959. Pres., CEO Fuji Bank Ltd., Tokyo; with Fuji Bank, 1959—2000, mng. dir., 1989—91, dep. pres., 1991—96, pres., CEO, 1996—2000; chmn., co-CEO Mizuho Holdings Inc., Tokyo, 2000—02. Office: Marunouchi Center Bldg 6-1 Marunouchi 1-chome Chiyoda-ku Tokyo 100-0005 Japan

YAMANOUCHI-RYNN, MIDORI, social sciences educator; b. Osaka City, Japan, Jan. 8, 1928; arrived in US, 1956, permanent resident; d. Shin'ichi and Fumiko (Urai) Yamanouchi; m. Edward J. Rynn, Oct. 10, 1975 (dec. July 29, 1987). Diploma, Tokyo Kasai U., 1948; student, U. Tampa, 1950—51; AB, Sophia U. Internat. Divsn., 1956; MA, Mich. State U., 1958, PhD, 1972; MA in LS, U. Mich., 1959. Chief rsch. assoc. Internat. Divsn. Sophia U., Tokyo, 1952—56; libr., bibliographer Mich. State U., East Lansing, 1959—63, 1964—67; asst. dir. R&D Sperry & Hutchinson Co., N.Y.C., 1963—64; asst. prof. sociology and anthropology Marshall U., Huntington, W.Va., 1967—70, Fisk U., Nashville, 1970—72; assoc. prof. Livingston Coll., Salisbury, NC, 1972—74; prof. U. Scranton, Pa., 1975—. Vis. prof. Frostburg State U., 1974—75. Translator: (Book) Listen to the Voices from the Sea, 2000; editor: (Jour.) Sociol. Viewpoint, 1989—91; assoc. editor (Jour.) Comparative Civilizations Rev., 1996—2001. Trustee Lacawac Sanctuary, Lake Ariel, Pa., 1993—; mem. adv. bd. Northeastern Intermediate Unit Sch. Bd., Scranton, Pa., 1998—; trustee Lackawanna Coll., 1995—2001, 2002—, Tokyo Kasei U., 1997—; mem. pres. coun. Cedar Crest Coll., 1996—2002; trustee Everhart Mus., Scranton, 2004—; mem. adv. bd. Scranton-Pocono Girl Scout Coun., 2004—; bd. dirs. Diversity Inst. Coll. Misericordia, Dallas, Pa., 1999—. Recipient Seeley Svc. medal, Lackawanna Coll., 2001, Ednl. Svc. award, Wilkes Barre (Pa.) Bd. Edn., 2002. Mem.: Assn. for Gen. and Liberal Studies (mem. exec. bd. 1975—78), Internat. Orgn. for Unification of Terminological Neologisms (del. UN 1995—, del. non-govt. orgn. 1995—, Disting. Contbn. award 2000), Internat. Soc. for Comparative Study of Civilizations (mem. exec. bd. 1978—, editor newsletter 1990—93), Pa. Sociol. Soc. (editor newsletter 1986—89, pres. 1990—91). Home: 220 Salem Pk Ln Lake Ariel PA 18436 Office: Univ Scranton 800 Linden St Scranton PA 18510-4605 Office Phone: 570-941-6137. E-mail: yamanouchi@scranton.edu.

YAMASHINA, TADASHI (GEORGE), transportation executive; arrived in U.S., 1993; m. Hiromi Yamashina; children: Kae, Kaki. BME, Waseda U., 1977. From engr. to project mgr. Toyota Motor Corp., Aichi, Japan, 1977—93; from exec. coord. to pres. Toyota Tech. Ctr., Ann Arbor, Mich., 1993—2001, pres., 2001—. Office: Toyota Technical Ctr USA Inc 1555 Woodridge Ave RR 7 Ann Arbor MI 48105

YAMATO, KEI C. international business consultant; b. Honokaa, Hawaii, Sept. 21, 1921; s. Kango and Shizuka (Tanaka) Y.; children: Karen, Marla, Kei Tracy. BA, U. Hawaii, 1946; LLD, Yale, 1950; DD, World Christianship Ministries, 1994. Ordained to ministry Ind. Universal Ch. of God, 1994. Pres. Internat. Bus. Mgmt. Co., 1950; founder Pacific-Asia Bus. Council, 1950; pres. Orchids of Hawaii Internat., Inc., 1951, Polynesian Products, Inc., Holiday Promotions Internat., Inc., 1952, Orchawaii Internat. Travel Corp., 1962, Pacific Area Landscaping, Inc., 1970—, Hawaii Hort. Enterprises, Inc., 1970—, Agrisystems, Inc., 1971-95; minister Ind. Universal Ch. God, Honolulu, 1995—. V.p., dir. Sperry & Hutchison Travel Awards, Inc., 1964, Copley Internat. Corp., 1967; all N.Y.C.; pres. Internat. Cons. Co., 1968, Asia-Pacific Corp., 1968; chmn. Asia Internat. Group of Cos., Asia Internat. Cons.; mng.

dir. Internat. Cons. Assocs., 1993; universal cons. svcs. God's Universal Ch. and Ministries. Bd. dirs. Internat. Execs. Assn., World Trade Club N.Y.C., Sales Execs. Club N.Y.C.; mem. Regional Export Expansion Council, U.S. Dept. Commerce; organizer Asia Pacific Inst.; pres. Saudi Arabia Pacific Asia Bus. Council, Arab Asian Assocs. Served to 1st lt. AUS, World War II, ETO. Decorated Silver Star, Purple Heart with 2 oak leaf clusters. Mem. Advt. Club N.Y.C., Nat. Indsl. Conf. Bd., Profl. Mgmt. Cons. Assn. Am., Sales Promotion Execs. Assn., Chgo. Execs. Club, Sales and Marketing Execs. Internat., N.Y. Hort. Soc., Asia Soc., Japan Soc., Am. Mgmt. Assn. (lectr.), 442d Regimental Combat Team Assn., Landscape Contractors Assn. Hawaii, Gen. Contractors Assn. Hawaii, Friends East-West Center, East-West Philosophers Conf., Hawaii Assn. Nurserymen, Hawaii Bot. Soc., Honolulu Execs. Assn., U. Hawaii Alumni Assn., Navy League, Nat. Fedn. Ind. Bus., Am. Assn. Nurserymen, Pacific Area Travel Assn., Assn. U.S. Army, Hawaii Visitors Bur., Hawaii C. of C., U.S. Arab C. of C., Saudi Arabia Bus. Council. Clubs: Rotary, Bankers. Home: PO Box 653 Honolulu HI 96809-0653

YAMAUCHI, EDWIN MASAO, history professor; b. Hilo, Hawaii, Feb. 1, 1937; s. Shokyo Yamauchi and Haruko (Owan) Yamauchi Higa; m. Kimie Honda, Aug. 31, 1962; children: Brian, Gail. Student, U. Hawaii, 1957-58, BA, Shelton Coll., 1960; MA, Brandeis U., 1962, PhD, 1964. Instr. Greek lang. Shelton Coll., Ringwood, N.J., 1960-61; grad. asst. Brandeis U., Waltham, Mass., 1962-63; asst. prof. Rutgers U., New Brunswick, N.J., 1964-69; assoc. prof. Miami U., Oxford, Ohio, 1969-73, prof. dept. history, 1973—, dir. grad. studies, 1978-82. Author: Pre-Christian Gnosticism, 1973, World of the First Christians, 1981, Foes from the North Frontier, 1982, Persia and the Bible, 1990, Africa and the Bible, 2004, 12 other books, 1966-99; sr. editor Christianity Today, 1992-94; editor: Africa and Africans in Antiquity, 2001; co-author 2 books, co-editor 2 books. Fellow NEH, 1968, Inst. for Holy Land Studies, Jerusalem, 1968, Inst. for Advanced Christian Studies, 1974-75; grantee Am. Philos. Soc., 1970. Fellow Am. Sci. Affiliation (pres. 1983), Inst. Bibl. Rsch. (chair 1984-86, pres. 1987-89); mem. Conf. on Faith and History (pres. 1974-76), Near East Archaeol. Soc. (v.p. 1978-79), Archaeol. Inst. Am. (chpt. pres. 1973-74), Evang. Theol. Soc. (v.p. 2003). Office: Miami Univ Dept History Oxford OH 45056 Office Phone: 513-529-5141. Business E-Mail: yamauce@muohio.edu.

YAMAUCHI, GLORIA, aerospace engineer; married, 1988. Aerospace engr. NASA. Avocations: fishing, golf, basketball, softball. Office: NASA Ames Rsch Ctr Bldg T12B Rm 104 Moffett Field CA 94035

YAMAYEE, ZIA AHMAD, engineering educator, dean; b. Herat, Afghanistan, Feb. 2, 1948; came to U.S., 1974; s. Sayed and Merjan Ahmad. BSEE, Kabul (Afghanistan) U., 1972; MSEE, Purdue U., 1976, PhD, 1978. Registered profl. engr., Calif., Wash. Mem. faculty of engring. Kabul U., 1978; engr. Systems Control, Inc., Palo Alto, Calif., 1979-81; sr. engr. Pacific N.W. Utilities, Portland, Oreg., 1981-83; assoc. prof. elec. engring. Clarkson U., Potsdam, N.Y., 1983-85; assoc. prof. Gonzaga U., Spokane, 1985-87, dean Sch. Engring., 1988-96; prof., chair elec. engring. dept. U. New Orleans, 1987-88. Part-time rsch. engr. La. Power and Light Co., New Orleans, 1987-88; sr. cons. Engring. and Cons. Svcs., Spokane, 1989-96. Contbr. articles, reports to profl. jours. Bd. dirs. Wash. State Math., Engring. Sci. Achievement, Seattle, 1989-96; mem. Spokane Intercollegiate Rsch. and Tech. Inst. Adv. Coun., 1990-96. NSF grantee. Mem. Am. Soc. Engring. Edn., IEEE (sr.). Office: University of Portland 5000 N Willamette Blvd Portland OR 97203-5798 Office Phone: 503-943-7314. E-mail: yamayee@up.edu.

YAMAZAKI, MAKOTO, economics educator; b. Tokyo, Dec. 19, 1948; s. Motoi and Mutsuko (Yamamoto) Y.; m. Abigail Elizabeth Burford, Aug. 4, 1984. BA in Law, Keio U., Japan, 1971; BA in Econs. and Polit. Sci., Wittenberg U., 1972-74; MA in Internat. Rels., The Fletcher Sch. of Law and Diplomacy, 1976; PhD in Econs., Duke U., 1984. Instr. Wittenberg U., Springfield, Ohio, 1972-74, asst. to program dir., 1973-75; vis. lectr. Tufts U., Medford, Mass., 1976, teaching asst. 1977-79; teaching asst. Duke U., Durham, N.C., 1982; asst. prof. W.Va. State Coll., Institute, 1984-85; vis. asst. prof. Wittenberg U., Springfield, Ohio, 1985-87; asst. prof. Aguinas Coll., Grand Rapids, Mich., 1987—; prin. Grand Rapids Japanese Sch., 1990—; pres. Global Trade Cons., Grand Rapids, 1990-91; chmn. M&M Hilmont Internat., Inc., 1991—, Living Space Internat., Inc., 1997—; faculty advisor Internat. Honor Soc. in Econs., 1988—, Student in Free Enterprise, 2002; exec. com. U.S./Japan Grassroots Seminar, 1993—; chmn. bus. adv. coun. Nat. Rep. Congl. Com., 2002; bd. mem. U.S. Japan Econ. Bus. and Cultural Form, 2003-, Green Build Japan, 2003-; Advisor Assn. Internat. des Etudients en Scis. Economiques Commerciales in French acronym, Grand Rapids, 1990. Recipient Nat. Leadership award Nat. Rep. Congl. com., 2002, Disting. Tchr. award Aquinas Coll., 2002; named Businessman of Yr., Nat. Rep. Congl. Com., 2002; Wittenberg U. scholar, 1972; Grad. scholar Duke U., 1980; recipient rsch. grants Wittenberg U., 1986, Aquinas Coll., 1988. Mem. Am. Econ. Assn., Grand Rapids Home Builders Assn. (lifetime design com., 1999), Organic Trade Assn., U.S.A. Track and Field, Omicron Delta Epsilon. Congregationalist. Avocations: tennis, running, swimming, cooking, gardening. Home: 1131 Fernridge Ave SE Grand Rapids MI 49546-3818 Office: Aguinas Coll Econs Dept Grand Rapids MI 49506 Office Phone: 616-459-8281.

YAMAZAKI, SHINJI, research scientist; b. Fuji, Shizuoka, Japan, Dec. 10, 1962; came to U.S., 1998; s. Mitsuru and Mie (Takeuchi) Y.; m. Yoshiko Nakaizumi, Aug. 5, 1993; 1 child, Yumi. BS in Pharmacy, Tokyo Coll. Pharmacy, 1985, MS in Molecular Pharmacology, 1987; PhD in Molecular Pharmacology, Tokyo U. Pharmacy & Life Sci., 1999. Scientist drug metabolism rsch. Upjohn Pharm., Ltd., Takasaki, Japan, 1987-88, scientist drug metabolism and analytical chemistry rsch. Tsukuba, Japan, 1988-96, Pharmacia & Upjohn Ltd., Tsukuba, 1996-98; rsch. scientist pharmacokinetics and bioanalytical rsch. Pharmacia & Upjohn Inc., Kalamazoo, 1998—2001, sr. rsch. scientist global drug metabolism, 2001—03; sr. prin. scientist pharmacokinetics, dynamics and metabolism Pfizer, Inc., San Diego, 2003—. Contbr. articles to profl. jours. Avocations: golf, soccer, wildlife. Office: Pharmacokinetics Dynamics & Metabolism LaJolla Labs Pfizer Inc 10777 Science Ctr Dr CB3 San Diego CA 92121 Office Phone: 858-622-8050. E-mail: shinji.yamazaki@pfizer.com.

YAMBRUSIC, EDWARD SLAVKO, lawyer, consultant; b. Conway, Pa., Mar. 9, 1933; s. Michael Misko and Slavica Sylvia (Yambrusic) Y.; m. Natalie Visniak, 1990. BA, Duquesne U., 1957; postgrad., Georgetown U. Law Ctr., 1959-61; JD, U. Balt., 1966; cert., The Hague (Netherlands) Acad. Internat. Law, 1967, 69; diploma, Ctr. Study and Rsch. Internat. Law and Internat. Rels., 1970; PhD in Pub. Internat. Law, Cath. U. Am., 1984. Bar: Md. 1969, U.S. Ct. Customs and Patent Appeals 1972, U.S. Supreme Ct. 1972, U.S. Ct. Internat. Trade 1988. Copyright examiner U.S. Copyright Office, Libr. of Congress, Washington, 1960-69; atty. adviser Office Register of Copyrights, 1969-98; pvt. practice internat. and immigration law, 1969—. Legal counsel Nat. Ethnic Studies Assembly, 1976—, Soc. Fed. Linguists, 1980; pres. AMCRO Internat. Consulting, Inc., 1995—. Author: Treat Interpretation: Theory and Reality, 1987, The Trade-Based Approaches to the Protection of Intellectual Property, 1990; contbr. articles to ofcl. newsletter Nat. Confedn. Am. Ethnic Groups, also legal jours. Pres. Nat. Confedn. Am. Ethnic Groups, Washington; nat. chmn. Croatian-Am. Bicentennial Com. nat. chmn. Nat. Pilgrimage of Croatian-Ams. to Nat. Shrine of Immaculate Conception, Washington; v.p. Croatian Acad. Am. Served to capt. U.S. Army, 1957-59. Duquesne U. Tamburitzans scholar, 1953-57; Hague Acad. Internat. Law fellow, 1970. Mem. ABA, Md. Bar Assn., Internat. Law Assn., Internat. Fiscal Assn., Am. Soc. Internat. Law, Croatian Cath. Union Am., Croatian Frat. Union Am. Republican. Roman Catholic. Certificate issued by the Librarian of Congress in recognition of 40 years of distinguished service to the people of the United States of America, 1957-98. Home and Office: 4720 Massachusetts Ave NW Washington DC 20016-2346

YAMIN, DIANNE ELIZABETH, judge; b. Danbury, Conn., June 4, 1961; d. Raymond Joseph and Linda May (Bucko) Goetz; m. Robert Joseph Yamin, Sept. 3, 1988; children: Samantha Blythe, Rebecca Anne. AB, Lehigh U., 1983; JD, Mercer U., 1986. Bar: Conn. 1986, U.S. Dist. Ct. Conn. 1989. Atty. Gerald Hecht & Assocs., Danbury, 1986-92; judge State Conn., Danbury, 1991—. Atty. Yamin & Yamin, Danbury, 1992—; chmn. ethics com. Conn. Probate Assembly, 1994-2003; mem. Conn. Coun. on Adoptions, 1992—; 1st v.p. Conn. Probate Assembly, 2004— Bd. dirs. Big Bros./Big Sisters, Danbury, 1987-94, Danbury Music Ctr., 1996-2004, Hispanic Ctr. Greater Danbury, 1999—; pres. Conn Brass Soc., Inc., 1991—; active Friends of Tarrywile Park, Inc., Danbury, 1993-99; pres. coun. women Lehigh U, 2000—. Recipient Outstanding Young Citizen award Conn. Jaycees, 1994, pro bono award Conn. Legal Svcs., 1993; named one of 21 Young Lawyers Leading US into the 21st Century, ABA Mag., 1995, Thayer Bowman award, 2004. Mem. ABA, Conn. Bar Assn., Danbury Bar Assn., Greater Danbury C. of C. (bd. dirs. 2003—), Omicron Delta Kappa. Republican. Roman Catholic. Avocations: ballet, volunteerism, travel, outdoor activities. Home: 66 Barnum Rd Danbury CT 06811-2938 Office: 155 Deer Hill Ave Danbury CT 06810-7726 Office Phone: 203-744-7090.

YAMIN, JOSEPH FRANCIS, lawyer, counselor; b. Detroit, Mar. 12, 1956; s. Raymond Samuel and Sadie Ann (John) Y. 1975; BA, U. Mich., 1978; J.D., London Sch. Econs., 1981; JD, Detroit Coll. Law, 1982. Bar: U.S. Ct. Appeals (6th cir.) 1982, U.S. Dist. Ct. (ea. dist.) Mich. 1982. Pvt. practice, Birmingham, Mich., 1981-93; ptnr. Beier Howlett PC, Bloomfield Hills, Mich., 1993—; bd. dir. Am. Wash Systems, Birmingham, 1979—; instr. Detroit Coll. Law Rev., 1984-86; case evaluation Wayne County, Oakland County. Pres. Pheobe Found., 2002—. Recipient Am. Jurisprudence Book award Am. Jurisprudence Soc., 1981. Mem. ABA, Oakland County Bar Assn., meditor State of Mich. Bar Assn., Law Rev., Phoebe Found., pres. 2002—, Chi Phi, Oakland County Real Property Sect. Roman Catholic. Office: Beier Howlett PC 200 E Long Lake Rd Ste 110 Bloomfield Hills MI 48304-2328

YAMIN, MICHAEL GEOFFREY, lawyer; b. NYC, Nov. 10, 1931; s. Michael and Ethel Yamin; m. Martina Schaap, Apr. 16, 1961; children: Michael Jeremy, Katrina. AB magna cum laude, Harvard U., 1953, LLB, 1958. Bar: NY 1959, U.S. Dist. Ct. (so. and ea. dists.) NY, U.S. Ct. Appeals (2d cir.) 1966, U.S. Supreme Ct. 1967. Assoc. Weil, Gotshal & Manges, NYC, 1958-65; sr. ptnr. Colton, Hartnick, Yamin & Sheresky, NYC, 1966-93, Kaufmann, Feiner, Yamin, Gildin & Robbins, LLP, NYC, 1993—. Trustee Gov.'s Com. Scholastic Achievement, 1976—; mem. Manhattan Cmty. Bd. 6, 1974—88, chmn., 1986—88; mem. Manhattan Borough Bd., 1986—88. Mem. ABA, NY State Bar Assn., Assn. Bar City of NY, Fed. Bar Coun., Am Fgn. Law Assn. (Am. br.), Internat. Law Assn., Societe de Legislation Comparee, Internat. Bar Assn., Harvard Faculty Club (Cambridge, Mass.), Harvard Club of NYC (trustee NY Found. 1981—, pres. 1999—, sub-chmn. schs. and scholarships com. 1972-93, bd. mgrs. 1985-88, 93-98, chair house com. 1992-95, v.p. 1995-98, chair comm. com. 1997-99, chair membership svcs. com. 1999-2000), Harvard Alumni Assn. (bd. dirs. 1995-98). Office: Kaufmann Feiner Yamin Gildin & Robbins LLP 777 3rd Ave New York NY 10017-1401 Office Phone: 212-755-3100.

YAMMARINO, FRANCIS JOSEPH, management consultant, educator; b. Buffalo, Dec. 25, 1954; s. Peter Anthony and Helen Ann (Giangrisostomi) Yammarino; m. Cathy Ann Apa, July 4, 1982; children: Kayla M., Anthony J. BS, SUNY-Buffalo, 1976, MBA, 1979, PhD, 1983. Svcs. coord. Buffalo Savs. Bank, 1972—76; rsch. assoc., instr. SUNY-Buffalo, 1977—79, rsch. fellow, 1979—81, project dir., 1980—81; asst. prof. mgmt. U. Ky., Lexington, 1982—85, SUNY-Binghamton, 1985—90, assoc. prof., 1990—95, prof., 1995—2003, disting. prof., 2003—, dir. Ctr. for Leadership Studies, 2000—. Mgmt. cons. Fune 500 cos., several orgns. and agys. Co-author (with F. Dansereau and J.A. Alutto): Theory Testing in Organizational Behavior: The Varient Approach, 1984; author: Multiple Level Approaches to Leadership, 1998, Research in Multi-Level Issues, 2002, 6 others; sr. editor Leadership Quar., mem. editl. rev. bd. 7 jours.; contbr. articles over 100 to profl. jours. Recipient rsch. and innovation awards, numerous grants, Corning Glass; grantee Rsch. grantee, Ctr. for Leadership Studies/SUNY-Binghamton. Fellow: Am. Psychol. Soc.; mem.: Internat. Assn. Applied Psychology, Acad. Mgmt., N.Y. Acad. Scis., Soc. for Human Resources Mgmt., Soc. Indsl. and Orgnl. Psychology, APA, Beta Gamma Sigma. Democrat. Office: SUNY Binghamton School Management PO Box 6000 Binghamton NY 13902-6000 Office Phone: 607-777-6066.

YAMMINE, RIAD NASSIF, retired oil company executive; b. Hammana, Lebanon, Apr. 12, 1934; came to U.S., 1952, naturalized, 1963; s. Nassib Nassif and Emilie (Daou) Y.; m. Beverly Ann Hosack, Sept. 14, 1954; children: Kathleen Yammine Gross, Cynthia Yammine Rotman, Michael. BS in Petroleum Engring., Pa. State U., 1956; postgrad. advanced mgmt. program, Harvard U., 1977. Registered profl. engr., Ohio. Engr. Trans-Arabian Pipe Line Co., Saudia Arabia, 1956-61; with Marathon Pipe Line Co., 1961-75, mgr. we. divsn., 1971-74, mgr. Ea. divsn. Martinsville, Ill., 1974-75; mktg. ops. divsn. mgr. Marathon Oil Co., 1975-83, pres., 1983-84; v.p. supply and transp. Marathon Petroleum Co., 1984-88, dir., 1984-90; pres. EMRO Mktg. Co., 1988-98; exec. v.p. Marathon Ashland Petroleum, 1998-99; ret. Bd. dirs. Marathon Oil Co.; chmn. bd. Findlay Devel. LLC. Patentee in field. Past trustee Wright State U. Found., Fisk U; bd. dirs. Findlay C. of C., bd. mgrs. Findlay Devel. LLC. Mem. ASME, Am. Petroleum Inst. (bd. dir.), Springfield and Clark C. of C. (bd. dirs.), Findlay C. of C. (bd. dirs.), Findlay Country Club. Republican. Home: 200 Penbrooke Dr Findlay OH 45840-8301

YAMPOLSKY, PHYLLIS, artist; b. Phila. d. Louis Jacob Yampolsky and Bassia Yampolsky Green; m. Peter Forakis, June 12, 1959 (div. 1964); children: Gia, Joseph Peter. Student, Phila. Mus. Sch. Arts, 1950-52, Inst. Allende, San Miguel de Allende, Mex., 1954-55, Ecole Beaux Arts, Fontainbleau, France, 1956, Hans Hofmann Atelier, N.Y.C., 1956-58. Founder, dir., tchr. Workshop Yampolsky, N.Y.C., 1956-66; art instr. 92d St. YMHA, N.Y.C., 1958-60; founder, dir. Hall of Issues, N.Y.C., 1960-61; 1st artist-in-residence N.Y.C., 1966-67; creator, dir. Portrait of Ten Towns N.Y. State Coun. Arts, 1967-70; founder, officer Northeast Windham Coun. Arts, Vt., 1978-79; instr. Vt. Acad., Saxton's River, 1979-81, Vt. C.C., Springfield, 1979-81; co-founder, instr. New Vt. Sch. Arts, 1981; founder, pres. Ind. Friends McCarren Pk., Inc., N.Y.C., 1988—. Creator, dir., prodr. Hoving Happenings, 1966, 67; cons. Model Cities, Columbus, Ohio, 1968, Province Ont. Coun. Arts, 1968-70, Phila. Bicentennial Commn., Smithsonian Inst. Bicentennial Travelling Festival Kit; cons., panelist, performance artists Arcosanti, Ariz., 1977-78, 80, 81; facilitator NEA, 1970-75; cons., organizer, program dir. Habitat II CBO Host Com., N.Y.C., 1995-96; spl. events dir. Youth Pavilion, World's Fair, San Antonio, 1968; writer, dir. art curriculum Marylerose Acad., Albany, 1969, Bennett Coll., 1970; presenter Habitat II, UN conf., Istanbul, Turkey, 1996. One-woman shows include Phila. Art Alliance, 1953, Judson Gallery, N.Y.C., 1960, 62, Walker Gallery, N.Y.C., 1974, Kulicke Gallery, N.Y.C., 1975, Graham Gallery, N.Y.C., 1977, O.K. Harris and Susan Caldwell Galleries, N.Y.C., 1978, Stryke Gallery, N.Y.C., Windam Coll., Vt., 1978, Marlboro Coll., Vt., 1981, A Place Apart, N.Y.C., 1984, City Bank Gallery, Bklyn., 1986, Loft Lawyers, N.Y.C., 1987, 479 Gallery, N.Y.C., 1996, Stephan Gang, 1999, The Cave, 2000; exhibited in group shows at Park Place Gallery, N.Y.C., Brata Gallery, Cornell U., Dallas Mus. Fine Arts, Mus. Erotic Art, San Francisco, Mus. Erotic Art, Stockholm, Whitney Mus., Weisner Gallery, N.Y.C., City Without Walls Gallery, Newark, Green Gallery, N.Y.C., Leo Castelli Gallery, N.Y.C., Allan Stone Gallery, N.Y.C., Franklin Furnace, N.Y.C., Dorsky Gallery, N.Y.C., Bklyn. Terminal Show, N.Y.C., Food Stamp Gallery, N.Y.C., ABC No Rio, N.Y.C., Blue Mountain Gallery, N.Y.C., Boriqua Coll., N.Y.C., Phila. Mus. Art, Holland-Goldowsky, Chgo., Peter David, Mpls., Mc Nay Inst., San Antonio, Tex., Stephen Gang Gallery, N.Y.C., The Cave, Bklyn., Bklyn. Brewery; represented in permenant collections Am. Town Hall Wall Sys. used in Robert Kennedy Presdl. Primary, 1968, Clinton Presdl. Campaign and Inaugural Festivities, 1993, 97, UN Women's Conf., Beijing, 1995, UN 50th Celebration, N.Y.C., 1995, V.P. Gore's Reinvention Revolution Conf., Washington, 1996-97, March Against Cancer, Washington, 1998, W.A.F.E. Festival/Conf. on the Environment, Bklyn., 1998, The Hague (The Netherlands) Appeal Peace Conf., 1999, Main St. Millennium, Washington, Dallas Mus. Fine Arts, Mus. Erotic Art, Pres. Clinton Libr.; contbr. articles to profl. jours. Recipient Cue Mag., 1967, Betsy Barlow Rogers award Ind. Friends McCarren Pk., 1995; Ecole Beaux Arts scholar, Hans Hofmann Atelier scholar; grantee Ind. Friends McCarren Pk., J.M. Kaplan Fund, Andy Warhol Found., N.Y. Found., Vincent Astor Found., Citizen's Com. N.Y.C. Inc., 1990—. Fax: 718-383-5785. E-mail: ifmp@earthlink.net.

YAMPOLSKY, VICTOR, conductor; b. Frunze, Kirgizskaj, SSR, Oct. 10, 1942; s. Vladimir and Fanny (Zaslavsky) Y. Student, Moscow Conservatory, 1961-66, Leningrad Conservatory, 1968-72. Violinist Moscow Radio Orch., 1965; violinist, asst. condr. Moscow Philharm. Orch., 1965-72; violinist Boston Symphony Orch., 1973-77; music dir. Atlantic Symphony Orch., Halifax, N.S., Can., 1977-83; condr. Tanglewood Inst., Boston U., 1977-84; prof. music Boston U., 1979-84; assoc. prof. music Northwestern U., 1984—, Carol R. and Arthur L. Rice Jr. prof. in music performance, 1993—; music dir. Peninsula Festival, Fish Creek, Wis., 1986—; hon. dir. Scotia Festival of Music, Halifax; music dir. Omaha (Nebr.) Symphony Orch., 1995—. Office: Omaha Symphony Orch 1605 Howard St Omaha NE 68102-2797

YAN, LIANSHAN, optical engineer, scientist; s. Peigui Yan and Xuelan Shi; m. Tianhong Wang. BE, Zhejiang U., 1996; PhD, U. So. Calif., L.A., 1999—2004. Engr. N. China Rsch. Inst. Electro-Optics, Beijing, 1994—99; sr. optical engr. Gen. Photonics Corp., Chino, Calif., 2001—. Contbr. over 70 articles to profl. jours. Recipient 1st class prize for high power solid state laser, 1996; Grad. fellowship, IEEE/Laser and Electro-Optical Soc., 2002. Mem.: Internat. Soc. for Optical Engring., Optical Soc. Am., IEEE Laser & Electro-Optics Soc., IEEE Comm. Soc. Achievements include patents for the variale polarization dependent loss source; the higher-order PMD compensation; patents pending for the all-order PMD emulator; the tunable pulse width generation of return to zero format for system optimization; the polarization stablization; the chromatic dispersion insensitive PMD monitoring; the PDL monitoring and compensation. Office: Univ So Calif 3740 McClintock Ave EEB 500 Los Angeles CA 90089-2565 Office Phone: 213-740-1488. Personal E-mail: ofc00@yahoo.com. Business E-Mail: oct00@yahoo.com.

YAN, QING, bioinformatics scientist; d. Chongli Yan and Shaoshan Zhang; m. Donglei Hu, June 23, 2002. MD in Internal Medicine, Nanjing U. of TCM, Nanjing, China, 1993; MS in Microbiology, Immunology, U. of Ariz., 1998; PhD in Biol. and Med. Informatics, U. of Calif. San Francisco, 2001. Diplomate in Chinese Herbology Nat. Certification Commn. for Acupuncture and Oriental Medicine, 2000. Bioinformatics scientist MedImmune, Inc., Mountain View, Calif., 2001—. Editor (author): (scientific book) Membrane Transporters: Methods and Protocols; author (scientific publ.): (article in book) Hypertension: Methods and Protocols, (article in jour.) AAPS Pharm Sci., Drug Information Jour., Biochemical, Biophysics Res. Cmty. Mem.: AAAS, Am. Chem. Soc., Drug Info. Assn. Achievements include first to design and develop the first human membrane transporter relational database for drug discovery and pharmacogenomics studies; design and develop web portal and the first influenza mutation database for viral vaccine studies; research in bioinformatics and drug information; pharmacogenomics; cancer rsch. Office: MedImmune Inc 297 N Bernardo Ave Mountain View CA 94043 Business E-Mail: yanq@medimmune.com. E-mail: qyan@itsa.ucsf.edu.

YAN, YING, statistician, researcher; b. Beijing, Feb. 9, 1960; arrived in U.S., 1985; d. Youguang Yan and Jingzhong Du; married; children: Alice Y. Wang, Carolyn Y. Wang. MA in Math., U. Wyo., 1990, MS in Stats., 1991, PhD in Stats., 1994. Rschr. Radian Corp., Research Triangle Park, NC, 1992—94, PPD, Inc., Cary, NC, 1994—96, Astra Zeneca, Del., 1996—97, Glaxo-Smith Kline, King of Prussia, Pa., 1997—. Mem.: Drug Info. Assn., Am. Statis. Assn. Office: 2301 Renaissance Blvd King Of Prussia PA 19406

YANAGISAWA, EIJI, otolaryngologist, educator; b. Yokohama, Japan, May 12, 1930; came to U.S., 1955; s. Jiro and Sue Yanagisawa; m. June Yanagisawa, Sept. 16, 1960; children: Ken, Kay, Amy Ray. MD, Nihon U., Tokyo, 1955. Intern Hosp. of St. Raphael, New Haven, 1962, U.S. Tokyo Army Hosp., 1955—56; resident in otolaryngology Yale-New Haven Hosp., 1956—59; instr. otolaryngology Yale U. Sch. Medicine, New Haven, 1959-61, 63-64, clin. instr., 1964-67, asst. clin. prof., 1967-72, assoc. clin. prof., 1972-83, clin. prof., 1983—; pvt. practice New Haven, 1964—. Author (with G. Gardner): The Surgical Atlas of Otology and Neuro-0tology, 1983; author: Color Atlas of Diagnostic Endoscopy in Otorhinolaryngology, 1997, Atlas of Rhinoscopy--Endoscopic Sinonasal Anatomy and Pathology, 2000; author: (with D.A. Christmas and J.P. Mirante) Powered Instrumentation in Otolaryngology and Head and Neck Surgery, 2001; contbg. author more than 250 chpts. and jour. articles, assoc. editor Ear, Nose & Throat Jour., 1999—, monthly contbr. Rhinoscopic Clinic sect. Ear, Nose and Throat Jour., 1993—. Mem.: AMA, ACS (com. mem. Clin. Congress, Otolaryngol. Movie Session 1984—2002), Am. Rhinologic Soc., New Eng. Otolaryngol. Soc. (pres. 1992), Triological Soc. (v.p., chmn. ea. sect. 1990), Am. Otol. Soc., Am. Broncho-Esophagological Assn. (pres. 1994), Am. Laryngol. Assn., Am. Acad. Otolaryngology-Head and Neck Surgery (chmn. continuing edn. through TV subcom. 1988—98, co-chmn. interactive multimedia faculty 1998—2000). Avocations: photography, videography, digital imaging. Office: So New Eng ENT and Facial Plastic Surg Group 98 York St New Haven CT 06511

YANAI, MICHIO, atmospheric scientist; b. Jan. 16, 1934; arrived in U.S., 1970; s. Kin (Watanabe) Yanai; m. Yoko Miyazaki, Apr. 25, 1965; children: Takashi, Satoshi. BS, U. Tokyo, 1956, MS, 1958, DSc, 1961. Rsch. meteorologist Meteorol. Rsch. Inst. Japan Meteorol. Agy., Tokyo, 1961-65; asst. prof. U. Tokyo, 1965-70; from assoc. prof. to prof. UCLA, 1969-99, prof. emeritus, 1999—. Fellow: Am. Meteorol. Soc. (assoc. editor Jour. Atmospheric Scis. 1988—90, mem. awards com. 1992, Jule Charney award 1986); mem.: Meteorol. Soc. Japan (councilor 2003, Soc. award 1962, Fujiwara award 1993), Royal Meteorol. Soc., Am. Geophys. Union. Achievements include discovery of large-scale wave in the equatorial stratosphere called the Yanai wave; development of method of diagnosing mass flux in cumulus ensemble called Q1-Q2 diagnosis; research in role of the Tibetan Plateau in the onset of the Asian summer monsoon. Office: UCLA Dept Atmos Scis 405 Hilgard Ave Los Angeles CA 90095-1565 E-mail: myanai@ucla.edu.

YANAI, SHUNJI, former diplomat; b. Tokyo, Jan. 15, 1937; Grad., U. Tokyo, 1961. Joined Ministry Fgn. Affairs Japan, 1961, dir. internat. convs. divsn. Treaties Bur., 1976, cabinet councilor Prime Mins. Office, 1977, dir. legal affairs divsn. Treaties Bur., 1977, dir. treaties divsn. Treaties Bur., 1978, french interpreter Imperial Household Agy., 1980, amb. Embassy of Japan Republic Korea, counselor min., 1981, dep. dir.-gen. Asian Affairs Bur., 1984, dep. dir.-gen. Treaties Bur., 1987, consul-gen. Japan, 1987, dir.-gen. Treaties Bur., 1990, exec. sec. Internat. Peace Cooperation Hdqrs. Prime Mins., 1992, dir.-gen. Fgn. Policy Bur., 1993, dep. min. fgn. affairs, 1995, vice-min. fgn. affairs, 1997; amb. E.& P. U.S., 1999. Office: Embassy of Japan 2520 Massachusetts Ave NW Washington DC 20008-2869 Fax: 202-328-2187.

YANCEY, ASA GREENWOOD, SR., physician; b. Atlanta, Aug. 19, 1916; s. Arthur H. and Daisy L. (Sherard) Y.; m. Carolyn E. Dunbar, Dec. 28, 1944; children: Arthur H. II, Carolyn L., Caren L., Asa Greenwood Jr. BS, Morehouse Coll., 1937, ScD (hon.), 1991; MD, U. Mich., 1941; ScD (hon.), Howard U., 1991. Diplomate Am. Bd. Surgery. Intern City Hosp., Cleve., 1941-42; resident Freedmen's Hosp., Washington, 1942-45, U.S. Marine Hosp., Boston, 1945; instr. surgery Meharry Med. Coll., 1946-48; chief surgery VA Hosp., Tuskegee, Ala., 1948-58; chief surgery of Hughes Spalding Pavilion, 1958-72; pvt. practice specializing in surgery Atlanta, 1958-86; med. dir. Grady Meml. Hosp., Atlanta, 1972-89; mem. staff Hughes Spalding Hosp., St. Joseph Hosp., Emory U. Hosp., up to 1986-88; asst. prof. surgery Emory U., 1958-72, assoc. prof., 1972-75, prof. surgery, 1975-86, prof. emeritus, 1986—, assoc. dean Emory U. Sch. Medicine, 1972-89; clin. prof. surgery Morehouse Sch. Medicine, 1985—. Contbr. articles to profl. jours. Mem. Atlanta Bd. Edn., 1967-77, Fulton-De Kalb Hosp. Authority, trustee Body for Grady Meml. Hosp., 1989-93. 1st lt. M.C., AUS, 1942. Fellow ACS, Am. Surg. Assn.; mem. Nat. Med. Assn. (1st v.p. 1988-89, trustee 1960-66, editorial bd. jour. 1964-80), Inst. Medicine of NAS, So. Surg. Assn. Baptist. Home and Office: 2845 Engle Rd NW Atlanta GA 30318-7216

YANCEY, CAROLYN DUNBAR, educational policy maker; b. Detroit, Feb. 10, 1921; d. Henry Steward and Annie Louise (Dye) Dunbar; m. Asa Greenwood Yancey Sr., Dec. 28, 1944; children: Arthur H. II, Carolyn L., Caren L., Asa Greenwood, Jr. BA, Wayne State U., 1941. Cert. tchr., Mich. Mem. Bd. Edn. Atlanta Pub. Schs., 1982-97, v.p. Bd. Edn., 1993. Mem. bd. regents Univ. Sys. of Ga., 1985-92; trustee Spelman Coll., Atlanta, 1972-2001; bd. dirs. Women's C. of C. of Atlanta, 1972-74. Pres. PTA, Frank L. Stanton Sch., Atlanta, 1960; active in voter registration Atlanta Voters League, 1963. Recipient Daniel James Gen. Edn. award Tuskegee Airmen, Inc., 1993, Achievement award Atlanta Med. Assn., 1982, Leadership award NAACP, 1981. Mem. Links Inc. (pres. 1968), Delta Sigma Theta. Congregationalist. Avocations: sewing, homemaking. Home: 2845 Engle Rd NW Atlanta GA 30318-7216

YANCEY, GARY, electronics company executive; Pres., CEO Applied Signal Tech., Sunnyvale, Calif. Office: Applied Signal Tech 400 W California Ave Sunnyvale CA 94086-5151

YANCEY, JAMES D. bank executive; AS, Columbus State U., 1964; grad. Sch. of Banking, La. State U.; grad. Stonier Sch. of Banking, Rutgers U.; D (hon.), Columbus State U., 1997. Various positions Columbus Bank and Trust Co., Synovus Finl. Corp., 1959—83, pres., 1983—90, vice chmn. bd., 1992; pres. Synovus, 1990, vice chmn. bd., 1992, pres., COO, 1997—. Bd. dirs. Synovus Finl. Corp., Columbus Bank & Trust Co., TSYS, Shoney's Inc. Former mem. Bus. Coun. Ga.; former campaign chmn. United Way; former pres. Met. Boys Club; former dir. YMCA; former vice chmn. Southern Open; former pres. Historic Columbus Found.; former bd. trustee Brookstone Sch.; former chmn. bd. trustees Columbus State U. Recipient Thomas Y. Whitley Dist. Alumnus award, Columbus State U. Alumni Assn., 1987. Mem.: Ga. C. of C. (former bd. dirs.). Office: Synovus Finl Corp PO Box 120 Columbus GA 31902

YANCEY, KIM BRUCE, dermatology researcher; b. Atlanta, Nov. 25, 1952; s. Andrew Jackson and Edrie (Johnson) Yancey. BS, U. Ga., 1974; MD, Med. Coll. Ga., 1978. Diplomate Am. Bd. Dermatology. Intern dept. internal medicine Med. Coll. Ga., Augusta, 1978-79, resident dept. dermatology, 1979-81; med. staff fellow dermatology br. NIH, Bethesda, Md., 1981-84, sr. staff fellow dermatology br., 1984-85, sr. investigator dermatology br., 1993—2000; asst. prof. dept. dermatology Uniformed Svcs. U. Health Scis., Bethesda, 1985-87, assoc. prof. dept. dermatology, 1987-93, acting chmn. dept. dermatology, 1990-93; prof., chair dept. dermatology Med. Coll. Wis., Milw., 2001—. Cons. Walter Reed Army Med. Ctr., Washington, 1985—2000. Author monographs and sci. manuscripts; mem. various editl. bds.; contbr. articles to profl. jours. Rsch. grantee NIH, 1986—, collaborative rsch. grantee NATO, 1988-93. Fellow: Am. Acad. Dermatology (editl. bd. 1986—93, 2004—); mem.: AMA, Assn. Profs. Dermatology (chmn. program com. 2004), Wis. Dermatol. Assn., Dermatology Found., Am. Fedn. Med. Rsch., Soc. Investigative Dermatology (bd. dirs. 1982—84, co-chmn. ea. region 1990—92, bd. dirs. 2004—), Am. Dermatol. Assn. (Young Leadership award 1986), Am. Bd. Dermatology, Am. Soc. Clin. Investigation. Methodist. Office: Med Coll Wis Dept Dermatology 8701 Watertown Plank Rd Milwaukee WI 53226

YANCEY, RICHARD CHARLES, investment banker; b. Spokane, Wash., May 28, 1926; s. George R. and M. Ruth (Yenney) Y.; m. Mary Anne Shaffer, Feb. 5, 1956; children: Leslie, Jennifer, Richard C. Jr. BA in Econs., Whitman Coll., Walla Walla, Wash., 1949; MBA with distinction, Harvard U., 1952. Assoc. Dillon, Read & Co. Inc., N.Y.C, 1952—63; v.p. Dillon, Read & Co., Inc., N.Y.C., 1963-75, mng. dir., 1975-89, dir., 1990; sr. adv., 1992; ret. Dillon, Read & Co., Inc., N.Y.C., 1992. Trustee, lead trustee W.M. Group of Funds, Seattle; mng. dir. Ad Media Ptnrs., Inc., N.Y.C.; dir. Czech and Slovak Am. Enterprise Fund, Massapequa, N.Y.; former mem. partnership bd. Whittle Comms. L.P., Knoxville, Tenn. Former bd. overseers Whitman Coll.; former trustee, former pres. Plymouth Ch. of Pilgrims, Bklyn.; former trustee N.Y. Infirmary-Beekman Downtown Hosp. Served with USNR, 1944-46, PTO. Mem. N.Y. Soc. Security Analysts, Assn. for Investment Mgmt. and Rsch., Harvard Club, Met. Club, N.Y.C., Pilgrims of the U.S. Republican. Home: 42 Monroe Pl Brooklyn NY 11201-2603 Office: Ad Media Ptnrs Inc 19th Fl 444 Madison Ave Fl 19 New York NY 10022-6903 Office Phone: 212-759-1870. Personal E-mail: rc1yancey@earthlink.net. Business E-Mail: ryancey@admediapartners.com.

YANCEY, ROBERT EARL, JR., retired oil company executive; b. Ashland, Ky., June 16, 1945; s. Robert E. Sr. and Estelline (Tackett) Y.; m. Nina McGee, June 16, 1962; children: Rob, Yvonne, Elizabeth. BS in Chem. Engring., Cornell U., 1967. Sr. v.p., group operating officer; supt. Catlettsburg (Ky.) Refinery, 1976-79; exec. asst. Ashland (Ky.) Petroleum Co., 1979-80, group v.p., 1980-81, sr. v.p., 1981-86, pres., 1986—; sr. v.p., group operating officer Ashland Inc., 1988-97; ret. Republican. Avocations: golf, hunting, fishing. Home: 504 Amanda Furnace Dr Ashland KY 41101-2193

YANCEY-JONES, FLORISTINE DARLENE, artist, educator; b. Pocahontas, Va., Dec. 24, 1945; d. Viola Phyllis Yancey-Carter; m. Richard C. Jones, Mar. 28; children: Mark, Brian, Todd. Student, Capital U. Lectr., tchr. Christopher Program, Columbus, 1993; artist, tchr. Children of the Future, Franklin U., Columbus, 1995; art exhbn. artist Columbus Mus. Art, 1996; lectr. Ohio State U. Coll. Art, Columbus, 1999; lectr. Black history Ohio State U., Columbus, 2000; artist in-sch. program Greater Columbus Arts Coun., 1992—2002; lectr., tchr. My Brothers Who Are We, Columbus, 1992—2003; Black history rsch. historian, 1973—; visual artist, clothes designer. Adv. bd. mem. Ace and Acme Art Gallery, Columbus, 1993—95. Author: (poetry) A Black Woman's Soul, 1973. Pres. Somerset Civic Assn., Columbus, Ohio, 1974—76; dir. food pantry New Hope Ch. of God, Columbus, 1992—95; coun. woman Pocahontas (Va.) Town Coun., 1984—86. Recipient commendation, Ohio Ho. of Reps., Columbus, 1992, Ednl. Coun. award, Franklin U., Columbus, 1993, Ednl. Svc. award, Fed. Govt. Am., Washington, 1995, Hon. Mention, Ace 25th Anniversary Art Exhbn., 2004. Mem.: Children of the Future (tchr.), Greater Columbus Arts Coun. (artist, tchr.), Ace Art Gallery. Jewish. Avocations: guitar, interior decorating, painting, gardening, reading. Home: 1637 Liv-moor Ct Columbus OH 43227

YANCIK, JOSEPH JOHN, government official; b. Mt. Olive, Ill., Dec. 1, 1930; s. Joseph John and Anna (Gubach) Y.; m. Rosemary Panich, Feb. 19, 1955; children— Geri Anne, Ellen Marie. BS, U. Ill., 1954; MS in Mining Engring., Mo. Sch. Mines, 1956; PhD, U. Mo., Rolla, 1960. Mining research engr. St. Joe Lead Co., Bonne Terre, Mo., 1955-58; mgr. research and devel. Monsanto Co., St. Louis, 1960-70; asst. dir. mining U.S. Bur. Mines, Washington, 1970-77; v.p. research Nat. Coal Assn., Washington, 1977-82; pres. Bituminous Coal Research, Inc., Washington, 1980-82; dir. Coal Export Office U.S. Dept. Commerce, Washington, 1982-84; dir. Office of Energy Internat. Trade Adminstrn., Washington, 1984-95; pvt. practice Mc Lean, Va., 1995—2003; ret., 2003. Cons. energy in internat. trade and investment; dir. energy affairs U.S.-Russia Bus. Coun., Washington, 1996—2002. Contbr. articles to profl. jours. Served with C.E. U.S. Army, 1950-52. Recipient Alumni Achievement award U. Mo.-Rolla, 1975, Silver Medal award U.S. Dept. Commerce, 1986, Gold Medal award Dept. Commerce, 1992. Mem. Cosmos Club (Washington). Roman Catholic. Home and Office: 1703 James Payne Cir Mc Lean VA 22101-4223

YANCOPOULOS, GEORGE, health facility administrator; BA, Columbia U., 1980, PhD, 1986, MD, 1987. Chief sci. officer, pres. Regeneron Labs., Tarrytown, NY, 1989—. Adj. prof. Columbia U., 1990—. Recipient Univ. medal for excellence, Columbia U., 2002; Howard Hughes fellow, 1987, Lucille P. Markey scholar, 1988—89. Office: Regeneron Labs 777 Old Saw Mill River Rd Tarrytown NY 10591

YANCY, DOROTHY COWSER, college president; 1 child. BA in History and Social Sci., Johnson C. Smith U.; MA in History, U. Mass.; PhD in Polit. Sci., Atlanta U. Cert. MNGT, Harvard U. Tchr. Albany State Coll., Hampton U., Evanston (Ill.) Twp. H.S.; dir. Afro-Am. studies program Barat Coll., Lake Forest, Ill.; prof. Sch. History, Sch. Mgmt. Ga. Inst. Tech., Atlanta, 1972-94. Lectr. Acad. Pub. Adminstrn. and Social Studies of Small Hural and Ulan Bator, Mongolia, 1991; apptd. spl. master Fla. Pub. Employee Rels. Commn.; mem. labor del. to Soviet Union and Europe, 1988, 90; cons. to govt. agys., unions and cos., including GM, AT&T Bell Labs; arbitrator fed. mediation and conciliation svs. Am. Arbitration Assn. Contbr. over 40 articles to profl. jours. Bd. advisors USAR Historically Black Colls. and Univs./Minority Instn.; bd. dirs. College Fund/UNCF; past mem. N.C. Post-Secondary Eligibility Commn.; former bd. dirs. Opera Carolina, Charlotte Urban League, Charlotte C. of C. Fulbright scholar; named one of Six Best Tchrs. in U.S., Newsweek on Campus, 1988. Mem. Assn. Social and Behavioral Scientists (past pres., Torchbearer award, Belle Ringer Image award), Indsl. Rels. Rsch. Assn. (past pres. Atlanta chpt.), Ctrl. Intercollegiate Athletic Assn. (past pres.), Links, Inc. (past mem. exec coun.), Coun. Ind. Colls. (former mem. governing bd.), Assn. for Study of African-Am. Life and History (exec. coun.), Omega Psi Phi, Phi Kappa Phi, Alpha Kappa Mu, Sigma Rho Sigma, Omicron Delta Kappa, Phi Beta Kappa (mem. Delta Ga. chpt.). Episcopalian. Office: 100 Beatties Ford Rd Charlotte NC 28216-5302 Business E-Mail: dcyancy@jcsu.edu.

YANCY, WILLIAM SAMUEL, pediatrician; b. Pittsboro, Miss, Aug. 17, 1939; s. Lester Truman and Maxyne (Lindsey) Y.; m. Susan Elizabeth Guest, June 19, 1965 (dec.); children: Amy Lynn Yancy, William Samuel Jr., James Michael. BA, Duke U., 1961, MD, 1965. Diplomate Am. Bd. Pediat. Resident pediat. Duke U. Med. Ctr., Durham, NC, 1965—68; resident pediat., then fellow adolescent medicine U. Rochester Med. Ctr., NY, 1966—67, 1970—71; pediatrician Durham Pediat., 1971—. Dir. adolescent medicine tng. program Duke U. Med. Ctr., 1971-99, dir. behavioral pediat. tng. program, 1978-90, assoc. clin. prof. psychiatry, 1982-2000, clin. prof. pediat., 1984—; dir. pediat. tng. program Durham Regional Hosp., 1977-80, med. coun., 1980-86, chmn. dept. pediat., 1980-86, chmn. nursery com., 1986-96; pediatrician Duke U. Affiliated Physicians, 1995—; bd. mem. Am. Bd. Pediat., 1992-2000; chmn. Coalition for Healthy NC Youth, 1991-95; editl. bd. Jour. Devel. and Behavioral Pediat., 1984—. Bd. dir. Child Advocacy Commn. Durham, 1973-76, 79-85, pres. 1973-74; bd. dir. Durham Cmty. Guidance Clinic, 1974-76; NC State Coordinating Coun., Raleigh, 1994-95; vestry St. Stephen's Episcopal Ch., Durham, 1985-87, 95-98. Lt. cmdr. US Navy, 1968-70. Fellow Am. Acad. Pediat. (com. on adolescence 1999-2003), Soc. Adolescent Medicine (exec. sec.-treas. 1978-83, pres. 1985-86, chmn. fin. com. 1989-93); mem. AMA, Internat. Assn. Adolescent Health, Soc. Devel. and Behavioral Pediat. (pres. 1984-85), NC Pediat. Soc. (chmn. com. on adolescents 1989-96), Beta Omega Sigma, Omicron Delta Kappa. Avocations: stamp collecting/philately, writing, golf. Home: 59 Kimberly Dr Durham NC 27707-5418 Office: Durham Pediatrics 2609 N Duke St Ste 1000 Durham NC 27704-3048 Business E-Mail: yancy002@mc.duke.edu.

YANDELL, CATHY MARLEEN, language educator; b. Anadarko, Okla., Dec. 27, 1949; d. Lloyd O. and Maurine (Dunn) Y.; m. Mark S. McNeil, Sept. 7, 1974; children: Elizabeth Yandell McNeil, Laura Yandell McNeil. Diplôme d'études, Inst. des Professeurs de Français à l'Etranger, Sorbonne, Paris, 1970; BA, U. N.Mex., 1971; MA, U. Calif., Berkeley, 1973, PhD, 1977. Tchg. asst. U. Calif., Berkeley, 1971-75, acting instr., 1976-77; asst. prof. Carleton Coll., Northfield, Minn., 1977-83, assoc. prof., 1983-89, prof. French, 1989—. Chair commn. on the status of women Carleton Coll., Northfield, 1983-85, ednl. policy com., 1985-86, 96-97, romance langs. and lits., 1990-94, chair faculty affairs com., 2000-02, pres. of faculty, 1991-94, Bryn-Jones disting. tchg. prof. humanities, 1996-99, mentor to jr. faculty, 1996—, W.I. and Hulda F. Daniell prof. French lit., lang. and culture, 1999—; dir. Paris French Studies Program, 1998, 2004. Author: Carpe Corpus: Time and Gender in Early Modern France, 2000; co-author: Vagabondages: Initiation à la litt. d'expression française, 1996; contbr. to Art & Argumentation: The Sixteenth Century Dialogue, 1993, French Texts/American Contexts: French Women Writers, 1994, Montaigne: A Collection of Essays, Vol. 4, Language and Meaning, 1995, Reflexivity in Women Writers of the Ancien Régime, 1998, High Anxiety, 2002, Ronsard, figure de la variété, 2002, Lectrices d'Ancien Régime, 2003; editor: Pontus de Tyard's Solitaire Second, ou prose de la musique, 1980; contbr. articles to profl. jours. Active exec. com., then mem. Amnesty Internat., Northfield, 1980—. Regents' Travelling fellow, U. Calif. at Berkeley, 1975—76, Faculty Devel. grantee, Carleton Coll., 1988, 1991, NEH Rsch. fellow., 1994—95, Mellon Faculty fellow, 2003. Mem. MLA (del. 1989-92, exec. com. French 16th century lit., 2001-04, 16th century studies coun. 2001-, pres. 2004). Democrat. Home: 514 5th St E Northfield MN 55057-2220 Office: Carleton College 1 N College St Northfield MN 55057-4044 Office Phone: 507-646-4245. E-mail: cyandell@carleton.edu.

YANDERS, ARMON FREDERICK, biological sciences educator, research administrator; b. Lincoln, Nebr., Apr. 12, 1928; s. Fred W. and Beatrice (Pate) Y.; m. Evelyn Louise Gatz, Aug. 1, 1948; children: Mark Frederick, Kent Michael. AB, Nebr. State Coll., Peru, 1948; MS, U. Nebr., 1950, PhD, 1953. Rsch. asso. Oak Ridge Nat. Lab. and Northwestern U., 1953-54; biophysicist U.S. Naval Radiol. Def. Lab., San Francisco, 1955-58; asso. geneticist Argonne (Ill.) Nat. Lab., 1958-59; with dept. zoology Mich. State U., 1959-69; prof., asst. dean Mich. State U. (Coll. Natural Sci.), 1963-69; prof. biol. scis. U. Mo., Columbia, 1969—, dean Coll. Arts and Scis., 1969-82, rsch. prof., dir. Environ. Trace Substances Rsch. Ctr., 1983-93, dir. Alzheimer's Disease and Related Disorders Program, 1994—, dir. Spinal Cord Injury Rsch. Program, 2002—, rsch. prof., dir. Environ. Trace Substances Rsch. Ctr. and Sinclair Comparative Medicine Rsch. Farm, 1984-94, prof. emeritus, 1994—. Trustee Argonne Univs. Assn., 1965-77, v.p., 1969-73, pres., 1973, 76-77, chmn. bd., 1973-75; bd. dirs. Coun. Colls. Arts and Scis., 1981-82; mem. adv. com. environ. hazards VA, Washington, 1985-2002, chmn. sci. coun., 1988-2000, chmn. of com., 1990-2002. Contbr. articles to profl. jours. Trustee Peru State Coll., 1992-2001. Served from ensign to lt. USNR, 1954-58. Recipient Disting. Svc. award Peru State Coll., 1989. Fellow AAAS; mem. AAUP (Robert W. Martin acad. freedom award 1971), Environ. Mutagen Soc., Genetics Soc. Am., Radiation Rsch. Soc., Soc. Environ. Toxicology and Chemistry. Home: 1204 Castle Bay Pl Columbia MO 65203-6257 Office: U of Mo 521 Clark Hall Columbia MO 65211-4420 Office Phone: 573-882-1640. E-mail: YandersA@umsystem.edu.

YANDLE, STEPHEN THOMAS, dean; b. Oakland, Calif., Mar. 7, 1947; s. Clyde Thomas and Jane Walker (Hess) Y.; m. Martha Anne Welch, June 26, 1971. BA, U. Va., 1969, JD, 1972. Bar: Va. 1972. Asst. dir. admissions U. Va. Law Sch., Charlottesville, 1972-76; from asst. to assoc. dean Northwestern U. Sch. Law, Chgo., 1976-85; assoc. dean Yale U. Law Sch., New Haven, 1985—2002; exec. dir. Housing Authority of New Haven, 2002—04; dep. cons. on legal edn. ABA, 2004—. Bd. dirs. The Access Group; lectr. in law Yale Law Sch., 2002—. Commr. New Haven Housing Authority, 1998-2002; trustee Nat. Assoc. for Law Placement Found. for Rsch. and Edn., 2000—. Capt. U.S. Army, 1972. Mem. Law Sch. Admission Coun. (programs, edn. and prelaw com. 1978-84), Assn. Am. Law Schs. (chmn. legal edn. and admissions sect. 1979, nominations com. 1987, chmn. adminstrn. of law schs. sect. 1991), Nat. Assn. for Law Placement (pres. 1984-85, co-chmn. Joint Nat. Assn. com. on placement 1986-88), New Haven Legal Assistance Assn. (bd. dirs., treas. 1992-98). Office: Yale Law Sch PO Box 208215 New Haven CT 06520-8215 E-mail: stephen.yandle@yale.edu.

YANDLE, SYLVESTER ELWOOD, II, sales executive; b. Lafayette, La., Sept. 14, 1932; s. Arthur Ray and Marie (Delhomme) Y.; m. Gretchen Ehrensing, June 28, 1957; children: Gretchen Marie, Sylvester E. III, Gladys Anne, Henry Arthur. Student, Southwestern La. Inst. Well logger Core Labs., Lafayette, La., 1954-56; salesman Security Rock Bits, Lafayette, La., 1956-61, Orbit Valve, New Orleans, 1961-62, So. Engine & Pump, New Orleans, 1962-66; owner, pres. Indsl. Pump Sales, Inc., Belle Chasse, La., 1967—, Commodore Boat Stores, Belle Chasse, La., 1978—, Hydro Damp Inc., Belle Chasse, La., 1992—. Inventor: Air bag for airlines (patent 1991), Hydro Damp (patent 1989), Indicators Studs for Railroads (patent pending), 2 others pending. Active mem. Aurora Civic Assn., La. Sgt. 1st class, M.C., USAR, 1948-59. Mem. New Orleans C.C., Airplane Owners & Pilots Assn. Republican. Roman Catholic. Avocations: duck carving, knife making, painting, inventing, flying. Home: 5883 Rhodes Ave New Orleans LA 70131-3925 Office: Indsl Pump Sales Inc 2814 Engineers Rd Belle Chasse LA 70037-3153

YANG, CHAO YUH, chemistry professor, medical educator; b. Pingtung, Taiwan, May 8, 1939; came to U.S., 1982; s. Shang-Sheng and Kuei-Mei (Lee) Y.; m. Manlan Lou Yang; children: Tseming, Tseliang, Thomas. BS, Tamkang U., Taipei, Taiwan, 1962; MS, Georg-August U., Goettingen, Germany, 1970, PhD, 1973. Tchr. Chiatung Agr. High Sch., Pingtung, Taiwan, 1963-64; chemist Kuantu Glass Plant, Taipei, 1964-68; postdoctoral fellow dept. molecular biology Max-Planck Inst. for Exptl. Medicine, Goettingen, 1973-75, scientist dept. immunochemistry, 1975-82; asst. prof. biochemistry Baylor Coll. Medicine, Houston, 1982-89, asst. prof. dept. medicine, 1983-86, rsch. assoc. prof. dept. medicine, 1986-90, rsch. assoc. prof. dept. biochemistry, 1989-91, rsch. prof. medicine, 1990-95; rsch. prof. biochemistry, 1991-95; prof. medicine and biochemistry, 1995—. Dir. peptide core Nat. Rsch. and Demonstration Ctr. in Arteriosclerosis, Baylor Coll. Medicine, 1984-96, internal adv. com., 1986-96; organizing com. 10th Internat. Conf. on Methods in Protein Structure Analysis, Snowbird, Utah, 1994; sci. com. Internat. Conf. on Methods in Protein Sequence Analysis, Berlin, 1988, Sweden, 1990; reviewer grants Biomed. Rsch. rev. Com., Nat. Inst. on Drug Abuse, NSF, Washington; lectr. in field. Reviewer papers for Jour. Chromatography, Jour. Lipid Rsch., Jour. Protein Chemistry, Molecular and Cellular Biochemistry, Biochemistry, Arteriosclerosis; contbr. articles to profl. jours. Pres. Taiwanese Am. Citizens League of Houston, 1988-90, Taiwanese Am. Assn. Houston, 1985-86. Grantee BRSG Funds, 1982-83, NIH, 1986-96, 2001—, AHA, 1985-90, 97-99, Meth. Hosp. Found., 1988-91, AHA Tex., 1997-2001, ADA, 2003—. Home: 4102 Levonshire Dr Houston TX 77025-3915 Office: Baylor Coll Medicine Dept Medicine/Atherosclerosis MSA601 6565 Fannin MS A601 Houston TX 77030-3411 Office Phone: 713-798-4210. Business E-Mail: cyang@bcm.tmc.edu.

YANG, CHEN NING, physicist, educator; b. Hefei, Anhwei, China, Sept. 22, 1922;, naturalized, 1964; s. Ke Chuan and Meng Hwa Lo; m. Chih Li Tu Yang, Aug. 26, 1950; children: Franklin, Gilbert, Eulee. BS, Nat. S.W. Assoc. U., China, 1942; PhD, U. Chgo., 1948; DSc (hon.), Princeton U., 1958, Bklyn. Poly. Inst., 1965, U. Wroclaw, Poland, 1974, Gustavus Adolphus Coll., 1975, U. Md., 1979, U. Durham, Eng., 1979, Fudan U., 1984, Swiss Fed. Inst. Tech., Switzerland, 1987, Moscow State U., 1992, Drexel U., 1995, Tsinghua U., Taiwan, 1996, Chinese U., Hong Kong, 1997, U. Michigan, 1998, SUNY, 1999. Instr. U. Chgo., 1948—49; mem. Inst. Advanced Study, Princeton, NJ, 1949—55, prof., 1955—66; Albert Einstein prof. SUNY, Stony Brook, 1966—99, prof. emeritus, 1999—, dir. Inst. Theoretical Physics, 1966—99, dir. emeritus C.N.Yang Inst. Theoretical Physics; disting. prof.-at-large Chinese U., Hong Kong, 1986—. Trustee Rockefeller U., 1970—76, Salk Inst., 1978—89, Ben Gurion U., 1980—. Recipient Nobel prize for Physics, 1957, Rumford prize, 1980, Nat. medal of Sci., 1986, Benjamin Franklin medal, 1993, Bower prize, 1994, Onsager prize, 1999, King Faisal Internat. prize, 2001. Mem.: NAS, AAAS (bd. dirs. 1975—79), Pontifical Acad. Scis., Am. Philos. Soc., Korean Acad. Sci. & Tech., Russian Acad. Scis., Russian Acad. Scis., Polish Acad. Scis., Royal Spanish Soc. Scis., Venezuelan Acad. Scis., Brazilian Acad. Scis., Academia Sinica, Chinese Acad. Scis., Royal Soc. London (fgn. mem.), Am. Phys. Soc., Sigma Xi. Office: SUNY Inst Theoretical Physics Stony Brook NY 11794-0001

YANG, DAGANG, mathematician, educator; PhD, SUNY, Stony Brook, 1986; BS, Zhe Jiang U., 1982. Vis. asst. prof. Purdue U., West Lafayette, Ind., 1987—89; assoc. prof. Tulane U., New Orleans, 1989—. Contbr. articles to profl. publs. Fellow, Sloan Found., 1984—85; grantee, NSF, 1987—. Mem.: Am. Math. Soc. Achievements include research in differential geometry, Einstein Manifolds. Office: Tulane U Dept Math New Orleans LA 70118 E-mail: dgy@tulane.edu.

YANG, DEBRA W. lawyer; b. L.A. Grad., Boston Coll. Lawyer; judge L.A. Mcpl. and Superior Cts.; fed. prosecutor; U.S. atty., 2002—. Adj. prof. U. So. Calif. Law Sch. Office: Ctrl Dist Calif US Courthouse Rm 1200 312 N Spring St Los Angeles CA 90012

YANG, DENNIS TAO, education educator; b. Beijing, Feb. 1, 1966;, US, 1985; m. Sally Liu, Dec. 12, 1993; children: Caton C., Alyce W. BA in econ., Univ. Calif. at Los Angeles, 1987; PhD, U. Chgo., 1994; internat. B, United World Coll., 1984. Asst. prof. econ. Duke U., 1993—2000; assoc. prof. econ. Va. Polytechnic Inst., 2001—. Cons. World Bank, Washington, 2003. Mem. editl. bd. Comparative Economic Studies, 2003—, China Economic Review, 2001—; co-editor: How Far Across the River?, 2003; author: Urban Biased Policies and Rising Income Inequality in China, 1999. Grant, Trent Found., 1998—99, CCK Foun., 1996—2000, fellow, Wolrd Bank Bejing U., 1996. Mem.: Population Assn. Am., Am. Econ. Assn. Avocations: golf, bridge, travel. Business E-Mail: deyang@vt.edu.

YANG, FAN, electrical engineering research scientist; b. Wuhan, Hubei Province, China, 1975; s. Zhixi Yang, Weidong Zhou; m. Jianxia Xue. Ph. D, UCLA, Los Angeles, 1999—2002; MS, Tsinghua University, Beijing, 1997—99, BS, 1992—97, MS, 1997—99, BS, 1992—97. Research scientist UCLA electrical engineering, Los Angeles, CA, 2002—02; Graduate student researcher UCLA electrical engineering Dept., Los Angeles, CA, 1999—2002; research assistant State key laboratory of microwave and digital communication, Beijing, CA, China, 1995—99; teaching assistant Tsinghua University, Beijing, CA, China, 1996—99; Research assistant State key laboratory of Microwave and Digital Communication, Beijing, CA, China, 1994—99. Publicity officer IEEE AP society, Los Angeles Chapter, Los Angeles, CA, 2002—02; Session chair 2001 IEEE AP-s International Symposium Committee, Boston, 2001—01; reviewer IEEE Transactions on Antenna and Propagation, Piscataway, NJ, 2001—01. Author: (jounal articles) IEEE Transactions on antenna and propagations, 2001 (Honorable mention of IEEE APS student paper competition, 2000), (journal papers) microwave and optical technology letters, 2001, electronic letters, 2001, microwave and wireless components letters, 2002, (papers and presentations) in various international symosium from 1997 to present. Vice president Chinese student and scholar association at UCLA, Los Angeles, CA, 2001—02. Mem.: IEEE. Office: UCLA Electrical Engineering Dept 420 Westwood Plaza Los Angeles CA 90095 Office Phone: (310)206-4801. Office Fax: (310)206-8495. Personal E-mail: ygfn@ee.ucla.edu. Business E-Mail: ygfn@ee.ucla.edu.

YANG, GUANGBIN, engineer; b. Jiexie, China, Aug. 22, 1964; s. Xitan and Meirong Y.; m. Ling Jin, Nov. 19, 1991; children: Benjamin, Laurence. BS, Hangzhou Inst. Elec. Engring., China, 1986, M of Engring., 1989; MS, Wayne State U., 1998, DPhil, 2000. Engr., team leader China Elec. Product Reliability & Environ. Testing, Guangzhou, China, 1989-95; rsch. asst. Wayne State U., Detroit, 1995-96; rschr. Ford Motor Co., Dearborn, Mich., 1996-98; reliability engr. Yazaki N.Am., Inc., Canton, Mich., 1998-2000, Ford Motor Co., Dearborn, Mich., 2000—. Mem. tech. com. Fault-Tolerance Computation Soc., Beijing, 1994-95; cons. in field. Contbr. articles to profl. jours. Recipient Engr. of Yr. award, IEEE Reliability Soc., 2002. Mem. IEEE (sr.), Internat. Soc. Sci. and Applied Tech. (organizer and chair invited sessions, mem. program com. Internat. Conf. on Reliability and Quality in Design), Am. Soc. Quality (sr.), IEEE Reliability Soc. (chair automotive sys. com., Engr. of the Yr. award 2002). Avocations: poetry, classical music. Office: Ford Motor Co 21500 Oakwood Blvd MD 25 Dearborn MI 48121 Business E-Mail: gyang@peoplepc.com.

YANG, HENRY S. (HONG YANG), metallurgist, materials engineer; b. Tai Xin, Jiang Su, China, Oct. 27, 1964; came to U.S., 1989; s. Xiao-Wen and Yan-Hua (Li) Y.; m. Xiao-Ping (Susan) Su, May 1, 1992; children: Jenny Su, Rachel Su. BS, Harbin (China) Inst. Tech., 1984; MPhil, U. Birmingham, Eng., 1987, PhD, 1989. Postdoctoral rsch. fellow U. Calif., Davis, 1989-92, staff rsch. assoc., 1992-93; staff rsch. metallurgist Kaiser Aluminum & Chem. Corp., Pleasanton, Calif., 1994-98; sr. metall. Kaiser Aluminum Engineered Products, L.A., 1999—. Instr. Laney Coll., Oakland, Calif., 1994-95. Contbr. articles to internat. sci. jours. Recipient Emsley award Inst. Materials, London, 1988, Pfeil medal and prize Inst. of Materials, London, 1993, Buehler Tch. Paper Merit award Internat. Metallographic Soc., 1997. Mem. The Minerals, Metals and Materials Soc., Materials Rsch. Soc. Christian. Achievements include contributions to the understanding of superplasticity in aluminum

alloys, titanium alloys, and intermetallics; study of physical and mechanical metallurgy problems of aluminum alloys. Office: Kaiser Aluminum Engrd Products 6250 Bandini Blvd Los Angeles CA 90040-3168

YANG, HENRY T. academic administrator, educator; b. Chungking, China, Nov. 29, 1940; s. Chen Pei and Wei Gen Yang; m. Dilling Tsui, Sept. 2, 1966; children: Maria, Martha. BSCE, Nat. Taiwan U., 1962; MSCE, W.Va. U., 1965; PhD, Cornell U., 1968; D honoris causa, Purdue U., 1996, Hong Kong U. Sci. and Tech., 2002. Structural engr. Gilbert Assocs., Reading, Pa., 1968—69; asst. prof. Sch. Aeros. and Astronautics, Purdue U., West Lafayette, Ind., 1969—72, assoc. prof., 1972—76, prof., 1976—94, Neil A. Armstrong Disting. prof., 1988—94, sch. head, 1979—84; dean engring. Purdue U., 1984—94; chancellor U. Calif., Santa Barbara, 1994—. Mem. sci. adv. bd. USAF, 1985—89; mem. aero. adv. com. NASA, 1985—89; mem. engring. adv. com. NSF, 1988—91; mem. mechanics bd. vis. ONR, 1990—93; mem. def. mfg. bd. DOD, 1998—99, def. sci. bd., 1989—91; mem. acad. adv. bd. NAE, 1991—94; mem. tech. adv. com. Pratt & Whitney, 1993—95; mem. Naval Rsch. Adv. Com., 1996—98. Recipient 12 Best Tchg. awards, Purdue U., 1971—94, Outstanding Engr. award, 1999. Fellow: AIAA, Am. Soc. Engring. Edn. (Centennial medal 1993, Benjamin Garver Lamme award 1998); mem.: NAE, Academia Sinica. Office: U Calif Chancellors Office Santa Barbara CA 93106

YANG, JERRY, Internet company executive; b. Taiwan; BS, MSEE, Stanford U., 1990. Co-creator (with David Filo) online navigational guide Yahoo!, Calif., 1994—; co-founder Yahoo!, Inc., Calif., 1995—, chief Yahoo, bd. dirs., 1996—. Bd. dirs. Cisco Systems, Inc., 2000—. Office: Yahoo! Inc 701 First Ave Sunnyvale CA 94089-1019*

YANG, JOHN, lawyer; AB, Washington U.; JD with honors, George Washington U. Bar: D.C., Ill. Ptnr. Wiley Rein & Fielding, Washington. Assoc. professorial lectr. law George Washington U. Law Sch., 1994—2000. Mem. editl. adv. bd.: Environ. Claims Jour., book rev. and articles editor: The George Washington Law Rev.; contbr. articles to profl. jours. Mem. citizens adv. coun. D.C. Met. Police Dept. Mem.: Nat. Asian Pacific Am. Legal Consortium (mem. nat. adv. coun. 1998—2000, bd. dirs. 2001—, treas. 2002—), Orgn. Chinese Am. (gen. counsel 2000—), Asian Pacific Am. Bar Assn. Greater Washington (bd. dirs. 1995—2001, pres. 1997—98), D.C. Bar (sec. 1998—99, gen. counsel 2000—02), Nat. Asian Pacific Am. Bar Assn. (S.E. regional gov. 1999—2001, pres.-elect). Office: Wiley Rein & Fielding 1776 K St NW Washington DC 20006

YANG, KEWU, chemist; b. Xian, Shanxi, China, Dec. 25, 1956; arrived in U.S., 1998; m. Fang Dong, July 22, 1982; 1 child, Yang Yang. BSc, Northwestern Normal U., Lanzhou, China, 1982; MSc, Lanzhou U., 1991; PhD, Chinese Acad. Scis., 1994. Nat. postdoctoral fellow Fudan U., Shanghai, 1994-96, prof. chemistry, 1996-98; rsch. chemist Miami U., Oxford, Ohio, 1998—. Contbr. 50 articles to profl. jours. Ind. rsch. grantee China Postdoctoral Sci. Found., 1994-96, Shanghai City Postdoctoral Sci. Found., 1995-97. Mem. AAAS, Am. Chem. Soc., Sigma Xi. Home: 616 Brill Dr Oxford OH 45056 Office: Dept of Chemistry Miami Univ High St Oxford OH 45056 E-mail: kewuyang@yahoo.com.

YANG, KEY PAIK, librarian, archivist; b. Naju, Chollo Namdo, Korea, Jan. 8, 1919; s. Yunmuk and Yunhui Yang; m. Hazel K. Yang; children: Won Kyung, A Kyung, Mal Kyung. Diploma, Song Sil Acad., Pyongyang, Korea, 1939; diploma in Commerce, Nihon U., Tokyo, 1943; BA in Polit. Sci., Monmouth Coll., 1949; MA in Pub. Adminstrn., Am. U., 1958; MSLS, Cath. U. Am., 1960; PhD (hon.), Dongguk U., Seoul, Korea, 1975. With Chosen Kinyu Kumiai, Seoul, 1939, Chosen Kinsoku Butshi Eidan, Seoul, 1943—45; chief Property Custodian Office, Seoul, 1945—46; head of sect. Pub. Works Divsn., Seoul, 1947—48, Pub. Info., Seoul, 1948—49; head Korean sect. Libr. of Congress, Washington, 1950—94, chief, Asian divsn., 1994—95; advisor Korean Embassy Archives, Washington. Mem. panel Bd. of U.S. Civil Svc. Examiners, 1955—55; chmn. Subcom. on East Asian Librs., 1980—80. Author: Physiology of Korean Culture, Art and Civilization, Introduction to Koreanology; co-author: The School of Yi Confucianism; contbr. articles to profl. jours.; author: Quotations to Ponder: Medley of Quotations on Traditional Society of Korea, China and Japan. Recipient Meritorious award, The Libr. of Congress, 1984; U.S. State Dept. sr. fellow, Korea, 1965, Fulbright Lectr., Korean U., Seoul, 1983, Harvard U. grantee in Korean Ecology, 1960. Mem.: Assn. of Asian Studies. Democrat-Npl. Home: 5104 Marlyn Drive Bethesda MD 20816

YANG, LI, computer scientist, educator; b. Heze, Shandong, China, Sept. 20, 1966; arrived in U.S., 2000; s. Mu Yang and Yunxia Dong; m. Xiaojie Wang, Dec. 8, 1995; children: Chang, Ann. BS, Shandong U., Jinan, China, 1985; M in Engring., U. Sci. and Tech. China, Hefei, China, 1988, PhD, 1992; postgrad., Chinese Acad. Scis., Beijing, 1994. Lectr. U. Sci. and Tech. China, Hefei, 1992; vis. scientist Nat. U. Singapore, 1994—95; tech. staff Inst. High Performance Computing, Singapore, 1995—99; asst. prof. Western Mich. U., Kalamazoo, 2000—02, assoc. prof., 2002—. Mem.: IEEE (sr.), Assn. for Computing Machinery. Office: Western Mich Univ Dept Computer Sci 1903 W Michigan Ave Kalamazoo MI 49008

YANG, LIANXIANG, optical engineer, educator; b. Shaoxing, Zhejiang, China, Nov. 27, 1959; s. Huiyuan Yang and Furong Cai; m. Yang Hu, July 26, 1959; 1 child, Yang. PhD, U. of Kassel, Germany, 1996. Lectr. and assoc. prof. Hefei (China) U. of Tech., 1986—91; rschr. and sr. rsch. fellow U. of Kassel, Germany, 1991—98; sr. engr. Dr. Ettemeyer GmbH, Neu Ulm, Germany, 1998—2000; r&d scientist JDS-Uniphase Corp., Ottawa, Canada, 2000—01; assoc. prof. Oakland U., Rochester, Mich., 2001—. Cons. Ettemeyer LLC, Tucker, Ga., 2001—, Ettemeyer AG, Elchingen, Bavaria, Germany, 2001—. Co-author: Digital Shearography. Recipient The Silver Medal award, The Chinese Nat. Com., 1987, 1st prize, Assn. of German Engrs., 1998; fellow Rsch. fellowship, Otto-Braun Found. of Germany, 1993—94, Daimler-Chrysler, 2003, Oakland U., 2003; grantee, German Nat. Rsch. Found., 1995—98; scholar, The Chinese Nat. Edn. Ministry, 1992. Fellow: The Soc. of Chinese Physicists (chmn. 1996); mem.: The Am. Soc. of Nondestructive Testing (corr.), The Internat. Soc. of Optical Engring. (corr.). Achievements include patents in field; patents pending for. Office: Oakland University Department of Mechanical Engineering Rochester MI 48309 E-mail: yang2@oakland.edu.

YANG, NINI, finance educator, researcher; BA, Beijing Inst. of Foriegn Lang. and Tourism, 1982; MA, SUNY at Buffalo, Amherst, N.Y., 1989, PhD, 1996. Cert. Translation Theory and Consecutive Interpretation UN. Prof. Clayton Coll. and State U., Atlanta, 1994—2001, San Francisco State U., 2001—. Governor's tchg. fellow U. Sys. Ga., 1999—; chair Ednl. Test Svc. Coll. Level Exam. Program Com. for Prins. Mgmt., Princeton, NJ, 1999—; spkr. in field. Contbr. articles to profl. jours. Recipient U.S. Fulbrighter, Fed., 2001; Governor's Tchg. fellow, State of Ga., 1999—. Mem.: Acad. Strategic Mgmt., Soc. for Human Resource Mgmt., Acad. Ednl. Leadership (Disting. Rsch. award 1999, 2002), Asian Acad. Mgmt., European Acad. Mgmt., Acad. Mgmt., Beta Gamma Sigma, Sigma Beta Delta. Office: San Francisco State Univ 1600 Holloway Ave San Francisco CA 94132

YANG, SONG-YU, research biochemist; b. Wu-Xi, Jiangsu, China, Oct. 27, 1938; came to U.S., 1981; s. Rong-Geng Zhong and Su-Fei Yang; m. Xue-Ying He, Jan. 1965; children: Ying-Zi, Yu-Xiao. MD, Beijing U. Med. Ctr., 1960; MS, CCNY, 1983; PhD, CUNY, 1984. Diplomate Beijing U. Med. Ctr. Instr. Peking Med. Coll./Beijing U. Med. Ctr., 1960-75; asst. prof. Shanghai Inst. Biochem. and Cell Biology, Acad. Sinica, 1975-80; tchg. asst. CCNY, 1981-84; rsch. assoc. Rsch. Found. of CUNY, 1984-88; rsch. scientist NYS OMRDD, 1988—; head med. biochem. lab. Inst. for Basic Rsch. in Devel. Disabilities, 1994—. Contbr. chpts. to books and numerous articles to profl. jours. Investigator Am. Heart Assn., N.Y.C., 1991-94. Recipient L.J. Curtman prize CCNY, 1984, Wall Street Fellowship award, 1991, NIH Rsch. award, 1994, Alzheimer's Assn. Rsch. award, 1999. Mem. AAAS, Am. Chemistry Soc., Am. Soc. Biochemistry and Molecular Biology, N.Y. Acad. Scis., Sigma Xi. Research contribution to the fatty acid beta-oxidation and the sex steroid hormone metabolism; enzymes and related genes. Office: NYS Inst Basic Rsch in Devel Disabilities Dept of Pharmacology 1050 Forest Hill Rd Staten Island NY 10314-6356 Personal E-mail: yang_songyu@yahoo.com

YANG, TSONG-TOH (T.T.), pharmacist, researcher; b. Taiwan, Mar. 1, 1949; s. Yen-Leng and Chhai-Shia Lin Yang; m. Lee-Ju Wu Yang, Aug. 26, 1951; children: Benson Pin-Sheng, Steven Shih-E. BS in Pharmacy, Kaohsiung Med. Coll., Kaohsiung, Taiwan, 1971; MS in Pharmacy, U. of R.I., 1979; PhD in Pharm. Sci., U. of So. Calif., L.A., 1984. Registered pharmacist Taiwan, Republic of China, 1971. Med. supply officer Chinese Army in Taiwan, Taiwan, 1971—73; prodn. supr. Sterling Products Internat. Inc., Taiwan, Taipei, 1973—77; tchg. asst. U. of R.I., Kingston, 1977—79, U. of So. Calif., L.A., 1979—81, U. of N.C., Chapel Hill, 1982—83; rsch. pharmacist Am. Cyanamid Co., Pearl River, NY, 1984—85; devel. fellow Schering-Plough Rsch. Inst., Kenilworth, NJ, 1985—. Recipient Pres.'s Award for Devel., Schering-Plough Rsch. Inst., 1994, 2002, The Twelfth DuPont Gold award for dry powder inhaler, DuPont, Campden & Chorleywood Food Rsch. Assn. in Eng., and Nat. Food Processors Assn. in Wash. DC, 1998. Mem.: Am. Chinese Pharm. Assn., Controlled Release Soc., Am. Assn. for Pharm. Scientists. Achievements include patents for Preparation of powder agglomerates; inhaler for powdered medications; invention of Twisthaler dry powder inhaler- device and formulation. Home: 9 Old Farm Rd Warren NJ 07059 Office: Schering-Plough Research Institute 2000 Galloping Hill Rd K-11-2-J4 Kenilworth NJ 07033 Personal E-mail: ttyangphd@yahoo.com. E-mail: tsong-toh.yang@spcorp.com.

YANG, WEN-CHING, chemical engineer; b. Taipei, Taiwan, Nov. 11, 1939; came to U.S., 1964; s. Ting-Lien and Ho (Lee) Y.; m. Rae Tien, Aug. 24, 1968; children: Evonne R., Peter T. BSChemE, Nat. Taiwan U., Taipei, 1962; MSChemE, U. Calif., Berkeley, 1965; PhD in Chem. Engring., Carnegie Mellon U., 1968. Sr. engr. rsch. and devel. ctr. Westinghouse Electric Co., Pitts., 1968-76, fellow engr., 1976-93, adv. engr. sci. and tech. ctr., 1993-98, Siemens Westinghouse Power Corp., Pitts., 1998—. Instr. U. Pitts., 1980, 83; chmn. rsch. rev. panel Office Fossil Energy, Dept. Energy, Washington, 1990; hon. guest prof. Tsinghua U., Beijing, 1996—; co-chair 10th Internat. Conf. on Fluidization, Beijing, 2001. Author: (with others) Encyclopedia of Fluid Mechanics, 1986, 92; editor spl. vol. Powder Tech. jour., 1987, 98; editor: Fluidization, Solids Handling, and Processing, 1999, Handbook of Fluidization and Fluid-Particle Systems, 2003; contbr. over 100 papers to sci. jours. Lt. Army Tank Corp., 1962-63. Fellow AIChE (programming chair and sec. group 3, editor 9 symposium series vols. 1987-88, 92-93, sec. particle tech. forum 1993—, Fluidized Processes Recognition award 1993, George Westinghouse Signature award of excellence 1995. Fluidization Lectureship award 2000); mem. Am. Chem. Soc., Chinese Am. Chem. Soc. (pres. Pitts. chpt. 1994), Orgn. Chinese Am. Achievements include patents in field; development of widely-used correlations and design equations in pneumatic transport and fluidization areas. Home: 2376 Mt Vernon Ave Export PA 15632-9028 Office: Siemens Westinghouse Power Corp Sci & Tech Ctr 1310 Beulah Rd Pittsburgh PA 15235-5068 E-mail: yangwc@adelphia.net.

YANG, XIANGZHONG, research scientist, administrator, educator; b. Weixian, Hebei, China, July 31, 1959; came to U.S., 1983; s. Wukui Yang and Fengrong Zhang; m. Xiuchun Tian, Jan. 5, 1986; 1 child, Andrew Chun. BS in Animal Sci. with honors, Beijing Agrl. U., 1982; diploma, Nanjing (China) Agrl. U., 1982; MS in Reproductive Physiology, Cornell U., 1986, PhD in Reproductive Physiology, 1990. Rsch. asst. Cornell U., Ithaca, NY, 1983-89, lab. program coord., 1987-90, postdoctoral fellow, 1990-91, sr. rsch. assoc., dir. Embryo Engring. Program, 1992-96; assoc. prof., head Transgenic Animal Facility Biotech Ctr./Animal Sci., U. Conn., Storrs, 1996-2000, prof., 2000—; dir. Ctr. Regenerative Biology U. Conn., 2001. Adj. prof. Beijing Agrl. U., 1992—; adj. prof. Cornell U., 1996—; hon. prof. Chinese Acad. Agrl. Scis., Beijing, 1991—, Beijing Agrl. U., 1992—, Xinjiang (China) Acad. Animal Scis., 1993—; dir. China-Cornell Fellowship Programs, Ithaca, 1992-96; dir. China Bridges Internat., Storrs, 1996—; chmn. local arrangement com. Reproduction in Farm Animals Symposium, Ithaca, 1992; mem. internat. program com. Ann. M.C. Chang Meml. Conf., 1992; cons. sci. dir. Baylor Ctr. Reproductive Health, Dallas, 1993-94; cons. Gencyme Transgenics, Inc., Framingham, Mass., 1993—, PPL Therapeutics, Blacksburg, Va. Author: Biotechnology of Preimplantational Embryos, 1993; editor-in-chief Agr. Scis. Overseas, 1990-94; contbr. numerous articles to sci. jours., abstracts, tech. papers to conf. procs. Grantee Conn. U. Biotech., 1993—, EAIC Inc., 1993-96, USDA, 1991-94, 92-95, 96-98, 2001-, Rockefeller Found., 1991-95, 92-97, 97—, Lingnan Found., 1995-97, 97-99, Vet Sch., 1993-94, 94-96, NIH, 2001-, Transpharm. Inc., 1994—, Baylor U., 1994-96, Genzyme Transgenic Corp., 1996—, Conn. Innovations Inc., Biotech. R & D Corp.; fellow China State Edn. Commn., 1983-85, Cornell U. Grad. Sch., 1985. Mem. Internat. Embryo Transfer Soc. (edn. com. mem. 1992-94), Soc. Study of Reproduction (com. chair 1991-93), NY State Acad. Scis., Chinese Agrl. Assn. Students and Scholars (founder, pres. 1988-89, conf. chair 1989), Am. Fertility Soc., Chinese Soc. and Tech. Assn., Sigma Xi. Office Phone: 860-486-8728. E-mail: jyang@canr.uconn.edu.

YANG, YANG, science educator; b. Kaohsiung, Taiwan, Nov. 7, 1958; came to U.S., 1985; s. Shun-Wen and Huang-Yin Yang; m. Danmei Lee, May 30, 1987; 1 child, Jonathan Lee Yang. BS in Physics, Nat. Cheng Kung U., 1982; MS in Physics, U. Mass., 1988, PhD in Physics, 1992. Rsch. asst. U. Mass., Lowell, 1989-91; rsch. assoc. U. Calif., Riverside, 1991-92; rsch. scientist UNIAX Corp., Santa Barbara, Calif., 1992-96; prof. UCLA, 1997—. Contbr. articles to profl. jours. Mem. Am. Phys. Soc., Material Rsch. Soc. Office: UCLA Dept Materials Sci Engring Los Angeles CA 90095-0001

YANG, YUNG Y. economics educator, consultant; arrived in U.S., 1970; s. Hoe W. Yang and Soon I. Song; m. Choongja Jane Kim, Dec. 16, 1944; children: Eugene W., Benjamin E., Laura E. PhD, U. of Oreg., 1974. Prof. econs. Calif. State U., Sacramento, 1974—. Mem.: Am. Econ. Assn., Korea Am. Econ. Assn. (pres. 2001—02). Achievements include research in international economic problems, particulary in the East Asian countries. Office: Calif State U - Sacramento 6000 J Street Sacramento CA 95819

YANGA, ISMAEL DURAN, surgeon; b. Bocaue, The Philippines, Feb. 5, 1932; s. Ismael Eusebio Yanga Sr. and Sofia Rodriguez Duran; m. Ruth Morter, Dec. 17, 1971; children: Michele Marie, I. David III. AA, U. Santo Thomas, Manila, 1951, MD, 1956. Diplomate Am. Bd. Surgery, Am. Bd. Disability Analysts. Rotating intern Mercy Hosp., Buffalo, N.Y., 1963; surg. resident meml. Hosp., Albany, N.Y., 1964, Hurley Med. Ctr., Flint, Mich., 1965-69, fellow in surgery, 1969-70; practice medicine specializing in surgery Howell, Mich. Chief med. staff McPherson Hosp., Howell, Mich., 1994, 95; pres. Dr. Yanga's Hosp., Inc., Bocaue Bulacan, Philippines, 2000, bd. dirs. Pres. mission bd. Christ for the Philippines. Fellow ACS, Am.Soc. Laser Medicine and Surgery (diplomate), Internat. Coll. Surgeons; mem AMA, Mich. State Med. Soc., Livingston County Med. Soc. (pres. 1979), Am. Bd. Disability Analysts, Livingston Physicians Group (pres. 1991-94), chmn. bd. dirs. 1994—), Livingston Physicians Orgn., Am. Coll. Managed Care Medicine (diplomate), Am. Coll. Med. Quality, Howell C. of C. Baptist. Office: 1315 Byron Rd Howell MI 48843-1008 E-mail: Iyanga@Ismi.net.

YANITY, JOSEPH BLAIR, JR., lawyer; b. Homer City, Pa., Nov. 11, 1925; s. Joseph Blair and Pierina Maria (Carcelli) Y.; m. Joyce Ann Gilham, Jan. 9, 1954; children: Joseph B., John M., Jennifer A. AB with high honors, Ea. Ky. U., 1949; JD, Washington and Lee U., 1952. Bar: Ohio 1953, U.S. Dist. Ct. (so. dist.) Ohio 1966. Ptnr. Lavelle & Yanity, Athens, Ohio, 1953-78, Yanity & De Veau, Athens, Ohio, 1978-85; pros. atty. County of Athens, 1958-61; of counsel Shostak Law Office, 2002—. Mem. Vets. Commn. Athens County, 1961-88; past v.p., trustee, Ohio Valley Health Svcs. Found., Athens, dir., AAA East Crtl. Pitts., 1995—. Served to 1st lt., U.S. Army, 1943-53, ETO. Recipient Outstanding Alumnus prize Ea. Ky. U., 1976, E.E. Davis award Ohio Valley Health Svcs. Found., 1981. Mem. ABA, Athens County Bar Assn. (pres. 1971), Ohio State Bar Assn., Am. Legion, Symposiarchs Club (pres. 1979), K.C. (grand Knight 1965), Elks (exalted ruler 1961). Office: PO Box 748 Athens OH 45701-0748 Home: 8800 Johnson Rd 120 The Plains OH 45780-1277

YANKWICH, PETER EWALD, chemistry educator; b. L.A., Oct. 20, 1923; s. Leon Rene and Helen (Werner) Y.; m. Elizabeth Pope Ingram, July 14, 1945; children: Alexandra Stone Yankwich, Leon Rene II, Richard Ingram. BS, U. Calif., Berkeley, 1943, PhD, 1945. Mem. sci. staff Radiation Lab., U. Calif., Berkeley, 1944-48; faculty U. Calif., 1947-48; mem. faculty U. Ill., Urbana, 1948-88, prof. chemistry, 1957-88; head div. phys. chemistry U. Ill., Urbana, 1962-67, v.p. acad. affairs, 1977-82. Mem. Adv. Coun. on Coll. Chemistry, 1961-68; NSF Sr. Postdoctoral fellow, 1960-61, exec. officer Directorate for Sci. and Engring. Edn., 1985-90, Directorate for Edn. and Human Resources, 1990-92, sr. staff assoc., 1992-99. Mem. Urbana Bd. Edn., 1958-73. Fellow AAAS, Am. Phys. Soc.; mem. Am. Chem. Soc. (chmn. phys. chemistry div. 1971-72, chem. edn. planning and coordinating com. 1974-77, chmn. edn. commn. 1977-81, bd. dirs. 1987-91), Phi Beta Kappa, Sigma Xi. Home: 2665 Tallant Rd Apt W305 Santa Barbara CA 93105-4889

YANNAS, IOANNIS VASSILIOS, polymer scientist, educator; b. Athens, Apr. 14, 1935; s. Vassilios Pavlos and Thalia (Sarafoglou) Yannas; m. Stamatia Frondistou (div. Oct. 1984); children: Tania, Alexis. AB, Harvard U., 1957; SM, MIT, 1959; MS, Princeton U., 1965, PhD, 1966. Asst. prof. mech. engring. MIT, Cambridge, 1966-68, duPont asst. prof., 1968-69, assoc. prof., 1969-78, prof. polymer sci. and engring. dept. mech. engring., 1978—, prof. dept. materials sci. and engring., 1983—; prof. Harvard-MIT Div. Health Scis. and Tech., Cambridge, 1978—. Vis. prof. Royal Inst. Tech., Stockholm, 1974. Author: (book) Tissue and Organ Regeneration in Adults, 2001; mem. editl. bd. Jour. Biomed. Materials Rsch., 1986—, Jour. Materials Sci. Materials Medicine, 1990—, Tissue Engring., 1994—; contbr. articles to profl. jours. Recipient Founders award, Soc. Biomaterials, 1982, Clemson award, 1992, Fred O. Conley award, Soc. Plastics Engrs., 1982, award in medicine and genetics, Sci. Digest/Cutty Sark, 1982, Doolittle award, Am. Chem. Soc., 1988; fellow, Shriners Burns Inst., Mass. Gen. Hosp., 1980—81; Pub. Health Svc. fellow, Princeton U., 1963. Fellow: Biomaterials Sci. and Engring., Am. Inst. Med. and Biol. Engrs. (founding mem.), Am. Inst. Chemists; mem.: Inst. Medicine Nat. Acad Scis. Achievements include patents in field. Office: MIT Bldg 3-332 77 Mass Ave Cambridge MA 02139-4307

YANNELIS, NICHOLAS C. economist, educator; s. Constantine D. and Olga G. Yannelis; m. Anne P. Villamil, July 30, 1982; children: Constantine Nicholas, Eleni Olga. PhD, U. of Rochester, N.Y., 1983. Commerce disting. alumni prof. of econs. U. of Ill., Champaign, 1988—. Co-editor: Economic Theory; editor: Studies in Economic Theory; assoc. editor Jour. of Math. Econs. Mem.: Soc. for Advancement of Econ. Theory (pres.). Office: University of Illinois Economics Depart 1206 Six South St Champaign IL 61820 E-mail: nyanneli@uiuc.edu.

YANNELLA, DONALD, literature and language professor; b. N.Y.C., May 12, 1934; s. Donald Joseph and Johanna (Meehan) Y.; m. Kathleen Malone, May 23, 1959; children: Susan Y. Harrigan, Katherine Y. Jennings, Donald III, Christopher, Clare. BS, Fordham U., 1956, MA, 1963, PhD, 1971. Teaching asst. dept. English Auburn U., 1956-57; prof. dept. English U. So. Miss., 1981-83, Rowan U. (formerly Glassboro State Coll.), 1964-81, 83-91, prof. emeritus, 1991—; prof. dept. English Barat Coll., 1991-94, disting prof. Am. lit., 1995—2000. Dir. grad. studies English Rowan U., 1973-81, co-dir. Am. studies program, 1974-81; chair dept. English U. So. Miss., 1981-83; v.p. acad. affairs, dean coll. Barat Coll., 1991-94; cons. in field. Author: American Prose to 1820, 1979, Ralph Waldo Emerson, 1982, The Perfect Prodigy: Melville on the Birth of Malcolm, 1986, Herman Melville's Malcolm Letter: "Man's Final Lore", 1992, New Essays on Billy Budd, 2002; contbr. articles to profl. jours. With U.S. Army, 1957-58. Recipient Merit awards Rowan U., 1979-80, 85-86; NEH fellow, 1978-79. Mem. AAUP (chpt. pres. 1968-69, mem. cons. group Coll. and Univ. Govt. 1969, v.p. N.J. State Conf. 1969-71, founding editor N.J. Conf. newsletter 1969-71, nat. spl. com. non-tenured faculty 1971-72, chair 1973-79), Modern Lang. Assn. (Am. lit. sect., sec.-treas. 1982-85, exec. com. 1982-86, 88, adv. coun. 1986-88, nominating com. 1987-89, chair 1989, award 1988), Melville Soc. (program chair 1972-73, acting sec.-treas. 1973-74, acting editor 1973-74, sec.-treas. 1975-89, editor 1976-89, pres. 1990), Nat. Project Ctr. Film & Humanities (adv. com. 1974-75). E-mail: yannellakd@aol.com.

YANNEY, PATRICK STEVEN, human resources specialist; b. Denver, Sept. 9, 1952; s. Merle Philip and Madeline Veronica Yanney; m. Stephanie Ann Robinson, Aug. 15, 1981; children: Mark Phillip, Luke Steven. BA, Colo. State U., 1974. Sr. Human Resource Profl.certification. Gatekeeper Glen Eyrie Conf. Ctr., 1974—76, reception ctr./bookstore mgr., 1977—78; adminstrv. asst. to dir. of adminstrv. svcs. The Navigators, 1978—79, pers. and facilities mgr., 1980—82, dir. adminstrv. svcs., 1983—91, pers. svcs. dir., 1992—99, assoc. human resources dir., 2000—. Chmn. supervisory com. Mountain Bell Credit Un ion, Colorado Springs, 1984—86; guest lectr. Webster U., Colorado Springs, 2003—04. Editor: ASTD newsletter, 1988—89; contbr. articles to profl. jours.; actor: Blue Cross as surgeon (TV comml.), 1998. Vol. mediator BBB, Colorado Springs, 1995—, 4th Jud. Dist. Small Claims Ct., Colorado Springs, 1997—. Named Outstanding Young Bus. and Profl. Person, Rotary Internat., 1986. Mem.: ASTD, Toastmasters (area gov. 1988—89). Avocations: Porsche racing, aviation, photography, camping, commercial acting. Office: The Navigators 3820 N 30th St Colorado Springs CO 80904 Office Phone: 719-594-2362. E-mail: pat.yanney@navigators.org.

YANNI, JOHN MICHAEL, pharmacologist; b. St. Mary's, Pa., Nov. 3, 1952; s. John Paul and Regina (Emmert) Y.; m. Nancy Jane Reedy, Sept. 22, 1979; children: Susan Elizabeth, Jennifer Ruth, Steven Reedy. BS, Allegheny Coll., 1974; MS, Va. Commonwealth U., 1979, PhD, 1982; AMP, Harvard U., 2000. Biologist A.H. Robins Co., Richmond, Va., 1980-82, sr. rsch. biologist, 1982-86, rsch. assoc., 1986-88; group leader Eastman Kodak Co., Rochester, N.Y., 1988-90; asst. dir. Alcon Labs., Inc., Ft. Worth, 1990-92, dir., 1992-93, sr. dir., 1993-2000, v.p. pharm rsch. R & D, 2001—. Contbr. articles to profl. jours.; patentee in field. Alden scholar Allegheny Coll., 1974. Mem. Am. Soc. Pharmacology and Exptl. Therapeutics, N.Y. Acad. Sci., Assn. for Rsch. in Vision and Ophthalmology, Soc. for Leukocyte Biology, Am. Acad. Allergy, Asthma and Immunology. Achievements include patents in area of allergy; described thromboxane A2's muco-secretory effect; identified antiallergic potential of Arylalkly-heterocyclic amines; discovered drugs Patanol and Emadine for treatment of ocular allergy; described secretory response of human conjunctival and choroidal mast cells. Office: Alcon Labs Inc 6201 South Fwy Fort Worth TX 76134-2099 Business E-Mail: john.yanni@alconlabs.com.

YANNUCCI, THOMAS DAVID, lawyer; b. Springfield, Ohio, Mar. 30, 1950; s. David Marion and Patricia (Wilson) Y.; m. Lisa Marie Copeland, June 30, 1972; children: Teresa, Andrea, Thomas D. Jr. AB, U. Notre Dame, 1972, JD, 1976. Bar: Ohio 1977, U.S. Ct. Appeals (D.C., 1st, 2d, 3d, 4th, 5th, 6th, 7th, 8th, 11th and 10th cirs.) 1980, U.S. Supreme Ct. 1980, D.C. 1981. Law clk. to presiding justice U.S. Ct. Appeals (D.C. cir.), Washington, 1976-77; trial atty. U.S. Dept. Justice, Washington, 1977-80; ptnr. Kirkland & Ellis, Washington, 1980—. Editor-in-chief U. Notre Dame Law Rev., 1975-76. Roman Catholic. Office: Kirkland & Ellis LLP 655 15th St NW Ste 1200 Washington DC 20005-5793 Office Phone: 202-879-5000. E-mail: tyannucci@kirkland.com.

YANO, ELIZABETH MARTIN, epidemiologist, researcher; d. William Oliver Martin and Marjorie Ann Turner; m. Grant Akira Yano, May 3, 1986; children: Michael, David, Steven. BS in Psychobiology, UCLA, 1983, MSPH in Epidemiology, 1986, PhD in Epidemiology, 1995. Rsch. analyst med. outcomes study RAND Corp., Santa Monica, Calif., 1984—86, rsch. epidemiologist, 1986—95; project mgr. dept. medicine UCLA, 1986—88, health svcs. rschr. Med. Treatment Effectiveness Program, 1993—94, assoc. prof. health svcs. Sch. Pub. Health, 1997—; sr. assoc. Arlene Fink Assocs., Inc.,

Pacific Palisades, Calif., 1986—95; assoc. chief pace evaluation Sepulveda (Calif.) VA Med. Ctr., 1989—94, assoc. chief evaluation and decision support, 1994—97; rsch. health scientist VA Health Svcs. R & D Ctr. Excellence, Sepulveda, 1993—97, asst. dir., 1997—99, assoc. dir., 1999—2002, sr. social scientist, 2002—, co-dir. VA associated health postdoctoral tng. program, 2002—. Mem. sci. rev. bd. VA Greater LA Healthcare Sys., 2002—; steering com. mem. nat. VA orgnl. survey VA Mgmt. Decision and Rsch. Ctr., Boston, 2001—; exec. com. mem. colorectal cancer quality enhancement rsch. initiative Ctr. for Chronic Disease Outcomes Rsch., Mpls., 2001—; mem. nat. ethics task force on gender disparities Dept. Vets., Washington, 2001—; presenter in field. Contbr. articles to profl. jours. Chair grant writing com. Carpenter Elem. Sch., Studio City, Calif., 2000. Recipient Achievement awards, UCLA Alumni Assn., 1980, 1981, Nat. Psychology Honors award, Psi Chi, 1982; grantee, VA HSR&D Svc., 1997—99, 1998—2002, VHA Survey of Women Veterans Health Programs and Practices, Dept. Vets. Affairs, 2001; Regents scholar, UCLA, 1979—83, Alumni scholar, UCLA Alumni Assn., 1979—83, UCLA Coll. Honors Meeker scholar, UCLA Coll. Honors Program, 1981—82, UCLA Marhoefer Med. scholar, UCLA, 1982—83, Health Policy fellow, RAND-UCLA, Inst. Medicine, Pew Meml. Trusts, 1986—89. Mem.: Acad. Health, Soc. for Gen. Internal Medicine. Office: VA Health Svcs R&D Ctr Excellence 16111 Plummer St 152 Sepulveda CA 91343 Office Phone: 818-895-9449. Business E-Mail: elizabeth.yano@med.va.gov.

YANOFF, ARTHUR SAMUEL, artist, art therapist educator; b. Boston, Mass., May 9, 1939; s. Jack and Sheila (Molensky) Yanoff; m. Carol Marie Meider (div.); 1 child, Lenya Alexis; m. Joan Elizabeth Zito, Jan. 10, 1977 (div.); 1 child, Almaisa Marishka. Student, Mus. Sch. of Fine Arts, Boston, 1958-61; studied with Jason Berger, Brookline, Mass., 1962-65. Instr. children's summer art program Temple Beth Jacob, Concord, NH, 1969; art design cons. Lillabulero Press, Northwood Narrows, 1967-74; art therapist for emotionally disturbed children N.H. Hosp., Concord, 1970-71, designer therapeutic program for children with learning disabilities, 1970-71; art instr. adult edn. program Coe-Brown Acad., Northwood, 1972; instr. Manchester Inst. Art, Concord, 1973-74, art therapist, 1975—. Instr. landscape painting Berkshire C.C., Great Barrington, Mass., 1997—; instr. Interlaken Sch. Art, Stockbridge, Mass., 1998—; artist in residence Joseph Eisner Camp, Great Barrington, 2002. Author: The Paste-Up Autobiography: A Visual Memoir; An Approach to Psychotherapy and Remedial Teaching, 1973; Brooks Sch., North Andover, Mass., 1966, one-man shows include B.E.L. Gallery, Westport, Conn., 1972, Boston Ctr. for Arts, 1974, Addison Gallery Am. Art, Andover, Mass., 1974, New Hampton Sch., N.H., 1976, Ithaca House Gallery, N.Y., 1976, Mus. Fine Arts, Boston, 1983, Babson Coll., Wellesley, Mass., 1983, Currier Mus. Art, Manchester, N.H., 1985, Concordia Coll., Bronxville, N.Y., 1986, Symposium '88 Le Centre D'Art, Baie-St-Paul, Que., 1999, Bobbie Lefenfeld Gallery, 2003, exhibited in group shows at Sarah Y. Rentschler Gallery, Hudson, N.Y., 2000, Western Wall Project, Deborah Davis Fine Art, Hudson, 2002—03, Perrala Gallery, Fulton Montgomery C.C., Johnstown, N.Y., 2003, C.W. White Gallery, Portland, Maine, 2003—, Deborah Davis Fine Art, 2003, 2004, Represented in permanent collections Congregation Ahavath Chesed, Jacksonville, Fla., Congregation Kesser Israel, Springfield, Mass., Mus. Fine Arts, Boston, Santa Fe, Addison Gallery Am. Art, Andover, New Hampton Sch., Commn. on Arts, Concord, N.H., N.H. Savs. Bank, Concord, Lee Bank, Lee, Mass., Hampshire Coll., Amherst, Mass., Yeshiva U. Mus., Babson Coll., MFA/Hines Indsl. Found., Cambridge, Mass., Rose Art Mus., Brandeis U., Waltham, Mass., Currier Mus. Art, Manchester, Le Centre D'Art, Baie-St-Paul, Chabad House Lubavitch of N.H., Manchester, Detroit Inst. Arts, Mus. Art, Ft. Lauderdale, Fla., Temple Beth Shalom, Santa Fe, exhibited in painting series, The Teaching of Isaac Luria, New Eng. Coll. Gallery, Henniker, N.H., 1995, Yeshiva U. Mus., N.Y.C., 1996—97, Koussevitzky Arts Festival, Berkshire C.C., Pittsfield, 1997, The Ea. Spirit in Contemporary Art, Coun. for Creative Projects, Warehouse Gallery, Lee, Mass., 1997, Gallery Talk: Renoir's Portraits and Landscapes, Sterling and Francine Clark Art Inst., Williamstown, Mass., 2000, exhibited in traveling show, Rural Artists with Urban Sensibilities, Perrella Gallery, Fulton Montgomery C.C., Johnstown, N.Y., 2003, Hudson Opera House, N.Y., 2004, exhibited in numerous shows, Mass., Va., N.H., Maine, Santa Fe. Recipient Prix, Rene Richard, Lingo Fine Arts Gallery, W. Stockbridge, Mass., 1999; grantee, Max and Anna Levnison Found. and Ctr. for Jewish Culture and Creativitiy, 1996—98; L.A. Meml. Found. Jewish Culture fellow, N.Y.C., 1989—90. Mem.: N.H. Art Assn., Am. Art Therapy Assn., Boston Painters and Sculptors, Am. Working Terrier Assn. (field trial judge), Greater Boston Kerry Blue Terrior Club (chmn. sheep guarding project), N.H. Sheep and Wool Growers Assn., Am. Southdown Breeders Assn., Livestock Guard Dog Assn. Hampshire Coll. Jewish. Avocation: study and evaluate terriers and other dogs for predator control and livestock protection. Home: 624 S Egremont Rd Great Barrington MA 01230-1930 Address: Deborah Davis Fine Arts Inc 345 Warren St Hudson NY 12534-

YANOFF, MYRON, ophthalmologist; b. Phila., Dec. 21, 1936; s. Jacob and Lillian S. (Fishman) Yanoff; m. Karin Michelle Lindblad, Aug. 8, 1980; 1 child, Alexis A.; children from previous marriage: Steven L., David A., Joanne M. AB, U. Pa., 1957, MD, 1961. Prof. ophthalmology and pathology U. Pa. Med. Sch., Phila.; William F. Norris and George E. de Schweinitz prof. ophthalmology, chmn. dept., dir. Scheie Eye Inst., 1977-86; chmn., prof. ophthalmology Drexel U., Phila., 1988—. 1st exch. vis. prof. U. Vienna, 1992. Author: Ocular Pathology, Textbook of Ophthalmology; contbr. articles to profl. jours. Served to maj. M.C. USAR. Recipient Humboldt award, 1988. Mem.: Am. Acad. Ophthalmology (Sr. Honor award 1995), Am. Ophthalmic Soc., Verhoeff Soc. Office: 219 N Broad St Fl 3 Philadelphia PA 19107 Office Phone: 215-832-0097.

YANOFSKY, CHARLES, biology professor; b. N.Y.C., Apr. 17, 1925; s. Frank and Jennie (Kopatz) Y.; m. Carol Cohen, June 19, 1949, (dec. Dec. 1990); children: Stephen David, Robert Howard, Martin Fred; m. Edna Crawford, Jan. 4, 1992. BS, CCNY, 1948; MS, Yale U., 1950, PhD, 1951, DSc (hon.), 1981, U. Chgo., 1980. Rsch. asst. Yale U., 1951-54; asst. prof. microbiology Western Res. U. Med. Sch., 1954-57; mem. faculty Stanford U., 1958—2000, prof. biology, 1961—2000, Herzstein prof. biology, 1966—2000, prof. emeritus, 2000—. Career investigator Am. Heart Assn., 1969-95. Served with AUS, 1944-46. Recipient Lederle Med. Faculty award, 1957, Eli Lilly award bacteriology, 1959, U.S. Steel Co. award molecular biology, 1964, Howard Taylor Ricketts award U. Chgo., 1966, Albert and Mary Lasker award, 1971, Townsend Harris medal Coll. City N.Y., 1973, Louisa Gross Horwitz prize in biology and biochemistry Columbia U., 1976, V.D. Mattia award Roche Inst., 1982, medal Genetics Soc. Am., 1983, Internat. award Gairdner Found., 1985, named Passano Laureate, Passano Found., 1992; recipient William C. Rose award in biochemistry and molecular biology, 1997, Abbott Lifetime Achievement award Am. Soc. Microbiology, 1998. Mem. NAS (Selman A. Waksman award in microbiology 1972), Am. Acad. Arts and Scis., Genetics Soc. Am. (pres. 1969, Thomas Hunt Morgan medal 1990), Am. Soc. Biol. Chemists (pres. 1984), Royal Soc. (fgn. mem.), Japanese Biochem. Soc. (hon.) Home: 725 Mayfield Ave Stanford CA 94305-1016 Office: Stanford U Dept Of Biological Sci Stanford CA 94305

YANSKY, BRIAN LEE, education educator, writer; s. William and Agnes Yansky; m. Frances Lee Hill, Dec. 18, 1987. BA, U. Tex., 1990; MFA, Vt. Coll. of Norwich U., 2002. Adj. faculty Austin CC, Austin, Tex., 1995—2002, asst. prof., 2002—. Author: (novels) My Road Trip to the Pretty Girl Capital of the World (Tex. Inst. Letters/ Best Young Adult Novel, 2003), (short stories) The Devil in Louisiana, Looking High and Low. Mem.: Nat. Assn. Devel. Edn. (assoc.). Avocations: reading, travel, film, martial arts. Home: 21 Kern Ramble Austin TX 78722 Personal E-mail: byansky@austincc.edu.

YANSOUNI, CYRIL J. computer company executive; BSEE, U. Louvian, Belgium; MSEE, Stanford U. Various tech. and mgmt. positions including v.p., gen. mgr. Hewlett-Packard Co., 1967-86; pres. Convergent Techs. (now Unisys Corp.), 1986-88; various sr. mgmt. positions including exec. v.p. Unisys Corp., 1988-91; CEO, chmn. Read-Rite, Milpitas, Calif., 1997-2000, chmn., 2000—. Dir. Informix Software, Inc., PeopleSoft, Inc., Raychem Corp., ActiveCard, Inc. Office: 345 Los Coches St Milpitas CA 95035-5428

YANTIS, STEVEN GEORGE, psychology educator; b. Oct. 24, 1955; BS in Psychology with honors, U. Wash., 1978; PhD in Exptl. Psychology, U. Mich., 1985. Postdoctoral fellow dept. psychology Stanford U., 1985-86; asst. prof. psychology Johns Hopkins U., Balt., 1986-92, assoc. prof. psychology and cognitive sci., 1992-95, prof. psychology, cognitive sci., 1995—. Mem. perception and cognition rsch. rev. com. NIMH, 1993-97, chair, 1996-97, spl. reviewer psychobiology and behavior rsch. rev. com. Mem. editl. bd. Jour. Exptl. Psychology: Human Perception and Performance, 1991—, Perception & Psychophysics, 1991—, Psychol. Bull., 1994—; contbr. articles to profl. jours. Recipient Troland Rsch. award NAS, 1996; NSF grad. fellow, 1981-84; Rackham Dissertation fellow, 1984-85. Mem. APA (Disting. Sci. award for Early Career Contbn. to Psychology 1994), Am. Psychol. Soc., Ea. Psychol. Assn., Psychonomic Soc. Office: Dept Psychology Ames 139 Johns Hopkins Univ Baltimore MD 21218-2686

YANUSHEVSKY, RAFAEL TOVIE, electromechanical engineer, scientist, consultant, educator; b. Kiev, Ukraine, Nov. 15, 1939; arrived in US, 1987; s. Tovie Isaac Yanushevsky and Beyla Efrime Kiperburg; m. Isabella Solomon Libel, Dec. 30, 1990; children: Camilla, Daniel. MS in Electromech. Engring., Kiev Poly. Inst., 1961; MS in Math, Kiev State U., 1964; PhD in Optimization Theory and Control, USSR Acad. Sci., 1967. Engr. Machine Tool Plant, Kiev, 1961—63; prof. Moscow State Auto. Tech. U., 1969—74; sr. scientist Inst. Control Sci., Moscow, 1964—76; prof. U. Md., College Park, 1988—92, U. D.C., 1988—97; sr. staff Sys. Engring. Group, Inc., Columbia, Md., 1998—2001; sr. scientist Tech. Svc. Corp., Silver Spring, Md., 2001—. Sr. cons. Analytic Sci. Corp., Arlington, Va., 1991—93, RTC, Bethesda, Md., 1993—. Author: Theory of Linear Optimal Multivariable Systems, 1973, Control Plants with Time-Lag, 1978, Optimal Control Systems, 1989, editor 20 books; contbr. articles to profl. jours. Recipient Letter of Appreciation, Dept. of Navy, 2002. Republican. Achievements include research in theory of differential difference systems. Avocations: music, tennis, soccer. Home: 5106 Danbury Rd Bethesda MD 20814 Office: Tech Svc Corp Washington Ops 962 Wayne Ave Ste 800 Silver Spring MD 20910 Office Phone: 301-576-2389.

YAO, BIN, mechanical engineering educator; b. Shaanxi, China, Dec. 23, 1968; came to U.S., 1992; s. Weikuan Yao and Qingrong Liu; m. Ying Xie, July 14, 1999 (div. 2003). PhD, U. Calif., Berkeley, 1996. Postdoctoral rschr. mech. engring. dept. U. Calif., Berkeley, 1996; asst. prof. Sch. Mech. Engring. Purdue U., West Lafayette, Ind., 1996—2002, assoc. prof. Sch. Mech. Engring., 2002—. Summer faculty sabbatical leave Advanced Hydraulics Group, Joliet (Ill.) plant, Caterpillar Inc., 1997. Contbr. numerous tech. articles to profl. publs. (NSF Career award 1998). Recipient D. Hugo Schuck Best Paper award Am. Automatic Control Coun., 2004; Regents fellow U. Calif., 1992. Mem. IEEE, ASME. Avocations: sports, travel, art, music. Office: Purdue U Sch Mech Engring West Lafayette IN 47907 Office Phone: 765-494-7746. Office Fax: 765-494-0539. E-mail: byao@ieee.org.

YAO, DAVID DA-WEI, engineering educator; b. Shanghai, July 14, 1950; came to U.S., 1983, naturalized, 1990; s. William Kang-Fu and Nancy Yun-Lan (Lu) Y.; m. Helen Zhi-Heng Chen, Jan. 31, 1979; children: Henry, John. MASc, U. Toronto, Ont., Can., 1981, PhD, 1983. Assoc. prof. systems engring. Harvard U., Cambridge, Mass., 1986-88; asst. prof. indsl. engring. and ops. rsch. Columbia U., N.Y.C., 1983-86, prof., 1988—, Thomas Alva Edison prof., 1992—. Acad. visitor AT&T Bell Labs., Holmdel, N.J., 1989, T.J. Watson Rsch. Ctr., IBM, Yorktown, N.Y., 1990—. Co-author: Monotone Structure in Discrete-Event Systems, 1994, Fundamentals of Queueing Networks, 2001, Dynamic Control of Quality in Production-Inventory Systems, 2002; contbr. over 150 articles to profl. jours. including Maths. Ops. Rsch., Jour. of Assn. Computing Machinery, Advances in Applied Probability. Recipient Presdl. Young Investigator award NSF, Washington, 1987-92, Guggenheim fellow John Simon Guggenheim Meml. Found., N.Y.C., 1991-92. Fellow IEEE; mem. Soc. Indsl. and Applied Math. (Outstanding Paper prize 2003), Ops. Rsch. Soc. Am. (George Nicholson prize 1983, Franz Edelman award 1999). Achievements include development of theory of algebraic structures in discrete-event systems, theory of stochastic convexity and its applications in queuing networks, stochastic network models for manufacturing systems and supply chains, methodologies in the optimization and control of stochastic discrete-event systems. Home: 1261 Underhill Ave Yorktown Heights NY 10598-5718 Office: Columbia U IEOR Dept 302 Mudd Bldg New York NY 10027-6699 Business E-Mail: yao@ieor.columbia.edu.

YAO, JOHN SEN, physician; b. Honolulu, Aug. 28, 1954; s. Hsin-Hung and Dorothy W. Yao; m. Pauline A. Mysliwiec, Oct. 16, 1993. MPH, Columbia U., 1978, MD, 1983; MBA, UCLA, 1998; MPA, Harvard U., 1999. Diplomate Am. Bd. Internal Medicine, Nat. Bd. Med. Examiners. Resident in internal medicine U. Calif.-San Francisco Med. Ctr., 1983-86, asst. clin. prof., 1988-94; chief med. officer USPHS, Calif., 1990-98; med. dir. Cigna Healthcare, inc., 1997-98; fellow in policy studies Harvard U., Cambridge, Mass., 1998—. Mem. exec. com. State of Calif. TB Control, 1994—; mem. steering com. Breast and Cervical Cancer Prevention, Stte of Calif., 1991-94; med. advisor State of Calif. Medicaid Reform com., 1994-95. Contbr. articles to profl. jours. Med. advisor Gov.'s Coun. on Exercise and Health, Calif., 19945; mem. Calif. HIV-AIDS Commn., 1990-93. Fellow ACP. Avocations: golf, tennis, skiing, classical music, opera. Office: PO Box 4675 El Dorado Hills CA 95762 E-mail: jyaomd@jyaomd.com.

YAO, TITO GO, pediatrician; b. Manila, May 30, 1943; arrived in U.S., 1970, naturalized, 1984; s. Vincente and Sin Keng (Go) Yao; m. Lilia Ytem, July 3, 1976; children: Robert, James, Richard. MD, Far Eastern U., Manila, 1969. Diplomate Am. Bd. Pediatrics, Am. Bd. Quality Assurance. Intern Evang. Deaconess Hosp., Milw., 1970-71; resident in pediatrics T.C. Thompson Children's Hosp., Chattanooga, 1971-72, Meth. Hosp., Bklyn., 1972-73; fellow St. Christopher Hosp. Children, Phila., 1973-74, Cook County Children's Hosp., Chgo., 1974-75; dir. GSK Med. Ctr., Chgo., 1976—; preceptor Rush Med. Coll., 2003—. Chmn. dept. pediat. St. Anne's Hosp., Chgo., 1986—88, Loretto Hosp., Chgo., 1988—; dir. RJ Med. Ctr., Chgo., 1980—; mem. staff Norwegian Am. Hosp., St. Anthony's Hosp., St. Mary Nazareth Hosp. Fellow: Am. Coll. Utilization Rev. Physicians, Am. Acad. Pediat. (life); mem.: AMA (life Physician Recognition award 1973—), Chgo. Pediatric Soc., Chgo. Med. Soc., Am. Assn. Individual Investors, Ill. Med. Assn., Assn. Philippine Physicians Practicing in Am. Office: 5351 W North Ave Chicago IL 60639-4350 also: 5140 W Chicago Ave Chicago IL 60651-2903 Office Phone: 773-889-4501. Personal E-mail: titogyao@aol.com.

YAPIJAKIS, CONSTANTINE, environmental engineer, educator, consultant; b. Drama, Macedonia, Greece, July 18, 1948; arrived in U.S., 1971; s. Nikos and Stella (Voyagi) Yapijakis; m. Lily Huang, July 10, 1993; 1 child, Nicole Isako. MS in Civil Engring., Nat. Tech. U., Athens, Greece, 1971; MS in Environ. Engring., NYU, 1973; PhD in Environ. Engring., Poly. U., N.Y.C., 1981. Registered profl. engr., N.Y., civil engr., Tech. Chamber of Greece. Jr. engr. Dr. Panaghiotakis' Cons. Group, Athens, 1969-71; intern engr. Dutch Pub. Wks. Dept., Amsterdam, 1970; environ. lab. asst. NYU, N.Y.C., 1971-73; environ. engr. City Planning Dept., N.Y.C., 1972, John J. Kassner & Co., N.Y.C., 1973, Hazen and Sawyer, P.C., N.Y.C., 1973-78; adj. prof. CCNY/Polytechnic U., 1977—; assoc. prof. Pratt Inst., N.Y.C., 1980-86; prof. environ. engring., environ. rsch. lab dir. The Cooper Union, N.Y.C., 1986—. Founding ptnr. Hellenic EnvironTech, Inc., Athens, Greece, 1991—; cons., presenter in field. Co-author: (book) Scale-up of Treatment Processes, 1983, Industrial Wastes Treatment Handbook, 1993, Hazardous Waste Site Remediation Mgmt., 1999, Water Quality-Reflection of Land Use, 1999, Environmental Engineering and Pollution Control, 2001, Handbook of Industrial and Hazardous Waste Treatment, 2004; contbr. articles to profl. jours. Recipient Earth Day award and medallion, City Club N.Y., 1995, Intern Egnr. award, Inst. Internat. Edn., 1972; grantee, NSF, 1988, 1992; scholar Intern. Engr., Internat. Assn. Students Tech. Edn., 1970, Sr. scholar, Fulbright Program, Greece, 1993—94, Fulbright Program, Aegean Initiative, 2002. Mem.: Assn. Environ. Engring. and Sci. Profs., Environ. Law Inst., N.Y. Water Environment Assn. (Met. chpt. bd. dirs. 1992—94, 2001—03, chmn. edn. com., Svc. award 1995, Membership award 1996—99, Svc. award 2004), N.Y. Acad. Scis. (judge h.s. sci. projects ann. competition 1994—), Internat. Assn. Water Quality, Am. Water Wks. Assn., Water Environment Fedn. (VIP Cir. 1994, Recruiters Recognition Club 1996). Achievements include development of design of preozonation - D.E. filtration process for New York City's water supply, design for rotating biological contractors for application to industrial and hazardous wastes; research in extensive lead contamination in surface soil of parks and playgrounds in New York City, perc pollution prevention study for 2000 drycleaners in N.Y.C; fast-rate bioremediation for protection of groundwater, enhanced solar evaporation for treatment of hazardous wastes; pollution prevention in the construction industry and brownfields development in N.Y.C. metro area. Avocations: travel, photography, reading, movies. Office: The Cooper Union Sch of Engring 51 Astor Pl New York NY 10003-7185 Office Phone: 212-353-4296.

YAPLE, HENRY MACK, librarian; b. Vicksburg, Mich., May 30, 1940; s. Henry J. and Pauline B. (Spencer) Y.; m. Marilyn Lou Bales, Dec. 31, 1971; children: Sean H., Kendra S. BA in English with hons., Kalamazoo Coll., 1963; MA, U. Idaho, 1966; postgrad., U. d'Aix-Marselle, France, 1965-66, U. Toronto, 1966-69; MLS, W. Mich. U., 1972. Order libr. Mich. State U., E. Lansing, 1972-74, humanities bibliographer, 1974-78; acquisitions libr. U. Wyo., Laramie, 1978-87; coll. libr. Whitman Coll., Walla Walla, Wash., 1987—. Mem. Wyo. Coun. for the Humanities, 1982-86. U. Toronto scholar, 1966-69; Rotary fellow, 1965, 66; U. Wyo. rsch. grantee, 1982, 86. Mem. ALA, Wyo. Libr. Assn. (pres. 1984-85), Nat. Ski Patrol System (sr. patroller 1978-95, nat. #6946 1988), Wash. Libr. Assn., Northwest Assn. of Pvt. Colls. and U. Librs. (pres. 1987-88, 94-95), Beta Phi Mu. Avocations: book collecting, skiing, kayaking. Home: 1889 Fern St Walla Walla WA 99362-9393 Office: Whitman Coll Penrose Libr 345 Boyer Ave Walla Walla WA 99362-2067 E-mail: yaple@whitman.edu.

YARBER, ROBERT EARL, writer, retired educator; b. East St. Louis, Ill., Sept. 28, 1929; s. Earl Yarber and Dorothy Anastasia Dwyer; m. Mary Roberta Winzerling, Nov. 27, 1952; children: Robert D., Charles C., Mary L. BA, McKendree Coll., 1951; MA, St. Louis U., 1953; postgrad., Exeter Coll. Oxford U., 1969. Prof. Mesa Coll., San Diego, 1963-89. Author: Writing for College, 1995, Reviewing Basic Grammar, 1996; contbr. articles to textbooks, revs., articles to profl. jours. Democrat. Roman Catholic. Home: 4125 Rochester Rd San Diego CA 92116-2123

YARBERRY, LONNIE STEPHEN, information scientist, director; b. Little Rock, June 30, 1957; s. Lonnie Ray Yarberry and Mary Lou Voss; m. Rhonda Ann Hunter, Sept. 4, 1998; children: Brian, Eric, Eric, Nikki. BS in Math. and Computer Sci., U. Ark., Little Rock, 1982, MS in Applied Math., 1986; PhD in Ops. Rsch., U. N.C., 1993. Cert. computer scientist Inst. for Certification of Computing Profls., 1986. Sys. analyst Savers Fed., Little Rock, 1982—86; micro computer cons. U. Ark., Little Rock, 1986—87; rsch. asst. U. N.C., Chapel Hill, NC, 1987—93; dir. info. tech. Baptist Health, Little Rock, 1994—. Adj. prof. Webster U., Little Rock, 1993—; cons. Yarberry & Assocs., Little Rock, 1982—. Contbr. articles to profl. jours. Mem.: Inst. Ops. Rsch. and the Mgmt. Scis., Phi Kappa Phi. Office: 904 Autumn Rd Ste 300 Little Rock AR 72112 E-mail: lsyarberry@baptist-health.org.

YARBOROUGH, CLINTON JOSEPH, lawyer; b. Ft. Leavenworth, Kans., Dec. 28, 1969; s. William Glenn and Betsy Yarborough; m. Patsy Lee, Aug. 16, 1997; child, CJ. BS, Coll. Charleston, 1991; JD, U. S.C., 1993. Bar: S.C. 1994, Ga. 1995, U.S. Dist. Ct. (so. dist.) S.C. 1995, U.S. Supreme Ct. 2000. Title abstractor Woodward, Leventis, Unger, Daves, Herndon & Cothran, Columbia, S.C., 1992-94; forclosure atty. Ronald C. Scott, P.A., Columbia, 1994-95; asst. pub. defender Defender Corp. Aiken County, Aiken, S.C., 1995-98; asst. dist. atty. Toombs Judicial Cir., Thomson, Ga., 1998-99; assoc. Jackson R. Massey & Assocs., P.C., Augusta, Ga., 1999-2000, Rogers, Townsend & Thomas, P.C., Columbia, SC, 2000—02; v.p. underwriting and claims counsel Atlantic Title Ins. Co., Columbia, 2002—03; assoc. state counsel First Am. Title Ins. Co., Columbia, 2003—. Mem. ABA, Sigma Chi, Rotary Internat. Roman Catholic. Avocations: archaeology, reading, anthropology, forestry. Office: PO Box 1462 Columbia SC 29202 Office Phone: 803-731-4409. Business E-Mail: cjyarborough@firstam.com.

YARBOROUGH, WILLIAM CALEB, retired race car driver; b. Timmonsville, S.C., Mar. 27, 1939; Named winner, Atlanta 500, 1967, 1968, 1974, Cam 2 Moto Oil 400, 1977, Capital City 400, 1976, Carolina 500, 1975, Daytona 500, 1968, 1977, 1983, 1984, Mazon-Dixon 500, 1969, Nat. 500, 1973, So. 500, 1968, 1973, 1974, 1978, Va. 500, 1974, 1977, Wilkes 400, 1974, Winston-Salem 500, 1974, champion, Winston Cup, 1976—78, Grand Nat. Champion, Champion Nat. Assn. Stock Car Auto Racing, 1976. Office: NASCAR 1801 W Internat Speedway Bd Daytona Beach FL 32114-1243

YARBOROUGH, WILLIAM GLENN, JR., military officer, forest farmer, defense and international business executive; b. June 21, 1940; s. William Glenn and Bessie (Rainsford) Y.; m. Betsy Gibson, Jan. 24, 1969; children: Bill, Clinton, Frank, Elizabeth. BS, U. S.C., 1961, MBA, 1969; postgrad., Command and Gen. Staff Coll., 1970, Naval War Coll., 1979, U. Va., 1983. Commd. to U.S. Army, advanced through grades to col., 1980, co. and troop comdr., squadron staff officer, 1961-71, strategist, 1971-73; chief of assignments Office Pers. Mgmt. Mil. Pers. Ctr., Washington, 1973-76; comdr. 1st Squadron 1st Cavalry, Europe, 1976-78; chief of staff, spl. asst. to chief of staff 1st Armored Divsn., Europe, 1978; br. chief Office of Chief of Staff, Washington, 1979-80; exec. to dep. comdg. gen. Material Devel. and Readiness Command, Washington, 1980-81; mil. dep. for asst. sec. for rsch., devel. and acquisition Washington, 1981-85; dir. ops. Ford Aerospace, Washington, 1986—89; army mktg. dir. Grumman Corp., Bethpage, NY, 1990-93; pres., CEO Allied Rsch. Corp., Vienna, Va., 1993—2001; founder & prin. WGY & Assocs. Bd. dirs. Carleton Techs., Eads N.Am. Def. Co., Am. Conversion Corp., Old Dominion Corp. Trustee Patton Mus.; bd. dirs. So Others Might Eat (Some), Easter Seals; bd. dirs. Moore Sch. Bus. U. S.C. Decorated Silver Star, Bronze Star medal with 4 oak leaf clusters and V device, Purple Heart, Legion of Merit. Mem. VFW, SAR, Assn. U.S. Army (George Washington chpt., v.p. membership), Am. Legion, Armed Forces Comms. and Electronics Assn., U.S. Army Armor Assn., Nat. Def. Indsl. Assn. (bd. dirs. N.Y. chpt.), Mil. Order of the World Wars, N.G. Assn., Res. Officers Assn., Soc. of the Purple Heart, Army-Navy Club, Army Navy Country Club, Belle-Meade Country Club, Tower Club. Home: Box 115 Thomson GA 30824 Office: Box 828 Mc Lean VA 22101 Office Phone: 703-748-1717. E-mail: wgyarc@aol.com.

YARBOROUGH, WILLIAM PELHAM, writer, lecturer, retired army officer, consultant; b. Seattle, May 12, 1912; s. Leroy W. and Addessia (Hooker) Y.; m. Norma Mae Tuttle, Dec. 26, 1936 (dec.); children: Norma Kay (dec.), William Lee, Patricia Mae. BS, U.S. Mil. Acad., 1936; grad., Command and Gen. Staff Coll., 1944, Brit. Staff Coll., 1950, Army War Coll., 1953. Commd. 2nd lt. U.S. Army, 1936, advanced through grades to lt. gen., 1968, ret., 1971, various assignments, 1936-42; exec. officer Paratroop Task Force, North Africa, 1942; comdr. 2d Bn., 504th Par. Inf. Regt., 82d Airborne Div., Sicily invasion, 1943, 509th Parachute Inf., Italy and France, 1943-44; comdg. officer 473 Inf., Italy, 1945; provost marshal 15th Army Group, ETO, 1945, Vienna Area Command and U.S. Forces, Austria, 1945-47; mem. staff, faculty U.S. Army Info. Sch., 1948-49; operations officer, gen. staff Joint Mil. Assistance Adv. Group, London, Eng., 1951-52; mem. faculty Army War Coll., 1953-56, 57; dep. chief Mil. Assistance and Adv. Group, Cambodia, 1956-57; comdg. officer 66th CIC Group, Stuttgart, Germany, 1958-60, 66th M.I. Group, Stuttgart, 1960; comdg. gen. U.S.A. Spl. Warfare Ctr.; also comdt. U.S. Army Spl. Warfare Sch., Ft. Bragg, 1961-65; sr. mem. UN Command Mil. Armistice Commn., Korea, 1965; asst. dep. chief staff DCSOPS for spl. operations Dept. Army, Washington; chmn. U.S. delegation Inter-Am. Def. Bd., Joint Brazil U.S. Def. Commn., Joint Mexican-U.S. Def. Commn.; Army mem. U.S. sect. permanent Joint Bd. on Def., Can.-U.S. Def. Commn., Washington, 1965; asst. chief of staff intelligence Dept. Army Washington, 1966-68; comdg. gen. I Corps Group, Korea, 1968-69; chief staff, also dep. comdr.-in-chief U.S. Army, Pacific, Hawaii, 1969-71. Contbr. Internat. Mil. and Def. Ency., 1993, MacMillan Ency. of the Am. Mil., 1994; William P. Yarborough collection papers and artifacts donated to Mugar Meml. Librs., Boston U. Decorated Disting. Svc. medal with three oak leaf clusters, Silver Star, Legion of Merit with three oak leaf clusters, Bronze Star, Joint Svc. Commendation medal with oak leaf clusters, Croix de Guerre with Palm

(France), Cross for Valor and Diploma (Italy), Order of Merit Second Class (Korea), Order of Ulchi (Korea). Fellow Co. Mil. Historians; mem. Kiwanis Club. Home: 160 Hillside Rd Southern Pines NC 28387-6727

YARBRO, ALAN DAVID, lawyer; b. Huntington, W.Va., Sept. 16, 1941; s. John David and Bernice (Bulette) Y.; m. Lee Merryman Myers, July 1961; children: Wendy, Jennifer, Caroline. AB magna cum laude, Harvard U., 1962, LLB cum laude, 1966. Bar: Md. 1966, U.S. Ct. Appeals (4th cir.) 1966, U.S. Dist. Ct. Md. 1966. Assoc. Venable Baetjer & Howard, Balt., 1966-72, ptnr., 1973-96, of counsel, 2002—; gen. counsel Mercantile Bankshares Corp., 1996—2002, corp. sec., 2002. Pres. W.S. Baer Corp., 1990—99. Trustee Children's Hosp., Balt., 1986-99, Children's Hosp. at Sinai Found., 1999—, Sinai Hosp. of Balt., 1999—; bd. dirs. The Park Heights St. Acad., Balt., 1986-89. Fellow Am. Bar Found., Md. Bar Found.; mem. ABA, Md. Bar Assn., Bar Assn. of Balt. (chmn. ethics com. 1988-89).

YARBROUGH, ALLYSON DEBRA, electrical engineer; b. Peterborough, England, Feb. 14, 1958; d. Freddy Dekhoma and Rosalind Mavis Y.; m. John Russell Scarpulla, May. 8, 1990. BSEE, N.Mex. State U., 1979; MSEE, Cornell U., 1985, PhD in Elec. Engring., 1988. Rsch. asst. Nat. Atmospheric and Ionospheric Ctr., Arecibo, P.R., 1979; microwave applications engr. Hewlett-Packard Co., Santa Rosa, Calif., 1979-82; assoc. prof. Calif. State U., L.A., 1988-89; tech. staff Aerospace Corp., El Segundo, Calif., 1989-93, sect. mgr., 1993-99, dept. dir., 1999—. Mem. IEEE, Microwave Theory and Techniques Soc., Alpha Kappa Alpha, Eta Kappa Nu. Democrat. Roman Catholic. Avocations: woodworking, sewing, collecting vintage radios. Home: 26821 Grays Lake Rd Palos Verdes Estates CA 90275 Office Phone: 310-375-9695. Personal E-mail: blue.onyx@verizon.net.

YARBROUGH, EDWARD MEACHAM, lawyer; b. Nashville, Dec. 17, 1943; s. Gurley McTyeire and Miriam (Mefford) Y. BA, Rhodes Coll., 1967; JD, Vanderbilt U., 1973. Bar: Tenn. 1973. Asst. dist. atty. Davidson County, Nashville, 1973-76; ptnr. Hollins, Wagster & Yarbrough, Nashville, 1976—. Chmn. com. Crime Commn., Nashville, 1981-82; mem. task force House Judiciary Com., Nashville, 1984; chmn. Crimestoppers Inc., Nashville, 1983-86; trustee United Way, Nashville, 1983-86, Belmont U., 1993-99, Cumberland Sci. Mus., 1996—; bd. dirs. Big Bros. Inc., Nashville, 1983-85; mem. nat. devel. bd. Lipscomb U., 2000—; vice chmn. deacons Forest Hills Bapt. Ch. Served to 1st lt. U.S. Army, 1969-71, Vietnam. Decorated Bronze Star; named Best Criminal Def. Atty., Bus. Nashville mag., 1999. Fellow Nat. Speleological Soc. (bd. dirs. 1960—); mem. ABA (bd. dirs. 1985), Tenn. Bar Assn., Nashville Bar Assn. (pres. 1983), Tenn. Criminal Def. Lawyers, Nashville Kiwanis (pres. 1992), Am. Legion, Richland Country Club, City Club (Nashville). Democrat. Baptist. Avocations: cave exploration, photography, skiing, golf, running. Home: 5230 Granny White Pike Nashville TN 37220-1715 Office: Hollins Wagster & Yarbrough Ste 2200 424 Church St Nashville TN 37219-2303

YARBROUGH, KAREN A. state representative; b. Wash., DC, Aug. 22, 1950; m. Henderson Yarbrough; children: Tami, Vicki, Carmen, Sara, Marcus, Henderson Jr. BA Bus. Admin., Chgo. State Univ., Chgo., Ill. 1993; MA Inner city Studies, NE Ill. Univ., Ill., 1996. Chief Exec. Officer Hathaway Ins. Agy., 1975—; Rep., Dist. 7 State House of Rep., 2000—. Candidate House of Rep., Dist. 7, Ill., 1998. Mem.: Juvenile Justice Reform, Ins. (Vice Chair), Appropriations - pub. safety, Maywood Chamber of Comm. (past pres. 1989—92, 1994—96), United Way of Suburban Chgo. (bd. exec. 1998—), Proviso Area United Way (v.p. 1987—2000), Profl. Indep. Ins. Agents (bd. mem. 1997—), Oak Park Young Men's Christian Assoc. (bd. mem. 1998), Elem. & Sec. Ed., Maywood Youth Mentoring Program (mem.), Maywood Live Theater (founder). Democrat. Bapt. Office: 292-S Straton Office Bldg Springfield IL 62706 also: 1030 South 17th Maywood IL 60153

YARBROUGH, KATHRYN DAVIS, public health nurse; b. Montrose, Colo., Aug. 31, 1947; d. L.O. and V. Jean (Dunn) Davis; m. James H. Yarbrough, Aug. 8, 1970; children: James, Jason. Diploma, Good Samaritan Hosp. Sch. Nursing, Phoenix, 1971; BSN, Kennesaw State Coll., 1996. RN, Ga.; cert. NAACOG. Supr. Cherokee County Health Dept., Canton, Ga., 1976-97. Den mother Boy Scouts Am., Canton, 1986-87; bd. dirs. Cancer soc., Canton, 1987—, Cherokee County Violence Ctr., 1990, First Steps Bd., 1993-97, Cherokee County Advocacy Ctr., 1994-97; HIV cons. ARC, Canton, 1988—, disaster vol., Cherokee County, 1993-99; co-chair Early Intervention Coun., Canton, 1991-93; mem. Leadership Cherokee, 1994, Interagy Coun., 1994; mem. Blue Ridge Jud. Cir. Domestic Violence Task Force, 1995. Mem.: ANA, Ga. Nurses Assn., Svc. League Cherokee County (hon.). Methodist. E-mail: Kyarbro216@aol.com.

YARBROUGH, MARTHA CORNELIA, music educator; b. Waycross, Ga., Feb. 8, 1940; d. Henry Elliott and Jessie (Sirmans) Y. BME, Stetson U., 1962; MME, Fla. State U., 1968, PhD, 1973. Choral dir. Ware County H.S., Waycross, 1962-64, Glynn Acad., Brunswick, Ga., 1964—70; asst. choral dir. Fla. State U., 1970-72; cons. in music Muscogee County Sch. Dist., Columbus, Ga., 1972-73; cons. in tchr. edn. Psycho-Edno. Cons., Inc., Tallahassee, 1972-73; asst. prof. music edn., dir. choruses and oratorio socs. Syracuse (NY) U., 1973-76; assoc. prof. music edn. Syracuse U., 1976-83, prof., 1983-86, acting asst. dean Coll. Visual and Performing Arts, 1980-82, acting dir. Sch. Music, 1980-82, chmn. music edn., 1982-86; prof. music La. State U., Baton Rouge, 1986—, coord. music edn., 1986—2000, Haymon prof. of music, 1995—. Artist-in-residence Sch. Music U. Ala., Tuscaloosa, 1989-90, 98, 2002; chair exec. com. Music Edn. Rsch. Coun., 1992-94. Co-author: Competency-Based Music Education, 1980; mem. editl. com.: Jour. Rsch. in Music Edn., editor-in-chief:, 2000—; contbr. chapters to books, articles to profl. jours. Mem. Music Educators Nat. Conf. (Sr. Rschr. award 1996), La. State Music Assn., Am. Ednl. Rsch. Assn., Soc. Rsch. Music Edn. (mem. exec. com. 1988-90, program chair 1990-92, chair 1992-94), AAUP, Coll. Music Soc., Pi Kappa Lambda, Phi Beta, Kappa Delta Pi. Office: Sch Music La State U Baton Rouge LA 70803-2504 Office Phone: 225-578-2481. Business E-Mail: cyarbro@lsu.edu.

YARCHOAN, ROBERT, clinical immunologist, researcher; b. N.Y.C., July 21, 1950; s. Zachary and Anne Mae (Veneroso) Y.; m. Giovana Tosato; children: Mark, John. BA magna cum laude, Amherst Coll., 1971; MD, U. Pa., 1975. Diplomate Am. Bd. Internal Medicine, Am. Bd. Allergy and Immunology. Resident in medicine U. Minn. Hosps., Mpls., 1975-78; clin. assoc. metabolism br. Nat. Cancer Inst., Bethesda, Md., 1978-80, investigator metabolism br., 1980-83, investigator clin. oncology program, 1983-87, sr. investigator clin. oncology program, 1988-91, chief retroviral diseases sect. medicine br., 1991-96, chief HIV and AIDS malignancy br., 1996—. Co-author: (chpt.) Cecil Textbook of Medicine, 1992, 95, 99; assoc. editor Jour. Immunology, 1985-89, AIDS Rsch. and Human Retroviruses, 1986-2004, AIDS, 1990-00, Jour. AIDS, 2000—, Jour. Human Virology, 2002—; sect. editor Thymus, 1992-97; contbr. articles to sci. jours.; patentee in field. Capt. USPHS, 1978—. Recipient Commendation medal USPHS, 1991, Asst. Sec. Health award U.S. govt. Dept. Health & Human Svcs., 1989, Inventors award U.S. Dept. Commerce, 1986, 87, Fed. Tech. Transfer Act award, 1999, 2000, 01, Outstanding Svc. medal USPHS, 2002. Fellow AAAS; mem. Am. Soc. Hematology, Am. Assn. Immunologists, Clin. Immunology Soc., Am. Soc. for Clin. Investigation, Internat. AIDS Soc. Achievements include co-inventor of therapies for AIDS and AIDS malignancies including ddI (didanosine) and ddC (zalcitabine) for AIDS and IL-12 for Kaposi's sarcoma; co-developer of therapies for AIDS and AIDS malignancies including AZT (zidovudine) for AIDS and paclitaxel for Kaposi's sarcoma; research in interactions between viruses and the immune system, therapy of AIDS and virally induced tumors; pathogenesis of AIDS and viral-induced tumors.

YARD, MOLLY, social activist; b. China; d. James Maxon and Mabelle Merriam (Hickcox) Y.; m. Sylvester Garrett; 3 children. AB, Swarthmore Coll., 1933, Hon. LLD, 1988. Chmn. Am. Student Union; active in Dem. party politics, Pa. and Calif., 1940s and 50s; active in civil rights movement, Pa., 1960s and 70s; staff mem. VISTA, 1960s; active NOW, from 1970s, polit. dir., 1985-87, pres., 1987-91.

YARD, SHERRY, chef; b. Bklyn. Pastry chef Spago, Beverly Hills, Calif. Recipient pastry chef of yr. award, So. Calif. Restaurant Writers Assn. Office: Spago 176 N Canon Dr Beverly Hills CA 90210

YARDE, RICHARD FOSTER, art educator; b. Boston, Oct. 29, 1939; s. Edgar St. Clair and Enid (Foster) Y.; m. Susan Donovan, July 8, 1967; children: Marcus, Owen. BFA in Painting cum laude, Boston U., 1962, MFA, 1964; DFA (hon., Mass. Coll. Arts, Boston, 1998. Asst. prof. art Boston U., 1965-71; assoc. prof. art Wellesley Coll., 1971-76; vis. assoc. prof. Amherst Coll., 1976-77, Mt. Holyoke Coll., 1980-81; vis. artist Mass. Coll. Art, 1977-80; prof. art U. Mass., Boston, 1981-90, Amherst, 1990—. Visual arts panelist Mass. Coun. Art and Humanities, 1976-78; bd. overseers Inst. Contemporary Art, Boston, 1991-2003; panelist Painting Mass. Cultural Coun. One-man shows include Studio Mus. in Harlem, San Diego Mus., Balt. Mus., Smith Coll. Mus. Art, Northampton, Mass., 1997, Mass. Coll. Art, 1996-99, Worcester Mus. Art, Mass., 2003; exhibited in group shows at Newport (RI) Art Mus., NAD, NYC, Mass., Smithsonian Inst., Washington, 1999, New Mus. Contemporary Art, NYC, 1999, Mus. Fine Arts, Boston, 1999, Master Drawings from the Smith Coll. Art Mus., Lacaixa, Madrid, Spain, 2002, DeCordova Mus., Lincoln, Mass., 2002, Inst. Contemporary Art, Boston, 2003, Heckscher Mus. Art, Huntington, NY, 2003, NAS, Washington, 2004, Sheldon Meml. Art Gallery U. Nebr., Lincoln. Recipient Alumni award for disting. contbn. to arts Boston U., 1987, Chancellor's award for disting. scholarship U. Mass., Boston, 1984, Acad. award in art Am. Acad. Arts and Letters, 1995, Disting. Tchg. award U. Mass. Amherst, 1997, Works on Paper award New Eng. Found. for the Arts, Boston, 1998; Nat. Endowment for Arts fellow, 1976, Samuel F. Conti faculty fellow U. Mass., 2000, When the Spirit Moves Group Exhib., Spelman Coll. Mus., 2000, Charles Wright Mus., 2000, Commonwealth Award, Artist Category, Mass. Cultural Council, 2001, William P. and Gertrude Schweitzer prize NAD, NY, others. Office: U Mass Amherst care Arts Dept Fine Arts Ctr Box 32150 Amherst MA 01003 Office Phone: 413-545-1902.

YARDLEY, JONATHAN, journalist; b. Pitts., Oct. 27, 1939; s. William Woolsey and Helen (Gregory) Y.; m. Rosemary Roberts, June 14, 1961 (div. 1975); children: James Barrett, William W. II.; m. Susan L. Hartt, Mar. 23, 1975 (div. 1998); m. Marie Arana, Mar. 21, 1999. AB, U. N.C., 1961; DHL (hon.), George Washington U., 1987. Writer N.Y. Times, 1961—64; editl. writer, book editor Greensboro (N.C.) Daily News, 1964—74; book editor Miami (Fla.) Herald, 1974—78, Washington Star, 1978—81; book critic Washington Post, 1981—. Author: Ring: A Biography of Ring Lardner, 1977, Our Kind of People: The Story of an American Family, 1989, Out of Step: Notes from a Purple Decade, 1991, States of Mind: A Personal Journey Through the Mid-Atlantic, 1993, Misfit: The Strange Life of Frederick Exley, 1997, Monday Morning Quarterback, 1998; editor: My Life as Author and Editor (H.L. Mencken), 1993, Selected Stories (Ring Lardner), 1997. Recipient Pulitzer prize for criticism, 1981, Disting. Alumnus award U. N.C., 1989; Nieman fellow in journalism Harvard U., 1968-69. Home: 100 5th St NE Washington DC 20002-5936 Office: Washington Post 1150 15th St NW Washington DC 20071-0001 Office Phone: 202-544-7779. E-mail: yardleyj@washpost.com.

YARED, GABRIEL, composer; b. Lebanon, 1949; Composer, orchestrator, 1973—. Composer for Johnny Hallyday, Charles Aznavour, Gilbert Becaud, Mireille Mathieu, Sylvie Vartan, Tania Maria, Francoise Hardy, (filmography) Sauve Qui Peut La Vie, 1980, Malevil, 1980, L'Invitation au voyage, 1981, Interdit au moins de treize ans, 1982, La Lune dans le carniveau, 1983 (Gran Prix de la SACEM, 1984), La Jave des ombres, 1983, La Scarlatine, 1983, Sarah, 1983, Les Petites guerres, 1983, Nemo, 1984, Hanna K, 1984 (Gran Prix de la SACEM, 1984), La Diagonale du fou, 1984, Tir à vue, 1984, Le Téléphone sonne toujours deux fois, 1985, Adieu Bonaparte, 1985, Scout toujours, 1985, 37 2 le Matin (nominee Césars, 1988, Victiores, 1988), Gandahar contre les hommes machines, 1987, Beyond Therapy, 1987, Agent Trouble, 1987, Clean and Sober, 1988, Le Testament d'un poète juif assassiné, Les Saisons du plasir, 1988, L'Homme voilé, 1988, Une Nuit à l'Assemblée nationale, 1988, La Romana, 1988, Camille Claudel, 1988 (nominee Césars, 1989, Victoire de la Musique, 1989), Tennessee Nights, 1989, Romero, 1989, Tennessee Waltz, 1989, Les Mille et une nuits, 1989, Vincent and Theo, 1990, Vincent et Théo, 1990, Tatie Danielle, 1990, La Putain du roi, 1990, L'Amant, 1991 (Victoire de la Musique, 1993, César de la Musique, 1993, nominee Internat. Musical Visual award, 1993), L'Arche et les déluges, 1991, IP5, 1991, Map of the Human Heart, 1992, Coeur de métisse, 1992 (nominee Australian Film Inst. award, 1993), La Fille de l'air, 1992, L'Instinct de l'ange (nominee Midem award l'ensemble de son oeuvre, 1993), Les Marmottes, 1993 (nominee Victoires, 1994), Des Feux mal étients, 1993, Profil bas, 1993 (nominee Midem award for l'ensemble de son oeuvre, 1994), Wings of Courage, 1994, Noir comme le souvenir, 1995 (nominee Victoires de la Musique, 1996), Hercule et Sherlock, 1996, English Patient, 1996 (Golden Globe award, 1996, First Golden Satellite award, 1997, Oscar, 1997, Brit. Acad. Arts and TV award, 1997, Indie award, 1997, Grammy awards, 1998, Victoire de la Musique, 1998, Gran Prix de la SACEM, 1998, nominee Acad. award, 1996, Comdr. des Arts et Lettres), Tonka, 1997, City of Angels, 1998 (Film and TV Music award, 1998, nominee Golden Satellite award, 1998, nominee Grammy awards, 1998), Message in a Bottle, 1999.

YARICK, PAUL E. food products executive; V.p., treas. Interstate Bakeries Corp., Kansas City, Mo. Office: Interstate Bakeries Corp PO Box 419627 Kansas City MO 64141-6627

YARICK-CROSS, DORIS, voice educator, soprano; d. Esmer Jasper and Ruth Burns; m. Richard Cross, June 21, 1963; children: Catherine Kalonia, Dylan Ma'is Cross. MA, Westminster Choir Sch. Soprano Chgo. Lyric Opera, Chgo., 1960; lyric soprano NYC Opera, NYC, 1960—64; soprano Santa Fe Opera, Santa Fe, 1960—70, San Francisco Opera, 1962—63, Sutherland Williamson Opera Co, Australia, 1965, Frankfurt Opera, Germany, 1966—78, Boston Opera, 1967; prof. U Tex., Austin, Tex., 1978—80, U. Conn., Storrs, Conn., 1980—83; prof., dir., head of voice and opera Yale Sch. of Music, Yale U., New Haven, 1983—. Profl. divsn. judge, coord. of collegiate divsn. MacAllister Competition, Indpls., 1995—2002; judge Met. Opera, Auditions, NYC, Fulbright Com., NYC; evaluator Conn. Coun. for the Arts, Westchester Coun. of the Arts, NY. Recipient Joy in Singing award, Joy in Singing, 1960.

YARINGTON, CHARLES THOMAS, JR., surgeon, educator, health facility administrator; b. Sayre, Pa., Apr. 26, 1934; s. C.T. and Florence (Hutchinson) Yarington; m. Barbara Taylor Johnson, Sept. 28, 1963; children: Leslie Anne, Jennifer Lynne, Barbara Jane. AB, Princeton U., 1956; MD, Hahnemann Med. Coll., 1960; grad., Army Command and Gen. Staff Coll., 1969, Air War Coll., 1973, Indsl. Coll. Armed Forces, 1974. Intern Rochester (NY) Gen. Hosp., 1960-61; resident Dartmouth Hosp., 1961-62, U. Rochester Strong Meml. Hosp., 1962-65; instr. otolaryngology U. Rochester Sch. Medicine, 1962-65; chief ENT U.S. Army Hosp., Ft. Carson, Colo., 1965—67; asst. prof. surgery W.Va. U. Sch. Medicine, 1967-68; assoc. prof., chmn. dept. otorhinolaryngology U. Nebr. Med. Ctr., 1968-69, prof., chmn. dept. otorhinolaryngology, 1969-74; clin. prof. otolaryngology U. Wash., Seattle, 1974—; clin. prof. surgery Uniformed Svcs. U. Health Scis., Bethesda, Md., 1985—; chief otolaryngology Virginia Mason Med. Ctr., Seattle, 1978-88, 92-95, chief dept. surgery, 1988-91; surgeon Mason Clinic, Seattle, 1974-97. Cons. Surg. Gen. USAF, Hunter Group Med. Mgmt. Cons., 1996-98, Seattle Multispecialty Panel, 1998—; pres. Virginia Mason Rsch. Ctr., Seattle, 1983-85; trustee Mason Clinic, 1988-91; adv. coun. Nat. Inst. Neurol. Diseases, Communicative Diseases, Stroke of NIH, Bethesda, Md., 1986-90; bd. dirs. Virginia Mason Hosp., Virginia Mason Med. Ctr., bd. govs., 1989-98. Author books and articles in field.; mem. editl. bd. Aviation, Space, Environ. Med. Jour., Otol. Clinics of N.Am., Mil. Medicine, Otolaryngology-Head and Neck Surgery. Trustee Seattle Opera Assn., 1983-89. Served to lt. to lt. col. USAR, 56-70, to brig. gen. USAF, 1970-86. Decorated D.S.M., Legion of Merit, comdr. Venerable Order St. John (Gt. Britain), companion with star Order Orthodox Hospitallers (Republic of Cypress), knight grand cross Mil. and Hospitaller Order of St. Lazarus; recipient Sir Henry Wellcome medal, 1984. Fellow ACS, Royal Soc. Medicine, Am. Acad. Otolaryngology (Barraquer Meml. award 1968, mem. standing com., bd. govs. 1982-88, Honor award 1974); mem. AMA, Am. Broncho-Esophagological Assn. (coun., treas. 1982-86, pres. 1987-88), Am. Laryngol. Assn., Pacific Coast Soc. Ophthalmology and Otolaryngology (coun., pres. 1987-88), Soc. Med. Cons. to Armed Forces, Am. Soc. Head and Neck Surgery, N.W. Acad. Head and Neck Surgery (pres. 1984-86), Am. Soc. Otology, Rhinology and Laryngology (v.p. 1992-93, coun. 1997-2000), Res. Officers Assn. (past pres. Seattle chpt., nat. officer), Soc. Colonial Wars, Sons Revolution (pres. Wash. 1985-87), Internat. Power Boat Assn. (comdr. 1999-2000), Seattle Yacht Club (trustee 2001—), Princeton Quadrangle Club, Broadmoor Golf Club, RAF Club (London), Sigma Xi.

YARINGTON, DAVID JON, retired educator; b. Auburn, N.Y., Sept. 13, 1936; s. Charles T. and Florence Yarington; m. Maybelle Yarington, Nov. 10, 1982; children: John, Susan. BA, Duke U., 1960; MEd, Cornell U., 1961; DEd, U. Pa., 1966. Cert. fundraising exec. Prof. Ohio U., Athens, 1964-66, U. Mass., Amherst, 1967-71; prof., head dept. Aquinas Coll., Grand Rapids, Mich., 1972-76; v.p. acad. affairs Lake Superior State U., Sault, Mich., 1976-78; dir. devel. Ea. Conn. State U., Willimantic, 1979-89, U. Maine, Orono, 1990-94; devel. officer Yale U., New Haven, 1995-97; ret., 1997. Rsch. fellow U. Pa., Phila., 1962-65. Author: Surviving In College, 1976, The Great American Reading Machine, 1977; contbr. articles to profl. jours. V.p. Rotary Internat., Willimantic, 1988, Bangor, 1994. With U.S. Army, 1956-58. U.S. Office Edn. fellow, 1966-67; rsch. grantee U.S. Office Edn. Mem. Peninsular Club. Methodist. Avocation: collecting rare books. Home: 0-1710 W Leonard Rd Grand Rapids MI 49544

YARIV, AMNON, electrical engineering educator, scientist; b. Tel Aviv, Apr. 13, 1930; arrived in U.S., 1951, naturalized, 1964; s. Shraga and Henya (Davidson) Y.; m. Frances Pokras, Apr. 10, 1972; children: Elizabeth, Dana, Gabriela. BS, U. Calif., Berkeley, 1954, MS, 1956, PhD, 1958. Mem. tech. staff Bell Telephone Labs., 1959-63; dir. laser research Watkins-Johnson Co., 1963-64; mem. faculty Calif. Inst. Tech., 1964—, Martin Summerfield prof. applied physics, 1966—. Co-founder Arroyo Optics, Inc. Author: Quantum Electronics, 1967, 75, 85, Introduction to Optical Electronics, 1971, 77, 89, Theory and Applications of Quantum Mechanics, Propagation of Light in Crystals. Served with Israeli Army, 1948-50. Recipient Pender award U. Pa., Harvey prize Technion, Israel, 1992. Fellow IEEE (Quantum Electronics award 1980), Am. Optical Soc. (Ives medal 1986, Esther Beller medal 1998), Am. Acad. Arts and Scis.; mem. NAS, NAE, Am. Phys. Soc. Office: 1201 E California Blvd Pasadena CA 91125-0001

YARMEY, RICHARD ANDREW, investment manager; b. Kingston, Pa., Aug. 23, 1948; s. Stanley Richard and Rose Mary (Rees) Y.; m. Jeanne Marie Cappelli, Aug. 5, 1972; children: Lynn Rees, Jessica Brett, Kristen Alexandra. BS, U. Scranton, 1970; JD, Cath. U., 1975. Bar: Pa. 1975, D.C. 1976, U.S. Ct. Appeals (5th cir.) 1976, U.S. Tax Ct. 1978, U.S. Ct. Appeals (D.C. cir.) 1980. Contract adjudicator GAO, Washington, 1970-73; program asst. EPA, Washington, 1973; assoc. Sharon, Pierson, et al, Washington, 1975-82; of counsel Pierson, Semmes et al, Washington, 1982-93; prin. Yarmey Capital Mgmt., 1989-95; sr. portfolio mgr. PNC Advisors, 1995—; mng. dir. Instl. Investment Group, 2000—02; portfolio mgr. Pvt. Investment Adv. Program Merrill Lynch, Wilkes-Barre, Pa., 2002—. Fin. cons. various pension plans, individuals and bus. concerns, 1976—; TV panelist, speaker, writer on portfolio mgmt.; instr. fin. mgmt. and investments continuing edn. Wilkes U., Wilkes-Barre. Mem. Pa. Bar Assn., Aircraft Owners and Pilots Assn., Alpha Sigma Nu. Democrat. Avocation: cabinetmaking. Office: 600 Balt Dr Wilkes Barre PA 18702 Office Phone: 570-829-8052. Business E-Mail: ryarmey@pclient.ml.com.

YARMO, FANNY F. not-for-profit fundraiser; b. Kansas City, Mo., Dec. 25, 1910; d. Sol and Della Fox; m. Al Yarmo (dec. Feb. 19, 1987); 1 child, Robert L.; m. Leo Sofnas, 1936 (dec. 1950). BS in Bus. summa cum laude, U. Kans., 1931. Ins. sec. Norman Hobart, Kansas City, 1931—32; Spanish translator Ismert Hincke Milling, Kansas City, 1932—35; pres. Fan-Ro Corp., Kansas City, 1954—75; regional treas. Sisterhood, Kansas City, 1989—90. Hon. fellow Truman Libr. Sch. for Democracy, Kansas City, 1992—, patron Truman Libr. Independence, Mo., 1999; patron vis. artists Kemper Art Mus., Kansas City, 1999—; charter patron Spencer Libr.--Nelson-Atkins Mus., Kansas City, 1999; TZDA art patron Jewish Cmty. Ctr., Overland Park, Kans., 1999—; life mem. Hadassah Menorah Hosp., 1945—; mem. Kansas City Historic Found., 1999—; charter patron Kemper Mus. Art; vol. Friends of O.P. Arts, Congregation Hesed Com.; mem. Nat. Wildlife Press, Friends of DAV; vice chmn. then life mem. chmn. NCJW, Kansas City; life mem. chmn. Brandeis U. Women, Kansas City, 1960; spl. gifts chmn. Fedn., Kansas City, 1965; mem. pres. coun. Art Inst., 1980—87; mem. nat. com. Kemper Art Mus., Kansas City, 2001—03; mem. univ. assocs. U. Mo., Kansas City, 1995—. Mem.: AAUW, Symphony Women's Assn., Mo. Reperatory Theatre Patron, Smithsonian Inst., Oakwood C.C. (life), Native Sons of Kansas City, Jewish War Vets Assn., Phi Chi Theta. Jewish. Avocations: bridge, Mah Jongg, Bible study, computers. Home: 102 E woodbridge Ln Kansas City MO 64145

YARNO, WENDY, pharmaceutical executive; BA, Portland State U., 1982; MBA, Temple U., 1988. Profl. rep. U.S. Human Health, 1983—85, mktg. analyst, 1985—87, product mgr. pediatric vaccines, 1988, assoc. dir. econ. affaris, 1989, sr. dir. mktg. planning, 1990—91, nat. account exec., 1991, sr. dir. managed health care affairs, 1992, project leader for U.S. Health Care Reform, 1992—93; v.p. ctrl. region Merck-Medco, 1994; v.p. hypertension and heart failure therapeutic bus. group U.S. Human Health, 1994—97; v.p. Ortho McNeil Pharm., Johnson & Johnson, 1997—98; v.p. worldwide human health Merck & Co., Inc., Whitehouse Station, NJ, 1999, v.p. human resources, 1999, sr. v.p. human resources, 2000—. Named Hon. Chairperson for Dinner of Hope, Somerset Hills Handicapped Riding Ctr. Office: Merck and Co Inc One Merck Dr Whitehouse Station NJ 08889-0100

YARNOLD, DAVID, editor; Grad., San Jose State U. City desk clk. San Jose (Calif.) Mercury News, 1977, copy editor, reporter, asst. mng. editor for graphics, picture editor, mng. editor, 1995—99, sr. v.p., editor, 2003—. Chmn. mng. editors diversity com. AP, 1999—. Mem. exec. com. Silicon Valley chpt. Am. Leadership Forum; bd. mem. RAFT. Recipient Leadership award, Columbia Grad. Sch. Journalism, 2002, Catalyst award, Nat. Assn. Minority Media Execs., 2003. Mem.: Am. Soc. Newspaper Editors (chair diversity com. 2003). Office: San Jose Mercury News 750 Ridder Park Dr San Jose CA 95190-0001

YAROS, CONSTANCE GREENBERG, painter, sculptor; b. Phila., Aug. 03; d. Harry William and Dorothy (Hofberg) Greenberg; m. Irvin Yaros, June 17, 1950 (dec. Nov. 6, 1983); children: Michael J. Yaros, Aimee Y. Silverman, Nancy S. Yaros. Student, Temple U., Tyler Sch. of Art, 1957-60, Blai Studio, 1976-81, Pa. Acad. Fine Arts, 1978-79, 87, Schuler Sch. of Art, 1990. One-woman shows include Tyler Alumni Gallery, 1992; exhibited in group shows including History Mus., Phila., 1984-88, Woodmere Art Mus., Phila., 1995, Am. Artists Profl. League, N.Y., 1993, Oil Painters Am., 1994, Art at the Armory, Phila., 1990-92, Artists Equity Assn. Triennial, 1984, 88, 91, Allied Artists of Am., 1988, Catherine Loriliard Wolfe Art Club, 1988, Salmagundi Art Club, 1988, Tyler Alumni Gallery-Diamond Club, Temple U., 1988-92, Phila. Sketch Club, 1987, Old York Rd. Art Guild, 1975; public collections at Temple U., Jefferson Park Hosp., Bd. City Trusts, Fed. Dist. Ct. House, Bd. City Trusts; numerous pvt. collections. Mem. Portrait Soc. Am., Am. Technion Assn., Greenpeace, Phila. Mus. Art, Allied Artists Am., Am. Soc. Classical Realism, Am. Soc. Portrait Artists, Am. Artist Profl. League, Pa. Acad. Fine Arts, Oil Painters Am., Artists Equity Assn., Woodmere Art Mus., Phila. Art Alliance, Archives of Women's Mus. of Art, Alumni Pa. Acad. Fine Arts, Alumni Tyler Sch. Art., Plastic Art Club. Avocations: music, ballet, exercise, photography, animal protection. Home and Office: 2401 Pennsylvania Ave Ste 4a5 Philadelphia PA 19130-3002

YAROWS, STEVEN ALLEN, internist; BS, U. Mich.; MD, Wayne State U., 1977. Diplomate Am. Bd. of Medicine, 1980, cert. specialist in hypertension Am. Soc. of Hypertension, 1999. Intern, resident Henry Ford Hosp., Detroit, 1977—81; dir. ICU Chelsea (Mich.) Cmty. Hosp., 1985, chief of medicine, 1988—. Bd. dir. Purple Rose Theater, Chelsea, 1990—2002, Huron Valley

Ambulance, Ann Arbor, Mich., 1990—97. Named one of Best Doctors in Am., Woodward White, 1999—2002. Fellow: ACP; mem.: Am. Heart Assn. (bd. dir. 2002). Office: Chelsea Internal Medicine PLLC 128 Van Buren Chelsea MI 48118 E-mail: syarows@cimmd.com.

YARRIGLE, CHARLENE SANDRA SHUEY, realtor, investment advisor; b. Redlands, Calif., July 25, 1940; d. Troy Frank and Anna (Miskew) Shuey; m. Robert Charles Yarrigle, Oct. 16, 1965 (div. July 1985); children: Stephanie Ann, Steven Charles. AA, San Bernardino (Calif.) Coll., 1965; student, Ariz. State U., 1965-66; BS, No.Mich. U., 1976; postgrad., No. Mich. U., 1976-77. Clk. Bungalow Grocery, Redlands, 1957-59; operator Pacific Tel. Co., San Bernardino, 1958-61; svc. rep. So. Calif. Gas, San Bernardino, 1961-66; tchr. bus. Gwinn (Mich.) HS, 1976-78; realtor, investment counselor Remax Fair Oaks, Calif., 1978—; broker, 1990—. Tchr. Project 100,000, Sheppard AFB, Wichita Falls, Tex., 1966—70. Vol. Easter Seal Soc., Humane Soc., Coventry Ho.; adv. mentally ill; tchr. family-to-family classes Nat. Alliance Mentally Ill., 1999—; mem. steering com., adv. bd. Sacramento Bd. Realtors, 1981—. Mem.: NAFE, Sacramento Assn. Realtors, Calif. Assn. Realtors (Outstanding Life Mem., Master's Club 1981—2003), Nat. Assn. Realtors (lic.), Nat. Alliance Female Execs., Calif. Alliance Mentally Ill (adv.), Nat. Alliance Mentally Ill (adv.). Republican. Avocations: financial planning for seniors, physical fitness, stock market, gardening. Office: Remax Gold Internat 5252 Sunrise Blvd Ste 6 Fair Oaks CA 95628-3535 E-mail: charrigle@aol.com.

YARRINGTON, GEORGE A. retired public relations executive, advertising executive, writer; b. Springfield, Mass., Oct. 20, 1906; s. George Timberlake and Jennie Elizabeth Yarrington; m. Katherine Peter Yarrington, Apr. 15, 1944. BA, Comml. Sci., Northeastern Univ., Boston, MA, 1930—34. Free-lance writer Self Employed, Belleville, Ill., 1972—2002; pub. rels. dir. Builders Assn., Boston, 1968—72; exec. dir. Quincy Taxpayers Assn., Quincy, 1953—68; instr. Burdette Coll., Boston, 1946—53; electronics instr. USAF, Scott Field, 1942—46; radio advt. writer CBS Sta. WMAS, Inc., Springfield, 1940—42; owner-mgr. Yarrington's Ser. Sta., Melrose, 1930—40; dept. store buyer Forbes & Wallace, Inc., Springfield, 1925—30. Pub. speaking instr. Dale Carnegie Inst., New York, NY, 1946—48; chmn. Old Colony Area Transp. Comm., Boston, 1958—60; chmn. adv. bd. News-Dem., Belleville, Ill., 1984—85. Author: (book) Tales of the 20th Century. Campaign mgr. Ronald Reagan for Pres., North Conway, NH, 1972; admn. asst. to Gov. Foster Furcolo, Mass., 1958—60; bd. dirs. Citizens for Modern Transit, St. Louis, 1982—92. Sargeant USAF, 1942—46, Scott Field, IL.

YARRINGTON, HUGH, corporate lawyer, communications company executive; BA, Randolph-Macon Coll.; JD, George Washington U. Assoc. Wilkinson, Cragun & Barker, Washington; v.p., gen. counsel Bur. Nat. Affairs, Inc., Washington; from sr. v.p., pub. to pres., CEO, exec. com. CCH Inc., Riverwoods, Ill. Mem. Info. Industry Assn. (bd. dirs. 1988—, chmn., treas., sec.). Office: CCH Inc 2700 Lake Cook Rd Riverwoods IL 60015-3867

YARRINGTON, PATRICIA, oil industry executive; b. Apr. 1956; B Polit. Sci., Pomona Coll., 1977; MBA, Northwestern U. With Chevron Corp., 1980—; sr. fin. analyst Chevron U.S.A. Inc., 1984—86, mgr. investor relations, 1986; various supervisory positions Chevron Products Co., Chevron U.S.A Prodn. Co., Chevron Rsch. and Tech. Co.; mgr. credit card enterprises Chevron Products Co., 1995—97, comptr., 1997—98; pres. Chevron Can. Ltd., Vancouver, Canada, 1998—2000; v.p. strategic planning Chevron Corp., 2000—01; v.p. pub. and govt. affairs ChevronTexaco Corp., San Ramon, Calif., 2002—. Bd. dirs. Chevron Phillips Chem. Co. Bd. dirs. ChevronTexaco Found. Office: ChevronTexaco Corp 6001 Bollinger Canyon Rd San Ramon CA 94583-2324

YARROW, ANDREW LOUIS, writer, journalist, educator, international relations consultant; b. Washington, June 11, 1957; s. Leon Jay and Marian Jeannette (Radke) Y.; 1 child, Richard. BA, UCLA, 1979; MA, Princeton U., 1981; MPA, Harvard U., 1994. Reporter N.Y. Times, N.Y.C., 1981-92; prof. Am. U., Washington, 1994-97; spl. asst. to sec. labor U.S. Dept. Labor, Washington, 1995-99; speechwriter Export-Import Bank, 1999—. Internat. rels. cons. World Bank, Washington, 1994-95, UNICEF, 1999—; cons. U.S. Dept. Edn., 2000—. Author: Latecomers: Children of Parents Over 35, 1991; contbr. articles to profl. jours. and popular mags. Inst. for Internat. Edn. fellow, Eng., 1979; recipient Visitors Program award European Union, Brussels, 1993; Rsch. grant Govt. France, 1992-93. Mem. Phi Beta Kappa. Democrat. Avocations: photography, creative writing. Home: 7509 Oldchester Rd Bethesda MD 20817- Office: Export-Import Bank Washington DC 20571 Personal E-mail: andrew_yarrow@hotmail.com.

YARROW, PETER, folksinger; b. N.Y.C., May 31, 1938; BA, Cornell U.; D (hon.), Nat. Lewis U., 2002, San Francisco State U., 2003. Mem. group: Peter, Paul, and Mary, 1962—, also solo performer, recording artist, Warner Bros.: albums with Peter, Paul, and Mary include: Peter, Paul, and Mary, Moving, In the Wind, In Concert, A Song Will Rise, See What Tomorrow Brings, Peter, Paul, and Mary Album, Album 1700, Late Again, Peter, Paul & Mommy, 10 Years Together: The Best Of, Reunion, Peter, Paul & Mommy, Too (Emmy nominee 1993), No Easy Walk to Freedom, Lifelines, Songs of Concience and Concern, In These Times, Carry It On; solo album: Peter, 1972, That's Enough for Me, 1973, Hard Times, 1975, Love Songs, 1975; on Broadway appearance: Peter, Paul, and Mary "From Bleecker to Broadway", 1986; TV spls. include: Reunion, Holiday Concert, Peter, Paul & Mommy, Too, Lifelines (PBS). Bd. dirs. Newport Folk Festival Found., Kerrville (Tex.) Folk Festival, 1971, Ctr. for Global Edn., Augsberg Coll.; chmn. bd. trustees Telluride Inst., 1997; founder, co-chair Oper. Respect, "Don't Laugh At Me", 1999 Recipient Emmy nominee for "Puff the Magic Dragon", 1979, Citizen Action Leadership award, Vista, 1979, Alfred Lowenstein award, 1982, Hospice Care of R.I. award, 1987, Nat. Emergency Civil Liberties Com. award, 1988, Interlochen Disting. Alumnus Arts award, 1992, Conn. Hospice award, 1993, Grammy award for prodr. Peter Paul & Mommy, Too, 1994, Kate Wolf Meml. award for the World Folk Music Assn., 1994, Tikkum Plam award, Ctrl. Synogogue, 1995, People for th Am. Way Defenders Democracy award, 1999, Ctrl. Sunagogue Shofar awartd, 1999, Spirit Crazy Horse award, 2000, AASC Sch. Counselor of Yr. award, 2001, Gandhi World Peace Flame, 2001,Rescuer of Humanity award, 2001, Starr Commonwealth Bd. Trustees Child Advocacy award, 2001, Good Neighbor award, 2002, N.Y. STate ASCS Educator of Yr. award, 2002; Congressional hon., 1999.

YARVIS, JEFFREY SCOTT, military officer, social worker; b. Morristown, N.J., Oct. 9, 1965; s. Stephen Harlen Yarvis and Arlene Haskin; m. Laura Suzanne Gabrielle Yarvis, Aug. 31, 1997; children: Jacob, Olivia. BA, Ind. U., 1988; MEd, Cambridge Coll., 1992; MSW, Boston Coll., 1994; PhD, U. Ga., 2004. Clin. social work diplomate Am. Bd. Examiners in Clin. Social Work, 1997, diplomate psychotherapy Am. Psychotherapy Assn., 1997, domestic violence counseling CDV-III ABFE, 1997, cert. sch. social work N.J., 1994, lic. master social worker-advanced clin. practitioner Tex., 1996, Acad. Cert. Social Workers NASW, 1996. With U.S. Army; occupl. social worker 85th Med. Detachment, Fort Hood, Tex., 1994—97; chief social work and family advocacy Dewitt Army Cmty. Hosp., Fort Belvoir, Va., 1997—99; instr. U.S. Army Med. Dept. Ctr. & Sch., Fort Sam Houston, Tex., 1999—. Tank platoon leader 1/63 Armor Bn., Fort Irwin, 1989—91; prevention team leader 47th Field Hosp., Port-au-Prince, Haiti, 1994—95, 85th Med. Detachment, Eagle Base, Bosnia-Herzegovina, 1997. Contbr. articles to profl. jours. Critical incident stress debriefing Bell-Coryell County Chpt. of ICISF, Killeen, 1994—97. Decorated 26 military decorations and badges; recipient Mental Health Profl. Yr. award, Internat. Critical Incidence Stress Found., Tex., 1997, Social Policy Grad. assistantship, Boston Coll. Grad. Sch. of Social Work, 1993—94. Mem.: Am. Soc. of Clin. Hypnosis, Assn. of Mil. Surgeons of the U.S., 5th U.S. Cavalry Assn., Nat. Guild of Hypnotists, Soc. for Social Work and Rsch., Assn. of U.S. Army, Nat. Assn. of Social Workers, Am. Legion. Democrat. Jewish. Avocations: running, boating. Home: CMR 442 Box 726 APO AE 09042 Office: 30th Med Brigade APO AE 09014 Heidelburg Germany Office Phone: 01104906221-2416. Personal E-mail: yarvis831@aol.com. Business E-Mail: armymsw@arches.uga.edu.

YARYAN, RUBY BELL, psychologist; b. Toledo, Apr. 28, 1938; d. John Sturges and Susan (Bell) Y.; m. John Frederick Buenz, Jr., Dec. 15, 1962 (div. 1968). AB, Stanford U., 1960; PhD, U. London, 1968. Lic. clin. psychologist; diplomate Am. Bd. Psychology, Am. Acad. Experts in Traumatic Stess. Rsch. dir., univ. radio and TV, U. Calif., San Francisco, 1968-70; dir. delinquency coun. U.S. Dept. Justice, Washington, 1970-73; evaluation dir. Office Criminal Justice Planning, Sacramento, Calif., 1973-76; CAO project mgr. San Diego County, 1977-92; dir. devel. svcs. Childhelp USA, Woodland Hills, Calif., 1992-94; rsch. coord. Neuropsychiat. Inst. and Hosp., UCLA, 1986-87; exec. dir. Centinela Child Guidance Clinic, Inglewood, Calif., 1987-89; clin. dir. Nat. Found. Emotionally Handicapped, North Hills, Calif., 1990-93; pvt. practice, Beverly Hills, Calif., 1973—; supr. psychologist Los Angeles County Dept. Mental Health, 1998—. Psychologist Sr. Psychology Svcs., North L.A. County, 1994-98; cons. White House Conf. Children, Washington, 1970; mem. Nat. Adv. Com. Criminal Justice Standards and Goals, Washington, 1973; clin. affiliation UCLA Med. Ctr. Contbr. articles to profl. jours.; chpts. to books and monographs in field. Chair Human Svcs. Commn., City of West Hollywood, Calif., 1986; first vice-chair United Way/Western Region, L.A., 1988; mem. planning-allocations-rsch. coun. United Way, San Diego, 1980-82. Grantee numerous fed., state and local govt. orgns. Mem. Am. Psychol. Assn., Western Psychol. Assn., Calif. Psychol. Assn., Am. Orthopsychiat. Assn., Am. Profl. Soc. on Abuse of Children, Phi Beta Kappa. Episcopalian. Avocations: painting, music, theater, writing, reading. Office: 337 S Beverly Dr Ste 107 Beverly Hills CA 90212-4307 Office Phone: 310-271-3921.

YASHER, MICHAEL, retired accountant; b. United, Pa., Aug. 17, 1928; s. Michael and Mary (Sasik) Y.; m. Margaret Jean Wallace, June 23, 1956 (dec. July 12, 1987); 1 child, Michael. BS, Penn State U., 1956; diploma, Air Command & Staff Coll., 1972, Nat. Defense U., 1977; MA, Ctrl. Mich. U., 1983. CPA, D.C.; cert. profl. contract mgr., D.C. Enlisted USAF, 1948; commd. 1st lt. U.S. GAO, Washington, 1956, advanced through grades to col., 1982; ret. USAF, 1988; mem. appropriations com. U.S. House of Reps., 1978-79; acct. to the comptroller U.S. Air Materials Command, 1979-83; acct., cons. E. K. Williams Co., Silver Spring, Md., 1985-98. Contbr. numerous papers and articles to profl. pubs. Treas. Boy Scouts Am., Rockville, Md., 1970; bd. dirs. Sr. Softball Assn., Montgomery County, Md., 1993—94, Montgomery County Sr. Sports Assn., 1999—2001; pres. Leisure World (Md.) Billiards Club, 1994—96, treas., 1997, 1999; commr., organizer Sr. Softball League, Montgomery County, 1994; participant Nat. Sr. Olympics, 1995—2003; news corr. Billiards Club-Leisure World, 2000—. Decorated with 14 mil. decorations; recipient Bronze medal softball Md., Md. Sr. Olympics, 1992, 1993, 1996—98, Silver medal softball Md., 1995, Silver medal softball, 2000, 2001, 2002, Gold medal softball, 1994, 1998, 1999, Bronze medal volleyball, 1993, 1995—97, Silver medal volleyball, 1998, 2000, 2002, Gold medal volleyball, 1999, 2001, Bronze medal Billiards, 1998, Gold medal Billiards, 2000, Bronze medal softball, Nat. Sr. Olympics, 1999, Meritorious Svc. award, U.S.G.A.O., 1975, USAF Outstanding Officer, Data Sys. Design Ctr., 1978, Silver medal softball, Md. Sr. Olympics, 2003, Silver medal volleyball, 2003, Silver medal 10 pin bowling doubles, 2003. Mem. AICPA, Nat. Capital Area Bowling Assn., Res. Officers Assn., Disabled Am. Vets. Comdrs. Club, Leisure World Billiards Club, Nat. Sr. Games Assn. (charter mem.), Am. Legion, VFW. Democrat. Roman Catholic. Avocations: coin collecting/numismatics, sports. Home: 15107 Interlachen Dr Apt 318 Silver Spring MD 20906-5629

YASHIN, ALEXEI, professional hockey player; b. Sverdlovsk, Russia, Nov. 5, 1973; Profl. hockey player Ottawa Senators, 1992—2001, NY Islanders, 2001—. Player CIS Jr. Team, 1992, World Jr. Championships, Russia Jr. Team, 1993, Russia Team World Championships, 1994, 96, NHL All-Star Game, 1994. Office: New York Islanders Nassau Veterans Memorial Coliseum Hempstead NY 11553

YASHON, DAVID, neurosurgeon, educator; b. Chgo., May 13, 1935; s. Samuel and Dorothy (Cutler) Y.; children— Jaclyn, Lisa, Steven. BS in Medicine, U. Ill., 1958, MD, 1960. Diplomate Am. Bd. Neurol. Surgery. Intern U. Ill., 1961, resident, 1961-64, asst. in neuroanatomy, 1960; clin. instr. neurosurgery U. Chgo., 1965-66; asst. prof. neurosurgery Case Western Res U., Cleve., 1966-69; assoc. prof. neurosurgery Ohio State U., Columbus, 1969-74, prof., 1974-89, prof. emeritus, 1989—; mem. staff St. Ann's Hosp., Children's Hosp., Grant Med. Ctr., Ohio State U. East Med. Ctr. Cons. Med. Research and Devel. Command, U.S. Army; mem. Neurology B Study Sect NIH. Author: Spinal Injury; contbr. articles to med. jours. Served as capt. U.S. Army, 1960-68. Fellow Royal Coll. Surgeons Can. (cert.), A.C.S.; mem. AMA, Am. Physiol. Soc., Congress Neurol. Surgeons, Am. Assn. Anatomists, Canadian, Ohio neurosurg. socs., Am. Assn. Neurol. Surgeons, Research Soc. Neurol. Surgeons, Acad. Medicine Columbus and Franklin County, Soc. for Neurosci., Soc. Univ. Surgeons, Am. Acad. Neurology, Assn. for Acad. Surgery, Am. Acad. Neurol. Surgery, Am. Assn. for Surgery of Trauma, Central Surg. Soc., Ohio Med. Soc., Columbus Surg. Soc., Sigma Xi, Alpha Omega Alpha. Address: 500 Columbia Pl Bexley OH 43209-1677 Office Phone: 614-224-1720. E-mail: dyashon@columbus.rr.com.

YASINITSKY, GREGORY WALTER, music educator; b. San Francisco, Oct. 3, 1953; s. Walter G. and Gloria S. Yasinitsky; m. Ann Marie Kelley, Jan. 15, 1977; 1 child, Laura A. DMA, Eastman Sch. of Music, 1995. Lectr. in music San Francisco (Calif.) State U., 1977—81, San Jose (Calif.) State U., 1978—82; prof. of music Wash. State U., Pullman, Wash., 1982—. Prin. saxophonist Spokane (Wash.) Symphony, 1991—. Composer, arranger, saxophonist: Music in Mixed Accents, 1995, Sittin' In With Greg Yasinitsky and Crosscurrent, 1995, Double Vision, 1995, Overdue, 1995, Cats in Rome, 1996, Masterclass: Jazz Duets, 1996, Intuition, 1997, Inside Track: Jazz @ WSU, 1997, America's Millennium Tribute to Adolphe Sax, Vol. I, 1998, Vol. II, 1999, Saxophone Jour. CD, 1999, Trios, 2000, First Flight, 2003, others; musician (Saxophone): Sarah Vaughan, Ella Fitzgerald, Lionel Hampton, Stan Getz, Mel Torme, Louis Bellson, Ray Charles, San Francisco Symphony, San Francisco Opera, albums; contbr. articles to profl. jours. Named Wash. State Composer of Yr., Washington State Music Tchrs. Assn., 2002—03; recipient Spl. awards for competition, ASCAP, 1986—2005, Jazz Educator award, Nat. Band Assn., 1989; grantee Composer Residencies, Meet the Composer, 1990, Wash. Artist Trust, 1990, 1992, 1996, Wash. State Composer in Residence, Commn. Project, 2000—03; Jazz Composition fellow, NEA, 1986. Mem.: Wash. Music Educators Assn. (jazz coord. 1997—98), Music Educators Nat. Conf., Soc. of Composers, Inc., Internat. Assn. for Jazz Edn. Home: 485 NW Robert Street Pullman WA 99163 Office: Washington State University Music Program PO Box 645300 Pullman WA 99164-5300 E-mail: yasinits@wsu.edu.

YASNYI, ALLAN DAVID, communications company executive; b. New Orleans, June 22, 1942; s. Ben Z. and Bertha R. (Michalove) Y.; m. Susan K. Manders; children: Benjamin Charles, Evelyn Judith, Brian Mallut. BBA, Tulane U., 1964. Free-lance exec. producer, producer, writer, actor, designer TV, motion picture and theatre, 1961-73; producer, performer the Second City; dir. fin. and adminstrn. Quinn Martin Prodns., Hollywood, Calif., 1973-76, v.p. fin., 1976-77, exec. v.p. fin. & corp. planning, 1977; vice chmn., CEO QM Prodn., Beverly Hills, Calif., 1977-78, chmn. bd., CEO, 1978-80; exec. dir. Susan Manders Fine Art, 2002—; pres., CEO The Synapse Comm. Group, Inc., 1981—, ASI Entertainment, 1998-99. Mng. dir. Susan Mandeers Fine Art, 2001—; exec. dir., adj. prof. U. So. Calif. Entertainment Tech. Ctr., 1994-99, exec. dir. emeritus, 1999—; participant IC IS Forum, 1990-95; exec. prodr. first live broadcast combining Intelsat, Intersputnik, The Voice of Am., and The Moscow World Radio Svc., 1990; resource guest Aspen Inst. Exec. Seminars, 1990; chmn. bd. dirs. Found. of Global Broadcasting, Washington, 1987-93; nat. adv. bd. DeSantis Ctr. Fla. Atlantic U., 1998-. Trustee Hollywood Arts Coun., 1980-83; exec. v.p., trustee Hollywood Hist. Trust, 1981-91; bd. dirs. Internat. Ctr. Intergative Studies, NYC, 1988-92; bd. dirs. Asthma and Allergy Found. Am., 1981-85. With US Army, 1964-66, Vietnam. Named to Tulane U. Hall of Fame. Mem. Acad. TV Arts and Sci., Inst. Noetic Sci., Hollywood Radio and TV Soc., Hollywood C. of C. (dir., vice chmn. 1978-93), Screen Actors Guild, Assn. Transpersonal Psychology (keynote spkr. 1988). Office: 4132 Fulton Ave Sherman Oaks CA 91423-4340 Office Phone: 818-995-0009.

YASSIN, ROBERT ALAN, museum administrator, curator; b. Malden, Mass., May 22, 1941; s. Harold Benjamin and Florence Gertrude (Hoffman) Y.; m. Marilyn Kramer, June 9, 1963; children: Fredric Giles, Aaron David. BA, Dartmouth Coll., 1962; postgrad., Boston U., 1962—63; MA, U. Mich., 1965, postgrad., 1968—70, PhD candidate, 1970; postgrad., Yale U., 1966—68. Asst. to dir. Mus. Art U. Mich., 1965-66, asst. dir., 1970-72, assoc. dir., 1972-73, acting dir., 1973, instr. dept. history of art, 1970-73; co-dir. Joint Program in Mus. Tng., 1970-73; chief curator Indpls. Mus. Art, 1973-75, 87-89, acting dir., 1975, dir., 1975-89; exec. dir. Tucson Mus. Art, 1990—2001, Palos Verdes (Calif.) Art Ctr., 2002—. Adj. prof. Herron Sch. Art Ind. U./Purdue U., 1975-89. Contbr. to mus. publs. Rufus Choate scholar, 1962, Samuel H. Kress Found. fellow, 1968—70, Ford Found. fellow, 1966—68. Mem.: Calif. Assn. Museums, Western Mus. Assn., Nat. Trust Hist. Preservation, Coll. Art Assn. Am., Am. Assn. Museums (bd. dirs. Internat. Coun. Mus. 1986—89). Jewish. Office: Palos Verdes Art Ctr 5504 W Crestridge Rd Rancho Palos Verdes CA 90275 Home: 7321 Marina Pacifica Dr N Long Beach CA 90803-3808 Office Phone: 310-541-2479. E-mail: rayassin@charter.net.

YASTINE, BARBARA A. diversified financial services company executive; BA in Journalism, NYU, 1981, MBA in Finance, 1987. Various communications and investor-relations positions W.R. Grace & Co.; dir. investor relations, Primerica Citigroup, 1987—91, v.p. investor relations and fin. planning & analysis, Traveler's Group, 1991, exec. v.p. fin. and insurance, CitiFinancial, chief admin. officer, global consumer group, 1998, chief auditor, CFO, global corp. and investment bank, 2000—02; CFO Credit Suisse First Boston, 2002—. Office: Credit Suisse First Boston 11 Madison Ave New York NY 10010-3629 Office Phone: 212-325-2000. Office Fax: 212-325-6665.

YASUDA, HIROTSUGU KOGE, engineering educator, director; b. Kyoto, Mar. 24, 1930; s. Mitsuo and Kei (Niwa) Y.; m. Gerda Lisbeth Schmidtke, Apr. 6, 1968; children: Ken Eric, Werner Akira, Lisbeth Kay. BSChemE, Kyoto U., 1953; MS in Polymer Chemistry, SUNY, Syracuse, 1959, PhD in Polymer and Phys. Chemistry, 1961. Rsch. assoc. Ophthalmic Plastic Lab., Mass. Eye & Ear Infirmary, Boston, 1962-63; head biomaterial sect. eye rsch. Cedar-Sinai Med. Ctr., L.A., 1963-65; vis. scientist Royal Inst. Tech., Stockholm, 1965-66; sr. chemist Rsch. Triangle Inst., Rsch. Triangle Pk., N.C., 1966-72, mgr. Polymer Rsch. Lab., 1972-78; prof. chem. engring. U. Mo., Rolla, 1978-88, dir. Thin Films Inst., 1974-88, prof. chem. engring. Columbia, 1988—, chmn. dept., 1988-90, James C. Dowell rsch. prof., 1989—2003, prof. emeritus, 2003—, dir. Ctr. for Surface and Plasma Techs., 1989—. Author: Plasma Polymerization, 1985, Luminous Chemical Vaper Deposition and Interface Engineering, 2004. Home: 1004 Lake Point Ln Columbia MO 65203-2900 Office: Ctr For Surface Sci & Plasma Tech Columbia MO 65211-0001 Office Phone: 573-882-9602. E-mail: yasudah@missouri.edu.

YASUDA, NOBUYOSHI, music educator; b. Takarazuka, Japan, Oct. 12, 1962; arrived in U.S., 1986; s. Masayoshi and Taeko Yasuda. MusB, Soai U., Osaka, Japan, 1986; MusM, Ind. U., 1988. Asst. prof. U. Wis., Eau Claire, 1991—; music dir. The Chippewa Valley Symphony, Eau Claire, 1993—; assoc. condr. The Grand Teton Music Festival, Jackson, Wyo., 1997—. Avocations: golf, hiking. Home: 3244 Old Orchard Rd Eau Claire WI 54703 Office: U Wis-Eau Claire Dept Music and Theatre Arts 105 Garfield Ave Eau Claire WI 54702-4004 E-mail: yasudan@uwec.edu.

YATES, ALBERT CARL, academic administrator, chemistry educator; b. Memphis, Tenn., Sept. 29, 1941; s. John Frank and Sadie L. (Shell) Y.; m. Ann Young; children: Steven, Stephanie, Aerin Alessandra, Sara Elizabeth. BS, Memphis State U., 1965; PhD, Ind. U., 1968. Research assoc. U. So. Calif., Los Angeles, 1968-69; prof. chemistry Ind. U., Bloomington, 1969-74; v.p. research, grad. dean U. Cin., 1974-81; exec. v.p., provost, prof. chemistry Washington State U., Pullman, 1981-90; pres. Colo. State U., Fort Collins, 1990—; chancellor Colo. State U. System, Fort Collins, 1990—. Mem. grad. record exam. bd. Princeton (N.J.) U., 1977-81; undergrad. assessment program coun. Ednl. Testing Svc., 1977-81, NRC, 1975-82, Office Edn., HEW, 1978-80; mem. exec. coun. acad. affairs Nat. Assn. State Univs. and Land Grant Colls., 1983-87, Am. Coun. on Edn., 1983-87, nat adv. coun. gen. med. scis. NIH, 1987-90. Contbr. research articles to Jour. Chem. Physics; research articls to Phys. Rev.; research articles to Jour. Physics, Phys. Rev. Letters, Chem. Physics Letters. Served with USN, 1959-62. Recipient univ., state and nat. honors and awards Mem. AAAS, Am. Phys. Soc., Am. Chem. Soc., Sigma Xi, Phi Lambda Upsilon. Home: 1744 Hillside Dr Fort Collins CO 80524-1965

YATES, DAVID JOHN C. chemist, researcher; b. Stoke-on-Trent, Staffordshire, Eng., Feb. 13, 1927; arrived in US, 1958; s. Eric John and Beatrice Victoria Y.; m. Natalie Chmelnitsky, June 22, 1983 BS with honors, U. Birmingham, U.K., 1949; PhD, U. Cambridge, Eng., 1955, Sc.D., 1968. Rsch. physicist Kodak Labs., Wealdstone, London, 1949-50; rsch. chemist Brit. Ceramic Rsch. Assn., Stoke-on-Trent, 1950-51; rsch. assoc. dept. colloid sci. U. Cambridge, 1951-58; lectr. Sch. Mines and dept. chemistry Columbia U., N.Y.C., 1958-60; sr. rsch. fellow Nat. Phys. Lab., Teddington, U.K., 1960-61; rsch. assoc. corp. labs. Exxon Rsch. and Engring., Annandale, N.J., 1961-86; rsch. prof. dept. of chem. engring. Lafayette Coll., Easton, Pa., 1986-87; rsch. prof. dept. materials sci. Rutgers U., Piscataway, N.J., 1987-88; cons. San Diego, 1988—. Contbr. over 70 articles to profl. jours., chpts. to books; 13 U.S. patents, numerous fgn. patents. Fellow Inst. of Physics (U.K.), Royal Soc. Chemistry (U.K.), N.Y. Catalysis Club (chmn. 1966-67). Clubs: N.Y. Catalysis (chmn. 1965-66). Avocations: photography, bicycling, gliding, travel, sports cars.

YATES, DONALD ALFRED, retired literature educator; b. Ayer, Mass., Apr. 11, 1930; s. Alfred Craig Yates and Bessie Mae Cambridge; m. Mary Dodd, June 24, 1951 (div. Mar. 1961); children: Brian Donald, Juliet Marie; m. Lynn P. Taylor, Mar. 31, 1962 (div. May 1975); 1 child, John Allan; m. Joanne Margaret Mueller, Mar. 21, 1977. AB in Spanish, U. Mich., 1951, MA in Spanish, 1954, PhD in Spanish, 1961. Tchg. fellow U. Mich., Ann Arbor, 1953-57; instr. Mich. State U., East Lansing, 1957-61, asst. prof. Spanish-Am. lit., 1961-64, assoc. prof., 1964-67, prof., 1967-83, prof. emeritus, 1983—. Pres. Internat. Inst. Latin-Am. Lit., Pitts., 1971-73. Author: Jorge Luis Borges: Life, Work & Criticism, 1985; editor, translator: Latin Blood: Best Crime Stories of Latin America, 1972; co-editor, translator: Labyrinths: Selected Writings of Jorge Luis Borges, 1962; co-editor: (textbook) Imaginación y Fantasía, 1960, 6th edit., 1999. With U.S. Army, 1951-53. Translation grantee NEA, 2000-01. Mem. MLA, Mystery Writers of Am., Baker St. Irregulars (The Greek Interpreter 1972), Sherlock Holmes Soc. London. Democrat. Home: 555 Canon Park Dr Saint Helena CA 94574-9726 E-mail: mrmelas72@earthlink.net.

YATES, ELLA GAINES, library consultant; b. Atlanta, June 14, 1927; d. Fred Douglas and Laura (Moore) Gaines; m. Joseph L. Sydnor (dec.); 1 child, Jerri Gaines Sydnor Lee; m. Clayton R. Yates (dec.). AB, Spelman Coll., Atlanta, 1949; MS in L.S, Atlanta U., 1951; JD, Atlanta Law Sch., 1979. 1954Asst. br. librarian Bklyn. Pub. Library, 1951; head children's dept. Orange (N.J.) Pub. Library, 1956—59; br. librarian East Orange (N.J.) Pub. Library, 1960—69; med. librarian Orange Meml. Hosp., 1967—69; asst. dir. Montclair (N.J.) Pub. Library, 1970—72, Atlanta-Fulton Pub. Library, 1972—76, dir., 1976—81; dir. learning resource ctr. Seattle Opportunities Industrialization Ctr., 1982—84; asst. dir. adminstrn. Friendship Force, Atlanta, 1984—86; state librarian Commonwealth of Va., 1986—90; library cons. Price Waterhouse, 1991; adv. bd. Library of Congress Center for the Book, 1977—85; interim dir. Atlanta-Fulton Pub. Libr., 1998—99; cons., dir. Woodruff Libr., Atlanta, 2000—02. Cons. in field; vis. lectr. U. Wash., Seattle, 1981-83; mem. Va. Records Adv. Bd., 1986-90; mem. Nagara Exec. Bd., 1987-91. Contbr. to profl. jours. Vice chmn. N.J. Women's Coun. on Human Rels., 1957-59; chmn. Friends Fulton County Jail, 1973-81; bd. dirs. United Cerebral Palsy Greater Atlanta, Inc., 1979-81 Coalition Against Censorship, Washington, 1981-84, YMCA Met. Atlanta, 1979-81, Exec. Women's Network, 1979-82, Freedom To Read Found., 1979-85, Va. Black History Mus., Richmond, 1990-91; sec., exec. dir. Va. Libr. Found. Bd., 1986-90. Recipient meritorious svc. award Atlanta U., 1977, Phoenix award City of Atlanta, 1980,

Serwa award Nat. Coalition 100 Black Women, 1989, Black Caucus award, 1989, disting. svc. award Clark-Atlanta U., 1991, ednl. support svc. award Tuskegee Airmen, 1993, Alumnae Achievement award Spelman Coll., 1998, Annie McPheters award Atlanta-Fulton Pub. Libr., 1998, Disting. Alumnae award Clark Atlanta U., 2001; named profl. woman of yr. NAACP N.J., 1972, outstanding chum of yr., 1976; named outstanding alumni Spelman Coll., 1977, named to alumni hall of fame, 1995. Mem. ALA (exec. bd. 1977-83, commn. freedom of access to info.), NAACP, Southeastern Libr. Assn., Nat. Assn. Govt. Archives and Records Adminstrn. (exec. bd. 1987-91), Delta Sigma Theta (Pinnacle leadership award 2001). Baptist. Home and Office: 1171 Oriole Dr SW Atlanta GA 30311-2424

YATES, GARY L. marriage and family therapist; b. Washington, Aug. 16, 1944; s. Lewis Edward and Norma Jean (Andruss) Y.; m. Cynthia Ann Pagay, Aug. 16, 1974; children: David, Jonathan, Daniel, Matthew, Nathan. BA, Am. U., 1967; MA, U. No. Colo., 1978. Tchr. St. Anthony's, Kailua, Hawaii, 1970-74, Acad. of Pacific, Honolulu, 1974-79; adminstr. Dept. Pub. Health, San Bernardino, Calif., 1979-81, Charles Drew Sch. of Medicine, L.A., 1981-82; assoc. dir. Divsn. of Adolescent Medicine/Children's Hosp., L.A., 1982-92; sr. program officer Calif. Wellness Found., Woodland Hills, Calif., 1992-93, program dir., 1993-94, pres., CEO, 1995—. Asst. clin. prof. U. So. Calif., 1988—; bd. dirs. Calif. Wellness Found., Grantmaker in Health, Hispanics in Philanthropy, So. Calif. Assn. Philanthropy, Coun. Found. Contbr. articles to profl. jours.; contbg. author: Multi Agency System of Care, 1990. Mem. L.A. Roundtable for Children, 1988-92, United Way Task Force on AIDS, L.A., 1988-92, San Bernardino Comm. Coun., 1980-82; chmn. Hawaii Sch. Counseling Assn., Honolulu, 1978-79. S(sgt.) U.S. Army, 1968-70. Recipient NACO Achievement award Nat. Assn. U.S. Counties, 1980, 3rd Century award Hollywood Coord. Coun., 1989, Gov.'s Victim's Svc. award Gov. of Calif., 1990, Commendation award Calif. State Senate, 1992, Hispanic Health Leadership award, 1999, L.A. Free Clinic Lenny Somberg award, 1998. Mem. Am. Assn. Humanistic Psychologists, Soc. for Adolescent Medicine, Calif. Assn. Marriage and Family Therapists, Am. Pub. Health Assn. Democrat. Methodist. Avocations: reading, walking. Office: Calif Wellness Found 6320 Canoga Ave Ste 1700 Woodland Hills CA 91367-2565

YATES, GWENDOLYN DRAPER, mathematician, educator; d. Thomas Winthrop Draper and Lillian Blunt Lee, Bertha Hunt Draper (Stepmother); 1 child, Jeanetta Denise Yates-Swanson. BS magna cum laude, Alcorn State U., 1970; MEd, Miss. Coll., 1976, Edn. Specialist, 1981. Cert. math. tchr. Miss. Math. tchr. Forest (Miss.) Mid. Sch., 1970—71, Vicksburg (Miss.)-Warren Schools, 1972—; math. instr. Alcorn State U., Lorman, Miss., 1979, computer literacy instr., 1989; math. instr. Miss. Coll., Clinton, 1988. Intern personnel asst. in environ. lab. Waterways Expt. Sta., Vicksburg, 1985—89, mem. math. faculty program info. tech. lab., 1990—98; pvt. math. tutor, Vicksburg, 1995—; math. tutor Homework Network, Vicksburg H.S., 2002—. Contbr. poems to lit. publs. Mem. pub. rels. com. Standfield Missionary Bapt. Ch., Vicksburg, 2000—03. Mem.: Alpha Kappa Alpha. Baptist. Avocations: gardening, travel, interior decorating, gospel music, investments. Personal E-mail: yateskhb@aol.com.

YATES, JAMES ARTHUR, plastic surgeon; b. Butler, Pa., June 5, 1935; s. Adolph Walter and Laura Marie (De Foggie) Y.; m. Debra Lynne Stringer, June 19, 1983; 1 child, Jamie Dale Yates Reynolds. BA, Cornell U., 1956; MD, U. Md., Balt., 1960. Diplomate Am. Bd. Plastic Surgery, Nat. Bd. Med. Examiners, Am. Bd. Surgery; lic. physician, Pa., Ohio, R.I. Intern Cleve. Clinic Hosp., 1960-61, resident in gen. surgery, 1961-62, U. Pitts. Med. Ctr., 1963-65; resident in plastic surgery R.I. Hosp., 1966-67, chief resident, 1967-68; pvt. practice Plastic Surg. Ctr. Ltd., Camp Hill, Pa., 1968—; med. dir. Grandview Surgery Ctr., Mechanicsburg and Camp Hill, Pa. Tchg. fellow gen. surgery U. Pitts. Med. Ctr., 1963-65, instr. gen. surgery, 1965-66; clin. instr. plastic surgery Milton S. Hershey (Pa.) Med. Ctr., 1968—; staff maxillofacial and plastic surgery dept. Harrisburg (Pa.) Hosp., 1968—; chief plastic and aesthetic surgery dept. Holy Spirit Hosp., Camp Hill, 1968—; staff Mechanicsburg Rehab. Hosp., Carlisle (Pa.) Hosp., Pinnacle Health Sys. Hosps.; med. dir. Grandview Surgery and Laser Ctr., Camp Hill, Grandview Surgery & Laser Ctr., Mechanicsburg; cons. Harrisburg State Hosp.; physician surveyor Am. Assn. Ambulatory Health Care; physician trainer plastic surgery residency program Am. Coll. Osteo. Surgery; bd. dirs., pres. Am. Assn. Accreditatiion of Ambulatory Surgery Facilities. Contbr. articles to profl. jours.; adv. bd. Town and Country Mag. Police commr. West Shore Regional Police Dept.; pres. Boro Coun. Lemoyne Boro; mem. credentialling com. Keystone Health Plan; mem. task force on ambulatory surgery Pa. Dept. Health; mem. coun. Lemoyne (Pa.) Borough Coun., pres.; credentialing officer Freedom Health Care HMO; commr. West Shore Regional Police. Fellow ACS; mem. AMA, Pa. Med. Soc., Am. Burn Assn., Am. Soc. Plastic and Reconstructive Surgeons, Am. Burn Victim Found., Am. Soc. Aesthetic Plastic Surgery, Vail Cosmetic Surgery Soc., Pa. Plastic Surgery Soc. (pres.-elect), Am. Soc. Automobile Medicine, Northeastern Soc. Plastic Surgeons, Royal Soc. Medicine, Lipolysis Soc. N.Am., Internat. Soc. Clin. Plastic Surgeons, South Ctrl. Pa. Regional Med. Dirs., Am. Coll. Physician Execs. Republican. Roman Catholic. Avocations: biking, skiing, model airplaning, ferrari sports cars. Home: 833 Kiehl Dr Lemoyne PA 17043-1201 Office: Plastic Surgery Ctr Ltd 205 Grandview Ave Camp Hill PA 17011-1708 Office Phone: 717-763-7814. Personal E-mail: jay5plas@msn.com.

YATES, JOHN MELVIN, retired ambassador; b. Superior, Mont., Nov. 25, 1939; s. Leon Glen and Violet May (McPheeters) Y.; m. Peggy Maureen Simpson, Mar. 26, 1961 (dec. Apr. 1986); children: Catherine Diener, John Simpson, Maureen Cole, Paul Marion, Leon Gregory; m. Mary Barbara Carlin, Jan. 30, 1988. AB, Stanford U., 1961; MA, Fletcher Sch. Law and Diplomacy, 1962, MAL.D., 1963, PhD, 1972. Fgn. service officer U.S. Dept. State, Washington, 1964—2002, Algiers, Algeria, 1964-66, Blantyre, Malawi, 1967-68, Bamako, Mali, 1969-71, New Delhi, 1973-75, Ankara, Turkey, 1975-77, Libreville, Gabon, 1977-80, Washington, 1971-73, 80-82; amb. to Republic of Cape Verde, Am. Embassy, 1983-86, counselor for polit. affairs, 1986-89, dep. chief of mission Lagos, Nigeria, 1989-91, Kinshasa, Zaire, 1991-93, chief of mission, 1993-95, amb. to Republic of Benin, Cotonou, 1995-98, amb. to Republic of Cameroon and Republic Equatorial Guinea, Yaounde, 1998—2001. Recipient Presdl. award for sustained superior accomplishment in conduct of fgn. policy. Mem. Am. Fgn. Service Assn. Address: 2020 Accra Pl Dulles VA 20189-2020 E-mail: johnmyates@hotmail.com.

YATES, JOHN ROBERT, JR., engineer, educator; b. Boston, Feb. 9, 1930; s. John Robert and Rosemary Natalie (Logue) Y.; m. Virginia Dianne Finocchio, July 3, 1954 (dec. Feb. 1988); children: Deborah A., John Robert, Thomas F., Catherine I.; m. Barbara Marandola, Dec. 28, 1990. AB, Northeastern U., 1954. Commd. 2d lt. USMC, 1954, advanced through grades to lt. col., 1970; action officer, constrn. team, joint logistics rev. bd. Office Sec. Def., 1969-70; engr. III Marine Amphibious Force, Fleet Marine Force, Okinawa, 1970-71; comdg. officer, marine barracks U.S. Naval Base, Boston, 1971-74, ret., 1974. Dir. engring. Soldiers' Home, Chelsea, Mass., 1974-85; energy conservation coord. Exec. Office of Human Svcs., Commonwealth of Mass.; faculty Energy Mgmt. in Healthcare Instns., HEW, 1977. Mem. exec. bd. USO Coun. New Eng., 1971-84, pres., 1988-94; trustee Charlestown YMCA, 1974—, pres. 1988-94, vice chmn., 1977-79, chmn., 1980-82. Decorated Joint Svc. Commendation medal, Navy Commendation medal, Army Commendation medal. Mem. Soc. Am. Mil. Engrs. (dir. Boston post), Am., New Eng. hosp. engrs. socs., Navy League U.S. (v.p. Mass. Bay coun.), Am. Legion, VFW, Bostonian Soc., Wardroom Club (Boston), Army-Navy Club (Washington). Roman Catholic. Home and Office: 39 Chapman Rd Boxford MA 01921-2330

YATES, JOHN THOMAS, JR., chemistry educator, research director; b. Winchester, Va., Aug. 3, 1935; s. John Thomas and Kathryn (Barnett) Y.; m. Kerin Joyce Narbut, Oct. 18, 1958; children: Geoffrey, Nathan. BS, Juniata Coll., 1956; PhD, MIT, 1960. Asst. prof. chemistry Antioch Coll., Yellow Springs, Ohio, 1960-63; NRC fellow, rsch. chemist Nat. Bur. Standards, Washington, 1963-82; R.K. Mellon prof. chemistry U. Pitts., 1982—, dir. Surface Sci. Ctr., 1982—. Co-dir. materials rsch. ctr. U. Pitts., 1994, R.K. Mellon prof. chemistry and physics, 1994—. Author: Experimental Innovations in Surface Science, 1997; co-author: The Surface Scientist's Guide to Organometallic Chemistry, 1987; co-editor: Vibrational Spectroscopy of Molecules on Surfaces, 1987, Chemical Perspectives of Microelectronic Materials, Vol. 131; assoc. editor: Studies in Surface Science and Catalysis, 1986; series editor: Methods of Surface Characterization, 1987; bd. editors Ann. Rev. Phys. Chemistry, 1983-85, Jour. Phys. Chemistry, 1983-88, Jour. Chem. Physics, 1984-87, Jour. Catalysis, 1987-91, Chem. Revs., Langmuir, Surface Sci., Applications of Surface Sci., Accounts Chem. Rsch.; assoc. editor Langmuir, 1991-98; contbr. revs. and articles to profl. jours.; inventor desorption spectrometer, 1981. Sherman Fairchild Disting. scholar Calif. Inst. Tech., 1977-78; recipient Silver medal Dept. Commerce-Nat. Bur. Stds., 1973, Stratton award, 1981, Gold medal Dept. Commerce Nat. Bur. Stds., 1981, Pres.'s Disting. Rsch. award U. Pitts., 1989, Proctor & Gamble award, 1989, Alexander von Humboldt Sr. Rsch. award, 1994, Linnett lectr. Cambridge U., 2000, named Among 100 Most Highly Cited Chemists in World 1984-, G.N. Lewis award U. Calif.-Berkeley, 2002; fellow Sidney Sussex Coll., 2000. Fellow Am. Phys. Soc. (bd. dirs. divsn. chem. physics 1991—, chmn. divsn. chem. physics 1989), Am. Vacuum Soc. (chmn. surface sci. divsn. 1973, 92, trustee 1975, bd. dirs. 1982-85, M.W. Welch award 1994, fellow 1994); mem. NAS, Am. Chem. Soc. (chmn. divsn. colloid and surface chemistry, Langmuir lectr. 1979, Kendall award in colloid of surface chemistry 1986, Morley prize Cleve. chpt. 1990, Peter Debye lectr. Cornell U. 1993, Pitts. award 1998, A.W. Adamson award 1999), Pitts.-Cleve. Catalysis Soc. Office: U Pitts Surface Sci Ctr Dept Chemistry Pittsburgh PA 15260

YATES, LEIGHTON DELEVAN, JR., lawyer; b. Atlanta, Sept. 4, 1946; s. Leighton Delevan and Stella Louise (Hill) Y.; m. Phyllis Jeanne Hummer, Dec. 22, 1968; children: Leighton Delevan III, Lauren Jeanne. BA, Hampden-Sydney Coll., Va., 1968; JD with high honors, U. Fla., 1973. Bar: Fla. 1974, U.S. Dist. Ct. (middle dist.) Fla. 1975. Assoc. Maguire, Voorhis & Wells, P.A., Orlando, Fla., 1974-77, shareholder, 1978-98, dept. chmn., 1985-90; ptnr. Holland & Knight LLP, Orlando, Fla., 1998—. Bd. dirs. Hubbard Constrn. Co., Winter Park, Fla., 1985—, Blythe Constrn., Inc., Charlotte, NC, 1999—; adminstrv. dir. SunTrust Bank, Orlando, Fla., 1990—. Exec. editor U. Fla. Law Rev., 1973. Mem. Fla. Bd. Bar Examiners, 1992-97, 2002—, vice chmn., 1995-96, chmn. 1996-97; chmn. Fla.'s Blood Ctrs., 1995—, vice chmn., 1980-95; chmn. Orlando Opera Co., 1994, pres., 1993. Fellow Am. Bar Found.; mem. ABA, Fla. Bar Assn., Orange County Bar Assn., Univ. Club of Orlando, Country Club of Orlando, Order of the Coif, Omicron Delta Kappa, Phi Kappa Phi. Republican. Presbyterian. Avocations: scuba diving, bicycling, music, reading. Home: 3218 S Osceola Ave Orlando FL 32806-6251 Office: Holland & Knight LLP 200 S Orange Ave Ste 2600 Orlando FL 32801-3453 Office Phone: 407-425-8500. Personal E-mail: lyates@cfl.rr.com. Business E-Mail: leighton.yates@hklaw.com.

YATES, MARY CARLIN, ambassador; b. Portland, Oreg., Dec. 1946; m. John Melvin Yates. BA in English, Oreg. State U.; M in Comparative East West Humanities, postgrad., NYU. Joined fgn. svc., 1980; press attaché for Amb. Pamela Harriman Dept. of State, sr. cultural attaché Am. Embassy, U.S. amb. to Burundi Washington, 1999—. Office: DOS Amb 2100 Bujumbura Pl Washington DC 20521

YATES, MICHAEL FRANCIS, management consultant; b. N.Y.C., Feb. 9, 1946; s. John Berchmans and Jane Ann (Gretz) Y.; m. Christine Mary Dallos, Jan. 14, 1967; children: Erik Michael, Alison. BA, U. Buffalo, 1968. Mgmt. trainee, dept. mgr. Sears, Roebuck & Co., Buffalo, 1968-69; cons. Rothman & D'Alessandro, Inc., N.Y.C., 1969-71; sr. cons. Martin & Segal & Co., Inc., N.Y.C., 1971-75, A.S. Hansen, Inc., N.Y.C., 1975-78; exec. v.p. A.M. D'Alessandro & Co., Inc., North Haledon, N.J., 1978-81; mng. dir. Alexander & Alexander Cons. Group, Inc., Lyndhurst, N.J., 1981-97; pres. Michael F. Yates & Co., Inc., Hampton, N.J., 1997—. Bd dirs. Am. Intercon, Inc. Host of Your Human Resources Resource, WALE AM, 2001—. Pres. Lincoln Sch. PTA, 1975-77, Bethlehem Twp. Rep. Club, mem. Hunterdon County com.; chmn. Bethlehem Twp. Econ. and Indsl. Devel. Bd., 1980-83; active Rep. Nat. Com. Mem. Am. Mgmt. Assn., Am. Compensation Assn., Soc. Human Resource Mgmt., Adminstrv. Mgmt. Soc., Aircraft Owners and Pilots Assn. Home: 519 Lannon Ln Glen Gardner NJ 08826-3817 Office: 2 Manor Dr Hampton NJ 08827-5409

YATES, RONALD EUGENE, newspaper editor, journalist, educator, author; b. Kansas City, Mo., Feb. 19, 1941; s. Guy Raymond and Willadene (Peterson) Y.; m. Ingeborg Zoelss, May 7, 1966; children: Jennifer Christina, Nicole Brigitte. BS (Gannett Newspapers scholar 1968-69, Angelo C. Scott Meml. scholar 1969), U. Kans., 1969. Reporter Kansas City (Kans.) Star, 1968; editor Univ. Daily Kansan, 1969; reporter, asst. city editor, fgn. corr. Chgo. Tribune, Chgo. and Tokyo, 1969-76, Asia and Latin Am. corr., 1976-82, met. editor, 1983—, nat. editor, 1984—, chief Asia corr., 1985—, sr. writer, 1992—; prof., chmn. dept. journalism U. Ill., Champaign, 1997—, dean Coll. Comm., 2003—. Contbr. articles to mags. Served with U.S. Army Intelligence, 1962-66. Recipient award for excellence in staff leadership William Allen White Sch. Journalism, 1968, Edward Scott Beck award for best fgn. reporting, 1975, 87, 89, Inter-Am. Press Assn. award for reporting on Latin Am., 1979, Peter Lisagor award for bus. and fin. reporting, 1993; named Outstanding Sr. U. Kans., 1969 Mem. Fgn. Corrs. Club of Japan (v.p. 1989—), Los Angeles Press, Sigma Delta Chi. Lutheran. Office: U Ill 810 S Wright St Champaign IL 61820 Office Phone: 217-333-2350.

YATES, STEVEN A. curator, artist, scholar; b. Chgo., Nov. 14, 1949; s. Thomas A. and Phyllis E. (Wilson) Y.; m. Lynne A. Smith, Aug. 5, 1972; children: Kelsey Victoria, Mackenzie Phyllis. BFA, U. Nebr., 1972; MA, U. N.Mex., 1975, MFA, 1978. Curatorial asst. Sheldon Meml. Art Gallery, 1972-73, U. Art Mus., U. N.Mex., 1973-75; faculty dept. art Claremont (Calif.) Colls. and Pomona, 1976; part-time faculty U. N.Mex., Albuquerque, 1976—, assoc. adj. prof. dept. art and art history; curator prints, drawings and photographs Mus. of N.Mex., Santa Fe, 1980-84; curator of photography Mus. Fine Arts, 1985—. Vis. prof. 19th and 20th century photography Santa Fe C.C., 1997-2002; frequent lectr. and essayist on contemporary and early modern history of photography and rsch. internationally; guest artist Tamarind Inst., Albuquerque, 1988; lectr., rschr., curator exhbns. internationally. One-man shows include Sheldon Meml. Art Gallery, Lincoln, Nebr., 1978, Gallery A-3, Moscow, 1996, Up and Down Gallery, Kharkov, Ukraine, 1997, U. Nebr., 1997, Mus. Photography, Riga, Latvia, 1998, Gallery A-3 Moscow, 2002; collaborative installation Ctr. for Contemprary Arts, Irving, Tex., 2000; group shows include San Francisco Mus. Modern Art, 1980, 81, 84, 86, 96, Cinema Ctr., Moscow, 1991, St. Petersburg, Russia, 1997, Photographic Icons: Film Form and Montage, A homage to Sergei Eisenstein adn Gustav Klucis, Latvia, 1998, Empires: Russia Past and Present, 1998; represented in permanent collections San Francisco Mus. Modern Art, Sheldon Art Gallery, Mint Mus., Art Mus. U. N.Mex., Ctr. for Creative Photography, Tucson; editor: The Essential Landscape, The New Mexico Photographic Survey, 1985; guest editor spl. issue Contemporary Photography, 1987, El Palacio, 1987, Poetics of Space: A Critical Photographic Anthology, 1995, Betty Hahn: Photography or Maybe Not, 1995, Theatre as Memory: L. Millet, 1999, The Avant-garde Document: A. Macijauskas, 2001, Idea Photographic: After Modernism, 2002, Poéticas del espacia, 2002, Alexander Rodchenko, Modern Photography, Film, and Photomontage, 2003; numerous mus. catalogs and pubs. nationally and internationally. Ford Found. fellow, 1977, Nat. Endowment Arts fellow, 1980; recipient Vreeland award U. Nebr., 1972, Outstanding Alumni Achievement award U. Nebr., 1994; Sr. Fulbright Scholars award USSR, 1991, Russian Fedn., 1995.

YATES, WILLIAM TENNYSON, II, educational consultant, management consultant; b. Tuskeegee, Ala., Mar. 26, 1944; s. William Tennyson Yates, Sr. and Dorothea Jordan Yates; m. Sue Wilson, Aug. 4, 1984. BS, Temple U., 1968; MS, Troy State U., 1975; PhD, St. Louis U., 1987. Commd. lt. USAF, 1969, advanced through grades to lt. col., 1985, ret., 1989; program dir., grant writer Woodrow Wilson Nat. Fellowship Found., Princeton, NJ, 1990—92; asst. v.p. Temple U., Phila., 1993—96; founding exec. dir. Moore Multi-Cultural Ctr., Cocoa, Fla., 1996—99; mgmt. cons. Phoenix Orgn., Indialantic, Fla., 1999—2001; regional v.p. Hire Golden, Inc., Valley Forge, Pa., 2001—. Mem. Civilian/Mil. Affairs Com., Melbourne, Fla., 1997—2002; v.p. Hosts of Brevard, Inc., Melbourne, 1999, pres., 2000—. Decorated Def. Meritorious Svc. medal, Air Force Meritorious Svc. medals (4), Air Force Commendetion Medal. Mem.: Rotary. Republican. Avocations: music, martial arts, computers, writing, photography.

YAU, OI YAN EUGENIA, music educator; arrived in U.S., 1990; d. Kwong Tong Yau and So Yuen Yuen. Honors diploma, Baptist U., Hong Kong, 1990; Master's, Tex. State U., 1992; DMA, U. Tex., 1997; MBA, Southwestern Coll., 2003. Dir. music program Olivet Coll., Mich., 1997—2001; dir. music Reformation Luth. Ch., Wichita, Kans., 2001—; asst. prof. music Southwestern Coll., Wihfield, Kans., 2001—. Bd. dirs. Opera Kans., Wichita, 2002—. Office: Dept Music Southwestern Coll 100 College Dr Winfield KS 67156

YAU, SHING-TUNG, mathematics professor; b. Swatow, China, Apr. 4, 1949; arrived in U.S., 1969; m. Yu-Yun Kuo; children: Isaac, Michael. PhD, U. Calif., Berkeley, 1971, Chinese U. Hong Kong, 1980, Harvard U., 1987. Mem. Inst. Advanced Study, Princeton, N.J., 1971-72; asst. prof. math. SUNY, Stony Brook, 1972-73; prof. math. Stanford (Calif.) U., 1974-79, Inst. Advanced Study, Princeton, 1979-84, U.Calif.-San Diego, La Jolla, 1984-87, Harvard U., Cambridge, Mass., 1987—. Vis. prof., chair math. dept. U. Tex., Austin, 1986; spl. chair Nat. Tsing Hua U., Hsinchu, Taiwan, 1991—; Wilson T.S. Wang Disting. vis. prof. Chinese U., Hong Kong, 1991—. Contbr. articles to profl. publs. Named Honorable prof., Fudan U. China, Academia Sinica China; recipient Sr. Scientist award, Humboldt Found. fellow, 1985, Crafoord prize, 1994, Veblen prize, 1981, Fields medal, 1982, Carty prize, 1980. Mem.: AAAS, NAS, Chinese Acad. Sci. (fgn. mem.), Acad. Sinica (Taiwan), Soc. Indsl. Applied Math., Am. Phys. Soc., Am. Math. Soc., Acad. Arts and Scis. Boston, N.Y. Acad. Scis. Office: Harvard U Dept Math 3d Fl Sci Ctr 1 Oxford St Cambridge MA 02138-2901

YAU, STEPHEN SIK-SANG, computer science and engineering educator, computer scientist, researcher; b. Wusei, Kiangsu, China, Aug. 6, 1935; arrived in U.S., 1958, naturalized, 1968; s. Pen-Chi and Wen-Chum (Shum) Y.; m. Vickie Liu, June 14, 1964; children: Andrew, Philip. BSEE, Nat. Taiwan U., China, 1958; MSEE, U. Ill., Urbana, 1959, PhD, 1961. Asst. prof. elec. engring. Northwestern U., Evanston, Ill., 1961-64, assoc. prof., 1964-68, prof., 1968-88, prof. computer scis., 1970-88, Walter P. Murphy prof. Elec. Engring. and Computer Sci., 1986-88, also chmn. dept. computer scis., 1972-77, chmn. dept. elec. engring. and computer sci., 1977-88; prof. computer and info. sci., chmn. dept. U. Fla., Gainesville, 1988-94; prof. computer sci. and engring. Ariz. State U., Tempe, 1994—, chmn. dept. computer sci. and engring., 1994—2001. Conf. chmn. IEEE Computer Conf., Chgo., 1967; gen. chmn. Nat. Computer Conf., Chgo., 1974, First Internat. Computer Software and Applications Conf., Chgo., 1977; Trustee Nat. Electronics Conf., Inc., 1965-68; chmn. organizing com. 11th World Computer Congress, Internat. Fedn. Info. Processing, San Francisco, 1989; gen. co-chmn. Internat. Symposium on Autonomous Decentralized Systems, Japan, 1993, gen. chmn., Phoenix, 1995; conf. co-chair 24th Ann. Internat. Computer Software and Applications Conf., Taipei, 2000. Editor-in-chief Computer mag., 1981-84; assoc. editor Jour. Info. Sci., 1983-99; editor IEEE Trans. on Software Engring., 1988-91; contbr. numerous articles on software engring., distributed and parallel processing systems, computer sci., elec. engring. and related fields to profl. pubis.; patentee in field. Recipient Louis E. Levy medal Franklin Inst., 1963, Golden Plate award Am. Acad. Achievement, 1964, The Silver Core award Internat. Fedn. Info. Processing, 1989, Spl. award, 1989. Fellow IEEE (mem. governing bd. Computer Soc. 1967-76, pres. 1974-75, dir. Inst. 1976-77, chmn. awards com., 1996-97; Richard E. Merwin award Computer Soc. 1981, Centennial medal 1984, Extraordinary Achievement award 1985, Outstanding Contbn. award Computer Sci. Soc. 1985, The Third Millennium medal 2000, Tsutomu Kanai award 2002), AAAS, Franklin Inst.; mem. Assn. for Computing Machinery, Am. Fedn. Info.-Processing Soc. (mem. exec. com. 1974-76, 79-82, dir. 1972-82, chmn. awards com. 1979-82, v.p. 1982-84, pres. 1984-86; chmn. Nat. Computer Conf. Bd. 1982-83, spl. award 1990), Am. Soc. Engring. Edn., Sigma Xi, Tau Beta Pi, Eta Kappa Nu, Pi Mu Epsilon. Office: Ariz State U PO Box 878809 Tempe AZ 85287-8809

YAVARKOVSKY, JEROME HAROLD, library director; b. N.Y.C., May 12, 1940; B Mech. Engring., Rensselaer Poly. Inst., 1960; MS in Mgmt., MIT, 1962; M Libr. Sci., Columbia U., 1971. Lic. pub. libr. Adminstrv. specialist Bell Labs., Murray Hill, N.J., 1963-64; systems analyst J.C. Penney Co., N.Y.C., 1965-67; tech. cons. Auerbach Assocs., N.Y.C., 1967-68; head programming Columbia U., N.Y.C., 1969-71, chief systems, 1971-72, asst. univ. libr., 1972-83; dean librs. Adelphi U., Garden City, N.Y., 1983-85; dir. N.Y. State Libr., Albany, 1985-95; univ. libr. Boston Coll., Chestnut Hill, 1995—. Office: Thomas P O'Neill Libr Boston Coll Chestnut Hill MA 02467

YAVORKOVSKY, LEONID LAZAR, oncologist, researcher, hematologist; b. Riga, Latvia, Mar. 8, 1955; s. Lazar Israel and Erna Jana Yavorkovsky; m. Karina A. Sidorenko; children: Gleb, Eva. MD, Riga Med. Inst., 1978; PhD, Latvian Acad. Medicine, Riga, 1986, DMS, 1992. Diplomate internal medicine, oncology, hematology. Postdoctoral fellow U. of Tex. Med. Sch., Houston, 1993—94; rsch. coord. Baylor Coll. of Medicine, Houston, 1995—96; med. resident NYU Med. Ctr., N.Y.C., 1996—98; tchg. asst. NYU Sch. of Medicine, N.Y.C., 1998—99; fellow in oncology/hematology NYU Med. Ctr., The Bklyn Hosp. Ctr., N.Y.C., 1999—2001; oncologist/hematologist The Permanente Med. Group, Inc., San Jose, Calif., 2001—. Author: (invention) Lithium carbonate for differentiation between myelodysplastic syndromes and aplastic anemia, 1986, (scientific contribution) Lithium Carbonate for Neutropenias: Indications and Efficacy, 1985. Recipient Author's Cert., 1986, Top award for best rsch. work in hematology, 2d USSR Hematology Congress, 1985; grantee rsch. grantee, Coun. Scis. of Latvian Republic, 1991. Mem.: Am. Soc. Clin. Oncology, Am. Soc. Hematology, Latvian Soc. Hematology (sec. 1990—93), European Assn. Cancer Rsch., Alumni Club, European Sch. Oncology. Achievements include invention of lithium carbonate for differentiation between myelodysplastic syndromes and aplastic anemia; lithium carbonate for neutropenias: indications and efficacy. Avocations: travel, classical music, stamp collecting/philately. Office: Permanente Med Group Inc 270 International Circle San Jose CA 95119 Office Phone: 408-972-6560. E-mail: leonid.yavorkovsky@kp.org.

YAVORSKY, WILLIAM D. semiconductor company executive; BS in Bus. Adminstrn., Bowling Green State U.; postgrad., Stanford U., U. Va. With Tektronix, Xerox Corp.; dir. internat. sales InFocus Corp., 1993—96, v.p. worldwide sales, 1996—2000, sr. v.p., gen. mgr., 2000—03; v.p. worldwide sales Pixelworks, Inc., Tualatin, Oreg., 2004—. Office: Pixelworks Inc Ste 300 8100 SW Nyberg Rd Tualatin OR 97062*

YAWORSKY, BOHDAN, criminal justice educator, consultant; s. Dmytro and Cornelia Yaworsky; m. Tedra L. Buckmaster, Sept. 19, 2000; children: Amy Gravett, Samantha Wall. BA, Rutgers U., New Brunswick, 1969; MA, Rutgers U., Newark, 1981, PhD, 1994. Drug counselor U.S. Army, Long Binh, Vietnam, 1970—71; tng. coord. Middlesex County Probation Dept., New Brunswick, 1973—78; dir. criminal justice planning Union County, Elizabeth, NJ, 1978—80, acting dir dept. pub. safety, 1980, asst. county adminstr., 1980—81; prof., chair dept. criminal justice New Jersey City U., Jersey City, 1981—. Disting. faculty mem. Nat. Coun. Juvenile & Family Ct. Judges, Reno; sr. cons. Office Internat. Criminal Justice, Chgo., Rutgers Ctr. Mgmt. Devel., Piscataway, NJ; cons., Hamburg, NJ, 1978—, Nat. Inst. Corrections, Longmont, Colo.; charter mem. N.J. Supreme Ct. Mcpl. Ct. Certification Bd., Trenton; charter mem. exec. com. N.J. Supreme Ct. State Adv. Bd. for Probation, Trenton; charter mem. N.J. Juvenile Intensive Supervision Program Adv. Bd., Trenton. Author: 100 criminal justice studies. Mem.: Am. Correctional Assn., Am. Probation and Parole Assn. (cons.), Acad. Criminal Justice Scis. Office: New Jersey City U Dept Criminal Justice Jersey City NJ 07305 E-mail: byaworsky@njcu.edu.

YAZDI, MAHVASH, utilities executive; BS in Indsl. Mgmt., Poly. U., Pomona; MBA, U. So. Calif.; grad. mgmt. info. tech. program, Harvard U. CIO Hughes Aircraft; joined Edison Internat., 1997, sr. v.p. bus. integration, CIO So. Calif. Edison subs., sr. v.p. bus. integration, CIO. Bd. dirs. Claremont

U. Consortium, Ptnrs. in Care Found., Columbus Newport Corp.; adv. dir. Lotus Corp., IBM Corp.; mem. So. Calif. Forum of the Trusteeship of the Internat. Women's Forum, 2003. Office: Edison Internat 2244 Walnut Grove Ave Rosemead CA 91770

YAZZIE, AARON FRANKLIN, events laborer; b. Ft. Defiance, Az., Apr. 30, 1962; s. Robert Franklin Yazzie Sr. and Sadie Mildred (Williams) Yazzie; life ptnr. Linda James, Jan. 20, 1965. Mechanic Ft. Sill, Lawton, Okla., 1985—87; parts washer Embassy Suites, Phoenix, 1996—98; staff rug racker Baker Bros., Super Floors, Phoenix, 1997—99; events set up crew Ariz. State U., West Phoenix, 1999—. Vol. Native Am. Student Organ., Phoenix, 2002—03. Pvt. U.S. Army, Korea. Recipient Mil. Svc. award, Dept. of Def., 1987. Mem.: Am. Indian Sci. and Engring. Soc. Democrat. Avocations: painting, bicycling, naturalist, pow wows. Office: Az State U Auxillary Svcs Integrative Studies Gerontology Tempe AZ 85287 Home: Rancho Santa fe Apts #2134 10201N 44th D Glendale AZ 85302 E-mail: aaronfyazzie62@hotmail.com.

YE, HENGCHUN, meteorologist, educator; m. Argyl Brian Houser; 1 child, Crysti Wang. BS, Hangzhou Univ., 1985, MS, 1988; PhD, U.Del., Newark, 1995. Asst. prof. Emporia State U., Kans., 1995—98, U. of Idaho, Moscow, Idaho, 1998—2001; assoc. prof. Calif. State U., LA, 2001—. Contbr. articles to research publications. Recipient Faculty Excellence Award, Alumni Assn. of UI, 2000, Faculty Recognition Award, UI and Wash. State Univ. Naval Res. Officer Tng. Corps, 2000, Faculty Excellent Award, Alumni Assn. of UI, 1999; grantee, NSF, 1999-2003, Coop. Inst. for Artic Rsch., 2001-2003. Mem.: Royal Meteorol. Soc., Am. Geophys. Union, Am. Meteorol. Soc., Am. Assn. Geographers. Achievements include research in Climate variability and change. Office: California State University Los Angeles 5151 State University Dr Los Angeles CA 90032-8222 E-mail: hye2@calstatela.edu.

YE, JUN, physicist, researcher; b. Shanghai, China, Nov. 7, 1967; s. Shanxiang Ye and Changhong Fan; m. Ying Zhang, June 22, 1993; 1 child, Shirley Eileen. PhD, U. of Colo., 1992—97. Assoc. fellow JILA, Nat. Inst. of Std. and Tech. and U. of Colo., Boulder, 1999—2001, fellow, 2001—. Author (principle researcher): (laser spectroscopy) Ultrasensitive and ultrahigh resolution laser absorption spectroscopy (Adolph Lomb Medal, Optical Soc. of Am., 1999, 1999); author: (principle investigator) (precision measurement) Precision Optical frequency metrology (Gold Medal, U. S. Dept. of Commerce, 2001); author: (researcher) (quantum optics and cold atoms) Trapping of a single atom in cavity QED. Recipient U. Fellowship, U. of Colo. at Boulder, 1993 - 1994, Selection to Frontiers of Engring. Symposium, NAE, 2000, Tech. Rev. Magazine's TR100 Young Innovator, Tech. Rev. Mag., 2002, Presdl. Early Career Award for Scientists and Engineers, U.S. Pres., 2003; fellow R. A. Millikan Prize Fellowship, Calif. Inst. of Tech., 1997 - 1999. Mem.: Optical Soc. of Am., Am. Phys. Soc. Achievements include invention of Cavity based ultrasensitive absorption spectroscopy; research in Highly stabilized lasers for precision measurements; Precision, wide bandwidth optical frequency comb; invention of Phase locking indepedent ultrafast lasers; patents for Comb generating optical cavity that includes an optical amplifier and an optical modulator; patents pending for A novel cavity ringdown heterodyne spectroscopy: 1 x 10-10 sensitivity with microwatt light power; Sub 10 - femtosecond active synchronization of two passively mode-locked Ti:sapphire oscillators; research in Cooling and trapping of alkaline earth atoms; Manipulation of cold molecules. Office: National Institute of Standards & Techno JILA Campus Box 440 Univ of Colorado Boulder CO 80309-0440 E-mail: ye@jila.colorado.edu.

YEADON, TAMMY PAMELA, information specialist; b. Bayonne, N.J., Feb. 3, 1967; d. Tom and Betty Yeadon. BS in Polymer and Plastics Engring., U. Detroit, 1989; MLS, Rutgers U., 1994. Engr. Whirlpool Corp., Benton Harbor, Mich., 1988, Ford Motor Co., Detroit, 1989-90, MedTech Group, South Plainfield, N.J., 1991; quality assurance analyst Block Drug, Jersey City, N.J., 1992-93; info. mgr. John Brown, Bridgewater, N.J., 1994-97; tech. knowledge specialist A.T. Kearney, N.Y.C., 1998-99; sys. mgr. Berkshire Capital Corp., 2000—. Computer cons. Tyrell the Collection, Linden, N.J., 1991—; libr. cons. The Penn of N.Y., 1998-99. Tutor Literacy Vols. of Am., Elizabeth, N.J., 1993; vol. Gay Men's Health Crisis, N.Y.C., 1993. Mem. ALA, Am. Soc. of Info. Scis., Spl. Libr. Assn.

YEAGER, ANSON ANDERS, writer, retired editor, retired columnist; b. Salt Lake City, June 5, 1919; s. Charles Franklin and Elise Marie (Thingelstad) Yeager; m. Ada May Bidwell, Sept. 10, 1944; children: Karen Ann, Anson Anders, Harry H., Terry Douglas, Ellen Elise. BS, S.D. State U., Brookings, 1947; LLD (hon.), Dakota State Coll., Madison, S.D., 1972; DPub.Svc. (hon.), S.D. State U., Brookings, 1991. Printer's devil, linotype operator Faith Ind. and Gazette (S.D.), 1935-38; printer S.D. State U., 1940-41; staff writer Argus Leader, Sioux Falls, SD, 1947-55, Sunday editor, 1955-60, exec. editor, 1961-77, assoc. editor, 1978-84, editor editl. page, 1961-84, columnist, 1984-98, author travel articles and commentary. Lectr. dept. journalism U. S.D., 1953—55. Contbr. to World Book Ency., 1966—84; author: Anson Yeager's Stories, 2000. Bd. dirs. Sioux Falls Area C. of C., 1964—70, Sioux Falls Devel. Found., 1967, Boys Club of Sioux Falls, 1966—68, S.D. State U. Found., 1987—99, chmn., 1988—89; bd. dirs. Sioux Coun., Boy Scouts Am., Sioux Falls, 1967—72, v.p., 1970—72; coun. mem. Ctr. for We. Studies, 2002—. Capt. U.S. Army, 1942—46, capt. U.S. Army, 1950—52, lt. col. U.S. Army, 1979, ret. U.S. Army, 1979, lt. col. S.D. Army N.G., 1961—64. Named Newsman of Yr., 1978; named to S.D. Newspaper Hall of Fame, 1994, S.D. Hall of Fame, 1998; recipient S.D. Sigma Delta Chi award, 1956, Editl. Excellence award, William Allen White Found., 1976, Disting. Alumni award, S.D. State U., 1980, Friend of Augustana Coll. award, 1980, Ralph D. Casey Minn. award for disting. svc. in journalism, U. Minn., 1981, Eminent Svc. award, East River Elec. Power Coop., 1984, Mass. Comms. award, S.D. State U., 1984, Les Helgeland Cmty. Svc. award, S.D. AP Mng. Editors, 1985, Disting. Svc. award, S.D. Press Assn., 1988, A.H. Pankow award, 1995, Jerome J. Lohr award, S.D. State U. Found., Western Am. award, Ctr. for Western Studies, Augustana Coll., 2000.

YEAGER, CAROLINE HALE, radiologist, consultant; b. Little Rock, Sept. 5, 1946; d. George Glenn and Crenor Burnelle (Hale) Y.; m. William Berg Singer, July 8, 1978; children: Adina Atkinson Singer, Sarah Rose Singer. BA, Ind. U., Bloomington, 1968; MD, Ind. U., Indpls., 1971. Diplomate Am. Bd. Radiology; med. lic. State of Calif. Intern Good Samaritan Hosp., Los Angeles, 1971-72; resident in radiology King Drew Med. Ctr. UCLA, Los Angeles, 1972-76; dir. radiology Hubert Humphrey Health Ctr., Los Angeles, 1976-77; asst. prof. radiology UCLA, Los Angeles, 1977-84, King Drew Med. Ctr. UCLA, Los Angeles, 1977-85, dir. ultrasound, 1977-84; ptnr. pvt. practice Beverly Breast Ctr., Beverly Hills, Calif., 1984-87; cons. Clarity Communications, Pasadena, Calif., 1981—; pvt. practice radiology Claude Humphrey Health Ctr., 1991-93; dir. sonograms and mammograms Rancho Los Amigos Med. Ctr., 1993-94. Trustee Assn. Teaching Physicians, L.A., 1976-81; cons. King Drew Med. Ctr., 1984, Gibraltar Savs., 1987, Cal Fed. Inc., 1986, Medical Faculty At Home Professions, 1989—, Mobil Diagnostics, 1991-92, Xerox Corp., 1990-91, Frozen Leopard, Inc., 1990-91. Author: (with others) Infectious Disease, 1978, Anatomy and Physiology for Medical Transcriptionists, 1992; contbr. articles to profl. jours. Trustee U. Synagogue, Los Angeles, 1975-79; mem. Friends of Pasadena Playhouse, 1987-90. Grantee for innovative tng. Nat. Fund for Med. Edn., 1980-81. Mem. Am. Inst. Ultrasound in Medicine, L.A. Radiology Soc. (ultrasound sect.), Nat. Soc. Performance and Instrn. (chmn. conf. Database 1991, publs. L.A. chpt. 1990, info. systems L.A. chpt. 1991, dir. adminstrn. L.A. chpt. 1992, Outstanding Achievement in Performance Improvement award L.A. chpt. 1990, bd. dirs. 1990-93, Pres. award for Outstanding Chpt. 1992, v.p. programs 1993), Stanford Profl. Women L.A. Jewish. Avocations: writing, humor, design. Home and Office: 3520 Yorkshire Rd Pasadena CA 91107-5440

YEAGER, JEANA, aviator; b. Fort Worth, Tex., May 18, 1952; Aviator Scaled Composites Inc., Mojave, Calif. Recipient Presdl. Citizen Medal of Honor, 1986, Collier Trophy, Nat. Aeronautic Assn., 1986, Ivan C. Kincheloe award, Soc. of Exptl. Test Pilots, 1987, Nat. Air and Space Mus. Trophy, 1987. Achievements include flying the Voyager aircraft around the world non-stop without refueling; set four separate speed records in the Rutan EZ planes. Office: Scaled Composites Inc 1624 Flight Line Mojave CA 93501 Office Phone: 661-824-4541. Office Fax: 661-824-4174.

YEAGER, JOSEPH HEIZER, JR., lawyer; b. Indpls., Jan. 8, 1957; s. Joseph Heizer and Marilyn Virginia (Hillyard) Y.; m. Candance A. Grass, June 2, 1984; children: Samuel, Henry. AB cum laude, Harvard U., 1979; JD cum laude, Ind. U., 1983. Bar: Ind. 1983, U.S. Dist. Ct., (so. and no. dist.) Ind. 1983, U.S. Ct. Appeals (7th cir.) 1986, U.S. Supreme Ct. 1996. Dir. ops. Penn and Schoen Assocs., N.Y.C., 1979-80; assoc. Baker & Daniels, Indpls., 1983-89, ptnr., 1990—. Bd. dirs. Indpls. Legal Aid Soc., 1990-99, pres. 1992-94; chmn. Indpls. Com. for UNICEF, 1986-91; mem. Indpls. Com. for Fgn. Affairs, 1986-91, Ind. Comm. for Continuing Legal Edn., 2003—. Mem. Ind. Bar Assn., Indpls. Bar Assn. (litigation sect. exec. com. 1985-86, 1996-2000, chair 1999), Cen. Ind. Regional Citizens League (bd. dirs. 1997-99). Democrat. Avocation: private pilot. Office: Baker & Daniels 300 N Meridian St Ste 2700 Indianapolis IN 46204-1782 Office Phone: 317-237-0300. Business E-Mail: jhyeager@bakerd.com.

YEAGER, KURT ERIC, research institute official; b. Cleve., Sept. 11, 1939; s. Joseph Ellsworth and Karolyn Kristine (Pedersen) Y.; m. Rosalie Ann McMillan, Feb. 5, 1960; children: Geoffrey, Phillip; m. Regina Ursula Querfurt, May 12, 1970; 1 dau., Victoria. BA in Chemistry, Kenyon Coll., 1961; postgrad., Ohio State U., 1961-62; MS in Physics, U. Calif., Davis, 1964; MS Wharton Sch. Bus., U. Pa., 1995. Tchg. asst. Ohio State U., 1961-62; officer, program mgr. Air Force Tech. Applications Ctr., Alexandria, Va., 1962-68; assoc. dept. dir. Mitre Corp., McLean, Va., 1968-72; dir. energy rsch. and devel. planning EPA, Washington, 1972-74; dir. fossil power plants dept. Electric Power Rsch. Inst., Palo Alto, Calif., 1974-79, dir. coal combustion systems, 1979-83, v.p. coal combustion systems, 1983-88, v.p. generation and storage, 1988-96, pres., CEO, 1996—. Mem. commerce tech. adv. bd., Oak Ridge fossil energy adv. bd. Nat. Acad. Engring.; mem. exec. bd. Nat. Coal Coun.; bd. dir. nat. coalition advanced mfg. U.S. Energy Assn. Contbr. articles to profl. jours. Pres. No. Va. Youth Football Assn., 1973-74. Capt. USAF, 1962-68. Decorated Air Force Commendation medals (2); recipient Outstanding Svc. award EPA, 1974; named Energy Policy Leader, Sci. Am., 2003. Fellow ASME (rsch. policy bd., trustee com. econ. devel.); mem. AAAS, Am. Chem. Soc., Palo Alto C. of C. Republican. Episcopalian. Business E-Mail: KYeager@EPRI.com.

YEAGER, MARK, real estate company executive; Degree, Lehigh U.; MBA in Mktg., Fairleigh Dickinson U. From v.p. to pres., CIO The Gale Co. Real Estate Investment Svcs. (formerly Sammis then Gale & Wentworth), Florham Pk., NJ, 1991; pres. The Gale Co. Real Estate Investment Svcs., CIO. Mem. Regional Bus. Partnership; mem. exec. com. Tri-County Scholarship Fund. Mem.: Nat. Assn. Indsl. and Office Properties (bd. dirs.). Office: The Gale Co Rela Estate Investment Services 100 Campus Drive Ste 200 Florham Park NJ 07932*

YEAGER, MARK LEONARD, lawyer; b. Chgo., Apr. 7, 1950; BA, U. Mich., 1972; JD, Northwestern U., 1975. Bar: Ill. 1975, Fla. 1985. Ptnr. McDermott, Will & Emery, Chgo., 1975—. Mem. ABA.

YEAGER, PETER CLEARY, sociologist, educator; b. Terre Haute, Ind., Nov. 29, 1949; s. Ralph Oscar and Dorothy (Cleary) Y.; m. Kathy Ellen Kram, Aug. 9, 1981; 1 child, Jason Kram Yeager. BA in Journalism, U. Minn., 1971; MS in Sociology, U. Wis., 1976, PhD in Sociology, 1981. Writer, photographer Sun Newspapers, Mpls., 1971-72; from lectr. to asst. prof. sociology Yale U., New Haven, 1979-82; from asst. to assoc. prof. sociology Boston U., 1982—. Rsch. fellow ethics and the professions program Harvard U., Cambridge, Mass., 1989-90. Co-author: Illegal Corporate Behavior, 1979, Corporate Crime, 1980 (named one of Choice's outstanding acad. books 1981); author: The Limits of Law, 1991. Bd. assessors 1st Parish in Framingham, Mass., 1992-94. Managerial Ethics Rsch. grantee Amsterdam Found., 1989-92, Human Resources Policy Inst. Boston U., 1986-87, 93-94. Mem. Am. Sociol. Assn., Am. Soc. Criminology, Law and Soc. Assn., Soc. for Study of Social Problems, Phi Beta Kappa, Kappa Tau Alpha. Avocations: hiking, reading, creative writing, tennis, travel. Office: Dept Sociology Boston U 96-100 Cummington St Boston MA 02215

YEAGER, PHILLIP CHARLES, transportation company executive; b. Bellevue, Ky., Nov. 15, 1927; s. Ferd A. and Helen (Koehler) Y.; m. Joyce E. Ruebusch, June 2, 1951; children: David P., Debra A. Yeager Jensen, Mark A. BA, U. Cin., 1951. Warehouse mgr. Pure Carbonic Co., Cin., 1950-52; trace clk., rate clk., asst. office mgr. Pa. R.R., Chgo., 1952-56, salesman Kansas City, Mo., 1956-59, asst. dir. Trailvan Phila., 1959-65, div. sales mgr. Milw., 1965-68; dir. Trailvan Penn-Ctrl. R.R., N.Y.C., 1968-71; pres. Hub City Terminals, Chgo., 1971-85; chmn. The Hub Group, Chgo., 1985—; also bd. dirs. Bd. dirs. 30 Hubcity terminals. Cpl. U.S. Army, 1946-47. Recipient Achievement award Intermodal Transp. Assn., 1991, Harry E. Salzberg medallion for outstanding achievement in transp.; named Chgo. Transp. Man of Yr., Chgo. Transp. Assn., 1990. Mem. N.Y. Traffic Club, Chgo. Traffic Club. Republican. Lutheran. Avocations: golf, biking, swimming.

YEAGER, RUTH, lawyer; Asst. U.S. Atty., Dept. Justice, Tyler, Tex., chief civil divsn., 1988—2002; U.S. Atty., Ea. Dist. Tex., 1993—94. Office: US Attys Office 110 N College Ave Ste 700 Tyler TX 75702-0204 E-mail: ruth.yeager@usdoj.gov.

YEAMANS, GEORGE THOMAS, librarian, educator; b. Nov. 7, 1929; s. James Norman and Dolphine Sophia (Manhart) Yeamans; m. Mary Ann Seng, Feb. 1, 1958; children: Debra, Susan, Julia. AB, U. Va., 1950; MLS, U. Ky., 1955; EdD, Ind. U., 1965. Asst. audio-visual dir. Ind. State U., Terre Haute, 1957—58; asst. film libr. Ball State U., Muncie, Ind., 1958—61, film libr., 1961—69, assoc. prof. libr. sci., 1969—72, prof., 1972—95, prof. emeritus, 1995—. Cons. Pendleton (Ind.) Sch. Corp., 1962, 67, Captioned Films for the Deaf Workshop, Muncie, 1963—65, Decatur (Ind.) Sch. Sys., 1978; adjudicator Ind. Media Fair, 1979—93, David Letterman Scholarship Program, 1993. Author: Projectionists' Programmed Primer, 1969, rev. edit., 1982, Mounting and Preserving Pictorial Materials, 1976, Tape Recording, 1978, Transparency Making, 1977, Photographic Principles, 1981, Computer Literacy — A Programmed Primer, 1985, Building Effective Creative Project Teams, 2000, Designing Dynamic Media Presentations, 1996;: rev. edit., 2000, Robert F. Kennedy Archival Project, 1968—2004; songwriter: Branson Bound, 1996; contbr. articles to profl. jours. Campaign worker Wilson for Mayor, Muncie, 1979. With USMC, 1950—52. Recipient Citations of Achievement, Internat. Biog. Assn., Cambridge, England, 1973, Am. Biog. Assn., 1976, Mayor James P. Carey award for achievement for disting. contbns. to Ball State U. and City of Muncie, 1988; Video Info. Sys. grantee, Ball State U., 1993. Mem.: ALA, NEA (del. assembly dept. audiovisual instrn. 1967), Audio-Visual Instrn. Dirs. Ind. (exec. bd. 1962—68, pres. 1966—67), Thomas Jefferson Soc. Alumni U. Va., Ind. Pub. Libr. Assn., Ind. Acad. Libr. Assn., Ind. Corp. and Network Libr. Assn., Ind. Libr. Fedn., Assn. Ednl. Comm. and Tech., Autisim Soc. Am., Assn. Ind. Media Educators (chmn. auditing com. 1979—81), Ind. Assn. Ednl. Comms. and Tech. (dist. dir. 1972—76), Am. Assn. Sch. Librs., Phi Delta Kappa. Republican. Unitarian-Universalist. Avocations: photography, stamp collecting/philately, coin collecting/numismatics, genealogy. Home: 4507 W Burton Dr Muncie IN 47304-3575

YEARA, JAMES CARROLL, secondary school educator, writer; s. CArroll Bertress and Betty Lou (Vanderbrook) Yeara; widowed; children: Jinny, Alice Elisabeth. BA, Nazareth Coll., 1981; MA, SUNY, Albany, 1986. Eng. tchr. Monoe H.S., Rochester, NY, 1980—81, Interim Jr. H.S., Rochester, 1981—82, Migrant Tutorial Outreach, Brockport, NY, 1982—83; Eng. and drama tchr. Averill Park (N.Y.) H.S., 1983—85, Bethlehem Ctrl. H.S., Delmar, NY, 1985—. Drama critic Metroland Mag., Albany, 1990—. Actor, dir.: Wit & Will Theatre, 1998—; Capital Repertory Theatre, 1998—, 2003; Lysistrata Project, 2003—; author: (plays) Haunted Albany, 2003—. Scholar, NEH, 1984, 1989, NEH, 1990, NEH, 1991, 1995. Avocations: theater, writing, bicycling. Home: 299 New Scotland S Rd Slingerlands NY 12159 Office: Bethlehem Ctrl HS 700 Delaware Ave Delmar NY 12054 Office Phone: 518-439-7698.

YEARGIN-ALLSOPP, MARSHALYN, medical epidemiologist, pediatrician; b. Greenville, S.C., May 17, 1948; d. Grady Andrew and Willie Mae (Blocker) Yeargin; m. Ralph Norman Allsopp, Apr. 5, 1975; children: Timothy Chandler, Whitney Marisha. Student Bennett Coll., 1964-66; BA, Sweet Briar Coll., 1968; MD, Emory U., 1972. Diplomate Am. Bd. Pediatrics. Intern Montefiore Hosp., Bronx, N.Y., 1972-73, resident, 1973-75; instr. pediatrics Albert Einstein Coll. Medicine, Bronx, 1975-77, asst. prof. pediatrics, 1977-78, 80-81; pediatrician Montefiore-Morrisania Comprehensive Health Care Ctr., Bronx, 1975-78, Louise Wise Adoption Agy., N.Y.C., 1975-80, Children's Evaluation and Rehab. Ctr., Rose F. Kennedy Ctr., Bronx, 1980-81; officer USPHS, 1981—, comdr., 1983—; epidemiologic intelligence surveillance officer birth defects br. Ctrs. for Disease Control, Atlanta, 1981-83, preventive medicine resident, 1982-84, med. epidemiologist, 1984—; pediatric cons. Clayton County Early Intervention Program, Jonesboro, Ga., 1983—; med. dir. Easter Seal Presch. Program, Atlanta, 1981-83; physician Com. on Handicapped, N.Y.C., 1979-81, United Cerebral Palsy Program, Bronx, 1980-81. Bd. overseers Sweet Briar Coll., 1981-89; bd. dirs. Neighborhood Arts Ctr., Atlanta, 1984-87; mem. prevention edn. com. Retarded Citizens, Atlanta, 1984-96; mem. fundraising campaign Greater Atlanta YWCA, 1985; bd. trustees Pace Acad., 1986—; co-chmn. Minority Atlanta Families in Ind. Schs., Inc., 1986—; chair, Bd. dirs. profl. adv. com. Cerebral Palsey Ctr., REACH, Inc., Atlanta, 1988—; mem. State of Ga. Interagy. Coun. for Edn. of the Handicapped Act., 1988-96; mem. sci. adv. bd. Nat. Alliance for Autism Rsch. Recipient Disting. Alumna award, Sweet Briar Coll., 1992. Fellow Am. Acad. Pediatrics, Am. Acad. Cerebral Palsy and Devel. Medicine; mem. AMA, Atlanta Med. Assn., Jack and Jill of Am., Phi Beta Kappa, Delta Sigma Theta. Office: Ctrs for Disease Control 4770 Buford Hwy NE Atlanta GA 30341-3717

YEARIAN, MASON RUSSELL, retired physicist; b. Lafayette, Ind., July 5, 1932; married; three children. BS, Purdue U., 1954; MS, Stanford U., 1956, PhD in Physics, 1959. Rsch. assoc. physics U. Pa., 1959-61; asst. prof. Stanford (Calif.) U., 1961—65, assoc. prof., 1965—70, assoc. dean, undergraduate studies, 1974—77, prof. physics, 1970—97, prof. emeritus physics, 1997—, dir. High Energy Physics Lab. W.W. Hansen Experimental Physics Lab., 1973-95. Mem. Coll. Bd. (physics), Educational Testing Svc., 1992—.

YEARWOOD, TRISHA, country music singer, songwriter; b. Monticello, Ga., 1964; m. Chris Latham (div.); m. Robert Reynolds, May 21, 1994 (div.). Degree in Music Bus., Belmont U. Intern MTM Records, demo singer, commercial jingles singer; recording artist MCA Records. Albums include Trisha Yearwood, 1991 (double platinum), Hearts in Armor, 1992 (Grammy nomination: Best Country Female Vocal, 1994 for "Walkaway Joe"), The Song Remembers When, 1993, Thinkin' About You, 1995, Everybody Knows, 1996, (songbook) A Collection of Hits, 1997, Where Your Road Leads, 1998, Real Live Woman, 2000; back-up vocalist Garth Brooks albums; opening act Garth Brooks Tour, 1991; TV appearances on TNN American Music Shop, The Tonight Show, Late Night with David Letterman, Good Morning America, A&E Live By Request, 1998 Academy Awards, 1996 Summer Olympic Closing Ceremonies. Named Best New Country Artist by Am. Music Awards, 1992, Top New Female Vocalist by Acad. Country Music, 1992, Top Female Vocalist of Yr., 1998; Top Female Vocalist of Yr., Country Mus. Assn., 1997, 98; first female in country music history to have debut single reach #1 on charts with She's in Love with the Love, 1991; recipient Grammy awards for best female country vocal, 1998, best country vocal collaboration (with Aaron Neville) 1994, (with Garth Brooks), 1998.

YEATMAN, HARRY CLAY, biologist, educator; b. Ashwood, Tenn., June 22, 1916; s. Trezevant Player and Mary (Wharton) Y.; m. Jean Hansford Anderson, Nov. 24, 1949; children— Henry Clay, Jean Hansford. AB, U. N.C., Chapel Hill, 1939, MA, 1942, PhD, 1953; student, Cornell U., summer 1937. Asst. prof. biology U. of South, Sewanee, Tenn., 1950-54, asso. prof., 1954-60, prof., 1960—, Kenan prof., 1980—, chmn. dept., 1972-76, elderhostel tchr., 1987-88. Vis. prof. marine biology Va. Inst. Marine Sci., Gloucester Point, summer 1967; cons. Smithsonian Instn., Sci. Applications, Inc., La Jolla, Calif., Ctrs. for Disease Control, Atlanta, WHO, Ecol. Analysts, Inc., Balt., Duke Power Co., Charlotte, N.C. Contbr. articles to profl. jours. Served with AUS, 1942-46. Gen. Edn. Bd. fellow, 1941-42; Brown Found. fellow, 1984 Fellow AAAS; mem. Soc. Systematic Biology (charter), Soc. Limnology and Oceanography (charter), Soc. Ichthyology and Herpetology, Tenn. Acad. Sci., Am. Micros. Soc., Am. Ornithologists Union, Tenn. Ornithol. Soc., Tenn. Archeol. Soc., Nat. Speleological Soc., Blue Key, Phi Beta Kappa, Sigma Xi, Omicron Delta Kappa, Sigma Nu. Republican. Episcopalian. Home: PO Box 356 Jumpoff Rd Sewanee TN 37375 Office: 735 University Ave Sewanee TN 37383-1000 Office Phone: 931-598-1000.

YEATS, ROBERT SHEPPARD, geologist, educator; b. Miami, Fla., Mar. 30, 1931; s. Robert Sheppard and Carolyn Elizabeth (Rountree) Y.; m. Lillian Eugenia Bowie, Dec. 30, 1952 (dec. Apr. 1991); children: Robert Bowie, David Claude, Stephen Paul, Kenneth James, Sara Elizabeth; m. Angela M. Hayes, Jan. 7, 1993. BA, U. Fla., 1952; MS, U. Wash., 1956, PhD, 1958. Registered geologist, Oreg., Calif., Wash. Geologist, petroleum exploration and prodn. Shell Oil Co., Ventura and L.A., Calif., 1958-67, Shell Devel. Co., Houston, 1967; assoc. prof. geology Ohio U., Athens, 1967-70, prof., 1970-77; prof. geology Oreg. State U., Corvallis, 1977-97, prof. oceanography, 1991-97, prof. emeritus, 1997—, chmn. dept., 1977-85; geologist U.S. Geol. Survey, 1968, 69, 75, Glomar Challenger scientist, 1971, co-chief scientist, 1973-74, 78; mem. Oreg. Bd. Geologist Examiners, 1981-83; chmn. Working Group 1 Internat. Lithosphere Program, 1987-90, chmn. task force group on paleoseismology, 1990-98; chmn. subcom. on Himalayan active faults Internat. Geol. Correlation Program, Project 206, 1984-92; mem. geophysics study com. NRC, 1987-94. Rschr. on Cenozoic tectonics of So. Calif., Oreg., New Zealand and Himalaya; active faults of Calif. Transverse Ranges, deep-sea drilling in Ea. Pacific; vis. scientist New Zealand Geol. Survey, 1983-84, 99, Geol. Survey of Japan, 1992, Inst. de Phys. du Globe de Paris, 1993; sr. cons. Earth Cons. Internat., 1997—, ptnr., 2001—. Author: The Geology of Earthquakes, 1997, Living with Earthquakes in the Pacific Northwest, 1998, 2d edit., 2004, Living with Earthquakes in California-A Survivor's Guide, 2001. Mem. Ojai (Calif.) City Planning Commn., 1961-62, Ojai City Coun., 1962-65. 1st lt. U.S. Army, 1952-54. Named Richard H. Jahns Disting. Lectr. in Engring. Geology, 1995; Ohio U. rsch. fellow, 1973-74; grantee NSF, U.S. Geol. Survey. Fellow AAAS, Geol. Soc. Am. (chmn. structural geology and tectonics divsn. 1984-85, Cordilleran sect. 1988-89, assoc. editor bull. 1987-89); mem. Am. Assn. Petroleum Geologists (Outstanding Educator award Pacific sect. 1991, Michel T. Halbouty human needs award 1998), Am. Geophys. Union, Seismol. Soc. Am., Oreg. Acad. Sci. Home: 1654 NW Crest Pl Corvallis OR 97330-1812 Office: Oreg State U Dept Geoscis Corvallis OR 97331-5506 Office Phone: 541-737-1226. E-mail: yeatsr@geo.oregonstate.edu.

YEATTS, DOROTHY ELIZABETH FREEMAN, nurse, educator, retired county official; b. Richmond, Va., Jan. 19, 1925; d. Robert Franklin and Elizabeth Bell (Wiggins) Freeman; m. Roy Earl Yeatts, Nov. 27, 1948; children: Martha Jane Yeatts Couch, Robert Patrick. Diploma in nursing, Stuart Circle Hosp., Richmond, Va., 1947; BS in Nursing, Coll. William and Mary, 1947; cert. pub. health nursing supr., U. N.C., 1974. RN, Va., N.C. Vis. nurse Instructive Vis. Nurses Assn., Richmond, 1947-49; maternity nurse N.C. Bapt. Hosp., Winston-Salem, 1969-71; pub. health nurse I, Forsyth County Health Dept., Winston-Salem, 1971-72, pub. health nurse coord., 1972-74, pub. health nurse supr., 1974-78. Sunday sch. tchr. Tuckahoe Presbyn. Ch., Richmond, 1954-57, Trinity Presbyn Ch., Winston-Salem, 1960-84; pres. Buckingham Park Garden Club, Richmond, 1956-58, Women of Trinity Presbyn. Ch., 1963-64; elder Trinity Presbyn. Ch., 1978-81, circle bible moderator, 1984-97; bd. dirs. Forsyth Cancer Soc., Winston-Salem, 1980-86;

instr. ARC, Winston-Salem, 1978-97, vol., 1993-97. Republican. Avocations: arts and crafts, fishing, stamp collecting/philately, woodcarving, sewing. Home: 310 Coventry Park Ln Winston Salem NC 27104-3676 E-mail: ryeatts@triad.rr.com.

YEAZEL, KEITH ARTHUR, lawyer; b. Fayetteville, N.C., Feb. 14, 1956; s. Russell E. and Barbara E. (Weaver) Y.; m. Deborah M. MacDonald, Aug. 30, 1986. BA, Ohio State U., 1983; JD, Capital U., 1989. Bar: Ohio 1989, U.S. Dist. Ct. (so. dist.) Ohio 1989, U.S. Ct. Appeals (6th cir.) 1990, U.S. Supreme Ct. 1992. Law clk. to judge George C. Smith U.S. Dist. Ct., Columbus, Ohio, 1988-89; prin. Keith A. Yeazel, Atty. at Law, Columbus, 1989—. Mem. Ohio Bar Assn., Columbus Bar Assn., Nat. Assn. Criminal Def. Lawyers, Ohio Assn. Criminal Def. Lawyers, Order of Curia. Republican. Lutheran. Office: 65 S 5th St Columbus OH 43215-4307

YEAZELL, RUTH BERNARD, English language educator; b. N.Y.C., Apr. 4, 1947; d. Walter and Annabelle (Reich) Bernard; m. Stephen C. Yeazell, Aug. 14, 1969 (div. 1980). BA with high honors, Swarthmore Coll., 1967; MPhil, Yale U., 1970, PhD, 1971. Asst. prof. English Boston U., 1971-74, UCLA, 1975-77, assoc. prof., 1977-80, prof., 1980-91, Yale U., New Haven, 1991—, dir. grad. studies, 1993-98, Chace family prof., 1995—, chair, 2000—. Author: Language and Knowledge in the Late Novels of Henry James, 1976, Death and Letters of Alice James, 1981, Fictions of Modesty: Women and Courtship in the English Novel, 1991, Harems of the Mind: Passages of Western Art and Literature, 2000; assoc. editor Nineteenth-Century Fiction, 1977-80; editor: Sex, Politics and Science in the 19th Century Novel, 1986, Henry James: A Collection of Critical Essays, 1994. Dir. Lewis Walpole Libr., 1996—. Woodrow Wilson fellow, 1967-68, Guggenheim fellow, 1979-80, NEH fellow, 1988-89, Pres.'s rsch. fellow U. Calif., 1988-89, Getty scholar, 2003-04 (declined). Mem. MLA (exec. coun. 1985-88), English Inst. (supervising com. 1983-86). Office: Yale U Dept English New Haven CT 06520-8302 Office Phone: 203-432-2232.

YECKE, CHERI PIERSON, education policy fellow, columnist, author; b. St. Paul, Feb. 5, 1955; d. Leo Sylvester and Marceline Mae (Intihar) Pierson; m. Dennis Joseph Yecke, Dec. 22, 1973; children: Anastasia, Tiffany. BA, U. Hawaii, 1975; MST, U. Wis., River Falls, 1984; PhD, U. Va., 2001. Apptd. mem. State Bd. Edn., 1995—98, dep. sec. edn., 1998—2001, sec. edn., 2001—02; dir. tchr. quality and pub. sch. choice US Dept. Edn., 2002—03; sr. adv. to White House on USA Freedom Corps., 2003; commr. edn. State of Minn., 2003—04; disting. sr. fellow for edn. and social policy Ctr. of the Am. Experiment, 2004—. Author: The War Against Excellence: The Rising Tide of Mediocrity in America's Middle Schools, 2003. Republican. Home: 2106 Arnold Palmer Dr Blaine MN 55449

YECKEL, ANITA T. state legislator; b. Salt Lake City, Nov. 12, 1942; m. Robert Yeckel; 2 children. BS in Polit. Sci., postgrad., U. Mo., St. Louis. With 1st Nat. Bank, St. Louis, 1960-68, Am. Home Savs. & Loans Assn., 1982-92; mem. Lindebergh Sch. Dist. Bd. Edn., 1990—, Mo. Senate from 1st dist., Jefferson City, 1996—. Mem. Kiwanis. Republican. Roman Catholic. Office: 8819 Gladlea Saint Louis MO 63127 Fax: 314-843-7542. E-mail: ayeckel@services.state.mo.us.

YEE, ALBERT HOY, writer, retired psychologist, educator; b. Santa Barbara, Calif., June 14, 1929; children: Lisa Diane, Hoyt Brian, Cynthia Rae. BA, U. Calif., Berkeley, 1952; MA, San Francisco State U., 1959; Ed.D., Stanford U., 1965. Post-doctoral research fellow U. Oreg., Eugene, 1966-67; assoc. prof. edn. U. Wis., Madison, 1967-70, prof., 1970-73; prof. ednl. psychology, dean grad. studies and research Calif. State U., Long Beach, 1973-79, originating founder Grad. Ctr., 1974; prof. edn. U. Mont., 1979-83, dean Sch. Edn., 1979-82; sr. lectr. psychology Chinese U. of Hong Kong, 1985-89; dean, prof. psychology Am. Coll., Singapore; sr. lectr. psychology Nat. U., Singapore, 1989-90; dir. program U. Md., Hongkong, 1990; disting. vis. prof. ednl. psychology spl. adviser coll. grad. studies and internat. programs Marist Coll., 1990-92; prof. ednl. psychology Fla. Internat. U., Miami, 1992-94, rsch. scholar, 1994-95. Chmn. 1st Fed. Adv. Com. for Asian and Pacific Island Ams., Bur. Census, 1976-81. Author: Man, Society and the World, 1968; co-author: Comprehensive Spelling Instruction: Theory, Research and Application, 1971; editor: Social Interaction in Educational Settings, 1971, Perspectives on Management Systems Approaches to Education: A Symposium, 1973, Search for Meaning, 1984, A Study on Possible Future Developments for Hong Kong: Strategic Planning and Innovations, 1985, A People Misruled: Hong Kong and the Chinese Stepping-Stone Syndrome, 1989, 2d edit., 1992; editor: East Asian Higher Education: Traditions and Transformations, 1994, Whither Hong Kong: China's Shadow or Visionary Gleam?, 1999, Yeee-Hah!: Remembrances and Longing, 2004. With AUS, 1952-55, Korea, Japan. Recipient Civic Commendation Madison, 1973; sr. Fulbright lectr. Tokyo and Tamagawa Univs., Japan; also 1st Fulbright scholar to People's Republic China, 1972. Fellow AAAS, Nat. Conf. Research in English, Am. Psychol. Assn., Am. Psychol. Soc.; mem. Calif. Coll. and Univ. Faculty Assn. (founder 1961), Chinese Hist. Soc. Am. and Orgn. of Chinese Americans (Bicentennial speaker), Asian-Am. Psychol. Assn. (pres. 1979-82, jour. editor 1981-82), Western Mont. Stanford Alumni Club (founding pres. 1997—). Home: 3822 Lincoln Rd Missoula MT 59802-3039 E-mail: alyee@montana.com.

YEE, ALFRED ALPHONSE, structural engineer, consultant; b. Honolulu, Aug. 5, 1925; s. Yun Sau and Kam Ngo (Lum) Y.; m. Janice Ching (div.); children: Lailan, Mark, Eric, Malcolm, Ian; m. Elizabeth Wong, June 24, 1975; children: Suling, Trevor, I'Ling. BSCE, Rose Hulman Inst. Tech., 1948, Dr. of Engring. (hon.), 1976; MEng in Structures, Yale U., 1949. Registered profl. engr., Hawaii, Calif., Guam, Tex., Minn., No. Marianas Islands. With civil engring. dept. Dept. Pub. Works, Terr. of Hawaii, Honolulu, 1949-51; structural engr. 14th Naval Dist., Pearl Harbor, Hawaii, 1951-54; pvt. practice structural engring. cons. Honolulu, 1954-55; structural engring. cons. Park & Yee Ltd., Honolulu, 1955-60; pres. Alfred A. Yee & Assocs. Inc., Honolulu, 1960-82; v.p., tech. adminstr. Alfred. A. Yee div. Leo A. Daly, Honolulu, 1982-89; pres. Applied Tech. Corp., Honolulu, 1984—. Patentee in concrete tech., land and sea structures; contbr. articles to profl. jours. Served with U.S. Army, 1946-47. Named Engr. of Yr., Hawaii Soc. Profl. Engrs., 1969, one of Men Who Made Marks in 1970, Honolulu, 1970. Mem. ASCE (hon.), NSPE, CASE, ACEC, NAE, Am. Concrete Inst. (hon.), Post-Tensioning Inst., Precast-Prestressed Concrete Inst. (PCI medal of honor award 1997), Prestressed Concrete Inst. (State of Art award 1991), Structural Engrs. Assn. Hawaii, Yale Sci. and Engring. Assn. (Martin P. Korn award 1965, Robert J. Lyman award 1984), Singapore Concrete Inst. Avocations: golf, swimming. Office: 1217 Palolo Ave Honolulu HI 96816-2525 E-mail: atc@lava.net.

YEE, CORDELL D.K. liberal arts educator, historian; b. L.A., Aug. 7, 1955; s. Yet-Lin and Sally L. Yee; m. Ingrid P.Y. Hsieh-Yee, Aug. 7, 1983; 1 child, Corinna Qixia. BA, Pomona Coll., 1977; MJ, U. Calif., Berkeley, 1979; MA, U. Wis., 1981, PhD, 1989. Tutor, prof. St. John's Coll., Annapolis, Md., 1989—. Exhibition and catalog, Space and Place: 400 Years of Chinese and Western Mapmaking, 1996; author: (book) The Word According to James Joyce: Reconstructing Representation, 1997; asst. editor (book) History of Cartography, vol. 2, book 2, 1994; co-author: (book) Approaches and Challenges in a Worldwide History of Cartography, 2001. Home: 1024 Harbor Dr Annapolis MD 21403 Office: St Johns College PO Box 2800 Annapolis MD 21403

YEE, DAVID, chemist; b. Albany, N.Y., Sept. 26, 1948; s. Fook On and King Sau (Seto) Y.; m. Vivien Chee-Nan Yeo, May 11, 1974; children: Daniel Ming-dao, Peter Ming-de. BS (cum laude), Rensselaer Polytech. Inst., 1970; MS, Cornell U., 1973, PhD, 1978. Fellow Max Planck Inst. for Exptl. Medicine, Göttingen, Germany, 1978—80; rsch. assoc. Harvard U., 1980—85; rsch. dir. Advance Biofactures Corp., Lynbrook, NY, 1985—99; sr. program mgr. Wolters Kluwer Health, Yardley, Pa., 2000—. Contbr. articles to profl. jours. including Analytical Chemistry, Jour. of Molecular Evolution, Biochemistry, Hoppe-Seyler's Zeitschrift für Physiologische Chemie, FEBS Letters, European Jour. Biochemistry; patentee in field. Mem. Am. Chem. Soc., Am. Sci. Affiliation. Office: 770 Township Line Rd Ste 300 Yardley PA 19067 Office Phone: 267-757-3521. E-mail: DQY@juno.com., dyee@pharma.wkhealth.com.

YEE, KEITH PHILIP, accountant, finance company executive; b. Luton, Eng., Apr. 26, 1958; came to the U.S., 1985; m. Ginny Sung, Feb. 9, 1985; children: Ashley, Brittany. BA in Acctg. with honors, Exeter (Eng.) U., 1979. CPA, Calif. Audit sr. Ernst & Whinney, London, 1979-83, investigation supr. Hong Kong, 1983-85, audit mgr. Memphis, 1985-86; audit sr. mgr. Ernst & Young, San Francisco, 1986-91, internat. resident, 1991-93, audit sr. mgr., 1993-95, Price Waterhouse, San Jose, Calif., 1995-97, Adaptec, Milpitas, Calif., 1997-98, Synnex Info. Tech., Fremont, Calif., 1998-2000, Tripath Tech., Inc., Santa Clara, Calif., 2000—. Vice chmn. adv. coun. for svcs. to srs. Salvation Army, San Francisco, 1989. Grad. leadership San Francisco program San Francisco C. of C., 1990. Fellow Inst. Chartered Accts. in Eng. and Wales; mem. AICPA, Asian Am. CPAs (mem. adv. bd. 1994-95), Calif. Soc. CPAs, Inst. for Internat. Edn. (student programs com. 1990-95), San Francisco C. of C. (internat. bus. devel. com. 1993-95), Palo Alto Tennis Club. Avocations: internat. travel, music, sports. Office: Tripath Tech Inc 2560 Orchard Pkwy San Jose CA 95131 E-mail: keith@tripath.com.

YEE, NANCY W. travel consultant; b. Honolulu, Nov. 6, 1917; d. Sai Ho and Ah Oi Sen Wong; m. Ken Yee, Dec. 2, 1941; children: Roy Jensen, Sylvia Mei-ling McCaffrey, Carolyn Mei-en Lee, Susan Mei-jen. BA in Edn. Music and Dance, U. Hawaii, 1941. Sr. translator U.S. Postal Censorship, Honolulu, 1941-45; pvt. tchr. English and civics Honolulu, 1945-50; radio announcer Chinese KGMB Radio/TV, Honolulu, 1946-56; ptnr. Ken's Electric Motor Svc., Honolulu, 1949-65, travel cons. Royal Adventure/Quality, Honolulu, 1957—; sec., officer mgr. KEMS Inc., Honolulu, 1965-85. Radio announcer Chinese, KAHU, Honolulu, 1956; chmn. Small Bus. Adminstrn. Adv. Bd., Honolulu, 1967-68; advisor Jr. Achievement, Honolulu, 1970-71; pres. Women's Propeller Club U.S., Honolulu, 1977-78. Den mother Cub Scouts, 1948-50; mem., choir mem. First Chinese Ch. of Christ, 1950-99; chmn. fund raiser, den mother Pacific Girl Scouts Am., 1958-68; mem. Honolulu Youth Symphony, 1967-71; sec. Ctrl. Dist. PTA, Honolulu, 1968; vol. Hawaii Heart Assn., Honolulu, 1970-73; vol. tchr. Chinese song and dance Mun Lun Sch., 1970; mem., pres. Mun Lun Sch. PTA, 1970, Palolo Home Aux, Honolulu, 1977-78, Associated Chinese U. Women, 1978. Named Chinese Model Mother of the Yr., United Chinese Soc., Honolulu, 1986, Hawaii Chinese Living Treasure, Chinese Youth Hawaii, Honolulu, 1995. Avocations: playing chinese butterfly harp, singing chinese operas, travel, cruising, volunteer work.

YEE, ROBERT DONALD, ophthalmologist; b. Beijing, Feb. 21, 1945; came to U.S., 1947, naturalized, 1947; s. James and Marian Y.M. (Li) Y.; m. Linda Margaret Neil, June 28, 1968; children: Jillian Neil, Allison Betram. AB, Harvard U., 1966; MD, 1970. Diplomate Am. Bd. Ophthalmology. Fullbright scholar, 1966; intern U. Rochester, N.Y., 1970-71; resident in ophthalmology Jules Stein Eye Inst. UCLA, 1971-74; fellow in neuro-ophthalmology Nat. Eye Inst., Bethesda, Md., 1974-76; chief ophthalmology Harbor-UCLA Med. Ctr., Torrance, Calif., 1976-78; asst. prof. ophthalmology Sch. Medicine UCLA, 1976-78, assoc. prof., 1978-82, prof., 1982-87; prof., dept. chmn. ophthalmology Ind. U. Sch. Medicine, Indpls., 1987—. Mem. residency rev. com. for ophthalmology Accrediation Coun. for Grad. Med. Edn., 1995-2002, vice-chmn., 1998-2000, chmn., 2000-2002. Mem. editorial bd. Investigative Ophthalmology and Visual Sci., 1982—, von Graefe's Archives of Ophthalmology, 1983-89; Feldman endowed chair ophthalmology UCLA, 1984-87; Grayson endowed chair ophthalmology Ind. U., 2003—. Author numerous med. research papers. Lt. comdr. USPHS, 1974—76. Grantee, NIH, 1976—84; scholar Dolly Green Rsch. scholar, 1984—86. Fellow: ACS, Am. Acad. Ophthalmology; mem.: AMA, Accreditation Cou. for Grad. Med. Edn. (residency rev. com., chair 2000—02), Indpls. Ophthal. Soc., Ind. Med. Soc., Chinese Am. Ophthal. Soc. (pres. 1996—98), Ind. Acad. Ophthalmology, Am. Ophthal Soc., Assn. Rsch. in Vision and Ophthalmology (chmn. eye movement sect. 1981, 1987, trustee 1996—2001, v.p. 2000—01), Phi Beta Kappa, Alpha Omega Alpha. Office: Ind U Med Ctr 702 Rotary Cir Indianapolis IN 46202-5133 Office Phone: 317-274-7101. E-mail: ryee@iupui.edu.

YEE, WAI GEN, computer scientist, educator; b. NYC, Jan. 6, 1973; PhD, Ga. Inst. Tech., Atlanta, 1997—2003. Programmer Lakeshore Technologies, Inc., Chgo., 1995—97; asst. prof. Ill. Inst. Tech., Chgo., 2003—. Avocation: sports. Office: Ill Inst Tech 10 W 31st St Chicago IL 60657

YEGGE, ROBERT BERNARD, law educator, dean; b. Denver, June 17, 1934; s. Ronald Van Kirk and Fairy (Hill) Y. AB magna cum laude, Princeton U., 1956; MA in Sociology, U. Denver, 1958, JD, 1959. Bar: Colo. 1959, D.C. 1978. Ptnr. Yegge, Hall and Evans, Denver, 1959-78; with Harding Shultz & Downs successor to Nelson and Harding, 1979—; prof. U. Denver Coll. Law, 1965—, dean, 1965-77, 97-98, dean emeritus, 1977—; asst. to pres. Denver Post, 1971-75; v.p., exec. dir. Nat. Ctr. Preventive Law, 1986-91. Author: Colorado Negotiable Instruments Law, 1960, Some Goals; Some Tasks, 1965, The American Lawyer: 1976, 1966, New Careers in Law, 1969, The Law Graduate, 1972, Tomorrow's Lawyer: A Shortage and Challenge, 1974, Declaration of Independence for Legal Education, 1976. Mng. trustee Denver Ctr. for Performing Arts, 1972-75; chmn. Colo. Coun. Arts and Humanities, 1968-80, chmn. emeritus, 1980—; mem. scholar selection com. Henry Luce Found., 1975—; Active nat. and local A.R.C., chmn. Denver region, 1985-88; trustee Denver Symphony Soc., Inst. of Ct. Mgmt., Denver Dumb Friends League, 1992—, chmn. 2000—, Met. Denver Legal Aid Soc., 1994-99, Colo. Legal Svcs., 2000—, Colo. Acad.; chmn. Colo. Prevention Ctr., 2000—; trustee, vice chmn. Nat. Assembly State Arts Agys.; vice chmn. Mexican-Am. Legal Edn. and Def. Fund, 1970-76. Recipient Disting. Svc. award Denver Jr. C. of C., 1965; Harrison Tweed award Am. Assn. Continuing Edn. Adminstrs., 1985, Alumni Faculty award U. Denver, 1993. Mem. ABA (chmn. lawyers conf. 1987-88, chmn. accreditation commn. for legal asst. programs 1980-90, standing com. legal assts. 1987-92, 98-2001, standing com. delivery legal svcs. 1992-95, 2001—, com. on Gavel award 1995-98, del. to jud. adminstrn. coun. 1989-95, Robert B. Yegge award 1996), Law and Soc. Assn. (life, pres. 1965-70), Colo. Bar Assn. (bd. govs. 1965-77, 97-98), Denver Bar Assn., D.C. Bar Assn., Am. Law Inst., Am. Judicature Soc. (bd. dirs. 1968-72, 75-85, Herbert Harley award 1985), Am. Acad. Polit. and Social Sci., Am. Sociol. Soc., Assn. Am. Law Schs., Order St. Ives, Phi Beta Kappa, Beta Theta Pi, Phi Delta Phi, Alpha Kappa Keta, Omicron Delta Kappa. Home: 3472 S Race St Englewood CO 80113-3138 Office: U Denver Coll Law 2255 E Evans Ave Denver CO 80208

YEGULALP, TUNCEL M. mining engineer, educator; b. Konya, Turkey, Nov. 5, 1937; came to U.S., 1963; s. Faik Suleyman and Selma Safiye (Karatay) Y.; m. Sevinc Guneri, July 5, 1963; children: Ali, Serdar. BS, Tech. U., Istanbul, 1961; DEngring. Sci., Columbia U., 1968. Mining engr. M.T.A., Ankara, Turkey, 1961-63, chief feasibility studies group, 1971; rsch. engr. Mobil Rsch., Paulsboro, N.J., 1967-69; chief sys. cons. Sisag Ltd., Ankara, 1971-72; asst. prof. Columbia U., N.Y.C., 1972-75; assoc. prof. Henry Krumb Sch. Mines, 1975-85, prof., 1985—. Dir. N.Y. Mining and Mineral Resources Inst. Rsch., 1987—; elected permanent mem. U.S. del. World Mining Congress, 1993. Author articles in field. Served to 2d lt. C.E. Turkish Army, 1969-71. Internat. AEC fellow, Vienna, 1963; Krumb fellow, Columbia U., 1964, Campbell fellow, 1965. Mem. AIME, Internat. Higher Edn. Acad. Scis., Turkish Studies Assn., Inst. for Ops. Rsch. and the Mgmt. Scis., Sigma Chi. Moslem. Office: Columbia U 924 SWM New York NY 10027 Office Phone: 212-854-2984. E-mail: yegulalp@columbia.edu.

YEH, GONG PING (G.P.), physicist; b. Taipei, Taiwan, Sept. 16, 1951; s. Huo Wang and Sung Yeh; m. Barbara Fernandes, Mar. 11, 1989. BS, MIT, 1975, PhD, 1984; MS, Calif. Inst. Tech., 1977. Postdoctoral rsch. assoc. MIT, Cambridge, Mass., 1984—85, Fermi Nat. Accelerator Lab., Batavia, Ill., 1985—89, assoc. scientist, 1989—95, scientist, 1995—2000, sr. scientist, 2000—. Leader Taiwan group Fermi Nat. Accelerator Lab., Batavia, 1993—; adj. faculty mem. Academia Sinica, Taipei, 1993—96; presdl. sci. and tech. adv. com. Govt. Taiwan, Taipei, 2000—; spl. advisor to min. sci. and tech. policy Govt. Japan, Tokyo, 2002—, co-leader project to create internat. grad. univ. sci. and tech. in Okinawa; internat. adv. com. Nat. Ctr. for High-Performance Computing, Hsinchu, Taiwan; sci. adv. Fermi Inst. Hadron Therapy, Taiwan, 2003—. Recipient Disting. Accomplishment award, Chinese Acad. and Profls. Assn., 1994, Outstanding Achievement award, Chinese Sci. and Tech. Assn., 1998; Internat. Sci. Rsch. grantee, Nat. Sci. Coun. and Academia Sinica, Taiwan, 1993—2003, Internat. Sci. and Tech. Collaboration grantee, Agy. for Internat. Sci. and Tech. Collaboration, Slovakia, 1999—2002, Internat. Collaboration grantee, Govt. Okinawa, 2000—. Mem.: Am. Phys. Soc. (assoc.). Achievements include discovery of the top quark; first to large scale computing using Linux and commodity computers; new initiatives in international collaborations. Office: Fermi Nat Accelerator Lab Mail Station 318 Batavia IL 60510-0500 Office Phone: 630-840-2358. Business E-Mail: gpyeh@fnal.gov.

YEH, HSU-CHONG, radiology educator; b. Taipei, Taiwan, Mar. 30, 1937; came to US, 1973; s. Ping-Hui and Ah-Chu (Chuang) Y.; m. Cha-Pying Yeh, Sept. 26, 1964; children: David, Benjamin. MD, Nat. Taiwan U., Taipei, 1962. Diplomate Am. Bd. Radiology. Rotating intern U. Alberta Hosp., Edmonton, Can., 1964-65; resident in diagnostic radiology Montreal Gen. Hosp., McGill U., Canada, 1969-72, fellow in diagnostic ultrasound, 1972-73; mem. active med. staff Soldier's Meml. Hosp., Campbellton, Canada, 1967-69; assoc. Mt. Sinai Sch. Medicine, NYC, 1973-75, asst. prof. radiology, 1976-78, assoc. prof., 1979-86, prof., 1986—. Cons. radiology VA Hosp., Bronx, NY, 1977-87. Author: Radiology of the Adrenals, 1982; contbg. author: Progress in Liver Disease, 1979, Frontiers in Liver Disease, 1981, Ultrasound Annual, 1982, 85, Ultrasound in Urology, 1984, Ultrasonography of the Urinary Tract, 1991, Surgical Management of Urologic Disease, 1991, contbr. articles to med. jour. 2d lt. Armored Corps, Taiwan Army, 1962-63. Fellow Soc. Radiologists in Ultrasound; mem. Am. Inst. Ultrasound in Medicine (sr.), Radiol. Soc. N.Am. (sci. exhibit award 1988-2000), Computerized Radiology Soc., Am. Roentgen Ray Soc. (sci. exhibit award 1988), NY Roentgen Ray Soc. Avocations: fine art painting, sculpture, jogging, movies. Office: Mt Sinai Med Ctr One Gustave L Levy Pl New York NY 10029-6574

YEH, KUO HSING, bank executive; b. Taipei, Taiwan, Republic of China, Feb. 1, 1932; m. Hsiu-Mei Yeh Tsang. BA, Nat. Taiwan U., 1954. Exec. v.p. Hwa Nan Comml. Bank, Ltd., Taiwan, 1955-81; pres. Banking Inst. Republic China, 1981-88; CEO Fin. Info. System Group Ministery Fin., Taiwan, 1984-88; pres. Chang Hwa Comml. Bank Ltd., Taiwan, 1988-94; chmn. Taipeibank, Taipei, 1994-97, Taiwan First Investment & Trust Co Ltd, Taipei, 1998, Cathay United Bank Co Ltd., Tapei, Taiwan, 1998—. Author: Theory and Practice of Lending Management, 1980; editor: Practice of Bank's Consumer Loan, 1983. Recipient Disting. Fin. Staffer award Ministry Fin., Taipei, 1974. Mem. Banker's Assn. Taiwan (chmn. 1988-92), Banker's Assn. Taipei (chmn. 1992-97), Taiwan U. Alumni Assn. (mng. dir. Taipei chpt. 1994), Taiwan U. Alumni Club, Taipei Yuen-Shan Club. Home: 3 Fl No 432 Chi Lin Rd Taipei 104 Taiwan Office: Cathay United Bank Co Ltd 218 Sec 2 Tun Hwa S Rd Taipei 104 Taiwan

YEH, MING-NENG, obstetrician, gynecologist; b. Taiwan, Oct. 13, 1938, came to U.S., 1966; s. Chao-Chieh and Pu-Tseng (Song) Y.; m. Lisa Lie-Yu Lin, Oct. 18, 1965; children: Angela, Rubina, Noreen, Janet. MD, Nat. Taiwan U., Taipei, 1964. Diplomate Am. Bd. Ob-Gyn. Intern Johnston-Willis Hosp., 1966-67; resident Bklyn.-Cumberland Hosp., 1967-68, St. Luke's Hosp. Ctr., N.Y.C., 1968-71; fellow fetal medicine Columbia-Presbyn. Med. Ctr., N.Y.C., 1971-73, attending obstetrician, 1987—; clin. prof. Columbia U., N.Y.C., 1987—. Fellow N.Y. Acad. Medicine, N.Y. Acad. Sci.; mem. Am. Fertility Soc., Am. Inst. Ultrasound Medicine, Am. Coll. Ob-Gyn., N.Y. Obstet. Soc., N.Y. Gyn. Soc. Office: Columbia-Presbyn Med Ctr 161 Fort Washington Ave New York NY 10032-3713

YEH, PAUL PAO, electrical and electronics engineer, educator; b. Sung Yang, Chekiang, China, Mar. 25, 1927; came to U.S., 1956, naturalized, 1963; s. Tsung Shan and Shu Huan (Mao) Y.; m. Beverley Pamela Eng, May 15, 1953; children: Judith Elaine, Paul Edmond, Richard Alvin, Ronald Timothy. Student, Nat. Cen. U., Nanking, China, 1946—49; B.A.Sc., U. Toronto, Ont., Can., 1951; MSEE, U. Pa., 1960, PhD, 1966. Registered profl. engr., Ont. Design engr. Can. Gen. Electric Co., Toronto, 1951-56; asst. prof. SUNY, Binghamton, 1956-57; sr. engr. H.K. Porter, ITE & Kuhlman, Phila. and Detroit, 1957-61; assoc. prof. N.J. Inst. Tech., Newark, 1961-66; supr. rsch. and devel. N.Am. Rockwell, Anaheim, Calif., 1966-70; sr. R&D engr. Skunk Works Lockheed Calif. Co., Burbank, Calif., 1970-72, 78-89; mem. tech. staff The Aerospace Corp., El Segundo, Calif., 1972-78; sr. R&D engr. Lockheed Advanced Devel. Co., Burbank, 1978-89; chief scientist Advanced Systems Rsch., Pasadena, Calif., 1989—. With Consol. Edison Co., N.Y.C., 1963-64, Pub. Svc. Elec. and Gas Co. N.J., 1965-66, Zhejiang Sci. and Tech. Exch. Ctr. with Fgn. Countries, 1995—; sr. lectr. State U. Calif., Long Beach, 1967-73; cons. prof. Chung Shan Inst. Sci. and Tech., 1989-92; vis. prof. Tsinghua U., 1993—, South China U. Sci. and Tech., 1997—; vis. chair prof. S.E. U., 1994—, Zhejiang U., 1994—; cons. prof. Northwestern Poly. U., 1993—, Shanghai U., 1994—; hon. prof. Beijing U. Aeronautics and Astronautics, 1993—, Zhejiang U. Sci. and Tech., 1994—; chair, prof. Nanjing U. Aeronautics & Astronautics, 1999—, Wuyi U., 1999—; rschr. power sys. design and control, 1951-66; investigator R&D Stealth tech. electronic warfare, anti-jam warfare, avionics, IR/EO Tech, nuclear hardening, anti-submarine warfare. Recipient Achievement award for anti-submarine warfare/magnetic anomaly detection sys. Lockheed Corp. Mem. IEEE (sr., life), Nat. Mgmt. Assn. (life), Nat. Def. Indsl. Assn., Assn. Old Crows, Chinese Am. Engring./Sci. Assn. So. Calif. (life; pres. 1969-71), Nat. Ctrl. U. Alumni Assn. (life; pres. 1977), Beijing Assn. for Sci. and Tech. Exchs. with Fgn. Countries, (hon. dir.), Assn. Profl. Engrs. of Ont., N.Y. Acad. Scis., Air Force Assn., Zhejiang Assn. for Sci. and Tech. Exchs. with Fgn. Countries (advisor), Armed Forces Comms. and Electronics Assn., U.S. Naval Inst., Assn. U.S. Army. Republican. Presbyterian. Achievements include patent for Non-Capacitive Transmission Cable. Home: 78278 Quail Run Palm Desert CA 92211 Office: Advanced Systems Rsch Inc 33 S Catalina Ave Ste 202 Pasadena CA 91106-2426 Office Phone: 760-200-4678. Business E-Mail: Drpaulpyeh@ieee.org.

YEH, RAYMOND WEI-HWA, architect, educator; b. Shanghai, Feb. 25, 1942; came to U.S., 1958, naturalized, 1976; s. Herbert Hwan-Ching and Joyce Bo-Ding (Kwan) Y.; m. Hsiao-Yen Chen, Sept. 16, 1967; children— Bryant Po Yung, Clement Chung-Yung, Emily Su-Yung. BA, U. Oreg., 1965, B.Arch., 1967; M.Arch., U. Minn., 1969. Cert. Nat. Coun. Archtl. Registration Bds.; registered architect, Tex., Okla., Calif., Hawaii. Draftsman, designer various archtl. firms, 1965-68; design architect Ellerbe Architects, St. Paul, 1968-70; v.p., dir. design Sorey, Hill, Binnicker, Oklahoma City, 1973-74; prin. architect Raymond W.H. Yeh & Assos., Norman, Okla., 1974-80; asst. prof. to prof. U. Okla., Norman, 1970-79; head dept. architecture, prof. Calif. Poly. State U., San Luis Obispo, 1979-83; dean Coll. Architecture U. Okla., Norman, 1983-92; prin. architect W.H. Raymond Yeh, Norman, 1983-93; dean sch. architecture U. Hawaii at Manoa, Honolulu, 1993—. Profl. adviser Neighborhood Conservation and Devel. Center, Oklahoma City, 1977 79 Works include: St. Thomas More U. Parish and Student Center, Norman, Summit Ridge Center Retirement Community, Harrah, Okla., (recipient Nat. Design award Guild Religious Architecture 1978). Nat. Endowment for Arts fellow, 1978-79 Fellow AIA (dir., pres. Okla. chpt. 1986, design awards, nat. com. chmn. 1989); mem. Calif. Coun. Archtl. Edn. (dir., pres. 1982-83), Okla. Found. for Architecture (founding chair bd. 1989-90), Asian Soc. Okla. (award of Excellence 1992), Asia Pacific Ctr. for Arch. (founding bd. dirs. 1996). Presbyterian. Office: U Hawaii Manoa Sch Architecture Honolulu HI 96822

YEH, YING CHIN, electrical engineer; b. Tainan, Taiwan, June 1, 1945; came to U.S., 1978; s. Tso Hsueh and Ai Lien (Yen) Y.; m. Su Chin Lee, Oct. 24, 1972; children: Karen Y.C., Cindy S.C. BSEE, Nat. Cheng Kung U., 1967; MSEE, Nat. Taiwan U., 1970; PhDEE, U. Ottawa, Can., 1973. Indsl. postdoctoral fellow RCA Ltd. R&D Lab., Montreal, Can., 1973-76; sr. engr. Canadair Ltd., Montreal, 1976-78; sr. mem. tech. staff Otis Elevator Co. R&D Ctr., Farmington, Conn., 1978-81; assoc. tech. fellow The Boeing Co., Comml. Airplane Group, Seattle, 1981—. Mem. Internat. Fedn. for Info. Processing Working Group on Dependable Computing and Fault Tolerance.

V.p. Taiwanese Am. Citizen League, Seattle, 1993-95. Mem. IEEE, Taiwanese Assn. for Greater Seattle (bd. dirs. 1998—). Achievements include development in 7J7 Control System Performance Study for synchronous PFC and Autonomous ARINC 629 operation; development 777 flight controls ARINC 629 Bus Requirement; design and validation testing of 777 PFC (primary flight computer) redundancy management. Office: Boeing Comml Airplane Group PO Box 3707 Seattle WA 98124-2207 E-mail: ying.c.yeh@boeing.com.

YELENICK, MARY THERESE, lawyer; b. Denver, May 17, 1954; d. John Andrew and Maesel Joyce (Reed) Y. B.A. magna cum laude, Colo. Coll., 1976; J.D. cum laude, Georgetown U., 1979. Bar: D.C. 1979, U.S. Dist. Ct. D.C. 1980, U.S. Ct. Appeals (D.C. cir.) 1981, N.Y. 1982, U.S. Dist. Ct. (so. and ea. dists.) N.Y. 1982, U.S. Supreme Ct. 1992, U.S. Ct. Appeals (5th cir.) 1995. Law clk. to presiding justices Superior Ct. D.C., 1979-81; ptnr. Chadbourne & Parke, LLP, N.Y.C., 1981—. Editor Jour. of Law and Policy Internat. Bus., 1978-79.; mem. Cath. Soc. Justice Lobby (bd. dirs., 2004—) Mem. Phi Beta Kappa. Democrat. Roman Catholic. Home: 310 E 46th St New York NY 10017-3002 Office: Chadbourne & Parke LLP 30 Rockefeller Plz Fl 31 New York NY 10112-0129

YELICH, LOUIS JAMES, engineering executive; b. Ironwood, Mich., July 20, 1928; s. Louis and Ann Catherine (Miller) Yelich; m. Barbara Catherine Den Dooven, Feb. 22, 1952; children: Louis J., Ann M., Mary B., Thomas E. BBA, U. Minn., 1954; MBA, No. Ill. U., 1963. Cost acctg. and data processing mgr. Badger Meter Mfg. Co., Milw., 1955—60; contr. Elgin (Ill.) Nat. Watch Co., 1960—65, Cleco Air Tools, Houston, 1966—69; v.p., contr. Hycel, Inc., Houston, 1970—71; pres. Modular Bldg. Sys., Inc., Houston, 1972—73; v.p. fin. NSW Corp., Houston, 1974—83; founder, pres. Hydro Pump & Equipment, Inc., Houston, 1983—. Established Perpetuity Ann. Scholarship Gogebic CC, Ironwood. Staff sgt. USAF, 1946—51. Recipient cert., Jr. Achievement, Milw., 1959, U. Minn. Found. plaque, 1999. Mem.: Assn. Chem. Industry Tex., Soc. Naval Arch. & Engrs., Rotary. Republican. Roman Catholic. Avocations: golf, skiing, coin collecting/numismatics. Home: PO Box 40294 Houston TX 77240 Office: Hydro Pump & Equipment PO Box 40294 Houston TX 77240 Office Phone: 281-232-8960. Business E-Mail: hydropump@msn.com.

YELICH, LYNNE, member of parliament; b. Mar. 24, 1953; m. Matt Yelich; 2 children. Grad., Kenaston HS, 1971. Farmer, Kenaston; mem. House of Commons, Ottawa, Canada, ofcl. opposition dep. critic for citizenship and immigration. Office: House of Commons Rm 686 Confederation Bldg Ottawa ON K1A 0A6 Canada Address: Unit #71 Market Mall 2325 Preston Ave Saskatoon SK S7J 2G2 Canada E-mail: yelic.l@parl.gc.ca.

YELIN, ROBERT BRUCE, musician, recording artist, composer, lyricist; b. Yonkers, N.Y., Sept. 25, 1944; s. Paul and Libby (Watinsky) Y.; m. Harriet Ann Hunter, Mar. 22, 1980. Student, NYU, 1962-65. Jazz guitarist, performer, educator, N.Y., 1962-80, 1981-85; pres. Arbee Why Music Publs., Colo., Conn., 1981-87; prof. jazz guitar studies U. Colo., Denver, 1982; pres. Chord Master Records, Colo., Conn., 1983-88; jazz performer, educator Conn., 1985-88. Pvt. guitar tchr., 1962-88. Jazz guitarist (solo guitar albums) Night Rain, 1981 (Reviewer's Choice 1982), Talents of the Heart, 1990, Robert Yelin Plays the Music of Jobim & Brazil, 1999; (jazz trio album) Song for My Wife, 1983; performer N.Y. Jazz Guitar Festival, 1976, Breckenridge (Colo.) Jazz Festival, 1982, Winter Park (Colo.) Jazz Festival, 1983; (CD recordings), Bossa, Ballads and Blues Vols. 1-5, 1997, Welcome to my World, 1999, Enchanted, The Beauty of the 14-String Guitar, 1999; jazz clubs, concerts nationwide, 1962—; author: Jazz Standards for Solo Guitar, 2002, Jazz Classics for Solo Guitar, 2002, Jazz Favorites for Solo Guitar, 2002; co-author: The Tal Farlow Jazz Guitar Method Book, 1973-74; contbg. editor Guitar Player mag., 1968-82, Frets mag. 1978-80; Wes Montgomery's Book, 1984-85(newsletter) The Jazz Guitar Soc. We. Australia, 1989—; contbg. cons., article writer Just Jazz Guitar, 1994—; arranger also; co-prodr. (videos) Legends of Jazz Guitar, vols. 1-3, 1995-96; commd. 1st 14-string archtop guitar. Donates audio and video tape recordings to music schs., colls., univs. and guitar socs. all over the world. Mem. Broadcast Musician, Inc. Clubs: Jazz Guitar Record Library and Club (pres. 1981—). Home and Office: 17583 Fieldbrook Cir E Boca Raton FL 33496-1534

YELISEEV, ALEXEI ARKADIEVICH, biochemist, researcher; b. Moscow, Nov. 3, 1959; s. Arkadii Aleksandrovich and Tatiana Georgievna (Sokolova) E.; m. Elena Dmitrievna Polonnikova, Aug. 20, 1985; children: Ekaterina, Tatiana. MS in Chemistry, Moscow State U., 1981; PhD in Biochemistry, Russian Acad. Scis., 1987. From trainee rschr. to sr. rschr. A.N. Bakh Inst. Biochemistry, Russian Acad. Scis., Moscow, 1981-92, sr. rschr., 1992—. Vis. rsch. scientist U. Tex., Houston, 1993-99; sr. rsch. scientist Roche Vitamins, Inc., 1999-2001; sr. scientist Kosan Bioscis., Inc., 2001—2003, staff scientist, Nat. Inst. of Health, 2003—. Contbr. chapters to books, articles to profl. jours. Rsch. fellow Alexander von Humboldt Stiftung, 1989-92, Internat. Union Biochemistry, 1992, Royal Soc. London, 1993; grantee Internat. Sci. Found., 1994-95. Mem. AAAS, Am. Soc. Microbiology, Russian Biochem. Soc. (lectureship 1987). Avocations: travel, music, books. Personal E-mail: alexeieliseev@aol.com. Business E-Mail: yeliseeva@mail.nih.gov.

YELLEN, JANET LOUISE, bank executive; b. Bklyn., Aug. 13, 1946; d. Julius and Anna Ruth (Blumenthal) Y.; m. George Arthur Akerlof, July 8, 1978; 1 child, Robert Joseph. BA in Econs. summa cum laude, Brown U., 1967; PhD, Yale U., 1971; hon. JD, Brown U., 1998; hon. LHD, Bard Coll., 2000. Asst. prof. econs. Harvard U., Cambridge, Mass., 1971-76; lectr. London Sch. Econs. and Polit. Sci., Washington, 1978-80; asst. prof. econs. Sch. Bus. Adminstrn., U. Calif., Berkeley, 1980-82, assoc. prof., 1982-85, prof. Haas Sch. Bus., 1985—, Bernard T. Rocca Jr. prof. internat. bus. and trade, 1992—, Eugene E. and Catherine M. Trefethem prof. bus., 1999—; cons. div. internat. fin., Bd. Govs. of FRS, Washington, 1974-75, economist trade and fin. studies sect., 1977-78, mem., 1994-97; chair coun. econ. advisers The Cabinet, Washington, 1997-99; pres., CEO Fed. Res. Bank San Francisco, 2004—. Mem. adv. panel in economics NSF, 1977—78, 1991—92, com. visitors, economics program, 1996, 2004; adv. bd. Women's Econ. Round Table, 1999—, Ctr. Internat. Polit. Economy, 1999—, Jerome Levy Economics Inst., 2002—, Calif. Assembly Select Com. on Asian Trade, 2003; bd. dirs. Economists Allied for Arms Reduction, 2002—, Delta Dental of Calif., 2003—; mem. amb. adv. coun. for Marshall Scholarships, 1996—, OECD, High-Level Sustainable Devel. Group, 1999—2001, NAS Panel, Ensuring Best Presidential Sci. and Tech. Appointments, 2000; chair Pres. Interagency Com. on Women's Bus. Enterprise, 1997—99, Econ. Policy Com. Orgn. for Econ. Coop. and Devel., 1997—99; rsch. fellow MIT, Cambridge, 1974; cons. Congl. Budget Office, 1975—76, mem. panel econ. advisers, 1993—94; rsch. affiliate Yale U., 1976; fellow Yale Corp., 2000—; rsch. assoc. Nat. Bureau Econ. Rsch., 1999—; prin. investigator Russell Sage Found. Grant on Sustainable Employment, 2000; sr. adviser Macroeconomic Advisers, 2003—; mem. Brookings Panel on Econ. Activity, 1987—88, 1990—91, sr. adviser, 1989—94, adv. bd., 1999—; Yrjö Jahnsson Found. lectr. on macroecon. theory, Helsinki, 1977—78; mem. Coun. on Fgn. Rels, 1976—81. Author: (monograph) (with Arrow and Shavell) The Limits of the Market in Resource Allocation, 1977; assoc. editor Jour. Econ. Perspectives, 1987-91; contbr. articles to profl. jours. Hon. Woodrow Wilson fellow, 1967, grad. fellow NSF, 1967-71, Guggenheim fellow, 1986-87, fellow, Am. Academy Arts and Sciences, 2001; grantee NSF, 1975-77, 90-94; Maria and Sidney Rolfe award for Nat. Econ. Svc., Women's Econ. Round Table, 1997, Wilbur Lucius Cross Medal, Yale U., 1997. Mem. Am. Econ. Assn. (adv. com. to Pres. 1986-87, nominating com. 1988-90, v.p. 2004-), Western Econ. Assn. (pres., 2003-04), Phi Beta Kappa. Office: Fed Res Bank San Francisco 101 Market St San Francisco CA 94105-1579

YELLIN, VICTOR FELL, composer, music educator; b. Boston, Dec. 14, 1924; s. Mendl and Sarah (Fell) Y.; m. Isabel Joseph, May 26, 1948; 1 son, Garo. AB cum laude, Harvard U., 1949, AM, 1952, PhD, 1957. Tchg. fellow Harvard U., Cambridge, Mass., 1952-56; asst. prof. NYU, NYC, 1956-58, assoc. prof., 1961-64, prof., 1964—; asst. prof. Williams Coll., Williamstown, Mass., 1958-60; assoc. prof. Ohio State U., Columbus, 1960-61; coord. NY Metro-Fulbright-Hayes Vis. Scholars, 1978-82. Mem. editl. adv. bd. Am. Music. Composer: (opera) Abaylar, 1974 (song cycle) Dark of the Moon, 1986; condr.: Mrs. H.H.A. Beach's Grand Mass in E-flat, NYC, 1982; author: Chadwick, Yankee Composer, 1990, Bye Bye Blues Variations for Violin and Piano, Tully Hall, NYC, 1992, for Cello and Piano, Merkin Hall, NYC, 2002, The Omnibus Idea, 1998; contbr. articles in Early Melodrama in Am., The Aethiop, Orchestral Restoration, Am. Music, A Celebration Am. Music, Jour. Musicology, Music in Early Va. Served with US Army, 1943-46, ETO. Recipient grant NEH, 1978. Mem. Am. Musicol. Soc., Sonneck Soc. Home: 52 Washington Mews New York NY 10003-6608 Office: NYU 100 Washington Sq E New York NY 10003-6688 Office Phone: 212-998-8314.

YELLIS, KENNETH, museum administrator; Rsch. historian Office of Small Exhibits, Nat. Portrait Gallery, curator edn.; dir. pub. programs Plimoth Plantation; dir. First Lights Mus. Consultants; asst. dir. pub. programs Peabody Mus. Natural History, Yale U. Office: Peabody Mus Natural History Yale Univ 170 Whitney Ave New Haven CT 06520-8118

YEMELYANOV, ALEXANDER M. mathematician, educator; b. Ivanovo, Russia, Jan. 31, 1953; s. Michael A. Kotik and Valentina L. Yemelyanova; m. Alla A. Zelenkevich, Nov. 12, 1961; 1 child, Alina Alexandrina Yemelyanova. MS in Math., Moscow State U., 1975; PhD, Russian Acad. Scis., Moscow, 1980; DS, Aviation Inst., Zhukovsky, Russia, 1990. Jr., then sr. rschr. All-Union Rsch. Info. Inst., Moscow, 1975—82; dir. computer support systems divsn. Moscow Rsch. Inst. of Planning and Mgmt., 1982—89; prof. Plekhanov Russian U. Econs., Moscow, 1989—2000; adj. prof. Va. Commonwealth U., Richmond, 2000—01; assoc. prof. computer sci. Ga. Southwestern State U., Americus, 2001—. Project leader Rsch. Aviation Inst., Moscow, 1988—2000; prof. Bauman Moscow State Tech. U., 1997—99. Contbr. articles to profl. publs. Grantee, Russian State Aviation Safety Program, 1989, 1992. Mem.: Human Factors and Ergonomics Soc., Assn. Computing Machinery. Achievements include rschr. in field. Office: Georgia Southwestern State U 800 Wheatley St Americus GA 31709-4379 Personal E-mail: ay@canes.gsw.edu. E-mail: ay@canes.gsw.edu.

YEMENIDJIAN, ALEX, film company executive; BA in acctg., Calif. State U., Northridge; M in bus. taxation, U. So. Calif. Mng. ptnr. Parks, Palmer, Turner & Yemenidjian; with MGM Grand Inc. (now MGM Mirage), Las Vegas, 1990—, pres., COO, 1995-99; chmn., CEO Metro-Goldwyn-Mayer Inc., Santa Monica, Calif., 1999—. Bd. dirs. MGM Grand Inc. (formerly MGM Grand Inc.), 1989-. Chmn. United Armenian Fund; bd. dirs. Kirk Kerkorian's Lincy Found. Office: MGM Studios Inc 2500 Broadway Santa Monica CA 90404-3065*

YEN, BING CHENG, retired civil engineer, retired engineering educator; arrived in U.S., 1959; s. Ding Y. and Shu J. Yen; m. Ann Margret Nielsen, June 21, 1964; children: Annette, Brigitte, Pei, Charlotte, Dagmarette. BS, Nat. Taiwan U., Taipei, 1956; PhD, U. Utah, Salt Lake City, 1963. Cert. civil engr., Calif., 1966, geotech. engr., Calif., 1994. Asst. prof. civil engring. U. Utah, Salt Lake City, 1963—64; asst. prof. to prof. civil engring. Calif. State U., Long Beach, 1964—89; pres. Bing Yen & Associates, Irvine, Calif., 1989—98. Cons. engring. dept. L.A. County, 1966—69; cons. Woodward Clyde Cons., 1970—79; ind. cons. U.S. and Europe, 1979—89. Contbr. articles to profl. jours., scientific papers. Recipient Outstanding Educator of Am., AAUP, 1972; grantee rsch., Nat. Sci. Found., 1980, U.S. Navy, 1979—88, State of Calif., 1979—88. Achievements include research in long term slope stability analyses under static and seismic loadings, holding capacity, soil-pipe interaction in soil mechanics.

YEN, GILI, economics researcher; b. Taipei, Taiwan, Mar. 8, 1953; s. Tzeng-song and Yueh-yun Yen; m. Eva Chung-Chiung; 1 child, Bernard Chih-hsun. BA, Nat. Taiwan U., Taipei, 1975, MA, 1978; PhD, Wash. U., 1983. Assoc. rsch. fellow Chung-Hua Instn. for Econ. Rsch., Taipei, 1983-86; assoc. prof. Inst. Indsl. Econs. Nat. Ctrl. U., Chung-li, 1985-87, prof., then dir., 1987-89, prof., founding dir. Inst. Fin. Mgmt., 1989-92; sr. rsch. fellow, divsn. dir. Taiwan Inst. Econ. Rsch., Taipei, 1992-93; sr. rsch. fellow Taiwan Rsch. Inst., Taipei, 1994—; 1st v.p. China Devel. Bank (formerly China Devel. Corp.), Taipei, 1994-97; dir., supr. China Steel Corp., Kaohsiung, 1990-97; dean Sch. Mgmt. Chaoyang U. of Tech., 1998—2001; prof. Dept. Bus. Adminstrn., 2001—. Advisor Exec. Yuan (the Adminstrv. Br. of the Ctrl. Govt.), Taipei, 1983-84, 89-90, Everfortune Bus. Group, 1999-2000, sr. advisor, 2001-03; adj. assoc. prof. Nat. Taiwan U., Taipei, 1985-87, adj. prof., 1987-93. Author: (collection of acad. papers) Empirical Studies on Business Finance and Government Policy in Taiwan, 1996; editor: New Directions in Regional Trade Liberalization and Investment Cooperations, APEC, 1994, Proceedings Annual Acad. Nat. Conf. Mgmt.-related Topics, 2000—; mem. editl. bd. Advances in Pacific Basin Bus., Econs., Fin., 1995—, Jour. Fin. Studies, 1993—; Review of Pacific Basin Fin. Markets and Policies, 1998—; contbr. approximately 40 articles to profl. jours. Recipient numerous rsch. awards Nat. Sci. Coun. Mem. Chinese Econ. Assn. (gov. 1991-94), Chinese Fin. Assn. (sec.-gen., exec. dir. 1992-96), Internat. Soc. for Instnl. Econs. (country rep. 1997). Avocations: reading, listening to music, playing table tennis, travel, playing mahjong. Home: 7th Floor-1 No 2 Ln 218 Gifeng Rd Taichung Taiwan Office Phone: 886-4-23323000 ext. 4351. E-mail: gyen@mail.cyut.edu.tw.

YEN, HENRY CHIN-YUAN, computer systems programmer, software engineer, consulting company executive; b. Mpls., Apr. 18, 1958; s. James and Elizabeth Y.; m. Michele Calen, Oct. 8, 1988; children: Andrew, Matthew. Sr. systems programmer Grumman Data Systems Corp., Bethpage, N.Y., 1978-83; mgr. Data Ctr. On-Line Software Internat., Inc., Ft. Lee, N.J., 1983-85, lead systems programmer, 1985-88; v.p. The Galamery Co., Inc., Del., 1988—, Aegis Info. Systems, Inc., Del., 1989—. Bd. dirs. Personal Computer Systems Corp. Bd. trustees Syosset Pub. Libr., NY, 2001—. Mem. IEEE, Assn. Computing Machinery, Network and Sys. Profls. Assn., Mensa (bd. dirs. greater N.Y. chpt. 2002-), Intertel. Avocations: bicycling, profl. musician. Home: PO Box 1 Hicksville NY 11802-0001 Office: Aegis Info Systems Inc PO Box 730 Hicksville NY 11802-0730 Business E-Mail: henry@AegisInfoSys.com.

YEN, SAMUEL S(HOW)-C(HIH), obstetrics and gynecology educator, reproductive endocrinologist; b. Beijing, Feb. 22, 1927; divorced; children: Carol Amanda, Dolores Amelia, Margaret Rae. BS, Cheeloo U., China, 1949; MD, U. Hong Kong, 1954, DSc, 1980. Diplomate Am. Bd. Ob-Gyn, Am. Bd. Reproductive Endocrinology. Intern Queen Mary Hosp., Hong Kong, 1954—55; resident Johns Hopkins U., Balt., 1956—60; fellow reproductive endocrinology Harvard Med. Sch., Boston, 1960—62; assoc. prof. reproductive biology Case Western Res. U., Cleve., 1967—70; prof. ob-gyn U. Calif., San Diego, 1972—83, chmn. dept. reproductive medicine, 1972—83, prof. reproductive medicine, 1983—; dir. reproductive endocrinology U. Calif. Med. Ctr., San Diego, 1983—98, W.R. Persons chair, 1987. Assoc. dir. obstetrics Univ. Hosp., Cleve., 1968—70; DeGroof lectr., 1987; Van Campenhaut lectr. Can. Fertility and Andrology Soc., 1995; bd. examiners Am. Bd. Ob-Gyn., 1973—78, Am. Bd. Reproductive Endocrinology, 1976—82; 1st Marilyn and John Huffman Meml. lectr. XII World Congress Adolescent Gynecology, Helsinki, 1998; James M. Cuaseo Meml. lectr. U. Pa., 1998; A. Marsh Panloon Jr. lectr. U. Utah, 2001; plenary lectr. 4th Internat. Congress Reproductive Endocrinology, Beijing, 2001, 9th World Congress Gynecol. Endocrinology, Hong Kong, 2001. Editor: Reproductive Endocrinology Physiology, Pathophysiology and Clinical Management, 1978, 1999, 2003. Named to Soc. of Scholars, Johns Hopkins U., 1992; recipient Axel Munthe Found. award, 1982, Simpson medal, U. Edinburgh, Scotland, 1996; fellow, Oglebay, 1968—69. Fellow: Royal Coll. Ob-Gyn. (ad eundem, London); mem.: Am. Fertility Soc., Endocrine Soc. (Rorer Clin. Investigator award 1992, Disting. Scientist award 1992), Soc. Gynecol. Investigation (pres. 1981, Disting. Scientist award 1992), Assn. Am. Physicians, NAS Inst. Medicine. Office: U Calif San Diego Reproductive Medicine # 0633 La Jolla CA 92093

YEN, TEH FU, civil and environmental engineering educator; b. Kun-Ming, China, Jan. 9, 1927; came to U.S., 1949; s. Kwang Pu and Ren (Liu) Y.; m. Shiao-Ping Siao, May 30, 1959 BS, Cen. China U., 1947; MS, W.Va. U., 1953; PhD, Va. Poly. Inst. and State U., 1956; hon. doctoral degree, Pepperdine U., 1982, Internat. U. Dubna, Russia, 1996, All Russian Petroleum Exploration Inst., St. Petersburg, Russia, 1999. Sr. research chemist Good Yr. Tire & Rubber Co., Akron, 1955-59; fellow Mellon Inst., Pitts., 1959-65; sr. fellow Carnegie-Mellon U., Pitts., 1965-68; assoc. prof. Calif. State U., Los Angeles, 1968-69, U. So. Calif., 1969-80, prof. civil engring. and environ. engring., 1980—. Hon. prof. Shanghai U. Sci. and Tech., 1986, U. Petroleum, Beijing, 1987, Daqing Petroleum Inst., 1992; cons. Universal Oil Products, 1968-76, Chevron Oil Field Rsch. Co., 1968-75, Finnigan Corp., 1976-77, GE, 1977-80, United Techs., 1978-79, TRW Inc., 1982-83, Exxon, 1981-82, DuPont, 1985-88, Min. Petroleum, Beijing, 1982—, Biogas Rsch. Inst.-UN, Chengdu, 1991. Author numerous tech. books; contbr. articles to profl. jours. Recipient Disting. Svc. award Tau Beta Pi, 1974, Imperial Crown Gold medal, Iran, 1976, Achievement award Chinese Engring. and Sci. Assocs. So. Calif., 1977, award Phi Kappa Phi, 1982, Outstanding Contbn. honor Pi Epsilon Tau, 1984, Svc. award Republic of Honduras, 1989, award in Petroleum Chem. Am. Chem. Soc., 1994, Kapitsa Gold medal Russian Fedn., 1995. Fellow Chem. Soc., Inst. Petroleum, Am. Inst. Chemists; mem. Am. Chem. Soc. (bd. dirs. 1993, councillor, founder and chmn. geochemistry divsn. 1979-81, Chinese Acad. Scis. (standing com.), Acad. Scis. Russian Fedn. (academician, fgn. mem.). Home: 2378 Morslay Rd Altadena CA 91001-2716 Office: U So Calif 3620 S Vermont Ave Rm 224A Los Angeles CA 90089-2531 Office Phone: 213-740-0586. Business E-Mail: tfyen@usc.edu.

YEN, WEN LIANG, retired aerospace engineer; b. Taipei, Taiwan, Dec. 13, 1937; came to U.S., 1963; s. Ping Ting and Mei Yen; m. Fina H. Kuo, Mar. 9, 1966; 1 child, AnnFrances. BS, Nat. Taiwan U., 1960; MS, Nat. Tsinghua U., Taiwan, 1962; PhD, Purdue U., 1969. Asst. prof. Ind. U.-Purdue U., Indpls., 1968-73, assoc. prof., 1973-80; mem. sci. staff Deutsches Elektronen-Synchrotron, Hamburg, Germany, 1978-80; programmer/analyst Computer Scis. Corp., Greenbelt, Md., 1980-82; sys. specialist Lockheed Engring. and Mgmt. Svcs. Co., Inc., Greenbelt, Md., 1982-87; sr. analyst Honeywell Tech. Solutions Inc., Greenbelt, Md., 1987—2002. Contbr. articles to profl. jours. Recipient Group Achievement award NASA, 1993. Achievements include development of spacecraft battery model which predicts whether the battery of a spacecraft will support proposed loads. Personal E-mail: wlyen2002@yahoo.com.

YEN, WEN-HSIUNG, language and music professional, educator; b. Tainan, Taiwan, June 26, 1934; came to U.S., 1969; m. Yuan-yuan Yen, Jan. 6, 1961; children: Tin-ju, Tin-jen, Tin-Tao. BA, Nat. Taiwan Normal U., 1960; MA, UCLA, 1971; PhD in Music, World U., 1988; Candidate Philosophy in Ethnomusicology, UCLA, 1995; cultural doctorate philosophy of music, The World Univ., 1988. Instr. Nat. Taichung Tchr. Coll., 1961-62; prof. Chinese Culture U., Taipei, 1964-69; lectr. West L.A. C.C., 1978-82; founder Chinese Culture Sch. L.A., 1976—. Grad. tchg. asst. U. Md., 1982-83; instr. L.A. City Coll., 1983—, Calif. State U. L.A., 1984—, Pasadena City Coll., 1989—; prof. Chinese Santa Monica (Calif.) Coll., 1986—, Calif. State U. Northridge, 1986—; founder Wen Yen Piano Studio, 1972—; founder, dir. Chinese Mus. Orch. So. Calif., 1974—; founder, pres. Chinese- Amer. Musicians Assn. of So. Calif., 1990—; co-chair Conf. Students of Chinese Lang. and Culture. Musician: musical compositions include Collection of Works by Mr. Yen, 1969, (recordings) Art Songs and Chinese Folk Songs, 1982; author: Taiwan Folk Songs, 1967, vol. 2, 1969, A Collection of Wen-hsiung Yen's Songs, 1968, vol. 2, 1987, vol. 3, 2000 (award Fedn. Overseas Assns., 2000, 2002), Achievement and Methodology for Comparative Musicology, 1968; translator: Chinese Musical Culture and Folk Songs, 1989, Silk and Bamboo Expresses Emotion and Meaning, 2000; composer: 100 songs and instrumental music; exhibitor traditional Chinese musical instruments and publs., Chinese Culture Ctr., 1995, 1996, Arcadia Pub. Libr., 1999, organizer concerts, contbr. articles to profl. jours. Bd. dirs. So. Calif. Coun. Chinese Sch., 1998—; bd. dirs. Chinese Studies Ctr., Calif. State U., L.A., 1990—; conducter Chinese Music Orch. So. Calif., 1974-; producer Chinese Art and Culture Festival, 1990-2003. Mem.: Chinese Writers Assn. So. Calif. (v.p. 2000), Fedn. Overseas Chinese Assns. (bd. dirs. (hon.) 2002), So. Calif. Coun. Chinese Schs. (v.p. 2000—, chmn. exec. com.), Chinese Am. PTA So. Calif. (supr. 1985—), Taiwan Benevloent Assn. Calif. (v.p. 1986, pres. 1987—89, bd. dirs.), Taiwan Benevolent Assn. Am. (bd. dirs.), Alumni Assn. Chinese Culture U. So. Calif., Soc. Asian Music (founder, pres.), Internat. Coun. Traditional Music, Coll. Music Soc., Soc. Ethnomusicology, Chinese Performing Arts Assn. of Am. (bd. dirs.), Chinese Choral Soc. So. Calif. (music dir.), Chinese-Am. Musicians Assn. So Calif. (pres.). Avocations: walking, ping pong/table tennis, tai chi chuan. Office: Chinese Culture Sch 615 Las Tunas Dr Ste B Arcadia CA 91007-8469 E-mail: wenhyen2000@yahoo.com.

YENA, JOHN A. academic administrator; BS, U. R.I., 1962, MBA, 1968; DBA (hon.), Detroit Coll. Bus., 1975; DHL honoris causa (hon.), Constantinian U., 1994, U. Bridgeport, 1999. Instr. econs. Johnson & Wales U., Providence, 1962, dir. student activities and athletics, 1965, dean of men, 1966, dir. Reading Inst., 1967, dean of Coll., 1968, v.p., 1969, pres., 1989—. Mem. Accrediting Commn. of Ind. Colls. and Schs.; mem. exec. adv. bd. Irwin Career Edn. Divsn., Homewood, Ill.; bd. dirs. EdVerifY, Inc. Bd. trustees Providence Found., NCCJ; apptd. exec. bd. United Way Southeastern New Eng., 1996; govtl. appointee bd. govs. R.I. Commodores, 1991; mayoral appointee Downcity Task Force, 1991; bd. dirs. Vocat. Resources, Inc., Children's Crusade, Corp. of Providence Pub. Libr., Providence/Warwick Conv. and Visitors Bur., R.I. Conv. Ctr. Authority, Coalition for Comty. Devel. in Providence, Food Bank R.I., 2000, Nat. Commn. for Coop. Edn., 2001, Kent County Hosp.; appointee nat. adv. com. Instnl. Quality and Integrity for the U.S. Dept. of Edn., 1998. Recipient Bus. Leadership award, Restaurant Bus. mag. Mem.: Am. Assn. Pres. of Ind. Colls. and Univs., Greater Providence C. of C. (bd. dirs.), Am. Coun. on Edn., R.I. Higher Ind. Edn. Assn. (chmn.), Assn. Ind. Colls. and Schs. (pres., treas. 1980—88, edn. credit and credentials commn. 1987—91), Hon. Order of Golden Toque (life). Office: 8 Abbot Park Pl Providence RI 02903

YENIKA-AGBAW, VIVIAN S. English studies educator, researcher; b. Tiko, Cameroon, Africa, May 21, 1959; came to U.S., 1991; d. Mathias Bayena and Teresa Joy Yenika; m. Steven Ekema Agbaw, June 30, 1984; children: Stephen Y., Michael L., Joy E. BA, U. Yaounde, Cameroon, 1983; MA, U. Conn., 1986; PhD, Pa. State U., 1996. Grad. asst. Pa. State U., University Park, 1993-96; asst. prof. Clarion (Pa.) U., 1997-98; assoc. prof. Bloomsburg (Pa.) U., 1998—; literacy cons., 2000—. Lit. cons. Bloomsburg U., 2000—; ad hoc reviewer Jour. Adolescent and Adult Literacy, 1997—. Contbg. author: Running for the Lives, 2000; contbr. articles to profl. jours. including Lang. Arts, Internat. Rev. Edn.; mem. editl. bd. Lang. Arts-Nat. Coun. Tchrs. English, 1998-2001. Program co-chair Columbia-Montour Women's Conf., Bloomsburg, 2000; chair acad. program com. 2002 Children's Lit. Assn. Conf. Grantee Bloomsburg U., 1998—. Mem. MLA, Internat. Reading Assn., Nat. Coun. Tchrs. English, Children's Lit. Assn., Comparative Internat. Edn. Soc. Home: 365 Hillside Dr Bloomsburg PA 17815 E-mail: vyenika@chusky.bloomu.edu.

YENKIN, BERNARD KALMAN, coatings and resins company executive; b. Columbus, Ohio, Dec. 2, 1930; s. Abe I. and Eleanore G. Yenkin; m. Miriam Schottenstein, Mar. 31, 1957; children: Leslie Mara, Jonathan, Allison Katsev, Amy. BA, Yale U., 1952; MBA, Harvard U., 1954. V.p. Yenkin-Majestic Paint Corp., Columbus, 1968-77, pres., 1977-85, chmn. bd., 1985—. Pres. Columbus Jewish Fedn., 1980-82, Pro Musica Chamber Orch., Columbus, 1983-85, Columbus Torah Acad., 1977-79; bd. v.p. Jewish Edn. Svc. N.Am., N.Y.C., 1991-95. Recipient Mayor's award for Vol. Svc. City of Columbus, 1984, Young Leadership award Columbus Jewish Fedn., 1965. Mem. Yale Club of Cen. Ohio (pres. 1979-81), Yale Club of N.Y., Athletic Club (Columbus). Office: Yenkin-Majestic Industries 1920 Leonard Ave Columbus OH 43219-2514

YEO, KIM ENG, artist; b. Singapore, Apr. 24, 1947; came to U.S., 1978; d. Cheng Chye and Seok Kim (Chew) Lee; m. Bock Cheng Yeo; children: Beng Lin, Beng Jene. Student, Nanyang Acad. Fine Arts, Singapore, 1963; BSc with honors, U. Singapore, 1968. Watercolor demonstrator Flushing Art League, N.Y.C., 1980-84; art instr. Poppenhusen Inst., N.Y.C., 1984; substitute art tchr. UN Internat. Sch., N.Y.C., 1984-85; freelance paper product designer, 1981-87; textile designer J. Brown Designs, N.Y.C., 1987-91; tchg. artist Flushing (N.Y.) Town Hall, 1995—2002; artist-in-residence Pub. Sch. 214, 165, Francis Lewis H.S., Flushing, 1997-2001. Art cons. Corp. Art Directions, N.Y.C.; visual arts panelist, Flushing Coun., 1985-87, Queen's Coun., 1998-99, 2001-04. One person shows at Alliance Francais, 1975-77, Bhirasri Inst. Modern Art, Bangkok, Thailand, 1975-77, Flushing Coun. on Arts, 1995, 2000; exhibited Mallette Gallery, L.I., N.Y., 1998, 99, Artfolio Gallery, Singapore, 2000, Langston Hughes Cmty. Libr. and Cultural Ctr., N.Y., 2004; exhibited in group shows at Womanart Gallery, N.Y.C., 1979-80, Nat. Art League, Douglastown, N.Y., 1979-86, Flushing Coun. on Arts, 1984-88, 96-2004, Postcrypt Art Gallery, N.Y.C., 1997, Singapore Watercolor Soc., 1997-99, 2001-03; represented in corp. and pvt. collections; artist greeting cards UNICEF, 1997-98; featured on QPATV Artists Series, 1993, QPTV Queens Jour., 2000. Benefit show UN Devel. Fund for Women Singapore, 1999. Mem. Flushing Art League (bd. dirs., treas. 1979-85, award 1986), Flushing Coun. on Arts. Buddhist. Avocations: gardening, bookmaking. Home: 16202 77th Ave Flushing NY 11366-1022 Fax: (718) 591-8483. E-mail: artist@kimengyeo.com.

YEO, RON, architect; b. Los Angeles, June 17, 1933; s. Clayton Erik and Rose G. (Westman) Y.; m. Birgitta S. Bergkvist, Sept. 29, 1962; children: Erik Elov, Katarina Kristina. B.Arch., U. So. Calif., 1959. Draftsman Montierth & Strickland (Architects), Long Beach, Calif., 1958-61; designer Gosta Edberg S.A.R. Arkitekt, Stockholm, 1962; partner Strickland & Yeo, Architects, Garden Grove, Calif., 1962-63; pres. Ron Yeo, Architect, Inc., Corona del Mar, Calif., 1963—. Cons., lectr. in field. Archtl. works include Garden Grove Civic and Cmty. Ctr., 1966, Hall Sculpture Studio, 1966, Garden Grove Cultural Ctr., 1978, Gem Theater, 1979, Festival Amphitheatre, 1983, Los Coyotes Paleontol. Interpretive Ctr., 1986, Calif. State U. Fullerton Alumni House, 1997, O'Neill Regional Pk. Nature Ctr., 1998, Upper Newport Bay Interpretive Ctr., 2000, Stough Canyon Nature Ctr., 2000. Mem. Orange County Planning Commn., 1972-73, 1975-76; chmn. Housing and Community Devel. Task Force, 1978, Orange County Fire Protection Planning Task Force, City of Newport Beach City Arts Commn., 1970-72; pres. Orange County Arts Alliance, 1980-81; gen. plan advisory com. Newport Beach, 2002-04. Fellow AIA; mem. Green Bldg. Coun., Internat. Conf. Bldg. Ofcls., Nat. Assn. for Interpretation (founding), Constrn. Specification Inst. Democrat. Office: Ron Yeo FAIA Architect Inc 500 Jasmine Ave Corona Del Mar CA 92625-2308

YEO, YEE-CHIA, engineering educator, consultant; m. Jiak Lui Ng. BEE, Nat. U., Singapore, 1996, MEE, 1997; MS, PhD, U. Calif., Berkeley, 2002. Asst. prof. Nat. U., Singapore; tech. cons. Taiwan Semiconductor Mfg. Co., Hsinchu, Taiwan, 2001—03. Contbr. chapters to books. NUS OGS scholar, Nat. U. of Singapore, 1998—2002. Mem.: IEEE (Paul Rappaport award 2002, EDS fellow 2001). Achievements include development of dual-metal gate CMOS process; patents pending for strained channel transistors, multiple-gate transistors, metal-gate electrodes, others. Office: Nat U Singapore 4 Engineering Dr 3 Singapore 117576 Singapore Office Phone: 65-6874-2298. E-mail: yeo@ieee.org.

YEOMANS, DONALD KEITH, astronomer; b. Rochester, NY, May 3, 1942; s. George E. and Jessie Y.; m. Laurie Robyn Ernst, June 20, 1970; children: Sarah, Keith. BA, Middlebury (Vt.) Coll., 1964; MS, U. Md., 1967, PhD, 1970. Supr. Computer Scis. Corp., Silver Spring, Md., 1973-76; sr. rsch. astronomer Jet Propulsion Lab., Pasadena, Calif., 1976-92, supr., 1992—. Discipline specialist Internat. Halley Watch, 1982-89; sci. investigator NASA Comet Mission, 1987-91, Near-Earth Asteroid Rendezvous Mission, 1994-2001, Multi-Comet Flyby Mission, 1997-2002, Comet Impact Mission, 1999—; project scientist for asteroid sample return mission, 1998—. Author: Comet Halley: Once in a Lifetime, 1985, The Distant Planets, 1989, Comets: A Chronological History of Observation, Science, Myth, and Folklore, 1991. Recipient Space Achievement award AIAA, 1985, Exceptional Svc. medal NASA, 1986, Achievement award Middlebury Coll. Alumni, 1987; named NASA/JPL Sr. Rsch. Scientist, 1993. Mem.: Am. Astron. Soc., Internat. Astron. Union. Democrat. Presbyterian. Avocations: tennis, history of astronomy. Office: Jet Propulsion Lab #301-150 4800 Oak Grove Dr Pasadena CA 91109-8001 Business E-Mail: donald.k.yeomans@jpl.nasa.gov.

YEOMANS, DONALD RALPH, Canadian government official, consultant; b. Toronto, Ont., Can., Mar. 25, 1925; s. Ralph and Louise (Weismiller) Y.; m. Catherine Simpson Williams, May 13, 1950; children: Patricia Ann, Nancy Louise, Jane Elizabeth. BASc, U. Toronto, 1947. Registered profl. engr., Ont.; cert. mgmt. acct. Mem. Bur. of Govt. Orgns., Ottawa, Ont., 1962-64; dep. sec. Treasury Bd., Ottawa, 1964-69; asst. dep. minister Dept. Supply and Services, Ottawa, 1969-75; assoc. exec. dir. Anti-Inflation Bd., Ottawa, 1975-76; asst. dep. minister Dept. Nat. Health-Welfare, Ottawa, 1976-77; commr. Correctional Services of Can., Ottawa, 1977-85; chmn. Tariff Bd., 1985-89; spl. advisor Can. Jud. Centre, 1989-92; mem. bd. govs. Carleton U., 1980-93, chmn., 1989-91. Spl. advisor Royal Com. Govt. Orgns., 1961, Royal Com. Fin. Accountability, 1977; assoc. Cons. and Audit Can., 1992-97; exec. counsellor Pub. Svc. Commn., 1990-95; cons. to govt. and industry, 1990-97, bd. dirs. Corrections Corp. Can.; mem. bd. govs. Can. Comprehensive Audit Found., 1989-94; mem. ind. adv. com. Auditor Gen. Can., 1989-95; chmn. Coun. Adminstrv. Tribunals, 1986; chmn. Coun. Chairs Ont. Univs., 1991-93; mem. Expert Com. on AIDS in Prisons, 1992-94; chmn. awards com. Am. Correctional Assn., 1992-97; bd. dirs. Corrections Corp. Can., Baker Group Internat., Inc. Recipient Centennial medal Govt. Can., 1967, Jubilee medal Govt. Can., 1977, E.R. Cass award Am. Corr. Assn., 1991, Corr. Svc. of Can. Exemplary Svc. medal, 2000, Founder's award Carleton U., 2000; Australian Commonwealth fellow, 1985. Fellow: Soc. Mgmt. Accts. Can. (pres. 1977); mem.: Fed. Superannuates Nat. Assn. (pres. Ottawa br. 1998—2000, bd. dirs., nat. regional dir. 2002—), Inst. Pub. Adminstrn. Can. (pres. 1974), Assn. State Correctional Adminstrs. (pres. 1983), Ottawa Heart Inst. Alumni Assn. (v.p.), Five Lakes (pres. 1975); Canadian (Ottawa, pres. 1978), Canadian Club (Ottawa, pres. 1978), Five Lakes Club (pres. 1975). Home and Office: 205-211 Second Ave Ottawa ON Canada K1S 2H8 Fax: 613-231-4557. E-mail: kdyeom@cyberus.ca.

YEOMANS, GORDON ALLAN, retired education educator; b. Cherry Valley, Ohio, Sept. 30, 1921; s. Ralph Carey Yeomans and Margaret Warner; m. Marjorie Jo Roberts, Feb. 27, 1949; 1 child, Lynne Leigh Yeomans Craver. BA, U. S.W. La., 1951; MA, La. State U., 1952, PhD, 1966. Instr. U. Miss., Oxford, 1952; assoc. prof. Samford U., Birmingham, Ala., 1952-66, U. S.W. La., Lafayette, 1966-67; prof., dept. head Miss. U. for Women, Columbus, 1967-68; prof. U. Tenn., Knoxville, 1968-87, prof. emeritus, 1987. Cons. Andersen Electric Corp., Leeds, Ala., 1958, John Williamson Co., Birmingham, 1960-61, Birmingham (Ala.) Trust Bank, 1962, Union Carbide Corp., Oak Ridge, Tenn., 1969-81, Magnavox Corp., Asheville, N.C., 1975. Author: A Handbook for Speakers, 1969; contbr. author: The Heart of the Valley, 1976, Pamphlets and The American Revolution, 1976; contbr. articles to profl. jours. Program chmn. Knoxville Religious Bicentennial, 1976; adv. coun. Knoxville Alcohol and Drug Rehab. Ctr.; mem. 1st United Meth. Ch., Knoxville, religious drama dir. With USAAF, 1940-45. Tchr. grantee Danforth Found., 1956-57, summer 1963, Rsch. grantee U. Tenn., 1974, 75; named Speech Tchr. of Yr., State of Tenn., 1984. Mem. Speech Communication Assn., So. Speech Communication Assn., East Tenn. Hist. Soc., Knoxville Civil War Roundtable. Democrat. Avocation: antiquarian book dealer and collector. Home: 805 Noragate Rd Knoxville TN 37919-7016

YEONAS, GEORGE C. real estate executive; m. Marjorie Yeonas; children: Christina, Constance. Grad., Georgetown U.; MBA, U. Pa. Divsn. ptnr. Trammel Crow; v.p. devel. NVR; v.p., gen. mgr. South Fla. divsn. The Arvida Co.; pres., COO, The Fortress Group, Inc., McClean, Va., 1996-99, CEO, 1999—. Office: The Fortress Group Inc 11350 Random Hills Rd #650-800 Fairfax VA 22030-6044

YEOSOCK, JOHN JOHN, army officer; b. Wilkes-Barre, Pa., Mar. 18, 1937; s. John A. and Elizabeth B. Yeosock; m. Betta Lynn Hoffner; children—John John, Elizabeth John BS in Indsl. Engring., Pa. State U., 1959; MS in Ops. Rsch., U.S. Naval Postgrad. Sch., Monterey, Calif., 1969; postgrad., Nat. War Coll., 1976. Commd. officer U.S. Army, 1959, advanced through grades to lt. gen.; brigade comdr. 194th Armored Brigade, Ft Knox, Ky., 1978-80; chief of staff 1st Cavalry div. U.S. Army, Ft. Hood, Tex., 1980-81, asst. div. comdr., 1983-84; project mgr. Saudi N.G., Riyadh, Saudi Arabia, 1981-83; dep. chief of staff ops. Forces Command., Atlanta, 1984-86; comdr. 1st Cavalry Div., Ft. Hood, 1986-88; asst. dep. chief of staff for ops. The Pentagon, Washington, 1988-89; comdr. 3d Army and dep. comdg. gen. Forces Command, Ft. McPherson, Ga., 1989—&; comdr. U.S., U.K., French Army Forces, Kuwaiti Theater Ops., Desert Storm, Saudi Arabia, 1990-91; internat. cons., 1993—. Decorated D.S.M. (3), Legion of Merit (2), Bronze Star with v (2), French Legion of Honor, King Faisal award Class II, King Abdul Aziz medal Class II (Saudi Arabia), Combat Infantryman badge; recipient Nat. Vets. award, 1994, AUSA Inspiration award Atlanta, 1992; named Outstanding Engring. Alumnus, Pa. State U., 1990, Disting. Alumni, 1992, Disting. Alumnus, Valley Forge Mil. Acad., 1994; named to Pi Kappa Phi Hall of Fame. Mem. Wilkes-Barre C. of C. (hon., Achievement award 1991)

YEOSOCK, MICHAEL MICHAEL, funeral director, civil engineer; b. Wilkes-Barre, Pa., July 28, 1962; s. Michael J. and Patricia A. (Sauerwein) Y.; m. Mary Jacqueline Clemente; children: Adriana Grace, Christopher Michael. Student, Pa. State U., 1980-82; BS, W.Va. U., 1984; diploma in mortuary sci., New Eng. Inst., 1985; MS in Environ. Engring., U. New Haven, 1993. Cert. engr.-in-tng.; lic. profl. engr., Pa., Conn., N.Y. Project mgr. M.J. Pasonick, Jr., Inc., Wilkes-Barre, 1986-89; asst. civil engr. in tng. City of Norwalk (Conn.) Dept. of Pub. Works, 1989—, sr. engr., 1994—; supr. Jan Fabian Funeral Chapel, Hanover, Pa., 1990-91. Bd. dirs. Norwalk (Conn.) Tree Alliance. Mem. IEEE, AIME, ASCE, Soc. Mining Engrs., Can. Mining and Metallurgy, N.Y. Acad. Scis., Am. Rock Mechanics Assn., Internat. Soc. Rock Mechanics, Geospatial Info. and Tech. Assn. Republican. Russian Orthodox. Avocations: flying, white-water rafting. Home: 5 Country Club Dr White Plains NY 10607 Office: City of Norwalk 125 East Ave Norwalk CT 06851-5702 E-mail: myeosock@aol.com.

YERGIN, DANIEL HOWARD, writer, consultant; b. Los Angeles, Feb. 6, 1947; s. Irving H. and Naomi Y.; m. Angela Stent, Aug. 10, 1975; children: Alexander George, Rebecca Isabella. BA, Yale U., Eng., 1968; MA with first class honors, Cambridge U., Eng., 1970, PhD, 1974; PhD (hon.), U. Mo., 1980, U. Houston, 1994. Contbg. editor New York mag., 1968-70; research fellow Harvard U., Cambridge, Mass., 1974-76, lectr. bus. sch., 1976-79, lectr. Kennedy Sch. Govt., 1979-83, research assoc., 1983-90; chmn. Cambridge Energy Research Assoc., Cambridge, 1982-98, also chmn., sec. energy task force on strategic energy R&D, 1998—. Mem. policy adv. com. Program on U.S.-Japan Rels., Harvard U.; mem. bd. energy experts Dallas Morning News; mem. internat. panel advisors Asia-Pacific Petroleum Conf.; fellow World Econ. Forum, Davos. Author: Shattered Peace: The Origins of the Cold War and the National Security State, 1977, rev. edit., 1990, The Prize: Epic Quest for Oil, Money and Power, 1991 (Pulitzer Prize for non-fiction 1992, Eccle prize 1992); co-author: Cold War, 1977, Energy Future, 1979, Global Insecurity, 1982, Future of Oil Prices: Perils of Prophecy, 1984, Russia 2010: And What It Means for the World, 1993, the Commanding Heights, 1998; contbg. editor Atlantic Monthly, 1977-83. Mem. adv. bd. Solar Energy Rsch. Inst., Golden, Colo., 1979-81; sec. Energy Adv. Bd. Fellow Univ. Consortium for World Order Studies, 1974-75, Rockefeller Found., 1975-79, German Marshall Fund, 1980-81, Harvard U., Ctr. for Bus. and Govt., 1997—; Marshall scholar Cambridge U., 1974; recipient U.S. Energy award, 1997. Mem. PEN, Coun. on Fgn. Rels. (com. on studies), Nat. Petroleum Coun., Internat. Assn. for Energy Econs., Am. Hist. Assn., Am. Polit. Assn., Royal Inst. Internat. Affairs, Assn. Marshall Scholars (bd. dirs. 1988-91), U.S. Energy Assn. (bd. dirs.), Nat. Petroleum Coun., Yale Club (N.Y.C.), Harvard Club (N.Y.C.). Office: Cambridge Energy Research Assoc 55 Cambridge Pkwy Cambridge MA 02142-1234

YERKES, DAVID NORTON, architect; b. Cambridge, Mass., Nov. 5, 1911; s. Robert Mearns and Ada (Watterson) Y.; m. Catharine Noyes, Oct. 7, 1939 (dec. 1969); 1 dau., Catharine; m. Sarah Hitchcock Satterlee, July 9, 1972. BA, Harvard U., 1933; M.F.A., Yale U., 1935. Draftsman, designer, Chgo. and Washington, 1937-39, Deigert & Yerkes and Assos., Washington, 1945-69, David N. Yerkes & Assos., Washington, 1970-80, Yerkes, Pappas and Parker, 1980-83. Mem. panel archtl. advisers Nat. Commn. Fine Arts, 1961-63, 79-82; vice chmn. Presdl. Inaugural Parade Com., 1965 Prin. works include Voice of America Studios, Washington, 1958, Nat. Arboretum Hdqrs. Bldg. Am. Embassy, Somalia, also Madeira Sch. Auditoriu, 1969; 4 stas. Washington subway sys., 1971-81, hdqrs., Nat. Trust Historic Preservation, Washington, 1977, suite, Time, Inc., Washington, 1980, also various schs., labs; paintings exhibited in New Eng. and Washington. Served to capt. AUS, 1943-45. Firm recipient numerous regional and nat. awards; recipient Kemper award AIA, 1972 Fellow AIA (bd. dirs. 1965-68, v.p. 1968-69, chmn. nat. honor awards jury 1966, chmn. Reynolds Meml. award jury 1969, pres. found. 1974-76) Home: 3050 Military Rd NW #449 Washington DC 20015

YERKES, SUSAN GAMBLE, newspaper columnist; b. Evanston, Ill., Sept. 5, 1959; d. Charles Tyson Yerkes and Darthea (Campbell) Higgins. BA in Liberal Arts (hon.), U. Austin, 1974; MA in Mass Comms., Wichita State U., 1976. Pub. affairs dir. anchor KAKE-TV, Wichita, Kans., 1977-81; freelance writer pub. rels. YS Comms. Global, 1981-84; metro columnist San Antonio Light, 1986-93; lifestyle columnist S.A. Express News, San Antonio, 1993—. Radio TV host WOAI-AM, San Antonio, 1993—; nat. assn. broadcast editls., Boston, 1978-81. Recipient 1st Place Column Writing Nat. Press Women, 1988, Tex. AP Mng. Editors, 1995, 97, Vivian Castelberry award Assn. for Women in Journalism, 1997. Mem. Internat. Women's Forum, Women in Comm., Pub. Rel. Soc. Am., Rotary, Phi Beta Kappa. Episcopalian. Avocations: Argentine tango, horseback riding, travel, reading, friends, the Internet. E-mail: syerkesexpress-news.net. Home: 68 Granburg Cir San Antonio TX 78218-3011 Office Phone: 210-287-7326. E-mail: syerkes@espress-news.net.

YERMAN, FREDRIC WARREN, lawyer; b. NYC, Jan. 8, 1943; s. Nat W. and Tina (Barotz) Y.; m. Ann R. Rochlin, May 31, 1965; children: Emily, Deborah. BA, CUNY, 1963; LLB, Columbia U., 1966. Bar: N.Y. 1967. Assoc. Kaye Scholer LLP, NYC, 1966—74, ptnr., 1974—, chmn. exec. com., 1990—92. Bd. dirs. United Way Tri-State, Jewish Bd. Family and Children Svcs., N.Y.C. Fellow Am. Coll. Trial Lawyers. Home: 31 Sheridan Rd Scarsdale NY 10583-1523 Office: Kaye Scholer LLP 425 Park Ave New York NY 10022-3506 Business E-Mail: fyerman@kayescholer.com.

YERRID, C. STEVEN, lawyer; b. Charleston, W.Va., Sept. 30, 1949; s. Charles George and Audrey Faye Yerrid; m. Sharon Wainman, Feb. 13, 2000. BA in History and Polit. Sci., La. State U., 1971; JD, Georgetown U., 1975. Bar: Fla. 1975, Va. 1975, U.S. Supreme Ct. 1979, D.C. 1984; cert. civil trial advocate Nat. Bd. Trial Advocacy. Aide U.S. Senator Ellender, Washington, 1971-73; ptnr. Holland & Knight, Tampa, Fla., 1975-86; pres. Stagg, Hardy & Yerrid, Tampa, 1986-89, Yerrid, Knopik & Krieger PA, Tampa, 1990-2000, The Yerrid Law Firm, Tampa, 2000—. Mediator and Cir. Ct. arbitrator Fla. and Fed. Cts. Mem. ABA, Va. Bar Assn., D.C. Bar Assn., Fla. Bar Assn. (chmn. admiralty law com. 1984-85, bd. cert. com. 1988-91, vice chmn. 1990-91, chmn. 1994-95, bd. cert. civil trial lawyer), Southeastern Admiralty Law Inst., Am. Judicature Soc., ATLA (sustaining), Am. Bd. Trial Advocates (advocate), Maritime Law Assn. (proctor), Tex. Trial Lawyers Assn., Acad. Fla. Trial Lawyer (designated continuing legal edn. speaker 1982—, bd. dirs. 1989-97, 2000-01), Inner Cir. Advocates, Internat. Soc. Barristers, Am. Inns. of Ct. (supporting fellow), Cousteau Soc., Centre Club, Tampa Club, Univ. Club, Grand Havana Club, Old Memorial Golf Club. Democrat. Avocations: fishing, tennis, boxing. Office: The Yerrid Law Firm 101 E Kennedy Blvd Ste 3910 Tampa FL 33602-5187 Office Phone: 813-222-8222.

YERUSHALMI, YOSEF HAYIM, historian, educator; b. NYC, May 20, 1932; s. Leon and Eva (Kaplan) Y.; m. Ophra Pearly, Jan. 4, 1959; 1 child, Ariel. BA, Yeshiva U., 1953; M in Hebrew Lit., Jewish Theol. Sem. Am., 1957; MA, Columbia U., 1961, PhD, 1966; MA (hon.), Harvard, 1970; DHL (hon.), Jewish Theol. Sem. Am., 1987; LHD (hon.), Hebrew Union Coll., 1996; PhD (hon.), U. Haifa, 1997, Ludwig Maximilians U., 1997; DHL (hon.), Spertus Inst., 2002; PhD (hon.), Ecole Pratique des Hautes Etudes Sorbonne Paris, 2003. Instr. Jewish history Rutgers U., New Brunswick, N.J., 1963-66; asst. prof. Hebrew and Jewish History Harvard U., 1966-70, prof., 1970-78, Jacob E. Safra prof. Jewish history and Sephardic civilization, 1978-80, chmn. dept. near eastern langs. and civilizations, 1978-80, Salo Wittmayer Baron Prof. of Jewish History, Culture, Soc.; dir. Ctr. for Israel and Jewish Studies Columbia U., N.Y.C., 1980—. Author: From Spanish Court to Italian Ghetto: Isaac Cardoso, A Study in Seventeenth-Century Marranism and Jewish Apologetics, 1971, Haggadah and History, 1975, The Lisbon Massacre of 1506, 1976, Zakhor: Jewish History and Jewish Memory, 1982, Freud's Moses: Judaism Terminable and Interminable, 1991, A Field in Anatot: Essays on Jewish History (in German), 1993, Servants of Kings and Not Servants of Servants: Some Aspects of the Political History of the Jews (in German), 1995, Sefardica: Essays on the History of the Jews, Marranos and New Christians of Hispano-Portuguese Origin (in French), 1998; author (in Hebrew): Spinoza on the Survival of the Jews, 1983; contbr. articles to profl. publs. on Spanish and Portuguese Jewry and history of psychoanalysis; chmn. publs. com. Jewish Publ. Soc., 1972-84; pres. Leo Baeck Inst., 1986-91. Bd. dirs. Conf. Jewish Social Studies, Psycho analytic Research and Devel. Fund, Editorial Bd., History and Memory. Recipient Newman medal CUNY, 1975, Nat. Jewish Book award, 1983, 92,Ansley award Columbia U. Press, 1968, medal of achievement in history Nat. Found. for Jewish Culture,1995; Kent fellow, 1963, travel fellow Nat. Found. for Jewish Culture, 1964, fellow NEH, 1976-77, Rockefeller fellow in humanities, 1983-84, Guggenheim fellow, 1989-90; Carl Friedrich von Siemens Stiftung fellow (Munich), 1996-97. Fellow Am. Acad. Jewish Research, Am. Acad. Arts and Scis., Acad. Portuguesa História Lisbon (hon.), Acad. Scis. Lisboa (hon.). Office: Columbia U 511 Fayerweather Hall 1180 Amsterdam Ave New York NY 10027-7039

YERXA, DONALD A. historian, educator, editor; b. Portland, Maine, July 19, 1950; s. Rex A. and Lois Wright Yerxa; m. Lois M. Hassinger, July 30, 1970. PhD, U. Maine, Orono, 1982. Prof. history Ea. Nazarene Coll., Quincy, Mass., 1977—. Co-author: Species of Origins: America's Search for a Creation Story; contbg. editor: Books & Culture, 1999—. Recipient Best Article in Naval History, USN Hist. Ctr., 1986; fellow, U. Maine, 1974—75; USN Predoctoral fellow, USN Hist. Ctr., 1975—76, John Templeton Found. grantee, John Templeton-Oxford U., 1999—2001. Mem.: World History Assn., Conf. Faith and History (exec. bd. 2003—04), Orgn. Am. Historians, Am. Hist. Assn., Colonial Soc. Mass., Hist. Soc. (asst. dir. 2001—04, editor Historically Speaking 2001—). Office: Historical Soc 656 Beacon St Mezzanine Boston MA 02215-2010 Personal E-mail: d.yerxa@comcast.net. E-mail: yerxad@bu.edu.

YESAIR, DAVID WAYNE, biochemist; b. Newbury, Mass., Sept. 9, 1932; s. Wayne and Roma Jackson (Arlin) Y.; m. Ruth Elizabeth Avery, June 6, 1954; children: Karen, Catherine, Peter. BS in Chemistry, U. Mass., 1954; PhD in Biochemistry, Cornell U., 1958. NSF postdoctoral fellow Nat. Inst. for Rsch., Shinfield, England, 1961-62; sr. scientist biochemistry group Arthur D. Little, Inc., Cambridge, Mass., 1962-66, head biochemistry/biomed. and pharmacology group, 1966-71, 72-77, mgr. biomolecular scis. sect., 1977-82, v.p., 1978-84; pres. BioMolecular Products, Inc., 1984—; founder, pres. Lym-Med Nutritional Products LLC, 2000, Lym-Drug Products, LLC, 2000. NIH sabbatical fellow L'Inst. de Chemie des Substances Naturelle, CNRS, Gif-Sur-Yvette, France, 1971-72; drug metabolism chmn. Gordon Rsch. Conf., 1983; mem. biotech. adv. bd. U. Conn., 1986-94; guest lectr. toxicology curriculum MIT, 1972-82. Contbr. numerous articles to profl. jours. and chpts. to books; holder more than 50 worldwide patents. Active Newbury Hist. Soc., Newburyport Maritime Mus., Sons and Daus. First Settlers of Newbury, pres., 1975, 76; active Newburyport Choral Soc.; class agt., Mass. capital fund chairperson Gov. Dummer Acad. Fellow Leukemia Soc. Am., NSF, NIH. Fellow Am. Inst. Chemists; mem. N.Y. Acad. Scis., Internat. Lecithin and Phospholipid Soc., AAAS, Am. Chem. Soc., Mass. Inst. Chemists, Am. Assn. for Cancer Rsch., Am. Soc. Toxicology, Am. Soc. Pharmacology Exptl. Therapeutics, Internat. Soc. for Studying Xenobiotics, Sigma Xi. Avocations: woodworking, antique furniture restoration, creative landscape gardening, choral singing, swimming. Office: BioMolecular Products Inc PO Box 929 Byfield MA 01922-0929

YESAWICH, PETER CHARLES, advertising executive; b. Ithaca, N.Y., Oct. 28, 1950; s. Paul Joseph Jr. and Elizabeth (Larkin) Y.; m. Paris Pyne; children: Peter Charles, Paul Christopher, Logan Baker. BS, Cornell U., 1972, MS, 1974, PhD, 1976; AMP, Yale U., 1994. Dir. rsch. Robinsons, Inc., Orlando, Fla., 1976-78, v.p., 1978-81, exec. v.p., 1981-83; pres., CEO Yesawich, Pepperdine & Brown, Orlando, 1983—. Vis. assoc. prof. Cornell U., Ithaca, 1977—, U. Ctrl. Fla., Orlando, 1988—; chmn. Pope Tourism Inst., Orlando, 1988-90. Contbr. articles to profl. jours. Recipient World Travel award Am. Assn. Travel Editors, 1985, Silver Medal award Am. Assn. Advt. Agys., 1992, Adrian award Hospitality Sales and Mktg. Assn. Internat., 1993; named Author of Yr. Cornell Quar., 1986. Mem. Cornell Hotel Soc., Am. Hotel & Motel Assn., Caribbean Hotel Assn., Hotel Sales Mktg. Assn., Am. Mktg. Assn. Avocations: jogging, writing. Office: Yesawich Pepperdine & Brown 423 S Keller Rd # 100 Orlando FL 32810-6102 Office Phone: 407-875-1111. E-mail: peter-yesawich@ypbr.com.

YESSIN, GERSON, musician, educator; b. Malden, Mass., Jan. 25, 1929; s. David and Ada Yessin; m. Anne B. Baker, Dec. 18, 1971; children: Thomas Edwin Ewart, Nancy Anne Shockey, Richard Lee Ewart, Gary Richard. BS, Juilliard Sch. Music, N.Y.C., 1950—53, MS, 1954—55; MusD, Fla. State U., Tallahassee, 1963—65. Cert. piano tchr. Fla. State Music Teachers Assn., 1960. Music dept. founding chair and prof. Jacksonville U., Jacksonville, Fla., 1958—71; music dept. founding chair and prof., 1971-1998, U. of North Fla., Jacksonville, Fla.; instr. Rollins Coll., Winter Pk, Fla., 1955—58; dir. Steinway Sch. of Piano, Jacksonville, Fla., 2003—. Pres. Fla. State Music Teachers Assn., 1960—62. Musician: (music recording) Bartok Sonata with Leopold Stokowsky, 2004, Premiers: Concerto by Chase, Concertino by Firestone, Concerto No. 4 by Villa-Lobos. Bd. mem. Jacksonville Symphony, Fla., 1964—70, Jacksonville Art Mus., Fla., Fla. Sch. Arts, Fla. Grantee, Fla. Arts Coun., 1958—59, Fla. Dept. State, 1962—63, Nat. Endowment for the Humanities, 1974—75. Mem.: Music Tchrs. Nat. Assn. Home: 693 Ponte Vedra Blvd #102 Ponte Vedra Beach FL 32082

YESSMAN, TIMOTHY, insurance company executive; b. 1959; Bachelor's Degree, Seton Hall U.; JD, Villanova U. Joined Travelers Ins., 1984, sr. v.p. spl. liability group, 1997—2001; exec. v.p. claims St. Paul Co., Inc., 2001—. Office: St Paul Cos Inc 385 Washington St Saint Paul MN 55102

YETERIAN, EDWARD HARRY, psychologist, educator, administrator; b. New Britain, Conn., Mar. 5, 1948; s. Arthur and Mary Yeterian; m. Margaret Emily Wellock, Sept. 13, 1975; children— Robert, Julie. BS, Trinity Coll., 1970; MA, U. Conn., 1974, PhD, 1975. Rsch. fellow Harvard Med. Sch., Boston, 1975-78, postdoctoral fellow, 1975-78; cons. Maine State Bur. Mental Retardation, Augusta, 1982—88; v.p. for acad. affairs, dean of faculty, dept. psychology Colby Coll., Waterville, Maine. Author book chpts.; contbr. articles to profl. jours. Mem. bd. fellows Trinity Coll., Hartford, Conn., 1986—93. NIMH fellow, 1977-78. Mem. Soc. for Neurosci., Eastern Psychol. Assn., Nat. Assn. for Armenian Studies and Rsch. Avocations: automobile repair and rebuilding; short-wave radio. Home: 86 Lake Ridge Dr Sidney ME 04330-2103 Office: VP Acad Affairs Dept Psychology Colby Coll Waterville ME 04901

YETMAN, GARY, investment company executive; Pres., COO Wagner Stott Clearing Corp., N.Y.C.; pres., CEO Merril Lynch Clearing Corp., New York, 1997—. Office: Merrill Lynch Pro 222 Broadway 6 New York NY 10038-2510

YETMAN, LEITH ELEANOR, academic administrator; b. Kellits, Clarendon, Jamaica, West Indies; came to U.S., 1967; d. 2nd child of 12 children of Percival Augustus and Grace Elizabeth (Anderson) Y.; m. Noel W. Miller, Apr.

8, 1961 (div. 1977); children: Donovan, Jo-Ann, Kirk, Lori-Anne; adopted children: LaFara, Samantha, Brandon Ryan. Attended, Bethlehem Teachers Coll., St. Elizabeth, Jamaica, 1960; BSC, Baruch Coll., 1976; MA, Columbia U., 1979. Cert. tchr., N.Y.; accredited Grace Inst. Bus. Tech., Bklyn., 1998. Legal sec. various law firms, N.Y.C., 1969-76; instr. Taylor Bus. Inst., N.Y.C., 1977-79; founder, pres., dir. N.Y. Inst. English and Bus. (formerly N.Y. Inst. Bus. Tech., N.Y.C., 1981—; founder Grace Inst. Bus. Tech., Bklyn., 1996. Founder Grace Inst. Bus. Tech., Bklyn., 1996. Recipient Outstanding Achievement award Baruch Coll. Alumni Assn., 1989, Outstanding Achievement award Baruch Coll. Alumni Assn., citations Hon. Virginia Fields, Gov. N.Y. State, Hon. George E. Pataki, letters of recognition and praise Ex-First Ladies Barbara Bush, Hillary Clinton, Ex-Pres. Bill Clinton, Senator Charles Rangel, Ex-Mayor David Dinkins, others; Leith E. Yetman Day proclaimed June 1, 1994 by Manhattan Borough Pres. Office: NY Inst English and Bus 248 W 35th St New York NY 10001 Office Phone: 212-725-9400. Personal E-mail: myiebo2@aol.com.

YETT, SALLY PUGH, elementary school educator, gifted and talented educator; b. St. Louis, Feb. 15, 1935; d. John D. and Esther Ruth Pugh; m. Donald Edward Yett, June 19, 1964; children: Stephen Edward, John Harold. BFA, Washington U., St. Louis, 1956; tchg. credential, Calif. State U., L.A., 1989. Cert. gen. clear multiple subject and art supplementary Calif. Dept. Edn. Recreation therapist ARC, San Antonio, 1956-58; dir. recreation therapy dept. Jewish Hosp., St. Louis, 1958-64; tchr. art-gifted class Juan Cabrillo Elem., Malibu, Calif., 1975-78; educator pre-kindergarten Malibu Meth. Pre-Sch., 1979-81; educator grades 9-12 Santa Monica (Calif.) Sch. Dist., 1981-89; spl. edn. educator grades 1-6 art L.A. Unified Sch. Dist.-Visual and Performing Arts Magnet, 1990—; resource tchr., art edn. advisor Calif. State U., L.A., 2001—, master tchr. Dominguez Hills, 2003—. Judge Making History, L.A., 1998—; participant UCLA Tchrs. and Scholars Symposium, 1999—2003; cons. edn. dept. Calif. State U., L.A.; state judge History Day in Calif., 2003. Exhibitions include Malibu Art Festival, 1976 (3rd place award), Malibu Art Assn. Show, 1984 (3rd place award), Roberts Art Gallery, 1989, CAEA State Conv.-Calif. State Bakersfield Exhibit, 2001; contbr. articles to profl. jours. PTA pres. Juan Cabrillo Elem., Malibu, 1976—78, Malibu Park Jr. HS; pres. Santa Monica Jr. Programs, 1979—81; 2d, 3d, and 4th v.p. Santa Monica/Malibu PTA Coun., 1982—85; pres. Malibu Art Assn., 1992—93. Nominee Tchr. of Yr., Walt Disney Co., Barbie Doll Art Educator of Yr., 2004; recipient Honoree Bravo award, L.A. Music Ctr.; grantee, Calif. Cmty. Found., 2003. Mem.: Internat. Studies Overseas Program, East West Players Orgn., Calif. Alliance Arts Edn., Ams. for the Arts, Smithsonian Inst., Huntington Mus., Gene Autrey Mus., Nat. Mus. Women, Mus. Natural History, Calif. Art Edn. Assn., Calif. Coun. Social Studies, Soc. Calligraphy (bd. dirs., pub. rels. 1987—91), Tchrs. and Writers Collaborative, Nat. Art Edn. Assn., L.A. Conservancy, Pacific Asia Mus., Craft and Folk Mus., UCLA Fowler Mus. Cultural History, L.A. County Art Mus., S.W. Mus., Mus. Contemporary Art, Shakespeare Festival/L.A., Metro. Mus. Art, People to People Internat. (Indigenous Art del. to New Zealand, Australia 1998), Art Mus. Long Beach, Smithsonian Nat. Mus. Am. Indian, Mus. L.Am. Art, UCLA Book Club, Kappa Alpha Theta. Avocations: travel, reading, calligraphy, hiking, gardening. Home: 2042 Hanscom Dr South Pasadena CA 91030-4012

YETTER, R. PAUL, lawyer; b. Milw., Aug. 5, 1958; s. Richard and Lobelia (Gutierrez) Y.; m. Patricia D. Yetter, May 6, 1983; children: Chris, Mark, Michael, Joseph, Thomas, Andrew, Daniel. BA, U. Tex., El Paso, 1980; JD, Columbia U., 1983. Bar: Tex. 1983, U.S. Dist. Ct. (so., ea., no. and we. dists.) Tex., U.S. Ct. Appeals (5th cir.); bd. cert. in civil trial law and personal injury trial law Tex. Bd. Legal Specialization. Law clk. to Hon. John R. Brown U.S. Ct. Appeals (5th cir.), Houston, 1983-84; assoc. Baker & Botts, L.L.P., Houston, 1984-89, ptnr., 1990-97; name ptnr. Yetter & Warden, L.L.P., Houston, 1997—. Chair state judiciary rels. com. State Bar, 1995-96; mem. Funding Parity Task Force, 1995-97; mem. ex officio Jud. Selection Task Force, 1995-97; chair Alliance for Jud. Funding, Inc., 1996—; mem. ex officio contbns. com. Tex. Ctr. for the Judiciary, mem. com. on admissions, So. Dist., Tex., 2000—. Contbr. articles to profl. jours. Recipient Presdl. citation State Bar Tex., 1996; Southwestern Legal Found. rsch. fellow. Fellow Tex. Bar Foun., Houston Bar Found. Office: Yetter & Warden LLP 909 Fannin Ste 3600 Houston TX 77010- Office Phone: 713-632-8000. E-mail: pyetter@yetterwarden.com.

YEUN, PAUL LORENZO, minister; b. Hong Kong, Apr. 14, 1944; came to U.S., 1960; s. Kaki Yeun and Carmen (Flores) Pio; m. Elisabeth Wendy Chan, June 19, 1971; children: Evangeline, Abigail. BA, Azusa Pacific U., 1968; MDiv, Asbury Sem., 1971, MA, 1974; DMin, Lexington Sem., 1977. Ordained to ministry Meth. Ch., 1973; cert. marriage and family therapist; lic. profl. counselor; cert. profl. mental health clergy. Parish pastor Aberdeen (Ohio) United Meth. Ch., 1971-72, Morrow (Ohio) United Meth. Ch., 1972-76, Albany (Ohio) United Meth. Ch., 1976-78, Oakland Park United Meth. Ch., Columbus, Ohio, 1978-81; group chaplain USAF, Rickenbacker AFB, Ohio, 1980-81, protestant chaplain George Air Force Base, Calif., 1981-84, installation chaplain Clark Air Base, Philippines, 1984-87; sr. protestant chaplain USAF, Davis Monthan AFB, Tucson, 1987—. Counselor Pastoral Counseling Ctr., Columbus, 1979-81; advisor Asian Pacific Fellowship, Tucson, 1987—; chair ch. and soc. South Dist. United Meth. Ch., Tucson, 1989-90; bd. dirs. Ariz. Marriage and Family Therapy, Tucson Met. Ministries. Author: Dealing with the Psychological needs of Aged, 1985, Meaning of our Membership Vows, 1987. Mem. Task Force in Credentialing, State of Ariz., 1989—. Lt. col. USAF, 1980—. Decorated Air Force Commendation medal, Air Force Meritorious Svc. medal with 4 oak leaf clusters; recipient award Air Force Best Sermons, 1985, Man of Achievement award; named to Ky. Cols. Mem. Am. Assn. Marriage and Family Therapy (clin.), Internt. Acad. Behavior, Medicine and Psychotherapy (diplomate), Asian Pacific Fellowship, Tucson Chaplain Assn. (steering com. 1987-90), Lions. Democrat. Office: 128 Buckingham Chambersburg PA 17201 Office Phone: 717-267-7749. Business E-Mail: pyeun@summithealth.org. *Authentic preaching is telling the stories of Jesus and His love the best we can with the expectation that those who heard may enter a loving relationship with God.*

YEUNG, EDWARD SZESHING, chemist; b. Hong Kong, Feb. 17, 1948; arrived in U.S., 1965; s. King Mai Luk and Yu Long Yeung; m. Anna Kunkwok Seto, Sept. 18, 1971; children: Rebecca Tze-Mai, Amanda Tze-Wen AB magna cum laude, Cornell U., 1968; PhD, U. Calif., Berkeley, 1972. Instr. chemistry Iowa State U., Ames, 1972-74, asst prof., 1974-77, assoc. prof, 1977-81, prof. chemistry, 1981-89, disting. prof., 1989—. Contbr. articles to profl. jours. Alfred P. Sloan fellow, 1974-76; recipient Am. Chem Soc. award in Analytical Chemistry, 1994. Fellow AAAS; mem. Soc. Applied Spectrosci. (Lester Strock award 1990), Am. Chem. Soc. (award in chem. instrumentation 1987, award in analytical chemistry 1994, award in chromatography 2002). Home: 1005 Jarrett Cir Ames IA 50014-3937 Office: Iowa State U Gilman Hall Ames IA 50011

YEUNG, RONALD WAI-CHUN, engineering educator, researcher; s. Foo and Pui Fong Yeung; m. Grace Y. Chow, Sept. 5, 1970; 1 child, Brian H. BSME, U. Calif., Berkeley, 1968; MS in Naval Architecture, U. of Calif., Berkeley, 1970, PhD in Engring., 1973. Naval arch. Advanced Marine Tech. Divsn., Litton Ship Sys., Culver City, Calif., 1970—71; instr. U. Calif. LA extension, Long Beach Naval Shipyard, 1970—71; asst., assoc. prof. MIT, Cambridge, Mass., 1974—82; prof. hydromechanics & ocean engring. U. Calif., Berkeley, 1982—, chair dept naval architecture & offshore engring., 1989—96, prof. disting. rank, 1994—; Humboldt prof. U. Hamburg, Germany, 1988, Mercator U., Duisburg, Germany, 1998—99. Prin. R. W. Yeung - Consulting Naval Architecture & Ocean Engring., Moraga, Calif., 1976—. Editor: Ocean Mechanics, 1999, Jour. Engring. Math.; contbr. articles to profl. jours. Recipient Gold medal, U. Calif., 1968, Disting. Scientist award, Alexander von Humboldt Found., 1988, Best Paper award in Recognition of Outstanding Originality and Significance, ASME, Offshore Mechanics and Arctic Engring., 1991, Georg Weinblum lectr., Naval Studies Bd., Soc. Naval Architecture and Marine Engrs. and Schiffbautechnische Gesellschaft, 2002—03, Best Paper award J.V. Wehausen symposium, ASME, Offshore Mech. and Arctic Engring., 2002, Kenneth Davidson medal Outstanding Sci. Accomplishment Ship Rsch., Soc. Naval Architecture and Marine Engrs. and Schiffbautechnische Gesellschaft, 2004; fellow Elected, Soc. Naval Architects & Marine Engrs., 1998; scholar Fulbright-Hayes Sr. scholar, U. Adelaide, Australian-Am. Edn. Found., 1981. Mem.: Japanese Soc. Naval Architects, Soc. Naval Architects & Marine Engrs. (No. Calif. exec. com. and acad. liaison), Am. Soc. Engring. Edn., Internat. Soc. Offshore and Polar Engrs. (chair hydrodynamics com. 2002—03), Phi Beta Kappa, Pi Tau Sigma, Tau Beta Pi. Home: 27 Indian Wells Moraga CA 94556-1020 Office: U Calif 6135 Etcheverry Hall Berkeley CA 94720-1740 Office Phone: 510-642-8347. E-mail: rwyeung@socrates.berkeley.edu.

YEUNG, WEI-JUN JEAN, research scientist; b. Taiwan, June 10, 1958; d. Chin-ching Lee and Show-Yu Hong; m. Bernard Yeung; children: Michael B., Anne M. PhD, U. of Alta., Can., 1991. Rsch. scientist U. of Mich., Ann Arbor, 1989—2001; sr. rsch. scientist NYU, N.Y.C., 2001—. Author: (book chpt.) Fathers As Potential Resource for Children's School Success, in Conley & Albright (Eds.) After the Bell: Solutions Outside the School. London, Routledge Press.; co-author (with M. Linver and J. Brooks-Gunn): (jour. article) How Money Matters for Young Childrens' Development: Parental Investment and Family Process, 2002; contbr. articles to profl. jours. Recipient Contemporary Am. Fathers' Involvement with Their Children grant, Nat. Inst. of Child Health and Human Devel., Nat. Inst. of Health, 2000, Wealth, Health, and Racial Disparity grant, 2003, The Panel Study of Income Dynamics ? Waves 30, 31 and 32 grant, NSF, 1997—2001, Responses of Baby-boomers to the Health Care Needs of Their Elderly Parents grant, Nat. Inst. of Aging, 2001, Long-Term Trends in Child Poverty and Welfare Receipt grant, NSF. Mem.: Am. Sociol. Assn. Achievements include research in Intergenerational transfers on children's achievement, teaching in sociology of the family. Office: NYU Dept Sociology 269 Mercer St New York NY 10012 Office Phone: 212-998-8381. E-mail: jean.yeung@nyu.edu.

YEVICK, GEORGE JOHANNUS, scientist; b. Berwick, Pa., May 8, 1922; s. John and Theresa Yevick; m. Miriam Amalia Lipschutz-Yevick, May 15, 1945; 1 child, David Owen. BS, Mass. Inst. Tech., Cambridge, 1942; PhD, Mass. Inst. Tech., 1947. Prof. physics Stevens Inst. Tech., Hoboken, NJ, 1947—92. Lectr. Lucent Corp., 1997-2001; founder, prin. investigator Personal Comms., Stanford, Conn., 1979-87. Contbr. articles to sci. jours.; patentee in field. Primary candidate of congress Dem. Party, Bergen County, N.J., 1964. Rsch. grantee U.S. Govt. Achievements include discovery of (with Jerome K. Percus) P.Y. equation, fundamental to the theory of liquids. Avocations: sculpture, painting, mosaic work. Home: 22 Pelham St Princeton NJ 08540-5315 Office: Stevens Inst Tech Hoboken NJ 07030 Office Phone: 201-216-5665. E-mail: gandonyevick@rcn.com.

YGLESIAS, HELEN BASSINE, author, educator; b. N.Y.C., Mar. 29, 1915; d. Solomon and Kate (Goldstein) Bassine; m. Bernard Cole, 1938 (div. 1950); children: Tamar Cole, Lewis Cole; m. Jose Yglesias, Aug. 19, 1950 (div. 1992); 1 child, Rafael. Student pub. schs.; LHD (hon.), U. Maine, 1996. Literary editor Nation Mag., 1965-70; adj. assoc. prof. writing Columbia Sch. Arts, N.Y.C., 1973—. Vis. prof. creative writing Writers Workshop, U. Iowa, Iowa City, 1980. Author: (novels) How She Died (Houghton Mifflin award), 1972, Family Feeling, 1976, Sweetsir, 1981, The Saviors, 1987, The Girls, 1999, (non-fiction) Starting: Early, Anew, Over and Late, 1978, Isabel Bishop, 1989. Home: Apt 1303 1261 5th Ave New York NY 10029-3866

YGLESIAS, KENNETH DALE, college president; b. Tampa, Fla. s. Jose and Julia Yglesias; m. Donna Carmen Belli, Nov., 1977. BA, U. South Fla., 1969; MA, Western Carolina U., 1973; EdD, U. So. Calif., 1977. Cert. tchr., Calif., Fla. Tchr., coach pub. schs., Tampa, 1969-73; tchr., dept. chmn. Am. Sch. Madrid, 1973-76; fgn. svc. officer USIA, Washington and Tel Aviv, 1977-79; assoc. prof. Pepperdine U., L.A., 1979-83; prof., dir. El Camino Coll., Torrance, Calif., 1981-83; adminstrv. dean Coastline Coll., Fountain Valley, Calif., 1983-88; v.p. Coast C.C. Dist., Costa Mesa, Calif., 1988-95; pres. Golden West Coll., Huntington Beach, Calif., 1995—2004; chancellor Coast Cmty. Coll. Dist., Costa Mesa, Calif., 2004—. Contbr. articles to profl. jours. Bd. dirs. C.C.'s for Internat. Devel., 1988-94, Orange County Marine Inst., Costa Mesa, 1990-93, United Way Orange County, Santa Ana, Calif., 1991-94. Mem. Am. Assn. for Higher Edn. (Hispanic caucus), Assn. Calif. C.C. Adminstrs., Phi Delta Kappa. Democrat. Roman Catholic. Avocations: basketball fan, walking. Office: Golden West Coll PO Box 2748 Huntington Beach CA 92647-0748

YGLESIAS, RAFAEL JOSE, novelist; b. N.Y.C., May 12, 1954; s. Jose and Helen (Bassine) Y.; m. Margaret Joskow, Oct. 15, 1977; children: Matthew, Nicholas. Author: Dr. Neruda's Cure for Evil, 1996, The Murderer Next Door, 1990, Only Children, 1988; screenwriter, author (film) Fearless, 1993; screenwriter (films) Death and the Maiden, 1995, Les Miserables, 1998, From Hell, 2001. Mem. The Author's Guild, Writer's Guild of Am., Acad. Motion Picture Arts and Scis.

YGUADO, ALEX ROCCO, economics professor; b. Lackawanna, N.Y., Jan. 17, 1939; s. Manuel and Rose (Barrillio) Y.; m. Patricia Ann Rieker; children: Gary Alexander, Melissa Rose, Charissa Ann. BA, San Fernando State Coll., Northridge, 1968; MA, Calif. State U., Northridge, 1970; MS, U. So. Calif., 1972. Contractor, L.A., 1962-69; instr. Calif. Poly. State U., San Luis Obispo, 1969-70, U. So. Calif., L.A., 1970-74; prof. econs. L.A. Mission Coll., San Fernando, Calif., 1975—, acad. senate pres., 1992-93, cluster chair profl. studies, 1993-2001, dean acad. affairs, 2001—. Cons. Community Service Orgn., Los Angeles, 1969-71. Author: Principles of Economics, 1978; contbr. chpts. in books. Served with U.S. Army, 1957-60. Recipient: Blue Ribbon landscape design City of Albuquerque, 1962, Cert. Appreciation Los Angeles Mission Coll., 1978; Fulbright scholar, 1986-87. Mem. Calif. Small Bus. Assn. Clubs: Newman (Los Angeles), Sierra Retreat (Malibu, sponsor). Democrat. Roman Catholic. Avocations: gardening, skiing, photography. Home: 25323 Oak Ridge Dr Santa Clarita CA 91350-3300 Office: LA Mission Coll 13356 Eldridge Ave Sylmar CA 91342-3200 Office Phone: 818-364-7624. Business E-Mail: yguadoar@laccd.edu.

YI, TAEIL, mathematician, educator; b. Seoul, South Korea, Dec. 16, 1962; s. Beomyoung and Bongwol Yi; m. Moonsil Kim, Nov. 20, 1962; children: Hanyong David, Changyong Peter. BS, Dankook U., Seoul, 1988, MS, 1990, U. Ill., 1994; MEd, U. Fla., 1997, PhD, 2000. Math. tchr. Yongmoon H.S., Seoul, 1988—90; instr. U. Fla., Gainesville, 2000—01; asst. prof. U. Tex., Brownsville, 2001—. Advisor math. honor club U. Tex., Brownsville, 2002—. Prodr.: (instructional video) Name That Move (Jim Harbin Award / Fla. Assn. for Media in Edn., 1995); contbr. articles to profl. jours. Condr. choir Korean Ch., Urbana/Champaign, Ill., 1993—94; chief editor Korean Bapt. Ch., Gainesville, Fla., 1996—2001, dir. gen. affair, 1997—2000; leader youth group Open Door Ch., Brownsville, Tex., 2001, sec. bd., 2002. Recipient Jim Harbin award, Fla. Assn. Media Edn., 1995. Mem.: Soc. Indsl. and Applied Math., Math. Assn. Am., Am. Math. Soc., Phi Kappa Phi (life). Achievements include development of an automated stereotactic radiosurgery algorithm for brain tumor treatment planning, which has been developed by a software company for broad usage. Avocations: golf, studying theology. Home: 5 Deer Haven Ct Brownsville TX 78520 Office: Univ Tex Brownsville 80 Fort Brown Brownsville TX 78520 Office Phone: 956-574-6621. Personal E-mail: tyi@utb.edu.

YIELDING, K. LEMONE, physician; b. Auburn, Ala., Mar. 25, 1931; s. Riley Lafayette and Bertie (Dees) Y.; m. Lerena Wade Hauge, Dec. 7, 1973; children: K. Lemone, Michael Lafon, Teresa Louise, Riley Lafayette, Katrina Elizabeth, Elaine Louise Blodgett, Laura Carlen Blodgett. BS, Ala. Poly. Inst., 1949; MS, U. Ala., 1952, MD, 1954. Intern U. Ala. Med. Center, 1954-55; clin. assoc. Nat. Inst. Arthritis and Metabolic Diseases, NIH, 1955-57, sr. investigator, 1958-64; resident med. service USPHS Hosp., Balt., 1957-58; physician in practice of oncology and emergency medicine, 1995—. Adj. asst. prof. medicine Georgetown U. Med. Sch., 1958-64; cons. USPHS, 1964-68, 75—; prof. biochemistry, assoc. prof. medicine, chief lab. molecular biology U. Ala. Med. Ctr., Birmingham, 1964-80; prof., chmn. dept. anatomy, prof. medicine U. So. Ala. Coll. Medicine, Mobile, 1980-87; dean grad. sch. U. Tex. Med. Br., Galveston, 1987-95, dean emeritus, 1995—; cons. Am. Heart Assn., Arthritis Found., NIH, NASA. Contbr. to profl. jours., books. Served with USPHS, 1955-64. Grantee USPHS, Am. Cancer Soc., Nat. Found.-March of Dimes, U.S. Army, Am. Inst. Cancer Research. Mem. Am. Soc. Biol. Chemistry, Am. Assn. Cancer Research, Am. Assn. Photobiology, Assn. Research Vision and Ophthalmology, Soc. Exptl. Biology and Medicine, Am. Soc. Pharm. and Exptl. Therapeutics, Am. Assn. Pathologists, So. Soc. Clin. Investigation, Am. Assn. Anatomy, Soc. Toxicology, Sigma Xi. E-mail: yielding@hiwaay.net.

YIGIT, NUYAN, journalist; b. Istanbul, Turkey, Oct. 25, 1927; s. Ibrahim Sureyya and Ayse (Mediha) Y.; m. Fatos, July 2, 1958; children: Ipek, Ibrahim Sureyya. BA in Arts and Philosophy, Robert Coll., 1948; postgrad., Istanbul U., 1951, Columbia U., 1961. Cub reporter, editor Cumhuriyet newspaper, Istanbul, 1948-60; asst. bur. chief Time and Life, Istanbul, 1957-59; dep. gen. mgr. Hurriyet News Agy., Istanbul, 1963; Istanbul corr. Reuters, 1965-70; London bur. chief Hurriyet newspaper, London, 1970-83; gen. mgr. Gunaydin Newspaper Group, Istanbul, 1983-90. Freelance journalist, Istanbul, 1996—. Author travelog, 1995, short stories, 1996. Candidate for Turkish Parliament, Dem. Party, Istanbul, 1991. 1st lt. Turkish Cavalry, 1952-54. Moslem. Avocations: sports writing and commenting, rowing, reading. Home: 437 Golden Isles Dr Hallandale FL 33009

YIH, MAE DUNN, state legislator; b. Shanghai, May 24, 1928; d. Chung Woo and Fung Wen (Feng) Dunn; m. Stephen W.H. Yih, 1953; children: Donald, Daniel. BA, Barnard Coll., 1951; postgrad., Columbia U., 1951-52. Asst. to bursar Barnard Coll., N.Y.C., 1952-54; mem. Oreg. Ho. Reps. from 36th dist., 1977-83, Oreg. Senate from 19th dist., 1983—. Mem. Clover Ridge Elem. Sch. Bd., Albany, Oreg., 1969-78, Albany Union H.S. Bd., 1975-79; mem. Joint Legis. Ways and Means Com., Senate Transp. Com., 1999, Senate pres. pro-temore, 1993. Episcopalian. Home: 34465 Yih Ln NE Albany OR 97321-9557 Office: Oreg Senate S 307 State Capitol Salem OR 97310-0001

YIN, GERALD ZHEYAO, technology and business executive; b. Beijing, Jan. 29, 1944; arrived in U.S., 1980; s. Huaixin and Halumi Yin; m. Elizabeth Yi; children: John Chengjiang, Christina. BS in Chem. Physics, U. Sci. and Tech. China, Beijing, 1967; postgrad., Beijing U., 1978-80; PhD in Chemistry, UCLA, 1984. Process engr. Lanzhou Oil Refinery, Lanzhou, People's Republic of China, 1968-73; mgr. rsch. staff Chinese Acad. Scis., Lanzhou, 1973-78; sr. process engr. Intel Corp. Santa Clara TD, Santa Clara, Calif., 1984-86; mgr., staff engr. R & D, Lam Rsch. Corp., Fremont, Calif., 1986-91; mng. dir. Etch New Product, Santa Clara, Calif., 1991—; chief tech. officer, gen. mgr. Etch Product Bus. Group; chief tech. officer, head Asia Sourcing and Procurement Applied Materials Asia, 1991—; v.p. Applied Materials, Inc., Santa Clara, 1996—. Author: Introducing Orthogonal Design to Semiconductor Industry, 1985. Recipient Nat. Acad. award, People's Republic of China, 1979, Nat. Acad. Invention award, 1980. Mem.: Silicon Valley Chinese Engring. Assn. (founder, first pres.), Am. Vacuum Soc., Am. Chem. Soc., Electrochem. Soc. Achievements include invention of Rainbow oxide etcher; 200 mm enhanced Electron Cyclotron Resonance reactor; High Density plasma source for Dielectric Etch; Decoupled Plasma Source and reactors for Conductor Etches; patents for 63 U.S. and foreign patents.

YIN, ZHIPING, engineer; m. Yongsheng Ma; children: Lina, Vincent. BS in Semicondr. Physics, Lanzhou U., China, 1982, MS in Semicondr. Physics, 1985; PhD in Physics, CUNY, 1991. Lectr. physics dept. Lanzhou U., 1985; scientist Solar Physics, L.I., 1991—92; rsch. fellow Nanyang Technol. U., Singapore, 1992—95; rsch. assoc. CCNY, N.Y.C., 1995—96; fellow Micron Tech., Inc., Boise, 1996—. Contbr. more than 20 sci. papers to profl. jours. Achievements include more than 30 patents in field. Avocations: badminton, music, travel, movies, playing with children. E-mail: zyin@micron.com.

YING, JACKIE, chemical engineer, educator; Prof. MIT, Cambridge, 1992—. Exec. dir. Inst. Bioengring. and Nanotech., Singapore, 2003—. Mem. editl. bd. Jour. Metastable and Nanostructured Materials, Nanoparticle Sci. and Tech., Jour. Electroceramics, Jour. Porous Materials, Materials Today, Molecular and Supramolecular Sci. Recipient Camille Dreyfus Tchr.-Scholar award, 1996, Exxon Solid-State Chemistry Fellowship award Am. Chem. Soc., 1997, Colburn award AIChE, 2000, TR100 Innovator award, 2000; David and Lucile Packard fellow, 1995. Business E-Mail: jyying@mit.edu.

YINGLING, GERALD PHILLIP, business executive; b. Pitts., Mar. 8, 1952; s. Roy Phillip and Mary Elvira (Lawall) Y.; 1 child, Jonathan Eric. BA, Calif. State U., San Francisco, 1977; cert. grad. rsch., Oita Nat. U., Japan, 1978-80. Asst. v.p. Denny's Internat., Inc., LaMirada, Calif., 1980-83; mgr. bus. devel., Asia-Pacific region Visa Internat., Tokyo, 1983-86; mng. dir. Asia-Pacific devel. State of Ga., Dept. Industry and Trade, Atlanta, 1986—; prin., owner Ga'ga Inc., Guam. Exec. mgr. Guam Internat. Airport Authority. Mem. cabinet Gov. Carl T.C. Gutierrez, Guam. With USMC, 1969-71. Mem. Ga. Indsl. Developers, Red Cross of Constantine, Masons. Methodist. Avocations: scuba diving, golf, hiking. Home: PO Box 12788 420 Farenholt Ave Tamuning GU 96913-3103

YINGLING, JOHN A. military officer; b. Alexandria, Va. BA, Wake Forest U., 1975. Commd. U.S. Army, 1974, advanced through grades to brig. gen.; firing platoon comdr. Weapons Support Detachment, 3d Bn., 81st Field Artillery; from battery exec. officer to comdr. A Battery, 3d Bn., 6th Field Artillery U.S. Army, comdr. C Battery, 1st Bn., 76th Field Artillery, bn. ops. officer; field artillery assignment officer Mil. Pers. Ctr., 1984—86; 1st corps officer ps. mgr., fire support officer 1st Brigade, 9th Inf. Divsn., Ft. Lewis, 1987—91; staff officer Joint Staff, Nat. Mil. Command Systems, Pentagon, 1991—93; comdr. 7th Bn., 8th Field Artillery, Red Dragons, 25th Inf. Divsn., 1993—95, 3d Inf. Divsn. Artillery, 1996—98; dir. Fire Support and Combined Ops. Dept., Ft. Sill, 1998—99; asst. divsn. comdr. 2d Inf. Divsn., 1999; chief of staff USAR Command, Ft. McPherson, Ga.; comdr. Joint Task Force, 2002—04. Decorated Legion of Merit with one oak leaf cluster, Meritorious Svc. medal with 4 oak leaf clusters, Joint Commendation medal, Army Commendation medal with 2 oak leaf clusters, many others. Office: Joint Task Force Bldg 11603 Fort Bliss TX 79918

YIOTIS, GAYLE, archivist, researcher, anthropologist, writer; d. Pedro and Margarette Rionda; m. Christos Fotios Yiotis; children: Fotios Christos, Peter Wesley. MA, George Washington U., Washington, 1992. Mus. specialist anthropology Smithsonian Instn., Washington, 1995—2003, archivist Nat. Mus. of Am. Indian, 2003—. Presenter Soc. for the Preservaton of Natural History Collections, 1999; alumni, network vol., Marquette U., Milw., 2000—, student career alumni network, 2000—. Contbr. articles to profl. jours. Mem.: Soc. of Am. Archivists. Avocations: historical research, writing, martial arts, collecting.

YIP, WINNIE, health economics educator; arrived in U.S., 1984; BA, U. Calif., Berkeley, 1988; PhD, MIT, 1994. Asst. prof. econs., Sch. Pub. Health Harvard U., Cambridge, Mass., 1994—2001, assoc. prof. internat. health econs., Sch. Pub. Health, 2001—. Cons. World Bank, Washington, 1995—96, Washington, 1999—2000, Govt. Hong Kong, 1997—99. Mem.: Internat. Health Econs. Assn., Am. Econ. Assn., Phi Beta Kappa. Office: Harvard Sch Pub Health 124 Mt Auburn St Ste 410 S Cambridge MA 02138 E-mail: wyip@hsph.harvard.edu.

YIP-SCHNEIDER, MICHELE TERRELL, researcher; b. Oakland, Calif., Nov. 19, 1960; d. Lawrence and Ruth Yip; m. Brian Mark Schneider, Nov. 10, 1990; children: Emma Rose Schneider, Justine Grace Schneider. BS, U. of Calif., Berkeley, 1982; PhD, U. of Calif., Davis, 1988. Postdoctoral fellow U. of Calif., LA, 1988—90, Ind. U. Sch. of Medicine, Indpls., 1991—97, rsch. assoc., 1997—2001, asst. scientist, 2001—. Author: (jour. pub.) Jour. of Pharmacology and Exptl. Therapeutics, Biochemistry Jour., Internat. Jour. of Oncology. Recipient Nat. Rsch. award, NIH, 1984—86; grantee Rsch. funding, Ctrl. Surg. Assn. Found., 2002—03; Grad. Opportunity Fellowship, U. of Calif., Davis, 1982—84, Cancer Rsch. Coordinating Com. Grant, U. of Calif., 1990—91. Mem.: Am. Gastroent. Assn., Am. Assn. for Cancer Rsch. (assoc.), Phi Beta Kappa. Achievements include patents pending for Use of

nonsteroidal anti-inflammatory drugs for the treatment of pancreatic cancer. Office: Ind Univ Sch of Medicine 1044 W Walnut St Building R4 Rm 041 Indianapolis IN 46202 E-mail: myipschn@iupui.edu.

YIU, FANG, structural engineer, researcher; b. Shanghai, Apr. 21, 1972; d. Boxian Yiu and Jingfang Hua. BS, Shanghai Inst. Ry. Tech., 1993; MS, Tongji U., Shanghai, 1995; PhD, Cornell U., 2003. Cost evaluation cert., cert. fundamental engr. Structural engr. Shanghai Posts & Telecoms. Design Inst., 1993-95; rsch. asst. dept. civil and environ. engring. Cornell U., Ithaca, NY, 1998—2002; sr. staff tech. profl. Mustang Engring., L.P., 2002—. Asst. engring. mgr. Shanghai Designing INst. Telecomms., Shanghai, 1993—95; peer advisor dept. civil and environ. engring. Cornell U., Ithaca, 1999—2000, engring. grad. student assn. rep., 2000—02. Referee: for profl. jours. Mem. civil engring. del. People to People Amb., Spokane, Wash., 2000—; treas. Chinese Students and Scholars Assn., Ithaca, 1998—99. Mem.: ASCE, Soc. Woman Engrs., Earthquake Engring. Rsch. Inst. (treas. 2000—). Mailing: Apt 714 Timber Creek Pl Dr Houston TX 77084 Office: 16001 Park Ten Pl Houston TX 77084 E-mail: fy16@cornell.edu.

YIZHONG, LI, business executive; Grad., Beijing Petroleum Inst., 1966. Various mgmt. and sr. engr. positions; pres Qilu Petrochem. Co., 1985-87; v.p. then mng. v.p. Old Sinopec, 1987-97; chmn., pres. China East United Petrochem. Group Ltd., 1997-98; chmn. Yizheng Chem. Fiber Co. Ltd.; pres. Sinopec Group Co., Beijing, 1998—2000, chmn, 2000—. Office: Sinopec Corp A6 Huixindong St Beijing China

YNDA, MARY LOU, artist, educator; b. Los Angeles, Apr. 4, 1936; d. Ernest Pastor Ynda and Mary Estella (Ruiz) Zapotocky, m. Gary Lynn Coleman, Sept. 1, 1956 (div. Feb. 1983); children: Debra Lynn, Lisa Annette, David Gary; m. Miles Ciletti, May 25, 1991. Student, Immaculate Heart Coll., Los Angeles, 1973-79; AA in Fine Arts, Los Angeles City Coll., 1976; BA, Calif. State U., L.A., 1993. Instr. Fashion Inst. Design, L.A., 1980-81; tchr. art to disabled First St. Gallery, Claremont, Calif., 1991-94; tchr. art Tierra Del Sol Found., Sunland, Calif., 1995-96. Exhibited in group shows at Double Rocking G Gallery, L.A., 1983, Improv Theater West, West Hollywood, Calif., 1983, Exposition Gallery Calif. State U., L.A., 1983, L.A. Art Core Gallery, 1985, Poly. Tech. Sch., Pasadena, Calif., 1986, Bad Eye Gallery, L.A., 1987, Art in the Hall VI West Hollywood City Hall, 1989, Echo Park Gallery, L.A., 1991, Art N Barbee Gallery, 1992, A Celebration of City Life, 1993, DADA Show Downtown Lives, L.A., 1994, 96, Spirit Exhbn. for Women's Caucus for Art, Santa Ana, Calif., 1995; designer Spoken Word CD Long Days and Monster Nights, 1994; contbg. author poetry Spoken Word Voices of the Angels, 1982; book rev. Yesterday and Tomorrow: California Women Artists, 1989. Archetypes and Contemporary Images in The Hispanic World. The City of Lancaster Mus./Art Gallery, Lancaster Calif. Mem. Women's Caucus for Art. Democrat. Avocations: mask making, fetish art, study of animal behavior.

YOAKAM, LYNN KELLY, harpist, educator; b. Little Rock, Ark., July 5, 1957; d. Vance Leonard and Donna Jo (Criner) Broadaway; m. Robert William Yoakam, Aug. 11, 1979; children: Amy Louise, Ryan William. BA, Harding U, 1979; A in Applied Arts/Music summa cum laude, Harding U., 2004; A in Applied Music summa cum laude, Lansing Cmty. Coll., 2004. Tchr. of arts East Lansing Cmty. Edn., Holt Cmty. Edn., East Lansing, Mich., 1989—95; sec. The Bug Man Pest Control, Mason, 1987—; music tchr. pvt. practice, Mason, Mich., 1990—; tai chi instr. Lansing (Mich.) Cmty. Coll., 2002—. Cert. in Duchess Lace Jusith de Kreijer, Etten Leur, Netherlands, 1999. CD, Shantih-Lost in Time, 1995. Shantih-Winds of Change, 2004. Dist. .ensemble chair CAMTA Capital Area Music Tchr. Assn., Lansing, 2000—; state chmn. non-competitive activities Mich. Music Tchr. Assn., Lansing, 2003—. Master: CAMTA; mem.: CALM Capitol Area Lace Makers, ASTA, MNTA, MMTA. Christian. Office: Ms Yoakam 120 W Sycamore Street Mason MI 48854

YOCAM, DELBERT WAYNE, retired software products company executive; b. Long Beach, Calif., Dec. 24, 1943; s. Royal Delbert and Mary Rose (Gross) Y.; m. Janet McVeigh, June 13, 1965; children— Eric Wayne, Christian Jeremy, Elizabeth Janelle. BA in Bus. Adminstrn., Calif. State U.-Fullerton, 1966; MBA, Calif. State U., Long Beach, 1971. Mktg.-supply changeover coordinator Automotive Assembly div. Ford Motor Co., Dearborn, Mich., 1966-72; prodn. control mgr. Control Data Corp., Hawthorne, Calif., 1972-74; prodn. and material control mgr. Bourns Inc., Riverside, Calif., 1974-76; corp. material mgr. Computer Automation Inc., Irvine, Calif., 1976-78; prodn. planning mgr. central staff Cannon Electric div. ITT, World hdqrs., Santa Ana, Calif., 1978-79; exec. v.p., COO Apple Computer, Inc., Cupertino, Calif., 1979-91; pres., COO, dir. Textronix Inc., Wilsonville, Oreg., 1992-95; chmn., CEO Borland Internat., Inc./Inprise Corp., Scotts Valley, Calif., 1996-2000, ret., 2000. Mem. faculty Cypress Coll., Calif., 1972-79; bd. dirs. Adobe Sys Inc., San Jose, Calif., Softricity, Inc., Boston; vice chmn. Tech. Ctr. Innovation, San Jose, Calif., 1989-90. Mem. Am. Electronics Assn. (nat. bd. dirs. 1988-89), Control Data Corp. Mgmt. Assn. (co-founder 1974), L.A. County Heart Assn. (active 1966). E-mail: yocam@aol.com.

YOCAM, ERIC WAYNE, engineer; b. Garden Grove, Calif., Aug. 23, 1966; s. Delbert Wayne and Janet Yocam; m. Siu Kuen Annie Choi, Nov. 5, 2000. BS in Computer Engring., U. Pacific, Stockton, Calif., 1990; MBA, U. San Diego, 1997; MS in Fin., Seattle U., 2002. Cert. software devel. profl., IEEE-Computer Soc., 2002, project mgmt. profl., PMI, 2002, E-commerce cons., tech. specialist, ICECC, 2002. Mem. of tech. staff Apple Computer/Claris Corp., Santa Clara, Calif., 1991—93, Media Vision Corp., Fremont, Calif., 1993—94; tech. mgr. Ray Dream Corp., Mountain View, Calif., 1994—96, Hewlett-Packard Co., Cupertino, Calif., 1997—97; data ctr. project mgr. Intuit Corp., San Diego, 1998—99; sr. program mgr. Microsoft Corp., Redmond, Wash., 1999—. Grad. fellowship, U. San Diego, 1997. Mem.: Sigma Xi. R-Consevative. Methodist. Avocations: private pilot, scuba diving, golf, skiing, surfing. Home: 210 239th Way SE Sammamish WA 98074-3685

YOCHELSON, ELLIS L(EON), paleontologist; b. Washington, Nov. 14, 1928; s. Morris Wolf and Fannie (Botkin) Y.; m. Sally Witt, June 10, 1950; children: Jeffrey, Abby, Charles. BS, U. Kans., 1949, MS, 1950; PhD, Columbia U., 1955. Paleontologist U.S. Geol. Survey, 1952-85, scientist emeritus, 1991—; biostratigrapher, specializing in Paleozoic gastropods and minor classes of extinct mollusks; lectr. night sch. George Washington U., 1962-65; lectr. Univ. Coll., U. Md., 1966-74; rsch. assoc. Smithsonian Instn., Washington, 1967—; lectr. U. Del., 1981; vis. prof. U. Md., 1986-87; organizer N.Am. Paleontol. Conv., 1969, 1996, editor proc., 1970-71. Co-editor: Essays in Paleontology and Stratigraphy, 1967; editor: Scientific Ideas of G.K. Gilbert, 1980; editorial bd. Nat. Geog. Rsch. and Exploration; contbr. numerous articles to profl. jours.; sec. Internat. Congress Carb. Stratigraphy, 1979. Author: Charles Doolittle Walcott, Paleontologist, 1998, Smithsonian Institution Secretary Charles Doolittle Walcott, 2001. Fellow AAAS (chmn. sect. E 1971); mem. Soc. Systematic Zoology (sec. 1961-66, councilor 1973), Internat. Paleontol. Assn. (treas. 1972-76), Paleontol. Soc. (pres. 1976), Geol. Soc. Am. (History Geology Divsn. award 2003), History of Earth Sci. Soc. (hon. life; sec.-treas. 1982-85, sec. 1986-87, pres. 1989), N.Am. Paleontol. Conv. (hon. life; sec.), Smithsonian Instn. (150th Anniversary com.), Sigma Xi. Office: Smithsonian Instn E-305A Mus Natural History Washington DC 20013-7012 E-mail: yochelson.ellis@nmnh.si.edu.

YOCKIM, JAMES CRAIG, former state senator, foundation administrator; b. Williston, N.D., Feb. 13, 1953; s. Daniel and Doris (Erickson) Y.; children: Jenna, Ericka. BSW, Pacific Luth. U., 1975; MSW, San Diego State U., 1979. Caseworker Dyslin Boys Ranch, Tacoma, 1975-77, head caseworker, program dir., 1979-80; landman Fayette Oil & Gas, Williston, 1980-82; owner Hy-Plains Energy, Williston, 1982-87; city fin. commr. City of Williston, 1984—88, 1998—2002; therapist Williston, 1983; senator N.D. State Senate, 1986-98; owner James C. Yockim Resources, Williston, 1987—. Dir. Bethel Luth. Found., 1993—; del. N.D. Dem. Conv., 1984, 86, 88, 90, 92, 94, 96, 98, 2000, 02, 04; dist. chmn. Dem. Party, Williston, 1988; caucus chmn. Dem. Caucus N.D. State Senate; mem. N.D. Legis. Coun., 1997-98; coun. pres. 1st Luth. Ch. Recipient Ruth Meiers award N.D. Mental Health Assn., 1989, Legislator of Yr. award N.D. Children's Caucus, 1989; named Outstanding Young North Dakotan N.D. Jaycees, 1988. Mem. NASW. Avocations: racquetball, golf. Home: 1123 2nd Ave E Williston ND 58801-4302 Office: PO Box 2344 Williston ND 58802-2344

YOCUM, BRIAN LEE, paramedic, educator; b. Montrose, Colo., Apr. 3, 1962; s. Robert William Yocum and Pamela Ann George. AAS with honors, Denver Tech. Coll., 1991; paramedic, St. Anthony Emegency Med.Svcs., Denver, 1993. Paramedic Broomfield (Colo.) Ambulance, 1991—, Reed Ambulance/Am. Med. Response, Denver, 1992-96, Medtrans of the Rockies, Denver, 1996—; Platte Valley Ambulance, Brighton, Colo., 1996—. Bd. dirs. Broomfield Ambulance. Mem. Elks. Avocations: fishing, mountain biking, inline skating. Home: 16666 6725 Rd Montrose CO 81401-9513

YODAIKEN, RALPH E. pathologist, occupational medicine physician, educator; b. Johannesburg, 1928; BS, U. Witwatersrand, Republic of South Africa, 1956; MPH, Johns Hopkins U., 1976. Diplomate Am. Bd. Pathology, Am. Bd. Forensic Medicine. Intern Coronation Hosp., Johannesburg, 1956-57; resident U. Witwatersrand Med. Ctr., 1957-58, Johannesburg Gen. Hosp., 1958; assoc. pathologist Buffalo Gen. Hosp., 1965 67; mem. staff Cin. Gen. Hosp., 1968-71; rsch. assoc. Johns Hopkins U. Sch. Hygiene and Pub. Health, Balt., 1976—; sr. staff mem. Nat. Inst. Occupational Safety and Health, Washington, 1977—, chmn. sr. adv. staff, 1983; dir. office occupational medicine Occupational Safety and Health Adminstrn., U.S. Dept. Labor, Washington, 1983-91, sr. med. advisor, 1991—98; clin. prof. preventive medicine U. Health Scis., Washington, 1983—. Lectr. U. Witwatersrand, 1958-63; asst. prof. pathology, SUNY Buffalo, 1963-67; assoc. prof. pathology U. Cin., 1968 71; prof. pathology, assoc. prof. medicine Emory U., Atlanta, 1971-75; adj. clin. prof. George Washington U., 1975—, sr. assoc. Johns Hopkins Sch. Hygiene and Pub. Health; clin. prof. preventive medicine uniformed svcs. U. Health Scis. Served to lt. Israeli Army, 1948-50. Fellow Coll. Am. Pathologists, Am. Coll. Occupl. and Environ. Health, Am. Coll. Forensic Medicine. Office Phone: 301-469-9210.

YODER, BRUCE ALAN, chemist; b. Seward, Nebr., Apr. 29, 1962; s. Elwood John and Elda Raye (Stutzman) Y. BS in Chemistry, Wayne State Coll., 1983. Lab. technician Wayne (Nebr.) State Coll., 1982-83, Harris Labs., Lincoln, Nebr., 1984, chemist, 1984; scientist Dorsey Labs., Lincoln, 1984-86, scientist A, 1986-88; product stability analyst Sandoz Pharms., Lincoln, 1988-89, Sandoz Rsch. Inst., Lincoln, 1989-91; mgr. lab. computer ops. Sandoz Pharms., Lincoln, 1991-97; pres., CEO Data Mgmt. Svcs., Inc., Lincoln, 1997—. Active Lancaster County Young Reps., Lincoln, 1988—, co-chmn., 1990-91, pres., 1991-93; mem. Nebr. Fedn. Young Reps., 1988—, exec. com., 1990—, chmn., 1998-99; exec. com. Lancaster County Rep. Party, 1990-97; mem. Def. Adv. Com. Lancaster County, 1992-00; active Lincoln Mayor's Cmty. Cabinet, 1992-93, Lincoln City Charter Revision Commn., 1994—, co-chmn., 1998-2000, chmn., 2000—, v.p., 1999-2000, pres., 2000—; trustee Wayne State Coll. Found., 1991—; advisor Jr. Achievement, 1993-97; bd. dirs. Lincoln Meadows Assn., 1998-99. Recipient Dwight M. Frost, MD award for overcoming a phys. disability Immanuel Rehab. Ctr., 1993, Verdi Smith award for outstanding voluntary contbns. to Lancaster County Rep. Party, 1995-96, First Dist. Outstanding Vol. award Nebr. Reps., 1996-97, Daniel D. Fahrnbruch Leadership award 2000. Mem. Internat. Soc. for Pharm. Engrs., Am. Inst. Chemists, Am. Chem. Soc., Lincoln Ind. Bus. Assn., Jaycees, Elephant Club. Mennonite. Achievements include design of a sample holder for solid dosage forms when using a hunter color instrument, design of a new computer system for Sandoz Pharmaceuticals laboratory computer operations, design of a new computer system for Novartis Consumer Health, Inc. Home: 2240 Winding Way Lincoln NE 68506-2846 Office: Novartis Consumer Health Inc 10401 Hwy 6 Lincoln NE 68517-9626

YODER, EDGAR PAUL, education educator; b. Millersburg, Ohio, June 20, 1946; s. Albert Daniel Yoder and Ella Marie (Bontrager) Erb; m. Deborah Jean Barnhart, June 12, 1971; children: Scott, Suzan. BSA, Ohio State U., 1968, MS, 1972, PhD, 1976. Cert. tchr., counselor, prin., Ohio, Va. Tchr. agr. and sci. Conotton Valley Schs., Bowerston, Ohio, 1968-69, East Holmes Schs., Berlin, Ohio, 1969-72; curriculum specialist Ohio State U., Columbus, 1972-74, project dir., 1974-76; asst. prin. Montgomery County Schs., Blacksburg, Va., 1976-77; asst. prof. Va. Poly. Inst. and State U., Blacksburg, 1977-78, Pa. State U., University Park, 1978-84, assoc. prof. tchr. edn., 1984-94, prof., 1994—, interim dept. head, 1995-98. Cons. Poland Ministry Edn., Warsaw, 1994, Swaziland Ministry Agr., Mbane, 1985, 87, U. Peredenyia, Kandy, Sri Lanka, 1984. Author text: Ag Supplies and Services, 1974; (with others) Undergraduate Education in Agriculture, 1989, also chpt. to book. Chmn. community svc. Sertoma Internat., Columbus, 1975; asst. dir. Va. HSA Assn., Blacksburg, 1978; sect. chmn. Am. Heart Assn., State College, Va., 1981; pres. Ferguson Twp. PTO, State College, 1983-84; bd. dirs. RAFT Drug Rehab. Ctr., Radford, 1976-78, Nat. Future Farmers Am., Alexandria, Va., 1981-83. Recipient hon. degree, Nat. Future Farmers Am., 1983. Mem. Nat. Assn. Coll. Tchrs. Agr. (pres., teacher fellow 1987, Regional Outstanding Teaching award 1992). Am. Assn. Agr. Educators (legis. chmn. 1985), Am. Assn. Ednl. Rsch., Am. Vocat. Edn. Rsch. Assn., Assn. Internat. Agr. and Extension Edn., Phi Delta Kappa, Gamma Sigma Delta (Teaching award of Merit 1987). Avocations: collecting sports memorabilia, restoring antiques, classic cars. Office: Penn State U Rm 323 Ag Adminstrn Coll Agricultural Scis University Park PA 16802

YODER, EDWIN MILTON, JR., columnist, educator, editor, writer; b. Greensboro, N.C., July 18, 1934; s. Edwin M. and Mytrice M. (Logue) Y.; m. Mary Jane Warwick, Nov. 1, 1958; children: Anne Daphne, Edwin Warwick. BA, U. N.C., 1956; BA, MA (Rhodes scholar), Oxford (Eng.) U., 1958; D.H.L. (hon.), Grinnell Coll., 1980, Elon Coll., 1986; DLitt (hon.), U. N.C., 1993, Richmond Coll., London. Editorial writer Charlotte (N.C.) News, 1958-61; editorial writer Greensboro Daily News, 1961-64, assoc. editor, 1965-75; asst. prof. history U. N.C., Greensboro, 1964-65; editorial page editor Washington Star, 1975-81; syndicated columnist Washington Post Writers Group, 1982-97; prof. journalism and humanities Washington and Lee U., 1992—2002, prof. emeritus, 2002—. Hon. fellow Jesus Coll., Oxford, Eng., 1998—. Author: Night of the Old South Ball, 1984, The Unmaking of a Whig, 1990, Joe Alsop's Cold War, 1995, The Historical Present, 1997; contbr. articles to periodicals. Trustee Inst. for Early Am. History and Culture, Nat. Humanities Ctr., 1991-97. Recipient awards editorial writing N.C. Press Assn., 1958, 61, 66, Walker Stone award Scripps-Howard Found., 1978, Pulitzer prize editorial writing, 1979; Disting. Alumnus award U. N.C., Chapel Hill, 1980 Mem. Nat. Conf. Editorial Writers, Am. Soc. Newspaper Editors. Democrat. Episcopalian. Home: 4001 Harris Pl Alexandria VA 22304-1720 E-mail: yoderem@aol.com.

YODER, JAMES DALE, adult education educator; b. Souderton, Pa., May 21, 1935; s. Lloyd Rickert and Viola Sell Yoder; m. Nicole Donnay Yoder, Sept. 8, 1957; children: Michelle, Beckie, Laurie. BA, Albright Coll., 1957; MA, Lehigh U., 1959, PhD, 1969. Tchr. Palisades H.S., Bethlehem, Pa., 1957—60; prof. Del. Valley Coll., Doylestown, Pa., 1963—65, Albright Coll., Reading, Pa., 1966—. Grad. asst. Lehigh U., Bethleham, Pa., 1961—62. Author: Pearl Buck's Living Legacy, 1999. Tennis coach Albright Coll., Reading, 1971—. Named Tennis Coach of Yr., Middle Atlantic Conf., 1997. Mem.: Orgn. Am. Historians. Home: 206 Neversink Rd Reading PA 19606 E-mail: dyoder6221@aol.com.

YODER, PATRICIA DOHERTY, public relations executive; b. Pitts., Oct. 30, 1939; d. John Addison and Camella Grace (Conti) Doherty; children: Shari Lynn, Wendy Ann; m. James Ronald Wolfe, Oct. 30, 1999. BA, Duquesne U., 1961. Press sec. U.S. Ho. of Reps., 1965-69; dir. Office of Pub. Info., City of Ft. Wayne, 1973-76; asst. mgr. pub. and corp. comm. Mellon Bank N.A., Pitts., 1977-79; v.p. pub. affairs Am. Waterways Operators Inc., Washington, 1980-83, sr. v.p., gen. mgr., 1983-86, exec. v.p., dir. banking, 1989-91; exec. v.p., dir. internat. banking Hill and Knowlton Inc., Pitts.; sr. v.p. corp. and pub. affairs PNC Fin. Svcs. Group, Pitts., 1987-89; v.p., mgr. corp. pub. rels. and advt. GE Capital Svcs. Corp., Stamford, Conn., 1991-95; corp. v.p. pub. affairs and comm. GTE Corp., Stamford, 1995-96; sr. v.p. corp. comm. Avis Group Holdings, Garden City, N.Y., 1996-99; prin. PDY Assocs., 1999—. Trustee Shadyside Hosp., Pressley Ridge Sch., Pitts., Ellis Sch.; bd. dirs. Children's Mus., Civic Light Opera, Pitts. Ballet Theatre, Jr. League of City of N.Y. Recipient Outstanding Woman Bus. and Industry, 1988, Disting. Alumni award Duquesne U., 1996. Mem. Pitts. Field Club, Duquesne Club, Indian Harbor Yacht Club, Boca Raton (Fla.) Resort Country Club. Roman Catholic. Home and Office: 500 SE 5th Ave Apt 601 Boca Raton FL 33432-5510 also: 535 E 86th St Apt 16E New York NY 10028-7533 E-mail: pdyoder@att.net.

YODER, RANDALL D. music educator; b. Lancaster, Pa., Jan. 21, 1949; s. David J. and Mary Lou Yoder; m. Leslee Ann Brenneman, Jan. 24, 1992; stepchildren: Dustin M. Kemper, Jelee Elizabeth Kemper. BS in Music Edn., Susquehanna U., 1971; MusM in Choral Conducting, Westminster Choir Coll., 1978. Tchr., choral dir. Northeastern Sch. Dist., Manchester, Pa., 1971—88, York (Pa.) City Schs., 1997—. Dir. The York County Honors Choir, 1998—2004; choral dir. Pa. Ambs. of Music, European Concert Tour, 2001, Sound of Am. Honor Choir, European Concert Tour, 2002, European Concert Tour, 04. Composer: (original music for documentary) Historic Pennsylvania, 1996 (Emmy award, 1997), Hershey Park Memories, 1998, (CD) Christmas Rose, 2000. Mem.: Music Educators Nat. Conf., Am. Choral Dirs. Assn. Avocation: travel.

YODER, RONNIE A. judge; b. Knoxville, Tenn., July 10, 1937; s. Raymond Abraham and Veryl Hope (Hostetler) Y.; m. Shirley Mae Grimes, June 28, 1961; children: Susan Elizabeth Torres, Mary Amanda Anderson, Elizabeth Anne Lee, John Anthony Gerhard. BA in Polit. Sci. with honors, U. Va., 1958, JD, 1961. Bar: Va. 1961, N.Y. 1963, D.C. 1965, U.S. Dist. Ct. D.C. 1965, U.S. Dist. Ct. (so. dist.) N.Y. 1969, U.S. Ct. Claims 1964, U.S. Supreme Ct. 1968. Assoc. Mudge Rose Guthrie & Alexander, N.Y.C. and Washington, 1962-70; of counsel Zuckert Scoutt & Rasenberger, Washington, 1970-72, ptnr., 1972-75; adminstrv. law judge U.S. Dept. Labor, Washington, 1976, CAB, Washington, 1976-84, U.S. Dept. Transp., Washington, 1985-98, acting chief adminstrv. law judge, 1999-2001, chief adminstv. law judge, 2001—. Adminstrv. law judge Nat. Transp. Safety Bd., 1979-80, Maritime Adminstrn., 1983, 86-88, FDIC, 1982-83, SBA, 1983, FAA, 1985—, Fed. Hwy. Adminstrn., 1985—, Fed. R.R. Adminstrn., 1993-95, Rsch. and Spl. Programs Adminstrn., 1991—, Surface Transp. Bd., 1996-97, Fed. Motor Carrier Safety Adminstrn., 2000—, Fed. Transp. Security Adminstrn., 2002—; mem. Adminstrv. Conf. of U.S., 1994-95. Mem. editorial bd. U. Va. Law Rev., 1959-61; contbr. articles to profl. jours. Sec., co-counsel Capital Headstart, 1966-68; narrator Lincoln Commn., 1985, 86; mem. permanent jud. commn. Nat. Capital Presbytery, 1985-91. Rockefeller fellow, 1961. Fellow: Am. Bar Found.; mem.: SAR, ATLA, FBA (jud. divsn. leadership coun. 1999—, bd. dirs. D.C. chpt. 1999—, pres.-elect D.C. chpt. 2002—03, pres. 2003—), ABA (exec. com. nat. conf. adminstrv. law judges 1980—83, mem. Nat. Ctr. for State Cts. working group on asbestos litig. 1982—84, exec. com. nat. conf. adminstrv. law judges 1985—89, reporter Model Code Jud. Conduct for Fed. Adminstrv. Law Judges 1989, exec. com. nat. conf. adminstrv. law judges 1990—96, sec. 1991—92, parliamentarian 1991—92, by govt. employees 1991—92, vice chmn. 1992—93, chmn.-elect 1993—94, jud. divsn. coun. 1994—95, chmn. 1994—95, vice chmn. social security com. sr. lawyers sect. 1996—2000, parliamentarian 1996—2001, exec. com. nat. conf. adminstrv. law judges 1997—2001, judges adv. com. on ethics and profl. responsibility 2001—04, exec. com. nat. conf. adminstrv. law judges 2002—04, parliamentarian 2002—, adminstrv. law sect., sec. sect. officers chmn. task force participation profl. assns, govt. employees sect., pub. contract law sect., litig. sect.), Prettyman Levanthal Am. Inn of Ct., Am. Guild Musical Artists, D.C. Bar Assn., Va. Bar Assn. (bd. govs. adminstrv. law sect. 1981—87), Nat. Assn. Adminstrv. Law Judges, Fed. Adminstrv. Law Judges Conf. (exec. com. 1976—81, 1985, 1987, 1999—), Am. Judicature Soc., Phi Eta Sigma, Phi Beta Kappa. Home: 1400 Summit Ave Alexandria VA 22302-2735 Office: Dept Transp Rm 5411 400 7th St SW Washington DC 20590-0001 E-mail: ronnie.yoder@ost.dot.gov, honron@aol.com.

YODER, STEPHEN ALAN, lawyer; b. Wilmington, Del., Aug. 9, 1953; s. Richard Esser and Jane Frances (Whitby) Y.; m. Louise Lea Whitney, Sept. 3, 1977; children: Salle Lea, Katharine Anne, Caroline Whitney. AB, Duke U., 1975; JD, Northwestern U., 1978. Bar: Pa. 1978, Calif. 1983. Assoc. Reed Smith Shaw McClay, Pitts., 1978-83, Pettit & Martin, San Francisco, 1983-84, Reed Smith, Pitts., 1984-86, ptnr., 1987-90; mng. counsel Mellon Bank, Pitts., 1990-92, asst. gen. counsel, 1992-95; gen. counsel Am. South Bancorp., Birmingham, Ala., 1995—. Trustee Birmingham Hist. Soc., 1996—, Ala. Eye Inst., Birmingham, 1996—. Office: Am South Bancorp 1901 6th Ave N Birmingham AL 35203-2618

YODER-WISE, PATRICIA SNYDER, education educator; b. Wadsworth, Ohio, July 2, 1941; d. Belford Grant and Leona Cora (Mohler) Snyder; m. Robert Thomas Wise, Feb. 17, 1973; children: Doreen Ellen, Deborah Ann. BSN, Ohio State U., 1963; MSN, Wayne State U., 1968; EdD, Tex. Tech. U., 1984. RN, Tex. Interim dir. nursing ctr. Tex. Tech. U. Health Sci. Ctr. Sch. Nursing, Lubbock, 1988-89, interim assoc. dean practice program, 1989-90, interim dean, prof., 1991-93, dean and prof., 1993-2000, prof., 2000—; clin. prof. U. Tex. Health Sci. Ctr., San Antonio, 1993—2000; pres. Tex. Woman's U., 2004—. Mem. rev. panel Nursing Outlook, 1993—; mem. adv. com. GlaxoWellcome, 1996-2000; v.p. ANCC, 2000-03, sec. 2003-04; mem. Nat. Quality Forum Provider Panel, 2001-04. Author (editor): Leading and Managing in Nursing, 1994 (Book of Yr. award, 1996, 1999, 2003); peer reviewer: Jour. Profl. Nursing, 1984—2003, mem. editl. bd.: Jour. Continuing Edn. in Nursing, 1978—; editor, 1988—. Participant Leadership Tex.-Found. for Women's Resources, 1997-98; mem. Leadership Tex., 1998-99, Leadership Am., 1999-2000. Recipient of Woman of Excellence in Medicine, YWCA, Lubbock, 1996. Fellow: Am. Acad. Nursing (chair Inst. for Nursing Leadership 1999—2002, mem. planning com. 2004); mem.: ANA (del. 1995—2000, chair constituent assembly 1998—2000, sec. 2000—02, 1st v.p. 2002—), Tex. Nurses Assn. (pres. 1995—99). Office: Texas Tech Univ HSC Sch Nursing 7309 93rd St Lubbock TX 79424-4939

YODOWITZ, EDWARD JAY, lawyer; b. N.Y.C., 1943; BS, Long Island U., 1965; JD, U. Balt., 1969. Bar: N.Y. 1972. With Skadden, Arps, Slate, Meagher & Flom, L.L.P., N.Y.C., 1969—, now sr. ptnr. Chmn. securities litigation seminar Practicing Law Inst., 1984-95; bd. trustees L.I. U., 1990-99. Mem.: ABA. Home: 105 Ocean Ave Lawrence NY 11559-2006 Office: Skadden Arps Slate Meagher & Flom LLP Four Times Sq New York NY 10036-6522 Business E-Mail: eyodowit@skadden.com.

YOFFIE, ERICH H. religious organization administrator; m. Amy Jacobson; 2 children. Grad., Brandeis U., Hebrew Union Coll., NYC, 1974. Ordained rabbi 74. Rabbi, Lynbrook, NJ; rabbi Durham, NC; dir. Midwest Coun. Union Am. Hebrew Congregations, NYC, 1980—92, v.p., dir. Commn. on Social Action, 1992—96, pres., 1996—; exec. dir. Assn. Reform Zionists of Am., 1983—. Exec. editor: Reform Judaism mag., 1992—96; contbr. articles to profl. jours. Religious leader Million Mom March, 2000; regional pres., nat. v.p. NAm. Fedn. Temple Youth; bd. dirs. many Jewish orgns. including Mazon: A Jewish Response to Hunger and the Jewish Agy. for Israel. Named to "Top Fifty List of Leadership", Forward Annual. Office: UAHC Hdqs 633 3rd Ave New York NY 10017-6706*

YOGANATHAN, AJIT PRITHIVIRAJ, biomedical engineer, educator; b. Colombo, Sri Lanka, Dec. 6, 1951; came to U.S., 1973; s. Ponniah and Mangay (Navaratnam) Y.; m. Tripti Yoganathan. BSChemE with honors, Univ. Coll., U. London, 1973; PhDChemE, Calif. Inst. Tech., 1978. Engring. asst. Shell Oil Refinery, Stanlow, Eng., 1972; tchg. asst. Calif. Inst. Tech., 1973-74, 1976, rsch. fellow, 1977-79; asst. prof. Ga. Inst. Tech., 1979-83, assoc. prof., 1983-88, chmn. bioengring. com., 1984-88, prof. chem. engring., 1988-94, dir. Bioengring. Ctr., 1989—, prof. mech. engring., 1989-94, co-dir. Emory U.-Ga. Tech. Biomed. Tech. Ctr., 1992—, Regents prof., 1994—, assoc. chair biomed. engring., 1998—; Wallace H. Coulter disting. faculty chair, 2004—. Adj. assoc. prof. U. Ala., 1985—. Founding fellow Am. Inst. Med. & Biol. Engring., 1992; recipient Edwin Walker prize Brit. Inst. Mech. Engrs., 1988, Humboldt fellowship, 1985, Am. Heart Assn.-Ga. Affiliate Rsch. Investigatorship award, 1980-83, Calif. Inst. Tech. fellowship, 1973-77, Goldsmid Medal and prize Univ. Coll., 1972-73, Brit. Coun. scholarship, 1971-73. Mem.

AIChE, ASME (Bioengring. div., H.R. Lissner award 1997), Biomed. Engring. Soc., Am. Soc. Echocardiography (dir. 1987-91). Office: Sch Biomed Engring Ga Tech/Emory Atlanta GA 30332-0535 E-mail: ajit.yoganathan@bme.gatech.edu.

YOGESWARAN, PARARAJASINGAM, physician; b. Jaffna, Sri Lanka, Dec. 6, 1963; arrived in U.S., 2000; s. Pararajasingam and Ahilandeswary Vallipurum; m. Anitha Yogeswaran, June 9, 1990; children: Vidhushei, Shaiesh. MD, Southampton (Eng.) Med. Sch., 1994. House officer in medicine and surgery Southampton (Eng.) Gen. Hosp., Southampton, England, 1994—94; sr. house officer in emergency medicine Bromley Hosp., Kent, England, 1996; sr. house officer medicine and gerontology Hillingdon Hosp., Uxbridge, England, 1996—96; registrar internal medicine Queen Elizabeth Hosp. II, Welwyngarden City, 1996—98; registrar radiology St. Mary's Hosp., Paddington, London, 1998—2000; resident internal medicine Coney Island Hosp., Bklyn., 2000—. Mem.: Royal Coll. Physicians (London). Home: 2610 Olean Pkwy #2B Brooklyn NY 11235 Office: Coney Island Hosp 2601 Ocean Pkwy Brooklyn NY 11235

YOGEV, RAM, pediatrician, educator; b. Rehovot, Israel, Oct. 27, 1942; came to U.S., 1975; s. Samuel and Jenny (Proper) Y.; m. Sara Frankel; children: Eldad, Shelly, Tomer. MD, Hebrew U., 1970. Diplomate Am. Bd. Pediatrics. Pediatric resident Hadassah Hosp., Israel, 1972-75, fellow pediatric infectious disease, 1975-77; asst. prof., assoc. prof., prof. Northwestern U., Chgo., 1977—. Dir. pediatric and maternal HIV infection Children's Meml. Hosp., Chgo., 1987—. Author, editor: Management of HIV Infection in Infants and Children, 1992; contbr. over 200 articles to profl. jours., books. Recipient Exceptional Merit award, Ill. Dept. Pub. Health, 1996, Jonas Salk award, March of Dimes, 1999, Pub. Svc. award, Chgo. Med. Soc., 2002, numerous grants in field. Mem. Am. Acad. Pediatrics. Office: Children's Meml Hosp 2300 N Childrens Plz Chicago IL 60614-3394 E-mail: r-yogev@northwestern.edu.

YOH, HAROLD L., III, company executive; b. L.A., Dec. 22, 1960; s. Harold L. Jr. and Mary Michael (Milus) Y.; m. Sharon Lynn Cructher, Oct. 13, 1984; children: Kristen, Catherine, Samantha. BSME, Duke U., 1983; MBA, U. Pa., 1990. Various positions to v.p., 1983-89; pres. Day Products, Bridgeport, N.Y., 1992-93; sr. v.p. Day & Zimmerman Internat., Phila., 1993-94; pres. Day & Zimmermann Internat.-Process & Indsl., Inc., Phila., 1995—; chmn., CEO Day & Zimmerman Internat, Phila. Office: Day & Zimmermann Internat 1818 Market St Fl 22 Philadelphia PA 19103-3638

YOH, HAROLD LIONEL, JR., retired engineering, construction and management company executive; b. Bryn Mawr, Pa., Dec. 12, 1936; s. Harold Lionel and Katherine (Hulme) Y.; m. Mary Michael Milus, June 20, 1959; children: Harold Lionel III, Michael Hulme, Karen Bogart, Jeffrey Milus, William Courtlandt. BS in Mech. Engring, Duke, 1958; MBA, U. Pa., 1962. Vice pres. H.L. Yoh Co. subs. Day & Zimmerman Group, Inc., Phila., 1960-63, sr. v.p. div. mgr., 1963-64, pres., 1964-76; v.p. adminstrn. Day & Zimmermann Group, Inc., Phila., 1961-69, sec., 1966-70, v.p., treas., 1969-76, vice chmn., CEO, 1976-80, chmn. bd., CEO, 1980—, also bd. dirs. Past pres., past dir. Nat. Tech. Services Assn.; bd. dirs. Continental Bancorp. Greater Phila First Corp. and several other privately held cos. Bd. dirs. Phila. Coll. Arts, Bryn Mawr Civic Assn., Phila. Indsl. Devel. Corp., The Haverford Sch.; past chmn. bd. dirs. Pop Warner Little Scholars; past Pa. State chmn. U.S. Savs. Bonds.; chmn. dean's council Sch. Engring. Duke U., chmn. univ. Greater Phila. Area Capital Campaign; Mid-Atlantic regional chmn. U.S. Olympics. Named Ambassador City of Phila., Silver Knight of D&Z Lone Star chpt. Mgmt. Nat. Mgmt. Assn., 1979-80; recipient Blue Devil award Duke U., Disting. Alumnus award Duke U., Robert Morris award Boy Scouts Am. Mem. ASME, Am. Def. Preparedness Assn. (dir.), Phila. C. of C. (chmn., dir.), Young President's Orgn. (internat. dir.), Phila. Pres.' Orgn., Chief Execs. Orgn., Navy League (life), Newcomen Soc., World Bus. Council, Sigma Nu. Clubs: Union League, Phila. Country (Phila.); Merion Golf (Ardmore, Pa.); University (Washington); Seaview Country (N.J.). Republican. Episcopalian. Avocations: golf, fishing.

YOH, JACK JAI-ICK, mechanical engineer; b. Seoul, Republic of Korea, Mar. 4, 1970; s. Sang Whan Yoh and Seung Hee Sohn; m. Eun Joung Jee, Dec. 28, 1995; children: David Doughyun, Chad Songhyun. BS, U. Calif., Berkeley, 1992; MS, UCLA, 1995; PhD, U. Ill., Urbana, 2001. Safety engr. U.S. Steel, Pitts., Calif., 1989—92; cons. Korean Air Inst. Adv. Tech., Seoul, 1993—95; grad. rschr. U. Ill., Urbana, 1998—2001; staff scientist Lawrence Livermore (Calif.) Nat. Lab., 2002—. Translator Sunday bilingual worship. Deacon Contra Costa Presbyn. Ch., Walnut Creek, Calif., 2002—03. Postdoctoral Rsch. fellow, US Air Force Rsch. Lab., 2001. Mem.: AIAA, ASME, Soc. Indsl. Applied Materials, Am. Phys. Soc. Achievements include research in high-order accurate multi-material hydro code; first to thermal explosion of energetic materials. Office: Lawrence Livermore Nat Lab PO Box 808 L-268 Livermore CA 94551

YOHALEM, HARRY MORTON, lawyer; b. Phila., Jan. 21, 1943; s. Morton Eugene and Florence (Mishnun) Y.; m. Martha Caroline Remy, June 9, 1967; children: Seth, Mark. BA with honors, U. Wis., 1965; JD cum laude, M in Internat. Affairs, Columbia U., 1969. Bar: NY 1969, DC 1981, Calif. 1992, U.S. Supreme Ct. 1985. Assoc. Shearman & Sterling, NYC, 1969-71; asst. counsel to gov. State of NY, Albany, 1971-73, counsel office planning svcs., 1973-75; asst. gen. counsel FEA, Washington, 1975-77; mem. staff White House Energy Policy and Planning Office, Washington, 1977; dep. gen. counsel for legal svcs. Dept. Energy, Washington, 1978-80, dep. under sec., 1980-81; ptnr. Rogers & Wells, Washington, 1981-91; gen. counsel Calif. Inst. Tech., Pasadena, 1991—. Editor comments Columbia Jour. Transnat. Law, 1967-68, rsch. editor, 1968-69. Prin. Coun. for Excellence in Govt., Washington, 1990—; pres. Opera Bel Canto, Washington, 1984-87; mem. Lawyers Com. for Arts, Washington, 1981-88; bd. visitors dept. English U. Wis., 1999—. Harlan Fiske Stone scholar Columbia U., 1967, 69. Mem.: DC Bar Assn., Calif. Bar Assn., Athenaeum, Phi Kappa Phi. Home: 702 E California Blvd Pasadena CA 91106 Office: Calif Inst Tech Mail Code 109-31 1200 E California Blvd Pasadena CA 91125 E-mail: harry.yohalem@caltech.edu.

YOHAY, STEVEN JACOB, healthcare company executive, consultant; b. N.Y.C., N.Y., Nov. 28, 1950; s. Nathan and Natalie (Modlinger) Y.; children: Charlotte, Paige. BS in Psychology, SUNY-Empire State Coll., Saratoga Springs, N.Y., 1977. Cert. addiction specialist, alcoholism and substance abuse counselor. Staff counselor-trainee AREBA Casriel Inst., N.Y.C., 1971-72, asst. resident dir., 1972-73, resident dir., 1973-75, exec. dir., 1975-82, pres., chief exec. officer, 1982—. Cons. Long Lane Sch., Middletown Conn., Brookside Acad., Mt. Freedom, N.J., The Key, Ghent, Belgium, New Ctr. for Psychotherapies, Boston, Psychiat. Engring. Standards Assn. Contbr. articles to profl. jours. Bd. dirs. N.Y. Regional Therapeutic Communities of Am. Recipient Community Svc. award Bronx Borough Pres.'s Officer, 1966; Regents scholar N.Y. State Bd. Regents, 1966. Fellow Am. Soc. New Identity Process; mem. Am. Coll. of Addiction Treatment Adminstrs., Am. Coll. Healthcare Adminstrs., Nat. Assn. Alcoholism and Drug Abuse Counselors, Alcohol and Drug Problems Assn. N.Am., Nat. Assn. Addiction Treatment Providers, N.Y. State Assn. Practicing Psychotherapists. Jewish. Avocations: motorboating, sailing, tennis, scuba diving, mountain biking. Home: 78 Hawser Dr Oak Beach NY 11702 Office: AREBA Casriel Inc 500 W 57th St New York NY 10019-2902

YOHN, SHARON A. manufacturing executive; b. Altoona, Pa., Mar. 1, 1952; AS in Retail cum laude, Harcum Jr. Coll. (Pa.), 1972; BSBA, Villanova U., 1976. V.p. legal dept. Items Internat., Inc., Altoona, Pa., 1987-95, v.p., 1995—. Active ch. choir and choral soc. Republican. Methodist. Avocations: needlecrafts, sewing, music, performing arts, travel. Office: Items Internat Inc 1540 E Pleasant Valley Blvd Altoona PA 16602-7224

YOHN, WILLIAM H(ENDRICKS), JR., federal judge; b. Pottstown, Pa., Nov. 20, 1935; s. William H. and Dorothy C. (Cornelius) Y.; m. Jean Louise Kochel, Mar. 16, 1963; children: William H. III, Bradley G., Elizabeth Y. Lemmon. AB, Princeton U., 1957; JD, Yale U., 1960. Bar: Pa. 1961, U.S. Dist. Ct. D.C. 1961. Ptnr. Wells Campbell Reynier & Yohn, Pottstown, 1961-71; mem., chmn. coms. Pa. House of Reps., Harrisburg, 1968-80; ptnr. Binder Yohn & Kalis, Pottstown, 1971-81; judge Montgomery County Ct. of Common Pleas, Norristown, Pa., 1981-91, U.S. Dist. Ct. (ea. dist.), Pa., 1991—. Asst. dist. atty., Montgomery County Dist. Atty. Office, 1962-65; instr. Am. Inst. of Banking, 1963-66; bd. dirs. Fed. Jud. Ctr., 1999-2003. Bd. dirs. Greater Pottstown Drug Abuse Prevention Program, 1970-76, Pottstown Meml. Med. Ctr., 1974-95, chmn., 1984-95; mem. exec. com. Yale Law Sch. Alumni Assn., 1998—. Cpl. USMCR, 1960-66. Mem. Pa. Bar Assn., Montgomery Bar Assn. (bd. dirs. 1967-70), Fed. Judge Assn. Republican. Office: US Dist Ct 14613 US Courthouse 601 Market St Philadelphia PA 19106-1713 Office Phone: 215-597-4361.

YOHO, BILLY LEE, lawyer; b. Huntington, W.Va., Oct. 24, 1925; s. Wilbert Wiley Yoho Sr. and Nellie Pansy (Bryan) Hawkins; m. Martha Sue Carroll; children: Kevin Richard, Karen Lee; m. Shirley Ann Stone Morris. BA, U. Md., 1950; LLD, U. Md., Balt., 1953. Bar: Md. 1953. Ptnr. Hoyert & Yoho Chartered, Lanham, Md., 1953—; gen. counsel City of College Park, Md., 1959-62; town atty. Town of Colmar Manor, Md., 1956-72; gen. counsel Prince George's Gen. Hosp., Cheverly, Md., 1955-74, MD22 Lions Rsch. Found., Balt., 1988—; ptnr. Hoyert & Yoho Chartered, Lanham, Md., 1987—. Mem. College Park airport program in saving the oldest airport in the world, 1968. With USN, 1943-47. Mem. ABA, Prince George's County Bar Assn. (pres. 1976-77), Md. Assn. Trial Attys., Lions Clubs Internat. (dist. gov. 1989-90, life mem.), NRA, U. Md. Alumni Assn. Democrat. Presbyterian. Avocations: computing, genealogy, christian study. Home: 5950 Westchester Park Dr College Park MD 20740-2802 Office Phone: 301-459-4200.

YOKEN, MEL B(ARTON), French language educator, radio commentator, writer; b. Fall River, Mass., June 25, 1939; s. Albert Benjamin and Sylvia Sarah (White) Y.; m. Cynthia Stein, June 20, 1976; children: Andrew Brett, David Ryan, Jonathan Barry. BA, U. Mass., 1960; MAT, Brown U., 1961, PhD, 1972. Instr. French U. Mass., Dartmouth, 1966-72, asst. prof., 1976-81, prof., 1981-2001, chancellor prof., 2001—. Dir. French summer study program French Inst., 1981-88; radio commentator Am. Field Svc., 1971—, pres., 1984-86, v.p., 2001—; vis. prof. Wheaton Coll., 1987, U. of Montreal, 1981-88; translator New Bedford Superior Ct., New Bedford, Mass., 1985—, Fall River Superior Ct., Fall River, Mass., 1985—; reader, cons. AP Exams in French, 1997—; mem. nominating com. Nobel Prize for lit., 1972—, Acad. Am. Poets, 1999—. Author: Claude Tillier, 1976, Speech is Plurality, 1978, Claude Tillier (1801-44): Fame and Fortune in His Novelistic Work, 1978, Entretiens Quebecois I, 1986, Entretiens Quebecois II, 1989, Letters of Robert Molloy, 1989, Festschrift in Honor of Stowell Goding, 1993, Entretiens Quebecois III, 1999; contbr. articles to profl. jours. Pres. Friends of Fall River Pub. Libr., 1972-80, pres., bd. dirs., 1972-80; pres. New Bedford Pub. Libr., 1980-82; bd. dirs. Am. Field Svc., 1980—, pres., 1984-86, v.p., 2001—; v.p. Friends of U. Mass. Libr., 1998—, pres., 1999—; dir. Boivin Ctr., 1999—. Decorated officier Ordre des Palmes académiques, Acad. Française, 2001—; recipient Disting. Svc. award City Fall River, 1974, 80, Excellence in Tchg. French award, 1984, 85, Gov.'s citation, 1986, Nat. Disting. Leadership award, 1990, Dist. Svc. award Mass. Foreign Lang. Assn., 1992, Medaille de Vermeil du Rayonnement de la Langue Française, L'Academie Française, 1993, Outstanding Cmty. Svc. award, 1997, Disting. Alumni award, Durfee H.S., 1998, Golden Apple award Fall River Herald News, 1998; Govt. of Que. grantee, 1981-85, 87-89, Can. Embassy grantee, 1986, 87, Southeastern Mass. U. grantee, 1985, 89, 90; named Hon. Life Mem., Fall River Pub. Libr., 2003; Mel Yoken Day proclaimed by Mayor of New Bedford, 1990. Mem. MLA (life), Am. Assn. Tchrs. French (life), Am. Coun. Tchrs. Fgn. Langs., Middlebury Amicale (life), N.E. MLA (coord. 1987-91), New Eng. Fgn. Lang. Assn., Mass. Fgn. Lang. Assn. (bd. dirs. 1985-90, disting. svc. award 1992), N.Y. State Assn. Fgn. Lang. Tchrs., Internat. Platform Assn., Francophone Assn. (v.p. 1990-98), Assn. Literary Scholars and Critics, Fall River C. of C., Brown U. Alumni Assn. (rep.), Richelieu Internat., Universal Manuscript Soc. (v.p. 1993-95). Avocations: travel, languages, baseball, postcards, meteorology. Home: 261 Carroll St New Bedford MA 02740-1412 Office: U Mass Dartmouth Lang Dept Old Westport Rd North Dartmouth MA 02747-2512 Business E-Mail: myoken@umassd.edu.

YOKLEY, RICHARD CLARENCE, protective services official; b. San Diego, Dec. 29, 1942; s. Clarence Ralph and Dorothy Junese (Sackman) Y.; m. Jean Elizabeth Liddle, July 25, 1964; children: Richard Clarence II, Karin Denise. Student, San Diego City Coll., 1967; AS, Miramar Coll., 1975; student, London Fire Brig. Tng. Acad., 1994, Fire Svc. Coll., Eng., 1994. Cert. fire officer, fire instr., fire investigator, Calif. Disc jockey Sta. KSDS-FM, San Diego, 1966-67; bldg. engr. Consolidated Systems, Inc., San Diego, 1968-72; with Bonita-Sunnyside Fire Dept., Calif., 1972-99, fire marshal, 1981-91, ops. chief, 1991-93, maintenance officer, 1993-99. Med. technician Hartson Ambulance, San Diego, 1978-80, Bay Gen. Hosp. (now Scripps Hosp.), Chula Vista, Calif., 1980-83, EMT-D Sea World of San Diego, 1997—2003, Seaworld Aviculture Dept. Penguin Encounter, 2003—; chmn. South Bay Emergency Med. Svc., 1988; mem. firefighter adv. coun. to San Diego Burn Inst., 1989, 1999, mem. Coun. of Courage, 1991-99; mem. Emergency Med. Care Com. for San Diego County, 2001--. Author: TV Firefighters, 2003; contbr. articles to jours., newspapers and mags. Asst. curator Firehouse Mus., San Diego, 1972-89, docent, 1990-93; scoutmaster troop 874 Boy Scouts Am., Bonita, Calif., 1978-79. With USAF, 1962-66. Recipient Heroism and Community Svc. award Firehouse Mag., N.Y.C., 1987, Star News Salutes award Chula Vista Star News, 1987, Golden Svc. award San Diego County Credit Union, 1988, SeaWorld San Diego Excellence award, 2000. Mem. Internat. Assn. Firefighters (pres. local chpt. 1981-82), Calif. State Firefighters Assn. (dep. dir. so. divsn. 1994-97), Calif. Fire Mechanics, San Diego County Fire Prevention Officers (v.p. 1984, pres. 1985), Bonita Bus. and Profl. Assn. (bd. dirs. 1991-93, Historian award 1987, Pioneer award 1997), Fire Mark Cir. of the Ams. (dir. 1994-2000, Exemplary Svc. award 2002), Smokey Bear Collectors Assn. (co-founder, dir. 1995-97, advisor 1998-2000), South Bay Commn., Bonita Hist. Mus. (co-founder 1986, adv. bd. 1997, v.p. 1998, 99, bd. dirs. 2003—), Sport Chalet Dive Club (v.p. 1991). Republican. Methodist. Avocations: scuba diving, visit fire departments of foreign countries, collect fire memorabilia, skiing. Office: Seaworld San Diego 500 Sea World Dr San Diego CA 92109-7904 Home: 8802 E Buckboard Rd Tucson AZ 85749

YOKOUCHI, KATHY, nursing administrator; Exec. officer Hawaii Bd. Nursing, Honolulu. Office: Hawaii Bd Nursing PO Box 3469 Honolulu HI 96801-3469

YOKUBAITIS, ROGER T. lawyer; b. Wharton, Tex., Jan. 9, 1945; Student, St. Louis U.; BA, JD, U. Houston, 1969. Bar: Tex. 1969; U.S. Dist. Ct. (so., we., ea. and no. dists.) Tex., U.S. Ct. Appeals (5th, 9th, 11th cirs.), U.S. Supreme Ct. Ptnr. Carmody & Yokubaitis, L.L.P., Houston, 1995—2000; prin. Roger T. Yokubaitis, P.L.L.C., Houston, 2000—. Mem. ABA, Houston Bar Assn., State Bar of Tex., Houston Bankruptcy Bar Assn., Am. Bankruptcy Inst., Fed. Bar Assn., Federalist Soc. Office: Roger T Yokubaitis PLLC 1177 W Loop S Ste 1650 Houston TX 77027-9086 Office Phone: 713-227-9000. E-mail: Yokubaitis@swbell.net.

YOLDAS, BULENT ERTURK, materials scientist, educator; b. Isaparta, Turkey, Feb. 19, 1938; arrived in U.S., 1958, naturalized; s. Mustafa and Hatice Yoldas; m. Lubomyra Anne Ivanycky; children: Erol, Kim. BS in Ceramic Engring, Ohio State U., Columbus, 1963; MS, Ohio State U., 1964, PhD, 1966. Sr. engr. Owens Ill. Tech. Ctr., Toledo, 1966—74; fellow scientist Westinghouse Rsch. Ctr., Pitts., 1974—84, PPG Industries R&D Ctr., Pitts., 1984—96; adj. prof. Carnegie Mellon U., Pitts., 1996—99. Mem. editl. bd. Jour. of Sol-gel Sci. of Tech., 2000—. Contbr. articles to profl. jours. Named one of top 100 Internat. Innovators, Tech. Mag. (pemier issue), 1981. Fellow: Am. Ceramic Soc.; mem.: AAAS, Materials Rsch. Soc. Achievements include invention of a radical glass forming method, 1980; image transfer technology, 1999; research in in ceramic and glass formation by chemical polymerization-so-called sol-gel technology; optical coatings and advanced materials; patents in field of 75. Avocations: gardening, hiking, music, poetry. Home: 16728 Adrienne Way Ramona CA 92065 E-mail: yoldas.pgh@worldnet.att.net.

YOLEN, JANE, author; b. N.Y.C., Feb. 11, 1939; d. Will Hyatt and Isabelle (Berlin) Y.; m. David Wilber Stemple, Sept. 2, 1962; children: Heidi Elisabet, Adam Douglas, Jason Frederic. BA, Smith Coll., 1960; EdM, U. Mass., 1978; LLD (hon.), Coll. of Our Lady of the Elms, 1980. Asst. editor This Week mag., 1960; mem. staff Saturday Rev., 1960; asst. editor Gold Medal Books, 1961, Rutledge Press, 1961-63; asst. juvenile editor A.A. Knopf, Inc., 1963-65; freelance writer, 1965—; lectr. dept. edn. Smith Coll., 1979-84; editor Jane Yolen books, imprint Harcourt Brace Jovanovich, 1988-97. Tchr. writers confs. Centrum, Cape Cod Writers Conf., Soc. Children's Book Writers, U. Mass.; mem. Mass. Coun. on Arts, 1974. Author: Pirates in Petticoats, 1963, The Witch Who Wasn't, 1964, The Emperor and the Kite, 1968, Writing Books for Children, 1973, The Girl Who Cried Flowers, 1974, The Hundredth Dove, 1978, The Dream Weaver, 1979, Commander Toad in Space, 1980, The Gift of Sarah Barker, 1981, Touch Magic, 1981, Dragon's Blood, 1982, Tales of Wonder, 1983, Heart's Blood, 1984, Cards of Grief, 1984, Dragonfield, 1985, Merlin's Booke, 1986, The Lullabye Songbook, 1986, Ring of Earth, 1986, Favorite Folktales From Around the World, 1986, Piggins, 1987, Owl Moon, 1987, Three Bears, 1987, A Sending of Dragons, 1987, The Devil's Arithmetic, 1988, Sister Light/Sister Dark, 1988, White Jenna, 1989, Dove Isabeau, 1989, Baby Bear's Bedtime Book, 1990, Tam Lin, 1990, Bird Watch, 1990, Sky Dogs, 1990, Wizard's Hall, 1991, All those Secrets of the World, 1991, Wings, 1991, Hark! A Christmas Sampler, 1991, Encounter, 1992, Briar Rose, 1992, Letting Swift River Go, 1992, What Rhymes with Moon, 1993, Welcome to the Greenhouse, 1993, Honkers, 1993, Here There Be Dragons, 1993, Grandad Bill's Song, 1994, Good Griselle, 1994, The Girl in the Golden Bower, 1994, Old Dame Counterpane, 1994, Old Macdonald's Songbook, 1994, Here There Be Unicorns, 1994, Beneath the Ghost Moon, 1994, The Wild Hunt, 1995, Ballad of the Pirate Queens, 1995, And Twelve Chinese Acrobats, 1995, Water Music, 1995, Among Angels, 1995, Here They Be Witches, 1995, O. Jerusalem, 1996, Welcome to the Sea of Sand, 1996, Passager, 1996, Hobby, 1996, Sacred Places, 1996, Here There Be Angels, 1996, Milk and Honey, 1996, Meet The Monsters, 1996, Once Upon Ice, 1997, Merlin, 1997, Child of Faerie, 1997, Twelve Impossible Things Before Breakfast, 1997, Miz Berlin Walks, 1997, Nocturne, 1997, Armageddon Summer, 1998, House/House, 1998, Prince of Egypt, 1998, Raising Yoder's Barn, 1998, The Wizard's Map, 1999, The Pictish Child, 1999, The Fairies' Ring, 1999, Moonball, 1999, Gray Heroes: Elder Tales From Around the World, 1999, How Does a Dinosaur Say Goodnight, 2000, Off We Go, 2000, Queen's Own Fool, 2000, Not One Damsel in Distress, 2000, Mirror/Mirror, 2000, Color Me a Rhyme, 2000, Welcome to the River of Grass, 2001, The Fish Prince and Other Merman Stories, 2001, Odysseus in the Serpent's Maze, 2001, Dear Mother/Dear Daughter, 2001, Hippolyta and the Curse of the Amazons, 2002, Wild Wings, 2002, Firebird, 2002, Horizons, 2002, Animal Train, 2002, Harvest Home, 2002, Girl in a Cage, 2002, Sword of the Rightful King, 2003, How Do Dinosaurs Get Well Soon, 2003, Take Joy, 2003, My Brothers' Flying Machine, 2003, Hoptoad, 2003, Mightier than the Sword, 2003, The Radiation Sonnets, 2003, The Flying Witch, 2003, Jason and the Gorgon's Blood, 2004, How Do Dinosaurs Clean their Rooms?, 2004, The Barefoot Book of Ballet Stories, 2004, Prince Across the Water, 2004, over 200 others. Mass. del. Dem. Nat. Conv., 1972; town coord. Robert Drinan's campaign, 1970; chmn. bd. trustees Hatfield (Mass.) Libr., 1978-83. Mem. Soc. Children's Book Writers (bd. dirs. 1974—), Children's Lit. Assn. (bd. dirs. 1977-79), Sci. Fiction Writers Am. (pres. 1986-88), Mystery Writers Am., Authors Guild. Democrat. Jewish/Quaker. Home: PO Box 27 Hatfield MA 01038-0027

YOLLICK, BERNARD LAWRENCE, otolaryngologist, surgeon; b. Toronto, Mar. 24, 1922; came to U.S., 1949; s. Samuel and Beatrice (Roth) Y.; m. Liny L. Pajgin, 1947; children: Ingrid, Eric Lyf. Sr. Matriculation, Harbord Collegiate Inst., Toronto, 1939; MD, U. Toronto, 1945. Diplomate Am. Bd. Surgery, Am. Bd. Otolaryngology. Intern Sunnybrook Hosp., Toronto, 1945-46; resident D.C. Gen. Hosp., Washington, 1950, St. Louis County Hosp., Clayton, Mo., 1952-53; Am. Cancer Soc. fellow M.D. Anderson Cancer Hosp., Houston, 1953-54; resident in pathology Cook County Hosp., Chgo., 1949; surgeon Houston, 1953-59; fellowship in otolaryngology VA Hosp., Dallas, 1960-63; asst. prof. anatomy Baylor Med. Sch., Houston, 1953-59; assoc. prof. anatomy U. Tex. Dental Sch., Houston, 1953-59, Baylor Coll. Dentistry, Dallas, 1987-90; mem. staff Children's Med. Ctr., Dallas, 1990—; mem. staff, chief dept. otolaryngology St. Paul Med. Ctr., Dallas, 1990-98. Cons. Tex. Workers Compensation Ins. Fund, 1996—, Dept. Defense, Dallas, 1997—; mem. otolaryngology staff Vets. Adminstrn. Hosp., Dallas, 1990—. Contbr. articles to profl. jours. Served to capt. Royal Can. Army Med. Corps, 1942-45. Recipient fellowship Am. Cancer Soc., 1953. Fellow Am. Coll. Surgeons; mem. Tex. Otolaryn. Assn. (pres. 1979).

YOLTON, JOHN WILLIAM, philosopher, educator; b. Birmingham, Ala., Nov. 10, 1921; s. Robert Elgene and Ella Maude (Holmes) Y.; m. Jean Sebastian, Sept. 5, 1945; children: Karin Frances Yolton Griffith, Pamela Holmes Yolton Smith. BA with honors, U. Cin., 1945, MA, 1946; postgrad., U. Calif., Berkeley, 1946-50; DPhil (Fulbright fellow), Balliol Coll., Oxford, Eng., 1952; LL.D. (hon.), York U., 1974; D.Litt. (hon.), McMaster U., 1976. Vis. lectr. philosophy Johns Hopkins U., 1952-53; asst. prof. Princeton U., 1953-57; assoc. prof. Kenyon Coll., 1957-61; prof. U. Md., 1961-63; prof. philosophy York U., Toronto, 1963-78, chmn. dept., 1963-73, acting dean grad. studies, 1967-68, acting pres., 1973-74; prof. philosophy Rutgers U., New Brunswick, N.J., 1978—, dean Rutgers Coll., 1978-85, John Locke prof. history of philosophy, 1989-92, prof. emeritus philosophy, 1992—. Cons. Bertrand Russell Archives, McMaster U., 1973-86. Author: John Locke and the Way of Ideas, 1956, Metaphysical Analysis, 1967, Locke and the Compass of Human Understanding, 1970, Thinking Matter, 1983, Perceptual Acquaintance from Descartes to Reid, 1984, Locke and French Materialism, 1991, Perception and Reality, 1996, Realism and Appearances, 2000, The Two Intellectual Worlds of JOhn Locke, 2004, other books; gen. editor Clarendon Edit. of Works of John Locke, Oxford U. Press, 1984-92, Blackwell's Companion to the Enlightenment, 1992, Locke Dictionary (Blackwell), 1993, Library of the History of Ideas, 5 books in field; mem. editl. bd. jours. in field; editor (with Jean S. Yolton) Some Thoughts Concerning Education, by Locke, 1989; v.p., bd. dirs. Jour. of the History of Ideas, 1991-98; contbr. articles to profl. jours. Mem. N.J. Com. for Humanities, 1978-85, treas., 1980-85. Am. Coun. Learned Socs. fellow, 1960-61; Can. Coun. fellow, 1968-69. Mem.: Hume Soc., Am. Soc. for 18th Century Studies, Can. Philos. Assn., Mind Assn., Am. Philos. Assn. Fax: 732-545-7134.

YONDA, ALFRED WILLIAM, mathematician; b. Cambridge, Mass., Aug. 10, 1919; s. Walter and Theophelia (Naruscewicz) Y.; m. Mary Jane McManus, Dec. 19, 1949 (dec.); children: Nancy, Kathryn, Elizabeth, John; m. Peggy A. Terrel, June 22, 1975. BS, U. Ala., 1952, MA in Math., 1954. Registered profl. engr. Mathematician rocket rsch. Redstone Arsenal, Huntsville, Ala., 1953, U.S. Army Ballistic Rsch. Labs., Aberdeen, Md., 1954-56; instr. math. U. Ala., Tuscaloosa, 1954, Temple U., Phila., 1956-57; assoc. scientist, rsch. & devel. divsn. Avco Corp., Wilmington, Mass., 1957-59; sr. mem. tech. staff RCA, Camden, N.J., 1959-66; mgr. computer analysis and programming dept. Raytheon Co. Space and Info. Systems Divsn., Sudbury, Mass., 1966-70, mgr. software systems lab., 1969-70, prin. engr. missiles systems divsn., 1970-73; mgr. sys. analysis & programming GTE Govt. Systems Corp., 1973-77, mgr. software engring. Atlantic ops., 1977-82, sr. mem. tech. staff Command Control & Comm. Sector, 1983-91; software systems engr. Yonda Software Systems Cons., 1991—. Contbr. articles to profl. jours. Pres. Milford Area Assn. Retarded Children, 1970-74, vice chmn. fin. com. Town of Medway, 1973; bd. dirs. Blackstone Valley Mental Health and Retardation Area, 1970-76; trustee Medway Libr., 1973-82, chmn., 1974-81. With USAAF, 1943-46. Hon. fellow Advanced Level Telecomm. Tng. Ctr., Ghaziabad, India, 1981. Mem. AAAS, IEEE, Math. Assn. Am., N.Y. Acad. Scis., Sigma Xi, Phi Eta Sigma, Pi Mu Epsilon (pres. Ala. chpt. 1953-54), Sigma Pi Sigma. Office: 1622 Worcester Rd Apt 225B Framingham MA 01702-4415 E-mail: awyonda@aol.com.

YONETANI, AYAKO, music educator, entertainer; d. Mitsuya and Yuko Yonetani. Mus B, Juilliard Sch., 1986; MusM, Julliard Sch., 1987, MusD, 1993. Asst. prof. of violin/viola U. of Ctrl. Fla., Orlando, 1993—98, assoc. prof. of violin, 1998—; asst. faculty Aspen Music Festival and Sch., Aspen,

Colo., 1989—2002. Concertmaster Aspen Music Festival and Sch., Colo., 2001—02. Translator: (book) Teaching Genius: Dorothy DeLay and the Making of a Musician. Avocations: opera, classical music. Office: U of Ctrl Fla Music P O Box 161354 Orlando FL 32816-1354 E-mail: yonetani@mail.ucf.edu.

YONEZU, TAKEHIKO, retired investment company executive; Retired CFO, exec. v.p., treas. Sumitomo Corp., Tokyo. Office: Sumitomo Corp 22 Hitotsubashi 1chome Chiyodaku Chiyoda Tokyo 1008 601 Japan

YONG, RAYMOND NEN-YIU, civil engineering educator; b. Singapore, Apr. 10, 1929; naturalized, 1966; s. Ngim Djin and Lucy (Loh) Y.; m. Florence Lechensky, July 8, 1961; children: Raymond T.M., Christopher T.K. BA in Math. and Physics, Washington and Jefferson Coll., 1950; BS, MIT, 1952; MS, Purdue U., 1954; MEngring., McGill U., Montreal, Que., Can., 1958, PhD, 1960. Mem. faculty McGill U., 1959-95, prof. civil engring., 1965-72, William Scott prof. civil engring. and applied mechanics, 1972-95; dir. Geotech Rsch. Ctr., 1973-95; assoc. mem. Ctr. for Medicine, Ethics and Law McGill U., 1991-95. Adj. prof. civil engring. U. Fla., Gainesville, 1984—; adj. rsch. prof. civil engring. Carleton U., Ottawa, 1990; disting. rsch. prof. U. Wales, Cardiff, 1995-2002, emeritus prof., sr. sci. advsisor, 2002—; sr. sci. dir. Geoenviron. Engring. Rsch. Ctr., Cardiff Sch. Engring., U. Wales,1995. Author: Soil Properties and Behavior, 1975 (Japanese edit. 1977), Introduction to Soil Behavior, 1966 (Japanese edit. 1974), Vehicle Traction Mechanics, 1985, Principles of Contaminant Transport in Soils, 1992 (Japanese edit. 1995), Geoenvironmental Engineering: Contaminated Soils, Pollutant Fate and Mitigation, 2001, Natural Attenuation of Contaminants in Soils, 2004. Decorated chevalier Ordre National du Que.; recipient Killam prize Can. Coun., 1985, ASTM Charles B. Dudley award, 1988, Can. Environ. Achievement award, Lifetime Achievement Environment Can., 1991. Fellow Royal Soc. Can., Engring. Inst. Can., Can. Soc. for Civil Engring.; mem. ASCE, ASTM (Charles B. Dudley award 1988), Inst. Civil Engrs., Soc. Rheology, Clay Minerals Soc., Internat. Soc. Terrain-Vehicle Systems (pres. 1993—), Can. Geotech. Soc. (R.F. Legget award 1993). E-mail: r.nyong@shaw.ca.

YONKMAN, FREDRICK ALBERS, lawyer, management consultant; b. Holland, Mich., Aug. 22, 1930; s. Fredrick Francis and Janet Dorothy (Albers) Y.; m. Kathleen VerMeulen, June 9, 1953 (div. Sept. 22, 1980); children: Sara, Margriet, Nina.; m. Barbara Anne Sullivan, Aug. 22, 1981 (div. Mar. 31, 1994); 1 child, Fredrick Ryan; m. Jewel Marie Humphrey, July 4, 1998. BA, Hope Coll., Holland, 1952; JD, U. Chgo., 1957. Bar: NY 1958, Mass. 1968, DC 1984. With Winthrop, Stimson, Putnam & Roberts, NYC, 1957-64; sec., gen. counsel Reuben H. Donnelley Corp., NYC, 1964-66, Dun & Bradstreet, Inc., NYC, 1966-68; ptnr. Sullivan & Worcester, Boston, 1968-72; gen. counsel Am. Express Co., NYC, 1972-78, exec. v.p., 1975-80; pres. Buck Cons., NYC, 1980-81; mgmt. cons., psychoanalyst, 1981—2003; counsel Peabody, Lambert & Myers, Washington, 1983-84; exec. dir. Asian Bus. Ctr., Rutgers U. Bus. Sch., Piscataway, NJ, 2003—. Chmn. Outward Bound, Inc., Garrison, NY, 1980-81; mem. bd. and chmn. audit com. Kennecott Corp., 1978-81; adj. prof. law Georgetown U., 1976-78; chmn. Georgetown Internat. Law Inst., 1980-81; vis. com. U. Chgo. Law Sch., 1980-82; mem. exec. com. Warner-Amex, 1978-80; bd. dirs. and advisors, Sageworks Inc., Raleigh, NC, 1998-2004. Bd. dirs. Washington Campus Program, 1976-81; bd. dirs. Young Audiences, 1978-83. With CIC, U.S.Army, 1952-54. Recipient Silver Anniversary award NCAA, 1977. Mem.: ABA, NY State Bar Assn. Methodist. Home: 5200 No Ocean Dr Apt 1410 Lauderdale By The Sea FL 33308 Office Phone: 954-876-0872.

YONTS, LARRY BRENT, lawyer; b. Greenville, Ky., Mar. 21, 1949; s. Larry Ray and Dorothy Nell (Sweeney) Y.; m. Janice Faye Covington, Nov. 20, 1976; children: Emily, Ellen, Harrison. BS, Murray State U., 1971; JD, U. Ky., 1975. Bar: Ky. 1976. Assoc. Streets & Cisney, Greenville, Ky., 1976-78; pvt. practice Greenville, 1978—; mem. for dist. 15 Ky. State Ho. of Reps, Greenville, Ky., 1996—. Bd. dris. Muhl Co. Indsl. Bd., Greenville. 1st lt. U.S. Army, 1971-77. Democrat. Baptist. Avocation: civil war-lincoln collector. Office: PO Box 370 Greenville KY 42345-1512

YONTS-SHEPARD, SUSAN, forest service administrator; BA in History and Polit. Sci., Transylvania U.; grad. sr. exec. fellow program, Kennedy Sch. Govt., Harvard U. Pub. affairs positions Washington and Idaho Panhandle Nat. Forest; with Washington Office in Land Mgmt. Planning, Legis. Affairs; program mgr. Nat. Appeals and Litigation; dep. dir. for strategic planning and resource assessment USDA Forest Svc., Washington, assoc. dep. chief for programs and litigation, 2002—. Mem. working group Columbia River Basin Team, No. Spotted Owl Team; agy. rep. to exec. office Pres., Coun. on Environ. Quality. Office: USDA Forest Service 1400 Independence Ave SW Washington DC 20250-0002

YONTZ, KENNETH FREDRIC, medical and chemical company executive; b. Sandusky, Ohio, July 21, 1944; s. Kenneth Willard and Dorothy (Kromer) Y.; m. Jean Ann Marshall, July 21, 1962 (div. Aug. 1982); children: Terri, Christine, Michael, Jennifer; m. Karen Glojek, July 7, 1984 (wid. Dec. 1994); m. Karen Mc Diarmid, Jan. 10, 1997. BSBA, Bowling Green State U., 1971; MBA, Eastern Mich. U., 1979. Fin. planning mgr. Ford Motor Co., Rawsonville, Mich., 1970-74; fin. mgr. Chemetron Corp., Chgo., 1974-76, pres. fire systems div., 1976-80; pres. electronics div. Allen Bradley Co., Milw., 1980-83, group. pres. electronics, 1983-85, exec. v.p., 1985-86; chmn. bd. Apogent Techs., Milw., 1986—, Sybron Dental Specialities, Milw., 1986—. Bd. dirs. Rockwell Int., Milw. Founder Karen Yontz Womens Cardiac Awareness Ctr. Mem. Bluemound Country Club, Muirfield Village Golf Club, Vintage Club (Indian Wells, Calif.), Tradition Golf Club (La Quinta, Calif.), Chenequa Country Club (Hartford, Wis.), Flint Hills Country Club (Wichita). Roman Catholic. *Positive results are seldom achieved from negative thoughts.*

YOO, CHOON WANG, financial consultant; b. Seoul, Korea, July 11, 1960; came to U.S., 1986; s. Seung Ahn and Song Hee (Kim) Y.; m. Yeong Mee Kwon, May 26, 1990; 1 child, Sean. BA in Econs., Korea U., 1986; MBA in Acctg., CUNY, 1989; MBA in Fin., C.W. Post Coll., 1991. Acctg. mgr. Kenney Transport, Inc., N.Y.C., 1986-89, controller, 1989-92; fin. cons. Equitable Fin. Co., N.Y.C., 1992-94; dist. mgr. Equitable/Equico Security Co., Paramus, N.J., 1994-95; pres. Hexagon Internat. Group Co., Ft. Lee, N.J., 1995—. Cons. Korean-Am. One-Hour Photo Assn., Massapequa, N.Y., 1993—, Korean Producers Assn., Bronx, 1995—, Pa. Merchant Group, Radnor, 1995—, 1st Security Co., Ltd., Seoul, Korea, 1995—, Hangil Merchant Bank, Seoul, 1996. Pres. Korean Am. 1.5 Generation Assn., 1994—. Young Poong Found. scholar, Seoul, 1984-86. Mem. Internat. Assn. Fin. Planning, Nat. Assn. Securities Dealers, Nat. Assn. Life Underwriters, Assn. Investment Mgmt. and Rsch. Presbyterian. Avocations: skiing, golf, tennis, art collecting. Office: Hexagon Internat Group Co 2175 Lemoine Ave Ste 400 Fort Lee NJ 07024-6033 Address: 576 Valley Rd # 173 Wayne NJ 07470-3526

YOO, GRACE, legal association administrator; Exec. dir. Nat. Asian Pacific Am. Bar Assn., Washington. Office: Nat Asian Pacific Am Bar Assn Ste 315 733 15th St NW Washington DC 20005

YOOD, HAROLD STANLEY, retired internist; b. Plainfield, N.J., Feb. 23, 1920; s. Raphael and Netta (Newcorn) Y.; m. Helen H. Hull, Nov. 8, 1941; children: Pamela, Patricia Yood Herskovitz, Paula Yood Peterson, Andrew H. BA, U. Va., 1940, MD, 1943. Intern Syracuse (N.Y.) U. Med. Ctr., 1943; pvt. practice Plainfield, N.J., 1946-91; med. dir. Cen. Jersey Individual Physicians Assn., 1987-2000; ret. Staff dept. medicine Muhlenberg Hosp., 1946—, pres. staff, 1980-86, cons., 1991-95, emeritus, 1995—. Contbr. articles to Jour. Med. Soc. N.J., Communication for Ciba, others. Pres. vol. med. staff Raritan Valley Hosp., Greenbrook, N.J., 1969; bd. govs. Muhlenberg Regional Med. Ctr., 1980-86, exec. com.; trustee, v.p. United Way Plainfield/Fanwood, 1975-81; bd. dirs. United Way Union County, 1978-81; pres. Jewish Community Ctr., Plainfield, 1970-71; v.p. Jewish Fedn. Cen. N.J., 1971-73, Cen. N.J. Jewish Home for Aged, 1973-80. Capt. M.C. AUS, 1944-45, ETO. Decorated Purple Heart, Combat Med. badge, Combat Glider badge. Fellow Am. Coll. Gastroenterology (sr.), Am. Coll. Angiology (ret.), Internat. Coll. Angiology (ret.); mem. AMA, Med. Soc. N.J. (governing coun. hosp. med. staff sect. 1983-92, chmn. 1988-90; trustee 1989-90), Union County Med. Soc., Lions (life). *Enjoyment in my profession, pleasure in relationship with patients, a belief in the necessity for civic and community volunteer involvement, a commitment to support causes that aid the unfortunate and do no harm to individuals.*

YOOK, CHONG CHUL, engineering educator; b. Kyngbuk, Sunsan, Korea, Jan. 1, 1926; s. Jae Kyun Yook and Choi (Shoon) Ie; m. Sook Kae Chang, Aug. 15, 1949; children: Myung-Hi, Oak-Soo, Sun-Hi. BS in Engring., Seoul (Republic of Korea) Nat. U., 1950; postgrad., Oak Ridge Inst., Argonne Internat. Inst., 1961, U. Ill., 1962; PhD in Nuclear Engring., Hanyang U., Seoul, 1967. Prof. Chung-Nam Nat. U., Taejon, Republic of Korea, 1957-64, dean Engring. Coll., 1962-64; prof. Hanyang U., 1964-91, prof. emeritus, 1991—. Mem. tech. adv. bd. Ministry of Sci. and Tech., Seoul, 1988-90; advisor inspection, testing and examination cons. ITEC Svc. Co., Ltd., Seoul, 1991—. Author: Radiation Safety Handling, 1982, East and West, 1991 (Panel award 1991); patent for applied measuring device of engine ring wear. Mem. energy and resources adv. com. Rep. of Korean Govt., Seoul, 1981-83. Mem. Korean Assn. for Radiation Protection (pres. Seoul chpt. 1977-79), Internat. Radiation Protection Assn. (rep. Netherlands chpt. 1977-80, adv. com. Fed. Republic of Germany 1978-81), Korean Atomic Energy Rsch. Inst. (standing com. Taejon chpt. 1989-90), Korean Radioisotapes Assn. (audit treas. Seoul chpt. 1985-91). Mem. Christian Ch. Avocations: reading, mountain climbing, swimming.

YOON, JAY MYOUNG, oncologist, hematologist, internist; b. Korea, Sept. 30, 1946; married. BA Coll. Liberal Arts & Sci. summa cum laude, Seoul Nat. U., 1967, MD summa cum laude, 1971. Diplomate Am. Bd. Internal Medicine, 1978, Am. Bd. Oncology, 1979, Am. Bd. Hematology, 1980. Intern Bklyn. Hosp. Ctr.-Cornell U., N.Y.C., 1974—75; resident in medicine Bronx-Lebanon Hosp.-Albert Einstein Coll. Medicine, N.Y.C., 1975-76; fellow in hematol. oncology Baystate Med. Ctr.-Tufts U. Sch. Medicine, Springfield, Mass., 1976-78; fellow in oncology Roswell Park Cancer Inst.-SUNY, Buffalo, 1978-79, rsch. clinician in oncology dept. surg. develop. oncology, 1979-80; rsch. instr. medicine SUNY, 1978—80; attending physician, med. oncologist St. Francis Hosp. and Health Ctr., Clarian Health Ptnrs., Beech Grove and Indpls., 1980-98; rsch. instr. medicine SUNY, 1978—80; prof. medicine Ulsan U. Med. Sch., 1997—98; CEO, pres. Yoon Clinic, P.C., Edmonds, Wash., 1999—; mem. med. staff Stevens Meml. Hosp., Edmonds, Wash., 1999—, Northwest Hosp., Seattle, 1999—, Swedish Med. Ctr., Seattle, 2000. Contbr. articles to profl. jours. Mem. AAAS, AMA, ADA, AACR, Am. Assn. Blood Banks, Am. Soc. Clin. Oncology, Am. Soc. Hematology, N.Y. Acad. Sci. Home: 11901 59th Ave W Mukilteo WA 98275-5569 Office: Yoon Clinic PC Edmonds Med and Profl Ctr 7631 212th St SW Ste 106 B Edmonds WA 98026-7565 Office Phone: 425-778-5551. Office Fax: 425-697-6222. Personal E-mail: jmyoon@msn.com. E-mail: yoonclinicpc@msn.com.

YOON, JI-WON, virology, immunology and diabetes educator, research administrator; b. Kang-Jin, Chonnam, Korea, Mar. 28, 1939; came to U.S., 1965; s. Baek-In and Duck-Soon (Lee) Y.; m. Chungja Rhim, Aug. 17, 1968; children: John W., James W. MS, U. Conn., 1971, PhD, 1973. Sr. investigator NIH, Bethesda, Md., 1978-84; prof., chief div. virology U. Calgary, Alta., Can., 1984—, assoc. dir. Diabetes Rsch. Ctr., 1985—90, dir., 1990—99, Julia McFarlane prof., 1990—99, dir. Lab. Viral and Immunopathogenesis of Diabetes, 1999—, Can. Rsch. Chair Diabetes, 2001—. Mem. editl. bd. Diabetologia, 1977, Ann. Rev. Advances Present Rsch. Animal Diabetes, 1990—, Diabetes Rsch. Clin. Practice, 1989—, Jour. Biomed. Rsch., 1992—, Jour. Exptl. Molecular Medicine, 1996—; mem. editl. adv. bd. Jour. Diabetologia, 1996—99; vis. prof. Diabetes Endocrinology Rsch. Ctr., Yale U., New Haven, 1997—, Can. rsch. chair in diabetes, 2001—03; prof. and dir. Ctr. for Immunologic Rsch., Chgo. Med. Sch., 2003; dir. Rosalind Franklin Diabetes Ctr. Chicago Med. Sch., 2004. Contbr. articles to New England Jour. Medicine, Jour. Virology, Sci., Nature, The Lancet, Jour. Diabetes, Jour. Immunology, Jour. Biochemistry, Jour. Exptl. Medicine. Rsch. fellow Sloan Kettering Cancer Inst., 1973-74, Staff fellow, Sr. Staff fellow NIH, 1974-76, 76-78; recipient NIH Dir. award, 1984, Heritage Med. Scientist award, Alberta Heritage Found. Med. Rsch., 1984, Lectrship. award, 3d Asian Symposium Childhood Diabetes, 1989, 8th Annual Meeting Childhood Diabetes, Osaka, Japan, 1990, 9th Korean/Can. Heritage award, 1989, 1st Compatriot award Fedn. Korean-Can. Assn., 1996. Mem. Am. Soc. Immunologists, Am. Diabetes Assn., Am. Soc. Microbiology, N.Y. Acad. Sci., Soc. Virology, Internat. Diabetes Fedn. Baptist. Achievements include first isolation of diabetogenic virus from patients with recent onset of IDDM; first demonstration of prevention of virus-induced diabetes by vaccination with nondiabetogenic virus in animals; discovery that autoimmune IDDM can be prevented by depletion of macrophages in autoimmune diabetic NOD mice, certain viral glycoproteins (rubella virus E2 glycoprotein) can induce organ-specific autoimmune disease; research on molecular identification of diabetogenic viral gene in animal models, discovery of a nontoxic organic compound with no side effects that completely prevents type I diabetes in NOD mice, discovery that bacterial superantigens such as staphylococcal enterotozins (SEC1, SEC3) can prevent autoimmune type I diabetes by activation of CD4+ suppressor T cells in NOD mice; research on the role of cloned T-Cells in the pathogenesis of autoimmune Type I Diabetes at cellular and molecular level, molecular role TGFB in prevention of Autoimmune IDDM, molecular role of macrophages in pathogenesis of virus-induced diabetes; developed the method for prevention of autoimmune type 1 diabetes in diabetic mice by immunogene therapy; developed a new method for prevention of autoimmune diabetes in mice by control of the finely tuned immune balance by treatment with human choriogonadotropin; developed an insulin gene therapy for the cure of autoimmune diabetes by the expression of modified insulin in hepatocytes under the control of glucose-sensitive promoter; developed a stem cell gene therapy for the possible cure of type 1 diabetes by neurogenesis of beta cells from the pancreatic stem cells using betacellulin with the albumin leader sequence for its secretion. Office: Rosalind Franklin Diabetes Ctr. Chicago Med Sch 3333 Green Bay Rd North Chicago IL 60064 Office Phone: 847-578-3436. Business E-Mail: Ji-Won.Yoon@rosalindfranklin.edu.

YOPCONKA, NATALIE ANN CATHERINE, computer specialist, educator, business owner; b. Taylor, Pa., July 21, 1942; d. Michael Joseph and Natalie Ann Lucille (Panek) Y. BS with high honors, U. Md., 1965; MBA, George Washington U., 1976, MA in Edn. and Human Devel., 1988, postgrad., 1990—96. Mgmt. analyst, adminstrv. trainee, computer programmer U.S. Dept. Commerce, Maritime Adminstrn., Washington, 1965-67; computer programmer, computer specialist U.S. Dept. Labor, Washington, 1967-78; instr. computer sci. Assn. for Computing Machinery, Washington, 1978; instr. computer sci. and mgmt. tech. Montgomery Coll., Takoma Park and Rockville, Md., 1979; sr. programmer analyst Dynamic Data Processing, Inc., Silver Spring, Md., 1979; instr. Nat. Bus. Sch., Inc., Alexandria, Va., 1980; cons. McLeod Corp., Washington, 1980; lectr. computer sci., coop. coord. U. Md., College Park, 1980-81; sr. adminstrv. applications analyst programmer Data Transformation Corp., Washington, 1981; sr. sys. analyst Singer Link Simulation Sys. Divsn., Silver Spring, 1981-82; accessory designer, 1982-83; market rschr. Washington Fin. Svc., 1982-83; lectr. computer info. and sys. sci. U. D.C., Rockville, Md., 1983; prof. computer programming and mgmt. info. sys. Benjamin Franklin U., Washington, 1983; rschr. Info. U.S.A., Potomac, Md., 1983-85; admissions rep. Brook-Wein Bus. Inst., Washington, 1985; pvt. distbr. Hyattsville, Md., 1979—86; distbr. AMWAY Corp., 1979—92. Pvt. distbr. Hyattsville and Columbia, Md., 1979-1992, distbr. AMWAY Corp., 1979-92, course developer, instr. Grad. Sch. USDA, Balt., 1986-87; field interviewer Nat. Drug Abuse Bur., 1989-90, chmn. Cert. for Computing Profls. Exam. Review Course for Balt. Washington, D.C. corridor, 1994-95; agent Kivex, Inc., 1996-97, Information Builders, Inc., 1997-2000, 3COM Corp., 1997-99, bus. owner, cons. Sys. and Edn. Enterprises, 1979—; pvt. cons. Columbia, Md., 1987—. Mem. Takoma Park Disability Com., Mayor's Com. on Energy, Housing and Planning, 1980-81; mem. Vision 2030 Balt./Howard County, 2002-2003; mem. Missionary Oblates of Immaculate Mary; mem. choir Our Lady of Sorrows Cath. Ch., 1977-82; mem. various choirs, St. John the Evangelist Cath. Ch., eucharistic min. 1990-2003, internet com., 1996-97, lector; mem. Balt. Wash. Corridor C. of C., 1996-97, Citizens Adv. Com. to Bd. Edn., Howard County, 1991-92; mem. computer adv. com. Bd. Edn. Howard County, 1993-95; chmn. Leukemia Soc. Md.; active Suburban Md. High Tech. Coun., 1994-95, Howard County High Tech. Coun., 1994-95. Recipient chmn./woman of the yr., Leukemia Soc. of Md., 1996. Mem. NAFE, IEEE (Balt. sect., carlier Wash. sect., computer soc., commn. soc., tech. com. on software engring., stds. com and groups, software standards assn., et. al), ASCD, IEEE, IEEE Computer Soc. (tech. com. on software engring., software engring. stds. coms. and groups), Software Stds. Assn., Nat. Info. Sys. Audit and Control Assn., Assn. for Computing Machinery (Wash. DC chpt., edn. com., instr. 1978-79, edn. com. 1980-81, profl. devel. com. 1982-83), Data Processing Mgmt. Assn. (chmn. cert. for computing profls. exam. rev. course for Balt.-Washington corridor 1994-95), Balt. Washington Info. Sys. Educators (consortium com. 1984-85, program com. for 1986 regional tng. conf. 1985-86, vendor com. 1988-89), Fed. Automatic Data Processing Users Group (various coms. 1976-1983), Armed Forces Comm. and Electronics Assn., Balt. Coun. Fgn. Affairs, Am. Assn. Ret. Persons (Howard County chpt.), Nat. Assn. Ret. Fed. Employees (sec. Howard County chpt.), Nat. Bus. Edn. Assn. (Wash. DC chpt.), U. Md. Howard County Alumni Club (scholarship com. 1989), Columbia (Md.) Assn., Phi Delta Gamma (scholarship com. 1977 78, social com. 1980-81, hospitality com. 1982-83, sec. 1989-90).

YORDAN, EDGARDO LUIS, gynecologist; b. Ponce, P.R., June 6, 1946; BA, Columbia U., 1968; MD, U. Md. Sch. Medicine, 1972. Diplomate Am. Bds. Obstetrics & Gynecology and Gynecol. Oncology. Intern U. Chgo. Hosps. and Clinics, 1972-73; resident in ob/gyn Columbia U.-Presbyn. Med. Ctr., N.Y.C., 1973-77, Meml. Sloan-Kettering Cancer Ctr., N.Y.C., 1976; fellow U. So. Calif.-L.A. County Med. Ctr., 1977-79, Rush-Presbyn. St. Luke's Med. Ctr., Chgo., 1980, assoc. prof., 1980—. Dir. gynecol., Luth. Gen. Hosp., Chgo., 1987—. Mem. Soc. Gynecol. Oncology, Western Assn. Gynecol. Oncology, Ctrl. Assn. OB-GYN, Am. Coll. Surgeons, Soc. Gynecol. Laparascopy, Chgo. Gynecol. Soc., Ctrl. Travel Club. Office: Rush Cancer Inst Rush Univ Med Ctr 1653 W Congress Pkwy Chicago IL 60612 also: Advocate Med Group Lutheran Gen Hosp 1700 Luther Ln Park Ridge IL 60068-1270 Office Phone: 312-942-6723. E-mail: edgardo.yordan@advocatehealth.com., edgardoyordan668@msn.com.

YORINKS, ADRIENNE BERG, artist, illustrator; b. N.Y.C., May 25, 1956; d. Jerome Sydney and Helene Berg; m. Douglas Keith Schoenberg, June 8, 2003. BS in Psychology Animal Behavior, U. Wis., 1977; M in Dance Edn., NYU, 1982. Illustrator: Stand for Children, 1998, The Alphabet Atlas, 1999, The Last Will & Testament of an Extremely Distinguished Dog, 2000, Quack, 2003; illustrator My Travels with Capt. Lewis an Clark, 2004, writer, illustrator A Quilt of States, 2005. Recipient Merit award, Ga. Coun. Arts. Mem.: Manhattan Quilters Guild. Avocations: hiking, tennis, dance. Home and Studio: 10 Edwards Pl Short Hills NJ 07078 Office Phone: 973-467-1001.

YORINKS, ARTHUR, children's author, writer, director; b. Roslyn, N.Y., Aug. 21, 1953; s. Alexander and Shirley (Kron) Y.; m. Adrienne Berg, Oct. 23, 1983. Writer, tchr. performer Am. Mime Theatre, 1969-79; instr. theatre arts Cornell U., Ithaca, N.Y., 1972-79; assoc. dir. New Works Project, N.Y.C., 1977—; founder, artistic dir. Moving Theatre, N.Y.C., 1979, The Night Kitchen, N.Y.C., 1990—. Author: (children's books) Sid and Sol, 1977, The Magic Meatballs, 1979, Louis the Fish, 1980 (Sch. Libr. Jour. Best Book Yr. Citation 1980), It Happened in Pinsk, 1983 (Booklist Children's Editor's Choice 1984, Biennale of Illustration plaque 1985), Hey, Al, 1986 (ALA Notable Book citation 1986, Caldecott medal 1987, Ky. Bluegrass award 1988), Bravo Minski, 1988 (Sch. Libr. Jour. Best Book Yr. Citation 1988), Company's Coming, 1988 (ALA Notable Book citation 1986), Oh, Brother, 1989 (Sch. Libr. Jour. Best Book Yr. Citation 1989), Ugh, 1990 (Sch. Libr. Jour. Best Book Yr. citation 1990), Christmas in July, 1991, Whitefish Will Rides Again, 1994, The Miami Giant, 1995, Frank & Joey Go To Work, 1996, Frank & Joey Eat Lunch, 1996, Harry & Lulu, 1999, The Alphabet Atlas, 1999, Tomatoes from Mars, 1999, The Flying Latke, 1999, The Flying Cow and Other Stories, 2000, Quack! There's a Duck on the Moon, 2002, (plays) Six, 1973, The Horse, 1978, Crackers, 1979, The King, 1980, Kissers, 1980, Piece for a Small Cafe, 1981, Piece for a Larger Cafe, 1982, So Sue Me, 1994, It's Alive!, 1995; (opera librettos) Leipziger Kerzenspiel, 1984, The Juniper Tree, 1985 (music by Philip Glass), The Fall of the House of Usher, 1988 (music by Philip Glass), (screenplay) Sid and Sol, 1982, It's a Miracle, 1991, Usher, 1991, Making Scents, 1993, (dance pieces) A Selection, 1999 (with Pilobolus Dance Co.). Office: The Night Kitchen 1350 Avenue Of The Americas New York NY 10019-4702

YORK, ALEXANDRA, lawyer; b. Jersey City, Feb. 9, 1939; d. Daniel Simpson and Regina (Norwich) S. BA, Tulane U., 1960; JD, Fordham U., 1976. Bar: N.Y. 1978, N.J., 1984; U.S. Dist. Ct. (so. and ea. dists.) N.Y. 1978, U.S. Dist. Ct. N.J. 1984, U.S. Ct. Appeals (2d cir.) 1987. Vol. Peace Corps, Philippines, 1961-63; legis. adviser Speaker of the Philippine House of Reps., Manila, 1964; speechwriter Mems. U.S. Congress, Washington, 1965; compliance officer U.S. Equal Employment Opportunity Commn., Washington, 1966-68; cons. N.Y.C. Dept. Consumer Affairs, 1969; cons., speechwriter N.Y.C. Dept. Air Resources, 1970-72; assoc. Shea and Gould, N.Y.C., 1977-79, Leopold Kaplan P.C., N.Y.C., 1980-86; asst. atty. gen. N.Y. State Dept. of Law, N.Y.C., 1987-93; spl. counsel external affairs Congress of Federated States of Micronesia, Pohnpei, 1993-95. Del. Federated States of Micronesia Internat. Climate Change Neg., Geneva, 1994; sr. policy adv. Philippine Sen. Com. Environment, 1996; U.N. devel. prog. cons. Philippine Dept. Environment and Natural Resources, 1996-97; mem., adv. com. environ. law, Practicing Law Inst., N.Y.C., 1991-93; prof. environ. policy, Ateneo de Manila U., Philippines, 1996-97; ofcl. del. UN Conf. on Environ. and Devel., Rio de Janiero, 1992; spkr. in field. Contbr. articles on environ. mgmt., internat. environ. law and climate change to profl. jours. Mem. ABA (natural resources sect., energy and environ. sect., internat. law and practice sect. 1990-93, program chair ann. meeting 1991, 92, chair subcom. on Human Rights and Environ., goal IX officer, 1992-93), Assn. of Bar of City of N.Y. (mem. internat. law com. 1990-93, mem., originator spl. com. internat. environ. law 1991, environ. com. 1987-90), Am. Soc. Internat. Law (environ. sect. 1991-92).

YORK, CANDACE A. marketing professional, writer; b. Lubbock, Tex., Mar. 7, 1954; d. Billy John and Francis Ann York; m. James R. Callahan, Feb. 23, 1947. BFA in Art History, U. Tex., 1976. Archival asst. S.W. collection Tex. Tech. U., Lubbock, 1976—77; claims analyst Met. Life, Austin, Tex., 1977—78; mktg. software engr., info. devel. IBM Corp., Austin, Tex., 1978—. Author: 155 Tips to Protect Your Home and Wealth From Fire, 2003, numerous poems, short stories; contbr. articles to profl. jours. Vol. Austin (Tex.) Cmty. Gardens, 2003—04, Tex. Sch. Blind, 2003. Named Internat. Poet of Merit, Internat. Libr. Poetry, 2001; recipient Excellence award, Soc. Tech. Comm., 1980, Honorable Mention award, Iliad Press, 2001, 1st pl. poetry in motion competition, 2001, 2nd place, Sol poet laureate competition, 2002. Mem.: Assn. Interactive Media, Pub. Rels. Soc. Am. (programs com. Austin chpt. 2003), Acad. Am. Poets, Internat. High IQ Soc. Avocations: poetry, photography, guitar, painting, tai chi. Home: 8210 Bent Tree Rd #213 Austin TX 78759 Personal E-mail: canyork@aol.com.

YORK, CAROLYN PLEASANTS STEARNS, English educator; b. High Point, N.C., Aug. 23, 1949; d. Frank Ellis and Jessie May (Pleasants) Stearns; m. Guy Aaron York, July 11, 1970; children: Adam Landon, Emily Pleasants, Jonathan Aaron. BA, U. N.C., Greensboro, 1971; MEd, U. N.C., Chapel Hill, 1985. Project Head Start asst. Forsyth County Schs., Winston-Salem, N.C., 1968; publicity dir. House in the Horseshoe Outdoor Drama, Southern Pines, N.C., 1975-76; chpt. I reading tchr. Lee County Schs., Sanford, N.C., 1977-86, English instr., 1987—. Reading instr. Ctrl. Carolina C.C., Sanford, 1985; reading chmn. So. Assn., Sanford, 1978; workshop dir., conf. spkr. N.C. Assn. Compensatory Educators, Raleigh, 1983; advisor, Internat. Thespian Soc., 2002-2003; writer-in-residence Peace Coll EDS Prog., 2003. Author: (poetry) Pleasantries, 1996, Weaver of Destiny, 1999; contbr. poems and stories to books; editor newsletter Creations, 1976; appeared on Friday Noon Poets Assn. Pub. TV Program, 1997; photographer Lee High Rev. lit. mag., 1998-99; advisor Internat. Thespian Soc., 2002-03. Founding mem. Lee County Arts Coun., Sanford, 1975; sec. Footlight Players, Lee County Recreation Dept., 2002; Sunday Sch. tchr., Bible sch. tchr. First Presbyn. Ch., Sanford, 1982,

86-89; bd. dirs. Child Devel. Ctr., Sanford, 1980-82; mem. adv. coun. Cmty. Playhouse of the Temple Theater, 1997-99; Builders Club sponsor Kiwanis Club of Lee County, Sanford, 1978-80. Recipient local and state prize N.C. Reading Assn., 1995, 1st prize Fields of Earth Poetry Symposium, 1996, 1st place Am. Scholastic Press Assn., 2000. Mem. N.C. Poetry Soc. (bd. dirs., 3d v.p. 1997-2003, workshop dir. 1993, 2d prize 1993, 1st prize 1999), San-Lee Writers (pres. 1993—, co-founder), Tri County English Alliance (coord., English Fair rep. 1995-2001), Lee County Reading Assn. (young authors' chmn. 1996-97; advisor lit. mag. Lee High Rev. 1998-99), Guild Am. Papercutters, Poetry Coun. NC (contest judge 2003). Avocations: snorkeling, playing the dulcimer, weaving, collecting antique valentines, cutting schrenschnitte. Home: 315 N Steele St Sanford NC 27330-3956 Personal E-mail: Yorkshome@wave-net.net.

YORK, COURTNEY CARTER, retired engineering executive, genealogist; b. Roland, Okla., Jan. 26, 1929; s. Jacob A. York and Rosa Pauline Bias; m. Gerlene Joy Gibson, Jan. 8, 1931 (dec.); children: Barbara Ann, Darlene Rosa; m. Roberta Louise Gale, Mar. 8, 1936. AA in Electronics, West Valley Coll., 1968. Signal dept. crew So. Pacific R.R., Calif., 1953-63; foreman, engr. Ampex Corp., Redwood City, Calif., 1963-73; engr. Vesatel-Printers, Sunnyvale, Calif., 1974-76; engring. corp mgr. Racal-Vadic, Sunnyvale, 1986; ret., 1986. Author 30 books on genealogy. Home: 2035 Smokey Dr Los Banos CA 93635-5107

YORK, DAVID P. lawyer; b. 1963; BA, Birmingham So. Coll.; JD, Samford U. Asst. dist. atty. Douglas Jud. Cir., 1990—91; assoc. atty. Johnston, Wilkins, Druhan & Holz, 1991—92; asst. dist. atty. 13th Jud. Cir., 1992—97; atty. Pierce, Ledyard, Latta, Wasden & Bowron, Mobile; U.S. atty. So. Dist. Ala. Office: River View Plz 63 S Royal St Mobile AL 36602

YORK, DOUGLAS ARTHUR, manufacturing and construction company executive; b. Centralia, Ill., June 5, 1940; s. Harry Bernice and Violet Alvera (Johnstone) Y.; m. Linda Kay McIntosh, Sept. 13, 1958; children: deborah Ann, Darren Anthony. Student, San Diego Jr. Coll., 1957. With Meredith & Simpson Constrn. Co./DBA Pressure Cool Co., Indio, Calif., 1958—, v.p., 1968—, sec., gen. mgr., 1976-82, pres., 1982—. Mem. Bldg. and Housing Appeals Bd., City of Indio, City of Coachella, Calif.; bd. dirs. Coachella Valley Wild Bird Ctr., Coachella Valley Mus.; mem. adv. com. Coachella Valley Enterprise Zone; trustee Eisenhower Med. Ctr., Rancho Mirage, Calif. Mem. ASHRAE, Internat. Conf. Bldg. Ofcls. Republican. Office: 83-801 Ave 45 Indio CA 92201

YORK, E. TRAVIS, academic administrator, former university chancellor, consultant; b. Mentone, Ala., July 4, 1922; s. E.T. and Leila (Hixon) Y.; m. Vermelle Cardwell, Dec. 26, 1946; children: Lisa Carol, Travis Loften. BS, Auburn U., 1942, MS, 1946, DSc (hon.), 1982; PhD, Cornell U., 1949; postgrad., George Washington U., 1957-59; DSc (hon.), U. Fla., 1984, Ohio State U., 1996, NC State U., 2003. Rsch. fellow Cornell U., Ithaca, 1946-49; Assoc. prof. N.C. State Coll., 1949-52, prof., 1952-56, head dept. agronomy, 1953-56; Eastern dir. Am. Potash Inst., 1956-59; dir. Ala. Extension Service, Auburn U., 1959-61; adminstr. Fed. Extension Service, U.S. Dept. Agr., 1961-63; provost for agr. U. Fla., 1963-67, v.p. agrl. affairs, 1967-73, exec. v.p., interim pres., 1973-74, Disting. Svc. prof., 1988-96. Chancellor State U. System of Fla., 1975-80, chancellor emeritus, 1980— Mem. Am. Food for Peace Coun., 1961-62, Freedom from Hunger Com., 1961-62, Pres.'s. Panel Vocat. Edn., 1961-62; chmn. coun. grad. edn. in agrl. scis. So. Regional Edn. Bd., 1964-66, mem., 1975-80, exec. com., 1978-80, mem. pres. coun., Pres.' Sci. Adv. Coun. Task Force on World Food Problems, 1966-67; senate, exec. com. Nat. Assn. State Univs. and Land Grant Colls., 1967-70; mem. Edn. Commn. of States, 1975-79, steering com., 1977-79, treas., exec. com., 1978-79; bd. dirs. Nat. 4-H Svc. Com., 1963-75, AV Med. Corp., Sante Fe, 1987-96; trustee, bd. dirs Hlth Improvement Inc mem., 1996-98, exec. com. Nat. 4-H Found., 1968-73; mem.-at-large nat. coun. Boy Scouts Am., 1962-75; dir., pres. Alpha Gamma Rho Edn. Found., 1965-72; bd. dirs. Nat. Ctr. for Voluntary Action, 1970-74; mem. Bd. for Internat. Food and Agrl. Devel., 1980-86, chmn., 1983-86; trustee Escuela Agrícola Panamericana, 1980-88, Found. for Agronomic Rsch., 1980-92; tech. adv. com., cons. Group for Internat. Agrl. Rsch., 1983-89; trustee Agronomic Sci. Found., 1989-92; chmn. bd. Internat. Fertilizer Devel. Ctr., 1999-. Officer AUS, 1943-45. Recipient B.B. Comer award excellence natural sci. Auburn U., 1942; disting. svc. award Fla. Vet. Med. Assn., 1966; Nat. 4-H Alumni award, 1967; George Washington honor medal award Freedoms Found., 1967; nat. ptnr. in 4-H award, 1970; disting. faculty award U. Fla., Fla. Blue Key, 1972; E.T. York, Jr. disting. svc. award U. Fla., 1973; honors medal U. Fla. Acad. Scis., 1974; E.T. York svc. award Fla. Bd. Regents, 1983, disting. svc. award Am. Farm Bur., 1991, Svc. Above Self award Rotary Internat., 1994, Medal of Honor, DAR, 1998; named to Fla. Agrl. Hall of Fame, 1990, Ala. Agrl. Hall of Honor, 1995, Internat. Adult and Continuing Edn. Hall of Fame, 1996; designated as Great Floridian, Fla. History Mus., 1997. Fellow AAAS, Am. Soc. Agronomy, Soil Sci. Soc. Am., AM. Crop Sci. Soc.; mem. Am. Soc. Hort. Sci. (hon.), Assn. So. Agrl. Scientists (pres. 1968), Blue Key, Rotary (dist. gov. 1981-82), Sigma Xi, Phi Kappa Phi, Alpha Zeta, Gamma Sigma Delta (Internat. Disting. Svc. award 1973), Omicron Delta Kappa, Phi Delta Kappa, Epsilon Sigma Phi, Alpha Gamma Rho (named to Hall of Fame 1982). Methodist. Home: 5200 SW 25th Blvd # 4216 Gainesville FL 32608-8925

YORK, HERBERT FRANK, physics educator, government official; b. Rochester, N.Y., Nov. 24, 1921; s. Herbert Frank and Nellie Elizabeth (Lang) Y.; m. Sybil Dunford, Sept. 28, 1947; children: David Winters, Rachel, Cynthia. AB, U. Rochester, 1942, MS, 1943; PhD, U. Calif., Berkeley, 1949; DSc (hon.), Case Inst. Tech., 1960; LL.D., U. San Diego, 1964, Claremont Grad. Sch., 1974. Physicist Radiation Lab., U. Calif., Berkeley, 1943-58, assoc. dir., 1954-58; asst. prof. physics dept. U. Calif., Berkeley, 1951-54, assoc. prof., 1954-59, prof., 1959-61; dir. Lawrence Radiation Lab., Livermore, 1952-58; chief scientist Advanced Rsch. Project Agy., U.S. Dept. Def., 1958; dir. advanced rsch. projects divsn. Inst. for Def. Analyses, 1958; dir. def. rsch. and engring. Office Sec. Def., 1958-61; chancellor U. Calif.-San Diego, 1961-64, 70-72, prof. physics, 1964—, chmn. dept. physics, 1968-69, dean grad. studies, 1969-70, dir. program on sci., tech. and pub. affairs, 1972-88; dir. Inst. Global Conflict and Cooperation, 1983-88, dir. emeritus, 1988—. Amb. Comprehensive Test Ban Negotiations, 1979-81; trustee Aerospace Corp., Inglewood, Calif., 1961-87; mem. Pres.'s Sci. Adv. Com., 1957-58, 64-68, vice chmn., 1965-67; trustee Inst. def. Analysis, 1963-96; gen. adv. com. ACDA, 1962-69; mem. Def. Sci. Bd., 1977-81; spl. rep. of sec. def. at space arms control talks, 1978-79; mem. coun. nat. labs. Pres. U. Calif., 1991—; mem. task force future nat. labs. Sec. Emergy, 1994-95; cons. Stockholm Internat. Peach Rsch. Inst.; rschr. in application atomic energy to nat. def. problems of arms control and disarmament, elem. particles. Author: Race to Oblivion, 1970, Arms Control, 1973, The Advisors, 1976, Making Weapons, Talking Peace, 1987, Does Strategic Defense Breed Offense?, 1987, (with S. Lakoff) A Shield in the Sky, 1989, Arms and the Physicist, 1994; also numerous articles on arms or disarmament; bd. dirs. Bull. Atomic Scientists. Trustee Bishop's Sch., La Jolla, Calif., 1963-65. Recipient E.O. Lawrence award AEC, 1962, Vannevar Bush award, 2000, Clark Kerr award, 2000, Enrico Fermi award, 2000; Guggenheim fellow, 1972. Fellow AAAS, Am. Phys. Soc. (forum on physics and soc. award 1976, Leo Szilard award 1994), Am. Acad. Arts and Sci.; mem. Fedn. Am. Scientists (chmn. 1970-71, exec. com. 1969-76, 95-2000, pub. svc. award 1992), Pugwash Movement 1969—, Phi Beta Kappa, Sigma Xi. Home: 6110 Camino De La Costa La Jolla CA 92037-6520 Office: U Calif San Diego Mail Code 0518 La Jolla CA 92093 E-mail: hyork@ucsd.edu.

YORK, JAMES ORISON, real estate executive; b. Brush, Colo., June 27, 1927; s. M. Orison and Marie L. (Kibble) Y.; m. Janice Marie Sjoberg, Aug. 1, 1959; children: Douglas James, Robert Orison. Student, U. Calif. at Berkeley, 1945-46; BA cum laude, U. Wash., 1949. Tchg. fellow U. Wash., Seattle, 1950-52; econ. rsch. analyst Larry Smith & Co. Real Estate, Seattle, 1953-60, ptrn., 1960-66, pres. San Francisco, 1966-71; pres., chief exec. officer R.H. Macy Properties, N.Y.C., also sr. v.p. planning and devel., dir. R.H. Macy & Co., Inc., 1971-88; chmn. James York Assocs. (real estate and venture capital), 1988—. Dir. emeritus UBP Properties, Inc.; chmn., N.Y.C. retail div. Am. Cancer Soc. Contbg. author: Shopping Towns-USA, 1960. Trustee ICSC Ednl. and Rsch. Found. With USNR, 1945-47. Recipient Disting. Alumnus award Econs. U. Wash., 1989. Fellow Phi Beta Kappa; mem. Am. Soc. Real Estate Counselors, Urban Land Inst., Internat. Real Estate Fedn., Internat. Council Shopping Centers, Lambda Alpha. Clubs: Olympic (San Francisco); American Yacht (Rye, N.Y.); Corinthian Yacht (Seattle); Union League (N.Y.C.); Knights of Malta, Order St. John, Washington Athletic (Seattle), Royal Victoria (B.C.) Yacht. Episcopalian. Home and Office: 4 Riverstone Laguna Niguel CA 92677-5309 also: Sunrise Country Club 6 Malaga Dr Rancho Mirage CA 92270-3820 E-mail: jysail@aol.com.

YORK, JAMES WESLEY, JR., theoretical physicist, educator; b. Raleigh, N.C., July 3, 1939; s. James Wesley and Mary Smedes (Poyner) York; m. Betty Louise Mattern, Aug. 19, 1961 (div. Apr. 1, 2002); children: Virginia York Setzer, Guilford Mattern; m. Sarah Williams Wolf, June 13, 2002. BS with high honors in Physics, N.C. State U., Raleigh, 1962, PhD in Physics, 1966. Asst. prof. N.C. State U., Raleigh, 1965-68; rsch. assoc. Princeton (N.J.) U., 1968-69, lectr., 1969-70, asst. prof., 1970-73; assoc. prof. U. N.C., Chapel Hill, 1973-77, prof. dept. physics, 1977-89, Agnew H. Bahnson, Jr. disting. prof. physics, 1989—2001, dir. Inst. Field Physics, 1984-90; vis. asst. prof. U. Md., College Park, 1972; prof. associe U. Paris, 1976; vis. scientist Harvard U., Cambridge, 1977; vis. prof. U. Tex., Austin, 1979, 87; prof. physics Cornell U., 2002—. Spkr. Internat. Symposium on Methods of Differential Geometry in Physics and Mechanics, Warsaw, 1976; spkr. conf., Cargèse, Corsica, 2002; Alfred Schild Meml. lectr. U. Tex., 1979; del. Seventh Internat. Congress on Math. Physics, Boulder, Colo., 1983, Tex. Symposium on Relativistic Astrophysics, Jerusalem, 1984, Marcel Grossman Meeting, Rome, 1985, Jerusalem, 97, NATO Advanced Study Inst., Les Houches, France, 1982, Huelva, Spain, 92, Paris, 92, Banff, Canada, 92, other internat. and nat. meetings; co-organizer sci. meetings including Neutron stars and pulsars, Princeton, 1969; Spacetime dynamics Aspen Ctr. for Theoretical Physics, 1981, Classical Problems in Gravitation, 1990, Cosmic Censorship, 1992; coord. lectr. Inst. Theoretical Physics, U. Calif., Santa Barbara, 2000—; mem. com. of visitors physics divsn NSF, 1991; plenary lectr. Fifth Can. Conf. on Gen. Relativity and Astrophysics, Waterloo, 1993, Directions in Gen. Relativity, College Park, Md., 1993, Pacific Coast Gravity Mtg., Salt Lake City, 1996, 2d Samos meeting, Greece, 1998; plenary lectr. 50 Years of the Cauchy Problem, Cargese, Corsica, 2002; hon. physics chmn. Cornelius Lanczos Internat. Centenary, Raleigh, NC, 1993; vis. prof. dept. physics N.C. State U., 1998—99, Inter-Instl. Disting. prof. physics, 2001—02. Mem. editl. bd. Jour. Math. Physics, 1989-92; contbr. chpts. to books, articles to sci. jours. Decorated Companion of St. Patrick, 1960; recipient 3d prize Gravity Rsch. Found. Essay award, 1975; Ford Found. fellow, 1962-65, NSF postdoctoral fellow, 1969-70; Battelle Found. grantee, 1967, Nat. Rsch. Com. France grantee, 1976, NSF grantee, 1974—, travel grantee, 1971, 76, 83, 84; U.S.A.-Israel Binat. Sci. Found. grantee, 1987-90, 90-93, Kenan Found. grantee, 1990, W.N. Reynolds Found. grantee, 1998; recipient Disting. Alumnus award, 1997, Marcel Grossmann prize, Rio de Janeiro, 2003; co-winner Dannie Heineman prize for math. physics Am. Phys. Soc., 2003. Fellow Am. Phys. Soc.; mem. AAAS, Internat. Soc. Gen. Relativity and Gravitation, Phi Beta Kapa, Sigma Xi, Phi Kappa Phi, Tau Beta Pi, Sigma Pi Sigma, Pi Mu Epsilon, Phi Eta Sigma. Avocations: literature, reading. Office: Cornell U 604 Space Scis Dept Physics Ithaca NY 14853 Business E-Mail: york@astro.cornell.edu. E-mail: jaswyork1@mac.com.

YORK, JEROME B. computer retail executive; b. Memphis, June 22, 1938; BS, U.S. Mil. Acad., 1960; MS, MIT, 1961; MBA, U. Mich., 1966. Various engring. positions GM Corp., Pontiac, Mich., 1962-67; various managerial positions Ford Motor Co., Deerborn, Mich., 1967-70; dir. strategic planning RCA Corp., Hertz Corp. (subs.), 1970-72, v.p., 1972-75; group v.p. Baker Industries, Inc., Parsippany, N.J., 1976-78; pres. Delta Truck Body Co., Inc., Montgomeryville, Pa., 1978-79; asst. contr. Chrysler de Mex. Chrysler Corp., Highland Park, Mich., 1979-82, mng. dir. Chrysler de Mex., 1982-85, v.p., gen. mgr. Dodge divsn., 1986-90, v.p., contr., 1989-90, exec. v.p., CFO, 1990-93; sr. v.p., CFO IBM Corp., Armonk, NY, 1993—95; vice chmn. Tracinda Corp., 1995—99; also bd. dirs. IBM Corp., Armonk, N.Y.; chmn., pres. & CEO Micro Warehouse, Inc., Norwalk, CT, 2000—. Bd. dirs. Tyco Internat. Ltd. Office: Micro Warehouse Gov Ed Inc 2 Enterprise Dr Ste 404 Shelton CT 06484-4672

YORK, KAREN KAY, accountant, farmer; b. Cedar Falls, Iowa, Jan. 30, 1950; d. Richard Arthur and Betty Lenore Wittren; m. Edward Louis York, June 28, 1969; 1 child, David Christian. AAS, McHenry C.C., Crystal Lake, Ill., 1978. Layout artist Black Dot Publ. Co., Crystal Lake, 1972-74; sch. bus. driver Sch. Dists. 47, 155, Crystal Lake, 1975-83; gen. acct., office mgr. Yornell Tool & Mold, Crystal Lake, 1976-87; staff acct. Scot Forge Co., Spring Grove, Ill., 1987—. Advisor and ednl. dir. Scot Forge Employee Ownership Coun., 1981—; spkr. in field. Contbr. articles to co. newsletter. Trustee Employee Ownership Found., 1998-99. Named Employee Owner of Yr. Employee Stock Ownership Assn., 1998, Ill. Employee Owner of Yr. Ill. Employee Ownership Assn., 1998. Mem. Nat. Employee Ownership (at-large bd. govs. 1992—). Avocations: raising and training horses, scuba diving, gardening, motorcycling. Office: Scot Forge Co 8001 Winn Rd # 8 Spring Grove IL 60081-9687

YORK, MICHAEL (MICHAEL YORK-JOHNSON), actor; b. Fulmer, Eng., Mar. 27, 1942; s. Joseph Gwynne and Florence Edith (Chown) Johnson; m. Patricia McCallum, Mar. 27, 1968. BA with honors in English, Univ. Coll., Oxford U. (Eng.), 1964; DFA (hon.), U. S.C. Profl. debut with Dundee Repertory Theatre, Scotland, 1964; mem. Nat. Theatre Co., London, 1965-66; TV film or miniseries appearances include: Much Ado About Nothing, The Forsyte Saga, Rebel in the Grave, True Patriot, Jesus of Nazareth, 1977, A Man Called Intrepid, 1979, The Phantom of the Opera, 1983, The Master of Ballantrae, 1984, Space, 1985, The Far Country, 1985, Are You My Mother, 1986, Ponce de Leon, 1987, Till We Meet Again, 1989, The Road to Avonlea, 1991, Gardens of the World, 1993; The Four Minute Mile, The Lady and the Highway Man, 1988, The Heat of the Day, 1988, The Hunt for Stolen War Treasure, 1989, The Night of the Fox, 1990, The Magic Paintbrush, 1993, David Copperfield's Christmas, 1994, Teklab, 1994, Fall From Grace, 1994, Not of This Earth, 1995, Duel of Hearts, September, 1995, A Young Connecticut Yankee in King Arthur's Court, 1995, A Knight in Camelot, (TV series) Knots Landing, 1987, SeaQuest, 1995, The Naked Truth, 1995, Babylon 5, 1995, The Ring, 1996, Un Coup De Baguette Magique, True Women, 1997, Sliders, 1997, The Magnificat, 1997, the Long way home, 1997, A Christmas Carol, 1997, The Search for Nazi Gold, 1998, The Ripper 1998, Dead Man's Gun, 1998, Perfect Little Angels, 1998, The Haunting of Hell House, 2000, The Lot, 2000, Founding Fathers, 2002, Liberty's Kids, 2002, Curb Your Enthusiasm, 2002, Founding Brothers, 2002, La Femme Musketeer, 2004; stage appearances include: Any Just Cause, 1967, Hamlet, 1970, Broadway prodns. of Outcry, 1973, Ring Round the Moon, 1975, Bent, 1980, Cyrano de Bergerac, 1981, Whisper in the Mind, 1990, The Crucible, 1991, Someone Who'll Watch Over Me, 1993, Nora, 1993, Ira Gershwin at 100, 1996; appeared in motion pictures including: The Taming of the Shrew, 1966, Accident, 1966, Red and Blue, 1967, Smashing Time, 1967, Romeo and Juliet, 1967, The Strange Affair, 1967, The Guru, 1968, Alfred the Great, 1968, Justine, 1969, Something for Everyone, 1969, Zeppelin, 1970, La Poudre D'Escampette, 1971, Cabaret, 1971, England Made Me, 1971, Lost Horizon, 1972, The Three Musketeers, 1973, Murder on the Orient Express, 1974, Great Expectations, 1974, Conduct Unbecoming, 1974, The Four Musketeers, 1975, Logan's Run, 1976, Seven Nights in Japan, The Last Remake of Beau Geste, 1977, The Island of Dr. Moreau, 1977, Fedora, 1977, The Riddle of the Sands, 1978, Final Assignment, 1980, The White Lions, Success is the Best Revenge, Perfect Little Angels, 1998,, 1984, Dawn, 1985, Vengeance, 1986, The Secret of the Sahara, 1987, Imbalances, 1987, Lethal Obsession, 1987, Midnight Cop, 1988, The Return of the Musketeers, 1989, The Long Shadow, 1991, Eline Vere, 1991, Wide Sargasso Sea, 1991, Rochade, 1991, Discretion Assured, Shadow of a Kiss, 1993, Gospa, 1994, Goodbye America, Austin Powers, Dark Planet, The Treat, 1997, Wrongfully Accused, 1998, One Hell of a Guy, 1998, Lovers and Liars, 1998, The Ghostly Rental, 1999, Austin Powers: The Spy Who Shagged Me, 1999, The Omega Code, 1999, Borstal Boy, 2000, Megiddo, 2001, Austin Powers in Goldmember, 2002, Moscow Heat, 2004; radio performances The Dark Tower, 1977, (recipient Peabody award), A Matter of Honor, 1986, Babbitt, 1987, The Crucible, 1988, Are You Now, UTZ, 1989, McTeague, 1992, Make and Break, 1993; recs. include: Mere Christianity, 1982, Anna Karenina, 1985, Don Quixote, 1986, The King Must Die, 1988, British Rock: The First Wave, UTZ, 1989, The Modigliani Scandal, 1989, The Mummy, 1989, Candide, 1989, The Vampire Lestat, 1989, The Berlin Stories, 1990, The Remains of the Day, 1990, City of Joy, 1991, Beyond Love, 1991, Memories, Dreams, Reflections, 1991, A Poet's Bible, 1992, Einstein's Dreams, 1993, Accidentally on Purpose, 1993, The English Patient, 1993, Fortune's Favorite, 1993, The Three Musketeers, 1993, Paradise Lost, 1993, The Book of Psalms, 1994, The Book of Virtues, 1994, The Magic Paw-Paw, 1994; contbr. (books) The Courage of Conviction, 1985, Voices of Survival, 1987; author: Accidentally on Purpose, 1992; co-author: A Shakespearean Actor Prepares,2000, Dispatches From Armageddon, 2002; (recs.) The Rubaiyat of Omar Khayyam, 1995, Aesop's Fables, 1995, The Poetry of Edgar Allen Poe, 1995, The Hunting of the Snark, Caesar's Women, 1996, Treasure Island, 1996, (Grammy Nomination) The Wind in the Willows, 1996, Rose, 1996, Daily Word, 1997, Les Miserables, 1998, Caesar, 1998, Brave New World, 1998, Titanic Hearings, 1998, The Fencing Master, 1999 (Audie award), Rikki Tikki Tavi, 1999, King Rat, 1999, Going Home: Jesus and Buddha, 2000, The Lion, The Witch and The Wardrobe, 2000, A Shakespearean Actor Prepares, 2002, Enoch Arden, 2003, The Theory of Everything, 2003, Creating True Peace, 2003, The Bounty, 2003. Chmn. Calif. Youth Theatre. Decorated officer Order Brit. Empire, chevalier Nat. Order Arts and Letters (France). Avocations: travel, music, art. Office: Innovative Artists 1505 Tenth St Santa Monica CA 90401

YORK, THEODORE ROBERT, retired consulting company executive; b. Mitchel Field, NY, May 4, 1926; s. Theodore and Helen (Zierak) Y.; m. Clara Kiefer, Jan. 3, 1952; children: Theodore R. II, Sharon L., Scott K., Krista A. Miller. BS, U.S. Mil. Acad., 1950; MBA, George Washington U., 1964; MPA, Nat. U., 1984. Commd. 2d lt. USAF, 1950, advanced through grades to col., 1970, ret., 1974; pres. T. R. York Cons., Fairfax, Va., 1974-79, T. R. Cons., San Diego, 1979-85; dir. Software Productivity Consortium, Herndon, Va., 1985-90; pres. ULTRAPLECS Intelligent Bldgs., Sandy, Utah, 1991—2002, ret., 2002. Decorated DFC, Air medal (5), Meritorius Svc. medal, Joint Svcs. Commendation medal, Air Force Commendation medal (5). Mem. Shriners, Masons. Avocations: computers, electronics. Personal E-mail: tedusma50@hotmail.com. *Success is measured in terms of help from others. I believe in building a team to manage any project. Always use the word "we" and forget the word "I" when addressing a successful project and loyalty will follow.*

YORK, TINA, painter; b. Germany, Feb. 9, 1951; Student, Sch. Mus. Fine Arts, Boston, 1967-71; studied with, George Dergalis, Wayland, Mass., 1967-75; BA cum laude, Brandeis U., 1978; postgrad., N.Y. Med. Coll., 1980-83. Contbr. works to numerous publs., 1987-2003; solo show include Gallery of Contemporary Art, Provincetown, Mass., 1969, Springfield (Mass.) Art Assn., 1971, Copley Soc., Boston, 1972, 73, Boston U., 1974, Mendler Gallery, Rockport, Mass., 1974, Cambridge (Mass.) Art Assn., 1975, Ames Gallery, N.Y.C., 1976, Gallery Seven, Boston, 1977, Brandeis U., Waltham, Mass., 1978, Rue Oker Gallery of Art, Sturbridge, Mass., 1979, Art Collectors Gallery, N.Y.C., 1981, 153 Gallery, Inc., N.Y.C., 1982, Creative Concepts, L.A., 1984, Alpha Contemporary Exhibits, L.A., 1985, Darraby Gallery, L.A., 1986, 8th St. Gallery, L.A., 1986, Koplin Gallery, L.A., 1987, Galerie Beverly Hills, Calif., 1988, Conv. Ctr., Rome, 1988, Merck, Sharpe & Dohme, Rahway, N.J., 1988, Erlgangen Kultur Borse, Germany, 1989, Arwell Gallery, Laguna, Calif., 1989, Deutsch-Amerikanisches Inst., Regensburg, Germany, 1990, Art in Pub. Bldgs., Nuremberg, Germany, 1990, Art Expo, N.Y.C., 1990, Amerikahaus, Nuremberg, 1990, Art 5, Nuremberg, 1990, Dresdner Bank, Nuremberg, 1990, Amer. Hosp. Assn., Washington, 1990, So. Med. Assn., Nashville, 1990, 94, 95, Studio Gallery, North Hollywood, Calif., 1991, 92, Galerie Lehman, Germany, Galerie Sud, Studio la Citta, Italy, Studio Gallery, Calif., 1991 La Foire Internat. d'Art Contemporain, Paris, 1992, 94, Med. Heritage Gall., Waco, Tex., 1991, Herbstmesse, Frankfurt, Germany, 1992, 93, Kunstforum Internat., Aachen, Germany, 1993, Kunstlerhaus, Germany, 1993, Ambiente, Frankfurt, 1993, 94, 95, 96, 97, 98, 2000, 01, 02, 03, ART/LA, 1993, 94, 95, Internat. Art Fair, Czechoslovakia, 1993, 94, 95, 96, 97, 98, 99, 2000, 01, 02, 03, Art Fair, Seattle, 1993, 94, Art Expo, Chgo., 1993, 94, Frankfurter Buchmesse, Frankfurt, Germany, 1993, Art Expo, N.Y.C., 1993, 94, 95, 96, Chgo. Trade Show, Chicago, 1993, 95, 97, Toronto Trade Show, 1993, Art Cologne, Germany, 1993, 94, 96, Centre d'Art Contemporain, Switzerland, Dresdner Bank, Germany, Galerie Littmann, Switzerland, Galerie Fischer, 1994 Art Asia, Hong Kong, 1994, 95, 96, Art Expo, Calif., 1994, 96, PPFA Toronto Trade Show, 1994, 95, Limited Edit. Expo, New Orleans, 1994, 95, Frankfurt Book Fair,1994, 97, 98, 2000, 03, Internat. Spring Fair, Birmingham, Eng., 1994, 95, Art Miami, 1994, 95, Exposition of Art, Sydney, Australia, 1993, Art Taipei, Taiwan, 1993, 94, 95, Art Santa Fe, 1993, 94, 95, NASA Ames Rsch. Ctr., Moffett Field, Calif., 1994, NASA Johnson Space Ctr., Houston, 1995, Galerie Rudelko, Germany, Scheffler Galerie, Germany, 1995, Studio Gall., Ariz., 1996, Jahns House, Germany, 1996, Internat. Contemporary Art Fair, Madrid, 1995, West Valley Mus. Art, Phoenix, 1998, Las Vegas Art Mus., 2000, Paul Joseph Galleries, Las Vegas, Nev., 2002, Rio Decor, 2003, Tina York Studio, Naples, Fla., 2003,; represented in permanent collections, Paul Joseph Galleries, Las Vegas, Rio Decor, Mus. of Art, Las Vegas, Downey (Calif.) Mus. Art, Mus. Fine Arts, Salt Lake City, Mcpl. Art Mus., Osaka, Japan, Regional Mus. Art, Bautzen, Germany, Carter Ctr., Atlanta, Kennedy Space Ctr., Fla., New Zealand Space Adminstrn., Auckland, NASA, Internat. Peace Acad., NY, USIA, BBC (Brit. Broadcasting Co.), Lagan Jute, Ltd., India, NIH, Universitet Kliment Orchridski, Bulgaria, Hiatt Internat., Beverly Hills, Calif., Paris, Gallery Dmovrosek, Yugoslavia, Columbia U., Nat. Cancer Inst., Md., Kulturamt der Stadt Nurnberg, Germany, Planetary Soc., Calif., Mayo Clin., Ariz.; represented on Artrain USA a show that travels through the entire U.S. for 5 yrs. Hon. mention: mixed media painting, Waltham Art League, Waltham, MA, 1969; first prize: painting, Arts Fest., Scituate, MA, 1969; hon. mention: works on paper, Springfield Art Assn., Springfield, MA, 1970; first prize: painting, Internatl. Show, Fall River, MA, 1971; third prize, mixed media painting, De Cordova Mus., Lincoln, MA, 1972; second prize, painting, Amer. Artists in Paris, Paris, 1975; first prize, mixed media painting, Inst. of Contemporary Art, 1979; gold medal, Painting, Spring Arts Fest., Los Angeles, CA, 1985; first prize, mixed media painting, One Fifty Three Gall., Inc., 1987. Studio: Tina York Studio 754 Waterloo Ct Naples FL 34120

YORK, VERMELLE CARDWELL, real estate broker and developer; b. Evergreen, Ala., Jan. 30, 1925; d. Frederick Lofton and Emmie Mildred (Pitts) Cardwell; m. E. Travis York, Jr., Dec. 26, 1946; children: Lisa, Travis. BS, Auburn U., 1946. Pres. Tralisa Corp., Gainesville, Fla., 1966—87, sec., treas., 1988—94, Caret Corp., Gainesville, Fla., 1979—86, pres., 1987—. Mem. devel. com. Harn Mus., Gainesville, 1990-96, Hospice House, Gainesville, 1992-96; co-chair March of Dimes, Gainesville, 1995, Red Ribbon Campaign, 1989, 90; bd. dirs. Keep Alachua County Beautiful, Phillips Ctr. Performing Arts U. Fla. Recipient President's Medallion, U. Fla., 1980; named Woman of Distinction Santa Fe C. C., 1988. Mem. Gainesville Builders Assn. (bd. dirs. 1997—), The Heritage Club (mem. amb. com. 1991-96), P.E.O. (pres. 1989-90), Surfside N. Club, (dir. 1988-91), Gainesville Women's Forum (membership chair 1994-96), Altrusa, Rotary, DAR, Phi Kappa Phi. Avocation: genealogy. Home and Office: 5200 SW 25th Blvd # 4216 Gainesville FL 32608-8925

YORKE, JAMES ALAN, chaos mathematician; b. Plainfield, N.J., Aug. 3, 1941; married; three children. AB in Math., Columbia U., 1963; PhD in Math., U. Md., 1966. Cmem. faculty U. Md., College Park, 1963—, prof., 1973—, dir. Inst. for Phys. Sci. and Tech. 1College Park, 0985—2001. Guggenheim fellow, 1980—81. Mem.: AAAS, Soc. Indsl. and Applied Math., Math. Assn. Am., Am. Phys. Soc., Am. Math. Soc. Office: U Md Inst For Phys Sci And Tech College Park MD 20742-2431

YORKE, MARIANNE, lawyer, real estate executive; b. Nov. 4, 1948; d. Joseph George and Catherine Veronica (Friel) Y. BA, West Chester U., 1971; JD, Temple U., 1980; MS in Ognl. Dynamics summa cum laude, U. Pa., 1987;

M in Corp. Real Estate, Internat. Assn. Corp. Real Estate Execs., 1996. Bar: Pa. 1981, N.Y. 1992. Mgr. CIGNA Corp., Phila., 1982-85, asst. dir., 1985-90; v.p. Chase Manhattan Bank, N.Y.C., 1990-92; real estate dir. Johnson & Johnson, 1992—. Real estate atty. Garfinkel & Volpicelli, Phila., 1980-82; prin., mng. ptnr. Yorke/Eisenman, Real Estate, Phila., 1976-89, prin., mng. ptnr. Yorke/Mac Lachlin Real Estate, Phila., 1989-2002; lectr. Women in the Arts, 1982-90; guest spkr. Wharton Sch. Bus. Class of 1989, U. Pa., grad. sch. arts and sci. Class of 1988; asst. prof. bus. law Rider U. Grad Sch., 2002 (eve.), asst. prof. legal environ., Rutgers U. 2003— (eve.) Contbr. articles to profl. jours. Solicitor Pa. Ballet, Phila., 1983-90, United Way, Phila., 1983-90; mem. steering com. U. Pa., 1986-90, dir. alumni assn., 1987-90; mem. adv. com. for econ. devel. Luth. Settlement House Adv., 1986-88; mem. Ctr. Adv. Bd., 2000—; bd. dirs. Hamilton Townhouse Assn., Phila., 1988-90, chmn. ins. com., 1989-90, 718 Broadway Inc., N.Y.C., 1990-94, Johnson Health Care Svcs. Recipient Live for Life Mgmt., Johnson Health Mgmt., 1995, Pres. Quality Process Excellence award, EthiconEndo Surgery, 2000, Process Excellence award, Ethicon, Inc., 2001. Mem. ABA (forum on constrn. 1982-90), Pa. Bar Assn. (condominium and zoning com. 1982-90), Assn. of Bar of City of NY (sects. on internat. law and real property law 1992-94), Phila. Bar Assn., Phila. Women Real Estate Atty., Nat. Assn. Corp. Real Estate Exec. (internat. coun. 1984—, comml. coun. 1984—), Internat. Atty., Roundtable, Women's Law Caucus, Phi Alpha Delta. Independent. Roman Catholic. Home: The Admiralty 33 Ocean Ave Monmouth Beach NJ 07750-1366 Office: Johnson & Johnson W H 7135 1 Johnson & Johnson Plz New Brunswick NJ 08933-0002

YORKE, THOMAS EDWARD, musician, vocalist; b. Wellingborough, England, Oct. 7, 1968; 1 child. Student in English and Art, Exeter (Eng.) U. Guitarist Flickernoise; orderly; vocalist, guitarist Radiohead, 1992—. Musician (and vocalist): (albums) Pablo Honey, 1993, The Bends, 1995, Ok Computer, 1997 (Grammy award, 97), Kid A, 2000 (Grammy award, 2000), Amnesiac, 2001, I Might Be Wrong: Live Recordings, 2001, Hail to the Thief, 2003. Office: Capital Records 1750 North Vine St 10th Floor Hollywood CA 90028

YORN, RICK, talent agent; Ptnr. Artists Mgmt. Group, Beverly Hills, Calif. Office: Artists Management Group 9465 Wilshire Blvd Ste 212 Beverly Hills CA 90212-2610

YORSZ, STANLEY, lawyer; b. Norwich, Conn., June 5, 1953; s. Stanley and Helen (Chimilewski) Y.; m. Margaret A. McLean, June 14, 1986. BA, Colgate U., 1975; JD, Dickinson U., 1978. Bar: Pa. 1978, U.S. Dist. Ct. (we. dist.) Pa. 1978, U.S. Ct. Appeals (3d cir.) 1980, U.S. Supreme Ct. 1980. Law clk. to judge Pa. Superior Ct., Pitts., 1978-80; assoc. Buchanan Ingersoll P.C., Pitts., 1980-86, ptnr., 1986—. Editor comments Dickinson Law Rev., 1978. Mem. ABA, Allegheny County Bar Assn., Pa. Bar Assn., Rivers Club. Roman Catholic. Avocations: tennis, squash, golf. Office: Buchanan Ingersoll PC 1 Oxford Ct Pittsburgh PA 15219-1407 Office Phone: 412-562-8841. E-mail: yorszs@bipc.com.

YOSELOFF, JULIEN DAVID, publishing company executive; b. N.Y.C., June 25, 1941; s. Thomas and Sara (Rothfuss) Y.; m. Darlene Starr Carbone, Aug. 6, 1967; children: Michael Ian, Anthony Alexander. BA, U. Pa., 1962; student, London Sch. Econs., 1962—63; MA, Rutgers U., 1994. With A.S. Barnes and Co., Inc., Cranbury, NJ, 1963-80; dir. Associated Univ. Presses, Inc., 1966—; pres. Rosemont Pub. and Printing Corp., 1985—. Served with AUS, 1964. Mem. Phi Beta Kappa Assocs., Phi Beta Kappa, Pi Sigma Alpha. Avocations: amateur radio, photography, bicycling. Office: 2010 Eastpark Blvd Cranbury NJ 08512-3518 Office Phone: 609-655-4770.

YOSELOFF, THOMAS, publisher; b. Sioux City, Iowa, Sept. 8, 1913; s. Morris and Sarah (Rabinowitz) Y.; m. Sara Rothfuss, Apr. 30, 1938 (div. 1964); children: Julien David, Mark Laurence; m. Lauretta Sellitti, Apr. 23, 1964; 1 dau., Tamar Rachel. AB, U. Iowa, 1934; LittD (hon.), Bucknell U., 1982; LHD (hon.), Fairleigh Dickinson U., 1982. Chmn. Rosemont Pub. & Printing Corp., 1969—, Associated Univ. Presses, 1969, Golden Cockerel Press, London, 1979—. Author: A Fellow of Infinite Jest, 1946, (with Lillian Stuckey) Merry Adventures of Till Eulenspiegel, 1944, Further Adventures of Till Eulenspiegel, 1957, The Time of My Life, 1979; Editor: Seven Poets in Search of an Answer, 1944, Voyage to America, 1961, Comic Almanac, 1963, The Man from the Mercury, 1986. Pres. Ctr. for War/Peace Studies, 1977-91. Recipient award of merit Bucknell U., 1975, award of merit U. Del., 1987. Mem. Phi Beta Kappa, Sigma Delta Chi, Delta Sigma Rho. Home: 27 Globeflower Ln West Windsor NJ 08550 Office: 2010 Eastpark Blvd #130 Cranbury NJ 08512-3518

YOSHIDA, AKIRA, biochemist; b. Okayama, Japan, May 10, 1924; came to U.S., 1961; s. Isao and Etsu (Kagawa) Y.; m. Michiko Suzuki, Nov. 10, 1954; 1 child, Emmy. MSc, U. Tokyo, 1947, DSc, 1954. Assoc. prof. U. Tokyo, 1952-60; sr. rsch. fellow U. pa., Phila., 1960-63; rsch. scientist NIH, Bethesda, Md., 1963-65; rsch. prof. U. Wash., Seattle, 1965-72; dir. dept. biochem. genetics City of Home Med. Ctr., Duarte, Calif., 1972—98, emeritus profl., 1998—. Contbr. more than 300 articles to profl. jours. Scholar Rockefeller Found., 1955-56; recipient Merit award Japanese Soc. Human Genetics, 1980, Achievement award City of Hope, 1981, Merit Grant award NIH, 1988. Mem. AAAS, Am. Soc. Biol. chemists, Am. Soc. Human Genetics (assoc. editor), Am. Soc. Hematology, N.Y. Acad. Scis. Home: 2140 Pinecrest Dr Altadena CA 91001-2121 Office: City of Hope Beckman Inst 1450 Duarte Rd Duarte CA 91010-3011 E-mail: ma3024@earthlink.net.

YOSHIDA, HIROYUKI, mathematician, computer scientist, educator, medical science educator; b. Yokote, Akita, Japan, Mar. 16, 1961; s. Tadashi Yoshida; m. Shinobu Muto. PhD, U. of Tokyo, 1989. Asst. prof. Tokyo Inst. of Polytechnics, Atsugi, Japan, 1989—93; from vis. rsch. assoc. to asst. prof. The U. of Chgo., Chgo., 1993—97, asst. prof., 1997—. Author: Windows Magic, 1992, The Best Guide to NeXT Computers, 1992; editor: Introduction to the BASIC Programming Language, 1992, Essential LAN Terminology 100, 1993, The Best Guide to the World Wide Web, 1996, Essential Network Terminology 100, 1997, The Internet Dictionary, 1997; contbr.: chpt. Wavelets in Signal and Image Analysis, 2001, Atlas of Virtual Colonoscopy, 2002; contbr. articles to profl. jours., Practical Applications of Soft Computing. Recipient Cum Laude award Edn. Exhibit, Radiol. Soc. of N.Am., 2000, Excellence in Design award Edn. Exhibit, 2002, Hon. Mention award, Internat. Soc. Optical Engring., 2002; grantee, Whitaker Found., 1995, Lewis Block Fund grant, The U. of Chgo., 1999, Am. Cancer Soc., 2000, NIH, 2000, Cancer Rsch. Found. of Am., 2001, Nat. Cancer Inst., 2003. Mem.: IEEE, Assn. for Computing Machinery, Inst. Electronics, Info. and Comm. Engrs., Info. Processing Soc. Japan, Internat. Soc.Optical Engring., Am. Assn. Physicists Medicine. Home: 5140 S Greenwood Ave 2 Chicago IL 60615 Office: U of Chicago Dept Radiology 5841 S Maryland Ave MC2026 Chicago IL 60637 Office Phone: 773-834-3154. Business E-Mail: yoshida@uchicago.edu.

YOSHIDA, ROLAND KIYOSHI, academic dean, special education educator; b. L.A., May 3, 1948; s. Robert and Yoshi (Kuniyuki) Y.; m. Sharon A. Stirler, Oct. 13, 1984. BA, U. So. Calif., 1970, MS, 1971, PhD, 1974. Specialist edn. program U.S. Dept. Edn., Washington, 1975-82; assoc. prof. spl. edn. Fordham U., N.Y.C., 1982-84, prof., 1985-87, Queens Coll. CUNY, Flushing, 1987—, dean, 1990—. Contbr. articles to profl. jours. Fellow APA; mem. Phi Beta Kappa. Home: 133 E Wall St Bethlehem PA 18018-6125 Office: CUNY Queens Coll 65-30 Kissena Blvd Flushing NY 11367-1575

YOSHIMURA, YOSHIKO, librarian; b. Tokyo, Oct. 21, 1933; arrived in U.S., 1958; d. Shigeru and Jun Yoshimura. BA, Tsuda Coll., Tokyo, Japan, 1956; MSLS, Syracuse U, 1961; AM, Harvard U, 1971. Libr. asst. Toyo Bunko Libr., Tokyo, 1956—58; cadet (intern) Syacuse (N.Y.) U Libr., 1958—61; sr. cataloger/acting sect. head Harvard-Yenching Libr., Cambridge, Mass., 1961—71; sr. Japanese cataloger Libr. of Congress, Washington, 1971—81, area specialist Japan, 1981—98. Author (compiler): Japanese Govt. Documents and Censored Pub., 1992, Censored Japanese Serials of the Pre- 1946 Period, 1994. Mem.: Council on East Asian Libr., Assn. Asian Studies. Avocations: tennis, skiing, concert (classical), travel, aromatherapy. Home: 2311 Pimmit Dr No 1215 Falls Church VA 22043

YOSHIZUMI, DONALD TETSURO, dentist; b. Honolulu, Feb. 18, 1930; s. Richard Kiyoshi and Hatsue (Tanouye) Yoshizumi; m. Barbara Fujiko Iwashita, June 25, 1955 (dec. Feb. 1998); children: Beth Ann E., Cara Leigh S., Erin Yuri. BS, U. Hawaii, 1952; DDS, U. Mo., 1960, grad. cert. prosthodontics, 1962, MS, 1963. Clin. instr. U. Mo. Sch. Dentistry, Kansas City, 1960—63; pvt. practice Santa Clara, Calif., 1963—70, San Jose, Calif., 1970—. Contbr. articles to profl. jours. With USAF, 1952—56. Mem.: ADA, Santa Clara County Dental Soc., Calif. Dental Assn., Delta Sigma Delta, Omicron Kappa Upsilon. Home: 5054 Parkfield Ave San Jose CA 95129-3225 Office: 2011 Forest Ave Ste 1 San Jose CA 95128-4813

YOSKIN, JON WILLIAM, II, insurance company executive; b. Phila., Oct. 16, 1939; s. Lewis William and Louise (Houck) Y.; m. Dorothea James, Sept. 25, 1961 (div. Mar. 1992); children: Nicholas, Dorothea, Maurice P.; m. Elizabeth Anne Groves, Sept 26, 1992. Pvt. practice, Phila., 1959-74; sr. v.p. Mid. Atlantic Gen. Investment Co., Phila., 1974-80; exec. v.p. Transatlantic Life Assurance Co., Phila., 1980-85, Meritor Life Ins. Co., Phila., 1985-88; owner, CEO Tri-Arc Fin. Svcs., Phila., 1988—; chmn., CEO Magellan Ins. Co. Ltd., Bermuda, 1996—. Bd. dirs. Annuity and Life Re (Holdings), Ltd. Bd. dirs. Concerto Soloist, Phila., 1990-92, Nat. Media Corp., 1994-98, Phila. Commn. to End. Homelessness, 1995—; mem. Spl. Olympics Adv. Com. Mem. Nat. Assn. Life Underwriters, Coun. Ins. Agts. and Brokers (bd. dirs.), Profl. Assn. Ins. Agts., Sons of Am. Revolution, Mil. Order Loyal Legion of U.S. Republican. Episcopalian. Avocation: big game hunting. Home: 1606 Pine St Philadelphia PA 19103 6711 Office: Tri-Arc Fin Svcs PO Box 6745 983 Old Eagle School Rd Ste 616 Wayne PA 19087-1711 E-mail: jyoskin@triarcfs.com.

YOSKOWITZ, IRVING BENJAMIN, lawyer, merchant banker; b. Bklyn., Dec. 2, 1945; s. Rubin and Jennie Y.; m. Carol L. Magil, Feb. 11, 1973; children: Stephen M., Robert J. BBA, CCNY, 1966; JD, Harvard U., 1969; postgrad., London Sch. Econs., 1971-72. Bar: N.Y. 1970, D.C. 1970, Conn. 1982. Programmer IBM, East Fishkill, N.Y., 1966; systems analyst Office Sec. Def., Washington, 1969-71; assoc. Arnold & Porter, Washington, 1972-73; atty. IBM, 1973-79, regional counsel, to 1979; dep. gen. counsel United Technologies Corp., Hartford, Conn., 1979-81, v.p. and gen. counsel, 1981-86, sr. v.p., gen. counsel, 1986-90, exec. v.p., gen. counsel, 1990-98; sr. ptnr. Global Tech. Ptnrs., L.L.C., Washington, 1998—; sr. counsel Crowell & Moring, Washington, 2001—. Bd. dirs. Equant, N.V., SIRVA Corp. Mem. editorial bd. Harvard Law Rev., 1968-69. With U.S. Army, 1969-71. Knox fellow, 1971-72 Mem. ABA, Am. Corp. Counsel Assn. (bd. dirs. 1982-85), Assn. Gen. Counsel.

YOSKOWITZ, MARLENE, lawyer, educator; BA, Rutgers U., 1964; MA, Kean U., 1968; JD cum laude, Seton Hall U., 1975. Bar: N.J. 1975, N.Y. 1983, U.S. Dist. Ct. 1975, U.S. Supreme Ct. 1983. With firm Timins & Lesniak, Elizabeth, N.J., 1987-88, Norman A. Cohen, Perth Amboy, N.J., 1977-92; sole practitioner Union, N.J., 1992—. Adj. instr. Kean U. N.J., Union, 1995—. Office: PO Box 484 Union NJ 07083-6132

YOST, DEE RENEE, librarian, educator; b. Auburn, Nebr., Apr. 13, 1951; d. Lawrence Welch Wattles and Joyce Arvene Kraft; m. Jonathan Daniel Yost, Sept. 1, 1973; children: Kyle Daniel, Kipp Lawrence. BA, Hastings (Nebr.) Coll., 1972; MA in Libr. Sci., U. Denver, 1973. Soc. editor Norfolk (Nebr.) Daily News, 1973—74; media specialist Norfolk Jr. High, 1974—78; music libr. Hastings Coll., 1978—79, pub. svcs. libr., assoc. prof. libr. sci., 2000—; asst. dir. Hastings Pub. Libr., 1979—89; adminstr. Republican Valley Libr. Sys., Hastings, 1989—2000. Mem. adv. bd. Nebr. Ednl. TV Coun. for Higher Edn., 2002—; mem. del. White Ho. Conf. on Librs., 1990. Bd. dirs., trustee Hastings Pub. Libr., 2002—; bd. dirs. Willa Cather Pioneer Meml. and Ednl. Found., Red Cloud, Nebr., 2003—. Recipient MAX award, Hastings C. of C., 1996. Mem.: ALA, Nebr. Libr. Assn. (pres., v.p., Meritorious Svc. award 1995), Alpha Chi. Republican. Lutheran. Avocations: reading, gardening, antiques. Home: 724 E 7th St Hastings NE 68901 Office: Perkins Libr Hastings Coll 705 E 7th St Hastings NE 68901-7620 Office Phone: 402-461-7411. Business E-Mail: dyost@hastings.edu.

YOST, EMERY JOSEPH, music industry producer, educator; b. Chgo., May 1, 1964; s. Thomas Joseph and Jean Ann (Kawa) Yost. BA in Music, Columbia Coll., 1988; MA, DePaul U., 2003. Cert. tchr. Ill. Music instr. Chgo. Pk. Dist., Chgo., 1989—; music tchr. Immaculate Heart of Mary Sch., Chgo., 1994—95; internat. recording and performance artist Smash/Polygram Records, Chgo., 1995—97; CEO Spl. Music by Spl. People Inc., Chgo., 1998—; cons. music programming Little City, Palatine, Ill., 1999—2000; pres., dir. House of Song, Chgo., 2000—; prodr. House of Song Records Records/Media Products, Chgo., 2001—. Prodr.: (Garifuna drum trg. DVD's and guitar method DVD's). Finalist Osterman awards, 1996, 1998; named Stan Greanias scholar, Spl. Childrens Charities, 1997, Anne Burke scholar, 1998. Mem.: Music Educators Nat. Conf., Nat. Acad. Recording Arts and Scis. Democrat. Office: Chgo Pk Dist 3420 N Long Chicago IL Home: 1909 N Kedzie Ave #2 Chicago IL 60647-3723 Office Phone: 312-742-7511.

YOST, GERALD B. lawyer; b. Harvey, Ill., Dec. 21, 1954; s. Richard Dennis and Marilyn Patricia (Moore) Y.; m. Kay Lynn Benton, Apr. 16, 1977; children: Matthew Brian, Benjamin Gerald, Andrew Richard. BA in Journalism, Drake U., 1976; student, Purdue U., 1975; JD, Hamline U., 1980. Bar: Minn. 1980, U.S. Dist. Ct. Minn. 1980, Wis. 1987. Assoc. Bergman, Street & Ulmen, Mpls., 1980—84; ptnr. Wasserman and Baill, Mpls., 1984—90, Yost, Stephenson & Sanford, Mpls., 1990—95, Yost & Baill LLP, Mpls., 1996—. Editor: Student Osteo. Med. Assn. Publ. mag., 1976; mem. Law Review Hamline U., 1978-80. Active YMCA, St. Paul. Recipient Am. Jurisprudence award, Lawyers Coop. Pub. Co., St. Paul, 1979. Mem. ABA, Minn. State Bar Assn., Wis. Bar Assn., Phi Alpha Delta, Sigma Delta Chi. Avocations: tennis, racquetball, boating and water skiing, jogging. Home: 422 Mt Curve Blvd Saint Paul MN 55105 Office: Yost & Baill LLP 2050 Pillsbury Ctr S 220 S 6th St Minneapolis MN 55402-1803 Office Phone: 612-338-6000. E-mail: gyost@yostbaill.com.

YOST, JAMES A. manufacturing executive; BSc in Computer Sci., Johns Hopkins U., 1971; MBA in Fin., U. Chgo. Controller Autolatina; various positions Ford Europe; v.p. corp. strategy Ford Motor Co.; v.p. fin. Hayes Lemmerz, Northville, Mich., 2002—, CFO, 2002—. Office: Hayes Lemmerz 15300 Centennial Drive Northville MI 48167*

YOST, LARRY D. automotive executive; Mgr. prodn. and inventory control Rockwell Internat., from 1971, pres. heavy vehicles sys. divsn., 1994-97; pres., CEO, Meritor Automotive Inc. (merger with Arvin Co.), Troy, Mich., 1997—, chmn., 1998—. Office: Arvin Meritor Inc 2135 W Maple Rd Troy MI 48084-7121

YOST, PAUL ALEXANDER, JR., foundation executive, retired coast guard officer; b. Phila., Jan. 3, 1929; s. Paul Alexander Sr. and Jeanne Moore (Bailey) Y.; m. Jan Worth, June 2, 1951; children: Linda L., Paul Alexander III, David J., Lisa L., Christopher J. BS, USCG Acad., 1951; MS, U. Conn., 1959; MA, George Washington U., 1964; grad., Naval War Coll., 1964. Commd. ensign USCG, 1951, advanced through grades to adm., 1986, comdr. 8th dist., 1978-81, chief staff hdqrs. Washington, 1981-84, comdr. 3d dist., maritime Atlantic def. zone, and Atlantic area N.Y.C., 1984-86, commandant Washington, 1986-90, ret., 1990; pres. James Madison Found., Washington, 1990—. Decorated D.S.M. with gold star, Silver Star, Legion of Merit combat "V" with gold star, Meritorious Service Medal. Office: James Madison Meml Fellowship Found 2000 K St NW Washington DC 20006-1809

YOST, R. DAVID, pharmaceutical executive; b. 1947; married. BS, USAF Acad., 1969; MBA, UCLA, 1970. From v.p. to pres. Kauffman-Lattimer Co., Columbus, Ohio, 1969-74; from group v.p. to group pres. cen. region Alco Health Systems Corp., Malvern, Pa., 1989-97; pres., CEO, chmn. AmeriSource Health Corp., Malvern, Pa., 1997—2001; pres., CEO Amerisource Bergen Corp. (formerly Amerisource Health Corp.), 2001—. Capt. USAF, 1969—74. Office: AmeriSource Bergen Corp 1300 Morris Dr Ste 100 Wayne PA 19087-5594

YOST, RICHARD ALAN, chemistry professor; b. Martins Ferry, Ohio, Mar. 31, 1953; s. Donald Errold and Jessie Lee (Hoover) Y.; m. Katherine Sarah Fitzgerald, June 16, 1979; children: Sarah Elizabeth, Michael Patrick, Matthew Jefferson. BS in Chemistry, U. Ariz., 1974; PhD in Analytical Chemistry, Mich. State U., 1979. Asst. prof. chemistry U. Fla., Gainesville, 1979-83, assoc. prof., 1983-89, prof., 1989—, head divsn. analytical chemistry, 1994—2000, assoc. dean rsch., 2000—01. Cons. Lawrence Livermore Nat. Lab., Finnigan MAT Corp., Bristol-Myers Squibb; mem. sci. adv. and rev. bd. Lawrence Livermore Nat. Lab., 1994-2003; fellow, mem. adv. bd. U. Fla. Inst. for Sci. and Health Policy, 1999-2001; founding mem. William R. Maples Forensic Sci. Ctr., U. Fla., 1999--; sr. mem. Shands Cancer Ctr., U. Fla., 2001—. Mem. editl. bd. Jour. Am. Soc. Mass Spectrometry, 1990-97, Internat. Jour. Mass Spectrometry, 1996—; patentee in field. Dist. commr. Boy Scouts Am., 1981-84. Fellow NSF, 1975-79, Am. Chem. Soc. Analytical Divsn., 1977-78. Mem. Am. Chem. Soc., Am. Soc. Mass Spectrometry (sec. 1997-99, Disting. Contbn. award 1993), Internat. Chemometrics Soc. (foundin mem. N.Am. chpt.), Internat. Mass Spectrometry Soc. (founder), Phi Beta Kappa, Phi Kappa Phi. Office: U Fla Dept Chemistry Gainesville FL 32611 Office Phone: 352-392-0557. E-mail: ryost@ufl.edu.

YOST, WILLIAM ALBERT, psychology educator, hearing researcher; b. Dallas, Sept. 21, 1944; s. William Jacque and Gladys (Funk) Y.; m. Lee Prater, June 15, 1969; children: Kelley Ann, Alyson Leigh BA, Colo. Coll., 1966, DSc (hon.), 1997; PhD, Ind. U., 1970. Assoc. prof. psychology U. Fla., Gainesville, 1971-77; dir. sensory physiology and perception program NSF, Washington, 1982-83; prof. psychology Loyola U., Chgo., 1979—, dir. Parmly Hearing Inst., 1977—2001, dir. interdisciplinary neurosci. minor, 1977—2001, prof. hearing scis., 1990—. Adj. prof. psychology and otolaryngology Loyola U., Chgo., 1990—, acting v.p. rsch., 1999—2001, assoc. v.p. rsch., dean Grad. Sch., 2001—04; individual expert bio-acoustics Am. Nat. Stds. Inst., 1983—; mem. study sect. Nat. Inst. Deafness and Other Communication Disorders, 1990—94; chair hearing bioacoustics and biomechanics com. NRC, 1992—2001, mem. bd. on behavioral cognitive and sensory scis., 1998—2004. Author: Fundamentals of Hearing, 1977, 4th edit., 2000; editor (with others) New Directions in Hearing Science, 1985, Directional Hearing, 1987, Auditory Processing of Complex Sounds, 1987, Classification of Complex Sounds, 1989, Psychoacoustics, 1993; assoc. editor Auditory Neurosci., 1994-97; ad hoc reviewer NSF, Air Force Office Sci. Rsch., Office Naval Rsch., 1981—; contbr. chpts. to books, articles to profl. jours. Pres. Evanston Tennis Assn., Ill., 1984, 90. Grantee NSF, 1974—, NIH, 1975—, AFOSR, 1983—, ONR, 1989-90. Fellow AAAS, Am. Phys. Soc., Acoustical Soc. Am. (assoc. editor jour. 1984-91, chair tech. com. 1990-94, exec. com. 1999—, v.p. 2002-04, pres. 2004—), Am. Speech-Lang.-Hearing Assn.; mem. NAS (exec. com. on hearing bioacoustics, biomechanics 1981-87, chmn. 1993-97), Assn. Rsch. in Otolaryngology (sec.-treas. 1984-87, pres.-elect 1987-88, pres. 1988-89), Nat. Inst. Deafness and Other Comm. Disorders (task force, rev. panel 1990-94, chmn. 1994), Am. Auditory Soc. (exec. bd. 1993-98). Office Phone: 773-508-2713. *I am fortunate that I am in an occupation that is so much fun. Teaching and research are very enjoyable. Most days for me are fun.*

YOSTE, CHARLES TODD, lawyer; b. Vicksburg, Miss., Nov. 11, 1948; s. Harry M. and Charlene (Todd) Y. BS, Miss. State U., 1971; JD, U. Miss., 1976. Bar: Miss. 1976, U.S. Dist. Ct. Miss. 1976, U.S. Ct. Appeals, 1982, U.S. Supreme Ct. 2002. Sole practice, Starkville, Miss., 1976—; city atty., 1979-85; pros. atty., 1977-79; city judge, 1981-82. Candidate for Congress 2d dist., Miss., 1980. Served to capt. U.S. Army, 1971-73. Recipient Outstanding Young Man award Starkville Jaycees, 1980. Mem. ABA, Miss. Bar Assn., Am. Trial Lawyers Assn., Miss. Trial Lawyers Assn. (bd. govs. 1988-94), Starkville C. of C. (pres. 1982), Am. Legion, Rotary, Am. Coll. Barristers, Internat. Acad. Litigators. Republican. Roman Catholic. Home: 902 Montgomery St Starkville MS 39759 Office: PO Box 80288 Starkville MS 39759-0488 E-mail: cyoste@netdoor.com.

YOTHER, MICHELE, publisher; b. Atlanta, Aug. 25, 1965; d. Carole (Spence) Marsh; m. Michael B. Yother, Mar. 17, 1990; children: Christina Michele, Grant Michael. BA in acctg. cum laude, Ga. State U., 1990. Asst. v.p. Bank Am., Atlanta, 1986-90; pres. Gallopade Internat. Inc., Atlanta, 1990—. Pres. Carole Marsh Family Interactive Multimedia, 1993—. Pub. over 10000 children's books, computer disks and activities. Equifax Bus. scholar Ga. State U., 1989. Mem. Women's Nat. Book Assn. (bd. dirs. 1994-95), Bank Am. Club (pres. 1989), Golden Key. Methodist. Home: 502 Rose Down Trce N Peachtree City GA 30269-3718 Office: Gallopade Internat Inc Ste 600 665 Highway 74 S Peachtree City GA 30269-3003

YOU, ALETA, education educator; b. Honolulu, Apr. 13, 1947; d. Richard W. and Eleanor (Chun) You; children: Aaron, Erika Mastny BS in Secondary Edn., Bradley U., 1970; MA in Speech Communication, U. Hawaii, 1971; PhD in Philosophy of Edn., Ariz. State U., 1975. Assoc. prof. student tchg., dir. Incarnate Word Coll., San Antonio, 1978-82; adj. assoc. prof. edn. The Coll. of N.J., Ewing, 1983-85; asst. dir. Princeton (N.J.) U., 1985-86; project dir. Rutgers U., New Brunswick, N.J., 1986-89, dir. program devel., 1989-94, sr. equity specialist, 1994—. Co-author: Science Teams Teachers Manual, 1992, (handbook) Linking Schools & Community Services, 1989; contbr. chpt. to book; project dir. (tchg. techniques video) Science Teams, 1994 (Bronze Apple award); contbr. articles to profl. jours.; editor Eisenhower Nat. Math. & Sci. Edn. newsletter, Rutgers U., 1991-94. Fellow Philosophy of Edn. Soc.; mem. AAUW, Nat. Alliance Bus., Nat. Assn. Ptnrs. in Edn., N.J. Assn. Ptnrs. in Edn. (exec. dir., New Brunswick, 1991-99). Avocations: reading, biblical research, travel, dance. Office: NJ Statewide Systemic Initiative Rutgers U 640 Bartholomew Rd Piscataway NJ 08854-8003

YOU, HARRY L. computer company executive; BA in Econs. cum laude, Harvard Coll.; MA in Econs., Yale U. Advisor to the bd. dirs. Lucky-Goldstar Internat., Seoul, Republic of Korea; economist, asst. to the dir. Internat. Monetary Fund; fed. res. liaison U.S. Treasury Dept.; v.p. Salomon Bros., Inc.; sr. v.p. gen. indsl. group Lehman Bros.; prin. gen. indsl. group, mng. dir. Morgan Stanley, 1996—2001; CFO Accenture Ltd., Bermuda, 2001—04; exec. v.p., CFO Oracle Corp., Redwood City, Calif., 2004—. Office: Oracle 500 Oracle Pkwy Redwood City CA 94065*

YOU, YALI, music educator; b. Xian, Shaanxi Province, China, July 31, 1962; d. Damin You and Fang Lin; m. Paul Steven Knuth, Aug. 9, 2002. Dr. of Musical Arts, U. of Cin., Cin., Ohio, 1989—96; MusM, Northwestern U., Evanston, Ill., 1986—87; BA, Shanghai Conservatory of Music, Shanghai, China, 1980—84. Cert. cello performance Northwestern U., 1988. Assoc. prof. of music Hamline U., St. Paul, Minn., 1996—; adj. prof. of music Concordia U., St. Paul, Minn., 1997—2001. Musician concert performances in various venues. Recipient Excellent Performance, 4th Chinese Nat. Chamber Music competition, 1985. Mem.: Am. Assoc. of Univ. Professors. Buddhism. Avocations: folk dancing, gardening, travel. Office: Hamline Univ 1536 Hewitt Ave Saint Paul MN 55104 Office Phone: 651-523-2439. Personal E-mail: yaliyou@piper.hamline.edu. E-mail: yyou@gw.hamline.edu.

YOUD, T. LESLIE, retired civil engineer; b. Spanish Fork, Utah, Apr. 2, 1938; s. Thomas Leslie and Mary (Evans) Y.; m. Denice Porter, June 26, 1962; children: Verlin, Lance, Melinda, Thomas, Emily. BS, Brigham Young U., 1964; PhD, Iowa State U., 1967. Rsch. civil engr. U.S. Geological Survey, Menlo Park, Calif., 1967-84; prof. Brigham Young U., Provo, Utah, 1984—2003; ret., 2003. Recipient Maeser Rsch. award Brigham Young U., 1991, Utah Engring. Educator of Yr., 1995, ASCE H. Bolton Seed medal, 2002. Mem. ASCE, Internat. Soc. for Soil Mechanics and Fnd. Engring., Earthquake Engring. Rsch. Inst. Mem. Lds Ch. Achievements include development of techniques for mapping earthquake induced liquefaction hazard and

techniques for estimating earthquake induced laterial spread displacements; inventor system for coupling accelerometers into bore hole casings. Home: 1132 E 1010 N Orem UT 84097-4306 Office: Brigham Young U Dept Civil Engring Provo UT 84602

YOUDELMAN, ROBERT ARTHUR, financial executive, lawyer; b. L.I., N.Y., Mar. 28, 1942; s. Jack and Marjorie Vivian (Baer) Y.; m. Karen Leita Schneier, July 30, 1966; children: Mara, Sondra. BBA in Acctg., Case Western Res. U., 1963; LLB, NYU, 1966, LLM in Taxation, 1975. Bar: N.Y. 1969, U.S. Tax Ct. Vol. U.S. Peace Corps, Salvador, Brasil, 1966-68; mgr. Arthur Andersen & Co., N.Y.C., 1969-77; v.p., dir. taxation The Allen Group Inc., Melville, N.Y., 1977-89, exec. v.p., CFO, 1989—. Mem. N.Y. State Hazardous Waste Task Force, Albany, 1985-87; pres. Residents for a More Beautiful Port Washington, N.Y., 1981-92; bd. dirs., treas. Transitional Housing Inc., 1997—; bd. dirs. Future Heights, 2001—. Recipient Individual Environ. Quality award for Region 2 EPA, 1992; named Citizen of Yr., Port Washington Rotary Club, 1989. Mem. ABA. Avocations: camping, hiking, environmental education and awareness. Office: Allen Telecom Inc 31225 Bainbridge Rd Ste A Solon OH 44139-2293

YOUGA, TONY, winery executive; CFO E.&J. Gallo Winery, Modesto, Calif. Office: E&J Gallo Winery PO Box 1130 Modesto CA 95353-1130 E-mail: tony.youga@ejgallo.com.

YOUKER, JAMES EDWARD, radiologist; b. Cooperstown, N.Y., Nov. 13, 1928; s. Bliss Jacob and Marian (Ostrander) Y.; children— Elizabeth Ann, James David. AB, Colgate U., 1950; MD, U. Buffalo, 1954. Diplomate: Am. Bd. Radiology. Intern U. Minn., Mpls., 1954-55, resident in radiology, 1955-56, 58-60; resident in pathology Georgetown U., Washington, 1958; pvt. practice medicine, specializing in radiology Corpus Christi, Tex., 1956-58; asst. prof. radiology Med. Coll. Va., Richmond, 1961-63; research fellow U. Lund, Malmo, Sweden, 1963-64; asst. prof. radiology U. Calif., San Francisco, 1964-67; asso. prof. U. Clif., 1967-68; prof., chmn. dept. radiology Med. Coll. Wis., Milw., 1968—; dir. dept. radiology Milwaukee County Gen. Hosp., Milw., 1968-96; chmn. dept. radiology Froedtert Meml. Luth. Hosp., 1979—. Served with Project Hope, Indonesia, 1961; cons./lectr. VA Hosp., Richmond, 1961-63, San Francisco, 1964-68, Martinez, Calif., 1964-68; cons./lectr. Letterman Army Med. Center, San Francisco, 1964-68, Oakknoll Naval Hosp., Oakladn, Calif., 1964-68, VA Hosp., Milwaukee, Wis., 1968—; vis. prof. U. Calif. Sch. Medicine, San Francisco, 1974, Stanford U. Sch. Medicine, Palo Alto, Calif., 1976; vis. physician dept. cardiology St. Vincent's Hosp., Melbourne, Australia, 1974-75; mem. com. diagnosis breast cancer task force NIH, 1975-79; Head Physicians for Ford; chmn. health and med. sci. tech. com. for program planning com. North Div. High Sch., 1979; bd. dirs. Med. Coll. Wis., 1986-88, mem. residency rev. commn. for radiology, 1985-90. Contbr. numerous articles to profl. jours. Served with M.C. USN, 1956-58. N.Y. State Regents scholar, 1946; Buffalo Found. scholar, 1952; grantee USPHS; grantee Squibb Pharms.; grantee Nat. Cancer Inst.; grantee others. Fellow Am. Coll. Radiology (bd. chancellors 1978—84, vice-chmn. commn. on cancer 1972-74, chmn./mem. numerous coms., v.p. 1983-84); mem. Am. Bd. Med. Specialties (pres. 2000), AMA, Am. Roentgen Ray Soc. (adv. com. research and edn.), Assn. Univ. Radiologists (chmn. govt. affairs com. 1978-79), Med. Soc. Milwaukee County (hosp. med. staff liaison com. 1978-79), Milw. Acad. Medicine, Milw. Roentgen Ray Soc., Soc. Chairmen Acad. Radiolgy Depts. (pres. 1972, coms.), Vail Creative Concepts Conf. (co-founder), Wis. Med. Soc., Wis. Radiol. Soc., Clubs: Univ. (Milw.); Chenequa Country. Republican. Office: Froedtert Meml Luth Hosp 9200 W Wisconsin Ave Milwaukee WI 53226-3522 E-mail: jyouker@mcw.edu.

YOUM, YOOSIK, education educator; s. Choong-Wook Youm and Jung-Shin Kim; m. Gyuseon Min, Dec. 5, 1993; 1 child, Seungonin Yoosik; 1 child, Seungho. PhD, U. of Chgo. Asst. prof. U. of Ill. at Chgo., Chicago, Ill., 2000—. Office: Univ of Il at Chicago 1007 W Harrison St MC312 Chicago IL 60607 E-mail: yoosik@uic.edu.

YOUMAN, ROGER JACOB, editor, writer; b. N.Y.C., Feb. 25, 1932; s. Robert Harold and Ida (Kellner) Y.; m. Lillian Frank, June 22, 1958; children: Nancy, Laura, Joshua, Andrew. BA, Swarthmore Coll., 1953. Desk asst. CBS News, N.Y.C., 1953; program editor TV Guide, N.Y.C., 1956, regional editor Memphis, 1956-57, Houston, 1957, asst. programming editor N.Y.C., 1957-60, assoc. editor Radnor, Pa., 1960-65, asst. mng. editor, 1965-72, mng. editor, 1972-76, exec. editor, 1976-79, 80-81, co-editor, 1981-90, editor, 1990-93, Panorama, 1979-80; editl. dir. TV Guide On Screen, 1993-96; freelance writer, editorial cons., 1996—. Del. U.S.-Soviet Bilateral Info. Talks, 1988, 90; adj. prof. Columbia U. Grad. Sch. Journalism, N.Y.C., 2002—. Author: How Sweet It Was, The Television Years, Tuscan Notes; contbr. articles to various publs. Served with AUS, 1954-55. Home: 752 Mancill Rd Wayne PA 19087-2043

YOUMANS, JULIAN RAY, neurosurgeon, educator; b. Baxley, Ga., Jan. 2, 1928; s. John Edward and Jennie Lou (Milton) Y.; children— Reed Nesbit, John Edward, Julian Milton. BS, Emory U., 1949, MD, 1952; MS, U. Mich., 1955, PhD, 1957. Diplomate: Am. Bd. Neurol. Surgery. Intern U. Mich. Hosp., Ann Arbor, 1952-53, resident in neurol. surgery, 1953-55, 56-58; fellow in neurology U. London, 1955-56; asst. prof. neurosurgery U. Miss., 1959-62, assoc. prof., 1962-63, Med. U. S.C., 1963-65, prof., 1965-67, chief div. neurosurgery, 1963-67; prof. U. Calif., Davis, 1967-91; prof. emeritus, 1991—; chmn. dept. neurosurgery U. Calif., 1967-82. Cons. USAF, U.S. VA, NRC. Editor: Neurological Surgery, 1973; contbr. articles to profl. jours. No. vice chmn. Republican State Central Com. of Calif., 1979-81. Served with U.S. Navy, 1944-46. Mem. ACS (bd. govs. 1972-78), Congress of Neurol. Surgeons (exec. com. 1967-70), Am. Acad. Neurology, Am. Assn. Neurol. Surgeons, Am. Assn. Surgery of Trauma, Pan-Pacific Surg. Assn., Western Neurosurg. Soc., Neurosurg. Soc. Am., Soc. Neurol. Surgeons, Soc. Univ. Neurosurgeons, N. Pacific Soc. Neurology and Psychiatry, Royal Soc. Medicine, Am. Trauma Soc., U.S. C. of C., Bohemian Club, Sutter Club, Rotary. Republican. Episcopalian.

YOUMANS, WILLIAM BARTON, retired physiologist; b. Cin., Feb. 3, 1910; s. Charles Trimble and Lucy May (Gardiner) Y.; m. Cynthia McCreary Holbrook, Nov. 24, 1932; children: William Barton, Carol Anne, Charles Gilbert. Student, Vanderbilt U., 1928—29; BS, Western Ky. State Coll., Bowling Green, 1932; MS, Western Ky. State Coll., 1933; PhD, U. Wis., 1938; MD, U. Oreg., 1944. Intern Henry Ford Hosp., Detroit, 1944-45; instr. biology Western Ky. U., Bowling Green, 1932-35; rsch. asst. physiology U. Wis., Madison, 1935-36, instr. physiology, 1936-38; instr. physiology to assoc. prof. physiology U. Oreg. Med. Sch., Portland, 1938-42, prof. physiology, 1942-46, head physiology dept., 1946-52; prof. and chmn. dept. physiology U. Wis., Madison, 1952-71, prof. physiology, 1971-76, prof. emeritus, 1976—. Mem. physiology study sect. USPHS, 1952-56, mem. tng. grant and fellowship rev. panels, 1956-60, 60-64. Author: Nervous and Neurohumoral Regulation of Intestinal Motility, 1949, Hemodynamics in Failure of the Circulation, 1951, Basic Medical Physiology, 1952, Fundamentals of Human Physiology, 1957, others; contbr. articles to profl. jours. including the Pharos. Recipient Meritorious Achievement award, U. Oreg. Med. Sch. Alumni Assn., 1967, Emeritus Faculty award, U. Wis. Med. Alumni Assn., 1985. Fellow AAAS; mem. Am. Physiol. Soc., Am. Soc. Pharmacology and Exptl. Therapeutics, Am. Heart Assn., Alpha Omega Alpha, Phi Sigma, Gamma Alpha. Avocations: tenor banjo, gardening, camping. Home: 3212 S Old Ridge Rd Columbia MO 65203-9513

YOUNA, GERARD, information technology executive; Degree in IT engring., Inst. Informatique d'Entreprise, Paris. Mng. dir. Tech Data France, 1989—99; regional mng. dir. Tech Data France, Israel, 1999—2000; sr. v.p. So. Europe Tech Data Corp., Clearwater, Fla., 2000—. Office: Tech Data Corp 5350 Tech Data Dr Clearwater FL 33760-3122

YOUNAN, JOSEPH, bishop; b. Hassakeh, Syria, Nov. 15, 1944; came to U.S., 1986; Student, Our Lady Deliverance Sem., Sharfet, Lebanon, Pontifical Coll. Propagation, Rome. Ordained priest Roman Cath. Ch., 1971. Served Syrian Caths. in U.S.; bishop Our Lady of Deliverance, Union City, N.J., 1996—. Roman Catholic. Office: Chancery Office Our Lady of Deliverance 502 Palisade Ave Union City NJ 07087-5213

YOUNATHAN, JANET N. chemist; b. Tallahassee, May 24, 1959; d. Ezzat Saad and Margaret Tims Younathan. BS, La. State U., 1981; PhD, U. Tex., 1985. Postdoctoral rsch. assoc. U.N.C., Chapel Hill, 1985—88; sr. rsch. scientist Eastman Kodak Co., Rochester, NY, 1988—2003. Contbr. articles to profl. jours. Tutor Literacy Vols. Am., Rochester, NY, 1989—2003; deacon Webster (N.Y.) Christian Ref. Ch., 1996—97, 2003—. Predoctoral fellow, Welch Found., 1982—85, Postdoctoral fellow, NIH, 1987—88. Mem.: Am. Chem. Soc., Iota Sigma Pi (chpt. pres. 1984—85), Phi Beta Kappa, Phi Kappa Phi. Achievements include patents in field.

YOUNESSI, HOUMAN, computer science educator; b. Tehran, May 28, 1963; s. Parviz and Farah Younessi; m. Sheyda Delavari; 1 child, Zhubin Daniel. PhD, Swinburne U. Tech., Melbourne, Australia, 1988. Mng. dir. Australian Bus. Cons. PL, Melbourne, 1987—96; sr. lectr. Swinburne U. Tech., Melbourne, Australia, 1992—99; prof. Rensselaer at Hartford, Conn., 1999—. Victorian dir. COTAR, Melbourne, 1998—99; mem. internat. adv. com. SQM, Southampton, 1995—; mem. The OPEN Consortium, Sydney, NSW, Australia, 1996—. Author: (book) The OPEN Process Specification, 1997, The OPEN Toolbox of Techniques, 1998, Object-oriented Defect Mangement of Software, 2002, (book chpt.) Handbook of Object Technology, 1998; contbr. articles to profl. jours. Mem.: IEEE. Avocations: tennis, skiing. Home: 34 Doria Ln South Windsor CT 06074 Office: Rensselaer at Hartford 275 Windsor St Hartford CT 06120

YOUNEY, JOHN WILLIAM, lawyer; b. Manchester, N.H., May 10, 1954; s. William John and Christine (Zoulias) Y.; m. Karol A. Kish. BS in Resource Devel., Mich. State U., 1975; JD, Western New Eng. Coll., 1980; LLM in Taxation, Boston U., 1981. Bar: Maine 1980, Mass. 1980. Sole practice, Boston and Skowhegan, Maine, 1980-81; sr. tax specialist Laventhol & Horwath, Tucson, 1981-83; mgr. Tax Computer Systems, Inc., Tucson, 1984; adminstrv. law judge Office of Appeals State of Ariz., Tucson, 1984-89; atty. Law Offices of Ron Cullenberg, Farmington, Maine, 1989-90; ptnr., prin. Merrill, Hyde, Fortier & Youney, P.A., Skowhegan, Maine, 1991—. Bus. and tax cons. 1980—. Rep. campaign coordinator, Augusta, Maine, 1976; campaign mgr. Laos for Congress Com., Tucson, 1982; Rep. Com. mem. Skowhegan, 1972-80, 89—; state committeeman Maine Rep. State Commn., 1992-98; chmn. assembly St. Demetrios Greek Orthodox Ch., 1986, Tucson, Ariz., parish coun. St. George Greek Orthodox Ch., Bangor, Maine, 1991-95. Recipient Eagle Scout award Boy Scouts Am., 1969. Mem. Maine Bar Assn., Somerset County Bar Assn., Mich. State U. Alumni Club (advisor Tucson chpt., bd. govs.), Am. Hellenic Ednl. Progressive Assn. (warden 1985-86, bd. govs. 1986-88), Masons, Lions (past pres., Dist. Cabinet 1994—, vice dist. gov. 1998-99, dist. gov. 1999-2000, MD Parlimentarian 2001—, USA/Can. Lions Leadership forum presenter, moderator and discussion leader.). Home: 161 Madison Ave Skowhegan ME 04976-1345 Office: Merrill Hyde Fortier & Youney PA PO Box 3100 Skowhegan ME 04976-3100 Office Phone: 207-474-3345.

YOUNG, ALBERT FREDERICK ANTONIO, grants coordinator; b. Kingston, Jamaica, Oct. 30, 1948; s. Naphtali and Enid Hyacinth Young; m. Monica Verona Christie, Dec. 30, 1970 (div. July 1999); children: Yvonne McKenzie, Albert Jr., Maree Gordon, Yvette; m. Lorna Romona Young, Oct. 1, 2000. MEd, Cambridge Coll., 1995; PhD, Columbus U., 2000. Lic. alcohol and drug counselor; cert., internat. cert. alcohol and drug counselor, cert. domestic violence counselor III. Substance abuse counselor Cmty. Health Svcs. Inc., Hartford, Conn., 1992—95; dir. chem. dependency program Cmty. Health Svcs., Hartford, Conn., 1995—2002; grants coord. and program mgr. Waterbury (Conn.) Hosp., 2002—. Mem. exec. com. Conn. HIV/AIDS Cmty. Planning Group, Hartford, 1999—2001. Mem. Ct. Common Coun. Mayor of Hartford Commn. on Alcohol and Drug Abuse, 1997—99. Mem.: Am. Coll. Profl. Mental Health Practitioners (diplomate), Nat. Assn. Forensic Counselors (cert.), ACA (cert.). Democrat. Seventh Day Adventist. Avocations: breeding and training German shepherd dogs, movies, walking. Home: 509 Burnside Ave Apt A3 East Hartford CT 06108

YOUNG, ALICE, lawyer; b. Washington, Apr. 7, 1950; d. John and Elizabeth (Jen) Y.; m. Thomas L. Shortall, Sept. 22, 1984; children: Amanda, Stephen. AB magna cum laude, Yale U., 1971; JD, Harvard U., 1974. Bar: N.Y. 1975. Assoc. Coudert Bros., NYC, 1974-81; mng. ptnr. Graham & James, NYC, 1981-87; ptnr. Milbank, Tweed, Hadley & McCloy, NYC, 1987-93; ptnr., chair Asia Pacific Practice Kaye, Scholer LLP, NYC, 1994—. Bd. dirs. Mizuho Trust and Banking Co., mem. exec. com., 2003—; spkr. Traphager Distinguished Alumni Speakers Forum, Harvard Law Sch., 2004. Contbr. articles to profl. jours. Bus. com. Nat. Com. on U.S.-China Rels., 1993—, U.S.-China Bus. Coun., 1993—, Com. of 100, 1993—, vice-chmn., 1999—; bd. overseers visitation com. to Law Sch. Harvard U., 1994—99, chair subcomm. on grad. program, 1996; trustee Lingnan Found., NYC, 1984—91, Pan-Asian Repertory Theatre, NYC, 1987—90, Aspen Inst., Colo., 1988—, Am. Assembly, 2000—; bus. com. Met. Mus. Art, NYC, 1989—94; active Coun. on Fgn. Rels., 1977—, Chmn.'s Forum, 2000—; trustee Asia Found., 2002—. Named one of Top 100 Minority Leaders, 1998, one of 40 Under 40 Crain's Bus., NY, 1989; Bates fellow Yale U., 1970, NDFL fellow Harvard U., 1967-68; recipient Star award NY Women's Agenda, 1992, Justice in Action award, Asia Am. Legal Defense and Edn. Fund, 2004. Mem. ABA, NY State Bar Assn. (fgn. investment com.), Assn. Bar City NY (spl. com. on rels. with Japanese bar, Union Internat. des Avocats), Nat. Asian Pacific Am. Bar Assn., Asian Am. Bar Assn. NY, Harvard Law Sch. Assn. NYC (trustee 1990-94), Japan Soc. (sec. 1989-97), Asia Soc. (pres.'s coun. 1984-2002). Office: Kaye Scholer LLP 425 Park Ave New York NY 10022-3506 E-mail: ayoung@kayescholer.com.

YOUNG, AMY Y. school librarian, writer; d. Sung-Ling Kwong and Daisy L Fung; m. Kenneth Young, Dec. 26, 1970; 1 child, Kenneth Scott. BS, Okla. Bapt. U., 1969; MLS, U. Calif., Berkeley, 1970. Cert. pub. libr. N.Y. State Edn. Dept., 1972, health scis. libr. Med. Libr. Assn. Acad. of Health Info. Profl., 1994. Corp. libr. Chem. Systems, Inc., N.Y.C., 1971; editor, revisor com. catalog, cataloger Queensborough Pub. Libr., Jamaica, NY, 1972—87; head dept. cataloging Health Scis. Libr., SUNY, Stony Brook, 1989—95, head serials dept. Thomas D. Greenley Libr. Farmingdale, 1995—97; catalog libr. N.Y. Inst. Tech., Old Westbury, 1997—. Mem. univ. residential appeals bd. SUNY, Stony Brook, 1990—91, libr. pers. policy com., 1991—92, faculty senate, senator-at-large, 1991—92, mentor program, 1991—95, budget com., Farmingdale, 1995—97, libr. pers. policies com., 1996—97; libr. pers. evaluation com. N.Y. Inst. of Tech., Old Westbury, 2001—. Editor (compiler): (book) Best of Nursing Humor, vol. 1, vol. 2. Christmas Fair organizer Presbyn. Ch. of Glen Cove, NY, 1990—92. Rsch. Fund grant, AAUP/N.Y. Inst. of Tech., 1997, Libr. Study Leave grant, N.Y. State United Univ. Professions, 1993-1994. Mem.: ALA, Nassau Libr. Assn. (exec. bd. and continuing edn. 1995), Med. Libr. Assn.

YOUNG, ANDRE See DR. DRE

YOUNG, ANDREW BRODBECK, lawyer; b. Phila., Feb. 8, 1907; s. Edward E. and Estelle (Brodbeck) Y.; m. Olive C. Sherley, Apr. 22, 1933; children: Andrew Oliver (dec.), Sherley. AB, Princeton U., 1928; LL.B., Harvard U., 1931. Bar: Pa. 1931. Ptnr. Stradley, Ronon, Stevens & Young, Phila., 1935-95, assoc., 1995—. Bd. dirs. Welex Inc., Holmes Investment Co., Phila.; lectr. finance U. Pa., 1939-66; lectr. various tax insts., 1953-81; mem. Mayor's Com. Exec. and Elective Salaries Phila. City Govt., 1959, Mayor's Com. Port Promotion Phila., 1959-63; mem. adv. coun. Phila. Cmty. Renewal Program, 1964-66; chmn., dir. Phila. Indsl. Devel. Corp., 1963-68, pres., 1963-70, chmn., 1970-86; mem. Mayor's Tax Study Commn., 1960, mem. Commr. Internal Revenue's Adv. Group, 1965; voting trustee Phila. Belt Line Ry. Co. Trustee Lovett Found.; mem. coun. pres.'s advisers LaSalle Coll., 1969-74. With Surgeon Gen.'s Office, AUS, 1942-45. Fellow Am. Bar Found.; mem. ABA (mem. ho. of dels. 1966-70, mem. council tax sect. 1958-70, chmn. sect. 1963-65), Pa. Bar Assn., Am. Law Inst. (tax adv. group, corps.-stockholders project 1957-59), Am. Coll. Tax Counsel, Am. Law Inst. (estate and gift tax project 1964-67), Phila. C. of C. (pres. 1958-60, chmn. bd. 1960-62, dir.), Am. Arbitration Assn. (nat. panel arbitrators), Phi Beta Kappa. Clubs: Philadelphia, Sunday Breakfast, Sunnybook Golf, Anglers, Wilderness. Republican. Episcopalian. Home: 613 Foulkeways Gwynedd PA 19436-1024 Office: Stradley Ronon 2600 One Commerce Sq 2005 Market St Philadelphia PA 19103-7042 E-mail: ayoung@stradley.com.

YOUNG, ANDREW JACKSON, civil rights leader, clergyman, former mayor, former ambassador, former congressman; b. New Orleans, Mar. 12, 1932; s. Andrew J. and Daisy (Fuller) Y.; m. Jean Childs, June 7, 1954 (dec. 1994); children— Andrea, Lisa Dru, Paula Jean, Andrew J. III; m. Carolyn M. 1996. Student, Dillard U., 1947-48; BS, Howard U., 1951; B.D., Hartford Theol. Sem., 1955; D.D. (hon.), Wesleyan U., 1970, United Theol. Sem. Twin Cities, 1970; LL.D. (hon.), Wilberforce U., 1971, Clark Coll., 1973, Yale U., 1973, Swarthmore Coll., Atlanta U., others; numerous other hon. degrees. Ordained to ministry Congl. Ch., 1955; pastor Thomasville, Ga., 1955-57; assoc. dir. dept. youth work Nat. Council Chs., 1957-61; mem. staff So. Christian Leadership Conf., 1961-70, adminstr. citizen edn. program, 1961-64, exec. dir., 1964-70, exec. v.p., 1967-70; bd. dirs., mem. 93d-95th Congresses from 5th Ga. Dist.; mem. Rules com.; U.S. ambassador to UN, 1977-79; mayor of Atlanta, 1982-89; co-chmn. Atlanta Com. for the Olympic Games, 1996; prof., Public Affairs Ga. State U., Atlanta. Chmn. Atlanta Community Relations Commn., 1970-72; chmn. bd. Delta Ministry of Miss.; bd. dirs. Martin Luther King, Jr. Center for Social Change, Robert F. Kennedy Meml. Found., Field Found., So. Christian Leadership Conf. Recipient Pax-Christi award St. John's U., 1970; Springarn medal.; Medal of Freedom, 1980, French Legion of Honor medal, 1982; co-recipient, Martin Luther King, Jr., Award for Public Svc. (Ebony mag.), 1990. Mem. Ams. Dem. Action.

YOUNG, ANN ELIZABETH O'QUINN, historian, educator; b. Waycross, Ga. d. James Foster and Pearl Elizabeth (Sasser) O'Quinn; m. Robert William Young, Aug. 18, 1968; children: Abigail Ann, Leslie Lynn. Student, Shorter Coll.; BA, MA, U. Ga., PhD, 1965. Asst. prof. history Kearney (Nebr.) State Coll. (name changed U. Nebr.-Kearney), 1965-69, assoc. prof., 1969-72, prof., 1972-00, prof. emeritus, 2000—. Participant Inst. on Islam, Middle East and World Politics, U. Mich., summer 1984, Coun. on Internat. Ednl. Exch., London, 1990, NEH Seminar NYU, 1993, faculty senate mem., 1985—, sec. 1993-94, pres., 1995-96. Conbg. author Dictionary of Georgia Biography; contbr. articles to profl. revs. Mem. NEA, PEO, Phi Alpha Theta, Delta Kappa Gamma (chpt. pres. 1978-79), Phi Mu. Republican. Presbyterian. Office: U Nebr at Kearney Dept History Kearney NE 68849-0001

YOUNG, ANNE B. neurologist, educator; AB, Vassar Coll., 1969; MD, Johns Hopkins U., 1973, PhD in Pharmacology, 1974. From asst. prof. to prof. chemistry Dept. Neurology, U. Mich., 1978-91; Julieanne Dorn prof. neurology Harvard Med. Sch., 1991—; chief neurology Mass. Gen. Hosp., 1991—. Fellow Scottish Rite Found., Lexington, 1973; med. intern Mt. Zion Hosp. & Med. Ctr., San Francisco; neurological resident Dept. Neurology U. Calif., San Francisco.; David Segal vis. prof. Columbia U., 1996; presdl. lectr. Am. Acad. Neurology, 1996. Contbr. numerous articles to profl. jours. Recipient Tchr./Investor Devel. award NIH, 1979-84, Facility Devel. award Merck, 1987-89, Milton Wexler award for Huntington's Rsch. Huntington's Dis. Soc. Am., 1989, Weinstein-Goldenson award United Cerebral Palsy Assn., Inc., 1990. Mem. Inst. Medicine-Nat. Acad. Science. Office: Dept Neurology Mass Gen 15 Parkman St Ste 835 Boston MA 02114-3117

YOUNG, ANNETTE D. state representative; b. Miss., June 25, 1952; d. Terry W. and Alice R. Douglas; m. Roger Allen Young (dec.); children: Robert, Kristina. Pres. Young Enterprises; mem. SC Ho. of Reps., 1991—; ho. majority leader, 1995. Mem. Givhans Sch. Improvement Coun., 1990; bd. dirs. YMCA; del. Rep. Nat. Conv., 1988; chmn. Dorchester Rep. Party, 1988—90; chmn. legis. del. Dorchester County, 1991—94. Named Rep. of Yr., Dorchester County, 1986—87; recipient, Archdale Women's Club, 1989. Mem.: Summerville C. of C. Republican. Office: State Capitol 308 C Blatt Bldg Columbia SC 29211

YOUNG, ARTHUR PRICE, librarian, educator; b. Boston, July 29, 1940; s. Arthur Price and Marion (Freeman) Y.; m. Patricia Dorothy Foss, June 26, 1965; children: John Marshall, Christopher Price. BA, Tufts U., 1962; MA in Tchg., U. Mass., 1964; MSLS, Syracuse U., 1969; PhD, U. Ill., 1976. Head reader svcs., social sci. bibliographer SUNY-Cortland, 1969-72; rsch. assoc. U. Ill. Libr. Rsch. Ctr., Urbana, 1972-75; asst. dean pub. svcs., assoc. prof. U. Ala., Tuscaloosa, 1976-81; dean librs., prof. U. R.I., Kingston, 1981-89; dir. Thomas Cooper Libr., U. S.C., Columbia, 1989-93; sr. fellow UCLA, 1991; dean librs., mem. adj. faculty dept. history No. Ill. U., DeKalb, 1993—. Mem. adj. faculty Syracuse (N.Y.) U., 1970-71, Dominican U., River Forest, Ill., 1994-96; pres. Consortium R.I. Acad. and Rsch. Librs., 1983-85; mem. bd. govs. Univ. Press New England, 1987-89; mem. exec. bd. Ill. Libr. Computer Sys. Orgn., 1995-99; chair Coun. Dirs. State Univ. Librs., 1994-95, 2001—; sr. fellow UCLA, 1991; pres. Ill. Libr. Assn., 2002. Author: Books for Sammies: American Library Association and World War I, 1981, American Library History: A Bibliography of Dissertations and Theses, 1988, Higher Education in American Life, 1636-1986: A Bibliography of Dissertations and Theses, 1988, Cities and Towns in American History: A Bibliography of Doctoral Dissertations, 1989, Academic Libraries: Research Perspectives, 1990, Religion and the American Experience, 1620-1900: A Bibliography of Doctoral Dissertations, 1992, Religion and the American Experience, The Twentieth Century: A Bibliography of Doctoral Dissertations, 1994; The Next Library Leadership: Attributes of Academic and Public Library Directors, 2003; editl. bd. various jours. Chair Coun. of Dirs. Ill. State Univ. Librs., 1994-95, 2001-02. Served to capt. USAF, 1964-68. Recipient Berner Nash award U. Ill., 1976. Mem. ALA (chmn. editl. bd., chair Libr. Rsch. Seminar I, 1996), Assn. Coll. and Rsch. Librs. (publs. in librarianship 1982-88, chmn. Jesse H. Shera Endowment Fund com. 1991-94), Ill. Libr. Assn., S.C. Libr. Assn. (chmn. libr. adminstrn. sect. 1991-92), Assn. Rsch. Librs. (scholarly commn. com. 1991-93), Orgn. Am. Historians, Am. Hist. Assn., Horatio Alger Soc. (pres. 1999-2000), Caxton Club (Chgo.), Phi Kappa Phi, Beta Phi Mu, Phi Delta Kappa. Episcopalian. Home: 912 Borden Ave Sycamore IL 60178-3200 Office Phone: 815-753-9801. Business E-Mail: ayoung@niu.edu.

YOUNG, BARBARA, psychiatrist, psychoanalyst, psychiatry educator, photographer; b. Chgo., Oct. 27, 1920; d. William Harvey and Blanche (DeBra) Y. AB, Knox Coll., 1942; MD, Johns Hopkins U., 1945; grad., Balt. Psychoanalytic Inst., 1955. Intern Univ. Hosps., Iowa City, Iowa, 1945-46, asst. resident in neurology, 1945-47; asst. resident in psychiatry Phipps Clinic, Johns Hopkins U. Hosp., Balt., 1947-49; staff psychiatrist Perry Point (Md.) VA Hosp., 1949-51; practice medicine specializing in psychiatry/psychoanalysis Balt., 1951—; instr. Johns Hopkins U., 1953-69, asst. prof. psychiatry, 1969—, prof. emeritus, 1997—; freelance photographer, 1958—. Lectr. dept. psychiatry Johns Hopkins U.; lectr. Lucy Daniels Found., Carey, N.C., dept. humanities Yale U. Med. Sch., Boston Inst. for Psychotherapy, local psychiat. and social orgns. Works represented in Mus. Modern Art, N.Y.C., Balt. Mus. Art, Santa Barbara (Calif.) Mus. Art, Eastman House, Rochester, N.Y., Yale U. Gallery of Art; photographer: The Plop-A-Lop Tree, 1995, Tales of Courage: Recovering LIfe After Catastrophe, 2003; contbr. articles to profl. jours. Mem. Am. Psychoanlytic Assn., Am. Psychiat. Assn., Balt.-Washington Soc. for Psychoanalysis. Democrat. Address: 5307 Herring Run Dr Baltimore MD 21214-1937 Office Phone: 410-426-3583.

YOUNG, BARNEY THORNTON, lawyer; b. Chillicothe, Tex., Aug. 10, 1934; s. Bayne and Helen Irene (Thornton) Y.; m. Sarah Elizabeth Taylor, Aug. 31, 1957; children: Jay Thornton, Sarah Elizabeth, Serena Taylor. BA, Yale U., 1955; LLB, U. Tex., 1958. Bar: Tex. 1958. Assoc. Thompson, Knight, Wright & Simmons, Dallas, 1958-65; ptnr. Rain, Harrell, Emery, Young & Doke, Dallas, 1965-87; mem. firm Locke Purnell Rain Harrell (A Profl. Corp.), 1987-98; of counsel Locke, Liddell & Sapp LLP, 1999—. Mem. adv. coun. Dallas Cmty. Chest Trust Fund, Inc., 1964-66; bd. dirs. Mental Health Assn. Dallas County, Inc., 1969-72, Trammell Crow Family Found., 1984-87; trustee Hockaday Sch., Dallas, 1971-77, 90—, chmn., 1994-96, Dallas Zool. Soc.,

1986-92, Lamplighter Sch., Dallas, 1976-99, chmn., 1983-86, St. Mark's Sch., Dallas, 1970—, pres., 1976-78, The Found. for Callier Ctr. and Comm. Disorders, 1988-99, Friends of Ctr. for Human Nutrition, 1988—, Dallas Hist. Soc., 1993-2001; bd. dirs. Susan G. Komen Breast Cancer Found., 2000—, Nat. Assn. Ind. Schs., 2000-04; mem. Yale Devel. Bd., 1984-91, 1998—. Fellow Tex. Bar Found., Dallas Bar Found.; mem. ABA, Tex. Bar Assn., Dallas Bar Assn., Am. Judicature Soc., Order of Coif, Phi Beta Kappa, Pi Sigma Alpha, Phi Gamma Delta, Phi Delta Phi, Dallas Country Club., Petroleum Club (Dallas), Yale Club (Dallas, N.Y.C.). Home: 6901 Turtle Creek Blvd Dallas TX 75205-1251 Office: Locke Liddell & Sapp LLP 2200 Ross Ave Ste 2200 Dallas TX 75201-6776 Office Phone: 214-740-8402. E-mail: byoung3@mindspring.com.

YOUNG, BOYD D. labor union administrator; b. Evadale, Tex. m. Charlie Faye Young; 1 child, Boyd D., Jr. Student, Abilene Christian U. Pres. Brotherhood Pulp, Sulphite & Paper Mill Workers Local 801, Tex., 1971-73; organizer United Paperworkers Internat. Union, 1973-75, rep., 1975-88, v.p., regional dir. region 6, 1988-96, pres., 1996—. Coord. exec. bd. United Paperworkers Internat. Union; chmn. Paper Industry Union-Mgmt. Pension Fund; past chmn. United Paperworkers Internat. Union Internat. Paper Coun., Boise-Cascade Coun., Gaylord Container Coun.; mem. nat. labor-mgmt. cooperative coms. Internat. Paper Co., Boise Cascade Corp., James River Corp.; mem. steering body So. Pulp & Paper Industry Labor-Mgmt. Com. Office: United Paperworkers Internat Union PO Box 1475 Nashville TN 37202-1475

YOUNG, BRUCE K. obstetrician, gynecologist, educator; b. N.Y.C., Aug. 11, 1938; s. Morton David and Cecile Barbara (Lebenson) Y.; m. Phyllis Ann Lipsius, Dec. 16, 1962; children: Kathryn Rachel, Caroline Sue. AB, Princeton U., 1959; MD, NYU, 1963. Diplomate Nat. Bd. Med. Examiners, Am. Bd. Ob-gyn.; cert. spl. competence in maternal-fetal medicine Am. Bd. Ob-gyn. Intern Montefiore Hosp., Bronx, N.Y., 1963-64; resident ob-gyn. Bellevue Hosp. Ctr., N.Y.C., 1964-68, NYU Hosp., 1964-68; chief obstetrics Bellevue Hosp., N.Y.C., 1970-95; dir. obstetrical svcs. NYU Hosps. Network, 1995—. Cons. N.J. Health Sys. Agy., Hoffman LaRoche Co., Kimberly Clark, Litton Ind., Revlon Corp., 1975—; dir. maternal and fetal medicine NYU Sch. Medicine Med. Ctr., N.Y.C., 1975—; prof. ob-gyn. NYU Sch. Medicine, 1980—, Herbert R. and Henry R. Silverman prof. ob-gyn., 1996—. Editor: Perinatal Medicine Today, Problems in Perinatal Medicine; mem. editl. bd. Diagnostic Gynecology and Obstetrics, Jour. Perinatal Medicine; contbr. chpts. to books and articles to profl. jours. Bd. dirs. N.Y. State Prenatal Diagnostic Ctr., N.Y.C., 1977-87; chair health professions bd. Greater N.Y. March of Dimes, N.Y.C., 1995—, v.p., dir., 1995—. Recipient Disting. Svc. in Med. Edn. award March of Dimes, 1985, Voluntary Svc. award March of Dimes, 1990, Program Excellence award March of Dimes, 1991. Fellow ACOG, Am. Fertility Soc., Am. Gynecol. and Obstet. Soc., Am. Assn. Gynecol. Laparoscopists, Soc. Laparoendoscopic Surgeons, N.Y. Perinatal Soc. (pres. 1997—), N.Y. Obstet. Soc. (treas. 1997—); mem. AMA, SPO, NYU Sch. Medicine Alumni Assn. (pres. 1995-96, citation 1996), Mar-a-Lago Club. Home: 530 1st Ave. Ste 5G New York NY 10016-6402

YOUNG, BRUCE KENNETH, film director; b. Reno, Dec. 1, 1960; s. Kenneth Evans and Mae Wittenmyer Y.; m. Jennifer Law, Aug. 7, 1993. BA, Washington and Lee U., 1982. Dir. (documentary film) Stolen Years, 1999 (Capital Region emmy, 1999). Mem. Nat. Press Club, White House News Photographers' Assn. Office: Evans-McCan Group PO Box 763 Lexington VA 24450 E-mail: bruce@evans-mccan.org.

YOUNG, BRYANT LLEWELLYN, lawyer, business executive; b. Rockford, Ill., Mar. 9, 1948; s. Llewellyn Anker and Florence Ruth Y. AB, Cornell U., 1970; JD, Stanford U., 1974. Bar: Calif. 1974, Nev. 1975, D.C. 1979. Law clk. U.S. Dist. Ct. (no. dist.) Calif., San Francisco, 1974-75; assoc. Dinkelspiel, Pelavin, Steefel & Levitt, San Francisco, 1975-77; White House fellow, spl. asst. to sec. HUD, Washington, 1977-78, spl. asst. to sec., 1978-79, acting dep. exec. asst. for ops. Office of Sec., 1979; from dep. gen. mgr. to acting gen. mgr. New Cmty. Devel. Corp., 1979-80; mgmt. cons. AVCO Corp., 1980; spl. asst. to chmn. bd., CEO U.S. Synthetic Fuels Corp., Washington, 1980-81, project dir., 1981; pres. Trident Mgmt. Corp., San Francisco, 1981-87; of counsel Pelavin, Norberg, Harlick & Beck, San Francisco, 1981-82, ptnr., 1982-87; mng. ptnr. bus. sect. Carroll, Burdick & McDonough, San Francisco, 1987-90; founding ptnr. Young, Vogl & Harlick, San Francisco, 1990-93, Young, Vogl, Harlick, Wilson & Simpson, LLP, San Francisco, 1993-99; pres. Young Enterprises, Inc., 1995—; mgr. SRY Industries LLC, 1997—, KML Hospitality Industries LLC, 1997—; ptnr. Young Vogl LLP, 1999—2001; prin. Law Offices of Bryant L. Young, 2002—. Dir. The Whitman Inst. Pub. affairs com. San Francisco Aid Retarded Citizens, Inc., 1977; U.S. co-chmn. New Towns Working Group, U.S.-USSR Agreement on Cooperation in Field of Housing and Other Constrn., 1979-80; treas., bd. dirs. White House Fellows Found., 1980-84; prin. Coun. Excellence in Govt., Washington, 1986-94; adv. com. Nat. Multi-Housing Coun., 1987-92; mem. Ross Sch. Found., 1994-97, sec., 1995-97; bd. dirs. Marin AIDS Project, 1996-97, sec., 1997; trustee Ross Sch., 1997-2003, pres. 2002-2003. Mem. ABA (real property, trust and probate law sects. 1975-96), White House Fellows Assn. (chmn. ann. meeting 1979, del. China 1980), Marin County Sch. Bds. Assn., Am. Field Svc. Returnees Assn., Can.-Am. C. of C. No. Calif. (v.p., bd. dirs. 1992), Chile-Calif. Found. (exec. com., bd. dirs. 1993-96). Office: 44 Montgomery St ste 4020 San Francisco CA 94104-4602 Office Phone: 415-291-1970. E-mail: bly@ebzlaw.net.

YOUNG, C. W. (BILL YOUNG), congressman; b. Harmarville, Pa., Dec. 16, 1930; m. Beverly Young; children: Robert, Billy, Patrick. Mem. Fla. State Senate, 1961—71, minority leader, 1967—71; mem. 92nd-108th Congresses from 10th dist. Fla., 1971—, chmn. ho. appropriations/intelligence coms., 1971—; mem. Fla. Constn. Revision Commn., 1965-67; chmn. So. Hwy. Policy Com., 1966-68; mem. Electoral Coll., 1968. Appropriations com., chmn. subcom. Def., Labor, HHS and Edn. Fla. Legislature. With Nat. Guard USAR, 1948—57. Named Most Valuable Senator, Capitol Press Corps, 1969. Republican. Methodist. Office: US Ho Reps 2407 Rayburn Ho Office Bldg Washington DC 20515-0910 E-mail: bill.young@mail.house.gov.

YOUNG, CARON L, county official; b. Montgomery, Ala., July 13, 1960; d. Willie Lee and Eugene Lewis; m. Willie H. Young, Nov. 10, 1991; children: Trameka Jevert Rowell, Karen Jevert, Sharon Denise. Remote clk. Montgomery County Probate Office, Montgomery, Ala., 1982—. Dir. Youth Dept., Montgomery, Ala., 2000—02. Home: 1135 Birdwood Ct Montgomery AL 36111 Office: Montgomery County Probate Office 3032 Woodley Rd Montgomery AL Office Phone: 334-281-9999. Personal E-mail: tayika03@hotmail.com.

YOUNG, CATHARINE M. state legislator; m. Dick Young; 3 children. BS magna cum laude in Mass Comm., SUNY, Fredonia. News reporter; state rep. State of N.Y., 1998—. Highest ranking Rep. mem. Govtl. Opers. Comt.; standing com. assignments include Aging, Health and Sml. Bus. Coms.; appt. Task Force on Ednl. Stds.; regional whip on issues of sexual assault reform; mem. Energy, Envrion. and Agr. Task Force/am. Legis. Exch. Coun. (ALEC). Dir. comms. and devel. Rehab. Ctr. Named Rep. Woman of Yr., 2000, Cattaraugus County Rep. Woman of yr.; recipient Bus. First's 40 Under Forty award, N.Y. Republican. Office: 700 Westgate Plaza West State St Olean NY 14760

YOUNG, CHARLES EDWARD, former academic administrator; b. San Bernardino, Calif., Dec. 30, 1931; s. Clayton Charles and Eula May (Walters) Young. AA, San Bernardino Coll., 1954; AB, U. Calif., Riverside, 1955; MA, UCLA, 1957, PhD, 1960; DHL (hon.), U. Judaism, L.A., 1969; DHL (hon.), Occidental Coll., L.A., 1997. Congl. fellow, Washington, 1958—59; adminstrv. analyst Office of the Pres., U. Calif., Berkeley, 1959—60; asst. prof. polit. sci. U. Calif., Davis, 1960, UCLA, 1960—66, assoc. prof., 1966—69, prof., 1969—97, asst. to chancellor, 1960—62, asst. chancellor, 1962—63, vice chancellor, adminstrn., 1963—68, chancellor, 1968—97, chancellor emeritus, 1997—; pres. U. Fla., Gainesville, 1999—2004. Bd. dirs. Intel Corp., Acad. TV Arts and Sci. Found., L.A. Met. Project; cons. Peace Corps., 1961—62, Ford Found. on Latin Am. Activities, 1964—66. Mem. Nat. Com. on U.S.-China Rels.; adminstrv. bd. Internat. Assn. Univs; mem. Knight Found. Commn. on Intercollegiate Athletics, Calif. Coun. on Sci. and Tech., Town Hall of Calif., Carnegie Comm. Task Force on Sci. and Tech. and the States, Pacific Coun. on Internat. Policy, NCAA Pres.'s Commn., Coun. for Govt.-Univ.-Industry Rsch. Roundtable and the Nat. Rsch. Coun. Adv. Bd.-Issues in Sci. and Tech.; chancellor's assocs. UCLA; coun. trustees L.A. Ednl. Alliance for Restructuring Now; past chair. Assn. Am. Univs., Nat. Assn. State Univs. and Land-Grant Colls.; past co-chair Calif. Campus Compact; trustee UCLA Found.; bd. dirs. Found. Internat. Exchange Sci. and Cultural Info. by Telecom., L.A. Internat. Visitors Coun., Greater L.A. Energy Coalition, L.A. World Affairs Coun. With USAF, 1951—52. Named Young Man of Year, Westwood Jr. C. of C., 1962; recipient Inter-Am. U. Cooperaton award, Inter-Am. Orgn. Higher Edn., Neil H. Jacoby Internat. award, UCLA Student Ctr., 1987, Edward A. Dickson Alumnus of Yr. award, UCLA Alumni Assn., 1994, Disting. Svc. award, U. Calif. Riverside Alumni Assn., 1996, Treasure of L.A. award, L.A. Ctrl. City Assn., 1996, Albert Schweitzer Leadership award, Hugh O'Brien Youth Found., 1996; fellow, UCLA Coll. Letters and Sci., 1996. Fellow: AAAS; mem.: Nat. Collegiate Athletic Assn. Pres. Commn.

YOUNG, CHARLES RANDALL, application developer, marketing professional; b. Phila., Dec. 18, 1950; s. Charles Calvin and Henrietta Emma (Sorber) Y.; m. Mary Frances Hoey, June 8, 1973. BS with honors in Math., Drexel U., 1973; MS in Computer and Info. Sci., Ohio State U., 1975. Programmer coop Princeton (NJ) Time Sharing Svcs., 1969-71; grad. tchg. asst. Ohio State U., Columbus, 1973-75; compiler programmer Burroughs, Paoli, Pa., 1975-76; simulation programmer Sperry, Blue Bell, Pa., 1976-78, computer security lead programmer, designer, 1978-84, operating sys. group mgr., 1984-89; disk program devel. mgr. Unisys, Blue Bell, Pa., 1989-91, compiler and posix program mgr., 1991-93, open/oltp program mktg. mgr., 1993-94, superserver, internet and security bus. product, mktg. dir., 1995—. Contbr. articles to profl. jours. Mem. IEEE, Assn. Shareware Profls. Reformed Episcopal. Avocations: swimming, opera, church bass soloist, tennis. Home: 412 Norristown Rd Ambler PA 19002-2737 Office: Unisys PO Box 500 Blue Bell PA 19424-0001

YOUNG, DALE LEE, banker; b. Palmyra, Nebr., Mar. 13, 1928; s. Mike P. and Grace (Clutter) Y.; m. Norma Marie Shalla, June 18, 1950; children—Shalla Ann, Philip Mike. BBA, U. Nebr., 1950. With FirsTier Bank N.A. (formerly First Nat. Bank & Trust Co.), Lincoln, Nebr., 1950-91, cashier, 1966-91, v.p., 1966-76, exec. v.p., 1976-92; sec. ISCO, Inc., Lincoln, 1991—, also bd. dirs. Bd. dirs. Lincoln Fed. Savs. Bank; sec., bd. dirs. Leasing Corp. Treas. Lincoln City Library Found.; bd. dirs., v.p. Lincoln Symphony; bd. dirs. Lincoln Community Services, ARC, Lincoln Found.; trustee Bryan Meml. Hosp., 1976-80; mem. Lincoln City Coun., 1991-98, elected mayor, 1998. Served with AUS, 1946-48, 50-51. Mem. Nebr. Art Assn., Omaha-Lincoln Soc. Fin. Analysts, Lincoln C. of C. (pres.), Theta Xi. Clubs: Nebraska, Lincoln Country, Univ. Presbyterian. Home: 3911 Firethorn Ct Lincoln NE 68520-1466 Office: PO Box 81008 Lincoln NE 68501-1008

YOUNG, DAVID MICHAEL, biochemistry and molecular biology educator, physician; b. Bluffton, Ind., Oct. 11, 1935; s. Eli and Ruth (Comer) Y.; m. Diane Tangeman, Dec. 28, 1957 (div. 1971); children: Peter Michael, Amy Katherine; m. Lucia Virginia Patat, Sept. 2, 1972; children: David Michael II, Allison Amelia. BS, Duke U., 1957, MD, 1959. Diplomate: Nat. Bd. Med. Examiners. Intern pediatrics dept. Duke U. Med. Ctr., Durham, N.C., 1958-60; staff scientist Lab Cellular Physiology and Metabolism Nat. Heart Inst., NIH, 1960-62; vis. scientist McCollum-Pratt Inst., Johns Hopkins U., Balt., 1962-63, asst. prof. biology, 1963-64; asst. prof. Harvard U. Med. Sch., Boston, 1965-72, assoc. prof. Biol. chemistry, 1972-79, tutor biochem. scis., 1966-76, mem. grad. program for advanced study in immunology, 1971-76, assoc. chmn. div. med. scis., chmn. program for cell biology, 1972-76; head Lab Phys. Biochemistry Mass. Gen. Hosp., Boston, 1965-79; prof. biochemistry U. Fla. Coll. Medicine, Gainesville, 1979—, prof. medicine, 1979-86, chmn. dept. biochemistry and molecular biology, 1979-81, prof. molecular biology, 1981-86, prof. pediatrics, 1986—. Mem. cell physiology study sect. NIH, Bethesda, Md., 1978-82, sect. chmn., 1980; acad. assoc. Nichols Inst., San Juan Capistrano, Calif., 1976—; vis. prof. biology Johns Hopkins U., 1994, 95. Editor-in-chief: Jour. Molecular and Cellular Biochemistry, 1983—; patentee nerve growth factor, nerve growth factor antibody. Served to sr. surgeon USPHS, 1959-63. USPHS spl. fellow, 1962; recipient career devel. award USPHS, 1967-72; NIHresearch grantee, 1964—; grantee John A. Hartford Found., 1968-73 Fellow AAAS; mem. Am. Soc. Biol. Chemists, Am. Chem. Soc., Biophys. Soc., Am. Soc. for Clin. Investigation, Am. Heart Assn. (research allocations com. 1976-79), Am. Soc. for Cell Biology, Alpha Omega Alpha Home: 29 Tenney Hl Blue Hill ME 04614-5948

YOUNG, DAVID NELSON, media and communications consultant; b. Baton Rouge, Nov. 12, 1953; s. Nelson Joseph and Agnes (LeBlanc) Young; m. Michéle Marie-Therese Bedél, May 7, 1979; children: Jason, Jessica. Student, La. State U., 1972, U. S.W. La., 1975. News editor Gonzales (La.) Weekly, 1976-77. Organizer Soviet/Am. Culinary Exch., 1989, Soviet/Am. High Sch. Basketball Excha., 1990; cons. in field. Host, Ascension Jour. TV Show. Bd. dirs. Ascension Cancer/Leukemia Soc., Gonzales, 1978—; organizer Societ/Am. High Sch. Basketball Exch.; nat. conmmitteeman La. Dem. Ctrl. Com., 1996-2000. Recipient Best-in-Depth Reporting award La. Newspaper Assn., 1984, Appreciation award USIA, 1988, Sovincentr Medal Honor, Moscow World Trade Ctr., 1988. Mem. East Ascension Genealogical Soc. (pres. 1980-81), East Ascension Sportsman League. Roman Catholic. Avocations: reading, computing, cooking. Office: DN Young & Assocs Inc 203 W Ascension St Gonzales LA 70737-2803

YOUNG, DAVID WILLIAM, management educator; b. L.A., Feb. 8, 1942; s. William Albert and Hilda Mary (Cook) Y.; m. Ernestine M.L. Van Schaik, Oct. 4, 1968 (div. 1975); m. Francesca Michela Larson, Jan. 28, 1984; children: Christian William, Anthony Edwin. BA, Occidental Coll., 1963; MA, UCLA, 1966; D in Bus. Adminstrn., Harvard U., 1977. Systems engr. IBM, Glendale, Calif., 1963-64; asst. to pres. Lundberg Survey, Inc., Hollywood, Calif., 1964-66; program economist U.S. AID, El Salvador, 1966-69; cons. Thomas Goldsmith & Assoc., Cambridge, Mass., 1969-71; mng. dir. Commonwealth Mgmt. Sys., Cambridge, 1971—; assoc. prof. mgmt. Harvard U. Sch. Pub. Health, Boston, 1976-85, adj. faculty mem., 1985—; prof. mgmt. Boston U. Sch. Mgmt., 1985—, chmn. dept. acctg., 1986-91, dir. acctg. MBA program, 1989-93, dir. inst. acctg. rsch. and edn., 1989-93, dir. health care mgmt. program, 1991-94; prin. The Crimson Group, Cambridge, 1994—. Vis. prof. mgmt. control Instituto de Estudios Superiores de la Empresa, Barcelona, Spain, 1984, 2004. Author: The Managerial Process in Human Service Agencies, 1979, Financial Control in Health Care, 1984, The Hospital Power Equilibrium, 1985, Management Control in Nonprofit Organizations, 1984, 7th edit., 2003, Introduction to Financial and Management Accounting: A User Perspective, 1994, Primer on Financial Accounting, 1998, Primer on Management Accounting, 1999, Managing Integrated Delivery Systems: A Framework for Action, 1999, The Manager's Guide to Creative Cost Cutting: 181 Ways to Build the Bottom Line, 2003, Techniques of Management Accounting,: An Essential Guide for Managers and Financial Professionals 2003, Management Accounting in Health Care Organizations, 2003; contbr. articles to profl. jours. Trustee Roxbury Comprehensive Cmty. Health Ctr., 1983-86, Art Inst., Boston, 1990-96, Mass. Eye and Ear Infirmary, Boston, 1990-92, Symmes Hosp., Arlington, 1993-94, The Atrium Sch., 1995-97, Youville Hosp., 1997-2000, Coolidge Corner Theatre Found., 2000—, Spaulding Rehab. Hosp., 2001—; commr., chair Mass. Hosp. Payment Sys., 1992-95. Milton Fund fellow Harvard Med. Sch., 1984. Mem.: Am. Acctg. Assn. Democrat. Office: Boston U Sch Mgmt 595 Commonwealth Ave Boston MA 02215-1704 Office Phone: 781-648-8417. E-mail: dwy204@cs.com.

YOUNG, DEBORAH (DEBORAH AYLING YANOWITZ), social worker, librarian; b. Syracuse, N.Y., June 27, 1950; d. David and Jean (AyLing) Y. Student, Pa. State U., Wilkes-Barre and Altoona; postgrad., Pa. State U., Wilkes-Barre, 1988; BA magna cum laude, Wilmington Coll., 1972; MSW, Western Mich. U., 1979; postgrad., Elmira Coll, 1983-84; MLS, U. Pitts., 1994. Cert. social worker, Mich., Pa., NY, Va.; cert. pub. libr., NY, Va., Pa., Mich.; cert. homemaker-home health aide Found. Hospice and Homecare. Homeworker Kalamazoo Pub. Schs., 1974-76; group leader, project coord. Kalamazoo Parks-Recreation Dept.-Youth Conservation Corps, 1977, 78; dir. summer camp Huntington Family Ctrs., Inc., Syracuse, 1980-82; agy. dir. Schuyler Head Start-Day Care, Inc., Watkins Glen, Montour Falls, N.Y., 1982-87; pvt. practice child and elder care, N.Y., 1988-90; social worker, discharge planner VA Med. Ctr., Altoona, Pa., 1990-91; libr. worker U. Pitts. Sch. Libr. and Info. Scis., 1993-94; vocat. worker Laurelton (Pa.) Ctr., 1994-95; children-young adult svcs. coord., reference libr. Petersburg (Va.) Pub. Libr., 1996-97; libr. dir. Berwick (Pa.) Pub. Libr., 1997-98, Hollidaysburg (Pa.) Free Pub. Libr., 1999—2002; part time Altoona Mirror Newspaper, 2003—. Vol. ARC, NY, 1965—, 1965—, 1965—; ref. and children's vol. helper Altoona Area Pub. Libr., 1992—96; caregiver Babysitter Heaven Referral Svc., Altoona, 1995—96; mem. Blair County Health and Welfare Coun., Altoona, 1990—95; help-line tel. worker Contact, Altoona, 1992; mem. choir Blessed Sacrament Cathedral, Altoona, 1991—2001; mem., rotating chmn. Watkins Glen Human Svcs. Com., 1982—87; bd. dirs. Mental Health Assn. Human Svcs. Coalition, Columbia and Montour counties, Pa., 1997, 1998; mem., past camp staffer Cir. Pines Ctr., Delton, Mich., 1967—. Scholar Wilmington Coll., 1968-72, Office Vocat. Rehab., Pa. Dept. Labor and Industry, 1993-94; grad. fellow Western Mich. U., 1976. Mem. NASW, ALA, Religious Soc. Friends and Brethren in Christ, Green Key Honor Soc. Democrat. Roman Catholic. Avocations: swimming, travel, cooking, reading, writing.

YOUNG, DEBORAH SCHWIND, lawyer; b. Buffalo, Feb. 28, 1955; d. Richard G. and Rhoda R. Schwind; m. Thomas Paul Young, May 23, 1981. BA, Dartmouth Coll., 1976; JD, SUNY, Buffalo, 1979. Bar: N.Y. 1980, U.S. Dist. Ct. (we. dist.) N.Y. 1980. Assoc. Harter, Secrest and Emery, Rochester, N.Y., 1979-83; asst. v.p., asst. counsel Chase Lincoln First Bank, Rochester, 1983-85, v.p., sr. counsel, 1985-92; v.p., sr. assoc. counsel The Chase Manhattan Bank, Rochester, 1993-96, v.p., asst. gen. counsel, 1997—2000, J.P. Morgan Chase & Co., Rochester, 2001—. Mem. pension com. Rochester Philharm. Orch., 1983-91; mem. Rochester-Monroe County Youth Bd., 1987-88. Mem. N.Y. Bar Assn. Office: JP Morgan Chase & Co 1 Chase Sq Rochester NY 14643-0002

YOUNG, DEIDRA JANE, educational researcher; b. Ottawa, Ont., Can., Nov. 19, 1955; came to Australia, 1970; d. Douglas Pedar and Elizabeth Alice (Allison) Holmberg; 1 child, Lauren. BS, U. Western Australia, Perth, 1977; diploma of edn., Murdoch U., Perth, 1988; M in Applied Sci., Curtin U., Perth, 1988, PhD, 1991. Postdoctoral rsch. fellow Curtin U. Tech., 1991-94, Australian rsch. fellow, 1995-2000; sec. Western Austrlian Inst. Ednl. Rsch., Perth, 1998-2000; dir. Academe Consultancies, Karrinyup, Australia, 2000—; sr. project officer Dept. Health Western Australia, 2004—. Sec. Western Australian Inst. Ednl. Rsch., Perth, 1998—2000. Author: How to Use HLM2, 1993, A Comparison of Student Performance in Metropolitan, Rural and Remote Western Australian Government Schools, 1994; contbr. numerous articles to profl. jours. and conf. procs., chpt. to book; conf. presenter in field; assoc. editor Education in Rural Australia. Recipient Brce Chopin Meml. award Internat. Assn. Ednl. Achievement, 1994; Rsch. fellow Nat. Drug Rsch. Inst., Australia, 2003—. Mem.: Australian Inst. Rsch. in Edn., Internat. Congress Sch. Effectiveness and Improvement, Am. Ednl. Rsch. Assn. (divsns. D and H, various spl. interest groups). Avocations: swimming, walking. Home: 18 George St Stirling WA 6021 Australia Office: Dept Health 189 Royal St East Perth WA 6004 Australia Office Phone: 61-8-922-2-4468. E-mail: deidrayoung@bigpond.com.

YOUNG, DIANE CAROLINE, pharmaceutical executive; b. Balt., Apr. 11, 1956; d. John Edwin and Violet Koski Young; m. Robert John Mich, Sept. 28, 1985; children: Shannon Mich, Ryan Mich. AB magna cum laude, Harvard U., 1977, MD, 1981. Diplomate Am. Bd. Internal Medicine, Am. Bd. Med. Oncology. Resident in internal medicine Johns Hopkins Hosp., Balt., 1981-83, Vanderbilt U. Hosp., Nashville, 1983-84; fellow in med. oncology Dana Farber Cancer Inst., Boston, 1984-87; instr. oncology Meml. Hosp., N.Y.C., 1987-88; asst. dir. R & D Hoffman-LaRoche, Nutley, N.J., 1988-90; dir. R & D Sandoz Pharms., East Hanover, N.J., 1990-92; from sr. dir. to v.p. global devel. Johnson & Johnson, Raritan, NJ, 1993—2002; v.p. clin. devel. oncology Novartis, East Hanover, 2002—. Contbr. articles to profl. jours. Fellow Cancer Rsch. Inst., Cambridge, Mass., 1987; recipient TWIN award YWCA, Raritan, 1996. Mem. AMA, Am. Soc. Hematology, Am. Soc. Clin. Oncology, Soc. Biologic Therapy, Am. Assn. Pharm. Physicians, Phi Beta Kappa. Avocations: swimming, tennis, golf, piano. Home: 76 Prospect Hill Ave Summit NJ 07901 Office Phone: 862-778-7378.

YOUNG, DONA DAVIS GAGLIANO, lawyer; b. Bklyn., Jan. 8, 1954; BA and MA in Polit. Sci., Drew U., 1976; JD, U. Conn., 1980. Bar: Conn. 1980, U.S. Dist. Ct. Conn. 1980. Joined The Phoenix Cos., Hartford, Conn., 1980, asst. counsel, 1981—83, assoc. counsel, 1983, dir. reinsurance adminstrn., 1983—84, dir. and asst. v.p. reinsurance adminstrn., 1984—85, 2nd v.p., ins. counsel, 1985-87, v.p., asst. gen. counsel, 1987-89, sr. v.p. individual sales and mktg., gen. counsel, 1989-94, exec. v.p., gen. counsel, 1994—2000, pres. and COO, 2000—02, chmn., pres., and CEO, 2003—, pres., CEO, chmn., 2003—. Bd. dirs. Wachovia Corp., 2000—, Sonoco Products Co., 1995—, Foot Locker Inc. Chair United Way Capital Area Cmty. Campaign, 2003; bd. dirs. Hartford Hosp.; bd. trustees Goodspeed Opera House Found. Inc. Named Laura A. Johnson Woman of Yr., Hartford Coll. for Women, 2002; recipient Leadership Award for Women in Bus., New England Coun., 1994, Antoinette Bascetta Women's Career Devel. Award, Trust House, Hartford, Conn., 2000, Outstanding Alumni Award, Drew U., 2001, Disting. Grad. Award, U. Conn. Sch. Law, 2002, Human Rels. Award, Nat. Conf. Cmty. and Justice, 2002. Mem. ABA, Hartford County Bar Assn., Conn. Bar Assn., N.Y. Bar Assn. Office: The Phoenix Cos Inc 1 American Row Hartford CT 06102

YOUNG, DONALD ALAN, physician; b. Oakland, Calif., Feb. 8, 1939; s. Leo Alan and Pearl Anita (Walker) Y.; children: Jennifer, Karen BA, U. Calif., Berkeley, 1960, MD, 1964. Diplomate Am. Bd. Internal Medicine. Intern, then resident in internal medicine U. Calif. Hosp., San Francisco, 1964-66; resident in internal medicine Parkland Hosp., Dallas, 1966-67; fellow chest diseases U. Calif. Hosp., San Francisco, 1967-68; mem. staff Palo Alto (Calif.) Med. Clinic, 1970-75; med. dir. Am. Lung Assn., 1975-77; scholar adminstrv. scholars program VA, Washington, 1977-80. Dep. dir. policy Bur. Program Policy Health Care Financing Adminstrn. HHS, Washington, 1980—84; exec. dir. Prospective Payment Assessment Commn., Washington, 1984—97; sr. v.p. Am. Assn. Health Plans, 1997—99; COO, med. dir., pres. Health Ins. Assocs. Am., 1999—2003; clin. instr. U. Calif. Med. Sch., San Francisco, 1968—70, Stanford U. Med. Sch., 1970—75; dep. asst. sec. for health Dept. Health and Human Svcs., OASPE, Washington, 2004—. Bd. visitors Ind. U. Served with M.C. AUS, 1968-70. Decorated Commendation medal.; Recipient Borden award, 1964 Home: 6109 Trotter Ridge Ct Columbia MD 21044-4919 Office: Ste 500 1201 F St NW Washington DC 20004

YOUNG, DONALD E. congressman; b. Meridian, Calif., June 9, 1933; m. Lula Fredson; children— Joni, Dawn. AA, Yuba Jr. Coll., 1952; BA ., Chico (Calif.) State Coll., 1958. Former educator, river boat capt.; mem. Fort Yukon City Council, 6 years, mayor, 4 years; mem. Alaska Ho. of Reps., 1966-70, Alaska Senate, 1970-73, U.S. Congress from Alaska, 1973—; now ranking mem. transp. & infrastructure com., chmn. resources com., steering com., homeland sec. com. With U.S. Army, 1955-57. Republican. Episcopalian. Office: US Ho Reps 2111 Rayburn Ho Ofc Bldg Washington DC 20515

YOUNG, DONALD STIRLING, clinical pathology educator; b. Belfast, N. Ireland, Dec. 17, 1933; s. John Stirling and Ruth Muir (Whipple) Y.; m. Silja Meret; children: Gordon, Robert, Peter. MB, ChB, U. Aberdeen, Scotland, 1957; PhD in Chem. Pathology, U. London, 1962. Terminable lectr. materia medica U. Aberdeen, 1958-59; fellow Postgrad. Med. Sch., U. London, 1959-62, registrar, 1962-64; vis. scientist NIH, Bethesda, Md., 1965-66, chief clin. chemistry service, 1966-77; head clin. chemistry sect. Mayo Clinic, Rochester, Minn., 1977-84; prof. pathology and lab. medicine U. Pa., 1984—,

vice chmn. lab. medicine dept. pathology and lab. medicine, 1994—; dir. William Pepper Lab. Hosp. of U. Pa., 1984—; dir. R. Philip Custer Lab., Presbyn. Med. Ctr., 1997—. Past bd. dirs. Nat. Com. Clin. Lab. Standards. Co-editor: Drug Interference and Drug Metabolism in Clinical Chemistry, 1976, Clinician and Chemist, 1979, Chemical Diagnosis of Disease, 1979, Drug Measurement and Drug Effects in Laboratory Health Science, 1980, Interpretation of Clinical Laboratory Tests, 1985, Effects of Preanalytical Variables on Clinical Laboratory Tests, 1997, Effects of Drugs on Clinical Laboratory Tests, 2000, Effects of Disease on Clinical Laboratory Tests, 2001. Recipient Dir.'s award NIH, 1977, Gerard B. Lambert award, 1974-75, MDS Health Group award Can. Soc. Clin. Chemists, 1978; Roman lectr. Australian Assn. Clin. Biochemists, 1979; Jendrassik award Hungarian Soc. Clin. Pathologists, 1985, ATB award Italian Soc. Clin. Biochemistry, 1987. Mem. Am. Assn. Clin. Chemistry (J.H. Roe award Capital sect. 1973, Bernard Gerulat award N.J. sect. 1977, Ames award 1977, Van Slyke award N.Y. met. sect. 1985, J.G. Reinhold award Phila. sect. 1993, past pres.), Internat. Fedn. Clin. Chemists (past pres.), Acad. Clin. Lab. Physicians and Scientists (past exec. com.), Assn. Clin. Biochemists (Ciba-Corning lectr. 1985). Achievements include research in clinical chemistry, optimized use of the clinical laboratory. Office: Hosp U Pa 3400 Spruce St Philadelphia PA 19104-4206 E-mail: donaldyo@mail.med.upenn.edu.

YOUNG, DOUGLAS REA, lawyer; b. L.A., July 21, 1948; s. James Douglas and Dorothy Belle (Rea) Y.; m. Terry Forrest, Jan. 19, 1974; 1 child, Megann Forrest. BA cum laude, Yale U., 1971; JD, U. Calif., Berkeley, 1976. Bar: Calif., 1976, U.S. Dist. Ct. (no. dist.) Calif. 1976, U.S. Ct. Appeals (6th and 9th cirs.) 1977, U.S. Dist. Ct. (ctrl. dist.) Calif. 1979, U.S. Dist. Ct. Hawaii, U.S. Dist. Ct. (so. dist.) Calif., U.S. Supreme Ct. 1982; cert. specialist in appellate law. Law clk. U.S. Dist. Ct. (no. dist.) Calif., San Francisco, 1976-77; assoc. Farella, Braun & Martel LLP, San Francisco, 1977-82, ptnr., 1983—. Spl. master U.S. Dist. Ct. (no. dist.) Calif., 1977-78, 88, 96, 2000; mem. Criminal Justice Act Def. Panel no. dist. Calif.; mem. faculty Calif. Continuing Edn. of Bar, Berkeley, 1982—, Nat. Inst. Trial Advocacy, Berkeley, 1984—, Practicing Law Inst., 1988—; adj. prof. Hastings Coll. Advocacy, 1985—; vis. lectr. law Boalt Hall/U. Calif., Berkeley, 1986; judge pro tem San Francisco Mcpl. Ct., 1984—, San Francisco Superior Ct., 1990—. Author: (with Purver and Davis) California Trial Handbook, ed edit., (with Hon. Richard Byrne, Purver and Davis), 3d edit., (with Purver, Davis and Kerper) The Trial Lawyers Book, (with Hon. Eugene Lynch, Taylor, Purver and Davis) California Negotiation and Settlement Handbook; contbr. articles to profl. jours. Bd. dirs. Berkeley Law Found., 1977-78, chmn., 1978-79; bd. dirs. San Francisco Legal Aid Soc., pres., 1993—; bd. dirs. Pub. Interest Clearinghouse, San Francisco, chmn., 1987—, treas., 1988—; chmn. Attys. Task Force for Children, Legal Svcs. for Children, 1987—; mem. State Bar Appellate Law Adv. Commn., 1994—. Recipient award of appreciation Berkeley Law Found., 1983, Criminal Justice Achievement award Criminal Trial Lawyers Assn. of No. Calif., 2002. Fellow Am. Coll. Trial Lawyers, Am. Acad. Appellate Lawyers; mem. ABA (Pro Bono Pub. award 1992), San Francisco Bar Assn. (founding chmn. litigation sect. 1988-89, award of appreciation 1989, bd. dirs. 1990-91, pres. 2001), Calif. Acad. Appellate Lawyers, McFetridge Am. Inn of Ct. (master), Lawyers Club San Francisco. Democrat. Office: Farella Braun & Martel 235 Montgomery St Ste 3000 San Francisco CA 94104-2902 Office Phone: 415-954-4400. E-mail: dyoung@fbm.com.

YOUNG, EDWIN HAROLD, chemical and metallurgical engineering educator; b. Detroit, Nov. 4, 1918; s. William George and Alice Pearl (Hicks) Y.; m. Ida Signe Soma, June 25, 1944; children: David Harold, Barbara Ellen. BS in Chem. Engring, U. Detroit, 1942; MS in Chem. Engring, U. Mich., 1949, MS in Metall. Engring, 1952. Chem. engr. Wright Air Devel. Center, Dayton, Ohio, 1942-43; instr. U. Mich., Ann Arbor, 1946-52, asst. prof., 1952-56, assoc. prof., 1956-59, prof. chem. and metall. engring., 1959-89, prof. emeritus chem. and metall. engring., 1989—. Mem. Mich. Bd. Registration for Profl. Engrs., 1963-78, chmn., 1969-70, 72-73, 75-76; mem. Mich. Bd. Registration for Architects, 1963-78 Author: (with L.E. Brownell) Process Equipment Design, 1959; contbr. articles to profl. jours. Dist. commr. Boy Scouts Am., 1961-64; mem. Wolverine coun., 1965-68. With USNR, 1943-46, to capt. Res. ret., 1978. Fellow ASME, ASHRAE, AIChE (Donald Q Kern award 1979), Am. Inst. Chemists, Engring. Soc. Detroit; mem. Am. Chem. Soc., Am. Soc. Engring. Edn., Nat. Soc. Profl. Engrs. (pres. 1968-69, award 1977), Mich. Soc. Profl. Engrs. (pres. 1962-63, Engr. of Year award 1976), Mich. Assn. of Professions (pres. 1966, Distinguished award 1970), Nat. Council Engring. Examiners, Naval Res. Assn., Res. Officers Assn., Sigma Xi, Tau Beta Pi, Phi Kappa Phi, Phi Lambda Upsilon, Alpha Chi Sigma. Republican. Baptist. Home: 609 Dartmoor Rd Ann Arbor MI 48103-4513 Personal E-mail: ehyoung@engin.umich.edu.

YOUNG, EDWIN S. W. federal agency official; b. Honolulu, Nov. 13, 1943; s. Hoon Kwan and Clara (Lee) Y.; m. Joan Tay, May 19, 1978. BA, U. Hawaii, 1966; MBA, U. Utah, 1975; MS, U. So. Calif., 1983. Asst. gen. mgr. Royal Men's Shops, Inc., Honolulu, 1973-75; mgmt. analyst U.S. Gen. Acctg. Office, Denver and Honolulu, 1976-83; audit mgr. USAF Audit Agy., L.A., 1983-84, 87-90; fgn. svc. officer Dept. State, 1984-87; with Office of Insp. Gen., Office Policy & Program Rev., Washington, 1984-87; divsn. dir., asst. dir., dir. prodn. Naval Audit Svc. Western Region, Vallejo, Calif., 1990-95; desk officer, planning and policy dir. Naval Audit Svc., Washington, 1995; regional inspector gen. for auditing, audit mgr. U.S. Small Bus. Adminstrn., L.A., 1995-2000; dir. internal audit Calif. State U., Fullerton, 2000—01; dep. city auditor City of Palo Alto, Calif., 2001—. U.S. govt. rep. Pacific and Asian Affairs Coun., Honolulu, 1978—83; USN audit svc. rep. World Affairs Coun. No. Calif., 1990—95; exec. dir. The Asian-Am. Found. Phoenix, 1990—; SBA rep. World Affairs Coun. So. Calif., 1995—2000; Calif. State Fullerton rep. World Affairs Coun., 2000—01; City of Palo Alto rep. World Affairs Coun. No. Calif., 2001—. Community coord. Kailua Neighborhood Bd., Honolulu, 1978-83; area rep. Urban Mass Transit Authority, Honolulu, 1978-83. Capt. USAF, 1966-72. Recipient Commendation awards U.S. Gen. Acctg. Office, 1980, USAF Audit Agy., 1983, 88, 90, USAF Acctg. and Fin. Ctr., 1984, U.S. Naval Audit Svc. award 1992, 94, 95, Nat. Assn. Local Auditors award/winner nat. award for best audit, 2004. Mem. Assn. Govt. Accts., Inst. Internal Auditors, Chinese C. of C., World Affairs Coun. Roman Catholic. Avocations: photography, skiing, swimming, tennis, snorkeling. E-mail: eswyoung@aol.com.

YOUNG, ESTELLE IRENE, dermatologist, educator; b. N.Y.C., Nov. 2, 1945; d. Sidney D. and Blanche (Krosney) Young. BA magna cum laude, Mt. Holyoke Coll., 1967; MD, Downstate Med. Ctr., 1971. Intern Lenox Hill Hosp., N.Y.C., 1971-72, resident in medicine, 1972-73; resident in dermatology Columbia Presbyn. Hosp., N.Y.C., 1973—74, NYU Hosp., 1974—75, Boston U. Hosp., 1975-76; asst. dermatologist Harvard U. Health Svcs., Cambridge, Mass., 1975-76; assoc. staff mem. dermatology Boston U. Med. Ctr., 1976-77; practice medicine specializing in dermatology Petersburg, Va., 1976-97; mem. staff Poplar Springs Hosp., 1976—2002, Southside Regional Med. Ctr. (formerly Petersburg Gen. Hosp.), 1976—2002, Ctrl. State Hosp., 1976—. Clin. instr. dept. dermatology Med. Coll. Va., 1976-87, asst. clinic prof., 1988-94, assoc. clin. prof., 1994-2002; sec. med. staff Petersburg Gen. Hosp., 1982. Contbr. articles to profl. jours. Fellow Am. Acad. Dermatology; mem. Va. Med. Soc., Va. Dermatology Soc., Tidewater Dermatology Soc. (pres. 1982-83), Physicians for Social Responsibility Soc., Tidewater Physicians for Social Responsibility (pres. 1990), Internat. Physicians for Prevention of Nuclear War, Southside Va. Med. Soc., Sigma Xi. Home and Office: PO Box 20182 New York NY 10021-0063 Fax: (212) 249-5948. E-mail: eiy112@aol.com.

YOUNG, EVERETT J. management consultant, agricultural economist; b. Webberville, Mich., Mar. 14, 1913; s. J.P. and Ullie Jospehine (Sigourney) Y.; m. Irene Elizabeth Olick, June 18, 1949. BS in Agrl. Econs., Mich. State U., 1939, MBA, 1960. Field rep. Mich. Fam Bur., Lansing, Mich., 1940-45; asst. exec. sec. Mich. Assn. Farmer Coops., Lansing., 1945-55; fin., mktg. advisor U.S. State Dept., Thailand, 1955-57; mktg. specialist Mich. Dept. Agrl., Lansing, 1957-58; mgr. Dairy Assn. Retail Inds., Detroit, 1961-63; ast. dir. Agrl. Coop. Devel. Internat., Washington, 1968-70; appraiser County of Eaton, Charlotte, Mich., 1974-83; farm mgr. 2 farms pvt. practice, Charlotte, 1972-96. Cons. E. Jay Young Mktg., Detroit, 1962-68, Experience, Inc., Mnpls., 1969-71, Africa, Asia Internat. Devel. Svcs., Washington, 1971-73; chief of party Internat. Coop. Devel. Assn., Uruguay, 1969-70. Author: Agricultural Cooperative, 1952; (USDA Aid Pub.) Food Mktg. in Developing Countries, 1970. Bd. dirs. Episc. Westrn Diocese Mich., Kalamzaoo, 1978-82; exec. com. Eaton County Rep. Club, Charlotte, 1983. Recipient Bishop's cross Episc. Ch., Kalamazoo, 1978. Mem. Internat. Assn. Agrl. Economists, Am. Fgn. Svc. Assn., Internat. Platform Assn., Circumnavigators Club (life), Shriners, Patriarch Mich. State U., Knights Templar, Lansing Farmers Club. Republican. Methodist. Avocations: travel, organ, french lang. Home: 1797 Packard Hwy Charlotte MI 48813-9717

YOUNG, FREDERIC HISGIN, information systems executive, data processing consultant; b. Boston, Sept. 7, 1936; s. Ralph Randel Jr. and Wilhelmina Amalia (Imberger) Y.; m. Carol Joan Costello, Sept. 7, 1963 (div. Dec. 1971); children: Tracy Jean, Jodi Ann; m. Kathleen Paula Thorne, Dec. 1, 1984. BBA, U. Mass., 1961; JD, Suffolk U., 1966. Mgr. systems and programs Matrix Corp., Burlington, Mass., 1968-69; sr. cons. Programming Dimensions, Inc., Burlington, 1969-70; bus. mgr. JTB Rehab. Ctr., North Reding, Mass., 1970-75; regional bus. mgr. Mass. Dept. Mental Health, Waltham, 1975-78, dir. personnel mgmt. Boston, 1978-81; prin. cons. Lafayette Assocs., Chelsea, Mass., 1980-81; asst. regional dir. Corp. for Applied Systems, Indpls., 1982-84; v.p. cons. svcs. HAS, Inc., Carmel, Ind., 1984-88; v.p. info. sytems Ind. Fed. Credit Union, Anderson, Ind., 1988-95; sys. cons. AIC, Inc., Indpls., 1995-96; sr. cons. Whittman-Hart, Inc., 1996-98; pres. FHY Assoc., Inc., Rio Rancho, N.Mex., 1999-2000; sr. cons. MarchFIRST, Spencer, Ind., 2000-01; divsn. mgr. PACE, 2001—. With USN, 1954-56. Republican. Avocation: woodworking. Home: 1840 Carmichael Ln Spencer IN 47460 Office Phone: 812-828-0992. E-mail: f-young@ccrtc.com.

YOUNG, GENEVIEVE LEMAN, publishing executive, editor; b. Geneva, Sept. 25, 1930; came to U.S., 1945, naturalized, 1968; d. Clarence Kuangson and Juliana Helen (Yen) Y.; m. Cedric Sun, 1955 (div. 1972); m. Gordon Parks, Aug. 26, 1973 (div. 1979). BA (Wellesley Coll. scholar), Wellesley Coll., 1952. Asst. editor Harper & Row (pubs.), N.Y.C., 1960-62, editor, 1962-64, asst. mng. editor, 1964-66, mng. editor, 1966-70; exec. editor J.B. Lippincott Co., N.Y.C., 1970-77, v.p., 1972-77; sr. editor Little, Brown & Co., N.Y.C., 1977-85; editor-in-chief Lit. Guild Am., N.Y.C., 1985-88; v.p., editorial dir. Bantam Books, N.Y.C., 1988-92. Alumna trustee Phillips Acad., Andover, Mass., 1975-78, class agt., 1979-85; mem. Wellesley Bus. Leadership Coun., 1989-98; mem. Youth Counseling League, 1986-98, pres., 1989-96, mem. com. of 100, 1991-93; mem. Literacy Ptnrs., Inc., N.Y.C., 1992-2001, sec., 1996-2001; mem. Andover Devel. Bd., 1993-98; trustee Jewish Bd. Family and Children's Svcs., 1996-98. Recipient Alumna Achievement award Wellesley Coll., 1982, Matrix award, 1988. Mem. Assn. Am. Pubs. (exec. coun. gen. pub. div. 1975-78, 85-87, freedom to read com. 1972-75), Women's Media Group (pres. 1981-82, 2d v.p. 1994-95), Century Assn. Home: 30 Park Ave New York NY 10016-3801

YOUNG, GEORGE CRESSLER, federal judge; b. Cin., Aug. 4, 1916; s. George Philip and Gladys (Cressler) Y.; m. Iris June Hart, Oct. 6, 1951; children: George Cressler, Barbara Ann. AB, U. Fla., 1938, LLB, 1940; postgrad., Harvard Law Sch., 1947. Bar: Fla. 1940. Practice in, Winter Haven, 1940-41; asso. firm Smathers, Thompson, Maxwell & Dyer, Miami, 1947; adminstrv., legislative asst. to Senator Smathers of Fla., 1948-52; asst. U.S. atty. Jacksonville, 1952; partner firm Knight, Kincaid, Young & Harris, Jacksonville, 1953-61; U.S. dist. judge No., Middle and So. dists. Fla., 1961-73; chief judge Middle Dist., 1973-81, sr. judge, 1981—. Mem. com. on adminstrn. fed. magistrates system Jud. Conf. U.S., 1973-80 Bd. dirs. Jacksonville United Cerebral Palsy Assn., 1953-60. Served to lt. (s.g.) USNR, 1942-46. Mem. Rollins Coll. Alumni Assn. (pres. 1968-69), ABA (spl. com. for adminstrn. criminal justice), Fla. Bar Assn. (gov. 1960-61), Jacksonville Bar Assn. (past pres.), Order of Coif, Fla. Blue Key, Phi Beta Kappa, Phi Kappa Phi, Phi Delta Phi, Sigma Alpha Epsilon. Home: 2424 Shrewsbury Rd Orlando FL 32803-1334 Office: George C Young US Courthouse and Fed Bldg 80 N Hughey Ave Orlando FL 32801-2278 Office Phone: 407-835-4280.

YOUNG, GEORGE HAYWOOD, III, investment banker; b. Washington, D.C., Feb. 10, 1959; s. George H. Jr. and Jeanne Marie (Collins) Y.; m. Adina Chouequet, Oct. 12, 1996; children: Nathalie Haywood, George Haywood IV. BA in Internat. Rels. with honors, Brown U., 1982; MPhil in Internat. Rels., Magdalene Coll., U. Cambridge, Eng., 1983; M in Pub. and Pvt. Mgmt., Yale U., 1987. Assoc. cons. Bain & Co., Boston, 1983-85; assoc. mergers and acquisitions dept. CS First Boston, N.Y.C., 1987-90, v.p., 1990-91, dir., 1992-94; White House fellow U.S. Dept. Treasury, Washington, 1991-92; sr. v.p. Lehman Bros., N.Y.C., 1994-96, mng. dir., 1996—, mng. dir., co-head of global comms. group, 2000—. Spkr. in field. Application reader White House Fellows Commn., N.Y.C., 1993—; mem. alumni coun. exec. com. Phillips Acad., Andover, Mass., 1994—98, vis. mem. fin. and investment com. bd. trustees, 1998—; mem. regional selection panel White House Fellows Commn., N.Y.C., 2002—; vol. Ch. of the Holy Trinity, N.Y.C., 1990—97. Mem. Coun. Fgn. Rels. (term membership selection com.), Assn. U.S. Army, Harrow Sch. Assn., Yale Golf Club, Metedeconk Nat. Golf Club. Roman Catholic. Home: 138 W 17th St Apt 8 New York NY 10011-5412 Office: Lehman Bros 745 7th Ave New York NY 10019-0001 E-mail: gyoung@lehman.com.

YOUNG, GLADYS, business owner; m. H. Timothy Kuhn; 3 children. Pres. Young Pontiac Cadillac Dealership, Escondido, Calif. Dir. Downtown Escondido Redevel., Palomar Coll. Pres.'s Assn.; contbr. St. Clare's Home, The North County Interfaith Crisis Ctr., Palomar Pomerado Hosp. Health Found., EYE Counseling and Crisis Ctr., Calif. Ctr. Arts. Recipient Quality Dealer award Time Mag., 1996. Mem. New Car Dealers Assn. (San Diego county chpt. award), Escondido Auto Park Assn. (pres.), Escondido C. of C. (dir.). Office: Young Pontiac Cadillac Dealership 1515 Auto Park Way N Escondido CA 92029-2098

YOUNG, GRACE MAY-EN, pediatrician, educator; b. Pitts. AB, Harvard U., 1977; MD, Columbia U., 1981. Diplomate Am. Bd. Pediat. Emergency Medicine, Am. Bd. Pediat. From intern to resident in pediat. Children's Nat. Med. Ctr., Washington, 1981-84, fellow in pediat. emergency medicine, 1986-87; asst. prof. pediat. George Washington U. Sch. Medicine, Washington, 1986-90, NYU Sch. Medicine, N.Y.C., 1990-93; assoc. prof. pediat. U. Md. Sch. Medicine, Balt., 1993—.

YOUNG, GWYNNE A. lawyer; b. Durham, N.C., 1950; AB, Duke U., 1971; JD, U. Fla., 1974. Bar: Fla. 1974. Asst. state atty. 13th Judicial Cir., Fla.; mem. Carlton, Fields, Ward, Emmanuel, Smith & Cutler P.A., Tampa, Fla. Instr. U. Fla. Coll. Law, 1974. Exec. editor U. Fla. Law Review, 1973-74. Pres. Jr. League Tampa, Inc., 1985-86; bd. dirs. Assn. Jr. Leagues, Inc., 1987-89, Duke U. Nat. Alumni Assn., 1993—, pres., 1999-2000; trustee Duke U., 1999—. Fellow Am. Bar Found.; mem. ABA., Office: Carlton Fields Ward Emmanuel Smith & Cutler PA 1 Harbour Pl 777 S Harbour Island Blvd Tampa FL 33602-5729

YOUNG, HENRY E. tissue engineering medical educator; b. Dayton, Ohio, Dec. 5, 1951; s. Henry O. and Lucille M. Y.; m. Valerie E. Achorn, May 16, 1976; 1 child, Katherine. BS in Biology, Ohio State U., 1974; MS in Zoology, U. Ark., 1977; PhD, Tex. Tech. U., 1983. Instr.biochemistry Rush-Presbyn.-St. Luke's Med. Ctr., Chgo., 1987-88; asst. prof. anatomy Mercer U. Sch. Medicine, Macon, Ga., 1988-95, asst. prof. surgery, 1988-94, assoc. prof. anatomy, pediatrics, 1995—2004, prof. anatomy, pediat., 2004—. Inventor in field. NIH Postdoctoral fellow biochemistry Case Western Res. U., Cleve., 1983-85, Muscular Dystrophy Assn. postdoctoral fellow, 1985-87; recipient Hooding award Excellence in Teaching and Rsch. Mercer U. Med. Sch., 1993, 94, Gender Equity award Am. Med. Women's Assn., 1997. Mem.: Am. Soc. Cell Biology, Stem Cells and Regen Medicine, Tissue Culture Soc., Am. Assn. Anatomists. Achievements include discovery of adult pluripotent stem cells; invention of muscle morphogenetic protein and scar inhibitory factor. Avocation: reading. Office: Mercer U Sch Medicine 1550 College St Macon GA 31207-1500 Office Phone: 478-301-4034.

YOUNG, HOBART PEYTON, economist, mathematician, educator; b. Evanston, Ill., Mar. 9, 1945; s. Hobart Paul and Louise (Buchwalter) Y.; m. Fernanda Toueg, Mar. 27, 1982; children: Hobart Patrick, Benjamin Morris Chandler. BA, Harvard Coll., 1966; PhD, U. Mich., 1970. Econ. Nat. Water Commn., Arlington, Va., 1971; from asst. to assoc. prof. CUNY, 1971-75; rsch. scholar, dep. chmn. systems and decision sci. Internat. Inst. for Applied Systems Analysis, Laxenburg, Austria, 1975-81; prof. pub. policy U. Md., College Park, 1981-94; prof. econ. Johns Hopkins Univ., 1994—; sr. fellow in econ. The Brookings Inst., 1998—. Adv. panel John D. and Catherine T. MacArthur Found., 1997-99; external faculty and mem. Sci Steering Com-.,Santa Fe Inst., 2001—. Author: Fair Representation, 1982, Equity, 1994, Individual Strategy and Social Structure, 1998, Strategic Learning and Its Limits, 2004; editor Cost Allocation, 1985, Fair Allocation, 1985, Negotiation Analysis, 1991, Social Dynamics, 2001; assoc. editor: Games and Economic Behavior, 1989—, Social Choice and Welfare, 1990-97. NSF grantee, 1975-86, 90-91, 96-2002, Office Naval Rsch. grantee, 1986-89, Russell Sage Found. grantee, 1989-91; Erskine fellow in Econs., 1990; recipient Lester R. Ford award Math. Assn. Am., 1976; Named Fulbright Disting. Chair in Econs., 2003-. Fellow Econometric Soc.; mem. Am. Polit. Sci. Assn., Ops. Rsch. Soc. Am., Cosmos Club, European Econ. Assn., v.p. Game Theory Soc., 2004— Episcopalian. Avocations: choral singing, canoeing. Office: Johns Hopkins Univ Dept Econ Baltimore MD 21218 also: The Brookings Instn 1775 Massachusetts Ave NW Washington DC 20036-2103 E-mail: pyoung@jhu.edu.

YOUNG, HOWARD THOMAS, foreign language educator; b. Cumberland, Md., Mar. 24, 1926; s. Samuel Phillip and Sarah Emmaline (Frederick) Y.; m. Carol Osborne, Oct. 5, 1949 (div. 1966); children: Laurie Margaret, Jennifer Anne; m. Edra Lee Airheart, May 23, 1981; 1 child, Timothy Howard. BS summa cum laude, Columbia U., 1950, MA, 1952, PhD, 1954. Lectr. Columbia U., N.Y.C., 1950-54; asst. prof. Romance langs. Pomona Coll., Claremont, Calif., 1954-60, assoc. prof., 1960-66, Smith prof. Romance langs., 1966-98, prof. emeritus, 1998—. Vis. prof. Middlebury Program in Spain, Madrid, 1986-87, U. Zaragoza, 1967-68, Columbia U., summer 2000; chief reader Spanish AP Ednl. Testing Svc., Princeton, 1975-78, chmn. Spanish lang. devel. commn., 1976-79; mem. fgn. lang. adv. commn. Coll. Bd., N.Y.C., 1980-83; mem. West Coast selection commn. Mellon Fellowships for Humanities, Princeton, 1984-86, European selection com., 1987, 90; trans. cons. Smithsonian Inst. Author: The Victorious Expression, 1964, Juan Ramón Jimènez, 1967, The Line in the Margin, 1980; editor: T.S. Eliot and Hispanic Modernity, 1995; contbr. London Times Higher Edn. Supplement; contbr. numerous articles and book revs. to profl. jours. Dir. NEH summer seminar for Sch. tchrs., 1993. Served with USNR, 1944-46, ETO. Fellow Del Amo Found., 1960-61, NEH, 1975, 89-90; Fulbright fellow; 1967-68; Rockefeller Study Ctr. scholar, 1976. Mem. MLA, Assn. Tchrs. Spanish and Portuguese, Am. Comparative Lit. Assn., Acad. Am. Poets, Assn. Lit. Scholars and Critics. Home: 447 W Redlands Ave Claremont CA 91711-1638 Office: Pomona Coll Romance Lang Dept 550 Harvard Ave Claremont CA 91711-6380 Business E-Mail: htyoung@pomona.edu.

YOUNG, HUBERT HOWELL, JR., lawyer, real estate investor and developer; b. Franklin, Va., May 30, 1945; s. Hubert Howell and Elizabeth Ann (Davidson) Y.; m. Christine P. Brooks, Dec. 31, 1964; 1 son, Hubert Howell, III. BA, Washington Lee U., 1967, LLB, magna cum laude, 1969. Bar: Va. 1969, U.S. Supreme Ct. 1972, Tex. 1974, U.S. Dist. Ct. Tex. 1974, U.S. Dist. Ct. (ea. dist.) Va. 1980. Assoc., Johnson, Bromberg, Leeds and Riggs, Dallas, 1973-75; gen. counsel Trammel Crow Co., Dallas, 1975-79; sole practice, Suffolk, Va., 1979—; gen. counsel Young Properties, Suffolk, 1979—; dir. Young Properties Devel. Corp., Trammel Crow Investment Corp., Suffolk Broadcasting Corp. Pres. Suffolk (Va.) Found. Trust, 1982-83; vice chmn. Suffolk Coalition for Sr. Citizen Housing, Inc., 1982-83; mem. Suffolk Substance and Abuse and Youth Coun., 1982-84; chmn. Suffolk Rep. Party, 1982-85; commr. Med. Coll. Hampton Roads, 1990-96; dir. Va. Symphony, 1991-94. Served as lt. JAG, USN, 1969-73. Designated col. Confederate Army The Lee-Jackson Meml. Inc., 1981. Mem. ABA, Suffolk Bar Assn. (pres. 1994), Property Owners and Mgrs. Assn. (pres. 1995-96). Club: Town Point, Sports, Ducks Unlimited (Suffolk). Office: Young Properties 444 N Main St Suffolk VA 23434-4425 Office Phone: 757-539-3479. Fax: 757-539-5130. Personal E-mail: yprop@msn.com.

YOUNG, HUGH DAVID, physics educator, writer, organist; b. Ames, Iowa, Nov. 3, 1930; s. Hugh Surber and Nellie Sibella (Peters) Y.; m. Alice Carroll, June 25, 1960; children: Gretchen Carroll, Rebecca Susan BS in Physics, Carnegie-Mellon U., 1952, MS in Physics, 1953, PhD in Physics, 1959, BFA in Music, 1972. From instr. to assoc. prof. physics Carnegie-Mellon U., Pitts., 1956-77, prof., 1977—; head dept. natural scis. Margaret Morrison Carnegie Coll., Carnegie-Mellon U., 1962-67, acad. coordinator, lectr. modern engring. mgrs. program, 1966-82. Vis. assoc. prof. physics U. Calif., Berkeley, 1967-68, vis. prof. physics, 1974; asst. organist St. Paul's Cathedral, Pitts., 1978-82 Author: Statistical Treatment of Experimental Data, 1962, Fundamentals of Mechanics and Heat, 2d edit., 1974, Fundamentals of Optics and Modern Physics, 2d edit., 1976; (with Sears and Zemansky) College Physics, 7th edit., 1990, University Physics, 9th edit., 1996. Bd. dirs. Renaissance and Baroque Soc., 1980-86. Recipient Ryan Tchg. award Carnegie Inst. Tech., 1965, Doherty award for excellence in edn. Carnegie Mellon U., 1997. Mem. Am. Assn. Physics Tchrs., Am. Phys. Soc., Am. Guild Organists (assoc.) Democrat. Avocations: organ, rock climbing. Home: 5746 Aylesboro Ave Pittsburgh PA 15217-1412 Office: Carnegie-Mellon Univ Dept Physics Pittsburgh PA 15213 Office Phone: 412-268-2759. Business E-Mail: hdy@andrew.cmu.edu.

YOUNG, J. WARREN, magazine publisher; Pub. Boys' Life Mag., Irving, Tex. Office: Boys' Life PO Box 152079 Irving TX 75015-2079

YOUNG, JACK ALLISON, financial executive; b. Aurora, Ill., Dec. 31, 1931; s. Neal A. and Gladys Young; m. Virginia Dawson, Jan. 24, 1959; children: Amy D., Andrew A. BS in Journalism, U. Ill., 1954. CLU; chartered fin. cons.; registered security rep. Advt. writer Caterpillar Tractor Co., 1956-58; inst. agent Equitable Life Assurance Soc., St. Geneva, Ill., 1958—, ins. broker, 1972—; pres. Jack A. Young and Assocs., 1978—, Creative Brokerage, Inc., 1982-95. Past pres., gen. securities prin. Chartered Planning, Ltd., 1984-2000; past trustee Equitable CLU Assn.; past chmn. Equitable Nat. Agents Forum. Bd. dirs. Tri-City Famiy Services, 1975-83, pres., 1979-81; trustee Delnor-Community Health System, 1985-97, chmn., 1988-91; bd. dirs. St. Charles Ctr. Phys. Rehab., 1991-97; chmn., pres. Delnor-Cmty. Health Care Found., 1986-88; dir. Kane County Bar Found., Inc., 1997-2000. Lt. (j.g.) USN, 1956. Named to Equitable Hall of Fame, 1978. Mem. Million Dollar Round Table (life), Am. Soc. C.L.U.s, Am. Coll. C.L.U. Golden Key Soc., Fox Valley Estate Planning Council, Internat. Assn. for Fin. Planning, Inc., Aurora Assn. Life Underwriters (past pres., nat. committeeman), Nat. Assn. Securities Dealers (registered prin.), Geneva Golf Club (pres. 1994). Home: 18 Campbell St Geneva IL 60134-2732 also: 2706 Laurel Dr Vero Beach FL 32960-5063 Office: 28 N Bennett St Geneva IL 60134-2207 E-mail: jayassoc@aol.com., yjackayoung@aol.com.

YOUNG, JACK PHILLIP, chemist; b. Huntington, Ind., Oct. 28, 1929; s. Jacob P. and Marie Young; m. Jean Elizabeth Kennedy, June 18, 1955; children: James, Mark, David, Timothy, Karen. BS, Ball State U., 1950; PhD, Ind. U., 1955. Chemist Kraus Lab., Huntington, Ind., 1950, Huntington Lab., 1952-53, Oak Ridge (Tenn.) Nat. Lab., 1955-82, sr. staff, 1982—2000; cons. Oak Ridge Nat. Lab., 2000—. Co-editor: Radiation and Public Perception, 1995; contbr. more than 200 articles to profl. jours. Patentee in field. Bd. dirs., pres. Children's Mus., Oak Ridge, 1983-89; bd. dirs. Oak Ridge Civic Music Assn., 1993-98. Recipient award Indsl. Rsch., 1983. Fellow AAAS; mem. Am. Chem. Soc. (local pres. 1993, D.A. Shirley award East Tenn. sect. 2003), Sigma Xi. Roman Catholic. Achievements include development of methods to

detect and identify single atoms, demonstration of the chemical consequences of radioactive transmutation and characterization of nuclear isomers. Office: Oak Ridge Nat Lab PO Box 2008 Oak Ridge TN 37831-2008 E-mail: youngjp@ornl.gov.

YOUNG, JACQUELINE EURN HAI, former state legislator, consultant; b. Honolulu, May 20, 1934; d. Paul Bai and Martha (Cho) Y.; m. Harry Valentine Daniels, Dec. 25, 1954 (div. 1978); children: Paula, Harry, Nani, Laura; m. Daniel Anderson, Sept. 25, 1978 (div. 1984); m. Everett Kleinjans, Sept. 4, 1988 (div. 1998). BS in Speech Pathology, Audiology, U. Hawaii, 1969; MS in Edn., Spl. Edn., Old Dominion U., 1972; advanced cert., Loyola Coll., 1977; PhD in Communication, Women's Studies, Union Inst., 1989. Dir. dept. speech and hearing Md. Sch. for the Blind, Balt., 1975-77; dir. deaf-blind project Easter Seal Soc. Oahu, Hawaii, 1977-78; project dir. equal ednl. opportunity programs Hawaii State Dept. Edn., Honolulu, 1978-85, state ednl. specialist, 1978-90; state rep. dist. 20 Hawaii State Legislature, Honolulu, 1990-92, state rep. dist. 51, 1992-94; vice-speaker Hawaii Ho. of Reps., Honolulu. Apptd. to U.S. Dept. Def. Adv. Commn. on Women in the Svc.; cons. spl. edn. U.S. Dept. Edn., dept. edn. Guam, Am. Samoa, Ponape, Palau, Marshall Islands, 1977-85; cons. to orgns. on issues relating to workplace diversity; adj. prof. commn., anthropology, mgmt. Hawaii Pacific U.; dir. mktg. Am. Cancer Soc. Hawaii Pacific, 1985—, dir. mktg., 1999—. TV writer, host, producer, 1992—. 1st v.p. Nat. Women's Polit. Caucus, 1988-90; chair Hawaii Women's Polit. Caucus, 1987-89; bd. dirs. YWCA Oahu, Kalihi Palama Immigrant Svc. Ctr., Hawaii Dem. Movement, Family Peace Ctr.; appointee Honolulu County Com. on the Status of Women, 1986-87; founding bd. dirs. Windward Spouse Abuse Shelter, 1993—; campaign dir. Protect Our Constn., 1998; trustee St. Louis Sch., 1997-99; mem. nat. adv. coun. ACLU, 2004. Recipient Outstanding Woman Leader award YWCA of Oahu, 1994, Pres.'s award Union Inst., 1993, Fellow of the Pacific award Hawaii-Pacific U., 1993, Headliner award Honolulu chpt. Women in Commn., 1993, Korean Am. Alliance Washington Spl. Recognition award, 1998, Hawaii Women Lawyers Disting. Svc. award, 1999, Disting. Equity Adv. award Hawaii chpt. Nat. Coalition for Sex Equity in Edn., 1998, NEA Mary Hatwood Futrell for advancing women's rights award, 1999, Friend of Social Work award Hawaii chpt. NASW, 1998, Allan Saunders award Hawaii chpt. ACLU, 1999; named one of Extraordinary Women Hawaii, Found. Hawaii Women's History, 2001. Home: 212 Luika Pl Kailua HI 96734-3237

YOUNG, JAMES E. banker; BS in Bus. Adminstrn., Tenn. State U., 1971. Mgmt. trainee Chase Manhttan Bank, N.Y.C., 1971-72, lending officer, from 1972, various lending positions corporate banking dept., v.p., team mgr. credit audit divsn., human resource specialist in charge EEO programs, until 1989; v.p., chief comml. loan officer City Nat. Bank N.J., 1989-90, sr. v.p. gen. adminstrn. and comml. loans, 1990-93; pres., CEO, bd. dirs. 1st So. Bancshares, Atlanta, from 1993, pres., CEO, bd. dirs. 1st So. Bank subs., from 1993; pres., CEO, Citizens Trust Bank, Atlanta, also bd. dirs. Mem. regional adv. bd. Fannie Mae; pres., CEO, bd. dirs. Citizens Bancshare Corp., Atlanta, Citizens Trust Bank Mortgage Svcs., Inc., Atlanta. Bd. dirs. Metro tlanta YMCA, Atlanta Neighborhood Devel. Partnership, DeKalb Conv. and Visitors Bur. Mem. Nat. Bankers Assn., DeKalb C. of C. Office: Citizens Trust Bank 75 Piedmont Ave Atlanta GA 30303

YOUNG, JAMES EARL, ceramics educator, educational administrator; b. Chgo., Dec. 20, 1922; s. James Alexander and Ellen (Chedister) Y.; children: Hugh Parker, Katherine Sue. BS, U. Ill., 1948; PhD, State U. N.Y. Coll. Ceramics Alfred U., 1962. Ceramic engr. Republic Steel Co., Chgo., 1948-52; ceramic engr. Armour Research Found., Chgo., 1952-55; research supr. Structural Clay Research Found., Geneva, Ill., 1955-57; research fellow State U. N.Y. Coll. Ceramics at Alfred U., 1957-61, asst. prof., 1961-63, assoc. prof., 1963-67, prof., chmn. dept., 1967-70; dean Coll. Arts and Scis., Rutgers U., Camden, N.J., 1970-73; provost Rutgers U., Newark, 1973-82; exec. dir. Commn. on State Colls. of N.J., 1982-84; prof. Rutgers U., 1984-93, prof. emeritus, 1993—. Contbr. articles to tech. jours. Served with AUS, 1943-46. Am. Council Edn. fellow acad. adminstrn., 1966-67 Mem. Am. Ceramic Soc. Home: 130 Kingsberry Dr Somerset NJ 08873-4309

YOUNG, JAMES EDWARD, lawyer; b. Painesville, Ohio, Apr. 20, 1946; s. James M. and Isabel P. (Rogers) Y. BBA, Ohio U., 1968; JD, Ohio State U., 1972. Bar: Ohio 1972. Law clk. to chief judge U.S. Ct. Appeals, Nashville, 1972-73; chief counsel City of Cleve., 1980-81, law dir., 1981-82; assoc. Jones, Day, Reavis & Pogue (now Jones Day), Cleve., 1973—79, ptnr., 1983—. Office: Jones Day 901 Lakeside Ave E Cleveland OH 44114-1190 Business E-Mail: jameseyoung@jonesday.com.

YOUNG, JAMES JULIUS, academic administrator, retired military officer; b. Fort Ringgold, Tex., Nov. 28, 1926; s. John Cooper and Violet Thelma (Ohl) Y.; m. June Agnes Hillstead, Dec. 17, 1948; children: Robert Michael, Steven Andrew, Patrick James, Mary Frances. BS, U. Md., 1960; M.H.A., Baylor U., 1962; PhD in Hosp. and Health Adminstrn, U. Iowa, 1969. Commd. 2d lt. U.S. Army, 1947, advanced through grades to brig. gen., 1977, comdr., med. ops. officer, dir. tng. field med. units in European Command, 1949-53; comdr. Mil. Med. Leadership Sch., 1953-54; med. advisor (Nationalist Army of China), 1955-57; asst. adminstr. Fitzsimons Army Med. Center, 1957-60; med. plans and ops. officer (US Forces), Korea, 1962-63; sr. field med. instr., chief field med. service Med. Field Service Sch., 1963-66; dir. health care orgn. and mgmt. analysis Office of Surgeon Gen., 1969-71; dir. med. plans and ops. directorate Office of the Surgeon, Military Assistance Command, Vietnam, 1971-72; exec. officer, chief adminstrv. services Silas Hays Army Hosp., 1973-74; military health analyst, military health care study OMB, Exec. Office of Pres., 1974-76; dep. dir. resources mgmt. and cons. for health care adminstrn. Office of Surgeon Gen., 1976-77; chief med. svcs. corps U.S. Army, 1977-81; dir. resources mgmt. Office of Surgeon Gen., 1977-81; ret., 1981; instr. U. Iowa, 1967-69; asst. prof., preceptor Baylor U., 1973-74; vice chancellor for health affairs W.Va. Bd. Regents, Charleston, 1982-87; dean sch. of allied health scis. U. Tex. Health Sci. Ctr., San Antonio, 1987-90, interim dean Sch. Medicine, 1988-89, dean Sch. Medicine, 1989—, dean emeritus, 2000—. Cons. to Min. of Health, Republic of Vietnam, 1971-72, 1989-2000; adj. prof. Baylor U., 1977-81, George Washington U., 1975-76, W.Va. U., 1986; prof. U. Tex. health Sci. Ctr., San Antonio, 1989-2000. Contbr. articles to profl. jours. Decorated D.S.M., Legion of Merit, Meritorious Service medal, others; recipient Walter Reed medallion for service, 1981; Army Med. Dept. medallion for contbn. to health service, 1981, Order of Mil. Med. Merit, 1981, U. Tex. Health Scis. Ctr. Hon. medallion Fountains of Progress, 2000; recipient Humanism in medicine award Health Care Foun. N.J., 2000. Mem. APHA, Coun. Deans, Assn. of Am. Med. Colls., Bexar Cty. Med. Soc., Tex. Med. Assn., Assn. Mil. Surgeons (chmn. med. svc. sect. 1978), Assn. U.S. Army, Interagy. Inst. Fed. Health Execs., Phi Kappa Tau. Roman Catholic. Home: 1610 Anchor Dr San Antonio TX 78213-1943 Personal E-mail: jyoung51@satx.rr.com.

YOUNG, JAMES MORNINGSTAR, internist, military officer; b. Massillon, Ohio, Oct. 28, 1929; s. Ralph Louis and Pauline Louise (Morningstar) Y.; m. Bettylu Jones, July 3, 1952; children: Anne Christine, Mark Andrew, Patricia Jane, Elizabeth Lynne, Judith Pamela, Claudia Dianne; m. Mariette M. Aubuchon, Oct. 11, 1970; children: Gretchen Camille, Jason Paul. AB, Duke U., 1951, MD, 1955. Diplomate Am. Bd. Internal Medicine. Intern Bethesda Naval Hosp., 1955-56, asst. dir. tissue bank, 1956-58, resident, 1958-61; commd. lt. (j.g.) USN, 1955, advanced through grades to lt. comdr., 1961, promoted to temporary rank capt., 1963; White House physician to Presidents Kennedy and Johnson, Washington, 1963-66. Asst. chief medicine and dir. of interns, Oakland (Calif.) Naval Hosp., 1966-69; chief medicine Naval Hosp. Boston, Chelsea, Mass., 1969-74; med. officer Naval Air Sta., South Weymouth, Mass., 1974-75; assoc. clin. prof. medicine Boston U. Sch. Medicine, 1969-75; v.p. med. affairs Mass. Blue Shield/Blue Cross, 1975-87; lectr. Harvard Sch. Pub. Health, 1987-90; sr. advisor Beijing Coll. Traditional Chinese Medicine, 1987-88; med. advisor U.S.-China People's Friendship Assn., Washington, 1988-90; cons. USPHS, Office Asst. Sec. for Health, Nat. Ctr. for Health Svcs., Rsch. and Health Care Tech. Assessment, HHS, 1985-90; v.p. for med. affairs Greenery Rehab. Group, Inc., 1988-90; assoc. med. dir. New. Eng. Rehab. Hosp., 1992-95, chief medicine, 1992-95. Contbr. articles to med. publs. Decorated knight comdr. with star Equestrian Order of the Holy Sepulchre of Jerusalem; named Disting. Citizen of Washington H.S., Massillon, Ohio, 1993. Fellow ACP, AMA, Alpha Omega Alpha, Omicron Delta Kappa, Beta Omega Sigma, Sigma Alpha Epsilon. Home: 77 Harvey Mill Rd Lee NH 03824-6302 Personal E-mail: jmyoung9@hotmail.com.

YOUNG, JAMES OLIVER, dentist, communication company executive; b. Parris Island, S.S., Apr. 19, 1945; s. William Oliver and Ruth Cherokee (Risner) Y.; m. Virginia Evelyn Koontz; children: Amy Robyn, Jenny Elizabeth, Thomas William. BS, Southeast State U., Okla., 1967; DDS, Baylor U., 1972. Ordained deacon Episc. Ch., 2001. Tchr. pub. schs., 1967-68; practice dentistry Ardmore, Okla., 1972-93; v.p. Cherokee Telephone Co., Calera, Okla., 1963-94, pres., 1994—. V.p. Cherokee Cellular, Inc., 1989—; pres. Comm. Equipment Co., Calera, 1984—, Ardmore Soup Kitchen, Inc., 1999—; bd. dirs. Good Shepherd Med. Clinic. Trustee Ardmore Devel. Authority, 1980-85; pres. Oak Hall Epis. Sch., 2002-03. Bd. dirs. Ardmore Cmty. Concerts Assn., 1980-90, Salvation Army, 1990-91; scoutmaster Boy Scouts Am., pres. Arbuckle Area Coun., 1994-95; Okla. state adv. bd. Easter Seal Soc. Named one of Outstanding Young Men Am., 1981. Fellow Acad. Gen. Dentistry, Acad. Dentistry Internat.; mem. ADA, Okla. Dental Assn., Ind. Dentists Southern Okla. (pres. 1986), Okla. C. of C. (bd. dirs. 1984-85), Masons. Republican. Avocations: skiing, sailing. Home: 2207 Ridgeway St Ardmore OK 73401-3405 Office: PO Box 445 Calera OK 74730-0445

YOUNG, JAMES R. railroad transportation executive; Grad., U. Nebraska. With Union Pacific Corp., 1978—, mgmt. fin. and ops., asst. v.p., re-engineering, Union Pacific R.R. Co., 1994—95, former v.p., fin. & quality, former sr. v.p. fin., exec. v.p., CFO, 1999—2004, pres., Union Pacific R.R. Co., 2004—. Office: Union Pacific 1416 Dodge St Omaha NE 68179

YOUNG, JAMES W. biotechnology company executive; BS Chemistry, Fordham U.; PhD Organic Chemistry, Cornell U. Sr. v.p. rsch. & devel. ALZA Crop.; pres. pharms. divsn. Affymax; sr. v.p., gen. mgr. pharms. divsn. Sepracor Corp.; CEO, dir. Sunesis Pharms., Inc., South San Francisco, 2000—. Office: Sunesis Pharms Inc 341 Oyster Point Blvd South San Francisco CA 94080

YOUNG, JAY ALFRED, chemical safety and health consultant, writer, editor; b. Huntington, Ind., Sept. 8, 1920; s. Jacob Phillip and Marie (Skully) Y.; m. Anne Elizabeth Neff, June 29, 1942 (dec. June 1962); children: John, Paul, Cecelia, Michael, Joseph, Andrea, Therese, Gregory, Thomas, Lucy, Margaret, Antonia; m. Mary Ann Owens, Aug. 15, 1962; children: James, Laurence; 4 stepchildren. BS, Ind. U., 1939; AM, Oberlin Coll., 1940; PhD, U. Notre Dame, 1950. Chief chemist Asbestos Mfg. Co., Huntington, Ind., 1941-42; ordnance engr. U.S. War Dept., Washington, 1942-44; from instr. to prof. chemistry King's Coll., Wilkes-Barre, Pa., 1949-69; vis. prof. Carleton U., Ottawa, Ont., Can., 1969-70, Fla. State U., Tallahassee, 1975-77; Hudson prof. Auburn (Ala.) U., 1970-75; mgr. tech. publs. Chem. Mfrs. Assn., Washington, 1977-80; chem. safety and health cons. Silver Spring, Md., 1980—. Pro bono cons. OSHA, EPA, Consumer Product Safety Commn., Washington, 1980—; invited lectr. chem. edn. and chem. health and safety U.S., Can., Mex., Brazil, Argentina, Chile, Great Britain, Norway, France, Italy, India, Indonesia, Australia, New Zealand, Japan, 1963—. Author: Practice in Thinking, 1958, Elements of General Chemistry, 1960, Chemical Concepts, 1963, Selected Principles of Chemistry, 1963, Arithmetic for Students of Science, 1968, Instructor's Guide for Chemistry, a Cultural Approach, 1971, Study Guide for General Chemistry, 1974, Fire!, 1977, Actions and Reactions, 1978, Chemistry, A Human Concern, 1978, Kitchen Chemistry, 1980, Electron Microscopy Safety Handbook, 1985; co-author: Study Guide for Continental Classroom Chemistry, NBC/TV, vols. I and II, 1959, 60, Keys to Chemistry, 1973, Chemistry Preparation Laboratory, 1973, Keys to Oxidation-Reduction, 1974, Things that Last, 1977, Principles of Laboratory Safety (with videotape), 1980, OSHA Hazard Communication Regulations, 1984, Chemical Safety Manual for Small Businesses, 1st edit., 1989, 2d edit., 1992, Developing a Chemical Hygiene Plan, 1990; editor: Guidelines and Recommendations for the Preparation and Continuing Education of Secondary School Teachers of Chemistry, 1977, Improving Safety in the Chemical Laboratory: A Practical Guide, 1st edit., 1989, 2d edit., 1992 (also contbr.), Safety in Academic Chemistry Laboratories, 7th edit., 2002, Chemical Safety for Teachers and Their Supervisors, Grades 7-12, 2001; co-editor: Heath Chemistry Laboratory Experiments, 1987, Handbook of Chemical Health and Safety, 2001 (also contbr.); contbr. and cons. numerous books; contbr. Encyclopedia Britannica, and over 100 articles to profl. jours. Tech. resource person to media and expert witness regarding chem. hazards, precautions, transp. incidents involving chems.; mem. NSF Coll. Chemistry Commn., 1962-68. Lt. USNR, 1944-46. Recipient Disting. Chemistry Alumnus award U. Notre Dame, 1968, Excellence in Chemistry Tchg. award Mfg. Chemists Assn., 1970. Fellow AAAS; mem. Am. Chem. Soc. (councilor 1963-87, policy com. 1970-81, sec. divsn. chem. edn. 1969-78, chmn. divsn. chem. health and safety 1979-80, mem. chem. safety com. 1982-2003, Chem. Health and Safety award 1991, Outstanding Svc. award 2003). Roman Catholic. Avocations: wood and metalworking, gardening. Home and Office: 12916 Allerton Ln Silver Spring MD 20904-3105

YOUNG, JAY MAITLAND, healthcare communications consultant; b. Louisville, Nov. 26, 1944; s. Clyde Dudley and Olive May (Tyas) Y. BA in Chemistry and Math. magna cum laude, Vanderbilt U., 1966; MS in Biochemistry, Yale U., 1967, MPhil in Phys. Chemistry, 1968, PhD in Chemistry, 1971. Cert. Am. Med. Writers Assn. Multi-disciplinary Core, 1999. Asst. prof. chemistry Bryn Mawr (Pa.) Coll., 1970-76; rsch. biochemist Abbott Labs., Ill., 1977-78, project mgr. physiol. diagnostics, 1978-80, project mgr. cancer product devel., 1980-82, internat. clin. specialist sci. affairs, 1982-85, clin. project mgr. physiol. diagnostic quality and sci. support, 1986-90, staff quality assurance and sci. support, 1990-93, fertility, pregnancy, thyroid mgr., quality and sci. support, 1993-95, fertility, pregnancy, thyroid, cancer mgr., product quality assurance, 1995-97, staff noninfectious disease diagnostics sci. affairs, 1997—2001; cons. and med. writer pharm. and diagnostic areas, 2002—. Cons. Inst. for Cancer Rsch., Fox Chase, Phila., 1974, vis. scientist, 1975-76; honors examiner Swarthmore Coll., 1973, 74, mem. vis. evaluation com., 1975; presenter to med. groups on cancer markers, viral hepatitis and epidemiology of AIDS, 1982-84. Contbr. articles to profl. jours.; patentee in field. Vol. Episcopal Ch. Outreach Commn. Named to Hon. Order Ky. Cols.; predoctoral fellow NSF, Yale U., 1966-70; postdoctoral fellow, NIH, U. Oxford, 1971-72; travel grantee NATO, 1974. Mem. Am. Med. Writers Assn. (Del. Valley chpt. program chair 2002-03, treas. 2003—, cert mem. Multi-disciplinary Core 1999). E-mail: maitland@mailbug.com.

YOUNG, JENNIFER B. federal agency administrator; b. Bellevue, Ohio; m. J. T. Young. Exec. asst. Ohio Human Svcs. Dept.; dir. health legis. Nat. Govs. Assn.; exec. dir. pub. programs Am. Assn. Health Plans; sr. health policy advisor House Com. on Ways and Means, Senate Fin. Com.; dep. aasst. sec. for health legis. U.S. Dept. Health and Human Svcs., Washington, asst. sec. for legis., 2003—. Office: US Dept HHS Asst Sec for Legis 200 Independence Ave SW Washington DC 20201

YOUNG, JESS RAY, retired internist; b. Fairfield, Ill., Feb. 4, 1928; s. Edgar S. and Clara B. (Musgrave) Y.; m. Gloria Wynn, July 10, 1953; children—James C., Patricia A. BS, Franciscan U., 1951; MD, St. Louis U., 1955. Intern Highland Alameda County Hosp., Oakland, Calif., 1955-56; resident in internal medicine Cleve. Clinic Hosp., 1956-59, mem. staff dept. vascular medicine, 1959-97, chmn. dept., 1976-97; ret., 1998. Co-author: Leg Ulcer, 1975, Peripheral Vascular Diseases, 1991, 1996; contbr. articles to profl. jours., chpts. to books. Served with AUS, 1946-47. Mem. AMA, Am. Heart Assn. (stroke council), Am. Coll. Cardiology, Internat. Cardiovascular Soc., ACP, Am. Fedn. Clic. Research, Ohio Soc. Internal Medicine, Soc. for Vascular Medicine and Rsch., Inter-Urban Club. Methodist. Home: 1503 Burlington Rd Cleveland OH 44118-1216 E-mail: jesyoung@aol.com.

YOUNG, JOAN CRAWFORD, advertising executive; b. Hobbs, N.Mex., July 30, 1931; d. William Bill and Ora Maydelle (Boone) Crawford; m. Herchelle B. Young, Nov. 23, 1971 (div.). BA, Hardin Simmons U., 1952; postgrad., Tex. Tech. U., 1953-54. Reporter Lubbock (Tex.) Avalanche-Jour., 1952-54; promotion dir. Sta. KCBD-TV, Lubbock, 1954-62; account exec. Ward Hicks Advt., Albuquerque, 1962-70; v.p. Mellekas & Assocs. Advt., Albuquerque, 1970-78; pres. J. Young Advt., Albuquerque, 1978—; dir. advt. So. Therapy, Austin, Tex., 1999—. Author: (with Louise Allen and Audre Lipscomb) Radio and TV Continuity Writing, 1962. Bd. dirs. N.Mex. Symphony Orch., 1970-73, United Way of Greater Albuquerque, 1985-89; bd. trustees N.Mex. Children's Found., 1994-96. Recipient Silver medal N.Mex. Advt. Fedn., 1977. Mem. N.Mex. Advt. Fedn. (bd. dirs. 1975-76), Am. Advt. Fedn., Greater Albuquerque C. of C. (bd. dirs. 1984), Albuquerque Petroleum Club (membership chmn. 1992-93, bd. dirs. 1993—, sec. 1994-95, v.p. 1995-97, pres. 1997-99). Republican. Office: 6009 Belfast Dr Austin TX 78723-1832

YOUNG, JOHN ALAN, electronics company executive; b. Nampa, Idaho, Apr. 24, 1932; s. Lloyd Arthur and Karen Eliza (Miller) Y.; m. Rosemary Murray, Aug. 1, 1954; children: Gregory, Peter, Diana. BSEE, Oreg. State U., 1953; MBA, Stanford U., 1958. Various mktg. and fin. positions Hewlett Packard Co. Inc., Palo Alto, Calif., 1958-63, gen. mgr. microwave divsn., 1963-68, v.p. electronic products group, 1968-74, exec. v.p., 1974-77, COO, 1977-78, pres., 1977-92, CEO, 1978-92; ret., 1992. Bd. dirs. ChevronTexaco Corp., Agere Sys., Affymetrix, Inc., Ciphergen, Lucent Technologies, Perlegen, Fluidigm. Chmn. ann. fund Stanford U., 1966-73, nat. chmn. corp. gifts, 1973-77, mem. adv. coun. Grad. Sch. Bus., 1967-73, 75-80, Univ. trustee, 1977-87; bd. dirs. Mid-Peninsula Urban Coalition, 1971-80, co-chmn., 1983-85; chmn. Pres.'s Commn. on Indsl. Competitiveness, 1983-85, Nat. Jr. Achievement, 1983-84; pres. Found. for Malcolm Baldrige Nat. Quality Award; mem. Adv. Com. on Trade Policy and Negotiations, 1988-92. With USAF, 1954-56. Mem. Nat. Acad. Engring., Coun. on Competitiveness (founder, founding chair computer systems policy project 1986), Bus. Coun. (co-chair pres. com. of advisors on sci. & tech. 1993-2001).

YOUNG, JOHN EDWARD, lawyer; b. Tulsa, July 11, 1935; s. Russell Edward and Frances Lucille (Wetmore) Y.; m. Mary Moore Nason, Dec. 27, 1966; children: Cynthia Nason Eberstadt, Abigail Brackett Moses. BS with honors, Calif. Inst. Tech., 1956; LLB magna cum laude, Harvard U., 1959. Bar: N.Y. 1961, U.S. Dist. Ct. (so. dist.) N.Y. 1973. Assoc. Cravath, Swaine & Moore LLP, N.Y.C., 1960-67, ptnr., 1968-95, resident ptnr. Paris, 1971-73, London, 1990-95, sr. counsel, 1996—. Editor Harvard Law Rev., 1958-59. Trustee Internat. Sculpture Ctr., 1997—, vice chmn., 2000—; trustee Royal Oak Found., 1997-2002, chmn., 1999-2002; gov. Am. Crafts Mus., 1997-2000; trustee Nat. Found. for Advancement of the Arts, 2003—. Sheldon Traveling fellow Harvard U., 1959-60. Mem. Assn. Bar City N.Y., Century Assn., Harvard Club of N.Y.C., N.Y. Yacht Club. Democrat. Episcopal. Home: 1088 Park Ave New York NY 10128-1132 Office: Cravath Swaine and Moore LLP 825 Eighth Ave New York NY 10019 E-mail: jeyoung@attglobal.net.

YOUNG, JOHN HARDIN, lawyer, corporate executive; b. Washington, Apr. 25, 1948; s. John D. and Laura Virginia (Gwathmey) Y.; m. Mary Frances (Farley) Crosby. JD, U. Va., 1973; BCL, Oxford (Eng.) U., 1976. Bar: Va. 1973, DC 1974, Pa. 1979, U.S. Dist. Ct. Va. 1974, U.S. Dist. Ct. DC 1974, U.S. Dist. Ct. Md. 1989, U.S. Ct. Fed. Claims 1974, U.S. Ct. Appeals (4th, 5th, Fed. and DC cirs.), Internat. Trade Ct. 1974, U.S. Supreme Ct. 1977. Ptnr., counsel Porter Wright Morris & Arthur, Washington, 1988—99, Sandler, Reiff & Young, PC, 2001—; exec. v.p. external affairs SECORIX, Inc., San Mateo, Wash., 2004—. Adv. bd. Antitrust Bull., 1980-1994; mem. U.S. Sec. State's adv. com. Pvt. internat. Law, 1987-95; chmn. Va. Retirement Sys. Rev. Bd., 1990-94; asst. atty. gen. Commonwealth of Va., 1976-78; Delmarva Adv. coun., 2004-; moderator Alexandria Forum, 1993-98, Fedn. Forum/TV Channel 10, 1989-91; sr. v.p., gen. counsel various tech. cos.; adj. faculty George Mason U. Sch. Law, 2003— Author: Young's Federal Rules of Evidence, Mastering Written Discovery; contbr. articles to profl. jours. Spl. counsel Dem. Nat. Com., 1998—99, chair nat. lawyers coun., 1998—; lead recount counsel for V.P. Gore Fla., 2000. Fellow: ABA (chmn. adminstrv. law and regulatory practice sect. 1999—2000, standing com. on continuing edn. of the bar 2002—04, standing com. on election law, fellow adminstrv. law 2001—), Am. Bar Found., Temple Bar Found. (bd. dirs., founder); mem.: Am. Inns of Ct. (bd. trustees 2004—), Comml. Bar Assn. U.K. (overseas), George Mason Am. Inn of Ct. (master 1990—, pres. 2002—03, Best Spl. Projects award 2003), Am. Law Inst., Phi Alpha Theta (history honors), Hon. Soc. Mid Temple U.K. Episcopalian. Office Phone: 202-479-1111. Business E-Mail: young@sandlerreiff.com.

YOUNG, JOHN WATTS, astronaut; b. San Francisco, Sept. 24, 1930; s. William H. Y.; m. Susy Feldman; children by previous marriage: Sandra, John. BS in Aero. Engring, Ga. Inst. Tech., 1952; LLD (hon.), Western State U., 1969; D Applied Sci. (hon.), Fla. Technol. U., 1970; DSc (hon.), U. S.C., 1981, Brown U., 1983; DEng (hon.), Glasgow U., 2001; PhD (hon.), Ga. Tech. U., 2003. Joined USN, 1952, advanced through grades to capt.; test pilot, program mgr. F4 weapons systems projects, 1959-62; then maintenance officer Fighter Squadron 143, Naval Air Sta., Miramar, Calif.; chief astronaut office Flight Ops. Directorate, 1974-87; spl. asst. dir. JSC for engring. ops., safety, 1987-96; assoc. dir. (tech.) JSC, 1996—. Decorated DFC (3), D.S.M. (2); recipient NASA Disting. Svc. medal (3), NASA Exceptional Svc. medal (2), NASA Engring. Achievement medal, 1988, NASA Outstanding Leadership medal, 1992, NASA Outstanding Achievement medal, 1994, AIAA Goddard Astronautics award, 2000, Congl. Space medal of honor, 1981; named Disting. Young Alumni Svc. award Ga. Tech. Acad. Disting. Engrs., 1994; named to Nat. Aviation Hall of Fame, 1988, Ga. Aviation Hall of Fame, 1998, Tex. Aviation Hall of Fame, 2003. Fellow Am. Astronautical Soc. (Flight Achievement award 1972, 81, 83, Space Flight award 1993), Soc. Exptl. Test Pilots (Iven Kincheloe award 1972, 81), AIAA (Haley Astronautics award 1973, 82, 84, NASA Disting. Exec. 1998, 2001, Rotary Space Trophy 2000, Houston Hall of Fame 2002); mem. Sigma Chi. Achievements include being an astronaut NASA, made 1st two-man 3 orbit flight, Gemini 3, Mar. 1965, Gemini 10 3 day flight, 1966, Apollo 10 8-day flight lunar landing dress rehearsal, 1969, Apollo 16 11 day lunar landing and surface exploration, 1972; comdr. 54 hour, 36 orbit 1st flight of Space Shuttle, 1981, and 10-day orbital flight 1st flight Space Lab, 1983; dir. space shuttle br., astronaut office, 1973-75. Office: NASA Johnson Space Ctr Houston TX 77058

YOUNG, JON NATHAN, archaeologist; b. Hibbing, Minn., May 30, 1938; s. Robert Nathan Young and Mary Elizabeth (Barrows) Roy; m. Karen Sue Johnson, June 5, 1961 (div. May 1980); children: Shawn Nathan, Kevin Leigh; m. Tucker Heitman, June 18, 1988 (div. Apr. 1996). BA magna cum laude, U. Ariz., 1960, PhD, 1967; MA, U. Ky., 1962. Archeologist Nat. Park Svc. Southwest Archeol. Ctr., Globe and Tucson, Ariz., 1967-75; exec., camp dir. YMCA of Metro. Tucson, 1976-77; asst. dir. Kit Carson Meml. Found., Taos, N.Mex., 1978; co-dir. Las Palomas de Taos, 1979; archeologist Nat. Forest Svc., Carson Nat. Forest, Taos, 1980-99, Taos Ski Valley, 2000—. Exec. order cons. U.S. Sec. Interior, 1973-75. Author: The Salado Culture in Southwestern Prehistory, 1967; co-author: Excavation of Mound 7, 1981, First-Day Road Log in Tectonic Development of the Southern Sangre de Cristo Mountains, 1990, The Gila Pueblo Salado, 1997. Active YMCA White Rag Soc.; mem. Kit Carson Hist. Mus. Grantee NEH, 1978; Ariz. Wilson Found., NSF, Ky. Rsch. Found. fellow, 1960-62; Baird Found., Bausch and Lomb, Elks; recipient cert. merit USDA, 1987, 89. Fellow AAAS, Am. Anthrop. Assn., Explorers Club, Royal Anthrop. Inst.; mem. Current Anthropology (assoc.), Ariz. Archaeol. and Hist. Soc., Ariz. Hist. Soc., Ctr. Anthropol. Studies, Coun. on Am.'s Mil. Past, Friends of Taos Pub. Libr., Friends of Taos Land Trust, New Mex. Heritage Preservation Alliance, Soc. Hist. Archaeology, Soc. Am. Archaeology, Southwest Forest Svc. Amigos, Harwood Found., Millicent Rogers Mus., Taos Archaeol. Soc., San Juan County Mus. Assn., Taos County Hist. Soc. (bd. dirs.), Taos Hist. Mus., Sigma Xi, Phi Beta Kappa, Alpha Kappa Delta, Phi Kappa Phi, Delta Chi. Home: HCR 74 Box 24826 El Prado NM 87529-9549

YOUNG, JUDITH ANNE, animal conservationist; b. LA, Feb. 11, 1953; d. John Mahlstedt Young and Cynthia Sheilds Tunnicciff. Grad. h.s., L.A. CEO Otter Conservation Ctr., Statesboro, Ga., 1983—. Copyright U.S. Govt., 1995. Avocations: animal keeping, water gardens, agriculture. Office Phone: 912-839-2100. Personal E-mail: judy@g-net.net.

YOUNG, KENNETH ALDEN, aerospace engineer, consultant; b. Austin, Tex., June 16, 1939; s. Richard Alden and Nell (Wallace) Young; m. Patricia Gail Freeman, Apr. 30, 1971; m. Eunice Tuttle, May 29, 1962 (div. Oct. 19, 1970); children: Brandi Lee, Holly Y., Richard A. BS in Aerospace Engring., U. Tex., 1962. Aerospace engr. Manned Spacecraft (now Johnson Space) Ctr., Houston, 1962—88; aerospace engr.-mgr. Grumman Aerospace Corp., Houston, 1988—94; aerospace systems intergation mgr. Loral/Lockheed Martin, Houston, 1994—2001; aerospace cons. Houston, 2001—. Mem.: NASA Alumni League. Avocations: golf, baseball, writing, lecturing. Home: 402 Pebblebrook Dr Seabrook TX 77586 Personal E-mail: kenyoung@houston.rr.com.

YOUNG, KENNETH EVANS, educational consultant; b. Toronto, Ont., Can., Mar. 21, 1922; s. John Osborne Wallace and Gwendolyn May (Evans) Y.; m. Mae Catherine Wittenmyer, July 1, 1945; 1 child, Bruce Kenneth. AB, San Francisco State Coll., 1943; MA, Stanford U., 1947, PhD, 1953; LLD (hon.), U. Nev., 1972. Instr. journalism and speech San Francisco State Coll., 1946-48; instr. journalism and English Calif. State Poly. Coll., San Luis Obispo, 1949-50; from asst. prof. to acting dean Coll. Arts and Scis. Kellogg-Voorhis Campus, Pomona, 1951-57; dean faculty U. Alaska, College, 1957-59; fellow in coll. adminstrn. U. Mich., Ann Arbor, 1959-60; exec. v.p. U. Nev., Reno, 1960-64; pres. SUNY, Cortland, 1964-68; v.p., dir. Washington office Am. Coll. Testing Program, 1968-75; pres. Council on Postsecondary Accreditation, Washington, 1975-80; exec. dir. Nat. Univ. Continuing Edn. Assn., Washington, 1980-84; dir. Inst. for Learning in Retirement, Am. U., Washington, 1984-89. Sr. assoc., cons. Diane U. Eisenberg Assocs., Washington, 1984-95; chmn. Evans-McCan Group, 1996—. Prin. editor: Understanding Accreditation, 1983; contbr. articles to profl. jours. Sgt. U.S. Army, 1943-45. Republican. Home: 5 Stratford Ln Lexington VA 24450-1778

YOUNG, LARRY, SR., protective services official, educator, investigator; b. Chgo., Aug. 11, 1947; s. Doris Hinds and Casey Young; children: Larry Jr., Aaron Lawrence, Georgette Buckhalter, Larry Anthony Deshon. BA in psychology, St. Xavier U., 1973—75; MA, Ctrl. Mich. U., 1977—79; MA psychology, U. No. Colo., 1982—90; AA in criminal justice, Laramie C.C., 1982—84. Juvenile probation officer Travis County Probation Dept., Austin, Tex., 1987—89; juvenile detention officer Bexar County Probation Dept., San Antonio, 1987—88; prof. St. Phillips C.C., San Antonio, 1988—89; investigator Tex. Edn. Agy., Austin, Tex., 1989—91; investigator/equal opportunity US Dept. Housing, Fort Worth, Tex., 1991—92; project mgr. Career Transition Ctr., Fort Worth, Tex., 1992—94; prof. Pikes Peak C.C., Colorado Springs, 1996—; probation officer/investigator 4th Jud. Dist. Probation Depart, Colorado Springs, 1996—. Author: (novels) Lick A Suspenseful Detective Novel. Civil svc. commr. City Colorado Springs, 1996—2004; minority edn. adv. mem. Pikes Peak C.C., Colorado Springs, 2004. Sgt. USAF, 1967—70, capt, ops. officer USAF, 1975—84, Cheyenne. Recipient Outstanding Young Man Am., US Jaycees, 1980, 1982. Independent. Avocations: writing, martial arts, bowling, acting, travel. Home: 808A Johanne Pl Colorado Springs CO 80906 Office: 4th Judicial Dist Probation Depart 326 S Tejon Colorado Springs CO 80903 Office Phone: 719-867-5391. Home Fax: 719-227-5107; Office Fax: 719-227-5107. Personal E-mail: doclarryyoung@aol.com. E-mail: larry.young@judicial.state.co.us.

YOUNG, LAURA, dance educator, choreographer; b. Boston, Aug. 5, 1947; d. James Vincent and Adelaide Janet Young; m. Anthony Charles Catanzaro, Sept. 26, 1970 (div. Nov. 1981); m. Christopher Edward Mehl, Aug. 23, 1987. Grad. H.S., Cohasset, Mass. Dancer Met. Opera Ballet, N.Y.C., 1971-73, Boston Ballet Co., 1963-65, prin. dancer, 1965-71, 73-89, ballet mistress, 1989-91. Guest tchr. Dance Tchrs. Club Boston, 1978—82, Dance Masters Assn., 1979, 90, 92, 93, Walnut Hill Sch., Natick, Mass., 1984—87, Natick, 1990—91, Granite State Ballet, 1993, Portland Ballet, Maine, Nat. Dance Theatre Bermuda, 1993, Worcester Performing Arts Sch., Mass., 1994, Alwin Sch. Dance Summer Intensive, Albuquerque, 1994—95, Ashland Youth Ballet, Ky., 1995, N.E. Regional Festival, 1996, Okla. Summer Arts Inst., 2000, Pitts. Ballet Theater Summer Program, 2000; asst. dir. Boston Ballet II, 1984—86, tchr., dir., 1986—96, dir. Summer Dance Program, 1986—94; dir. DanceLab, 2001—; 1st hon. mem. Dance Masters Assn., Chpt. 5, 1992; mem. faculty Boston Conservatory, 1990—94; prin. Boston Ballet Sch., 1993—. Choreographer (ballets) Occasional Waltzes, 1984, Albinoni Suite, 1986, Champ Dances, 1987, A Place of Sound and Mind, 1988, Deadlock, 1989, Rumpelstiltskin, 1989. Recipient Leadership award Greater Boston C. of C., 1987; named Disting. Bostonian Boston's 350th Jubilee Com., 1980. Mem. Am. Guild Mus. Artists, Dance Masters Am. (hon.). Office: Boston Ballet Co 19 Clarendon St Boston MA 02116-6100 Office Phone: 617-456-6261. E-mail: lyoung@bostonballet.com.

YOUNG, LAUREN SUE JONES, education educator; b. San Diego, July 21, 1947; d. Warren Calvin and Lola Esther Jones; 1 child, Forest McRay Young. AB, Occidental Coll., 1969; MS, San Diego State U., 1971; EdM, Harvard U., 1979, EdD, 1984. Adminstrv. asst. Child Devel. Research Unit, Nairobi, Kenya, 1969-70; asst. prof. San Diego State U., 1974—78, assoc. dir. Tchr. Corps., 1971—78; co-chmn. and mem. Harvard Ednl. Review, Cambridge, Mass., 1979-81; research assoc. The Huron Inst., Cambridge, 1980-82, Atari Cambridge Research Lab., Cambridge, 1982-84; policy analyst N.Y. State Dept. Social Services, Albany, 1984-85, spl. asst. to commr., 1985-87; assoc. prof. Mich. State U., East Lansing, 1987-2001; sr. program officer, dir. The Spencer Found., Chgo., 1998—. Cons. Am. Insts. for Rsch., Cambridge, 1980, Tchr. Corps, Boston area, 1978-80, instr., Pago Pago, Am. Samoa, 1979; rsch. assoc. A Study of H.S.'s, Cambridge, 1980-82; disting. visitor John D. and Catherine T. MacArthur Found., 1995-96. Co-editor: Too Little, Too Late, 1988; mem. editorial bd. Evaluation Rev. Jour., L.A., 1984-88, Jour. Negro Edn. Team mem. Operation Crossroads Africa, Morogoro, Tanzania, 1968; mem. program adv. bd. Spencer Found., 1992. Recipent Danforth Found. fellow, St. Louis, 1978-84, tchr. scholar award, M.S.U., 1993. Mem. Am. Ednl. Research Assn. Office: The Spender Found 875 N Michigan Ave Ste 3930 Chicago IL 60611-1803

YOUNG, LAURENCE R. biomedical researcher, biomedical engineer, aeronautical engineer, aerospace engineer; AB, Amherst Coll., 1957; Cert. in Applied Math., Sorbonne, Paris, 1958; MSEE, MIT, ScD in Instrumentation, 1962. With Sperry Gyroscope Co., 1957—58; rsch. staff MIT, Cambridge, 1958—62, faculty, 1962—, Apollo prof. astronautics, 1995—2003, prof. health scis. and tech., 2003, Harvard - MIT, 2003—; dir. Nat. Space Biomed. Rsch. Inst., Houston, 1997—2001. Rschr. in eye movement Sch. Medicine, U. P.R., 1961; payload specialist Spacelab Life Scis. 2, NASA, alt. payload specialist, 1993; chmn. Harvard-MIT Com. on Biomed. Engring. and Physics and Interdeptl. PhD Program in Biomed. Engring.; vis. prof. Swiss Fed. Inst. Tech., 1972—73, Zurich Kantonsspital, 1972—73, Conservatoire des Arts et Metiers, Paris, College de France, Paris, 2002; vis. scientist NASA Ames Rsch. Ctr., 1987—88; vis. prof. elec. engring. Stanford U.; lectr. Harvard Med. Sch., Boston; chmn. airlift panel Air Force Sci. Adv. Bd.; mem. space medicine and biology com. NAS; mem. life sci. adv. com. NASA; mem. tng. com. on biomed. engring. NIH; mem. numerous coms. NRC. Contbr. over 200 articles to profl. jours. Recipient Air Force Decoration for Exceptional Civilian Svc., Dryden Lectureship in Rsch., AIAA, 1982, Jeffries award, 1992, Paul Hansen award, Aerospace Human Factors Assn., 1995, Pub. Svc. Group Achievement award, NASA, Award of Merit, U.S. Ski Assn., Best Rsch. Paper award, Am. Acad. Orthop. Surgeons. Fellow: IEEE; mem.: ASTM (chair ski injury statistics subcom., com. on snow skiing chmn.), Internat. Soc. for Skiing Safety (dir.), Biomed. Engring. Soc., Aerospace Med. Assn., Human Factors Soc., Barany Soc. (pres. 1979, Alza Lectr. 1984), Nat. Acad. Engring., Inst. of Medicine of NAS, Explorers Club. Achievements include research in in instrumentation (eye movement measurement) and basic and applied research in field of vestibular function; psychophysical work on semicircular canal and otolith function led to models which are applied to flight simulator motion control and are being extended to include visually-induced motion effects; in ski injurys. Home: 217 Thorndike St Apt 108 Cambridge MA 02141 Office: MIT Rm 37-219 77 Massachusettes Ave Cambridge MA 02139-4307

YOUNG, LAWRENCE, electrical engineering educator; b. Hull, Eng., July 5, 1925; arrived in Can., 1955; naturalized, 1972; s. Herbert and Dora Y.; m. Margaret Elisabeth Jane, Jan. 5, 1951. BA, Cambridge (Eng.) U., 1946, PhD, 1950, ScD, 1963. Asst. lectr. Imperial Coll., London, 1952-55; mem. research staff B.C. Research Council, 1955-63; assoc. prof. U. B.C., Vancouver, 1963-65, prof. dept. elec. engring., 1965-90, prof. emeritus, 1990—. Author: Anodic Oxide Films, 1961; contbr. articles to profl. jours. Recipient Callinan award Dielectrics div. Electrochemical Soc., 1983, Can. Electrochem. Gold medal, 1990. Fellow IEEE, Royal Soc. Can., Electrochem. Soc. Office: U BC Dept Elec Engring Vancouver BC Canada V6T 1W5 Business E-Mail: youngl@interchange.ubc.ca.

YOUNG, LEO, electrical engineer; b. Vienna, Aug. 18, 1926; came to U.S., 1953, naturalized, 1958; s. Samuel and Marie Y.; m. Fay Merskey, Jan. 4, 1953 (dec. May 1981); children— Philip Michael, Sarah Anne, Joseph David; m. Ruth Breslow, Jan. 2, 1983 (dec. Nov. 1996); m. Jo-Ellen Turner, July 9, 1999. BA, Cambridge U., 1946, MA, 1950; MS, Johns Hopkins U., 1956, D.Engring. (Westinghouse-B.G. Lamme grad. scholar), 1959, D.H.L. (hon.), 1989. Lab. mgr. Decca Radar, Ltd., Surbiton, Eng., 1951-53; adv. engr. Westinghouse Electric Corp., Balt., 1953-60; staff scientist, program mgr. Stanford Rsch. Inst., Menlo Park, Calif., 1960-73; staff cons., assoc. supt. Naval Rsch. Lab., Washington, 1973-81; dir. rsch. Office of Undersec. for Def. Rsch. and Engring., Dept. Def., 1981-94; cons. to dir. def. rsch. and engring. Dept. Def., 1994—2002; bd. dirs. Filtronic-Comtek (U.K.), 1994—. Mem. NSF delegation to Japan, 1995, 99; chair NSF Rev. Panel on Critical Techs., 1997; chair adv. com. dept. elec. and computer engring. Johns Hopkins U., 2003. Author: Microwave Filters, 1964, Systems of Units in Electricity and Magnetism, 1969, Advances in Microwaves, Vols. 1-8, 1966-74, Everything You Should Know About Pensions Plans, 1976; also articles; patentee in field. Recipient Woodrow Wilson award for Disting. Govt. Svc., 2001. Fellow: IEEE (pres. 1980, Disting. Contbns. to Engring. Professionalism award 1993, Pinnacle award 1995, Centennial award), AAAS; mem.: NAE, Electromagnetics Acad., Royal Acad. Engring. U.K., Microwave Soc. (life; pres. 1969, Microwave prize 1963, Microwave Career award 1988), Sigma Xi. Personal E-mail: youngturner@earthlink.net. *It has been my goal to serve the public and my belief that engineering and science improve the quality of life. I have enjoyed doing engineering research and am fortunate in receiving recognition.*

YOUNG, LEROY, plastic surgeon; b. Oneida, Ky., Oct. 14, 1945; BS, U. Ky., Lexington, 1966, MD, 1970. Cert. in Surgery 1978, in Plastic Surgery 1981. Intern U. Ky. Med. Ctr., Lexington, 1970—71, resident, gen. surgery, 1973—77; resident, plastic surgery Barnes Hosp., Washington U., St. Louis, 1977—79; attending physician, surgery Barnes Hosp., St. Louis, 1979—, St. Louis Children's Hosp., 1979—, Barnes-Jewish West County Hosp., St. Louis, 1990—; prof., plastic reconstructive surgery Washington U. Sch. Medicine, St. Louis, 1990—. Mem.: Am. Soc. for Aesthetic Plastic Surgery (chair, nonsurg. procedures com., co-chair, breast surgery com.), Am. Bd. Plastic Surgery (examiner), Plastic Surgery Edn. Found. (chair, silicone implant rsch. com.), Am. Soc. Plastic Surgeons (bd. dirs.). Office: 1040 N Mason Rd Ste 206 Saint Louis MO 63141-6366 Address: Ste 17424 One Barnes Hosp Plz Saint Louis MO 63110*

YOUNG, LIH YING H. economist, consultant, advocate; d. Hua S. and Lin W. Huang; m. Kan Hua Young; children: Albert M., Janice M. BA, Nat. Taiwan U., 1963; MA, CUNY, 1968, PhD, 1977. Pvt. instr., Taipei, Taiwan, 1959—63; loan ofcl. Bank of China, Taipei, 1963—65; economist U.S. Dept. Health and Human Svcs., Rockville, Md., 1978—84, program analyst Washington, 1984—86; economist OMNIX, Potomac, Md., 1986—. Adj. prof. Bloomfield Coll., NJ. Prodr.: (broadcast television program) Twilight of Judiciaries (I): Donna Briggs: Uncommon Lawyer, Twilight of Judiciaries (II): Civic Forum, Twilight of Judiciaries (III): People's Voice and Protest!, Federal Shambles: Civic Forum 1, Federal Shambles: Civic Forum 2, Leroy W. Warren Jr.: Uncommon Citizen; co-prodr. (broadcast tv program) The Spot (Studio interview segment law enforcement), prodr., host Citizen Times (broadcast studio series). Mem. exec. and steering coms. Nat. Women's Polit. Caucus, ACLU, NAACP; candidate for numerous pub. offices, including Md. state sen., state comptroller, U.S. Congress, mayor of Rockville, city coun. Md., 1994—; testified on various issues before local and fed. govt. bodies on social issues. Recipient Certificates for Prestigious High Exam. and Spl. Examinations, Taiwan Ctrl. Govt., 1963. Mem.: Am. Econ. Assn., Am. Statis. Assn. Avocation: reading. Home: 1121 Pipestem Pl Potomac MD 20854 Office: Lih Young For Comptroller - Maryland 1121 Pipestem Pl Potomac MD 20854 Personal E-mail: lyoung2k@yahoo.com.

YOUNG, LIONEL WESLEY, radiologist; b. New Orleans, Mar. 14, 1932; s. Charles Henry and Ethel Elsie (Johnson) Y.: m. Florence Inez Brown, June 24, 1957; children: Tina Inez, Lionel Thomas, Owen Christopher. BS in Biology, St. Benedict's Coll., Atchison, Kans., 1953; MD, Howard U., 1957. Diplomate Am. Bd. Radiology. Intern Detroit Receiving Hosp., Wayne State Univ. Coll. of Medicine, 1957-58; resident Strong Meml. Hosp., U. Rochester (N.Y.) Med. Ctr., 1958-61; pediatric radiologist, assoc. prof. radiology and pediatrics U. Rochester Med. Ctr., 1965-75; prof. radiology and pediatrics U. Pitts., 1975-86; dir. radiology and pediatrics Children's Hosp. of Pitts., 1980-86; chmn. radiology Children's Hosp. Med. Ctr. of Akron (Ohio), 1986-91, Children's Hosp. and Northeastern Ohio U. Coll. Medicine, Rootstown, 1987-91; dir. Divsn. Pediat. Radiology Loma Linda (Calif.) U. Med. Ctr. and Children's Hosp., 1991—. Pres. Akron Pediatric Radiologists, 1986—. Lt. comdr. USN, 1961-63. Mem. Am. Coll. Radiology (mem. coun., steering com.), Soc. for Pediatric Radiology. Democrat. Roman Catholic. Avocation: music. Office: Divsn Pediatric Radiology Loma Linda U Childrens Hosp 11234 Anderson St Loma Linda CA 92354-2804

YOUNG, LOWELL SUNG-YI, medical administrator, educator; b. Honolulu, Dec. 5, 1938; AB, Princeton U., 1960; MD, Harvard U., 1964. Di;omate Am. Bd. Internal Medicine with subspecialty in infectious diseases. Intern, jr. asst. resident, sr. asst. resident med. divsn. Bellevue Hosp. and Meml. Hosp., N.Y.C., 1964-67; fellow in medicine Cornell U. Med. Coll., 1965-67; epidemic intelligence officer bacterial diseases br. Nat. Communicable Disease Ctr., Atlanta, 1967-69, chief spl. pathogens sect., 1968-69; spl. postdoctoral rsch. fellow Nat. Inst. Allergy and Infectious Diseases, 1969-70; rsch. fellow in medicine Meml. Hosp./Cornell U. Med. Coll., 1969-70; clin. asst. physicisn infectious disease svc. dept. medicine Meml. Hosp., 1970-72, assoc. dir. microbiology lab., 1971-72; instr. in medicine Cornell U. Med. Coll., 1970-72; asst. clinician Sloan-Kettering Inst. for Cancer Rsch., 1971-72; chief divsn. infectious disease Calif. Pacific Med. Ctr., San Francisco, 1985-99; dir. Kuzell Inst., San Francisco, 1985—. Adj. prof. pharmacy U. of Pacific, San Francisco, 1989—; mem. microbiology and invectious diseases adv. com. Nat. Inst. Allergy and Infectious Diseases, 1981-85, mem. allergy and immunology rsch. com., 1975-79; mem. staff Calif. Pacific Med. Ctr., Mt. Zion Hosp. and Med. Ctr., U. Calif., San Francisco; mem. sci. adv. bd. Am. Found. for AIDS Rsch. Mem. editl. bd. Infection, Infectious Diseases in Clin. Practice, Diagnostic Microbiology and Infectious Diseases, Antimicrobial Agts. and Chemotherapy, Infection and Immunity; contbr. numerous articles to profl. jours., chpts. to books. Recipient Alexander D. Langmuir prize Epidemic Intelligence Svc., 1970, Garrod medal Brit. Soc., 1992. Fellow ACP (mem. med. self-assessment com.), Infectious Diseases Soc. Am. (councillor 1983-85); mem. Am. Soc. for Clin. Investigation, Am. Fedn. for Clin. Rsch., Am. Soc. for Microbiology, Western Soc. for Clin. Rsch., Internat. Immunocompromised Host Soc., Brit. Soc. Antimicrobial Chemotherapy. Office: Kuzell Inst 2200 Webster St Ste 305 San Francisco CA 94115-1821 also: Calif Pacific Med Ctr 2100 Webster St Ste 326 San Francisco CA 94115-2378 Office Phone: 415-600-1734. Business E-Mail: kiaid@cooper.cpmc.org.

YOUNG, LUCY CLEAVER, physician; b. Aug. 8, 1943; d. Oliver B. and Ada (Smith) Cleaver; m. Lynn H. Young, Feb. 4, 1968 (div. 1977); m. Lynn H. Young, Apr. 2, 1986; 1 child, Clinton Oliver. BS in Chemistry, Wheaton (Ill.) Coll., 1965; MD, Ohio State U., 1969. Diplomate Am. Bd. Family Practice, Bd. Ins. Medicine. Rotating intern Riverside Meth. Hosp., Columbus, Ohio, 1969-70; resident Trumbull Meml. Hosp., Warren, Ohio, 1970-71; practice medicine specializing in family practice West Chicago, Ill., 1971-73, Paw Paw and Mendota, Ill., 1973-78; co-founder, med. dir. Wholistic Health Ctr. of Mendota, 1976-78; asst. med. dir. Gt. Lakes head office Met. Life Ins. Co., Aurora, Ill., 1979-80; med. dir. Commonwealth Life Ins. Co., Louisville, 1980-85; locum tenens family practice Kron Med. Corp. of Chapel Hill, NC, 1986-89; physician Red Bird Mission & Med. Ctr., Beverly, Ky., 1989-90; family practice floater Ochsner Clinic satellites, New Orleans, 1990—. Assoc. prof. U. Ill. Abraham Lincoln Sch. Medicine, 1976-79; faculty monitor MacNeal Meml. Hosp. Family Practice Ctr. (Ill.), 1979-80; faculty preceptor U. Louisville Family Practice Dept., 1981-85; clin. faculty preceptor La. State U. Sch. Medicine, 1992—; mem. staffs Ctrl. DuPage Hosp., Winfield, Ill., 1971-73, Mendota Cmty. Hosp., 1973-80, Ochsner Found. Hosp., New Orleans, 1991—. Vol. Red Bird Med. Ctr., 1985—; part-time worship coord. Hosanna Luth. Ch., Mandeville, La., 1996-97; musician, lay preacher, nursing home visitor, 1990—. Fellow Am. Acad. Family Practice; mem. Christian Med. and Dental Assns. (del. to Ho. 1995-2000). Lutheran. Home: PO Box 0730 Madisonville LA 70447-0730 Office: Ochsner Clinic 2810 E Causeway Approach Mandeville LA 70448

YOUNG, LUCY H.Y. physician, retina surgeon; b. Taipei, Taiwan, Dec. 8, 1957; came to U.S., 1974; d. TsenMen Young and PeiLan Liu; m. Henning A. Gaissert, Aug. 12, 1989; children: Anna Gaissert, Philipp Gaissert, Henry Gaissert. BS in Biology, U. Wis., 1977, MD, 1981; PhD, Harvard U., 1984. Diplomate Am. Bd. Ophthalmology. Intern Framingham (Mass.) Union Hosp., 1984-85; resident in ophthalmology Mass. Eye and Ear Infirmary, Boston, 1985-88, retina fellow, 1988-90; instr. in ophthalmology Mass. Eye and Ear Infirmary/Harvard U., Boston, 1990-92, asst. prof. ophthalmology, 1992-97, assoc. prof., 1998—. Contbr. articles to profl. jours. Grantee Mass. Lions Eye Rsch. Fund, NIH, Cancer Rsch. Inst. Fellow ACS; mem. Am. Acad. Ophthalmology, Assn. for Rsch. in Vision and Ophthalmology, New Eng. Ophthal. Soc., Retina Soc., Macula Soc., Mass. Soc. Eye Physicians and Surgeons, Soc. for Neurosci. Office: Mass Eye and Ear Infirmary 243 Charles St Boston MA 02114-3096

YOUNG, M. DENDY, finance company executive; Pres., CEO Falcon, 1989-94; prin., cons. The Exeter Group, 1994-95; pres., CEO Govt. Tech. Svcs., Inc., Chantilly, Va., 1995-98, CEO, dir., 1995—, chmn. bd. dirs., 1998—. Office: Govt Tech Svcs Inc 3901 Stonecroft Blvd Chantilly VA 20151-1032

YOUNG, MARGARET ALETHA MCMULLEN (MRS. HERBERT WILSON YOUNG), social worker; b. Vossburg, Miss., June 13, 1916; d. Grady Garland and Virgie Aletha (Moore) McMullen; m. Herbert Wilson Young, Aug. 19, 1959. BA cum laude, Columbia Bible Coll., 1949; grad., Massey Bus. Coll., 1958; MSW, Fla. State U., 1965; postgrad., Jacksonville U., 1961-62; MA in Old Testament, Tyndale U., 1967, Columbia Internat. U., 1992. Dir. Christian edn. Eau Claire Presbyn. Ch., Columbia, S.C., 1946-51; tchr. Massey Bus. Coll., Jacksonville, Fla., 1954-57, office mgr., 1957-59; social worker, unit supr. Fla. divsn. Family Svcs., St. Petersburg, 1960-66, dist. casework supr., 1966-71; social worker, project supr., program supr. Project Playpen, Inc., 1971-81, pres. bd., 1982-83, cons., 1986-89; pvt. practice family counselor, 1982—. Mem. coun. Child Devel. Ctr., 1983-89; mem. transitional housing com. Religious Cmty. Svcs., 1984-90. Mem. Acad. Cert. Social Workers, Nat. Assn. Social Workers (pres. Tampa Bay chpt. 1973-74), Fla. Assn. for Health and Social Svcs. (pres. chpt. 1971), Nature Conservancy, Rotary Ann (pres. 1970-71), Eta Beta Rho. Democrat. Presbyterian. Home: Presbyterian Home 201 W 9th North St Unit 151 Summerville SC 29483-6712

YOUNG, MARGARET HELEN, educational association administrator, writer; b. Oberlin, Ohio, Mar. 29, 1966; d. David Pollock and Chloe (Hamilton) Young. BA, Yale U., 1988; MA, U. Calif., Davis, 1993. Sch. prodns. coord. Open Door Theater Co., Phila., 1988—90; instr. Allegheny Coll., Meadville, Pa., 1993—95, Mohican Outdoor Sch., Danville, Ohio, 1999; KIDS smART coord. Oberlin Early Childhood Ctr., 2000—03; instr. Oberlin Coll., 2003; edn. coord. Firelands Assn. for the Visual Arts, Oberlin, 2003—. Arts edn. cons. Oberlin Coll. Ctr. for Svc. and Learning, 2000—; cons. on environ./bioregional lit. Allegheny Coll., 1995—96; artist-in-residence Ohio Arts Coun. Arts in Edn., 2000—. Author: Willow From the Willow, 2002 (Cleve. Poets Series winner, 2002). Recipient Ellen Hansen Meml. award, U. Calif.-Davis, 1993, Elmore Willets Fiction prize, Yale U., 1988, Disting. Achievement award, Ednl. Press Assn., 1991, 1st prize poetry contest, Antietam Rev., 1998; Walter Rumsey Marvin grant, Ohioana Libr. Assn., 1994. Mem.: Ohio Assn. for Edn. of Young Children. Avocations: permaculture, gardening, cooking. Home: 261 W Lorain St Oberlin OH 44074

YOUNG, MARLENE ANNETTE, lawyer; b. Portland, Oreg., Mar. 3, 1946; d. Hardy Shelby and Eunice Jean (Gregory) Y.; m. Abdullah Samir Rifai, June 3, 1973 (div. May 1981); m. John Hollister Stein, Jan. 1, 1986. BS, Portland State U., 1967; PhD, Georgetown U., 1973; JD, Willamette U., 1975. Bar: Oreg. 1975. Dir. research Multnomah County Sheriff's Office, Portland, 1975-77; sole practice Wilsonville, Oreg., 1975-81; exec. dir. Applied Systems Research & Data, Wilsonville, 1976-81, Nat. Orgn. Victim Assistance, Washington, 1981—. Instr. Essex Community Coll., 1971-73, U. Utah, 1976-78, Portland State U., 1979; cons. U. Research Corp., Washington, 1979-83, ABT Assocs., Boston, 1984—. Author: Victim Service System, 1983; (manuals) Patrol Officers and Crime Victims, 1984, Prosecutors: Attorneys for the People, Advocates for the Victims, 1984; editor: Justice and Older Americans, 1977; contbr. articles to profl. jours. Mem. Ways and Means Com., Wilsonville City, 1977-79, planning commn., 1979-81; Bd. visitors Willamette Coll. Law, Salem, Oreg., 1981-83; bd. dirs. Chemeketa Community Coll., Salem, 1979. Recipient Presdl. award Nat. Orgn. Victim Assistance, Washington, 1981, 92, Pub.Policy award World Fedn. Mental Health, Washington, 1983, Found. for Improvementof Justice award, 1988. Mem. ABA (criminal justice sect., adv. bd. 1981-90), Am. Profl. Soc. Abuse of Children (bd. dirs. 1986—), Soc. Traumatic Stress Studies (bd. dirs. 1985—, treas.), World Soc. Victimology (adv. bd. 1979—, exec. com. 1986—, v.p., Hans Von Hentig award 1985). Democrat. Methodist. Avocations: piano, running, gardening, pets. Office: Nat Orgn Victim Assistance 1757 Park Rd NW Washington DC 20010-2101

YOUNG, MARVIN OSCAR, lawyer; b. Union, Mo., Apr. 4, 1929; s. Otto Christopher and Irene Adelheide (Barlage) Y.; m. Sue Carol Mathews, Aug. 23, 1952; children: Victoria Leigh, Kendall Marvin. AB, Westminster Coll., 1951; JD, U. Mich., 1954; LLD, Westminster Coll., 1989. Bar: Mo. 1954. Practice law firm Thompson, Mitchell, Thompson Douglas, St. Louis, 1954-55, 57-58; atty. Mo. Farmers Assn., Columbia, 1958-67; exec. v.p. First Mo. Corp., Columbia, 1965-68; v.p. ops. MFA-Central Coop., Columbia, 1967-68; v.p., gen. counsel, sec. Peabody Coal Co., St. Louis, 1968-82; gen. counsel Peabody Holding Co., Inc., St. Louis, 1983-85; also dir., sec. subs. and affiliates Peabody Coal Co.; ptnr. Gallop, Johnson & Neuman, St. Louis, 1986—, chmn. corp. dept., 1988-90, chmn. energy dept., 1990—. City atty. Warson Woods, Mo., 1990—; spkr. in field. Assoc. editor Mich. Law Rev., 1953-54; contbr. articles to profl. jours. Pres. Warson Woods PTA, 1974-75; trustee Met. Sewer Dist. St. Louis, 1974-80, chmn. 1978-80; active Mo. Energy Coun., 1973-77, Mo. Environ. Improvement and Energy Resources Athority, 1983-87, vice-chmn. 1986-87; trustee Eastern Mineral Law Found., 1983-98; pres. Alumni Assn. Westminster Coll., Fulton, Mo., 1978-80, trustee coll., 1977—, exec. com., 1978-2003, chmn. 1986-90, chmn. investment com., 1998-2002; chmn. Churchill Meml. and Libr., Fulton, 1992-2000; mem. chancellor's coun. adv. bd. U. Mo., St. Louis, 1992—; trustee Stages—St. Louis, 2001—; lawyers adv. coun. Gt. Plains Legal Found., Kansas City, Mo., 1976-84; mem. Rep. Com. Boone County, Mo., 1962-68, chmn. legis. dist. com., 1962-64, 66-68; alt. del. Rep. Nat. Conv., 1968; pres. Clayton Twp. Rep. Club, 1973-77; sr. warden Episcopal Ch., 1988-89. Capt. USAF, 1955-57. Recipient alumni award of merit, 1972; named Coal Lawyer of Yr., Nat. Coal Assn., 1994; Churchill fellow, 1990. Mem. ABA, Mo. Bar Assn., Bar Assn. Met. St. Louis, Barristers Soc., Round Table Club St. Louis, John Marshall Rep. Lawyers Club, 1977, Mo. Athletic Club, Shamrock Club St. Louis County, Rotary (bd. dirs. St. Louis club 1993-95), Masons, Order of Coif,

Shriners. Home: 555 Flanders Dr Saint Louis MO 63122-1617 Office: Gallop Johnson & Neuman LC 101 S Hanley Rd Ste 1600 Saint Louis MO 63105-3489 Office Phone: 314-615-6210. E-mail: moyoung@gjn.com.

YOUNG, MARVIN RICHARD, dermatologist, educator; b. Monroe, Wash., Apr. 5, 1935; s. Julian Giliat and Margaret Alice (Anderson) Y.; m. Judith Yvonne Heitkemper, Dec. 27, 1958; children: John Edward, Leslie Elizabeth. BA, U. Oreg., Eugene, 1957; MD, Oreg. Health Scis. U., Portland, 1959. Diplomate Am. Bd. Dermatology. Intern Phila. Gen. Hosp., 1959-60; dermatology resident Oreg. Health Sci. U., 1960-65; pvt. practice Seattle, 1965-88, Minor & James Med., Seattle, 1988-96, Alaska, 1996—; clin. instr., asst. prof., assoc. prof., clin. prof. derm. U. Wash. Sch. Medicine, 1965—. Contbr. med. articles to profl. jours. Lt. comdr. USNR, 1960-62. Fellow Am. Acad. Dermatology; mem. AMA, Seattle Dermatol. Soc. (pres. 1975), Wash. State Med. Assn. (pres. 1991), King County Med. Soc. (pres. 1984). Avocations: jazz pianist, fly fishing, flying.

YOUNG, MARY ANN, lawyer; b. Alton, Ill., May 1, 1952; d. William Jerome and Barbara Ann (Blocher) Y. Student, St. Mary of the Plains Coll., 1970-71; BA in Econs., Washburn (Kans.) U., 1974; JD, U. Mo., 1976. Bar: Mo. 1977. Pvt. practice, Holden, Mo., 1977-84, Warrensburg, Mo., 1984—. Atty. City of Holden, 1978-80, asst. prosecutor Johnson County, Mo., 1978-80, 83-88; bd. dirs. Indsl. Svc. Contactors Sheltered Workshop, Warrensburg. Mem. Rep. Women, Johnson County, 1988-89, CLIMB, Johnson County, 1989—, Task Force for Drug Free Mo., Johnson County, 1989—; 2d. v.p. Johnson County Rep. Women, 1989—. Mem. Mo. Bar Assn., Johnson County Bar Assn., Johnson County C. of C., Mo. Farm Bur. Roman Catholic. Avocations: antique collecting, gardening. Office: 307 N Holden St Warrensburg MO 64093-1705

YOUNG, MERWIN CRAWFORD, political science educator; b. Phila., Nov. 7, 1931; s. Ralph Aubrey and Louise (Merwin) Y.; m. Rebecca Conrad, Aug. 17, 1957; children: Eva Colcord, Louise Conrad, Estelle Merwin, Emily Harriet. BA, U. Mich., 1953; postgrad., Inst. Hist. Rsch. U. London, 1955-56, Inst d'Etudes Politiques, U. Paris, 1956-57; PhD, Harvard U., 1964; DSc (hon.), Fla. Internat. U., 1998. Asst. prof. polit. sci. U. Wis., Madison, 1963-66, assoc. prof., 1966-69, prof., 1969—2001, emeritus, 2001—, Rupert Emerson prof., 1983; H. Edwin Young prof., 1994; chmn. African Studies Program U. Wis., Madison, 1964-68, chmn. dept. polit. sci., 1969-72, 84-87, assoc. dean Grad. Sch., 1968-71, acting dean Coll. Letters and Sci., 1992-93. Vis. prof. Makerere U. Coll., Kampala, Uganda, 1965-66; dean Faculty of Social Sci. Nat. U., Lubumbashi, Zaire, 1973-75; Fulbright prof. U. Dakar, Senegal, 1987-88. Author: Politics in the Congo, 1965, The Politics of Cultural Pluralism, 1976 (Herskovits prize 1977, Ralph Bunche prize 1979), Ideology and Development in Africa, 1982, The African Colonial State in Comparative Perspective, 1994 (Gregory Luebbert prize 1995); co-author: Cooperatives and Development, 1981, The Rise and Decline of the Zairian State, 1985; editor: The Rising Tide of Cultural Pluralism: The Nation-State at Bay?, 1993, Ethnic Diversity and Public Policy, 1998, The Accommodation of Cultural Diversity, 1999; co-editor: Dilemmas of Democracy in Nigeria, 1995, Beyond State Crisis? Postcolonial Africa and Post-Soviet Eurasia in Comparative Perspective, 2002. Served to 1st lt. U.S. Army, 1953-55. Fellow Woodrow Wilson Internat. Ctr. for Scholars, 1983—84; Social Sci. Rsch. fellow, 1967—68, Ford Faculty fellow, 1972—73; Guggenheim Found. fellow, 1977—78, vis. fellow, Inst. for Advanced Study, Princeton, 1980—81. Mem. AAAS, Am. Acad. Arts and Scis., Am. Polit. Sci. Assn., African Studies Assn. (pres. 1982-83, Disting. Africanist award 1991), Coun. Fgn. Rels. Home: 639 Crandall St Madison WI 53711-1836 Office: U Wis Dept Polit Sci North Hall 1050 Bascom Mall Madison WI 53706-1389 Office Phone: 608-263-2040. Business E-Mail: young@polisci.wisc.edu.

YOUNG, MICHAEL CHUNG-EN, allergist, immunologist, pediatrician; b. Chgo., July 10, 1953; s. Koon C. and Siu Fun (Hui) Y.; m. Karen Lee Young, Apr. 7, 1979; 1 child, Liane. AB cum laude, Harvard Coll., 1975; MD, Yale U., 1979. Diplomate Am. Bd. Allergy and Immunology, Am. Bd. Pediatrics, Nat. Bd. Med. Examiners. Resident pediat. Children's Hosp., Boston, 1979—82, fellow in allergy and immunology, 1982—84, asst. in medicine (immunology), attending physician, 1984—; clin. instr. pediat. Harvard Med. Sch., Boston, 1985—2001, asst. clin. prof. pediat., 2002—. Mem. active staff South Shore Hosp., South Weymouth, Mass., 1985—. Author: Peanut Allergy Answer Book, Fair Winds Press, 2001; contbr. articles to profl. jours. Named physician honoree, Asthma and Allergy Found. Am., 2001; named to Guide to Top Doctors, Ctr. for the Study of Svcs.; recipient Nat. Rsch. Svc. award, NIH, 1982—84. Fellow Am. Coll. Allergy and Immunology (Parke Davis Allergy Fellows award 1983), Am. Acad. Allergy and Immunology, Am. Coll. Chest Physicians, Am. Acad. Pediatrics; mem. New Eng. Soc. Allergy, Mass. Allergy Soc. (pres. 1992-94), Mass. Med. Soc. Office: South Shore Allergy & Asthma Specialists 851 Main St South Weymouth MA 02190-1612

YOUNG, MICHAEL KENT, dean, lawyer, educator; b. Sacramento, Nov. 4, 1949; s. Vance Lynn and Ethelyn M. (Sowards) Young; m. Suzan Kay Stewart, June 1, 1972; children: Stewart, Kathryn, Andrew. BA summa cum laude, Brigham Young U., 1973; JD magna cum laude, Harvard U., 1976. Bar: Calif. 1976, N.Y. 1985. Law clk. to Justice Benjamin Kaplan, Supreme Jud. Ct. Mass., Boston, 1976-77; assoc. prof., prof., Fuyo prof. Japanese law Columbia U., N.Y.C., 1978-98; dir. Ctr. Japanese Legal Studies Ctr. for Korean Legal Studies, N.Y.C., 1985-98; dir. Program Internat. Human Rights and Religious Liberties Columbia U., N.Y.C., 1995-98; dep. legal advisor U.S. Dept. State, Washington, 1989-91, dep. under sec. for econ. affairs, 1991-93, amb. for trade and environ. affairs, 1992-93; law clk. to Justice William H. Rehnquist U.S. Supreme Ct., Washington, 1977-78; dean, Lobingier prof. comparative law and jurisprudence George Washington U. Sch. of Law, Washington, 1998—2004; pres. U. Utah, Salt Lake City, 2004—. Chair U.S. Commn. on Internat. Religious Freedom, 2001—02, 2003—04, vice chair, 2002—03; vis. scholar law faculty U. Tokyo, 1978—80, 1983; vis. prof. Waseda U., 1989; chmn. bd. advisors Japan Soc., 1996—98; counsel select subcom. on arms transfers to Bosnia U.S. Ho. of Reps., 1996; mem. steering com. Law Profs. for Dole, 1996; mem. com. on internat. jud. rels. U.S. Jud. Conf., 1999—; mem. Brown v. Bd. Edn. 50th Anniversary Commemoration Com.; chair NAFTA labor agreement adv. com. Dept. of Labor, 2002—; mem. trade and environ. policy adv. com. U.S. Trade Rep. Office, 2003—. Author: Fundamentals of U.S. Trade Law, 2001, Japanese Law in Context, 2001. Bd. visitors USAF Acad., 2000—02. Fellow, POSCO Rsch. Inst., 1995—98, Japan Found., 1979—80, Fulbright, 1983—84. Fellow: Am. Bar Found.; mem.: Coun. Fgn. Rels. Mem. Lds Ch. Avocation: Avocations: skiing, scuba diving, photography. Home: 1480 Military Way Salt Lake City UT 84103 Office Phone: 801-581-5701. E-mail: president@utah.edu.

YOUNG, MICHAEL R. manufacturing executive; b. 1945; With Rockwell Internat. Corp., until 1983, Bristol Compressor Co., 1983-88, York Internat. Corp., 1988—, pres., COO, now pres., CEO. Office: York Internat Corp 631 S Richland Ave York PA 17403-3445

YOUNG, MICHAEL WARREN, geneticist, educator; b. Miami, Fla., Mar. 28, 1949; s. Lloyd George and Mildred (Tillery) Y.; m. Laurel Ann Eckhardt, Dec. 27, 1978; children: Natalie, Arissa. BA, U. Tex., 1971, PhD, 1975. NIH postdoctoral fellow Stanford (Calif.) U. Med. Sch., 1975-77; asst. prof. genetics The Rockefeller U., N.Y.C., 1978-83, assoc. prof., 1984-88, prof., 1988—, dir. Levy/White Ctr. Mind, Brain and Behavioral Studies, 2000—02, v.p. for acad. affairs, 2004—; head Rockefeller unit NSF Sci. and Tech. Ctr. Biol. Timing, 1991—2001. Investigator Howard Hughes Med. Inst., N.Y.C., 1987-96; adv. panel on genetic biology NSF, Washington, 1983-87; spl. advisor Am. Cancer Soc., N.Y.C., 1985—; spl. reviewer genetics study sect. NIH, Bethesda, Md., 1990—, cell biology study sect., 1993-97. Contbr. articles to profl. jours. Meyer Found. fellow, N.Y.C., 1978-83. Fellow N.Y. Sci. Soc. Fellows; mem. AAAS, Genetics Soc. Am., Am. Soc. Microbiologists, N.Y. Acad. Scis., Harvey Soc. (treas. 2001-04). Achievements include research on transposable DNA elements, molecular genetics of nerve and muscle development, biological clocks, molecular control of circadian rhythms. Home: 51 Greenwoods Rd Old Tappan NJ 07675-7018 Office: The Rockefeller Univ 1230 York Ave New York NY 10021-6399

YOUNG, MILTON EARL, retired petroleum company executive; b. San Angelo, Tex., Dec. 3, 1929; s. Edward Earl and Annie Mae Y.; m. Clara Louise Sens, June 1, 1957; children— Vanessa, Bradley. AA, San Angelo Coll., 1950; BS in Petroleum Engring, U. Tex., 1953. Various positions Continental Oil Co., 1953-73; v.p. for prodn., drilling, engring. Tesoro Petroleum Corp., San Antonio, 1973-74, sr. v.p., 1974-85, group v.p. exploration and prodn., 1985-86, retired, 1986. Served with USNR, 1948-49. Mem. Soc. Petroleum Engrs. Republican. Lutheran. Home: 1932 Frazar Rd Sealy TX 77474-8439

YOUNG, NANCY MELINDA, otolaryngologist; b. N.Y.C., 1956; m. Mitchell L. Marinello; children: Samantha, Michelle, Lindsey. BA, Wesleyan U., 1978; MD, NYU, 1982. Resident in gen. surgery Montefiore Hosp., Bronx, 1982-84; resident in otolarnygology-head and neck surgery Northwestern Meml. Hosp., Chgo., 1984-87; fellow in neurotology Chgo. Otology Group-Hinsdale Hosp., 1987-88; head sect. neurotology and otology Children's Meml. Hosp., Chgo., 1988—. Asst. prof. Northwestern U., 1990-2002, assoc. prof., 2002; mem. med. adv. bd. Advanced Bionics Corp., Sylmar, Calif., 1997—, Cochlear Corp., Englewood, Colo. Bd. dirs. Chgo. Hearing Soc., 1992-97, Anixter Ctr., 1997—.Bd. mem. Am. Auditory Soc. Fellow Am. Acad. Otolaryngology-Head & Neck Surgery, mem. ACS, AMA, Am. Neurol. Soc., Chgo. Med. Soc., Ill. Med. Soc. Office: Dept Otolaryngology 2300 Children Plz # 25 Chicago IL 60614-3318

YOUNG, OLIVIA KNOWLES, retired librarian; b. Benton, Ark., Sept. 3, 1922; d. Wesley Taylor and Med Belle (Crawford) Knowles; m. Calvin B. Young, Oct. 6, 1951; 1 child, Brigham Taylor. BA, Tenn. Tech. U., 1942, BS in Libr. Sci., 1946. Head periodicals and documents dept. Peabody Coll. Library, Nashville, 1946-49; area libr. U.S. Army, Austria, 1949-51; libr. Cairo Pub. Libr., Ga., 1955-57, Caney Fork Regional Libr., Sparta, Tenn., 1957-58; chief libr. Ft. Stewart (Ga.) U.S. Army, 1959-63; dir. Watauga Regional Libr., Johnson City, Tenn., 1963-70; dir. devel. and extension Tenn. State Libr. and Archives, Nashville, 1971-82, state libr. and archivist, 1982-85; ret., 1985. Mem. Tenn. Library Assn. (treas. 1970, Honor award 1985), Southeastern Library Assn., ALA, Boone Tree Library Assn. (pres. 1968), Altrusa Club (sec. 1967). Methodist. Home: 203 E Everett St Sparta TN 38583

YOUNG, PATRICIA JANEAN, speech pathology/audiology services professional; b. San Diego, Nov. 30, 1953; d. Bernarr E. and Janean Romig Young. AA, Palomar C.C., San Marcos, Calif., 1976; BA, Calif. State U., Chico, 1978; MA, Calif. State U., Long Beach, 1981. Cert. clin. competence Am. Speech-Lang.-Hearing Assn., lic. speech pathologist Calif., cert. tchr. Calif. Mgmt. trainee Robinson's Dept. Store, LA, 1976—78; speech and hearing screening coord. Riverview Hearing, Speech, Lang. Ctrs., Long Beach, 1978—81, speech pathologist, 1981—84; speech pathologist, dir. Speech Pathology Svcs., Carlsbad and Temecula, Calif., 1984—; speech pathologist, augmentative comm. coord. Lake Elsinore (Calif.) Unified Sch. Dist., 1998—. Prodr. TV shows on comm. disorders Long Beach Cable TV, 1983; coord. pub. svc. announcement and interviewee for Disabilities Awareness Week ABC TV, San Diego, 1986, San Diego, 88. Contbr. poetry to lit. publs.; author: (game) Match This!, 1995. Named to Outstanding Young Women Am. Mem.: Calif. Speech-Lang-Hearing Assn. (region rep., Outstanding Achievement award 1987), Am. Speech-Lang-Hearing Assn., Zeta Tau Alpha. Avocations: writing, theater, decorating. Home: 31935 Calle Espinoza Temecula CA 92592 Office: Lake Elsinore Unified Sch Dist 545 Chaney St Lake Elsinore CA 92530 Office Phone: 951-253-7000 5390.

YOUNG, PATRICK, writer, editor; b. Ladysmith, Wis., Oct. 19, 1937; s. Rodney and Janice (Wolf) Y.; m. Leah Ruth Figelman, Oct. 8, 1966; 1 child, Justine Young Gottshall. BA, U. Colo., 1960. Reporter UPI, Washington, 1961-62; journalist USN, 1963-64; staff writer Nat. Observer, Silver Spring, Md., 1965-77; free-lance writer Laurel, Md., 1977-79; mem. sr. staff Pres.'s Commn. on the Accident at Three Mile Island, Washington, 1979; chief sci. and med. writer Newhouse News Svc., Washington, 1980-88; editor Sci. News, Washington, 1988-95; ind. writer, editor, cons., 1995—. Sci. writer in residence U. Wis., 1986. Author: Asthma and Allergies, 1980, Drugs and Pregnancy, 1987, Schizophrenia, 1988; co-author: Keeping Young Athletes Healthy, 1991. With USN, 1963-64. Recipient Howard W. Blakeslee award Am. Heart Assn., 1971, Sci. Writing award in physics and astronomy Am. Inst. Physics, 1974, James T. Grady award Am. Chem. Soc., 1977. Mem. Nat. Assn. Sci. Writers, Nat. Press Club, Am. Assn. Adv. Sci. Office Phone: 301-498-4251. E-mail: young@nasw.org.

YOUNG, PAUL ANDREW, anatomist; b. St. Louis, Oct. 3, 1926; s. Nicholas A. and Olive A. (Langford) Y.; m. Catherine Ann Hofmeister, May 14, 1949; children— Paul, Robert, David, Ann, Carol, Richard, James, Steven, Kevin, Michael. BS, St. Louis U., 1947, MS, 1953; PhD, U. Buffalo, 1957. Asst. in anatomy U. Buffalo, 1953, instr. anatomy, 1957; asst. prof. anatomy St. Louis U., 1957, asso. prof., 1966, prof., 1972—, chmn. dept., 1973—2004. Author: (with B.D. Bhagat and D.E. Biggerstaff) Fundamentals of Visceral Innervation, 1977, (with P.H. Young) Basic Clinical Neuroanatomy, 1996, also computer assisted neurological anatomy tutorials; contbr. articles to profl. pubs. Recipient Golden Apple award, Student AMA, 1974, 2000, Tchg. award, Acad. Sci. St. Louis, 1993, Emerson Excellence in Tchg. award, 2001. Mem. Am. Assn. Anatomists, Am. Assn. Clin. Anatomists, Soc. Neurosci., Sigma Xi, Alpha Omega Alpha. Office: St Louis U Ctr for Anatomical Sci and Edn 1402 S Grand Blvd Saint Louis MO 63104-1004 Office Phone: 314-977-8025. Personal E-mail: payoun5@aol.com. Business E-Mail: youngpa@slu.edu.

YOUNG, PAUL GARLIN, principal; b. Lancaster, Ohio, Mar. 5, 1950; s. Mary Winifred and Howard Grove Young; m. Gertrude Faith VanAuken, June 8, 1974; children: Katherine Gertrude, Mary Ellen. BFA, Ohio U., 1972, MusM, 1973, PhD, 1992. Cert. elem. prin. Ohio, 2001. Dir. bands Fairfield Union H.S., Lancaster, Ohio, 1973—84; tchr. 4th grade Bremen Elem. Sch., 1984—86; prin. Glenford Elem. Sch., 1986—87, Sanderson Elem. Sch., Lancaster, 1987—90, Medill Elem. Sch., 1990, West Elem. Sch., 1996—. Pres. NAESP, Alexandria, Va., 2002—. Sec. West After Sch. Ctr., Inc., Lancaster, 1998—2002. Mem.: ASCD, Ohio Assn. Elem. Sch. Administrators (pres. 1996—97), Nat. Assn. Elem. Sch. Prins. (pres. 2002—03), Phi Delta Kappa, Phi Mu Alpha Sinfonia (life; pres. 1971—72). R-Consevative. United Methodist. Avocations: running, gardening, travel, reading, writing. Home: 485 Crestview Dr Lancaster OH 43130 Office: West Elem Sch 625 Garfield Ave Lancaster OH 43130 Personal E-mail: pyoung6@columbus.rr.com. E-mail: p_young@lancaster.k12.oh.us.

YOUNG, PAUL RAY, medical board executive, physician; b. Fairfield, Nebr., June 27, 1932; s. Earl Edward and Louisa May (Saunders) Young; m. Irene Marie Gray (div. 1971); children: Michael, Susan, Jean, James; m. Faye Elizabeth Hall, Oct. 28, 1972. BA, U. Nebr., Lincoln, 1953; MD, U. Nebr., Omaha, 1958. Diplomate Am. Bd. Family Practice. Intern Rsch. Hosp., Kansas City, Mo., 1958—59, dir. continuing med. edn., 1967—71; pvt. practice Raytown, Mo., 1961—67; assoc. prof. family practice U. Mo. Coll. Medicine, Columbia, 1971—75; chmn. dept. U. Nebr. Coll. Medicine, 1975—80, U. Tex. Med. Br., Galveston, 1980—88; dep. dir. Am. Bd. Family Practice, Lexington, Ky., 1988—90, exec. dir., 1990—97, sr. exec., 1998—. Chmn. RRC for Family Practice, Chgo., 1979—87. Founding editor: Family Practice Recert, 1979, Jour. Am. Bd. Family Practice, 1987. Pres. Nicholas J. Piscano Meml. Found., 1990—97. Capt. M.C. USAF, 1959—61. Fellow: Am. Acad. Family Physicians; mem.: Soc. Tchrs. Family Practice (bd. dirs. 1970—72), Alpha Omega Alpha. Office: Am Bd Family Practice Inc 2228 Young Dr Lexington KY 40505-4219 E-mail: pyoung@abfp.org.

YOUNG, PETER ROBERT, librarian; b. Washington, Aug. 13, 1944; s. Ju Chin and Jane Kathrine (Lybrand) Y.; m. Mary Sue Townsend, Mar. 25, 1978; children: Kathryn, Timothy; children from previous marriage: Robert, Jonathan. AB Philosophy, Coll. Wooster, Ohio, 1966; grad., George Washington U., 1967; MSLS Libr. Svc., Columbia U., 1968. Adminstrv. libr. Am. U. Libr., Washington, 1968; head cataloger, reference libr. Franklin & Marshall Coll. Libr., Lancaster, Pa., 1971-74; asst. libr. pub. svcs. Rice U. Librs., Houston, Tex., 1974-76; asst. dir. Grand Rapids (Mich.) Pub. Libr., 1978; sales support libr. CL Systems Inc., Newtonville, Mass., 1976-78, libr. systems analyst, 1978-80; customer svcs. officer Cataloging Distbn. Svc. Libr. Congress, Washington, 1980-84, asst. chief Marc edit. divsn., 1984-85, chief Copyright Cataloging divsn., 1985-88; dir. acad. info. svcs. The Faxon Co., Westwood, Mass., 1988-89, dir. Faxon Inst. Advanced Studies Scholarly and Sci. Communication, 1989-90; exec. dir. U.S. Nat. Commn. Librs. and Info. Sci., Washington, 1990-97; chief cataloging distbn. svc. Libr. of Congress, Washington, 1997—. Exec. bd. Fed. Libr. and Info. Ctr. com., 1993-96; adv. bd. Highsmith Press, 1991-99; co chair libr. stats. standard revision com. Nat. Standards Info. Office, 1989-93; libr. adminstrs. devel. program U. Md., 1984; implementation task force libr. data Nat. Ctr. Edn. Stats. U.S. Office Edn., 1988, adv. coun. edn. stats. Office Edn. Rsch. and Improvement, 1990—; lectr. in field. Edit. bd. Serials Review, 1990—; contbr. articles to profl. jours. With U.S. Army, 1968-70, Vietnam. Mem. ALA (pub. policy for pub. librs. com. 1993—, com. rsch. and stats. 1990—, coun. 2000—, various coms., assns.), Internat. Stds. Orgn. (libr. stats. and libr. performance indicators stds. 1998—), Chinese Am. Libr. Assn. (chair pub. rels. com. 1987-88, pres. 1989-90), U.S. Nat. Commn. Librs. and Info. Sci. (stats. task force 1988-89). Office: Libr of Congress John Adams Bldg Stop Code 4910 Washington DC 20540-0001

YOUNG, PHILIP HOWARD, library director; b. Ithaca, N.Y., Oct. 7, 1953; s. Charles Robert and Betty Irene (Osborne) Young; m. Nancy Ann Stutsman, Aug. 18, 1979. BA, U. Va., 1975; PhD, U. Pa., 1980; MLS, Ind. U., 1983. Asst. prof. history Appalachian State U., Boone, NC, 1980-82; reference asst. Lilly Libr. Ind. U., Bloomington, 1982-83; adminstr., info. specialist Ind. Corp. Sci. & Tech., Indpls., 1983-85, dir. Krannert Meml. Libr. U. Indpls., 1985—. Mem.: Archeol. Inst. Am., Am. Libr. Assn., Phi Beta Kappa, Beta Phi Mu, Phi Alpha Theta. Democrat. Home: 4332 Silver Springs Dr Greenwood IN 46142-9623 Office: U Indpls Krannert Meml Libr 1400 E Hanna Ave Indianapolis IN 46227-3630

YOUNG, QUENTIN HAYSE, family counselor; b. Panama City, Fla., Mar. 1, 1944; s. Mayo Beckford Young and Rose Mary Kama; m. Mary C. Grith, June 13, 1964 (div. July 1972); children: Jeff, Samantha; m. Ginger Bialas-Lucas, Aug. 18, 2001. Degree in mech. design, Cen. Design Coll., 1968. Machine operator Plastics Fabrication, Wichita, Kans., 1965-67; metal fabricator Beach Aircraft, Wichita, 1967-69; with aircraft design dept. Fairchild, San Antonio, 1969-70; mem. bd. design Data Point, San Antonio, 1970-72; officer Ga. Correctional Officer, Alto, 1972-73; dir. rsch. So. Steel, San Antonio, 1973-84; exec. v.p. design ADTEC, San Antonio, 1984-90; sr. design engr. R.R. Brink, Shorewood, Ill., 1990-2000; instr. native Am. Indian studies Coll. of DuPage, Glen Ellyn, Ill., 1997—; family counselor Balance Thru the 4 Winds of the Lakota, Winfield, Ill., 2000—. Advanced open water instr. Scuba Schs. Internat., 1980—. Patentee lock designs, child restraint. With U.S. Army, 1962-65. Mem. ACA, Monroe Inst. Avocations: rock climbing, scuba diving, art. Home: 0S425 Florida Ln Winfield IL 60190 Office: Balance Thru the 4 Winds of the Lakota PO Box 606 Winfield IL 60190 Office Phone: 630-933-9953. E-mail: wicasa54@aol.com.

YOUNG, R. JAMES, insurance company executive; V.p. fin. and planning The Allstate Corp., Northbrook, Ill., 1997-2000, v.p. property and casualty ops., 2000—. Office: The Allstate Corp 2775 Sanders Rd # F6 Northbrook IL 60062-6110

YOUNG, RAY G. automotive executive; B in Bus. Adminstrn., U. Western Ontario, 1984; M Bus. Adminstrn., U. Chgo., 1986. Joined GM Can., 1986, dir. capital markets and fgn. exchange, 1988—93; regional treas. GM Europe, Brussels, 1993—96; v.p. fin. CAMI Automotive, 1996—2001; v.p., CFO GM N. Am., 2001—. Office: GM Corp PO Box 300 300 Renaissance Ctr Detroit MI 48265-3000

YOUNG, RAYMOND HENRY, lawyer; b. Boston, Sept. 28, 1927; s. Raymond H. and Clara Elms (Oakman) Y.; m. Louisa Breda, Sept. 1, 1951; children: Christopher, Pamela, Amy. AB, Yale U., 1947, LLB, 1950. Bar: Mass. 1951. Assoc. Warner, Stackpole, Stetson & Bradlee, Boston, 1950-52; pvt. practice Boston, 1952-64; ptnr. Young & Bayle, Boston, 1964—. Mem. ABA (past sec. sect. real property, probate and trust law, mem. commn. legal problems of the elderly), Am. Coll. Trust and Estate Counsel (mem. joint editorial bd. for trust and estate acts), Am. Law Inst. (advisor for restatement property 3d donative transfers, cons. restatement trusts 3d), Nat. Commn. on Nat. Probate Ct. Standards, Internat. Acad. Trust and Estate Law (past pres.), Mass. Bar Assn., Boston Bar Assn. (past pres.), Boston Estate Planning Coun. (past pres., Estate Planner of Yr. award 1991), Boston Probate and Estate Planning Forum. Home: 122 Garfield St Watertown MA 02472-4916 Office: Young & Bayle 150 Federal St Boston MA 02110-1713

YOUNG, REBECCA MARY CONRAD, retired state legislator; b. Clairton, Pa., Feb. 28, 1934; d. Walter Emerson and Harriet Averill (Colcord) Conrad; m. Merwin Crawford Young, Aug. 17, 1957; children: Eve, Louise, Estelle, Emily. BA, U. Mich., 1955; MA in Teaching, Harvard U., 1963; JD, U. Wis., 1983. Bar: Wis. 1983. Commr. State Hwy. Commn., Madison, Wis., 1974-76; dep. sec. Wis. Dept. of Adminstrn., Madison, 1976-77; assoc. Wadsack, Julian & Lawton, Madison, 1983-84; elected rep. Wis. State Assembly, Madison, 1985-99. Translator: Katanga Secession, 1966. Supr. Dane County Bd., Madison, 1970-74; mem. Madison Sch. Bd., 1979-85. Recipient Wis. NOW Feminist of Yr. award, 1996, Eunice Zoghlin Edgar Lifetime Achievement award ACLU, 1997, Outstanding Legislator award Wis. Counties Assn., 1998, Voice for Choice award Planned Parenthood Wis., 1998, Luan Gilbert award for outstanding activities in domestic violence intervention and prevention Domestic Violence Intervention Svc., 1998. Mem. LWV. Democrat. Avocations: board games, hiking. Home: 639 Crandall St Madison WI 53711-1836

YOUNG, RICHARD ALAN, association executive; b. Oak Park, Ill., Mar. 17, 1935; m. Carol Ann Schellinger, June 28, 1958; children: Steven, Karen, Christopher. BA, U. Iowa, 1958; MS, PhD, Western State U., 2000. Chief engr. Cardox Corp., Chgo., 1958-61; asst. chief engr. Goodman Mfg. Co., Chgo., 1961-63; plant and environ. engr. Signode Corp., Glenview, Ill., 1963-68; editor Pollution Engring. Tech. Pub. Co., Barrington, Ill., 1968-81; exec. dir. Nat. Registry of Environ. Profls., 1988—; pub. Cahners Pub. Co., Des Plaines, Ill., 1990-95. Adj. prof. George Williams Coll.; mcpl. pollution control adviser and enforcement officer for 24 cities and state govts; ofcl rep. and pollution control expert U.S. Govt. at tech. transfer meetings; exec. dir. Internat. Certification Accreditation Bd., 1999—. Editor 26 books on environ. engring.; pollution engring.; series editor, Marcel Dekker Inc., N.Y.C.; contbr. articles to profl. jours.; patentee in field. Recipient Jesse H. Neal certificate for outstanding editorial writing Am. Bus. Press, Inc., 1971, Outstanding Service award Western Soc. Engrs., Charles Ellet award as Most Outstanding Engr. of Yr. 1970; Environ. Quality award EPA, 1976 Mem. Internat. Assn. for Pollution Control (dir.), Am. Soc. Bus. Press Editors (Editl. Excellence award 1980, Design Excellence award 1982), Am. Inst. Plant Engrs. (past nat. chmn. environ. quality), Internat. Congress Environ. Profls. (mng. dir.), Nat. Inst. Hazardous Materials Mgmts. (dir. 1984-88, cert. hazardous materials mgr.).

YOUNG, RICHARD ALLEN, molecular biologist, educator; b. Pitts., Mar. 12, 1954; s. Allen Young and Jane (Moore) Stockhausen. BS in Biol. Sci., Ind. U., 1975; PhD in Molecular Biology, Biochemistry, Yale U., 1979. Postdoctoral fellow Swiss Inst. Exptl. Cancer Research, Lausanne, Switzerland, 1979-80, Stanford (Calif.) U., 1981-84; assoc. prof. biology MIT, Cambridge, 1984—, now prof.; mem. Whitehead Inst. Biomed. Research, Cambridge, 1984—. Cons., com. mem. WHO, Geneva, Switzerland, 1983-89, chmn. biology subcom., 1987-90. Grantee WHO, NIH, 1984—; recipient Molecular Parasitology award Burroughs Wellcome Co., 1987, Chiron Corp. Biotechnology award Am. Society for Microbiology, 1994 Fellow Molecular Medicine Soc. (charter); mem. AAAS, Am. Acad. Microbiology, Genetics Soc. Am. Avocations: skiing, mountain climbing. Office: Whitehead Inst Biomed Research 9 Cambridge Ctr Cambridge MA 02142-1479

YOUNG, RICHARD D. state legislator; b. Dec. 2, 1942; m. Elaine Thacker; 5 children. AA, Vincennes U., 1992. Mem. Ind. Senate from 47th dist., 1988—; mem. agr., small bus., edn., fin. and natural resource coms.; minority

leader, 1996—. Farmer. Mem. Farm Bur., Crawford County C. of C., Lions.' Democrat. Home: 10347 E Daugherty Ln Milltown IN 47145-9801 Office: Ind Senate State Capitol 200 W Washington St Indianapolis IN 46204-2728

YOUNG, RICHARD WILLIAM, corporate director; b. Ridgewood, N.Y., Oct. 17, 1926; s. Charles Michael and Louise Margaret (Baust) Y.; m. Sheila deLisser, Sept. 11, 1949; children: Christine, Noreen, Brian, Eileen. AB, Dartmouth Coll., 1946, A.M., 1947; PhD, Columbia U., 1950; DSc (hon.), Regis Coll., 2002. Sr. rsch. chemist Chemotherapy div. Am. Cyanamid Co., Conn., 1950-56, group leader pesticide chems. Agrl. div., 1956-58, dir. chem. Agrl. div., 1958-60, dir. chem. rsch. cen. rsch. div., 1960-62; asst. dir. rsch. Polaroid Corp., Cambridge, Mass., 1962-69, v.p., 1963-69, sr. v.p. rsch. and devel., 1969-72, sr. v.p., pres. Internat. div., 1972-80, exec. v.p., dir. worldwide mktg., 1980-82; pres. Houghton Mifflin Co., Boston, 1982-85; chmn., CEO Mentor O & O, Inc., Norwell, Mass., 1985-92. Bd. dirs. Bay State Milling Corp., Quincy, Mass., Instron Corp., Canton, Mass., Oceantrawl Inc., Seattle, Mentor Corp., Santa Barbara, Calif. Patentee in field. Chmn. bd. trustees Regis Coll., Weston, Mass.; trustee Mass. Eye and Ear Infirmary, Boston, 1963-90, Trinitas Found., Quincy; mem. corp. Northeastern U., Boston, 1960-92. Mem. Am. Chem. Soc. Home: 4 Scotch Pine Cir Wellesley Hills MA 02481-1222 Office: Trinitas Found 100 Congress St Quincy MA 02169-0906

YOUNG, ROBERT A., III, freight systems executive; b. Ft. Smith, Ark., Sept. 23, 1940; s. Robert A. and Vivian (Curtis) Y.; m. Mary Carleton McRae; children: Tracy, Christy, Robert A. IV (dec.), Stephen BA in Econs., Washington and Lee U., 1963. Supr. terminal ops. Ark. Best Freight, Ft. Smith, 1964-65; pres. Data-Tronics Inc, Ft. Smith, 1965-67; sr. v.p. Nat. Bank of Commerce, Dallas, 1967-70; v.p. fin. Ark. Best Corp., Ft. Smith, 1970-73, exec. v.p., 1973, pres., chief operating officer, 1973-88, chief exec. officer, pres., 1988—; pres. ABF Freight Systems, Inc., Ft. Smith, 1979-94. Bd. dirs. First Nat. Bank, Ft. Smith. Pres. United Way, Ft. Smith, 1981; chmn. bd. dirs. Sparks Regional Med. Ctr., Ft. Smith, 1995, chair, 1999; bd. dirs. ATA Found., Inc., Ft. Smith Boys Club; chmn. bd. trustees Lyon Coll., Sparks Regional Med. Ctr., Ft. Smith. Recipient Silver Beaver award Boy Scouts Am. Mem. Am. Trucking Assn. (vice chmn.), Phi Delta Theta. Presbyterian. Office: Ark Best Corp PO Box 10048 Fort Smith AR 72917-0048 also: Ark Best Corp 3801 Old Greenwood Rd Fort Smith AR 72903-5937

YOUNG, ROBERT BRUCE, lawyer; b. Chgo., June 23, 1936; s. James T. and Julia A. (Frey) Y.; m. Janice C. Crowhurst, Aug. 12, 1961; children: Robert W., William J., Leslie B. BS in Engring., Millikin U., 1959; JD, John Marshall Law Sch., 1978. Bar: Ill. 1978, U.S. Dist. Ct. (no. dist.) Ill. 1978. Assoc. Gifford, Detuno & Gifford, Ltd., Chgo., 1978—91; mng. ptnr. Young & Gildea, Ltd., Chgo., 1991—2004; pvt. practice Lemont, Ill., 2004—. With U.S. Army, 1959-61. Mem. ABA, Ill. Bar Assn., Chgo. Bar Assn., Workers Compensation Lawyers Assn. Home: 13827 Steeples Rd Lemont IL 60558

YOUNG, ROBERT CRABILL, medical researcher, science facility administrator, internist; b. Columbus, Ohio, 1940; MD, Cornell U., 1965. Diplomate Am. Bd. Internal Medicine, subspecialty bds. hematology and med. oncology. Intern N.Y. Hosp., N.Y.C., 1965-66, resident, 1966-67; sr. resident Yale-New Haven Med. Ctr., 1969-70; sr. investigator, attending physician med. br. Nat. Cancer Inst., Bethesda, Md., 1971—, chief med. br., 1974-88; pres. Fox Chase Cancer Ctr., Phila., 1988—. Clin. prof. medicine Georgetown U., from 1974, assoc. prof., 1976-84; clin. prof. medicine George Washington U., 1984—; bd. Sci. Advisors, Nat. Cancer Inst., 1996—; bd. Nat. Cancer Policy, 1997-99; chmn. bd. Nat. Comprehensive Cancer Network. Assoc. editor Jour. Clin. Oncology; chmn. editl. bd. Oncology Times. Sr. surgeon USPHS, 1967-69. Fellow ACP; mem. Am. Soc. Hematology, Am. Assn. Cancer Rsch., Am. Soc. Clin. Oncology (pres. 1990), Am. Cancer Soc. (bd. dir. 1995-99, 1st v.p. 1999-2000, pres. 2002), Internat. Gynecol. Cancer Soc. (pres.-elect 1998, pres. 2000). Office: Fox Chase Cancer Ctr 7701 Burholme Ave Ste 2 Philadelphia PA 19111-2497

YOUNG, ROBERT CRAIG, banker; b. N.Y.C., Mar. 15, 1960; s. Robert J. and Gloria L. (Sandhop) Y.; m. Anke Ott, Dec. 2, 2000. BS cum laude, NYU, 1982, MBA, 1985. Asst. v.p. Chem. Bank, N.Y.C., 1982-86; project mgr. GE Credit Corp., Stamford, Conn., 1986-87; dir. Merrill Lynch & Co., N.Y.C., 1987-94; sr. v.p. Greenwich (Conn.) Capital Markets, Inc., 1994-97; mng. dir. Nomura Securities, N.Y.C., 1997-2001; divsn. dir. Macquarie, N.Y.C., 2001—. Home: 98 Revere Rd Manhasset NY 11030-2733 Office: Macquarie 600 5th Ave New York NY 10020 E-mail: reverecap@aol.com.

YOUNG, ROBERT EDWARD, computer company executive; b. L.A., Nov. 28, 1943; s. David and Sue Young; m. Lucia Young. Student, E. Los Angeles Coll., 1973, Santa Monica Coll., 1975; BA, UCLA, 1978. Cert. securities analyst N.Y. Inst. Fin., 1972. Computer operator Rocketdyne Corp., Canoga Park, Calif., 1963-65; computer ops. supr. Hughes Aircraft Corp., El Segundo, Calif., 1965-67; with investment securities dept. Smith, Tilton & Co., Inc., Santa Ana, Calif., 1967-70, Morton Seidel & Co., Inc., L.A., 1970-78; sales mgr. of comml. interior constrn. NICO Constrn. Co., Inc., L.A., 1978-80; sales mgr. Strauss Constrn. Co., Inc., L.A., 1981-82; v.p., instl. investment officer FCA Asset Mgmt./Am. Savs., Los Angeles, 1982-87; pres., chief exec. officer Avalon Fin. Group, Inc., Los Angeles, 1988-90; prin. Robert Young & Co., 1991-2000; pres. youngbob.com, Inc., 2000—. Bd. dirs. RESA Prodns. 1973-80, Edu Care, L.A., 1981-90, ASC Edn. Svcs. Inc., L.A., chmn. fin. com.; mktg. cons. Shebania Enterprises, L.A., 1978-79; sales tng. cons. Versailles Gallery, L.A., Schwartz Constrn., L.A., 1982; cons. PC Etcetera, L.A., 1990-91; guest lectr. Pryor Seminars, 2000-02. Photographer: prin. works include Man at Work or Play UN, Geneva, 1976, Cat of Yr. photo, 1977, Photomontage U. So. Calif. Early Childhood Edn. Ctr., 1977; producer weekly pub. affairs prog. for family fin. planning sta. KPOL Radio, 1974, Stocks and Bonds Show KWHY-TV, 1975-78, MacRadio show, Am. Radio Network, 1989, WinRadio Show, 1990, MacWin Radio, 1991-93. Fin. cons. Hofheinz Fund, Houston, 1988. Served with USCGR, 1964-70. Mem. Archtl. Hist. Soc. (life mem. So. Calif. chpt.), Reel Sports Club, Masons, Marine Venice Yacht Club (commodore). Avocations: fishing, computers, sailing. Home: 249 Loma Ave Long Beach CA 90803 E-mail: bob@youngbob.com.

YOUNG, ROBERT P., JR., state supreme court justice; Bachelor's degree cum laude, Harvard Coll., 1974; JD, Harvard U., 1977. With Dickinson, Wright, Moon, Van Dusen & Freeman, 1977-1992; v.p., corp. sec., gen. counsel AAA Mich., 1992; appt. Mich. Ct. Appeals 1st Dist., 1995; justice Mich. Supreme Ct., 1998—. Mem. Mich. Civil Svc. Commn.; bd. trustees Cen. Mich. U. Office: PO Box 30052 Lansing MI 48909-7552

YOUNG, ROGER AUSTIN, natural gas distribution company executive; b. Boston, Feb. 2, 1946; s. Robert Harris McCarter and Gloria Bond (Tenney) Y.; m. Linda Furste, Sept. 6, 1975; children: Catherine Simms, Geoffrey Furste. BA, Princeton U., 1968. Systems analyst Orange and Rockland Utilities, Inc., Spring Valley, N.Y., 1968-72; asst. v.p. Bay State Gas Co., Boston, 1972-75, v.p., 1975-80, exec. v.p. Canton, Mass., 1980-81, pres. Westborough, Mass., 1981-90, pres., chief exec. officer, 1990-96, CEO, 1996-99, chmn., bd. dirs., 1999—. Past chmn., bd. trustees, mem. exec. com. Inst. Gas Tech.; regional bd. dirs. Bank Boston. Bd. dirs. Watts Industries, Inc., North Andover. Mem. New Eng. Gas Assn. (chmn. 1984-85). Clubs: The Country (Brookline, Mass.); Colonial (Princeton, N.J.). Congregationalist. Office: Bay State Gas Co 300 Friberg Pkwy Westborough MA 01581-3900 Home: PO Box 775816 Steamboat Springs CO 80477-5816

YOUNG, ROMA SKEEN, lawyer; b. Vancouver, Wash., Feb. 21, 1950; d. Carroll Hallam and Dorothy Elizabeth (Miller) Skeen; m. Robert Hugh Young, Jr., May 20,1978; children: Matthew Hallam, Brian Robert. BA, Sweetbriar Coll., 1971; JD, Georgetown U., 1978. Bar: Pa. 1978. Mem. staff U.S. Senate Energy Com., Washington, 1972-75; lobbyist Marathon Oil Co., Washington, 1975-78; assoc. Pepper, Hamilton & Scheetz, Phila., 1978-84, Wolf, Block, Schorr and Solis-Cohen, Phila., 1984-89, ptnr., 1989—. Office: Wolf Block Schorr and Solis-Cohen 15th And Chestnut St Fl 12 Philadelphia PA 19102-2625

YOUNG, RONALD FARIS, commodity trader; b. Schenectady, Dec. 17, 1939; s. James Vernon and Dorothy (Girod) Y.; m. Anne Randolph Kendig, Feb. 23, 1963; children: Margaret Randolph Reynolds, Anne Corbin. BA, U. Va., 1962; MBA, Harvard U., 1966. Grain trader Continental Grain Co., 1966-70; pres. Conti-Commodities, Chgo., 1970; v.p. commodity sales Du-Pont, Glore Forgan, Chgo., 1971-72; self-employed commodity trader Chgo. Bd. Trade, 1972-78; ind. trader Va. Trading Co., 1978-90, pres., 1978-84, dep. chmn., 1984-89; pres. Randolph Ptnrs., Ltd., 1983-91. Chmn. bd. Chgo. Bd. Trade, 1978, dir., 1975—77, 1980, 2003. Bd. dirs. Princeton Fund, 1981-82, Lake Forest Hosp., 1981-84, Lake Forest Country Day Sch., 1981-86. Served with USMCR, 1959-65. Mem. Racquet Club (bd. dirs. 1989-97), Onwentsia Club (Lake Forest, Ill., bd. dirs. 1981-90, pres. 1991-93), Everglades Cub (Palm Beach, Fla.), Bath and Tennis Club (Palm Beach). Republican. Episcopalian. Home: 531 N Mayflower Rd Lake Forest IL 60045

YOUNG, ROY ALTON, university administrator, educator; b. McAlister, N.Mex., Mar. 1, 1921; s. John Arthur and Etta Julia (Sprinkle) Y.; m. Marilyn Ruth Sandman, May 22, 1950; children: Janet Elizabeth, Randall Owen. BS, N.Mex. A&M Coll., 1941; MS, Iowa State U., 1942, PhD, 1948; LLD (hon.), N.Mex. State U., 1978. Tchg. fellow Iowa State U., 1941-42, instr., 1946-47, Indsl. fellow, 1947-48; asst. prof. Oreg. State U., 1948-50, assoc. prof., 1950-53, prof., 1953—, head dept. botany and plant pathology, 1958-66, dean rsch., 1966-70, acting pres., 1969-70, v.p. rsch. and grad. studies, 1970-76, dir. Office for Natural Resources Policy, 1986-90; chancellor U. Nebr., Lincoln, 1976-80; mng. dir., pres. Boyce Thompson Inst. Plant Rsch., Cornell U., Ithaca, N.Y., 1980-86. Mem. Commn. on Undergrad. Edn. in Biol. Scis., 1963-68; mem. Gov.'s Sci. Coun., 1987-90; cons. State Exptl. Stas. divsn. USDA; chmn. subcom. plant pathogens, agriculture bd. NAS-NRC, 1965-68; mem. exec. com. study on problems of pest control, 1972-75; mem. exec. com. Nat. Govs.' Coun. on Sci. and Tech., 1970-74; mem. U.S. com. man and biosphere UNESCO, 1973-82; mem. com. to rev. U.S. component Internat. Biol. Program, NAS, 1974-76; mem. adv. panel on postdoctoral fellowships in environ. sci. Rockefeller Found., 1974-78; bd. dirs. Pacific Power & Light Co., 1974-91, PacifiCorp., 1984-91, Boyce Thompson Inst. for Plant Rsch., 1975-93, Boyce Thompson Southwestern Arboretum, 1981-92, Oreg. Grad. Inst., 1987-94; mem. adv. com. Directorate for Engring. and Applied Sci., NSF, 1977-81; mem. sea grant adv. panel, 1978-80; mem. policy adv. com. Office of Grants, USDA, 1985-86. Trustee Ithaca Coll., 1982-89. Lt. USNR, 1943-46. Recipient Disting. Svc. award Oreg. State U., 1978. Fellow AAAS (exec. com. Pacific div. 1963-67, pres. div. 1971), Am. Phytopathology Soc. (pres. Pacific div. 1957, chmn. spl. com. to develop plans for endowment 1984-86, bd. dirs. 1986-88); mem. Oreg. Acad. Sci., Nat. Assn. State Univs. and Land Grant Colls. (chmn. coun. for rsch. policy and adminstrn. 1970, chmn. standing com. on environment and energy 1974-82, chmn. com. on environment 1984-86), Sigma Xi, Phi Kappa Phi, Phi Sigma, Sigma Alpha Epsilon. Home: 3605 NW Van Buren Ave Corvallis OR 97330-4950

YOUNG, RUSSELL DAWSON, physics consultant; b. Huntington, N.Y., Aug. 17, 1923; s. C. Halsey and Edna (Dawson) Y.; m. Carol Vaughn Jones, Aug. 14, 1954; children: Bessmarie, Gale, Janet, Shari. BS in Physics, Rensselaer Poly. Inst., Troy, N.Y., 1953; PhD in Physics, Pa. State U., 1959. Rsch. assoc. Pa. State U., State College, 1959-61; project leader Nat. Bur. Stds., Gaithersburg, Md., 1961-73, chief optics and micrometrology, 1973-78, chief mech. processing div., 1975-80, ind. sys. div. chief, 1980-81, chief mech. prodn. div., 1980-81; pres. R.D. Young Cons., Pasadena, Md., 1981—. Contbr. articles to profl. jours.; inventor in field of instrumentation. 1st lt. Signal Corps, U.S. Army, 1943-46. Recipient Edward V. Condon award Dept. Commerce, 1974, Silver medal 1979, Gaede-Langmuir award 1994, Presdl. citation 1986, Washington Acad. Scis. award 1988. Fellow Internat. Inst. Prodn. Engring. Rsch., Nat. Inst. Standards and Tech. Avocation: boating. Home: 852 Riverside Dr Pasadena MD 21122-1730 E-mail: cryoung@aol.com.

YOUNG, RUTH BROOKS, retired elementary education educator; b. Balt., Aug. 30, 1933; d. Benjamin Franklin and Ora Estelle Brooks; m. David Donald Young Sr., 1952; children: David Donald Jr. (dec.), Gerard Brooks Sr., Mark Douglas (dec.), Elizabeth Allyson Mack. BS, Coppin State Tchrs. Coll., 1958; MS, Morgan State Coll., 1975. Cert. tchr., Md. Tchr. Balt. City Pub. Schs., 1958-98, supervising tchr., 1968-72, sch. test coord., 1990-96; ret., 1998. Mem. Phi Delta Kappa. Democrat. Lutheran.

YOUNG, SCOTT THOMAS, business management educator; b. Oak Park, Ill., Dec. 28, 1949; s. Thomas Menzies and Grace (Butler) Y.; children: Reginald, Galen; m. Luciana Pagotto. BA, U. Ga., 1974; MBA, Ga. Coll., 1982; PhD, Ga. State U., 1987. Prof. U. Utah, Salt Lake City, 1987—, chmn. mgmt. dept., 1994-97, assoc. dean David Eccles Sch. Bus., 1997-99; prof. and chair dept. mgmt. DePaul U., Chgo., 2003—. Mgmt. cons. to numerous orgns.; lectr., speaker, cons. on ops., quality and project mgmt. Author: Managing Global Operations; contbr. numerous articles to profl. jours. With U.S. Army, 1971-73. Decorated Commendation medal; grantee Nat. Assn. Purchasing Mgmt., 1986. Mem. Decision Sci. Inst., Acad. Mgmt., Prodn. and Ops. Mgmt. Soc. Avocation: marathon running. Office: DePaul U Coll Commerce 1 E Jackson Blvd Chicago IL 60604 E-mail: syoung16@depaul.edu.

YOUNG, SEAN (MARY SEAN YOUNG), actress; b. Louisville, Ky., Nov. 20, 1959; Appeared in films: Jane Austen in Manhattan, 1980, Stripes, 1981, Blade Runner, 1982, Young Doctors in Love, 1982, Dune, 1984, Baby-Secret of Lost Legend, 1985, Blood and Orchids, 1986, No Way Out, 1987, Wall Street, 1987, The Boost, 1988, Cousins, 1989, Fire Birds, 1990, A Kiss Before Dying, 1991, Once Upon a Crime, 1992, Love Crimes, 1992, Fatal Instinct, 1993, Ace Ventura Pet Detective, 1994, Witness to the Execution, 1994, Even Cowgirls Get the Blues, 1994, Blue Ice, 1994, Dr. Jekyll and Ms. Hyde, 1995, Mirage, 1995, The Proprietor, 1996, Motel Blue, 1997, Exception to the Rule, 1997, The Invader, 1997, Men, 1997, Out of Control, 1998, Special Delivery, 1999, In the Shadow of the Cobra, 2001, Before I Say Goodbye, 2003.

YOUNG, SHELDON MIKE, lawyer, author; b. Cleve., Aug. 27, 1926; s. Jack and Ray Y.; m. Margery Ann Polster, Dec. 25, 1948 (div. 1988); children: Jeffrey, Martin, Janet; m. Bette Abel Roth, Nov. 11, 1988. BA, Ohio State U., 1948, JD, 1951; LLM, Case Western Res. U., 1962. Bar: Ohio 1951, U.S. Dist. Ct. (no. dist.) Ohio. Gen. counsel Eugene M. Klein & Assocs., Actuaries, Cleve., 1952-72; assoc. Shapiro, Persky & Marken, Cleve., 1972-74; counsel pension tech. svcs. dept. CNA Ins., Chgo., 1974-76; ptnr. Weiss & Young, Cleve., 1976; of counsel Arter & Hadden, Cleve., 1977-85, Squire, Sanders & Dempsey, Cleve., 1985-87; pvt. practice Columbus, 1987-91; of counsel Schwartz, Kelm, Warren & Rubenstein, Columbus, 1991—93, Walter & Haverfield, Columbus, 1993—. Instr. Case Western Res. U. Law Sch., 1962-82, 85, U. Akron Law Sch., 1984, 88. Author: Pension and Profit Sharing Plans, 7 vols., 1977-93, (novel) Toledoth-City of Generations, 2003; freelance writer for newspapers and mags.; contbr. articles to profl. jours. Served with USN, WWII. Recipient award Nathan Burkan Meml. Copyright Competition, 1951. Fellow Am. Coll. Employee Benefits Counsels (charter); mem. ABA (chair obsolete pension rev. rule taskforce), Cleve. Bar Assn., Columbus Bar Assn., Masons. Jewish. Home and Office: Walter Haverfield 4776 Smoketalk Ln Westerville OH 43081-7838 Office Phone: 614-898-1096. Office Fax: 614-898-7190. Business E-Mail: yomike@asacomp.com.

YOUNG, STEPHEN K. academic administrator; DDS, U. Mo., 1971; MS in oral pathology, U. Mich., 1974. Diplomate Am. Bd. Oral Pathology. Asst. prof., oral and maxillofacial surgery U. Okla. Coll. Dentistry, David Ross Boyd prof., adj. prof., pathology, assoc. dean, dean, 1999—. Contbr. articles to profl. jours. Chair Nat. Cancer Inst.'s Ad Hoc Cancer Edn. Grant Review Com. Recipient President award, Okla. Dental Assn., 1988. Office: 1001 Stanton L Young Blvd Rm 507 Oklahoma City OK 73190*

YOUNG, STEVE, correspondent, anchor; Grad., Emerson Coll., 1962. Sr. tech. corr. CBS News; with CNN, 1987—; anchor Tech Talk CNN Fin. News, N.Y.C., reporter The Moneyline Newshour, reporter Moneyweek. Adj. faculty Grad. Sch. Journalism, Columbia U., 1969-73. Co-author: (textbook) Broadcast Writing, Editing and Reporting. Co-recipient George Foster Peabody award, 1987; recipient Best TV Bus. Reporting From Abroad award, Overseas Press Club, 1995. Office: CNN 5 Penn Plz Fl 20 New York NY 10001-1810

YOUNG, STEVE G. former labor union administrator; Student, Berklee Coll. Music. Pres. Local 9-535, Boston, 1987; mem. exec. bd. Am. Fedn. Musicians U.S. and Can., 1989-91, v.p., 1991-95, pres., 1995—2001. Mem. faculty Berklee Coll. Music, Boston. Plays bassoon, sax, clarinet, flute; performed with Boston Ballet, Opera Co. Boston, Boston Symphony and Pops; performer Marlboro Music Festival.

YOUNG, STEVEN, former professional football player; b. Salt Lake City, Oct. 11, 1961; JD, Brigham Young, 1993. With L.A. Express, USFL, 1984—85, Tampa Bay Buccaneers, 1985—87; quarterback San Francisco 49ers, 1987—2000; panelist ESPN Sunday NFL Countdown, 2001—. Founder, mgr. Forever Young Found. benefitting Bay Area and Utah youth-oriented charities, 1993—. Named MVP, NFL, 1992, Player of Yr., 1994, All-Am. team quarterback, The Sporting News, 1983, Top-rated quarterback, NFL, 1991, NFL MVP, The Sporting News, 1992, NFL All-Pro team quarterback, 1992, Bay Area Sports Hall of Fame Profl. Athlete of Yr., 1992, Superbowl MVP, 1994; recipient Davey O'Brien award, 1983. Achievements include played in Pro Bowl, 1992, 93; highest rate passer NFL, 1991-93. Mailing: Forever Young Foundation PO Box 527 Park City UT 84060

YOUNG, SUSAN BABSON, retired library director; b. Boston, June 22, 1939; d. David Leaveau and Katherine Lockhart (Allen) Babson; m. Thomas Herbert Young III, June 17, 1961; children: Thomas Herbert IV, Nathaniel Allen. BA, Vassar Coll., 1961; MLS, SUNY, Albany, 1983. Cert. sch. media specialist, Mass. English and history tchr. St. Anthony's H.S., Long Beach, Calif., 1962-63; asst. dir. Geier Libr. Berkshire Sch., Sheffield, Mass., 1968-72, dir., 1972-95; ret., 1995. Contbr. articles to profl. jours. Chair Friends of the Bushnell-Sage Meml. Libr. Capital Fund, Sheffield, Mass., 1995—, trustee, 1994—; mem. Arts Coun., Sheffield, 1983-90, 95-2000; mem. So. Berkshire Regional Sch. Com., 1998-2004. Mem. Am. Needlepoint Guild (1st pl. Nat. Exhibit award 1980, 85, 2d Internat. Exhibit award 1982), Embroiders Guild Am., Sheffield Garden Club (pres. 1996-98), Phi Beta Mu. Republican. Home: 321 Boardman St Sheffield MA 01257-9515 E-mail: syoung@campram.com.

YOUNG, SUSAN JEAN, music specialist; b. Chgo., Nov. 9, 1940; d. Walter Lawrence and Grace Helen (Blue) Pennie; m. Peter R. Young Jr., June 23, 1962; children: Laura Jane, Beth Ann. B.Mus.Ed (scholar), Northwestern U., 1962; M.Mus.ED (grad.scholar), Am. Conservatory of Music, Chgo., 1974; cert. advanced study in gen. adminstrn., Nat.-Louis U., 1995. Music specialist Skokie (Ill.) Sch. Dist., 1962-63, Northbrook (Ill.) Sch. Dist. # 28, 1974—. Lectr. music edn. North Park Coll., 1995-96, Northwestern U., 1997—; pvt. piano tchr., 1963-74; pres. Stevenson High Choral Guild, 1979-81; music dir., choir dir. Wheeling Community Ch., 1981-93; choir dir. Ivanhoe United Ch. of Christ, 1995-96; dir. Y'all Come Choir, 1991—; music dir. Northbrook Children's Theatre, 1981-88, Glenview Community Theatre, Northbrook Community Theatre. Mem. ASCD, Music Educators Nat. Conf., Ill. Music Educators Assn. (chmn. Jr. High Choral Fest 1987-90, Mary E. Hoffman award for tchg. excellence 2003), Music Tchrs. Nat. Assn., Ill. Music Tchrs. Assn., Nat. Registered Music Educator, Am. Choral Dirs. Assn., Soc. Am. Musicians, Delta Kappa Gamma (pres. Beta Tau chpt. 1992-96, Ill. State music chmn. 1995-99, internat. music rep. 2002—), Mu Phi Epsilon, NICE, ISTE. Home: 3161 N Southern Hills Dr Wadsworth IL 60083-9289 Office: 1475 Maple Ave Northbrook IL 60062-5418

YOUNG, TERESA GAIL HILGER, retired adult education educator; b. Modesto, Calif., Mar. 4, 1948; d. Richard George and Jessie Dennie (Dennis) Long; m. Charles Ray Young, June 22, 1974; 1 child, Gregory Paul. BS in Edn., Abilene (Tex.) Christian U., 1970; MEd in Curriculum, Tarleton State U., Stephenville, Tex., 1976; postgrad., Tex. Tech U., 1990-92. Cert. supr., mid-mgmt., supt., Tex. Tchr. sci. Tex. Youth Coun., Gatesville, 1970-73, Gatesville Ind. Sch. Dist., 1973-81; coord. Edn. and Tng. Ctr., Cen. Tex. Coll., Gatesville, 1983; tchr. Tex. Dept. of Criminal Justice-ID, 1984—2002; ret., 2003. Conf. presenter. Trustee Jonesboro (Tex.) Ind. Sch. Dist., 1988-96. Teacher of the Year for Region II of Tex. Dept. of Criminal Justice, 1997-98. Mem. Am. Fedn. Tchrs., Assn. Tex. Profl. Educators. E-mail: tyoung@htcomp.net.

YOUNG, TERRI L. ophthalmologist; b. Sacramento, 1959; AB in Biochemistry and Sociology, Bowdoin Coll., Brunswick, Maine, 1981; MD in Medicine, Harvard U., 1986. Postdoctoral in pediat. Children's Hosp. Boston, 1986—87; resident in ophthalmology U. Ill., Chgo., 1987—90; clin. instr. ophthalmology U. Ill. Sch. Medicine, Chgo., 1989—90; extern in strabismus and adult motility disorders U. Iowa, 1991; fellow in pediatric ophthalmology, strabismus and adult motility disorders U. Pa. and Children's Hosp. Phila., 1990—92; clin. instr. opthalmology U. Pa., 1990—92; instr. neurobiology and ophthalmology Harvard Med. Sch., 1992—94; asst. prof. ophthalmology U. Minn., 1994—2000, asst. prof. pediat., 1998—2000, assoc. prof. pediat., 2000; dir.Ophthalmic Genetics Rsch. Ctr., Children's Hosp. Phila., 2000—; assoc. prof. ophthalmology and pediat. U. Pa., 2001—. Recipient Surdna Undergrad. Rsch. fellowship, Bowdoin Coll., 1980—81, Stanley J. Sarnoff Soc. Cardiovascular Rsch. award and fellowship, Harvard Med. Sch., 1983—84, Commonwealth Fund Rsch. fellowship, 1985, George and Mary Knox Harvaard Med. Grad. award, 1984, Grad. Kaiser Merit award, Nat. Med. Fellowship, 1986, Keeshin Prize Rsch. award, Inst. Medicine Chgo., 1990, Honor award, Am. Acad. Ophthalmology, 1998, Robert Wood Johnson Faculty Devel. award, 1992—97, Honor award, Am. Acad. Ophthalmology, 1998, Am. Assn. Pediatric Ophthalmology and Strabismus, 2002; selected as part of, NIH's "Changing the Face of Medicine" exhbn., 2003. Office: Childrens Hosp of Phila 34th St and Civic Ctr Blvd Philadelphia PA 19104-4399

YOUNG, TOMMIE MORTON, social psychology educator, writer; b. Nashville; BA cum laude, Tenn. State U., 1951; MA, Vanderbilt U., 1955; PhD, Duke U., 1977; postgrad., U. Okla., 1967, U. Nebr., 1968. Coord. Young Adult Program Lucy Thurman br. YWCA, 1951-52; instr. edn. Tenn. State U., Nashville, 1956-59; instr. coord. media program Prairie View Coll. (Tex.), 1959-61; asst. prof. edn., assoc. prof. English, dir. IMC Ctr. U. Ark., Pine Bluff, 1965-69; asst. prof. English and edn., dir. learning lab N.C. Central U., Durham, 1969-74; prof., dir./chairperson libr. /dir. Afro-Am. Family Project, prof. philosophy sociol. found. N.C. Agrl. and Tech. State U., Greensboro, 1975—92; adj. prof. langs., lit. and philosophy, dir. schs. history project Tenn. State U., Nashville, 1994—. Dir. workshops, grants; pres., dir. Ednl. Cons. Svcs.; owner Historic Black Nashville Tours. Author: Afro-Am. Genealogy Sourcebook, 1987, Oral Histories of Former All-Black Public Schs., 1991, After School Program for At-Risk Youth and Their Families, 1997, Sable Scenes, 1996, Genealogist's Guide to Discovering Your African Ancestors, 1997, A Sister Speaks, 1998, Nashville, Tennessee, 2000; contbr. poem to Poetry: American Heritage; contbr. rsch. papers, articles to profl. jours. Nat. chmn. Com. to Re-Elect the Pres.; past sec. Fedn. Colored Women's Clubs; bd. dirs. Southwestern div. ARC, Nashville area, 1994-, dir. Volun-Teens; chairperson schs. div. Durham County Unit Am. Cancer Soc.; past mem. adv. bd., bd. dirs. YMCA, Atlanta; chair Guilford County Commn. on Needs of Children; bd. advisors NIH, N.C. Coun. of the Arts; mem. Guilford County Involvement Coun.; chmn. N.C. adv. com. U.S. Civil Rights Com.; mem. exec. planning com. Greensboro; hon. staff mem. 54th Legis. Dist., Nashville, 1996; pres. Davidson County Dem. Women, 2003-04; rep. dist. I exec. com. Davidson County Dem. Party; chair resolutions com. Nat. Fedn. Dem. Women. Recipient awards ARC, 1968, 73, NAACP, 1973, HEW, 1978, U.S. Commn. on Civil Rights, 1982, cert. of Accomplishement Contributing to Youth Devel. Bus. and Profl. Women, 2000; named Disting. Alumni Tenn. State U., 1994. Mem. AAUW (honor award 1983, pres. Greensboro br., chairperson internat. rels. com.), ALA (divsn. coll. and rsch. librs., past chair), NAACP (life, 1st v.p. Durahm br., exec. bd. Greensboro br. dir. parent edn./child advocacy program, Woman of Yr. 1992), NEA, LWV (bd. dirs. Nashville), Assn. Childhood Ednl. Internat., Comperative and Internat. Edn. Assn., Archives Assoc., Internat. Platform Assn., Nat. Hist. Soc., Greenboro Jr. League (community adv. bd. 1991—), African Am. Gen. Soc. Tenn. (founder

1994), Zeta Phi Beta (chairperson polit. action com. eastern region, nat. grammateus, Polit. and Civic Svc. award 1974, Outstanding Social-Polit. Svc. award 1982, Woman of Yr. 1977), Comm. on Status of Women (Woman of Achievement 1991), Phi Kappa Phi (Disting. Alumni award Tenn. State U. 1994, Disting. Alumni NAFEO award, 1995, Carl Rowan-Oprah Winfrey lectr. Tenn. State U., 1995, Excellence in Journlism award SPJ, 1995, Tenn. Outstanding Achievement award, 1997), 100 Black Women, Steering Com., Tenn. Trust for Historic Preservation, 1999 (named Woman of Distinction Top Ladies, 2001). Home: PO Box 281613 Nashville TN 37228-8506

YOUNG, TZAY Y. electrical and computer engineering educator; b. Shanghai, Jan. 11, 1933; came to U.S., 1958; s. Chao-Hsiung and Chiu-Ming (Chu) Y.; m. Lily Liu, Dec. 27, 1965; children: Debbie Chia-Pei, Arthur Chia-Kai. BS, Nat. Taiwan U., Taipei, 1955; MS, U. Vt., 1959; DEng, Johns Hopkins U., 1962. Rsch. assoc. Johns Hopkins U., Balt., 1962-63; mem. tech. staff Bell Labs., Murray Hill, N.J., 1963-64; asst. prof. Carnegie-Mellon U., Pitts., 1964-68, assoc. prof., 1968-74; prof. elec. and computer engrng. U. Miami, Coral Gables, Fla., 1974—2003, acting chmn. dept., 1988-91, chmn. dept., 1991-2000, prof. emeritus, 2004—. Sr. postdoctoral rsch. assoc. NAS, NASA, Goddard Space Flight Ctr., Md., 1972-73. Author: (with T.W. Calvert) Classification, Estimation and Pattern Recognition, 1974; editor; (with K.S. Fu) Handbook of Pattern Recognition and Image Processing, 1986; editor: Handbook of Pattern Recognition and Image Processing, vol. 2, Computer Vision, 1994; also numerous articles. Rsch. grantee NSF, NASA, FHTIC, also indsl. grants. Fellow IEEE (assoc. editor Trans. Computers 1974-76; editorial bd. Trans. Pattern Analysis and Machine Intelligence 1979-84, adv. bd. 1984-90); mem. Sigma Xi, Eta Kappa Nu, Omicron Delta Kappa. Office: U Miami Dept Elec & Computer Engring Coral Gables FL 33124 E-mail: tyoung@miami.edu.

YOUNG, VERA LEE HALL, educational administrator, association executive; b. Natchitoches, La., Jan. 9, 1944; d. Sidney and Gertrude (Bell) H.; m. Willie L. Young, Aug. 21, 1965 (div. June 1971). BS, Grambling State U., 1967; MS, Bank St. Coll., 1977; PhD with distinction, Century U., 1985. Cert. tchr., La., N.J., N.Y. Ednl. cons. family day care program N.Y.C. Community Sch. Dist. 6; ednl. dir. Leslie Freeman Daycare Ctr., Bklyn., 1973-74; tchr. West N.Y. Bd. of Edn., 1978—; exec. dir., founder Operation Super Inst., Ft. Lee, N.J., 1986—. Lectr., tchr., panelist and cons. in field; participant Statewide Child Care Adv. Coun. Conf., N.J., 1980, State Ill. Tchrs. Conf., 1987, U. S.C. Tchrs. Conf., Georgetown, 1989; discussant Speaking for Schools radio program, N.J., N.Y.; program developer N.Y. Pub. Schs., 1996; del. 24th Internat. Congree Arts and Comms., 1997; instr. Funda C.C., Soweto, South Africa, 1998. Author: A Day Care Solution in America: The Learning Center, 1985; contbr. articles to field. Recipient Internat. Order of Merit award (# 320 of 500 world-wide), Internat. Biog. Ctr., Cambridge, Eng.; named Educator or Yr., Black Achievement and Awards, 1988; Dept. Labor grantee, Jerusalem, 1982-83 Mem. NEA, Nat. Alliance Bus., N.J. Edn. Assn. (conf. participant 1987), N.J. Women Bus. Ownership Orgn., Internat. Platform Assn., Internat. Reading Assn., Minority & Women Owned Bus. N.Y., Bank St. Coll. Alumni Assn., Gambling Coll. Alumni Assn. Mem. Dutch Reform Ch. Avocations: reading, travel, sports. Office: Operation Super 229 Main St # 1834 Fort Lee NJ 07024-5709

YOUNG, VERNON LEWIS, lawyer; b. Seaman, Ohio, Oct. 13, 1919; s. Ezra S. and Anna (Bloom) Y.; m. Eileen Humble, Sept. 20, 1941; children: Robert, Loretta, Bettie Jo, Jon W., Denise L. Student, Alfred Holbrook Coll., 1938-39; JD, Ohio No. U., 1942. Bar: Ohio 1942. Employee War Dept., 1942; sole practice West Union, Ohio, 1942-50, 78-81; ptnr. Young & Young, West Union, 1959-78, Young & Caldwell, 1978—81, 1995—2003, Young-Caldwell & BUBP, West Union, 1981-95. Spl. counsel Office of Atty. Gen., State of Ohio, West Union, solicitor Cities of Jamestown, Seaman, Winchester, Manchester, Ohio; pros. atty. Adams County, Ohio, 1952-56, acting county judge, 1968-79. Mayor City of Seaman, 1944-46; mem. Adams County Health Bd., West Union, 1968-75; chmn. membership com. Eastern Shore Inst. Lifelong Learning, Fairhope, Ala., 1983-84; mem. Rep. Presdl. Task Force, 1980-94. Mem.: Adams County Bar Assn. (former pres.), Jr. Bar (pres. Ohio No. U. 1941—42), Ohio State Bar Assn., Ohio No. Univ., Lions (pres. 1950—51, dist. gov. 1951—52), Masons (32 degrees), Sigma Delta Kappa (chancellor 1940). Avocations: fishing, hunting, gardening. Home: 10 Hickory Dr Seaman OH 45679-9762

YOUNG, VICTORIA E. occupational health nurse, lawyer; b. Concord, Mich., Apr. 20, 1933; d. Arthur Raymond and Edith Louise (Hands) Y. Diploma, Mercy Sch. Nursing, Jackson, Mich., 1954; JD, U. West Los Angeles, Culver City, Calif., 1973; BSN, UCLA, 1960, MPH in Adminstrn., 1966. Bar: Calif., U.S. Dist. Ct., Calif.; RN, Calif.; cert. pub. health nurse, pediatric nurse practitioner. Pub. health nurse L.A. City and Los Angeles County Health Dept.; exec. dir. Santa Monica (Calif.) Vis. Nurse Assn.; sch. nurse practitioner L.A. Unified Schs.; relief nurse L.A. Times. Vol. Moorpark City Hall, Moorpark Sr. Ctr; mem. Disaster Assistance Response Team, Moorpark. Ret. capt. USNR, Desert Storm. Mem. Nat. Assn. Pediatric Nurse Assocs. and Practitioners, Calif. Bar Assn., Fleet Res. Assn., Moorpark Woman's Fortnightly Club (treas. 1998-99). Home: 4359 Brookdale Ln Moorpark CA 93021-2302

YOUNG, VIRGIL MONROE, education educator; b. Santa Rosa, Calif., Sept. 24, 1936; s. Virgil M. and Vesta May (Huyett) Williams; stepson Louis H. Young; m. Katherine Ann Young, Dec. 20, 1964; 1 child, Susan Annette. BS, U. Idaho, 1958, EdD, 1967. Cert. advanced secondary edn. educator, sch. supt., Idaho. Tchr. Moscow (Idaho) Sch. Dist., 1959-63; adminstrv. asst. to supt. Coeur d'Alene (Idaho) Sch. Dist., 1965-67; prof. edn. Boise (Idaho) State U., 1967-96, head dept. edn., 1989-96, prof. emeritus, 1996—. Author: (elem. textbook) The Story of Idaho, 4 edits.; co-author: The Story of the Idaho Guide and Resource Book, 1993; author: (with others) Year 2000 Grolier Multimedia Encyclopedia, 2000; designer, author ednl. Internet websites, 1999—. Capt. USAR. Mem. N.W. Assn. Tchr. Educators (past pres.), Idaho Assn. Colls. Tchr. Edn. (past pres.), Phi Delta Kappa (past pres.).

YOUNG, WILLIAM BENJAMIN, retired special education educator; b. Wichita, Kans., Jan. 30, 1929; s. Ernest William and Florence Belle (McCann) Y.; m. La Vona P., Feb., 1949 (div. 1973); children: Lynda, David, Timothy; m. Patricia Sue Reber, Aug., 1974. Student, Southwestern Coll., Winfield, Kans., 1947-48; B in Gen. Edn., U. Omaha, 1961; MS in Pers. Counseling, Miami U., Oxford, Ohio, 1965; PhD in Exceptional Edn., Adminstrn. and Counseling, Ohio State U., 1972. Cert. elem. and secondary adminstr., tchr., counselor, psychologist, psychometrist, spl. edn., mental retardation, learning disabled/behavior disordered, emotionally handicapped, Ind.; cert. K-12 guidance counselor and edn. leadership, Fla.; lic sexologist, flight instr.; lic. Coast Guard capt. Enlisted USAF, 1948, commd. 2nd lt., 1955, advanced through grades to capt., 1960, ret., 1966; numerous teaching and counseling positions as civilian, 1966-91; co-owner, instr. Ft. Wayne (Ind.) Ground Schs., 1984-88; marriage and family counselor, pvt. practice, 1966-91; tchr., counselor, behavior specialist Broward County Schs., Ft. Lauderdale, Fla., 1989-99; ret., 1999. Cons., internat. presenter/lectr. learning and behavior problems. Vol. instr. AARP Safe Driving Course; vol. support group leader for dementia caregivers support. Mem. ACA, Coun. for Exceptional Children, Coun. Behavior Disorders, Fla. Counseling Assn., 32 degree Masons. Avocations: travel, golf, swimming. Home and Office: 1101 SW 70th Ter Plantation FL 33317-4135 E-mail: wby130@aol.com.

YOUNG, WILLIAM F. legal educator; b. 1925; BA, U. Tex., 1947, LLB, 1949. Bar: Tex. 1949. Grad. fellow Harvard U., 1951-52; prof. U. Tex., 1949-56, Columbia U., 1956-95, emeritus, 1996—. Mem. Am. Law Inst., Order of Coif. Office: Columbia U Sch Law 435 W 116th St New York NY 10027-7201

YOUNG, WILLIAM GLOVER, federal judge; b. Huntington, NY, Sept. 23, 1940; s. Woodhull Benjamin and Margaret Jean (Wilkes) Y.; m. Beverly June Bigelow, Aug. 5, 1967; children: Mark Edward, Jeffrey Woodhull, Todd Russell. AB, Harvard U., 1962, LLB, 1967; LLD, New Eng. Sch. Law, 2001. Bar: Mass. 1967, U.S. Supreme Ct. 1970. Law clk. to chief justice Supreme Jud. Ct., Mass., 1967-68; spl. asst. atty. gen. Mass., 1969-72; chief legal counsel to gov., 1972-74; asso. firm Bingham, Dana and Gould, Boston, 1968-72, ptnr., 1975-78; assoc. justice Superior Ct., Commonwealth of Mass., Boston, 1978-85; judge U.S. Dist. Ct. Mass., Boston, 1985-99, chief judge, 1999 . Mem. budget com., 1987-2001, chmn. economy subcom., 1991-2001; lectr. part time Boston Coll. Law Sch., 1968-90, Boston U. Law Sch., 1979—, Harvard Law Sch., 1979—1990. Served to capt. U.S. Army, 1962-64. Mem. Am. Law Inst., Mass. Bar Assn., Boston Bar Assn., Harvard Alumni (pres. 1976-77) Office: US Courthouse Rm 5710 Boston MA 02210 Office Phone: 617-748-9138. Personal E-mail: bjbg2y3@earthlink.net. Business E-Mail: william_young@mad.uscourts.gov.

YOUNG, WILLIAM H. labor union administrator; b. 1947; m. Debbie Young; 3 children. Local branch pres. Nat. Assn. Letter Carriers, 1971—78, regional adminstrv. asst., 1978—86, nat. bus. agent San Francisco region, 1986—90, asst. sec.-treas., 1990—94, v.p., 1994—98, exec. v.p., 1998—2002, nat. pres., 2002—. Officer Calif. State Assn., 1972—; v.p. Am. Fedn. Labor, Coun. Indsl. Orgn. (AFL-CIO). Nat. v.p. Muscular Dystrophy Assn. (MDA); mem. adv. bd. Walter P. Reuther Libr. Labor and Urban Affairs, Wayne State U., Detroit. Office: Nat Assn Letter Carriers 100 Ind Ave NW Washington DC 20001-2144 Office Phone: 202-393-4695.

YOUNG, WILLIAM SHERBAN, investment broker; b. Augusta, Maine, Sept. 19, 1947; m. Jeanne Aschenbrenner, June 20, 1970; 1 child, Stephan Sherban. BA, U. Balt., 1974; MA, Morgan U., 1982. Cert. fin. planner. Account exec. Md. Nat. Bank, Balt., 1974-76; div. mgr. Jefferson-Pilot Co., Balt., 1976-81; ptnr. Stewart-Young & Assocs., Balt., 1981-83; dir. equity dept. First Fin. Group, Balt., 1983 . Bd. dirs. Balt. Choral Arts, 1990. With U.S. Army, 1965-68. Mem. Inst. Cert. Fin. Planners, Am. Jujitsu Assn., Balt. Coun. on Fgn. Rels. Republican. Avocations: chess, black belt jujitsu. Office: 401 Washington Ave Ste 6 Towson MD 21204-4821 E-mail: wyoung@glic.com.

YOUNG, WILLIAM WEBB, military officer, poet; b. St. Louis, Aug. 4, 1962; s. Raymond Andrew and Betty Rosella (Myers) Young; children: Jamie Elizabeth, Christen Lee, Sara Rayan. Commd. ensign USN, 1987; Gulf War/Cold War vet. Svc. officer Three Rivers Serenity Group, Poplar Bluff, Mo., 1989—2002; dist. 8 spl. needs com. chmn. S.E. Mo. AA, Poplar Bluff, Mo., 2001—. Author numerous poems. Local stream team coord. Mo. Dept. Conservation, Butler County, Mo., 1997—2002, frontiers program leader, 1998—2002; water quality monitoring vol. Mo. Dept. Natural Resources, Butler County, Mo., 1999—2002. Decorated Order of the Spanish Main, numerous medals; recipient Iliad Lit. award, Internat. Poet of Merit, 1996, Editors Choice award, 1996, Americanism award, Grande Voiture of N.J. Navy, 1990, Loyalty Day award, VFW, 1990, Battle "E" Award Persian Excursion, 1991. Fellow: K.C. (1st degree crusader, Altar Server award 1981); mem.: Internat. Soc. Poets, Disabled Am. Vets. (life Golden Anchor award 1988), Amherst Soc., Iraqi Desert Yacht Club, Gulf of Oman Yacht Club, Gulf of Sidra Yacht Club, Persian Gulf Yacht Club, Persian Gulf Health Club (life; adminstr.), Am. Legion (honor guard). Roman Catholic. Avocation: art. Home: 201 W Lexington Ave Poplar Bluff MO 63901

YOUNGBERG, CHARLOTTE ANNE, education specialist, clergywoman; b. Hampton, Iowa, May 8, 1937; d. Sebo and Marion Bradford (Boutin-Clock) Reysack; m. Paul Gordon Neal, Mar. 29, 1969 (div. Jan. 1984); children: Rachel Elizabeth, Kory Bradford; m. Lyle Edwin Youngberg, June 30, 1990; stepchildren: Lynn Eugene, Lori Ann. BA, U. No. Iowa, 1958; MEd, DePaul U., 1966; postgrad., No. Ill. U.; DD in Christian Counseling, Christian Bible Coll. and Sem., Independence, Mo., 2000, DD in Theology, 2003. Cert. K-14 tchr. and supr. in guidance, counseling, elem. supervising, K-9 elem. tchr., spl. K-12 learning disabilities. Elem. tchr. Des Moines Ind. Sch. Dist., 1958-59, Glenview (Ill.) Pub. Schs., 1959-61; elem. tchr., psychol. ednl. diagnostician Schaumburg Dist. Schs., Hoffman Estates, Ill., 1961-69; supr. learning disabilities and behavior disorders Springfield (Ill.) Pub. Schs., 1969-73; psycho-ednl. diagnostician Barrington (Ill.) Sch. Dist. 220, 1973-77; ednl. strategist Area Edn. Agy. 7, Cedar Falls, Iowa, 1978-90; tchr. spl. edn., testing evaluator Verona (Mo.) Pub. Schs., 1990—2004, dir. spl. edn., 1992—95. Ednl. cons. Spl. Edn. Dist. Lake County, Gurnee, Ill., summer 1968. Mem. Mo. Tchrs. Assn., Phi Delta Kappa. Home: PO Box 147 Verona MO 65769-0147

YOUNGBLOOD, BETTY J. academic administrator; b. Detroit; m. Ralph P. Youngblood; 1 child. BA in Political Sci., Oakland U., Rochester, Mich.; MA in South Asian Studies, PhD in Political Sci., U. Minn. Formerly mem. faculty State U. West Ga., Tex. Tech. U.; various adminstrv. positions Kennesaw State U., Marietta, Ga.; v.p. acad. affairs MacMurray Coll., Jacksonville, Ill., Wesley Coll., Dover, Del.; vice chancellor acad. affairs, dean faculty, prof. polit. sci. U. Wis.-Superior, 1990-91, acting chancellor, 1991-92, chancellor, 1992—95; pres. We. Oreg. U., 1995—2002, Lake Superior State U., Mich., 2002—. Cons., evaluator North Ctrl. Assn. Colls. and Schs. Contbr. articles to profl. jours. Bd. dirs. United Way, Sault Ste. Marie. Rsch. grantee for study in N.W. India. Mem. Sault Ste. Marie C. of C., War Meml. Hosp., Rotary. Office: Lake Superior State Univ 650 W Easterday Ave Sault Sainte Marie MI 49783

YOUNGBLOOD, DAISY, ceramist; b. Asheville, NC; Student, Va. Commonwealth U., 1963—66. Exhibitions include, N.Y.C., San Francisco, Calif., Milian, Italy, Represented in permanent collections, Toledo Mus. of Art. Grantee fellow, MacArthur Found., 2003.

YOUNGBLOOD, DEBORAH SUE, lawyer, speech pathology/audiology services professional; b. Fairview, Okla., July 29, 1954; d. G. Dean and Beatrice J. (Hiebert) White. BS with honors, Okla. State U., 1976, MA with honors, 1979; JD cum laude, Boston Coll. Law Sch., 1991; MPH in Health Care Mgmt., Harvard U., 1992. Bar: Colo., U.S. Ct. Appeals (10th cir.). Jud. law clk. Colo. Supreme Ct., 1992-94; assoc. atty. Patton Boggs, L.L.P., Denver, 1994—97; sr. assoc. atty. Vaglica & Meinhold, L.L.C., Colorado Springs, 1997-99; pvt. practice speech-lang. pathologist North Conway, NH, 1999—2001, Sun Valley, Idaho, 2001—. Mem. leadership coun. Harvard Sch. Pub. Health, 2003—. Mem. leadership coun. Harvard Sch. Pub. Health, 2003—. Recipient LEXIS Legal Rsch. and Writing Award, Boston Coll. Law Sch. Mem.: Harvard Sch. Pub. Health Leadership (coun. 2003—), Minoru Yasui Am. Inns of Ct. (exec. coun. 1995—97), Colo. Bar Assn., Sun Valley Edn. Found. (bd. dirs.), Phi Kappa Phi. Office: 118 W Bullion St Hailey ID 83333 E-mail: youngblood@peoplepc.com.

YOUNGBLOOD, ELAINE MICHELE, lawyer; b. Schenectady, NY, Jan. 9, 1944; d. Roy W. and Mary Louise (Read) Ortoleva; m. William Gerald Youngblood, Feb. 14, 1970; children: Flagg Khristian, Megan Michele. BA, Wake Forest Coll., 1965; JD, Albany Law Sch., 1969. Bar: Tex. 1970, Tenn. 1978, U.S. Dist. Ct. (no. dist.) Tex. 1971, U.S. Dist. Ct. (so. dist.) Tex. 1972, U.S. Dist. Ct. (mid. dist.) Tenn. 1978, U.S. Dist. Ct. (we. dist.) Tenn. 1998, U.S. Dist. Ct. (ea. dist.) Tenn. 2001. Assoc. Fanning & Harper, Dallas, 1969-70, Crocker & Murphy, Dallas, 1970-71, McClure & Burch, Houston, 1972-75, Brown, Bradshaw & Plummer, Houston, 1975-76; with Seligmann & Youngblood, Nashville, 1977-88; pvt. practice Nashville, 1987—94; of counsel Ortale, Kelley Herbert & Crawford, Nashville, 1994—. Contbr. articles to profl. jours. Active Com. Women in Govt., Dallas, 1969—71; vestry Ch. of Advent, 1991. Fellow: Congress Fellows Ctr. Intl. Studies, Nashville Bar Found.; mem.: LAW (treas. 2001), Nashville Bar Assn. (chair fee dispute com. 1990—), Tenn. Bar Assn., Alumnae Club, Cable Club Nashville (charter), Davidson County Rep. Women's Club, Pi Beta Phi (v.p. 2002, pres. 2003, bd. dirs., counsel Christmas Village bd.). Episcopalian. Address: PO Box 198985 Nashville TN 37219-8985 E-mail: eyoungblood@ortalekelley.com.

YOUNG-COOMBS, ESTHER ELIZABETH (BETSEY EVELETH, BETSEY L. EVELETH), poet; b. Auburn, Maine, Aug. 18, 1938; d. Charles Henry Eveleth and Grace Lillian Hodgkins Eveleth; m. Roy Wilson Young, Nov. 28, 1987 (dec. Feb. 7, 1997); m. Orrin Franklin Coombs, Sept. 2000; children: Sherri, Janet, Larry, John Wood, Kimberly Farrington. Grad., Newspaper Inst. Am., Writer's Inst. Children's Lit., Writer's Digest Short Story Course. Writer, poet, columnist Bear Facts of Maine, Norway, 1989 98, writer animal stories series, 2000—. Contbr. poetry to anthologies; author: (poetry) Best New Poets of 1986 and 1987. Avocations: reading, music, embroidery. Home: PO Box 596 Dover Foxcroft ME 04426

YOUNGDAHL, PAUL FREDERICK, mechanical engineer; b. Brockway, Pa., Oct. 8, 1921; s. Harry Ludwig and Esther Marie (Carlson) Y.; m. Elinor Louise Jensen, Nov. 27, 1943; children: Mark Erik, Marcia Linnea, Melinda Louise. Student Pa. State U., 1938-40; BS in Engring., U. Mich., 1942, MS in Engring., 1949, PhD, 1962. Indsl. and devel. engr. DuPont, Bridgeport, Conn., 1942-43, Carneys Point, N.J., 1946-48; dir. research Mech. Handling Systems, Detroit, 1953-62; prof. U. Mich., Ann Arbor, 1962-74; cons. mech. engr., Palo Alto, Calif., 1974—; dir. Liquid Drive Corp., Holly, Mich. Contbr. articles to profl. jours. With USNR, 1943-46. Mem. Mich. Soc. Profl. Engrs., Nat. Soc. Profl. Engrs., ASME, Am. Soc. Engring. Edn., Mich. Assn. Professions, Sigma Xi, Tau Beta Pi, Phi Kappa Phi, Pi Tau Sigma. Methodist. Address: 151 Del Mesa Carmel Carmel CA 93923

YOUNGER, JUDITH TESS, law educator; b. N.Y.C., Dec. 20, 1933; d. Sidney and Kate (Greenbaum) Weintraub; m. Irving Younger, Jan. 21, 1955; children: Rebecca, Abigail M. BS, Cornell U., 1954; JD, NYU, 1958; LLD (hon.), Hofstra U., 1974. Bar: N.Y. 1958, U.S. Supreme Ct 1962, D.C. 1983, Minn. 1985. Law clk. to judge U.S. Dist. Ct., 1958-60; assoc. firm Chadbourne, Parke, Whiteside & Wolff, N.Y.C., 1960-62; mem. firm Younger and Younger, and (successors), 1962-67, adj. asst. prof. NYU Sch. Law, 1967-69; asst. atty. gen. State of N.Y., 1969-70; assoc. prof. Hofstra U. Sch. Law, 1970-72, prof., assoc. dean, 1972-74; dean, prof. Syracuse Coll. Law, 1974-75; dep. dean, prof. law Cornell Law Sch., 1975-78, prof. law, 1975-85; vis. prof. U. Minn. Law Sch., Mpls., 1984-85, prof., 1985-91, Joseph E. Wargo Anoka County Bar Assn. prof. family law, 1991—. Of counsel Popham, Haik, Schnobrich & Kaufman, Ltd., Mpls., 1989-95; cons. NOW, 1972-74, Suffolk County for Revision of Its Real Property Tax Act, 1972-73; mem. N.Y. Gov.'s Panel To Screen Candidates of Ct. of Claims Judges, 1973-74; mem. Minn. Lawyers' Profl. Responsibility Bd., 1991-93. Contbr. articles to profl. jours. Trustee Cornell U., 1973-78. Mem.: AAUP (v.p. Cornell U. chpt. 1978—79), ABA (council legal edn. 1975—79), Minn. Bar Assn., Assn. of Bar of City of N.Y., Am. Law Inst. (adv. restatement property 1982—84). Home: 3520 W Calhoun Pkwy Minneapolis MN 55416-4657 Office: U Minn Law Sch Minneapolis MN 55455 Office Phone: 612-625-5844. Business E-Mail: young001@umn.edu.

YOUNGER, LAURIE, broadcast executive; B in Comm., Queens Coll.; MBA, UCLA. Former dir. bus. affairs 20th Century Fox; dir. bus. affairs network TV divsn. The Walt Disney Co., 1985—86, v.p. bus. affairs, 1986—90; sr. v.p. bus. affairs and adminstrn. Walt Disney TV and Telecomm.; sr. v.p. ABC, Inc., 1996—98, sr. v.p., CFO, 1998—2003, exec. v.p., CFO, 2003—; exec. v.p. ABC TV Distbn., 2000—03; pres. Buena Vista Worldwide TV Distbn., 2003—. Named one of 100 Most Powerful Women in Hollywood, Hollywood Reporter, 2003. Office: ABC Inc 500 S Buena Vista St Burbank CA 91521-4775

YOUNGER, STEPHEN P. lawyer; b. NYC, May 9, 1956; s. George D. and Doris Anne (Hill) Y.; m. Prudence Madden, Aug. 7, 1982; children: Millicent, Willard, Coleman, Emery. BA, Harvard Coll., 1977; JD magna cum laude, Albany Law Sch., 1982. Bar: N.Y. 1983, U.S. Dist. Ct. (so. and ea. dists.) N.Y. 1986, U.S. Ct. Appeals (2d cir.) 1986, U.S. Tax Ct. 1989. Law clk. to assoc. judge N.Y. State Ct. Appeals, Albany, 1982-84; assoc. Patterson Belknap Webb & Tyler, N.Y.C., 1985-91, ptnr., 1991—. Asst. counsel N.Y. State Commn. on Jud. Nomination, 1994—; spl. asst. N.Y. Corp. Counsel's Office, N.Y.C., 1990; staff counsel Gov.'s Commn. on Liability Ins., N.Y.C., 1986-87. Editor-in-chief Albany Law Rev., 1981-82. Active, mem. strategic planning com.Glen Ridge Congl. Ch.; trustee, mem. com. on trustees Albany Law Sch., 1994—; trustee, mem. strategic planning com. Sorrento V.I.A., 1996-2003; trustee NY Theol. Sem., 2002—, sec. 2004—. Mem. Bar Assn. City NY (com. on arbitration 1995-98), NY State Bar Assn. (chair securities litigation com. 1998-2004, chmn.-elect, comml. and fed. litigation sect.), CPR Inst. Dispute Resolution (exec. com. 2003—), Harvard Club of the City of NY, Albany Law Sch. Nat. Alumni Coun. (pres. 1992-93), Sorrento Yacht Club (commodore 1996-99), Stuyvesant Alumni Assn. (bd. dirs. 1997-2000), Hist. Soc. NY State Cts. (treas. 2002—). Congregationalist. Avocations: sailing, golf. Home: 26 Hillcrest Rd Glen Ridge NJ 07028 Office: Patterson Belknap & Tyler LLP 1133 Ave of Ams New York NY 10036 Office Phone: 212-336-2685.

YOUNG III, HARMON GRIFFITH, music educator; b. Charleston, W.Va., July 29, 1951; s. Harmon Griffith Young II and Phyllis Hall Young. BS, W.Va. Wesleyan Coll., 1973; MA, W.Va. U., 1974, MA, 1980; PhD, U. Fla., Gainesville, FL, 1995; postgrad., Westminster Choir Coll., Ohio U. Prof. music W.Va. U., Parkersburg, W.Va., 1975—. W.Va pres. Am. Choral Directors Assn., 1993—95; pres. W.Va. Coun. Cultural Coordinators, W.Va., 1995—99; project dir., condr. Continental Harmony, W.Va., 1999—2000; coll. chorale condr. W.Va. U., Parkersburg, 1975—, artistic dir. disting. performance series, 1980—. Finalist Prof. of Yr., Faculty Merit Found. W.Va., 2000. Mem.: Internat. Fedn. Choral Music, Soc. Am. Music, Am. Choral Directors Assn. (life W.Va. chpt. Disting. Svc. award 2004), Pi Kappa Lambda, Phi Kappa Phi, Omicron Delta Kappa. United Methodist. Achievements include Commissioned and conducted premieres of choral works by eight American composers; Prepared choruses for numerous performances including collaborations with Robert Shaw and Dave Brubeck. Home: 75 Reamer Road Clendenin WV 25045 Office: West Virginia University Parkersburg 300 Campus Drive Parkersburg WV 26104 Office Phone: 304-424-8248. E-mail: hg.young@mail.wvu.edu.

YOUNGMAN, OWEN RALPH, newspaper executive; b. Chgo., Apr. 24, 1953; s. Ralph Elmer and Charlotte Earldine (Ottoson) Y.; m. Linda Ann Erlandson, Aug. 24, 1975. Sportswriter Ashtabula (Ohio) Star-Beacon, 1969-71; office clk. Chgo. Tribune, 1971-73, transcriber, 1973-75, copy editor, slotman, 1976-79, copy chief, news editor, 1979-83, dep. sports editor, 1984-86, assoc. met. editor, 1986-88, assoc. features editor, 1988-90, dep. fin. editor, 1990-91, assoc. mng. editor, 1991-93, features editor, 1993-95, mng. editor, features, 1995, dir. interactive media, 1996-99, dir. planning and devel., 1999, v.p. devel., 2000—. Bd. dirs. Swedish Covenant Hosp., Legacy.com Mem. Newspaper Assn. Am. New Media Fedn., Am. Soc. Newspaper Editors, Presidents Club of North Park U., Arts Club of Chgo. Avocation: vocal and instrumental music. Home: 40 Kenmore Ave Deerfield IL 60015-4750 Office: Chicago Tribune 435 N Michigan Ave Chicago IL 60611-4066 Office Phone: 312-222-4179. Business E-Mail: oyoungman@tribune.com.

YOUNGMAN, PAUL A. language educator; b. Rochester, N.Y., May 3, 1965; s. Peter A. and Susan W. Youngman; m. Julia Furr, Aug. 11, 1988; children: Alexander P., Madeleine O. BS in Bus. Adminstrn., Washington and Lee U., Lexington, Va., 1987; MA in German Lit., U. N.C., 1995, PhD in German Lit., 2003. Cert. K-12 German language N.C. Tchr. East Chapel Hill H.S., Chapel Hill, NC, 1996—2003; prof. German lit. U. N.C., Charlotte, 2003—. Chair ECHHS Sch. Governance Com., Chapel Hill, 1998—2000, East Found., Chapel Hill, 1999—2003. Capt. U.S. Army, 1987—93. Decorated Bronze Star with "V" device; named Tchr. of the Yr., East Chapel Hill H.S., 2002. Mem.: MLA, Am. Assn. Tchrs. German, Phi Delta Kappa. Episcopalian. Avocations: reading, exercise. Home: 404 Holly Ln Chapel Hill NC 27517-3017

YOUNG-POHLMAN, COLETTE LISA, music educator; b. Honolulu, July 20, 1952; d. Richard Ah On and Winifred Oi Chin Chang Young; m. Kurt I. Pohlman, Oct. 5, 1985; 1 child, Vinson Sterling Pohlman. EdB, U. Hawaii-Manoa, Honolulu, 1974, postgrad., 1975. Part-time tchr. dept. edn. Kalani High, Honolulu, 1978—79; chpt. 1 reading tchr. McKinley High, Honolulu, 1979—80, basic skills tchr., 1980—81; part-time tchg. asst. pvt. preschs., Honolulu, 1981—82; part-time tchr. dept. edn., chpt. 1 reading Ala Wai Elem. and Palolo Elem., 1982—83; classroom tchr. Heeia Elem., Kaneohe, Hawaii, 1990; part-time tchr. dept. edn. Wailupe Valley Elem., Honolulu, 1990—91;

instrnl. resource augmentation tchr. Maemae Elem., Honolulu, 1991—92; project tchr. Title I reading Washington Intermediate, Honolulu, 1992—94; instrnl. resource augmentation tchr. Accelerated Gifted & Talented Performing Arts, Kailua, Hawaii, 1994—97; classroom tchr. Mokapu Elem., Kailua, 1997—2002, instrnl. resource augmentation music tchr., 2002—, Ann. Winter Concert and Talent Showcase, 2002—. Dir., choreographer, scripting/editing of musical play productions in elem. sch. settings, Honolulu. Dir.(choreographer, writer): (multicultural musical plays) Little Firefly, the Rough-face Girl, Double Happiness, Souled Out; composer: There's Something About a Pet, 1998 (2d Pl. award, 1998); composer: (choreographer) (new sch. song dance) Enchantment of Mokapu, 2000, Reading Rap, 2003; prodr. (dir.): (monthly TV program Olelo Cablevision) Nakeiki Hanoli o Mokapu, The Happy Children of Mokapu. Mem., tchr. Boy Scouts Am. Troop 113, 1999—. Mem.: Hawaii State Tchrs. Assn., Hawaii Music Educators Assn., Hawaii Orff Schulwerk Assn., Am. Orff Schulwerk Assn., Music Educators Nat. Conf., Nat. Tchr. Assn. Avocations: composing songs, poetry, singing, keyboard, storytelling. Home: 45-427 Loli'i St Kaneohe HI 96744-5911

YOUNGQUIST, WALTER LEWELLYN, geologist, consultant; b. Mpls., May 5, 1921; s. Walter Raymond and Selma Regina (Knock) Y.; m. Elizabeth Salome Pearson, Dec. 11, 1943; children: John, Karen, Louise, Robert. BA, Gustavus Adolphus Coll., St. Peter, Minn., 1942; MSc, U. Iowa, 1943, PhD, 1948. Registered profl. geologist, Oreg. Jr. geologist U.S. Geol. Survey, 1943-44; rsch. assoc. U. Iowa, Iowa City, 1945-48; asst. prof. geology U. Idaho, Moscow, 1948-51; sr. geologist Internat. Petroleum Co., Talara, Peru, 1951-54; prof. geology U. Kans., Lawrence, 1954-57, U. Oreg., Eugene, 1957-66; cons. geologist Minerals dept. Exxon Corp., Houston, 1968-73; geothermal cons. Eugene Water & Electric Bd., 1973-92; ind. cons. Eugene, 1992—. Author: Investing in Natural Resources, 1980, Mineral Resources and the Destinies of Nations, 1990, GeoDestinies, 1997; co-author: Ordovician Cephalopod Fauna of Baffin Island, 1954. Ensign, USNR, 1944-45. Recipient Lowden Prize in Geology, U. Iowa, 1943, Journalist award, Am. Assn. Petroleum Geology, 2000, Disting. Alumni award Gustavus Adolphus Coll., 2002. Fellow AAAS, Geol. Soc. Am.; mem. Am. Assn. Petroleum Geologists, Geothermal Resources Coun., N.W. Energy Assn., N.Y. Acad. Scis., Sigma Xi. Lutheran. Avocations: fly-tying, photography, fishing. Office: PO Box 5501 Eugene OR 97405-0501

YOUNGS, JACK MARVIN, cost engineer; b. Bklyn., May 2, 1941; s. Jack William and Virginia May (Clark) Y.; m. Alexandra Marie Robertson, Oct. 31, 1964; 1 child, Christine Marie. B in Engring., CCNY, 1964; MBA, San Diego State U., 1973. Mass properties engr. Gen. Dynamics Corp., San Diego, 1964-68, rsch. engr., 1968-69, sr. rsch. engr., 1969-80, sr. cost devel. engr., 1980-81, cost devel. engring. specialist, 1981-95; prin. estimator Martin Marietta Astronautics, 1994-95; estimating adminstr. Lockheed Martin Astronautics, 1995-96; prin., owner Youngs Group, 1996—. Dist. dir. Scripps Ranch Civic Assn, 1976-79; pres. Scripps Ranch Swim Team, 1980-82, dir., 1986-87; judge Greater San Diego Sci. and Engring. Fair, 1981-98, sweepstakes judge, 1999; mem. Princeton U. Parents Assn. Recipient 5th pl. award World Body Surfing Championships, 1987, 6th pl. award, 1988, 2d pl. award, 1999. Mem. AIAA, N.Y. Acad. Scis., Alumni Assn., CUNY, Bklyn. Tech. H.S. Alumni Assn., Inst. Cost Analysis (cert., charter, treas. Greater San Diego chpt. 1986-90), Soc. Cost Estimating and Analysis (cert. cost estimator/analyst, pres. San Diego chpt. 1990-91), Internat. Soc. Parametric Analysts (bd. dirs. San Diego chpt. 1987-90), Nat. Mgmt. Assn. (space sys. divsn. charter 1985, Award of Honor Convair chpt. 1975), Assn. MBA Execs., San Diego State U. Bus. Alumni Assn. (charter 1986), Convair Alumni Assn., Scripps Ranch Swim and Racquet Club (dir. 1977-80, treas. 1978-79, pres. 1979-80), Beta Gamma Sigma, Chi Epsilon, Sigma Iota Epsilon. Lutheran. Achievements include research in life cycle costing and econ. analysis. Office: 11461 Tribuna Ave San Diego CA 92131-1907 E-mail: youngsgroup@hotmail.com.

YOUNGS, ROBERT RIGGS, engineer; b. Riverside, Calif., Aug. 20, 1947; s. James Porter and Gwendolyn Gloria (Miller) Y.; m. Susan Ann Cohen, Feb. 10, 1974; children: Sarah Gwen Cohen Youngs, Noah James Cohen Youngs. BS, Calif. State Poly. Coll., 1967; MS, U. Calif., Berkeley, 1973, PhD, 1982. Staff engr. Pacific Found. Engrs., Bloomington, Calif., 1970-72; staff to project engr. Woodward Clyde Consultants, Oakland, Calif., 1974-84; sr. to prin. engr. Geometrix Consultants, Oakland, 1985—. Contbr. articles to profl. jours. Mem. Am. Soc. Engrs., Seismol. Soc. Am., Earthquake Engring. Rsch. Inst. Avocations: fishing, science fiction. Home: 1147 High Ct Berkeley CA 94708-1624 Office: Geomatrix Consultants 2101 Webster St Fl 12 Oakland CA 94612-3027

YOUNGS, WILLIAM ELLIS, photographer, motion picture engineer, projectionist; b. Miami, Fla., Apr. 30, 1916; s. Edward Ray and Maude Myrtle (Burd) Y.; m. Mary Helen Still, Aug. 28, 1948; 1 child, Renee Helen. Student, Nat. Radio Inst., 1952. Film technician Washington Motion Picture Co., 1934-35, U.S. Dept. State, Washington, 1948-53; night service mgr. MGM Film Exchange, Washington, 1936-41; mgr., projectionist Calvert Theatre, Prince Frederick, Md., 1941-42; research asst. Exec. Office of the President, Washington, 1942; photo lab technician Office War Info., Washington, 1942-43; br. chief, advisor film and equipment USIA, Washington, 1953-78; engr., projectionist Motion Picture Assn. Am., Washington, 1979-94; photographer, chaplain Vets. Commn., Falls Church, Va., 1997—. Advisor Stephens Coll., Columbia, Mo., 1973-75. Columnist Falls Church (Va.) Sun-Echo, 1953-55. Pres. Greenway Downs Civic Assn., Falls Church, 1953-54; pres. Second (Indian Head) Div. Assn. D.C. br., 1953-57; hon. recruiter USN, 1984; chaplain, photographer Vets. Common, U.S.A., Arlington/Falls Church, Va., 1997—. With U.S. Army, 1943-45, ETO. Fellow Soc. Motion Picture and TV Engrs. (life; nat. membership chmn. 1969, Outstanding Svc. award 1979); mem. Washington Film and Video Coun. (life; pres. 1967-68), Univ. Film and Video Assn., SAR (pres. Fairfax Resolves 1991-92, chaplain emeritus 2002, Va. ofcl. photographer, nat. mem. mag. adv. com. SAR/DAR liaison com. 1990—, historian 1993-94, editor 1994—, Meritorious Svc. medal 1991, Va. medal, 1994, Pres. Gen.'s citation for Disting. Svc. and Silver Good Citizenship medal 1994, Patriot medal 1996), Presbyterian. Avocations: photography, pub. relations, hist. and tech. writing. Home: 1436 Mayflower Dr Mc Lean VA 22101-5614

YOUNGSTROM, PAUL CLARENCE, anesthesiologist; b. Cedar Rapids, Iowa, Dec. 4, 1950; s. Clarence Swan and Hilda (Konga) Y.; m. Karen Jane Daykin, Aug. 18, 1973; children: Erica, Christiane, Andrew. BA in Econs., Yale U., 1972; MD, McGill U., 1976. Cert. anesthesiology. Intern U. Hosps., Cleve., 1976-77, resident in anesthesiology, 1977-79; staff anesthesiologist Cleve. Clinic, 1993—. Cons. Agy. for Health Care Policy and Rsch., Washington, 1993-94. Author: Operative Obstetrics, Common and Uncommon Obstetric Syndromes and Conditions. Elder St. Peter's Luth. Ch., Shaker Heights, 1994—. Lt. col. M.C., USAFR. Mem. Am. Soc. Anesthesiologists, Am. Soc. for Regional Anesthesia, Internat. Anesthesia Rsch. Soc., Soc. Obstetric Anesthesia and Perinatology. E-mail: paul.youngstrom.es.72@aya.yale.edu.

YOUNGWOOD, ALFRED DONALD, lawyer; b. NYC, Apr. 27, 1938; s. Milton and Lillian (Ginsburg) Y.; m. Judith Goldfarb, June 24, 1963; children: Jonathan David, Stephen Michael. BA magna cum laude, Yale U., 1959; LLB magna cum laude, Harvard U., 1962. Bar: NY 1962, DC 1970, US Tax Ct. 1964, US Ct. Appeals (2d cir.) 1969. Law clk. to judge US Dist. Ct. NY, NY, 1962-63; assoc. Paul, Weiss, Rifkind, Wharton & Garrison LLP, NYC, 1964-70, ptnr., 1970—, chair, 1999—. Pres. Ctrl. Synagogue, N.Y.C., 2003—. Fulbright scholar, London, 1963-64. Fellow Am. Coll. Tax Counsel; mem. ABA, NY State Bar Assn. (chmn. tax sect. 1978-79, exec. com. 1971—, ho. of dels. 1979-80), Assn. of Bar of City of NY, Coun. on Fgn. Rels. Home: 1125 Park Ave New York NY 10128-1243 Office: Paul Weiss Rifkind Wharton & Garrison LLP 1285 Avenue Of The Americas New York NY 10019-6064 Business E-Mail: ayoungwood@paulweiss.com.

YOUNG-ZOOK, MONICA M. language educator; b. Sacramento, Sept. 2, 1968; d. Albert Miebach Young and D'vonne Marie Hutchins; m. Daniel S. Zook, Aug. 12, 2000. BA, Calif. State U., 1994, MA, 1997; PhD with distinction, NYU, 2002. Tchg. asst. NYU, NYC, 1998—2002; asst. prof. English Macon (Ga.) State Coll., 2003—. Adj. instr. lit. and composition NYU, N.Y.C., 2000—03, Eugene Lang. Coll., 2002—03; participant The Dickens U., Santa Cruz, Calif., 2001; organizer Gradnotes, Sacramento, 1995—97. Sgt. USAF, 1987—91. Recipient 2 pl., Bazzannella Writing Contest, Sacramento, 1993. Mem.: Victorian & Edwardian Study Group, Modern Lang. Assn., Sigma Tau Delta. Office: Macon State Coll 100 Coll Sta Dr Macon GA 31206 Office Phone: 478-471-5735. Business E-Mail: myoung@mail.maconstate.edu.

YOUNKER, KATHLEEN TEUBER, pianist, music educator; b. St. Cloud, Minn., Jan. 22, 1947; d. Hans Richard and Philomena (Hortsch) T.; m. Daniel William Younker, July 19, 1968; children: Laura, Jonathan. BA in History and Philosophy, St. Cloud State U., 1968; ARCT in Piano Performance, Royal Conservatory Toronto, Ont., Can., 1983; BA in Music, Bishop's U., Lennoxville, Que., Can., 1984; pvt. piano student, Rose Goldblatt, Montreal, 1985-95; MA in Spl. Studies, St. Cloud State U., 2002. Self-employed piano tchr., Lennoxville, 1978—97, St. Cloud, 1997—; sch. music tchr. Eastern Twps. Regional Sch. Bd., Lennoxville, 1982-86; ch. organist Peace United Ch. of Christ, St. Cloud, 1998-99; accompanist Sauk Rapids (Minn.) Rice HS, 1999—2000. Mem Music Tchrs. Nat Assn., Nat. Guild Piano Tchrs., Can. Fedn. Music Tcrs. Assns. (com. mem., ex officio nat. conv. 1997), Minn. Music Tchrs. Assn. (com. mem. state conv. 1999-01, com. mem. piano exam devel. com. 2002—), Eastern Twps. Music Tchrs. Assn. (pres. 1989-91), Que. Music Tchrs. Assn. (pres. provincial coun. 1993-97). Avocations: home restoration, pets, reading, gardening, cooking, entertaining.

YOUNT, GEORGE STUART, paper company executive; b. L.A., Mar. 4, 1949; s. Stanley George and Agnes (Pratt) Y.; m. Geraldine Marie Silvio, July 18, 1970; children: Trisha Marie, Christopher George. Postgrad., Harvard U., 1983-86. Mgmt. trainee Fortifiber Corp., L.A., 1969-71, asst. to v.p. ops., 1971-75, adminstrv. v.p., treas., sec., 1975-85, exec. v.p., sec., CFO, bd. dirs., 1985-90, chmn., CEO, 1991—; pres., dir. Fonzia Corp., 1993—. Bd. dirs. Stanwall Corp., pres., 1989—, Thompson & Co. Ins. Svcs., Pasadena, Calif., 1996—, Parasol Found., 1999—, Tracerton Enterprises, Inc., 2001-2004; past pres. Hollister Ranch Cattle Coop., Gaviota, Calif., 1986-88; trustee Sierra Nev. Coll., 1999-2002,(vice Chair, 2002); adv. bd. Med. Tech. Internat., Inc., 2004-. Team leader L.A. United Way, 1981-86; bd. dirs. Big Bros. Greater L.A., 1984-87, L.A. coun. Boy Scouts Am., 1992—; mem. Young Pres. Orgn., 1991, forum moderator, 1993-95, chpt. forum officer, 1997-99; presdl. appointee Tahoe Regional Planning Agy. Governing Bd., 2002—. Mem. Am. Paper Inst. (dir. 1993-95, splty. coaters and extrusion sect. 1990—), Chief Execs. Orgn., World Presidents Orgn., Jonathan Club (L.A.), Rotary (bd. dirs. L.A. club 1992-94), Internat. Wine and Food Soc., Chaine des Rotisseurs Food and Wine Soc., Wine and Food Soc., Conferie des Chevaliers du Tastevin Wine and Food Soc. Avocations: scuba diving, electronics, cattle ranching, computers. Office: Fortifiber Corp 1001 Tahoe Blvd Incline Village NV 89451-9309

YOUNT, GWENDOLYN AUDREY, humanities educator; b. Indpls., July 24, 1957; d. August de Alba and Hena Yount; 1 child, Clark. AA, L.A. City Coll., 1977; BA, UCLA, 1979, MA, 1982, Candidate in Philosophy, 1987. Cert. C.C. lifetime credential Calif., bilingual cert. competence. Ednl. aide Alexander Hamilton H.S., Los Angeles, 1975—76; tchg. fellow UCLA, 1981—88; instr. L.A. Unified Sch. Dist., 1982—90; prof. Institut Franco-Americain de Mgmt., Paris, 1983—84; instr. Santa Monica (Calif.) Coll., 1987—88; lectr. U. of Calif., Riverside, 1988—91; instr. Beverly Hills (Calif.) Adult Sch., 1986—88; assoc. prof. Riverside (Calif.) C.C., 1990—. Dir. RCC Study Abroad Program in Spain, Salamanca, Spain, 1998—2002, RCC Study Abroad Program in Costa Rica, San Jose, Costa Rica, 1993, UCLA Spanish Program in Mex., Guadalajara, Mexico, 1987. Dancer (ballet performance) Celebrate Dance, 2000; actor: (mus. theater) La Cage Aux Folles, 1998; singer: (vocal performance) Montreux Jazz Festival, 1993. Adminstr. G. Yount scholarship Riverside County Found., 1998—2003; sen. Acad. Senate, Riverside, 1997—2003; mem. Spanish lang. steering com. Riverside Pub. Libr., 1989—91; charter mem. Mus. of Tolerance, L.A., 1994—2003. Named Most Influential Instr., RCC Disabled Student Svcs., 1993, 1998, Tchr. of Distinction, LDS Ch., 1998, 2000, 2001, 2002, Tchr. of the Yr., Riverside C.C., 1999—2000, 2000—01, 2002—03; grantee Univ. grantee for grad. study, UCLA, 1979. Mem.: Philol Soc. of the Pacific Coast, Assn. for Tchrs. of Spanish, Sigma Tau Sigma, Alpha Mu Gamma (pres. 1977—78), Sigma Delta Pi (v.p. 1985—86). Liberal. Avocations: travel, reading, studying. Office: Riverside C C 4800 Magnolia Ave Riverside CA 92506 Office Phone: 909-222-8371. Business E-Mail: gwen.yount@rcc.edu.

YOUNT, ROBIN, retired professional baseball player; b. Danville, Ill., Sept. 16, 1955; Shortstop, outfielder Milw. Brewers, 1974—93. Named Am. League Player of Decade for 1980s, USA Today, 1989; named to Baseball Hall of Fame, 1999; recipient Most Valuable Player awards as shortstop, 1982, Most Valuable Player awards as centerfield, 1989. Achievements include being a 3-time All-Star; being ranked 15th on all-time hits list; being the 3d youngest player to amass 3000 hits; being one of only 3 players to amass over 3,000 hits; making 250 home runs, 200 stolen bases and 100 triples in career lifetime. Office: c/o Nat Baseball Hall of Fame PO Box 590 Cooperstown NY 13326-0590

YOUNTS, PATTY LOU, interior design executive,inventor, researcher; b. Lexington, N.C., Feb. 20, 1950; d. Wayne Lohr and Rosetta Mae (Myers) Y. BS, U. N.C., Greensboro, 1972; postgrad., Wake Forest U., Winston-Salem, N.C., 1976. Apprentice draftsman and interior designer Paul T. Briggs, AIA, Lexington, 1971, in-house designer, specifer, 1972-74; part-time interior designer Watkins Office Interiors, Winston-Salem, 1972-74; ptnr. IN-Ex Designs, Inc., 1974-75, corp. officer, head, 1975-81, pres., owner, 1981—. Pres. Decorative Panel Koncepts, Inc., 1986—, J.P. Walls, Inc., 1989—, pres., 1990—; bd. dir. Industry Gen. Tire, GF Bus. Systems, Armstrong Industries, Mid-State Tile; guest speaker univs. Adv. bd. Lexington Meml Hosp., 1984—, Western Carolina U., 1983—; mem. N.C. Entrepreneurial Devel. Bd., 1996-99, N.C. Econ. Devel. Bd., 1997-98. Patentee novel wall system, 1990. Recipient N.C. AIA awards for Sch. Planning, 1977, 79; Sperry and Hutchinson scholar, 1968-72, hon. scholar U. N.C., Greensboro, 1971-72. Mem. Inst. Bus. Designers (mem., chmn. various coms., pres. Carolinas chpt. 1977-80, 82-84), Am. Soc. Interior Designers, Color Mktg. Group (chairholder 1985, bd. dirs. 1989-91), Lexington C. of C. (com. chmn. 1980, bd. dirs. 1981-84, 92—, pres. 1990), Rotary. Democrat. Mem. United Ch. of Christ. Achievements include patents for predecorated monolithic wallboard called instawall. Avocations: water-skiing, golf. Office: Design Cons 302 W Center St Lexington NC 27292-2710 E-mail: pyounts@hotmail.com.

YOUREE, CHERYL ANN, secondary school educator; b. L.A., Oct. 14, 1950; d. James William Catlett and Thelma Dolores (Closs) Courts; m. Thomas Eugene Youree, Jan. 19, 1975 (div. Dec. 1992); children: Anna Louise, Daniel Paul. BA in Drama, Calif. State U., Chico, 1973; MA in Theatre, Tex. A&M, 1990. Secondary tchrs. cert., Tex. Theatre, pub. speaking and English tchr. Bonham (Tex.) H.S., 1985—. Actress (movie) When The Time Comes, 1987; cons. (video) Sam Rayburn, 1995; puppeteer, vocal coach (video) Don't Make That Trash, 1995; dir. (commls.) Fannin County Family Crisis Ctr., 1999. Pres. Fannin County Arts Coun., Bonham, 1983; mem. adv. bd., cmty. svc. chmn. Rotary Club Internat., Bonham, 1991-92, mem., 1991-96; del. to People's Republic of China, People to People Internat., Spokane, Wash., 1993. Mem. Ednl. Theatre Assn., Assn. Tex. Profl. Educators, Tex. Edn. Theatre Assn., Alpha Psi Omega. Avocations: travel, knitting, theatre directing. Office: Bonham HS PO Box 490 Bonham TX 75418-0490 E-mail: c_youree@bhs.bonhamisd.org.

YOURZAK, ROBERT JOSEPH, management consultant, engineer, educator; b. Mpls., Aug. 27, 1947; s. Ruth Phyllis Sorenson. BCE, U. Minn., 1969; MSCE, U. Wash., 1971, MBA, 1975. Registered profl. engr., Wash., Minn. Surveyor N.C. Hoium & Assocs., Mpls., 1965-68, Lot Surveys Co., Mpls., 1968-69; site layout engr. Sheehy Constrn. Co., St. Paul, 1968; structural engring. aide Dunham Assocs., Mpls., 1969; aircraft and aerospace structural engr., program rep. Boeing Co., Seattle, 1969-75; engr., estimator Howard S. Wright Constrn. Co., Seattle, 1976-77; dir. project devel. and adminstrn. DeLeuw Cather & Co., Seattle, 1977-78; sr. mgmt. cons. Alexander Grant & Co., Mpls., 1978-79; mgr. project sys. dept., project mgr. Henningson, Durham & Richardson, Mpls., 1979-80; dir. project mgmt., regional offices Ellerbe Assocs., Inc., Mpls., 1980-81; pres. Robert Yourzak & Assocs., Inc., Mpls., 1982—. Lectr. engring. mgmt. U. Wash., 1977-78; lectr., adj. asst. prof. dept. civil and mineral engring. and mech./indsl. engring. Ctr. for Devel. of Tech. Leadership, Inst. Tech.; mem. strategic mgmt. and orgn. dept., mgmt. scis. dept. Sch. Mgmt., U. Minn., 1979-90, 96—; bd. adv. inst. tech., 1989-93; founding mem., membership com., mem. U. of Minn. com. Minn. High Tech. Coun., 1983-95; instr. principles mgmt. dept. bus. and pub. policy Concordia U., 1997, instr. constrn. mgmt., constrn. estimating and scheduling, bldg. orgn. and tech., project mgmt. and planning skills, and supervision and applied leadership Inver Hills C.C., 1998—; instr. introduction to engring. and design, statics, mechanics of materials, ops. mgmt. North Hennepin C.C., 2002—; adj. instr. ops. mgmt. Hamline U., St. Paul, 2001; spkr. in field. Author: Project Management and Motivating and Managing the Project Team, 1984, (with others) Field Guide to Project Management, 1998, 2004 (sec. edition). Chmn. regional art group experience Seattle Art Mus., 1975-78; mem. Pacific N.W. Arts Coun., 1977-78, ex-officio adviser Mus. Week, 1976; bd. dirs. Friends of the Rep. Seattle Repertory Theatre, 1973-77; mem. Symphonics Seattle Symphony Orch., 1975-78. Named Outstanding Young Man of Am., U.S. Jaycees, 1978; scholar Boeing Co., 1967-68, Sheehy Constrn. Co., summer 1967. Fellow ASCE (chmn. continuing edn. subcom. Seattle chpt. 1976-79, chmn. program com. 1978, mem. transp. and urban planning tech. group 1978, Edmund Friedman Young Engr. award 1979, chmn. continuing edn. subcom. 1979-80, chmn. energy com. Minn. chpt. 1980-81, bd. dirs. 1981-89, sec. 1981-83, v.p. profl. svcs. 1983-84, v.p. info. svcs. 1984-85, pres. 1986-87, past pres. 1987-89, spkr.), PMI Project Mgmt. Inst. (cert. project mgmt. prof., spkr., founding pres. 1985, chmn., adv. com. 1987-89, bd. dirs. 1984-86, program com. chmn. and organizing com. mem. Minn. chpt. 1984, spkr., project mgr. internat. mktg. program 1985-86, chmn. internat. mktg. standing com. 1986, long range and strategic planning com. 1988-93, chmn. 1992, v.p. pub. rels. 1987-88, ex-officio dir. 1989, 92, internat. pres. 1990, chmn. bd. 1991, ex-officio chmn. 1992, internat. bd. dirs., chmn. nominating com. 1992, PMI fellow 1995, chmn. exec. dir. selection com. 1996-97, Robert J. Yourzak Scholarship Award established Minn. chpt. 1998—), Inst. Indsl. Engrs. (pres. Twin Cities chpt. 1985-86, chmn. program com. 1983-84, bd. dirs. 1985-88, awards com., chmn. 1984-89, fellow 1999, spkr.); mem. ASTD (So. Minn. chpt.), Am. Cons. Engrs. Coun. (peer reviewer 1986-89), Am. Arbitration Assn. (mem. Mpls. panel of constrn. arbitrators), Minn. Surveyors and Engrs. Soc., Cons. Engrs. Coun. Minn. (chmn. pub. rels. com. 1983-85, vice chmn. 1988, chmn. 1989, program com. chmn. Midwest engrs. conf. and exposition 1985-90, spkr., Honor award 1992), Inst. Mgmt. Cons. (cert. mgmt. cons.), Mpls. Soc. Fine Arts, Internat. Facility Mgmt. Assn., Am. Soc. Engring. Edn., Rainer Club (co-chmn. Oktoberfest), Sierra club, Chowder Soc., Mountaineers, North Star Ski Touring, Chi Epsilon (life). Office: 7320 Gallagher Dr Ste 325 Minneapolis MN 55435-4510

YOUSEF, FATHI SALAAMA, communication studies educator, management consultant; b. Cairo, Jan. 2, 1934; arrived in U.S., 1968, naturalized, 1973; s. Salaama and Rose (Tadros) Yousef; m. Marjan El-Faizy Lowies, June 24, 1994. BA, Ain Shams U., Cairo, 1955; MA, U. Minn., 1970, PhD, 1972. Svc. ctr. supt. Shell Oil Co., Cairo, 1955-61; indsl., mgmt. tng. instr. ARAMCO, Dhahran, Saudi Arabia, 1961-68; tchg. assoc. U. Minn., Mpls., 1968-72; comm. studies prof. emeritus Calif. State U., Long Beach, 1972—. With orgn. and indsl. engring. dept. ARAMCO, 1978—80. Co-author: An Introduction to Intercultural Communication, 1975, 1985; contbr. Grantee, NSF, 1981, 1982, 1983. Mem.: Assn. Egyptian Am. Scholars. Democrat. Office: Calif State U Dept Comm Studies Long Beach CA 90840-2407 E-mail: fyousef@csulb.edu.

YOUSSEF, MOUSTAFA AMIN, computer scientist, researcher; b. Alexandria, Egypt; BSc(hon.), Alexandria U., Egypt, 1992—97, MSc, 1997—99, U. of Md., Coll. Pk., 2000—02, PhD, 2000—04. Lectr. Alexandria U., Egypt, 1997—2000; tchg. asst. U. of Md., Coll. Pk., Md., 2000—02, rsch. asst., 2002—. Designer (PC World middle east magazine context) What You See Is What You Get HTML editor under OS/2 oper. sys. (First Prize, 1996), game under DOS oper. sys. (First Prize, 1995), Electric Circuits Analyzer (First Prize, 1994). Recipient Ministry Cert. of Honor, Egyptian Ministry of Edn., 1992, Faculty Cert. of Honor, Faculty of Engring., Alexandria U., Egypt, 1993-1997, Prof. Dr. Abdelsamie Moustafa Award., Alexandria U., Egypt, 1997, Prof. Dr. Naim Aboutaleb Award, 1997, Cert. of Honor, Gen. Egyptian Soc. For the Talented, 1997, Taha Hussien Medal of Honor, Egyptian Ministry of Edn., 1999, Elected mem. honor soc., Phi Kappa Phi, 2002; fellow Grad. Fellow, U. of Md., Coll. Pk., 2001—02; grantee Travel Grant, ACM Sig Comm, 2002, NSF Travel Grant, IEEE Info Comm., 2004. Mem.: The Soc. for Modeling and Simulation Internat., IEEE Comm. Soc., IEEE Computer Soc., IEEE, Phi Kappa Phi, Gen. Egyptian Soc. For the Talented (life). Achievements include patents pending for Nuzzer Technology: providing phys. security using Wi-Fi; Horus: an RF-based location determination sys; Energy Aware: mgmt. for cluster based sensor networks; Koolspan: securing WI-FI networks at the edge. Office: Univ MD at Coll Pk AV William's Bldg College Park MD 20742

YOUST, DAVID BENNETT, career development educator; b. May 14, 1938; s. Howard Page and Agnes (Bennett) Y.; m. Faye Phillips; children: Stacy Sillen, Shawna Sannier, Liesl Berger, Genny Phillips, Elizabeth Curley. BS, SUNY-Albany, 1959; MS, Syracuse (N.Y.) U., 1961; PhD, Mich. State U., 1969. Cert. career counselor Nat. Bd. Counselor Cert. Tchr. sci. North Syracuse schs., 1959-61; adminstr. student pers. Mich. State U., 1961-63; counselor, prin., program dir. Rochester (N.Y.) schs., 1963-70; sr. rsch. technologist Eastman Kodak Co., Rochester, 1970-72; asst. dean Nat. Tech. Inst. for the Deaf, Rochester Inst. Tech., 1972-74; mem. faculty Empire State Coll., SUNY, Rochester, 1974-78; exec. dir. Career Devel. Coun., Corning, N.Y., 1978-84; mgr. engring. tng. Corning Inc., N.Y., 1984-90; ptnr. Phillips Tng. Sys., Inc., 1989—. Former adj. faculty Corning C.C., Elmira Coll., C.W. Post Coll.; mediator cmty. dispute resolution Bd. of Dir. Cmty. Dispute Resolution Ctr., Ithaca, NY; instr. MSF motorcycle safety; EEO mediator U.S. Postal Svc. Author guide, articles in field; former mem. editl. bd. Career Devel. Quar. Former bd. dirs. 171 Cedar Arts Ctr. Mem. ASTD, ACA, Nat. Career Devel. Assn. (Merit award 1970, 84), Am. Ednl. Rsch. Assn., Assn. Measurement and Evaluation in Guidance. Republican. E-mail: youst@empacc.net.

YOUTCHEFF, JOHN SHELDON, physicist; b. Newark, Apr. 16, 1925; s. Slav Joseph and Florence Catherine (Davidson) Y.; m. Elsie Marianne, June 17, 1950; children: Karen Janette, John Sheldon, Mark Allen, Heidi Mary Anne, Lisa Ellen. AB, Columbia U., 1949, BS, 1950; PhD, UCLA, 1953. Registered profl. engr., Calif., D.C. Ops. analyst Gen. Elec. Co., Ithaca, N.Y., 1953-56, cons., engr. missile & space divsn. Phila., 1956-64, mgr. advanced reliability programs, 1964-72; mgr. reliability and maintainability Litton Industries, College Park, Md., 1972-73; program mgr. U.S. Postal Svc. Headquarters, Washington, 1973—. Instr. U. Pa., 1965-66, Villanova U., 1957—. Lt. USAAF, 1943-46; to comdr. USNR, 1946—. Fellow AAAS, Br. Interplanetary Soc., AIAA, Explorers Club; mem. IEEE (sr.), Ops. Rsch. Soc., Rsch. Soc. Am., Am. Math. Soc., Am. Physics Soc., Am. Cehm. Soc., Am. Astron. Soc., Am. Geol. Socl., Nat. Soc. Profl. Engrs., Engring. and Tech. Socs., Coun. Del. Vly. (spkrs. bur.), USCG Aux. (flotilla comdr.), Res. Officers Assn., Am. Legion, Optimists Internat. (pres. Valley Forge chpt. 1970-71). Roman Catholic. Home: 1400 S Joyce St Apt 1406 Arlington VA 22202-1852 Office: L'Enfant Plz Washington DC 20260

YOVICH, DANIEL JOHN, education educator; b. Chgo., Mar. 5, 1930; s. Milan D. and Sophie (Dorociak) Y.; m. Anita Barbara Moreland, Feb. 7, 1959; children: Daniel, Amy, David, Julie Ann. Ph.B., DePaul U., 1952; MA, Governors State U., 1975, MS, 1976. Cert. reality therapist, cert. profl. mgr., PMA instr. Formulator Nat. Lead Co., 1950-52, 56-59; researcher Montgomery Ward, Chgo., 1959-62; tech. dir. Riley Bros., Inc., Burlington, Iowa, 1962-66, Mortell Co., Kankakee, Ill., 1966-70; exec. dir. Dan Yovich Assos., 1970-79; asst. prof. Purdue U., Hammond, Ind., 1979-84, assoc. prof., 1984-90, prof., 1990-2000, prof. emeritus, 2000—. Instr. Army Security Agy.

Sch., 1954—56, Napoleon Hill Acad., 1965—66, Kankakee C.C. Continuing Edn., 1976; cons. Learning House, 1964—; assoc. Hill, Zediker & Assocs. Psychologists, Kankakee, 1975—79; mem. adv. bd. Nat. Congress Inventor Orgns., 1984; vis. prof. Grand Valley State U., 2000—, Northwood U., 2001—. Author: Applied Creativity; prdr., moderator: (program) Careers Unlimited, Sta. WCIU-TV, Chgo., 1967; contbr. articles to profl. jours.; patentee game Krypto, coating Sanitane. Mem. cmty. adv. coun. Governors State U., 1978; mem. Hammond (Ind.) Hist. Soc. Served to 1st lt. AUS, 1952-56. Recipient Outstanding Citizen Award News Pub. Co. Am., 1971, Outstanding Tchr. award Purdue U., 1980, 82, 83, Faculty Service award Nat. U. Continuing Edn. Assn., 1984, Disting. Service award Purdue U.-Calumet Alumni Assn., 1988, Arthur Young award Venture Mag., 1988, Entrepreneurial Edn. award Inc. Mag., 1990, Indiana Spirit of Innovation award, 1996. Mem. ASTD, World Future Soc., Nat. Mgmt. Assn., Am. Soc. Profl. Supervision (exec. sec. 1986), Inventors and Entrepreneurs Soc. Am. (founder, exec. dir. 1984, prodr. Salute Vet. Recognition Programs 1999—), Global Intuition Network, Internat. Creativity Network, Infantry Officer Cand. Sch. Alumni Assn. (life), Napoleon Hill Found., Inst. Reality Therapy, Inst. Contemporary Living, Soc. Am. Inventors (life), Am. Legion, K.C., Vets. of the Battle of the Bulge (historian), Army and Navy Club of Grand Rapids. Home: 3527 Whispering Brook Dr SE Kentwood MI 49508-3733 E-mail: danyovich@aol.com.

YOVITS, MARSHALL CLINTON, computer and information science educator, university dean; b. Bklyn., May 16, 1923; s. Louis Frederick and Rebecca (Gerber) Y.; m. Anita S. Friedman, Aug. 2, 1952; children: Bruce J., Mara F., Steven. BS, Union Coll., Schenectady, 1944, MS, 1948, Yale U., 1949, PhD, 1951. Sr. physicist John Hopkins U., 1951-56; physicist electronics br. Office Naval Rsch., Washington, 1956, head info. systems br., 1956-62, dir. Naval Analysis Group, 1962-66, prof., chmn. dept. computer and info. sci. Ohio State U., 1966-78, prof., 1978-79; prof. computer and info. sci. Sch. of Sci., Ind. U., Purdue U., Indpls., 1980—, dean., 1980-88; prof. emeritus Ind. U., Purdue U., Indpls., 1993—. Gen. chmn. Computer Sci. conf. NSF, 1973 Editor: (with Scott Cameron) Self-Organizing Systems, Proc. Interdisciplinary Conf., 1960, Large-Capacity Memory Techniques for Computing Systems, 1961 (with George T. Jacobi, Gordon D. Goldstein) Self-Organizing Systems, 1962, (with D.M. Gilford, R.H. Wilcox, E. Staveley, H.D. Lerner) Research Program Effectiveness, 1966, Advances in Computers, Vol. 11, 1971; editor: series Advances in Computers, Vols. 13-40; contbr. rsch. articles to profl. jours. AEC fellow, 1950-51, Indpls. Ctr. Advanced Rsch. fellow, 1988-89; recipient Navy Superior Civilian Service award, 1964; Navy Outstanding Performance award, 1961 Fellow AAAS (chmn. coun. sect. T 1985-88, chmn. 1996-98), IEEE (computer soc. chmn. awards com. 1989, bd. govs. 1988-89, computer pioneer award 1990), Assn. for Computing Machinery (coun., gen. chmn. computer sci. conf. 1982), EDUCOM (nominating com.), Sigma Xi. Home: 9016 Dewberry Ct Indianapolis IN 46260-1527 E-mail: myovits@iupui.edu.

YOW, ASUKA TAGA, music educator, researcher; b. Osaka City, Japan, May 29, 1978; arrived in US, 1994; d. Haruki and Makie Taga; m. Thomas Jeremy Yow, May 31, 2003. MusB, U. Memphis, 2001; MusM, Mich. State U., 2003. Grad. asst., opera pianist, accompanist Mich. State U., East Lansing, 2001—03; tchr. Memphis City Sch. Group Piano, 2003—, Lausanne Music Conservatory, 2003—. Catherine Herrick Cobb scholar, Mich. State U., 2001—03. Fellow: Music Tchrs. Nat. Assn. Avocations: music, movies, travel. Home: 2457 Union Ave #2 Memphis TN 38112

YRIGOYEN, CHARLES, JR., church denomination executive; b. Phila., Dec. 9, 1937; s. Charles and Erma Mae (Suters) Y.; m. Jeanette Alice Brittingham, Dec. 13, 1958; children: Debra Jean, Charles III. BS in Econs., U. Pa., 1959; BD, Lancaster (Pa.) Theol. Sem., 1962; ThM, Ea. Bapt. Theol. Sem., Phila., 1964; PhD, Temple U., 1973; DD (hon.), Albright Coll., 1987. Ordained to ministry United Meth. Ch., 1960. Pastor various chs. Meth. Ch., Pa., 1958-66, campus min., 1966-68; chaplain, prof. religion Albright Coll., Reading, Pa., 1968-82; gen. sec. Gen. Com. on Archives and History, United Meth. Ch., Madison, NJ, 1982—. Vis. scholar Union Theol. Sem., N.Y.C., 1980, adj. prof., 1982-93, 2000—; adj. prof. ch. history Drew U., Madison, 1982—; adj. prof. Moravian Theol. Sem., Bethlehem, Pa., 1994-02; exec. com. World Meth. Coun., 1986—; bd. dirs. Wesley Works Editl. Project; adj. prof. Luth. Theol. Sem., Phila., 1999. Author: Acts for Our Time, 1987, John Wesley: Holiness of Heart and Life, 1996, Belief Matters: United Methodism's Doctrinal Standards, 2001; editor: Reformed and Catholic, 1978, Catholic and Reformed, 1979, Historical Dictionary of Methodism, 1996, The Global Impact of the Wesleyan Traditions and Their Related Movements, 2002, Meth. History Jour., 1982—. Mem. alumni coun. Lancaster Theol. Sem., 2002—. Masland fellow Union Theol. Sem., 1975, 80. Mem. World Meth. Hist. Soc. (gen. sec. 1987—), Wesley Hist. Soc., Wesleyan Theol. Soc., Am. Soc. Ch. History, Charles Wesley Soc., Oxford Inst. Meth. Theol. Studies, Mercersburg Soc. (bd. dirs.), United Meth. Hist. Soc. Republican. Methodist. Home: 2 Hemlock Ln Morristown NJ 07960-6774 Office: Gen Com on Archives and History PO Box 127 Madison NJ 07940-0127 Office Phone: 973-408-3189. E-mail: cyrigoyen@gcah.org.

YRIZARRY, MAGDA N. communications executive; married; 2 children. Joined Bell Atlantic (predecessor to Verizon), 1991—; dir. cmty. affairs Bklyn. and S.I. Bell Atlantic; v.p. pub. policy and strategic affairs Verizon Comm., Washington, 2003—. Bd. mem. LULAC Nat. Edn. Svcs. Ctrs.; mem. corp. adv. bd. USHCC, Nat. Hispanic Caucus of State Legislators, Nat. Coun. LaRaza. Former trustee, pres. N.Y.C. Cmty. Sch. Bd. 9; former mem. Bd. Edn. Com. on Bilingual and Spl. Edn., NY; former vol. N.Y. State Mentoring Program, Sch.-Based Mgmt., Jr. Achievement. Recipient Pres. award, U.S. Hispanic C. of C. Found., Nat. Hispanic Corp. Achievers award, 1998, Corp. Rep. of the Yr. award, Am. GI Forum, 2003. Mem.: ASPIRA (chairperson N.Y., exec. bd. mem.), 100 Hispanic Women (founding mem.), Nat. Hispanic Leadership Inst. Office: Verizon Pub Policy and Strategic Affairs 1710 H St NW Washington DC 20006*

YSSELDYKE, JAMES EDWARD, psychology educator, dean; b. Grand Rapids, Mich., Jan. 1, 1944; 2 children. Student in psychology, Calvin Coll., 1962-65; BA in Psychology and Biology, Western Mich. U., 1966; MA in Sch. Psychology, U. Ill., 1968, PhD, 1971. Lic. cons. psychologist, Minn. Tchr. spl. edn. Kent County Juvenile Ct. Ctr., Grand Rapids, 1966-67; rsch. asst. U. Ill. Inst. Rsch. on Exceptional Children, 1969-70, tchg. asst. dept. ednl. psychology, 1970; sch. psychology intern Oakland County Schs., Pontiac, Mich., 1970-71; asst. prof. sch. psychology Pa. State U., 1971-75, assoc. prof., 1975, U. Minn., Mpls., 1975-79, prof., 1979-91, dir. Inst. Rsch. on Learning Disabilities, 1977-83, dir. Nat. Sch. Psychology Insvc. Tng. Network, 1977-83, dir. sch. psychology program, 1987-93, dir. Nat. Ctr. on Ednl. Outcomes, 1991-99, assoc. dean for rsch., 2000—. Emma Birkmaier endowed prof. U. Minn., 1998-2000; advisor, cons. and researcher in field. Author: (with J. Salvia) Assessment in Special and Remedial Education, 1985, 9th edit., 2003, (with B. Algozzine and M. Thurlow) Critical Issues in Special and Remedial Education, 1992, 3d edit., 2000, Strategies and Tactics for Effective Instruction, 1997, (with S.L. Christenson) Functional Assessment of Academic Behavior, 2003; editor: Exceptional Children, 1984-90; assoc. editor: The School Psychologist, 1972-75, mem. editorial bd., cons. editor numerous jours.; contbr. chpts. to books and articles to jours. Recipient Disting. Tchg. award U. Minn., 1988, Disting. Alumni award U. Ill. Coll. Edn., 1998; fellow NIMH, 1967-69; grantee in field. Fellow APA (Lightner Witmer award 1973); mem. APA, NASP, Am. Ednl. Rsch. Assn., Coun. for Exceptional Children (Rsch. award 1995), Coun. for Ednl. Diagnostic Svcs. Office: Coll of Edn and Human Devel 104 Burton Hall 178 Pillsbury Dr SE Minneapolis MN 55455-0296 Business E-Mail: jim@umn.edu.

YSURSA, BEN T. state official; b. Boise, Idaho, June 10, 1949; m. Penny Ysursa; children: Shawn Del, Matthew, Andrew. BA, Gonzaga U., 1971; JD, St. Louis U. Law Sch., 1974. Dep. sec. state Idaho Sec. State's Office, 1974—76, chief dep., 1976—2002; sec. state State of Idaho, 2002—. Mem. Basque Ctr., St. John's Parish; pres. Adh County Lincoln Day, 1990. Mem.: Reagan-Bush Idaho Com. (treas. 1984), NHSS (secs. state 2003), Idaho State Bar Assn. Republican. Roman Catholic. Office: Office Sec State 700 W Jefferson Rm 203 PO Box 83720 Boise ID 83720-0080

YTTREHUS, ROLV BERGER, composer, educator; b. Duluth, Minn., Mar. 12, 1926; s. Chris and Petra (Andal) Y. BA, U. Minn., Duluth, 1950; MusM, U. Mich., 1953; diploma, Acad. Santa Cecilia, Rome, 1962; studies with Nadia Boulanger, Paris, 1954-55; studies with Roger Sessions, Princeton, N.J., 1957-60; studies with Aaron Copland, Tanglewood, 1958; studies with Goffredo Petrassi, 1960—62. Instr. music U. Mo., Columbia, 1963-68; asst. prof. Purdue U., West Lafayette, Ind., 1968-69; assoc. prof. U. Wis., Oshkosh, 1969-77; prof. Rutgers U., New Brunswick, N.J., 1977-96; prof. emeritus, 1996—; recorded with Composers Recs., Inc., 1st Edition Records, Centaur Records, MMC Records. Lectr. Internat. Ferienkurse Für Neue Musik, Darmstadt, Germany, 1994. Composer: Music for Winds, Percussion and Viola, 1961, Expressioni Per Orchestra, 1962, Music for Winds, Percussion, Cello and Voices, 1969, Quintet, 1973, Sextet, 1974, Gradus Ad Parnassum, 1979, Sonata for Percussion and Piano, 1983, Explorations for Solo Piano, 1985, Sonata for Cello and Piano, 1988, Raritan Variation (solo piano), 1989, Symphony No. 1, 1998, Espressioni per Orchestra performed by Philharm. Orch., Augsburg, Germany, 1996, Symphony No. 1, 1998 (performed with Warsaw Nat. Philharm. Orch. on Warsaw Autumn Festival 1998), Plectrum Spectrum, 2000; CRI CD 843 the Music of Rolv Yttrehus issued 2000. Served with USN, 1944-46, PTO. Recipient award Minn. Fedn. Music Clubs, 1957, Margaret Lee Crofts award, Tanglewood, Mass., 1958, award N.J. Coun. on Arts, 1989; Fulbright scholar, 1954, scholar Govt. of Italy, 1960-62; fellow Composers Conf., 1971, 72, 75; grantee Nat. Endowment for Arts, 1976. Mem. Internat. Soc. Contemporary Music (bd. dirs. 1979—), Am. Composers Alliance (rec. award 1985), Composers Guild N.J. (pres. 1985-92). Avocation: reading. Home: One Woods Circle East Brunswick NJ 08816 E-mail: yttrehus@rci.rutgers.edu.

YU, AITING TOBEY, engineering executive; b. Chekiang, China, Jan. 6, 1921; came to U.S., 1945, naturalized, 1955; s. H.K. and A. (Chow) Y.; m. Natalie Kwok, Nov. 10, 1951; children: Pamela, Leonard T. BS, Nat. Cen. U., Chungking, China, 1943; SM, MIT, 1946; PhD, Lehigh U., 1949; MBA, Columbia U., 1972. Registered profl. engr., Fla. Asst. prof. engring. NYU, 1949-51; design engr. Hewitt-Robins Inc., 1951-54, chief design engr., 1955-58, engring. mgr., 1958-59, dir. systems engring., 1967-68, v.p. ops., 1968-71; tech. dir. West S.Am. Overseas Corp., N.Y.C., 1959-67; prin. A.T. Yu Cons. Engrs., 1971-72; co-founder, chmn. Orba Corp., Mountain Lakes, N.J., 1972—, now chmn. emeritus. Contbr. articles to profl. jours; patentee in field. Recipient nat. outstanding engring. achievement awards by ASCE, NSPE, AIME, ASME; inducted into Nat. Mining Hall of Fame, 1998. Mem. NAE, AIME (chmn. minerals processing div., SME pres. 1986), NSPE, Nat. Acad. Engring., Sigma Xi. Home: 36750 Us Highway 19 N Palm Harbor FL 34684-1239 also: 4303A Hana Hwy Haiku HI 96708-5303 Office: Orba Corp 1250 W Sam Houston Pkwy S Houston TX 77042-1916

YU, ANDREW, minister; b. Fu-Yang, Chekian, China, Feb. 28, 1927; came to the U.S., 1972; s. Kung-Chu Yu and Mei-Chen Liu; m. Julie Yu, July 13, 1957; children: Peter, Ruth. BTh, Taiwan Bapt. Theol. Sem., Taipei, 1957; postgrad., Tanghai U., Taichung, Taiwan, 1965; MA in Ministry Studies, Moody Bible Inst., 1991; postgrad., Bibl. Archaeology Soc., 1993, Fuller Theol. Sem., 1996, Fuqua Internat. Sch. Christian Comm., 1998. Cert. pastoral counseling. Jour. clk. Bankers Trust Co., N.Y.C., 1972-80; pastoral coounselor Am. Assn. Christian Counseling, Forest, Va., 1991—; minister Manhattan Chinese Bapt. Ch., N.Y.C., 1980—, sr. pastor, 1986—. Author: Rekinling the Fires of Revial, 1993, A Master Piece of Spirituality, 1995, The Poem of Draw Wings, 2001; editor Chinese Christian Workers, 1999—; chief editor: Chinese Newsletter, N.Y., 2002-. Mem. positive thinking divsn. Guideposts Norman Vincent Peal Ctr. for Positive Thinking, Paulling, NY, 2003. Recipient Lifetime Royal Patronage status Kevin, Prince Regent Princepality of Hutt River Province, Australia, 1994, Cert. of Appreciation, Ronald Reagan Presdl. Found., 2003. Mem. Poetry Soc. Am., Am. Bible Soc., Chinese Writers Assn. N.Y. Avocations: reading, writing, music, travel, collecting. Home: Apt 20E 675 Water St New York NY 10002 Office: Manhattan Chinese Bapt Ch 236 W 72nd St New York NY 10023

YU, ANTHONY C. religion and literature educator; b. Hong Kong, Oct. 6, 1938; came to U.S., 1956, naturalized, 1976; s. P.C. and Norma (Au) Y.; m. Priscilla Tang, Sept. 18, 1963; 1 son, Christopher Dietrich. BA, Houghton Coll., 1960; STB, Fuller Theol. Sem., 1963; PhD, U. Chgo., 1969, DLitt, 1996. Instr. U. Ill., Chgo., 1967-68; asst. prof. U. Chgo., 1968-74, assoc. prof., 1974-78, prof., 1978—. Assoc. vis. prof. Ind. U., Bloomington, 1975; Whitney J. Oates short-term vis. fellow Princeton U., 1986; disting. vis. prof. Faculty of Arts, U. Alta., Can., 1992; mem. joint com. on study Chinese civilization Am. Coun. Learned Socs., 1980-86, bd. dirs., 1986-94; regional chmn. Mellon Fellowship in Humanities, 1982-92; bd. dirs. Ill. Humanities Coun., 1995-97; vis. prof. dept. religion Chinese U. Hong Kong, 1997; mem. com. social thought U. Chgo., 2004—. Asst. editor Jour. Asian Studies, 1975-78; co-editor Jour. Religion, 1980—; author, editor: Parnassus Revisited, 1973; editor, translator: The Journey to the West, 4 vols., 1977-83, Essays on The Journey to the West and Other Studies (in Chinese), 1989; co-editor (with Mary Gerhart) Morphologies of Faith: Essays on Religion and Culture in Honor of Nathan A. Scott, Jr., 1990, Rereading the Stone: Desire and the Making of Fiction in Dream of the Red Chamber, 1997. Recipient Gordon J. Laing prize, 1983; Danforth fellow, 1960-67; Guggenheim fellow, 1976-77; NEH translation grantee, 1977-82; Am. Coun. Learned Socs. sr. fellow, 1986-87; Masterworks Study grant NEH Seminar for Pub. Sch. Tchrs., 1992; elected academician Academia Sinica, 1998; Phi Beta Kappa vis. scholar 2001-02. Fellow Am. Acad. Arts and Scis.; mem. MLA (exec. coun. 1998—2001), Assn. for Asian Studies, Am. Acad. Religion (bd. dirs. 1995-97), Am. Comparative Lit. Assn., Milton Soc. Am., Arts Club. Home: 950 N Clark St Unit G Chicago IL 60610-8702 Office: U Chicago 1025 E 58th St Chicago IL 60637-1509 E-mail: acyu@midway.uchicago.edu.

YU, CHACK YUNG, pediatrics educator, molecular biologist; b. Guangdong, People Republic of China, Dec. 24, 1957; s. Hung Ho and Shui-Wo (Kwok) Y.; m. Lai-Chu, Apr. 23, 1987; children: Gayang Heidi, Gakit Richard. BS, Chinese U. Hong Kong, 1981, MPhil, 1983; DPhil, Oxford U., England, 1988. Asst. prof. Ohio State U., Columbus, 1990-96, assoc. prof., 1996—. Contbr. articles to profl. jours. Grantee NIH, Bethesda, Md., 1994—, March of Dimes, 1992-94; postdoctoral fellow Med. Rsch. Coun. Lab. Molecular Biology, Cambridge, England, 1987-90. Mem. AAAS, Am. Assn. Immunologists, Am. Soc. Human Genetics, Am. Soc. Microbiology, Am. Soc. Biochemistry and Molecular Biology, Soc. for Pediat. Rsch. Office: Children's Rsch Inst 700 Childrens Dr Columbus OH 43205-2664 E-mail: cyu@chi.osu.edu.

YU, FEI, internist; b. Beijing, Mar. 12, 1956; came to U.S., 1990; d. Longshan and Dan (Zheng) Y.; m. Xiangqun Fu, Jan. 7, 1984; 1 child, Danni. MD, Beijing Med. U., 1982; PhD in Med. Sci., Beijing Union Med. Coll., 1989. Diplomate Am. Bd. Internal Medicine. Intern The People's Hosp., Beijing Med. U., 1981-82; resident in internal medicine Jishuitan Hosp., Beijing, 1983-84, Beijing Union Med. Coll. Hosp., 1984-87; clin. fellow hematology dept. internal medicine Beijing Union Med. Coll., Chinese Acad. Med. Scis., 1987-89; rsch. fellow dept. devel. cell biology Sloan-Ketterng Inst. Cancer Rsch., N.Y.C., 1991-93; rsch. fellow dept. internal medicine Columbia U. Coll. Physicians and Surgeons, N.Y.C., 1993—95; resident in medicine N.Y. Meth. Hosp., Bklyn., 1996-99; physician Regal Med. PC, Clifton, NJ, 2000—02, Clifton Med. & Rehab. Ctr., 2003; pvt. practice Englewood Cliffs, NJ, 2003—. Contbr. articles to profl. jours. Mem. AMA, ACP. Avocations: music, swimming, novel reading, travel, stamp collecting/philately. Office: 385 Sylvan Ave 25 Englewood Cliffs NJ 07632 Office Phone: 201-567-0686. Personal E-mail: drfeiyu@aol.com.

YU, GEORGE TZUCHIAO, political science educator; b. London, May 16, 1931; s. Wangteh and Ying (Ho) Y.; m. Priscilla Chang, Aug. 11, 1957; children: Anthony, Phillip. AB, U. Calif., Berkeley, 1954, MA, 1957, PhD, 1961. Asst. prof. polit. sci. U. N.C., Chapel Hill, 1961-65; assoc. prof. polit. sci. U. Ill., Urbana, 1965-70, prof., 1970—, head dept., 1987-92, dir. Ctr. for East Asian and Pacific Studies, 1992—, dir. grad. studies, 1981-85, chair Asian Am. studies com., 1997—2002. Vis. sr. lectr. polit. sci. Univ. Coll., Nairobi, 1968. Author: The Chinese Anarchist Movement, 1961, 65, Party Politics in Republican China, 1966, China and Tanzania, 1970, China's African Policy, 1975, Intra-Asian International Relations, 1977, Modern China and Its Revolutionary Process, 1985, American Studies in China, 1993, China in Transition, 1994, Asia's New World Order, 1997, Mongolia and Northeast Asia, 1999. Grantee, Social Sci. Rsch. Coun., 1967—68, 1970—71, NEH, 1978—81, 1984—86, Earhart Found., 1976—77, 1981—83, 1988, Ford Found., 1985—87, 1989, 1992, Freeman Found., 1996, 1997, 1999, 2001—03. Mem. Assn. Asian Studies. Office: 702 S Wright St Urbana IL 61801-3631 Business E-Mail: g-yu@uiuc.edu.

YU, JEN, medical educator; b. Taipei, Taiwan, Jan. 23, 1943; came to U.S., 1969; s. Chin Chuan and Shiu Lan (Lin) Y.; m. Janet Chen, June 16, 1973; children: Benjamin, Christopher. MD, Nat. Taiwan U., 1968; PhD in Physiology, U. Pa., 1972. Diplomate Am. Bd. Phys. Medicine and Rehab. Intern Phila. Gen. Hosp., 1972-73; resident in phys. medicine and rehab. Hosp. of U. Pa., 1973-75; asst. prof. dept. phys. medicine and rehab. U. Pa. Sch. Medicine, Phila., 1975-76, U. Tex. Health Sci. Ctr., San Antonio, 1976-79, assoc. prof., 1979-81; prof. dept. phys. medicine and rehab. U. Calif. Irvine Coll. Medicine, 1981-82, prof., chmn. dept. phys. medicine and rehab., 1982—. Contbr. articles to profl. jours. Mem. Am. Acad. Phys. Medicine and Rehab., Am. Congress Rehab. Medicine, Assn. Acad. Physiatrists, Am. Assn. Anatomists, Soc. for Neurosci. Office: U Calif Irvine Med Ctr Dept Phys Medicine & Rehab 101 The City Dr Orange CA 92868-3201 Office Phone: 714-456-6504. Business E-Mail: jyu@uci.edu.

YU, JESSICA, director, producer, writer, editor; b. 1966; BA in English with honors, Yale U. Bd. dirs. Internat. Documentary Assn. Prodr.(dir.): Home Base: A Chinatown Callen Heinlenville, Sour Death Balls, 1992, Breathing Lessons: The Life and Work of Mark O'Brien, 1996 (Acad. award for best documentary short subject, 1997), Better Late, 1997 (TV films) Men of Re-enaction, 1998; dir.: (documentaries, feature) The Living Museum, 1998; contbr. articles. Recipient Edward R. Murrow award, Skeptics Soc., 1995, 24 film festival awards. Fellow: Yaddo, MacDowell Colony; mem.: Phi Beta Kappa.

YU, JIANG W. research scientist; b. Beijing, Nov. 8, 1956; came to U.S., 1980; s. Daosheng Wu and Baoqing Shen. Student, Peking U., Beijing, 1978-80; BA, SUNY, Albany, 1983, PhD, 1990. Rsch. scientist N.Y. State Office of Alcoholism and Substance Abuse Svcs., Albany, N.Y., 1988—. Dir. Sci. Rsch. Consulting, Albany, 1991-99. Contbr. rsch. articles to profl. jours. Mem. APHA, Internat. Coun. on Alcohol, Drugs and Traffic Safety, Am. Sociol. Assn., Am. Soc. Criminology, Acad. Criminal Justice Scis., Rsch. Soc. on Alcoholism. Avocations: tennis, skiing, inline skating. Home: 173 Williamsburg Ct Albany NY 12203-5507 Office: N Y State Office Alcoholism and Substance Abuse Svcs 1450 Western Ave Albany NY 12203-3539

YU, JIYUAN, philosopher, educator; b. Zhuji, Zhejiang, China, July 5, 1964; arrived in U.S., 1997; m. Yajie Zhang, Feb. 22, 1989; 1 child, Norman. BA, Shandong U., Jinan, China, 1983; MA, Renmin U., Beijing, 1986; PhD, Guelph (Can.) U., 1994. Rsch. fellow U. Oxford, England, 1994—97; asst. prof. SUNY, Buffalo, 1997—2003, assoc. prof., 2003—. Author: Structure of Being in Aristotle, 2003; editor: Rationality and Happiness, 2003; co-author: Blackwell Dictionary of Philosophy, 2004; mem. History Philosophy Quar., 2001—. Fellow, Nat. Humanities Ctr., 2003—04. Office: SUNY Buffalo NY 14260 Office Phone: 716-645-2444. Office Fax: 716-645-6139. Business E-Mail: jyyu@acsu.buffalo.edu.

YU, JOHN JUNYAO, mechanical engineer, researcher; PhD in Mech. Engring., U. Alta., Edmonton, Alberta, CANADA, 1997. Lic. Alta., 1999. Faculty mem. Shanghai Jiao Tong U., Shanghai, 1985—92; rsch. assoc. U. Alta., Edmonton, Canada, 1997—98; rsch. engr. Bently Rotor Dynamics Rsch. Corp., Minden, Nev., 1998—99, sr. rsch. engr., 1999—2000, rsch. scientist, 2000—02; machinery diagnostic specialist GE Power Sys.-Bently Nev., Minden, Nev., 2002—. Contbr. scientific papers more than 40 (IGTI 2001 John P. Davis Award, 2003). Recipient PhD Dissertation Fellowship, U. Alta., 1996-1997. Mem.: ASME (chair 2003, rotordynamics session chair ASME/IGTI Turbo Expo 2003, 2004), IGTI Dynamics and Structure Com. Achievements include development of rolling element bearing defect detection methodology; Gas bearing design code; discovery of dry-whip generated spontenuously. Home: 1839 Bougainvillea Dr Minden NV 89423 Office: GE Power Sys - Bently Nevada 1631 Bently Pkwy S Minden NV 89423 Office Phone: 775-215-1225. Personal E-mail: john.yu@charter.net. Business E-Mail: john.yu@ps.ge.com.

YU, JUN, biologist; s. Guofan Yu and Qingzhen Xu; m. Cong Xu; children: Yuezhou, Yueyang. PhD, NYU, 1990. Rsch. asst. prof. N.Y. U., 1990—93; sr. fellow U. Wash., 1993—98; assoc. dir. Beijing Genomics Inst. Chinese Acad. Scis., 1998—. Named Rsch. Leader of the Yr., Sci. Am., 2002. E-mail: junyu@genomics.org.cn.

YU, LINDA, newswoman, television anchorwoman; b. Xian, China, Dec. 1, 1946; BA in Journalism, U. So. Calif., 1968. With Sta. KTLA-TV, Los Angeles, Sta. KABC-TV, Los Angeles; news anchor, reporter Sta. KATU-TV, Portland, Oreg.; gen. assignment reporter Sta. KGO-TV, San Francisco; with Sta. WMAQ-TV, Chgo., 1979-84, gen. assignment reporter, weekend anchor, 1979-80, co-anchor Monday-Friday edit. NEWSCENTERS, 4:30 PM, 1980-81, co-anchor NEWSCENTER5, 10:00 PM, 1981-84; co-anchor Eyewitness News, WLS-TV, Chgo., 1984—; spl.: Linda Yu in China, 1980; anchor WLS-TV, Chgo., 1984—. Recipient Chgo. Emmy award, 1981, 82, 87. Office: Sta WLS-TV 190 N State St Chicago IL 60601-3302

YU, MAY HUANG, librarian, educator, real estate agent; b. Chengdu, Sichuan, China, June 24; came to the U.S., 1989; s. Dazhou Huang and Jiangzhen Yu; m. Lixin Yu; 1 child, Michael. Student, Beijing U., 1988; LLB, State Normal U. Sichuan, Chengdu, 1982; MLS, SUNY, Albany, 1996. Cert. pub. libr., N.Y. Tchr. Fuxing H.S., Qingcheng, Sichuan, China, 1975-78; asst. prof. State Normal U. Sichuan, Chengdu, 1982-89; libr., instr. Alcorn State (Miss.) U., 1996—97; web developer, metadata libr. Fla. State U., Tallahassee, 1998—2000; head media dept. Alcorn State (Miss.) U., media libr., instr., 2000—. Spl. corr. Jour. Ethics, Chengdu, 1985-89; gen. sec. Sichuan State Ethics Assn., Chengdu, 1985-89. Editor: The Dictionary of Ethics, 1987. Named Outstanding Rschr., Assn. Philosophy and Social Scis. Sichuan State, 1987. Mem. ALA, Internat. Fedn. Libr. Assns. and Instns. Avocations: ping pong/table tennis, movies, travel. Office: JD Boyd Libr 1000 ASU Dr Alcorn State MS 39096-7510 Fax: 601-877-3885.

YU, MEI-YING WONG, chemist, researcher; d. H-C and C-S (Chen) Wong; m. Tsann-wang Yu, Jan. 9, 1971; 1 child, Irene. BS in Pharmacy, Kaohsiung Med. Coll., Kaohsiung, Taiwan, 1959—64; MS in Pharmacology, U. of Ala., Birmingham, 1964—68, PhD in Pharmacology, 1968—70. Pharmacist Taiwanese Pharmacist Assn./Taiwan, 1964. Postdoctoral fellow Baylor Coll. of Medicine, 1970—71; rsch. assoc. U. of Tex., 1971—74; sr. staff fellow Nat. Inst. of Child Health and Human Devel., 1974—80; inspector FDA, 1980—99, sr. staff fellow, 1980—81, rsch. chemist, 1981—2000, supervisory rsch. chemist, 2000—. Author (regulatory reviewer): (research and review) Numerous Sci. Journals. Operation com. mem. Kaohsiung Med. U. Alumni Assn., 2002. Recipient James H Nakano Citation Award and Charles Shepard Sci. Award, Ctr. for Disease Control and Prevention (CDC), 1997. Mem.: Am. Soc. Pharmacology and Exptl. Therapeutics (ASPET)/FASEB. Achievements include research in Establish independent research programs regarding safety, purity, and potency of blood and blood products. Home: 7809 Ivymount Terr Potomac MD 20854 Office: Food and Drug Administration 1401 Rockville Pike Rockville MD 20852-1448 E-mail: yu@cber.fda.gov.

YU, MEI-YU, medical researcher; b. Chongqing, China, Feb. 21, 1944; d. Wencheng Yu and Xiuying Pan; m. Bo-nan Jiang, Dec. 26, 1968; children: Bo, Hao. MD, Shanghai Med. U., 1968; MA, U. Tex. Austin, 1983, PhD, 1986.

Physcian Changha Railway Hosp., Changsha, China, 1969-81; rschr. U. Tex., Austin, 1981-86; post-doctoral fellow U. Mich., Ann Arbor, 1987-89, asst. rsch. scientist, 1990-95, project dir., 1996—. Project dir., Healthy Asian Ams. project, 1996—; adminstr., Internat. Learning program, 1996—. Recipient fellowship, The Population Coun., N.Y., 1983-85, postdoctoral fellowship, NIA, 1987-89. Mem. Nat. Asian Women's Health Orgn's. Nat. Policy Coun., Internat. Coun. Women's Health Issues. Avocations: travel, danicng, music, movies. Office: U Mich Sch Nursing 400 N Ingalls St Ann Arbor MI 48109-0482 Fax: 734-647-9966. E-mail: yujiang@umich.edu.

YU, OLIVER SHUKIANG, corporate executive, educator, technology strategist; b. Chendu, Sichuan, China, July 8, 1939; arrived in U.S., 1961; s. Cecil S. and Nan S. Yu; m. Joanna S. Chu, June 1, 1985; children: Amy S., Christopher S., Hamilton S. MS, Ga. Inst. of Tech., 1963, Stanford U., 1967, PhD, 1972. Mgr. planning analysis Electric Power Rsch. Inst., Palo Alto, Calif., 1974—89; dir. energy and tech. strategies SRI Internat., Menlo Park, Calif., 1989—2000; pres., CEO The STARS Group, Los Altos, Calif., 2000—. Dir. Silicon Valley bus. stars program San Jose State U., 2002—; cons. assoc. prof. Stanford U., 1984—86; sr. tech. advisor Taiwan Power Co., Taipei, 1979—. Author: (book) Introduction to Technology Management, 1998. With Taiwanese Navy, 1959—61. Named Hon. Fellow, East-West Ctr., 1981; recipient Fulbright fellowship, U.S. State Dept., 1961. Mem.: IEEE, Inst. for Ops. Rsch. and Mgmt. Sci. (coun. mem., chair meeting com. 1985—91). Achievements include research in Technology Portfolio Planning and Management Methodology. Office: The STARS Group 470 Santa Barbara Dr Los Altos CA 94022 E-mail: oliveryu@starstrategygroup.com.

YU, PAUL, academic administrator; m. Ellen Yu; children: Gregory, Nicholas. BA in Philosophy, U. Mich., 1965, MA in Philosophy, 1967, PhD in Philosophy, 1973. Mem. faculty philosophy Ctrl. Mich. U., 1969—80, chair philosophy, 1981—87, assoc. dean Coll. Arts and Scis., 1987—89; dean Coll. Liberal Arts and Scis. Butler U., 1989—91, v.p. acad. affairs, 1991—92, provost, sr. v.p. acad. affairs, 1992—97; pres. SUNY, Brockport, 1997—2004, San Jose (Calif.) State U., 2004—. Fulbright lectr. philosophy Nat. Taiwan U., 1980—81; vis. scholar Chinese Acad. Social Scis., Beijing, 1990; bd. dirs. Am. Assn. Univ. Adminstrs., 1998—2001; mem. exec. com. Commn. on the Liberal Arts Agenda Am. Assn. State Colls. and Univs., 1998—2001, co-chair Forum on the Liberal Arts Agenda, 2001—02; mem. Commn. on Internat. Edn. Am. Coun. on Edn., 2000—02. Recipient Disting. Faculty award, Mich. Assn. Governing Bds., 1982, Disting. Hoosier award, Office of Evan Bayn, Gov. Ind., 1990. Mem.: Am. Philos. Assn. Office: San Jose State Univ Office of the Pres Tower Hall 206A One Washington Sq San Jose CA 95192-0002*

YU, PAULINE RUTH, former dean, educational association administrator; b. Rochester, N.Y., Mar. 5, 1949; d. Paul N. and Iling (Tang) Y.; m. Theodore D. Huters, Aug. 23, 1975 (div. Feb. 2000); children: Emily Elizabeth, Matthew Charles, Alexander David. BA in History and Lit. magna cum laude, Harvard U., 1971; MA in Comparative Lit., Stanford U., 1973, PhD in Comparative Lit., 1976. Asst. prof., then assoc. prof. U. Minn., Mpls., 1976-85; assoc. prof., then prof. Columbia U., N.Y.C., 1985-89; prof., founding chair dept. East Asian langs. and lit. U. Calif., Irvine, 1989-94; dean humanities UCLA, 1994—2003, prof. East Asian langs. and culture, 1994—2003; pres. Am. Coun. Learned Socs., N.Y.C., 2003—. Author: The Poetry of Wang Wei, 1980, The Reading of Imagery in the Chinese Poetic Tradition, 1987; editor and contbg. author: Voices of the Song Lyric in China, 1994, Culture and State in Chinese History: Conventions, Accommodations, and Critiques, 1997, Ways with Words: Writing about Reading Texts from Early China, 2000; editor, contbr.: The Longman Anthology; mem. editl. bd. Tang Studies, Chinese Lit., Comparative Lit. Studies, 1993—. Mem. nat. adv. bd. Woodrow Wilson Found., 2004—; trustee Nat. Humanities Ctr., 2000; bd. dirs. The Teagle Found., 2003—; mem. adv. coun. Dept. East Asian Studies, Princeton U., 2003—; bd. overseers Harvard U., 2003—. Guggenheim fellow, 1983-84, ACLS fellow, 1983-84; recipient Profl. Achievement award U. Calif. at Irvine Alumni Assn., 1993. Fellow Am. Acad. Arts and Scis.; mem. MLA, ACLS (bd. dirs. 1998-), Assn. Asian Studies (mem. China and Inner Asia coun. 1982-85), Am. Comparative Lit. Assn., Am. Oriental Soc., Woodrow Wilson Found. (nat. adv. bd 2004-), Phi Beta Kappa Soc. (senator 1997-). Office: Am Coun Learned Societies 633 Third Ave New York NY 10017-6795 E-mail: paulineyu@acls.org.

YU, ROBERT KUAN-JEN, biochemistry educator; b. Chungking, China, Jan. 27, 1938; came to U.S., 1962; m. Helen Chow, July 1, 1972; children: David S., Jennifer S. BS, Tunghai U., Taiwan, 1960; PhD, U. Ill., 1967; Med.ScD. (hon.), Tokyo, 1980; MA (hon.), Yale U., 1985. Rsch. assoc., instr. Albert Einstein Coll. Medicine, Bronx, 1967-72; asst. prof. Yale U., New Haven, 1973-75, assoc. prof., 1975-82, prof., 1983-88; prof. biochemistry, chmn. dept. Med. Coll. Va. Va. Commonwealth U., Richmond, 1988-2000; dir. Inst. Mol. Med. Genetics Med. Coll., Augusta, Ga., 2000—. Mem. study sect. NIH, Washington, 1980-84, 96—; mem. Bd. Lab. Svcs., Va., 1994-98. Editor: Gangioside Structure Function and Biomedical Potential, 1984, New Trends in Ganglioside Research, 1988; contbr. over 500 articles to profl. publs. Josiah Macy scholar, 1979; grantee NIH, 1975—; recipient Va. Outstanding Scientist of Yr. award, 1995, Jacob Javits award NIH, 1984-91, Alexander von Humboldt award, 1990, GRA Eminent scholar, 2000, Tunghai U. Dist. Alumnus award, 2003, Achievement award, Chinese Assn. Engrs. and Scientists of So. Calif., 2004, Academecian award Academia Sinica, 2004. Mem. AAAS, Am. Soc. Cell Biology, Am. Soc. Neurochemistry (mem. coun. 1983-86, 91-95, pres. 2001-03), Internat. Soc. Neurochemistry, Soc. Neurosci., Am. Soc. Biochemistry and Molecular Biology, Am. Chem. Soc., N.Y. Acad. Sci. Home: 821 River Bluff Rd North Augusta SC 29841-6056 Office: IMMAG Med Coll Ga 1120 15th St Augusta GA 30912-0004 Office Phone: 706-721-0699. Business E-Mail: ryu@mcg.edu.

YU, ROGER HONG, physics educator; b. Shanghai, Apr. 19, 1960; came to U.S., 1987; s. Rei Qian and Wei-Zen (Zhang) Y.; m. Ting Shi, Sept. 8, 1990; children: William S., John S. BS, Shanghai U. Sci. & Tech., 1982; MS, U. Mo., 1987; PhD, Mont. State U., 1990. Lectr. physics Shanghai U. Sci., 1982-85; tchg. asst. U. Mo., Kansas City, 1985-86, rsch. asst., 1986-87; tchg. asst. Mont. State U., Bozeman, 1987-88, rsch. asst., 1988-90; prof. physics Ctrl. Wash. U., Ellensburg, 1990—, dist. prof. rsch., chmn. dept. physics, 1997-2000; dean sch. natural scis. St. Edward's U., Austin, Tex., 2000—. Dir. undergrad. rsch. program Ctrl. Wash. U., Ellensburg, 1998—. Contbr. articles to profl. jours.; referee Phys. Rev. B. Mem. Am. Phys. Soc., Acoustic Soc. Am., Coun. Undergrad. Rsch., Associated Western Univs. (rsch. and edn. com.). Office: Sch Natural Scis St Edward's U Austin TX 78704 E-mail: rogery@admin.stedwards.edu.

YU, SHAN, artist; b. Fuzhou, Fujian, China, Oct. 24, 1949; came to the U.S., 1986; s. Yiqiang Chen and Juan Yue Yu; m. Hui Ling Du, Oct. 5, 1980; 1 child, Han. BA, Fujian Art Sch., Fuzhou, 1980; postgrad., Shanghai (China) Theater Acad., 1985-86; MFA, Boston U., 1989. Art tchr. Fujian Art Sch., Fuzhou, 1980-85; chief set designer Visual Design Assn., Cambridge, Mass., 1989-92; sr. set designer V.D.A. Inc., Somerville, Mass., 1992-99; pres. Ea. Decor & Art, Somerville, 1993—. Dir. Watercolor Soc., Fuzhou, 1984-85. One-man shows include Hong Kong Art Ctr., 1989, The Market Barn Gallery, Falmouth, Mass, 1989, CCI Gallery, Boston, 1993, 1998, Fuzhou Art Acad. Gallery, China, 2003, Hong Kong Art and Design Gallery, 2003, exhibited in group shows at The East and West Gallery, Chgo., 1990, Creative Arts Workshop Gallery, New Haven, 1992, Hewlett-Packard Co., Andover, Mass, 1994, Kane Gallery, Boston, 1995, Wilson Gallery, 1997, Am. Watercolor Soc., N.Y.C., 1999, Fuzhou Art Acad. Gallery, China, 2003, Hong Kong Art & Design Gallery, 2003, executed murals, Children's Mus., Boston, 1995, Mus. Sci., 1998—2000, The Children's Mus. at Mus. Ctr., Cin., 1998, Angel Mounds Historic Stie Mus., Evansville, Ind., 2000, Ind. State Mus., Indpls., 2001, Dinosaurs Exhibit Nat. tour, 2002, Royal BC Mus., 2003, Nat. Great Rivers Mus., Alton, Ill., 2003, Seacoast Sci. Ctr., Rye, NH, 2004; author: Liaoning Art Press, 1997, Landscape Paintings by Yu Shan, 1997. Fellow Asian Culture Coun., N.Y.C., 1986-89; internat. scholar Boston U., 1989. Mem. Internat. Soc., Nat. Soc. Mural Painters. Avocations: music, drama, film, photography, video. Home: 45 Robinson St Somerville MA 02145 Office: Eastern Decor and Art Ste B 45 Robinson St Somerville MA 02145 E-mail: yushannet1@aol.com.

YU, SHAN PING, neuroscientist, educator; s. Yong-niang Yu; m. Ling Wei; 1 child, Steven S. MS, Inst. of Pharmacology and Toxicology, Beijing, China, 1982; MD, Capital Inst. of Medicine, Bejing, China, 1982; PhD, SUNY, 1990. Rsch. asst. neuropharmacology Inst. Pharmacology and Toxicology, Beijing, 1982—84; vis. rschr. Lund U., Sweden, 1985—86; postdoctoral rschr. Howard Hughes Med. Inst., Stony Brook, NY, 1990—92; asst. prof. Wash. U., St. Louis, 1992—98, assoc. prof., 1998—2002, Med. U. S.C., Charleston, 2002—. Contbr. articles to profl. jours. Recipient Grant-in-Aid award, Am. Heart Assn., 1999, Am. Heart Assn. and Bugher award, 2001; Oversea fellow, WHO, 1985, Rsch. grantee, NSF, 1999, NIH, 2001. Mem.: Soc. for Neuroscience. Achievements include discovery of Potassium channel regulation in neuronal apoptosis and novel regulations of glutamate receptors. Home: 1214 Waterfront Dr Mount Pleasant SC 29464 Office: Med Univ of SC 280 Calhoun St Charleston SC 29425 Office Phone: 843-792-2992. Personal E-mail: yusp@musc.edu.

YU, SHIAO-LING S. humanities educator; d. Yueh Sheng and Mei-ying Ching; m. Yun S. Yu, Apr. 17, 1960; children: Lawrence H., Michael H., Mark H., David H. BA, Caldwell Coll., 1958; MA, U. Kans., 1977; PhD, U. Wis., Madison, 1978—83. Asst. prof. Oreg. State U., Corvallis, 1987—91, assoc. prof., 1991—. Vis. asst. prof. Ohio State U., Columbus, 1983—84, U. Kans., Lawrence, 1984—86. Author: (novels) Chinese Drama After the Cultural Revolution (Nat. Endowment for the Arts Fellowship, 1994); contbr. (books) Routledge Encyclopedia of Contemporary Chinese Culture, The Unbroken Chain: An Anthology of Taiwan Fiction Since 1926, Theater and Society: An Anthology of Contemporary Chinese Drama, Nativism Overseas: Contemporary Chinese Women writers, Revenge East and West, Encyclopedia of Modern Drama; contbr. articles to profl. jours. Mem. So. Poverty Law Ctr., Montgomery, Ala., 2002—03. Charlotte W. Newcombe Dissertation Fellowship, Woodrow Wilson Nat. Fellowship Found., 1982. Mem.: MLA (mem. del. assembly 2003—), Assn. Asian Performance (vice chair and conf. planner 1998—2001), Assn. Asian Studies. Office: Oregon State Univ Corvallis OR 97331 Personal E-mail: syu@orst.edu.

YU, WEI-WEN, retired engineering educator; b. Shandong, China, July 10, 1924; arrived in U.S., 1954; s. Chi-tung and Mong-shih Yu; m. Yueh-hsin Wang, Sept. 6, 1953; children: Julie H.H., Dorothy H.L., Gordon H.I. BS, Nat. Taiwan U., 1950; MS, Okla. State U., 1955; PhD, Cornell U., 1960. Registered profl. engr., Mo. Structural engr. T.H. McKaig & Assocs., Buffalo, 1955—56, 1959—60; rsch. engr. Am. Iron and Steel Inst., N.Y.C., 1960—67; staff engr. TRW Sys., Redondo Beach, Calif., 1967—68; assoc. prof. U. Mo., Rolla, 1968—72, prof., 1972—82, Curator's prof., 1982—92, Curator's prof. emeritus, 1992—. Dir. Ctr. for Cold-Formed Steel Structures, Rolla, 1990—2000; founding dir. Wei-Wen Yu Ctr. for Cold-Formed Steel Structures, Rolla, 2001—. Author: Cold-Formed Steel Structures, 1973, Cold-Formed Steel Design, 1985, 1991, 2000; guest editor: Spl. Issue on Recent Devels. in Thin-Walled Structures, 1998; editor (and co-editor): Recent Rsch. and Devel. in Cold-Formed Steel Design and Constrn., 1971—; guest editor Spl. issue on Cold-Formed Steel Structures, 1993. Recipient Alumni Merit award, U. Mo. Sch. of Mines and Metallurgy/U. Mo.-Rolla Alumni Assn., 1979, Arch T. Colwell Merit award, Soc. Automotive Engrs., 1988. Fellow: ASCE (Shortridge Hardesty award 2001); mem.: U. Mo.-Rolla Acad. Civil Engrs. (hon.), Chi-Epsilon (chpt. honor). Achievements include research in Cold-formed steel structures. Avocations: reading, gardening. Office: U Mo Rolla Dept Civil Engring Rolla MO 65409

YU, XIAO NAN, dancer; b. Dalian, China; Student, Nat. Ballet Sch., 1995—96. Apprentice Nat. Ballet Can., Toronto, Canada, 1996—2000, first soloist, 2000—. Dancer (ballets) Onegin, Cinderella, Odette/Odile, Swan Lake, Jewels, The Fairy's Kiss, Les Sylphides, Soloist La Bayadère, dancer One Hundred Words for Snow. Office: Walter Carsen Ctr Nat Ballet Canada 470 Queens Quay West Toronto ON Canada M5V 3K4

YU, YI-HAO, endocrinologist, educator, physician, research scientist; s. Shi-Qing Yu, Hui-Ling Gan; m. Yiying Zhang; 1 child, Irene. BS, Fudan U., Shanghai, China; MS, PhD, MD, NYU. Diplomate Am. Bd. Internal Medicine. Rsch. asst. prof. NYU Sch. Medicine, N.Y.C.; resident physician Columbia Presbyn. Hosp., N.Y.C., 1996—98, physician, endocrine fellow, 1998—2001; Markey rsch. fellow Columbia U. Coll. Physicians and Surgeons, N.Y.C., 1998—2001; staff physician Columbia Presbyn. Med. Ctr., 2001—, dir. adult nutrition and TPN svc.; asst. prof. medicine Columbia U. Coll. Physicians and Surgeons. Cons. Physicians Cons. Network, Mt. Arlington, NJ; mem. com. Nat. Bd. Nutrition Support Certification, Inc., CNSP. Contbr. articles, sci. papers, books in field. Fellow, China-U.S. Biochemistry Exam. and Application/Ray Wu Soc., in Atherosclerosis, NIH, 1998—2001; grantee NIH, 2001—, Pfizer, 2002—; rsch. grantee, Endocrine Fellows Found., 1999. Mem.: ACP, AMA, AAAS, Am. Soc. Parenteral and Enteral Nutrition, Am.-Chinese Med. Assn. (med. cons. 2001—), Am. Assn. Clin. Endocrinologists, Am. Soc. Cell Biology, N.Y. U. Alumni, Fudan Alumnin U.S. Avocations: Chinese calligraphy, travel, hiking, swimming. Office: Columbia Univ P&S 630 West 168th St PH10-305J New York NY 10032 Office Fax: 212-305-3213. Business E-Mail: yy102@columbia.edu.

YUAN, CHUN, physicist, educator; b. Beijing, Aug. 23, 1957; s. Zhenwu Yuan and Shunying Cheng; m. Tong Zhu, Dec. 17, 1987; children: Eric, Isabelle. BSc, Beijing Normal U., China, 1982; PhD, U. Utah, 1988. Sr. sys. analyst GE Med. Sys., Waukesha, Wis., 1988—91; asst. prof. U. Wash., Seattle, 1991—97, assoc. prof., 1997—2001, prof., 2001—. Adv. bd. Vulnerable Plaque Orgn., Houston, 2001—; vis. prof. The Post Grad. Med. Coll. of People's Liberation Army, Beijing, 2001—. Contbr. articles to profl. jours. Recipient Rsch. Career Develop. award, NIH, 1996—2000, RO1 award, 1998—. Mem.: AAAS, Am. Asn. Physicists in Medicine, Soc. Cardiovasc. Magnetic Resonance (Best Presentation Award 1999), Internat. Soc. Magnetic Resonance in Medicine (student stipend com. 1997—2000). Avocations: skiing, tennis, hiking, bicycling, music. Office: Univ Wash PO Box 357115 1959 Pacific Ave N Seattle WA 98195 Office Phone: 206-685-3536. Office Fax: 206-543-3495. Business E-Mail: cyuan@u.washington.edu.

YUAN, JIAN, network technician, researcher, engineering educator; s. Zhenbing Yuan and Huiming Su; m. Hongwu Wang, Feb. 4, 1970; children: Henry, Caleb W. PhD, U. Electronic Sci. Tech., China, 1998. Guest rschr. NIST, Gaithersburg, Md., 2000—; assoc. prof. Tsinghua U., Beijing, 2004—. Mem.: IEEE (assoc.). Achievements include patents for a new countermeasure against FH-SS communications. Office: NIST 820 W Diamond Ave Rm 465 Gaithersburg MD

YUAN, JUNYING, medical educator, researcher; b. Shanghai; BS, Fudan U., Shanghai, 1982; PhD in Neuroscience, Harvard U., 1989. Postdoctoral trainee in devel. biology MIT, 1989—90; instr. medicine Harvard U., 1990—91, asst. prof. medicine and program in neuroscience, 1992—96, asst. prof. cell biology and program in neuroscience, 1996—; asst. geneticist Cardiovasc. Rsch. Ctr. Mass. Gen. Hosp., 1990—96. Mem. editl. bd.: Current Biology, 1996, ad hoc reviewer: NIH Human Embryology and Devel. 2 Study Sect., 1995, regular reviewer:, 1996—; patentee in field, —; contbr. articles to profl. jours.; presenter in field, —. Recipient Wilson S. Stone Meml. award, MD Anderson Cancer Ctr. U. Tex., 1994, Established Investigator award, Am. Heart Assn., 1996—; fellow Ryan, Harvard Med. Sch., 1985—89. Office: Harvard Med Sch Dept Cell Biology 240 Longwood Ave Boston MA 02115-5701

YUAN, SHAO WEN, aerospace engineer, educator; b. Shanghai, Apr. 16, 1914; came to U.S., 1934, naturalized, 1954; s. Ti An and Chieh-huang (Chien) Y.; m. Hui Chih Hu, Nov. 5, 1950. BS, U. Mich., 1936; ME, Stanford U., 1939; MS, Calif. Inst. Tech., 1937, PhD, 1941. Rsch. engr. Glenn Martin Co., 1942-43; chief of rsch. Helicopter div. McDonnell Aircraft Corp., 1943-45; instr. Washington U., St. Louis, 1944-45; adj. prof. Poly. Inst. Bklyn., 1946-49, assoc. prof., 1949-54, prof., 1954-57; ptnr. von Kármán, Yuan & Arnold Assocs., 1955-63; prof. aerospace engring. U. Tex., 1958-68; prof., chmn. mech. engring. div. George Washington U., 1968-78, chmn. civil, mech. and environ. dept., 1973-78, 80-81, prof. emeritus, 1984; pres. RISE, Inc., 1977-85. Canadair Chair prof. U. Laval, Can., 1957-58; chmn. adv. com. Joint Inst. for Advancement of Flight Sci., 1970-84; hon. prof. Zhejiang U., 1987—; cons. Edo Aircraft Corp., Aerojet Corp., Cornell Aero. Lab., Dept. of Interior, Oak Ridge Nat. Lab., N.Am., Aviation, Inc., Fairchild-Hiller Corp., McDonnell-Douglas Corp., The World Bank; hon. adviser Nat. Center Research of China, Taiwan, 1958-68; chmn., founder 1st U.S.-China Conf. on Energy, Resources, and Environment, 1982; founder Consortium of Univs. for Promoting Grad. Aerospace Studies, 1984; founder Disting. Lecture Series on Founds. of Aerospace Research and Devel., 1986. Author: Foundations of Fluid Mechanics, 1967; Contbr. to: High Speed Aerodynamics and Jet Propulsion series, 1959, Energy, Resources, and Environment: Procs. at 1st U.S.-China Conf., 1982. Founder Yuan Engring. Libr., Zhejiang U., China. Recipient Outstanding Achievements and Contbns. award George Washington U., 1981; named Outstanding Educator of Am., 1970, Outstanding Chinese American, 1983, others; Yuan Engring. Libr. established, 2002. Fellow AAAS, AIAA, Internat. Biog. Assn; mem. ASME (life), Am. Soc. Engring. Edn., Soc. Engring. Sci. (bd. dirs. 1973-78, pres. 1977), Torchbearers Caltech, Founding Grant Soc. of Stanford U. (charter), John Montieth Soc. of U. Mich. (charter), Sigma Xi, Phi Kappa Phi, Phi Tau Phi, Sigma Gamma Tau, Pi Tau Sigma, Tau Beta Pi, Tau Xi Sigma. Achievements include patents in field. Home: 1400 Geary Blvd Apt 1505 San Francisco CA 94109-9309 E-mail: tianyuan@aol.com. *As engineers and scientists, we are concerned with that "something beyond"; consequently, the utmost achievement of an engineer is to create what has never been, for the improvement of quality of life.*

YUDOF, MARK GEORGE, law educator, university system chancellor; b. Phila., Oct. 30, 1944; s. Jack and Eleanor (Parris) Y.; m. Judith Lynn Gomel, July 11, 1965; children: Seth Adam, Samara Lisa. BA, U. Pa., 1965, LLB, 1968. Bar: Pa. 1970, U.S. Supreme Ct. 1974, U.S. Dist. Ct. (we. dist.) Tex. 1975, U.S. Ct. Appeals (5th cir.) 1976, Tex. 1980. Law clk. to judge U.S. Ct. Appeals (5th cir.), 1968-69; assoc. gen. counsel to ABA study FTC, 1969; rsch. assoc. Harvard Ctr. Law and Edn., 1969-70, sr. staff atty., 1970-71; lectr. Harvard Grad. Sch. Edn., 1970-71; asst. prof. law U. Tex., Austin, 1971-74, prof., 1974—97, 2002—, assoc. dean, 1979-84, James A. Elkins Cent. chair in law, 1983-97, dean, 1984-94, exec. v.p., provost, 1994-97, John Jeffers rsch. chair in law, 1991-94; pres. U. Minn., 1997—2002; chancellor U. Tex. Sys., 2002—. Jamail regents chair higher edn. leadership, 2002—, Wright chair fed. courts, 2002—. Of counsel Pennzoil vs. Texaco, 1987. Author: When Government Speaks, 1983 (Scribes Book award 1983, cert. merit ABA 1983), (with others) Educational Policy and the Law, 1992, (with others) Gender Justice, 1986. Mem. Tex. Gov.'s Task Force on Sch. Fin., 1989-90, Tex. Gov.'s Select Com. on Edn., 1988; bd. dirs. Freedom to Read Found., 1989-91; mem. Austin Cable Commn., 1981-84, chmn., 1982; mem. nat. panel on sch. desegregation rsch. Ford Found., 1977-80; mem. state exec. com. Univ. Interscholastic League, 1983-86; bd. dirs. Jewish Children's Regional Svc., 1980-86; mem. Gov.'s Select Task Force on Pub. Edn., 1995; mem. Telecomms. Infrastructure Fund Bd., State of Tex., 1995-97; adv. bd. Nat. Inst. for Literacy, 2002-. Recipient Tchg. Excellence award, 1975, Most Meritorious Book award Scribes, 1983, Humanitarian award Austin region NCCJ, 1988, Antidefamation League Jurisprudence award, 1991, James Wilson award U. Pa. Law Sch., 2004; hon. fellow Queen Mary and Westfield Coll., U. London. Fellow: Am. Acad. Arts & Sci., Am. Bar Found., Tex. Bar Found.; mem.: Edn. Testing Svc. (mem. bd. dirs. 2000—02), Am. Coun. Edn. (mem. com. on leadership and instl. effectiveness 2000), Assn. Am. Law Schs. (chmn. law and edn. sect. 1983—84, exec. com. 1988—90), Tex. Bar Found., Am. Law Inst. Avocation: collecting antique maps. Office: U Texas System 601 Colorado St Austin TX 78701-2904 Office Phone: 512-499-4201. E-mail: myudof@utsystem.edu.

YUE, AGNES KAU-WAH, otolaryngologist; b. Shanghai, Peoples Republic China, Dec. 1, 1947; came to U.S., 1967; d. Chen Kia and Nee Yuan (Ying0; m. Gerald Kumata, Sept. 25, 1982; children: Julie, Allison Benjamin. BA, Wellesley Coll., 1970; MD, Med. Coll. Pa., 1974; postgrad., Yale U., 1974-78. Intern Yale-New Haven Hosp., 1974-75, resident, 1975-78; fellow U. Tex. M.D. Anderson Cancer Ctr., Houston, 1978-79; asst. prof. U. Wash., Seattle, 1979-82; physician Pacific Med. Ctr., Seattle, 1979-90; pvt. practice Seattle, 1991—. Fellow Am. Acad. Otolaryngology; mem. Northwest Acad. Otolaryngology. Avocations: sailing, opera, cooking. Office: 1801 NW Market St Ste 410 Seattle WA 98107-3909 Office Phone: 206-782-1090.

YUE, ALFRED SHUI-CHOH, metallurgical engineer, educator; b. China, Nov. 12, 1920; s. Choy Noon-woo and Sze Man-hun (Tom) Y.; m. Virginia Chin-wen Tang, May 21, 1944; children: Mary, Raymond Yuan, John, Ling Tsao, David, Nancy Chang. BS, Chao-tung U., 1942; MS, Ill. Inst. Tech., 1950; PhD, Purdue U., 1956. Assoc. engr. Taiwan Aluminum Co., 1942-47; instr. Purdue U., 1952-56; research engr. Dow Chem. Co., Midland, Mich., 1956-62; sr. mem. Lockheed, Palo Alto Research Lab., 1962-69; now cons.; prof. engring. and applied sci. U. Calif., Los Angeles, 1969—. Hon. prof. Xian Jiao-tong U., China, 1980; cons. LTV Aerospace Co., Lockheed Missile & Space Co., Atlantic Richfield Co.; Sec.-gen. Chinese Culture Assn. in, U.S.A., 1967, also; bd. dirs. Chinese scholar to U.S.A. Fellow AIAA (assoc.); mem. AAAS, AIME, Am. Soc. Metals, Materials Rsch. Soc., Sigma Xi, Sigma Pi Sigma, Tau Beta Pi, Phi Tau Phi (pres. 1978-82) E-mail: yuealfred@aol.com., asyue@yahoo.com.

YUECHIMING, ROGER YUE YUEN SHING, mathematics professor; b. Mauritius, Feb. 25, 1937; s. James and Marie Yuechiming; m. Renée Bethery, Nov. 9, 1963; children: Françoise, Marianne, Isabelle. BSc with 1st class honours, U. Manchester, Eng., 1964, PhD, 1967. Asst. U. Strasbourg, France, 1967-69; lectr. math. U. Paris VII, 1970—. Participant math. confs. and seminars in numerous countries; referee various math. jours. Contbr. over 90 articles on ring theory to sci. jours. of numerous countries. Mem. French Math. Soc., Am. Math. Soc., London Math. Soc., Belgian Math. Soc., Japan Math. Soc. Achievements include introduction of concept of p-injective modules and the more generalized notion of YJ-injectivity, new approaches in ring and module theory leading to a better understanding of von Neumann regular rings, V-rings, self-injective rings and generalizations. Home: 38 rue du Surmelin 75020 Paris France Office: U Paris VII Unité Mixte de Rsch 9994 CNRS 2 Pl Jussieu 75251 Paris France

YUEN, BENSON BOLDEN, airline management consultant, software executive; b. Hong Kong, Nov. 20, 1960; arrived in U.S., 1968; s. Eugene Howard and Janet Yuen. BSBA in Fin. summa cum laude, U. Cen. Fla., 1983. Mgr. market planning and automation Fla. Express, Inc., Orlando, 1983-85, dir. pricing, 1986-87; dir. customer svc. Seabrook Mktg., Inc., Houston, 1988-91, v.p. customer svc., 1992-94; v.p. consulting svcs. PROS Strategic Solutions, Inc., Houston, 1994-96, sr. v.p. mktg. and consulting svcs., 1996-99; sr. v.p. PROS Revenue Mgmt., Inc., Houston, 2000, pres. travel and transp., 2000—. Cons. airline revenue mgmt., mktg. automation, bus. mgmt., sys. devel. and bus. process engring. to more than 100 transp. cos. worldwide, pres. travel and transp. divsn. PROS Revenue Mgmt., Inc., 2000—. Designer (software) Passenger Revenue Forecast and Optimization System, 1989, Group Revenue Optimization and Management System Version 3, 1990-94, Version 4, 1995—, Holiday Mgmt. Module, Network Pricing Analysis Sys., Hub Complex Optimization; mem. editl. bd. Jour. Revenue and Pricing Mgmt.; contbr. articles to profl. jours. Avocations: travel, music. Office: PROS Revenue Mgmt Inc 3100 Main St Ste 900 Houston TX 77002-9312 Office Phone: 713-335-5202. Business E-Mail: byuen@prosrm.com.

YUEN, HENRY C. former consumer electronics manufacturing company executi; b. China, 1951; BS in Maths., U. Wisc.; D, Calif. Inst. Tech., 1973; LLB, Loyola U. Rsch. scientist TRW Inc.; various faculty positions Calif. Inst. Tech., NYU; co-founder Gemstar Internat. Group Ltd., 1989, CEO, chmn. bd. dirs., 1999—2002. Contbr. articles to profl. jours. Recipient Nat. Entrepreneur of Yr. award Ernst & Young USA Today and NASDAQ, 1996, Disting. Alumni award Calif. Inst. Tech., 1999, Disting. Alumni award Loyola Law Sch., 1999.

YUEN, WING HO, electrical engineer, researcher; b. Hong Kong, July 22, 1973; arrived in U.S., 1997; s. Siu Sing Yuen and Yuen Wah Wong. BSEE, Hong Kong U. Sci. and Tech., 1995; MPhil, Chinese U. of Hong Kong, 1997; PhD, Rutgers U., 2003. Tchg. asst. Chinese U. of Hong Kong, 1995—97; rsch. asst. Wireless Info. Networking Lab., Rutgers U., Piscataway, NJ, 1997—. Contbr. articles to profl. publs. Recipient award, Sir Edward Youde Meml. Fund, 1990. Mem.: IEEE. Home: 1306 Mindy Ln Piscataway NJ 08854 Office: WINLAB Rutgers U 73 Brett Rd Piscataway NJ 08854 Office Phone: 732-306-5907. Business E-Mail: andyyuen@winlab.rutgers.edu.

YUFIK, YAN MARK, director research development; b. Jan. 22, 1946; MS, Odessa Poly. U., 1968; PhD, Kalinin U., 1973; postgrad, U. Calif., 1981. Sr. scientist General Atomic, Calif., 1981-83; sr. advisor, v.p. R&D NCR Co., Ohio, 1983-85; sr. scientist FMC Co., Calif., 1985-87; dir. R&D Inst. Med. Cybernetics, 1987—. Home: 12204 St Taures Rd Potomac MD 20854

YUHNKE, ROBERT E. lawyer, educator, consultant; b. Buffalo, Dec 13, 1943; s. Edward L. and Marjorie T. Y.; m. Stephanie Mines; 1 stepdaughter, Rachel Erdman. BS, Canisius Coll., 1965; student, Columbia U., 1968-69; JD, Yale U., 1972. Bar: Pa 1972, U.S. Supreme Ct. 1977, Ill. 1980, Colo. 1981, U.S. Ct. Appeals (D.C. cir.) 1979, (7th cir.) 1983, (9th cir.) 1986, (10th cir.) 1985, (11th cir.) 2000, (5th cir.) 2001. Spl. asst. atty. gen. Pa. Dept. Environ. Resources, Harrisburg, 1972-78; asst. regional solicitor U.S. Dept. Interior, Denver, 1978-79; pvt. practice Chgo., 1979-80; sr. atty. Environ. Def. Fund, Boulder, 1980-92; prin. Robert E Yuhnke & Assocs., 1992—. Founder, treas. DOM Project, Eldorado Springs, Colo., 1993—; adj. prof. environ. law U. Colo. Sch. Law, Boulder, 1998—. Contbr. articles to profl. jours. Tenor Rocky Mountain Chorale, Boulder, 1994—. 1st lt. U.S. Army Res., 1965-68. Avocations: flute, paddling, yoga. trout fishing. Office: 2910-D County Road 67 Boulder CO 80303 9639

YUKI, GODA, science educator; PhD Biochemistry, Stanford U. Asst. prof. biology U. Calif., La Jolla. Recipient young investigator award, Nat. Alliance Rsch. Schizophrenia & Depression; fellow, Sloan Found. Office: 9500 Gilman Dr 1123 A Pac Hall La Jolla CA 92093

YULE, JOE See ROONEY, MICKEY

YULISH, CHARLES BARRY, public relations executive; b. Cleve., Oct. 14, 1936; s. Isadore and Shirley Yulish; m. Barbara Pearlman, Aug. 22, 1973 (div. 1995); 1 child, Alexi Jules-Nicholas; m. Cynthia Brown Fleek, Oct. 28, 1995. AA in Govt., U. Fla., 1957; BS in Polit. Sci., Kent State U., 1959; MPA, Maxwell Sch., Syracuse U., 1963; postgrad., NYU, 1961-63, New Sch. Social Rsch., 1963-64. Spl. projects officer U.S. AEC, Washington and N.Y.C., 1961-63; pub. affairs mgr. Atomic Indsl. Forum, N.Y.C., 1963-66; pres., chief exec. officer Charles Yulish Assocs. Inc., N.Y.C., 1966-83; exec. v.p. Wesley, Brown & Bartle Inc., N.Y.C., 1984-87; vice chmn., ptnr. Holt, Ross & Yulish, Edison, N.J., 1988-92; exec. v.p., mng. dir. E. Bruce Harrison Co., Washington, 1993-95; v.p. corp. comm. USEC Inc., Bethesda, Md., 1995—. Writer, dir. (film) Energy: We Have the Choices, 1978 (Golden Eagle award); editor: Hard vs. Soft Energy Paths, 1980; author over 60 articles on classical music. Founder, bd. dirs. Serge Koussevitsky Archives Soc., N.Y.C., 1977; bd. dirs. Imperial Russia Hist. Soc., 1986, U.K. and U.S. Friends of Benjamin Franklin. Maxwell fellow Syracuse U., 1960. Mem. Internat. Assn. Pub. Participation Practitioners, Soc. Profl. Mgmt. Cons. (cert.). Home: 1438 Q St NW Washington DC 20009-3808

YULY, RUDY LEROY, writer, graphics designer; s. Donald LeRoy Yuly and Dixie Lee Lang; m. Shelly Kaye Newcomer, Sept. 27, 1996; 1 child, John Elvis Newcomer. BA, We. Wash. U., 1981. Registered Counselor Wash., 1999. Mng. editor Trailblazer Mag., Bellevue, Wash., 1984—87; dir. of pub. Seattle Seafair, 1987—88; owner Rudy Yuly Pub., Seattle, 1988—. Graphic designer, cons. Eddie Bauer Corp. Social Responsibility, Redmond, Wash., 1995—2000; graphic designer/cons. Starbucks Corp. Social Responsibility, Seattle, 2000—; writer, editl. cons. Seattle U., 2000—; interim dir. pub. rels. Jewish Fedn. Greater Seattle, 1994; prodn. mgr. Rocket Mag., Seattle, 1996—97. Co-author (book) World Business Desk Reference; composer (singer, Tiny Hat Orch.): (compact disc) Put a Hat On It, Noon at Nine, Funhaus, Naked, 2004; editor: (literary journal) Jeopardy; author: (novel) Crime Scene Cleaners. Graphic designer/cons. Eastside Domestic Violence Program, Seattle, 2002—04; graphic designer/pub. cons. Issaquah Sch. Dist., Wash., 1994—2004; graphic designer, cons. Cath. Archdiocese of Seattle, 1993—93; graphic designer, pub. cons. Jewish Fedn. Greater Seattle, 1989—94. Recipient Gold award, Newspaper Advt., Nat. Coun. Jewish Fedns., 1992, Silver Award, Coun. for Advancement and Support of Edn., 2002; scholar, Gannett Found., 1980—81, Women in Comm., 1980—81; State Finalist Rhodes Scholarship, 1981, Quarterfinalist, Nicholl Fellowship in Screenwriting, Acad. Awards Found., 2003. Mem.: Am. Screenwriters Assn., Willamette Writers. Democrat-Npl. Avocations: film, music, yoga, astronomy, history. Personal E-mail: rudyyuly@comcast.net.

YUMOTO, FUTOSHI, statistician, researcher; b. Gifu, Japan, Sept. 24, 1970; s. Kazuaki and Atsuko Yumoto; m. Rieko Imazeki, Dec. 26, 2000. MA in Counseling Psychology, 2002. Lic. profl. counselor Dept. Profl. Regulation, State of Ill., 2001. Substance abuse specialist Chgo. (Ill.) Health Outreach, 2001—03; rsch. assoc. Stoelting Co., Wood Dale, Ill., 2002—. Rschr. Adler Sch. Profl. Psychology, 2000—03. Contbr. articles to profl. jours. Mem.: Am. Educatoinal Rsch. Assn. Office: Stoelting Co 620 Wheat Lane Wood Dale IL 60191 Home: 2811 Nicholson St Apt 304 Hyattsville MD 20782-2812 Personal E-mail: fyumoto@hotmail.com. Business E-Mail: toshi@stoeltingco.com.

YUN, DANIEL DUWHAN, physician, foundation administrator; b. Chinjoo, Korea, Jan. 20, 1933; came to U.S., 1959; naturalized, 1972; s. Kapryong and Woo Im Yun; m. Rebecca Sungja Choi, Apr. 13, 1959; children: Samuel, Lois, Caroline, Judith. BS Coll. Sci. and Engring., Yon-Sei U., 1954, MD, 1958; student, U. Pa., 1963; PhD, Barrington U., 1995. Intern Quincy (Mass.) City Hosp., 1960; resident and fellow Presbyn.-U. Pa. Med. Ctr., Phila., 1961-65; med. dir. Paddon Meml. Hosp., Newfoundland, Labrador, Can., 1965-66; dir. spl. care unit Elkins Park (Pa.) Hosp., 1967-79; founder, pres. Philip Jaisohn Meml. Found., Inc., Elkins Park, Pa., 1975-85, also med. dir., trustee. Clin. prof. medicine U. Xochicalco, 1978; faculty Allegheny U. Health Scis., Phila.; bd. dirs. Elkins Park Hosp. Mem. Bd. Asian Studies Found., U.S. Senatorial Bus. Adv. Bd.; mem. home safety com. Mayor's Commn. on Svcs. to Aging, Phila.; trustee United Way of Southeastern Pa., co-founder Rep. Presdl. Task Force; mem. U.S. Congl. Adv. Bd.; cons. on Korean affairs Phila. City Coun.; hon. mem. adv. coun. Peaceful Unification Policy of Korea; trustee Albright Coll., Reading, Pa., 1997—; chmn. bd. Korean-Am. Christian Broadcasting of Phila.; mem. Phila. Internat. City Coord. Com.; commr. Pa. Human Rels. Commn., 1991—; founder, pres. Korean Heritage Found., 1991—; amb. City of Phila., 1991. Recipient Phila. award Human Rights award, 1981, Disting. Cmty. Svc. award Phila. Dist. Atty., 1981, medal of Merit Presdl. Task Force, 1981, Medal of Nat. Order, Republic of Korea, 1984, Nat. Dong Baek medal Republic of Korea, 1987, award City Coun. Phila., 1987, Gov.'s Pa. Heritage awards, 1990, commendation award Pa. Senate, 1991, award Asian Law Ctr., 1991, Rep. Senatorial Medal of Freedom, 1994; named to Legion of Honor, The Chapel of Four Chaplains; named Amb. City of Phila., 1991. Mem. AMA, Am. Soc. Internal Medicine, Am. Coll. Cardiology, Am. Heart Assn. (mem. coun. on clin. cardiology), Pa. Med. Soc., Phila. County Med. Soc., Royal Soc. Health, Am. Coll. Internat. Physicians, World Med. Assn., Fedn. State Med. Bds., Am. Law Enforcement Officers' Assn., Am. Fedn. Police, Internat. Culture Soc. Korea (hon.), Am. Soc. Contemporary Medicine and Surgery. Home: 3903 Somers Dr Huntingdon Valley PA 19006-1913 Office: 60 Township Line Rd Elkins Park PA 19027-2220

YUN, JAMES KYOON, electrical engineer; b. Andong, South Korea, Oct. 26, 1965; came to U.S., 1973; s. Joh Kyong and Karen Suk (Kim) Y. BSEE, U. Ill., 1987, MSEE, 1989. System engr. GE Co., Syracuse, N.Y., 1989-91, software engr., 1991-93, Martin Marietta Corp., Syracuse, 1993-95; sr. mem. engring. staff Lockheed Martin Corp., Moorestown, N.J., 1995—. Cons. Silver Knight Co., Liverpool, N.Y., 1994—. Inventor seal indicator. Mem. IEEE, Assn. for Computing Machinery, Tau Beta Pi, Eta Kappa Nu.

YUN, LIANG, marine engineer, educator; b. Shanghai, July 15, 1932; s. KunLin and Yun Ya (Sun) Y.; m. Li Hui Qiu, Jan. 1, 1962; children: Gang, Xiao. Grad., Dalian (China) U. Tech., 1953. Asst. prof. Mil. Engring. Acad. China, Harbin, 1953-56, lectr., 1956-66, Harbin Shipbldg. Engring. Inst., 1966-73; dir. air cushion vehicle divsn. Marine Design & Rsch. Inst. China, Shanghai, 1973-85, dep. chief engr., prof., sr. engr., 1980—; tech. dir. China Air Cushion Tech. Corp., Shanghai, 1984-86, Flying Dragon Sci. and Tech. Ltd., Hong Kong, 2000—, Engain Tech Ltd., Hong Kong, 2000—. Prof. Harbin Shipbldg. Engring. U., 1988—, Wu Han (China) Transport Engring. U., 1990—; dir. Advanced Marine Vessel, Internat. Advanced Vehicles Assocs., Inc. Author: Theory and Design of Air Cushion Vehicle (in Chinese), 1990, 2000, (in English), 1993, 98. Rcipient 2nd class nat. award nat. Def. Com. China, Beijing, 1980, 2nd class nat. award China State Shipbldg. Corp., Beijing, 1992, 1st class nat. award Kwang-Hua Sci. & Tech. Found., Beijing, 1994., 1st class nat. award China State Shipbuilding Corp., 2002. Fellow Royal Instn. Naval Architects; mem. China Soc. Naval Architects and Marine Engrs. (standing dir. 1993-97, chmn. high performance vehicle subcom. 1984—, vice chmn. cons. ship design com. 1992-2002, cons. ship design com. 2002—). Home: 175 Gao Xiong Rd Apt 501 Shanghai 200011 China Office: Marine Design & Rsch Inst 1688 Xi Zang Nan Rd 200011 Shanghai China Mailing: 55 Brook St Woodbridge NJ 07095 E-mail: yunxiao@online.sh.cn., yunliango1@netzero.net.

YUN, YOUNG JAE, neurosurgeon; b. Seoul, Republic of Korea, Aug. 4, 1943; s. Pyung S. and Soo Yu; m. Choon Hui Yoon; children: Helena, Peter. BS, Yonsei U., MD, 1967. Resident SUNY; cons. neurosurgeon Mt. St. Mary's Hosp., Lewiston, Niagara Falls MMC. Mem.: AMA, Am. Coll. Surgeons, Am. Assn. Neurosurgeons, Can. Med. Soc., N.Y. State Neurosrugery Soc., N.Y. State Med. Soc. Home: 703 Mountainview Dr Lewiston NY 14092 Office: Niagara Neurosurgery 734 Main St Niagara Falls NY 14301

YUND, MARY ALICE, biotechnology consultant; b. Xenia, Ohio, Feb. 12, 1943; d. John Edward and Ethel Louise Stallard; m. E. William Yund, June 11, 1966. BA, Knox Coll., 1965; PhD, Harvard U., 1970. Asst. rsch. geneticist U. Calif., Berkeley, 1975-88; pvt. practice cons. Berkeley, 1988-97; biotech. cons. Tech. Forecasters, Inc., Alameda, Calif., 1997—. Mem. devel. biology adv. panel NSF, Washington, 1983-87; vis. scientist NSF/ CSIRO U.S./ Australia Coop. Sci. Progam, North Ryde, Australia, 1980; co-chair women in Biosci. Conf., Stanford, Calif., 1993; organizer sci. seminar series and confs. in field. Contbr. articles, revs. to profl. jours., chpts. to books. Cons., counselor Bay Area Biosci. Ctr., Oakland, Calif., 1992—. Rsch. grantee NSF, NIH, 1975-86. Mem. AAAS, Genetics Soc. Am., Soc. for Developmental Biology, Am. Soc. Zoologists, Assn. for Women in Sci. (chpt. officer 1991—), Phi Beta Kappa, Sigma Xi. Achievements include first identification and characterization of ecdysteroid receptors. Office: 723 Woodhaven Rd Berkeley CA 94708-1540

YUNG, WAI KWAN ALFRED, neurology and neuro-oncology educator; b. Hong Kong; BS, U. Minn., 1971; MD, U. Chgo., 1975. Intern in neurology U. Calif., San Diego, 1975—76; asst. resident neurology UCSD, 1976—78, chief resident neurology, 1978, MSKCC, 1978—79, fellow neurology, 1978—81; clin. fellow neurology NY Hosp., 1979—81; prof. neurology Dept. Neurology, U. Tex. Med. Sch., Houston, 1992—; prof. of tumor biology dept. tumor biology M.D. Anderson Cancer Ctr., Houston, 1992—, prof. neurology dept. of neuro-oncology, 1992—, chmn. dept. neuro-oncology, 1999—. Florence M. Thomas prof. of cancer rsch. M.D. Anderson Cancer Ctr., Houston, 1996-2002, chmn. Margaret and Ben Love chair in clin. cancer care, 2002—. Office: MD Anderson Cancer Ctr Box 431 1515 Holcombe Blvd Houston TX 77030-4009 Office Phone: 713-794-1285.

YUNGINGER, JOHN W. allergist; MD. Exec. sec. Am. Bd. Allergy and Immunology, Phila. Office: Am Bd Allergy and Immunology 510 Walnut St Ste 1701 Philadelphia PA 19106-3601 E-mail: abai@abai.org.

YUNIS, JORGE JOSE, anatomy, pathology, and microbiology educator; b. Sincelejo, Colombia, Oct. 5, 1933; s. José and Victoria (Turbay) Yunis. MD, Complutense U., Madrid, 1956, PhD, 1957; D (hon.), UCLA, 1997. Gen. practice medicine, Barranquilla, Colombia, 1957-59; resident in clin. pathology U. Minn., Mpls., 1959-62, resident in anat. pathology, 1962-64, mem. faculty, 1965-89, prof., 1969-89, dir. grad. studies of lab. medicine, 1969-74, dir. grad. studies of pathology, 1972-74, chmn. human genetics com. for health scis., 1972-77; mem. faculty Hahnemann U., Phila., 1989-92, prof. dept. neoplastic diseases, 1989-92, vice chmn., assoc. dir. Inst. for Cancer and Blood Diseases, 1989-92, dir. Human Genetics and Molecular Biology Div., 1989-92, prof. dept. pathology, 1991-92; prof. depts. anatomy, pathology, microbiology & immunology Thomas Jefferson U. Med. Coll., Phila., 1993—; dir. cancer biol., dept. anatomy, pathology, cell biology Thomas Jefferson U. Med. Col., Phila., 1993—. Vis. prof. numerous univs. Author: Human Chromosome Method, 1965, 1975, Biochemical Methods in Red Cell Genetics, 1969, Molecular Pathology, 1975, New Chromosomal Syndromes, 1977, Molecular Structure Human Chromosomes, 1995, Esencia Humana, 1995, Así es la Vida, 1997, The Myth of God, 2002; contbr. more than 250 articles to profl. jours. Named Clin. Prof. of Yr. Harvard Med. Sch., 1987; honored by Colombian Parliament, Bogota, 1986, 93, Colombian Med. Schs. Assn., 1993. Mem. Leukemia Soc. Am. (trustee 1983-88), Colombian Acad. Medicine. Avocations: poetry, religion, literature, photography. Office Phone: 305-858-7684. Personal E-mail: jorgeyunis@aol.com.

YURASKO, FRANK NOEL, judge; b. Rahway, NJ, Dec. 22, 1938; s. Frank H. and Estelle (Yurasko) mm. Mary Byrd, July 23, 1966 (dec. 1991); children: Elizabeth Anne, Suzanne, Frank; m. Rosalee Yurasko, May 1997. BA, Brown U., 1960; cert., London Sch. Econs., 1961; student, Gray's Inn., London, 1960—61; JD, Yale U., 1964. Bar: NJ 1964, U.S. Dist. Ct. NJ 1965, U.S. Supreme Ct. 1969, Fla. 1979, U.S. Ct. Appeals 1980, cert.: NJ (civil trial atty.). Judge's law clk. NJ Dept. Judiciary, Trenton, 1964-66; ptnr. Graham, Yurasko, Golden, Lintner & Rothchild, Somerville, NJ, 1966-80; pvt. practice Somerville, 1980—. Judge Montgomery Twp. (NJ) Mcpl. Ct., 1973-84; twp. atty. Hillsborough Twp. (NJ), 1973-2000; atty. Green Brook (NJ) Bd. Adjustment, 1973-2001. Trustee Gill/St. Bernard Sch., Bernardsville, NJ; mem. alumni bd. trustees Peddie Sch., Hightstown, NJ. Mem. ABA, Am. Jud. Soc., NJ Bar Assn., Fla. Bar Assn., Somerset County Bar Assn., Mercer County Bar Assn., Assn. Trial Lawyers Am., Trial Attys. NJ, NJ Fedn. Planning Ofcls., Fed. Bar Assn. Office: PO Box 1041 139 W End Ave Somerville NJ 08876-1809 Office Phone: 908-231-0220. E-mail: fyurasko@compuserve.com.

YURCHAK, KATHERINE SASSO, writer; b. Atlantic Highlands, N.J., June 23, 1921; d. Anthony Sasso and Theresa Sommese; m. Nicholas Yurchak, Feb. 21, 1954; 1 child, John Marshall. BA, Bloomsburg U., 1995. Columnist E. Lycoming Shopper and News, Hughesville, Pa., 1995—; freelance writer monthly periodicals, popular mags. Spkr. in field. Translator (from Italian): Prolific Writings of Giuseppe Petrelli, 1968-1989; contbr. articles to profl. jours. Mem. Soc. Profl. Journalists, Phi Kappa Phi. Avocations: reading, writing, walking.

YURCHENCO, HENRIETTA WEISS, ethnomusicologist, writer; b. New Haven, Mar. 22, 1916; d. Edward and Rebecca (Bernblum) Weiss; m. Basil Yurchenco, June 1936 (div. 1955); 1 child, Peter; m. Irving Levine, 1965 (div. 1979). Student, Yale U., 1935-36; student piano scholarship, Mannes Coll. Music, 1936-38. Radio producer WNYC, WBAI, others, 1939-69; writer, critic, tchr., folk music editor Am. Record Guide and Musical Am., 1959-70. Prof. music CCNY, 1962-86, Bklyn. Coll., 1966-69, New Sch. for Social Rsch., 1961-68; co-dir. project for study of women in music, Grad. Ctr. CUNY; mem. exec. com. Panamerican Musical Rsch. Arts. Author: A Fiesta of Folk Songs From Spain and Latin America, 1967, A Mighty Hard Road: A Biography of Woody Guthrie, 1970, !Hablamos! Puerto Ricans Speak, 1971, Around the World in 80 Years: A Memoir, 2003, in Spanish, 2004; contbr. articles to profl. jours.; 15 field recs. from Mexico, P.R., John's Island, S.C., Guatemala, Ecuador, Morocco, issued by Libr. Congress, Folkways, Nonesuch, Folkways/Smithsonian, Global Village, Rounder Records; collections in Libr. Congress, Discoteca Hebrew U., Jerusalem, Arias Montana Inst., Madrid, Inst. Nacional Indigenista, Mexico City; collections in Am. Sephardic Found. Recipient award Nat. Inst. Fine Arts, Mex., 2003, grants-in-aid Am. Philos. Soc., 1954, 56, 57, 65, 67, 89, grants-in-aid CUNY Faculty Rsch. Fund, 1970, 83, 87; NEH grantee, 1984. Mem. Internat. Council Traditional Music (com. on women's studies), Soc. Ethnomusicology, Soc. Asian Music, Sonneck Soc., Internat. Assn. Study of Popular Music, Am. Musicologists Soc. Achievements include research in folk, tribal and popular music for Library of Congress, Mexico, Guatemala, P.R., Spain, Morocco, Balearic Islands, John's Island, S.C., Ireland, 1941-83. Home: 360 W 22d St New York NY 10011-2600 Office: 139th St And Convent Ave New York NY 10031 Personal E-mail: hyurchenco@aol.com.

YURCHUCK, ROGER ALEXANDER, retired lawyer; b. Amityville, N.Y., June 9, 1938; s. Alexander and Ella Marie (Munley) Y.; m. Sally Ward, Apr. 14, 1961 (div. 1972); children: Scott, Lauren; m. Susan Holland, June 1, 1985. AB cum laude, Northwestern U., 1959; LLB, Harvard U., 1962. Bar: Ohio 1962. Assoc. Vorys, Sater Seymour and Pease, Columbus, Ohio, 1962-68, ptnr., 1969—71, 1973—2002, ptnr. Cin. office, 1984—2002; v.p., gen. counsel Fed. Home Loan Mortgage Corp., Washington, 1971-73. Vice chmn., bd. dirs. Securities Investors Protection Corp., Washington, 1982-88. Del. Rep. Nat. Conv., 1980, 84. Mem. Ohio Bar Assn., Queen City Club (Cin.), Phi Beta Kappa. Republican. Episcopalian. Office Phone: 513-723-4013. Business E-Mail: rayurchuck@ussp.com.

YURENEV, ALEKSEY PAVLOVICH (ALEXEI PAVLOVICH YURENEV), cardiologist, researcher; b. Moscow, Jan. 20, 1945; s. Pavel Nikolaevich Yurenev and Nina Petrovna Obnorskaya; m. Lilia Grigorievna (Lipkina); children: Yulia, Elena, Inna, Aleksey. MD 2d., Moscow Med. Inst., 0967; candidate in Med. Sci., Cardiology Rsch. Ctr., Moscow, 1972, D in Med. Sci., 1984. prof. cardiology 1990—. Resident Cardiology Rsch. Ctr., Moscow, 1967—69, fellow, 1969—72, jr., sr. rschr., 1972—84, chief outpatient clinic, 1984—2002. Chief cardiologist Moscow Health Dept., 1987-2000; chief, chair cardiology, Moscow Med. Acad., 1989-2003; chmn. editl. bd., JAMA, Russia, 1998-2003. Co-author: The Hypertensive Heart, 1994; contbr. articles to profl. journals, chpt. to book. Fellow Am. Coll. Cardiology, Am. Heart Assn., Moscow Assn. Cardiologists (pres. 1990-2003), Internat. Acad. Informatisation (pres. clin. medicine bd. 1994—), Lions Club Internat. (charter mem., Melvin Johns Fellow, dist. gov., 1995-96). Achievements include patents in field. Avocations: history, music, literature, art. Home: 135 Fifth Ave Apt 2C Pelham NY 10803

YURIKO, (YURIKO KIKUCHI), dancer, choreographer; b. San Jose, Calif., 1920; m. Charles Kikuchi, 1946. Student, UCLA, Martha Graham Sch. Mem. Martha Graham Dance Co., 1944-67; dance tchr. N.Y.C., 1945—; dir., founder Yuriko Dance Co., 1967-74; assoc. artistic dir. Martha Graham Dance Co., 1991—. Artistic dir. dance company Time and Talents Club, Bombay, 1974; organizer Modern Dance Sch., Ctr. Internat. de la Danse, Paris, 1975; resident guest tchr., modern dance cons. Ballet Nacional de Cuba, 1976; ind. modern dance choreographer Warsaw Weiklki Classic Ballet Co., 1977, 78, Australian Dance Theater's Concert at Adelaide Festival of the Arts, 1978; guest tchr., choreographer Akar Modern Dance Co., Switzerland, 1981; guest tchr. Nat. U. Costa Rica, Nat. Ballet of Mexico, Martha Graham Sch. Contemporary Dance; guest artist and tchr. various cities including London, Paris, Mexico City, Zurich, Tokyo and Cologne, Germany; founder & dir., The Arigato Project. Dancer premiere prodns. Appalachian Spring, Cave of the Heart, Dark Meadow, Embattled Garden, Clytemnestra; appeared on Broadway as Eliza in The King and I, 1951; performed feature role The Small House of Uncle Thomas, Sandhog, Flower Drug Song; dir., re-staged Broadway prodn. of The King and I, 1977, London prodn., 1979, dir. Toyko prodn., 1978; dir. Madame Butterfly. Recipient Bessie award N.Y. Dance and Performance, 1991; grantee N.Y. State Arts Coun., Nat. Endowment for the Arts; Guggenheim fellow for choreography, 1968; commissioned to choreograph and perform Judith Symphony.*

YURIST, SVETLAN JOSEPH, mechanical engineer; b. Kharkov, USSR, Nov. 20, 1931; came to U.S., 1979, naturalized, 1985; s. Joseph A. and Rosalia S. (Zoilman) Y.; m. Imma Lea Erlikh, Oct. 11, 1960; 1 child, Eugene. MSME with honors, Poly. Inst. Odessa, USSR, 1954. Engr., designer Welding Equipment Plant, Novaya Utka, USSR, 1954-56; sr. tech. engr. Heavy Duty Automotive Crane Plant, Odessa, USSR, 1956-60, asst. chief metallugist, 1971-78; supr. rsch. lab. Inst. Spl. Methods in Foundry Industry, Odessa, 1960-66, project engr. sci. rsch., 1966-70; engr. designer Teledyne Cast Product, Pomona, Calif., 1979-81; sr. mech. engr. Walt Elliot Disney Enterprises, Glendale, Calif., 1981-83; foundry liaison engr. Pacific Pumps divsn. Dresser Industries, Inc., Huntington Park, Calif., 1984-86; casting engr. Superior Industries Internat., Inc., Van Nuys, Calif., 1986-89; mech. engr. TAMCO Steel, Ramcho Cucamonga, Calif., 1989-96. Contbr. reports, articles to collections All Union Confs. Spl. Methods in Foundry, USSR. Recipient award for design of automatic lines for casting electric motor parts USSR Ministry Machine Bldg. and Handtools Mfr., 1966, for equipment for permanent mold casting All Union Exhbn. of Nat. Econ. Achievements, 1966-70. Mem. Am. Foundrymen's Soc. Achievements include patents for permanent mold casting. Home: 1718 Downs St Oceanside CA 92054-6191

YURKO, MICHIKO KATHLEEN, music educator, writer; b. Cottonwood, Ariz., Jan. 19, 1951; d. Stanley Meredith and Mary Sumie Fujii Henshall; m. Richard Joseph Yurko, Sept. 18, 1971 (div. Apr. 19, 1993); children: Meredith Kathleen, David Richard Edward, Andrew Henry Joseph; m. Cristian Ianculescu, May 8, 2004. MusB, Ohio U., 1973, postgrad. in Music Theory, 1973—74. Pvt. piano studio, Rockville, Md., 1973—2002; chair Suzuki piano dept., chair music mind games theory dept. Levine Sch. of Music, Washington, 1994—. Lectr., presenter in field. Author: (manual) Music Mind Games, 1992, (music game) Musopoly, 1992, Music Mind Games Materials, 1992, No H in Snake: Music Theory for Children, 1979; composer: Twinkle Variations. Mem.: Suzuki Assn. of the Ams. (bd. dirs. 1976—79, registered tchr. trainer, bd. dirs. 1986—89). Democrat. Avocations: composition, travel, photography, cooking, origami. Office: Levine Sch of Music 2801 Upton St NW Washington DC 20008 Office Phone: 202-686-8000. E-mail: myurko@levineschool.org.

YURT, ROGER WILLIAM, surgeon, educator; b. Louisville, June 8, 1945; s. Albert William and Mary Louise (McGrath) Y.; m. Joan A. Terry, Sept. 3, 1971; children: Jennifer, Daniel, Gregory. BS in Biology, Loyola U., New Orleans, 1967; MS, U. Miami, 1972. Diplomate Nat. Bd. Med. Examiners. Intern. Parkland Meml. Hosp.-Southwestern Med. Sch., U. Tex., Dallas, 1972-73, resident, 1973-74; postdoctoral trainee NIH, 1975-77; resident, chief resident N.Y. Hosp.-Cornell Med. Ctr., N.Y.C., 1977-79, acting dir. Burn Ctr., dir. rsch., 1982-83, dir. Trauma Ctr., 1992-99, prof. surgery, 1982-92, 92—, The Johnson & Johnson disting. prof. surgery, 1995—; vice chmn. dept. surgery Cornell U. Med. Coll., N.Y.C., 1987—, acting chmn., 1991-93, dir. Burn Ctr., 1995—. Acting surgeon-in-chief The N.Y. Hosp., 1991-93; clin. asst. prof. surgery Uniformed Svcs. U. Health Sci., Bethesda, Md., 1980-82; clin. asst. prof. gen. surgery Health Sci. Ctr., U. Tex., San Antonio, 1981-82; chmn. burn com., Regional Emer. Med. Svcs. N.Y., 1982-84, mem. trauma ctr. adv. com., 1984-89, chmn., 1995-98, mem. burn ctr. adv. com., chmn., 1996-2000, mem. sp. ref. ctr. com., chmn., 1996—, N.Y. Bklyn. ACS Com. Trauma, 1994—; dir. Mulhearn Rsch.Lab., N.Y.C., 1982—. Editor: Infections in Surgery, 1981-88; contbr. articles to med. jours. Maj. M.C., U.S. Army, 1979-82. Recipient Hewitt award, Royal Soc. medicine, 2003, Irma Hirschl Trust Career Scientist award, 1984-88; grantee United Health Found., 1968-69, NIH, 1984-87; fellow Sch. Medicine, U. Miami, summer, 1969-71, USPHS, 1973-75, postdoctoral fellow medicine Robert B. Brigham Hosp.-Harvard U. Med. Sch., Boston, 1974-77. Mem. Am. Surg. Infection Soc. (charter, chmn. membership com., sec. 1987-90, pres. 1991-92), Am. Surg. Assn., Assn. Acad. Surgery, Soc. U. Surgeons, Internat. Surg. Soc., Am. Assn. Surgery Trauma, Alpha Omega Alpha, Omicron Delta Kappa. Roman Catholic. Office: NY Hosp Cornell Med Ctr Dir The Burn Ctr 525 E 68th St Rm L-706 New York NY 10021-4885

YUSKO, DAVE, automotive executive; CFO Potamkin Cos. (now Planet Automotive Group Inc.), Coral Gables, Fla. Office: Planet Automotive Group Inc Ste 600 2333 Ponce De Leon Blvd Coral Gables FL 33134

YUSPEH, ALAN RALPH, lawyer, healthcare company executive; b. New Orleans, June 13, 1949; s. Michel and Rose Fay (Rabenovitz) Y.; m. Janet Horn, June 8, 1975. BA, Yale U., 1971; MBA, Harvard U., 1973; JD, Georgetown U., 1978. Bar: DC 1978. Mgmt. cons. McKinsey & Co., Washington, 1973-74; adminstrv. asst., legis. asst. Office of U.S. Senator J. Bennett Johnston, Washington, 1974-78; atty. Shaw, Pittman, Potts & Trowbridge, Washington, 1978-79, Ginsburg, Feldman, Weil and Bress, Washington, 1979-82; gen. counsel Com. on Armed Svcs.-U.S. Senate, Washington, 1982-85; ptnr. Preston, Thorgrimson, Ellis & Holman, Washington, 1985-88, Miller & Chevalier, Washington, 1988-91, Howrey & Simon, Washington, 1991-97; sr. v.p. ethics, compliance and corp. responsibility HCA, Nashville, 1997—. Coord. Def. Industry Initiative on Bus., Ethics and Conduct, 1987-97; pres. Health Care Compliance Assn., 2002. Editor Law and Policy in Internat. Bus. Jour., 1978-79, Nat. Contract Mgmt. Jour., 1988-92; assoc. editor Pub. Contract Law Jour., 1987-91. Chmn. bd. ethics, City of Balt., 1988-96, planning commn., 1996-97; bd. dirs. Ethics Officer Assn.; chmn. bd. dirs. Tenn. Repertory Theater; bd. dirs. YMCA Mid. Tenn. Camp, 2002—, Balt. Housing Authority, 1996-97. 1st lt. USAR, 1971-77. Office: HCA One Park Plaza Nashville TN 37203 Home: 126 Third Ave N Franklin TN 37064 Office Phone: 615-344-1005. Business E-Mail: alan.yuspeh@hcahealthcare.com.

YUSSOUFF, MOHAMMED, retired physicist, educator; b. Cuttack, India, Aug. 14, 1942; arrived in U.S., 1991; s. Haji and Nurunnisa Fakhruddin; m. Farhana Begum, Apr. 6, 1969; children: Ashraf, Zeenat, Mustafa. MSc, Delhi U., 1963; PhD, Indian Inst. Tech., Kanpur, 1967. Prof. physics Indian Inst. Tech., Kanpur, 1967-90; vis. prof. physics Mich. State U., East Lansing, 1991—; ret., 1999. Guest scientist Ford Rsch., Dearborn, Mich., 1991-97, GM Tech. Ctr., Warren, Mich., 1997-98, Delphi Tech. Ctr., Warren, 1999—; vis. scientist U. Köln, Germany, 1972-74, U. Western Ont., London, Can., 1990-91; Humboldt scientist Atomic Energy Agy, Jülich, Germany, 1979-81; vis. prof. U. Konstanz, Germany, 1986-89; mem. com. physics examination Pub. Svc. Commn., Delhi, India, 1976-86, rsch. grants Univ. Grants Commn., Delhi, 1985-90; dir. Internat. Sch. on Band Structure, Indian Inst. Tech., 1986; creator Slow Pace program for tchg. sci. and engring. to deficient students with poor econ. or sch. backgrounds. Editor: Electronic Band Structure and Its Applications, 1987, The Physics of Materials, 1987. Mem.: Am. Phys. Soc., Internat. Ctr. Theoretical Physics (assoc.). Moslem. Achievements include patents for monitoring the catalytic converters in cars; research in theory of freezing; kinetic model of catalysis; theory of disordered systems, chanelling, clusters, electronic structure, ionic conductors, exhaust gas sensors, superconductors, zeolites; fundamental rate constants of catalytic reactions and foundations of quantum theory. Home: 5920 Crystal Lake Dr Romulus MI 48174 E-mail: yussouf2@hotmail.com.

YUSTER-FREEMAN, LEIGH CAROL, broadcast executive; b. Trenton, N.J., July 23, 1949; d. Leon Carl and Helen Loretta (Wisniewski) Markiewicz; m. Charles Yuster (div. Apr. 1985); stepchildren: Sarah, Elizabeth, Jared, Alexandra; m. Richard N. Freeman; 1 child, Jessica Lee Freeman. Profl. dancer, 1967—71; editor R.R. Bowker, N.Y.C., 1971—72, from ISBN agy. editl. coord. to dir. prod. devel., 1972—89, dir. product devel., pub. Ulrich's Database, 1989—90, assoc. pub. Bowker Bus. Rsch., A&I Pub. New Providence, NJ, 1990—91, also pub. Ulrich's Database, 1990—91, pub. Broadcasting & Cable Yearbook, 1991—97; mng. dir. Reed Reference Pub., New Providence, 1992—94, v.p. bibliographies, 1994—96, v.p. directories, 1996; v.p. Database Pub. R.R. Bowker, New Providence, 1996—99, sr. mng. dir. prodn., 1999—2000; project mgr. workforce devel. NJN Pub. TV, Trenton, NJ, 2000—. Ptnr. Eagle Bakery, Trenton, NJ, 1991—92. Recipient Climate of Excellence award, Cahners Pub. Co., Newton, Mass., 1987, cert. of Appreciation, Consortium of Univ. Film Ctrs., Kent, Ohio, 1986. Mem.: Actors Equity Assn. Jewish. Avocations: gardening, dance, music, children and children's issues, community services. Home: 19 Theodora Dr Hillsborough NJ 08844-4723 E-mail: lfreeman@njn.org.

YZAGUIRRE, RAUL HUMBERTO, civil rights leader; b. San Juan, Tex., July 22, 1939; s. Ruben Antonio and Eva Linda (Morin) Y.; m. Audrey H. Bristow, Jan. 2, 1965; children: Regina Dolores, Raul Humberto, Elisa Almalinda, Roberto Hayse, Rebecca Morin, Benjamin Ruben. Student, U. Md., 1963-64; BS, George Washington U., 1968. Registered med. technologist. Student and community activist, 1963-65; active War on Poverty, 1969-74; founder, exec. dir. Interstate Research Assocs (Hispanic cons. firm), Washington, 1969-73; v.p. Center for Community Change, Washington, 1974; community organizer in S.Tex., 1974; pres. Nat. Council of La Raza, Washington, 1974—. Lectr. Harvard U., U. Notre Dame, U. Tex., others.; commr. U.S. Nat. Commn. for UNESCO, 1983—; chmn. bd. dirs. Associated SW Investors, 1976—. Co-chmn. Nat. Urban Coalition, 1975-83; co-chmn. Working Com. on Concerns of Hispanics and Blacks, 1979—, sec. ind. sector, 1983-84; sec., chmn. Forum of Nat. Hispanic Orgns., 1976-79; chmn. adv. com. I.N.S.; former trustee Common Cause; co-founder, chmn. Nat. Neighborhood Coalition, 1977—; immediate past chair Ind. Sector; bd. dirs. Enterprise Found., Nat. Dem. Insts. Served with USAF, 1959-62. Recipient Rockefeller Public Service award, 1979, Common Cause Pub. Service award, 1986; fellow Inst. Politics John F. Kennedy Sch. Govt. Mem. Am. GI Forum, Hispanic Assn. Corp. Responsibility (co-founder, chmn. bd. dirs.). Democrat. Roman Catholic. Office: Nat Coun La Raza 1111 19th St NW Ste 1000 Washington DC 20036-3622 *The civil rights struggle of the 80's will be the transformation of America to a truly pluralistic society where cultural differences will not only be tolerated, but indeed valued.*

YZERMAN, STEVE, professional hockey player; b. Cranbrook, B.C., Can., May 9, 1965; With Detroit Red Wings, 1983—. Mem. Stanley Cup Champion, 1997, 98, 2002, Can. Olympic Hockey Team, 2002. Named Sporting News NHL Rookie of Yr., NHL All-Rookie Team, 1983—84, 1988—93; recipient Lester B. Pearson award, 1988—89, Olympic Gold medal, 2002. Achievements include Youngest person ever to play in NHL All-Star game, 1984. Office: Detroit Red Wings 600 Civic Center Dr Detroit MI 48226-4419

Z, CHRIS, internist, medical educator; b. Corning, N.Y., Sept. 10, 1960; s. Chris and Potoula Rouldis; m. Maria Eugenia Hallas, May 24, 1987. BA with distinction, U. Va., 1982, MD, 1986. Diplomate Am. Bd. Internal Medicine. Resident U. Calif., San Francisco, 1988-91; assoc. Yater Med. Group, Washington, 1991-92; asst. clin. prof. Georgetown U., Washington, 1993-95; assoc. Duke U. Affiliated Physicians, Durham, N.C., 1995-96; asst. clin. prof. dept. medicine Duke U., Durham, 1996-2000, Emory U., Atlanta, 2001—. Gen. Internal Medicine fellow Georgetown U., 1992-93. Fellow: ACP; mem.: AMA. Avocations: music, piano, flute, bonsai, golf. Office: Emory U 1525 Clifton Rd NE Atlanta GA 30322

ZABANAL, EDUARDO OLEGARIO, lawyer; b. Legazpi City, Albay, The Philippines, Aug. 8, 1952; came to U.S., 1986; s. Jose Agas and Maria Soledad (Olegario) Z.; m. Leorosie Rebodos Nabor, June 18, 1983; children: Shalimar Rosary, Angelica Almira, Regina Tatiana, Lorelei Blossom, Eduardo Olegario, Jr. BA, Aquinas U., The Philippines, 1972; BL, U. The Philippines, 1978. Bar: Hawaii 1990, The Philippines 1979, U.S. Dist. Ct. Hawaii 1990, U.S. Ct. Appeals (9th cir.) 2002. Assoc. Pacis & Reyes, Manila, 1979-86; pvt. practice Honolulu, 1990—. Contbr. articles to profl. jours. Bd. dirs. Kahaluu Neighborhood Bd., Honolulu, 1991-93; active Filipino Coalition for Solidarity, Honolulu, 1991—. Recipient recognition among Disting. Filipinos in Oahu, FIL-AM Courier, 1995, Outstanding Vol. award HSBA. Mem. ABA, ATLA, Hawaii State Bar Assn., Am. Civil Immigration Lawyers Assn., Hawaii Filipino Lawyers Assn., Integrated Bar The Philippines, Philippine Bar Assn., Filipino C. of C. Hawaii. Roman Catholic. Avocations: jogging, travel, reading. Home: 91-1146 Lanakoi St Kapolei HI 96707-2907 E-mail: e.zabanal@worldnet.att.net.

ZABEL, SHELDON ALTER, lawyer, law educator; b. Omaha, Apr. 25, 1941; s. Louis Julius and Anne (Rothenberg) Z.; m. Roberta Jean Butz, May 10, 1975; children: Andrew Louis, Douglas Patrick, Robert Stewart Warren. AB cum laude, Princeton U., 1963; JD cum laude, Northwestern U., 1966. Bar: Ill. 1966, U.S. Supreme Ct. 1976. Law clk. to presiding justice Ill. Supreme Ct., 1966-67; assoc. Schiff, Hardin LLP, Chgo., 1967-73, ptnr., 1973—. Instr. environ. law Loyola U., Chgo. Mem. governing bd. Chgo. Zool. Soc. Mem. ABA, Chgo. Bar Assn., Chgo. Coun. Lawyers, Order of Coif, Union League Club, Met. Club (Chgo.) Jewish. Avocations: skiing, squash. Office: Schiff Hardin LLP Sears Tower 233 S Wacker Dr Ste 6600 Chicago IL 60606-6473 Office Phone: 312-258-5540. E-mail: szabel@schiffhardin.com.

ZABEL, VIVIAN ELLOUISE, secondary school educator; b. Randolph AFB, Tex., July 28, 1943; d. Raymond Louis and Dolly Veneta (Lyles) Gilbert; m. Robert Lee Zabel, Feb. 18, 1962; children: René Lynne, Robert Lee Jr., Randel Louis, Regina Louise. BA in English and Speech, Panhandle State U., 1977; postgrad., U. Ctrl. Okla., 1987-92. Cert. tchr., Okla. Tchr. English, drama, speech, debate Buffalo (Okla.) H.S., 1977-79; tchr. English, drama, speech Schulter (Okla.) H.S., 1979-80; tchr. English Morris (Okla.) H.S., 1980-81; tchr. speech, drama, debate Okla. Christian Schs., Edmond, 1981-82; tchr. English, drama, debate, speech/debate coach Braman (Okla.) H.S., 1982-83; debate coach Pawhuska (Okla.) H.S., 1983-84; tchr. English, French, drama, speech and debate coach Luther (Okla.) H.S., 1984-95; tchr. debate, forensics, yearbook, newspaper, mag., creative writing, competitive speech Deer Creek H.S., Edmond, Okla., 1995—2001; ret., 2001. Dir. drama Nazarene Youth Impact Team, Collinsville, Okla., 1979-81; tchr. h.s. Sun. sch. class Edmond Ch. of Nazarene, 1991-94; mem. cmty.-sch. rels. com. Luther Pub. Schs., 1991-92, supt.'s adv. com., 1992-94. Editor: Potpourri mag., 1975—77; author (as Vivian Gilbert Zabel): Reflected Images, Writing Poetry; author: poetry, short stories, novels. Adult supr. Texas County 4-H, Adams, Okla., 1975-77; double diamond coach NFL; adjudicator and tournament dir. qualifying OSSAA Tournaments. Recipient Disting. Svc. award NFL, 1994, Editor's Choice award for poetry, 1997, 1998, 1999, Tchr. of Excellence, 1996, Outstanding Poet award, 1997, 1998, 1999, 2001. Mem. Nat. Debate Coaches Assn., Nat. Fedn. Interscholastic Speech and Debate Assn., Okla. Speech Theatre Comms. Assn., Okla. Tchrs. English, Internat. Soc. Poets. Republican. Nazarene. Home: 2912 Rankin Ter Edmond OK 73013-5344 E-mail: vzabel@juno.com. *Children are our future, yet we are living in an age of throw-away children. We must find a way to save these children, to give them purpose, training, and love so that they have a promising future, and so will we.*

ZABREK, ALBERT SAMUEL, architect; b. Wash., DC, July 12, 1933; s. Louis and Dora Zabrek; life ptnr. Anne Leona Goldman; children: Robin Lynn Olson, Scott M. Cert. Architectural Draftsman Columbia Tech. Inst., 1955. Chmn., CEO Imperial Tempra Corp. Est., 1966; founder I.T. Rsch. Found., 1972; dedicated Arts Scis. and Humanities, Montgomery Village, Md., 1972—2003; design, engr., cons., product rsch. ZBK/Imperial, Montgomery Village, Md., 2003—. Candidate for pres. South Village Bd. Dirs., Montgomery Village. Seaman US Coast Guard, 1950—53. Recipient Recognition for Contributing to the Advancement of Am. Architecture, 1978. Achievements include patents for Triune Energy Sys., that create indep. electric power on demand; energy sys. program for peace through econ., 1972-2003. Avocations: pvt. pilot, golf, gourmet health food, exercise. Home and Office: Imperial Tempra 18755 Walkers Choice Rd Montgomery Village MD 20886 E-mail: zbk.imperial@comcast.net.

ZABRISKIE, JOHN L. healthcare and agricultural products manufacturing company executive; b. 1940; With Merck & Co., Inc., Whitehouse Station, NJ, 1965-93, past exec. v.p., past pres. mfg. divsn.; chmn., CEO Upjohn Co., Kalamazoo, 1993-95, also bd. dirs.; pres., CEO Pharmacia & Upjohn, Inc., Windsor, U.K., 1995-97, NEN Life Science Product Inc, Boston, 1997-99, chmn., 1999—. Office: Alphagene Inc 10 Cedar St Ste 31 Woburn MA 01801-6365

ZABRISKIE, SHERRY LAFOLLETTE, filmmaker, author, actress; b. Madison, Wis., Feb. 22, 1936; d. Philip Fox and Isabel (Bacon) LaFollette; m. George Albert Zabriskie, feb. 10, 1962; children: Oliver LaFollette, Tavia LaFollette. Student, Bennington (Vt.) Coll., 1958, Stella Adler, N.Y.C., 1959, Uta Hagen, 1959. Filmmaker Zabriskie Prodns., N.Y.C., 1962—; profl. chef Sherry's Specialties, Sharon, Conn., 1978—. Actress in Tall Story, Broadway, N.Y.C., 1959, various summer stock, 1953-62, Late Night with Conar O'Brian, N.Y.C., 1998—; Voice of Cheer opposite Alfred Drake as Voice of Gloom in Exxon's Great Energy Answer Hunt, 1975; co-author: (book) Belle Biography of Belle Case LaFollette, 1984, (screenplay) Summerdog, 1977, (cookbooks) Empanandas, 1982, Pancakes, 1983. Justice of the Peace, State of Conn., Salisbury, 1977-82; active fundraising various polit. campaigns. Recipient Golden Eagle award Coun. of Internat. Events, Washington, 1964, Silver Spoon award Woman's Day, 1978; Josephine Bay/Michael Paul Found. grantee, 1988. Mem. Actors Equity, Screen Actors Guild, Am. Fedn. Radio and TV Artists, The Authors Guild. Democrat. Avocations: travel, food, wine, gardening, walking, theater. Home: 14 Schermerhorn St Brooklyn NY 11201-4803 Office: PO Box 75 Laingsburg MI 48848-0075

ZABRODSKY, ALEXANDER, network technician; s. Andrew and Tatianna Zabrodsky. BArch, U. of Idaho, 1990. Software programmer and animation coord. U. of Idaho, Moscow, 1990—92; asst. mgr. and sr. cad Swisher-Hall Architects, Las Vegas, Nev., 1996—97; cad mgr., asst. design mgr., network adminstr. Steven Langford Architects, Irvine, Calif., 1997—99; bldg. designer, cad coord. Carlson Design - Constrn., Inc., Framingham, Mass., 1999—2000; sr. archtl. coord., cad coord. Wimberly, Allison, Tong & Goo Architecture & Planning, Newport Beach, Calif., 1999—2000; tech. designer cad mgmt. AZCADD, Corona Del Mar, Calif., 2001—; bldg. designer, cad coord. Charles Schwab Data Ctr., 1999; sr. archtl. coord., cad coord. Caesars Palace So. Tower, Retail Podium Base, Las Vegas, Nev., 2000. Lighting design lab. tech. NW Daylighting Forum, Seattle, 1991; software programmer DOE - Bonneville Power Admin, Moscow, 1991—92. Tchr./counselorl devel. of human soul and spirit Believers Fellowship, Moscow, Idaho, 1988—93; tv show devel. of human soul and spirit KLOV-TV, Lewiston, Idaho, 1992—94; tchr. spiritual truths Grush Fellowship, Cheney, Pa., 1985—87. Recipient Bronze Medal, Tau Sigma Delta, 1990, Nat. Collegiate Architecture & Design award, US Achievement Acad., 1988; scholar AAF scholar - Advanced Study & Rsch., AIA, 1992, Catherine Brandt scholar, U. of Idaho, 1988—90, Sch. Gold Medal for Excellence in the Study of Architecture from the Henry Adams fund, AIA, 1990, Ann. Fine Arts award, Phi Kappa Phi, 1988, AIA scholar, 1988, Va. Mowry scholar, U. of Idaho, 1989—90. Achievements include research in Co-author of 3-D Scientific Visualization Software -; development of visual software, 360 degree view - Slice; design of geometric art - Triangular Infinity; invention of visualization of mathematical data - natural and electrical illumination in a building; three dimensial simulation software program, flagship product, light scapes, illuminatin analysis prediction tool of natural daylight and elec. lighting. Office: AZware PO Box 663 Corona Del Mar CA 92625 Office Phone: 800-445-8373. E-mail: azbuild@yahoo.com.

ZABSKY, JOHN MITCHELL, engineering executive; b. Joplin, Mo., Apr. 18, 1933; s. Joseph Anthony and Joan (Lucas) Z. AS, Joplin Jr. Coll., 1953; BSME, U. Mo., 1956; MSME, U. Kans., 1965. Profl. engr., Mo. System engr. Bendix KCD, Kansas City, Mo., 1958-62; rsch. engr. Rocketdyne, Neosho, Mo., 1962-65, Boeing Co., Huntsville, Ala., 1965-66; prin. rsch. engr., scientist Honeywell Inc., St. Paul, 1966-71; chief engr. Pressure Tank & Pipe Fabrication Co., Nashville, 1971-72, Engring. for Industry, Danville, Va., 1972-73; area mgr. fluid machinery Dresser Adv. Tech. Ctr., Irvine, Calif., 1973-85; v.p. ops. ATI, Laguna Niguel, Calif., 1985-93; pres. Cytoprobe, San Diego, 1993-94, v.p. ops., 1994-95; v.p. engring. KleenAir Sys., Inc., Irvine, Calif., 1995—. Cons. Oral Care Products, L.A., 1990-92. Patentee in field. Pres. Mpls.-St. Paul Singletons, 1969-72. Mem.: ASME, AIAA, Soc. Automotive Engrs., Soc. Mfg. Engrs., Mo. Soc. Profl. Engrs. Home: 3640 S Main St Apt C Santa Ana CA 92707-5726 Office: Kleenair Sys Inc 1711 Langley Irvine CA 92614 E-mail: jzabsky@adelphia.net.

ZACARIAS, FERNANDO R. K. physician; b. Sept. 9, 1944; MD, U. Mexico, Mexico City, 1969; DPH, Harvard U., 1986. Intern St. Francis Gen. Hosp., Pitts.; resident in family medicine U. Miami; resident in internal medicine, infectious diseases Grady Meml. Hosp. Emory U., Atlanta; assoc. researcher Mexican Social Security Inst., 1975-79; prof. cmty. medicine U. Mex., 1978-79; prof. microbiology and parasitology U. Anáhuac, Mexico City, 1976-79; vis. scientist Ctrs. for Disease Control, Atlanta, 1982-84; regional advisor on STD and AIDS Pan Am. Health Orgn., Washington, 1984-89, sr. regional advisor on AIDS/STD, 1989-93, coord. AIDS/STD program, 1993—.

ZACCAGNINO, JOSEPH ANTHONY, hospital administrator; b. New Rochelle, N.Y., June 16, 1946; BS, U. Conn., 1968; MPH hospital admin., Yale U., 1970. Adminstrv. resident Yale-New Haven (Conn.) Hosp., 1970-71, adminstrv. asst., 1971-72, asst. dir., 1972-75, assoc. dir., 1975-77, v.p. adminstrn., 1977-78, exec. v.p., COO, 1978-91, pres., CEO, 1991—. Mem. NEHA, Am. Hosp. Assn. (mem. com. svc.), Conn. Hosp. Assn. (trustee). Office: Yale-New Haven Hosp 20 York St New Haven CT 06510-3220

ZACCARIA, ADRIAN, utilities executive; b. 1944; BS, U.S. Merchant Marine Acad., 1966. Engr. Raytheon Co., Lexington, Mass., 1967-68, Gen. Dynamics Corp., Falls Ch., Va., 1968-71; with Bechtel Power Corp., San Francisco, 1974—, now pres. Office: Bechtel Power Corp PO Box 193965 50 Beale St San Francisco CA 94105-1813

ZACCARO, JOHN F. health/medical products executive; Co-founder, vice chmn., COO Physician Computer Network; co-founder, shareholder, vice chmn. drkoop.com. Prodr. Internat. Health and Med. Films Competition, AMA; spkr. in field. Author: Climb Your Own Mountain: The Ultimate Guide to Personal and Career Success, Climb Your Own Mountain: The Ultimate Success Guide. Achievements include developed the sealed air solar pool blanket. Office: drkoop com inc 8920 Business Park Dr Ste 200 Austin TX 78759-7405

ZACCHINO, NARDA, newspaper editor; b. San Diego, 1947; BA in english lit., UCLA. Assoc. editor L.A. Times, Calif. Office: Los Angeles Times Times Mirror Sq Los Angeles CA 90053

ZACCONE, SUZANNE MARIA, sales executive; b. Chgo., Oct. 23, 1957; d. Dominic Robert and Lorretta F. (Urban) Zaccone. Grad. high sch., Downers Grove, Ill. Sales sec. Brookeridge Realty, Downers Grove, 1975-76; sales cons. Kafka Estates Inc., Downers Grove, 1975-76; adminstrv. asst. Chem. Dist., Inc., Oak Brook, Ill., 1976-77; sales rep., mgr. Anographics Corp., Burr Ridge, Ill., 1977-85; pres., owner Graphic Solutions, Inc., Burr Ridge, 1985—. Bd. dirs. Di Trolio Flexigraphic Inst. Curriculum adv. bd. mem. Sch. Dist. 99, 1997, 1998, 1999, 2000, 2001; bd. dirs. Ditrolio Flexographic Inst. Named Supplier of Yr. Through Preferred Supplied, Gen. Binding Corp., 1988—99; recipient Supplier Mem. award, Internat. Bottled Water Assn., 1987—88, Supplier award for excellence U.S., SBA, 1990, Top Performer Supplier award, Cutler Hammer Westinghouse Divsn., 1993—99, Blue Chip Enterprise Initiative award, 1994. Mem.: NAFE, Ditrolio Flexographic Inst. (bd. dirs.), World Label Assn. (1st pl. in World Championship 1994—96, 2002), Women in Packaging (exec. bd.), Inst. Packaging Profls., Women Entrepreneurs DuPage County (past pres.), Tag and Label Mfrs. Inst. (chmn. pub. rels. and mktg. com., bd. dirs., pres. 1998—2000, Best Managed Co. award 1992, 1st place award in U.S. for Screen Printing 1994—97, 1999—2001, Best Managed Co. award 2001—03). Avocation: Avocations: reading, sailing, cooking, needlepoint, scuba diving. Office: Graphic Solutions Inc 311 Shore Dr Burr Ridge IL 60521-5859 Office Phone: 630-325-8181.

ZACEK, JOSEPH FREDERICK, history educator, international studies consultant, Central and East European culture and affairs specialist; b. Stickney, Ill., Dec. 18, 1930; s. Joseph and Emilie (Dvorak) Z.; m. Judith Ellen Cohen (div. 1975); 1 child, Natalie Ann; m. Jane Perlberg Shapiro; stepchildren: Leslie Helen, Peter Carl. BA summa cum laude, U. Ill., Champaign-Urbana, 1952, MA in History, 1953, PhD in History, 1962; cert., Columbia U. Inst. on East Cen. Europe, 1962. Asst. prof. history Occidental Coll., L.A., 1962-65; asst. prof., dir. Russian & East European Programs UCLA, 1965-68; assoc. prof. SUNY at Albany, 1968-71, dir. Russian & East European Programs, 1968-77, 91-92, prof., 1971—2001, chair dept. history, 1974-77, prof. emeritus, 2001—. Mem. selection com. for East Europe Internat. Rsch. and Exch. Bd., Princeton, N.J., 1978-81; nat. bd. cons. NEH, Washington, 1975—; vis. scholar IREX Comenius U., Bratislava, and Charles U., Prague, Czechoslovakia, 1973, Columbia U., 1977-78, U. Ill, Champaign-Urbana, 1987. Author: Palacky: The Historian as Scholar and Nationalist, 1970; editor, co-author: Frantisek Palacky, 1798-1876: A Centennial Appreciation, 1981, The Enlightenment and the National Revivals in Eastern Europe, 1983, The Intimate Palacky, 1984; also numerous periodical articles and chpts. in multi-authored books. With M.I., U.S. Army, 1954-57. Fgn. Area Tng. fellow Ford Found., Columbia U., 1960-62, Sr. Humanities fellow Rockefeller Found., 1977-78, fellow Russian Rsch. Ctr. Harvard U., 1986-91; rsch. grantee Am. Coun. Learned Soc./Soc. Sci. Rsch. Coun., 1965, Am. Philos. Soc., 1968; recipient Comenius medal Govt. of Czech and Slovak Fed. Republic, 1992, Medal of Comenius Pedagogical Inst. in Prague, 1992, Josef Hlávka medal of Czechoslovak Acad. of Scis. in Prague, 1992; also other grad. and postdoctoral awards and grants. Mem. Am. Hist. Assn., Am. Assn. for Advancement Slavic Studies, Western Slavic Conf., Czechoslovak History Conf., Slovak Studies Assn., Consortium on Revolutionary Europe, Assn. for Study of Ethnicity and Nationalism, Phi Beta Kappa. Avocations: travel, gardening, music. Home: 22 Sandhurst Dr Slingerlands NY 12159-9418

ZACHARAKIS, ANDREW, business educator; b. Colorado Springs, Dec. 15, 1963; s. Theodore and Norma Zacharakis; m. Julie Lambert; children: Lillie, Sophie. PhD, U. Colo., 1995. Prof. mgmt. Bentley Coll., Waltham, Mass., 1995-98; prof. entrepreneurship, dir. Entrepreneurship Ctr. Babson Coll., Wellesley, Mass., 1998—. Author: 3 books in field; contbr. articles to profl. jours. Office: Babson Coll Arthur M Blank Ctr Entrepre Babson Park MA 02457

ZACHARIAS, DONALD WAYNE, academic administrator; b. Salem, Ind., Sept. 28, 1935; s. William Otto and Estelle Mae (Newlon) Z.; m. Tommie Kline Dekle, Aug. 16, 1959; children: Alan, Eric, Leslie. BA, Georgetown (Ky.) Coll., 1957, LLD (hon.), 1983; MA, Ind. U., 1959, PhD, 1963. Asst. prof. communication and theatre Ind. U., 1963-69; assoc. prof. U. Tex., Austin, 1969-72, prof., 1972-79, asst. to pres., 1974-77; exec. asst. to chancellor U. Tex. System, 1978-79; pres. Western Ky. U., 1979-85, Miss. State U., Starkville, 1985-97, pres. emeritus, 1998—. Bd. dirs. First Fed. Savs. & Loan Assn., Bowling Green, Ky., Inst. for Tech. Devel., Sanderson Farms, Inc., Miss. Econ. Coun.; dir. John Grisham Libr., Starkville, 1998. Author: In Pursuit of Peace: Speeches of the Sixties, 1970. Bd. dirs. Greenview Hosp.; pres. Southeastern Conf., 1989-91. With U.S. Army, 1959-60. Named Mississippian of Yr. Data Processing Mgmt. Assn.; recipient Teaching award Ind. U. Found., 1963, Cactus Teaching award U. Tex., 1971, Justin Smith Morrill award U.S. Dept. Agriculture, 1992, Disting. Teaching award Honors Program, 2000. Mem. Inst. Tech. Devel. (bd. dirs. 1985-92), Nat. Assn. State Univs. and Land-Grant Colls. (exec. com. 1990-92), Phi Kappa Phi (pres. 1978). Democrat. Episcopalian.

ZACHARY, LOUIS GEORGE, chemical company consultant; b. Aug. 14, 1927; s. George E. and Angelike (Hantsis) Zacharakis; m. Lillie Vletas, Apr. 20, 1955; children: Leslie A., Louis George. Prodn. supr. Dewey & Almy Co., Acton, Mass., 1951-52; salesman chem. divsn. Union Camp Corp., Wayne, N.J., 1952-59, sales mgr. chem. divsn., 1959-62, gen. mgr. chem. ops., 1962-66, gen. mgr. chem. divsn., 1970-78, v.p., 1974-78, Drake Mgmt. Co., N.Y.C., 1966-70; sr. v.p. GAF Corp., N.Y.C., 1978-82, mem. office of chmn., 1981-82; cons., 1983-84; chmn., CEO Universal Die Casting, Inc., Saline, Mich., 1984-90; acting pres. chem. divsn. Church & Dwight Inc., 1990-91; v.p. Nat. Exec. Svc. Corp., N.Y.C., 1993-96. Mem. vis. com. chem. engring. dept. Johns Hopkins U., Balt., 1981-83. Co-editor: Tall Oil and Its Uses, 1965.

With USN, 1945-46. Mem. Chem. Mfrs. Assn. (dir. 1979-83), Synthetic Organic Chem. Mfrs. Assn., Soc. Chem. Industry, Harvard Club N.J. (exec. com.; trustee 2000—). Home: 227 Oak Ridge Ave Summit NJ 07901-3258

ZACHEM, TYLER, investment company executive; BA magna cum laude, U. Rochester; MBA first yr. honors, Harvard Bus. Sch. Cons. McKinsey & Co.; with McDonald & Co., Cleveland; ptnr. McCown De Leeuw & Co.; mng. dir. DB Capital Ptnrs.; ptnr. MidOcean Ptnrs. Bd. dirs. Infocrossing, Inc., Newroads, Inc. Mem.: Phi Beta Kappa. Office: MidOcean Ptnrs 320 Park Ave Ste 1700 New York NY 10022 Office Phone: 212-497-1400.

ZACHERT, VIRGINIA, psychologist, educator; b. Jacksonville, Ala., Mar. 1, 1920; d. R.E. and Cora H. (Massee) Z. Student, Norman Jr. Coll., 1937; AB, Ga. State Woman's Coll., 1940; MA, Emory U., 1947; PhD, Purdue U., 1949. Diplomate: Am. Bd. Profl. Psychologists. Statistician Davison-Paxon Co., Atlanta, 1941-44; research psychologist Mil. Contracts, Auburn Research Found., Ala. Poly. Inst.; indsl. and research psychologist Sturm & O'Brien (cons. engrs.), 1958-59; research project dir. Western Design, Biloxi, Miss., 1960-61; self-employed cons. psychologist Norman Park, Ga., 1961-71, Good Hope, Ga., 1971-99. Rsch. assoc. med. edn. Med. Coll. Ga., Augusta, 1963-65, assoc. prof., 1965-70, rsch. prof., 1970-84, rsch. prof. emeritus, 1984—, chief learning materials divsn., 1973-84, faculty senate, 1976-84, acad. coun., 1976-82, pres. acad. coun., 1983, sec., 1978; mem. Ga. Bd. Examiners Psychologists, 1974-79, v.p., 1977, pres. 1978; adv. bd. Comdr. Gen. ATC USAF, 1967-70; cons. Ga. Silver Haired Legislature, 1980-86, senator, 1987-93, pres. protem, 1987-88, pres., 1989-93, rep., spkr. protem, 1993-96, spkr., 1997-98, Nat. Silver-Haired Congress rep., 1995—, spkr. 1997-99; govs. appointee White House Conf. on Aging, 1971, 96, Ga. Coun. on Aging, 1988-96; U.S. Senate mem. Fed. Coun. on the Aging, 1990-93; senator appointee White House Conf. on Aging, 1995; Ga. Health Decision's appointee to Ga. Coalition for Health, 1996-98. Author: (with P.I. Wilds) Essentials of Gynecology-Oncology, 1967, Applications of Gynecology-Oncology, 1967. Del. White House Conf. on Aging, 1981, 95. Served as aerologist USN, 1944-46;aviation psychologist USAF, 1949-54. Recipient Jane Kennedy Excellence Aging award, 1999. Fellow AAAS, Am. Psychol. Assn.; mem. AAUP (chpt. pres. 1977-80), Sigma Xi. (chpt. pres. 1980-81) Baptist. Home: 4275 Owens Rd # 403 Evans GA 30809 *It's really quite simple-I find, if I wish to be understood or heard, that simplicity is necessary but not ever easy. Simplicity is basic, essential and always the major factor in my search for truth.*

ZACHMANN, WILLIAM FRANCIS, computer and communications industry market research company executive; b. Cleve., Oct. 19, 1942; s. Kurt Wilhelm and Jean (O'Konski) Z.; m. Elizabeth Ann Loftus, June 7, 1980. BA, Harvard U., 1966. Programmer, analyst Cambridge (Mass.) Computer Assocs., 1967-69; sys. rsch. officer 1st Nat. Bank, Boston, 1969-74; dir. rsch. Forum Corp., Boston, 1974-75; coord. personnel adminstrn. Harvard U., Cambridge, 1976-77; mgr. tech. support CallData Sys., Boston, 1977-79; v.p. tech. assessment Internat. Data Corp., Framingham, Mass., 1979-83, v.p. corp. rsch., 1983-87, sr. v.p., 1987-88; pres. Canopus Rsch., Duxbury, Mass., 1988—, editor, pub. Canopus report, 1992—, host Canopus rsch. forum, 1992-99; v.p. Meta Group, Stamford, Conn., 2000—02; chmn., CEO Canopus Rsch. Inc., Duxbury, 2002—. Mem. Harvard (Boston), Harvard Faculty (Cambridge), Compuserve. Author: Keys to Application Development Productivity, 1981; contbg. editor Computer Industry Report, 1982-88, Communications and Distributed Resources Report, 1983-87, PC World mag., 1987-88; columnist On Communications mag., 1984-86, Software News mag., 1984-86, Computerworld mag., 1986-88, Infoworld mag., 1987-88, Micromarketworld mag., 1985-87, PC Mag., 1988-92, PC Week mag., 1988-92, MacUser mag., 1988-89, Windows World, 1992-95, Ad Week's Marketing Computers, 1993-95, Computing Pro, 1996-99, CIO mag., 1999-2002; columnist, sr. contbg. editor OS/2 Professional, 1992-94. Mem. City Mgrs. Adv. Com. on Cable TV, Cambridge, 1979-93; mem. Duxbury Econ. Devel. Com., 1992-95; mem. Planning Bd., Duxbury, 1995-2001, vice chmn., 1996-2000. Home: 160 Standish St Duxbury MA 02332-5065 Office: Canopus Rsch Inc PO Box 2805 Duxbury MA 02331-2805 E-mail: wfz@canopusresearch.com.

ZACHOS, KIMON STEPHEN, lawyer; b. Concord, N.H., Nov. 20, 1930; s. Stephen and Sophia (Bacogiannis) Z.; m. Anne Colby, July 5, 1959; children: Ellen, Elizabeth, Sarah. BA, Wesleyan U., 1952; JD, NYU, 1955; LLM, Boston U., 1968; LLD (hon.), N.H. Coll., 1992, St. Anselm Coll., 1994. Bar: N.H. 1955, U.S. Dist. Ct. N.H. 1957, U.S. Supreme Ct. 1963. Ptnr. Sheehan, Phinney, Bass & Green, Manchester, N.H., 1957—. White House fellow, spl. asst. to atty. gen. Nicholas deB. Katzenbach, Washington, 1965-66; bd. dirs. New Eng. Tel., Bank of Ireland 1st Holdings Inc., Citizens Bank N.H., Hitchiner Mfg. Co., Inc., also others. Dep. speaker N.H. Ho. Reps., 1969-74; active various charitable and ednl. orgns. Named Man of Yr., Manchester C. of C., 1985, Disting. Citizen, Boy Scouts Am., 1987, Bus. Leader of Yr., New Hampshire Assn. C of C., 1994; recipient Brotherhood award NCCJ, 1966, Disting. Alumnus award, Wesleyan U., 1997, Lifetime Achievement award N.H. Bus. and Industry Assn., 2000. Mem. ABA, N.H. Bar Assn. Republican. Greek Orthodox. Avocation: stamp collecting/philately. Home: 2093 Elm St Manchester NH 03104-2316 Office: Sheehan Phinney Bass & Green 1000 Elm St Manchester NH 03101-1792 Office Phone: 603-627-8104. E-mail: kzachos@sheehan.com.

ZACHRY, HENRY BARTELL, JR., construction executive; CEO Zachry Constrn. Corp., San Antonio, 1984—. Office: Zachry Constrn Corp 527 Logwood San Antonio TX 78221

ZACK, ARNOLD MARSHALL, lawyer, mediator, arbitrator; b. Lynn, Mass., Oct. 7, 1931; s. Samuel George and Bess Ethel (Freedman) Z.; m. Norma Eta Wilner, Aug. 10, 1969; children: Jonathan Samuel, Rachel Ann. AB, Tufts Coll., 1953; LLB, Yale U., 1956; MPA, Harvard U., 1961. Asst. to Saul Wallen (arbitrator), 1956-63; cons. govt. South Africa UN Mission to Congo, 1960; cons. U.S. Peace Corps, 1961-63, Labor Dept., 1962-79, Pres.'s Study Commn. on Nat. Service Corps, 1962-63, U.S. AID, 1963—, Friedrich Ebert Stiftung, 1963-64, Nat. Center for Dispute Settlement, 1968-76. Cons. IMF, 2000—02, Govt. Italy, 2002—, Internat. Labor Orgn., 1961—; mem. steering com. Permanent Ct. Arbitration, 2002—; vis. Fulbright lectr. Haile Selassie U., Addis Ababa, Ethiopia, 1963—64; referee Nat. R.R. Adjustment Bd., 1964—; mem. faculty Labor and Worklife Program Harvard Law Sch., 1985—; full time mediator/arbitrator, Boston, 1968—; bd. dirs. Ctr. for Socio-Legal Studies faculty of law U. Natal, South Africa, 1986—92; mem. Fgn. Svc. Labor Rels. Bd., 1982—84, Presdl. Emergency Bds. 221 and 222; chair Presdl. Emergency Bd. 232, 234; chmn. Essential Industries Dispute Settlement Bd. Bermuda, 1993—2000; chair Essential Svcs. Dispute Settlement Bd. Bermuda, 1996—2000; vis. lectr. Yale Law Sch., 1995—96; permanent arbitrator Am. Airlines & APA, IRS & NTEU, Commonwealth Mass., Capital ABC and NABET, Overseas Fedn. Tchrs., Def. Dept.; judge Adminstrv. Tribunal Asian Devel. Bank, 2004—. Author: Labor Training in Developing Countries, 1964, Ethiopia's High Level Manpower-Analysis and Projections, 1964, Handbook on Grievance Arbitration in the Public Sector, 1974, Handbook on Fact Finding and Arbitration in the Public Sector, 1974, Grievance Arbitration, A Practical Guide, 1977; (with R. Bloch) Arbitration of Discipline and Discharge Cases, 1979, (with R. Bloch) The Agreement in Negotiation and Arbitration, 1983, 2d edition, 1995, Arbitration in Practice, 1984, Mediation in the Public Sector, 1985, Grievance Arbitration: Cases on the Merits in Discipline Discharge and Contract Interpretation, 1989, Handbook on Grievance Arbitration: Issues on Procedure and Ethics, 1992, (with J. Dunlop) Mediation and Arbitration of Employment Disputes, 1997, Arbitration Discipline and Discharge Cases, 2000; contbr. articles to profl. jours. Bd. visitors Harvard U. Recipient Whitney North Seymour medal for oustanding contbn. to arbitration, 1980, Cushing Gavin award, 1986, Mildred Spaulding award, 1987, Disting. Svc. award for arbitration of labor-mgmt. disputes, 1989, Pioneer award Assn. Conflict Resolution, 2003, Willoughby Abner award, Assn. for Conflict Resolution, 2004; Wertheim fellow Harvard U., 1996-97. Fellow: African Studies Assn.; mem.: ABA (mem. coun. labor and employment law sect. 2000—), Coll. Labor and Employment Lawyers, Internat. Soc. for Labor Law and Social Security (bd. dirs.), Indsl. Rels. Rsch. Assn. (bd. dirs.), Am. Arbitration Assn. (dir. Labor-Mgmt. Inst. 1966—68), Nat. Acad. Arbitrators (treas. 1972—75, bd. govs. 1977—79, v.p. 1980—82, pres. Rsch. and Edn. Found. 1989—91, pres. 1994—95), Yale Law Sch. Assn., Yale Club (N.Y.C.), Harvard Club. Address: 170 W Canton St Boston MA 02118-1216 Business E-Mail: azack@law.harvard.edu.

ZACK, DANIEL GERARD, retired library director; b. Waukegan, Ill., Oct. 1, 1943; s. Raymond Gerard and Rosanna Marie (Atkinson) Z.; m. Mary Frances Anthony, Aug. 25, 1966; children: Jennifer Lee, Rebecca Jane. BA in Psychology, Western Ill. U., 1967; MS in Libr. Sci., U. Ill., 1975. Editor IBM Corp., Rochester, Minn., 1968-70, Memorex Corp., Mpls., 1970-74; rsch. assoc. Libr. Rsch. Ctr. U. Ill., Urbana, 1974-75; asst. dir. Portage County Pub. Libr., Stevens Point, Wis., 1976-78; dir. Burlington (Iowa) Pub. Libr., 1978-87, Gail Borden Pub. Libr., Elgin, Ill., 1987—2004; ret., 2004. Trustee Batavia (Ill.) Pub. Libr., 1997-2003; founder Friends of Ill. Libr., 1990, bd. dirs. 1990-97. Mem. ALA, ACLU, Ill. Libr. Assn. (mgr. pub. libr. forum 1991-92, 2002-03, exec. bd. dirs. 1992-95, pub. policy com. 1995-98), Pub. Libr. Assn. (intellectual freedom com. 1993-96), Kiwanis.

ZACK, GEORGE J. conductor, music director; b. Pine Bluff, Ark., July 8, 1936; s. George Peter and Eugenia (Paschal) Z.; m. Kerry Sheehan, Oct. 4, 1970; children: Katherine Eugenia, Melissa Sheehan. Student, Am. Conservatory Music, Chgo., 1957, 58; MusB cum laude in Music Theory and Composition, Wichita State U., 1958; MusM in Music Theory and Viola, U. Mich., 1960; PhD in Music Theory, Fla. State U., 1972; studies with Dr. Richard Lert, Stella Roberts, Gustav Meier. Instr. music U. Mich., Ann Arbor, 1962-64; assoc. prof. Hiram (Ohio) Coll., 1964-72; music dir. Music Theater Soc., Lexington, Ky., 1972-75, Lexington Philharm., 1972—, Wooster (Ohio) Symphony, 1973-75, Warren (Ohio) Chamber Orch., 1967—99. Artist-in-residence Ea. Ky. U., James Madison U.; guest condr. State Orch. Salonika, Greece, 1981, 83-84, 84-85, Louisville Orch., 1978; condr. N.E. Ohio All State Orch., 1969, Men and Boy's Choir Festival, 1975, 76, N.Y. All-State Orch., 1975, Ky. All-State Orch., 1974, 76, South Bend, Inc., Youngstown, Ohio, Albuquerque Chamber Orch., Monterey County Symphony, Calif., Amarillo, Tex., Bridgeport, Conn., Santa Cruz, Calif., Stockton, Calif., Charleston, S.C., Modesto, Calif., Las Vegas, Nev.; guest speaker various civic orgns. Dir. (radio program) George Zack's Enhancement of Music, Sta. WEKU-FM, 1975—; dir., producer (radio program) The Enhancement of Music, Sta. WBKY-FM, 1973-75, (TV program) Form in Music, NBC, 1965; co-host (TV program) Ky. Morning, 1979. Commr. Picnic with The Pops, Lexington, 1982—. Recipient Orpheus award Phi Mu Alpha, 1976, Hellenic award, 1993, Humanitarian award Nat. Conf., 1994, Optimist Cup, 1999; named Gov. Artist of Yr., State of Ky., 1994. Mem. Am. Symphony Orch. League, Condr.'s Guild, Am. Fedn. Musicians (hon. mem. chpt. 554-635 local 118), Cen. Ky. Youth Music Soc. (bd. dirs., condr.), NCCJ (bd. dirs., co-chmn.). Greek Orthodox. Home: 237 Woodspoint Rd Lexington KY 40502-1905 Office: Lexington Philharm Artsplace 161 N Mill St Lexington KY 40507-1125

ZACK, STEPHEN NEIL, lawyer; b. Detroit, Dec. 2, 1947; s. Benn Zack and Anita (Rabinovich) Petluck; children: Jason, Tracey. BA, U. Fla., 1969, JD, 1971. Bar: Fla. 1972, D.C., N.Y., U.S. Dist. Ct. (no. and so. dists.) Fla., U.S. Ct. Appeals (5th and 11th cirs.). Sr. ptnr. Floyd, Pearson, Richman, Greer, Weil, Zack & Brumbaugh P.A., Miami, Fla., 1972-91, Zack, Hanzman & Ponce P.A., Miami, 1991—95, Zack Kosnitzky P.A., 1995—2002, Boies, Schiller & Flexner LLP, Miami, 2002—. Legis. aide to Congressman Claude Pepper, 1971-72; chmn. environ. rev. bd. City of Miami, 1978-79, Fla. law ctr. council U. Fla., 1982; mem. Speakers Adv. Com. on Future, Jud. Nomination Commn. for 11th Cir.; spl. counsel, criminal justice advisor to Gov. Bob Graham, 1986; bd. dirs. Jewish Family Services, 1984—. Named to Hall of Fame, U. Fla. Mem. ABA, ALTA, Fla. Bar Assn. (pres. young lawyers sect. 1975-76, bd. govs. 1977-88, chmn. internat. law sect. 1981-82), Acad. Fla. Trial Lawyers (bd. dirs. 1982-86), Dade County Bar Assn. (pres. young lawyers sect. 1975-76), Cuban-Am. Lawyers Assn., Federacion Interamericana de Abogados, Blue Key (pres. Fla. chpt.), Omicron Delta Kappa. Office: Boies Schiller & Flexner LLP Bank of Amer Tower 100 SE 2nd St Ste 2800 Miami FL 33131-2115 E-mail: szack@bsfllp.com.*

ZACKHEIM, ADRIAN WALTER, editor; b. N.Y.C., Sept. 19, 1951; s. Albert Alex and Mary Elizabeth (Cooper) Z.; m. Sarah Babst Parsons, Sept. 1, 1985; children: Adrian Alex, David Parsons. BA, Grinnell Coll., 1973; MA, U. Toronto, Ont., Can., 1975. Editor St. Martins Press, N.Y.C., 1977-79, Doubleday & Co., Inc., N.Y.C., 1979-84, sr. editor, 1984-85, William Morrow & Co., Inc., N.Y.C., 1986-89, sr. editor, v.p., 1989-90, exec. editor, v.p., 1990-91, editorial dir., v.p., 1991-94; pub. dir., v.p. HarperBus, 1994-97; exec. editor, v.p. Harper Collins, 1994-97, pub. HarperBus., sr. v.p. Harper Collins adult trade, 1997-99; editor-in-chief Harper Info., 1999—2001; pub. Portfolio, Penguin Group (USA), N.Y.C., 2001—. Office: PPI 375 Hudson St New York NY 10014

ZADEL, C. WILLIAM, business executive; b. Chgo., May 22, 1943; s. Charles William and Mary Anna (Klestik) Z.; m. Elizabeth Ann Nickla, June 12, 1965; children: Bartholomew Charles, Elizabeth Jill, David Tyler. BS, U.S. Mil. Acad., 1965; MBA, U. Chgo., 1974. Various mktg. and mfg. positions Quaker Oats Co., Chgo., 1969-74; mfg. supt. Johnson & Johnson, Chgo., 1974-77; med. products gen. mgr. Abbott Labs., North Chicago, 1977-83; v.p. bus. devel. Corning (N.Y.) Glass Works, 1983-85; sr. v.p. Americas Ciba Corning Diagnostics Corp., Medfield, Mass., 1985-86, pres. and CEO, 1986-96; chmn., pres. and CEO Millipore Corp., Bedford, MA, 1996—. Bd. dirs. Kulicke & Soffa Industries, Willow Grove, Pa., Health Industry Mfrs. Assn., Washington, Mass. High Tech. Coun., Boston (chmn.), Maritech, Inc., Am. Bus. Conf. Bd. dirs. South Shooore Hosp. Health & Edn. Found., Weymouth, Mass., 1994—; trustee Archbishop Williams H.S. Endowment Campaign, Braintree, Mass., 1993—. Capt. USMC, 1965-69, Cuba, Vietnam. Mem. West Point Soc. of New Eng., U. Chgo. Grad. Sch. of Bus. Club of Boston (bd. dirs. 1988-93), Cohasset Golf Club, Grand Harbor Golf and Beach Club, Linville Ridge Country Club. Avocations: golf, reading, music. Office: Millipore Corp 80 Ashby Rd Bedford MA 01730-2237 Home: 80 Ashby Rd Bedford MA 01730-2237

ZADRA, SHARON KAY, business development professional; b. Reno, Nev., May 6, 1956; d. Peter Joseph Zadra and Darlene Janet Mello-Zadra. BA, U. Nev., 1978. Advt. dir. Circus Circus Hotel Casino, Reno, 1978—79; mktg. dir. Harolds Club/Summa Corp., Reno, 1979—84, Caesars Resort Casino, Reno, 1984—87; pres. Olsen & Zadra, Reno, 1989—96, Mktg. Synergists, Reno, 1994—; coun. mem. City of Reno, 2002—. Bd. mem. Redevelopment Agy., Reno, 2002—, Conv. and Visitors Authority, Reno, 2002—, Employers Ins. Co., Reno, 2000—01. Bd. mem./liaison Econ. Develop. Authority of Western Nev., 2002—, Airport Authority, 2002—; co-founder Reno Balloon Races, 1982—95. Recipient Woman of Achievement, Nev. Women's Fund, 2003, honoree, Outstanding Young Women of Am., 1983. Mem.: MADD and Washoe Cty. Victims Impact Panel (adv.), Ct. Apptd. Spl. Advocates (bd. mem. 1997—), Washoe Health Systems (adv. mem. 1996—). Avocations: cooking, ceramics, travel, classical music, jewelry making. Office: Marketing Synergists 600 So Arlington Ave Ste 5 Reno NV 89509

ZAERA, FRANCISCO, chemistry professor, consultant; b. Caracas, Venezuela, May 11, 1958; s. Francisco and Everys Zaera; m. Encarnacion Montecino. Licenciate, Simon Bolivar U., Caracas, 1979; PhD, U. Calif., Berkeley, 1984. Tchg. asst. Open Univ. divsn. Simon Bolivar U., Caracas, 1975—78, rsch. asst., 1978—79, prof., 1979—80; rsch. asst. U. Calif., Berkeley, 1980—84; asst. chemist Brookhaven Nat. Lab., Upton, NY, 1984—86; prof. chemistry U. Calif., Riverside, Calif., 1986—. Cons. Mex. Inst. Petroleum, Mexico City, 2001—03, Venezuelan Inst. Petroleum Tech., Los Teques, Miranda, Venezuela, 1993—98; vis. prof. Venezuelan Inst. Sci. Rsch., Caracas, 1993; Gran Mariscal de Ayacucho vis. prof., 93; presenter in field. Contbr. reports to profl. jours.; editor: Jour. Molecular Catalysis; assoc. editor: Encyclopedia of Chemical Physics and Physical Chemistry, 1998—2001, guest editor: Jour. Phys. Chemistry, 2001, mem. editl. bd.: Langmuir, 2000. Recipient Innovation Recognition Program award, Union Carbide, 1994, 1995. Fellow: AAAS; mem.: Am. Vacuum Soc., Calif. Catalysis Soc. (pres. 1991—92, sec.-treas. 1990—91), N.Am. Catalysis Soc. (Paul H. Emmett award 2003), Am. Chem. Soc. (treas. colloids divsn. 1997—98, George A. Olah award in hydrocarbon or petroleum chemistry 2001). Office: U Calif Dept Chemistry Riverside CA 92521 Business E-Mail: francisco.zaera@ucr.edu.

ZAFERSON, WILLIAM S. philosophy educator, publisher; b. Kalavrita, Greece, Feb. 10, 1925; came to U.S., 1953; s. Steven A. and Katharine (Michael) Z.; m. Toni Adelgunde Humberg, Oct. 15, 1955. BA in Lit. cum laude, U. Athens, Greece, 1952; MA in Classical Lang. and Lit., U. Chgo., 1965; DPhil magna cum laude, U. Athens, 1976; postgrad., Truman Coll., 2000; Internat. Scholar in Tr origin. classical texts. Asst. prof. U. Upper Iowa, Fayette, 1966-68, Marymount Coll., Salina, Kans., 1968-70; prof. philosophy St. Mary's U., San Antonio, Tex., 1970-72. Internat. scholar translating original classical texts. Author: The Meaning of Metempsychosis, 1965, The Universe, Its Elements and Justice, 1974, A Hymn to Health, 1975, The Platonic View of Moral Law and the Influence of the Tragedians on Plato's Thoughts, 1976, The Perfect Family, 1986, The Heraclitean Logos, 1996; author, pub.: The Songs of the Muses for Gods and Men, 1999, (70 philos. poems set to music) Hephaestus, 2000, (poem set to music) Hermes to King Odysseus, 2001, (lyrics and music) Mother Gaea's Reprobation, 2001, (lyrics and music) Pluto and Persephone (A Look into the Elusinian Mysteries Verifying Every Soul's Immortality), 2002, (poem set to music) Hymn to the Earth: Mother of All, 2002, (music) The Throne of Virtue, 2002, The Titans (War of Ideologies. Vice versus Virtue, words & music), 2003, others. A. Daniel L. Shorey fellow, U. Chgo., 1955. Mem. NRTA, AAUP, Am. Philos. Assn. (ctrl. divsn. emeritus), U. Chgo. Alumni Assn., Am. Assn. Learned Socs., Goethe-Institut Chgo., Nat. Assn. Scholars. Avocations: poetry, classical music, opera, hiking, swimming.

ZAFFARONI, ALEJANDRO C. biochemist, medical research company executive; b. Montevideo, Uruguay, Feb. 27, 1923; arrived in U.S., 44; s. Carlos and Luisa (Alfaro) Zaffaroni; m. Lyda Russomanno, July 5, 1946; children: Alejandro A., Elisa. B., U. Montevideo, 1943; PhD in Biochemistry, U. Rochester, 1949; Doctorate (hon.), U. Republic, Montevideo, 1983; M.Divinity, Cen. Bapt. Seminary, 1987. Dir. biochem. research Syntex S.A., Mexico City, 1951—54, v.p., dir. research, 1954—56; exec. v.p., dir. Syntex Corp., Palo Alto, Calif., 1956—68; pres. Syntex Labs. Inc., Palo Alto, Calif., 1962—68, Syntex Research, Palo Alto, Calif., 1962—68; founder, co-chmn. ALZA Corp., Palo Alto, Calif., 1968—, also CEO, till 1998, founder, dir. emeritus, 1998—99, ret., 1999; founder, mem. policy bd. and exec. com. DNAX Research Inst. of Molecular and Cellular Biology, Inc., Palo Alto, Calif., 1980—, chmn., 1980—82; founder, chmn., chief exec. officer Affymax, N.V., Palo Alto, 1989—. Chmn. Internat. Psoriasis Research Found., Palo Alto; incorporator Neuroscis. Research Found. MIT, Brookline, Mass.; bd. govs. Weizmann Inst. Sci., Rehovot, Israel; mem. pharm. panel of com. on tech. and internat. econs. and trade issues Nat. Acad. Engring. Office of Fgn. Sec. and Assembly of Engring., Washington; hon. prof. biochemistry Nat. U. Mex., 1957, U. Montevideo, 1959. Contbr. numerous articles to profl. jours.; patentee in field. Recipient Barren medal, Barren Found., Chgo., 1974, Pres.'s award, Weizmann Inst. Sci., 1978, Chem. Pioneer award, Am. Inst. Chemists, Inc., 1979, National Medal of Technology, 1995. Fellow: Am. Pharm. Assn., Am. Acad. Arts and Scis.; mem.: AAAS, NAE, Christian Legal Soc. (Mo. bd. dirs. 1973—), N.Y. Acad. Scis., Internat. Soc. Research in Biology of Reproduction, Endocrine Soc., Biochem. Soc. Eng., Sociedad Mexicana de Nutricion y Endocrinologia, Soc. Exptl. Biology and Medicine, Internat. Soc. Study of Biol. Rhythms, Internat. Soc. Chronobiology, Internat. Pharm. Fedn., Calif. Pharmacists Assn., Biomed. Engring. Soc., Am. Soc. Pharmacology and Exptl. Therapeutics, Am. Soc. Microbiology, Am. Soc. Biol. Chemists, Inc., Am. Inst. Chemists, Inc., Am. Found. Pharm. Edn., Am. Chem. Soc., Tau Kappa Epsilon (internat. pres. 1953—57).

ZAFFIRINI, JUDITH, state legislator, small business owner; b. Laredo, Tex., Feb. 13, 1946; d. George and Nieves Pappas; m. Carlos Zaffirini, 1965; 1 child, Carlos Jr. BS, U. Tex., 1967, MA, 1970, PhD, 1978. Committeewoman Tex. State Dem. Exec. Com., 1978-84; mem. Tex. State Senate, 1987—, pres. pro tempore, 1997; owner Zaffirini Comms., Laredo, 1998—. Del. Dem. Nat. Conv., 1980, 84. Recipient Medal of Excellence Nat. League United Latin Am. Citizens, 1987, Jose Maria Morelos y Pavon Medal of Merit for leadership in strengthening U.S.-Mex. rels., 1987; named Woman of Achievement Tex. Press Women, 1980, Gov. of Tex. for a Day, Apr. 19, 1997, Ten Best Legislators Tex. Monthly Mag., 1997, 2001, Disting. Alumnus U. Tex., 2003; inductee Nat. Hispanic Hal of Fame, 1987. Democrat. Roman Catholic. Home: PO Box 627 Laredo TX 78042-0627 Office: 1407 Washington St Laredo TX 78040-4411 Office Phone: 956-724-8379. E-mail: judith.zaffirini@senate.state.tx.us.

ZAFIROPOULO, ARTHUR, electronics executive; Pres. Kayex; v.p. lab. elecs., founder, pres. Drytek; pres. internat. ops. Gen. Signal Semiconductor Equipment Groups; CEO, pres., chmn. Ultratech Stepper, San Jose, Calif., 1990—. Patentee in field. Office: 3050 Zanker Rd San Jose CA 95134-2126

ZAFIROVSKI, MIKE S. communications executive; b. Macedonia; came to U.S., 1970; m. Robin Zafirovski; 3 children. BA in Math., Edinboro U., 1975. Mem. fin. leadership program GE, 1975-78, corp. audit staff, 1978-81, various, 1981-86; pres., CEO GE Capital Auto Actions, 1986-89, Avis Fleet Svcs., 1992-94, GE Capital Mortgage Ins. and Mortgage Svcs., 1994-96, GE Lighting Europe, 1996-99, GE Lighting, 1999—2000; pres., personal comm. sector Motorola, Inc., 2000—02, pres., COO, 2002—. Bd. dir. Motorola, Inc., Econ. Club Chgo. Bd. dir. United Way of Lake County, Children's Meml. Hosp. Chgo. Office: Motorola, Inc 1303 E Algonquin Rd Schaumburg IL 60196*

ZAFREN, HERBERT CECIL, librarian, educator; b. Balt., Aug. 25, 1925; s. Morris and Sadie Mildred (Edlavitch) Z.; m. Miriam Koenigsberg, Feb. 11, 1951; children: Ken, Edie. AB, Johns Hopkins U., 1944, postgrad., 1946-49; diploma, Balt. Hebrew Coll., 1944, LittD (hon.), 1969; AM in Libr. Sci, U. Mich., 1950. Jr. instr. Johns Hopkins U., Balt., 1947-49; bibliog. searcher Law Libr. U. Mich., Ann Arbor, 1949-50; libr. Hebrew Union Coll.-Jewish Inst. Religion, Cin., 1950-91, prof. Jewish bibliography, 1968-95, prof. emeritus, 1996—; exec. dir. Am. Jewish Periodical Ctr., Cin., 1956-80, co-dir., 1980-96, dir., 1996—2002, dir. libs. Cin., L.A., N.Y.C., Jerusalem, 1966-94; dir. emeritus librs. Hebrew Union Coll.-Jewish Inst. Religion, Cin., 1994—. Mem. exec. bd. Jewish Book Coun. Am., 1979-96. Editor Studies in Bibliography and Booklore, 1953—2002, Bibliographica Judaica, 1969-92; compiler: A Gathering of Broadsides, 1967. With USN, 1944-46. Mem. ALA, Assn. Jewish Librs. (founder, nat. pres. 1965-66), World Coun. on Jewish Archives (v.p. 1977-81), Assn. Jewish Studies, Spl. Librs. Assn. (pres. Cin. chpt. 1953-54), Coun. Archives and Rsch. Librs. in Jewish Studies (pres. 1974-78, 89-91), Am. Hist. Assn., Israel Bibliophiles, World Union Jewish Studies, AAUP (chpt. pres. 1964-68), Grolier Club (N.Y.C.), Phi Beta Kappa, Beta Phi Mu. Office: Hebrew Union Coll- Jewish Inst Religion 3101 Clifton Ave Cincinnati OH 45220-2488

ZAGANO, PHYLLIS, religious studies educator; BA in English, Marymount Coll., 1969; MS in Pub. Rels., Boston U., 1970; MA in English, L.I.U., 1972; PhD in English, SUNY, Stony Brook, 1979; MA in Theology, St. John's U., Jamaica, N.Y., 1990. Program officer Nat. Humanities Ctr., N.Y.C., 1979-80; asst. prof. comms. Fordham U., Bronx, N.Y., 1980-84; rschr. Archdiocese of N.Y., 1984-86; ind. rschr. N.Y.C., 1986-88; assoc. prof. comm. Boston U., 1988—98, adj. assoc. prof. theology, 1988—98, dir. inst. for democratic comm., 1988—98; spl. assoc. prof. religious studies Hofstra U., Hempstead, NY, 2003—. Author: Religion and Public Affairs, 1987, Social Impact of the Mass Media, 1991, Woman to Woman, 1993, On Prayer, 1994, Ita Ford: Missionary Martyr, 1996, Twentieth Century Apostles, 1999, Things New and Old, 1999, Holy Saturday: An Argument for the Restoration of the Formale Diaconate in the Catholic Church, 2000 (Book award Catholic Press Assn. 2001, Coll. Theology Soc. 2002), Dorothy Day: In My Own Words, 2003, Called to Serve: A Spirituality for Deacons, 2004; monthly radio host Boston U. World of Ideas, 1992-97. Lector, lay minister Ch. St. Vincent Ferrer, NYC, 1980-92, Our Lady of the Miraculous Medal Ch., 1996—, Newman Ctr., Boston U., 1992-96. Comdr. USNR, 1976—. Faculty Rsch. grantee Fordham U., 1983, Rsch. grantee Nat. Inst. Peace, 1989, Rsch. grantee Wabash Ctr.,

2003; Coolidge fellow Episcopal Divinity Sch., 1987; recipient citation for heroism Nassau County (N.Y.) Fire Commn., 1995. Mem. Am. Acad. Religion (co-chair Roman Cath. Studies, 1991-2001), Am. Cath. Philos. Assn., Assn. Profs. Religious Studies, Naval Res. Assn., Soc. for Study of Christian Spirituality. Roman Catholic. Office: 115 Hofstra Univ Hempstead NY 11549 Office Phone: 516-463-5612.

ZAGAR, ROBERT JOHN, psychologist, researcher; b. Great Lakes, Ill., Nov. 26, 1948; s. Anthony John and Helen Gertrude (Kurzynowski) Z.; m. Agata. MS in Psychology, Ill. Inst. Tech., Chgo., 1975; PhD in Psychology, Northwestern U., 1981; MPH in Pub. Health, U. Ill. Med. Ctr., Chgo., 1982; postgrad., DePaul U., 1982-83, Barry U., 1984-85. Clin. psychologist, Ill.; sch. psychologist, Ill. Sch. psychologist Chgo. Pub. Schs., 1991-93; asst. prof. Nat. Louis U., Evanston, Ill., 1991-93; psychologist Juvenile Divsn. Cir. Ct., Chgo., 1985-91; economist Ill. Dept. Labor, 1986-87; pvt. practice Chgo., 1992—. Cons. psychologist But. Disability Determination, Chgo., 1992—, Dept. Children and Family Svcs., 1992—, Juvenile Divsn. Cir. Ct., 1992—; asst. prof. Ill. Sch. Profl. Psychology, 1989—91; sch. psychologist Aurora Pub. Schs., Ill., 1989—91; asst. prof. Forest Sch. Profl. Psychology, Wheeling, 1988—89; sch. psychology Chgo. Pub. Schs., 1999—, Woodstock, 2000—01; invited spkr. Nat. Summit Youth Violence, U.S. Dept. Dept. Corrections, others; asst prof. Lewis U., 1998—. Contbr. articles to profl. jours. in field of neuropsychol. tests, forensic exams. and aggress. Mem. APA, APHA, Am. Psychol. Soc., Fla. Psychol. Assn., Ill. Psychol. Assn., Nat. Assn. Sch. Psychologists. Roman Catholic. Home: 5507 N Winthrop Ave Chicago IL 60640-1412 also: 8642 226th Ave Salem WI 53168-9356 E-mail: drzagar@msn.com.

ZAGASKI, CHESTER ANTHONY, JR., author, researcher; b. Manchester, Conn., Mar. 28, 1949; s. Chester Anthony Sr. and Lenora M.; m. Suzanne M. Celata, Apr. 1979 (div. Apr. 1989); children: Jason Paul, Brian Matthew. BA, U. S.C., 1971; postgrad., Northeastern U. Sch. Law, Wilbraham, Mass., 1971-72, U. Conn., 1973-75. Career trainee Hartford (Conn.) Ins. Co., 1971; spl. agt. Am. Group, Worcester, Mass., 1973-76; supr. underwriter Interstate Nat./Chgo. Ins., Boston, underwriting mgr. Phila., 1977-79; reins. mgr. N.Am. Reins. (Swiss Re), Phila., 1979-80; asst. v.p. Falcon Ins. Co./Comml. Union Group, Boston, 1980-82; acct. exec. Frank B. Hall & Co., Boston, 1982-84; surplus lines broker Stewart Smith East (USA), Boston, 1984-86; sr. underwriting cons. CNA Ins. Co., Quincy, Mass., 1986-89. Former ind. ins. and risk mgmt. cons. to several prominent firms and groups; organizational cons. Omnium Capital, Montreal, 1st Physicians Ins. Co. Vt., 1995, 96; instr., lectr. Inst. Libr. Assn. Boston, Tufts U., 1984-88; former advisor govt. and bus. groups, 1982-90, including New Eng. Coun., Inc., SBA New Eng., Commonwealth of Mass., Dept. Environ. Protection, Joint Ins. Com. of Mass. Legis., U.S. Congl. Subcom., U.S. SEC; lead organizer, cons. A Spl. Purpose Ins. Co., 1983; provider expert testimony before state and fed. legis. coms., among others; workshop and seminar leader. Author: Environmental Risk and Insurance, 1992; contbr. profl. bus. mags. and jours. (40 plus); involved in prodn. (films) A Civil Action, 1997. Mem. Quincy City Rep. Com., 1989-91; del. State Conv., Boston, 1990; advisor nat. Bush/Quayle Campaigns, 1989, 92; charter mem., sponsor WWII Meml., Washington, 1997. Recipient Citation of Merit Mass. Legis. Spl. Commn. Liability Release Hazardous Materials Rep. Emmett Hayes, 1986. Mem. Harvard Sq. Script Writers, Cape Cod Writers Ctr. Roman Catholic. Achievements include discovery of Mayflower Providence as Crown Colony 1623 "coinage" and historical artifacts from that period in a collection of other "proof quality for period" original sets kept for eventual photo displays; in writings and possible trade and exhibits; discovery of Royal Crown artifacts and British East India Tea Co. and Mass. Bay Co. pieces from 1620 with exceptions; and colleciton of the full lost dark masterpiece in cameo The Adoration of the Shepherds by Giorgionine.

ZAGAT, NINA, publishing executive; m. Tim Zagat, 1965; children: Ted, John. AB, Vassar Coll., 1963; LLB, Yale U.; attended, Le Cordon Bleu Ecole de Cuisine. Atty. Sherman and Sterling, N.Y.C., 1966—90; co-founder, co-pub. Zagat Survey, N.Y.C., 1979—; co-chair, co-founder Zagat.com, 1999—. Served on White House Conference on Travel and Tourism; mem. Who's Who of Food and Beverage in Am.; mem. of the corp. Culinary Institute of Am., 1994—, established lecture series, 2001. Office: Zagat Survey 4 Columbus Circle New York NY 10019*

ZAGAT, TIM, publishing executive; m. Nina Zagat, 1965; children: Ted, John. BA, Harvard U., 1961; LLB, Yale U., 1966. Assoc. Hughes, Hubbard & Reed; ptnr. Pomerantz, Levy, Haudek & Block, 1976—82; chief litigation counsel Gulf & Western Industries Inc., 1980—87; co-founder, publisher Zagat Survey, 1979—. Office: Zagat Survey 4 Columbus Circle New York NY 10019

ZAGEL, JAMES BLOCK, federal judge; b. Chgo., Mar. 4, 1941; s. Samuel and Ethel (Samuels) Z.; m. Margaret Maxwell, May 27, 1979. BA, MA in Philosophy, U. Chgo., 1962; JD, Harvard U., 1965. Bar: Ill. 1965, U.S. Dist. Ct. (no. dist.) Ill. 1965, U.S. Supreme Ct. 1970, U.S. Ct. Appeals (7th cir.) 1972. Asst. state atty. Cook County, 1965—69; asst. atty. gen. criminal justice divsn. State of Ill., Springfield, 1970-77; chief prosecuting atty. Ill. Jud. Inquiry Bd., Springfield, 1973-75; exec. dir. Ill. Law Enforcement Commn., Springfield, 1977-79; dir. Ill. Dept. Revenue, Springfield, 1979-80, Ill. Dept. State Police, Springfield, 1980-87; judge U.S. Dist. Ct. (no. dist.) Ill., Chgo., 1987—. Co-author: Criminal Law and Its Administration, 1989, Cases and Comments on Criminal Procedure, 1992, Author's Money to Burn, 2002. Named Outstanding Young Citizen, Chgo. Jaycees, 1977; recipient Disting. Svc. Merit award Assn. Commerce and Industry, 1983. Mem. Chgo. Bar Assn., Jud. Conf. of U.S. (codes of conduct com. 1987-92). Office: US Dist Ct 219 S Dearborn St Ste 2588 Chicago IL 60604-1801

ZAGER, BERNARD SOLOMON, physician, consultant; b. Detroit, Nov. 3, 1926; s. Philip and Lena Zager; m. Denise Acheson, Sept. 11, 1953; children: Robert, Gerald, Martin. BS, Wayne State U., 1947; MD, Northwestern U., 1950. Diplomate Am. Bd. Preventive Medicine and Occpl. Medicine. Intern Detroit Grace Hosp., 1949-50, resident in surgery, 1952-56; chief physician AAD Ford Motor Co., Utica, Mich., 1964-68; med. dir. Nuc. Energy Divsn. GE, San Jose, Calif., 1968-87; occupl. medicine cons. Reno, 1987—. Capt. US Army, 1950-52. Home and Office: 1210 Bridlewood Way Reno NV 89509-7116 Office Phone: 775-329-8940. E-mail: bernzag@aol.com.

ZAGER, RICHARD A. medical educator, researcher; s. Max and Ruth Zager; m. Brenda K. Burger, Apr. 15, 1973; children: David, Michael, Amy. BS, Northwestern U., 1965, MD, 1969. Diplomate Am. Bd. of Internal Medicine, 1974. Asst. chief of medicine VA, Roxbury, Mass., 1976—80; assoc. prof. of medicine Ohio State U., Columbus, 1980—85; chief of nephrology Harborview Med. Ctr., Seattle, 1985—2000; head of nephrology Fred Hutchinson Cancer Rsch. Ctr., Seattle, 1990—. Cons. Abbott Labs., Chgo., 1995—; mem. NIH Study Sect., Bethesda, Md., 2002—. Contbr. over 130 articles to profl. jours.; reviewer: articles in 20 profl. jours.; contbr. chapters to books; mem. editl. bd.: Kidney Internat., 1992, Jour. of Am. Soc. of Nephrology, 1996—2002. Lt. comdr. USPHS, 1971—73. Named Hon. Chmn., US Congress, State of Wash. Physicians, 2002; recipient Merit award, 2002; grantee, NIH, 2000. Mem.: Internat. Soc. of Nephrology, Am. Soc. of Nephrology. Avocations: skiing, fishing, gardening, piano. Office: Fred Hutchinson Cancer Research Center 1100 Fairview Ave N PO Box 19024 Seattle WA 98109-1024

ZAGER, RONALD I. chemist, consultant; b. N.Y.C., Dec. 27, 1934; s. Joseph and Theodora Zager; m. Judith Ellen Bilt, Dec. 24, 1961 (div. July 1975); children: Scott Lawrence, Joseph Daniel; m. Anne Coykendall Chase, 1995. BS, Bklyn. Coll., 1955; MS in Chemistry, Stevens Inst. Tech., 1969. Chemist Charles Pfizer & Co., N.Y.C., 1956-58, Halocarbon Products, Hackensack, N.J., 1958-66; devel. chemist Tenneco Chems., Garfield, N.J., 1966-71; sr. chemist Givaudan Corp., Clifton, N.J., 1971-77; tech. dir. Internat. Flavors and Fragrances, Union Beach, N.J., 1977-88; cons. Highlands, N.J., 1988-92, Glen, N.H., 1993—; pres. Ronald Zager Assocs LLC. Overseas tech. cons. Unistar Program, UN, 1992. Mem. Am. Chem. Soc., Assn. Cons. Chemists and Chem. Engrs. (v.p. 1990-92, pres. 1993-94). Achievements include research in aroma chemicals and organic fluorocarbons. Office: Ronald Zager Assocs LLC Box 1200 85 Glen Ledge Rd Glen NH 03838 E-mail: rzager@chemconsultants.com.

ZAGER, STEVEN MARK, lawyer; b. Memphis, Nov. 16, 1958; s. Jack and Sylvia (Bloomfield) Z.; m. Debra D'Angelo; children: Samantha, Amanda, Kathryn, Jackson. BA, Vanderbilt U., 1979, JD, 1983. Bar: Tex. 1984, U.S. Dist. Ct. (all dists.) Tex. 1984, U.S. Dist. Ct. Ariz. 1992, U.S. Dist. Ct. (D.C.) 1998, U.S. Ct. Appeals (5th, 6th, and 11th cirs.) 1983, U.S. Ct. Appeals (D.C. cir.) 1991, U.S. Ct. Appeals (Fed. cir.) 1997, U.S. Supreme Ct. 1991. Assoc. Fulbright & Jaworski, Houston, 1983-86, Weil, Gotshal & Manges, Houston, 1986-90, ptnr., 1990-98, head Houston office litigation sect., 1994-96; head natl. litigation grp., 2001—03; mng. ptnr. Tex. offices Brobeck, Phleger & Harrison, 1999—2001, firm ops. com., 1999—2003, Akin, Gump, Strauss, Hauer & Feld, LLP, Houston, 2003—. Adj. prof. U. Houston Sch. Law, 1990—95; nat. adv. bd. NALP, 1996—99. Contbr. articles to Tex. Bar Jour., Texas Lawyer, Houston Lawyer. Bd. dirs., exec. com. Alley Theatre, Houston, 1988-96, Tex. Accts. and Lawyers for the Arts, Houston, 1984-88; adv. bd. Montgomery Bell Acad., 1996—; bd. dirs. Vol. Legal Svcs. Ctrl. Tex., 2000-01, TV Sta. KLRU, 2001-03. Named Outstanding Young Man in Am., U.S. Jaycees, 1983, Best Civil Def. Trial Lawyer in Tex., Tex. Lawyer, 2003; named one of 45 Best Lawyers Under 45 in Am., Tex. Super Lawyers, Tex. Monthly Mag., 2003, 2004; recipient Frank J. Scurlock award, State Bar Tex., 1991, Outstanding Pro Bono Svc., Professionalism award, Tex. Ctr. for Legal Ethics, 2002. Mem. ABA (litigation sect.), State Bar Tex. (dir. 1997-98, Frank J. Scurlock award 1991), Houston Bar Assn. (sec. 1996-97, v.p. 1997-98, bd. dirs. 1993-96, 2004, chair law and arts com. 1994, chair adminstrn. of justice com. 1995, rodeo com. 1997, chair law and media com. 2004, chair cmty. svc. task force 2004, Outstanding Young Lawyer in Houston 1991, Pres.'s award 1996-98), Houston Vol. Lawyers Program (bd. dirs. 1997-98, chair 1998), Travis County Bar Assn. (bd. dirs. 2001-03, chair bench bar program 2000, chair, 2003, mem. jud. affairs com. 1999-2000), Fed. Bar Assn. Office: Akin Gump Strauss Hauer & Feld 1111 Louisiana 44th Flr Houston TX 77002 Office Phone: 713-220-8109.

ZAGHLOUL, DINA AMAL, quality assurance professional, consultant; b. Omaha, Oct. 6, 1975; d. F. Omar and Hoda Z. BS in Biochemistry, U. Nebr., 1996; postgrad., Concord Law Sch., Calif. Quality assurance chemist Cargill, Blair, Nebr., 1996—97; validation specialist PharmTech, Libertyville, Ill., 1997—98; cons. Interim Tech., Oak Brook, Ill., 1998—99; sr. cons. Whittman-Hart, Chgo., 1999; quality assurance mgr. U.S. Office Products IT, Des Plaines, Ill., 1999—2000; cons. Interim Tech. Cons., Scottsdale, Ariz., 2000—; ind. cons. Scottsdale, 2000—. Mem. Am. Chem. Soc., Alpha Lambda Delta, Phi Lambda Upsilon, Phi Eta Sigma. Avocations: sports, reading. Personal E-mail: dzaghloul@msn.com.

ZAGNOLI, ROLAND CANDIANO, management and marketing consultant, pharmacist; b. Highland Park, Ill., Nov. 6, 1931; s. Valerio Walter and Maria Adalgisa (Solignani) Z.; m. Virginia Louise Rizzo, Oct. 7, 1961; children: Roland Christopher, Lisa Louise, Regina Marie, Laurette Rene, Annia Lynn. BS in Pharmacy, U. Mich., 1955; MBA, Harvard U., 1957; LLB, LaSalle Extension U., 1963. RPh, Fla., Ill., Tenn.; registered consulting pharmacist, Fla. Tech. & adminstrv. rotation trainee Abbott Labs., Inc., North Chgo., 1957-59, corp. product mgr., 1959-63, dir. product mgmt. & new mktg. devel. Ross pediatric div. Columbus, Ohio, 1963-65, dir. product mgmt. internat. div. North Chgo., 1965-67, dir. mktg. & sales diagnostics div. North Chgo. & Los Angeles, 1967-70, dual mgr. Amp-Vial project & mfg. hosp. div. North Chgo. & Rocky Mountain, N.C., 1970-73; pres., gen. mgr. Health Care Industries, Inc., Michigan City, Ind., 1973-76, pres., chmn. bd., CEO, 1976-81; pres., CEO M/PIC Cons., Deltona, Fla., 1982—. Med. Inventors Corp., Orlando, Fla., 1988-99. Charter mem. Pharmacy Advancement Com. U. Mich., 1976-91; mem. Ctrl. Fla. Inventors Coun., Orlando, 1984-89; charter mem., bd. advisors Southtech Growth Fund, Ltd., Orlando, 1988-89; advisor Internat. Med. Techs., Winter Springs, Fla., 1989-92. Inventor Dye Pharm. Chem. (tablets dye-coating stability), 1958; patentee, 1959. Charter mem. Ctrl. Fla. Coun. High Tech., Orlando, 1984-94; gen. chmn. Notre Dame Parish Festival, Michigan City, 1977-79; pres. Evans Scholars Alumni, 1961-62; mem., cons. Mktg. & Mgmt. Ctrl. Fla. Innovation, Corp. 1995-2002; fund raiser various orgns. Evans Scholar of Yr. Western Golf Assn., 1954; won 8 golf tournament weekend championships at 7 sites in 4 states; William Douglas McAdams fellow, 1955-57. Mem. Am. Pharm. Assn., Ctrl. Fla. Soc. Hosp. Pharmacists, Fla. Soc. Hosp. Pharmacists, Ctrl. Fla. Pharmacy Assn. (v.p. 1990-91), Fla. Pharmacy Assn., Assn. Univ. Tech. Mgrs., Volusia County Pharmacists Assn., Walnut Hill County Club (Columbus), Pottawattamie Country Club (Michigan City), Kiwanis, Rotary, Phi Eta Sigma, Rho Chi. Home and Office: 1936 Saxon Blvd Deltona FL 32725-4582 Office Phone: 386-789-5479. E-mail: megasus1@earthlink.net.

ZAGORIA, SAM D(AVID), reporter, government official, educator; b. Somerville, N.J., Apr. 9, 1919; s. Nathan and Rebecca (Shapiro) Z.; m. Sylvia Bomse, Dec. 21, 1941; children: Paul, Marjorie Zagoria Isacks, Ronald. BL in Journalism, Rutgers U., 1941. With New Brunswick (N.J.) Daily Home News, 1940-41, N.J. Def. Coun., Trenton, 1941-42, Fed. Office Govt. Reports, Newark, 1942; reporter Washington Post, 1946-55; adminstrv. asst. to Senator Clifford P. Case, Washington, 1955-65; pres. Washington Newspaper Guild, 1953; mem. NLRB, Washington, 1965-69; dir. Labor-Mgmt. Rels. Svc. U.S. Conf. of Mayors, Washington, 1970-78; mem. U.S. Consumer Product Safety Commn., 1978-84; ombudsman Washington Post, 1984-86; arbitrator, 1986—. Fulbright lectr., Copenhagen, 1987; vis. prof. Fla. Atlantic U., Boca Raton, 1988—91; adj. prof. Wake Forest U., Winston-Salem, NC, 1993—2001. Author: Public Workers, Public Unions, 1972, The Ombudsman: How Good Governments Handle Citizens' Grievances, 1988. Campaign mgr. reelection Senator Case, 1960; campaign mgr. race for gov., former Sec. of Labor James P. Mitchell, 1961. With USAAF, 1942-45. Nieman fellow Harvard U., 1954. Mem. Common Cause, Nat. Consumers League, Rutgers U. Alumni Assn. Jewish. Home and Office: 3101 S Ocean Blvd Apt 622 Highland Beach FL 33487-2524 also: 2864 Wynfield Crossing Ln Winston Salem NC 27103-6597 Office Phone: 561-274-6376.

ZAGORIN, JANET SUSAN, legal firm administrator, marketing professional; b. Lakewood, NJ; d. Irving C. and Dorothy (Tarshish) Z. BA, Douglass Coll., 1975; MLS, Rutgers U., 1977. Asst. law libr. N.J. Atty. Gen., Trenton, 1977-78; head of reference sect. Cardozo U. Law Sch., N.Y.C., 1978-79; law and legis. svcs. libr. FTC, Washington, 1979-81; dir. of reference Paul Weiss Rifkind, N.Y.C., 1981-82; libr. dir. Riker Danzig Scherer & Hyland, Morristown, N.J., 1982; libr., profl. devel. dir. Baker & McKenzie, N.Y.C., 1982-96; dir. practice devel. and info. svcs. Stroock & Stroock & Lavan LLP, N.Y.C., 1996-98; dir. practice devel. Cadwalader, Wickersham & Taft, N.Y.C., 1998-99, Gibson, Dunn & Crutcher, N.Y.C., 1999—2001, Sidley Austin Brown & Wood, N.Y.C., 2001—. Bd. dirs. N.Y. Cares, 1998—. Mem. ABA (vice chmn. standing com. Law Libr. Congress 1995-96, chmn. 1996—, mem. law 2000 steering com. Libr. Congress), Fin. Women's Assn. (mem. bd. dirs. 1993-95, 99—), Bus. Women's Network, Am. Assn. Law Librs. (chair fgn. comparative internat. law com. 1990-91, vice chair pvt. law librs. 1990-91, chair 1991—, chair com. on recruitment 1991), Spl. Librs. Assn., Hadassah. Office Phone: 212-839-8797. Business E-Mail: jzagorin@sidley.com.

ZAGORIN, PEREZ, historian, educator; b. Chgo., May 29, 1920; s. Solomon Novitz and Mildred (Ginsburg) Z.; m. Honoré Desmond Sharrer, May 29, 1947; 1 son, Adam. AB, U. Chgo., 1941; A.M., Harvard U., 1947, PhD, 1952. Various positions OWI, U.S. Govt., U.P. Syndicate, CIO, 1942-46; instr. Amherst Coll., 1947-49; lectr. Vassar Coll., 1951-53; from asst. prof. to prof. history McGill U., 1955-65; prof. U. Rochester, 1965—, Joseph C. Wilson prof. history, 1982-90, Joseph C. Wilson prof. history emeritus, 1990—, chmn. dept., 1968-69, acting chmn. dept., 1988-89; vis. prof. Johns Hopkins, 1964-65; Amundsen vis. prof. U. Pitts., 1964; William Andrews Clark Meml. Library prof. UCLA, 1975-76. Thompson lectr. history Vassar Coll., 1987. Author: A History of Political Thought in the English Revolution, 1954, 2d edit., 2000, The Court and the Country, 1969, Culture and Politics from Puritanism to the Englightenment, 1980, Rebels and Rulers 1500-1660, 2 vols., 1982, 2d edit., 2003, Ways of Lying: Dissimulation, Persecution, and Conformity in Early Modern Europe, 1990, Milton Aristocrat and Rebel: The Poet and His Politics, 1992, Francis Bacon, 1998, The English Revolution: Politics, Events, Ideas, 1998, How the Idea of Religious Toleration Came to the West, 2003; co-editor: Philosophy Science and Religion in England 1640-1700, 1991, Guide to Historical Literature, 1994, Thucydides. An Introduction For The Common Reader, 2004; contbr. numerous articles in hist. ours.; mem. editl. bd. Jour. of the History of Ideas. Sheldon travel fellow Harvard U., 1949-50, Fulbright fellow 1949-50, faculty rsch. fellow Social Sci. Rsch. Coun., 1958-59, 61-62, sr. rsch. fellow Folger Shakespeare Libr., 1964-65, fellow Inst. Advanced Study, Princeton, N.J., 1972-73, sr. fellow Nat. Humanities Ctr., 1978-79, fellow Ctr. Advanced Study in Behavioral Scis., 1983-84, Guggenheim fellow, 1983-84, Edgar F. Shannon Ctr. for Advanced Studies fellow U. Va., 1994—, Fellow Royal Hist. Soc., Am. Acad. Arts and Scis.; mem. Am. Hist. Assn. (chmn. Gershoy and Schuyler prize com. 1982-84). Home: 2990 Beaumont Farm Rd Charlottesville VA 22901-8717 Office: U Rochester Dept History Rochester NY 14627 E-mail: pz3p@virginia.edu.

ZAHARIA, ERIC STAFFORD, health facility administrator; b. Pomona, Calif., Aug. 24, 1948; s. Edgar A. and Dorothy (Stafford) Zaharia; m. Caryle Koentz, Dec. 23, 1967; children: Tye W., Tieg A. BA, Pomona Coll., 1970; MEd, U. Ariz.-Tucson, 1973; PhD, George Peabody Coll., 1978. Mental retardation worker Ariz. Tng. Program, Tucson, 1970-71, unit dir., 1971-73; dir. residential svcs. Willmar State Hosp., (Minn.), 1973-76; rsch. asst. Inst. on Mental Retardation and Intellectual Devel., Nashville, 1976-78; dir. mental retardation program svcs. Dept. Mental Health/Mental Retardation, State of Tenn., Nashville, 1978-79; dir. Caswell Ctr., Kinston, N.C., 1979-86; program adminstr. Colo. Divsn. of Devel. Disabilities, Denver, 1986-90; dir. Utah divsn. Svcs. for People with Disabilities, Salt Lake City, 1990-95; ind. cons. Park City, Utah, 1995-2000; dir. Ariz. Divsn. Devel. Disabilities, Phoenix, 2000—. Mem. adj. faculty East Carolina U., Greenville, 1979—86; bd. dirs. Neuse Enterprises Inc., Kinston. Chmn. Big Bros./Sisters Kinston Inc., 1980—83; mem. N.C. Coalition for Cmty. Svc., 1982—85. Mem.: Assn. Retarded Citizens, Nat. Assn. Supts., Am. Assn. Mental Retardation, Kinston C. of C. (bd. dirs. 1983—86), Pub. Residential Facilities. Home: 1352 N Hibbert Mesa AZ 85201

ZAHEDI, CAVEH, filmmaker, video artist, video specialist; b. Washington, Apr. 29, 1960; BA in Philosophy, Yale U., 1981; MFA in Film Prodn., UCLA, 1991. Filmmaker Sundance Inst., Park City, Utah, 1991, Mus. Modern Art, N.Y.C., 1991, Lincoln Ctr., Pesaro, Italy, 1991, WDR-TV, Koln, Germany, 1992, Centro Galego Arte Contemporanea, Santiago, Spain, 1996, Sundance Channel, 2000, I Don't Hate Las Vegas Anymore, I Was Possessed by God, In the Bathtub of the World; co-dir.: A Little Stiff; performer: Citizen Ruth, 1996, Treasure Island, 1999, Waking Life, 2001, A Sign From God, 2000; contbr. articles to profl. jours. Named Atlanta Film Festival Best Feature, Image Film and Video Ctr., 1997, Guggenheim fellow, 1997; recipient Rotterdam Film Festival Critics award, Assn. Dutch Critics, 1994; fellow, NEA, 1996. Mem.: Film Arts Found.

ZAHEDI, SINA, electrical engineer, researcher; b. Tehran, Tehran, Iran, July 8, 1976; s. Masoud Zahedi and Parivash Abedian. BS, Sharif U. Tech., Tehran, Iran, 1998, MS, 2000; postgrad. in PhD program, Stanford U., 2000—. Rsch. asst. Sharif U. Tech., 1997—2000, Stanford U., Stanford, Calif., 2000—. Pres. Persian Student Assn., Stanford U., Stanford, Calif., 2002—03. Mem.: IEEE (sec. student br., Sharif U. Tech. 1997—98, chmn. comm. student br. 1998—99). Office: Stanford University Packard Bldg 257 Stanford CA 94305 E-mail: szahedi@stanford.edu.

ZAHL, PAUL FRANCIS MATTHEW, dean; b. N.Y.C., May 24, 1951; m. Mary McLean Cappleman, Dec. 29, 1973; children: John Arthur, David William Franklin, Simeon McLean. Student, U. N.C., 1968-70; AB magna cum laude, Harvard Coll., 1972; MPhil in Theology, U. Nottingham, Eng., 1975; diploma in pastoral studies, St. John's Theol. Coll., Nottingham, 1975; ThD, Eberhard-Karls-Univ., Tübingen, Germany, 1994. Ordained min. Protestant Episcopal Ch., 1976. Deacon in tng. Good Shepherd Episcopal Ch., Silver Spring, Md., 1975-76; curate Grace Ch., N.Y.C., 1976-82; rector St. Mary's Ch., Scarborough, N.Y., 1982-88, St. James' Ch., Charleston, S.C., 1988-92; fellow Episcopal Ch. Found., 1993-95; dean Cathedral Ch. of the Advent, Birmingham, Ala., 1995—. Tchr. Gen. Theol. Sem., N.Y.C., 1979-82, The King's Coll., Briarcliff Manor, N.Y., 1985-88, Coll. Charleston, S.C., 1990-92, U. Tübingen, Germany, 1992-93; vis. scholar Wycliffe Hall, Oxford, Eng., 1994-95. Author: Who Will Deliver Us?, 1983, Die Rechtfertigungslehre Ernst Kasemanns, 1996, Protestant Face of Anglicanism, 1998; co-author: The Collects of Thomas Cranmer, 1999; columnist The Anglican Digest, 1986—; contbr. articles to profl. jours. Mem. Phi Beta Kappa. Episcopalian. Office: Cath Church of the Advent 2017 6th Ave N Birmingham AL 35203-2701

ZAHLER, ADAM TROY, theater director; b. Houston, Nov. 30, 1955; s. Burton Ross and Suzanne Troy Zahler, Michal Frank Zahler (Stepmother); m. Amy Bernstein, July 30, 1988; children: Michal Celia, Naomi Esther. BA (magna cum laude), U. Vt., 1977; MFA, U. Va., 1996. Founding artistic dir. Second Stage, Burlington, Vt., 1978—81; assoc. dir. Vt. Repertory Theatre, Winooski, Vt., 1987—88; founding artistic dir. The Open Stage, Burlington, Vt., 1988—93; producing assoc. New Repertory Theatre, Newton Highlands, Mass., 1997—. V.p. Burlington (Vt.) Arts Round Table, 1991—92, pres., 1992—93; adj. prof. U. Mass., Lowell, 2000—; chair Theatre Arts Mktg. Alliance, Boston, 2003. Dir.: (stage play) Wit (IRNE Award Best Acting, 2002), Rose (IRNE Award Best Solo Performance, 2001), Stonewall Jackson's House (Elliot Norton award for Best Prodn. Small Theatre, 2001, Elliot Norton award for Best Actress Small Theatre, 2001), (stage play on tour) To Bed With Betsy. Mem.: Theatre Arts Mktg. Alliance. Avocations: gourmet cooking, birdwatching, vegetable gardening. Personal E-mail: adamzahler@rcn.com.

ZAHLER, NOEL BARRY, composer, music educator; b. NYC, May 10, 1951; s. Murray Gustav Zahler and Marion Horowitz; m. Clara Tatar, Aug. 24, 1975; children: Mathieu Pierce, Metisse Petra. BA, MA, CUNY Queens Coll., 1970—74; MFA, Princeton U., 1974—76; Certificato di Perfezionamento, L'Accademia Musicale Chigiana, 1976—77; D of musical arts, Columbia U., 1982—88. Preceptor Columbia U., NYC, 1984—86; asst. prof. music Conn. Coll., New London, 1984—90, assoc. prof. music, 1990—94, prof. music, 1994—2000, Sylvia Pasternack Marx prof. music, 2000—04; prof., dir. Sch. Music U. Minn., Mpls./St. Paul, 2004—. Dir. Cummings Electronic and Digital Sound Studios, New London, 1984—; founding dir. Ammerman Ctr. Arts and Tech., New London; v.p. Am. Composers Alliance, New York, Conn., 2002—. Composer: (concerto) Concerto for clarinet, chamber orchestra and interactive computer, (string quartet) String Quartet I, (fanfare) Olin Fanfare, (flute and interactive computer) Within The Dome Of Time, (solo guitar) reCollections, (solo piano) Piano Études, (video soundtrack) Scuiller's dream, (orchestral) Symphony, (video soundtrack) Gothic Tempest (Silver Medal, Swiss Internat. Video Competition, 1988), (chamber opera) Automata, (piano trio) Trio (NEA Consortium Commn., 1984), (chamber orchestra) Agarttha (Aaron Copland Found. Grant for rec., 2000), (electronic) Electronic Study No. 4, (song with mixed ensemble) All Night, (solo violoncello) Rhapsody for violoncello alone, (chamber orchestra) Harlequin (NYSCA Rec. Award, 1981), (mixed ensemble) Charms, (solo violin) Tableau, (song cycle) Four Songs of Departure (NYSCA rec. grant, 1980), (solo piano) Regions I (NYSCA rec. grant, 1980), (song cycle) Three Yeats Songs for soprano and chamber orchestra, (electronic) Electronic Study No. 3, (song) Tears, (electronic) Computer Syudy No. 2, (flute and piano) Sonatina for flute and piano, (electronic) Kriss Kross, Computer Study No. I, (duo for violin and cello) Study for violin and cello, (interactive music for dance) Au Volant, (documentary soundtrack) Movement and Magic (CPTV Award for Best Documentary Yr., 1999), (song cycle) Songs from Salamandra, (solo clarinet) For clarinet alone, (virtual reality soundscape) Cézanne Set. Elected mem. Waterford Bd. Edn., Conn., 1995—99; dir. Laban/Bartenieff Inst. Movement Studies, Inc., NYC, 1987—89, TechConn, Groton, Conn., 1990—94, Thames Valley Music Sch., Conn., 1992—2000. Recipient Best Documentary Yr., Conn. Pub. TV, 2000, Best Soundtrack for exptl. video, Conn. Public TV/Conn. Commn. Arts, 1988, Individual Artists Award, State Conn. Commn.

Arts, 1985; fellow Fullbright-Hays Full Grant, US Congress, 1976-1977, Residency, Composers Conf., 1976, Atlantic Ctr. Arts, 1997, Associated Kyoto Program, 1990, MacDowell Colony, 1983 and 1979; grantee Rsch. Grant at CNUCE, Italian NRC, 1977, Consortium Commn., Nat. Endowment arts, 1983-1984, Composers Grant, Meet the Composer, 1978 to date; scholar Summer Electronic Music Conf. at Dartmouth Coll. and U. NH, Nat. Endowment Arts, 1972; Grant for Rec., NY State Coun. Arts, 1981. Mem.: Conn. Composers, Inc. (corr.; pres. 1987—89), Composers Guild (corr.; dir. 1996—2000), Soc. Composers, Inc. (corr.; regional chair 1997—2000), Am. Composers Alliance (corr.; v.p. 2002—), Soc. Electro Acoustic Music US (assoc.), Internat. Computer Music Assn. (assoc.), Coll. Music Soc. (assoc.), Broadcast Music, Inc. (assoc.). Achievements include research in Score Follow, a computer program that listens to and follows a live performer, providing accompaniment or spatialization of sound. Office: Univ Minn Sch Music 2106 Fourth St S Minneapolis MN 55455 Office Phone: 612-624-5740. Business E-Mail: nbz2@umn.edu.

ZAHN, CARL FREDERICK, museum publications director, designer, photographer; b. Louisville, Mar. 9, 1928; s. Fred Joseph and Myrtle (Fulks) Z.; m. Betty Jane Woodrow, Nov. 18, 1950 (div. July 1977); children: Lisa, Karen, Richard; m. Felicitas Magdalena Fuhlrott, July 30, 1979 (dec. Mar. 1999). BA, Harvard Coll., 1948. Asst. in conservation Fogg Art Mus., Cambridge, Mass., 1949-50; with art dept. Benton & Bowles Inc., N.Y.C., 1950-51; design asst. Inst. Contemporary Art, Boston, 1951-56; dir. publs. Mus. Fine Arts, Boston, 1956—; also dir. exhbns., 1995-96; ret., 1997; co-founder Mus. Pub. Ptnrs., 2000. Exhibitions include: Addison Gallery Am. Art, Andover, Mass., 1959, Am. Inst. Graphic Arts, N.Y.C., 1960—, Rose Art Mus. Brandeis U., Waltham, Mass., 1969; author: Introduction to Hermann Zapf and His Design Philosophy, 1987, Books and Such Designed by Carl Zahn at the Museum of Fine Arts, Boston, 1956-97, 1997; co-author Weston's Westons: Portraits and Nudes, 1989; co-editor: Eye of the Beholder: Masterpieces from the Isabella Stewart Gardner Museum, 2003. Mem. Soc. Printers, Bund Deutscher Buchkünstler, Mink Meadows Golf Club, East Chop Tennis Club (bd. dirs. 1970-72), Longwood Cricket Club. Home: 39 Cedarwood Rd Jamaica Plain MA 02130-3021 also: 1808 Par Pl Sarasota FL 34240-9689 E-mail: czbird@comcast.net.

ZAHN, PAULA, newscaster; b. Omaha, Feb. 24, 1956; m. Richard Cohen; children: Haley Brynne, Jared Brandon, Austin Bryce. BA in journalism, Stephens Coll., Columbia, Mo., 1978. With Sta. WFAA-TV, Dallas, 1978, Sta. KFMB-TV, San Diego, 1979—81, Sta. KPRC-TV, Houston, 1981—83, Sta. WHDH-TV, Boston, 1983—85; anchor, reporter Sta. KCBS-TV, L.A., 1985—87; anchor The Health Show ABC News, N.Y.C., 1987—88, co-anchor World News This Morning, 1988—90; co-anchor CBS This Morning CBS News, N.Y.C., 1990—96, anchor CBS Evening News Sat. edit., 1996—99; anchor The Fox Report with Paula Zahn Fox News Network, N.Y.C., 1999, anchor The Edge with Paula Zahn, 1999—2001; co-anchor American Morning CNN, 2001—03, co-anchor People in the News, 2002—, anchor Paula Zahn Now, 2003—. Primetime co-host Olympic Winter Games, Albertville, France, 1992; co-anchor Olympic Winter Games, Lillehammer, Norway, 94. Musician (Cellist): Carnegie Hall Debut, 1992. Named Newscaster of Yr., Am. Women in Radio and TV, 1983; recipient Broadcasting Award, Nat. Commn. Working Women, 1982, Spirit Achievement Award, Albert Einstein Coll. Medicine, 1993, Cancer Awareness Award, Congl. Families Action for Cancer Awareness, 1994, Emmy award for outstanding coverage of a continuing news story, 1994, Spirit of Life Award, City of Hope Cancer Ctr., 2003. Office: CNN 820 1st St NE Washington DC 20002-4243

ZAHN, RICHARD GREGORY, construction executive; s. Richard John and Maria Jose Zahn; m. Marnie Blake Savarese, Sept. 25, 2002; children: Richard Gregory Jr., Codie Thomas, Madison Ann Marie. BA in Mktg., Regis U., 1991, MBA in Mgmt., 2001, PhD in Bus. Mgmt., 2003. Lic. gen. contractor Fla., CMR. With psychol. ops. SOCOM Spl. Ops. Command U.S. Army, Ft. Bragg, NC, 1985—97; sheriff's dep. Cumberland County Sheriff's Office, Fayetteville, NC, 1990—91; mgr. Glidden Paint Co., Fayetteville, 1991—95; regional mgr. Jones Blair Paint, Dallas, 1995—97; dir. ops. Hersh Reconstrn., Inc., Longwood, Fla., 1997—99, exec. v.p., 1999—2001, CEO, owner, 2001—. Mem. air quality bd. ADG Apt. Group, Miami, Fla., 2002—; mold cons. IAQA, Longwood, 2002—. Comdr. Civil Air Patrol, Myrtle Beach, SC, 1986; active DeBary (Fla.) Art League, 2001. Staff sgt. U.S. Army, 1985—97. Decorated Commendation medal with valor U.S. Army; recipient Tampa Bay (Fla.) Renovator of Yr. award, Tampa Apt. Assn., 2000, Renovation of Yr. award, Nat. Apt. Assn., Atlanta, 2001. Mem.: Strategic Mgmt. Soc., Am. Mgmt. Soc. Republican. Avocations: boating, scuba diving, golf, mountain biking. Home: 1951 Elkhorn Ct Longwood FL 32750 Office: Hersh Reconstrn Inc 688 Florida Ctrl Pky Longwood FL 32750

ZAHND, RICHARD H. professional sports executive, lawyer; b. N.Y.C., July 22, 1946; s. Hugo and Rose (Genovese) Z.; m. Phyllis Beth Workman, Aug. 13, 1978; children: Andrew Richard, Melissa Dawn. AB, NYU, 1968, JD, 1971. Bar: N.Y. 1972. Assoc. Paul, Weiss, Rifkind, Wharton & Garrison, N.Y.C., 1971-74; staff atty. Madison Square Garden Corp., N.Y.C., 1974-75; v.p. legal affairs Madison Square Garden Center, Inc., N.Y.C., 1975-79; v.p., gen. counsel Madison Square Garden Corp., N.Y.C., 1979-86; v.p. N.Y. Knickerbockers Basketball Club, N.Y.C., 1979-86, N.Y. Rangers Hockey Club, N.Y.C., 1979-86; ptnr. Morrison & Foerster, N.Y.C., 1986-91; exec. v.p., gen. counsel NHL Enterprises, L.P., N.Y.C., 1992—. Served to capt. U.S. Army, 1972. John Norton Pomeroy scholar NYU Law Sch., 1969; Mortimer Bishop scholar NYU Law Sch., 1969; Judge Jacob Markowitz scholar NYU Law Sch., 1970; recipient Am. Jurisprudence prize NYU Law Sch., 1969. Episcopalian. Office: NHL Enterprises LP Fl 46 1251 Ave of the Americas New York NY 10020-1104 Office Phone: 212-789-2023. Business E-Mail: rzahnd@nhl.com.

ZAHNER, DOROTHY SIMKIN, elementary school educator; b. Chengdu, Szechuan, China, May 01; d. Robert Louis and Margaret Isadore (Timberlake) Simkin; divorced; children: Mary De Avilan, Robert Louis. BA in Sociology, Whittier Coll.; MLS, U. So. Calif., L.A. Cert. tchr. Calif., Ariz. Tchr. LA and Pasadena Sch., Calif., 1969-93; dir., owner Betty Ingram Sch., North Hollywood, Calif., 1976-79; dir. Foothill Nursery Sch., La Crescenta, Calif., 1970s; tchr. L.A. Unified Sch. Dist.; guest tchr. Washington Unified Sch. Dist., Phoenix, 1994-97. Guest tchr. Osborn Sch. Dist., 1998-2000, Madison Sch. Dist., Phoenix, 1999-2001. Author: poems pub. in U.S. and Europe. Bd. dirs. Ariz. Tenants Assn., Phoenix, 1994, 95; vol. Am. Friends Svc. Com., Phila., Calif., 1985—, Common Cause, LA, 1990, Internat. Rescue Com., Dem. Candidates, LA and Phoenix. Mem.: Ariz. State Poetry Soc. (pres. 2002—03, chmn. 2004), Alameda Writers Group, Phoenix Poetry Soc. (pres. 1998, anthology editl. co. 2001, com. mem., Poet of Yr. 2000, poetry awards 1995, 2000), Phoenix Writers Club (sec. 1998). Avocations: theater, films, music, swimming, reading.

ZAHNER, MARY ANNE, art educator; b. Dover, Ohio, Mar. 30, 1938; d. Alfred James and Anna Elizabeth (Stewart) Riggle; m. Gordon Dean Zahner, Aug. 27, 1960 (dec. Mar. 1967); 1 child, Anne Colette Krach; m. John Charles Opalek, Aug. 21, 1982. BFA, Ohio U., 1960, MA, 1969; PhD, Ohio State U., 1987. Cert. tchr., Ohio. Instr. art Springfield Twp. Schs., Akron, Ohio, 1960-61, Logan (Ohio) H.S., 1961-62, Dover H.S., 1967-68, chair art dept., 1969-71; teaching asst. Ohio State U., Columbus, 1980-82; from instr. art edn. to asst. prof. U. Dayton, 1971-74, asst. prof., 1974-91, assoc. prof., 1991-2000, prof., 2000—. Faculty rights, governance and svc. com. U. Dayton, 1992-93, arts series com., 1995-98; higher edn. steering com. Ohio Dept. Edn., 1995, adv. com., tchr. preparation programs, 1997; exec. bd. Western Regional Profl. Devel. Ctr., 1996—2004; reviewer Harcourt, Brace, 1993-98, Prentice Hall Inc., 1996-99. Author: (book) Barkan, 2003; contbr. chpts. to books; author procs.; exhibited in group show at Westbeth Gallery, N.Y., 1995. Sec. Kettering (Ohio) Arts Coun., 1990, mem., 1988-93; mem. discretionary support com. Miami Valley Arts Coun., Dayton, 1992; coord. 3d congl. art contest sponsored by Tony P. Hall, Dayton, 1993-95; mem.-at-large edn. com. Culture Works: The Arts and Culture Alliance of the Miami Valley, 1996. Recipient Best of Show award Canton Art Inst., 1969, Inst. Faculty award The Ohio Partnership for the Visual Arts, 1989. Fellow Ohio Art Edn. Assn. (mem. editl. bd. Ohio Art Edn. Jour. 1986—, editor newsletter Artline 1988, workshop coord. 1992, 97, cons. tchr. insvc. for Dayton Pub. Schs. 1995, Outstanding Art Tchr. western dist. 1992, 96); mem. ASCD, Nat. Art Edn. Assn., Assn. Tchr. Educators, Ohio Alliance for Arts Edn., Univ. Coun. for Art Edn., Phi Delta Kappa, Phi Kappa Phi, Delta Kappa Gamma. Democrat. Avocations: music, theater, physical fitness. Office: U Dayton 300 College Park Dayton OH 45469-0001 Office Phone: 937-229-3207. E-mail: mary.zahner@notes.udayton.edu.

ZAHNER-KRACH, ANNE COLETTE, preschool educator; b. Mansfield, Ohio, May 15, 1962; d. Gordon Dean and Mary Anne (Riggle) Zahner; m. David Krach, 2001; 1 child, Sarah Rose Krach. BS in Journalism, Ohio U., 1984; MS in Tchg., U. Dayton, 1992. Staff writer Huber Heights (Ohio) Courier, 1984-87, editor, 1987; preschool tchr. Cath. Social Svcs., Dayton, Ohio, 1993-97, Butler County Bd. Mental Retardation, Fairfield, Ohio, 1997—. Reporter Athens Mag., 1983, Athena Yearbook, 1983. Sec. Local Profl. Devel. Com., 2003—. Mem. Sigma Delta Chi, Alpha Gamma Delta (house chair 1983-84, corr. sec. 1982-83, newsletter editor 1997). Democrat. Roman Catholic. Avocations: travel, photography, exercise. Office: Butler County Bd Mental Retardation Janet Clemmons Ctr 282 N Fair Ave Hamilton OH 45011-4222 Home: 5967 Kensingston T Liberty Township OH 45044-8632

ZAHRA, ELLIS E. lawyer; V.p., gen. counsel Winn-Dixie Stores Inc., Jacksonville, Fla. Office: Winn-Dixie Stores Inc PO Box B Jacksonville FL 32203-0297

ZAHRT, WILLIAM DIETRICH, II, lawyer; b. Dayton, Ohio, July 12, 1944; s. Kenton William and Orpha Catharine (Wagner) Z.; m. Patricia Ann Marek, June 10, 1969; children: Justin William, Alitheia Patricia. BS in Physics, Yale U., 1966, JD, 1969, M of Pub. and Pvt. Mgmt., 1990. Bar: N.Y. 1970, Ohio 1972, Tex. 1982, N.C. 1992, Calif. 2004, NDCA 2004, 9th cir. Ct. Appeals 2004, U.S. Ct. Appeals (Fed. cir.) 1977, US Paten & Trademark Office 1971. Assoc. Kenyon & Kenyon, N.Y.C., 1969-71, Biebel, French & Nauman, Dayton, 1971-80; sr. patent atty. Schlumberger Well Svcs., Houston, 1980-82; sole practice Kingwood, Tex., 1982-85, 88-90; patent atty. Shell Oil Co., Houston, 1985-88; sr. patent counsel Raychem Corp., Fuquay-Varina, N.C., 1990-97; asst. gen. counsel Advanced Micro Devices, Sunnyvale, Calif., 1997-2000; assoc. gen. counsel, legal dir. intellectual property Palm, Inc., Santa Clara, Calif., 2000—02; of counsel Law Offices of Mikio Ishimaru, Sunnyvale, 2002—. Mem. ABA, Am. Intellectual Property Law Assn., Silicon Valley Intellectual Property Law Assn., Dayton Racquet Club, Masons. Anglican. Home: 629 Villa Centre Way San Jose CA 95128-5138 Office: 1110 Sunnyvale-Saratoga Rd Ste A1 Sunnyvale CA 94087

ZAIDI, EMILY LOUISE, retired elementary school educator; b. Hoquiam, Wash., Apr. 20, 1924; d. Burdick Newton and Emily Caroline (Williams) Johnston; m. M. Baqar Abbas Zaidi, June 12, 1949 (dec. Dec. 1983). BA in Edn. and Social Studies, Ea. Wash. State U., 1948; MEd, U. Wash., 1964, EdD, 1974. Tchr. 4th grade Hoquiam Schs., 1948-49; tchr. grades 5-6 Lake Washington Sch. Dist., Kirkland, Wash., 1949-51; tchr. grades 2-3 Port Angeles (Wash.) Schs., 1951-54; tchr. grade 2 Seattle Schs., 1954-55; tchr., reading specialist Northshore Sch. Dist., Bothell, Wash., 1955-69, Sacramento City Schs., 1969-87; ret. Mem. Calif. State Instructional Materials Panel, Sacramento, 1975. Mem. Sacramento Opera Assn., 1986—, Sacramento Ballet Assn., 1987-2000. Fulbright Commn. Exchange Tchr., 1961-62. Mem. Reading Club. Democrat. Avocations: writing, children's literature, reading, travel. Home: 4230 N River Way Sacramento CA 95864-6055

ZAIDI, IQBAL MEHDI, biochemist, scientist; b. Bijnor, India, June 30, 1957; s. Iqbal Haider and Habib (Zehra) Z.; m. Nuzhat Shikoh, Jan. 2, 1993; 1 child, Shan Zehra. BS in Chemistry with honors, Aligarh Med. U., 1976, MS in Biochemistry, 1978, PhD in Biochemistry, 1984. Cert. in radiation. Rsch. fellow Indsl. Toxicology Rsch. Ctr., Lucknow, India, 1979-83; rsch. affiliate NY State Health Dept., Albany, 1984-91; scientist Applied Biosystems, Applera Corp., Foster City, Calif., 1991—. Contbr. articles to profl. jours. Mem. AAAS, Am. Chem. Soc. (biochem. tech. divsn. 1992—), Shia Assn. Bay Area, NY Acad. Scis. Avocations: photography, swimming, travel, natural history. Office: Applied Biosystems 850 Lincoln Centre Dr Foster City CA 94404-1128 E-mail: zaidins22@yahoo.com.

ZAIKOW, LARRY J. JAMES, painter; b. Red Lake, Ont., Can., Dec. 25, 1951; s. Jim DeMetor and Alice Helen (Dutka) Z. Grad., Red Lake H.S. With Poetry Co., Sacramento, Calif., 1987-92. Author: Who's Who in Poetry, 1992. Avocation: writing poetry and songs. Home: 334 Howey St Red Lake ON Canada

ZAIMAN, JOEL HIRSH, rabbi; b. Chgo., Mar. 10, 1938; s. Solomon and Ruth (Levy) Z.; m. Ann Shanok, July 1, 1959; children: Elana Beth, Sarina, Ari Lev. BS, DePaul U., 1957; Master of Hebrew Letters, Jewish Theol. Sem., N.Y.C., 1962. Assoc. rabbi Temple Emanu-El, Providence, 1962-73, sr. rabbi, 1973-80, Chizuk Amuno Congregation, Balt., Md., 1980—. Pres. Balt. Bd. Rabbis, 1985-87; 1st v.p. Synagogue Coun. Am., 1988, pres., 1989-91. Contbr. articles to profl. jours. Chmn. edn. com. Kreiger Schecter Day Sch., Balt., 1983; bd. dirs. Balt. Bd. Jewish Edn., Md. Commn. on Hereditary and Congenital Disorders, Assoc. Jewish Charities and Welfare Fund, Levindale Hebrew Geriat. Ctr. and Hosp., Balt., 1984—, long range planning com.; v.p. Balt. Jewish Coun., 1992-94, pres., 1994-96; chancellors rabbinic cabinet Jewish Theol. Sem.; bd. dirs., patient care adv. com. Sinai Hosp., 1991; bd. dirs., chmn. program com. Inst. Christian and Jewish Studies; adv. coun. Md. Health Care Decisions Act, 1994—. Fellow Pearlstone Inst. Jewish Living (program planning com.); mem. Rabbinical Assembly (exec. council, long range planning com.), United Synagogue Commn. Jewish Edn. (chmn.), Md. Jewish Hist. Soc. (bd. dirs.), Associated Jewish Fedn. Balt. (bd. dirs. 1991—). Jewish. Home: 1 Talton Ct Baltimore MD 21208-3109 Office: Chizuk Amuno Congregation 8100 Stevenson Rd Baltimore MD 21208-1899 E-mail: jhzaiman@chizukamuno.org.

ZAIMAN, K(OICHI) ROBERT, dentist; b. Cin., Oct. 19, 1944; s. Noboru Gary and Toshiko (Matsuyama) Zaiman; m. Kimberly Ann Sass, Nov. 6, 1976; children: Kara Jean, Matthew Robert. Student, Creighton U., Omaha, 1962-64, DDS, 1968. Asst. prof. Creighton U. Sch. Dentistry, Omaha, 1971-73, assoc. prof., 1973-75; pvt. practice dentistry Omaha, 1971—. Dir. Chicano and Native-Am. Free Clinic Creighton U., Omaha, 1970—75. Mem. bd. elders King of Kings Luth. Ch., 1990—95; past v.p., bd. dirs. Japanese-Am. Citizens League, Omaha, 1977—86. Fellow: Internat. Coll. Dentistry, Acad. Continuing Edn., Acad. Gen. Dentistry (nat. del. 1971—76, pres. 1976—77), Pierre Fauchard Internat. Hon. Acad.; mem.: ADA, Omaha Dental Study Club (pres. 1999—2001), Nebr. Dental Assn. (del. 1971—94, 1996—), Omaha Dist. Dental Soc. (bd. dirs. 1968, treas. 1980—85, peer rev. 1996—), Delta Sigma Delta (pres. 1973—74). Office: 10841 Q St Ste 109 Omaha NE 68137-3741 Office Phone: 402-339-4999.

ZAIS, MITCHELL M. career military officer; b. Ft. Bragg, N.C. Grad. in engrng., U.S. Mil. Acad., West Point, Md.; MS, PHD, U. Wash. Commd. infantry U.S. Army, advanced through grades to brigadier gen.; infantry svc. airborne, air assault, mechanized, ceremonial standard, Bradley, light infantry, other, Vietnam, Korea, U.S.; comdr. 2 rifle cos., infantry battalion, light infantry brigade; chief war plans Chmn. Joint Chiefs of Staff; social aide The White House, Washington; exec. officer to comdr. in chief U.S. So. Command, Panama; commanding gen. Coalition Joint Task Force, Kuwait, Joint Task Force Provide Refuge for Kosovar Refugees in U.S.; dep. comdg. gen. maneuvers Ft. Riley, Kans.; chief of staff USAR Command, Ft. McPherson, Ga. Asst. prof. U.S. Mil. Acad.

ZAISER, KENT AMES, lawyer; b. St. Petersburg, Fla., June 10, 1945; s. Robert Alan and Marion (Brown) Z. AB, Duke U., 1967; postgrad., U. Calif., Berkeley, 1971; JD, U. Fla., 1972. Bar: Fla. 1973, U.S. Dist. Ct. (no. dist.) Fla. 1974, U.S. Supreme Ct. 1978, U.S. Dist. Ct. (so. dist.) Fla. 1980, U.S. Dist. Ct. (mid. dist.) Fla. 1981, U.S. Ct. Appeals (11th cir.) 1981. Rsch. aide Fla. Supreme Ct., Tallahassee, 1973-75, adminstrv. asst. to chief justice, 1975-76; asst. gen. counsel Fla. Dept. Natural Resources, Tallahassee, 1976-80; asst. atty. gen. Fla. Dept. Legal Affairs, Tallahassee, 1980-85; dep. gen. counsel S.W. Fla. Water Mgmt. Dist., Brooksville, 1985-89, gen. counsel, 1989-92; ptnr. Foley and Lardner, Tallahassee, 1992-93; prin. Kent A. Zaiser, P.A., Tallahassee, 1994—. Cons. Fla. State Cts. Adminstr., Tallahassee, 1975; mem. Fla. New Motor Vehicle Arbitration Bd., 1998-99. Contbg. author: Environmental Regulation and Litigation in Florida, 1980-84. Campaign chmn. Vince Fechtel for State Rep. of Fla., Leesburg, 1972. Mem. Tallahassee Bar Assn., Jefferson County Bar Assn., Govs. Club. Democrat. Episcopalian. Home: 3286 Longleaf Rd Tallahassee FL 32310-6406 Office: PO Box 6045 Tallahassee FL 32314-6045 Office Phone: 850-576-7600.

ZAITZEFF, ROGER MICHAEL, lawyer; b. Detroit, June 25, 1940; s. Peter and Mary (Fedchenia) Z.; children: Zachary, Natasha, Zoe, Peter. BA with high honors and high distinction, U. Mich., 1962; MA with distinction, U. Calif., Berkeley, 1963, JD, 1969. Bar: N.Y. 1970, U.S. Dist. Ct. (so. dist.) N.Y. 1975, U.S. Ct. Appeals (2d cir.) 1975, D.C. 1985. Assoc. Seward & Kissel, N.Y.C., 1969-77, ptnr., 1977-94, Latham & Watkins, N.Y.C., 1994-2000, LeBoeuf Lamb Greene & MacRae, N.Y.C., 2000—02, Swidler Berlin Shereff Friedman, N.Y.C., 2002—. Contbr. articles to profl. jours. Mem. Tribar Opinion Com., 1990-93. Heller grantee U. Mich., 1962; recipient William Jennings Bryan Prize. Fellow: Am. Bar Found. (life); mem.: Phi Beta Kappa Assocs. Office: Swidler Berlin Shereff Friedman 405 Lexington Ave 11th Fl New York NY 10174 Office Phone: 212-891-9385.

ZAJAC, ALFRED, physicist, researcher; b. Vienna, Feb. 18, 1917, came to U.S., 1948; s. Joseph and Frances (Nevrkla) Z.; m. Dorothy Chmielowiec, Sept. 2, 1950; children: Mark, Andrew. BS, St. Andrew's U., 1948; MS, NYU, 1952; PhD, Polytechnic Inst. Bklyn., 1957. Prof. physics Polytechnic Inst. Bklyn., 1957-64, Adelphi (N.Y.) U., 1964-87, Hofstra U., Hempstead, N.Y., 1987—. Author: Basic Principles and Laws of Mechanics, 1964; co-author: Optics, 1970. Mem. Polish Army Vets. Post 123 (treas.), Hejnal Chorus (co-dir.). Democrat. Roman Catholic. Avocations: choral singing, bee keeping. Home: 60-26 60th Rd Maspeth NY 11378 Office: Hofstra Univ Hempstead NY 11550

ZAJAC, CLAIRE MARIE, lawyer; b. Meriden, Conn., July 16, 1959; BA, Cath. U. Am., Washington, 1981; JD, U. Conn., 1984. Bar: Conn., Minn. Commd. U.S. Army, JAG Corps, 1985—, advanced through grades to lt. col.; sr. health plan counsel Health Ptnrs., Inc., Mpls., 1988—. Adj. faculty U. Wis.-River Falls, 2002—. Office: Univ Wisconsin-River Falls 410 S 3d St River Falls WI 54022-5013

ZAJAC, JOHN, semiconductor equipment company executive; b. NYC, July 21, 1946; s. John Andrew and Catherine (Canepa) Z.; m. Vera Barbagallo, Jan. 13, 1973; children: Jennifer, Michelle. AAS, NYU, 1966; BEE, U. Ky., 1968. Project engr. B.C.D. Computing, N.Y.C., 1968-70; v.p. Beacon Systems, Commack, N.Y., 1970-73, E.T. Systems, Santa Clara, Calif., 1973-77; v.p. research and devel. Eaton Corp., Sunnyvale, Calif., 1977-81; pres. Semitech/Gen. Signal, Los Gatos, Calif., 1981-83; mgr. advanced product div. Tegal/Motorola Inc., Novato, Calif., 1983-86; v.p. research and devel. U.S. Alcohol Inc., San Jose, Calif., 1986—2002; staff scientist Mattson Tech., Fremont, Calif., 1994—2002; dir. R&D Silicon Etch Tech., 2003—04; v.p. R&D Zajac Optimum Output Motors, Inc., San Jose, 2004—. Author: The Delicate Balance, 1988, A Thief's Way to Heaven, 1999, Pyramids, Prophecy and 666, 2000; holder of 25 patents in field; guest TV and radio. Office Phone: 408-428-9213. Personal E-mail: zajacjohn@earthlink.net.

ZAJICEK, JERONYM, retired music educator; b. Krasne, Brezno, Czechoslovakia, Nov. 10, 1926; came to U.S., 1952; s. Frantisek Zajicek and Emilie (Lauterkranz) Zajickova. Studied with, Otakar Jeremias, Prague, Czechoslovakia, 1946—49; student, Charles U., Prague, Czechoslovakia, 1946-49; MusB, Roosevelt U., 1957, MusM, 1958; studied with, K.B. Jirak, Paul A. Pisk; PhD, Charles U., Prague, 1990. Music program dir. for Czechoslovak sect. Radio Free Europe, Munich, 1950-52; prof. theory and composition Loop Coll., Chgo., 1964-96; ret. Composer Clarinet Sonata, 1958, Sinfonietta for Large Orch., 1958, Cello Sonata, 1975; recorded Concertino for Flute and String Orch., 1963, Willie Schwegler Flute and Cologne Radio Orch., String Quartet, 1963, Sonatina for flute, clarinet and bassoon, 1996, Pater Noster for mixed chorus, 1990, Twenty Czech Carols, 2001, Twenty Moravian Carols for four part children chorus, 2002. Oliver Ditson fellow, 1956, 57; 1st prize Violin Sonata Internat. Soc. for Contemporary Music (Chgo. chpt. 1964); named hon. citizen Hrochuv Tynec, Czech Republic, 1998. Roman Catholic. Home: 4230 Prescott Ave Lyons IL 60534-1537 Office: Harold Washington Coll 30 E Lake St Chicago IL 60601-2403

ZAJONC, ROBERT B(OLESLAW), psychology educator; b. Lodz, Poland, Nov. 23, 1923; came to U.S., 1949, naturalized, 1953; s. Mieczyslaw and Anna (Kwiatkowska) Z.; m. Donna Benson, June 20, 1953 (div. 1981); children: Peter Clifford, Michael Anton, Joseph Robert; m. Hazel Markus, May 25, 1982; 1 child, Krysia Courcelle Rose PhD, U. Mich., 1955; Dr. hon. causa, U. Louvain, 1984, U. Warsaw, 1989. Asst. prof. psychology U. Mich., 1955-60, assoc. prof., 1960-63, prof., 1963-94, Charles Horton Cooley Disting. prof. psychology, 1983-94, rsch. scientist Inst. for Social Rsch., 1960-83, dir., 1989-94; prof. psychology Stanford (Calif.) U., 1994—. Directeur d'études Maison des Sciences de L'Homme, Paris, 1985-86; vis. prof. U. Oxford, 1971-72. Author: Social Psychology: An Experimental Approach, 1965; editor: Animal Social Psychology, 1970; assoc. editor: Jour. Personality and Social Psychology, 1960-66. Guggenheim fellow, 1978-79; Fulbright fellow, 1962-63; recipient Disting. Prof. award of social sci., 1983. Fellow AAAS (co-recipient Psychol. prize 1976), APA (Disting. Sci. Contbrn. award 1978), Japan Soc. Promotion of Sci., N.Y. Acad. Scis.; mem. Soc. for Exptl. Social Psychology (Disting. Scientist award 1986), Polish Acad. Scis. (fgn.). Office: Stanford U Dept Psychology Jordan Hall Stanford CA 94305

ZAK, ROBERT JOSEPH, lawyer; b. Steubenville, Ohio, July 29, 1946; s. Joseph and Pearl (Munyas) Zak; m. Kristy Hubbard Winkler, Sept. 13, 1980; children: Elizabeth Adele, Robert Joseph Jr, Barbara Ann. BS, W.Va. U., 1968, JD, 1975. Bar: WVa 1975, US Dist Ct (so dist) WVa 1975, US Dist Ct (no dist) WVa 1989, US Ct Appeals (4th cir) 1990. Staff atty. Pub. Svc. Commn. of W.Va., Charleston, 1975-76; assoc. Preiser & Wilson L.C., Charleston, 1976-81, ptnr., 1981-85; sr. ptnr. Zak & Assocs., Charleston, 1985—. Hearing examiner W.Va. Bd. Regents, Charleston, 1987—90; spl. asst. atty. gen. State of W.Va., 1987—90; mem. Workers Compensation Appeals Bd., 1991—97, 2001—04. Chmn. West Va. Support Enforcement Commn., 2003—. With U.S. Army, 1969—71, Vietnam. Fellow: Am Acad Matrimonial Lawyers; mem.: Order Barristers. Republican. Presbyterian. Office: Zak & Assocs 607 Ohio Ave Charleston WV 25302-2228 Office Phone: 304-345-0745. E-mail: zakslaw@hotmail.com.

ZAKANITCH, ROBERT RAHWAY, artist; b. Elizabeth, NJ; s. Andrew and Mary Z. Student, Newark (N.J.) Sch. Fine and Indsl. Art, 1954-57. Vis. artist, lectr. Sch. Art Inst. Chgo., 1976, U. Calif., San Diego, 1974; lectr. in field. One-man shows include Henri Gallery, Alexandria, Va., 1965, Reese Palley Gallery, N.Y.C., 1970—71, Cunningham Ward, 1973—74, Holly Solomon Gallery, 1977, Robert Miller Gallery, 1978—79, 1981, 1984—85, 1988, Galerie Liatowitsch, Basel, Switzerland, 1978, Galerie Rudolf Zwirner, Cologne, Germany, 1979, Daniel Templon Gallery, N.Y.C., 1980, Bruno Bischofberger Gallery, Zurich, 1980, James Mayor Gallery, London, 1981, Marcus Gallery, 1984, Inst. Contemporary Art, Phila., 1981, Akira Ikeda Gallery, Nagoya, Japan, 1981, Daniel Templon Gallery, Paris, 1982, 1987, 1991, McIntosh-Drysdale Gallery, Washington, 1983, Harcus Gallery, Boston, 1984, 1987, 1989, Delahunty Gallery, Dallas, 1984, Helander/Rubinstein Gallery, Palm Beach, Fla., 1985, 1989, Asher Faure Gallery, L.A., 1985, Yares Gallery, Scottsdale, Ariz., 1987, Sidney Janis Gallery, N.Y.C., 1990, Jason McCoy Gallery, 1994—95, Guild Hall, East Hampton, N.Y., 1995, Hirschl & Adler, N.Y.C., 1995, Patricia Faure Gallery, L.A., 1997, Santa Monica, Calif., 2003, Locks Gallery, Phila., 1997, 1999, Spike Gallery, N.Y.C., 2003, Patricia Faure Gallery, L.A., 2003, exhibited in group shows at Franklin Gallery,

Cornell U., 1978, Va. Mus. Fine Arts, 1979, Palais des Beaux-Arts, Brussels, 1979, Inst. Contemporary Art, U. Pa., 1979, New Mus., N.Y., 1979, Galerie Daniel Templon, Paris, 1980, Nat. Gallery Art, Washington, 1980, Indpls. Mus. Art, 1980, San Francisco Art Inst., 1980, Whitney Mus. Am. Art, N.Y.C., 1981, Jacksonville Art Mus., 1981, Galeria Civica, Italy, 1982, Mus. Fine Arts, Boston, 1982, Fay Gold Gallery, Atlanta, 1982, High Mus. Art, 1983, Meml. Art Gallery, Rochester, N.Y., 1983, Kunstmuseum, Luzern, 1983. With U.S. Army, 1958-60. John Simon Guggenheim fellow, 1995. Studio: 119 N 11th St Brooklyn NY 11211-1163 E-mail: robertraw@earthlink.net.

ZAKHEIM, BARBARA JANE, development professional; b. London, Jan. 31, 1953; d. David Sloma and Sarah Frances (Leifer) Portnoi; m. Dov Solomon Zakheim, Aug. 20, 1972 (div. 1990); children: Keith Samuel, Roger Israel, Scott Elisha; m. Ronald Kleinfeldt, Dec. 13, 1992. BA, Oxford U., Eng., 1974, MA, 1978. Economist Maxima Corp., Silver Spring, Md., 1979, U.S. Dept. Energy, Washington, 1979-80; sr. project analyst Applied Mgmt. Scis., Silver Spring, 1980-83, staff assoc., 1983-85; prin. analyst NUS Corp., Gaithersburg, Md., 1985-87, cons. analyst, 1987-89; pres. Keith R. Scott Assocs., Inc., 1989-96, African Treasures, Inc., 1990-93; dir. policy and econ. studies Sanford Cohen & Assocs., Inc., 1993-96, v.p. info. & comm. svcs. divsn., 1996-2000, COO, 2000—02; dir. devel. Save A Child's Heart Found., U.S., Inc., 2002—. U.S. rep. Coll. Petroleum Studies, Oxford, 1984-93; N.Am. rep. Twirltrade Internat. Ltd., London, 1985—; mem. adv. com. on women in bus. Theodore Roosevelt Nat. Bank, Washington, 1991-92; profl. team mem. Venture Ptnrs. Internat., Inc., N.Y.C., 1990-94. Contbr. articles to profl. jours. Bd. dirs. SE Hebrew Congregation, Silver Spring, 1977-78; sec. Stonington Woods Homeowners' Assn., 1997-98, pres., 1998-99; founder, pres. Greater Washington Jewish Coalition Against Domestic Abuse, 1999—; bd. dirs. Jewish Cmty. Coun. Greater Washington, 2002—. Mem. NAFE, Hadassah, Jewish Women Internat. Republican. Avocations: reading, travel, theater, music, ballroom dancing. Home and Office: 11247 Watermill Ln Silver Spring MD 20902-3439 E-mail: bzakheim@aol.com.

ZAKHEIM, DOV SOLOMON, economist, government official; b. Dec. 18, 1948; s. Zvi Hirsh and Bella (Rabinowitz) Zakheim; m. Barbara Jane Portnoi, Aug. 20, 1972 (div. 1990); children: Keith Samuel, Roger Israel, Scott Elisha; m. Deborah Bing Lowy, May 26, 1991. Student, London Sch. Econs., 1968-69; BA summa cum laude, Columbia U., 1970; DPhil, Oxford U., 1974. Rsch. fellow St. Antony's Coll. Oxford U., 1974; asst. to mng. dir. U.K. br. Internat. Credit Bank Geneva, 1974-75; assoc. analyst Nat. Security and Internat. Affairs Congl. Budget Office, Washington, 1975-78, prin. analyst, 1978-81; spl. asst. to asst. sec. def. (internat. security policy) Dept. Def., Washington, 1981-82, spl. asst. to under sec. def., 1982-83, asst. under sec. def. (policy and resources), 1983-85, dep. under sec. def. for planning and resources, 1985-87; exec. v.p. Sys. Planning Corp., Arlington, Va., 1987-90, corp. v.p., 1990-2001; CEO SPC Int Inc, 1998—2001; under-sec. def. (comptr. and CFO) U.S. Govt., 2001—04; v.p. Booz Allen Hamilton, McLean, Va., 2004—. Consult to secy def and undersecy def, 1987—2000; adj prof Nat Def Univ, 1992, Columbia Univ, 1995—96, Yeshiva Univ, 1995—96; adj prof, presidential fellow Trinity Col, Conn., 1998; guest lectr War Coll. Author: (book) Flight of the Lavi; contbr. articles to profl jours. Mem US Comn Preservation Am's Heritage Abroad, 1991—95; mem bd visitors Dept Def Overseas Regulatory Ctrs, 1998; mem Secy Def Task Force Def Reform; mem bd deps Brit Jews, 1971—72; mem Chief Rabbi's Chaplaincy Bd, England, 1971—72; bd dirs Friends of Jewish Chapel, US Naval Acad, 1997—. Fellow, NSF, 1970—73, Kellet, Columbia Col, 1974. Mem.: Royal Inst Int Affairs (UK), Int Inst Strategic Studies, Coun Foreign Relations, United Oxford and Cambridge Univ Club, Columbia Club, Phi Beta Kappa. Home: 817 Lamberton Dr Silver Spring MD 20902-3038 Office: Booz Allen Hamilton 8283 Greensboro Dr Mc Lean VA 22102 Office Phone: 703-902-7000. Business E-Mail: zakheim_dov@bah.com.

ZAKIAN, MICHAEL, museum director; BA, Columbia U., 1979; MA, Rutgers U., 1984, PhD, 1994. Assoc. curator Palm Springs Desert Mus., 1986—95; dir. Frederick R. Weisman Mus. Art, Malibu, Calif., 1995—. Office: The Frederick R Weisman Art Museum Pepperdine U 24255 Pacific Coast Hwy Malibu CA 90263

ZAKIM, DAVID, biochemist; b. Paterson, N.J., July 10, 1935; s. Sam and Ruth (Sorokin) Zakim; m. Nancy Jane Levine, June 12, 1957 (div. 1976); children: Michael, Eric, Thomas; m. Dagmar Aurelia Stanke, July 30, 1978; children: Tamara, Robert. AB in Chemistry, Cornell U., 1956; MD summa cum laude, SUNY, Bklyn., 1961. Diplomate Am Bd Internal Med. Intern N.Y. Hosp., N.Y.C., 1961-62, asst. resident, 1962-63, fellow, 1963-65; asst. prof. to prof. medicine and pharmacology U. Calif., San Francisco, 1968-83; Vincent Astor Disting. prof. medicine Cornell U. Med. Coll., N.Y.C., 1983-2000; prof. biochemistry Cornell U. Grad. Sch. Med. Sci., N.Y.C., 1983-2000, prof. emeritus, 2000—; chief scientist, chmn. Zmedix Corp., San Francisco. Editor: (book) Hepatology: A Textbook of Liver Disease, 1982, Hepatology: A Textbook of Liver Disease, 4th edit., 2002, Disorders of Acid Secretion, 1991, (series) Current Topics in Gastroenterology, 1985, Gastroenterology Medicine Today, 1992—95; contbr. articles to profl. jours. Capt U.S. Army, 1965—68. Named Distinguished Alumnus, SUNY-Brooklyn, 1986. Mem.: Am. Soc. Clin. Investigation, Am. Soc. Biol. Chemists, Am. Assn. Physicians. Office Phone: 415-595-8820. E-mail: dzakim@pacbell.net., david@zmedix.net.

ZAKIN, JACQUES LOUIS, chemical engineering educator; b. N.Y.C., Jan. 28, 1927; s. Mordecai and Ada Davies (Fishbein) Z.; m. Laura Pienkny, June 11, 1950; children: Richard Joseph, David Fredric, Barbara Ellen, Emily Anne, Susan Beth. BSChemE, Cornell U., 1949; MChemE, Columbia U., 1950; DEng. Sci., NYU, 1959. Chem. engr. Flintkote Research Labs., Whippany, N.J., 1950-51; research technologist, research dept. Socony-Mobil, Bklyn., 1951-53, sr. research technologist, 1953-56, supervising technologist, 1959-62; assoc. prof. chem. engring. U. Mo., Rolla, 1962-65, prof., 1965-77, dir. minority engring. program, 1974-77, dir. women in engring. program, 1975-77; chmn. dept. chem. engring. Ohio State U., Columbus, 1977-94, Helen C. Kurtz prof. chem. engring., 1994-2000, Helen C. Kurtz prof. emeritus, 2000—. Chmn. sci. manpower and resources com. Coun. Chem. Rsch., 1984-86, governing bd., 1986-89; exec. com., 1988-89; adv. bd. State of Ohio Alternative Fuels, 1992-93; vis. prof. Technion, 1968-69, 94-95, Hebrew U., 1987; disting. vis. prof. Mex. Acad. Scis. and Mex.-USA Found. for Scis., 1999. Co-editor: Proc. Turbulence Symposium, 1969, 71, 73, 75, 77, 79, 81, 83; contbr. articles to profl. jours.; patentee in field. Bd. dirs. Rolla Community Concert Assn., 1966-77, 2d v.p., 1975-77; bd. dirs. Ozark Mental Health Assn., 1976-77; trustee Ohio State Hillel Found., 1981-84, treas., 1984-89, pres., 1989-92; trustee Congregation Beth Tikvah, 1983; bd. trustees Columbus Jewish Fedn., 1989-92; co-chmn. Academics and Scientists for Soviet Refuseniks. With USNR, 1945-46. Recipient Outstanding Rsch. award U. Mo., 1970, Josef Hlavka Meml. medal Czechoslovakian Acad. Sci., 1992, Clara M. and Peter L. Scott Faculty award, 1996, Rsch. award Japanese Govt., 2001; named Outstanding Educator of Yr., Ohio Soc. Profl. Engrs., 1994, Tech. Person of Yr., Columbus Tech. Coun., 1987; Am. Chem. Soc. Petroleum Rsch. Fund Internat. fellow, 1968-69, Socony-Mobil Employee Incentive fellow NYU, 1956-59, Sr. Fulbright Rsch. fellow Technion, 1994-95. Fellow Am. Inst. Chem. Engrs.; mem. Am. Chem. Soc., Soc. of Rheology, Am. Soc. Engring. Edn., Sigma Xi, Phi Lambda Upsilon, Phi Eta Sigma, Alpha Chi Sigma, Tau Beta Pi, Phi Kappa Phi. Jewish. Office: Ohio State U 140 W 19th Ave Columbus OH 43210-1110 Business E-Mail: zakin.1@osu.edu.

ZAKY-AL-HASHIMI, HAJJAH SAKINA NURA, writer; d. Thimimian Jirjis IBN Abdullah Al-Hashimi and Waliyah Rabah Bint Walid; m. Yahya IBN Yahya, Dec. 25, 1964 (dec. Apr. 1969); children: Mustafa, Fatimah; m. Gamal Baghat Zaky, July 12, 1990. Student, Portland State U., 1971—73; PhD, Omdurman U., Sudan, 1980; student, Fresno City Coll., 2003. Cert. astrologer. Regional mgr. R.K.O. Industries, Riverside, Calif., 1984—89; editor Astral Light 2000 Publs., Jersey City, 1990—2000; reporter Fresno City Coll. Rampage, Calif., 2000—03. Author: Doves of Light, A Journey to Truth, 1999, Celestial Blue, A Spiritual Awakening, 2000, A Journey Through Death, 2001. Mem.: NOW (treas. 1970—72), Future Tchrs. Am. (sec. 1962—64), Am. Fedn. Astrologers. Independent. Orthodox Islam. Avocations: researching religious history, writing, reading. Personal E-mail: sakinazaky@hotmail.com.

ZALAZNICK, SHELDON, editor, journalist; b. Bronx, N.Y., Aug. 6, 1928; s. Samuel and Esther Leah (Schneiderman) Z.; m. Vera Altobelli, Apr. 4, 1953; 1 dau., Andrea. BA, NYU, 1948; MA, Tchrs. Coll. Columbia, 1950. Tchr. English Benjamin Franklin H.S., N.Y.C., 1950-52; assoc. editor Newsweek mag., 1952-56; v.p. Manning Pub. Relations Co., 1956-59; sr. editor Forbes mag., 1959-63, mng. editor, 1976-89; founding editor New York mag. sect. N.Y. Herald Tribune, N.Y.C., 1963-64; Sunday editor N.Y. Herald Tribune, 1964-66; staff writer Gen. Learning Corp., 1966-67; assoc. editor Fortune mag., 1967-69; v.p., editl. dir. New York mag., 1969-76. Home: 458 W 246th St Bronx NY 10471-3330 E-mail: zalaznick@optonline.net.

ZALDASTANI, OTHAR, structural engineer; b. Tbilisi, Republic of Georgia, Aug. 10, 1922; came to U.S., 1946, naturalized, 1956; s. Soliko Nicholas and Mariam Vachnadze (Hirsely) Z.; m. Elizabeth Reily Bailey, June 22, 1963; children: Elizabeth, Anne, Alexander. Diplome d'Ingenieur, Ecole Nat. des Ponts/Chausees, Paris, 1945; Licencie es Scis., Sorbonne, Paris, 1946; MS in Geotech. Engring., Harvard U., 1947, DSc in Aerodynamics, 1950. Registered prof. engr., Mass., R.I. Tenn., Mo., N.H. Mem. faculty Harvard U., Cambridge, Mass., 1947-50; ptnr. Nichols, Norton and Zaldastani, Boston, 1952-63; pres. Nichols, Norton and Zaldastani, Inc., Boston, 1976-88, chmn., 1989-97, dir., 1997—, Ga. Coastal Devel. Found. Inc., Boston, 1998—. Gordon McKay vis. lectr. structural mechanics Harvard U., 1961; trustee, 1st v.p. Mass. Constrn. Industry Bd., 1973-76; mem. Mass. Designer Selection Bd., 1976-80. Contbr. author: Advances in Applied Mechanics, vol. 3, 1953; patentee sound-absorbing block, prestressed concrete beam and deck system. Trustee Wheelock Coll., Boston, 1975-81, mem. corp., 1984-93; trustee Boston U. Med. Ctr., 1976—, Brooks Sch., North Andover, Mass., 1986-95. Recipient awards from various ogrns. and agys. including Prestressed Concrete Inst., Cons. Engrs. Coun. New Eng., Am. Inst. Steel Constrn. Fellow ASCE (Ralph W. Horne award), AIAA (assoc.), Am. Concrete Inst.; mem. Georgian Assn. in U.S. (pres. 1958-65, hon. citizen Republic of Georgia 1997), Sigma Xi, Harvard Club, Harvard Faculty Club, Somerset Club (Boston), Country Club (brookline, Mass.), Rolling Rock Club (Ligonier, Pa.). Home: 70 Suffolk Rd Chestnut Hill MA 02467 Office: Zaldastani Assocs Inc 70 Federal St Boston MA 02110-1906 E-mail: otharz@aol.com.

ZALESKI, JAMES VINCENT, electronics executive; b. Kenosha, Wis., Oct. 8, 1943; s. Louis Edward and Lena Louise (Bellotti) Zalewski; m. Beverly Rae Neumann, Nov. 8, 1969. BBA, BSME, U. Wis., 1966, MS, 1967. Project engr. AC Electronics div. GM, Milw., 1968-73; ops. mgr. Applied Computer Sci., Inc., Milw., 1970-72; sect. mgr. Delco Electronics div. GM, Santa Barbara, Calif., 1973-84, dept. mgr., 1984-85, chief engr., 1985-87; pres., chief exec. officer Vetronix Corp., Santa Barbara, Calif., 1984—; chief exec. officer Vetronix Japan, Ltd., Kawagoe, Japan, 1990—; pres., chief exec. Vetronix Sales Corp., Santa Barbara, CA, 1997—. Contbr. articles to profl. jours.; patentee in field. Named Entrepreneur of Yr. Greater L.A. Inc. mag., 1995. Mem. Soc. Automotive Engrs., Evans Scholars Assn., Mensa. Avocation: backpacking. Office: Vetronix Corp 2030 Alameda Padre Serra Santa Barbara CA 93103-1716

ZALESKI, JAN FRANCISZEK, biochemist; b. Bytom, Poland, Feb. 3, 1949; came to U.S., 1979; s. Stanislaw and Maria (Fliska) Z.; m. Margaret M. Toczkowska, Dec. 28, 1971; children: Marta, Monika. MS in Biochemistry, U. Warsaw, Poland, 1971, PhD in Biochemistry, 1978. Rsch. assoc., asst. prof., assoc. prof. U. Warsaw Inst. Biochemistry, 1971-82; vis. scientist Roswell Park Meml. Inst., Buffalo, 1979-82; assoc. scientist Okla. Med. Rsch. Found., Oklahoma City, 1982-85; rsch. assoc. U. Pa. Med. Sch., Phila., 1985-88; vis. scientist Great Lakes Lab., Buffalo, 1988; rsch. assoc. prof. Rutgers U. Sch. Pharmacy, New Brunswick, N.J., 1989-97. Cons. J.A. Haley Vets. Hosp., Tampa, 1985, Great Lakes Lab., Buffalo, 1988, Wyeth-Ayerst Rsch., Princeton, 1994. Contbr. articles to profl. jours., chpts. to books. Co-recipient awards Ministry Sci. and Higher Edn., Warsaw, 1978, Polish Acad. Scis., Warsaw, 1979. Mem. AAAS, Internat. Soc. Study of Xenobiotics, Am. Soc. Biochemistry and Molecular Biology. Avocations: antique and modern prints collecting, photography, basketball, gardening. Personal E-mail: jmzaleski@comcast.net.

ZALESKI, JEAN, artist; b. Birkirkara, Malta; d. John M. and Carolina (Micallef) Busuttil; children: Jeffrey, Philip, Susan. Student, Art Students League, N.Y.C., 1955—58, New Sch., 1967—69, Moore Coll. Art, Phila., 1970—71, Parsons Sch. Design, N.Y.C., 1974—75, Pratt Inst., 1976—77. Dir. art Studio 733, Great Neck, NY, 1963-67; sr. art instr. Hussian Coll. Art, Phila., 1970-71; dir. Naples (Italy) Art Studio, 1972-74; corp. sec. Women in The Arts, N.Y.C., 1974-75, exec. coord., 1976-78. Adj. lectr. Bklyn. Coll., 1974-75, Hofstra U., 1977-82, Cooper Union, 1986—. One-woman shows include Neikrug Gallery, N.Y.C., 1970, Wallnuts Gallery, Phila., 1971, Il Gabbiano Gallery, Naples, Italy, 1973, Adelphi U., Garden City, N.Y., 1975, Women in Arts Gallery, N.Y.C., 1975, Alonzo Gallery, 1979—80, Va. Ctr. for Creative Arts, Sweet Briar, 1981, Hodgell Galleries, Sarasota, Fla., 1982—83, Elaine Starkman Gallery, N.Y.C., 1986, Romano Gallery, Barnegat Light, N.J., 1987—88, Citicorp Ctr., N.Y.C., 1988—89, Z Gallery, 1991, Sweet Briar Coll., Va., 1993, Trinity Coll., Hartford, Conn., 1996, Myungsook Lee Gallery, N.Y.C., 1997—98, Slater Mus., Norwich, Conn., 1999, Four Decades of Painting, Retrospective Westbeth Gallery, N.Y.C., 2000, St. James Cavalier Contemporary Art Ctr., Valletta, Malta, 2002, exhibited in group shows at Art U.S.A., N.Y.C., 1969, Internat. Art Exhbn., Cannes, France, 1969, Frick Mus., Pitts., 1970, NAD, N.Y.C., 1970—71, Phila. Mus. Art, 1971, Am. Women Artists, Palazzo Vecchio, Florence, Italy, 1972, Internat. Women's Arts Festival, Milan, 1973 (Gold medal), Bklyn. Mus., 1975, Sweet Briar Coll., Va., 1977, CUNY, 1978, Va. Ctr., 1988, Mus. Hudson Highlands, 1982, Pace U. Gallery, N.Y.C., 1982, Bayly Mus., Charlottesville, Va., 1986, Allbright Knox Mus., Buffalo, 1986, E Starkman Gallery, N.Y.C., 1987, Nabisco, 1989, Queens Coll., N.Y., 1991—92, Mus. City of N.Y., 1993, Nat. Mus. Fine Arts, Malta, 2000, Mediterranean Conf. Ctr., 2001, Westbeth Gallery, NYC, 2002—04, Represented in permanent collections N.Y. Pub. Libr., Met. Mus. Art, Va. Ctr. for Creative Arts, Nat. Mus. Women in Arts, Mus. City of N.Y., Nat. Mus. Malta; author: Winged Spirits, 1995; co-author: COW/LINES, 1983. Recipient Susan B. Anthony award NOW, 1986; MacDowell fellow, 1971—, Ragdale fellow, 1986—, Va. Ctr. for Creative Arts fellow, 1976—, Tyrone Guthrie Ctr. fellow, 1991; grantee NEA/Brown U., 1982, Artists Space, 1988; invited to White House by Pres. Carter, 1977. Mem. Artists Equity, Women in the Arts. Democrat. Roman Catholic. Achievements include represented Malta in UN art exhibition celebrating entry of 25 countries to E.U. 2004. Avocations: music, opera, writing. E-mail: valletta@aol.com.

ZALESKI, LINDA C. retail executive; Pres. Data Projections, Houston, 1987—. Recipient Entrepreneur Yr. award, 1996, Blue Chip Enterprise Initative award, Nations Bus. Mag. and U.S. Chamber Commerce, 1995. Office: Data Projections 3036 Rogerdale Rd Houston TX 77042-4121 Fax: 713-781-3338. E-mail: getinfo@dpict.com.

ZALEZNIK, ABRAHAM, psychoanalyst, management specialist, educator; b. Phila., Jan. 30, 1924; s. Isadore and Anna (Appelbaum) Z.; m. Elizabeth Ann Aron, June 24, 1945; children: Dori Faith, Ira Harry. AB in Econs., Alma Coll., 1945, DLitt (hon.), 1992; MBA, Harvard U., 1947, DCS, 1951; grad., Boston Psychoanalytic Soc. and Inst., 1965; D (hon.), U. Montreal, 1999; prof. (hon.), Haute Etude Commercial, France, 2001. Research asst. Harvard U. Grad. Sch. Bus. Adminstrn., 1947-48, instr., 1948-51, asst. prof., 1951-56, assoc. prof., 1956-61, prof., 1961—, Cahners-Rabb prof. social psychology of mgmt., 1967-83, Konosuke Matsushita prof. leadership, 1983-90, Konosuke Matsushita prof. leadership emeritus, 1990—; research fellow Boston Psychoanalytic Soc. and Inst., 1965-68, mem. faculty, 1972—; pvt. practice psychoanalysis Boston, 1968—. Cons. in field. Author: Human Dilemmas of Leadership, 1966, (with Manfred F.R. Kets de Vries) Power and the Corporate Mind, 1975, The Managerial Mystique, 1989, An Executive Guide to Motivating People, 1990, Learning Leadership, 1992; contbr. articles to profl. jours. Bd. overseers Beth Israel Hosp., Boston, 1968— . Served with USN, 1942-46. Mem. Boston Psychoanalytic Soc., Am. Psychoanalytic Assn. (cert.), Am. Sociol. Assn., Tavern Club (Boston), Belmont Country Club (Mass.). Home: 170 N Ocean Blvd Palm Beach FL 33480-3946 Office: Harvard University Business School Boston MA 02163 Office Phone: 617-495-6285. E-mail: azaleznik@hbs.edu.

ZALL, PAUL MAXWELL, retired English language educator, consultant; b. Lowell, Mass., Aug. 3, 1922; s. Nathan and Bertha (Rubin) Z.; m. Elisabeth Weisz, June 21, 1948; children: Jonathan, Barnaby, Andrew. BA, Swarthmore Coll., 1948; AM, Harvard U., 1950, PhD, 1951. Teaching fellow Harvard U., 1950-51; instr. Cornell U., 1951-55, U. Oreg., 1955-56; research editor Boeing Co., 1956-57; asst. prof. Calif. State Coll., Los Angeles, 1957-61, asso. prof., 1961-64, prof. English, 1964-86; research scholar, cons. to library docents Huntington Library, San Marino, Calif., 1986-96; acting chmn. dept. Calif. State Coll., 1969-71. Cons. in report writing, proposal preparation and brochures to industry and govt. agys., 1957-99. Author: Elements of Technical Report Writing, 1962, Hundred Merry Tales, 1963, Nest of Ninnies, 1970, Weakly Blast, 1960-85, Literary Criticism of William Wordsworth, 1966, (with John Durham) Plain Style, 1967, Simple Cobler of Aggawam in America, 1969; (with J.R. Trevor) Proverb to Poem, 1970, Selected Satires of Peter Pindar, 1971, Comical Spirit of Seventy Six, 1976, (with Leonard Franco) Practical Writing, 1978, Ben Franklin Laughing, 1980; (with J.A.L. Lemay) Autobiography of Benjamin Franklin, 1981; Norton Critical Edition of Franklin's Autobiography, 1986, Abe Lincoln Laughing, 1983, 95; (with E. Birdsall) Descriptive Sketches, 1984, Mark Twain Laughing, 1985, Being Here, 1987, George Washington Laughing, 1989, Franklin's Autobiography: Model Life, 1989, Founding Mothers, 1991, Becoming American, 1993, 98, Lincoln's Legacy, 1994, Wit and Wisdom of the Founding Fathers, 1996, Blue and Gray Laughing, 1996, Lincoln on Lincoln, 1999, 2003, Dolley Madison, 2001, Franklin on Franklin, 2001, Jefferson on Jefferson, 2002, Washington on Washington, 2003, Adams on Adams, 2004. Pres. Friends of South Pasadena Library, 1967-70. Served with USAAF, 1942-45, ETO. Am. Philos. Soc. fellow, 1964, 66; John Carter Brown Libr. rsch. grantee, Huntington Libr. rsch. grantee, fellow, 1993. Home: 1911 Leman Ln South Pasadena CA 91030-4628 Office: Huntington Libr San Marino CA 91108 Fax: 626-449-5720.

ZALLEN, HAROLD, corporate executive, scientist, former university official; b. Boston, Apr. 7, 1926; s. Joseph and Lillian L. (Stahl) Z.; m. Eugenia Malone, Aug. 23, 1959. BS in Pharmacy, Northeastern U., Boston, 1951; EdM in Sci. and Math., Boston U., 1954; MS in Organic Synthetic Medicinal Chemistry, Purdue U., 1959, PhD in Analytical Medicinal Chemistry and Nucleonics, 1960. Registered pharmacist, Mass., Ind. With USAAF, 1943-46, combat flier, sgt. 487th bomb group H, 839th bomb squadron; commd. 1st lt. U.S. Army, 1955, advanced through grades to col.(P), 1986; ret.; mgr. Shoppers World Pharmacy, Inc., Framingham, Mass., 1951-53; asst. prof. phys. sci. Portia Law Sch. Calvin Coolidge Coll., Boston, 1952-54; tchr. physics and chemistry Natick (Mass.) High Sch., 1955-56; asst. prof. microbiology Lowell Gen. Hosp. Sch. Nursing, Mass., 1955-56; grad. instr., asst. radiol. control officer Purdue U., West Lafayette, Ind., 1957-58; assoc. prof. chemistry Coll. Pharmacy Mercer U., Atlanta, 1960-61; assoc. prof. to prof., head dept. radiol. scis., dir. Office Radiol. Safety Auburn U., Ala., 1961-66; specialist phys. sci. rsch. div. higher edn. rsch. Bur. Rsch., U.S. Office Edn., 1966-67, head curriculum higher edn. rsch., 1967; head instructional sci. equipment program, assoc. program dir., then dir. spl. projects program NSF, Washington, 1967-72; asst. dean, dir. rsch. and grad. studies Okla. State U., Stillwater, 1972-73, prof. chemistry, 1972-73, rsch. prof. biochemistry and molecular biology, 1973-75; assoc. v.p. for adminstrn. and fin., CEO Health Scis. Ctr. Campus U. Okla., Oklahoma City and Tulsa, 1973-75, assoc. v.p. for systems planning, procedure devel. and spl. projects, cen. adminstrn. Norman, 1975—; exec. v.p. Acad. World Inc., 1975—; pres., CEO Malone, Zallen & Assocs. div. AcaWorld Corp., Greenville, N.C.; v.p., dir. nuclear divsn. Vachon, Nix & Assocs., Atlanta; pres., CEO Computer Profls. Inc., Computer Distbrs. Corp., Malone Group Internat., Columbus, Ga.; sci. advisor Litton Corp./Army Rsch. Inst., 1991, Omega Tng. Group Inc./GIAT Industries, France, 1992—, Wetzel Internat., Inc., 1994—; chmn. bd. dirs. Cons. Unltd., Columbus, Ga. Asst. dean, dir. rsch. and grad. studies Okla. State U., Stillwater, 1972-73; analytical chemist Communicable Diseases Ctr. USPHS, Atlanta, 1962; spl. lectr. NSF Radiobiology Inst., Tuskegee U., 1963-64, head instrnl. sci. equipment program, assoc. program dir., dir. spl. projects program, 1967-72; pres. Pres.'s Sci. and Technol. Adv. Commn., Washington; v.p. Okla. Coll. Osteo. Medicine and Surgery, Tulsa; cons. Okla. State Regents for Higher Edn.; Gov. N.C. primary alt. to So. States Energy Bd., 1984-90, exec. com. bd., 1986; bd. vis. Tex. Christian U., Ft. Worth, 1973-76; adv. coun. Coll. Sci. and Math. Auburn U., 2003—; cons. in field. Author 4 books in field, 1986-89; editor, pub. Jour. Internat 6800 Computer Ctr.; contbr. articles to profl. jours. Hon. chmn. bus. adv. coun., Ala., 2003; rep. candidate NC Gen. Assembly, 1986; mem. nat. rep. congl. com. Recipient Mayoralty cert. of merit for outstanding svc. and Key to City, City of New Orleans, 1973, Most Outstanding Alumni award Northeastern U., 1996, Comdg. Gen. award for excellence U.S. Army Inf. Ctr., 1998; GE sci. fellow Union U., Schenectady, NY., 1955, fellow Purdue Rsch. Found., 1958, Elks Cancer Soc., 1959, Am. Cancer Soc., 1960. Mem. Am. Chem. Soc. (bd. dirs., chmn. Auburn sect. 1966), Am. Soc. Engring. Edn. (long range planning com.), Nat. Coun. Univ. Adminstrs., Soc. Rsch. Adminstrs. (pres. So. sect. from 1974, chmn. publs. com.), Health Physics Soc., Greenville (N.C.) Area C. of C. (chmn. rsch.), Columbus Club, Rotary (chmn. bull. com. Auburn 1963, bd. dirs. Auburn 1964, bd. dirs. Stillwater 1972-73, Greenville 1981-86, charter pres. Greenville, N.C. Morning club 1986, Paul Harris fellow), Masons (32 degree), Shriners, Rotary Club of Auburn (chair classification), Sigma Xi, Phi Lambda Upsilon, Rho Chi, Phi Delta Kappa, Delta Sigma Theta, Beta Phi (past nat. sec.).Rotary Int., Svc. above Self award, 1986 Baptist. Office: Malone Group Internat PO Box 3682 Auburn AL 36831-3682 Personal E-mail: zallen1780@hotmail.com.

ZALMAN, MARVIN, law educator; b. Bronx, Jan. 9, 1942; s. Harry and Violet Bar David Zalman; m. Greta Ann Durst, July 28, 1966; children: Amy Ruth, Seth Philip. BA, Cornell U., 1963; JD, Bklyn. Law Sch., 1966; MA, SUNY, Albany, 1971, PhD, 1977. Bar: N.Y. 1966. Lectr. law, Peace Corps vol. Ahmadu Bello U., Zaria, Nigeria, 1967—69; assoc. prof. Mich. State U., East Lansing, 1971—80; project leader Mich. Felony Sentencing project, State Ct. Adminstrv. Office, Lansing, 1978—79; chmn. dept. criminal justice Wayne State U., Detroit, 1980—87, 2001—03, prof. criminal justice law, 1987—. Exec. dir. N.Y. State Com. on Sentencing Guidelines, Albany, 1984; mem. Mich. State Bar Prison and Corrections Com., 1976—84. Contbr. articles to legal and criminal justice jours. Mem. pub. safety and justice com. New Detroit, Inc., 1981—84. Mem.: Law and Soc. Assn., Acad. Criminal Justice Scis. (chmn. awards com. 1983—84), Am. Soc. Criminology. Jewish. Home: 26260 Pembroke Rd Huntington Woods MI 48070-1625 Office: Dept Criminal Justice Wayne State U Detroit MI 48202 Office Phone: 313-577-6087. Business E-Mail: aa1887@wayne.edu.

ZALOZNIK, ARLENE JOYCE, oncologist, retired military officer; b. Pitts., Jan. 30, 1948; d. Ernest and Frances Elizabeth (Augustin) Z. BS, Carlow Coll., 1969; MS, Duquesne U., 1972; MD, Med. Coll. Pa., 1976. Diplomate Am. Bd. Internal Medicine, Am. Bd. Oncology. Commd. U.S. Army, 1976, advanced through grades to col.; intern then resident in internal medicine Madigan Army Med. Ctr., Tacoma, 1976-77; fellow in hematology and oncology Fitzsimons Army Med. Ctr., Aurora, Colo., 1979-81, staff oncology, 1981-82, asst. chief med. oncology, 1982-84, chief hematology and oncology, 1984-86, Brooke Army Med. Ctr., Ft. Sam Houston, Tex., 1986-90; assoc. prof., chief divsn. hematology/oncology divsn. Tex. Tech. U. Health Scis., El Paso, 1997—. Clin. instr. dept. medicine U. Colo. Health Sci. Ctr., 1982-86. Contbr. articles to books and profl. jours. Active profl. edn. com. Aurora-Adams Unit Am. Cancer Soc., 1983-86, pres., 1983-86, active Colo. divsn., 1984-86. Fellow ACP; mem. AMA, Am. Soc. Clin. Oncology. Home: 324 Sharondale Dr El Paso TX 79912-4250 Office: Tex Tech U Health Scis Hematol/Oncol Divsn 4800 Alberta Ave El Paso TX 79905-2709 Office Phone: 915-545-6619. E-mail: arlene.zaloznik@ttuhsc.edu.

ZALTA, EDWARD, otorhinolaryngologist, physician; b. Houston, Mar. 2, 1930; s. Nouri Louis and Marie Zahde (Lizmi) Z.; m. Carolyn Mary Gordon, Oct. 8, 1971; 1 child, Ryan David; children by previous marriage: Nouri Allan,

Lori Ann, Barry Thomas, Marci Louise. BS, Tulane U., 1952, MD, 1956. Diplomate Am. Bd. Quality Assurance and Utilization Rev. Physicians. Intern Brooke Army Hosp., San Antonio, 1956-57; resident in otolaryngology U.S. Army Hosp., Ft. Campbell, Ky., 1957-60; practice medicine specializing in otolaryngology Glendora, West Covina and San Dimas, Calif., 1960-82. ENT cons. City of Hope Med. Ctr., 1961-76; mem. staff Foothill Presbyn.; past pres. L.A. Found. Cmty. Svc., L.A. Poison Info. Ctr., So. Calif. Physicians Coun., Inc.; founder, chmn. bd. dirs. CAPP CARE, INC.; founder Inter-Hosp. Coun. Continuing Med. Edn.; trustee U.S. Pharmacopeial Conv., Inc.; mem. adv. bd. Global Health Sys., Inc. Author: (with others) Medicine and Your Money; mem. editl. staff Jour. Assn. Managed Healthcare Orgns., Managed Care Interface, Mng. Employee Health Benefits; mem. editl. adv. bd. Inside Medicaid Managed Care, Disease Mgmt. News, Managed Care Outlook; contbr. articles to profl. jours. Pres. bd. govs. Glendora Unified Sch. Dist., 1965-71; mem. Calif. Cancer Adv. Coun., 1967-71, Commn. of Californias, L.A. County Commn. on Economy and Efficiency. Served to capt. M.C. AUS, 1957-60. Recipient Award of Merit Order St. Lazarus, 1981 Mem. AMA, Calif. Med. Assn., Am. Acad. Otolaryngology, Am. Coun. Otolaryngology, Am. Assn. Preferred Provider Orgns. (past pres.), Am. Coll. Med. Quality, L.A. County Med. Assn. (pres. 1980-81), Kappa Nu, Phi Delta Epsilon, Glendora CountryClub, Centurion Club, Sea Bluff Beach and Racquet Club; Center Club (Costa Mesa, Calif.), Pacific Golf Club (San Juan, Capistrano). Republican. Jewish. Home: 3 Morning Dove Laguna Niguel CA 92677 Office: Ste 1123 27136 B Paseo Espada San Juan Capistrano CA 92675 E-mail: edzalta@cox.net.

ZALTMAN, MARK ALLEN, federal agency administrator; b. Revere, Mass., Apr. 27, 1948; s. Isadore and Ethel Zaltman; m. Donna Jean Matthews, Jan. 13, 1974; 1 child, Rebecca. BA magna cum laude, U. Mass., 1970; MA, Binghamton U., 1974, PhD, 1995. Claims examiner Social Security Adminstrn., Chgo., 1974-90; labor rels. specialist Dept. Housing Urban Devel., Chgo., 1990-98, Region V human resources coord., 1998—. Tchg. asst. U. Wis., Milw., 1971-72, Binghamton (N.Y.) U., 1972-74; del. Milw. County Labor Coun., 1971-72. Author: Suburban/Rural Conflict in Late 19th Century Chicago, 1998; contbr. articles to profl. jours. Chief steward Am. Fedn. Govt. Employees Local 1395, Chgo., 1974—75, v.p., 1975—79, exec. v.p., 1979—83; mem. adv. bd. fed. sector labor rels. and labor law program Chgo.-Kent Coll. Law, 1998—; bd. dirs. Temple Menorah, Chgo., 2000—. Recipient Achievement award Am. Fedn. Govt. Employees Local 1395, 1976. Mem. Phi Beta Kappa, Phi Eta Sigma. Avocations: reading, travel. Office Phone: 312-353-5950 x2557.

ZALUTSKY, MORTON HERMAN, lawyer; b. Schenectady, Mar. 8, 1935; s. Albert and Gertrude (Daffner) Z.; m. Audrey Englebardt, June 16, 1957; children: Jane, Diane, Samuel BA, Yale U., 1957; JD, U. Chgo., 1960. Bar: Oreg. 1961. Law clk. to presiding judge Oreg. Supreme Ct., 1960-61; assoc. Hart, Davidson, Veazie & Hanlon, 1961-63, Veatch & Lovett, 1963-64, Morrison, Bailey, Dunn, Cohen & Miller, 1964-69; prin. Morton H. Zalutsky, P.C., 1970-76; ptnr. Dahl, Zalutsky, Nichols & Hinson, 1977-79, Zalutsky & Klarquist, P.C., Portland, Oreg., 1980-85, Zalutsky, Klarquist & Johnson, Inc., Portland, 1985-94; Zalutsky & Klarquist, P.C., Portland, 1994—. Instr. Portland State U., 1961-64, Northwestern Sch. of Law, 1969-70; assoc. prof. U. Miami Law Sch.; lectr. Practising Law Inst., 1971—, Oreg. State Bar Continuing Legal Edn. Program, 1970, Am. Law Inst.-ABA Continuing Legal Edn. Program, 1973—, 34th, 37th NYU ann. insts. fed. taxation, So. Fed. Tax Inst., U. Miami Inst. Estate Planning, Southwestern Legal Found., Internat. Foun. Employee Benefit Plans, numerous other profl. orgns.; dir. A-E-F-C Pension Plan, 1994-99, chmn., 1989-99. Author: (with others) The Professional Corporation in Oregon, 1970, 82; contbg. author: The Dentist and the Law, 3d edit.; editor-in-chief (retirement plans) Matthew Bender's Federal Tax Service, 1987-90; contbr. to numerous publs. in field. Mem. vis. com. U. Chgo. Law Sch., 1986-88. Mem. ABA (vice chair profl. svcs. 1987-89, mem. coun. tax sect. 1985-87, spl. coord. 1980-85), Am. Law Inst., Am. Bar Retirement Assn. (trustee, bd. dirs., vice chair 1990-91, chair 1991-92), Am. Coll. Employee Benefits Coun. (charter mem.), Am. Coll. Tax Coun. (charter mem.), Multnomah County Bar Assn., Am. Tax Lawyers (charter mem.), Oreg. Estate Planning Coun. Jewish. Home: 3118 SW Fairmount Blvd Portland OR 97201-1466 Office: 215 SW Washington St Fl 3 Portland OR 97204-2636 E-mail: mort@erisalaw.com.

ZAMAN, NAVEED, mathematician, educator; b. Gujrat, Pakistan, Sept. 6, 1966; s. Mohammad Zaman and M. Bagum; m. Shaista Akram, June 22, 2002. BS in Math. and Physics, Punjab U., Lahore, Pakistan, 1987; MS in Math., Quaid-i-Azam U., Islamabad, Pakistan, 1990, MPhil in Math., 1992; PhD in Math., U. Ky., Lexington, 2000. Instr. U. Ky., Lexington, 1998—2000; asst. prof. math. W.Va. State Coll., Institute, W.Va., 2000—. Bd. dirs. NASA Space Grant Consortium, W.Va., 2001—; referee Math. Mag., Washington, 2001—, Ctrl. European Sci. Jour., 2001—. Contbr. articles to profl. jours. Mem.: Math. Assn. Am., Am. Math. Soc. Avocations: cricket, basketball, golf. Office: WVa State Coll Rt 25 and Barron Dr Institute WV 25112 E-mail: zamanna@mail.wvsc.edu.

ZAMARIN, RONALD GEORGE, lawyer; b. NYC, May 2, 1946; s. Leonard Leon and Laura Aileen (Gargus) Z.; m. Kathleen Veronica Durkin, July 20, 1968; children: Ryan, Chad, Jennifer. BA, UCLA, 1969, JD, 1972. Bar: Ill. 1972, U.S. Ct. Appeals (7th cir.) 1972, Fed. Trial Bar. Assoc. Isham, Lincoln & Beale, Chgo., 1972-79, ptnr., 1980-88; pvt. practice Des Plaines, Ill., 1988—2003, Palatine, Ill., 2003—. Coop. atty. ACLU, Chgo., 1982—; litigating mem. Lawyers Com. for Civil Rights under Law, Chgo., 1974-78. Co-author: Media Law Handbook, 1982. Trustee, treas. Palatine Pub. Libr. Dist. (Ill.), 1980-89; co-chair Citizens Com. for the Palatine Libr., 1990-95, Citizens Com. for the Palatine Park Dist., 1994—; co-founder Palatine Pub. Libr. Found.; mem. Palatine Adv. Bd., 1978-79; mem. bd. commrs. Palatine Boys' Baseball, 1983-98, sec., 1986-98. Mem.: ABA (forum on comm. law), First Amendment Lawyers Assn. Democrat. Office: Suite 700 800 E Northwest Hwy Palatine IL 60074 Home: 200 White Branch Ct Buffalo Grove IL 60089 Office Phone: 847-705-3895. Personal E-mail: rgzlaw@comcast.net.

ZAMARRA, GALEN, chef; Chef Bouley Bakery, N.Y.C. Named Grey Poupon Rising Star Chef of Yr., James Beard Found., 2001. Office: Bouley Bakery 120 W Broadway New York NY 10013

ZAMBIE, ALLAN JOHN, lawyer; b. Cleve., June 9, 1935; s. Anton J. and Martha (Adamski) Z.; m. Nancy Hall, Sept. 22, 1973. Student, Ohio U., 1953-54; BA, Denison U., 1957; LL.B., Western Res. U. (now Case Western Res. U.), 1960. Bar: Ohio 1960. Asso. firm Hribar and Conway, Euclid, Ohio, 1961-63; staff atty. The Higbee Co., Cleve., 1963-67, asst. sec., 1967-69, sec., 1969-74, v.p.-sec., 1974-88, gen. counsel, 1978-88; v.p., sec., gen. counsel The Lamson & Sessions Co., Cleve., 1989-94; of counsel Conway, Marken, Wyner, Kurant & Kern Co., LPA, Cleve., 1994-95; v.p.-sec. John P. Murphy Found., Cleve., 1996-2000, exec. v.p., 2001—. V.p., sec. Kulas Found., 2001. Trustee Cleve. Music Sch. Settlement, pres. bd. trustees, 1980—82, treas., 1996—2001; trustee N.E. Ohio affiliate Am. Heart Assn., 1989—96. Served with U.S. Army, 1960—61. Mem. Ohio Bar Assn., Cleve. Bar Assn., Am. Soc. Corporate Secs. (nat. v.p. 1977—) Home: 2953 Litchfield Rd Cleveland OH 44120-1738 Office: 50 Pub Sq Ste 924 Cleveland OH 44113-2203 Office Phone: 216-623-4772. E-mail: azambie@murphykulas.org.

ZAMBITO, JOHN R. executive search firm executive; b. Clinton, Iowa, Feb. 17, 1960; s. John R. and Donna (Snell) Z.; m. Jamy S. Nelson, Sept. 14, 1985; children: Molly, Ben, Max. BA in Polit. Sci., Ohio State U., 1985. Salesman Edward Don Co., Columbus, 1985-87, Michaels, Inc., Columbus, 1987-90; acct. exec. MRI (Mgmt. Recruiters, Internat.) of Columbus Downtown, 1990-94, sales mgr., 1994-96, gen. mgr., 1996—; pres. Zambito Exec. Search, LLC, 2003. Dir. adv. bd. Mgmt. Recruiters, Inc., Cleve., 1999—. Contbr. articles to mags., newspapers, internet news, radio shows. Fundraiser Upper Arlington (Ohio) Civic Assn., 1997, 99; chief Indian Guides and Princesses YMCA, Upper Arlington, 1996, 97, 99; donor ARC, Upper Arlington, 1985—. Mem. Athletic Club Columbus, Heritage Golf Club, Kiwanis, Rotary, Ohio State U. Alumni Assn., President's Club, Phi Kappa Tau. Avocations: golf, tennis, running, reading, squash. Home: 2705 Abington Rd Upper Arlington OH 43221-3020 Office: Zambito Exec Search 1335 Dblin Rd Ste 200A Columbus OH 43215

ZAMBONE, ALANA MARIA, special education educator, consultant; b. Vineland, NJ, Sept. 17, 1952; d. L. Alan and Joyce (Bernero) Z. AB in Spl. Edn. and Elem. Edn., U. N.C., Chapel Hill, 1974; MS in Human Devel. Liaison, George Peabody Coll. Tchrs., 1978; PhD in Spl. Edn., Vanderbilt U., 1984. Cert. spl. edn., elem. edn., visual impairments, mental retardation, N.C. Tchr., counselor Orange County Assn. for Retarded Citizens, Chapel Hill, N.C., 1973-74; lead tchr. Shelbyville-Bedford (Tenn.) County Adult Svc. Ctr., 1974; program coord. Dickson (Tenn.) County Adult Svcs., 1974-75; dept. head, habilitative svcs. CloverBottom Devel. Ctr., Nashville, Tenn., 1975-76; exec. dir. Waves, Inc. Adult Svcs., Fairview, Tenn., 1976-77; from vocat. cons. to liaison, Peabody Tchrs. Coll. Vanderbilt U., 1977-80; chairperson, bd. dirs. Residential Svcs., Inc., Nashville, 1976-80; asst. prof., coord., dept. curriculum N.C. State U., Raleigh, N.C., 1981-84; coord. and asst. prof., div. spl. edn. Minot (N.D.) State U., 1984-86; coord. internat. outreach svcs. Hilton-Perkins Internat. Program Perkins Sch. for the Blind, Watertown, Mass., 1989-94, assoc. prof., dir. Inst. for Visually Impaired Pa. Coll. Optometry, Phila., 1994—. Co-founder, sr. rsch. fellow Walker-Wheelock Inst. for Equity in Edn., sr. project dir. exceptional needs assessment devel. lab. Edn. Devel. Corp., Newton, Mass., 1998—; co-coord. grad. program tchrs. of students with spl. needs, grad. faculty infant toddler program evaluator Danforth cmty. devel. project Wheelock Coll., 1995-98; nat. cons. Am. Found. for the Blind, NYC, 1986-89; adj. asst. prof. div. spl. edn., Columbia U., 1987—; co-dir. model infant/toddler program, sch. medicine, U. N.C., Chapel Hill, 1983-84; project dir., mem. grad. faculty severe and multiple disabilities Simmons Coll., 1990—; bd. dirs. ND Coun. for the Arts, Specialized Svcs. for Children, Inc.; adv. bd. Blind Babies Found.; adv. com. Robert E. Miller, Inc., Community Residential Svcs. for Disabled Children; sch. edn. rep. to fac. N.C. State U., sch. edn. fac. senate, others. Grantee Busch Found., N.D. Coun. Arts, Nat. Coun. on the Arts, Dean's Grant Program, Burlington/No. Found., Kate B. Reynolds Found., Nat. Rural Spl. Edn. Consortium, U.S. Office Human Devel. Svcs., U.S. Office of Spl. Edn. Mem. Coun. for Exceptional Children (past dir. div. visual handicaps), Assn. for Retarded Citizens, Assn. for Persons with Severe Handicaps, Am. Assn. Mental Deficiency, Am. Assn. for Applied Behavior Analysis, Nat. Assn. for Parents of the Visually Impaired, Internat. Assn. for the Edn. of the Deaf-Blind, Assn. for the Edn. and Rehab. of the Blind and Visually Impaired (pre-sch. div., multihandicaps div., chairperson multiple disabilities div.), Internat. Coun. Educators of Children and Youth Who Are Blinded or Visually Impaired (co-coord. functions curriculum devel. project 1993—). Avocation: scuba diving. Office: Inst for Equity in Schs Affiliate Walker Home & Sch 1968 Central Ave Needham MA 02492-1410 also: Edn Devel Corp 35 Chapel St Newton MA 02458-1010 also: NC Ctrl Univ Sch Edn 712 Cecil Ave Durham NC 27707 E-mail: azambone@earthlink.net.

ZAMBORSKY, DONALD A. lawyer; b. Allentown, Pa., Dec. 21, 1947; s. Edward J. and Helen A. (Gresko) Z.; m. Joan E. Gallo, July 19, 1969; children: Sonia, Eric, Laura, David. BA, U. Pa., 1969; JD, Villanova U., 1972. Law clk. to Hon. Martin Coyne County Ct., Allentown, Pa., 1972-73; ptnr. Zamborsky & Zamborsky, Allentown, 1973-92; pvt. practice Allentown, 1992-97; ptnr. Tallman, Hudders & Sorrentino, P.C., Allentown, 1998—. Mental health rev. officer Lehigh County Ct., Allentown, 1977—; adj. prof. Cedar Crest Coll., Allentown, 1978-93, Pa. State U., Fogelsville, 1978-92. Mem. Lehigh Valley Estate Planning Coun., pres., 1982-83. Mem. Lehigh Country Club (bd. dirs. 1993-97, sec. 1999-2001). Roman Catholic. Avocations: golf, paddle tennis. Office: 1611 Pond Rd Ste 300 Allentown PA 18104-2258 E-mail: dzamborsky@thslaw.com.

ZAMBRANO, EDUARDO VICENTE, pathologist, researcher; b. Guayaquil, Guayas, Ecuador, Sept. 13, 1965; arrived in U.S., 1997; s. Jose Vicente Zambrano and Ana Julia Tola; life ptnr. Samantha Mary Boris. MD, Cath. U., Guayaquil, 1992; MS, Vrije U., Brussels, 1994; grad. profl. cert., U. New Haven, 2001. Prof. of biology Sch. of Medicine, Universidad Catolica, Guayaquil, Ecuador, 1995—97; resident in anat. and clin. pathology Yale-New Haven Hosp., Yale U., New Haven, 1997—2002, adminstrv. chief resident in pathology, 2001—02, attending pathologist, 2003; clin. fellow in pathology Children's Hosp., Harvard U., Boston, 2002—03. Rschr. Ctr. for Human Genetics, U. of Louvain, Leuven, Belgium, 1993—95; acting dir. Inst. of Tropical Molecular Biology, Cath. U., Guayaquil, 1995—97; instr. of lab. courses Yale U. Sch. of Medicine, New Haven, 1999—2002; ad-hoc reviewer Pediat. and Devel. Pathology Jour., New Haven. Author: (textbook) Introduccion a la Biologia Molecular; contbr. articles, sci. papers, abstracts, poster presentations. Vol. support and cmty. programs for the Hispanic population Hispanos Unidos, New Haven, 2000—01. Named Disting. Guest, Mayoralty of the City of Managua, Nicaragua, 2001; recipient Clin. fellowship in pathology, Harvard Med. Sch., 2002—03. Mem.: Ecuadorian Coll. of Surgeons, Latin Am. Pathology Found. (chair of admissions com. 2000—), Soc. for Pediat. Pathology, U.S. and Can. Acad. of Pathology, Coll. of Am. Pathologists (inspector 2001). Achievements include one of first to develop human molecular genetics in Ecuador. Avocations: travel, reading, hiking, soccer, running. Office: Children's Hosp Boston 300 Longwood Ave Boston MA 02115 Home: 50 Aiken St Apt 296 Norwalk CT 06851-2022 Personal E-mail: eduardozambranot@hotmail.com. E-mail: eduardo.zambrano@tch.harvard.edu.

ZAMECNIK, PAUL CHARLES, oncologist, medical research scientist; b. Cleve., Ohio, Nov. 22, 1912; married; 3 children. AB, Dartmouth Coll., 1933; MD, Harvard U., 1936; DSc (hon.), U. Utrecht, 1966, Columbia U., 1971, Harvard U., 1982, Roger Williams Coll., 1983, Dartmouth Coll., 1988, U. Mass., 1994. Resident Huntington Meml. Hosp. Harvard U., Boston, 1936—37; intern U. Hosps., Cleve., 1938—39; Moseley traveling fellow Carlsberg Labs. Harvard U., Copenhagen, 1939—40; Finney-Howell fellow Rockefeller Inst., 1941—42; instr., assoc. prof. medicine Harvard U., 1942—56, Collis P. Huntington prof. oncologic medicine, 1956—79; dir. J.C. Warren Labs., 1956—79; chmn. exec. com. Dept. Medicine Harvard U., 1956—61; emeritus prof. oncological medicine Sch. Medicine, 1979—; prin. sci. Worcester Found. Experimental Biology, 1979—97; physician Mass. Gen. Hosp., 1956—79, hon. physician, 1979—, sr. scientist, 1998—. Vis. fellow dept. chemistry Calif. Tech. U., 1952; vis. Commonwealth scholar in chemistry U. Cambridge, 1962. Recipient Warren Triennial prize, Mass. Gen. Hosp., 1946, 1950, 1999, James Ewing award, 1962, Borden award, 1965, Am. Cancer Soc. Nat. award, 1968, Passano award, 1970, Nat. medal of sci., NSF, 1991, Hudson Hoagland award, 1992, City of Medicine award, Durham, N.C., 1995, Enterprize 2000 award, City of Worcester, Mass., 1996, Lasker award for Special Achievement in Medicine, Lasker Found., 1996, Am. Soc. Biochemistry and Molecular Biology-Merck award, 1997. Mem.: NAS, Mass. Med. Soc. (annual lectr. 1998, Ann. Orator 1998), Nat. Acad. Medicine, Assn. Am. Physicians, Am. Assn. Cancer Rsch. (pres. 1964—65), Am. Soc. Biol. Chemists, Am. Acad. Arts and Scis., Interurban Club. Office: Mass Gen Hosp Charlestown 149 13th St Rm 1494005 Charlestown MA 02129-2020*

ZAMFIR, NICOLAE VICTOR, physicist, researcher; b. Brasov, Romania, Mar. 24, 1952; arrived in U.S., 1992; s. Nicolae Zamfir, Livia Zamfir; m. Ecaterina Edita Petre; children: Radu Bogdan, Ioana Livia. Masters Degree (magna cum laude), U. Bucharest, Romania, 1976; PhD, Ctrl. Inst. Physics, Bucharest, Romania, 1984. Physicist Inst. Physics and Nuc. Engring., Magurele, Romania, 1978—84, sr. rschr. Bucharest, 1984—; physicist Brookhaven Nat. Lab., Upton, NY, 1994—97; sr. rsch. scientist Yale U., New Haven, 1997—2004; dir. Nat. Inst. Physics and Nuc. Engring., Bucharest, 2004—. Cons. Clark U., Worcester, Mass., 1992—2003; mem. adv. com. 7 Internat. Confs. Contbr. over 160 articles to profl. jours.;, co-editor 7 internat. conf. proceedings. Recipient Hurmuzescu award in physics, Romanian Acad., 1984. Mem.: AAAS, Am. Phys. Soc. Achievements include research in evolution of nuclear collectivity, phase/shape transition and phase coexistence in nuclei, octupole collectivity in nuclear structure. Office: Yale Univ Physics Dept New Haven CT 06520-8124 also: Nat Inst Physics and Nuc Engring Bucharest Romania Business E-Mail: zamfir@tandem.nipne.ro.

ZAMKA, GEORGE D. astronaut; b. Jersey City, N.J., June 29, 1962; s. Conrad and Sofia Zamka; m. Elisa P. Walker; 1 child. BS in Math., U.S. Naval Acad., 1984; MS in Engring. Mgmt., Fla. Inst. Tech., 1997. Commd. 2d lt USMC, 1984, advanced through grades to lt. col.; with Navy Attack Squadron, Marine All Weather Attacki Squadron, VMA, El Toro, Calif.; squadron weapons and tactics instr.; with Marine All Weather Fighter Attack Squadron VMFA, El Toro; forward air contr. 1st Bn., 5th Marines, Camp Pendleton, Calif.; with 31st Marine Expeditionary Unit, USS Belleau Wood, Western Pacific; test pilot/project officer Naval Strike Aircraft Test Squadron; aircraft maintenance officer VMFA; astronaut NASA, Houston, 1998, with Astronaut Office. Decorated 6 Navy Strike Air medals, Navy Commendation medal with Combat V. Mem.: Soc. Exptl. Test Pilots, Marine Corps Assn., U.S. Naval Acad. Alumni Assn. Achievements include logged over 3,000 flight hours in over 30 different aircraft. Office: Astronaut Office /CB NASA Johnson Space Ctr Houston TX 77058

ZAMMIT, JOSEPH PAUL, lawyer; b. N.Y.C., May 19, 1948; s. John and Farla (Rudolph) Z.; m. Dorothy Therese O'Neill, June 6, 1970; children: Michael, Paul, Brian. AB, Fordham U., 1968; JD, Harvard U., 1971; LLM, NYU, 1974. Bar: N.Y. 1972, U.S. Dist. Ct. (so. and ea. dists.) N.Y. 1973, U.S. Dist. Ct. (no. dist.) Ala. 1989, U.S. Dist. Ct. (we. dist.) N.Y., 1991, U.S. Ct. Appeals (2d cir.) 1973, U.S. Supreme Ct. 1978, U.S. Dist. Ct. (no. dist.) N.Y. 1983, U.S. Ct. Appeals (11th cir.) 1987, U.S. Ct. Appeals (fed. cir.) 1995. Assoc. Reavis & McGrath, N.Y.C., 1971-74; asst. prof. law St. John's U., Jamaica, N.Y., 1974-76, assoc. prof., 1976-78; assoc. Reavis & McGrath, N.Y.C., 1978-79, ptnr., 1979-88, Fulbright & Jaworski L.L.P. (formerly Fulbright Jaworski & Reavis McGrath), N.Y.C., 1989—. Adj. assoc. prof. St. John's U., Jamaica, 1979-83, adj. prof., 1984—; mem. panel comml. arbitrators tech. panel Am. Arbitration Assn., N.Y.C., 1977—. Bd. editors E-commerce Law and Strategy, 1987—; contbr. articles to profl. jours. Mem.: ABA, Computer Law Assn., Assn. Bar City of N.Y. (chmn. comml. liability subcom. 1981—87, chmn. com. on computer law 1995—98, fed. cts. com. 1998—2001, info. tech. law com. 2004—), N.Y. State Bar Assn., Phi Beta Kappa. Office: Fulbright & Jaworski LLP 666 5th Ave Fl 31 New York NY 10103-0001 Office Phone: 212-318-3000. Personal E-mail: jzammit@fulbright.com.

ZAMORA, MARJORIE DIXON, retired political science educator; b. Farm Randolph, N.Y., Nov. 8, 1933; d. Wendell Hadley and Jessie (Mercer) Dixon; m. Cornelio Raul Zamora, Dec. 20, 1969; 1 child, Daniel Cornelio. BA, Earlham Coll., 1956; MA, U. Ill., 1968; postgrad., U. Ill., Chgo., 1989—. Tchr. Ridge, Sch., Godsman Sch., Stenson Sch., various cities, 1956-62; with U.S. Peace Corps, tchr. Palmares High Sch., Costa Rica, 1963-64; reporter Lerner Newspaper, Chgo., 1965; dormitory counselor U. Ill., Urbana, 1966-68, 86; instr. Chgo. City Coll., 1968-69; prof. polit. sci. Moraine Valley C.C., Palos Hills, Ill., 1969-94, prof. emeritus, 1994—. Rschr. U. Ill., Chgo., 1985-88. Author short stories; contbr. articles on Costa Rican polit. bus. cycle and economy, land reform to publs. in U.S., Cen. Am.; contbr. short stories to mags. Dir. Coalition for a U.S. Dept. of Peace, 2001—; rep. Beijing Plus Five Regional Steering Com., 1999; appointed to planning com. for a dept. of peace bill Rep. D. Kucinich. Mem. AAUW (elected-pres. Western Spring area chpt. 1999, Ill. congressional liaison 2000—), Western Springs Band and Orch. Assn. (pres. 1990-91), Am. Assn. Ret. Persons, State Cmty. Coll. Retirees Assn. Mem. Soc. Of Friends. Avocations: skiing, swimming, writing fiction, nonfiction and filmscripts, symphonic music, scuba. Home: 3820 Lawn Ave Western Springs IL 60558-1141

ZANARDELLI, JOHN JOSEPH, healthcare services executive; b. Monongahela, Pa., July 27, 1950; s. John and Linda (Lazzari) Z.; m. Suzanne King, Jan. 29, 1972; children: Brandon John, Stephen William, Robyn Lynn. Student, Davis & Elkins Coll., 1968; AA, C.C. Allegheny Cty, Pitts., 1970; AS in Acctg., C.C. Allegheny Cty., Pitts., 1991; BS in Edn., California State Coll. Pa., 1972; MPH, U. Pitts., 1979, cert. acct., 1994; cert. non-profit mgmt., Harvard U., 1998; cert. gen. mgmt., Carnegie Mellon U., 1999. Rsch. asst. grad. sch. pub. health U. Pitts., 1973-78; adminstrv. resident Ctrl. Med. Ctr. and Hosp., Pitts., 1978-79; vice-chmn., sec., dir. Allegheny Mountain Health Enterprises, Inc., Oil City, Pa., 1985-88; exec. v.p. Oil City Area Health Ctr., Inc., 1979-88; exec. v.p., COO Grane Healthcare, Inc., Pitts., 1988-90; adminstr., COO Southwood Psychiat. Hosp., Inc., Pitts., 1990-91; exec. dir. Allegheny divsn. Presbyn. Sr.Care, Pitts., Pa., 1991-92; exec. dir., CEO United Meth. Svcs. for Aging, 1993—. Preceptor, mentor health adminstrn. program U. Pitts. Grad. Sch. Pub. Health, 1980—, vis. faculty, 1997—98; adj. asst. prof. health svcs. adminstrn. Grad. Sch. Pub. Health, 1998—2001, adj. assoc. prof. health policy and mgmt., 2001—; pres. HCCP, Inc., Pitts., 1983—; bd. dirs. Faith-Based Network, Inc., 1998—; co-chair pub. rels. and mktg. com. Davis and Elkins Coll., 2000—02; co-chair exec.-in-residence com. U. Pitts. Grad. Sch. Pub. Health, 2001—02, exec. in residence, health adminstrn. program, 2001—03; preceptor, Initiative on Social Enterprise, Harvard Bus. Sch., 2001—; mem. planning com. and faculty for longterm care program U. Pitts. Inst. on Aging, 2002. Fellow: Am. Coll. Healthcare Execs.; mem.: Delta Omega (Omicron chpt., pres. 2000—01). Home: 2997 Greenwald Rd Bethel Park PA 15102-1615 Office: Asbury Heights 700 Bower Hill Rd Pittsburgh PA 15243-2040 Office Phone: 412-571-5134. E-mail: johnzan@alumni.pitt.edu., jzanardelli@asburyheights.org.

ZAND, DALE EZRA, business management educator; b. N.Y.C., July 22, 1926; m. Charlotte Edith Rosenfeld, Oct. 16, 1949; children: Fern, Mark, Karen, Jonathan, Matthew. BEE, Cooper Union, 1945; MBA, NYU, 1949, PhD, 1954. Asst. to v.p. Spectator Bags, 1947-49; v.p. Glo-Cold Co., 1949-50; mem. faculty Stern Sch. Bus., NYU, N.Y.C., 1950—, prof. mgmt., 1963—, chmn. dept., 1968—, sr. faculty fellow, 1999—. Cons. to industry, 1951—; bd. dirs. Newfield Exploration Co., Inst. Applied Behavioral Sci. Author: Information, Organization, and Power, 1981, The Leadership Triad, 1997, also articles. Served with USNR, 1945. Ford Found. fellow, 1959-60 Mem. Am. Psychol. Soc., Inst. Mgmt. Sci., Acad. Mgmt., Internat. Assn. Applied Social Scientists. Office: NYU 40 W 4th St # T723 New York NY 10012-0157

ZAND, LLOYD CRAIG, radiologist; b. N.Y.C., May 1, 1942; s. Walter Paul and Estelle Leone Zand; m. Mardan Jeanne Foster, June 9, 1968; children: Jason Matthew, Jory Meagan. AB, U. Ill., 1964; MD, Chgo. Med. Sch., 1968. Intern U. Minn., Mpls., 1968-69; resident in radiology U. Miami, Fla., Fla., 1969-70, 72-74, clin. instr., 1973-80; attending radiologist North Shore Med. Ctr., Miami, 1974-97, chmn. dept. radiology, 1989-97, chmn. dept. medicine, 1995-98; pres. Mar-J Enterprises, Inc., Miami, 1990—; chmn. Diagnostic Network, Inc., 1993-96. Chmn. Med. Resources Devel. Corp., Miami, 1985—88; mem. adv. bd. 3M Corp., Mpls., 1988—90; bd. dirs. MTR, Inc., Atlanta, Disabled Sports USA. Trustee Zool. Soc. Fla., Miami, 1996—; pres. bd. Cmty. Crusade Against Drugs, 2001—. Lt. comdr. USNR, 1970—72. Mem. AMA, Am. Coll. Radiology, Radiology Soc. of Fla., Soc. Cardiovascular and Interventional Radiology. Avocations: flying, photography. Office: 10501 Snapper Creek Rd Coral Gables FL 33156-3452

ZANDER, ARLEN RAY, retired physics educator; b. Shiner, Tex., Dec. 12, 1940; s. Elton A. and Lillie G. (Malina) Z.; m. Dorothy Marie Mayer, Feb. 1, 1964; children: Melanie, Aaron, Bryan. BS in Physics, U. Tex., 1964; PhD in Physics, Fla. State U., 1970. Asst. prof. physics East Tex. State U., Commerce, 1970-74, assoc. prof. physics, 1975-79, prof. physics, 1980-89, coord. external grants, 1974-77, asst. dean arts and sci., 1982-86, dean arts and sci., 1986-89; provost, v.p. acad. affairs U. La., Monroe, 1989-2000. Liaison superconducting super collider E. Tex. State U., Commerce, 1987-89; lectr. fgn. countries; commentator weekly radio show Sci. Update, 1981-82. Contbr. articles to profl. jours.; author weekly newspaper column Halley's Comet (Sci. Writing award Coun. for Advancement and Support of Edn. 1986), 1985-86. Campaign chmn. United Way, Commerce, 1988; bd. govs. Monroe Symphony Orch., 1991. Numerous grants various agys.; NATO fellow, 1982. Mem. Am. Assn. Physics Tchrs., West Monroe C. of C. (chmn. 1994), Lions (bd. dirs. internat. youth camp 1983-86), Sigma Xi. Avocations: jogging, reading, racquetball, classical music. Home: 100 Bluff Dr West Monroe LA 71291-9434 Office: U La-Monroe 700 University Ave Monroe LA 71209-9000 E-mail: zander@ulm.edu.

ZANDER, BENJAMIN, conductor, educator; b. London, Mar. 9, 1939; Diploma, State Conservatory, Cologne, 1960; BA, London Univ., 1964; studied cello with, Gaspar Cassadó. Prof. chamber music, performance and analysis New Eng. Conservatory of Music, Boston, 1967—, condr. Youth Philharm. Orch., 1972—; mus. dir., condr. Boston Philharm. Orch., 1979—; artistic dir. Walnut Hill High Sch. for the Performing Arts. Address: New England Conservatory of Music 290 Huntington Ave Boston MA 02115-5018

ZANDER, EDWARD, electronics executive; BSEE, Rensselaer Poly. Inst.; MBA, Boston U. Formerly with Apollo, Data Gen., Raytheon; with Sun Microsystems Inc., Palo Alto, Calif., 1987—2002, COO, 1998—2002, pres., COO, 1999—2002; with Silver Lake Ptnrs., 2002—03; chmn., CEO Motorola Inc., Schaumburg, Ill., 2004—. Bd. dirs. Documentum, Inc., Portal Software, Inc., Rhythms Netconnections, inc. Mem. sci. adv. bd. Rensselaer Poly. Inst., Troy, NY; bd. dirs. Jason Found. for Edn. Office: Motorola Inc 1303 E Algonquin Rd Schaumburg IL 60196

ZANDER, GAILLIENNE GLASHOW, psychologist; b. Bklyn., Apr. 7, 1932; d. Saul and Anna (Karasik) G.; m. A.J. Zander, Aug. 5, 1952; children: Elizabeth L., Caroline M., Catherine A. MusB, U. Wis., 1953, MS, 1970; PhD, Marquette U., 1984. Diplomate Am. Bd. Forensic Examiners, Am. Acad. Pain Mgmt.; cert. Am. Soc. Clin. Hypnosis. Music tchr. Wis. Sch. Systems, 1953-65; psychol. asst. Vernon Psychol. Labs., Chgo., 1965-70; psychologist Milw. Pub. Schs., 1970-92, CESA 19, Kenosha, Wis., 1977-78; pvt. practice psychology Milw., 1980—. Fellow Am. Orthopsychiat. Assn.; mem. APA, Wis. Psychol. Assn. Home: 13750 Carson Ct Brookfield WI 53005-4989 also: A Healing Ctr 20860 Watertown Rd Waukesha WI 53186-1872 Office Phone: 262-821-6117. Personal E-mail: zanderga@aol.com.

ZANE, PHILLIP CRAIG, lawyer; b. N.Y.C., Sept. 25, 1961; s. Martin I.L. and Rosalind Carol (Siegler) Z.; m. Denise Janine Wydra; 1 child, Christopher Abelard. BA, Pomona Coll., 1983; postgrad., U. Mich., 1985-88; JD cum laude, NYU, 1991. Bar: Ill. 1991, D.C. 1996, U.S. Dist. Ct. (no. dist.) Ill. 1991, U.S. Ct. Appeals (7th cir.) 1994, U.S. Ct. Appeals (8th cir.) 1993, U.S. Ct. Appeals (9th cir.) 1996, U.S. Fed. Cir. Ct. 1994, U.S. Dist. Ct. D.C. 2000. Assoc. Mayer, Brown & Platt, Chgo., 1991-93; judicial law clerk to Hon. Morris S. Arnold 8th Cir. Ct. Appeals, Little Rock, 1993-94; assoc. Mayer, Brown & Platt, Chgo., 1994-95, Morgan, Lewis & Bockius, Washington, 1996-2000, of counsel, 2000—. Staff editor NYU Rev. of Law and Social Change, 1989-90, critical legal studies editor, 1990-91; editor Sherman Act Almanac, 1998; contbr. articles to profl. jours. Sec. gen. coun. Arthur F. Burns Fellowship Program, Inc., 1998—. Fellow Thomas J. Watson Found., 1983-84; fgn. lang. area studies fellow U. Mich., Ann Arbor, 1986, 87-88. Mem. ABA (vice chair Sherman Act sect. one com. 1999-2001), Ill. State Bar Assn. (spl. com. on Law Day in Moscow & Kiev 1992) Democrat. Avocation: legal history. Office: Morgan Lewis & Bockius LLP 1111 Pennsylvania Ave NW Washington DC 20004 E-mail: pzane@morganlewis.com.

ZANE, WILLIAM ANTHONY, chemicals executive; b. Hazleton, Pa., Oct. 15, 1950; s. William Richard and Mary An (Maylath) Z.; m. Jean Marie Holy, Feb. 22, 1975; children: William P., Michael J., Andrew A. BSChE, Pa. State U., 1972. Sales rep. Diamond Shamrock Chem. Co., Omaha, Pitts., Dayton, Ohio, 1972-77, mktg. mgr. chlorine Cleve., 1978-80, product mgr. internat., 1981-82, dist. sales mgr., 1982-84, Midwest regional mgr. splty. chem. divsn. Chgo., 1985-87; nat. sales mgr. Cognis Corp. (formerly Henkel Corp.), Chgo., 1988-89, N.Am. sales mgr. Phila., 1989-94, bus. dir., 1993-94, bus. dir. coating resins and additives, 1994-95, v.p., gen. mgr. plastic and polymer chem. divsn., 1995-98, v.p. coatings and inks divsn. and plastic/polymer divsn., 1998—2001; v.p. global graphic arts North Am. Polymer coating Ink, 2001—. Treas. Methacton H.S. Basketball Club, Fairview Village, 1995-96. Mem. Medinah Country Club (non-resident). Republican. Roman Catholic. Avocations: golf, skiing, running, family activities. Home: 3067 Sunny Ayre Dr Lansdale PA 19446-5828 Office: Cognis Corp 300 Brookside Ave Ambler PA 19002-3497 E-mail: waz34869@aol.com., bill.zane@cognis-us.com.

ZANECCHIA, THOMAS EDWARD, financial executive; b. Bklyn., Dec. 29, 1954; s. Armando Luigi and Irma Elda (Martinuzzi) Z.; m. Deborah Sue Newhouse, June 18, 1977; children: Natalie Newhouse, Katie Lynn. BS in Commerce, U. Va., 1976; MBA in Fin., U. Pa., 1981. CPA, Colo. Sr. acct. Coopers & Lybrand, Boston, 1976-79; staff cons. Wharton Applied Rsch. Ctr., Phila., 1979-81; pres., shareholder Asset Mgmt. Group, Denver, 1981-93; founder, pres. Wealth Mgmt. Cons., Inc., Denver, 1993—; co-founder, pres. Branzan Investment Advisors, Inc., 2001—. Bd. advisors F&B Mfg., Inc., 1994—, Denver Family Bus. Coun., 2001—; guest lectr. U. Denver, 1996—2004; bd. dirs. Am. Materials Corp.; spkr. in field. Contbr. articles to profl. jours.; recognized in J.K. Lasser's Estate Planning for Baby Boomers and Retirees. Bd. dirs. Hospice Metro Denver, 1989-94, bd. advisers Denver Entrepreneurship Acad., 1992-94; mem. Body of Knowledge com. Family Firm Inst., 1995-96, mentor com., 2001-03. Named one of Best Fin. Advisors, Worth Mag., 1998—2004. Fellow Family Firm Inst.; mem. AICPA, Colo. Soc. CPAs. Avocations: golf, skiing. Home: 4930 S Gaylord St Englewood CO 80113 Office: Wealth Mgmt Cons Inc 475 17th St Ste 570 Denver CO 80202-4015 E-mail: tez1@wealth-manage.com.

ZANES, GEORGE WILLIAM, management, marketing, human resources consultant; b. Laconia, N.H., May 13, 1926; s. Robert Lewis and Mina (Edgerly) z.; m. Anne Schuetz, Dec. 21, 1957 (div. 1970); children: Laura, David, Scott, Hugh; m. Ruth Weissman, June 17, 1970; stepchildren: Glenn, Lee. BS, U. N.H., 1952. Dir. indsl. rels., cons. I.P.C. Inc., Bristol, N.H., 1953-56; dir. spl. projects Am. Rsch. Bur. Inc., Beltsville, Md., 1957-60, Alfred Politz Rsch. Inc., N.Y.C., 1960-62; v.p. Simulmatics Corp., N.Y.C., 1962-63; group rsch. mgr. Foote Cone & Belding Inc., N.Y.C., 1963-65; v.p. Trendex Inc., N.Y.C., 1965-67; pres. Zanes & Assocs. Inc., Ft. Lee, N.J., 1967-80, chmn., chief exec. officer, 1980-88; also bd. dirs., pres. The Mktg. Rsch. Workshop Inc., Ft. Lee, N.J., 1974-88. Cons. Strategic Resource Group Inc., 1988-89; sec. treas. Unlimited Resources, Inc.; cons., ceo G & R Enterprises, Tallahassee, Fla., Alpharetta, Ga., 1989—, bd. dirs. Ad Net, Inc. Mem. F. Lee Rent Leveling Bd., past pres., Jaycees, Bristol, N.H. With U.S. Army, 1944-47; ETO, capt. USAR, 1947-60. Mem. Am. Mktg. Assn. (v.p. programs Atlanta chpt. 1993-94), Greater North Fulton C. of C., Acacia.

ZANETTI, RICHARD JOSEPH, publisher; b. Weehawken, N.J., Mar. 22, 1939; s. Mario and Lucille (Coco) Z.; m. Norma Diane Nesheim, June 28, 1969; children: Joseph, Michael. BSChemE, Bucknell U., Lewisburg, Pa., 1961, MSChemE, 1964; MBA, Fairfield U., 1998. Technologist Mobil Oil Corp., Bklyn., 1964-66; dept. editor Chem. Week mag., N.Y.C., 1980-84; from assoc. editor to editor-in-chief Chem. Engring. mag., N.Y.C., 1984-97, pub., 1997—. Lectr. in field. Producer, dir. documentary film: Standups, 1979. Cons. Manhattan Coll., Riverdale, N.Y., 1989—. 1st lt. U.S. Army, 1964-65. Recipient Hammer award Nat. Performance Rev. Mem. Am. Bus. Press, Tau Beta Pi, Omicron Delta Kappa. Avocations: fiction writing, fishing, stamp collecting/philately. Office: Chemical Week Assoc 110 William St New York NY 10038-3901

ZANETTI, TERESA A. state representative; b. Columbus, Ga., Jan. 20, 1958; m. Gregory Zanetti; children: Daniel, Michael. BA, Harvard U., 1979; MA, St. John's Coll., 1987. Test adminstr. Army Edn. Ctrs., Augsburg, Germany, 1982—85; bur. chief N.Mex. State Dept. Regulation and Licensing, 1989—90; faculty Albuquerque Acad., 1990—97; columnist Albuquerque Tribune, 2000—02; state rep. dist. 15 N.Mex. Ho. of Reps., Santa Fe, 2002—. Mem. N.Mex. State. Bd. Edn., 2001—02. Named Rookie of the Yr., Greater Albuquerque C. of C., 2002. Republican. Office: State Capitol Room 202B Santa Fe NM 87503

ZANFAGNA, PHILIP EDWARD, government executive, urban planner; b. Lawrence, Mass., Dec. 5, 1936; s. Philip Edward and Edna Edith (Hill) Z.; m. Joan Elizabeth Criswell, Sept. 9, 1961; children: Deborah Carol Bass, Gary Philip. BA, Ohio Wesleyan U., 1958; MDiv, Yale U., 1961; JD, George Washington U., 1964. Certified in sr. exec. svcs., acquisition profl. Sr. negotiator USN, Washington, 1964-72; dep. dir. contracts dept. Navy USMC, Washington, 1972-80, dir. contracts, 1980-90, asst. chief of staff installations and logistics, 1990—, dep. asst. commandant, 2000. Pres. Lewinsville Inc., McLean, Va., 1980-95. Commr., vice chmn. Fairfax (Va.) County Planning Commn., 1973-77; active Dulles Airport Planning Com., Fairfax, 1975-76, Fairfax Blue Ribbon commn., 1986-87; pres. Dranesville Dist. Coun., McLean, 1982-83; chmn. bd. dirs. McLean Citizens Assn., 1979-81; trustee McLean Found., 1980-86; bd. dirs. McLean Citizen's Assn., 1996—. Recipient Presdl. Rank award for meritorious pub. svc., 1993, 1998. Mem. Sr. Exec. Assn., Yale U. Alumni Assn., Fed. Exec. Inst. Assn., Nat. Def. U. Alumni Assn., Harvard U. Sch. Govt. Alumni Assn. Presbyterian. Avocations: travel, music, photography, sports, teaching theology.

ZANI, FREDERICK CAESAR, retired corporate consultant; b. Medford, Mass., June 9, 1929; s. John and Catherine (Voluletti) Zani; m. Dorothy Ann Menezes, Feb. 20, 1960; children: Gregory Robert, Elizabeth Ruth. BS, Salem State Coll., 1954; M.Ed., Boston U., 1959, cert. in advanced grad. studies, 1967; PhD (hon.), World U., 1986. Lic. sch. psychologist. Tchr., 1954—60; tchr. pub. schs., 1960—65; guidance counselor Attleboro, Mass. public schs., 1965—90; ret. Former owner, exec. dir. Zani Group Internat. Consulting Co., 1990—. Contbr. articles to profl. jours. Recipient Outstanding Svc. award, Bristol County Tchrs. Assn. . Mem.: Ret. State, County and Mcpl. Employees Assn., Boston Children's Hosp. Med. Center Parent Orgn. for Exceptional Children, Mass. Sch. Psychologists Assn., Mass. Ret. Tchrs. Assn., Mass. Tchrs. Assn., Attleboro Tchrs. Assn., Mass. Assn. Children with Learning Disabilities (v.p. Attleboro chpt. 1969—70), Ret. Nat. Educators Assn., Christian Edn. Assn., Internat. Platform Assn. Mem. Assembly Of God. Ch. Home and Office: 115 Holmes Rd North Attleboro MA 02760-4441 E-mail: fcz1@aol.com.

ZANJACOMO, PAULO REGIS, engineering executive; s. Expedicto and Alzira Zanjacomo; m. Hilda Hortensia Valero Tonone, Mar. 27, 1999. BSc in Computer Scis., U. Sao Paulo, 1990, MSc in Applied Math., 1992; PhD in Indsl. Engring., Ga. Inst. Tech., 1998. Asst. prof. U. Sao Paulo, 1992—94; sr. engr. for rsch. and product design Energy Imperium, Atlanta, 1999—99; dir. rsch. and design Altra Energy Technologies, Houston, 1999—2000; chief tech. officer Delfin Energy, Atlanta, 2000—, Stats. and Research Autom. Trading Desk Charleston, SC, 2002—. Contbr. articles to profl. jours. Mem.: INFORMS.

ZANNA, MARTIN THOMAS, physician; b. Mpls., Apr. 2, 1947; s. Peter J. and Mary L. (Peck) Z. AB, Harvard U., 1969, MPH, 1976; MD, U. Minn., 1973. Diplomate Am. Bd. Preventive Medicine. Resident in pub. health N.J. State Dept. Health, 1974-77, acting dir. chronic disease svcs., 1976-79, dir. chronic disease svcs., 1979-81; med. adminstr. Fla. Dept. Health and Rehab. Svcs., Tallahassee, 1981-82; med. cons. N.J. Medicaid, Trenton, 1982—, chief med. cons., 1990-96; med. cons. N.J. State Dept. Health and Sr. Svcs., 1996—. Mem. Fla. Cancer Coun., 1981-82, Fla. Bd. Med. Examiners, 1982, N.J. Hypertension Study Group, 1977-81; chmn. grad. med. edn. com. N.J. State Dept. Health & Sr. Svcs., 1993—; diabetes adv. coun. exec. com. N.J. Dept. Health, 2001—. Contbr. articles to profl. jours. Participant Fla. Gov.'s Mission to Haiti, 1982; mem. divsn. profl. edn. Am. Cancer Soc., 1976-81. Fellow Am. Coll. Preventive Medicine; mem. APHA, Harvard Club (Boston), Harvard Faculty Club (Cambridge), Harvard Club (Washington). Home: # 11 201 Salem Ct Apt 11 Princeton NJ 08540-7039 Office: NJ State Dept Health & Sr Svcs PO Box 807 Trenton NJ 08625-0722

ZANNIERI, NINA, museum director; b. Summit, N.J., Feb. 1, 1955; d. Angelo Joseph and Louise Mary (Brumm) Z.; m. Douglas M. Vogel, Oct. 29, 1994. BA, Boston Coll., 1977; postgrad., Coll. of William & Mary, 1977-78; MA, Brown U., 1980. Curatorial asst. R.I. Hist. Soc., Providence, 1980-81, asst. curator, 1981-83, curator, 1983-86; dir. Paul Revere Meml. Assn., Boston, 1986—. Gen. editor: (exhbn. catalog) Paul Revere: The Man Behind the Myth, 1988; collaborator: (house guide) A Most Magnificent Mansion; project dir.: (exhbn. catalog) Let Virtue Be A Guide To Thee, 1983 Mem. Am. Assn. Mus.'s (bd. dirs. 1999-02, vice-chair 2002-03), New Eng. Mus. Assn. (pres. 1998-02), Am. Assn. State and Local History, Phi Beta Kappa. Office: Paul Revere Meml Assn The Paul Revere House 19 North Sq Boston MA 02113-2405*

ZANUCK, LILI FINI, film director, producer; b. Leominster, Mass., Apr. 2, 1954; m. Richard Zanuck, Sept. 23, 1978. Rsch. asst. World Bank, Washington, 1970-78; office mgr. Carnation Co., L.A., 1977-78; rsch. and devel. Zanuck-Brown Co., 1978-89; co-founder, co-owner Zanuck Co., 1989—. Prodr. films Cocoon, 1985, Cocoon: The Return, 1988, Driving Miss Daisy, 1989 (Acad. award 1989), Rich in Love, 1993, Clean Slate, 1994, Wild Bill, 1995, Dvojnik, 1995, Mulholland Falls, 1996, True Crime, 1999, Reign of Fire, 2002; dir. film Rush, 1991, TV miniseries From the Earth to the Moon (Part 3), 1998. Mem.: Calif. Film Commn. Office: The Zanuck Company 9465 Wilshire Blvd Beverly Hills CA 90212-2612

ZANUCK, RICHARD DARRYL, motion picture company executive; b. Beverly Hills, Calif., Dec. 13, 1934; s. Darryl F. and Virginia (Fox) Z.; m. Lili Gentle; children: Virginia, Janet; m. Linda Harrison, Oct. 26, 1969; children: Harrison Richard, Dean Francis; m. Lili Fini, Sept. 23, 1978. Grad., Harvard Mil. Acad., 1952; BA, Stanford, 1956. Story, prodn. asst. Darryl F. Zanuck Prodns., 1956, v.p., 1956-62; president's prodn. rep. 20th Century-Fox Studios, Beverly Hills, 1962-63, v.p. charge prodn., 1963-69, pres., 1969-71, dir., 1966-71; founder, pres., owner Zanuck Co., Beverly Hills, 1989—. Chmn. 20th Century-Fox Television, Inc.; sr. exec. v.p. Warner Bros., Inc., 1971-72; co-founder, pres. Zanuck/Brown Co., 1972-88. Producer: The Sting, 1973 (Acad. award), The Sugarland Express, 1974, Jaws, 1975, Jaws 2, 1978, The Island, 1980, Neighbors, 1982, The Verdict, 1983, Cocoon, 1985, Cocoon, the Return, 1988, Driving Miss Daisy, 1989 (Acad. award, Irving G. Thalberg award 1991), Rush, 1991, Rich in Love, 1992, Mulholland Falls, 1996, Deep Impact, 1998, True Crime, 1999, Rules of Engagement, 1999, Planet of the Apes, 2000, Road to Perdition, 2001, Big Fish, 2003; prodr. Acad. Award Show, 2000. Nat. chmn. Fibrosis Assn., 1966-68; mem. organizing com. 1984 Olympics; trustee Harvard Sch. 2d lt. U.S. Army. Named Producer of Yr., Nat. Assn. Theatre Owners, 1974, '85, Producers Guild Am., 1989; recipient Irving Thalberg award, 1991, Lifetime Achievement award, Producers Guild Am., 1993. Mem. Acad. Motion Picture Arts and Scis. (bd. govs.), Screen Producers Guild, Phi Gamma Delta. Office: Zanuck Co 9465 Wilshire Blvd Ste 930 Beverly Hills CA 90212-2608

ZAPAPAS, JAMES RICHARD, pharmaceutical company executive; b. Martinsville, Ind., July 15, 1926; s. James K. and Bertha (Gardner) Z.; m. Patricia A. Ryan, Aug. 30, 1947; children: Marianne Zapapas McGriff, Patricia Zapapas Parry, Gail Zapapas Rodecker, James R., Carol, Julie. BS in Pharmacy, Purdue U., 1947, ScD hon., 1979. Dir. dry products ops. Eli Lilly & Co., Indpls., 1967-70, dir. pers., 1970-73, dir. pers. and pub. rels., 1973-74, v.p. prodn. ops., 1974-75, group v.p., dir., 1976-77, pres. Elizabeth Arden Inc., 1975-76, chmn. bd., 1977-86, ret., 1986. Bd. dirs., group v.p. Eli Lilly & Co., 1976-86. Republican. Roman Catholic.

ZAPEL, ARTHUR LEWIS, book publishing executive; b. Chgo., 1921; m. Janet Michel (dec.); children: Linda (dec.), Mark, Theodore, Michelle; m. Cynthia Rogers Pisor, 1986; stepchildren: Dawn, Anthony. BA in English, U. Wis., 1946. Writer, prodr. Westinghouse Radio Stas.; film writer Galbreath Studios, Ft. Wayne; creative dir. Kling Studios, Chgo., 1952-54; writer, prodr. TV commls. J. Walter Thompson Advt., Chgo., 1954-73, v.p. TV and radio prodn., 1954-73; founder, pres. Arthur Meriwether, Inc., 1973-83; pres. Meriwether Pub. Ltd., 1969-90, chmn., 1990-97. Pres. Westcliffe (Colo.) Ctr. for the Arts. Author: Sweet Uncertainty, 2001; illustrator: 'Twas the Night Before, The Jabberwock mystery; created game A Can of Squirms; wrote plays and musical comedy scripts for ednl. use in schs. and chs.; supr. editing and prodn. 2500 plays and musicals, 1970-99; exec. editor 210 books on theater skills for secular and religious use. Founding pres. Art Students League of Colorado Springs, 1992; past pres. Colo. Springs Symphony Coun.; past bd. dirs. Colorado Springs Opera Festival. Recipient numerous awards Freedoms Found., Valley Forge, Art Dirs. Club N.Y., Art Dirs. Chgo., Hollywood Advt., 1960-67, Gold Records Radio Ad Bur., 1959-60, XV Festival Internat. Du Film Publicitaire Venise, 1968, Gold Camera award U.S. Indsl. Film Festival, 1983, Dukane award, 1983, Gold award Houston Internat. Film Festival, 1984, 2d pl. award Best New Fiction, Colo. Ind. Publishers Assoc., 2002. Office: Meriwether Pub Ltd 885 Elkton Dr Colorado Springs CO 80907-3576 Personal E-mail: merpcds@aol.com.

ZAPF, HERMANN, book and type designer; b. Nuremberg, Germany, Nov. 8, 1918; s. Hermann and Magdalene (Schlamp) Zapf; m. Gudrun von Hesse, Aug. 18, 1951; 1 child, Christian Ludwig. D in Fine Arts(hon.), U. Ill., 2003. Freelance designer, 1938—; type dir. D. Stempel AG, type foundry, Frankfurt, Fed. Republic of Germany, 1947-56; design cons. Mergenthaler Linotype Co., N.Y.C. and Frankfurt, 1957-74; cons. Hallmark Internat., Kansas City, Mo., 1966-73; v.p. Design Processing Internat. Inc., N.Y.C., 1977-86; prof. typographic computer programs Rochester (N.Y.) Inst. Tech., 1977-87; chmn. Zapf, Burns & Co., N.Y.C., 1987-91. Instr. lettering Werkkunstschule, Offenbach, Fed. Republic Germany., 1948-50; prof. graphic design Carnegie Inst. Tech., 1960; instr. typography Technische Hochschule, Darmstadt, Fed. Republic Germany, 1972-81. Author: William Morris, 1948, Pen and Graver, 1952, Manuale Typographicum, 1954, 1968, About Alphabets, 1960, 1970, Typographic Variations, 1964, Orbis Typographicus, 1980, Hora fugit/Carpe diem, 1984, Hermann Zapf and His Design Philosophy, 1987, ABC-XYZapf, 1989, Poetry Through Typography, 1993, August Rosenberger, 1996, (film) The Art of Hermann Zapf, German version Die Welt der Buchstaben von Hermann Zapf, (CD-ROM) The World of Alphabets, 2001; designer types Palatino, Melior, Optima, ITC Zapf Chancery, ITC Zapf Internat., Digiset Marconi, Digiset Edison, Digiset Aurelia, Pan-Nigerian, URW-Roman and San Serif, Renaissance Roman, Linotype Zapfino. Hon. pres. Edward Johnston Found., Ditchling, Eng.; hon. curator Computer Mus., Boston. Named hon. citizen, State of Tex., 1970, hon. Royal Designer for Industry, London, 1985; recipient Silver medal, Brussels, 1962, 1st prize typography, Biennale Brno, Czechoslovakia, 1966, Gold medal, Type Dirs. Club, N.Y., Frederic W. Goudy award, Inst. Tech. Rochester, 1969, Silver medal, Internat. Book Exhbn., Leipzig, 1971, Gold medal, 1989, Johannes Gutenberg prize, Mainz, Fed. German Republic, 1974, Gold medal, Museo Bodoniano, Parma, Italy, 1975, J.H. Merck award, Darmstadt, 1978, Robert Hunter Middleton award, 1987, Euro Design award, 1994, Wadim Lazursky award, Acad. of Graphic Arts, Moscow, 1996, SOTA Typography award, 2003. Mem. Royal Soc. Arts, Am. Math. Soc., Alliance Graphique Internationale, Bund Deutscher Grafik Designer, Internat. Gutenberg Gesellschaft; hon. mem. Type Dirs. Club N.Y.C., Soc. Typographique de France, Soc. Typographic Arts, Double Crown Club, Soc. Scribes and Illuminators, Friends of Calligraphy, Soc. Printers, Soc. Graphic Designers Can., Bund Deutscher Buchkünstler, Grafiska Inst., Typophiles, Alpha Beta Club (Hong Kong), Soc. of Calligraphy, Wynkyn de Worde Soc., Letter Exchange, Caxton Club, Monterey Calligrapher's Guild, Washington Calligraphers Guild, Eesti Kalligraafide Koondis (Tallinn, Estonia), Chgo. Calligraphy Collective, Typographers Internat. Assn., Art Dirs. Club Kans. City, Alcuin Soc., Goudy Internat. Ctr., Brno Biennale Assn., Soc. Scribes N.Y., Grolier Club (hon.), Dante e.V. (German TEX Group), Gamma Epsilon Tau.

ZAPFFE, NINA BYROM, retired elementary education educator; b. Independence, Mo., Aug. 17, 1925; d. Richmond Douglas and Nina Belle (Howell) Byrom; m. Robert Glenn Fessler, June 25, 1946 (dec. June 1947); 1 child, Robert Glenn Fessler Zapffe; m. Fred Zapffe, July 1, 1952 (dec. Dec. 1999); children: Paul Douglas, Carl Raymond. BA, So. Meth. U., 1946. Fin. sec. Tyler St. Meth. Ch., Dallas, 1948-49; tchr. Dallas Ind. Sch. Dist., 1949-52, Norman (Okla.) Pub. Schs., 1966-74; cert. chief reader for GED Writing Skills Test Part II GED Testing Svc., Am. Coun. on Edn., Washington, 1990-98. Adv. com. (Acad. Resource Ctr.) Moore-Norman Tech. Ctr., 1988—. Adv. bd. Norman Salvation Army, 1978-90, chmn., 1986; organizer, historian Norman Salvation Army Womens Aux., 1983-2000, pres., 1985; organizer, past pres. Norman Literacy Coun., 1976—; organizing com., past pres. Norman Interfaith Coun., 1974-93; organizing com., past treas. Friends of the Norman Libr., 1979—; mem. McFarlin Meml. United Meth. Ch., historian 2-in-1 Sunday Sch. class, 1990-2002, lay leader, 1980-81, adminstrv. bd., 2001-2004. Named Woman of Yr., Norman Bus. and Profl. Women, 1999; named to Literacy Hall of Fame, Pioneer Libr. Sys., Norman, 1995; recipient medal of appreciation, SAR, 2002. Mem. DAR (regent Black Beaver chpt. 1998-2000, state literacy chmn. 2000-2002, sec. 2002-2004), Nat. Soc. Daus. 1812 (state treas. 1996-2000, sec. 2002-2004), Old Regime Study Club (pres. 1998-99), Coterie Club (pres. 1996, 2002), Delta Delta Delta Alumnae. Independent. Avocation: genealogy. Home: 2717 Walnut Rd Norman OK 73072-6940

ZAPHIRIOU, GEORGE ARISTOTLE, lawyer, educator; b. July 10, 1919; came to U.S., 1973, naturalized, 1977; s. Aristotle George and Callie Constantine (Economou) Z.; m. Peaches J. Griffin, June 1, 1973; children: Ari, Marie. JD, U. Athens, 1940; LLM, U. London, 1950. Bar: Supreme Ct. Greece 1946, Eng. 1956, Ill. 1975, Va. 1983. Gen. counsel Counties Ship Mgmt. and R & K Ltd., London, 1951-61; practicing barrister, lectr. City of London Poly., 1961-73; vis. prof. Ill. Inst. Tech.-Chgo. Kent Coll. Law, 1973-76; pvt. practice Northbrook, Ill., 1976-78; prof. law George Mason U. Sch. Law, 1978-94, prof. law emeritus, adj. prof., 1994—. Prof. internat. transactions George Mason U. Internat. Inst., 1992-94; mem. Odin, Feldman & Pittelman P.C., Fairfax, Va., 1994-96; mem. study group on internat. elec. commerce conv. and other pvt. internat. law convs. U.S. Dept. of State. Author: Transfer of Chattels in Private International Law, 1956, U.S. edit., 1981, European Business Law, 1970; co-author: Declining Jurisdiction in Private International Law, 1995; joint editor: Jour. Bus. Law, London, 1962-73; bd. dirs. and bd. editors Am. Jour. Comp. Law of Am. Soc. Comparative Law, 1980-94; contbr. articles to profl. jours. Mem.: ABA (sect. internat. law and practice and dispute resolution), George Mason Am. Inn of Ct. (founder, master, emeritus), Am. Arbitration Assn. (panel comml. arbitrators), Chgo. Bar Assn., Ill. Bar Assn. Home: 400 Green Pasture Dr Rockville MD 20852-4233 E-mail: gzaphiri@gmu.edu.

ZAPOL, WARREN MYRON, anesthesiologist; b. N.Y.C., Mar. 16, 1942; BS, MIT, 1962; MD, U. Rochester, 1966; MA (hon.), Harvard U., 1990. Cert. in anesthesiology. Intern Harvard Surgical Unit/Boston City Hosp., 1966-67; resident in anesthesiology Mass. Gen. Hosp., Boston, 1970-72, anesthesiologist-in-chief, 1994—; Reginald Jenney prof. anesthesiology Harvard Med. Sch., 1991—. Mem. Am. Heart Assn., Am. Phys. Soc., Am. Thoracic Soc., Am. Soc. Anesthesiologists, Inst. of Medicine/NAS, Polar Rsch. Bd./NAS. Office: Mass Gen Hosp 55 Fruit St Boston MA 02114

ZAPP, JOHN S. retired medical association administrator; Exec. dir. ADA, 1993—2002.

ZAPPA, GAIL, record producer; m. Frank Zappa (dec.); children: Moon, Dweezil, Ahmet, Diva. Recipient (with Frank Zappa) Best Recording Package-Boxed Grammy award for Frank Zappa's Civilization, Phaze III, 1996.

ZAPPE, JOHN PAUL, city editor, educator, newspaper executive; b. N.Y.C., July 30, 1952; s. John Paul and Carolyn (Pikor) Z. BA, Marist Coll., 1978; JD, Syracuse (N.Y.) U., 1978. Reporter Poughkeepsie Jour., 1973-75, Nev. State Jour., Reno, 1979-80; prin. Am. Media Bold, Oakland, Calif., 1981-83; reporter Press-Telegram, Long Beach, Calif., 1983-88, city editor, 1988-97, webmaster PT Connect, 1995-97, mgr. new media, 1997-98; dir. new media Riverside (Calif.) Press-Enterprise, 1998-2000; v.p. new media L.A. Newspaper Group, Woodland Hills, Calif., 2000—03; prin. Zappe Media Svcs., 2003—; consulting gen. mgr. Mother Lode Internet, 2003—04; assoc. editor Classified Intelligence Report/Advanced Interactive Media Group, 2004—. Tchr. Syracuse U., 1976-78, Calif. State U., 1985-87, U. So. Calif., 2003—; cons. Am. Media Bold, 1981-83; consulting gen. mgr. Mother Lode Internet, 2003-04. Assoc. editor: Advanced Interactive Media Classified Intelligence Report, 2003—. Chmn. Local 69 Newspaper Guild, Long Beach, 1984-87. Mem. Investigative Editors and Reporters, NAA New Media Fedn. Office Phone: 562-252-0686. Personal E-mail: jzappe@charter.net.

ZAR, JERROLD H(OWARD), biologist, statistician; b. Chgo., June 28, 1941; s. Max and Sarah (Brody) Z.; m. Carol Bachenheimer, Jan. 15, 1967; children: David Michael, Adam Joseph BS, No. Ill. U., 1962; MS, U. Ill., Urbana, 1964, PhD, 1967. NSF fellow marine sci. Duke U. Marine Lab., Beaufort, N.C., 1965; research assoc. dept. zoology U. Ill., Urbana, 1967-68; asst. prof. dept. biol. scis. No. Ill. U., DeKalb, 1968-71, assoc. prof., 1971-78, prof., 1978—2002, prof. emeritus, 2002—, chmn. dept. biol. scis., 1978-84, vice provost grad. studies and research, dean Grad. Sch., 1984—2002. Vis. scientist Argonne Nat. Lab., 1974; cons. EPA, also other govt. agys. and industries; founder, dir. ENCAP, Inc., 1974-93. Author: Biostatistical Analysis, 1974, 4th edit., 1999. NIH fellow U. Ill. Urbana, 1965-67. Fellow AAAS; mem. Am. Inst. Biol. Scis., Am. Ornithologists Union, Am. Physiol. Soc., Am. Statis. Assn., Biometric Soc., Cooper Ornithol. Soc., Ecol. Soc. Am., Nat. Assn. Biol. Tchrs., Wilson Ornithol. Soc. Office: No Ill U Dept Biol Scis Dekalb IL 60115 E-mail: jhzar@niu.edu.

ZAR, JUDITH L. (MICKEY MCBRIDE), writer; b. Evanston, Wyo., May 12, 1942; d. Jack LaDoy and Cecile Marie McBride; m. James Courtney Zar, May 14, 1977; children: Richelle, Jack Richard, Chet Edward. Hosp. ward clk., 1981. Substitute tchr. St. Peter's Tuller Sch., San Pedro, Calif., 1967—74, kindergarten tchr., 1974—77; tchr. Adult Phonics Reading, Torrance, Calif., 1985—86; asst. Paine Webber, Palos Verdes, Calif., 1986—87; journalist San Pedro (Calif.) Weekly, 1987—88; novelist, 1988—. Author (as Mickey McBride): (plays) The Phone Call, 1998, (novels) Two Kinds of Miracles, 2001, Command Performance, 2002, Scream Once for Help--A San Pedro Mystery, 2003, Art to Die For--A Harry Calle Mystery, 2003, Stealer of Wishes--A Harry Calle Mystery, 2004. Chmn. March of Dimes, San Pedro, Calif., 1966; mem. Jr. C. of C., San Pedro, Calif., 1966. Avocations: horticulture, knitting, painting, gourmet cooking. Home: 1843 Jaybrook Dr Rancho Palos Verdes CA 90275 Personal E-mail: jjzar@juno.com.

ZARAGOZA, LAWRENCE JAY, government manager; b. Santa Maria, Calif., Mar. 4, 1952; s. Julio and Helen Zaragoza; m. Karen Lynn Feldmann, Nov. 9, 1996; 1 child, Matthew Lawrence. BA in Biology, UCLA, 1975; MA, Calif. State U., Long Beach, 1977; D of Environ. Sci. and Engring., UCLA, 1982. Environ. health scientist Office of Air Quality Planning and Standards/EPA, Research Triangle Park, N.C., 1979-86; environ. protection specialist Office of Solid Waster and Emergency Response/EPA, Washington, 1986-89, Office of Emergency and Remedial Response/EPA, Washington, 1989-99, dir. Regions 5/7 Accelerated Response Ctr., 1999—. Co-chair tech. rev. workgroup for lead/EPA, 1997-99. Author articles. Chair archtl. rev. com. Wessynton Homes Assn., Alexandria, Va., 1998-99; v.p. Arlington County Civic Fedn., 1994; chair Air Quality Pub. Adv. Com., Washington, 1998, 99; pres. Colonial Villages Cmty. Svcs. Assn., Arlington, 1992-95. Recipient Environ. award Arlington County Bd., 1992. Mem. AAAS. Avocations: bicycling, kayak paddling. Office: US EPA 5204 G 1200 Pennsylvania Ave NW Washington DC 20460-0001 Fax: (703) 603-9133. E-mail: Zaragoza.Larry@EPA.Gov.

ZARB, FRANK GUSTAVE, investment executive; b. N.Y.C., Feb. 17, 1935; s. Gustave and Rosemary (Antinoro) Z.; m. Patricia Koster, Mar. 31, 1957; children: Krista Anne, Frank, Jr. BBA, Hofstra U., 1957, MBA, 1962, L.H.D., 1975. Trainee Cities Service Oil Co., N.Y.C., 1957-62; gen. partner Goodbody & Co., N.Y.C., 1962-69; exec. v.p. CBWL-Hayden Stone, Inc. (investment banking), N.Y.C., 1969-71; asst. sec. U.S. Dept. Labor, Washington, 1971-72; exec. v.p. Hayden Stone, Inc., N.Y.C., 1972-73; assoc. dir. Office of Mgmt. and Budget, Washington, 1973-74; asst. to Pres. for Energy Affairs U.S., 1974-77; adminstr. Fed. Energy Adminstrn., Washington, 1974-77; adv. U.S. Congress, 1977-78; gen. ptnr. Lazard Freres & Co., N.Y.C., 1977-88; chmn., pres. chief exec. officer Smith, Barney, Harris, Upham & Co., Inc., N.Y.C., 1988-93; vice chmn., group chief exec. The Travelers Inc., N.Y.C., 1993-94; chmn., pres., CEO, Alexander & Alexander Svcs. Inc., N.Y.C., 1994-97; pres. Nat. Assn. Securities Dealers, 1997-98, chmn., CEO, 1997—. Bd. dirs. CS First Boston, Inc., Coun. on Fgn. Rels.; former chmn. N.Y. Stock Exch. Nominating Com.; chmn. L.I. Power Authority, 1996-97. Author: The Stockmarket Handbook, 1969, Handbook of Financial Markets, The Municipal Bond Handbook Mem. bd. trustees Gerald R. Ford Found.; mem. and former chmn. bd. trustees Hofstra U. Recipient Disting. Scholar award Hofstra U., 1974; bus. sch. named in his honor Hofstra U. Mem. Coun. Fgn. Rels. Home: 60 Tiffany Rd Oyster Bay NY 11771-1908

ZARBIN, MARCO ATTILIO, ophthalmologist, surgeon, educator; b. Milan, Nov. 20, 1956; came to the U.S., 1958; s. Gino Franco and Adriana Virginia (Corasaniti) Z. BA summa cum laude, Dartmouth Coll., 1978; MD, PhD, Johns Hopkins U., 1984. Diplomate Am. Bd. Ophthalmology. Resident Johns Hopkins Hosp., Balt., 1985-88, fellow vitreoretinal surgery, 1988-89, chief resident opthalmology, 1989, fellow retinal vascular disease, 1990; asst. prof. ophthalmology U. Calif., San Francisco, 1990-93; chair dept. ophthalmology N.J. Med. Sch., Newark, 1994—, prof., 1998—. Mem. sci. adv. bd. Found. Fighting Blindness, Hunt Valley, Md., 1995—. Mem. editl. bd. Investigative Ophthalmology and Visual Sci., Survey of Ophthalmology. Fellow Am. Acad. Ophthalmology (Honor award 1995), Retina Soc. (exec. com. 1998), Macula Soc.; mem. Assn. for Rsch. in Vision and Ophthalmology, Assn. U. Prof. Ophthalmology (bd. dirs. 2000—), Am. Opthalmological Soc., Phi Beta Kappa, Alpha Omega Alpha. Avocations: ancient history, opera. Office: NJ Med Sch Dept Ophthalmology 90 Bergen St Newark NJ 07103-2425 Office Phone: 973-972-2038.

ZARDETTO-SMITH, ANDREA, medical educator; BS in Biology, Coll. of St. Elizabeth, 1978; MS in Physiology, Loyola U. of Chgo., 1983, PhD, 1990. Rsch. biologist G.D. Searle, Skokie, Ill., 1978—83; postdoctoral fellow dept. internal medicine U. Iowa, 1990—91; postdoctoral rschr. NIH, 1990—92; assoc. dept. anatomy U. Iowa, 1993—96; prof. phys. and occupl. therapy and pharm. sci. Creighton U., Omaha, 1996—2002; prof. biology and neuroscience U. Nebr., Omaha, 2002—. Prin. investigator Brains Rule! Nat. Neurosci. Expositions, a Sci. Edn. Drug Abuse Partnership Award Nat. Inst. on Drug Abuse. Grantee NSF, 1996—98. Mem.: AAAS, Assn. of Women in Sci. (pres. ea. Iowa chpt. 1994—96), Women in Neurosci. (past pres.), Am. Assn. Clin. Anatomists, Am. Assn. Anatomists, Soc. for Neurosci. (com. neuroscience literacy). Achievements include research in on the role of various neurotransmitters in brainstem and forebrain circuits that modulate body fluid balance and how they affect overall control of blood pressure; development of model program for improving neuroscience literacy. Office: Univ Nebraska 3001 Dodge St ASH 347 Omaha NE 68182

ZARE, RICHARD NEIL, chemistry professor; b. Cleveland, Nov. 19, 1939; s. Milton and Dorothy (Amdur) Zare; m. Susan Leigh (Shively), Apr. 20, 1963; children: Bethany Jean, Bonnie Sue, Rachel Amdur. BA, Harvard U., 1961; post grad., U. Calif., Berkeley, 1961—63; PhD (hon.), Harvard U., 1964; DS (hon.), U. Ariz., 1990, Northwestern U., 1993, ETH, Zürich, 1993, Columbia U., 2000, State U. West Ga., 2001; DP (hon.), Uppsala U., Sweden, 2000; PhD U. York (hon.), 2001; PhD (hon.), Hunan U., 2002. Postdoctoral fellow Harvard U., 1964; rsch. assoc. Joint Inst. for Lab. Astrophysics, 1964—65; asst. prof., chemistry MIT, 1965—66; asst. prof., dept. physics and astrophysics U. Colo., 1966—68, assoc. prof. physics, astrophysics, chemistry, 1968—69; prof. chemistry Columbia U., 1969—77, Higgins prof. natural sci., 1975—77; prof. Stanford U., 1977—, Shell, disting. prof. chemistry, 1980—85, Marguerite Blake Wilbur prof., natural sci., 1987—, prof., physics, 1992—. Cons. Aeronomy Lab, NOAA, 1966—77; radio standards physics divsn. Nat. Bur. Std., 1968—77, Lawrence Livermore Lab., U. Calif., 1974—, SRI, Internat., 1974—, Los Alamos Sci. Lab., U. Calif., 1975—; fellow adj. Joint Inst. Lab. Astrophysics, U. Colo.; sci. adv. com. IBM, 1977—92; chmn. commn. on phys., scis., and math applications Nat. Rsch. Coun., 1992—95; chmn. bd. dir. Ann. Rev., Inc., 1995—. Contbr. articles to profl. jour.; editor: Chem. Physics Letters, 1982—85. Named Calif. Scientist of Yr., 1997; recipient Fresenius Award, Phi Lambda Upsilon, 1974, Michael Polanyi Medal, 1979, Nat. Medal Sci., 1983, Spectroscopy Soc. Pitts. Award, 1983, Michelson-Morley Award, Case Inst. Tech., Case We. Res. U., 1986, ISCO Award for significant contbn. to instrumentation for biochemical separations, 1990, Ea. Analytical Symposium Award, 1997, Exceptional Sci. Achievement Award, NASA, 1997, Space award Aviation Week and Space Tech., 1997, Disting. Svc. Award, Nat. Sci. Bd., 1998, Centennial Medal, Harvard U., The Welch Award, 1999, Faraday Medal, Royal Soc. Chemistry, 2001, Bing Fellowship Tchg. Award, 1996; fellow Non-resident fellow, Joint Inst. for Lab. Astrophysics, 1970—, Alfred P. Sloan fellow, 1967—69, Christensen fellow, St. Catherine's Coll. Oxford U., 1982, Stanford U., 1984—86, Fellow: AAAS, Inst. of Physics, Royal Soc. Chemistry (hon.), Calif. Acad. Sci. (hon.); mem.: NAS (coun. mem., Chem. Sci. Award 1991), Royal Soc. London, Chem. Soc. London, Am. Philos. Soc., Am. Chem. Soc. (Harrison Howe Award 1985, Remsen Award 1985, Kirkwood Award 1986, Willard Gibbs Medal 1990, Peter Debye Award in phys. chemistry 1991, Linus Pauling Medal 1993, Dannie-Heineman Prize 1993, The Harvey Prize 1993, Analytical Chemistry Divsn. Award in chem. instrumentation 1995, Analytical Chemistry Award 1998, G.M. Kosalapoff Award 1998, E. Bright Wilson award in spectroscopy 1999, Nobel Laureate Signature Award 2000, Charles Lathrop Parsons award 2001, Madison Marshall award 2001), Am. Phys. Soc. (Earle K. Plyler prize 1981, Irving Langmuir Prize 1985, Arthur L. Schawlow prize in laser sci. 2000), Am. Acad. Arts and Scis., Phi Beta Delta, Phi Beta Kappa. Achievements include research in laser chemistry and chem. physics. Office: Stanford U Dept Chemistry Stanford CA 94305-5080

ZARELLA, PETER T. state supreme court justice; BS, Northeastern U., 1972; JD, Suffolk U., 1975. Bar: Mass. 1975, Conn. 1977, U.S. Dist. Ct. Mass. 1976, U.S. Dist. Ct. Conn. 1977, U.S. Supreme Ct. 1985, U.S. Ct. Appeals (2nd cir.) 1985, U.S. Dist. Ct., So. Dist. N.Y. 1990. Pvt. practice, 1977—96; ptnr. Brown, Paindiris & Zarella, Hartford, Conn., 1978—96; judge Superior Ct., 1996—99, Appellate Ct., 1999—2001; assoc. justice Conn. Supreme Ct., 2001—. Chmn. Criminal Justice Commn., 2001—; chmn. rules com. Superior Ct., 2001—. Mem Ethics Commn., Town of West Hartford, Conn., 1992—95, mem. Charter Revision Commn., 1995—96. Mem.: Conn. Bar Assn. (mem. exec. com. coml. law and bankruptcy sect. 1985—90, mem. banking law com. 1990—94). Office: Conn Supreme Ct 231 Capitol Ave Hartford CT 06106

ZAREM, ABE MORDECAI, management consulting executive; b. Chgo., Mar. 7, 1917; s. I.H. and Lea (Kaufman) Z.; m. Esther Mariam Moskovitz, Oct. 4, 1941; children: Janet Ruth, David Michael, Mark Charles. BS in Elec. Engring, Ill. Inst. Tech., 1939, LL.D. (hon.), 1968; MS in Elec. Engring, Calif. Inst. Tech., 1940, PhD, 1944; LL.D., U. Calif. at Santa Cruz, 1967. Design engr. very high voltage power transmission system Allis Chalmers Rsch. div., 1944; group leader Ultra Micro Time Program Manhattan Dist. Project/CalTech, 1944—45; initiator, group mgr. Microtime & Electro Optical Phys. Rsch., U.S. Naval Test Sta., 1945-48; assoc. dir., mgr. L.A. div. Stanford Rsch. Inst., 1948-56; mem. faculty UCLA, 1956-61; founder, chmn., pres. Electro-Optical Systems, Inc., Pasadena, Calif., 1956-67; v.p. Xerox Corp., L.A., 1963-67, sr. v.p., dir. corp. devel., bd. dirs., 1967-69; mgmt. and engring. cons., 1969-79; founder, chmn. Xerox Devel. Corp., L.A., 1975-80; chmn. strategic bus. planning, techno-econ. and venture capital, pres., owner Abe M. Zarem & Co., 1981—; founder, mng. dir., Frontier Assoc., 1980—. Mem. adv. com. competitive tech. program State of Calif., 1989; mem. Calif. Coun. Sci. and Tech., chmn. advanced sci. & tech. programs com., 1989-97, disting. fellow 1997—; cons., disting. vis. exec. in sci. and tech., sr. advisor on tech. transfer and commercialization and strategic planning studies Jet Propulsion Lab./Calif. Inst. of Tech., 1997—; cons., advisor, chair of sr. adv. bd. UCLA Brain Rsch. Inst., 1997—; mem. adv. bd. dept. urology UCLA, 1994—. Author: Utilization of Solar Energy, 1963. Traffic and parking commr. City of Beverly Hills, 1971-72, planning commr., 1972-73; Bd. dirs. Music Center Opera Assn., Los Angeles, 1968—; nat. trustee City of Hope; trustee Calif. Inst. Arts, 1973-76. Named Outstanding Young Elec. Engr. in U.S. Eta Kappa Nu, 1948; One of America's Ten Outstanding Young Men U.S. Jr. C. of C., 1950; recipient Albert F. Sperry medal Instrument Soc. Am., 1969 Fellow AIAA, IEEE; sci. mem. (a founder) Solar Energy Soc.; mem. Nat. Acad. Engring. Achievements include inventing World's fastest high-speed camera, automatic oscillograph. Home: 9640 Lomitas Ave Beverly Hills CA 90210-3333 *I have always had a Vision, Mission & Series of Strategic Objectives - The principal one having been instilled by loving parents & family who encouraged me. I was born to identify talent and to challenge it to do more than it would have done if it had not met me. I am mentor and tormentor. I build and stretch people.*

ZAREM, HARVEY ALAN, plastic surgeon; b. Savannah, Ga., Feb. 13, 1932; s. Harry A. and Rose (Gold) Z.; m. Beth McCanghey, July 11, 1981; children: Harold, Allison, Melissa, Kathryn, Michael, Robert. BA, Yale U., 1953; MD, Columbia U., 1957. Diplomate Am. Bd. Surgery, Am. Bd. Plastic Surgery; lic. physician, Md., Ill., Calif. Intern Johns Hopkins Hosp., Balt., 1957-58, resident in plastic surgery, 1964-66; rsch. fellow Peter Bent Brigham Hosp., Boston, 1958-59, asst. resident in surgery, 1959-61; resident in surgery then chief resident Boston City Hosp., 1961-63; postdoctoral fellow NYU, N.Y.C., 1963-64; from asst. prof. to assoc. prof. surgery U. Chgo., 1966-73; prof. surgery U. Calif., L.A., 1973-87, prof. emeritus, 1987—; mem. med. staff Pacific Surgicenter, Santa Monica, Calif., 1987—. Physician Sepulveda (Calif.) VA Hosp., 1974—; mem. med. staff St. Johns Hosp., Santa Monica, Calif., 1987—, Santa Monica Hosp., 1988—; vis. prof. So. Ill. U., 1983, Lackaland AFB, 1986, Creighton U., 1987, Comesa, Milan, 1989, Baylor Coll. Medicine, 1990; Kazanjian vis. prof. Mass. Gen. Hosp., 1986, 88; cons. and presenter in field. Contbr. numerous articles to profl. jours. Grantee NIH, 1964-75, NIH, 1967-72, Sheldon and Carol Appel Family Found., 1982—, Chantal Pharms., 1983-84, Mentor Corp./Heyer-Schulte Products, 1985—, Michael Jackson Burn Found., 1986-87. Fellow ACS; mem. AMA, Am. Soc. Plastic Reconstructive Sugeons, Inc., Am. Burn Assn., Am. Cleft Palat Assn., Am. Assn. Plastic Surgeons, Am. Soc. Aesthetic Plastic Surgery, Am. Assn. Hand Surgery, Am. Assn. Surgery of Trauma, Calif. Med. Asssn., Calif. Soc. Plastic Surgeons, New Eng. Soc. Plastic Surgeons (hon.), L.A. Cunty Med. Assn., Johns Hopkins Med. and Surg. Soc., Plastic Surgery Rsch. Coun., Soc. Head and Neck Surgeons (sr.), Soc. U. Surgeons, N.W. Soc. Plastic Surgeons (hon.), others. Office: Pacific Surgicenter 1301 20th St Ste 470 Santa Monica CA 90404-2082

ZAREMSKI, MILES JAY, lawyer; b. Chgo., Aug. 16, 1948; s. Samuel and Ann (Levine) Z.; m. Elena Chinita Resnik, July 19, 1970; children: Jason Lane, Lauren Devra. BS, U. Ill., 1970; JD, Case Western Res. U., 1973. Bar: Ill. 1973, Pa. 2000, Ind. 2000, U.S. Dist. Ct. (no. dist.) Ill. 1973, U.S. Dist. Ct. Nebr. 1996, U.S. Dist. Ct. (ea. dist.) Tenn. 1997, U.S. Dist. Ct. (no. dist.) Ind. 2001, U.S. Ct. Appeals (7th cir.) 1973, U.S. Ct. Appeals (8th cir.) 1988, U.S. Ct. Appeals (6th cir.) 1998, U.S. Ct. Appeals (9th cir.) 2002, U.S. Supreme Ct. 1977. Spl. asst. state's atty. Lake County, Ill., 1980-82; ptnr. Kamensky & Rubinstein, Lincolnwood, Chgo., Ill., 2000—. Arbitrator, mandatory arbitration programs Cook and Lake Counties, Ill., 1990—; asst. prof. med. jurisprudence Rosalind Franklin U. Medicine and Sci., 1991—; adj. faculty U. Chgo. Law Sch., 1999—2001; advisor to congressman and staffs on patient rights, 1999—; adj. asst. prof. Case Western Res. Law Sch., 2001—03. Editor: Medical and Hospital Negligence, 4 vols., 1988, supplement, 1993, 95-99; contbr. chpts. in books and articles to profl. jours.; author: Reengineering Healthcare Liability Litigation, 1997, supplement, 1999; patentee in field. Oversight com. law sch. Case Western Res. U., Cleve., 1985-99, alumni bd. dirs., 1996-99, pres. oversight com., 2002-03; mem. exec. com. law sch. ctr for health care Loyola U., Chgo., 1987-89; mem. lakefront commn. City of Highland Park, Ill., 1982-84; bd. dirs., officer Regional Organ Bank Ill., Chgo., 1986-91, The Lambs, Libertyville, Ill., 1982-84, Jocelyn Ctr. for Mental Health, 1994-96; field play marshall U.S. Olympics Baseball, Atlanta, 1996. Named one of Outstanding Young Men in Am., U.S. Jaycees, 1979. Fellow: Am. Bar Found., Am. Coll. Legal Medicine (assoc. in law 1973—91, editl. bd. Jour. Legal Medicine 1981—, chair legal com. 1996—98, chair Amicus com. 1997—2003, bd. govs., sec. 1999—2000, treas. 2000—01, pres.-elect 2001—02, pres. 2002—03); mem.: ABA (editor-in-chief Forum 1979—81, vice chmn. 1979—90, chmn. med. and law com. 1984—85, editl. bd. Forum on Health Law 1989—91, spl. com. on med. profl. liability 1991—95, 1998—, chmn. spl. com. on med. profl. liability 2000—03, chmn. std. com. med. profl. liability 2003—, various coms. tort, trial and ins. practice sect.), World Congress Med. Law, Ill. Assn. Healthcare Attys., Quality Mgmt. Health Care (editl. bd.), Am. Soc. Writers on Legal Subjects (scribes), Am. Health Law Assn. (vice chair hosp. liability com. 1999—2001), Am. Soc. Law and Medicine (editor-in-chief 1981—83, bd. editors 1983—86), Lake County Bar Assn., Ill. Bar Assn. (1st and 3d prizes 1978—79). Jewish. Avocations: baseball, soccer, coaching athletic teams. Office: Kamensky & Rubinstein 7250 N Cicero Ave Ste 200 Lincolnwood IL 60712 Office Phone: 847-568-5602. E-mail: mzaremski@kr-law.com. *"Success is a journey; not a destination." "A man may make many mistakes but he isn't a failure until he starts blaming someone else." John R. Wooden.*

ZARET, BARRY LEWIS, cardiologist, medical educator; b. N.Y.C., Oct. 3, 1940; s. Irving Z. and Beatrice (Fader) Zaret; m. Myrna Zimmerman, June 23, 1963; children: Adam L., Elliot C., Owen M. BS, Queens Coll., 1962; MD, NYU, 1966; MA, Yale U., 1982. Diplomate Am. Bd. Internal Medicine. Intern Bellevue Hosp., N.Y.C., 1966-67, resident, 1967-79; rsch. fellow John Hopkins U., Balt., 1969-71; asst. prof. medicine Yale U., New Haven, 1973-76, assoc. prof. medicine and diagnostic radiology, 1976, chief sect. cardiology, 1978—2004, assoc. prof. medicine and diagnostic radiology, 1980-82, prof. medicine and diagnostic radiology, 1982-84, Robert W. Berliner prof. medicine, 1984—, assoc. chair clin. affairs dept. internal medicine, 1994—2004; mem. staff Yale-New Haven Med. Ctr.; med. dir. Yale-New Haven Med. Hosp. Heart Ctr., 1999—2004. Mem. cardiovasc. subsplty. bd. Am Bd. Internal Medicine, 2002—. Mem. editl. bd. Am. Jour. Cardiology, 1977—. Jour. Am. Coll. Cardiology, 1986-91, 92-97, Jour. Cardiac Imaging, 1986—, Circulation, 1993; assoc. editor: Yearbook of Nuc. Medicine, 1980-95; editor-in-chief Jour. Nuc. Cardiology, 1993-2004; contbr. articles to profl. jours. Recipient Casimir Funk award Soc. Mil. Surgeons, 1973; recipient Herrman Blumgart Pioneer award New Eng. chpt. Soc. Nuc. Medicine, 1978, Solomon Berson Alumni Achievement award in clin. sci. NYU Sch. Medicine, 1998, Ellis Island medal Honor, 2004. Fellow Am. Coll. Cardiology, Coun. Clin. Cardiology, Am. Heart Assn., Coun. Circulation, Am. Heart Assn., Am. Physiology Soc.; mem. Am. Soc. Clin. Investigation, Am. Fedn. Clin. Rsch., Assn. Am. Physicians, Soc. Nuc. Medicine, Am. Soc. Nuc. Cardiology, Assn. Univ. Cardiologists, Assn. Profs. Cardiology (pres. 1992), Phi Beta Kappa, Alpha Omega Alpha, Interurban Clin. Club. Jewish. Home: 15 Cassway Rd Woodbridge CT 06525-1214 Office: 333 Cedar St # 3fmp New Haven CT 06520-8017 Office Phone: 203-785-4127.

ZARGES, THOMAS H. engineering executive; Degree in engring., Va. Mil. Inst. V.p. bus. devel. United Engrs. & Constructors, 1990; pres., CEO power and indsl./mfg. divsns. Washington Group, 1991; sr. exec. v.p. ops. Washington Group Internat., Boise, Idaho, 2002—. Office: Washington Group Internat PO Box 73 Boise ID 83729

ZARGHAMI, CYMA, broadcast executive; m. George Zarghami; 1 child, Liam. Exec. v.p. Nickelodeon, gen. mgr., 1996—. Directs co. initiatives Big Help and Kids Pick the Pres. Campaign; launched Nick Jr., SNICK, Nicktoons. Office: Nickelodeon 1515 Broadway New York NY 10036

ZARICZNYJ, BASILIUS, orthopedic surgeon; b. Ukraine, Aug. 31, 1924; came to U.S., 1951; m. Stefania Pidburny, Aug. 21, 1954; children: Marta, Stephanie Christine, Andrea Maria, Mark B. MD, U. Bonn, Germany, 1951; MD (hon.), Odessa State Med. U., Ukraine, 1996. Diplomate Am. Bd. Orthopedic Surgery. Resident St. Luke's Hosp., Chgo., 1954-56, Univ. Hosps., Oklahoma City, 1955-56; fellow in orthopedics Northwestern U., Chgo., 1957; asst. prof. Sch. Medicine U. Okla., Oklahoma City, 1957-58; orthopedic surgeon Springfield, Ill., 1958—; clin. prof. Sch. Medicine So. Ill. U., Springfield, Ill., 1973-85, acting chmn. divsn. orthopedic surgery, 1972-75, chief sports medicine sect., 1975-82, program chmn. sports injury symposium, 1977-79, 82, 83. Mem. sports medicine com. Ill. State Med. Soc., 1979-80; chmn. dept. orthopedic surgery St. John's and Meml. Hosps., Springfield, 1970-79; program chmn. Med. Congress of World Fedn. of Ukrainian Med. Assn., Dniepropetrovsk, 1994, Odessa, Ukraine, 1996; presenter Am. Acad. Orthopedic Surgeons, Miami, Fla., 1961, N.Y., 1969, San Francisco, 1971, Washington, 1972, Las Vegas, 1973, 77, Anaheim, Calif., 1983, Chgo. Orthopedic Soc., 1967, 76, O'Donoghue Okla. Orthopedic Alumni Assn., Oklahoma City, 1972, 75, 78, Internat. Soc. for Orthopedic Surgery and Traumatology, XII World Congress, Tel Aviv, 1972, Copenhagen, 1975, Kyoto, Japan, 1978, So. Ill U. Sch. Medicine, Springfield, 1977, 79, 80, 82, Ill. State Orthopedic Soc., Chgo., 1978, ACS, Chgo., 1979, Am. Orthopedic Soc. for Sports Medicine, Atlanta, 1980, Big Sky, Mont., 1980, Lake Tahoe, Nev., 1981, Clin. Orthopedic Soc., Chgo., 1987, World Fedn. Ukrainian Med. Assn., Kiev, Ukraine, 1990, U. Lviv, Ukraine, 1990, 11th Congress of Orthopedic Surgeons of Ukraine, Kharkiv, 1991, Congress of World Fedn. of Ukrainian Med. Assn., Kharkiv, 1992, Dniprópetrovsk, 1994, Odessa, 1996, Ukraine, among others. Mem. editl. bd. Jour. Ukrainan Med. Assn. N.Am., 1977-95; contbr. articles to profl. jours. and med. textbooks. Fellow Am. Acad. Orthopedic Surgery; mem. AMA, Ill. Orthopedic Soc., Internat. Soc. Orthopedic Surgery and Traumatology, Am. Orthopedic Soc. for Sports Medicine, Internat. Soc. of the Knee, Mid-Am. Orthopedic Assn., Ukrainian Acad. and Profl. Assn. Pres. 1985-89), Sangamon County Med. Soc., Chgo. Orthopedic Soc. Avocations: golf, walking, chess. Home and Office: 125 Oakmont Dr Springfield IL 62704-3118

ZARING, ALLEN G. homebuilding company executive; Student, Babson Coll. Founder, chmn., CEO Zaring Homes, 1964—. With U.S. Army. Recipient High Achievement award Profl. Builders Mag.; named Builder of Yr., Home Builders Assn. Greater Cin., 1995, Ams. Best Builder. Office: 625 Eden Park Dr #1250 Cincinnati OH 45202-6024 Fax: 513-247-2667.

ZARINS, BERTRAM, orthopaedic surgeon; b. Latvia, June 22, 1942; came to U.S., 1946, naturalized, 1956; s. Richard Arthur and Maria (Rozenbergs) Z. AB in Chemistry, Lafayette Coll., 1963; MD, SUNY, Syracuse, 1967. Diplomate Am. Bd. Orthop. Surgery. Clin. instr. orthop. surgery Harvard Med. Sch., Boston, 1976—, asst. clin. prof., 1982—; orthop. surgeon Mass. Gen. Hosp., Boston, 1982-95; assoc. clin. prof. Harvard Med. Sch., Boston, 1996—; chief sports medicine svc. Mass. Gen. Hosp., Boston, 1982—; team physician Boston Bruins Hockey Team, 1976—. Chmn. edn. com. Sports Medicine Coun., U.S. Olympic Com., 1980-92; team physician New England Patriots football team, 1982—; head physician USA Olympic teams XIV Winter Olympic Games, Sarajevo, Yugoslavia, 1984; cons. editor for sports medicine Jour. of Bone and Joint Surgery, 1999—. Contbr. articles to profl. jours. Team physician N.E. Revolution profl. soccer team, 1996—. Lt. comdr. M.C., USNR, 1973-75. Fellow ACS, Am. Acad. Orthop. Surgeons (chmn. com. on sports medicine 1993-97), Am. Coll. Sports Medicine; mem. AMA, Internat. Arthroscopy Assn. (bd. dirs. 1991-95), Arthroscopy Assn. N.Am., N.Am. Trauma Assn. (pres. 1977), Internat. Soc. of Arthroscopy, Knee Surgery and Orthopaedic Sports Medicine, Am. Shoulder and Elbow Surgeons, Herodicus Soc., Brookline (Mass.) Country Club, Somerset Club. Office: Mass Gen Hosp Ambulatory Care Ctr Ste 514 Boston MA 02114 Business E-Mail: bzarins@partners.org.

ZARINS, CHRISTOPHER KRISTAPS, surgery educator, vascular surgeon; b. Tukums, Latvia, Dec. 2, 1943; came to U.S., 1946; s. Richard A. and Maria (Rozenbergs) Z.; m. Zinta Zarins, July 8, 1967; children: Daina, Sascha, Karina. BA, Lehigh U., 1964; MD, Johns Hopkins U., 1968. Surgery residency U. Mich., Ann Arbor, 1968-74; asst. prof. surgery U. Chgo., 1976-79, assoc. prof. surgery, 1979-82, prof. surgery, 1983-93, chief of vascular surgery, 1978-93; prof. surgery, chmn. divsn. vascular surgery Stanford (Calif.) U., 1993—, acting chmn. dept. of surgery, 1995-97. Author: Essays In Surgery, 1986, Atlas of Vascular Surgery, 1988; editor Jour. of Surg. Rsch., 1982-95; contbr. articles to profl. jours. Pres. Latvian Med. Found., Boston, 1991. Lt. comdr. USN, 1974-76. Grantee NIH, NSF. Mem. Am. Surg. Soc., Soc. for Clin. Surgery, Soc. for Vascular Surgery (pres. 1998-99), Internat. Soc. for Cardiovascular Surgery, Soc. of Univ. Surgeons, Latvian Nat. Acad. of Scis., Latvian Vascular Surg. Soc. (pres. 1989), Soc. for Vascular Surgery (pres. 1998-99). Avocations: triathlons, skiing. Office: Stanford U Med Ctr Divsn Vascular Surgery 300 Pasteur Dr # H3630 Palo Alto CA 94304-2203

ZARKIN, HERBERT J. retail company executive; Exec. vice-pres. Zayre Corp., Framingham, Mass., until 1986; pres. Zayre Corp., HomeClub subs., Framingham, Mass., 1986-88; chmn. Zayre Corp., Zayre Stores div., Framing-

ham, Mass., 1988; pres., CEO Waban Inc, Natick, 1988-95, chmn. bd., 1997-98; chmn. BJ's Wholesale Club Inc., 1998—, HomeBase, Irvine, Calif., 1999—2001. Address: HomeBase 3345 Michelson Dr Irvine CA 92612 Office: BJs Wholesale Club Inc 1 Mercer Rd Natick MA 01760-2400

ZARO, BRAD A. research company executive, biologist; b. San Jose, Calif., Dec. 4, 1949; s. Raymond J. and Irene R. Z.; children: Amy C., Kristen E. BA in Zoology, San Jose State U., 1974, MA in Biology, 1981. Chemist, Dept. Drug Metabolism Syntex Rsch., Inc., Palo Alto, Calif., 1976-78, chemist II, Dept. Drug Metabolism, 1978-81, chemist III, Dept. Drug Metabolism, 1981-84, clin. rsch. assoc. I, Inst. of Clin. Medicine, 1984-85, clin. rsch. assoc. II, Inst. of Clin. Medicine, 1985-87, sen. clin. rsch. assoc., Inst. of Clin. Medicine, 1985-87; sen. clin. rsch. assoc. Triton Biosciences, Inc., Alameda, Calif., 1988, mgr. clin. trials, 1988; pres., CEO Clinimetrics Rsch. Assoc., Inc., San Jose, 1988—. Contbr. articles to scholarly jours. Mem. AAAS, Am. Coll. Clin. Pharmacology, Am. Soc. Pharmacognosy, Assn. Clin. Rsch. Profls., Drug Info. Assn. Democrat. Roman Catholic. Avocations: scuba diving, skiing, flying airplanes. Office: Clinimetrics Rsch Assocs 5285 Hellyer Ave San Jose CA 95138

ZARR, MELVYN, lawyer, law educator; b. Worcester, Mass., Aug. 29, 1936; m. Gail Sclar, Aug. 29, 1971. AB, Clark U., 1958; LL.B., Harvard U., 1963. Bar: Mass. bar 1964, Maine bar 1973. Staff atty. NAACP Legal Def. & Edn. Fund, Inc., N.Y.C., 1963-69; co-dir. Mass. Law Reform Inst., Boston, 1970-73; prof. law U. Maine, 1973—; U.S. magistrate, Portland, Maine, 1977-82. Mem. Am. Law Inst. Home: 19 Mckinley Rd Falmouth ME 04105-1913 Office: U Maine Sch Law 246 Deering Ave Portland ME 04102-2837 Business E-Mail: mzarr@usm.maine.edu.

ZARRA, ERNEST JOSEPH, III, educator, researcher; b. Montclair, N.J., Dec. 14, 1955; s. Ernest Joseph Jr. and Faith Zarra; m. Susan Sembrat, May 29, 1976; children: Elya Joelle, Jonathan Joseph. BA, Northeastern Bible Coll., 1978; MA, Simon Greenleaf U., 1981; MABS, Grace Grad. Sch., Long Beach, Calif., 1986; MEd, Calif. State U., Bakersfield, 1988; PhD, U. So. Calif., 1999. Cert. tchr., N.J., Calif. Pvt. sch. tchr., 1978-89; pastor Millington Bapt. Ch., Basking Ridge, N.J., 1994-95; tchr., GATE coord. Fruitvale Sch. Dist. Pub. Sch., Bakersfield, Calif., 1989-94, 95-00; tchr. govt. and econs. Centennial H.S., Bakersfield, Calif., 2000—, girls varsity soccer coach, 2000—. Adj. faculty Calif. State U., Bakersfield, 1998—, Pt. Loma Nazarene U.; lectr. U. Pa., Bakersfield Coll., Fresno Pacific U., U. San Diego, others; presenter in field. Author: It Should Never Happen Here, 1997; contbr. articles to profl. jours. Youth coach Am. Youth Soccer Orgn., Kern County, Calif., 1993—; youth and adults tchr. Laurelglen Bible Ch., Bakersfield, 1984—; presenter to law enforcement officers Kern County Sheriffs Dept., 1988. Named All-Am. Soccer Player Nat. Christian Coll. Athletic Assn., 1978, All-State. All Dist., All Conf.; drafted Dallas Tornado (NASL), 1978. Mem. ASCD, Am. Ednl. Rsch. Assn., Evang. Theol. Soc., Link Inst., Kappa Delta Pi (Character Edn. Partnership). Republican. Mennonite Brethren. Avocations: athletics, writing, travel, ministry, debate. Home: 400 Sinaloa Ave Bakersfield CA 93312-9334

ZARTMAN, DAVID LESTER, animal sciences educator, researcher; b. Albuquerque, July 6, 1940; s. Lester Grant and Mary Elizabeth (Kitchel) Z.; m. Micheal Aline Plemmons, July 6, 1963; children: Kami Renee, Dalan Lee. BS, N.Mex. State U., 1962; MS, Ohio State U., 1966, PhD, 1968. Cert. dairy cattle specialist, Am. Registry Profl. Animal Scientists. Jr. ptnr. Marlea Guernsey Farm, Albuquerque, 1962-64; grad. rsch. assoc. Ohio State U., Columbus, 1964-68; asst. prof. dairy sci. N.Mex. State U., Las Cruces, 1968-71, assoc. prof., 1971-79, prof., 1979-84, Ohio State U., Columbus, 1984—. Chmn. dept. Ohio State U., Columbus, 1984-99; pres. Mary K. Zartman, Inc., Albuquerque, 1976-84; cons. Bio-Med. Electronics, Inc., San Diego, 1984-89, Zartemp, Inc., Northbrook, Ill., 1990, Recom Applied Solutions, 1993-2000, Am. Registry of Profl. Animal Scientists, 1996—, Midwest Univs. Consortium for Internat. Assistance, 2004. Contbr. articles to profl. jours.; patentee in field. Recipient State Regional Outstanding Young Farmer award Jaycees, 1963, Disting. Rsch. award N.Mex. State U. Coll. Agr. and Home Econs., 1983, Outstanding Svc. award Ohio Poultry Assn., 1999, Grazier of Yr. award Gt. Lakes Internat. Grazing Conf., 2001, hon. state degree Ohio FFA, 2000, The Jack Tucker Disting. Svc. award Ohio Forage and Grassland Coun., 2004; course acclaimed by Humane Soc. of U.S.; named one of Top 100 Agr. Alumni, N.Mex. State U. Centennial, 1987; spl. postdoctoral fellow NIH, New Zealand, 1973; Fulbright-Hayes lectr., Malaysia, 1976. Fellow AAAS; mem. Am. Dairy Sci. Assn., Am. Soc. Animal Sci., Dairy Shrine Club, Ohio Farm Bur., Sigma Xi, Gamma Sigma Delta, Alpha Gamma Rho (1st Outstanding Alumnus N.Mex. chpt. 1985), Alpha Zeta, Phi Kappa Phi. Home: 7671 Deer Creek Dr Worthington OH 43085-1551 Office: Ohio State U 2027 Coffey Rd Columbus OH 43210-1043 Office Phone: 614-292-1387. Business E-Mail: zartman.3@osu.edu.

ZARUTSKIE, ANDREW JOHN, town official; b. Newburgh, NY, Feb. 16, 1950; s. Steve and Eleanor L. Zarutskie. AA, Orange County C.C., 1969; BA, Am. U., 1971; postgrad., SUNY, New Paltz, 1971-73. Asst. for urban renewal dept. City of Newburgh, N.Y., 1971-72; asst. assessor Town of Newburgh, 1972-73; dist. office asst. U.S. Congressman Benjamin A. Gilman, Newburgh, 1973-77, grants and project coord. Washington, 1977-83, pres. sec., 1983-2001; town clk. Town of Newburgh, 2001—. Contbr. articles to profl. publs. Mem. Orange County Rep. Com., 1971—, exec. com., 1979-83; bd. dirs. Meals on Wheels, Newburgh, 1975-77. Mem. Rep. Comm. Assn., Orange County Hist. Soc., KC, Kiwanis. Roman Catholic. also: PO Box 10185 Newburgh NY 12552

ZARWYN, BERTHOLD, physical scientist; b. Vienna, Aug. 22, 1921; came to U.S., 1949, naturalized, 1955; s. Joseph and Bronislawa Regina (Unger) Zarwyn. ME, Gliwice, Poland, 1946; ScD, UN Univ., Munich, 1947; PhD, NYU, 1954; ScD in Engring., Columbia U., 1963. Project engr. Curtiss-Wright Corp., Woodridge, NJ, 1951-55; staff scientist AMF Corp., N.Y.C., 1955-57; chief scientist Link Aviation Co., Binghamton, NY, 1957-58; head rsch. staff Am. Bosch-Arma Corp., Garden City, NY, 1958-63; corp. cons. Cutler-Hammer Corp., Deer Park, NY, 1963-65; chief engr. Bell Aerosystems Corp., Niagara Falls, NY, 1965-66; sr. cons. Mitre Corp., Bedford, Mass., 1966-68; spl. asst. to commdg. gen., acting chief engr. Hdqs. U.S. Army Materiel Command, Arlington, Va., 1968-71; chief phys. scis. br. U.S. Army Devel. and Readiness Command, Alexandria, Va., 1971-75; phys. scientist U.S. Army Harry Diamond Labs., Washington, 1975-78; chief sys. analysis br. U.S. Army Elec. Rsch. and Devel. Command, Adelphi, Md., 1978-79, chief tech. divsn., 1979-81, asst. tech. dir., 1981-85; spl. asst. to dep. chief of staff for tech. & program mgmt. U.S. Army Lab. Command, Adelphi, Md., 1985-87; pres. Pan-Tech. Corp., Delray Beach, Fla., 1987—. Adj. faculty, lectr., cons. in field; dir. Film Microelectronics Co. Inc., Burlington, Mass., 1965-67. Mem. editl. bd. Bavarian Soc. Engrs., 1947-49, transl. panel Russian Jour. Applied Math. and Mechanics with Pergamon Inst., 1956-57; inventor nuc. gyroscope, microwave holography, other items. Mem. IEEE, Am. Phys. Soc., N.Y. Acad. Scis., Sigma Xi. Home and Office: Pan-Tech Corp 7589 Mansfield Hollow Rd Delray Beach FL 33446-3314

ZARYCHTA, WILLIAM ALEX, physician assistant; BS, West Chester U., 1993—96; AAS, Gloucester County Coll., 1997—99; BS, MCP, Hahnemann U., 1999—2001; M in physician asst. studies, U. Of Nebr., 2001—02. Cert. physician asst. Nat. Comm. On Certification Of Physician Assistants, 2001, registered paramedic Nat. Registry of Emergency Med. Technicians, 1993; RN, Pa., 1999. Paramedic Mercy Health Sys., Darby, Pa., 1993—99; emergency dept. RN Mercy Fitzgerald Hosp., Darby, Pa., 1999—2000; emergency medicine physician asst. Brandywine Emergency Physician Associates, Wayne, Pa., 2001—04; deployed to S.W. Asia with U.S. Army supporting Operation Enduring Freedom, 2004—. Clin. instr. Arcadia U., Glenside, Pa., 2001—, Drexel U., Phila., 2001—. Med. screening Spl. Olympics, Phila., 2000, Mid Atlantic Powerboat Assn., Ocean City, Md., 2001. 1st lt. U.S. Army, 1990. Decorated Army Commendation medal U.S. Army, Armed Forces Res. medal Dept Of Def., Army Achievement medal U.S. Army, Army Res. Component Achievement medal, Mil. Outstanding Vol. Svc. medal. Fellow: Pa. Soc. of Physician Assistants, Soc. of Army Physician Assistants, Soc. Of Emergency Medicine Physician Assistants, Am. Acad. Of Physician Assistants; mem.: Am. Coll. Clinicians (charter), Phi Theta Kappa. Office: Brandywine Hosp 201 Reeceville Rd Coatesville PA 19320

ZASLAVSKY, THOMAS, mathematics professor; b. Bklyn., Jan. 16, 1944; s. Sam and Claudia Z. BS, CCNY, 1965; PhD, MIT, 1974. Staff sci. Arcon Corp., Wakefield, Mass., 1972-73; instr. MIT, Cambridge, Mass., 1975-77; asst. prof. Ohio State U., Columbus, 1977-84; visiting researcher U. Evansville (Ind.), 1984-85; assoc. prof. math. SUNY, Binghamton, 1985-88, prof. math., 1988—. Contbr. articles to profl. jours. Office: Binghanton Univ SUNY Dept Math Scis Binghamton NY 13902-6000

ZATAR, WAEL ABDELHALIM, civil engineer, educator; s. Abdelhalim Mohamed Zatar and Yossr Hassan Elsheihy; m. Gehan Elhady Elsayed, Apr. 24, 1973; 1 child, Ahmed Wael Abdelhalim Mohamed Zatar. B. Eng. in Civil Engring., Cairo U., 1990, MS in Civil Engring., 1994; DEng in Civil Engring., Saitama U., Saitama Ken, 1999. Registered EIT, Oreg., 1999. Design engr. Dars Cons. and Engrs., Cairo, 1990—91, Ferrometalco Internat. Co., Cairo, 1990—93, sr. design engr., 1993—96; rsch. asst. Dept. of Civil Engring., Saitama U., Japan, 1996—99, tchg. asst., 1996—99; faculty fellow Saitama U., 1999—2001; vis. prof. U. of Ky., Lexington, 2001—03; civil engring. prof. W.Va. U. Inst. of Tech., Montgomery, 2004—. Asst. editor Design Specification of Prestressed Concrete Hwy. Bridges, Tokyo, 2001—02, Newsletter of Japan Soc. for Civil Engrs., Tokyo, 1997—2001; reviewer Computer-Aided Civil and Infrastructure Engring., Cin., 2001—. Contbr. articles to profl. jours. Named Ideal Engr., Ferrometalco internat. GMBH Co., 1994; fellow Cairo U. Distinction fellow, Cairo U., 1992—93; grantee, Ky. Transp. Cabinet grantee, 1999—2002, FRP grantee, 2000—02, Ky. Transp. Cabinet grantee, 2002—04, 2001—03, Japan Soc. for the Promotion of Sciences grantee, 1999—2001, Met. Expy. Pub. Corp. and Japan Engring. Cons. grantee, 1999—2001, Ministry of Edn., Culture and Sci. grantee, 2001, 2000—01, 1996—99,; scholar PhD scholar, Ministry of Edn., Culture and Sci., 1996—99. Fellow: Japan Soc. for the Promotion of Sciences (life Outstanding Rschr. Award 1999); mem.: Japan Prestressed Concrete Engring. Assn. (assoc.), Japan Soc. of Civil Engrs. (assoc.), Japan Concrete Inst. (assoc.), Am. Roadway and Transp. Builders Assn. (assoc.), Inst. of Transp. Engrs. (assoc.), Am. Concrete Inst. (assoc. Commended as a finalist to Am. Concrete Inst. Honors and Awards Com. 2002), ASCE (assoc.), Egyptian Syndicate of Engrs. (life). Achievements include invention of Role of prestressing concrete bridge piers in mitigation of seismic damage; development of Health monitoring of structures; first to Strengthening of Viaduct structures for enhanced seismic behavior; Inelstic behavior of girders of viaduct structures; Strut and tie models for continous concrete structures; research in seismic ranking of bridges in the US; Applivcation Of Fiber Reinforced Polymers To Bridges; Ductile behavior of structures; Evaluation of infrastructures in seismic regions; development of Contolled Cracking of bridge decks. Avocations: sightseeing, travel, soccer, tennis, squash. Office: West Virginia University Tech 405 Fayette Pike Montgomery WV 25136 Office Phone: 304-442-3370. Office Fax: 304-442-3391. E-mail: wael.zatar@mail.wvu.edu.

ZATLIN, GABRIEL STANLEY, physician; b. N.Y.C., Dec. 5, 1935; s. Samuel and Bernice (Morgenstern) Z.; m. Linda M. Gertner, Dec. 29, 1959 (div. 1973); children: Jonathan Reid, Andrew Evan; m. Lorna G. Schofield, May 14, 1983; 1 child, Sarah Schofield. BS, U. Miami, Coral Gables, Fla., 1956; MD, Washington U., St. Louis, 1960. Diplomate Am. Bd. Pediatrics, Am. Bd. Family Practice. Intern St. Louis Children's Hosp., 1960-61, resident, 1961-62, Children's Hosp. Med. Ctr., Boston, 1965-66, Downstate Med. Ctr., Bklyn., 1979-81; Epidemiologist Ctrs. for Disease Control, Atlanta, 1962-64; pvt. practice Atlanta, 1966-73; cons. Pertamina, Jakarta, Indonesia, 1974-76; field dir. African Health Tng. Project, Yaounde, Cameroun, 1976-77; assoc. dir. Brown U. Health Svcs., Providence, 1977-79; asst. prof. Downstate Med. Ctr., Bklyn., 1981-82; assoc. dir. St. Mary Hosp. Family Practice, Hoboken, N.J., 1982-88, dir., 1988-92; clin. assoc. prof. Downstate Med. Ctr., Bklyn., 1992-95, dir. family practice residency program, 1993-95; faculty family practice residency program Beth Israel Hosp., 1997—. Clin. asst. prof. Albert Einstein Sch. Medicine, 1997—. Contbr. articles to profl. jours. With USPHS, 1962-64. Fellow Am. Acad. Pediatrics; mem. Am. Acad. Family Practice. Avocation: gardening. Office: Inst for Urban Family Prac 16 E 16th St New York NY 10003-3105 Office Phone: 212-924-7744.

ZATLIN, PHYLLIS, Spanish language educator, translator; b. Green Bay, Wis., Dec. 31, 1938; d. Frank L. and Ellen Mary (Butler) Z.; m. George Boring Kelly, Aug. 20, 1962; children: William, Lee. BA, Rollins Coll., 1960; postgrad., U. Grenoble, France, 1960-61; MA, U. Fla., 1962, PhD, 1965. Cert. Spanish to English translator Am. Translators Assn. Instr. Rutgers U., New Brunswick, N.J., 1963-66, asst. prof., 1966-71, assoc. prof., 1971-79, assoc. dean, 1974-80, prof. Spanish, 1979—, chair dept. Spanish, grad. dir., 1980-87. Mem. discipline adv. com. Coun. Internat. Exch. Scholars', 1990—93; spkr. in field. Co-author: Lengua y Lectura: Un Repaso y Una Continuación, 1970; author: Elena Quiroga, 1977, Víctor Ruiz Iriarte, 1980, Jaime Salom, 1982, Cross Cultural-Approaches to Theatre: The Spanish-French Connection, 1994, The Novels and Plays of Eduardo Manet: An Adventure in Multiculturalism, 2000; editor: (Francisco Ayala) El Rapto, 1971, (Víctor Ruiz Iriarte) El Landó de Seis Caballos, 1979, (Jaime Salom) La Piel del Limón, 1980, (Antonio Gala) Noviembre y un Poco de Yerba. Petra Regalada, 1981, (Francisco Nieva) Combate de Opalos y Tasia. Sombra y Quimera de Larra. La Magosta, 1990, El teatro alternativo español, 2001; co-editor: The Contemporary Spanish Theater. A Collection of Critical Essays, 1988, Homenaje (A Tribute to Martha T. Halsey), 1995; co-editor: Entre Actos: Diálogos sobre teatro español, 1999, Un escenario propio (A Stage of Their Own), 1998; co-guest editor jour. Art Teatral. Cuadernos de Minipiezas Ilustradas, 1996; translator play edits.: (J.L. Alonso de Santos) Going Down to Marrakesh, 1992, Hostages in the Barrio, 1997, (Paloma Pedrero) Parting Gestures (The Color of August, A Night Divided, The Voucher, With Tonight in the Subway, 1999, (Jaime Salom) A Bonfire at Dawn, 1992, The Other William, 2004, (Jean-Paul Daumas) The Elephant Graveyard, 1994, (Eduardo Manet) Lady Strass, 1992, 97, also performances; assoc. editor Estreno, 1992-2001, editor Estreno Plays, 1998—; mem. editl. bd. Western European Stages, Espana Contemporanea, others. State pres. Women's Equity Action League, N.J., 1971-72, nat. bd. dirs., Washington, 1973, 76-77. Fellow Fulbright Found., 1960-61, Woodrow Wilson Found., 1961-62; recipient Disting. Alumna award Rollins Coll., 1985, Profl. award Fgn. Lang. Educators of N.J., 1989, Outstanding Alumna award Romance Langs., U. Fla., 2003. Mem. AAUP (mem. nat. coun. 1987-90), MLA (mem. commn. on status of women 1978-81), Dramatists Guild, Soc. Gen. de Autores y Editores (Profl. award 1997). Democrat. Avocations: biking, jogging, travel. Home: 5 Timber Rd East Brunswick NJ 08816-2941 Office: Rutgers Univ 105 George St New Brunswick NJ 08901-1414 E-mail: pzatlin@spanport.rutgers.edu.

ZATSIORSKY, VLADIMIR MOISEEVICH (MICHAILOVICH), biomechanics educator, researcher; b. Leningrad, Russia, Dec. 26, 1932; came to U.S., 1990; s. Moisey T. and Berta L. (Bardenstein) Z.; m. Rita Y. Zatsiorsky, Oct. 27, 1960; children: Betty V. Ulitsky, Michael V. PhD, Lesgaft Inst. Phys. Culture, Leningrad, 1961; DSc, Ctrl. Inst. Phys. Culture, Moscow, 1969; D honoris causa, Acad. Phys. Culture, Wroclaw, Poland, 1999, Russian State U. Physical Culture, 2003. Asst. prof. Lvov (Ukraine) Inst. Phys. Culture, 1954—57; asst. prof., assoc. prof., prof. Ctrl. Inst. Phys. Culture, Moscow, 1959—90; vis. prof. UCLA, 1990, U. Calgary, Canada, 1991; prof. kinesiology Pa. State U., University Park, 1991—. Med. commn. Internat. Olympic Com., 1982—. Author (15 books including): Science and Practice of Strength Training, 1995, Kinematics of Human Motion, 1998, Kinetics of Human Motion, 2002; editor: Biomechanics in Sport, 2000, Classics in Movement Science, 2001 (all books published in English, Russian, German, Italian, Spanish, Portuguese, Chinese, Japanese, Polish, Romanian, Czech, Serbo-Croatian & Bulgarian). Recipient J. Dyson award Internat. Soc. of Sport Biomechanics, 1992. Fellow: Am. Acad. Kinesiology; mem.: Internat. Soc. Sport Kinetics (hon.). Avocations: reading, music. Office: Pa State U 39 Rec Bldg University Park PA 16802 Business E-Mail: vxz1@psu.edu.

ZATZ, IRVING J. structural engineer; b. May 27, 1953; s. Hyman and Frances Zatz; m. Janet Gwen Share, Aug. 15, 1976; children: Jonathan, Eric. BS, Cornell U., 1975; M in Engring., 1976. Structural engr. Goodkind & O'Dea, Inc., Clifton, N.J., 1976-77, Grumman Aerospace Corp., Bethpage, N.Y., 1977-80; sr. project engr. engring. analysis divsn. Princeton (N.J.) U. Plasma Physics Lab., 1980—. Univ. fellow Cornell U., 1975-76. Contbr. articles to profl. jours. Bd. dirs. Princeton Oaks Homeowners Assn. (v.p. 1992-94, pres. 1994-97); mgr. West Windsor Little League; mem. West Windsor Rd. Design Com., West Windsor Transp. Com. Recipient 1st Pl. award, James F. Lincoln Engring. Design Competition, 1975, Cmty. Svc. award, West Windsor Twp., 1994. Mem. AIAA, ASCE (exec. com. met. sect. 1978-80), ASME, Am. Concrete Inst., Tau Beta Pi, Chi Epsilon (chpt. treas. 1974-75, pres. 1975-76). Home: 8 Huntington Dr Princeton Junction NJ 08550-2122 Office: Princeton Plasma Physics Lab PO Box 451 Princeton NJ 08543-0451 Office Phone: 609-243-2054. E-mail: zatz@pppl.gov.

ZAUDERER, MARK CARL, lawyer; b. Jan. 26, 1946; BA, Union Coll., 1967; JD, NYU, 1971. Bar: N.Y. 1972. Law clk. U.S. Dist. Ct., Newark, 1971—72; ptnr. Piper Rudnick, N.Y.C., 2003—. Faculty chmn. Practicing Law Inst. Program., Litigating Comml. Cases up to Trial, N.Y.C. and San Francisco, 1986, faculty mem. Deposition Skills Tng. Program, N.Y., 1986, 88-90; adv. com. on civil practice to Chief Adminstrn. Judge N.Y. State Ctrs., 1992—; trustee bd. advisors Union Coll., 1993—; chief Judge's Task Force on Comml. Cts., 1995—; chmn. Chief Judge's Commn. on Jury, 2003—. Author, moderator practising law inst. satellite TV program Deposition Strategy and Tactics, 1989; contbr. articles to profl. jours. Fellow N.Y. Bar Found.; mem. ABA, N.Y. State Bar Assn. (chmn. program strategy and tactics in bus. and comml. litigation N.Y.C., Buffalo and Rochester, N.Y., 1990-91, 94, faculty 1992-94), Assn. of Bar of City of N.Y. (com. state cts. superior jurisdiction 1983-87, profl. discipline com. 1987-88, judiciary com. 1988-91, chmn. com. complex civil litigation, comml. and fed. litigation sect., mem. exec. com. 1991—, chair 1996-97), Fed. Bar Coun. (trustee 1998—). Home: 11 Avon Rd Larchmont NY 10538-1420 Office: 1251 Ave of Americas New York NY 10020-1104 Office Phone: 212-835-6075. E-mail: mark.zauderer@piperrudnick.com.

ZAVADA, BARBARA JOHANNA, artist; b. Jena, Thueringen, Germany, June 20, 1938; came to U.S., 1953; d. Paul Egon and Johanna Helene (Kuehlich) Weber; m. Gerhard Manfred Grote, Mar. 6, 1971 (div. Jan. 1975); 1 child, Erika Barbara. Cert., Traphagen Sch. Fashions, N.Y.C., 1960; studied with, Karl Bobeck, Berlin, 1962; Assoc., Rochester (N.Y.) Inst. Tech., 1966; postgrad., Art Students League, N.Y.C., 1970. Painter, Europe and U.S.A., 1960—; fashion designer H & U Schmidt, Berlin, 1961-62, Dave Goldberg, N.Y.C., 1967-71; graphic designer Zavada Assocs., Stamford, Conn., 1974-90; now lectr. on abstract expressionism. One-woman shows include Mus. Art Sci. and Industry, 1974, Bruce Mus., 1976, Conn. Women's Bank, Greenwich, 1985, Stamford (Conn.) Landmark Tower Rotunda, 1985, So. Conn. State U., New Haven, 1990, Edge of Cedars Mus., Blanding, Utah, 1996, 1999, We. Colo. Ctr. Arts, 1998, Zavada Fine Art Studio, Gallery Arroyo Seco, N.Mex., 1998—, State of Utah, Iron Mission State Park, 2000—, pmwgallery.com, —, artprice.com, Saint-Romain-au-Mont-d'Or, France, graphics, Scholarship Fund, Greenwich (Conn.) Acad., 1985—90, lithographs, various Luth. chs., 2002. Vice pres. Ind. German Lang. Sch., Westport, Conn., 1981-83; search and rescue pilot CAP, Rochester, N.Y., 1964-68, N.Y.C., 1969-70. Recipient 1st prize N.Y.C. Fashion Competition, 1960, Faber Birren Color award, Stamford, 1981. Mem. Am. Acad. Women Artists, The Art Ctr. at Fuller Lodge, Friends of Contemporary Art, Mus. N.Mex. Found. Avocations: travel, hiking, skiing, gardening. Home: HC 64 Box 3001 Castle Valley UT 84532-9614 also: 24 Meyers Rd Espanola NM 87532-9609 E-mail: bjzavada@yahoo.com.

ZAVALA, ALBERT, research psychologist; b. Chgo., Mar. 10, 1930; s. Edward and Maria Soledad (Herrejon) Z.; div.; children: Camille, Sally, Elena, Jenifer, Alexis. BA, Willamette U., 1959; MA, Mich. State U., 1961; PhD, Kans. State U., 1966. Prof., head life scis. Carlspan, Buffalo, 1967-73; prof. SUNY, Buffalo, 1968-78; exec. dir. Corp. IV, Cheektowaga, N.Y., 1973-77; dir. projects Inpsych, Cupertino, Calif., 1978-80; sr. rsch. psychologist SRI Internat., Menlo Park, Calif., 1980-85; sr. staff engr. Lockheed Missiles and Space Co., Sunnyvale, Calif., 1985-94; sr. engr. Nova Mgmt. Monterey, Calif., 1994-97; bid mgr. Siemens Info. and Network Comm., Inc., Santa Clara, Calif., 1997-2000; sr. staff engr. Hernandez Engring., Inc., Santa Clara, Calif., 2000—. Author: (with J.J. Paley) Personal Appearance Identification, 1972; contbr. numerous articles to profl. jours. Mem. Erie County (N.Y.) Sheriff's Sci. staff, 1972-78. With U.S. Army, 1955-57. Dunlap fellow, 1964, fellow Greater Kans. City Mental Health Found., 1962-63. Mem. APA, Human Factors Soc., Sigma Xi, Psi Chi, Phi Kappa Phi.

ZAVALIANGOS, ANTONIOS, mechanical engineer, educator; b. Volos, Greece, Mar. 26, 1963; s. Ioannis Zavaliangos and Artemis Samaras; m. Athina Petropulu, Aug. 19, 1989; children: Artemis, Panayiotis. BS in Mech. Engring., Nat. Tech. U. of Athens, 1980—86; MS in Engring., Columbia U., N.Y.C., 1986—87; PhD in Mech. Engring., MIT, Cambridge, Mass., 1987—92. Mem. rsch. faculty, dept. materials engring. Drexel U., Phila., 1992—94, asst. prof., 1994—98, assoc. prof., 1998—. Cons. Merck Inc. & Co., Blue Bell, Pa., Komareck Rsch., Ala. Contbr. articles to profl. jours. Recipient Career Award, NSF, 1996. Mem.: SOR, TMS, ASM, ASME. Office: Drexel Univ Dept Materials Sci & Engring 32nd & Chestnut Sts Philadelphia PA 19010 Business E-Mail: azavalia@coe.drexel.edu.

ZAVON, MITCHELL RALPH, occupational medicine physician; b. N.Y.C., May 9, 1923; s. Irving and Claire (Gutterman) Z.; m. Betty Berthold, June 24, 1976; children by previous marriage: Peter, Dan, Juliet, Barbara. Student, Cornell U., 1940-43, Harvard U., 1943-44; MD, Boston U., 1949; postgrad., Duke U., 1951-52, U. Cin., 1956-58. Diplomate Am. Bd. Med. Examiners, Am. Bd. Preventive Medicine, Am. Bd. Indsl. Hygiene. Intern Wilson Meml. Hosp., Johnson City, N.Y., 1949-50; surgeon USPHS, Washington, 1950-56; from instr. to asst. clin. prof. U. Cin., 1952-74, from asst. prof. to clin. prof. indsl. medicine, 1956-71; asst. health commr. Cin. Health Dept., 1956-74; med. dir. Ethyl Corp., Baton Rouge, 1974-76; dir. health Occidental Chem. Corp., Niagara Falls, N.Y., 1976-86; pres., med. dir. Agatha Corp., Sarasota, Fla., 1968—. Mem., cons., del. Threshold Limits Com., 1962-87; mem., cons. Biol. Indeces Com., 1982-96; pres. Place-to-Be, 1978-83; mem. cons. staff Mt. St. Mary's Hosp., 1980-94; med. dir. Buffalo Union Occupl. Health Ctr., 1996-98; mem. sci. adv. bd. Internat. Joint Commn. (U.S./Can.), 1977-80; pres. Am. Assn. Poison Control Ctrs., 1962-64. Contbr. articles to profl. jours. Bd. dirs. HART; mem. Cincinnatus Assocs., 1969-77; mem. Niagara County (N.Y.) Bd. Health, 1994-00, pres., 1997. Fellow APHA, Am. Coll. Occupl. and Environ. Medicine, Am. Indsl. Hygiene Assn.; mem. AMA, AAAS, N.Y. State Med. Soc., Niagara County Med. Soc., Am. Conf. Govtl. Indsl. Hygienists. Unitarian Universalist. Home and Office: 4559 Trails Dr Sarasota FL 34232-3450 Office Phone: 941-378-7015. Personal E-mail: zavonm@cs.com.

ZAWACKI, BRUCE EDWIN, surgeon, educator, ethicist; b. Northampton, Mass., Dec. 6, 1935; BS, Coll. of Holy Cross, 1957; MD, Harvard U., 1961; MA, U. So. Calif., 1986. Diplomate Am. Bd. Surgery. Intern in surgery Mass. Gen. Hosp., 1961—62, resident in surgery, 1962—65; vis. scholar in trauma surgery Birmingham Accident Hosp., Birmingham, England, 1966; resident in surgery Mass. Gen. Hosp., 1967; gen. surgeon So. Calif. Permanente Med. Group, Panorama City, 1969-71; dir. burn ctr. L.A. County and U. So. Calif. Med. Ctr., L.A., 1971-98; assoc. prof. surgery U. So. Calif. Sch. Medicine, L.A., 1975-98, assoc. prof. emeritus, 1998—; assoc. prof. religion U. So. Calif. Sch. Religion, L.A., 1992-98; assoc. for edn. Pacific Ctr. for Health Policy and Ethics, 1997—; adj. assoc. prof. religion U. So. Calif., 2001—02. Contbr. articles to profl. jours. Served to maj. U.S. Army, 1967-68. Mem. Am. Burn Assn. (2d v.p., bd. trustees 1992-93; Harvey Stuart Allen Disting. Svc. award 1996), Am. Soc. Bioethics and Humanities, L.A. Surg. Soc., Internat. Soc. for Burn Injuries. Achievements include first to describe the natural history of reversible burn injury, the independence of burn hypermetabolism from evaporative water loss and an autonomous role for burn patients without precedent for survival.

ZAWADA, EDWARD THADDEUS, JR., physician, educator; b. Chgo., Oct. 3, 1947; s. Edward Thaddeus and Evelyn Mary (Kovarek) Z.; m. Nancy Ann Stephen, Mar. 26, 1977; children: Elizabeth, Nicholas, Victoria, Alexandra. BS summa cum laude, Loyola U., Chgo., 1969; MD summa cum laude, Loyola-Stritch Sch. Medicine, 1973. Diplomate Am. Bd. Internal Medicine, Am. Bd. Nephrology, Am. Bd. Nutrition, Am. Bd. Critical Care, Am. Bd. Geriatrics, Am. Bd. Clin. Pharm., Am. Bd. Forensic Examiners, Am. Bd. Forensic Medicine; specialist Hypertension, Am. Soc. Hypertension. Intern UCLA Hosp., 1973, resident, 1974-76; asst. prof. medicine UCLA, 1978-79, U. Utah, Salt Lake City, 1979-81; assoc. prof. medicine Med. Coll. Va., Richmond, 1981-83; assoc. prof. medicine, physiology & pharmacology U. S.D. Sch. Medicine, Sioux Falls, 1983-86, Freeman prof., chmn. dept. Internal Medicine, 1987—2002, prof. emeritus, 2002—, chief div. nephrology and hypertension, 1983-88, pres. univ. physician's practice plan, 1992—95; v.p. sci. affairs, dir. dialysis, critical care Avera Health Sys., 2002—, dir. e-icu, 2002—. Chief renal sect. Salt Lake VA Med. Ctr., 1980-81; asst. chief med. service McGuire VA Med. Ctr., Richmond, 1981-83. Editor: Geriatric Nephrology and Urology, 1984; contbr. articles to profl. publs. Pres. Minnehaha div. Am. Heart Assn., 1984-87, pres. Dakota affiliate Am. Heart Assn., 1989-91. VA Hosp. System grantee, 1981-85, 85-88; Health and Human Svcs. grantee Pub. Health Scvs. Rsch. Adminstrn. Bureau Health Profl., 1993—. Fellow ACP, Am. Coll. Chest Physicians, Am. Coll. Nutrition, Am. Coll. Clin. Pharmacology, Internat. Coll. Angiology, Am. Coll. Angiology, Am. Coll. Clin. Pharmacology, Am. Coll. Forensic Examiners, Royal Soc. Medicine, Soc. for Vascular Medicine and Biology; mem. Internat. Soc. Nephrology, Am. Soc. Nephrology, Am. Soc. Pharmacology and Exptl. Therapeutics, Am. Physiol. Soc., Am. Inst. Nutrition, Am. Soc. Clin. Nutrition, Am. Geriatric Soc., Am. Soc. Transplant Physicians, Westward Ho Country Club. Democrat. Roman Catholic. Avocations: golf, tennis, skiing, cinema, music. Home: 2908 S Duchess Ave Sioux Falls SD 57103 4826 Office: North Ctrl Kidney Inst 911 E 20th St Ste 601 Sioux Falls SD 57105 Office Phone: 605 322-5800. Business E-Mail: edward.zawada@mckennan.org.

ZAWAIDEH, SAMER K. orthodontist; b. Amman, Jordan, June 23, 1967; s. Kamel Michael Zawaideh and Violette M. Baqae'en; m. Salma Al-Nims, 2002. BDS, U. Jordan, Amman, 1989; DMSc, Harvard U., 1997. Tchg. and rsch. asst. orthodontic dept. U. Jordan, 1989-93; acting dir. postdoctoral orthodontic program dept. growth and devel. Harvard U. Sch. Dental Medicine, Boston, 1997-98, dir. postdoctoral orthodontics, 1998—2000, dir. grad. orthodontics dept. growth and devel., 2000—; orthodontist Harvard Dental Ctr., 1997—. Editl. advisor Orthodontic Products Mag., 1999—. Author articles, abstracts in field. Recipient Coenraad Moorrees award, Harvard Soc., 1997; scholar, Fulbright Found., 1993—95, U. Jordan, 1995—97. Mem.: ADA, NE Soc. Orthodontists, Connective Tissue Oncology Soc., Jordan Dental Assn., Am. Assn. Orthodontists, Harvard Soc. Advancement of Orthodontics. Avocations: cooking, swimming, travel. Office: Harvard Sch Dental Medicine Dept Growth and Devel 188 Longwood Ave Boston MA 02115-5819 Home: 166 Woodside Ave West Harrison NY 10604-2021 E-mail: samerzawaideh@post.harvard.edu.

ZAWISTOWSKI, STEPHEN LOUIS, psychologist, educator; b. Lackawanna, N.Y., July 28, 1955; s. Louis Henry and Alice Theresa (Bartus) Z.; m. Jane Elaine Clark, May 26, 1979; 1 child, Matthew. BA, Canisius Coll., 1977; AM, U. Ill., 1979, PhD, 1983. Cert. tech. animal rescue specialist, Am. Humane Assn./Rescue 3. Vis. asst. prof. Ind. U., Bloomington, 1983-84, postdoctoral fellow, 1984-85; asst. prof. St. John's U., N.Y.C., 1985-88; sr. v.p. ASPCA, N.Y.C., 1988—. Mem. com rev. Smithsonian Instn. Nat. Zoo NRC, 2003—04; adj. prof. U. Ill. Vet. Coll., 2004. Author: Animal Shelter Medicine for Veterinarians and Staff, 2004, co-editor, 2004; co-author: Animal Rights Handbook, 1990; editor Animal Behavior Cons. Newsletter; co-editor: For Kids Who Love Animals, 1991; contbg. editor Animal Watch Mag.; co-exec. prodr. (film) Question of Respect, 1990 (Silver Apple award 1990); writer, host ASPCA pet check segments, PBS; mem. bd. editors Psychologists for the Ethical Treatment of Animals, 1988-95; founding co-editor Jour. Applied Animal Welfare Sci.; contbg. editor, sci. advisor Animaland Mag., 1998-2000; script cons. Animal Rescue Kid, 1997; contbr. articles to profl. jours. Scoutmaster Boy Scouts Am., S.I., 1988-98; asst. coach S.I. Youth Soccer, 1986-95; bd. dirs. Nat. Coun. on Pet Population Study and Policy, v.p., 1995-96, 99-2000, pres., 1996-97, advisor, 2004—; mem. steering com. N.Y. State Watchable Wildlife Program; mem. Nat. Humane Dog Tng. Task Force; bd. dirs. United for Wildlife, 1999-2001, Harmony Inst. Cmty. Adv. Bd.; mem. sci. adv. com. Humane Farm Animal Care, 2003—. Recipient Stan Lesny scholarship Kosciuszki Found., 1977, U. Ill. Grad. fellowship, 1977, Postdoctoral fellowship NSF, 1984, Patrick Daley award for contbns. to edn. St. John's U.; named Psychologist of Yr., Psychologists for Ethical Treatment of Animals, 1989. Mem. NAS (nat. rsch. coun. panel for rev. of the nat. zoo), World Soc. for Protection of Animals (sci. adv. panel 2003—), Animal Behavior Soc. (cert. applied animal behaviorist, chmn. bd. profl. cert. 1998—, devel. com. 1995-98, animal welfare com. 1989-95), Assn. for Contraception of Cats and Dogs, Order of Arrow (mem. exec. bd. 1996-98), Sigma Xi. Achievements include research in genetics and animal learning, animal behavior and welfare. Office: ASPCA 424 E 92nd St New York NY 10128-6804 Office Phone: 212-876-7700 x4401.

ZAX, LEONARD A. lawyer; b. Paterson, N.J., July 16, 1950; s. Harry and Shirley Jeanne (Hollander) Z.; m. Helen Kemp, May 25, 1980; children: David Hollander, Laura Alexandra. BA, U. Chgo., 1971; M of City Planning, JD, Harvard U., 1975. Bar: N.J. 1978, D.C. 1978. Spl. asst. to gen. counsel HUD, 1975-76, spl. asst. to sec., 1976-77; lectr., mem. faculty Harvard U., Cambridge, Mass., 1977-78; assoc. Fried, Frank, Harris, Shriver & Kampelman, Washington, 1977-82, ptnr., 1982-95, Latham & Watkins, Washington, 1995—, also chmn. real estate group. Co-chmn. Mayor's Downtown Housing Commn., Washington, 1986-89, D.C. Enterprise Zones Study Commn., 1986-89; D.C. Downtown Interactive Retail Task Force, 1996-98; co-chmn. Washington adv. com. Asian Real Estate Assn., Washington, 1991-92. Contbg. author Nat. Law Jour., N.Y. Times, L.A. Times, Harvard Law Bull., Real Estate Fin. Jour., Urban Land, Washington Business Jour., Washington Post; editor: Real Estate and the RTC: A Guide to Asset Purchases and Contracting, Urban Land Inst., 1990. Trustee Nat. Bldg. Mus., D.C. Preservation League, 1988-95; mem. Fannie Mae Nat. Adv. Coun., 1994-95; mem. vis. com. Harvard Design Sch., 2000—. Mem. ABA (chmn. com. on housing and urban devel. law 1986-89, steering com. representation of the Homeless Project 1988-91, governing bd. forum com. affordable housing and community devel. 1991-94), D.C. Bar Assn., Urban Land Inst., Nat. Multi Housing Coun. Home: 4511 28th St NW Washington DC 20008-1035 Office: Latham & Watkins 555 11thSt NW Ste 1000 Washington DC 20004-1304

ZAX, MELVIN, psychologist, educator; b. Cambridge, Mass., Apr. 14, 1928; s. Joseph and Sadie (Kirshner) Z.; m. Ruth Leah Vogel, Apr. 23, 1977; children: Jeffrey S., David B., Jonathan B. AB, Boston U., 1951, A.M., 1952; PhD, U. Tenn., 1955. Clin. psychologist U. Tenn., Knoxville, 1955-56; staff psychologist St. Elizabeths Hosp., Washington, 1956-57; asst. prof. psychology U. Rochester, N.Y., 1957-62, assoc. prof. psychology, 1962-67, prof., 1967-93, prof. emeritus, 1993—; pvt. practice, 1973—. Chmn. exptl. and spl. tng. rev. com. NIMH, 1970-71. Author: (with G. Stricker) Patterns of Psychopathology, 1963, (with E.L. Cowen) Abnormal Psychology: Changing Conceptions, 1972, (with G.A. Specter) An Introduction to Community Psychology, 1974, (with M. Nichols) Catharsis in Psychotherapy, 1977; editor: (with Stricker) The Study of Abnormal Behavior: Selected Readings, 1964, (with Cowen and E.A. Gardner) Emergent Approaches to Mental Health Problems, 1967, (with D. Dorr and J. Bonner) The Psychology of Discipline, 1983; adv. editor Jour. Cons. and Clin. Psychology, 1965-81; contbr. articles to profl. jours. Served with AUS, 1946-47. NIMH spl. research fellow Psykologisk Inst., Copenhagen, 1966-67 Fellow Am. Psychol. Assn.; mem. Eastern Psychol. Assn., AAUP, Phi Beta Kappa, Sigma Xi, Phi Kappa Phi. Home: 27 Sky Ridge Dr Rochester NY 14625-2167 Office: 625 Panorama Trl Bldg 2 Rochester NY 14625-2432 Office Phone: 585-385-6370.

ZAYAS, ELINOR ABRAMS, music educator; b. Bay Shore, N.Y., Feb. 25, 1954; d. Alfred and Rosaline Abrams; m. Robert Zayas, Jr., June 12, 1983; 1 child, Alison Rose. MusB, Manhattan Sch. Music, 1976, MusM, 1978; advanced cert. in sch. dist. adminstrn., SUNY, Stony Brook, 2003. Freelance musician, N.Y.C., 1978—85; music faculty Guitar Study Ctr., N.Y.C., 1981—83; musical dir. Gateway Playhouse, Bellport, NY, 1991—99; prof. music Five Towns Coll., Dix Hills, NY, 1994—96; adj. instr. Hofstra U., Hempstead, NY, 1996—98; music tchr. Massapequa (N.Y.) Pub. Schs., 1997—99, Sachem Ctrl. Sch. Dist., Holbrook, NY, 1999—. Artistic dir., pianist Nepenthe Chamber Ensemble, Brightwaters, NY, 1986—. Prodr.: (CD rec.) Nepenthe Chamber Ensemble, 1999. Campaign vol. Re-election Rep. Steve Israel, Hauppauge, NY, 2003; bd. mem. B'Nai Israel Reform Temple Sisterhood, Oakdale, NY, 1998. Mem.: Suffolk County Music Educators Assn., Phi Delta Kappa. Avocations: sailing, attending concerts and museums, reading, travel. Home: 480 Ackerson Blvd Brightwaters NY 11718

ZAYAS-BAZAN, EDUARDO, foreign language educator; b. Camagüey, Cuba, Nov. 17, 1935; came to U.S., 1962, naturalized, 1969; s. Manuel Eduardo and Aida Modesta (Loret de Mola); children: Eduardo, Elena María. Dr. en Derecho, U. Nacional José Martí, 1958; MS, Kans. State Tchrs.' Coll., 1966. Social worker Cuban Refugee Asst. Program, 1962-64; Spanish tchr. Plattsmouth High Sch., 1964-65, Topeka West High Sch., 1965-66; Spanish instr. Appalachian State U., 1966-68; asst. prof. East Tenn. State U., Johnson City, 1968-73, assoc. prof. 1973 79, prof., 1979-99, chmn. fgn. lang. dept., 1973-93, prof. emeritus, 1999—. Author (with P. Ferreiro): Cómo dominar la redacción, 1989; author: (with G. Fernández de la Torriente) Cómo aumentar su vocabulario 3; author: Cómo escribir cartas eficaces, 1989; author: (with N.A. Humbach and José B. Fernández) Nuestro mundo, 1990; author: (with José Fernández) iArriba!, 1993, 1997; author: (with Carolyn M. Novak) No se equivoque con el inglés, 1993; author: El inglés que usted no sabe que sabe, Primera y Segunda Serie, 1993; author: (with Susan Bacon and Dulce García) Conexiones, 1999; author: (with Susan Bacon and Dulce García), 2002; editor (with Anthony G. Lozano): Del amor a la revolución, 1975; editor: (with L. Suárez) De aquí y de allá, 1980; editor: (with G. J. Fernández) Así somos, 1983; translator: Secret Report on Cuban Revolution, 1981; author (with Susan Bacon): iArriba!, 2001, 2004. Pres. Sister Cities Internat., Johnson City, 1971-76. Recipient Disting. Faculty award E. Tenn. State U., 1978 Mem.: Cuban Cultural Heritage Assn. (bd. dirs. 2000—02, sec. 2003—), Nat. Assn. Cuban-Am. Educators (pres. 1991—93, chair bd. dirs. 1994—2002, pres. 2002—), Tenn. Fgn. Lang. Teaching Assn. (pres. 1980, Jacqueline Elliott award 1989), Am. Assn. Tchrs. Spanish and Portuguese (pres. 1985, assoc. editor Hispania 1994—98), Am. Coun. Tchrs. Fgn. Langs., Municipality of Camagüey in Exile (editor El Camagüeyano Libre 2002—, pres. 2000—02), Sigma Delta Pi (Premio Martel 1984). Home: 7540 SW 52 Ct Miami FL 33143

ZAYDON, JEMILLE ANN, language educator, communications educator; b. Peckville, Pa., Feb. 21; d. Joseph and Catherine Ann (Hazzouri) Zaydon. Student, Barry Coll. for Women; BS, Marywood U.; MS in Edn., Wilkes U.; doctoral candidate, Temple U. Tchr. St. Hugh Elem. Sch., Coconut Grove, Fla., Allapattah Elem. Sch., Miami, Columbus Elem. Sch., Westfield, N.J.; comm. instr. Keystone Job Corps, Drums, Pa.; vol. instr. Keystone Rehab. Ctr., Scranton, Pa.; curriculum cons. for mentally retarded Vienna; prof. English and reading Lackawanna Jr. Coll., Scranton, head dept. English, speech and reading, chmn. dept. arts, humanities and social studies; assoc. prof. Marywood U., Wilkes U. Adj. prof. English U. Scranton, comm. instr. Lackawanna County Vocat. Tech. Sch. Editor: Lebanese Am. Jour. Supr. recreation program, Hazleton, Pa.; founder, adviser Keystone Kourier; sec. Fedn. Youth, Willim W. Scranton; coord. annual Christmas for Mentally Retarded Keystone City Residence; supr. students Heart Fund campaign; developer program mentally retarded Allied Svcs. Handicapped Scranton; class rep. Marywood U. Fund Dr.; gen. faculty coord. Am. Cancer Soc.; active ARC, March of Dimes, Heart Fund, Leukemia and United Fund drs., Sickle Cell Anemia Found.; exec. bd. Northeastern Pa. Environ. Coun., co-chmn. pub. edn. and funding; bd. women Lackawanna County Commrs., 2003—; mem. bd. Lackawanna County Commn., 2003—; instr. Confraternity Christian Doctrine; bd. dirs. Michael F. Harrity Meml. Fund. Named Tchr. of the Yr., Tchr. We Will Never Forget, Dade County Allpattah Elem. Students, 1991, N.E. Woman, Scranton Sunday Times, 1993; recipient Faculty Mem. of the Yr. award, Keystone Job Corps, Humanitarian award, Outstanding Educators award, 1992, Educators award, Dade County; Svc. scholar, Barry Coll. Mem.: NEA, Pa. State Edn. Assn., Theta Chi Beta (charter pres.), Sigma Tau Delta, Beta Lambda Tau, Lambda Iota Tau (life). Home: 608 N Main Ave Scranton PA 18504-1870

ZAZZALI, JAMES R. state supreme court associate justice; b. Newark, N.J., June 17, 1937; m. Eileen Fitzsimmons; children: Mara, James Jr., Robert, Courtney, Kevin. BA, JD, Georgetown U. Bar: NJ, NY, DC. Law clk. U.S. Dist. Ct. Judge Lawrence A. Whipple, 1964—65; from asst. prosecutor to chief appellate sect. Essex County Prosecutor's Office, 1965—68; ptnr. Zazzali, Fagella, & Nowak, Newark; atty. gen. State of NJ, 1981—82; gen. counsel NJ Sports and Exposition Authority; assoc. justice NJ Supreme Ct., 2000—. Adj. prof. Seton Hall Law Sch., 1984—; commr. NJ State Commn. of Investigation, 1984—94, chmn., 1990—94; vice-chair Disciplinary Rev Bd., 1984—2000. Democrat. Office: NJ Supreme Court Hughes Justice Complex PO BOX 23 Trenton NJ 08625-0023

ZBAR, LLOYD IRWIN STANLEY, otolaryngologist, educator; b. Jersey City, June 2, 1939; m. Margo Wally, Mar. 25, 1965; children: Ross I.S., Brett I.W. MD, Queen's U., Kingston, Ont., Can., 1964. Cert. in otolaryngology. Intern Beth Israel/Harvard, Boston, 1964; resident in surgery French Hosp., N.Y.C., 1965-66; resident in otolaryngology Bellevue Hosp. Ctr.-NYU, N.Y.C., 1966-69, fellow in otolaryngology, 1969-70; chmn. med. edn. com. Mountainside Hosp., Montclair, N.J., 1979-89, dir. otolaryngology, 1990-97, 99—. Sec. med. bd. Mountainside Hosp., Glen Ridge, N.J., 1986-90, clin. assoc. prof. otolaryngology NYU Sch. Medicine. Contbr. rev. to New Eng. Jour. Medicine, 1988. Mem. exec. bd. Boy Scouts of Am., Essex County, N.J., 1984-95; pres. Mountainside Physicians Scholarship Loan Fund, 1972-85. Fellow ACS, Am. Acad. Otolaryngology-Head and Neck Surgery, Royal Soc. Medicine. Office: 200 Highland Ave Glen Ridge NJ 07028-1528 Office Phone: 973-744-2424. Office Fax: 973-743-3111. Personal E-mail: liszmd@yahoo.com.

ZDANIS, RICHARD ALBERT, academic administrator; b. Balt., July 15, 1935; s. Albert Francis and Elsie (Kral) Z.; m. Barbara Rosenberger, June 5, 1955; children: Michael Richard, Carole Lynn. BA, Johns Hopkins U., 1957, PhD in Physics, 1960. Rsch. assoc. Princeton (N.J.) U., 1960-61, instr., 1961-62; asst. prof., then assoc. prof. Johns Hopkins U., Balt., 1962-69, prof., 1969-88, assoc. provost, 1975-79, v.p. for adminstrv. svcs., 1977-79, vice provost, 1979-88; provost Case Western Res. U., Cleve., 1988-2000, retired, 2000. Cons. Naval Ordnance Lab., 1967-68, 69-74. Bd. dirs. Great Lakes Mus., 1990-, Cleve. Edn. Found., 1990-96; mem. governing coun. Ohio LINK, 1994-2000; mem. Cleve. Initiative for Edn., 1999-2004. Mem.: Associated Univs. Inc. (bd. dirs.), Am. Phys. Soc.

ZDANSKY, JANICE CECELIA, mathematician; b. Corpus Christi, TX, Nov. 22, 1956; d. Anton Frank and Rita Joline (Kocurek) Zdansky; m. Donald Francis Phillipp, June 4, 1983; children: Tara Phillipp, Kindra Phillipp, April Phillipp, Colton Phillipp, Dustin Phillipp. BS math, geology, TX A&M U, Kingsville, Tx, 1978; MS, TX A&M U, Kingsville, TX, 1981; PhD EDCI, TX A&M U, Coll. Sta., TX, 1994—. Asst. prof. U of TX, Brownsville, Tex., 1981—. Com. mem. St. Joseph Acad., Brownsville, Tex., 2002—. Grantee MISP, Dept. of Edn., 1990. Mem.: NCTM. Avocations: camping, fishing, gardening, coaching. Home: 12895 FM 3067 LaFeria TX 78559 Office: Univ of TX 80 Fort Brown Brownsville TX 78520

ZDEBLICK, MARK JAMES, information technology executive; s. William and Mary Zdeblick; m. Melanie C. Smitt; children: Daniel, Grace. Student, U. Paris, No. III, Versailles, France, 1981—82; B of Fine and Applied Arts, Arch., BSCE, U. Ill., 1982; MS Aeronautics and Astronautics, Stanford U., 1984, PhD, 1988. Founder, dir., chief tech. officer Redwood Microsystems, Menlo Park, Calif., 1989—97; consulting prof. Stanford (Calif.) U., 1997—98; pres. Aspire Tech., Portola Valley, Calif., 1998—2000; chief tech. officer optical switch program K2 Optronics, Inc., Sunnyvale, Calif., 2000—01; entrepreneur in residence Spring Ridge Ventures, Atherton, Calif., 2001—02; CEO Vivomems, Inc., Atherton, 2001—02. Contbr. articles to profl. jours. Pres. Ladera Cmty. Assn., 1994—95; judge Santa Cruz County Sci. Fair, 2001, IEEE Sect. 6 for Intel Sci. Fair, 2001; Bd. dirs. Ladera Cmty. Assn., 1992—95; bd dirs. Palo Alto Adult Soccer League, 1990—91. Recipient Commendation for Excellence in Tech. Comms., Laser Focus World, 2001, Trip to Nixon's Inauguration Competition, Park Ridge Newspaper Svc., 1973, Sawyer Cup, Phi Gamma Delta, 1981. Mem.: IEEE, Sensors and Materials Jour. (assoc. editor 1993—2002), Phi Eta Sigma, Tau Beta Pi. Achievements include patents for integrated microminiature electric-to-fluidic valve pressure/flow regulator; method of making an integrated scanning tunneling microscope; microfabricated cantilever stylus with integrated conical tip; microfabricated microscope assembly; integrated variable focal length lens and its application; microfabricated cantilever stylus with integrated pyramidal tip; integrated scanning tunneling microscope; integrated mass storage device. Avocations: soccer, hiking, travel, swimming. Home: 300 La Mesa Dr Menlo Park CA 94028 Office: Vivomems, Inc 3351 El Camino Real Menlo Park CA 94027 Personal E-mail: mark.zdeblick@stanfordalumni.org. Business E-Mail: mzdeblick@stvc.com.

ZEARFOSS, HERBERT KEYSER, retired lawyer; b. Montandon, Pa., Oct. 13, 1929; s. Dean Wilson and Susan Lesher (Keyser) Z.; m. Thelma Mary McCarthy, Dec. 19, 1953 (dec. 1984); children: Timothy McCarthy, Jonathan Andrew, Sarah Creighton; m. Suzanne VanderVeer, Nov. 14, 1992. AB, Bucknell U., 1951; postgrad., Yale U., 1951-53; JD, Am. U., 1958. Bar: Pa. 1959, U.S. Dist. Ct. (mid. dist.) Pa. 1959, U.S. Dist. Ct. (ea. dist.) Pa. 1975, U.S. Supreme Ct. 1975. Ptnr. Fetter & Zearfoss, Lewisburg, Pa., 1959-60; asst. counsel Fidelity Mut. Life Ins. Co., Phila., 1960-67, sr. v.p., gen. counsel, 1978-82; sec., mgr. Ins. Fedn. of Pa. Inc., 1967-68; ptnr. Zearfoss & Campbell, 1968-78; sr. v.p., sec., gen. counsel Provident Indemnity Life Ins. Co. and parent co. Provident Am. Corp., Norristown, Pa., 1982-87; sole practice Radnor, Pa., 1987-91; adj. faculty Cabrini Coll., 1988-90; asst. gen. counsel, asst. sec. Teleflex Inc., Limerick, Pa., 1991-2001. Author: The Life Insurance Law of Pennsylvania, 1983; book rev. editor Am. U. Law Rev., 1956-58. Rep. Pa. Gen. Assembly from 167th dist., 1968-78; justice of the Peace, Radnor Twp., Delaware County, Pa., 1966-67; v.p. Valley Forge coun. Boy Scouts Am., 1982-86; treas. Netherlands-Am. Amity Trust, Inc., 1981-86, Civil War and Underground R.R. Mus. Phila., 2003—; bd. dirs. Am. Revolution Patriots Fund, 2002—. Lt. comdr. USNR, 1954-58. Decorated officer Order of Orange-Nassau (Netherlands); recipient Silver Beaver award Boy Scouts Am., 1989. Mem. ABA, Pa. Bar Assn., Assn. Life Ins. Counsel, Netherlands Soc. Phila. (pres. 1979-83), SAR (pres. Phila. Continental chpt. 1986-87), Colonial Soc. Pa. (gov. 1988-91), Del. Soc. Cin. (pres. 1996-99), Soc. Colonial Wars in the Commonwealth of Pa. (gov. 2004—), Pa. Geneal. Soc. (counsel 1987-91, pres. 1995—), Soc. War 1812 (pres. gen. 1996-99), Mil. Order Loyal Legion U.S. (comdr., Pa. comdr. 1999-2001, judge adv.-in-chief 2001—), Sovereign Mil. Order Temple Jerusalem (grand officer), Priory of Phila. (prior 1994-98), Yale Club Phila., Phila. Club, Penn Club, Merion Cricket Club, Omicron Delta Kappa, Phi Alpha Delta, Phi Alpha Theta, Tau Kappa Alpha, Pi Sigma Alpha. Republican. Presbyterian. Home: 532 Candace Ln Villanova PA 19085-1702 Personal E-mail: hzcarfoss@aol.com.

ZEBROSKI, EDWIN LEOPOLD, risk management consultant; b. Chgo., Apr. 1, 1921; s. Peter Paul and Sophie (Rydz) Z.; m. Gisela Karin Rudolph, Sept. 6, 1969; children: Lars, Zoe, Susan, Peggy. BS, U. Chgo., 1941; PhD, U. Calif., Berkeley, 1947. Registered prof. engr., Calif. Project engr. Gen. Electric Co., Schenectady, N.Y., 1947-53, mgr. devel. engring. San Jose, Calif., 1958-73; mgr. engring. SRI Internat., Menlo Park, Calif., 1954-58, dir. systems and materials dept., 1974-79; dir. nuclear safety analysis ctr. EPRI, Palo Alto, Calif., 1979-81; v.p. engring. INPO, Atlanta, 1981-83; chief nuclear scientist EPRI, 1982—88; dir. risk mgmt. svcs. APTECH Engring. Svcs., Sunnyvale, Calif., 1988-97; safety and risk mgmt. advisor DOE-Sandia Nat. Lab., 2000—. Vis. prof. Purdue U., West Lafayette, Ind., 1977-78; cons. OTA, Washington, 1980, 82-83, Dept. Energy, Washington, 1985-90, panels Nat. Rsch. Coun., 1990—, Electricite de France, 1986-87, Dept. Interior, Washington, 1987-89, EPRI, Palo Alto, 1988-98, Acad. Sci., USSR, 1987, Karlsruhe Lab., Germany, 1988; mem. commn. engring. edn. NRC, Washington, 1970-73; mem. NAS-NRC Panel on Decision-Making in Govt. Agy., 1997-98; mem. NAS-NRC Panel on High Level Waste R&D, 2001; mem. NAE Panel on Countering Terrorism, 2002—03. Contbr. chpts. to books, numerous articles to profl. jours.; patentee in field. Bd. dirs. Unitarian Ch., Palo Alto, 2004—, Stevenson House, Palo Alto, 2003—. Recipient Charles A. Coffin award Gen. Electric Co., Schenectady, 1954, Edward Teller award, 2002. Fellow AAAS, Am. Nuclear Soc. (bd. exec. com. 1969-71), Am. Inst. Chemists; mem. NAE (chmn. energy com. 1984-86, chmn. mem. com. 1986-87, policy com. 1995-96), Am. Phys. Soc., Soc. for Risk Analysis. Avocations: safety and risk management, public sector decision processes, music, writing. Office: ELGIS Consulting 1546 Plateau Ave Los Altos CA 94024-5320 E-mail: edzeb@sbcglobal.net.

ZEBROWITZ, LESLIE ANN, psychology educator; b. Detroit, Nov. 8, 1944; d. Aaron Harry and Esther (Milgrom) Z.; m. A. Verne McArthur (div. July 1988); children: Caleb Jonathan McArthur, Loren Zachary McArthur. BA, U. Wis., 1966; MS, Yale U., 1968, PhD, 1970. Asst. prof. psychology Brandeis U., Waltham, Mass., 1970-76, assoc. prof., 1976-82, prof., 1982—, chmn. dept., 1986-91, Manuel Yellen prof. social rels., 1989—. Vis. scholar Henry Murray Rsch. Ctr. Radcliffe Coll., Cambridge, Mass., 1991-92, vis Erskine fellow, U. Canterbury, 1996; program dir. social psychology, NSF, Arlington, Va., 1994-95. Author: Social Perception, 1991, Reading Faces, 1997; editor: (with Gillian Rhodes) Facial Attractiveness, 2003; contbr. numerous articles to sci. jours. Ford. Found. faculty fellow, 1973-74; rsch. grantee NIMH, 1975-81, 87-97, NSF, 1997-2002. Fellow Am. Psychol. Assn., Am. Psychol. Soc. (charter), Soc. for Exptl. Social Psychology, Ea. Psychol. Assn., Phi Beta Kappa. Office: Brandeis U Dept Of Psychology Waltham MA 02454

ZECH, RONALD H. financial services executive; BSEE, Valparaiso, 1965; MBA, Wis. U., 1965. V.p., gen. mgr. First Nat. Bank of Chgo., San Francisco, 1996—; v.p. fin. GATX Capital Corp., 1977, pres., CEO, 1984-94. Office: GATX Corp 500 W Monroe St Chicago IL 60661

ZECHMAN, EDWIN KERPER, JR., medical facility administrator; b. Harrisburg, Pa., Jan. 22, 1948; married. BA, MA, Shippensburg U., 1970; M Health Adminstrn., Ohio State U., 1974. Asst. adminstr. Children's Hosp. Med. Ctr., Akron, Ohio, 1974-78, assoc. adminstr., 1978-80; exec. dir. Children's Hosp., New Orleans, 1980-81, Children's Hosp. of Ala., birmingham, 1981-85; pres. Children's Hosp., Pitts., 1985-94; pres., CEO Children's Nat. Med. Ctr., Washington, 1994—. Recipient various cmty. svc. awards. Mem. AMA, Am. Hosp. Assn., Am. Coll. Healthcare Execs. Office: Children's Nat Med Ctr 111 Michigan Ave NW Washington DC 20010-2916

ZECKHAUSER, RICHARD JAY, economist, educator; b. Phila., Nov. 1, 1940; s. Julius Nathaniel and Estelle (Borgenicht) Z.; m. Nancy Mackell Hoover, Sept. 9, 1967; children: Bryn Gordon, Benjamin Rennell. AB, Harvard U., 1962, PhD, 1969. Jr. fellow Soc. Fellows Harvard U., 1965-68, mem. faculty, 1968—, prof. polit. econ. Kennedy Sch., 1972—, now Frank P. Ramsey prof. polit. economy. Bd. dirs. Comm. Group Ins., Mass., Digi-Block, Inc.; founder, bd. dirs. Niederhoffer, Cross & Zeckhauser, 1968—84. Co-author: A Primer for Policy Analysis, 1978, Demographic Dimensions of the New Republic, 1981, The Early Admissions Game: Joining the Elite, 2003; editor or co-editor Benefit-Cost and Policy Analysis, 1974, What Role for Government, 1982, Principals and Agents: The Structure of Business, 1985, Am. Soc. Pub. and Pvt. Responsibilities, 1986, Privatization and State-Owned Enterprise: Lessons from the United Kingdom, Canada and the United States, 1988, Strategy and Choice, 1991, Wise Choices, Games, Decisions, and Negotiations, 1996; contbr. more than 200 articles to profl. jours. and books; rsch. on fin., coll. admissions and healthcare. Bd. dirs. Commonwealth Sch. Fellow Econometric Soc., Assn. for Pub. Policy and Mgmt., Am. Acad. Arts and Scis, Inst. of Medicine/Nat. Acad. Scis. Achievements include winning numerous regional and nat. contract bridge competitions (finalist World Pairs

Championship 1998, 2d pl. U.S. Mixed-Teams Championship 2003, 3d pl. U.S. Open Pairs Championship 2004). Office: Harvard U John F Kennedy Sch Govt 79 JFK St Cambridge MA 02138-5801

ZEDILLO PONCE DE LEON, ERNESTO, former president of Mexico; b. Mexico City, Apr. 27, 1951; s. Rodolfo Zedillo Castillo and Martha Alicia Ponce de Leon; m. Nilda Patricia Velasco Nuñez; children: Ernesto, Emiliano, Carlos, Nild Patricia, Rodrigo. Student, Instituto Politécnico Nacional, Bradford U., U. Colo.; MA, Yale U., 1977, PhD, 1981, LLD (hon.), 2001. With Partido Revolucionario Institucional, 1971—, Instituto de Estudios Políticos, Económicos y Sociales; econ. rschr. Dirreción Gen. de Programación Económica y Social; lectr. Colegio de Mex., 1978-80; dep. mgr. finance and econ. rsch., advisor to bd. dirs. Banco de Mex.; dep. sec. for planning and budget Govt. Mex., Mexico City, 1985-88, sec. for planning and budget, 1988-92, sec. public edn., 1992-93; campaign mgr. presdl. nominee Luis Donald Colosio Partido Revolucionario Institucional, 1993-94; pres. Govt. Mex., Mexico City, 1994—2000; chair, high level panel financing for devel. UN; prof., internat. economics, politics Yale U.; dir. Yale Ctr. Study of Globalization, 2002—. Recipient Wilbur Cross Medal, Yale U., 2001. Office: Yale U Ctr Study of Globalization Betts Hall New Haven CT 06520

ZEDLER, JOY BUSWELL, ecological sciences educator; b. Sioux Falls, S.D., Oct. 15, 1943; d. Francis H. and Charlotte (Johnson) Buswell; m. Paul H. Zedler, June 26, 1965; children: Emily and Sarah (twins). BS, Augustana Coll., 1964; MS, U. Wis., 1966, PhD, 1968. Instr. U. Mo., Columbia, 1968-69; prof. San Diego State U., 1969-97; Aldo Leopold prof. restoration ecology, arboretum, botany U. Wis., Madison, 1998—. Mem. Nat. Wetland Tech. Com., Water Sci. Tech. Bd. Nat. Rsch. Coun., 1991-94; dir. Pacific Estuarine Rsch. Lab., 1985—, Coastal and Marine Inst., 1991-93; gov. bd. The Nature Conservancy, 1995—; trustee Environ. Def. Fund, 1998—. Author: Ecology of Southern California Coastal Wetlands, 1982, Salt Marsh Restoration, 1984; co-author: A Manual for Assessing Natural and Restored Wetlands, 1990, Ecology of Tijuana Estuary, 1992, Tidal Wetland Restoration, 1996; editor: Handbook for Restoring Tidal Wetlands, 2000. Fellow San Diego Natural History Mus.; mem. Ecol. Soc. Am. (mem. pub. affairs com. 1988-90), Soc. Wetlands Scientists, Soc. Ecol. Restoration. Achievements include pioneering studies of impacts of freshwater inflows to coastal wetlands in southwestern U.S. and Australia; contributions to understanding of coastal wetland functioning; development of methods for improving restoration projects in wetlands; identification of shortcomings of wetland restoration projects; role of diversity in the function restored ecosystems, improving the science of restoration ecology. Office: U Wis Botany Dept Madison WI 53706

ZEDROSSER, JOSEPH JOHN, lawyer; b. Milw., Jan. 24, 1938; s. Joseph and Rose (Zollner) Z.; m. Antonina Krass, Sept. 6, 1997. AB, Marquette U., 1959; LLB, Harvard U., 1963. Bar: N.Y. 1964, U.S. Dist. Ct. (so. dist.) N.Y. 1966, U.S. Dist. Ct. (ea. dist.) N.Y. 1971, U.S. Ct. Appeals (2d cir.) 1971, U.S. Ct. Appeals (D.C. Cir.) 1975, U.S. Supreme Ct. 1975. Assoc. William G. Mulligan, N.Y.C., 1964-67, Christy, Bauman, Frey and Christy and successors, N.Y.C., 1967-71; dir. cmty. devel. unit Bedford-Stuyvesant Cmty. Legal Svcs. Corp., N.Y.C., 1971-73; assoc. fed. defender svcs. unit Legal Aid Soc., N.Y.C., 1973-74; asst. atty. gen. Environ. Protection Bur., N.Y. State Dept. Law, N.Y.C., 1974-80; regional counsel EPA, N.Y.C., 1980-82; assoc. prof. St. John's U. Sch. Law, N.Y.C., 1982-86; ptnr. Rivkin, Radler, Dunne & Bayh, Uniondale, N.Y., 1986-89, Breed, Abbott & Morgan, N.Y.C., 1989-93, Whitman Breed Abbott & Morgan, N.Y.C., 1993-95; v.p. CPR Inst. for Dispute Resolution, N.Y.C., 1996; sr. investigative counsel com. on investigations, taxation, and gov. ops. N.Y. State Senate, 1998-99; asst. atty. gen. Environ. Protection Bur. N.Y. State Office Atty. Gen., N.Y.C., 1999—. Lectr., contbr. to course handbooks for courses sponsored by Practicing Law Inst. and other assns. Lt. USNR, 1965-74, USAR, 1963-65. Mem. ABA, Assn. of Bar of City of N.Y., N.Y. State Bar Assn., Alpha Sigma Nu. Roman Catholic. Home: 45 E End Ave Apt 11F New York NY 10028-7982

ZEECK, DAVID, newspaper editor; m. Valarie S. Zeeck; children: Phillip, Michael. BJ, U. Mo.; MBA, Rockhurst Coll. Various positions The Kans. City Star, 1974—94; exec. editor The News Tribune, Tacoma, 1994—. Bd. dir. Am. Soc. Newspaper Editors; instr. in field. Presbyn. Office: The News Tribune 1950 South St Tacoma WA 98405 Mailing: PO Box 11000 Tacoma WA 98411 E-mail: david.zeeck@mail.tribnet.com.

ZEFF, OPHELIA HOPE, lawyer; b. Oak Park, Ill., Aug. 19, 1934; d. Bernard Allen and Esther (Levinsohn) Gurvis; m. David Zeff, Dec. 29, 1957 (div. 1983); children: Sally Lyn Zeff Propper, Betsy Zeff Russell, Ellen, Adam; m. John Canterbury Davis, Sept. 18, 1987. BA, Calif. State U., 1956; JD, U. Pacific, 1975. Bar: Calif. 1975. Reporter Placerville (Calif.) Mountain Dem., 1956-57, Salinas Californian, 1957-59; corr. Modesto (Calif.) Bee, 1962-64; atty. ALRB, Sacramento, 1975-76, Yolo County Counsel, Woodland, Calif., 1976-78, Law Office of O.H. Zeff, Woodland, 1978-85; employee rels. officer Yolo County, 1985-87; ptnr. Littler, Mendelson, Fastiff, Tichy & Mathiason, Sacramento, 1987-98, Atkinson, Andelson, Loya, Ruud & Romo, Sacramento, 1998—. Mem. Vallejo (Calif.) Sch. Bd., 1971-74, pres., 1974; mem. Woodland Libr. Bd., 1982; v.p. LWV, Vallejo, 1972; mem. LWV, Sacramento, 1987—. Recipient Am. Jurisprudence Lawyer Coop. Pub., 1974. Mem. Sacramento County Bar, Sacramento Women Lawyers, Indsl. Rels. Assn. No. Calif., Traynor Soc. (life). Democrat. Jewish. Avocations: hiking, skiing, biking, reading, travel. Office: Atkinson Andelson Loya Ruud & Romo 555 Capitol Mall Ste 645 Sacramento CA 95814-4502

ZEFF, STEPHEN ADDAM, accounting educator; b. Chgo., July 26, 1933; s. Roy David and Hazel (Sex) Zeff. BS, U. Colo., 1955, MS, 1957; MBA, U. Mich., 1960, PhD, 1962; D in Econs. honoris causa, Turku Sch. Econs. and Bus. Adminstrn., Finland, 1990. Instr. U. Colo., 1955-57; teaching fellow, instr. U. Mich., 1958-61; asst. prof. acctg. Tulane U., New Orleans, 1961-63, assoc. prof., 1963-67, prof., 1967-77, W.R. Irby prof., 1977-78; prof. acctg. Rice U., 1978-79, Herbert S. Autrey prof., 1979—. Prof. acctg. U. Maastricht, The Netherlands, 1992-95; vis. assoc. prof. U. Calif.-Berkeley, 1964-65, U. Chgo., 1966; vis. prof. Instituto Tecnológico y de Estudios Superiores de Monterrey, Mex., 1969, Victoria U., Wellington, New Zealand, 1976, Harvard U., 1977-78, Northwestern U., 1982, 83, U. Tex.-Austin, 1986, Free U. Amsterdam, 1990, 91, U. Nijenrode, 1994-97; spl. lectr., hon. sr. fulbright scholar Monash U., Australia, 1972. Author: Uses of Accounting for Small Business, 1962, American Accounting Association, Its First 50 Years, 1966, Forging Accounting Principles in Five Countries: A History and an Analysis of Trends, 1972, Forging Accounting Principles in Australia, 1973, Forging Accounting Principles in New Zealand, 1979, Company Financial Reporting: A Historical and Comparative Study of the Dutch Regulatory Process, 1992, Henry Rand Hatfield: Humanist, Scholar and Accounting Educator, 2000; editor: Business Schools and the Challenge of International Business, 1968, Asset Appreciation, Business Income and Price-Level Accounting: 1918-1935, 1976, The Accounting Postulates and Principles Controversy of the 1960s, 1982, The U.S. Accounting Profession in the 1890s and Early 1900s, 1988; co-editor: Essays in Honor of William A. Paton: Pioneer Accounting Theorist, 1979, Sourcebook on Accounting Principles and Auditing Procedures 1917-1953, 1984, Milestones in the British Accounting Literature, 1996, Accounting Reseach, 1948-58, 1996, Readings and Notes on Financial Accounting, 5th edit., 1997; book rev. editor Acctg. Rev., 1962-66, editor, 1977-82; rev. editor Acctg. Horizons, 1995-97, The Internat. Jour. of Acctg., 1997-2003; founder, editor Boletín Interamericano de Contabilidad, 1968-71; contbr. articles to profl. jours. Named to Acctg. Hall of Fame, Ohio State U., 2002; recipient Hourglass award, Acad. Acctg. Historians, 1973, 2001. Mem.: AAUP, Fin. Execs. Internat., Inst. Mgmt. Accts., Am. Econ. Assn., European Acctg. Assn. (exec. com. 1981—2004), Am. Acctg. Assn. (dir. edn. 1969—71, pres. 1985—86, named Outstanding Acctg. Educator 1988, Outstanding Internat. Acctg. Educator 1999), Tex. Soc. CPAs (hon.), Harvard Club of N.Y.C. Home: 4545 Acacia St Bellaire TX 77401-3701 Office: Rice University MS 531 PO Box 2932 Houston TX 77252-2932 E-mail: sazeff@rice.edu.

ZEFFREN, EUGENE, toiletries company executive; b. St. Louis, Nov. 21, 1941; s. Harry Morris and Bess (Dennis) Z.; m. Steccia Leigh Stern, Feb. 2, 1964; children: Maryl Renee, Bradley Cruvant. AB, Washington U., 1963; MS, U. Chgo., 1965, PhD, 1967. Research chemist Procter & Gamble Co., Cin., 1967-75, sect. head, 1975-77, assoc. dir., 1977-79; v.p. R & D, Helene Curtis, Inc., Chgo., 1979-95; pres. Helene Curtis USA, Chgo., 1995-96; sr. v.p. Helene Curtis bus. unit Unilever Home and Personal Care USA, Chgo., 1996-98, exec. v.p., COO hair and deodorant bus. unit, 1998-2000; sr. v.p. brand devel. Unilever Home and Personal Care N.Am., 2000—02; chmn. NFG Stuff, Inc., 2002—. Mem. vis. com. for phys. scis. U. Chgo., 1995—; active Wash. U. Nat. Coun. for Arts and Scis., 1997—; pres. bd. dirs. River North Dance Co., 1998-2000, chmn. 2000—. Co-author: The Study of Enzyme Mechanisms, 1973; contbr. articles to profl. jours.; patentee in field of enzymes and hair care. Bd. dirs. Goodman Theatre, 1999—, Children's Meml. Inst. for Edn. and Rsch., 2002—; trustee Spertus Inst. Jewish Studies, 2002—. Mem. AAAS, Am. Chem. Soc., Soc. Cosmetic Chemists, Cosmetic Toiletry and Fragrance Assn. (sci. adv. com. 1979-95, vice chmn. 1984-88, chmn. 1988-90, bd. dirs. 1996-02), Soap and Detergent Assn. (bd. dirs., exec. com. bd. 2000-02), Indsl. Rsch. Inst., Omicron Delta Kappa. Republican. Jewish. Avocations: tennis, skiing, reading adventure and espionage novels.

ZEGARELLI, EDWARD VICTOR, retired dental educator, researcher; b. Utica, N.Y., Sept. 9, 1912; s. Frank Anthony and Maria Josephine (Ambroselli) Z.; m. Irene Marie Ceconi, June 17, 1939; children: Edward V., David J., Philip E., Peter J. AB, Columbia U., 1934, DDS, 1937, DSc (hon.), 1983; MS, U. Chgo., 1942. Staff Sch. Dental and Oral Surgery, Columbia U., 1937-78, asst. instr., then successively instr., asst. prof., asso. prof., head diagnosis and roentgenology, 1947-58, chmn. com. dental research, 1956-78, Dr. Edwin S. Robinson prof. dentistry, 1958, prof. dentistry, dir. div. stomatology, 1958-78, acting dean, 1973, dean, 1974-78, dean emeritus, 1979—; Edward V. Zegarelli prof. dentistry, 1993—; chmn. sect. hosp. dental services Columbia-Presbyn. Med. Center; dir. and attending dentist dental service Presbyn. Hosp., 1974-79, also mem. exec. com. of med. bd., 1974-76; police surgeon N.Y.C., 1968-89; chmn. exam. com. N.E. Regional Bd. Dental Examiners, 1969-90. Cons. VA, Washington; Weisberger Meml. lectr. Harvard U., 1969, Mershon Meml. lectr., 1970, Ralph L. Spaulding Meml. lectr., 1972; deans com. Montrose VA Hosp.; cons. East Orange, Kingsbridge VA hosps., Westchester Med. Ctr., Valhalla, N.Y., USPHS, Phelps Meml. Hosp., Tarrytown, N.Y., Vassar Bros. Hosp., Poughkeepsie, Bur. Medicine, FDA, Council on Dental Therapeutics; area cons. VA; cons.-lectr. U.S. Naval Dental Sch., Bethesda, Md., 1970-78; pres. N.Y. State Bd. Dental Examiners, 1970-71; chmn. exam. rev. com. N.E. Regional Bd. Dental Examiners, 1969-90; Samuel Charles Miller Meml. lectr., 1976; mem. council deans Am. Assn. Dental Schs., 1973-79; mem. postgrad. edn. com. N.Y.C. Cancer Com.; mem. profl. edn. and grants com. N.Y.C. div. Am. Cancer Soc., 1963-73; chmn. panel on drugs in dentistry NAS, NRC, FDA; mem. N.Y. State Health Research Council, N.Y. Commn. on Health Manpower; chmn. bd. govs. (dental) Gen. Health Ins., N.Y.C. Contbg. author: The Thyroid, Medical Roentgenology, Current Pediatric Therapy, Cancer of Head and Neck; author: (with others) Pharmacotherapeutics of Oral Disease, 1964, Clinical Stomatology, 1966, Diagnosis of Diseases of Mouth and Jaws, 1969, 2d edit., 1978; also articles on mouth, jaw bone disease. Bd. dirs. Hist. Soc. Tarrytowns, 1983, United Way Tarrytowns, 1983, YMCA of Tarrytowns, 1984, Phelps Meml. Hosp. Hospice Agy, 1986. Recipient Austin Sniffen medal 9th Dist. Dental Soc., 1961; Columbia U. Dental Alumni Research award, 1963; Jarvie-Burkhart medal N.Y. Dental Soc., 1970; Samuel J. Miller medal Am. Acad. Oral Medicine, 1976; Henry Spenadel award 1st Dist. Dental Soc., 1979; Man of Yr. award C. of C. Tarrytowns and Irvington, 1983; Man of Achievement award Americans for Italian Migration, 1984; named Disting. Practitioner mem. Nat. Acads. Practice, 1986. Fellow Am. Coll. Dentists (William J. Gies medal 1981), N.Y. Acad. Dentistry, Internat. Coll. Dentists, 9th Dist. Dental Soc.; mem. Am. Acad. Oral Pathology, Am. Assn. for Cancer Edn. (charter), Am. Assn. Dental Examiners (Dentist Citizen of Yr. award 1978), Orgn. Tchrs. Oral Diagnosis, N.Y. Acad. Scis., N.Y. Dental Soc. (chmn. council sci. research 1956-71), Greater N.Y. Acad. Prosthodontics (hon.), Guatemala Dental Soc. (hon.), Am. Dental Assn. (mem. council dental therapeutics 1963-69, vice chmn. 1969), Columbia Dental Alumni Assn., William Jarvie Research Soc., Internat. Assn. Dental Research, AAAS, Nat. Italian-Am. Found., Sigma Xi (chpt. pres. 1974-76), Omicron Kappa Upsilon (sec. treas. Columbia chpt. 1944-57, pres. 1959-60), Sigma Phi Alpha., Knight Malta. Lodges: Rotary (pres. 1985-86) (Tarrytown). Home: 120 Gory Brook Rd Sleepy Hollow NY 10591-1724

ZEGAS, ALAN LEE, lawyer; b. Newark, Oct. 28, 1952; s. Norman and Harriet (Lava) Z.; m. Tina Hannah Burk, Aug. 22, 1976; children: Rachel Sarah, Leah Ariel, Joelle Shira. BS, U. Pa., 1974; MBA, Harvard U., 1978; JD, Rutgers U., 1981. Bar: N.J. 1981, U.S. Dist. Ct. N.J. 1981, N.Y. 1982, U.S. Ct. Appeals (3d cir.) 1982. Law clk. to Hon. H. Lee Sarokin U.S. Dist. Ct. N.J., Newark, 1981-83; assoc. Robinson, Wayne, Levin, Riccio & La Sala, Newark, 1983-84; pvt. practice Chatham, N.J., 1984—. Adj. prof. law Rutgers U., Newark, 1983-88; reader N.J. Bd. Bar Examiners, Trenton, 1985; pres. Assn. Criminal Def. Lawyers N.J., 1998-99. Editor-in-chief Rutgers U. Law Rev., 1980-81; editor (pamphlet) Law Tips for the Elderly, 1983. Mem. N.J. Bar Assn. (dist. rep. young lawyers div. 1983-85, vice chmn. 1985-86, trustee 1986-88, chmn. criminal law sect. 1996-97), Essex County Bar Assn. (chmn. lawyers referral service 1986—), Rutgers U. Law Sch. Alumni Assn. (rep. 1983—), U. Pa. Alumni Assn. (sec. 1986-87), Harvard U. Bus. Sch. Alumni Assn., Assn. Criminal Def. Lawyers of N.J. (pres. 1998-99). Home: 476 South St New Providence NJ 07974-2132 Office: 552 Main St Chatham NJ 07928-2120

ZEGLIS, JOHN D. communications executive, lawyer; BS, U. Ill., 1969; JD, Harvard U., 1972. Bar; Ill. Assoc. Sidley & Austin, 1973—78, partner, 1978—84; corporate v.p., gen. attorney AT&T, 1984—86, vice chmn., pres., 1997—99, gen. counsel, 1986—97; chmn., CEO AT&T Wireless, Redmond, Wash., 1999—. Mem. ABA (vice chmn. communications of pub. utility law sect). Office: AT&T 900 US Highway 202/206 Bedminster NJ 07921-2691

ZEHEL, WENDELL EVANS, surgeon; b. Brownsville, Pa., Mar. 6, 1934; s. Michael and Emma (Evans) Z.; m. Joan Leasure, Nov. 1, 1958; children: Lori Ann, Wendell Charles. BA, Washington and Jefferson Coll., 1956; MD, U. Pitts., 1960; postgrad. in bioengring., Carnegie-Mellon U., 1968-75. Diplomate Am. Bd. Surgery. Intern Shadyside Hosp., Pitts., 1960-61; resident in surgery U. Pitts., VA Hosp., 1963-66, Wilmington (Del.) Med. Ctr., 1966-68; pvt. practice Pitts., 1968—; surgeon St. Clair Hosp., Pitts., 1968—. Served with USAF, 1961-63. Fellow ACS; mem. Assn. Advancement of Med. Instrumentation. Home: 553 Harrogate Rd Pittsburgh PA 15241-2028 Office: 110 Fort Couch Rd Ste 3D Pittsburgh PA 15241-1030 Fax: 412-835-7159.

ZEHNDER, FREDERICK JOHN, retired automotive executive; b. Detroit, Feb. 11, 1926; s. Frederick Ernest and Katherine Josephine (Raymann) Z.; m. Adele Louise Leslie, May 15, 1970; children: Frederick J. Jr., Leslie, John, Linda. BS, U.S. Merchant Marine Acad., 1947; MBA, U. Mich., 1951. Credit analyst Comerica Bank, Detroit, 1951-53; from budget analyst to usedvehicle mgr. truck ops. Ford Motor Co., Detroit, 1953—76, used vehicle mgr. truck ops., 1976-80; ops. mgr. Ford Dealer Ops. div. Ford Motor Co., Detroit, 1980-90, ret., 1990. Served to lt. USNR, 1947-67. Mem. U. Mich. Club, Delta Sigma Pi. Republican. Lutheran. Avocations: boating, photography.

ZEHR, NORMAN ROBERT, retired association administrator; b. Niagara Falls, May 19, 1930; s. George Andrew and Ina kate (Morrell) Zehr; m. Janet Hutchinson, Apr. 24, 1976; children: Jeannette Ann, Leslie. Engr. of mines, Colo. Sch. Mines, 1952, MS, 1956. Sales trainee Ingersoll-Rand Co., NYC, 1955—56, sales engr. Lima, Peru, 1956—64, regional mgr. mining and constrn. sales, 1964—68, gen. sales mgr. Latin Am. NYC, 1968—69, gen. mgr. Latin Am. ops., 1969—71, v.p., 1975—83, Ingersoll Rand Internat., Woodcliff Lake, NJ, 1971—72, pres., 1972—83; exec. dir. Colo. Sch. Mines Alumni Assn., 1984—95; ret., 1995. Mem. editl. bd. Encyclopedia of the Korean War, 2000. With U.S. Army, 1952—54. Recipient Disting. Achievement medal, Colo. Sch. Mines, 1977. Mem.: AIME, Nat. Soc. Pershing Rifles, Scabbard and Blade, Mining Club, Sigma Nu.

ZEHRING, KAREN, information executive; b. Washington, Dec. 5, 1945; d. Robert William Zehring and Gretchen (Lorenz) Proos; m. George Lang, 1970 (div. 1979); m. Peter Frank Davis (div. 1995); children: Jesse, Antonia; stepsons: Timothy, Nicholas. BA, U. Denver, 1967; grad., Yale U., 1967-68. Assoc. pub. mktg. and sales Instl. Investor mag., N.Y.C., 1968-74; co-owner, co-creator Cafe des Artistes Restaurant, N.Y.C., 1975-79; owner, pub. The Corp. Fin. Letter, N.Y.C., 1976-78; group dir. planning and devel. Bus. Week mag., N.Y.C., 1977-78; owner, pub., exec. editor Corp. Fin. Sourcebook The Corp. Fin. Bluebook, N.Y.C., 1979-84; chmn., pres., pub., editor-in-chief Corp. Fin. mag., N.Y.C., 1986-90; cons. Karen Zehring & Assocs., Castine, Maine, 1990-94; CEO SourceCapital InterNetwork, N.Y.C., 1998—2001; mng. ptnr. Creative Devel. Ptnrs., N.Y.C., 1995-98, 2001—. Mem.: The Internat. Women's Forum. Unitarian Universalist.

ZEHRING, PEGGY JOHNSON, artist; b. Hutchinson, Kans., Jan. 4, 1941; d. Phillip E. and Bernice (Ashley) Johnson; m. R. David Zehring, July 27, 1963; children: Lisa, Geoff. BS, U. Kans., 1963; BA, U. Ill., 1977. Instr. Bellevue (Wash.) C.C., 1979-93, Sch. Visual Concepts, Seattle, 1985-86, Seattle Ctrl. C.C., 1987-97, North Seattle C.C., 1987-97, Coupeville (Wash.) Art Ctr., 1993—. Juror and lectr. Eastside Assn. Fine Art, Mercer Island Visual Arts League, Nat. League Am. Artists & Pen Women; lectr. Women Painters of Washington, Bellevue Art Mus., N.W. Watercolor Soc., Hutchinson Art Assn., Kans. One-woman shows include King County Arts Commn., Seattle, Blake Gallery, Seattle, Bellevue (Wash.) C.C., PACCAR, Bellevue, Pacific N.W. Bell, Seattle, U. Ill., Chgo., Hutchinson Art Assn.; exhibited in group shows at COCA Annual, Seattle, Seattle Art Mus. Sales & Rental Gallery, LewAllen Fine Art, Santa Fe, Bellevue Art Mus., Diablo Valley Coll., Elizabeth Prince Gallery, Prescott, Ariz.; represented in selected collections City of Lynnwood, Wash., Pacific NW Bell, PACCAR, Delitte, Haskins & Sells, Opti-Copy, Kansas City, Harper & Assocs., Bellevue and numerous other pvt. collections; work published in The Artistic Touch I, II and III, The Encyclopedia of Living Artists. Pres. The LaVeta (Colo.) Sch. of Arts. Recipient 1st pl. award Ariz. Internat., Snowgrass Art Inst., Cashmere, Wash., Kans. State Fair, Hutchinson, SPACe, La Veta, Colo., Honorable Mention award W. Wash. State Fair, 2d pl. award Ea. N.Mex. U., Portales, Snowgrass Art Inst., Cashmere, Wash., Merit award Mont. Inst. of the Arts, Butte; named finalist Pierce County Libr. Project, Gig Harbor, Wash., 3rd place Greeley Nat. Juried show. Home: PO Box 967 La Veta CO 81055-0967 E-mail: zehrings@rmi.net.

ZEID, PAULA KLEIN, metals broker; b. Chgo., Oct. 16, 1941; d. Arthur A. and Rosalyn (Davidson) Schwartz; m. Sanford David Klein, Dec. 18, 1960 (div. 1981); children: Gregory Scott, Julie Ann. Student, Mich. State U., 1959-60; BA, Governors State U., 1974, MA, 1975. Mem. editl. staff Okinawa Morning Star, Machinato, 1960-63; exec. dir. Bloom Twp. Com. on Youth, Chicago Heights, Ill., 1975-81; dir. fund devel. and pub. rels. South Chgo. Cmty. Hosp., 1981-84; v.p. South Chgo. Health Care Found., 1982-84; dir. devel. and pub. rels. Chgo. Crime Commn., 1985-88; broker, buyer, trader Universal Scrap Metals, Chgo., 1988—; pres. Klein Trading Co., Chgo., 1997—; v.p. USM Processing Ltd. Trustee Chgo. Sinai Congregation. Mem. Inst. Scrap Recycling Industries, Indsl. Coun. of N.W. Chgo. Jewish. Home: 1908 N Dayton St Chicago IL 60614-5029 Office: Universal Scrap Metals 2500 W Fulton St Chicago IL 60612-2104 Office Phone: 312-666-0011. E-mail: pklein@universalscrap.com.

ZEID, PHILIP L. metal recycling executive; b. Chgo., July 27, 1943; s. Samuel P. and Mary S. (Stamler) Z.; m. Donna M. Winston, Dec. 16, 1966 (div. Feb. 1978); 1 child, Jason I.; m. Paula S. Klein, Oct. 13, 1991. BA, Drake U., 1966; postgrad., U. Kans., 1966. Sales mgr. Random House, Inc., Chgo., 1969-74; v.p., dir. mktg. dept. Coronet Films, Chgo., 1974-82; sr. mgr. MCI Communications, Chgo., 1982-84; pres. Universal Scrap Metals, Inc., Chgo., 1984—, also bd. dirs. Pres., bd. dirs. USM Processing Ltd., 1997—. Mem. exec. com. Jewish United Fund. Mem. Assn. Media Producers (statis. com. 1980-82, speakers bur., chmn. trade show com., lobbyist Washington chpt. 1981-82), Sales and Mktg. Execs. Assn., Inst. Scrap Recycling Industries. Avocations: photography, art collecting, skiing, tennis, travel. Home: 1908 N Dayton St Chicago IL 60614-5029 Office: Universal Scrap Metals Inc 2500 W Fulton St Chicago IL 60612-2104

ZEIDENSTEIN, GEORGE, population educator; b. Pitts., July 29, 1929; s. Max and Sophia (Cohen) Z.; m. Sondra F. Auerbach, Jan. 25, 1953; children: Laura, Louis Peter. BA, U. Pitts., 1951; JD cum laude, Harvard U., 1954. Bar: N.Y. 1954. Pvt. practice, N.Y.C., 1954—65; vol. lawyer Lawyers Constl. Def. Com., Holly Springs, Miss., 1965; ptnr. Spear and Hill, 1962—65; country dir. Kathmandu, Nepal, Peace Corps, Nepal, 1965—68; regional dir. designate Office E. Asia and Pacific, Washington, 1968; pres. Bklyn. Linear City Devel. Corp., N.Y.C., 1968—69; sr. program officer Asia and Pacific Ford Found., 1969—71, dep. head Asia and Pacific, 1971—72, rep., 1972—76; pres., trustee Population Coun., N.Y.C., 1976—93; disting. fellow Harvard Ctr. Population and Devel. Studies, Cambridge, Mass., 1993—. Chmn. Himalayas coun. Asia Soc., 1970-72; assoc. seminar tradition and change in South and S.E. Asia, Columbia U., 1971-73, assoc. seminar on tech. and pub. issues, 1981-85; coun. Overseas Devel. Coun., 1979-93; chmn. Appraisal Group Global Com. Parliamentarians on Population and Devel., 1985-86; bd. visitors Grad. Sch. Pub. Health, U. Pitts., 1988—; advisor to chair Ind. Commn. on Population and Quality of Life, 1993-95. Vice chmn. bd. trustees, chmn. program com. Save the Children Fedn., 1991-95, Internat. Ctr. Rsch. on Women, 1993—; chmn. Internat. HIV/AIDS Alliance, 1993—; bd. dirs. Earthforce, 1993-95; active Britton Woods Com., 1992—. Decorated knight comdr. Order of Lion (Finland, Senegal). Home: 795 East St N Goshen CT 06756-1130 Office: Harvard Ctr Population Devel Studies 9 Bow St Cambridge MA 02138-5103

ZEIDLER, FRANK P. former association administrator, mayor, arbitrator, mediator, fact-finder; b. Milw., Sept. 20, 1912; s. Michael and Clara (Nitschke) Z.; m. Agnes Reinke; children: Clara, Dorothy, Michael, Anita, Mary, Jeannette. Student, Marquette U., 1930, U. Wis. Extension Div., 1930-70, U. Chgo., 1937; LLD (hon.), U. Wis., 1958, St. Olaf Coll., 1988; LHD (hon.), Carthage Coll., 1983, Mt. Mary Coll., 1993, U. Wis.-Milw., 1990. Dir. Milw. Pub. Schs., 1941-48; mayor City of Milw., 1948-60; dir. Wis. Dept. Resource Devel., 1963-64. Sec. emeritus Pub. Enterprise Com.; mem. U.S. nat. commn. UNESCO, 1953, 56, 59. Author: Shakespeare's plays in modern verse. Pres. Ctrl. North Cmty. Coun.; pres. Greater Milw. UN Assn., pres.; nat. chmn. Socialist Party U.S.A., 1973-83; Socialist Party candidate for Pres. U.S., 1976; convenor Dem. Socialist Conf.; past pres. Luth. Social Action Conf.; bd. dirs. Goethe House, Milw., Milw. Theol. Inst.; mem. exec. coun. Luth. Ch. Am., 1980-82; hon. mem. cabinet Interfaith Conf. Greater Milw.; chmn. Norman Thomas Inst. for Peace and Social Justice. Named One of 10 Outstanding Young Men, Nat. Jr. C. of C., 1949; recipient Eugene V. Debs award, 1977. Mem. Milw. World Federalist Assn. (bd. dirs.), Nat. Model R.R. Assn. (founder). Home: 2921 N 2nd St Milwaukee WI 53212-2411

ZEIDMAN, FRED S. corporate financial executive; BSBA, Washington U.; MBA, NYU. Chmn. US Holocaust Meml. Coun., Washington, 2002—07; mng. partner WoodRock & Co., Houston. Mem.: Bd. of Regents, Tex So. U. (vice chmn.), Anti Defamation League (chmn.), Am Isreal Public Affairs Com. (exec. com.), Jewish Inst. Nat. Sec. Affairs (vp, dir.), Isreal Bonds. Office: 100 Raoul Wallenberg Pl SW Washington DC 20024

ZEIEN, ALFRED M. former consumer products company executive; b. N.Y.C., Feb. 25, 1930; s. Alphonse and Betty (Barthelemy) Z.; m. Joyce Valerie Lawrence, Dec. 26, 1952; children: Scott, Grey, Claudia BS, Webb Inst.; MBA postgrad., Harvard U. Group v.p. Gillette Co., Boston, 1973-74; div. gen. mgr. Braun AG, Frankfurt, Federal Republic of Germany, 1974-76; sr. v.p. Gillette Co., Boston, 1978-81, vice chmn., 1981-90, pres., 1990-91, chmn., chief exec. officer, 1991-99; chmn. bd. Braun AG, Frankfurt, Federal Republic of Germany, 1976-78. Bd. dirs. Polaroid Corp., Cambridge, Mass., EMC Corp. Trustee Woods Hole Oceanographic Inst. & Marine Biology Lab. Avocations: sailing; tennis.

ZEIGER, LARRY See KING, LARRY

ZEIGER, ROBERT S. allergist; b. Bklyn., July 31, 1942; s. Murray and Mildred Z.; m. Karen P. Zeiger, June 25, 1967; children: Joanna, Laurie. BA with honors, Tulane U., 1963; MD, PhD, SUNY, Bklyn., 1969. Diplomate Am. Bd. Pediatrics, Am. Bd. Allergy-Immunology. Intern pediatrics Harriet Lane Johns Hopkins Hosp., Balt., 1969-70; staff assoc. NIH, Bethesda, Md., 1970-72; resident pediatrics Boston Children's Hosp., 1972-73, allergy fellow, 1973-75; instr. Harvard Med. Sch., Boston, 1975-76; chief of allergy Kaiser Permanente, San Diego, 1976—; clin. assoc. prof. U. Calif., San Diego, 1980-87, clin. prof., 1987—. Editorial bd. Family Practice Survey, 1983-85, Jour. Allergy Clin. Immunology, 1985-91, Pediatric Allergy Immunology Jour., 1990—; author: Nasal Manifestations of Systemic Diseases, 1990; contbr. articles to profl. jours. Lt. comdr. USPHS, 1970-72. Phizer Honor scholar Phizer Corp., 1967-69, Charles A. Janeway scholar Harvard U., 1975; Hood Found. grantee, 1975-77. Fellow Am. Acad. Pediatrics, Am. Acad. Allergy Clin. Immunology (Travel award 1975), Phi Beta Kappa, Alpha Omega Alpha. Democrat. Avocations: tennis, travel, golf, cinema. Office: Kaiser Permanente 7060 Clairemont Mesa Blvd San Diego CA 92111-1003 also: U Calif San Diego Dept Pediat 9500 Gilman Dr La Jolla CA 92093-0833

ZEIGLER, ANN DEPENDER, lawyer; b. Spokane, Wash., June 7, 1947; d. F. Norman and Dorothy (Wolter) dePender; m. Paul Stewart Zeigler, June 20, 1970; 1 child, Kate Elizabeth. BA magna cum laude, Ft, Wright Coll. Holy Names, Spokane, 1969; MFA in Creative Writing, U. Mont., 1975; JD, U. Houston, 1984. Bar: Tex. 1984. Course adminstr. legal communications U. Houston, 1982-84; assoc. Dula, Shields & Egbert, 1984-87; ind. project atty., 1987; assoc. Dow, Cogburn & Friedman, 1987-90; assoc. bankruptcy sect./avoidance litigation Hughes, Watters & Askanase, Houston, 1990—. Co-editor: Insurance Guide-Arts Nonprofits, 1993, Basic Issues in Estate Planning-Representing the Artist, 1994, Leading the Arts Nonprofit: Duties of Officers and Directors, 1999; editl. bd. Houston Lawyer, 1999—, guest editor spl. hist. issue 2000, 01, guest editor 40th ann. issue, 2003; assoc. editor Keeping Up With, 2002-03; contbr. articles to profl. jours. Mem. publs. com., writer Tex. Accts. and Lawyers for Arts, Houston, 1988—; mem. Supreme Ct. of Tex. Unauthorized Practice of Law Com., Houston; vol. Houston Lawyers for Hunger Relief, 1988-90. Mem. ABA, State Bar Tex., Houston Bar Assn. (chair law and the arts com. 1996-97, co-chair ann. fiction contest), Can. Bar Assn., Phi Alpha Delta. Democrat. Home: 4038 Cheena Dr Houston TX 77025-4702 Office: Hughes Watters & Askanase 1415 Louisiana St Fl 37 Houston TX 77002-7360 Office Phone: 713-759-0818. E-mail: azeigler@hwa.com.

ZEIGLER, EARLE FREDERICK, physical education-kinesiology educator; b. NYC, Aug. 20, 1919; s. Clarence Mattison and Margery Christina (Beyerkohler) Shinkle; m. Bertha M. Bell, June 25, 1941 (dec. Feb. 1998); c. Donald H., Barbara A; m. Anne K. Rogers, Feb. 27, 1999. AB, Bates Coll., 1940; AM, Yale U., 1944, PhD, 1951; LLD, U. Windsor, 1975; DSc, U. Lethbridge, Alta, Can., 1997. Assoc. phys. dir., aquatic dir. Bridgeport (Conn.) YMCA, 1941-43; instr. German U. Conn., Storrs, 1943-47; coach, instr. phys. edn. Yale U., 1943-49; asst. prof. U. Western Ont. (Can.), London, 1949-50, prof., chmn. dept. phys., health and recreation edn., 1950-56, assoc. prof. Sch. Edn.; supr. phys. edn. and athletics U. Mich., Ann Arbor, 1956-63, chmn. dept. phys. edn. Sch. Edn., 1961-63; prof. dept. phys. edn. for men Coll. Phys. Edn., U. Ill., Urbana, 1963-72, head dept. phys. edn. for men, chmn. grad. dept., 1964-68; prof. dept. phys. and health edn. U. Western Ont., London, 1971-89, prof. emeritus, 1989—, dean faculty phys. edn., 1972-77. Author: A History of Professional Preparation for Physical Education in the United States, 1951, Administration of Physical Education and Athletics, 1959, The Case Method Approach: An Instructional Manual, 1959, Philosophical Foundations for Physical, Health, and Recreation Education, 1964, A Brief Introduction to the Philosophy of Religion, 1965, (with H.J. VanderZwaag) Physical Education: Progressivism or Essentialism, 1968, Problems in the History and Philosophy of Physical Education and Sport, 1968, (with M.L. Howell and M. Trekell) Research in the History and Philosophy of Physical Education and Sport, 1971, Personalizing Physical Education and Sport Philosophy, 1975, Physical Education and Sport Philosophy, 1977, Issues in North American Physical Education and Sport, 1979, Decision-Making in Physical Education and Athletics Administration, 1982, (with G.W. Bowie) Management Competency Development in Sport and Physical Education, 1983, Ethics and Morality in Sport and Physical Education, 1984, (with J. Campbell) Strategic Market Planning: An Aid to the Evaluation of an Athletics/Recreation Program, 1984, Assessing Sport and Physical Education: Diagnosis and Projection, 1986, (with G. Bowie and R. Paris) Competency Development in Sport and Physical Education Management, 1988, (with A. Mikalachki and G. Leyshon) Change Process in Sport and Physical Education Management, 1988, Introduction to Sport and Physical Education Philosophy, 1989, Sport and Physical Education: Past, Present, Future, 1990, Professional Ethics for Sport Managers, 1992, Critical Thinking for the Professions of Health, Physical Education, Recreation, and Dance, 1994, A Selected, Annotated Bibliography of Completed Research on Management Theory and Practice in Physical Education and Athletics to 1972, 1995, (with G.W. Bowie) Developing Management Competency in Sport and Physical Education, 1995, Who Knows What's Right Anymore?, 2002, Whatever Happend to "The Good Life"?, 2002, Socio-Cultural Foundations of Physical Education and Educational Sport, 2003;, A Way Out of Ethical Confusion, 2004, Through the Eyes of a Concerned Liberal, 2004; author, editor: A History of Sport and Physical Education to 1900, 1973, A History of Physical Education and Sport in the United States and Canada, 1975, (with M.J. Spaeth) Administrative Theory and Practice in Physical Education and Athletics, 1975, History of Physical Education and Sport, 1979, rev. edit., 1988, Physical Education and Sport: An Introduction, 1982, Physical Education and Kinesiology in North America: Professionalism and Scholarly Foundations, 1994; contbr. 404 articles to profl. jours. Recipient Outstanding Tchr. award U. Western Ont., 1987, Disting. Svc. award Internat. Soc. Comparative Phys. Edn. and Sport, 1988; named to Univ. Western Ont.'s Wall of Wrestling Fame, 1991, Univ. Western Ont.'s W Club Hall of Fame, 1995, Univ. Western Ont.'s Swimming Wall of Honor, 2000; named first Human Movement Scis. and Edn. scholar U. Memphis, 1994. Fellow: N.Am. Soc. Health, Phys. Edn., Recreation, Sport and Dance Profls. (Canadian and U.S. br.), Am. Acad. Kinesiology and Phys. Edn. (pres. 1981—82); mem.: N.Am. Soc. for Sport Mgmt. (hon. past pres. 1986—87, founder Earle Zeigler Lecture 1988), Philosophic Soc. for Study of Sport (pres. 1974—75), Soc. Mcpl. Recreation Dirs. Ont. (Honor award 1956), Ont. Recreation Assn. (v.p., dir. 1955—56), Can. Profl. Schs. Conf. (pres. 1953—55), Internat. Soc. for Comparative Phys. Edn. and Sport (Earle Zeigler award established in his honor), N.Am. Soc. Sport History (life), Nat. Assn. Phys. Edn. in Higher Edn., Am. Philos. Assn., Can. Assn. Health, Phys. Edn. and Recreation (v.p. 1955—56, 1983—85, Honor award 1975, Spl. Presidential citation 1986), Internat. Assn. Profl. Schs. Phys. Edn., Philosophy Edn. Soc., AAHPERD (Alliance scholar 1977—78, Disting. Svc. award 1979, Honor award 1981, Gulick award 1990), Phi Epsilon Kappa (life). Home: 105 8560 Currie Rd Richmond BC Canada V6Y 1M2 also: PO Box 630 Point Roberts WA 98281-0630 Fax: 604-270-8414. E-mail: zeigrog@axion.net. *Ever since the Platonic tradition split what was once before believed to be a unified organism into mind and body, and then Christianity added a spiritual dimension that shattered a unified concept of the organism even further, purposeful human movement in sport, dance, play, and exercise has been regarded as inferior to so-called intellectual attainments. My life purpose is to work toward redressing that imbalance by promoting a type of education that restores the Greek Classical Ideal.*

ZEIGLER, L(UTHER) HARMON, political science educator; b. Savannah, Ga., Mar. 9, 1936; s. Luther H. and Sarah Louise (Betts) Z.; m. Patricia Lynn Duffy, Dec. 20, 1956; children: Michael, Amanda. BA, Emory U., 1957; MA, U. Ill., 1958, PhD, 1960. Asst. prof. Fla. State U., Tallahassee, 1960-61, Emory U., Atlanta, 1961-63, U. Ga., Athens, 1963-64; assoc. prof. U. Oreg., Eugene, 1964-67, prof. dept. polit. sci., 1967-85, chmn., 1982-85; Philip M. Phibbs disting. prof. Am. politics U. Puget Sound, Tacoma, Wash., 1985-92. Affiliate prof. U. Wash., 1986-92. Author: The Irony of Democracy, 1970, 10th edit., 1997, 11th edit., 2000, 12th edit., 2003, Governing American Schools, 1974, Professionals Versus the Public: Attitudes, Commnication and Response in Local School Districts, 1980, American Politics in the Media Age, 1983, Women, Public Opinion and Politics: The Changing Attitudes of American Women, 1984, Pluralism, Corporatism and Confucianism, 1988, The Political Community, 1990, Political Parties in Industrial Democracies, 1992. Fellow Ford Found., 1969; Guggenheim fellow, 1969-70; Fulbright-Hays grantee W. Germ., 1977; sr. scholar Australia, 1978 Mem. Am. Polit. Sci. Assn. E-mail: harmonzeigler@hotmail.com.

ZEIKUS, J. GREGORY, microbiologist, educator; BA, U. S.Fla., 1967; MS, Indiana U., 1968, PhD, 1970; Doctor of Honoris Causa in Applied Biol. Scis. (hon.), U. Gent, Belgium, 1992. Postdoctoral fellow Lab. Thermal Biology USPHS, W. Yellowstone, Mont., 1970; NIH postdoctoral fellow dept. microbiology U. Ill., Urbana-Champaign; from asst. to assoc. prof. dept. bacteriology U. Wis., Madison, 1972—80, prof. dept. bacteriology, 1980—84; prof. biochemistry Mich. State U., E. Lansing, 1984—86, prof. microbiology and biochemistry, 1986—; exec. dir. Mich. Biotechnology Inst., E. Lansing, 1984—86; pres. MBI Internat., E. Lansing, 1986—2002, v.p. tech. acquisition and pres. emeritus, 2002—. Grantee, U.S. Dept. Energy, 1980—, U.S. Dept. Agr., 1989—, 1996—99, NSF, 1995—98. Office: Dept Microbiology and Molecular Genetics Mich State U 410 Biochemistry East Lansing MI 48824

ZEILBERGER, DORON, researcher, mathematics educator; b. Haifa, Israel, July 2, 1950; s. Yehuda Heinz and Ruth (Alexander) Z.; m. Jane Deborah LeGrange, June 3, 1979; children: Celia, Tamar, Hadas. BS with first class hons., U. London, 1972; PhD, Weizmann Inst., Rehovot, Israel, 1976. Mem. Inst. for Advanced Study, Princeton, N.J., 1977-78, 93; vis. asst. prof. Ga. Inst. Tech., Atlanta, 1978-79; lectr. U. Ill., Urbana, 1979-80; sr. scientist Weizmann Inst., Rehovot, Israel, 1980-82; lectr. U. Pa., Phila., 1982-83; assoc. prof. Drexel U., Phila., 1983-88, prof., 1988-90, Temple U., Phila., 1990-99, Laura H. Carnell prof., 1999-2001; bd. govs prof. Rutgers U., New Brunswick, N.J., 2001 –. Mem. editl. bd. Elec. Jour. of Combinations, others, editor-in-chief Advances in Applied Math.; contbr. numerous articles to profl. jours. Mem. Am. Math. Soc. (Leroy P. Steele Prize 1998), Math. Assn. Am. (Lester R. Ford award 1990). Business E-Mail: zeilberg@math.rutgers.edu.

ZEILE, TODD EDWARD, professional baseball player; b. Van Nuys, Calif., Sept. 9, 1965; m. Juliane McNamara. Student, UCLA, 1989. With St. Louis Cardinals, 1995, Chgo. Cubs, 1995, Phila. Phillies, 1995—96, Balt. Orioles, 1996, L.A. Dodgers, 1996, Fla. Marlins, 1996—98; 3rd baseman Tex. Rangers, 1998—99; 1st baseman, infielder N.Y. Mets, 1999—. Named Midwest League co-Most Valuable Player, 1987. Achievements include being holder of Nat. League single-season record for fewest putouts by third baseman, 1993; sharing Am. League single-game record for most errors by first baseman, 1996. Office: New York Mets 12301 Roosevelt Ave Flushing NY 11368-1699

ZEILIG, NANCY MEEKS, writer, editor; b. Nashville, Apr. 28, 1943; d. Edward Harvey and Nancy Evelyn (Self) Meeks; m. Lanny Kenneth Fielder, Aug. 20, 1964 (div. Dec. 1970); m. Charles Elliot Zeilig, Jan. 6, 1974 (div. Dec. 1989); 1 child, Sasha Rebecca. BA, Birmingham-So. Coll., 1964; postgrad., Vanderbilt U., 1971-73. Editorial asst. Reuben H. Donnelley, N.Y.C., 1969-70; asst. editor Vanderbilt U., Nashville, 1970-74; editor U. Minn., St. Paul, 1975; asst. editor McGraw-Hill Inc., Mpls., 1975-76; mng. editor Denver mag., 1976-80; editor Jour. Am. Water Works Assn., Denver, 1981—99; owner Nancy Zeilig Writing & Editing, Denver, 2000—. Editor, co-pub.: WomanSource, 1982, rev. edit., 1984; contbr. articles to trade and consumer mags. Co-chair arts adv. com. Denver Sch. Arts, 1994-96. Avocations: travel, reading British and Am. fiction, cooking. Subject of NBC News documentary Women Like Us, 1980. Office Phone: 303-758-7750. E-mail: nzeilig@earthlink.net.

ZEILINGER, ELNA RAE, elementary educator, gifted-talented education educator; b. Tempe, Ariz., Mar. 24, 1937; d. Clayborn Eddie and Ruby Elna (Laird) Simpson; m. Philip Thomas Zeilinger, June 13, 1970; children: Shari, Chris. BA in Edn., Ariz. State U., 1958, MA in Edn., 1966, EdS, 1980. Bookkeeper First Nat. Bank of Tempe, 1955-56; with registrar's office Ariz. State U., 1956-58; piano tchr., recreation dir. City of Tempe; tchr. Thew Sch., Tempe, 1958-61; elem. tchr. Mitchell Sch., Tempe, 1962-74, intern prin., 1976, personnel intern, 1977; specialist gifted edn. Tempe Elem. Schs., Tempe, 1977-86; elem. tchr. Holdeman Sch., Tempe, 1986-89; tchr. grades 1-12 and adult reading, lang. arts, English Zeilinger Tutoring Svc., 1991—. Grad. asst. ednl. adminstrn., Iota Workshop coordinator Ariz. State U., 1978; presenter Ariz. Gifted Conf., 1978-81; condr. survey of gifted programs, 1980; reporter pub. rels. Tempe Sch. Dist., 1978-80, Access com. for gifted programs, 1981-83. Author: Leadership Role of the Principal in Gifted Programs: A Handbook, 1980; Classified Personnel Handbook, 1977, also reports, monographs and paintings. Active Tempe Hist. Assn., liaison, 1975, Tempe Art League; freedom train com. Ariz. Bicentennial Commn., 1975-76; bd. dirs. Maple Property Owners Assn., 1994-2002; storyteller Tempe Hist. Mus., 1997—; dir. pagentry Daus. of the Nile, 2002-03. Named Outstanding Leader in Elem. and Secondary Schs., 1976' Ariz. Cattle Growers scholar, 1954-55; Elks scholar, 1954-55; recipient Judges award Tempe Art League, 1970, Best of Show, Scottsdale Art League, 1976. Mem.: Daus. of the Nile (dir. pageantry 2002—03). Democrat. Congregationalist.

ZEILSTRA, DONALD J. research and development company executive; b. Oak Pk., Ill, Nov. 8, 1953; s. Donald William Zeilstra and Verna Jabaay; m. Janna Doesburg Zeilstra, Sept. 10, 1977; children: Donald A., Jacob T. BA, Calvin Coll., 1975; MA, U. Chgo.; Dr. of Mgmt., Case Western Reserve U., 2003. Cert. Fund Raising Exec. CFRE Internat., Fundraising Mgmt. Ctr. in Philanthropy Ind. U. Comm. devel. Christian Reformed World Relief, Middlesboro, Ky., 1977—79; coord. Christian Reformed World Relief, Appalachian Devel. Projects, Knoxville, Tenn., 1980—84; regional dir. Christian Reformed World Relief, Oak Park, Ill., 1984—92, dir. of devel. Grand Rapids, Mich., 1993—98; cons. Ketchum Inc., Dallas, 1998—2001, sr. cons., 2001—02, sr. cons., staff supr., 2002—03, v.p., 2003—. Mem. Assn. of Fundraising Profl., Edn. Com., West Mich. Chpt., Grand Rapids, Mich., 2001—03, CFRE Internat., Job Analysis Task Force, 2002—03; chair CFRE Internat., Profl. Practice Task Force, Alexandria, Va., 2003—. Contbr. articles various profl. jours. Mem.: Assn. of Funraising Profl., Assn. for Rsch. on Non-Profit Organ., Acad. of Mgmt. Home: 2730 Elmwood Dr SE Grand Rapids MI 49506 Office: Ketchum Inc 5151 Beltline Rd Ste 900 Dallas TX 75254 E-mail: dzeilstra@viscern.com.

ZEINE, RANA R. pathologist, research scientist; b. Beirut, May 13, 1962; arrived in U.S., 1998; d. Ramsey and Omayma Zeine; m. Hinhark Gan, July 1, 1989. BS in Biology, Am. U. Beirut, 1983, MD, 1987; PhD, McGill U., Montreal, Can., 1993. Rsch. fellow Ottawa (Can.) U., 1995—98; rsch. assoc. Albert Einstein Coll., NY, 1998—2000, resident in neuropathology, 2004; resident in pathology Montefiore Med. Ctr./Albert Einstein Coll. Medicine, Bronx, NY, 2000—04; rsch. project mgr. Ctr. for Dementia Rsch. Nathan Kline Inst., NY, 2004—. Presenter in field. Author numerous abstracts in neuroimmunology field; contbr. articles to profl. jours. Recipient Recognition award, AMA, 2003; fellow, Multiple Sclerosis Soc. Can., 1996—98. Mem.: Coll. Am. Pathologists, NY Acad. Scis. Mem. Baha'I Faith. Avocations: ballet, piano, swimming. Office Phone: 845-398-2176. E-mail: rzeine@nki.rfmh.org.

ZEISEL, LAURA, Office: Drake Sommers Loeb et al 1 Corwin Ct Newburgh NY 12550 E-mail: lzeisel@dsltc.com.

ZEISEL, STEVEN H. nutritionist, scientist, educator; b. N.Y.C., July 16, 1950; BS in Life Sci., MIT, 1971; MD, Harvard Med. Sch., 1975; PhD in Nutrition, MIT, 1980. Asst. in medicine Children's Hosp., Boston, 1980-81; asst. prof. pathology and pediatrics Boston U. Sch. Medicine, 1982-87, assoc. prof., 1987-90, prof., 1990; prof. dept. pediatrics U. N.C., Chapel Hill, 1990—, prof., chair dept. nutrition, 1990—; chair med. edn. com. Am. Soc. Clin. Nutrition, 1995-96. Chair joint membership com. AIN/ASCN, 1992-94; chmn. adv. bd. Gen. Clin. Rsch. Ctr., U. N.C., 1998—; mem. Inst. of Medicine panel on folate and B Vitamins, 1997-98; mem. sci. adv. bd. Monsanto Corp., 1998—; mem. sci. coun. Dannon Inst.; bd. dirs. Interactive Info. Editor-in-chief Jour. Nutritional Biochemistry. Mem. Internat. Soc. for Rsch. on Human Milk and Lactation, Am. Soc. Nutritional Scis., Am. Soc. Clin. Nutrition (councilor 1991-94, chmn. residency edn. and subspecialty tng. com. 1995-97), Am. Soc. Parenteral and Enteral Nutrition, Am. Coll. Nutrition, Am. Pub. Health Assn., Soc. Pediatric Rsch. Office: UNC Dept Nutrition # 7400 Sch Pub Health/Sch Medicine 2212 Mcgavran Greenberg Hal Chapel Hill NC 27599-0001 Fax: 919-966-7216.

ZEITELHACK, GLORIA JEANNE, artist; b. San Diego, June 24, 1952; d. Leon Mathew and Claire Irene (Morel) Morissette; m. Don Roger Zeitelhack, Sept. 3, 1977. Artist, Tomahawk, Wis., Alto, N.Mex.; owner Many Moons Jewelry Gallery, Ruidoso, N.Mex. Inventor mother of pearl shell landscapes for jewelery, 1977— (technique copyrighted 2001). Avocations: art, music, dance. Home and Office: PO Box 419 Alto NM 88312-0419: Many Moons Jewelry Gallery Time Sq 2501 Sudderth Ruidoso NM 88345

ZEITLIN, HERBERT ZAKARY, retired academic administrator, real estate consultant; b. N.Y.C., Jan. 14; s. Leonard and Martha Josephine (Soff) Zeitlin; m. Eugenia F. Pawlik, July 3, 1949; children: Mark Clyde, Joyce Therese Zeitlin Harris, Ann Victoria, Clare Katherine. BS, NYU, 1947, MA, 1949; EdD, Stanford U., 1956. Tchr. Mepham High Sch., Bellmore, NY, 1946-47, Nassau County Vocat. Edn. Extension Bd., Mineola, NY; electronics instr., adj. faculty Mephan C.C., 1946-49; tchr., counselor, dir. testing Phoenix Union High Sch. and Coll. Dist., 1949-57; dean eve. coll., prin. high sch. Antelope Valley Union High Sch. and Coll. Dist., Lancaster, Calif., 1957-62; dean instrn. Southwestern Coll., Chula Vista, Calif., 1962-64; pres., supt., cons. Triton Coll., River Grove, Ill., 1964—79; dean, pres. West L.A. Coll., 1976-80; pres. Trident Consultants, L.A., mgmt. cons., 1976—; adj. faculty Ariz. State U., Flagstaff, 1953-55, No. Ill. U., DeKalb, 1971 76, U. Calif., Santa Barbara, 1979. Author: Turbulent Birth of Triton College, 2001, Corruption: How to Fight It and Win, 2003; editor: in field. Pres. Antelope Valley Breeze & Sage, 1959—60, Bon Vivant Homeowners Assn., 1982—84; mayor Upper Woodland Hills, Calif. With USAAF, 1942—46. Named Adminstr. of the Yr., Triton Coll. Faculty Assn., 1974, Most Influential Educator in Ill., Chgo. Sun Times; recipient Spl. commendation, Chgo. Tribune, Richard Ogilvie, former Gov. Ill., Spl. Achievement award for visionary accomplishment, Ill. Sch. Adminstrs. Assn., 1976. Mem.: Ariz. State Vocat. Assn. (pres. 1952—53), Ariz. Vocat. Guidance Assn. (pres. 1951—52), Maywood Ill. Rotary (pres. 1972—73), Antelope Valley Rotary (pres. 1962). Office: Paramount Properties 21031 Ventura Blvd Woodland Hills CA 91364-1845 Mailing: Trident Cons PO Box 571412 Tarzana CA 91357 Office Phone: 816-999-2030 x 2902. Personal E-mail: Herbertzzeitlin@aol.com. *I always felt that being the president of an organization, having held many presidencies in my lifetime, was like being the quarterback on the football team. You had a choice of running with the ball and taking some bruises or passing it to someone who should score. I was lucky most of the time in selecting some very fine receivers.*

ZEITLIN, JIDE JAMES, investment banker; b. Ibadan, Nigeria; came to U.S., 1976; s. Arnold S. and Marian E. (Frank) Z. BA, Amherst Coll., 1985; MBA, Harvard U., 1987. V.p. Goldman, Sachs & Co., N.Y.C., 1987—. Exec. prodr.: (documentary) Adrift, 2002. Bd. trustees, treas. The Milton Academy. Office: Goldman Sachs & Co 85 Broad St New York NY 10004-2456*

ZEITLIN, LAURIE, printing company executive; BA in Econs., Duke U., 1984; MBA in Fin., U. Pa., 1989. Rsch. asst. Touche Ross & Co., 1985—87; sr. mng. consulting Deloitte & Touche LLP, 1989—95; dir. info. tech., sr. mgr. application devel., v.p. info. tech. Home Depot, Inc., Atlanta, 1995—2003; sr. v.p., chief info. officer Kinko's Inc., Dallas, 2003—. Office: Kinkos 13155 Noel Rd Ste 1600 Dallas TX 75240 E-mail: laurie.zeitlin@fedexkinkos.com.

ZEITLIN, MARILYN AUDREY, museum director; b. Newark, July 14, 1941; d. Sidney M. and Theresa Feigenblatt) Litchfield; widowed; children: Charles C. Sweedler, Milo Sweedler. Student, Vanderbilt U., 1963-65; AB in Humanities, Harvard U., 1966, MA in Teaching of English, 1967; postgrad., Cornell U., 1971-74. Dir. Ctr. Gallery, Bucknell U., Lewisburg, Pa., 1975-78; Freedman Gallery, Albright Coll., Reading, Pa., 1978-81; Anderson Gallery, Va. Commonwealth U., Richmond, 1981-87; curator, acting co-dir. Contemporary Arts Mus., Houston, 1987-90; exec. dir. Washington Projects for the Arts, 1990-92; dir. Univ. Art Mus., Ariz. State U., Tempe, 1992—. Juror Dallas Mus. of Arts, McKnight Awards, Mpls.; grant evaluator IMS; grant evaluator, panelist NEH; lectr., cons. in field. Editor, contbr. essays to art publs. Bd. dirs. Cultural Alliance Washington; curator, commr. for U.S. for 1995 Venice Biennale. Samuel H. Kress fellow, 1972-73. Mem. Assn. Coll. and Univ. Mus. and Galleries (v.p. 1986-88), Am. Assn. Mus., Coll. Art Assn. (U.S. commr. Venice Biennale 1995). Office: Ariz State U Art Mus PO Box 872911 Tempe AZ 85287-2911

ZEITLIN, MAURICE, sociology educator, writer; b. Detroit, Feb. 24, 1935; s. Albert J. and Rose (Goldberg) Zeitlin; m. Marilyn Geller, Mar. 1, 1959; children: Michelle, Carla, Erica. BA cum laude, Wayne State U., 1957; MA, U. Calif., Berkeley, 1960, PhD, 1964. Instr. anthropology and sociology Princeton (N.J.) U., 1961-64; rsch. assoc. Ctr. Internat. Studies, 1962-64; from asst. prof. to assoc. prof. sociology U. Wis., Madison, 1964—70, prof., 1970-77; dir. Ctr. Social Orgn., 1974-76; prof. sociology UCLA, 1977—, rsch. assoc. Inst. Inds. Rels. Vis. prof. polit. sci. and sociology Hebrew U., Jerusalem, 1971—72. Author (with R. Scheer): Cuba: An American Tragedy, 1963, 1964, Revolutionary Politics and the Cuban Working Class, 1967, 1970, The Civil War with Chile, 1984; author: (with R. E. Ratcliff) Landlords and Capitalists, 1988, The Large Corporation and Contemporary Classes, 1989; author: (with J. Stepan-Norris) Talking Union, 1996, Left Out: Reds and America's Industrial Unions, 2003; Latin Am. editor: Ramparts mag., 1967—73, editor-in-chief: Political Power and Social Theory, 1980—90; mem. editl. adv. bd. Progressive mag., 1985—96; editor (with J. Petras): Latin America: Reform or Revolution?, 1968, American Society, Inc., 1970, 1977, Father Camilo Torres: Revolutionary Writings, 1972, Classes Class Conflict, and the State, 1980, How Mighty a Force?, 1983, Insurgent Workers: The Origins of Industrial Unionism, 1987. Chmn. Madison Citizens for a Vote on Vietnam, 1967—68, Am. Com. for Chile, 1973—75; mem. exec. bd. U.S. Com. Justice to Latin Am. Polit. Prisoners, 1977—84; mem. exec. com. Calif. Campaign for Econ .Democracy, 1983—86. Named to Ten Best Censored list, 1978; recipient Project Censored award, Top Censored Story, 1981, Inaugural Disting. Publ. award in Labor Studies, Soc. for Study Social Problems, 1996; Ford Found. fellow, 1965—67, 1970—71, Guggenheim fellow, 1981—82, NSF grantee, 1981, 1982, 1998. Mem.: Internat. Sociol. Assn. (mem. editl. bd. 1977—81), Am. Sociol. Assn. (mem. governing coun. 1977—80, Disting. Contbn. Scholarship award in Polit. Sociology 1992, 1996, 2002, Max Weber Disting. Book award in Orgns., Occuptaions and Work 2004). Democrat. Jewish. Office: UCLA Dept Sociology 264 Haines Hall Los Angeles CA 90095-1551 Office Phone: 310-825-3968. Business E-Mail: zeitlin@soc.ucla.edu. *Personal philosophy: "If I am not for myself who will be? and when I am for myself, what am I?" Hillel, the Elder.*

ZEKMAN, PAMELA LOIS (MRS. FREDRIC SOLL), reporter; b. Chgo., Oct. 22, 1944; d. Theodore Nathan and Lois Jane (Bernstein) Z.; m. Fredric Soll, Nov. 29, 1975. BA, U. Calif. at Berkeley, 1965. Social worker Dept. Public Aid Cook County, Chgo., 1965-66; reporter City News Bur., Chgo., 1966-70, Chgo. Tribune, 1970-75, Chgo. Sun-Times, 1975-81; investigative reporter Sta. WBBM-TV, Chgo., 1981—. Recipient Pulitzer Prize awarded to Chicago Tribune for gen. local reporting on vote fraud series, 1973; Community Service award for vote fraud series UPI, 1972; Feature Series award for nursing home abuses series AP, 1971; Pub. Service award for slumlord series UPI, 1973; Newswriting award AP, 1973; In Depth Reporting award for police brutality series AP, 1974; Investigative Reporting awards Inland Daily Press Assn., 1974, 78; Investigative Reporting award for series on city waste AP, 1975; Pulitzer Prize for pub. service for series on hosp. abuses, 1976; Investigative Reporting award for series on baby selling, 1976; Pub. Service award for series on currency exchange abuses UPI, 1976; Investigative Reporting award for series on abuses in home for retarded children AP, 1977; Soc. Midland Authors Golden Rake award; UPI Public Service award; Ill. AP award; Nat. Headliners Club award; Sweepstakes award for Mirage Tavern investigative project, 1978; Nat. Disting. Service award for series on med. abuses in abortion clinics Sigma Delta Chi, 1979; named Journalist of Yr. No.

Ill. U., 1979; recipient George Foster Peabody Broadcasting award, 1982, 85, RTNDA Investigative Reporting award, 1983, DuPont Columbia award 1982, 87. Office: WBBM-TV 630 N McClurg Ct Chicago IL 60611-4495

ZEKMAN, TERRI MARGARET, graphic designer; b. Chgo., Sept. 13, 1950; d. Theodore Nathan and Lois (Bernstein) Z.; m. Alan Daniels, Apr. 12, 1980; children: Jesse Logan, Dakota Caitlin. BFA, Washington U., St. Louis, 1971; postgrad, Art Inst. Chgo., 1974-75. Graphic designer (on retainer) greeting cards and related products Recycled Paper Products Co., Chgo., 1970—, Jillson Roberts, Inc., Calif.; apprenticed graphic designer Helmuth, Obata & Kassabaum, St. Louis, 1970-71; graphic designer Container Corp., Chgo., 1971; graphic designer, art dir., photographer Cuerden Advt. Design, Denver, 1971-74; art dir. D'Arcy, McManus & Masius Advt., Chgo., 1975-76; freelance graphic designer Chgo., 1976-77; art dir. Garfield Linn Advt., Chgo., 1977-78; graphic designer Keiser Design Group, Van Noy & Co., Los Angeles, 1978-79; owner and operator graphic design studio Los Angeles, 1979—. Art and photography tchr. Ctr. for Early Edn., L.A., 1996—, Buckley Sch., Sherman Oaks, 1996—; 3d grade tchr. asst., 1999—. Recipient cert. of merit St. Louis Outdoor Poster Contest, 1970, Denver Art Dirs. Club, 1973 Office Phone: 818-789-9611. Personal E-mail: redzek50@aol.com.

ZELBY, ANDREW S. neurosurgeon; s. Leon W. and Rachel Zelby; m. Cynthia W. Zelby, 1960; children: Elaine, Karen, Allison. BS in Physiology, Okla. State U., Stillwater, 1983; MD, U. Okla., Oklahoma City, 1987. Diplomate Am. Bd. Neurol. Surgeons. Asst. prof. Loyola U. Chgo. Med. Ctr., Maywood, Ill., 1994—96; pvt. practice neurosurgeon Neurol. Surgery and Spine Surgery, Maywood, Ill., 1996—; clin. assoc. prof. U. Chgo., 1998—. Hon. chmn. Physicians Adv. Bd., Washington, 2003. Fellow: ACS; mem.: Am. Assn. Neurol. Surgeons. Avocations: skiing, scuba diving, golf. Office: Neurol Surgeons & Spine Surgery SC Ste 302 1701 S First Ave Maywood IL 60153

ZELBY, LEON WOLF, electrical engineering educator, consulting engineer; b. Sosnowiec, Poland, Mar. 26, 1925; came to U.S., 1946, naturalized, 1951; s. Herszel and Helen (Wajnryb) Zylberberg; m. Rachel Kupfermintz, Dec. 28, 1954; children: Laurie Susan, Andrew Stephen. BSEE, Moore Sch. Elec. Engring., 1956; MS, Calif. Inst. Tech., 1957; PhD, U. Pa., 1961. Registered profl. engr., Pa., Okla. Mem. staff RCA, Hughes R & D Labs., Lincoln Lab., MIT, Sandia Corp., Argonne (Ill.) Nat. Labs., Inst. for Energy Analysis; mem. faculty U. Pa., 1959-67, assoc. prof., 1964-67; assoc. dir. plasma engring. Inst. Direct Energy Conversion, 1962-67; prof. U. Okla., Norman, 1967-95, dir. Sch. Elec. Engring., 1967-71; ret., 1995. Cons. RCA, 1961-67, Moore Sch. Elec. Engring., 1967-68, also pvt. firms. Editor Tech. and Soc. mag., 1990-93; contbr. articles on energy-associated problems and issues to profl. jours. With AUS, 1946-47. Cons. Electrodynamic Corp. fellow Calif. Inst. Tech., 1957, Mpls.-Honeywell fellow U. Pa., 1957-58, Harrison fellow, 1958. Mem. IEEE, Franklin Inst., Sigma Xi, Tau Beta Pi, Eta Kappa Nu, Pi Mu Epsilon, Sigma Tau, Phi Kappa Phi. Home: 1009 Whispering Pines Dr Norman OK 73072-6912 Office Phone: 405-325-4290. Business E-Mail: zelby@ou.edu. *To learn as much, and to experience as much as possible, without harm to others; read, study, vary professional and recreational activities within constraints of the system.*

ZELDES, BENJAMIN, optometrist; b. New Britain, Conn., Oct. 23, 1924; m. Edith R. Zeldes. Student, U. Conn., 1945—48; BS, OD, Ill. Coll. Optometry, 1950, postgrad., 1954, Gesell Inst. Child Devel., 1961—62. Pvt. practice, Newington, Conn., 1957—. Optometric cons. Mediplex of Newington and Mediplex of Wethersfield; cons. Hartford (Conn.) Easter Seal Rehab. Ctr., 1970—73, Continuous Progress Ednl. Consultants, 1970—73. Mem. Conn. Comprehensive Health Planning Adv. Coun., 1970—73; mem. adv. bd. Conn. Assn. Children with Perceptual Learning Disabilities, 1966—68; mem. Physicians Task Force on Mental Retardation, 1964—65; chmn. religious sch. com. Temple Sinai, Newington. Fellow: Am. Acad. Optometry; mem.: Nat. Eye Rsch. Found. (fellow internat. orthokeratology sect.), Hartford County Optometric Assn., Conn. Assn. Optometrists (chmn. ins. com. 1959—76, exec. coun. 1970—82, pres. 1976, commn. on personal health svcs., chmn. children's vision), New Eng. Coun. Optometrists (chmn. ins. com. 1965—84, 1986, pres.), Am. Optometric Assn. (ins. com. 1983—84, key person, polit. action com.), Lions (past pres. Newington chpt., chmn. eye rsch.). Home: 107 Lake Shore Blvd Stafford Springs CT 06076 Office: 1268 Main St Newington CT 06111

ZELDIN, RICHARD PACKER, publisher; b. Worcester, Mass., Aug. 7, 1918; s. M. and Virginia (Gealt) Z.; m. Virginia Graves, Nov. 25, 1950; children— Elizabeth Ann, Richard Shepherd. BS, West Chester U., Pa., 1942; grad. exec. program bus. adminstrn., Columbia U., 1966. Gen. mgr. profl. and reference book div. McGraw-Hill Book Co., Inc., 1948-68; v.p., publishing dir. Litton Ednl. Pub. Co., Inc., 1968-70; pres. R.R. Bowker Co., 1970-76, Xerox Coll. Pub., Xerox Individualized Pub., 1970-76; pub. John Wiley & Sons, Inc., 1976-83; v.p. Moseley Assocs. Inc., N.Y.C., 1983—. Sec.-treas. sci., tech. and med. book pubs. group Assn. Am. Pubs., 1966-70; mem. adv. com. comml. publs. AEC, 1966-70 Author: A Tennis Guide to the USA, 1980, Business Forms on File, 1984, Personal Forms on File, 1984; contbr. Scholarly Publishing, Books, Journals, Publishers and Libraries in the 20th Century, 2002. Served to lt. USNR, 1942-46. Recipient Disting. Alumni award West Chester U., 1974. Mem. Info. Industry Assn. (sec. 1973—), IEEE, Am. Soc. Info. Sci., Soc. for Scholarly Pub. Clubs: Dutch Treat (N.Y.C.), Pubs. Lunch (N.Y.C.). Home: 20 Fairfield Dr Eatontown NJ 07724-3114 Office: Moseley Assocs Inc 342 Madison Ave Rm 1414 New York NY 10173-1423

ZELEKE, ASSEFA, electrical engineer; b. Finoteselam, Gojjam, Ethiopia, Aug. 12, 1963; arrived in U.S., 1991; s. Zeleke Desta and Tiruwork Tizazu. BSc in Elect. Engring., Kiev Polytech Inst., Kiev, Ukraine, 1983; MSc in Nuc. Powerplant Design Analysis, Moscow Power Engring. Inst., Moscow, Russia, 1986; PhD (hon.), Parkwood Univ., London, Eng., 1990, Dr, 1994. Power plant constrn. Ministry of Energy and Mines, Addis Ababa, Ethiopia, 1990—91; design analysis EEEtechnology, Alexandrea, Va., 1991—. Rschr. (experimental engring.), —. Mem.: N.Y. Acad. of Sci. Avocations: tennis, jogging, reading. E-mail: assefa@peoplepc.com.

ZELEN, MARVIN, statistics educator; b. N.Y.C., June 21, 1927; m. Thelma Geier, Sept. 10, 1950; children: Deborah, Sandra. BS, CCNY, 1949; MS, U. N.C., 1951; PhD, Am. U., 1957; MA (hon.), Harvard U., 1977; Docteur Honoris Causa, U. Victor Segalen, 2003. Stat. eng. lab. Nat. Bureau of Standards, 1952-61; assoc. prof. Univ. Md., 1960-61; head, stat. and applied Math. section Nat. Cancer Inst., 1963-66; leading prof. State U., Buffalo, 1967-77; pres. Frontier Sci. and Tech. Rsch. Found., Boston, 1975—; chmn. dept. biostats. Dana Farber Cancer Inst., Boston, 1977-98; prof. Harvard U. Sch. Pub. Health, Boston, 1977—; chmn. dept. biostat. Harvard U., 1980-90. Vis. prof. Univ. Wis., 1961-63, vis. assoc. prof. Univ. Calif., 1958. Sgt. U.S. Army, 1945-46. Fulbright scholar, 1965-66. Fellow Am. Acad. Arts and Sci., AAAS, Inst. Math. Stats., Am. Statis. Assn.; mem. Internat. Stats. Inst. Home: 230 Eliot St Chestnut Hill MA 02467-1447 Office: Harvard Sch Pub Health 677 Huntington Ave Boston MA 02115-6096 Business E-Mail: zelen@hsph.harvard.edu.

ZELENAK, EDWARD MICHAEL, lawyer, musician; b. Dearborn, Mich., Aug. 28, 1953; s. Edward Patrick and Irene Elaine (Maruska) Z.; m. Angeline Rose Cianfarani, May 24, 1986; children: Amelia Mary Rose and Edward Patrick (twins), Elliott William. BA, Wayne State U., 1975, JD, 1977. Bar: Mich. 1977, US Dist. Ct. (ea. dist.) Mich. 1977, 6th Cir. Ct. of Appeals 1987. Leader Ed Zelenak Orch., Lincoln Pk., Mich., 1971—; dir. pub. affairs Sta. WDRQ, Southfield, Mich., 1977-83, host talk show, 1978-83; instr. Wayne State U., Detroit, 1977-84; pvt. practice Lincoln Pk., 1977—; atty. Cities of Lincoln Pk. and Southgate (Mich.), 1978—. Hon. consul Slovak Republic, 2001—; corr. RKO Network, 1980-83; host talk show United Cable TV Mich., Woodhaven, 1980—, Sta. WXYT, 1988-94; host The Legal Huddle, Am. Radio Network, 2003-04; gen. counsel Pat Paulsen for Pres., 1996; hon. consul Slovakia, 2001. Composer, performer (album) C. B. Polka, 1977. Alt. del. Dem. Nat. Conv., Miami, Fla., 1972, mem. staff Dem. Nat. Conv., NYC, 1976; exec. bd. 16th Dist. Dems., Dearborn, 1975-87; gen. counsel First Cath. Slovak Union US and Can., 1988-99, Pat Paulsen for Pres. Campaign, 1996; spl. counsel City of Ecorse, Mich., 1989—; bd. dirs. People's Cmty. Svcs. of Detroit, 1992-98; dir. Downriver Coun. for the Arts, 1997—; mem. Congress on New Urbanism, Seaside Inst. Recipient Commendation Mich. State Senate, 1982; named One of Five Outstanding Young Michiganders, Mich. Jaycees, 1990. Mem. Am. Fedn. Musicians, State Bar Mich., Wayne State U. Law Sch. Alumni Assn. (dir. 1998—, sec., v.p. 2001, pres. 2002), Downriver Bar Assn., Slovak League Am. (nat. dir. 1985—, del. meeting with Vaclav Havel and Alexander Dubcek conf. in Czecho-Slovakia 1990), Wayne State U. Law Alumni Assn. (mem. exec. com., v.p. 2001, pres. 2002), Slovak Cath. Sokol Club, First Cath. Slovak Union, KC (fin. com. Robert Jones chpt. 1987-96), Kiwanis (pres. local chpt. 1981-82), Rotary Internat. Home: 711 Saint Johns Blvd Lincoln Park MI 48146-4925 Office: 2933 Fort St Lincoln Park MI 48146-2425 Office Phone: 313-386-6400. E-mail: zband@comcast.net.

ZELENKA, DONALD JOHN, lawyer; b. Akron, Ohio, Feb. 16, 1952; s. Donald Banser and Jane (Cunningham) Z.; m. Leslie Rock, May 24, 1975. BA in Arts and Scis., Ohio State U., 1974; JD, U. S.C., 1977. Bar: S.C. 1977, U.S. Ct. Appeals (4th cir.) 1978, Va. 1980, U.S. Dist. Ct. S.C. 1981, U.S. Supreme Ct. 1983, U.S. Ct. Appeals (11th cir.) 1985. Law clk., research asst. U.S. Ct. Appeals (4th cir.), Richmond, Va., 1977-79; from asst. to chief dep. atty. gen. S.C. Atty. Gen., Columbia, 1979-94; asst. dep. atty. gen. supr. Capital Litigation/Fed. Habeas Corpus unit S.C. Atty. Gen., 1995—. Tchr., instr. clin. programs U. S.C. Law Sch., Columbia, 1983-84. Mem. Sentencing Guidelines Commn., Columbia, 1983-89, S.C. Victim-Witness Task Force. Recipient Silver Scales of Justice award S.C. Victim Assistance Network, 1991. Mem. ABA (pub. sector lawyers divsn.), Richland County Bar Assn., Assn. Govt. Attys. in Capital Litigation (exec. bd. dirs. 1985—, pres. 1992-93, Excellence award 1995), S.C. Bar Assn. (criminal law sect.), Nat. Dist. Attys. Assn. Methodist. Home: 320 Hunters Blind Dr Columbia SC 29212-1610 Office: SC Atty Gen PO Box 11549 Columbia SC 29211-1549

ZELEPUKIN, VALERI, professional hockey player; b. Vosdresensk, Russia, Sept. 17, 1968; married. Hockey player VOSK/USSR, 1984-87, 89-90, CSKA/USSR, 1987-88, SKA/USSR, 1987-88, KHIM/USSR, 1990-91, NJER/NHL, 1991-92, 93-97, 1997-98, EDMO/NHL, 1997-98, RUSS/OLYMP, 1997-98, PHIL/NHL, 1998—, Chgo. Blackhawks, 2000. Recipient ice hockey Silver medal Olympic Games, Nagano, Japan, 1998. Avocation: tennis. Office: Chgo Blackhawks United Ctr 1901 W Madison Chicago IL 60612

ZELEZNAK, SHIRLEY ANNE, psychotherapist; b. Ft. Dodge, Iowa; d. Melvin Peter and Illiah Mary (Olson) Hood; m. Donald John Zeleznak, June 14, 1969; children: Kristine Anne, Ryan John. BA, Briar Cliff Coll., 1967; MS in Clin. and Ednl. Psychology and Counseling, Winona State U., 1972. Cert. hypnotherapist, psychotherapist. Secondary tchr., Rochester, Minn., 1969-74; secondary tchr./counselor Mankato, Minn., 1974-77; task force dir. Heart Assn., Mankato, 1978-82; mental health counselor Scottsdale, Ariz., 1985—. Tchr. Maricopa County C.C., Scottsdale, 1986-89; motivational speaker, Mankato, 1974-84; sch. cons. Paradise Valley/Scottsdale Sch. Dist., 1987—; bd. dirs. Home Base, Phoenix; psychotherapist St. Maria Goretti Ch., Scottsdale, 1986—; crisis intervention counselor, police dept., Phoenix, 1993—. Author: Series for Junior High Students, 1981 (books), 1982-83 (software programs). Chef A'La Heart, Minn. Heart Assn., Mankato, 1979-81; motivational speaker Gang Awareness, Scottsdale, 1992—. Recipient Appreciation award Minn. Heart Assn., 1981. Mem. Mental Health Counselors, Nat. Ctr. for Learning Disabilities, Am. Counseling Assn., Phoenix Scottish Rite Found., Inst. for Developmental and Behavioral Neurology. Roman Catholic. Avocations: golf, tennis, power walking.

ZELICKSON, SUE, newspaper and cookbook editor, television reporter and host, food consultant; b. Mpls., Sept. 13, 1934; d. Harry M. and Bernice (Gross) Zipperman; m. Alvin S. Zelickson, Aug. 21, 1956; children— Barry M., Brian D. B.S. in Edn., U. Minn., 1956. Cert. elem. tchr., S.C., Minn. Tchr. various schs. Mpls., S.C., Golden Valley, Minn., 1956-79; writer, editor, columnist Mpls.-St. Paul Mag., 1980—, Buylines, Mpls., 1984—; TV-radio reporter Sta. WCCO-KSTP, Mpls, 1980—, Lifestyles with Sue Zelickson Sta. WCCO cable; restaurant developer, cons. Mpls., 1978—; v.p. Passage Tours, Mpls., 1984-88. Coordinator, editor: Much Ado About Food, 1978; Minnesota Heritage Cookbook, 1979; Lee Ann Chin's Chinese Cuisine, 1981; Collins Back Room Cooking Secrets, 1981; The Governor's Table Cookbook, 1981; Chocolate Days & Chocolate Nights, 1982; Food for Show, Food on the Go, 1983; Wild Rice Star of The North, 1985; Look What's Cooking Now, 1985. Contbr. articles to Sun Newspaper, Post Publs., Mpls., Tribune. Public relations, promoter, fundraiser Mpls. Boys & Girls Club, Mpls. Inst. Arts, Hennepin County Med. Soc. Aux., Ronald McDonald House, Bonaventure Mall, Women's Assn. Minn. Symphony Orchestra, Council Jewish Women, Mt. Sinai Hosp., Brandeis U. Women, Minn. Opera Assn., Guthrie Theatre, Sholom Home, Am. Cancer Soc., M.S. Soc., March of Dimes, Am. Heart Assn.; bd. dirs. U. Minn. Alumni Bd., Golden Valley State Bank. Recipient Outstanding Achievement award There's Living Proof Am. Cancer Soc., Duluth, Minn., 1984; Outstanding Achievement award Boys & Girls Club Minn., 1984. Mem. Nat. Council Jewish Women, Women's Assn. Minn. Orch., numerous others. Avocations: reading, travel; writing; painting. Home and Office: 101 Ardmore Dr Minneapolis MN 55422-5209

ZELIGER, BERNARD, dean; Provost and dean Touro U. Coll. Osteo. Medicine. Office: 832 Walnut Ave Vallejo CA 94592

ZELIKOW, HOWARD MONROE, management and financial consultant; b. Bklyn., Apr. 17, 1934; s. Herman and Mae (Rebell) Z.; m. Doris Brown, June 10, 1956 (div. Aug. 1987); children: Lori Ann Zelikow Florio, Daniel M.; m. Marcie Peskin Rosenblum, Dec. 12, 1987. BA, Dartmouth Coll., 1955; MBA, Amost Tuck Sch., 1956. Acct. Ernst & Ernst, N.Y.C., 1956-61; controller Kratter Corp., N.Y.C., 1961-64; mgr. J.H. Cohn, CPAs, Newark, 1964-65; ptnr. Zelikow & Rebell CPAs, N.Y.C., 1965-70; v.p. Oxbow Constrn. Corp., Port Washington, N.Y., 1970-76; exec. v.p., treas., chief fin. officer Progressive Ins. Cos., Mayfield Village, Ohio, 1976-87; prin. ZKA Assocs., Cleve., 1987-96; ptnr., mng. dir. Kayne Anderson Investment Mgmt., L.A., 1988—. Trustee Village of Great Neck Estates, Great Neck, N.Y., 1975-76. Mem. Hillcrest Club, Phi Beta Kappa. Jewish. Home: 10114 Empyrean Way Los Angeles CA 90067-3830 Office: Kayne Anderson Investment Mgmt 1800 Avenue Of The Stars Los Angeles CA 90067-4212 Business E-Mail: hzelikow@kayne.com.

ZELIN, JEROME, retired retail executive; b. Bklyn., Dec. 24, 1930; s. Isidore and Ida (Roffman) Z.; m. Muriel Altsher, Dec. 18, 1955; children— Dorothy, Michael, Steven. BS magna cum laude, N.Y.U., 1952. Acct. Seymour Schwartz CPA, 1954-57; partner firm Schwartz, Zelin & Weiss CPAs, N.Y.C., 1958-61; vice chmn., pres., exec. v.p., treas., financial v.p., dir. Unishops, Inc. (retail co.), Jersey City, 1961-74; exec. v.p. Masters, Inc., Westbury, N.Y., 1974-97; cons. Master's, Inc., Westbury, N.Y., 1997-2000; ret. Trustee Temple Sholom of Flatbush. Served with AUS, 1952-54. Mem. N.Y. Soc. CPAs, Am. Inst. CPAs, Beta Gamma Sigma, Tau Alpha Omega. Jewish. Home: 225 Arkansas Dr Brooklyn NY 11234-6901 E-mail: j.zelin1000@aol.com.

ZELIN, MADELEINE, think-tank executive; Prof. History and East Asian Langs. and Cultures Columbia U., dir. East Asian Inst., dir. Columbia East Asian Nat. Resource Ctr. Mem. adv. bd. Jour. Chinese Law, Chinese History Assn., bd. dirs. Chinese Bus. History Soc., curriculum com., sub. com. East Asian Langs. Presenter in field. Office: East Asian Inst Columbia U Mail Code 3333 420 W 118th St New York NY 10027-7213

ZELINSKI, JOSEPH JOHN, engineering educator, consultant; b. Glen Lyon, Pa., Dec. 30, 1922; s. John Joseph and Lottie Mary (Oshinski) Z.; m. Mildred G. Sirois, July 22, 1946; children: Douglas John, Peter David. BS, Pa. State U., 1944, PhD, 1950. Grad. fellow Pa. State U., University Park, 1946-50; project supr. applied physics lab. Johns Hopkins U., Silver Spring, Md., 1950-58; staff scientist Space Tech. Labs. (now TRW, Inc.), Redondo Beach, Calif., 1958-60; head chem. tech. div. Ops. Evaluation Group MIT, Cambridge, 1960-62; prin. rsch. scientist Avco Everett (Mass.) Rsch. Lab., 1962-64; prof. mech. engring. Northeastern U., Boston, 1964-85, prof. emeritus, 1985—; pres. World Edn. Resources, Ltd., Tampa, Fla., 1984—. Cons. Avco Everett Rsch. Lab., 1964-71, Pratt & Whitney Aircraft, East Hartford, Conn., 1966-70, Modern Electric Products and Phys. Scis. Co., Inc., Boston, 1980-82, Morrison, Mahoney and Miller, Boston, 1984; vice-chmn., chmn. exec. com. Univ. Grad. Coun., Northeastern U., Boston, 1980-84, dir. mech. engring. grad. program, 1982-85; del. 4th World Conf. Continuing Engring. Edn., Beijing China People to People, Spokane, Wash., 1989. Contbr. articles to profl. jours. Prin. Confraternity Christian Doctrine, Andover, Mass., 1961-64; pres. Andover Edn. Coun., 1962-64; vice chmn. Dem. Town Com., Boxford, Mass., 1980-84. Lt. (j.g.) USNR, 1943-46, PTO. Mem. AAAS, ASME, Am. Chem. Soc., N.Y. Acad. Scis., Combustion Inst. Democrat. Roman Catholic. Achievements include U.S. and foreign patents for coal combustion system for magnetohydrodynamic power generation, for fuel-cooled combustion systems for jet engines flying at high Mach numbers; prediction of optical observables of re-entry vehicles from analysis of decomposition mechanisms of heat-shield materials; invention of high-temperature furnace for production of crystalline graphite; development and verification of a design method for ramjet combustors.

ZELINSKY, PAUL O. illustrator, painter, author; b. Evanston, Ill., Feb. 14, 1953; s. Daniel and Zelda B. (Oser) Z.; m. Deborah M. Hallen, Dec. 31, 1981; children: Anna H., Rachel L. BA summa cum laude, Yale U., 1974; MFA in Painting, Tyler Sch. Art, 1976. Art instr. San Diego State U., 1976; freelance illustrator/author, 1977—. Illustrator: Emily Upham's Revenge, 1978, How I Hunted the Little Fellows, 1979, The History of Helpless Harry, 1980, What Amanda Saw, 1981, Ralph S. Mouse, 1982, The Song in the Walnut Grove, 1982, The Sun's Asleep Behind the Hill, 1982, Zoo Doings, 1983, Hansel and Gretel, 1984 (Caldecott Honor 1985), The Story of Mrs. Lovewright and Purrless her Cat, 1985, The Random House Book of Humor for Children, 1988, Strider, 1991, The Enchanted Castle, 1992, Dear Mr. Henshaw, 1993, More Rootabagas, 1993, Swamp Angel, 1994 (Caldecott Honor 1995), Five Children and It, 1999, Awful Ogre's Awful Day, 2001, Doodler Doodling, 2004; illustrator, adapter: The Maid and the Mouse and the Odd-shaped House, 1981, Rumpelstiltskin 1986 (Caldecott Honor 1987), Rapunzel, 1997 (Caldecott Honor 1998); illustrator, author: The Lion and the Stoat, 1984; illustrator, adapter, designer: The Wheels on the Bus, 1990, Knick-Knack Paddywhack!, 2002. Recipient Caldecott Honor for Best Illustrated Book N.Y. Times Book Rev., 1981, 85, 94, 2001, 02. Mem. PEN, Graphic Artists Guild, Author's Guild, Soc. Children's Book Writers and Illustrators, Phi Beta Kappa.

ZELIS, ROBERT FELIX, cardiologist, educator; b. Perth Amboy, NJ, Aug. 5, 1939; s. Felix Andrew and Rita Marie (Jurasz) Z.; m. Gail Ann Heelon, Sept. 10, 1960; children: Robert Felix, Kathleen, Karen, David. BS cum laude, U. Mass., 1960; MD with honors, U. Chgo., 1964. Diplomate: Am. Bd. Internal Medicine (cardiovascular disease). Intern, then asst. resident in medicine Beth Israel Hosp., Harvard U. Med. Sch., 1964-66; clin. assoc. (lt. comdr. USPHS) cardiology br. Nat. Heart Inst., NIH, Bethesda, Md., 1966-68; mem. faculty U. Calif. Med. Sch., Davis, 1968-74, asst. assoc. prof. medicine, 1972-74, chief lab. clin. physiology, 1968-74, asst. chief sect. cardiovasc. medicine, 1970-74; prof. medicine and cellular/molecular physiology Milton S. Hershey (Pa.) Med. Ctr., Pa. State U. Coll. Medicine, 1974—, chief divsn. cardiology, 1974-84, dir. cardiology rsch., 1984—. Editor: The Peripheral Circulations, 1975; co-editor: Calcium Blockers, 1982; mem. editorial bd. Annals Internal Medicine, 1976-79, Am. Jour. Physiology, 1976-79, Circulation, 1979-82, Am. Heart Jour., 1980-90, Am. Jour. Cardiology, 1983-86, Jour. Cardiovasc. Pharmacology, 1991-2001, Jour. Am. Coll. Cardiology, 1994-99; contbr. articles to profl. jours. Walter S. Barr fellow, 1960-64; recipient Borden Rsch. award, 1964, Palmer award for Faculty Mentoring Pa. State U., 1997, Disting. Educator award Pa. State U. Coll. Medicine, 2003, Disting. Svc. award U. Chgo. Med. and Biol. Scis. Alumni Assn., 2004. Fellow A.C.P., Am. Coll. Chest Physicians, Am. Coll. Cardiology (gov. Eastern Pa. 1977-80); mem. Am. Fedn. Clin. Research (pres. 1977-78), Am. Soc. Clin. Investigation (nat. council 1981-85, v.p. 1984-85), Am. Physiol. Soc., Assn. Am. Physicians, Assn. Univ. Cardiologists, Am. Soc. Pharmacology and Exptl. Therapeutics, Am. Heart Assn. (nat. fellow councils circulation, arteriosclerosis, clin. cardiology and epidemiology, v.p. for community programs 1979-81, award of merit 1983 v.p., exec. com. Pa. 1976-79, pres. Pa. affiliate 1979-80, Charles T. Mears Humanitarian award 1984), Western Soc. Clin. Research, Sigma Xi, Alpha Omega Alpha, Phi Eta Sigma. Roman Catholic. Home: 815 Verden Dr Hummelstown PA 17036-9700 Office: MS Hershey Med Ctr Cardiology Divsn HO-47 PO Box 850 Hershey PA 17033-0850 Office Phone: 717-531-1790.

ZELKOWITZ, MARVIN VICTOR, computer science educator; b. Bklyn., Aug. 7, 1945; s. Philip and Tillie Zelkowitz; m. Cindy Sonia Dectrow, May 24, 1970; children: Elena Rochelle, Aaron Daniel. BS in Math., Rensselaer Poly. Inst., 1967; MS in Computer Sci., Cornell U., 1969, PhD in Computer Sci., 1971. Instr. math. Ithaca (N.Y.) Coll., 1970; asst. to assoc. prof. U. Md., College Park, 1971-90, prof., 1990—, assoc. chmn. for edn., 1982-85, acting chmn., 1985, assoc. chmn. for facilities, 1987-88. Systems programmer RCA Computer Systems Divsn., 1969; computer scientist faculty Nat. Inst. Standards and Tech., Gaithersburg, Md., 1976-98; co-dir. Fraunhofer Ctr.-Md., 1997-2002, chief scientist, 2004—; spkr. in field. Series editor: Ablex Software Engineering Series, 1986-97; co-author: Software Specification: Formal Methods, 1994, Programming Languages Design and Implementation, 1996, 4th ed., 2001; editor: Advances in Computers, 1994—; contbr. chpts. to books, articles to profl. jours. Mem. math. adv. com. Howard County, Md., 1992-97. Recipient Software Engring. Lab. grant NASA/Goddard, 1976-2002, Cert. Recognition, Nat. Bur. Standards, Gaithersburg, 1981, Cert. Appreciation Navy Next Generation Computing Resources program, Washington, 1993. Fellow Computer Soc. of IEEE (Meritorious Svc. award 1992, 99, cert. of appreciation 1980), Assn. for Computing Machinery (Svc. award 1996, Sigsoft Disting. Svc. award 2000), Nat. Capital Area Skeptics (bd. dirs. 1992—, chmn. 2003—), Tech. Com. on Software Engring. (chmn. 1981-83), Assn. for Computing Machinery (chmn. spl. interest group on software engring. 1979-81). Avocations: jogging, model railroading. Office: Univ Md Dept Computer Sci College Park MD 20742-0001 Business E-Mail: mvz@cs.umd.edu.

ZELL, GLENN, lawyer; b. N.Y.C., N.Y., Nov. 2, 1934; s. Joseph and Rose (Hyman) Z.; m. Gloria Wynne, Apr. 16, 1961; children: Jeffrey, Rodney, Barbara. BS, N.Y.U., 1954; LLB, Emory U., 1965. Bar: Ga. 1965. Pvt. practice Zell & Zell, P.C., Atlanta, 1965—. Mem. Ga. Bar Assn., Ga. Assn. Criminal Def. Lawyers. Jewish. Office: Zell & Zell PC 729 Piedmont Ave NE Atlanta GA 30308 Office Phone: 404-523-4611.

ZELL, SAMUEL, transportation leasing company executive; b. Chgo., Sept. 28, 1941; married. BA, U. Mich., 1963, JD, 1966. With Yates Holleb and Michelson, 1966-68; pres. Equity Fin. and Mgmt. Co., 1968—; chmn. Great Am. Mgmt. and Investment Inc., 1981—, also chief exec. officer; also co-chmn. Revco D.S.; chmn. Equity Group Investments, LLC, 1976—. Chmn. Delta Queen Steamboat Co., New Orleans, 1984—, Eagle Industries Inc.; chmn. Itel Corp., 1985—, bd. dirs. Office: Davel Communications Group Inc 10120 Windhorst Rd Tampa FL 33619*

ZELLER, CHRISTOPHER LEE, archaeologist, preservationist; b. Northampton, Pa., Nov. 25, 1956; s. Karl Fredrich and Joan Veron (Hagenbuch) Zeller; m. Christi Joanne Wiggins, Apr. 24, 1982 (div. Mar. 11, 2004); 1 child, Kaeti Grace. BA in Anthropology, Ft. Lewis Coll., 1980. Fireline archaeologist U.S. Forest Svc., cert. Ski patroller Nat. Ski Patrol, EMT Colo. Preservation tech., foreman San Juan Stabilization, Mancos, Colo., 1977—81; archaeologist Bur. Land Mgmt., Durango, Colo., 1982; stabilization specialist Paul Nickens and Assocs., Montrose, Colo., 1983; ind. contractor, stabilization specialist Woods Canyon Archaeol. Cons., Yellow Jacket, Colo., 1985—87; ind. contractor, project dir. Four Corners Rsch. Inst., Durango, 1986—87; owner, operator Petro Graphics, Durango, 1987—. Ski patroller Durango Mountain Resort, 1974—. Achievements include invention of toboggan

platform; conducted over 70 major preservation projects involving over 60 archaeological and historic sites in American Southwest. Avocations: fine art, trout fishing, camping. Office: Petro Graphics Po Box 745 Durango CO 81302

ZELLER, JOSEPH PAUL, advertising executive; b. Crestline, Ohio, Mar. 19, 1940; s. Paul Edward and Grace Beatrice (Kinstle) Z.; m. Nancy Jane Schmidt, June 17, 1961; children: Laurie, Joe. BA, U. Notre Dame, 1962; MFA, Ohio U., 1963. Mgr.radio/television Drewrys Ltd. USA, Inc., South Bend, Ind., 1963-64; media supr. Tatham-Laird & Kudner, Chgo., 1964-67; v.p. assoc. media dir. J. Walter Thompson Co., Chgo., 1967-77; v.p. media dir, v.p. Campbell-Mithun, Chgo., 1977-80; sr. v.p., dir. media, fin., chmn. media coun. D'Arcy Masius Benton & Bowles, Chgo., 1980-96, sr. v.p., 1996-2000; pres. Fox River Trading Co., East Dundee, Ill., 2000—. Chmn. Z Prop, 1986—; dir. circle Desert Caballeros Mus., 1994-96; founder Native Am. Images web mag., 1999. Pres. Amateur Hockey Assn. Ill., 1985. Mem. Broadcast Pioneers, Chgo. Advt. Club, Moose. Roman Catholic. Avocations: amateur hockey, photography, country music. E-mail: jzeller@prodigy.net., trader@rivertradingpost.com.

ZELLER, MARILYNN KAY, retired librarian; b. Scottsbluff, Nebr., Mar. 1, 1940; d. William Harold and Dorothy Elizabeth (Wilkins) Richards; m. Robert Jerome Zeller, May 21, 1966; children: Kevin Jerome and Renae Kay. BS, Calvary Bible Coll., 1983; MLS, U. Mo., Columbia, 1989. Cert. libr. File clk. Waddell & Reed, Kansas City, Mo., 1962-65; payroll clk. Century Fin. Co., Kansas City, Mo., 1965-67, Percy Kent Bag Co., Independence, Mo., 1968-70; accounts receivable Swansons on the Pla, Kansas City, 1971-73; clk. casualty ins. Mill Mutuals, Kansas City, 1977-80; registrar's asst. Calvary Bible Coll., Kansas City, 1980-85, libr. asst., 1985-88, asst. libr., 1988-89, head libr., 1989—96. Chairperson libr. com. Calvary Bible Coll., Kansas City, 1989-96; libr. rep. Friends of the Hilda Kroeker Libr., Kansas City, 1989-96. Author: History of the Christian Librarian's Association, 1989. Mem. Christian Librs. Assn. Avocations: walking, reading, crocheting, sewing, swimming. Home: 401 13th Ave N Greenwood MO 64034-9750

ZELLER, MICHAEL EDWARD, physicist, researcher; b. San Francisco, Oct. 8, 1939; s. Edward Michael and Marie (Eschen) Z.; m. Linda Marie Smith, June 12, 1960; children: Jeffrey, Daniel. BS, Stanford U., 1961; MS, UCLA, 1964, PhD, 1968. Rsch. assoc. UCLA, 1968-69; instr. physics Yale U., New Haven, 1969-70, asst. prof., 1970-76, assoc. prof., 1976-82, prof., 1982—, chmn., 1989-95, Henry Ford II prof., 1996—. Recipient DeVane medal Phi Beta Kappa, 1980. Fellow Am. Phys. Soc.; mem. N.Y. Acad. Sci., Sigma Xi, Sigma Pi Sigma. Democrat. Jewish. Home: 135 Newton Rd Woodbridge CT 06525-1534 Office: Yale U Physics Dept 260 Whitney Ave New Haven CT 06511-8903

ZELLERBACH, WILLIAM JOSEPH, retired paper company executive; b. San Francisco, Sept. 15, 1920; s. Harold Lionel and Doris (Joseph) Z.; m. Margery Haber, Feb. 25, 1946; children: John William, Thomas Harold, Charles Ralph, Nancy. BS, Wharton Sch., U. Pa., 1942; grad., Advanced Mgmt. Program, Harvard U., 1958. With Crown Zellerbach Corp. and subs., 1946-85; officer, dir. Crown Zellerbach Corp., 1960-85. Mem gen. adv. com. fgn. assistance programs AID, 1965-68; chmn. bd. Zellerbach Family Found. Served as lt. USNR, 1942-46. Mem. Nat. Paper Trade Assn. (pres. 1970) Clubs: Villa Taverna (San Francisco), Presidio Golf (San Francisco), Pacific Union (San Francisco), Commonwealth (San Francisco); Peninsula Country (San Mateo, Calif.). Office: 120 Montgomery St Ste 1960 San Francisco CA 94104-4323

ZELLIOT, ELEANOR MAE, history educator; b. Des Moines, Oct. 7, 1926; d. Ernest A. and Minnie (Hadley) Z. BA, William Penn Coll., 1948; MA, Bryn Mawr (Pa.) Coll., 1949; PhD, U. Pa., 1969. Assoc. editor The Am. Friend, Richmond, Iowa, 1950-58; tchr. Scattergood Sch., West Branch, Iowa, 1958-60; editor Pendle Hill Pubs., Wallingford, Pa., 1960-62; acting instr., asst. prof. U. Minn., Mpls., 1966-69; researcher South Asia Hist. Atlas, Mpls., 1966-69; from asst. prof. to assoc. prof. Carleton Coll., Northfield, Minn., 1969-79, prof., 1979-97, dept. chair, 1989-92, Laird Bell prof., 1993-97, prof. emerita, 1997—. Pres. Midwest Conf. on Asian Affairs, 1996-97. Author: From Untouchable to Dalit, 1992, 96, 2000; editor: Experience of Hinduism, 1988, Untouchable Saints, 2004; editor jour. issue Marathi Sampler, 1982; contbr. articles to profl. jours. Mem. Dem. Farmer Labor Party, Minn., LWV. Fellowship NEH, 1987, Fulbright, 1992. Mem. Minn. Consortium for South Asia, Am. Inst. of Indian Studies (v.p. 1994-97, bd. trustees, fellowship 1985, 89), Assn. of Asian Studies (Disting. Svc. award 1999). Mem. Soc. Of Friends. Avocations: walking, cooking. Address: Carleton Coll Dept History Northfield MN 55057 E-mail: ezelliot@carleton.edu.

ZELLNER, ARNOLD, economics and statistics educator; b. Bklyn., Jan. 2, 1927; s. Israel and Doris (Kleiman) Z.; m. Agnes Marie Sumares, June 20, 1953; children— David S., Philip A., Samuel N., Daniel A., Michael A. AB in Physics, Harvard, 1949; PhD in Econs., U. Calif. at Berkeley, 1957; PhD (hon.), Autonomous U. Madrid, 1986, Tech. U. Lisbon, 1991, U. Kiel, 1998. Asst., then assoc. prof. econs. U. Wash., 1955-60; Fulbright vis. prof. Netherlands Sch. Econs., Rotterdam, 1960-61; assoc. prof., then prof. econs. U. Wis., 1961-66; H.G.B. Alexander disting. service prof. econs. and statistics U. Chgo., 1966-96, prof. emeritus, 1996—; dir. H.G.B. Alexander Rsch. Found., 1973—. Cons. Battelle Meml. Inst., 1964—71; vis. rsch. prof. U. Calif., Berkeley, 1971, Berkeley, 96, adj. prof., 1998—; trustee Nat. Opinion Rsch. Corp., 1973—80; bd. dirs. Nat. Bur. Econ. Rsch., 1980—; seminar leader NSF-NBER Seminar on Bayesian Inference in Econometrics and Stats., 1970—95; vis. prof. Am. U., Cairo, 1997, Hebrew U., 1997, U. Calif., Berkeley, 1997—2003. Co-author: Systems Simulation for Regional Analysis, 1969, Estimating the Parameters of the Markov Probability Model, 1970; author: Bayesian Inference in Econometrics, 1971, Basic Issues in Econometrics, 1984, Bayesian Analysis in Econometrics and Statistics: The Zellner View and Papers, 1997, Statistics, Econometrics and Forecasting, 2004; editor: Economic Statistics and Econometrics, 1968, Seasonal Analysis of Economic Time Series, 1978, Simplicity, Inference and Modelling, 2001; assoc. editor: Econometrica, 1962-68; co-editor: Studies in Bayesian Econometrics and Statistics, 1975, Jour. Econometrics, 1972—, founding editor ASA Jour. Bus. and Econ. Stats., 1983; contbr. articles to profl. jours. Pres. Leonard J. Savage Meml. Trust Fund, Chgo., 1977-2000. Served with AUS, 1951-53. Fellow AAAS, Am. Acad. Arts and Scis., Am. Econ. Assn., Internat. Inst. of Forecasters, Econometric Soc., Am. Statis. Assn. (pres. elect 1990—, pres. 1991—, chmn. bus. and econs. sect. 1980, chmn. Bayesian statis. sci. sect. 1993); mem. Internat. Statis. Inst., Internat. Soc. Bayesian Analysis (co-pres. 1993, pres. 1994-96, Founders award 1998), Soc. Actuaries (trustee, rsch. found., 1994-98). Avocations: golf, tennis, travel, grandchildren. Home: 5628 S Dorchester Ave Chicago IL 60637-1722 Office: U Chgo Grad Sch Bus 1101 E 58th St Chicago IL 60637-1511 Office Phone: 773-702-7145. Business E-Mail: arnold.zellner@gsb.uchicago.edu.

ZELLWEGER, RENEE, actress; b. Katy, Tex., Apr. 25, 1969; BA in English, U. Tex. Actress feature films including Reality Bites, 1994, Love and a .45, 1994, 8 Seconds, 1994, The Low Life, 1995, Empire Records, 1995, The Whole Wide World, 1996, Jerry Maguire, 1996, Texas Chainsaw Massacre: The Next Generation, 1997, Deceiver, 1997, One True Thing, 1998, A Price Above Rubies, 1998, The Bachelor, 1999, Nurse Betty, 2000 (Golden Globe award for best actress in a comedy or musical 2000), Me, Myself & Irene, 2000, Bridget Jones's Diary, 2001 (nominee Best Actress SAG award, Broadcast Film Critics Assn. award, Brit. Acad. Award and Acad. award 2001; Golden Globe award nominee best actress in a comedy or musical, 2001), White Oleander, 2002, Chicago, 2002 (Golden Globe award for best supporting actress in a comedy or musical, 2002, SAG award for Best Actress, 2003, Academy award nominee Best Actress, 2003), Down With Love, 2003, Cold Mountain, 2003 (Golden Globe for best supporting actress, 2004, Screen Actors Guild Award for best supporting actress, 2004, Acad. Award for best supporting actress, 2004). TV including Shake, Rattle and Rock Movie, 1993, Murder in the Heartland mini-series, 1994. Office: Byant Joel CAA 9830 Wilshire Blvd Beverly Hills CA 90212*

ZELMAN, SUSAN TAVE, school system administrator; DEd, U. Mich.; D in Pub. Edn. (hon.), U. Rio Grande, Ohio; D in Humanities (hon.), Youngstown U. Assoc. prof. edn. Emmanuel Coll., Boston, chair dept. edn.; assoc commr. ednl. dept. personnel Mo. Dept. Edn., Jefferson City, 1988—94; dep. commr. Mo. Dept. Elem. and Secondary Edn., Jefferson City, 1994—99; supt. pub. instrn. Ohio Dept Edn., Columbus, 1999—. Rschr. Edn. Tech. Ctr. Harvard Grad. Sch. Edn. Recipient Nat. Sci. Rsch. Opportunity award, Columbus Tchrs. Coll. Office: Ohio Dept Edn 25 S Front St Columbus OH 43215-4183

ZELMANOV, EFIM ISAAKOVICH, mathematician, educator; b. USSR, Sept. 7, 1955; MS, Novosibirsk State U., 1977, PhD in Math., 1980; doctoral scientist, Leningrad U., St. Petersburg, Russia, 1985. Jr. rschr. Inst. of Math., Acad. of Scis. of USSR, Novosibirsk, 1980-85, sr. rschr., 1985-86, leading rschr., 1986-90; prof. math. U. Wis., Madison, 1990-94, U. Chgo., 1994-95; prof. Yale U., New Haven, 1995—. Recipient Fields medal Inst. de Matematica Pura e Aplicada, 1994, Coll. de France medal, 1992, Andre Aizenstadt prize, 1996. Office: Yale U Dept Math PO Box 208283 10 Hillhouse Ave New Haven CT 06520-8283

ZELMANOWITZ, JULIUS MARTIN, mathematics educator, university administrator; b. N.Y.C., Feb. 20, 1941; s. Morris and Tillie (Holtz) Z.; m. Joan R. Traubel, June 24, 1962; 1 child, Dawn Michèle. AB, Harvard U., 1962; MS, U. Wis., 1963, PhD, 1966. Asst. prof. U. Calif., Santa Barbara, 1966-73, assoc. prof., 1973-77, prof. maths., 1977—, assoc. vice chancellor acad. affairs, 1985-87, assoc. vice chancellor acad. personnel, 1988-98; assoc. prof. Carnegie-Mellon U., Pitts., 1970-71; interim vice provost acad. initiatives U. Calif., 1999-2000, v.p. acad. initiatives, 2000—. Vis. asst. prof. UCLA, 1969-70, vis. assoc. prof. 1973-74, vis. prof. U. Rome, 1977, McGill U., Montreal, Quebec, 1982-83, 87 88, U. Munich, 1983, 88. Contbr. articles to profl. jours. Sr. rsch. grantee Italian Nat. Rsch. Coun., Rome, 1977, Palermo, 1988; named Milw. Prof. of Maths. The Technion, Haifa, Israel, 1979; Fulbright sr. fellow, Munich, 1983. Mem. Am. Math. Soc., Math. Assn. Am. Home: 2040 Franklin St # 1407 San Francisco CA 94109-2982 Office: Off Pres Acad Initiatives 1111 Franklin St Oakland CA 94607-5200 Office Phone: 510-987-9414. Business E-Mail: julius.zelmanowitz@ucop.edu.

ZELNAK, STEPHEN P., JR., construction materials company executive; BS, Ga. Inst. Tech.; M Adminstrv. Sci. and Bus. Adminstrn., U. Ala. With Martin Marietta Corp., Raleigh, N.C., 1981—, head aggregates ops., 1982-92, pres. materials group, 1992-93; pres. Martin Marietta Materials, Raleigh, 1993—, chmn. bd. dirs., 1997—. Former chmn. N.C. Citizens for Bus. and Industry. Office: Martin Marietta Materials Inc 2710 Wycliff Rd Raleigh NC 27607

ZELNICK, CARL ROBERT ROBERT, writer, educator; b. NYC, Aug. 9, 1940; s. David Isadore and Lillian (Ostrow) Z.; m. Pamela Margaret Sharp, Dec. 30, 1967; children: Eva Michal, Dara Yael, Marni Ruth. BS, Cornell U., 1961; LLB, U. Va., 1964. Bar: NY 1965, DC 1966. Law assoc. H. Charles Ephraim, Washington, 1966-67; corr./columnist Anchorage Daily News, 1968-76; assoc. editor Environ. Law Reporter, 1971-72; spl. corr. Christian Sci. Monitor, 1973-77; corr./bur. chief Nat. Pub. Radio, Washington, 1972-76; exec. editor Frost/Nixon Interviews, Washington, 1976-77; dir. news coverage ABC-TV, Washington, 1977-81; dep. bur. chief ABC News, Washington, 1981-82, Moscow bur. chief, corr., 1982-84, corr., 1984-86; ABC News Pentagon corr. Washington, 1986-94; media fellow Hoover Instn., Stanford U., 1998. Mem. Citizens Commn. on Race, 1998—2003; vis. prof. Boston U., 1998—2000, prof., 2000—, chmn. dept. journalism, 2002—; rsch. fellow Hoover Instn., 2002—. Author: Backfire--A Reporter Looks at Affirmative Action, 1996, Gore--A Political Life, 1999, Winning Florida: How the Bush Team Fought the Battle, 2000, Swing Dance: Justice O'Connor and the Michigan Muddle, 2004; contbr. articles to newspapers and mags. Served with USMC, 1964-65. Recipient Gavel awards Am. Bar Assn., 1969, 74, Du Pont award Columbia U. Sch. Journalism, 1984, Emmy award, 1984, 92; rsch. fellow Hooer Inst., 2001—. Mem. Council on Fgn. Relations, Phi Epsilon Pi, Pi Delta Phi. Jewish. Office: Boston U Coll Comm 640 Commonwealth Ave Boston MA 02215-2422 E-mail: bzelnick@bu.edu.

ZELNICK, RONALD STUART, surgeon; b. N.Y.C., Dec. 6, 1958; BS, George Washington U., 1980; MD, Albany Med. Coll., 1984. Diplomate Am. Bd. Surgery, Am. Bd. Colon Rectal Surgery. Resident gen. surgery L.I. Jewish Hosp., New Hyde Park, N.Y., 1984-89; fellowship colon and rectal surgery Henry Ford Hosp., Detroit, 1989-90; pvt. practice Jupiter, Fla., 1991—. Fellow ACS, Am. Soc. Colon Rectal Surgeons; mem. Fla. Surg. Soc., Fla. Colon Rectal Surgery Soc. Office: Ste 105 210 Jupiter Lakes Blvd #3105 Jupiter FL 33458

ZELNICK, STRAUSS, entertainment company executive; b. Boston, June 26, 1957; s. Allan Zelnick and Elsa Lee Strauss; m. Wendy Belzberg, 1990; children: Cooper, Lucas, Leigh. BA summa cum laude, Wesleyan U., Middletown, Ct., 1979; MBA, JD cum laude, Harvard U., 1983. Bar: N.Y. 1984. Dir. internat. TV Columbia Pictures Internat. Corp., N.Y.C., 1983-85, v.p. internat. TV, 1985-86; sr. v.p. corp. devel. Vestron Inc., Stamford, Conn., 1986-87, exec. v.p., 1987, pres., chief oper. officer, 1988-89, Twentieth Century Fox, L.A., 1989-93; pres., CEO Crystal Dynamics, Palo Alto, Calif., 1993-95; pres., CEO, BMG Entertainment N.Am., N.Y.C., 1995-98, BMG Entertainment, N.Y.C., 1998—. Trustee Wesleyan U., 1992—; mem. contemporary arts coun. Mus. Modern Art, 1989, Young Pres. Orgn.; chmn. Covenant House Calif., 1992-95; bd. dirs. Covenant House, N.Y.C., 1995-2000. Mem. N.Y. State Bar Assn., Harvard Club, Phi Beta Kappa. Avocations: squash, sailing, skiing. Office: BMG Entertainment 1540 Broadway Ste 9W New York NY 10036-4074

ZELON, LAURIE DEE, lawyer; b. Durham, N.C., Nov. 15, 1952; d. Irving and Doris Miriam (Baker) Z.; m. David L. George, Dec. 30, 1979; children: Jeremy, Daniel. BA in English with distinction, Cornell U., 1974; JD, Harvard U., 1977. Bar: Calif. 1977, U.S. Ct. Appeals (9th cir.) 1978, U.S. Supreme Ct. 1989. Assoc. Beardsley, Hufstedler & Kemble, L.A., 1977-81, Hufstedler, Miller, Carlson & Beardsley, L.A., 1981-82, ptnr., 1983-88, Hufstedler, Miller, Kaus & Beardsley, L.A., 1988-90, Hufstedler, Kaus & Ettinger, L.A., 1990-91, Morrison & Foerster, L.A., 1991-2000; judge L.A. Superior Ct., 2000—03; assoc. justice Calif. Ct. Appeal, L.A., 2003—. Contbg. author: West's California Litigation Forms: Civil Procedure Before Trial, 1996; editor-in-chief Harvard Civil Rights and Civil Liberties Law Rev., 1976-77 Bd. dirs. N.Y. Civil Liberties Union, 1973-74. Mem. ABA (chmn. young lawyers divsn. pro bono project 1981-83, delivery and pro bono projects com. 1983-85, subgrant competition-subgrant monitoring project 1985-86, chair standing com. on lawyers pub. svc. responsibility 1987-90, chair law firm pro bono project 1989-91, standing com. legal aid and indigent defendants 1991-97, chmn. 1993-97, mem. ho. dels. 1993—, state del. 1998—, commn. on ethics 2000 1997-2002), Calif. Bar Assn. (bd. dirs. appellate project 1995-2000, chair comm. on access to justice 1997-99), L.A. County Bar Assn. (trustee 1989-91, v.p. 1992-93, sr. v.p. 1993-94, pres.-elect 1994-95, pres. 1995-96, fed. cts. and practices com. 1984-93, vice chmn. 1987-88, chmn. 1988-89, chmn. judiciary com. 1991-92, chmn. real estate litigation subsect. 1991-92), Women Lawyers Assn. L.A., Calif. Women Lawyers Assn. Democrat. Office: Calif Ct of Appeal 2d Appellate Dist 300 S Spring St Los Angeles CA 90013

ZEMAN, GREGORY OSWALD, physician; b. Chgo., 1936; MD, Loyola U., 1960. Diplomate Am. Bd. Internal Medicine, 1968, Am. Bd. Allergy and Immunology, 1974. Intern St. Joseph Hosp., Chgo., 1960-61; resident Hines VA Hosp., 1963-65; with MacNeal Hosp., Berwyn, Ill., Hinsdale Hosp., Elmhurst Hosp. Allergy fellow U. Ill. Rsch.-Edn. Hosp., Chgo., 1965-66. Fellow ACP, Am. Acad. Allergy & Immunology, Am. Coll. Allergy & Immunology. Office: 720 Milburn St Evanston IL 60201

ZEMANIAN, ARMEN HUMPARTSOUM, electrical engineer, mathematician; b. Bridgewater, Mass., Apr. 16, 1925; s. Parsegh and Filor (Paparian) Z.; m. Edna Odell Williamson Zemanian, July 12, 1958; children: Peter, Thomas, Lewis, Susan. BEE, CCNY, 1947; ScD in Engring., NYU, 1953; prof. honoris causa, Dubna (Russia) U., 1996. Registered profl. engr., N.Y. Tutor CCNY, 1947-48; engr. The Maintenance Co., N.Y.C., 1948-52; from asst. to assoc. prof. NYU, 1952-62; prof. SUNY, Stony Brook, 1962-83, leading prof., 1983-98, distinguished prof., 1998—. Author: Distribution Theory and Transform Analysis, 1965, Generalized Integral Transformations, 1968, Realizability Theory for Continuous Linear Systems, 1972, Infinite Electrical Networks, 1991, Transfiniteness for Graphs, Electrical Networks and Random Walks, 1996; Pristine Transfinite Graphs and Permissive Electrical Networks, 2001; co-author: Electronics, 1961; co-founder, editor-in-chief emeritus Circuits, Systems and Signal Processing, 1982—. NSF sr. faculty fellow in sci., 1975-76; recipient Sci. award Armenian Students Assns. Am., 1982; Academician (fgn. mem.) Armenian Acad. Scis., 1990, Academician (fgn. mem.) Armenian Acad. Engrs., 1994. Fellow IEEE, IEEE Circuits and Systems Soc. (Golden Jubilee medal 2000), Am. Math. Soc., Russian Acad. Natural Scis. (fgn. mem.; Kapitsa Gold medal 1996), Sigma Xi, Tau Beta Pi, Eta Kappa Nu. Democrat. Presbyterian. Office: SUNY Electrical Engring Dept Stony Brook NY 11794-0001 E-mail: Zeman@ee.sunysb.edu.

ZEMECKIS, ROBERT L. film director; b. Chgo., May 14, 1952; m. Mary Ellen Trainor. Ed., U. So. Calif. Cinema Sch. Dir. (films) I Wanna Hold Your Hand (also writer), 1978, Used Cars, 1980, Romancing the Stone, 1984, Back to the Future (also writer), 1985, Who Framed Roger Rabbit?, 1988, Back to the Future Part II (also writer), 1989, Back to the Future Part III (also writer), 1990, Death Becomes Her (also prodr.), 1992, Forrest Gump, 1994 (Best Dir. Acad. award), Contact, 1996 (TV series episode) Amazing Stories; co-screenwriter 1941, 1979, Trespass (also exec. prodr.), 1992; prodr. (films) Contact, 1997, (TV series) Johnny Bago, 1993, The House on Haunted Hill, 1999; exec. prodr. (film) The Public Eye, 1992, Tales from the Crypt Presents: Demon Knight, 1995, The Frighteners, 1996, Tales from the Crypt Presents: Bordello of Blood, 1996 (also writer), The 20th Century: The Pursuit of Happiness, 1999 (TV), What Lies Beneath, 2000, (TV series) Tales from the Crypt, 1989, W.E.I.R.D. World, 1995, Perversions of Science, 1997; writer (films) 1941, 1979, Used Cars, 1980; TV guest appearances include Parker Lewis Can't Lose, 1990; prodr., dir. Cast Away, 2000; prodr. Thirteen Ghosts, 2001, Ritual, 2001, Ghost Ship, 2002; exec. prodr. Matchstick Men, 2003. Mem. Dirs. Guild Am. Office: care Gelfand Rennert & Feldman 1880 Century Park E Ste 900 Los Angeles CA 90067-1609 also: Creative Artists Agy c/o Karen Sage 9830 Wilshire Blvd Beverly Hills CA 90212-1804 also: South Side Amusement Bugalow 127 100 Universal City Plz Universal Cty CA 91608-1002

ZEMENS, ANNA JO C. library director; b. Detroit, May 17, 1940; d. Joseph Leo and Hortense E. (Marlow) Zemens; m. Robert Richmond, Apr. 4, 1966 (div. Jan. 1974); children: Allen Richmond, Terri Jo Richmond. BA in sociology, U. Mich., 1962; MA in lib. sci., U. Chgo., 1970. Ref. lib. Chgo. (Ill) Pub. Lib., 1964—65, Evanston (Ill) Pub. Lib, 1968—69, Loyola Univ., Chgo., 1972—74; lib. dir. Pk. Forest So. (Ill) Pub. Lib. Dist., 1974—77; asst. dir. Newberry Lib., Indian Hist. Ctr., Chgo., 1977—79; br. lib. Richmond (Calif) Pub. Lib., 1981—92; lib. dir. Patten U., Oakland, Calif., 1992—. Del. Newberry Lib., Whitehouse Preconference on Indian Lib. Svc., Denver, 1978; spkr. Am. Lib. Assn. Annual Conference, Chgo., 1978. Editor: Chgo. Geneal. Soc., 1975, Calif. Geneal. Soc., 1983—84. Mem. Am. Lib. Assn., 1992—99, Calif. Lib. Assn., 1992—99. Regents scholar, U. Mich., 1958—62, LaVerne Noyes scholar, U. Chgo., 1964—65. Mem.: Lancaster Mennonite Hist. Soc. Avocations: genealogy, European history, British mystery reading, Americana antiques. Office: Patten U Lib 2433 Coolidge Ave Oakland CA 94601 E-mail: Ann.Zemens@patten.edu.

ZEMM, SANDRA PHYLLIS, lawyer; b. Chgo., Aug. 18, 1947; d. Walter Stanley and Bernice Phyllis (Churas) Z. BS, U. Ill., 1969; JD, Fla. State U., 1974. Bar: Fla. 74, Ill. 75. With fin. dept. Sinclair Oil, Chgo., 1969-70; indsl. rels. advisor Conco Inc., Mendota, Ill., 1970-72; assoc. Seyfarth, Shaw, Fairweather & Geraldson, Chgo., 1975-82, ptnr., 1982—. Mem. Art Inst. Alliance, Chgo., 1993—; bd. dirs. Chgo. Residential Inc., 1993—97, pres., 1995—97. Mem. Ill. State Bar Assn., Fla. State Bar Assn., Univ. Club Chgo. (bd. dirs. 1991-94); Nat. Coll. of Labor and Employment Lawyers. Office: Seyfarth Shaw 55 E Monroe St Ste 4200 Chicago IL 60603-5863

ZEMPLENYI, TIBOR KAROL, cardiologist, educator; b. Part Lupča, Czechoslovakia, July 16, 1916; came to U.S., 1968, naturalized, 1974; s. David Dezider and Irene (Pollak) Z.; m. Hana Bendová, Aug. 13, 1952; 1 son, Jan. MD, Charles U., Prague, Czechoslovakia, 1946, Docent Habilit., 1966; CSc. (PhD), Czechoslovak Acad. Sci., 1960, DSc., 1964. Clin. asst. with dept medicine Prague Motol Clinic and Charles U., 1946-52; head atherosclerosis rsch. Inst. for Cardiovascular Rsch., Prague, 1952-68; assoc. prof. medicine Charles U., 1966-68, U. So. Calif., L.A., 1969-75, prof., 1975-92, prof. emeritus, 1992—. Attending physician L.A. County- U.So. Calif. Med. Ctr. Author: Enzyme Biochemistry of the Arterial Wall, 1968; editl. bd. Atherosclerosis, 1962-75, Cor et Vasa, 1993—; adv. bd. Advances in Lipid Rsch., 1963-66; contbr. articles to numerous profl. jours. WHO fellow for study in Sweden and Gt. Britain, 1959. Fellow Am. Heart Assn., Am. Coll. Cardiology; mem. Western Soc. for Clin. Rsch., Longevity Assn. (mem. sci. bd.), European Atherosclerosis Group, Italian Soc. for Atherosclerosis (hon.). Office: 3400 Loadstone Dr Sherman Oaks CA 91403-4512

ZEMTSOV, ALEXANDER, dermatology and biochemistry educator, inventor; b. Baku, USSR, Nov. 9, 1959; came to U.S., 1977; s. Ilya and Marya (Dubinsky) Z.; m. Tali Giveon, Oct. 17, 1987; children: Raquel Karen, Gregory Ethan. BA magna cum laude, Temple U., 1981; MSc, U. Pa., 1982; MD with honors, NYU, 1986. Diplomate Am. Bd. Dermatology. Intern, then resident Cleve. Clinic Hosp. Found., 1989-90; assoc. prof. biochemistry and molecular biology Ind. U. Sch. Medicine, Muncie, 1995—. Editor Skin Rsch. and Tech. Jour.; contbr. articles to profl. jours. and books; patentee in field. Recipient Am. Soc. Dermatol. Surgery award, 1989; Cert. Appreciation, Ohio Dermatol. Soc., 1990. Fellow Am. Acad. Dermatology, Am. Contact Dermatitis Soc.; mem. Soc. Magnetic Resonance, Internat. Soc. for Digital Imaging of Skin (pres.), Kiwanis. Jewish. Avocations: stamp collecting/philately, hiking, swimming. Office: U Dermatology Ctr 2525 W University Ave Ste 402 Muncie IN 47303-3409 E-mail: uniderm@aol.com.

ZEN, E-AN, research geologist, educator; b. Peking, China, May 31, 1928; came to U.S., 1946, naturalized, 1963; s. Hung-chun and Heng-chi'h (Chen) Z. AB, Cornell U., 1951; MA, Harvard U., 1952, PhD, 1955. Rsch. fellow Woods Hole Oceanographic Inst., 1955-56, rsch. assoc., 1956-58; asst. prof. U. N.C., 1958-59; geologist U.S. Geol. Survey, 1959-80, rsch. geologist, 1981-89, scientist emeritus, 1990—; sr. scientist Va. Mus. Natural History. Adj. prof. geology U. Md., 1990—; vis. assoc. prof. Calif. Inst. Tech., 1962; Crosby vis. prof. MIT, 1973; Harry H. Hess sr. vis. fellow Princeton U., 1981; counselor 28th Internat. Geol. Congress. 1986-89. Contbr. articles to profl. jours. Recipient Maj. John Coke medal Geol. Soc. London, 1992, Outstanding Contbn. to Pub. Understanding of Geology award Am. Geol. Inst., 1994, Thomas Jefferson medal Va. Mus. Natural History Found., 1996. Fellow: AAAS, Mineral Soc. Am. (coun. 1975—77, pres. 1975—76, Roebling medal 1991), Geol. Soc. Am. (councillor 1985—88, v.p. 1991, ores. 1992, Day medal 1986), Am. Acad. Arts and Scis.; mem.: NAS, Geol. Soc. Washington (pres. 1973), Va. Mus. Natural History (sr. scientist). Office: U Md Dept Geology College Park MD 20742-0001

ZENDLE, HOWARD MARK, software development researcher; b. Binghamton, N.Y., June 8, 1949; s. Abraham and Evelyn (Hershowitz) Z. BA in Physics summa cum laude, SUNY, Binghamton, 1972, MA in Physics, 1976; MSEE, Syracuse U., 1987. With IBM, Owego, NY, 1974—94, staff programmer, 1978-83, mgr. microprocessor application software, 1979-81, mgr. tactical avionics software, 1981-82, adv. programmer, 1983-86, sr. programmer, 1986-94, Loral, Owego, NY, 1994-96, Lockheed Martin, Owego, NY, 1996—. Mem. Fed. Sector div. Mktg. Conf. IBM, 1991. Sec. Men's Club Beth David Synagogue, Binghamton, 1984-85, v.p., 1986-88; bd. dirs. Jewish Cmty. Ctr., Binghamton, 1983-86. Mem. IEEE, Assn. Computing Machinery, Ctrl. Electric Railfan's Assn., Masons, Phi Beta Kappa, Sigma Pi Sigma.

Republican. Avocations: railfanning, research into history of industrial development in america. Home: 5 Leigh St Johnson City NY 13790-1608 Office: Lockheed Martin 1801 State Route 17C Owego NY 13827-3998 E-mail: hzendle@stny.rr.com.

ZENG, AMY Z. finance educator, engineering educator; arrived in U.S., 1990; d. Decheng Zeng and Zicheng Luo; m. Tianming Zhang, July 16, 1965; children: Catherine M. Zhang, Alexander T. Zhang. BS in Engring., Beijing U. Aeronautics and Astronautics, 1990; MS in Engring., U. Wash., 1992; PhD in Bus. Adminstrn., Pa. State U., 1996. Asst. prof. U. N.C., Wilmington, 1996—99, Worcester (Mass.) Poly. Inst., 1999—2003, assoc. prof., 2003—. Contbr. chapters to books, articles to profl. jours. and conf. proceedings. Recipient Best Paper Reviewer award, Ops. Mgmt. Divsn. at Acad. Mgmt., 2002; Tchg. Innovation grantee, NSF, 2002—03. Mem.: Coun. Logistics Mgmt., APICS-The Ednl. Soc. Resource Mgmt. (Rsch. Study in Global Supply Chain Mgmt. grantee 2000), Inst. for Ops. Rsch. and Mgmt. Sci., Prodn. and Ops. Mgmt. Soc., Decision Scis. Inst., Beta Gamma Sigma, Phi Kappa Phi. Achievements include research expertise in analyzing the decisions in supply and distribution networks in supply chain management and bus. logistics; teaching experiences in operations management, business logistics, and supply chain management. Office: Worcester Poly Inst 100 Institute Rd Worcester MA 01609 Office Phone: 508-831-6117. E-mail: azeng@wpi.edu.

ZENG, HONG, audio system architect, researcher; b. Changchun, Jilin, China, Feb. 20, 1958; arrived in France, 1990; s. Peiwei Zeng and Shige Chen; m. Yuzhi Guo, Jan. 14, 1983 (div. Nov. 2000); 1 child, Yu; m. Jie Li, Aug. 8, 2001; 1 child, Aisling. B in Elec. Engring., Changchun Coll. Geology; M in Elec. Engring., U. Pierre & Marie Curie, Paris, 1991, D in Physics, 1996. Asst. engr. Hangzhou (China) Applied Acoustics Rsch. Inst., 1982-85, rsch. engr., dir. magnetic signal processing sect., 1985-90; rsch. engr. French Nat. Sci. Rsch. Ctr., Paris, 1990-95; sys. engr. O1dB Co., Lyon, France, 1995-98; sr. software engr., project team leader ATI Technologies, Inc., Toronto, 1998-2001; audio sys. arch. ViXS Sys. Inc., Toronto, 2001—. Contbr. articles to profl. jours.; inventor in field. Recipient Sci. and Tech. award China Shipbuilding Industry Corp., Beijing, 1989. Mem. IEEE. Home: 815 Grandview Way Toronto ON Canada M2N 6V5 Office: ViXS Systems Inc 2235 Sheppard Ave E # 1705 Toronto ON Canada M2J 5B5 E-mail: hongzeng@ieee.org., hzeng@vixs.com.

ZENG, HONGLIU HENRY, geophysicist, geologist; b. Nidu, Jiangxi, China, Jan. 5, 1957; arrived in U.S., 1989; s. Zhikang Zeng and Lianrong Chen; m. Yan Phoebe Yang, Feb. 20, 1961; children: Luying, Leo. BA, U. Petroleum, Dongying, 1982, MA, 1985; PhD, U. Tex., 1994. Advanced geoscientist Texaco Inc., New Orleans, 1994—96; rsch. scientist Bur. Econ. Geology, Jackson Sch. Geosci., U. Tex., Austin, 1997—. Lectr. U. Petroleum, Beijing, 1995—99. Contbr. articles to profl. jours. Mem.: Soc. Exploration Geophysicists, Am. Assn. Petroleum Geologists. Achievements include invention of stratal slicing, a 3-D seismic data interpretation technique; Seismic frequency control on seismic stratigraphy, a seimic data interpretation therory; research in on seismic sedimentology, seismic stratigraphy, reservoir characterization, and special seismic processing, as applied to petroleum prospecting. Office: Bur Econ Geology Bldg 130 10100 Burnet Rd Austin TX 78758-4445 Office Phone: 512-475-6382. Business E-Mail: hongliu.zeng@beg.utexas.edu.

ZENG, LIANG, education educator; b. Chongren, China, Nov. 30, 1972; d. Yi Zeng and Shuzhen Liu. PhD in theoretical physics, Zhejiang U., 1996—98; Postdoctoral Studies in Quantitative Methods and Stats. Analysis, U. of Tex. Pan Am., 1998—99. Grad. tchg. asst. Zhejiang U., Hangzhou, China, 1996—98; asst. prof. U. of Tex. Pan Am., 1999—. Textbook pre-revision reviewer for applied stats. for the behavioral sciences Houghton Mifflin Co., Boston, 2000—; conf. proposal reviewer Am. Ednl. Rsch. Assn., Washington, D.C., 2001—; dissertation com. mem. Ednl. Leadership Doctoral Program, U. of Tex. Pan Am., 2000—; thesis com. mem. Coll. of Edn. and Coll. of Health Sciences and Human Services, U. of Tex. Pan Am., 1999—; mem. Faculty Senate and Academic Computer Coun. at the U. of Tex. Pan Am.; presenter in field. Assoc. editor: Jour. of Probability and Statis. Sci., 2002; contbr. articles to profl. jours. Program holder and narrator of Chinese costume show People's Republic of China in Houston and U. of Tex. Pan Am., 2002. Recipient Sch. Vol. award, Edinburg Consol. Ind. Sch. Dist., 2000; scholar, Alumni Fund of Jiangxi Normal U.; grant, Nat. Natural Sci. Found. of China, 1997—99, Nat. Ctr. for Ednl. Stats., U.S. Dept. of Edn., 2001, 2002. Mem.: Chinese Physics Assn., Internat. Chinese Stats. Assn., Am. Ednl. Rsch. Assn., Am. Statis. Assn., Am. Assn. for the Advancements of Sci., NY Acad. of Sciences. Achievements include research in quantum optics; structural equation modeling to examine a theoretical model predicting performance on a teacher certification test (ExCET). Avocations: music, swimming, travel. Home: 1609 W McIntyre St Apt 4 Edinburg TX 78541 Office: Department of Educational Psychology University of Texas Pan American Edinburg TX 78539 E-mail: zengl@panam.edu.

ZENG, WEI, environmental engineer; s. Qinghua Zeng and Chengrui Ni; m. Tongrui Liu; 1 child, Tony X. B in Engring., Tsinghua U., Beijing, 1992; PhD, U. Ga., 2000. Asst. engr. China Inst. Water Resources and Hydropower Rsch., Beijing, 1992—96; rsch. asst. U. Ga., Athens, 1996—2000; environ. engr. Ga. Dept. Natural Resources, Atlanta, 2000—. Reviewer ASCE Press, 2003. Contbr. articles to profl. jours. Mem.: Am. Geophys. Union, Am. Water Resources Assn. Office: Ga Dept Natural Resources 2 Martin Luther King Dr SE 1058 E Atlanta GA 30334 Business E-Mail: wei_zeng@dnr.state.ga.us.

ZENGER, JOHN HANCOCK, training company executive; b. Salt Lake City, Nov. 13, 1931; s. John H. and L. (Hancock) Z.; m. Dixie Robison, June 1, 1955 (div. 1978); children: Mark R., Robin, Todd R., Blake R., Mitchell R., Drew R.; m. Holly Olsen, June 29, 1979; stepchildren: Roger, Kirk, Lori, Michael. BS, Brigham Young U., 1955; MBA, UCLA, 1957; DBA, U. So. Calif., 1963. Asst. prof. Grad Sch. Bus. U. So. Calif., L.A., 1966—67; exec. v.p. Blanfield-Smith and Co., Pasadena, Calif., 1965—67; v.p. human resources Syntex Corp., Palo Alto, Calif., 1967—77; pres. Zenger-Miller Inc., Cupertino, Calif., 1977—92; group v.p. Times Mirror Co., San Jose, 1992—97; pres., CEO Provant, Inc.; CEO Zenger Folkman Corp., 2003—. Chmn. Palo Alto Human Rels. Coun., 1961-66; trustee Utah Valley State Coll., chmn., 2003-04; pres. Midway Boosters, Inc. Ford Found. fellow, 1962-63; recipient Disting. Svc. award Brigham Young U., 1983; named to Human Resources Devel. Hall of Fame, 1994. Mem. Brigham Young U. Alumni Assn. (pres. 1981). Republican. Mem. Lds Ch. Avocation: magic. Home: 275 Luzern Rd Midway UT 84049-1268 Office Phone: 801-705-9494. E-mail: jzenger@zfcorp.com.

ZENKER, WENDY, financial executive; BA, Radcliffe Coll., 1974. Exec. asst. to comptr. Dept. of Edn., Washington, 1981-87, chief grants ofcl., 1987-89; chief mgmt. integrity br. Office of Fed. Fin. Mgmt., Office of Mgmt. and Budget, Washington, 1989-98; COO Corp. for Nat. Svc., Washington, 1998—. Office: Corp for Nat Svc 1201 New York Ave NW Washington DC 20525-0001

ZENNER, SHELDON TOBY, lawyer; b. Chgo., Jan. 11, 1953; s. Max and Clara (Goldner) Z.; m. Ellen June Morgan, Sept. 2, 1984; children: Elie, Nathaniel. BA, Northwestern U., 1974, JD, 1978. Bar: U.S. Dist. Ct. (no. dist.) Ill. 1978. Assoc. Shadur, Krupp & Miller, Chgo., 1978-80; law clk. to judge U.S. Dist. Ct. (no. dist.) Ill., Chgo., 1980-81; asst. U.S. atty., dep. chief spl. prosecutions div. No. Dist. of Ill., Chgo., 1981-89; ptnr. Katten Muchin & Zavis, Chgo., 1989—. Adj. faculty Medill Sch. Journalism, Northwestern U., 1982-89, Sch. of Law, 1986—; instr. Nat. Inst. Trial Attys., 1989—; mem. practitioners adv. com. U.S. Sentencing Commn.; bd. dirs. Legal Assistance Found.; mem. editl. adv. bd. Northwestern U. Magazine. Mem. Phi Beta Kappa. Office: Katten Muchin Zavis Rosenman 525 W Monroe St Ste 1500 Chicago IL 60661-3693

ZENTALL, THOMAS R. psychologist, educator; b. Bezier, Herault, France, Sept. 29, 1940; came to the U.S., 1942; s. Robert Sigmund and Elizabeth Aigner Zentall; m. Sydney Snider, Aug. 29, 1965 (div.); m. Melodie Rae, June 4, 1988; children: Gabriel Clay, Shannon Rae. BA, BSEE, Union Coll., 1963; PhD, U. Calif., Berkeley, 1969. Asst. prof. U. Pitts., 1969-75; prof. U. Ky., Lexington, 1975—. Editor: Social Learning, 1988, Animal Cognition, 1993, Stimulus Class Formation, 1996; assoc. editor Psychonomic Bull. and Rev., 1998-2002, Animal Learning & Behavior, 2002-. Fellow APA (exec. com. divsn. 6 1998-2001, exec. com. divsn. 3 1999—), Am. Psychol. Soc., Midwestern Psychol. Assn. (sec.-treas. 1998-2001, pres. 2002—), Psychonomic Soc. (governing bd. 2001-2003), Comparative Cognition Soc. (pres. 2004—). Office: Dept Psychology Univ Ky Lexington KY 40506-0044 E-mail: zentall@uky.edu.

ZENTZ, PATRICK JAMES, artist, rancher; b. Cando, N.D., Jan. 22, 1947; s. Clifford Wayne and Sybil Mae (Dehrer) Z.; m. Susan Grace Hedley, Dec. 7, 1968; children: Keenan, Jesse, Tyson. BA in Biology, Westmont Coll., 1969; MFA in Sculpture, U. Mont., 1974. Juror Nev. State Coun. on the Arts Grants Program, Las Vegas, 1989, Nev. State Coun. on the Arts, Artists Fellowship Program, Reno, 1990, Wash State Commn. on the Arts, Olympia, 1992; artist adv. task force Western States Arts Fedn., Portland, 1991; del. Japan-Am. Grassroots Summit, Tokyo and Kyoto, Japan; vis. artist program U. Ill., Carbondale, 1994, Oxbow Sch., Napa, Calif., 1999, U. Idaho, MOscow, 2003; lectr. in field. Exhibited in group shows Western State Arts Found., Bklyn. Mus., 1986, No. Ariz. U., 1987, Mont. State U., 1987, Washington Project for the Arts, 1987, Curtis Ctr., Phila., 1987, Aspen Art Mus., 1988, Missoula Mus. of the Arts, 1989, Beall Park Art Ctr., Bozeman, Mont., 1989, John Michael Kohler Art Ctr., 1989, Henry Art Gallery, U. Wash., Seattle, 1989, Seattle Art Mus., 1989, The Ctr. on Contemporary Art, Seattle, 1990, Hockaday Ctr. for the Arts, Kalispell, Mont., Contemporary Arts Mus., Houston, 1990, Boulder Art Ctr., 1991, U. Mont., 1992, Beam Art Gallery, U. Nev., 1992, Internat. Sculpture Ctr., Phila., 1992, Cheney Cowles Mus., Spokane, Wash., 1994, San Antonio Mus. of Art, 1994, Rubelle & Norman Schaffer Gallery, Pratt Inst., Bklyn., 1994, Boise Art Mus., 1995, Neuberger Mus. of Art, SUNY, Purchase, 1997, Sheppard Gallery, U. Nev., Reno, 1998, Tarble Art Ctr., Ea. Ill. U., 1998, McAllen (Tex.) Internat. Mus., 1999, Yellowstone Art Mus., Billings, Mont., 1999, Miami U., Oxford, Ohio, Soyama Space, Seattle, 1999, Mont. State U. Sch. Arch., Bozeman, 2000, U. Mont. Mus. Art and Culture, Missoula, 2000, Outes Park Art Ctr., Fallon, Nev., 2001, Paris Gibson Sq. Mus., Grant Falls, Mont., 2002; represented in permanent collections U. Med. Ctr. U. Wash., Seattle, 1990, Richard Tam Alumni Ctr. U. Nev., Las Vegas, 1991, Snake River Correctional Instn., Ontario, Oreg., 1993, Yellowstone Art Mus., Billings, Mont., 1992, Western State Hosp., Ft. Steilecom, Wash., 1993, Salt Palace, Salt Lake City, 1994, TRI-MET Westside Light Rail Sys., Portland, 1995, Mus. of Fine Art, U. Mont., Missoula, 1997, FDA, College Park, Md., 1999, Edgewood Coll., Madison, Wis., 1999, Miami U., Oxford, Ohio, Reno/Sparks Conv. Ctr., Wash. State U., Spokane, Boise City Arts Commn., Idaho, Weber State U., Ogden, Utah, U. Mont. Recreational Ctr., Missoula, 2003, Cultural Devel. Authority, King Co., Seattle, 2003. Grantee Art Matters, Inc., 1988, LEF Found., 1992; fellowship Nat. Endowment for the Arts, 1990.

ZEOLLA, KIM ANNE, minister; b. Pittsburgh, Pa., Jan. 21, 1961; d. Edward William Logue and Melody Joy Long; m. Allen Lee Zeolla, Sept. 8, 1984; children: April Nicole, Daniel Nicholas, Jonathan Michael. Student, Dayspring Bible Sch., 1982—84, Greater Works Bible Sch., 2003. Minister women's groups, retreats, families, 1998—. V.p. min. develop., exec. bd. Murrysville Aglow Lighthouse, Murrysville, Pa., 2003—; prayer chairperson Pure Freedom (abstinence retreat), 2004—; coord. Cornerstone Min., Drug Awareness Seminar, Export, Pa., 2004. Judge fine arts Assemblies of God sign lang., human vidoe, comedy categories and drama categories, Pa., Del., 2001—; interpreter deaf Our Lady of Joy C.C.D. Class, Plum Boro, Pa., 2002—; v.p. min. devel. Murrysville Aglow Lighthouse, Murrysville, Pa., 2003; choreographer Mar. for Jesus, Pitts., 1997—98; leadership United for Christ Marriage Ministries, Pitts., 1988—94, Dayspring Christian Ctr., Pitts., 1988—99; jr./sr. high, new life bible study tchr. Pitts., 1995—2003; fin. sec. Murrsville Aglow Lighthouse, Murrysville, Pa., 2002—03. Conservative-R. Full Gospel. Home: 128 Alcan Dr Pittsburgh PA 15239 Personal E-mail: kimmwaone@yahoo.com.

ZEPEDA, OFELIA, linguist, educator; b. Stanfield, Ariz., Mar. 24, 1954; BA, U. Ariz., 1980, MA, 1981, PhD, 1984. Tchr. O'odham and linguistics U. Ariz., 1979-92, assoc. prof. linguistics, 1992-98, full prof., 1998—. Tchr. O'odham and Pima, Am. Indian Lang. Devel. Inst., 1980—, co-dir., 1989—. Author: A Papago Grammar, 1983, Ocean Power: Poems From the Desert, 1995, Earth Movement, 1997; editor: Mat Hekid o Ju: When It Rains: Papago and Pima Poetry, 1982; co-editor: South Corner of Time, 1980; contbr.: Returning the Gift, 1994, Home Places, 1995; series editor Sun Tracks Fellow MacArthur, 1999—; grantee, NSF, 1986, NEH, 1992. Office: U Ariz Douglass Bldg Rm 222 Tucson AZ 85721-0001 E-mail: ofelia@u.arizona.edu.

ZEPEDA, SUSAN GHOZEIL, foundation executive; b. NYC, Aug. 8, 1946; d. Harry S. and Anne (Golden) Kantor; m. Isaac Ghozeil, Jan. 29, 1967 (div. Oct. 1979); children: Daniel Jacob, Adam Leo; m. Fernando Zepeda, Jan. 2, 1983 (div. Feb. 1998); children: Paloma Andrea, Sofia Elisa. BA, Brown U., 1967; MA, U. Ariz., 1971, postgrad., 1971-75; PhD, Internat. Coll., 1985. Rsch. assoc. div. bus. and econ. rsch. U. Ariz., Tucson, 1971-73, rsch. assoc. Coll. Medicine, 1975-76; assoc. dir. Pima Alcoholism Consortium, Tucson, 1976-79, exec. dir., 1979-80; dep. dir. pub. health Orange County Health Care Agy., Santa Ana, Calif., 1980-89, dir. policy, planning, 1989-90; dir. pub. fin. Orange County, 1990-92; dir. San Luis Obispo County Health Agy., 1993-99; CEO The Healthcare Found. for Orange County, Santa Ana, Calif., 1999—. Cons. Tucson Sch. Dist., 1973-75, U.S. Dept. Labor, Washington, 1976-79, Indian Health Svc., Rockville, Md., 1984-85; ptnr. Zepeda Assocs., Fullerton, Calif., 1987-93; presenter in field. Mem. Fullerton Planning Commn., 1984-91, chmn., 1990-91; mem. Calif. Task Force on Comparable Worth, 1984-85, Calif. Dist. Appeal Bd. No. 510, L.A., 1986—. Recipient Woman of Achievement award Orange County Bd. Suprs., 1988, Disting. Achievement awards Nat. Assn. Counties, 1985, 86, 87, 89. Mem. APHA, Health Funders Partnership of Orange County (chair 2000-02), County Health Execs. Assn. Calif. (v.p. 1998-99), Nat. Assn. County and City Health Ofcls. (bd. dirs.), Ctrl. Coast Hosp. Coun. (chair 1996), County Alcohol Program Adminstrs. Assn. Calif. (v.p. 1983, pres. 1984-85), So. Calif. Grantmakers (bd. dirs. 2004—), Grantmakers in Health (bd. dirs. 2004-), Rotary Santa Ana (pres. 2001-02). Avocation: fiber arts. Office: The Healthcare Found for Orange County 1450 N Tustin Ave Ste 103 Santa Ana CA 92705-8653 Home: 208 Almador Irvine CA 92614 Office Phone: 714-245-1650. E-mail: szepeda@hfoc.org.

ZEPF, THOMAS HERMAN, physics educator, researcher; b. Cin., Feb. 13, 1935; s. Paul A. and Agnes J. (Schulz) Z. BS summa cum laude, Xavier U., 1957; MS, St. Louis U., 1960, PhD, 1963. Asst. prof. physics Creighton U., Omaha, 1962-67, assoc. prof., 1967-75, prof., 1975—2002, prof. emeritus, 2002—, acting chmn. dept. physics, 1963-66, chmn., 1966-73, 81-93, coord. allied health programs, 1975-76, coord. pre-health scis. advising, 1976-81. Cons. physicist VA Hosp., Omaha, 1966-71; vis. prof. physics St. Louis U., 1973-74; program evaluator Am. Coun. on Edn., 1988-2002. Contbr. articles and abstracts to Surface Sci., Bull. Am. Phys. Soc., Proceedings Nebr. Acad. Sci., The Physics Tchr. Jour., others. Recipient Cert. Recognition award Phi Beta Kappa U. Cin. chpt., 1953. Mem. AAAS, Am. Phys. Soc., Am. Assn. Physics Tchrs. (pres. Nebr. sect. 1978), Nebr. Acad. Sci. (life, chmn. physics sect. 1985—), Internat. Brotherhood Magicians, Soc. Am. Magicians (pres. assembly #7, 1964-65), KC, Sigma Xi (Achievement award for rsch. St. Louis chpt. 1963, pres. Omaha chpt. 1993-94), Sigma Pi Sigma. Roman Catholic. Office: Creighton U Dept Physics Omaha NE 68178-0001 *The real magic we all have at our disposal - is the ability to comprehend our world, to understand how things behave. This understanding, which we gain through science, enables us to predict outcomes and exert a measure of control over nature. It's a sacred trust. It makes the scientist a kind of modern day magician.*

ZEPNICK, SEYMOUR, civil engineer, consultant; b. NYC, Mar. 16, 1927; s. Leo and Rose Z.; m. Isabelle Federofsky Zepnick, Dec. 24, 1950; children: Glen Reed, Ira Mark, Eileen Lynda. BSCE, CCNY, 1950. Registered profl. engr., NY, NJ, Mass., Conn., .Va., Del., Calif., Md., Ala., Colo. Structural engr. Gussow & Skidmore, NYC, 1950-51, H.K. Furgerson, NYC, 1951-53, Vitro Corp., NYC, 1953-55; ptnr. Firm of Dermot Reddy, NYC, 1955-88. Ptnr., 1974-88, dir. engring., 1968-74, chief engr., 1967-68, Firm of S. Zepnick; pvt. practice, 1988-96; bd. dirs. Devenco Inc., NYC, 1974-88. Contbr. articles to profl. jours. Pres. Bnai Brith Colossus Lodge, 1968, 69. Recipient ASCE award, NYC, 1989, Merit award, Phase 2 Culvert Design, Newark Internat. Airport. Fellow ASCE (chmn. bd. structures 1973, vice chmn. 1972), Technical Publications: 1.precast, prestressed concrete-new design vistas. concrete industry board, 1967, 2.Tower reconstruction for higher power transmission-electrical world, 1969 Home and Office: 6087 Millington Way Delray Beach FL 33484-2487

ZEPOS, NICHOLAS S. academic administrator; BA, U. Wis., 1976, JD, 1979. Joined faculty Vanderbilt U., Nashville, 1987, assoc. dean rsch. Law Sch., assoc. provost, 1999, vice chancellor for instnl. planning and advancement, 2000, provost, vice chancellor for acad. affairs, 2001—. Contbr. articles to publs. Office: Vanderbilt Univ 131 21st Ave South Nashville TN 37203-1181*

ZEPPELIN, MARY FRANCES, special education educator, elementary school educator, consultant; b. Detroit, Aug. 24, 1958; d. Robert Francis Singelyn and Doris Jean Hunt; m. Mark A. Hague, Apr. 23, 1982 (div. Feb. 2001); children: Jason, Samantha, Lauren, Alexander. BA, Oakland U., 1993, EdM, 1998, postgrad. 7th grade math/lang. arts tchr. Mason Middle Sch., Waterford, Mich., 1993—2000; spl. instr. Oakland U., Rochester, Mich., 1998—. Math. cons. Zeppelin Consulting, Waterford, Mich., 1999—. Co-author: Making Sense of Exponents A Constructivist Approach, 1999. Mem.: Detroit Area Coun. Tchrs. Math. (v.p. elem. 2002—). Avocations: pottery, painting, swimming, weightlifting, music. Office: Oakland Univ ED Bldg 475A Rochester MI 48309

ZERBE, DARELL, metal products executive; PhD in Indsl. Engring. Named an IT Inspiration, Enterprise Systems, 2001. Office: Ryerson Tull 2621 W 15th St Chicago IL 60608*

ZERBE, KATHRYN JANE, psychiatrist; b. Harrisburg, Pa., Oct. 17, 1951; d. Grover Franklin and Ethel (Schreckengaust) Z. BS with BA equivalent cum laude, Duke U., 1973; MD, Temple U., 1978. Diplomate Am. Bd. Psychiatry, 1984. Resident Karl Menninger Sch. Psychiatry, Topeka, 1982, dean, dir. edn. and rsch., 1992-97; staff psychiatrist Menninger Found., Topeka, 1982-2001; v.p. edn. and rsch. The Menninger Clinic, Topeka, 1993-97, prof., 1997-2001, Jack Aron chair in psychiat. edn., 1997-2001, apptd. tng. and supr. analyst, 1995—; prof. psychiatry, prof. ob-gyn. Oreg. Health Scis. Univ., Portland, 2001—, dir. behavioral medicine dept. women's health, 2001—, prof. psychiatry, prof. ob-gyn., dir. behavioral medicine, women's health, chmn. psychotherapy, dir. outpatient clinic, 2003—, vice chair for psychotherapy, 2003; tng. and supr. analyst Oreg. Psychoanalytic Ctr., 2002—. Instr. numerous seminars and courses. Author: The Body Betrayed: Women, Eating Disorders and Treatment, 1993, Women's Mental Health in Primary Care, 1999, numerous articles profl. rsch. papers; editor: Womens Mental Health: Primary Care Clinics, 2001, Bull. of Menninger Clinic, 1998—2001; assoc. editor:, 1996—98, mem. editl. bd.: Eating Disorders Rev., Eating Disorders: The Jour. of Treatment and Prevention Postgrad. Medicine; editor (sect.): Current Women's Health; contbr. book revs. and articles to profl. jours. Probation officer Juvenile divsn. Dauphin County, Pa., 1973. Recipient Ann. Laughlin Merit award The Nat. Psychiat. Endowment Fund, 1982, Outstanding Paper of Profl. Programs award The Menninger Found. Alumni Assn., 1982, Writing award Topeka Inst. for Psychoanalysis, 1985, 90, Mentorship award, 1997, Women Helping Women award, 1995, Tchr. of Yr. award, 1988, 96, 99; named one of Outstanding Young Women in Am., 1986, 88; Seeley fellow, 1979-82; Hilde Bruch lectureship, 1996. Fellow Am. Psychiat. Assn.; mem. AMA, Am. Coll. Psychiatrists, Am. Med. Women's Assn., Oreg. Med. Assn., Oreg. Psychiat. Assn., Sigma Xi, Alpha Omega Alpha. Avocations: writing, reading, art history, travel. Office: Oreg Health and Scis U Adult Psychiatry 3181 SW Sam Jackson Park Rd Portland OR 97239-3098 Office Phone: 503-494-1009. Business E-Mail: zerbek@ohsu.edu.

ZERBS, STEPHEN TAYLOR, communications engineer; b. Churdan, Iowa, May 5, 1946; s. Hobert Frank and LaVon Monica (Mantz) Z.; m. Patricia Lynn Tvrdik, Mar. 28, 1976; children: Rick Andrew, Steve Matthew. AAS in Electronics Tech., Iowa State U., 1967; BS, U. Nebr., 1984, cert. advanced mgmt., 1995; MBA in Global Tech., Tufts U., 1995. Engring. assoc. Western Elec., Omaha, Nebr., 1967-82; planning engr. Western Elec./AT&T, Omaha, 1983-91; sr. engr. AT&T/Lucent Technologies, Omaha, 1992—. Inventor and patentee in field with numerous U.S. and Fgn. Patents. Elected mem. Sanitary Improvement Dist. 29, Gretna, Nebr., 1980-82. Recipient Outstanding Recognition Jr. Achievement Omaha, 1969. Mem. IEEE, Tel. Pioneers Am., Am. Legion (assoc.) Office: Lucent Techs 120th and I Streets Omaha NE 68137

ZERCHER, CRAIG ALLEN, special education educator, researcher; s. Chris Robert and Barbara Eloise Zercher; m. Christine Joy Nakagawa, June 26, 1982; children: Jackie Miya, Mia Marissa, Emma Christine. BA in Psychology, U. Calif., Berkeley, 1982; MA in Spl. Edn., San Francisco State U., 1990; PhD in Spl. Edn., U. Calif. and San Francisco State U., 2003. Respite worker Cmty. Assn. for the Retarded, Palo Alto, Calif., 1977—82; profound disability specialist Assn. for Retarded Citizens, San Leandro, Calif., 1982—83; dir. therapeutic preschool program Zonta Svcs., San Jose, Calif., 1985—93, dir. resources for early assessment children's mental health, 1990—93; early childhood tchr. Santa Clara County Office, San Jose, 1993—94; rsch. assoc. San Francisco State U. Early Childhood Rsch. Inst. on Inclusion, 1994—99; lectr. spl. edn. San Francisco State U., 1997—; edn. rschr. SRI Internat., Menlo Park, Calif., 2000—. Preschool disability and behavior cons. various local sch. dists. and day care assns., San Francisco and Bay Area, 1990—. Contbr. chapters to books, articles to profl. jours. Named Non-Profit Program of the Yr., United Way Santa Clara County, 1992; Spl. Edn. Leadership scholar, San Francisco State U., 1994—98. Mem.: Coun. for Exceptional Children, Soc. for Rsch. in Child Devel., Phi Beta Kappa. Achievements include development of innovative multidisciplinary programs for the treatment of young children with behavior disorders; research in examining the peer conflicts of preschool children with problem behavior; peer culture and mixed qualitative and quantitative research methods in the study of young children with disabilities; influence of cultural and linguistic diversity in the early education of children with disabilities. Avocations: running, history, studying theology and the history of christian dogma, swimming. Office: SRI Internat 333 Ravenswood Ave Menlo Park CA 94025 Personal E-mail: jzz10@aol.com.

ZERELLA, JOSEPH T. retired pediatric surgeon; b. Youngstown, Ohio, Mar. 7, 1941; s. Atilio and Ann (Capuzello) Z.; m. Diana Isabelle Talbot, Aug. 5, 1967; children: Ann, Michael, Mark. BS, Northwestern U., 1962, MD, 1966. Diplomate Am. Bd. Surgery, Am. Bd. Pediatric Surgery. Intern Med. Coll. Wis., Milw., 1966-67, resident in surgery, 1967-68, 70-73; tng. fellow in pediatric surgery Children's Hosp. Med. Ctr., Cin., 1973-75; staff pediatric surgeon Phoenix Children's Hosp., 1975—; pvt. practice medicine, specializing in pediatric surgery Phoenix, 1975—. Mem. staff Good Samaritan Hosp., Phoenix, 1975—, sect. chief pediatric surgery, 1979—; mem. staff St. Joseph's Hosp., Phoenix, 1975—, sect. chief pediatric surgery, 1980—. Contbr. articles to profl. jours. Served as capt. U.S. Army, 1968-70. Served as capt. USAR, 1968—70. Fellow ACS, Am. Acad. Pediatrics, Am. Pediatric Surg. Assn., Pacific Assn. Pediatric Surgeons. Roman Catholic. Office: Saguaro Childrens Surgery Ltd 1301 E Mcdowell Rd Ste 100 Phoenix AZ 85006-2605 Mailing: 8426 N 15th Dr Phoenix AZ 85021

ZERHOUNI, ELIAS ADAM, Director National Institutes of Health; b. Algeria, Apr. 12, 1951; s. Mohamed and Yamna (Raahmouni) Z.; m. Nadia Azza, Oct. 25, 1975; children: Djillali, Yasmin, Adam. MD, U. Algiers, 1975.

Diplomate Am. Bd. Radiology. Asst. dir. body CT Johns Hopkins Hospital, Balt., 1978—81; vice chmn., dir. body imaging De Paul Hospital, Norfolk, Va., 1982—85; co-dir. MRI and body CT, coord. clinical research Johns Hopkins Med. Institutions, Balt., 1985—88, dir. thoracic imaging and MRI, 1988—96; dir. Advanced Med. Imaging Inst., Norfolk, Va., 1991—92; radiologist-in-chief Johns Hopkins Hospital, Balt., 1996—; dir. Nat. Inst. of Health Dept HHS, Bethesda, Md., 2002—. Resident in diagnostic radiology Johns Hopkins U., Balt., 1975—79, instr., 1978—79, asst. prof. radiology, 1979—81, Ea. Va. Med. Sch., Norfolk, Va., 1981—83, assoc. prof. radiology, 1983—85; cons. Nat. Cancer Inst., NHLBI, 1985—88; assoc. prof. radiology Johns Hopkins U., Balt., 1985—92, prof. radiology, 1992; centennial lectr. Swedish Royal Acad. Radiology, Stockholm, 1994; prof. biomed. engring. Johns Hopkins U., Balt., 1995, chmn. radiology, 1996—, exec. vice dean, vice dean clinical affairs, 1996—99, vice dean research, 1999—2000, exec. vice dean, 2000—02; assoc. editor, mem. of the editorial bd. Journal of Surgical and Radiological Anatomy, 1980—86; assoc. editor Radiology, 1983—90; mem. editorial bd. Topics in Clinical MRI, 1990—96; assoc. editor, mem. of the editorial bd. Journal of Thoracic Imaging, 1990—97. Patentee in field. Recipient Lauterbur award for MRI research, 1989, 93, Hounsfield award for CT Imaging, 1991. Mem.: Inst. of Med., NAS, Soc. for Chmn. of Academic Radiology Dept., Soc. for Cardiovascular Magnetic Resonance, N. Am. Soc. for Cardiac Imaging, Balt. City Med. Soc., Am. Assn. for the Advancement of Sci., Am. Coll. of Radiology, Am. Heart Assn., Internat. Soc. for Magnetic Resonance in Med. (bd. of trustees 1995—98), Fleischner Soc. (Fleischner Soc. medal 1997), Assn. of U. Radiologists, Soc.of Computed Body Tomography, Soc. of Thoracic Radiology (founding member), Radiological Soc. of N.Am., Am. Roentgen Ray Soc. Avocations: swimming, windsurfing, music. Office: Dept HHS NIH 1 Center Dr MSC 0148 Bldg 1 Bethesda MD 20892-0148*

ZERIN, STEVEN DAVID, lawyer; b. N.Y.C., Oct. 1, 1953; s. Stanley Robert and Cecilie Paula (Goldberg) Z.; children: Alexander James, J. Oliver. BS, Syracuse U., 1974; JD, St. Johns U., 1977. Bar: N.Y. 1978, U.S. Dist. Ct. (so. dist.) N.Y. 1985, U.S. Supreme Ct. 1986. Of coun. Sperry, Weinberg, Wels, Waldman & Rubenstein, N.Y.C., 1982-85; ptnr. Wels & Zerin, N.Y.C., 1985—. Trustee, mem. bd. govs. Daytop Village. Mem. ABA (exec. mem. and lectr. family law sect.), N.Y. State Bar Assn. (exec. com. family law sect.), Assn. of Bar of City of N.Y. Democrat. Home: 12 E 88th St New York NY 10128-0535 Office: Wels & Zerin 600 Madison Ave Fl 22 New York NY 10022-1615 Office Phone: 212-838-8608. E-mail: szerin@welsandzerin.com.

ZERMAN, MELVYN BERNARD, publishing company executive, author; b. N.Y.C., July 10, 1930; s. Abraham and Ida (Belsky) Zirman; m. Miriam Baron, Jan. 2, 1985 (dec.); children: Andrew, Jared, Lenore. BA, U. Mich., 1952; MA, Columbia U., 1953. With Oxford Book Co., N.Y.C., 1953-55; asst. editor Abelard-Schuman, Pubs., N.Y.C., 1955-57; office mgr., salesman Harper & Row, N.Y.C., 1957-61, sales rep., 1961-69, sales mgr., 1969-79, Random House, Inc., N.Y.C., 1979-83, sales cons., 1983-87; pres., pub. Limelight Edits., N.Y.C., 1983—. Mem. exec. com. N.Y.Is Book Country, N.Y.C., 1985—. Author: Call the Final Witness, 1977, Beyond a Reasonable Doubt, 1981 (Freedoms Found. medal 1981), Taking on the Press, 1986. Mem. Phi Beta Kappa. Democrat. Avocations: book collecting, travel. Office: Limelight Edits 118 E 30th St New York NY 10016-7303

ZERR, RICHARD KEVIN, lawyer; b. St. Charles, Mo., Apr. 10, 1949; s. Elmer George and Lillian Grace (Gross) Z.; m. Martha Jo Zerr, Mar. 19, 1969 (div. June 1976); m. Judy Ann Yeager, Aug. 8, 1978; 1 child, Richard Kevin Jr. AB in Polit. Sci., U. Mo., 1971; JD, U. Ark., 1974. Bar: Mo. 1974, U.S. Dist. Ct. (we. dist.) Mo. 1974, U.S. Dist. Ct. (ea. dist.) Mo. 1983, U.S. Ct. Appeals (8th cir.) 1985, U.S. Supreme Ct. 1985. Asst. to pros. atty. County of St. Charles, 1974; magistrate judge City of St. Charles, 1975-78; assoc. judge Cir. Ct., St. Charles, 1979-82; ptnr. Zerr Fralily & Wolff PC, St. Charles, 2003. Bd. dirs. St. Charles County Police Acad., 1978-88, Legal Svcs. Ea. Mo., 1978—. Bd. dir. St. Charles City-County Libr. Dist., 1991—. Mem. ABA (state chmn. small claims ct. com. 1978-82), Mo. Bar Assn. (bd. govs. 1999—), St. Charles County Bar Assn., Metro. St. Louis Bar Assn., U. Mo. Columbia Alumni Assn. (nat. bd. dirs. 1994—). Lodges: Kiwanis. Democrat. Roman Catholic. Avocation: college football officiating. Home: 176 Huntington Downs Saint Charles MO 63301-8700 Office: Zerr Fralily & Wulff PC 2777 W Clay St Saint Charles MO 63301-2539 E-mail: rzerr@btzlaw.com.

ZERVAS, NICHOLAS THEMISTOCLES, neurosurgeon; b. Lynn, Mass., Mar. 9, 1929; s. Themistocles and Demetra P. (Stasinopoulos) Z.; m. Thalia Poleway, Feb. 15, 1959; children: T. Nicholas, Christopher Louis, Rhea. AB, Harvard U., 1950; MD, U. Chgo., 1954. Intern N.Y. Hosp., 1955; resident in neurology Montreal Neurol. Inst., 1956; resident in neurosurgery Mass. Gen. Hosp., Boston, 1958-62; fellow in stereotaxic cerebral surgery U. Paris, 1960-61; asst. attending surgeon, asso. neurosurgery Jefferson Med. Coll., Phila., 1962-67; asso. prof. surgery Harvard U., 1971-77; also chief neurosurg. service Beth Israel Hosp., Boston, 1967-77; prof. surgery Harvard U., 1977-200; also chief neurosurg. service Mass. Gen. Hosp., 1977-2000; Higgins prof. neurosurgery Harvard U., 1986-2000. Contbr. numerous articles to sci. jours. Chmn. Mass. Coun. Arts and Humanities, 1983-91; trustee Boston Symphony Orch., 1990—, vice chmn., 1993—, pres., 1994-2002. Capt. M.C. AUS, 1956-58, 87-2002. Fellow Am. Acad. Arts and Scis.; mem. Am. Acad. Neurol. Surgery (pres. 1990-91), Am. Assn. Neurol. Surgeons, Soc. Neurol. Surgeons, Am. Neurol. Assn., Am. Bd. Neurol. Surgery (chmn. 1990-91), Inst. Medicine Nat. Acad. Scis., Sigma Xi. Home: 100 Canton Ave Milton MA 02186-3507 Office: Mass Gen Hosp Attn Barbara Perrier 55 Fruit St Boston MA 02114-2620

ZERZAN, CHARLES JOSEPH, JR., retired gastroenterologist; b. Portland, Oreg., Dec. 1, 1921; s. Charles Joseph and Margaret Cecelia (Mahony) Z.; m. Joan Margaret Kathan, Feb. 7, 1948; children: Charles Joseph, Michael, Kathryn, Paul, Joan, Margaret, Terrance, Phillip, Thomas, Rose, Kevin, Gregory. BA, Wilamette U., 1948; MD, Marquette U., 1951. Diplomate Am. Bd. Internal Medicine. Commd. 2d lt. U.S. Army, 1940, advanced through grades to capt., 1945, ret., 1946, re-enlisted, 1951, advanced through grades to lt. col., M.C., 1965; intern Madigan Gen. Hosp., Ft. Lewis, Wash., 1951-52; resident in internal medicine Letterman Gen. Hosp., San Francisco, 1953-56, Walter Reed Gen. Hosp., San Francisco, 1960-61; chief of medicine Rodriquez Army Hosp., 1957-60, U.S. Army Hosp., Fort Gordon, Calif., 1962-65; chief gastroenterology Fitzsimmons Gen. Hosp., Denver, 1965-66; chief profl. svcs. U.S. Army Hosp., Ft. Carson, Colo., 1967-68; dir. continuing med. edn. U. Oreg., Portland, 1968-73; ptnr. Permanente Clinic, Portland, 1973-92, ret., 1992. Assoc. clin. prof. medicine U. Oreg., 1973-97; individual practice medicine, specializing in gastroenterology, Portland, 1968-92; staff Northwest Permanente, P.C., ret., 1992, dir., 1980-83. Decorated Legion of Merit, Army Commendation medal with oak leaf cluster; Meritorious Alumnus award Oreg. Health Scis. U., 1990. Fellow ACP; mem. Am. Gastroenterol. Assn., Oreg. Med. Assn. (del. Clackamas County), Ret. Officers Assn., China-Burma-India Vet. Assn., Burma Star Assn. Republican. Roman Catholic. Home and Office: 6364 SE Mcnary Rd Portland OR 97267-5119

ZESCH, HAL, energy executive; BBA in Acctg., U. Tex., Austin. CPA. Audit and consulting mgr. Deloitte & Touche; various pos., including v.p. best bus. practices, asst. corp. controller, controller for natural gas ops., and dir. corp. acctg. Valero Energy Corp., San Antonio, v.p. SAP systems integration, v.p., chief info officer, 2003. Office: Valero Corp Hdqrs One Valero Place San Antonio TX 78212-3186

ZESCHUK, GREG, application developer; MD, U. Alta., Can., 1995. Joint CEO BioWare Corp., Edmonton, Canada, 1995—. Software developer (electronic game) Baldur's Gate. Office: BioWare Corp 302 10508 82d Ave Edmonton AB T6E 6H2 Canada

ZETA-JONES, CATHERINE, actress; b. Swansea, Wales, Sept. 25, 1969; d. Dai and Pat Jones; m. Michael Douglas, Nov. 18, 2000; children: Dylan Michael, Carys Zeta. Film appearances include Les 1001 nuits (Italy), 1990, Christopher Columbus: The Discovery, 1992, Splitting Heirs, 1993, Blue Juice, 1995, The Phantom, 1996, The Mask of Zorro, 1998, Entrapment, 1999, The Haunting, 1999, High Fidelity, 2000, Traffic, 2000, America's Sweethearts, 2001, Chicago, 2002 (Best Sup. Actress Academy award, 2003, Best Actress in Sup. Role, British Acad. Film Award (BAFTA) 2003), Sinbad: Legend of the Seven Seas (voice only), 2003, Intolerable Cruelty, 2003, The Terminal, 2004; (T.V. films) Out of the Blue, 1991, The Cinder Path, 1994, The Return of the Native, 1994, Catherine the Great, 1995, Titanic, 1996,; (T.V. series) The Darling Buds of May, 1991; (T.V. appearances) The Adventures of Young Indiana Jones: Daredevils of the Desert, 1992. Office: c/o ICM 8942 Wilshire Blvd Beverly Hills CA 90211

ZEUGNER, JOHN FINN, history educator, writer; b. N.Y.C., Oct. 7, 1938; s. Orland Kump and Ethel (Finn) Z.; m. Alice Chatfield Valentine, Sept. 7, 1968; children: Emily Valentine, Maxwell Finn, Laura Ruth. AB, Harvard U., 1959; MA, Fla. State U., 1968, PhD, 1971. Night mgr. Beach Cart, Sarasota, Fla., 1960-67; asst. prof. history Worcester Poly. Inst., Mass., 1971-74, assoc. prof., 1974-82, prof., 1982—; Fulbright lectr. Osaka U., Kobe U., Japan, 1976-78. Vis. prof. Keio U., Tokyo, 1981-83; Bryant Drake guest prof. Kobe Coll., Japan, 1994-95. Contbr. articles, short stores to profl. publs. With USCG, 1961—62. Named Paris Fletcher Disting. Prof. Humanities, Worcester Poly. Inst., 1985; grantee NEA, 1970 Mem. Orgn. Am. Historians, Soc. Historians Am. Fgn. Rels. Avocations: tennis; chess. Home: 31 William St Worcester MA 01609-2313 Office: Worcester Poly Inst Humanities & Arts Dept Worcester MA 01609 Office Phone: 508-831-5246. Business E-Mail: jzeugner@wpi.edu.

ZEUSCHNER, ERWIN ARNOLD, investment advisory company executive; b. Freiburg, Germany, Nov. 17, 1935; came to U.S., 1936; s. Reinhold Hermann and Helene Barbara (Maas) Z.; m. Christa Elfreide Ellmers, June 20, 1959 (dec. Aug. 1971); children— Peter Erwin, Suzanne Christina, Andrea Ellmers; m. Margaret Anne Finn, Mar. 25, 1972; 1 dau., Elizabeth Nora. BA in Econs., Queens Coll., 1957; MBA in Fin, NYU, 1964. Sr. v.p. Chase Manhattan Bank, N.Y.C., 1970-72; sr. v.p., dir. Chase Investors Mgmt. Corp., 1972-80; sr. v.p. Chase Manhattan Corp., 1970-80; ptnr. David J. Greene & Co. (investment advs.), N.Y.C., 1980—. Trustee Marymount Manhattan Coll., 1997. Served to capt. USAF, 1958-60. Mem. N.Y. Soc. Security Analysts (dir.) Home: 1 Middle Dr Manhasset NY 11030-1414 Office: 599 Lexington Ave New York NY 10022-6030

ZEVNIK-SAWATZKY, DONNA DEE, retired litigation coordinator; b. Tulsa, Dec. 15, 1946; d. Robert Joseph Z. and Dorothy Dee (Robertson) Zink; m. Kenneth Sawatzky, May 30, 1965; children: K. Brian, Kaira D. Student, U. Ctrl. Okla., 1977, Okla. State U., 1984. Cert. AIDS educator, State of Okla., 1995-97. Sec. Farmers Ins. Co., Oklahoma City, 1974-80; office mgr. S.A.F.E., Inc., Oklahoma City, 1980-83; jr. acct. Southeast Exploration Corp., Oklahoma City, 1983-84; acct. Young Bros., Inc., Oklahoma City, 1984-88, The Denman Co., Inc., Oklahoma City, 1988-89; litig. coord. ACLU Okla., Oklahoma City, 1994—2003; ret., 2003; founder, owner, CEO Otherwhere Arts, 1999—2001. Author and illustrator: That Place--Otherwhere, 1994, Something for Otherwhere, 1995; author: At Our House, 1979-83; columnist Putnam City-N.W. News, Warr Acres, Okla., 1979-83; designer stage sets Miss Warr Acres Pageant, 1971-88. Bd. dirs. Miss Warr Acres Pageant, 1984-88, Warr Acres C. of C., 1981-85; treas. ACLU of Okla., 1995—, bd. dirs., 1994—; child welfare adv. Okla. State Dept. Human Svcs., Oklahoma City, 1987-89; coord. AIDS clinic Triangle Assn., Oklahoma City, 1994-97; founder Circle of Friends with Arachnoiditis World Wide Web Chronic Pain Support Group, 1997. Named Honorary Mayor of Warr Acres, 1971, Super Citizen, 1973, Outstanding Vol. Okla. State Dept. Human Svcs., 1988; recipient Svc. award Warr Acres C. of C., 1979, Legis. Commendation State of Okla., 1988, numerous Okla. Newspaper Column of Month awards Okla. Press Assn., Oklahoma City, 1981-82. Mem. NAFE, ACLU (Exec. Dir. Vol. Svc. award 1996), Nat. Notary Assn., Am. Inst. Profl. Bookkeepers, Amnesty Internat., The Interfaith Alliance, Pflag, Human Rights Campaign, Okla. Coalition to Abolish the Death Penalty. Democrat. Methodist. Avocations: painting, writing, photography, family. Office: 3000 Paseo Dr Oklahoma City OK 73103

ZEVON, SUSAN JANE, editor; b. N.Y.C., July 23, 1944; d. Louis and Rhea (Alter) Z. BA, Smith Coll., 1966. Asst. editor trends and environments House & Garden, N.Y.C., 1970-80; account supr. Jessica Dee Comm., N.Y.C., 1981-84; sr. editor architecture House Beautiful, N.Y.C., 1985—. Author: Inside Architecture, 1997, Outside Architecture, 1999; (with others) Decorating On The Cheap, 1984. Bd. dirs. The Cornerstone Learning Ctr., 1999—. Mem. Archtl. League N.Y., Smith Coll. N.Y. Club (v.p. 1987-88, pres. 1988-89), The Mcpl. Art Soc., Internat. Furnishings and Design Assn. Avocations: films, lit., gymnastics, art. Office: House Beautiful 1700 Broadway New York NY 10019-5905

ZEVTCHIN, J. MARK, financial executive, consultant; b. Coatesville, Pa., Oct. 29, 1957; s. Michael Fredrick and Ethel Deloris Zevtchin. BA, Salem (W.Va.) Internat. U., 1980. Pres. Maxwell Industries, Exton, Pa., 1989-90; prin. JMZ Fin. Svcs., Parkersburg, Pa., 1984—; contr., adminstrn. mgr. Macke Bldg. Svcs., Bala Cynwyd, Pa., 1986; CFO, Brighter Cmty. Inc., York, Pa., 1991-92; contr. Pilz Am. Inc., Concordville, Pa., 1995-96. Cons. PPL, Allentown, Pa., 1998-2000, JP Morgan Chase, Wilmington, Del., 2000-2001; informal advisor Dept. Def., Washington, 1980—, Dept. Justice, Washington, 1980—, NSC, Washington, 1990—, IRS, Washington, 1995—. Mem. Nature Conservancy, UN Assn. (bd. dirs.), World Affairs Coun. Phila., Internat. Visitors Assn. Avocations: herpetology, ecology, scuba diving, politics, international affairs. Home and Office: 3013 Lincoln Hwy Parkesburg PA 19365 E-mail: jmarkz@ohesco.com.

ZEWAIL, AHMED HASSAN, chemistry and physics educator, editor, consultant; b. Damanhour, Egypt, Feb. 26, 1946; arrived in U.S., 1969, 1982; s. Hassan A. Zewail and Rawhia Dar; m. Dema Zewail; children: Maha, Amani, Nabeel, Hani. BS, Alexandria U., Egypt, 1967, MS, 1969; PhD, U. Pa., 1974; MA (hon.), Oxford U., 1991; DSc (hon.), Am. U., Cairo, 1993, Katholieke U., Leuven, Belgium, U. Pa., U. Lausanne, Switzerland, 1997; DU (hon.), Swinburne U., Australia, 1999; HDA Sc (hon.), Arab Acad. for Sci. and Tech., Egypt, 1999, Alexandria U., 1999; DSc (hon.), U. New Brunswick, Canada, 2000; DHC (hon.), U. Rome, Italy, 2000, U. de Liège, Belgium, 2000. Teaching asst. U. Pa., Phila., 1969—70; IBM fellow U. Calif., Berkeley, 1974—76; asst. prof. chem. physics Calif. Inst. Tech., Pasadena, 1976—78, assoc. prof., 1978—82, prof., 1982—89, Linus Pauling prof. chem. physics, 1990—94, Linus Pauling prof. chemistry and prof. physics, 1995—, dir. NSF Lab. for Molecular Scis., 1996—. Cons. Xerox Corp., Webster, NY, 1977—80, ARCO Solar, Inc., Calif., 1978—81. Editor Laser Chemistry, 1980—85, Jour. Phys. Chemistry, 1985—90, Chem. Physics Letters, 1991—; editor: International Series Monographs on Chemistry, 1992—, Advances in Laser Spectroscopy, 1977—, 1978—, Photochemistry and Photobiology, 1983—, Ultrafast Phenomena, 1990—, 1993—, 1994—, The Chemical Bond: Structure and Dynamics, 1992, Femtochemistry-Ultrafst Dynamics of the Chemical Bond, 1994; contbr. numerous articles to sci. jours., patentee in solar energy field. Recipient Tchr.-Scholar award, Dreyfus Found., 1979—85, Alexander von Humboldt Sr. U.S. Scientist award, 1983, John Simon Guggenheim Meml. Found. award, 1987, King Faisal Internat. prize in sci., 1989, NASA award, 1991, 1st AMM Achievement award, 1991, Nobel Laureate Signature award, 1992, Carl Zeiss award, Cairo U. Medal and Shield of Honor, 1992, U. Qatar medal, 1993, Niles award of honor Bonner Chemiepreis, Germany, 1994, Order of Merit first class, Egypt, 1995, Cdl. de France medal Leonardo Da Vinci award of excellence, France, 1995, J.G. Kirwood medal, Yale U., 1996, Beijing U. medal, 1996, Robert A. Welch award in chemistry, 1997, Pitts. Spectroscopy award, 1997, Benjamin Franklin medal, 1999, Paul Karrer Gold medal, Zurich, 1999, Roentgen prize, Germany, 1999, E.O. Lawrence award, U.S. Govt., 1999, Merski award, U. Nebr., 1999, Nobel prize in Chemistry, 1999, Egypt Postage Stamp with portrait issued, 1999, Grand Collar of the Nile, Highest Award, 2000, Order of Zayed, United Arab Emirates, 2000, Ahmed Zewail fellow established, U. Pa., 2000, Order of Cedar, Lebanon, 2000, Order of ISESCO 1st class, Saudi Arabia, 2000, Order of merit, Tunisia, 2000, Insignia Pontifical Acad., Vatican, 2000. Mem.: NAS (Chem. Sci. award 1996), AAAS, Third World Acad. Scis., European Acad. Arts, Scis. and Humanities, Royal Danish Acad. Scis. and Letters, Pontifical Acad. Sci., Am. Phys. Soc. (Herbert P. Broida prize 1995), Am. Philos. Soc., Am. Chem. Soc. (Buck-Whitney medal 1985, Harrison-Howe award 1989, Hoechst prize 1990, Peter Debye award 1997, Linus Pauling medal 1997, 1st E.B. Wilson award 1997, William H. Nichols award 1998, Richard C. Tolman medal 1998), Am. Acad. Arts and Scis. (Royal Netherlands Acad. Arts and Scis. medal 1993), Sigma Xi (Earle K. Plyler prize 1993, Wolf prize 1993). Office: Arthur Amos Noyes Lab of Chem Physics Mail Code 127-72 Pasadena CA 91125

ZEX, DAMON, artist; b. Columbus, Ohio, July 11, 1963; s. Arnold Hobart Zaner, Rhoda Lee Zaner. BA, Ohio State U., 1985, MFA, 1991. Sales rep. FAZ Art Products, Columbus, Ohio, 1984—86; dir. gallery Artreach Gallery, Columbus, 1986—87; designer Contemporary Glass, Columbus, 1987—88; comml. designer Columbus Arts & Entertainment Mag., Columbus, 1988—89, Ohio Transmission Corp., Columbus, 1989—91; videographer, tech. dir. Cmty. 21 TV, Columbus, 1992—2001; co-owner Damon Zex Ltd., Columbus, 2001—. Expert art witness U.S. Fed. Ct., Columbus, 1999. Zex Cards, 1991; actor: Zex TV, 1993—2001 (Comedy award, 1994, 1997, 1998). Avocations: chess, yoga, dance, astrology, weight training. Home: Apt 361A 2913 Neil Ave Columbus OH 43202-2043 Office Phone: 614-262-0274. E-mail: zex@zexart.com.

ZEXTER, ELEANOR M. secondary school educator; b. Providence, R.I., Sept. 7, 1936; d. Morris and Anna Rae (Cantor) Marks; m. D. Ronald Zexter, Dec. 24, 1958; children: Françine Deborah, Judith Blair. BA, Brown U., 1958, MAT, 1962. Cert. tchr. R.I., Calif. Tchr. French and English Hope H.S., Providence, 1959—69, Nathan Bishop Mid. Sch., Providence, 1970—93; tchr. English and social studies Harkham Hillel Hebrew Acad., Beverly Hills, Calif., 1993—99. Mktg. dir. DRZ Sales; grant writer Nathan Bishop Mid. Sch., Providence, 1980-93, choral dir., 1985-93, founder Famous Authors, 1987-93; cons. substance abuse program, Brown U., 1987-93; ednl. cons. Vol. tutor Harkham Hillel Hebrew Acad., 1993-99, French club coord., Harkham Hillel Acad., 1993-99. Recipient Citizen Citation for outstanding efforts with Providence children, Mayor, 1990, McClorin award, 1991. Mem. Am. Assn. French Tchrs., Alliance Francaise, R.I. Assn. Foreign Language, Beverly Hills Country Club (tennis team capt.). Avocations: tennis, antique collecting, reading clubs, bridge, travel. Home: 8544 Burton Way Apt 401 Los Angeles CA 90048-3390

ZGUTA, RUSSELL, history professor; b. Ukraine, Oct. 3, 1941; came to U.S., 1949; s. Stephen and Pauline Zguta; m. Nancy Anne Splinter, Aug. 30, 1969; children: Larissa, Gregory, Katherine, Ellen. BA, St. Francis Coll., Pa., 1964; MA, Pa. State U., 1965, PhD, 1967. Asst. prof. history U. Mo., Columbia, 1967-74, assoc. prof., 1974-79, prof., 1979—, chmn. dept. history, 1989-91, chmn. dept. econs., 1991-95. Author: Russian Minstrels, 1978; contbr. articles to profl. jours. Fulbright-Hays fellow, Helsinki, 1969-70, fellow Am. Coun. on Edn., 1986-87; younger humanist grantee NEH, 1974-75, grantee Nat. Libr. Medicine, 1978-79. Mem. Am. Hist. Assn., Am. Assn. for Advancement Slavic Studies, Am. Assn. for History Medicine, Am. Assn. for Ukrainian Studies, Early Slavic Studies Assn., Slavonic and East European Folklore Assn. Avocations: jogging, reading. Home: 500 Thilly Ave Columbia MO 65203-3461 Office: U Mo Dept History Columbia MO 65211-0001 Office Phone: 573-882-9458. E-mail: zgutar@missouri.edu.

ZHA, JIANYING, writer, educator; b. Beijing; M of Philosophy in Comparative Lit., Columbia U. Writer. Vis. scholar Rice U. Author: (book) China Pop: How Soap Operas, Tabloids and Best Sellers Are Transforming a Culture, 1995 (Guggenheim fellowship, 2003). Office: The New Press 4th Fl 38 Greene St New York NY 10013

ZHABOTINSKY, ANATOL MARKOVITCH, biophysicist, educator; b. Moscow, Jan. 17, 1938; MS in Physics, Moscow State U., Russia, 1961; PhD in Biophysics, Inst. of Biophysics, Moscow, Russia, 1965; DSc in Biophysics, Inst. of Biophysics, Puschino, Russia, 1965—71. Rsch. assoc. Inst. of Oncology, Moscow, 1961—62; grad. rsch. assoc. Inst. of Biophysics, Moscow, 1962—65, rsch. assoc. Puschino, 1965—68, sr. rsch. assoc., 1968—73; lab. head Inst. of Biol. Testing of Chem. Compounds, Kupavna, 1973—89, Nat. Sci. Ctr. of Hematology, Moscow, 1989—91; sr. rsch. assoc. Brandeis U., Waltham, Mass., 1991—92, sr. scientist, 1992—94, adj. prof. chemistry, 1994—2002, prof. chemistry, 2002—. Contbr. scientific papers on chemical oscillations, waves to sci. jours. Recipient Lenin prize, 1980. Mem.: Am. Chem. Soc. Achievements include discovery of Belousov-Zhabotinsky class of oscillating chemical reactions; periodic chemical waves in homogeneous systems. Office: Brandeis U Dept Chemistry 415 South St Waltham MA 02454-9110

ZHAI, SHUMIN, computer scientist; b. Harbin, Heilongjiang, China, Apr. 1, 1961; arrived in US, 1966; s. Zhen-Huan Zhai and Run-Qing Wei. PhD, U. Toronto, Can., 1995. Lectr. Xidian U., Xi'an, China, 1984—89; rsch. scientist U. of Toronto, Toronto, Canada, 1995—96; rsch. staff mem. Almaden rsch. ctr. IBM, San Jose, Calif., 1996—. Contbr. scientific papers (Best Paper, IEEE Computer Soc., 2003). Mem.: Assn. for Computing Machinery. Achievements include research in novel methods of human-computer interaction, 80 papers, 12 US patents. Home: 995 Foxchase Dr #564 San Jose CA 95123 Office: IBM Almaden Rsch Ctr 650 Harry Road B-2 San Jose CA 95120 E-mail: zhai@us.ibm.com.

ZHAMNOV, ALEXEI, professional hockey player; b. Moscow, Oct. 1, 1970; Ctr. Winnipeg Jets, 1992—96, Chgo. Blackhawks, 1996—2004, Philadelphia Flyers, 2004—. Player NHL All-Star game, 2002, Russian Olympic Team, 1992, 98, 2002, Team Russia, World Cup of Hockey, 1996. Office: c/o Philadelphia Flyers 3601 South Broad St Philadelphia PA 19148

ZHANG, CHARLES C. financial planner; MA in Econs., Western Mich. U., 1991; MBA, Northwestern U., 2004. ChFC; CFP; CLU; chartered mutual fund counselor; cert. fund specialist. Sr. fin. advisor Am. Express Fin. Advisors, Inc., Kalamazoo, 1991—. Adj. prof. finance Western Mich. U. Mem. Am. Soc. CLU and ChFC, Inst. cert. Fin. Planners, Internat. Assn. Fin. Planning. Office: Am Express Fin Advisors Inc 1302 W Milham Portage MI 49024 E-mail: charles.c.zhang@aexp.com.

ZHANG, CHUNLONG, environmental educator; b. Lanxi, Zhejiang, China, May 4, 1964; s. Yunfeng Pan and Peile Zhang; m. Shuou Zhao; 1 child, Richard. PhD, Louisiana State University, Baton Rouge, 1993—97. Asst. prof. Hangzhou University, Hangzhou, China, 1986—91, University of Houston-Clear Lake, Houston, 2000—02. Environmental engineering consultant Tyndall Air Force Base, Tyndall, Fl, 1999—99. Author: (original research) Environmental Science and Technology, 2001; original research, Environmental Science and Technology, 2003, Jour. of Hazardous Materials, 2001; author: Journal of Hazardous Materials, 1998, Bulletin of Environmental Contamination and Toxicology, 2000, Journal of Contaminant Hydrology, 1999, Journal of Environmental Science and Health, 1998, Environmental Science and Technology, 1999;: Water Research, 1999, Journal of Hazardous Materials, 2001;: Bioremediation Journal, 1998, Dissertation, 1997 (Outstanding dissertation in the field of engineering and physical science, 1997), Separation Science and Technology, 1996. Mem.: Society of Environental Toxicology and Chemistry, American Chemical Society, Association of Environmental Engineering and Science Professors. Office: University Of Houston - Clear Lake 2700 Bay Area Blvd Houston TX 77058 Office Phone: 281-283-3746. Business E-Mail: zhang@cl.uh.edu.

ZHANG, DAOWEI, forest economist, researcher, educator; b. Rudian, China, Nov. 6, 1963; s. Qingxiang Zhang; m. Zilun Fan, Sept. 2, 1992; children: Xinrei, Ting Dan. PhD, U. B.C., Vancouver, Can., 1994. Asst. prof. forestry Auburn (Ala.) U., 1994-99, assoc. prof. forestry, 1999—2003, prof. forestry, 2003—. Bd. dirs. Pinchot Inst. Conservation, Washington, 2000—. Recipient Forestry Ext. Jour. Publs., So. Ext. Forest Resources Specialists,

1997, Rsch. Recognition award, Ala. Agr. Experiment Sta., 2001, Dir.'s Rsch. award, 2002. Mem. Soc. Am. Foresters. Avocation: swimming. Office: Auburn U Sch Forestry&Wildlife Scis Auburn AL 36849 Fax: (334) 844-1084. E-mail: zhangd1@auburn.edu.

ZHANG, DONGXIAO, research scientist; b. Wuning, Jiangxi, China, Mar. 15, 1967; m. Liheng Zhang, May 3, 1967; children: Benjamin Ary, Grace Danyi. MS, U. Ariz., 1992, PhD, 1993. Asst. rsch. scientist U. Ariz., Tucson, 1994—95; sr. hydrologist Daniel B. Stephens & Assocs. Inc., Albuquerque, 1995—96; sr. rsch. scientist Los Alamos Nat. Lab., N.Mex., 1996—. Author: Stochastic Methods for Flow in Porous Media: Coping with Uncertainties; editor: Theory, Modeling and Field Investigation in Hydrogeology; assoc. editor: Water Resources Rsch., 2001—. Mem.: Soc. Petroleum Engrs. (mem. editl. bd. jour. 2002—), Geol. Soc. Am., Am. Geophys. Union. Office: Los Alamos National Lab PO Box 1663 Los Alamos NM 87545 Personal E-mail: dzhang601@msn.com. Business E-Mail: donzhang@lanl.gov.

ZHANG, G. Z. (GUANGZHI ZHANG), electro-optics engineer; b. Linqu, China, May 23, 1963; arrived in U.S., 1997; s. Sengjie Zhang and Zhaofend Zeng; m. Hong Gao, May 1, 1989; 1 child, Bohan. BSc, Shandong U., Jinan, China, 1983; MSc, Tsinghua U., Beijing, 1988; PhD in Sci., U. Electro-Comms., Tokyo, 1995. Elec. engr. Ministry Metallogical Industry, Beijing, 1983-91; postdoctoral fellow U. Toronto, Canada, 1995-97; sr. electro-optics engr. New Focus Inc., San Jose, Calif., 1997—. Contbr. articles to profl. jours. Recipient Sci. and Tech. award, Ministry of Metallogical Industry, Beijing, 1992, 1999. Mem.: Optical Soc. Achievements include first to method to produce broad-band frequent tunable single-mode laser with external feedback and mode-hop free orientation; research in high-conversion efficiency nonlinear optical generations using electromagnetically induced transparency; development and engineering on single-frequency tunable lasers, ultra-low antireflection optical coating; nonlinear optics, fiber optical components, and optoelectronic instruments for fiber optical network, automation industry, biotechnology and in-situ imaging and metrology; 2 U.S. patents for various tunable laser configurations for noise suppression, power enhancement and laser stability improvement. Avocations: sports, fishing, hiking. Office: Bookham-New Focus 2584 Junction Ave San Jose CA 95134 Office Phone: 408-919-1558. E-mail: guangzhi.zhang@bookham.com.

ZHANG, JIE, education educator, researcher; b. Jinan, Shandong, China, Nov. 10, 1955; s. Leyu Zhang and Xiuyu Feng; m. Xuehong Lu; children: Mengmeng, Yuanyuan. BA in Brit. and Am. Lang. and Lit., Shandong U., 1982; MA in tchg. ESL, Brigham Young U., 1988, PhD, 1992. Asst. prof. Beijing Inst. of Chem. Tech., 1982—86; instr. Brigham Young U., Provo, Utah, 1987—91, part-time instr., 1990; adj. instr. UT Valley State Coll., 1991; vis. asst. prof. Weber State U., Ogden, Utah, 1991—93; asst. prof. Ga. So. U., Statesboro, 1993—97, SUNY, Buffalo, 1997—99, assoc. prof., 1999—2004, prof., 2004—. Dir. Ctr. for China Studies at SUNY Coll. at Buffalo, 2000. Mem. bd. of dirs. Chinese Sch. Assn. in the US, 1999. Home: 192 Halston Pkwy East Amherst NY 14051 Office: SUNY College at Buffalo 1300 Elmwood Ave Buffalo NY 14222 Personal E-mail: zhangj@buffalostate.edu.

ZHANG, KEHONG, neuropharmacologist, educator; b. Tumen, Jilin Province, China, Nov. 4, 1964; married. PhD, La. State U., 1997. Asst. prof. psychiatry and neurosci. Harvard Med. Sch./McLean Hosp., Belmont, Mass., 1999—. Contbr. articles to profl. jours. Recipient Branfman Found. award, Branfman Found., 2002, Livingston award, Harvard Med. Sch., 2000, Alfred Pope Young Investigator award, 2001, Travel award, Am. Coll. Neuropharmacology, 2002; fellow, Pharm. Rsch,. and Mfrs. Am/ion, 1995. Mem.: ASPET, Soc. Neurosci. Home: 27A Wycoma Way Waltham MA 02453-2605 Office: Harvard Med Sch McLean Hosp 115 Mill St Belmont MA 02478 Office Phone: 617-855-3222. Business E-Mail: kz@mclean.harvard.edu.

ZHANG, LI, engineer, researcher; b. Beijing, Nov. 8, 1969; s. Qicheng Zhang and Liuying. MS in Nuclear Engring., MS in Elec. Engring and Computer Sci., MIT, 1996, PhD in Radiol. Scis., 1998. Tchg. asst. MIT, Cambridge, 1993-94, rsch. asst., 1994-98; sys. engr. Robotic Vision Sys., Inc., Hauppauge, N.Y., 1998; tech. mgr. Youngtech Inc., Edison, NJ, 1998—2001; project leader ADP Inc., Parsippany, NJ, 2001—02; pres. Internat. Innovative Imaging Sys., LLC, Piscataway, NJ, 2003—. Dir. electronics Beijing Perfect Electronics Engring. Corp., Beijing, 1992-93; project mgr. AT&T, Bedminster, N.J., 1998-99. Mem. AAAS, IEEE, SPIE, Assn. for Computing Machinery, Health Physics Soc., Am. Nuclear Soc., N.Y. Acad. Scis., Sigma Xi. Achievements include creation and research for explosive detection and nuclear medicine imaging. Avocations: hiking, travel, movies, Broadway shows, computer/internet surfing. Office: IIIS LLC 136A Pleasantview Dr Piscataway NJ 08854 E-mail: lizhang@alum.mit.edu.

ZHANG, LIN, research scientist, educator; s. Huasheng Zhang and Youzhi Zhu; m. Lan Hu, Feb. 28, 1988; children: Yintong, Sarah. BS, Fudan U., Shanghai, China, 1984, MS, 1987, PhD, 1997, Tex. A&M U., College Station, 2003. Asst. prof. Shandong U. of Sci. & Tech., Taian, China, 1987—94; rsch. asst. Tex. A&M U., College Station, Tex., 1997—2003, post doctoral rsch. assoc., 2003—. Recipient Excenllent Sci. Tech. Achievements, Nat. Ednl. Com. China, 1992, Minitry Coal Industry China, 1994; grantee Guanghua Scholoarship, Guanghua Found., China, 1996. Mem.: Am. Math. Soc., Soc. Indsl. and Applied Math., Internat. Assn. for Computational Mechanics, U.S. Assn. for Computational Mechanics. Achievements include research in Error estimations of the finite element solutions; Superconvergence of finite element solutions. Office Phone: 979-845-0714.

ZHANG, LIPING, research scientist; d. Changsheng Zhang and Aiye Xu; m. Ruwen Cui, Dec. 10, 1988; 1 child, Ting Cui. PhD, Zhejiang U., Hangzhou, 1996. Asst. prof. Shanxi Agrl. U., Taigu, China, 1989—93; assoc. prof. Zhejiang Agrl. U., Hangzhou, China, 1996—99, U. Tex. Med. Br., Galveston, Tex., 1999—. Author: (book) The Plant Nutrition Molecular Physiology. Named outstanding tchr., Shanxi Agrl. U., 1992; recipient Leadership award Young Scientist sci. and tech., Zhejiang Agrl. U., 1998, 2nd prize progress sci. and tech. establishment and classification Vitis Germplasm, Com. Sci. and Tech. Zhejiang Province, 1999. Achievements include research in the disease resistance gens in tomatoes. Office Phone: 409-772-3368.

ZHANG, MING, policy analyst; b. Jiangsu, China, 1962; arrived in U.S., 1988; m. Jiping Wu, 1993; children: Oak, Sky. BA, Nanjing U., 1983, MA, 1986; cert., Johns Hopkins U.-Nanjing U., 1987; PhD, Purdue U., 1994. Rsch. fellow Nat. Def. U., Washington, 1994—97; rsch. analyst Libr. Congress, Washington, 1995—97; dir. rsch. IHS Internat., Arlington, Va., 1998—. Cons. Carnegie Endowment, Washington, 1998—99; non-resident sr. fellow Atlantic Coun. U.S., Washington, 2000—; pres. Crossroads Initiative LLC, Va., 2002—; spkr. in field. Author: Major Powers at a Crossroads, 1995, China's Changing Nuclear Posture, 1999, A Triad of Another Kind, 1999. Grantee Tchg. grant, Rockefeller Bros. Fund, 1991, Travel grant, Am. Polit. Sci. Assn., 1993, Rsch. grant, NDU Found., 1994—97. Mem.: Internat. Studies Assn. Avocations: basketball, travel. Home: 3126 Borge St Oakton VA 22124 E-mail: mingzhang28@aol.com.

ZHANG, NENGLI, thermophysics scientist; b. Sichuan, China, Jan. 8, 1940; arrived in US, 1989; s. Sunxian Zhang and Huirong Xiong; m. Xiaohui Sun, Jan. 29, 1968; 1 child, Chi. BS equivalent in thermophysics, Tsinghua U., Beijing, 1962; PhD equivalent in thermophysics, Tsinghua U., 1984. Rsch. asst. Tsinghua U., Beijing, 1962—78, asst. prof., 1978—80; vis. scholar U. Mich., Ann Arbor, 1981—83; assoc. prof. Tsinghua U., 1984—89; rsch. assoc. U. Mich., 1989—93; sr. rsch. assoc. NRC at NASA Lewis Rsch. Ctr., Cleve., 1994—98; sr. scientist Ohio Aerospace Inst. at NASA Glenn Rsch. Ctr., Cleve., 1989—. Concurrent deputy chief engr. Hai Hua New Tech. Devel. Ctr., Beijing, 1984—88; cons. Beijing Inst. of Rubber Industry, 1984—86, Da peng Sci.-Tech. Industry Ltd., Co., 1987—89. Author: Process System Engineering (in chinese), 1982; contbr. articles various profl. jours. Recipient Achievements in Sci. award, Beijing Sci.-Tech. Com., 1983, Nat. Sci-Tech. Progress award, Nat. Sci.-Tech. Com., 1985, Achievement in Sci. award, China State Edn. Com., 1988, Achievement in Natural Sci. award, Nat. Sci-Tech. Com., 1989, 3 NASA Tech Innovations awards, NASA, 1998. Mem.: Am. Assn. for Advancement of Sci., Am. Soc. of Mech. Engrs. Achievements include patents for innovative heat pipe systems using new working fluids; shadowgraphic method to measure contact angles with flow visualization in a sessile drop; discovery of thermal instability in evaporating sessile drops; identifying the profiles near three-phase contact line through caustic-diffraction of wave; convective instability in transient evaporating thin liquid layer. Avocations: music, gardening, sports. Home: 34671 Plantation Pl North Ridgeville OH 44039 Office: Ohio Aerospace Inst NASA Glenn Rsch Ctr 21000 Brookpark Rd Cleveland OH 44135 Office Phone: 216-433-8750. E-mail: nengli.zhang@grc.nasa.gov.

ZHANG, SHENGLIANG, materials scientist, physicist; b. Zhangjiagang, Jiangsu Province, China, May 21, 1964; s. Xiangxing Zhang and Yongdi Wang; m. Qian Zhou, Mar. 20, 1993; 1 child, Gloria. BS, Nanjing U., 1984, MS, 1987; PhD, U. Rochester, 2001. Vis. rschr. Kyoto U., 1986—88; lectr. Nanjing U., 1988—93; sr. project engr. Xerox Corp., Webster, NY, 1999—2001, tech. specialist, 2001—. Contbr. articles to profl. jours.; patents in field (Xerox Inventor's awards, 2003). Japanese Govt. Monbusho scholar, 1988. Mem.: AIChe, ASM Internat., Materials Rsch. Soc. Avocations: fishing, hiking. Home: 161 Chartwell Ct Rochester NY 14618 Office: Xerox Corporation 800 Phillips Rd Bldg 111-30N Webster NY 14580 Office Phone: 585-422-9511. Personal E-mail: johnslz@yahoo.com. E-mail: john.s.zhang@usa.xerox.com.

ZHANG, SHENGMAN, corporate financial executive; b. China; With Ministry of Fin., China; exec. dir. for China The World Bank, Washington, 1994—95, and sec., 1995—97; mng. dir. World Bank Group, 1997—, chair crisis mgmt. com. Office: The World Bank Group 1818 H St NW Washington DC 20433

ZHANG, SHU, statistician; arrived in US, 1986; d. Xiongfei Zhang and Zhunian Cui. MD, Beijing Med. Sch. Chinese Medicine, 1983; MS, U. Minn., 1988; ScD, Harvard U., 1997. Biostatistician Harvard Med. Sch., Boston, 1988—90, Trilogy Corp., Waukegan, Ill., 1990—93; sr. biostatistician Pfizer, Inc., Groton, Conn., 1997—2001; prin. biostatistician Sepracor, Inc., Marlborough, Mass., 2001—. Contbr. articles to profl. jours. and ency. Recipient Student Travel award, Internat. Biometric Soc., 1998, Presentation Award, Fourth World Conf. on Acupuncture, 1996; grantee, Nat. Inst. Environ. Health Scis., 1993—97. Mem.: Am. Statis. Assn.

ZHANG, TIANXI, research scientist, researcher; b. Leping, Jiangxi, People's Republic of China, Dec. 3, 1962; parents Leiyun Zhang and Huiying Xu; m. Yirong Sun; children: Meirui, Robert. BS, Jiangxi U., China, 1983; PhD (hon.), Chinese Acad. Scis., Beijing, 1999. Asst. Nanchang U., Jiangxi, 1983—91, lectr., 1991—94; postdoctoral rsch. assoc. Peking U., Bejing, 1999—2001, N.C. State U., 2001—03; rsch. assoc. Clarkson U., 2003—. Contbr. articles to 29 profl. jour. pubs. Hydrometallurgy, Jour. Colloid and Interface Sci., Biotech. Press, Jour. Jiangxi Polytech. U., Jour. Nanchang U., Chinese Jour. Process Engring., others. Mem.: Am. Chem. Soc., Chemistry and Chem. Engring. Soc. Jiangxi Province (Top prize rsch. project 1989). Avocations: reading, swimming, jogging. Home: 13 Larnard St Apt 1 Potsdam NY 13676 Office: Clarkson U 8 Clarkson Ave Potsdam NY 13699 Office Phone: 315-268-7742. E-mail: zhangtianxi@hotmail.com.

ZHANG, XIANGDONG, research scientist, educator; arrived in U.S., 2000; PhD, Nanjing U., China, 1992. Rsch. fellow Inst. Ocean Sci., Sydney, Canada, 1997—99; asst. prof. Internat. Arctic Rsch. Ctr., U. Alaska, Fairbanks, 2000—. Author: Arctic Climate Change and Variability, 2001, 3d edit., 2004; contbr. articles pub. to prof. jour. Mem.: Am. Geophys. Union. Achievements include research in Arctic sea ice and freshwater changes. Office: Internat Arctic Rsch Ctr Univ Alaska Fairbanks 930 Koyukuk Dr Fairbanks AK 99775 Office Phone: 907-474-2675. Business E-Mail: xdz@iarc.uaf.edu.

ZHANG, XIAODONG, computer scientist, educator, researcher; b. Beijing, July 16, 1958; came to the U.S., 1983; s. Min and Yishan (Jiang) Z.; m. Yan Meng, July 20, 1985; 1 child, Simon. BS, Beijing (China) Poly. U., 1982; MS, U. Colo., 1985, PhD, 1989. Rsch. asst. Beijing (China) Poly. U., 1982-83, Environ. Rsch. Lab., Boulder, Colo., 1983-85, U. Colo., Boulder, 1985-89; tech. staff Toplogix Inc., Denver, 1989; asst. prof. U. Tex., San Antonio, 1989-92, assoc. prof., 1993-97, chair computer sci., 1993, dir. high performance computing and software lab., 1993—; prof. Coll. William and Mary, Williamsburg, Va., 1997—, dir. grad. studies, 1999-2001, chair computer sci., 2003—, Lettie Pate Evans prof. of computer sci., 2003—; prog. dir. NSF, Arlington, Va., 2001—. Vis. scientist Rice U., 1990-91; guest prof. Wuhan U., China, 1995-97; guest rsch. prof. U. Sci. and Tech. of China, 1997—, guest prof. Northwestern Poly. U., China, 1998—; tech. cons. NASA ICASE, 1998—; mem. overseas expert assessor Chinese Acad. Scis., 1999—; adv. panelist NSF, 1995, 96, 97, 99, 2000; program chair 4th Internat. Workshop on Modeling, Analysis and Simulation of Computer and Telecomm. Systems; keynote spkr. 8th Internat. Conf. on Parallel and Distributed Computer Sys., 1996. Co-author: Multiprocessor Performance, 1994; editor Jour. of Parallel Computing, 1994-95; contbr. articles to profl. jours. Recipient Disting. Rsch. Achievement award U. Tex., 1993, Best Paper award 9th Internat. Conf. on Supercomputing, 1995; grantee NSF, 1990—, Southwestern Bell, 1992-97, USAF, 1993-97, AFOSR, 1995—, ONR, 1995-97, Sun Microsystems, 1998. Mem. IEEE (sr., chmn. tech. com. on supercomputing applications, disting. visitor, program coms., program com. 7th Symposium on Parallel and Distributed Processing 1995, 8th Symposium, 1996, 4th Internat. Symposium on High Performance Computer Arch. 1998, Supercomputing '99, others, mem. steering com. Supercomputing '96, '97, 98, 99, High Performance Computing Asia '97, 98, 99, 2000, internat. conf. on parallel processing 2000, editl. bd. Transactions on Parallel and Distributed Sys. IEEE Micro), Assn. Computing Machinery (nat. lectr., program coms., program com. 10th Internat. Conf. on Supercomputing), Soc. Indsl. and Applied Math. Office: Coll William and Mary Computer Sci Williamsburg VA 23187

ZHANG, XIN, science educator; arrived in U.S., 1998; d. Yugui Zhang and Qiuyun Chen. BS, Northeastern U., Shenyang, China, 1991, MS, 1994; PhD, Hong Kong U. of Sci. and Tech., 1998. Rsch. scientist MIT, Cambridge, Mass., 1998—2001; Fraunhofer asst. prof. Boston U., 2001—. Contbr. articles to profl. jours. Recipient Faculty Career award, NSF, 2003—; grantee, Air Force Rsch. Lab., 2002—, Def. Advanced Rsch. Projects Agy., 2002—03, Army Rsch. Lab., 2003—04, Air Force of Sci. Rsch., 2003—. Mem.: ASME, IEEE. Achievements include patents pending for uncooled cantilever microbolometer focal plane arrays with mK temperature resolution; development of micro gas turbine engines; research in MEMS micro-pumps for a cryogenic heat transport system; micro/nanomachined structures and devices for cell migration and bio traction force measurements; flexible fabrication of 3-D multilayer microstructures using direct laser writing; massively parallel cell analysis and sorting chip for cancer evaluation; laser-assisted wafer-lever nanostructures for biomedical applications; uncooled double cantilever microbolometer arrays; residual stress and fracture of power MEMS structures and devices; reliability of MEMS structures and materials under cryogenic operations. Office: Boston U MFG Dept 15 Saint Mary's St Brookline MA 02446 Office Phone: 617-358-2702. Personal E-mail: xinz@bu.edu.

ZHANG, XUEMEI, reliability scientist; b. Qingdao City, Shandong, China, Jan. 16, 1969; parents Fengliang Zhang and Hongzhen Su. M in Mech. and Sys. Engring., Beijing Inst. Tech., 1994; M in Indsl. Engring., Rutgers U., 1997, M in Stats., 1998, PhD in Indsl. Engring., 1999. Rsch. asst. Rutgers U., New Brunswick, N.J., 1996-97, tchg. asst., 1997-98, rsch. asst., 1998-99; reliability scientist Bell Labs., Holmdel, N.J., 1999—. Author: (book chpts.) Recent Advances in Reliability and Quality Engineering, 1999, Handbook of Statistics on Reliability, 2000, (modeling and toolkit devel.) Software Reliability Assessment Tools, 1999; contbr. papers to profl. jours. Marion Johnson fellow Rutgers U., 1995-96. Mem. IEEE, Inst. Indsl. Engrs., Inst. Ops. Rsch. and Mgmt. Sci. Office: Bell Labs 101 Crawfords Corner Rd Holmdel NJ 07733-1985 Home: 20 Berkley Ct Morganville NJ 07751-4249 Fax: (732) 949-0019. E-mail: xzhang4@lucent.com.

ZHANG, YAO, statistician; s. Zhehua and Yaqin Zhang; m. Yifan Wang. PhD in Stats., Iowa State U., 2002; BS in Physics, Wuhan U., 1993; MS in Physics, Iowa State U., 1999. Rsch. asst. Ames Lab., Iowa State U., Ames, Iowa, 1996—98; rsch. asst. statis. lab. Iowa State U., Ames, 1998—2000; sr. statistician Pfizer Global R & D, Groton, Conn., 2001—. Contbr. articles to profl. jours. Recipient 1st-class scholarship, Wuhan U., 1989—93, Snedecor award, Iowa State U., 2001. Mem.: Math. Assn. of Am., Am. Statis. Assn., Phi Kappa Phi, Gamma Sigma Delta. Achievements include research in new statistical methods. Home: 52 Scotch Cap Rd Quaker Hill CT 06375-1431

ZHANG, YOUXUE, geology educator; b. Huarong County, Hunan, China, Sept. 17, 1957; came to U.S., 1983; s. Zaiyi Zhang and Dezhen Wu; m. Zhengjiu Xu; children: Dan, Ray. BS in Geol. Scis., Peking U., Beijing, 1982; MA in Geol. Scis., Columbia U., 1985, MPhil, 1987, PhD in Geol. Scis., 1989. Grad. rsch. asst. Columbia U., N.Y.C., 1983-88; postdoctoral fellow Calif. Inst. Tech., 1988-91; asst. prof. geology U. Mich., Ann Arbor, 1991-97, assoc. prof., 1997—2004, prof., 2004—. Contbr. articles to profl. jours. Named Young Investigator, NSF, 1994. Mem. AAAS, Am. Geophys. Union, Geochem. Soc. (F.W. Clarke medal 1993), Mineral. Soc. Am., Sigma Xi. Office: Dept Geol Sci U Mich Ann Arbor MI 48109-1063 E-mail: youxue@umich.edu.

ZHANG, ZHONGJIAN, research scientist; b. Zhengzhou, Henan, China, Dec. 14, 1956; s. Weimin Zhang and Guangrong Cui; m. Juan Zhang, Jan. 7, 1986; 1 child, Feipeng. MS, Xian (China) Med. U., 1986; PhD, U. Miami, 1992. Rsch. assoc. U. Miami, 1993-94; intramural rsch. tng. Award fellow NIH, Bethesda, Md., 1994-98, staff rsch. scientist, 1998—. Contbr. articles to profl. jours. Achievements include patents for domestic and internat.

ZHANG, ZHUKAI, Internet company executive, consultant; b. Chengdu, Sichuan, China; arrived in U.S., 2001; s. Shihao Zhang and Zhongying Liu. BA in Design, Hunan U., Changsha, China, 1999; M in Design and Planning, I.I.T., Chgo., 2003. Design mgr. TCL Group, Guangdong, China; CEO San Stone, LLC, Chgo.; pres., CEO Altimiti Inc., Chgo., myperiod.com Inc., Chgo. Home and Office: 3343 S Union Ave #2 Chicago IL 60616 Office Phone: 773-247-4269. Fax: 773-247-4269. E-mail: david88chicago@hotmail.com.

ZHAO, FANG LI, medical researcher; b. Wugong, Shaan Xi, China, Jan. 3, 1963; s. Huoan Zhao and Yu Ling Zhou; m. Jinzhu Gu, Dec. 19, 1989; 1 child, Guanchao. BA, Shaanxi Teachers U., China, 1984; MA, Xi'an Med. U., China, 1987, PhD, 1997. Asst. rschr. Xi'an Med. U., China, China, 1987—93, 1997—98; postdoctoral rschr. Ohio State U., Ohio, 1998—. Contbr. articles to profl. jours. Mem.: Assn. Chemoreception Sci. Avocations: movies, science novels, political news. Office: Oral Biology College of Dentistry 3 at W 12th Avenue Columbus OH 43218-2357

ZHAO, GUANG-QUAN, developmental reproductive biologist, researcher; b. Qingdao, Shandong, China, Feb. 21, 1963; came to U.S., 1988; s. Feng-Yue and Xiu-Yun Song Z.; m. Xiaoxia (Sasha) Qi, Dec. 26, 1987; children: Dawn, Erica. MD, Shandong Med. U., 1984; PhD, U. Tex. Grad. Sch. Biomedical Sci., 1993. Clin. resident Shandong Med. Univ., Jinan, China, 1984-88; grad. rsch. asst. Univ. Tex. Anderson Cancer Ctr., Houston, 1988-93; rsch. assoc. Howard Hughes Med. Instit., Nashville, 1993-97; asst. prof. Univ. Mo., Columbia, 1997-2001, Univ. Tex. Southwestern Med. Ctr., Dallas, 2001—. Author numerous jour. articles. Recipient rsch. grant NIH. Mem. Soc. Devel. Biology, Soc. Study Reproduction.

ZHAO, HONG, biomedical engineer, educator; b. Beijing, He Bei, China, Dec. 10, 1959; d. Yongkai Zhao and Hengyun Liu; m. Weijian Guo; 1 child, Jiannan. MD(hon.), Beijing Med. U., 1983; Master (hon.), Inst. Nat. Polytechnique de Lorraine, Nancy, France, 1998; PhD in Biomed. Engring. (hon.), U. Henri Poincaré, Nancy, France, 2002. Asst. prof. Beijing Heart, Lung, Blood Vessel Med. Ctr., 1986—92; assoc. prof. Inst. Clin. Med. Sci., China-Japan Friendship Hosp., Beijing, 1993—2002; scientist BioChain Inst., Inc., Calif., 2002—. Contbr. articles to profl. jours. Recipient Young Investigator award, Fourth Asian Congress for Microcirculation, 2000. Mem.: Société Française de Biorhéologie Fondamentale et Clinique.

ZHAO, HONGWEI, biostatistician; b. China; DSc, Harvard Sch. of Pub. Health, Boston, 1997. Asst. prof. U. of Rochester, NY, 1998—2003, assoc. prof., 2003—. Recipient Internat. Scientist of Yr., Internat. Biog. Ctr., Cambridge Eng., 2002. Mem.: Am. Statis. Assn. Office: Univ of Rochester 601 Elmwood Ave Box 630 Rochester NY 14642

ZHAO, JIA, lawyer; b. Shanghai, Sept. 23, 1940; came to U.S., 1980; BA, Beijing Fgn. Studies U., 1963; JD, Harvard U., 1983. Bar: Ill. 1985, D.C. 1986. U.S. desk officer dept. Am. and Oceanic Affairs, Fgn. Ministry People's Republic of China, 1972; atty. Arnold & Porter, Washington, Covington & Burling, Washington, Pillsbury, Madison & Sutro, San Francisco; 1st sec. dept. treaty and law, Am. and oceanic affairs Chinese Fgn. Ministry, 1986—88; with Baker & McKenzie, Chgo., 1988—, ptnr., 1994—. Mem. ABA, D.C. Bar, Chgo. Bar Assn., Beijing Fgn. Econ. Law Assn. Office: Baker and McKenzie One Prudential Plz 130 E Randolph Dr Chicago IL 60601

ZHAO, JIWEI, lawyer; b. Macheng City, Hubei, May 21, 1966; arrived in U.S., 1996; s. Bin Fu Zhao and Yuan Hua Jiang; m. Xuefei Feng Zhao, Sept. 18, 1993; 1 child, Virginia F. BS, Northeastern U., Shenyang China, 1988; MS, Northeastern U., Shenyang, 1991; JD, Rutgers U., Camden, N.J., 2001. Bar: N.J. 2001, N.Y. 2002. V.p. Qinhuanadao Empire Trading Co., China, 1993—96; CEO Mighty Dragon Inc., Edison, NJ, 1996—2001; pvt. practice Law Office of Jiwei Zhao, Esq., Edison, 2001—02; of counsel Kline & Gast, P.A., Edison, 2002—. Chmn. bd. dirs. Mighty Dragon, Inc., Edison, 0199—2002; adv. bd. Huaxia Chinese Sch. USA, Edison, 2002—; bd. dirs. The Am. Chinese Times, Edison, 2001—. Author: A Review of China Coastal City Development, 1994; editor: Handbook for Chinese Economists, 1991. Legal counsel Chinese Culture Day of N.J., Jersey City, 2002—; gen. counsel N.J. Chinese Dancing Assn., Livingston, NJ. Fellow: Rutgers Alumni Assn.; mem.: Am. Immigration Lawyers Assnj., N.Y. State Bar Assn., N.J. State Bar Assn. Avocations: reading, soccer. Office: Law Offices of Jiwei Zhao Esq 1967 Lincoln Hwy Ste 22 Edison NJ 08817

ZHAO, MINGJUN, physicist, research scientist; b. Shaanxi, China, July 13, 1957; came to U.S., 1994; s. Yong Zhao and Fengying Xue; m. Shihong Chen, July 31, 1984; 1 child, Bowen. BS, Shaanxi Normal U., Xian, 1982; PhD, Xian Inst. Optics/Prec. Mechs., Chinese Acad. Scis., Xian, 1989. Faculty Xian Inst. Petroleum, 1982-86; postdoctoral fellow Xian Inst. Optics & Precision Mechanics Academia Sinica, Xian, 1990-92; Internat. Ctr. for Theoretical Physics fellow Inst. Nat. Optics, Firenze, Italy, 1992-93; rsch. fellow Inst. Phys. and Chem. Rsch., Wako-shi, Japan, 1993-94; rsch. assoc. N.Mex. State U., Las Cruces, 1994-96; rsch. engr. U. Calif., Santa Barbara, 1996; rsch. scientist Phys. Optics Corp., Torrance, Calif., 1996—. Contbr. articles to profl. jours. including Chinese Physics-Letter, Optics Comm., Optics Letter. Recipient 2d pl. natural scis. award Shaanxi Province, 1992, Excellent award Chinese Acad. Scis., 1991, Excellent award of Pres. Scholarship, 1989. Mem. AAAS, Internat. Soc. for Optical Engring., N.Y. Acad. Scis. Achievements include main contribution to nonlinear optics, especially in field of photorefractive multi-wave mixing, phase conjugation, created pertubation approximation theory for analysis of phase distortion in degenerate four-wave mixing, developed photorefractive spatial light modulator base on home-made BSO crystal; realization of self-pumped phase conjugation of diffusely reflected light in a KNSBN crystal, and dynamics pattern formation and storage; demonstrated system which combined ultrasound generation and double phase conjugation for non-destructive evaluation application, and micro-optical and liquid crystal for 3-D display, optical limiting and optical switching and its applications in communications, and laser plasma diagnostics. Home: Apt 176 39639 Leslie St Fremont CA 94538-2249

ZHAO, QUANSHENG, university administrator, educator; BA, Peking U., 1981; MA, U. Calif., Berkeley, 1982, PhD, 1987. Prof. Fletcher Sch. of Law and Diplomacy, Tufts U., Old Dominion U., Hong Kong U. of Sci. and Tech.,

Aoyama Gakuin U., Tokyo; assoc.-in rsch. Fairbank Ctr. for East Asian Rsch., Harvard U., 1993—; prof., divsn. dir. Am. U., Washington, 1996—. Dir. divsn. comparative and regional studies Sch. of Internat. Svcs., 1999—. Author: Interpreting Chinese Fgn. Policy, 1996, Japanese Policymaking, 1993 (Outstanding Acad. book Choice), (in Chinese) Understanding Chinese Fgn. Policy, 1999; co-editor: Politics of Divided Nations: China, Korea, Germany and Vietnam, 1991; editl. advisor: Jour. of Strategic Studies, 2000—, Jour. of Contemporary China, —, mem. editl. advisory bd.: The China Rev., Hong Kong Jour. of Social Sciences; editor: Future Trends in East Asian Internat. Rels., 2002. Mem. Am. Polit. Sci. Assn. (chair conf. group on China studies 1992—). Avocations: swimming, skiing. Office: CRS/SIS Am U 4400 Massachusetts Ave NW Washington DC 20016 Office Phone: 202-885-1662.

ZHAO, RONGGUO, chemist; b. China; PhD, U. Tenn, 2001. Sr. chemist China Textile Acad., Beijing, 1995—96; grad. rsch. asst. U. Tenn., Knoxville, 1996—2001; dir. R&D Biax Fiberfilm Corp., Greenville, Wis., 2001—. Presenter in field. Author: Melt Blown Technologies and Product Developments; contbr. articles to profl. jours. Recipient Best Student Paper award, INDA-Assn. Nonwoven Fabrics Industry, 2002; Ida A. Anders scholar, U. Tenn., Knoxville, 1998—2001. Mem.: Fiber Soc., Sigma XI. Achievements include patents pending for microfibers and nowovens. Office: N992 Quality DrSuite B Greenville WI 54942 Personal E-mail: rzhao@biax-fiberfilm.com. E-mail: rzhao@biax-fiberfilm.com.

ZHAO, WEI (WAYNE), materials scientist, researcher, transmission electron microscopist; s. Zuyao Zhao and Dingru Liu; m. Yi (Merry) Sun, Jan. 28, 1992; 1 child, Allen Aquila. B in Engring., Harbin Inst. Tech., 1987; M in Engring., NE Forestry U., Harbin, 1989; PhD, U. Tenn., Knoxville, 1999. Asst. prof. Tianjin (China) U., 1989—91, lectr., prin. investigator, 1992—95, postdoc. rsch. faculty U. Pa., Phila., 1999—2001; sr. TEM engr. Infineon Tech. Richmond, Sandston, Va., 2001—03, TEM analyst Intl. Sematech, Austin, Tex., 2003—04; staff scientist, supr. electron microscopy grp. Kerr McGee Chemical, LLC., Oklahoma City, 2004—. Grad. tchg. and rsch. asst. NE Forestry U., Harbin, 1987—89; grad. rsch. asst. U. Tenn., Knoxville, Tenn., 1996—99. Contbr. articles to profl. jours. Mem.: Microscopy Soc. Am., Materials Rsch. Soc. Achievements include discovery of stacking sequence effects on mechanical performance for a plain-weave Nicalon fiber-fabric reinforced SiC ceramic-matrix composite; first to computer-aided modeling on effects of lamina stacking sequence and laminate layup for plain-weave Nicalon/SiC ceramic-matrix composite; introduce SEM/XEDS linescan technique to semi-quantify fiber/matrix interfacial oxidation behavior for a Nicalon/SiC ceramic-matrix composite; discovery of fiber orientation effects on mechanical properties for a crow-foot woven Nextel fiber-fabric reinforced Blackglas low-cost ceramic-matrix composite; first to initiate combined SEM/XEDS elemental mapping, ultrasonic, and x-ray computed tomography characterization on fiber and void distributions in a crow-foot woven Nextel/Blackglas ceramic-matrix composite; research in atomic-scale high-resolution transmission electron microscopy in nanometer semiconductor wafer process development; analytical transmission electron microscopy in physical failure analysis for nanometer semiconductor wafer and device process integration; materials science issues in advanced metallization for nanometer semiconductor wafer integration; development of advanced surface coatings to nonometer titanium dioxide pigment and particle physics; first to introduce polycrystallined diamond compact and tungsten carbide composite blank onto woodworking tools in China; research in synthesis of diamond thin film by combustion flames techniques. Office: Tech Ctr Kerr McGee Chemical POB 25861 Oklahoma City OK 73125 Personal E-mail: wayne_zhaowei@yahoo.com.

ZHAO, WENYI, systems analyst; b. Zigong, Sichuan, China, Feb. 24, 1969; s. Zhili Zhao and Anrong Zhang; m. Ying Liu, Dec. 2, 1971. BA, Tsinghua Univ.; PhD, U. Md., 2000. Mem. tech. staff Sarnoff Corp., Princeton, NJ, 2000—. Contbr. articles to profl. jours. Mem.: IEEE. Office: Sarnoff Corp 201 Washington Rd Princeton NJ 08540

ZHAO, YICHUAN, education educator; arrived in U.S.A., 1997; s. Huasong Zhao and Zhaoying Lin; m. Yu Qiu, Nov. 7, 1965; 1 child, Qiyan. MS, Peking U., China, 1991, U. Utrecht, Netherlands, 1997, Fla. State U., 1999, PhD, 2002. Instr. U. Electronic Sci. and Tech. of China, Chengdu, 1991—96; asst. prof. Ga. State U., 2002—. Cons. Fla. Dept. Law Enforcement, Tallahassee, 1999. Author: Statistics and Probability Letters, 2002. Mem.: Internat. Chinese Statis. Assn. (student rsch. paper award 2002), Inst. Math. Statis., Am. Statis. Assn. (R.L. Anderson student paper award 2002). Avocations: swimming, tennis, ping pong/table tennis, chess. Home: 10303 Ashford Gables Dr Dunwoody GA 30338 Office: Ga State Univ Atlanta GA 30303

ZHAO, ZHEN, music educator; b. Tian Jin, China, Aug. 27, 1947; arrived in U.S., 1985; parents Tian Qi Zhao and Pei Ying Gong; m. Yang Zhong Zhang, Apr. 29, 1976; 1 child, William Wen Wei Zhang. MusB, U. Tex., 1991, MusM, 1994. Pvt. piano tchr., Austin, Tex., 1995—. Contbr. articles to profl. jours. Mem.: Nat. Guild Piano Tchrs., Music Tchrs. Nat. Assn., Tex. Music Tchrs. Assn., Austin Dist. Music Tchrs. Assn. Achievements include established the Zhen Zhao piano studio; her students have won numerous competitions. Avocations: ping pong/table tennis, tai chi, travel, photography.

ZHAO, ZHONGSHAN, structural engineer, researcher; b. Zhejiang Province, China, Oct. 5, 1963; s. Zongrong Zhao and Chunchai Zhang; m. Qinglin Shen Zhao, Apr. 13, 1971; 1 child, Audrey Y. B in Bridge Engring., Tongji U., China, 1985; M in Engring., U. of Tokyo, 1992; PhD, Tex. Tech U., 1997. Rsch. asst. Tongji U., Shanghai, 1985—90; structural engr. Wind Engring. Inst., 1992—94; rsch. assoc. Tex. Tech U., Lubbock, 1998—2000; structural engr. Mustang Engring., LP, Houston, 2000—. Contbr. articles to profl. jours. Recipient John B. Hawley award, ASCE, Tex. Sect., 1999. Achievements include patents for Cable stay aerodynamic damper band and method of use. Office: Mustang Engring LP 16001 Park Ten Pl Houston TX 77084

ZHARIKOV, ALEXANDER NIKOLAEVICH, trade union federation executive; b. Michailov, Rjazan, Russia, Jan. 2, 1945; s. Nikolaj Philippovich and Claudia Egorovna (Gorodnicheva) Z.; m. Eva Svachova; children: Michail, Anette. Student, Shipbldg. Inst., Leningrad, Russia, 1969. Sec. Student Orgn. Shipbldg. Inst., Leningrad, 1967-70; dir. student dept. Leningrad City Youth Orgn., Leningrad, 1970-71, sec., 1971-74; vice chmn. Com. Youth Orgns. USSR, Moscow, 1974-76; chmn. Student Coun. USSR, Moscow, 1976-78; v.p. Internat. Union Students, Prague, Czechoslovakia, 1978-84; officer Internat. Dept. Ctrl. Com. CPSU, Moscow, 1984-88; dir. internat. dept. All Union Ctrl. Coun. Trade Unions, Moscow, 1988-90; gen. sec. World Fedn. Trade Unions, Prague, 1990—. Co-author: International Union of Students, 1978. Mem. City Com. Leningrad Youth Orgn., 1970-71, sec., 1971-74; mem. Ctrl. Com. Youth Orgn. USSR, Moscow, 1978-84. Capt. Russian mil., 1962-66. Office: Branická 112 14700 Prague 4 Czech Republic E-mail: wftu@login.cz.

ZHDANKIN, VIKTOR VLADIMIROVICH, chemistry professor; b. Sverdlovsk, Russia, June 6, 1956; came to U.S., 1990; s. Vladimir M. and Rimma V. (Lukanina) Z.; m. Olga Y. Geraskina, Sept. 20, 1980; children: Vasili V., Vladimir V. BS, MS, Moscow State U., 1978, PhD, 1981, DSc, 1987. Rsch. fellow Moscow State U., 1982-86; vis. scientist U. Minn., Duluth, 1987-88; rsch. prof. Moscow State U., 1988-89; instr., sr. rsch. assoc. U. Utah, Salt Lake City, 1990-93; asst. prof. U. Minn., Duluth, 1993-96, assoc. prof., 1996-99, prof., 1999—. Panel mem. Internat. Sci. Found., Washington, 1993-95. Contbr. articles to profl. jours.; mem. editl. bd. Russian Jour. Organic Chemistry, 1989-93, Jour. Mendeleev Chem. Soc., 1989-95, Mendeleev Comm., 1998—, Arkivoc, 2003—. Grantee, Rsch. Corp., 1993—96, Petroleum Rsch. Fund/Am. Chem. Soc., 1994—96, NSF, 1995—, Civilian R&D Found., 2000—02, NIH, 2002—. Mem. Am. Chem. Soc., Coun. Undergrad. Rsch., Sigma Xi. Achievements include discovery of new phenomena in physical-organic chemistry; preparation of new iodine reagents; development of organic chemistry of xenon. Office: U Minn Dept Chemistry 10 University Dr Duluth MN 55812-2403 Business E-Mail: vzhdanki@d.umn.edu.

ZHDANOV, MICHAEL SEMENOVICH, geophysicist, educator; b. Moscow, Oct. 2, 1946; m. Olga Nikolaevna Zhdanov; 1 child, Elena. MSc in Geophysics, Moscow State Oil and Gas U., 1968; MSc in Math., Moscow State U., 1969, PhD in Physics and Math., 1970, D of Scis., 1978. From asst. to full prof. dept. geophysics Moscow Gubkin State U. of Oil and Gas, 1970—92; head of dept., dep. dir. Inst. Terrestrial Magnetism, Ionosphere and Radio Wave Propagation USSR Acad. Scis., Moscow, 1978—90; dir. Inst. Geoelectromagnetic Rsch. Russian Acad. Scis., Moscow, 1991—92; prof. dept. geology and geophysics U. Utah., Salt Lake City, 1993—. Lansdown vis. prof. U. Victoria, B.C., Canada, 1991; Gauss prof. Gettingen Acad. Scis., Gettingen, Germany; vis. prof. Colo. Sch. Mines, Golden. Author: Advanced Theory of Deep Geomagnetic Sounding, 1984, Integral Transforms in Geophysics, 1988, The Geoelectrical Methods in Geophysical Exploration, 1994, Geophysical Inverse Theory and Regularization Problems, 2002; patentee in field. Named Hon. Prof., China Nat. Ctr. of Geol. Exploration Tech., 1997; recipient award for outstanding achievement in the devel. of sci. and tech., Russian Acad. Natural Scis., 2000. Fellow: Electromagnetics Acad. U.S.A., Acad. Natural Scis. Russia; mem.: Am. Geophys. Union, Soc. Exploration Geophysics. Office: U Utah 135 S 1460 E Rm 719 Salt Lake City UT 84112

ZHENG, GANG, mathematician, statistician, researcher; arrived in U.S., 1994; s. Chang-Gen Zheng; m. Liu Ling-Xian. BS in Applied Math., Fudan U., Shanghai, 1987; MS in Math., Mich. Technol. U., 1996; PhD in Stats., George Washington U., 2000. Lectr. Shanghai Second Poly. U., 1987—94; math. statistician Nat. Heart, Lung and Blood Inst., Bethesda, Md., 2000—. Contbr. articles to profl. jours. Fellow: The Royal Statis. Soc.; mem.: Internat. Biometrics Soc., Inst. Math. Stats., Internat. Chinese Statis. Assn. (life), Internat. Indian Statis. Assn. (life), Am. Statis. Assn. Office: National Heart Lung and Blood Institute 6701 Rockledge Dr MSC 7938 Room 8223 Bethesda MD 20892-7938 Office Phone: 301-435-1287.

ZHENG, MIN, engineer; d. ZiYing Zhao and Shuzhong Zheng; m. Xiangdong Bi, Apr. 19, 1995. PhD, Inst. Physics, Chinese Acad. Scis., 1997. Postdoc. rsch. assoc. Ctr. Materials Rsch. and Analysis, Dept. Physics, U. Nebr., Lincoln, 1998—2000; staff R&D engr. Maxtor Corp./MMC Tech., San Jose, Calif., 2000—. Postdoc. fellow Max-Planck-Instt. Mikrostrucktur, Halle/Saale, Germany, 1997—98. Contbr. articles to profl. jours., The Royal Fellowship fellow, 1997. Mem.: Sigma Xi. Achievements include patents pending for. Home: 284 Rio Verde Pl #3 Milpitas CA 95035 Office: MMC Technology 2001 Fortune Dr San Jose CA 95131 E-mail: zhengmin70@hotmail.com.

ZHENG, QI, statistician, biomathematician; b. Lanxi, Zhejiang, China, July 8, 1958; arrived in U.S., 1988; s. Huanming Zheng and Sulan Zhuge; m. Huiping Hu, May 12, 1987; children: Yan, Eric Hugh. BS in math., Zhejiang U., 1978—82; PhD in stats., Tex. A&M U., 1988—93, postgrad., 1993. Cert. independent Mathematica trainer. Post-doc Nat. Ctr. Toxicological Rsch., Jefferson, Ark., 1994—96, staff fellow, 1996—2002; rsch. scientist Tex. A&M U., College Station, 2002—03, assoc. prof. dept. epidemiology and biostats. Sch. Rural Pub. Health, 2003—. Contbr. articles to jour. (Commendable Svc. award, FDA, 1997). Grantee Mathematica Vis. Scholar Grant, Wolfram Rsch. Inc., 1995, 1997. Mem.: Am. Statis. Assn., Phi Kappa Phi. Achievements include research in directed mutation hypothesis; irrelevancy of dispersion index in the molecular clock controversy; schochastic modeling of carcinogtenesis; development of first comprehensive computer software SALVADOR for estimating mutation rates using data from fluctuation experiments. Avocations: reading, mountain hiking. Office: Tex A&M U Sys Health Sci Ctr Sch Rural Pub Health Dept Epidemiology and Biostats College Station TX 77843 Personal E-mail: qzheng@#srph.tamu.edu.

ZHENG, QI-HUANG, chemist, educator; b. Quanzhou, China, Sept. 30, 1964; came to U.S., 1994; s. Yinglin Zheng and Houqing Qiu; m. Yiming Yang, Apr. 2, 1988; 1 child, Xiazhe Zheng. BS, Xiamen (China) U., 1984, MS, 1987; PhD, Zhongshan U., Guangzhou, China, 1990. Asst. prof. Zhongshan U., 1990-92, assoc. prof., 1992-97; rsch. assoc. Ind. U., Indpls., 1997-99, asst. scientist, 1999-2000, asst. prof., 2001—. Vis. scholar U. Chgo., 1994; v.p. Conland Group Co., Zhaoqing, China, 1990-91. Author: Encyclopedia of the Science and Technology Reviews, 1993; contbr. articles to profl. jours. Recipient China Young Chemist prize Chinese Chem. Soc., 1991, Outstanding Tchr. award Guangdong Province, China, 1992, Outstanding Youth award Haizhu Dist., China, 1993; grantee Susan G. Komen Breast Cancer Found., 2000, Nat. Natural Sci. Found. China, 1993. Mem. Am. Chem. Soc. Office: Ind U Dept Radiology 975 W Walnut St Rm 028C Indianapolis IN 46202-5121 E-mail: gzheng@iupui.edu.

ZHENG, ROBERT ZHIWEI, educational technology educator; b. Shanghai, May 4, 1958; came to U.S., 1994; s. Zushen Zheng and Yuefeng You; m. Shaowen Hu, May 10, 1992; 1 child, Joanna. BA, Shanghai Tchrs. U., China, 1983; MA, Fudan U., Shanghai, China, 1989; EdD, Baylor U., 1998. Tchr. Shanghai Jian-she H.S., China, 1983—86; lectr. Fudan U., Shanghai, 1989—94; grad. asst. Baylor U., Waco, Tex., 1994—98; instrl. designer Vincennes U., Ind., 1999; asst. prof. edn. in ednl. tech. Marian Coll., Fond du Lac, Wis., 1999—2002; asst. prof. edn. Temple U., Phila., 2002—. Tech. coord. Marian-Chegwin Ptnr. Program, Fond du Lac, 1999-2002. Grantee, U.S. Dept. Edn., 2001—. Mem. Internat. Soc. Tech. Edn., Assn. Ednl. Comm. & Tech., Phi Delta Kappa. Baptist. Avocations: fishing, photography, travel, reading. Office: Coll Edn Temple Univ Philadelphia PA 19122 E-mail: robert.zheng@temple.edu.

ZHENG, WENXIN, fiber optic communication specialist; b. Beijing, Nov. 13, 1953; arrived in Sweden, 1985; s. Zhidong and Luyuan (Chen) Z.; m. Baihua Sun, June 1, 1982; 1 child, Jan. MSEE, North China Inst. Electric Power, Beijing, 1982; PhD in Elec. Engring., Royal Inst. of Tech., Stockholm, 1989. Lectr. North China Inst. of Electric Power, 1983-85; guest rschr. Royal Inst. of Tech., Stockholm, 1985-89; rsch. engr. Ericsson Cables AB, Stockholm, 1989-94, sr. specialist, 1994-98; sr. prin. engr. CIENA Corp., Elkridge, Md., 1998—. Author: Radar Cross Sections of Complex Objects, 1989; inventor in fiber optic comms.; contbr. articles to profl. jours. Mem. IEEE, Lasers and Electro-Optics Soc. Home: 9608 John Randolph Ct Ellicott City MD 21042 Office: Ciena Corp 6671R Santa Barbara Rd Elkridge MD 21075

ZHEUTLIN, DALE, sculptor, educator; b. Newark, July 27, 1948; BFA, R.I. Sch. Design, 1970; MFA, Columbia U., 1972. Group exhbns. include Gallery at Hastings-on-Hudson, N.Y., 1980, Craftsman's Gallery, Scarsdale, N.Y., 1980, 83, Thorpe Intermedia Gallery, Sparkhill, N.Y., 1980, Foundations Gallery, N.Y.C., 1981, Meyer, Breier, Weiss Gallery, San Francisco, 1981, Nat. Arts Club, N.Y.C., 1981, Ten Downtown, N.Y.C., 1981, Hudson River Mus., Yonkers, N.Y., 1981, Holsten Gallery, Palm Beach, Fla., 1982, Robertson Ctr. for Arts and Scis., Binghamton, N.Y., 1982, Cooper/Lynn Gallery, N.Y.C., 1982, Bronx Mus. Arts, N.Y., 1982, Departure Gallery, N.Y.C., 1983, Aldrich Mus., Riegefield, Conn., 1983, Plum Gallery, Kensington, Md., 1984, Newport (R.I.) Art Mus., 1984, Renwick Gallery, Washington, 1984, Ariel Gallery, N.Y.C., 1985, Artquest 1985, L.A., 1985, Greenwich House, N.Y.C., 1985, Henry St. Settlement, N.Y.C., 1986, Hudson River Mus., Yonkers, N.Y., 1986, Palo Alto (Calif.) Cultural Ctr., 1986, Artisan Space, N.Y.C., 1987, Boody Fine Art, St. Louis, 1987, Wita Gardiner Gallery, San Diego, 1987, Joan Robey Gallery, Denver, 1987, Works Gallery, N.Y.C., 1988, Maple Hill Gallery, Portland, Maine, 1988, Castle Mus. Vallauris, France, 1988, Robert Martin Gallery, White Plains, N.Y., 1989, Moviehouse Studio Gallery, Millerton, N.Y., 1989, Katonah (N.Y.) Mus., 1989, Nicolaysen Art Mus., Casper, Wyo., 1989, Tajimi City Spl. Exhbn. Hall, Mino, Japan, 1989, Internat. Ceramics Mus., Faenza, Italy, 1989, San Angelo (Tex.) Mus. Art, 1990, Hudson River Mus., 1991, Wheeler Seidel Gallery, N.Y.C., 1992, Sotheby's, N.Y.C., 1993, Am. Craft Mus., N.Y.C., 1993, Internat. Ceramics Mus., Faenza, Italy, 1995; represented in permanent collections Aetna, Hartford, Conn., Apple Computer, Inc., Norwalk, Conn., Chase Manhattan Bank, N.Y.C., Deloitte and Touche, Wilton, Conn., ITT, Hartford, Peat, Marwick and Main, Indpls., British Airways, IBM, Citibank Tower, others. Recipient Sculpture award Hudson River Mus., Pauline Law prize Nat. Assn. Women Artists.

ZHITNIK, ALEXEI, professional hockey player; b. Kiev, Russia, Oct. 10, 1972; m. Luda Zhitnik. Defense L.A. Hockey Team, Buffalo Sabres, 1995—. Mem. def. team Russia World Championships, Austria, 1996, World Cup Tournament, 1996, World Championships, Italy, 1993—94; rep. Gold medal unified team Albertville Winter Olympics, France, 1992. Office: Buffalo Sabres Marine Midland Arena One Seymour H Knox III Plz Buffalo NY 14203

ZHIYOU, WEN, research scientist; b. TianJin, Tianjin, China, May 23, 1971; s. Wen Fu, and He Xiuying; m. Yang Jianhua, June 28, 1973. PhD, U. Hong Kong, 2001. Postdoctoral rsch. assoc. Wash. State U., Pullman, Wash., 2001—. Contbr. articles various profl. jours. Mem.: AAAS.

ZHONG, DALONG, materials scientist, consultant; s. Dashan Zhong; m. Xiaolan Zhang, Nov. 6, 1996. BS metallurgy, Ctrl. South U. Tech., Changsha, Hunan, China, 1993, MS metallurgy, 1996; PhD in materials sci., Colo. Sch. Mines, 2001. Tchg./rsch. asst. Colo. Sch. Mines, Golden, 1997—2001, lab mgr. advanced coatings & surface engring. lab., 1999—, rsch. assoc., 2001—. Pvt. cons, Protonetics Internat. Inc., Golden, Colo., 2001—, MVSystems, Inc., Golden, Colo., 2001—; referee Thin Solid Films, 2001—, Tribology Internat., 2001—, Jour. Materials Synthesis and Processing, 2001—, Jour. Applied Physics, 2002—, Surface & Coating Tech., 2002—, Acta Materialia, 2002—; presentor invited papers at confs. Contbr. articles to profl. jours. Fellow Zhao Tiancong fellow, Ctrl. South U. Tech., 1994, Li Found. fellow, Colo. Sch. Mines, 1997—2000. Mem.: Am. Vacuum Soc., Materials Rsch. Soc., The Minerals, Metals & Materials Soc. Office: Colorado Sch Mines 1500 Illinois St Golden CO 80401 Office Phone: 303-273-3178, Office Fax: 303-273-3057. Business E-Mail: dazhong@mines.edu.

ZHOU, BING-NAN, chemist, educator; b. Shanghai, Jan. 31, 1934; came to U.S., 1993; m. Xiu-Ying Chen, Feb. 11, 1958; children: Cindy Qin, Hong. MD, Shanghai Med. U., 1954; PhD, Shanghai Inst. Materia Medica, 1964. Vis. scientist Czechoslovak Acad. Scis., Prague, 1962-64; postdoctoral fellow U. Wis., Madison, 1981-83; prof. Shanghai Inst. Materia Medica, 1988—99; sr. rsch. scientist dept. chemistry Va. Tech., 1994—2002; sr. rsch. scientist R&D Tahitian Noni Internat., Inc., Provo, Utah, 2002—. Reviewer The Sci. Found. for New Drug Rsch. in China, Beijing, 1987-92, NSF of China, Beijing, 1988-94; vis. prof. chemistry U. B.C., Vancouver, Can., 1986, U. Ill., Chgo., 1987-94; dir. dept. phytochemistry Nat. Lab. Drug Rsch., Shanghai, 1989-94. Author: Extraction and Separation of Active Compounds from Chinese Herbs, 2d edit., 1981, Bioactive Natural Products, 1981, The Chemistry of Natural Products, 1993, The Strategies for Development of Natural Organic Chemistry in China, 1995; contbr. over 150 articles to profl. jours. Home: 138 W Thorneberry Way Pleasant Grove UT 84062 Office: Tahitian Noni Internat (Marinda Inc) R&D 737 East 1180 South American Fork UT 84003

ZHOU, CHENG JI, neuroscientist; b. Jinyun, Zhejiang, China, Mar. 8, 1966; arrived in Japan, 1993; came to U.S., 2001. m. Xinyin Han; children: Tian, Ryan, Kenny. BS, Waseda U., Tokyo, 1998, MS, 1999, PhD, 2001. Cert. med. engr., China. Med. technologist Lishui Bihu Hosp., Lishui City, Zhejiang, 1984-88; med. engr. Lishui Zhongyi Hosp., Lishui City, 1988-92; rschr. Showa U. Med. Sch., Tokyo, 1998-2001; with dept. neurology U. Calif., San Francisco, 2001—. Contbr. articles to profl. jours. Mem.: AAAS, Am. Soc. Cell Biology, Soc. Neurosci., Soc. Devel. Biology, Chinese Students Assn. Waseda U. (ex-pres. 1996), N.Y. Acad. Scis., Clin. Electron Microscopy Soc. Japan, Japanese Assn. Anatomists. E-mail: zhoucj@itsa.ucsf.edu.

ZHOU, DESHENG, petroleum engineer; b. Wusheng, Sichuan, China, Nov. 19, 1963; s. Lisheng Zhou and Hongyu Luong; m. Xiaoping Zhang, Sept. 5, 1988; children: Ruoyao, Jennifer Aileen. BS, Beijing U., Aeronautics and Astronautics, China, 1985; MS, S.W. Petroleum Inst., China, 1988; D in Engring., S.W. Petroleum Inst., 1992; PhD, La. State U., 2000. Cert. petroleum engineer, China. Engr. China Nat. Petroleum Corp., Nanchong, China, 1988—94, vice chmn. petroleum-mech. engring. dept., 1994—96; from rsch. assoc. to rsch. asst. La. State U., Baton Rouge, 1996—2000; sr. petroleum engr. IHS Energy, Dallas, 2000—. Rschr. and software developer (second class award of Tech. and Sci. Progress by China Nat. Petroleum Corp., 1996); contbr. numerous articles to profl. jours. Mem.: China Soc. Petroleum Engrs. (dir. Nanchong divsn. 1994—96), Nat. Petroleum Engring. Honor Soc. Achievements include patents for parabolic tooth of roller cone bit; design of designed three types of roller cone bits: XHP1s, XHP2s, and XHP3s; research in projects for China National Petroleum Corporation as computer simulation of rock-bit interaction, project for US Minerals Management Service: leak-off tests in shallow marine sediments. Home: 7510 David Dr Frisco TX 75034 Office: IHS Energy 18333 Preston Rd Ste 300 Dallas TX 75252 Personal E-mail: deshzhou@yahoo.com. E-mail: desheng.zhou@ihsenergy.com.

ZHOU, JIAN-ZHONG (JOE), librarian; s. Zhi-yao Zhou and Xi-ling Ding; m. Min Yang, June 19, 1965; children: Glen W, Allan Y, Milan M. MBA, U. Del., 1996; MLIS, Dominican U., 1990; BS in Physics, Beijing Normal U., 1985. Reference dept. head Calif. State U, Sacramento, 2000—; head physics libr. U. Del., Newark, 1990—2000. Chmn. of bd. dir. SacramentoChinese.org, Sacramento, 2002—04; strategic initiatives bd. mem. Libr. Info. Tech. Assn., Chgo., 1998—2000; bd. mem. New Castle County Libr. Sys., Wilmington, Del., 1999—2000; cons. Chinese Acad. Scis., Beijing, 1990—2000; adv. coun. mem. Internat. Channel Networks. Compiler, editor: of first desk-top laser printer publ. in China Chinese-English Annotated Physics Bibliography, 1986; contbr. more than 10 articles to libr. and info. tech. jours.; reviewer: of lit. in libr. sci. and info. tech. Editor and compiler for the organ.'s bylaw and point-based-credit sys. Sacramento Chinese Orgn. web site, Sacramento, 2001—. Fellow, Frye Inst., 2001; Faculty R & D grantee, Calif. State U. Sys., 2001. Mem.: ALA (assoc.; internat. rels. com. chair 1992—96), Assn. of Am. U. Professors (assoc.). Office: California State University Sacramento 2000 State University Dr E Sacramento CA 95819-6039

ZHOU, JUHUA, molecular biologist; b. Dongyang, Zhejiang, China, Apr. 21, 1963; arrived in U.S., 1994; s. Fude Zhou, Yujuan Shan; m. Yin Zhong; 1 child, Beibei. MS, Zhejiang U., 1988; BS, Zhejiang U., Hangzhou, China, 1983; PhD, U.La., 1999. Assoc. prof. Zhejiang U. (Formerly Hangzhou University), Hangzhou, China, 1988—94; postdoctoral fellow ctr. for cell & gene therapy Baylor Coll. Medicine, Houston, 1999—. Vice dir. divsn. plant physiology Zhejiang U., Hangzhou, Zhejiang, China, 1988—94. Contbr. articles to profl. jours. Grantee, Zhejiang Provincial Natural Sci. Found., 1992, Chinese Natural Sci. Found., 1994. Mem.: AAAS, N.Y. Acad. Scis., Sigma Xi. Home: 5606 Bissonnet St Apt 114 Houston TX 77081 Office: Baylor Coll Medicine One Baylor Plaza N1120 Houston TX 77030 Office Phone: 7137985064. Office Fax: 7137981362. Personal E-mail: juhuaz@hotmail.com. Business E-Mail: jzhou@bcm.tmc.edu.

ZHOU, SOPHIA HUAI, biomedical engineering scientist; b. Huaiyin, Jiangsu, China, Dec. 6, 1953; MS, Dalhousie U., Halifax, Can., 1987, PhD, 1991. Profl. engr., Nova Scotia. Rsch. assoc. U. Alta., Edmonton, Canada, 1991-93, asst. prof., 1993-94, St. Louis U., 1994-95; engring. scientist Hewlett-Packard Co., Andover, Mass., 1995-99; prin. scientist Agilent Techs. Inc., Andover, Mass., 1999—2001; sr. rsch. mgr. Advanced Algorithm Rsch. Ctr.; prin. scientist Philips Med Sys., Oxnard, Calif., 2001—. Contbr. articles to profl. jours. Fellow Am. Coll. Cardiology; mem. NY Acad. Sci., Soc. Women Engrs., Internat. Soc. Electrocardiology, Internat. Soc. Computerized Electrocardiology, Am. Heart Assn. Achievements include design and development of automated ECG interpretations. Office: Philips Med Sys 1201 N Rice Ave Oxnard CA 93030 E-mail: sophia.zhou@philips.com.

ZHOU, WEI, engineer, educator; b. China, Jan. 23, 1965; s. Qishun Zhang and Cuiying Zhou; m. Hui Chen. BEng, Tsinghua U., Beijing, 1980—85; PhD, U. Cambridge, 1987—91. Guest scientist Fraunhofer Inst. Mechanics of Materials, Freiburg, Germany, 1991—92; lectr. Nanyang Tech. U., 1992—97, sr. lectr., 1998—99, prof., 2000—; vis. scholar in applied physics Harvard U., Cambridge, Mass., 2002. Cons. Def. Sci. Orgn., 1999—2003, Singapore Techs. Engring. Ltd., 1995—, Def. Materials Orgn., 1996—97; pres. Singapore Fracture Group, 1998—99; chmn. Consulting Com., Singapore Weld-

ing Soc., 1998—2001. Fellow, Mech. Engring. Lab., Tsukuba, Japan, 1995; scholar The Sino-British Friendship Scholarship, The Chinese and Brit. Governments, 1987—91. Mem.: MRS, TMS (life). Office: Nanyang Tech Univ 50 Nanyang Ave Singapore 639798 Singapore Office Phone: 6790 4700. Office Fax: 6791 1859. Personal E-mail: wzhou@cantab.net. E-mail: mwzhou@ntu.edu.sg.

ZHOU, XIN (JOSEPH ZHOU), medical educator; b. Qingdao, Shandong, China, Sept. 20, 1963; came to U.S., 1988; m. Jian Wang, May 18, 1988; children: Jason K., Jaclyn W. MD, Beijing (China) Med. U., 1986. Diplomate Am. Bd. Pathology. Resident internal medicine China-Japan Friendship Hosp., Beijing, 1986—88; nephrology rsch. fellow U. So. Calif., LA, 1988—90, U. Calif., Irvine, 1990—91, asst. prof., 1991—95, pathology resident and fellow, 1995—98; asst. prof. U. Tex. Southwestern Med. Ctr., Dallas, 1998—2002, assoc. prof., 2002—. Dir. renal rsch. lab. U. Calif., Irvine, Calif., 1990—95; dir. divsn. renal pathology U. Tex. Southwestern Med. Ctr., 1998—. Bd. dirs. med. jours.:; contbr. articles, chapters to books. Mem.: Chinese Am. Soc. Nephrology (pres.-elect 2001—02, pres. 2002—), Internat. Acad. Pathology, Renal Pathology Soc., Coll. of Am. Pathologists (Tng. in Tech. award 1997), Am. Soc. Nephrology, Internat. Soc. Nephrology. Home: 3617 McFarlin Blvd Dallas TX 75205 Office: U Tex Southwestern Med Ctr Dept Pathology 5323 Harry Hines Blvd Dallas TX 75390-9073 Office Phone: 214-648-3536.

ZHOU, XINZHANG, materials scientist, ceramist; b. Wuhan, Hubei, China, Jan. 2, 1969; s. Yuanxing Zhou and Jichun Jiang; m. Yuhong Liu; 1 child, Nathan. PhD, Rutgers U., New Brunswick, N.J., 2002. Quality assurance engr. Yangtze Optical Fibre and Cable Co. Ltd., Wuhan, China, 1995—97; postdoctoral rschr. U. Calif., Davis, Calif., 2003—. Contbr. articles pub. to profl. jour. Grantee Rsch. Funds, Office of Naval Rsch., 1997-2004. Mem.: Am. Ceramic Soc. (ohio 1989). Achievements include patents pending for spray deposited nanostructured ceramics coatings and preforms. Office: Univ Calif Davis CHMS 1 shields Ave Davis CA 95616 Office Phone: 530-752-6290. Business E-Mail: xinzhou@ucdavis.edu.

ZHOU, XU, research scientist, educator; b. Shenyang, Peoples Republic of China, Nov. 1, 1965; arrived in U.S., 2000; d. Shulian Zhou and Defang Wu; m. Zaiyong Sun, Aug. 15, 1993. PhD, Northwestern Poly. U., Xi'an, Shaanxi, China, 1991—94. Vis. rsch. scientist U. Ill., Urbana, 2001—02; rsch. asst. prof. U. Vt., Burlington, 2002—. Postdoctoral assoc. Rutgers U., Piscataway, NJ, 2000—01. Alexendar von Humboldt fellow, Germany, 1995. Office: U Vt 231-C Votey Bldg 33 Colchester Ave Burlington VT 05401 E-mail: xzhou@emba.uvm.edu.

ZHOU, YUANXIN, mechanical engineer, educator; b. Laian, Anhui Peovince, China, Sept. 22, 1972; arrived in U.S., 2001; s. Banglu Zhou and Sufang Zhang; m. Ying Wang, July 24, 1971. BS, U. Sci. and Tech. China, 1995; PhD, U. Sci. and Tech. China, Hefei, Anhui, China, 2000. Lectorate U. Sci. and Tech. China, Hefei, 2000—01; postdoctoral investigator U. Mich., Dearborn, 2001—. Recipient Spl. Prize of Pres. Scholarship, Chinese Acad. Sci., 2000. Mem.: AAAS, ASME, Am. Soc. Composite. Achievements include development of tensile impact recovery experimental technique; Monte Carlo Numerical Model. Business E-Mail: yxzhou@engin.umd.umich.edu.

ZHU, DONGMING, materials scientist; b. Hefei, Anhui, China, Dec. 2, 1962; arrived in U.S., 1989; s. ZhengSe Zhu and Jingjuan Xu; m. Huixiang Deng; 1 child, Shirley. BS, Hefei U. of Tech., China, 1984, MS, 1988; PhD, U. of Minn., 1996. Sec. of rsch. inst. forecast & devel. Hefei U. Tech., Hefei, China, 1988—90, asst. prof., 1988—90; rsch. & tchg. asst. U. Minn., Mpls., 1990—96; sr. materials scientist U.S. Army Rsch. Lab./NASA Glenn Rsch. Ctr., Cleve., 1996—. Contbr. articles to profl. jours. Bd. dir. Commonwealth Ter. Coop. U. Student Family Housing Sys. U. of Minn., Mpls., 1992—93. Rsch. Assoc. Fellowship, Nat. Rsch. Coun./Nat. Acad. Sci. & Nat. Acad. Engring., 1996. Mem.: ASM Internat., Am. Ceramic Soc. (chmn. nominating/awards com. engiring ceranmic divsn. 2001—03, Best Paper award 2002). Home: 1915 Salem Parkway Westlake OH 44145 Office: NASA Glenn Rsch Ctr 21000 Brookpark Road Mail Stop 24-1 Cleveland OH 44135 Business E-Mail: Dongming.Zhu@grc.nasa.gov.

ZHU, HUA, biochemist, researcher; b. Xiaogan, Hubei, China, Nov. 5, 1965; came to U.S., 1994; d. Chaoqun Zhu and Yuanying Long; married, May 7, 1997; children: Jessica Xiaoman Yao, Stephanie Xiaoru Yao. BA in Agronomy, Hua Zhong Agrl. U., Wuhan, China, 1985; M in Botany, Northwestern Agrl. U., Yang Ling, China, 1991; PhD in Botany, Chinese Acad. Sci., Beijing, 1994; M in Biochemistry, U. Okla., 1997, PhD in Biochemistry, 2001. Rsch. asst. dept. botany and microbiology U. Okla., Norman, 1994-96, rsch. asst. dept. biochemistry and chemistry, 1996—2001; rsch. scientist Advanced Ctr. for Genome Tech., U. Okla., Norman, 2001—02; rsch. assoc. Civil Aerospace Med. Inst., FAA, Oklahoma City, 2002—; rsch. assoc. NRC, NAS FAA, Oklahoma City, 2003—. V.p. Soc. Chinese Scholar and Students of U. Okla., 1996-97. Mem. AAAS, Am. Chemistry Soc., Microscopy Soc. Am., Botanic Soc. China. Avocations: bedminton, swimming, travel, music, movies. Office: Toxicology Accident Lab CAMI FAA/AAM-610 Biochemistry 6500 S MacArthur Blvd Oklahoma City OK 73125 E-mail: zhuhua9863@yahoo.com.

ZHU, JIAN ZHONG, research scientist; b. Zhengzhou, Henan, China, Oct. 25, 1955; arrived in U.S., 1991; m. Song Yu, Aug. 17, 1997; 1 child, Jiang Wei. BSc, Harbin Engring. U., China, 1978; MSc, Tianjin U., China, 1982; PhD, U. Coll. Swansea, Eng., 1987. Lectr. Harbin Engring. U., China, 1978—80, Tianjin U., China, 1983; rsch. asst. Univ. Coll. Swansea, 1986—87, sr. rsch. asst., 1987—91; sr. scientist UES-Software, Inc., Annapolis, Md., 1991—2002, Procast Inc., Columbia, Md., 2003—. Contbr. articles to profl. jours.; mem. editl. bd. Commun. Numerical Meth. Engring. Named one of Highly Cited Rschrs., ISI Thomson Scientific, 2000. Mem.: U.S. Assn. for Computational Mechanics, Internat. Assn. for Computational Mechanics, ASME. Mailing: ProCAST Inc Suite 140 5850 Waterloo Rd Columbia MD 21045-1941

ZHU, KANGMIN, epidemiologist; b. Wuhan, Hubei, China, Nov. 10, 1956; came to U.S., 1988; s. Guangzhong Zhu and Kaiqiong Li; m. Min Dai, Feb. 4, 1985; children: Jingcai, Gene Lee. MD, Tongji Med. U., Wuhan, 1982, MPH, 1985; PhD, U. Wash., 1994. Tchg. asst. Tongji Med. U., 1985-87, lectr., 1987-88; rsch. asst., assoc. U. Wash./Fred Hutchinson Cancer Rsch. Ctr., Seattle, 1988-94; asst. prof. Meharry Med. Coll., Nashville, 1994-98, assoc. prof., 1998-2000, Pa. State Med. Coll., Hershey, 2000—. Rschr. in field. Contbr. articles to profl. jours. Recipient Innovative Devel. and Exploratory award U.S. Dept. Def., 1996, New Investigator award U.S. Dept. Def., 1996, IDEA award U.S. Dept. Def., 1997, Concept award U.S. Dept. Def., 2001. Mem.: Am. Assn. Cancer Rsch. (Hist. Black Colls. and Univs. faculty award in cancer rsch. 1998, Hist. Black Colls. and Univs. faculty award in cancer rsch. 1998), Soc. for Epidemiol. Rsch. Home: 5921 Mystic Ocean Ln Clarksville MD 21029-1263

ZHU, PETER C. chemist; b. Jiashan, China, May 8, 1957; came to U.S., 1987; s. Sanguan and Mingbao (Shen) Z.; m. June Zhu, Aug. 7, 1998. BS, Jiangxi Coll. Chinese Medicine, Nanchang, China, 1981, MS, 1987; PhD, Miss. State U., 1993. Instr. Jiangxi Coll Chinese Medicine, Nanchang, China, 1981-85; rsch. scientist 1st Chem. Corp., Mississippi State, Miss., 1990-92; sr. rsch. chemist 3M Health Care, Tustin, Calif., 1994-99, Terumo Med. Corp., Tustin, 1999-2000; prin. scientist ASP, Johnson & Johnson, Irvine, Calif., 2000—04, rsch. fellow, 2004—. Adj. chemistry prof. Irvine Valley Coll., 1997—; cons. and rschr. in field. Postdoctoral fellow U. Calif., Santa Barbara, 1993-94. Mem. Am. Chem. Soc. (divsn. organic chemistry, divsn. polymer, divsn. medicinal chemistry, divsn. carbohydrate chemistry, divsn. analytical chemistry, divsn. environ. chemistry). Achievements include new biocides discoveries, nanochemistry application, nanobeads chemistry, attachment chemistry, DNA attachment, new chemistry application in molecular biology; development of new chemistry of cyclic ketene acetals, including synthetic procedures and new reactions; invented pure monoacetylation of diols via cyclic ketene acetals; first cationically polymerized cyclic ketene acetals and obtained stable polymers and copolymers; developed new chemistry which led to a chemical oxygen sensor used for open-heart surgery, of new glucose and CO2 chemical sensor for medical use; invented several industrial processes of speciality chemicals; discovered a new silicone reaction; isolated one anticancer agent from a plant; development of a new preparative TLC methods, analytical methods of amine in organic and inorganic polymers, a synthetic procedure to introduce PhSe group. Office: ASP Biocides Rsch Johnson & Johnson 33 Technology Dr Irvine CA 92618 E-mail: pzhu1@aspus.jnj.com.

ZHU, XIANKUI, mechanical engineer, researcher; b. Zhongxiang, Hubei, China, Aug. 29, 1962; s. Mingjing Zhu and Fengying Wu; m. Lin Zhang; children: Julia, Jesse. BS, Hohai U., Nanjing, China, 1984; MS, Hohai U., Nanjing, China, 1987; PhD, Tsinghus U., Beijing, 1995. Rsch. asst. Hohai U., 1984—87; asst. prof. Wuhan U., China, 1987—91; rsch. asst. Tsinghua U., Beijing, 1991—95, postdoctoral rschr., 1995—96; rsch. prof. U. SC, Columbia, 1997—2001; prin. rsch. scientist Battelle, Columbus, 2002—. Contbr. Jour. of the Mechanics and Physics of Solids. Grantee, NASA, 2000, NSF, 2001, USAF, 2001, US Dept. Engring., 2001, PRCI, 2002. Mem.: ASME, ASTM, Am. Acad. Mechs. Home: 2049 Ridgeview Rd Columbus OH 43221 Office: Battelle 505 King Ave Columbus OH 43201 Personal E-mail: xkuizhu@yahoo.com. Business E-Mail: zhux@battelle.org.

ZHU, XIN LIANG, molecular biologist, researcher; b. Aug. 26, 1930; s. Zhong-Han and Hui-Wen (Wu) Z.; m. Hui Ying Bai; children: Cheng Zhao, Cheng Lang. MD, ZheJiang Med. U., Hang Zhou, 1953; PhD, Shanghai Inst. Cell Biology, 1960. Rsch. instr. Sch. Medicine La. State U., New Orleans, 1991-93; rsch. scientist ARC, Portland, Oreg., 1993-95; rsch. scientist in internal medicine Wash. U., St. Louis, 1995-96; rsch. assoc. in biochemistry Kirksville (Mo.) Coll. Osteo. Medicine, 1996—. Vis. scholar in cell biology Roche Inst. Molecular Biology, Nutley, N.J., 1980-82; vis. scholar in cell genetics Cornell U., N.Y.C., 1982-83; vis. scholar in biochemistry St. Louis U., 1987-91. Mem. editl. bd. Jour. Biochemistry, 1984-87. Mem. Am. Soc. Hematology. Home: 4553 A Gibon Ave Saint Louis MO 63110

ZHU, YILIANG, research scientist, educator; B.Sc., Shanghai U., 1982; M.Sc., Queen's U. at Kingston, Ont., Can., 1987; Ph.D., U. Toronto, Ont., 1991. Rsch. scientist Environ. Health Ctr. Health Can., Ottawa, 1991—93; assoc. prof., asst. prof. U. South Fla., Tampa, 1993—. Principle biostatistician Shriner's Hosps. for Chindren, Tampa, 1997—2000; CEO Scinfo Assocs., Tampa, 2000—; vis. scientist Nat. Ctr. for Environ. Assessment, U.S. EPA, Research Triangle Park, NC, 2000—01. Exec. com. mem. Asian Am. Coalition Fla., Tampa, 2001—02; founding pres. Chinese Am. Assn. Tampa Bay, 2001—02; pres. USF Asian Faculty and Staff Alliance, Tampa, 1997—98. Grantee, NSF, 1999—2002. Mem.: Am. Statis. Assn. Office: Coll Pub Health Univ S Fla 13201 Bruce B Downs Blvd Tampa FL 33612 E-mail: yzhu@hsc.usf.edu.

ZHU, YONG, research scientist; b. Shanghai, Oct. 30, 1947; s. Shuping Chu and Zhiping Wang; m. Shaokui Wang, Apr. 22, 1977; 1 child, Shenke. B of Engr., East China Inst. Chem. Tech., Shanghai, 1981; postgrad., Tianhin Inst. Textile Engring., 1982; PhD in Organic Chemistry, U. Ill., 1992. Laborer Qingdao (China) Cigarette Manufacture, 1968-72; rsch. asst. Qingdao Inst. Light Industry, 1972-77; asst. prof., head dept. Shandong Inst. Textile Engring., China, 1983-87; vis. scientist U. Ill., Urbana, 1987-88, tchg./rsch. asst., 1988-92, postdoctoral rsch. assoc., 1992-93; scientist Procter and Gamble Far East, Kobe, Japan, 1993-95; sr. staff scientist Procter and Gamble Co., Cin., 1995—. Cons. Qingdao Manufacture of Dyeing Auxiliaries, 1983-87, Jiaonan (China) Manufacture of Fragrances, 1984-87. Patentee in field; contbr. chpts. to books and articles to profl. jours. Recipient Edn. scholarship Chinese Edn. Assn., 1987. Mem. Am. Chem. Soc. (vol. in pub. outreach 1991-95), Inter-Am. Photochem. Soc., Chinese Color-Optical Soc., Shandong Textile Engring. Assn. Avocations: volleyball, swimming, music, violin, travel.

ZHU, YUDONG, medical imaging researcher; b. Shanghai, Feb. 16, 1969; arrived in U.S., 1991; s. Xingzhong Zhu and Wenzhen Yin; m. Yaxing Zhang, Sept. 6, 1994; 1 child, Kimberly. Diploma, Shanghai Jiao Tong U., 1991; MSEE, Vanderbilt U., 1993; PhD in Elec. Engring., Stanford U., 1998. Rsch. asst. dept. elec. engring. Vanderbilt U., Nashville, 1992-93; rsch. asst. Lucas MRS Imaging Ctr. Stanford U., Palo Alto, Calif., 1993-98, postdoctoral fellow, 1998; sr. scientist electronic sys. lab. GE Corp. R&D Ctr., Schenectady, N.Y., 1998—. Contbr. articles to profl. jours., chapters to books. Univ. scholar, Vanderbilt U., 1991. Mem.: IEEE, Internat. Soc. Magnetic Resonance in Medicine, Sigma Xi. Achievements include nine patents in field; six patents pending. Office: GE Corp R&D Ctr Bldg K1 Rm NMR129 Schenectady NY 12309 E-mail: zhu@crd.ge.com.

ZI, GOANGSEUP, engineering educator; b. Suncheon, Jenlanam Do, Korea, Apr. 5, 1969; s. Gyu-Yul Zi and Myung-Ja Kim; m. Soo Yun Cho, Jan. 29, 1994; children: Haeun, Evelyn Hayoon. BSc, Hanyang U., Korea, 1994, MSc, 1996, PhD, Northwestern U., 2002. 1st Grade Civil Engineer, KSCE / Seoul, Korea, 1994. Engr. Korea Infrastructure Safety and Tech., Anyang, Republic of Korea, 1996—97; postdoctoral fellow Northwestern U., Evanston, Ill., 2002—04; asst. prof. Korea U., Seoul, Republic of Korea, 2004—. Rsch., edn. Korea U., Seoul, Korea (South), 2004—. V.p. Korean Student Assn., Northwestern U., Evanston, Ill., 1998—99. Sgt. Korean Army, 1989—91, South Korea. Recipient Industry Stipend of Excellence, Larfarge and EDF, 2001; Walter P. Murphy hon. fellowship, Northwestern U., McCormick Sch. Engring., 1998-1999. Achievements include research in size effect of negative-positive geometries, development of Constitutive models, analysis of radionuclide decontamination using microwaves, computational mechanics. Office: Korea U Anam Dong 5Ga 1 South Korea Seoul 136-701 Republic of Korea Personal E-mail: g-zi@korea.ac.kr.

ZIADEH, FARHAT J. Middle Eastern studies educator; b. Ramallah, Palestine, Apr. 8, 1917; s. Jacob and Nimeh Farah Z.; m. Suad Salem, July 24, 1949; children— Shireen, Susan, Rhonda, Deena, Reema. BA, Am. U., Beirut, 1937; LL.B., U. London, 1940. Bar: Barrister-at-law Lincoln's Inn 1946. Instr. Princeton U., 1943-45, lectr. Oriental studies, 1948-54, asst. prof., 1954-58, asso. prof., 1958-66; magistrate Govt. of Palestine, 1947-48; editor Voice of Am., USIA, 1950-54; prof. U. Wash., Seattle, 1966—, prof., chmn. dept. Near Eastern lang. and lit., 1970-82, dir. Ctr. Arabic Study Abroad, 1983-89. Adj. prof. U. Wash. Law Sch., 1978-87, prof. emeritus, 1987— Author: Reader in Modern Literary Arabic, 1964, Lawyers, The Rule of Law and Liberalism in Modern Egypt, 1968, Property Law in the Arab World, 1979; contbr. articles to profl. jours. Mem. Middle East Studies Assn. (pres. 1979-80), Am. Oriental Soc. (past pres. western br.), Am. Research Center in Egypt (past bd. govs., exec. com.), Am. Assn. Tchrs. Arabic (past pres.) Eastern Orthodox. Office: Univ Wash Mid Eastern Studies Dept Seattle WA 98195-0001 Office Phone: 206-543-4959. E-mail: farhat@u.washington.edu.

ZIBART, MICHAEL ALAN, wholesale book company executive; b. Nashville, Mar. 12, 1947; s. Alan Walter and Joy (Hughes) Z.; m. Margaret Anne Boyd, Dec. 27, 1976; children: Emily Joy, Mary Claire. BA, Vanderbilt U., 1969. Mgmt. trainee Zibart Bros. Books, Nashville, 1961-69; property mgr. Pollack Co., Nashville, 1966-69; buyer Ingram Book Co., Nashville, 1970-75, mgr. trade dept., 1976, v.p., 1976-85, exec. v.p., 1985-88; founder, pres. ProMotion, Inc., Nashville, 1988—. Author: Almanac on Bookselling, 3d edit., 1980; pub. (monthly book review) BookPage, 1988—. Office: ProMotion Inc 2143 Belcourt Ave Nashville TN 37212-3503 Office Phone: 615-292-8926.

ZICHEK, MELVIN EDDIE, retired minister; b. Lincoln, Nebr., May 5, 1918; s. Eddie and Agnes (Varga) Zichek; m. Dorothy Virginia Patrick, May 28, 1942; 1 child, Shannon Elaine. AB, Nebr. Ctrl. Coll., 1942; MA, U. Nebr., 1953; DLitt, McKinley-Roosevelt Ednl. Inst., 1955. Ordained to ministry Christian Ch., 1942. Min. Christian chs., Brock, Nebr., 1941, Ulysses, Nebr., 1942—43, Elmwood, Nebr., 1943—47, Central City, Nebr., 1947—83; rural tchr. Merrick County, Nebr., 1937—40; prin. Alvo (Nebr.) Consol. HS, 1943—47; supt. Archer (Nebr.) Pub. Schs., 1948—57; head dept. English and speech Central City (Nebr.) HS, 1957—63; supt. Marquette (Nebr.) Consol. Schs., 1963—79; ret., 1983. With U.S. Army, 1942. Mem.: Grand Island Ret. Tchrs. Assn. Republican. Home: 2730 N North Rd Grand Island NE 68803-1143

ZICHEK, SHANNON ELAINE, retired secondary school educator; b. Lincoln, Nebr., May 29, 1944; d. Melvin Eddie and Dorothy Virginia (Patrick) Zichek. AA, York (Nebr.) Coll., 1965; BA, U. Nebr., Kearney, 1968; postgrad., U. Okla., Edmond, 1970—75, U. Nebr., Kearney, 1980—82, U. Nebr., 1989, postgrad., 1992. Tchr. history and English, N.W. H.S., Grand Island, Nebr., 1948-1999, ret., 1999. Republican. Home: 2730 N North Rd Grand Island NE 68803-1143

ZICHERMAN, DAVID L. lawyer, educator, financial consultant; b. N.Y.C., Oct. 12, 1961; BA in Psychology magna cum laude, W.Va. U., 1984; JD, MPIA, U. Pitts., 1989. Bar: Del. 1990, Pa. 1990, D.C. 1990; cert. Sr. Advisor, fin. mgr., chartered retirement plans specialist, cert. mediator. Assoc. Richards, Layton & Finger, Wilmington, Del., 1989-92, Klehr Harrison et al, Phila., 1992-94, Kelly Grimes Pietrangelo & Vakil, P.C., Media, Pa., 1994-97; fin. cons. Merrill Lynch, 1998—2003, Sr. Advisory Svcs., Inc., 2004—; pvt. practice Law Offices of David L. Zicherman, Esq., 2004—. Adj. prof. Widener U. Law Ctr., Wilmington, 1993-95. Editor: State Legislation Forum newsletter, 1991-93; editor Delaware County Legal Jour., 1995-97; contbr. chpt. to book, articles to profl. jours. Bd. dirs. Nat. Tay Sachs and Allied Diseases Assn. Delaware Valley, 1998-2001; mem. tech. com. Rose Tree Media Edn. Found., 1998-2000. Avocations: sports, photography, creative writing, travel. Office: 41 University Dr Ste 400 Newtown PA 18940 Home: 140 Livery Dr Churchville PA 18966-1175 Office Phone: 267-757-8707.

ZICK, JOHN WALTER, retired accounting company executive; b. Highland Park, Ill., Sept. 21, 1925; s. Walter Ernest and Helen Ann (Wiedenhoeft) Z.; m. Mary Ann Sutter, Dec. 11, 1948; children: Sharon, Catherine, John W. (dec.). BS, Northwestern U., 1948. With Price Waterhouse, Chgo., 1948-73, N.Y.C., 1973-86, partner, 1960-86, partner in charge N.Y.C. office, 1973-76, regional mng. partner, 1976-78, co-chmn., ops., dept. sr. partner, 1978-86. Bd. dirs. Mid-Am. chpt. ARC, 1968-73, Medic Alert Found. U.S., 1994-99; founding mem., elder Winnetka (Ill.) Presbyterian Ch., 1956-67; bd. auditors New Trier Twp., Ill., 1969-73; trustee Carnegie Hall Soc. and Corp., 1980—; mem. corp. Greenwich Hosp. Assn., 1980-89. Served with USN, 1943-46. Mem. AICPA (treas. and dir. 1974-77), Ill. Soc. CPAs (pres. 1971-72) Clubs: Pine Valley Golf; Union League (N.Y.C.); Blind Brook; Burning Tree (Washington).

ZICKUS, ANNE, state legislator; b. Apr. 6, 1939; m. Charles Zickus, 1958; children: Kathy, Chuck. Alderman City of Palos Hills, Ill., 1973-75; state rep. Dist. 47, Ill., 1989-90, Dist. 48, Ill., 1993—; dir. Ill. State Crime Commn., 1997. Dir. Helping Hand Rehab. Ctr., 1995—. Mem. Suburban Assn. Realtors, Nat. Assn. Realtors. Republican. Home: 7909 W 112th St Palos Hills IL 60465-2731

ZIEBARTH, ROBERT CHARLES, management consultant; b. Evanston, Ill., Sept. 12, 1936; s. Charles A. and Marian (Miller) Z.; m. Patience Arnold Kirkpatrick, Aug. 28, 1971; children— Dana Kirkpatrick, Scott Kirkpatrick, Christopher, Nicholas. AB, Princeton, 1958; MBA, Harvard, 1964. With Bell & Howell Co., Chgo., 1964-73, treas., chief fin. officer, 1969-73; mgmt. cons. Ziebarth Co., 1973—. Mem. dirs. adv. bd. Arkwright Boston Ins. Co., devel. com. Nat. Assn. Ind. Schs.; bd. dirs. M.B.A. Resources, Inc., Telemedia, Inc., Corp. Resources, Inc., Nordemann Grimm Inc. Assoc. Community Renewal Soc., Citizens Coun. Gateway House; mem. Ill. Bd. Higher Edn., Ill. Joint Edn. Commn.; trustee Choate Sch.; trustee, pres. Latin Sch.Chgo., Chgo. Maternity Ctr.; bd. dirs. Harvard Bus. Sch. Fund, U.S.O., Inc., Prentice Women's Hosp., Northwestern Meml. Corp., Found. for Reproductive Rsch. and Edn., Endowments Inc., Bond Portfolio Endowments Inc. Served to lt. USNR, 1958-62. Mem. Naval Hist. Found., Art Inst. Chgo., Chgo. Hist. Soc., Mus. Modern Art. Clubs: Mid-Am. (Chgo.), Racquet (Chgo.), Saddle and Cycle (Chgo.), Economic (Chgo.), Executives (Chgo.). Presbyterian. Office: PO Box 4569 Ketchum ID 83340-4569

ZIEGAUS, ALAN JAMES, public relations executive; b. Bremerton, Wash., May 8, 1948; s. Alan Moon and Dorothy (Lamont) Z.; m. Constance Jean Carver, 1972; children: Jennifer, Ashley. BJ, San Diego State U., 1970. Staff writer San Diego Tribune, 1972-77; exec. asst. San Diego City Council, 1977-78; v.p. Gable Agy., San Diego, 1978-80; pres. Stoorza, Ziegaus & Metzger, San Diego, 1980-2000. Mem. planning com. County San Diego, 1980-82; mem. sewage task force City of San Diego, 1986-88, civil svc. com., 1992—; trustee armed forces YMCA, San Diego, 1984—. Recipient Best Investigative Series award AP, 1975. Mem. San Diego Press Club (Best News Story award 1973). Office: Stoorza Ziegaus & Metzger 225 Broadway Fl 18 San Diego CA 92101-5005 Home: 11343 Breckenridge Way San Diego CA 92131-2953

ZIEGEL, BARI A. marketing professional; b. N.Y.C., Nov. 25, 1959; d. Leonard and Norma (Nemeth) Z.; m. Steven M. Rosman, Sept. 8, 1984; children: Michal Sima Ziegel Rosman, Ilan Chaim Ziegel Rosman. BBA, Hofstra U., 1980. Ops., sales rep. Unitours, Inc., N.Y.C., 1980-82; adminstrv. asst. Bozell and Jacobs, Inc., N.Y.C., 1982-83, Parfums Stern, Inc., N.Y.C., 1983-85; mgmt. assoc. Citicorp Indsl. Credit, Inc., Harrison, N.Y., 1985-87, mktg. officer Rye, N.Y., 1987-88; area mgr. Lucent Techs. Product Fin., Plainview, N.Y., 1988-2000; regional sales dir. Expanets Fin. Svcs., Pt. Washington, N.Y., 2000—. Mem. NAFE, Women in Equipment Leasing. Jewish. Office: Expanets Fin Svcs 49 Shore Rd Port Washington NY 11050

ZIEGELAAR, BOB W. transportation executive; Dir. Bangor (Maine) Internat. Airport, 1991—2001; pres. Telford Aviation, Rockland, Maine, 2001—, CEO, 2001—. Office: Telford Aviation Inc PO Box 686 Rockland ME 04841

ZIEGENHAGEN, DAVID MACKENZIE, consultant, retired healthcare company executive; b. Mpls., May 25, 1936; s. Elmer Herbert Ziegenhagen and Margaret Ruth (Mackenzie) Kruger; m. Mary Ange Kinsella, Nov. 26, 1966 (div. Dec. 1982); children: Marc, Eric; m. Mary Kinsella, Feb. 7, 2002. BA, U. Minn., 1962. Assoc. dir. Thailand Peace Corps, Bangkok, 1963-65, Thailand program officer Washington, 1966-67, dir. Western Samoa Apia, 1967-70; exec. dir. Mental Health Assn. Minn., Mpls., 1970-76; co-founder, pres. Current Newspapers, Inc., Burnsville, Minn., 1975-84; sr. program officer The St. Paul Found., 1982—85; pres. DMZ Assocs., Cloverdale, Calif., 2000—; exec. dir. Minn. Bd. Med. Practice, St. Paul, 1985-88; CEO, pres. Stratis Health, Bloomington, Minn., 1988-2000. Field dir. Am. Refugee Com., Bangkok, 1979; dir. Health Edn. Rsch. Found., St. Paul, 1993—99; mem. Citizens League, Mpls., 1975—2000, dir., 1988—95; mem. Adminstrs. in Medicine, Washington, 1985—88; dir. Walk-In Counseling Ctr., Mpls., 1990—99, Ctr. for Clin. Quality Evaluation, Washington, 1990—99. Mem. Cloverdale Planning Commn., 2000—, Sonoma County Civil Grand Jury, 2001—. Mem. Nat. Mental Health Staff Coun. (pres. 1970-76). Avocations: travel, international development, arts. Office Phone: 707-894-0894.

ZIEGER, ROBERT HARMAN, history educator, historian; b. Englewood, NJ, Aug. 2, 1938; s. John H. Zieger and Grace Elizabeth Harman; m. Gay Annette Pitman, June 30, 1962; 1 child, Robert E. BA, Montclair State Coll., 1960; MA, U. Wyo., 1961; PhD, U. Md., 1965. From asst. to assoc. prof. history U. Wis., Stevens Point, 1964-73; assoc. prof. history Kans. State U., Manhattan, 1973-77; prof. history Wayne State U., Detroit, 1977-86, U. Fla., Gainesville, 1986—98, disting. prof. history, 1998—. Author: Rebuilding the Pulp and Paper Workers' Union, 1984 (Taft award 1985), American Workers, American Unions, 1920-85, 1986, 2d rev. edit., 1994, John L. Lewis: Labor Leader, 1988, Republicans and Labor, 1919-1929, 1969, The CIO, 1935-55 (Taft award 1996), America's Great War, 2000; (with Gilbert J. Gall) American Workers, American Unions, 2002; editor: Organized Labor in the 20th Century South, 1991, Southern Labor in Transition, 1940-1995, 1997; mem. editl. bd. Am. Communist History, 2003—. Grantee NEH, 1972, 83, Faculty Enrichment Programme award Can. Govt., 1985, Rsch. grantee Am.

Philos. Soc., 1974, 80, Am. Coun. Learned Soc., 1982, Rockefeller Archives Ctr., 1994. Mem. Orgn. Am. Historians, So. Hist. Assn., Historians of Am. Communism (pres. 1990-92). Democrat. Unitarian Universalist. Avocations: baseball, tennis. Home: 2025 NW 18th Ln Gainesville FL 32605-3959 Office: Univ Fla Dept History Gainesville FL 32611 Office Phone: 352-392-0271. Business E-Mail: zieger@ufl.edu.

ZIEGLER, ANN E. retail executive; b. 1958; BA, Coll. William and Mary; JD, U. Chgo. With Skadden, Arps, Slate, Meagher & Flom; asst. counsel Sara Lee Corp., 1993—94, exec. dir. corp. devel., 1994—2000, v.p., 1997—2000, sr. v.p. corp. devel., 2000—01, sr. v.p. mergers and acquisitions, 2001—, CFO bakery group, 2003—, sr. v.p. adminstrn. bakery group. Bd. dirs. Unitrin, Inc. Office: Sara Lee Corp 3 First Nat Plaza Chicago IL 60602-4260

ZIEGLER, ARTHUR P., JR., foundation executive; b. Pitts., June 20, 1937; s. Arthur P. and Vinnie (DeWinter) Ziegler. BA, U. Pitts., 1958, MA, 1959; postgrad., Union Theol. Sem., NYC, 1960, Western Res. U., 1961. Instr. Carnegie Mellon U., Pitts., 1961-64, Pa. State U., 1961-63; pres. Pitts. History, Landmarks, 1964—, Cranston Devel. Corp., 1980-87. Trustee Allegheny Found., Pitts., 1975—, Walden Trust, 1990—, Sarah Scaife Found., 2000—; trustee emeritus Nat. Trust, Washington; chmn. Allegheny County Hist. Properties Commn., Pa. Editor: (novels) A Critical Edition of Lord of the Flies, 1964; author: (book) Historic Preservation of Inner City Areas, 1971, Revolving Funds for Historic Preservation, 1975; co-author: Allegheny, 1975, Historic Preservation for Small Towns, 1980, Landmark Architecture of Allegheny County, 1987. Mem. N.E. regional, Pitts. adv. coun. Fannie Mae; advisor 10,000 Friends of Pa.; dir. Riverlife Task Force, Harbor Gardens, Pitts.; advisor, sustainable architecture program Carnegie Mellon U.; mem. bd. advisors The Waterfront Ctr.; bd. dirs. Preservation Pa., Preservation Action. Recipient Crowninshield award, Nat. Trust, Nat. Recognition award, Ptnrs. for a livable Cmty., Pvt. Sector award, Pres. of the US, Otto Haas award, Preservation, Pa., Pa. Man of Yr. in Arts award, Pitts., Jaycees, Golden Quill award, Remax Renaissance award. Mem.: HYP Club, City Club. Avocation: gardening. Office: One Station Sq Ste 450 Pittsburgh PA 15219

ZIEGLER, CHARLES EDWARD, political science educator, department chairman; b. Plymouth, Ind., Oct. 17, 1953; s. Charles A. and Justine D. Ziegler; m. Janna Shakhmuratovna Tajibaeva, Oct. 14, 1995; 1 child, Alan Taj. PhD, U. Ill., 1979, AM, 1975—77; BA, Purdue U., 1975. Asst. prof. St. Leo Coll., St. Leo, Fla., 1979—80, U. Louisville, Ky., 1980—86, prof., 1993—, prof., chair, dept. of polit. sci., 1998—, assoc. prof., 1986—93; legislative asst. U.S. Senate, Washington, 1989. Exec. dir. Louisville Com. on Fgn. Rels., Louisville, 1990—; pres. Ky. Polit. Sci. Assn., Ky., 1997—98. Author: (book) Environmental Policy in the USSR, 1987, Foreign Policy and East Asia, 1993, The History of Russia, 1999; editor: The Russian Far East, 2002. Mem., exec. com. Am. Committees on Fgn. Rels., Washington, 1995—98. Sr. Fulbright scholar Pusan Nat. U., Republic of Korea, 1995, Nat. fellow Hoover Instn., 1985-86, Internat. Affairs fellow Coun. on Fgn. Rels., 1987-88. Mem.: So. Conf. on Slavic Studies, Internat. Inst. for Strategic Studies, Nat. Com. on United States-China Rels., Am. Assn. for the Advancement of Slavic Studies, Am. Polit. Sci. Assn. Avocation: 4th degree junior master in taekwondo. Office: U Louisville Dept Polit Sci Louisville KY 40292-0001 Office Phone: 502-852-3248. Business E-Mail: ceziegler@louisville.edu.

ZIEGLER, DANIEL MARTIN, chemistry professor; b. Quinter, Kans., July 6, 1927; s. Anton T. and Clara (Weissbeck) Z.; m. Mary Alice Weir, Aug. 19, 1952; children: Daniel L., Paul W., Mary Claire, James M. BS in Chemistry, St. Benedicts Coll., 1949; PhD in Chemistry, Loyola U., 1955; postdoctoral, U. Wis., 1955-58; DSc (hon.), Benedectine Coll., 2001. Asst. prof. Inst. Enzyme Rsch. U. Wis., Madison, 1958-61; asst. prof. chemistry U. Tex., Austin, 1961-62, assoc. prof. chemistry, 1962-69, prof. chemistry, 1969-97, Roger J. Williams Centennial prof. in biochemistry, 1990-97, prof. emeritus, 1997—. Editor jour. Biol. Chemistry, 1979-83, 85-90, 93-98; mem. editl. bd. Analyt. Biochemistry, 1989-91, Arch. Biochem. Biophys., 1966-71; contbr. articles to profl. jours. Recipient Bernard B. Brodie award Am. Soc. Pharmacol. Exptl. Therapy, 1990, Alexander von Humboldt award, Germany, 1991; estab. investigator Am. Heart Assn., 1960-65. Mem. Internat. Soc. for the Study of Xenobiotics (hon. life). Home: 6704 Shoal Creek Blvd Austin TX 78757-4379 Office: U Tex Dept Chemistry/Biochemistry Austin TX 78712 Business E-Mail: dziegler@mail.utexas.edu. E-mail: dziegler3@austin.rr.com.

ZIEGLER, DEWEY KIPER, neurologist, educator; b. Omaha, May 31, 1920; s. Isidor and Pearl (Kiper) Z.; m. Mar. 30, 1954; children: Amy, Laura, Sara. BA, Harvard U., 1941, MD, 1945. Diplomate Am. Bd. Psychiatry and Neurology (bd. dirs. 1974-83, exec. com. 1978-82). Intern in medicine Boston City Hosp., 1945-46; asst. resident then chief resident in neurology N.Y. Neurol. Inst.-Columbia U. Coll. Physicians and Surgeons, 1948-51; resident in psychiatry Boston Psychopathic Hosp., 1951-53; asst. chief neurol. service Montefiore Hosp., N.Y.C.; and asst. prof. neurology Columbia U., 1953-55; asst. prof. U. Minn., 1955-56; asso. clin. prof. U. Kans. Med. Sch., 1956-64, chief dept. neurology, 1968-85; prof. U. Kans. Med. Center, 1964-89, prof. emeritus, 1989—. Cons. Social Security Adminstrn., 1975—; mem. com. on certification and co-certification Am. Bd. Med. Specialties, 1979-82 Author: In Divided and Distinguished Worlds, 1942; Contbr. numerous articles to profl. jours. Served to lt., j.g., M.C. USNR, 1946-48. Fellow Am. Acad. Neurology (pres. 1979-81); mem. AMA, Am. Neurol. Assn. (v.p. 1972-73), Am. Headache Assn. Jewish. Home: 8347 Delmar Ln Shawnee Mission KS 66207-1821 Office: Kans U Med Ctr 3900 Rainbow Blvd Kansas City KS 66103-2918 Office Phone: 913-588-6922. Business E-Mail: dziegler@kumc.edu.

ZIEGLER, DONALD EMIL, federal judge; b. Pitts., Oct. 1, 1936; s. Emil Nicholas and Elizabeth Ziegler; m. Claudia J. Chermak, May 1, 1965; 1 son, Scott Emil. BA, Duquesne U., 1958; LL.B., Georgetown U., 1961. Bar: Pa. 1962, U.S. Supreme Ct. 1967. Practice law, Pitts., 1962-74; judge Ct. of Common Pleas of Allegheny County, Pa., 1974-78, U.S. Dist. Ct. (we. dist.) Pa., Pitts., 1978—, chief judge, 1994-2001. Mem. Jud. Conf. U.S., 1997-2000. Treas. Big Bros. of Allegheny County, 1969-74. Mem. ABA, Pa. Bar Assn., Allegheny County Bar Assn., Am. Judicature Soc., St. Thomas More Soc. Clubs: Oakmont Country. Democrat. Roman Catholic. Office: 100 Ross St Ste 105 Pittsburgh PA 15219-2013

ZIEGLER, DONALD ROBERT, accountant; b. Lancaster, Pa., Nov. 15, 1932; s. John Jacob and Esther Mae (McKelly) Z.; m. Suzanne Foster; children: D. Rand, Scott F., Kurt J. BS in Econ. Acctg., Franklin and Marshall Coll., 1954. CPA, Pa. Mgr., sr. staff mem. Price Waterhouse, Phila., 1954-67, ptnr., 1967-92, sr. practice ptnr., 1978-92, mng. ptnr. Mid-Atlantic area, 1985-88, vice chmn. S.E. region, 1988-92, mem. policy bd. N.Y.C., 1980-88, mem. mgmt. com., 1986-92. Author: (with others) Managing and Accounting for Inventories, 1980; contbg. author various books in field. Trustee Franklin and Marshall Coll., 1983—, mem. alumni exec. coun., 1979—83, mem. exec. com., 1995—, chmn. audit com., 1989—2003, vice-chmn. bd. trustees, 2002—, mem. Phila. alumni coun.; trustee Pa. Ballet, 1988—92, 1994—95, mem. devel. and fin. coms., vice chmn. bd. trustees, 1989—92, chmn. exec. com., 1989—91; bd. dirs. Beebe Med. Ctr., 2000—, Beebe Med. Found., 2001—, So. Del. Surgery Ctr., 2003—. With U.S. Army, 1955—57. Recipient Outstanding Soldier award U.S. Army, 1955, Disting. Svc. Alumni medal Franklin and Marshall Coll., 1991. Mem. AICPA (auditing stds. com. 1973-76, chmn. subcom. fraud 1976-80), Pa. Inst. CPAs (Phila. chpt. exec. coun.), Rehoboth Beach Country Club (bd. govs. 2000—, treas. 2003—), Phila. Aviation Club (bd. govs. and treas. 1969-90), Royal Blackheath Golf Club (U.K.). Home: One West St Dewey Beach DE 19971 Office: Pricewaterhouse-Coopers LLP Two Commerce Sq 2001 Market St Ste 1700 Philadelphia PA 19103-7042 Personal E-mail: drsfzig@aol.com.

ZIEGLER, EARL KELLER, minister; b. Sheridan, Pa., Mar. 4, 1929; s. Abraham Hoffman and Rhoda Bucher (Keller) Z.; m. Vivian Zug Snyder, Aug. 12, 1951; children: Karen Louise, Randall Earl, Doreen Kay Creighton, Michael Wayne, Konnae Ziegler Berces, Sulien Nicodemus. BA, Elizabethtown (Pa.) Coll., 1951; MDiv, Bethany Theol. Sem., Chgo., 1954; DDiv, Lancaster (Pa.) Theol. Sem., 1982. Ordained to ministry Ch. of the Brethren, 1950. Pastor Woodbury (Pa.) Congregation, Pa., 1954-60, Black Rock Ch. of Brethren, Brodbecks, Pa., 1960-70, Mechanic Grove Ch. of Brethren, Quarryville, Pa., 1970-83, Atlantic N.E. Dist. Exec., Harrisburg, Pa., 1983-89, Lampeter (Pa.) Ch. of the Brethren, 1989-99; moderator Ch. of the Brethren, Elgin, Ill., 1993-94; interim pastor Florin Ch. of the Brethren, Mt. Joy, Pa., 1999—2001. Moderator various dists., Pa., 1959—; mem. Gen. Bd., Ch. of Brethren, 1975-80; chmn. Parish Ministerial Commn., 1979-80; dir. Family Life Inst., 1961, 64, mem. Nat. Korean Cons. Com., 1988-91, Denominational Structure Com., 1990-91, others; adj. prof. ch. history Evang. Sem., Myerstown, Pa., 1988—. Author: Divorce Among the Church of the Brethren Clergy, 1981; contbr. articles to profl. jours. Pres. Manheim Elem. PTA, 1964-65; trustee Elizabethtown Coll., 1965-83; bd. dirs. Cmty. Choir, Lineboro, Md., 1966-70, Solanco Community Men's Chorus, Quarryville, 1976-83, Samaritan Counseling Ctr., Lancaster, Pa., 1992-98, Pa. Coun. Chs., 1983-89, 2000—, Hope Internat. Trustees, 2000—. Recipient Alumni citation, Elizabethtown Coll. Alumni Assn., 1964, award for Outstanding Ch. Planting in Azua Province of Dominican Republic, 1990, Award of Appreciation, Germantown Ch. of Brethren, 1990. Mem. Lampeter Willow St. Ministerium (pres. 1989-91). Republican. Mem. Brethren Ch. *"You shall have what your faith expects," were the words of Jesus to two blind men. These words challenge the potential within each of us, a faith that conquers, a spirit that soars. Between the possible and the impossible is the measure of one's will.*

ZIEGLER, EKHARD ERICH, pediatrics educator; b. Saalfelden, Austria, Apr. 12, 1940; children: Stefan, Gabriele, Lena. MD, U. Innsbruck, Austria, 1964. Diplomate: Am. Bd. Pediatrics. Intern U. Innsbruck, 1966-67, resident in pediatrics, 1967-68 70-71, resident in pharmacology, 1964-66, asst. dept. pediatrics, 1970-73; vis. instr. pediatrics U. Iowa, Iowa City, 1968-70, asst. prof. pediatrics, 1973-76, assoc. prof., 1976-81, prof., 1981—. Mem. nutrition study sect. NIH, 1988-92. Recipient Nutrition award Am. Acad. Pediactrics, 1988. Mem. Am. Soc. Clin. Nutrition, Soc. Pediatric Research, Soc. Exptl. Biology and Medicine, N.Am. Soc. Pediatric Gastroenterology, Midwest Soc. Pediatric Research, Am. Pediatric Soc., The Nutrition Soc., N.Y. Acad. Scis., Am. Acad. Pediatrics., Am. Dietetic Assn. (hon.). Clubs: Univ. Athletic (Iowa City). Office: U Iowa Dept Pediatrics Iowa City IA 52242 Office Phone: 319-356-2836. E-mail: ekhard-ziegler@uiowa.edu.

ZIEGLER, GWENDOLYN WOODS, minister, consultant; d. William Darnell and Christine Anna Woods; children: Geraldine, Tonia Elaine, Faith Evangeline, Charity Elise. BTh, United Bible Coll., Orlando, Fla., 1988, EdM, 1990. Pastoral lic. Deliverance Evangelistic Ctrs., Inc./N.J., 1970, Evangelistic lic. Deliverance Evangelistic Ctrs., Inc./N.J., 1967. Pres./cons. G. Chafto Industries, Washington, 1990—; v.p. In The Midst, Inc., Severn, Md., 1999—2002. Spl. asst. to the pres. We Can Do Ministries, Inc., Newark, 1990—92; tchr./radio broadcaster Positive Proof Ministries, Orange, NJ, 1995—97; cons./radio broadcaster Global Ministries, South Orange, NJ, 1997—98. Author: (non-fiction book) Judgment Work - A Conclusion To The Matter, 2003. Mem.: N.Am. Bookdealers Exch. Independent. Office: G Chafto Industries 3161 Beaverwood Lane Silver Spring MD 20906 Office Phone: 301-758-5386. E-mail: gwen_ziegler@hotmail.com.

ZIEGLER, HENRY STEINWAY, lawyer; b. Utica, NY, June 21, 1933; s. Frederick J. and Alice (Cantwell) Z.; m. Patricia Blackmore (div.); children: Frederick S., Alicia P., Timothy O.; m. Jourdan Arpelle, Apr. 6, 1991. AB, Harvard U., 1955; LLB, Columbia U., 1958. Bar: N.Y. 1961, U.S. Dist. Ct. (ea. and so. dists.) N.Y. 1962, U.S. Ct. Appeals (2d cir.) 1963, U.S. Tax Ct. 1972. Assoc. Shearman & Sterling, N.Y.C., 1958-67, ptnr., 1967-92; chmn. CEO Deutsche Bank Trust Co., 1995-97, Trust Estate Planning dir., 1998-99; sr. v.p. Fiduciary Trust Co. Internat., N.Y.C., 1999—2003; cons., governance and transfer of family wealth, 2003—. Pres. Chamber Music Soc. of Lincoln Ctr., Inc., 1983-89, Christopher D. Smithers Found.; bd. dirs. Lincoln Ctr. for Performing Arts, N.Y.C., 1985-89; hon. trustee St. Lukes-Roosevelt Hosp. Ctr.; bd. regents, Am. Coll. Trust Estate Counsel, 1988-94. With U.S. Army, 1958-60, 61-62. Mem. ABA (former vice chmn. internat. com. on property probate and trust law), Acad. internat. Trust and Estate Law (mem. exec. coun., v.p.), N.Y. State Bar Assn., Assn. Bar City of N.Y., Century Assn., Order St. John of Jerusalem. Clubs: Racquet and Tennis, Knickerbocker. Republican. Avocation: music. Home: 55 Liberty St Apt # 7A New York NY 10005 E-mail: hziegler@ftci.com.

ZIEGLER, JACK (JACK DENMORE), cartoonist; b. N.Y.C., July 13, 1942; s. John Denmore and Kathleen Miriam (Clark) Z.; m. Jean Ann Rice, Apr. 20, 1968 (div. 1995); children: Jessica, Benjamin, Maxwell; m. Kelli Joseph, Aug. 1996. BA in Communication Arts, Fordham U., 1964. Free-lance cartoonist, N.Y.C., 1972—; cartoonist The New Yorker, N.Y.C., 1974—. Author: Hamburger Madness, 1978, Filthy Little Things, 1981, Marital Blitz, 1987, Celebrity Cartoons of the Rich and Famous, 1987, Worst Case Scenarios, 1990, Mr. Knocky, 1993, The Essential Jack Ziegler, 2000, How's The Squid?, 2004; illustrator: (children's books) Lily of the Forest, 1987, Flying Boy, 1988, Annie's Pet, 1989, Eli and the Dimplemeyers, 1994 (adult books) Waiting Games, 1983, The Joy of Stress, 1984, That's Incurable!, 1984, Modern Superstitions, 1985, The No-Sex Handbook, 1990, There'll Be a Slight Delay, 1991, Byte Me!, 1996. Democrat.

ZIEGLER, JAMES L. marketing executive; b. Fort Benning, Ga., Sept. 10, 1965; s. Gordon L. and Kum S. Ziegler. BS, US Mil. Acad., 1989; MBA, U. Chgo., 1998. Sales Pfizer, Inc, Dallas, 1993—96; biotech. exec. Amgen, Inc., Thousand Oaks, Calif., 2000—. Bd. mem. West Point Soc. LA, 2000—03. Capt. U.S. Army, 1989—93. Decorated Army Achievement Medal U.S. Army, Army Commendation Medal; recipient Disting. Contbn., Nat. Hispanic Med. Assn., 2003, President's award, Nat. Med. Assn., 2004, Significant Achievement award, Assn. of Am. Indian Physicians, 2002. Personal E-mail: jziegle@gsb.uchicago.edu.

ZIEGLER, JAMES RUSSELL, computer consultant; b. Warren, Pa., Oct. 10, 1922; s. LeRoy Curtis and Daisy (Gesin) Z.; m. Maxine Evelym Hogue, Feb. 10, 1952 (dec. Nov. 1968); children: Evalinde Aurelia, Charlotte Elaine, Curtis Wayman, Bruce Allan; m. Florence M. Bowler, 1969 (div. 1975); 1 child, Scott. BSEE, Pa. State U., 1943, MA in Math., 1948. UHF wave guide rsch. Norden Corp., N.Y.C., 1943-44; instr. math. Pa. State coll., 1946-48, U. Calif., L.A., 1948-54; rsch. assoc. statistician tchrs. characteristics study Am. Coun. Edn., 1951-54; mgr. programming svcs., electronic computers Nat. Cash Register Co., Hawthorne, Calif., 1954-68; pres. Turn-Key Computer Applications, 1968-75; dir. So. Fed. Savs. & Loan Assn., L.A., 1968-69; adv. dir. Coast Fed. Savs. & Loan Assn., L.A., 1969-74; sr. cons. analyst NCR Co., San Diego, 1975-78, San Diego Cash Register Co., 1978-80. Computer cons. Yemen Arab Rep. Nat. Water and Sewerage Authority, 1980-87; tech. cons. Office Naval Rsch. Study; data processing cons. psychol. rsch. projects U. So. Calif., also U. Utah. Author: Time Sharing Data Processing Systems, 1967; contbr. articles to profl. jours. With USMCR, 1944-46; PTO. Mem. Masons, Tau Beta Pi, Sigma Tau, Eta Kappa Nu. Republican. Methodist. Home: 1050 Pinecrest Ave Escondido CA 92025-3853

ZIEGLER, JOHN ALAN, historian, political scientist, educator; b. Belleville, Ill., Jan. 28, 1933; s. John Wendell and Georgia Elizabeth (Reppel) Z.; m. Carol Ruth Alcorn, June 15, 1963; children: Mimi, Robin. BS, So. Ill. U., 1955, MS, 1956; Rotary Found. fellow, St. Andrews (Scotland) U., 1956-57; PhD, Syracuse U., 1970. Asst. prof. polit. sci. and social sci. Calif. State U., Hayward, 1966-72; lectr. Am. civilization Calif. State Poly. U., Pomona, 1972-74; assoc. prof. polit. sci. Hendrix Coll., Conway, Ark., 1974-84, prof., 1984-91, Harold and Lucy Cabe Disting. prof. history and politics, 1991-98, emeritus prof., 1998—, legendary lectr., 1998. Coord. and founder Hendrix-Oxford program, 1979-98, head social sci. area, 1978-82, chmn. dept. polit. sci. and history, 1974-83; guest lectr. St. Peter's Coll., Oxford U., 1983, 90, 94, Clare Coll., Cambridge U., 1988, 89, Dundee U., 1994; Churchill life fellow Westminster Coll., Fulton, Mo.; participant Wilton Pk. Confs., Wiston House Internat. Conf. Ctr., Sussex, England, 1979—. Author: Experimentalism and Institutional Change, In Search of the Special Relationship with Britain. With AUS, 1957-60. Mem. AAUP, Friends Churchill Meml. (life), Am. Friends Wilton Park, ACLU, Royal Oak Found., Soc. Sussex Downsmen (life), Dundee (Scotland) Curling Club. Mem. United Ch. of Christ. Home: PO Box 1045 Conway AR 72033-1045 Office: Hendrix Coll Conway AR 72032 E-mail: johnziegler@webtv.net.

ZIEGLER, JOHN AUGUSTUS, JR., lawyer; b. Grosse Pointe, Mich., Feb. 9, 1934; s. John Augustus and Monnabell M. Ziegler; m. G. Kay Brubeck; children: John Augustus III, Laura, Lisa, Adeline. AB, U. Mich., JD, 1957. Bar: Mich. 1957. Since practiced in, Detroit; assoc. Dickinson, Wright, McKean & Cudlip, 1957-65, ptnr., 1965-68, Parsons, Tennent, Hammond, Hardig & Ziegelman, 1969-70, Ziegler, Dykhouse & Wise, 1970-77; pres., CEO Nat. Hockey League, 1977-92, chmn. bd. govs., 1976-78; of counsel Dickinson, Wright, PLLC, Bloomfield Hills, 1992—99. Office: 375 Park Ave Ste 2004 New York NY 10152-2099

ZIEGLER, R. W., JR., lawyer, consultant; b. Pitts. children: Caroline, Gretchen, Jeremy, Benjamin, Phoebe, Polly. Student, Carnegie Tech., U. Pitts.; JD, Duquesne U., 1972. Bar: Pa. 1972, Calif. 1981, U.S. Ct. Appeals (3d cir.) 1977, U.S. Dist. Ct. (we. dist.) Pa. 1972, U.S. Supreme Ct. 1977, U.S. Tax Ct. 1978, Calif. 1982, U.S. Dist. Ct. (no. dist.) Calif. 1982, U.S. Ct. Appeals (9th cir.) 1982. Ptnr. Ziegler & Ombres, Pitts., 1973-79; pres. Ziegler Ross Inc., San Francisco, 1979—. Lectr. for Bar Assns. Author: Law Practice Management; editor: Law Office Guide in Computing. Mem. ABA, Am. Mgmt. Assn., Pa. State Bar Assn., Calif. State Bar Assn., Assn. of Legal Admin., Young Presidents' Org., Am. Assn. of Law Librarians., San Francisco Bar Assn. Office: 220 Montgomery St Ste 900 San Francisco CA 94104-5413 Office Phone: 415-732-0300.

ZIEGLER, RICHARD FERDINAND, lawyer; b. Elizabeth, N.J., Aug. 1, 1949; m. Carolyn Lewis; children: Anna B., David A., Andrew P. D-J. BA in History summa cum laude, Yale u., 1971; JD magna cum laude, Harvard U., 1975. Bar: N.Y. 1976, U.S. Dist. Ct. (so. and ea. dists.) N.Y. 1976, U.S. Dist. Ct. (ea. dist.) Mich. 1982, U.S. Supreme Ct. 1984, U.S. Dist. Ct. (no. dist.) N.Y. 1987. Law clk. to judge U.S. Dist. Ct. (so. dist.), N.Y.C., 1975-76; assoc. Paul, Weiss, Rifkind, Wharton & Garrison, N.Y.C., 1976-77; asst. U.S. atty. U.S. Dept. Justice (so. dist.) N.Y., N.Y.C., 1977-80; assoc. Cleary, Gottlieb, Steen & Hamilton, N.Y.C., 1980-83, ptnr., 1983—2002; sr. v.p. legal affairs, gen. counsel 3M Co., St. Paul, 2003—. Lectr. law Columbia Law Sch., 1997—. Mem. ABA, Assn. Bar City of N.Y., Fed. Bar Coun., N.Y. State Bar Assn. (chmn. com. on profl. ethics, 1995-98). Office: 3M Ctr PO Box 33428 Saint Paul MN 55133-3428*

ZIEGLER, RICHARD J. dean, educator; BS in biology, Muhlenberg Coll., 1965; PhD in microbiology, Temple U., 1970. Rsch. assoc. in microbiology Rockefeller U., 1970—71; asst. prof. microbiology U. Minn.-Duluth, 1971—77, assoc. prof. microbiology, 1977—89; prof. microbiology Sch. Medicine, U. Minn.-Duluth, 1989—, interim dean, 1997—98, dean, 1998—. Recipient James H. Sova award, Minn. Med. Found., 2000. Office: UMD Sch Medicine 1035 Univ Dr Duluth MN 55812 Business E-Mail: rziegler@d.umn.edu.

ZIEGLER, ROBERT OLIVER, retired music and special education educator; b. Cullman, Ala., Sept. 6, 1939; s. Mary Catherine (Taylor) McDonald; adopted Edgar and Kathryn Ziegler; m. Gladys L. Friese, May 3, 1962 (div. Jan. 1970); children: Robert, Edgar, Lesha, Kathy. BS, U. Ala., Tuscaloosa, 1961, MA, 1964, PhD, 1970. Cert. spl. edn. tchr., sch. counselor, music tchr., Ga. Band dir. Phillips Jr. H.S., Mobile, Ala., 1961-62, Wiggins (Colo.) H.S., 1962-63, Eastwood Jr. H.S., Tuscaloosa, 1963-65, McAdory H.S., McCalla, Ala., 1966-70, Calera (Ala.) H.S., 1971-72; prof. music edn. Tift Coll., Forsyth, Ga., 1972-78; jr. H.S. counselor Clayton County Schs., Jonesboro, Ga., 1978-80; elem. sch. counselor Rockdale County Schs., Conyers, Ga., 1980-82; spl. edn. tchr. Henderson Jr. H.S., Jackson, Ga., 1982-87, Clayton County Schs., Jonesboro, Ga., 1987-92, gen. music tchr., 1996-99; spl. edn. tchr. City Schs. of Decatur, Ga., 1992-96; elem. sch. music tchr. Clayton County Schs., 1996-99. Clarinetist Mobile (Ala.) Symphony Orch., 1961-62; vis. lectr. Stillman Coll., Tuscaloosa, Ala., 1970-71; prof. grad. sch. Mercer U., Macon, 1972-74; vis. lectr. in music Wesleyan Coll., Macon, Ga., 1975-76; acting head music dept. Tift Coll., Forsyth, Ga., 1976-77; curriculum cons. South Metro Psychoedul. Ctr., Atlanta City Schs., 1989. Contbr. articles to profl. publs. Minister of music, choir dir. United Meth. Ch., 1961-90, lay leader, 1989-94; mem. South Metro Concert Band, Morrow, Ga., 1978—, Tara Wind Band, Jonesboro, Ga., 1987-88. Recipient Cert. of Appreciation United Meth. Ch., 1990, Spl. Mission Recognition award United Meth. Women, 1983; U. Ala. grantee, 1960-61 Mem. Profl. Assn. Ga. Educators (bldg. rep. 1994-96), Soc. for Preservation and Encouragement of Barber Shop Quartet Singing in Am. (founding mem., co-dir. Fayetteville chpt. 1990, co-founder, 1st dir. So. Crescent Chorus 2001). Avocations: tennis, ragtime piano playing, singing gospel music. Home: 9228 Overlook Dr Tampa FL 33617-5422 E-mail: bobmzieg@aol.com.

ZIEGLER, STEVE, health care services/centers executive; CPA. Acct. Pearlman, Nebben & Assocs.; regional controller, reimbursement mgr. Life Care Ctrs. of Am., Cleveland, Tenn., v.p., CFO, 1996—. Office: Life Care Ctrs of Am PO Box 3480 Cleveland TN 37320-3480

ZIEGLER, WILLIAM, III, diversified industry executive; b. N.Y.C., June 26, 1928; s. William and Helen (Murphy) Z.; m. Jane Elizabeth Troy, Feb. 22, 1952; children: Melissa Jane, William Troy, Peter Martin, Cynthia Curtis, Helen Matilda, Karl Huttig. BA, Harvard U., 1950; MBA, Columbia U., 1962. Chmn. bd., dir. Swisher Internat. Group, 1966—; pres. Hay Island Holding Corp., Darien, Conn., 1995—. Pres. E. Matilda Ziegler Found. for Blind; v.p. Matilda Ziegler Pub. Co. for Blind; trustee Maritime Aquarium, Norwalk, Conn.; mem. adv. bd. Yale Eye Ctr. Lt. comdr. USNR, 1952-54. Mem. N.Y. Yacht Club, Noroton (Conn.) Yacht Club. Home: 161 Long Neck Point Rd Darien CT 06820-5815 Office: Swisher Internat Group 20 Thorndal Cir Darien CT 06820-5421

ZIEGLER, WILLIAM ALEXANDER, lawyer; b. N.Y.C., July 15, 1924; s. William Alexander and Sally (Cootes) Z.; m. Glenn Crawley, Feb. 10, 1950; children: Richard S., Daryl A. Henning, Susan G. Barrows, W. Thomas. AB, Harvard U., 1944, JD, 1949. Bar: N.Y. 1949, U.S. Tax Ct. 1950, U.S. Dist. Ct. (so. dist.) N.Y. 1949, U.S. Dist. Ct. (ea. dist.) N.Y. 1957, U.S. Dist. Ct. (no. dist.) Ohio 1973, U.S. Dist. Ct. (ea. dist.) Mich. 1983, U.S. Ct. Apppeals (1st cir.) 1963, U.S. Ct. Appeals (2d cir.) 1957, U.S. Ct. Appeals (3d cir.) 1986, U.S. Ct. Appeals (4th cir.) 1979, U.S. Ct. Appeals (5th cir.) 1987, U.S. Ct. Appeals (6th cir.) 1984, U.S. Ct. Appeals (7th cir.) 1992, U.S. Ct. Appeals (8th cir.) 1981, U.S. Ct. Appeals (9th cir.) 1973, U.S. Ct. Appeals (10th and 11th cirs.) 1983, U.S. Ct. Appeals (D.C. cir.) 1972, U.S. Supreme Ct. 1972. Assoc. Sullivan & Cromwell, N.Y.C., 1949-56, ptnr., 1957-89. Bd. dirs. Std. Comml. Corp. Bd. dirs. Wilton (Conn.) Land Conservation Trust. Mem. Assn. Bar City N.Y., Riverside Country Club (Mont.), Harvard Club of N.Y.C., Harvard Club of Fairfield Country (bd. dirs.), Harvard Club Mont.

ZIEHLER, TONY JOSEPH, insurance agent; b. Anderson, Ind., June 20, 1936; s. Joseph Anthony and Julie Ann (Kette) Z.; m. Alice Mae Pattison, Apr. 2, 1956 (div. 1972); children: Susan Z. Brown, Kathryn Z. Dwyer, Jane Z. Bee, Patricia Z. Koty, Michael; m. Barbara Buys Wood, Feb. 28, 1981; stepchildren: David Wayne Wood, Brent Douglas Wood. BSBA, U. Ariz., 1958. CLU. Prin. mng. ptnr. Ziehler Ins. Group, LLC, Tucson, 1958—. Mem. Fed. Jud. Magistrate Selection Com., 1998—. Employee edn. chmn. So. Ariz. Div. Am. Cancer Soc.; co-chmn. Medic-Alert Found., Pima County, Ariz.; chmn. Tucson Festival Soc.; mem. Salpointe High Sch. Found., others. Recipient William Wisdom award U. Ariz., Tucson, 1958. Mem. Greater Tucson Assn. Life Underwriters (pres. 1963-64, Agt. of Yr. 1975), Ariz. Assn. Life Underwriters (pres. 1970-71, Agt. of Yr. 1980), So. Ariz. CLU Soc. (pres. 1968-69), Salvation Army (pres. adv. bd. 1984-85), Univ. of Ariz. Found. (mem. planned giving com.), Rotary, (com. chmn.), Tucson Conquistadores (pres. 1985-86), Los Charros del Desierto, Golden Key Soc., MIllion Dollar

Round Table, Tucson Country Club, others. Republican. Avocations: travel, trail riding, belgian draft horses, mountain hiking, sports. Home: 8741 E Woodland Rd Tucson AZ 85749-9575 Office: 6992 E Broadway Blvd Tucson AZ 85710-2803

ZIELINSKI, MELISSA L. museum director; BS, Coll. William an Mary, 1978; MS, N.C. State U., 1983. Park svc. ranger, interpreter Cape Hatteras Nat. Seashore, Buxton, N.C., 1980, 81; exhibits intern N.C. Mus. Natural Scis., Raleigh, 1980-81, 81-82, asst. curator pub. programs, 1984-92; vol. svcs. coord. N.C. State U., 1981-82, 82-83, lab. instr. vertebrate zoology lab., 1983; naturalist Durant Nature Park Raleigh (N.C.) Parks and Recreation Dept., 1983-84; mus. educator Humboldt State U. Natural History Mus., Arcata, Calif., 1992-93, dir., 1993—. Co-author, editor, illustrator vertebrate zoology lab. text, 1983-84. Sch. edn. program dir. Friends of the Dunes The Nature Conservancy, Arcata, Calif., 1993-94, mem. Mem. Am. Mus. Natural History, Nat. Assn. Interpretation, Nat. Marine Educators Assn., Guild of Natural Sci. Illustrators, Nat. Audubon Soc. Home: 1363 Mill Creek Rd Mckinleyville CA 95519-4448 Office: Humboldt State U Natural History Mus 1315 G St Arcata CA 95521-5820

ZIELINSKI, PAUL BERNARD, grant program administrator, civil engineer; b. West Allis, Wis., Sept. 9, 1932; s. Stanley Charles and Lottie Charlotte (Pliszkiewicz) Z.; m. Monica Theresa Beres, July 13, 1957; children: Daniel Paul, Gregory John, Robert Mathias, Sarah Ann. BSCE, Marquette U., 1956; MS, U. Wis., 1961, PhD, 1965. Registered profl. engr., Wis., S.C. Asst. instr. engrng. mechanics Marquette U., Milw., 1956-59, asst. prof., 1964-67; instr. civil engrng. U. Wis., Madison, 1959-64; from asst. prof. to prof. Clemson (S.C.) U., 1967-78, prof. environ. and systems engrng., 1978-82, prof. civil engrng., 1982-90, prof. emeritus, 1991—; dir. S.C. Water Resources Rsch. Inst., Clemson, 1978-90; assoc. dir. associateship grant program Nat. Rsch. Coun., Washington, 1990—. Cons. Am. Pub. Works Assn., Chgo., 1973-76, Nat. Coun. Examiners of Engrng. and Surveying, Clemson, 1973—; cons. swirl devices for storm water separation; com. on exams for profl. engrs. Author numerous publs. on hydraulics and water resources rsch. Chmn. Clemson City Planning Commn., 1971-74; ex-officio mem. S.C. Water Resources Commn., Columbia, 1978-90. Mem. ASCE, Sigma Xi. Roman Catholic. Home: 2111 Wisconsin Ave NW Apt 717 Washington DC 20007-2278 Office: Nat Rsch Coun 500 Fifth St NW GR322 Washington DC 20001 Office Phone: 202-334-3196.

ZIEMAN, MARK, newspaper editor; b. El Dorado, Kan., Jan. 17, 1945; m. Kristi Zieman (div.); children: Glynnis, Gracie. Degree in Journalism, Kans. U., 1983. Mem. staff Houston bur. The Wall St. Jour., 1984—86; columnist Kans. City (Mo.) Star, 1986—89, editor projects desk, 1989—92, mng. editor, 1992—97, v.p, editor, 1997—. Recipient Pulitzer prize, 1992. Office: The Kansas City Star 1729 Grand Blvd Kansas City MO 64108-1458

ZIEMBA, KAREN, actress; Appeared in Broadway plays A Chorus Line, 42nd Street, Crazy for You, Chicago, Never Gonna Dance (Tony nom. best featured actress in a play, 2004), Contact (Tony award); (off-Broadway) And the World Goes 'Round (Drama Desk award) I Do! I Do!; (musical) Steel Pier (Tony award nominee); (tour) Crazy for You (Joseph Jefferson award), Chicago (1998-99); (regional play) Much Ado About Nothing, House and Garden, The Foreigner, Fifth of July; (opera) The Most Happy Fella, 110 in the Shade; singer Allegro, Grand Night for Singing; (TV show) Sondheim: A Celebration at Carnegie Hall, Evening at Pops, My Favorite Broadway: The Leading Ladies, Law and Order; album recs. include And the World Goes 'Round, Fifty Million Frenchmen, Lost in Boston II, Shakespeare on Broadway, 110 In The Shade, The Most Happy FElla, Ziegfeld Follies of 1936.

ZIEMER, JAMES L. automotive executive; BBA, MBA, U. Wis., Milw. With Harley-Davidson, Inc., Milw., 1972—, v.p., contr., CFO, 1987—. Office: Harley-Davidson Inc PO Box 653 3700 W Juneau Ave Milwaukee WI 53201-0653

ZIEMER, RODGER EDMUND, electrical engineering educator, consultant; b. Sargeant, Minn., Aug. 22, 1937; s. Arnold Edmund and Ruth Ann (Rush) Z.; m. Sandra Lorann Person, June 23, 1960; children: Mark Edmund, Amy Lorann, Norma Jean, Sandra Lynn. BS, U. Minn., 1960, MS, 1962, PhD, 1965. Registered profl. engr., Mo. Research asst. U. Minn., Mpls., 1960-62, research assoc., 1962; prof. elec. engring. U. Mo., Rolla, 1968-83, U. Colo., Colorado Springs, 1984—, chmn. dept. elec. engring., 1984-93; program dir. comms. rsch. NSF, 1998-2001. Cons. Emerson Electric Co., St. Louis, 1972-84, Mid-Am. Regional Coun., Kansas City, Mo., 1974, Motorola, Inc., Scottsdale, Ariz., 1980-84, Martin Marietta, Orlando, 1980-81, TRW, Colorado Springs, summer, 1985, Sperry, Phoenix, 1986, Pericle Communications, summer, 1994, Motorola, Schaumburg, 1995, Scottsdale, 1996, Arlington Heights, 1997. Author: Principles of Communications, 1976, Principles of Communications, 2d edit., 1985, Principles of Communications, 3d edit., 1990, Principles of Communications, 4th edit., 1995, Principles of Communications, 5th edit., 2002, Signals and Systems, 1983, Signals and Systems, 2d edit., 1989, Signals and Systems, 3d edit., 1993, Signals and Systems, 4th edit., 1998, Digital Communications and Spread Spectrum Systems, 1985, Introduction to Digital Communication, 1992, Introduction to Digital Communication, 2d edit., 2001, Introduction to Spread Spectrum Communications, 1995, Elements of Engineering Probability and Statistics, 1997; editor: IEEE Jour. on Selected Areas in Comms., 1989, 1992, 1995, IEEE Comm. Mag., 1991. Served to capt. USAF, 1965-68. Scholar Western Electric, 1957-59; trainee NASA, 1962-65 Fellow IEEE (life; Third Millenium award 2000); mem. Am. Soc. Engring. Edn., Armed Forces Comms. and Electronics Assn., Sigma Xi, Tau Beta Pi, Eta Kappa Nu. Lutheran. Home: 8315 Pilot Ct Colorado Springs CO 80920-4412 Office: Univ Colo PO Box 7150 Colorado Springs CO 80933-7150 Office Phone: 719-262-3350. E-mail: ziemer@eas.uccs.edu.

ZIEMSKI, CONNIE MARIE, social studies educator; b. Endicott, NY, May 2, 1966; d. Paul Quentin and Mary Ellen Burgess; m. James Ziemski, June 19, 1997; children: Eileen Mary Kennedy, Colleen Ann Kennedy, Shannon Maureen Kennedy. BS in secondary edn., Lock Haven U., 1984—89; student, SUNY Binghamton, 2002—; MA in History. Tchr. Harpursville Ctrl. Schools, NY, 2000—. Mem. Libertarian Party, 2001—02. Libertarian. Roman Catholic. Home: 33 Kabanek Rd Binghamton NY 13903

ZIENTEK, LINDA REICHWEIN, mathematician, educator; b. Houston, Oct. 31, 1965; d. Kenneth John and Harriet Kay Reichwein; m. Gilbert Zientek, July 30, 1984; children: Jason Wayne, Jacob John, Jenna Marie. BS in Math., Sam Houston State U., 1995, MS in Math., 1997; postgrad., Tex. A&M U. Math. instr. Blinn Coll., Brenham, Tex., 1997—. Mem.: Math Assn. of Am. (assoc.), Tex. Math. Assn. Two Yr. Colls. (pres.), Tex. C.C. Tchrs. Assn. (sec. 2002, chair math. sect. 2004). Home: 5420 Larkspur Ln Chappell Hill TX 77426 Office: Blinn College 902 College Ave Brenham TX 77833 Office Phone: 979-830-4437. Personal E-mail: zientek@alpha1.net. E-mail: lzientek@blinn.edu.

ZIERDT, CHARLES HENRY, microbiologist; b. Pitts., Apr. 24, 1922; s. Conrad Henry and Nancy Leora (Harshberger) Zierdt; m. Margaret May Wise, June 1, 1942 (div. 1962); children: Charles Henry Jr., Carolyn, Douglas, Richard; m. Willadene Smith, Sept. 30, 1967. BS, Pa. State U., 1943; MS, U. Mich., 1945; PhD, George Washington U., 1967. Rsch. assoc. Parke-Davis & Co., Detroit, 1945—48; microbiologist Henry Ford Hosp., Detroit, 1948—53, USPHS, Detroit, 1953—56; rsch. microbiologist NIH, Bethesda, Md., 1956—. Scientist sponsor U. Md., 1975—; instr. Found. Advanced Edn. Scis., Bethesda, Md., 1978—. Author: Glucose Nonfermenting Gram Negative Bacteria in Clinical Microbiology, 1978, Non-fermentative Gram Negative Rods: Laboratory Identification and Clinical Aspects, 1985, McGraw-Hill Yearbook of Science and Technology, 1986, Diagnostic Procedures for Bacterial Infections, 1987; contbr. articles to profl. jours. Fellow: Am. Acad. Microbiology; mem.: Mensa, Avanti Owners Assn. Internat., U.S. Fedn. Culture Collections (membership chmn. 1985), Am. Soc. Microbiology (chpt. pres. 1976), Antique Auto Club Am. (pres. Sugar Loaf Mountain region 1997), Model T Ford Club Internat., Model A Ford Club Am. (Fairfax, Va. chpt. pres. 1985), Sigma Xi. Achievements include the classification and pathogenesis of Blastocystis Hominis, an intestinal protozoan parasite of man. Avocations: gardening, antique car restoration, church historian. Home: 4100 Norbeck Rd Rockville MD 20853-1869 Office: NIH Bethesda MD 20816 Office Phone: 301-496-4433.

ZIERDT, JOHN GRAHAM, JR., transportation company executive; b. Warner Robins, Ga., July 22, 1943; s. John Graham and Elizabeth (Matthews) Z.; m. Regina Astor, June 18, 1966; children: John III, Karen, Michael. BS in Engring., U.S. Mil. Acad., 1966; MS in Engring., Ariz. State U., 1972. Commd. 2d lt. U.S. Army, 1966, advanced through grades to brig. gen., 1991, battalion comdr. 702d Maintenance Battalion, 1984-85, brigade comdr. 46th Support Group Ft. Bragg, N.C., 1988-89, comdg. gen. 1st Corps Support Command, 1989-91, dir. logistics U.S. Army Forces Command Atlanta, 1991-95, ret., 1995; pres., CEO TransCor Am., Inc., Nashville, 1995—. Author: Acquisition Management: The Role and The Reality, 1987. Decorated Legion of Merit with 2 oak leaf clusters, Bronze Star with oak leaf cluster, Disting. Svc. medal; Nat. security fellow Kennedy Sch. Govt., Harvard U., 1986-87. Republican. Roman Catholic. Home: 516 Midway Cir Brentwood TN 37027-5179 Office: TransCor Am Inc 646 Melrose Ave Nashville TN 37211-2161

ZIERING, CRAIG L. osteopath; b. 1960; DO, Southeastern U. Health Scis., Miami Beach, Fla. Diplomate Am. Bd. Dermatology, Am. Bd. Hair Restoration Surgery, lic. physician Fla., N.Y., Ohio, Ill., Mich., Pa. Clin. dir. Advanced Laser Ctrs.; founder, med. dir. Ziering Med., L.A. Resident in dermatology Ohio U./Grandview Med. Ctr. Mem.: Am. Osteo. Coll. of Dermatology (exec. bd. pres. 1999), Am. Soc. Hair Transplant Surgeons (charter), N.Am. Soc. Phlebology, Am. Soc. for Laser Medicine and Surgery, World Hair Soc., Am. Osteo. Assn., N.Am. Acad. Cosmetic and Restorative Surgery, Am. Acad. Dermatology, Am. Acad. Facial, Plastic and Reconstructive Surgery, Am. Soc. Dermatologic Surgery, Am. Acad. Cosmetic Surgery, Internat. Soc. Hair Restoration Surgery, Am. Hair Loss Coun. Office: Ziering Medical 8500 Wilshire Blvd #1010 Los Angeles CA 90211

ZIERING, MICHAEL, medical products executive; b. 1957; V.p. adminstrn. Diagnostic Products Corp., pres., dir., COO, 1994-99, pres., COO, CEO, 1999—. Office: Diagnostic Products Corp 5700 W 96th St Los Angeles CA 90045-5544

ZIERING, WILLIAM MARK, lawyer; b. New Britain, Conn., Feb. 4, 1931; s. Jacob Max and Esther (Freedman) Z.; m. Harriet Koskoff, Aug. 20, 1958 (div. Sept. 1993); 1 son, Benjamin. BA, Yale U., 1952; JD, Harvard U., 1955. Bar: Conn. 1955, Calif. 1962. Assoc. Koskoff & McMahon, Plainville, Conn., 1959-60; sr. trial atty. SEC, San Francisco, 1960-65; pvt. practice law San Francisco, 1965—; ptnr. Bremer & Ziering, 1972-77. Instr. Golden Gate U. Law Sch., San Francisco, 1968-75 Vice pres., bd. dirs. Calif. League Handicapped, 1972— . Served to comdr. USNR, 1955-58. Mem. ABA, Calif. Bar Assn., San Francisco Bar Assn. (past chmn. securities, corps. and banking), Navy League (dir.) Clubs: Commonwealth. Home: 440 Davis Ct Apt 620 San Francisco CA 94111-2418 E-mail: wmziering@sbcglobal.net.

ZIERLER, NEAL, retired mathematician; b. Balt., Sept. 17, 1926; children: Robert Eugene, Joan Mariye, Ann M. AB, Johns Hopkins U., 1945; AM, Harvard U., 1949, PhD, 1959. Mathematician, physicist Ballistic Rsch. Labs., Aberdeen, Md., 1951; mem. tech. staff instrumentation lab. MIT, Cambridge, Mass., 1952-54, mem. tech. staff Lincoln Lab. Lexington, Mass., 1954-60; supr. info. processing group of jet propulsion lab. Calif. Inst. Tech., Pasadena, 1960-61; sr. scientist ARCON Corp., Lexington, 1961-62; head sub-dept. process analysis MITRE Corp., Bedford, Mass., 1962-65; tech. staff Ctr. for Comm. Rsch. Inst. Def. Analysis, Princeton, N.J., 1965-96. Patentee error-detecting and -correcting devices; contbr. articles to profl. jours. Lt. USN, 1944-46. Fellow IEEE; mem. Am. Math. Soc., Math. Assn. Am., Am. Physics Soc. Avocations: tennis, skiing, photography. E-mail: nzierler@ieee.org.

ZIESE, DENNIS RUSSELL, protective services official, retired military officer; b. Bklyn., Jan. 18, 1950; s. Russell Arthur and Joan Elizabeth Ziese; m. Kazuko Katashi, Apr. 23, 1971 (div. June 1985); children: Diane, John, Kathy; m. Linda Nell Pohl, May 18, 1999; children: Eric Pohl, Evan Pohl. AS, Columbia Coll., 1992, BA, 1993; MA, Lincoln U., 1996. Master sgt. USMC, Washington, 1967—89, served in Vietnam, ret., 1989; functional unit mgr. Mo. Dept. Corrections, Jefferson City, 1990—. Decorated Vietnam Cross of Galantry, Combat Action medal USMC, Naval Commendation medal with combat V; recipient Conspicuous Svc. medal, State of NY, 1973. Mem.: VFW, USMC League, KC. Republican. Roman Catholic. Avocations: golf, fishing, hunting, reading.

ZIESE, NANCYLEE HANSON, social worker; m. J. A. Ziese; 1 child, G. Graham. BA in Sociology, Morningside Coll., 1960; MSW, U. Iowa, 1982, cert. in aging studies, 1986; EFM, U. of the South, 1996. Social worker Florence Crittenton Home, Sioux City, 1960-65, L.A. County, 1965; social worker, supr. Polk County Dept. Social Welfare, Des Moines, 1966-69; social worker, community liaison Tommy Dale Meml., Sioux City, Iowa, 1977-79; dir. internships Briar Cliff Coll., Sioux City, 1981-83; dir. continuing edn. Coe Coll., Cedar Rapids, Iowa, 1983-85; exec. dir. Profl. Women's Network, Cedar Rapids, 1985-87; pvt. practice counselor, consultant, speaker, writer Woman-place Counseling, Cedar Rapids, 1985-87, 99—; adoption coord. Hillcrest Family Svcs., Cedar Rapids, 1987-99. Bd. dirs. Young Parent's Network M.E.L.D., Cedar Rapids, pres., 1994—96; cons. cmty. improvement, recycling; spkr. in field; gov. apptd. mem. Iowa State Child Advocacy Bd., 2002—. Contbr. articles to newspapers. Steering bd. Iowa Women's Polit. Caucus, 1987—93, pres., 1992—93; dep. gen. conv. ECUSA, 1997—2003; past chair Iowa Birth Defects Inst. Adv. Com. Iowa Assn. Adoption Agys.; bd. dirs. Linn County Adolescent Pregnancy Prevention Coalition, treas., 1992—96; steering com. mem. ERA Iowa 1992, 1991—95; gov.'s com. Adoption Reform in Iowa, 1993—94; lt. gov.'s com. spl. needs Adoption in Iowa, 1994; bd. dirs., pub. policy chair AAUW, 1995—2002, pres., 2000—01; co-founder, pres. Iowa Breast Cancer Action, 1998—2000; mem. to chmn. Cedar Rapids Civil Rights Commn., 2000—04; cons. med. ethics com. for In-Vitro Fertilization Adoption Program, U. Iowa, 1995; bd. dirs. commn. mem. Human Needs, commn. on ministry Episcopal Diocese Iowa, 1996—99, standing com., 2000—; v.p. Sioux City Sch. Bd., 1978—83; bd. dirs., pres. Friends of Iowa Pub. TV, 1978—88; bd. dirs., pres. Family Svc. Boys and Girls Home, Sioux City, 1973—81; bd. dirs. Goodwill Industries S.E. Iowa, 2003—. Named Woman of Yr., Linn County, Cedar Rapids, 1995; recipient Outstanding Svc. awards, Sioux City C. of C., 1976, Siouxland Arts Coun., 1977. Mem.: Profl. Women's Network Cedar Rapids (bd. mem., Woman of Yr. 1997), NASW, Rotary Internat. Avocation: women's movement, human needs advocacy, reading. Home and Office: 1759 Applewood Pl NE Cedar Rapids IA 52402-3321 E-mail: znancylee@earthlink.net.

ZIESER, JOHN S. lawyer, publishing executive; m. Adele Zieser; children: John, Philip, Allison. BBA, MBA, U. Iowa; JD, Cornell U. With Sullivan & Cromwell; assoc. gen. counsel First Data Corp., 1993—99; group pres. First Data Mcht. Svcs. subs. First Data Corp.; v.p. corp. and employee svcs. group, gen. counsel Meredith Corp., Des Moines, 1999—, also sec. bd. dirs. Office: Meredith Corp 1716 Locust St Des Moines IA 50309-3023

ZIETLOW, RUTH ANN, reference librarian; b. Richland Center, Wis., Apr. 5, 1960; d. James Eldon and Dixie Ann (Doudna) Z.; m. David Robert Voigt, Aug. 22, 1992; children: Eleanor Ruth, Isabel Anna, Carl James. BA in English, U. Nebr., 1987; MA in Libr. Studies, U. Wis., 1990; cert. in info. sys., U. St. Thomas, St. Paul, 1995. English instr. Guangzhou (China) English Lang. Ctr. Zhongshan U., 1987-88; adminstrv. asst. Helm Group, Lincoln, Nebr., 1988-89; circulatio supr. Sch. Edn. U. Wis., Madison, 1990-91; libr. specialist St. Paul Pub. Libr., 1991-92; reference librarian coordinator extention library svcs. U. St. Thomas, 1991—. Author manual: Electronic Communication and Information Resources Manual, 1995. Mem. Minn. Libr. Assn. (chair Distance Learning Roundtable 1999-2000). Avocations: gardening, reading. Office: U St Thomas O'Shaughnessey-Frey Libr 2115 Summit Ave Saint Paul MN 55105-1048 E-mail: razietlow@stthomas.edu.

ZIETZ, JOACHIM, economics professor; b. Bergen, Fed. Republic Germany, Oct. 14, 1953; came to U.S., 1978; s. Werner and Gisela Zietz; m. Emily J. Norman, 1996; children: Michael, Olivia. Diplom-Volkswirt, U. Goettingen, Fed. Republic Germany, 1978; Dr. rer. pol., U. Goettingen, 1982. Rsch. asst. Internat. Food Policy Rsch. Inst., Washington, 1979-81; asst. prof. econs. U. Balt., 1981-85; rsch. fellow Kiel Inst. World Econs., Fed. Republic Germany, 1985-87; assoc. prof. U. Detroit, 1987-89; prof. dept. econs. and fin. Mid. Tenn. State U., Murfreesboro, 1989—. Cons. Internat. Food Policy Rsch. Inst., 1981-90, World Food Programme, Rome, 1983-84, World Bank, Washington, 1984, 93, Orgn. for Econ. Coop. and Devel., Paris, 1989. Editor: Jour. Econs. and Fin., 1999—2003. Mem. Am. Econ. Assn., Royal Econ. Soc., Acad. Econs. and Fin., So. Econ. Assn., Cosmos Club. Office: Mid Tenn State U Dept Econs and Fin PO Box 129 Murfreesboro TN 37132-0129 Office Phone: 615-898-5619. E-mail: jzietz@mtsu.edu.

ZIETZ, KARYL LYNN KOPELMAN, writer, opera critic, television correspondent, producer, documentary filmmaker; b. N.Y.C., Oct. 11, 1943; d. Bernard and Vera Jean (Wantman) Kopelman; m. Neil J. Stone, Aug. 16, 1970 (div. 1975); m. Joachim Zietz, July 19, 1978 (div. 1994). BA in Chemistry, U. Pa., 1965; MA in Film and Broadcast Journalism, Am. U., 1980; spl. cert., Goettinger U., Germany, 1976. Rschr. Columbia Coll. Physicians and Surgeons, N.Y.C., 1967-70, NIH, Bethesda, Md., 1971-72; producer, writer Am. Chem. Soc., Washington, 1976-78; prodr., rschr. Zweites Deutsches Fernsehen, Mainz, Germany, 1978-89; prodr. ORF-Austrian TV, 1980-84; prodr., reporter European Television Svc., Cologne, Germany, 1985-88; prodr., dir., corr. KOPE Prodns., Washington, 1985—. Lectr. Smithsonian Inst., Arts Club, Chautauqua Instn., 1998, Italian Cultural Soc., 1999, Balt. Opera Guild, 2000, Italian Cultural Inst. (part of Italian Embassy), Washington, 2002, Italian Opera House Lectr. Series, Washington, 2003; site reporter NEA, 1994—95. Author: Opera! Guide to Western Europe's Great Houses, 1991, Eastern Europe's and USSR's Great Opera Houses, 1992, Opera-Going in South America, 1993, Opera Companies and Houses of the United States: A Comprehensive, Illustrated Reference, 1994, The National Trust Guide to Great Opera Houses in America, 1996, Italian Opera Directory, 1998, Opera Companies and Houses of Western Europe, Canada, Australia, New Zealand: A Comprehensive Illustrated Reference, 1999, Breve Storia dei Teatri d'Opera Italiani, 2001; prodr. (video) An Amish Portrait for USIA; prodr., dir., writer, interviewer documentary films; opera critic, contbr. articles to Opera Now, Orpheus Oper Internat., Toronto Globe and Mail, Opera News, Musica and Arte: Quaderno del Museo Teatrale alla Scala, Opera-Opera. Mem. Music Critics Assn., Coun. Internat. Nontheatrical Events, Internat. Platform Assn., Am. Women in Radio and TV, Author's Guild, Assn. Ind. Video and Filmakers, Washington Ind. Writers, Contemporary Authors, Cosmos Club. Avocations: sailing, jogging, bicycling, tennis, foreign languages. Office: KOPE Prodns Palisades Sta PO Box 40103 Washington DC 20016-0103 Personal E-mail: rifiuti4u@aol.com.

ZIFCHAK, WILLIAM C. lawyer; b. 1948; BA, Harvard U., 1970; JD, Columbia U., 1973. Bar: N.Y. 1974, U.S. Ct. Appeals (2d cir.) 1975, U.S. Ct. Appeals (3d cir., D.C. cir.) 1983, U.S. Dist. Ct. (so. dist.) N.Y. 1984. Ptnr., co-chair labor and employment law dept. Kaye, Scholer, Fierman, Hays & Handler, N.Y.C. Planning com. NYU Ann. Nat. Conf. Labor, 1991-97. Contbr. articles to profl. jours. Mem. ABA (sect. labor and employment law 1975—, subcom. antitrust, RICO and labor rels. law), Assn. Bar City of N.Y. (sec. com. labor and employment law 1984-87), N.Y. State Bar (comml.-fed. litig. sect. co-chair labor and employment law com. 1995-97). Office: Kaye Scholer LLP 425 Park Ave New York NY 10022-3506

ZIFF, LARZER, English language educator; b. Holyoke, Mass., Oct. 2, 1927; s. Isadore Menden and Sara (Rosenbloom) Z.; m. Ruth Rosalind Geisenberger; children— Joshua, Oliver, Joel, Abigail. Student, Middlebury Coll., 1945-47; MA, U. Chgo., 1951, PhD, 1955; MA (hon.), U. Oxford, Eng., U. Pa. Prof. English U. Calif., Berkeley, 1956-73; univ. lectr. Oxford U., Eng., 1973-78; prof. English U. Pa., 1978-81; Caroline Donovan prof. English Johns Hopkins U., Balt., 1981—, chair dept., 1991-95. Dir. U. Calif. Edn. Abroad Program, U.K., Ireland, 1969-71; cons. and lectr. in field. Author: The Career of John Cotton, 1962; The American 1890's, 1968; Puritanism in America, 1973; Literary Democracy, 1981; Writing in the New Nation, 1991, Return Passages, 2000, Mark Twain: Life and Legacy, 2004; also articles, essays in profl. jours.; mem. editl. bds. including ELH, 1981—94. Recipient numerous awards for excellence in English including Christian Gauss award, the American 1890's, 1967; Fulbright fellow, 1959-60, fellow Am. Coun. Learned Socs., 1963-64, Newberry Libr., 1964, NEH, 1967-68, Guggenheim fellow, 1977-78, Woodrow Wilson Internat. Ctr. for Scholars, 1986-87; Fulbright Disting. Sr. Lectr., 1993. Fellow Am. Acad. Arts and Scis., Soc. Am. Historians; mem. MLA, Am. Antiquarian Soc. Office: Johns Hopkins U Dept English Baltimore MD 21218 E-mail: lziff@attglobal.net.

ZIFFREN, KENNETH, lawyer; b. Chgo., June 24, 1940; BA, Northwestern U., 1962; JD, UCLA, 1965. Bar: Calif. 1967. Law clerk to Chief Justice Warren, 1965—66; ptnr. Ziffren, Brittenham, Branca & Fischer, L.A. Mem.: ABA, L.A. Copyright Soc., Beverly Hills Bar Assn., L.A. County Bar Assn. (pres. 1977—78), State Bar Calif. Office: Ziffren Brittenham Branca & Fischer 1801 Century Park W Los Angeles CA 90067-6406

ZIGLAR, JAMES W. federal agency administrator, investment banker, lawyer, educator; b. Pascagoula, Miss., Dec. 8, 1945; married; 3 children. BA, George Washington U., 1968, JD, 1972. Bar: Va. 1972, D.C. 1973, N.Y. 1975, Ariz. 1977. Staff asst. Senator James Eastland, Washington, 1964-71; spl. asst. Dept. of Justice, Washington, 1971-72; law clk. to assoc. justice Harry Blackmun U.S. Supreme Ct., Washington, 1972-73; assoc. Mudge, Rose, Guthrie et al, N.Y.C., 1973-77; ptnr. O'Connor, Cavanagh, Anderson et al, Phoenix, 1977-80; sr. v.p. Dillon, Read & Co., N.Y.C., 1980-84; mng. dir. Paine Webber, Inc., Washington, 1984—87, 1990—98; asst. sec. Dept. of Interior, Washington, 1987-88; mng. dir. Drexel Burnham Lambert Inc., N.Y.C., 1989-90; sgt. at arms U.S. Senate, Washington, 1998—2001; commr. immigration and naturalization serv. U.S. Dept. Justice, Washington, 2001—02; resident fellow Inst. of Politics Harvard U., Cambridge, Mass., 2003. Disting. vis. prof. Law Sch. George Washington U., 2003—. Office: 2000 H St NW Washington DC 20052

ZIGLER, EDWARD FRANK, psychologist, educator; b. Kansas City, Mo., Mar. 1, 1930; s. Louis and Gertrude (Gleitman) Z.; m. Bernice Gorelick, Aug. 28, 1955; 1 child, Scott. BA, U. Mo.-Kansas City, 1954; PhD, U. Tex., 1958; MA (hon.), Yale, 1967; DSc (hon.), Boston Coll., 1985; LHD (hon.), Bank St. Coll. Edn., 1989, U. New Haven, 1991, St. Joseph Coll., 1991; PhD (hon.), Hon. degree, CUNY, 1995; LLD (hon.), Gonzaga U., 1995; HHD, Park U., 2000; LHD, McGill U., 2001. Psychol. intern Worcester (Mass.) State Hosp., 1957-59; asst. prof. psychology U. Mo., 1958-59; mem. faculty Yale U., 1959—, prof. psychology and child study center, 1967—, Sterling prof., 1976—, dir. child devel. program, 1961-76, chmn. dept. psychology, 1973-74; head psychology sect. Yale Child Study Center, 1967—; dir. Bush Center in Child Devel. and Social Policy, 1977—. Chief Children's Bur. NEW, Washington, 1970-72; cons. in field, 1962—; mem. nat. steering com. Project Head Start, 1965-70, chmn. 15th anniversary Head Start com., 1980; mem. nat. adv. com. Nat. Lab. Early Childhood Edn., 1967-70; nat. rsch. adv. bd. Nat. Assn. Retarded Children, 1968-73; nat. rsch. coun. Project Follow-Through, 1968-70; chmn. adv. com. Vietnamese Children's Resettlement, 1975; mem. Pres.'s Com. on Mental Retardation, 1980; joint appointee Yale U. Sch. Medicine, 1982—, chmn. Yale Infant Care Leave Commn., 1983-85, Parents as Tchrs., 1986—; mem. adv. com. Head Start Quality and Expansion, 1993; mem. adv. com. on svcs. for families with infants and toddlers HHS, 1994; mem. 25th Anniversary hon. com. Children's Def. Fund, 1997; mem. program com. Head Start's 5th Nat. Rsch. Conf., 1998—; mem. nat. adv. panel hon. chair, hist. mentor Nat. Head Start Assn.: Fulfilling the Promise 2010 Project 1998-2000; mem. adv. com. Head Start Rsch. and Evaluation for Adminstrn. for Children and Families, 1999—, Nat. Partnership's Family

Leave Income Initiative, 1999—. Author, co-author, editor books and monographs; contbr. articles to profl. jours. With AUS, 1951-53. Recipient Gunnar Dybwad Disting. scholar in behavioral and social sci. award Nat. Assn. Retarded Children, 1964, 69, Social Sci. Aux. award, 1962, Alumni Achievement award U. Mo., 1965, Alumnus of Yr. award, 1972, C. Anderson Aldrich award Am. Acad. Pediatrics, 1985, Nat. Achievement award Assn. for Advancement of Psychology, 1985, Dorothea Lynde Dix Humanitarian award for svc. to handicapped Elwyn Inst., 1987, Sci. Leadership award Joseph P. Kennedy Jr. Found., 1990, Mensa Edn. and Rsch. Found. award for excellence, 1990, Nat. Head Start Assn. award, 1990 Founders award, 1995, Bldg. dedication Edward Zigler Head Start Ctr., 1990, As They Grow award in edn. Parents mag., 1990, Excellence in Edn. award Pi Lambda Theta, 1991, Friend of Edn. award Conn. Edn. Assn., 1991, Loyola-Mellon Social Sci. award 1991, Pres.'s award Conn. Assn. Human Svcs., 1991, Harold W. McGraw, Jr. prize in edn., 1992, Disting. Achievement in Rsch. award Internat. Assn. Sci. Study of Mental Deficiency, 1992, Disting. Svc. award Coun. Chief State Sch. Officers, 1993, Outstanding Fed. Leadership in Support of Head Start Rsch., Adminstrn. on Children, Youth and Families, 1993, Child and Family Advocacy award Parents as Tchrs. Nat. Ctr., 1994, Nat. Distinction award U. Pa. Edn. Alumni Assn., 1994, Disting. Fellow award So. Conn. State U. chpt. Phi Delta Kappa, 1997, Lifetime Achievement award in Applied and Preventive Psychology Am Assn. Applied and Preventive Psychology, 1998, Recognition award Coun. for Early Childhood Profls., Child Devel. Assocs., 1999, Heinz award pub. policy, 1999, Nat. Head Start Assn. award appreciation, 2000, Disting. Svc. medal Tchrs. Coll. Columbia U., 2000, Disting. Alumnus U. Tex., 2000, Key to the City, Independence, Mo., 2000, Nat. Head Start Assn. award appreciation, 2000, Disting. Svc. medal Tchrs. Coll. Columbia U., 2000, Lifetime Mentoring award, ACYF, 2000, Lifetime Contbn. psychology award CT Psychol. Assn., 2000, Lifetime Commitment to comty. svc. award Ct dept. higher edn. and CT commn. on nat. and comty. svc., 2001, Florence Halpern award disting. profl. contbns. in clin. psychology APA, 2001, Bridges Over Barrtiers awrd, Family REsources Youth Svcs. Coalition Ky., 2002, others; named Hon. Commr. Internat. Yr. of Child, 1979. Fellow Am. Orthopsychiat. Assn. (Blanche F. Ittleson award 1989, pres. 1993-94), APA (pres. divsn. 7, 1974-75, G. Stanley Hall award 1979, award for disting. contbns. to psychology in pub. interest 1982, Nicholas Hobbs award 1985, award for disting. profl. contbns. to knowledge 1986, Edgar A. Doll award 1986, award for disting. contbn. to cmty. psychology and cmty. mental health 1989, pres.-elect divsn. 37 1997, pres. 1998, past pres. 1999, Bronfenbrenner Lifetime Contbn. award divsn. 7 1998, Florence Halpern award for disting. profl. contbns. in clin. psychology divsn. 12 2001); mem. Inst. Medicine of NAS, AAAS, Am. Acad. Mental Retardation (Career Rsch. award 1982), Soc. Psychol. Study Social Issues (Kurt Lewin meml. award 1995), Zero to Three (Dolley Madison award 1995), P.R. Head Start Assn. (Outstanding Leadership award 1995, True Father of Headstart recognition award 1996, award of appreciation for lifelong support and participation 1997), Am. Psychol. Found. (gold medal for life contbn. 1997, Parents Child Care award for advocacy 1998, Heinz award in pub. policy, 1999). Home: 177 Ridgewood Ave North Haven CT 06473-4442 Office: Yale U Dept Psychology PO Box 208205 2 Hillhouse Ave New Haven CT 06520-8205 E-mail: edward.zigler@yale.edu.

ZIKMUND, BARBARA BROWN, minister, church history educator; b. Ann Arbor, Mich., Oct. 16, 1939; d. Henry Daniels and Helen Langworthy Brown; m. Joseph Zikmund II, Aug. 26, 1961; 1 child, Brian Joseph. BA, Beloit Coll., 1961; BDiv, Duke U., 1964, PhD, 1969; D in Div (hon.), Doane Coll., 1984, Chgo. Theol. Sem., 1985, Ursinus Coll., 1989; LHD, U. Hartford, 1998. Ordained to ministry United Ch. of Christ, 1964. Instr. Albright Coll., Reading, Pa., 1966-67, Temple U., Phila., 1967-68, Ursinus Coll., Collegeville, Pa., 1968-69; asst. prof. religious studies Albion Coll., Mich., 1970-75; asst. prof. ch. history, dir. studies Chgo. Theol. Sem., 1975-80; dean and assoc. prof. ch. history Pacific Sch. Religion, Berkeley, Calif., 1981-85, dean and prof. ch. history, 1985-90; pres. Hartford (Conn.) Sem., 1990-2000. Prof. grad. sch. am. studies Doshisha U., Kyoto, Japan, 2000—; chmn. United Ch. of Christ Hist. Coun., 1983-85, mem. coun. for ecumenism, 1983-89; mem. Nat. Coun. Chs. Commn. on Faith and Order, 1979-87, World Coun. of Chs. Programme Theol. Edn., 1984-91, Nat. Coun. Chs. Working Group on Inter-Faith Rels., 1992-96, Nat. Coun. Chs. Commn. on Inter-faith Rels., 1996—, chair Commn. on Inter-faith Rels., 2000—, World Orgn. Confs. Theol. Instns., sec. treas., 1992-96, pres., 1996-2000. Author: Discovering the Church, 1983, Clergy Women: An Uphill Calling, 1998; editor: Hidden Histories in the UCC, 1984, vol. 2, 1987; (with Manschreck) American Religous Experiment, 1976; mem. editl. bd. Jour. Ecumenical Studies, 1987—, Mid-Stream, 1991—; series editor: Living Theological Heritage of the United Church of Christ; contbr. articles to profl. jours. Mem. City Coun., Albion, Mich., 1972-75; elector Wadsworth Atheneum, 1994-2000; corporator St. Francis Hosp., 1994-2000, Hartford Hosp., 1996-2000; pres. Greater Hartford Consortium for Higher Edn., 1994-96. Woodrow Wilson fellow, 1964-66; NEH grantee, 1974-75; vis. scholar Schlesinger Libr. Women's History, Radcliffe Coll., 1988-89, Disting. Alumna, Duke Divinity Sch., 1994; recipient Disting. Svc. Citation Beloit Coll., 1986. Mem. Assn. Theol. Schs. (v.p. 1984-86, pres. 1986-88, issues implementation grantee 1983-84, Disting. Svc. award 2004), Am. Soc. Ch. History (coun. 1983-85, pres. elect 1996-97, pres. 1997-98), Internat. Assn. Women Ministers (v.p. 1977-79), AAUW (v.p. 1973-75), Greater Hartford C. of C. (bd. dirs. 1992-95). Democrat. Office: Grad Sch Am Studies Doshisha U Kyoto 602-8580 Japan Business E-Mail: bbz@hartsem.edu.

ZIL, J. S. psychiatrist, physiologist; b. Chgo. s. Stephen Vincent and Marillyn Charlotte (Jackson) Z.; 1 child, Charlene-Elena. BS magna cum laude, U. Redlands, 1969; MD, U. Calif., San Diego, 1973; MPH, Yale U., 1977; JD with honors, Jefferson Coll., 1985. Med. clk. Clinica de Casa de Todos, Tijuana, Mexico, 1968—70; intern, resident in psychiatry and neurology U. Ariz., 1973-75; fellow in psychiatry, advanced fellow in social, cmty. and forensic psychiatry, Yale cmty. cons. to Conn. State Dept. Corrections, 1975-77; instr. psychiatry Yale U., 1976-77; instr. physiology U. Mass., 1976-77; unit chief Inpatient and Day Hosp., Conn. Mental Health Ctr., Yale-New Haven Hosp., 1975—77; asst. prof. psychiatry U. Calif., San Francisco, 1977-82, assoc. prof. psychiatry and internal medicine, 1982—86, vice-chmn. dept. psychiatry, 1983-86; prof. natural sci. Calif. State U., 1985-87; assoc. prof. bioengring. and internal medicine U. Calif., Berkeley, San Francisco, 1982-92, clin. faculty Davis, 1991-99, legis. liaison Ctrl. Office, 1988—; med. dir. Sierra Vista Hosp., 2003—. Chief psychiatry and neurology VA Med. Ctr., Calif., 1977—86; prin. investigator Sleep Rsch. and Physiology Lab., 1980—86; chmn. dept. psychiatry and neurology U. Calif., San Francisco, Ctrl. San Joaquin Valley Med. Edn. Program and Affiliated Hosps. and Clinics, 1983—86; chief psychiatrist State Calif. Dept. Corrections, 1986—89, chief forensic Psychiatrist, 1986—2003; chmn. State of Calif. Inter-Agy. Tech. Adv. Com. on Mentally Ill Inmates & Parolees, 1986—92; mem. med. adv. com. Calif. State Pers. Bd., 1986—95; apptd. councilor Calif. State Mental Health Plan, 1988—93; cons. Nat. Inst. Corrections, 1992—94; invited faculty contbr. and editor Am. Coll. Psychiatrist's Resident in Tng. Exam, 1981—86; commr. physician's adv. bd. Pres. Commn. on Bus., U.S. Ho. of Reps., 2002—. Author: Suicide Prevention handbook, 1987, 4th edit., 1996, The Case of the Sleepwalking Rapist, 1992, Mentally Disordered Criminal Offenders, 5 vols., 1989, 2nd edit., 1992; contbg. author The Measurement Mandate: On the Road to Performance Improvement in Health Care, 1993, Psychiatric Services in Jails and Prisons, 2nd edit., 2000, assoc. editor Corrective and Social Psychiatry Jour., 1978—97, referee, 1980—, reviewer, 1981—; contbr. articles to profl. jours. Nat. Merit scholar, 1965; recipient Nat. Recognition award Bank of Am., 1965, Julian Lee Roberts award U. Redlands, 1969, Kendall award Internat. Symposium in Biochemistry Rsch., 1970, Campus-Wide Profl. Achievement award U. Redlands, 1994, U. Calif., 1995-1996. Fellow Royal Soc. Health, Am. Assn. Social Psychiatry; mem. AAUP, APHA, Am. Psychiat. Assn., Am. Assn. Mental Health Profls. in Corrections (nat. pres. 2002—), Nat. Coun. on Crime and Delinquency, Calif. Scholarship Fedn. (past pres.), Delta Alpha, Alpha Epsilon Delta. Office: PO Box 160208 Sacramento CA 95816-0208 Personal E-mail: corrmentalhealth@aol.com.

ZILBER, IRENE, counselor; b. Gomel, Belarus, Sept. 2, 1978; d. Lyubov and Michael Zilber. BS, Cornell U., 2000; postgrad., U. Pa., 2001—02; MEd, Harvard U., 2004. Rsch., statis. analyst Cornell U., Ithaca, 1997—99; peer counselor Empathy and Referral Svcs., Ithaca, 1997—2000; rsch. coord. Children's Hosp. Phila., 2000—03; rsch. asst. U. Pa. Med. Ctr., Phila., 2000—03; mental health counselor Maimonides Med. Ctr., Bkyn.; clin. counselor YouthCare, Charlestown, Mass., 2003—. Recipient 1st, 2d, and 3d pl., Ballroom Dance Competition, Internat. and Std. styles, 2000—02; scholar, Cornell U., 1996—2000. Mem.: APA. Home: The Liberty Apt 504 152 Temple St New Haven CT 06510 Personal E-mail: irenezilber@yahoo.com.

ZILBERT, ALLEN BRUCE, education educator, computer consultant; b. Bronx, NY, May 26, 1957; s. Murray and Perla Z.; m. Barbara Dale Palley, July 1, 1984; children: Heather Robynne, Jared Lee. BA in Econ., CUNY, 1978; MBA, St. Johns U., 1980, advanced profl. cert., 1982; MEd in Adminstrv. Computer Systems Edn., Columbia U., 1986, EdD, 1988; postgrad., Kennedy-Western U., 1995—. Instr. bus. computer info. systems & quantitative methods Hofstra U., Hempstead, NY, 1981-83; asst. prof. info. systems Pace U. Sch. Computer Sci. and Info. Systems, N.Y.C., 1983-89; dir. ancillary systems Advanced Med. Systems, Rockville Centre, 1989-90; asst. prof. mgmt. Long Island U. Sch. Bus., Coll. Mgmt., Brookville, 1990-94; asst. prof. mgmt. info. sys. Sy Syms Sch. Bus., David Zysman prof. of mgmt. info. sys. Yeshiva U., N.Y.C., 1994-2000; assoc. prof. math./computer sci. Molloy Coll., Rockville Centre, 2000—03, dir. computer sci. and computer info. systems programs, 2000—03; assoc. prof. computer info. sys. Briarcliffe Coll., Patchogue/ Bethpage, 2003—, chair computer info. sys. dept., 2003—04, dir. acad. portal and web sys., 2004—. Curriculum com. Pace U. Sch. Computer Sci. and Info. Sys., 1983-89; chmn. personal computer resources com. Advanced Med. Sys., 1989-90; campuswide computer com. L.I. U., 1991-94, chmn., 1993-94, chmn. scholarship awards com., 1990-91; assembly collegiate schs. bus. curriculum planning com. Coll. Mgmt., 1993-94, chmn. computer needs, usage and stds. com., 1990-93, chmn. mgmt. dept. computer com., chmn. scholar awards com., 1992-93; book and software reviewer. Contbr. articles to profl. jours. Mem. IEEE, Assn. for Computer Tng. and Support, Assn. for Computing Machinery, Assn. of Info. Tech. Profls., Internat. Assn. for Computer Info. Sys., Internat. Assn. Mgmt., Info. Resources Mgmt. Assn., Control Commn. Armenian Agrl. Acad., Armenian Agrl. Acad. Trade-Union, Armenia Libr. Union. Office Phone: 631-730-2033. Business E-Mail: azilbert@bcl.edu.

ZILKHA, EZRA KHEDOURI, banker; b. Baghdad, Iraq, July 31, 1925; arrived in U.S., 1941, naturalized, 1950; s. Khedouri A. and Louise (Bashi) Z.; m. Cecile Iny, Feb. 6, 1950; children: Elias Donald, Donna, Bettina Louise. Grad., Hill Sch., Pottstown, Pa., 1943; AB, Wesleyan U., Middletown, Conn., 1947, LLD (hon.), 1987. Dir. Zilkha & Sons, Inc., NYC, 1946—, chmn., pres., 1956—. Dir. Cigna Corp., Phila., 1968—96, INA Life Ins. Co. of NY, 1973—87, Cambridge Assocs., Boston, 1988—2000, Revlon, Inc., 1981—95, Blyth Eastman Dillon & Co., 1976—79, Chgo. Milw. Corp., 1981—96, Mothercare, Ltd., England, 1970—82; vice chmn. bd. Fortune Bancorp, 1990—94, Handy & Harman, 1969—88; chmn. bd. Fidelity Internat. Bank., 1968—79; chmn. Union Holdings, 1984—90. Trustee emeritus, former chmn. investment com. Wesleyan U.; hon. trustee, former chmn. investment com. Brookings Inst., Washington; trustee Spence Sch., NYC, French Inst., NYC, Lycee Francais de NY; trustee Am. Soc. French Legion of Honor; former mem. exec. com., former chmn. bd., Internat. Ctr. for Disabled, NYC. Decorated officier Legion d'Honneur, officier Ordre Nat. du Merite (France); recipient Freedom of Human Spirit award Internat. Ctr. for Disabled, 1989, Pilier d'Or award French Inst./Alliance Francaise, 1995, Charles de Ferry de Fontnouvelle award Lycee Francais de N.Y., 2003. Mem.: Coun. Fgn. Rels., The Brook Club, Polo Club, Travellers Club, Meadow Club, Knickerbocker Club, Racquet & Tennis Club. Office Phone: 212-758-7750.

ZILLMAN, DONALD NORMAN, law educator, university official; b. Madison, Wis., May 19, 1944; s. Theodore William and Helen Ward Zillman; m. Linda Goforth, June 8, 1968. BS, U. Wis., 1966, JD, 1969; LLM, U. Va., 1973. Staff atty. Defenders, Inc., San Diego, 1970; prof. law Ariz. State U., 1974-79, U. Utah, Salt Lake City, 1979-90; dean, Godfrey prof. law U. Maine Law Sch., Portland, 1991-98, Godfrey prof. law, 1998—; interim provost, acad. v.p. U. Maine, 1999—2000. Disting. vis. prof. U.S. Mil. Acad., 1990; interim pres. U. Maine, Ft. Kent, 2001—02. Co-author: The Military in American Society, 1980, Energy Law, 1983, Constitutional Law for the Citizen-Soldier, 1991, Maine Tort Law, 1993, Energy Law and Policy for the 21st Century, Human Rights in Natural Resources Development, 2002, Energy Security, 2004. Special asst. atty. gen. State of Ariz., 1978. Maj. U.S. Army, 1970-74. Mem. Am. Law Inst., Rotary Club. Avocations: athletics, theater, reading. E-mail: zillman@usm.maine.edu.

ZILLY, THOMAS SAMUEL, federal judge; b. Detroit, Jan. 1, 1935; s. George Samuel and Bernice M. (McWhinney) Z.; divorced; children: John, Peter, Paul, Luke; m. Jane Greller Noland, Oct. 8, 1988; stepchildren: Allison Noland, Jennifer Noland. BA, U. Mich., 1956; LLD, Cornell U., 1962. Bar: Wash. 1962, U.S. Ct. Appeals (9th cir.) 1962, U.S. Supreme Ct. 1976. Ptnr. Lane, Powell, Moss & Miller, Seattle, 1962-88; dist. judge U.S. Dist. Ct. (we. dist.) Wash., Seattle, 1988—. Judge pro tem Seattle Mcpl. Ct., 1972-80; mem. adv. com. bankruptcy rules U.S. Judicial Conf. Contbr. articles to profl. jours. Mem. Cen. Area Sch. Council, Seattle, 1969-70; scoutmaster Thunderbird Dist. council Boy Scouts Am. Seattle, 1976-84; bd. dirs. East Madison YMCA. Served to lt. (j.g.) USN, 1956-59. Recipient Tuahku Dist. Service to Youth award Boy Scouts Am., 1983. Mem. ABA, Wash. State Bar Assn., Seattle-King County Bar Assn. (treas. 1979-80, trustee 1980-83, sec. 1983-84, 2d v.p. 1984-85, 1st v.p. 1985-86, pres. 1986-87). Office: US Dist Ct 410 US Courthouse 1010 5th Ave Seattle WA 98104-1189

ZILM, KARL MILLER, education educator; b. Carlinville, Ill., Feb. 22, 1948; s. Henry George and Mary Loehr Zilm; m. Sharon Kaye Henning, May 28, 1983; children: Kristin Marie, John Henning. MS, Purdue U., 1972. Prof. Lewis & Clark C.C., Godfrey, Ill., 1973—. Pres. Ill. Math. Assn. of Cmty. Colleges, 1996—97. Author: (textbook supplements) Graphing Calculator Keystroke Guides. Dir., bd. of spiritual ministry Faith Luth. Ch., Godfrey, Ill., 1991—2003. Mem.: Math. Assn. of Am. (com. on the two-year coll. 1997—2003), Am. Math. Assn. of Two-Year Colleges. Lutheran Church-Missouri Synod. Office: Lewis & Clark Cmty Coll 5800 Godfrey Rd Godfrey IL 62035 E-mail: kzilm@lc.edu.

ZILVETI, CARLOS BENJAMIN, preventive medicine physician, pediatrician; b. Sucre, Bolivia, June 14, 1928; came to U.S., 1956; s. Carlos and Marina (De La Reza) Z.; m. Halina J. Daszewski, Sept. 8, 1957 (div. Sept. 1976); 1 child: Carlos Joseph III; m. Vita Palazzolo, Sept. 5, 1987. BS, Sacred Heart Coll., Sucre, Bolivia, 1946; MD, U. San Francisco Xavier, Sucre, Bolivia, 1954; MPH, Yale U., 1966. Physician in rural medicine Bolivian Power Co., La Paz, 1955; intern Hosp. Obrero Victor Paz Estenssoro, La Paz, 1956; asst. resident in pediats. St. Luke's Hosp., Meml. Cancer Ctr., Woman's Hosp., N.Y.C., 1957-58; resident and chief resident in pediats. Hosp. of St. Raphael, New Haven, 1958-59; pvt. practice New Haven and Branford, Conn., 1960-63; dir. maternal-child health New Haven Dept. Health, 1964-74; regional med. officer South and Ctrl. Am. Peace Corps, Bogota, Colombia, 1975-76; regional med. officer, sci. attache in West Africa U.S. Dept. of State, Liberia, Ghana, Togo, Sierra Leone, 1976-79; reserve appt. of maj., advanced to col. USAF, San Antonio, 1979-91, chief environ. medicine Wilford Hall Med. Ctr., 1979-83, cons. preventive and occupl. medicine, 1983-91, cons. aerospace-preventive medicine Wilford Hall Med. Ctr. Lackland AFB, Tex., 1984-91, ret. col., 1991. Cons. FDA, HEW, Washington, 1966-75; cons. to Headstart Am. Acad. Pediats., Stanford-Norwalk, Conn., 1968-75; regional med. officer, sci. attache West Africa U.S. Dept. State. Contbr. articles to profl. jours. Chmn. gov.'s task force Conn. State Dept. Health, Hartford, 1969-75. Fellow Am. Acad. Pediats. (emeritus), Am. Coll. Preventive Medicine (emeritus); mem. APHA, AMA, New Eng. Pub. Health Assn., Conn. Acad. Preventive Medicine, Am. Occupl. Med. Assn. Avocations: long distance swimming, tennis, golf, international travel, classical music. Home: 9222 Dover Rdg San Antonio TX 78250-3557

ZIMAN, RICHARD S. real estate company executive; Bachelor's Degree, JD, U. So. Calif. Ptnr. Loeb & Loeb, 1971—80; founder, mng. gen. ptnr. Pacific Fin. Group, Beverly Hills, Calif., 1979; founder Arden Realty Inc. (formerly Arden Realty Group Inc.), L.A., chmn., CEO. Office: Arden Realty Inc Ste 400 11601 Wilshire Blvd Los Angeles CA 90025*

ZIMAND, HARVEY FOLKS, lawyer; b. N.Y.C., Aug. 28, 1928; s. Savel and Gertrude (Folks) Z.; m. Ingeborg Rockosch, 1963 (div. 1980); children—Patricia Folks Carpenter, Stephanie Folks; m. Noel French, Apr. 30, 1983 BA, Colgate U., 1950; postgrad., Oxford U., Eng., 1950; MA, U. Chgo., 1951; postgrad., Columbia U., 1952-53; LL.B., Yale U., 1957. Bar: N.Y. 1957. Rapporteur Council for Fgn. Relations, N.Y.C., 1952-53; atty. Dept. Navy, Washington, 1956-70; ptnr. Kelley Drye & Warren, N.Y.C., 1970—. Dir. Toronto-Dominion Trust Co., N.Y.C., 1975-83. Bd. editors The Chase Jour. Bd. dirs. Virginia Day Nursery, N.Y.C., 1980-84. Served to cpl. U.S. Army, 1951-53 Fellow N.Y. Bar Found., Am. Coll. Trust and Estate Counsel; mem. ABA, N.Y. State Bar Assn., Assn. Bar City of N.Y., Estate Planning Coun., Univ. Club. Clubs: Yale (N.Y.C.); Randolph Mountain (N.H.). Republican. Episcopalian. Home: 120 E 81st St New York NY 10028-1428 Office: Kelley Drye & Warren LLP 101 Park Ave New York NY 10178-0002 Business E-Mail: hzimand@kelleydrye.com.

ZIMBALIST, ANDREW S. economist, educator; b. N.Y.C., Oct. 16, 1947; s. Samuel A. and Dorothy H. Zimbalist; m. Shelley Abend Zimbalist; children: Jeffrey, Michael, Alex, Ella. BA, U. Wis., 1969; MA, Harvard U., 1972, PhD, 1974. Tchg. fellow Harvard U., Cambridge, Mass., 1971—74; from asst. to prof. Smith Coll., Northampton, Mass., 1974—. Vis. prof. Harvard U., 1978—79, Doshisha U., Kyoto, 1985; vis. prof U. Geneva, 2003; dir. LASA Cuba Task Force study group on transition and reform, 1990—91; chmn. LASA Task Force on Scholarly Rels. with Cuba, 1993—94; mem. working group on Cuba Atlantic Coun. of U.S., 1994—95; project cons. Ford Found., 1990, MacArthur Found., 1992; mem. adv. bd. Eco Consult, 1992—96; chmn. Cable Adv. Bd., Northampton, 1993—94; bd. dirs. Network on East-West-South Rsch. Coop. on Tech. Transfer, 1988—94; mem. adv. bd. Western Mass. Civil Liberties Union, 1988—94; mem. editl. bd. L.Am. Perspectives, 1988—98, Jour. Sports Econs., 1999—; series editor L.Am. Econ. Devel. Book Series, Westview Press, 1987—94; cons. in field.; commentator bus. of sports Nat. Pub. Radio. Author: Baseball and Billions: A Probing Look Inside the Big Business of Our National Pastime, 1992, Japanese edit., 1993, paperback edit., 1994, Unpaid Professionals: Commercialism and Conflict in Big-Time College Sports, 2001, May the Best Team Win: Baseball Economics and Public Policy, 2003; author: (with Juan Espinosa) Economic Democracy: Workers' Participation in Chilean Industry, 1970-73, 1978; author: (with H. Sherman and S. Brown) Comparing Economic Systems: A Political Approach, 1984; author: (with Claes Brundenius) The Cuban Economy: Measurement Development and Political Change in the Twentieth Century, 1991; author: (with Roger Noll) Sports, Jobs and Taxes: The Economic Impact of Sports Teams and Stadiums, 1997; editor: Case Studies on the Labor Process, 1981, Comparative Economic Systems: An Assessment of Knowledge, Theory and Method, 1983, Cuba's Socialist Economy Toward the 1990s, 1987, Cuban Political Economy: Controveries in Cubanology, 1988, The Economics of Sport I and II, 2001; co-editor: Cuba in Transition: Crisis and Transformation, 1992, author articles, revs. to profl. publs. Mem. Drake Group for Coll. Athletic Reform. Fellow Doherty L.Am. fellow, 1972—73, Harvard U. Dept. Econs., 1979, Picker fellow in internat. studies, 1982—83, 1985—86; grantee, Harvard Inst. Internat. Devel., 1973—74, MacArthur Found., 1990, 1992—96, Ford Found., 1990—91; scholar, Doshisha U., 1985. Mem.: Soc. for Am. Baseball Rsch., L.Am. Scholars Assn., Am. Econ. Assn., Assn. for Comparative Econ. Studies (editl. bd. jour. Comparative Econ. Studies 1987—90). Office: Smith Coll Dept Econs Northampton MA 01063 Office Phone: 413-585-3622. Business E-Mail: azimbali@smith.edu.

ZIMBLE, JAMES ALLEN, military officer, obstetrician, gynecologist, educator; b. Phila., Oct. 12, 1933; s. Nathan Norman and Mary Jay (Klaits) Z.; m. Judith Ann Goldberg, Sept. 17, 1961 (div. Apr. 1970); children: Amy B., Jennifer L.; m. Janet Mary Bailey, June 19, 1970 (dec. Dec. 1994); 1 child, Daniel A.; stepchildren: David T., Jennifer G., Melinda S. Richards; m. Mona C. Melton, Feb. 23, 1996; stepchildren: David P., Findley, Emily E. Zadjura. BS, Franklin and Marshall Coll., 1955; MD, U. Pa., 1959; ScD, SUNY Sch. Medicine, 1990. Diplomate Am. Bd. Ob-Gyn, Nat. Bd. Med. Examiners. Intern U.S. Naval Hosp., St. Albans, N.Y., 1959-60, resident, 1963-66; commd. ensign U.S. Navy, 1956, advanced through grades to vice adm., 1987, med. officer in USS John Marshall, 1961-63; staff U.S. Naval Hosp., Camp Pendleton, Calif., 1966-70, Phila., 1970-72, chief obstetrics and gynecology, dir. clin. services Lemoore, Calif., 1972-76; dir. clin. services Naval Regional Med. Ctr., Long Beach, Calif., 1976-78, comdg. officer Orlando, Fla., 1978-81; med. officer Hdqrs. U.S. Marine Corps, Washington, 1981-83; fleet surgeon to comdr. in chief Atlantic Fleet, med. advisor to Supreme Allied Command, Norfolk, Va., 1983-86; dep. asst. sec. of def. for strategic planning and med. program mgmt. Dept. Def., 1986-87; surgeon gen. USN, Washington, 1987-91; chief Bur. Medicine and Surgery, 1987-91; pres. Uniformed Svcs. U. Health Scis., Bethesda, Md., 1991—. Assoc. clin. faculty U. Calif.-Irvine, 1977-78; assoc. prof. dept. mil. medicine Uniformed Svc. U. Health Scis., Bethesda, Md., 1983—. Contbr. articles to profl. jours. Decorated Def. Meritorious Svc. medal (5), Legion of Merit (3), Navy Meritorious Svc. medal, Navy Disting. Svc. medal, Def. Superior Svc. medal; recipient Surgeon Gen.'s medal, Frank Brown Berry prize Fed. Healthcare, 2001. Disting. fellow Am. Coll. Physician Execs.; fellow ACS, Am. Coll. Ob-Gyn, Assn. Mil. Surgeons U.S.; mem. AMA (del.), Uniformed Svcs. U. Health Scis. (bd. regents), Nat. Libr. Medicine (bd. regents), NRA, Interagy, Inst. for Fed. Health Care Execs., U.S. Naval Inst., Rsch. Officers Assn., Naval Hist. Found. (trustee), Armed Forces Radiol. Rsch. Inst. (bd. govs.), Am. Hosp. Assn. (del.). Republican. Jewish. Office: USUHS 4301 Jones Bridge Rd Bethesda MD 20814-4799

ZIMENT, IRWIN, medical educator; b. England, 1936; MB BChir, Cambridge U., 1961. Intern, resident, England, 1961-64, 1964-65; resident Bronx Mcpl. Hosp. Ctr., 1965-66; dir. respiratory therpay Harbor Gen. Hosp., Torrance, Calif., 1968-75; chief medicine Olive View-UCLA Med. Ctr., 1975—2001, med. dir., 1994-97; prof. medicine UCLA Sch. Medicine, 1980—2001, prof. emeritus clin. medicine, 2002—. Contbr. articles to profl. jours. Trustee Chest Found., 2000—. Infectious Disease fellow Wadsworth VA Hosp., L.A., 1966-68. Mem. Am. Thoracic Soc. (clin. problems assembly chmn. 1981-82, resp. bd. med. advisors 1986-90), Am. Coll. Chest Physicians (mem. editl. bd. 1997-2000), Nat. Assn. Med. Dir. Respiratory Care (founding mem., vice pres. 1978, treas. 1979-81, bd. dirs. 1983-89, 98—), Calif Thoracic Soc. (pres. 1980-81, various coms. 1970-85), L.A. Lung Assn. (various coms. 1969-86). Office: Olive View UCLA Med Ctr Dept Med Rm 2B 182 14445 Olive View Dr Sylmar CA 91342-1437

ZIMET, CARL NORMAN, psychologist, educator; b. Vienna, June 3, 1925; came to U.S., 1943, naturalized, 1945; s. Leon and Gisela (Kosser) Z.; m. Sara F. Goodman, June 4, 1950; children: Andrew, Gregory. BA, Cornell U., 1949; PhD, Syracuse U., 1953; postdoctoral fellow, Standard U., 1953-55. Diplomate in clin. psychology Am. Bd. Profl. Psychology (trustee 1966-74). Instr., then asst. prof. psychology and psychiatry Yale U., 1955-63; mem. faculty U. Colo. Med. Center, 1963—, prof. clin. psychology, 1965—, head div., 1963—. Mem. Colo. Bd. Psychol. Examiners, 1966-72, Colo. Mental Health Planning Commn., 1964-66; mem. acad. adv. com. John F. Kennedy Child Devel. Center, U. Colo., 1966-68; chmn. Council for Nat. Register of Health Service Providers in Psychology, 1975-85, pres., mem. exec. bd. div. psychotherapy, 1970-89; chair exec. com. Assn. Psychol. Internship Ctrs., 1988-91. Bd. editors: Jour. Clin. Psychology, 1962-91, Jour. Clin. and Cons. Psychology, 1964-73, Psychotherapy, 1967—, Profl. Psychology, 1969-75. With USNR, 1943-46. Recipient Disting. Service award Colo. Psychol. Assn., 1976 Fellow: APA (coun. reps. 1969—72, 1973—76, bd. dirs. 1985—88, Disting. award for profl. contbn., div. psychotherapy and div. clin. psychology 1987), Soc. Personality Assessment (pres. 1975—76, 1975—76, chair gen. psychol. svcs. 1987—97, bd. dirs.); mem.: Med. Sch. Profs. Psychology (pres. 1992—94, bd.

dirs. 2004—), Denver Psychoanalytic (trustee 1968—71), Am. Acad. Clin. Psychology (pres. 1993—2001). Home: 400 E 3rd Ave # 901 Denver CO 80203 Office Phone: 303-315-8611. Business E-Mail: carl.zimet@uchsc.edu.

ZIMET, LLOYD, sport psychologist, health planner, educator; b. Bklyn., Oct. 5, 1951; s. Victor R. and Marcia Z. BA, Whittier (Calif.) Coll., 1973; MA, U. Md., 1983, PhD, 1984; MPH, NYU, 1989. Head basketball coach Aarhus (Denmark) U., 1973—78, 1980—82, 1985—86; resident dir. U. Md., College Park, 1978—80; sports supr. Montgomery County (Md.) Dept. of Recreation, 1978, 1982—84; dir. health promotion Optimal Fitness Inc., N.Y.C., 1986—91; internat. cons. cmty. and occupational health, 1984—; dir. World of Discovery Day Camp, Bklyn., 1997—2000. Dir. edn. AIDS Ctr. of Queens (N.Y.) County, 1989-90; bd. dirs. Patricia Manning Meml. Fund childhood cancer Am. Cancer Soc., Queens, 1988-95; mem. AIDS adv. com. N.Y.C. Bd. of Edn., 1989-90; mem. adv. bd. Adolescent Health Network, Queens, 1989-90; keynote speaker NYU Health Edn. Alumni, 1990, USPHS Region II Conf., 1991.; prevention specialist Hillsborough County., Fla., 2004; mem. AIDS Adv. Com. Hillsborough County Sch. Dist., Fla, 2004, student health adv. com., 2004. Bd. govs. U.S. Amateur Boxing Fedn., Colorado Springs, Colo., 1988-91; bd. dirs. Met. Amateur Boxing Fedn., N.Y.C., 1988-91; mem. USA Boxing Nat. Scholarship com., 1984-88. Fellow: Soc. Pub. Health Educators; mem.: AAHPERD, APHA, APA.

ZIMET, MATTHEW, graphic arts and science educator; b. Bklyn., Aug. 29, 1947; s. Sidney and Rebecca (Wishnofsky) Z.; m. Yvonne Streisinger, Oct. 16, 1994; children: Timnah, Jacob, Abraham, Nathan. MS, U. Mass., 1976, PhD, 1980. Prof. Vt. Tech. Coll., Randolph, 1984—. Illustrator: Zero, 2000, Black Holes & Timewarps, 1996. Mem. Sigma Xi. Jewish. Avocations: art, canoeing, cross country skiing. Office: Vt Tech Coll Main St Randolph VT 05061 E-mail: mzimet.fac@vtc.edu.

ZIMM, BRUNO HASBROUCK, physical chemistry educator; b. Woodstock, N.Y., Oct. 31, 1920; s. Bruno L. and Louise S. (Hasbrouck) Z.; m. Georgianna S. Grevatt, June 17, 1944; children: Louis H., Carl B. Grad., Kent (Conn.) Sch., 1938; AB, Columbia U., 1941, MS, 1943, PhD, 1944. Research assoc. Columbia U., 1944; research assoc., instr. Polytech. Inst. Bklyn., 1944-46; instr. chemistry U. Calif. at Berkeley, 1946-47, asst. prof., 1947-50, assoc. prof., 1950-51; vis. lectr. Harvard U., 1950-51; research assoc. research lab. Gen. Electric Co., 1951-60; prof. chemistry U. Calif., San Diego, 1960-91, prof. emeritus, 1991—. Assoc. editor: Jour. Chem. Physics, 1947-49; adv. bd.: Jour. Polymer Sci., 1953-62, Jour. Bio-Rheology, 1962-73, Jour. Biopolymers, 1963—, Jour. Phys. Chemistry, 1963-68, Jour. Biophys. Chemistry, 1973—. Recipient Bingham Medal Soc. Rheology, 1960, High Polymer Physics prize Am. Phys. Soc., 1963; Kirkwood medal Yale U., 1982 Mem. Biophys. Soc., Am. Soc. Biol. Chemists and Molecular Biologists, Am. Chem. Soc. (Baekeland award 1957), Nat. Acad. Scis. (award in Chem. Scis. 1981), Am. Acad. Arts and Scis., Am. Phys. Soc.

ZIMMAN STETSON, NANCY See STUART, NANCY

ZIMMER, DONALD WILLIAM, professional baseball coach, former professional baseball manager; b. Cin., Jan. 17, 1931; s. Harold Lesley and Lorraine Bertha (Ernst) Z.; m. Jean Carol Bauerle, Aug. 16, 1951; children: Thomas Jeffrey, Donna Jean. Student Pub. Schs., Cin. Baseball player Dodger Farm Clubs, 1949-54, Bklyn. Dodgers, 1954-57, L.A. Dodgers, 1958-59, 1963, Chgo. Cubs, 1960-61, N.Y. Mets, 1962, Cin. Reds, 1962, Washington Senators, 1963-65, Toei Flyers, Tokyo, 1966; mgr. Cin. Reds Farm Clubs, Knoxville and Buffalo, 1967, Indpls., 1968, San Diego Padre Farm Clubs, Key West, Fla., 1969, Padre Farm Club, Salt Lake City, 1970; coach Montreal Expos, Canada, 1971; mgr. San Diego Padres, 1972-73; coach Boston Red Sox, 1974-76, 1992, mgr., 1976-80, Tex. Rangers, 1981-82; coach Chgo. Cubs, 1984, 85, 86, mgr., 1988-91; coach San Francisco Giants, 1987, Colo. Rockies, Denver, 1993-95, N.Y. Yankees, 1983, 1986, 1996—2003; sr. baseball advisor Tampa Bay Devil Rays, 2004—. Mem. minor league All-Star Teams, Hornell, N.Y., 1950, Elmira, N.Y., 1951, Mobile, Ala., 1952, St. Paul, 1953; player World Series teams 1955, 56, 59; coach World Series teams 1975, 96, 98, 99, 2000, 01, 03; mem. adv. bd. Baseball Assistance Team. Recipient Bill Stern award NBC, 1949; named St. Paul Rookie of Yr., 1953, All Star Team Player, 1961, All Star Coach, 1978, 81, 90, 97, 99, 2000, 01, 02, 03; named Nat. League Mgr. of Yr. 1989. Mem. Profl. Baseball Players Assn. (life), Maj. League Baseball Players Alumni Assn., Old Time Ball Players Wis. Office: c/o Tampa Bay Devil Rays 1 Tropicana Drive Saint Petersburg FL 33705 Office Phone: 727-825-3137.

ZIMMER, GEORGE, men's apparel executive; CEO Men's Wearhouse, Freemont, Calif. Office: Mens Wearhouse 40650 Encyclopedia Cir Fremont CA 94538-2453

ZIMMER, JANIE LOUISE, mathematics educator, administrator; b. Balt., Sept. 25, 1943; d. Joseph Max and Anna Margaret (Vogtmann) Zimmer; m. Gordon Henry Stills, Jan. 7, 1972 (div. May 1978); 1 child, Sanova Stills; m. William Broaddus Long, Jr., Nov. 17, 1984; children: W. Michael, Calvin, Travon. BA in Math., Trinity Coll., Washington, 1966; MEd, Loyola Coll., Balt., 1973; postgrad., U. Md., 1982—. Tchr. math. Norfolk (Va.) Cath. H.S., 1966-69, Balt. City Pub. Schs., 1969-73, math. specialist, 1980-83; chmn. dept. math. Edmondson H.S., Balt., 1973-80; math. supr. Howard County Pub. Schs., Ellicott City, Md., 1983-91, exec. supr. math., 1991-92, curriculum coord., 1992-2000; math. assoc. Rsch. for Better Schs., Phila., 2000—. Cons. Md. Math. League, 1987-2000; prof. U. Md., Balt. County, 1989-95; clown/mathemagician Md., 1981—. Columnist in math. jour., 1986-98; editor: State Functional Math Guide, 1984, IMAGES: Improving Measurement and Geometry in the Elementary Schools, 2002; contbr. Mathematical Connections: A Bridge to Algebra and Geometry, 1992. Recipient Outstanding Math. Educator award Md. Coun. Tchrs. of Math., 1991, Outstanding Svc. award Md. Coun. Tchrs. Math., 1985, United Cerebral Palsy, 1974, Citizenship award K.C., 1961, Outstanding Alumna of Yr. award Maryvale Trinity Coll. Prep Sch., 1983. Mem. Md. Assn. Supervision and Curriculum Devel. (bd. mem. 1999-2000), Md. Coun. Tchrs. Math. (rep. 1986-94, pres. 1984-85), Nat. Coun. Tchrs. Math. (regional svcs. com. 1994-97, chair 1997-98, chair regional conf. 1991, bd. dir. 2002—), Nat. Assn. Sci. Tchrs., Pa. Sci. Tchrs. Assn., Nat. Mid. Sch. Assn., Pa. Coun. Tchrs. of Math., Pa. Coun. Suprs. of Math., Nat. Coun. Suprs. of Math., Md. Coun. Suprs. of Math., Clowns of Am. Internat., Freestate Clown Alley, Phi Delta Kappa. Democrat. Roman Catholic. Avocations: clowning, dance, skiing, reading. Home: 125 N Maple St Woodbury NJ 08096-1838 Office: Rsch for Better Schs 112 N Broad St Philadelphia PA 19107 E-mail: zimmer@rbs.org.

ZIMMER, LARRY WILLIAM, JR., sports announcer; b. New Orleans, La., Nov. 13, 1935; s. Lawrence W. Sr. and Theodora (Ahrens) Z.; m. Dawn M. Caillouet, June 4, 1955 (div. June 1972); children: Larry III, Tracey; m. Brigitte Bastian, Nov. 17, 1972. Student, La. State U., 1953-55; BJ, U. Mo., 1957. Sports dir. KFRU Radio, Columbia, Mo., 1960-66; asst. mgr. programming WAAM Radio, Ann Arbor, Mich., 1966-71; broadcaster football, basketball Mich., 1966-70; sportscaster, sports dir. KOA Radio, Denver, 1971—; broadcaster Denver Broncos Football, 1971-96; broadcaster football, basketball U. Colo. Buffaloes, 1971—; broadcaster Denver Rockets, 1972-74. Adj. prof. journalism U. Colo., 2001—. Bd. mem. Colo. Ski Mus. and Hall of Fame, Vail, 1981-2000, Opera Colo., Denver, 1985—, Colo. chap. Nat. Football Found; adv. bd. Jefferson Co. Youth Advocacy Ctr. 1st lt. US Army, 1958-60. Named Colo. Sportscaster of the Yr., Nat. Sportscasters and Sportswriters Assn., Salisbury, NC, 1988, 90, 91, 2001, 02, Broadcaster of the Yr., Colo. Broadcaster's Assn., Denver, 1995; recipient Powerade award for best radio/TV sports story of yr. Nat. Sportscasters and Sportswriters Assn., 2000. Avocations: skiing, jogging, opera. Office: KOA Radio 4695 S Monaco St Denver CO 80237-3403 E-mail: larryzimmer@clearchannel.com.

ZIMMER, LAWRENCE JOSEPH, psychiatrist, internist; b. Port Huron, Mich., Mar. 15, 1946; MD, Wayne State U., 1971; grad., Cin. Psychoanalytic Inst., 2000. Diplomate Am. Bd. Psychiatry, Am. Bd. Internal Medicine and Cardiovascular Disease. Rotating intern U. Cin., 1971-72, resident in internal medicine, 1972-74, 75-76, fellow in cardiology, 1974-75, 76-77, resident in psychiatry, 1986-89; pvt. practice Cin., 1989—2001, Ft. Gratiot, Mich., 2001—. Adj. asst. clin. prof. U. Cin., 1989—2001. Mem.: ACP, Am. Psychoanalytic Assn. Office: Blue Water Mental Health Clinic 1501 Krafft Rd Fort Gratiot MI 48059 Office Phone: 810-985-5122.

ZIMMER, MARKUS BERNHARD, federal court administrator; b. Basel, Switzerland; came to U.S., 1948; s. Max Bernhard and Elisabeth (Sulzmann) Z.; m. Shelley Elaine Melcomian, Jan. 5, 1976; children: Jessica, Christopher. BA in Philosophy, U. Utah, 1971, MA in Philosophy, 1975; MEd, Harvard U., 1977; EdD in Philosophy of Edn., 1980. Rsch. asst. Harvard Law Sch., Cambridge, Mass., 1977-78; teaching fellow law and ethics Harvard U., Cambridge, Mass.; asst. divsn. dir. Div. Continuing Edn. and Tng., Fed. Jud. Ctr., Washington, 1983-84, chief legal svcs. tng. br., 1984-87, chief mgmt. tng. br., 1984-87; adj. assoc. prof. mgmt. U. Md., College Park, 1985-87; clk. of ct., dist. ct. adminstr. U.S. Dist. Ct., Dist. Utah, Salt Lake City, 1987—. Fed. dist. ct. clks. adv. com. Adminstrv. Office US Cts., 1990-96, fed. dist. ct. case mgmt. and stats. umbrella group, 1992-98, dist. ct. efficiencies task force, 1992-93, ct. adminstrn. adv. coun., 1995-96, chmn. tech. panel on automation, 1999-2002; interagy. adv. group on tng. and devel. Office of Pers. Mgmt., Washington, 1984-87; ABA Cen. and East European Law Initiative ct. adminstrn. cons. Bulgarian Ministry Justice, Sofia, 1992, cons. Constnl. Ct. Bosnia and Herzegovina, 1995, legal specialist, Skopje, Macedonia, 1997, faculty, Jud. Tng. Inst., Prague, Czech Republic, 2000-01; ct. cons., Zagreb, Croatia, 1994; spkr., Workshop on US Jud. Conf., Budapest, Hungary, 1998, ct. cons., Warsaw, Poland, 1998, Romania, 1999, Slovak Republic, 2000, Azerbaigan, 2002, Kosovo, 2003, Bahrain, 2003; chair US Dist. Cts. Civil/Criminal User Group, 1995-98; ad hoc task force on budget allotment simplification US Cts., 1996-98; dist. clk. liaison US Jud. Conf. IT Com., 1999-2001, 03—, internat. jud. rels. com., 2002—; adv. roundtable on law on cts. Coun. Europe, Rep. of Montenegro, 2001; jud. edn. cons., Kigali, Rwanda, 2002cons. in field. Contbr. articles to profl. jours. Exec. bd. Utah Combined Fed. Campaign, 1989—, bd. chmn. and statewide campaign dir., 1992, 2002. Fulbright fellow, 1972-73; recipient U.S. Cts. Dir.'s award for outstanding leadership, 1994, Roy B. Gibson Freedom of Info. award, Utah chpt. Soc. Profl. Journalists, 2000. Mem. ABA (CEELI ct. adminstrn. working group 1991-94, Russian jury trial working group 1993-94), ASTD (dir. justice sys. trainers 1984-86), Fed. Ct. Clks. Assn. (exec. bd. 1991-92). Office: U S Dist Ct 120 Frank E Moss Courthouse 350 S Main St Ste 150 Salt Lake City UT 84101-2180 E-mail: markus_zimmer@utd.uscourts.gov.

ZIMMER, RICHARD ALAN, educational association administrator, lawyer, former congressman; b. Newark, N.J., Aug. 16, 1944; s. William and Evelyn (Schlank Rader) Zimmer; m. Marfy Goodspeed Zimmer, Dec. 27, 1965; children: Carl William, Benjamin Goodspeed. BA, Yale U., 1966, LLB, 1969. Bar: N.Y. 1971, U.S. Dist. Cts. (so. and ea. dists.) N.Y. 1974, N.J. 1975, U.S. Dist. Ct. N.J. 1975, U.S. Supreme Ct. 1980. Assoc. Cravath, Swaine and Moore, N.Y.C., 1969—75; gen. atty. Johnson & Johnson, New Brunswick, NJ, 1976—91; mem. N.J. Gen. Assembly, 1982—87, chmn. state govt. com., 1986—87; mem. N.J. Senate, 1987—91, 102nd-104th Congresses from 12th N.J. dist., Washington, 1991—97; with Dechert, Princeton, NJ, 1997—2001; of counsel Gibson, Dunn & Crutcher, Washington, 2001—. Lectr. pub. and internat. affairs Woodrow Wilson Sch., Princeton U., 1997—2000. Chmn. Citizens for a Better N.J., 1997—2000, Study Commn. on the Implementation of the Death Penalty, 1997—98; trustee Freedom House Found., 1997—2001. Republican. Office: Gibson Dunn & Crutcher 1050 Connecticut Ave NW Washington DC 20036-5306 E-mail: rzimmer@gibsondunn.com.

ZIMMER, ROBERT J. mathematician; b. N.Y.C., Nov. 5, 1947; s. Max S. and Harriet (Brokaw) Z.; m. Terese Schwartzman, Oct. 27, 1974; children—David, Benjamin, Alexander. AB, Brandeis U., 1968; PhD, Harvard U., 1975. Asst. prof. U.S. Naval Acad., Annapolis, Md., 1975-77; instr. U. Chgo., 1977-79, assoc. prof., 1979-80, prof. math, 1980—; prof. math. U. Calif.-Berkeley, 1981-83, chmn. math dept., 1991-95, assoc. provost for rsch. & edn., 1995—. Author: Ergodic Theory and Semisimple Groups, 1984, Essential Results of Functional Analysis; contbr. articles to profl. jours. Sloan Found. fellow, 1979-83 Office: U Chicago Dept Math 5734 S University Ave Chicago IL 60637-1514

ZIMMERER, KATHY LOUISE, university art gallery director; b. Whittier, Calif., Dec. 9, 1951; BA cum laude, U. Calif., Berkeley, 1974; MA, Williams Coll., 1976. From tour guide to curatorial asst. Sterling and Francine Clark Inst., Williamstown, Mass., 1975-76; spl. asst. dept. modern art L.A. County Mus. Art, 1976-77; mus. edn. fellow Fine Arts Mus. San Francisco, 1977-78; dir. coll. art gallery SUNY, New Paltz, 1978-80; cons. in field, 1980-81; dir. univ. art gallery Calif. State U., Dominguez Hills, 1982—. Project dir. Painted Light: California Impressionist Paintings from the Gardena H.S./L.A. Unified Sch. Dist., 1996—. Mem. Internat. Assn. Art Critics, Art Table. Office: Univ Art Gallery Calif State U 1000 E Victoria St Carson CA 90747-0001 E-mail: kzimmerer@csudh.edu.

ZIMMERMAN, AMY J. television producer, television director; b. N.Y.C., Nov. 4, 1961; d. Arthur S. and Louise (Weild) Zimmerman. BA in Journalism and History, U. So. Calif., 1983. Writer, photographer Thoroughbred Calif. Mag., Arcadia, 1981-85; prodr. Hammond Prodns., Lexington, Ky., 1985; assoc. prodr. NBC Sports, N.Y.C., 1986—; dir. broadcasting Santa Anita Pk., Arcadia, 1986—, acting dir. ops., 1999; prodr., dir. Fox Sports Net, L.A., 1996—2002; cons. Fox Sports, L.A., 1998—2002; exec. prodr. Horse Racing TV Network, 2002—. Assoc. prodr.: (TV series) Breeders' Cup, 1992 (Emmy award Best Live Sports Spl., 1992); exec. prodr.: Santa Anita Tonight: One on One, 1993 (Eclipse award hon. mention local TV), Santa Anita Today, 1996 (Eclipse award hon. mention local TV), Inside Santa Anita, 1998; exec. prodr., dir.: Best of Santa Anita, 1999 (Eclipse award local TV); assoc. prodr., editor: A Cup of Courage, 1988 (Eclipse award hon. mention local TV); exec. prodr.: Mec Broadingcasting, 2004—. Bd. dirs. U. So. Calif. Panhellenic, 1982—83, Sterling Assn. Aviva Ctr., Hollywood, Calif., 1998—2002. Named Outstanding Woman in Thoroughbred Racing, Calif. State Assembly, 2004. Mem.: Nat. Thoroughbred Racing Assn. (racing and TV task force, Internat. Simulcast award 2000, 2001), Turf Publicists Assn., Alpha Gamma Delta. Office: Santa Anita Park 285 W Huntington Dr Arcadia CA 91007-3439 E-mail: azimmerman@santaanita.com.

ZIMMERMAN, BERNARD, investment banker; b. Bklyn., Dec. 7, 1932; s. Jacob and Pearl (Schechner) Z.; m. Joyce M. Singer, Dec. 24, 1960; children: Wayne Jay, Ellen Holly. BBA, CCNY, 1954; MBA, NYU, 1957. CPA NY. Fin. exec. consumer products Spartans Industries, Inc., NYC, 1961-65; sr. v.p. Scheinman, Hochstin, and Trotta, Inc., NYC, 1965-72; pres. Bernard Zimmerman and Co., Inc., Weston, Conn., 1972—; pres., CEO FCCC, Inc. (formerly First Conn. Capital Corp.), Norwalk, 2003—. Pres. Beacon Hill Mgmt., Inc., Boston, 1994-97; sr. v.p. corp. fin. Gruntal & Co., Inc., 1983-84; pres., chmn. bd., pres. St. Lawrence Seaway Corp., Indpls., 1985-93, fin. cons.; sr. v.p. The Zimmerman Group, Inc., 1991-96; chmn. bd. dirs., pres. Beacon Hill Mut. Fund, Inc., Boston, 1994-97; Liquidating trustee Unity Buying Svc. Co. Liquidating Trust, Hicksville, NY; bd. dirs. Sbarro, Inc., Melville, NY; fin. cons. Beautiful Visions-U.S.A., Ltd., Bethpage, NY, Task Mgmt. Co., Ridgefield, Conn., 1998-99; pres. and CEO FCCC, Inc., Norwalk, Conn., 2003—; chmn. of bd. and pres. GVC Venture Corp., NYC, 2004—. Bd. dirs. Inst. Cancer Rsch. and Molecular Medicine, Temple U., Phila., 1995-; trustee Sharro Family Found., Melville, 1993—; mem. Nat. Assn. Corp. Dir. Blue Ribbon Commn. on Corp. Governance-Best Practice Com., 1997. With AUS, 1955-57. Mem.: NY State Soc. CPAs. Home and Office: 18 High Meadow Rd Weston CT 06883-2946 Office Phone: 203-226-5165.

ZIMMERMAN, BERNARD, judge; b. Munich, Bavaria, Fed. Republic Germany, May 31, 1946; came to U.S., 1949; s. Sam and Roza (Spodek) Z.; m. Grace L. Suarez, Oct. 23, 1976; children: Elizabeth, Adam, David, Dara Bylah. AB, U. Rochester, 1967; JD, U. Chgo., 1970. Bar: Calif. 1971, La. 1971, U.S. Supreme Ct. 1975, U.S. Dist. Ct. (no., ea., cen. and so. dists.) Calif., U.S. Dist. Ct. (ea. dist.) La., U.S. Ct. Appeals (9th cir.). Law. clk. chief judge U.S. Dist. Ct. (ea. dist.) La., New Orleans, 1970-71; asst. prof. law La. State U., Baton Rouge, 1971-72; ptnr. Pillsbury, Madison & Sutro, San Francisco, 1972-95; legal cons. 3d Constnl. Conv. Commonwealth of the No. Mariana Islands, Northern Mariana Islands, 1995; U.S. magistrate judge U.S. Dist. Ct. (no. dist.) Calif., 1995—. Dep. pub. defender City of San Francisco, 1975; arbitrator U.S. Dist. Ct., San Francisco, AAA; judge pro tem San Francisco Superior and Mcpl. Cts. Bd. dirs., mem. exec. com. San Francisco Lawyers' Com. on Urban Affairs, 1984-95, treas., 1987; mem. regional bd. Anti-Defamation League, 1989-95. Mem. Phi Beta Kappa. Clubs: Olympic (San Francisco). Democrat. Jewish. Office: 450 Golden Gate Ave San Francisco CA 94102-3661 Office Phone: 415-522-4093.

ZIMMERMAN, CAROLE LEE, public relations professional; b. Roxboro, NC, Aug. 28, 1948; d. Ray Richard and Annie Theresa (O'Briant) Zimmerman; m. Richard A. Hoehn, Oct. 26, 1991; 1 child, Kristin Nicole Sizemore. BS in Edn., Fla. State U., 1970; publs. specialist cert., George Washington U., 1980; MA in Pub. Comm., Am. U., 1993. Accredited in pub. rels. Tchr. Gadsden County Pub. Schs., Quincy, Fla., 1971-72, Am. schs., Kaiserslautern and Darmstadt, Germany, 1974-76; editor, writer USLICO Corp., Arlington, Va., 1980-84; dir. comm. Bread for the World, Washington, 1984-95, Nat. Coun. for Sci. and Environment, Washington, 1995-97; dir. comm. and mktg. APHA, Washington, 1997—2002; dep. exec. dir. comm. and member svcs. Am. Pub. Human Svcs. Assn., Washington, 2002—. Bd. dirs. N Street Village, 2000—. Scholar, Pub. Health Leadership Inst., 2001—02. Mem.: Assn. Women in Comm. (bd. dirs. 1996—98), Pub. Rels. Soc. Am., Am. Soc. Assn. Execs. Democrat. Office: Am Pub Human Svcs Assn 810 First St NE Washington DC 20002

ZIMMERMAN, CONNIE ANN, public administrator; AA, HACC, 1978; BS in Pub. Policy, Pa. State U., 2002. Exec. sec. DER, 1993—95, adminstrv. asst., 1995—99; pers. officer PennDOT Bureau of Design, Harrisburg, 1999—. V.p. Women's Legis. Exchange, 2001—; bd. dirs. Ctrl. Pa. Women Execs., Harrisburg, Pa., 1997—, YWCA of Greater Harrisburg, 2002—. Mem.: Am. Soc. Pub. Adminstrn., Sierra Club, Mitgleider Deutscher Verein, St. Lawrence Fraternal Union, Pi Gamma Mu. Roman Catholic. Avocations: golf, dance, music. Home: 933 Highland St Steelton PA 17113-1537

ZIMMERMAN, DAVID ALAN, cardiologist; b. Akron, Ohio, Sept. 22, 1962; s. Henry Edward and Betty Jane (Young) Z; m. Karlyn Marie Hooton, June 4, 1994. BS summa cum laude, Ohio State U., 1985; MD, Duke U., 1991. Diplomate in internal medicine and cardiovascular disease Am. Bd. Internal Medicine. Intern Ohio State U., Columbus, 1991-92, resident, 1992-94; fellow transplantation cardiology Ochsner Med. Found., New Orleans, 1995-96; fellow in cardiology Tulane U., New Orleans, 1996-2000; cardiologist Kennestone Cardiovasc. Cons., Marietta, Ga., 2000—. Named one of America's Top Physicians, Consumer's Rsch. Coun., 2003. Mem. AMA; fellow Am. Coll. Cardiology.

ZIMMERMAN, DAVID CARL, controller, corporate financial executive; b. Harrisburg, Pa., July 9, 1957; s. Raymond S. and Alice Hoke Z.; m. JoAnn G. Zimmerman. BBA, Ga. State U., 1981; MBA, Montclair State U., 2001. Field auditor Grand Union, Atlanta, 1981-89, sr. field auditor Wayne, N.J., 1989-96, acctg. mgr., 1996-99; CFO, controller Dowel Assocs., Morristown, NJ, 1999—2002; CFO Atkins Companies, West Orange, NJ, 2002—. Mem. AICPA, N.J. Soc. CPAs, Ga. CPAs, Phi Kappa Phi, Alpha Epsilon Lambda, Beta Gamma Sigma. Avocation: golf. Home: 74 Donald Pl Waldwick NJ 07463 Office: 101 Old Short Hills Rd Ste PH1 West Orange NJ 07052 Business E-Mail: davidz@atkinscompanies.com.

ZIMMERMAN, D(ONALD) PATRICK, lawyer; b. Albany, N.Y., Mar. 20, 1942; s. Bernard M. and Helen M. (Eshelman) Z. Student, Lawrenceville Sch., 1960, McDonogh Sch.; BA, Rollins Coll., 1964; JD, Dickinson Sch. Law, 1967. Bar: Pa. 1968, U.S. Supreme Ct. 1971. Atty. Legal Aid, 1968-69; pub. defender Lancaster County, Pa., 1969-72; pvt. practice Lancaster, 1974—. Instr. Ct. Common Pleas for Constables, 1976-; solicitor Lancaster County Dep. Sheriff Assn., 1977-, Lancaster County Constable Assn., 1975-; sheriff solicitor Lancaster County Sheriff Office 2004-; instr. sheriff's dept. Lancaster County for Dep. Sheriffs, 1978-85; of counsel to Dep. Sheriff Assn. Pa., 1979-81; spl. counsel Pa. State Constables Assn., 1981; chmn. Bd. Arbitrators Lancaster County, 1975-81; spl. counsel Legislative Com. to Constable Assn. Pa., 1982; bd. dirs. Sheriff Solicitors Assn. Author: The Pennsylvania Landlord and Tenant Handbook, 1982, revised edit., 1993; editor (with J. Hatfield and A. Taylor) Pennsylvania Constable Handbook, 1998; contbr. articles to profl. jours. Mem. pastoral coun. St. Anthony's Cath. Ch., 1995-98. Recipient Ofcl. Commendation of Merit, Lancaster County Sheriff's Dept., 1979, Ofcl. Commendation of Merit, F.O.P. State Police Lodge 66, 1985, Disting. Svc. award, 1987, Cert. of Appreciation, Lancaster Crime Commn., 2003; named Extraordinary Min., 2002. Mem. ABA, ATLA, Pa. Bar Assn., Acad. Family Mediators, Lancaster County Bar Assn., W. Hensel Brown Inn of Ct., Lancaster County Constables Assn. (Outstanding Leadership award 1988, Disting. Svc. award as solicitor 1998, 25 Yrs. Dedicated Svc. award 2000). Office: 214 E King St Lancaster PA 17602-2977

ZIMMERMAN, EARL ABRAM, physician, scientist, educator, neuroendocrinology researcher; b. Harrisburg, Pa., May 5, 1937; s. Earl Beckley and Hazel Marie (Myers) Z. BS in Chemistry, Franklin and Marshall Coll., 1959; MD, U. Pa., 1963. Diplomate Am. Bd. Psychiatry and Neurology, Am. Bd. Internal Medicine. Intern Presbyn. Hosp., N.Y.C., 1963-64, resident, 1964-65, Neurol. Inst. CPMC, N.Y.C., 1965-68, research fellow endocrinology, 1970-72; asst. prof. to prof. neurology Columbia U., N.Y.C., 1972-85; prof., chmn. dept. neurology Oreg. Health Sci. U., Portland, 1985-2000; chmn. dept. neurology Albany (N.Y.) Med. Coll., 2000—; clin. dir. neuroscis. Advanced Imaging Rsch. Ctr. AMC/GE. Dir. neurology Helen Hayes Hosp., Haverstraw, N.Y., 1982-83 Mem. editl. bd. Jour. Histochem. Cytochemistry, 1980-85, 87, Neuroendocrinology, 1985-88, Annals of Neurology, 1985-91, Western Jour. Medicine, 1993-98, Jour. Clin. Endocrinal Metabolism, 1995-99; contbr. numerous articles to profl. jours. Maj. USAF, 1968-70 Rsch. grantee NIH, 1977—. Mem. Am. Neurol. Assn. (program chmn. 1980-82), Am. Acad. Neurology (Wartenber lectr. 1985), Endocrine Soc. Democrat. Mem. United Ch. of Christ Avocations: woodworking, gardening, theater, music, art, skiing, tennis. Office: Albany Med Coll Dept Neurology 47 New Scotland Ave Albany NY 12208 Office Phone: 518-262-0801. E-mail: zimmere@mail.amc.edu.

ZIMMERMAN, EDWIN MORTON, lawyer; b. N.Y.C., June 11, 1924; s. Benjamin and Tobie (Fuchs) Z.; m. Caroline Abbot, July 3, 1956; children: Sarah Abbot, Lyle Benjamin, Miriam Appleton. AB, Columbia U., 1944, LLB, 1949. Bar: N.Y. 1949, D.C. 1969, U.S. Supreme Ct 1969. With Hoover Commn. Reorgn. Exec. Br., 1948; law clk. to Hon. Stanley F. Reed U.S. Supreme Ct., 1950-51; law clk. to Judge Simon H. Rifkind U.S. Dist. Ct., 1949-50; pvt. practice law N.Y.C., 1951-59; prof. law Stanford U., 1959-69; with Justice Dept., 1965-69, asst. atty. gen. charge antitrust div., 1968-69; mem. Covington & Burling, Washington, 1969-94, sr. counsel, 1994—. Mem. coun. Adminstrv. Conf. U.S., 1975—78; mem. mfg. studies bd. Nat. Acad. Sci., 1983—87; adj. prof. George Washington Sch. Law, 1996—2001. Trustee Textile Mus., 1983—, pres. bd. trustees, 1987-96; mem. Folger Poetry Bd., 1990—; mem. adv. bd. Partisan Rev., 1996-2003. 1st lt. AUS, 1944-46. Mem. ABA, Assn. of Bar of City of N.Y., Am. Law Inst., Coun. Fgn. Rels., Phi Beta Kappa. Home: 1820 Kalorama Sq NW Washington DC 20008-4022 Office: Covington & Burling PO Box 7566 1201 Pennsylvania Ave NW Washington DC 20004-2401 Business E-Mail: ezimmerman@cov.com.

ZIMMERMAN, GEORGE OGUREK, physicist, researcher; b. Poland, Oct. 20, 1935; s. Charles and Carolin Olga (Fisher) Z.; m. Isa Kaftal, Oct. 4, 1964. BS, Yale U., 1958, MS, 1959, PhD (Univ. Wilson fellow 1959-60, D.N. Clark fellow 1959-61), 1963. Research assoc. Yale U., 1962-63; asst. prof. physics Boston U., 1963-68, assoc. prof., 1968-74, prof., 1974—2001, assoc. chmn. dept. physics, 1971-72, chmn. dept., 1973-83, chmn. faculty coun., 1985-86, dir. honors program in sci. and engring. for HS students, 1978—. Mem. staff Nat. Magnet Lab., Cambridge, Mass., 1964, vis. scientist, 1964-70; assoc. physicist U. Calif., San Diego, 1973; vis. scientist Brookhaven Nat. Lab., 1980; vis. scholar Harvard U., 1988, Kamerling Onnes Laboratorium, Leiden, The Netherlands, 1988, Imperial Coll., London, 1997; pres. Zerres Corp.,

1992-97; pres., bd. dirs. Kenmore Tower Corp., 1996—, pres. Super Solder Corp., 1997-99; co-chair internat. symposium on Jahn-Teller Effect, 1999-2000; participant numerous physics teaching improvement programs for secondary sch. tchrs. and students; lectr. in field, prof. emeritus, 2001—. Contbr. articles on low temperature physics, phase transitions and superconductivity to profl. jours.; patentee in field. Chmn. Boston U. Planning Com., 1999. Rsch. Corp. grantee, 1964-65, Air Force Office Sci. Rsch. grantee, 1966-86, NSF grantee, 1975-95. Mem. AAAS, Am. Phys. Soc., N.Y. Acad. Scis., Phi Beta Kappa, Sigma Xi. Home: 566 Commonwealth Ave Boston MA 02215-2520 Office: Boston U Dept Physics Boston MA 02215 *Administration is easier than science because in administration one can create one's own reality, while in science reality is unalterable.*

ZIMMERMAN, GIDEON K. minister; b. Lehr, N.D., Aug. 18, 1920; m. Eleanor Pekrul; children: Paul, Mark (dec.), Thomas. Diploma, N.Am. Baptist Sem., Rochester, N.Y., 1943; BA, Wesley Coll., U. N.D., 1951; postgrad., Bethany Bibl. Sem., 1958-59, Chgo. Lutheran Sem., 1959-61; BD, N.Am. Bapt. Sem., Sioux Falls, S.D., 1960, DD, 1971. Pastor First Bapt. Ch., Auburn, Mich., 1943-47, Grace Bapt. Ch., Grand Forks, N.D., 1947-51, Temple Bapt. Ch., Milw., 1951-55; gen. sec. dept. Christian edn. N. Am. Bapt. Conf., 1955-68, exec. sec., 1968-79, estate planning counselor, 1979-85. Home: 3721 Bardstown Rd Apt 601 Louisville KY 40218-2261

ZIMMERMAN, GOLDA, lawyer, educator; b. Syracuse, N.Y., Sept. 25, 1949; d. Julius and Sara (Lavine) Z.; m. David C. Kapell, Sept. 18, 1977; children: Jermy S., Bethany R. BS in Edn., Boston U., 1971; MS in Ednl. Adminstrn., U. Kans., 1974; JD, Syracuse U., 1980. Bar: N.Y. 1984, U.S. Dist. Ct. (no. dist.) N.Y. 1984, U.S. Tax Ct. 1984. Elem. tchr. St. John's Sch., Lawrence, Kans., 1971-73; adminstrv. asst. U. Kans., Lawrence, 1973-75; sr. sys. analyst, student data sys. Syracuse U., 1975-77; pvt. practice law Syracuse, 1984—. Adj. prof. adoption law Coll. Law Syracuse U., 1989-99; mem. bd. visitors Syracuse U. Coll. Law, 1988—2003; spkr. various groups on intercoutry and domestic adoption. Author (with Sandra Crowther): Five Career Education Module for Pre-Service and In-Service Teachers, 1974; author: Adoption Law in N.Y., 1997, supplement, 2000; editor-in-chief: Adoption Law in New York, 1997; translator: Adoption Law in the 21st Century: Procedures and Pracitices, N.Y. State Bar Assn., 2004. Mem.: Boston U. Alumni Assn., Onondaga County Bar Assn. (bd. dirs. 2002—), N.Y. State Bar Assn. (family law sect.), Women's Bar Assn. State of N.Y. (N.Y. chpt. 1985—87, state dir. 1987—89), Am. Acad. Adoption Attys. (bd. dirs.). Democrat. Office: 711 E Genesee St # 200 Syracuse NY 13210-1540 Office Phone: 415-475-3322.

ZIMMERMAN, HAROLD SAMUEL, retired state legislator, newspaper editor and publisher, state administrator; b. Valley City, N.D., June 1, 1923; s. Samuel Alwin and Lulu (Wylie) Z.; m. Julianne Williams, Sept. 12, 1946; children: Karen, Steven, Judi Jean (dec.). BA, U. Wash., 1947. News editor Sedro-Woolley (Wash.) Courier-Times, 1947-50; editor, pub. Advocate, Castle Rock, Wash., 1950-57; pub. Post-Record, Camas, Wash., 1957-80; assoc. pub., columnist, dir. Eagle Publs., Camas, 1980-88. Mem. Wash. Ho. of Reps., 1967-80; mem. Wash. Senate, 1981-88, Wash. State Environ. Hearings Bd., Lacey, 1988-93. Mem. Grange, Lions, Kiwanis, Sigma Delta Chi, Sigma Chi. Republican. United Methodist. E-mail: hszim@aol.com.

ZIMMERMAN, HELENE LORETTA, retired business educator; b. Rochester, N.Y., Feb. 26, 1933; d. Henry Charles and Loretta Catherine (Hobert) Z. BS, SUNY, Albany, 1953, MS, 1959; PhD, U. N.D., 1969. Cert. records mgr. Bus. tchr., chmn. bus. dept. Williamson (N.Y.) Cen. Sch., 1953-69; asst. prof. U. Ky., Lexington, 1969-70; assoc. prof. bus. Cen. Mich. U., Mt. Pleasant, 1970-74, prof., 1974-98. Author General Business, 1977; contbg. author to records mgmt. text book, 1987. Sec. Isabella County Christmas Outreach, Mt. Pleasant, 1983—. Mem.: AAUW (pres. 1984—86), Mich. Bus. Edn. Assn. (bd. dirs. 1985—90, pres. 1988—89, bd. dirs. 1995—97), Nat. Bus. Edn. Assn., Internat. Soc. Bus. Edn. (internat. v.p. English speaking nations 1986—88, editor Internat. Rev. 1997—), Inst. Cert. Records Mgrs. (sec. 1985—89, exam. devel. com. 1993—2002), Assn. Records Mgmt. and Adminstrn., Gen. Fedn. Women's Clubs (1st v.p. Mt. Pleasant chpt. 2002—03, Mt. Pleasant area Internat. rels. com. 2003—, pres. 2004—), Delta Kappa Gamma (state pres. 1987—89, internat. fin. com. 1990—94, internat. ad hoc com. on tech. 1996—2000). Avocations: travel, crafts. E-mail: zimmerhl@cmich.edu.

ZIMMERMAN, HOWARD ELLIOT, chemist, educator; b. N.Y.C., July 5, 1926; s. Charles and May (Cohen) Zimmerman; m. Jane Kirschenheiter, June 3, 1950 (dec. Jan. 1975); children: Robert, Steven, James; m. Martha L. Bailey Kaufman, Nov. 7, 1975 (div. Oct. 1990); 1 stepchild, Peter B. Kaufman; m. Peggy J. Vick, Oct. 1991; 1 stepchild, Tanya Kaufman. BS, Yale U., 1950, PhD, 1953. NRC fellow Harvard U., 1953-54; faculty Northwestern U., 1954-60, asst. prof., 1955-60; assoc. prof. U. Wis., Madison, 1960-61, prof. chemistry, 1961—, Arthur C. Cope and Hilldale prof. chemistry, 1975—. Chmn. 4th Internat. Union Pure and Applied Chemistry Symposium on Photochemistry, 1972; organizer, chmn. Organic Photochemistry, 1972, Organic Photochemistry Symposium at Pacifichem Honolulu, 1995, Organic Photochemistry Symposium at Pacifichem, 2000. Honolulu, 00. Author: (book) Quantum Mechanics for Organic Chemists, 1975; mem. editl. bd.: Jour. Organic Chemistry, 1967—71, Molecular Photochemistry, 1969—75, Jour. Am. Chem. Soc., 1982—85, Revs. Reactive Intermediates, 1984—89; contbr. articles to profl. jours. and chpts. to profl. texts. Recipient Halpern award for photochemistry, N.Y. Acad. Scis., 1979, Chem. Pioneer award, Am. Inst. Chemists, 1986, Sr. Alexander vonHumboldt award, 1988, Hilldale award, U. Wis., 1988—89, 1990. Mem.: NAS, Inter-Am. Photochemistry Assn. (co-chmn. orgnic divsn. 1977—79, exec. com. 1979—86), German Chem. Soc., Chem. Soc. London, Am. Chem. Soc. (James Flack Norris award 1976, Arthur C. Cope Scholar award 1991), Phi Beta Kappa, Sigma Xi. Achievements include guiding 86 of his research students into professorships. Home: 7813 Westchester Dr Middleton WI 53562-3671 Office: U Wis Chemistry Dept 1101 University Ave Madison WI 53706-1322 Business E-Mail: Zimmerman@chem.wisc.edu.

ZIMMERMAN, JAMES ALLEN, historian, educator; b. Peoria, Ill., May 12, 1933; s. Levi Benjamin and Ann Zimmerman; m. Kathryn Marie Gallagher, Feb. 9, 1936; children: Karen Marie Dunkelberger, Ann Elizabeth, Maria Lynn Thompson, James Edward. BS, Ill. State U., 1955; MA, U. Ill., 1961, PhD, 1971. Educator Carl Sandburg H.S., Orland Park, Ill., 1957—61, edn. adminstr., 1961—67; asst. prof. Mankato (Minn.) State U., 1970—73, Tri-State U., Angola, Ind., 1973—75, assoc. prof., chair, 1975—81, prof., dean, 1981—84, prof., v.p. for acad. affairs, 1984—90, prof., interim pres., 1990, univ. prof. arts and scis., 1990—. Contbr. articles to profl. jours. Active Ind. Acad. Social Scis., Ind. Consortium Internat. Programs. Specialist third class U.S. Army, 1955—57. Recipient Cert. for Svc. in the White House, Pres. Dwight D. Eisenhower, 1957; grantee, State Ill. Programs for Tchrs. Gifted Students, 1957, Ind. Endowment for the Humanities, Am. Philos. Soc. Mem.: NEA (life), Orgn. Ind. Historians, Soc. for Historians Am. Fgn. Rels., Orgn. Am. Historians (life). Roman Catholic. Home: 306 Stonyridge Dr Angola IN 46703 Office: Tri-State Univ 1 University Ave Angola IN 46703 Business E-Mail: zimmermanj@tristate.edu.

ZIMMERMAN, JAMES M. retail company executive; b. 1944; Chmn. Rich's Dept. Store div. Federated Dept. Stores, 1984-88; pres., COO Federated and Allied Dept. Stores, Cin., 1988-97; chmn., CEO Federated Dept. Stores, Cin., 1997—. Office: Federated Department Stores Inc 7 W 7th St Cincinnati OH 45202-2424

ZIMMERMAN, JEAN, lawyer; b. Berkeley, Calif., Dec. 3, 1947; d. Donald Scheel Zimmerman and Phebe Jean (Reed) Doan; m. Gilson Berryman Gray III, Nov. 25, 1982; children: Charles Donald Buffum and Catherine Elisabeth (Phebe (twins); stepchildren: Alison Travis, Laura Rebecca, Gilson Berryman. BSBA, U. Md., 1970; JD, Emory U., 1975. Bar: Ga. 1975, D.C. 1976, N.Y. 1980. Asst. mgr. investments FNMA, Washington, 1970-73; assoc. counsel Fuqua Industries Inc., Atlanta, 1976-79; assoc. Sage Gray Todd & Sims, N.Y.C., 1979-84; from assoc. counsel to sr. v.p., gen. counsel, sec. IBJ Whitehall Bank & Trust Co., N.Y.C., 1984—99; sr. v.p., gen. counsel, sec., bd. dirs. IBJ Schroder Bus. Credit Corp., N.Y.C., 1996-98, Innovest Capital Mgmt., Inc., N.Y.C., 1997-99; sr. v.p., gen. counsel, sec. Innovest Corp., N.Y.C., 1997-99; from gen. counsel, sec. to exec. v.p. ops. and legal ArrowSight, Inc. (formerly ParentWatch.com), N.Y.C., 2001—. From asst. sec. to sr. v.p., gen. counsel, sec., bd. dirs. IBJ Whitehall Bus. Credit Corp., IBJ Whitehall Capital Corp., IBJ Whitehall Securities, Inc., Delphi Asset Mgmt., Inc., Innovest Asset Mgmt., Inc., N.Y.C., 1997-99; from asst. sec. to v.p., gen. counsel, sec. IBJ Schroder Internat. Bank, Miami, Fla., 1989-98; sr. v.p., gen. counsel, sec. Execution Svcs., N.Y.C., 1991-93. Founder, officer ERA Ga., Atlanta, 1977-79; bd. dirs. Ct. Apptd. Spl. Advs., 1988-94. Named one of Outstanding Atlantans, 1978-79; recipient Disting. Alumni award Emory U. Sch. Law, 1999. Mem.: ABA, LWV, Am. Soc. Corp. Secs., Inc., Ga. Assn. Women Lawyers (bd. dirs. 1977—79), Assn. Bar City N.Y., Assn. Emory Alumni (N.Y. pres. 1999—2003, bd. govs. 2001—), DAR. E-mail: jzimmer642@aol.com., jean/zimmerman@arrowsight.com.

ZIMMERMAN, JO ANN, health services and educational consultant, former lieutenant governor; b. Van Buren County, Iowa, Dec. 24, 1936; d. Russell and Hazel (Ward) McIntosh; m. A. Tom Zimmerman, Aug. 26, 1956; children: Andrew, Lisa, Don and Ron (twins), Beth. Diploma, Broadlawns Sch. of Nursing, Des Moines, 1958; BA with honors, Drake U., 1973; postgrad., Iowa State U., 1973—75. RN, Iowa. Asst. head nurse maternity dept. Broadlawns Med. Ctr., Des Moines, 1958—59, weekend supr. nursing svcs., 1960—61, supr. maternity dept., 1966—68; instr. maternity nursing Broadlawns Sch. Nursing, 1968—71; health planner, community rels. assoc. Iowa Health Systems Agy., Des Moines, 1978—82; mem. Iowa Ho. Reps., 1982—86; lt. gov., pres. of Senate, State of Iowa, 1987—91; cons. health svcs., grant writing and continuing edn. Zimmerman & Assocs., Des Moines, 1991—2000; dir. patient care svcs. Nursing Svcs. Iowa, 1996—98; nurse case mgr. Olsten Health Svcs. (now Gentiva Health Svcs.), 1998—2004; founder JAZ Tours, 2002—. Ops. dir. Medlink Svcs., Inc., Des Moines, 1992-96. Contbr. articles to profl. jours. Mem. advanced registered nurse practioner task force on cert. nurse mid-wives Iowa Bd. Nursing, 1980-81, Waukee, Polk County, Iowa Health Edn. Coord. Coun., Iowa Women's Polit. Caucus, Dallas County Women's Polit. Caucus; chmn. Des Moines Area Maternity Nursing Conf. Group. 1969-70, task force on sch. health svcs. Iowa Dept. Health, 1982, task force health edn. Iowa Dept. Pub. Instruction, 1979, adv. com. health edn. assessment tool, 1980-81, Nat. Lt. Govs., chair com. on Agrl. and Rural Devel., 1989; Dallas County Dem. Ctrl. Com., 1972-84, 98—; bd. dirs. Waukee Cmty. Sch. Bd., 1976-79, pres. 1978-79; bd. dirs. Iowa PTA, 1979-83, chair Health Com., 1980-84; mem. steering com. ERA, Iowa, 1991-92; founder Dem. Activist Women's Network (DAWN), 1992; mem. Disciples of Christ Mission Group to El Salvadore, 2003, 04; originated health com. with outreach First Christian Ch., 2004. Mem. ANA, LWV (health chmn. met. Des Moines chpt.), Iowa Nurses Assn., Iowa League for Nursing (bd. dirs. 1979-83), Family Centered Childbirth Edn. Assn. (childbirth instr., advisor), Iowa Cattleman's Assn., Am. Lung Assn. (bd. dirs. Iowa 1988-92), Dem. Activist Women's Network (founder 1992). Mem. Christian Ch. Avocations: gardening, sewing, reading, bridge, breeding british white cattle. Office: Gentiva Health Svcs 3737 Westown Pkwy Ste 2C West Des Moines IA 50266-1028 E-mail: atzzzzz@aol.com.

ZIMMERMAN, JOHN, public relations executive; Dir. pub. and consumer affairs Meijer, Inc., Grand Rapids, Mich., 1994—. Office: Meijer Inc 2929 Walker Ave NW Grand Rapids MI 49544-9428

ZIMMERMAN, JORDAN, marketing professional; b. NJ; MBA, U. South Fla. Chmn, CEO Zimmerman & Ptnrs., Ft. Lauderdale, Fla., 1984—; pres., co-owner Fla. Panthers, 2001—. Achievements include led Just Say No marketing initiative during the Carter administration which is one of the most recognizable anit-drug campaigns to date. Office: 2200 West Commerical Blvd Fort Lauderdale FL 33309

ZIMMERMAN, JOSEPH FRANCIS, political scientist, educator; b. Keene, N.H., June 29, 1928; s. John Joseph and May Veronica (Gallagher) Z.; m. Margaret Bernardette Brennan, Aug. 2, 1958; 1 child, Deirdre Ann. BA, U. N.H., 1950; MA, Syracuse U., 1951, PhD, 1954. Instr. govt. Worcester Poly. Inst., 1954—55, asst. prof., 1955-57, assoc. prof., 1957-62, prof., 1962-65; lectr. Clark U., Worcester, Mass., 1957-65; prof. polit. sci. SUNY, Albany, 1965—. Staff dir. N.Y. State Joint Legis. Com. Transp., 1967-68, rsch. dir., 1968-73; rsch. dir. N.Y. State Select Legis. Com. Transp., 1977-82, Legis. Commn. on Critical Transp. Problems, 1982-95. Author: State and Local Government, 1962, The Massachusetts Town Meeting: A Tenacious Institution, 1967, The Federated City: Community Control in Large Cities, 1972, Pragmatic Federalism, The Reassignment of Functional Responsibility, 1976, (with Frank W. Prescott) The Politics of the Veto of Legislation in New York, 1980, The Government and Politics of the Empire State, 1981, Local Discretionary Authority, 1981, (with Deirdre A. Zimmerman) The Politics of Subnational Governance, 1983, State-Local Relations: A Partnership Approach, 1983, 2d edit., 1995 (CHOICE award as outstandin acad. book, 1984), Participatory Democracy: Populism Revived, 1986, Federal Preemption: The Silent Revolution, 1990, Contemporary American Federalism, 1992, (with Wilma Rule) United States Electoral System: Their Impact Upon Women and Minorities, 1992, (with Wilma Rule) Electoral Systems in Comparative Perspective: Their Impact on Women Minorities, 1994, Curbing Unethical Behavior of Government, 1994, Interstate Relations: The Neglected Dimension of Federalism, 1996, The Recall: Tribunal of the People, 1997, The New England Town Meeting: Democracy in Action, 1999; The Initiative: Citizen Law-Making, 1999, (with Wilma Rule) The U.S. House of Representatives: Reform or Rebuild?, 2000, The Referendum: The People Decide Public Policy, 2001 Interstate Cooperation: Compacts and Administrative Agreements, 2002, Interstate Economic Relations, 2004; contbr. articles to profl. publs. Pres. Citizens' Plan E Assn., Worcester, 1960-62, Citizens for Neighborhood Improvement Worcester, 1957-59. Served to capt. USAF, 1951-53. Named 1 of 3 Outstanding Young Men Worcester Jr. C. of C., 1959, 61, 1 of 3 Outstanding Young Men Mass, Jr. C. of C., 1961, disting. citizen award Nat. Conf. on Govt., 1986. Mem. Am. Polit. Sci. Assn. (Outstanding Academician sect. intergovtl. adminstrn. 1997), Am. Soc. Pub. Adminstrn. (Outstanding Federalism Academician 1997), Nat. Mcpl. League. Clubs: German-Am. Social. Roman Catholic. Home: 82 Greenock Rd Delmar NY 12054-4414 Office: SUNY Rockefeller College 135 Western Ave Albany NY 12222

ZIMMERMAN, KATHLEEN MARIE, artist; b. Floral Park, NY, Apr. 24, 1923; d. Harold G. and Evelyn M. (Andrade) Z.; m. Ralph S. Iwamoto, Nov. 23, 1963. Student, Art Students League, N.Y.C., 1942—44, Nat. Acad. Sch. Fine Arts, 1944—47, Nat. Acad. Sch. Fine Arts, 1950—54. Tchr. drawing and painting Midtown Sch. Art, N.Y.C., 1947-52. Illustrator (with Ralph S. Iwamoto) Diet for a Small Planet, 1971; one-woman shows include Westbeth Gallery, N.Y.C., 1973, 1974, St. Mary's Coll., St. Mary's City, Md., 1990, Broome St. Gallery, N.Y.C., 2002, exhibited in group shows at Woodstock Art Gallery, N.Y., 1945, Nat. Arts Club, N.Y.C., 1948—56, 1984, Emily Lowe Award Show, 1951, Contemporary Arts Gallery, N.Y.C., 1952, 1960, Village Art Ctr., 1956—61, Allied Artists Ann., N.Y.C., 1956, 1978, 1980—91, 1993—2003, Studio Gallery, 1957—60, Nat. Assn. Women Artists, N.Y.C., 1957—85, 1987—98, 2000, 2003, Art USA, 1958, ACA Gallery, 1958—59, City Ctr. Gallery, 1960, Janet Nessler Gallery, N.Y.C., 1961, Silvermine Guild, Conn., 1962, Pioneer Gallery, Cooperstown, N.Y., 1962—63, Audubon Artists, N.Y.C., 1963—2003, NAD, 1969—2001, 2003, Women Artists Award Winners, N.Y.C., 1974, Am. Watercolor Soc., 1975—78, 1980, Cheyenne (Wyo.) Western Galleries, 1975—77, Edward-Dean Mus., Cherry Valley, Calif., 1975—77, Frye Mus., Seattle, 1975—76, 1997, Boise Gallery Art, 1975, Central Wyo. Mus. Art, 1975—76, Willamette U., 1975, Yellowstone Art Ctr., Billings, Mont., 1975, Utah State U., 1975, Applewood Art Gallery, Colo., 1976, Charleston Art Gallery, W.Va., 1976, Kent State U., 1976, Cin. Art Club, 1976, Martello Mus., Key West, Fla., 1976, Buecker Gallery, N.Y.C., 1976, Anchorage Fine Arts Mus., 1976, Davis and Long Gallery, N.Y.C., 1977, Butler Inst. Am. Art, 1978, 2000, Washington Square East Gallery, NYU, 1979, Internat. Festival Women Artists, Copenhagen, 1980, Westbeth Gallery, N.Y.C., 1980, 1983, 1999—2004, City Gallery, 1981, Bergen Cmty. Mus., Paramus, N.J., 1983, Kenkeleba Gallery, N.Y.C., 1985, Adelphi U., Garden City, N.Y., 1987, Lotos Club, N.Y.C., 1987, Temperance Hall Gallery, Bellport, N.Y., 1987, Monmouth Mus., Lincroft, N.J., 1987, Marbella Gallery, N.Y.C., 1989, Knickerbocker Artists, 1990, Brownstone Gallery, N.Y.C., 1993, Viridian Gallery, 1995, Sundance Gallery, Bridgehampton, N.Y., 1996, Mcpl. Art Ctr., Athens, Greece, 1996, ISE Art Found., N.Y.C., 1996, Nat. Soc. Painters in Casein & Acrylic, 1997-2001, 2004, Zimmerli Mus., Rutgers U., New Brunswick, N.J., 1998, Gallery OneTwentyEight, N.Y.C., 2001—03, Broome St. Gallery, 2002—03, Nat. Acad. Mus., 2003, Lecei Gallery, West Concord, Mass., 2003, Represented in permanent collections Butler Inst. Am. Art, Youngstown, Ohio, Sheldon Swope Art Gallery, Terre Haute, Ind., Lauren Rogers Mus. Art, Laurel, Miss., U. Wyo. Art Mus., Laramie, U. Miami Lowe Art Mus., Coral Gables, Fla., N.C. Mus. Art, Raleigh, Swarthmore Coll., Pa., Erie Art Mus., Nat. Acad. Design, N.Y.C., Zimmerli Mus., Rutgers U., New Brunswick, Nat. Mus. Women in the Arts, Washington; bibliography James Mellow, N.Y. Times Art Rev., 1973, Hilton Kramer, N.Y. Times Rev., 1977, Helen A. Harrison, N.Y. Times Rev., 1987, William Zimmer, N.Y. Times Rev., 1999, Terry Teachout, Washington Post Review, 2003, Ken Johnson, N.Y. Times Rev., 2003, contbr. (bibliography) The Art of Collage, 1978, Mastering Color & Design in Watercolor, 1981, The Collage Handbook, 1985, Painting Without a Brush, 1992, Collage Techniques, 1994. John F. and Anna Lee Stacey scholar, 1954; recipient Nat. Soc. Painters in Casein and Acrylic award 1997, Liquitex Art award, 1999, Winsor & Newton award 2001, Howard Mandel Meml. award, 2004. Mem.: NAD (Henry Ward Ranger Fund purchase prize 1976, cert. of merit 1980, Henry Ward Ranger Fund purchase prize 1982, L.G. Sawyer prize 1988, Ogden Pleissner Meml. award 1991, William A. Paton prize 1993, 1997, Zellah W. Pike prize 2001), N.Y. Artists Equity Assn. (Dr. Maury Leibovitz award 1985), Allied Artists Am. (Silver medal 1981, Jane Peterson award 1985, Creative Watercolor prize 1989, Silver medal 1991, Creative Watercolor prize 1997, Mary Lou Fitzgerald Meml. award 1998, John Young-Hunter Meml. award 2002, Pauline Law Meml. award 2003), Nat. Assn. Women Artists (14 prizes 1957—), Am. Watercolor Soc. (Barse Miller Meml. award 1976), Audubon Artists (John Wenger Meml. award 1978, Ralph Fabri medal 1981, J&E Liskin Meml. award 1987, Dick Blick award 1994, Gold Medal of Honor 2001, Art Students League award 2002). Home: 463 West St Apt 1110A New York NY 10014-2040

ZIMMERMAN, KENT M. lawyer; BA in Polit. Sci., Washington U., 1994; JD, Ill. Inst. Tech., 1998. TV prodr. KPLR, 1994—96; assoc. Bullwinkel Ptnrs., 1998—99; v.p., gen. counsel Hubbard One, Chgo., 1999—. Office: Hubbard One 6th Fl 247 S State Chicago IL 60604*

ZIMMERMAN, LARRY JOHN, anthropologist, educator; b. Anamosa, Iowa, May 24, 1947; s. August Dietrich and Minnie Heiken Zimmerman; m. Karen Louise Pike, July 18, 1970; children: Dietrich, Alice. BA, U. Iowa, 1969, MA, 1971; PhD, U. Kans., Lawrence, 1976. Disting. regents prof. anthropology U. SD, Vermillion, 1974-96; prof., chair Am. Indian and Native studies U. Iowa, Iowa City, 1998—2001, adj. prof. anthropology, 2001—02; head arch. Minn. Hist. Soc., St. Paul, 2002—. Harrington lectr. Coll. Arts and Scis., U. SD, 1992. Author: Native North America, 2000, Presenting The Past, 2003; editor: (books) Indians and Anthropologists, 1997, Ethical Issues in Archaeology, 2003. Named Tchr. of Yr., U. SD Student Assn., 1980, Nat. Lectr., Sigma Xi, 1991-92. Fellow Am. Anthrop. Assn. Avocations: travel, reading. Home: 1827 Trailway Drive 7 Eagan MN 55122-3226 Office: Minn Hist Soc Dept Archaeology 345 Kellogg Blvd W Saint Paul MN 55102-1906 Office Phone: 612-970-2843. Personal E-mail: oneota@earthlink.net. Business E-Mail: larry.zimmerman@mnhs.org.

ZIMMERMAN, LAWRENCE A. corporate financial executive; b. NY, Dec. 2, 1942; BS in Fin., NYU, 1965; MBA, Adelphi U., 1967. From dir. budgets to corp. contr. IBM Corp., 1988—94, v.p. fin. Europe, Middle East and Africa ops., 1994—96, v.p. fin. and planning server and tech. divsn., 1996—98; exec. v.p., CFO Sys. Software Assoc., Inc., Chgo., 1999; corp. sr. v.p., CFO Xerox Corp., Stamford, Conn., 2002—. Office: Xerox Corp 800 Long Ridge Rd Stamford CT 06904

ZIMMERMAN, LYNN DIANN, language educator, literary forensic consultant; b. Steubenville, Ohio, Mar. 16, 1968; d. Don Omar and Jonnie Marie Zimmerman; m. Jack Michael Hall, Jan. 21, 1995; children: Ian Blair children: Jacob Riley. PhD in English, Kent State U., Ohio, 2003. English prof. John Carroll U., Univ. Heights, Ohio, 1991—93, Kent State U., Ohio, 1995—. Lit. forensic consulting, Lorain, Ohio, 2001—. Grantee Pringle Fellowship, 2000; scholar Tchg. Fellowship, Kent State U., 1995—2000. Democrat. Mem. United Church Of Christ. Achievements include research in Narrative Theory and Strategies; Disarming Militia Discourse. Avocations: travel, reading. Personal E-mail: ldzimmerman@att.net.

ZIMMERMAN, MARLIN U., JR., chemical engineer; b. Akron, Ohio, Aug. 2, 1923; s. Marlin Ulrich and Helen (Nelson) Z. BChemE, Johns Hopkins U., 1944; MBA, Harvard U., 1966. Registered profl. engr., Ohio. Jr. engr. Standard Oil Co. (Ohio), Cleve., 1944-46, engr., 1946-48, sr. engr., 1948-49, process engr. Lima (Ohio) refinery, 1949-50, group engr., 1951-55, group supr., 1956-60, supr. process sys. sect., 1961-63, head acrylonitrile task force, 1961, tech. specialist, 1964-66; mgr. long term planning Norton Co., Worcester, Mass., 1966-69; cons. John Van Der Valk & Assocs., N.Y.C., 1970-73; pvt. practice cons. chem. engr. ammonia-urea Hackensack, N.J., 1974—. Head task force to help commercialize Sohio acrylonitrile process. Contbr. articles to profl. jours. Baker scholar, 1966. Mem. AIChE, Johns Hopkins Club, Tudor and Stuart Club, Tau Beta Pi, Omicron Delta Kappa, Beta Theta Pi. Methodist. Achievements include patent for process improvement of Tosco shale process for oil recovery; patent for pig handling for gasoline blender meter testing loop, others. Avocations: travel, photography, reading, investing, computer programming. Office: 229 Union St Hackensack NJ 07601

ZIMMERMAN, MARTIN B. automotive executive; b. New York City, June 19, 1946; B(hon.), Dartsmouth Coll.; D in Econ., Mass. Inst. of Tech. Faculty mem. Sloan Sch. of Mgmt., Mass. Inst. of Tech.; prof. bus. econ. dept. Univ. Mich. Grad. Sch. Bus. Admin., 1983—85, prof. and chmn. bus. econ. dept., 1985; co. chief economist Ford Motor Co., Dearborn, Mich., 1987—94, exec. dir. govtl. rels. and corp. econ., 1994—99, v.p. govtl. affairs, 1999—2001, group v.p., corp. affairs, 2001—. Sr. economist President's Coun. of Econ. Advisors, 1985—86; adv. coun. Nat. Aeronautic and Space Admin., 1988—92. Serves on bd. of the Citizens Rsch Coun. of Mich., Cmty. Found. of S.E. Mich. and Detroit Met. Visitors and Conv. Bur. Recipient Blue Chip Econ. Forecasting Award. Mem.: Citizens Rsch. Coun. of Mich., Bus. for Soc. Responsibility (bd. dir.), The Panel of Econ. Advisors to the Congl. Budget Office, Com. for Econ. Devel. (bd. of trustees), Nat. Assn. Bus. Economists, Phi Betta Kappa. Office: Ford Motor Co One American Rd Dearborn MI 48123-1899

ZIMMERMAN, MARY ALICE, performing arts educator; BA, MA, PhD, Northwestern U. Asst. prof. performance studies Northwestern U., Evanston, Ill.; artistic assoc. Goodman and Seattle Repertory Theater; mem. Lookingglass Theater Company, Chicago. Dir.: (plays) The Notebooks of Leonardo da Vinci, The Odyssey, Arabian Nights, Journey to the West, Metamorphoses (Tony award for best director, 2002), Secret in the Wings, Eleven Rooms of Proust, Measure for Measure, Henry VIII, A Midsummer Night's Dream, All's Well That Ends Well. Active Lookingglass Theatre Co. Recipient MacArthur Fellowship, 1998, 20 Joseph Jefferson Awards for best direction. Office: Dept Performance Studies Northwestern U 1920 Campus D Evanston IL 60208

ZIMMERMAN, MICHAEL, agricultural products, grain company executive; BA, Trinity Coll., 1972; MBA, Harvard U., 1976. Various sr. investment banking positions Salomon Brothers, 1976-96; pres. ContiInvestments, 1996—, sr. v.p. investments & strategy, 1996-99; exec. v.p., CFO Conti Group, 1999—. Office: Conti Group 277 Park Ave New York NY 10172

ZIMMERMAN, MICHAEL DAVID, lawyer; b. Chgo., Oct. 21, 1943; s. Elizabeth Porter; m. Lynne Mariani (dec. 1994); children: Evangeline Albright, Alessandra Mariani, Morgan Elisabeth; m. Diane Hamilton, 1998. BS,

U. Utah, 1966, JD, 1969, PhD (hon.), 2001. Bar: Calif. 1971, Utah 1978. Law clk. to Chief Justice Warren Earl Burger U.S. Supreme Ct., Washington, 1969-70; assoc. O'Melveny & Myers, L.A., 1970-76; assoc. prof. law U. Utah, 1976-78, adj. prof. law, 1978-84, 89-93; of counsel Kruse, Landa, Zimmerman & Maycock, Salt Lake City, 1978-80; spl. counsel Gov. of Utah, Salt Lake City, 1978-80; ptnr. Watkiss & Campbell, Salt Lake City, 1980-84; assoc. justice Supreme Ct. Utah, Salt Lake City, 1984-93, 98-00, chief justice, 1994-98; atty., mediator, arbitrator, of counsel Snell & Wilmer, Salt Lake City, 2000—. Co-moderator Justice Soc. Program of Snowbird Inst. for Arts and Humanities, 1991, 92, 93, 94, 95, 97, 98; moderator, Tanner lecture panel dept. philosophy U. Utah, 1994; faculty Judging Sci. Program Duke U., 1992, 93; bd. dirs. Conf. of Chief Justices, 1995-98. Note editor: Utah Law Rev., 1968-69; contbr. numerous articles to legal publs. Mem. Project 2000, Coalition for Utah's Future, 1985—96; trustee Hubert and Eliza B. Michael Found., 1994—98; bd. dirs. Rowland-Hall St. Mark's Sch., 1997—; bd. assoc. Utah Mus. Natural History Found., 1995—; bd. dirs. Summit Inst. for Arts and Humanities, 1998—, chair, 1999—; bd. dirs. Hansen Planetarium, 1997—, Snowbird Inst. for Arts and Humanities, 1989—98, Deer valley Inst. for Arts and Humanities, 1996—98, Kanzeon Zen Ctr., 1999—, chair, 2000—; bd. dirs. Utah Coun. on Conflict Resoultion, 1999—, chair, 1999—; bd. dirs. Pvt. Adjudication Ctr.; mem. Duke U., 2000—; co-dir. Registry of Ind. Sci. and Tech. Advisors, Duke U., 2000—; chair Utah Jud. Coun. Task Force on Racial and Ethnic Fairness in the Jud. Sys., 1996. Named Utah State Bar Appellate Ct. Judge of Yr., 1998; recipient Excellence in Ethics Award, Ctr. for Study of Ethics, 1994, Disting. Svc. Award Utah State Bar, 1998, Individual Achievement Award Downtown Alliance, 1997, The Peter W. Billings, Sr. American Arbitration Assoc. Outstanding Dispute Resolution Svc. Award, 1997, participant Justice and Soc. Program of Aspen Inst. for Humanistic Studies, 1998, co-moderator, 1989. Fellow: Am. Bar Found.; mem.: Gov. Radiation Exposure Study Mgmt. Com., Ririe-Woodbury Dance Co. (exec. bd. 1982—84), U.S. Dept. of Energy Dose Assessment Adv. Group of the Off-Site Radiation Exposure Reconstruction Project (Utah citizen rep. 1980—84), Utah Legal Svc. Corp. (Bd. of Trustees 1985—87), U. Utah Master of Pub. Adminstrn. Program Practitioners' Adv. Com. (mem 1985—89), U.S. Vet. Adminstrn. Adv. Com. on Environ. Hazzards (e.g., agent orange, nuclear radiation 1985—89), Nat. Endowment for the Humanities Scholar in Residence at Utah Valley Cmty. Coll. (Orem, Utah 1990), Order of Coif, Am. Judicature Soc. (bd. dirs. 1995—2001), Am. Inns of Ct. VII, Utah Jud. Coun. (supreme ct. rep. 1986—91, chair 1994—98), Jud. Conf. U.S. (adv. com. civil rules 1985—91), Salt Lake County Bar Assn., Utah Bar Assn., Am. Law Inst., ABA (faculty mem. appellate judges' seminar 1993), Phi Kappa Phi. Office: Snell & Wilmer 15 West South Temple Ste 1200 Salt Lake City UT 84101

ZIMMERMAN, NANCY PICCIANO, library science educator; b. Jeannette, Pa., July 29, 1951; d. Daniel Joseph and Helen Elizabeth (Lipinski) Picciano; m. Lee W. Zimmerman, Aug. 10, 1974; children: Matthew, Renée. BA in English, Carlow Coll., Pitts., 1973; MLS in Libr. Sci., U. Pitts., 1974; MS in Computer Edn. and Cognitive Sys., U. North Tex., 1992; PhD in Libr. and Info. Studies, Tex. Woman's U., 1992. Lic. libr. media specialist, K-12, lang. arts/English 7-12. Libr. media specialist Fairfield (Calif.)-Suisun Sch. Dist., 1976-78; reference libr. Pikes Peak Libr. Dist., Colorado Springs, Colo., 1983; libr. media specialist North Pole (Alaska) H.S., 1984-85, Prince William County Schs., Woodbridge, Va., 1985-89; dir. info. retrieval lab. Tex. Woman's U., Denton, 1989-91; adj. prof., rsch. assoc. U. North Tex., Denton, 1991-92; from asst. to assoc. prof. Sch. Info. and Libr. Studies SUNY, Buffalo, 1993-99; assoc. prof. Sch. Libr. and Info. Scis. U. S.C., Columbia, 1999—. ALISE/OCLC rsch. grantee, 1994, 2004. Mem. ALA (coun. 2000—, chair Libr. Rsch. Round Table 1995-96), Am. Assn. Sch. Librs. (treas. 1996-99, pres. 2002-2003, exec. bd. 1996-99, 2001-04), Internat. Assn. Sch. Librs., N.Y. Libr. Assn. (pres. 1999), Nat. Bd. for Profl. Tchg. Stds. (sch. libr. media com. 1997-2000), Phi Delta Kappa, Beta Phi Mu (nat. exec. com. 1994-99). Office: U SC Sch Libr and Info Scis 217 Davis Coll Columbia SC 29208-0001 Office Phone: 803-777-1215.

ZIMMERMAN, PAUL ALBERT, retired college president, minister; b. Danville, Ill., June 25, 1918; s. Albert Carl and Hanna Marie (Haffner) Z.; m. Genevieve Emmaline Bahls, June 11, 1944; children— Karmin (Mrs. Raymond Philp), Thomas. Student, Concordia Coll., Ft. Wayne, Ind., 1936-39; BA, Concordia Sem., St. Louis, 1941, M.Div., 1944; MA, U. Ill., 1947, PhD, 1951; D.D., Concordia Sem., Springfield, Ill., 1975; LLD (hon.), Concordia Coll., Ann Arbor, Mich., 1994. Prof. theology and sci. Bethany Coll., Mankato, Minn., 1944-53; prof. Concordia Tchrs. Coll., Seward, Nebr., 1953-54, pres., 1954-61, Concordia Luth. Jr. Coll., Ann Arbor, Mich., 1961-73, Concordia Coll., River Forest, Ill., 1973-83, ret., 1983; pastor St. Luke's Luth. Ch., Harrison, Mich., 1983-88. Author and editor: Darwin, Evolution and Creation, 1959, Rock Strata and the Bible Record, 1971, Creation, Evolution and God's Word, 1972. Chmn. Washtenaw County Red Cross, 1968-70; pres. Ann Arbor Found., 1970-71; mem. Citizens Com. Study Taxation, Ann Arbor, 1972; mem. adv. bd. St. Joseph Mercy Community, 1969-72; chmn. Luth. Ch. Mo. Synod's Bd. for Mission Services, 1982-92, Mission Task Force, 1990-91, adminstrv. asst. pres. Mo. Synod, 1972-73, 93-94, mem. curriculum commn. bd. higher edn., 1963-73, mem. task force constl. revision Mo. Synod, chmn. com. adjudication procedures Mo. Synod, Mo. Synod com. on structure, 1995-98. Fellow Creation Rsch. Assn. Lutheran. Home: 2798 Princeton Dr Traverse City MI 49684-9131

ZIMMERMAN, RAYMOND, retail chain executive; b. Memphis, Tenn., 1933; married. V.p. Service Mdse. Co., Inc., Nashville, from 1959, pres., 1973-1981, chmn. bd. dirs., 1981-98, 99—, chief exec. officer, until 1997. Address: 2968 Foster Creighton Dr Nashville TN 37204-3719

ZIMMERMAN, ROBERT ALLEN See DYLAN, BOB

ZIMMERMAN, ROBERT S., JR., federal agency administrator; m. Jean Zimmerman; children: Wendy, Steven. B in Sociology, King's Coll.; MPH, U. Tenn. Developer, dir. Bur. Primary Care Resources and Sys. Devel. Pa. Dept. Health, 1993—95; dep. sec. for med. assistance programs Pa. Dept. Pub. Welfare, 1997—99; sec. Pa. Dept. Health, 1999—2003; regional rep. Region III U.S. Dept. Health and Human Svcs., Phila., 2003—. Office: US Dept HHS Pub Ledger Bldg Ste 436 150 S Independence Mall West Philadelphia PA 19106-3499

ZIMMERMAN, ROGER JOSEPH, fishery biologist; b. Alice, Tex., Dec. 2, 1941; s. Walter George and Laura Virgie (Heine) Z.; m. Domenica Marie DeCaro, Dec. 28, 1976; children: Kathryn, Robert. BS in Biology, Tex. A&I Coll., 1966, MA in Biology and Geology, 1969; PhD in Marine Scis., U.P.R., Mayaguez, 1979. Tchg. asst. biology dept. U. South Fla., Tampa, 1971, rsch. assoc. marine sci. dept. St. Petersburg, 1971-73; rsch. assoc. P.R. Nuclear Ctr. U. P.R., 1974-75, grad. fellow, 1975-78, marine benthic ecologist Ctr. for Energy & Environ. Rsch., 1978-81; fishery ecologist fishery mgmt. divsn. NOAA/NMFS Galveston (Tex.) Lab., 1981-91, divsn. chief fishery ecology divsn., 1991-93, lab. dir., 1993—. Rsch. fellow U.S. Nat. Mus. Natural History, Smithsonian Instn., Washington and Harbor Beach, Fla., summer 1975, 76; vis. instr. marine biology dept. Tex. A&M U., Galveston, summer 1988, 89; vis. instr. biology dept. Corpus Christi (Tex.) State U., 1986; tchg. asst. biology U. South Fla., 1970; lectr.-counselor Tex. A&I U., 1969, lab. coord., tchg. asst., 1968-69; OAS and U.S. AID advisor to Instuto de Pesca de Ecuador, 1985-88; mem. com. coastal ocean estuarine habitat rsch. planning com. NOAA 1987, sci. adv. com., 1989; chair predator-prey com. S.E. Fisheries Sci. Ctr., 1990-91; coord. climate and global change ecol. sys. and dynamics work group NMFS, 1990, spl. asst. to office of sr. scientist, 1990; mem. sci. adv. com. Galveston Bay project Nat. Estuary Program, 1993-96, mgmt. com. Coastal Bend project, 1994-98; bd. dirs. Gulf of Mex. regional marine rsch. program NMFS-SEFSC, 1992-93; rep. programs on coastal fisheries and estuarine ecology SERSC, 1992-95; grad. student advisor, adj. wildlife and fisheries dept. and biology dept. Tex. A&M U., dept. biology Corpus Christi State U., dept. marine scis. La. State U., 1985-89, dept. biology U. Houston, 1983-85; presenter workshops in field. Reviewer for jours. in field, including Fishery Bull., Contbns. to Marine Sci., Marine Ecology Progress Series, Jour. Exptl. Marine Biology and Ecology, Marine Biology, Bull. Marine Sci., Jour. Wetlands Ecology and Mgmt., Estuaries, Coastal and Shelf Sci., also various proposals; editl. reviewer SEFSC Galveston Lab., 1984—; contbr. numerous articles to profl. publs.; author abstracts, revs. in field. Mem. Estuarine Rsch. Fedn., Gulf Estuarine Rsch. Soc., Crustacean Soc., Am. Fisheries Soc., Assn. Marine Labs. of the Caribbean. Office: Nat Marine Fisheries Svc SE Fisheries Sci Ctr 4700 Avenue U Galveston TX 77551-6901

ZIMMERMAN, S(AMUEL) MORTON (MORT ZIMMERMAN), engineering executive; b. Paterson, N.J., Mar. 18, 1927; s. Solomon Zimmerman and Miriam (Feder) Glatzer; m. Marion Patricia Boque, Sept. 15, 1951 (dec. 1993); children: Judy, Suzy, Sharon, Dan; m. Rosalie Fitzgerald, June 1, 1998. Student, Ga. Inst. Tech., 1942-44, 46-48, Oglethorpe U., 1948-51; BSEE, Pacific Internat. U., L.A., 1958. Pres. Comml. Electronics Corp., Dallas, 1954-56, Electron Corp. subs. LTV Corp., 1956-65; chmn. bd., pres. Capital Bancshares, Inc., 1965-66; chmn. bd. Capital Nat. Bank Tampa (formerly Springs Nat. Bank), Fla., 1965, Capital Nat. Bank Miami (name now Peoples Downtown Bank), Fla., 1966, Merc. Nat. Bank Miami Beach (name now Barnett Bank), Fla., 1967, Underwriters Bank & Trust Co. N.Y. (name now Banco Cen.), 1968; chmn. bd., pres. Capital Gen. Corp., 1967, Comml. Tech., Inc., 1977—, Petro Imperial Corp. and subs. DOL Resources and Tech.-Star, Dallas, 1983—; founder, chmn. bd. Atmospheric & Magnetic Tech., Inc. (now Atmospheric Water Tech., Inc.), 1997—. Chmn. bd., pres. Trans Exchange Corp., 1965—, Electric & Gas Tech., Inc., 1985—; also chmn. 8 subs. cos.; chmn. bd. Video Sci. Tech., Inc., 1981-92, Interfed. Capital, Inc., 1990—, Dynamic Funding Inc., 2000—, Logic Metals Tech., Inc., 2002—. Patentee: TV camera video amplifier and blanking circuits, electronic thermometer, video x-ray image system and methods, video system and method for presentation and reproduction x-ray film images, electromagnetic radio frequency lighting system, laser display of electronically generated image signal; additional patents pending; U.S. copyrights on electronic atmosphere dew point generator of pure refrigeration drinking water, 2001, hydrogen peroxide electrical power generator, 2001. Petty officer USN, 1942-45. Recipient Interfaith award City of N.Y. Mem. IEEE, Brookhaven Country Club. Republican. Jewish. Home: 5901 Yardley Ct Dallas TX 75248-2138 Office: Electric & Gas Tech Inc 13636 Neutron Rd Dallas TX 75244-4410 Fax: 972 991-3265. Office Phone: 972-934-8797. E-mail: mortzim@webtv.net.

ZIMMERMAN, SOL SHEA, pediatrician; b. N.Y.C., June 25, 1948; s. Isaac and Estera (Berkowicz) Z.; m. Diana F. Zimmerman, Aug. 8, 1971; children: Jeffrey, Steven, Andrew. AB, Columbia U., 1968; MD, NYU, 1972. Diplomate Am. Bd. Pediats.; pediat. critical care medicine. Intern dept. pediats. NYU-Bellevue Hosp. Ctr., N.Y.C., 1972-73, resident dept. pediats., 1973-75, chief resident dept. pediats., 1977-78, asst. prof. clin. pediats., 1978-83, assoc. prof. clin. pediats., 1983—, dir. pediat. critical care medicine, 1978-98, assoc. dir. dept. pediats., 1985—; assoc. chair dept. pediats. NYU Sch. of Medicine, N.Y.C., 1997—, assoc. prof. pediat., 2002—. Pres. Pediat. Assocs. N.Y.C., P.C., 1978—; v.p. Univ. Physicians Network, 1996—; chmn. bd. mgrs. Univ. MSO, 1998—; assoc. prof. pediat. NYU-Bellevue Hosp. Ctr., 2002. Editor, author: (textbook) Critical Care Pediatrics, 1985. Chmn. com. on heart, health in the young N.Y.C. affiliate Am. Heart Assn., 1987-93. Maj. USAF MC, 1975-77. Fellow Am. Acad. Pediats., Am. Coll. Chest Physicians, Critical Care Medicine; mem. N.Y. Soc. Pediat. Critical Care Medicine (v.p. 1989-91, pres. 1991-93), Alpha Omega Alpha. Office: Pediat Assocs NYC PC 317 E 34th St New York NY 10016-4974 also: 20 Plaza St E Brooklyn NY 11238-4955

ZIMMERMAN, WILLIAM EDWIN, newspaper editor, publisher, writer; b. Bklyn., Feb. 2, 1941; s. George and Ruth (Edelbaum) Z.; m. Teodorina Bello, Dec. 13, 1969; 1 child, Carlota Pastora. BA, Queens Coll., 1962. Pres. Guarionex Press, Ltd., N.Y.C., 1979—; with Am. Banker, N.Y.C., 1962-82, editor, sr. v.p., 1982-89; editor in chief Banking Week, 1986-89; dep. editor Sunday Bus. sect. The N.Y. Times, 1989; spl. projects editor, editor Student Briefing Page Newsday, L.I., N.Y., 1989—. Author: How to Tape Instant Oral Biographies, 1979, A Book of Questions to Keep Thoughts and Feelings, 1984, Make Beliefs, 1987, Life Lines: A Book of Hope, 1990, The Little Book of Joy, 1995, Dogmas: Simple Truths from a Wise Pet, 1995, Make Beliefs for Kids of All Ages, 1996, A Book of Sunshine, 1997, Cat-e-chisms: Feline Answers to Life's Big Questions, 1997, My Life: An Open Book, 2000, Lunch Box Letters, 2000, Idea Catcher for Kids, 2000, Butterfly Wishes, 2002, My Paper Memory Quilt, 2004. Mem. Am. Oral History Assn., Am. Soc. Bus. Writers, Am. Soc. Bus. Press Editors, N.Y. Fin. Writers Assn., Overseas Press Club, Deadline Club, Dowtown Athletic Club, N.Y. Athletic Club, Sigma Delta Chi. Democrat. Jewish. Office: Newsday Inc 2 Park Ave New York NY 10016-5679 Personal E-mail: wmz@aol.com.

ZIMMERMAN, ZORA DEVRNJA, comparative literature and folklore educator; b. Marienbad, Czechoslovakia, May 12, 1945; came to U.S., 1951; d. Milutin Devrnja and Dorothea Wohlgemuth; m. Thomas Lee Zimmerman, Sept. 12, 1976; children: Anna, Elizabeth. BA, SUNY, Buffalo, 1967, PhD, 1974. From asst. prof. to assoc. prof. Iowa State U., Ames, 1974-84, prof. English, 1985—, assoc. dean Coll. Liberal Arts and Scis., 1990—. Author: (book) Serbian Folk Poetry: Ancient Legends, Romantic Songs, 1986; editor: (poetry book) Arc from Now, 1978; contbr. articles to profl. jours., chpts. to books. NEH summer fellow Ind. U., 1979. Office: Iowa State U Coll Liberal Arts and Scis 202 Carrie Chapman Catt Hl Ames IA 50011-0001 Business E-Mail: zdzimme@iastate.edu.

ZIMMERMANN, FRANK MARTIN, physicist, surface scientist, educator; b. Karlsruhe, Germany, May 6, 1964; came to U.S., 1987; s. Manfred Eugen and Herta Zimmermann; m. Yeong-Ah Soh, Oct. 29, 1995 (div. Sept. 2, 2003); 1 child, Ingrid Hana (div. Sept. 2, 2003). MS in Physics, Cornell U., 1993, PhD in Physics, 1995. Rsch. asst. solid state physics Ariz. State U., 1988-89; rsch. asst. surface sci. Cornell U., 1990-95; asst. prof. physics dept. physics and astronomy and lab. surface modification Rutgers U., Piscataway, N.J., 1995-2001, assoc. prof., 2001—. Lectr., presenter in field. Contbr. numerous articles to profl. jours. including Surface Sci. Reports and Phys. Rev. Lett. Fulbright fellow, 1987-88, Internat. Rsch. fellow Sci. and Tech. Agy., Japan, 1996, 98; Rutgers bd. trustees rsch. fellow for scholarly excellence, 2001. Mem. Am. Phys. Soc., Am. Vacuum Soc. (Grad. Rsch. award 1994, Morton M. Traum award 1995), Am. Chem. Soc. (Victor K. LaMer award 1996), Phi Kappa Phi. Achievements include elucidation of mechanisms and dynamics of thermal and photochemical desorption and adsorption using laser spectroscopy. Avocations: whitewater kayaking, downhill skiing, bicycling. Office: Rutgers U Dept Physics 136 Frelinghuysen Rd Piscataway NJ 08854-8019

ZIMMERMANN, JOHN PAUL, plastic surgeon; b. Milw., Mar. 9, 1945; s. Paul August and Edith Josephine (Tutsch) Z.; m. Bianca Maria Schaldach, June 13, 1970; cbildren: Veronica, Jean-Paul. BS in Biology, Chemistry, Marquette U., 1966; MD, Med. Coll. Wis., 1970. Diplomate Am Bd. Plastic Surgery. Internship surgery Stanford U. Sch. of Medicine, Calif., 1970-71, residency in gen. surgery, plastic & reconstructive surgery, 1974-79; flight surgeon USAF, 1971-73; fellowship head & neck surgery Roswell Park Meml. Cancer Inst., Buffalo, N.Y., 1977; pvt. practice Napa, Calif., 1979—. Dir. Aesthetic Surgery Ctr. of Napa Valley, Calif., 1993—; clinical asst. prof. of plastic surgery Stanford U. Sch. of Medicine, Calif., 1993—; bd. dirs. Interplast, Palo Alto, Calif. (pres., bd. dirs. 1991-94, chmn. bd. dirs. 1994-95). Mem. Am. Soc. Plastic Surgeons, Am. Soc. Aesthetic Plastic Surgeons, Lipoplasty Soc., Calif. Soc. Plastic Surgeons (bd. dirs.), Calif. Med. Assn., Napa County Med. Assn. Republican. Roman Catholic. Avocations: sailing, golf, direct care of indigent patientsthrough interplast. Office: Plastic Reconstructive Surgery Ctr 3443 Villa Ln Ste 10 Napa CA 94558-6417

ZIMMERMANN, ROBERT A. molecular biologist, science educator; b. Phila., July 17, 1937; s. William and Margaret (Lukens) Z.; m. Athleen B. Kammerer; 1 child, Hannah Kelly. BA, Amherst Coll., 1959; PhD, MIT, 1964. Rsch. fellow Med. Sch. Harvard U., Boston, 1966-69; rsch. assoc. U. Geneva, 1970-73; assoc. prof. U. Mass., Amherst, 1973-77, prof. dept. biochemistry and molecular biology, 1977—, head dept. biochemistry, 1979-86, dir. program in molecular and cellular biology, 1985-88, dir. NIH chemistry-biology interface tng. program, 1995-2000, adj. prof. dept. chemistry, 2001—. Cons. WHO, Geneva, 1975-78; mem. molecular biology study sect. NIH, Washington, 1978-82; mem. molecular biochemistry panel NSF, Washington, 1994-97. Editor: Ribosomal RNA, 1994; assoc. editor RNA, 1996—; translator, editor: Introduction to Molecular Biology, 1971; contbr. over 90 articles to sci. jours. Participant U.S.-U.S.S.R. Interacad. Exch., 1965-66. Helen Hay Whitney Found. fellow, 1968-71, European Molecular Biology Orgn. sr. fellow, 1971-72; recipient Rsch. Career Devel. award NIH, 1975-80. Mem. AAAS, RNA Soc., Am. Chem. Soc., Am. Soc. Biochemistry and Molecular Biology, Sigma Xi. Office: Univ Mass Dept Biochem and Molec Biol Amherst MA 01003

ZIMMERMANN, ROBERT LAURENCE, marketing professional; b. Mpls., Jan. 1, 1932; s. Lawrence and Bertha Mabel (Foss) Z. BA, U. Minn., 1954, MA, 1965, PhD, 1970. Asst. prof. psychology U. Winnepeg, Man., Can., 1968-69; research assoc. psychiatry research unit U. Minn., Mpls., 1969-75; sr. scientist biometrics lab. George Washington U., Washington, 1975-76; pvt. cons. research design and data analysis Mpls., 1976-84; sr. research mgr. Maritz Market Rsch., Mpls., 1984—. Clin. asst. prof. psychiatry dept. U. Minn., Mpls., 1976-90; external rev. officer FDA, Washington, 1974-77. Contbr. numerous articles to profl. jours. Fellow NIMH, 1958, 61, 69-71; merit fellow State of Minn. Mem. AAAS, Com. on Space Rsch., Nat. Space Soc., Nat. Space Found., The Planetary Soc., ACLU, Amnesty Internat., Ctr. Pub. Integrity, Oxfam. Democrat. Avocation: writing. Home: 1920 S 1st St Apt 1104 Minneapolis MN 55454-1048 Office: Maritz Market Rsch Inc 7701 France Ave S Minneapolis MN 55435-5288

ZIMMERMANN, THOMAS CALLANDER PRICE, retired historian, educator; b. Bryn Mawr, Pa., Aug. 22, 1934; s. R.Z. and Susan (Goodman) Z.; m. Margaret Upham Ferris. BA, Williams Coll., 1956, Oxford U., 1958, MA, 1964; AM, Harvard U., 1960, PhD, 1964. Asst. prof. Reed Coll., Portland, Oreg., 1964-67, assoc. prof., 1967-73, prof. history, 1973-77, chmn. dept. history, 1973-75; v.p. acad. affairs Davidson (N.C.) Coll., 1977-86, Charles A. Dana prof. History, 1986-99, Charles A. Dana prof. history emeritus, 1999-2000, ret., 2000. Mem. Oreg. Com. for Humanities NEH, 1971—77; mem. Region 14 selection com. Woodrow Wilson Nat. Fellowship Found., Princeton, NJ, 1967—70. Author: Paolo Giovio: The Historian and the Crisis of Sixteenth-Century Italy, 1995 (Helen and Howard R. Marraro Book prize Am. Hist. Assn. 1996, Presdl. Book award Am. Assn. for Italian Studies 1997); co-editor of collected works of Paolo Giovio, 1985; contbr. articles to profl. jours. Pres. Am. Alpine Club, N.Y.C., 1979-82, bd. dirs., 1975-83; bd. dirs. Charlotte Opera Assn., N.C., 1980-82, N.C. Outward Bound Sch., Morganton, 1978-81; bd. advisors Lowell Obs., 1988-93; mem. Rome Prize Jury (Post-Classical Humanistic Studies) Am. Acad. in Rome, 1993. Danforth fellow, 1956-62, Fulbright fellow, Italy, 1962-64, Villa "I Tatti" fellow Harvard U. Ctr., 1970-71; Am. Council of Learned Socs. fellow, N.Y.C., 1975-76. Mem. Renaissance Soc. Am., Sixteenth Century Studies Conf., Soc. Italian Hist. Studies, Am. Assn. Italian Studies, Phi Beta Kappa.

ZIMMERS, VIVIAN ELEANOR, development and administrative consultant; b. St. Louis, Oct. 19, 1946; d. John Dominic and Aurea Genevieve (Schottel) Baron; m. John Paul Hargis, Aug. 21, 1964 (div. Mar. 1968); m. Filomeno Mariano Ramos, June 30, 1973 (dec.); children: William S. Ramos, Kiersten E. Ramos, Leilani A. Ramos; m. Ronald Franklin Zimmers, Sept. 27, 1997 (dec.). Student, St. Louis U., 1968-69, U. Hawaii, 1986-87; BA in Mgmt., Nat. Louis U., 1991. Co-founder, owner, pres. Batts Ramos and Assocs., Inc., St. Louis, 1991—. Cons. Hawaii Govtl. Affairs Com., Honolulu, 1975—76; mem. govtl. affairs com. St. Louis Assn. Realtors, 1996—97. Bd. dirs. Mo. Orthopedically Disabled, 1993—, pres., 1997—; active Assoc. Pres.'s Youth Opportunity Program, St. Louis, 1968; vol. literacy coun., rschr. Vols. in Probation and Parole. Mem.: Mililani Mchts. Assn. (pres. 1985), St. Louis Real Estate Bd., Nat. Assn. Realtors (mem. com. pub. rels. 1987), Rotary. Democrat. Roman Catholic. Home: 70 Willow Dr Eureka MO 63025-2198

ZIMMETT, MARK PAUL, lawyer, educator; b. Waukegan, Ill., July 4, 1950; s. Nelson H. Zimmett and Roslyn (Yastrow) Zimmett Grodzin; m. Joan Robin Urken, June 11, 1972; children: Nora Helene, Lili Eleanor. BA, Johns Hopkins U., 1972; JD, NYU, 1975. Bar: N.Y. 1976, U.S. Dist. Ct. (so. and ea. dists.) N.Y. 1976, U.S. Dist. Ct. (no. dist.) Calif. 1980, U.S. Ct. Appeals (2d cir.) 1980, U.S. Supreme Ct. 1981, U.S. Ct. Appeals (5th cir.) 1986, U.S. Ct. Appeals (9th cir.) 1988. Assoc. Shearman & Sterling, N.Y.C., 1975-83, ptnr., 1984-90; adj. assoc. prof. internat. law NYU, 1986-88; lectr. internat. comml. litig. and arbitration Practicing Law Inst., 2000—02. Author: Letters of Credit, New York Practice Guide Business and Commerical Law, 1990; contbr. articles to profl. jours. Mem. ABA (subcom. on letters of credit, com. on uniform comml. code sect. bus. law), N.Y. State Bar Assn., Assn. of the Bar of the City of N.Y., N.Y. County Lawyers Assn. (com. on bus. bankruptcy law), Citizens Union. Democrat. Jewish. Office: 126 E 56th St New York NY 10022-3613

ZIMMIE, THOMAS FRANK, civil engineer, educator; b. Scranton, Pa., Jan. 24, 1939; s. Thomas and Stella Josephine (Price) Z.; m. Patricia Joyce Kelly, June 8, 1962 (div. 1979); 1 child, David Thomas; m. Judith Anne Braden, July 13, 1989. BSCE, Worcester Poly. Inst., 1960; MSCE, U. Conn., 1962, PhD in Geotech. Engring., 1972. Registered profl. engr., N.Y., Conn. Staff engr. Union Carbide Corp. (Linde div.), Buffalo, 1964-68; profl. engr. Town of Mansfield, Conn., 1968-72; ptnr. Wang and Zimmie Cons., Troy, N.Y., 1973-80; v.p. Arch Engring. Cons., Troy, 1984-88; program dir. NSF, Washington, 1988-90; pres., CEO Civrotech Engrs., Inc., Troy, 1993—; prof. dept. civil engring Rensselaer Poly. Inst., Troy, 1973—. Postdoctoral researcher Norwegian Geotech. Inst., Oslo, 1972-73; geotech. engr. N.Y. Dept. Environ. Conservation, Albany, 1983-85; town engr. Town of North Greenbush, N.Y., 1985-88. Editor: Permeability and Groundwater Contamination, 1981. 1st lt. U.S. Army, 1962-64. Fellow Am. Coll. of Forensic Examiner, fellow ASCE (cert., Outstanding Svc. award 1986, 87); mem. ASTM (Spl. Svc. award 1980, Charles Dudley award 1984), Transp. Rsch. Bd., Am. Rd. and Transp. Builders Assn. Achievements include research in environmental geotechnology. Home: 39 Zelenke Dr Wynantskill NY 12198-8627 Office: Rensselaer Poly Inst Civil Engring Dept Soil Mechanics Lab Troy NY 12180 Office Phone: 518-276-6939. Business E-Mail: zimmit@rpi.edu.

ZIMNY, MAX, labor union administrator, lawyer; b. Bklyn., Mar. 9, 1925; s. Joseph and Rebecca (Nadelman) Z.; m. Bernice Nelson, June 26, 1948; children: Stuart, Andrew. Student, Bklyn. Coll., 1942—47, LLB cum laude, 1950; postgrad., NYU Grad. Sch. Labor Law, 1950—52. Bar: N.Y. 1950, U.S. Dist. Ct. (so. and ea. dists.) N.Y. 1951, U.S. Ct. Appeals (2nd cir.) 1955, U.S. Supreme Ct. 1962, U.S. Ct. Appeals (D.C. cir.) 1968, U.S. Ct. Appeals (4th cir.) 1969, U.S. Ct. Appeals (9th cir.) 1975, U.S. Ct. Appeals (8th cir.) 1980, U.S. Dist. Ct. (no. dist.) N.Y. 1983, U.S. Ct. Appeals (6th cir.) 1987, U.S. Ct. Appeals (7th cir.) 1988, U.S. Ct. Appeals (3rd and 5th cirs.) 1991. Mem. Zimny & Goldberg, N.Y.C., 1950—52; asst. gen. counsel Textiles Workers Union Am., N.Y.C., 1952—58, Internat. Ladies' Garment Workers' Union, N.Y.C., 1958—63, assoc. gen. counsel, 1963—72, gen. counsel, 1972—95, Union of Needletrades, Indsl. and Textile Employees, 1995—2001. Mem. Vladeck, Elias, Vladeck, Zimny and Englehard, N.Y.C., 1976-78; lectr. NYU Sch. Law, Stetson U. Sch. Law, Indsl. Rels. Rsch. Inst., Nat. Acad. Arbitrators. Editor: Labor Arbitrator Development, 1983, Arbitration: A Guide for Advocates, 1990, Arbitration Casebook, 1997. Mediator, fact finder N.Y. Pub. Employment Rels. Bd., 1968—; chmn. Consumer Adv. Coun. City of N.Y.; mem. Levittown (N.Y.) Bd. Edn.; chmn. Profls. for Histadrut, N.Y.C.; arbitrator NYS disciplinary panel; Bd. dirs. Nat. Resources Ctr. for Consumers Legal Svcs., Lawyers Coord. Com. AFL-CIO; bd. dirs. Corsi Labor Mgmt. Inst.; mediator, arbitrator Am. Arbitration Assn.; labor, employment and comml. panels, arbitrator labor and mgmt. panel Fed. Mediation and Conciliation Svc.; arbitrator N.Y.C. Office of Collective Bargaining, Electric Boat, Groton, Conn.; mem. nat. adv. coun., chair com. on rules and procedures, chair nat. task force on ADR in employment and due process protocol; mem. steering com. ctr. for Law and Econ. Policy Columbia U. Sch. Law; adv. com. NYU and Fordham Conf. on Labor, 1985—. With U.S. Army, 1943—46. Fellow: Coll. Labor and Employment Lawyers; mem.: ABA (chmn. com. on arbitration 1977—81, coun. labor sect. 1989—, chair labor and employment

sect., pub. rels. com.), Commn. Healthcare Dispute Resolution, N.Y. State Bar Assn., Bar Assn. City of N.Y. (labor com.), B'nai B'rith Club (pres. lodge), Order of Coif. Office Phone: 516-731-4358. E-mail: maxzimny@optonline.net.

ZIMPHER, NANCY LUSK, academic administrator; b. Gallipolis, Ohio, Oct. 29, 1946; d. Aven Denzle and Elsie Gordon (Hammond) L.; 1 child from a previous marriage, William Fletcher Zimpher; m. Kenneth R. Howey, May 8, 1987. BS, Ohio State U., 1968, MA, 1971, PhD, 1976. Cert. K-12 Tchr., Ohio. English tchr. Montgomery County Schs., Md., 1968, Reynoldsburg (Ohio) Schs., 1970; substitute tchr. Rolla (Mo.) City Schs., 1970-71; tchr. Phelps County Schs., Mo., 1971-72; grad. teaching assoc. Coll. Edn. Ohio State U., Columbus, 1972-73; dir. Coll. of Edn. Ohio State U., Columbus, 1973-74, grad. adminstrn. asst. to dean, 1974-76, dir. field experiences alumni rels., 1976-80, coord. undergraduate programs, 1980-84; asst. prof. Ednl. Policy and Leadership Ohio State U., 1984-86, assoc. prof., 1986-91, full prof., 1991-98, assoc. dean, 1992, dean, 1993, exec. dean, 1994; chancellor, prof. curriculum and instrn. U. Wis., Milw., 1998—2003; pres. U. Cincinnati, 2003—. Prin. investigator U.S. Office Edn. Field Devel. Grant, 1981-83, 85-88, co-principal investigator Metro. Life Found. Grant. 1989—, 1992—; cons. The Holmes Group, Lansing, Mich., 1991—. Book rev., editor: Journal of Teacher Education, 1986-89; co-author: Book Profiles of Preservice Teacher Education, 1989, RATE Profiles, 1987-92. Chair Faculty Compensation and Benefits Commn., 1989-90, Fiscal Com., 1991-92, Spousal Equivalency Com., 1990-91, Search Com., v.p. for Fin., 1992, Ohio State U; pres., chair bd. dirs. Holmes Partnership, 1997; chair edn. vision coun. United Way Franklin County, 1997; chair bd. dirs. United Way Franklin County, 1998. Fellow Com. for Instnl. Coop., Acad. Leadership Program. 1989-90; recipient Disting. Rsch. award, Disting. Teacher Educator award Assn. Tchr. Educators, 1990, Adams Professorshi Coll. Edn. Ind. State U., 1990—, Alumni Disting. Tchg. award, The Ohio State U., 1992, Chief Exec. Leadership award Coun. for the Advancement and Support Edn., 2003, Career Woman of Achievement award YWCA, 2004, Profl. Achievement award Ohio State U., 2004; named YWCA Woman of Achievement, 1997. Mem. AAUP, Am. Edn. Rsch. Assn., Am. Assn. Coll. Teacher Edn. Rsch. Comm., Assn. Tchr. Educators, ASCD, Phi Delta Kappa. Episcopalian. Avocations: watercolorist, golf, sewing. Office: Univ Cin 625 Univ Pavilion PO Box 210063 Cincinnati OH 45221-0063

ZINBERG, DOROTHY SHORE, science policy educator; b. Boston; m. Norman E Zinberg (dec.); children: Sarah Zinberg Mandel, Anne. BA, MA, Boston U.; PhD, Harvard U., 1966. Research chemist Lever Bros., Cambridge; sr. research assoc. Daniel Yankelovich, Inc., N.Y.C., and; Cambridge Center for Research in Behavioral Scis., 1966-68; NSF research sociologist dept. chemistry U. Coll. London, 1968-69; lectr. Harvard U., 1960—. Mem. adv. com. Office Sci. Pers. NRC, Washington, 1971—74, bd. on engring. edn., 1991; spl. adviser Aspen Inst.; cons. MacArthur Found., 1989—93; vis. scholar NAS, China, 1987, Nat. Inst. Sci. and Tech., Tokyo, 1991; vis. lectr. Inst. for Human Scis., Vienna, 1995; mem. adv. bd. Erik Erikson Inst. for Edn. and Rsch., 1996—; vis. prof. Imperial Coll., London, 2001—. Columnist: London Times Higher Educ Supplement, 1993—2001, NY Times Syndication, 1994—96. Mem. internat. sci. exchs. NAS, 1994—96, mem comt int relations, 1977—80, mem comt int human resources; chmn adv coun int div NSF, 1978—81; mem coun Int Exchange Scholars, 1978—81; mem comt int exchange engrs NAE, 1987—88; mem adv panel Office Technology Assessment Educ and Employment Scientists and Engrs, 1986—88; trustee Simon's Rock Col, 1971—75; mem panel sci and tech policy NATO, 1995—99; bd. dirs. Fine Arts Workshop, Provincetown, Mass., 1970—86, Bill T. Jones Found for Dance Promotion, 1997—99; bd dirs Gen Scanning, Inc, 1998—99; bd dirs eng educ NRC, 1990—95. Fellow: AAAS (mem comt sci freedom and responsibility 1972—74, comt opportunities in sci 1973—76, comt sci, eng, and pub policy 1982—88, comt exchange scientists with Fed Republic Germany 1987—91, 1991); mem.: NAS (mem comt to evaluate Int Sci and Technology Ctr Moscow 1995—97), Int Sci Policy Found (mem adv bd 1988—), Coun Foreign Relations, Fedn Am Scientists (mem coun 1980—85). Home: 3 Acacia St Cambridge MA 02138-4818 Office: Harvard U 79 JF Kennedy St Cambridge MA 02138 Office Phone: 617-495-1406. E-mail: dorothy_zinberg@harvard.edu.

ZINCZENKO, DAVID, publishing executive; s. Bohdan Zinczenko and Janice Sobieski. B, Moravian Coll. Assoc. editor Men's Journal, 1991—93; editl. dir. Men's Health Internat.; assoc. editor then sr. editor Men's Health, 1993; editor-in-chief Men's Health Mag., 2000—. Nominee ASME Nat. Mag. award; named Folio's 1999 Thirty Under 30, one of People Mag. 50 Most Eligible Bachelors, 2002; recipient 6 gold medals in Folio Mag. CDMA competition. Office: Men's Health 733 Third Ave New York NY 10017 also: Men's Health Roadale 33 E Minor St Emmaus PA 18098

ZINDER, NEWTON DONALD, stock market analyst, consultant; b. N.Y.C., Aug. 12, 1927; s. Paul and Jennie (Feld) Z.; m. Clarice Katz, Dec. 26, 1954; children— Marla, Andrea, Pamela. BA, NYU, 1948, MBA, 1957; MA, Columbia U., 1949. Securities analyst Ira Haupt & Co., N.Y.C., 1953-60; securities analyst E.F. Hutton & Co., N.Y.C., 1960-63, stock market analyst, 1963-88, Shearson Lehman Bros., N.Y.C., 1988-92; investment cons., 1993—. Served with USN, 1945-46 Mem. Market Technicians Assn. Home: 1734 Roland Ave Wantagh NY 11793-2856 E-mail: newtwiz@webtv.net.

ZINDER, NORTON DAVID, genetics educator, university dean; b. N.Y.C., Nov. 7, 1928; s. Harry Jean and (Gottesman) Z.; m. Marilyn Estreicher, Dec. 24, 1949; children— Stephen, Michael. AB, Columbia U., 1947; MS, U. Wis., 1949, PhD, 1952. Asst. Rockefeller U., N.Y.C., 1952-56, asso., 1956-58, asso. prof. genetics, 1958-64, prof., 1964-99, prof. emeritus, 1999—, John D. Rockefeller Jr. prof., 1977—, dean grad. and postgrad. studies, 1993-95. Cons. genetic-biology NSF, 1962-66, Office Tech. Assessment, Washington, 1979-81, Chas. Pfizer & Co., 1963-67; chmn. ad hoc com. to rev. viral cancer program Nat. Cancer Inst., 1973-74; mem. vis. com. dept. biology Harvard U., 1975-81, sect. virology Yale U., 1975-83, dept. biochemistry Princeton U., 1975-86; mem. sci. adv. bd. Carter-Wallace Inc., 1982-85, Genetic Systems Corp., 1981-86; mem.adv. com. Alliance Internat. Health Care Trust, 1984—; trustee Cold Spring Harbor Lab., 1967-85, sec. to bd., 1980-85; chmn. com. to rev. Army chem. weapons stockpile disposal program, NAS/NRC, 1987-91; chmn. program adv. com. on human genome, NIH, 1988-91, other affiliations; mem. adv. com. Celera Genomics, 1998—. Assoc. editor: Virology; sect. editor Intervirology, 1973-90. Recipient Eli Lilly award in microbiology and immunology, 1962, U.S. Steel Found. award in molecular biology, 1966, medal of excellence Columbia U., 1969, award in sci. freedom & responsibility AAAS, 1982; Am. Cancer Soc. scholar, 1955-58. Fellow Am. Acad. Arts and Scis. (coun. 1984-87); mem. NAS (mem. coun. 1988-91, exec. com. Assembly of Life Scis. 1975-78, bd. army sci. and tech. 1981), Soc. Am. Biol. Chemists, Genetics Soc. Am., Am. Soc. for Microbiology, Council Fgn. Relations, Harvey Soc., Sigma Xi. Achievements include spl. research in microbial genetics. Home: 450 E 63rd St New York NY 10021-7928 Office: Rockefeller U 1230 York Ave New York NY 10021-6399

ZINGALE, DONALD PAUL, academic administrator, educator; b. Bklyn., Aug. 3, 1946; s. Charles and Helen (Puglisi) Z. BS in Health, Phys. Edn., Bklyn. Coll., 1967; MS in Phys. Edn., U. Mass., 1969; PhD in Phys. Edn., Ohio State U., 1973; MSW, Calif. State U., Sacramento, 1984. Lic. clin. social worker, Calif.; lic. marriage and family counselor, Calif.; cert. health and phys. edn. instr. secondary schs., N.Y.C., N.Y.; cert. Alpine ski instr. Prof., assoc. dean health, human svcs. Calif. State U., Sacramento, 1973-93, assoc. v.p. rsch. and grad. studies, 1993-95, dean L.A., 1995—96; dean Coll. Health and Human Svcs. San Francisco State U., 1996—2004; v.p. academic affairs The Calif. Maritime Acad., 2004—. Contbr. articles to profl. jours. and publs. Mem.: APHA, Nat. Coun. U. Rsch. Adminstrs., Am. Assn. Higher Edn., Am. Assn. Health Phys. Edn., Recreation and Dance, Profl. Ski Instrs. Am. Roman Catholic. Avocations: alpine skiing, sailing, travel, cooking, home renovation. Office: Coll Health & Human Svcs San Francisco State U 1600 Holloway Ave San Francisco CA 94132

ZINGALES, LUIGI G. finance educator; b. Padova, Italy, Aug. 2, 1963; arrived in U.S., 1988; children: Giueseppe, Gloria. B.Econs. summa cum laude, U. Bocconi, Milan, Italy, 1987; PhD in Econs., MIT, 1992. From asst. prof. to prof. fin., now Robert C. McCormack prof. entrepreneurship and fin. U. Chgo., 1992—. Faculty rsch. assoc. Nat. Bur. Econ. Rsch., 1994—; rsch. fellow Ctr. for Econ. Policy Rsch., 1997—. Contbr. articles to profl. jours.; co-author: Saving Capitalism from the Capitalists, 2003. Recipient Brattle prize, 2000, Bernacer prize, 2003, Nasdaq award for best paper in capital formation, 2002; grantee Econs. grantee, NSF, 1995—97. Fellow: European Corp. Governance Inst. Office: Univ of Chicago Grad Sch Bus 1101 E 58th St Chicago IL 60637

ZINGARO, JOHN CHARLES, minister; b. Ellwood City, Pa., Apr. 4, 1954; s. Pat Charles and Norma Lena Zingaro. BA in Journalism and Comm., Point Park Coll., 1976; MDiv, Pitts. Theol. Sem., 1993. Ordained min. Presbyn. Ch., 1994. Freelance journalist, Pitts., 1982—87; English tchr. Mpechi Secondary Sch., Tanzania, 1987—89; student chaplain Shadyside Hosp., Pitts., 1991; student pastor Trinity Presbyn. Ch., Pitts., 1992; camp counselor Camp Crestfield, Slippery Rock, Pa., 1993; pastor Bryn Mawr Presbyn. Ch., Cottage Grove, Wis., 1994—. Author, editor: Thielemann: The Preacher's Preacher, 1999; author: Harry Potter Sermons, 2001, Spellman: One Man's Influence, 2003; contbr. articles to profl. jours. Bd. mem. Health Systems Agy. S.W. Pa., Pitts., 1980—82, United Ministries in Higher Edn., Madison, Wis., 1995—98. Presbyterian. Avocations: bicycling, chess. Home: 237 N Main St Cottage Grove WI 53527 Office: Bryn Mawr Presbyn Ch 229 N Main St Cottage Grove WI 53527 Office Phone: 608-839-4768.

ZINGG, PAUL JOSEPH, academic administrator; b. Newark, July 22, 1947; s. Carl William Zingg and Dolores Lucking Dulebohn; m. Candace A. Slater, Aug. 9, 1980. BA history, Belmont Abbey Coll., Belmont, N.C., 1968; MA history, U. Richmond, Va., 1969; PhD history, U. Ga., 1974. Chair and asst. prof., dept. of history and polit. sci. St. Bernard's Coll., Cullman, Ala., 1975-77; dean, academic affairs Daniel Hale Williams U., Chgo., 1977-78; adj asst./assoc. prof., dept. of Am. civilization U. Pa., Phila., 1978—86, asst. dean, academic affairs, Coll. of Arts and Sciences, 1978—79, vice dean, undergraduate studies and admissions, Coll. of Arts and Sciences, 1979—83, Am. Coun. on Edn. Fellow in Academic Adminstrn. and spl. asst. to the pres., 1983—84, exec. asst. to pres., 1984—86; cons. U. Calif., Berkeley, 1986; dean liberal arts and prof., dept. of history St. Mary's Coll., Moraga, Calif., 1986-93; prof., dept. of history Calif. Poly. State U., San Luis Obispo, Calif., 1993—2003, dean liberal arts, 1993-95, provost and acad. v.p., 1995—2003; pres. Calif. State U., Chico, 2004—. Vis. instr. history Ga. Coll., Milledgeville, 1971; cons., contbr. on exhibits Oakland Mus., 1992-94, Calif. Hist. Soc., 2004, PBS-TV documentary film Baseball, 1991-93; editorial cons. U. Nebr. Press, 1994—, U. Ill. Press, 1995-, others. Author: Pride of the Palestra, 1987, Harry Hooper, 1887-1974: An American Baseball Life, 1993, Runs, Hits and and Era: The Pacific Coast League, 1903-1958, 1994, 2nd edit., 1996, A Good Round: A Journey Through the Landscapes and Memory of Golf, 1999; editor, co-author: The Academic Penn, 1986; editor, contbr.: The Sporting Image: Readings in American Sport History; editor: In Search of the American National Character, 1984; contbr. numerous articles to profl. jours. Mem. Calif. Hist. Soc, 2000-, commn. on human resources and social change Nat. Assn. State Univs. and Land-Grant Colls., 1994-2004, commn. on academic affairs, 1995-2004; charter mem., Calif. Coun., Oakland Mus., 1995—; mem. Ctrl. Coast Performing Arts Ctr. Commn., San Luis Obispo, 1993-2004; bd. dirs. Hearst Art Gallery, Moraga, Calif., 1988-90 NEH summer fellow, 1975, summer rsch. grant, 1989, Ctr. for Internat. Study and Rsch. fellow, 1980-82, Am. Coun. on Edn. fellow, 1983-84; U.Pa. Rsch. Found. awards, 1983-85, faculty mem. of the yr., 1984, grantee St. Mary's Coll., 1987, 90, 91, 93, alumni faculty scholarship award, 1992. Mem. Orgn. Am. Historians, Soc. for History Edn., N.Am. Soc. for Study of Sport, Am. Studies Assn., Soc. for Am. Baseball Rsch., Am. Coun. on Edn., Assn. Am. Colls. and Univs., Am. Assn. Higher Edn., Nat. Assn. State Univs. and Land-Grant Colls., Merion Golf Club, U. Calif. Golf Club, Phi Alpha Theta, Phi Beta Delta Avocations: golf, labrador retrievers, baseball, hiking. Office: Calif State U 400 W First St Chico CA 95929-0155 Office Phone: 530-898-5201. E-mail: pzingg@csuchico.edu.*

ZINGHER, HARRY LEE, chemical engineer; b. Rushville, Ill., Dec. 18, 1956; s. Henry Cherry and Dessie Z. BS in Chem. Engring., U. Ill., 1980; MS in Chem. Engring., U. Iowa, 1985; PhD in Chem. Engring., Ohio State U., 1989; MD, U. Ill., 1990. Registered profl. engr. Resident U. Ill. Hosps. and Clinics, Chgo.; chem. engr. Nat. Starch & Chem., Meredosia, Ill., 1977, Marathon Oil Co., Robinson, Ill., 1979-80, Monsanto Chem., Texas City, Tex., 1980, Ill. EPA, Springfield, 1989-90; profl. cons. chem. engr. Rushville, Ill., 1990—. Recipient scholarship Marathon Oil Co., U. Ill., 1976-80, fellowships U. Iowa, 1984-85, Dow Chem., Ohio State U., 1985-89; Nobel Prize Laureate, N.Y. Acad. Sci., 1994. Mem. AAAS, Am. Chem. Soc., N.Y. Acad. Scis., U. Ill. Alumni Assn., U. Iowa Alumni Assn., Pres.'s Club Ohio State U., Tau Beta Pi. Achievements include partial patenting including computer calculations of electrophoresis modeling and partial patenting on peristaltic pump. Office: Monsanto Chem Corp 417 W Washington St Rushville IL 62681-1355

ZINI, JAMES E. physician; m. Judy Zini; children: Heather, Brett. MDiv, Eden Theol. Sem., St. Louis, 1972; DO, U. Health Scis., Coll. Osteo. Medicine, Kansas City, Mo., 1976. Intern Normandy Osteo. Hosp., St. Louis; pvt. practice Mountain View, Ark. Med. examiner FAA; med. dir. Searcy County Nursing & Rehab. Ctr., Marshall, Ark., Stone County Skilled Nursing Facility, Mountain View. Recipient Flight Safety award, FAA, 1998, Disting. Citizen award, Mountain View C. of C., 1997. Mem.: Ark. Osteo. Med. Assn. (v.p. ex-officio, Physician of Yr. award 1989), Ark. Osteo. Found., Ark. Med. Soc., Am. Osteo. Assn. (rep. to Commn. on Lab. Accreditation Bd., rep. to Ctrs. for Disease Control and Prevention). Office: Am Osteo Assn 142 E Ontario St Chicago IL 60611

ZINK, CHARLES TALBOTT, lawyer; b. Long Beach, Calif., Oct. 27, 1937; s. William Talbott and Nellie Grace (Hoskins) Z.; m. Deborah Sidney Burks, Nov. 26, 1983. AB, Princeton U., 1959; LLB, U. Va., 1965. Bar: Ga. 1965. Mng. ptnr. Hansell & Post, Atlanta, 1965-89; ptnr. Jones, Day, Reavis & Poque, Atlanta, 1989-93, Long, Aldridge & Norman, Atlanta, 1993—2002, McKenna Long & Aldridge LLP, 2002—. Lectr. N.W. Ctr. for Profl. Edn., Washington, Atlanta and Tampa, Fla., 1983—; mem. faculty Atlanta Coll. Trial Advocacy, 1985, mem. exec. com., 1984—, pres., 1985, 86. Bd. dirs. Atlanta Humane Soc., 1983—. Lt. (j.g.) USN, 1959-62. Mem. Atlanta Tax Forum, Capital City Club. Republican. Episcopalian. Office: 303 Peachtree St NE # 5300 Atlanta GA 30303-3002

ZINK, JOAN WILSON, writer, poet, composer; b. Tulsa, Dec. 17, 1928; d. Paul Almus and Gladys Emily Wilson; m. David Daniel Zink, Feb. 5, 1948; children: Laurie Zink Menard, David Paul; m. Lawrence Eugene Dalen, June 24, 1990. BA, U. Colo., 1958. Contbg. author The Ancient Stone's Speak, 1979, The Stones of Atlantis, 1978; author: (book of poetry) The Road Less Travelled, 1980; co-author (with David Zink): (book) You Are the Mystery, 1976, You Are the Mystery, new edit., 2001; contbr. articles to profl. jours., poetry to profl. pubs. Mem.: Nat. League Am. Pen Women, SPUR. Home: 4011 Saxon Dr New Smyrna Beach FL 32169

ZINK, LEE BERKEY, retired academic administrator, economist, educator; b. Salem, Ind., June 7, 1930; s. Otto C. and Lera (Berkey) Z.; m. Patricia Louise Patton, Aug. 16, 1964; children: Kevin Patrick, Barry Lee. BA in Econs. magna cum laude, Ind. U., 1959; PhD in Econs., Okla. State U., 1967. Field rep. GM Acceptance Corp., Louisville, Ky., 1953-54; asst. mgr. Dougherty Motor Sales, Salem, 1954-56; asst. prof. econs. Southeastern State Coll., Durant, Okla., 1964-67, spl. asst. to dir. Tech. Use Studies Ctr., 1964-65, dir., 1965-68, assoc. prof. of Econs., 1967-68; dir., prin. rsch. economist, bur. bus. and econ. rsch. U. N.Mex., Albuquerque, 1968-77; prof. bus. adminstrn. N.Mex. Highlands U., Kirtland, 1974-81; dir. Inst. Applied Rsch. Svcs. U. N.Mex., Albuquerque, 1975-2000, dir. Nat. Energy Info. Ctr. affiliate/U.S. Dept. Energy, 1978-87, assoc. v.p. rsch., bus. and govt. rels., 1988-2000; ret. Mem. Gov.'s adv. com. statis. standards for Okla., 1964-66, sci. and industry Okla., 1965-66, statewide planning com. implemenation of Tech. Svcs. Act, Okla., 1965-66; cons. majority leader U.S. Ho. Reps., 1964-68, So. Okla. Devel. Assn., 1965-68, Gov. Okla., 1965-68; Kiamichi Econ. Devel. Dist., Okla., 1967-68, N.Mex. Corp. Commn., 1969-74, N.Mex. State Planning Office, 1971, Ohio State U. Evaluation Ctr., 1972, others; mem. Gov.'s adv. com. N.Mex. Dept. Devel., 1971; adv. panel spl. tech. assistance program Office Econ. Opportunity, 1972-74; mem. Albuquerque adv. coun. U.S. Small Bus. Adminstrn., 1974-81, chmn. 1977-79; chmn. Gov.'s Coun. Econ. Advisors, 1975-78; sec. econ. devel. Gov.'s Cabinet, 1975-76, policy advisor, 1976-78; econ. devel. task force We. Interstate Commn. Higher Edn., 1979. Mem. edit. review bd. Review of Regional Economics and Business, 1976-85; bd. edit. contbrs. The Albuquerque Tribune, 1979-82; mem. edit. adv. bd. The Southwest Review of Management and Economics, 1981-85; contbr. articles to profl. jours. Organizing pres. Kiamichi Econ. Devel. Dist., Okla., 1966-67; active Monte Vista Christian Ch., 1968—; exec. dir. N.Mex. Coun. Econ. Edn., 1969-75, chmn. operating com., 1976-86; pres. East Holiday Park Neighborhood Assn., 1978-94; adv. coun. city growth and devel. Greater Albuquerque Leadership Devel. Program, 1980-82; adv. bd. U.S. Armed Svcs., 1980-87; adv. bd. econ. devel. City of Albuquerque, 1980-84; community advisor NCAA Vols. for Youth, 1981-85; mem. Bernalillo county Human Svcs. Coalition, 1982-85; apptd. by Gov.-elect Anaya N.Mex. Jobs Task Force, 1982-83; apptd. chmn. by mayor Better Albuquerque Bond Coms., 1983-87, 93-95; trustee U. Albuquerque, 1983-86; bd. dirs. Nat. Tng. Inst. Cmty. Econ. Devel., 1979-82, Inst. Study Cmty. Econ. Devel., 1980-82, Albuquerque Conv. and Vis. Bur., 1984-87, Consumer Credit Counseling Svc. N.Mex., 1985-94, pres. 1989-90, Better Bus. Bur. N.Mex., 1992—; pres. adv. coun. UNICEF, Albuquerque, 1985-95; mem. employment and tng. needs task force City of Albuquerque, 1987-88; evaluation team Congressman Lujan's South Valley task force, 1987; apptd. chmn. by Mayor Saavedra and city coun. pub. forum com. recycling, 1991. 2d lt. U.S. Army, 1951-53, Germany; lt. col. USAR, 1953-71. Fellow Nat. Defense Edn. Act, 1959-62; grantee Nat. Aeronautics and Space Adminstrn., 1964-68, N.Mex. Dept. Devel., 1968-80, HEW, 1968-76, 1971-72, Bank N. Mex., 1969-77, The Albuquerque Model Cities Agy., 1969-70, Four Corners Regional Commn., 1969-80, U.S. Forest Svc., 1974-77, U.S. Dept. Commerce, 1975-79, 1976-2000, N.Mex. Energy Resources Bd., 1976-77, The Navajo Nation, 1976-78, U.S. Army Corps. Engrs., 1976-78, U.S. Dept. Energy, 1978-87. Mem. Am. Assembly Collegiate Schs. Bus. (rsch., statis., publs. com. 1976-77, small bus. adminstrn. liasion com. 1976-78), Am. Soc. Info. Sci. (frontier chpt. exec. com. 1972-73, chmn.-elect 1972, chmn. 1973), Assn. Univ. Bus. and Econ. Rsch. (exec. com. 1971-78, v.p. 1975-76, pres. 1976-77), Mid continent Rsch. and Devel. Coun. (bd. dirs. 1965-69), Fedn. Rocky Mountain States (chmn. bus. rsch. com. 1969-75), Rocky Mountain Coun. Bus. Bus. and Econ. Rsch. (chmn. 1969-77), N.Mex. Coun. Econ. Edn. (bd. dirs. 1969-90), Am. Guild Organists (dean Albuquerque chpt. 1996-98), Greater Albuquerque C. of C. (edn. com. 1968-73, bd. dirs. 1970-76, 78-82, chmn. growth com. 1972, v.p. 1973-74, pres. 1981), U. N.Mex. Retiree Assn. (pres. 2003—), Phi Kappa Phi, Phi Beta Kappa (alpha chpt. exec. com., sec. 1973-75), Golden Key (hon.). Democrat. Avocation: pipe organs. Home: 3741 Mount Rainier Dr NE Albuquerque NM 87111-4399 Personal E-mail: drLBZ@aol.com. Business E-Mail: leezink@unm.edu.

ZINK, WALTER EARL, II, lawyer; b. Lincoln, Nebr., Nov. 20, 1947; s. Walter Earl and Marjorie Ellen (Hull) Z.; m. Carol Ann Thomas, June 26, 1971; children: Walter, Robert, Carmela. BA in Edn., Nebr. Wesleyan U., 1970; JD with distinction, Nebr. Coll. Law, 1974. Bar: Nebr. 1974, U.S. Dist. Ct. Nebr. 1974. Ptnr. Baylor, Evnen, Curtiss, Grimit & Witt, Lincoln, 1974—. Adj. prof. law Nebr. Coll. Law, Lincoln, 1978-82; brig. gen., asst. adj. gen. Army, NEARNG, asst. Div. Cmdr, 75th Dir (TS), 2001-; mem. Army Res. Forces Policy Bd., 2002—. Bd. dirs. Camp Kitaki YMCA, Lincoln, 1980-92. Mem. ABA, Nebr. Bar Assn. (vice chmn. young lawyers 1982-83), Fedn. Ins. Corp. Counsel (workers' compensation chair 1995-97), Assn. Def. Trial Attys., Am. Bd. Trial Advocates, Internat. Assn. Def. Counsel (past mem. exec. com., past chair employment law and membership com.), N.G. Assn. U.S., Res. Officers Assn. (v.p. Army 1984-85) mem.: Army Reserve Forces Policy Bd., Hillcrest Country Club (pres. 1994-96), Blue Key, Kappa Delta Pi. Home: 1420 Broadmoore Dr Lincoln NE 68506-1511 Office: Baylor Evnen Curtiss Grimit & Witt 206 S 13th St Ste 1200 Lincoln NE 68508-2077 Office Phone: 402-475-1075. Business E-Mail: wzink@baylorlaw.com.

ZINKE, MICHAEL DUANE, finance and accountancy manager; b. Mendota, Ill., Oct. 13, 1954; s. Elmer H. and Barbara A. (Williams) Z.; m. Cathy L. Myers, July 22, 1978; children: Duane M., Brian M. AA cum laude, Ill. Valley Community Coll., 1974; BS, No. Ill. U., 1976; MBA, Cen. State U., Edmond, Okla., 1988. Comptr. Office World, Oklahoma City, 1977-79; credit analyst C.I.T. Corp., Oklahoma City, 1979-80, sr. credit analyst, 1980-81, dist. credit mgr., 1982-84; credit mgr. Macklanburg-Duncan Co., Oklahoma City, 1984-87, mgr. credit, payroll, accounts payable, gen. acctg., 1987-90; credit mgr. N.Am. Chem. Co., Mission, Kans., 1991-92, N.Am. Salt Co. and N.Am. Chem. Co., Overland Park, Kans., 1992—98; dir. acctg. and credit IMC Salt, Inc., 1998—2001; controller N.Am. Compass Minerals Group, Inc., 2001—. Chmn. unsecured creditors com. H.E. Leonhardt Lumber, Oklahoma City, 1989-90; mem. unsecured creditors com. O'Hommel Co., Overland Park, Kans., 1991—. Author rsch. papers. Membership drive vol. Oklahoma City C. of C., 1989; rep. Napco Constrn. to Oklahoma City C. of C., 1990-91; dist. sec.-treas. Am. Bus. Clubs, Oklahoma City, 1985-86; bearer of U.S. Olympic Festival Torch, 1989; leader Boy Scouts Am., 1994—. Mem. Nat. Assn. Credit Mgmt., Nat. Chem. Creditors Assn., Fin. Credit and Internat. Bus. Assn., Inst. Mgmt. Acctg., Internat. Trade Club Greater Kansas City. Democrat. Lutheran. Avocations: fishing, hunting, reading. Home: 8800 Candlelight Ln Lenexa KS 66215-3432 Office: Compass Minerals Group 8300 College Blvd Overland Park KS 66210-1841 E-mail: mzinke54@aol.com.

ZINKERNAGEL, ROLF MARTIN, immunology educator; b. Basle, Switzerland, Jan. 6, 1944; s. Robert W. and Suzanne (Staehlin) Zinkernagel; m. Kathrin G. Ludin, Mar. 11, 1968; children: Christine, Annelies, Martin. MD, U. Basel, 1968. Intern in surgery Claraspital, Basel, 1968—69; postdoctoral Inst. Biochemistry, Lausanne, 1970—72, Dept. Microbiology, ANU, Canberra, Australia, 1973—75; asst. prof. Dept. Immunopathology, Scripps U., La Jolla, Calif., 1975—80, mem., 1978—79; assoc. prof. Dept. Pathology, Div. Exptl. Pathology, U. Zurich, 1979—92; full prof. Dept. Pathology, Inst. Exptl. Immunology, U. Zurich, 1992—. Editl. bd. Exptl. Cell Biology, 1976—88, Immunogenetics, 1977—, Parasite Immunology, 1978—84, Jour. of Immunology, 1978—80, Thymus, 1979—89, Jour. of Exptl. Medicine, 1981—84, Cellular Immunology, 1983—, Jour. of Environ. Pathology Toxicology and Oncology, 1981—, Internat. Jour. of Microbiology, 1983—, and others. Co-recipient Nobel Prize for medicine, 1996; recipient Albert Lasker award for Basic Med. Rsch., 1995. Mem.: others, Deutsche Gesellschaft fur Virologie, Deutsche Gesellschaft fur Immunologie, ENI European Network of Immunol. Instns., Internat. Soc. for Antiviral Rsch., Acadmia Euopea, Swiss Soc. of Cell and Molecular Biology, Swiss Soc. of Microbiology, Swiss Soc. of Pathology, Am. Assn. of Pathologists, Am. Assn of Immunologists, Australian Soc. for Immunology, Swiss Soc. of Allergy and Immunology, Soc. Francaise d'Immunolgie (hon.), Scandinavian Soc. of Immunology (hon.). Achievements include discovery of of MHC-restricted T cell recognition; of the thymus role in determining MHC-restricted T-cell specficity; NK-cell activity in virus infections, T-cell epitope escape virus mutants, tolerances to viruses; research in on role of virus-specific T-cells in causing immunopathology. Office: Univ Hosp Inst Exptl Immunology Schmelzbergstr 12 CH-8091 Zurich Switzerland Fax: 41-1-255 44 20. E-mail: Rolf.Zinkernagel@pty.usz.ch.

ZINKHAM, W. ROBERT, lawyer; b. Balt., May 30, 1955; s. William H. and Claire A. Z.; m. Theresa McGeehan, July 7, 1985; children: Natalie Anne, Elizabeth Claire. BA, Johns Hopkins U., 1977; JD, U. Md., Balt., 1980. Law clerk to chief judge Md. Ct. Appeals, Balt., 1980-81; assoc. Venable, Baetjer and Howard, Balt., 1981-88, ptnr., 1989—. Bd. dirs. Greater Balt. Med. Ctr. Found., 1992—. Editor Md. Law Rev., 1979. Chmn. Johns Hopkins Hosp. Psychiat. Day Hosp., Balt., 1982-92; pres. Mt. Washington Hills Assn., Balt., 1984-87. Mem. ABA, Am. Acad. Hosp. Attys., Nat. Health Lawyers Assn., Md. Bar Assn., Balt. Bar Assn. Republican. Office: Venable 2 Hopkins Plz Ste 1800 Baltimore MD 21201-2982 E-mail: wrzinkham@venable.com.

ZINMAN, DAVID JOEL, conductor; b. N.Y.C., July 9, 1936; s. Samuel and Rachel Ilo (Samuels) Z.; m. Leslie Heyman (dec.); children: Paul Pierre, Rachel Linda; m. Mary Ingham, May 19, 1974; 1 child, Raphael. MusB, Oberlin (Ohio) Conservatory, 1958; MA, U. Minn., 1961. Asst. to Pierre Monteux, 1961-64; guest condr. U.S. and Europe; music dir. Netherlands Chamber Orch., 1964-77, Rochester (N.Y.) Philharm. Orch., 1974-85; prin. guest condr. Rotterdam (Netherlands) Philharm. Orch., 1977-79; chief condr. Rotterdam Philharm. Orch., 1979-82; prin. guest condr., music dir. designate Balt. Symphony Orch., 1983-85, music dir., 1985—98, Tonhalle Orch., Zurich, Switzerland, 1995; music dir. designate Aspen (Colo.) Music Festival and Sch., 1997, music dir., 1998—; program dir. Am. Acad. Conducting, Aspen, 1998—. Adj. prof. Eastman Sch. Music, Rochester. Rec. artist Phillips, Nonesuch, Decca/London, Decca/Argo, Angel/EMI, Telarc, Sony Classical. Recipient Grand Prix du Disque, 1967, 82, Edison award, 1967, 3 Grammy awards, 1990, Grammophone best selling record award, 1993, Grammophone award, 1994, Deutschen Schallplatten prize, George Peabody medal for outstanding contbn. to music in Am., 1996. Office: PO Box 161 Millville DE 19970 Office Phone: 302-541-8087.

ZINN, BEN T. engineer, educator, consultant; b. Tel Aviv, Apr. 21, 1937; came to U.S., 1957; s. Samuel and Fridah (Gelbfish) Cynowicz; children: Edward R., Leslie H. BS in Mech. Engring. cum laude, NYU, 1961; MS in Mech. Engring., Stanford U., 1962; MS in Aerospace Engring., Princeton U., 1963, PhD in Aerospace Engring. and Mech. Scis., 1965. Asst. research Princeton U., 1964-65; asst. prof. Ga. Inst. Tech., Atlanta, 1965-67, assoc. prof., 1967-70, prof., 1970-73, Regents prof., 1973—, joint prof. Schs. Aerospace Engring. and Mech. Engring., 1996—, Disting. prof., 1990, Davis S. Lewis, Jr. chair Sch. Aerospace Engring., 1992—. Research scientist research div. Am. Standard Co., New Brunswick, N.J., summer 1976; cons. Brasilian Space Research Inst., Sao Jose dos Campos, Brazil, Aetna Casualty & Sr. Co., Atlanta Recipient David Orr Mech. Engring. prize NYU, 1961; recipient Founder's Day NYU, 1961, Cert. of Recognition NASA, 1974; Ford fellow, 1962-63 Fellow AIAA (assoc. editor jour. 1982—, Propellants and Combustion award 1996, Pendray Aerospace Lit. award 2000), ASME, Combustion Inst. (past. pres. Eastern sect.), Nat. Fire Acad. (bd. visitors 1979-82), Am. Tech. Soc. (v.p. Atlanta chpt. 1980-84, pres. 1984-86); mem. Nat. Acad. Engring., Sigma Xi (rsch. award 1969, sustained rsch. award 1976), Tau Beta Pi, Pi Tau Sigma Office: Ga Inst Tech Aerospace Engri Atlanta GA 30332-0001

ZINN, GESA, education educator; b. Moelln, Germany, Sept. 15, 1961; d. Volker Herman Zinn; m. Michael John Mullins, June 28, 1983; children: Saskia Mullins, Mikaela Zinn Mullins. BA English, Calif. State U., Sacramento, 1986; MLitt German, U. Minn., Mpls., 1986, DLitt German, 1996. Asst. prof. german U. Louisville, Louisville, 1996—2001; asst. prof. german studies U. Minn., Duluth, Minn., 2001—. Contbr. articles to profl. jour. (Best Article Award, 2001). Grantee Grant-in-Aid, U. Minn., 2003-2005, Rsch. on Women Grant, U. Louisville, 1998/99, Harold Meml. Film Stipend, U. Minn., 1993-94; Harold Meml. Film Fellowship, U. Minn., 1993-1994. Mem.: Assn. of Teachers of German (Curriculum Devel. 2002—03), Women in German, MLA (Midwestern, Atlantic), Order of the Ky. Colonels. Avocation: travel. Office: Univ Minn 10 Univ Dr Duluth MN 55812

ZINN, KEITH MARSHALL, ophthalmologist, educator; b. Bklyn., Oct. 15, 1940; s. Victor Zinn and Eve (Lane) Z.; m. Elaine H. Kirban, Apr. 8, 1979. Student, NYU, Bronx, 1961; MD, SUNY, Bklyn., 1965. Diplomate Am. Bd. Ophthalmology; lic. physician, NY, Calif. Intern St. Lukes Hosp., NYC, 1965-66; research assoc. NIH, Bethesda, Md., 1966-68; post-doctoral fellow Retina Found., Boston, 1968-69; post-doctoral fellow dept. ophthalmology Harvard U. Med. Sch., Boston, 1968; asst. resident chief resident dept. ophthalmology Mount Sinai Hosp., NYC, 1969-71, ednl. fellow dept. ophthalmology, 1971-72; chief clin. fellow retina service Mass. Eye & Ear Infirmary, Harvard U. Med. Sch., Boston, 1972-73, Heed fellow dept. ophthalmology, 1972-73; research assoc. dept. retina research Retina Found., Boston, 1972-73; mem. faculty Lancaster Post-Grad. Course Ophthalmology, Harvard U. Med. Sch., Boston, 1970-90; consulting mng. dir. HT Capital Advisors, LLC, 2000—. Guest faculty dept. ophthalmology Harvard U. Med. Sch., Boston, 1969-84; asst. prof. dept. ophthalmology Mt. Sinai Sch. medicine, NYC, assoc. clin. prof., 1976-80, clin. prof., 1980—; attending ophthalmic surgeon NYC, 1980—; attending ophthalmic surgeon Manhattan Eye Ear & Throat Hosp., NYC, 1981—; surgeon cons. Hosp. Joint Diseases, NYC, 1975-83, Patrolmen's Benevolent Assn., NYC, 1977—; lectr. field. Author: The Pupil, 1972, Ocular Fine Structure for the Clinician, 1973, The Developing Visual System, 1975, The Retinal Pigment Epithelium, 1975; author-editor: The Retinal Epithelium, 1979, Clinical Atlas of Peripheral Retinal Disorders, 1988; numerous audio-visual teaching progs. in ophthalmology; contbg. editor Mt. Sinai Jour. Medicine, 1975—; assoc. mem. editorial bd. Ophthalmic Surgery, 1980-89; mem. faculty editorial bd. Clin. Opththalmology Update, 1982—; inventor field. Served lt. comdr. USPHS, 1966-68. Recipient numerous awards excellence medicine, including: Joseph Globus award Mount Sinai Jour. Medicine, 1979, Abraham Kornzweig Teaching award Mount Sinai Sch. Medicine, 1982. Fellow Am. Acad. Ophthalmology, Otolaryngology, ACS, Internat. Coll. Surgeons, Internat. Eye Found., Soc. Eye Surgeons, NY Acad. Medicine, NY Diabetes Assn., NY Heart Assn., NY Soc. Clin. Ophthalmology, Soc. Heed Fellows, Retina Soc., Ophthalmic Soc. UK, Oxford Ophthal. Congress, Brit. Am. Retinal Group; mem. AMA (Physicians Recognition award 1971, 76, 81, 82, 85), Ophthalmic Laser Surg. Soc. (v.p. 1986-88, pres. 1988-90), Am. Intraocular Lens Implant Soc., NY Acad. Medicine (trustee 1989-90, sec. 1985-86, chmn. ophthalmology sect. 1987-88, David Warfield fellowship com. 1990-92), Am. Bd. Laser Surgery (bd. dirs. 1987—), others. Office: 1044 5th Ave New York NY 10028-0108 Office Phone: 212-535-5030.

ZINN, RAY, computer company executive; CEO Micrel, San Jose, Calif. Office: Micrel 1849 Fortune Dr San Jose CA 95131-1724

ZINN, WILLIAM, musician, composer; b. N.Y.C., Nov. 19, 1924; s.:Philip and Anna (Miller) Z.; m. Sophia Kalish, July 11, 1948; children: Karen Louise Heau, David Benjamin. Student, SUNY, 1952-54. Violinist Balt. Symphony, 1944-45, Indpls. Symphony, 1945-46, Ft. Wayne Philharm., 1946-47, Pitts. Symphony, 1947-49, Mpls. Symphony, 1950-51; concertmaster New Britain (Conn.) Symphony, 1968-90, Queens Symphony, 1969-71, Ridgefield (Conn.) Symphony, 1973-76, Chappaqua (N.Y.) Symphony, 1976, Yonkers Philharm., 1993—. Soloist with orchs. on records, on radio, TV, and in recitals, 1993-2003; founder Masterwork Piano Trio, Masterwork Piano Quartet, Classical String Quartet, Zinn's Ragtime String Quartet, Excelsior String Quartet, Queens Festival Orch., Bayside, N.Y., 1965, Assn. Musical William Zinn, Caracas, Venezuela, 1968, Vitametrics of Am., 1976, Internat. Symphony for World Peace, 1978, Big Apple Chamber Pops, 1983, Excelsior Composer's Festival Competition, 1984; tchr. mech. drafting Mondell Inst., 1956; coach ensembles for Chamber Music Assocs., 1973-78; engr. N.Y.C. Bd. Edn., 1951-57, Bodin-Zinn Corp., 1957-58, Chem. Constrn. Corp., 1958-59; pres. Zinn Originals, Inc., 1959-68, Sparx, Inc., Trademark Hall of Fame, Inc., Nice Realty Corp., MFW Restaurant Corp.; co-founder Excelsior Music Pub. Co., Visionary Music Pub. Co., Nat. Music Promotion Agy., Telecomm. Svcs., 1982, Assoc. Sci. Publs., 1985, Barclay House Pubs., 1985, Excelsior Typographers and Engravers Unltd., 1985, Empco Recs. Internat., 1985, Imperial Editions, 1986, Missing Link Publs., 1986, Krazy Klassics Kompany, 1986, New Age Publs., 1987, Krazy Klassics Komix, 1988, Zinn Pub. Group, 1989, Zinn Comm., 1989, Decca Books, 1993, Arlington House, 1993, Zinn Labs., Inc.; sec. treas Spark Industries, Inc., Music Clearing House, 1989, Innovation Records, 1991, Krazy Klassics Records, 1991, Hanover House, 1991; pres. Zinn Labs., Inc., 1994, Caramoor Press Internat. Corp., 1996, Dunhill Pub. Co., 1996, ZinnPrint Internat., Inc., 1996, Barclay Holdings Group, Inc., 1998; adj. prof. NYU, 1987—; cons. Worldwide Leisure Corp., 1997. Author: (with Edward Gordon) Themography, 1947, (with George S. Grosser) Vitametrics I, The Human Formula for Self-Evaluation, 1976, Vitametrics II, The Human Formula for Self-Improvement, 1978, The Lost Chord, 1981, To Whom It May Concern, 1995, 1,001 Original Wise Sayings of William Zinn, 1996, 2,600 Wise Sayings, 1997, 3,500 Wise Sayings, 1998, 4,100 Wise Sayings, 1999, 6,000 Wise Sayings, 2000, 6,700 wise sayings, 2001, 10,000 Wise Sayings, 2002, 11,000 Wise Sayings, 2003, 12,500 Wise Sayings, 2004; composer (perpetual movement for woodwinds, strings and percussion) Chromatique, 1946, Piccolo Concerto, 1948, Violin Concerto, 1950, String Quartet, 1963, (piano solo) Chopinesque, 1965, (ballet) Night Creatures, 1966, Andante for Strings, 1967, Concerto for Octahorn, 1976, The International Anthem for World Peace, 1977, String Symphony, 1977, Romance for French Horn or Viola and Piano, 1981, Concerto for Violin/Viola/Cello/Double Bass and Orch., 1985, Kol Nidrei Meml. for String Quartet or String Orchestra, 1985, six concert duos for violin and viola, 1988, 15 Leroy Anderson favorites for string quartet or string orch., 1988, also songs including Mia, 1989, Aloha Hawaii, 1989, The Willows, 1990 (winner Hawaiian Nat. Song Contest 1990), Our Song of Love, 1990, Symphony in Ragtime, 1990, In Old Hawaii, 1991, Christmas in Hawaii, 1991, A Tribute to the Masters for String Quartet or String Orchestra (14 original works in the style of Bach, Vivaldi, Mozart, Beethoven, Brahms, Rossini, Chopin, Schubert, J. Strauss, Jr., Tschaikowsky, Dvorak, Debussy, Mendelssohn, Sousa), 1991, A Stroll in a Japansese Garden for Violin, Cello, Harp trio in 24 movements, 1996; arranger numerous operatic arias for string quartet or string orch.; orginator Musiphonics, 1981, 24 Paganini Caprices for String Quartet, 1992, 10 Sousa marches for string quartet, 1992, The Merry Widow Waltz for string quartet or string orch., 1992, Mozart Symphony # 40, 1992; arranger 21 Henry Mancini songs for string quartet/string orch., 1992, 16 Duke Ellington songs for string quartet/string orch., 1993, Gold and Silver Waltz, Skater's Waltz for string quartet and string orch., 8 arias from Porgy & Bess for string quartet/string orch., 1992, A Tribute to Fritz Kreisler for violin and piano, 1994, 16 arrangements of Fritz Kreisler works for string quartet/string orch., 1994, 12 classic Jewish favorites for string quartet/string orch., 1995, 12 Jewish Songs for String Quartet/String Orch., 1995, 6 duets for violin and viola, vol. II, 1996, An elegy for Mother Teresa, 1997, concerto Hebraic for piano ands string orch., Let Freedom Ring, a Tribute to Martin Luther King, Jr., for orchestra, chorus, and narrator; 24 Etudes for solo cello, 1998, Hebraic Lament of Atonement for solo cello and string quartet or string orch., 1999, A Symphonic Portrait of Yonkers, 1999, The Seven Seasons for orchestra: seven symphonic works commemorating the Jewish holidays of Rosh Hashanah, Yom Kippur, Sukkot, Hanukkah, Purim, Passover, Shavuot, 2000, Siegfried Idyll Rhapsody solo violin and orch. (original Wagner orch.), 2001, A Requiem for Jerome G. Sala for soloists, chorus and orch., 2001; 6 Bach cello solo suites converted to duets with original part added, 2002, Dance of the Hours Fantasy for solo violin and orch. or piano, 2002, Meditation for solo violin or flute, harp and string orch., 2002, 28 Beethoven Bagatelles arranged for string quartet or string orch., 2002, Beethoven: Pathetique Sonata, slow movement arranged for string quarter or string orch., 2002, arranged for violin and piano The Carnival of the Animals, Nutcracker Suite, 2003, In Hallowed Ground, 9/11/2001 for solo voice chorus, string orch., bass clarinet, 2003, Peter & the Wolf for violin and piano, 2004, String Trio, 2004, A Klezmer Symphony, 2004, 6 Dvorak waltzs for quartet or string orch., 2004, others; pioneer multi-styles of music for string quartet and string orch.; composer over 500 works; developer numerous products for home, personal, automobile, and novelty use. Chmn., bd. dirs. Let Us Remember to Remember, 1984. Recipient 41st Hawaiian Nat. Song Contest award, 1990, Mayor and City Coun. citations for Yonkers 2000, a Symphonic Portrait. Mem. ASCAP, Internat. Platform Assn., Nat. Coun. Women of U.S., Am. Fedn. Musicians, N.Y. Humanist Assn. Home: 35-19 215th Pl Bayside NY 11361-1725

ZINNEN, ROBERT OLIVER, general management executive; b. Racine, Wis., June 28, 1929; s. Aloys Henry and Mabel Helen (Holy) Z.; m. Darlene Mary Weyers, Aug. 25, 1956; children: Claudia Jane, Robert O. BBA, U. Wis., 1951, JD, 1956. Bar: Wis. 1956, Ill. 1959, Mass. 1982; CPA, Ill. Tax accountant Price Waterhouse, Chgo., 1956-59; mem. firm Tenney & Bentley, Chgo., 1959-64; assoc. dir. taxes Allstate Cos., Skokie, Ill., 1964-65; v.p. fin. Do-All Co., Des Plaines, Ill., 1965-67; dir. taxes Quaker Oats Co., Chgo., 1967-71; internat. atty. Am. Hosp. Supply Corp., 1971-75; fin. cons. Alexander Proudfoot Co., Chgo., 1975-76; v.p. fin. Milton Bradley Co., Springfield, Mass., 1976-82; co-owner, exec. v.p. Roadmaster Corp., Olney, Ill., 1982-88, cons., 1988—. Mem. Housing and Traffic Commns., Highland Park, Ill., 1963-66; chmn. Congl. Action Com., Springfield; bd. dirs. Assoc. Industries, Mass. Served with U.S. Army, 1951-53. Mem. Toy Mfrs. Am. (bd. dirs. 1984-88), Quail Creek Country Club, Moorings Country Club, Longmeadow Country Club. Republican. Roman Catholic. E-mail: cyberzinn@sprintmail.com.

ZINNER, MICHAEL JEFFREY, surgeon, educator; b. Miami, Fla., Apr. 2, 1945; s. Doran D. and Eve Zinner; m. Rhonda Zinner; children: Darren, Daniel. BEE, Johns Hopkins U., 1967; MD, U. Fla., 1971; postgrad., NIH Found. for Edn. in the Scis., Bethesda, Md., 1973-74. Diplomate Am. Bd. Surgery (bd. dirs. 1988-94). Intern The Johns Hopkins Hosp., Balt., 1971-72, jr. asst. resident in surgery, 1972-73, sr. asst. resident, 1976-79, asst. chief of svc. in surgery, 1979-80; registrar thoracic surgery Frenchay Hosp., Bristol, Eng., 1977; instr. The Johns Hopkins U. Sch. Medicine, Balt., 1978-80; asst. prof. surgery Downstate Med. Ctr., Bklyn., 1980-83, assoc. prof., 1983-85; assoc. dir. surg. residency program, coord. residency program The Johns Hopkins Med. Instns., Balt., 1985-88, assoc. prof., vice chmn. dept. surgery, 1985-88, prof., 1988; prof., chmn. dept. surgery UCLA Sch. Medicine, 1988-94; mem. staff Kings County Hosp., Bklyn., 1980-85, chief gen. surgery and oncology, 1983-85; mem. staff Balt. VA Hosp., 1985-88, Johns Hopkins Hosp., 1985-88, Wadsworth VA Hosp., L.A., 1988-94; chief of surgery UCLA Med. Ctr., 1988-94; surgeon-in-chief Brigham and Womens Hosp., Boston, 1994—; prof. Harvard Med. Sch., 1994—. Bd. dirs. Sisters of Mercy Health Sys., 1992—98, Ptnrs. Health Care Sys., 1996—2000, Brigham and Women's Hosp., 1996—. Contbr. over 200 articles to profl. jours.; lectr. in field. Maj. M.C., U.S. Army, 1973-76. Rsch. grantee NIH, 1982-86, 88—; merit rev. grantee VA, 1988-91; grantee numerous univers., founds., pharm. cos., 1978—. Fellow ACS (com. on rsch. and edn. 1988, adv. com. on gen. surgery 1988); mem. IEEE, NIH (ad hoc, study sect., surgery and biomed. engring. 1986), Am. Fedn. Clin. Rsch., Assn. Acad. Surgery (com. on issues 1980-82, recorder 1982-84, exec. coun. 1982-88, pres. 1985-86), Am. Physiol. Soc., Am. Gastroenterol. Assn., Am. Pancreatic Assn., Soc. Univ. Surgeons (com. on publs. 1984-86, com. on edn., 1986-87, exec. coun. 1986-92, pres. 1987-88), Soc. Critical Care Medicine, Surg. Biology Club, Collegium Internationale Chirugiae Digestival (bd. dirs. 1990-96), Soc. Surgery of Alimentary Tract, Soc. Clin. Surgery, Alpha Omega Alpha. Avocations: fishing, boating. Office: Brigham and Womens Hosp Dept Surgery 75 Francis St Boston MA 02115-6106

ZINSER, ELISABETH ANN, academic administrator; b. Meadville, Pa., Feb. 20, 1940; d. Merle and Fae Zinser. BS, Stanford U., 1964; MS, U. Calif., San Francisco, 1966, MIT, 1982; PhD, U. Calif., Berkeley, 1972. Nurse VA Hosp., Palo Alto, Calif., 1964-65, San Francisco, 1969-70; instr. Sch. Nursing U. Calif., San Francisco, 1966-69; pre-doctoral fellow Nat. Inst. Health, Edn. and Welfare, 1971-72; adminstr. Sch. Medicine U. Wash., Seattle, 1972-75, Coun. Higher Edn., State of Ky., 1975-77; prof., dean. Coll. Nursing U. N.D., Grand Forks, 1977-83; vice chancellor acad. affairs U. N.C., Greensboro, 1983-89; pres. Gallaudet U., Washington, 1988, U. Idaho, Moscow, 1989-95; chancellor U. Ky., Lexington, 1995—. Bd. dirs. Am. Coun. Edn., Washington, 1995-98; chmn. commn. on outreach and tech. transfer; bd. dirs. Nat. Assn. State Univs. and Land Grant Colls., Am. Assn. Colls. and Univs., 1999—, Ctr. Acad. Integrity, 1998—; co-chair Bd. Oceans and Atmosphere, 1998—; cons. in field. Primary author: (with others) Contemporary Issues in Higher Education, 1985, Higher Education Research, 1988; spkr. in field. Bd. dirs. Humana Hosp., Greensboro, 1986-88; v.p., bd. dirs. Ea. Music Festival, Greensboro, 1987-89; trustee N.C. Coun. Econ. Edn., 1985-89, Greensboro Day Sch., 1987-89; ann. mem. Truman Found. Panel; bd. dirs. YMCA, Lexington, 1999—. Leadership fellow Bush Found., 1981-82. Office: U Ky 111 Adminstrn Bldg Lexington KY 40506-0001

ZINTER, STEVEN L. state supreme court justice; m. Sandra Zinter; 2 children. Doctorate, Univ. So. Dakota, 1975, BS, 1972. Pvt. practice, 1978—86; practice as asst. atty. gen. State So. Dakota; cir. judge State of So. Dakota, 1987—97; presiding judge Sixth Judicial Cir., 1997—2002; judge Supreme Court, 2002—. Mem. Harry S. Found.; trustee So. Dakota Retirement Sys.; elect. pres. So. Dakota Corrections Commn. Mem.: Am. Bar Assn. Office: Supreme Court S Dakota 500 State Capital Bldg E Capitol Ave Pierre SD 57501-5070

ZINTERHOFER, LOUIS, pathologist; b. Detroit, Nov. 13, 1942; s. Louis Zinterhofer and Martha Madsen Greenlee, Ralph Greenlee (Stepfather); m. Susan Alderman, June 15, 1968; children: Eric Zintrerhofer, Nina Stanford. BS, U. of Notre Dame, 1967; MD, Tulane U., 1967. Diplomate Am. Bd. of Pathology, 1972, lic. Am. Bd. of Pathology, 1975. Resident Yale Med. Sch., New Haven, 1967—71; attending pathologist Monmouth Med. Ctr., Long Branch, NJ, 1973—89, chmn. Dept. Pathology, 1989—; dir. Dept. Pathology Irvington (N.J.) Gen. Hosp., 2001—. Clin. lab. insp. Coll. of Am. Pathologists, Northfield, Ill. Contbr. articles to profl. jours. Maj. USAF, 1971—73. Mem.: Am. Soc. for Clin. Chemistry, Am. Soc. of Clin. Pathologists, Coll. of Am. Pathologists, Kenwood Country Club. Home: 53 Shrewsbury Drive Rumson NJ 07760 Office: Monmouth Medical Center - Pathology 300 Second Ave Long Branch NJ 07740

ZINZ, DAVID ALBERT, humanities educator; b. Philipsburg, Pa., Nov. 2, 1952; s. Albert Calvin and Dolores Aleda (Helwig) Zinz, Leroy Peters (Stepfather); m. Glenda L. Zinz; children: Kristeen Buffalo, Ryan Bonsall. Student, Pa. State U., 1970—72; diploma in profl. photography, Sch. Modern Photography, 1976; student, Winona Sch. Profl. Photography, 1974—75, Nat. Radio Inst., 1980—82; Cert. in Bibl. Studies, Moody Bible Inst., 1991; MDiv, N.Am. Bapt. Sem., 1994; postgrad., Kilian C.C., Niobara Sch. Ministry. Owner David A. Zinz Photography, Winburne, Pa., 1973—87; photog. lab. specialist T.V.G.T. Engrs. and Surveyors, Orchard Park, N.Y. and Lanse, Pa., 1976—79; advanced indsl. photographer HRB Systems, Signal Intelligence Specialists, State College, Pa., 1980—89; instr. spiritual formation and Christian history North Am. Bapt. Sem., 1995—96; cabinetmaker/craftsman Don's Custom Cabinetry, 1994—2001; sales specialist, dept. profl. The Home Depot, 2001—; assoc. prof. ethics Colo. Tech. U., Sioux Falls campus, 1994—2003; assoc. prof. philosophy and religion Kilian C.C., 2000—. Scoutmaster Boy Scouts Am., Kylertown, Pa., 1986—91, mem. staff Camp Mountain Run, 1990, provisional scoutmaster/camp commr., dir. first yr. camper program, 1991, program dir., acting camp dir., 1992, camp dir., 1993, asst. dist. commr. Susquehanna Dist., 1989—90, dist. commr., 1990—91, mem. dist. com. Ctrl. Dist., Sioux Coun., 1994—; oblate of St. Benedict Blue Cloud Abbey, Marvin, SD, 1999—. Mem.: Am. Benedictine Acad., Ctr. for Bioethics and Human Dignity, Soc. Christian Philosophers, Christian Motorcyclist Assn., Cross Road Riders Christian Motorcycle Club (pres. local chpt. 1984—85, sec.-treas. 1986—88), Tetonwana Lodge OA (Vigil Honor 1994—), Ah' Tic Lodge OA (advisor planning/activities com. 1988—91, Vigil Honor 1991). Home: 4808 W 38th St Sioux Falls SD 57106

ZIOLKOWSKA-BOEHM, ALEKSANDRA, writer; b. Lodz, Poland, Apr. 15, 1949; arrived in US, 1990; d. Henryk and Antonina Zofia (Laskiewicz) Z.; m. C. Norman Boehm Jr., June 8, 1990; 1 child, Thomas Tomczyk. M in Lit., U. Lodz, 1973; PhD, U. Warsaw, Poland, 1978. Pvt. asst. Melchior Wankowicz, Warsaw, 1972-74; repertoire rsch. staff Warsaw TV Theater, 1977-81. Author: Blisko Wankowicza, 1975, 1978, 1988, Z Miejsca Na Miejsce, 1983, 1986, 1997, Senator Haidasz, 1983, Dreams and Reality, 1984, Kanada, Kanada, 1986, Diecezja Lodzka I Jej Biskupi, 1987, Moje I Zaslyszane, 1988, Kanadyjski Senator, 1989, Na Tropach Wankowicza, 1989, 1999, Proces M. Wankowicza, 1964, 1990, Nie Tyllko Ameryka, 1992, Korzenie Sa Polskie, 1992, Ulica Zolwiego Strumienia, 1995, Amerykanie Z Wyboru, 1998, The Roots are Polish, 2000;: 2d edit., 2004, Korespondencja J. Giedroyc-Wankowicz, 2000, Podroze Z Moja Kotka, 2002; author: (with Szymon Kobylinski) Nie minelo nic, procz. lat., 2003. Recipient Kontrasty award, 1980, Zloty Exlibris award Ksiaznica Pomorska, 2001; scholar Oxford (Eng.) Lang. Ctr., 1975, Ont. Ministry of Culture, Toronto, 1981-83, Can. Polish Rsch. Inst., Toronto, 1981-83, A. Mickiewicz Found., Toronto, 1981-83, Inst. Internat. Edn., Washington, 1985. Mem. Am. PEN Club, Polish Writers Union, Polish Writers Union Abroad, Polish Inst. Arts and Sci., Zaiks, Kosciuszko Found. (scholar 1990). Avocations: travel, birdwatching, domestic pets. Home: 11 Ridgewood Cir Wilmington DE 19809-2860

ZIOLKOWSKI, JAN MICHAEL, medievalist educator; b. New Haven, Nov. 17, 1956; s. Theodore J. and Yetta (Goldstein) Z.; m. Elizabeth Ann Hillenius; children: Saskia Elizabeth, Ada Margaret, Yetta Joy. AB summa cum laude, Princeton U., 1977; PhD, U. Cambridge, Eng., 1982; MA (hon.), Harvard U., 1987. Asst. prof. Harvard U., Cambridge, Mass., 1981-84, John L. Loeb assoc. prof. of the humanities, 1984-87, prof. medieval Latin and comparative lit., 1987—2002, Arthur Kingsley Porter prof. medieval Latin, 2002—. Author: Alan of Lille's Grammar of Sex, 1985, Nigel of Canterbury, Miracles of the Virgin Mary, 1986, Jezebel: A Norman Latin Poem, 1989, On Philology, 1990, Talking Animals: Medieval Latin Beast Poetry, 1993, Nigel of Canterbury, The Passion of St. Lawrence, 1994, The Cambridge Songs, 1994, 98, Obscenity: Social Control and Artistic Creation in the European Middle Ages, 1998, The Medieval Craft of Memory, 2002; editor Comparative Literature Studies. Pres. Internationales Mittellateiner Komitee, 2000—. Fellow Guggenheim Found., 1987-88, ACLS, 1986, Rome Prize fellow, Am. Acad. in Rome, 1980-81; Marshall scholar, 1977-80. Mem. Medieval Acad. Am. (councillor 1991-94), Dante Soc. Am. (councillor 2004—), Am. Philol. Assn., Phi Beta Kappa. Home: 930 Centre St Newton MA 02459-1266 Office: Harvard Univ Classics 221 Boylston Hall Cambridge MA 02138

ZIOLKOWSKI, THEODORE JOSEPH, comparative literature educator; b. Birmingham, Ala., Sept. 30, 1932; s. Miecislaw and Cecilia (Jankowski) Z.; m. Yetta Bart Goldstein, Mar. 26, 1951; children: Margaret Cecilia, Jan Michael, Eric Josef. AB, Duke U., 1951, AM, 1952; student, U. Innsbruck, Austria, 1952-53; PhD, Yale U., 1957; DrPhil honoris causa (hon.), U. Greifswald, 2001. Instr., then asst. prof. Yale U., New Haven, 1956-62; assoc. prof. Columbia U., N.Y.C., 1962-64; prof. Germanic langs. and lit. Princeton (N.J.) U., 1964-69, chmn., 1973-79, Class of 1900 prof. modern langs., 1969-2001, prof. comparative lit., 1975-2001, dean Grad. Sch., 1979-92, prof. emeritus, 2001. Vis. prof. Rutgers U., 1966, Yale U., 1967, 75, CUNY, 1971, Bristol U., 1987, U. Munich, 1992; vis. scholar U. Ctr. in Va., 1971, Piedmont U. Ctr., N.C., 1971; Dancy Meml. lectr. U. Montevallo, 1973; Christopher Longest lectr. U. Miss., 1979; Patten Found. lectr. Ind. U., 1980; vis. lectr. Österreichische Akademie der Wissenschaften, 1992; vis. lectr. Korean Ministry of Edn., 1996; chmn. N.Y. State Doctoral Evaluation Program in German, 1975-80; nat. rev. panel for U.S. Nat. Grad. Fellows Program, 1985-87, 91—; chmn. overseers vis. com. on German Harvard U., 1982-88; mem. selection com. for Bennett award, 1988; with German-Am. Acad. Coun., 1993-99; chmn. N.Y. State Humanities Screening Com., 1996; chmn. bd. German-Am. Ctr. for Vis. Scholars, 1997-99; forum assembly spkr. Brigham Young U; mem. evaluation team Rosenzweig Zentrum of Hebrew U., Jerusalem, 1999; mem. search com. for chair in German, Bristol U., 1999; mem. search com. for dean Internat. U. Bremen, 1999-00. Author: Hermann Broch, 1964, The Novels of Hermann Hesse, 1965, Hermann Hesse, 1966, Dimensions of the Modern Novel, 1969, Fictional Transfigurations of Jesus, 1972 (James Russell Lowell prize for criticism), Disenchanted Images, 1977, Der Schriftsteller Hermann Hesse, 1979, The Classical German Elegy, 1980, Varieties of Literary Thematics, 1983, German Romanticism and Its Institutions, 1990, Virgil and the Moderns, 1993, The Mirror of Justice, 1997 (Christian Gauss prize), Das Wunderjahr in Jena, 1998, The View from the Tower, 1998, The Sin of Knowledge, 2000, Berlin: Aufstieg einer Kulturmetropole um 1810, 2002, Hesitant Heroes, 2004, Clio the Romantic Muse, 2004; also articles and revs.; editor: Hermann Hesse, Autobiographical Writing, 1972, Hermann Hesse, Stories of Five Decades, 1972, Hesse: A Collection of Critical Essays, 1972, Hermann Hesse, My Belief: Selected Essays, 1974, Hermann Hesse, Tales of Student Life, 1976, Hermann Hesse, Pictor's Metamorphoses and Other Fantasies, 1982, Hermann Hesse, Soul of the Age: Selected Letters, 1891-1962, 1991; mem. editl. bd. Germanic Rev., 1962-95, Publs. MLA, 1971-75, Arbitrium, 1983-, 17th Century Studies, 1985-, Germanistik, 1987-, Jahrbuch für Internat. Germanistik, 1997-, World Literature Today, 1998-, Etudes Germaniques, 1998-, Publications of the English Goethe Society, 2003-, Spectrum Lit./Comparative Studies, 2004-; mem. editl. bd. Princeton U. Press, 1972-75, trustee, 1982-95; translator (with Yetta Ziolkowski): The

Poetics of Quotation (Herman Meyer) 1968, Hermann Hesse: A Pictorial Biography, 1975. Decorated comdr.'s cross Order of Merit (Germany); recipient Howard T. Behrman award for disting. achievement in humanities, 1978, Wilbur Lucius Cross medal Yale U., 1982, Goethe Inst. gold medal, 1987, Henry Allen Moe prize in humanities, 1988, Festschrift Themes and Structures (ed. Alexander Stephan), 1997, Jakob-und-Wilhelm Grimm prize for German Studies, 1998, Humboldt Sr. Rsch. prize, 1998; Mellon Emeritus Faculty fellow, 2003; Fulbright rsch. grantee, 1958-59, grantee Am. Philos. Soc., 1959, NEH grantee, 1978, Guggenheim fellow, 1964-65, Am. Coun. Learned Socs. fellow, 1972, 76; resident fellow Bellagio Study Ctr., 1993. Mem. MLA (exec. coun. 1976-77, pres. 1985), Acad. Lit. Studies, Am. Comparative Lit. Assn., Am. Acad. Arts and Scis., Assn. Lit. Scholars and Critics, Authors Guild, Am. Assn. Tchrs. German (hon. life), Yale Grad. Sch. Assn. (pres. 1974-76), Assn. Grad. Schs. (v.p. 1989-90, pres. 1990-91), Heinrich von Kleist Gesellschaft, Goethe-Gesellschaft, Novalis-Gesellschaft, Internat. Vereinigung für Germanistik (exec. coun. 1985-95, treas. 1990-95), Am. Philos. Soc. (councillor 1991-97), Göttingen Akademie der Wissenschaften, Austrian Akademie der Wissenschaften, Deutsche Akademie für Sprache und Dichtung, Phi Beta Kappa. Home: 36 Bainbridge St Princeton NJ 08540-3902 Office: Princeton U Dept German Princeton NJ 08544-0001 E-mail: tjziol@aol.com.

ZIOLO, RONALD F. research scientist, educator, academic administrator, writer; s. Charles F. Ziolo and Sophia H. Deane; m. Nina R. Zia, June 17, 1967; children: Karen M., Melissa S., Kristin L. BSc, UCLA, LA, 1964—66; PhD, Temple U., 1966—70. Post doctoral rsch. fellow Calif. Inst. Tech., Pasadena, 1971—72; assoc. scientist Xerox Corp., Webster, NY, 1972—75, scientist, 1976—82, sr. scientist, 1983—92, sr. rsch. scientist, mgr., 1993—96, dir., sr. rsch. fellow U. Barcelona Xerox Lab, 1997—2003; invited prof., dept. physics U. Barcelona, 2003—. Co-founder U. Barcelona Xerox Lab; advisor US govt. and internat. funding review bd.; cons. CONCYTEC, Mexico. Author over 100 sci. jour. articles, tech. publ., reviews; editor: (proceedings) Metastable Phases and Microstructures. Recipient Discover Awards Technol. Innovation nominations, Discover Mag., 1994, 1995; grantee Invited Professorship, U. Barcelona, Spanish Ministry Edn., Culture and Sports, 2004; Brite Durham Coop. Rsch. Grant, European Union, 1998-2000. Mem.: AAAS, Am. Crystallographic Assn., Materials Rsch. Soc., Am. Inst. Physics, Am. Phys. Soc., Am. Chem. Soc., Sigma Xi (life), Alpha Chi Sigma. Achievements include research in nanostructured materials and condensed matter physics, quantum magnetization, nonlinear optical effects, biomedical applications, nano and molecular magnets; discovery of matrix synthesis of nanostructured materials, free-rotor nanomagnets, nanoparticle synthesis via matrix milling tech; first to optically transparent magnetic materials, colored magnetic material nanotechnology, transparent aqueous ferrofluids; development of opically transparent electronically conducting ground plane tech; patents for over 120 issued; patents pending for terahertz generation and superradiance from molecular magnets, polymer microspheres for biomedical applications.

ZIOMEK, JONATHAN S. journalist, educator; b. Newport News, Va., July 28, 1947; s. Stanley Walter and Joy Carmen (Schmidt) Z.; m. Rosalie Ziomek, Aug. 14, 1977; children: Joseph, Jennifer; 1 stepchild, Daniel. BA in Sociology, U. Ill., 1970, MS in Journalism, 1982. Reporter, labor writer, feature writer, Sun. fin. editor Chgo. Sun-Times, 1970-78; press sec. for U.S. Senate campaign, Chgo., 1979-80; asst. prof. Medill Sch. Journalism, Northwestern U., Evanston, Ill., 1983-88; dir. grad. editl. programs Medill Sch. Journalism/Northwestern U., Evanston, Ill., 1988—, asst. dean, assoc. prof., 1994—. Presenter writing workshops; corp. writing cons. Contbr. articles to various mags.; editor: Chgo. Journalist Newsletter, 1991-93. Participant Internat. Visitors Ctr., Chgo., 1988—; fact-finder USIA, Bulgaria and Yugoslavia, 1990; rapporteur Aspen Inst., Journalism and Soc. Seminar, 2004. Mem. Assn. for Edn. in Journalism and Mass Communications, Soc. Profl. Journalists, Nat. Assn. Sci. Writers, Chgo. Headline Club. Home: 2149 Hartrey Ave Evanston IL 60201-2571 Office: Northwestern Univ Medill Sch Journalism Evanston IL 60208-0001

ZIPES, DOUGLAS PETER, cardiologist, researcher; b. White Plains, NY, Feb. 27, 1939; s. Robert Samuel and Josephine Helen (Weber) Z.; m. Marilyn Joan Jacobus, Feb. 18, 1961; children: Debra, Jeffrey, David. BA cum laude, Dartmouth Coll., 1961, B of Med. Sci., 1962; MD cum laude, Harvard Med. Sch., 1964. Diplomate Am. Bd. Internal Medicine, mem. subsplty. bd. cardiovasc. disease 1989-99, chmn., 1995-99, chmn. com. cert. in clin. cardiac electrophysiology 1989-96, bd. dirs. 1995-2003, exec. com. 1999-2003, chmn. bd. 2002-03. Intern, resident, fellow in cardiology Duke U. Med. Ctr., Durham, N.C., 1964-68; vis. scientist Masonic Med. Rsch. Lab., Utica, N.Y., 1970-71; from asst. prof. medicine to dir. emeritus Ind. U., Indpls., 1970—2004, dir. emeritus Krannert Inst. Cardiology Sch. Medicine, 2004—, chmn. Cardiovascular Disease Krannert Inst. Cardiology, 2004—. Bd. dirs. Inst. for Clin. Evaluation; cardiology adv. com NIH, 1991—94; mem. med. adv. bd. ABCNews.com, 2000—; mem. dean's coun. Dartmouth Med. Sch., Ind. Med. Sch.; cons. in field. Author: Comprehensive Cardiac Care, 7th edit., 1991; editor: Slow Inward Current, 1980, Cardiac Electrophysiology and Arrhythmias, 1985, Nonpharmacological Therapy of Tachyarrhythmias, 1987, Cardiac Electrophysiology From Cell to Bedside, 1990, 4th edit., 2004; co-editor: Treatment of Heart Diseases, 1992, Ablation of Cardiac Arrhythmias, 1994, 2d edit., 2002, Antiarrhythmic Therapy: A Pathophysiologic Approach, 1994, Heart Disease, A Textbook of Cardiovascular Medicine, 7th edit., 2004, Thoracic Vein Arrhythmias, 2004; mem. editl. bd. Circulation, 1974-78, 83-, Am. Jour. Cardiology, 1979-82, 88-, Am. Jour. Medicine, 1979-90, Jour. Am. Coll. Cardiology, 1983, 2002-, Am. Heart Jour., 1977-97, PACE, 1977-, Circulation Rsch., 1983-90, Am. Jour. Noninvasive Cardiology, 1985-89, Jour. Electrophysiology, 1987-89, Cardiovasc. Drugs and Therapy, 1986-93, Japanese Heart Jour., 1989-, Jour. Cardiovasc. Pharmacology and Therapeutics, 1994-, Jour. Cardiovasc. Pharmacology, 1995—, Cardiovasc. Therapeutics, 1995, Current Clin. Trials, 1995-98, Jour. Interventional Cardiac Electrophysiology, 1996-, Am. Heart Hosp. Jour., Jour. Am. Coll. Cardiology; editor-in-chief: Progress in Cardiology, 1988-92, Jour. Cardiovasc. Electrophysiology, 1990-2004, Cardiology in Rev., 1992-2002, Contemporary Treatments of Cardiovasc. Disease, 1996-98, Am. Coll. Cardiology Extended Learning, 1997-, Ind. Jour. Pacing and Electrophysiology Online, 2001-; founding editor Heart Rhythm, 2004-; contbr. articles to profl. jours.; patentee cardioverter, elec. prevention of arrhythmia, discrimination of atrial fibrillation, fixation of implantable devices, and pericardial delivery of therapeutic and diagnostic agents. Pres., bd. dirs. Indpls. Opera Co., 1983-85; mem. study sect. NIH, Washington, 1977-81; mem. nat. merit rev. bd. VA, 1982-85, Cardiology Adv. Com. NHLBL, 1991-98, chmn. steering com. AVID; chmn. Data and Safety Monitoring Bd. AFFIRM, 1996-2002; bd. dirs. Am. Bd. Internal Medicine Found., 2002-04; chmn. Am. Bd. Internal Medicine, 2002-03. Recipient Disting. Achievement award Am. Heart Assn., 1989, Sagamore of the Wabash award, Gov. Ind., 2001. Master Am. Coll. Cardiology (chmn. ACC/AHA subcom. to assess EP studies, chmn. young investigators award com. 1988-94, trustee 1992-97, chair nominating com. 2003, Disting. Scientist award 1996, chmn. devel. com. 1996-2001, sci. sessions program com. 1996-98, v.p. 1999-2000, pres. 2001-02, co-chair ventricular arrythmias guidelines 2003-); fellow ACP, Am. Heart Assn. (exec. com. 1980-88, sci. sessions program 1983-86, chmn. various coms., chmn. 1995, bd. dirs. Internat. Cardiology Found. 1993-98, bd. dirs. 1994-96, chmn. emergency cardiac care com. 1995-96; Herrick award 1997, Cor Vitae award 2004); mem. Am. Soc. Clin. Investigation, Assn. Univ. Cardiologists (v.p. 1994, pres. 1995), Assn. Am. Physicians, Am. Physiol. Soc., Cardiac Electrophysiology Soc. (pres. 1985-86), N.Am. Soc. Pacing and Electrophysiology (pres. 1988-90, trustee 1990—, endowed lectr. 2004, Disting. Scientist award 1995), InterAm. Soc. Cardiology (1st v.p. 1995-98), Ind. Cardiac Electrophysiology Soc. (founder). Home: 10614 Winterwood Carmel IN 46032-9688 Office: Ind U Sch Medicine 1100 W Michigan St Indianapolis IN 46202-5208 Office Phone: 317-962-0555. Business E-Mail: dzipes@iupui.edu.

ZIPF, ROBERT EUGENE, JR., legal medicine consultant, pathologist; b. Sept. 18, 1940; s. Robert Eugene and Meriam (Murr) Z.; m. Nancy J. Gaskell, Sept. 11, 1965; children: Karin Lorene, Marjorie Kristine. BA, DePauw U., 1962; MD, Ohio State U., 1966. Diplomate Am. Bd. Pathology. Intern Miami Valley Hosp., Dayton, Ohio, 1966-67; dir. forensic pathology Duke U. Med. Ctr., Durham, N.C., 1967-72; dir. radioisotope pathology Riverside Meth. Hosp., Columbus, 1974-78; dep. coroner, forensic pathologist Franklin County, Columbus, 1974-78; regional forensic pathologist State of N.C., Rocky Mount, 1978—. Clin. asst. prof. East Caroline U. Med. Sch., Greenville, N.C., 1979—; adj. prof. Atlantic Christian Coll., Wilson, N.C., 1980-89, dir. Sch. Med. Tech., 1983-89; dir. clin. and diagnostic labs. Nash Gen. Hosp., Rocky Mount, 1978—; dir. forensic toxicology lab. Nash Health Care Sys., Rocky Mount, 1990—; cons. in field. Contbr. articles to profl. jours. Trustee United Fund, 1979-84; mem. Mayor's Com. on Drug and Substance Abuse, 1987—. Maj. USAF, 1972-74. Fellow Am. Soc. Clin. Pathologist, Am. Acad. Forensic Scientists; mem. SMS (clin. adv. bd. 1988-91, lab. advisors bd. 1989-91), Assn. Clin. Scientists, Am. Coll. Nuclear Medicine, N.C. Med. Soc., N.Y. Acad. Scis. (pres. Lab. Users Group 1988-90, 92), Nash County Med. Soc. (pres. 1995). Home: 120 Newby Ct Rocky Mount NC 27804-3322 Office: Nash Gen Hosp Pathology Lab Rocky Mount NC 27804 E-mail: rezpath@email.com

ZIPORI-BECKENSTEIN, PNINIT, business administration educator, researcher; b. Tel Aviv, Oct. 22, 1947; d. Shmaya and Tirza Beckenstein; m. Dov Zipori, June 1, 1971 (div. 1993); children: Sigal, Dan. MSc with honors, Tel Aviv U., 1970; PhD, Weizman Inst. Sci., Rehovot, Israel, 1976; MBA, Bar-Ilan U., Ramat-Gan, Israel, 1985; PhD (hon)., Weizman Inst. Sci., 1977. Researcher Leiden (The Netherlands) U., 1976-78; with software mktg. dept. Med. Corp., Palo Alto, Calif., 1985-87; dir. mktg. Orgenics Ltd., Yavne, Israel, 1987; health editor Globes Econs. Newspaper, Tel Aviv, 1988-90; exec. Med. Mktg., Rehovot, 1988-97; lectr. Sch. Bus. Adminstrn., Israel, 1990-97. Researcher Sheba Med. Ctr., Tel-Hashomer, Israel, 1993-97. Author: Effective Interpersonal Communication, 1996, Effective Coping with Obstacles, 1997; contbr. articles to profl. jours. Mem. municipality edn. com., Rehovot, 1980; mem. leadership com. Meretz Polit. Party, Tel Aviv, 1997; legis. activist for disabled, 1993—. Mem. Biochemistry Soc. Jewish. Avocations: solo travel, swimming, painting. Home: 4 Hagra St 76310 Rehovot Israel Office: Med Mktg Ltd 23A Weizman St 76282 Rehovot Israel Office Phone: 972-8-9474789.

ZIPP, JOEL FREDERICK, lawyer; b. Shaker Heights, Ohio, Feb. 12, 1948; s. Jack David and Eleanor Adele Zipp; m. Elizabeth Ann Frieden, Dec. 4, 1976; 1 child, Carlyn Leigh. BS, U. Wis., 1970, MS, 1972; JD, Case Western Res. U., 1975. Bar: Ohio 1975, D.C. 1976, U.S. Claims Ct., U.S. Ct. Appeals (D.C. cir.) 1976, U.S. Ct. Appeals (5th cir.) 1979, U.S. Ct. Appeals (11th cir.) 1983, U.S. Supreme Ct. 1983. Trial atty. Fed. Energy Regulation Com., Washington, 1975-79, asst. dir. office of enforcement, 1979; assoc. Morley & Caskin, Washington, 1979-80; ptnr. Morley, Caskin & Generelly, Washington, 1981-98; mng. ptnr. Cameron McKenna LLP, Washington, 1998—2003; gen. counsel, sec. Portland Natural Gas Transmission Sys., 1993-99; ptnr. Bracewell & Patterson, Washington, 2003—. Notes editor: Energy Law Jour., 1990—98; contbr. articles to profl. jours. Bd. dirs. Westmoreland Children's Ctr., Washington, 1987—88, Found. Energy Law Jour., 1999—2001. Fellow Smithsonian, 1969. Mem.: ABA, Energy Bar Assn. (v.p. 1989—99, past com. chair ann. meeting 1992, 1993, bd. dirs. 1993—96, pres. 2000—01, bd. dirs. 2001—02, mem. nominations com. 2002—). Jewish. Avocations: skiing, running, bicycling. Home: 9216 Burning Tree Rd Bethesda MD 20817-2251 Office: Bracewell & Patterson 2000 K St NW Washington DC 20006-1872 Office Phone: 202-828-5811. E-mail: Joel.Zipp@bracepatt.com.

ZIPPIN, CALVIN, epidemiologist, educator; b. Albany, N.Y., July 17, 1926; s. Samuel and Jennie (Perkel) Z.; m. Patricia Jayne Schubert, Feb. 9, 1964; children: David Benjamin, Jennifer Dorothy. AB magna cum laude, SUNY, Albany, 1947; ScD, Johns Hopkins U., Balt., 1953. Rsch. asst. Sterling-Winthrop Rsch. Inst., Rensselaer, NY, 1947-50, Johns Hopkins U., Balt., 1950—53; instr. biostats. Sch. Pub. Health, U. Calif., Berkeley, 1953-55; asst. to full rsch. biostatistician Sch. Medicine U. Calif., San Francisco, 1955-67, asst. prof. preventive medicine, 1958-60; post doctoral fellow London Sch. Hygiene and Tropical Medicine, 1964-65; prof. epidemiology U. Calif., San Francisco, 1967-91, prof. emeritus, 1991—. Vis. assoc. prof. stats. Stanford U., 1962; adv. WHO, 1969—; vis research worker Middlesex Hosp. Med. Sch., London, 1975; various coms. Am. Cancer Soc. and Nat. Cancer Inst., 1956—; faculty adviser Regional Cancer Centre, Trivandrum, India, 1983—; cons., lectr., vis. prof. in field. Co-author book, book chpts.; author or co-author papers primarily on biometry and epidemiology of cancer; editorial advisor Jour. Stats. in Medicine, Boston, 1981-86. Mem., alt. mem. Dem. Ctrl. Com., Marin County, Calif., 1987-96. Recipient Disting. Alumnus award SUNY, Albany, 1969, Lifetime Achievement and Leadership award Nat. Cancer Inst., 2003, also awards, fellowships and grants for work in cancer biometry and epidemiology. Fellow Am. Statis. Assn., Am. Coll. Epidemiology, Royal Statis. Soc. Gt. Britain; mem. Biometric Soc. (mem. internat. coun. 1978-81, pres. Western N.Am. region 1979-80), Calif. Cancer Registrars Assn. (hon.), Internat. Assn. Cancer Registries (hon.), B'nai B'rith (pres. Golden Gate lodge 1970-71, pres. Greater San Francisco Bay area coun. 1974-75), Phi Beta Kappa, Sigma Xi, Delta Omega. Office: Univ Calif Dept Epidemiology Biostats San Francisco CA 94143-0560 Office Phone: 415-476-1374. Business E-Mail: czippin@itsa.ucsf.edu.

ZIRINSKY, SUSAN, television producer; Grad., Am. U. Sr. prodr. CBS Evening News, 1986-91, sr. broadcast prodr., 1991-93; sr. prodr. Eye to Eye, 1993-94, exec. prodr., 1994-95, CBS News, 48 Hours, N.Y.C., 1996—. Sr. prodr. CBS News coverage of 1992 Olympic Winter Games, Campaign '96. Office: CBS News 48 Hours 524 W 57th St Fl 5 New York NY 10019-2924

ZIRKIND, RALPH, physicist, educator; b. N.Y.C., Oct. 20, 1918; s. Isaac and Zicel (Lifshitz) Z.; m. Ann Goldman, Nov. 22, 1940; children: Sheila Zirkind Knopf, Elaine Zirkind Gorman, Edward I. BS, CCNY, 1940; MS, Ill. Inst. Tech., 1945; postgrad., George Washington U., 1946-47; PhD, U. Md., 1950; D.Sc., U. R.I., 1968. Physicist Navy Dept., 1945-50, chief physicist, 1951-60; physicist Oak Ridge Nat. Lab., 1950-51, Advanced Research Project Agy., Washington, 1960-63; prof. Poly. Inst. Bklyn., 1963-70, U. R.I., Kingston, 1970-72, adj. prof., 1972—; physicist Advanced Research Projects Agy., Arlington, Va., 1972-74; cons. Advanced Rsch. Projects Agy., Arlington, Va., 1974—. Lectr. U. Md., 1947-48, 48-50, George Washington U., 1952-53, U. Mich., 1964, 66, Haifa Inst. Tech., 1971; cons. ACDA, Jet Propulsion Lab., Calif. Inst. Tech.; cons. to industry, 1974—. Contbg. author: Jet Propulsion Series, 1952, FAR Infrared Properties of Materials, 1968, NAS Study Biology and Exploration of Mars, 1966; editor: Electromagnetic Sensing of Earth, 1967, Procs. SPIE-Developments in Electronic Imagining Techniques, vol. 32, 1972; mem. editl. bd. Infrared Physics, 1963—; contbr. articles profl. jours. Recipient Meritorious Civilian Svc. award Navy Dept., 1957; Meritorious Civilian Svc. award Dept. Def., 1970; Outstanding Educator of Am. medal, 1972; Maj. Contbn. award BMDO/AIAA, 1994; Spl. Lifetime Achievement Award for Pioneering Work in Sensors, SPIE, 2002. Mem. Am. Phys. Soc., N.Y. Acad. Scis., Sigma Xi, Sigma Pi Sigma (SPIE Aerosense Lifetime Achievement award 2002), Eta Kappa Nu. Home: 820 Hillsboro Dr Silver Spring MD 20902-3202 Office: 4001 Fairfax Dr Ste 700 Arlington VA 22203-1618 Business E-Mail: rzirkind@starsociates.com.

ZIRKLE, WILLIAM DENMAN, investment company executive; b. Roanoke, Va., Dec. 6, 1938; s. William Isaiah and Dorothy Hutcheson (Smythe) Z.; m. Dagmar Helene Agnes von Maltzahn, Oct. 10, 1970 (dec. Sept. 1987); children: Micaela, Sigrid Anne, Luise Bettina, William Wade. BS, Va. Poly. Inst., 1960; MBA, U. Pa., 1962. Program mgr. IBM Corp., White Plains, N.Y., 1973-76; asst. v.p. Conrail, Phila., 1976-80, asst. treas., 1980-83; mktg. dir. Morgan Stanley Asset Mgmt., N.Y.C., 1983-86; mng. dir. Marinvest, N.Y.C., 1986-89; sr. v.p. Lynch & Mayer Inc., N.Y.C., 1989-97; exec. v.p. Templeton Worldwide, Ft. Lauderdale, Fla., 1997—2002; CEO Carret and Co., N.Y., 2002—04; pres. Shenandoah Valley Holdings, LLC., Edinburg, Va., 2004—. Mem. bus. adv. council Va. Poly. Inst., Blacksburg, 1979—, mem. pres.'s adv. coun., 1997—. Trustee Randolph-Macon Woman's Coll., 1995-2000; chmn. Prayer Book Soc. Episcopal Ch., 1998-2003. Served to lt. col. U.S. Army, 1960-64, with Res. 1964-86. Mem. Am. Inst. Mktg. and Sales Execs., World Affairs Coun. Phila., Sons Confederate Vets., Alpha Kappa Psi, Omicron Delta Kappa. Clubs: Econ. Club N.Y., Army & Navy (Washington); Merion Cricket (Haverford, Pa.); Phila.; Union (N.Y.). Republican. Anglican. Avocations: tennis, backpacking, fishing. Home: 12097 S Middle Rd Edinburg VA 22824-3847 Office: Shenandoah Valley Holdings LLC PO Box 96 Edinburg VA 22824 Office Phone: 540-335-9322. Personal E-mail: wdzirkl@attglobal.net.

ZIRPS, FOTENA ANATOLIA, psychologist, researcher; b. Pitts., Mar. 27, 1958; d. George T. and Barbara F. (Skinner) Z. BA, U. Akron, 1983, MA, 1987; PhD, Fla. State U., 1990. Sch. psychologist Canton (Ohio) City Schs., 1985-86, Leon County Schs., Tallahassee, 1986-88, program evaluator, 1988-90; cons. Evaluation Systems Design, Inc., Tallahassee, 1990-91; pres. Zirps, Vella and Assocs., Inc., Tallahassee, 1991—; dir. program evaluation Families First, Atlanta, 1991-94; assoc. prof. Fla. Mental Health Inst. U. South Fla., 1995-97; Fla. mental health coord. Fla. Mental Health Inst.-U. South Fla., 1995-97; coord. spl. studies for children Comprehensive Cmty. Mental Health Program-U. South Fla., 1995-97; pres. Fla. Inst. Quality Improvement, Brandon, 1997-99; dir. standards and evaluation Fla. Dept. Children & Families, Tallahassee, 1999—. Tchr. Fla. State U., Tallahassee, summers 1988-91, grant coord., 1989-90; cons. hild Welfare League Am.; coord. spl. studies Comprehensive Cmty. Mental Health Svcs. Children with Severe Emotional Disturbances; adj. faculty Sch. Social Work, Univ. South Fla. Author: Sun and Moon, 1991, Doing It Right the First Time: A Model Quality Assurance for Human Services Agencies, 1994, rev. edit., 1997, Accountability & Accreditation: A Primer on Outcomes, 1998; (with others) Computer Models of Reading, 1989; author, cartoonist: (slides show/audio tape) Human Rights, 1986; co-inventor: (games) Beauty Pageant, Alien Abduction; editor, co-author: Quality Improvement Program and Program Evaluation in Child Welfare: Managing into the Next Century; panel standards writers Coun. on Accreditation Svcs. for Families and Children, Inc. Chmn. grad. student adv. com. Fla. State, 1986-88. Mem. Am. Psychol. Assn., Am. Evaluation Assn., Am. Ednl. Rsch. Assn. (Disting. Presenter 1991), Nat. Coun. Rsch. in Child Welfare (chair quality improvement subcom.), Fla. Ednl. Rsch. Assn. (Disting. Author 1990). Mem. Soc. Of Friends. Avocations: running, racquetball, tennis, reading. Office: Fla Dept Children & Families 417 Williams St Apt C Tallahassee FL 32303-6381

ZIRPS, GEORGE THOMAS, marine engineer, consultant; b. Nyack, N.Y., Apr. 24, 1932; s. Thomas House and Anna Zirps; m. Barbara Faye Skinner, June 30, 1957; children: Fotena Anatolia, Thomas Christos. B in Marine Engring., Maritime Coll., 1954; A in Computer Engring. Tech., Aiken (S.C.) Tech. Coll., 1999, A in Electronics Engring. Tech., 2000. Registered profl. engr., Pa. Mech. engr. U.S. Naval Shipyard, Bklyn., 1954-55; engring. officer U.S.S. Chambers USN, Newport, R.I., 1955-57; engring. mgr. Westinghouse Plant Apparatus Divsn., Pitts., 1957-69; sr. project engr. Exxon Rsch. and Engring. Co., Florham Park, N.J., 1969-71; program mgr., product devel. mgr., engring. mgr. Babcock & Wilcox Co., Barberton, Ohio, 1971-87; sr. fellow engr., vice chair pressur eqt. protection com. Westinghouse Savannah River Co., Aiken, S.C., 1989-95. Cons. Zirps Consulting, North Canton, Ohio, 1987—. Contbr. articles to profl. jours. including Power, Sci. Am.; inventor vernier throttling/block valves, others. Capt. USNR 1954-84, ret. Mem. ASME (nat. bd. com. for pressure relief devices), Phi Theta Kappa. Democrat. Greek Orthodox. Avocation: computer programming. Home: 4 Inverness St E Aiken SC 29803-5946 E-mail: gtzirps@aol.com.

ZISCHKE, DOUGLAS ARTHUR, foreign service officer; b. Sioux Falls, S.D., May 24, 1929; s. Arthur Gustav and Alice Minetta (Wedeking) Z.; m. Janice Mae Kuehnemann, June 8, 1957; children: Mark Douglas, Deborah Jan, Todd Lincoln. BS in Journalism cum laude, U. Wis., 1951, MS, 1952. Joined U.S. Fgn. Svc., 1957; tech. editor Forest Svc., Madison, 1955-57; asst. info. officer USIS, Montevideo, Uruguay, 1957-58, La Paz, Bolivia, 1958-59; asst. cultural affairs officer, br. pub. affairs officer Mexico, 1960-65; info. specialist, 1965-67; pub. affairs officer Tegucigalpa, Honduras, 1967-69; dep. pub. affairs officer Buenos Aires, 1969-71; pub. affairs officer Guatemala City, Guatemala, 1971—74; assigned to U.S. Army War Coll., 1974-75; dep. pub. affairs officer Am. embassy Tehran, Iran, 1975-78; cultural coord. USICA, Washington, 1979-80; internat. cons., 1980-86; fgn. affairs advisor State Dept., 1986-98. Author monograph. Bd. dirs. Boy Scouts Am; dir. Lutheran Ch. 1973-74. Served with Signal Corps, AUS, 1953-55. Mem. Diplomatic and Consular Officers Ret.

ZISKIN, LAURA, television producer, film producer; Co-founder Frogwood Films; pres. Fox 2000, Beverly Hills, Calif. Films include: (assoc. prodr.) Eyes of Laura Mars, 1978; (prodr.) Murphy's Romance, 1985, No Way Out, 1987, D.O.A., 1988, Everybody's An American, 1988, The Rescue, 1988, What About Bob?, 1991, The Doctor, 1991, Hero, 1992, To Die For, 1995, Spiderman, 2002; (exec. prodr.) Pretty Woman, 1990, As Good As it Gets, 1997; (TV) Fail Safe, 2000, Dinner with Friends, 2001, 74th Ann. Acad. awards, 2002, Tarzan, 2003, The Spaces, 2003., prodr.(TV) How I Learned to Drive, 2001. Office: Culver Studios 9336 Washington Blvd Culver City CA 90232-2600

ZISKIND, DEBORAH ZISKIND, public relations and legal marketing executive; b. Pitts., Mar. 4, 1961; d. Gerald N. and Norma Jean (Morris) Ziskind. BA in Internat. Rels., Tufts U., 1983. Litigation specialist, sr. case mgr., pub. affairs and client devel. assoc. Weil, Gotshal & Manges, N.Y.C., 1989-94; mgr. mktg. Reed Smith Shaw & McClay, Pitts., Phila., N.Y.C., Washington and Princeton, N.J., 1994-96; pres., CEO, Ziskind Pub. Rels. Assocs., Pitts., 1996—; founder, chmn. The Global Conf. Inst., 1996—. Pub. rels. cons. Pitts. Chamber Music Soc., U. Pitts. dept. music, 1983-85; antitrust case mgr. cons. Dickie, McCamey & Chilcote, 1985-87; exec. May Corp., Pitts., 1987-89. Contbg. columnist The Chronicle, Pitts., 1977—; columnist Resident Publs., N.Y.C., 1991-94, Actor's Resource, N.Y.C., 1992-94; bd. editors Strategies: The Journal of Legal Marketing; mem. Legal Mktg. Assn., 1992—; exec. editor for Yr. 2000, Strategies, The Jour. Legal Mktg. Mem. exec. com. New Leadership bd. Pitts. Symphony Orch., 1994—. MacJannet scholar in internat. law and economics Tufts U. and Ctr. for European Studies, Talloires, France, 1981. Mem. Tufts Media and Comm. Group, Pitts. Filmmakers (bd. dirs. 1996—), Tufts Media and Comms. Group. Avocations: international politics, music, writing, piano performance, legal ethics. Office: 4415 5th Ave Pittsburgh PA 15213-2654 Home: 50 E Bellevue Pl Apt 1901 Chicago IL 60611-1169

ZISMAN, BARRY STUART, lawyer; b. N.Y.C., Sept. 18, 1937; s. Harry and Florence Rita (Tucker) Z.; m. Maureen Frances Brumond, Dec. 30, 1979; children: Michael Glenn, Marlene Ann. AB, Columbia U., 1958, JD, 1961. Bar: D.C. 1962, N.Y. 1965, Tex. 1986, U.S. Dist. Ct. (ea. and so. dists.) N.Y. 1967, U.S. Ct. Appeals (D.C. cir.) 1967, U.S. Dist. Ct. (no. and so. dists.) Tex. 1986, U.S. Ct. Appeals (5th cir.) 1988, U.S. Supreme Ct. 1967. With U.S. Govt., 1962-66; pvt. practice Syosset, N.Y., 1966-71; sr. counsel CBS Inc., N.Y.C., 1972-75; asst. gen. counsel, asst. sec. M. Lowenstein & Sons, N.Y.C., 1975-79; gen. counsel Grumman Allied Indsl. Inc., Bethpage, N.Y., 1979-83; asst. gen. counsel Grumman Corp., Bethpage, 1982-83; sr. atty. FDIC, Dallas, 1984-87; of counsel Arter & Hadden, Dallas, 1987-88, ptnr., 1988, Winstead, McGuire, Sechrest & Minick, Dallas, 1988-90, Arter & Hadden, Dallas and Washington, 1990-91, Rubinstein & Perry, Dallas, 1991-93, The Zisman Law Firm, P.C., Dallas, 1993—. Advisor in field; vice-chmn. Assn. of Bank and Thrift Receivership Coun. Editor and author: Banks and Thrifts: Government Enforcement and Receivership Law, 1991. With U.S. Army, 1961-62. Home: 905 Murl Dr Irving TX 75062-4441 Office: 1412 Main St Fl 23 Dallas TX 75202 Office Phone: 214-745-1300. Personal E-mail: zislaw@aol.com.

ZISSER, MARTIN SHEPHERD, fur apparel manufacturer, investor, trader; b. Bklyn., Jan. 30, 1942; s. Irving and Jean (Shepherd) Z. Student, NYU, 1960-63. Wall St. invester and trader. Sec. treas. Fur Dressers Union Local 2A, N.Y.C., 1989-92; v.p. UFCW Local 174, N.Y.C., 1992—. Recipient Ofcl. Brit. Coat of Arms, Queen Elizabeth II. Mem. Internat. Soc. Philosophical Enquiry, Mensa. Republican. Jewish. Avocations: study of history, politics, world current events, economics. Home: 1219 E 80th St Brooklyn NY 11236-4165

ZISSU, MICHAEL JEROME, lawyer; b. N.Y.C., June 3, 1934; s. Leonard and Ruth Edith (Katz) Z.; m. Maria Theresia Duffner, June 27, 1960 (div. Feb. 1971); children: Audrey Lynn Zissu Hensley, Erik March; m. Patricia Joan Murphy, Feb. 20, 1971 (div. 1977); 1 child, Jacob Royal. AB, Dartmouth Coll., 1956; postgrad., U. Chgo., 1956-58; LLB, New Eng. Law Sch., 1962. Bar: Mass. Supreme Jud. Ct. 1963, N.Y. (app. divsn. 1st dept.) 1964. Assoc. Zissu, Marcus & Stein, N.Y.C., 1962-68, Regan Goldfarb Powell & Quinn, N.Y.C., 1968-71; ptnr. Zissu & Harris, N.Y.C., 1972-82, Murphy & Zissu, N.Y.C., 1985-96. With U.S. Army, 1958-60. Mem. Assn. of the Bar of the City of N.Y., Copyright Soc. USA. Jewish. Home: 12800 Vonn Rd Apt 7603 Largo FL 33774-2590 Office: 375 Riverside Dr Apt 9E New York NY 10025-2120

ZISSU, ROGER L. lawyer; b. Oceanside, NY, Feb. 16, 1939; s. Leonard Zissu and Ruth Zissu Kahn; married. Student, Sorbonne U., Paris, 1958-59, Inst. d'Etudes Politiques, 1958-59; AB summa cum laude, Dartmouth Coll., 1960; LLB cum laude, Harvard U., 1963. Bar: N.Y. 1963, U.S. Dist. Ct. (ea. and so. dists.) N.Y. 1965, U.S. Dist. Ct. (no. dist.) N.Y. 1989, U.S. Ct. Appeals (2d cir.) 1965, U.S. Ct. Appeals (9th cir.) 1999, U.S. Tax Ct. 1972, U.S. Supreme Ct. 1974. Law clk. U.S. Dist. Ct. Ea. Dist. N.Y., Bklyn., 1963-65; assoc. Davis, Polk & Wardwell, N.Y.C., 1965-70; corp. counsel Vornado, Inc., Garfield, N.J., 1970-73; assoc. Cowan, Liebowitz & Latman PC, N.Y.C., 1973, ptnr., 1974-90, Weiss, David, Fross, Zelnick & Lehrman PC, N.Y.C., 1990-97, Fross, Zelnick, Lehrman & Zissu PC, N.Y.C., 1997—. Lectr. in field. Class agt. Dartmouth Coll. Alumni Fund, Hanover, N.H., 1960—; bd. dirs. Vol. Lawyers for the Arts, 1987-90. Mem. ABA, Assn. of Bar of City of NY (chmn. copyright and literary property com. 1989-92, judiciary com. 1995-98, 2003), NY State Bar Assn., Copyright Soc. USA (trustee 1981, 83-86, 92—, treas. 1988-90, v.p. 1990-92, pres. 1992-94), Phi Beta Kappa, Alpha Delta Phi. Avocations: swimming, tennis, cross country skiing. Office: Fross Zelnick Lehrman & Zissu PC 866 United Nations Plz New York NY 10017-1822 Office Phone: 212-813-5900.

ZITELLI, BASIL J. pediatrician, educator; b. Pitts., June 21, 1946; m. Suzanne Mary Drake, July 8, 1972; children: Matthew, Daniel, Benjamin, Anne. BS, U. Pitts., 1967, MD, 1971. Cert. Pediatrics Md., 1976. Clin. instr., pediat. Jefferson Med. Sch., Phila., 1974—76; chief resident, pediat. Johns Hopkins Hosp., Balt., 1976—78; asst. prof. pediat. Children's Hosp. of Pitts., 1978, assoc. prof. pediat., prof. pediat., 1992—. Chief, divsn. Diagnostic referral svc. Children's Hosp. Pitts., 2002. Editor: Atlas of Pediatric Physical Diagnosis, 2002, Common & Chronic Symptoms in Pediatrics, 1997, Harriet Lane Handbook, 1978. Mem. Internat. Child Health Found., Pitts. Lt. commd. USN, 1974—76. Fellow: Am. Acad. of Pediat. Office: Children's Hosp of Pitts 3705 Fifth Ave Pittsburgh PA 15213

ZITO, BARRY, professional baseball player; b. Las Vegas, Nev., May 13, 1978; Student, U. Calif., Santa Barbara, Pierce Jr. Coll., U. So. Calif. Pitcher Oakland A's, 2000—. Named to, Am. League All-Star team, 2002, 2003; recipient Am. League Cy Young award, 2002. Achievements include has appeared on TV shows including JAG, Arli$$, and the Chris Isaak Show; led American League in Wins, 2002. Office: c/o Oakland Athletics Network Assocs Coliseum 7000 Coliseum Way Oakland CA 94621*

ZITO, CHRISTOPHER RICHARD, molecular biologist, biochemist; b. New Haven, CTConn., Nov. 21, 1975; s. Andrew Richard and Ann (Panico) Zito. BS in Biol. Sci., Albertus Magnus Coll., New Haven, 1997; MS in Cellular and Molecular Biology, U.of New Haven, 1998; postgrad., Wesleyan U., Middletown. Assoc. rsch. scientist Dept. Pharmacology, Yale U., New Haven, 1994—97; ind. rsch. scientist Dept. Ob-Gyn., Yale U., 1997—99; rsch. scientist, tchg. asst. Wesleyan U., Middletown, Conn., 1999—. Molecular biology cons. Yale U., New Haven, 1997—, radiation safety lab. cons., 2000—, hazardous waste lab. instr., 2000—. Contbr. articles to sci. jours. Vol. North Haven Rep. Election Com., North Haven, 1994—2000; bd. dirs. St. Tarsius Squire Cir., New Haven, 1994—97, Albertus Magnus Coll. Campus Min., New Haven, 1994—97; counselor K.C., Hamden, 1994—97. Recipient The June Veckerelli Mem.l Award for Academic Excellence in Sci., Albertus Magnus Coll., 1997, Annual Acad. Rsch. Assistantship award, U. of New Haven, 1997—98; fellow Annual Doctoral Acad. Rsch. fellow, Wesleyan U./NIH, 1999—2001. Mem.: K.C. (3rd Degree Member 1994—, Squire Circle Counselor of the Year Award 1996 & 1997). Roman Catholic. Avocations: basketball, classical and contemporary piano, acoustic guitar, computers. Home: 197 Maple Ave North Haven CT 06473-3324 Office: Wesleyan Univ Lawn Ave Middletown CT 06459 Personal E-mail: crzito@iconn.net. Business E-Mail: czito@wesleyan.edu.

ZITO, GEORGE VINCENT, sociologist, sociology educator; b. N.Y.C., Dec. 5, 1923; s. John Joseph And Margaret (Sapatella) Z.; m. Dorothea Rose Lutz, Apr. 29, 1944; children: Darlene A., George Robinson, Dorothea, Pamela G. BA, Syracuse U., 1970, MA and PhD, 1972. Asst. sr. engr. Bendix Corp., Teterboro, N.J., 1947-69; asst. prof. sociology grad. faculty New Sch. Social Rsch., N.Y.C., 1973-76; assoc. prof. Lemoyne Coll., Syracuse, N.Y., 1976-77, Syracuse U., 1977-94, prof. emeritus, 1994—. Rsch. dir. Law Enforcement Assistance Adminstrn. Victimization, Newark, 1974-75; rsch. assoc. Maxwell Policy Ctr., Syracuse, N.Y., 1977-79; program evaluator history-pub. policy NEH grant U. DC, 1981-83. Author: Methodology and Meanings, 1975, Systems of Discourse, 1984, Sociology of Shakespeare, 1991, The Death of Meaning, 1993, others; contbr. 15 articles to profl. jours. Trustee Northvale (N.J.) Pub. Libr., 1965; advisor Syracuse Taiwan Assn., 1994; mem. Mayor's Neighborhood Com., Syracuse, 1989-94. Invited scholar Taiwan, 1991. Mem. Am. Sociol. Assn., N.Y. State Sociol. Assn. (Leadership scholar 1982, pres. 1980, 92), Ea. Sociol. Assn. (mem. coms. 1975-96), Assn. Sociology of Rels. (chair sessions 1992). Democrat. Mem. Unitarian Ch. Avocations: military miniatures, canoeing, sketching, travel, computers. Home: 822 Lancaster Ave Syracuse NY 13210-2924

ZITO, JUDI, information technology executive; married; 4 children. BBA U. So. Fla.; M in Comm. and Leadership, Seton Hall U. Cert. in telecom. U. Miami. Sys. analyst Miami-Dade County, Fla., 1981, programming sys. supr., div. dir., IT Dept.; mgr. Miami-Dade County Comm. Dept., 2001—03; chief info. officer Miami Dade County, Fla., 2003—. Named one of Computer World's 100 Premier IT Leaders, 2004; recipient Quiet Storm award, Women's Power Caucus, 2003. Office: 111 NW 1st St Miami FL 33128

ZITRIN, ARTHUR, physician; b. Bklyn., Apr. 10, 1918; s. William and Lillian (Elbaum) Z.; m. Charlotte Marker, Oct. 4, 1942; children— Richard Alan, Elizabeth Ann. BS, City Coll. N.Y., 1938; MS, N.Y. U., 1941, MD, 1945; certificate psychoanalytic medicine, Columbia, 1955. Diplomate: Am. Bd. Psychiatry and Neurology. Research fellow animal behavior Am. Museum Natural History, 1939-42; intern King County Hosp., 1945-46; resident psychiatry Bellevue Hosp., 1948-51; instr. physiology Hunter Coll., N.Y.C., 1948-49; mem. faculty N.Y.U. Sch. Medicine, 1949-97, prof. psychiatry, 1967-97, prof. emeritus, 1997—; mem. staff Bellevue Hosp., N.Y.C., 1951—, dir. psychiatry, 1955-68, N.Y.C. Dept. Hosps., 1962- 64; pvt. practice, 1949—; attending psychiatrist Univ. Hosp., N.Y.C. Cons. psychiatrist Manhattan Va Hosp. Author papers in field. Served to capt., M.C. AUS, 1946- 48. Fellow Am. Psychiat. Assn. (life), N.Y. Acad. Medicine; mem. AMA, N.Y. Soc. Clin. Psychiatry (pres. 1966- 67), Am. Psychoanalytic Assn. (life), Sigma Xi, Alpha Omega Alpha. Home: 56 Ruxton Rd Great Neck NY 11023-1529 Office: 550 1st Ave New York NY 10016-6402

ZITT, MYRON J. allergist, immunologist; b. N.Y.C., Sept. 15, 1939; s. Arthur and Bertha (Grossman) Z.; m. Jeanne Patricia Schwartz, Oct. 9, 1966; 1 child, Jonathan. BS, Trinity Coll., 1960; MD, SUNY, Bklyn., 1965. Bd. cert. Am. Bd. Internal Medicine, Am. Bd. Allergy & Immunology. Intern L.I. Coll. Hosp., Bklyn., 1965-66, resident, 1966-68; chief allergy-immunology Queens L.I. Med. Group, North Babylon, NY, 1972—. Dir. adult allergy clinic Nassau County Med. Ctr., East Meadow, N.Y., 1979—; assoc. clin. prof. SUNY, Stony Brook, 1984—. Mem. edit. bd. Annals of Allergy-Asthma-Immunology, 1995—. Maj. USAF, 1969-72. Allergy-Immunology fellow Duke U., Durham, N.C., 1968-69. Fellow Am. Coll. Allergy, Asthma & Immunology (regent 1992-95, v.p. 2002-03, pres.-elect 2003-04), Am. Acad. Allergy, Asthma & Immunology, Nassau Acad. Medicine; mem. Am. Thoracic Soc., L.I. Allergy Soc. (pres. 1989-91). Home: 9 Cypress Dr Woodbury NY 11797-1501 Office: Queens LI Med Group 300 Bay Shore Rd North Babylon NY 11703-2823

ZITTO, RICHARD JOSEPH, physics educator; b. Lisbon, Ohio, Sept. 1, 1945; s. Tony Joseph and Olive Lucille (Davison) Z.; m. Pamela Daryl Irons, July 22, 1967; children: Angela Marie, Elena Michelle. BS in Sci. Edn., Ohio State U., 1968, MA in Phys. Sci. Edn., 1978. Tchr. sci. Kenton (Ohio) Jr. H.S., 1968-70, tchr. physics and sci. Kenton Sr. H.S., 1970-76; tchr. physics Boardman H.S., Youngstown, Ohio, 1976-99; physics educator Youngstown State U., 1981—, coord. Physics Olympics, 1994—. Dir. Youngstown Area Physics Alliance, 1987—. Trustee Hardin Meml. Hosp., Kenton, 1971-76; bd. dirs. Blue Cross of Lima, Ohio, 1973-76, Nat. Multiple Sclerosis Soc. N.E. Ohio, 1981-91; trustee Columbiana Pub. Libr., 1990—, pres., 1993-95, 2000—. Recipient Outstanding Young Educator award Kenton Jaycees, 1972, Outstanding Sci. Tchr. Youngstown State U. Sigma Xi, 1980, Career Educator award Ohio State U. Coll. Edn., 1997; A. Jennings scholar Martha Holden Jennings Found. Fellow Ohio Acad. Sci.; mem. ASCD, Am. Assn. Physics Tchrs. (physics tchg. resource agt. 1986—, pres. Ohio sect. 1989-90, mem. physics in high schs. com. 1991-94, History and Philosophy com. 1999-2002), Ont. Assn. Physics Tchrs., Nat. Sci. Tchrs. Assn., N.E. Ohio Edn. Assn. (co-chmn. sci. workshop 1979—), Sci. Edn. Coun. Ohio, United Tchg. Profession, Lions, Rotary (sec. 1978-79), Elks. Republican. Presbyterian. Avocations: woodworking, tennis, history of science, collecting antique physics apparatus. Office: Physics & Astronomy Dept Youngstown State Univ Youngstown OH 44555-0001 E-mail: rjzitto@ysu.edu.

ZITTRAIN, JONATHAN L. law educator; b. Pitts., Dec. 24, 1969; s. Lester and Ruth Zittrain. BS, Yale U., 1991; JD, Harvard U., 1995, MPA, 1995. Bar: Pa. 1995, D.C. 1996, U. S. Ct. Appeals (D.C. cir.) 1996. Chief forum adminstr. Compuserve Info. Svc., 1984—86; editl. columnist Computer Shopper, 1986-90; program mgr. Microsoft Corp., Redmond, Wash., 1990; with U.S. Dept. State, Washington, 1991; staff U.S. Senate Select Com. on Intelligence, Washington, 1992, 94; law clk. U.S. Ct. Appeals, Washington, 1995; exec. dir. Berkman Ctr. for Internet & Society, Harvard Law Sch., Cambridge, Mass., 1997—2000, faculty co-dir., 2000—; lectr. law Harvard Law Sch., Cambridge, Mass., 1997—99, asst. prof., 2000—, Jack N. and Lillian R. Berkman asst. prof. for entrepreneurial legal studies, 2001—. Office: Berkman Ctr for Internet & Society Harvard Law Sch Baker House 1587 Massachusetts Ave Cambridge MA 02138 Business E-Mail: zittrain@law.harvard.edu.

ZITTRAIN, LESTER EUGENE, lawyer; b. Norfolk, Va., Mar. 27, 1931; s. Leonard and Lee Zittrain; m. Ruth Ann Cohen, Aug. 20, 1957; children: Laura Zittrain Eisenberg, Jeffrey, Jonathan. BA, Washington and Lee U., 1952; JD, U. Va., 1955. Bar: Va. 1955, Pa. 1959, U.S. Supreme Ct. 1970. Ptnr. Zittrain and Zittrain, Pitts., 1959—. Former mem. exec. bd. and trustee Tree of Life Congregation, Pitts. Lt. USN, 1955-58. Fellow: Pa. Bar Found. (life); mem.: ATLA, ABA, Allegheny County Bar Assn. (judiciary com. 1983—86, chmn. 1986, mem. lawyers ins. com. 1984—, bench-bar conf. com. 1986—88, ct. rules com. 1987—, women in law com. 1988—, law libr. com. 1988—, bd. govs. 1988—2001, by-laws com. 1990—, chmn. civil litigation sect. 1986, Amram award 1998), Acad. Trial Lawyers Allegheny County (bd. govs. 1981—85, treas. 1986—88), Pa. Assn. Trial Lawyers, Pa. Bar Assn. (jud. selection reform com., mem. ho. of dels. from Allegheny County). Home: 136 Thornberry Dr Pittsburgh PA 15235-5061 Office: Zittrain & Zittrain 201 Franklin Ctr Profl Bldg 4240 Greensburg Pike Pittsburgh PA 15221-4297 Fax: 412-271-2300. E-mail: razlez@mindspring.com.

ZITZNER, DUANE E. computer company executive; b. 1947; BS, Univ. Wisc., Madison, Wisc., 1970; grad. studies, Univ. Minn., Mpls. With IBM, 1973—89; sec. mgr. Hewlett-Packard Co., Palo Alto, Calif., 1989—90, rsch. and devel. mgr., 1990—91, gen. mgr., 1991—93, pres. computing systems, 1993—2002, exec. v.p. personal sys. group, 2002—. Bd. dirs. Entone Tech. Office: Hewlett-Packard Co 3000 Hanover St Palo Alto CA 94304

ZIVELONGHI, KURT DANIEL, painter, computer graphics artist, designer; b. Barstow, Calif., Oct. 3, 1960; s. Vincent Otto and Beverly Dean (Schwind) Z. Student, Pasadena (Calif.) City Coll., 1984-85, Art Students League, N.Y.C., 1988-89; BFA, Art Ctr. Coll. of Design, 1993. Self employed fine artist, Pomona, Calif., 1990—. Art dir. movies Seagull's Journey, Gizmo LLC, The Innocent Bystander, Mad Dogs Prodns., 1998. One-man show at Coll. of Design Art Ctr., Pasadena, Calif., 1993; group shows include Flux Gallery, Eagle Rock, Calif., 1993, Art Students League, N.Y.C., 1989, Artexpo, N.Y., 2000, Marbella, Spain, 2000, AR+21, Las Vegas, 2000, 10th Internat. Biennial Portraiture-Drawings-Graphics, Tuzla, 2002, Aaron Gallery, Washington, 2003, Scottsdale Art Festival, 2003, Orlando Gallery, 2004, Orlando (Fla.) Gallery, 2004; exhibits at Orlando (Fla.) Gallery, 2004. Mem.: Am. Acad. Poets. Avocations: piano, weightlifting, theater, cinema. Personal E-mail: kzivelonghi@earthlink.net.

ZIVIN, NORMAN H. lawyer; b. Chgo., Aug. 10, 1944; s. Alfred E. and Irene (Scher) Z.; m. Lynn F., Dec. 27, 1967; children: Alison, Stephen, Michael. E.M. in Mining Engring., Colo. Sch. Mines, 1965; JD cum laude, Columbia U., 1968. Bar: N.Y. 1968, Ill. 1970, U.S. Supreme Ct. 1975. Assoc. Cooper & Dunham LLP (and predecessor firms), N.Y.C., 1968-70, 71-75, ptnr., 1976—. Mem. Bd. Ethics New Castle (N.Y.), 1974-79. Mem. ABA, Assn. of Bar of City of N.Y., Am. Intellectual Property Law Assn., N.Y. Intellectual Property Law Assn., Soc. Mining Engrs., U.S. Trademark Assn., Fed. Bar Coun., Town Club of Newcastle (pres. 1982-84). Home: 3 Valley Ln Chappaqua NY 10514-2002 Office: Cooper & Dunham LLP Ste 2200 1185 Avenue Of The Americas New York NY 10036-2615 Office Phone: 212-278-0400. E-mail: nzivin@cooperdunham.com.

ZIZI, artist; b. China, 1954; came to U.S., 1985; Grad., Guanzhou Fine Arts Acad., 1979. Chief-in-designer The North Guandong Acad. of Design, China. Hon. curator Borong Mus. Art, China. Exhibited in shows including Fed. Hall Nat. Meml., N.Y.C., 1997, Shogun Chinese Art Mus., China, 1997, Wisser Meml. Libr. N.Y. Inst. of Tech., 1998, Chung Cheng Art Gallery St. John's U., N.Y.C., 1998, others; represented in permanent collections Abney Gallery, N.Y.C., Agroa Gallery, N.Y.C., Kent Gallery, London, Comm. Art Gallery, Phila., Yunbei Fine Arts Mus., China, Xuboreng Fine Arts Mus., China, Ink Painting Mus., Japan, Xin-Shenzhou Gallery, Singapore, Mus. of Arts Collection, Calif., TV Univ., China, Shaogun Tchrs.' Coll., China, Asia Art Sch., London, Guangzhou Fine Arts Acad., China, Modern Art Hall, Paris, Immigrants' Project Theater, Bklyn., Fine Arts Edn. Ctr., N.Y.C., Acad. Oriental Arts, China. Recipient 1st prize in watercolor Queens Artists Alliance's 1st Nat. Exhbn., Award of Excellence Town of Oyster Bay, 2d Pl. Rongwood Manor Arts Assn., Award of Excellence New Age Fine Arts Ctr., Artist Showcase award Manhattan Arts Internat. 5th Ann. Competition, 1st place London Kent Ann. Competition, 1996, Silver medal Chinese Art Exhibition by Comtemporary Famous Artists in China, 1997, Lakeland Bank award Ringwood Manor Assn. Arts's 33rd Annual Exbhn., N.J., 1998, award of excellence Internat. Arts League's 19998 Annual Competition, N.Y., 1998, award for excellence Xin-Shen Zhou Art Inst.'s 5th Internat. Competition, Singapore, 1998. Address: 94-46 85 Rd # 2H Woodhaven NY 11421 Home: 9446 85th Rd Apt 2H Woodhaven NY 11421-1712 Fax: 718-846-6540.

ZIZIC, THOMAS MICHAEL, physician, educator; b. Milw., Dec. 9, 1939; s. Michael Mitchell Zizic and Dorothy (Batas) Ciric; m. Karen Owens, June 15, 1962 (div. Sept. 1967); m. Martha Ann Ardos, Nov. 22, 1967; children: Lara Ann, Kristine Michelle. BS, U. Wis., 1961; MD, Johns Hopkins U., 1965. Intern Johns Hopkins Hosp., Balt., 1965-66, asst. resident, 1966-67, fellow in internal medicine, 1969-71, instr. dept. medicine, 1971-73, asst. prof. medicine, 1971-81, assoc. prof. medicine, 1981—; pres., CEO Bionicare Med. Techs., Inc., 2002—. Pvt. practice, Balt., 1988—; co-dir. Chesapeake Osteoporosis Ctr., Balt., 1988—; dir. med. affairs Murray Electronics, 1993—; v.p. med. quality care Physicians Quality Care, 1995—; pres. U.S. Osteoporosis Network, Inc., 1996—; co-founder, dir. Creative Environ. Solutions, Inc., 1996—; cons. in field. Contbr. numerous articles and abstracts to profl. jours. V.p. Md. chpt. Arthritis Found., Balt., 1976-77; chmn. Md. Commn. on Arthritis and Related Diseases, 1986-90. Fellow Am. Coll. Rheumatology, 1986; Md. Soc. Rheumatic Diseases (pres. 1975-76), D.C. Rheumatism Assn., Balt. City Med. Soc., Johns Hopkins Hosp. Med. Soc., Arthritis Found. (fellow 1971-73, v.p. 1976-77, med. and sci. com. 1977-79, chmn. profl. edn. com. 1977-78, govtl. affairs com. 1979-83), Phi Beta Kappa, Phi Kappa Phi, Phi Eta Sigma. Avocations: skiing, tennis. Office: 5601 Loch Raven Blvd Baltimore MD 21239-2905 Office Phone: 410-472-1888. E-mail: drzizic@bionicare.com. *Give 100% today. We have only the present. Plan for the future but don't live in the future. The future never comes. We have only today.*

ZLAKET, THOMAS ANDREW, attorney, former state supreme court chief justice; b. May 30, 1941; AB in Polit. Sci., U. Notre Dame, 1962; LLB, U. Ariz., 1965; LLM, U. Va., 2001. Bar: Ariz. 1965, U.S. Dist. Ct. Ariz. 1967, U.S. Ct. Appeals (9th cir.) 1969, Calif. 1976. Atty. Lesher Scruggs Rucker Kimble & Lindamood, Tucson, 1965-68, Maud & Zlaket, 1968-70, Estes Browning Maud and Zlaket, 1970-73, Slutes Estes Zlaket Sakrison & Wasley, 1973-82, Zlaket & Zlaket, 1982-92; judge pro tempore Pima County (Ariz.) Superior Ct., 1983—; justice Ariz. Supreme Ct., 1992—2002, vice chief justice, 1996—97, chief justice, 1997—2002. Fellow Am. Coll. Trial Lawyers, Am. Bar Found., Ariz. Bar Found.; mem. ABA, Pima County Bar Assn., Am. Bd. Trial Advocates, Ariz. Coll. Trial Advocacy, U. Ariz. Law Coll. Assn., Ariz. Law Rev. Assn. Office: 310 S Williams Blvd Ste 170 Tucson AZ 85711 E-mail: tazlaket@qwest.net.

ZLATKIN, MICHAEL BRIAN, physician; b. Montreal, Que., Can., Mar. 20, 1957; came to U.S., 1986; s. Ralph and Gertrude (Rosen) Z.; m. Paula Roanne Ralph, May 30, 1982 (div. Jan. 1992); children: Nancy, Robert; m. Marilyn Judith Bohan, June 5, 1994; children: Alyssa, Chad. BSc with great distinction, McGill U., Montreal, Can., 1977; MD, Queens U., Kingston, Ont., Can., 1981. Intern Royal Victoria Hosp. McGill U., Montreal, 1981-82, resident diagnostic radiology Jewish Gen. Hosp., 1982-85, chief resident diagnostic radiology Jewish Gen. Hosp., 1985-86; fellow osteoradiology U. Calif., San Diego, 1986-87; asst. prof. radiology Hosp. U. Pa., 1987-89; dir. musculoskeletal imaging Memorial Healthcare System, Fla., 1989-99, Health S. Drs. Hosp., Coral Gables, Fla., 1995-97; pres. Specialists in Diagnostic Imaging. PA, Sunrise, Fla. Clin. assoc. prof. Sch. Medicine U. Miami, Coral Gables, 1989—. Author: Magnetic Resonance Imaging of the Shoulder, 1991, Clinical Magnetic Resonance Imaging, 2d. edit., 1996. Frances C. C. Lynch scholar Carleton U., 1974-75; Univ. Entrance scholar McGill U., 1975-76, Univ. scholar, 1976-77; named one of Best Drs. in Am., 1998, one of Outstanding Young Men of Am., 1998. Fellow Royal Coll. Physicians (Can.), Am. Bd. Radiology; mem. AMA, Internat. Soc. Magnetic Resonance Imaging Medicine, Internat. Skeletal Soc., Am. Roentgen Ray Soc., Radiologic Soc. N.Am., Am. Coll. Radiologists. Avocations: tennis, swimming, skiing, reading, movies. Address: 2529 Sanctuary Dr Weston FL 33327-1534

ZLATOFF-MIRSKY, EVERETT IGOR, violinist; b. Evanston, Ill., Dec. 29, 1937; s. Alexander Igor and Evelyn Ola (Hill) Z.-M.; m. Janet Dalbey, Jan. 28, 1976; children from previous marriage— Tania, Laura. B.Mus., Chgo. Mus. Coll., Roosevelt U., 1960, M.Mus., 1961. Mem. faculty dept. music Roosevelt U., Chgo., 1961-66. Founding mem., violinist, violist Music of the Baroque, 1971-2003. Violinist orch. Lyric Opera of Chgo., 1974-2003; concert master, pers. mgr., 1974-2003, violinist, violist, Contemporary Chamber Players U. Chgo., 1964-82, solo violinist, Bach Soc., 1966-83; violist, violinist, Lexington String Quartet, 1966-81; rec. artist numerous recs., radio-TV and films; solo violinist appearing throughout U.S. Recipient Olive Ditson award Franklin Honor Soc., 1961 Mem. Nat. Acad. Rec. Arts and Scis. Republican. Roman Catholic. Home: 1600 Old Pecos Trail Santa Fe NM 87505 E-mail: jdzm@aol.com.

ZLATOS, CHRISTY, librarian; b. Decatur, Ill., June 4, 1956; d. Rudolph and Iva Dene Ebersole Zlatos; m. Michael Boyd Nelson, Dec. 22, 1995. AB, U. Ill., 1978, MSLS, 1979. Reference libr. U. So. Ind., Evansville, 1980-82, Auburn (Ala.) U., 1983-89, Northeastern U., Boston, 1989-91, Wash. State U., Pullman, 1991-92, head edn. libr., 1991-95, head media materials svcs., 1995—. Book rev. editor Jour. Acad. Librarianship, 1995—. Editor: Coming of Age in Reference Services; A Case History of Washington State University Libraries, 1999. Mem. ALA (various coms.). Republican. Episcopalian. Avocation: collecting american pottery. Office: Wash State U Libraries New Library Rm 1 Pullman WA 99164-0001

ZLOBIN, ANDREW, molecular biologist, virologist; b. Moscow, Sept. 11, 1953; arrived in U.S., 1994; s. Julian Andrew Zlobin and Inna Ivanovna Zlobina; 1 child from previous marriage, Catrina Zlobina. MS in Biology, Moscow State U., 1975; PhD in Molecular Biology, Inst. Virology, Ministry of Health, Moscow, 1981. Sci. officer Edinburgh (Scotland) U., 1992—94; rsch. assoc. Rockefeller U., N.Y.C., 1995—97, Loyola U. Med. Ctr., Chgo., 1997—. Office: Loyola U Med Ctr 21605 1st Ave Maywood IL 60153 Office Phone: 708-327-3170. Business E-Mail: azlobin@lumc.edu.

ZLOCH, WILLIAM J. federal judge; b. 1944; Judge U.S. Dist. Ct. (so. dist.) Fla., Ft. Lauderdale, 1985—. Office: US Dist Ct 299 E Broward Blvd Fort Lauderdale FL 33301-1944

ZLOTNICK, NORMAN LEE, lawyer; b. Bklyn., Nov. 2, 1947; s. Harry S. and Frances Zlotnick; m. JoAnn L. Zlotnick, Nov. 26, 1976; m. Sharon Harris, Mar. 12, 2000. BA in History, CCNY, 1969; JD, Rutgers U., 1972. Bar: N.J. 1972, U.S. Dist. Ct. N.J. 1972, U.S. Ct. Appeals (3d cir.) 1974, U.S. Supreme Ct. 1976, N.Y. 1990. Assoc. Perskie & Callinan, 1972-77; ptnr. Perskie, Bloom & Zlotnick, P.A., 1977-79, Bloom & Zlotnick, 1979-82, Marione, Biel, Zlotnick & Feinberg, P.A., Atlantic City, 1982—. Contbr. Rutgers-Camden Law Jour. Mem. ABA, ATLA, N.J. Bar Assn., N.Y. Bar Assn., Cape May County Bar Assn., Atlantic County Bar Assn. (N.J. Supreme Ct. spl. ethics master, Atlantic County civil case arbitrator, cert. civil trial atty.). Office: 3201 Atlantic Ave Atlantic City NJ 08401-6216 Address: 20 Devon Dr Egg Harbor Township NJ 08234-7569 E-mail: normanzlotnick@mbzflaw.com.

ZLOTOLOW-STAMBLER, ERNEST, real estate executive, architectural executive; b. Buenos Aires, Sept. 27, 1943; came to US, 1981; m. Laura I. Chotti; children: Dan A., Vanessa E., Paul J. BAS, Buenos Aires Nat. Coll., 1960; license architecture, U. Buenos Aires, 1968. Lic. architect; registered profl. engr., Argentina. Prof. U. Buenos Aires, 1964-81; mng. ptnr. Zlotolow, Chotti & Assocs., Buenos Aires, 1968-81; pres. Imparsa Corp., Buenos Aires, 1970-86; mng. ptnr. Archeting Assocs., Buenos Aires, 1970-81; prof. U. Belgrano, Buenos Aires, 1976-80; v.p. Playa de la Gruta Corp., Montevideo, Uruguay, 1976-78; project mgr. Kravco Corp., King of Prussia, Pa., 1981-84; chmn. Zlotolow-Evantash-Reider Ltd., Southeastern, Pa., 1985—2002; pres. Meridian Real Corp., Wayne, Pa., 1985—, U.S.E.S. Corp., 1989—. Gen. ptnr., One Jenkintown (Pa.) Sta. Assoc., 1984-89. Contbr. articles to profl. publ. Paul Harris fellow, 1987, Guy Gundaker fellow, 1990, Paul Vaughan fellow, 1991. Mem. AIA (assoc.), Urban Land Inst., Nat. Trust Historic Preservation, Pa. Soc. Architects, Sociedad Ctrl. Arquitectos (Argentina), Rotary (pres. 1990-91, chmn. charitable found. 1990-91, chmn. cmty. svc. 1998--), Gundaker Found. (bd. dir. 1992-1999, v.p. 1996-97, pres. 1997-98); Green Hills Landowners Assn. (bd. dir. 1994-97). Avocations: macroeconomics, computer science, cmty. svc. Office: Meridian Real Corp PO Box 589 Southeastern PA 19399-0589

ZLOTOWSKI, MARTIN, psychologist; b. Lodz, Poland, Aug. 10, 1934; s. Pawel and Helen Zlotowski; m. Judith Ann Lifschitz, May 17, 1974; children: David, Steven, Laura. BA, NYU, 1955; MA, Mich. State U., 1958, PhD, 1960. Rsch. assoc. Grad. Sch. Pub. Health U. Pitts., 1960-61; rsch. assoc., lectr. Boston U., 1961-62; staff psychologist VA Hosp., Coatesville, Pa., 1962-65, unit chief, 1965-73; clin. dir. St. Mary Providence, 1966-70; assoc. prof. spl. edn. West Chester (Pa.) U., 1973—2003. Grad. coord., 1987-2000; dir. Counseling Assocs., Paoli, Pa., 1973-85, exec. dir., 1985—. Pres. Chester County Family Acad., 1999-2002, bd. trustees 2002-; v.p. Victim Witness Svcs. Chester County, 1976-77. Fellow Phila. Soc. Clin. Psychologists (pres. 1978-79, sec. human svcs. ctr. 1982), Phila. Psychol. Assn., Am. Orthopsy-

chiat. Assn. (life); mem. APA, Pa. Fedn. Coun. Exceptional Children (pres. Pa. divsn. behavior disorders 2000-). Democrat. Jewish. Home: 241 Tozzey Pine Ct West Chester PA 19380 Office Phone: 610-647-8270. Personal E-mail: MZlotowski@aol.com.

ZLOWE, FLORENCE MARKOWITZ, artist; b. Allentown, Pa. d. Morris and Anna (Mandel) Markowitz; m. Irwin Zlowe, May 1, 1936. Student, Pa. Mus. Coll. Art, Phila., 1929-33; fine arts courses, NYU, 1950-53. One woman show, Charles Z. Mann Gallery, N.Y.C., 1968, Community Gallery, N.Y.C., 1978; exhibited in group shows, Nat. Acad., Riverside Mus., N.Y., Nat. Arts Club, Pen and Brush Club, Lever House, Jersey City Mus., Norfolk (Va.) Mus., Fort Lauderdale (Fla.) Mus., Joe and Emily Lowe Mus., Fla.; represented in permanent collections, Norfolk Mus., Fort Lauderdale Mus., Joe and Emily Lowe Mus., Wilson Pub. Co., N.Y.C., Phila. Mus. Art, Butler Inst. Am. Art, Minn. Mus. Art, St. Paul, Cooper-Hewitt Mus. Design, Smithsonian Instn., N.Y.C., Tweed Mus., Duluth, Minn., Evansville (Ind.) Mus., Lakeview (Ill.) Center Arts and Scis., Ga. Mus. Art, Athens, Slater Meml. Mus., Norwich, Conn. Mem. Am. Soc. Contemporary Artists (dir., treas.), N.J. Soc. Painters and Sculptors, Nat. Assn. Women Artists (1st prize ann. 1958, 12 additional awards for oils 1958-84), League Present Day Artists, Artists Equity Assn. N.Y. Home: 2 Franklin Town Blvd Apt 1606 Philadelphia PA 19103 1230

ZNAMIEROWSKI, DAVID M, investment company executive; BA, Colby Coll.; MBA, Amos Tuck Sch. of Bus., Dartmouth Coll. V.p. corp. fin. Salomon Bros., 1986—91; portfolio mgr., v.p, investment strategy and policy Aetna Life & Casulty Co., 1991—96; dir., risk mgmt. strategy Hartford Life, Conn., 1996—97, sr. v.p., dir., life investment strategy, 1997—99, sr. v.p., chief investment officer, 1999—2001; chief investment officer The Hartford Fin Svcs. Group, Inc., Conn., 2001—; pres. Hartford Investment Mgmt. Co. (HIMCO), Conn., 2001—. Mem. bd. govs. Investment Co. Inst., Am. Coun. of Life Ins.; dir., pres. Hartford sponsored mutual funds. Office: Hartford Fin Svc Group Inc Hartford Plaza 690 Asylum Ave Hartford CT 06115

ZOBEL, LOUISE PURWIN, author, educator, lecturer, writing consultant; b. Laredo, Tex., Jan. 10, 1922; d. Leo Max and Ethel Catherine (Levy) Purwin; m. Jerome Fremont Zobel, Nov. 14, 1943; children: Lenore Zobel Harris, Janice A., Robert E., Audrey Zobel Dollinger. BA cum laude, Stanford U., 1943, MA, 1976. Cert. adult edn. and community coll. tchr., Calif. Freelance mag. writer and author, Palo Alto, Calif., 1942—; writer, editor, broadcastor UP Bur., San Francisco, 1943; lectr. on writing, history, travel No. Calif., 1964—; lectr., educator U. Calif. campuses, other colls. and univs., 1969—; writing cons. to pvt. clients, 1969—; editorial asst. Assn. Coll. Unions Internat., Palo Alto, 1972-73; acting asst. prof. journalism San Jose State U., 1976. Coord. TV shows; TV personality publicity and public rels. campaigns; tchr. corr. classes Writer's Digest Sch.; tchr. online writing classes for Writingschool.com, 1999—; spkr., presenter in field. Author: The Travel Writer's Handbook, 1980, (hard cover), 1982, (paperback) 83, 84, 85, rev. edits., 1992, 94, 97, 2002; author, narrator (cassette) Let's Have Fun in Japan, 1982; contbr. articles to mags. and newspapers; writer advertorials. Bd. dirs., publicity chair Friends of Palo Alto Libr., 1985—; officer Santa Clara County Med. Aux., Esther Clark Aux., others; past pres. PTA. Recipient award for excellence in journalism Sigma Delta Chi, 1943, awards Writers Digest, 1967-95, Armed Forces Writers League, 1972, Nat. Writers Club, 1976, All Nippon Airways and Japanese Nat. Tourist Orgn., 1997. Mem. Am. Soc. Journalists and Authors, Travel Journalists Guild, Internat. Food, Wine and Travel Writers Assn., Pacific Asia Travel Assn., Calif. Writers Club (v.p. 1988-89), AAUW (v.p. 1955-57, Nat. writing award 1969), Stanford Alumni Assn., Phi Beta Kappa. Avocations: travel, reading, writing, photography. Home and Office: 23350 Sereno Ct Unit 30 Cupertino CA 95014-6543 E-mail: lzobelwriter@cs.com.

ZOBEL, RYA WEICKERT, federal judge; b. Germany, Dec. 18, 1931; AB, Radcliffe Coll., 1953; LLB, Harvard U., 1956. Bar: Mass. 1956, U.S. Dist. Ct. Mass., 1956, U.S. Ct. Appeals (1st cir.) 1967. Assoc. Hill & Barlow, Boston, 1967-73, Goodwin, Procter & Hoar, Boston, 1973-76, ptnr., 1976-79; judge U.S. Dist. Ct. Mass., Boston, 1979—; dir. Fed. Jud. Ctr., Washington, 1995-99. Mem. Boston Bar Assn., Am. Bar Found., Mass. Bar Assn., Am. Law Inst. Office: US District Ct 1 Courthouse Way Boston MA 02210-3002

ZOBELL, CHARLES W. newspaper managing editor; b. Provo, Utah, Mar. 17, 1950; m. Marilyn M. Earl, May 5, 1978; children: David, Rebecca. BA in Comm., Brigham Young U., 1974. Reporter Las Vegas Rev.-Jour., 1975-78; dir. Office Intergovtl. Rels. City of Las Vegas, 1978-80; city editor Las Vegas Rev.-Jour., 1980-92, mng. editor, 1992—. Vol. rep. Mormon Ch., Argentina, 2 yrs. Office: Las Vegas Review Jour Donrey Med Grp PO Box 70 1111 W Bonanza Rd Las Vegas NV 89125

ZOBELL, KARL, lawyer; b. La Jolla, Calif., Jan. 9, 1932; s. Claude E. and Margaret (Harding) ZoB.; m. Barbara Arth, Nov. 22, 1968; children: Bonnie, Elizabeth, Karen, Claude, Mary. Student, Utah State U., 1949-51, Columbia U., 1951-52, AB, 1953, student of law, 1952-54; JD, Stanford U., 1958. Bar: Calif. 1959. Assoc., lawyer Gray Cary Ware & Freidenrich (formerly Gray, Cary, Ames and Frye), San Diego, 1959-64, ptnr., lawyer, 1964—, chmn., 1989-90. Bd. dirs., founder La Jolla (Calif.) Bank and Trust Co.; v.p. bd. dirs. Geisel-Seuss Enterprises, Inc., The Copley Press Inc. Trustee La Jolla Town Coun., 1962-87, chmn. bd. trustees, 1967-68, pres. 1976-77, 80-81, v.p., 1986-87; trustee La Jollans Inc., 1964-80, founder, 1964, pres. 1965-68, 73-76, 78-79, Dr. Seuss Found., 1992—, James C. Copley Charitable Found., 1992—; mem. charter rev. com. City San Diego, 1968, 73; chmn. City of San Diego Planning Commn., 1988-93; trustee La Jolla Mus. Art, 1964-72, San Diego Mus. Contemporary Art, 1990-92; pres. 1967-70, bd. dirs Scripps Meml. Hosp. Found., 1980-84, bd. overseers, Stanford Law Sch., 1977-80, U. Calif., San Diego, 1974-76. Served to lt. USCG, 1954-57. Fellow Am. Coll. Trust and Estate Counsel; mem. ABA, Calif. Bar, La Jolla Beach and Volleyball Club (pres. 1982-90), La Jolla Beach and Tennis Club, Lambda Alpha. Republican. Home: Po Box 1 7585 Country Club Dr La Jolla CA 92037-3731 Office: Gray Cary Ware & Freidenrich 1200 Prospect St Ste 575 La Jolla CA 92037-3645 Business E-Mail: kzobell@graycary.com.

ZOBRIST, BENEDICT KARL, library director, historian; b. Moline, Ill., Aug. 21, 1921; s. Benedict and Lila Agnas (Colson) Z.; m. Donna Mae Anderson, Oct. 23, 1948; children: Benedict Karl II, Markham Lee, Erik Christian. AB, Augustana Coll., Rock Island, Ill., 1946; postgrad., Stanford U., 1946-47; MA, Northwestern U., 1948, PhD, 1953; postgrad., U. Ill., 1961, Tunghai U., Taiwan, 1962, Columbia U., 1962-63, Fed. Exec. Inst., Charlottesville, Va., 1974, Hebrew U., Israel, 1978; LHD, Avila Coll., 1995. Manuscript specialist in recent Am. history Library of Congress, Washington, 1952-53; asst. reference librarian Newberry Library, Chgo., 1953-54; command historian Ordnance Weapons Command, Rock Island Arsenal, 1954-60; prof. history, chmn. dept. Augustana Coll., 1960-69, asst. dean faculty, 1964-69, asso. dean, dir. grad. studies, 1969; asst. dir. Harry S. Truman Libr., Independence, Mo., 1969-71, dir., 1971-94. Exec. sec. Harry S. Truman Libr. Inst., Independence, 1971-94; mem. steering com. Harry S. Truman Statue Com., Independence, 1973-76; dir., regent Harry S. Truman Good Neighbor Award Found., 1974—; mem. Independence Truman Award Commn., 1975-94, Mo. Hist. Records Adv. Bd., 1978—; adj. prof. history U. Mo.-Kansas City, 1975-94, Ottawa U., Kansas City, 1977-94, U. Mo. St. Louis, 1987-94; chmn. Independence Commn. Bicentennial of U.S. Constitution, 1987, Uptown Independence, Inc., 1989-94; mem. adv. coun. Truman Little White House State Historic Site, Key West, Fla., 1987-94. Contbr. articles, revs. to profl. jours. Trustee Heritage League of Greater Kansas City, 1981—, Liberty Meml. Assn., Kansas City, Mo., 1990-2002, Black Archives Mid-Am., Inc., Kansas City, 1992-94; mem. Truman Nat. Centennial Com., 1982-84. Served with AUS, 1942-46. Recipient Outstanding Alumni Achievement award Augustana Coll., 1975, Bronze Good Citizenship medal Kans. SAR, 1986, People's Choice award Independence (Mo.) Neighborhood Councils, 1987, Mid-Am. Regional Council award for contbns. to met. community, 1987, Citizen Achievement award Black Archives of Mid-Am., 1988, Silver Good Citizenship medal Mo. SAR, 1988, Special Recognition award City of Independence, 1988, Outstanding Civic Leader in Independence, 1989, Gold Medal of Honor DAR, 1990, Spl. Commendation award Nat. Park Svc., 1993; named World Citizen of Yr. by Kans. City Mayor's UN Day Com., 1994. Mem. AAUP, Am. Hist. Assn., Jackson County (Mo.) Hist. Soc. (v.p. 1972-82, 93-95), Orgn. Am. Historians, Assn. Asian Studies, Am. Assn. State, Local History, Soc. Am. Archivists, U.S. Power Squadron, Am. Legion, La Societe des 40 Hommes et 8 Chevaux, VFW. Home: 71B T St Lake Lotawana MO 64086-9728

ZOBRIST, GEORGE WINSTON, computer scientist, educator; b. Highland, Ill., Feb. 13, 1934; s. George H. and Lillie C. (Augustin) Z.; m. Freida Groverlyn Rich, Mar. 29, 1955; children: Barbara Jayne, George William, Jean Anne. BS, U. Mo., 1958, PhD, 1965; MS, Wichita State U., 1961. Registered profl. engr., Mo., Fla. Electronic scientist U.S. Naval Ordnance Test Sta., China Lake, Calif., 1958-59; rsch. engr. Boeing Co., Wichita, 1959-60; instr. Wichita State U., 1960-61; assoc. prof. U. Mo., Columbia, 1961-69, U. So. Fla., Tampa, 1969-70; chmn. elec. engring. dept. U. Miami, Coral Gables, Fla., 1970-71; prof. U. South Fla., Tampa, 1971-72, 73-76; prof., chmn. dept. elec. engring. U. Toledo, 1976-79; dir. computer sci. and engring. Samborn, Steketee, Otis, Evans, Inc., Toledo, 1979-82; prof. computer sci. Grad. Engring Ctr. U. Mo., St. Louis, 1982-85, prof. computer sci. Rolla, 1985-99, chmn. dept., 1994-99, prof. emeritus, 1999—. Rsch. prof. U. Edinburgh, Scotland, 1972-73; lectr. U. Western Cape, South Africa, 1995 summer; cons. Wilcox Electric Co., Bendix Corp., both Kansas City, Mo., 1966-68, ICC, Miami, 1970-71, Def. Comm. Agy., Washington, 1971, 72, U.S. Naval Rsch. Labs., Washington, 1971, Med. Svc. Bur., Miami, 1970-71, NASA, Kennedy Space Ctr., Fla., 1973-76, 88, 89, 93, 94, Prestolite Corp., Toledo, 1977-79, IBM, Lexington, Ky., 1983-86, Wright-Patterson AFB, Ohio, 1986, PAFB, Fla., 1987, McDonnell Douglas, Mo., 1989, Digital Systems Cons., Mo., 1989, Oak Ridge Nat. Labs., 1992. Author: Network Computer Analysis, 1969, Progress in Computer Aided VLSI Design, 1988-90; editor Internat. Jour. Computer Aided VLSI Design, 1989-91, Object Oriented Simulation IEEE Press, 1996, Computer Sci. and Computer Engring. Monograph series, 1989-91, Internat. Jour. Computer Simulation, 1990-96, VLSI Design, 1992-2002; editor IEEE Potentials Mag., 1996-99, 2003; assoc. editor, 1984-96, 99—; contbr. articles to profl. jours. Served with USAF, 1951-55. Named Young Engr. of Yr. ctrl. chpt. Mo. Soc. Profl. Engrs., 1967; NSF summer fellow, 1962, 64; NASA, IBM, DOE, UES/AFOSR, McDonnell Douglas rsch. grantee, 1967-88. Fellow IEEE (life, mem. IEEE Press editl. bd. 1998—); mem. Am. Legion, Rotary, Sigma Xi, Tau Beta Pi, Phi Eta Sigma, Eta Kappa Nu, Pi Mu Epsilon, Upsilon Pi Epsilon. Home: 12030 Country Club Dr Rolla MO 65401-7469 Office: U Mo Rolla Dept Compuer Sci 1870 Miner Cir Rolla MO 65409-0001 E-mail: zobrist@umr.edu.

ZOELLECK, ROBERT BRUCE, federal official; b. Evergreen Park, Ill., July 25, 1953; s. William T. and Gladys Zoellick; m. Sherry Lynn Ferguson, June 28, 1980. BA with honors, Swarthmore Coll., 1975; M in Pub. Policy, JD magna cum laude, Harvard U., 1981. Bar: D.C. 1981. Spl. asst. to asst. atty. gen. criminal div. U.S. Dept. Justice, Washington, 1978-79; pvt. practice law, 1981-82; law clk. to Judge Patricia M. Wald, U.S. Ct. Appeals for D.C. Cir., Washington, 1982-83; v.p., asst. to chmn. and chief exec. officer of bd. Fannie Mae, Washington, 1983-85; from spl. asst. to Dep. Sec., Dep. Asst. Sec. for Fin. Instns. Policy, to counselor to sec. and exec. sec. U.S. Treasury Dept., Washington, 1985-88; counselor of Dept. with rank under sec. U.S. Dept. State, Washington, 1989-92, under sec. for econ. and agrl. affairs, 1991-92; dep. chief of staff, asst. to Pres. White House, Washington, 1992-93; exec. v.p. housing and law Fannie Mae, Washington, 1993-97; Olin prof. nat. security U.S. Naval Acad., 1997-98; pres., CEO-designate Ctr. Strategic & Internat. Studies, Washington, 1998-99; resident fellow German Marshall Fund U.S., Washington, 1999—; rsch. scholar Belfer Ctr. Sci. and Internat. Affairs Harvard U.; sr. internat. advisor Goldman Sachs; U.S. Trade Rep. Washington, 2001—. Bd. dirs. Alliance Capital, Jones Intercable, Said Holdings, Coun. Fgn. Rels., German Marshall Fund U.S., European Inst., Eurasia Found., Nat. Bur. Asian Rsch., Am. Coun. Germany, Am. Inst. Contemporary German Studies, Overseas Devel. Coun. Mem. Trade Deficit Rev. Commn.; dir. strategy group fgn. policy Aspen Inst.; mem. adv. bd. Johns Hopkins Sch. Advanced Internat. Studies, Law & Econs. Ctr. George Mason U.; mem. adv. com. Inst. Internat. Econs. Decorated Knight Comdr.'s Cross (for work on German unification, Germany); recipient Alexander Hamilton award U.S. Treasury Dept., 1988, Disting. Svc. award U.S. State Dept, 1992; fellow Luce Found., Hong Kong, 1980. Mem. D.C. Bar Assn., Phi Beta Kappa.*

ZOELLER, DONALD J. lawyer; b. Queens Village, N.Y., Mar. 18, 1930; s. Henry Adolph and Marion Elizabeth (Brodie) Z.; m. Susan Josephine Campisi, Sept. 3, 1955; children— Paul Joseph, Jean Marie, Diane Marie AB, Fordham Coll., 1951; LL.B., Fordham Sch. Law, N.Y.C., 1958. Bar: N.Y. 1959, D.C. 1967. Law clk. to judge U.S. Dist. Ct. (so. dist.) N.Y., N.Y.C., 1958-59; assoc. Mudge Rose Guthrie Alexander & Ferdon, N.Y.C., 1959-68, ptnr., 1968-95, exec. ptnr., 1991-95, chmn. exec. com., 1995; counsel Carter, Ledyard & Milburn, N.Y.C., 1995-96, ptnr., 1997-98, of counsel, 1999—2003, ret., 2003. Adj. prof. law Fordham U. Law Sch., 1989—; lectr. in field. Contbr. articles to legal publs. 1st lt. U.S. Army, 1951-53, Korea. Mem. ABA, N.Y. State Bar Assn., Bar Assn. City of N.Y., Inst. Jud. Adminstrn., Am. Judicature Soc., Fed. Bar Coun. Republican. Roman Catholic. Avocations: skiing, swimming, tennis, reading. Business E-Mail: dzoeller@optonline.net. *Notable cases include: Matsushita Electric Indsl. Co. Ltd. et al vs. Zenith Radio Corp. et al, 475 U.S. 574, 89 L. edit. 2d 538, 106, s.ct. 1438.*

ZOELLER, JACK CARL, financial executive; b. Buffalo, Feb. 26, 1949; s. Ronald Carl and Margaret Lillian (Wademan) Z.; m. Kathryn Louise Helmke, Apr. 25, 1981; children: Andrew, Alexander, Charles (dec.). BS, U.S. Mil. Acad., 1970; M of Pub. Policy, Harvard U., 1972; M of Letters, Oxford (Eng.) U., 1974. Program budget officer Army Chief of Staff's Office, Pentagon, Washington, 1978-80; v.p. E.F. Hutton & Co., Inc., N.Y.C., 1982; pres. E.F. Hutton Indemnity Group, N.Y.C., 1983-85, Capital Risk Mgmt., Iselin, N.J., 1985-87; exec. v.p., bd. dirs. ComFed Mortgage Co., Lowell, Mass., 1987-88, pres., 1988-91, ComFed Savs. Bank, Lowell, 1990-91; chmn. chief exec. officer ComFed Bancorp., Cambridge, Mass., 1990-95; pres. The Zoeller Group, Washington, 1993-95. Bd. dirs. N.Am. Health Plans, Inc., Amherst, NY, 1995—99; pres. AtlantiCare Risk Mgmt. Corp., 1995—, N.Am. Health & Life Ins., Barbados, 1996—; chmn., CEO AtlantiCare, Inc., 1995—. Mem. exec. com. Lowell Devel. and Fin. Corp., 1989-91, class gift com. U.S. Mil. Acad., 1990-95; youth sports coach, 1990-96; Am. chmn. 750th Ann. Campaign Univ. Coll., Oxford, Eng., 1998-2002; parent group leader Maret Sch., Washington, 1998-2003. Served to capt. U.S. Army, 1970-80. Decorated Meritorious Svc. medals; Rhodes scholar Oxford U., 1972. Mem. DC Captive Ins. Coun., West Point Soc. N.Y. (bd. govs. 1985-87), West Point Soc. D.C., Am. Friends Univ Coll. Oxford, Inc. (v.p. 1999—), Fed. Nat. Mortgage Assn. (N.E. regional adv. bd. 1990-91), New Eng. Hist. Geneal. Soc., Soc. Mayflower Descs. Home: 2810 31st St NW Washington DC 20008-3523 Office: AtlantiCare Inc 1025 Connecticut Ave NW Ste 1000 Washington DC 20036

ZOGHBI, HUDA Y. pediatric neurology and genetics educator; b. June 29, 1955; BSc, Am. U. Beirut, 1976; MD, Meharry Med. Coll., 1979. Prof. pediat. neurology and geriatrics Baylor Coll. Medicine, Houston, 1994—; investigator Howard Hughes Med. Inst., 1996—. Elected mem. Inst. of Medicine, 2000. Office: T 807 1 Baylor Plz Houston TX 77030-3411

ZOGHBY, JERIAD MARCUS, lead analytical specialist, consultant; b. Mobile, Ala., Aug. 19, 1969; s. John Henry and Joy Bethea Zoghby; m. Jennifer Marie Alaniz, Dec. 5, 1998. BSc in Applied Math. with Stats., Tex. A&M U., 1995; MSc in Ops. Rsch., U. Tex., 1997, PhD in Ops. Rsch., 2002. Ops. analyst Advanced Micro Devices, Austin, Tex., 1997—99; sr. ops. analyst Garden.com, Austin, 1999—2000; strategic ops. and capacity planning mgr. Fujitsu Microelectronics, Inc., Gresham, Oreg., 2000—02; lead quantitative analyst H.E.B. Grocery Co., San Antonio, 2002—. Mentor Semiconductor Rsch. Corp., San Jose, Calif., 1998—99. Contbr. articles to profl. jours. Mem.: IEEE, Inst. for Ops. Rsch. and Mgmt. Sci. Roman Catholic. Achievements include patents for Processing System Having a Scheduling System Based On a Composite Ratio of Process Scheduling Factors. Avocation: basketball. Home: 7327 Beartrap Ln San Antonio TX 78249 Office: HEB 646 South Main Ave San Antonio TX 78283 Personal E-mail: jeriad@hotmail.com. E-mail: zoghby.jeriad@heb.com.

ZOGRAFI, GEORGE, pharmacologist, educator; b. N.Y.C., Mar. 13, 1936; married; 4 children. BS, Columbia U., 1956; MS, U. Mich., 1958, PhD in Pharm. Chemistry, 1961; DS (hon.), Columbia U., 1976. Asst. prof. pharmacology Columbia U., N.Y.C., 1961-64; from asst. prof. to assoc. prof. U. Mich., Ann Arbor, 1964-72; rsch. fellow Am. Found. Pharm. Edn., 1970-71; Pheiffer rsch. fellow Utrecht (The Netherlands) U., 1970-71; prof. pharmacology U. Wis., Madison, 1972—, dean, 1975-80. Mem. AAAS, NAS (Inst. Medicine), Am. Pharm. Assn. (Ebert prize 1984), Am. Chem. Soc., Am. Assn. Pharm. Scientists, Internat. Pharm. Fedn., Internat. Assn. Colloid and Interface Scientists, Am. Inst. Hist. Pharm., Sigma Xi. Office: U Wis Sch Pharmacology 425 N Charter St Madison WI 53706-1508

ZOHN, ANDREW ELIOT, musician, music educator; b. Planefield, NJ, May 18, 1970; s. Kenneth Edward and Virginia Elizabeth Zohn; m. Kristin Miller Zohn, Aug. 6, 1994. MusB, NC Sch. of the Arts, 1991; MusM, U. Tex., 1998; Mus D, Fla. State, 1997. Asst. prof. music Columbus (Ga.)State U., 1999—. Res. artist Mediterranean Guitar Festival, Cervo, Italy, 1999—, Guitare LaChine Festival, Montreal, Canada, 2001—. Composer: (12 solo guitar works) Les Productions d'Oz, 1998—, (4 solo guitar arrangements) Tuscany Pubs., 1998—; performer: (cd) A Guitar Recital, 1999. Recipient bronze medal, Guitar Found. Am. Internat. Competition, 1992, 1993, winner Nat. Collegiate Competition, Music Tchrs. Nat. Assn., 1993.

ZOHN, MARTIN STEVEN, lawyer; b. Denver, Oct. 22, 1947; s. William and Alice Zohn; m. Carol Falender, June 6, 1980; children: David Joseph, Daniel Robert. BA, Ind. U., 1969; JD, Harvard U., 1972. Bar: Calif. 1972, Ind. 1973, U.S. Ct. Claims 1980, U.S. Supreme Ct. 1980, U.S. Ct. Appeals (9th cir.) 1981. Assoc. Cadick, Burns, Duck & Neighbors, Indpls., 1972-77, ptnr., 1977-80, Pacht, Ross, Warne, Bernhard & Sears, Inc., L.A., 1980-86, Shea & Gould, L.A., 1986-89, Proskauer Rose LLP, L.A., 1989—. Pres. Indpls. Settlements, Inc., 1977-79. Bd. dirs. Pub. Counsel, 2001—. Mem. Fin. Lawyers Conf., L.A. County Bar Assn. (exec. com. prejudgment remedies sect. 1985-92, exec. com. bankruptcy sect. 2001-02), Beverly Hills Bar Assn. (exec. com. bus. law sect. 1985-92, exec. com. bankruptcy sect. 2003—), Phi Beta Kappa. Office Phone: 310-284-5648. E-mail: mzohn@proskauer.com.

ZOHOURI, SAEED, electronics company executive; MS in Chemistry, Manchester U., Eng.; D in Chemistry, Stanford U. former chemistry instr. Razi U., Iran. Various positions to chief technology officer, pres. N.Am. Solectron Corp., Milpitas, Calif., 1980-99, sr. v.p., CEO, 1999—. Office: Solectron Corp 777 Gibraltar Dr Milpitas CA 95035

ZOIS, CONSTANTINE NICHOLAS ATHANASIOS, meteorology educator; b. Newark, Feb. 21, 1938; s. Athanasios Konstantinos and Asimina (Speros-Blekas) Z.; m. Elyse Stein, Dec. 26, 1971; children: Jennifer, Jonathan. *Great-grandfather Haralambos Zois was a goatherd in Greece. Grandfather A. Blekas went to sea as a cabin boy at age 8. Grandfather Konstantinos Zois was a goatherd in Greece. Blekas eventually came to U.S.A. and worked on the Pennsylvania Railroad. Konstantinos remained in Greece, but his son, Athanasios, came to the U.S.A. in 1918 at age 20. Athanasios met Asimina Blekas at the Washington Florist, where they both worked. They married and had two children, Constantine N.A. Zois and K. Barbara Zois. Constantine N.A. Zois married Elyse Stein in 1971. They had two children, Jennifer and Jonathan.* BA, Rutgers U., 1961; MS, Fla. State U., 1965; PhD, Rutgers U., 1980. Draftsman Babcock and Wilcox Corp., Newark, 1956; designer Foster Wheeler Corp., Carteret, NJ, 1956; instr. Rutgers U., New Brunswick, NJ, 1961-62; grad. asst. Fla. State U., Tallahassee, 1962-65; rsch. meteorologist Nat. Weather Svc., Garden City, LI, NY, 1965-67; prof. Kean Coll. NJ, Union, 1967—. Founder meteorology program Kean Coll., NJ; cons. Connell, Foley, Geiser, Roseland, NJ, 1986-88; chmn. Kean Coll. All-Coll. Promotion com., 1991-93. Author, editor: Papers in Marine Science, 1971; author: Observation of the Newark NJ Nocturnal Heat Island and Its Consideration in Terms of a Physical Model, 1980, Dynamical and Physical Oceanography, 1988, Atmospheric Dynamics: Exercises and Problems, 1988, Climatology Workbook, 1988, Weather Map Folio, 1989; contbg. author: Outcomes Assessment at Kean College of NJ, 1992, Synoptic Meterology-Exercises and Readings, Vols. 1-3, 1995, Weather Folio, Vol. 2; NWS Map Anthology, 2003. Mem. AAAS, Nat. Weather Assn., Am. Meteorol. Soc. (pres. NJ chpt. 1980-81), NY Acad. Scis. (vice chmn. atmospheric scis. sect. 1986-87, chmn. 1987-88, adv. com. atmospheric sci. sect., 1988—), NJ Marine Scis. Consortium, Phi Beta Kappa. Republican. Greek Orthodox. Avocations: guitar, banjo, fishing, baseball, snorkeling. Home: 2798 Carol Rd Union NJ 07083-4831 Office: Kean Coll of NJ Dept Meterology Morris Ave Union NJ 07083-7117 Office Phone: 908-737-3693. *It is water that consecrates the atmosphere as a cathedral of wonderment, as it is water that incarnates the sea as an oasis of life.*

ZOLA, GARY PHILLIP, rabbi, historian, religious educational administrator; b. Chgo., Feb. 17, 1952; m. Stefani Paula Rothberg; children: Amanda Roi, Jorin Benjamin, Jeremy Micah, Samantha Leigh. BA in Am. History with distinction, U. Mich., 1973; MA in Counseling Psychology, Northwestern U., 1976; PhD in Am. Jewish History, Hebrew Union Coll., Cin., 1991. Ordained rabbi, 1982. Dir. informal edn. and youth activities Temple Israel, Mpls., 1973-74; regional youth dir., asst. camp dir. Olin-Sang-Ruby Union Inst., UAHC, Chgo., 1974-77; student pulpit B'nai Israel Congregation, Williamson, W.Va., 1978-79; mem. student pulpit Anshe Sholom Congregation, Olympia Fields, Ill., 1979-80, Columbus Hebrew Congregation, Columbus, Ind., 1981-82; rabbi for high holy days Chgo. Jewish Experience, Chgo., 1982-94; nat. dir. admissions Hebrew Union Coll.-Jewish Inst. Religion, Cin., 1982-89, nat. dean admissions and student affairs, 1989-91, nat. dean admissions, student affairs and alumni rels., 1991-98; exec. dir. Jacob Rader Marcus Ctr. Am. Jewish Archives at Hebrew Union Coll., Cin., 1998—; assoc. prof. Am. Jewish Experience Hewbrew Union Coll. Jewish Inst. of Religion. Del. Emerging Leaders Conf., Am. Coun. for Internat. Leadership, 1989, 91; bd. dirs. Am. Jewish Com., Cin., 1982—, mem. exec. com., 1984—; bd. dirs. Hillel U. Cin., 1991-94, Jewish Fedn., Cin., 1993-95; pres. Greater Cin. Bd. Rabbis, 1993-95, Jewish Cmty. Rels. Coun., (bd. dir.,1994—); founding mem. Kehillah of Cin., Jewish Think Tank; pres. Martin Luther King Jr. Coalition Cin., 2003—; chair Commn. for Commemorating 350 Years of Am. Jewish History. Author: Isaac Harby of Charleston, 1994; editor: Hebrew Union College--Jewish Institute of Religion--A Centennial History, 1875-1975, (Michael A. Meyer), 1992, Women Rabbis: Exploration and Celebration, 1996, The Dynamics of American Jewish History, 2003; editor: The American Jewish Archives Jour., 1998—; contbr. numerous scholarly articles to profl. jours.; mem. editl. bd. Reform Judaism. Bd. dirs. ethics com. Jewish Hosp., Cin.; life mem. N.Am. Fedn. Temple Youth; active NCCJ. Mem. Ctrl. Conf. Am. Rabbis, Orgn. Am. Historians, Assn. Jewish Studies, So. Jewish Hist. Soc., Am. Jewish Hist. Soc., N.Am. Fedn. Temple Youth (life). Office: Hebrew Union Coll Jewish Inst Religion 3101 Clifton Ave Cincinnati OH 45220-2404

ZOLA, MICHAEL S. lawyer; b. Madison, Wis., Dec. 15, 1942; s. Emanuel and Harriet (Sher) Zola; 1 child, Emanuel David. BS cum laude, U. Wis., 1964; LLB, Columbia U., 1967. Bar: D.C. 1968, Wis. 1968, U.S. Dist. Ct. (we. dist.) Wis. 1968, Calif. 1969, U.S. Dist. Ct. (no. dist.) Calif. 1969, U. S. Ct. Appeals (9th cir.) 1969, Hawaii 1981, U.S. Dist. Ct. Hawaii 1981. Law clk. to judge U.S. Dist. Ct. (we. dist.) Wis., 1967—68; mng. atty. San Francisco Neighborhood Legal Assistance Found., 1968—70; sole practice Calistoga, Calif., 1970—73; directing atty. Mendocino Legal Svcs., Ukiah, Calif., 1973—76; state chief of legal svcs. State of Calif., Sacramento, 1976—78, dep. state pub. defender, 1978—79; sole practice Kailua-Kona, Hawaii, 1981—. Mem. adv. bd. Kona Salvation Army, 1983—93; chmn. Mendocino County Dem. Ctrl. Com., Ukiah, 1975—76; pres. Kona Beth Shalom Congregation, 1991—94. Reginald Heber Smith Poverty Law fellow, 1968—70. Mem.: Legal Aid Soc. Hawaii (bd. dirs. 1985—86), Nat. Assn.

Criminal Def. Lawyers, Hawaii Assn. Criminal Def. Lawyers (bd. dirs. 1989—), Rotary Club Kona (pres. 1998—99). Office: 75-5744 Alii Dr Ste 223 Kailua Kona HI 96740-1740 E-mail: zolalaw@aol.com.

ZOLLAR, ALFRED, computer company executive; M in Applied Math., U. Calif., San Diego. Sys. engr. trainee IBM, San Francisco, 1977, gen. mgr. e-network software, sr. v.p. develop. tivoli software, lab dir. software group, DB2 product mgr. Santa Teresa, Calif., gen. mgr. network computing software divsn., gen. mgr. lotus software, 2000—. Bd. dirs. Chubb Corp.; mem. Leadership Coun. of Ctr. Bus. and Govt., John F. Kennedy Sch. Govt., Harvard U. Mem.: Greater Boston C. of C. (exec. com.). Office: IBM 1 Rodgers St Cambridge MA 02142

ZOLLAR, JAWOLE WILLA JO, artist, choreographer; b. Kansas City, Kans., Dec. 21, 1950; d. Alfred Jr. and Dorothy Delores Zollar; 1 child, Elizabeth Herron. BA in Dance, U. Mo., Kansas City, 1975; MFA in Dance, Fla. State U., 1979. Faculty Fla. State U., Tallahassee, 1977-80; artistic dir. Urban Bush Women, N.Y.C., 1984—; prof. dance Fla. State U., 1997—. Named Outstanding Alumni, U. Mo., 1993, Regent's lectr. dept. dance and worlds culture, UCLA, 1995—96, Alumna of Yr., Fla. State U., Tallahassee, 1997; recipient N.Y. Dance Performance award, 1992, Capezio award outstanding achievement in dance, 1994, Doris Duke awad, Am. Dance Festival, 1997; Choreography fellow, NEA, 1992, 1993, 1994, Worlds of Thought resident scholar, Mankato State U., 1994. Mem.: Internat. Assn. Blacks in Dance, Assn. Am. Cultures. Office: Urban Bush Women # 4B 138 S Oxford St Brooklyn NY 11217 also: care IMG Artists 420 W 45th St Fl 6 New York NY 10036-3503

ZOLLARS, WILLIAM D. freight company executive; With Kodak; sr. v.p. Ryder Integrated Logistics Ryder Sys., Inc.; pres. Yellow Freight Sys., 1996-99; chmn., pres., CEO Yellow Corp., Overland Park, Kans., 1999—. Office: Yellow Corp 10990 Roe Ave Overland Park KS 66211-1213

ZOLLER, MICHAEL, otolaryngologist, head and neck surgeon, educator; b. New Orleans, July 21, 1947; s. Harry and Mildred (Daitch) Z.; m. Linda Kramer, Dec. 21, 1974; children: Rebecca, Jonathan. BS, U. New Orleans, 1971; MD, Tulane U., 1972. Resident in gen. surgery Jewish Hosp., St. Louis, Washington U. Sch. Medicine, 1972—74; resident in otolaryngology Mass. Eye and Ear Infirmary, Harvard U. Med. Sch., Boston, 1974—77; pres. Ear, Nose and Throat Assocs., Savannah, Ga., 1977—2004; chmn. eye, ear, nose and throat dept. Candler Hosp., 1996—98. Asst. clin. prof. surgery Med. Coll. Ga., Augusta, 1982—96, assoc. clin. prof. surgery, 1996—2003; assoc. prof. surgery Mercer Med. Sch., 2000—04; dir. otology otoneurology dept. St. Joseph's Hosp., Savannah, 1994—2004. Chmn. med. divsn. United Way, Savannah, 1990, chmn. profl. divsn., 1991, 94-2001, vice chmn. campaign, 2002, chmn. campaign, 2003, bd. dirs., 2002-04, vice chmn. bd. dirs., 2004—; mem. allocation panel, 1997-2002; bd. dirs. Am. Cancer Soc., Savannah, 1993-2000, pres. Chatham County unit, 1996-97, chmn. bd., 1997-98; bd. dirs. Savannah Country Day Sch., 1993-97, chmn. ann. campaign, 1995-96; bd. dirs. Candler Hosp. Found., 2001-04; pres. Savannah Jewish Fedn., 1991-93; active Savannah Jewish Fedn. Endowment Bd., 1995-99; mem. med. adv. bd. South Coll., 1996-2000; mem. parents coun. Washington U., St. Louis, 1997-2001, Tulane U., 2002-04; bd. dirs. Leadership Savannah, 1996-98. Recipient Young Leadership award Savannah Jewish Fedn., 1985, Boss of Yr. award Savannah Jaycees, 1993, Celebrate Savannah award for outstanding contbns. to Savannah, Ga. Guardian, 1996; Harvard U. Med. Sch. fellow, 1976-77. Fellow: ACS; mem.: AMA, Ga. Soc. Otolaryngology (pres. bd. trustees 1997—98, editor newsletter 1998—2001), Med. Assn. Ga. (mem. ho. of dels. 1990—2004, bd. dirs. 1995—2004, editl. bd. 2001—04, Ga. Cup award 1993, Ayest-Wyeth Cmty. Svc. award 1996, Cmty. Svc. award 2001), 1st Dist. Med. Assn. (pres. 1987—88), Ga. Med. Soc. (pres. 1992, chmn. bd. trustees 1997, chmn. endowment fund 2004, John B. Rabun Cmty. Svc. award 1995, Hero's award 2001), Am. Neurotology Soc., Am. Soc. Head and Neck Surgery, Am. Acad. Otolaryngology and Head and Neck Surgery (tonsils and adenoids com. 1996—99, sleep disorders com. 1996—2002, pediat. otolaryngology com. 2003—04). Office: Ear Nose and Throat Assocs Savannah 5201 Frederick St Savannah GA 31405-4501 Personal E-mail: MZ47ent@aol.com.

ZOLNO, MARK S. lawyer; BA Polit. Sci., No. Ill. Univ., 1965; JD, John Marshall Law Sch., 1978; MA cum laude Internat. Rels., Universidad de las Américas, Mexico, 1974. Bar: Ill. 1978, U.S. Dist. Ct. (no. dist.) Ill. 1979, U.S. Ct. Internat. Trade 1979, U.S. Ct. Appeals (fed. cir.) 1979. With U.S. Customs Svc., Dept. Commerce, U.S. Trade Rep's. Office, Internat. Trade Commn., Fed. Trade Commn., FDA; ptnr. Katten, Muchin, Zavis & Rosenman, Chgo., 1988—. Past chmn. Chgo. Bar Assn. Customs and U.S. Trade Law Com.; lectr. in field. Contbr. articles to profl. jours. Office: Katten Muchin Zavis & Rosenman 525 W Monroe St Ste 1600 Chicago IL 60661-3693

ZOMPARELLI, WENDY, newspaper publisher; b. Chgo., 1950; d. Rocco and Eileen Zomparelli; m. André Spies; 1 child, Samuel Z. Spies. BA, Cornell U., 1971. Staff writer Raleigh (N.C.) Times, 1978-80; writer, copy editor Raleigh (N.C.) News and Observer, 1982-84; staff writer Roanoke (Va.) Times, 1984-85, asst. features editor, 1985, features editor, 1985-92, asst. to pres. and pub., 1992-95, editor, 1995-98, v.p., gen. mgr., 1998-2000, pres., pub., 2000—. Mem. Pulitzer Prize journalism awards jury, 1998-99. Mem.: Soc. Profl. Journalists, Am. Soc. Newspaper Editors, Phi Beta Kappa. Office: The Roanoke Times PO Box 2491 201 Campbell Ave SW Roanoke VA 24011-1100 E-mail: wendy.zomparelli@roanoke.com.

ZONANA, VICTOR, lawyer, educator; b. Zagazig, Eqypt, Aug. 28, 1940; s. Isaac A. and Fortunee (Cohen Beyda) Z.; m. Mary Linda Haynie, Aug. 22, 1964; children: David A., Nancy B. Zonana Dickinson. BS in Econs., Hofstra U., 1961; LLB, NYU, 1964, LLM, 1966. Bar: N.Y. 1965. Assoc. Kaye, Scholer, Fierman, Hays & Handler, N.Y.C., 1966-69; prof. NYU, 1969-80, adj. prof., 1981—, Charles S. Lyon vis. prof., 1994; dep. tax legis. counsel U.S. Dept. Treasury, 1975-76; cons. to asst. commr. IRS, 1975, office of chief counsel, 1994; counsel, ptnr. Kaye, Scholer, Fierman, Hays & Handler, N.Y.C., 1980-87, Arnold & Porter, N.Y.C., 1988—2001; prof. Bklyn. Law Sch., 1996—2002; prin. KPMG LLP, London, 2002—. Mem., chmn. adv. bd. NYU Tax Inst. Fellow Am. Coll. Tax Counsel; mem. ABA, N.Y. State Bar Assn. (co-chmn. com. on fgn. activities of U.S. taxpayers, chmn. com. on depreciation and investment credit, co-chmn. com. tax acctg. matters, com. tax policy). Office: KPMG LLP 8 Salisbury Sq London EC4Y 8BB England Office Phone: +44 (0)207 694 1737.

ZONDER, ADAM STEVEN, theater educator, production manager; s. Geoffrey Steven and Rosalie Ann Zonder. BA, Bucknell U., 1994; MFA, U. Conn., 1997. Prodn. mgr. Hangar Theatre, Ithaca, NY, 1996—; project mgr. Quinlan Scenic Studios, Marcus Hook, Pa., 1997—98; prodn. mgr. J. Howard Wood Theatre, Sanibel Island, Fla., 1998—99; asst. prof./prodn. mgr./tech. dir. SUNY dept. theatre U. Albany, 1999—. Vice commr. for edn. tech. prodn. com. U.S. Inst. for Theatre Tech., Syracuse, NY, 2002—, job descriptions project leader, 2002—. Technical director (theatrical production) Noises Off (Merit Award for Tech. Direction, 2003). Mem.: U.S. Inst. for Theatre Tech. (vice commr. for edn. tech. prodn. com. 2002—04). Office: Univ Albany PAC 262 1400 Washington Ave Albany NY 12222

ZONE, RAY, writer; b. Cleve., Ohio, May 16, 1947; s. Lawrence Gerald Miller and Betty Jean Hoskinson; children: Johnny Ray, Jimmy Ray. Grad. h.s., Alta Loma, Calif. Historian Am. Soc. of Cinematographers, Hollywood, Calif., 2002—; pres. The 3-D Zone, L.A., 1983—. Stereographic cons. Walt Disney Co., Burbank, Calif., 1986—94, L.A. Pub. Librs., 1997—, L.A. Unified Sch. Dist., 1988—, Colonial Williamsburg Found., Va., 1999, Tokyo Met. Mus. of Photography, 1995, Pacific Sci. Ctr., Seattle, 1998—99, Ft. Wayne (Ind.) Mus. of Art, 1986—87, CMP Publs., Manhasset, NY, 1988—89, Henry Schein Vet. Supply, Port Washington, NY, 1995, RCA/Columbia Home Video, Burbank, Calif., 1986—89, Warner Bros., L.A., 1990—96, DC Comics, N.Y.C., 1986—, Wildstorm Comics, La Jolla, Calif., 1997—98, Nat. Geog. Soc., Washington, 1987, John Wiley & Sons, N.Y.C., 1995, Artech Ho., Norwood, Mass., 1990, Waite Group Press, Mill Valley, Calif., 1991, Bantam, Doubleday, Dell, N.Y.C., 1995. Contbr. photographs, art revs. L.A. Reader; 3-D art, 3-D Comic Books (Am. Comic Book award, 1985, Inkpot award for outstanding achievement in Comic arts, 1987), VARBusiness Mag., 1989 (Ozzie-Gold award of excellence, 1989); art critic: articles Art Alternatives, Juxtapoz, contbg. editor, photographer: articles American Cinematographer; articles, The Hollywood Reporter; contbr. articles to profl. publs., mags., and newspapers, book revs. International Documentary; journalism, art revs., L.A. Weekly; editor: (book) Writer of Light, the Cinematography of Vittorio Storaro, New Wave King, the Cinematography of Laszlo Kovacs; art revs., ArtScene, the monthly digest to Art in Southern California, Art Week, Art Gallery International; stereographic historian: articles, interviews Stereo World (William C. Darrah Fellow award, 2000). 3-D news editor, program dir. Stereo Club of So. Calif., L.A., 2000—02. Recipient In Recognition of Outstanding Dedication to the Field of 3-D Photography, Stereo Club of So. Calif., 1986—88, Customer Svc. award, Comics Buyer's Guide, 1990—94, Cert. of Recognition, Wilson Acad., 1992, Cert. of Appreciation, Ariz. State Fair, 1992, Nat. Stereoscopic Assn., 1995, Recognition of Generosity and Support, Cultural Ctrs. of Calif. Poly., 1999, Appreciation award, Pasadena Stereo Club, 1999. Mem.: Stereoscopic Soc. Am. (gen. sec. 2002), Nat. Stereoscopic Assn. (corr.; contbg. writer, presenter 1983—2002), Ohio Stereo Photography Soc. (assoc.), Third Dimension Soc. (assoc.), Internat. Stereoscopic Union (assoc.), Detroit Stereo Club (corr.), Cascade Stereo Club (assoc.). Achievements include first to Polychromatic Anaglyphs for 4-color printing; First polychromatic anaglyphs printed on fabric; Produced hundreds of stereographic conversions for printing applications; Produced first anaglyphs for continuous roll form silk screen printing on fabric; Produced or published over 130 3-D comic books. Avocations: stereo photography, painting, hand analysis, movies, art museums. Office: 3-D Zone PO Box 741159 Los Angeles CA 90004 Personal E-mail: r3dzone@earthlink.net. E-mail: r3dzone@earthlink.net.

ZONGOLOWICZ, HELEN MICHAELINE, education and psychology educator; b. Kenosha, Wis., July 22, 1936; d. Edmund S. and Helen (Ostrowski) Z. EdB, Dominican Coll., 1966; MA, Cardinal Stritch Coll., 1973; EdD, U. No. Colo., 1977. Tchr. elem. schs., Kenosha, 1956-58, Center Line, Mich., 1958-59, Taft, Calif., 1960-61, Lake Wales, Fla., 1962-63, Albuquerque, 1963-65; tchr., asst. prin. St. Mary's Sch., Taft, 1965-69; asst. sch. supt. Diocese of Fresno, Calif., 1969-70; tchr. primary grades Greasewood Boarding Sch., Ganado, Ariz., 1970-72, coord. spl. projects, 1972-75, liaison to parent adv. coun., 1972-75, 1972-75, ltchr. supr., 1972-76; ednl. specialist Ft. Defiance Agy., Navajo Area, Ariz., 1974-75, ednl. diagnostician, 1979-80; asst. prof. Auburn (Ala.) U., 1977-79, U.Mex.-Gallup, 1981-94, prof. edn. and psychology, 1994—, dir. child care ctr., pres. faculty senate, 1995-97; prin. Chuska Sch., 1980-93, chair dept. psychology/edn. CDA dir., 1995-2001, chair behavioral and social scis. dept, 1996—2001, chair psychology/edn. dept., 1995-2001, asst. dean instrn., 2001—, acting dean instrn., 2002—04. Vis. prof. U. Colo., 1976; mem. N.Mex. State Articulation Task Force, 1994—. Recipient Spl. Achievement award U.S. Dept. Interior, 1971, 73, Points of Light award, 1990, Superior Performance award, 1982, Achievement award Navajo Nation, 1993; named Prin. of Yr. Bur. of Indian Affairs, 1990, Navajo Area Sch. Bd. Assn., 1991. Mem. AAUW, ASCD, NAFE, Nat. Assn. Edn. of Young Children, Nat. Staff Devel. Coun., Am. Assn. Mental Deficiency, Coun. for Exceptional Children, Coun. for Basic Edn., Am. Ednl. Rsch. Assn., Internat. Reading Assn., Assn. for Children with Learning Disabilities, Nat. Coun. Tchrs. of English, Assn. Childhood Edn. Internat., Kappa Delta Pi, Phi Delta Kappa. Address: 604 Mckee Dr Gallup NM 87301-4830 Office Phone: 505-863-7541. E-mail: hzons@gallup.unm.edu.

ZOOGMAN, NICHOLAS JAY, lawyer; b. N.Y.C., Apr. 2, 1947; s. Morris William and Hannah (Stern) Z.; m. Carla Ganz, June 7, 1970; children: Sarah Elizabeth, Peter William. BA, NYU, 1967; MA, Harvard U., 1969, JD, 1973. Bar: N.Y. 1974, U.S. Dist. Ct. (so. and ea. dists.) N.Y. 1974, U.S. Ct. Appeals (2d cir.) 1975, U.S. Supreme Ct. 1979, U.S. Dist. Ct. (ea. dist.) Mich. 1988, U.S. Ct. Appeals (D.C. cir.) 1990, U.S. Ct. Appeals (6th cir.) 1993, U.S. Ct. Appeals (5th cir.) 1997. Assoc. Donovan Leisure Newton & Irvine, N.Y.C., 1973-75; ptnr. Anderson Kill & Olick, N.Y.C., 1976-2000; counsel Dickstein Shapiro Morin & Oshinsky, N.Y.C., 2000—. Mem. ABA, N.Y. State Bar Assn., Assn. Bar City of N.Y., Phi Beta Kappa, Pi Sigma Alpha. Office: Dickstein Shapiro Morin & Oshinsky 1177 Avenue of Americas New York NY 10036-2714 Office Phone: 212-835-1400. Business E-Mail: zoogmann@dsmo.com.

ZOOK, BERNARD CHARLES, pathology educator, administrator, researcher; b. Beach, N.D., Nov. 1, 1935; s. Frank N. and Elizabeth Ferne (Kramer) Z.; m. Elinore A. Schillo, Oct. 1, 1955; children: Bernita, Melinda, Andrew. BS, Colo. State U., 1962, DVM, 1963; postgrad., Harvard U., 1963-68, Northeastern U., 1966. Diplomate Am. Coll. Vet. Pathologists. From rsch. fellow to asst. in pathology Med. Sch. Harvard U., Boston, 1963-68; from. rsch. fellow to assoc. pathologist Angell Meml. Animal Hosp., Boston, 1963-69; asst. prof. George Washington U., Washington, 1969-74, dir. Animal Rsch. Facility, 1972—2001, assoc. prof., 1974-83, prof. pathology, 1983—. Cons. comml. orgns. Contbr. articles on heart disease, poisoning, radiation injury, and other med. conditions to profl. jours. Mem. St. John's Choir, 1993—. Rsch. fellow Smithsonian Instn., 1969—; grantee NIH, 1967-68, Murray Corp., 1981-85, Nat. Cancer Inst., 1975-86, Population Coun., 1981-85, Motorola Corp., 1991-2002, Sabin Vaccine Inst., 2001-2004. Mem. Am. Coll. Vet. Pathology, Soc. Toxicologic Pathologists, Nat. Soc. Med. Rsch. (bd. dirs. 1981-86), Bridge Club, KC, Beta Beta Beta, Phi Zeta. Republican. Roman Catholic. Avocations: music, painting. Office: George Washington U Med Ctr 2300 I St NW Washington DC 20037-2336 Business E-Mail: resbcz@gwumc.edu.

ZOOK, ELVIN GLENN, plastic surgeon, educator; b. Huntington County, Ind., Mar. 21, 1937; s. Glenn Hardman and Ruth (Barton) Z.; m. Sharon Kay Neher, Dec. 11, 1960; children— Tara E., Leigh A., Nicole L. BA, Manchester Coll., 1959; MD, Ind. U., 1963. Diplomate Am. Bd. Surgery, Am. Bd. Thoracic Surgery, Am. Bd. Plastic Surgery. Intern Meth. Hosp., Indpls., 1963-64; resident in gen. and thoracic surgery Ind. U. Med. Center, Indpls., 1964-69; resident in plastic surgery Ind. U. Hosp., Indpls., 1969-71, asst. prof. plastic surgery, 1971-73; asso. prof. surgery So. Ill. U., Springfield, 1973-75, prof., 1975—, chmn. div. plastic surgery, 1973—. Mem. staff Meml. Med. Center, St. Johns Hosp., Springfield. Contbr. articles to med. jours. Mem. Assn. Acad. Surgery, Am. Soc. Plastic Surgery (sec. 1988-91, v.p. 1991-92, pres.-elect 1992-93, pres. 1993-94), Midwestern Soc. Plastic Surgery (pres. 1986-87), ACS, Sangamon County Med. Soc. (pres. 1987), Am. Cleft Palate Assn., Am. Assn. Plastic Surgery (trustee 1987-90), Plastic Surgery Rsch. Coun. (chmn. 1981), Am. Burn Assn., Ill. Surg. Soc., Am. Soc. Surgery Hand (coun.), Am. Bd. of Plastic Surgery (sec.-treas. 1988-91, chmn. 1991-92), Am. Soc. Aesthetic Plastic Surgery, Am. Soc. Surgery of Trauma, Assn. Acad. Chmn. Plastic Surgery (pes. 1986-87), Am. Surg. Assn., RRC for Plastic Surgery, Sangamo Club, Springfield Med. Club, Island Bay Yacht Club. Clubs: Sangamo, Springfield Med, Island Bay Yacht. Presbyterian. Home: 7235 Mansion Rd Chatham IL 62629-8763 Office: 747 N Rutledge St Springfield IL 62702-6700 E-mail: ezook@siumed.edu. *Do the best possible in all that is possible.*

ZOOK, THERESA FUETTERER, gemologist, consultant; b. Barberton, Ohio, Mar. 12, 1919; d. Charles Theodore and Ethel May (Knisely) Fuetterer; m. Donovan Quay Zook, June 21, 1941; children: Theodore Alan, Jacqueline Deborah Zook Cochran. AB, Ohio U., 1941; MA in Pub. Adminstrn., Am. U., 1946. Adminstrv. intern Nat. Inst. Pub. Affairs, Washington, 1941-42; mgmt. intern USDA, Washington, 1941-42; adminstrv. analyst Office Emergency Mgmt., Washington, 1942-43, Office Price Adminstrn., Washington, 1943-45; founder Zook and Zook Mgmt. Cons., Arlington, Va., 1945-47; tchr. ancient history and U.S. govt. Fairfax County Pub. Sch., Va., 1963-64; founder, pres. Associated Gem Cons. Lab., Alexandria, 1974—, Alpha Gate Crafts Ltd., Alexandria, 1977—. Color cons. Internat. Com. on Color in Gems, Bangkok, 1983. Author: Directory of Selected Color Resources Annotated Guide, 1982, Reunion of Descendants of David and Magdalena (Blough) Zook, 1983, Basic Machine Knitting, 1979; contbr. articles to profl. jours. Bd. dirs. Am. Embassy Com. on Edn., Montevideo, Uruguay, 1962; co-founder Workshop of Arts, Santiago, Chile, 1958; mem. Nat. Trust for Hist. Preservation, Nat. Mus. Women in Arts, Nat. Mus. Am. Indian, Am. Horticulture Soc., Textile Mus. Fellow Gemmological Assn. of Gt. Britain (diplomate); mem. AAUW, DAR, Nat. Geneal. Soc., Inter-Soc. Color Coun. (chmn. com. color in gemstones 1982-84, Appreciation cert. 1984), Accredited Gemological Assn. (co-founder, v.p.), Phi Beta Kappa, Tau Kappa Alpha, Kappa Delta Pi. Avocations: garden design, knitting, fabric creation, genealogy, music. Home: Sunrise Ste 215 8033 Holland Rd Alexandria VA 22306-3130

ZOOK, TOM, state senator; b. Miles City, Mont., Jan. 29, 1932; m. Isabel Zook. Diploma, Custer County H.S. Rancher; Rep. rep. dist. 3 Mont. Ho. of Reps., 1988-2000; Rep. senator dist. 2 Mont. State Senate, 2000—. Mem. adv. bd. Fed. Intermediate Credit Bank, Spokane; chair appropriations Mont. State Senate, joint appropriations subcom. on long-range planning. Mem. Miles City PCA; trustee Sch. Bd. With USN, 1951-55. Office: HC 40 Miles City MT 59301-9806 also: Capitol Station Helena MT 59620

ZOON, KATHRYN CHRISTINE, biochemist; b. Yonkers, N.Y., Nov. 6, 1948; d. August R. and Violet T. (Pollock) Egloff; m. Robert A. Zoon, Aug. 22, 1970; children: Christine K., Jennifer R. BS, Rensselaer Poly. Inst., 1970; PhD, Johns Hopkins U., 1975. Rsch. chemist divsn. biochem. biophys. Bur. Biologics FDA, Bethesda, Md., 1980-84, rsch. chemist divsn. virology, 1984-88, rsch. chemist divsn. cytokine biology Ctr. Biologics, 1988—92, divsn. dir., 1989-92; dir. Ctr. Biologics Evaluation and Rsch., 1992—2003; dep. dir. Ctr. for Cancer Rsch. Nat. Cancer Inst., NIH, 2003—04; dep. dir. planning and devel. divsn. intramural rsch. NIAID, NIH, 2004—. Lectr. NIH, 1994, Reigelman Lectureship, 1994; chmn. expert com. on biol. standardization WHO, 1997-98, 99, 2000, 01; mem. adv. com. of CMR, 2000-03. Contbr. articles to rsch. in biol. chemistry to sci. jours.; sect. editor Jour. Interferon and Cytokine Rsch., 1980—. Bd. dirs. Found. Advanced Edn. Scis., 1996—. 1st v.p., 1999-2003; mem. adv. bd. Def. Advance Rsch. Projects Agy., 1998-2000, Inst. Medicine Nat. Acad. Sci., 2002—. Recipient Person of the Yr. award Biopharm, 1992, Pub. Svc. and Genetic Engring. News award, 1995, Presdl. Meritorious Exec. Rank award, 1994, Grateful Patient award Nat. Assn. Cancer Patients, 1997, Rensselaer Alumni Assn. award, 1997, Sec.'s award for disting. svc. Dept. Health and Human Svcs., 2001, 03, Disting. Alumnus award Johns Hopkins U., 2003; N.Y. State Regents fellow, 1970, Interferon rsch. fellow NIH, Bethesda, 1975-77, staff fellow, 1979-80. Mem. Am. Soc. Biochem. and Molecular Biology, Intenat. Soc. Interferon and Cytokine Rsch. (pres. elect 1998-99, pres. 2000-01), Internat. Assn. Biol. Standardization (mem. adv. coun. 2000—), Inst. of Medicine. Roman Catholic. Office: Ctr for Cancer Rsch NCI/NIH Bldg 31A Rm 3A11 31 Center Dr Bethesda MD 20892 Office Phone: 301-496-4346. Office Fax: 301-496-0775. Personal E-mail: kzoon@comcast.net. Business E-Mail: kzoon@niaid.nih.gov.

ZOPF, EVELYN LANOEL MONTGOMERY, guidance counselor; b. Laurel, Miss., July 10, 1932; d. Arthur LaNoel and Ruby Lee (Lewis) Montgomery; m. Paul Edward Zopf Jr., Aug. 5, 1956; 1 child, Eric Paul. MusB in Edn., U. So. Miss., 1953, MA, 1954. Guidance counselor U. So. Miss., 1953-54, U. Fla., 1954-56; tchr. New Orleans City Schs., 1956-57; pub. sch. music tchr., band dir., choral dir. Putnam County Schs., Fla., 1957-59; pvt. music tchr. voice, piano, clarinet and trumpet, 1953-61; substitute tchr. Guilford County Schs., 1959-93; mem. arts series com. Guilford Coll., 1973-77; interim choir dir. New Garden Friends Meeting, 1961, chmn. music com., 1974-76; adviser to fgn. students, 1954-56, 59-62; mem. First Internat. Congress on Quaker Edn. Com., 1987-88, Guilford Coll.'s Sesquicentennial Com., 1985-87; speaker various religious and art groups. Vol. ARC, Boy Scouts Am.; mem. U. Fla. Union Bd., 1955-56; precinct del. County Dem. Conv., 1977, 79, precinct worker, 1980, campaign worker, 1980; bd. dirs. Greensboro Friends of Music, 1970-71, Greensboro chpt. N.C. Symphony Bd., 1979-93, mem. feeder bd. The Guilford Coll. Friends of the Lib. Bd., 1993-94, mem. exec. bd., 1994-95. Mem. United Soc. of Friends Women (pres. 1979-81), Internat. Fellowship Quaker Women, Guilford Coll. Community Chorus, Phi Mu. Clubs: Women's Soc. (dir. 1978-82), Guilford Coll. Arts Appreciation (v.p. 1980-81, pres. 1981-82), Guilford Gourmet. Home: 815 George White Rd Greensboro NC 27410-3317

ZOPF, PAUL EDWARD, JR., sociologist; b. Bridgeport, Conn., July 9, 1931; s. Paul Edward and Hilda Ernestine (Russell) Z.; m. Evelyn Lanoel Montgomery, Aug. 5, 1956; 1 child, Eric Paul. BS, U. Conn., 1953; MS, U. Fla., 1955, PhD, 1966. Asst. prof. sociology Guilford Coll., Greensboro, NC, 1959-66, assoc. prof., 1966-70, prof., 1970-72, Dana prof. sociology, 1972-93, Dana prof. sociology emeritus, 1993—, chief coll. marshal, 1997—. Cons. U.S. Dept. Agrl., local govt. agys. Author: North Carolina: A Demographic Profile, 1967, Demography: Principles and Methods, 1970, 76, Principles of Inductive Rural Sociology, 1970, Profile of Women in Greensboro: 1990, 1977, Sociocultural Systems, 1978, Cultural Accumulation in Latin America, 1980, Population: An Introduction to Social Demography, 1984, Income and Poverty Status of Women in Greensboro, 1985, America's Older Population, 1986, American Women in Poverty, 1989, Mortality Patterns and Trends in the United States, 1992; editor Guilford Coll. Self-Study Accreditation Report; contbr. articles to profl. jours. Recipient Teaching Excellence award Guilford Coll., 1978; grantee Kenan Found., 1970-79, Guilford Coll., 1979-93. Mem. Am. Sociol. Assn., Internat. Union Sci. Study Population, So. Sociol. Soc., Rural Sociol. Soc., Population Reference Bur. Mem. Soc. Of Friends. Home: 815 George White Rd Greensboro NC 27410-3317 Office: Guilford Coll Dept Sociology Greensboro NC 27410 *In my role as professor, researcher and author, I have oriented my activities to the service of students, my institution, my professional discipline, and various community agencies. I have found that pursuing various professional processes that I enjoy and can handle adequately, is the real reward. Honors, if they come, are a by-product of that pursuit; they would be elusive and perpetually inadequate if they were the principal reason for my efforts.*

ZOPP, ANDREA LYNNE, lawyer, retail executive; b. Rochester, N.Y., Jan. 25, 1957; d. Reuben K. and P. Greta (Hurst) Davis; m. William E. Zopp, Jr., Oct. 7, 1989; children: Alyssa, Kelsey. BA cum laude, Harvard Coll., 1978; JD, Harvard U., 1981. Bar: Ill. 1981, U.S. Dist. Ct. (no. dist.) Ill. 1981, U.S. Ct. Appeals (7th cir.) 1982. Law clk. Hon. George N. Leighton, U.S. Dist. Ct., Chgo., 1981-83; asst. U.S. atty. U.S. Atty.'s Office, Chgo., 1983-86, dept. chief OCDETF, 1986-88, dep. chief criminal lit., 1988-90; ptnr. McDermott, Will & Emery, Chgo., 1990-91; chief narcotics prosecutions bur. Cook County State's Attys. Office, Chgo., 1991-92, first asst. state's atty., 1992—96; ptnr. Sonnenschein Nath & Rosenthal, 1997—2000; v.p., dep. gen. counsel Sara Lee Corp., 2000—03; sr. v.p., gen. counsel Sears, Roebuck & Co., Hoffman Estates, Ill., 2003—. Mem. Gov.'s Commn. on Capital Punishment, State of Illinois, 2000—. Bd. dirs. Aux. Bd., Art Inst. Chgo., 1987—; bd. dirs. Chgo. Regional Bd. of Jr. Achievement, 1991—, Chgo. Area Project, 1992—. Fellow Leadership Greater Chgo., 1989-90; Kizzy Scholarship Fund award, 1991-92. Fellow Am. Bar Found., Am. Coll. Trial Lawyers; Mem. ABA, Chgo. Bar Assn., Chgo. Inn of Ct., Cook County Bar Assn., Black Women Lawyers Assn., Leadership Greater Chgo. (bd. dirs.). Avocations: running, music, theater. Office: Sears Roebuck & Co 3333 Beverly Rd Hoffman Estates IL 60179*

ZORE, EDWARD JOHN, financial services executive; b. Milw., July 5, 1945; s. Joseph F. and Marie A. Z.; m. Diane Widemshek, Aug. 19, 1967; children: Annemarie, Kathryn. BS, U. Wis.-Milw., 1968, MS, 1970. With Northwestern Mut., Milw., 1969—, pres., 2000—, CEO, 2001—. Republican. Roman Catholic. Office: Northwestern Mutual 720 E Wisconsin Ave Milwaukee WI 53202-4703

ZORICK, NANCY LEE, artist, actress; b. Chgo., July 24, 1946; d. William Russel and Wilma Beatrice (Fithian) Noble; m. Peter Michael Zorick, Aug. 8, 1980. Student, Art Inst. Chgo., 1965-67, Second City Workshop, Chgo., 1967-68, Am. Acad. Art, 1971. Comml. artist Embosograph Display Co., Chgo., 1964-66, Stevens-Biondi-DiCiccio, Chgo., 1966-68. Illustrator: (book) Making Weight, 1991, (children's book) The Little Acorn, 1996; exhibns. include Fontana (Calif.) Arts Assn., 1988, Riverside County Art Exhibnn., 1990; appeared in plays My Sweet Charlie, Chgo., 1968, Harold, Chgo., 1969, films include Medium Cool, 1968, Jackson County Jail, 1976, Outside

Chance, 1978; appeared in commercial Tastee Freeze, 1969. Mem Des Arts, 1981, historian, 1983—85, parliamentarian, 1986—93, 1996—, pres., 1993—95. Named to Taft Alumni Hall of Fame, Chgo., 2000; recipient 1st Place in Fine Arts, Nat. Date Festival, 1983, 2d place, Riverside Nat. Date Festival, 1993, 1996, 2001, 3d place, 2004, Best of Show in Fine Arts, Des-Arts Show, 1988, 1st place, Des Arts, 1986, 1990, 1992, 1993, 1996, 1997, 1998, 2000, 2001, 2003, 2004, Best of Show in Fine Arts, Fontana (Calif.) Arts Assn., 1988. Avocations: teaching sunday school, ballet and art, volunteering. Home: 51-555 Monroe St #31 Indio CA 92201

ZORKIN, MELISSA WAGGENER, public relations executive; b. 1954; BA Eng., Lewis & Clark Coll. With Tektronix Inc., Beaverton, Oreg., 1975-80, Regis McKenna, Portland, 1980-83; founder Waggener Edstrom, Inc., 1983—, now pres. and CEO. Named Person of Yr., Media, Inc.; named one of 100 Most Influential People of the 20th Century in Pub. Rels., 50 Most Powerful Women in the Field, PR Week, 1999; recipient Alumni award, Lewis and Clark Coll. Office: Waggener Edstrom Inc 3 Centerpointe Dr Ste 300 Lake Oswego OR 97035-8663

ZORKO, MARK A. financial executive; b. Cleve., Mar. 11, 1952; s. Frank A. and Dorothy E. (Bever) Z.; m. Sue A. Langdon, Sept. 6, 1975; children: Jennifer, Andrew. BS in Acctg., Ohio State U., 1976; MBA in Mgmt. Info Systems, U. Minn., 1977. CPA; CPIM. Sr. staff cons. Arthur Andersen & Co., Mpls., 1978-80; fin. mgr. Honeywell, Inc., Mpls. and Brussels, 1980-87; corp. contr. Zenith Data Systems Corp., St. Joseph, Mich., 1987-91; CFO Inverness Castings Group, Inc., Bangor, Mich., 1991-93; v.p. fin., sec., CFO Comptronix Corp., Huntsville, Ala., 1993-94; v.p., CFO and chief info. officer Network Svcs. Co., Mt. Prospect, Ill., 1995-99; ptnr. Tatum CFO Ptnrs, LLP, Chgo., 2000—. Bd. dirs. Intellimedia Corp. Treas., bd. dirs. United Way, St. Joseph, 1988-93. Sgt. USMC, 1970-73. Mem. AICPA, Fin. Execs. Inst. (pres. Chgo chpt.), Nat. Assn. Corp. Dirs., Assn. for Corp. Growth, Opportunity Internat. (bd. govs.). Methodist. Avocations: sailing, skiing, golf, triathlon. Office: Tatum CFO Partners LLP 9 Greenbriar Ln Chicago IL 60047 Office Phone: 847-777-0560. E-mail: mzorko@attglobal.net.

ZORN, ROBERT LYNN, education educator; b. Youngstown, Ohio, Mar. 22, 1938; s. Robert S. and Frances L. Zorn; BS in Edn., Kent State U., 1959; MEd, Westminster Coll., 1964; PhD, U. Pitts., 1970; m. Joan M. Wilkos, Apr. 26, 1957; children: Deborah Lynn, Patricia Lynn. Tchr., West Branch (Ohio) Schs., 1961-62; elem. prin. Poland (Ohio) Schs., 1962-67, supt. schs., 1976—; HS unit prin. Boardman (Ohio) Schs., 1967-70; dir. adminstrv. services Mahoning County (Ohio) Schs., 1970-73, asst. supt., 1973-76; adj. prof. edn. Westminster Coll., 1985—; chmn. Ohi Adv. Com. to State Dept. Edn.; chmn. McGuffey Hist. Soc. Nat. Educator's Hall of Fame. Chmn. Mahoning County chpt. Am. Cancer Soc.; pres. bd. trustees Poland Methodist Ch.; trustee Mahoning County chpt. Am. Heart Assn. Served to lt. USAF, 1959-61. Mem. Doctoral Assn. Educators (life), Am. Assn. Sch. Adminstrs., Ohio PTA (life, Educator of Yr. 1980-81), Phi Delta Kappa. Republican. Clubs: Fonderlac County, Rotary, Protestant Men's. Author: Speed Reading, 1989, rev. edit., 1997; contbr. articles to profl. jours. Office: 30 Riverside Dr Youngstown OH 44514-2049 Office Phone: 330-757-7000. Business E-Mail: pola-r2@access-k12.org.

ZORNES, MILFORD, artist; b. Camargo, Okla., Jan. 25, 1908; s. James Francis and Clara Delphine (Lindsay) Z.; m. Gloria Codd, 1935; 1 son, Franz Milford; m. Patricia Mary Palmer, Nov. 8, 1942; 1 dau., Maria Patricia. Student, Otis Art Inst., Los Angeles, 1929, Pomona Coll., 1930-34. Instr. art Pomona Coll., 1946-50; art dir. Vortox and Padua Hills Theatre, Claremont, 1954-66. Exhibited, Calif. Watercolor Soc., Met. Mus., Am. Watercolor Soc., Corcoran Gallery, Bklyn. Mus., Denver Mus., Cleve. Mus., L.A. Mus., Brooks Gallery, London, Bombay Art Assn., Chgo. Art Inst., Butler Mus., Gallery Modern Masters, Washington, Santa Barbara (Calif.) Mus., Cin. Mus., Laguna (Calif.) Art Gallery, Oklahoma City Mus., Springville (Utah) Mus., Claremont (Calif.) Fine Arts, Anderson Art Gallery, Sunset Beach, Calif.; represented in permanent collections at L.A. Mus., White House Collection, Met. Mus., Pentagon Bldg., Butler Mus., UCLA, Nat. Acad., San Diego Mus., L.A. County Fair, Home Savs. and Loan Assn., L.A., Corcoran Gallery, Washington; mem. art com., Nat. Orange Show, San Bernardino, Calif., 1963-65; author: A Journey to Nicaragua, 1977, The California Style: California Watercolor Artists, 1925-1955, 1985; subject of book by Gordon McClelland: Milford Zornes, Hillcrest Press, 1991. Served with U.S. Army, 1943-45, CBI. Recipient Paul Prescott Barrow award Pomona Coll., 1987, David Prescott Burrows award, 1991, A Most Disting. Citizen award So. Utah State Coll., 1988, Am. Artist Achievement award Am. Artist Mag., 1994; named Nat. Academician. Mem. NAD, Am. Watercolor Soc., Southwestern Watercolor Soc., Watercolor West, Nat. Watercolor Soc., Utah Watercolor Soc. Address: 2136 Brescia Ave Claremont CA 91711-1804 *It has been my effort in life to have awareness: not to have all knowledge because no one can encompass all knowledge; not to have only wealth or only success, because there is no dimension of completeness of wealth or success; not to achieve complete goodness, because goodness and right are relative; not to enjoy the epitomy in taste because taste is a gratification of self alone; but rather to seek and achieve understanding of relative values and a concept of the completeness of life. With this as my effort and my inner goal, I find success within the areas of my limited abilities, my meager knowledge, and my frail grasp of the infinite.*

ZORNOW, DAVID M. lawyer; b. N.Y.C., Mar. 31, 1955; s. Jack and Marion (Gilden) Z.; m. Martha Malkin, July 21, 1985; children: Samuel Morris, Hannah Jane, Ethan Lewis. AB summa cum laude, Harvard U., 1976; JD, Yale U., 1980. Bar: N.Y. 1981, D.C. 1988, U.S. Ct. Appeals (3d cir.) 1982, U.S. Dist. Ct. (so. dist.) N.Y. 1983, U.S. Ct. Appeals (2d cir.) 1984, U.S. Dist. Ct. D.C. 1989, U.S. Ct. Appeals (D.C. cir.) 1989, U.S. Dist. Ct. Ariz. 1990, U.S. Dist. Ct. (ea. dist.) N.Y. 1993. Law clerk to Judge Herbert J. Stern U.S. Dist. Ct. N.J., Newark, 1980-82; assoc. Kramer Levin Kamin Nessen & Frankel, N.Y.C., 1982-83; asst. U.S. atty. so. dist. N.Y. U.S. Atty.'s Office, N.Y.C., 1983-87; assoc. counsel Office Ind. Counsel-Iran/Contra Investigation, Washington, 1987-89; ptnr. Skadden Arps Slate Meagher & Flom LLP, N.Y.C., 1989—. Chmn. N.Y.C. Civilian Complaint Rev. Bd., 1994-96; vis. faculty Trial Advocacy Workshop Harvard Law Sch., Cambridge, Mass., 1988. Mem. ABA (com. on white collar crime), Fed. Bar Coun., Assn. of Bar of City of N.Y., N.Y. Coun. Def. Lawyers. Office: Skadden Arps Slate Meagher & Flom LLP 4 Times Sq Fl 39 New York NY 10036-6595 E-mail: dzornow@skadden.com.

ZOROWITZ, RICHARD DAVID, physiatrics educator; b. Teaneck, N.J., Nov. 23, 1958; s. Irving Monroe and Selma Doris Zorowitz; m. Candace Stair, June 25, 1989; children: Samuel, Joel. BS, Northwestern U., 1981; MD, Tulane U., 1985. Diplomate Am. Bd. Phys. Medicine and Rehab., Spinal Cord Injury Medicine. Internal medicine intern L.I. Jewish Med. Ctr., 1986; resident in phys. medicine and rehab. Northwestern U., 1986-89; asst. prof. phys. medicine and rehab. U. Medicine Dentistry N.J.-N.J. Med. Sch., Newark, 1991-95; asst. prof. rehab. medicine U. Pa., Phila., 1995-2001, assoc. prof. phys. medicine and rehab., 2001—; med. dir. Piersol rehab. unit Hosp. U. Pa., Phila., 1997—. Dir. stroke svcs. Kessler Inst. for Rehab., East Orange, N.J., 1992-95. Cubmaster pack 36 Cub Scouts Am., Cherry Hill, N.J., 1999—. Recipient career achievement award for stroke caregiving Nat. Stroke and Quality of Life Med. Edn. Inst., 1996. Mem. Am. Acad. Phys. Medicine and Rehab., Assn. Acad. Physiatrists, Am. Heart Assn. (fellow stroke coun., Operation Stroke Inst. award S.E. Pa. region 2001, Outstanding Leadership award Pa.-Del. affiliate 2002), Nat. Stroke Assn., (Visionary in Practice Soc. award 2002, Excellence in Stroke Edn. award 2001), Phi Eta Sigma, Tau Beta Pi. Democrat. Avocations: swimming, music, theater. Office: U Pa Med Ctr 3400 Spruce St Philadelphia PA 19104-4283

ZOROWSKI, CARL FRANK, engineering educator, university administrator; b. Pitts., July 14, 1930; s. Stanley and Mary Josephine (Kozuch) Z.; m. Sarah Jane Crossley, Aug. 7, 1954 (dec. 1983); children: Kathleen Ann, Karl Alan, Kristine Alaine; m. Louise Parrish Lockwood, Apr. 13, 1985. BSME, Carnegie Inst. Tech., 1952, MSME, 1953, PhD, 1956. Instr. Carnegie Inst. Tech., Pitts., 1952-56, asst. prof., 1956-61, assoc. prof., 1961-62; prof. dept. mech. and aero. engring. N.C. State U., Raleigh, 1964-66; R.J. Reynolds Industries prof., 1966-97; assoc. dept. head, 1964-72; dept. head, 1972-79; assoc. dean acad. affairs Sch. Engring., 1979-85; dir. Integrated Mfg. Sys. Inst., 1986-92; dept. head, 1992-93; dir. Succeed/NSF Coalition, 1993-97; assoc. dean acad. affairs, 1993-94; R.J. Reynolds Industries emeritus prof., 1997—. Contbr. articles to profl. jours.; patentee in field. 2d lt. USAR, 1952-58. Recipient Rsch. award Sigma Xi, 1967. Fellow ASME (Richards Meml. award 1975), Fellow Am. Soc. Engring. Edn. (We. Electric award 1968); mem. Fiber Soc. (Achievement award 1970). Home: 103 Windyrush Ln Cary NC 27511-9758 Office: NC State U PO Box 7901 Raleigh NC 27695-0001 Office Phone: 919-515-6597. E-mail: zorowski@eos.ncsu.edu., zorowski@mindspring.com.

ZORTHIAN, BARRY, communications executive; b. Kutahia, Turkey, Oct. 8, 1920;, naturalized, US, 1930; s. Herbert Peter and Annaly (Markarian) Zorthian; m. Margaret Aylaian, June 6, 1948; children: Gregory Jannig, Stephen Arnak. BA, Yale U., 1941; LLB, N.Y. U., 1953; LLD (hon.), Ind. Inst. Tech., 1970. Bar: NY 1953. Newspaper reporter, 1936-42; newspaper and radio reporter, 1947-48; news and policy editor USIA, 1948-56, program mgr. Voice of Am., 1956-61; dep. pub. affairs. officer USIS, India, 1961-64; min.-counselor for info. Am. Embassy, Vietnam, 1964-68; v.p. Time, Inc., 1969-79, v.p. govt. affairs, 1974-79; pres. Time-Life Broadcast, 1969-73, Washington/Balt. Regional Assn., 1979-81; sr. v.p. Gray and Co., Washington, 1981-84; ptnr. Alcalde & Fay, Arlington, Va., 1984—. Bd dirs Am. Univ. Armenia, Armenian Gen Benvolent Union, Internat. Rsch. and Exchs. With USMC, 1942—46, col USMCR, 1946—73. Mem.: Marine Corps Res. Officers Assn., Washington Inst. Fgn. Affairs, Am. Fgn. Svc. Assn., Coun. Fgn. Rels., Congl. Country Club (Washington), Met. Club (Washington), Burning Tree Club (Washington), Century Assn. Club (N.Y.C.). Home: 4201 Cathedral Ave NW Apt 405E Washington DC 20016-4914 Office: Alcalde & Fay 2111 Wilson Blvd Ste 850 Arlington VA 22201-3051 Office Phone: 703-841-8646. Personal E-mail: barzor2@aol.com.

ZORTMAN, MARK ALBERT, secondary school educator, director; b. York, Pa., Dec. 10, 1960; s. Harry E. Zortman, Jr and Joan Raubenhold Zortman; m. Nancy-Ann Zupp, May 23, 1987; children: Zachary, Sean, Chelsea. M, West Chester U., 1987. Tchr., dir. Ctrl. York H.S. Performing Arts Dept., Pa., 1982—. Guest dir., musical dir., performer York Little Theater, 1982—. Musician: (vocalist, violinist, percussionist) with the York Symphony, Bob Clay Orch., Harrisburg Singers, Harrisburg Oratorio Soc. Asst. scout master Boy Scouts Am. Troop #25; coun. pres. Grace United Ch. Christ; dir., and v.p. artistic support York Little Theater, 1985—90; dir. TOP Prodns., Pa. Mem.: NEA (assoc.), Ctrl. York Edn. Assn. (assoc.), Pennsylvania's Music Educator's Assn. (assoc.), Music Educator's Nat. Conf. (assoc.), Am. Choral Dirs. Assn. (assoc.), Edni. Theater Assn. (assoc.), Phi Mu Alpha (assoc.). Avocations: theater, music, scouting, camping. Office: Central York High School 300 E 7th Ave York PA 17404 Personal E-mail: mzortman@cysd.k12.pa.us. E-mail: mzortman@cysd.k12.pa.us.

ZOSS, ABRAHAM OSCAR, chemical company executive; b. South Bend, Ind., Feb. 17, 1917; s. Harry and Fannie (Friedman) Z.; m. Betty Jane Hurwich, Dec. 24, 1939; children: Roger, Joel, Hope; m. Magda Szanto, May 26, 1978. BSChemE, U. Notre Dame, 1938, MS, 1939, PhD, 1941. With Gen. Aniline & Film Corp., Easton, Pa., 1941—47, from tech. mgr. to plant mgr. Linden, NJ, 1947—57; from mfr. mfg. adminstrn. to prodn. mgr. chem. divsn. Minn. Mining & Mfg. Co., St. Paul, 1957—60; v.p. Photek, Inc., West Kingston, RI, 1960—62; asst. corp. tech. dir. Celanese Corp., N.Y.C., 1962—65, corp. tech. dir., 1965—66, corp. dir. comml. devel., 1966—69; v.p. corp. devel. Tenneco Chems., Inc., N.Y.C., 1969—71, Universal Oil Products Co., Des Plaines, Ill., 1971—72; group v.p. Engelhard Industries divsn. Engelhard Minerals & Chem. Corp., Murray Hill, NJ, 1972—74, v.p. bus. devel., 1974—77; v.p. corp. devel. CPS Chem. Co., Inc., Old Bridge, NJ, 1977, dir., v.p., chief adminstrv. officer, 1978—84; pres. Bus. Devel. Internat., NJ, 1984—. Mem. field info. agy. Office Tech. Svc., Commerce Dept., Europe, 1946; tchg. asst. U. Notre Dame, 1939-41. Contbr. articles to profl. jours.; patentee in field. Active Met. Mus. Art., N.Y.C. Recipient Centennial Sci. award U. Notre Dame, 1965, accredited Profl. Chemist, 1980. Fellow AAAS, Am. Inst. Chemists; mem. AIChE, Am. Chem. Soc., N.Y. Acad. Scis., Comml. Devel. Assn., Soc. Chem. Industry, Soc. Chimie Industrielle (pres. Am. sect.), Chemists Club (N.Y.C.). Achievements include pioneering research in stereospecific polymerization. Home and Office: 333 Elmwood Ave Ste D538 Maplewood NJ 07040-2449 Office Phone: 973-762-5802. Personal E-mail: aozoss@aol.com.

ZOTOS, FREDERIC P. research and development company executive; BS in Mech. Engring., Northeastern U., 1987, JD, MBA, 1993, MSEE, 1994. Bar: Mass., Conn., registered: (patent atty.). Intellectual property assoc. Pepe & Hazard, Hartford, Conn., 1994—96; asst. to pres. and patent counsel Competitive Technologies, Inc., Fairfield, Conn., 1996—98; ind. patent atty., tech. lic. cons. Cohasset, Mass., 1998—99; dir. due diligence, internal legal counsel Licent Capital, LLC, Jericho, NY, 1999—2000; dir. Atlantic Tech. Ventures, Inc., N.Y.C., 1999—, pres., 2000—. Co-chair Fairfield-Westchester. Mem.: Lic. Exec. Soc. (chair N.Y.C. chpts., mem. fin. markets com.). Office: Atlantic Technology Ventures, Inc 787 7th Ave New York NY 10019-6018

ZOU, XIAOLEI, meteorologist, educator; b. Jiang Ying, China, May 5, 1960; d. Shixi Zou and Jingan Li; m. Yuanzheng Yao; children: Yimei (Laura) Yao, Yige (Noah) Yao. PhD in Meteorology, Acad. Sinica, Beijing, China, 1988. Fellow U. Ill. Urbana-Champaign, 1989—89, Fla. State U., Tallahassee, 1989—93; scientist Nat. Ctr. Atmospheric Rsch., Boulder, Colo., 1993—97; prof. Fla. State U., Tallahassee, 1997—. Mem.: Royal Meteorol. Soc., Am. Geophy. Union, Am. Meteorol. Soc. Office: Fla State Univ 404 Love Bldg Tallahassee FL 32306 Office Phone: 850-644-6025. Office Fax: 850-644-9642. Business E-Mail: zou@met.fsu.edu.

ZOU, ZHEN, English and Chinese educator, translator and critic, computer technologist; b. Ganzhou, Jiangxi, China, Sept. 12, 1954; came to U.S., 1998; s. Xunqing and Jilie (Li) Z.; m. Ling Wang, Sept. 4, 1982; 1 child, Jia. BA, Jiangxi Normal U., 1982; MA, Peking U., Beijing, 1989, PhD, 1999. Lectr. Jiangxi Normal U., Nanchang, 1982-86; tchg. asst. Peking U., Beijing, 1986-89, asst. prof., 1989-95, assoc. prof., 1997—, dir. grad. English tchg. divsn., 1989-91; vis. scholar SUNY, New Paltz, 1991-92; tchg. asst. Purdue U., West Lafayette, Ind., 1995-97, tchr. and rsch. asst., coord., 1998-2000; asst. edn. specialist U. Minn., Mpls., 2000—04, lead tchr., 2001—02, assoc. edn. specialist, 2004—. Chief editor: An English Listening and Speaking Course for Graduate Students, 1996; contbr. articles to profl. jours. Grantee Purdue Rsch. Found., 1999; Winner Translation Contest, English Rev. Mag., 1983; Guanghua award Peking U., 1993-94. Mem. MLA, Chinese Lang. Tchrs. Assn., Peking U. Lit. and Translation Rsch. Soc. (v.p.). Avocations: swimming, skating, ping pong/table tennis. Office: U Minn Lang Ctr 51 Folwell Hall 9 Pleasant St SE Minneapolis MN 55455 Personal E-mail: zzou6@hotmail.com.

ZOUB, BURTON IRVING, lawyer; b. Chgo., Feb. 1, 1926; s. Morris B. and Taubie M. (Gertz) Z.; m. Barbara H. Zoub, Nov. 14, 1954 (div. 1971); children: Jeffrey R., Debra J., Andrew S.; m. Eleanor Weiss, Apr. 19, 1986. BS, U. Ill., 1948; JD, Northwestern U., 1952. Bar: Ill. 1952. Lawyer Ruttenberg & Ruttenberg, Chgo., 1952-54; pvt. practice Chgo., 1954—. Pres. Acad. of Family Mediators, Lexington, Ma., 1987-88; founding pres. Meditation Coun. of Ill., 1982. Author: Mediating Child Custody Disputes, 1992. With U.S. Army, 1944-46. Mem. Chgo. Bar Assn. (chmn. matrimonial law com. 1974-75). Avocations: tennis, swimming, gardening, travelogues. Office: 155 N Michigan Ave Chicago IL 60601-7511

ZOUBAREFF, KATHY OLGA, administrative assistant; b. Hassalt, Belgium; d. Vladimir F. and Kataryna (Sarcov) Z. Grad. in TV acting, J.R. Powers Sch.-Model Agy.; BA in Polit. Sci., Wayne State U.; postgrad., Ann Parsley Sch. Dance, Clinton Twp., Mich., 1990-95, Mary Skiba Sch. Dance, 1995—; A in Gen. Studies, Drama, Macomb Community Coll.; fitness and nutrition cert., Internat. Corr. Schs. Ctr., Scranton, Pa.; voice studies, Ctr. for Creative Studies, Detroit, 1994—; drama studies, Wayne State U., 1994—; broadcasting studies, Macomb C.C., Warren, Mich., 2001. Acct./adminstrv. asst. Univ. Orthopaedic Assocs. Detroit, P.C., 1990-96, office mgr., 1996-98; with The Zoubareff Co., 1998—. Actress, dancer, fashion, TV comml. and photog. model/film screen extra, Hawaiian Tropic Pageants; fragrance model; swimsuit model Ujena; nat. spokesperson Dryell, Physique, Pantene, Oil of O'Lay, Vidal Sassoon, others. Mem. Renaissance Ctr. Fashion Panel, Detroit, 1989-91; rsch. bd. advisors Am. Biog. Inst.; mem. Internat. Biog. Centre Adv. Coun., 1992, St. Clair Shores Players. Avocations: art, drawing, exercising, reading, singing. Home: 38579 Delta Dr Clinton Township MI 48036-1711 Office: Univ Orthopaedics 28800 Ryan Rd Warren MI 48092

ZRULL, JOEL PETER, psychiatry educator; b. Detroit, Jan. 10, 1932; s. Arthur Benjamin and Mildred (Bazy) Z.; m. Nancy Jane Eichenlaub, June 19, 1954; children: Mark Christian, Lisa Carol. BA with honors, U. Mich., 1953, MD, 1957. Diplomate Am. Bd. Psychiatry, Am. Bd. Child Psychiatry. From instr. to assoc. prof. psychiatry U. Mich. Med. Sch., Ann Arbor, 1962-73; prof., chief child psychiatry Med. Coll. Ohio, Toledo, 1973-75, prof., chmn. dept. psychiatry, 1975-97, prof. emeritus, 1997—. Cons. Monroe (mich.) County Intermediate Sch. Dist., 1961—; pres. Associated Physicians MCO, Inc., Toledo, 1983-84, 87-90; chief of staff Med. Coll. Hosps., Toledo, 1984-86; mem. com. on cert. in child psychiatry Am. Bd. Psychiatry and Neurology, 1986-91, chmn. 1990-91. Editor: Adult Psychiatry: New Directions in Therapy, 1983; contbr. articles to profl. jours. Grantee NIMH, 1974-76, Ohio Dept. Mental Health, 1978-86. Fellow Am. Psychiat. Assn. (life, Agnes Purcell McGavin award for disting. career achievement in child and adolescent psychology 2003), Am. Acad. Child and Adolescent Psychiatry (chmn. com. tng. 1984-87, chmn. comm. memls. and awards 1992-95), Am. Coll. Psychiatrists, Am. Ortho-Psychiat. Assn.; mem. AMA, Soc. Profs. of Child and Adolescent Psychiatry (sec. treas. 1989-92, pres.-elect 1992-94, pres. 1994-96). Roman Catholic. Avocations: tennis, bridge. Home: 6133 Wyandotte Rd W Maumee OH 43537-1334 Office: Med Coll Ohio Kobacker Ctr 3130 Glendale Ave Toledo OH 43614-5811*

ZSCHAU, JULIUS JAMES, lawyer; b. Peoria, Ill., Apr. 1, 1940; s. Raymond Johann Ernst and Rosamond Lillian (Malicoat) Z.; m. Leila Joan Krueger, Aug. 7, 1971; children: Kristen Elisabeth, Kimberly Erna, Kira Jamie, Karla Johanna. BS, U. Ill., Champaign, 1964, JD, 1966; LLM, John Marshall Law Sch., 1978. Bar: Ill. 1966, Fla. 1975. Atty. Ill. Central Gulf R.R. Co., Chgo., 1966-68; assoc. Coin & Sheerin, Chgo., 1968-70, Snyder, Clarke et al, Waukegan, Ill., 1970-72; counsel Ill. Ctr. Corp., Chgo., 1972-74; v.p., gen. counsel, sec. Am. Agronomics Corp., Tampa, Fla., 1974-76; pres. Sorota & Zschau, Clearwater, Fla., 1976-90; shareholder Baynard, Harrell, Ostow & Ulrich PA, 1990-94, Johnson, Blakely, Pope, Bokor, Ruppel and Burns, Clearwater, 1994—2002, Pennington Moore Wilkinson Bell & Dunbar PA, 2002—. Bd. dirs. Attys. Title Ins. Fund, Inc., chmn. bd. dirs., 1994—95; chmn. com. on land trusts Fla. Bar, chmn.-elect Real Property, Probate and Trust Law sect., vice chair grievance com., 1985—87, chair leadership conf., 1987; chmn. Jud. Nominating Commn. of 6th Jud. Dist., 1991—94; mem. jud. nominating com. U.S. Ct. Appeals (2d dist.). Bd. dirs. Nat. Attys. Title Assurance Fund, Attys. Title Ins. Fund, Attys. Title Guaranty Fund of Colo., treas.; mem. Pinellas County Exec. Com., Tampa Regional Planning Coun., 1988-92. Served to capt. USNR, 1962-92. Fellow: Am. Bar Found. (life); mem.: ABA (chmn. standing com. lawyers title guaranty funds 1991, chmn. land trust com.), Fla. Bar Found. (chmn. jud. nominations procedures com. 1992—93, legal aid to poor com.), Fla. Coun. Bar Assn. (past pres., past chmn. vol. bar liaison com.), Clearwater Bar Assn. (past pres.), Chgo. Bar Assn., Ill. Bar Assn., Am. Coll. Real Estate Lawyers (chmn. condominium com.), Clearwater C. of C. (bd. govs., exec. com., past v.p.), Countryside Country Club, Shriners, Scottish Rite, Masons. Republican. Home: 1910 Saddlehill Rd N Dunedin FL 34698-2437 Office: Pennington Moore et al 133 N Fort Harrison Clearwater FL 33607 Office Phone: 727-747-9553. Business E-Mail: jayz@penningtonlaw.com.

ZSCHAU, MARILYN, singer; b. Chgo., Feb. 9, 1944; d. Edwin Arthur Eugene and Helen Elizabeth (Kelly) Z. BA in Radio, TV and Motion Pictures, U. N.C., 1959; grad., Juilliard Sch. Music, 1965; studied opera theatre with Christopher West, studied voice with Florence Page Kimball, studied with John Lester. Toured with Met. Nat. Co., 1965-66; debut, Vienna Volksoper, in Die Tote Stadt, 1967, Vienna Staatsoper, in Ariadne auf Naxos, 1971; with N.Y.C. Opera in La Fanciulla del West, 1978; debut Royal Opera, covent Garden in La Boheme, 1982, Met. Opera, in La Boheme, 1985, La Scala, in Die Frau ohne Schatten, 1986; has toured and sung in many countries including S.Am., Japan, and Australia. Office: 4245 Wilshire Blvd Oakland CA 94602-3549 Office Phone: 510-484-7742. E-mail: marilynzschau@yahoo.com.

ZSIGMOND, ELEMER KALMAN, anesthesiologist; b. Budapest, Hungary, May 16, 1930; came to U.S., 1956, naturalized, 1966; m. Kathryn Fogarasi; 1 child, Zoltan William. MD, U. Budapest, 1955. Diplomate: Am. Bd. Anesthesiology. Intern Med. Clinics, U. Budapest, 1954-55, Allegheny Gen. Hosp., Pitts., 1960-61, resident in anesthesiology, 1961-63, clin. anesthesiologist, dir. anesthesiology research labs., 1966-68; prof. anesthesiology Med. Sch., U. Mich., Ann Arbor, 1968-79, U. Ill. Med. Sch., Chgo., 1979-95, prof. emeritus, 1995—; mem. staff Univ. Hosp., U. Ill., Chgo. Contbr. over 380 articles on anesthesiology, neuropharmacology, and pulmonary physiology to profl. jours. Fellow Am. Coll. Anesthesiologists, Am. Coll. Clin. Pharmacologists; mem. AAAS, AMA, Am. Soc. Anesthesiologists, Internat. Anesthesia Research Soc., Hungarian Acad. Sci., N.Y. Acad. Sci., Ill. Med. Soc., Cook County Med. Soc. Home: 6611 N Longmeadow Ave Chicago IL 60646-3207 Office: U Ill Med Ctr 1740 W Taylor St Ste EEI317 Chicago IL 60612-7232 E-mail: ezsigmon@uic.edu., elmerzsigmond@aol.com. *My father's motto for one of his books has been my principle: "Every man represents as much worth to society as he is willing to give from himself to his fellowman.".*

ZSIGMOND, VILMOS, cinematographer, director; b. Szeged, Hungary, June 16, 1930; came to U.S., 1957, naturalized, 1962; s. Vilmos and Bozena (Illichmann) Z.; children: Julia, Susi. MA, U. Film and Theater Arts, Budapest, Hungary, 1955. Free-lance cinematographer for numerous commls., also ednl., documentary and low-budget feature films, 1965-71; now dir., cinematographer on commls. (winner several nat. and internat. awards); feature films, 1971-; films include McCabe and Mrs. Miller, 1971; Images, 1972, Deliverance, 1972, The Long Goodbye, 1973, Scarecrow, 1973, Cinderella Liberty, 1973, The Sugarland Express, 1974, Obsession, 1976, Close Encounters of the Third Kind, 1977 (Acad. award 1977), The Last Waltz, 1978, The Rose, 1978, The Deerhunter, 1978 (Acad. award nomination and Brit. Acad. award), Heavens Gate, 1979, The Border, 1980, Blow Out, 1980, Jinxed, 1981, Table for Five, 1982, The River, 1983 (Acad. award nomination), No Small Affair, 1984, Real Genius, 1985, Witches of Eastwick, 1986, Journey to Spirit Island, 1988, Fatman and Little Boy, 1989, Two Jakes, 1989, Bonfire of the Vanities, 1990, Stalin, 1991 (CableAce award, Direction of Photography and/or Lighting Direction in a Dramatic/Theatrical Special/Movie or Miniseries, ASC award, Emmy award), Sliver, 1992; dir. The Long Shadow, 1992, Intersection, 1993, Maverick, 1993, The Crossing Guard, 1994, Assassins, 1995, The Ghost and the Darkness, 1996 (ASC Award nomination), Fantasy for a New Age, 1997, Playing By Heart, 1998, The Body, 1999, The Mists of Avalon, 2000, Life as a House, 2001, (opera film) Bank Ban, 2002, Jersey Girl, 2003, Melinda and Melinda, 2004. Recipient lifetime achievement award Worldfest, Flagstaff, 1998. Mem. Acad. Motion Picture Arts and Scis., Dirs. Guild, Am. Soc. Cinematographers (lifetime achievement award 1998). Office: Feinstein & Berson 16255 Ventura Blvd Ste 625 Encino CA 91436-2418 E-mail: vilmoszsigmond@hotmail.com.

ZUBER, RANDOLPH CLARK, urologist; b. Dallas, Apr. 4, 1941; s. Oran H. and Minnie M. (Cuthbertson) Z.; m. Billie Gayle Schumacher, June 20, 1964; children: Randolph Blake, Rustin Kurt. AAPS, Amarillo Jr. Coll., 1961; BA, U. Tex., 1963; MD, U. Tex., Galveston, 1967. Diplomate Am. Bd. Urology. Intern Kans. U. Med. Ctr., 1967—68, resident in urology, 1969—72; practice medicine specializing in urology Kerrville, Tex., 1974—2003; part-time urology practice South Tex. VA Hosp., Kerrville, Tex., 2003—. Bishop Ch. of Christ, 1983-93; mem. urologic cultural exchange to Peoples Republic

of China People to People Found., 1987. Founding dir., past pres. Hill County Right to Life; chmn. steering com. Kerr County YMCA, 1990. Served to maj. USAF, 1972-74. Recipient Disting. Leadership award, cert. of excellence Leadership Kerr County, 1989. Fellow ACS; mem. Am. Urol. Assn. (Tex. rep., bd. dirs. south ctrl. sect. 1990-96), Tex. Urol. Soc. (pres. 1988-89, bd. dirs. 1996-98), Tex. Med. Assn. Office: South Tex VA Hosp Kerrville TX 78028 E-mail: 2Zubers@hctc.net.

ZUBKOFF, MICHAEL, medical educator; b. N.Y.C., June 2, 1944; s. Harry and Catherine (O'Brien) Z.; children: Steven, Joel, Lisa; m. Leslee Ann Michaels, 1991. BA, Am. Internat. Coll., 1965, LLD (hon.), 1981; MA, cert. Internat. Fellow program, Columbia U., 1966, PhD, 1968; MA (hon.), Dartmouth Coll., 1980. Research assoc. conservation human resources Columbia U., N.Y.C., 1966-67; assoc. prof. econs. Fisk U., Nashville, 1967-70; assoc. prof. health econs., assoc. chmn. dept. family and community health Meharry Med. Coll., Nashville, 1967-75; assoc. prof. econs. Vanderbilt U., Nashville, 1970-75; prof. econs. and mgmt. Amos Tuck Sch. Bus., prof. chmn. dept. cmty. and family medicine Med. Sch. Dartmouth Coll., Hanover, NH, 1975—. Mem. inst. medicine Nat. Acad. Scis., 1982—, mem. assembly engrs. inst. med. com. on tech. and health care, 1977-79, grad. med. ednl. nat. adv. com., 1977-81., com. on grad.-med. edn. programs for mil. services Nat. Acad. Scis., 1980-82., nat. research council commn. on human resources Nat. Acad. Scis., 1980-84, com. on aging soc. Nat. Acad. Scis., 1984-89; corr. com. human rights Nat. Acad. Scis., 1983—, nat. rsch. coun. com. computer tech. and svc. sector productivity Nat. Acad. Scis., 1991-94; instr. econs. Harvard U., Yale U., and Columbia U., 1967-68. Co-author: Urban Health Services: The Case of New York, 1971, Consumer Incentives for Health Care, 1974, Health: A Victim of Cause of Inflation, 1976, Framework for Government Intervention in the Health Sector, 1978, Hospital Cost Containment: Selected Notes for Public Policy, 1980, Problem Based Learning of Social Science & Humanities by Fourth Year Medical Students, 1986, The Medical Outcomes Study: An Application of Methods for Monitoring the Results of Medical Care, 1989, Measuring Functional Status & Well Being: The Medical Outcomes Study Approach, 1992, Health Society & The Physician: Problem Based Learning of Social Sciences & Humanities, 1993; contbr. numerous articles to profl. jours. Del., health spokesman White House Summit on Inflation, 1974. Fellow Woodrow Wilson Found., 1964-66, Fulbright Found., 1967-68, USPHS, 1966-67. Mem. Am. Econ. Assn., Am. Pub. Health Assn. Home: RR 1 Fairlee VT 05045-9801 Office: Dartmouth Med Sch Dept Comty & Family Med HB7250 Hanover NH 03755

ZUBOV, LYNN, special education educator, researcher; b. Bklyn., Dec. 3, 1960; d. David P. Roche III. BS in Spl. Edn., St. John's U., Jamaica, N.Y., 1983; MS in Spl. Edn., St. John's U., 1988, EdS in Supervision and Adminstrn., 1990; PhD in Spl. Edn., Vanderbilt U., Nashville, 1996. Tchr. asst. Little Village Sch., Garden City, N.Y., 1981-82; tchr. of emotionally disturbed J.H.S. 8, Jamaica, N.Y., 1983-86, Poseidon, Los Angeles, 1986-87; ednl. coord., mainstream coord. P.S. 80, Jamaica, N.Y., 1987-91; rsch. asst. Peabody Coll. Vanderbilt U., Nashville, 1991-95; asst. prof., program dir. Canisius Coll., Buffalo, 1995-99; asst. prof., program coord. Winston-Salem State U., 1999—. Spl. edn. cons. Paul J. Cooper, Bklyn., 1991; mem. project Basics I.H.S. 8, Jamaica, N.Y., 1983-86; sec. Pupil-Pers. Commn., P.S. 80, Jamaica, 1987-91. Cons., instr. How To Use The Apple Computer, How to Make Inclusion Work, Developing Positive Behavioral Support Plans Through the Use of a Functional Analysis of Behavior; co-author: Handbook for the Special Education Paraprofessional, 1990. Mem. CEC, N.Y. State Coun. for Exceptional Children (past pres.). Republican. Roman Catholic. Home: 229 Engleman Ave Burlington NC 27215-4801 Office: Winston-Salem State U 601 Martin Luther King Jr CB 19360 Winston Salem NC 27157 E-mail: zubovle@wssu.edu.

ZUBOV, SERGEI, professional hockey player; b. Moscow, July 22, 1970; Hockey player Rangers, 1992-95, Penguins, 1995-96; defense Dallas Stars, 1996—. Office: Amer Airlines Ctr 2500 Victory Ln Dallas TX 75219

ZUBRITSKY, ALEXANDER NICKOLAEVICH, pathologist; b. Severo-Kurilsk, Sakhalin, Russia, Mar. 14, 1949; s. Nickolay Alexandrovich and Kaleriya Andreevna (Chechulina) Z.; children: Vladimir, Sergey Yashin. MD, Med. Inst., 1974. Hosp. attendant dept. pathology City Hosp. N21, Sverdlovsk, Russia, 1965-67; hosp. attendant Medico-Legal Morgue N1, Sverdlovsk, 1967-68; nurse Sta. of Emergencies Care N1, Sverdlovsk, 1971-72; head pathology dept. Ctrl. Regional Hosp., Neviyansk, Russia, 1975-76; chief pathology dept., head pathologist Sverdlovsk Rd. Hosp., 1976-83; lectr. path. anatomy Med. Sch. Sverdlovsk Rd., 1976-77; chief dept. pathology mcpl. instn. Taldom Ctrl. Regional Hosp., 1983—. Contbr. articles to profl. jours. Recipient award Am. Coll. Chest Physicians, 1990, Pathology Rsch. Practice award, Taldom-Innsbruck, 1993, Internat. Peace prize UCC, 2003, 21st Century award IBC, 2003; named Internat. Man of Yr., 1994-95, 2003. Mem.: AAAS, N.Y. Acad. Sci., Internat. Soc. Diagnostic Quantitative Pathology, Internat. Soc. Heart Rsch. (European sect.), Internat. Union Against Tb and Lung Disease, European Soc. Pathology. Avocations: music, walking. Home: Prospekt Mira101B/79 129085 Moscow Russia Office Phone: (7-096)-20-6-02-57.

ZUBROFF, LEONARD SAUL, surgeon; b. Minersville, Pa., Mar. 27, 1925; s. Abe and Fannie (Freedline) Z. BA, Wayne State U., 1945, MD, 1949. Diplomate Am. Bd. Surgery. Intern Garfield Hosp., Washington, 1949-50, resident in surgery, 1951-55, chief resident surgery, 1954-55; pvt. practice medicine specializing in surgery, 1958-76; med. dir. Chevrolet Gear and Axle Plant, Forge Plant, GM, Detroit, 1977-78; divsnl. med. dir. Detroit Diesel Allison divsn., Detroit, 1978-87; regional med. dir. GM, 1987-89; ret., 1989. Chief of surgery, chief profl. svcs. N.E. Air Command, Pepperell AFB, Newfoundland. With USAF, 1956—58. Mem.: Le Vine Found. (trustee). Home and Office: 22511 S Bellwood Dr Southfield MI 48034-2116

ZUCARO, ALDO CHARLES, insurance company executive; b. Grenoble, France, Apr. 2, 1939; s. Louis and Lucy Zucaro; m. Gloria J. Ward, Oct. 12, 1963; children: Lucy, Louis, Faye. BS in Acctg, Queens Coll., N.Y.C., 1962. C.P.A., N.Y., Ill. Ptnr. Coopers & Lybrand (and predecessor), Chgo. and N.Y.C., 1962-76; exec. v.p., chief fin. officer Old Republic Internat. Corp., Chgo., 1976-81, pres., 1981—, chief exec. officer, 1990—, also chmn. bd. dirs., 1993—, chmn. of the bd., 1993—. Pres., bd. dirs. Old Republic Life Ins. Co., Old Republic Life of N.Y., Old Republic Ins. Co., Internat. Bus. and Merc. Reassurance Co., Republic Mortgage Ins. Co., Old Republic Nat. Title Ins. Co., Home Owners Life Ins. Co. Editor: Financial Accounting Practices of the Insurance Industry, 1975, 76. Mem. AICPAs. Roman Catholic. Office: Old Republic Internat Corp 307 N Michigan Ave Chicago IL 60601-5311

ZUCCARELLO, MARIO, neurosurgeon, researcher; b. Catania, Italy, Apr. 25, 1952; m. Gabriella Tempesta, May 25, 1985; 1 child, Marco. Undergrad., U. Padova, Italy, 1970-76, MD, 1976. Intern U. Hosp., Padova, Italy, 1976-80, resident in neurosurgery, 1976-80; instr. neurosurgery Padova, 1981-84; rsch. fellow U. Va., Charlottesville, 1984-85; clin. fellow neurosurgery U. Cin., 1985-88, assoc. prof. neurosurgery, 1990-99, prof., 1999—, dir. cerebrovascular surgery; asst. prof. neurosurgery Genova, Italy, 1988-90; chief neurosurgery VAMC, Cin., 1990—, vice chmn., 2004—. Contbr. articles to profl. jours. Capt. Italian Army, 1981-82. Recipient U. Cin. Rsch. award, 1995; Max Planck scholar, 1977-78, NATO scholar, 1984; VA Merit Rev. grantee Veteran Adminstrn. Med. Ctr., 1991—. Roman Catholic. Avocations: soccer, classical music, skiing, history, geography. Home: 231 Bethesda Ave Cincinnati OH 45229-2827 Office: U Cin 231 Bethesda Ave Cincinnati OH 45229-2827 Fax: 513-558-7702. E-mail: zuccarm@e-mail.uc.edu.

ZUCCOTTI, JOHN EUGENE, real estate company executive; b. N.Y.C., June 23, 1937; AB in History, Princeton U., 1959; LLB, Yale U., 1963. Bar: N.Y. 1963, D.C. 1970. Asst. to under sec. and sec. HUD, Washington, 1967-69; sec., counsel Nat. Corp. for Housing Partnerships, Washington, 1969-70; spl. counsel to housing subcom. Banking and Currency Com. U.S. Ho. of Reps., Washington, 1970-73; ptnr. Tufo, Johnston and Zuccotti, N.Y.C., 1970-72; chmn. N.Y.C. Planning Commn., 1973-75, mem., 1971-73; 1st dep. mayor City of N.Y., 1975-77; sr. ptnr. Tufo, Johnston, Zuccotti and Allegaert, N.Y.C., 1977-86, Brown & Wood, N.Y.C., 1986-89; pres., chief exec. officer Olympia and York Cos. (U.S.A.), 1989—. Impartial arbitrator between MTA/TWU, 1981-90. Office: World Financial Properties Inc 1 Liberty Plz 165 Broadway New York NY 10006-1404*

ZUCK, ALFRED CHRISTIAN, consulting mechanical engineer; b. Ridgefield, N.J., Dec. 16, 1924; s. Frederick William and Margaret Christine (Umland) Z.; m. Vilma Hudson, May 6, 1951; children: Allyson, Jon, Randall. M.E., Poly. Inst. Bklyn., 1960. Registered profl. engr., 21 states including N.Y.; nat. council engring. examiners; lic. profl. planner, N.J. From designer to sr. v.p. Syska & Hennessy, Inc., N.Y.C., 1946-78; prin. Edwards & Zuck (P.C.), N.Y.C., 1978-91, ret., 1991. Mem. nat. panel Am. Arbitration Assn, Nat. Council Engring. Examiners. Served with AUS, 1943-46; to 1st lt. USAF, 1951-52; to capt. N.J. Air N.G., 1947-56. Decorated Bronze Star (2) Fellow Am. Cons. Engrs. Council (past mem. Nat. Ethical Practices Com.); mem. NSPE, N.Y. State Soc. Profl. Engrs. (past chmn. profl. engrs. in pvt. practice program), Am. Soc. Mil. Engrs., Nat. Council Engring. Examiners, N.Y. Assn. Cons. Engrs. (past v.p., bd. dirs.), ASHRAE, N.Y. Bldg. Congress. (bd. govs.). Clubs: N.Y. Athletic. Lutheran. Home: 80 N Walnut St Ridgewood NJ 07450-3224 Office: Edwards & Zuck PC 330 W 42nd St Fl 27 New York NY 10036-6949

ZUCK, ALFRED MILLER, public administration educator; b. East Petersburg, Pa., Aug. 27, 1934; s. Walter Newton and Mary (Miller) Z.; m. Geraldine Connelly, July 21, 1957; children: Susan, David. BA, Franklin and Marshall Coll., 1957; MPA, Syracuse U., 1958. Dir. fed. program Presdl. Commn. on Youth Opportunities, Washington, 1967-68; dir evaluation Employment and Tng. Adminstrn., Dept. Labor, Washington, 1968-70, dir adminstrn. and mgmt., 1970-75; comptroller U.S. Dept. Labor, Washington, 1975-77; exec. dir. Commn. on Exec., Legis. and Jud. Salaries, Washington, 1980; asst. sec. Dept. Labor, Washington, 1977-83, acting sec., 1981; asst. adminstr. EPA, Washington, 1983; exec. dir. Nat. Assn. Schs. of Pub. Affairs and Adminstrn., Washington, 1983-97; disting. prof. Am. U., Washington, 1996—. Pres. Internat. Inst. Adminstrv. Scis., Brussels, 1989-92, Am. Consortium for Internat. Pub. Adminstrn., Washington, 1984-89; bd. dirs. Pub./Pvt. Venture, Inc., Phila., 1984-90. Recipient Presdl. Disting. Exec. award Pres. of U.S., 1980; Disting. Alumni award Franklin and Marshall Coll., 1980. Fellow Nat. Acad. Pub. Adminstrn. (trustee 1989-95, chmn. bd. trustees 1993-95); mem . Phi Beta Kappa.

ZUCKER, ALEXANDER, physicist, administrator; b. Zagreb, Yugoslavia, Aug. 1, 1924; came to U.S., 1939; s. William and Bertha (Klopfer) Z.; m. Joan-Ellen Jamieson, Nov. 28, 1953; children: Rebecca, Claire, Susannah. BA, U. Vt., Burlington, 1947; MS, Yale U., New Haven, 1948, PhD, 1950. Physicist Oak Ridge Nat. Lab., Tenn., 1950-60, assoc. dir. electro-nuclear div., 1972-75, dir. heavy ion project, 1988, assoc. dir. phys. scis., 1973-88, acting lab. dir., 1988, assoc. dir. for nuclear techs., 1989-93; exec. dir., environ. studies bd. NAS-NAE, Washington, 1970-72; prof. physics U. Tenn., 1996—. Mem. U.S. del. to USSR on Peaceful Uses of Atomic Energy, 1963; Ford prof. physics U. Tenn., Knoxville, 1968-73; U.S. del. to Pugwash Conf., 1971; research coordination council Gas Research Inst., Chgo., 1978-85; com. Army manpower Nat. Research Council, Washington, 1982-83; adv. panel on technologies to reduce U.S. materials import vulnerability Office of Technology Assessment, Washington, 1982-85; council on energy engring. research Dept. of Energy, Washington, 1983—; industry, nat. lab. steel initiative White House, Washington, 1984 Editor Internat. Jour. Nuclear Sci. Applications, 1980—; cons. editor Ency. and Yearbook of Sci. and Tech. McGraw-Hill Pub. Co., 1989; mem. editorial bd. Science, 1981-82; contbr. articles to profl. jours. Guggenheim fellow, 1966-67; Fulbright-Hays Research scholar, 1966-67 Fellow Am. Phys. Soc., AAAS, Sigma Xi; mem. ASME, Nat. Acad. Scis. (nuclear physics del. to People's Republic of China 1979), Internat. Union Pure and Applied Physics (mem.-at-large U.S. nat. com. 1976-78) Achievements include research in nuclear physics with heavy ions and protons; accelerators, especially cyclotrons; materials research programs, especially high-temperature materials and surfaces; nuclear power reactors, especially gas-cooled reactors; research reactor with ultra high neutron flux. Office: Oak Ridge Nat Lab PO Box 2008 Oak Ridge TN 37831-2008

ZUCKER, ALFRED JOHN, English language educator, academic administrator; b. Hartford, Sept. 25, 1940; s. Samuel and Rose (Zucker) Z.; m. Sallie Lea Friedheim, Dec. 25, 1966; children: Mary Anne, John James Jr., James Patrick, Patrick Jonathan, Anne-Marie Kathleen, Kathleen Mary. AA, L.A. Valley Coll., 1960; AB in English, UCLA, 1962, AB in Speech, MA in English, 1962, MA in Speech, 1963, PhD, 1966; postgrad., U. So. Calif., Harvard U.; MA in history, 2000, MA in Polit. Sci., 2004. Prof. English and history, chmn. div. humanities L.A. S.W. Coll., 1968-72; prof. English El Camino Coll., 1985—, L.A. Valley Coll., 1989—, chmn. dept. English, honors sponsor, 1997—. Contbr. articles to profl. jours. Mem. L.A. Coll. Dist. Senate, 1969—. Mem. AAUP, L.A. Coll. Tchrs. Assn. (dir.), Calif. Jr. Coll. Assn., Calif. Tchrs. Assn., World Affairs Coun., Calif. Scholarship Fedn., Mensa, KC, Gold Key, Phi Beta Kappa, Phi Delta Kappa (pres. UCLA chpt. 1966-67, v.p. 1967-68), Tau Alpha Epsilon, Phi Theta Kappa, Phi Alpha Theta, Phi Kappa Phi, Phi Delta Gamma. Office: 5800 Fulton Ave Van Nuys CA 91401-4062 Office Phone: 818-947-2343. E-mail: zuckeraj@lavc.edu.

ZUCKER, ARNOLD HARRIS, psychiatrist; b. Bklyn., July 29, 1930; s. Charles Israel and Bertha (Leff) Z.; m. Marilyn Pistreich, June 10, 1962; children: Harvey, Deborah, Shoshanna, David. BA, Bklyn. Coll., 1950; MD, SUNY, Bklyn., 1954; cert. psychoanalysis, Columbia U. Psychoanalytic Ctr, 1971. Diplomate, Am. Bd. Psychiatry and Neurology. Intern USPHS, Staten Island, N.Y., 1954-55; resident Kings County Hosp., Bklyn., 1955-56, Southwestern Med. Sch., Dallas, 1958-59, Albert Einstein Coll. Medicine, Bronx, N.Y., 1959-60, asst. clin. prof. psychiatry, 1960-72; pvt. practice Mt. Vernon, NY, 1960—2000. Assoc. attending psychiatrist, Mt. Vernon Hosp.; assoc. prof. pastoral counseling, Iona Coll., New Rochelle, N.Y., 1968-2000. Contbr. articles to profl. jours. Surgeon, USPHS, 1956-58. Fellow Am. Psychiat. Assn. (life), Am. Acad. Psychoanalysis (life); mem. Am. Psychoanalytic Assn., Assn. Psychoanalytic Medicine, AMA, Westchester Psychoanalytic Soc., Phi Beta Kappa. Democrat. Jewish. Avocation: religious studies. Office: 120 E Prospect Ave Mount Vernon NY 10550-2212 Office Phone: 914-668-2332.

ZUCKER, HOWARD ALAN, pediatric cardiologist, intensivist, anesthesiologist, government agency administrator; b. NYC, Sept. 6, 1959; s. Saul and Phyllis (Goldblatt) Zucker. BS, McGill U., Montreal, 1979; MD, George Washington U., 1982; JD, Fordham U., 2000; LLM, Columbia U., 2001. Pediatric intern Johns Hopkins Hosp., Balt., 1982-83, pediatric resident, 1983-85; anesthesiology resident Hosp. of U. Pa., Phila., 1985-87; pediatric critical care fellow Children's Hosp. of Phila., 1987-88; asst. prof. anesthesiology and pediatrics Yale U. Sch. Medicine, New Haven, 1988-90; pediatric cardiology fellow Children's Hosp., Harvard Med. Sch., Boston, 1990-92; assoc. prof. clin. pediat. and clin. anesthesiology N.Y. Presbyn. Hosp. and Children's Hosp., N.Y.C., 1992—2001; dir. pediatric transport Columbia Presbyn. Med. Ctr. Babies and Children's Hosp. N.Y., N.Y.C., 1992—2001; White House fellow, 2001—02; dep. asst. sec. for health designee HHS. Adj. assoc. prof. pediat. Cornell U. Weill Coll. Medicine, 2000—01; involved with crew tng. NASA Space Shuttle STS-1 Mission, 1978—80; rsch. affiliate Man-vehicle Lab MIT; White House fellow, 2001—02; coun. on fgn. relations, 2003—. Participant med. missions to China Children China Pediat. Found.; chmn. bd. Terre Verte Found., Inc.; bd. dirs. Little Hearts Pediat. Found. Named Person of the Week, ABC World News Tonight, 1993; fellow, White House, 2001—02. Fellow: Am. Coll. Critical Care Medicine, Am. Coll. Legal Medicine, Am. Coll. Cardiology, Am. Coll. Chest Physicians, Am. Acad. Pediat.; mem.: AMA, Soc. Critical Care Medicine, Am. Heart Assn., Am. Soc. Anesthesiologists (mem. coun. fgn. rels. 2003—), Coun. Fgn. Rels. Jewish. Achievements include research in in adaptation to zero gravity, cardiac critical care. Home: 100 Winston Dr Apt 12G Cliffside Park NJ 07010-3240

ZUCKER, JEFFREY, broadcast executive; m. Caryn Zucker; children: Andrew, Elizabeth, Peter. BA in Am. History, Harvard Coll., 1986. Rschr., 1988 Olympic Games, Seoul, Korea NBC Sports, 1986—88; field prodr. NBC News, 1989; exec. prodr. Today, 1992—93, Now with Tom Brokaw and Katie Couric, NBC Nightly News with Tom Brokaw, 1993, Today, 1994—2000; pres. NBC Entertainment, 2000—03, NBC Entertainment, News and Cable Group, 2003—. Exec. prodr.: (news segments) Russian coup, 1991, Persian Gulf War, 1991, 1993 and 1997 presdl. inaugurations, the bombing of Centennial Olympic Pk., 1996, 1996 and 2000 polit. conventions, Decision 2000; writer: The Games of the XXIV Olympiad (Emmy award, outstanding writing, 1988); supervising prodr.: "Senator Edward Kennedy" Today (Emmy award, outstanding interview, 1991); exec. prodr.: "California Fire" Now with Tom Brokaw and Katie Couric (Emmy award, outstanding coverage of a single breaking news story, 1993), "Tragedy in Rwanda" Now with Tom Brokaw and Katie Couric (Emmy award, outstanding background/analysis of a single current story, 1994), "The Brain" Now with Tom Brokaw and Katie Couric (Emmy award, outstanding informational or cultural program, 1994). Office: NBC 3000 W Alameda Ave Burbank CA 91523-0002 also: 30 Rockefeller Plz New York NY

ZUCKER, JERRY, chemical manufacturing executive; b. Tel-Aviv, Israel, Aug. 24, 1949; s. Leon and Zipora (Shlifkovitz) Z.; m. Anita Goldberg, June 21, 1970; children: Jonathan Michael, Andrea Michelle, Jeffrey Mark. BS, U. Fla., 1968, MEE, 1972. Electronics design engr. Vital Industries, Inc., Gainesville, Fla., 1968-71; devel. engring. group dir. Cons. Engrs., Inc., Gainesville, 1971-73; supr. process engring. and tech. svcs. Hudson Pulp & Paper Corp. (now Ga. Pacific), Palatka, Fla., 1973-78; dir. mfg. and tech. svcs. Raybestos Manhattan, Inc., North Charleston, S.C., 1978-82; chmn. bd., pres., CEO InterTech Group, Inc., 1983—; chmn., CEO Polymer Group, Inc., 1996—2003. Bd. dirs. High Tech. Coatings Corp., Advanced Chem. Techs., Inc., Tighitco, Inc., Ecosys, Inc., Polymer Group, Inc., FiberTech Group, Inc., ConX Inc., Tycon Inc., Worthington Products Inc., Aerospace Def. Inc., Technetics Group, Inc., Thantex, Inc., Global Golf, Inc., Fabrene, Inc., Polymer Group, Inc., Daramic, Inc., RemGrit Corp., Polyionix, Inc.; cons. phosphate mining, pulp and paper and sugar industries. Contbr. articles to tech. hours.; patentee in electrochem., mech. and chem. fields. Bd. dirs. Roper Hosp., Trident United Way, Charleston Jewish Fedn.; pres. Hotline Inc., Hebrew Benevolent Soc., Hebrew Orphan Soc., Orgn. Rehab. Tng., S.C. Aquarium; pres. Synagogue Emanuel; trustee S.C. Rsch. Inst., U. S.C., Med. U. S.C. Rsch. Inst. Mem. IEEE, TAPPI (nat. elec. engring. com. 1977-95), Am. Chem. Soc. Jewish. Office: The InterTech Group Inc PO Box 5205 4838 Jenkins Ave North Charleston SC 29405-4816

ZUCKER, LEONARD CHARLES, trucking executive, rabbi; b. Bronx, N.Y., June 13, 1933; s. Ralph Gilbert and Elsie (Himmelstein) Z.; m. Elaine Trachtman, Dec. 25, 1955 (dec. Aug. 1998); children: Anne, Esther Lynne, Rhea Miriam, Ronald Gary; m. Marilyn Stennstien, Dec. 12, 1999. BA, Yeshiva U., 1951; postgrad., Acad. Advanced Traffic, 1955. Ordained rabbi, 1957. With Charlton Bros. Transp. Co., Inc., Phila., 1953-58; sales mgr. Phila.-Pits. Carriers, Phila., 1958-61; dist. sales rep. Preston Trucking Co., Inc., 1961-65; v.p. Drake Motor Lines Inc., Cherry Hill, N.J., 1965-76; exec. v.p., COO Pinto Trucking Svc., Inc., Phila., 1976-83, pres., 1984-86, L. Zucker Assocs., 1986—. Rabbi Congregation B'nai Tikvah, Turnersville, N.J., 1975-97, Golden Lakes Temple, West Palm Beach, Fla., 1998—; chaplain Fedn. Jewish Agys. of Atlantic County, 1987-93; pres. Tri County Bd. Rabbis, 1995-97; mem. Phila. Bd. Rabbis, Palm Beach County Bd. Rabbis. Author: Why Be a Transportation Specialist, 1971, Safety Guide for the Motor Carrier, 1973. Bd. dirs. Motor Transport Labor Rels., Phila., 1973-76. With U.S. Army, 1953-55. Mem. Assn. ICC Practitioners, Transp. Law Practitioners U.S., Air Cargo Club, Nat. Fedn. Men's Clubs, Fifth Wheel Club, Traffic and Transp. Club, Delta Nu Alpha. Democrat. Jewish. Home: 119 Lake Nancy Dr West Palm Beach FL 33411-9202 Office: PO Box 210064 Royal Palm Beach FL 33421

ZUCKER, LYNNE GOODMAN, sociology educator, consultant; b. Dayton, Ohio, May 10, 1945; d. Robert Alfred and Sieglinde Goodman; m. Joel Steven Zucker, June 5, 1966 (div. Sept. 1991); children: Joshua, Danielle; m. Michael Rucker Darby, Feb. 14, 1992; children: Margaret, David. AB, Wells Coll., 1966; MA, Stanford U., 1969, PhD, 1974. Instr. dept. sociology Stanford U., Palo Alto, Calif., 1972-73; lectr. dept. sociology and urban studies program San Francisco State U., 1974; lectr. dept. sociology UCLA, 1974-75, asst. prof., 1975-81, assoc. prof., 1981-89, prof., 1989—, mem. affiliated faculty Sch. Edn., 1984—, program dir. for orgnl. rsch. Inst. for Social Rsch., 1986—2000, prof. policy studies Sch. Pub. Policy and Social Rsch., 1996—, dir. Ctr. for Internat. Sci., Tech. and Cultural Policy, 1996—. Mem. com. on evaluation employment and tng. programs NAS-NRC, 1977-80; mem. vis. faculty dept. sociology U. Chgo., 1982; mem. sociology panel NSF, 1984-87, mem. young presdl. scholar award panel, 1989-91; fellow program on non-profit orgns. Inst. for Social and Policy Studies, Yale U., New Haven, 1986; mem. vis. faculty program in orgnl. behavior Harvard U. Bus. Sch., Boston, 1987; economist stats. of income IRS, U.S. Treasury Dept., Washington, 1989-94; cons. sociologist Am. Inst. Physics, N.Y.C., 1980-95; prin. Dumbarton Group, L.A., 1992—; Hightower lectr. Emory U. Bus. Sch., 1993; rsch. assoc. Nat. Bur. Econ. Rsch., Cambridge, Mass., 1994—. Author: (with Freeman and Jones) Social Problems: A Policy Perspective, 1979, (monograph) The Impact of Proposition 13 on Public Funding and Services for Education and Health in California, 1982, (with Meyer) Permanently Failing Orgniazation, 1989; editor: Institutional Patterns and Organizations: Cultures and Environments, 1988; mem. editl. bd. Am. Jour. Sociology, 1985-87, 95-97, Adminstrv. Sci. Quar., 1982-86, Am. Sociol. Rev., 1980-83, Pacific Sociol. Rev., 1977-83, Symbolic Interaction, 1986-91. Bd. dirs. Opera Assocs., L.A., 1994—. Regents faculty fellow U. Calif., 1976, fellow Calif. Coun. on Sci. and Tech., 2000—. Mem. Macro Orgnl. Behavior Soc., Am. Sociol. Assn. (co-chmn. com. on archives 1994—), Alpha Kappa. Delta. Episcopalian. Avocations: art, opera, hiking. Office: UCLA Dept Sociology Box 951441 Los Angeles CA 90095-1551 Fax: 310-454-2748.

ZUCKER, ROBERT A(LPERT), psychologist; b. N.Y.C., Dec. 9, 1935; s. Morris and Sophie (Alpert) Z.; m. Martine Latil; children: Lisa, Alex, Eleanor; m. Kristine Ellen Freeark, Mar. 10, 1979; 1 child, Katherine. B.C.E., CCNY, 1956; postgrad., UCLA, 1956-58; PhD, Harvard U., 1966. Diplomate Am. Bd. Profl. Psychology (clin.); lic. psychologist, Mich. From instr. to asst. prof. psychology Rutgers U., 1963-68; from asst. prof. to assoc. prof. to prof. Mich. State U., 1968-94; prof. psychology in psychiatry and psychology U. Mich., 1994—, dir. Addiction Rsch. Ctr., 1994—, dir. substance abuse sect. Dept. Psychiatry, 1994—, faculty assoc. RCGD Inst. for Social Rsch., 1996—. Vis. prof. U. Tex., Austin, 1975; vis. rsch. prof. psychology in psychiatry U. Mich., 1990-91; vis. scholar Nat. Inst. Alcohol Abuse and Alcoholism, 1980; dir. clin. tng. Mich. State U., 1982-94; lectr. Nebr. Symposium on Motivation, 1986; cons. in field. Co-author, editor: Further Explorations in Personality, 1981, Personality and the Prediction of Behavior, 1984, The Emergence of Personality, 1987, Studying Persons and Lives, 1990, Personality Structure in the Life Course, 1992, The Development of Alcohol Problems: Exploring the Biopsychosocial Matrix of Risk, 1994, Alcohol Problems Among Adolescents: Current Directions in Prevention Research, 1995, Alcohol Problems and Aging, 1998, Multiproblem Youth: Intervention and Treatment, 2004; contbr. chpts. and articles to profl. publs. Bd. dirs. Nat. Coun. on Alcoholism-Mich., 1978-82; mem. Psychosocial Initial Rev. Group, Nat. Inst. Alcohol Abuse and Alcoholism, 1989-92; mem. HPRB study sect. Ctr. for Sci. Rev., NIH, 1998-2000. Fellow Inst. Children Youth and Families, 1993, grantee NIH, 2003—; recipient Excellence in Clin. Rsch. award Blue Cross-Blue Shield Mich. Found., 1997. Fellow AAAS, APA (pres. addictions divsn. 50 1997-98), APS, Am. Orthopsychiat. Assn.; mem. Midwestern Psychol. Assn., Rsch. Soc. on Alcoholism (sec., bd. dirs. 2000-03). Office: Univ Mich Addiction Rsch Ctr 2025 Traverwood Dr Ste A Bldg 3 Ann Arbor MI 48105-3318 Office Phone: 734-998-7454. Business E-Mail: zuckerra@umich.edu.

ZUCKER, STEFAN, tenor, writer, editor, radio broadcaster; b. N.Y.C. BS, Columbia U., 1967; postgrad., NYU, 1967-72. Freelance tenor concerts and operas in U.S. and Europe, 1965—; philosophy lectr. Coll. Ins., 1972; tenor RCA Records, N.Y.C., 1972-77; guest singer radio and TV programs U.S. and

Europe, 1975—; radio producer, host WKCR-FM, N.Y.C., 1980-94; opera critic N.Y. Tribune, 1983-84; host web radio program Opera Fanatic www-.belcantosociety.org, 2002—. Lectr. The Mannes Coll. Music, 2000—. Author: The Origins of Modern Tenor Singing, 1997; appeared in film Opera Fanatic: Stefan and the Divas, 1998; record producer including Rossini's Rivals: Music By Then-Famous, Now-Obscure, Italian Composers, 1984; restorer films of opera singers, 1987—; singer, producer, stage dir., adminstr. various operas, 1967—; editor Opera Fanatic mag., 1986—; commentator and singer (TV series) Bel canto: Tenors of the 78 Era, 1996-97; contbr. articles to Internat. Dictionary of Opera, Opera News, The Opera Quar., Am. Record Guide, Opera Fanatic, Globe & Mail, News World, Professione Musica, others. Pres. Bel Canto Soc., Inc., 1985—. Named Worlds Highest Tenor by Guinness Book of World Records, 1979—; subject of record Stefan Zucker: The World's Highest Tenor, 1981. Mem. NYU Philosophy Assn. (pres. 1969-72, v.p. 1968), Music Critics Assn., Assn. Furtherment Bel Canto (pres. 1967-80). Office: Bel Canto Soc Inc 11 Riverside Dr New York NY 10023-2504

ZUCKER, WILLIAM, retired business educator; b. Bridgeport, Conn., July 21, 1917; s. Meyer and Ida Lena (Elovitz) Z.; m. Kathlyn Saltman, Jan. 16, 1944; children— Peter Bayard, Alison Beth, Jeremy Michael, David Laurence AB, Johns Hopkins U., 1938, AM, Harvard U., 1940, PhD, 1951. Sec. Commerce and Industry Assn. of N.Y., N.Y.C., 1944-59; v.p. Downtown Lower Manhattan Assn., N.Y.C., 1959-64; pres. Southeastern Pa. Econ. Devel. Corp., Phila., 1964-73; adj. prof. Wharton Sch. U. Pa., Phila., 1972-83, assoc. dir. Entrepreneurial Ctr., Wharton Sch., 1973-83, dir. exec. edn. Wharton Sch., 1977-83, dir. Wharton Real Estate Ctr., 1983-88, Meshulam Riklis prof. creative mgmt. Wharton Sch., 1983-88, prof. emeritus, 1988—; pres. Advisery Co., Phila., 1993-94. Lectr. CCNY, 1936-38; vis. prof. Columbia U. Grad. Sch. Bus., N.Y.C., 1988-91; adj. prof. Drexel U., PHila., 1997— Author: Local Development Corporations, 1980, REITS, 1975; editor Real Estate Fin. Jour., 1985-98; contbr. articles to profl. jours. Mem. New Canaan Bd. Edn., Conn., 1961-64, New Canaan Bd. Fin., 1958-61 Democrat. Jewish. Home: Cathedral Village 600 E Cathedral Rd Apt L105 Philadelphia PA 19128-1942 Office: U Pa 2000 Steinberg Dietrich Hal Philadelphia PA 19104

ZUCKER-FRANKLIN, DOROTHEA, internist, educator; b. Berlin, Aug. 9, 1930; came to U.S., 1949; d. Julian J. and Gertrude Zucker; m. Edward C. Franklin (dec.); 1 child, Deborah Julie. BA, CUNY, 1952, PhD in Sci. (hon.), 1996; MD, N.Y. Med. Coll., 1956 Diplomate Am. Bd. Medicine. Intern Phila. Gen. Hosp., 1956-57; resident in internal medicine Montefiore Hosp., N.Y.C., 1957-59, postdoctoral fellow in hematology, 1959-61; postdoctoral fellow in electron microscopy NYU Sch. Medicine, N.Y.C., 1961-63, asst. prof. medicine, 1963-67, assoc. prof., 1968-74, prof. medicine, 1974—; assoc. attending physician Bellevue Hosp., 1968-74, attending physician, 1974—. Assoc. attending physician Univ. Hosp., Tisch Hosp., 1968—74, attending physician, 1974—; cons. physician Manhattan VA Hosp., 1970—; meml. editl. bd. numerous publs., including Blood, 1963—76, 1980—86, Am. Jour. Pathology, 1979—, Ultrastructure Pathology, 1979—, Blood Cells, 1980, Am. Jour. Medicine, 1981—87, Hematology Oncology, 1982—, Jour. AIDS Rsch., 1987—, Hematopathology and Molecular Hematology, 1987—, others; meml. bd. reviewing editors Jour. Lab. and Clin. Medicine, 1990—; mem. hematology panel Health Rsch. Coun. City of N.Y., 1971—74; mem. pathology tng. com. Nat. Inst. Med. Scis., 1971—74; mem. allergy and immunology rsch. com. Nat. Inst. Allergy and Infectious Diseases, 1974—81; mem. U.S.-Israel Binat. Sci. Found., 1980—; mem. ad hoc promotion com. Harvard Med. Sch., 1981, 83; mem. blood products adv. com. FDA, 1981—86; mem. sci. adv. bd. and sci. rev. panel Israel Cancer Rsch. Found., 1982—90; mem. grant rev. panel VA AIDS Ctr., 1988—89; vis. fellow Assn. Claude Bernard, 1974—75. Co-author: The Physiology and Pathology of Leukocytes, 1962, Amyloidosis, 1986, Atlas of Blood Cells: Function and Pathology, 2 vols., 1981, 3d edit., 2003, Thrombopoiesis and Thrombopoietins: Molecular, Cellular, Preclinical and Clinical Biology, 1996; contbr. over 300 articles to profl. jours. Bd. dirs. Henry M. and Lillian Stratton Found., Inc., 1987-95. Named to Hall of Fame, Hunter Coll., 1977, Internat. Profl. and Bus. Women, 1994. Fellow: AAAS, N.Y. Acad. Scis.; mem.: NTLV and Related Viruses, Internat. Retrovirology Assn., N.Y. Soc. Study of Blood (chair program com. 1976—80, pres. 1981—82), N.Y. Soc. Electron Microscopists (program chair 1984, pres. 1984—85), Am. Soc. Cell Biology (program com. internat. congress 1976), Am. Soc. Exptl. Pathology, Am. Assn. Immunologists, Am. Acad. Arts and Scis., Reticuloendothelial Soc. (life; program com. 1974—76, nominating com. 1976—78, pres. 1984—85), Am. Soc. Physiology, Federated Socs. Exptl. Biology and Medicine, Am. Soc. Hematology (program com. 1973, edn. com. 1974—78, chair subcom. on leukocyte physiology 1977, chair subcom. on immunohematology 1984, com. on advanced learning resources 1986—, exec. coun. 1987—91, pres.-elect 1992, v.p. 1993, pres. 1994—95, chair adv. bd. 1996, com. on govt. affairs 2001), Am. Soc. Clin. Investigation, Am. Fedn. Clin. Rsch., Am. Assn. Physicians, Inst. Medicine NAS, Alpha Omega Alpha, Phi Beta Kappa. Office: NYU Med Ctr 550 1st Ave New York NY 10016-6402 Office Phone: 212-263-5634. E-mail: dorothea.zucker-franklin@med.nyu.edu.

ZUCKERKANDL, EMILE, molecular evolutionary biologist, scientific institute executive; b. Vienna, July 4, 1922; came to U.S., 1975; s. Frederic and Gertrude (Stekel) Z.; m. Jane Gammon Metz, June 2,1950 MS, U. Ill., 1947; PhD, Sorbonne, Paris, 1959. Postdoctoral rsch. fellow Calif. Inst. Tech., Pasadena, 1959-64; rsch. dir. CNRS, Montpellier, France, 1967-80, dir. Ctr. Macromolecular Biochemistry, 1965-75; pres. Linus Pauling Inst., Palo Alto, Calif., 1980-92, Inst. Molecular Med. Scis., Palo Alto, Calif., 1992—. Cons. in genetics Stanford U., 1963, vis. prof., 1964; vis. prof. U. Del., 1976 Contbg. author: Horizons in Biochemistry, 1962, Evolving Genes and Proteins, 1965; co-author: Genetique des Populations, 1976; editor Jour. Molecular Evolution, 1971-2000. Decorated Hon. Cross for Sci. and Art (Austria), Order of Merit (France). Fellow AAAS; mem. Societe de Chimie Biologique, Internat. Soc. Study Origin of Life, Internat. Soc. Molecular Evolution. Home: 565 Arastradero Rd Ph A Palo Alto CA 94306-4323 Office: Inst Molecular Med Scis PO Box 20452 Stanford CA 94309-0452

ZUCKERMAN, BARRY, medical educator; Prof., chmn. dept. pediatrics Boston U. Sch. Medicine. Mem. Nat. Commn. on Children, Carnegie Commn. on Mtg. the Needs of Young Children.; bd. dirs. Zero to Three, Nat. Ctr. for Clin. Infant Programs, Nat. Ctr. Children in Poverty. Recipient Nat. Leadership Award Children's Def. Fund, 1994. Office: Boston University 850 Harrison Ave Boston MA 02118-4001

ZUCKERMAN, BRIAN D. lawyer; m. Jennifer Zuckerman; children: Jake, Mason. BA, SUNY, Binghampton, N.Y., 1991; JD, Temple U., 1994. Assoc. Klehr, Harrison, Harvey, Branzburg & Ellers, Phila., 1994—97; atty. Pepper Hamilton, Phila., 1997—99, Pep Boys, Phila., 1999—. Office: The Pep Boys 3111 W Allegheny Ave Philadelphia PA 19132*

ZUCKERMAN, HARRIET, sociologist, educator; b. N.Y.C., July 19, 1937; d. Harry and Anne D. (Wiener) Z; m. Robert K. Merton, 1993. AB, Vassar Coll., 1958; PhD, Columbia U., 1965. Asst. prof. sociology Columbia U., 1965-72, assoc. prof., 1972-78, prof., 1978-92; prof. emerita, 1993—; sr. rsch. scholar, 1993—; chmn. dept. Columbia U., 1978-81; v.p. Andrew W. Mellon Found., 1991-98, sr. v.p., 1998—. Vis. scholar Russell Sage Found., 1971-72, 85-87; mem. adv. bd. Social Sci. Citation Index, Inst. Sci. Information, 1972-98; dir. Annual Revs., Inc., 1974-; trustee Am. Savs. Bank, 1978-83 Author: Scientific Elite: Nobel Laureates in the United States, 1977, rev. edit., 1996; co-editor: Toward A Metric of Science: The Advent of Science Indictors, 1978, The Outer Circle: Women in the Scientific Community, 1991; mem. editorial bd. Scientometrics, 1977-, Am. Jour. Sociology, 1972-74, 77-79, Am. Sociol. Rev, 1972-74, 87-91, Sci., 1985-86; contbr. articles to profl. jours. Bd. dirs. Social Sci. Rsch. Coun., 1974-76, AAAS, 1980-84, Women's Forum, 1989-91; trustee Ctr. for Advanced Study in Behavioral Scis., 1976-88, 89-2001, 03—; mem. ednl. adv. bd. John Simon Guggenheim Meml. Found., 1986-93, mem. com. on selection, 1989-91. Woodrow Wilson fellow, 1958-59; Ctr. for Advanced Study in Behavioral Scis. fellow, 1973-74; Guggenheim fellow, 1980-81; Phi Beta Kappa vis. scholar, 1982-83; recipient Dean's award for Disting. Achievement Columbia U. Grad. Sch., 1998. Mem. Am. Philos. Soc. (councillor 1997-03, chmn. Class III membership com. 2002—), Am. Acad. Arts and Scis. (chmn. class III membership com. 1991-94), Soc. Social Studies Sci. (pres. 1989-91), The Century Assn., Coun. on Fgn. Rels.

ZUCKERMAN, HERBERT LAWRENCE, lawyer; b. Newark, June 11, 1928; s. David and Adele Zuckerman; m. Janet Albert, Sept. 10, 1950; children: Julia, Elizabeth, William. BSBA, Lehigh U., 1949; JD, Rutgers U., 1953. Acct. Zuckerman & Black, Newark, 1949-56; pvt. practice law Newark, 1956-71; ptnr. Zuckerman, Aronson & Horn, Newark, 1971-81; ptnr., v.p. Sills Cummis, Newark, 1981-98, sr.counsel, 1998—. Bd. dirs. Am. Jewish Com., 1990—; vol. The Hospice, Glen Ridge, N.J., 1985-93. Fellow Coll. of Tax Counsel; mem. ABA, N.J. Bar Assn., Fed. Bar Assn., Essex County Bar Assn., Mental Health Assn. (bd. dirs. 1997-99), Mensa. Avocations: tennis, music, theater, opera, reading. Office: Sills Cummis 1 Riverfront Plz 13th Fl Newark NJ 07102-5400 Office Phone: 973-643-7000. E-mail: hzuckerman@sillscummis.com.

ZUCKERMAN, MARC ABRAHAM, accountant, educator; b. N.Y.C., May 30, 1951; s. Henry and Rela (Ast) Z.; m. Sue Carol Kezurer, Dec. 6, 1981; 1 child, Sam David. BA cum laude, CUNY, Bronx, 1973; MA, Columbia U., 1974; MBA, Manhattan Coll., 1984. Cert. mgmt. acct., cash mgr., credit executive. Dir. corp. credit Clinton Swan Clothes, N.Y.C., 1978-80; dir. fin. Lord Jeff, Norwood, N.J., 1980-88; dir. corp. credit Bernard Chaus, Inc., Secaucus, N.J., 1988-89; asst. treas. Warnaco, Bridgeport, Conn., 1989; treas. Bernard Chaus, Inc., Secaucus, 1989-95; corp. contr. Precision Custom Coatings, Totowa, N.J., 1996-99; v.p. ops., CFO Triboro Quilt Mfg. Corp., 1999—. Pres. Meadowlands Fin. Group, 1991-95; adj. prof. fin. Contbr. articles to profl. jours. Pack com. mem. Ridgewood Boy Scouts Am., 1997-2000, treas. 1997-2000. Mem. Inst. Mgmt. Accts., Treas. Mgmt. Assn., Treas. Mgmt. Assn. N.J., Nat. Assn. Credit Mgmt., N.J. Corp. Treas. Mgmt. Assn. (treas. 1996—), Nat. Apparel Mfrs. Credit Assn. (bd. dirs. 1993-95), Bergen Rockland Inst. Mgmt. Accts. (bd. dirs. 1996-97). Avocations: jogging, golf. Home: 153 Lincoln Ave Ridgewood NJ 07450-4105 Office: Triboro Quilt Mfg Corp 172 South Broadway White Plains NY 10605

ZUCKERMAN, MARVIN, psychologist; b. Chgo., Mar. 21, 1928; s. Eli and Sophia (Pilder) Z.; children: April B. Zuckerman Schanoes, Steven H. BA, NYU, 1949, PhD, 1954. Rsch. assoc. Inst. Psychiat. Rsch., Ind. U. Med. Ctr., 1956-59; asst. prof. psychology Bklyn. Coll., 1959-62; rsch. assoc. Albert Einstein Med. Ctr., Phila., 1963-69; prof. psychology U. Del., Newark, 1969—2002, prof. emeritus, 2002—. Author: (with C.D. Spielberger) Emotions and Anxiety, 1976, Sensation Seeking: Beyond the Optimal Level of Arousal, 1979, Biological Bases of Sensation Seeking, Impulsivity and Anxiety, 1983, Psychobiology of Personality, 1991, Behavioral Expressions and Biosocial Bases of Sensation Seeking, 1994, Vulnerability to Psychopathology, 1999. Fellow APA, Am. Psychol. Soc.; mem. Internat. Soc. Study Individual Differences (past pres.). Home: 1500 Locust St Apt 4013 Philadelphia PA 19102-4326 Business E-Mail: zuckerma@udel.edu.

ZUCKERMAN, MORTIMER BENJAMIN, publisher, editor, real estate developer; b. Montreal, June 4, 1937; arrived in U.S., 1961, naturalized, 1977; s. Abraham and Esther Zuckerman. BA in Econs. and Polit. Theory with 1st class honors, McGill U., Montreal, 1957, LLB with honors, 1961; MBA with distinction, U. Pa., 1962; LLM, Harvard U., 1962. Sr. v.p. Cabot, Cabot & Forbes, Boston, 1965—69; chmn. bd. Boston Properties Co., 1970—; pres., chmn. bd. Atlantic Monthly Co., Boston, 1980—; chmn., editor-in-chief US News & World Report, 1984—; chmn., co-pub. NY Daily News, 1993—. Dir., mem. exec. com. Stride Rite Corp., 1970—83; dir. Property Capital Trust Co., 1979—80, RET Income Found., 1976—79; pub. interest dir. Fed Home Loan Bank of Boston, 1972—73; lectr., then assoc. prof. Harvard U. Grad. Sch. Design, 1966—74; vis. lectr. city and regional planning Yale U., 1967—69. Mem. Coun. on Fgn. Rels.; founder Zuckerman Fellowships Harvard U., 2004—; pres. bd. trustees Sidney Farber Cancer Inst., Boston, 1980; trustee Mus. Sci., 1980, Beth Israel Hosp., 1975, Ford Hall Forum, 1979—83, Urban Inst., Russell Sage Found., 1985—86; chmn. bd. visitors Boston U. Sch. Medicine, 1978—79; adv. bd. Ctr. Strategic and Internat. Studies, Wharton Sch.; bd. dirs. Wolf Trap Found., Tennis Hall of Fame. Mem.: Internat. Inst. Strategic Studies, Harmonie (N.Y.C.), Harvard Club (Boston and N.Y.C.). Office: New York Daily News 450 W 33rd St Fl 3 New York NY 10001-2681 also: US News & World Report 1050 Thomas Jefferson St NW Washington DC 20007-3817 Address: Boston Properties 599 Lexington Ave Rm 1800 New York NY 10022-6030*

ZUCKERMAN, NANCY CAROL, learning disabilities specialist, consultant; b. Jersey City, Aug. 14, 1951; d. Bernard Milton and Shirley (Stepner) Solomon; m. Marshall Howard Zuckerman, Aug. 20, 1978; 1 child, Seth Michael. BA, Rider U., 1973; MEd, William Paterson Coll., 1977. Cert. elem. tchr., spl. edn. and learning disabilities tchr., prin., N.J. Tchr. elem. edn. North Bergen (N.J.) Bd. Edn., 1973-76; tchr. state compensatory edn. Bayonne (N.J.) Bd. Edn., 1977, tchr. cons. learning disabilities, 1977—. Chairperson Child Study Team, Bayonne, 1988-99. Mem. adv. bd., sec., asst. pack leader Cub Scouts Pack 35, Bayonne, 1996-2000, com. chair Troop 35, 2002—; bd. dirs. Temple Beth Am, Bayonne, 1975-79, 97—, edn. chmn., 1975-79. Mem. CEC, Assn. Learning Consultants, Pi Lambda Theta. Jewish. Home: 21 E 35th St Bayonne NJ 07002-3924 Office: Bayonne Bd Edn Bayonne NJ 07002 E-mail: N@LDTC@aol.com.

ZUCKERMAN, PAUL HERBERT, lawyer; b. Bklyn., Mar. 7, 1935; s. Max B. and Minnie (Mendelson) Z.; m. Sara Shiffman, Aug. 25, 1963; children: David Isaac, Daniel Mark. BS in Econs., Wharton Sch., U. Pa., 1957; MBA in Corp. Fin., NYU, 1964; JD, Bklyn. Law Sch., 1967. Bar: N.Y. 1968, U.S. Dist. Ct. (so. and ea. dists.) N.Y. 1975, U.S. Tax Ct. 1977, U.S. Ct. Appeals (2d cir.) 1972, U.S. Supreme Ct. 1973. Security analyst U.S. Trust Co., N.Y.C., 1962-66; sr. security analyst CNA Mgmt. Rsch. Corp., N.Y.C., 1966-71, mgr. dept. investment rsch., 1971-73; sole practice N.Y.C., 1973—. Speaker and writer in field; radio, TV appearances. Hon. trustee Sutton Place Synagogue. Served to lt. (j.g.) USN, 1957—60. Mem. Assn. Bar City N.Y., Wharton Bus. Sch. (N.Y.C.). Office: 8th Fl 226 W 26th St New York NY 10001-6785 Office Phone: 212-367-1900. E-mail: EstatesWillsTrus@cs.com.

ZUCKERMAN, RICHARD ENGLE, lawyer, law educator; b. Yonkers, N.Y., Aug. 2, 1945; s. Julius and Roslyn (Ehrlich) Z.; m. Denise Ellen Spoon, July 14, 1968; children: Julie Ann, Lindsay Beth. BA, U. Mich., 1967; JD cum laude, Southwestern U., 1974. Bar: Calif. 1974, Mich. 1976, Nev. 1986, U.S. Dist. Ct. (ea. and we. dists.) Mich. 1977, U.S. Ct. Appeals (6th cir.) 1977, U.S. Ct. Appeals (9th cir.) 1982, U.S. Ct. Appeals (2d and 7th cirs.) 1994, U.S. Tax Ct. 1980, U. S. Supreme Ct. 1985, U.S. Ct. Appeals (4th cir.) 2001. Spl. atty. organized crime and racketeering sect. U.S. Dept. Justice, Detroit, 1974-77; sr. ptnr. Raymond, Rupp, Wienberg, Stone & Zuckerman, P.C., Troy, Mich., 1977-87, Honigman, Miller, Schwartz & Cohn, Detroit, 1987—, chair litigation dept., 1996—2002, also bd. dirs., 1999—2003. Adj. prof. Detroit Coll. Law, 1978—98, 2004—; mem. Mich. Atty. Grievance Commn. (Mich. Supreme Ct. appointee), 1995—2001, vice chair, 1999—2000, chair, 2000—01. Served to lt. USN, 1967-71, Vietnam. Mem. ABA (grand jury com. criminal justice sect.), Fed. Bar Assn. (chmn. criminal law sect. Detroit chpt. 1985-90, bd. dirs. 1985-94, co-chair criminal def. com. 1990-95), Knollwood Country Club (West Bloomfield, Mich.), Std. Club, Am. Inns Ct. (master of bench 1995-97), Tam O'Shanter Country Club. Republican. Jewish. Office: Honigman Miller Schwartz & Cohn 2290 First National Bldg Detroit MI 48226 E-mail: rez@honigman.com.

ZUCKERMAN, SIDNEY, retired allergist, immunologist; b. N.Y.C., May 2, 1918; s. Max and Rose (Katz) Z.; m. Irene Elinor Cohen, Oct. 27, 1945; children: Elaine, Laurie, Jed, Amy. BA, Columbia Coll., 1939; MD, N.Y. Med. Coll., 1943. Diplomate Am. Bd. Internal Medicine, Am. Bd. Allergy and Immunology. Chief medicine 172 Sta. Hosp. US Army Med. Corps., Sendai, Japan, 1945-47; med. dir. Ford Instrument Co. divsn. Sperry Corp., N.Y.C., 1947-60; pvt. practice N.Y.C., 1947-91; med. dir. Unysis Corp., Great Neck, NY, 1960-90. Capt. U.S. Army Med. Corps., 1945-47, Japan. Fellow ACP, Am. Coll. Allergy, Asthma and Immunology, Am. Acad. Allergy, Asthma and Immunology, Am. Coll. Occupational and Environ. Medicine, Am. Assn. Cert. Allergists; mem. Masons (jr. warden), Soc. Columbia Grads. Avocations: woodworking, golf. Home: 4140 Bocaire Blvd Boca Raton FL 33487-1148

ZUCKERMAN, STUART, psychiatrist, forensic examiner, educator; b. Syracuse, N.Y., Feb. 18, 1933; s. George and Cassie Zuckerman. Student, U. Kans., 1950—51; BS, U. Ala., 1954; DO, Phila. Coll. Osteo. Medicine, 1958. Diplomate Am. Osteo. Bd. Neurology and Psychiatry, Am. Nat. Bd. Psychiatry, Am. Coll. Forensic Medicine, Bd. Forensic Medicine, Bd. Forensic Examiner; cert. correctional health profl. Rotating intern Hosps. Phila. Coll. Osteo. Medicine, 1958-59; psychiat. fellow, resident Phila. Mental Health Clinic, 1959-62, Psychoanalytic Studies Inst., Phila., 1959-62, chief resident, 1962; chief divsn. neuropsychiatry Grandview Hosp., Dayton, Ohio, 1962-65; asst. med. dir., chief children's and adolescent's unit NJ State Hosp., Ancora, 1967-70; chief outpatient dept. Atlantic City, 1970-72; practice specializing in neuropsychiatry Atlantic City, 1965—98; founding prof. psychiatry, chmn. dept. Ohio U. Coll. Osteo. Medicine, Athens, 1976-77, clin. prof., 1977; mem. faculty U. Pa. Sch. Medicine, Phila. Coll. Osteo. Medicine, 1972-76, with Benjamin Franklin scholar spl. studies faculty; lectr. U. Pa., 1977-79; prof. dept. psychiatry, charter faculty Sch. Medicine, Marshall U., 1977-78, clin. prof., 1979-80, NY Coll. Osteo. Medicine, 1979—96; chief mental hygiene VA Hosp., Huntington, W.Va., 1978-79; liaison psychiatrist, acting chief VA Med. Ctr., Perry Point, Md., 1979-80; med. dir. Mental Health Clinic of Ocean County, Toms River, NJ, 1980-85, Ventnor (NJ) Mental Health Ctr.; chief psychiatrist NJ Dept. Corrections So. State Correctional Facility, 1985-96 Physician Atlantic City Beach Patrol, 1961-63; attending psychiatrist Atlantic City, Shore Meml., Kessler Meml., Washington Meml., Atlantic County Mental hosps., 1965-76; attending psychiatrist, asst. dir. dept. psychiatry Phila. Gen. Hosp., 1972-76; med. dir. Shawnee Mental Health Center, (Adams, Lawrence, Scioto counties), Portsmouth, Ohio, 1977-78; cons. psychiatrist Athens Mental Health and Mental Retardation Ctr., 1976-77, Scioto Meml. Hosp., So. Hills Hosp., Mercy Hosp., Portsmouth, 1977-78, Lansdowne Cmty. Mental Health Center, (Greenup, Carter counties), Ashland, Ky., 1977-78, Atlantic City Med. Ctr., 1984-97, Cmty. Meml. Hosp., Toms River, NJ, 1984-91, So. Ocean County Hosp., Manahawkin, NJ, 1984-91, Paul-Kimball Med Ctr., Lakewood, NJ, 1984-97, Obleness Meml. Hosp., Clin. Svcs. of Athens, Vinton, Hocking Counties, Hudson Health Ctr., Ohio U., 1976-77; cons. Bayside State Prison, Leesburg, NJ, 1989-96, Atlantic County Justice System, Mays Landing, NJ, 1992-93; cons. child study spl. svcs. South Jersey Sch. Systems; chmn. profl. adv. com. Atlantic County Mental Health Bd., 1969-71; mem. nominating com. Mental Health Assn., Atlantic County, 1972-75; exam. psychiatrist Jersey Police and Fire Depts.; mem. profl. adv. com. NJ Dept. Corrections; cons. NJ Dept. Pub. Adv.; mem. splty. adv. panel NJ State Bd. Med. Examiners, 1998-2000. Mem. adv. bd. Osteo. Physician, 1975-98; assoc. editor Bull. Am. Coll. Neuropsychiatrists, 1963-70, Jour. Corr. Health Editl. Bd.; contbr. articles to profl. jours. Bd. dir. Atlantic County Family Svcs. Assn., 1968-74, Cape May County Drug Abuse Coun., 1973-76, Nat. Comm. Correctional Health Care, 1988-97; mem. Ventnor City Beautification Com., 1996—; sponsor, house physician Friends of the Pops Ocean City (N.J.) Music Pier. Fellow Am. Coll. Forensic Psychiatry, Am. Coll. Neuropsychiatrists (bd. reps.), Am. Acad. Disability Evaluating Physicians (charter), Acad. Psychosomatic Medicine, Acad. Medicine NJ, Coll. Physicians of Phila.; mem. AMA (Physicians Recognition award 1985-2000), AAUP, Am. Bd. Forensic Examiners (cert. 1994), Am. Coll. Forensic Medicine (bd. cert. 1996), World Psychiat. Assn., Am. Psychiat. Assn., NJ (confidentiality, pub. psychiatry com., gen. hosp. psychiatry com., law com., mkgt. benefits com.) Psychiat. Assn., Am. Assn. Psychiatrists in Alcohol and Addictions (founder), APHA, NJ Pub. Health Assn., Am. Osteo. Assn. (hosp. inspection team 1971-75, bd. reps.), Am. Assn. CMHC Psychiatrists, Am. Assn. Psychiatrists in Pvt. Practice, Internat. Assn. Med. Specialists, Am. Soc. Law and Medicine, Am. Acad. Clin. Psychiatrists, Corp. Advancement Psychiatry, Am. Med. Writers Assn., Nat. Coun. Cmty. Mental Health Ctrs., Nat. Alliance Mentally Ill (profl. assoc. mem.), Met. Coll. Mental Health Assn., Am. Soc. Criminology., South Jersey Neuropsychiat. Soc., Psychiat. Outpatients Ctrs. Am., Am. Coll. Legal Medicine, Acad. Psychiatry and Law (pub. info. com., edn. com., internat. affairs com.), Am. Acad. Forensic Scis., Am. Assn. Acad. Psychiatry, Am. Coll. Emergency Physicians (charter mem.), Am. Acad. Psychotherapists, Am. Assn. Mental Deficiency, Am. Assn. Psychiat. Services for Children, NJ (chmn. com. on confidentiality, liaison com. health human svcs., corrections), Fla. assns. osteo. physicians and surgeons, NJ Hosp. Assn., Am. Vocat. Assn., Am. Assn. Group Therapy, Am. Soc. Clin. Psychopharmacology, Assn. Mil. Surgeons U.S. (v.p. ret.), Nat. Assn. VA Physicians pres. 1978-79), Am. Assn. Psychiat. Adminstrs., Am. Assn. Adolescent Psychiatry, World Med. Assn., Am. Assn. Mental Health Adminstrs., Am. Assn. Gen. Hosp. Psychiatrists, Human Factors Soc., Orthopsychiat. Assn., Am. Physicians Fellowship, Assn. for Rsch. Nervous and Mental Diseases, Atlantic County Osteo. Med. Soc. (pres. 1970-72), NJ Assn. Mil. Surgeons U.S. (v.p.), Am. Assn. Correctional Health Care, Am. Coll. Forensic Psychiatry (diplomate 1984), Soc. of Correctional Physicians (charter). Home: # 502 700 Ocean Royale Way Juno Beach FL 33408 Office Phone: 561-848-2222.

ZUCKMAN, HARVEY LYLE, law educator; b. Mpls., Apr. 14, 1934; s. George and Elizabeth (Polinsky) Z.; m. Charlotte Anne Snyder, Jan. 27, 1962; children: Jill Belinda, Beth Nancy, Michael Scott. AB, U. So. Calif., 1956; LL.B., NYU, 1959. Bar: Calif. 1960, D.C. 1973, U.S. Supreme Ct. 1963. Atty. civil div. appellate sect. U.S. Dept. Justice, Washington, 1963-67; prof. law St. Louis U., 1967-70, Columbus Sch. Law of Cath. U. Am., 1970—; dir. Inst. for Communications Law Studies Columbus Sch. Law, Cath. U. Am., 1981-01; adj. prof. communications Am. U., 1976-81. Cons. Bur. Nat. Affairs., 1974-81 Producer: Am. Law Inst.-ABA Legal Edn. TV series, 1973-74; co-author: Mass Communications Law, 1977, 5th edit., 2000, Modern Communication Law, 3 vols., 1999; editor ABA newsletter Comm. Lawyer, 1981-86. Served with U.S. Army Judge Adv. Gen., 1960-63. Mem. ABA (forum com. on comm. law, co-chmn. nat. celebration of 200th anniversary of 1st amendment 1991), D.C. Bar chairperson com. on continuing legal edn. 1975-83), Fed. Comm. Bar Assn., Am. Law Inst. (life), Assn. Am. Law Schs. (sects. family law and mass comm.), Cosmos Club. Democrat. Office: Cath U Am Columbus Sch Law 3600 John Mccormick Rd NE Washington DC 20064-0001 Fax: 202-319-4459. E-mail: zuckman@law.edu.

ZUEHLKE, RICHARD WILLIAM, technical communications consultant, writer; b. Milw., June 17, 1933; s. Harold Babcock and Phoebe Blanche (Frykman) Z.; m. Carol Sue Yates, Dec. 26, 1955; children: Kenneth Richard, William Woodfill, Deanne Elizabeth. BS, Lawrence Coll., 1955; PhD, U. Minn., 1960. Instr. chemistry Lawrence U., 1958-62, asst. prof., 1962-68; Eliphalet Remington prof. chemistry U. Bridgeport, 1968-79, chmn. dept., 1968-73; vis. prof. U. R.I., 1976-77, 79-80, assoc. marine scientist, 1980-85; owner, pres. The Right Connection, Inc., 1983-91; pres. TetraR Cons., Inc., 1985-88. Cons. Kimberly-Clark Corp., 1960-62, United Illuminating Co., 1969-75, Chem. Specialties Corp., 1970-73, Sperry Remington Corp., 1976-79; NSF Sci. Faculty fellow U. Pitts., 1966-67; asst. to dir. Gordon Rsch. Confs., 1990-94; cons., writer in field. Fellow Am. Inst. Chemists; mem. Am. Chem. Soc., AAAS, Rotary, Sigma Xi, Sigma Phi Epsilon. Congregationalist. Home: PO Box 52 Wilmot NH 03287-0052 Office: PO Box 784 New London NH 03257-0784 E-mail: rzuehlke@tds.net.

ZUERLEIN, DAMIAN JOSEPH, priest; b. Norfolk, Nebr., May 28, 1955; s. Victor Damian and Elizabeth P. (Wegener) Z. BA, U. St. Thomas, St. Paul, 1977; MDiv, St. Paul Sem., 1981. Ordained priest Roman Cath. Ch., 1981. Tchr. Norfolk Cath. HS, 1981—85; asst. pastor Sacred Heart/St. Mary's Parish, Norfolk, 1981—85; assoc. pastor St. Pius X Cath. Ch., Omaha, 1985-88, Mary Our Queen Cath. Ch., Omaha, 1988-90; pastor Our Lady of Guadalupe Parish, Omaha, 1990—2004, St. Agnes Parish, Omaha, 1997—2004, St. Francis of Assisi Parish, Omaha, 2002—03, St. Columbkille Parish, Papillion, Nebr., 2004—. Cons. Archdiocesan Vocations Office, Omaha, 1985-95; chmn., co-founder Omaha Together One Cmty., 1991-95; co-founder Weaving, Women's Advocacy Group, Omaha, 1988—. Presenter (video) Loving Your Marriage, 1990, El Matrimonio: Una Jornada Para Todo Una Vida, 1995; co-author: (manual) Hispanic Pastoral Plan, 1991. Bd. dirs. United Cath. Social Svcs., Omaha, 1990-96, Chicano Awareness Ctr., Omaha,

1991-98, Omaha Food Bank, 2000—, Vis. Nurse Assn., 1996-2000, Omaha 100 Inc., 1991-96, chair, 1991-93; advisor Mayor P.J. Morgan, Omaha, 1991-95; active Gov. Nelson's Urban Adv. Task Force, 1994, Domestic Violence Coord. Coun. Gtr. Omaha, 1996—, Nat. Campaign for Human Devel. Adv. Bd., 1997-2000, Nebr. Gov.'s Task Force on Immigration, 1999-2000; founder, dir. Guadalupe-Ines Mission Sch., 1998-2004; pres. Omaha Presbyn. Coun., 2003-; del. Omaha City Charter Review Conv., 2003; pres. Greater Omaha Clergy Assn., 1987-88; bd. dirs. South Omaha Neighborhood Assn., 1992, pres. 1994-98. Mem. Pax Cristi, Amnesty Internat., Fontenelle Forest Assn. Avocations: canoeing the bwca, skiing, travel, hiking. Home and Office: 200 E 6 St Papillion NE 68046 Office Phone: 402-339-3285. Personal E-mail: damzuer@aol.com.

ZUFRYDEN, FRED S. academic administrator, marketing educator, researcher; b. Grenoble, France, June 13, 1943; came to U.S., 1956; s. Henri and Cecile (Frymer) Z.; m. Toby Marlene Levin, Dec. 24, 1967; 1 child, Ryan BA in Math., UCLA, 1965, MBA, 1966, PhD in Bus. Adminstrn., 1971. Rsch. engr. mil. ops. and systems analysis group N.Am. Aviation, Inc., L.A., 1966-67; rsch. assoc. resources rsch. dept. Planning Rsch. Corp., L.A., 1967-68; ops. rsch. specialist data systems div. Litton Systems, Inc., L.A., 1968-70; asst. prof. dept. mgmt. scis. Sch. Bus. and Econs., U. Calif., Northridge, 1970-71; asst. prof. dept. mktg. Grad. Sch. Bus. U. So. Calif., L.A., 1971-75, assoc. prof., 1975-82, prof., 1982—, Ernst Hahn prof. mktg., 1991—, chmn. mktg. dept., 1987-90, rsch. dir. internat. bus. econs. and rsch. Grad. Sch. Bus., 1983—. Mem. editorial bd. Jour. Advt. Rsch., 1981—, Mktg. Sci., 1979—, Jour. Mktg., 1978—; mem. cons. and planning com. Mktg. Sci. Jour., 1979; referee Jour. Mktg. Rsch., Mgmt. Sci., Decision Sci., Jour. Internat. Rsch. in Mktg.; mem. abstract writing staff International Abstracts in Operations Rsch./Mgmt. Sci., 1973; contbr. articles to profl. jours. including Jour. Mktg. Rsch., Mktg. Sci., Jour. Operational Rsch. Soc., Mgmt. Sci., Decision Scis., Jour. Mktg., Jour. Advt. Rsch., Jour. Internat. Rsch. in Mktg., Jour. Royal Statis. Soc., Interfaces, Rsch. in Mktg., Jour. of Mktg. Rsch. Soc., Jour. of Bus., others Rsch. grantee U. So. Calif., 1973, 75, 76, 77, 78, A.C. Nielsen Co., 1988-90. Mem. Am. Mktg. Assn. (cert. recognition 1974), Ops. Rsch. Soc. Am., Inst. Mgmt. Sci., Omega Rho, Beta Gamma Sigma

ZUG, ELIZABETH E. concert pianist, educator; b. Phila., Oct. 8, 1907; d. Nathan Walter and Amelia Elizabeth (Nelson) Zug. BA in Music, Irving Coll., 1928. Mem. faculty Nat. Guild Piano Tchrs., 1949. Judge piano auditions Yr. in Music, Nat. Guild Piano Tchrs., 1949. Debut N.Y. Town Hall, 1938; concert pianist, S.Am. tour, 1941. Named Outstanding N.Y. Debut as Pianist, 1938, Judge of the Yr. Nat. Guild Piano Tchrs., 1949. Mem. Music Tchrs. Nat. Assn., Pa. Music Tchrs. Assn. United Ch. Christ. Avocations: writing, designing, landscaping. Studio: 12 N 4th St Reading PA 19601-3910

ZUGAZAGOITIA, JULIAN, museum director; b. Mexico City; Grad., l'Ecole du Louvre; PhD in Aesthetics, Sorbonne, Paris. Cons., spl. advisor to dir. Getty Conservation Inst., L.A.; dir. visual arts Spoleto Festival, Italy, 1997—99; asst. to the dir. Guggenheim Mus., N.Y.C., 1999—2002; exec. dir. El Museo del Barno, N.Y.C., 2002—. Office: El Museo del Barrio 1230 Fifth Ave New York NY 10029*

ZUGGER, THOMAS W. music educator, musician; b. Buffalo, N.Y., Feb. 8, 1964; s. Virginia and Eugene Zugger. MusB in Edn., U. Mich., 1988; MusM in Trombone Performance, Mich. State U., 1993; MusD in Trombone Performance, Ohio State U., 1998. Prin. trombone Adrian Symphony Orch., Mich., 1989—94; asst. prof. of music Adrian Coll., Mich., 1990—92; asst. band dir. Walled Lake Pub. Schs., Mich., 1993—95; grad. tchg. assoc. Ohio State U., Columbus, 1995—98; asst. prof. music Capital U., Columbus, Ohio, 1998—, Mt. Vernon Nazarene U., Ohio, 1998—2001. Substitute trombonist with orchestras including Richmond, Ind. Symphony, W.Va. Symphony, Columbus, Ohio Symphony, Pro Musica Chamber Orch., 1999—. Composer (9 published compositions 6 arrangements). Music scholarship, Mich. State U., 1991-1993, Grad. Tchg. fellowship, Ohio State U., 1995-1998, Grad. Rsch. fellowship, 1998. Mem.: Ohio Music Educators Assn. (assoc.), Music Educators Nat. Conf. (assoc.), Am. Music Soc. (assoc.), Internat. Trombone Assn. (assoc.; bd. dirs. Press 2003—), Phi Kappa Phi. Dfl. Avocations: marathon running, travel, photography, philosophy. Home: 5728 Blendonbrook Ln Gahanna OH 43230 Office: Capital Univ Conservatory of Music 2199 E Main St Columbus OH 43209 Office Phone: 614-236-6274. Business E-Mail: tzugger@capital.edu.

ZUGIBE, FREDERICK THOMAS, retired pathologist; b. Garnerville, N.Y., May 28, 1928; s. Benjamin and Anna (Zarick) Z.; m. Catherine Frances O'Leary, Apr. 7, 1951; children: Frederick T., Thomas P., Cathryn T. Blaber, Theresa A. Mandracchia, Mary E. Raleigh, Matthew M., Kevin J. BS, St. Francis Coll., 1951; MS, U. Chgo., 1959, PhD, 1960; MD, W.Va. U., 1968. Diplomate Am. Bd. Pathology-Anatomic, Am. Bd. Pathology-Forensic, Am. Bd. Family Practice. Rsch. histologist Lederle Labs., Pearl River, N.Y., 1950-52, rsch. chemist, 1953-55; rsch. assoc. ophthalmic rsch. Columbia U., N.Y.C., 1955-56; dir. cardiovascular rsch. U.S. VA, Pitts., 1960—65; chief med. examiner County of Rockland, Pomona, NY, 1969—2003. Adj. assoc. prof. pathology Columbia U., 1972—; bd. dirs. Hudson Techs. Inc., Hillburn, N.Y., Rockland Westchester Found. for Sudden Infant Death, White Plains, N.Y.; med. dir. Rockland County Emergency Med. Svcs. N.Y.S. Dept. Health, Pomona, 1990-2003; supervising med. officer disaster med. assistance team Nat. Disaster Med. Assistance, Pomona, 1992-2003; expert on crucifixion and Shroud of Turin. Author: Eat, Drink and Lower Your Cholesterol, 1964, Diagnostic Histochemistry, 1970, The Cross and Shroud: A Medical Inquiry into Crucifixion, 1988, 14 Days to a Healthy Heart, 1986; contbr. numerous articles to profl. jours. and chpts. to books; appeared in TV documentaries on Discovery Channel, History Channel, Learning Channel, In Search Of, Nat. Geographic, CNN, CBC, others. Named Knight by His Royal Highness Dom Duarte Pio, Duke of Braganca, Head of Royal House Portugal, 2002, Dr. Frederick T. Zugibe Forensic Unit (formerly Rockland County Med. Examiner's Office), legis. action, 2003; named one of 25 people in Rockland County, N.Y. who most influenced this region in the 20th century; recipient Disting. Citizens award, Assn. Visually Impaired, 1998, Physician Recognition awards, more than 68 law enforcement, govtl. and med. awards, 1971—, numerous others, Presdl. Tribute, 1998, Spl. Congressional Recognition award, 1998; Dr. Frederick T. Zugibe Forensic Unit named in his honor, Rockland County Med. Examiners Office, 2003. Fellow Coll. Am. Pathologists (emeritus), Am. Coll. Cardiology (emeritus), Am. Acad. Forensic Scis., N.Y. Cardiology Soc., Coun. Arteriosclerosis of Am. Heart Assn., Assn. Scientists and Scholars Internat. for the Shroud of Turin (pres., founder), Sigma Xi. Roman Catholic. Achievements include first to describe glycoprotein storage disease (Zugibe-Gilbert Syndrome), the defect in the syndrome of the sea blue histocyte and arthrodentoosteodysplasia. an acroosteolysis syndrome, a mask to eliminate odors of putrefaction, and a demummifaction technique for fingerprinting; invented ac/dc cardiopulmonary resuscitator, many others. Home: 1 Angelus Dr Garnerville NY 10923-2022 Office: Rockland County Health Comp Office Med Examiner Pomona NY 10970 E-mail: ftzugibe@msn.com.

ZUHDI, NABIL (BILL ZUHDI), lawyer, litigator, consultant, producer; b. N.Y.C., June 8, 1955; s. Nazih and Lamya Zuhdi; child from previous marriage: Noah; m. Darla L. Boyd, May 19, 1984. BS, U. Ctrl. Okla., 1979; JD, U. Okla., 1982. Bar: Okla. 1982, U.S. Dist. Ct. (we. dist.) Okla. 1982, U.S. Ct. Appeals (10th cir.) 1989, U.S. Supreme Ct. 1990, Tex. 1991, U.S. Dist. Ct. (no. dist.) Tex. 1998. Assoc. Linn & Helms, Oklahoma City, 1982-85; ptnr. Zuhdi & Denum, Oklahoma City, 1985-87; assoc. Law Firm Darrell Keith, Ft. Worth, 1994; pvt. practice Oklahoma City, 1987—. Pres. Zuhdi Entertainment Group, Inc., Okla. City, 1986—, Amerisphere, Inc., Okla. City, 1996—, criminal justice act panel We. Dist. Okla., 1985—, spl. death penalty habeas corpus panel, 1998, criminal justice act voluntary panel No. Dist. Tex., 1998. Producer: (concerts) Frank Sinatra, Julio Igleas. Patron Okla. Heart Ctr., Oklahoma City, 1994—. Mem. ABA, ATLA, State Bar Tex., Oklahoma Bar Assn., Oklahoma County Bar Assn., Phi Alpha Delta, Alpha Chi. Republican. Avocations: boxing, film, prodr. of concerts including Frank Sinatra and others. Office: PO Box 1077 Oklahoma City OK 73101-1077

ZUHDI, NAZIH, former surgeon, administrator; b. Beirut, May 19, 1925; arrived in U.S., 1950; s. Omar and Lutfiye (Atef) Z.; children by previous marriage: Omar, Nabil; m. Annette McMichael; children: Adam, Leyla, Zachariah BA, Am. U., Beirut, 1946, MD, 1950. Diplomate Am. Bd. Surgery, Am. Bd. Thoracic Surgery. Intern St. Vincent's Hosp., SI, NY, 1950-51, Presbyn.-Columbia Med. Ctr., NYC, 1951-52; resident Kings County SUNY Med. Ctr., NYC, 1952-56; fellow SUNY Downstate Med. Ctr., Bklyn., 1953-54; resident Univ. Hosp., Mpls., 1956, Okla. City, 1957-58, practice surgery specializing in cardiovasc. and thoracic, 1958-87, adminstr., 1985-99, ret., 1999. Founder, dir. Oklahoma Transplantation Inst. (renamed Nazih Zuhdi transplant Inst., Aug., 1999) Bapt. Med. Ctr., 1984-99, chmn. dept. transplantation, 1994-99; transplantation surgeon in chief Bapt. Hosp., Okla. City, 1984-99; founder, chmn. Okla. Cardiovasc. Inst., Okla. City, 1983-84, Okla. Heart Ctr., Okla. City, 1984-85 Contbg. author Cardiac Surgery, 1967, 2d edit., 1972; contbr. articles to profl. jour.; developer numerous med. devices, techniques, rsch. and publs. on cardiopulmonary bypass, internal hypothermia, assisted circulation, heart surgery and transplantation of thoracic organs; developer heart-lung machines; designer, use of exptl. plastic bypass hearts; originator use of banked citrated blood for cardiopulmonary bypass for open heart surgery, of clin. non-hemic primes of heart-lung machines producing intentional hemodilution, at present, the universally accepted principle of cardiopulmonary bypass for partial and total body perfusion; researcher in cardiovasc. studies. Founder Islamic Ctr., Inc., Oklahoma City. Named to Okla. Hall of Fame, 1994. Fellow ACS; mem. AMA, NCCJ (Humanitarian award 1996), Am. Thoracic Soc., Okla. Thoracic Soc., So. Med. Assn., Okla. Med. Assn., Internat. Coll. Angiology, Am. Coll. Chest Physicians, Oklahoma City C. of C., Oklahoma County Med. Soc., Oklahoma City Clin. Soc., Okla. Surg. Assn., Oklahoma City Surg. Soc., Southwestern Surg. Congress, Am. Coll. Cardiology, Am. Soc. Artificial Internal Organs, Soc. Thoracic Surgeons (founding mem.), Am. Assn. for Thoracic Surgery, Internat. Cardiovasc. Soc., Okla. State Heart Assn., Osler Soc., So. Thoracic Surg. Assn., Lillehei Surg. Soc., Internat. Soc. Heart Transplantation, Dwight Harken's Founder's Group Cardiac Surgery, Westaby's Pioneers in Cardiac Surgery, Internat. Soc. Cardiothoracic Surgery (Japan, founding mem.), Am. Soc. Transplant Surgeons, Milestones of Cardiology of Am. Coll. Cardiology, Okla. City Golf and Country Club, Okla. Hall of Fame. Achievements include first to use banked citrated blood for cardiopulmonary bypass for open heart surgery; invention of experimental and clinical non-hemic primes of heart-lung machines producing intentional hemodilution. Home: 7305 Lancet Ct Oklahoma City OK 73120-1430 Personal E-mail: nzmd@aol.com.

ZUICHES, JAMES JOSEPH, sociologist, educator; b. Eau Claire, Wis., Mar. 24, 1943; s. William Homer and Bronnie Monica (Stich) Z.; m. Carol Ann Kurilo, Aug. 19, 1967; children:; James Daniel, Joseph Kurilo. BA in Philosophy, U. Portland, 1967; MS in Sociology, U. Wis., 1969, PhD in Sociology, 1973. Instr., asst. prof., assoc. prof. sociology Mich. State U., East Lansing, 1971-82, prof., 1982; assoc. program dir. in sociology NSF, Washington, 1979-80, program dir. in sociology, 1980-82; assoc. dir. rsch. Cornell U., Ithaca, N.Y., 1982-86; assoc. dean Coll. Agr. and Home Econs., Wash. State U., Pullman, 1986-94, dir. Agrl. Rsch. Ctr., 1986-94; program dir. food sys. and rural devel. W.K. Kellogg Found., Battle Creek, Mich., 1994-95; dean Coll. Agr. and Home Econs. Wash. State U., Pullman, 1995—2003, prof. Dept. Cmty. and Rural Sociology, 1986—. Mem. adv. subcom. NSF, 1977-79; sci. adv. com. USDA Nat. Rsch. Initiative, Washington, 1992-93; com. on future land grant univ. bd. on agr., NRC, Washington, 1994-96; pub. Wash. Land and People Mag., 1987-92; mem. Bd. Natural Resources, Wash. State, 1995-2003. Co-editor: The Demography of Rural Life, 1993; contbr. articles to profl. jours. Pres., bd. dirs. Edgewood Village Children's Ctr., East Lansing, 1978-79. Recipient sustained superior performance award NSF, 1981; rsch. grantee NIMH, 1973, ERDA, 1978. Fellow AAAS; mem. Rural Sociol. Soc. (pres. 1992-93, editor 50th Anniversary Rsch. Series, 5 vols. 1988-93), Am. Sociol. Assn., Population Assn. Am. Roman Catholic. Avocations: skiing, swimming, hiking, reading. Office Phone: 509-335-8540.

ZUICK, ERNEST RONALD, JR., career officer, advertising executive; b. San Bernardino, Calif., Nov. 2, 1935; s. Ernest Ronald Sr. and Catherine Louise (Leach) Z.; m. Johnnie Fern Lemons, Aug. 19, 1966. BA, Fresno State U., 1964, MA, 1968; MPA, Auburn U., 1974; postgrad., Air Command and Staff Coll., 1974, Air War Coll., 1982. Cert. tchr., Calif. Joined Calif. Air N.G., 1958, advanced through grades to col., 1984; advt. acct. exec., sports and polit. cartoonist Turlock (Calif.) Jour., 1956-62; advt. acct. exec. Fresno (Calif.) Bee, 1965-76; various assignments Calif. Mil. Dept., Sacramento, 1976-85, dir. legis., 1985-95, spl. projects dir., 1999—2001; dir. Media Svcs., 2001—04. Mem. ancillary staff Res. Forces Policy Bd., Office of Sec. of Def., 1982-95. Contbr. articles to profl. jours. Mem. N.G. Assn. Calif. (pres. 1983-84). Avocations: writing, cartooning, video production.

ZUIDEMA, GEORGE DALE, surgeon, educator; b. Holland, Mich., Mar. 8, 1928; s. Jacob and Reka (Dalman) Z.; m. Joan K. Houtman, June 2, 1953; children: Karen Sue, David Jay, Nancy Ruth, Sarah Kay. AB, Hope Coll., 1949, D.Sc. (hon.), 1969; MD, Johns Hopkins U., 1953. Diplomate: Am. Bd. Surgery. Intern Mass. Gen. Hosp., 1953-54, asst. resident surgeon, then chief resident surgeon, 1954, 57, 58, 59; asst. prof. surgery, then assoc. prof. U. Mich. Sch. Medicine, 1960-64; prof. surgery, dir. dept. Johns Hopkins Sch. Medicine; also surgeon in chief Johns Hopkins Hosp., 1964-84; prof. surgery, vice provost med. affairs U. Mich., 1984-94. Cons. Walter Reed Army Med. Center, Sinai Hosp., Balt., Balt. City Hosp., Clin. Center of NIH; chmn. Study on Surg. Services for U.S., 1970-75 Editor: (with O.H. Gauer) Gravitational Stress in Aerospace Medicine, 1961; (with G.L. Nardi) Surgery-A Concise Guide to Clinical Practice, 1961, 4th edit., 1982; (with R.D. Judge and F. Fitzgerald) Physical Diagnosis, 1963, 6th edit., 1997; (with W.F. Ballinger and R.B. Rutherford) Management of Trauma, 1968, 4th edit., 1985; (with L. Schlossberg) Atlas of Human Functional Anatomy, 1977, 4th edit., 1997, Shackelford's Surgery of the Alimentary Tract, 5th edit., 2001; editor Jour. Surg. Rsch., 1966-72, assoc. editor, mem. editl. bd., 1972—; mem. editl. bd. Surgery Ann., 1968-75, Surgery, 1970-97, co-editor in chief, 1975-97. Bd. dirs. Md. divsn. Am. Cancer Soc., 1964-68; trustee William Beaumont Hosp., Royal Oak, Mich., 1984-94, Hope Coll., Holland, Mich, 1987—. Capt. M.C., USAF, 1954-56. John and Mary R. Markle scholar academic medicine, 1961-66; recipient Henry Russell award U. Mich., 1963 Fellow ACS, Royal Coll. Surgeons Ireland (hon.); mem. Assn. Am. Med. Colls., Ctrl. Soc. Clin. Rsch., Soc. Univ. Surgeons, Am. Surg. Assn., So. Surg. Assn., Soc. Clin. Surgery, Soc. Vascular Surgery, Internat. Cardiovascular Surgery, Halsted Soc., Nat. Inst. Medicine, Assn. Acad. Surgeons (pres. 1967-69), Allen O. Whipple Soc., Coun. on Grad. Med. Edn., Phi Beta Kappa, Tri Beta, Alpha Omega Alpha. Home: 983 Willow View Ct Holland MI 49424-6615

ZUK, CARMEN VEIGA, psychiatrist; b. Buenos Aires, Mar. 5, 1939; came to U.S., 1971; d. Carlos and Carmen Villella Veiga; m. Gerald Harvey, May 7, 1974; children: Cary Elizabeth and Gabrielle Ann (twins). MD, U. Buenos Aires, 1964, cert. psychiatry, 1969. Diplomate Am. Bd. Psychiatry and Neurology. Intern Med. Coll. of Pa., Phila., 1974-75; resident in psychiatry Norristown (Pa.) State Hosp., 1977-79; child psychiatry fellowship Med. Coll. Pa. and Ea. Pa. Psychiat. Inst., Phila., 1979-81; dir. child and adolescent unit Hosp. of Med. Coll. Ga., Augusta, 1981-83; dir. treatment team New Orleans Adolescent Hosp., 1983-85; assoc. Psychiatry Med. Group, Calif., 1985-86; mental health psychiatrist L.A. County Dept. Mental Health San Fernando Mental Health Svcs., 1986-88; psychiatrist-ptnr. So. Calif. Permanente Med. Group, Van Nuys, Calif., 1988-98, ptnr., 1988-98; staff psychiatrist Santa Clarita Child and Family Ctr., 1999—2002. Asst. prof. dept. psychiatry Med. Coll. Ga., 1981-83; clin. asst. prof. dept. psychiatry and neurology Tulane U., 1983-85. Contbr. articles to profl. pubs. Mem. AMA, Internat. Soc. for Adolescent Psychiatry. Avocations: reading, cooking, gardening, swimming, music. Home: 7620 Hollister Ave #219 Goleta CA 93117 Office: Santa Clarita Child and Family Ctr 21545 Redview Dr Santa Clarita CA 91350-2617 E-mail: CarmenZuk@msn.com.

ZUK, GERALD HARVEY, psychologist, consultant; b. Chgo., Oct. 25, 1929; s. Albert and Gladys (Gross) Z.; m. Carmen Veiga, May 7, 1974; children: Cary and Gabrielle (twins). BA, L.A. State Coll., 1951; PhD, U. Chgo., 1955. Lic. psychologist, Calif. Asst. rsch. psychologist Inst. Child Welfare/U. Calif., Berkeley, 1955-56; clin. psychologist Pacific State Hosp., Pomona, Calif., 1956-57; chief psychologist St. Christopher's Hosp. for Children, Phila., 1957-61; assoc. dir., dir. tng. program dept. family psychiatry Ea. Pa. Psychiat. Inst., Phila., 1961-80; prof. dept. psychiatry, dir. family therapy program Med. Coll. Ga., 1981-83; clin. prof. dept. psychiatry and neurology Tulane U. Sch. Medicine, New Orleans, 1983-85; assoc. and dir. family therapy tng. program Beck Psychiat. Med. Group, Los Angeles County, 1985-86; pvt. practice Los Angeles County, 1986—. Cons. and presenter in field. Author: Family Therapy: A Triadic-Based Approach, 1972, 2d edit., 1981, Process and Practice in Family Therapy, 1975, 2d edit., 1986; editor: Family Therapy Approaches for Adolescents, 1985; co-editor: Family Therapy and Disturbed Families, 1967; founding editor Internat. Jour. Family Therapy, 1979-86; mem. editl. bd. Family Process, Psychotherapy: Theory, Rsch. and Practice, Jour. Marriage and Family Counseling, Terapia Familiar; contbr. articles to profl. jours. Fellow APA. Avocation: classical music. Home and Office: Zuk Cons 7620 Hollister Ave # 219 Goleta CA 93117-2442 Personal E-mail: geraldzuk@msn.com.

ZUK, JUDITH, botanic garden administrator; b. Canandaigua, N.Y., Sept. 11, 1951; BA, Rutgers U., 1973; MS, U. Del., 1976. CEO, pres. Bklyn. Botanic Garden, 1990—. Bd. dirs. Botanic Gardens Conservation Internat., Greenwood Cemetery; mem. regional adv. bd. JP Morgan Chase. Mem. Phi Beta Kappa. Office: Bklyn Botanic Garden 1000 Washington Ave Brooklyn NY 11225-1008 Office Phone: 718-623-7269. E-mail: judithzuk@bbg.org.

ZUKAUKAS, CHARLES LAWRENCE, surgeon; b. Newark, 1921; s. Andrew Joseph and Anna (Naudzeus) Z.; m. Leonora Brust, Aug. 2, 1947; children: Maryanne Tashjian, Andrea Aikins. BA, Rutgers U., 1943; MD, U. Pa., 1946. Diplomate Am. Bd. Surgery. Intern St. Lukes Hosp., N.Y.C., 1946-47; resident in surgery NYU-Bellevue Hosp., N.Y.C., 1949-53; ret., 1991; dir. surg. emeritus Monmouth Med. Ctr., Long Branch, N.J., 1992—; prof. surg. emeritus Hahnemann U., 1993—. Cons. in surgery Jersey Shore Med. Ctr., 1970-89, Freehold (N.J.) Med. Ctr., 1977-80. Trustee Monmouth Med. Ctr., 1982-88, YMCA; dir. Long Branch Pub. Health Nursing Assn. Capt. U.S. Army, 1947-49. Named Physician of Yr., Am. Cancer Soc., N.J. divsn., 1977; recipient N.J. C. of C. award. Fellow ACS (pres. N.J. chpt. 1974, gov. at large 1984-87), Acad. Medicine N.J.; mem. AMA, S.E. Surg. Congress, N.J. State Med. Soc. (Golden Merit award), Soc. Surgeons N.J. (pres. 1985-86), Rotary. Roman Catholic. Home: 609 Westwood Ave Long Branch NJ 07740-5008 E-mail: doctorz@comcast.net.

ZUKERMAN, MICHAEL, lawyer; b. Bklyn., Oct. 3, 1940; s. Charles Morris and Gertrude Ethel Zukerman; m. Claire J. Goldsmith, June 25, 1961 (div. 1986); children: Steven, Amy; m. Elaine DeMasi, Nov. 21, 1986 (div. 1999); children: Jaclyn, Laura; m. Janey Alexander, Feb. 2, 2001. BS, U. Fla., 1961; LLB, St. John's U., 1964; LLM, NYU, 1966. Bar: NY 1965, Pa. 1983, U.S. Tax Ct. 1984. Credit analyst, loan officer Franklin Nat. Bank, 1964-66; assoc. Jaffin, Schneider, Kimmel & Galpeer, N.Y.C., 1966-67; ptnr. Zukerman, Licht & Friedman and predecessors, N.Y.C., 1967-79, Baskin & Sears, P.C., N.Y.C., 1979-85, Graubard, Moskowitz, Dannett, Horowitz & Mollen, N.Y.C., 1985-86, Gersten, Savage, Kaplowitz & Zukerman, N.Y.C., 1986-89; of counsel Olshan, Grundman, Frome & Rosenzweig, N.Y.C., 1990-95, Graham & James, N.Y.C., 1995-2000, Bryan Cave LLP, 2000—03; exec. v.p. Brookhill Group, 1986-89; counsel Sonnenschein Nath and Rosenthal, N.Y.C., 2003—04; of counsel Warshaw Burstein Cohen Schlessinger & Kuh LLP, N.Y.C., 2004—. Pres. First Ptnrs. Credit Corp., N.Y.C., 1988—93; bd. dirs. Interjurist Ltd., Whitestone Realty Capital, Inc.; mng. dir. Nat. Aspbergers Rsch. Found., 1993—, trustee, 2001—; lectr. in field. Contbr. articles to profl. jours. Trustee Temple Beth Torah, Melville, N.Y., 1972-80, YMHA Suffolk County, Hauppague, N.Y., 1980-85; bd. dirs. Dayton Mgmt. Corp., 1974-2001, Suffolk Jewish Cmty. Planning Bd., Hauppague, 1982-85, Congregation Bnai Elohim, 1994, 2nd v.p., 1995; co-chmn. bus. adv. coun. Town of Greenburgh, 1992. Mem.: ABA. Home: 915 Cherry Ln Valley Stream NY 11581-2722 Office: Warshaw Burstein Cohen Schlessinger & Kuh LLP 11th Fl 555 Fifth Ave New York NY 10017 Office Phone: 212-984-7836. E-mail: mzukerman@whitestonerealty.com.

ZUKERMAN, PINCHAS, concert violinist, violist, conductor; b. Tel Aviv, July 16, 1948; came to U.S., 1962; s. Yehuda and Miriam (Lieberman) Z.; m. Eugenia Rich, May 26, 1968 (div.); children: Natalia, Arianna; m. Tuesday Weld, 1985 (div.); m. Amanda Forsyth, Mar. 2004. Student, Juilliard Sch. Music, 1965-68; MusD (hon.), Brown U., 1989. Ind. concert violinist, 1968—. With impresario, Sol Hurok, 1967-76; condr., soloist English Chamber Orch., 1974, Mostly Mozart Festival, N.Y.C., 1975; guest condr., soloist Los Angeles Philharm., Boston Symphony, Chgo. Symphony, Pitts. Symphony, Phila. Orch., N.Y. Philharm.; music dir. South Bank Festival, London, 1978-80, St. Paul Chamber Orch., 1980-87, Nat. Arts Ctr. Orch., 1998—; prin. festival condr. Dallas Internat. Summer Music Festival, 1990-94; prin. guest condr. Dallas Symphony, 1993-95; toured with Isaac Stern; mem. trio with Daniel Barenboim and Jacqueline du Pre; (rec. artist) CBS, EMI, Philips Classics labels, RCA Victor Red Seal, BMG Classics. Winner Internat. Levintritt Competition, 1967, Medal of Arts, 1983, Isaac Stern award Nat. Arts Awards, 2002. Office: care Kirshbaum Demler & Assoc 711 W End Ave Apt 5KN New York NY 10025-6821

ZULAUF, SANDER (WILLIAM), poet, educator, editor; b. Paterson, N.J., Nov. 5, 1946; s. S. William Z. and Marion Ann Zulauf; m. Christianne Beresford, June 15, 1968 (div. 1976); 1 child, Scott; m. Madeline Ruth Slocum, May 26, 1979; stepchildren: Michael, Mary Beth. BA, Gettysburg Coll., 1968; MA, Ind. U., 1973. Tchr. Martin Luther King Sch., Paterson, NJ, 1968—69, Hanover Park Regional H.S., East Hanover, NJ, 1969-71; prof. County Coll. Morris, Randolph, NJ, 1973—. Editor, pub. Ars Poetica, Lake Hopatcong, N.J., 1996-99. Author poems, including collection Succasunna New Jersey, 1987; editor: Jour. N.J. Poets, 1989—; founding editor Index Am. Periodical Verse, 1971—82. Sec.-treas. Forest South Homeowners Assn., Byram Twp., 1989—94; committeeman County Com., Byram Twp., NJ, 1994—; lay eucharistic min. St. Dunstan's Episcopal Ch., Succasunna, 1974—. Named 1st Poet Laureate, Diocese of Newark, 1999—; recipient Allen Ginsberg award, Poetry Ctr., Passaic, N.J., 1993, 2001, 2002, Excellence in Print award, Jour. N.J. Poets Pub. Radio's Poet and the Poem, 2002; fellow NEH, Princeton, 1987; grantee N.J. Arts Coun., 1992—93. Mem. Acad. Am. Poets, Poetry Soc. Am., Poets House, Kenneth Burke Soc., Thoreau Soc., Associated Writing Programs, Skylands Writers & Artists Assn. (sec. treas. 1994-98, v.p. 1999-2000). Democrat. Episcopalian. Avocations: camping, boating, environmental preservation, gardening, travel. Office: County Coll Morris 214 Center Grove Rd Randolph NJ 07869-2086 E-mail: szulauf@ccm.edu., sanderzpoet@msn.com.

ZULCH, JOAN CAROLYN, retired medical publishing company executive; b. Great Neck, N.Y., Apr. 10, 1931; d. Walter Howard and Edna Ruth (Howard) Z. BS in Biology, Allegheny Coll., 1952; postgrad., Hunter Coll., 1954. Med. sec. E.R. Squibb & Sons, N.Y.C., 1952; with Macmillan Pub. Co., N.Y.C., 1952-88, editorial asst. med. dept., 1952-56, asst. editor med. dept., 1956-58, editor med. dept., 1958-61, med. editor coll. and profl. div., 1961-75, sr. editor medicine, coll. and profl. div., 1975-78, exec. editor med. books, profl. books div., 1978-79, editor-in-chief, 1979-80, asst. v.p., editor-in-chief profl. books div., 1980-82, v.p., pub. med., nursing, health sci. dept., 1982-85, v.p., pub. med. books, sci., tech., med. dept., 1985-88. Recipient Best Illustrated Med. Book award Assn. Med. Illustrators, 1977, Outstanding Book in Health Sci. award Assn. Am. Pubs., 1982. Mem. AAAS, Post Libr. Assn., L.I.U. (rec. sec. 1990-93, exec. coun. 1990—), Friends of Locust Valley Libr. (pres. 1991-93, 94-96, 98-2000, 2004—, treas. 1993-94, 96-98, 2000-02, 1st v.p. 2002-04), Locust Valley C. of C. (bd. dirs. 1997—), Alpha Gamma Delta, Delta Sigma Rho. Republican. Home: 36 Wood Ln Lattingtown PO Box 547 Locust Valley NY 11560-0547

ZULKER, CHARLES BATES, broadcasting company executive; b. Pleasantville, N.J., Dec. 20, 1926; s. William John and Virginia (Carr) Z.; m. Virginia Wright, June 24, 1949; children: Connie Lee, Timothy Scott Charles. Adminstrv. officer Princeton (N.J.) U., 1950-60; asst. mgr. Sta. WPEL, Montrose, Pa., 1960-65; gen. mgr. Sta. WCHR, Trenton, N.J., 1965—. Trustee

Princeton Evang. Fellowship, 1973-83; bd. council Word of Life Internat., Schroon Lake, N.Y., 1974-82; mem. exec. bd. Upper Makefield Community Assn., 1972-79; deacon Westerly Rd. Ch., Princeton, 1999-2002. With U.S. Army, 1945-46. Mem. Wooden Canoe Heritage Assn. of Am., Nat. Religious Broadcasters, Nat. Assn. of Broadcasters, Squam Lakes Assn. (Holderness, N.H.). Office: 119 Locktown Rd Flemington NJ 08822-4715 Office Phone: 215-493-4252. E-mail: cbzulker@earthlink.com.

ZUMBACH, STEVEN ELMER, lawyer; b. Jan. 12, 1950; s. Elmer J. and Mary C. (Frese) Zumbach; m. Kathy J. Case, June 5, 1971; children: Stephanie L., Mathew J. BS, Iowa State U., 1973, PhD, 1980; JD, U. Iowa, 1975. CPA; bar: Iowa 1975. Assoc. Belin Lamson McCormick Zumbach Flynn, P.C., Des Moines, 1977—, ptnr., 1980—. Lectr. law Drake U., Des Moines, 1980—84; mem. Iowa Bd. Regents, 1973—77; bd. govs. Iowa State U. Found., Ames, Iowa, 1986—. Chmn. Greater Des Moines Partnership, 2003. Fellow: Am. Coll. Trust and Estate Counsel; mem.: Iowa Soc. CPAs, Iowa State U. Alumni Assn. (pres. 1986—87), Gamma Sigma Delta, Omocron Delta Kappa, Phi Kappa Phi, Order of Colf. Republican. Home: 708 38th St West Des Moines IA 50265-3176 Office: Belin Lamson McCormick Zumbach Flynn PC 666 Walnut St Ste 2000 Des Moines IA 50309-3989 Office Phone: 515-283-4625. E-mail: sezumbach@belinlaw.com.

ZUMBANO, ANTHONY RALPH, risk, claims management executive; b. Jersey City, May 11, 1947; s. Carl R. and Catherine (Guddemi) Z.; children: Carl Robert, Brian Joseph; m. Kathy E. Kenny, Oct. 7, 1989. BS, St. Peter's Coll., Jersey City, 1969; Dipl. Claims Law, Am. Ednl. Inst., Basking Ridge, N.J., 1973. Supr. Travelers Ins. Co., Morris Plains, N.J., 1969-78; v.p. Marsh & McLennan Inc., N.Y.C., 1978-84; pres., chief exec. officer AMNA Corp., Ft. Lauderdale, Fla., 1984-92; pres., CEO PLCM Group, Inc., Ft. Lauderdale, 1993-98; pres. Cambridge Profl. Liability Svcs., 1999—. Contbr. articles to profl. jours. Vol. Broward County Spl. Olympics, Ft. Lauderdale, 1991—; bd. pres. Las Olas Villas, Ft. Lauderdale, 1986-88. Mem. Am. Soc. for Healthcare Risk Mgmt., Fla. Med. Malpractice Claims Coun., Tower Club. Republican. Roman Catholic. Avocations: boating, tennis, chess, home restoration. Office: PLCM Group Inc 805 E Broward Blvd Ste 300 Fort Lauderdale FL 33301-2046

ZUMBRUN, ALVIN JOHN THOMAS, law and criminology educator; s. Orrell Sylvester Tilton and Mary Kathryn (Sprinkle) Z.; m. Marianne Jane Nolan; children: Mary Susan, Alvin J.T. Jr., Steven M., Diane, MaryAnn, Mary Kathleen. BA, U. Md., 1952, MA, 1956; MEd in Spl. Edn., Coppin State U., 1972, MEd in Adminstrn., 1974; JD, U. Balt., 1970. Probation officer Supreme Bench of Balt., 1950-52; budget and program dir. Cmty. Chest, Balt., 1953-55; mng. dir. Criminal Justice Commn., Balt., 1956-59; exec. dir., criminologist Md. Crime Investigating Com., Balt., 1960—93; dept. chmn., prof. criminal justice Catonsville (Md.) C.C., 1968-94; dept. chmn., dir. grad. program, prof. criminal justice U. Balt., 1974-76. Adj. prof. criminal justice U. Md., Hood Coll., Coppin State U., Md. State Police Acad., Balt. County Police Acad., 1969—; mem. adv. bd. U. Balt. Criminal Justice Program, 1976-94; cons. Am. Edn. Assn., Washington, 1980-1985; mem. senate Catonsville C.C., 1970-83; mem. Nat. Disaster Med. System, 1993—; mem. acad. stds. senate com. U. Md., College Park, 1997-99. Author: Maryland Crime Report, 5 vols., 1959-94, Directory of Criminal Justice Agencies, 22 vols., 1962-94, Civil Disturbance Riots of 1968, 69, also rsch. in field. Mem. scholarship com. Md. Troopers Assn., Pikesville, 1990-93; mem. adv. bd. articulation com. U. Md., College Park, 1977-94; lay pres., mem. coun. Salem Luth. Ch., Catonsville, 1956-59, 65-68; pres. Maplewoods Home Owners Assn., 1996-97. Served to lt. (j.g.) USN. Recipient Superior Pub. Svc. award Afro Am. Newspaper, 1962, Excellence in Teaching award Md. State Bd. C.C.s, 1987, Superior Ednl. Svcs. award Balt. County Police Chief, 1994, Gov.'s citation for ednl. achievements Gov. of Md., 1994, Hon. Trooper 25 Yrs. Acad. Teaching Md. State Police, 1995. Mem. VFW (life), Am. Legion (life), Md. Acad. Criminal Justice Profs. (pres. 1971-94), Internat. Soc. Criminology, Nat. Dist. Attys. Assn., Internat. Assn. Chiefs of Police, Maplewoods Homeowners Assn. (pres. 1995-96). Avocations: walking, biking, family activities, world travel. Home and Office: 438 Maple Forest Rd Catonsville MD 21228-1783 Personal E-mail: azumbrun@comcast.net.

ZUMBRUNNEN, DAVID ARNOLD, mechanical engineering and materials science educator, consultant; b. Salt Lake City, Sept. 3, 1955; m. Elizabeth Buck. B in Mech. Engring., U. Minn., 1977; MS in Mech. Engring., Purdue U., 1984, PhD in Mech. Engring., 1988. Registered profl. engr., Ind., S.C. Rsch. leader NSF Ctr. for Advanced Engring. Fibers and Films. Lt. USN, 1977—82. Presdl. Faculty Fellow The White House/NSF, 1992-97. Mem.: AAAS, ASME, Polymer Processing Soc., Material Rsch. Soc., SPE, Am. Chem. Soc., AIChemE. Achievements include invention of structured materials formed by chaotic advection. Office: Clemson U Dept Mech Engring Clemson SC 29634-0921 Office Phone: 864-656-5625. E-mail: zdavid@ces.clemson.edu.

ZUMERCHIK, JOHN, urologist; b. Chgo., Nov. 29, 1932; s. John and Anna (Marchuk) Z.; m. Eileen Heraty, June 14, 1958; children: Cheryl Ann, John Francis, David Lee, Steven Jay, Patricia Eileen, James Jacob, Janine Marie. AA, Wilson Jr. Coll., Chgo., 1953; student, U. Ill., Chgo., 1953-54; MD, Loyola U., 1958. Diplomate Am. Bd. Urology. Rotating intern Cook County Hosp., Chgo., 1958-59, urology resident, 1960-63; gen. surg. resident MacNeal Meml. Hosp., Berwyn, Ill., 1959-60; pvt. practice Drs. Ross-Zumerchik Partnership, Evergreen Park, Ill., 1964-67, Drs. Ross, Zumerchik, Boctor, Evergreen Park, 1970-83, Southwest Urology Assocs., Evergreen Park, 1983—. Staff urologist Little Co. of Mary Hosp., chmn. divsn. urology, dept. surgery, 1977-80, 82-84; staff urologist Ingalls Meml. Hsop.; mem. resident edn. attending staff dept. urology Cook County Hosp., 1961-85, grad. edn. asst. prof., 1963-85; clin. instr. urology med. student edn. Loyola U. Chgo., 19562-72. Pres. 98th and Kedzie Corp., Evergreen Park, 1988, 96-97. Lt. col. M.C. U.S. Army, 1968-70. Fellow ACS (mem. examining com. 1978-84, 92-96); mem. AMA, Am. Urol. Assn. (north ctrl. sect.), Am. Assn. Clin. Urologists, Chgo. Urol. Soc. (exec. com. 1987), Ill. Urol. Soc., Ill. Med. Soc., Chgo. Med. Soc., Pan-Pacific Surg. Assn., Royal Soc. Medicine, Am. Soc. Andrology, Am. Fertility Soc., Am. Inst. Ultrasound in Medicine, Endourology Soc. Avocations: tennis, skiing, biking, photography, carpentry. Office: Southwest Urology Assocs 9760 S Kedzie Ave Evergreen Park IL 60805-3123

ZUMWALT, RICHARD DOWLING, flour mill executive; b. Amarillo, Tex., Dec. 1, 1912; s. Richard Dowling and Cora Bell (Pate) Z.; m. Florine Anita Nelson, Oct. 23, 1938; 1 dau., Alexandra Anita (Mrs. Klaus Schwabe). Student, Met. Bus. Coll., 1930; ext. student, Tex. Tech. Coll., 1931, Dallas Coll., 1949. With Pearlstone Mill & Elevator Co., summers 1929/30, J. C. Crouch Grain Co., 1931-44, Burrus Mills, Inc., Dallas, 1944-83, exec. v.p., 1956-64, pres., 1964-83; sec.-treas. Zumwalt Inc., 1973—; ret. gen. mgr. Burrus milling dept. Cargill, Inc. Past pres. Bulgur Assos., Washington, Dallas Grain Exch. Mem. Millers Nat. Fedn., Tex. Mfrs. Assn. (past dir.). Home: 7353 Blairview Dr Dallas TX 75230-5416

ZUMWALT, ROGER CARL, hospital administrator; b. Eugene, Oreg., Oct. 26, 1943; s. Robert Walter and Jean Elaine (Adams) Z.; children: Kathryn Nicole Zumwalt DeWeber, Timothy Robert. Student, Boise State U., 1963—65; BA, We. Oreg. U., 1969; postgrad., U. Iowa, 1969—71; MA cum laude, Oreg. State U., 1973. Adminstr. Coulee Cmty. Hosp., Grand Coulee, Wash., 1973-75, Eastmoreland Hosp., Portland, Oreg., 1975-81; exec. dir. Cmty. Hosp., Grand Junction, Colo., 1981-97; pres., healthcare cons. accreditation Zumwalt Consulting, Salem, Oreg., 1997—; dir. adminstrv. svcs. divsn. SAIF Corp., Salem, 1998—. Chmn., bd. dirs. Alphabet House Pediat. Rehab. and Edn., 1998-2000, Castle Rock Med. Group, Inc., Denver, 1998—; part owner, chmn. bd. dirs. Castle Rock (Colo.) Med. Ctr., 1998--, N.W. Okla. Regional Med. Ctr. Cherokee, 2000; spkr. numerous local and nat. presentations, subjects including healthcare, hosp. mktg./success/costs, 1981-97; CEO Cmty. Med. Plz., 1984-97, Cmty. Health Care Providers Orgn., 1986-97, Cmty. Hosp. Found., 1988-97; guest lectr. Mesa State Coll., 1993-98, Colo. Christian Coll., 1996-98. Newspaper columnist, 1973-75; contbr. articles, presentations to profl. publs. Commr. Multnomah County Health Care Commn., Portland, 1978-81; health cons. Grant County Housing Auth., Grand Coulee, 1974-75; mem. pk. bd. City of Tigard, Oreg., 1976-78; caucus rep. Mesa County Rep. Party, Grand Junction, 1988; mem. adv. com., pres.'s office Mesa State Coll., Grand Junction, 1989; bd. dirs. Hospice of Grand Valley, Grand Junction, 1992-97, mem. devel. com., 1993-97, vice chmn. bd. dirs., 1994-97; bd. dirs. Grand Valley Hospice, 1992-96; com. mem. Salem Coalition on Youth Literacy, 2000—. Fellow Coll. Osteo. Healthcare Execs. (bd. dirs. 1985-88, pres. 1987, examiner 1989—, Disting. Svc. award 1989); mem. Am. Osteo. Healthcare Assn. (bd. dirs. 1987-98, treas. 1992-93, 1st v.p. 1994-95, 2d v.p. 1993-94, vice chairperson 1994-95, chmn. 1996-97, chairperson 1997-98, past chmn. 1998), Am. Osteo. Assn. (ex-officio mem. bd. dirs. 1996), Bur. Healthcare Facilities Accreditation (v.p. 1994, advisor 1995-98, accreditation cons. 1995—, accreditation surveyer 1978—, accreditation survey instr. 1994—), Joint Commn. on Am. Healthcare Orgn. (task force on small and rural hosps. 1994-98), Colo. Hosp. Assn. (bd. dirs. 1987-92), Mountain States Vol. Hosp. Assn. (bd. dirs. 1984-98, exec. com. 1991-98, v.p. 1993, vice chmn. bd. dirs. 1997-98), We. Coll. Ind. Practice Assn. (Medicine Mauls Measles com., fin. com. 1991-92), We. Colo. Health Care Alliance (bd. dirs. 1989-94, v.p. 1992, chmn. bd. dirs. 1993), Mesa County Mental Health Assn. (bd. dirs. 1988-89, 91-92), Grand Junction C. of C. (bd. dirs. 1991-93), Rotary (Grand Coolee, Wash. 1973-75, Portland 1975-81, Grand Junction 1981-98, Salem 1998—, chmn. fund raising com. 2000-01, bd. dirs. 2001-02), Masons, Shriners (pres. Grand Junction club 1989, bd. dirs. El Jebel 1986-90, 1st v.p. Western Colo. club 1989). Republican. Methodist. Avocations: golf, camping, fishing, hunting. Home: 592 Meadowbrook Ln Stayton OR 97383 Office: SAIF Corp 440 Church St SE PWB 2 Salem OR 97312-2000 Fax: 503-315-3086. E-mail: rogzum@saif.com., rogzum@netzero.net.

ZUMWALT, ROSS EUGENE, forensic pathologist, educator; b. Goodrich, Mich., July 18, 1943; s. Paul Lawrence and Lila Ann (Birky) Z.; m. Theresa Ann Schar, Sept. 12, 1970 (div. Apr. 1988); children: Christopher Todd, Tenley Ann; m. Cheryl Lynn Willman, Sept. 4, 1988; 1 child, David Willman Zumwalt. BA, Wabash Coll., 1967; MD, U. Ill., 1971. Diplomate in anat. and forensic pathology Am. Bd. Pathology. Intern, resident in pathology Mary Bassett Hosp., Cooperstown, N.Y., 1971-73; resident in anat. and forensic pathology Southwestern Med. Sch., Dallas, 1973-76; asst. med. examiner Dallas County, Dallas, 1974-76; staff pathologist, dir. labs. Naval Regional Med. Ctr., Camp Lejeune, N.C., 1976-78; dep. coroner Cuyahoga County, Cleve., 1978-80, Hamilton County, Cin., 1980-86; assoc. prof. pathology U. Cin. Sch. Medicine, 1980-86; prof. pathology U. N.Mex. Sch. Medicine, Albuquerque, 1987—, chief med. investigator Office of Med. Investigator, Albuquerque, 1991—; pres. Am. Bd. of Pathology, Tampa, 2000—01. Trustee Am. Bd. Pathology, Tampa, Fla., 1993—. Lt. comdr. USN, 1976-78. Fellow Am. Acad. Forensic Scis., Coll. Am. Pathologists; mem. AMA, Nat. Assn. Med. Examiners (bd. dirs. 1984-96, pres. 1995-96), Am. Soc. Clin. Pathologists, Am. and Can. Acad. Pathologists. Avocation: golf. Office Phone: 505-272-0710. Business E-Mail: rzumwalt@salud.unm.edu.

ZUNG, THOMAS TSE-KWAI, architect; b. Shanghai, Feb. 8, 1933; came to the U.S., 1937, naturalized, 1954; 1 child, Thomas Bates. Student, Drew U., 1950-51, Va. Poly. Inst., 1951-53, Columbia U., 1955-57; BArch, U. Mich., 1960; MS in Design Sci., Internat. Coll., 1982. Project arch. Edward Durell Stone, Arch., N.Y.C., 1958, 60-65; arch. Cleve., 1967—. Pres. Buckminster Fuller, Sadao and Zung, Archs., 1979—; disting. sr. fellow Stanford U. Librs. Author-editor: Buckminster Fuller, Anthology for the New Millennium; prin. works include City Cleve. Pub. Utilities Bldg., Cleve. State U. Geodesic Elongated Dome, Mayfran, Inc., Sawmill Creek Lodge, U. Akron Guzzetta Hall, Music, Speech and Theater Arts Ctr., Alumni Ctr. Bowling Green State U., U. Akron Master Plan-West, City of East Cleveland, Superior Euclid beautification plan, student recreation ctr. Bowling Green State U., Glenville Pub. Libr., campus bldg. Tex. Wesleyan Coll., recreation, health and phys. edn. bldg. Wittenberg U., Medina Res. Park Office, arena, health, phys. edn. complex U. Akron, Dyke Coll., Lima State Prizon, Cleve. Children's Christian Home, State of Ohio Pre-Release Ctr. Cleve., Lorain-Grafton State Prison, Mayfield H.S., Asian Village Project, Cleve. Metroparks Tropical Rainforest Bldg., Student Union Wittenberg U., YWCA, Salem, Ohio, China Internat. Trade Ctr., People's Rep. China, additions to Cleve. Hopkins Internat. Airport, Ohio State U. Coll. of Dentistry-Postle Hall and Hist. Costume and Textile Mus., Master Plan Schreiner Coll. and Cailloux Student Ctr., Griffin Welcome Ctr., Master Plan Walsh Univ., Walsh Student Union, Columbus, Western Res. Psychiat. Hosp., Ohio, Trumbull State Prison, Ohio Dept. Transp. Prototypical Rest Stop Design; patentee in field. Trustee Pace Assn., 1970-73, Karamu House, 1974-80, Cleve. Inst. Music, 1979-86, Chinese Cultural Assn., 1980-84, Ohio Arts Coun., 1982-84; task force chmn. Greater Cleve. Growth Assn., 1970; mem. Coun. Human Rels., 1972, Leadership Cleve. Class '77; cubmaster local Boy Scouts Am., 1977-79; vestryman St. Christopher-by-River, 1980-83; bd. dirs. Buckminster Fuller Inst., 1983—, Pearl S. Buck Found., 1989-98, cons. arch. hist. house com.; mem. Adv. Coun. Aging, State of Ohio, 1997—. With Signal Corps, U.S. Army, 1953-55. Decorated 5 medals; recipient Pub. Works award, State of Ohio, 1971, Design award, Korean Inst. Constrn. Tech., 1984, Ohio Valley ABC Design Excellence award, Wittenberg U. Student Union, 1989, others; Disting. sr. fellow, Stanford U. Librs. Mem. AIA (dir. Cleve. chpt. 1980, Design award Cleve. chpt. 1972, Design award 1989), Am. Soc. Planning Ofcls., English Speaking Union (trustee 1972-75), Ohio Soc. Archs., Ohio Assn. Minority Archs. and Engrs. (trustee 1982-90), Hermit Club, City Club (dir. 1972-74, v.p. 1974), Rotary. Office: Buckminster Fuller Sadao & Zung 1 Bratenahl Pl Cleveland OH 44108-1181

ZUNGER, ALEX, research scientist; BSc, MSc, Tel Aviv U., PhD in chemical physics, 1976. Post doctoral Northwestern U., 1975—77; IBM fellow U. of Calif., 1977—78; prin. scientist Nat. Renewable Energy Lab., 1984—91, inst. rsch. fellow, 1991—. Founder and head Nat. Renewable Energy Lab., Solid State Theory Group, 1978—; adj. prof. physics U. of Colo. at Boulder. Named the 39th most cited physicist out of more than 500,000 physicists examined, Inst. of Sci. Info.; recipient John Bardeen award, 2001, Annesur Rahman award, Am. Physical Soc., 2001, DOE-BES award for sustained rsch. in solid state physics, 1997, Outstanding achievement award, IBM fellowship, 1980. Office: Nat Renewable Energy Lab Mail Stop 3213 OfficeSERF/W1009 Ctr 5900 1617 Cole Blvd Golden CO 80401

ZUNGOLO, EILEEN H. dean; BS, MEd, EdD, Columbia U. Prof., dean Sch. Nursing Northeastern U., Boston, assoc. dean Bouve Coll. Health Scis. Office: Northeastern Univ Sch Nursing 360 Huntington Ave Boston MA 02115-5000 E-mail: ezungolo@lynx.dac.neu.edu.

ZUNIGA, FANNY, aerospace engineer; Postgrad., Stanford U., 2001—; BS in Aero. Engring., Syracuse U.; MS in Aero. Engring., U. So. Calif. Aerospace engr. sys. analysis br. NASA Ames Rsch. Ctr., 1990—. Office: NASA Ames Rsch Ctr Mail Stop 247-4 Bldg 258 Rm 120 Moffett Field CA 94035

ZUNZ, OLIVIER JEAN, history professor; b. Paris, July 19, 1946; s. Jean R. and Monique M. (Blin) Z.; m. Christine M. Crommen, July 3, 1970; children: Emmanuel, Sophie. Licence in history and geography, U. Paris X, 1968, M in History, 1969; Doctorat-ès-Lettres, U. Paris I, Panthéon-Sorbonne, 1982. Scientist Ctr. Nat. de la Recherche Scientifique, Paris, 1976-78; asst. prof. dept. history U. Va., Charlottesville, 1978-83, assoc. prof., 1983-88, prof., 1988-99, Commonwealth prof., 1999—. Vis. prof. Ecole des Hautes Etudes en Scis., Sociales, Paris, 1985—, Coll. France, 1997; dir. seminar for Coll. Tchrs. NEH, 1989, 92. Author: The Changing Face of Inequality: Urbanization, Industrial Development, and Immigrants in Detroit, 1980-1920, 1982, Making America Corporate, 1870-1920, 1990, Why the American Century?, 1998; editor, co-author: Reliving the Past: The Worlds of Social History, 1985; editor: Alexis de Tocqueville, Democracy in America (transl. A. Goldhammer), 2004; co-editor: (with David Ward) The Landscape of Modernity: Essays on New York City, 1900-1940, 1992, (with Leonard Schoppa and Nobuhiro Hiwatari): Social Contracts under Stress: The Middle Classes of America, Europe, and Japan at the Turn of the Century, 2002, (with Alan S. Kahan): The Tocqueville Reader: A Life in Letters and Politics, 2002; mem. editl. bd. Revs. in Am. History, 1990-98; contbr. articles, book revs. to profl. jours. Jr. fellow Mich. Soc. Fellows, 1973-76, John Simon Guggenheim Meml. Found. fellow, 1986-87; grantee U. Mich.-Ford Found. Population Devel. Fund, 1974-76, NSF, 1976-78, NEH, 1979-81, 84-87; also recipient numerous rsch. grants. Mem. Am. Hist. Assn., Orgn. Am. Historians, The Tocqueville Soc. (pres. 2001—). Home: 1368 Hilltop Rd Charlottesville VA 22903-1225 Office: U Va Corcoran Dept of History PO Box 400180 Randall Hall Charlottesville VA 22904-4180 Business E-Mail: oz@virginia.edu.

ZUO, MING JIAN, industrial engineering educator; BSc, Shandong (China) Inst. Tech., 1982; MSc, Iowa State U., 1986, PhD, 1989. Asst. prof. indsl. engring. U. Windsor, Ont., Can., 1989-90; prof. U. Alta., Edmonton, Can., 1990—; assoc. prof. City U. of Hong Kong, China, 1996-98. Guest editor spl. issue Jour. IIE Transactions on Quality and Reliability Engring., 1997; author: Contemporary Engineering Economics: A Canadian Perspective, 1995, 2001, Optimal Reliability Modeling: Principles and Applications, 2002; assoc. editor IEEE Transactions on Reliability, 2002—. Mem. IEEE (sr.), Inst. Indsl. Engrs. Avocations: basketball, badminton, travel. Home: 3006-105A St Edmonton AB Canada T6J3A5 Office: U Alberta Dept Mech Engring Edmonton AB Canada T6G2G8

ZUPAN, MARK A. dean, business professor; b. Rochester, N.Y., July 28, 1959; s. Janez and Maria (Močnik) Zupak; m. Carol Shuherk; children: Will, Walker. BA in econs., Harvard U., 1981; MA, MIT, 1984, PhD in econs. Teaching fellow Harvard U., MIT, Cambridge, 1983-86; asst. prof. to prof. econs. Sch. Bus. Adminstrn., U. So. Calif., 1986—97, assoc. dean masters programs; dean, prof. econs. Eller Coll. Bus. and Pub. Adminstrn., U. Arizona, 1997—2004; dean Simon Grad. Sch. Bus., U. Rochester, NY, 2004—. Vis. prof. Amos Tuck Sch. Bus. Adminstrn., Dartmouth Coll.; mem. editl. bd. Public Choice, Jour. Bus. Econs., Rsch. in Law and Econs. Co-author: (with E.K. Browning) Microeconomic Theory and Applications, (with T. W. Gilligan, A. M. Marino) Microeconomic Cases and Applications; Contbr. articles to profl. jours. Mem. Phi Beta Kappa. Lodges: Rotary. Office: William E Simon Grad Sch Bus Adminstrn U Rochester CS-2202H Carol Simon Hall Rochester NY 14627-0107

ZUPSIC, MATTHEW MICHAEL, insurance company executive; b. Pitts., Aug. 30, 1950; s. Joseph Matthew and Antoinette (Birsic) Z.; children: Tina Elizabeth, Matthew Quay. BA, Marietta Coll., 1972. Mktg. rep. Hartford Ins., Pitts., 1972-76; ins. agt. Githens Ins. Ctr., Belle Vernon, Pa., 1976-77; v.p., ptnr. Burchill Ins. Agy., Inc., Pitts., 1977-88; pres. Harte, Hawke & Zupsic Ins. Agy., Pitts., 1989—. Mem. Pa. Assn. Ind. Ins. Agts. (bd. dirs. 1980-88), Ind. Ins. Agts. Pitts. (treas. 1983, 1st v.p. 1984-86, pres. 1986-88), B&S Investment Club (pres 1985-87). Democrat. Roman Catholic. Avocations: sailing, skiing, boating, gardening. Office Phone: 724-940-7540.

ZURAITIS, MARITA, insurance company executive; V.p. ceded-reins. USF&G Comml. Ins. Group, br. v.p., regional v.p., sr. v.p.; sr. v.p. U.S. ins. ops. The St. Paul Co., Inc., St. Paul, 1998—2001, exec. v.p. Comml. Lines Group, 2001—02, CEO Comml. Lines Group, 2003—. Office: The Saint Paul Cos Inc 385 Washington St Saint Paul MN 55102*

ZURAW, KATHLEEN ANN, special education and physical education educator; b. Bay City, Mich., Sept. 29, 1960; d. John Luke and Clara Josephine (Kilian) Z. AA with high honors, Delta Community Coll., 1980; BS with high honors, Mich. State U., 1984, MA, 1987. Cert. spl. edn., mentally impaired phys. edn. grade K-12, adaptive phys. edn. tchr., Mich. Summer water safety instr. Camp Midicha, Columbia, Mich., 1982, Bay Cliff Health Camp, Big Bay, Mich., 1983; summer spl. edn. tchr. Jefferson Orthopedic Sch., Honolulu, 1984, 85, 86, Ingham Intermediate Sch. Dist., Mason, Mich., 1987; spl. edn. tchr. Bay Arenac Intermediate Sch. Dist., Bay City, 1985-87, Berrien County Intermediate Sch. Dist., Berrien Springs, Mich., 1987—. Mem. citizen amb program fitness delegation People's Republic China, 1991. Area 17 coach Mich. Spl. Olympics, Berrien Springs, 1987—; mem. YMCA, St. Joseph, Mich., 1987—, Y-Ptnrs., 1989, Coun. Exceptional Children; participant Citizen Ambassador Delegation to People's Republic of China, 1991. Mem. Am. Alliance Health, Phys. Edn., Recreation and Dance, Phi Theta Kappa, Phi Kappa Phi, Phi Delta Kappa. Roman Catholic. Avocations: sports, crafts. Home: 7306 W S Saginaw Rd Bay City MI 48706

ZURAWSKI, JEANETTE, rehabilitation services professional; b. June 30, 1951; Student, U. Wis., 1969-70, Portland C.C., 1974-78; BS in Chemistry, Portland State U., 1981; MD, Oreg. Health Scis. U., 1985; postgrad. in acupuncture, UCLA, 2000. Diplomate Am. Bd. Phys. Medicine and Rehab. Resident U. Kans. Med. Ctr., Kansas City, 1985-89; med. dir. rehab. svcs. North Miss Med. Ctr., Tupelo, 1989-97; pvt. practice Tupelo, Miss. Past mem. adv. com. Medicare Carrier; presenter in field; bd. dirs. Gilbert's Home Health Care Agy. Past chair pers. com., exec. bd. mem., co-chair fund raising com. Big Brothers/Big Sisters, Lee County, Miss. Mem. AMA, Am. Acad. Phys. Medicine and Rehab. (chairperson edn. com., mem. exec. coun. resident physician sect.), Am. Med. Women's Assn., Am. Bus. Women's Assn. (chair membership com., treas., recipient Woman of the Year), Miss. State Med. Assn., Assn. Acad. Physiatrists, Am. Med. Acupuncture Assn. (bd. eligible), Iota Sigma Pi. Office: 1010 N Eason Blvd Tupelo MS 38804-7532

ZURCHER, VICKIE LEE, geneticist; b. Millersburg, Ohio, Apr. 9, 1956; d. Carl Frederick and Fae Marie (Tressell) Z.; m. David Blaine Joyce, May 29, 1982; children: Katherine Michelle, Michael David. BA in Biology with honors, Coll. of Wooster, 1978; MD, U. Cinn., 1982. Diplomate Am. Bd. Pediatrics, Am. Bd. Med. Genetics. Intern, then resident in pediatrics Children's Meml. Hosp., Chgo., 1982-85, attending physician, 1985-86; mem. staff Children's Meml. Hosp./Prentice Women's Hosp., Chgo., 1985-86; fellow in clin. genetics U. Hosps. Cleve., 1986-89; instr. in pediatrics Case Western Res. U., Cleve., 1991-95, instr. in genetics, 1992-95; mem. staff Univ. Hosp. Clevel., 1995—2002. Adj. instr. genetics Case Western Res. U., 1995—2002. Contbr. articles to profl. jours. Mem. orch. MGP Cmty. Theater, Avon Lake, 1994—; mem. bell choir Avon Lake Presbyn. Ch., 1993—. Fellow Am. Acad. Pediatrics, Am. Coll. Med. Genetics (founding); mem. Am. Soc. Human Genetics, Phi Beta Kappa. Avocations: piano, accordion, clarinet, travel. Address: 31708 Sailors Cv Avon Lake OH 44012-2931 E-mail: DJoycefamily@comcast.net.

ZURHEIDE, CHARLES HENRY, consulting electrical engineer; b. St. Louis, May 9, 1923; s. Charles Henry and Ollie C. (Kirk) Z.; m. Ruth M. Plueck, June 25, 1949; children— Barbara Anne, Pamela S. BS in Elec. Engring, U. Mo., Columbia, 1944. Registered profl. engr., Mo. Distbn. engr. Laclede Power & Light Co., St. Louis, 1944-45; sub-sta. engr., then indsl. engr. Union Electric Co., St. Louis, 1945-51; chief elec. engr. Fruin-Colnon Contracting Co., St. Louis, 1951-54; a founder, treas., v.p. Smith-Zurheide, Inc., St. Louis, 1954-65; pres. Zurheide-Herrmann, Inc., St. Louis, 1965—, chmn. bd., 1988—2002; ret. Chmn. Elec. Code Rev. Commn., St. Louis, 1965-, Mo. Bd. Profl. Engrs., 1977-82, St. Louis Indsl. Devel. Commn., 1965-67; mem. adv. panel region 6 GSA, 1977—; plan commn., City of Ferguson, Mo., 1968-73; tech. adv. com. St. Louis C. of C., 1977; mem. Mo. Pub. Svc. Commn. Task Force on Retail Wheeling of Electricity, 1998. Recipient Dist. Svc. in Engring. award, U. Mo., 1976. Fellow Am. Cons. Engrs. Council; mem. Mo. Soc. Profl. Engrs. (Engr. of Year award 1970), Cons. Engrs. Council Mo., IEEE, Illuminating Engring. Soc., Engrs. Club St. Louis (Achievement award 2003), Tau Alpha Pi. Clubs: Norwood Hills Country, Mo. Athletic. Home: 14336 Spyglass Rdg Chesterfield MO 63017-2140 Office: Zurheide-Herrmann Inc 4333 Clayton Ave Saint Louis MO 63110-1684 E-mail: czurheide@zhideas.com.

ZURICK, JOHN, consultant, former dance company director; MFA in Theatre Arts, Brandeis U. Acting v.p. mktg. InterLearn, Inc.; creator Power of Once; regional mgr./full-time cons. Mills/James Prodns.; co-founder/pres./COO Finis; ptnr. Y&Z Mgmt., Boston; dir. mktg. Cin. Symphony Orch., 1983-88; instr. ESI Internat., Arlington, Va.; founder, past pres. MillennialMinds, Cin.; exec. dir. Cin. Ballet, 1998—2001; consultant Ballet Internationale, Ind., 2001—. Vol. v.p. mktg. Greater Cin. Arts & Edn. Ctr. Office: Ballet Internationale 502 N Capitol Avenue, Suite B Indianapolis IN 46204

ZURIER, REBECCA, art history educator; AB, Harvard U., 1978; PhD, Yale U., 1988. Assoc. prof. U. Mich., Ann Arbor; Schragis fellow in modern arts Syracuse U., 1990—92. Guest curator Metropolitan Lives: The Ashcan Artists and Their New York Nat. Mus. Am. Art, Smithsonian Instn., 1995; guest curator Yale U. Art Gallery, 1986; vis. appts. U. So. Calif., Emory U., U. Pa., George Washington U., 1988—90. Author: The American Firehouse: An Architectural and Social History, 1982, Art for the Masses (1911-1917): A Radical Magazine and Its Graphics, 1988 (Alfred H. Barr award Coll. Art Assn., 1996); co-author (with Robert W. Snyder and Virginia Mecklenburg): Metropolitan Lives, 1995. Charles Warren Ctr. for Studies in Am. History, Harvard U. fellow, 1999, Getty Postdoctoral grantee, 1993. Office: Univ Mich Art History Dept 519 S State St Ann Arbor MI 48109-1357

ZURIER, ROBERT BURTON, medical educator, clinical investigator; b. Passaic, N.J., Feb. 19, 1934; s. Milton and Lillian (Matzner) Z.; m. Catherine Elizabeth Miers, June 3, 1962; 1 child, Adam Wheaton. BS, Rutgers U., 1955; MD, U. Tex. Southwestern Med. Sch., Dallas, 1962; MA (hon.), U. Pa., 1981. Intern, then resident in medicine Boston City Hosp., 1962-64; fellow in medicine St. Lukes Hosp., N.Y.C., 1964-66; fellow in rheumatology NYU, 1970-73; pvt. practice internal medicine Holden, Mass., 1967-70; asst. prof. medicine U. Conn., Farmington, 1973-76, assoc. prof., 1976-80; prof., chief. rheumatology U. Pa., Phila., 1980-91; prof. medicine, dir. rheumatology div. U. Mass. Med. Ctr., Worcester, 1991—. Served to capt. USAR, 1956-68. Guggenheim Found. fellow, 1986. Mem. AAAS, Am. Coll. Rheumatology (master), Am. Soc. Clin. Investigation, Interurban Clin. Club (pres. 1989-90). Office: U Mass Med Ctr 55 Lake Ave N Worcester MA 01655-0002 Office Phone: 508-856-6246. E-mail: robert.zurier@umassmed.edu.

ZURKOWSKI, PAUL GEORGE, publisher; b. Milw., Nov. 8, 1932; s. Stanley Frank and Martha (Bednarz) Z.; m. Margaret Ann Becker, July 9, 1960; children: Paul Coleman, Pamela Carol, Patricia Christine, Peggy Catherine, Paula Claire, Peter Christopher. BA, U. Wis., Whitewater, 1954; LLB, U. Wis., Madison, 1957. Bar: Wis. 1957, U.S. Supreme Ct. 1961. Publisher Our Ads (shopping guide), Palmyra, Wis., 1950-55; investigator legal firm Swingen & Stern, Madison, 1955-58; atty. HHFA, Washington, 1958; examiner ICC, 1958-59; congl. legis. asst., 1959-61, 64-69; individual legal practice, also congl. home sec., 1961; exec. dir. Info. Industry Assn., Washington, 1969, pres., 1972-89. Pub. Holy Redeemer News, 1984-87, Today's Parish, 1987-90, Our Parish Times, 1990—, Family Beach Times, 1995-96, Interparish Community Guide and Business Directory, 1997—. Pres. Parish Cmty. Svcs. Inc., Md., 1991—; founder, lifetime mem. Cath. Bus. Network, 1993, pres., 1993-94, 2000-01, sec., 1994-96, edn. v.p., 1996-97, program v.p. 1997-98, bd. dirs. Prince Georges, 2002, bd. dirs. D.C., 2002--; founder, sec. Holy Land Christian Ecumenical Found., 1999-2000; founder Catholic Bus. Network USA, Nat. Assn. CBNs. Decorated Army Commendation medal; recipient Disting. Alumni Svc. award U. Wis., Whitewater, 1974, Outstanding Svc. award Cath. Bus. Network, 1994; named to Info. Industry Hall of Fame, 1988, Founders award Cath. Bus. Network Montgomery County, 2000, 1st Paul G. Zurkowski Founders award, CBN-MC. Office: PO Box 30104 Bethesda MD 20824 Office Phone: 301-931-8222. E-mail: info@ourparishtimes.com.

ZUSPAN, FREDERICK PAUL, obstetrician, gynecologist, educator; b. Richwood, Ohio, Jan. 20, 1922; s. Irl Goff and Kathryn (Speyer) Z.; m. Mary Jane Cox, Nov. 23, 1943; children: Mark Frederick, Kathryn Jane, Bethany Anne. BA, Ohio State U., 1947, MD, 1951. Intern Univ. Hosps., Columbus, Ohio, 1951-52, resident, 1952-54, Western Res. U., Cleve., 1954-56, Oblebay fellow, 1958-60, asst. prof., 1958-60; chmn. dept. ob-gyn. McDowell (Ky.) Meml. Hosp., 1956-58, chief clin. svcs., 1957-58; prof., chmn. dept. ob-gyn. Med. Coll. Ga., Augusta, 1960-66; Joseph Boliver DeLee prof. ob-gyn., chmn. dept. U. Chgo., 1966-75; obstetrician, gynecologist in chief Chgo. Lying-In Hosp., 1966-75; prof., chmn. dept. ob-gyn. Ohio State U., Columbus, 1975-87, R.L. Meiling prof. ob-gyn. Sch. Medicine, 1984-90, prof. emeritus, 1991—. Founding editor Lying In, Jour. Reproductive Medicine; editor-in-chief emeritus Am. Jour. Ob-Gyn. Ob-Gyn. Reports, (with Lindheimer and Katz) Hypertension in Pregnancy, 1976, Current Developments in Perinatology, 1977, (with Quilligan) Operative Obstetrics, 1981, 89, Manual of Practical Obstetrics, 1981, 90, 2000, Clin. and Exptl. Hypertension in Pregnancy, 1979-86; editor: (with Christian) Controversies in Obstetrics and Gynecology, (with Rayburn) Drug Therapy in Ob-Gyn., 1981, 3rd edit., 1992; contbr. articles to med. jours., chpts. to books. Pres. Barren Found., 1974-76. With USNR, 1942-43; 1st lt. USMCR, 1943-45. Decorated DFC, Air medal with 10 oak leaf clusters. Mem.: Perinatal Rsch. Soc., Soc. Perinatal Obstetrics, Am. Gynecology and Obstetrics Soc. (pres. 1986—87), Internat. Soc. Study of Hypertension in Pregnancy (pres. 1981—83), Soc. Gynecol. Investigation (Pres.'s award 2001), Am. Soc. Clin. Exptl. Hypnosis (exec. sec. 1968, v.p. 1970), Ctrl. Assn. Ob-Gyn. (Cert. of Merit, Rsch. prize 1970), South Atlantic Assn. Ob-Gyn. (Found. prize for rsch. 1962), Assn. Profs. Gynecology and Obstetrics, Am. Coll. Ob-Gyn., Am. Acad. Reproductive Medicine (pres.), Columbus Ob-Gyn. Soc. (pres. 1984—85), Chgo. Gynecol. Soc., Am. Assn. Ob-Gyn., Soc. Gynecol. Investigation, Alpha Omega Alpha, Sigma Xi, Alpha Kappa Kappa. Home: 10520 Button Willow Dr Las Vegas NV 89134-7346 E-mail: fpzus@aol.com. *The strength of our nation rests in the quality of our offspring. Every fetus has the privilege of being wellborn.*

ZUSSY, NANCY LOUISE, librarian; b. Tampa, Fla., Mar. 4, 1947; d. John David and Patsy Ruth (Stone) Roche; m. R. Mark Allen, Dec. 20, 1986. BA in Edn., U. Fla., 1969; MLS, U. So. Fla., 1977, MS in Pub. Mgmt., 1980. Cert. librarian, Wash. Ednl. evaluator State of Ga., Atlanta, 1969-70; media specialist DeKalb County Schs., Decatur, Ga., 1970-71; researcher Ga. State Libr., Atlanta, 1971; asst. to dir. reference Clearwater (Fla.) Pub. Libr., 1972-78, dir. librs., 1978-81; dep. state libr. Wash. State Libr., Olympia, 1981-86, state libr., 1986—2002; owner Nancy Zussy Allen Massage Therapy, 2003—. Chmn. Consortium Automated Librs., Olympia, 1982-97; cons. various pub. librs., Wash. and other U.S. states, Uzbekistan, Russia, 1981—; exec. officer Wash. Libr. Network, 1986-90; v.p. WLN (non-profit orgn.), 1990-93. Contbr. articles to profl. jours. Treas. Thurston-Mason Community Mental Health Bd., Olympia, 1983-85, bd. dirs., 1982-85; mem. race com. Seafair Hydroplane Race, Seattle, 1986—, mem. milk carton derby team, 1994—, announcer, prodr. air show; co-chair Pub. Info. Access Policy Task Force, 1995-96; mem. Gov.'s Work Group on Comml. Access to Govt. Electronic Records, 1996-97; mem. K-20 Telecomms. Oversight and Policy Com., 1996-2002. Mem. ALA, Assn. Specialized and Coop. Libr. Agys. (legis. com. 1983-86, chmn. 1985-87, vice chmn. state libr. agys. sect. 1985-86, chmn. 1986-87, chmn. govt. affairs com. Libr. Adminstrn. and Mgmt. Assn., 1986-87), Freedom To Read Found. (bd. dirs. 1987-91), Chief Officers of State Libr. Agys. (bd. dirs.-at-large 1987-90, v.p., pres.-elect 1990-92, pres. 1992-94), Wash. Libr. Assn. (co-founder legis. planning com. 1982-2002, fed. rels. coord. 1984-2002), Fla. Libr. Assn. (legis. and planning com. 1978-81), Pacific N.W. Libr. Assn., Rotary (bd. dirs. 1995-96), Phi Kappa Phi, Phi Beta Mu. Avocations: hiking, barbershop chorus/quartet, hydroplane boat racing, cross country skiing. Office: 1722 Harrison Ave NW Olympia WA 98502

ZUTAUT, STEVEN ERIC, systems analyst, application developer; s. James and Magdaline Zutaut. BS in Computer Sci./Chemistry, U. Ala., Huntsville, 1984, PhD in Materials Sci., 1993. Journeyman knowledge-based applications developer Minn., cert. internet application developer Oracle Corp., profl. Microsoft Corp., developer for JavaTM 2 Platform Sun Microsystems, Inc. Assoc. systems analyst Unisys, Montgomery, Ala., 1984—87; knowledge engr. PEAKSolutions Corp., Bloomington, Minn., 1987—89; rsch. assoc. U. Ala., Huntsville, 1993—96; rsch. scientist Nichols Rsch. Corp., Huntsville, 1996—99; sr. cons. Computer Scis. Corp., Huntsville, 1999—2001; software developer (cons.) AEROTEK, Huntsville, 2001—02; sr. systems analyst III Teledyne Solutions, Inc., Huntsville, 2002—. Contbr. articles to profl. jours. Mem.: IEEE, Assn. Computing Machinery. Home: 7801 Regent Pl SW Apt 6 Huntsville AL 35802-1471 Personal E-mail: sezutaut@msn.com.

ZVARA, CHRISTINE C. middle school education educator; BS in Physical Edn. and Adaptive Physical Edn., U. Wis. Mid. and secondary physical edn. specialist grades 6-12 Gibraltar Schs., Fish Creek, Wis. Coord. Dance for Heart Event; mem. swim team bd. Door County YMCA, 1991-95; vol. Sister Bay Fall Classic Run, 1988-91; mem. Sturgeon Bay Sch. Booster Club, 1992—, Sturgeon Bay Band Parents Club, 1991—, Friends of Gibraltar PTO, 1982—. Named Coord. of Yr. Wis. Northeast Dist. Jump Rope for Heart, 1993. Home: 205 S 10th Ave Sturgeon Bay WI 54235-1803 Office: Gibraltar Sch RR 1 Box 205-g Fish Creek WI 54212-9801

ZVETINA, JAMES RAYMOND, pulmonologist; b. Chgo., Oct. 14, 1913; s. John and Jennie (Albrecht) Z.; m. Florence Courtney, Feb. 4, 1944. BS, Loyola U., 1940; MD, U. Ill., 1943. Intern West Suburban Hosp., Oak Park, Ill., 1944, resident physician, 1944-45; asst. ward med. officer USNH, NOB, Norfolk, Va., 1945; staff physician Pulmonary TB Svc. VA Med. Hosp., Hines, Ill., 1946-54; asst. chief Pulmonary Svc. VA Med. Hosp., Hines, Ill., 1954-68, sect. chief, 1968-88, attending physician, 1988-91, cons., 1992—; clin. prof. medicine Coll. Medicine, U. Ill., Chgo., 1978—. Mem. adv. bd. Coll. Medicine, U. Ill., 1985—; rep. Rsch. Conf. in Pulmonary Disease, VA Armed Forces, 1946-74. Contbr. articles to profl. jours. V.p. Chgo. Cath. Physicians, 1979, pres., 1978. Comdr. USNR, 1945-46, med. officer USNR, ret. Recipient Svc. award 40 Yrs. VA Adminstrn., 1985, Svc. award 30 Yrs. U. Ill. Med. Sch., 1978. Fellow Am. Coll. Chest Physicians; mem. AMA, Ill. State Med. Soc. (Fifty Yr. club), Chgo. Med. Soc., Third Order of St. Dominic. Roman Catholic. Achievements include research in area of pulmonary infections. Home: 96 Forest Ave Riverside IL 60546-1977 Office: VA Hines Hines IL 60141

ZWADIUK, OLEH, radio executive; b. Lviv, Ukraine, Feb. 17, 1934; Grad., Hunter Coll. Sr. corr. Radio Free Europe, Radio Libr., Washington, dep. dir., dir. Washington news bur., 1989—2002; ret., 2002. Office: Radio Free Europe 1201 Connecticut Ave NW Washington DC 20036-2609

ZWAHLEN, FRED CASPER, JR., journalism educator; b. Portland, Oreg., Nov. 11, 1924; s. Fred and Katherine (Meyer) Z.; m. Grace Eleanor DeMoss, June 24, 1959; children: Molly, Skip. BA, Oreg. State U., 1949; MA, Stanford U., 1952. Reporter San Francisco News, 1949-50; acting editor Stanford Alumni Rev., Palo Alto, Calif., 1950; successively instr. journalism, news bur. asst., prof. journalism, chmn. journalism dept. Oreg. State U., Corvallis, 1950-91, prof. emeritus, 1991—. Swiss tour guide, 1991—; corres. Portland Oregonian, 1950-67. Author: (with others) Handbook of Photography, 1984, 5th edit., 2002, Two Centuries of Shadow Catchers, A History of Photography, 1996. Coord. E.E. Wilson Scholarship Fund, 1964-2000; active budget com. Corvallis Sch. Dist., 1979. Recipient Achievement award Sch. Journalism U. Oregon, 1988. Mem. Assn. for Edn. in Journalism and Mass Comm. (conv. chmn. 1983, Pres.' award 1988), Oreg. Newspaper Pubs. Assn. (hon. life 1998, bd. dirs. 1980-85, student loan fund named in his honor 1988), Soc. Profl. Journalists (nat. svc. citation 1988), Corvallis Country Club, Shriners, Masons, Delta Tau Delta. Republican. Presbyterian. Avocations: photography, sightseeing, travel. Home: 240 SW 7th St Corvallis OR 97333-4551 E-mail: fredz@peak.org.

ZWANGER, JEROME, physician; b. N.Y.C., Apr. 4, 1923; m. Bernice E. Lomazov, May 22, 1955; children: Susan, Roberta, Melissa, Betsy. AB, U. Pa., 1943; MD, Chgo. Med. Sch., 1947. Diplomate Am. Bd. Radiology. Intern Wyckoff Heights Hosp., Bklyn., 1947-49; resident L.I. Coll. Hosp., Bklyn., 1949-52; practice medicine specializing in radiology; asst. dir. dept. radiology L.I. Coll. Hosp., N.Y.C., 1953-54; radiologist L.I. Jewish Hosp., 1955-60; dir. radiology North Shore U. Hosp., Plainview, NY, 1961—, also bd. dirs. Asst. prof. clin. radiology SUNY, Stony Brook, 1974-80; governing bd. Nassau-Suffolk Health Systems Agy.; mem. N.Y. State Bd. Medicine, Bd. Profl. Med. Conduct N.Y. State Dept. Health. Mem. vis. com. Met. Mus. Art, Phila. Art Mus.; bd. overseers Sch. Arts and Scis., U. Pa. Fellow: Nassau Acad. Medicine (founding fellow, past pres.), Am. Coll. Radiology (councilor 1975—); mem.: AMA, Soc. for Breast Imaging, Am. Inst. Ultrasound in Medicine, L.I. Radiol. Soc. (past pres.), N.Y. State Radiol. Soc. (pres. 1986—87), Radiol. Soc. N.Am., Nassau County Med. Soc. (pres.), Med. Soc. N.Y., U. Pa. Alumni Assn. (bd. overseers 1997). Office: 126 Hicksville Rd Massapequa NY 11758-5822

ZWASS, VLADIMIR, computer science and information systems educator; b. Lvov, USSR, Feb. 3, 1946; came to U.S., 1970, naturalized, 1979; s. Adam and Friderike (Getzler) Z.; m. Alicia Kogut, Apr. 24, 1977; 1 child, Joshua Jonathan MS, Moscow Inst. Energetics, 1969; MPhil, Columbia U., 1974, PhD, 1975. Mem. profl. staff IAEA, Vienna, Austria, 1970; asst. prof. computer sci. Fairleigh Dickinson U., Teaneck, N.J., 1975-79, assoc. prof., 1979-84, prof., 1984—, prof. computer sci. and mgmt. info. sys., 1990—, disting. prof. computer sci. and mgmt. info. sys., 1999—, chmn. com. computer sci., 1976—. Cons. U.S. Govt., Met. Life Ins. Co., Citibank, Diebold Group; seminar assoc. Columbia U., 1986—; speaker nat. and internat. meetings. Author: Introduction to Computer Science, 1981, Programming in Fortran, 1981, Programming in Pascal, 1985, Programming in Basic, 1986, Management Information Systems, 1992, Foundations of Information Systems, 1998; editor-in-chief: Jour. Mgmt. Info. Sys., 1983—, Internat. Jour. Electronic Commerce, 1996—, Advances in Mgmt. Info. Systems, —; contbr. articles to profl. jours. and publs., Ency. Britannica, N.Y. Times, chpts. to books, chapters to books. Columbia U. fellow, 1970-71; Helena Rubinstein Found. scholar, 1971-75; grantee USN, other agys. Mem. IEEE, Assn. Computer Machinery, Assn. for Info. Sys., Sigma Xi, Eta Kappa Nu. Home: 19 Warewoods Rd Saddle River NJ 07458-2712 Office: Sch Computer Sci and Info Sys Fairleigh Dickinson U Teaneck NJ 07666 Personal E-mail: zwass@fdu.edu.

ZWEBACK, STANLEY, psychologist, educator; s. Harry and Belle Zweback; m. Dianne Barbara Fain, Dec. 24, 1964; children: Franklin Edward, Jessica Ellen. PhD, U. Md., 1972. Diplomate Am. Bd. Profl. Disability Consultants. Assoc. prof. psychology Towson (Md.) U., 1970—; dir. svcs. Pers. Screening Sys., Severna Park, Md., 1985—. Cons. Balt. City Pub. Sch. Sys., 1999—2003; dir. svcs. Drs. Zweback, Driscoll and Associates, Severna Park, 1989—98; psychol. cons. Arthur Slade Regional Sch., Glen Burnie, Md., 1973—. Contbr. articles to profl. jours. Pres. Bello Machre, Inc., Pasadena, Md., 1987—96. Experienced Tchr. fellow in sch. psychology, US Office of Edn., 1967—68. Mem.: APA (mem. continuing edn. com. 1989—89). Office: Towson U 8000 York Rd Towson MD 21252 Personal E-mail: dizwe@comcast.net. E-mail: zweback@towson.edu.

ZWEBEN, STUART HARVEY, information scientist, educator; b. Bronx, N.Y., Apr. 21, 1948; s. Max D. and Ruth (Schwartz) Z.; m. Rochelle T. Small, June 13, 1971; 1 child, Naomi. BS, CUNY, 1968; MS, Purdue U., 1971, PhD, 1974. Systems analyst IBM Corp., Kingston, N.Y., 1969-70; asst. prof. Ohio State U., Columbus, 1974-80, from vice chmn. to acting chmn. computer sci. dept., 1982-84, assoc. prof., 1980-92, prof., 1992—, chmn., 1994—. Pres. Computing Scis. Accreditation Bd., Stamford, Conn., 1989-91, v.p. 1987-89, sec.-treas. 1986-87; sec.-treas. Fedn. on Computing in the U.S., Washington, 1992. Contbr. articles to profl. jours. Rsch. grantee NSF, 1981-83, 88-90, 91-93, 93-97, Army Rsch. Office, 1980-83, Dept. Edn., 1983-85, Applied Info. Tech. Rsch. Ctr., 1990-91, Honda R&D, 1998—; equipment grantee AT&T Bell Labs, 1984, 86-88. Fellow Assn. for Computing Machinery (pres. 1994-96, v.p. 1992-94, coun. mem. 1982-88, chpt. bd. chmn. 1982-85, publications bd. 1988-92, fin. com. 1990-92, nominating com. chmn. 1999-2000, fellows com. chmn. 2003, constn. and bylaws chmn. 1988-92, Recognition of Svc. award 1980, 85, 87, 88, Outstanding Contbn. award 1997); mem. AAUP, IEEE Computer Soc. (assoc. editor 1990-98), Computing Rsch. Assn. (bd. dirs. 1997-2004), Coun. Sci. Soc. Presidents (sec. 1998), Columbus Tech. Coun. (Tech. Person of Yr. award 2000). Avocations: sports, stamp collecting/philately. Office: Ohio State U Computer Scis 2015 Neil Ave Columbus OH 43210-1210 Office Phone: 614-292-9526. Business E-Mail: Zweben@cse.ohio-state.edu.

ZWECKER, WILLIAM RENE, JR., (BILL ZWECKER), newspaper columnist, television reporter; b. Chgo., Dec. 25, 1949; s. William Rene and Margaret Rishel (Bushee) Z.; m. Deborah Heidrich Bunn Alley, Sept. 1, 1973 (div. July 1977); 1 child, Brayton. AB in History cum laude, Princeton U., 1971. Legis. asst. U.S. Senator Charles Percy, Washington, 1971-73; asst. officer First Nat. Bank of Chgo., 1973-75; adminstrv. v.p. Krancer & Frank, Inc., Chgo., 1975-77; pres. Animal Accents, Inc., Chgo., 1977-83; mgr. Saks Fifth Ave, Chgo. and Oak Brook, Ill., 1983-86; regional v.p. BMW (N) Holding Corp., Chgo., 1986-87; assoc. editor, columnist Lerner Newspapers, Chgo., 1987-92; columnist Chgo. Sun-Times, 1992—; corr. The Joan Rivers Show, N.Y.C., 1990-94. Host, producer Cast of Characters, Group W Cable TV, Chgo., 1988-90; entertainment reporter, film critic WMAQ-TV, NBC, Chgo., 1994-2000, WPNT-FM Radio, Chgo., 1993-95, WTMX-FM Radio, Chgo., 1999—; entertainment reporter WFLD-TV (Fox), Chgo., 2000-2003, WBBM-TV (CBS), Chgo., 2003—. Author numerous articles on lifestyle, fashion, travel in Chgo. Daily News, Crain's Chgo. Bus., Town and Country, Chgo., others. Bd. dirs. Greater N. Michigan Ave Assn., Chgo., 1980-85, Mental Health Assn. Greater Chgo., 1983-88; founding bd. dirs. Aux. bd. Lincoln Park Zoo, Chgo., 1979-89; bd. trustees Chgo. Acad. of Arts, 2004-. Recipient Tradition of Excellence alumni awrd Oak Park-River Forest H.S., 1995, Peter Lisagor award in journalism, 1991, 99; named Man of Vision Midwest Eye-Banks, 2000, Lifetime Achievement award Israel Film Festival, 2003. Mem. Soc. Profl. Journalists (bd. dirs. 1992-94), North Dearborn Assn. (bd. dirs. 1993-97), Rotary Club of Chgo., Arts Club of Chgo. Episcopalian. Office: Chgo Sun-Times 401 N Wabash Ave Chicago IL 60611-5642 Office Phone: 312-321-2820. E-mail: bzwecker@suntimes.com.

ZWEIFEL, DAVID ALAN, newspaper editor; b. Monroe, Wis., May 19, 1940; s. Cloyence John and Uva Lorraine (Skinner) Z.; m. Sandra Louise Holz, Sept. 7, 1968; children: Daniel Mark, Kristin Lynn. BJ, U. Wis., 1962. Reporter The Capital Times, Madison, Wis., 1962-71, city editor, 1971-78, mng. editor, 1978-83, editor, 1983—. V.p. Simpson St. Free Press, 2001—; bd. dirs. Swiss Am. Ctr., Friends of Monona Terrace, Capital Times Co., Madison Newspapers Inc., William T. Evjue Charitable Trust. V.p. Alliance for Children and Youth, Madison, 1983—; bd. dirs. United Cerebral Palsy Dane County, Madison, 1984-91. Lt. U.S. Army, 1963-65; col. USNG, ret. Named Investigative Reporter of Yr. Madison Press Club, 1972; Disting. Journalism grad., U. Wis., 2003 Mem.: Soc. Profl. Journalists (Spl. Achievement award 1992, 1996), Wis. Freedom of Info. Coun. (pres. 1986—2000), Wis. AP (pres. 1987—88), Am. Soc. Newspaper Editors (com. freedom of info., Pulitzer Prize juror 2000, 2001), U. Wis. Alumni Assn., Wis. N.G. Assn. (trustee 1975—81), Elks. Avocations: running, bowling, book collecting. Home: 5714 Tecumseh Ave Monona WI 53716-2964 Office: The Capital Times PO Box 8060 Madison WI 53708-8060

ZWEIFEL, DONALD EDWIN, retired newspaper editor, lobbyist, consultant; b. L.A., Nov. 30, 1940; s. Robert Fredrick and Eugenia Bedford (White) Z.; m. Donna Jean Croslin; 1 son, Phillip Matthew. Student, Orange Coast Coll., 1963-67, 90-92, U. Calif., Irvine, 1968-70, Western State U. Coll. Law, 1973, Irvine U. Coll. Law, 1974-75, Rancho Santiago Jr. Coll., 1988, Chapman U., 1989, 93-97; grad., Aviation Ground Sch., 1990; student, USAF Air U., 1994—95, USAF Air. U., 2000—01. Cert. student pilot 1989, registered lobbyist Calif. State Legis., 2002. Devel. tech. Hughes Aircraft, Newport Beach, Calif., 1963-64; co-founder Sta. KUCI-FM, Irvine, Calif., 1970; owner, mgr. Zweifel Jaguar Car Sales and Svc., Santa Ana, Calif., 1975-76; pres. Zweifel & Assocs. Inc., Santa Ana, 1977-86, Zweifel South Coast Exotic Cars, Orange, Calif., 1987-96, ret., 1996; assoc. editor Compliance News Pub. Co., Long Beach, Calif., 1998—. Mem. small bus. coun. Cal Trans, 2002—. Co-author: Challenge 2000, Regaining the America's Cup, 1996; editor: (coll. textbook) The Dream Is Alive, Space Flight and Operations In Earth Orbit. Vol. emergency coord. emergency mgmt. divsn. Orange County Fire Authority, 1985-87, Navy Relief Soc., 1993, 1st. lt. CAP Squadron 88 Group VII, 1993-95, sr. programs officer, 1993-94, asst. transp. officer Calif. Wing Hdqrs., 1994-95, Group VII Facilities officer, 1994-95, 2000-02, squadron pers. officer, 1993-95, 2000-02, Calif. wing rep. to Orange County Vol. Orgns. Active in Disaster, ARC, 1994-95, Calif. wing vol. Office Emergency Svcs., Calif., 1994-96, 2000-21, grad. Squadron Leadership Sch., 1993, Wing Supply Officers Sch., 1995, squadron safety officer, pub. affairs officer, asst. aerospace edn. officer, 1998-2001; program coord. Young Astronaut Coun., 1989-90; cadet CAP, USAF aux., Long Beach, Calif., 1953-59; mem. Orange County Homeless Issues Taskforce, 1994-95, 1997-2000, Orange County Homeless Svc. Providers for the Reuse of Marine Corps Air Sta., Tustin, Calif., 1994-95; mem. legis. com. Orange County Vets. Adv. Coun., 1998—; chmn. tech. rev. subcom. Marine Corps Air Sta., El Toro, Calif., 1998-2001; apptd. to CalEPA DTSC Adv. Group Mil. Base Closure, 1995-99, CalEPA Dept. Toxic Substances Control Adv. Group pro-bono cons., Orange County Citizen's Adv. Commn. and El Toro Local Redevel. Authority, 1996-2001; vol. mediator Victim-Offender Reconciliation program, 1995-96; restoration adv. bd. MCAS Tustin, 1994—, co-chair RAB, MCR, Tustin, 2003—; mem. restoration adv. bd. MCAS, El Toro, Calif., 1994—; mem. Freedom Com. of Orange County, Cmty. ER Response Team for City of Placentia, 2003—; mem. homeless vets. com. United Vets. Orgn. Orange County; fed. advocate for Disabled Veteran Bus. Enterprise, 2004—. With Army N.G. (hon. discharge), 1958-59. Recipient 6 certs. achievement Fed. Emergency Mgmt. Agy., 1989-96, 2 certs. appreciation CAP, 2 certs commendation, 1994, cert. appreciation Southwest Divsn. Naval Facilities Engring. Commd., 2000, Meritorious Svc. award, Calif. State Assembly Restoration Adv. Bd. Assemblyman John Campbell, 2001,Orange County Walk of Honor, 1998, Congres. Medal of Honor, 2004 Mem. Air Force Assn. (vice-chmn. civilian recruitment Calif. state membership com. 1988-89, 90-91, v.p. membership, Gen. Doolittle chpt. bd. dirs. 1987-89, 90-92, Exceptional Svc. award Gen. Jimmy Doolittle chpt. 1988, 91, Calif. Meritorious Svc. award 1988, v.p. membership Gen. Curtis E. LeMay Orange County chpt. 2000-02), Calif. Assn. for Aerospace Edn. (fellow), Marine Corps Hist. Found. (life), Aerospace Edn. Found. (Gen. Jimmy Doolittle fellow 1988, Gen. Ira Eaker fellow 1989, Pres.'s award 1988), U.S. Naval Inst., AIAA (Cert. of Appreciation 1989, L.A. chpt. hist. com. 1989), Gulf & Vietnam Vets. Strategic Studies Archives (cons., co-founder 1983—, dir.), Marine Corps League (assoc., capt. Heinsey detachment 2000-02), Confederate Air Force (col.1989), AmVets (nat. jr. coord. com. 2003—, Calif. jr. coord. 2003—, 2d vice comdr. Dist. II, Dept. Calif 2003-04), Masons, Saddleback Master Chorale of Orange County. Avocations: sailing, travel, flying. Home: 386 Hawaii Way Placentia CA 92870-6036 Personal E-mail: dzweifel@sbcglobal.net.

ZWEIFEL, RICHARD GEORGE, curator; b. L.A., Nov. 5, 1926; s. Harold Charles and Kathleen Marguerite (Garland) Z.; m. Frances Ann Wimsatt, July 30, 1956; children: Matthew Karl, Kenneth Paul, Ellen Katrina. BA, UCLA, 1950; PhD, U. Calif. at Berkeley, 1954. Mem. staff Am. Mus. Natural History, N.Y.C., 1954-89, chmn. curator dept. herpetology, 1968-80, curator emeritus, 1989—; sci. attaché Gondwana, 1974-75. Served with AUS, 1945-46. Mem. Soc. Study Amphibious and Reptiles, Am. Soc. Ichthyologists and Herpetologists. Home: PO Box 16354 Portal AZ 85632-1354

ZWEIG, JANET, artist; BA, Cornell U., 1971; MFA, SUNY, Rochester, 1981. Faculty RISD, 1982—; asst. prof. Boston U., 1983-84. Resident Nexus Press, Atlanta, 1981, Jacob's Pillow Dance Festival, 1986, Macdowell Colony, Peterborough, NH, 1989, Peterborough, 90, Peterborough, 93, Peterborough, 94; resident Nat. Studio program PS1 Mus., Long Island, NY, 1990—91; resident Blue Mountain Ctr., 1997, Djerassi Resident Artists Program, 1998; guest lectr. numerous instns. MIT, Sch. Mus. Fine Arts, Boston U., Wesleyan U., Worcester Art Mus., Hartford Atheneum, NYU, Harvard U., U. Mass., Folger Shakespeare Libr., Brown U., Sarah Lawrence Coll., SUNY, Purchase, Temple U. Rome, Bard Coll., Photog. Resource Ctr., Boston, Moore Coll. Art, Phila., 1980—; adj. faculty Cooper Union, Anderson Ranch Art Ctr., Emerson Coll., Mass. Coll. Art, Sch. Mus. Fine Arts, Boston, Visual Studies Workshop Summer Inst., 1982—; juror Cultural Edn. Collaborative, Boston, 1986, Ill. State Coun. on the Arts Visual Arts Fellowships, 1987; juror The Bunting Inst. Radcliffe Coll., 1992; juror Am. Acad. Rome, 1995; vis. critic Yale U., 1991. Prin. works include sculptures at List Visual Art Ctr. MIT, Cambridge, Mass., The Art Gallery U. Md., 1989, 1990, PS 1 Mus., Inst. Contemporary Art, Long Island, 1990, 1991, Wallace Gallery SUNY, Old Westbury, 1991, The Artists Mus., Lodz, Poland, 1992, The Ulrich Mus. Wichita State U., 1992, Diverse Works, Houston, 1992, Sala 1, Rome, 1993, Huntington Gallery Mass. Coll. Art, 1993, RISD Mus., Providence, 1994, DeCordova Mus., Lincoln, Mass., Computer Mus., Boston, 1994, Big Orbit Gallery, Buffalo, N.Y., 1995, Anderson Gallery, Buffalo, 1995, Motel Fine Arts, N.Y.C., 1997, 1997, Snug

Harbor Cultural Ctr., S.I., N.Y., 1995, Eighth Floor Gallery, N.Y.C., 1997, Cooper Union and the Coll. Art Assn., 1997, The Rotunda Gallery, Bklyn., 1998, Neuberger Mus. Art, Purchase, 1998, Represented in permanent collections Mus. Modern Art, Whitney Mus., Boston Mus. Fine Arts, Internat. Ctr. Photography, Calif. Inst. Arts, The Houghton Libr. Harvard, Cleve. Art Inst., Wellesley Coll. Libr., Visual Studies Workshop, Mus. Contemporary Art, Chgo., Art Inst. Chgo., Walker Art Ctr., Pompidou Ctr., RISD. Recipient Englehard award, Englehard Found. Inst. Contemporary Art, Boston, 1991; fellow in new genres category, Mass. Artists Found., 1985, visual arts fellow, NEA, 1985, 1994, The Rome Prize fellow, Am. Acad. Rome, 1991—92, grantee, Art Matters, Inc., 1986—90, Faculty Devel. Fund grantee, RISD, 1987, 1990, Individual Artists grantee, Artists Space, N.Y., 1990, grantee, Arts Internat., N.Y., 1992. Home: 54 Willow St Apt 4A Brooklyn NY 11201-6955 E-mail: jzweig@quicklink.com.

ZWEIG, STEVEN FREDERICK, statistician; s. Sammuel and Shirley Zweig. BS in Animal Sci., U. of Ga., 1979; MA in Econ., Va. Commonwealth U., 1985; MS in Biostatistics, Med. Coll. of Va., 1993. Retail mgr. Pk. Drug Store, Petersburg, Va., 1980—91; cons. InfoStat Cons., Columbus, 1994—96; statis. Covance, Inc., Princeton, NJ, 1996—2000, sr. statistician Target Rsch. Associates, New Providence, NJ, 2000—01; mgr. of biostatistics MDS Pharma Services, King of Prussia, Pa., 2001—03, SFBCI/New Drug Svcs. MNGR Biostats., Kennett Sq, Pa., 2003—04; cons. biostatistician Premier Rsch., Phila., 2004—. Sec. Columbus Jaycees, Columbus, Ohio, 1994—96. Recipient Dan O'Kane award, Columbus Jaycees, 1996. Mem.: Drug Info. Assn., Am. Statis. Assn. Home: 10 Sunflower Lane Yardville NJ 08620-3002 Personal E-mail: stevenfzweig@nctscape.net.

ZWEIMAN, BURTON, physician, scientist, educator; b. N.Y.C., June 7, 1931; s. Charles and Gertrude (Levine) Z.; m. Claire Traig, Dec. 30, 1962; children: Amy Beth, Diane Susan. AB, U. Pa., 1952, MD, 1956. Diplomate Am. Bd. Internal Medicine, Am. Bd. Allergy & Immunology. Intern Mt. Sinai Hosp., N.Y.C.; Hosp. U. Pa., Bellevue Hosp. Ctr. Hosp. U. Pa., Bellevue Hosp. Center, 1957-60; fellow NYU Sch. Medicine, 1960-61; mem. faculty dept. medicine U. Pa. Sch. Medicine, Phila., 1963—, prof. medicine, chief allergy and immunology divsn., 1975-98. Cons. U.S. Army, NIH; co-chmn. Am. Bd. Allergy and Immunology, 1979-81 Editor Jour. Allergy Clin. Immunology, 1988-93; contbr. articles to med. jours. Served with M.C., USNR, 1961-63. Allergy Found. Am. fellow, 1959-61 Fellow ACP, Am. Acad. Allergy, Asthma and Immunology (past pres.); mem. Am. Assn. Immunologists, Am. Fedn. Clin. Rsch., Phi Beta Kappa, Alpha Omega Alpha. Office: Hosp U Pa 527 Maloney Bldg 34th & Spruce St Philadelphia PA 19104 E-mail: bzweiman@mail.med.upenn.edu.

ZWERDLING, ALEX, English educator; b. Breslau, Germany, June 21, 1932; came to U.S., 1941, naturalized, 1946; s. Norbert and Fanni (Alt) Z.; m. Florence Goldberg, Mar. 23, 1969; 1 son, Antony Daniel. BA, Cornell U., 1953; postgrad. (Fulbright scholar), U. Munich, Germany, 1953-54; MA, Princeton U., 1956, PhD, 1960. Instr. English Swarthmore Coll., 1957-61; asst. prof. English U. Calif., Berkeley, 1961-67, asso. prof., 1967-73, prof., 1973-86, prof. English, 1988—, chmn. grad. studies, 1985-86; univ. prof. George Washington U., 1986-88. Vis. prof. Northwestern U., 1977; dir. edn. abroad program U. Calif., London, 1996-98; mem. advanced placement exam. com. Ednl. Testing Svc., 1975-79; mem. fellowship panel Nat. Endowment for Humanities, 1977-82, 84-87, Nat. Humanities Ctr., 1989-90; fellow Ctr. for Advanced Study in Behavioral Scis., 1964-65. Author: Yeats and the Heroic Ideal, 1965, Orwell and the Left, 1974, Virginia Woolf and the Real World, 1986, Improvised Europeans: American Literary Expatriates and the Siege of London, 1998; mem. adv. com. PMLA, 1978-82. Am. Coun. Learned Socs. fellow, 1964-65; NEH fellow, 1973-74; Guggenheim fellow, 1977-78; Woodrow Wilson Ctr. fellow, 1991-92, fellow Nat. Humanities Ctr., 1992-93. Mem. MLA (chmn. 20th Century Brit. lit. div. 1969-70, 85-86, Berkeley Citation, 2003). Office: U Calif Dept English Berkeley CA 94720-1030

ZWERLING, GARY LESLIE, investment bank executive; b. N.Y.C., Aug. 6, 1949; s. Seymour Joseph and Evelyn Rhoda (Posner) Z.; m. Marierose Miraglia, Aug. 25, 1974; children: Cara Marisa, Craig Harris. BEngring., SUNY, Stony Brook, 1970; MBA, SUNY, Albany, 1972. V.p. Chase Manhattan Bank, N.Y.C., 1972-78; ptnr. Goldman, Sachs & Co., N.Y.C., 1978-96; ret., 1996. Mem. bd. overseers Babson Coll., Mus. Jewish Heritage-A Living Meml. to the Holocaust; trustee Jewish Fedn. North Jersey; bd. govs. N.Y. chpt. Arthritis Found. Mem. Thoroughbred Owners and Breeders Assn., Nat. Thoroughbred Racing Assn. Jewish. Avocation: skiing.

ZWERLING, LEONARD JOSEPH, physician, educator; b. Bklyn., May 15, 1944; s. David Louis and Ray (Mooney) Z.; m. Holly Gail Margolin, June 4, 1972; children: Jared, Margo. BA, Columbia Coll., 1965; MD cum laude, Boston U., 1969. Diplomate Am. Bd. Internal Medicine, Am. Bd. Cardiovasc. Disease, Bd. Nuclear Cardiology. Intern Mt. Sinai Hosp., N.Y.C., 1969-70, resident, 1970-72; fellow cardiology Beth Israel Hosp., Boston, 1972-73, Mass. Gen. Hosp., Boston, 1975-76; pvt. practice Cardiovasc. Medicine Assocs., P.A., Miami, Fla., 1976—; clinical fellow medicine Harvard, 1972-76. Staff assoc. medicine MIT Arteriosclerosis Ctr., 1975-76; clin. asst. prof. medicine U. Miami Med. Sch., 1976-83, clin. assoc. prof., 1983-91, clin. prof., 1991—; med. dir. home health care svcs. Bapt. Health; active staff. Bapt. Hosp., South Miami Hosp. Author: (chpt.) Recent Advances in Studies on Cardiac Structure and metabolism, Vol. 5, Basic Functions of Cations in Mycardial Activity, 1975, The Care of the Post MI Patient, 1986. Lt. USNR, 1973-75. Recipient Boston Women's Club award, 1969, Maimonides award Boston Med. Soc., 1969, Univ. Hosp. award, 1969. Fellow ACP, Am. Coll. Cardiology, Am. Heart Assn. (coun. clin. cardiology); mem. Am. Soc. Echocardiography and Nuclear Cardiology, Alpha Omega Alpha. Home: 8300 Cheryl Ln Miami FL 33143-8610 Office: Cardiovasc Medicine Assocs 6200 SW 73d St Ste 210 Miami FL 33143

ZWERLING, LISA, painter, educator; d. David Robinson and Pauline Ormond. BA, Sarah Lawrence Coll.; BFA, Cooper Union; Masters, NYU. Adj. full prof. NYU, N.Y.C., 1980—. Painter, N.Y.C., 1974—. Paintings, The Four Seasons, one-woman shows include First St. Gallery, NY, 1976, 1980, 1982, 1986, 1990, 1992, 1994, 1997, 1999, 2002, exhibitions include Frye Art Mus., Seattle, 2000, 1978. Grantee, Pollock-Krasner Found., 1995, 1997, Gottlieb Found., 2003; Travel grant, Nat. Endowment for Arts, 1996. Avocations: travel, movies.

ZWERLING, PHILIP, language educator, playwright; b. N.Y.C., Nov. 5, 1948; s. David and Mildred Zwerling; m. Susan Graham Neal, May 21, 1995; children: Gabriel Benjamin Valdes, Jesse Harry, Morena Kate, Seth Asher; m. Connie Martin, June 16, 1968 (div. June 0, 1985). BA, St. Lawrence U., 1970; MDiv, Harvard U., 1974; MFA in Creative Writing, U. New Orleans, 1998; PhD in Dramatic Art, U. Calif., 2003. Min. First Unitarian Ch., Ashby, Mass., 1971—73, Cmty. Ch., Boston, 1974—78, First Unitarian Ch., L.A, 1978—89, Tucson, 1989—93; staff writer The Desert Leaf, 1989—99, The Valley Voice, Goleta, Calif., 1998—2002; asst. prof. English and creative writing Ursinus Coll., Collegeville, Pa., 2003—. Author: Nicaragua: A New Kind of Revolution, (plays) Dr. Sex (Am. Coll. Theatre Festival Excellence Playwriting award, 1997), Soul Play (Sherrill C. Corwin-Metropolitan Theatres Corp. Writing award Best Full Length Stage Play, 199). Dir. City at Peace, Isla Vista, Calif., 2000—01; bd. mem. Ind. Theatre Awards Com., Santa Barbara, 1999—2001; local bargaining team chair Assn. Grad. Student Employees/UAW, 1999—2000; founder, treas. Clergy for Choice, Tucson, 1992—93; bd. mem. Family Student Housing Tenants' Assn., 2000—01. Recipient Clarence Skiner award Best Sermon Social Justice, Unitarian Universalist Assn., 1980, 1982, Nat. Critics Inst. Winner, Region V!, Am. Coll. Theatre Festival, 1998, Nat. Critics Inst. Winner, Region VI, 1999, Outstanding Achievement in Creativity, Lakefront Players, U. New Orleans, 1998, Nat. Critics Inst. cert. Achievement, Eugene O'Neill Theatre Ctr., 1999. Mem.: Pedagogy and Theatre Oppressed, Assn. Theatre Higher Edn., Dramatists Guild. Office: Ursinus College Main Street Collegeville PA 19426

ZWICK, EDWARD M. director, producer, scriptwriter; b. Winnetka, Il., Oct. 8, 1952; s. Allen and Ruth Ellen (Reich) Z.; m. Lynn Liberty Godshall, Oct. 24, 1982. BA, Harvard U., 1974; MFA, Am. Film Inst., 1976. Editor, feature writer The New Republic, Rolling Stone, 1972-74; co-founder The Bedford Falls Co., 1985. Writer, prodr., dir.: (TV series) Family, 1976-80 (Humanitas prize 1980), (TV spl.) Spl. Bull., 1983 (Emmy award for outstanding drama spl. 1983, Dir. Guild award 1983, Writers Guild award 1983, Humanitas prize 1983); dir.: (TV movies) Paper Dolls, 1982, Having It All, 1982, Extreme Close-Up, 1990, (films) About Last Night, 1986, Glory, 1989, Leaving Normal, 1992, Legends of the Fall, 1994, Courage Under Fire, 1995, The Seige, 1998, The Last Samurai (also prodr.), 2003; prodr. Shakespeare in Love, 1998 (Oscar award for best picture, 1998, BAFTA award for best picture, 1999, Golden Satellite award for best picture, 1998), Traffic, 2000 (NY Film Critics Circle award for best picture, 2000, Golden Satellite award for best picture, 2000), I Am Sam, 2001, Women Vs. Men (TV movie), 2002, Abandon, 2002, Lone Star State of Mind (exec. prodr.), 2002; co-creator, exec. prodr.: (with Marshall Herskovitz) Thirtysomething, 1987-91 (Emmy award for outstanding drama series 1988), Dream Street, 1989, My So-Called Life, 1994-95, Relativity, 1996-97, co-creator, prodr. Once and Again, 2000, author: Literature and Liberalism, 1975. Office: USA Films 9333 Wilshire Blvd Beverly Hills CA 90210

ZWICK, REBECCA, education educator; BA in Psychology and Edn., Antioch Coll., 1974; MA in Quantitative Methods, U. Calif., Berkeley, 1981; PhD in Quantitative Methods, 1983; MS in Stats., Rutgers U., 1989. NIMH postdoctoral fellow L.L. Thurstone Psychometric Lab. U. N.C., Chapel Hill, 1983—84; rsch. scientist Psychometrics Rsch. Group Ednl. Testing Svc., Princeton, NJ, 1984—89, dir. data analysis and scale devel. Nat. Assessment Ednl. Progress, 1990—91, sr. rsch. scientist Rsch. Stats. Group, 1991—95, prin. rsch. scientist Rsch. Stats. Group, 1995—96; prof. dept. edn. U. Calif., Santa Barbara, 1996—. Cons., workshop presenter on psychometrics and stats. Clin. Svcs. Rsch. Tng. Program U. Calif., San Francisco, 1986—; sr. fellow Consortium of Univs. U.S. Def. Dept., 1998—; tech. design team Nat. Assessment of Adult Literacy, 1999—; reviewer for reports or proposals Nat. Ctr. for Edn. Stats., 1998, 2001, Nat. Acad. Scis., 1999, NSF, 2000, Nat. Inst. Statis. Scis., 2002, Springer Pubs., 2002. Editor: (spl. issue) Jour. Ednl. Stats., 1992, Jour. Ednl. Measurement, 1995—98; cons. editor: Jour. Consulting and Clin. Psychology, 1985—89, Psychol. Assessment, 1988—91, reviewer: Jour. Am. Statis. Assn., Psychometrika, Psychol. Methods, Applied Psychol. Measurement, Applied Measurement in Edn., Multivariate Behavioral Rsch., Jour. Ednl. Measurement, Jour. Ednl. and Behavioral Stats., Ednl. Measurement: Issues and Practice, Can. Jour. Behavioral Scis., Jour. Math. Psychology. Fellow: APA; mem.: Psychometric Soc., Nat. Coun. on Measurement in Edn. (chair publs. com. 2001—03, faculty advisor grad. student issues com. 1999—2001), Am. Stats. Assn., Am. Ednl. Rsch. Assn. (sec.-treas. 1988—90, program chair conv. 1995, pres. ednl. statisticians spl. interest group 1995—96), Soc. for Multivariate Experimental Psychology. Office: Univ Calif Santa Barbara 2216 Phelps Hall Santa Barbara CA 93106-9490

ZWICKER, CHARLES, economist, educator, accountant, consultant; b. N.Y.C., Apr. 13, 1912; s. Harry and Sarah Zwicker; m. Mildred Waldman, Oct. 25, 1941; children: Peter, Robert. BS, NYU, 1933, MBA, 1950. CPA, N.Y. Ptnr. Zwicker, Sturmer & Co. CPAs, N.Y.C., 1947-50, Rosenblum, Zwicker & Co., CPAs, N.Y.C., 1950-55, Zwicker & Simon CPAs, Garden City and N.Y.C., 1956-82; prof. emeritus L.I. U., Brookville, 1957-80, dean Sch. Accountancy, 1973-80; dir. First Nat. Bank L.I., Glen Head, NY, 1977—83, Charles Zwicker Tax Inst., Waterbury, Conn., 1980-98; prof. Teikyo Post U., Nat. U., San Diego, 1987-88. Author: (with others) Handbook for Auditors, 1971, Encyclopedia of Accounting Systems, 1976. Mem. nat. adv. bd. Ctr. for Study of Presidency, N.Y.C. and Washington, 1963-99; mem. adv. coun. Coll. of Mgmt., L.I. U., Brookville, 1998—. Recipient Cert. Recognition IRS, 1975-76, Acct. of Yr., Adelphi U., 1974, citations Ctr. Tax Studies, 1968, Teikyo Post U., 1989. Mem. AICPA, N.Y. State Soc. CPA, Sphinx, Quill, Delta Sigma Pi, Kappa Delta Rho. Avocations: golf, reading, travel. Office: CW Post/LI U Northern Blvd Greenvale NY 11548 also: 308 Applewood Southbury CT 06488-1375

ZWICKEY, SHEILA KAYE, lawyer; b. Chgo., July 9, 1951; d. Ewald Arthur Zwickey and Kathryn Allene (Hurst) Zaiden. BS, U. Wis., 1973; MSW, U. Ind., 1975, JD, 1981. Social worker Dept. of Corrections/State of Ind., Indpls., 1975-81; dep. pub. defender State of Ind., Indpls., 1981-85; pub. defender Rush County, Rushville, Ind., 1985-90, Wayne County, Richmond, Ind., 1986-90; prosecuting atty. Rush County/State of Ill., Rushville, 1991—; pvt. practice Batesville, Ind., 1991—. Bd. dirs. Ind. Pub. Defender's Coun., Indpls. Bd. dirs. Rush City Humane Soc., 1988-89; officer Rush County/Ind. Dem. Women's Club, 1991—. Mem. Kiwanis, Rush City Bar Assn. (pres. 1988-89). Democrat. Roman Catholic. Office: Prosecutors Office Rush County Ct House Rushville IN 46173

ZWICKLER, ALLEN, investment advisor, educator; b. N.Y.C., Mar. 18, 1958; s. Seymour Zwickler and Sandra Lewin; m. Ellen Karen Pikitch; children: Scott Emlen, Adam, Randi. BS Mgmt., SUNY, Binghamton, 1979; MBA, NYU, 1986. Registered rep. N.Y. Stock Exch., 1979. Rsch. analyst Ladenburg Thalmann, N.Y.C., 1981—89; investment advisor First Manhattan, N.Y.C., 1989—. Lectr. NYU Sch. Continuing Edn., N.Y.C., 2000—. Trustee Phil Zwickler Charitable and Meml. Found., N.Y.C., 1992—; bd. dirs. Metro Club Sch. Mgmt. SUNY, Binghamton. Avocations: scuba diving, basketball. Home: 420 E 72 St Apt 12-L New York NY 10021 Office: First Manhattan Co 437 Madison Ave New York NY 10022-7001

ZWIENER, DAVID K. insurance company executive; Bachelor's Degree, Duke U.; MBA in Fin. and Mktg., Northwestern U. Asst. treas. internat. ops. Kimberly Clark; sr. v.p., treas. Heller Internat. Corp., exec. v.p. capital markets; CFO, exec. v.p. ITT Fin.; pres., CFO, Hartford Fin. Svcs. Group, 1995—. Office: Hartford Plaza 690 Asylum Ave Hartford CT 06105-3845

ZWIERLEIN, RONALD EDWARD, athletics director; m. Cindy Cromer, Sept. 7, 1968; children: Heidi, Heather, Chad. BS, Bowling Green (Ohio) State U., 1968, MS; PhD in Athletic, Phys. Edn., Recreation, Ohio State U. Head swimming and diving coach Monroe H.S., Rochester, N.Y., Fremont (Ohio) Ross H.S., John Carroll U., University Heights, Ohio, 1975-81, athletic dir., 1977-81; head swimming and diving coach, instr. Bowling Green State U., 1981-1984, assoc. dir. Student Recreation Ctr., 1984--92, dir. recreational sports, 1992-94, dir. intercollegiate athletics, 1994-99, athletic dir., sr. assoc. v.p., 2000—. Mem. Nat. Assn. Collegiate Dirs. Athletics (mem. Mission & Values Com.). Office: Bowling Green State U Perry Stadium Bowling Green OH 43403-0001

ZWIKELMAIER, KURT E. pharmaceutical executive; b. Dallas, Dec. 5, 1954; s. Robert and Pearl Zwikelmaier; m. Madeline Axum; children: Virginia, Elise. BS in Chemistry, U. Mo., 1976; MBA, U. New Orleans, 1984. Cert. mgmt. acct. Rsch. chemist Monsanto Co., St. Louis, 1976—79, budget analyst, 1980—81. Cost acct. Monsanto Co., New Orleans, 1981—84, payroll acct., St. Louis, 1985—94, HRIT specialist, 1994—96, mgr. Ctr. for Employee Svcs., 1996—97, HRIT specialist - Europe/Africa, Brussels, 1998—99; sr. mgr. HRIT ops. Pharmacia Corp., St. Louis, 1999—. Sr. warden St. Timothy's Episcopal Ch., St. Louis, 2002. Mem.: Phi Beta Kappa. Episcopalian. Avocations: travel, foreign languages. Home: 11970 Greenwalk Saint Louis MO 63146

ZWILICH, ELLEN TAAFFE, composer; b. Miami, Fla., Apr. 30, 1939; d. Edward Porter and Ruth (Howard) Taaffe; m. Joseph Zwilich, June 22, 1969 (dec. June 1979). MusB, Fla. State U., 1960, MusM, 1962; D Mus. Arts, Juilliard Sch., 1975; studies with Roger Sessions and Elliott Carter; MusD (hon.), Oberlin Coll., 1987, Converse Coll., 1994; LHD (hon.), Manhattanville Coll., 1991, Marymount Manhattan Coll., 1994, N.Y. New Sch., Mannes, 1995. Francis Eppes disting. prof. Fla. State U., 1999—. Composer in residence Santa Fe Chamber Music Festival, 1990, Am. Acad. Rome, 1990; first Composer's Chair, Carnegie Hall, 1995-99. Premiere, Symposium for Orch., Pierre Boulez, N.Y.C., 1975, Chamber Symphony and Passages, Boston Musica Viva, Richard Pittman, 1979, 82. Symphony 1, Gunther Schuller, Am. Composers Orch., 1982; violinist Am. Symphony, N.Y.C., 1965-73; composer: Sonata in Three Movements, 1973-74; String Quartet, 1974; Clarino Quartet, 1977; Chamber Symphony, 1979; Passages (for Soprano and Chamber Ensemble), 1981; String Trio, 1982; Symphony 1:3 Movements for Orch., 1982 (Grammy nomination New World Records, 1987); Divertimento, 1983; Einsame Nacht, 1971; Emlekezet, 1978; Im Nebel, 1972; Passages for Soprano and Orch., 1982; Trompeten, 1974; Fantasy for Harpsichord, 1983; Intrada, 1983; Prologue and Variations, 1983; Double Quartet for Strings, Chamber Music Soc. of Lincoln Ctr., 1984; Celebration for Orch., Indpls. Symphony, John Nelson, 1984; Symphony #2 (Cello Symphony) San Francisco Symphony, Edo De Waart, 1985, Symphony #2 Louisville Orch. recording, L.L. Smith (Grammy nomination 1991); Concerto Grosso 1985, Handel Festival Orch., Steven Simon, 1986; Concerto for Piano and Orch., Detroit Symphony, Gunther Herbig, Marc-André Hamelin, 1986; Images for 2 Pianos and Orch., Nat. Symphony Orch., F. Machetti, 1987; Tanzspiel, Peter Martins N.Y.C. Ballet, 1987; Praeludium Boston chpt. AGO, 1987; Trio for piano, violin and cello; Kalichstein, Laredo, Robinson trio, 1987; Symbolon, Zubin Mehta and the N.Y. Philharm., Leningrad and Moscow (USSR), N.Y.C. (Koussevitsky Internat. Rec. award nominee 1990), 1988; concerto for trombone and orch. J. Friedman, Sir Georg Solti, Chgo. Symphony, 1989, concerto for trombone and orch. Christian Lindberg, James De Priest, Malmö Symphony, concerto for flute and orch. D.A. Dwyer, Seija Ozawa, Boston Symphony, 1990, quintet for clarinet and string quartet David Schiffrin, Chamber Music N.W., Lincoln Ctr. Chamber Mus. Soc., 1990; concerto for oboe and orch. John Mack, Christoph von Dohnanyi, Cleve. Orch., 1991; concerto for bass trombone strings, timpani and cymbals Chgo. Symphony Orch. Ch. Vernon, Daniel Barenboim, 1991; concerto for violin, violoncello and orch. Jaime Laredo, Sharon Robinson, Louisville Orch., L. Smith, 1991; Immigrant Voices Peter Leonard, St. Lukes Orch., N.Y. Internat. Festival of the Arts Chorus, Ellis Island, 1991, concerto for flute and orch, D.A. Dwyer, J. Sedares, London Symphony Orch., 1992, Symphony # 3 (Grammy nominee 1993), J. Ling, N.Y. Philharmonic, 1993, concerto for bassoon and orch., Nancy Goeres, Lorin Maazel, Pitts. Symphony, 1993, concerto for horn and string Orch., David Jolley, Rochester Philharm., L.L. Smith., 1993, Fantasy for Orch., JoAnn Falletta, Long Beach Symphony Orch., 1994, American Concerto Doc Severinsen, J. Falletta San Diego Symphony, 1994, A Simple Magnificat, 1994, Triple Concerto Kalichstein, Laredo, Robinson Trio Zdenek Macal, Minn. Orch., 1995, for piano and orch., Peanuts Gallery, 1996, violin concerto, Pamela Frank, H. Wolff, 1997; String Quartet # 2, 1998, Emerson Quartet; Upbeat! 1998, Nat. Symphony Orch., conducted by Anthony Aibel, Symphony # 4 (orch., chorus, children's chorus) Mich. State U., L. Gregorian 2000, Lament for solo piano Carnegie Hall, 2000, Millenium Fantasy for Piano & Orch., J. Biegel, J. Cobos-Lopez, Cin. Symphony, 2000, Lament for Cello & Piano, Met. Mus., N.Y.C., 2000, Partita for Violin & String Orch., Carnegie Hall, 2001, One Nation, 2002, Openings for Orch., 2002 JoAnn Falletta Va. Symphony, Clarinet Concerto, D. Shifrin, Chamber Music Soc. of Lincoln Ctr., Buffalo Philharm, 2002; New World Records: Music By Ellen Taaffe Zwilich; N.Y. Philharm. conducted by Zubin Mehta. Bd. dirs. Copland Fund. Named Martha Baird Rockefeller Fund rec. grantee, 1977, 1979, 1982, Guggenheim fellow, 1981; named to, Fla. Artists Hall of Fame, 1994; recipient Elizabeth Sprague Coolidge Chamber Music prize, 1974, Gold medal, G.B. Viotti, Vercelli, Italy, 1975, citation, Ernst von Dohnanyi, 1981, Pulitzer prize, 1983, Composers award, Lancaster Symphony Orch., Arturo Toscanini Music Critics award, 1987, Alfred I. DuPont award, 1991, Performing Arts award, Miami Ctr. Performing Arts, 2000, named, Musical Am. Composer of Yr., 1999. Mem.: AAAL (Acad. award 1984), Guggenheim Found. (bd. dirs.), MacDowell Colony (bd. dirs.), BMI Found., Am. Music Ctr. (bd. dirs., v.p. 1982—84), Am. Fedn. Musicians (hon.; life). Home: 600 W 246th St Bronx NY 10471-3611 Office: care Music Assocs Am 224 King St Englewood NJ 07631-3026

ZWILLENBERG, PAUL, management consultant; BA with distinction, Duke U.; grad., U. Glasgow Bus. Sch. Founder,. mng. dir. Associated New Media; v.p. global mktg. dir. Digital Equipment Corp.; chmn., CEO kpe Europe, 2001—. Named one of Digital Europe 25, Time Mag., 2000. Office: 20 Exch Pl 9th Fl New York NY 10005

ZWILLING, MARK C. music director; b. Albuquerque, Apr. 5, 1960; s. Daniel Zwilling and June Byles Housiaux. MusB, B in Music Edn., Ea. N.Mex. U., 1982; MusM, DePaul U., 1990. Tchr. Las Lunas (N.Mex.) Schs., 1982—85; music dir. First Presbyn. Ch., Roswell, N.Mex., 1985—87, Trinity-First United Meth. Ch., El Paso, 1987—90, First Presbyn. Ch., Las Vegas, Nev., 1990—99, Cathedral of Hope, Dallas, 1999—2000, St. Andrew United Meth. Ch., Littleton, Colo., 2000—. Music dir. MGM Grand Hotel, Las Vegas, 1994—98; Presbyn. Assn. Musicians exec. nat. bd. mem. Presbyn. Ch. USA, Louisville, 1996—99. Mem.: Music Tchrs., Am. Choral Dirs., Am. Guild Organists. Democrat. Home: 758 Monroe St Denver CO 80206 Office: St Andrew United Meth Ch 6325 S University Blvd Littleton CO 80121

ZWILLING, MICHAEL LOUIS, mathematician, educator; PhD, Case Western Res. U., 1987. Math. prof. Mt. Union Coll., Alliance, Ohio, 1981—. Math. dept. chair Mt. Union Coll., 1997—2003. Mem.: Math. Assn. Am. Office: Mount Union College 1972 Clark Avenue Alliance OH 44601

ZWINGE, RANDALL JAMES HAMILTON See RANDI, JAMES

ZWISLOCKI, JOZEF JOHN, neuroscience educator, researcher; b. Lwow, Poland, Mar. 19, 1922; arrived in U.S., 1951; s. Tadeusz and Helena (Moscicki) Z.; m. Ruth Gerber, Oct. 29, 1945 (div. May 1954); m. Sylvia Claire Goldman, July 11, 1954 (dec. July 17, 1992); m. Jadwiga M. Morrison, Dec. 2, 1993. Diploma, Fed. Tech. Inst., Zurich, Switzerland, 1944, ScD, 1948; D honoris causa, U. Adam Mickiewicz, Poznán, Poland, 1991, Syracuse (NY) U., 2004. Head electroacoustic lab. dept. otolaryngology U. Basel, Basel, Switzerland, 1945-51; rsch. fellow psychoacoustic lab. Harvard U., Cambridge, Mass., 1951-57; dir. Bioacoustic Lab. Syracuse U., 1958-63, founder, dir. Lab. of Sensory Communication, 1963-73, founder dir. Inst. for Sensory Rsch., 1973—84, prof. neurosci., 1984—88, disting. prof. neurosci., 1988—92, disting. prof. emeritus, 1992—; prof. communicative disorders dept. spl. edn. Syracuse U. Sch. Edn., 1982—92; rsch. prof. SUNY Health Sci. Ctr., Syracuse, 1967—. Affiliate prof. bioengring. L.C. Smith Coll. Engring., Syracuse U., 1986-92; Carhart Meml. lectr. Am. Auditory Soc., 1992; mem. exec. coun. Com. Hearing, Bioacoustics and Biomechanics, NRC, Washington, 1965-68, chmn., 1967-68; mem. rev. panel on communicative scis. NIH, Bethesda, Md., 1966-70, chmn., 1969-70; mem. Communicative Disorders Program Project rev. com. NIH, Bethesda, 1971-75; chmn. Bd. Sci. Advs. Ctr. Health Scis., U. Wis., Madison, 1975-78. Inventor acoustic ear simulator, acoustic bridge, several types of ear defenders; contbr. articles to profl. jours.; author: Auditory Sound Transmission: An Autobiographical Perspective, 2002. Recipient Faculty Rsch. award Syracuse chpt. Sigma Xi, 1973, Internat. Ctr. Ricerche e Studi Amplifon prize, 1976, Javits Neurosci. Investigator award NIH, 1984, Kwiek medal Acoustics Inst., A. Mickiewicz U., Poland, 1991, medal Acoustical Soc. Poland, 1991, Hugh Knowles prize Northwestern U., 1992. Fellow Acoustical Soc. Am. (chmn. tech. com. on psychol. and physiol. acoustics 1962, 63, exec. coun. 1982-85, recipient 1st Bekesy medal 1985, chmn. long-range planning com. 1983-86, nominating com. 1986-87, mem. com. on tutorials 1988-91, com. on meetings 1988-91, chmn. spring meeting, 1989), Am. Speech and Hearing Assn., The Polish Inst. of Arts and Scis. of Am.; mem. NAS, Polish Acad. Scis., Internat. Soc. Audiology (v.p. 1967-72), Internat. Union of Physiol. Scis. (commn. on auditory physiology 1982-89), Internat. Union Pure and Applied Physics (Commn. on Acoustics 1982-89), Collegium Oto Rhino Laryngologicum Amicitiae Sacrum, Assn. for Rsch. in Otolaryngology (award of merit 1988), Am. Otol. Soc. (assoc.), Hearing Rsch. (editl. bd.). Avocations: skiing, tennis, trout fishing, inventions. Office Phone: 315-443-9718. Business E-Mail: joe_zwislocki@isr.syr.edu.

ZWOYER, EUGENE MILTON, retired consulting engineering executive; b. Plainfield, N.J., Sept. 8, 1926; s. Paul Ellsworth and Marie Susan (Britt) Z.; m. Dorothy Lucille Seward, Feb. 23, 1946; children: Gregory, Jeffrey, Douglas. Student, U. Notre Dame, 1944, Mo. Valley Coll., 1944-45; BS, U. N.Mex., 1947; MS, Ill. Inst. Tech., 1949; PhD, U. Ill., 1953. Mem. faculty U. N.Mex.,

Albuquerque, 1948-71, prof. civil engring., dir. Eric Wang Civil Engring. Rsch. Facility, 1961-70; rsch. assoc. U. Ill., Urbana, 1951-53; owner, cons. engr. Eugene Zwoyer & Assocs., Albuquerque, 1954-72; exec. dir., sec. ASCE, N.Y.C., 1972-82; pres. Am. Assn. Engring. Socs., N.Y.C., 1982-84; exec. v.p. T.Y. Lin Internat., San Francisco, 1984-86, pres., 1986-89; owner Eugene Zwoyer Cons. Engr., 1989—2002; COO, treas. Polar Molecular Corp., Saginaw, Mich., 1990, exec. v.p., 1991-92; ret., 2002. Trustee Small Bus. Research Corp., 1976-80; trustee Engring. Info., Inc., 1981-84; internat. trustee People-to-People Internat. 1974-86; v.p. World Fedn. Engring. Orgns., 1982-85. Served to lt. (j.g.) USN, 1944-46. Named Outstanding Engr. of Yr. Albuquerque chpt. N.Mex Soc. Profl. Engrs., 1969, One Who Served the Best Interests of the Constrn. Industry, Engring. News Record, 1980; recipient Disting. Alumnus award the Civil Engring. Alumni Assn. at U. Ill., 1979, Disting. Alumnus award Engring. Coll. Alumni Assn., U. N.Mex., 1982, Can.-Am. Civil Engring. Amity award Am. Soc. Civil Engrs., 1988, Award for Outstanding Profl. Contbns. and Leadership Coll. Engring. U. N.Mex., 1989 Mem. AAAS, ASCE (dist. bd. dirs. 1968-71), NSPE, Am. Soc. Engring. Edn., Nat. Acad. Code Adminstrn. (trustee, mem. exec. com. 1973-79), Engrs. Joint Coun. (bd. dirs. 1978-79), Engring. Soc. Commn. on Energy (bd. dirs. 1977-82), Sigma Xi, Sigma Tau, Chi Epsilon. Home: 6363 Christie Ave Apt 1326 Emeryville CA 94608-1940

ZYCHICK, JOEL DAVID, lawyer; b. Cleve., June 23, 1954; s. Eugene K. and Myra (Rotblatt) Z. BBA, George Washington U., 1976; JD, Case We. Res. U., 1979; LLM in Taxation, NYU, 1979. Bar: Ohio 1979, N.Y. 1985, D.C. 1985, U.S. Tax Ct. 1980, U.S. Ct. Claims 1980, U.S. Ct. Appeals (fed. cir.) 1982. Assoc. Jones, Day, Reavis & Pogue, Cleve., 1980-83, Milbank, Tweed, Hadley & McCloy, N.Y.C., 1983-85; ptnr. Hertzog, Calamari & Gleason, N.Y.C., 1986-98; pres. Zcounsel LLC; pres., CEO, GETKO Group, Inc., Westbury, NY, 1998—2001. Former gen. counsel, dir. The Egg Factory, LLC, Va. Contbr. articles to profl. jours. Dir., treas. Northside Ctr. for Child Devel., N.Y.C. Mem. ABA (past sec., dir. coun. tax sect., nominating com., former chmn. sales and fin. trans. com., past vice chmn. regulations com. govt. submissions), Am. Coll. Tax Counsel, N.Y. State Bar Assn. Avocations: hiking, music, travel. Home: PO Box 1097 Amagansett NY 11930-1097 Office Phone: 516-680-2715. E-mail: JZ@Zcounsel.com.

ZYGOCKI, RHONDA I. oil industry executive; b. St. John's, Nfld., July 1957; B.Civil Engring., Meml. U. of Nfld., 1980. Petroleum engr. Chevron Can. Resources, Calgary, Canada, gen. mgr. strategic bus. svcs., 1993—94;

profit ctr. mgr. Chevron U.S.A. Prodn. Co., Houston, 1994—97; CFO Chevron Can. Resources, Calgary, 1997—99; mgr. strategic planning Chevron Corp., San Ramon, Calif., 1999—2000, advisor to chmn. bd., 2000—01; mng. dir. ChevronTexaco Australia Pty. Ltd., Perth, Australia, 2001—03; v.p. health, environment and safety Chevron Texaco Corp., San Ramon, 2003—. Mem.: Engrs. Without Borders (bd. dirs.), Internat. Petroleum Industry Environ. Conservation Assn. (bd. dirs.), Internat. Assn. Oil and Gas Prodrs. (bd. dirs.). Office: Chevron Texaco Corp 6001 Bollinger Canyon Rd San Ramon CA 94583-2324*

ZYROFF, ELLEN SLOTOROFF, information scientist, classicist, educator; b. Atlantic City, N.J., Aug. 1, 1946; d. Joseph George and Sylvia Beverly (Roth) Slotoroff; m. Jack Zyroff, June 21, 1970; children: Dena Rachel, David Aaron. AB, Barnard Coll., 1968; MA, The Johns Hopkins U., 1969, PhD, 1971; MS, Columbia U., 1973. Instr. The Johns Hopkins U., Balt., 1970-71, Yeshiva U., N.Y.C., 1971-72, Bklyn Coll., 1971-72; libr., instr. U. Calif., 1979, 81, 91, San Diego State U., 1981-85, 94; prof. San Diego Mesa Coll., 1981-95; dir. The Reference Desk Rsch. Svcs., La Jolla, Calif., 1983—; prin. libr. San Diego County Libr., 1985—. V.p. Archaeol. Soc. Am., Balt., 1970-71. Author: The Author's Apostrophe in Epic from Homer Through Lucan, 1971, Cooperative Library Instruction for Maximum Benefit, 1989; contbr. articles to profl. jours. Pres. Women's Am. ORT, San Diego, 1979-81, Zionist Orgn. of Am., San Diego dist., 1997-2000; mem. adv. bd. With Israel Now. Mem.: ALA (chair divsn. and roundtable coms. 1982—, coun. 2003—), Libr. Congress Cataloging in Publs. Adv. Group, Assn. Jewish Librs., Am. Classical League, Calif. Libr. Assn. (assembly 1993—99, editor Calif. Librs. 1997—99, pres. mgmt. sect. 2000—01), Am. Philol. Assn., Toastmasters, Beta Phi Mu. Office: PO Box 12122 La Jolla CA 92039-2122 E-mail: eszyroff@hotmail.com.

ZYSKIND, JUDITH WEAVER, molecular biology educator, entrepreneur; b. Cin., July 2, 1939; d. Max Correy Weaver and Mary Catherine Landis; m. George Zyskind, May 2, 1964 (dec. Sept. 13, 1974); children: Aviva, Joy; m. Douglas Wemp Smith, Aug. 16, 1975. BS, U. Dayton, 1961; MS, Iowa State U., 1964, PhD, 1968. Lectr. genetics dept. Iowa State U., Ames, 1970-72, postdoctoral fellow in biochemistry, 1972-74, U. Calif.-San Diego, La Jolla, 1974-77, asst. rsch. biologist, 1977-82; assoc.prof. biology San Diego State U., 1982-86, prof. biology, 1986—2002, prof. emeritus, 2002—; chief sci. officer Elitra Pharms., San Diego, 1997-99, also bd. dirs.; prof. emeritus San Diego State U., 2002—. Mem. editl. bd. Jour. Molecular

Microbiology and Biotech., Norfolk, Eng., 1998—. Contbr. over 60 articles, revs. to profl. publs. Bd. dirs. San Diego State U. Found., 1997— Recipient Women Who Mean Bus. award in biotech. San Diego Bus. Jour., 1997; grantee NIH, NSF, 1983—. Fellow Am. Acad. Microbiology; mem. AAAS, Am. Soc. Biochemistry and Molecular Biology, Am. soc. Microbiology, Assn. for Women in Sci., Sigma Xi. Achievements include patents in field of 4. Avocations: backpacking, trekking, photography. Office: San Diego State U Biology Dept 5500 Campanile Dr San Diego CA 92182-4614

ZYSMAN, JOHN ADLER, political scientist, educator; b. Omaha, Mar. 23, 1946; s. Evelyn Zysman; m. Victoria Rehn; 1 child, Lara. PhD of Polit. Sci., MIT, Boston, MA, 1973; BA, Harvard Coll., 1968. Lectr. Dept. Polit. Sci. MIT, Boston, 1973—74; asst. prof. Dept. Polit. Sci. U. Calif.-Berkeley, 1974—82, assoc. prof. Dept. Polit. Sci., 1982—87, prof. Dept. Polit. Sci., 1987—; co-dir. Berkeley Roundtable on Internat. Economy, 1982—. Office: BRIE / Univ of California 2234 Piedmont Avenue Berkeley CA 94720-2322 Office Phone: (510) 642 3067. Office Fax: (510) 643 6617. Business E-Mail: johnz@socrates.berkeley.edu.

ZYWICKI, ROBERT ALBERT, retired electrical distribution company executive; b. Chgo., Sept. 23, 1930; s. Martin Albert and Margaret Irene (Mackowski) Z.; m. Barbara Joan Hagerty; children: Robert, Cheryl, Cindy, Carrie. B in Commerce, Northwestern U., 1966. Teller Chgo. Title and Trust Bank, Chgo., 1949-50; painter Getz Molding Co., Chgo., 1950-51; purchasing agt. Woodworker's Tool Works, Chgo., 1953-54; serviceman Addressograph Multigraph, Chgo., 1954-55; mem. Chgo. Fire Dept., 1955-62; v.p. Anixter Bros. Inc., Skokie, Ill., 1955-87; co-owner A-Z Industries, Northbrook, Ill., 1987—2003; ret., 2003. Served as cpl. U.S. Army, 1951-53. Mem. Am. Legion (comdr.). Republican. Roman Catholic. Avocations: thoroughbred horse racing, classical music, baseball card collecting, tennis. Home: 1330 Sprucewood Ln Deerfield IL 60015-4771 Personal E-mail: peter1330@comcast.net. *Love your family, respect your friends and co-workers, value your customers and suppliers. Always keep each in its proper perspective. Most of all, remember - love, value and respect are all two-way streets.*

Geographic Index

Tieszen, Ralph Leland, Sr., *hospital administrator, educator*
Todd, Judith F. *lawyer*
Tomkins, Mark E. *manufacturing executive*
Tonkery, Dan *Internet company executive*
Trechsel, Gail *museum director*
Trimmier, Charles Stephen, Jr., *lawyer*
Tucker, Russell B. *insurance company executive*
Tucker, Thomas James *retired investment manager*
Turner, Kevin Paul *music educator*
Uddin, Nasim *civil engineer, educator*
Vickers, Selwyn M. *surgeon*
Vinson, Laurence Duncan, Jr., *lawyer*
Vyazovkin, Sergey *chemist, educator*
Warnock, David Gene *nephrologist*
Warren, William Michael, Jr., *utilities company executive*
Weatherly, Robert Stone, Jr., *banker*
Weeks, Arthur Andrew *retired lawyer, law educator*
Weinsier, Roland Louis *nutrition educator and director*
Wells, Alan Hilary *biomedical researcher*
Wells, Huey Thomas, Jr., *lawyer*
Westerfield, Richard *music director*
Wheeler, Cathy Jo *federal agency administrator*
Wheeler, Ruric E. *mathematics professor*
Whigham, Mark Anthony *computer scientist*
Wilson, James Charles, Jr., *lawyer*
Wrinkle, John Newton *lawyer*
Yoder, Stephen Alan *lawyer*
Zahl, Paul Francis Matthew *dean*

Chelsea
Culpepper, Michael Irving *researcher, educator*

Clanton
Jackson, John Hollis, Jr., *lawyer*

Columbiana
Armistead, William Cole, Jr., *marketing professional*

Cordova
Anthony, Yancey Lamar *minister*

Cottonwood
Smith, Christopher M. *music educator*

Dadeville
Barnes, Ben Blair *computer company executive, electrical engineer*
Oliver, John Percy, II, *lawyer, consultant*

Daphne
Baugh, Charles Milton *biochemistry educator, college dean*
Curreri, Peter William *health policy consultant*
Jeffreys, Elystan Geoffrey *geological engineer, petroleum consultant and appraiser, gemologist*

Decatur
Belser, Howard McGriff, Jr., *lawyer*
Blackburn, John Gilmer *lawyer*
Caddell, John A. *lawyer*
Little, Thomas Walker *retired protective services official*
Mardis, Elizabeth Williams *occupational health nurse*
Mason, Loretta Ann *accountant assistant*
Michelini, Sylvia Hamilton *auditor*
O'Brien, Richard Alan *research scientist*
Sandlin, Anathalee Gray *writer, music company owner*
Smith, Trina *academic administrator*
Smith, Troy Alvin *aerospace research engineer*
Talley, Richard Woodrow *accountant*

Demopolis
Lloyd, Hugh Adams *lawyer*

Dothan
Bailey, Chip *investment advisor, former state senator*
Cross, Steven Jasper *finance educator*
Fleming, Jennie M *retired education educator*
Fletcher, Sarah Lee *retired elementary school educator*
Flowers, V. Anne *academic administrator emerita*
Marks, Marilyn *trailer company executive*
Mocker, Hans Walter *physicist*
Palko, Lorri M. *automotive company executive*
Peterson, Roger *community bank executive, retired international investment banker, retired manufacturing executive, retired Air Force officer*
Wright, Burton *sociologist*

Duncanville
Prescott, Perry Don *psychology educator, counselor*

Enterprise
Garrett, Thomas W. *retired career officer*
Stagliano, James Joseph *physical science educator, scientist*

Eutaw
Turner, Marvin Lesere *musician*

Evergreen
Dailey, Marilyn *elementary school educator*

Fairfield
Hamrick, Leon Columbus *surgeon, medical director*

Fairhope
Hart, Eric Mullins *consumer products company executive*
Mozley, Paul David *retired obstetrics and gynecology educator*
Ottensmeyer, David Joseph *retired neurosurgeon, retired healthcare executive*

Florala
Duplechin, D. James *lawyer*

Florence
Badger, Phillip Charles *agricultural engineer*
Foote, Avon Edward *web developer/producer, communications educator*
Foote, Dorothy Gargis *nursing educator*
Johnson, Johnny Ray *mathematics professor*
McDermott, David (John) *writer, marketing professional, artist*
Thompson, Ermis Armenter *retired education educator*
Williams, Joyce Hall *secondary school educator*

Foley
Kingston, George Willis *retired naval officer, small business owner*
Pfeifer, William Lee, Jr., *lawyer*
Russell, Ralph Timothy *insurance company executive, mayor*
St. John, Henry Sewell, Jr., *utility company executive*

Fort Payne
Whitemire, Steve L. *judge*

Fort Rucker
Fraser, Stuart *engineer*
Stewart, John Edward *psychologist, researcher*

Gadsden
Arnold, Don Carl *pastor, religious organization executive*
Grimm, James R. (Ronald Grimm) *multi-industry executive*
Smothers, Jimmy *editor, sportswriter*

Gordo
McKnight, William Baldwin *physics educator*

Greensboro
Massey, James Earl *clergyman, educator*

Gulf Shores
Wallace, John Loys *aviation services executive*

Hamilton
Vinson, Leila Terry Walker *retired gerontological social worker*

Hanceville
Hazard, Lynn Marchetti *occupational therapist*

Hartselle
Slate, Joe Hutson *psychologist, educator*

Hayden
King, Vickie Ruth *minister, shop owner*

Hoover
Bishop, Joan H. *health facility administrator*
Lathem, Gina Cooley *small business owner*

Huntsville
Allan, Barry David *research chemist, government official*
Archuleta, Nancy E. *engineering executive*
Baldaia, Peter *curator*
Bass, Clayton *museum director*
Bearden, Thomas Eugene *research scientist, researcher*
Bendickson, Marcus J. *engineering company executive*
Bolte, James T. *transportation executive*
Bounds, Sarah Etheline *historian*
Brandon, Walter Wiley, Jr., *retired physicist, retired aerospace engineer*
Childs, Rand Hampton *information technology executive, consultant*
Collazo, Francisco J. *architectural firm executive*
Cornatzer, William Eugene *retired biochemistry educator*
Costes, Nicholas Constantine *aerospace technologist, educator, retired government official*
Dahm, Werner K. *aerodynamicist*
Daussman, Grover Frederick *electrical engineer, consultant*
Decher, Rudolf *physicist, researcher*
Dimmock, John Oliver *physics educator*
Dunar, Andrew J. *historian, educator*
Durnya, Louis Richard *lawyer*
Fargerson, Gordon Shawn *minister*
Francis, Herbert Edward, Jr., *writer*
Franz, Frank Andrew *university president, physics educator*
Freas, George Wilson, II, *computer consultant*
Gabig, Jerome S., Jr., *lawyer*
Gillani, Noor V. *atmospheric scientist, researcher, educator*
Graves, Benjamin Barnes *business administration educator*
Gray, Ronald W. *business executive*
Hawley, Harold Patrick *educational consultant*
Ho, Joseph Xiaomin *aerospace scientist*
Huber, Donald Simon *physician*
Huckaby, Gary Carlton *lawyer*
Hughes, Kaylene *historian, educator*
Hunter, Herbert Erwin *aerospace engineer*
Ingram, Shirley Jean *social worker*
King, Olin B. *electronics systems company executive*
Krueger, Kathleen Susan *special education administrator*
Lundquist, Charles Arthur *university official*
Mathews, Fred Leroy *librarian*
Mazumder, Sandip *engineer, researcher*
McAuley, Van Alfon *aerospace mathematician*
McCaleb, John E. *public health environmentalist, biologist*
McIntyre-Ivy, Joan Carol *data processing executive*
Meadlock, James W. *computer graphics company executive*
Mohan, Annette Imelda *producer, educator*
Mohan, Tungesh Nath *television and film producer, film educator*
Mok, Wai Yin *library and information scientist, educator*
Moore, Ann Roy *school system administrator*
Moore, Fletcher Brooks *retired engineering company executive*
Morgan, Beverly Hammersley *middle school educator, artist*
Morgan, Ethel Branman *accountant, retired electronics engineer*
Morgan, John Derald *electrical engineer*
Motz, Kenneth Lee *former farm organization official*
Norman, Ralph Louis *physicist, consultant*
Nuessle, William Raymond *surgeon*
Paciesas, William Simon *astrophysicist, educator*
Parnell, Thomas Alfred *physicist*
Pastrick, Harold Lee *aeronautical engineer*
Pittman, William Claude *electrical engineer*
Plunkett, Sara L. *communications company executive*
Pruitt, Alice Fay *mathematician, engineer*
Reece, Wanda G. *space station training engineer, writer*
Richardson, Patrick William *lawyer*
Robinson, Helen Margaret *emergency physician, internist*
Sackheim, Robert Lewis *aerospace engineer, educator*
Sapp, A. Eugene, Jr., *former electronics executive*
Schroer, Bernard Jon *industrial engineering educator*
Schumann, J. Paul *federal agency administrator*
Smith, Robert Earl *space scientist*
Snodgrass, Jonathan Wayne *music educator, pastor*
Spencer, William David *music educator*
Steinbuchel, Carla Faye *pediatrics nurse, nursing educator*
Stephenson, Arthur G. *aerospace engineer*
Stewart, Verlindsey Laquetta *accounting educator*
Stuhlinger, Ernst *physicist*
Tietke, Wilhelm *gastroenterologist, educator*
Traylor, Orba Forest *economist, lawyer, educator*
Tucker, Richard A. *airport terminal executive*
Urias, John M. *military officer, government agency administrator*
Vaughan, Otha H., Jr., *retired aerospace engineer*
Vaughan, William Walton *atmospheric scientist*
Watson, Raymond Coke, Jr., *engineering executive, academic administrator*
Williams, Phillip Wayne *former state official and army officer, securities and diversified company executive, consultant*
Williamson, Donald Ray *retired career Army officer*
Wright, John Collins *retired chemistry educator*
Wu, Susan Ying Chu Lin (Ying-chu Lin) *engineering company executive, engineer*
Zutaut, Steven Eric *systems analyst, application developer*

Hurtsboro
Bouilliant-Linet, Francis Jacques *global management consultant*

Irondale
Karr, Beverly Ann *counselor*

Jacksonville
Dunaway, Carolyn Bennett *retired sociology educator*
Dunaway, William Preston *retired educator*
Hubbard, William James *library director*
Merrill, Martha *library media educator*
Spector, Daniel Earl *historian, educator*

Jasper
Bevill, Tom *retired congressman, lawyer*
Rowland, David Jack *retired academic administrator*
Thomas, Steven Allen *lawyer*

Lillian
Burnette, Ollen Lawrence, Jr., *historian*

Livingston
Green, Asa Norman *university president*
Schellhammer, Richard Charles *historian*

Loachapoka
Schafer, Elizabeth Diane *historian, writer*
Schafer, Robert Louis *agricultural engineer, researcher*

Madison
Brannan, Eulie Ross *educational consultant*
Cazavan, Larry O. *television executive*
Dannenberg, Konrad K. *aeronautical engineer*
Emerson, William Kary *engineering company executive*
Stone, Frank Bruce *contractor*
Vo, Hieu N. *architect*

Marion
Street, Deborra Lynn *director of fine arts*

Maxwell AFB
Lester, Richard I. *military educator*

Maylene
Copes, Marvin Lee *college president*

Mc Calla
Kes, Vicki *museum director*

Meridianville
Oberhausen, Joyce Ann Wynn *aircraft company executive, artist*

Mobile
Armbrecht, William Henry, III, *retired lawyer*
Atkinson, William James, Jr., *retired cardiologist*
Baxley, Phillip Kent *lawyer*
Bertagnolli-Comstock, Amanda K. *mathematician, educator*
Blackburn, Dale Aaron *science educator*
Bostwick, Robert Otis *municipal staff member*
Braswell, Louis Erskine *lawyer*
Brogdon, Byron Gilliam *physician, radiology educator*
Butler, Charles Randolph, Jr., *federal judge*
Byrd, Gwendolyn Pauline *school system superintendent*
Campbell, Robert Craig, III, *lawyer, educator*
Clark, Jack *retired hospital company executive, accountant*
Clark, Veronica Ann Wilds (Ronni Patriquin Clark) *journalist*
Clausell, Deborah Deloris *artist*
Cohen, Michael Victor *cardiologist*
Cox, Emmett Ripley *judge*
Cunningham, Julian Antonia *retired protective services official*
DeBakey, Ernest George *physician, surgeon*
Delaney, Thomas Caldwell, Jr., *city official*
Edwards, Jack *former congressman, lawyer*
Eichold, Samuel *medical educator, medical museum curator*
Finkbohner, George Wheeler, Jr., *lawyer*
French, Elizabeth Irene *biology professor, violinist*
Gandy, Maurice Edward *English language educator, writer*
Gordon, James Oliver *small business owner, chiropractor*
Graddick, Charles Allen *lawyer*
Granade, Callie Virginia Smith S. *lawyer, federal district judge*
Habib, Thomas Mark *musician, educator*
Hamid, Michael *electrical engineering educator, consultant*
Hamner, Eugenie Lambert *English educator*
Harris, Benjamin Harte, Jr., *lawyer*
Helmsing, Frederick George *lawyer*
Higginbotham, Prieur Jay *city official*
Holland, Lyman Faith, Jr., *lawyer*
Holmes, Broox Garrett *lawyer*
Howard, Alex T., Jr., *federal judge*
Hsiao, Kuang-Ting *mechanical engineer, educator, researcher*
Jones, Joseph Seymour *small business owner, poet*
Kargleder, Charles Leonard *language educator*
Kreisberg, Robert A. *dean, medical educator*
Lee, Christopher Luke *municipal official*
Lipscomb, Oscar Hugh *archbishop*
Littleton, Jesse Talbot, III, *radiology educator*
LoCicero, Joseph *thoracic surgeon, researcher*
McCleery, Winston Theodore *computer consulting company executive*
McConnell, Roger *investment representative, political party official*
McCoy, Douglas Leon *lawyer*
Milling, Bert William, Jr., *magistrate judge*
Murchison, David Roderick *lawyer*
Peebles, E(mory) B(ush), III, *lawyer*
Perry, Nelson Allen *retired radiation safety engineer, radiological consultant*
Phan, Anh-Vu *adult education educator, researcher*
Pierce, Donald Fay *lawyer*
Pitcock, James Kent *head and neck surgical oncologist*
Pittman, Virgil *federal judge*
Quina, Marion Albert, Jr., *lawyer*
Rewak, William John *former academic administrator, clergyman*
Richelson, Paul William *curator*
Rodning, Charles Bernard *surgeon*
Roedder, William Chapman, Jr., *lawyer*
Smith, Jesse Graham, Jr., *dermatologist, educator*
Steadman, John Marcellus, III, *English educator*
Taylor, Aubrey Elmo *physiologist, educator*
Vulevich, Edward, Jr., *prosecutor*
York, David P. *lawyer*

Montevallo
Jarrett, Cynthia S. *accountant*
McChesney, Robert Michael, Sr., *political science educator*
Simone, Sam Paul *education educator, researcher*

Montgomery
Adams, Robert Barry *pathologist*
Aleinikov, Andrei Grigoryevich *scientist, researcher, educator, consultant*
Baker, Jimmy H. *former state finance administrator*
Barnes, Harrey McGwinn, III, *internist, oncologist*
Barron, Lowell Ray *state legislator*
Baxley, Lucy *lieutenant governor*
Bennett, James Ronald *state official*
Black, Robert Coleman *judge, lawyer*
Blount, Winton Malcolm, III, *investment executive*
Bright, Bobby *mayor*
Brown, Jean Williams *state supreme court justice*
Byars, Walter Ryland, Jr., *lawyer*
Calhoun, Gregory B. *retail food and beverage company executive*
Campbell, Maria Bouchelle *lawyer, consultant*
Canary, Leura *prosecutor*
Carnes, Edward E. *federal judge*
Cassels, Martha Beasley *realtor, developer*
Cauthen, Florence M. *protective services official*
Copeland, Jacqueline Turner *music educator*
Cornett, Lloyd Harvey, Jr., *retired historian*
Cox, Cathy A. *elementary school educator*
Darby, Larry Eugene *lawyer*
Dees, Morris Seligman, Jr., *lawyer*
De Ment, Ira *judge*
Dillon, Jean Katherine *executive secretary, small business owner*
Dixon, Larry Dean *state legislator*
Dubina, Joel Fredrick *federal judge*
Ely, Robert Eugene *lawyer, author, educator*
Escott-Russell, Sundra *state legislator*
Eubanks, Ronald W. *lawyer, broadcaster*
Figures, Vivian Davis *state legislator*
Frazer, David Hugh, Jr., *allergist*
Frazer, Nimrod Thompson *financial services company executive*
Frazer, Stuart Harrison, III, *cotton merchant*
Gerard, William Blake *literature educator*
Givhan, Edgar Gilmore *physician, writer*
Godbold, John Cooper *judge*
Gregory, William Stanley *lawyer*
Gribben, Alan *English language educator, research consultant*
Hammett, Seth *state legislator*
Hamner, Reginald Turner *lawyer*
Harwood, Robert Bernard, Jr., *state supreme court justice*
Hester, Douglas Benjamin *lawyer, federal official*
Hobbs, Truman McGill *federal judge*
Hoffman, Richard William *retired banker*
Holifield, Leonard Cleve *security firm executive, educator*
Hooper, Perry Ollie *retired state supreme court judge*
Houston, James Gorman, Jr., *state supreme court justice*
Hunker, Fred Dominic *internist, medical educator*
Ivey, Kay Ellen *state official*
Johnson, Mark Matthew *museum administrator*
Johnstone, Douglas Inge *state supreme court justice*
Kennedy, Yvonne *state legislator*
Kim, Ki Hang *mathematician*
King, Troy *state attorney general*
Kline, John Alvin *academic administrator*
Kloess, Lawrence Herman, Jr., *retired lawyer*
Langford, Charles Douglas *lawyer*
Laurie, Robin Garrett *lawyer*
Lawson, Thomas Seay, Jr., *lawyer*
Lee, Harry Antonius *allergist, immunologist*
Leslie, Henry Arthur *lawyer, retired banker*
Lewis, Joseph Brady (Jay Lewis) *lawyer*
Lowder, Robert E. *bank executive*
Lowe, Brian Wesley *music educator*
Lyons, Champ, Jr., *state supreme court justice*
Maddox, Alva Hugh *retired state supreme court justice*

Mandry, Christine M. *public adminstator*
May, Cecil Richard, Jr., *academic administrator*
McFadden, Frank Hampton *lawyer, business executive, former judge*
McLeod, Purser L., Jr., *financial executive*
McPherson, Vanzetta Penn *magistrate judge*
Murkett, Philip Tillotson *human resource executive*
Myers, Ira Lee *physician*
Nachman, Merton Roland, Jr., *lawyer*
Napier, Cameron Mayson Freeman *historic preservationist*
Pan, Chai-Fu *engineering educator*
Parker, Susan D. *state official, auditor*
Prestwood, Alvin Tennyson *lawyer*
Richardson, Edward R. *school system administrator*
Riley, Robert *governor*
Ritvo, Roger Alan *vice chancellor, health management-policy educator*
Salmon, Joseph Thaddeus *lawyer*
Sass, Neil Leslie *toxicologist*
Schloss, Samuel Leopold, Jr., *retired food service executive, consultant*
See, Harold Frend *judge, law educator*
Shepard, Judith Bethea *librarian*
Smith, Harri Anne *state legislator*
Smith, Maury Drane *lawyer*
Steele, Rodney Redfearn *judge*
Stevenson, Bryan Allen *lawyer*
Stuart, Lyn (Jacquelyn L. Stuart) *judge*
Taylor, Watson Robbins *construction company executive*
Taylor, Watson Robbins, Jr., *investment banker*
Thompson, Myron H. *federal judge*
Uzzell-Baggett, Karon Lynette *career officer*
Volz, Charles Harvie, Jr., *lawyer*
Wendzel, Robert Leroy *political science educator*
Williamson, Donald Ellis *state official*
Wood, James Jerry *lawyer*
Woodall, Thomas A. *state supreme court justice*
Worley, Nancy L. *secretary of state*
Young, Caron L *county official*

Muscle Shoals
Ownby, Terry Scott *music educator, director*
Roy, Amit H. *agricultural executive*

Normal
Dawkins, Jimmie Angela *art educator*
Edwards, Matthew E. *physicist, educator*
Gibson, John Thomas *academic administrator, consultant*
Hall, Doris Spooner *music educator*
Kearns, Nancy J. *language educator*

Opelika
Jenkins, Richard Lee *manufacturing executive*
Samford, Yetta Glenn, Jr., *lawyer, director*
Smith-Sanders, Carol Ann *music therapist, psychologist*

Orange Beach
Adams, Daniel Fenton *law educator*
Conrad, Marcel Edward *hematologist, educator*
Owens, Marsha *library director*

Owens Cross Roads
Williams, Lowell Craig *lawyer, employee relations executive*

Oxford
Johnson, Mary Murphy *social worker, writer*

Ozark
DuBose, Elizabeth (Bettye DuBose) *community health nurse*

Pelham
Harvey, James Mathews, Jr., *communications specialist*
Lee, James A. *health facility finance executive*
Turner, Malcolm Elijah *biomathematician, educator*

Pell City
Passey, George Edward *psychology educator*

Phenix City
Jinright, Noah Franklin *vocational school educator, security firm executive*

Point Clear
Englund, Gage Bush *dancer, educator*
Holt, Thaddeus *lawyer*

Prattville
Burrows, Henry Peter, III, *secondary school educator*
Lambert, Meg Stringer *construction executive, architect, interior designer*

Ramer
Napier, John Hawkins, III, *historian*

Redstone Arsenal
Parlier, Greg H. *military officer, engineer*

Roanoke
Terry, Roy D. *apparel manufacturing company executive*

Scottsboro
Flarity, Edith Lynne *medical/surgical nurse*

Seale
Harris-Stokes, Joyce A. *secondary school educator*

Selma
Galloway, Robert Michael
Price, Tina S. *administrative assistant*

Semmes
McCann, Clarence David, Jr., *museum curator and director, artist*
Phelps, James Franklin *retired county official*

Sheffield
Hamby, Gene Malcolm, Jr., *lawyer*

Shoal Creek
Ahearn, John Francis, Jr., *retired oil and gas company executive*

Somerville
Johnson, Loyd *agricultural engineer, researcher*

Spanish Fort
Benjamin, Regina Marcia *physician, administrator*
van Aken, John Henry *retired marine surveyor, engineer, consultant*

Sulligent
Burleson, Emily Jane *nursing administrator*

Talladega
Jeffers, Trellie Lee James *language educator, dean*
Schwinghamer, Mary Denise *veterinarian*
Swain, Mary Madgalene *pediatrics nurse*
Weaver, Robert Cooper *small business owner, volunteer*

Tallassee
Baker, Barry Gorden *computer technician*

Thomasville
Davis, Gene *retired civil engineer*

Troy
Davidson, Barry Sheldon *academic administrator, education educator*
McPherson, Milton Monroe *history professor*
Mitchell, Norma Taylor *history professor*
Rinehart, James Forrest *international relations professor*

Trussville
Best, Frederick Napier *artist, designer, educator*
Jacobson, James Edmund *retired newspaper editor*

Tuscaloosa
Aziz, Nasrullah *mathematician, educator*
Baklanoff, Eric Nicholas *economist, educator*
Barfield, Robert F. *retired mechanical engineer, educator, dean*
Beito, David Timothy *humanities educator*
Bickley, John S. *insurance association executive, educator, writer*
Blackburn, John Leslie *small business owner*
Bonner, Judy L. *academic administrator*
Bryan, Colgan Hobson *aerospace engineering educator*
Cava, Michael Patrick *chemist, educator*
Cook, Camille Wright *retired law educator*
Cramer, Dale Lewis *retired economics educator*
Crowley, John W(illiam) *English language educator*
Dalton, Margaret Stieg *library and information sciences educator*
Darden, William Howard, Jr., *biology professor*
Delpar, Helen *historian*
De Souza, Ismenia Sales *language educator*
Diehl, Richard A. *museum director*
England, John Henry, Jr., *judge*
Filler, Daniel M. *law educator*
Fish, Mary Martha *economics professor*
Fonseca, Daniel J. *engineering educator*
Fowler, Conrad Murphree *retired manufacturing company executive*
Freyer, Tony Allan *historian, educator*
Greene, Timothy James *industrial engineering educator*
Griffin, Marvin Anthony *industrial engineer, educator*
Gup, Benton Eugene *banking educator*
Hocutt, Max Oliver *retired philosophy educator*
Hubbard, Perry *lawyer, educator*
Janiga-Perkins, Constance Gabrielle *language educator*
Koger, Michael Pigott *physician, writer*
LaMoreaux, Philip Elmer *geologist, hydrogeologist, consultant*
Lumpkin, Thomas Riley *physician, educator*
Mancini, Ernest Anthony *geologist, educator, researcher*
Martone, Michael *writer*
Mayer, Morris Lehman *marketing educator*
Morley, Lloyd Albert *electrical engineering educator*
Moynihan, Gary Peter *industrial engineering educator*
Mysore, Shrikanth Bhaskar *operations research specialist*
Orcutt, Ben Avis *retired social work educator*
Pieroni, Robert Edward *internist, educator, military officer*
Polites, Michael Edward *aerospace engineer, educator*
Randall, Kenneth C. *dean, law educator*
Ray, Paul S. *engineering educator, researcher*
Reinhart, Kellee Connely *journalist*
Ross, Daniel J.J. *publishing executive*
Shabazz, Amilcar *historian, humanities educator*
Sinclair, Robert Ewald *retired physician*
Thomas, Joab Langston *retired university president, biology educator*
Vincent, John Bertram *chemist, educator*

Tuscumbia
Heflin, Howell Thomas *former senator, lawyer, former state supreme court chief justice*
Hutchens, Eugene Garlington *college administrator*

Tuskegee
Gray, Fred David *lawyer*
Green, Elbert P. *retired university official*
Payton, Benjamin Franklin *college president*

Tuskegee Institute
Cooley, Fannie Richardson *counselor, educator*
Datiri, Benjamin Chumang *soil and environmental scientist*
Hill, Walter A. *agricultural sciences educator, researcher*
Madison, Willie Clarence *park administrator*
White, Ymistye Laymonde *artist, composer, publishing executive*

Union Grove
Drew, Thomas Paul *chaplain*
Roberts, Lynn Novak *government employee*

Vestavia Hills
Coleman, Travis Brent *music educator*

Wadley
Caldwell, Ann B. *music educator*

Warrior
Johnson, Barbara L. *retired municipal official*

ALASKA

Anchorage
Anthony, Susan *secondary school educator*
Ashcraft, Charles Olin *business educator*
Baker, Grant Cody *civil engineering educator*
Ballard, Kirsten Kay *environmentalist, writer*
Behrend, Donald Fraser *environmental educator, university administrator*
Bond, Marc Douglas *lawyer*
Bowers, Paul D. *transportation company executive*
Bowie, Phyllis *secondary school educator*
Brady, Carl Franklin *retired aircraft charter company executive*
Branson, Albert Harold (Harry Branson) *judge, educator*
Braund-Allen, Julianna Elise *librarian*
Brown, Dean Naomi *state official, geologist*
Bryner, Alexander O. *state supreme court chief justice*
Burgess, Timothy M. *prosecutor*
Burke, Marianne King *state agency administrator, financial executive, consultant*
Butler, Rex Lamont *lawyer*
Byrd, Milton Bruce *college president, former business executive*
Cantor, James Elliot *lawyer*
Chapman, James Paul *university official*
Charles, George P. *religious studies educator*
Christensen, Ronald E. *physician*
Conway, George A. *medical epidemiologist, physician*
Cowell, Fuller A. *newspaper publisher*
Cuddy, Daniel Hon *bank executive*
Davis, Bettye Jean *academic administrator, state official*
Demarco, Patricia M. *state agency administrator*
DeTerra, Sandra Lee Shivers *secondary school educator*
Dougherty, Patrick *editor*
Duncan, Ronald A. *telecommunications company executive*
Ealy, Jonathan Bruce *lawyer*
Eastaugh, Robert L. *state supreme court justice*
Ebell, C. Walter (Cecil Walter Ebell) *lawyer*
Fabe, Dana Anderson *state supreme court justice*
Faulkner, Sewell Ford *real estate executive*
Fleming, Carolyn Elizabeth *religious organization administrator, interior designer*
Gamble, Patrick K. *retired military officer, rail transportation executive*
Gazaway, Barbara Ann *music educator, art educator*
Greenstein, Marla Nan *lawyer*
Gruenberg, Max F., Jr., *lawyer*
Hayes, George Nicholas *lawyer*
Hickel, Walter Joseph *investment firm executive, forum administrator*
Hill, Erik Bryan *newspaper photographer*
Hughes, Mary Katherine *lawyer*
Ippolito, Maria F. *psychologist, educator*
Jay, Christopher Edward *stockbroker*
Jones, Jewel *social services administrator*
Jones, Mark Logan *educational association executive, educator*
Kelly, Maxine Ann *retired property developer*
Kim, Taesoo *language educator*
Knowles, Tony *former governor*
Lacy, Gregory Lawrence *protective services official*
Leman, Loren Dwight *lieutenant governor, civil engineer*
Linxwiler, James David *lawyer*
Maimon, Elaine Plaskow *academic administrator*
Maki, Alan Walter *biologist, environmental scientist*
Mandell, Gordon Keith *aerospace engineer*
Matsui, Dorothy Nobuko *elementary school educator*
Metzger, Yale Hyder *lawyer, educator*
Mitchell, Michael Kiehl *elementary school educator, secondary school educator, security officer, minister*
Narang, Deborah Lynn *education educator*
Nielsen, Jennifer Lee *molecular ecologist, researcher*
North, Douglas McKay *academic administrator*
Obermeyer, Theresa Nangle *sociology educator*
Oesting, David W. *lawyer*
O'Regan, Deborah *association executive, lawyer*
Ostrovsky, Lawrence Zelig *lawyer*
Pagano, Rosanne V. *journalism professor, media consultant*
Park, Gloria *family physician, consultant*
Parker, Walter Bruce *arctic research specialist, consultant*
Pearson, Larry Lester *journalism educator*
Porcaro, Michael Francis *advertising agency executive*
Pressley, James Ray *electrical engineer*
Rasmuson, Edward Bernard *banker*
Reed, Frank Metcalf *bank executive, director*
Riendl, Robin Wendy *financial consultant*
Roberts, John Derham *lawyer*
Rogers, Donald Robert *retired pathologist*
Rollins, Alden Milton *documents librarian*
Rose, David Allan *portfolio manager*
Ross, Wayne Anthony *lawyer*
Rosston, Richard Mark *lawyer*
Ruedrich, Randy *political party official*
Rylander, Robert Allan *financial service executive*
Sandvik, Helvi *state agency administrator*
Schnell, Roger Thomas *small business owner, retired state official*
Sedwick, Deborah *state agency administrator*
Sells, Colin David *meteorologist*
Shively, John Terry *business executive*
Singleton, James Keith *federal judge*
Strohmeyer, John *writer, former editor*
Sturgulewski, Arliss *state legislator, director*
Suddock, Frances Suter Thorson *grief educator, writer*
Sullivan, George Murray *transportation consultant, former mayor*
Teague, Bruce Williams *chiropractor*
Thomas, Howard Paul *civil engineer, consultant*
Thomas, Lowell, Jr., *writer, lecturer, former lieutenant governor, former state senator*
Thompson, G. Nanette *state agency administrator*
Thorsness, Julia Marie *hospice administrator*
Tobin, William Joseph *newspaper editor*
von der Heydt, James Arnold *federal judge*
Walther, Dale Jay *lawyer*
Wedel-Cowgill, Millie Redmond *secondary school educator, performing arts educator, communications educator, education educator*
Wilkniss, Peter E. *foundation administrator, researcher*
Willard-Jones, Donna C. *lawyer*
Williams, Deborah Lee *foundation administrator*
Williams, Eleanor Joyce *retired government air traffic control specialist*
Wood, Darryl Scott *criminologist, educator*

Arctic Village
Tritt, Lincoln C. (Lincoln C. Gwich'in) *writer, educator, musician*

Bethel
Cooke, Christopher Robert *former state judge, lawyer*

Big Lake
DeLoach, Robert Edgar *corporate executive*

Cordova
Bugbee-Jackson, Joan *sculptor, educator*

Delta Junction
Noble, Alice L. *writer, researcher*

Denali National Park
Swenson, Richard Allen *business owner, animal trainer*

Eagle River
Cotten, Samuel Richard *fisheries consultant, fisherman, former state legislator*
Lange, Ron Q. *music educator*

Fairbanks
Alexander, Vera *dean, marine science educator*
Beistline, Earl Hoover *mining consultant*
Blake, Robert Philip *human services administrator, music therapist*
Bodwell, Lori *lawyer*
Cole, Terrence M. *historian, educator*
Doran, Timothy Patrick *educational administrator*
Duffy, Lawrence Kevin *biochemist, educator*
Fathauer, Theodore Frederick *meteorologist*
Gold, Carol *education educator*
Hamilton, Mark R. *academic administrator*
Heckman, Jyotsna (Jo) L. *bank executive*
Helfferich, Merritt Randolph *industry and education consultant*
Hess, Richard Christian, Jr., *obstetrician/gynecologist, educator*
Jonaitis, Aldona Claire *museum administrator, art historian*
Kessel, Brina *ornithologist, educator, researcher*
Kleinfeld, Andrew J. *federal judge*
Lan, Ping *business educator*
Lind, Marshall L. *academic administrator*
Lingle, Craig Stanley *glaciologist, educator*
Nagabhushana, Nagendra *materials scientist, educator*
Nakoneczny, Michael Martin *artist*
Reichardt, Paul Bernard *provost, chemistry educator*
Roederer, Juan Gualterio *physics educator*
Schamel, Douglas L. *science educator, researcher*
Schendel, William Burnett *lawyer*
Thompson, Daniel Emerson *vending machine service company executive*
Tilsworth, Timothy *retired environmental/civil engineering educator*
Wackerbauer, Renate Anna *physicist*
Weller, Gunter Ernst *geophysics educator*
Wichmann, Henry, Jr., *accounting educator, researcher*
Zhang, Xiangdong *research scientist, educator*

Girdwood
Trautner, John James *real estate executive*

Haines
Kaufman, David Graham *construction executive*

Homer
Phillips, Gail *state legislator*

Indian
Wright, Gordon Brooks *musician, conductor, educator*

Juneau
Carpeneti, Walter L. *judge*
Cissna, Sharon *state representative*
Collins, Patricia A. *lawyer, judge*
Dahlstrom, Nancy *state representative*
Daughhetee, Mark *curator, photographer*
Elton, Kim Steven *state legislator, pollster*
Green, Lyda N. *state legislator*
Guess, Gretchen *state senator*
Heinze, Cheryll Boren *state representative*
Kapsner, Mary *state representative*
Kohring, Victor H. *state legislator*
Kott, Pete *state representative*
Lincoln, Georgianna *state legislator*
Mackie, Jerry *state legislator, business owner*
Masek, Beverly *state representative*
McGuire, Lesil L. *state representative*
Miller, Mike *state legislator, small business owner*
Murkowski, Frank Hughes *governor*
Perdue, Karen *state agency administrator*
Phillips, Randy *state legislator, marketing professional*
Pugh, John Robert *chancellor, former state health administrator*
Renkes, Gregg *state attorney general*
Ruotsala, James Alfred *historian, writer*
Schorr, Alan Edward *librarian, publisher*
Shepard, Beatrice L. *retired microbiologist, historian*
Smith, Charles Anthony *business executive*
Smith, George Vinal *librarian*
Stevens, Gary Lee *state senator*
Therriault, Gene *state senator*
Usera, Vincent L. *state agency administrator*
Ward, Jerry *state legislator, real estate executive*
Wilson, Peggy *state representative, registered nurse*

Kodiak
Jamin, Matthew Daniel *lawyer, magistrate judge*
Selby, Jerome M. *mayor*

Kotzebue
Dakai, Steven Henry *alcohol/drug abuse services professional*
O'Brien, Annmarie *education educator*

Lake Clark Park
Kroll, Henry F. *writer, small business owner*

Nondalton
Gay, Sarah Elizabeth *lawyer*

North Pole
James, Jeannette Adeline *state legislator, accountant*
McGee, Michael Vanhook *writer*

Salcha
Rice, Julian Casavant *lawyer*

Sitka
Blood, Lawrence Preston *chamber of commerce executive*

Soldotna
Franzmann, Albert Wilhelm *wildlife veterinarian, consultant*
Moore, Hubert J. *addictions counselor, consultant*

Tuntutuliak
Daniel, Barbara Ann *retired elementary school educator*

Valdez
Devens, John Searle *natural resources administrator*
Todd, Kathleen Gail *physician*

Wasilla
Brunke, Dawn Baumann *writer, editor*

ARIZONA

Amado
Criswell, Stephen *astronomer*

Anthem
MacMillan, Hoke *former state attorney general*
Palenque, Stephanie Maher *small business owner, writer, book indexer*

Apache Junction
Bracken, Harry McFarland *philosophy educator*
Campbell, John Carl *retired engineering educator*
Maher, John *adult education educator, writer*
Ransom, Evelyn Naill *language educator, linguist*

Arizona City
Donovan, Willard Patrick *retired elementary education educator*

Benson
Erden, Sybil Isolde *artist*

Bisbee
Behney, Charles Augustus, Jr., *veterinarian*
Eppele, David Louis *columnist, author*
Gustavson, Carrie *museum director*
Milton, John P. *ecologist, educator, author, photographer*

Bullhead City
Hicks, Norm *airport authority executive*
Jones, Vernon Quentin *surveyor*

Camp Verde
Wagner, Gary Wayne *educational administrator*

Carefree
Alexander, Judd Harris *retired paper company executive*
Chase, James Keller *retired artist, museum director, educator*
Garr, Carl Robert *manufacturing executive*
Hook, William Franklin *retired radiologist*
Howell, William Robert *retail company executive*
Mangouni, Norman *publishing executive*
Putney, Mark William *lawyer, utilities executive*
Smoot, David Paul *finance company executive*

Casa Grande
Houle, Joseph Adrien *orthopedic surgeon*
Kapsos, Philip John *anesthesiologist*
Khan, Habib Urrehman *neurologist*
Landers, Patricia Glover *reading specialist*

Cave Creek
Boat, Ronald Allen *business executive*
O'Reilly, Thomas Eugene *retired human resources consultant*
Skarbek, Andrew Alexander *investment advisor, artist*

Chandler
Anderson, Darl *retail executive*
Anderson, Melanie Sue *special education educator*
Barnard, Annette Williamson *elementary school principal*
Basha, Edward N., Jr., *grocery chain owner*
Brunello-McCay, Rosanne *sales executive*
Caccamo, Robert *councilman, retired principal*
Canham, Jeanne M. *secondary school educator*
Carpenter, Ron D. *music educator*
Casteel, Camille *school system administrator*
Dunn, Boyd *mayor, lawyer*
Eckstat, Arthur Gene *consultant*
Elliott, Lee Ann *company executive, former government official*
Faust, Donny D. *music educator*
Fordemwalt, James Newton *microelectronics engineering educator, consultant*
Fowler, Reggie *retail executive*
Goyer, Robert Stanton *communication educator*
Graham, Anita Louise *correctional and legal nurse consultant, community health nurse*
Joyce, Kenneth Thomas *electronics company executive*
McGinnis, Robert William *electronics company executive*
Meieran, Eugene Stuart *material scientist*
Rossi, Mark Antony *political consultant, writer*
Rowe, Ernest Ras *education educator, academic administrator*
Simon, Diane Rose *music educator, writer, poet*

Chino Valley
Norton, Douglas Ray *former auditor general*

Clarkdale
Eide, Joel Sylvester *art consultant, appraiser*

Cornville
White, Judith Louise *social worker, counselor*

Cortaro
Wyatt, Roland Gratts *music educator, voice educator, consultant*

Cottonwood
Masters, Arlene Elizabeth *singer*

Davis Monthan AFB
Foglesong, Robert H. *lieutenant general United States Air Force*
Miller, Charles Wallace *historian, environmental geologist, educator*
Woods, Sharhonda Michele *military officer*

Duncan
Ouzts, Eugene Thomas *minister, secondary education educator*

Eloy
O'Leary, Thomas Michael *lawyer*

Flagstaff
Baron, Patricia Burrell *university director*
Bolin, Richard Luddington *industrial development consultant*
Braunstein, Ethan Malcolm *skeletal radiologist, paleopathologist, educator*
Collins, Galen Robert *technology educator*
Cortner, Hanna Joan *research scientist, educator*
Cothran, Dan Allen *political scientist, educator*
Cowser, Danny Lee *lawyer, mental health specialist*
Edgerton, Debra *artist, educator*
Evans, Ronald Allen *lodging chain executive*
Haeger, John Denis *academic administrator*
Hammond, Howard David *retired botanist, editor*
Levin, Mike Douglas *performing arts educator*
McDonald, Craydon Dean *psychologist*
Millis, Robert Lowell *astronomer, science observatory director*
Price, Peter Wilfrid *ecology educator, researcher*
Putnam, William Lowell *science association administrator*
Roe, Richard C. *industry consultant, former home furnishings manufacturing executive*
Shoemaker, Carolyn Spellman *planetary astronomer*
Slobodchikoff, Constantine Nicholas *biologist, educator*
Smith, Zachary Alden *political science and public administration educator*
Titus, Timothy Neal *aerospace scientist, military officer*
Weidenaar, Gary Alan *music educator*
Weston, Laurie Beth *psychiatrist*
Wolf, Arthur Henry *museum administrator*

Fort Huachuca
Adams, Frank *education specialist*

Fountain Hills
Israel, Robert Allan *statistician*
Lacy, Herman Edgar *management consultant*
Tyl, Noel Jan *baritone, astrologer, writer*
Wright, C. T. Enus *former academic administrator*

Gila Bend
Barnes, William Wayne *geographer, writer*

Gilbert
Earnhardt, Hal J., III, *automotive executive*
Kenney, Thomas Frederick *broadcast executive*
Stabler, Scott Lawrence *historian, educator*
Stephenson, Frank Alex *engineer, consultant*
Stroble-Thompson, Colette Mary Houle *plastering and stucco company executive*

Glendale
Altersitz, Janet Kinahan *principal*
Amador, Fred L. *counselor*
Avila, Lidia D. *principal*
Cole, James W. *academic administrator*
Edwards, Vicki Ann *elementary school principal*
Hamilton, Darded Cole *plastics company executive*
Haran, Robert Emmet *political scientist*
Howell, Llewellyn Donald *management educator*
Jordan, Melanie Alison *research scientist, educator*
Joseph, Gregory Nelson *media critic, writer, actor*
Lack, Larry Henry *small business owner*
Mathis, F. John *economist, educator*
McDonald, Barbara Ann *retired psychotherapist*
Michael, Cecil Francis, Jr., *pediatrician*
Scruggs, Elaine M. *mayor*
Staczek, John Joseph *academic administrator, consultant*
Stauffer, Thomas Michael *former university president*
Thomas, Bruce Larry *counselor*
Thrasher, Jacqueline F. *elementary school educator*
Uhlmann, Elenore Arlene *interior designer, writer*

Goodyear
Borton, George Robert *retired airline captain*
Carlson, Norman A. *government official*
Eppen, Gary Dean *business educator*
McBride, Janet Marie *small business owner*
Taylor, Richard L., Jr., *engineer, consultant*

Grand Canyon
Breecher-Breen, Sheila Rae *lawyer*
Bryant, Leland Marshal *business and nonprofit executive*

Green Valley
Bennett, Bradley Frederick *retired military officer, science association director*
Brewington, Arthur William *retired English language educator*
de Soto, Ernest Frank *artist, publisher*
Dingle, Albert Nelson *meteorology educator*
Lusk, Harlan Gilbert *national park superintendent, business executive*
Macafee, Susan Diane *reporter*
Moser, Robert Harlan *internist, educator, writer*
Page, John Henry, Jr., *artist, educator*
Pike, George Harold, Jr., *religious organization executive, clergyman*
Smith, Raymond Lloyd *former university president, consultant*

Hereford
Hirth, John Price *metallurgical engineering educator*
Schenk, Quentin Frederick *retired social work educator, mayor, psychologist*
Seeland, Arthur David *bishop*

Kingman
Basinger, Richard Lee *lawyer*
Hlavac, Dana Paul *lawyer, consultant*
Jones, Barbara Christine *linguist, creative arts designer, educator*

Kykotsmovi
Honan, Raena *writer*

Lake Havasu City
Brydon, Ruth Vickery *history educator*
Hurt, Nathan Hampton, Jr., *mechanical engineer*

Lake Montezuma
Burkee, Irvin *artist*
Loveland, John Bigelow *small business owner*

Lakeside
Stidham, Lucas Wesley *music educator*

Laveen
Wade, Tyra V. *manufacturing executive*

Litchfield Park
McKeighen, Ronald Eugene *physicist*

Marana
Green, Laura Lorraine *foundation administrator*

Mesa
Allen, David Harlow *business educator, logistician, consultant*
Baxter, Gene Kenneth *mechanical engineer, engineering company executive*
Boyd, Leona Potter *retired social worker*
Brown, Wayne J. *former mayor*
Burgess, Robert Kingsley *aeronautical engineer*
Cassalata, Richard William *secondary school educator*
Christiansen, Larry K. *college president*
DeRosa, Francis Dominic *chemical company executive*
Dillenberg, Jack *dean*
Dorland, Elizabeth M. *chemistry professor*
Duvall, Debra *school system administrator*
Evans, Don A. *healthcare company executive*
Fiorino, John Wayne *podiatrist*
Gantz, Nancy Rollins *hospital administrator, nursing administrator, consultant*
Garwood, John Delvert *former college administrator*
Gottry, Steven Roger *communications executive, author, screenwriter*
Hagen, Nicholas Steward *medical educator, consultant*
Hawker, Keno *mayor, trucking company executive*
Johnson, Doug *advertising and public relations executive*
Kaida, Tamarra *art and photography educator*
Kiefer, Don Russell *writer, researcher*
Kim, Kai Y. *art educator, artist*
Linxwiler, Louis Major, Jr., *retired finance company executive*
Luth, William Clair *retired research manager*
McGill, John J. *radiologist*
Moorhead, Nila Katherine *music educator*
Murphy, Edward Francis *sales executive*
Pierce, Byron James *research scientist*
Porter, Christy Lee *music educator*
Ramirez, Janice L. *assistant school superintendent*
Rummel, Robert Wiland *aeronautical engineer, writer*
St. Cyr, Margaret Ann (Peggy St. Cyr) *writer*
Skoldberg, Phyllis Linnea *music educator, musician*
Thompson, Ronald MacKinnon *former family physician, artist, writer*
Tindle, Charles Dwight Wood *broadcasting company executive*
Trejos, Franklin Anthony *physician assistant*
Wong, Willie *former mayor, automotive executive*
Zaharia, Eric Stafford *health facility administrator*

Miami
Ladendorff, Linda Hardin-Reed *early childhood education educator*

Oracle
Garmany, Catharine Doremus *astronomer*

Oro Valley
McConnell, Robert Eastwood *architect, educator*

Paradise Valley
Blumer, Harry Maynard *architect*
Buffmire, Donald K. *retired internist*
Burkholder, Peter Miller *physician, educator*
Chrisman, William Herring *property tax consultant*
Day, Richard Putnam *marketing, strategic planning and employee benefits consultant, arbitrator*
Hazard, Robert Culver, Jr., *hotel executive*
Joaquim, Richard Ralph *hotel executive*
Lorenzen, Robert Frederick *ophthalmologist*
McKennon, Keith Robert *chemical company executive*
Morris, Stephen Owens *psychiatrist*
Moya, Sara Dreier *educational association administrator*
Ratkowski, Donald J. *mechanical engineer, consultant*
Russell, Paul Edgar *electrical engineering educator*
Salmon, Matt *former congressman, communications company executive*
Swanson, Robert Killen *management consultant*
Targovnik, Selma E. Kaplan *physician*
Tubman, William Charles *lawyer*
Unruh, James Arlen *bank executive*

Parker
Carnicom, Gene E. *health services administrator*
Grazier, Diana Lynn *community health nurse, medical/surgical nurse, writer*

Patagonia
Bonner, Herbert Dwight *construction management educator*
La Noue, Terence David *artist, educator*

Payson
Hershberger, Robert Glen *architect, educator*
Lasys, Joan *medical nurse, writer, educator, publisher*

Peoria
Bailey, Claudia Jean *retired professor, librarian, artist*
Cook, Mary Margaret *steamfitter, educator*
Engelhardt, Thomas Francis *lawyer, consultant*
Gould, Dorothy Mae *executive secretary, soprano*
McMahon, Maribeth Lovette *physicist*
Schindler, William Stanley *retired public relations executive, consultant*

Phoenix
Agler, Brian *professional basketball coach*
Aguirre, Linda *state senator*
Allen, Janice Faye Clement *nursing administrator*
Allen, John Rybolt L. *chemist, biochemist*
Allen, Robert Eugene Barton *lawyer*
Alsentzer, William James, Jr., *lawyer*
Ammon, John Richard *anesthesiologist*
Andersen, Ronald Meredith *lawyer*
Anderson, Gary Gene *music educator*
Anderson, Ib *performing company executive*
Anderson, Lawrence Ohaco *magistrate judge, lawyer*
Armstrong, Nelson William, Jr., *gaming company executive*
Arzberger, Marsha *state senator*
Avila, Bridgett Bernice *writer*
Bachus, Benson Floyd *mechanical engineer, consultant*
Bain, C. Randall *lawyer*
Baker, William Dunlap *lawyer*
Bakker, Thomas Gordon *lawyer*
Ballinger, James K. *art museum executive*
Begam, Robert George *lawyer*
Beggs, Harry Mark *lawyer*
Bell, Jay Stuart *professional baseball player*
Bergamo, Ron *marketing executive*
Bidwill, William V. *professional football executive*
Bivens, Donald Wayne *lawyer, judge*
Blanchard, Charles Alan *lawyer, former state senator*
Blevins, Willard Ahart *electrical engineer*
Bodensteiner, John Burton *neurologist*
Bodney, David Jeremy *lawyer*
Bolin, Vernon Spencer *microbiologist, consultant*
Bouma, John Jacob *lawyer*
Brenly, Bob *professional sports team executive, broadcaster*
Brewer, Charles Moulton *lawyer*
Brewer, Janice Kay *state official*
Broomfield, Robert Cameron *federal judge*
Brown, Jack A. *state legislator, rancher, real estate broker*
Brunacini, Alan Vincent *protective services official*
Bryant, Andrew *electronics executive*
Burke, Timothy John *lawyer*
Burns, Brenda *state senator*
Bushee, Ward *newspaper editor*
Calderon, Ernest *lawyer*
Campbell, Jon R. *financial services executive*
Canby, William Cameron, Jr., *judge*
Carroll, Earl Hamblin *federal judge*
Carter, Ronald Martin, Sr., *pharmaceutical company executive*
Case, David Leon *lawyer*
Castleberry, W. Thomas *financial company executive*
Chanen, Steven Robert *lawyer*
Charlton, John Kipp *pediatrician*
Charlton, Paul *lawyer*
Chavez, Nelba R. *state agency administrator, former federal agency administrator*
Cheifetz, Lorna Gale *psychologist*
Cheuvront, Kenneth David *state senator, construction executive, small business owner*
Church, Steve *communications executive*
Cirillo, Edward J. *state legislator, retired financial manager*
Clark, John *corporate financial executive*
Clark-Johnson, Sue *publishing executive*
Clark-Johnson, Susan *publishing executive*
Clements, John Robert *real estate professional*
Coghill, William Thomas, Jr., *retired lawyer*
Cohen, Jon Stephan *lawyer*
Colangelo, Jerry John *professional sports team executive*
Cole, George Thomas *lawyer*
Cole, John *controller*
Comus, Louis Francis, Jr., *lawyer*
Condo, James Robert *lawyer*
Conrad, John Regis *lawyer, engineering executive, consultant*
Cook, Douglas Neilson *theater educator, producer, artistic director*
Cooledge, Richard Calvin *lawyer*
Coor, Lattie Finch *university president*
Coppersmith, Sam *lawyer*
Corson, Kimball Jay *lawyer*
Crane, Ross *electronics executive*
Crockett, Clyll Webb *lawyer*
Culnon, Sharon Darlene *reading specialist, special education educator*
Curcio, Christopher Frank *recreation director*
Curry, J. Stanton *lawyer, educator*
Daniel, James Richard *accountant, corporate financial executive*
Daniels, Lori S. *state legislator, insurance agent*
D'Antoni, Mike *professional athletics coach*
Davies, David George *lawyer, educator*
Dawson, John Joseph *lawyer*
Day, Ann *state legislator*
DeBartolo, Jack, Jr., *architect*
DelParigi, Angelo *research scientist*
deMatties, Nicholas Frank *artist, art educator*
De Michele, O. Mark *real estate company executive*
Derdenger, Patrick *lawyer*
Derouin, James Gilbert *lawyer*
Desser, Kenneth Barry *cardiologist, educator*
Dewane, John Richard *retired manufacturing company executive, consultant, business owner*

Dickey, Ginny Grace state agency administrator
Dignac, Geny (Eugenia M. Bermudez) sculptor
Doto, Irene Louise statistician
Drain, Albert Sterling business management consultant
Drnjevic, Jonathan Mark language educator
DuMoulin, Diana Cristaudo small business owner, writer, musician
Dunipace, Ian Douglas lawyer
DuVal, Merlin Kearfott health consultant
Early, Robert Joseph magazine editor
Edens, Gary Denton broadcast executive
Ehmann, Anthony Valentine lawyer
Elliott, Steve newspaper editor
Ellison, Cyril Lee literary agent, retired publisher
Elmore, James Walter architect, retired university dean
Enzor, Gary R. trucking executive
Erwin, Barbara F. school system administrator
Everett, James Joseph lawyer
Everett, Paul Marvin physicist
Fannin, Paul Robert political party official
Feder, Bruce lawyer
Felnstein, Allen Lewis lawyer
Feldberg, Harley marketing professional
Felicetta, James Vincent endocrinologist, educator
Fishburne, John Ingram, Jr., obstetrician/gynecologist, educator
Fitzgerald, Joan principal
Fleenor, Geneva Lucille retired elementary school educator
Flickinger, Don Jacob patent agent
Foley, William Patrick, II, title insurance company executive
Forshey, Timothy Allan lawyer
Foutz, Claudia state agency administrator
Franke, William Augustus corporate executive
Fraser, Martin automobile parts executive
Freyermuth, Clifford L. structural engineering consultant
Fugiel, Frank Paul insurance company executive
Gaffney, Donald Lee lawyer
Gaines, Francis Pendleton, III, judge
Gall, Donald Alan data processing executive
Gallagher, Michael L. lawyer
Gallagher, Philip electronics executive
Garagiola, Joe, Jr., baseball team executive
Genrich, Mark L. retired foundation administrator
Gerard, Susan state senator
Giedt, Bruce Alan paper company executive
Gilbert, Donald Roy lawyer
Gillom, Jennifer professional basketball player
Giltner, Phil food distributing executive
Gladner, Marc Stefan lawyer
Goddard, Terry state attorney general
Goldberg, Morris internist
Goldstein, Stuart Wolf lawyer
Gomez, David Frederick lawyer
Gordon, Phil mayor
Grace, Sue state legislator
Granato, Heather Breuninger editor
Gray, Charles Dale (Chuck Gray) state legislator, entrepreneur
Green, Dennis professional football coach
Griller, Gordon Moore legal association administrator
Grinell, Sheila museum director
Gwozdz, Kim Elizabeth interior designer
Haga, David L. lawyer
Halpern, Barry David lawyer
Hamada, Richard computer company executive
Hammerschlag, Carl A psychiatrist
Hammond, Larry Austin lawyer
Harrison, Mark Isaac lawyer
Hartley, Mary state legislator
Hawkins, Jasper Stillwell, Jr., architect
Hay, John Leonard lawyer
Hayden, William Robert lawyer
Hedberg, John Charles investor
Helling, Ricky Allen professional baseball player
Hellon, Toni state senator
Henze, Tom lawyer
Hicks, William Albert, III, lawyer
Hirsch, Steven A. lawyer
Hoecker, Thomas Ralph lawyer
Hoerber, Michael David music educator, conductor
Horner, Harry Charles, Jr., sales executive, theatrical and film consultant
Hotz, Jeffrey Alan anesthesiologist, educator
Houseworth, Richard Court state agency administrator
Hovis, John corporate financial executive
Howard, William Matthew arbitrator, writer, lawyer
Huntwork, James Roden lawyer
Huppenthal, John state senator, planning analyst
Hurwitz, Andrew D. judge
Hutchinson, Edna M. home care nurse
Inman, William Peter lawyer
Jacobson, Edward (Julian Edward Jacobson) lawyer
James, Charles E., Jr., lawyer
Jenkins, Maynard automotive executive
Jewett, Patrick electronics executive
Jirauch, Charles W. lawyer
Johnson, Kevin Maurice professional basketball player
Johnson, Randy (Randall David Johnson) professional baseball player
Johnson, Robert D. aerospace transportation executive
Johnston, Logan Truax, III, lawyer
Jones, Charles E. chief justice supreme court
Jones, Isola Charlayne mezzo soprano, voice educator
Jovicic, Dusko financial analyst
Kamins, Edward electronics executive
Karabatsos, Elizabeth Ann career counseling services executive
Karnas, Fred G., Jr., policy advisor
Kimball, Bruce Arnold soil scientist
Kitzman, Jerry Matson pharmaceutical executive
Klahr, Gary Peter retired lawyer
Klausner, Jack Daniel lawyer
Klein, R. Kent lawyer
Klepinger, John William trailer manufacturing company executive
Klor de Alva, Jorge education company executive
Knoller, Guy David lawyer
Koester, Berthold Karl lawyer, law educator, retired honorary German consul
Kossek, Sebastian Alexander information technology executive
Krietor, David airport authority executive
Kurn, Neal lawyer
Kuzma, George Martin retired bishop
Laufer, Nathan cardiologist
LaValle, Jennifer Suzette marketing communications specialist, consultant
Lawlis, Patricia Kite air force officer, computer consultant
Lawrence, William Henry, Jr., neurologist
Leach, John F. editor, journalism educator
Lee, Richard H(arlo) lawyer
Leiby, John Severn historian, educator
Lemon, Leslie Gene retired diversified services company executive, lawyer
Levetown, Robert Alexander lawyer
Levin, Warren Mayer family practice physician
Lewis, Orme, Jr., real estate company executive, land use adviser
Long, Michael Alan musician, writer
Lovely, Randy editor
Lovett, William Lee surgeon
Lubin, Stanley lawyer
Lundeen, Bradley Curtis lawyer
Mardian, Daniel construction company director
Marion, Shawn professional basketball player
Martensen, Barbara electronics executive
Martin, Douglas Kenton state agency administrator
Martone, Frederick J. judge
Martori, Joseph Peter lawyer
Mathis, Virginia federal judge
McClennen, Crane judge
Mc Clennen, Louis lawyer, educator
McClennen, Miriam J. former state official
McConnell, Albert Lynn dean
McGregor, Ruth Van Roekel state supreme court justice
McKay, Kay academic administrator
McLoone, James Brian psychiatrist, educator
McNamee, Stephen M. federal judge
McRae, Hamilton Eugene, III, lawyer
Merritt, Nancy-Jo lawyer
Metzler, Jerry Don retired nursing administrator
Miller, Janice electronics executive
Miller, Michael Jon survey engineer
Mitchell, Wayne Lee health care administrator
Motsenbocker, Rex Alan construction company executive
Mousel, Craig Lawrence lawyer
Moyer, Alan Dean retired newspaper editor
Moyes, Jerry C. transportation executive
Mullen, Daniel Robert finance executive
Myers, Robert David judge
Napolitano, Janet Ann governor
Newman, Lois Mae marketing executive
Nijinsky, Tamara actress, puppeteer, author, librarian, educator
Noone, Palmer academic administrator
Norris, John Steven healthcare company executive
North, Warren James government official
Olmsted, Thomas James archbishop
Olsen, Alfred Jon lawyer
Orr, Steven R. health facility administrator
Palacios, Christina academic administrator
Papp, Harry science association administrator
Perry, Lee Rowan retired lawyer
Peru, Ramiro G. metal products executive
Petersen, David A. state legislator, financial advisor
Phillips, James Harold lawyer
Pietzsch, Michael Edward lawyer
Pillalamarri, Seshasayi computer scientist and engineer, researcher
Platt, Warren E. lawyer
Pogson, Stephen Walter lawyer
Powell, Suzanne K. K. nurse, consultant
Prewitt, Alan Jay playwright, performing company executive
Proffitt, Dennis Lewis finance educator
Pyle, Thomas Alton instructional television and motion picture executive
Quddus, Mohammed Tanvir electrical engineer, researcher
Ragland, Samuel Connelly industrial engineer, management consultant
Ralston, Barbara Jo bank executive
Rapier, David electronics executive
Rathwell, Peter John lawyer
Reed, Wallace Allison anesthesiologist
Reyes, Anna Maria broadcast executive
Richardson, Judy McEwen education administrator, consultant, cartoonist
Rister, Gene Arnold humanities educator
Roof, Sally Jean-Marie library and information scientist, educator
Rose, Scott A. lawyer
Rosenblatt, Paul Gerhardt judge
Roush, Charles Dow lawyer
Rubeli, Paul E. gaming company executive
Rudd, Gerald Patrick ophthalmologist
Rudolph, Gilbert Lawrence lawyer
Ryan, Michael D. state supreme court justice
Sage, Webster LeGene, Jr., ophthalmologist
Salmonson, Marty Lee stockbroker, consulting engineer
Sanders, Barry R. lawyer
Savage, Stephen Michael lawyer
Schatt, Paul newspaper editor
Schiffner, Charles Robert architect
Schroeder, Mary Murphy federal judge
Seiler, Steven Lawrence health facility administrator
Sertich, Kelli Ann land use planner
Sexson, Richmond Lockwood professional baseball player
Sharp, Linda professional basketball coach
Shaw, Richard Glenn financial analyst
Sherk, Kenneth John lawyer
Silver, Roslyn Olson federal judge
Silverman, Alan Henry lawyer
Silverman, Barry G. federal judge
Singer, Jeffrey Alan surgeon
Smith, Emmitt J., III, professional football player
Smith, George marketing professional
Smith, Gordon finance company executive
Smock, Timothy Robert lawyer
Snell, Richard holding company executive
Snider, Timothy R. mining executive
Sochacki, Andrzej mechanical engineer, researcher, tourism educator
Solomon, John Davis aviation executive
Steckler, Phyllis Betty publishing company executive
Stegmayer, Joseph Henry housing industry executive
Stern, Richard David investment company executive
Stern, Stanley psychiatrist
Stewart, Nancy Sue Spurlock education educator
Stone, Hazel Anne Decker artist
Storey, Norman C. lawyer
Stoudemire, Amare Carsares professional basketball player
Strand, Roger Gordon federal judge
Swafford, Leslie Eugene physician assistant, consultant
Swann, Eric Jerrod professional football player
Swartz, Jack chamber of commerce executive
Swartz, Melvin Jay lawyer, writer
Takata, Lisa D. city manager, artist
Taurasi, Diana college basketball player
Taylor, Elizabeth Jane investment consultant, real estate and international marketing executive
Teague, Robert Cole physician
Teets, John William retired diversified company executive
Tennen, Leslie Irwin lawyer, consultant, inventor
Theodore, Nicholas neurosurgeon, researcher
Thomas, Jim Gus music educator
Thompson, Herbert Ernest tool and die company executive
Thompson, Joel Erik lawyer
Thompson, Terence William lawyer
Thorne, Ann LaRayne secondary school educator
Tribble, Richard Walter brokerage executive
Tsang, Raymond electronics executive
Turi, Louis publishing executive
Udall, Calvin Hunt lawyer
Udall, Vesta Hammond special education educator
Ulrich, Paul Graham lawyer, writer, editor
Underwood, Paul Lester cardiologist
Upson, Donald V. retired corporate financial executive
Vallee, Roy electronics company executive
Van Fleet, David Dominic educator
Van Haren, Peter lawyer
Waas, Andrea Sue nonprofit foundation administrator
Walker, Richard K. lawyer
Wall, Donald Arthur lawyer
Wall, Gerard W. physiologist, researcher
Weiers, Jim state representative
Weisenburger, Theodore Maurice retired judge, poet, educator, writer
Welborn, R. Michael bank executive
Welliver, Charles Harold hospital administrator
Wells, GladysAnn library director
Wheaton, Marilyn music educator, pianist, organist
Wheeler, Steven M. lawyer
Whisler, James Steven lawyer, mining and manufacturing executive
White, Edward Allen electronics company executive
Whitlow, William La Fond minister, theology school planter
Williams, Quinn Patrick lawyer
Wilmer, Charles Mark lawyer
Winslow, Paul David architect
Winthrop, Lawrence Fredrick judge
Wold, Kimberly G. legislative staff member
Wolf, G. Van Velsor, Jr., lawyer
Wolfe, William Downing nuclear energy industry executive
Wright, Richard Oscar, III, pathologist, educator, clinical ethicist
Yamamoto, Alice M. educator
Zerella, Joseph T. retired pediatric surgeon

Picacho
Cortright, Lewis Stephen elementary school educator

Pinetop
Colgate, Catharine Pamella secondary school educator

Portal
Zweifel, Richard George curator

Prescott
Anderson, Parker Lynn columnist, playwright
Anderson, Walter Lee environmental educator, artist, photographer
Bennett, Kenneth R. oil company executive, state legislator
Bieniawski, Zdzislaw Tadeusz Richard engineering educator emeritus, writer, consultant
Chamberlain, David Alanson lawyer, consultant, writer
Chesson, Eugene civil engineering educator, consultant
Garvey, Daniel Edward foundation administrator, educator, academic administrator
Gose, Celeste Marlene writer
Gose, Richard Vernie lawyer
Kahne, Stephen James systems engineer, educator, academic administrator, engineering executive
Madden, Paul Robert lawyer, director
Parkhurst, Charles Lloyd electronics company executive
Schaeffer, Reiner Horst military officer, foreign language professional
Stasack, Edward Armen artist
Stuart, Spencer Raymond management consultant
Waldock, William David aeronautical science and aviation safety educator
Waterer, Bonnie Clausing retired secondary school educator

Rio Rico
Lowell, J(ames) David geological consultant, cattle rancher

Rio Verde
Ramsey, David Selmer retired health facility administrator
Scott, Louis Edward advertising agency executive
Vanselow, Neal Arthur academic administrator, internist

Sacaton
Stephenson, Larry Kirk stategic planner, geography educator

San Carlos
Talgo, Harrison chief administrator tribal government

Scottsdale
Afsary, Cyrus artist
Amonte, Anthony Lewis professional hockey player
Ash, Fayola Foltz musician, music educator
Baack, Paula D. music educator
Baker, Jeffrey Charles telecommunications executive
Barnett, Michael professional sports team executive
Baum, Herbert Merrill consumer products company executive
Berman, Gizel sculptor
Birkelbach, Albert Ottmar retired oil company executive
Blinder, Martin S. business consultant, art dealer
Boucher, Brain professional hockey player
Braun, Stephen Hughes psychologist
Breyne, Matthew M. finance company executive
Broe, Carolyn Waters conductor, violist, music educator
Brown, Frederick Lee health care executive
Brown, Shirley Margaret Kern (Peggy Brown) interior designer
Buri, Charles Edward lawyer
Burr, Edward Benjamin life insurance company executive, financial executive
Cai, Weizhong (Will) electronics engineer, researcher, physicist
Carpenter, Peter Rockefeller retired bank executive
Carter, Carla Cifelli management consultant
Casper, Eric Michael lawyer
Cawley, Leo Patrick pathologist, immunologist
Chaurasia, Vishal physician, writer, computer programmer
Clement, Richard William plastic and reconstructive surgeon
Coffinger, Maralin Katharyne retired career officer, consultant
Cormie, Donald Mercer investment company executive
Coutts, Lawrence Robert publisher
Dahl, Mark Victor dermatologist, educator
Dalton, Phyllis Irene library consultant
Dean, Leslie Alan (Cap Dean) economist, consultant
Doan, Shane professional hockey player
Dobronski, Mark William judge, justice of the peace
Doede, John Henry investment company executive
Donaldson, Scott English language educator, writer
Dorland, Byrl Brown retired volunteer
Drake, Albert Estern retired statistics educator, farming administrator
Evans, Tommy Nicholas obstetrician/gynecologist, educator
Faer, A.M. magazine publishing consultant, poet
Ferree, John Newton, Jr., fundraising specialist, consultant
Fisher, John Richard engineering consultant, former naval officer
Francis, Robert professional hockey coach
Fratt, Dorothy artist
Freedman, Stanley Marvin manufacturing executive
French, Lyle Albert surgeon
Friedman, Shelly Arnold cosmetic surgeon
Friesen, Oris Dewayne software engineer, historian
Fuhr, Grant professional hockey player
Gans, Eugene Howard cosmetic and pharmaceutical company executive, consultant
Garcia-Buñuel, Luis neurologist
Garfield, Ernest bank consultant
Getz, Bert Atwater investment company executive
Gilson, Arnold Leslie retired engineering executive, consultant
Gookin, Thomas Allen Jaudon civil engineer
Grant, Merwin Darwin lawyer
Grenell, James Henry retired manufacturing company executive
Gretzky, Wayne Douglas retired professional hockey player, businessman
Grier, James Edward hotel executive, lawyer
Gwinn, Mary Dolores business developer, philosopher, writer
Hadder, Donald Everett, Sr., urban planner
Hanneman, Le Roy C., Jr., real estate executive
Hansen, Donald W. insurance and financial services executive
Hathaway, Peter S corporate financial executive
Highet, Mac travel company executive
Hill, Louis Allen, Jr., former university dean, consultant
Hockmuth, Joseph Frank physicist, psychotherapist
Holliger, Fred Lee oil company executive
Howard, William Gates, Jr., electronics company executive
Hull, Brett A. professional hockey player
Hutchison, Stanley Philip retired lawyer
Jacobson, Frank Joel cultural organization administrator
Jeffe, Sidney David automotive engineer
Jesky, T. J. pharmaceutical products executive
Kaufman, Jeffrey Allen publisher
Kilgore, L(eRoy) Wilson minister
Kinney, Carolyn physician
Kinsinger, Jack Burl chemist, educator
Kizziar, Janet Wright psychologist, writer, lecturer
Krupp, Clarence William lawyer, personnel and hospital administrator
Land, George A. philosopher, writer, educator, consultant, speaker
Lang, Margo Terzian artist
Lavenson, Susan Barker hotel corporate executive, consultant
La Vista, Frank William author, educator, speaker
Leighton, William D. plastic and reconstructive surgeon
Lemieux, Claude professional hockey player
Leonard, George Edmund real estate, bank, high tech and consulting executive
Lewis, John Christopher allergist
Lillestol, Jane Brush development consultant
Lillo, Joseph Leonard osteopath, family practice physician
Lindgren, D(erbin) Kenneth, Jr., retired lawyer
Lloyd, Eugene Walter retired construction company executive
Lloyd, Sally-Heath Fahnestock artist
Lowry, Edward Francis, Jr., lawyer
MacKinnon, Sally Anne retired fast food company executive
Maggard, Woodrow Wilson, Jr., management consultant
Manross, Mary mayor
Marks, Merton Eleazer lawyer, international arbitrator, mediator, consultant
Marshall, Jonathan charitable foundation administrator, journalist
Mc Gill, Archie Joseph venture capitalist
Meland, N. Bradly plastic surgeon
Milanovich, Norma JoAnne training and development company executive
Mohraz, Judy Jolley foundation administrator
Molever, Keith chemist, consumer products company executive

Morrison, James William, Jr., *lobbyist, government relations consultant*
Murian, Richard Miller *book company executive*
Nadler, Henry Louis *pediatrician, geneticist, medical educator*
Nelson, Florence Ely *civic leader*
Newman, Ursula Irene *music educator*
Nielsen, Greg Ross *lawyer*
Northey, William Thomas *microbiologist, educator*
Numminen, Teppo *professional hockey player*
O'Brien, John Conway *economist, educator, writer*
Orford, Robert Raymond *consulting physician*
Overgaard, Cordell Jersild *lawyer, business executive, director*
Pacheco, Manuel Trinidad *retired academic administrator*
Peterson, John Willard *composer, music publisher*
Quayle, Dan (James Danforth Quayle) *former vice president United States, entrepreneur*
Quayle, Marilyn Tucker *wife of former vice president of United States, lawyer*
Quigley, Jerome Harold *management consultant*
Rethore, Bernard Gabriel *retired manufacturing and mining company executive*
Reznick, Richard Howard *pediatrician*
Roberts, Jean Reed *lawyer*
Rutes, Walter Alan *architect*
Ryan, Thomas W. *treasurer manufacturing company*
Sanderson, David R. *physician*
Sapp, Donald Gene *retired minister*
Schmitz, Shirley Gertrude *marketing and sales executive*
Scholder, Fritz *artist*
Slager, Donald W. *waste management executive*
Smith, David Burnell *lawyer*
Steier, Jeffrey David *neurologist*
Stines, Fred, Jr., *publisher*
Stone, Alan Jay *retired academic administrator*
Stott, Brian *software company executive, consultant*
Taylor, James C. *writer*
Timmons, Evelyn Deering *pharmacist*
Titus, Jon Alan *lawyer*
Travers, Paul *company executive*
Tyner, Neal Edward *retired insurance company executive*
Vairo, Robert John *insurance company executive*
Van Brunt, Gary T. *consumer products company executive*
Vanier, Jerre Lynn *art director*
Van Weelden, Thomas H. *waste industry company executive*
Walsh, Edward Joseph *toiletries and food company executive*
Washburn, Jerry Martin *accountant, corporate executive*
Watkins, Eugene Leonard *surgeon, educator*
Weaver, Linda Marie *pharmacist, education educator*
Weil, Louis Arthur, III, *retired newspaper publishing executive*
Weisman, Avery *psychiatrist*
Whittington, Thomas Lee *lawyer*
Williamson, R. Max *diversified financial services company executive*
Wolfgang, Bonnie Arlene *musician, bassoonist*
Wong, Joe Bing *retired architect*

Sedona
Bell, Robert Matthew *pharmaceutical company consultant*
Briney, Allan King *retired radiologist*
Catterton, Marianne Rose *occupational therapist*
Chicorel, Marietta Eva *publishing company executive, consultant*
Copeland, Suzanne Johnson *real estate executive*
Dansby, John Walter *retired oil company executive*
Frankel, Jennie Louise *writer, composer, playwright*
Hawkins, David Ramon *psychiatrist, writer, researcher, religious studies educator*
Mastor, Helen *career planning administrator, educator*
McLeod, Lorna A. *personnel director*
Metzner, Richard Joel *psychiatrist, psychopharmacologist, educator*
Reno, Joseph Harry *retired orthopedic surgeon*
Sasmor, James Cecil *publishing representative, educator*
Shors, Clayton Marion *cardiologist*
Wolfe, Al *marketing and advertising consultant*

Show Low
Pershing, Robert George *telecommunications company executive*

Sierra Vista
Boughan, Zanetta Louise *music educator*
Bowen, Harry Ernest *management consultant*
Lutes, Todd Oakley *political science educator*
Plummer, Val J. *education educator, chaplain*
Ponder, Herman *geologist*

Sonoita
Cook, William Howard *architect*
Hanson, Thor *retired health agency executive and naval officer*
Scott, William Coryell *medical executive*

South Tucson
Eckstrom, Daniel William *retired county official*

Springerville
Geisler, Sherry Lynn *magistrate*

Sun City
Black, Robert Frederick *former oil company executive*
Blanchet, Jeanne Ellene Maxant *artist, educator, performer*
Buchman, Elwood *internist, pharmaceutical company medical director*
Coffman, Harold Emerson *retired agricultural products supplier, retail merchant*
Cooper, Vivian M. *minister, writer*
Crisman, Mary Frances Borden *librarian*
Davies, Percy (Pete) Charles *mechanical engineer*
Hamilton, Ronald Ray *minister*
Keesling, Karen Ruth *lawyer*
Lapsley, James Norvell, Jr., *minister, pastoral theology educator*
Nicchi, Vincent, Jr., *cardiologist*
Oppenheimer, Max, Jr., *foreign language educator, consultant*
Randall, Claire *church executive*
Reynolds, John Francis *insurance company executive*
Smith, Stanford Sidney *former state treasurer*
Tijmann, Willem Bert *civil engineer, consultant*
Treece, James Lyle *lawyer*
Vander Molen, Jack Jacobus *engineering executive, industrial facility planner, consultant*

Sun City West
Berkenkamp, Fred Julius *management consultant*
Brown, Ruth Geisler *engineering supervisor*
Czarny, Frank Silvey *social problems specialist, human and organizational systems consultant*
Forti, Lenore Steimle *business consultant*
Hartzog, Ira Barnes *aviation executive*
Holloway, Diane Elaine *psychological consultant, psychotherapist, writer*
Nordin, John Algot *economist, educator*
Person, Robert John *financial management consultant*
Schrag, Adele Frisbie *business education educator*
Stevens, George Richard *business consultant, public policy commentator*
Williams, William Harrison *retired librarian*

Sun Lakes
Johnson, Marian Ilene *education educator*
Sharpless, Joseph Benjamin *retired county official*
Smith, Eleanor Jane *retired university chancellor, consultant*
Thompson, Loring Moore *retired college administrator, writer*

Sunsites
Datcu, Ioana *artist*

Surprise
Bradford, Mariah *elementary school educator, consultant*
Clark, Lloyd *historian, writer, educator*
Eastman, Donna Kelly *composer*
Fennelly, Jane Corey *lawyer*
Horner, Jennie Linn *retired educational administrator, nurse*
Jackson, Randy *information technology executive*
Koessel, Donald Ray *retired bank executive*
Lazar, Max Seymour *retired pharmaceutical company executive*
Lucchetti, Lynn L. *career officer*
Orenstein, Fran M. *director, writer*
Veigel, Jon Michael *science administrator*
Wargo, Andrea Ann *retired public health official, commissioned officer*

Tempe
Adelson, Roger Dean *history educator, editor, historian*
Alisky, Marvin Howard *political science educator*
Amin, Omar Mohamed *parasitologist*
Anand, Suresh Chandra *physician*
Balanis, Constantine Apostle *electrical engineering educator*
Bender, Paul *lawyer, educator*
Berman, Neil Sheldon *chemical engineering educator*
Black, John Arthur, Jr., *electrical engineer, computer scientist, publisher*
Blankenship, Robert Eugene *biochemistry educator*
Boren, Kenneth Ray *endocrinologist, nephrologist*
Brack, O. M., Jr., *English language educator*
Buseck, Peter R. *geochemistry educator*
Carpenter, Ray Warren *materials scientist and engineer, educator*
Chawla, Nikhilesh *engineering educator*
Ching, Anthony Bartholomew *lawyer, educator, consultant*
Chiriac, Victor Adrian *aerospace engineer, researcher*
Chung, Young Sir *materials scientist*
Cochran, Mary Leffler *volunteer*
Codell, Julie Francia *academic administrator, educator*
Cortright, Barbara Jean *writer*
Cowley, John Maxwell *physics educator*
Crow, Michael *academic administrator*
Crown, Eric J. *information systems executive*
Crown, Timothy A. *computer technology company executive*
Durand, Barbara *dean*
Fanning, Francis Gerard *lawyer*
Ferry, David Keane *electrical engineering educator*
García, Peter Joseph *humanities educator*
Garzon, Amalia *Spanish educator, translator*
Giuliano, Neil Gerard *mayor, academic administrator*
Glick, Milton Don *chemist, university administrator*
Gordon, Leonard *retired sociology educator*
Goronkin, Herbert *physicist*
Green, Monica H. *history professor*
Haggerson, Nelson Lionel, Jr., *education educator*
Harris, Warren Lynn *computer engineer*
Haygood, Robert Collins *industrial psychologist, educator, consultant*
Herald, Cherry Lou *research educator, research director*
Hickson, Robin Julian *mining company executive*
Honegger, Gitta *language educator*
Huntsman, Edward *business consultant, marketing executive*
Iverson, Peter James *historian, educator*
Jefferson, Myra LaVerne Tull *sales executive*
Jennings, Marianne Moody *lawyer, educator*
Johanson, Donald Carl *physical anthropologist*
Jungbluth, Kirk E. *real estate appraiser*
Juvet, Richard Spalding, Jr., *chemistry professor*
Karady, George Gyorgy *electrical engineering educator, consultant*
Kaufman, Herbert Mark *finance educator*
Kerr, Derek J. *transportation executive*
Knox, Robert Lee *economics professor*
Krahenbuhl, Gary Stuart *university administrator*
Landschoot, Thomas V. *musician, educator*
Laybourne, Stanley *computer technology company executive*
Lockard, Joseph Franklin *literature educator, writer*
Lohr, Dennis E. *research scientist, education educator*
Lombardi, Eugene Patsy *retired orchestra conductor, violinist, educator*
MacKinnon, Stephen R. *Asian studies administrator, educator*
Mahajan, Subhash *electronic materials educator*
Matheson, Alan Adams *law educator*
Mays, Larry W. *civil engineering educator, hydrologist*
McKelvy, Michael John *materials chemist, research scientist*
Meehan, Robert Henry *human resources executive, electronics company executive, business educator*
Metros, Mary Teresa *librarian*
Montero, Darrel Martin *social worker, sociologist, educator*
Moore, Carleton Bryant *geochemistry educator*
Morrison, John Haddow, Jr., *engineering company executive*
Moya, Patrick Robert *lawyer*
Pany, Kurt Joseph *accounting educator, consultant*
Parker, W. Douglas *transportation executive*
Penley, Larry Edward *management educator*
Pettit, George Robert *chemist, educator, cancer researcher*
Picraux, Samuel Thomas *applied science and physics researcher*
Playford, Nancy Jean *medical staff administrator*
Prescott, Edward C. *economist, educator*
Raby, William Louis *writer, consultant*
Rankin, William Parkman *communications educator, academic administrator*
Reckers, Philip Merle *accounting and business educator*
Richards, Gale Lee *communications educator*
Rivers, Patrick A. *education educator, researcher*
Robertson, Samuel Harry, III, *transportation safety research engineer, educator*
Rowley, Beverley Davies *medical sociologist*
Roy, Asim *business educator*
Ruiz, Vicki Lynn *history professor, department chairman*
Sackton, Frank Joseph *public affairs educator*
Schatzki, George *law educator*
Schneller, Eugene Stewart *health administration and policy educator*
Schroder, Dieter Karl *electrical engineering educator*
Shah, Jami J. *mechanical engineering educator, researcher*
Shaw, Milton Clayton *mechanical engineering educator*
Shimpock, Kathy Elizabeth *lawyer, writer*
Simon, Sheldon Weiss *political science educator*
Smith, Branson M. *computer technology company executive*
Smith, David John *physicist, researcher*
Smith, Harvey Alvin *mathematics educator, consultant*
Spritzer, Ralph Simon *lawyer, educator*
Starrfield, Sumner Grosby *astrophysics educator, researcher*
Strom, Robert Duane *psychologist, educator*
Theodore, David *research scientist*
Tillman, Hoyt Cleveland *historian, educator, writer*
Tohe, Laura *English educator*
Tseng, Ampere An-Pei *mechanical engineer, educator, administrator*
Uttal, William R(eichenstein) *psychology and engineering educator, research scientist*
Wallen, Carl Joseph, Jr., *education educator*
Walters, Kathy *elementary school educator*
Weigend, Guido Gustav *geographer, educator*
Wetsel, William David *literature educator*
White, Patricia Denise *dean*
Williams, James Eugene *management consultant*
Wills, J. Robert *academic administrator, drama educator, writer*
Winicov, Ilga Butelis *biochemist, educator*
Wong, Timothy C. *language and literature educator*
Wytko, Joseph Rudolph *music educator*
Yau, Stephen Sik-sang *computer science and engineering educator, computer scientist, researcher*
Yazzie, Aaron Franklin *events laborer*
Zeitlin, Marilyn Audrey *museum director*

Tolleson
Etchart, Mike *agricultural products company executive*

Tubac
Assunto, Richard Anthony *human resources specialist*
Chilcote, Samuel Day, Jr., *trade association administrator*
Miller, Frederick Robeson *banker, director*
Pardue, A. Michael *retired plastic and reconstructive surgeon*

Tucson
Acker, Loren Calvin *medical instrument company executive*
Acker, Robert Flint *microbiologist*
Adjarian, Maude Madeleine *literature educator, researcher*
Alberts, David Samuel *physician, pharmacologist, educator*
Alpert, Joseph Stephen *physician, educator*
Angel, James Roger Prior *astronomer*
Arcus, Sam George *social worker, educator, writer*
Arnell, Walter James William *engineering educator, consultant*
Augello, William Joseph *lawyer*
Aurand, Charles Henry, Jr., *music educator, educator*
Axinn, George Harold *rural sociology educator*
Barrett, Bruce Richard *physics educator*
Bartlett, David Carson *state legislator*
Barton, Stanley Faulkner *management consultant*
Basford, Robert Eugene *retired biochemistry educator, researcher*
Batterbury, Simon Peregrine John *geographer, educator*
Bechtel, Robert Bernard *social sciences educator, consultant*
Ben-Asher, M. David *physician*
Berliner, David Charles *psychologist*
Bernmúdez, Carmen *trust company executive*
Best, Gary Thorman *commercial real estate broker*
Betteridge, Frances Carpenter *retired lawyer, mediator*
Birdman, Jerome Moseley *drama educator, consultant*
Birkinbine, John, II, *philatelist*
Bjorhovde, Reidar *structural engineer, educator*
Blackman, Jeffrey William *lawyer*
Block, Michael Kent *economics and law educator, public policy association executive, former government official, consultant*
Bloembergen, Nicolaas *physicist, researcher*
Bodinson, Holt *conservationist*
Bonvicini, Joan M. *women's college basketball coach*
Bootman, J. Lyle *pharmacy educator, dean*
Boswell, Susan G. *lawyer*
Boyle, Christopher George *English educator, counselor*
Boyle, Michael Frederick *retired television producer, actor*
Boyse, Edward Arthur *microbiologist, medical researcher*
Bradley, Gilbert Francis *retired bank executive*
Brainerd, Charles J(on) *experimental psychologist, applied mathematician, educator*
Brammer, J. William, Jr., *judge, lawyer*
Brasswel, Kerry *tax accountant*
Breiger, Ronald Louis *social sciences educator*
Broadfoot, Albert Lyle *physicist*
Browning, William Docker *federal judge*
Brunton, Daniel William *mechanical engineer*
Brusca, Richard Charles *biologist, researcher, educator*
Bryan, Gordon Redman, Jr., *retired naval officer*
Burg, Walter A. *airport terminal executive*
Butcher, Russell Devereux *author, photographer*
Cain, Vernon *retired information services executive*
Cameron, Alastair Graham Walter *astrophysicist, educator*
Capp, Michael Paul *physician, educator*
Carleton, Willard Tracy *retired finance educator*
Carman, Mary Ann *realtor, writer, retired medical/surgical nurse*
Carter, L. Philip *neurosurgeon, consultant*
Chandola, Anoop C. *educator, writer*
Chapman, Reginald Frederick *entomologist*
Clarke, James Weston *political science educator, writer*
Conant, Howard Somers *artist, educator*
Contractor, Dinshaw N. *civil engineer, educator*
Cook, Paul Christopher *engineering psychologist*
Cooper, Corinne *communications consultant, lawyer*
Corrigan, James John, Jr., *pediatrician, educator, dean*
Crawford, David L. *astronomer*
Crawford, Richard Eben, Jr., *former investment advisor*
Crooks, Roselyn June *artist, writer*
Dalen, James Eugene *cardiologist, educator*
Daley, Richard Halbert *museum director*
Davis, Cathy *publishing executive*
Davis, George Herbert *geologist, educator*
Davis, Stanley Nelson *hydrologist, educator*
Deal, Mike Gary *art educator*
DeLuca, Dominick *medical educator, researcher*
Dessler, Alexander Jack *astrophysicist, educator*
Deutsch, Maurice Mayer *healthcare educator, consultant, medical librarian*
De Young, David Spencer *astrophysicist, educator*
Dinnerstein, Leonard *historian, educator*
Donoghue, John Charles *application developer, consultant*
Dunn, Floyd *biophysics and biomedical engeering educator*
Dyer-Raffler, Joy Ann *special education diagnostician, educator*
Eberhardt, Marty Lampert *botanical garden administrator*
Eckhardt, August Gottlieb *retired law educator*
Eigel, James Anthony *environmental engineer*
Elliott, Sean P. *pediatrician, infectious disease specialist*
Emerson, Kirk *government agency administrator*
Erickson, Robert Porter *genetics researcher, educator, clinician*
Ewy, Gordon Allen *cardiologist, clinician, researcher, educator*
Fajardo, Sarah Elizabeth Johnson *financial consultant*
Feldman, Stanley George *lawyer*
Finley, Dorothy Hunt *beverage distribution company executive*
Flint, Willis Wolfschmidt (Willi Wolfschmidt) *artist, sculptor*
Fontana, Bernard Lee *retired anthropologist, writer, consultant*
Fortman, Marvin *law educator, consultant*
Francesconi, Louise L. *electronics executive*
Fredericksen, Dick Hartman *retired computer programmer*
Fritts, Harold Clark *dendrochronology educator, researcher*
Froman, Sandra Sue *lawyer*
Gaither, William Samuel *civil engineering executive, consultant*
Ganapol, Barry Douglas *nuclear engineering educator, consultant*
Ganguly, Jibamitra *science educator*
Gantz, David Alfred *lawyer, university official*
Garner, Girolama Thomasina *retired educational administrator, educator*
Gatenby, Robert A. *radiologist*
Gerba, Charles Peter *microbiologist, educator*
Girardeau, Marvin Denham *physics educator*
Glueck, Mary Audrey *retired psychiatric and mental health nurse*
Gonzales, Richard Joseph *lawyer*
Gottfredson, Michael Ryan *criminal justice educator*
Graham, Anna Regina *pathologist, educator*
Grams, Theodore Carl William *librarian, educator*
Grand, Marcia *civic worker*
Green, Richard Frederick *astronomer*
Green, Robert Scott *biotechnology company executive*
Gruhl, James *energy scientist, artist*
Gutsche, Carl David *chemistry professor*
Hale, William Bryan, Jr., *newspaper editor*
Hall, Henry Kingston, Jr., *chemistry professor*
Haney, Robert Locke *retired insurance company executive*
Harrington, Roger Fuller *electrical engineering educator, consultant*
Harris, David Thomas *immunology educator*
Harrison, Edward Robert *physicist, educator, science administrator*
Hattery, Robert Ralph *radiologist, educator*
Hawke, Robert Francis *dentist*
Hay, Richard Le Roy *geology educator*
Haynes, Caleb Vance, Jr., *geology and archaeology educator*
Hays, James Fred *geologist, educator*
Hayt, Therese D. *newspaper executive*
Heaphy, John Merrill *lawyer*
Hechler, Pauline Urbano King *fundraiser*
Heller, Frederick *retired mining company executive*
Hellon, Michael Thomas *tax consultant, political party official*
Herrnstadt, Richard Lawrence *American literature educator*
Hess, Richard Neal *plastic surgeon*

Hildebrand, John G(rant) *neurobiologist, educator*
Hill, Henry Allen *physicist, researcher*
Horan, Mary Ann Theresa *retired medical/surgical nurse*
Horne, William McHenry *management educator*
Houser, Harold Byron *epidemiologist*
Hubbard, William Bogel *planetary sciences educator*
Huestis, Douglas William *physician, pathologist*
Hull, Herbert Mitchell *plant physiologist, researcher*
Humphrey, John Julius *university program director, historian, writer*
Hunten, Donald Mount *planetary scientist, educator*
Hutchinson, Charles Smith, Jr., *book publisher*
Ingram, Helen Moyer *political science educator*
Isaak, G. Eugene *lawyer*
Jacobs, William Russell, II, *lawyer*
Jamison, Harrison Clyde *retired oil company executive*
Jefferies, John Trevor *astrophysicist, observatory administrator*
Jeter, Wayburn Stewart *retired microbiology educator, microbiologist*
Johnson, John Gray *retired university chancellor*
Jones, Frank Wyman *management consultant, mechanical engineer*
Jones, Roger Clyde *retired electrical engineering educator*
Jones, William Randolph *history educator*
Joseph, David Martin *medical administrator*
Jurkowitz, Daniel S. *lawyer, prosecutor, judge*
Kaliher, Michael Dennis *historian, librarian*
Kaltenbach, C(arl) Colin *dean, educator*
Kamilli, Robert Joseph *geologist*
Karkoschka, Erich *planetary science researcher, writer*
Kassman, Andrew Lance *orthodontist*
Kaszniak, Alfred Wayne *neuropsychologist*
Kay, Margarita *retired social sciences educator, retired nursing educator*
Kearney, Joseph Laurence *retired athletic conference administrator*
Kececioglu, Dimitri Basil *reliability engineering educator, consultant*
Kellogg, Frederick *historian*
Kennicutt, Robert Charles, Jr., *astronomer*
Kerwin, William James *electrical engineering educator, consultant*
Kessler, John Otto *physicist, researcher*
Kimble, William Earl *lawyer*
King, James Edward *retired museum director, consultant*
King, Joseph Willet *child psychiatrist*
Kingsolver, Barbara Ellen *writer*
Kischer, Clayton Ward *human embryologist, educator*
Kissinger, Karen G. *energy executive*
Kozolchyk, Boris *law educator, consultant*
Lacagnina, Michael Anthony *judge*
Lai, LiWen *molecular geneticist, educator*
Laird, Wilbur David, Jr., *bookseller, editor*
Lamb, Willis Eugene, Jr., *physicist, researcher*
Lanham, Sandra *conservationist*
Larson, L. Jean *educational administrator*
Larwood, Laurie *psychologist*
Lascelles, Susan *artist*
Law, John Harold *biochemistry educator*
Ledin, Patricia Ann *nurse, nurse legal consultant*
Lehrling, Terry James *real estate broker*
Leonard, Michael A. *retired automotive executive*
Lesher, Stephen Harrison *lawyer*
Levenson, Alan Ira *psychiatrist, physician, educator*
Levine, Norman *physician*
Lewis, Wilbur H. *educational management consultant*
Likins, Peter William *university administrator*
Lomicka, William Henry *investor*
Longacre, William Atlas *anthropology educator*
Longan, George Baker, III, *real estate company executive*
Lovejoy, Jean Hastings *social services counselor*
Magee, Wayne Edward *biochemistry educator, researcher*
Marcus, Frank Isadore *cardiologist, educator*
Markman, Sherman *investment banker, venture capitalist, financial consultant*
Marquez, Alfredo C. *federal judge*
Marshall, Robert Herman *economics professor*
Martin, June Johnson Caldwell *journalist*
Martin, Loren Winston *allergist*
Martin, Marci *writer, former advertising specialist*
Mason, Judith Ann *freelance writer*
Massaro, Toni Marie *dean, law educator*
Matthew, Neil Edward *artist, educator*
McCormick, Floyd Guy, Jr., *agricultural educator, college administrator*
Meehan, Michael Joseph *lawyer*
Meeker, Robert Eldon *retired manufacturing company executive*
Meislin, Harvey Warren *emergency healthcare physician, professional society administrator*
Mense, Allan Tate *research and development engineering executive*
Mercker, Mary Alice *aviation school administrator*
Miller, Elizabeth Rodriguez *city official*
Mixon, Billie Louise *language educator*
Mondragon, Marc Rene *dentist, pharmacist, consultant*
Morrison, Roger Barron *geologist*
Morrow, James Franklin *lawyer*
Mould, Jeremy Richard *astronomer*
Myers, Donald Earl *mathematics professor*
Nelson, Edward Humphrey *architect*
Nelson, Mark A. *music educator*
Neugebauer, Marcia *physicist, administrator*
Neuman, Shlomo P. *hydrology educator*
Nixon, Robert Obey, Sr., *business educator*
Noonan, James C. *lawyer, mediator, arbitrator*
O'Brien, Kevin James *investment banking executive*
Ogilvie, T(homas) Francis *engineer, educator*
Oro, Robert John *dentist, consultant, writer*
Osborne, John Edwards *lawyer*
Ostromencki, Nancy Lee *music educator*
Pace, Thomas M. *lawyer*
Pacholczyk, Andrzej Grzegorz *astrophysicist*
Parmenter, Robert Haley *physics educator*
Pearson, Gary Dean *dentist*
Peeler, Stuart Thorne *petroleum industry executive and independent oil operator*
Peirce, Karen Patricia *education educator*
Perret, Gary William *priest, educator*
Peters, Charles William *research and development company manager*
Poelstra, Edward M. *management consultant*
Pollack, Irwin William *psychiatrist, educator*
Prewitt, Charles Thompson *geochemist*
Prince, John Luther, III, *engineering educator*
Ratoff, Michael Barton (Nico Ratoff) *writer, poet, publishing executive*
Rees, Jay Carlyle *conductor, composer, music educator*
Reinius, Michele Reed *executive recruiter*
Reitan, Ralph Meldahl *clinical neuropsychologist, former educator*
Riggs, Lew *foundation executive*
Roemer, Elizabeth *astronomer, educator*
Rogers, Lee Frank *radiologist*
Roll, John McCarthy *judge*
Rose, Hugh *management consultant*
Ross, Robert *medical association administrator*
Rufe, Laurie J. *museum director*
Ruscher, Charles B. *finance educator, consultant*
Sakall, Daniel *education educator*
Samet, Dee-Dee *lawyer*
Sampliner, Richard Evan *physician*
Schaefer, John Paul *chemist*
Schannep, John Dwight *brokerage firm executive*
Schevill, Edward *social services agency director*
Schorr, S. L. *lawyer*
Schulz, Renate Adele *German studies and second language acquisition educator*
Schumacher, Michael John *allergist*
Scott, Shirley *city council*
Scotti, James Vernon *astronomer*
Seaman, Arlene Anna *retired musician, educator*
Seehausen, Richard Ferdinand *architect*
Shannon, Robert Rennie *optical sciences center administrator, educator*
Sheldon, Richard Neil *retired historian*
Shropshire, Donald Gray *hospital executive*
Simmons, Sarah R. *lawyer*
Slack, Donald Carl *agricultural engineer, educator*
Smerdon, Ernest Thomas *engineering educator*
Smith, David Wayne *psychologist, educator*
Smith, Kenneth Rodger *university dean, economics educator*
Snyder, Richard Gerald *research scientist, administrator, educator, consultant*
Soren, David *archaeologist, educator, writer*
Sprague, Ann Louise *space scientist*
Staubitz, Arthur Frederick *lawyer, healthcare products company executive*
Stearns, Elliott Edmund, Jr., *retired surgeon*
Stein, Daniel L. *physicist, educator*
Stini, William Arthur *anthropologist, educator*
Stoffle, Carla Joy *university library dean*
Strausfeld, Nicholas James *neurobiology and evolutionary biology researcher, educator*
Strittmatter, Peter Albert *astronomer, educator*
Strong, John William *lawyer, educator*
Stubblefield, Thomas Mason *agricultural economist, educator*
Sweeney, Joseph Dudley *law educator, political organization worker*
Swerdlove, Dorothy Louise *librarian, consultant*
Tang, Esther Don *development consultant, retired social worker*
Taveggia, Thomas Charles *business educator*
Theodorou, Andreas A. *pediatrician, educator*
Thompson, Kathleen Shambaugh *marriage and family counselor*
Thompson, Raymond Harris *retired anthropologist, educator*
Thomson, Donald Arthur *education educator*
Tifft, William Grant *astronomer, educator*
Tindall, Robert Emmett *lawyer, educator*
Tirrell, John Albert *organization executive, consultant*
Tombaugh, Dorothy Elve *retired secondary school educator, author, lecturer*
Treadwell-Rubin, Pamela A. *lawyer*
Underwood, Jane Hainline Hammons *anthropologist, educator*
Vaillancourt, Allison M *human resources specialist*
Valentine, Anna Mae *retired nurse*
Vincent, Thomas Lange *political science professor*
Volgy, Thomas John *political science educator, organization official*
Wahlke, John Charles *political science educator*
Walker, Ronald Hugh *retired management consultant*
Walkup, Robert E. *mayor*
Wallach, Leslie Rothaus *architect*
Wang, Wei *chemist, researcher*
Weber, Charles Walter *nutrition educator*
Weil, Andrew Thomas *physician, educator*
Whitaker, Ewen Adair *retired astronomer*
White, Herbert Spencer *research library educator, university dean*
Wickham, John Adams, Jr., *retired army officer*
Willert, Sister St. Joan *health care corporation executive*
Williams, Alan Keiser *management consultant*
Willott, Elizabeth *biochemist, educator, ecologist, researcher*
Willoughby, Stephen Schuyler *mathematics professor*
Wise, Evan M. *management consultant*
Witte, Marlys Hearst *internist, educator*
Wolfe, William Jerome *librarian, English language educator*
Wolff, Sidney Carne *astronomer, observatory administrator*
Woods, James Melvin *writer*
Woolfenden, James Manning *nuclear medicine physician, educator*
Woosley, Raymond *pharmacologist, educator*
Wyant, James Clair *engineering company executive, educator*
Zepeda, Ofelia *linguist, educator*
Ziehler, Tony Joseph *insurance agent*
Zlaket, Thomas Andrew *attorney, former state supreme court chief justice*

Tumacacori
Myers, Clay *retired investment management company executive*

Vail
Cardieri, Alexander M. *music specialist, music educator*
Reichlin, Seymour *physician, educator*

Waddell
Turner, Warren Austin *state legislator*

West Sedona
Eggert, Robert John, Sr., *economist*

Wickenburg
Henry, John Charles *county official*

Wikieup
Brattstrom, Bayard Holmes *biology professor*

Window Rock
Deschinny, Isabel *elementary school educator*

Yarnell
Rogers, Barbara Jean *writer, costume designer*

Yuma
Hossler, David Joseph *lawyer, law educator*
Houggard, Santa Carol Hall *family nurse practitioner*
Hudson, John Irvin *retired career officer*
Hunt, Gerald Wallace *lawyer*
Kiley, Thomas *rehabilitation counselor*
Norton, Dunbar Sutton *economic developer*

ARKANSAS

Arkadelphia
Addington, Ronald Paul *mass media educator*
Cai, Lei *music educator, pianist*
Dunn, Charles DeWitt *academic administrator*
Elrod, Ben Moody *academic administrator*
Fullerton, John C., III, *surgeon*
Grant, Daniel Ross *retired academic administrator*
Graves, John William *historian*
Grogan, Michael Wayne *columnist, editor-in-chief, poet*
Trofimova, Irina (Irene) Alexeevna *language educator*
Webster, Robert Lee *accounting educator, researcher*
Worth, Fred *mathematician, educator*

Ashdown
Edmonson, Phyllis Denty *artist*

Batesville
Carius, Robert Wilhelm *mathematics and science educator, retired naval officer*
Harkey, John Norman *judge*

Bella Vista
Johnson, A(lyn) William *chemistry educator, writer, researcher, consultant*
Medin, Alice Louise *librarian*
Medin, Myron James, Jr., *city manager*
Pogue, William Reid *former astronaut, foundation executive, business and aerospace consultant*
Sautter, Chester Arthur *physicist, educator*

Bentonville
Connolly, Robert *retail executive*
Coughlin, Thomas Martin *wholesale goods company executive*
Degn, Doug *retail executive*
Dible, David D. *retail executive*
Dillman, Linda *retail executive*
Duke, Michael *retail executive*
Fitzsimmons, J. Jay *retail executive*
Ford, Rollin *retail executive*
Glass, David D. *retail executive, professional sports team executive*
Harris, Don S. *retail executive*
Haworth, Jim H. *retail executive*
Herkert, Craig R. *retail executive*
Higham, Paul H. *marketing professional*
Hyde, Thomas D. *lawyer*
Mars, Tom *lawyer*
McMillon, Doug *retail executive*
Menzer, John *department store executive*
Menzner, John B. *retail executive*
Schoewe, Thomas M. *retail executive*
Scott, Lee (Harold Lee Scott Jr.) *retail executive*
Spragg, Gregg *retail executive*
Swanson, Celia *retail executive*
Turner, Kevin *retail executive*
Walton, S. Robson *discount department store chain executive*

Berryville
Brown, Frances Louise (Grandma Fran) *artist, art gallery owner*
Prpich, Michael Frank *food company manager*

Black Rock
Plunkett, Joseph Charles *electrical engineer, consultant*

Blytheville
Baker, Carlene Poff *real estate agent, reporter*
Fulling, Sharon S. *college nursing program director*
Slowik, Richard Andrew *air force officer*

Camden
Bradshaw, Otabel *retired primary school educator*
Owen, Larry Gene *academic administrator, educator, electronic and computer integrated manufacturing consultant*

Cedarville
Whitaker, Ruth Reed *state legislator, retired newspaper editor*

Cherokee Village
Burke, Richard Kitchens *lawyer, educator*
Hollingsworth, John Alexander *retired science and mathematics educator, writer, consultant*
Payne, Howard James *retired insurance company executive*

Conway
Brodman, James William *historian, educator*
Cloyd, J. Timothy *academic administrator*
Daugherty, Billy Joe *retired banker*
Hatcher, Joe Branch *management consultant*
Hays, Steele *retired state supreme court judge*
Horton, Joseph Julian, Jr., *economics and finance educator*
Johnson, James Douglas (Jim Johnson) *lawyer*
Kline, Rodger S. *marketing professional*
Leffler, Jean Riise *religious organization administrator*
McNew, Bennie Banks *retired finance educator*
Moore, Herff Leo, Jr., *management educator*
Showell, Jeffrey Adams *music educator, academic administrator, musician*
Spatz, Kenneth Chris(topher), Jr., *statistics educator*
Thompson, Winfred Lee *university president, lawyer*
Ziegler, John Alan *historian, political scientist, educator*

Crossett
Hubbell, Billy James *lawyer*

De Valls Bluff
Arnold, Elliott O. (Bill Arnold) *secondary school educator*

De Witt
Davenport, Heath Shane *information technology manager, educator*

Dumas
Schexnayder, Charlotte Tillar *state legislator*

El Dorado
Barnes, Harry Francis *federal judge*
Deming, Claiborne P. *oil industry executive*
Hardy, Charlotte B. *insurance agent*
Lee, Vernon Roy *minister*
McNutt, Jack Wray *oil company executive*
Nelson, Jerry R. *food company executive*
Nolan, William C., Jr., *energy executive*
Tommey, Charles Eldon *retired surgeon*
Watkins, Jerry West *retired oil company executive, lawyer*
Wynne, William Joseph *lawyer*

Eureka Springs
McCullough, V. Beth *pharmacist, educator*

Fayetteville
Andrews, John Frank *civil and environmental engineering educator*
Banks, David Russell *former health care executive*
Bassett, Woodson William, Jr., *lawyer*
Brown, Connell Jean *retired animal science educator*
Caldwell, Sarah *opera producer, conductor, stage director and administrator*
Commer, John Andrew *video director*
Edmark, David Stanley *communications director*
Ellstrand, Alan Edwin *finance educator*
Epley, Lewis Everett, Jr., *lawyer*
Farley, Roy Carl *counselor educator*
Fink, William James *retired surgeon*
Gaddy, James Leoma *chemical engineer, educator*
Hay, Robert Dean *retired management educator*
Hendren, Jimm Larry *federal judge*
Jackson, Robert Lee *real estate agent*
Jones, Louis, Jr., (Bucky Jones) *academic administrator*
Jones, Phillip John *librarian*
Kellogg, David Wayne *agriculture educator, researcher*
Kester, Charles Melvin *lawyer*
Khavinson, Dmitry *mathematician, educator*
LeFevre, Elbert Walter, Jr., *civil engineering educator*
Levine, Daniel Blank *classical studies educator*
Madison, Sue Wood *state legislator*
Mc Gimsey, Charles Robert, III, *anthropologist*
Morris, Justin Roy *food scientist, consultant, enologist, research director, science administrator*
Mullen, Maureen Ann *social worker*
Musacchia, X(avier) J(oseph) *physiology and biophysics educator*
Musick, Gerald Joe *retired entomology educator*
Nance, Cynthia Eleanor *law educator*
Pearson, Charles Thomas, Jr., *lawyer, director*
Pettus, E. Lamar *lawyer*
Purvis, Hoyt Hughes *political scientist, academic administrator, educator*
Rhoads, Robert K. *lawyer, retail executive*
Riggs, Robert Dale *plant pathology and nematology educator, researcher*
Rosenberg, Leon Joseph *marketing educator*
Rossetti, Manuel David *engineering educator, consultant*
Scharlau, Charles Edward, III, *natural gas company executive*
Schoppmeyer, Martin William *education educator*
Shafer, Carol Larsen *retired book reviewer*
Smith, Lavenski R. (Vence Smith) *federal judge*
Smith, Robert Victor *university administrator*
Smith, Stephen Austin *communications educator*
Steele, Kenneth Franklin, Jr., *science educator*
Studer, Patricia S. *psychologist*
Van Patten, James Jeffers *education educator*
VanWinkle, John Ragan *lawyer*
Waters, H. Franklin *federal judge*
Williams, Doyle Z. *university dean, educator*
Williams, Miller *poet, fiction writer, translator*
Wilson, Charles Banks *artist*

Foreman
Horn, Barbara B. *state legislator*

Forrest City
Coleman, Catherine Towne *counseling administrator*

Fort Smith
Boreham, Roland Stanford, Jr., *electric motor company executive*
Coleman, Michael Dortch *nephrologist*
Cromwell, William M. *lawyer*
Daily, Thomas A. *lawyer*
Davidson, Robert *trucking executive*
Decker, Josephine I. *health clinic official*
Drolshagen, Leo Francis, III, *radiologist, physician*
Floyd, William R. *health facility administrator*
Gean, Thomas C. *prosecutor*
Gooden, Benny L. *school system administrator*
Guest, Gordon D. *architectural firm executive*
Hembree, Hugh Lawson, III, *diversified holding company executive*
Howard, Jeff David *volunteer, retired military officer*
Howell, James Tennyson *allergist, immunologist, pediatrician*
Husarik, Stephen *music educator*
Pendergrass, Ewell Dean *communications executive*
Snider, James Rhodes *radiologist*
Tabakin, Scott M. *healthcare executive*
Young, Robert A., III, *freight systems executive*

Greenwood
Walters, Bill *former state senator, lawyer*

Harrison
Garrison, F. Sheridan *transportation executive*
Street, Susan Lee *elementary school educator*

Heber Springs
Niehaus, Sherry M. *social welfare administrator*
Rawlings, Paul C. *retired government official*

Helena
Kontos, George John, Jr., *surgeon*
Roscopf, Charles Buford *lawyer*

Hermitage
Heilman, Thomas Lewis *science educator*

Higden
George, James Edward *accountant*

Hindsville
Bayley, Carolyn Sue *primary school educator, writer, artist*

Hot Springs National Park
Brunner, John Harry *surgeon*
Plummer, Jack Moore *psychologist*
Ray, Arliss Dean *retired environmental consultant*
Schnipper, Don Martin *lawyer*
Schroeder, Donald Perry *retired food products company executive*

Hot Springs Village
Cawood, Jenny Lind *social worker, poet*
Lihs, Marilyn Louise *retired accountant*
Smith, W. Preston *publishing executive, educator, real estate broker*

Huntsville
Carr, Gerald Paul *former astronaut, retired business executive, former marine officer*

Jacksonville
Lawrence-Cox, Nancy Nell *artist, retired executive secretary*

Jefferson
Casciano, Daniel Anthony *biologist, educator*
Schwetz, Bernard Anthony *toxicologist*

Jonesboro
Allen, William Julius *art history educator*
Bartee, Neale *music educator, musician, conductor*
Deacon, John C. *lawyer*
Douglas, John T. *pharmacist, state agency administrator*
Elkins, Francis Clark *history educator, university official*
Jones, Kenneth Bruce *surgeon*
McNeill, Paul Deane *lawyer*
Smith, Eugene Wilson *retired university president and educator*
Tims, Robert Austin *data processing official, pilot*

Leachville
Adams, Eddie *textiles executive*

Little Rock
Adams, Rose Ann *nonprofit administrator*
Anand, Kanwaljeet Singh *pediatrician, researcher*
Anderson, Joel E., Jr., *university administrator*
Anderson, Philip Sidney *lawyer*
Apuya, Jesus Serra *anesthesiologist*
Arnold, Morris Sheppard *judge*
Arnold, Richard Sheppard *federal judge*
Barnes, Robert Webster *medical educator*
Bates, Joseph Henry *internist, educator*
Beebe, Mike *state attorney general*
Bell, James Winfred *retired publishing executive*
Bemis, Michael B. *utility company executive*
Bhattacharyya, Abhijit *engineering educator*
Bissada, Nabil Kaddis *urologist, educator, researcher, author*
Bowen, William Harvey *bunker, lawyer*
Brack, Robert Louis *retired music educator*
Braithwaite, Wilfred John *physics educator*
Briscoe, David Lloyd *academic sociologist, educator*
Bruce, Thomas Allen *physician, educator*
Burruss, Terry Gene *architect*
Caldwell, Bettye McDonald *education educator, director*
Campbell, George Emerson *lawyer*
Campbell, Gilbert Sadler *surgery educator, surgeon*
Cheek, James Richard *ambassador*
Cherry, Sandra Wilson *lawyer*
Chesser, Thelma Jo Sykes *early childhood educator, administrator*
Chiang, Chia-Chu *computer scientist, educator*
Corbin, Donald L. *state supreme court justice*
Cox, Frank *advertising executive*
Cross, J. Bruce *lawyer*
Cummins, H. E. Bud, III, *lawyer*
Daniels, Charlie *state official*
Darsey, Jerome Anthony (Jerry Darsey) *chemistry professor, consultant*
Dickey, Betty C. *judge*
Dillard, William, II, *department store chain executive*
Drummond, Winslow *lawyer*
Elders, (Minnie) Joycelyn *public health administrator, endocrinologist*
Fahoum, Yousef Arfan *financial analyst, educator*
Ferguson, John Lewis *state historian*
Ferrer, Thomas John *surgeon*
Fisher, Jimmie Lou *state official*
Fitzhugh, Kathryn Corrothers *law librarian*
Fogleman, John Albert *lawyer, retired judge*
Ford, Joe Thomas *telephone company executive, former state senator*
Ford, Scott T. *telecommunications company executive*
Frantz, Francis X. *telecommunications industry executive, lawyer*
Freeman, James I. *retail department store company executive*
Fribourgh, James Henry *retired university administrator*
Gardner, Jeffrey R. *communications executive*
Gardner, Kathleen D. *gas company executive, lawyer*
Glaze, Thomas A. *state supreme court justice*
Good, Mary Lowe (Mrs. Billy Jewel Good) *investment company executive, educator*
Goodner, Norman Wesley *governmental relations specialist*
Green, Johnnie D. *government finance officer, finance educator*
Greenberg, Paul *editor*
Greene, Tristan Dorian *state agency administrator*
Gulley, Wilbur Paul, Jr., *retired savings and loan association executive*
Gunter, Russell Allen *lawyer*
Hannah, Jim *state supreme court justice*
Hargis, David Michael *lawyer*
Harmon, Kay Madelon *occupational therapist*
Hart, Ronald Wilson *radiobiologist, educator, toxicologist, researcher, corporate advisor*
Hathaway, Charles E. *academic administrator*
Haught, William Dixon *lawyer, writer*
Hester, D. Micah *education educator*
Hickingbotham, Frank D. *food product executive*
Hill, Jim B. *state legislator*
Hinson, Jack Allsbrook *research toxicologist, educator*
Hough, Aubrey Johnston, Jr., *pathologist, physician, educator*
Huckabee, Michael Dale *governor*
Hussman, Walter E., Jr., *publishing executive*
Imber, Annabelle Clinton *state supreme court justice*
Ingram, Dale *consumer products company executive*
Itkin, David *music director, conductor*
Jacobi, Sandra E. *medical/surgical nurse, researcher*
Jansen, G. Thomas *dermatologist*
Jennings, Alston *lawyer*
Julian, Jim Lee *lawyer*
Kaza, Greg John *economist, educator*
Kemp, Stephen Frank *pediatric endocrinologist, educator, composer*
Kibbe-Reed, Trudie *academic administrator*
Kilgore, Nancy *educational association administrator*
Lang, Nicholas Paul *surgeon*
Ledbetter, Calvin Reville, Jr., (Cal Ledbetter) *political science educator, university dean, former legislator*
Levy, Eugene Pfeifer *architect*
Lewis, Johanna Miller *historian, educator*
Light, Jo Knight *stockbroker*
Lipe, Linda Bon *lawyer*
Lucy, Dennis Durwood, Jr., *neurologist, educator*
Malone, David Roy *educational association administrator, director*
May, Ronald Alan *lawyer*
McCaleb, Annette Watts *executive secretary*
McCoy, Stuart Sherman *manufacturing executive*
McKnight, William Edwin *minister*
McSwain, Byrdie Engle *laboratory scientist, immunohematologist*
Mehta, Jawahar Lal *cardiologist*
Moore, Helen Lucille *adult education educator, consultant*
Mrak, Robert Emil *neuropathologist, educator, electron microscopist*
Mulkey, Jack Clarendon *library director*
Munoz, Olivier *artistic director*
Murphey, Arthur Gage, Jr., *law educator*
Nelson, Edward Sheffield *lawyer, retired utilities executive*
Nunn, Patarica Dian *poet*
Orsini, Tom *retired telecommunications company executive*
Pollan, Carolyn Joan *state legislator, job research administrator*
Portis, Charles McColl *reporter, writer*
Priest, Sharon Devlin *association executive, former state secretary of state*
Pryor, David Hampton *former senator*
Raney, Miriam Day *actress*
Reasoner, Stephen M. *federal judge*
Reece, E. Albert *dean, obstetrician, gynecologist, perinatologist*
Reeves, Rosser Scott, III, *retired investment company executive*
Roaf, Andree Layton *judge*
Robison, Judy A. *grants officer, research administrator*
Rockefeller, Winthrop P *lieutenant governor*
Ross, Robert Dwain *lawyer*
Schwartz, Deborah S. *airport manager*
Scivally, Bart Murnane *accountant, auditor*
Sharma, Rajesh *research scientist*
Shaw, Robert *newspaper editor*
Shell, Robert J. *construction executive*
Sherman, Jerome Kalman *retired anatomy educator*
Sherman, William Farrar *lawyer, former state legislator*
Smith, Griffin *editor*
Sotomora-von Ahn, Ricardo Federico *pediatrician, educator*
Stockburger, Jean Dawson *lawyer*
Stroud, John Fred, Jr., *judge*
Thomas, Lestene *nurse*
Thomas, Thorp *retired lawyer*
Thornton, Ray *state supreme court justice, former congressman*
Townsend, James Willis *computer scientist*
Truemper, John James, Jr., *retired architect*
Truex, Dorothy Adine *retired university administrator*
Vickery, William *arts administrator*
Ward, Harry Pfeffer *hematologist, retired academic administrator*
Weiss, Richard A. *state official*
Wenger, Galen Rosenberger *pharmacology educator*
Westbrook, Kent Coleman *surgeon, educator*
Whiteside, Charles B., III, *investment company executive*
Wilson, I. Dodd *dean*
Wilson, William R., Jr., *judge*
Witherspoon, Carolyn Brack *lawyer*
Wright, Robert Ross, III, *law educator*
Wright, Susan Webber *judge*
Yarberry, Lonnie Stephen *information scientist, director*

Lonoke
Ross, Philip Rowland *retired library director*

Lowell
Garrison, Wayne *transportation executive*
Hunt, J. B. (Johnnie Bryan Hunt) *retired transportation executive*
Thompson, Kirk *transportation executive*
Walton, Jerry W. *trucking executive*

Magnolia
Avard, Joseph L. *mathematician, educator*
Campbell, Robert Gordon *music educator*
Gamble, Steven G. *academic administrator*
Juniker, Anthony Michael *economic developer, consultant*

Malvern
Dodd, Jerry Lee *lawyer*
Schultz, Marvin E. *historian, educator*

Marion
Hughes, Michael Randolph *evangelist*

Marked Tree
Everett, Mike *lawyer*

Mena
Eddleman, Floyd Eugene *retired English language educator*

Monticello
Babin, Claude Hunter *history professor*
Ball, William Kenneth *lawyer*
Cain, Michael Dean *research forester*

Morrilton
Johnson, Bob W. *state senator*
Lord, Penny *writer*
Lord, Robert *writer*

Mountain Home
Baker, Robert Leon *naval medical officer*
Preis, Christy Charlene *mathematics professor*

Nashville
Hall, Jaree Elayne *elementary school educator, musician*

North Little Rock
Clothier, Jeffrey Lane *neuropsychiatrist, educator*
Givens, John Kenneth *manufacturing executive*
Lawson, William Bradford *psychiatrist*
Patty, Claibourne Watkins, Jr., *lawyer*
Wilson, LaVerne *nursing administrator*

Osceola
Wilson, Ralph Edwin *lawyer, justice*

Palmer
Knight, William R. *research scientist, educator*

Paragould
Cox, Loretta C. *language educator*

Paris
Cleveland, Herschel *state representative*

Pine Bluff
Bradford, Jay Turner *insurance executive, state legislator*
Davis, Lawrence A., Jr., *academic administrator*
Economos, Cora Matheny *librarian*
Engle, Carole Ruth *aquaculture economics educator*
Gullett, Brenda B. *state legislator*
Jones, John Harris *lawyer*
Long, Edward Arlo *business consultant, retired manufacturing company executive*
Perschbacher, Peter Wesley *environmental scientist, educator*
Seawell, William Thomas *former airline executive*
Sewald, Carl Martin *music educator*
Strode, Joseph Arlin *lawyer*
Tai, Chong-Soo Stephen *political scientist, educator*
Walker, Richard Brian *chemistry professor*

Quitman
Martindale, Carla Joy *retired librarian*

Rogers
Angleman, Sharon Ann *journalist*
Cooper, John Alfred, Jr., *community development company executive*
Myers, Dane Jacob *lawyer, podiatrist*
Spainhower, James Ivan *retired college president*
Summerlin, William Talley *allergist, immunologist, dermatologist*
Wright, I. Melissa *secondary school educator*

Roland
Frazer, Randy *parks and recreation director*

Russellville
Finan, Marcel Bassil *mathematics educator, researcher*
Morris, Lois Lawson *retired education educator*
Trusty, Sharon *state legislator*

Scott
Rolingson, Martha *research archeologist*

Scranton
Uzman, Betty Ben Geren *retired pathologist*

Searcy
Burks, David Basil *academic administrator, educator*
Hughes, Thomas Morgan, III, *lawyer*

Sherwood
Eddy, Nancy C. *counselor*
Keaton, Frances Marlene *insurance sales representative*

Siloam Springs
Lewis, Cecil Dwain *minister*
McMennamy, Roger Neal *automotive executive*
Oliver, Gary Jackson *psychologist, educator*
Roby, Warren B. *humanities educator*

Springdale
Baker, Mike *food products executive*
Baledge, Les R. *food products executive, lawyer*
Beach, Jean Mrha *food products executive*
Cordell, Beulah Faye *special education educator*
Dunn, Jeri R. *food products executive*
Hankins, Steven G. *food company executive*
Hudson, R. Read *lawyer, food products executive*
Huett, Greg *food products executive*
Igli, Kevin J. *food products executive*
Leatherby, Dennis *food products executive*
Lee, Greg W. *food company executive*
Parks, Michelle *journalist*
Phillips, Linda Lou *pharmacist*
Pless, Rodney S. *food products executive*
Richards, Dusty *writer*
Rose, Kenneth L. *food products executive*
Schaffer, Archie, III, *food products executive*
Tyson, Donald John *food company executive*
Tyson, John H. *food products executive*
Van Bebber, David L. *food products executive*

State University
Comeau, Matthew J. *athletic training program director, educator*
Darwin, John Scott *language educator*
Lott, Rick *language educator, poet*
McClain, Veda *education educator, department chairman*
Milner, Clyde A., II, *historian*
Schichler, Robert Lawrence *English language educator*
Wyatt, Leslie, III, *academic administrator*

Stuttgart
Bell, Richard Eugene *grain and food company executive*

Subiaco
Pirrera, Aaron Charles *priest, headmaster*

Van Buren
Stone, David Mark *plastic surgeon*

Warren
Claycomb, Hugh Murray *lawyer, author*

West Memphis
Coley, Jeannette Cabell *writer*

White Hall
Scott, Vicki Sue *school system administrator*

Winslow
Burggraf, Frank Bernard, Jr., *landscape architect, retired educator*

CALIFORNIA

Acton
Butman, Harry Raymond *clergyman, writer*

Agoura Hills
Chagall, David *journalist, writer*
Currie, Malcolm Roderick *aerospace and automotive executive, scientist*
deCiutiis, Alfred Charles Maria *oncologist, television producer*
Gressak, Anthony Raymond, Jr., *sales executive*
Havlicek, Michael W *medical association administrator*
Homer, Raymond Rodney *film producer, director*
Klugman, Jack *actor*
Kuzmanovic, Jane Violet *academic administrator*
Merchant, Roland Samuel, Sr., *health facility administrator, educator*
Meyler, Nicholas James *management consultant*
Powers, J. D., III, *marketing executive*
Schmidt, Frank Broaker *executive recruiter*
Teresi, Joseph *publishing executive*

Alameda
Bartalini, C. Richard *judge*
Billings, Thomas Neal *computer and publishing executive, management consultant, entrepreneur, journalist, writer*
Boyer, Ford Sylvester *relationship consultant, minister*
Carter, Roberta Eccleston *therapist, counselor*
Collins, Kerry *professional football player*
Davis, Allen *professional football team executive*
Gannon, Rich *professional football player*
Grzanka, Leonard Gerald *writer, consultant*
Harbaugh, James Joseph *former professional football player*
Herrera, John *professional football team executive*
Hwang, Michael Tian-Chung *university president*
Kohgadai, Shukrullah *foundation administrator, editor*
Luther, John Stafford *biology professor, consultant*
Monahan, John *medical products executive*
Ngo, Tung Thanh *writer, photographer*
Potash, Jeremy Warner *public relations executive*
Rice, Jerry Lee *professional football player*
Sapp, Warren Carlos *professional football player*
Stonehouse, James Adam *lawyer*
Turner, Norv *professional football coach*
Vaughn, Donna Becker *retired social worker*
Whorton, M. Donald *occupational and environmental health physician, epidemiologist*

Alamo
Baker, William P. (Bill Baker) *former congressman*
Bouret, Pierre George *brokerage house executive*
Liggett, Lawrence Melvin *vacuum equipment manufacturing company executive*
Madden, Palmer Brown *lawyer*
Reed, John Theodore *writer, publisher*
Schreiber, John T. *lawyer*
Shiffer, James David *retired utility executive, consultant*
Whalen, John Sydney *management consultant*

Albany
Boris, Ruthanna *dancer, choreographer, dance therapist, educator*
Daniels, Lydia M. *health care administrator*
Eastwood, DeLyle *chemist*
Madgalene, David *editor, writer*
Schwimmer, Sigmund *food enzymologist*
Thomsen, Peggy Jean *mayor, educator*

Alhambra
Austin, Elizabeth Ruth *retired elementary school educator*
Birch, Tobeylynn *librarian*
Duke, Donald Norman *publishing executive*
Fried, Elaine June *insurance company executive*
Im, Jaemo *research scientist*
Knighton, Barbara McLeod *occupational health specialist, risk specialist*
Schuster, Darleen Victoria *director*

Suzuki, Bob H. *retired academic administrator*
Xie, Bin *epidemiologist, research scientist*

Aliso Viejo

Boeckmann, Alan L. *engineering and construction management company executive*
Carroll, Adeline F. *special education educator*
Cohen, Sasha (Alexandra Pauline Cohen) *ice skater*
Dunn, Dana-Lori *counselor*
Fisher, Lawrence N. *lawyer, engineering company executive*
Hawkins, Gregory J. *consumer products company executive*
Otero-Smart, Ingrid Amarillys *advertising executive*
Rollans, James O. *service company executive*
Trivelpiece, Craig Evan *computer electronics executive*

Alpine

Cole, George Arthur *marketing professional*
Doliber, Darrel Lee *retired engineering consultant, innkeeper*
Greenberg, Byron Stanley *newspaper and business executive, consultant*
Oliverio, Ponzio *protective services official, educator*
Roberts, Dwight Loren *engineering consultant, writer*

Alta Loma

Haskvitz, Alan Paul *elementary education educator, consultant*

Altadena

Burden, Jean Prussing *retired poet, writer, editor*
Coles, Donald Earl *retired aeronautics educator*
Dutton, Pauline Mae *fine arts and reference librarian*
Johnson, Kristen Marie *art director*
Montanez, Mary Ann Chavez *counselor, consultant, writer*
Willans, Jean Stone *bishop, religious organization executive*

Alviso

Ramsay, Michael *information technology executive*

Anaheim

Anderson, Garret *professional baseball player*
Barry, Sandra *school system administrator*
Baumgartner, Anton Edward *automotive sales professional*
Bennett, Genevieve *artist*
Brownhill, H. Bud *small business owner, canine behavior therapist*
Davis, Robert L. *information technology executive*
Elchert, Kenneth Clarence *aerospace engineer*
Fenton, Donald Mason *retired oil company executive*
Frank, Judith Ann (Jann Frank) *retired entrepreneur, small business owner*
Gaglani, Jitendra A. *aerospace engineer*
Glaus, Troy *professional baseball player*
Gobar, Alfred Julian *retired economic consultant, educator*
Goodspeed, Kathryn Ann *pre-school educator*
Gregg, James R. *optometrist, educator*
Guajardo, Elisa *counselor, educator*
Guerrero, Vladimir *professional baseball player*
Halligan, Joseph William *snack food industry executive*
Jantolak, Laura Jean *elementary school educator*
Jung, Charlene *city treasurer*
Kallay, Michael Frank, II, *medical devices company official*
Kelley, Lee *publishing executive*
Kishiyama, Craig Akira *orthodontist*
Laderman, Kathleen Ann *magazine publisher*
Lano, Charles Jack *retired financial executive*
Latham, Chad J. *management consultant*
Linhart, Eddie Gene *aerospace executive*
Nelipovich, Sandra Grassi *artist*
O'Berry, Carl Gerald *former career officer, electrical engineer*
Pringle, Curt *mayor*
Rizzo, James *editor*
Salmon, Timothy James *professional baseball player*
Stegemeier, Richard Joseph *oil company executive*
Sykora, Petr *professional hockey player*
Unan, George Vincent *adult education educator*
Uyehara, Otto Arthur *mechanical engineering educator emeritus, consultant*
Watson, Oliver Lee, III, *aerospace engineering manager*

Anaheim Hills

Warring, Jerome Thomas *management consultant*

Angwin

Maxwell, Donald Malcolm *clergyman, religious educator*

Antelope

Nenov, Ivo P. *mathematical and software researcher*

Antioch

Adams, Liliana Osses *music performer, harpist*
Archuleta, Keith Anthony *entrepreneur, business and management consultant*
Granik, Vladimir *mechanics researcher, educator*
Molina, Ron Joseph *music educator*

Apple Valley

Beller, Gerald Stephen *professional magician, former insurance company executive*
Lavallee, Charles Phillip *music educator, musician*
Mays, George Walter, Jr., *educational technology educator, consultant, tutor*
Watkin, Virginia Ruth *financial professional*

Aptos

Bohn, Ralph Carl *educational consultant, retired educator*
Heron, David Winston *librarian*
Hirsch, Bette G(ross) *college administrator, foreign language educator*
Trounstine, Philip John *communications consultant, institute administrator*

Arcadia

Baltz, Patricia Ann (Pann Baltz) *elementary school educator*

Belnap, David F. *journalist*
Coulombe, Charles Aquila *writer, educator*
Danziger, Louis *graphic designer, educator*
Fisher, Alan J. *otolaryngologist, plastic surgeon*
Gamboa, George Charles *retired oral surgeon, educator*
Gelber, Louise C(arp) *lawyer*
Seitz, Charles Lewis *computer scientist and engineer*
Sloane, Beverly LeBov *writer, consultant*
Soleimani, Massoud *internist, rheumatologist*
Stangeland, Roger Earl *retail chain store executive*
Yen, Wen-Hsiung *language and music professional, educator*
Zimmerman, Amy J. *television producer, television director*

Arcata

Bailey, Stephen Fairchild *retired museum director, ornithologist*
Bowker, Lee Harrington *sociologist, educator, writer*
Emenhiser, JeDon Allen *political science educator, academic administrator*
Janssen-Pellatz, Eunice Charlene *healthcare facility administrator*
Land-Weber, Ellen *photography educator*
McCrone, Alistair William *retired academic administrator*
Zielinski, Melissa L. *museum director*

Arroyo Grande

Bekey, Shirley White *psychotherapist*
Grisez, James Louis *physician, plastic surgeon*
Hoffmann, Jon Arnold *retired aeronautical engineer, educator*
Mott, Robert Lewis *writer, sound effects artist*
Oseguera, Palma Marie *retired career officer*

Artesia

Dhamija, Kailash Raj *physician, consultant*

Atascadero

Locke, Virginia Otis *writer*
Ogier, Walter Thomas *retired physics educator*
Rios, Evelyn Deerwester *columnist, musician, artist, writer*

Atherton

Bales, Royal Eugene *philosophy educator*
Barker, Robert Jeffery *financial executive*
Coleman, Robert Griffin *geology educator*
Ferris, Robert Albert *lawyer, venture capitalist*
Fried, John H. *chemist*
Gill, Stephen Paschall *retired physicist, mathematician*
Goodman, Sam Richard *electronics company executive*
Hogan, Clarence Lester *retired electronics executive*
Lane, Joan Fletcher *educational administrator*
Levinthal, Elliott Charles *physicist, researcher*
Lowry, Larry Lorn *engineering company executive*
Morel-Seytoux, Hubert Jean *civil engineer, educator*
Phipps, Allen Mayhew *management consultant*
Sollman, George Henry *venture capitalist*
Starr, Chauncey *research institute executive*
Weston, Jane Sara *plastic surgeon, educator*

Auburn

Henrikson, Donald Merle *forensic pathologist*
Hess, Patrick Henry *chemist, researcher*
Jeske, Howard Leigh *retired life insurance company executive, lawyer*
Lyon, Bruce Arnold *lawyer, educator*
Rothwell, Elaine B. *artist*
Sanborn, Dorothy Chappell *retired librarian*

Avila Beach

McLaren, Archie Campbell, Jr., *marketing executive*

Azusa

Aguilar, Gladys Maria *counselor, educator*
Gray, Paul Wesley *university dean*
Kostoulas, Ioannis Georgiou *physicist*
Lee, Chang Soo *education educator*
Liegler, Rosemary Menke *dean*
Vest, R. Lamar *church administrator*

Bakersfield

Akers, Tom, Jr., *cotton broker, consultant*
Arciniega, Tomas Abel *university president*
Ashburn, Roy *state senator*
Bacon, Leonard Anthony *accounting educator*
Beene, Richard Stuart *newspaper editor*
Bernard, Alexander *protective services official*
Burns, Sarah Chloe *historian, educator*
Duquette, Diane Rhea *library director*
Enriquez, Carola Rupert *museum director*
Fiedler, Joseph Robert *mathematician, educator*
Florez, Dean R. *state senator*
Frazier, Jo Frances *religious organization administrator*
Fuller, Jean *school system administrator*
Grimm, Bob *food products executive*
Hall, Harvey L. *mayor, medical transportation company executive*
Hancock, Tapp *elementary school educator*
Jenner, Mike *newspaper editor*
Karcher, Steven Michael *lawyer*
Kegley, Jacquelyn Ann *philosophy educator*
Kennedy, Joseph Paul, Jr., *retired elementary school educator*
Lundquist, Gene Alan *cotton company executive*
Martin, George Francis *lawyer*
McAlister, Michael H. *architect*
Peterson, Pamela Carmelle *English language educator*
Provencio, Roberto Enrique *music educator, music minister*
Prunes, Fernando *plastic surgeon, educator*
Reep, Edward Arnold *artist*
Saucier, Bonnie L. *dean, pediatrics nurse*
Sawyer, Nelson Baldwin, Jr., *credit union executive*
Schmidt, Joanne (Josephine Anne Schmidt) *language educator*
Singer, George Milton *clinical psychologist*
Sio, Jimmy Ong *embryologist*
Thomason, Scott *automobile executive*
Tornstrom, Robert Ernest *lawyer, oil company executive*
Wong, Wayne D. *nutritionist*
Zarra, Ernest Joseph, III, *educator, researcher*

Baldwin Park

Snyder, Esther *food service executive*

Banning

Finley, Margaret Mavis *retired elementary school educator*
Gladden, Garnett Lee *educator, health consultant, psychologist*

Barstow

Nyborg, Kenneth Wayne *retired social sciences educator, small business owner*

Bay Point

Karasch, Jack (John) *writer, educator*

Bayside

Cocks, George Gosson *retired chemical microscopy educator*
LaPlantz, David Milton *artist, retired educator*

Bell

Jackman, Hugh *actor*
Turner, Laraine Elizabeth *elementary school educator*

Bell Canyon

Labbett, John Edgar *senior financial executive*

Bellflower

Bermudez, Rudy *state official*
de Thouars, Victor Ivan Charles *professional martial artist, educator*
Lee, Paul Yue-Yan *surgeon*
Martin, Melissa Carol *radiological physicist*

Belmont

Endriz, John Guiry *retired electronics executive*
MacLennan, Amy Marie *poet*
Musmann, Lois S. *conductor, music educator*

Belvedere

Gale, Daniel Bailey *architect*
Hugenberg, Patricia Ellen Petrie *product designer*
Wallerstein, Robert Solomon *psychiatrist*

Belvedere Tiburon

Behrman, Richard Elliot *pediatrician, neonatologist, university dean*
Bremer, William Richard *lawyer*
Buell, Edward Rick, II, *lawyer*
Collins, Dennis Arthur *retired foundation administrator*
Kramer, Lawrence Stephen *journalist*
Rayner, Arno Alfred *investment company executive, consultant*
Rosenthal, Robert Jon *newspaper editor, journalist*

Ben Lomond

Sikora, James Robert *educational business consultant, financial analyst*

Benicia

Farnham, Timothy *training and education administrator*
Gauger, Harold Charles *artist, writer*
Nelson, Elmer Kingsholm, Jr., (Kim Nelson) *educator, writer, mediator, consultant*
Szabo, Peter John *investment company executive, financial planner, mining engineer, lawyer*
von Studnitz, Gilbert Alfred *state official*

Berkeley

Abbott, Myles Bruce *pediatrician*
Abel, Carlos Alberto *immunologist*
Adelman, Irma Glicman *economics professor*
Ahrendt, Rebekah Susannah *language educator, musician*
Akerlof, George Arthur *economics professor*
Alhadeff, David Albert *economics professor*
Allison, James Patrick *immunology educator, medical association administrator*
Alter, Robert Bernard *comparative literature educator, critic*
Anderson, William Scovil *classics educator*
Arveson, William Barnes *mathematics professor*
Attwood, David Thomas *physicist, researcher*
Auerbach, Alan Jeffrey *economist, educator*
Bagdikian, Ben Haig *journalist, emeritus university educator*
Bajcsy, Ruzena *computer engineer*
Bajcsy, Ruzena Kucerova *computer science educator*
Baldwin, Bruce Gregg *botany educator, researcher*
Barkin, Ronald S. *medical products executive*
Barnes, Thomas G. *law educator*
Barrett, Reginald Haughton *biology professor, wildlife management educator*
Bartlett, Neil *chemist, emeritus educator*
Barton, Babette B. *lawyer, educator*
Bastrenta, Brigitte Elisabeth *school administrator*
Baumrind, Diana *research psychologist*
Bellah, Robert Neelly *sociologist, educator*
Bendix, Jane *artist, author, anthropological illustrator*
Benedict, Burton *retired museum director, anthropology educator*
Benson, Sally M. *atmospheric scientist*
Berck, Peter *agricultural economics educator*
Bergman, George Mark *mathematician, educator*
Bergman, Robert George *chemist, educator*
Berring, Robert Charles, Jr., *law educator, law librarian, former dean*
Bertozzi, Carolyn R. *chemistry professor*
Bickel, Peter John *statistician, educator*
Birdsall, Charles Kennedy *electrical engineer*
Birgeneau, Robert Joseph *academic administrator, physicist, researcher*
Bissell, Mina J. *research laboratory administrator, biochemist*
Bloom, Robert *language professional educator*
Blume, James Beryl *investment advisor*
Bogy, David B(eauregard) *mechanical engineering educator*
Bolt, Bruce Alan *seismologist*
Booth, Stephen Walter *English language educator*
Borcherds, Richard Ewen *mathematics professor*
Bowker, Albert Hosmer *retired university chancellor*
Bragg, Robert Henry *physicist, researcher*
Brandes, Stanley Howard *anthropology educator, writer*
Brenner, Sydney *molecular biologist, researcher*
Breslauer, George William *political science educator*
Brocchini, Ronald Gene *architect*

Brooke, Tal (Robert Taliaferro) *writer*
Browne, G.M. Walter Shawn *journalist, publisher, organizer*
Buckland, Michael Keeble *librarian, educator*
Bucklin, Louis Pierre *business educator, consultant*
Budinger, Thomas Francis *radiologist, educator*
Buffler, Patricia Ann *epidemiologist, educator, dean emerita*
Burger, Edmund Ganes *architect*
Burnside, Mary Beth *biology professor, researcher*
Bustamante, Carlos J. *biophysicist, educator*
Buxbaum, Richard M. *law educator, lawyer*
Cairns, Elton James *chemical engineering educator*
Callenbach, Ernest *writer, editor*
Cantor, Rusty Sumner *artist*
Cardwell, Kenneth Harvey *architect, educator*
Carmichael, Ian Stuart Edward *geologist, educator*
Carpenter, Kenneth John *nutrition educator*
Casida, John Edward *entomology educator*
Castello, John L. *pharmaceutical executive*
Cerny, Joseph, III, *chemistry educator, scientific laboratory administrator, university dean and official*
Chamberlain, Bob *computer company executive*
Chamberlain, Owen *nuclear physicist*
Chamberlin, Michael John *biochemistry educator*
Chapela, Ignacio H. *biologist, researcher*
Cheit, Earl Frank *economist, educator*
Chern, Shiing-Shen *mathematics professor*
Chew, Geoffrey Foucar *physicist*
Choper, Jesse Herbert *law educator, university dean*
Chorin, Alexandre Joel *mathematician, educator*
Cieslak, William *academic administrator*
Clarke, John *physics educator*
Cline, Thomas Warren *geneticist, educator*
Cohn, Theodore Elliot *optometry educator, vision scientist, biomedical engineer*
Colson, Elizabeth Florence *anthropologist*
Consey, Kevin Edward *museum administrator*
Cooper, Michael David *information scientist, educator*
Cooper, William Secord *information science educator*
Costa, Gustavo *Italian studies scholar*
Day, Lucille Lang *museum administrator, educator, writer*
De Goff, Victoria Joan *lawyer*
Diamond, Marian Cleeves *anatomy educator*
Diamond, Richard Martin *nuclear chemist*
Dietrich, William E. *geophysicist, educator*
Dina, Dino *medical company executive*
diSessa, Andrea A. *education educator*
Dornfeld, David Alan *engineering educator*
Drechsel, Edwin Jared *retired magazine editor*
Dresher, Paul Joseph *composer, music educator, performer*
Duhl, Leonard *psychiatrist, educator*
Dundes, Alan *writer, folklorist, educator*
Edwards, Susan M. *hotel executive*
Efimova, Alla *curator*
Eisenberg, Melvin A. *law educator*
Enoch, Jay Martin *optometrist, vision scientist*
Ervin-Tripp, Susan Moore *psychology professor*
Feeley, Malcolm McCollum *law educator, political scientist*
Filippou, Filip C. *engineering educator*
Fleming, Graham Richard *chemistry educator*
Foster, George McClelland, Jr., *anthropologist, educator*
Fowler, Thomas Kenneth *physicist*
Fréchet, Jean Marie Joseph *chemistry professor*
Freedman, David Amiel *statistics educator, consultant*
Freedman, Mervin Burton *psychologist, educator*
Freedman, Sarah Warshauer *education educator*
Freeling, Michael Richard *genetics educator, researcher*
Frickey, Philip Paul *law educator*
Frisch, Joseph *mechanical engineer, educator, consultant*
Fuerstenau, Douglas Winston *mineral engineering educator*
Gaillard, Mary Katharine *physics educator*
Gall, Donald Arthur *minister*
Gallagher, M. Catherine *English literature educator*
Garrison, William Louis *civil engineering educator*
Genn, Nancy *artist*
Gilbert, Neil Robin *social work educator, writer, consultant*
Glaser, Donald Arthur *physicist*
Glenn, Evelyn Nakano *social sciences educator*
Goldhaber, Gerson *physicist, researcher*
Graham, Susan Lois *computer science educator, consultant*
Greif, Ralph *mechanical engineer, educator*
Grimes, Michael David *podiatrist*
Grossman, Elmer Roy *pediatrician*
Guest, Barbara *author, poet*
Hafter, Ervin R. *psychology educator*
Hahn, Erwin Louis *physicist, researcher*
Halbach, Edward Christian, Jr., *law educator*
Haley, George Patrick *lawyer*
Hamilton, Randy Haskell *city manager*
Hang, Bo *biochemist*
Harlan, Robert Dale *information studies educator, academic administrator*
Harris, Eva *molecular biology educator*
Harris, Michael Gene *optometrist, educator, lawyer*
Hartman, Robert Leroy *artist, educator*
Hazen, Terry Clyde *microbial ecologist, educator*
Heathcock, Clayton Howell *chemistry educator, researcher*
Helson, Henry Berge *publisher, retired mathematics educator*
Herr, Richard *history professor*
Hertelendy, Paul *critic, writer, poet*
Hill, Lorie Elizabeth *psychotherapist*
Hodges, David Albert *electrical engineering educator*
Hoffman, Darleane Christian *chemistry professor*
Holder, Harold D. *public health administrator, communications specialist, educator*
Hout, Michael *sociologist, educator*
Howell, Francis Clark *paleo-anthropologist*
Hsu, Chieh Su *applied mechanics engineering educator, researcher*
Hu, Teh-wei *economics professor*
Hull, Glynda *language educator*
Hyman, Edward Jay *forensic psychologist, cognitive and information scientist, consultant, educator, television news commentator*
Imbrie, Andrew Welsh *composer, educator*
Ivry, Richard *psychology educator*
Jackson, J(ohn) David *physicist, researcher*
Janney, Daniel S. *health products executive*

Jeanloz, Raymond *geophysicist, educator*
Jensen, Arthur Robert *psychology educator*
Johnson, Mary Katherine (Katie Johnson) *elementary school educator*
Johnson, Ned Keith *ornithologist, educator*
Johnston, Harold S(ledge) *chemistry professor*
Jones, Vaughan Frederick Randal *mathematician, educator*
Joyce, Rosemary Alexandria *anthropology educator*
Judge, George Garrett *economics professor*
Kaplansky, Irving *mathematician, educator, research institute director*
Karlinsky, Simon *language educator, writer*
Karp, Richard Manning *computer sciences educator*
Kasten, Karl Albert *painter, printmaker, educator*
Kastenberg, William Edward *engineering educator, science educator*
Katzen, Mollie *writer*
Kay, Herma Hill *education educator*
Kerman, Joseph Wilfred *musicologist, critic*
Kerth, Leroy T. *physics educator*
King, C. Judson *academic administrator*
Kirch, Patrick Vinton *anthropology educator, archaeologist*
Kirz, Janos *physicist*
Klinman, Judith Pollock *biochemist, educator*
Kluger, Richard *author, editor*
Koshland, Daniel Edward, Jr., *biochemist, educator*
Kuh, Ernest Shiu-Jen *electrical engineering educator*
Kurtzman, Ralph Harold *biochemist, researcher, consultant*
LaBelle, Thomas Jeffrey *academic administrator*
Lambert, Nadine Murphy *psychologist, educator*
Landau, Martin *political science educator*
Langridge, Robert *biophysicist, educator*
Lashof, Joyce Cohen *public health educator*
Lee, Ronald Demos *demographer, economist, educator*
Lehmkuhl, Lynn *publishing executive*
Leitmann, George *mechanical engineer, educator*
Leonard, Thomas *dean, educator, librarian*
Leopold, Luna Bergere *geology educator*
Lesser, Wendy *editor, writer, consultant*
Lester, William Alexander, Jr., *chemist, educator*
Letiche, John Marion *economist, educator*
Levine, Mark David *science administrator, director*
Levine, Michael Steven *science educator*
Lewis, Andrea Elen *editor*
Lewis, Edwin Reynolds *biomedical engineering educator*
Lichterman, Martin *history professor*
Lidicker, William Zander, Jr., *zoologist, educator*
Linn, Stuart Michael *biochemist, educator*
Lipps, Jere Henry *paleontology educator*
Litwack, Leon Frank *historian, educator*
Long, Anthony Arthur *classics educator*
Louie, Steven Gwon Sheng *physics educator, researcher*
Lu, Adolph *physicist, researcher*
Luker, Kristin *sociology educator*
Ma, Chung-Pei Michelle *astronomer, educator*
Maisel, Sherman Joseph *economist, educator*
Mandelstam, Stanley *physicist*
Margen, Sheldon *public health educator*
Marletta, Michael A. *biochemistry educator, researcher, protein chemist*
Martin, G. Steven *biochemist, educator*
Maslach, Christina *psychology educator*
Maslach, George James *former university official*
Matsumura, Vera Yoshi *pianist*
Matthews, Mildred Shapley *scientific editor, freelance writer*
May, Adolf Darlington *civil engineering educator*
McCoy, Charles Sherwood *university president, former theology educator*
McFadden, Daniel Little *economist, educator*
McKee, Christopher Fulton *physicist, astronomer, educator*
McLaughlin, Sylvia Cranmer *volunteer, environmentalist*
McMains, Sara A. *engineering educator*
McNulty, John Kent *lawyer, educator*
Meltzer, David *author, musician, educator*
Messinger, Sheldon L(eopold) *law educator*
Meyer, Barbara Jean *science educator*
Middlekauff, Robert Lawrence *history educator, administrator*
Miles, Raymond Edward *former university dean, organizational behavior and industrial relations educator*
Miller, William Hughes *theoretical chemist, educator*
Minkus, Jerome Bernard *mathematician, educator*
Minudri, Regina Ursula *librarian, consultant*
Mishkin, Paul J. *lawyer, educator*
Miyasaki, George Joji *artist*
Monismith, Carl Leroy *civil engineering educator*
Moran, Rachel *lawyer, educator*
Mudge, Lewis Seymour *theologian, educator, university dean*
Muir, William Ker, Jr., *political science educator*
Mukherjee, Bharati (Mrs. Clark Blaise) *author, English educator*
Muller, Richard Stephen *electrical engineer, educator*
Murayama, Hitoshi *physicist, educator*
Muscatine, Charles *English educator, author*
Myers, Miles Alvin *educational association administrator, educator*
Nader, Laura *anthropology educator*
Nagler, Michael Nicholas *peace and conflict studies educator*
Narasimhan, Thiruppudaimarudhur Narayanaiyer *science educator, research scientist*
Newman, John Scott *chemical engineer, educator*
Newton, A. Richard *engineering educator*
Odermatt, Diana B. *development consultant*
Ogg, Wilson Reid *lawyer, retired judge, poet, publishing executive, educator*
Olsen, Donald Emmanuel *architect, educator*
Ott, David Michael *engineering company executive*
Pagni, Patrick John *mechanical and fire safety engineering science educator*
Pawsey, Stuart Frederick *structural engineer, retired*
Penzien, Joseph *structural engineering educator*
Peterson, Andrea Lenore *law educator*
Pham, Quang Xuan *statistics educator*
Phillips, Norman Edgar *chemistry professor*
Pigford, Thomas Harrington *nuclear engineering educator*
Pines, Alexander *chemistry educator, researcher, consultant*
Pister, Karl Stark *engineering educator*
Polak, Elijah *engineering educator, computer scientist*
Poor, Clarence Alexander *retired physician*
Pope, Alexander H. *former lawyer, county assessor and non-profit administrator*
Portnoy, Daniel *microbiology educator*
Post, Robert Charles *law educator*
Quail, Peter Hugh *biologist, educator*
Quigley, John Michael *economist, educator*
Quinn, Nigel William Trevelyan *scientist, engineer*
Rajkumar, Lakshmanaswamy *biologist, researcher*
Rakas, Jasenka Milan *aviation engineer*
Ranney, Austin (Joseph Ranney) *political science educator*
Rappaport, Stuart Ramon *lawyer*
Rasmussen, John Oscar *nuclear research scientist*
Ratner, Marina *mathematician, educator, researcher*
Rauch, Irmengard *linguist, educator*
Rausser, Gordon C(lyde) *agricultural and resource economics educator*
Raymond, Kenneth Norman *chemistry educator, research chemist*
Reich, Michael *economics professor*
Reid, Frances Evelyn Kroll *cinematographer, director, film company executive*
Reidhaar, Donald Laverne *lawyer*
Renz, Christopher David *priest*
Rex, Walter Edwin, III, *humanities educator*
Rice, Robert Arnot *school administrator*
Richardson, John David *physicist*
Rippe, Lynn E. *contract administrator*
Ritchie, Robert Oliver *materials science educator*
Rosenzweig, Mark Richard *psychology educator*
Russell, Charlie L. *writer*
Samuelson, Pamela Ann *law educator*
Schachman, Howard Kapnek *molecular biologist, educator*
Scheiber, Harry N. *law educator*
Schekman, Randy W. *molecular biology administrator, biochemist*
Schultz, E. Eugene, Jr., *computer engineer*
Scotchmer, Suzanne Andersen *economics professor*
Scott, Peter Dale *writer, retired English language educator*
Seitz, Walter Stanley *cardiovascular research consultant*
Selz, Peter Howard *art historian, educator*
Séquin, Carlo H. *computer science educator*
Sessler, Andrew Marienhoff *physicist*
Shahani, Sapna *broadcast executive*
Shank, Charles Vernon *science administrator, educator*
Shannon, Chris *economics professor*
Shannon, Thomas Frederic *German language educator*
Shen, Yuen-Ron *physics educator*
Shortell, Stephen Michael *dean, health services researcher*
Shugart, Howard Alan *physicist, researcher*
Simpson, David William *artist, educator*
Sloane, Thomas O. *speech educator*
Smith, Kirk Robert *environmental health sciences educator, researcher*
Smolensky, Eugene *economics professor*
Sorensen, Linda *lawyer*
Sparks, John Edward *lawyer*
Spieler, Helmuth *physicist*
Spinrad, Hyron *astronomer*
Sposito, Garrison *soil scientist, educator, reseacher*
Staubus, George Joseph *accounting educator*
Steiner, Herbert Max *physics educator*
Stewart, Patricia Rhodes *former clinical psychologist, researcher*
Stoller, Claude *architect*
Strauss, Herbert Leopold *chemistry professor*
Streitwieser, Andrew, Jr., *chemistry professor*
Sulloway, Frank Jones *social sciences educator, historian*
Sussman, Wendy Rodriguez *artist, educator*
Swope, Alan Joseph *psychologist, educator*
Syme, Sherman Leonard *epidemiologist, educator*
Talbot, Stephen Henderson *television producer, documentary filmmaker, writer*
Tanner, Lee E. *retired materials scientist, photographer, writer, curator*
Taylor, John Lockhart *former city official*
Teeguarden, Dennis Earl *forest economist, educator*
Temko, Allan Bernard *writer*
Tempelis, Constantine Harry *immunologist, educator*
Thomas, Lisa *food service executive*
Thompson, Anthony Wayne *metallurgist, educator, consultant*
Thompson, Bernadette Maria *poet*
Thow, John H. *music educator, composer*
Tjian, Robert Tse Nan *biochemistry educator, biology researcher, virology researcher*
Torykian, Joan Marie *archivist*
Townes, Charles Hard *physics educator*
Trilling, George Henry *physicist, researcher*
Troxel, David B. *pathologist*
Tutashinda, Kweli (Brian P. Altheimer) *chiropractic physician, educator*
Tyson, Laura D'Andrea *dean, economist, educator*
Valentine, James William *paleobiology educator, writer*
Varian, Hal Ronald *economics professor*
Vojta, Paul Alan *mathematics professor*
Wachs, Martin *urban planning educator, author, consultant*
Wahl, Bernt Rainer *mathematician, writer, application developer*
Wake, David Burton *biology professor*
Wake, Marvalee Hendricks *biology professor*
Wakeman, Frederic Evans, Jr., *historian, educator*
Walker, Peter *landscape architect*
Waters, Alice *executive chef, restaurant owner, writer*
Weber, Eicke Richard *physicist*
Welch, Claude (Claude Raymond Welch) *theology educator*
Westheimer, Gerald *optometrist, educator*
Whinnery, John Roy *electrical engineer, educator*
White, Richard Manning *electrical engineering educator*
Wiegel, Robert Louis *consulting engineering executive*
Williamson, Oliver Eaton *economics and law educator*
Wilson, W(illiam) Daniel *language professional, educator*
Wilton, Peter Campbell *marketing educator*
Winkelstein, Warren, Jr., *physician, educator*
Wolf, Joseph Albert *mathematician, educator*
Wolfram, Charles William *law educator*
Woodhouse, Thomas Edwin *lawyer*
Xi, Xuemei *electrical engineer, researcher*
Yeung, Ronald Wai-Chun *engineering educator, researcher*
Yund, Mary Alice *biotechnology consultant*
Zwerdling, Alex *English educator*
Zysman, John Adler *political scientist, educator*

Berry Creek

Miller, Joseph Arthur *manufacturing engineer, consultant*

Beverly Hills

Adams, Joey Lauren *actress*
Alexander, Jason (Jay Scott Greenspan) *actor*
Allen, Debbie *actress, choreographer, dancer, television director*
Allen, Howard Norman *cardiologist, educator*
Allen, Joan *actress*
Allen, Ted *television personality*
Allen, Tim (Timothy Allen Dick) *actor, comedian*
Ambrose, Lauren *actress*
Ames, Edmund Dantes *singer, actor, producer*
Amiel, Jon *film director, film producer*
Anders, Allison *film director, screenwriter*
Anderson, Gillian *actress*
Anderson, Kenneth Allen *lawyer, hotel executive*
Anderson, Pamela *actress*
Anderson, Wes *film director*
Aniston, Jennifer *actress*
Ann-Margret, (Ann-Margret Olsson) *actress, performer*
Arieff, Allen Ives *physician*
Armstrong, Gillian May *film director*
Arnold, Tom *actor, comedian, producer*
Astin, Sean Patrick *actor, film director, film producer, writer*
August, Bille *film director*
Avary, Roger Roberts (Frank Brauner) *film director, producer, writer*
Azaria, Hank *actor*
Bacon, Kevin *actor*
Badham, John MacDonald *motion picture director*
Bailey, John *cinematographer*
Baker, Kathy Whitton *actress*
Ball, Alan *screenwriter*
Bancroft, Anne (Mrs. Mel Brooks) *actress, scriptwriter, television director*
Banderas, Antonio *actor*
Bao, Katherine Sung *pediatric cardiologist*
Basichis, Gordon Allen *writer, scriptwriter, marketing consultant, media consultant*
Bass, Ronald *screenwriter*
Bassett, Angela *actress*
Bates, Kathy *actress*
Bay, Michael Benjamin *film director*
Beal, John Everett *composer, conductor*
Beatty, (Henry) Warren *actor, producer, director*
Becker, Harold *film director, producer*
Bedelia, Bonnie *actress*
Bello, Maria Elana *actress*
Belushi, James A. *actor*
Bening, Annette *actress*
Berg, Jeffrey Spencer *talent agency executive*
Bergman, Andrew *motion picture director*
Bergman, Nancy Palm *real estate investment company executive*
Berkus, James *talent agent*
Berney, Bob *film company executive*
Berry, Halle M. *actress*
Bird, Antonia *film director*
Blanchett, Cate *actress*
Bogdanovich, Peter *film director, writer, producer, actor*
Bollenbach, Stephen Frasier *hotel executive*
Bonham-Carter, Helena *actress*
Bosworth, Kate *actress*
Boyle, Lara Flynn *actress*
Bradshaw, Terry *sports announcer, former professional football player*
Braff, Zach *actor, director, scriptwriter*
Branch, Michelle *musician*
Bratt, Benjamin *actor*
Braun, Zev *motion picture and television producer*
Brenneman, Amy *actress*
Bridges, Jeff *actor*
Brillstein, Bernie J. *producer, talent manager*
Brockie, Pamela *motion picture executive*
Broderick, Matthew *actor*
Brokaw, Norman Robert *talent agency executive*
Buchberg, Akiva *product designer, inventor, consultant*
Burnett, Carol *actress, comedienne, singer*
Burnett, Charles *film director, screenwriter, producer*
Burnham, John Ludwig *agent*
Burns, Edward J., Jr., *actor, film director*
Burns, Marvin Gerald *lawyer*
Burstyn, Ellen (Edna Rae Gillooly) *actress*
Buscemi, Steve *actor*
Busfield, Timothy *actor*
Bynes, Amanda *actress*
Byrne, Gabriel *actor*
Caan, James *actor, director*
Campbell, Neve *actress*
Cantor, Alan Bruce *management consultant, computer software engineer*
Capshaw, Kate (Kathy Sue Nail) *actress*
Carpenter, John Howard *director, screenwriter*
Carreras, José *tenor*
Carrey, Jim *actor*
Carroll, Diahann *actress, singer*
Carter, Chris *producer, director*
Carter, Dixie *actress*
Carter, Lynda *actress, entertainer*
Casey, Sue (Suzanne Marguerite Philips) *actress, real estate broker*
Castellaneta, Dan (Daniel Louis) *actor*
Caster, Andrew Ian *ophthalmologist*
Castle-Hughes, Keisha *actress*
Caton-Jones, Michael *film director, film producer*
Cattrall, Kim *actress*
Catz, Boris *endocrinologist, educator*
Caviezel, James Patrick *actor*
Channing, Carol *actress*
Chapelle, Dave *comedian*
Chase, David *scriptwriter, television producer, television director*
Cheadle, Don *actor*
Cher, (Cherilyn Sarkisian) *singer, actress*
Christensen, Hayden *actor*
Chritton, George A. *theater producer*
Clooney, George *actor*
Close, Glenn *actress*
Coen, Ethan *film director, writer*
Coen, Joel *film director, writer*
Cole, Natalie Maria *singer*
Collette, Toni *actress*
Columbus, Chris *film director, screenwriter*
Connelly, Jennifer *actress*
Connery, Sir Sean (Thomas Connery) *actor*
Corbett, John *actor*
Corman, Eugene Harold *motion picture producer*
Corwin, Stanley Joel *book publisher*
Covitz, Carl D. *state official, real estate and investment executive*
Cox Arquette, Courteney *actress*
Crawford, Cindy (Cynthia Ann Crawford) *model, actress*
Crowe, Cameron *screenwriter, film director*
Crowe, Russell *actor*
Cruz, Penelope *actress*
Culkin, Macaulay *actor*
Curtis, Jamie Lee *actress*
Cusack, Joan *actress*
Cusack, John *actor*
Dahl, John *film director*
Daly, Tyne *actress*
Damon, Matthew Paige *actor*
Darabont, Frank *screenwriter, director*
David, Clive *event planning executive*
David, Larry *television scriptwriter, producer, actor*
DeBont, Jan *cinematographer, director*
Delaney, Kim *actress*
Demme, Jonathan *director, producer, writer*
De Niro, Robert *actor, film producer, film director, restaurant owner*
Dennehy, Brian *actor*
Dennis, Karen Marie *plastic surgeon*
Depp, Johnny *actor*
Dern, Bruce MacLeish *actor*
DeVito, Danny Michael *actor, director, producer*
Diaz, Cameron *actress*
Diesel, Vin (Mark Vincent) *actor*
Dillon, Matt *actor*
Donaldson, Roger *film director, film producer*
Donati, Enrico *artist*
Dorff, Stephen *actor*
Dotrice, Roy Louis *actor*
Douglas, Michael Kirk *actor, film producer, director*
Dragan, Alexandra *mechanical engineer, consultant, environmental engineer, researcher, engineering educator*
Drescher, Fran *actress*
Dreyfuss, Richard Stephan *actor*
Driver, Minnie *actress*
Duchovny, David *actor*
Dunaway, Faye (Dorothy Dunaway) *actress*
Duncan, Michael Clarke *actor*
Dussault, Nancy *actress, singer*
Duvall, Robert *actor*
Duvall, Shelley *actress*
Eastwood, Clint *actor, film director, former mayor*
Eden, Barbara Jean *actress*
Emmerich, Roland *director, producer, writer*
Evans, Louise *investor, retired psychologist*
Everett, Rupert *actor*
Factor, Max, III, *arbitrator, mediator*
Falco, Edie *actress*
Farrelly, Bobby (Robert Leo Rarrelly Jr.) *writer, producer, director*
Fein, William *ophthalmologist*
Feldshuh, Tovah S. *actress*
Fernandez, Giselle *newscaster, journalist*
Ferrell, Will *actor*
Filicia, Thom *television personality, interior designer*
Finstad, Suzanne Elaine *writer, producer, lawyer*
Fisher, (Donald) Garth *plastic surgeon*
Flaum, Marshall Allen *television producer, writer, director*
Fleder, Gary *film director, producer*
Foch, Nina *actress, creative consultant, film director, educator*
Foley, David *television and film actor*
Foley, James *film director*
Fonda, Jane *actress*
Foster, Lawrence *concert and opera conductor*
Fox, Michael J. *actor*
Fox, Vivica *actress*
Foxx, Jamie *actor, comedian*
Fraser, Brendan *actor*
Friedman, Robert Lee *film company executive*
Garofalo, Janeane *actress, comedienne*
Garr, Teri (Ann) *actress*
Gelbart, Larry *writer, producer*
Gellar, Sarah Michelle *actress*
Gerber, William Norman *motion picture executive*
Gilpin, Peri *actress*
Glazer, Guilford *real estate developer*
Glover, John *actor*
Glover, Savion *actor, dancer*
Goldman, William *writer, scriptwriter*
Goldsmith, Bram *banker*
Goodman, John *actor*
Goodman, Mark Paul *physician*
Graham, Heather *actress*
Graham, Lauren *actress*
Grant, Hugh *actor*
Grant, Michael Ernest *educational administrator, institutional management educator*
Graves, Peter *actor*
Grazer, Brian *film company executive*
Green, Seth *actor*
Gregg, Rodman Walter *motion picture and television producer, publisher*
Grey, Brad *producer, agent*
Griffin, Anthony *plastic surgeon*
Griffin, Merv Edward *former entertainer, television producer, entrepreneur*
Griffiths, Rachel *actress*
Gyllenhaal, Jake *actor*
Gyllenhaal, Maggie *actress*
Hackford, Taylor *film director, producer*
Hackman, Gene (Eugene Alden Hackman) *actor*
Hallstrom, Lasse *director*
Hamilton, Laurell K. *writer*
Hamilton, Lisa Gay *actress*
Hanks, Tom *actor, producer, director*
Hannah, Daryl *actress*
Hanson, Curtis *film director, scriptwriter*
Harden, Marcia Gay *actress*
Harmon, Angie (Angie Sehorn) *actress*
Harrelson, Woody *actor*
Hart, Matthew J. *hotel/recreation executive*
Hartnett, Josh *actor*
Haskell, Peter Abraham *actor*
Hawn, Goldie *actress*
Haworth, Randal Digby *plastic surgeon*
Heaton, Patricia *actress*

Bloomberg, Stu *television producer*
Bower, Richard James *minister*
Braverman, Alan N. *lawyer*
Bright, Kevin S. *producer*
Bush, Billy *television personality*
Clapton, Eric *musician*
Cohen, Valerie A. *entertainment company executive*
Cole, Paula *pop singer, songwriter*
Cook, Richard W. *motion picture company executive*
Costner, Kevin *actor*
Crane, David *producer*
Cunningham, Robert D. *lawyer*
Daniels, Susanne *broadcast executive*
DeMent, Iris *vocalist, songwriter*
DiBonaventura, Lorenzo *film company executive*
Donner, Richard *film director, producer*
Doud, Jacqueline Powers *academic administrator*
Eisner, Michael Dammann *entertainment company executive*
Evanitsky, Stephan E. *film company executive*
Fishburne, Laurence, III, *actor*
Franco, James *actor*
Frank, Amélie Lorraine *marketing professional*
Gibson, Mel *actor, film director, producer*
Gold, Stanley Phillip *diversified investments executive*
Goldstein, Kenneth F. *entertainment executive, software publisher*
Granlund, Thomas Arthur *engineering executive, consultant*
Hartshorn, Terry O. *health facility administrator*
Hashe, Janis Helene *editor*
Henley, Don *singer, drummer, songwriter*
Horn, Alan *motion picture company executive*
Iger, Robert A. *broadcast executive*
Jacobson, Nina *film company executive*
Janney, Allison *actress*
Janollari, David *television broadcasting executive, cable producer, television producer*
Jonas, Tony *television executive*
Joseff, Joan Castle *manufacturing executive*
Jovovich, Milla (Natasha Militza Jovovich) *model, actress*
Kauffman, Marta *producer, writer*
Kaye, Jhani *radio station manager, owner production company*
Kellner, Jamie *broadcast executive*
Kinney, Kathy *actress*
Lamas, Lorenzo *actor, director*
Lang, K. D. (Katherine Dawn Lang) *country music singer, composer*
Lang, Laurie *entertainment company executive*
Lee, Paul *broadcast executive*
Letterie, Kathleen *broadcast executive*
Levinson, Barry L. *film director*
Mack, Kelly *newscaster*
Madison, Paula *broadcast executive*
Marinelli, Janice *broadcast executive*
McGraw, Tim *country music singer*
McPherson, Stephen *broadcast executive*
Mc Vie, Christine Perfect *musician*
McVie, John *musician*
Meyer, Barry Michael *motion picture executive*
Michel, Donald Charles *editor*
Miller, Clifford Albert *merchant banker, business consultant*
Milmore, Jennifer *actress*
Mitchell, Joni (Roberta Joan Anderson) *singer, songwriter*
Mooney, Andrew P. *consumer products company executive*
Murphy, Peter E. *corporate financial officer*
Nagra, Parminder *actress*
Neill, Ve *make-up artist*
Neumann, Nancy Ruth *studio educator*
Nielsen, Kenneth Ray *academic administrator*
O'Dell, Nancy *television personality*
Pedowitz, Mark *broadcast executive*
Petty, Tom (Thomas Earl Petty) *rock guitarist, band leader, composer*
Raulinaitis, Pranas Algis *electronics executive, consultant*
Rawlinson, Joseph Eli *foundation executive, lawyer*
Razouk, Rashad Elias *retired chemistry educator*
Remini, Leah *actress*
Renner, Andrew Ihor *surgeon*
Rimes, LeAnn *country music singer*
Robertson, Richard Trafton *entertainment company executive*
Ross, Rich *broadcast executive*
Roth, Peter *broadcast executive*
Ruiz, Michele *newscaster*
Rzeznik, Johnny *singer, musician*
Sajak, Pat *television game show host*
Schneider, Peter *theater producer*
Schumacher, Joel *director, writer*
Schumacher, Thomas *film company executive*
Shapiro, Angela *broadcast executive*
Sherbert, Sharon Debra *financial services executive*
Silver, Joel *film producer*
Sklar, Martin A. *recreational facility executive*
Staggs, Thomas *entertainment company executive*
Stainton, David *recreational facility executive*
Steel, Shawn *political party official*
Stewart, Roderick David *singer*
Stiles, Ryan *actor*
Sweeney, Anne M. *cable television company executive*
Sweeny, Anne *broadcast executive*
Taubin, Dawn *film company executive*
Thomas-Graham, Pamela *communications executive*
Thompson, Lea *actress*
Thyret, Russ *recording industry executive*
Valdez, Denise *newscaster*
Wachowski, Andy *film director*
Wachowski, Larry *film director*
Wallau, Alex *broadcast executive*
Wells, John Marcum *producer, writer*
Williams, Colleen *newscaster*
Wise, Helena Sunny *lawyer*
Wonder, Stevie (Stevland Morris) *singer, musician, composer*
Younger, Laurie *broadcast executive*
Zucker, Jeffrey *broadcast executive*

Burlingame
Cotchett, Joseph Winters *lawyer, author*
Garnett, Katrina A. *information technology executive*
Hubbard, Gregory Scott *physicist*
McGraw, Benjamin F., III, *biotechnology executive*
Mendelson, Lee M. *film company executive, writer, producer, director*
Mhatra, Nagesh *health products executive*
Ocheltree, Richard Lawrence *lawyer, retired forest products company executive*
Schwantes, Robert Sidney *international relations executive*
Stofflet, Mary Kirk *museum curator, writer*

Calabasas
Anderson, Joe D. *diversified financial services company executive*
Bernhard, Sandra *actress, comedienne, singer*
Boone, Thomas H. *diversified financial services company executive*
Bursten, Stuart Lowell *physician, biochemist*
Carner, Charles Robert, Jr., *screenwriter, director*
Christensen, Donn Wayne *insurance executive*
Cohen, William *construction executive*
Garcia, Carlos M. *financial services company executive*
Goldfield, Emily Dawson *finance company executive, artist*
Grimwade, Richard Llewellyn *lawyer*
Iacobellis, Sam Frank *retired aerospace company executive*
Isham, Mark *composer, jazz musician*
Kurland, Stanford L. *financial lending company executive*
Landau, Martin *actor*
Laney, Michael L. *manufacturing executive*
Levy, Dena Christine *television producer, director*
McLaughlin, Thomas Keith *diversified financial services company executive*
Menteer, David Hilton *producer, production manager*
Milne, Gordon A. *construction executive, mortgage company executive*
Moule, William Nelson *electrical engineer, consultant*
Mozilo, Angelo R. *diversified financial services company executive*
Phillips, Teddy Steve, Sr., *conductor, saxophone player, production company executive*
Sambol, David *diversified financial services company executive*
Samuels, Sandor E. *diversified financial services company executive*
Sieracki, Eric P. *diversified financial services company executive*
Sloan, Michael Dana *information systems specialist*
Stark, Martin J. *management consultant*

California City
Friedl, Rick *lawyer, former academic administrator*
Paiva, Clifford Anthony *physicist, consultant*

Calimesa
McNulty, James Francis, Jr., *lawyer, consultant*

Camarillo
Alexander, John Charles *editor, writer*
Boskovich, George, Jr., *food products executive*
Cobb, Roy Lampkin, Jr., *retired computer sciences corporation executive*
Cobb, Shirley Ann Dodson *public relations consultant, journalist*
Ford, Paul Francis *theology studies educator, writer*
MacAlister, Robert Stuart *oil industry executive, consultant*
Rush, Richard R. *academic administrator*
Sullivan, Michael Evan *investment and management company executive*
Weiss, Carl *aerospace company executive*

Cambria
Harden, Marvin *artist, educator*
Morse, Richard Jay *human resources specialist, consultant*
Salaverria, Helena Clara *retired language educator*

Cameron Park
Vorce-Tish, Helene R. *writer*

Camp Pendleton
Prato, Kimberly *public affairs officer*

Campbell
Bass, Lewis *lawyer*
Beizer, Lance Kurt *lawyer*
Castello, Raymond Vincent *lawyer*
Levy, Salomon *mechanical engineer*
Nicholson, Joseph Bruce *real estate developer*
Roberts, George P. *computer company executive*
Ross, Hugh Courtney *electrical engineer*

Canoga Park
Alexander, Sue *writer*
Brandenburg, Stanley C. *financial company executive*
Hawes, Bess Lomax *retired anthropologist*
Lederer, Marion Irvine *cultural administrator*
Meier, Sue A. *marriage and family therapist, director*
Rosenfeld, Sarena Margaret *artist*

Canyon Lake
Schilling, Frederick Augustus, Jr., *geologist, consultant*
Sparks, Dale Boyd *allergist, health facility administrator*

Capistrano Beach
Gregory, George G. *retired lawyer*

Capitola
Jackson, Kingsbury Temple *educational contract consultant*
Wolff, Jean Walton *writer*

Cardiff
Cowan, William Maxwell *neurobiologist*

Carlsbad
Allison, Stephen Galender *broadcast executive*
Aschenbrenner, Frank Aloysious *former diversified manufacturing company executive*
Benjamin, Theresa Mary *retired psychotherapist*
Bennett, C. Frank *molecular pharmacologist*
Carlo, Dennis J. *biotechnology company executive*
Chopra, Deepak *preventive medicine physician, writer*
Conway, Daniel Edward *management consultant*
Craig, Jenny *weight management executive*
Crooke, Stanley Thomas *pharmaceutical executive*
Cuthbert, Emilie Ann (Emilie Winthrop) *interior designer*
Farrell, Warren Thomas *author*
Fikes, Jay Courtney *anthropology educator, art dealer*
Glavin, James B. *biotechnology executive*
Halberg, Charles John August, Jr., *mathematics professor*
Hale, David Fredrick *biotechnology executive*
Hammes, Michael Noel *automotive company executive*
Howard, Robert Staples *newspaper publisher*
Kauderer, Bernard Marvin *retired naval officer, consultant*
Lange, Clifford E. *librarian*
Lu, Taijin *physical chemist, researcher*
Missett, Judi Sheppard *dancer, jazzercise company executive*
Mitchell, Thomas Edward, Jr., *communications cabling executive*
Nahavandi, Amir Nezameddin *retired engineering firm executive*
Owen, Charles Theodore *journalist, publishing executive*
Robb, Robert *biotechnology company executive*
Royston, Ivor *scientific director*
Smith, Warren James *optical scientist, consultant, lecturer, author*
Somit, Albert *political educator*
Turner, Lyle C. *biotechnology company executive*
Wilson, Donald Grey *management consultant*

Carmel
Alich, John Arthur, Jr., *manufacturing executive*
Alsberg, Dietrich Anselm *electrical engineer, consultant*
Aurner, Robert Ray, II, *retail executive*
Barton, Hugh Perry *bank executive*
Bengert, W. Raymond *lawyer, chemical engineer*
Chung, Kyung Cho *Korean specialist, educator, writer*
Creighton, John Wallis, Jr., *novelist, publisher, former management educator, consultant*
Didion, James J. *real estate company executive*
Dobey, James Kenneth *banker*
Epel, David *biologist, educator*
Epstein-Shepherd, Bee *coach, hypnotist, speaker*
Evans, Charlotte Mortimer *communications consultant, writer*
Faul, June Patricia *education specialist*
Felch, William Campbell *internist, editor*
Flanagan, Michael Brendan *obstetrician and gynecologist*
Gordon, David Jamieson *tenor*
Hamilton, Lyman Critchfield, Jr., *telecommunications industry executive*
Hobbs, C. Fredric *artist, filmmaker, author*
Jacobs, Ralph, Jr., *artist*
Koeppel, Gary Merle *publishing executive, art gallery owner, writer*
Lockton, David Ballard *business executive*
Mollman, John Peter *book publisher, consultant electronic publishing*
Pasten, Laura Jean *veterinarian*
Pippi, Mikel Eugene *cultural attache, television producer, arts administrator, television director*
Robinson, John Minor *lawyer, retired business executive*
Smith, Gordon Paul *management consultant*
Vagnini, Livio Lee *chemist, forensic consultant*
Youngdahl, Paul Frederick *mechanical engineer*

Carmel Valley
Chapman, Robert Galbraith *retired hematologist, administrator*
Kasson, James Matthews *electronics executive*
Meckel, Peter Timothy *arts administrator, educator*
Wolfe, Maurice Raymond *retired museum director, educator*

Carmichael
Areen, Gordon E. *finance company executive*
Cunningham, Brenda R. *secondary school educator, editor*
Halpenny, Diana Doris *lawyer*
Hellmuth, William Frederick *economics professor*
Rich, Albert Clark *solar energy manufacturing executive*
Wolfe, Bruce McLaren *surgery educator*

Carpinteria
Fisher, John Crocker *physicist*
Hansen, Robert William *artist, educator*
Lopker, Pamela *technology industry executive*
Schmidhauser, John Richard *political science educator*
Wheeler, John Harvey *political scientist, writer*

Carson
Bensussen, Gale *health products company executive*
Cienfuegos, Mauricio *professional soccer player*
Del Prado, Sergio *professional soccer team executive*
Fisher, Farah Lee *education educator*
Hirsch, Gilah Yelin *artist, writer*
Mori, Allen Anthony *academic administrator, consultant*
Oropeza, Jenny *state official*
Palmer, Beverly Blazey *psychologist, educator*
Schmid, Sigi *professional soccer coach*
Stuart, Nancy Giovinazzo *secondary school educator*
Suchenek, Marek Andrzej *computer science educator*
Zimmerer, Kathy Louise *university art gallery director*

Castaic
Burkhart, Stephanie Gloria *protective services official, writer*
Holmes, Dale Arthur *optics scientist*
La Cava, Donald Leon *communications executive*

Castro Valley
Erwin, Frances Suzanne *artist*
Morrison, Glenn Leslie *minister*
Thorburn, Lisa A. *acoustical consulting company executive*

Cathedral City
Berry, Ester Lorée *vocational nurse*
Garcia, Bonnie *state official*
Jackman, Robert Alan *retail executive*
Satcher, Clement Michael *elementary school educator*

Cayucos
Shahan, Sherry Jean *writer, educator*
Theurer, Byron W. *aerospace engineer, business owner*

Cazadero
Tuggle, Mike *writer, secondary school educator*

Ceres
Abbott, Dan-San *parachute designer*

Chatsworth
Bhartia, Prakash *defense research management executive, researcher, educator*
Dunwich, Gerina *writer, magazine editor, astrologer*
Faerber, Charles N. *editor*
Klein, Jeffrey S. *lawyer, media executive*
Levine, Arnold Milton *retired electrical engineer, documentary filmmaker*
Miller, Robert Steven *secondary school educator*
Schwab, Howard Joel *judge*
Stephenson, Irene Hamlen *biorhythm analyst, consultant, editor, educator*
Wilson, Darlene Anderson *elementary school educator*

Chico
Akimoto, Martin Wayne *mental health services professional*
Allen, Charles William *mechanical engineering educator*
Cooper, Erwin *writer*
Ediger, Robert Ike *botanist, educator*
Esteban, Manuel Antonio *academic administrator, language educator*
Hanton, E. Michael *public and personnel relations consultant*
Keene, Rick *state legislator*
Kistner, David Harold *biology professor*
Livingston, Myran Jay *author, film writer, director and producer*
Loker, William Meverell *anthropologist, educator*
McNall, Scott Grant *sociologist, educator, academic administrator*
Moore Jr, Cletus B. *financial consultant, hotel executive*
Patton, Thomas Edward *artist, educator*
Ritter, Dale William *obstetrician, gynecologist*
Schmidt, Diane Ellen *political scientist*
Schweitzer, Sandra Lynn *lawyer, nurse*
Shahid-García, María de Lourdes *foreign language educator*
Smith, Valene Smith *anthropologist, educator*
Spear, Paul Stanley *psychology educator, musician*
Ward, Chester Lawrence *physician, consultant*
Zingg, Paul Joseph *academic administrator*

China Lake
Bennett, Jean Louise McPherson *physicist, research scientist*

Chino
Determan, John David *lawyer*
Forsyth, Barbara Jean *elementary reading specialist, writer, poet*
Hall, Marshall Howard *artist*
Kennedy, Mark Alan *secondary school educator*
Van Wagner, Ellen *lawyer, law educator*

Chino Hills
Burge, Willard, Jr., *software company executive*
Nash, Sylvia Dotseth *consultant*
Ofner, William Bernard *investor*
Sanders, Nancy Ida *writer*
Teng, Chen *import/export company executive, wholesale distribution executive*

Chula Vista
Blankfort, Lowell Arnold *newspaper publisher*
Briggs, Franklin Henry *retired naval officer*
Cohen, Elaine Helena *pediatrician, cardiologist, educator*
Gongora, Eduardo *plastic surgeon*
Heise, Steven Anthony *surveyor, consultant*
Madigan, Laurie Anne *municipal official*
Moreno-Ducheny, Denise *state senator*
Ryan, Candace Irene *writer, director, editor*
Smith, Peggy O'Doniel *retired physicist*
Weiss-Cornwell, Amy *interior designer*
Worthington, George Rhodes *retired naval officer*

Citrus Heights
Daves, Sandra Lynn *poet, lyricist*
Leisey, Donald Eugene *educational materials company executive, educator*
Osaki, Mark Stephen *writer, development administrator*

City Of Commerce
Johnson, Keith Liddell *chemical company executive*
Lynch, Martin Andrew *retail company executive*
Martin, Richard J. *food wholesale executive*
Plamann, Alfred A. *wholesale distribution executive*

City Of Industry
Cavanaugh, Janis Lynn *protective services official, educator*
Pacheco, Robert *state official*
Perry, William Joseph *food processing company executive*
Requeno, Nestor Danilo *human services administrator*

Claremont
Ackerman, Gerald Martin *art historian, consultant*
Albaum, Jean Stirling *psychologist, educator*
Alexander, John David, Jr., *college administrator*
Ansell, Edward Orin *lawyer*
Atlas, Jay David *philosopher, consultant, linguist*
Bekavac, Nancy Yavor *academic administrator, lawyer*
Benjamin, Karl Stanley *artist, art educator*
Blizzard, Alan *artist*
Borcherding, Thomas Earl *economist*
Burns, Richard Dean *history educator, publisher, writer*
Christian, Suzanne Hall *financial planner*
Csikszentmihalyi, Mihaly *psychology educator*
Davis, Nathaniel *humanities educator*

Doty, Horace Jay, Jr., *theater administrator, arts consultant*
Douglass, Enid Hart *educational program director*
Dunye, Cheryl *artist, filmmaker*
Dym, Clive Lionel *engineering educator*
Eagleton, Robert Don *physics educator*
Espinosa, Gaston E. *writer, educator*
Ferguson, Cleve Robert *lawyer, educator*
Filson, Darren *economics professor, consultant*
Forti, William Bell *finance educator*
Gann, Pamela Brooks *academic administrator*
Genung, Dan Baldwin *minister, writer*
Goodrich, Norma Lorre (Mrs. John H. Howard) *French and comparative literature educator*
Hafif, Gregory Keith *lawyer*
Halpern, Diane F. *psychology educator, professional association executive*
Hansch, Corwin Herman *chemistry professor*
Hartford, Margaret Elizabeth (Betty Hartford) *social work educator, gerontologist, writer*
Helliwell, Thomas McCaffree *physicist, researcher*
Henriksen, Melvin *mathematician, educator*
Johnson, Jerome Linné *cardiologist, educator*
Kates, Gary *academic administrator*
Kucheman, Clark Arthur *philosophy and religious studies educator*
Lachowicz, Rachel *artist, art educator*
Lasswell, Marcia Lee *psychologist, educator*
Leeb, Charles Samuel *clinical psychologist*
Liggett, Thomas Jackson *retired seminary president*
Likens, James Dean *economics professor*
Maguire, John David *academic administrator, educator, writer*
Martin, Jay Herbert *psychoanalyst, English and political science educator*
McKirahan, Richard Duncan *classics and philosophy educator*
Molinder, John Irving *engineering educator, consultant*
Monson, James Edward *electrical engineer, educator*
Moss, Myra Ellen (Myra Moss Rolle) *philosophy educator*
Myhre, Janet *mathematician, educator*
Neumann, Harry *philosophy educator*
Oxtoby, David William *college president, chemistry educator*
Pedersen, Richard Foote *diplomat and academic administrator*
Pinney, Thomas Clive *retired English language educator*
Platt, Joseph Beaven *former college president*
Presecan, Nicholas Lee *environmental and civil engineer, consultant*
Rankaitis, Susan *artist*
Reynolds, Margaret Ann *minister, educator*
Riggs, Henry Earle *academic administrator, engineering educator*
Riley, Judith Merkle *writer, educator*
Rossum, Ralph Arthur *political science educator*
Sanders, James Alvin *minister, religious studies educator*
Shimkhada, Deepak *art historian*
Sontag, Frederick Earl *philosophy educator*
Stanley, Peter William *former academic administrator*
Strauss, Jon Calvert *academic administrator*
Tanenbaum, Basil Samuel *engineering educator*
Tilden, Wesley Roderick *writer, retired computer programmer*
Ulitin, Vladimir Gregor *retired Russian language and literature educator*
Valdez, Arnold *dentist, lawyer*
Wachtel, Albert *writer, educator*
Wettack, F. Sheldon *academic administrator*
Wheeler, Geraldine Hartshorn *historian, writer*
Wolf, Kenneth Baxter *writer, educator*
Woodress, James Leslie, Jr., *English language educator*
Young, Howard Thomas *foreign language educator*
Zornes, Milford *artist*

Clayton
Bower, Fay Louise *academic administrator, nursing educator*

Clearlake
Schoenherr, Bob *communications educator, consultant*

Clovis
Brahma, Chandra Sekhar *civil engineering educator*
Ninnis, William Raymond, Jr., *lawyer*
Shields, Allan Edwin *writer, photographer, retired educator*
Smith, William Clarke *clergyman*
Terrell, Howard Bruce *psychiatrist*

Coachella
Barker, Douglas P. *food products executive*

Coalinga
Frame, Ted Ronald *lawyer*

Cobb
Budzinski, James Edward *interior designer*

Colton
Brown, Jack H. *supermarket company executive*
Smith, Phillip J. *food products executive*

Colusa
Carter, Jane Foster *agricultural products executive*

Compton
Beauchamp, Patrick L. *distributing company executive*
Dymally, Mervyn Malcolm *retired congressman*
Janeway, Barbara *public relations executive*
Maradiaga Kieffer-Aanonsen, Nora Ludmila *language educator*
Shiloh, Allen *writer*
Wang, Charles Ping *engineering executive*

Concord
Crandall, Ira Carlton *consulting electrical engineer*
Fuld, Fred, III, *computer consultant, financial consultant*
Headding, Lillian Susan (Sally Headding) *writer, forensic clairvoyant*
Hearst, John Eugene *chemistry educator, researcher, consultant*
Lee, Low Kee *electronics engineer, consultant*
Middleton, Michael John *civil engineer*
Miller, John Nelson *banker, educator*
Misner, Charlotte Blanche Ruckman *retired community organization administrator*
Mitchell, Carol Denise *small business owner, writer*
Rohra, Srikrishin Assardas *cardiologist*
Scarpulla, Teresa *artist*
Schwartz, Eric *lawyer*
Thompson, Jeremiah Beiseker *international medical business executive, sinologist*

Cool
Trybul, Theodore Nicholas *engineering educator*

Corona
Amato, Carol Joy *writer, anthropologist*
Chao, Allen Y. *pharmaceutical executive*
Everett Nollkamper, Pamela Irene *legal management company executive, educator*
Hall, Harlan *federal agency administrator*
Haynes, Moses Alfred *physician*
Rankin, Alex C. *management executive*
Shaffer, Audrey Jeanne *health information administrator, educator*
Tillman, Joseph Nathaniel *engineering executive*
Weisemann, Claus *pharmaceutical executive*

Corona Del Mar
Allen, Russell G. *lawyer*
Britten, Roy John *biophysicist*
Delap, Tony *artist*
Helphand, Ben J. *actuary, consultant*
Hinderaker, Ivan *political science educator*
Indiek, Victor Henry *finance corporation executive*
Karson, Burton Lewis *musician, educator*
Morisseau, Nan Kruger *television personality*
Muller, David Webster *architectural designer*
O'Brien, John William, Jr., *investment management consultant, finance educator*
Terrell, A. John *retired university telecommunications director*
Tobis, Jerome Sanford *physician*
Wolf, Karl Everett *aerospace and communications corporation executive*
Yeo, Ron *architect*
Zabrodsky, Alexander *network technician*

Coronado
Axelson, Joseph Allen *professional athletics executive, publisher*
Baumer, Edward Ferdinand *financial services executive*
Betts, Barbara Lang *lawyer, rancher, realtor*
Butcher, Bobby Gene *retired military officer*
Crilly, Eugene Richard *engineering consultant*
Dalton, Matt *retired foundry executive*
Heisner, John Richard *lawyer*
Hostler, Charles Warren *former ambassador, international affairs consultant*
Hubbard, Donald *marine artist, writer*
Mock, David Clinton, Jr., *internist*
Neblett, Carol *soprano*
Sack, Edgar Albert *electronics company executive*
Smith, Albert Cromwell, Jr., *investment company executive, writer*
Stames, William Alexander *realtor, cost management executive*
Stockdale, James Bond *writer, research scholar, retired naval officer*
Wagener, Hobart D. *retired architect*

Corte Madera
Dalpino, Ida Jane *retired secondary school educator*
Epstein, William Louis *dermatologist, educator*
Scott, John Walter *chemical engineer, research management executive*
Serber, William *radiation oncologist, educator*

Costa Mesa
Alexiou, James *electronics executive*
Anderson, Jon David *lawyer*
Bartletti, Don *photographer, editor*
Brady, John Patrick, Jr., *electronics educator, consultant*
Caldwell, Courtney Lynn *lawyer, real estate consultant*
Chambers-Belida, Candace R. *radio personality, writer, television producer*
Cohen, Stanley *commercial real estate developer*
Cox, Fred B. *software company executive*
Currie, Robert Emil *lawyer*
Daniels, James Walter *lawyer*
DeMille, Dianne Lynne *mathematics educator, administrator*
Dempster, Murray Wayne *academic administrator, religion educator, minister*
Dougherty, Betsey Olenick *architect*
Giannini, Valerio Louis *investment banker*
Gimple, W. Thomas *sales executive*
Guilford, Andrew John *lawyer*
Hara, Tadao *educational administrator*
Hay, Howard Clinton *lawyer*
Hazewinkel, Van *manufacturing executive*
Hepp, David Worthington *draftsman*
Jones, H(arold) Gilbert, Jr., *lawyer*
Kiang, Assumpta (Amy Kiang) *brokerage house executive*
Labbe, Armand Joseph *curator, anthropologist*
Lattanzio, Stephen Paul *astronomy educator*
Lerner, Sandy *cosmetics executive*
Maddox, Ken *state official*
Marshall, Ellen Ruth *lawyer*
McEnary, John Walter *music educator*
Metzger, Vernon Arthur *management educator, consultant*
Mohajer, Dineh *cosmetics company executive*
Muller, Jerome Kenneth *photographer, art director, editor*
Mumford, Lawrence R. *composer, educator*
Panic, Milan *pharmaceutical and health products company executive*
Phelps, Aaron K(ay) *lawyer*
Ratcliff, Donald Earl *minister, educator*
Reich, Peter Lester *legal educator, legal and historical consultant*
Scarborough, Stephen J. *construction executive*
Svendsen, Arthur E. *construction executive*
Sykes, Jolene *former publishing executive*
Tanner, R. Marshall *lawyer*
Tennyson, Peter Joseph *lawyer*
Thierstein, Hans *biotechnology company executive*
Tillman, Barbara Ann *education educator, consultant*
Williams, William Corey *theology educator, consultant*

Cotati
Hill, Debora Elizabeth *writer, journalist, screenwriter*
Robertson, William Abbott *arbitrator, mediator, lawyer*

Coto De Caza
Bezar, Gilbert Edward *retired aerospace company executive, volunteer*
Sheehy, Jerome Joseph *electrical engineer*

Crescent City
Carter, Neville Louis *geophysicist, educator*
Potter, Scott Michael *artist, writer*
Ruffer, Joyce Sellars *poet, artist*

Crestline
Merrill, Steven William *research and development executive*
Noble, Lawrence Alan *artist*

Crockett
Leporiere, Ralph Dennis *retired quality engineer*
Silverman, Mervyn F. *health science association administrator, consultant*

Cromberg
Kolb, Ken Lloyd *writer*

Culver City
Boonshaft, Hope Judith *public affairs executive*
Brooks, James L. *writer, director, producer*
Brooks, Mel *producer, director, writer, actor*
Chaffin, Cean *producer*
Chammou, Eliezer *education educator, school librarian*
Chow, Judy *librarian, educator*
Clodius, Albert Howard *history educator*
Coolio, (Artis Ivey Jr.) *popular musician*
Dutt, Birendra *research specialist*
Evans, Linda *actress*
Ewing, Michael Snyder *producer, film company executive*
Fisher, Lucy *film producer*
Friedland, David L. *industrial and organizational psychologist*
Grant, Joan Julien *artist*
Guber, Peter *executive producer*
Hall, Barbara *television producer*
Harris, Mel *broadcast executive*
Holt, Dennis F. *media buying company executive*
Kaufman, Richard Stuart *conductor, music director*
Lenk, Edward C. (Toby) *Internet company executive*
Leve, Alan Donald *electronic materials manufacturing company owner, executive*
Lynton, Michael *film company executive*
Maltzman, Irving Myron *psychology educator*
Marcus, Richard Andrew *accountant, mayor*
Mark, Laurence Maurice *film producer*
Mastro, Danny Frank *protective services official*
Maxwell-Brogdon, Florence Morency *school administrator, educational consultant*
Michaels, Helene *broadcast executive*
Moss, Eric Owen *architect*
Netzel, Paul Arthur *fund raising management executive, consultant*
Neufeld, Mace *film company executive*
Pascal, Amy *film company executive*
Sakai, Richard *motion picture and television executive, producer*
Sussman, Deborah Evelyn *designer, company executive*
Tisch, Steven Elliot *television and movie producer*
Trebek, Alex *television game show host*
Wayans, Damon *actor*
Wick, Douglas *producer*
Wigan, Gareth *film company executive*
Wilson, David *artist*
Ziskin, Laura *television producer, film producer*

Cupertino
Berg, Karl *real estate company executive*
Carnie, Kay C. *artist, educator*
Cheeseman, Douglas Taylor, Jr., *wildlife tour executive, photographer, educator*
Chung, Jin Soo *ocean mining and ocean engineer*
Clyde, Robert Allan *computer software engineer*
Compton, Dale Leonard *retired space agency executive, consultant*
Cook, Timothy D. *computer company executive*
Dalrymple, Cheryl *retired computer company executive*
Devlin, Mike *software company executive*
Edson, William Alden *retired electrical engineer, researcher*
Fan, Chien *aerospace engineer, researcher*
Fletcher, Homer Lee *librarian*
Flynn, Ralph Melvin, Jr., *sales executive, marketing consultant*
Geddes, Barbara Sheryl *communications executive, consultant*
Hall, Brenda *human resources executive*
Haskell, Barry Geoffry *computer company researcher*
Heinen, Nancy R. *computer company executive*
Jelinch, Frank Anthony *lawyer*
Knapp, George Griff Prather *retired insurance executive*
Lam, Cheung-Wei *electrical engineer*
Lyon, Mary Lou *retired secondary school educator*
Mathias, Leslie Michael *electronic manufacturing company executive*
McCormick, Yumi *language educator, translator*
Thompson, John W. *information technology executive*
Tice, Bradley Scott *humanities educator*
Zobel, Louise Purwin *author, educator, lecturer, writing consultant*

Cypress
Bloom, Julian *artist, editor*
Bowlus, Brad A. *health care company executive*
Cao, Dac-Buu *software engineer*
Dorn, Marian Margaret *sports management administrator, educator*
Edmonds, Ivy Gordon *writer*
Garrett, Sharon *health services company executive*
Henrickson, Leslie Ann *educational consultant, education educator*
Konowiecki, Joseph S. *health care company executive*
Olschwang, Alan Paul *lawyer*
Scott, Gregory W. *health care company executive*
Waite, Verner Stuart *retired surgeon*

Daly City
Baladi, Naoum Abboud *surgeon*
Batlin, Robert Alfred *retired newspaper editor*
Dee, Jon Facundo *financial services executive*
Kennedy, Gwendolyn Debra *artist, scriptwriter, playwright*
Malifrando, Frank *foundation executive director, theater producer, consultant*

Dana Point
Fabricant, Jill Diane *technology company executive*
Kesselhaut, Arthur Melvyn *financial consultant*
Olvera, Carlos Nelson *mechanical engineer, executive*
Parker, John Marchbank *consulting geologist*
Walker, Doris Isaak *writer, historian, educator*

Danville
Bergsten, James Robert *computer technology architect*
Candland, D. Stuart *lawyer*
Cross, Christopher T. *education consultant*
Phelps, Orme Wheelock *economics educator emeritus*

Darwin
Palazzo, Robert Paul *lawyer, accountant*

Davis
Addicott, Fredrick Taylor *botanist*
Akesson, Norman Berndt *agricultural engineer, emeritus educator*
Ardans, Alexander Andrew *veterinarian, laboratory director, educator*
Ateh, Comfort Muyang *science educator, researcher*
Barbour, Michael G(eorge) *botany educator, ecological consultant*
Barthold, Stephen W. *veterinarian*
Bartosic, Florian *law educator, lawyer, arbitrator*
Baskin, Ronald Joseph *cell biologist, physiologist, biophysicist educator, dean*
Bellie, Sivakumar *engineer, researcher*
Bennett, Alan B. *research and development company executive, educator*
Bernd, Clifford Albrecht *language educator*
Biggart, Nicole Woolsey *dean*
Brandt, Harry *mechanical engineering educator*
Brower, Daniel Roberts *historian, educator, writer*
Brown, Hershel M. *retired newspaper publisher*
Bunch, Richard Alan *writer, educator, poet, philosopher*
Burri, Betty Jane *research chemist*
Cahill, Thomas Andrew *physicist, researcher*
Cardiff, Robert Darrell *pathology educator*
Carter, Colin Andre *education educator*
Chancellor, William Joseph *agricultural engineering educator*
Chang, Daniel Pan Yih *environmental engineering educator*
Cheney, James Addison *civil engineering educator*
Cohen, Lawrence Edward *sociology educator, criminologist*
Colvin, Harry Walter, Jr., *physiology educator*
Conn, Eric Edward *plant biochemist*
Day, Howard Wilman *geology educator*
DePaoli, Geri M. (Joan DePaoli) *artist, art historian*
Druzhnikov, Yuri Ilya *literature educator, writer*
Enders, Allen Coffin *anatomy educator*
Epstein, Emanuel *plant physiologist*
Fannjiang, Albert *mathematician, educator*
Feeney, Floyd Fulton *legal educator*
Frankel, Edwin N. *food scientist, educator*
Freedland, Richard Allan *retired biologist, educator*
Gardner, Murray Briggs *pathologist, educator*
German, Bruce J. *science educator, science administrator*
Gifford, Ernest Milton *biologist, educator*
Gottlieb, Leslie *geneticist, educator*
Groth, Alexander Jacob *political science educator*
Gubler, Walter Douglas *plant pathologist, educator*
Halsted, Charles Hopkinson *internist*
Handel, Darrell Dale *composer, retired music educator*
Hastings, Alan *environmental biology educator*
Hendrickx, Andrew George *research physiologist*
Hess, Charles Edward *environmental horticulture educator*
Hess, Ronald Andrew *aerospace engineer, educator*
Hinshaw, Virginia *academic administrator*
Hoffman, Michael Jerome *humanities educator, educator*
Hollinger, Mannfred Alan *pharmacologist, educator, toxicologist*
Hope, Hakon *research scientist*
Horwitz, Barbara Ann *physiologist, educator, consultant*
Hristova, Krassimira Radoykova *microbiologist, researcher*
Imwinkelried, Edward John *law educator*
Jensen, Hanne Margrete *pathology educator*
Jones, Edward George *neuroscience professor*
Jungerman, John Albert *physics educator*
Kado, Clarence Isao *molecular biologist*
Kavvas, M. Levent *civil engineering educator*
Kester, Dale Emmert *pomologist, educator*
Kofranek, Anton Miles *floriculturist, educator*
Krener, Arthur J. *systems engineering educator*
Krubitzer, Leah *psychology educator, neuroscientist*
Kuhl, Tonya L. *science educator*
Lescroart, John Thomas *writer, composer, singer*
Lipscomb, Paul Rogers *retired orthopedic surgeon, educator*
Liu, Gang-Yu *chemist, educator*
Lucas, William John *science educator*
Luciw, Paul A. *medical educator*
Major, Clarence Lee *poet, novelist, educator, artist*
Mann, Susan Louise *education educator*
Marino, Miguel Angel *engineering educator*
Mason, William A(lvin) *psychologist, educator, researcher*
McHenry, Henry Malcolm *anthropologist, educator*
Meyer, Margaret Eleanor *microbiologist, educator*
Moyle, Peter Briggs *fisheries and biology educator*
Mukherjee, Amiya K. *metallurgy and materials science educator*
Mulase, Motohico *mathematics professor*
Murphy, Frederick Augustus *virologist, researcher*
Murphy, Terence Martin *biology professor*
Musolf, Lloyd Daryl *political science educator, institute administrator*

Nash, Charles Presley *chemistry professor*
Osburn, Bennie I. *dean*
Overstreet, James Wilkins *obstetrics and gynecology educator, administrator*
Owings, Donald Henry *psychology educator*
Palmer, Philip Edward Stephen *radiologist*
Pan, Ning *engineering educator*
Perschbacher, Rex Robert *dean, law educator*
Pritchard, William Roy *former university system administrator*
Qualset, Calvin O. *plant genetics and agronomy educator*
Rappaport, Lawrence *plant physiology and horticulture educator*
Rhode, Edward Albert *veterinary medicine educator, veterinary cardiologist*
Richman, David Paul *neurologist, educator, researcher*
Rooks, George Malcolm *writer, educator, company executive*
Rost, Thomas Lowell *plant biology educator*
Roth, John Roger *geneticist, biology educator*
Rothchild, Donald Sylvester *political science educator*
Sanderson, Janet A. *ambassador*
Sandoval, Jonathan Hough *education educator*
Schenker, Marc Benet *preventive medicine educator*
Schneeman, Barbara Olds *nutritionist, educator*
Schoener, Thomas William *zoology educator, researcher*
Shackelford, James Floyd *materials science educator, researcher*
Sharrow, Marilyn Jane *library administrator*
Sillman, Arnold Joel *physiologist, educator*
Simonton, Dean Keith *psychology educator*
Skinner, G(eorge) William *anthropologist, educator*
Smith, Michael Peter *social science educator, researcher*
Sperling, Daniel *engineering educator, transportation studies director*
Spindler, George Dearborn *anthropologist, educator, writer, editor*
Springer, Sally Pearl *university administrator*
Stern, Judith Schneider *nutritionist, researcher, educator*
Stewart, James Ian *agricultural water scientist, cropping system developer, consultant*
Stumpf, Paul Karl *biochemistry educator emeritus*
Tang, Feng *research scientist*
Tchobanoglous, George *civil engineering educator*
Thurston, William Paul *mathematician*
Traill, David Angus *classics educator*
Troy, Frederic Arthur, II, *medical biochemistry educator*
Tsai, Chih-Ling *management educator*
Turcotte, Donald Lawson *geophysical sciences educator*
Turnlund, Judith Rae *nutritionist*
Van Alfen, Neal K. *plant pathologist*
Vanderhoef, Larry Neil *academic administrator*
Volman, David Herschel *chemistry professor*
Waddington, Raymond Bruce, Jr., *English language educator*
Wang, Shih-Ho *electrical engineer, educator*
Watt, Kenneth Edmund Ferguson *zoology educator*
Wegelin, Jacob Andreas *statistician*
Williamson, Alan Bacher *English literature educator, poet, writer*
Willis, Frank Roy *history educator*
Wolk, Bruce Alan *law educator*
Wydick, Richard Crews *lawyer, educator*
Zhou, Xinzhang *materials scientist, ceramist*

Deer Park
Hodgkin, John E. *pulmonologist*

Del Mar
Boynton, Robert Merrill *retired psychology educator*
Faludi, Susan C. *journalist, scholarly writer*
Farquhar, Marilyn Gist *cell biologist, pathologist, educator*
Fricke, Martin Paul *science company executive*
Johnson, Mary Evans *musicologist, musician*
Lesko, Ronald Michael *osteopathic physician*
Marx, Michael William *language educator, writer*
Morton, Frederic *author*
Mullen, George D. *artist*
Randall, Chandler Corydon *church rector*
Scherger, Joseph Edward *family physician, educator*
Seitman, John Michael *arbitrator, mediator, lawyer*
Smith, Robert Hamil *writer, fund raiser*
Walshok, Mary Lindenstein *academic administrator, sociology educator*
Wilkinson, Eugene Parks *nuclear engineer, director*

Delano
Caratan, Anton G. *food products executive*
Caratan, George *food products executive*
Salmassi, Sadegh *family practice physician*

Desert Hot Springs
Fulton, Norman Robert *credit manager*
Halasz, Stephen Joseph *retired electro-optical systems engineer*
Laws, Maurice Wesley *set decorator, museum exhibit designer*

Diamond Bar
Dogg, Snoop (Calvin Broadus) *vocalist, actor*
Johnson, Leonidas Alexander *optometrist, minister*
Mirisola, Lisa Heinemann *air quality engineer*

Dinuba
Leps, Thomas MacMaster *civil engineer, consultant*

Dixon
Hanowell, Ernest Goddin *physician*

Dobbins
Giles, Marjorie Briggs *publishing executive, writer*

Downey
Baumann, Theodore Robert *aerospace engineer, consultant, military officer*
Brooks, Lillian Drilling Ashton (Lillian Hazel Church) *adult education educator*
Diaz, Consuelo *health facility administrator*
Gong, Henry, Jr., *internist, researcher, educator*
Hackney, Jack Dean *physician*
Mishal, Devadatt M. *obstetrician/gynecologist*
Perry, Jacquelin *orthopedic surgeon*
Robles, Darline P. *school system administrator*
Shapiro, Richard Stanley *physician*

Wayman, Joseph McKelden *editor, researcher*

Duarte
Driskill, James Lawrence *minister*
Probst, John Elwin *chaplain, minister*
Riggs, Arthur D. *health facility administrator, research scientist*
Sleeter, John William Higgs *retired physician, health service administrator*
Vaughn, James English, Jr., *neurobiologist*
Weiss, Lawrence Martin *pathologist, researcher*
Yoshida, Akira *biochemist*

Dublin
Chen, John S. *computer company executive*
Mettinger, Karl Lennart *pharmaceutical executive*
Rubinfeld, Joseph *biotechnology company executive*
Whetten, John D. *food products executive*

East Palo Alto
Bates, William, III, *lawyer*
Furbush, David Malcolm *lawyer*
Lesser, Henry *lawyer*

Edwards
Brand, Vance Devoe *astronaut*
Larson, Jo Ann *government agency administrator*
McCarthy, Marianne *government agency administrator*
Petersen, Kevin *federal agency administrator*

Edwards AFB
Baer-Riedhart, Jenny *aeronautical engineer*

El Cajon
Anthony, Roy Sanford, Jr., *secondary school educator*
Bazzi, Michael J. *priest, educator*
Cossairt, Joseph Arthur, Jr., *writer*
Hollingsworth, Dennis *state senator*
Ostermeyer, Maryann *secondary school educator, writer*
Silverberg, Lewis Henry *legal consultant*
Swanson-Perrelet, Donna Kay *speech pathology/audiology services professional*
Thigpen, Mary Cecelia *city official, consultant*
Thomas, Esther Merlene *elementary and adult education educator*

El Centro
Steensgaard, Anthony Harvey *federal agency administrator*

El Cerrito
Alpen, Edward Lewis *biophysicist, educator*
Conti, Isabella *psychologist, consultant*
Hargis, Barbara Louise *artist*
Herzberg, Dorothy Crews *secondary school educator*
Kao, Yasuko Watanabe *retired library administrator*
Komatsu, Shigego Richard *architect*
Kuo, Ping-chia *historian, educator*
Maxwell, John E. *priest, educator*
Mendoza, Lydia *vocalist*
Wilson, Edward Lawrence *civil engineering educator, structural engineering consultant*

El Dorado Hills
Bartlett, Robert Watkins *educator, consultant, metallurgist*
Sparks, Robert Dean *medical administrator, gastroenterologist*
Yao, John Sen *physician*

El Granada
Heere, Karen R. *astrophysicist*

El Macero
Andrews, Neil Corbly *surgeon*
Stowell, Robert Eugene *pathologist, retired educator*

El Monte
Hwang, Tzu-Yang *minister*

El Segundo
Abbassian-Kashi, Mandana *industrial engineer, systems engineer*
Agrawal, Suphal P. *engineering company executive*
Bauer, Jerome Leo, Jr., *chemical engineer*
Bell, George F. *computer company executive*
Bernstein, Harvey N. *computer company executive*
Brown, Lorraine Ann *event coordinator, minister, hypnotist, therapeutic touch practitioner*
Bryant, Kobe *professional basketball player*
Byears, Latasha *professional basketball player*
Carey, Chase *broadcast executive*
Codon, Dennis P. *lawyer*
Cofoni, Paul M. *computer company executive*
Conrad, Paul Francis *editorial cartoonist*
Cordner, Tom *advertising executive*
Dallas, Terry G. *gas industry executive*
DeBuck, Donald *computer company executive*
Divac, Vlade *professional basketball player*
Eckert, Robert A. *manufacturing executive*
Farr, Kevin M. *consumer products executive*
Fisk, Hayward D. *computer company executive*
Gambaro, Ernest Umberto *lawyer, consultant, engineer*
Harper, David Taylor *civilian military employee*
Honeycutt, Van B. *computer company executive*
Hunter, Larry Dean *lawyer*
Imle, John F., Jr., *oil company executive*
Jacobs, Michael Moises *aerospace engineer, consultant*
Katz, Lew *advertising executive*
Kelble, Jack R. *electronics executive*
Laphen, Michael W. *computer company executive*
Leslie, Lisa DeShaun *professional basketball player*
Level, Leon Jules *computer company executive*
Malone, Karl *professional basketball player*
Manchester, Craig *construction executive*
McCarty, Shirley Carolyn *aerospace executive*
McDonald, Rosa Nell *engineering executive*
McQuillin, Richard Ross *management consultant*
Milton-Jones, DeLisha *professional basketball player*
Muhlbach, Robert Arthur *lawyer*
Musk, Elon *aerospace transportation executive*
Odom, Lamar Joseph *professional basketball player*
Pearce, Harry Jonathan *lawyer*
Puckett, Allen Emerson *aeronautical engineer*

Richmond, Mitchell James *professional basketball player*
Rosen, Harold A. *retired aeronautical engineer*
Rosenfield, Gene *construction executive*
Seymour, Scott *science administrator*
Sterling, Warren Martin *engineering director*
Thiry, Kent J. *health facility administrator*
Toler, Penny *former professional basketball player, sports team executive*
Tomjanovich, Rudolph *professional basketball coach*
Tucker, Paul Thomas *computer company executive*
Weatherspoon, Teresa Gaye *professional basketball player*
Webb, Darryl Willard *systems engineer*
Williamson, Charles R. *energy company executive*
Willis, Judy Ann *lawyer*
Wirta, Raymond E. *real estate company executive*

Elk Grove
Garth-Lewis, Kimberley *state official, public policy educator*
McDavid, Douglas Warren *executive research consultant*
McDonald, William Hector, Jr., *writer*
McIntyre, Mary Maureen *social services consultant*
Moe, Janet Anne *elementary school educator, church organist*
Romano, Sheila June *telecommunications industry executive, artist, writer*
Sparks, Jack Norman *college dean*
Vang, Timothy Teng *religious organization administrator*

Emeryville
Arguedas, Cristina C. *lawyer*
Bax, Simon Tristan *film company executive*
Choi, Doo-Sup *molecular biologist*
Goldstein, Jack *health science executive, microbiologist*
Gombocz, Erich Alfred *biochemist*
Houghton, Michael *geneticist*
Howe, Drayton Ford, Jr., *lawyer*
Hurst, Deborah *pediatric hematologist*
Jobs, Steven Paul *computer company executive*
Loving, Deborah June Pierre *lawyer, real estate broker*
Masri, Merle Sid *biochemist, consultant*
Mather, Ann *film company executive*
McEachern, Alexander *electronics company executive*
Moran, Mark *medical products executive*
Penhoet, Edward *medical association administrator, biochemicals company executive, former dean*
Pien, Howard *pharmaceutical executive*
Reuter, William Charles *historian, educator*
Smith, Christopher Allen *technology company executive, finance professional*
Spadora, Hope Georgeanne *real estate company executive*
Zwoyer, Eugene Milton *retired consulting engineering executive*

Encinitas
Ford, William Francis *retired bank holding company executive*
Frank, Michael Victor *risk assessment engineer*
Litvin, Inessa Elizabeth *piano educator*
Payne, James Richard *environmental chemist*
Rockwell, Elizabeth Goode *dance company director, consultant, educator*
Wigmore, John Grant *lawyer*

Encino
Baker, William Morris *cultural organization administrator*
Conway, Tim *comedian*
Dor, Yoram *accountant*
Franklin, Bonnie Gail *actress*
Friedman, George Jerry *aerospace engineer, engineering executive*
Glickman, Daniel Robert *motion picture executive, former congressman*
Greenberg, Allan *advertising and marketing research consultant*
Hawthorne, Marion Frederick *chemistry professor*
Holman, Harland Eugene *retired motion picture company executive*
House-Hendrick, Karen Sue *nursing consultant*
Ingels, Marty *theatrical agent, television and motion picture production executive*
Knuth, Eldon Luverne *engineering educator*
Laba, Marvin *management consultant*
Lesavoy, Malcolm A. *plastic surgeon, educator*
Lombardini, Carol Ann *lawyer*
Medak, Peter *film director*
Parrott, Dennis Beecher *retired insurance executive*
Phelps, Michael Edward *biophysics educator*
Pryor, Richard *actor, writer*
Rance, Quentin E. *interior designer*
Rawitch, Robert Joe *journalist, educator*
Ribac, Catalino Tagatac *retired accountant*
Saginor, Sidney V. *management consultant*
Seiden, Paul *insurance agent, consultant*
Shire, David Lee *composer*
Smith, Selma Moidel *lawyer, composer*
Taylor, Renee *actress, writer*
Vogel, Susan Carol *nursing administrator*
Westmore, Michael George *make-up artist, writer*
Zsigmond, Vilmos *cinematographer, director*

Escalon
Barton, Gerald Lee *farming company executive*

Escondido
Briggs, Edward Samuel *naval officer*
Damsbo, Ann Marie *psychologist*
de la Torre, Jack Carlos *clinical neuroscientist*
Dotto, Peter Attilius *retired marine corps officer, defense consultant*
Duguid, Iain Moir *education educator*
Ehrhart, Joseph Edward *retired television broadcast engineer*
Ellenberger, William Joseph *retired engineering consultant*
Everton, Marta Ve *retired ophthalmologist*
Friedman, Alan Howard *writer, educator*
Garcia, Luis F. *social worker, photographer*
Gentile, Robert Dale *optometrist, consultant*
Ghandhi, Sorab Khushro *electrical engineering educator*
Godone-Maresca, Lillian *lawyer*
Grew, Raymond Edward *mechanical engineer*
Hannam-Oosterbaan, Maria Gertrude *secondary school educator*

Kelley, George Lorenze *psychologist, consultant*
Kennedy, Robert Philip *civil engineer*
Linzey, Verna May *minister, writer*
Mayer, James Hock *mediator, lawyer*
McCarberg, Bill Harold *physician*
Mogul, Leslie Anne *business development and marketing consultant*
Moore, Marc Anthony *university administrator, writer, retired military officer*
Newman, Barry Ingalls *retired banker, lawyer*
Pantos, William Pantazes *mechanical engineer, consultant*
Sanders, Adrian Lionel *educational consultant*
Tomomatsu, Hideo *chemist*
Young, Gladys *business owner*
Ziegler, James Russell *computer consultant*

Etna
Auxentios, *clergyman*

Eureka
Berg, Patty *state legislator*
Clark, Dwight William *lawyer*

Fair Oaks
Agerbek, Sven *mechanical engineer*
Carrier, Lynne Thomson *journalist*
Chernev, Melvin *retired beverage company executive*
Davidson, Diane (Marie Davidson) *publisher*
Lemke, Herman Ernest Frederick, Jr., *retired elementary education educator, consultant*
Maskall, Martha Josephine *web site designer, publishing executive, health consultant*
Papa, Michael Joseph *real estate broker*
Stewart, William Thomas *communications educator*
Yarrigle, Charlene Sandra Shuey *realtor, investment advisor*

Fairfax
Ross, Sue *entrepreneur, author, fundraising executive*
Urquhart, Karin May *foundation administrator, environmentalist*

Fairfield
Haas, Richard *lawyer*
Martin, Clyde Verne *psychiatrist*
Munn, William Charles, II, *psychiatrist*
Stevenson, James D(onald), Jr., *psychologist, counselor*

Fallbrook
David, Ward S. *bank officer, retired federal agency executive*
Freeman, Harry Lynwood *retired accountant*
Harsha, Philip Thomas *retired aerospace engineer*
Loeber, Thomas Stanton *retired biologist*
Ragland, Jack Whitney *artist*
Sorbello, Joseph Charles *retired lawyer*
Tanner, John Douglas, Jr., *retired history educator, writer*

Felicity
Istel, Jacques Andre *mayor*

Felton
Wughalter, Emily Hope *physical education educator*

Flintridge
Johnston, Oliver Martin, Jr., *animator*

Folsom
Anderson, Jeffrey Lee *physician, anesthesiologist, consultant*
Campbell, Ann Marie *artist*
Ettlich, William F. *electrical engineer*
Ewing, Russell Charles, II, *physician*
Jefferds, William John *military advisor*
Majorkumar, Govindaraju *human factors engineer*
Peck, Ellie Enriquez *retired state administrator*
Peck, Raymond Charles, Sr., *behavior research specialist, consultant*
Regan, William Joseph, Jr., *energy company executive*
Ryu, Woong Hwan *electrical engineer*
Sarraf, Shirley A. *secondary school educator*

Fontana
Johna, Samir *surgeon*
Resch, Charlotte Susanna *plastic surgeon*
Tong, Freda Madeline *writer*

Forestville
Kielsmeier, Catherine Jane *school system administrator*

Foster City
Bischofberger, Norbert W. *medical products company executive*
Butcher, C. Preston *real estate company executive*
Denny, James M. *health care services company executive*
Goldenstein, Lissa A. *biotechnology company executive*
Ham, Lee Edward *civil engineer*
Hotz, Henry Palmer *retired physicist*
Inouye, Michael K. *medical products company executive*
Jeffrey, John Orval *lawyer*
Lonnquist, George Eric *lawyer*
Lutvak, Mark Allen *computer company executive*
Martin, John C. *medical products executive*
McHenry, Julie *communications executive*
Miller, Jon Philip *marketing and business development professional, pharmaceutical executive*
Rudolph, John *construction executive*
Shaheen, George T. *management consultant*
Thomlinson, Ralph *demographer, educator*
Wilson, Lerry *public relations executive*
Zaidi, Iqbal Mehdi *biochemist, scientist*

Fountain Valley
Armstrong, Jeffrey Lee *oceanographer*
Berman, Steven Richard *computer company executive*
Crecelius, Daniel Neil *history professor*
Davis, Jeremy Matthew *chemist*
Einstein, Stephen Jan *rabbi*
Hosokawa, Koichi *engineering company executive*
Kieu, Quynh Dinh *pediatrician, not-for-profit developer*

Melchior, Ib Jorgen *author, television and motion picture writer, director*
Miles, Joanna *actress, playwright, director*
Minnelli, Liza *singer, actress*
Mkhitarian, Marine *chemical engineer*
O'Brien, Edward John *musician, vocalist*
Parks, Robert Myers *appliance manufacturing company executive*
Perth, Rod *network entertainment executive*
Sacre, Antonio *playwright*
Salzman, David Elliot *entertainment industry executive*
Seacrest, Ryan *television and radio personality*
Selway, Phillip James *musician*
Warren, Diane *song writer*
Yorke, Thomas Edward *musician, vocalist*

Hopland
Jones, Milton Bennion *retired agronomist, educator*

Huntington Beach
Agadjanyan, Michael Grant *education educator*
Boardman, Connie *former mayor, biologist, educator*
Burson, Thomas Daniel *retired aerospace company executive*
Cook, Debbie *lawyer, councilman*
Davidson-Shepard, Gay *secondary school educator*
De Massa, Jessie G. *media specialist*
Fajardo, Frederick Joseph *public relations executive*
Flakes, Susan *playwright, screenwriter, director*
Garrels, Sherry Ann *lawyer*
Grooms, Henry Randall *civil engineer*
Hamilton, Allen Philip *financial advisor*
Harman, Thomas *state official*
Jensen, Dennis Lowell *lawyer*
Kovach, Ronald *footwear manufacturing executive*
Lans, Carl Gustav *architect, economist*
Leveton, Ian Sinclair *civil engineer*
Licata, Paul James *health products executive*
Martin, Wilfred Wesley Finny *psychologist, property owner and manager*
Nash, Richard Eugene *aerospace engineer*
Nguyen, Han Van *mechanical engineer*
Nikas, Richard John *lawyer*
Pacino, Frank George *physician, educator*
Pieper, Michael Joseph *freelance/self-employed television producer*
Schaffner-Irvin, Kristen *oil executive*
Shishkoff, Muriel Mendelsohn *education writer*
Stillman, Alfred William, Jr., *electrical engineer*
Welsh, William Daniel *geriatric medicine family practice physician*
Williamson, Edwin Lee *wardrobe and costume consultant*
Winterowd, Walter Ross *English educator*
Yglesias, Kenneth Dale *college president*

Hydesville
Shulman, Adley M. *lawyer, educator*

Idyllwild
Gawecki, Marcia Elizabeth *artist, writer*
Schneider, Paul *writer*

Imperial
Lokey, Frank Marion, Jr., *broadcast executive, consultant*

Imperial Beach
Merkin, William Leslie *retired lawyer*

Indian Wells
Hrabal, Antonin *physician, medical educator*
Jorgensen, Gordon David *retired engineering company executive*
Kelley, John Paul *communications consultant*
McDermott, Thomas John, Jr., *lawyer*
Munyon, William Harry, Jr., *architect*
Trotter, F(rederick) Thomas *retired academic administrator*

Indio
Bailey, Higgins D. *health products executive*
De Salva, Christopher Joseph *lawyer, consultant*
Garra, Raymond Hamilton, II, *marketing executive*
Houghton, Robert Charles *secondary school educator*
Tachovsky, Thomas G. *medical company executive*
York, Douglas Arthur *manufacturing and construction company executive*
Zorick, Nancy Lee *artist, actress*

Inglewood
Buss, Jeanie *professional sports team executive*
Cato, Gloria Maxine *retired secondary education educator, school program administrator*
Dixon, Tamecka *professional basketball player*
Epstein, Marsha Ann *public health administrator, physician*
Horton, Jerome E. *state official*
Patmore, Kimberly S. *financial services executive*
Sludikoff, Stanley Robert *publisher, writer*

Inverness
Welpott, Jack Warren *photographer, educator*

Inyokern
Bass, Nancy Agnes *airport executive*

Irvine
Agran, Larry *mayor, lawyer*
Alcone, Matt *advertising executive*
Allnut, Robert I. *pharmaceutical executive*
Alspach, Philip Halliday *manufacturing executive*
Ang, Alfredo Hua-Sing *civil engineering educator*
Anido, Vincente *biotechnology company executive*
Aswad, Dana William *biochemist, educator*
Ayala, Francisco José *geneticist, educator*
Baab, Carlton *advertising executive*
Bander, Myron *physics educator, university dean*
Bartkus, Richard Anthony *magazine publisher*
Bean, Frank D(awson) *sociology and demography educator*
Beard, Ronald Stratton *lawyer*
Belic Weiss, Zoran *artist, designer, educator*
Black, William Rea *lawyer*
Boyd, Carolyn Patricia *history professor*
Broadhurst, Norman Neil *food products executive*
Burton, Michael Ladd *anthropology educator*
Bystritskii, Vitaly Mikhailovich *physicist, researcher*
Campbell, John B. T., III, *state official*
Chang, Ying Chih *engineering educator, researcher*
Chelapati, Chunduri Venkata *civil engineering educator*
Cho, Zang Hee *physics educator*
Chronley, James Andrew *real estate executive*
Cicerone, Ralph John *academic administrator, geophysicist*
Clark, Bruce Robert *geologist, consultant*
Clark, Karen Heath *lawyer*
Click, James H. *automotive executive*
Copeland, Lawrence R. *construction company executive*
Cortney, Michael C. *construction executive, civil engineer*
Cotman, Carl W. *health science association administrator*
Creatura, Mark Anthony *lawyer*
Crowley, Daniel Francis, Jr., *transportation and logistics executive*
Curtis, Jesse William, Jr., *retired federal judge*
Danziger, James Norris *political science educator*
Davis, Clifton Duncan *actor, composer*
Davis, William W., Sr., *computer company executive*
de la Maza, Luis M. *pathology educator*
Demetrescu, Mihai Constantin *research scientist, educator, computer company executive*
Dzyaloshinskii, Igor Ekhielievich *physicist*
Farrar, Donald Keith *retired financial executive*
Feldstein, Paul Joseph *management educator*
Fleischer, Everly Borah *academic administrator*
Fouste, Donna H. *association executive*
Friedenberg, Richard Myron *radiology educator, physician*
George, Kattunilathu Oommen *physician, educator*
Godfrey, Raymond Michael *information systems educator*
Gupta, Sudhir *immunologist, educator*
Halvorsen, Clay A. *construction executive*
Hine, Robert Van Norden, Jr., *historian, educator*
Hoffman, Donald David *cognitive and computer science educator*
Huang, Taosheng *biomedical researcher, educator, medical geneticist*
Hubert, Judd David *language educator*
Huff, C(larence) Ronald *public policy and criminology educator*
Hurst, Charles Wilson *lawyer*
Jones, Joie Pierce *entrepreneur, acoustician, educator, writer, scientist*
Kaneda, Masayoshi *mathematics educator, researcher*
Kaplan, Arline Ray *editor, writer*
Kim, Han Pyong *dentist, researcher*
Kluger, Ruth *German language educator, editor*
Knobbe, Louis Joseph *lawyer, educator*
Kobsa, Alfred *computer scientist, educator*
Korc, Murray *endocrinologist*
Kraemer, Kenneth Leo *architect, educator, urban planner*
Lathrop, Richard Harold *computer science educator*
Lave, Charles Arthur *economics professor*
Leber, Mike *advertising executive*
Le Bon, Douglas Kent *investment manager*
Lee, Eva *medical educator*
Lenhoff, Howard Maer *biological sciences educator, academic administrator, activist*
Lesonsky, Rieva *editor*
Lightburn, Jeffrey Caldwell *corporate communications executive*
Lillyman, William John *German language educator, academic administrator*
Lin, Amy Yuh-Mei *industrial engineer, real estate investor*
Lorimer, Mark W. *transportation company executive*
Luce, R(obert) Duncan *psychology educator*
Luzko, Daniel *music educator*
Madden, James Cooper, V, *management consultant*
Maradudin, Alexei A. *physics educator*
Margolis, Julius *economist, educator*
McCubbin, Sharon A *elementary school educator*
McDaniel, Thomas R. *utilities executive*
Mc Gaugh, James Lafayette *psychobiologist*
McLaughlin, Calvin Sturgis *biochemistry educator*
McNeil, Robert G. *biotechnology company executive*
Monroe, Kristen Renwick *political scientist, educator*
Mussallem, Michael A. *healthcare company executive*
Mussey, Joseph Arthur *health and medical product executive*
Nalcioglu, Orhan *physics educator, radiological sciences educator*
Nowick, Arthur Stanley *metallurgy and materials science educator*
Oliver, Travis *advertising agency executive*
Olson, Gene L. *food products executive*
Orme, Melissa Emily *mechanical engineering educator*
Overman, Larry Eugene *chemistry educator*
Paine, David M. *public relations executive*
Parnes, Andrew H. *financial executive*
Peltason, Jack Walter *foundation executive, educator*
Phalen, Robert Franklynn *environmental scientist*
Pitcher, Thomas B. *lawyer*
Power, Francis William *newspaper publisher*
Premchand, Arigapudi *retired financial consultant*
Pyott, David Edmund Ian *pharmaceutical executive*
Quilligan, Edward James *obstetrician, gynecologist, educator*
Rachlis, Arnold Israel *rabbi, religion educator*
Reisman, Richard S. *publisher*
Rowland, Frank Sherwood *chemistry professor*
Ruttenberg, Susann I. *health sciences administrator*
Ruyter, Nancy Lee Chalfa *dance educator*
Rynn, Nathan *physics educator, consultant*
Saari, Donald Gene *mathematician, economist*
Samueli, Henry *electrical engineering educator, entrepreneur*
Schonfeld, William Rost *political science educator, researcher*
Seller, Gregory Erol *marketing executive, writer, consultant*
Shen, Ba-Zhong *mathematician, computer scientist*
Shirilau, Mark Steven *utilities executive*
Shrotriya, Rajesh C. *medical company executive*
Shusterman, Neal Douglas *writer, screenwriter*
Simmon, Vincent Fowler *biotechnology executive*
Sirignano, William Alfonso *aerospace and mechanical engineer, educator*
Smith, Harold Raymond *neurologist, sleep medicine specialist, educator*
Smith, Vincent C. *information technology executive*
Specter, Richard Bruce *lawyer*
Sperling, George *cognitive scientist, educator*
Stack, Geoffrey Lawrence *real estate developer*
Stanbridge, Eric John *biology professor*
Stein, M(eyer) L(ewis) *journalist, magazine editor, writer*
Steward, Oswald *neuroscience educator, researcher*
Stubberud, Allen Roger *electrical engineering educator*
Tachner, Leonard *lawyer*
Tetef, Merry Lynn *internist, oncologist*
Ting, Albert Chia *bioengineering researcher*
Ufimtsev, Pyotr Yakovlevich *physicist, electrical engineer, educator*
van-den-Noort, Stanley *neurologist, educator*
Wallis, Richard Fisher *physicist, researcher*
Wan, Frederic Yui-Ming *mathematician, educator*
Weinstein, Gerald D. *dermatology educator*
Werlin, Lawrence B. *obstetrician, gynecologist, reproductive endocrinologist*
Wertheim, Jay Philip *lawyer*
West, Robert Lee, Jr., *marketing professional*
Wetterau, Mark S. *food products/distributor executive*
White, Douglas Richie *anthropology educator*
White, Stephen Halley *biophysicist, educator*
Wilkeson, Kevin M. *architect*
Wintrode, Ralph Charles *lawyer*
Xu, Tao *electrical engineer, biomedical researcher*
Zabsky, John Mitchell *engineering executive*
Zhu, Peter C. *chemist*

Irwindale
Lu, Guiyang *electrical engineer*

Jackson
Halvorson, Frank Elsworth *sales executive*
Halvorson, William *former automotive executive*

Jacumba
Johnson, Crane *writer, lawyer*

Jamul
Harwood, Ivan Richmond *retired pediatric pulmonologist*
Smith, Akili *professional football player*

Janesville
Lathrop, Lawrence Erwin, Jr., *retired business owner, retired state forest ranger*

Kaweah
Foster, Joseph Kevin, IV, *entertainer, scribe*

Keene
Rodriguez, Arturo Salvador *labor union official*

Kelseyville
Fletcher, Leland Vernon *artist*

Kensington
Appelman, Evan Hugh *retired chemist*
Connick, Robert Elwell *retired chemistry educator*
Huddle, Franklin Pierce, Jr., *diplomat*
Littlejohn, David *writer*
Oppenheim, Antoni Kazimierz *mechanical engineer*
Stent, Gunther Siegmund *molecular biologist, educator*

Kentfield
Blum, Joan Kurley *fundraising executive*
Bruyn, Henry Bicker *physician*
Edgar, James Macmillan, Jr., *management consultant*
Halprin, Anna Schuman (Mrs. Lawrence Halprin) *dancer*
Ramirez, Archimedes *neurosurgeon, educator*
Schmid, Rudi (Rudolf Schmid) *internist, educator, academic administrator*

Kenwood
Podboy, John Watts *clinical, forensic psychologist*

King City
Ettinger, Steve Joel *music educator*

Kingsburg
Quaday-Gray, Ailene Diann *retired speech pathology/audiology services professional*

La Canada
Paniccia, Patricia Lynn *journalist, writer, lawyer, educator*
Tookey, Robert Clarence *actuary, consultant*

La Canada Flintridge
Baines, Kevin Hays *planetary scientist, astronomer*
Byrne, George Melvin *physician*
Costello, Francis William *lawyer*
Lamson, Robert Woodrow *retired school system administrator*
Macmillan, Robert Smith *electronics engineer*
Wallace, James Wendell *lawyer*

La Crescenta
Fisk, Irwin Wesley *financial investigator*
Loehwing, Lord Rudi Charles, Jr., *publicist, radio broadcasting executive, journalist*
Otoshi, Tom Yasuo *electrical engineer, consultant*
Purcell, Lee *actress, film producer*
Riccardi, Vincent Michael *pediatrician, researcher, educator, entrepreneur*

La Habra
Ahn, Peter Pyung-choo *dean*
Chase, Cochrane *advertising agency executive*
Oliver, Joyce Anne *journalist, editorial and film consultant, columnist*
Schoppa, Elroy *accountant, financial planner*

La Habra Heights
Agajanian, Gilda *pianist*

La Honda
Henderson, D. Austin *computer scientist*

La Jolla
Alvariño De Leira, Angeles (Angeles Alvariño) *biologist, oceanographer*
Andre, Michael Paul *physicist, educator*
Anthony, Harry Antoniades *city planner, architect, educator*
Antin, David *poet, critic*
Armstrong, Elizabeth Neilson *curator*
Arnold, James Richard *chemist, educator*
Asmus, John Fredrich *physicist*
Atkinson, Richard Chatham *retired academic administrator, educator*
Backus, George Edward *theoretical geophysicist*
Bailey, David Nelson *pathology educator, dean, academic administrator*
Baldridge, Kim *science educator*
Bardwick, Judith Marcia *management consultant*
Barlow, Carrolee *physician, scientist, educator*
Barnett, Faith Hemenway *neurosurgeon, researcher*
Barrett-Connor, Elizabeth Louise *epidemiologist, educator*
Bavasi, Peter Joseph *sports management executive*
Beebe, Mary Livingstone *curator*
Berger, Wolfgang H. *oceanographer, marine geologist*
Beutler, Ernest *physician, research scientist*
Blanchard, Daniel G. *cardiologist*
Blantz, Roland C. *nephrologist, educator*
Block, Melvin August *surgeon, educator*
Bloom, Floyd Elliott *internist, research scientist*
Boger, Dale L. *chemistry professor*
Bourgeois, Suzanne Hélène *retired science educator*
Brooks, Charles Lee, III, *computational biophysicist, educator*
Brown, Stuart I. *ophthalmologist, educator*
Buchholz, Debby *lawyer*
Buchta, Richard Michael *pediatrician*
Buckingham, Michael John *oceanography educator*
Bunch, James Raymond *mathematician, educator*
Burbidge, E. Margaret *astronomer, educator*
Burbidge, Geoffrey *astrophysicist, educator*
Burgin, George Hans *computer scientist, educator*
Butterfield, Alexander Porter *government agency administrator, air transportation executive*
Cain, William Stanley *experimental psychologist, educator, researcher*
Carmichael, David Burton *physician*
Carty, Heidi Marlene *educator, researcher*
Case, Kenneth Myron *physics educator*
Cavenee, Webster K. *director*
Chandler, Marsha *academic administrator, educator*
Chang, William Shen Chie *electrical engineering educator*
Chien, Shu *physiology and bioengineering educator*
Chisari, Francis V. *pathologist*
Chrispeels, Maarten Jan *biology professor*
Coburn, Marjorie Foster *psychologist, educator*
Coler, Myron A(braham) *chemical engineer, educator*
Copley, David C. *newspaper publishing company executive*
Counts, Stanley Thomas *retired naval officer, retired electronics company executive*
Covell, Ruth Marie *medical educator, medical school administrator*
Cowhey, Peter Francis *international relations educator, consultant*
Cox, Charles Shipley *oceanography researcher, educator*
Crawford, Vincent Paul *economist, educator*
Dalessio, Donald John *internist, neurologist, educator*
Davies, Hugh Marlais *museum director*
Degryse, Bernard *cell biologist*
Dixon, Frank James *medical scientist, educator*
Dixon, Jack Edward *biological chemistry educator, consultant*
Dorsey, Dolores Florence *retired corporate treasurer, business executive*
Drake, Hudson Billings *aerospace and electronics company executive*
Driscoll, Charles Frederick *physics educator*
Edelman, Gerald Maurice *biochemist, neuroscientist, educator*
Edgington, Thomas S. *pathologist, educator, molecular biologist, vascular biologist*
Edwards, Charles Cornell *surgeon, research administrator*
Elander, Richard Paul *consultant, retired pharmaceutical executive*
Elgamal, Ahmed *geotechnical and structural engineering educator*
Engvall, Eva *biochemist*
Erie, Steven Philip *political science educator*
Evans, Ronald M. *microbiologist, educator*
Falk, Julia S. *linguist, educator, dean*
Fantino, Edmund *psychology educator*
Farson, Richard Evans *psychologist*
Fisher, Frederick Hendrick *oceanographer emeritus*
Foley, L(ewis) Michael *real estate executive*
Fowler, Raymond Dalton *psychologist, educator*
Foxe, Marye Anne *university chancellor, chemistry educator*
Freedman, David Noel *religious studies educator*
Freedman, Jonathan Borwick *journalist, writer, lecturer, educator*
Friedmann, Theodore *physician*
Fritz, Chris *health facility administrator*
Fung, Yuan-Cheng Bertram *bioengineering educator, writer*
Garland, Cedric Frank *epidemiologist, educator*
Geckler, Richard Delph *metal products company executive, retired*
Geiduschek, E(rnest) Peter *biophysics and molecular biology educator*
Gerber, Michael Lewis *cardiac surgeon*
Gilbert, James Freeman *geophysics educator*
Gill, Gordon N. *medical educator*
Gittes, Ruben Foster *urological surgeon*
Glass, Christopher Kevin *physician*
Graham, Ronald Lewis *mathematician*
Granger, Clive William John *economist, educator*
Grobstein, Ruth H. *health facility administrator*
Guillemin, Roger C. L. *physiologist*
Halkin, Hubert *mathematics educator, research mathematician*
Hall, Harold Robert *retired computer engineer*
Hallin, Daniel Clark *communications educator*
Hamburger, Robert N. *pediatrician, educator, consultant*
Han, Jiahuai *medical researcher*
Harkins, Edwin L. *music educator, performer*
Harris, Philip Robert *management and space psychologist*
Harris, T. George *editor*
Harrison, Larry J. *health facility administrator*
Havis, Allan Stuart *playwright, theatre educator*
Haxo, Francis Theodore *marine biologist*
Helinski, Donald Raymond *biologist, educator*

Hench, Philip Kahler *physician*
Hendler, Sheldon Saul *internist, educator, biochemist, writer*
Henig, Suzanne *retired educator, writer, editor*
Hirsch, Jorge E. *science educator*
Hofmann, Alan Frederick *biomedical researcher, educator*
Holmes, Edward Warren *dean, physician, medical educator*
Horner, Anthony Adam *pediatrician, educator*
Hunter, Tony (Anthony Rex Hunter) *molecular biologist, educator*
Iddings, Kathleen *poet, editor, publisher, consultant*
Imana, Jorge Garron *artist*
Itano, Harvey Akio *biochemistry educator*
Jaffer, Adrian Michael *physician*
Janda, Kim D. *chemist, educator*
Jeub, Michael Leonard *financial consultant*
Jones, Charlie *television sports announcer*
Joris-Quinton, Liesbet *internal medicine physician*
Judd, Lewis Lund *psychiatrist, educator*
Kadonaga, James Takuro *biochemist*
Kaplan, Robert Malcolm *health researcher, educator*
Karin, Sidney *computer science and engineering educator*
Katzman, Robert *neurologist, medical educator*
Keeling, Charles David *oceanography educator*
Kent, Paula *public relations, marketing and management consultant, lecturer*
Kirchheimer, Arthur E(dward) *lawyer, business executive*
Kitada, Shinichi *biochemist*
Knowlton, Nancy *biologist*
Koldner, Richard David *biochemist, educator*
Koob, George *health science association administrator*
Kripke, Daniel Frederick *psychiatrist, educator*
Lal, Devendra *nuclear geophysics educator*
Lane, Sylvia *economist, educator*
Langacker, Ronald Wayne *linguistics educator*
Lauer, James Lothar *physicist, researcher*
Lee, Jerry Carlton *university administrator*
Levy, Ralph *engineering executive, consultant*
Lewin, Ralph Arnold *biologist*
Lewis, Carson McLaughl *retired plastic surgeon*
Lewis, George *music educator*
Lindenberg, Katja *chemistry professor*
Low, Mary Louise (Molly Low) *documentary photographer*
Lowe, Lisa *education educator, department chairman*
Lubarda, Vlado *mechanical engineer, researcher, educator*
Machina, Mark Joseph *economist*
Madsen, Richard Paul *sociology educator, writer*
Malhotra, Vivek *medical educator*
Mandler, George *psychologist, educator*
Mandler, Jean Matter *psychologist, educator*
Martin, James John, Jr., *retired consulting research firm executive, systems analyst*
Masouredis, Serafeim Panagiotis *pathologist, educator*
Masys, Daniel Richard *medical school director*
Mayer, John M. *medical researcher, educator*
McCammon, James Andrew *chemistry professor*
McDonald, Marianne *classicist*
McIlwain, Carl Edwin *physicist*
Mendoza, Stanley Atran *pediatric nephrologist, educator*
Merrim, Louise Meyerowitz *artist, actress*
Miller, David R. *academic administrator*
Milstein, Laurence Bennett *electrical engineering educator, researcher*
Mirsky, Phyllis Simon *librarian*
Miyoshi, Masao *literature educator, writer*
Moossa, A. R. *surgery educator*
Munk, Walter Heinrich *geophysics educator*
Nakamura, Robert Motoharu *pathologist*
Newmark, Leonard Daniel *linguistics educator*
Nicolaou, K. C. *chemistry professor*
North, Kathryn E. Keesey (Mrs. Eugene C. North) *retired secondary school educator*
Olafson, Frederick Arlan *philosophy educator*
Oldstone, Michael Beauregard Alan *immunologist, educator*
O'Neil, Thomas Michael *physicist, researcher*
Oreskes, Naomi *science historian*
Pashler, Harold E. *psychologist, educator*
Pasler, Jann C. *music educator*
Patton, Stuart *biochemist, educator*
Penner, Stanford Solomon *engineering educator*
Petersen, Richard Herman *federal agency administrator, aeronautical engineer*
Pratt, George Janes, Jr., *psychologist, author*
Purdy, Kevin Moore *estate planner*
Rajasekar, Arcot *computer scientist*
Rapaport, Samuel I. *educator, physician*
Rearden, Carole Ann *clinical pathologist, educator*
Rebek, Julius, Jr., *chemistry educator, consultant*
Reynolds, Roger Lee *composer, educator*
Richman, Douglas Daniel *medical virologist, educator, internist*
Ride, Sally Kristen *physics educator, scientist, former astronaut*
Rinaker, Samuel Mayo, Jr., *retired utilities executive*
Ripley, Stuart McKinnon *real estate consultant*
Rosen, Judah Ben *computer scientist*
Rosenblatt, Murray *mathematics professor*
Rosenfeld, Michael G. *medical educator*
Rotenberg, Manuel *physics educator*
Rubin, Lewis J. *physician, researcher*
Rudee, Mervyn Lea *engineering educator, researcher*
Ruoslahti, Erkki *medical research administrator*
Saldivar, Enrique *bioengineer, researcher*
Savoia, Maria Christina *vice dean*
Schmid-Schoenbein, Geert Wilfried Wilfried *biomedical engineer, educator*
Schneider, Benjamin *psychology educator, consultant*
Schneider, Gerald L. *plastic surgeon*
Schroeder, Julian Ivan *biology professor*
Sclater, John George *geophysics educator*
Shabaik, Ahmed *pathologist, educator*
Sham, Lu Jeu *physics educator*
Sharpless, K. Barry *chemist, educator*
Shor, George G., Jr., *geophysicist, oceanographic administrator, engineer*
Shuler, Kurt Egon *chemist, educator*
Singer, Robert *plastic surgeon*
Sinha, Sunil Kumar *physicist*
Smith, Richard Alan *neurologist, medical association administrator*
Sobel, Joel Kenneth *economist*
Somerville, Richard Chapin James *atmospheric scientist, educator*
Sorge, Joseph Anthony *molecular biologist*
Spiegelberg, Hans Leonhard *medical educator*
Spiess, Fred Noel *oceanographer, educator*
Spiro, Melford Elliot *anthropology educator*
Squire, Larry Ryan *neuroscientist, psychologist, educator*
Starr, Ross Marc *economist, educator*
Stefan, Vladislav Alexander *academic administrator, educator, research scientist, writer*
Steinberg, Daniel *preventive medicine physician, educator*
Stevens, Paul Irving *manufacturing executive*
Stone, Donald Diamond *investment and sales executive*
Stone, William Ross *research and development company executive, physicist*
Takabe, Kazuaki *gastroenterology surgeon, research scientist*
Tan, Eng Meng *immunologist, biomedical researcher*
Tarin, David *oncologist, researcher*
Taylor, Palmer W. *pharmacology educator*
Taylor, Susan Serota *biochemistry researcher*
Terras, Audrey Anne *mathematics professor*
Terry, Robert Davis *neuropathologist, educator*
Thal, Leon Joel *neuroscientist*
Thiemens, Mark H. *chemistry professor*
Thomas, Charles Allen, Jr., *molecular biologist, educator*
Tietz, Norbert Wolfgang *clinical chemistry educator, administrator*
Timmermann, Allan Gilling *economics professor*
Todd, Harry Williams *aircraft propulsion system company executive*
Toledo, Franck Marc *geneticist, molecular biologist*
Tsien, Roger Yonchien *chemist, cell biologist*
Tuszynski, Mark H. *neurologist*
Vale, Wylie W. *biochemist*
Van Lint, Victor Anton Jacobus *physicist*
Verma, Inder M. *biochemist*
Vogt, Peter K. *oncologist*
Waddy, Lawrence Heber *religious writer*
Walker, Richard Hugh *orthopaedic surgeon*
Watson, Kenneth Marshall *physics educator*
Weiner, Ferne *psychologist*
West, John Burnard *physiologist, educator*
Whitaker, Eileen Monaghan (Eileen Monaghan) *artist*
White, Michelle Jo *economics professor*
Wilkie, Donald Walter *retired biologist, aquarium museum director*
Wilkins, Floyd, Jr., *retired lawyer, consultant*
Williams, Forman Arthur *engineering science educator, combustion theorist*
Wilson, Bonnie Jean *lawyer, educator, investor*
Wilson, Ian Andrew *molecular biology educator*
Wolf, Jack Keil *electrical engineer, educator*
Wolynes, Peter Guy *chemistry researcher, educator*
Wong-Staal, Flossie *geneticist, medical educator*
Wright, Andrew *English literature educator*
Wulbert, Daniel Eliot *mathematician, educator*
Yaksh, Tony L. *pharmacologist, educator, health facility administrator*
Yen, Samuel S(how)-C(hih) *obstetrics and gynecology educator, reproductive endocrinologist*
York, Herbert Frank *physics educator, government official*
Yuki, Goda *science educator*
ZoBell, Karl *lawyer*
Zyroff, Ellen Slotoroff *information scientist, classicist, educator*

La Mesa
Behrend, Albert James *surgeon*
Boghairi, Anoushiravan *cardiologist*
Browne, Juanita Maria *academic administrator, social sciences educator*
Freeland, Robert Frederick *retired librarian*
Hansen, Grant Lewis *retired aerospace and information systems executive*
La Suer, Jay *state official*
Mitry, Darryl Joseph *writer, educator*
Schmidt, James Craig *retired bank executive, savings and loan association executive*
Trujillo, Solomon D. *telecommunications executive*

La Mirada
Krotinger, Sheila M. *secondary school educator*
Lock, William Rowland *director, educator, conductor*
Pennoyer, F. Douglas *dean*
Salinger, Charles *dermatologist*

La Palma
Knowles, Marie L. *transportation executive*
Thelander, Beverly *oil company executive*

La Puente
Hitchcock, Frederick E. "Fritz", Jr., *automotive company executive*

La Quinta
Adolph, Diane Joyce *retired underwriter*
Calvin, James Willard *thoracic and vascular surgeon*
Farber, Patricia Ann *secondary school educator*
Gassman, Andrea C. *journalist, artist*
Mathre, Lawrence Gerhard *minister, federal agency administrator*
Peden, Lynn Ellen *marketing executive*
Pitkin, Roy Macbeth *retired obstetrician, educator*
Tebbs, Carol Ann *secondary school educator, academic administrator*

La Verne
Fleck, Raymond Anthony, Jr., *retired university administrator*
Hwang, Cordelia Jong *chemist*
Jones, Jay H. *biology and biochemistry educator*
Marcus, Kenneth Hearne *historian, educator*
McDonough-Treichler, Judith Dianne *medical educator, consultant*
Morgan, Stephen Charles *academic administrator*
Neher, Robert Trostle *biology professor*

LaPuente
Rojo De Santos, Anita *shop owner, writer*

Lafayette
Cobb, George Edward *surgeon*
Davies, Paul Lewis, Jr., *retired lawyer*
Dethero, J. Hambright *banker*
Krueger, Robert Edward *manufacturing executive, mechanical engineer*
Lewis, Sheldon Noah *technology consultant*
Monheit, Molly Jane *artist*
Morehouse, Valerie Jeanne *librarian*
Peirano, Lawrence Edward *civil engineer*
Shurtleff, Akiko Aoyagi *artist, consultant*

Laguna Beach
Arnold, John David *management counselor, catalyst*
Benford, Gregory Albert *physicist, writer*
Bent, Alan Edward *political science educator, administrator*
Castro, Charles Edward *chemist, consultant*
Dale, Leon Andrew *economist, educator*
Englund, Robert *actor, director, producer*
Forry, Steven *not-for-profit fundraiser*
Frenzel, Frances Johnson *registered nurse, educator, lecturer, poet, real estate broker*
Fry, Edward Bernard *education educator, retired*
Ghiselin, Brewster *author, English language educator emeritus*
Hanauer, Joe Franklin *real estate executive*
Martinez, Vera *academic administrator*
Powers, Runa Skötte *artist*
Richard, Robert Max *cardiologist*
Taylor, James Walter *business and management educator*
Taylor, Theodore Langhans *author*
Wong, Wallace *medical supplies company executive, real estate investor*

Laguna Hills
Hammond, R. Philip *chemical engineer*
Ierardi, Stephen John *physician*
Miller, Eldon Earl *corporate business publications consultant, retired manufacturing company executive*
Reinglass, Michelle Annette *lawyer*
Rossiter, Bryant William *chemistry consultant*
Wheatley, Melvin Ernest, Jr., *retired bishop*
Widyolar, Sheila Gayle *dermatologist*

Laguna Niguel
Axon, Donald Carlton *architect*
Bates, Patricia C. *state official*
Bauer, Barbara A. *financial consultant*
Carr, Bernard Francis *hospital administrator*
Cifarelli, Thomas Abitabile *lawyer*
Eber, Lorenz *aeronautical engineer, civil engineer*
Freeland, Darryl Creighton *psychologist, educator*
Greenberg, Lenore *public relations professional*
Ricci, Robert Ronald *manufacturing executive*
Smith, Leslie Roper *hospital administrator, health facility administrator*
Teitelbaum, Harry *English educator*
Teitelbaum, Marilyn Leah *retired special education educator*
York, James Orison *real estate executive*

Laguna Woods
Badgley, John Roy *architect*
Berk, Jack Edward *gastroenterologist, educator*
Hussey, William Bertrand *retired foreign service officer*
Leonard, Elizabeth Adney *social worker*
McClure, Hal H. *film producer*
Waaland, Irving Theodore *retired aerospace design executive*

Lagunitas
Holman, Arthur Stearns *artist*

Lake Arrowhead
Beckman, James Wallace Bim *economist, marketing professional, educator*
Fitzgerald, John Charles, Jr., *investment banker*

Lake Elsinore
Corral, Jeanie Beleyn *journalist, school board administrator*
Young, Patricia Janean *speech pathology/audiology services professional*

Lake Forest
Blackley, Daniel John *theater educator, theater director*
Boccia, Judy Elaine Stacy *home health agency executive, consultant*
Earhart, Donald Marion *management consultant, health care company executive*
Haggerty, Charles A. *retired electronics executive*
Hopp, Terry A. *computer company executive*
Kabilamany, Caleb K. *religious studies educator, civil engineer, consultant*
Massengill, Matthew H. *retail company executive*
Milligan, Steve *retail executive*
Shakeel, Arif *retail executive*
Smith, William Hugh, Sr., *retired audit manager, consultant*

Lake View Terrace
Coolidge, Martha *film director*
Mann, Alfred *pharmaceutical executive*
McCraven, Eva Stewart Mapes *health service administrator*

Lakewood
Carr, Firpo Wycoff *bible scholar, educator, writer*
Woodson-Glenn, Yolanda *social worker*

Lancaster
Bell, Gary Lynn *owner production company, video and audio producer*
Ellsworth, Richard German *psychologist*
Emch, Brian Kelly *photographer*
Fluckey, Allison Evans *psychology professor*
Hodges, Vernon Wray *mechanical engineer*
Kiersch, George Alfred *geological consultant, retired educator*
Kottraba, Carin *psychologist*
Mellor, Karen Susann *entomologist*
Walsh, Patricia Maack *special education educator*

Landers
Dougherty, Raleigh Gordon *manufacturer representative*
Landers, Vernette Trosper *writer, educator, association executive*

Larkspur
Amico, Charles William *management consultant*
Aster, Richard (Rick) F., Jr., *diversified financial services company executive*
Dellar, Michael D. *restaurant owner, hospitality industry consultant*
Greenberg, Myron Silver *lawyer*
Napoles, Veronica *graphic designer, consultant*
Ogden, Bradley M. *chef, restaurateur*
Price, Tom *automotive sales executive*
Ratner, David Louis *retired law educator*
Saxe, Steven Louis *lawyer*
Saxton, Lloyd *psychologist, writer*

Lawndale
Matsushima, Teresa Takaki *school nurse practitioner*

Lincoln
Chong, Vernon *retired surgeon, retired military officer*
Dorn, Mary Ann *retired auditor*
Helzer, James Dennis *retired health facility administrator*

Littleriver
Van Dyck, Wendy *dancer*

Littlerock
Haas, Sir Russell (Duke of Elbasan) *ambassador*

Livermore
Alder, Berni Julian *physicist, researcher*
Anastasio, Michael R. *science foundation director*
Beller, Harry R. *microbiologist, chemist, researcher*
Brown, Cathie *city official*
Darter, Thomas Eugene, Jr., *composer, musician, writer*
Fodor, Imola Katalin *mathematician, researcher*
Glenzer, Siegfried Heinz *physicist, educator, researcher*
Haga, Enoch John *computer educator, author*
Hiskes, Dolores G. *language educator*
Holzrichter, John F. *physicist*
Hooper, Edwin Bickford *physicist*
Johnson, Roy Ragnar *electrical engineer, researcher*
Kidder, Ray Edward *physicist, consultant*
King, Ray John *electrical engineer, educator, business executive*
Kirkwood, Robert Keith *applied physicist*
Kumar, Mukul *research scientist*
Lambert, Michael Allen *physicist*
Lassila, David H. *materials scientist, researcher*
Leith, Cecil Eldon, Jr., *retired physicist*
Love, Sandra Rae *information specialist*
Max, Claire Ellen *physicist*
Mirkarimi, Paul B. *materials scientist, researcher*
Nuckolls, John Hopkins *physicist, researcher*
Santer, Benjamin *atmospheric scientist, meteorologist*
Schock, Robert Norman *geophysicist*
Seward, James Pickett *internist, educator*
Spiller, Eberhard Adolf *physicist, researcher*
Tarter, Curtis Bruce *physicist, science administrator*
Tripodes, James G. *nuclear safety and environmental regulatory affairs professional*
Weber, Stephen Vance *physics researcher, astrophysicist*
Weyhenmeyer, Constanze Elisabeth *environmental scientist, researcher*
Yoh, Jack Jai-ick *mechanical engineer*

Livingston
Carter, Paul *food products executive*
Foster, Ron *agricultural products supplier, agricultural products executive*
Fox, Robert August *food company executive*

Lodi
Bishop-Graham, Barbara *secondary school educator, journalist*
Elkins, Carl *food products executive*
Reinold, Christy Diane *school counselor, consultant*

Loma Linda
Bailey, Leonard Lee *surgeon*
Behrens, Berel Lyn *physician, academic and healthcare administrator*
Betancourt, Hector Mainhard *psychology scientist, educator*
Bleidt, Barry Anthony *pharmacy educator*
Boyne, Philip J. *dental association administrator, oral surgeon*
Briggs, Burton A. *medical educator*
Bull, Brian Stanley *pathology educator, medical consultant, business executive*
Bullock, Weldon Kimball *health facility administrator, pathologist, pathology educator*
Bunnell, William Paul *orthopaedic surgery educator*
Chan, Philip J. *medical educator*
Coggin, Charlotte Joan *cardiologist, educator*
Condon, Stanley Charles *gastroenterologist*
Dayes, Lloyd Albert *neurosurgeon, minister*
Edwards, Lincoln Paul *pharmacologist, educator*
Fechter, Laurence David *toxicology educator, researcher*
Feller, Ralph Paul *dentist, educator*
Fodor, Istvan *molecular biologist, researcher*
Goodacre, Charles J. *academic administrator*
Hardesty, Robert Alan *plastic surgeon*
Hinshaw, David B., Jr., *radiologist*
King, Helen Emori *dean*
Kirk, Gerald Arthur *nuclear radiologist*
Klooster, Judson *academic administrator, dentistry educator*
Lewis, Victor Wayne, I, *minister*
Llaurado, Josep G. *nuclear medicine physician, scientist*
Longo, Lawrence Daniel *physiologist, educator, obstetrician, gynecologist*
Mace, John Weldon *pediatrician*
Pendergraft, Janice Gayle *volunteer*
Reeve, Ivan Leon *physician*
Rendell-Baker, Leslie *anesthesiologist, educator*
Roberts, Walter Herbert Beatty *anatomist, educator*
Schwab, Ernest Roe, III *physiology educator, researcher*
Slater, James Munro *radiation oncologist*
Slattery, Charles Wilbur *biochemistry educator*
Smith, Aida Marissa *medical reference librarian*
Stilson, Walter Leslie *radiologist, educator*
Strother, Allen *biochemical pharmacologist, researcher*
Taylor, Barry Llewellyn *microbiologist, educator*
Wareham, Ellsworth Edwin *cardiothoracic surgeon, educator*

Young, Lionel Wesley *radiologist*

Lomita
Balcom, Orville *engineer*

Lompoc
Bongiorno, James William *electronics company executive*
Keller, Janice N. *lawyer, councilwoman*
Means, James Andrew *engineer*
Wagner, Geraldine Marie *nursing educator, consultant*

Long Beach
Adler, Jeffrey D. *political consultant, public affairs consultant, crisis management expert*
Aldrich, David Lawrence *public relations executive*
Bauer, Roger Duane *chemistry educator, science consultant*
Beebe, Sandra E. *retired English language educator, artist, writer*
Berenato, Joseph C. *manufacturing executive*
Binkiewicz, Donna *historian, educator*
Bond, Frances Curtis *retired editor*
Brown, Lester B. *social worker, educator*
Brown, Roxanne (Jerene Roxanne Brown) *sales executive*
Bursley, Kathleen A. *lawyer*
Calhoun, John R. *lawyer*
Collins, Aristide J., Jr., *academic administrator*
Cook, Karla Joan *elementary school educator*
Cotner, Douglas Monroe *provost, mathematics and environmental science educator*
Culton, Paul Melvin *retired counselor, educator, interpreter*
Davies, Grace Lucille *real estate educator*
Davis, Mark Hezekiah, Jr., *electrical engineer*
Deukmejian, George *lawyer, former governor*
Dillon, Michael Earl *engineering executive, mechanical engineer, educator*
Engle, Robert Irwin *music educator, musician, composer, writer, translator*
Fagan, Frederic *neurosurgeon*
Ferreri, Michael Victor *optometrist*
Fiebert, Martin Stephen *psychology educator, psychologist*
Fischler, Sandy Lynn *event producer*
Fleming, Jane Williams *retired educator, writer*
Friis, Robert Harold *epidemiologist, health science educator*
Fuller, Jack Arthur *lawyer*
Glenn, Constance White *art museum director, educator, consultant*
Haile, Lawrence Barclay *lawyer*
Halili, Antonio Marquez *facilities maintenance mechanic*
Hancock, John Walker, III, *banker*
Heiser, James S. *manufacturing executive*
Helwick, Christine *lawyer*
Hennen, Thomas Waldo *lawyer*
Hershberger, Scott Laurence *psychologist, educator, statistician, researcher*
Higginson, John *retired career officer*
Hu, Chi Yu *physicist, educator*
Karentte, Betty *state legislator*
Karnette, Betty *state senator*
Keller, J(ames) Wesley *credit union executive*
Kumar, Rajendra *electrical engineering educator*
Kwaan, Jack Hau Ming *retired physician*
Lathrop, Irvin Tunis *retired academic dean, educator*
Lauda, Donald Paul *dean*
Lee, Isaiah Chong-Pie *social worker, educator*
Lodwick, Michael Wayne *lawyer*
Loganbill, G. Bruce *logopedic pathologist*
Lowenthal, Alan *state official*
Lowentrout, Peter Murray *religious studies educator*
MacDonald, Patricia Geneve *theater director*
Macer, George Armen, Jr., *orthopedic hand surgeon*
Marks, Melvin I. *physician, educator, hospital administrator, consultant*
Maxson, Robert C. *university president*
McDonough, Patrick Dennis *academic administrator*
McGaughey, Charles Gilbert *retired research biochemist*
Mezyk, Stephen *chemist, educator*
Mills, Don Harper *pathology and psychiatry educator, lawyer*
Molina, Joseph Mario *medical administrator*
Moroso, Michael Joseph *aerospace engineer*
Mullins, Ruth Gladys *nurse*
Myers, John Wescott *aviation executive*
Nageotte, Michael Patrick *obstetrician*
Nelson, Harold Bernhard *museum director*
Nguyen, Huong Tran *English language professional, federal agency official*
O'Neill, Beverly Lewis *mayor, former college president*
Perkowitz, Simon (Sy) *architect, architectural firm executive*
Pineda, Anselmo *neurosurgery educator*
Pizzo, Pia *artist, educator*
Proust, Joycelyn Ann *retired librarian*
Pullman, Alan *architect*
Reed, Charles Bass *chief academic administrator*
Reichard, Gary Warren *university administrator, history educator*
Rosenberg, Jill *realtor, civic leader*
Ruszkiewicz, Carolyn Mae *newspaper editor*
Rutherford, Vicky Lynn *special education educator*
Sato, Eunice Noda *former mayor, consultant*
Schroeder, Arnold Leon *mathematics professor*
Schubel, Jerry Robert *marine science educator, scientist, university dean*
Sinclitico, Dennis J. *lawyer*
Singhal, Meena *education educator*
Sosoka, John Richard *consulting firm executive, engineer*
Stemmer, Edward Alan *surgeon, educator*
Stevens, Mark *publishing executive*
Strafaci, Samuel Anthony *academic administrator, consultant*
Strait, Viola Edwina Washington *librarian*
Tai, Kwok-Keung *biologist, researcher*
Tang, Paul Chi Lung *philosophy educator*
Tucker, Marcus Othello *judge*
Viola, Bill *artist, writer*
Welch, Ronnie Scott *health facility administrator*
Wells, James H. *plastic surgeon*
Wise, George Edward *lawyer*
Wollmer, Richard Dietrich *statistics and operations research educator*
Worcester, Howard Lester *internist*
Writer, Sharon Lisle *secondary school educator*
Wyse, Matthew F. *small business owner*
Young, Robert Edward *computer company executive*
Yousef, Fathi Salaama *communication studies educator, management consultant*

Los Alamitos
Aberman, Harold Mark *veterinarian*
Booth, John Nicholls *minister, writer, photographer*
Dunne, Donald Redmond *military officer*
Eckelman, Richard Joel *engineering specialist*
Nemirow, Lawrence H. *lawyer*
Spiegel, Marilyn Harriet *real estate executive*
Weinberger, Frank *information management consultant*

Los Altos
Abrams, Arthur Jay *physician*
Beer, Clara Louise Johnson *retired electronics executive*
Carlson, Warren Ore *civil engineer, consultant*
Carsten, Jack Craig *venture capitalist*
Collins, Gordon Dent *recording company executive*
Farber, Geraldine Ossman *civic worker*
Fong, Bernadine Chuck *academic administrator*
Fraknoi, Andrew *astronomy educator, astronomical society executive*
Gough, William Cabot *engineer*
Hahn, Harold Thomas *physical chemist, chemical engineer*
King, Chi-Yu *research scientist*
Martin, Leonardo S.J. *retired urologist, surgeon*
Moll, John Lewis *retired electronics engineer*
Nivison, David Shepherd *Chinese and philosophy educator*
Orman, Nanette Hector *psychiatrist*
Orr, Susan Packard *business owner*
Peterson, Victor Lowell *aerospace engineer, consultant*
Sharpe, Roland Leonard *structural engineer, consultant*
Sherwood, Patricia Waring *artist, educator*
Spangler, Dorothy Benita *artist*
Weir, Robert H. *lawyer*
Wilbur, Colburn Sloan *foundation consultant and trustee, former executive*
Yu, Oliver Shukiang *corporate executive, educator, technology strategist*
Zebroski, Edwin Leopold *risk management consultant*

Los Altos Hills
Fondahl, John Walker *civil engineering educator*
Robbins, Doren Gurstein *poet, educator, artist*
Wheeler, Frank Knowles Blasdell *retired military officer, business consultant*

Los Angeles
Aaron, Benjamin *law educator, arbitrator*
Abdul, Paula (Julie) *singer, dancer, choreographer*
Abrams, Norman *law educator, academic administrator*
Abramson, Leslie Hope *lawyer*
Adamek, Charles Andrew *lawyer*
Adams, Thomas Merritt *lawyer*
Adamson, Arthur Wilson *chemistry educator*
Adell, Hirsch *lawyer*
Ades, Leslie J. *entrepreneur, educator, writer*
Adler, Erwin Ellery *lawyer*
Adler, Fred Peter *retired electronics company executive*
Adler, Sara *arbitrator, mediator*
Agarwal, Sanjay Kumar *physician*
Agnew, John A. *education educator*
Alarcon, Arthur Lawrence *federal judge*
Alexander, Kenneth Sidney *mathematician, educator*
Alkalay, Arie L. *pediatrician, neonatologist*
Alkon, Ellen Skillen *physician*
Alkon, Paul Kent *English language educator*
Allen, Michael John Bridgman *English educator*
Allen, Sharon *accounting firm executive*
Allen, Suzanne *financial planning executive, insurance agent, writer*
Allen, William Richard *retired economist*
Allison, Jason *professional hockey player*
Allison, Laird Burl *business educator*
Allred, Gloria Rachel *lawyer*
Alpers, Edward Alter *history professor*
Alvarez, Rodolfo *sociology educator, consultant*
Amkraut, David M.h. *lawyer, judge*
Anawalt, Patricia Rieff *anthropologist, researcher*
Andersen, Ronald Max *health services educator, researcher*
Anderson, Charles David *lawyer*
Anderson, Herbert W. *consumer products company executive*
Anderson, John Edward *diversified holding company executive, lawyer*
Anderson, W. French *biochemist, physician*
Angel, Arthur Ronald *lawyer, consultant*
Angelo, Christopher Edmond *lawyer, consultant*
Angeloff, Dann Valentino *investment banking executive*
Ansell, Benjamin Jesse *physician*
Antin, Michael *lawyer*
Antonovich, Michael Dennis *county official*
Apfel, Gary *lawyer*
Apple, Jacki (Jacqueline B. Apple) *artist, writer, educator*
April, Rand Scott *lawyer*
Apt, Charles *artist*
Apt, Leonard *physician*
Apuzzo, Michael Lawrence John *neurological surgeon*
Arkoz, David X. *lawyer*
Armstrong, Lloyd, Jr., *university official, physics educator*
Armstrong, Orville *judge*
Arnkra, Joe *legal administrator, writer*
Arnold, Dennis B. *lawyer*
Aronowitz, Joel Alan *plastic and reconstructive surgeon*
Arzube, Juan Alfredo *bishop*
Ash, Lawrence Robert *public health educator, administrator*
Ash, Roy Lawrence *business executive*
Ashley, Sharon Anita *pediatric anesthesiologist*
Ashwell, Rachel *entrepreneur, interior designer*
Askin, Richard Henry, Jr., *entertainment company executive*
Astin, Alexander William *education educator*
Atchley, Raymond Deval *technology company executive*
Avedon, Loren Rains *actor*
Azad, Susan S. *lawyer*
Baca, Judith F. *art educator*
Badie, Ronald Peter *banker*
Bahr, Ehrhard *Germanic languages and literature educator*
Bain, Conrad Stafford *actor*
Baird, Lourdes G. *federal judge*
Bakaly, Charles George, Jr., *lawyer, mediator*
Bakeman, Carol Ann *travel manager, singer*
Baker, Robert Frank *molecular biologist, educator*
Ballard, Glen *composer*
Ballhaus, William Francis, Jr., *aerospace industry executive, research scientist*
Baquet, Dean Paul *newspaper editor*
Barberie, Jillian *newscaster, meteorologist*
Barker, Robert William (Bob Barker) *television personality*
Barker, Wiley Franklin *surgeon, educator*
Barnett, Marilyn *advertising agency executive*
Baron, Melvin Farrell *pharmacy educator*
Barren de Serres, Bruce Willard (H.R.H. The Duke Bruce Willard Barren de Serres) *merchant banker*
Barrett, Cynthia Townsend *neonatologist*
Barrett, Jane Hayes *lawyer*
Barron, Stephanie *curator*
Barsky, Wayne Mitchell *lawyer*
Barsugli, Jesse Benjamin *lab administrator*
Bart, Peter Benton *newspaper editor, film producer, novelist*
Bartchy, S(tuart) Scott *history educator, researcher*
Barton, Alan Joel *lawyer*
Basil, Douglas Constantine *writer, educator*
Bates, Marcia Jeanne *information scientist educator*
Baum, Michael Lin *lawyer*
Baumann, Richard Gordon *lawyer*
Baumgarten, Ronald Neal *lawyer*
Beart, Robert W., Jr., *colon and rectal surgeon, educator*
Becker, Donald Paul *surgeon, neurosurgeon*
Begley, Ed, Jr., *actor*
Bekey, George Albert *computer scientist, educator, engineer*
Bell, Lee Phillip *television personality, television producer*
Benatar, Pat (Pat Andrzejewski) *rock singer*
Bender, Charles William *lawyer*
Bender, Dean *public relations executive*
Bendix, Helen Irene *lawyer*
Benedict, Cheyann *apparel designer*
Bennett, Charles Franklin, Jr., *biogeographer, educator*
Bennett, Fred Gilbert *lawyer*
Bennis, Warren Gameliel *business administration educator*
Benson, Sidney William *chemistry researcher*
Berek, Jonathan Samuel *surgeon, cancer researcher, gynecologist, writer*
Berenbaum, Michael Gary *theology educator*
Bergman, Emily Anne *librarian*
Bergman, Marilyn Keith *lyricist, writer*
Berman, Gail *broadcast executive*
Berman, Geoffrey Louis *management company executive*
Berman, Jennifer R. *urologist*
Berman, Richard Keith *television producer, film producer*
Bernacchi, Richard Lloyd *lawyer*
Bernstein, Leslie *academic administrator, biostatistician*
Bernstein, Sol *cardiologist, educator*
Bernstein, William *film company executive*
Berry, Nancy *recording industry executive*
Berry, Stephen Joseph *reporter*
Bessman, Samuel Paul *pediatrician, biochemist*
Bharitkar, Sunil Ganpat *research scientist, technology specialist*
Bhaumik, Mani Lal *physicist*
Bhidayasiri, Roongroj *neurologist, researcher*
Bianchi, Carisa *advertising company executive*
Bice, Scott Haas *dean, lawyer, educator*
Biel, Jessica *actress, model*
Biggs, Jason *actor*
Biles, John Alexander *pharmacology educator, chemistry educator*
Billig, Franklin Anthony *chemist*
Binder, Gordon M. *venture capitalist*
Birren, James Emmett *university research center executive*
Bishop, Sidney Willard *lawyer*
Black, Donna Ruth *lawyer*
Black, Lisa Hartman *actress, singer*
Black, Sandra Eilene *economist, educator*
Blahd, William Henry *physician, nuclear medicine physician*
Blencowe, Paul Sherwood *lawyer, private investor*
Blendell, Elizabeth A. *lawyer*
Bloch, Paul *public relations executive*
Bloom, Claire *actress*
Blumberg, Grace Ganz *law educator, lawyer*
Bobrow, Michael Lawrence *architect*
Bodey, Bela *immunologist, pathologist, oncologist*
Bodkin, Henry Grattan, Jr., *lawyer*
Boehm, Barry William *computer science educator*
Bohle, Sue *public relations executive*
Boime, Albert Isaac *art history educator*
Bok, Dean *cell biologist, educator*
Boles, Richard Gregory *clinical geneticist, researcher*
Bomes, Stephen D. *lawyer*
Bondareff, William *psychiatry educator*
Bonesteel, Michael John *lawyer*
Boras, Kim *lawyer*
Borda, Deborah *symphony orchestra executive*
Bordy, Michael Jeffrey *lawyer*
Borenstein, Daniel Bernard *psychiatrist, educator*
Borsting, Jack Raymond *business administration educator*
Bortman, David *lawyer*
Bosl, Phillip L. *lawyer*
Boswell, James Douglas *medical research executive*
Bottjer, David John *earth scientist, biologist, educator*
Bouju, Jean-Marc *photojournalist*
Boxer, Lester *lawyer*
Boyd, Malcolm *minister, writer*
Boyer, Paul D. *biochemist, educator*
Boyle, Barbara Dorman *motion picture company executive*
Boyle, Danny *film director*
Brackmann, Derald E. *otolaryngologist*
Bradley, Lawrence D., Jr., *lawyer*
Bradshaw, Murray Charles *musicologist, educator*
Braginsky, Stanislav Iosifovich *physicist, geophysicist, researcher*
Branca, John Gregory *lawyer, consultant*
Brand, Elton *professional basketball player*
Bratton, William J. *police chief, former police commissioner*
Braudrick, Arthur C., Jr., *lawyer*
Brault, Lisa J. *prosecutor*
Braun, David A(dlai) *lawyer*
Braunstein, Glenn David *physician, educator*
Bremond, Duane Benjamin *marketing professional*
Breslow, Lester *preventive medicine physician, educator*
Bressan, Paul Louis *lawyer*
Breuer, Stephen Ernest *religious organization administrator*
Brian, Brad D. *lawyer*
Bringardner, John Michael *lawyer, clergyman*
Brittenham, Skip *lawyer*
Broad, Eli *financial services executive*
Brodwin, Martin George *counselor, educator*
Brolin, James (James Brunderlin) *actor*
Brown, Carol *make-up artist*
Brown, James Kevin *professional baseball player*
Brown, Kathleen *bank executive, lawyer*
Brubaker, William Rogers *sociology educator*
Bruce, William A. *airport executive*
Bryan, Karen Smith *lawyer*
Brynes, Russell Kermit *pathologist, educator*
Buchman, Mark Edward *banker*
Buchwald, Nathaniel Avrom *neurophysiologist*
Buffington, Gary Lee Roy *safety engineer, construction executive*
Bufford, Samuel Lawrence *federal judge*
Burch, Robert Dale *lawyer*
Burghdorf, Roger *business executive*
Burke, Robert Bertram *lawyer, political consultant, lobbyist*
Burke, Yvonne Watson Brathwaite (Mrs. William A. Burke) *lawyer*
Burkle, Ronald W. *former food service executive, business investor*
Burns, Robert Ignatius *historian, educator, clergyman*
Burrows, James *television and motion picture director, producer*
Burton, Tim *film director*
Bush, Wes *science administrator*
Butler, Brett *comedienne, actress*
Buzzi, Ruth *comedienne*
Byrd, Christine Waterman Swent *lawyer*
Byrnes, James Bernard *museum director, consultant*
Caine, Michael *actor*
Caldwell, Alethea Otti *health care systems executive*
Calman, Craig David *writer, actor, director*
Campbell, Jennifer Louise *lawyer*
Campion, Robert Thomas *manufacturing executive*
Campo, Todd Russell *principal, law enforcement educator*
Camron, Roxanne *retired magazine editor, consultant*
Cannon, Dyan *actress*
Caprioli, Joseph *ophthalmologist*
Caram, Eve La Salle *English educator, writer*
Carlin, George Denis *comedian, actor*
Carlson, Robert Edwin *lawyer*
Carnesale, Albert *academic administrator*
Caroompas, Carole Jean *artist, educator*
Carothers, A.J. *scriptwriter*
Carr, James Patrick *lawyer*
Carr, Willard Zeller, Jr., *lawyer*
Carrey, Neil *lawyer, educator*
Carroll, Ellen A. *judge, lawyer*
Carroll, John Sawyer *newspaper editor*
Carroll, Pete *college football coach*
Carroll, Raoul Lord *lawyer, investment banker*
Carter, Emily Ann *physical chemist, researcher, educator*
Cartwright, Brian Grant *lawyer*
Caskie, William Wirt *accountant, securities broker*
Cassavetes, Nick *film director, actor*
Castro, Leonard Edward *lawyer*
Catanzarite, David M. *theater educator, director*
Cates, Gilbert *film, theater, television producer and director*
Cecere, Domenico *homebuilding company executive*
Cedillo, Gilbert A. *state senator*
Cerrell, Joseph Robert *political scientist, public relations consultant*
Chambers, Mortimer Hardin, Jr., *retired history educator*
Champagne, Duane Willard *sociology educator*
Champlin, Charles Davenport *television host, book critic, writer*
Chan, David Ronald *tax specialist, lawyer*
Chandor, Stebbins Bryant *pathologist*
Chang, Edward H. *computer company executive*
Chang, Henry C. *library administrator*
Chapman, Carolyn *broadcasting director*
Chapman, Rosalyn M. *federal judge*
Chapman Collins, Janice *elementary school educator, supervisor, educational consultant*
Charles, Ray *musician, composer, lyricist, arranger, conductor*
Chavez, Victor Edwin *judge*
Chazen, Stephen I. *oil company executive*
Chedid, John G. *retired bishop*
Cheeseboro, Margrit *economics educator*
Chemerinsky, Erwin *law educator*
Chen, Francis F. *physics and engineering educator*
Chen, Irvin Shao Yu *microbiologist, educator*
Chen, Peter Wei-Teh *mental health services administrator*
Chen, William *surgeon*
Cheng, Tsen-Chung *electrical engineering educator*
Chernin, Peter *motion picture company executive*
Cherry, James Donald *pediatrician*
Chiate, Kenneth Reed *lawyer*
Chick, Laura *councilwoman*
Chiklis, Michael *actor*
Cho, Margaret *comedienne, actress*
Chobotov, Vladimir Alexander *aerospace engineer, educator*
Chopra, Inder Jit *physician, endocrinologist*
Christ, Roxanne E. *lawyer*
Christol, Carl Q(uimby) *lawyer, political science educator*
Christophe, Caloz *research scientist*
Chu, Morgan *lawyer*
Chui, Helena Chang *physician*
Chuksorji, Jean Caulfield *nursing educator*
Churgin, Amy *publishing executive*
Cicciarelli, James Carl *immunology educator*
Cislowski, Joseph A. *association executive*
Clark, Burton Robert *sociologist, educator*
Clark, R(ufus) Bradbury *lawyer, director*
Clark, William Arthur V. *geographer*
Clarke, Peter *communications and health educator*

Jacobson, Marcus J. *retired mechanical engineer*
Jacobson, Sidney *editor*
Jacoby, Neil Herman, Jr., *astronautical engineer, scientific consultant*
Jaffe, Sigmund *chemist, educator*
Jagger, Sir Mick (Michael Philip Jagger) *singer, musician*
Jaggers, Velma Mary Lee *foundation administrator, educator*
Jalali, Behnaz *psychiatrist, educator*
James, William Langford *aerospace engineer*
Jansson, Bruce Stevenson *social sciences educator, researcher*
Jarrell, Leeann *investment company executive*
Jarvik, Lissy F. *psychiatrist*
Jenders, Robert Allen *medical educator, researcher*
Jennings, Willbur *musician, popular*
Jin, Yan *university educator, researcher, consultant*
Johnson, Cage Saul *hematologist, educator*
Johnson, Carole A. *writer, artist*
Johnson, Charles Floyd *television executive, producer*
Johnson, Davey (David Allen Johnson) *professional baseball team manager*
Johnson, E. Eric *insurance executive*
Johnson, Earl, Jr., *judge, author*
Johnson, John Malcolm, Jr., *reporter*
Johnson, Jonathan Edwin, II, *lawyer*
Johnson, Philip Leslie *lawyer*
Johnson, Stephen *architectural firm executive*
Johnston, Roy G. *consulting structural engineer*
Johnston, Ynez *artist, educator*
Jones, Gerald Paul *software educator*
Jones, Neil Ford *surgeon, educator*
Jones, Peter Anthony *medical research administrator*
Jones, Quincy *producer, composer, arranger, conductor, trumpeter*
Jones, Tom *singer*
Jordan, Martha B. *lawyer*
Jordan, Robert Leon *lawyer, educator*
Jordan, Thomas Hillman *geophysicist, educator*
Ju, Jiann-Wen *mechanics educator, researcher*
Kaback, Elaine *career counselor, family therapist, consultant*
Kaczmarek, Jane *actress*
Kadison, Stuart *lawyer, educator, writer*
Kalaba, Robert Edwin *applied mathematician*
Kallet, Judith S. *publishing executive*
Kamil, Elaine Scheiner *pediatric nephrologist, educator*
Kamine, Bernard S. *lawyer*
Kandal, Terry R. *sociology educator, consultant*
Kanoff, Mary Ellen *lawyer*
Kaplan, Andy *broadcast executive*
Kaplan, Isaac Raymond *chemistry professor*
Kaplan, Nadia *writer*
Kaplowitz, Neil *physician, educator*
Karatz, Bruce E. *construction executive*
Karmarkar, Uday Sadashiv *management educator*
Karros, Eric Peter *professional baseball player*
Karst, Kenneth Leslie *law educator*
Kassner, Michael Ernest *materials science educator, researcher*
Kast, W. Martin *microbiology and immunology educator*
Katchur, Marlene Martha *nursing administrator*
Katz, Ronald Lewis *physician, educator*
Katzin, Carolyn Fernanda *nutritionist, consultant*
Kaunitz, Jonathan Davidson *physician*
Kedes, Laurence H. *biochemistry educator, physician, researcher*
Keenan, Edward L. *linguist, educator*
Keith, David *symphony orchestra conductor*
Kelleher, Robert Joseph *judge*
Kellerman, Sally Claire *actress*
Kelley, David E. *producer, writer*
Kelley, Harold Harding *psychology educator*
Kelly, Arthur Paul *physician*
Kelly, Henry Ansgar *English language educator*
Kelly, Pamela B. *lawyer*
Kelly, Robert Edward *engineer, educator*
Kennard, Lydia H. *airport terminal executive*
Kenoff, Jay Stewart *lawyer*
Khawli, Leslie Albert *research scientist, educator*
Kiekhofer, William Henry *lawyer*
Kim, Jeongbin John *mechanical engineering educator*
Kim, Ke Bom *stockbroker, financial planner*
Kimmel, Jimmy (James Christian Kimmel) *television personality*
Kindel, James Horace, Jr., *lawyer*
King, Peter Nelson *lawyer*
King-Ning, Tu *materials science and engineering educator*
Kipke, Michele Diane *education and social services administrator, former hospital director*
Kirwan, Betty Jane Jane *lawyer*
Kirwan, R. DeWitt *lawyer*
Kivelson, Margaret Galland *physicist*
Klauss, Kenneth Karl *composer, educator*
Kleeman, Charles Richard *medical educator, nephrologist, researcher*
Kleiman, Evan *chef*
Klein, Benjamin *economics educator, consultant*
Kleingartner, Archie *founding dean, educator*
Kline, Lee B. *retired architect*
Kline, Richard Stephen *public relations executive*
Klinger, Marilyn Sydney *lawyer*
Kloner, Robert A. *cardiologist, researcher, educator*
Knapp, Cleon Talboys *publishing executive*
Knight, Henry L. *minister*
Knittle, William Joseph, Jr., *media executive, psychologist, religious leader, management and marketing consultant, educator*
Knopoff, Leon *geophysics educator*
Knox, Gertie R. *company executive, accountant*
Kobe, Lan *medical physicist*
Koffler, Stephen Alexander *investment banker*
Koga, Rokutaro (Rocky Koga) *physicist*
Kolve, V. A. *English literature educator*
Korsch, Barbara M. *pediatrician*
Kraft, Scott Corey *correspondent*
Kramer, Barry Alan *psychiatrist, educator*
Kranwinkle, Conrad Douglas *broadcast executive*
Krupka, Robert George *lawyer*
Krupp, Edwin Charles *astronomer*
Kuang, Jun *aeronautical engineer, researcher, fluid mechanics engineer*
Kuechle, John Merrill *lawyer*
Kuehl, Hans Henry *electrical engineering educator*
Kupietzky, Moshe J. *lawyer*
Kupper, Ketti *artist*
Kurtz, Swoosie *actress*
Kyles, Cedric Antonio (Cedric the Entertainer) *comedian, actor*
La Force, James Clayburn, Jr., *economist, educator*
Lagasse, Emeril *chef*
Lagier, Christophe Philippe *language educator*
Laird, David *humanities educator emeritus*
Lake, Randall Alan *forensic specialist, educator*
Lamb, H. Richard *psychiatry educator*
Landers, Audrey *actress, singer*
Langguth, Arthur John *writer, journalism educator*
Lansing, Sherry Lee (Heimann) *motion picture executive*
Lapatin, Kenneth D.S. *archaeologist, art historian*
Lappen, Chester I. *lawyer*
Lark, Raymond *artist, art scholar*
Larkin, Thomas Ernest, Jr., *investment management company executive*
Larson, Gary *cartoonist*
Lasorda, Thomas Charles (Tommy Lasorda) *professional baseball team manager*
Latham, Joseph Al, Jr., *lawyer*
Lattimore, Steven *classicist professor*
Latzer, Richard Neal *investment company executive*
Lauchengco, Jose Yujuico, Jr., *lawyer*
Laurance, Dale R. *oil company executive*
Lavin, Laurence Michael *lawyer*
Lavin, Stephen Michael *university basketball coach*
Lavin, Sylvia *architecture educator*
Lavine, Adrienne Gail *mechanical engineering educator*
Lawrence, Sanford Hull *physician, immunochemist, author*
Lawton, Eric *lawyer, photographer, visual artist, author*
Layton, Harry Christopher *artist, lecturer, consultant*
Lazano, Monica *publishing executive*
Lazareff, Jorge Antonio *neurosurgeon, researcher*
Lazarus, Mell *cartoonist*
Leach, Anthony Raymond *financial executive*
Leahy, T. Liam *business development, technology investor*
Leal, George D. *engineering company executive*
LeBeau, Mary Delle *dancer, educator, writer*
Lechago, Juan *pathologist, educator*
Ledger, Heath *actor*
Leeves, Jane *actress*
Leff, Daniel V. *venture capitalist*
Leibow, Ronald Louis *lawyer*
Leijonhufvud, Axel Stig Bengt *economics professor*
Leiweke, Timothy *sports executive, marketing professional*
Lem, Richard Douglas *painter*
LeMaster, Susan M. *marketing executive, writer*
Lesser, Ian O. *foreign affairs expert*
Lesser, Joan L. *lawyer*
Letwin, Leon *law educator*
Leung, Frankie Fook-Lun *lawyer*
Levenson, Laurie L. *law educator*
Levey, Gerald Saul *dean, internist, educator*
Levine, Jesse E. *publishing executive*
Levine, Meldon Edises *lawyer, former congressman*
Levine, Michael *public relations executive, writer, talk show host*
Levine, Philip *classics educator*
Levine, Raphael David *chemistry professor*
Levine, Thomas Jeffrey Pello *lawyer*
Levinsohn, Gary *producer*
Levy, Alan David *real estate executive*
Lewin, Klaus Jonathan *pathologist, educator*
Lewis, Charles Edwin *epidemiologist, educator*
Lewis, Cherie Sue *lawyer, English language and journalism educator*
Lewis, Tommi *magazine editor*
Leyritz, James Joseph *professional baseball player*
Lieber, David Leo *university president*
Lieber, Michael Randall *biochemist, educator*
Light, Ivan Hubert *sociology educator*
Lim, David Jong-Jai *otolaryngology educator, researcher*
Lin, Thomas Wen-shyoung *accounting educator, researcher, consultant*
Lin, Tung Hua *civil engineering educator*
Linde, Leonard M. *pediatric cardiologist*
Lindholm, Dwight Henry *lawyer*
Lindley, F(rancis) Haynes, Jr., *foundation executive, lawyer*
Linsk, Michael Stephen *real estate executive*
Lionnet, Francoise *French and comparative literature educator*
Lipsig, Ethan *lawyer*
Litewka, Albert Bernard *communications and publishing company executive*
Litvack, Sanford Martin *lawyer*
Livingston, Larry J. *conductor, music educator*
Ljubimov, Alexander V. *molecular biologist, cell biologist, researcher*
Lloyd-Jones, Dadiva Bocobo *nursing assistant, writer*
Lockhart, Sharon *artist*
Logan, Nancy Jane *broadcast sales and marketing executive*
London, Andrew Barry *film editor*
Long, Gregory Alan *lawyer*
Looney, Claudia Arlene *healthcare administrator*
Lopez, George *actor, comedian*
LoPucki, Lynn Michael *law educator*
Lorizzo, Robert P. *science administrator*
Lototsky, Sergey *mathematician, educator*
Lovitz, Jon *actor, comedian*
Lowenthal, Abraham Frederic *international relations educator*
Lozano-Centanino, Monica Cecilia *publishing executive*
Lu, John Kuew-Hsiung *physiology educator, endocrinologist*
Ludlam, James Edward *lawyer*
Lund, James Louis *lawyer*
Lunden, Joan *television personality*
Lunt, Owen Raynal *biologist, educator*
Lynch, Beverly Pfeifer *education and information studies educator*
Lynch, Patrick *lawyer*
Macavinta-Tenazas, Gemorsita *family physician*
Mack, J. Curtis, II, *civic organization administrator*
MacLachlan, Kyle *actor*
MacLaughlin, Francis Joseph *lawyer*
MacLeod, William Bentley *economics and law educator*
Mager, Artur *retired aerospace company executive, consultant*
Maguire, Tobey (Tobias Vincent Maguire) *actor*
Mahony, Roger Michael *archbishop*
Maki, Kazumi *physicist, researcher*
Malamuth, Neil Moshe *psychology and communication educator*
Malcolm, Dawn Grace *family physician*
Malden, Karl (Malden Sekulovich) *actor*
Malick, Terrence (David Whitney II) *film director*
Mall, William John, Jr., *aerospace executive, retired Air Force general*
Malone, Nancy *actress*
Maloney, Kristen *gymnast*
Maloney, Robert Keller *ophthalmologist, medical educator*
Maltin, Leonard *television commentator, writer*
Maltzan, Michael Thomas *architect*
Mamer, John William *business educator*
Man, Lawrence Kong *architect, art dealer*
Mancino, Douglas Michael *lawyer*
Mandal, Ashis K. *cardiothoracic surgeon*
Mandles, Martinn H. *facility services company executive*
Manella, Nora M. *federal judge*
Mann, Nancy Louise (Nancy Louise Robbins) *entrepreneur*
Mann, Wesley F. *editor, writer, reporter*
Maquet, Jacques Jerome Pierre *anthropologist, writer*
March, Kathleen Patricia *judge*
Marciano, Maurice *apparel executive*
Marcus, Stephen Howard *lawyer*
Margulies, Lee *newspaper editor*
Markland, Francis Swaby, Jr., *biochemist, educator*
Marmarelis, Vasilis Zissis *engineering educator, writer, consultant*
Maronde, Robert Francis *internist, clinical pharmacologist, educator*
Marshall, Consuelo Bland *federal judge*
Marshall, Mary Jones *civic worker*
Marshall-Daniels, Meryl *communications executive, mediator*
Martin, Ann *newscaster*
Martin, J(ohn) Edward *architectural engineer*
Martin, Nanice S. *software company executive*
Martin, Shane Patrick *education educator, consultant*
Martinez, Jean *newscaster*
Martinez, Miguel Acevedo *urologist, consultant, lecturer*
Mason, Andrew *film producer*
Mason, Cheryl White *lawyer*
Mathias, Alice Irene *business management consultant*
Matthews, Melony Kerry *opera singer, actress*
Mavis, Darrell *lawyer, educator*
Maxworthy, Tony *mechanical and aerospace engineering educator*
May, Lawrence Edward *lawyer*
McAniff, Edward John *lawyer*
McCabe, Edward R. B. *academic administrator, educator, physician*
McCann, John David *physician, educator*
McCarthy, Nobu *actress, performing company executive, educator*
McCluggage, Kerry *film and television executive*
McClure, William Owen *biologist*
McCombs, Jeffrey Scott *economist, educator*
McCullagh, Grant Gibson *retired architect*
McDonough, Richard Aloysius, IV, *investment banker*
McGowen, Gerald Ellis *biologist*
McGraw, Phillip C. *psychologist, television personality*
McKinzie, Carl Wayne *lawyer*
McLane, Frederick Berg *lawyer*
McLean, Ian Small *astronomer, physics educator*
McLinn, Anna Ruth *educator*
McNamara, Aida Shahid *insurance executive*
Mc Pherson, Rolf Kennedy *clergyman, religious organization administrator*
McQueen, Justice Ellis (L. Q. Jones) *actor, director*
Medearis, Miller *lawyer*
Meier, Stephen Charles *foundation executive*
Meisinger, Louis M. *lawyer*
Mellinkoff, Sherman Mussoff *medical educator*
Mellor, Ronald John *history professor*
Melnick, Michael *geneticist, educator*
Mendel, Jerry Marc *electrical engineering educator*
Menes, Paul Ira *lawyer*
Merlis, George *television producer*
Mersel, Marjorie Kathryn Pedersen *lawyer*
Messerli, Douglas *writer, publisher*
Messner, Michael A. *sociologist, educator*
Mestres, Ricardo A., III, *motion picture company executive*
Metheny, Patrick Bruce *musician*
Metzger, Robert Streicher *lawyer*
Meyer, Michael Edwin *lawyer*
Michael, William Burton *psychologist, educator*
Michelson, Sonia *music educator, author*
Mihan, Richard *retired dermatologist*
Milchan, Arnon *film producer*
Miles, Jack (John Russiano) *journalist, educator*
Millard, Neal Steven *lawyer, educator*
Miller, Bruce *advertising executive*
Miller, Milton Allen *lawyer*
Miller, Timothy Alden *plastic and reconstructive surgeon*
Mintz, Marshall Gary *lawyer*
Mishell, Daniel R., Jr., *obstetrician, gynecologist, educator*
Mitchell, Theodore Reed *academic administrator*
Mock, Theodore Jaye *accounting educator*
Moe, Stanley Allen *architect, consultant*
Moffatt, Robert Henry *accountant, publisher, writer, consultant*
Mohr, John Luther *biologist, environmental consultant*
Molleur, Richard Raymond *lawyer*
Moloney, Stephen Michael *lawyer*
Mondino, Bartly J. *ophthalmologist*
Monforte-Muñoz, Hector L. *pathologist*
Montoya, Velma *economist, policy consultant*
More, Philip Harvey Birnbaum *business administration educator*
Morgan, Dirck *broadcast journalist*
Morgenthaler-Lever, Alisa *lawyer*
Morgner, Aurelius *economist, educator*
Morin, JoyAnn Hauge *education educator*
Morisky, Donald E. *director, medical educator*
Morris, Sharon Hutson *city manager*
Morrison, Donald Graham *business educator, consultant*
Morrow, Winston Vaughan *financial executive*
Moser, Franklin George *neuroradiologist, researcher*
Moshfegh, Moussa *surgeon*
Mosich, Anelis Nick *accountant, writer, educator, consultant*
Mosk, Richard Mitchell *judge*
Moskowitz, Joel Steven *lawyer*
Moussavi, Ramyar *podiatrist*
Moxley, John Howard, III, *internist*
Moy, Ronald Leonard *dermatologist, surgeon*
Mracky, Ronald Sydney *marketing and media executive, tourism consultant*
Mueller, Carl Richard *theater arts educator, author*
Muldaur, Diana Charlton *actress*
Mullan, John H. *science administrator*
Mulligan, Robert *film director, producer*
Munitz, Barry *arts and foundation administrator*
Muntz, Eric Phillip *aerospace and mechanical engineering and radiology educator, consultant*
Murcutt, Glen *architect*
Murphree, A. Linn *pediatric ophthalmologist*
Murray, Alice Pearl *data processing company executive*
Murray, Andy *professional hockey coach*
Myers, Albert F. *aerospace executive*
Myers, Barton *architect*
Nadler, Gerald *management consultant, educator*
Nagy, Bob *editor*
Nakanishi, Don Toshiaki *Asian American studies educator, writer*
Naqvi, Tasneem Zehra *cardiologist, researcher, consultant*
Nathwani, Bharat N. *pathologist, consultant*
Nazario, Sonia *reporter*
Neelin, J. David *meteorologist, educator*
Neely, Sally Schultz *lawyer*
Neil, Daniel *journalist*
Neiter, Gerald Irving *lawyer*
Nelligan, Kate (Patricia Colleen Nelligan) *actress*
Nelson, Bryce Eames *journalist, educator*
Nelson, Grant Steel *lawyer, educator*
Nelson, Howard Joseph *geographer, educator*
Nelson, Marvin Dale, Jr., *radiologist, educator*
Neufeld, Elizabeth Fondal *biochemist, educator*
Neufeld, Timothy Lee *lawyer*
Neutra, Dion *architect*
Newhall, Eric Luther *American literature educator*
Newhart, Bob *entertainer*
Newman, Anita Nadine *surgeon*
Newman, Michael Rodney *lawyer*
Newman, Randy *singer, songwriter, musician*
Newman, Richard G. *engineering company executive*
Nicholas, Frederick M. *lawyer*
Nicholas, William Richard *lawyer*
Nicholson, Jack *actor*
Nielsen, Leslie *actor*
Niemeth, Charles Frederick *lawyer*
Nimni, Marcel Ephraim *biochemistry educator*
Nissenson, Allen Richard *physician, educator*
Nobe, Ken *chemical engineering educator*
Noble, Douglas *architecture educator*
Noble, Ernest Pascal *pharmacologist, biochemist, educator*
Noble, James Wilkes *actor*
Nobumoto, Karen S. *prosecutor*
Nocas, Andrew James *lawyer*
Noce, Walter William, Jr., *hospital administrator*
Nochimson, David *lawyer*
Noguchi, Thomas Tsunetomi *writer, pathologist*
Norris, William Albert *retired judge*
O'Brien, Pat *television personality*
Ochoa, Arthur J. *lawyer, hospital administrator*
Ochs, Elinor *linguistics educator*
O'Connell, Kevin *lawyer*
O'Connell, Taaffe Cannon *actress, publishing executive*
O'Connor, Kevin Thomas *religious organization administrator*
O'Day, Anita Belle Colton *entertainer, musician, vocalist*
O'Donnell, Pierce Henry *lawyer*
O'Hara, Maureen (Maureen FitzSimons) *actress*
Ohlgren, Joel R. *lawyer*
Ohlmeyer, Donald Winfred, Jr., *film and television producer*
Okrent, David *engineering educator*
Olah, George Andrew *chemist, educator*
Oldham, Granville Murl, Jr., *conductor, educator*
O'Leary, Prentice Lee *lawyer*
Oliver, Anthony Thomas, Jr., *lawyer*
Oliver, Dale Hugh *lawyer*
Olivier, Kathy Ricks *college basketball coach*
Olmos, Edward James *actor*
Olsen, Ashley Fuller *actress*
Olsen, Frances Elisabeth *law educator, theorist*
Olsen, Mary-Kate *actress*
Olson, Ronald Leroy *lawyer*
O'Neil, William J. *newspaper executive*
O'Neil, William Scott *publishing executive*
O'Neill, Russell Richard *engineering educator*
Orbach, Jerry *actor, singer*
Ordin, Andrea Sheridan *lawyer*
O'Reilly, Richard Brooks *journalist*
Orme, Antony Ronald *geography educator*
Orsatti, Alfred Kendall *organization executive*
O'Toole, James Joseph *business educator*
Owen, Michael Lee *lawyer*
Ownbey, Vance Scott *corporate financial executive*
Palevsky, Max *industrialist*
Palffy, Zigmund (Ziggy Palffy) *professional hockey player*
Palmer, Pamela S. *lawyer*
Palmer, Roger Cain *information scientist*
Palmieri, Victor Henry *lawyer, business executive*
Parisi, Paula Elizabeth *writer, photographer, editor*
Park, Chan Ho *professional baseball player*
Park, Lee (Lee Parklee) *artist*
Park, No-Hee *academic administrator*
Parker, Alice Cline *computer engineering educator, consultant*
Parker, Robert George *radiation oncology educator, academic administrator*
Parkinson, Dian *actress*
Parks, Michael Christopher *journalist*
Parmelee, Arthur Hawley, Jr., *pediatric medical educator*
Pasich, Kirk Alan *lawyer*
Pastor, Jennifer *sculptor*
Patrick, Robert *playwright*
Patterson, Charles Ernest *lawyer*
Patzakis, Michael J. *orthopaedic surgeon, educator*
Paul, Charles S. *motion picture and television company executive*
Paulson, Donald Robert *chemistry professor*
Paxton, Bill *actor, writer, director*
Pearl, Judea *computer scientist, educator*
Peck, Austin H., Jr., *lawyer*

Welch, Lloyd Richard *electrical engineering educator, communications consultant*
Welch, Raquel *actress*
Wells, Annie *photographer*
Westerfield, Randolph W. *university dean, business educator*
Westheimer, David Kaplan *novelist*
Weston, John Frederick *business educator, consultant*
Wexler, Robert *university administrator*
Whitaker, Forest *actor, director, producer*
White, Brett *real estate company executive*
White, Christopher Todd *language educator*
White, Kelvin Lewis *historian, researcher*
White, Meg (Megan Martha White) *musician, vocalist*
White, Robert Joel *lawyer*
White-Whitfield, Lisa Denise *social worker, grant writer*
Whitten, Charles Alexander, Jr., *physics educator*
Whybrow, Peter Charles *psychiatrist, educator, director, author*
Wiggins, Marianne *writer*
Wilcox, Rand Roger *psychology educator*
Wilkerson, LuAnn *dean, medical educator*
Wilkinson, Alan Herbert *nephrologist, educator*
Williams, Bradley Robert *pharmacy and gerontology educator, consultant*
Williams, Carlton L. *communications executive*
Williams, Clarence J, III, *photographer*
Williams, Harold Marvin *foundation official, former government official, former university dean, former corporate executive*
Williams, Julie Ford *mutual fund officer*
Williams, Paul Hamilton *composer, singer*
Williams, Richard Thomas *lawyer*
Williams, Ronald Dean *minister, religious organization administrator*
Williams, Theodore Earle *retired industrial distribution company executive*
Willison, Bruce Gray *dean*
Willner, Alan Eli *electrical engineer, educator*
Wilson, Charles Zachary, Jr., *newspaper publisher*
Wilson, Donald Kenneth, Jr., *lawyer, publisher*
Wilson, Gayle Ann *civic worker*
Wilson, Miriam Geisendorfer *retired physician, educator*
Wincor, Michael Z. *psychopharmacology educator, clinician, researcher*
Wine, Mark Philip *lawyer*
Winet, Howard *research scientist, medical educator*
Winkler, Howard Leslie *business, finance, government relations consultant*
Winter, Donald C. *science administrator*
Winters, Barbara Jo *musician*
Winters, Dean *actor*
Wise, Robert *film producer, director*
Withers, Hubert Rodney *radiotherapist, radiobiologist, educator*
Wittrock, Merlin Carl *educational psychologist*
Wlaschin, Ken *cultural organization administrator, writer*
Wohl, Robert *historian, educator*
Wolfen, Werner F. *lawyer*
Wong, James Bok *economist, engineer, technologist*
Wood, Nancy Elizabeth *psychologist, educator*
Woodland, Irwin Francis *lawyer*
Woodley, David Timothy *dermatology educator*
Woodruff, Fay *paleoceanographer, geological researcher*
Wortham, Thomas Richard *English language educator*
Wright, Connie Hotchkiss *educational association administrator, researcher*
Wright, Ernest Marshall *physiologist, consultant*
Wright, Kenneth Brooks *lawyer*
Wright, Sandra *science administrator*
Wu, Li-Pei *banker*
Wudl, Fred *chemistry professor*
Wylie, Pamela Jane *writer, producer, consultant, small business owner*
Xue, Yongkang *science educator*
Yablonovitch, Eli *electrical engineering educator*
Yaffe, Sumner Jason *pediatrician, educator, science administrator*
Yager, Thomas C. *retired judge*
Yamaguchi, Colleen S. *lawyer*
Yan, Lianshan *optical engineer, scientist*
Yanai, Michio *atmospheric scientist*
Yang, Debra W. *lawyer*
Yang, Fan *electrical engineering research scientist*
Yang, Henry S. (Hong Yang) *metallurgist, materials engineer*
Yang, Yang *science educator*
Ye, Hengchun *meteorologist, educator*
Yen, Teh Fu *civil and environmental engineering educator*
Zacchino, Narda *newspaper editor*
Zeitlin, Maurice *sociology educator, writer*
Zelikow, Howard Monroe *management and financial consultant*
Zelon, Laurie Dee *lawyer*
Zemeckis, Robert L. *film director*
Zexter, Eleanor M. *secondary school educator*
Ziering, Craig L. *osteopath*
Ziering, Michael *medical products executive*
Ziffren, Kenneth *lawyer*
Ziman, Richard S. *real estate company executive*
Zone, Ray *writer*
Zucker, Lynne Goodman *sociology educator, consultant*

Los Banos

York, Courtney Carter *retired engineering executive, genealogist*

Los Gatos

Carson, Sol Kent *artist, educator*
Chapson, Lois Jester *interior designer*
Conaway, Margaret Grimes (Peggy Conaway) *library administrator*
Dahlberg, Thomas Robert *writer, lawyer, educator, software company executive*
Dunham, Anne *educational institute director*
Foy, Wade Hampton *retired research scientist*
Hastings, Reed *film company executive, educational association administrator*
Kazan, Benjamin *research engineer*
Meyers, Ann Elizabeth *sports broadcaster*
Naymark, Sherman *consulting nuclear engineer*
Rissanen, Jorma Johannes *computer scientist*
Rosenheim, Donald Edwin *electrical engineer*
Rudolph, Allen *secondary school educator, consultant*

Sawyer, Malcolm James, Jr., *religious studies educator*

Los Osos

Just, Faye Jordan *antique restoration company executive*
Kreitzer, Jacalyn Bower *vocalist, voice educator*
Topp, Alphonso Axel, Jr., *environmental scientist, consultant*

Lynwood

Dove, Donald Augustine *city planner, educator*
Legesse, Solomon *technology executive*
Nelson, Maurice S., Jr., *metal products company executive*
Sterling, Arthur James *legal assistant*

Madera

Curry, Cynthia J. R. *geneticist*
Glynn, James A. *sociology educator, author*

Malibu

Almond, Paul *film director, producer, screenwriter, novelist*
Ancker, Clinton James, Jr., *emeritus systems and industrial engineering educator*
Baskin, Otis Wayne *business educator*
Bedrosian, Edward *electrical engineer*
Benton, Andrew Keith *university administrator, lawyer*
Bowman, Bruce *art educator*
Carson, Johnny *television personality*
Dankanyin, Robert John *international business executive*
de la Rocha, Raquelle *lawyer, educator, state agency administrator*
DeMieri, Joseph L. *retired bank executive*
Ensign, Richard Papworth *transportation executive*
Harris, Ed(ward Allen) *actor*
Hill, Lawrence Sidney *finance educator*
Hunt, Valerie Virginia *electrophysiologist, educator*
Jenden, Donald James *pharmacologist, educator*
Keach, Stacy, Jr., *actor, director, producer, writer, musician, composer*
Kirby, Deborah Janice *electrical engineer, researcher*
Liu, David Shiao-Kung *physical scientist*
Marshall, Donald Glenn *English language and literature educator*
McCall, Elizabeth Kaye *columnist, consultant, writer*
Morgenstern, Leon *surgeon*
Murphy, Benjamin Edward *actor*
Palacio, June Rose Payne *nutritional science educator*
Pepper, David M. *physicist, educator, writer, inventor*
Phillips, Ronald Frank *university administrator*
Raine, Melinda L. *library manager*
Smith, Yvonne Smart *advertising executive*
Starr, Kenneth Winston *dean, lawyer*
Tellem, Susan Mary *public relations executive*
Tippens, Darryl Lee *literature educator, writer*
Wilson, Rita *actress*
Zakian, Michael *museum director*

Mammoth Lakes

Fitzgerald, Timothy K. *writer, political organizer, non-profit administrator*
Mager, Ingrid Irina *artist*

Manhattan Beach

Blanton, John Arthur *architect, writer*
Deutsch, Barry Joseph *consulting and management development company executive*
Hallett, James M. *lawyer*
Magner, Rachel Harris *retired banker*
Pettersen, Thomas Morgan *accountant, finance executive*
Schoenfeld, Lawrence Jon *real estate developer, asset lender*
Williams, Emma *rail transportation executive*

Manteca

Hirning, Fredric Carl *pharmacist*
Meckler, Mary McStroul *mortgage company executive, writer*
Talmage, Kenneth Kellogg *business executive*
Tonn, Elverne Meryl *pediatric dentist, dental benefits consultant, forensic odontologist*

Marina

Cornell, Annie Aiko *nurse, administrator, retired military officer*
Madsen, Roy I., Jr., *language educator*
Mettee-McCutchon, Ila *municipal official, retired career army officer*
Shane, William Whitney *astronomer*

Marina Del Rey

Allmon, Michael Bryan *financial consultant*
Annotico, Richard Anthony *legal administrator, real estate investor*
Banks, Ernest (Ernie Banks) *retired professional baseball player*
Fash, Michael William *cinematographer, director*
Gold, Carol Sapin *international management consultant, speaker*
Gregg, Lucius Perry, Jr., *aerospace executive*
Haddad, Edmonde Alex *public affairs executive*
Lindheim, Richard David *television company executive, university official*
Masotti, Louis Henry *real estate educator, consultant*
Minanel, Shelley *writer, artist*
Neuman, Clifford *computer scientist, educator*
Stebbins, Gregory Kellogg *foundation executive*

Marina del Rey

Abebe, Henok *engineer, researcher*

Mariposa

Bruce, John Anthony *artist*
Rogers, Earl Leslie *artist, educator*
Sutherland, Gail Russell *retired industrial equipment manufacturing company executive*

Marshall

Evans, Robert James *architect*

Martinez

Barnard, William Marion *psychiatrist*
Canciamilla, Joseph *state legislator*

Kimbrell, Deborah Ann *geneticist, educator*
McKnight, Lenore Ravin *child psychiatrist, educator*
Meyer, Jarold Alan *oil company research executive*
Sepulveda, Eduardo Solideo *chemical engineer*
Tetrault, Jeanne L. *building inspector*
Thomas, Walter Dill, Jr., *retired forest pathologist, consultant*
Tong, Siu Wing *computer programmer*
Williams, Charles Judson *lawyer, writer*
Withrow, Sherrie Anne (Jimie Jean Pearl) *financial specialist*

Marysville

Gray, Katherine *marriage, family and child therapist, writer, educator*
Larson, Billy Dell *finance company executive*
Myers, Elmer *psychiatric social worker*

Mckinleyville

Berry, Glenn *educator, artist*
Peithman, Roscoe Edward *physicist, educator*
Schoettger, Theodore Leo *city official*
Thueson, David Orel *pharmaceutical executive, researcher, writer, educator*

Mendocino

Bilas, Richard A. *economist*
Masterson, William A. *retired judge*
Woelfel, Robert William *broadcast executive, mayor*

Menifee

Balow, Irving Henry *retired education educator*
Morshed, Moqbul Monty *civil and environmental engineer*

Menlo Park

Allison, Anthony Clifford *research scientist, consultant*
Alsop, Stewart *communications executive*
Altman, Drew E. *foundation executive*
Bader, W(illiam) Reece *lawyer*
Baez, Joan Chandos *folk singer*
Balkanski, Alexandre *investment company executive*
Banks, Peter Morgan *physics educator, investor, business consultant*
Barkas, Alexander E. *biotechnology company executive*
Belaroff, Joseph K. *pharmaceutical executive*
Bourne, Charles Percy *information scientist, educator*
Bowes, William K., Jr., *venture capital investment company executive*
Boyarski, Adam Michael *physicist*
Bremser, George, Jr., *electronics company executive*
Brest, Paul A. *law educator*
Brown, Charles Dickson *not-for-profit fundraiser, consultant*
Bukry, John David *geologist*
Bynum, Gretchen Luepke *geologist*
Carlson, Curtis R. *electronics research industry executive*
Chamberlain, Paul Edward *investment banker*
Chapin, June Roediger *education educator*
Clair, Theodore Nat *educational psychologist*
Coats, William Sloan, III, *lawyer*
Collins, Nancy Whisnant *foundation administrator*
Copeland, Eric *venture capital company executive*
Coward, David Hand *physicist, researcher*
Crane, Hewitt David *science advisor*
Creswell, Donald Creston *business executive*
Davies, Paul Lewis, III, *venture capitalist*
Doerr, John *communications executive*
Drell, Sidney David *physicist, researcher*
Dyer, Charles Arnold *lawyer*
Fenton, Noel John *venture capitalist*
Funkhouser, Lawrence William *retired geologist*
Goodreau, Robert Charles *surgeon*
Grimes, Michael D. *investment banker*
Gunderson, Robert Vernon, Jr., *lawyer*
Harris, Edward Day, Jr., *physician*
Haslam, Robert Thomas, III, *lawyer*
Hazen, Paul Mandeville *banker*
Healy, Cynthia *pharmacologist, life scientist, researcher*
Holmquest, Donald Lee *physician, astronaut, lawyer*
Holzer, Thomas Lequear *geologist*
Honey, Richard Churchill *retired electrical engineer*
Jackson, Jeanne Pellegren *apparel executive*
Jorgensen, Paul J. *research company executive*
Kalinske, Thomas J. *education, video game and toy company executive*
Kamin, William Stephen *food company executive, photographer*
Karel, Steven *human resources specialist*
Kashnow, Richard A. *electronics executive*
Kaufman, Christopher Lee *lawyer*
Keeley, Michael Clark *economist*
Kelly, Daniel Grady, Jr., *lawyer*
Khosla, Vinod *investment company executive*
Kirk, Cassius Lamb, Jr., *retired lawyer, investor*
Kovachy, Edward Miklos, Jr., *psychiatrist, consultant*
Kurtzig, Sandra L. *software company executive*
Kuwabara, James Shigeru *research hydrologist*
Kvamme, Mark D. *marketing professional*
Lachenbruch, Arthur Herold *geophysicist, researcher*
Lane, Laurence William, Jr., *retired ambassador, publisher*
LaPorte, Kathleen Darken *venture capitalist*
Lindzey, Gardner *psychologist, educator*
Lucas, Donald Leo *investor*
Lynch, Charles Allen *investment executive, corporate director*
Lynch, Kevin J. *publishing executive, media planner*
Madding, Bruce Wallace *foundation executive*
Madison, James Raymond *lawyer*
McCarthy, Roger Lee *mechanical engineer*
McCown, George E. *venture banking company executive*
McDonald, Warren George *retired accountant, former savings and loan executive*
McGarr, Arthur Francis *geophysicist*
Mendelson, Alan Charles *lawyer*
Messmer, Harold Maximilian, Jr., (Max Messmer) *financial services executive*
Middleton, Teresa Muir *Internet company executive, researcher*
Montana, Joseph C., Jr., *former professional football player*
Mulgaonkar, Prasanna G. *computer scientist*

Neumann, Peter Gabriel *computer scientist*
Nichols, William Ford, Jr., *foundation executive, business executive*
Okkarma, Thomas B. *biotechnology company executive*
Pallotti, Marianne Marguerite *foundation administrator*
Penzias, Arno Allan *astrophysicist, technology consultant, research scientist, information systems specialist*
Reamy, Michaelin *marriage and family therapist, educator, consultant*
Richter, Burton *physicist, educator*
Roberts, George R. *investment banking company executive*
Ross, Bernard *engineering consultant, educator*
Saffo, Paul *communications executive*
Saifer, Mark Gary Pierce *pharmaceutical executive*
Schmidt, Chauncey Everett *banker, director*
Scholes, Myron S. *financier, former law and finance educator*
Scifres, Donald Ray *finance company executive*
Smith, Marshall Savidge *foundation executive*
Taylor, Richard Edward *physicist, researcher*
Taylor, Robert P. *lawyer*
Terman, Donna Lea *lawyer, foundation administrator*
Tiet, Quyen Q. *clinical psychologist, researcher*
Vane, Sylvia Brakke *anthropologist, writer, publishing executive, researcher*
Wachtel, John Steven *obstetrician, gynecologist*
Waddell, M. Keith *human resources specialist*
Walsh, William Desmond *investor*
White, Cecil Ray *librarian, consultant*
Wilson, James N. *health products executive*
Wolfson, Mark Alan *investor, business educator*
Zdeblick, Mark James *information technology executive*
Zercher, Craig Allen *special education educator, researcher*

Merced

Boese, Sandra Jean *publishing executive*
Denham, Jeffrey *state senator*
Elliott, Gordon Jefferson *retired English language educator*
Tomlinson-Keasey, Carol Ann *university administrator*

Mill Valley

Bolen, Jean Shinoda *psychiatrist, writer*
Burke, Kathleen J. *foundation administrator*
Cohn, Bruce *film and television company executive*
D'Amico, Michael *architect, urban planner*
Fuller, Glenn R. *park ranger*
Gianturco, Paola *communications consulting company executive*
Harner, Michael James *anthropologist, educator, author*
Harris, Jeffrey Saul *physician, executive, consultant*
Hoffman, John Douglas *lawyer, mediator*
Jones, Pirkle *photographer, educator*
Kolb, Felix Oscar *physician*
Leslie, Jacques Robert, Jr., *journalist*
Maubert, Jacques Claude *retired school superintendent*
McNamara, Stephen *newspaper executive*
Meyers, Robert Allen *chemist, publisher*
Mumford, Christopher Greene *corporate financial executive*
Nemir, Donald Philip *lawyer*
Padula, Fred David *filmmaker*
Premo, Paul Mark *oil company executive*
Rutledge, Louis C *entomologist*
Selvig, Jettie Pierce *lawyer*
Ware, David Joseph *financial consultant*

Millbrae

Chow, Eileen Siu-Ha *computer retailing, investment company executive*
Lande, James Avra *lawyer*
Mank, Edward Warren *marketing professional*
Rosenthal, Herbert Marshall *lawyer*

Milpitas

Cannon, Michael R. *electronics executive*
Chiu, Peter Yee-Chew *physician*
Corrigan, Wilfred J. *computer company executive*
Evans, Susan A. *chemist*
Everett, David *electronics executive*
Granchelli, Ralph S. *company executive*
Gray, Bruce *computer and electronics company executive*
Hawkins, Jeff *information technology executive*
Levinson, Marina *information technology executive*
Levy, Kenneth *executive*
Lin Chien, Chester *electronics executive*
London, Craig *electronics executive*
Moore, George W. *electronics executive*
O'Connor, Kevin *electronics executive*
Onetto, Marc *manufacturing executive*
Park, Chong S. *computer company executive*
Patel, Kiran *manufacturing executive*
Rabbat, Guy *electronics company executive, inventor*
Roddick, David Bruce *construction company executive*
Rollinson, Frederick (Rick), III, *manufacturing executive*
Stephens, Bob *electronic executive*
Swanson, Robert H. Jr. *electronics executive*
Tang, Joe *electronics executive*
Treichel, Helmuth W.A. *technology executive*
Tufano, Paul J *computer company executive*
Wang, Susan S. *manufacturing executive*
Yansouni, Cyril J. *computer company executive*
Zohouri, Saeed *electronics company executive*

Mission Hills

Cramer, Frank Brown *engineering executive, combustion engineer, systems consultant*
Weber, Francis Joseph *archivist, museum director*

Mission Viejo

Duringer, David Robert *lawyer*
Faley, Robert Lawrence *retired instruments company executive*
Glasky, Alvin Jerald *retired medical research scientist*
Hafner-Eaton, Chris *health services researcher, medical educator, policy analyst*
Harris, Ruby Lee *real estate agent*
Hodge, Kathleen O'Connell *academic administrator*
Ruben, Audrey H. *lawyer, arbitrator, actress*

Ruben, Robert Joseph *lawyer*
Tuohey, Conrad Gravier *lawyer*

Modesto
Barnes, William David *non-profit charities consultant, publisher*
Berry, John Charles *clinical psychologist, educational administrator*
Bucknam, Mary Olivia Caswell *artist, educator*
Chan, Alexander *internist*
Cimino, Lewis R., Jr., *surgeon*
Freedman, Louis *vintager executive*
Gallo, Ernest *vintner*
Gallo, Joseph E. *vintner*
Khanna, Kanwal *rheumatologist*
Lewis, Marshall Edward *psychiatrist, administrator, educator*
Martin, Anne Louise *music educator*
Mattos, William Harold *trade association executive, newspaper publisher*
Miller, Raymond Elmo *speech educator*
Moe, Andrew Irving *veterinarian*
Morrison, Robert Lee *physical scientist*
Murphy, John Thomas *lawyer*
Norton, Max C. *writer, educator*
Piccinini, Robert M. *grocery store chain executive*
Ponko, Anne Marie *adult nurse practitioner*
Riesenbeck, Ronald *supermarket executive*
Sabatino, Carmen *mayor*
Smith, Chester *broadcast executive*
Smith, Heather Lynn *psychotherapist, recreational therapist*
Suntra, Charles Ratapol *surgeon, educator*
Turner-Silvia, JoAnn *writer, vocalist, actress, music producer*
Vasche, Mark *newspaper editor*
Whiteside, Carol Gordon *foundation executive*
Youga, Tony *winery executive*

Moffett Field
Bakes, Emma *astrophysicist*
Bilimoria, Karl D. *aerospace engineer*
Bingham, Nancy F. *government agency administrator*
Clearwater, Yvonne A. *psychologist*
Cohen, Malcolm Martin *psychologist, researcher*
Denery, Dallas G. *aeronautical engineer, researcher*
Dismukes, Robert Key *medical scientist*
Dolci, Wendy Whiting *government agency administrator*
Friedmann, E(merich) Imre *biologist, educator*
Friedmann, Roseli Ocampo *microbiologist, educator*
Grymes, Rose *government agency administrator*
Harper, Lynn D. *biologist*
Hughes, Gregory L. *human services manager*
Kerr, Andrew W. *aerodynamics researcher*
Kittel, Peter *research scientist*
Kwong, Jennifer *writer*
Lissauer, Jack Jonathan *astronomy educator*
Mallis, Melissa Mercedes *research psychologist*
Morrison, David *science administrator, researcher*
Park, Chul *aerospace engineer*
Pendleton, Yvonne *astrophysicist*
Shaw, Tianna *biomedical engineer*
Statler, Irving Carl *aerospace engineer*
Whiting, Ellis Eugene *retired research scientist*
Yamauchi, Gloria *aerospace engineer*
Zuniga, Fanny *aerospace engineer*

Mojave
Melvill, Michael W. *aircraft company executive, experimental test pilot*
Rutan, Elbert L. (Burt Rutan) *aircraft designer, aircraft company executive*
Rutan, Richard Glenn (Dick Rutan) *aircraft company executive, aviator*
Shelby, Tim Otto *secondary school educator*
Yeager, Jeana *aviator*

Monarch Beach
Dougherty, Elmer Lloyd, Jr., *retired chemical engineering educator, consultant*
Mackaig, Janet Brownlee *artist, printmaker, educator*

Monrovia
Andary, Thomas Joseph *biochemist, researcher*
Brown, Gwendolyn (Williams) *music educator*
Comings, David Edward *physician, medical genetics scientist*
Deliman, Robert Michael *surgeon*
Edwards, Kenneth Neil *chemical engineering executive*
Jalbert, Janelle Jennifer *executive recruiter, secondary school educator*
Jemelian, John Nazar *management consultant*
Kimnach, Myron William *botanist, horticulturist*
Mountjoy, Dennis Lee *state official*
Pray, Ralph Emerson *metallurgical engineer*
Salaman, Maureen Kennedy *writer, nutritionist*
Stevens, Gary *retired jockey*

Montclair
Negrete McLeod, Gloria *state official*

Monte Nido
Brandewie, Richard Anthony *laser and optics consultant*

Monte Sereno
Allan, Lionel Manning *lawyer*

Montebello
Calderon, Ronald *state official*

Montecito
Coln, William Alexander, III, *retired pilot*
Meghreblian, Robert Vartan *manufacturing executive, physicist*
Shehata, Said Ahmed *surgeon, researcher*
Wheelon, Albert Dewell *physicist*

Monterey
Astore, William Joseph *historian, dean*
Bhaskar, Surindar Nath *pathologist, periodontist*
Black, Robert Lincoln *pediatrician, educator*
Boger, Dan Calvin *economics professor, consultant*
Bomberger, Russell Branson *lawyer, writer*
Browder, John Glen *former congressman, educator*
Butler, Jon Terry *computer engineering educator, researcher*
Davis, Craig Alphin *lawyer, manufacturing company executive*
de la Vega Montalvo, Guido Enrique *language educator, consultant*
Denning, Peter James *computer scientist, engineer*
Fenton, Lewis Lowry *lawyer*
Franke, Jack Emil *foreign language educator*
Gaver, Donald Paul *mathematics professor, consultant*
Gotshall, Cordia Ann *publishing company executive, distributing executive*
Haddad, Louis Nicholas *paralegal*
Hanlon, James Allison *confectionery company executive*
Hennessy, Robert Thomas *information technology executive*
Hoivik, Thomas Harry *military educator, international consultant*
Kadushin, Karen Donna *dean*
Lehr, Jeffrey Marvin *immunologist, allergist*
Lewis, Sharyn Lee *sculptor*
Marto, Paul James *retired mechanical engineering educator, consultant, researcher*
Matthews, David Fort *career officer*
Meyers, Gerald A. *metal products executive*
Miller, Richard Connelly *publishing executive, writer*
Newberry, Conrad Floyde *aerospace engineering educator*
Oder, Broeck Newton *school emergency management consultant*
Packard, Julie *aquarium administrator*
Peet, Phyllis Irene *women's studies educator*
Reese, William Albert, III, *psychologist, clinical neuropsychologist*
Reneker, Maxine Hohman *librarian*
Rowe, Neil Charles *science educator*
Sarpkaya, Turgut *mechanical engineering educator*
Schrady, David Alan *civilian military employee, educator*
Shull, Harrison *chemist, educator*
Shultz, Jeanne Marie *training director, workforce improvement analyst*
Sunde, Douglas *plastic surgeon*

Monterey Park
Amezcua, Charlie Anthony *social science counselor*
Hogan, Kelley Maureen *theater educator, actress*
Ly, Allan Q. *medical technician*
Montag, David Moses *telecommunications industry executive*
Moreno, Ernest H. *college president*
Sekiguchi, Eugene *dentist, dental association executive*
Smith, Betty Denny *county official, administrator, fashion executive*
Stapleton, Jean *journalism educator*
Szeto, Paul (Cheuk-Ching Szeto) *religious mission executive*
Tsao, Gus *information technology executive*
Wilson, Linda *librarian*

Moorpark
Bahn, Gilbert Schuyler *retired mechanical engineer, researcher, novelist*
Kessner, Dolly Eugenio *music educator, concert pianist*
Young, Victoria E. *occupational health nurse, lawyer*

Moraga
Allen, Richard Garrett *healthcare and education consultant*
Haag, Carol Ann Gunderson *marketing professional, consultant, hotel executive*
Hansen, George Eric *political scientist, educator*
Kilbourne, George William *lawyer*
O'Brien, Bea Jae *artist*
Peterson, Gene David *music educator*
Silcox, Frances Eleanor *museum and exhibits planning consultant*

Moreno Valley
Hadfield, Tomi Senger *hospital administrator*
White, Charles R. *former mayor*

Morgan Hill
Foster, John Robert *lawyer*
Freimark, Robert (Bob Freimark) *artist*
McGuire, Thomas Roger *distribution company executive*
O'Handley, Douglas Alexander *retired astronomer*
Tan, Lucas G. *anesthesiologist*

Morro Bay
Chandler, Bruce Frederick *internist*
Scholer, Margaret D. *adult education educator*

Moss Landing
Brewer, Peter George *ocean geochemist*
Clague, David A. *geologist*
Lange, Lester Henry *mathematics professor*

Mount Shasta
Mann, Karen *consultant, educator*
Mariner, William Martin *chiropractor*
Stienstra, Stephani Ann *editor, writer*

Mountain View
Abel, Elizabeth A. *dermatologist*
Barksdale, James Love *communications company executive*
Belluzzo, Richard E. *former computer company executive*
Bennett, Stephen M. *computer company executive*
Bills, Robert Howard *political party executive*
Brin, Sergey *information technology executive*
Chandramouli, Ramamurti *electrical engineer*
Clarke, C. Boyd *medical products executive*
Craig, Joan Carmen *secondary school educator, performing arts educator*
de Geus, Aart J. *computer software company executive*
Di Muccio, Mary-Jo *retired librarian*
Dixit, Anindya *business executive and information technology strategy consultant*
Drexler, Jerome *technology company executive*
East, John *computer company executive*
Edsell, Patrick L. *computer company executive*
Garlick, Larry *executive*
Johnson, Conor Deane *mechanical engineer*
Kisner, Daniel *electronics executive*
Kobza, Dennis Jerome *architect*
Koo, George Ping Shan *business consultant*
Kordestani, Omid *Internet company executive*
Lowen, Robert Marshall *plastic surgeon*
Malachowsky, Chris Alan *electrical engineer*
Mansfield, Elaine Schultz *molecular geneticist, automation specialist*
Otus, Simone *public relations executive*
Page, Larry *information technology executive*
Pasahow, Lynn H(arold) *lawyer*
Perrella, Anthony Joseph *electronics engineer*
Perry, Michael S. *biotechnology company executive*
Polese, Kim *software company executive*
Qureishi, A. Salam *computer software and services company executive*
Reidel, Art *health products executive*
Schmidt, Eric Emerson *information technology executive*
Sclavos, Stratton *information technology executive*
Serra, Patricia Janet *social services administrator*
Sultanov, Namig, 2d Baronet, *musician, music educator*
Tarter, Jill Cornell *science foundation director, astronomer, researcher*
Urman, Jeffrey David *physician, educator*
Warren, Richard Wayne *obstetrician, gynecologist*
Yan, Qing *bioinformatics scientist*

Murrieta
Cloud, Mark F. *video producer, director, writer, musician*
Geffe, Philip Reinhold *electrical engineer, consultant*
Lake, Bruce Meno *applied physicist*
McClellan, Barry Dean *city manager*
Plachno, Ronald John *electrical engineer*

Napa
Anderson, Richard Elliott *internist, educator*
Battisti, Paul Oreste *retired county supervisor*
Brough, Bruce Alvin *public relations executive, communications executive*
Chiarella, Peter Ralph *vintner*
Chung, Dae Hyun *retired geophysicist*
Eissmann, Walter James *consulting company executive*
Gillespie, Marcia Lou *tax specialist, accountant, musician*
Kuntz, Charles Powers *lawyer*
Loar, Peggy Ann *foundation administrator, museum administrator*
Morgese, Vincent John *neurosurgeon*
Silver, Diane S. *dermatologist*
Snow, Tower Charles, Jr., *lawyer*
Wahl, Howard Wayne *retired construction company executive, engineer*
Zimmermann, John Paul *plastic surgeon*

National City
Beauchamp, Miles Philip *newspaper editor, columnist, education consultant*
Morgan, Jacob Richard *cardiologist*

Nevada City
Whitsel, Richard Harry *retired biologist, entomologist*

Newark
Balmuth, Michael A. *retail executive*
Call, John G. *corporate financial executive*
Ferber, Norman Alan *retail executive*
Gupta, Anju *risk management consultant*
Mueller, Nancy *food products executive*
Peters, James C. *retail executive*
Shah, Haresh Chandulal *civil engineering educator*

Newbury Park
Bleiberg, Leon William *surgical podiatrist*
Fenton, Dennis Michael *research scientist*
Lindsey, Joanne M. *flight attendant, poet*
McCune, Sara Miller *foundation executive, publisher*
Stadler, Katherine Loy *advertising sales executive*

Newhall
Baity, Cameron B. *film director, writer*
Stein, Karl N. *plastic and reconstructive surgeon*

Newman
Carlsen, Janet Haws *retired insurance company executive*

Newport Beach
Adams, William George *lawyer*
Amyes, Edwin Westby *neurosurgeon*
Baskin, Scott David *lawyer*
Bennett, Bruce W. *construction company executive, civil engineer*
Bissell, George Arthur *architect*
Bren, Donald L. *real estate company executive*
Brown, Ernest Christopher *lawyer, engineer*
Brown, Giles Tyler *history educator, lecturer*
Bruggeman, Terrance John *financial corporate executive*
Bryant, Thomas Lee *magazine editor*
Cable, Wade H. *executive*
Cano, Kristin Maria *lawyer*
Carman, Ernest Day *lawyer*
Carmichael, David Richard *lawyer*
Casey, Thomas Clark *retired trust company executive, investment advisor*
Chiu, John Tang *physician*
Connolly, John Earle *surgeon, educator*
Crean, John C. *retired housing and recreational vehicles manufacturing company executive*
Dean, Paul John *magazine editor*
de Garcia, Lucia *marketing professional*
Di Massa, Ernani Vincenzo, Jr., *broadcast executive, television producer, writer*
Fawcett, John Scott *real estate developer*
Frederick, Dolliver H. *merchant banker*
Fries, Arthur Lawrence *life health insurance broker, disability claim consultant*
Gellman, Gloria Gae Seeburger Schick *marketing professional*
Gerken, Walter Bland *insurance company executive*
Gross, William H. (Bill Gross) *financial analyst, investment company executive*
Hinshaw, Ernest Theodore, Jr., *private investor, former Olympics executive, former finance company executive*
Jeffers, Michael Bogue *lawyer*
Johnson, William Stanley *metal distribution company executive*
Jones, Roger Wayne *electronics executive*
Kenney, William John, Jr., *real estate development executive*
Kolyer, John McNaughton *materials specialist, chemist*
Kraus, John Walter *former aerospace engineering company executive*
Lawless, William Burns *lawyer, retired judge, academic administrator*
Lawson, Thomas Cheney *fraud examiner*
Lyon, William *builder*
Mallory, Frank Linus *lawyer*
Mandel, Maurice, II, *lawyer, educator, mediator*
Marcoux, Carl Henry *former insurance executive, writer, historian*
Martin, Joseph Chekel *not-for-profit developer*
Matteucci, Dominick Vincent *real estate developer*
Mc Culloch, Samuel Clyde *history professor*
McMahon, Brian *publishing executive*
Millar, Richard William, Jr., *lawyer*
Mink, Maxine Mock *real estate company executive*
Mortensen, Arvid LeGrande *lawyer*
Parks, Fredrick Scott *systems engineer*
Pepe, Stephen Phillip *lawyer*
Phillips, Layn R. *lawyer*
Poole, Thomas Richard *endowment capital campaign director, fund raising counsel*
Randolph, Steven *financial advisor*
Richardson, Walter John *architect*
Rogers, Robert Reed *manufacturing executive*
Savopoulos, Marios A. *architect, director*
Schafer, Glenn S *insurance company executive*
Schiff, Laurie *lawyer*
Schnapp, Roger Herbert *lawyer, consultant*
Schumacher, Stephen Joseph *lawyer, educator*
Shamoun, John Milam *plastic surgeon*
Shohet, Jack A. *otolaryngologist*
Shonk, Albert Davenport, Jr., *advertising executive*
Solmer, Richard *surgeon*
Spitz, Barbara Salomon *artist*
Steinberg, Leigh W. *sports agent*
Stephens, Michael Dean *hospital administrator*
Stoutenborough, J. Todd *architect*
Sutton, Thomas C. *insurance company executive*
Thorp, Edward Oakley *investment management company executive*
Tracy, James Jared, Jr., *accountant, financial executive, law firm administrator*
Tran, Khanh T. *insurance company executive*
Viehe, Richard B. *podiatrist*
Vine, Naomi *museum administrator*
Wagner, John Leo *lawyer, former magistrate judge*
Webb, H. Lawrence *real estate executive*
Weissbard, Samuel Held *lawyer*
Wentworth, Diana von Welanetz *author*
Wentworth, Theodore Sumner *lawyer*
Whittemore, Paul Baxter *psychologist*
Woollatt, Paul G. *financial company executive*

Newport Coast
Afifi, Alaa Youssef *cardiothoracic surgeon*
Evanoff, George C. *retired publishing executive*
Pavony, William H. *retail executive, consultant*
Swan, Peer Alden *public utility executive*

Norco
Eisen, Hilda *food products executive*

North Hills
Boeckmann, Herbert F., II, *automotive executive*

North Hollywood
Balmuth, Bernard Allen *retired film editor*
Boulanger, Donald Richard *financial services executive*
Busch, Estelle Winston *theater director*
Campos, Luis *puzzle writer*
Chang, Wung *business advisor, researcher, lecturer*
de la Houssaye, Brette Angelo-Pepe *electronics engineer, researcher*
Downey, Roma *actress*
Fanning, Dakota *actress*
Gallardo, Sandra Silvana *producer*
Holmes, Michael *performing company executive, performing arts educator*
Kreger, Melvin Joseph *lawyer*
Kuter, Kay E. *writer, actor*
Miller, Philip Gray *artist*
Price, Joe (Joe Allen) *artist, former educator, actor*
Reynolds, Debbie (Mary Frances Reynolds) *actress*
Runquist, Lisa A. *lawyer*
Schlosser, Anne Griffin *librarian*
Shapiro, Larry *lawyer, Internet company executive*
Stone, Sharon *actress*
Taravella, Rosie *actress*
Thomas, Tony *producer*
Toplitt, Gloria H. *voice educator, singer, actress*
Toussieng, Yolanda *make-up artist*
Wadsworth, Steve *recreational facility executive*

North Palm Springs
Mowry, Frank Henry *journalist, photojournalist*

Northridge
Avsharian, Roupen *prosecutor, department chairman, educator*
Bassler, Robert Covey *artist, educator*
Bradshaw, Richard Rotherwood *engineering executive*
Cartwright, Nancy *actress, television producer*
Chen, Joseph Tao *historian, educator*
Curzon, Susan Carol *university administrator*
Dart, John Seward *journalist, writer*
Falk, Heinrich Richard *theater and humanities educator*
Kiddoo, Robert James *engineering service company executive*
Koester, Jolene *academic administrator*
Koistinen, Paul Abraham Carl *historian, educator*
Lewis, Louise Miller *gallery director, art history educator*
Logan, Lee Robert *orthodontist*
Loudon, Craig Michael *video specialist*
McHenry, Leemon Benton *education educator, writer*
Mitchell, James Andrew *education educator*
Mitchell, Rie Rogers *psychologist, counselor, educator*
Orenstein, Michael (Ian Orenstein) *philatelic dealer, columnist*
Reagan, Janet Thompson *psychologist, educator*
Roberts, Teri Alane *accountant, educator, civic activist*
Roscigno, John Anthony *music educator, conductor*
Smathers, James Burton *medical physicist, educator*
Sparling, Mary Lee *biology professor*
Stampke, Stuart Reh *physicist, researcher*

Torgow, Eugene N. *electrical engineer*
Walcher, Alan Ernest *lawyer*
Weatherup, Wendy Gaines *graphic designer, writer*

Norwalk
Armstrong, David Ligon *psychiatrist*
Bao, Joseph Yue-Se *orthopedist, microsurgeon, educator*
Betancourt, David Apodaca *music educator*
Gould, D. Joy *social services administrator*
Matsuura, Kenneth Ray *counselor, articulation officer*
Schreiner, Gregory Lee *music educator*

Novato
Bibeault, Donald Bertrand *business executive, investor*
Bugental, James Frederick Thomas *retired psychologist, educator*
Carendi, Jan R. *insurance company executive*
Criswell, Eleanor Camp *psychologist*
Fraser, Margot *consumer products company executive*
Hanahan, Donald James *biochemist, educator*
Jaeger, Patsy Elaine *retired secondary education educator, artist*
Kratka-Schneider, Dorothy Maryjohanna *psychotherapist*
Patterson, W. Morgan *college president*
Price, Frederic D. *pharmaceutical executive*
Thompson, Peter Layard Hailey, Sr., *landscape and golf course architect, architectural firm executive*
White, Linda Lee Locy *secondary educator*

Nuevo
Wagner, Cheri J. *business owner*

Oak Park
Caldwell, Stratton Franklin *kinesiology educator*
Vinson, William Theodore *lawyer, diversified corporation executive*

Oakdale
Saletta, Mary Elizabeth (Betty Saletta) *sculptor, rancher*

Oakhurst
Cantwell, Christopher William *artist*

Oakland
Alba, Benny *artist*
Alford, Joan Franz *entrepreneur*
Al Malik, Amir Isa *entrepreneur, consultant, musician*
Ames, Bruce N(athan) *biochemist and molecular biology educator, department chairman*
Anderson, Robert Thomas *anthropologist, researcher, physician*
Anderson, Brother Timothy Mel *academic administrator*
Andrasick, James Stephen *diversified company executive*
Appier, Kevin (Robert Kevin Appier) *professional baseball player*
Armstrong, Saundra Brown *federal judge*
Bacon, Robert Dale *lawyer*
Beasley, Bruce Miller *sculptor*
Benton-Hardy, Lisa Renee *psychiatrist, educator*
Berry, Kathleen A. *English language educator*
Berry, Phillip Samuel *lawyer*
Bonutti, Alexander Carl *architect, urban designer*
Bouska Lee, Carla Ann *nursing and health care educator*
Brevetti, Francine Clelia *journalist*
Brown, Jerry (Edmund Gerald Brown Jr.) *mayor, former governor*
Brown, Karen *performing company executive*
Brust, David *physicist*
Bryant, Arthur H. *lawyer*
Carwell, Hattie Virginia *health physicist*
Chodorow, Nancy Julia *psychoanalyst, psychotherapist, educator*
Clemons, Robert Earl *non-profit organization administrator*
Cohan, Christopher *professional sports team executive*
Cole, Joan Hays *social worker, clinical psychologist*
Collen, Morris Frank *medical association administrator, physician, researcher*
Cowens, David William (Dave Cowens) *professional basketball coach, insurance executive, retired professional basketball player*
Crane, Robert Meredith *health care executive*
Cronk, William F., III, *food products executive*
Dailey, Garrett Clark *publisher, lawyer*
DeFazio, Lynette Stevens *dancer, educator, choreographer, violinist, actress*
Deming, Willis Riley *lawyer*
DeMoro, Rose Ann *nursing administrator*
De Vos, George Alphonse *psychologist, anthropologist*
Dibble, David Van Vlack *visually impaired educator, lawyer*
DiStefano, Tony E. *communications executive*
Drexel, Baron Jerome *lawyer*
Dynes, Robert C. *academic administrator*
Earle, Sylvia Alice *research biologist, oceanographer*
Ejabat, Mory *communications executive*
Elkin, Lynne Osman *author, DNA historian, educator*
Elliott, Jack *folk musician*
Farrell, Kenneth Royden *economist*
Finkle, Bernard J. *biochemist, researcher*
Foley, Jack (John Wayne Harold Foley) *poet, writer, editor*
Foster (Anderson), Margaret Howard *editor, archivist*
George, Donald Warner *online columnist and editor, freelance writer*
Givant, Steven Roger *mathematician, computer scientist, educator*
Gomes, Wayne Reginald *academic administrator*
Gonzalez, Arthur Padilla *artist, educator*
Granoff, Dan Martin *research scientist*
Griffin, Betty Jo *elementary school educator*
Gruber, Ronald P. *plastic surgeon, researcher*
Hafey, Joseph Michael *health association executive*
Hafter, Ruth Anne *library director, educator*
Haiman, Franklyn Saul *author, communications educator*
Halpern, Mark *writer*
Halvorson, George Charles *health care insurance company executive*
Haskell, Arthur Jacob *retired steamship company executive*
Hawkins, Robert B. *think-tank executive*
Heinrich, Daniel J. *chemicals executive*
Henkin, Leon Albert *mathematician, educator*
Hilsinger, Raymond L., Jr., *otolaryngologist*
Holmgren, Janet L. *college president*
Holst, James E. *lawyer*
Howatt, Sister Helen Clare *former human services director, former college library director*
Isaac Nash, Eva Mae *secondary school educator*
Jakubowsky, Frank Raymond *religious writer*
Jensen, D. Lowell *federal judge, lawyer, government official*
Johnson, Kenneth F. *lawyer*
Johnston, Gerald E. *manufacturing company executive*
Kahn, Timothy F. *food products company executive*
Kettell, Russell Willard *banker*
Killebrew, Ellen Jane (Mrs. Edward S. Graves) *cardiologist, educator*
Kint, Arne Tonis *industrial engineer, mechanical engineer*
Klatsky, Arthur Louis *cardiologist, epidemiologist*
Knox, Helene Margrethe *writer*
Koch, Richard Phillips (Terry Koch) *lawyer*
Koplin, Donald Leroy *health products executive, consumer advocate*
Krause, Marcella Elizabeth Mason (Mrs. Eugene Fitch Krause) *retired secondary school educator*
Lake, Suzanne *singer, music educator*
Lazar, John Edward *administrator non-profit organization*
Lee, Jong Hyuk *accountant*
Le Noir, Michael A. *allergist*
Linford, Rulon Kesler *retired physicist, engineer*
Macmeeken, John Peebles *foundation executive, educator*
Massachi, Dalya Faith *writer, consultant*
Matschullat, Robert W. *chemicals executive*
Matsumoto, George *architect*
Mayers, Eugene David *retired philosopher, educator*
McDonnell, John L., Jr., *lawyer*
McKinney, Judson Thad *broadcast executive*
Michael, Gary G. *retired retail supermarket and drug chain executive, university administrator*
Miller, Barry *research administrator, psychologist*
Miller, Kirk Edward *lawyer, health foundation executive*
Miller, Thomas Robbins *lawyer, publisher*
Montgomery, Mike *professional baseball coach*
Morris, Ronald Lew *oil and gas company executive*
Musihin, Konstantin K. *electrical engineer*
Nathan, Laura E. *sociology educator*
Neeley, Beverly Evon *sociologist, consultant*
Nelson, Shirley W. *bank executive*
Newsome, Randall Jackson *judge*
Ng, Lawrence Ming-Loy *pediatrician*
Nicol, Robert Duncan *architect*
O'Hara, Delia Iglauer *family nurse practitioner*
Ong, George E. *lawyer*
Ostrander, Willis Frederick *real estate appraiser*
Patton, Dennis David *radiologist, educator*
Peters, Arnold Stevens *legal association administrator, mechanical engineer*
Quinby, William Albert *lawyer, arbitrator, mediator*
Randisi, Elaine Marie *accountant, educator, writer*
Rath, Alan T. *sculptor*
Reese, Charles Woodrow, Jr., *lawyer*
Rhein, Timothy J. *retired transportation company executive*
Rice, Frances Mae *physician*
Richardson, Jason Anthoney *professional basketball player*
Rogers, T. Gary *food products company executive*
Roster, Michael *lawyer*
Sandler, Herbert M. *savings and loan association executive*
Sandler, Marion Osher *savings and loan association executive*
Saunders, Ward Bishop, Jr., *retired aluminum company executive*
Schacht, Henry Mevis *writer, consultant*
Schrag, Peter *editor, writer*
Shapiro, David W. *prosecutor*
Sharpton, Thomas *physician*
Silverberg, Robert *author*
Slack, Vickie *human services administrator*
Smith, Eldred Reid *library educator*
Smith, Mark D. *foundation administrator*
Steele, Richard Donald *researcher, linguist, physicist*
Stewart, John Lincoln *university administrator*
Stromme, Gary L. *law librarian*
Sun, Peter P. *neurosurgeon*
Tchaikovsky, Leslie J. *federal judge*
Teufel, William Lockwood *emergency physician*
Theroux, David Jon *economist, educator, research and development company executive*
Turner, Tom *writer, editor*
Tyndall, David Gordon *business educator*
Wade, Bill *airport executive*
Warrick, Brooke *marketing executive*
Weinmann, Robert Lewis *neurologist*
West, Natalie Elsa *lawyer*
Wilken, Claudia *judge*
Williams, Carol H. *advertising executive*
Wills, John Arthur *computer programmer, analyst*
Willson, Clyde D. *biologist, educator*
Wood, James Michael *lawyer*
Wood, Larry (Mary Laird) *journalist, writer, public relations executive, educator, environmental consultant*
Woodbury, Marda Liggett *librarian, writer*
Youngs, Robert Riggs *engineer*
Zelmanowitz, Julius Martin *mathematics educator, university administrator*
Zemens, Anna Jo C. *library director*
Zito, Barry *professional baseball player*
Zschau, Marilyn *singer*

Occidental
Rumsey, Victor Henry *electrical engineering educator emeritus*

Oceano
Scott, Donald Michael *writer, educator*

Oceanside
Beck, Marilyn Mohr *columnist*
Bell, Sharon Kaye *small business owner*
Curtin, Thomas Lee *ophthalmologist*
Delienne, Jacquelyn E. *e-commerce consultant, publisher*
Downer, William John, Jr., *retired health facility administrator*
Garfin, Louis *retired actuary*
Hertweck, E. Romayne *psychology educator*
LaRosa, John Paul *education educator*
Lyon, Richard *mayor emeritus, retired naval officer*
McIntyre, Louise S. *income tax consultant*
McLean, Arthur Frederick *mechanical engineer*
Munson, Lucille Marguerite (Mrs. Arthur E. Munson) *real estate broker*
Peckham, Donald *computer company executive*
Pena, Maria Geges *academic services administrator*
Roberts, James McGregor *retired professional association executive*
Sarkisian, Pamela Outlaw *artist*
Sullivan, Patrick James *lawyer*
Swoger, James Wesley *magician*
Yurist, Svetlan Joseph *mechanical engineer*

Ojai
Cusumano, James Anthony *filmmaker, retired pharmaceutical company executive, former recording artist*
Paxton, Glenn Gilbert *composer*
Shagam, Marvin Hückel-Berri *private school educator*

Ontario
Ariss, David William, Sr., *real estate developer, consultant*
Dastrup-Hamill, Faye Myers *city official*
Dunn, Donald Jack *law librarian, law educator, dean, lawyer*
Endsley, Donal E. *architectural firm executive*
Gilliam, James L. *architectural firm executive*
Hull, Jane Laurel Leek *retired nurse, administrator*
Kain, Robert J. *architectural firm executive*
Küeng, Christian Roulland *elementary school educator, principal*
McGehee, Sharon *school system administrator*
Ovitt, Gary C. *mayor*
Peters, Jacqueline Mary *secondary school educator*
Previtti, James P. *real estate executive*
Rappaport, Michael Paul *columnist*
Rosenzweig, Herbert Stephen *stockbroker*
Soto, Nell *state senator*
Taylor, Chris R. *architect*

Orange
Anzel, Sanford Harold *orthopedic surgeon*
Armentrout, Steven Alexander *oncologist*
Ballard, Jeffrey Lawrence *surgeon, educator*
Barr, Ronald Jeffrey *dermatologist, pathologist*
Batchelor, James Kent *lawyer*
Booth, Donald Richard *economist, educator*
Brown, Tod David *bishop*
Chang, Jae Chan *hematologist, oncologist, educator*
Cinat, Marianne Eva *surgeon*
Cooper, Steven Harold *education educator*
Crumley, Roger Lee *surgeon, educator, otolaryngologist*
Cumiford, William Lloyd *historian, educator, curator*
Dimick, Neil Francis *medical products wholesale executive*
DiSaia, Philip John *obstetrician, gynecologist, radiology educator*
Doti, Frank John *law educator, consultant*
Doti, James L. *academic administrator*
Fischel, Richard Jeffrey *thoracic surgeon*
Fisher, Mark Jay *neurologist, neuroscientist, educator*
Fisk, Edward Ray *retired civil engineer, author, educator*
Godeke, Raymond Dwight Cook *insurance company executive, accountant*
Hamann, Dennis *food products executive*
Hamilton, Harry Lemuel, Jr., *atmospheric science professor*
Hubbell, Floyd Allan *internist, educator*
Kaempen, Charles Edward *manufacturing executive*
Kelley, Robert Paul, Jr., *management consultation executive*
Kim, Moon Hyun *endocrinologist, educator*
Klassen, Henry John *ophthalmologist*
Lungren, Daniel Edward *former state attorney general*
Martin, Mike W. *philosophy educator*
Matthews, Joseph Virgil *pianist, music educator*
Mc Farland, Norman Francis *bishop*
Milliken, Jeffrey *cardiothoracic surgeon*
Monsees, James Eugene *engineering executive, consultant*
Morgan, Beverly Carver *pediatrician, educator*
Mosier, Harry David, Jr., *physician, educator*
Rowen, Marshall *radiologist*
Sawdei, Milan A. *lawyer*
Scherman, Carol E. *human resources professional*
Shirvani, Hamid *architect, educator, author, administrator, philosopher*
Smith, Ronald Edward *ophthalmologist*
Spitzer, Todd *state official*
Stuewe, Isabel *elementary school educator*
Talbott, George Robert *physicist, mathematician, educator*
Todsen, Dana Rognar *health care executive*
Torres, Rudy Arnold *artist*
Tuggle, Francis Douglas *dean, consultant*
Underwood, Vernon O., Jr., *grocery stores executive*
Vatcher, James Gordon *retired physician*
Vaziri, Nosratola Dabir *internist, educator, nephrologist*
Wilson, Archie Fredric *medical educator*
Wong, Brian Jet-Fei *surgeon*
Yu, Jen *medical educator*

Orinda
Amoroso, Richard Louis *cosmologist, educator*
Epperson, Stella Marie *artist*
Fisher, Robert Morton *foundation administrator, university administrator*
Heftmann, Erich *biochemist*
Hetland, John Robert *lawyer, educator*
Mikalow, Alfred Alexander, II, *deep sea diver, marine surveyor, marine diving consultant*
Somerset, Harold Richard *retail executive*
Strong, Susan Clancey *writer, communication consultant, editor*
Trowbridge, Thomas, Jr., *mortgage banking company executive*
Woolsey, David Arthur *leasing and commercial company executive*

Oroville
Cella, Paul *civil engineer, consultant*
Chandy, Mammen G. *surgeon*
Curry, William Sims *county official*
Davis, Frederick Charles *county official*
Likley, Katherine *retired retail executive, writer*

Oxnard
Auston, David Henry *former academic administrator, electrical engineer, educator*
Dimitriadis, Andre C. *health care executive*
Engels, Gerhard *music educator, composer*
Gill, David *food products executive*
Hiepler, Mark O. *lawyer*
Hill, Alice Lorraine *history, genealogy and social researcher, educator*
Kavli, Fred *retired manufacturing executive, retired engineering executive*
Kirschbaum, Alan Ira *air force officer, systems integration specialist*
Lopez, Manuel M. *mayor*
O'Connell, Hugh Mellen, Jr., *retired architect*
Perrier, Barbara Sue *artist*
Sweet, Harvey *theatrical set designer, lighting designer*
Takasugi, Nao *state official, business developer*
Zhou, Sophia Huai *biomedical engineering scientist*

Pacific Grove
Davis, Robert Edward *retired communication educator*
Elinson, Henry David *artist, language educator*
Haider, Paul Randall *psychology consultant*
Longman, Anne Strickland *special education educator, consultant*

Pacific Palisades
Beck, John Christian *physician, educator*
Bilson, Wesley *healthcare company executive*
Cale, Charles Griffin *lawyer, private investor*
Casady, Dorothea Jane *artist, educator, sculptor*
Chesney, Lee Roy, Jr., *artist*
Claes, Daniel John *physician*
Diehl, Richard Kurth *retail business consultant*
Flattery, Thomas Long *lawyer, legal administrator*
Garwood, Victor Paul *retired speech communication educator, audiologist*
Georges, Robert Augustus *retired educator, researcher, writer*
Griver, Jeanette A *human factors scientist, consultant*
Hadges, Thomas Richard *media consultant*
Hagenbuch, Rodney Dale *financial consultant*
Herman, Elvin E. *retired consulting electronic engineer*
Hoffenberg, Marvin *retired political science educator, consultant*
Holberg, Eva Maria *volunteer*
Horowitz, Edward Jay *lawyer*
Humphreys, Robert Lee *advertising executive*
Jennings, Marcella Grady *rancher, investor*
Jones, Edgar Allan, Jr., *law educator, arbitrator, lawyer*
Kalis, Murray *advertising agency executive, writer*
Katz, George Gershon *psychologist*
Kirkgaard, Valerie Anne *media group executive, syndicated talk radio host, writer, producer, consultant*
Klein, Joseph Mark *retired mining company executive*
Longaker, Richard Pancoast *political science educator emeritus*
Love, Susan Margaret *surgeon, educator, writer*
Mendel, Dennis D. *lawyer*
Middleton, James Arthur *oil and gas company executive*
Mulryan, Henry Trist *mineral company executive, consultant*
Price, Frank *motion picture and television company executive*
Sevilla, Stanley *lawyer*
Tourtellotte, Wallace William *neurologist, educator*
Verrone, Patric Miller *lawyer, writer*

Pacifica
Kelly, Kevin *editor*

Palm Desert
Ayling, Henry Faithful *writer, editor, consultant*
Bass, Betty Zoe Passmore (Mrs. Eric Bass) *artist*
Baxter, Betty Carpenter *educational administrator*
Bernhard, Herbert Ashley *lawyer*
Bratrud, Linda Kay *secondary school educator*
Cedar, Paul Arnold *church executive, minister*
DeMarco, Ralph John *real estate developer*
Dugan, Robert Perry, Jr., *retired minister, religious organization administrator*
Epstein, Marvin Morris *retired construction company executive*
Friesz, Mary Lee *freelance/self-employed poet*
Goldberg, Martin Stanford *retired lawyer*
Heydman, Abby Maria *academic executive*
Hoffmann, Joan Carol *retired academic dean*
Kaufman, Charlotte King *artist*
Kern, Paul Alfred *advertising executive, consultant, realtor, financial analyst*
Krallinger, Joseph Charles *entrepreneur, business advisor, author*
Miller, Donald Ross *management consultant*
Olson, Phillip David LeRoy *agriculturist, chemist*
Osborne, Bartley Porter, Jr., *aeronautical engineer*
Pierno, Anthony Robert *lawyer*
Ponder, Catherine *clergywoman, author*
Sausman, Karen *zoological park administrator*
Sexson, Stephen Bruce *education writer, educator*
Stenhouse, Everett Ray *clergy administrator*
Vander Naald Egenes, Joan Elizabeth *small business owner, educator*
West, Hugh Sterling *aircraft leasing company executive*

Palm Springs
Arnold, Stanley Norman *manufacturing consultant*
Boyajian, Timothy Edward *public health officer, educator, consultant*
Brain, Jesse *manufacturing executive*
Coffey, Nancy Ann *real estate broker*
Diodosio, Charles Joseph *lawyer*
Dupree, Stanley M. *lawyer*
FitzGerald, John Edward, III, *lawyer*
Gaede, James Ernest *physician, medical educator*
Gerard, James Wilson *publishing consultant*
Gordon, Stewart Lynell *musician, educator*
Hartman, Rosemary Jane *retired special education educator*
Jones, Milton Wakefield *publisher*

Jumonville, Felix Joseph, Jr., *physical education educator, realtor*
Kimberling, John Farrell *retired lawyer*
Loya, Ranaldo *senior physician assistant*
Martin, Ann Bodenhamer *minister, writer*
Martin, Lisa Ann *literary agent, writer*
Owings, Thalia Kelley *elementary school educator*
Petermann, Hans Jürgen *research scientist*
Racina, Thom (Thomas Frank Raucina) *television writer, editor*
Rupracht, William George *chaplain*
Underwood, Thomas Woodbrook *communications company executive*
Weil, Max Harry *internist, cardiologist, educator, medical researcher*
Wiesner, John Joseph *retail chain store executive*
Wilson, Myron Robert, Jr., *retired psychiatrist*

Palmdale
Anderson, R(obert) Gregg *real estate company executive*
Farr, Donald Eugene *engineering scientist*
Kilanowski, Dana Marcotte *historian, writer, filmmaker, archaeologist*

Palo Alto
Adamson, Geoffrey David *reproductive endocrinologist, surgeon*
Andersen, Torben Brender *optical researcher, astronomer, software engineer*
Anderson, Charles Arthur *former research institute administrator*
Arnold Quinn, Helen Rhoda *physicist*
Aschwanden, Markus Josef *astrophysicist*
Babb, Richard Rankin *gastroenterologist, educator*
Bagshaw, Malcolm A. *radiation oncologist, educator*
Balzhiser, Richard Earl *research and development company executive*
Barnholt, Edward W. *computer company executive*
Baron, Frederick David *lawyer*
Baskins, Ann O. *lawyer, computer company executive*
Baum, Brandon *lawyer, law educator*
Benton, Lee F. *lawyer*
Berry, Robert Emanuel *aerospace company executive*
Beutler, Larry Edward *psychology educator*
Blackmore, Peter *computer company executive*
Blessing-Moore, Joann Catherine *allergist*
Bohrnstedt, George William *educational researcher*
Botcheva, Luba *psychologist, researcher*
Botstein, David *geneticist, educator*
Bradley, Donald Edward *lawyer*
Breyer, James William *venture capitalist*
Briggs, Winslow Russell *plant biologist, educator*
Britton, M(elvin) C(reed), Jr., *rheumatologist*
Brown, David Randolph *electrical engineer*
Brown, H. William *urban economist, private banker*
Byrd, Thomas Russell *medical educator*
Calvin, Allen David *psychologist, educator*
Casati, Fabio *engineer*
Chen, Stephen Shi-hua *pathologist, biochemist*
Climan, Richard Elliot *lawyer*
Cohen, Karl Paley *nuclear energy consultant*
Colligan, John C. (Bud Colligan) *multimedia company executive*
Cooke, John P. *cardiologist, medical educator, medical researcher*
Couder, Alain *personal computer manufacturing company executive*
Coughran, William M., Jr., *management consultant, researcher*
Cutler, Leonard Samuel *physicist*
Dabbagh, Karim *research scientist*
Dafoe, Donald Cameron *surgeon, educator*
Daniels, John R. *oncologist, educator*
Davidson, Gordon K. *lawyer*
DeLustro, Frank Anthony *biomedical company executive, research immunologist*
Dement, William Charles *medical researcher, medical educator*
Denzel, Nora *information technology executive*
Desai, Kavin Hirendra *pediatrician*
Diamond, Diana Louise *editor, graphic artist*
Druyan, Lara Catherine *venture capitalist*
Dunn, Debra L. *computer company executive*
Dwyer, John Charles *lawyer*
Eggers, Alfred John, Jr., *research corporation executive*
Eng, Lawrence Fook *biochemistry educator, neurochemist*
Ernst, Wallace Gary *geology educator*
Estrin, Judith *computer company executive*
Faxon, Thomas Baker *retired lawyer*
Fiorina, Carleton S. (Carly Fiorina) *computer company executive*
Flory, Curt Alan *research physicist*
Forbes, Alfred Dean *religious studies researcher*
Forno, Lysia S. *neuropathologist*
Fortmann, Stephen Paul *medical educator, researcher, epidemiologist*
Friedman, Paul A. *biotechnology company executive*
Fries, James Franklin *internal medicine educator*
Gerety, Robert John *microbiologist, pharmaceutical company executive, pediatrician, vaccinologist*
Glauthier, T. J. *non-profit executive*
Goff, Harry Russell *retired manufacturing company executive*
Gong, Mamie Poggio *elementary school educator*
Greene, Diane *information technology executive*
Halluin, Albert Price *lawyer*
Hamilton, David Mike *publishing executive*
Hammett, Benjamin Cowles *psychologist*
Haque, Promod *venture capitalist*
Harkonen, Wesley Scott *physician, pharmaceutical company executive*
Hays, Marguerite Thompson *nuclear medicine physician, educator*
Hecht, Lee *software company executive*
Hentz, Vincent R. *surgeon*
Herrick, Tracy Grant *fiduciary*
Heuman, Donna *lawyer*
Hinckley, Robert Craig *lawyer*
Hodge, Philip Gibson, Jr., *mechanical and aerospace engineering educator*
Holman, Halsted Reid *medical educator, physician*
Huberman, Bernardo A *physicist*
Hubert, Helen Betty *epidemiologist*
Illes, Judy *medical researcher, neuroethicist*
Ivy, Benjamin Franklin, III, *financial and real estate investment advisor*
Jackson, Cynthia L. *lawyer*
Johnson, Allison *corporate communications specialist*
Johnson, Craig W. *lawyer*
Johnson, Noble Marshall *research scientist*
Joshi, Vyomesh *computer company executive*
Kay, Alan C. *computer scientist*
Keeffe, Emmet Britton *medical educator*
Keller, Arthur Michael *computer science researcher*
Kim, Wan Hee *electrical engineering educator, business executive*
Kincaid, Judith Wells *electronics company executive*
Kohler, Fred Christopher *tax specialist*
Kung, Frank F. *biotechnology and life sciences investor, venture capitalist*
Lampman, Richard H. *computer company executive*
Lane, Alfred Thomas *medical educator*
Lange, Louis G. *health products executive*
Laurie, Ronald Sheldon *lawyer*
Lee, Virginia Fern *community volunteer*
Lehman, Michael Evans *computer company executive*
Lender, Adam *electrical engineer*
Linna, Timo Juhani *immunologist, researcher, educator*
Litt, Iris Figarsky *pediatrics educator*
Lo, Yee On *composer*
Loewenstein, Walter Bernard *nuclear power technologist*
Loveless, Edward Eugene *education educator, musician*
Luh, Howard H. *aerospace engineer*
Muffly, Roy Herrick *internist, educator, retired dean*
Massey, Henry P., Jr., *lawyer*
Matthews, Zakee *psychiatrist, educator*
Mayo, Robert N. *computer science researcher*
McCall, Jennifer Jordan *lawyer*
McCluskey, Lois Thornhill *photographer*
Mcglynn, Martin M *biotechnology company executive*
McHugh, Maura *professional basketball coach*
McHugh, Stuart Lawrence *materials engineer*
McIntyre, Robert Wheeler *retired conservation organization executive*
McKinney, Harry Webb *computer company executive*
Michie, Sara H. *pathologist, educator*
Miller, Michael Patiky *lawyer*
Moffitt, Donald Eugene *transportation company executive*
Mommsen, Katharina *retired German language and literature educator*
Moore, Cassandra Chrones *real estate broker and policy analyst*
Moos, Rudolf H. *psychologist, researcher*
Mosher, Roger L. *lawyer*
Murray, Dave *marketing professional, editor*
Neale-May, Donovan *marketing professional*
Nelson-Walker, Roberta *management software company executive*
Ning, Shoucheng *cancer biologist, head and neck surgeon*
Nopar, Alan Scott *lawyer*
Nordlund, Donald Craig *lawyer*
O'Brien, Raymond Francis *transportation executive*
Parker, James Wesley *former career naval officer, investment company executive*
Patten, Valerie Lynn *lawyer*
Patterson, Robert Edward *lawyer*
Perl, Martin Lewis *physicist, educator, chemical engineer*
Phair, Joseph Baschon *lawyer*
Pizzo, Philip A. *pediatrics educator, university administrator*
Quate, Calvin Forrest *engineering educator*
Ratnathicam, Chutta *transportation executive*
Rehman, Saifur *web site design company executive*
Renda, Patrick Blake *investment company executive*
Rich, Lesley Mosher *artist*
Richardson, Tom (Edward Thompson Richardson) *artist*
Rinsky, Arthur C. *lawyer*
Robinson, Agnes Claflin *educational administrator*
Robinson, Shane V. *computer company executive*
Rosaldo, Renato Ignacio, Jr., *cultural anthropology educator*
Rosenthal, Arnon *science association director*
Saegesser, Marguerite M. *artist*
Salvatierra, Oscar, Jr., *transplant surgeon, urologist, educator*
Sanders, William John *research scientist*
Saxena, Arjun Nath *physicist*
Schrier, Stanley Leonard *hematologist, educator*
Schulz, Michael *physicist*
Schurman, David Jay *orthopedic surgeon, educator*
Schwartz, John J. *biotechnology company executive*
Scitovsky, Anne Aickelin *economist, researcher*
Seethaler, William Charles *international business executive, consultant*
Shuer, Lawrence Mendel *neurosurgery educator*
Shulman, Ron E. *lawyer*
Silverman, Norman Henry *cardiologist, educator*
Simon, James Lowell *lawyer*
Skeff, Kelley Michael *health facility administrator*
Skoll, Jeffrey *philanthropist, Internet company executive*
Skoog, Douglas Arvid *retired chemistry educator, writer*
Smith, Glenn A. *lawyer*
Sonsini, Larry W. *lawyer*
Spanner, Robert Alan *lawyer*
Staprans, Armand *electronics executive*
Stein, Isaac *investment company executive*
Stephens, Bess *computer company executive*
Strober, Samuel *immunologist, educator*
Sullivan, Patrick Henry *management consultant*
Sundheim, George (Duf) *lawyer, political organization worker*
Sunshine, Philip *pediatrician*
Survilo, Francine Marion *painter, sculptor*
Swain, Judith Lea *cardiovascular physician, educator*
Taimuty, Samuel Isaac *physicist*
Tanner, Douglas Alan *lawyer*
Taylor, John Joseph *nuclear engineer, researcher*
Ticknor, Carolyn M. *computer company executive*
Tiffany, Joseph Raymond, II, *lawyer*
Trumbull, Terry Alan *energy and environmental consultant, lawyer*
Tsien, Richard Winyu *biology professor*
Tucker, Brian *seismologist*
Tune, Bruce Malcolm *pediatrics educator, renal toxicologist*
Urquhart, John *medical researcher, educator*
Van Atta, David Murray *lawyer*
Varney, Robert Nathan *retired physicist, researcher*
Vassar, Richard Holt *aerospace engineer*
Walker, Carolyn Peyton *English language educator*
Waller, Peter William *public relations executive*
Watson, David Colquitt *electrical engineer, educator*
Wayman, Robert Paul *computer company executive*
Weng, Wen-Kai *oncologist, medical researcher*
Wheeler, Raymond Louis *lawyer*
Whitfield, Roy A. *pharmaceutical executive*
Wick, Michael M. *biotechnology executive*
Willem, Karen J. *business software company financial executive*
Winfield, Roy A. *pharmaceutical company executive*
Winkleby, Marilyn A. *medical researcher*
Winkler, Michael *computer company executive*
Wong, Y(ing) Wood *real estate investment company executive, real estate development company executive, venture capital investment company executive*
Wright, Kirby Michael *writer, editor*
Zarins, Christopher Kristaps *surgery educator, vascular surgeon*
Zitzner, Duane E. *computer company executive*

Palos Verdes Estates
Abbott, A. Dwight *retired astronautical engineer*
Blackman, Lee L. *lawyer*
Brigden, Ann Smith *mediator, educator*
DeLuce, Richard David *lawyer*
Lazzaro, Anthony Derek *university administrator*
Mackenbach, Frederick W. *welding products manufacturing company executive*
Mennis, Edmund Addi *investment management consultant*
Paulikas, George Algis *retired physicist*
Perry, Robert Michael *engineering company executive*
Raue, Jorg Emil *electrical engineer*
Sharp, Jane Shriver *artist*
Smith, Stephen Randolph *aerospace executive*
Yarbrough, Allyson Debra *electrical engineer*

Palos Verdes Peninsula
Bailey-Klein, Katheryn Elizabeth *music educator, musician*
Christie, Hans Frederick *retired utility company subsidiaries executive, consultant*
Denke, Paul Herman *retired aircraft engineer*
Grant, Robert Ulysses *retired manufacturing company executive*
Greenberg, Kate *telecommunications industry executive*
Leone, William Charles *retired manufacturing executive*
Lowi, Alvin, Jr., *mechanical engineer, consultant*
Manning, Christopher Ashley *finance educator, consultant*
Mirels, Harold *aerospace engineer*
Narasimhan, Padma Mandyam *physician*
Pfund, Edward Theodore, Jr., *electronics company executive*
Rechtin, Eberhardt *retired aerospace executive, retired educator*
Seide, Paul *civil engineering educator*
Slayden, James Bragdon *retired department store executive*
Slusser, Robert Wyman *aerospace company executive*
Thomas, Claudewell Sidney *psychiatry educator*
Thomas, Hayward *manufacturing executive*
Vanderlip, Elin Brekke *philanthropic executive*
Wilson, Theodore Henry *retired electronics company executive, aerospace engineer*

Panorama City
Bass, Harold Neal *pediatrician, medical geneticist*
Chen, Edward M. *judge*
Jacob, Peter James *obstetrician-gynecologist*
Janis, Elinor Raiden *artist, educator*
Jasso, Nancy *dermatologist*
Sue, Michael Alvin *allergist*

Paradise
Barr, Donald Roy *statistics and operations research educator, statistician*
Bernstein, Elizabeth Ann *retired executive secretary*
Haws, Hale Louis *medical consultant*

Paramount
Cohn, Lawrence Steven *physician, educator*
Hall, Howard Harry *lawyer*
Williams, Vivian Lewie *retired counseling administrator*

Pasadena
Abelson, John Norman *biology professor*
Ahrens, Thomas J. *geophysicist*
Albee, Arden Leroy *geologist, educator*
Allen, Clarence Roderic *geologist, educator*
Almore-Randle, Allie Louise *special education educator*
Anderson, Don Lynn *geophysicist*
Arnott, Robert Douglas *investment company executive*
Axelson, Charles Frederic *retired accounting educator*
Baltimore, David *academic administrator, microbiologist, educator*
Barnes, Charles Andrew *physicist, researcher*
Baskin, John Spencer *physicist*
Bean, Maurice Darrow *retired diplomat*
Beauchamp, Jesse Lee (Jack Beauchamp) *chemistry professor*
Beer, Reinhard *atmospheric scientist*
Bejczy, Antal Károly *research scientist, research facility administrator*
Bishop, Robert Calvin *pharmaceutical company executive*
Bogaard, William Joseph *mayor, lawyer, educator*
Boochever, Robert *judge*
Borodin, Alexei *mathematician*
Bower, Curtis A. *engineering executive*
Breckinridge, James Bernard *optical engineer*
Brenner, Anita Susan *lawyer*
Bridges, William Bruce *electrical engineer, researcher, engineering educator*
Brogden-Stirbl, Shona Marie *writer, researcher*
Brooks, Edward Howard *retired academic administrator*
Brotman, Richard Dennis *counselor*
Bugga, Ratnakumar Venkata *electrochemist, researcher*
Bunting, Anne Evelyn (Eve Bunting) *author*
Buratti, Bonnie J. *aerospace scientist*
Caine, Stephen Howard *data processing executive*
Caldwell, Kim A. *company executive*
Call, Merlin Wendell *lawyer*
Calleton, Theodore Edward *lawyer, educator*
Carregal, Enrique J. *anesthesiologist, educator*
Chahine, Moustafa Toufic *atmospheric scientist*
Chan, Peter Wing Kwong *pharmacist*
Chan, Sunney Ignatius *chemist, educator*
Chiang, Wen-Li *hydrodynamicist*
Ching, Jianye *civil engineer, researcher*
Cooray, Asantha Roshan *astrophysicist, researcher*
Crowley, John Crane *real estate developer*
Dallas, Saterios (Sam Dallas) *aerospace engineer, researcher, consultant*
D'Angelo, Robert William *lawyer*
Davidson, Eric Harris *molecular and developmental biologist, educator*
Davis, Edmond Ray *lawyer*
DeMartino, Frank A. *engineering company executive*
Dervan, Peter Brendan *chemistry educator*
Dickinson, Michael *physiologist*
Dressler, Alan Michael *astronomer*
Drutchas, Gerrick Gilbert (Baron Khabarovsky) *investigator*
Dyck, Peter *neurosurgeon, educator*
Elachi, Charles *aerospace engineer*
Elliot, David Clephan *historian, educator*
Ellis, Richard Salisbury *astronomer, educator*
Ellner, Carolyn Lipton *not-profit organization executive, dean, consultant*
Everhart, Thomas Eugene *retired university president, engineering educator*
Fast, Henryk *mathematician, educator*
Ferber, Robert Rudolf *physics researcher, educator, science administrator*
Fernandez, Ferdinand Francis *federal judge*
Fisher, Raymond Corley *judge*
Franklin, Joel Nicholas *mathematician, educator*
Frautschi, Steven Clark *physicist, researcher*
Fredericks, Ward Arthur *venture capitalist, consultant*
Freedman, Wendy Laurel *astronomer, educator*
Fu, Lee-Lueng *oceanographer*
Gill, Gene *artist*
Gillis, Christine Diest-Lorgion *financial planner, stockbroker*
Gilman, Richard Carleton *retired college president*
Glovsky, Myron Michael *medical educator*
Goei, Bernard Thwan-Poo (Bert Goei) *architectural and engineering firm executive*
Goldreich, Peter Martin *astrophysics and planetary physics educator*
Goodwin, Alfred Theodore *federal judge*
Gould, Roy Walter *engineering educator*
Gray, Harry Barkus *chemistry professor*
Gref, Lynn G. *mathematician*
Gurnis, Michael Christopher *geological sciences educator*
Haight, James Theron *lawyer, corporate executive*
Hall, Cynthia Holcomb *federal judge*
Hall, William E. *engineering and construction company executive*
Harmsen, Tyrus George *librarian*
Harris, Jennifer A. *aerospace engineer*
Harvey, Joseph Paul, Jr., *orthopedist, educator*
Heindl, Clifford Joseph *physicist, researcher*
Helin, Eleanor Francis *astronomer, geologist*
Hemann, Raymond Glenn *research company executive*
Hicklin, Ronald Lee *music production company executive*
Hilbert, Robert S(aul) *optical engineer*
Hitlin, David George *physicist, researcher*
Hoffmann, Michael R. *dean*
Holmes, Louis Ira *physician assistant, educator, photojournalist*
Horak, Jan-Christopher *film studies educator, curator*
Horner, Althea Jane *psychologist*
Hornung, Hans Georg *aeronautical engineering educator, science facility administrator*
Horowitz, Norman Harold *biologist, emeritus educator*
Housner, George William *retired civil engineering educator, consultant*
Hunt, Gordon *lawyer*
Hunter, Milton *retired army officer*
Hwang, Li-San *technology executive*
Iturbide, Graciela *photographer*
Jacobs, Joseph John *engineering company executive*
Janssen, Michael Allen *astronomer*
Jennings, Paul Christian *civil engineering educator, academic administrator*
Johnson, Barbara Jean *retired judge, lawyer*
Jun, Insoo *nuclear scientist, researcher*
Kahle, Anne B. *geophysicist*
Kaplan, Gary *executive recruiter*
Keller, Herbert Bishop *mathematics professor*
Knowles, James Kenyon *applied mechanics educator*
Koelzer, George Joseph *lawyer*
Konishi, Masakazu *neurobiologist, educator*
Kornfield, Julia Ann *chemical engineering educator*
Kousser, J(oseph) Morgan *history educator*
Kozinski, Alex *federal judge*
Lake, Kevin Bruce *medical association administrator*
Lewis, Nathan Saul *chemistry professor*
Liebau, Frederic Jack, Jr., *investment manager*
Liebe, Carl Christian *aerospace engineer, researcher*
Liepmann, Hans Wolfgang *physicist, researcher*
Lingenfelter, Sherwood Galen *university provost, anthropology educator*
List, Ericson John *environmental engineering science educator, engineering consultant*
Logan, Francis Dummer *retired lawyer*
Lopes, Rosaly Mutel Crocce *astronomer, planetary geologist*
Magnes, Harry Alan *physician*
Marcus, Rudolph Arthur *chemist, educator*
Marlen, James S. *chemical, plastics and building materials manufacturing company executive*
Martin, Craig Lee *engineering company executive*
Mathies, Allen Wray, Jr., *former pediatrician, hospital administrator*
Matsko, Andrey B. *research scientist*
Mc Carthy, Frank Martin *oral surgeon, surgical sciences educator*
Mc Koy, Basil Vincent Charles *theoretical chemist, educator*
McNulty, James F. *engineering, construction company executive*
Means, Tina *police officer, consultant*

Menefee, John William, III, *cinematographer, producer*
Meye, Robert Paul *retired seminary educator, administrator, writer*
Meyerowitz, Elliot Martin *biologist, educator*
Mosher, Sally Ekenberg *lawyer, musician*
Mueth, Joseph Edward *lawyer*
Munger, Edwin Stanton *political geography educator*
Myers, R(alph) Chandler *lawyer*
Nackel, John George *technology executive*
Neal, Philip Mark *diversified manufacturing executive*
Nelson, Dorothy Wright (Mrs. James F. Nelson) *federal judge*
Neugebauer, Gerry *retired astrophysicist, educator*
Newell, Michael Alfred *electrical engineer*
Newman, Marjorie Yospin *psychiatrist*
O'Bryant, Daniel R. *manufacturing executive*
O'Connor, William Charles *automobile agency finance executive*
Oemler, Augustus, Jr., *astronomer, educator*
Opel, William *medical research administrator*
Paez, Richard A. *federal judge*
Parilis, Edward S. *physicist, researcher, consultant*
Parker, Robert Allan Ridley *federal agency administrator, astronaut*
Parr, James Allan *literature professor*
Pashgian, Margaret Helen *artist*
Patton, Richard Weston *retired mortgage company executive*
Pelletier, Sandra Maureen *mathematician, educator*
Pings, Cornelius John *educational consultant, director*
Pitts, Ferris Newcomb *physician, psychiatry educator*
Pleasants, John *online services company executive*
Politzer, Hugh David *physicist, educator*
Poon, Peter Tin-Yau *engineer, physicist*
Preskill, John Phillip *physics educator*
Roberts, John D. *chemist, educator*
Robinson, Roger *actor, director*
Roshko, Anatol *aeronautical engineer*
Rymer, Pamela Ann *federal judge*
Sabersky, Rolf Heinrich *mechanical engineer*
Sackmann, Inge-Juliana *astrophysicist*
Saffman, Philip G. *mathematician, educator*
Sanchez, Pauline Stella *artist*
Sandage, Allan Rex *astronomer*
Sanders, Gary Hilton *physicist*
Sargent, Wallace Leslie William *astronomer, educator*
Schander, Mary Lea *retired protective services official, educator, consultant*
Schlinger, Warren Gleason *retired chemical engineer*
Schmidt, Maarten *astronomy educator*
Schwarz, John Henry *theoretical physicist, educator*
Scott, David Clinton *research scientist*
Scott, Ronald Fraser *civil engineering educator, engineering consultant*
Scudder, Thayer *anthropologist, educator*
Seinfeld, John Hersh *chemical engineering educator*
Sekanina, Zdenek *astronomer*
Shaw, Anthony *pediatric surgeon, retired educator*
Shimada, Katsunori *retired electrical engineer*
Short, Elizabeth M. *internist, educator, retired federal agency administrator*
Shuster, Marguerite *minister, educator*
Siemon-Burgeson, Marilyn M. (Marilyn Burgeson) *education administrator*
Smith, Edward John *geophysicist, physicist*
Smith, Michael Robert *electro-optical engineer, physicist*
Spector, Phil *record company executive*
Spilker, Linda Joyce *aerospace scientist*
Staehle, Robert L. *foundation executive*
Stevens, Roy W. *sales and marketing executive*
Stolper, Edward Manin *secondary school educator*
Stone, Edward C. *physicist, researcher*
Suh, Jung Sook Ky *management consultant, educator*
Tanner, Dee Boshard *retired lawyer*
Tan-Wang, Grace *aeronautical engineer*
Tashima, Atsushi Wallace *federal judge*
Thomas, Joseph Fleshman *retired architect*
Thorne, Kip Stephen *physicist, researcher*
Tolaney, Murli *environmental engineering executive*
Tollenaere, Lawrence Robert *retired industrial products company executive*
Tombrello, Thomas Anthony, Jr., *physics educator, consultant*
Torres, Ralph Chon *minister*
Varshavsky, Alexander Jacob *molecular biologist*
Vogt, Rochus Eugen *physicist, researcher*
Wasserburg, Gerald Joseph *geology and geophysics educator*
Watkins, John Francis *management consultant*
Watson, Noel G. *construction executive*
Webster, Christopher R. *chemist, physicist, research scientist*
Weinman, Glenn Alan *lawyer*
Weisbin, Charles Richard *nuclear engineer*
Wennberg, Paul *chemist*
White-Thomson, Ian leonard *retired mining executive*
Wise, Mark B. *education educator*
Wong, Raymond Shiu-Loong *radiologist*
Wood, Lincoln Jackson *aerospace engineer*
Worby, Rachael Beth *conductor*
Worby, Rachel *conductor*
Wyatt, Joseph Lucian, Jr., *lawyer, writer*
Yariv, Amnon *electrical engineering educator, scientist*
Yeager, Caroline Hale *radiologist, consultant*
Yeh, Paul Pao *electrical and electronics engineer, educator*
Yeomans, Donald Keith *astronomer*
Yohalem, Harry Morton *lawyer*
Zewail, Ahmed Hassan *chemistry and physics educator, editor, consultant*

Paso Robles
Baron, Adelaide Josephine *newswriter, artist*
Boxer, Jerome Harvey *computer and management consultant, vintner, accountant*
Brown, Benjamin Andrew *retired journalist*
Webster, David Arthur *retired life insurance company executive*

Pauma Valley
Lewis, Gerald Jorgensen *judge*

Pebble Beach
Dallmann, William Charles *speech educator, writer*
Hoffman, Sharon Lynn *adult education educator*
Mauz, Henry Herrward, Jr., *retired naval officer*
Mortensen, Gordon Louis *artist, printmaker*
Neville, Roy Gerald *scientist, chemical management and environmental consultant*

Penn Valley
Accardi, James Leonard *musician*
Longan, Suzanne M. *retired elementary school educator*
Nix, Barbara Lois *real estate broker*
Throner, Guy Charles, Jr., *engineering executive, scientist, engineer, inventor, consultant*

Penryn
Bryson, Vern Elrick *nuclear engineer*

Perris
Tankersley, Michael Leonard (Mujahide Abdullah Rafi Rashid) *computer systems administrator*

Petaluma
Eller, Leslie Robert *lawyer*
Frederickson, Arman Frederick *minerals and petroleum company executive*
Guadarrama, Belinda *computer company executive*
Hass, Robert L. *writer, literature educator*
Immel, Barbara K. *management consultant*
McChesney, Robert Pearson *artist*
Mulkern-Kolosey, Sandy Kathleen *college counselor, educator, realtor*
O'Hare, Sandra Fernandez *education educator*
Paul, Amy *lawyer*
Pronzini, Bill John (William Pronzini) *writer*
Reichek, Jesse *artist*
Sebold, Alice *writer*
Skalagard, Hans Martin *artist*
Spiegelman, Art *author, cartoonist*

Pico Rivera
Collanton, Greg *manufacturing executive, controller*
Cowan, Richard *manufacturing executive*

Piedmont
Aderton, Jane Reynolds *lawyer*
Hughes, James Paul *physician*
Mayeri, Beverly *artist, ceramic sculptor, educator*
Montgomery, Theodore Ashton *physician*
Oser, Judi *lawyer, artist*
Putter, Irving *French language educator*
Reich, Stanley Benjamin *radiologist, medical educator*

Pinedale
Falcone, Patricia Jeanne Lalim *investor, foundation administrator*

Pinole
Grogan, Stanley Joseph *educational and security consultant*
Harvey, Elinor B. *child psychiatrist*
Naughton, James Lee *internist*

Pittsburg
Kaiper, Donald Dixon *historian, educator*
Schmalenberger, Jerry Lew *pastor, religious studies educator*
Williams, Elizabeth A. *financial planner, business consultant*
Williscroft-Barcus, Beverly Ruth *lawyer*

Pixely
Golden, Raymond Lee *retired theology studies educator, retired minister*

Placentia
Evans, Winthrop Shattuck *retired lawyer*
Zweifel, Donald Edwin *retired newspaper editor, lobbyist, consultant*

Placerville
Bonser, Quentin *retired surgeon*
Wall, Sonja Eloise *nursing administrator*
Wickline, Marian Elizabeth *former corporate librarian*
Wilkinson, Rosemary Regina Challoner *poet, writer*

Playa Del Rey
Cairns, Diane Patricia *motion picture executive*
McNeill, Daniel Richard *writer*
Mishelevich, David Jacob *medical company executive, consultant*
Weir, Alexander, Jr., *utility consultant, inventor*

Playa Vista
Noh, Jun-yong *computer scientist, researcher*

Pleasant Hill
Ashby, Denise Stewart *speech educator, communication consultant*
Edelstein, Mark Gerson *college president*
Hassid, Sami *architect, educator*
Hollister, Arthur Clair, Jr., *epidemiologist, consultant, retired public health service officer*
Richard, Robert Carter *psychologist*

Pleasanton
Bergquist, Rick *software company executive*
Bjorkholm, John Ernst *retired physicist*
Bond, David F. *food products executive*
Burd, Steven A. *food service executive*
Caldwell, Nanci *software company executive*
Ching, David T. *food products executive*
Conway, Craig A. *computer software executive*
Denavit, Jacques *retired physicist*
Dubois, Guy *software company executive*
Edwards, Robert L. *corporate financial executive*
Everette, Bruce L. *retail executive*
Goddard, John Wesley *cable television company executive*
Gordon, Robert A. *food products executive*
Gregoire, Michael P. *software company executive*
Gupta, Ram *software company executive*
Heizer, Ruth Bradfute *philosophy educator*
Hisaka, Eric Toru *plastic surgeon*
Jackson, Lawrence *food service executive*
Magelitz, Larry L. *construction company executive*
Novak, Randi Ruth *engineer, computer scientist*
Opperwall, Stephen Gabriel *lawyer*
Parker, Kevin T. *computer company executive*
Payack, Paul JJ *marketing executive*
Renda, Larree M. *retail executive*
Roshong, Dee Ann Daniels *dean, educator*
Ross, Michael Charles *lawyer*
Scott, G. Judson, Jr., *lawyer*
Shen, Mason Ming-Sun *medical center administrator*
Smith, Gary *marketing executive*
Staley, John Fredric *lawyer*
Stallings, Charles Henry *retired physicist*
Van Dreser, Merton Lawrence *ceramics engineer*
Weiss, Robert Stephen *medical manufacturing company financial executive*
Whisnand, Rex James *association housing executive*
Wilmington, W. Phillip *software company executive*
Wu, Jia Hao *transportation executive, researcher, consultant*

Point Mugu
Fisk, Charles John *meteorologist, researcher, consultant*

Point Richmond
Edginton, John Arthur *lawyer*

Pollock Pines
Johnson, Stanford Leland *marketing, international business educator*
Rickard, Margaret Lynn *retired library director*

Pomona
Agvanian, Youri *mathematician, educator, physicist*
Aurilia, Antonio *physicist, researcher*
Bidlack, Wayne Ross *nutritional biochemist, toxicologist, food scientist*
Brown, Ronald G. *automotive company executive*
Charney, George *academic administrator*
Cortez, Edward S. *mayor*
Cranston, John Welch *historian, educator*
Demery, Dorothy Jean *secondary school educator*
Dishman, Rose Marie Rice *academic administrator, researcher*
Driebe, Michael D. *corporate financial executive*
Evans, William McKee *historian, educator*
Garrity, Rodman Fox *psychologist, educator*
Hogarty, Charles J. *automotive executive*
Keating, Eugene Kneeland *animal scientist, educator*
Kopplin, David F. *music educator, composer*
Kucij, Timothy Michael *engineer, minister, musician*
Lenz, Craig *academic administrator*
Lin, Lianlian *management educator, researcher*
Mezey, Robert *poet*
Patten, Thomas Henry, Jr., *management, human resources educator*
Perez, Francisco, Jr., *music educator*
Rhodes, Rhonda Lynn *business educator*
Teague, Lavette Cox, Jr., *systems educator, consultant*
Tunison, Elizabeth Lamb *education educator*
Vo, Huu Dinh *pediatrician, educator*
Wirsig, Woodrow *magazine editor, trade association administrator*

Port Hueneme
Schneider, Arthur Paul *retired videotape and film editor, author*

Porterville
Hayes, Shirley Ann *special education educator*
Mullen, Rod *nonprofit organization executive*

Portola Valley
Carnochan, Walter Bliss *retired humanities educator*
Cooper, John Joseph *lawyer*
Fogarty, Thomas James *surgery educator*
Garsh, Thomas Burton *publisher*
Kuo, Franklin F. *computer scientist, electrical engineer*
Nycum, Susan Hubbell *lawyer*
Piaget, Gerald Warren *psychologist, educator*
Purl, O. Thomas *retired electronics company executive*
Ward, Robert Edward *retired political science educator and university administrator*

Poway
Barnhart, Douglas Edward *construction company executive*
Bradley, R. Todd *computer company executive*
Inouye, Wayne Ryo *computer company executive*
Kubilus, Norbert John *information technology executive*
Mueller, Gerhard G(ottlob) *retired financial accounting standard setter, retired educator*
Phillips, Steve *computer company executive*
Robino, David J. *computer company executive*
Sherwood, Rod(erick), III, *computer company executive*
Turner, David G. *information technology executive*
Uke, Alan Kurt *company executive*
Waitt, Theodore W. *computer company executive*

Prather
Coren, Lance Scott *consulting firm executive*

Quartz Hill
McKain, Mary Margaret *musician*
Nettelhorst, Robin Paul *academic administrator, writer*

Ramona
Hoffman, Wayne Melvin *retired airline official*
Van Zant, Susan Lucille *principal*
Yoldas, Bulent Erturk *materials scientist, educator*

Rancho Cordova
Carleone, Joseph *business executive*

Rancho Cucamonga
Alvarez, Tirso Reyes, Jr., *engineer*
Dutton, Robert D. *state official*
Merino, Akindotun *small business owner, consultant*

Rancho Dominguez
Corominas, Juan M. *language educator, priest*
Janura, Jan Arol *apparel manufacturing executive*

Rancho Mirage
Abel, Michael L. *marketing executive*
Brimble, Alan *business executive*
Cone, Lawrence Arthur *medical educator*
Ford, Betty Ann (Elizabeth Ann Ford) *former First Lady of the United States, health facility executive*
Ford, Gerald Rudolph, Jr., *38th President of the United States*
Fromm, Erwin Frederick *retired insurance company executive*
Greenbaum, James Richard *liquor distributing company executive, real estate developer*
Jacobson, John D. D. *anesthesiologist*
Kramer, Gordon *mechanical engineer*
Leydorf, Frederick Leroy *lawyer*
Olderman, Murray *columnist, cartoonist*
Reuben, Don Harold *lawyer*
Sheldon, Deena Lynn *television camera operator*
Steele, Charles Glen *retired accountant*
Wyatt, Lenore *civic worker*

Rancho Murieta
Irelan, Robert Withers *retired metal products executive*

Rancho Palos Verdes
Frassinelli, Guido Joseph *retired aerospace engineer*
Hillinger, Charles *journalist, writer*
Kwan, Benjamin Ching Kee *ophthalmologist*
Loether, Herman John *sociologist, educator*
Rubenstein, Leonard Samuel *communications executive, ceramist, painter, photographer*
Savage, Terry Richard *information systems executive*
Schimmenti, John Joseph *lawyer*
Smirnov, Alexei Vladimirovich *research scientist, consultant*
Swank, Damon Raynard *lawyer*
Yassin, Robert Alan *museum administrator, curator*
Zar, Judith L. (Mickey McBride) *writer*

Rancho Santa Fe
Affeldt, John Ellsworth *retired physician*
Best, Jacob Hilmer, Jr., *retired hotel chain executive*
Bow, Stephen Tyler, Jr., *management consultant*
Byrd, Betty Rantze *writer*
Carr, David Turner *physician*
Creutz, Edward Chester *physicist, museum consultant*
Dieffenbach, Otto Weaver, III, *real estate company executive*
Jordan, Charles Morrell *retired automotive designer*
Kessler, A. D. *financial, investment and real estate advisor, consultant, writer, broadcaster*
LaBonté, C(larence) Joseph *financial and marketing executive*
Levy, Michael Lee *neurosurgeon*
Matthews, Leonard Sarver *advertising and marketing executive*
Peterson, Nad A. *retired lawyer*
Polster, Leonard H. *investment company executive*
Rockoff, S. David *radiologist, physician, educator*
Ruiz, Ramon Eduardo *history professor*
Simon, William Leonard *film and television writer and producer, writer*
Step, Eugene Lee *retired pharmaceutical company executive*
Woolley, Roger Swire *lawyer*

Rancho Santa Margarita
Aguilera, Donna Conant *psychologist, researcher*
Curtis, John Joseph *lawyer, writer*
Newton, Michelle Marie *sales executive*
Parth, Frank R. *consulting company executive, educator*

Red Bluff
Kennedy, James William, Jr., (Sarge Kennedy) *special education administrator, consultant*
Peters, Michael Morgan *playwright, consultant, theater director, theater critic, educator*

Redding
Emerson, Red *lumber company executive*
Emmerson, Archie Aldis (Red Emmerson) *sawmill owner*
Emmerson, Mark *paper/lumber company executive*
La Malfa, Doug *state representative*
Lawrence, Marjorie Diane Long *computer company executive, consultant*
McColm, George Lester *international agricultural consultant, journalist*
Nicholas, David Robert *minister, college president*
Peterson, Robyn Gayle *museum curator*
Potter, James Vincent *association executive*
Renard, Ronald Lee *allergist*
Spawn, Kevin Lewis *education educator*
Streiff, Arlyne Bastunas *business owner, educator*
Waterbury, Elizabeth Floria *conductor*

Redlands
Adey, William Ross *physician*
Appleton, James Robert *university president, educator*
Bangasser, Ronald Paul *physician*
Burgess, Charlotte Gaylord *dean*
Burgess, Larry Eugene *library director, history educator*
Coleman, Arlene Florence *retired pediatrics nurse*
Dexter, James Riley *internist, pulmonologist, critical care specialist*
Griesemer, Allan David *retired museum director*
Hanson, Gerald Warner *retired county official*
Heiss, David James *editor*
Huntley, William Barney *religious studies professor*
Pick, James Block *business educator, demographer*
Sagmeister, Edward Frank *retired military officer, business owner*
Shimoff, Paul Martin *lawyer*
Skomal, Edward Nelson *aerospace company executive, electromagnetic environments consultant*
Skoog, William Arthur *former oncologist, educator*

Redondo Beach
Abernethy, Robert John *real estate developer*
Ball, William Paul *physicist, engineer*
Battles, Roxy Edith *novelist, consultant, educator*
Brodsky, Robert Fox *aerospace engineer, educator, author*
Contescu, Cristian Ion *chemist, researcher*
Dockstader, Jack Lee *retired electronics executive*
Foster, John Stuart, Jr., *physicist, former defense industry executive*
Grzesik, Jan Alexander *electronics engineer, mathematician*
Kagiwada, Reynold Shigeru *electronics executive*
Kich, Rolf *communications scientist, consultant*

McWilliams, Margaret Ann home economics educator, author
Mulvey, Gerald John meteorologist
Oh, Angela E. lawyer
Richards, Denise actress
Shellhorn, Ruth Patricia landscape architect

Redwood City
Alexander, Theron behavioral scientist, psychologist, writer
Bell, Frank Ouray, Jr., lawyer
Bell, George media executive
Bloom, Gary L. database company executive
Coddington, Clinton Hays lawyer
Cooperman, Daniel computer company executive, lawyer
Davidson, Mary Ann information technology executive
Ellis, Eldon Eugene surgeon
Ellison, Lawrence J. computer company executive
Hagart-Alexander, Claud software engineer
Hanf, Michael W. construction executive
Hawkins, Trip electronics company executive
Hearst, William Randolph, III, newspaper publisher
Henley, Jeffrey O. computer software company executive
Howard, Russell J. biotechnology company executive
Johnson, James Harding advertising executive
Katz, Safra computer company executive
Lane, Raymond J. software systems consulting company executive
Mandel, Martin Louis lawyer
Matthews, William health products executive
Mattrick, Don A. interactive entertainment software company executive
McFarland, Kevin John foundation administrator
Millard, Richard Steven lawyer
Nosler, Peter Cole construction company executive
O'Keefe, Donald Martin detective-lieutenant
Phillips, Charles computer company executive
Probst, Lawrence F., III, computer company executive
Rohde, James Vincent software systems company executive
Selick, Howard E. (Barry Selick) biotechnology executive
Sharpnack, Rayona management consultant
Simon, Nicholas J., III, medical products executive
Smith, Nancy L. information technology executive
Spangler, Nita Reifschneider volunteer
Tight, Dexter Corwin lawyer
Verhoeven, Charles K. lawyer
Wang, Chen Chi electronics company, real estate, finance company, investment services, and international trade executive
Wilhelm, Robert Oscar lawyer, civil engineer, developer
Williams, Duston electronics company executive
Woods, Jacqueline F. telecommunications industry executive
You, Harry L. computer company executive

Reedley
Carey, Ernestine Gilbreth (Mrs. Charles E. Carey) writer, lecturer
Dick, Henry Henry minister

Rescue
Ackerly, Wendy Saunders construction company executive
Frey, Charles Frederick surgeon, educator

Reseda
Chavez, Albert Blas finance company executive

Rialto
Jackson, Betty Eileen music and elementary school educator

Richmond
Anderson, Vera Strong retired dentist
Arnon, Stephen Soulé epidemiologist, research scientist
Cohen, Abraham Ezekiel retired health care company executive
Corbin, Rosemary MacGowan former mayor
Cushnie, Michele academic administrator
Dolberg, David Spencer lawyer
Freiman, Paul E. pharmaceutical company executive
Jenkins, Everett Wilbur, Jr., lawyer, author, historian
Lanphier, Edward O., II, medical company executive
Lasseter, John P. film director, computer animator
Moehle, Jack P. civil engineer, engineering executive
Quenneville, Kathleen lawyer
Renton, Hollings C. health products executive
Richards, Gerald Thomas lawyer, consultant, educator, writer
Robles, Eliodoro Gonzales consulting company executive, educator
Shladover, Steven Elliot transportation research professional
Terrill, Karen Stapleton retired medical planning consultant
Wessel, Henry photographer

Ridgecrest
Bennett, Harold Earl physicist, optics researcher
Paik, Sun Hye cell biologist, research scientist

Riverbank
Cooley, Stacy Raelyn administrative assistant

Riverside
Anderson, Jolene Slover small business owner, publishing executive, consultant
Atkinson, Roger chemist, educator, science administrator
Auth, Judith library director
Becker, Jörn Ole plant pathologist, researcher
Beni, Gerardo electrical and computer engineering educator, robotics scientist
Benoit, John J. state official
Bielucke, Edward Anthony, III, transportation executive, writer
Boldt, William Gregory academic administrator, consultant
Bricker, Neal S. physician, educator
Calfee, Robert Chilton psychologist, educational researcher
Carpenter, Mark Warren social sciences educator
Caudill, Edward B. automotive executive
Chamberlain, Willard Thomas retired metals company executive
Chang, Janice May lawyer, naturopathic doctor, psychologist
Chang, Sylvia Tan health facility administrator, educator
Czekanski, James P. military officer
Darling, Scott Edward lawyer
Deal, Kevin Paul furniture designer
Deese, E(thel) Helen English educator
Elliott, Emory Bernard English language educator, educational administrator
Embleton, Tom William horticultural science educator
Erwin, Donald Carroll plant pathology educator
Fagundo, Ana Maria creative writing and Spanish literature educator
Geraty, Lawrence Thomas academic administrator, archaeologist, educator
Giroir, Leo Jean Jr. accountant
Green, Harry Western, II, geology-geophysics educator
Griffin, Keith Broadwell retired economics educator
Grimm, Reinhold humanities educator
Hackwood, Susan electrical and computer engineering educator
Hall, Anthony Elmitt crop ecologist
Hendrick, Irving Guilford education educator
Holmes, Dallas Scott judge, educator
Jackson, Marguerite Faye Thurston rhetoric and intercultural communications and language educator
James, Etta recording artist
Jung, Timothy Tae Kun otolaryngologist
Jury, William A. soil scientist, educator
Kummer, Glenn F. retired manufacturing executive
Linaweaver, Walter Ellsworth, Jr., physician
Marlatt, Michael James lawyer
McClanahan, Michael Nelson systems analyst
Mc Cormac, Weston Arthur retired educator, retired career officer
McLaughlin, Leighton Bates, II, journalism educator, former newspaperman
Meadows, Joyce Katherine nurse
Mulchandani, Ashok Kimatrai chemical engineer, educator
Oakes, Judy Dianne real estate broker
O'Reilly, Patrick James public relations executive
Page, Albert Lee soil science educator, researcher
Petrinovich, Lewis Franklin psychology educator
Phillips, Virginia A. judge
Plowman, Boyd R. automotive executive
Pratt, John Jackson property manager, retired telephone installer
Prosser, Michael Joseph college librarian
Rabenstein, Dallas Leroy chemistry professor
Raikhel, Natasha V. plant cell biology educator
Rainey, Susan J. school system administrator
Ratliff, Louis Jackson, Jr., mathematics professor
Rodrigue, George P. newspaper editor
Rosenthal, Robert psychology educator
Ross, Delmer Gerrard historian, educator
Saito, William Hiroyuki software company executive
Schaible, Siegfried mathematician, educator
Sherman, Irwin William biological sciences educator
Shoji, Hiromu orthopedic surgeon, educator
Siambanes, David orthopedic surgeon
Smith, Dorothy Ottinger jewelry designer, civic worker
Smith, Jeffry Alan health administrator, physician, consultant
Smith, Richard Charles not-for-profit administrator, educator
Sokolsky, Robert Lawrence journalist, entertainment writer
Stewart, Richard A. former mayor
Stone, Herman Hull internist
Taylor, R. Ervin, Jr., archaeologist
Timlin, Robert J. judge
Turk, Austin Theodore sociology educator
Ullah, Aman economist, educator
Van Gundy, Seymour Dean nematologist, plant pathologist, educator
Van Wagenen, Jeffrey Anthony prosecutor, consultant
Warren, David Hardy psychology educator
Warren, Katherine Virginia art gallery director
Yacoub, Ignatius I. university dean
Yount, Gwendolyn Audrey humanities educator
Zaera, Francisco chemistry professor, consultant

Rocklin
Dwyer, Darrell James finance company executive
Hyde, Geraldine Veola retired secondary school educator
Lee, W. Bruce management consultant
Tal, Jacob electronics executive
Tovar, Nicholas Mario mechanical engineer
Womack, Joseph Darryl academic administrator

Rodeo
Emmanuel, Jorge Agustin chemical engineer, environmental consultant

Rohnert Park
Arminana, Ruben academic administrator, educator
Babula, William university dean
Byrne, Noel Thomas sociologist, educator
Haslam, Gerald William writer, educator
Johnson, Herman Leonall retired research nutritionist, researcher
Leeder, Elaine sociologist, educator, writer
Rosin, R. Thomas anthropologist, educator
Shinagawa, Larry Hatime American studies educator
Trowbridge, Dale Brian chemistry professor

Rolling Hills
Rumbaugh, Charles Earl arbitrator, mediator, educator, lawyer, speaker

Rolling Hills Estates
Bellis, Carroll Joseph surgeon, educator
Castor, Wilbur (Webb) Wright futurist, writer, consultant, playwright, actor
Chuang, Harold Hwa-Ming banker, consultant, finance educator
Diaz-Zubieta, Agustin nuclear engineer, engineering executive
Price, Lia Scott writer
Wong, Sun Yet engineering consultant

Rosemead
Bryson, John E. utilities company executive
Craver, Theodore F., Sr., utilites/energy executive
Danner, Bryant Craig lawyer
Featherstone, Diane L. utilities executive
Fohrer, Alan J. utilities company executive
Foster, Robert G. utilities executive
Goddard, Jo Ann investment advisor
McKinney, Michael Wayne government and public affairs representative
Moody, Wesley C. utilities executive
Noonan, Thomas M. utilities executive
Parsky, Barbara utilities executive
Rosenblum, Richard Mark utilities executive
Ryder, Beverly utilities executive
Smith, Anthony L. utilities executive
Yazdi, Mahvash utilities executive

Roseville
Ammon, Donald R. hospital administrator
Grant, Barbara venture capitalist
Jammal, Joseph Jamil cardiologist
Madden, Wanda Lois nurse
Wright, Carole Yvonne chiropractor

Ross
Godwin, Sara writer
Matan, Lillian Kathleen secondary school educator, consultant, interior designer
Nicholson, William Joseph forest products consultant
Pierce, Carole Jean artist

Rowland Heights
Cordova, John Michael mathematician, educator
Cruz, Wilfredo Vargas software safety and reliability consultant

Running Springs
Fangerow, Kay Elizabeth nurse
Liddle, Sidney George retired mechanical engineer, researcher

Rutherford
Staglin, Garen Kent computer service company executive, venture capitalist

Sacramento
Adelman, Rick professional basketball coach
Aghazarian, Greg G. state representative
Alberson, Barbara health services professional
Aldrich, Thomas Albert former brewing executive, consultant
Alpert, Deirdre Whittleton (Dede Alpert) state legislator
Amezcua, Esther Hernandez elementary school educator
Arkin, Michael Barry lawyer, arbitrator, writer
Armacost, Mary Jane healthcare company executive
Avendaño, Fausto language educator, writer
Baccigaluppi, Roger John agricultural company executive
Bailey, Michael Glenn engineer
Baltake, Joe film critic
Behrman, Bruce Ward social sciences educator
Bell, Wayne S. lawyer, state agency official
Belyn, David Neves journalist, editor
Betts, Bert A. former state treasurer, accountant
Blake, D. Steven lawyer
Block, Alvin Gilbert publishing executive
Bobrow, Susan Lukin lawyer
Bogren, Hugo Gunnar radiology educator
Bradshaw, Merlin E. language educator
Brewer, Roy Edward lawyer
Brittan, Martin R. biologist, educator
Brookman, Anthony Raymond lawyer
Brown, Craig L. state agency administrator
Bruce, Thomas Edward psychology educator, thanatologist
Burton, John state official
Burton, Randall James lawyer
Bustamante, Cruz M. lieutenant governor
Carr, Gerald Francis German educator
Chapman, Michael William orthopedist, educator
Chason, Robert health facility administrator
Chu, Judy May psychology educator, city official
Cogdill, David state representative
Cohn, Rebecca state representative
Cole, Glen David minister
Condon, Frank theater director, playwright
Connell, Kathleen state official
Corbett, Ellen M. mayor
Covin, David L. political science educator
Cox, Dave state legislator
Crimmins, Philip Patrick retired metallurgical engineer, lawyer
Cunningham, Mary Elizabeth (Mary Cunningham-Lusby) physician
Dager, William Erling pharmacist specialist, educator
Day, James McAdam, Jr., lawyer
Diaz, Manny state representative
Dobie, Robert Alan otologist
Drachnik, Catherine Meldyn recreational therapist, artist, counselor
Drummond, Marshall "Mark" Edward academic administrator
Dunnett, Dennis George retired state official
Ellis, William Gene neuropathologist
Evans, David Alun otolaryngologist
Fargo, Heather mayor
Farrell, Francine Annette psychotherapist, educator, author
Felderstein, Steven Howard lawyer
Forsyth, Raymond Arthur civil engineer, consultant
Foster, Douglas Taylor lawyer, investor
Franz, Jennifer Danton public opinion and marketing researcher
Friedman, Kenni healthcare company official, councilwoman
Friedman, Morton Lee lawyer
Frommer, Dario F. state representative
Gage, B. Timothy state finance department administrator
Gardner, Jerry Lee financial consultant
Gerringer, Elizabeth (The Marchioness de Roe Devon) writer, lawyer
Gerth, Donald Rogers university president, educator
Gillan, Kayla J. lawyer
Glackin, William Charles arts critic, editor
Goldberg, Jackie councilwoman
Goode, Barry Paul lawyer
Gore, Robert William performing arts educator
Gray, John Douglas education educator, researcher
Gray, Walter P., III, historian, archivist, consultant
Gray-Fuson, Joan Lorraine lawyer
Griffith, Yolanda Evette professional basketball player
Hackney, Robert Ward plant pathologist, nematologist, parasitologist, molecular geneticist, commercial arbitrator
Hall, Terry L. aerospace executive
Hallenbeck, Harry C. architect
Hancock, Loni state legislator, former mayor
Hardmon, Lady professional athlete
Heaphy, Janis Besler newspaper executive
Hendricks, Chris publishing executive
Hendrickson, George M. prosecutor
Holmes, Robert Eugene legislative staff member, journalist
Horton, Shirley A. state legislator, former mayor
Houpt, James Edward lawyer
Howard, Dina Elaine performing company executive, writer
Hughes, Teresa P. state legislator
Hull, Frederick Albert artist, writer
Hunter, Patricia Rae (Tricia Hunter) state official
Jackson, Richard Joseph epidemiologist, educator, pediatrician, preventive medicine physician
Janigian, Bruce Jasper lawyer, educator
Johnson, Van R. health facility administrator
Jones, Mark Alan broadcast technician
Karlton, Lawrence K. federal judge
Kawamoto, Walter family life research and service executive
Keiner, Christian Mark lawyer
Kennedy, B. L. poet, archivist
Kerri, Kenneth Donald civil engineering educator
Killian, Richard M. library director
Knudson, Thomas Jeffery journalist
Koretz, Paul state representative
Kuehl, Sheila James state legislator
Lam, Siuwa Monica education educator, consultant
Lathi, Bhagawandas Pannalal retired electrical engineering educator
Lee, Michael Gregory lawyer
Leong, Albin B. pediatric pulmonologist, allergist, educator
Levi, David F. federal judge
Levine, Lloyd E. state representative
Lieber, Sally J. state representative
Lilla, James A. plastic surgeon
Lim, Alan Young plastic surgeon
Lionakis, George architect
Lippold, Roland Will retired surgeon
Liu, Carol state representative
Lockyer, Bill state attorney general
Loewy, Erich Hans H. bioethicist, educator
Lucas, Donna communications executive
Lucchetti, David J. manufacturing executive
Lukenbill, Gregg real estate developer, sports promoter
Lundstrom, Marjie newspaper editor and columnist
Lynch, Peter John retired dermatologist
Mack, Edward Gibson retired business executive
Maitoza, Colleen professional sports team executive
Majesty, Melvin Sidney psychologist, consultant
Malkin, Harold Marshall medical researcher
Malloy, Michael Patrick law educator, consultant
Maze, Bill state representative
Mazzaferro, James Joseph music educator
McCarthy, Kevin state representative
McClatchy, James B. newspaper publisher, editor
McElroy, Leo Francis communications consultant, journalist
McGrath, William Arthur arbitrator, mediator, lawyer
Meindl, Robert James English language educator, poet
Merwin, Edwin Preston healthcare educator, consultant
Mette, Joseph P. museum director and park facilities superintendent
Montanez, Cindy state representative
Morgan-Prager, Karole lawyer, publishing executive
Morrow, Bill state legislator
Muehleisen, Gene retired protective services administrator, state official
Myrrdin, Terry A. state agency administrator
Nagy, Stephen Mears, Jr., physician, allergist
Newland, Chester Albert public administration educator
Nice, Carter conductor, music director
Norman, Ben Eric mathematician, educator
Nunez, Fabian state representative
Nye, Gene Warren retired art educator
O'Leary, Marion Hugh university dean, chemist
Owen, Allan Jacobs lawyer
Parra, Nicole M. state representative
Patino, Douglas Xavier foundation, government agency, and university administrator
Pavley, Fran J. state representative
Penicheiro, Ticha Nunes professional basketball player
Perata, Don state legislator
Peterson, Roy Martin, Jr., environmental scientist
Piper, Jami Kathleen music educator, composer
Post, August Alan economist, artist
Proud, Robert Donald (Robert Payton) broadcast executive
Purdy, James Aaron medical physics educator
Quinn, Francis A. bishop
Radford, R. S. lawyer, law educator
Reyes, Sarah state representative
Reynolds, Jerry Owen sports team executive
Richards, John Ray emergency physician, educator
Richman, Keith Stuart state representative
Robbins, Stephen J. M. lawyer
Roberts, James E. civil engineer
Roberts, Paul Dale state agency administrator, writer
Rodriguez, Rick newspaper executive editor
Root, Gerald Edward legal administrator
Rosenberg, Dan Yale retired plant pathologist
Rosenfeld, Arthur H. physics educator, research director
Ross, Jean M. think-tank executive
Ross, Terence William architect
Rounds, Barbara Lynn psychiatrist
Runner, Sharon state representative
Sanborn, Kathy career planning administrator, consultant
Schwartz, Milton Lewis federal judge
Schwarzenegger, Arnold Alois governor
Scott, McGregor W. lawyer
Shapero, Harris Joel pediatrician
Sharma, Arjun Dutta cardiologist
Shelley, Kevin state official

Sherwood, Robert Petersen *retired sociology educator*
Shirey, John Frederick *local government administrator*
Shoemaker, Cameron David James *dean, educator*
Shriver, Maria Owings *news correspondent*
Silva, Joseph, Jr., *dean, medical educator*
Simeroth, Dean Conrad *chemical engineer*
Simitian, Joe *state representative*
Skoor, John Brian *art educator, art consultant*
Smith, Marie B. *college president*
Spann, Lawrence Henry (Chip Spann) *physician associate*
Speed, Cynthia Agnes *retired mathematics educator*
Stall, William Read *writer*
Starr, Kevin *librarian, educator*
Steinberg, Darrell S. *state legislator*
Stevenson, Thomas Ray *plastic surgeon*
Strickland, Anthony *state representative*
Styne, Dennis Michael *physician, educator*
Swatt, Stephen Benton *communications executive, consultant*
Taylor, Walter Wallace *retired lawyer*
Terhaar, Joyce *editor*
Thomas, Laura Marlene *artist, retired private antique dealer*
Torres, Art *former state legislator*
Totton, Gayle *professional sports team executive*
Tung, Prabhas *plastic surgeon*
Ubaldi, Michael Vincent *lawyer*
Van Camp, Brian Ralph *judge*
Venosdel, Daniel Paul *agricultural association administrator*
Walsh, Denny Jay *reporter*
Wasserman, Barry L(ee) *architect*
Webber, Chris, III, (Mayce Edward Christopher Webber) *professional basketball player*
Wesson, Herb J. *state representative*
Wickland, J. Al, Jr., *petroleum product executive, real estate executive*
Wile, Philip Hodges *law educator*
Willis, Edward Oliver *management consultant, state official*
Wilson, E. Dotson *legislative staff member*
Wisner, David Hamilton *surgeon, educator*
Wolfe, Robert A. *aerospace executive*
Wolfman, Earl Frank, Jr., *surgeon, educator*
Wolkov, Harvey Brian *oncologist, researcher*
Woo, Sharon Y. *healthcare organization executive*
Wright, Cathie *state legislator*
Yang, Yung Y. *economics educator, consultant*
Zaidi, Emily Louise *retired elementary school educator*
Zeff, Ophelia Hope *lawyer*
Zhou, Jian-zhong (Joe) *librarian*
Zil, J. S. *psychiatrist, physiologist*

Saint Helena
Herber, Steven Carlton *physician*
Sone, Hiro *chef, restaurant owner, writer*
Wiggins, Rita Cassidy *poet*
Yates, Donald Alfred *retired literature educator*

Salinas
Bans, Phil *retired corporate security professional*
Chester, Lynne *foundation administrator, artist*
Drever, Mark *food products executive*
Esquivel, Joe G. *food products executive*
Esquivel, Mary *agricultural products company executive*
Jeffries, Russell Morden *communications company official*
Liebersbach, Norbert John *protective services official*
Mehta, Siddarth N. *credit services company executive*
Phillips, John P(aul) *retired neurosurgeon*
Puckett, Richard Edward *artist, consultant, former recreation executivve, former hotel executive*
Rosen, Jacqueline I. *flutist, music educator*
Sprude, Margaret *credit services company executive*
Stevens, Wilbur Hunt *accountant*
Taylor, Steven Bruce *agriculture company executive*
Wong, Walter Foo *county official*
Wu, Wayne Wen-Yau *artist*

San Andreas
Breed, Allen Forbes *correctional administrator*

San Anselmo
Chiaverini, John Edward *construction company executive*
Crawley, Cheryl K. *school system administrator*
Ellenberger, Diane Marie *nurse, consultant*
Harper Haines, Jan Frances *writer, educator*
Murphy, Barry Ames *lawyer*
Torbet, Laura *writer, artist, photographer, graphic designer*
Truett, Harold Joseph, III, (Tim Truett) *lawyer*

San Bernardino
Burgess, Michael *library director, writer*
Caballero, Sharon *academic administrator*
Curry, Paul Russell *law enforcement official, lobbyist*
De Haas, David Dana *emergency physician*
Estes, James Paul *financial services company executive*
Fullerton, Robert Victor *lawyer*
Giralt-Cabrales, Carlos Ignacio *consul of Mexico*
Gorenberg, Alan Eugene *physician*
Hwang, Young S. *education educator*
Kirkland, Bertha Theresa *project engineer*
Maul, Terry Lee *psychologist, educator*
McAfee, I. Paul, III, *editor*
McNally, Sean Patrick *prosecutor*
Mian, Lal Shah *entomologist, educator*
Neighbors, Ira Arthell *social work educator*
Ruml, Treadwell *English language educator*
Seitz, Victoria Ann *marketing educator*
Turpin, Joseph Ovila *counselor, educator*
Valles, Judith *mayor, former academic administrator*
Willis, Harold Wendt, Sr., *real estate developer*

San Bruno
Bradley, Charles William *podiatrist, educator*
Hariton, Lorraine Jill *information technology executive*
Rozman, James D. *church administrator*

San Carlos
Dafforn, Geoffrey Alan *biochemist*
Eby, Michael John *marketing research and technology consultant*
Foster, Mark Edward *lawyer, consultant, international lobbyist*
Gutow, Bernard Sidney *packaging manufacturing company executive*
Lee, John Jin *lawyer*
Oliver, Nancy Lebkicher *artist, retired elementary education educator*
Robinson, Neil *materials engineer, consultant*
Schumacher, Henry Jerold *museum administrator, former career officer, business executive*
Sullivan, Shirley Ross (Shirley Ross Davis) *art collector*
Symons, Robert Spencer *electronic engineer*

San Clemente
Clark, Earnest Hubert, Jr., *tool company executive*
Ditty, Marilyn Louise *gerontologist, educator*
Fisher, Myron R. *lawyer*
Geyser, Lynne M. *lawyer, writer*
Kim, Edward William *ophthalmic surgeon*
Petruzzi, Christopher Robert *business educator, consultant*
Steinberg, Howard *chemical company executive, consultant*
Wolfram, Thomas *physicist, educator*

San Diego
Aaron, Cynthia G. *judge*
Acosta, Gary E. *real estate company executive*
Adams, Loretta *marketing executive*
Alch, Mark Lee *organization executive, educator*
Alcosser, Sandra Beth *English language educator, writer*
Alksne, John F. *medical educator, former dean*
Amstadt, Nancy Hollis *retired language educator*
Anderson, Karl Richard *aerospace engineer, consultant*
Anderson, Paul Maurice *electrical engineering educator, researcher, consultant*
Angyal, Charles *architect*
Arova, Sonia *artistic director, ballet educator*
Atkinson, D. Scott *curator*
Auld, Robert Henry, Jr., *biomedical engineer, educator, consultant, author*
Backes, Jack Abraham *retired application developer*
Bakko, Orville Edwin *retired health care executive, consultant*
Balakin, Konstantin V. *chemist, researcher*
bar-Lev, Zev *linguist, educator*
Barone, Angela Maria *artist, researcher*
Barton, Thomas Donald *lawyer, educator*
Bartus, Raymond Thomas *neuroscientist, pharmaceutical executive, writer*
Basso, Robert J. *manufacturing engineer, inventor*
Batey, Sharyn Rebecca *clinical research scientist*
Bauer, Judy Marie *minister*
Baum, Stephen L. *utilities company executive*
Baxter, Robert Hampton *insurance executive*
Beaumont, Mona *artist*
Bejarano, David *protective services official*
Bell, Gene *newspaper publishing executive*
Benedyk, Mika Ono *editor, writer*
Bernstein, Sanford Irwin *biology professor*
Beyster, John Robert *engineering company executive*
Birndorf, Howard C. *health products executive*
Blade, Melinda Kim *archaeologist, educator, research scientist*
Blakemore, Claude Coulehan *banker*
Bleiler, Charles Arthur *lawyer*
Bliesner, James Douglas *municipal/county official, consultant*
Bochy, Bruce *professional sports team manager, coach*
Boggs, William S. *lawyer*
Bonn, Ronald Sheldon *TV news producer, journalism educator*
Boone, Bret Robert *professional baseball player*
Bot, Adrian Ion *immunologist*
Bowens, Thella *senior aviation director*
Bowie, Peter Wentworth *judge, educator*
Brandes, Raymond Stewart *history educator*
Brennan-Sparks, Jennifer Anne *writer*
Brewster, Rudi Milton *judge*
Brierton, Cheryl Lynn *lawyer*
Brom, Robert H. *bishop*
Bronn, Mark R. *pharmaceutical executive*
Brooks, John White *lawyer*
Brown, LaMar Bevan *lawyer*
Brumfield, Jack *communications executive*
Bryan, John Rodney *management consultant*
Burge, David Russell *concert pianist, composer, piano educator*
Burns, Larry Alan *judge*
Bussard, Robert William *physicist*
Cabrera, Quincy Rodolfo *minister, educator*
Calabrese, Philip George *mathematician, researcher, small business owner*
Campbell, Ian David *opera company director*
Cantor, Charles Robert *biochemistry educator*
Caughlin, Stephenie Jane *organic farmer*
Chambers, Henry George *orthopedic surgeon*
Charat, Jennifer Nicole *editor*
Chatroo, Arthur Jay *lawyer*
Chiplin, John *medical company executive*
Chory, Joanne *plant biologist*
Chou, Kuo-Chen *biophysical chemist*
Chun Fat, George *writer*
Cline, Stephanie E. *food service executive*
Cobble, James Wikle *chemistry professor*
Cobbs Hoffman, Elizabeth Anne *history educator*
Cogan, Mary Jo Gleber *lawyer*
Colella, Samuel D. *biotechnology executive*
Comrie, Sandra Melton *human resource executive*
Conant, Kim Untiedt *elementary school educator*
Conly, John Franklin *engineering educator, researcher*
Contreras, Thomas J., Jr., *career officer*
Cook, Joseph C., Jr., *pharmaceutical executive*
Cook, Stephen Barton *art educator, artist*
Corbett, Luke Robinson *lawyer*
Crisci, Mathew G. *marketing executive, writer*
Crocitti, John Joseph *historian, educator*
Crumpler, Hugh Allan *author*
Cunningham, Chester Grant *writer*
Dahlberg, Kenneth C. *manufacturing executive*
Damoose, George Lynn *lawyer*
Darcy, Thomas E. *science company executive*
Darmstandler, Harry Max *real estate executive, retired air force officer*
Da Rosa, Alison *travel editor*
David, Judy Breiner *advertising executive, consultant, public relations executive, television producer*
Davies, Thomas Mockett, Jr., *history educator*
Davis, John Warren *real estate broker, contractor*
Dean, Richard Anthony *mechanical engineer, engineering executive*
Delawie, Homer Torrence *retired architect*
Del Castillo, Adelaida Rebecca *social sciences educator, researcher*
DeMaria, Anthony Nicholas *cardiologist, educator*
DiRuscio, Lawrence William *advertising executive*
Doan, Tai Danh *social worker, director*
Dorne, David J. *lawyer*
Dostart, Paul Joseph *lawyer, investor, director, entrepreneur*
Downing, David Charles *retired minister*
Drummond, John C. *anesthesiologist, educator*
Duddles, Charles Weller *food company executive*
Dulbecco, Renato *biologist, educator*
Dumanis, Bonnie M. *prosecutor*
Dunlop, Marianne *retired English as second language educator*
Dunn, David Joseph *financial executive*
Dyer, Charles Richard *law librarian, law educator*
Earl, Christopher D. *health products executive*
Early, Teri Wilson (Denise Wilson) *elementary school educator, educator*
Ebbeling, William Leonard *physician*
Eckhart, Walter *molecular biologist, educator*
Edwards, Darrel *psychologist*
Edwards-Tate, Laurie Ellen *human services administrator, educator*
Eger, John Mitchell *lawyer, educator*
Eigner, William Whitling *lawyer*
Elliott, Graham *science educator*
Ellsworth, Robert Fred *investment executive, former government official*
Emerick, Robert Earl *retired sociologist, educator*
Engle, Steven B. *biotechnology company executive*
Evans, Ersel Arthur *consulting engineer executive*
Evans, John Joseph *management consultant, executive, educator, writer*
Everett, Hobart Ray, Jr., *engineer, naval officer, consultant, researcher*
Fagan, Peter Ledford *lawyer, naval officer*
Farmer, Janene Elizabeth *artist, educator*
Fauchier, Dan R(ay) *mediator, arbitrator, educator, construction management consultant,*
Fike, Edward Lake *newspaper editor*
Flatley, Jay T. *biotechnology company executive*
Fleischmann, Paul *religious organization administrator, minister*
Flettner, Marianne *opera administrator*
Flutie, Douglas Richard (Doug Flutie) *professional football player*
Foreman, John Patrick *electrical engineer*
Francisco, Edith Gaba *medical/surgical nurse*
Friedman, Arthur Daniel *electrical engineering and computer science educator, investment management company executive*
Friedman, Gary E. *lawyer*
Friedman, Paul Jay *radiologist, educator*
Gaal, Peter *electrical engineer, researcher*
Gage, Fred H. *neuroscientist, medical educator*
Garfin, Steven R. *orthopedic surgeon*
Gastil, Russell Gordon *geologist, educator*
Gazell, James Albert *public administration educator*
Gengor, Virginia Anderson *financial planning executive, educator*
Georgakakos, Konstantine Peter *research hydrologist*
Getis, Arthur *geography educator*
Gilbertson, Oswald Irving *marketing executive*
Gilleland, John Rogers *technology company executive*
Golding, Brage *university president*
Golding, Susan G. *former mayor*
Goldstein, Mark Kingston Levin *information technology executive, researcher*
Goltz, Robert William *physician, educator*
Gonzalez, Irma Elsa *federal judge*
Goodall, Jackson Wallace, Jr., *restaurant company executive*
Greene, Howard E., Jr., *pharmaceutical executive*
Greenwood, Richard Hopson *lawyer, minister*
Grey, Howard M. *science administrator, educator*
Grosser, T.J. *administrator, developer, fundraiser*
Guinn, Stanley Willis *lawyer*
Gupta, Madhu Sudan *electrical engineering educator*
Gwynn, Anthony Keith (Tony Gwynn) *former professional baseball player*
Hacksell, Uli *pharmaceutical executive*
Haener, Juan A. *physicist*
Hager, Michael W. *museum director*
Hales, Alfred Washington *mathematics educator, consultant*
Harris, James Michael *sales executive*
Harutunian, Albert T(heodore), III, *judge*
Haverly, Pamela Sue *nursing administrator*
Hayes, Claude Quinten Christopher *research scientist, inventor*
Hayes, Robert Emmet *retired insurance company executive*
Hays, Diana Joyce Watkins *consumer products company executive*
Heer, David Macalpine *sociology educator*
Heidrich, Robert Wesley *lawyer*
Heinemann, Stephen F. *molecular neurobiologist educator*
Henderson, John Drews *architect*
Herring, Charles David *lawyer, educator*
Higgs, Craig DeWitt *lawyer*
Hixson, Harry F., Jr., *health products executive*
Hofflund, Paul *lawyer*
Hoffman, Trevor William *professional baseball player*
Hoffner, John F. *food service executive*
Hoston, Germaine Annette *political science educator*
Huff, Marilyn L. *federal judge*
Hunt, Barnabas John *priest, religious organization administrator*
Ingle, M(orton) Blakeman *chemicals executive*
Inoue, Michael Shigeru *industrial engineer, electrical engineer*
Intriere, Anthony Donald *retired internist, gastroenterologist*
Ito, Carl Susumu *computer engineer*
Iversen, Leslie Lars *pharmaceutical executive*
Jacob, Dianne *county official*
Jacobs, Irwin Mark *communications executive*
Jacobs, Paul E. *communications executive*
Jacoby, Irving *physician*
Jagoda, Barry Lionel *writer, media adviser, communications consultant*
Jamieson, Stuart William *surgeon, educator*
Jennings, Jackie *construction executive, contractor*
Jenson, Ronald Allen *religious executive, educator*
Johnson, Kenneth Owen *retired speech pathology/audiology services professional*
Johnson, M. Ross *pharmaceutical executive*
Jones, Napoleon A., Jr., *judge*
Kaback, Michael *medical educator*
Kadous, Tamer Adel *research scientist*
Kahan, David Michael *education educator*
Kaplan, George Willard *urologist*
Kassel, Daniel Brian *biotechnologist, researcher*
Kaufman, Julian Mortimer *broadcasting company executive, consultant*
Kaweski, Susan *plastic surgeon, naval officer*
Keep, Judith N. *federal judge*
Kehoe, Christine T. *state official*
Keitel, William E. *communications executive*
Kelly, Karla Rosemarie *lawyer*
Kendrick, Ronald H. *banker*
Kitchen, James R. *academic administrator*
Klamerus, Karen Jean *pharmacist, researcher*
Klein, Herbert George *newspaper editor*
Klein, Saul D. *real estate company executive*
Klesko, Ryan *professional baseball player*
Klinedinst, John David *lawyer*
Knuth, Dean Leslie *research and development company executive, golf consultant, writer*
Koenig, Harold Martin *former United States Navy surgeon general*
Kranzler, Jay D. *pharmaceutical executive*
Krejci, Robert Harry *not-for-profit developer, consultant*
Kronewitter, Frank Dell *software engineer, researcher*
Kruggel, John Louis *plastic surgeon*
Krulak, Victor Harold *newspaper executive*
Krull, Kathleen *writer*
Krupchak, Tamara *artist*
Kuntz, William Richard, Jr., *lawyer*
Kyle, Robert Campbell, II, *publishing executive*
Lam, Carol C. *lawyer*
Lane, Gloria Julian *foundation administrator*
Lang, Linda A. *food service executive*
Langer, Eva Marie *video specialist*
L'Annunziata, Michael Frank *chemist, consultant, nuclear scientist*
Lansdowne, William M. *police chief*
Lao, Lang Li *nuclear fusion research physicist*
Larson, Arvid Gunnar *electrical engineer*
Larson, Mark Devin *communications executive*
Larson, Vernon Dale *audiologist, researcher*
Lathrop, Mitchell Lee *lawyer*
Lau, Maureen Treacy *television producer*
LeBeau, Charles Paul *lawyer*
Lederer, Richard Henry *writer, educator, columnist*
Leopold, George Robert *radiologist*
Lerach, William S. *lawyer*
Levy, Jerome *dermatologist, retired military officer*
Lewis, Alan James *pharmaceutical executive, pharmacologist*
Lewis, Shirley Jeane *psychotherapist, educator*
Lieber, Richard Louis *biomedical engineering scientist, educator*
Lief, Jack *pharmaceutical executive*
Litrownik, Alan Jay *psychologist, educator*
Livingston, Stanley C. *architect*
Longenecker, Martha W. *museum director*
Loper, Warren Edward *computer scientist*
Loria, Emile *medical company executive*
Lucchino, Lawrence *sports team executive, lawyer*
Lum, Rodger G. *city health department administrator*
Lundy-Slade, Bettie B. *retired electronics professional*
Lynberg, Terence Ellsworth *minister, education educator*
Lyons, Gary A. *medical company executive*
Lyons, Mary E. *academic administrator*
Madhavan, Murugappa Chettiar *economics educator, international consultant*
Magadan, David Joseph *professional baseball player*
Magnuson, Harold Joseph *physician*
Mahdavi, Kamal B. *writer, researcher*
Mahon, Maxine *performing company executive*
Maier, Paul Victor *pharmaceutical executive*
Maier-Lorentz, Madeline Marie *nurse educator*
Markowitz, Harry Max *finance and economics educator*
Masliah, Eliezer *neuroscientist, educator*
Mayer, George Roy *education educator*
McBrayer, Sandra L. *educational director, homeless outreach educator*
McCarty, Judy *councilman*
McClellan, Craig Rene *lawyer*
Mc Comic, Robert Barry *real estate development company executive, lawyer*
McGinnis, Robert E. *lawyer*
McKeown, Mary Margaret *federal judge*
McKeown, Michael Eugene *psychologist, consultant*
McLeod, Douglas Bailey *mathematician, educator*
McLeod, John Hugh, Jr., *mechanical and electrical engineer*
McNamara, Kevin Michael *floorcovering company executive*
Mebane, Julie Shaffer *lawyer*
Meerson, Felix Zalmanovich *cardiologist*
Mestechkin, Mikhail Markovich *math physicist*
Mittermiller, James Joseph *lawyer*
Molina Villacorta, Rafael Antonio *technology management investment company executive*
Moores, John *professional sports team executive*
Moos, Walter Hamilton *pharmaceutical company executive*
Morgan, Neil *writer, newspaper editor, lecturer, columnist*
Morris, Grant Harold *law educator*
Mosteller, James Wilbur, III, *data processing executive*
Murphy, Dick *mayor, former superior court judge*
Myers, Douglas George *zoological society administrator*
Naschak, Bruce Stephen *education educator, consultant*
Naslund, Eric *architectural firm executive*
Nassif, Thomas Anthony *business executive, former ambassador*
Nelson, Craig Alan *management consultant*
Nenner, Victoria Corich *nurse, educator*
Neuman, Tom S. *emergency medical physician, educator*
Neumann, Linda Kay *marketing professional*
Nevin, Phillip *professional baseball player*
Nguyen, Khue Vu *molecular biologist, researcher*
Noehren, Robert *organist, organ builder*
Norling, Richard Arthur *health care executive*

North, Robert L. *computer software executvie*
Noziska, Charles Brant *lawyer*
Nugent, Robert J., Jr., *fast food company executive*
O'Brien, Jack George *artistic director*
Ojeda, Norma *social sciences educator, researcher*
O'Laughlin, Joanie *broadcast executive*
Oldham, Maxine Jernigan *real estate broker*
Olefsky, Jerrold M. *medical educator, researcher*
Olevsky, Eugene A. *research scientist, educator*
O'Malley, Edward *psychiatrist, consultant*
Osby, Robert Edward *protective services official*
Overton, Marcus Lee *performing arts administrator, actor, writer*
Owen-Towle, Carolyn Sheets *clergywoman*
Paderewski, Sir Clarence Joseph *architect*
Padovani, Roberto *communications executive*
Pagan, Keith Areatus *music educator, academic administrator*
Paget, John Arthur *mechanical engineer*
Pan, Henry Yue-Ming *clinical pharmacologist*
Panetta, Joseph Daniel *biotechnology executive*
Parthemore, Jacqueline Gail *internist, educator, hospital administrator*
Partida, Gilbert A. *lawyer*
Pastoor, Robertus Antonius *academic administrator*
Paupp, Terrence Edward *research associate, educator*
Payne, Margaret Anne *lawyer*
Pecsok, Robert Louis *chemist, educator*
Peebles, Carol Lynn *immunology researcher*
Perrault, Jacques *biology professor*
Petersen, Martin Eugene *curator*
Peterson, Richard Hermann *retired history educator*
Pfiffner, Patrick Meehan *musician, educator*
Phillips, Wade *professional football team coach*
Pierson, Albert Chadwick *business management educator*
Pigliucci, Riccardo *pharmaceutical executive*
Pincus, Howard J. *geologist, engineer, educator*
Pincus, Robert Lawrence *art critic, cultural historian*
Pitt, William Alexander *cardiologist*
Plescia, George A. *state official*
Pohan, Cathy Ann *education educator, consultant*
Porter, Louisa S. *federal judge*
Prescott, Lawrence Malcolm *medical and health science writer*
Price, Robert E. *manufacturing executive*
Proehl, Gerald T. *pharmaceutical executive*
Pugh, Richard Crawford *lawyer, educator*
Purcifull, Robert Otis *insurance company executive*
Pyatt, Kedar Davis, Jr., *research and development company executive*
Quadros, Paul D. *health products executive*
Radke, Jan Rodger *pulmonologist, physician executive*
Rahmani, Reza Mossaver *writer, retired Iranian Air Force officer, banker, tour operator*
Ransom, Bryan Kenneth *music educator*
Rastetter, William H. *biotechnology company executive*
Ray, Albert *family physician, educator*
Ray, Gene Wells *industrial executive*
Reading, James Edward *transportation executive*
Reese, Michael *mathematics professor*
Rehmus, Charles Martin *law educator, arbitrator*
Reich, Jack W. *health products executive*
Reid, Robert Tilden *medical association administrator, internist*
Reif, Louis Raymond *lawyer, utilities executive*
Reinhard, Christopher John *merchant banking, venture capital and biotechnology executive*
Repetti, Anamaria *healthcare foundation executive*
Resnik, Robert *medical educator*
Reynolds, Rosina Widdowson *actress, theater director*
Rezin, Joyce June *pediatric nurse practitioner*
Rhoades, John Skylstead, Sr., *federal judge*
Rice, Clare I. *electronics company executive*
Riedy, Mark Joseph *finance educator*
Riffenburgh, Gerrye H. *artist, educator*
Robbins, Eleanora Iberall *biogeologist, researcher*
Robertson, Michael *Internet company executive*
Robins, Mitchell James *management consultant*
Robinson, David E. *pharmaceuticals executive*
Rodgers, Janet Ahalt *nursing educator, dean*
Rodríguez-Figueroa, R. Vilmarie *pharmaceutical executive*
Rohn, William R. *biotechnology company executive*
Roper, William Alford, Jr., *diversified technology services company executive*
Roseman, Charles Sanford *lawyer*
Rosen, Peter *health facility administrator, emergency physician, educator*
Ross, John, Jr., *cardiologist, educator*
Ross, Terry D. *lawyer*
Roth, Duane J. *pharmaceutical executive*
Roth, Theodore D. *pharmaceutical executive*
Rotter, Paul Talbott *retired insurance executive*
Rowe, Peter A. *newspaper columnist*
Russell, Cristel Antonia *finance educator*
St. Clair, Hal Kay *electrical engineer*
St. George, William Ross *lawyer, retired naval officer, consultant*
Saito, Frank Kiyoji *import and export firm executive*
Samant, Vijay B. *biotechnology company executive*
Samuelson, Derrick William *lawyer*
Sanders, Jerry *social services executive*
Santee, Dale William *lawyer, air force officer*
Sasaran, Laura Jeanne *humanities educator*
Sasidharan, Vinod *travel and tourism educator, researcher*
Sauer, David Andrew *librarian, technical writer*
Schmidt, Joseph David *urologist*
Schmidt, Terry L. *health care executive*
Schmidt, Thomas Charles *biomedical engineer, researcher*
Schottenheimer, Martin Edward *professional football coach*
Schoville, Dennis A(rnold) *lawyer*
Schrock, Donald E. *communications executive*
Schuhsler, Helmut *biotechnology company executive*
Schultz, Kenneth Robert *nuclear engineer, researcher*
Schwartz, Alfred *university dean*
Scott, Bonnie Kime *English literature and cultural educator*
Scripps, Robert P. *publishing executive*
Seagren, Stephen Linner *oncologist*
Seidenwurm, Richard Lewis *lawyer*
Sejnowski, Terrence Joseph *science educator*
Sell, Robert Emerson *electrical engineer*
Shapiro, Philip Alan *lawyer*
Shawver, Laura K. *biotechnology company executive*
Shearer, William Kennedy *lawyer, publisher*
Shedroff, Sharon D. *psychologist, researcher, anthropologist, consultant*
Sheldon, Lois Elizabeth *social services administrator*
Shippey, Sandra Lee *lawyer*
Shneour, Elie Alexis *biophysicist, researcher, historian*
Short, Jay Milton *biotechnology company executive*
Skelly, John Joshua *retired clergyman, fundraiser*
Skwara, Erich Wolfgang *novelist, poet, educator, literary critic*
Slate, John Butler *biomedical engineer*
Smith, Raymond Edward *retired health care administrator*
Smith, Steven Ray *law educator*
Snyder, David Richard *lawyer*
Sobol, Robert E. *medical company executive*
Spanos, Alexander Gus *construction company owner, professional sports team owner*
Spanos, Dean A. *professional sports team executive*
Spira, Patricia Goodsitt *association executive*
Stallings, Valerie Aileen *retired councilwoman, consultant*
Stambaugh, Larry G. *finance executive*
Standifird, Stephen Scott *finance educator*
Stapleton, Michael *information technology executive*
Steen, Paul Joseph *retired broadcasting executive*
Stein, Franklin Joseph *import/export company executive*
Sterrett, James Kelley, II, *lawyer*
Stevens, William C., Jr., *pharmaceutical executive*
Stoessinger, John George *political science educator*
Storer, Norman William *sociologist, educator*
Sturman, George *poet*
Sullivan, Michelle Cornejo *lawyer*
Sulpizio, Richard *communications company executive*
Sutton, Keith H. *information technology executive*
Suycott, Mark Leland *aerospace engineer, retired military officer*
Swank, William George *historian, writer*
Swanson, Mary Catherine *educational reform program founder*
Taylor, George Allen *advertising agency executive*
Teguh, Collin *physician, educator*
Tennent, Valentine Leslie *accountant*
Thoman, David Scott *surgeon*
Thomas, Robert McGuffey *automotive executive, educator*
Thompson, David Renwick *federal judge*
Thompson, Gordon, Jr., *federal judge*
Tidwell, Geoffrey Morgan *medical company executive*
Tillinghast, Charles Carpenter, III, *marketing company executive*
Timoshchuk, Victor Arkadyevich *research scientist*
Todd, John J. *computer company executive*
Tom, Lawrence *technology executive*
Tragen, Irving Glenne *consultant*
Travaglini, Joseph *educational consultant*
Trembley, Mark Michel *geographer, educator*
Tricoles, Gus Peter *electromagnetic engineer, physicist, consultant*
Tsybakov, Boris Solomon *information theory and communication networks researcher, educator*
Turov, Daniel *financial writer, investment executive*
Turrentine, Howard Boyd *federal judge*
Ulen, Gene Eldridge *elementary school educator*
Valdez, Jose Carbajal, Jr., *poet, lyricist*
Vanderbilt, Kermit *English language educator*
Van Kirk, Jaye Frances *psychology educator*
Van Schoik, D. Rick *think-tank executive*
Van Tassel, Lowell Thomas *mathematics professor*
Vasudevan, Sriram *risk management professional*
Vause, Edwin Hamilton *research foundation administrator*
Velo, Ani Piro *mathematician, educator*
Walker, Donald Ezzell *retired academic administrator*
Wallace, J. Clifford *federal judge*
Walton, Bill (William Theodore Walton III) *sportscaster, former professional basketball player*
Ward, Charles Raymond *systems engineer*
Ward-Steinman, David *composer, music educator, pianist*
Ware, Carl *immunologist*
Warner, John Hilliard, Jr., *technical services, military and commercial systems and software company executive*
Wasserman, Stephen Ira *allergist, immunologist, educator*
Wawrytko, Sandra Ann *humanities educator*
Weaver, Michael James *lawyer*
Weber, Stephen Lewis *university president*
Weeks, John Robert *geographer, sociology educator*
Weidner, Lauren Finder *lawyer*
Wells, David Lee *professional baseball player*
Welsh, Anne Marie *theater critic, writer, educator*
Wertheim, Robert Halley *national security consultant*
White, Vance R.(Randy) *medical company executive*
Whittington, Anne Elizabeth *diabetes educator*
Widder, Kenneth Jon *pathologist, educator*
Wierenga, Wendell D. *biotechnology company executive*
Wiesler, James Ballard *retired banker*
Wildenthal, Bryan Hobson, II, *law educator*
Williams, Carolyn *secondary school educator*
Willis, Norman Hunt *author, writer, director, producer*
Wilson, Hugh Steven *lawyer*
Wilson, Jerry Clark *language educator*
Winders, Glenda *publishing executive*
Winner, Karin E. *editor*
Wojcik, Martin Henry *not-for-profit executive*
Wolfe, Deborah Ann *lawyer*
Woods, Randall E. *pharmaceutical executive*
Yamazaki, Shinji *research scientist*
Yarber, Robert Earl *writer, retired educator*
Yokley, Richard Clarence *protective services official*
Youngs, Jack Marvin *cost engineer*
Zeiger, Robert S. *allergist*
Ziegaus, Alan James *public relations executive*
Zyskind, Judith Weaver *molecular biology educator, entrepreneur*

San Fernando
Douglass, Ramona Elizabeth *medical sales professional*

San Francisco
Abbas, Abul K. *pathologist, educator*
Abbott, Barry Alexander *lawyer*
Abramson, Norman *engineering educator*
Achtenberg, Roberta *former federal official*
Acker, Frederick Wayne *lawyer*
Ackerman, Arlene *school system administrator*
Adler, Nancy Elinor *psychologist, educator*
Ainsworth, Kent P. *engineering company executive*
Aldrich, Michael Ray *library curator, health educator*
Alexander, Robert C. *lawyer*
Alexis, Geraldine M. *lawyer*
Alou, Felipe Rojas *professional baseball manager*
Amend, William John Conrad, Jr., *physician, educator*
Anderson, Edward Virgil *lawyer*
Anschutz, Philip F. *transportation executive, communications executive*
Arbuthnot, Robert Murray *lawyer*
Armacost, Samuel Henry *bank executive*
Ascher, Nancy Louise *surgeon*
Atkins, Howard Ian *bank executive*
August-deWilde, Katherine *banker*
Babcock, Jo *artist, educator*
Bachman, David Christian *orthopedic surgeon*
Bainton, Dorothy Ford *pathology educator, researcher*
Baker, Cameron *lawyer*
Barbagelata, Robert Dominic *lawyer*
Barber, Malcolm *auction house executive*
Bardsley, Kay *historian, archivist, dance professional*
Bargmann, Cornelia I. *neuroscientist, science educator*
Barlow, William Pusey, Jr., *accountant*
Barondes, Samuel Herbert *psychiatrist, educator*
Barzelatto, Jose S. *social welfare organization executive*
Batterman, Boris William *physicist, educator, academic director*
Bauch, Thomas Jay *financial/investment advisor, lawyer, retired apparel executive*
Baumhefner, Clarence Herman *retired bank executive*
Baxter, Marvin Ray *state supreme court justice*
Baxter, Ralph H., Jr., *lawyer*
Bea, Carlos Tiburcio *federal judge*
Beall, Dennis Ray *artist, educator*
Bechtel, Riley Peart *engineering company executive*
Bechtel, Stephen Davison, Jr., *engineering company executive*
Bee, Robert Norman *banker*
Behrens, M. Kathleen *medical researcher*
Bell, Chester Gordon *computer engineering company executive*
Benet, Leslie Zachary *pharmacokineticist, educator*
Benioff, Marc *Internet company executive*
Bennett, William *oboist*
Bensinger, David August *dentist, university dean*
Bentley, Lisa *publisher*
Bergen, David M. *apparel executive*
Berger, Mitchel Stuart *neurosurgeon*
Bernstein, Gerald William *management consultant, researcher*
Bernstein, Harold Seth *pediatric cardiologist, molecular geneticist*
Bertolami, Charles Nicholas *dean, dental educator, oral surgeon*
Berzon, Marsha S. *federal judge*
Bishop, John Michael *academic administrator, biomedical researcher, educator*
Bitterman, Mary Gayle Foley *foundation executive*
Blackburn, Elizabeth Helen *molecular biologist*
Blakey, Scott Chaloner *journalist, writer*
Blanc, Maureen *public relations executive*
Blatt, Lawrence M. *pharmaceutical company executive*
Bleich, Jeffrey Laurence *lawyer, law educator*
Block, David Jeffrey *lawyer, investment manager*
Boehlke, Christine *public relations executive*
Boles, Roger *otolaryngologist*
Bondarook, Nina *public relations consultant*
Bondoc, Rommel *lawyer*
Bonds, Barry Lamar *professional baseball player*
Bonney, John Dennis *retired oil company executive*
Borowsky, Philip *lawyer*
Bostwick, James Stephen *lawyer*
Bothwell, Anthony Peirson Xavier, Sr., *lawyer, educator*
Botkin, Daniel Benjamin *biologist, environmental scientist, writer*
Bourne, Henry R. *medicine, cellular and molecular pharmacology educator*
Boutin, Peter Rucker *lawyer*
Boven, Douglas George *lawyer*
Boyden, Jaclyne White *university vice dean*
Boyle, Antonia Barnes *electronic learning consultant, writer*
Bracken, Thomas Robert James *real estate investment executive*
Bradford, David S. *surgeon*
Bratton, Christopher Alan *video and art educator*
Breall, Susan *judge*
Brechka, Frank Tilson *retired librarian, historian*
Breeden, David *clarinetist*
Brice, Charles Steven *airline executive*
Brickner, David *religious organization administrator, consultant*
Bridges, Robert Lysle *retired lawyer*
Briggs, Barry *business executive*
Brinkley, Susan *executive pastry chef*
Briscoe, John *lawyer*
Broadway, Nancy Ruth *landscape design and construction company executive, consultant, model and actress*
Bronstein, Phil *executive editor*
Brotman, Martin *gastroenterologist*
Brown, Amos Cleophilus *minister*
Brown, Donald Malcolm *plastic surgeon*
Brown, Donald Wesley *lawyer*
Brown, Eric Joel *biomedical researcher, researcher*
Brown, Janice Rogers *state supreme court justice*
Browning, James Robert *federal judge*
Bruen, James A. *lawyer*
Buccieri, Shirley H. *lawyer*
Buckner, John Knowles *investor*
Bull, Henrik Helkand *architect*
Burden, James Ewers *lawyer*
Burkey, Marcia B. *corporate financial executive*
Burlingame, Alma Lyman *chemist, educator*
Burns, Brian Patrick *lawyer*
Burt, Rick *lawyer*
Bushnell, Roderick Paul *lawyer*
Butenhoff, Susan G. *public relations executive*
Butz, Otto William *political science educator*
Bybee, Jay Scott *federal judge, federal agency administrator*
Byers, Brett Douglas *lawyer, investment company executive*
Cabraser, Elizabeth Joan *lawyer*
Caccamo, Aldo M. *oil industry executive*
Callahan, Michael L. *emergency physician, educator*
Callahan, Consuelo Maria *federal judge*
Callahan, Patricia R. *bank executive*
Callan, Terrence A. *lawyer*
Callison, Russell James *lawyer*
Calvin, Carolina *apparel executive, designer*
Calvin, Dorothy Ver Strate *computer company executive*
Cameron, Heather Anne *publishing executive*
Campbell, André Renay *surgical educator, internist*
Campbell, Jeffrey C. *pharmaceutical executive*
Campbell, Scott Robert *lawyer, former food company executive*
Canales, James Earl, Jr., *foundation administrator*
Caniparoli, Val William *choreographer, dancer*
Capozzi, Angelo *surgeon*
Carmi, Sofia *artist, educator*
Carrow, Robert Duane *lawyer, barrister*
Casey, Bernard J. *lawyer*
Cassman, Marvin *biochemist*
Cepeda, Orlando *retired professional baseball player*
Chang, Patti *foundation administrator*
Chapin, Dwight Allan *columnist, writer*
Chase, Marilyn *journalist*
Chater, Shirley Sears *health educator*
Chatterjee, Sharmila *marketing educator*
Cheatham, Robert William *lawyer*
Cheng, Wan-Lee *mechanical engineer, industrial technology educator*
Chesney, Margaret A. *medical educator, medical researcher*
Chesney, Maxine M. *judge*
Chicotel, Richard A. *real estate company executive*
Chin, Ming *state supreme court justice*
Chin, Sue Soone Marian (Suchin Chin) *conceptual artist, portraitist, photographer, community affairs activist*
Chou, Erwin C. *economist*
Cirese, Robert Charles *economist, real estate investment counselor*
Cisneros, Evelyn *dancer*
Clarey, Patricia *association executive*
Clements, John Allen *physiologist*
Clever, Linda Hawes *physician*
Cline, Fred Albert, Jr., *retired librarian, conservationist*
Clopton, Karen Valentia *lawyer, president civil services commission*
Cluff, Lloyd Sterling *earthquake geologist*
Cobbs, Price Mashaw *social psychiatrist*
Coffin, Judy Sue *lawyer*
Cohler, Charles B. *lawyer*
Cohn, Nathan *lawyer*
Coleman, Thomas Young *lawyer*
Colton, Roy Charles *management consultant*
Condy, Charles T. *restaurateur*
Connelly, Theodore Sample *communications executive*
Conti, Samuel *federal judge*
Coombe, George William, Jr., *lawyer, retired banker*
Corcoran, Maureen Elizabeth *lawyer*
Corrigan, Robert Anthony *academic administrator*
Costa, Walter Henry *architect*
Costa-Zalessow, Natalia *foreign language educator*
Cowan, Stephen A. *lawyer*
Coye, Molly Joel *state agency administrator*
Cranston, Mary B. *lawyer*
Crawford, Michael Howard *cardiologist, educator, researcher*
Crawford, Roy Edgington, III, *lawyer*
Crist, Paul Grant *lawyer*
Crittenden, Mary Rita *clinical psychology educator*
Cruse, Allan Baird *mathematician, computer scientist, educator*
Dachs, Alan Mark *investment company executive*
Darbee, Peter A. *electric power company executive*
D'Arpino, Tony *poet*
Da Silva, Delio P. *investment advisor*
David, George *psychiatrist, economic theory lecturer*
Dawson, Chandler Robert *ophthalmologist, educator*
Dawson, Peter A. *corporate financial executive*
Deane, Elaine *lawyer*
DeFeo, Phillip D. *brokerage house executive*
Deicken, Raymond Friedrich *neuropsychiatrist, clinical neuroscientist*
Delaney, Martin *not-for-profit developer*
Del Campo, Martin Bernardelli *architect*
Dell, Robert Michael *lawyer*
Dellas, Robert Dennis *investment banker*
Demarest, David Franklin, Jr., *banker, retired government official*
DeMuro, Paul Robert *lawyer*
Dennehy, Raymond Leo *philosopher, educator*
D'Errico, Didi *public relations executive*
Des Jardins, Traci *chef, restaurant owner*
DeSoto, Lewis Damien *art educator*
Dickey, Glenn Ernest, Jr., *sports columnist*
Dickinson, Eleanor Creekmore *artist, educator*
Dickinson, Wade *physicist, oil and gas company executive, educator*
Diekmann, Gilmore Frederick, Jr., *lawyer*
Dill, Kenneth Austin *pharmaceutical chemistry educator*
Dillon, William Patrick *neuroradiologist, radiologist*
Dodds, Christopher V. *finance company executive*
Dodge, Peter Hampton *architect*
Dolan, Brian Patrick *humanities educator*
Dolby, Ray Milton *engineering company executive, electrical engineer*
Donnally, Patricia Broderick *writer*
Dowling, Meaghan Hundley *editor*
Dracup, Kathleen Anne *nursing educator*
Draper, William Henry, III, *venture capitalist*
Dryden, Robert Eugene *lawyer*
Du Bain, Myron *financial services executive*
DuBose, Francis Marquis *clergyman*
Duffy, Jan *law educator, lawyer*
Dugoni, Arthur A. *orthodontics educator, dean*
Duncan, Deborah L. *finance company executive*
Dunn, Patricia C. *investment company executive*
Dunn, Richard Joseph *retired investment counselor*
Dunne, Kevin Joseph *lawyer*

Duscha, Julius Carl *journalist*
Dyson, Tim *public relations executive*
Eastham, Thomas *foundation administrator*
Eddington, Thomas L. *human resources consultant*
Edwards, C. Webb *bank executive*
Edwards, Robin Morse *lawyer*
Ehrlich, Susan Patricia *bank executive*
Eliaz, Rom Ezer *chemical engineer, educator*
Ellery, Tracey *internet company executive*
Ellis, John *urban designer*
Enfield, Donald Michael *insurance company executive*
Eng, Catherine *health care facility administrator, physician, medical educator*
Engleman, Ephraim Philip *rheumatologist*
Epstein, Charles Joseph *physician, medical geneticist, pediatrics and biochemistry educator*
Epstein, John Howard *dermatologist*
Erskine, John Morse *surgeon*
Estes, Carroll Lynn *sociologist, educator*
Etheridge, Melissa Lou *singer, songwriter*
Everett-Thorp, Kate *digital marketing executive*
Evers, William Dohrmann *lawyer*
Falk, Steven B. *newspaper publishing executive*
Falvey, Mary C. *management consultant*
Feller, Lloyd Harris *lawyer*
Fergus, Gary Scott *lawyer*
Ferlinghetti, Lawrence *poet*
Fernald, Thomas A. *publishing executive*
Ferris, Russell James, II, *writer*
Fessel, Walford Jeffrey *rheumatologist*
Festinger, Richard *music educator, composer*
Field, John Louis *architect*
Fielder, David R. *medical research administrator*
Fields, Howard Lincoln *neurology and physiology educator*
Filly, Roy A. *radiologist*
Finberg, James Michael *lawyer*
Finberg, Laurence *pediatrician, educator, dean*
Finck, Kevin William *lawyer*
Fisher, Donald G. *casual apparel chain stores executive*
Fishman, Robert Allen *neurologist, educator, department chair*
Fledderman, Harry L. *lawyer*
Fleishhacker, David *school administrator*
Fletcher, William A. *federal judge, law educator*
Flittie, Clifford Gilliland *retired petroleum company executive*
Fogel, Paul David *lawyer*
Fohrman, Burton H. *lawyer*
Folkman, David H. *retail, wholesale and consumer products consultant*
Fong, Heather J. *protective services official*
Foster, David Scott *lawyer*
Fox, Patrick John *sociology educator*
Fox, Steve *editor-in-chief*
Frank, Anthony Melchior *federal official, former financial executive*
Freeman, Tom M. *lawyer*
Freitag, Peter Roy *transportation specialist*
Freud, Nicholas S. *lawyer*
Freund, Fredric S. *real estate broker, property manager*
Frick, Oscar Lionel *physician, educator*
Friedman, K. Bruce *lawyer*
Friedman, Tully Michael *corporate financial executive*
Friedrichs, Edward Charles *architect*
Friese, Robert Charles *lawyer*
Fujii, Sharon M. *federal agency administrator*
Fuller, James William *financial director*
Furst, Arthur *toxicologist, educator*
Furth, Frederick Paul *lawyer*
Futch, Dorothy Helen *librarian, paralegal*
Gale, Michael Johnathan *entrepreneur*
Ganem, Donald E. *immunologist*
Ganong, William F(rancis) *physiologist, physician*
Garchik, Leah Lieberman *journalist*
Gardner, James Harkins *venture capitalist*
Garvey, Joanne Marie *lawyer*
Gekelman, Diana *dentist, dental educator, researcher*
Gelhaus, Robert Joseph *lawyer, publisher*
Gellin, Gerald Alan *dermatologist*
Gemello, John Michael *economics educator, consultant, academic administrator*
George, Ronald M. *state supreme court chief justice*
German, William *newspaper editor*
Gerwick, Ben Clifford, Jr., *construction engineer, educator*
Gibbs, Patricia Hellman *physician*
Gibson, Virginia Lee *lawyer*
Gillette, Frankie Jacobs *retired savings and loan executive, social worker, government administrator*
Gillette, James R. *construction executive*
Giovinco, Joseph *nonprofit administrator, writer*
Glazer, Jack Henry *lawyer*
Glynn, Robert D., Jr., *electric power and gas industry executive*
Gold, Herbert *author*
Goldberg, Robert Lewis *preventive and occupational medicine physician, internet executive*
Goldstein, David Baird *energy program director, physicist*
Goldstein, Sydney Rachel *photographer, writer, producer*
Goldstine, Stephen Joseph *college administrator*
Goodby, Jeffrey *advertising agency executive*
Gooding, Charles Arthur *radiologist, physician, educator*
Gooding, Gretchen Ann Wagner *physician, educator*
Gordon, Judith *communications consultant, writer*
Gore, Andrew *editor-in-chief periodical*
Gotway, Michael B. *radiologist, health facility administrator*
Gowdy, Franklin Brockway *lawyer*
Graber, Susan P. *federal judge*
Gradinger, Gilbert Paul *plastic surgeon*
Graw, LeRoy Harry *purchasing and contract management company executive*
Graysmith, Robert *political cartoonist, author*
Green, Robert Leonard *hospital management company executive*
Greenawald, Sheri *performing company executive*
Greene, Warner Craig *medical educator, medical association administrator*
Greenspan, Francis S. *physician*
Greenspan, John S. *dental and medical educator, scientist, administrator*
Gregory, Sara Susan (Sudie) *musician, singer, lyricist, poet, recording industry executive, sound recording engineer, archivist*
Gresham, Zane Oliver *lawyer*
Grodsky, Gerold Morton *biochemistry educator*
Grohe, Linda Squires *dean*
Gropman, Saul I. *music educator*
Grose, Andrew Peter *foundation executive*
Grossman, William *medical researcher, educator*
Grubb, David H. *construction company executive*
Grubb, Edgar Harold *financial services industrial executive*
Gruber, George Michael *accountant, financial systems consultant*
Grumbach, Melvin Malcolm *pediatrician, educator*
Guggenhime, Richard Johnson *lawyer*
Gund, George, III, *financier, professional sports team executive*
Guo, Su *science educator*
Gust, Anne Baldwin *retail apparel company executive*
Haas, Peter E., Sr., *apparel company executive*
Haas, Raymond P. *lawyer*
Haas, Robert Douglas *apparel manufacturing company executive*
Haerle, Paul Raymond *judge*
Hagenbuch, John Jacob *investor*
Hale, Cecil *communications educator, business educator*
Hall, Paul J. *lawyer*
Hall, Shannon *marketing professional, public relations executive, writer, photographer*
Halliday, John Meech *investment company executive*
Hallinan, Terence *prosecutor*
Halloran, Michael James *lawyer*
Hamilton, Joan Nice *editor-in-chief*
Hammergren, John H. *pharmaceutical executive*
Hansen, Carol Louise *English language educator*
Hara, George *software company executive*
Harlan, Neil Eugene *retired healthcare company executive*
Harrington, Charlene Ann *sociology and health policy educator*
Harris, Daniel Y. *private school educator, poet, artist*
Harvey, Glen H. *educational association administrator*
Hastings, Edward Walton *theater director*
Hauser, Stephen L. *medical educator*
Havel, Richard Joseph *physician, educator*
Hawkins, Richard *pharmaceutical and cosmetics company executive*
Hawthorne, Mark R. *investigator, educator*
Heilbron, David Michael *lawyer*
Hellman, F(rederick) Warren *investment advisor*
Henderson, Horace Edward *World War II historian, peace advocate*
Henderson, Isaac Craig *oncologist, researcher*
Henke, Dan *law educator*
Henshaw, Guy Runals *management consultant*
Henson, Ray David *law educator, consultant*
Herbert, Chesley C. *psychiatrist, educator*
Hering, William Marshall *medical organization executive*
Hernandez, Aileen C(larke) *urban consultant*
Herrera, Dennis J. *lawyer*
Herringer, Frank Casper *diversified financial services company executive*
Hershman, Lynn Lester *artist*
Hewitt, Conrad W. *bank executive*
Heyneman, Donald *parasitology and tropical medicine educator*
Higashida, Randall Takeo *radiologist, neurosurgeon, medical educator*
Highsmith, Stefan *biochemistry educator*
Hill, Emma *apparel executive*
Hill, Thomas Quinton *communication specialist, graphic designer*
Hills, Austin Edward *vineyard executive*
Hilton, Stanley Goumas *lawyer, educator, writer*
Hinman, Frank, Jr., *urologist, educator*
Hinman, Harvey DeForest *lawyer*
Hisert, George A. *lawyer*
Ho, Doreen Woo *bank executive*
Hochschild, Adam *writer, commentator, journalist*
Hoffman, Julien Ivor Ellis *pediatric cardiologist, educator*
Hoffman, William Yanes *plastic surgeon*
Hofmann, John Richard, Jr., *retired lawyer*
Hoganson, Susan Cook *non-profit organization executive*
Holden, Frederick Douglass, Jr., *lawyer*
Holmes, Irvin R., Jr., *marketing professional*
Holzemer, William L. *nursing educator*
Homer, Barry Wayne *lawyer*
Horn, Sabrina *public relations executive*
Horner, George F. *biotechnology company executive*
Howard, Carl *lawyer*
Howard, David E. *artist*
Hoyt, David A. *bank executive*
Hsieh, Michael Thomas *venture capitalist*
Hsu, John Chao-Chun *retired pediatrician*
Hubbell, Linda *publishing executive*
Hudner, Philip *lawyer, rancher*
Hudson, Darril *political scientist, educator*
Hudson, Mark Woodbridge *lawyer*
Hui, Helen Yuen Hing *lawyer*
Hynes, Aedhmar *public relations executive*
Ikeda, Clyde Junichi *plastic and reconstructive surgeon*
Illston, Susan Y. *federal judge*
Inman, Robert Anthony *writer*
Islambouly, Hagar Abdel-Hamid *consul general*
Jablons, David M. *surgeon, educator*
James, David Lee *lawyer, international advisor, author*
James, Maria-Elena *federal judge*
James, Thomas Larry *chemistry professor*
Jarvis, Donald Bertram *judge*
Jenkins, Margaret Ludmilla *choreographer, dancer*
Jewett, George Frederick, Jr., *forest products company executive*
Johnson, Camille *media executive*
Jones, Frances Mary *law librarian*
Jones, J. Gilbert *private investigator*
Jones, Stanton William *management consultant*
Jonsen, Albert R(upert) *retired medical ethics educator*
Judd, Bruce Diven *architect*
Julian, Paul C. *health products executive*
Kan, Yuet Wai *hematologist, educator*
Kane, Mary Kay *dean*
Kao, John Sterling *mathematician, educator*
Kaplan, Selna L. *medical educator*
Kapor, Mitchell David *software developer, foundation executive*
Kari, Ross *bank executive*
Kasanin, Mark Owen *lawyer*
Katz, Hilliard Joel *physician*
Katz, Mitchell H. *city health department administrator*
Katzung, Bertram George *pharmacologist*
Keeney, Ralph Lyons *decision and risk analyst, educator*
Keller, Edward Lowell *electrical engineer, educator*
Keller, Hubert *chef, restaurant owner*
Kelley, Michael Garhart Roosevelt *historian, educator, writer*
Kelly, Alan *public relations executive*
Kelly, J. Michael *lawyer*
Kelly, James Anthony *priest*
Kelly, Regis Baker *biochemistry educator, biophysics educator*
Kendall, Robert Daniel *priest, theology educator*
Kennard, Joyce L. *judge*
Kenyon, Cynthia J. *medical researcher*
Keogh, Keith *food company executive*
Kerman, Barry Martin *ophthalmologist, educator*
Kern, John McDougall *lawyer*
Kessler, David Aaron *dean, medical educator*
Khosla, Ved Mitter *oral and maxillofacial surgeon, educator*
Kiefer, Renata Gertrud *physician, epidemiologist, economist, international health management consultant*
King, Alonzo *artistic director, choreographer*
King, Talmadge E. *physician*
Kirincic, Paul E. *human services administrator*
Kirschner, Ruth Fay *writer, artist*
Klammer, Joseph Francis *retired management consultant*
Klein, Marc S. *newspaper editor and publisher*
Klitten, Martin R. *oil industry executive*
Knapp, Charles Lincoln *law educator*
Knebel, Jack Gillen *lawyer*
Koda-Kimble, Mary Anne *medical educator, pharmacologist, dean*
Koeppel, John A. *lawyer*
Koffel, Martin M. *engineering company executive*
Kolkey, Daniel Miles *former judge, lawyer*
Koo, John Ying Ming *psychiatrist, dermatologist*
Kornblum, Guy Orville *lawyer*
Kovacevich, Richard M. *bank executive*
Kozloff, Lloyd M. *university dean, educator, scientist*
Kramer, Steven G. *ophthalmologist, educator*
Kraus, Krandall Anthony *writer*
Kriken, John Lund *architect*
Krippner, Stanley Curtis *psychologist*
Kuhl, Paul Beach *lawyer*
Kunz, Heidi *healthcare company executive*
Kurtz, Larry *corporate communications executive*
Lacovara, Michael *lawyer*
Ladar, Jerrold Morton *lawyer*
La Farge, Timothy *retired plant geneticist*
Lam, Fung *obstetrician, gynecologist, medical educator*
Lamberson, John Roger *insurance company executive*
Landis, Richard Gordon *retired food company executive*
Lane, Fielding H. *lawyer*
Lane, Mary B. *education educator, writer*
Langton, Daniel Joseph *English, writing educator, poet*
Lanier, Lewis *microbiologist, educator, immunologist, educator*
Lara, Adair *columnist, writer*
Laret, Mark R. *school system administrator, health facility executive*
Larson, John William *lawyer*
Laspa, Jude *engineering company executive*
La Vine, Robert L. *lawyer*
LeBlanc, Tina *dancer*
Leddy, William *architect*
Lee, Iara *filmmaker*
Lee, Pamela Anne *bank executive, accountant, business analyst*
Lee, Philip Randolph Randolph *medical educator*
Lee, Richard Diebold *law educator, legal publisher, consultant*
Lee, Yikuan *finance educator*
Leno, Mark *state legislator*
Leondakis, Niki Anna *food service executive*
Leshy, John David *lawyer, legal educator, government official*
Lester, W. Howard *retail executive*
Levada, William Joseph *archbishop*
Leviton, Alan Edward *curator*
Levy, Jay A. *medical educator*
Lin, Robert Kwanhwan *language educator, consultant*
Liu, Xiao *ophthalmologist, neurobiologist*
Livsey, Robert Callister *lawyer*
Lo, Bernard *education educator*
Lolli, Andrew Ralph *industrial engineer, former army officer*
Lombardi, David Ennis, Jr., *lawyer, lecturer, mediator*
Lopes, James Louis *lawyer*
Lord, Mia W. *advocate*
Louderback, Jim *editor-in-chief*
Low, Donald *diplomat, financial investor*
Low, Randall *internist, cardiologist*
Lu, Ying *statistician, educator*
Lucia, Marilyn Reed *physician*
Luft, Harold S. *health economist*
Luft, Rene Wilfred *civil engineer*
Luikart, John Ford *investment banker*
Lynch, Loretta *state agency administrator*
Lynch, Timothy Jeremiah-Mahoney *lawyer, educator, theologian, realtor, writer*
Lyon, David William *research executive*
MacGowan, Eugenia *lawyer*
MacNaughton, Angus Athole *finance company executive*
Maddox, Lyndell E. *utilities company executive*
Madson, David John *fundraising executive*
Maffre, Muriel *ballet dancer*
Magnuson, Robert G. *former communications executive*
Magowan, Peter Alden *professional sports team executive, retail executive*
Mahley, Robert W. *health facility administrator*
Mahoney, David L. *former pharmaceutical wholesale and healthcare management company executive*
Mahoney, Michael James *investment and software executive*
Maier, Peter Klaus *lawyer*
Mandra, York T. *geology educator*
Mann, Bruce Alan *lawyer, bank executive, investment banker*
Manning, Jerome Alan *retired lawyer*
Maracek, Leigh *association administrator*
Marcus, Richard Leon *lawyer, educator*
Marcus, Robert *aluminum company executive*
Marduel, Alix *venture capitalist*
Marineau, Philip Albert *apparel executive*
Márquez-Magaña, Leticia Maria *biology professor*
Marshall, Grayson William, Jr., *biomaterials scientist, health sciences educator*
Marshall, Raymond Charles *lawyer*
Marston, Michael *urban economist, asset management executive*
Martel, John Sheldon *lawyer, writer*
Martin, David William, Jr., *biomedical research company executive, educator*
Martin, Fred *artist, college administrator*
Martin, John L. *airport executive*
Marzke, Ronald Oscar *physics and astronomy educator*
Mason, Dean Towle *cardiologist*
Mason, Greg *publishing executive*
Massaro, Mike *advertising executive*
Mathes, Stephen John *plastic and reconstructive surgeon, educator*
Mattern, Douglas James *think-tank executive*
Mattes, Martin Anthony *lawyer*
Matthews, Gilbert Elliott *investment banker*
Matthews, Philip Richard *lawyer*
Matzke, Richard H. *oil industry executive*
McAninch, Jack Weldon *urological surgeon, educator*
McClintock, Jessica *fashion designer*
McCollam, Sharon L. *retail executive*
McCovey, Willie Lee *former professional baseball player*
McElhinny, Harold John *lawyer*
McEvoy, Nan Tucker *publishing company executive, olive rancher*
McGettigan, Charles Carroll, Jr., *investment banker*
McGuire, William Albert *humanities educator*
McKean, Kevin S. *editor-in-chief, writer*
McKeever, Michael Pierce, Sr., *economics and business educator*
McKelvey, Judith Grant *lawyer, educator, university dean*
Mc Laughlin, Jerome Michael *lawyer, shipping company executive*
McNamara, Margaret M. *pediatrician*
McWhinney, Deborah *finance company executive*
Meadows, John Frederick *lawyer*
Mehta, Shailesh J. *banker*
Merrill, Harvie Martin *manufacturing executive, director*
Messina, Louis Michael *vascular surgeon, educator*
Metz, Mary Seawell *foundation administrator, retired academic administrator*
Meyers, David L. *food products executive*
Meyerson, Ivan D. *lawyer, holding company executive*
Miles, Donald F. *lawyer*
Miller, Walter Luther *pediatrician, educator*
Miller, William Napier Cripps *lawyer*
Millstein, David J. *lawyer*
Mina, Michael *chef, restaurant owner*
Minar, Paul G. *design consultant*
Ming, Jenny J. *retail apparel company executive*
Minnick, Malcolm David *lawyer*
Minor, Halsey *multimedia company executive*
Minton, Torri *journalist*
Mitchell, Bruce Tyson *lawyer*
Moe, Michael *diversified financial services company executive*
Moreno, Albert F. *apparel executive, lawyer*
Moreno, Carlos R. *state supreme court justice*
Morgan, Christina *venture capital firm executive*
Morgan, David O. *physiologist, educator*
Moris, Lamberto Giuliano *architect*
Morrissey, John Carroll, Sr., *lawyer*
Morris-Tyndall, Lucy *construction executive*
Moser, R. Kevin *clinical psychologist, educator*
Muegge, Lyn *advertising executive*
Munio, David J. *bank executive*
Muñoz, Calise I. *federal agency administrator*
Muranaka, Hideo *artist, educator*
Murphy, Kathleen Anne Foley *communications executive*
Murray, Kathleen Anne *lawyer*
Murray, Michael J. *bank executive*
Musfelt, Duane Clark *lawyer*
Mustacchi, Piero *preventive medicine physician, educator*
Naegele, Carl Joseph *university academic administrator, educator*
Nedelman, Adam *entrepreneur*
Needleman, Jacob *philosophy educator, writer*
Nen, Robert Allen (Robb Nen) *professional baseball player*
Neve, Victoria J. *music educator*
Newacheck, Paul W. *medical educator, researcher*
Newfield, Philippa *anesthesiologist*
Newirth, Richard Scott *cultural organization administrator*
Newman, Francis A. *medical device company executive*
Newsom, Gavin *mayor*
Nguyen, Ann Cac Khue *pharmaceutical and medicinal chemist*
Nichols, William J. *film studies educator*
Nix, Katherine Jean *medical care manager*
Noonan, John T., Jr., *federal judge, law educator*
Oakes, Nancy *chef, restaurant owner*
O'Connor, G(eorge) Richard *ophthalmologist*
O'Connor, Sheila Anne *freelance writer*
Odgers, Richard William *lawyer*
Odom, Richard B. *dermatologist, educator*
Offer, Stuart Jay *lawyer*
Okeke, Christian Nwachukwu *law educator*
Olsen, Steven Kent *dentist*
Olson, Robert Howard *lawyer*
Oman, Mark C. *bank executive*
O'Neill, Brian *national recreation area administrator*
O'Rourke, Dennis *advertising executive*
O'Shea, Erin K. *biomedical researcher*
Ostler, Clyde W. *banker*
Owades, Ruth Markowitz *marketing company executive*
Owen, Marc *health products executive*
Owsley, John Quincy, III, *plastic surgeon, educator*
Palmer, Venrice Romito *lawyer, educator*
Parker, Derek *architectural firm executive*
Parker, Diana Lynne *restaurant manager, special events director*

Morgan, Marilyn federal judge
Morgridge, John P. computer systems network executive
Morrison, William Fosdick business educator, retired electrical company executive
Myer, Warren Hitesh mortgage broker, internet advertising executive
Naegele, Joseph Loyola, Sr., lawyer
Nardi, Glen publishing executive
Near, Timothy theater director
Neptune, John Addison retired chemistry educator, consultant
Norberg, Deborah Dorsey museum administrator
Ogawa, Joichi Raphael director, consultant
Okerlund, Arlene Naylor university official
Omidyar, Pierre M. Internet company executive
Osland, Joyce Marie finance educator, consultant
Parkin, Stuart Stephen Papworth materials scientist
Pellegrini, Robert J. psychology educator
Perlegos, George electronic executive
Porter, John Paul artist, educator
Powell, Dennis computer systems network executive
Quon, Malcolm Yee defence systems company executive
Raghavan, Asuri business executive
Ricart, Glenn Internet company executive
Richardson, James computer company executive
Roelandts, Willem P. data processing executive
Rosenblum, Frank Michael civil engineer, consultant, surveyor
Rosendin, Raymond Joseph electrical contracting company executive
Rossi, Steven B. newspaper publishing company executive
Rothblatt, Donald Noah urban and regional planner, educator
Ryland, V. Wallace business developer
Sauers, William Dale lawyer, playwright
Sauvageau, Yvon application developer
Schaller, Anthony Josef technology management executive
Scheinman, A. Daniel computer system networks executive
Schmidt, Cyril James librarian
Schroeder, Kenneth L. electronics executive
Schroeder, William John electronics executive
Scott, Edward William, Jr., computer software company executive
Selanne, Teemu professional hockey player
Shannon, David M. lawyer
Shatney, Clayton Henry surgeon
Shaw, Charles Alden engineering executive
Shuster, Diana former artistic director
Simon, Ralph E. electronics executive
Slater, Stewart Eugene theatre producer
Smith, David Eugene business administration educator
Sola, Jure electronics executive
Stapleton, Beverly Cooper aerospace company executive
Stein, Arthur Oscar retired pediatrician, small business owner
Stein, John C. lawyer
Steinberg, Charles Allan electronics manufacturing company executive
Stevens, David Alec medical educator
Stevenson, Karen lawyer
Stewart, Melinda Jane judge
Straus, Jozef manufacturing executive
Stutzman, Thomas Chase, Sr., lawyer
Takeuchi, Tetsuya materials engineer
Tanaka, Richard Koichi, Jr., architect, planner
Tatipamula, Mallikarjun telecommunications and networking engineer
Togasaki, Shinobu computer scientist
Tonseth, Ralph G. airport executive
Towery, James E. lawyer
Tran, Jack Nhuan Ngoc gas and oil reservoir engineer
Tretz, Christophe Robert electrical engineer
Ulmer, David information technology executive
Vinderschmitt, Bernard V. data processing executive
Volpi, Mike computer company executive
Voth, Alden H. political science educator
Warnock, John Edward computer company executive
Webb, Maynard Internet company executive
Weiner, Claire Zundell theatrical director
Weinhardt, J. W. computer company executive
Whitman, Margaret C. (Meg Whitman) internet company executive
Whyte, Ronald M. judge
Wickramasinghe, Hemantha Kumar electrical engineer, physicist
Wiens, Beverly Jo psychology professor
Williams, Jouston L. service industry executive
Wilson, Ronald Lawrence professional hockey coach
Winters, Harold Franklin physicist
Wolak, Edmund L. engineering program manager
Woldt, Harold Frederick, Jr., newspaper publishing executive
Woolls, Esther Blanche library science educator
Wozniak, Curtis S. electronics company executive
Yarnold, David editor
Yavorkovsky, Leonid Lazar oncologist, researcher, hematologist
Yee, Keith Philip accountant, finance company executive
Yoshizumi, Donald Tetsuro dentist
Yu, Paul academic administrator
Zafiropoulo, Arthur electronics executive
Zaro, Brad A. research company executive, biologist
Zhai, Shumin computer scientist
Zhang, G. Z. (Guangzhi Zhang) electro-optics engineer
Zheng, Min engineer
Zinn, Ray computer company executive

San Juan Bautista
Fort, Robert Bradley minister

San Juan Capistrano
Braunstein, Herbert pathologist, educator
Burns, Toni Anthony artist
Carlson, Lawrence Arvid retired English language educator, real estate agent
Fisher, Delbert Arthur pediatric endocrinologist, educator, health facility administrator
Larwood, Susan Elizabeth elementary school educator
Peterson, Fred McCrae retired librarian
Suzuki, Yasuhiko retired law educator
Warren, Rick Duane minister, writer
White, Beverly Jane cytogeneticist
Zalta, Edward otorhinolaryngologist, physician

San Leandro
Wycoff, Charles Coleman writer, retired anesthesiologist

San Lorenzo
Thompson, Lyle Eugene electrical engineer

San Luis Obispo
Anderson, Warren Ronald electrical engineering educator
Bailey, Philip Sigmon, Jr., university official and dean, chemistry educator
Baker, Warren J(oseph) university president
Blakeslee, Diane Pusey financial planner
Bunge, Russell Kenneth writer, poet, editor
Daly, John Paul lawyer
Deasy, Cornelius Michael retired architect
DuFresne, Armand Frederick management and engineering consultant
Ericson, Jon Meyer academic administrator, rhetoric theory educator
Fairbanks, William Louis, II, anthropologist, educator
Fraser, Bruce Douglas, Jr., architect, artist
Geringer, John Michael economist, educator
Girard, Sally F. education educator
Grismore, Roger physics educator, researcher
Hafemeister, David Walter physicist
Haile, Allen Cleveland educator and administrator
Jamieson, James Bradshaw foundation administrator
LaScola, Russell A. philosophy educator
Lynch, Joseph James philosophy educator
Piirto, Douglas Donald forester, educator, academic administrator
Pinkel, Donald Paul pediatrician
Sena, James Anthony finance educator, department chairman
Shlaudeman, Harry Walter retired diplomat
Sullivan, Thomas James retired manufacturing company executive
Weaver, Karl E. psychiatrist
Williams, David Alexander retired chief pilot

San Luis Rey
Melbourne, Robert Ernest civil engineer

San Marcos
Ball, Betty Jewel retired social worker, consultant
Baringer, Sandra Kay literature educator
Barnes, Howard G. communications executive, film and video producer
Berry, Dawn Bradley writer, lawyer, jeweler
Coleman, Dorothy Jones retired educator
Coleman, Roger Dixon bacteriologist
Haynes, Karen Sue academic administrator, educator
Houk, Benjamin Noah performing company executive, choreographer
Jones, William Henry retired military officer
Lilly, Martin Stephen university dean
Page, Leslie Andrew consumer products company executive
Purdy, Alan Harris biomedical engineer
Sheath, Robert Gordon botanist, educator
Wingert, Hannelore Christiane real estate agent, chemical company executive

San Marino
Benzer, Seymour neuroscience educator
Cranston, Howard Stephen lawyer, management consultant
Footman, Gordon Elliott educational administrator
Galbraith, James Marshall lawyer, business executive
Gouw, Julia Suryapranata accountant
Grantham, Richard Robert financial consultant
Lashley, Virginia Stephenson Hughes retired computer science educator
McDermott, Irene Elizabeth librarian, columnist
Mortimer, Wendell Reed, Jr., judge
Robertson, Mary Louise archivist, art historian
Rolle, Andrew historian, writer
Terry, Roger retired pathologist, consultant
Tomich, Lillian lawyer
Travis, Albert Hartman retired ancient language educator
Zall, Paul Maxwell retired English language educator, consultant

San Mateo
Aadahl, Jorg business executive
Baio, James R. diversified financial services company executive
Bell, Leo S. retired physician
Brzozowsky, Keith William software consultant
Chong, Rachelle B. lawyer, federal communications commissioner
Ginn, Sam L. telephone company executive
Graham, Howard Holmes financial executive
Grecsek, Matthew Thomas software developer
Grill, Lawrence J. lawyer, accountant, corporate/banking executive
Halperin, Robert Milton retired electrical machinery company executive
Helfert, Erich Anton management consultant, writer, educator
Holmes, John Richard physicist, researcher
Hoops, Alan R. health care company executive
Hopkins, Cecilia Ann business educator
Hur, Stephen Ponyi civil engineer, management consultant, educator
Huxley, Mary Atsuko artist
Johnson, Charles Bartlett mutual fund executive
Johnson, Gregory E. diversified financial services company executive
Johnson, Rupert Harris, Jr., finance company executive
Jones, Louis Worth retired management analyst, journalist
Kenney, William Fitzgerald lawyer
Kertzman, Mitchell E. software company executive
Lawrie, J. Michael software company executive
McLucas, Kate magazine editor
Monaco, Daniel Joseph lawyer
Most, Nathan mutual fund executive
Mullin, Gene state legislator
Nizard, Michael editor-in-chief
O'Reilly, Terence John lawyer
Reed, Sandy former magazine editor
Sadilek, Vladimir architect
Sellers, Donald R. biotechnology company executive
Siebel, Thomas M. software company executive
Slabach, Stephen Hall lawyer
Strohm, David venture capitalist
Trabitz, Eugene Leonard aerospace company executive
Van Kirk, John Ellsworth retired cardiologist
Visbal, Jonathan Ralph communications executive
Wong, Otto epidemiologist

San Pablo
Woodruff, Kay Herrin pathologist, educator

San Pedro
Bowling, Lance Christopher record producer, publishing executive
Crutchfield, William Richard artist, educator
Daniels, Kathleen Angela educational administrator
Ellis, George Edwin, Jr., chemical engineer
Gaines, Jerry Lee retired secondary education educator
Kline, Frank Menefee psychiatrist
McCarty, Frederick Briggs electrical engineer, consultant
McMullen, Sharon Joy Abel life coach, marriage and family therapist
Plutchak, Noel Bernard meteorologist, management consultant
Russell, Thomas Arthur lawyer
Simmons, William physicist, retired aerospace research executive

San Rafael
Adcock, Muriel W. special education educator
Amada, Gerald retired psychotherapist
Barker, Celeste Arlette computer scientist
Bartz, Carol software company executive
Brett, Peter D. writer
Brubeck, David Warren musician
Burks, Rocky Alan disability access coordinator, consultant
Chilvers, Robert Merritt lawyer
Clark, Charles Sutter interior designer
Djordjevich, Miroslav-Michael bank executive
Douglas, James construction engineering executive
Drexler, Kenneth lawyer
Evenhuis, Henk J. research company executive
Fink, Joseph Richard academic administrator
Finkelstein, James Arthur management consultant
Freitas, David Prince lawyer
Friesecke, Raymond Francis health company executive
Greene, John Clifford dentist, retired dean
Gryson, Joseph Anthony orthodontist
Hart, John writer
Henry, Joseph Louis dean
Hoyt, Michael F. psychologist, writer
Keegan, Jane Ann insurance executive, consultant
Latno, Arthur Clement, Jr., telephone company executive
Lucas, George W., Jr., film director, producer, screenwriter
Morgan, Michael Brewster publishing company executive
Nelson, James Carmer, Jr., writer, editor, advertising executive
Neuburger, Karen apparel executive
Noah, Nuer filmmaker
Parker, Pam apparel manufacturing company executive
Pomerantz, Martin Arthur astronomer, educator
Purcell, Stuart McLeod, III, financial planner
Roulac, Stephen E. real estate consultant
Sansweet, Stephen Jay journalist, author, marketing executive
Santana, Carlos guitarist
Thomas, Mary Ann McCrary counselor, school system administrator
Tosti, Donald Thomas psychologist, consultant
Trepp, Leo rabbi
Turner, William Weyand writer
Wilson, Ian Holroyde management consultant, futurist

San Ramon
Bethancourt, John E. oil industry executive
Bruns, George H. electronics executive
Crowe, Stephen J. comptroller
Dennis, Patricia Diaz lawyer
Derr, Kenneth T. retired oil company executive
Gass, John D. oil industry executive
James, Charles Albert lawyer
Kalicki, Jan H. economist, political scientist
King Hauser, Ann Marie B. retired controller, artist
Kirkland, George L. oil industry executive
Krattebol, David M. oil industry executive
Laidlaw, William Samuel Hugh oil company executive
Litman, Robert Barry physician, writer, television and radio commentator
McDonald, John W. oil industry executive
Moore, Justin Edward information technology executive
Morrison, Cheryl Lynn petroleum engineer, project manager
O'Reilly, David J. oil company executive
Peebles, Lucretia Neal Drane policy and administration educator
Preston, Alan R. human resources specialist
Robertson, Peter James oil company executive
Schofield, James Roy computer programmer
Shapiro, Fania computer company executive
Su, George Shenghui (Sheng-Hui Su) chemist, medical researcher, educator
Vaughn, John Rolland auditor
Watson, John S. oil company executive
Welch, Thomas Andrew international and domestic commercial arbitrator
Wilcox, Raymond I. oil industry executive
Woertz, Patricia A. petroleum industry executive
Yarrington, Patricia oil industry executive
Zygocki, Rhonda I. oil industry executive

Sand City
Coile, Russell Cleven electrical engineer, consultant

Sanger
Albertson, David food products executive

Santa Ana
Abramo, Guy P. information technology executive
Adams, John M. library director
Amoroso, Frank retired communication system engineer, consultant
Anderson, James E., Jr., lawyer, information technology executive
Anderson, N. Christian, III, newspaper publisher
Andres, Eugen Charles lawyer
Bailey, Don Matthew aerospace and electronics company executive
Balzer, Robert Lawrence journalist
Barr, James Norman federal judge
Bauer, Bruce F. former aerospace engineer
Beal, Dennis academic administrator
Boyd, Larry C. computer company executive
Boynton, William Lewis retired electronic manufacturing company official
Brusic, Ken editor
Callahan, Daniel J. lawyer
Capizzi, Michael Robert prosecutor
Carter, Curtis William communications executive
Chenhalls, Anne Marie nurse, educator
Chudzinski, Mark Adam lawyer
Correa, Lou state official
Daly, Tom county official
Dean, William Evans aerospace industry executive
DeRoy, Craig I. lawyer
Dillard, John Martin lawyer, pilot
Ellis, Gregory Scott elementary school educator
Ferguson, Warren John federal judge
Flastrup, Asger information technology executive
Folick, Jeffrey M. healthcare systems company executive
Foster, Kent B. information technology executive
Freeman, James Michael musician, vocalist
Frost, Winston Lyle lawyer, educator
Gudea, Darlene publishing company executive
Harley, Robison Dooling, Jr., lawyer, educator
Kato, Terri Emi elementary school and gifted and talented educator
Katz, Tonnie newspaper editor
Kelly, James Patrick, Jr., retired engineering and construction executive
Klemens, Thomas A. insurance company executive
Koppen, Hans T. information technology executive
Kropp, William Rudolph physicist
Lehrer, John editor
Lyons, Linda health science association administrator
Mei, Tom Y. K. lawyer
Moore, David Gene academic administrator
Mosich, Nicholas Joseph lawyer
Murai, Kevin information technology executive
Myers, Marilyn Gladys pediatric hematologist and oncologist
Phanstiel, Howard G. managed health care company executive
Prizio, Betty J. volunteer, retired property manager
Pulido, Miguel Angel mayor
Reed, David Andrew managed health care company executive
Re Velle, Jack B(oyer) statistician, consultant
Ricketts, James F. treasurer
Rusciano, Gissela Liliana purchasing agent
Schmitz, Stephen E. mental health specialist, writer
Schub, Craig S. health science association administrator
Spierkel, Gregory M. information technology executive
Storer, Maryruth law librarian
Stotler, Alicemarie Huber federal judge
Tanaka, Richard I. computer products company executive
Toeppe, William Joseph, Jr., retired aerospace engineer
Treshie, R. David former newspaper publishing executive
Vaccaro, Jerome Vincent psychiatrist, educator, healthcare executive
Washburn, Lawrence Robert manufacturing executive
Weiermiller, Kathy publishing executive
Wilson, Beth A. college official
Zepeda, Susan Ghozeil foundation executive

Santa Barbara
Abbinante, Christopher finance company executive
Ackerman, Marshall publishing company executive
Adizes, Ichak management consultant, writer
Ahlers, Guenter physicist, researcher
Aigner, Dennis John economics educator, consultant
Albanese, Catherine religious studies educator
Aldisert, Ruggero John judge
Allaway, William Harris retired academic administrator
Anderson, Carol Ann retired secondary school educator, lawyer, political organization worker
Anderson, Donald Meredith bank executive
Atwater, Tanya Maria marine geophysicist, educator
Avalle-Arce, Juan Bautista Spanish language educator
Aylesworth, Owen Roy firefighter
Badash, Lawrence science history educator
Barber, Jerry Randel medical device company executive
Barry, Robert Michael education educator
Bartlett, James Lowell, III, investment company executive
Ben-Dor, Gisselle conductor, musician
Bischel, Margaret DeMeritt physician, managed care consultant
Bock, Russell Samuel writer
Boehm, Eric Hartzell information management executive
Bohn, Henning economist, educator
Bowers, Michael Thomas chemistry professor
Boyan, Norman J. retired education educator
Brantingham, Barney journalist, writer
Brilliant, Ashleigh Ellwood writer, cartoonist, publisher, educator
Brodhead, James E(aston) actor, writer
Brown, J'Amy Maroney journalist, media relations consultant, investor
Brown, Stephen F. health facility administrator
Brownlee, Wilson Elliot, Jr., history educator
Bruch, John Clarence, Jr., engineer, educator
Bruice, Thomas C. chemist, educator
Burgee, John Henry architect
Campbell, Robert Charles minister, theology educator
Campbell, William Steen publishing executive, writer, speaker
Casey, Mary A. telecommunications company executive
Chafe, Wallace LeSeur linguist, educator
Charness, Gary real estate broker, educator
Chmelka, Bradley Floyd chemical engineering educator
Christman, Arthur Castner, Jr., scientific advisor
Cirone, William Joseph educational administrator

McGurk, Christopher J. *film company executive*
McMillan, M. Sean *lawyer*
Milken, Michael R. *think-tank executive, philanthropist*
Milliken, Mary Sue *chef, television personality, writer*
Minghella, Anthony *film director, screenwriter*
Monosson, Ira Howard *physician*
Mora, Philippe *screenwriter, producer, director, painter*
Morgan, Kermit Johnson *lawyer*
Muller, Edward Robert *lawyer*
Osbourne, Sharon Arden *music manager, actress, television personality*
Ovitz, Michael S. *communications executive*
Ozaki, Joseph *finance company executive*
Palmatier, Malcolm Arthur *editor, consultant*
Park, Edward Cahill, Jr., *retired physicist*
Patel, Chandra Kumar Naranbhai *communications company executive, educator, researcher, entrepreneur*
Pezzullo, Ralph Michael *writer, playwright*
Pieton, Richard *anesthesiologist*
Postaer, Larry *advertising executive*
Preble, Laurence George *lawyer*
Prewoznik, Jerome Frank *lawyer*
Price, David *golf courses facilities executive*
Quinn, Patricia K. *literary agent*
Rand, Robert Wheeler *neurosurgeon, educator*
Recendez, Elijio Marco *personal care industry executive, small business owner*
Redford, Robert (Charles Robert Redford) *actor, director*
Remsing, Dennis *advertising agency executive*
Resnick, Jeffrey I. *plastic surgeon*
Rice, Donald Blessing *business executive, former secretary of air force*
Rich, Michael David *research corporation executive, lawyer*
Rifkin, Arnold *film company executive*
Risman, Michael *lawyer, business executive, securities company executive, real estate developer*
Rivin, Arthur Udell *medical educator*
Roberts, Tony (David Anthony Roberts) *actor*
Röckenwagner, Hans *chef, restaurateur*
Roney, Alice Lorraine Mann *poet*
Roney, Robert Kenneth *retired aerospace company executive*
Rubin, Gerrold Robert *advertising executive*
Russell, Marlou *psychologist*
Ryan, Jane Frances *corporate communications executive*
Safa, Afshin Akhavan *oncologist, researcher*
Salveson, Melvin Erwin *business executive, educator*
Schultz, Victor M. *physician*
Selvaggio, Piero *restauranteur*
Shamban, Ava T. *dermatologist*
Sherman, Zachary *civil engineer, aerospace engineer, consultant*
Shim, Elisabeth K. *dermatologist, writer*
Shipbaugh, Calvin LeRoy *physicist*
Simon, Diane Meyer *environmental services administrator, consultant*
Simpson, India.Arie *musician*
Singer, Frederick Raphael *medical researcher*
Sipos, Thomas M. *writer*
Smith, Anna Deavere *actress, educator, playwright*
Smith, James Patrick *economist*
Snedaker, Catherine Raupagh (Kit Snedaker) *editor*
Spataro, Janie Dempsey Watts *writer*
Stern, Walter Eugene *neurosurgeon, educator*
Stewart, Patrick *actor*
Stone, Oliver *screenwriter, director*
Summer, Donna (La Donna Adrian Gaines) *singer, songwriter, actress*
Sun, Li *statistician*
Suschitzky, Peter *cinematographer*
Sussman, Peter Alan *entertainment company executive*
Tennant, John Randall *management advisory company executive*
Thompson, Dennis Peters *plastic surgeon*
Thomson, James Alan *think-tank executive*
Timmer, Barbara *state agency administrator*
Tinturin, Peter *composer*
Unterman, Thomas *venture capitalist, lawyer*
Vega, Benjamin Urbizo *retired judge, television producer*
Ware, Willis Howard *computer scientist*
Warick, Lawrence Herbert *psychiatrist*
Watanabe, Ken *actor*
Watson, Doc (Arthel Lane Watson) *vocalist, guitarist, banjoist, recording artist*
Weinberger, Martin Andrew *computer company executive*
Wells, Kenneth B. *medical educator*
Wexler, Haskell *film producer, cameraman*
Whalley, Tom *recording industry executive*
Wilder, Gene *actor, film director, writer*
Williams, Kathleen *advertising executive*
Winkler, Henry Franklin *actor*
Wolf, Charles, Jr., *economist, educator*
Yemenidjian, Alex *film company executive*
York, Michael (Michael York-Johnson) *actor*
Zarem, Harvey Alan *plastic surgeon*

Santa Paula

Dillard, Michael L. *food products company executive*
Edwards, Samuel Roger *internist*
Kay, Hazel T. *local commissioner*

Santa Rosa

Adams, Delphine Szyndrowski *lawyer*
Aman, Reinhold Albert *philologist, publisher*
Anderson, Edwin C., Jr. *lawyer*
Andriano-Moore, Richard Count *retired military officer, secondary school educator, elementary school educator*
Biderman, Charles Israel *diversified financial services company executive*
Bowen, James Thomas *career officer*
Brigham, John Allen, Jr., *financial executive, environmentalist, polition*
Callum, Myles *magazine editor, writer*
Cavanagh, John Charles *advertising agency executive*
Christiansen, Peggy *principal*
Courteau, Girard Robert *retired prosecutor*
Daniel, Gary Wayne *motivation and behavior consultant*
Elam, John Richard *mortgage company executive*
Fields, Tina Rae *artist, ecopsychologist*
Guglielmino, Jude Patch *writer, humanitarian aid worker*
Hinch, Stephen Walter *telecommunications industry executive*
Ingerman, Michael Leigh *development director*
King, Gwendolyn Bair *former government staff member, public speaker*
Leong, Stephanie Mei *financial planner*
Leuty, Gerald Johnston *osteopathic physician and surgeon*
Lewis, Alvin Edward *pathology educator*
Monk, Diana Charla *artist, stable owner*
Morris, Jack G. *architecture educator, writer*
O'Connor, Paul Daniel *lawyer*
Ogg, Robert Danforth *corporate executive*
Pearson, Roger Lee *library director*
Person, Evert Bertil *newspaper and radio executive*
Rabinowitsh, Steve *urban planner educator, city council member*
Rosaschi, Jim *librarian*
Schafer, John Francis *retired plant pathologist*
Smith, Betty L. *results coach, seminar leader*
Smith, Thomas Kent *retired radiologist, viticulturist*
Swofford, Robert Lee *newspaper editor, journalist*
Trucker, Albert *plastic surgeon*
Walsh, Daniel Francis *bishop*
Webb, Charles Richard *retired university president*
Wiggins, Patricia Ann *computer systems analyst, state legislator*

Santa Ynez

Rymer, Ilona Suto *artist, retired art educator*

Santee

Morris, Henry Madison, Jr., *education educator*
Morris, Henry Madison, III, *minister, speaker, writer, consultant*
Peters, Raymond Eugene *historian, writer*
Schenk, Susan Kirkpatrick *nursing educator, consultant, small business owner*

Saratoga

Baratta-Lorton, Robert *mathematics educator*
Chisholm, Margaret Elizabeth *retired library education administrator*
Cisneros, Rebecca G. *language educator*
Dalton, Peter John *electronics executive*
Henderson, William Darryl *army officer, writer*
Houston, Elizabeth Reece Manasco *correctional education consultant*
Houston, Joseph Brantley, Jr., *optical instrument company executive*
Ogle, David William *art educator, sculptor, ceramist, printmaker*
Reagan, Joseph Bernard *retired aerospace executive, management consultant*
Syvertson, Clarence Alfred *engineering and research management consultant*

Saugus

Grishman, Lee Howard *college program administrator*

Sausalito

Apatoff, Michael John *entrepreneur*
Berkman, William Roger *lawyer, army reserve officer*
Brand, Stewart *editor, writer*
Casals, Rosemary *retired professional tennis player*
Gordon, Robert Eugene *lawyer*
Groah, Linda Kay *nursing administrator, educator*
Hansen, Charles Morton *editor, retired military officer*
Hyde, Catherine Ryan *writer, short story writer*
Jeffrey, Francis *software developer, forecaster, bioethicist*
Klott, David Lee *lawyer*
Ornish, Dean *medical educator, administrator*
Robertson, J. Martin *lawyer*

Scotia

Hise, Mark Allen *dentist*

Scotts Valley

Allen, Louis Alexander *management consultant*
Crandell, K(enneth) James *management and strategic planning consultant, entrepreneur*
Hernandez, Martin David *marketing professional*
Janssen, James Robert *consulting software engineer*
Luczo, Stephen J. *computer equipment company executive*
Pope, Charles C. *data processing executive*

Seal Beach

Olechno-Huszcza, Czeslaw *retired translator and educator*
Osgood, Frank William *urban and economic planner, writer*
Robinson, Michael R. *aeronautical engineer*
Rossi, Mario Alexander *architect*
Wiley, Dianne *aeronautical engineer*

Seaside

Anderson, David Louis *history educator*
Gales, Samuel Joel *retired civilian military employee, counselor*
May, James Harvey *communications educator*
Mendoza, Ruben G. *anthropologist, educator, archaeologist*
Paget, Ruth Pennington *academic administrator, educator, writer*
Panetta, Leon Edward *federal official, former congressman*
Segall, Daniel Owen *psychologist, researcher*
Stringer, Charles Columbus, Jr., *minister, protective services official, writer*

Sebastopol

Arnold, Marsha Diane *writer*
Marler, Joan *writer, educator*
McCarthy, Thomas Edward *retired telecommunications executive*
Norman, Arnold McCallum, Jr., *engineer*
O'Reilly, Tim *company executive*
Sabsay, David *library consultant*
Slater, Michael *communications executive*
Snyder, Allegra Fuller *dance educator*
Wall, Larry *computer scientist, web programmer*

Selma

Janian, Paulette *lawyer*

Sepulveda

Burton, Paul Floyd *social worker*
Yano, Elizabeth Martin *epidemiologist, researcher*

Shadow Hills

Bangs, Cate (Cathryn Margaret Bangs) *film production designer, interior designer*

Shaver Lake

Hatmaker, Grace Marie *nurse, writer*

Sherman Oaks

Alcott-Jardine, Susan *artist, writer*
Atwood, Colleen *costume designer*
Beck, Brent Alan *graphics designer*
Bergman, Alan *lyricist, writer*
Caren, Robert Poston *aerospace company executive*
Clark, Susan (Nora Goulding) *actress*
Cook, Paul Maxwell *technology company executive*
Crump, Gerald Franklin *retired lawyer*
Dawson, David Smith *television executive*
Elfman, Danny *composer*
Ellison, Harlan Jay *author, screenwriter*
Feldman, Phillip *lawyer*
Gibbs, Antony (Tony Gibbs) *film editor*
Goldenthal, Elliot *composer*
Hershman, Jerome Marshall *endocrinologist*
Holden, William Willard *insurance executive*
Hoover, Richard *set designer, art director, actor*
Horner, James *composer*
Howe, Daniel Walker *historian, educator*
Karras, Alex *actor, former professional football player*
Kerr, Gib *financial planner*
Koonce, John Peter *investment company executive, educator*
Krueger, Kenneth John *nutritionist, educator*
LeBlanc, Rena *writer*
Leighton, Carolyn *foundation administrator*
Levin, Evanne Lynn *lawyer, educator*
Lindgren, Timothy Joseph *supply company executive*
Little, Carole *women's apparel company executive*
Milgrim, Darrow A. *insurance company executive*
Norwood, Brandy Rayana (Brandy) *singer, actress*
O'Neill, Sallie Boyd *educational consultant, business owner, sculptor*
Platus, Libby *artist, sculptor, speaker*
Powell, Sandy *costume designer*
Reiner, Thomas Karl *manufacturing executive*
Schlessinger, Laura *radio talk show host*
Shore, Howard Leslie *composer*
Weiss, Julie *costume designer*
Williams, John Towner *composer, conductor*
Winkler, Lee B. *business consultant*
Wood, Evan Rachel *actress*
Yasnyi, Allan David *communications company executive*
Zemplenyi, Tibor Karol *cardiologist, educator*

Shingle Springs

Sorensen, Raymond Andrew *physics educator*

Sierra Madre

Converse, Elizabeth *artist, writer*
Nation, Earl F. *retired urologist, educator*

Signal Hill

Vandament, William Eugene *retired academic administrator*

Silverado

Mamer, James Michael *secondary school educator*

Simi Valley

Hochheiser, Marilyn *author, actress*
Loomis, Jennifer MacKenzie *information technology consultant*
Mow, William *apparel executive*
Ritacco, Patsy Richard *sales executive*
Trager, D. David *retired pharmacist, general consultant*

Solana Beach

Agnew, Harold Melvin *physicist*
Arledge, Charles Stone *former aerospace executive, entrepreneur*
Beard, Ann Southard *diplomat, oil company executive*
Beck-von-Peccoz, Michele *retired secondary school educator, writer*
Brody, Arthur *industrial executive*
Derbes, Daniel William *manufacturing executive*
Friedman, Maurice Stanley *religious educator*
Gildred, Theodore E. *former diplomat, real estate developer*

Somerset

Carr, Les *psychologist, educator*

Somis

Kehoe, Vincent Jeffré-Roux *photographer, author, cosmetic company executive*
Premack, Ann J. *writer*

Sonoma

Beckmann, Jon Michael *publishing company executive*
Fellows, Alice Combs *artist*
Gelpi, Armand Philippe *internist*
Herron, Ellen Patricia *retired judge*
Kizer, Carolyn Ashley *poet, educator*
Markey, William Alan *healthcare administrator, consultant*
Muchmore, Robert Boyer *engineering consultant executive*
Obninsky, Victor Peter *lawyer*
Sasaki, Y(asunaga) Tito *engineering executive*
Stadtman, Verne August *former foundation executive, editor*

Sonora

Carter, John Robert *music educator*
Chandler, E(dwin) Russell *clergyman, writer*
Clarke, Paula Katherine *anthropology educator, sociology educator*
Mathias, Betty Jane *communications and community affairs consultant, writer, editor, lecturer*
Sharboneau, Lorna Rosina *artist, educator, author, poet, illustrator*
Wheeler, Elton Samuel *financial executive*

Soquel

Goodman, Charles Schaffner, Jr., *food product executive, consultant*
Murray, Barbara Olivia *writer, retired psychologist*

South Gate

Firebaugh, Marco Antonio *state official*

South Laguna

Mowlavi, Arian S. *plastic surgeon*

South Lake Tahoe

Dean, John Randall *financial consultant, general building contractor*
Nason, Rochelle *conservation organization administrator*
Williams, Mark Didrik *music educator, composer*

South Pasadena

Askin, Walter Miller *artist, educator*
Finnell, Michael Hartman *corporate executive*
Fuller, Kathy J. *special education educator, consultant, researcher*
Girvigian, Raymond *architect*
Glad, Dain Sturgis *aerospace engineer, consultant*
Kopp, Eugene Howard *electrical engineer*
Mantell, Suzanne Ruth *editor*
Whang, Sukoo Jack *pathologist, microbiologist*
White, W. Robin *writer*
Yett, Sally Pugh *elementary school educator, gifted and talented educator*

South San Francisco

Caro, Ivor *dermatologist*
Desmond-Hellmann, Susan *medical products manufacturing executive*
Dixit, Vishva M. *pathology educator*
Exuzides, Alex *statistician, researcher*
Gerritsen, Mary Ellen *vascular and cell biologist*
Goodman, Corey Scott *neurobiology educator, researcher, biotechnology company executive*
Gower, James M. *biotechnology company executive*
Grannuci, Leo *retired marketing professional*
Hull, Cordell William *business executive*
Humphrey, Patrick Paul *pharmacologist*
Korman, Leo *wholesale distribution executive*
Lieberburg, Ivan *pharmaceutical executive*
Lindsay, Ronald M. *research and development company executive*
Lipsky, Ian David *biotechnologist*
Mertens, Lynne G. *retail executive*
Morris, Arlene Myers *marketing professional*
Niehaus, Ed *engineering executive*
Potter, Myrtle S. *research and development company executive*
Ryan, William *executive*
Scangos, George A. *medical company executive*
Tananbaum, James *medical engineering company executive*
Walker, John P. *pharmaceutical executive*
Wong, Carrie *public relations executive*
Young, James W. *biotechnology company executive*

Spring Valley

Long, David Michael, Jr., *biomedical researcher, cardiothoracic surgeon*

Stanford

Abrams, Herbert LeRoy *radiologist, educator*
Allen, Matthew Arnold *physicist*
Amemiya, Takeshi *economist, statistician*
Anderson, Theodore Wilbur *statistics educator*
Andreopoulos, Spyros George *writer*
Arrow, Kenneth Joseph *economist, educator*
Arvin, Ann Margaret *microbiology and immunology educator, researcher*
Aziz, Khalid *petroleum engineering educator*
Babcock, Barbara Allen *law educator, lawyer*
Baker, Keith Michael *history professor*
Baker, Patricia Ann *publishing executive*
Baldwin, Robert Lesh *biochemist, educator*
Ball, Arnetha *education educator*
Bandura, Albert *psychologist, educator*
Barron, Brigid *education educator*
Barton, John Hays *law educator*
Bauer, Eugene Andrew *dermatologist, educator*
Baylor, Denis Aristide *neuroscientist, educator*
Beaver, William Henry *accounting educator*
Berg, Paul *biochemist, educator*
Berger, Joseph *author, educator, counselor*
Bienenstock, Arthur Irwin *physicist, educator, federal official*
Blandford, Roger David *astronomy educator*
Blaschke, Terrence Francis *medicine and molecular pharmacology educator*
Blau, Helen Margaret *pharmacology educator*
Boaler, Jo *education educator*
Boudart, Michel *chemical engineer, chemist, educator, consultant*
Bracewell, Ronald Newbold *engineering educator*
Brauman, John I. *chemist, educator*
Bridges, Edwin Maxwell *education educator*
Brinegar, Claude Stout *retired oil company executive*
Brody, Richard Alan *political science educator, researcher*
Brown, Byron William, Jr., *biostatistician, educator*
Brown, J. Martin *oncologist, educator*
Brown, Patrick O. *molecular biologist, educator*
Bryson, Arthur Earl, Jr., *retired aerospace engineering educator*
Bube, Richard Howard *materials scientist, educator*
Bueno de Mesquita, Bruce James *political science educator*
Bunzel, John Harvey *political science educator, researcher*
Butcher, Eugene C. *science educator*
Byer, Robert Louis *applied physics educator, university dean*
Byerwalter, Mariann *academic administrator*
Campbell, Allan McCulloch *bacteriology educator*
Cannon, Robert Hamilton, Jr., *aerospace engineering educator*
Carlsmith, James Merrill *psychologist, educator*
Carstensen, Laura Lee *gerontology educator*
Casper, Gerhard *law educator, former academic administrator*
Chase, Robert Arthur *surgeon, educator*
Chrissochoidis, Ilias *musicologist*
Cohen, Albert *musician, educator*
Cohen, Elizabeth G. *education and sociology educator, researcher*
Cohen, Harvey Joel *pediatric hematology and oncology educator*
Cohen, Paul Joseph *mathematician*
Cohen, Stanley Norman *geneticist, educator*
Cohen, William *law educator*

Sylmar
Bridges, Robert McSteen *mechanical engineer*
Corry, Dalila Boudjellal *internist, educator*
Foster, Dudley Edwards, Jr., *musician, educator*
Froelich, Beverly Lorraine *foundation administrator*
Hayes, Cynthia Ann (C.A. Hayes) *writer*
Liu, Paul Ishen *pathologist, educator*
Madni, Asad Mohamed *engineering executive*
Powers, Mala *actress*
Roth, Joe *motion picture company executive*
Scheib, Gerald Paul *fine art educator, jeweler, metalsmith*
Tully, Susan Balsley *pediatrician, medical educator*
Yguado, Alex Rocco *economics professor*
Ziment, Irwin *medical educator*

Tarzana
Firestone, Morton H. *business management executive*
Gentile, Joseph F. *lawyer, educator*
Goldberg, Harvey *financial executive*
Handelsman, Yehuda *endocrinologist, internal medicine physician*
Hansen, Robert Clinton *electrical engineering consultant*
Jones, Dean Carroll *actor*
Kagan, Stephen Bruce (Sandy Kagan) *chief financial officer*
Lauter, James Donald *retired stockbroker*
Lindley, Charles Alexander *aerospace engineer, consultant*
Neece, Olivia Helene Ernst *investment company executive, consultant*
Portney, Joseph Nathaniel *retired aerospace executive, navigation consultant*
Richman, Peter Mark *actor, painter, writer, producer*
Rinsch, Maryann Elizabeth *occupational therapist*
Smith, Mark Lee *architect*
Weil, Leonard *banker*

Tehachapi
Melsheimer, Harold *obstetrician, gynecologist*
Mitchell, Betty Jo *writer, publisher*
Smith-Thompson, Patricia Ann *public relations consultant, educator*
Sprinkle, Martha Clare *elementary school educator*

Temecula
Angel, Michael Gonzalez *cultural organization administrator*
Bathaee, Soussan *engineering technician*
Keenan, Retha Ellen Vornholt *retired nursing educator*
May, Brian Thomas *mathematician, educator*
Minogue, Robert Brophy *retired nuclear engineer*
Rosenstein, Robert Bryce *lawyer, financial advisor*
Steiling, Daniel Paul *retired railroad conductor, writer, geographer, educator*

Temple City
Anderson, Paulette Elizabeth *retired elementary school educator*

Templeton
Abernathy, Shields B. *allergist, immunologist, internist, medical missionary*
Foster-Wells, Karen Margaret *artist*
Gandsey, Louis John *petroleum and environmental consultant*
Guenther, Robert Stanley, II, *investment and property executive*

The Sea Ranch
Baas, Jacquelynn *museum consultant, art historian*
Hayflick, Leonard *microbiologist, cell biologist, gerontologist, educator, writer*

Thousand Oaks
Brogden, Stephen Richard *library director*
Calborn, Keith W. *wholesale distribution executive*
Dayem, Hassan *information technology executive*
Falberg, Kathryn E. *pharmaceutical executive*
Farshidi, Ardeshir B. *cardiologist, educator*
Ferber, Samuel *publishing executive*
Gary, Russell Lee *sound recording engineer, music company executive*
Gaus, Clifton R. *healthcare executive*
Geiser, Thomas Christopher *lawyer*
Gillette, Dennis C. *academic administrator, mayor*
Gregory, Calvin *real estate investor*
Herman, Joan Elizabeth *healthcare company executive*
Heyer, Carol Ann *illustrator*
Hudson, Barbara *religious writer, actor*
Johnson, Shirley Amagna *health system executive*
Keller, James Robert *business development director*
Loren, Sophia *actress*
Malmuth, Norman David *research scientist, program manager*
Morrow, George J. *pharmaceutical company executive*
Nanula, Richard *health products executive*
Odre, Steven M. *lawyer*
O'Rourke, John A. *insurance company executive*
Ponder, Ron J. *insurance company executive*
Reaves, Michaela Crawford *history educator*
Rife, Douglas M. *publishing executive*
Rooney, Mickey (Joe Yule Jr.) *actor*
Rosenblatt, Alice F. *health products executive*
Schaeffer, Leonard David *healthcare executive*
Sharer, Kevin W. *healthcare products company executive*
Sherman, Gerald *nuclear physicist, financial estate adviser, financial company executive*
Shi, Zhi-Qing *endocrinologist*
Sladek, Lyle Virgil *mathematician, educator*
Sloane, J.P. *television producer, writer, entertainer, theologian*
Souza, Lawrence M. *health facility administrator*
Stolina, Marina *immunologist, research scientist*
Trover, Ellen Lloyd *lawyer, rancher*
Vizcaino, Henry P. *mining engineer, consultant*
Walker, Lorenzo Giles *surgeon, educator*
Washburn, Nan *conductor*
Weinberg, D. Mark *health insurance company executive*
Wiktorowicz, Andrew Charles *engineer*
Williams, Henry Newton *retired lawyer*

Tiburon
Barron-Druckrey, Eleanor *psychologist*
McAmis, Edwin Earl *lawyer*
Widman, Gary Lee *lawyer, former government official*

Toluca Lake
Hardy, Wayne Russell *insurance and investment broker*
Litwack, Gerald *biochemistry researcher, educator, administrator*
Morton, Hugh Wesley *producer, director*

Topanga
Bridgewater, Dee Dee *jazz singer, diplomat*

Torrance
Adelsman, Jean (Harriette Adelsman) *newspaper editor*
Amemiya, Koichi *motor vehicle company executive*
Ananth, Jambur *psychiatrist, educator*
Anderson, Marilyn Wheeler *English language educator*
Antkiewicz, Charmian Elizabeth *controller*
Birnbaumer, Diane Margaret *emergency physician, educator*
Brasel, Jo Anne *pediatrician, educator*
Brass, Eric Paul *internal medicine and pharmacology educator, director*
Bryan, Sharon Ann *lawyer*
Carey, Kathryn Ann *foundation administrator, editor, consultant*
Emmanouilides, George Christos *physician, educator*
Esmond, Donald V. *transportation executive*
Funo, Yukitoshi *automotive executive*
Gran, Robert *engineering company executive*
Hammer, Terence Michael *physician*
Helford, Irwin *consumer products company executive*
Horwich, Harvey *printer, publisher*
Howell, Irvin Wendell, Jr., *physician, consultant*
Howroyd, Janice Bryant *personnel placement executive*
Illingworth, Davis (Dave), Jr., *transportation executive*
Imbarus, Aura *language educator, consultant*
Johnson, Einar William *lawyer*
Kallman, Burton Jay *foods association director*
Kasari, Leonard Samuel *quality control professional, concrete consultant*
Kaufman, Sanford Paul *lawyer*
Keller, Margaret Anne Eikrem *pediatrician, educator*
Kerstiens, Gene J. *mathemagenician, consultant*
Kishita, Kazutaka *adhesive company executive, chemist*
Kohan, Betsy Burns *lawyer*
Kram, Harry Bernard *surgeon*
Kuc, Joseph A. *research scientist*
Kuykendall, Steven Thomas *former congressman*
Lee, Francis Cho-Kuen *aerospace engineering analyst*
Lieberman, Robert Arthur *physicist*
Mann, Michael Martin *electronics company executive*
McIntyre, Patricia Bowne *councilman*
McNamara, Brenda Norma *secondary school educator*
Mehringer, Charles Mark *medical educator*
Mehrotra, Rajnish *nephrologist, researcher, medical educator*
Mende, Howard Shigeharu *mechanical engineer*
Miller, Milton Howard *psychiatrist*
Moore, Christopher M. *lawyer*
Myhre, Byron Arnold *pathologist, educator*
Petillon, Lee Ritchey *lawyer*
Press, James E. *transportation executive*
Rogers, Howard H. *retired chemist*
Shitabata, Paul Kent *pathologist*
Signorovitch, Dennis J. *communications executive*
Sorstokke, Susan Eileen *systems engineer*
Sperling, Irene R. *publishing executive*
Stabile, Bruce Edward *surgeon*
Stringer, William Warner *physician*
Sun, Nora Chi-Jun *pathologist*
Tanaka, Kouichi Robert *hematologist, educator*
Van Emburgh, Joanne *lawyer*
Wafer, Thomas J., Jr., *newspaper publisher*
Walker, Dan *mayor, business consultant*
Yamamoto, Akimasa *transportation executive*

Trabuco Canyon
Addy, Jo Alison Phears *economist*
Jessup, R. Judd *health care executive*
Larson, Harry Thomas *electronics engineer, executive, consultant*

Tracy
Coursey, David *columnist, management consultant*
Harris, Kathleen Renee *marketing professional*
Kiggins, Mildred L.

Travis AFB
Kelly, Christopher A. *brigadier general United States air force*

Trinidad
Conant, Ralph Wendell *educator, consultant, author*
Marshall, William Edward *historical association executive*

Truckee
Sanwick, James Arthur *corporate financial executive*
Turner, George Pearce *consulting company executive*

Tujunga
Lathe, Robert Edward *management and financial consultant*
Pozzo, Mary Lou *retired librarian, writer*

Tulare
Birtcil, Robert Franklin, Jr., *dental educator*

Turlock
Ahlem, Lloyd Harold *psychologist*
Arias, Joe *agricultural products company executive*
Harris, Randall Duane *management consultant, educator*
Hughes, Marvalene *academic administrator*
Stensether, John Eldon *minister*
Tereshchenko, Alexander Pavlovich *research scientist, educator*

Tustin
Abu-Mostafa, Ayman Said *computer consultant*
Clauson, Gary Lewis *chemist*
Coronel, Raul Angulo *sculptor*
Crouch, Paul Franklin *minister, religious organization administrator*
Hester, Norman Eric *chemical company technical executive, chemist*
Kollias, Jim Harry *music educator*
Kraft, Henry Robert *lawyer*
Legere, Edward J. *health products executive*
Madory, Richard Eugene *lawyer*
Maeschen, David Michael *software engineer*
Prasad, Birendra (Brian) *mechanical engineer*
Schectman, Stephen Barry *pharmaceutical executive*

Twain Harte
Kinsinger, Robert Earl *property company executive, educational consultant*

Twentynine Palms
Clemente, Patrocinio Ablola *secondary school educator*
Fultz, Philip Nathaniel *management analyst*

Ukiah
Lohrli, Anne *retired English language educator, writer*
McClintock, Richard Polson *dermatologist*
Newell, Barbara Ann *coatings company executive*
Patel, Bharat *financial executive*
Sager, Madeline Dean *lawyer*
Toms, Michael Anthony *broadcast journalist, editor, writer, producer*
Van Dusen, Wilson M. *writer, psychologist*

Union City
Cross, Elizabeth *apparel manufacturing company executive*
Reyes, Luzviminda Canuto *social welfare administrator*

Universal City
Crow, Sheryl *singer, songwriter, musician*
Fleishman, Susan Nahley *film company executive*
Geffen, David *recording company executive, producer*
Gill, Libby *television executive*
Golper, John Bruce *lawyer*
Hahn, Helene B. *motion picture company executive*
Hammer, Bonnie *broadcast executive*
Menendez, Belinda *broadcast executive*
Merkerson, S. Epatha *actress*
Meyer, Ron *film company executive*
Nelson, Ronald L. *film company executive*
Parent, Mary *film company executive*
Peter, Arnold Philimon *lawyer, business executive*
Randall, Karen *film company executive*
Rapke, Jack *agent*
Reitman, Ivan *film director, producer*
Rocco, Nikki *film company executive*
Schulz, Diana *film company executive*
Snider, Stacey *film company executive*
Stuber, Scott *film company executive*
Torres, Jacqueline *television director, actress*
Wolf, Dick (Richard A. Wolf) *television producer, film company executive*

Upland
Berger, Stanley Christ *secondary school educator*
Cullen, Robert John *financial planner, investment advisor*
Goodman, John M. *construction executive*
Horton, Michael L. *mortgage company executive, publishing executive*
Jordan, Charles Wesley *retired bishop*
Lewis, Goldy Sarah *real estate developer, corporation executive*
Likens, John David *rehabilitation services professional*

Upper Lake
Twitchell, Kent *artist*

Vacaville
Lougoria, Steve *security firm executive, consultant*
Wolk, Lois *state legislator*

Valencia
Anguiano, Lupe *advocate*
Cusamano, Gary M. *real estate executive*
Finley, Greg Ronald *actor, scriptwriter*
Fogel, Jennifer Lynn *technical associate, researcher*
Garside, Marlene Elizabeth *retired advertising executive*
Heinisch, Robert Craig *sales and marketing executive, consultant*
House, David L. *electronics components company executive*
Lee, Thomas L. *real estate executive*
Levy, Ezra Cesar *aerospace scientist, real estate broker*
McQuown, Mark *scriptwriter*
Millar, Michael William *musician*
Parks, Suzan Lori *playwright*
Pocrass, Richard Dale *management consultant*
Webb, Margot *writer*
Werkheiser, Steven Lawrence *financial executive*
Windsor, William Earl *consulting engineer, sales representative*

Vallejo
Brooks, William George *retired aeronautical engineer*
Brown, Earl Kent *historian, clergyman*
Crosley-Mayers, Diane *social worker*
Gunn, Alexander N., II, *surgeon*
Landauer, Elvie Ann Whitney *humanities educator, writer*
McGowan, Thomas Randolph *retired religious organization administrator*
Murillo, Carol Ann *secondary school educator*
Toms, Kathleen Moore *nurse*
Womack, Thomas Houston *manufacturing executive*
Zeliger, Bernard *dean*

Valley Center
Andersen, Robert *health products, business executive*
Camp, Joseph Shelton, Jr., *film producer, director, writer*

Valley Springs
Anema-Garten, Durlynn C. *communications educator, counselor, writer*
Vitrac, Jean-Jacques Charles *international business consultant*

Valley Village
Barkin, Elaine Radoff *composer*
Diller, Phyllis *actress, writer*

Van Nuys
Altshiller, Arthur Leonard *secondary school educator*
Arabian, Armand *retired arbitrator, mediator, lawyer*
Becker, Frawley *writer, dialogue director, location manager*
Boone, Deborah Ann (Debby Boone) *singer*
Cook, Jenik Esterm (Jenik Esterm Cook Simonian) *artist, educator*
Farman, Richard Donald *energy company executive*
Fox, James Michael *orthopedic surgeon*
Graham, Roger John *photography and journalism educator*
Greenberg, Daniel *electronics rental company executive*
Harnsberger, Lindsey Carleton *music company executive, composer*
Hertzberg, Robert M. *former state legislator*
Iacocca, Lee (Lido Anthony Iacocca) *former automotive manufacturing executive, venture capitalist*
McLain, Christopher M. *lawyer*
Schell, George Aaron *lawyer*
Seymour, Jeffrey Alan *governmental relations consultant*
Westall, Andrew Jon *legislative staff member, urban planner*
Zucker, Alfred John *English language educator, academic administrator*

Vandenberg Afb
Hamel, Michael A. *career officer*
Huggins, Elaine Jacqueline *nurse, retired army officer*

Venice
Alf, Martha Joanne *artist*
Beal, Jason Eliot *architect*
Bill, Tony *producer, director*
Chipman, Jack *artist*
Eliot, Alexander *author, mythologist*
Eversley, Frederick John *sculptor, engineer*
Fracassi, Philip D. *bookstore retailer, publisher*
Padilla, Mario René *literature educator, writer, actor*

Ventura
Abul-Haj, Suleiman Kahil *pathologist*
Bowles, Walter Donald *economist, educator*
Downs, Floella McIntyre *civic worker, ferry pilot, instructor and flight examiner*
Gallagher, Timothy J. *newspaper editor*
Gartner, Harold Henry, III, *lawyer*
Gay, Marilyn Fanelli Martin *television producer, writer, talk show hostess, journalist*
Gaynor, Joseph *chemical engineer, technical-management consultant*
Greene, Warren W. *anesthesiologist*
Greig, William Taber, II, *publishing company executive*
Howry, Joe R. *newspaper editor*
Jaeger, Kenneth Michael *secondary school educator*
Kreissman, Starrett *librarian*
Lovell, Frederick Warren *pathologist, medical legal consultant*
Naurath, David Allison *engineering psychologist, researcher*
Nusbaum, Bennett *printing/copying company executive*
Renger, Marilyn Hanson *elementary school educator*
Smith, Bill *city manager*
Tamke, George William *printing/copying company executive*
Villaveces, James Walter *allergist, immunologist*

Vernon
Kim, Ho Gill *poet*

Victorville
Dilliard, Maxine K. *retired school psychologist*
Quadri, Fazle Rab *lawyer, government official*
Scott, Deborah Elizabeth *school system administrator, poet*
Sedeño, Eugene Raymond *electronics engineer, consultant*

Villa Park
Britton, Thomas Warren, Jr., *retired management consultant*
Hawe, David Lee *manufacturing consultant, venture capitalist*
Murphy, Patrick Christopher *music educator*

Visalia
Crowe, Daniel Walston *lawyer*
Crowe, John T. *lawyer*
Daniels, Madeline Marie *forensic psychologist, educator, author*
Hart, Timothy Ray *lawyer, dean*
Hsu, Shu-Dean *hematologist, oncologist*
Neeley, James Kame *credit agency executive*
Nevin, David Wright *real estate broker, mortgage broker*
O'Leary, Deanna Kay *analyst, consultant*
Phillipe, Chester Tolleson *alcohol/drug abuse services professional, educator, substance abuse facility administrator*
Riegel, Byron William *ophthalmologist*
Singh, Daljit *dean, business and public administration educator*

Vista
Cavanaugh, Kenneth Clinton *retired housing consultant*
Ferguson, Margaret Ann *tax consultant*
Fuhlrodt, Norman Theodore *retired insurance company executive*
Linhart, Letty Lemon *editor*
Owen, Daniel Hugh *writer*
Tadeo, Elvia *artist*
Wyland, Mark *state official*

Walnut
Budzak, Stephen Howard *tax specialist, consultant*
Cheng, Shide *engineer, researcher*
Humphreys, Roy *construction executive*
McKee, Catherine Lynch *law educator, lawyer*
Muszynski, Jane *interior designer, colorist, space planner*
Shea, John F. *construction executive, contractor*
Shontere, James G. *construction executive*
Smith, Harry Mendell, Jr., *science educator*

Walnut Creek
Anderberg, Roy A. *journalist*
Arnold, William Thomas *software developer, chemist*
Bryant, Warren F. *retail executive*
Burnison, Boyd Edward *lawyer*
Burns, Francis Raymond *medical facility administrator, researcher*
Cannon, Grace Bert *retired immunologist*
Carson, Jay Wilmer *pathologist, educator*
Cassidy, John Joseph *hydraulic and hydrologic engineer*
Chu, Valentin Yuan-ling *author*
Curtin, Daniel Joseph, Jr., *lawyer*
da Roza, Victoria Cecilia *human resources administrator*
Dea, Norman *secondary school educator*
De Benedictis, Dario *retired lawyer, retired arbitrator, retired mediator*
Derby, Steven Leo *lawyer*
Dreiling, Richard *retail executive*
Foster, Bonnie Gayle *operating room nurse, real estate agent*
Gardner, Trudi York *lawyer, insurance company executive*
Garlough, William Glenn *marketing executive*
Gill, Margaret Gaskins *lawyer*
Ginsburg, Gerald J. *lawyer, business executive*
Hamlin, Kenneth Eldred, Jr., *retired pharmaceutical company executive*
Hammond, Charles Edgar *data processing executive*
Hanschen, Peter Walter *lawyer*
Hanson, Robert Duane *civil engineering educator*
Horner, Clifford R. *lawyer*
Keith, Bruce Edgar *political analyst, genealogist*
Laddon, Michael M *retail executive*
Lilly, Luella Jean *academic administrator*
McCauley, Bruce Gordon *financial consultant*
McGrath, Don John *banker*
Medak, Walter Hans *lawyer*
Moore, John David *management consultant*
Nolan, David Charles *lawyer, arbitrator, mediator*
Nolan, Janiece Simmons *health care company executive*
Ogilby, Barry Ray *lawyer*
Pagter, Carl Richard *lawyer*
Palmer, William Joseph *accountant*
Pfeiffer, Phyllis Kramer *publishing executive*
Rainey, William Joel *lawyer*
Rathjen, Jon Laurence *lawyer, arbitrator, mediator*
Reimann, Arline Lynn *artist*
Rhody, Ronald Edward *banker, communications executive*
Satz, Louis K. *publishing executive*
Schneider, Gisela Helga *medical technician*
Seaborg, David Michael *evolutionary biologist*
Shastid, Jon Barton *wine company executive*
Sheen, Portia Yunn-ling *retired physician*
Skaggs, Sanford Merle *lawyer*
Stapp, Olivia Brewer *opera singer*
Trousdale, Stephen Richard *newspaper editor*
Willson, Prentiss, Jr., *lawyer*
Wu, Tse Cheng *research chemist*

Waterford
Reed, Thomas W. *secondary school educator*

Watsonville
Brown, Alan Charlton *retired aeronautical engineer*
Costanzo, Patrick M. *construction executive*
Dehner, David Anthony *music educator, voice educator*
Franich, Steven *automotive company executive*
Hernandez, Jo Farb *music director, consultant*
Repass, Randy *electrical company executive*

Weimar
Ing, Clarence Sinn Fook *preventive medicine physician, ophthalmic surgeon*
Kerschner, Lee R(onald) *academic administrator, political science educator*

West Covina
Ebiner, Robert Maurice *lawyer*
Fuller, George Stuart *secondary school educator*
Lavruk, Alexander E. *music educator, sales consultant*
McHale, Edward Robertson *retired lawyer*
Musich, Robert Lorin *motivational speaker*
Shanks, Sanford H. *sales executive, writer*
Torres, Esteban Edward *former congressman, business executive*
Tuck, Edward Fenton *venture capitalist*

West Hills
Hyde, M. Deborah *neurosurgeon*

West Hollywood
Annakin, Kenneth Cooper *film director, writer*
Baker, Anita *singer*
Cage, Nicolas (Nicolas Coppola) *actor*
De Line, Donald *film company executive*
De Palma, Brian Russell *film director, writer*
Eger, Denise Leese *rabbi*
Einstein, Clifford Jay *advertising executive*
Goin, Suzanne *food company executive, chef*
Grasshoff, Alex *writer, producer, director*
Harper, Robert *actor*
Hodal, Melanie *public relations executive*
Hoffenblum, Allan Ernest *political consultant*
Innes, Laura *actress*
Madonna, (Madonna Louise Veronica Ciccone) *singer, actress, producer*
Morris, Brian *advertising executive*
Perry, Troy D. *clergyman, religious organization administrator*
Schnabel, Timothy Brian *writer, publishing executive*
Shaye, Robert Kenneth *cinema company executive*
Sherman, Robert B(ernard) *composer, lyricist, screenwriter*
Slade, Bernard *playwright*
Stein, Benjamin J. *television personality, writer, lawyer, economist*
Thomas, Rob *singer, songwriter*
Wilson, Nancy Linda *religious organization administrator*

West Los Angeles
Hirschhorn, Charles *media company executive*

West Point
tenZeldam, Justine Cubbage *publishing executive, editor-in-chief*

West Sacramento
Anderson, William Wallace *financial executive*
Coyne, William J. *retail executive*
D'Arezzo, Dave *food products executive*
Lloyd, Sharon *marketing professional*
Searson, Dee *retail products executive*
Solomon, Russell M. *retail products executive*
Teel, James E. *supermarket and drug store retail executive*
Teel, Joyce Raley *retail executive*
Wilson, Eric F.G. *information technology executive*

Westlake Village
Caligiuri, Joseph Frank *retired engineering executive*
Carter, C. Michael *lawyer*
Colburn, Keith W. *electronics executive*
DeLorenzo, David A. *food products executive*
Detterman, Robert Linwood *financial planner*
Gibson, John Robert *software engineer*
Hoefflin, Richard Michael *lawyer, judicial administrator*
Levine, Donald Arthur *anesthesiologist*
Long, W. Michael *real estate company executive*
Lullo, Thomas A. *electronics executive*
Masry, Edward L. *lawyer*
Munson, John Backus *computer systems consultant, retired computer engineering company executive*
Murdock, David H. *diversified company executive*
Nichols, Steven *apparel executive*
Powlick, George *shoe and clothing manufacturing executive*
Smyth, Glen Miller *management consultant*
Troxell, Lucy Davis *management consultant*
Valentine, Gene C. *securities dealer*
Weiss, Barbara G. *artist*
Wester, Aaron Micah *web production manager, consultant*

Westminster
Allen, Merrill James *marine biologist*
Armstrong, Gene Lee *systems engineering consultant, retired aerospace company executive*
Nguyen, Duoc Tan *small business owner*
Nguyen, Lan Thi Hoang *physician, educator*

Whittier
Arenowitz, Albert Harold *psychiatrist*
Drake, E. Maylon *academic administrator*
Gosfield, Margaret *secondary school educator, school system administrator, consultant, editor*
Guerrero, Donna Marie *sales executive*
Korf, Jean Prinz *retired theater educator*
Loughrin, Jay Richardson *mass communications educator, consultant*
Meardy, William Herman *retired educational association administrator*
Prickett, David Clinton *physician*
Rosenstein, Mary Elisabeth Mallory *retired social worker*
Spencer, Williametta *composer, retired music educator*

Willits
Akins, George Charles *accountant*

Wilmington
Hamai, James Yutaka *business executive*
Hatch, Ronald Ray *engineer*

Wilton
Felts, Margaret Clemen *environmental engineer, consultant*
Harrison, George Harry, III, (Hank Harrison) *publishing executive, author*

Windsor
Sparks, Bennett Sher *military officer*

Woodland
Spisak, John Francis *environmental company executive*
Squires, Richard Felt *research scientist*

Woodland Hills
Anastasi, Michael Anton *journalist*
Babayans, Emil *financial planner*
Barrett, Robert Matthew *law educator, lawyer*
Berger, Phil *musician*
Brann, Alton Joseph *manufacturing executive*
Brown, Michael R. *former defense industry executive*
Chiodini, John Allen *musician, composer*
Colby, David C. *healthcare management company executive*
Deters, Thomas C. *publishing executive, educator*
Dreier, R. Chad *construction and mortgage company executive*
Ennis, Thomas Michael *management consultant*
Erwin, Steven P. *insurance company executive*
Even, Randolph M. *lawyer*
Feiman, Thomas E. *investment manager*
Fox, Stuart Ira *physiologist*
Funari, Robert Glenn *health care services executive*
Gellert, Jay M. *health and medical products executive*
Glick, Earl A. *lawyer*
Greaves, Roger F. *health maintenance organization executive*
Harmon, David *finance company executive*
Harris, Barbara S. *publishing executive*
Helwig, David S. *insurance company executive*
Herdeg, Howard Brian *physician*
Hokana, Gregory Howard *engineering executive*
Holland, Kathleen *political science educator*
John Robert, Bruce *healthcare company executive*
Johnson-Champ, Debra Sue *lawyer, educator, writer, artist*
Kaufman, Albert I. *lawyer*
Lax, Kathleen Thompson *judge*
Levy, Norman *motion picture company executive*
Lin, Lawrence Shuh Liang *lawyer*
Lund, Robert W. *newspaper editor*
Monteau, Norman Keith *gemologist*
Morishita, Akihiko *trading company executive*
Mund, Geraldine *judge*
Murphy, Irene Helen *publishing executive*
O'Connor, Brian D. A. *music educator, French Horn musician*
Pendergrass, Teddy (Theodore D. Pendergrass) *musician*
Pettit, John W. *administrator*
Piersol, Allan Gerald *mechanical engineer*
Pregerson, Harry *federal judge*
Rafter, Tracy *publishing executive*
Randall, Craig *financial and business management consultant, accountant, computer specialist*
Rich, Marvin P. *health association executive*
Rolin, Christopher Ernest *lawyer*
Schor, Suzi *lawyer, psychologist*
Schuchet, John R. *newspaper executive*
Siever-Henderson, Patricia *history university educator*
Stahlecker, Barbara Jean *marketing professional, consultant*
Stratton, Gregory Alexander *computer specialist, administrator, mayor*
Tellez, Cora *healthcare company executive*
Tuthill, Walter Warren *financial executive, international business consultant*
Vokshoor, Amir *neurosurgeon*
Weider, Joseph *wholesale distribution executive*
Westen, Brodie Curtis *lawyer*
Wiesner, Carol A. *financial services company executive*
Yates, Gary L. *marriage and family therapist*
Zeitlin, Herbert Zakary *retired academic administrator, real estate consultant*

Woodside
Arthur, Greer Martin *maritime container leasing firm executive*
Ashley, Holt *aerospace scientist, educator*
Blum, Richard Hosmer Adams *medical educator, writer*
Fisher, Kenneth Lawrence *investment management firm executive*
Freitas, Antoinette Juni *insurance company executive*
Gates, Milo Sedgwick *retired construction company executive*
Klein, August Stone *retired physicist*
Liebowitz, Daniel S. F. *retired medical educator*
Markkula, A.C., Jr., *entrepreneur, computer company executive*

Wrightwood
Caudron, John Armand *accident reconstructionist, forensic examiner*
Frame, John Fayette *sculptor*

Yorba Linda
Lynch, Frank Thomas *aeronautical engineer, consultant*
Medland, Maurice Blue *writer*
Naulty, Susan Louise *archivist*
Porcello, Leonard Joseph *engineering research and development executive*
Sperling, Scott Edward *software consultant, Bible expositor*
Stavropoulos, Rose Mary Grant *community activist, volunteer*
Vilardi, Agnes Francine *real estate broker*

Yosemite National Park
Forgang, David M. *curator*

Yountville
Bedell, Jay Dee *educator, writer*
Keller, Thomas A. *chef*

Yreka
Nelson, Steven Leslie *surgeon*
Smith, Vin *sports editor, business owner, novelist*

Yuba City
Kemmerly, Jack Dale *retired state official, aviation consultant*

Yucaipa
Bogh, Russell *state official*
D'Amelio, Dan Anthony *writer, journalist, educator*
Gomez, Louis Salazar *college president*
Lardy, Leonard Anthony *English educator*

Yucca Valley
Dockendorff, Robert Lawrence *computer graphics designer*
Styles, Beverly (Juanita Robins Carpenter) *entertainer, composer, musician*

COLORADO

Alamosa
Garcia, Castelar Medardo *lawyer*

Allenspark
Newman, Dean Gordon *business consultant*

Arvada
Bert, Carol Lois *retired educational assistant*
Ferguson, Lloyd Elbert *retired manufacturing engineer*
Glodava, Mila Garcia *entrepreneur, educator, consultant*
Halley, Diane Esther *artist*
Holden, George Fredric *brewing company executive, public policy specialist, writer*
Howard, Barry Christopher *minister*
Johnson, Christian Kent *lawyer*
Kreis, Elizabeth Susan *lawyer*
Meiklejohn, Mindy June (Lorraine Meiklejohn) *political organizer, realtor*
Peck, Kenneth E. *lawyer*
Pettit, Claud Martin *religious organization administrator*
Reed, Joan-Marie *special education educator*
Smith, Paul Tillman *engineering executive, writer*
Yamamoto, Kaoru *retired psychology and education educator*

Aspen
Berkeley, (Ed)ward *performing arts association administrator, music educator*
Clauson, F.L. Stan, Jr., *city planner, consultant*
Hardy, Gordon Alfred *music educator, music school president*
Hayes, Mary Eshbaugh *editor, writer*
Jennings, Richard Milburn *resort developer*
Manosevitz, Martin *psychologist*
Mitchell, Karen Frances *artist, jewelry designer*
Oden, Robert Rudolph *surgeon*
Roth, Don *music executive*
Soldner, Paul Edmund *artist, ceramist, educator*
Williams, Rhys A *surgeon*

Aurora
Battaglia, Frederick Camillo *physician*
Bauman, Earl William *accountant*
Beckman, L. David *university chancellor*
Brown, Anne Sherwin *speech pathologist, educator*
Dooley, J. Gordon *food scientist*
Du, Yiping P. *education educator*
Fisher, Patricia Anne *writer, publishing executive*
Fisk, Charles Carroll *retired civil engineer, consultant*
Grace, William Pershing *petroleum geologist, real estate developer*
Green, Larry Alton *physician, educator*
Hampton, Clyde Robert *lawyer, educator*
Heisler, Traciann *music educator, musician*
Heller, Austin Norman *chemical and environmental engineer*
Hodges, Robert Stanley *biochemist, educator, researcher in biotechnology*
Hughes, Christopher Adam *conductor, educator*
Katz, Michael Jeffery *lawyer*
Khanna, Kishanlal K. *lawyer, educator*
Lassen, Betty Jane *gifted and talented educator*
Lochmiller, Kurtis L. *real estate entrepreneur*
Mellette, Julian Ramsey, Jr., *dermatologist, dermatologic surgeon*
Miller, Sarah Pearl *librarian*
Moser, Jeffery Richard *state agency administrator, public affairs and public management executive, artist, writer, former state official*
Nelson, Marvin Ray *retired life insurance company executive*
Nichols, Clyde Richard *minister, consumer products company executive*
Nolen, James Allen *property manager, writer*
Nora, Audrey Hart *physician*
Onyeuku, Alfred Eme *small business owner, consultant*
Osterberg, Jorj O. *retired civil engineer*
Reitan, Harold Theodore *management consultant*
Reynolds, Robert Harrison *retired export company executive*
Robertson, James Mueller *civil engineer, educator*
Schwartz, Lawrence *aeronautical engineer*
Sheffield, Nancy *city agency administrator*
Sorenson, Katherine Ann *elementary school educator*
Stauffer, Scott William *lawyer, accountant*
Stifel, Frederick Benton *minister, biochemist, nutritionist*
Tauer, Paul E. *mayor, educator*
Ton, Paul *investor, educator*
Walker, Joyce Marie *secondary school educator*
Whelchel, Anita E. *publishing executive*

Basalt
Weill, Hans *medical educator*

Bayfield
Haug, Edward Joseph, Jr., *engineering educator, director*

Berthoud
Davis, Donald Alan *news correspondent, writer, lecturer*

Black Hawk
Jones, Linda May *tour guide, writer*

Boulder
Adler, Patricia Ann *sociologist, educator*
Albritton, Daniel Lee *atmospheric scientist*
Anderson, Ronald Delaine *education educator*
Araujo-Pradere, Eduardo A. *geophysicist, researcher*
Armstrong, David Michael *biology professor*
Arnold, Janet Nina *health care consultant*
Avery, Susan Kathryn *electrical engineering educator, research administrator*
Bangs, F(rank) Kendrick *former business educator*
Barchilon, Jacques *foreign language educator, researcher, writer*
Barnes, Frank Stephenson *electrical engineer, educator*
Bartlett, David Farnham *physics educator*
Baugh, L. Darrell *financial executive*
Baughn, William Hubert *former business educator and academic administrator*
Beer, Francis Anthony *political science educator*
Begelman, Mitchell Craig *astrophysicist, educator, writer*
Beylkin, Gregory *mathematician*
Bickman, Martin *literature educator, writer*
Bintliff, Barbara Ann *law educator, library director*
Bolomey, Roger Henry *sculptor*
Borko, Hilda *education educator*
Borysenko, Joan *psychologist, biologist*
Bourne, Lyle Eugene, Jr., *psychology educator*
Boydston, James Christopher *composer*
Braddock, David Lawrence *health science educator*
Breddan, Joe *systems engineering consultant*
Bruff, Harold Hastings *dean*
Budd, David A. *geologist, educator*
Buechner, John C. *academic administrator*
Burke, Thomas Sebastian, Jr., *educator, writer*
Burns, Daniel Hobart *management consultant*
Byerly, Radford, Jr., *science policy official*
Byyny, Richard Lee *academic administrator, physician*
Caccamise, Donna Jean *research scientist, director*
Cai, Xiao-Chuan *computer science educator*
Carlson, Rhonda *writer, law educator*
Cathey, Wade Thomas *retired electrical engineering educator*
Chappell, Charles Franklin *meteorologist, consultant*
Clark, Melvin Eugene *chemical company executive*
Clifford, Steven Francis *science research director*
Clos, Lynne Mobley *magazine publisher, paleontologist*

Conti, Peter Selby *astronomy educator*
Conway, Robert Edward *corporate executive*
Cooper, John *physicist, educator*
Copeland, Poppy Carlson *psychotherapist*
Cornell, Eric Allin *physics educator*
Corotis, Ross Barry *civil engineering educator, academic administrator*
Cristol, Stanley Jerome *chemistry professor*
Cziczo, Daniel James *research scientist, educator*
Danilov, Victor Joseph *museum administrator, educator, consultant, writer*
Deaktor, Darryl Barnett *lawyer*
Demos, Steven *food products executive*
Dilley, Barbara Jean *college administrator, choreographer, educator*
DiStefano, Philip *academic administrator*
Dubin, Mark William *educator, neuroscientist*
Dubofsky, Jean Eberhart *lawyer, retired state supreme court justice*
Duckworth, Guy *musician, pianist, educator*
Dudhia, Jimy *atmospheric scientist*
Dumas, Jeffrey Mack *lawyer*
Dunn, Gordon Harold *physicist, researcher*
Echohawk, John Ernest *lawyer*
Eldridge, Thomas Engle *restaurant executive*
El Mallakh, Dorothea Hendry *editor, publishing executive*
Enarson, Harold L. *retired academic administrator*
Engel, Barbara Alpern *history professor*
Fenster, Herbert Lawrence *lawyer*
Ferguson, Eldon Earl *retired physicist*
Fiflis, Ted James *lawyer, educator*
Fink, Robert Russell *music theorist, former university dean*
Fleming, Rex James *meteorologist*
Flowers, William Harold, Jr., *lawyer*
Garstang, Roy Henry *astrophysicist, educator*
Getches, David Harding *law educator, state environmental executive, lawyer, dean*
Glasergreen, Lawson Scott *designer*
Glover, Fred William *mathematical optimization, artificial intelligence and optimization research director, educator*
Gonzalez-del-Valle, Luis Tomas *Spanish language educator*
Gossard, Earl Everett *physicist*
Gray, William R. *lawyer*
Greenberg, Edward Seymour *political science educator, writer*
Greschik, Gyula *structural engineer*
Hanna, William Johnson *electrical engineering educator*
Hauser, Ray Louis *research engineer, entrepreneur*
Healy, Alice Fenvessy *psychology educator, researcher*
Heath, Josephine Ward *foundation administrator*
Hermann, Allen Max *physics educator*
Hess, John Warren *professional society administrator*
Hill, David Allan *electrical engineer*
Hill, Melvin James *retired oil company executive*
Hoffman, Charles Fenno, III, *architect*
Hoffman, Elizabeth *academic administrator*
Hofmann, David John *atmospheric science researcher, educator*
Hogg, David Clarence *physicist*
Holdsworth, Janet Nott *women's health nurse*
Holzer, Thomas E. *physicist*
Hubbard, Eleanor A. *sociologist, educator*
Hurd, Jerrie *writer*
Jerritts, Stephen G. *management consultant*
Jessor, Richard *psychologist, educator*
Jin, Deborah *physicist, educator*
Johnston, Laurance Scott *foundation director*
Joselyn, Jo Ann *space scientist*
Joy, Edward Bennett *electrical engineer, educator*
Jurafsky, Daniel *linguist*
Kabos, Pavel J.D. *physicist*
Kahn, Herta Hess (Mrs. Howard Kahn) *retired securities trader*
Kapteyn, Henry Cornelius *physics and engineering educator*
Kellogg, William Welch *meteorologist, researcher*
Kenney, Belinda Jill Forseman *technology company executive*
Kerr, Baine Perkins, Jr., *lawyer, writer*
Kessinger, Cathy Jeanne *meteorologist, researcher*
Kinder, Eugene J(oseph) *psychiatrist, psychoanalyst*
King, Edward Louis *retired chemistry educator*
Kintsch, Walter *psychology educator, director*
Kisslinger, Carl *geophysicist, educator*
Knoelker, Michael *science observatory director*
Korevaar, David *musician, educator*
Lally, Vincent Edward *atmospheric scientist*
Lefkoff, Kyle *pharmaceutical executive*
LeMone, Margaret Anne *atmospheric scientist*
Limerick, Patricia Nelson *history professor*
Lineberger, William Carl *chemistry educator*
Low, Boon Chye *physicist*
MacDonald, Alexander Edward *meteorologist*
Madden, Alice Donnelly *lawyer*
Mahajan, Roop L. *engineering educator*
Mahanthappa, Kalyana Thipperudraiah *physicist, researcher*
Mahlman, Jerry David *climate and atmospheric scientist*
Malde, Harold Edwin *retired federal government geologist*
Mancino, John Gregory *software company executive*
Mehalchin, John Joseph *entrepreneur, finance executive*
Meier, Mark Frederick *research scientist, glaciologist, educator*
Meier, Thomas Joseph *museum director, author*
Melicher, Ronald William *finance educator*
Menken, Jane Ava *demographer, educator*
Menn, Lise *linguistics educator*
Meyer, Andrea Peroutka *small business owner*
Middleton-Downing, Laura *psychiatric social worker, artist, small business owner*
Mitchell, Joan LaVerne *research scientist*
Monarchi, David Edward *management scientist, information scientist, educator*
Mooney, William Piatt *actor*
Moses, Raphael Jacob *lawyer*
Mulhern, Martin Robert *engineer*
Murino, Clifford John *atmospheric and oceanic research institute executive*
Mycielski, Jan *mathematician, educator*
Neinas, Charles Merrill *economist, consultant, sports association executive*
O'Brien, Elmer John *librarian, educator*
Pace, Norman R. *science educator, microbiologist*
Pankove, Jacques Isaac *physicist, researcher*
Peacock, Neil T. *engineer*
Peters, Max Stone *chemical engineer, educator*
Porzak, Glenn E. *lawyer*
Prescott, David Marshall *biology educator*
Ramirez, W. Fred *chemical engineering educator*
Randa, James Paul *physicist, electrical engineer*
Ranniger, Leslie Jean *lawyer*
Reitsema, Harold James *aerospace engineer*
Rienner, Lynne Carol *publishing executive*
Riis, Thomas Laurence *music educator*
Rinehart, Amy Hutchinson *publishing executive, consultant*
Robin, Howard W. *biotechnology company executive*
Rodriguez, Juan Alfonso *technology corporation executive*
Roellig, Leonard Oscar *physics educator*
Rood, David S. *linguistics educator*
Sable, Barbara Kinsey *retired music educator*
Sani, Robert LeRoy *chemical engineering educator*
Sarson, John Christopher *television producer, director, writer*
Schneider, Nicholas McCord *planetary scientist, educator, textbook author*
Serafin, Robert Joseph *science center administrator, electrical engineer*
Sirotkin, Phillip Leonard *education administrator*
Smith, Ernest Ketcham *electrical engineer*
Smith, Joel B. *environmental analyst*
Smythe, William Rodman *physicist, researcher*
Snow, Theodore Peck *astrophysics educator*
Sodal, Ingvar Edmund *electrical engineer, scientist*
Staehelin, Lucas Andrew *cell biology educator*
Stanton, William John, Jr., *marketing educator, author*
Stepanek, Joseph Edward *industrial development consultant*
Steuben, Norton Leslie *lawyer, educator*
Tatarskii, Valerian Il'Ich *physics researcher*
Thomas, Daniel Foley *retired financial services company executive*
Timmerhaus, Klaus Dieter *chemical engineering educator*
Tolbert, Bert Mills *biochemist, educator*
Tolbert, Margaret A. *geochemistry educator*
Trenberth, Kevin Edward *atmospheric scientist*
Truce, William Everett *chemist, educator*
Uberoi, Mahinder Singh *aerospace engineer, researcher*
Uhrik, Carl Thomas *computer scientist, educator*
Underwood, Anthony Paul *lawyer*
Valdovino, Luis Hector *art educator*
Waldman, Anne Lesley *poet, performer, editor, publisher, educational administrator*
Walker, Deward Edgar, Jr., *anthropologist, educator*
Ward, Denitta Dawn *lawyer*
Washington, Warren Morton *meteorologist*
White, Gilbert F(owler) *geographer, educator*
Wieman, Carl E. *physics educator*
Wittemyer, John *lawyer*
Wood, William Barry, III, *biologist, educator*
Ye, Jun *physicist, researcher*
Yuhnke, Robert E. *lawyer, educator, consultant*

Breckenridge

Ehrhorn, Richard William *electronics company executive*
Fromm, Jeffery Bernard *lawyer*

Brighton

Rinkenberger, Richard Krug *physical scientist, geologist, consultant*
Wagner, Samuel Albin Mar *records management executive, educator*

Broomfield

Crawford, Caren Lee *computer engineer*
Crowe, James Quell *communications executive*
Flanders, Eleanor Carlson *community volunteer*
Hoover, R. David *packaging company executive*
Jonsen, Eric Richard *lawyer*
King, Robert *retail company executive*
O'Hara, Kevin J. *information technology executive*
Patel, Sunit *telecommunications industry executive*
Scott, John Atwood, Jr., *hypnoanalyst, psychologist, marriage and family therapist*
Seabrook, Raymond J. *corporate financial executive*
Stortz, Thomas C. *lawyer, communications executive*
Williams, John James, Jr., *architect*
Woodard, Donald Marvin *marketing professional*

Buena Vista

Goddard, Hazel Bryan *religious organization administrator*
Herb, Edmund Michael *optometrist, educator*

Calhan

Fuller, Janice Marie *secondary school educator*
Henderson, Freda LaVerne *elementary school educator*

Canon City

Fisher, Neal Foster *artist, writer*
Fredrickson, Bryan Timothy *lawyer*
Honaker, Charles Ray *health facility administrator*
McCaslin, Kathleen Denise *child abuse educator*
Mohr, Gary Alan *physician*
Williamson, Edward Henry *chaplain, army officer*

Carbondale

Cowgill, Ursula Moser *biologist, educator, environmental consultant*

Castle Rock

Barnard, Rollin Dwight *retired financial executive*
Thornbury, John Rousseau *radiologist, physician*

Centennial

Barnthouse, William Joseph *lawyer*
Brown, Steven Harry *engineering executive*
Bryan, A(lonzo) J(ay) *retired service club official*
Goughnour, Roy Robert *civil engineer, consultant*
Haley, John David *petroleum consulting company executive*
Hunt, Gerald G., Jr., *architect, real estate broker*
Milliken, Douglas Gordon *financial consultant, municipal official*
Milliken, John Gordon *research economist*
Morley, Judy Mattivi *historian, educator, preservation consultant*
Ulevich, Neal Hirsh *photojournalist*

Cherry Hills Village

Stapleton, Katharine Hall (Katie Stapleton) *food broadcaster, writer*
Sutton, Robert Edward *investment company executive*

Clifton

Konola, Claudette June *finance company executive, financial consultant*

Colorado City

Stelle, Robert E. *physician, retired educator*

Colorado Springs

Adams, Bernard Schroder *retired college president*
Adams, Deborah Rowland *lawyer*
Adnet, Jacques Jim Pierre *astronautical and electrical engineer, consultant*
Anderson, Paul Nathaniel *oncologist, educator*
Arsenault, Samantha *Olympic athlete*
Barton, Gregory Mark *Olympic athlete, kayak racer*
Beard, Amanda *swimmer, Olympic athlete*
Bedford, Barbara J. *Olympic athlete*
Benko, Lindsay *Olympic athlete*
Bennett, Brooke *Olympic athlete*
Blackburn, Alexander Lambert *author, English literature educator*
Bobek, Nicole *professional figure skater*
Bohanon, Kathleen Sue *neonatologist, educator*
Bowen, Clotilde Marion Dent *retired career officer, psychiatrist*
Bowers, Larry Donald *chemistry and pathology educator*
Brander, Bruce George *international journalist, author*
Bressan, Robert Ralph *accountant*
Brooks, Glenn Ellis *political science educator, educational administrator*
Buckner-Davis, Annett *professional volleyball player*
Budington, William Stone *retired librarian*
Buell, Bruce Temple *lawyer*
Bybee, Rodger Wayne *science education administrator*
Cameron, Paul Drummond *research facility administrator*
Cash, Swin (Swintayla Marie Cash) *professional basketball player*
Celeste, Richard F. *academic administrator, former ambassador, former governor*
Chestnutt, Ellen Joanne *state official*
Christensen, C. Lewis *real estate developer*
Cimino, Jay *automotive company executive*
Clay, Bryan Ezra *Olympic track and field athlete*
Comes, Robert George *research scientist*
Corry, Charles Elmo *geophysicist, not-for-profit developer*
Corwin, Amber *figure skater*
Coughlin, Natalie *Olympic athlete*
Cramer, Owen Carver *classics educator*
Crocker, Ian *Olympic athlete*
Cutone, Kathaleen Kelly *figure skater, former skating judge, athletic representative*
Dassanowsky, Robert von *educator, producer, writer, editor*
Delph, Kathleen Anne *foundation administrator, development director*
D'Entremont, Amy *professional figure skater*
DiPadova, Regina Maria *counselor*
Dolan, Tom *Olympic athlete*
Drennan, Jerry M. *career officer*
Driscoll, David Lee *chiropractor*
Duvall, Lawrence Delbert *insurance company executive*
Engfer, Susan Marvel *zoological park executive*
Ervin, Anthony *Olympic athlete*
Evans, Janet *former Olympic swimmer*
Fagin, Barry Steven *computer science educator, writer*
Fahey, Henry Martin *information technology executive*
Farrer, Claire Anne Rafferty *anthropologist, educator, folklorist*
Fleming, Terri *newspaper editor*
Fortune, James Michael *computer support manager*
Freeman, J. P. Ladyhawk *vicar, underwater exploration, security and transportation executive, educator, fashion model, legislative advocate*
Gaddis, Larry Roy *lawyer*
Gardner, Donald Gene *management consultant, educator*
Gatlin, Justin *track and field athlete, Olympic track and field athlete*
Geraci, Richard V. *military officer, government agency administrator*
Gifford, Marilyn Joyce *emergency physician, consultant*
Goehring, Kenneth *artist*
Granato, Catherine (Cammi Granato) *Olympic athlete*
Greenlaw, Roger Lee *interior designer*
Guy, Mildred Dorothy *retired secondary school educator*
Haas, Julian L. *researcher, educator*
Halber, Diane *professional figure skater*
Hall, Gary, Jr., *Olympic athlete*
Hallenbeck, Kenneth Luster *retired numismatist*
Hamilton, Tyler *professional cyclist, Olympic athlete*
Hamm, Morgan *Olympic athlete*
Hamm, Paul *Olympic athlete*
Hanifen, Richard Charles *retired bishop*
Hawley, Nanci Elizabeth *association administrator*
Hayes, Joanna *Olympic track and field athlete*
Heilman, John Edward *engineering consultant*
Herron, Sherry Shelton *biology professor*
Hill, Christopher Vaughan *historian, educator*
Hinkle, Betty Ruth *educational administrator*
Hoffman, John Raleigh *physicist*
Hughes, Sarah *figure skater*
Hyman, Misty Dawn *Olympic athlete*
Johnson, Henry Fred *clergy*
Kettner-Polley, Richard Brian *director*
Killian, George Ernest *educational association administrator*
King, Peter Joseph, Jr., *retired gas company executive*
Krayzelburg, Lenny *Olympic athlete*
Kubida, William Joseph *lawyer*
Kupets, Courtney *Olympic athlete*
Kwan, Karen *professional figure skater*
Kwan, Michelle *professional figure skater*
Lang, Naomi *ice skater*
LeMieux, Linda Dailey *museum director*
Littlejohn, John Joseph *petroleum engineer*
Lokken, Steven Lee *chiropractor, nutritionist, internist*
Loux, Gordon Dale *company executive*
Makepeace, Mary Lou *former mayor*
Malchow, Thomas A *Olympic athlete*
Mattoon, James Richard *biology professor*
Matzke, Rex Kay *education educator*
May, Misty *Olympic athlete*
McCool, Courtney *Olympic athlete*
McCready, Guy Michael *lawyer*
McDonough, Ann Patrice *ice skater*
McElhany, Andy *state senator*
McMillan, Larry Donald *engineering executive*
Mehlis, David Lee *publishing executive*
Meyerrose, Dale William *career officer*
Miller, Zoya Dickins (Mrs. Hilliard Eve Miller Jr.) *civic worker*
Milton, Richard Henry *retired diplomat, children's advocate*
Morris, Steven Lynn *engineering consultant, retired career officer*
Munz, Diana *Olympic athlete*
Murphy, James Rodney *playwright*
Nikodinov, Angela *professional figure skater, Olympic athlete*
Noyes, Richard Hall *bookseller*
Olin, Kent Oliver *banker*
Olivas, Phil *secondary school educator*
Olson, Kenneth Paul *vocational consultant*
Oman, Virginia Mills *psychotherapist*
Orner, Linda Price *family therapist, counselor*
Owen, Thomas James *artist, educator*
Pappas, Tom *Olympic track and field athlete*
Partridge, William J. *military officer, government agency administrator*
Patterson, Carly *Olympic athlete*
Peirsol, Aaron *Olympic athlete*
Phelps, Michael *Olympic athlete*
Pickett, David Franklin, Jr., *technology company executive*
Pickle, Joseph Wesley, Jr., *religious studies educator*
Prochaska, Frank Joseph *industrial engineer, educator*
Quann, Megan *Olympic athlete*
Redding, Rogers Walker *physics educator, university official*
Reinitz, Neale Robert *retired literature educator*
Rhodes, Daisy Chun *writer, researcher, oral historian*
Riley, Ruth Ellen *professional basketball player*
Rivera, Lionel *mayor*
Rogers, Steven Ray *physicist*
Rouse, Jeff *Olympic athlete, swimmer*
Sceats, D(onald) James, Jr., *neurological surgeon*
Schultz, Richard Dale *national athletic organization executive*
Schwartz, Donald *chemistry professor*
Scott, Tiffany *ice skater*
Shambo, James Alan *accountant*
Shealy, Courtney *Olympic athlete*
Sheffield, Alden Daniel, Jr., *lawyer*
Shockley-Zalabak, Pamela Sue *academic administrator*
Simerville, James Jasper *pediatrician*
Simmons, George Finlay *retired mathematics professor*
Sinclair, William Donald *state legislator, former church official*
Skora, Wayne Philip *retired air force officer*
Spicer, Ronald L. *financial services educator*
Stahl, Philip Anthony *physics educator*
Standing Bear, Zugguelgeres Galafach *criminologist, forensic scientist, educator*
Stavig, Mark Luther *English language educator*
Stevenson, Bruce Warren *food products executive, researcher*
Storms, William Wallace *physician*
Swanson, Victoria Clare Heldman *lawyer*
Tindall, Jon W. *research scientist*
Todd, Harold Wade *retired association executive, retired air force officer*
Torres, Dara *Olympic athlete*
Tucker, Frank Hammond *history professor*
Tueting, Sarah *professional hockey player*
Vallado, David Anthony *aerospace engineer*
Vandenberg, Sara E. *secondary school educator*
Walsh, Kerri Lee *Olympic athlete*
Wariner, Jeremy *Olympic track and field athlete*
Watts, Oliver Edward *engineering consultancy company executive*
West, Ralph Leland *veterinarian*
Whalin, W. Terry *writer, editor*
Wheeler, Stephen Frederick *legal administrator*
White, Gayle Clay *aerospace company executive*
Williams, Joyce Marilyn *artist, business owner*
Williamson, Paul Michael *music educator*
Wong, Bert Yuan Shu *internist, cardiologist*
Woolridge, Orlando *former professional basketball coach, Olympic coach*
Wright, Laura Keith *editor, writer*
Yanney, Patrick Steven *human resources specialist*
Young, Larry, Sr., *protective services official, educator, investigator*
Zapel, Arthur Lewis *book publishing executive*
Ziemer, Rodger Edmund *electrical engineering educator, consultant*

Columbine Valley

Gagin, Lawrence Vincent *ceramics engineer, consultant*
Plusk, Ronald Frank *manufacturing executive*
Wittbrodt, Edwin Stanley *consultant, former bank executive, former air force officer*

Commerce City

Baker, Maria Luise *retired secondary school educator*
Hayes, James Anthony *city planner, business owner*

Craig

Chason, Renee Lynn *coach, legal coordinator*
Gray, Ann Maynard *broadcasting company executive*

Crested Butte

Fletcher, Donn Wallace *retired investor*

Crestone

Jaynes, Jefferson S. *artist*
Temple, Lee Brett *architect, songwriter, writer*
Wooten-Green, Ronald Clarence *writer*

Cripple Creek
Swanson, Erik Christian *museum director*

Delta
Lowell, Lauretta Jane *craftsperson, poet*
Wendt, John Arthur Frederic, Jr., *lawyer*

Denver
Abo, Ronald Kent *freelance/self-employed architect*
Abram, Donald Eugene *retired federal judge*
Abu-Hejleh, Naser M. *civil engineer, researcher*
Accurso, Frank Joseph *physician, educator*
Adelman, Jonathan Reuben *political science educator, consultant*
Adkins, Jeanne M. *state agency administrator*
Adler, Charles Spencer *psychiatrist*
Ahern, Arleen Fleming *retired librarian*
Aikawa, Jerry Kazuo *physician, educator*
Albig, Irina S. *music educator*
Allen, Barry K. *communications executive, human resources specialist*
Allen, Richard *computer software executive*
Alomar, Sandy, Jr., (Santos Velazquez Alomar) *professional baseball player*
Alsop, Marin *conductor*
Anderson, Donald H. *gas industry executive*
Anderson, John David *architect*
Anderson, Norma V. *state legislator*
Anthony, Carmelo F. *professional basketball player*
Arend, William Phelps *medical researcher*
Ashton, Rick James *librarian*
Asphaug, Rolf Gunnar *lawyer*
Austin, H(arry) Gregory *lawyer*
Avi, (Avi Wortis) *author*
Avrit, Richard Calvin *defense consultant, career officer*
Axley, Hartman *underwriter*
Babiniec, Dennis Henry *lawyer*
Bader, Gerald Louis, Jr., *lawyer*
Baer, Rich *communications executive, lawyer*
Baer, Richard N. (Rich Baer) *lawyer*
Bain, Donald Knight *lawyer*
Balboa, Marcelo *professional soccer player*
Barbour, Alton Bradford *human communication studies educator*
Barnhart, Arthur L. *state official*
Bates, James Robert *newspaper editor*
Baumgartner, Bruce *airport terminal executive*
Bearden, Thomas Howard *news program producer, correspondent*
Belitz, Paul Edward *lawyer*
Bender, Michael Lee *judge*
Benson, Robert Eugene *lawyer*
Benton, Auburn Edgar *lawyer*
Beresford, Thomas Patrick *psychiatry educator, alcoholism researcher*
Berg, Gordon Hercher *banker*
Berry, Gayle *state representative*
Beuerlein, Steve Taylor *professional football player*
Bialasiewicz, Jan Tadeusz *electrical engineering educator*
Blair, Andrew Lane, Jr., *lawyer, educator*
Blatter, Frank Edward *travel agency executive*
Blitz, Stephen M. *lawyer*
Borodkin, Alice *state representative*
Bosworth, Bruce Leighton *school administrator, educator, consultant*
Bourque, Ray *professional hockey player*
Boyd, Betty Ann *state representative*
Bradburn, James Henry *architectural firm executive*
Brantigan, Charles Otto *surgeon*
Breeskin, Michael Wayne *lawyer*
Brimhall, Dennis C. *hospital executive*
Britton, Dennis A. *former newspaper editor, newspaper executive*
Britz, John Dominic, II, *political scientist, consultant*
Brom, Libor *journalist, educator*
Brown, Hank *foundation administrator, former university administrator, former senator*
Brown, Keith Lapham *retired ambassador*
Browne, Spencer Ivan *mortgage company executive, internet executive*
Brownlee, Judith Marilyn *priestess, psychotherapist, psychic*
Buckstein, Caryl Sue *writer*
Bufe, Charles Glenn *geophysicist, researcher*
Bunn, Paul A., Jr., *oncologist, educator*
Burke, Gay Ann Wolesensky *lawyer*
Burrell, Calvin Archie *minister*
Burrows, Bertha Jean *retired academic administrator*
Burshtan, John Willis *television producer*
Butcher, Dorothy *state representative*
Butler, David *lawyer*
Byrne, Thomas J. *lawyer*
Cain, Douglas Mylchreest *lawyer*
Caldwell, Richard A. *director*
Campbell, Leonard M. *lawyer*
Campbell, William J. *lawyer*
Carrigan, Jim R. *arbitrator, mediator, retired judge*
Carroll, Kim Marie *nurse*
Cashman, Michael Richard *small business owner*
Cassidy, Samuel H. *lawyer, lieutenant governor, state legislator, humanities educator*
Ceci, Jesse Arthur *violinist*
Chamberlain, Adrian Ramond *transportation engineer*
Chaput, Charles J. *archbishop*
Charlip, Ralph Blair *military officer, health facility administrator*
Chavez, Jeanette *editor*
Cheroutes, Michael Louis *lawyer*
Childs, John David *retired computer hardware and services company executive*
Chlouber, Ken *state legislator*
Churchill, Mair Elisa Annabelle *medical educator*
Clapp, Lauri *state representative*
Clark, Gary R. *newspaper editor*
Clayton, Mack Louis *surgeon, educator*
Clinch, Nicholas Bayard, III, *business executive*
Coan, Patricia A. *magistrate judge*
Coats, Nathan B. *state supreme court justice*
Cobban, William Aubrey *paleontologist*
Cohen, Jeffrey *lawyer*
Cohn, Aaron I. *anesthesiologist, educator*
Coleman, Fran Natividad *state representative*
Colvis, John Paris *aerospace engineer, mathematician*
Conger, John Janeway *psychologist, educator*
Conover, Frederic King *lawyer*
Conroy, Mary Elizabeth *history professor*
Cook, Albert Thomas Thornton, Jr., *financial advisor*
Cook, Frank Richardson *aeronautical engineer, social scientist*
Cooke, Paul Lewis *state fire marshal*
Coombe, Bob *academic administrator*
Cooper, Paul Douglas *lawyer*
Cope, Thomas Field *lawyer*
Copeland, Eugene Leroy *lawyer, writer*
Covar, Ronina A. *medical educator*
Cox, Louis Anthony, Jr., *telecommunications executive*
Cox, William Vaughan *lawyer*
Crowley, Thomas James *psychiatry educator*
Cruciotti, Augie *communications executive*
Cuba, Stanley L. *government official*
Cubbison, Christopher Allen *newspaper editor*
Curl, Layton Seth *psychologist, consultant, educator*
Dance, Francis Esburn Xavier *communications educator*
Dancik, Jo Marie *accountant, accounting company executive*
Daniels, Martha K. *artist*
Danos, Robert McClure *retired oil company executive*
Davidson, Donetta *secretary of state*
Davis, Jerry Ray *retired railroad company executive*
Davis, R. Steven *lawyer*
Dean, Doug *state representative*
Dean, James Benwell *lawyer*
Decatur, Raylene *former museum director*
Decker, Peter Randolph *rancher, former state official*
Deitrich, Richard Adam *pharmacology educator*
Dennis, Ginette E. (Gigi) *state legislator*
Devine, Sharon Jean *lawyer*
Doida, Stanley Y. *dentist*
Dominick, Peter Hoyt, Jr., *architect*
Dowdle, Patrick Dennis *lawyer*
Drake, Sylvie (Jurras Drake) *theater critic*
Driggs, Margaret *educator*
Ducker, Bruce *novelist, lawyer*
Dugan, Michael Joseph *former career officer, health agency executive*
Dunham, Joan Roberts *administrative assistant*
Dunham, Stephen Sampson *lawyer*
Dunn, Randy Edwin *lawyer*
DuVivier, Katharine Keyes *lawyer, educator*
Dyer, Edward James "Jim" *public utilities commissioner*
Eaton, Gareth Richard *chemistry educator, university dean*
Ebel, David M. *federal judge*
Edelman, Joel *health facility administrator*
Ehret, Josephine Mary *microbiologist, researcher*
Eickhoff, Theodore Carl *epidemiologist*
Elliman, Donald M., Jr., *magazine company executive*
Emery, Henry Alfred *petroleum engineer*
Engdahl, Todd Philip *editor*
Engels, Patricia A. *communications executive*
Enright, Cynthia Lee *illustrator*
Eppler, Jerome Cannon *private financial advisor*
Epps, Mary Ellen *state legislator*
Ernewein, Philippe *educational consultant, educator*
Esposito, Joseph John *publishing company executive*
Evans, Mike *professional basketball coach*
Faatz, Jeanne Ryan *councilperson*
Fails, Thomas Glenn *geologist*
Fasel, Ida *English language educator, writer*
Fay, Richard James *mechanical engineer, executive, educator*
Featherstone, Bruce Alan *lawyer*
Felser, Louis A. *retired corporate financial executive, writer*
Felter, Edwin Lester, Jr., *judge*
Fennessey, Paul Vincent *pediatrics and pharmacology educator, research administrator*
Fentress, Curtis Worth *architectural firm executive*
Fielden, C. Franklin, III, *early childhood education consultant*
Figa, Phillip Sam *judge*
Filley, Christopher Mark *neurologist, researcher*
Fitz-Gerald, Joan *state senator*
Fletcher, Courtney Vance *pharmacologist, educator*
Fogg, Janet *architectural firm executive*
Forsberg, Peter *professional hockey player*
Frederick, Robert Allen *history educator*
Fredmann, Martin *ballet artistic director, educator, choreographer*
Freiheit, Clayton Fredric *zoo director*
Fulkerson, Richard *state agency administrator*
Fulkerson, William Measey, Jr., *college president*
Fuller, Robert Kenneth *architect, urban designer*
Gabow, Patricia Anne *internist, health facility executive*
Gampel, Elaine Susan *investment company executive, consultant*
Garcia, June Marie *librarian*
Gates, Charles Cassius *rubber company executive*
Gates, Chris *not-for-profit developer, political organization worker*
Gehres, James *retired lawyer*
George, Russell Lloyd *lawyer, former state legislator*
Gibbs, Ronald Steven *obstetrician/gynecologist*
Gibson, Elisabeth Jane *retired principal*
Giffin, Glenn Orlando, II, *music critic, writer, newspaper editor*
Gilbert, Alan Jay *lawyer, educator*
Gloss, Lawrence Robert *fundraising executive*
Goeken, Deborah *editor*
Golitz, Loren Eugene *dermatologist, clinical administrator, educator, pathologist*
Gordon, Ken *state senator*
Graham, Pamela Smith *artist, distributing company executive*
Grant, Patrick Alexander *lawyer, association executive*
Grant, William West, III, *banker*
Greyson, Clifford Russell *internist*
Gries, Robbie Rice *geologist, gas and petroleum company executive*
Grilly, Gerald E. *publishing executive*
Grissom, Garth Clyde *lawyer, director*
Haase, Gerald Martin *pediatric surgeon*
Haddon, Harold Alan *lawyer*
Halaby, Theodore S. *political organization worker, retired lawyer*
Halgren, Lee A. *academic administrator*
Haliw, Jerome Michael *civil engineer*
Hall, Larry Dean *business executive, lawyer*
Hall, Richard Murray, Jr., *finance executive, consultant*
Hankinson, Tim *soccer coach*
Hansen, Bruce D. *mining executive*
Hardaway, Timothy Duane *professional basketball player*
Harmsen, Dorothy *food products executive*
Harris, Dale Ray *lawyer*
Harris, Robert Adron *pharmacologist*
Hautzinger, James Edward *lawyer*
Havekost, Daniel John *architect*
Hawley, Robert Cross *lawyer*
Hefley, Lynn A. *state representative*
Heiserman, Robert Gifford *lawyer*
Helton, Todd *professional baseball player*
Hendrix, Lynn Parker *lawyer*
Hensen, Stephen Jerome *lawyer*
Hernandez, Robert Michael *state legislator, software engineer*
Hetzel, Fredrick William *biophysicist, educator*
Hickenlooper, John W. *mayor*
Hirschfeld, Arlene *civic worker, homemaker*
Hoagland, Donald Wright *lawyer*
Hobbs, Gregory James, Jr., *state supreme court justice*
Hodge, Mary *state representative*
Hodges, Joseph Gilluly, Jr., *lawyer*
Hoehn, Margaret Maier *neurologist*
Hoehn, Robert J. *plastic surgeon, educator*
Hoffman, Daniel Steven *lawyer, law educator*
Hoffman, Murray Stanley *internist, cardiologist, educator*
Hogan, Curtis Jule *union executive, industrial relations consultant*
Holme, Howard Kelley *lawyer, executive*
Holme, Richard Phillips *lawyer*
Holmes, Randall Kent *microbiology educator, academic administrator, internist, infectious disease physician*
Holtz, Clifford S. *communications executive*
Hopfenbeck, George Martin, Jr., *lawyer*
Hoppe, Phyllis Diane *state representative*
Horwitz, Kathryn Bloch *molecular biologist, educator, breast cancer researcher*
Houtsma, Peter C. *lawyer*
Howard, W. Scott *language educator*
Howse, Cathy L. *writer, researcher, entrepreneur*
Huang, Linda Chen *plastic surgeon*
Hughes, Bradley Richard *business executive*
Hughes, J(ohnson) Donald *history educator, editor*
Hurdle, Clint *professional athletics manager*
Hynek, Frederick James *architect*
Imhoff, Walter Francis *investment banker*
Imig, William Graff *lawyer, lobbyist*
Irwin, R. Robert *lawyer*
Jacobs, Paul Alan *lawyer*
Jafek, Bruce William *otolaryngologist, educator*
Jahn, Cheri E. *state representative*
Jarles, Ruth Sewell *education educator*
Johnson, Candice Elaine Brown *pediatrics educator*
Johnson, Geraldine Esch *language specialist*
Johnson, Harold Earl *human resources specialist*
Johnson, Walter Earl *geophysicist*
Johnston, Gwinavere Adams *public relations consultant*
Johnston, Richard Boles, Jr., *pediatrician, educator, biomedical researcher*
Johnston, Van Robert *management educator*
Jones, M. Douglas, Jr., *pediatrician, educator*
Jones, Richard Michael *lawyer*
Joyce, Mary Holt *retired social worker*
Judson, Franklyn Nevin *physician, educator*
Kahn, Edwin Sam *lawyer*
Kane, John Lawrence, Jr., *judge*
Kaplan, Sheila *academic administrator*
Kariya, Paul *professional hockey player*
Karsh, Philip Howard *advertising executive*
Keatinge, Robert Reed *lawyer*
Keithley, Roger Lee *judge*
Keller, Glen Elven, Jr., *lawyer*
Keller, Maryanne *state senator*
Kerwin, Mary Ann Collins *lawyer*
Kestenbaum, Richard *psychologist*
Kindt, Glenn W. *neurosurgeon, educator*
Kintzele, John Alfred *lawyer*
Kirshbaum, Howard M. *retired judge, arbiter*
Klipping, Robert Samuel *geophysicist*
Klump, Ron *food products executive*
Knaus, Tim *political organization administrator*
Knights, Ronald Michael *business educator*
Koul, Hari Krishen *research scientist, rights activist*
Krendl, Cathy Stricklin *lawyer*
Krieger, Marcia Smith *federal judge*
Krikos, George Alexander *pathologist, educator*
Kruger, Paula *telecommunications industry executive*
Krugman, Richard David *pediatrician, academic administrator, educator*
Krysiak, William J. *gas industry executive*
Kung, Malgorzata Laptas *architect*
Kurtz, Maxine *personnel consultant, lawyer*
Lacy, Elsie *state legislator*
LaMendola, Walter Franklin *technology educator, business executive*
Lamm, Richard Douglas *lawyer, former governor of Colorado*
Lance, Keith Curry *library and information scientist*
Landesman, Howard M. *academic administrator*
Landon, Susan Melinda *petroleum geologist*
La Rosa, Francisco Guillermo *pathologist, researcher, educator*
Larsen, Gary Loy *physician, researcher*
Lassonde, Peirre *mining executive*
Law, John Manning *retired lawyer*
Lazarus, Steven S. *management consultant, marketing consultant*
Lee, Lela A. *dermatology educator, researcher*
Leprino, James G. *food products executive*
Leraaen, Allen Keith *financial executive*
Lerman, Eileen R. *lawyer*
Levinson, Shauna T. *financial services executive*
Lillehei, Kevin Owen *neurosurgeon, educator*
Lincoln, Alexander, III, *financial analyst, lawyer, private investor*
Lindenfeld, JoAnn *physician, educator*
Livingston, Johnston Redmond *manufacturing executive*
Lockspeiser, Nancy Flanders *artist, designer*
Logan, James Scott, Sr., *federal agency administrator*
Long, Francis Mark *retired electrical engineer*
Low, Andrew M. *lawyer*
Low, John Wayland *lawyer*
Low, Merry Cook *civic worker*
Lubeck, Marvin Jay *ophthalmologist*
Lucero, Carlos *federal judge*
Lundy, Barbara Jean *training executive*
Lutsky, Sheldon Jay *financial and marketing consultant, writer*
Lutz, John Shafroth *lawyer*
Lytle, Gary R. *communications executive*
Macey, William Blackmore *oil company executive*
MacGregor, George Lescher, Jr., *freelance writer*
Mackey, Pamela Robillard *lawyer*
Mackinnon, Peggy Louise *public relations executive*
Maldonado, Kirk Francis *lawyer*
Mandarich, David D. *real estate corporation executive*
Marcum, Walter Phillip *manufacturing executive*
Markovchick, Vincent J. *surgeon*
Marquess, Lawrence Wade *lawyer*
Marshall, Rosemary *state representative*
Martin, Dallas Rea *lawyer*
Martin, J. Landis *manufacturing company executive, lawyer*
Martin, Kenyon *professional basketball player*
Martin, Richard Jay *medical educator*
Martinez, Alex J. *state supreme court justice*
Martz, Clyde Ollen *lawyer, educator*
Mathews, Laurie A. *state agency administrator*
Matsukage, Fay Mariko *lawyer*
Maul, Carol Elaine *small business owner*
Mauro, Richard Frank *lawyer, investment manager*
Maurstad, David Ingolf *federal agency administrator, insurance company executive*
May, Ron *state senator*
Maytham, Thomas Northrup *art and museum consultant*
McAtee, Patricia Anne Rooney *medical educator*
McCabe, John L. *lawyer*
McCandless, Bruce, II, *aerospace engineer, retired astronaut*
McConnell, Michael Theodore *lawyer*
McDonald, Kirk *publishing executive*
McDonnell, Barbara *lawyer*
McElhinney, James Lancel *artist, educator*
McFadyen, Liane *state representative*
McGuane, Frank L., Jr., *lawyer*
McIntosh, Carolyn Leigh *lawyer*
McKenna, Frederick Gregory *lawyer, consultant*
McMichael, Donald Earl *lawyer*
McMorris, Jerry *transportation company executive, sports team executive*
McVaney, C. Edward *computer software executive*
McWilliams, Robert Hugh *federal judge*
Meiklejohn, Alvin J., Jr., *state legislator, lawyer, accountant*
Meininger, Steven Robert *music educator*
Mendez, Celestino Galo *mathematics professor*
Mendez, William Humbert *family medicine physician*
Merker, Steven Joseph *lawyer*
Merritt, Jeralyn E. *lawyer*
Messer, Donald Edward *theological school president, theology educator*
Meurlin, Keith W. *airport manager*
Miller, Gale Timothy *lawyer*
Miller, Robert Nolen *lawyer*
Miller, Walker David *judge*
Minger, Terrell John *public administration and natural resource institute executive*
Mitchem, Allen P. *lawyer*
Mizel, Larry A. *housing construction company executive*
Moore, Ernest Eugene, Jr., *surgeon, educator*
Moore, George Eugene *surgeon*
Moore, Gregory L. *editor*
Morales, John Paul *television services producer*
Moulton, Jennifer T. *city official, architect*
Mueller, Kathryn Lucile *occupational and environmental medicine educator*
Mullarkey, Mary J. *state supreme court chief justice*
Mullineaux, Donal Ray *geologist*
Murane, William Edward *lawyer*
Murdock, Pamela Ervilla *travel and advertising company executive*
Murdy, Wayne William *mining company executive, financial officer*
Myhren, Trygve Edward *communications company executive*
Nelson, Bernard William *foundation executive, educator, physician*
Nelson, Nevin Mary *interior designer*
Nelson, Sarah Milledge *archaeology educator*
Nemiro, Beverly Mirium Anderson *author, educator*
Neumann, Herschel *physics educator*
Neumeyer, Zachary T. *hotel executive*
Newcom, Jennings Jay *lawyer*
Newman, Bob *radio personality, security consultant*
Nichol, Alice J. *state legislator*
Nicholson, Will Faust, Jr., *bank holding company executive*
Norman, John Edward *petroleum landman*
Norton, Jane E. *lieutenant governor*
Notebaert, Richard C. *telecommunications industry executive*
Nottingham, Edward Willis, Jr., *federal judge*
Novins, Douglas K. *psychiatrist, educator*
Nuñez, Joe C. *federal agency administrator*
Nutting, Paul Albert *medical educator, medical science administrator*
Oakes, Terry Louis *retail clothing store executive*
Obermeier, Tom *architectural firm executive*
O'Conner, Loretta Rae *lawyer*
O'Keefe, Edward Franklin *lawyer*
Olsen, M. Kent *lawyer, educator*
Orullian, B. LaRae *bank executive*
Osborn, Susan Chaney *writer, educator*
Outlaw, Lanny F. *gas company executive*
Owen, David Turner *state legislator, owner, operator*
Owens, Bill *governor*
Owens, Marvin Franklin, Jr., *oil company executive*
Pack, Stuart Harris *lawyer*
Page, Polly E. *state agency administrator*
Palmer, David Gilbert *lawyer*
Parker, Catherine Susanne *psychotherapist*
Pascoe, Donald Monte *lawyer*
Pearson, Michelle Line *private school educator, not-for-profit fundraiser*
Perez, Jean-Yves *engineering company executive*
Perington, Philip *management investment company executive*
Perlmutter, Leonard Michael *concrete construction company executive*
Petty, Thomas Lee *physician, educator*
Pfenninger, Karl H. *cell biology and neuroscience educator*
Pfnister, Allan Orel *humanities educator*
Piland, Neill Finnes *health services economist, researcher*
Piper, Steven Lee *economist*

Plummer, Ora Beatrice *nursing educator, trainer*
Pointer, Marsha G. *principal*
Poirot, James Wesley *engineering company executive*
Pomerantz, Marvin *thoracic surgeon*
Ponzi, James Doughlas *police officer, computer specialist*
Porfilio, John Carbone *federal judge*
Porter, J. Reid *engineering executive*
Potter, Gary Thomas *lawyer*
Price, Kathleen McCormick *book editor, writer*
Prochnow, James R. *lawyer*
Prosser, John Martin *architect, educator, urban design consultant*
Puck, Theodore Thomas *geneticist, biophysicist, educator*
Quenneville, Joel *professional hockey coach*
Quiat, Gerald M. *lawyer*
Rabinovitch, Nathan *pediatrician, educator*
Rael, Henry Sylvester, Sr., *retired health administrator, financial and management consultant*
Ragland, Bob *artist, educator*
Ragsdale, Ann F. *state representative*
Rainer, William Gerald *cardiac surgeon*
Ramji, Al-Noor *telecommunications industry executive*
Raughton, Jimmie Leonard *education consultant, public administrator, urban planner*
Ray, Bruce David *lawyer, writer*
Reeves, Peggy *state legislator*
Reidy, Mike *food products executive*
Rench, Stephen Charles *lawyer*
Repine, John Edward *internist, educator*
Rhodes, Pamela *state representative*
Rice, Nancy E. *judge*
Rich, Robert Stephen *lawyer*
Richardson, Elizabeth Hall *retired ecologist*
Ritchie, Daniel Lee *academic administrator*
Robertson, Lawrence Marshall, Jr., *neurosurgeon*
Robins, Judy Roselyn *interior designer*
Robinson, Cleo Parker *artistic director*
Rockwell, Bruce McKee *retired banker and foundation executive*
Roellig, Mark D. *telecommunications industry executive, lawyer*
Roesler, John Bruce *lawyer*
Rogers, Joe *former lieutenant governor*
Ronning, Charlotte Jean *foreign language educator*
Rothman, Paul Alan *publishing executive*
Rovira, Luis Dario *state supreme court justice*
Rowe, Tina L. *government official*
Rubin, Cathy Ann *retired educator*
Ruge, Daniel August *retired neurosurgeon, educator*
Rupert, Dorothy *state legislator*
Ruppert, John Lawrence *lawyer*
Sakic, Joe (Joseph Steve Sakic) *professional hockey player*
Salazar, Kenneth L. *state attorney general*
Saltz, Howard Joel *newspaper editor*
Samuels, Donald L. *lawyer*
Sandler, Thomas R. *accountant*
Sandoval, Paula E. *state senator*
Satter, Raymond Nathan *judge*
Sattler, Bruce Weimer *lawyer*
Sayre, John Marshall *lawyer, former government official*
Scheid, Steven L. *investment company executive*
Schiff, Donald Wilfred *pediatrician, educator*
Schrier, Robert William *physician, educator*
Schultz, Janet K. *nursing consultant, business executive*
Schwartz, Cherie Anne Karo *storyteller, writer*
Scudder, Richard B. *newspaper executive*
Seawell, Donald Ray *lawyer, publisher, arts center executive, producer*
Seiple, John W., Jr., *corporate financial executive*
Shaffer, Oren George *former manufacturing company executive*
Sharp, Lewis I. *museum director*
Sheeran, Michael John Leo *priest, college administrator*
Shepherd, John Frederic *lawyer*
Shore, James H(enry) *psychiatrist*
Shreve, Theodore Norris *construction company executive*
Shwayder, Elizabeth Yanish *sculptor*
Silverman, Arnold *pediatrician, educator*
Singleton, William Dean *publishing executive*
Smith, Daniel Timothy *lawyer*
Smith, Dwight Morrell *chemistry professor, academic administrator*
Smith, Laurie Hyson *lawyer*
Smith, Sallye Wrye *librarian*
Smith, William French, II, *safety engineer, special projects administrator*
Snyder, Charles Royce *sociologist, educator*
Spence, Nancy Joan *state representative*
Spies, Allan *telecommunications executive*
Spradley, Lola *state representative*
Springer, Jeffrey Alan *lawyer*
Stafford, Debbie *state representative*
Steefel, David Simon *lawyer*
Steenhagen, Robert Lewis *landscape architect, consultant*
Stephens, Larry Dean *engineer, consultant*
Stephenson, Arthur Emmet, Jr., *corporate and investment company executive*
Stockton, Kevin W. *insurance and investment professional*
Storey, Brit Allan *historian*
Strand, Melford Lien *anesthesiologist*
Strenski, Robert Francis *lawyer*
Studevant, Laura *medical association administrator*
Sujansky, Eva Borska *pediatrician, geneticist, educator*
Suthers, John William *prosecutor*
Swihart, Steven Taylor *judge*
Szefler, Stanley James *pediatrics and pharmacology educator*
Takeda, Yasuhiko *pathologist*
Takis, Stephanie *state senator*
Talman, Louis A. *mathematician*
Tanabe, Charles Y. *lawyer*
Tanner, Gloria Travis *state legislator*
Tate, Penfield *state senator*
Taussig, Lynn Max *healthcare administrator, pulmonologist, pediatrician, educator*
Taylor, Edward Stewart *physician, educator*
Taylor, Julia Fisher *communications executive*
Taylor, Teresa *communications executive*
Temple, John R. *publishing executive*
Thomasch, Roger Paul *lawyer*
Thompson, Cathy Joanne *nursing educator, consultant, acute care nurse practitioner*
Thompson, Joseph Paul *retired systems administrator*
Thompson, Lohren Matthew *oil company executive*
Tisdale, Douglas Michael *lawyer*
Trueblood, Harry Albert, Jr., *oil company executive*
Truhlar, Robert J. *lawyer*
Tupa, Ron *state senator*
Tyler, Kenneth Laurence *neurologist, researcher*
Tymkovich, Timothy Michael *federal judge*
Ulrich, Theodore Albert *lawyer*
Veiga, Jennifer *state representative*
Vigil, Jeffrey L. *infant and child products manufacturing executive*
Vogel, Robert Lee *retired college administrator, clergyman*
Volpe, Richard Gerard *insurance accounts executive, consultant*
Vosevich, Kathi Ann *writer, editor, scholar*
Wade, Karen *federal agency administrator*
Wagner, Judith Buck *investment firm executive*
Waldstein, Gail P. *pediatric pathologist, writer*
Walker, Joan H. *marketing and communications executive*
Walker, Larry Kenneth Robert *professional baseball player*
Walker, Radford *computer system architect*
Walker, Timothy Blake *lawyer, educator*
Ward, Lester Lowe, Jr., *arts executive, lawyer*
Weatherley-White, Roy Christopher Anthony *surgeon, consultant*
Wedgle, Richard Jay *lawyer*
Weihaupt, John George *geosciences educator, scientist, university administrator*
Weil, Jack Baum *clothing manufacturing company executive*
Weinshienk, Zita Leeson *federal judge*
Weston, William Lee *dermatologist*
Wetzel, Jodi (Joy Lynn Wetzel) *history and women's studies educator*
Wheeler, Malcolm Edward *lawyer, educator*
White, John David *composer, theorist, cellist*
White, Joyce Louise *librarian*
Wiggs, Eugene Overbey *ophthalmologist, educator*
Wilkinson, Joan Kristine *nurse, pediatric clinical specialist*
Wilks, Lewis O. *telecommunications company executive*
Williams, Andrea Irene *arbitrator, mediator, consultant*
Williams, Michael Anthony *lawyer*
Williams, Suzanne *state representative*
Williams, Tambor *state representative*
Windels, Sue *state senator*
Winters, Richard Allen *mineral economist*
Wirkler, Norman Edward *retired architectural, engineering, construction management firm executive*
Witt, Catherine Lewis *neonatal nurse practitioner, writer*
Woerner, Robert Eugene *federal agency administrator, editor*
Wohlgenant, Richard Glen *lawyer, director*
Wolman, Jonathan Paley *journalist*
Woodward, Lester Ray *lawyer*
Wright, Carole Dean *reading specialist*
Wunnicke, Brooke *lawyer*
Yegge, Robert Bernard *law educator, dean*
Zanecchia, Thomas Edward *financial executive*
Zimet, Carl Norman *psychologist, educator*
Zimmer, Larry William, Jr., *sports announcer*

Dillon

Becker, Quinn Henderson *orthopedic surgeon, military officer*
Follett, Robert John Richard *publisher*
Roder, Hans Martin *retired physicist, consultant*
Townsend, James Douglas *accountant*

Dolores

Kreyche, Gerald Francis *retired philosophy educator*

Durango

Ballantine, Morley Cowles (Mrs. Arthur Atwood Ballantine) *editor*
Burnham, Bryson Payne *retired lawyer*
Fogleman, Ronald Robert *retired air force officer, consultant*
Foster, James Henry *advertising and public relations executive*
Jones, Joel Mackey *academic administrator*
Korns, Leota Elsie *writer, mountain land developer, insurance broker*
Langoni, Richard Allen *civil engineer*
Reid-Bills, Mae *magazine editor, historian*
Van Mols, Brian *publishing executive*
Wigton, Chester Mahlon *family physician*
Zeller, Christopher Lee *archaeologist, preservationist*

Edwards

Chambers, Joan Louise *retired librarian, retired dean*

Eldorado Springs

Lovins, L. Hunter *public policy institute executive*

Englewood

Ahearn, Joseph August *military officer, civil engineer*
Bailey, Champ *professional football player*
Baratta, Robert M. *holding company executive*
Barbezat, Eugene LaVar *computer systems engineer, retired air force officer*
Bartee, Roy McKinley, II, *anesthesiologist*
Bennett, Robert R. *communications executive*
Bingham, Paris Edward, Jr., *electrical engineer, computer consultant*
Bondi, Bert Roger *accountant, financial planner*
Bowlen, Pat(rick)(Dennis) *professional sports team executive, holding company executive, lawyer*
Bradshaw, Beverly Jean *psychotherapist, consultant, educator*
Brennan, Joann *photographer, educator*
Campbell, Michael L. *recreational facility executive*
Chavez, Lloyd G. *automotive executive*
Cooper, Steven Jon *healthcare management consultant, educator*
Davis, Terrell *former professional football player*
DeMuth, Alan Cornelius *lawyer*
DeMuth, Laurence Wheeler, Jr., *lawyer, utilities executive*
Erickson, William Hurt *retired state supreme court justice*
Gertz, David Lee *homebuilding company executive*
Grant, Paul *chemical engineer, manufacturer's representative, real estate broker*
Graves, Nada Proctor *retired elementary school educator*
Griese, Brian *professional football player*
Guggenheim-Boucard, Alan Andre Albert Paul Edouard *business executive, international consultant*
Iapalucci, Samuel H. *financial executive*
Jones, Glenn Robert *cable systems executive*
Karstaedt, Arthur R., III, *lawyer*
Keegan, James Joseph *financial executive*
Keesling, Ruth Morris *foundation administrator*
Knize, David Maurice *plastic surgeon*
Kristin, Karen *artist*
Lamb, Darlis Carol *sculptor*
Lambert, Shirley Anne *marketing professional, publisher*
Lessey, Samuel Kenric, Jr., *foundation administrator*
Lidstone, Herrick Kenley, Jr., *lawyer*
Lubetkin, Alvin Nat *sporting goods retail company executive*
Lynch, John Terrence *professional football player*
Mahoney, Gerald Francis *manufacturing executive*
Makowski, Edgar Leonard *obstetrician and gynecologist*
Malone, John C. *telecommunications executive*
McGlockton, Chester *professional football player*
McGraw, Jack Wilson *federal agency administrator*
Miles, Amy E. *recreational facility executive*
Moran, Gregory Allan *real estate developer, real estate agent*
Neiser, Brent Allen *foundation executive, public affairs and personal finance consultant, speaker*
Oshman, Marilyn *retail executive*
Peters, Janice C. *cable company executive*
Peterson, Ralph Randall *engineering executive*
Plummer, Jason Steven (Jake Plummer) *professional football player*
Reese, Monte Nelson *agricultural association executive*
Rosser, Edwin Michael *mortgage company executive*
Shanahan, Mike *professional football coach*
Shannon, Malcolm Lloyd, Jr., *lawyer*
Shields, Marlene Sue *elementary school educator*
Sideman, Jill *engineering executive*
Smith, Neil *professional football player*
Smith, Rod *professional football player*
Somers, Daniel E. *telecommunications industry executive*
Spencer, Margaret Gilliam *lawyer*
Steinhauser, John William *retired lawyer*
Van Loucks, Mark Louis *venture capitalist, business advisor*
Woodward, John Simpson, Jr., *orthopedic surgeon*

Erie

Alpers, John Hardesty, Jr., *financial planning executive, retired military officer*
Plehaty, Phyllis Juliette *curator*

Estes Park

Cope, James Dudley *retired trade association executive*
Guest, Linda Sand *education educator*
Marr, James Joseph *venture capitalist*
Ojalvo, Morris *civil engineer, educator*
Piper, Mark Harry *retired banker*
Webb, Richard C. *engineering company executive*

Evergreen

Dobbs, Gregory Allan *journalist*
Haun, John Daniel *petroleum geologist, educator*
Heyl, Allen Van, Jr., *geologist*
Jackson, William Richard *entrepreneur*
McEldowney, Roland Conant *mining executive, photographer*
Rodolff, Dale Ward *engineer, sales executive, consultant*

Falcon AFB

Dylewski, Gary R. *retired career officer*

Fort Carson

Stanbro, Heather Aspen *emergency medical technician*

Fort Collins

Abt, Steven R. *civil engineering educator, dean*
Anderson, John Albert *physician*
Baldwin, Lionel Vernon *retired university president*
Bamburg, James Robert *biochemistry educator*
Benjamin, Stephen Alfred *veterinary medicine educator, environmental pathologist, researcher*
Bennett, Thomas LeRoy, Jr., *clinical neuropsychology educator*
Bernstein, Elliot Roy *chemistry professor*
Butki, Brian David *psychologist, educator*
Carlson, Alan Douglas *lawyer*
Cermak, Jack Edward *engineer, educator*
Chorpenning, H. R., III, *minister*
Christiansen, Norman Juhl *retired newspaper publisher*
Collet, Vicki S. *literature educator*
Downey, Arthur Harold, Jr., *lawyer, mediator*
Eitzen, David Stanley *sociologist, educator*
Emslie, William Arthur *electrical engineer*
Estep, Donald Joseph *mathematician, educator*
Evans, Norman Allen *retired civil engineering educator*
Ewing, Jack Robert *accountant*
Follett, Ronald Francis *soil scientist*
Gadaleta, Sabino *research scientist*
Gandy, H. Conway *retired judge, state official*
Garvey, Daniel Cyril *mechanical engineer*
Gillette, Edward LeRoy *radiation oncology educator*
Grandin, Temple *industrial designer*
Grigg, Neil S. *civil engineering educator*
Hallahan, Kirk Edward *journalism educator*
Han, Binbing *research scientist*
Harper, Judson Morse *retired university administrator, consultant, educator*
Heird, James C. *agricultural studies educator*
Hjelmfelt, David Charles *lawyer*
Hultgren, Glenn M. *chiropractor*
Jensen, Margaret *real estate broker*
Johnson, Donald Edward, Jr., *lawyer*
Johnson, Robert Britten *geology educator*
Karbula, John Charles *principal*
Keim, Wayne Franklin *retired genetics educator, plant geneticist*
Kenney, Wes, III, *conductor*
Kinnison, Robert Wheelock *retired accountant*
Kohli, Sandeep *materials scientist, researcher*
Kosoy, Michael Y. *biomedical researcher*
Kraus, David (Dirk) Bruce *musician, educator*
Lameiro, Gerard Francis *corporate strategist*
Loy, Ivan *mathematician, educator*
Lumb, William Valjean *veterinarian*
MacLauchlin, Robert Kerwin *communications artist, educator*
Maher, Thomas George *academic administrator, producer, media educator*
Matthies, Frederick John *civil and environmental engineer*
May, Stephen James *communications educator, writer*
Mc Clellan, William Monson *library administrator, retired*
McComb, David Glendinning *history educator*
Meyers, Albert Irving *emeritus chemistry educator*
Mielke, Paul William, Jr., *statistician, consultant*
Moorcroft, William Herbert *retired bio-psychologist, educator, researcher*
Mortvedt, John Jacob *soil scientist, researcher*
Nicholls, Peter J. *academic administrator*
Niswender, Gordon Dean *physiologist, educator*
Nobe, Kenneth Charles *international agricultural and water resource economics consultant*
Ogg, James Elvis *microbiologist, educator*
Ozawa, Terutomo *economics educator, consultant*
Patton, Carl Elliott *physics educator*
Perryman, Lance *dean*
Peterson, Gary Andrew *agronomics researcher*
Phemister, Robert David *veterinary medical educator*
Reif, John Steven *epidemiologist, veterinarian*
Richardson, Everett Vern *hydraulic engineer, educator, administrator, consultant*
Roberts, Archibald Edward *retired career officer, writer*
Roehrig, John T. *immunologist, educator*
Roesner, Larry August *civil engineer*
Rogers, Garth Winfield *lawyer*
Rollin, Bernard Elliot *philosophy educator, consultant*
Rolston, Holmes, III, *theologian, educator, philosopher*
Sandborn, Virgil Alvin *civil engineer, educator*
Savage, Eldon Paul *retired environmental health educator*
Schendel, Winfried George *insurance company executive*
Seidel, George Elias, Jr., *animal scientist, educator*
Shively, Robert William *urban planner*
Smith, Dwight Raymond *ecology and wildlife educator, writer*
Smith, Ralph Earl *virologist*
Sons, Raymond William *journalist*
Sprague, Amaris Jeanne *real estate broker*
Suinn, Richard Michael *psychologist*
Terauds, Juris *retired science educator, research scientist*
Thierstein, Gerald E. (Gerry Thierstein) *retired agricultural engineer*
Tremblay, William Andrew *English language educator, writer*
Tyler, Gail Madeleine *nurse*
Vonder Haar, Thomas H. *meteorology educator*
Watz, Martin Charles *brewery consultant*
Yates, Albert Carl *academic administrator, chemistry educator*

Fort Garland

Boyer, Lester Leroy, Jr., *architecture educator, consultant*
Moullette, John Brinkley *retired corporate trainer, consultant*

Fort Morgan

Raines, Louis Edward *school administrator*

Fowler

Fox, Jonathan Randall *banker, real estate broker, insurance agent*

Fraser

Hibbs, John David *computer company executive, electrical engineer, small business owner*

Frisco

Helmer, David Alan *lawyer*

Fruita

Bowles, Kelley Kay *secondary school educator, writer*

Georgetown

Hildebrandt-Willard, Claudia Joan *banker*
Stern, Mort(imer) P(hillip) *journalism and communications educator, academic administrator, consultant*

Golden

Alberts, Celia Anne *lawyer*
Baron, Robert Charles *publishing executive*
Bickart, Theodore Albert *university president emeritus*
Boumann, Robert Lyle *lawyer*
Christensen, Robert Wayne *oral maxillofacial surgeon, minister*
Coors, Jeffrey H. *technology manufacturing executive*
Coors, Peter Hanson *brewery company executive*
Dickinson, Carol Rittgers *arts administrator, writer, executive director*
Duke, Michael B. *aerospace scientist*
Eckley, Wilton Earl, Jr., *humanities educator, educator*
Eiberger, Carl Frederick *lawyer*
Fleener, Terry Noel *marketing professional*
Gosink, Joan P. *engineering educator*
Hamilton, Warren Bell *geologist, researcher, geophysicist, educator*
Hopper, Sally Hunter *former state legislator*
Karlin, Joel Marvin *allergist*
Kiely, W. Leo, III, *brewery company executive*
Klug, John Joseph *secondary school educator, director*
Kopel, David Benjamin *lawyer*
Krauss, George *metallurgist*
Lindsay, Nathan James *space systems consultant, retired military officer*
Lott, Brenda Louise *insurance company executive*

Mathews, E. Anne Jones *library educator and administrator, consultant*
Matthews, Thomas Michael *former energy company executive*
Myers, Daryl Ronald *engineer*
Olson, Marian Katherine *management executive, consultant, publisher*
Payton, Roger *logistics company executive*
Petrick, Alfred, Jr., *mineral economics educator, consultant*
Phillipson, Donald E. *lawyer*
Rodgers, Frederic Barker *judge*
Scott, Gregory Kellam *judge trial referee, former state supreme court justice, lawyer*
Shea, Dion Warren Joseph *university official, fund raiser*
Sloan, Earle Dendy, Jr., *chemical engineering educator*
Speer, John Gordon *metallurgist, educator, materials scientist, educator*
Spurck, Richard Francis *materials engineer*
Stewart, Frank Maurice, Jr., *federal agency administrator*
Trefny, John Ulric *college president*
Truly, Richard H. *academic administrator, former federal agency administrator, former astronaut*
Weimer, Robert Jay *geology educator, energy consultant, civic leader*
Wolf, Timothy Van de Wint *food products company executive*
Zhong, Dalong *materials scientist, consultant*
Zunger, Alex *research scientist*

Granby
Johnson, William Potter *publishing executive, director*

Grand Junction
Bacon, Phillip *geographer, author, consultant*
Bishop, Tilman Malcolm *retired state legislator, college administrator*
Griff, Harry *lawyer*
Janson, Richard Anthony *plastic surgeon*
Layton, Robert Glenn *radiologist*
Morton, Louis George *retired social sciences educator*
Nelson, Paul William *real estate broker*
Nizalowski, John Anthony *writer, educator*
Pantenburg, Michel *hospital administrator, health educator, holistic health coordinator*
Rutz, Richard Frederick *physicist, researcher*
Rybak, James Patrick *engineering educator*
Skogen, Haven Sherman *investment company executive*
Tavossi, Hasson M. *physics and engineering educator, consultant*

Greeley
Bond, Richard Randolph *foundation administrator, legislator*
Carrico, Stephen J. *construction company executive*
Conway, Rebecca Ann Koppes *lawyer*
Cook, Donald E. *pediatrician, educator*
Duff, William Leroy, Jr., *university dean emeritus, business educator*
Ebomoyi, William Ehigie *epidemiologist*
Frey, Henry Charles *lawyer*
James, Philip J. *agricultural products executive*
Jaouen, Richard Matthie *plastic surgeon*
Jenkins, Virginia *visual arts educator, artist*
Kelsey, Michael Loyal *geography educator*
Knott, Alexander Waller *historian, educator*
Miller, Diane Wilmarth *retired human resources director*
Morgensen, Jerry Lynn *construction company executive*
Schrenk, Gary Dale *foundation executive*
Simons, John S. *food products executive*
Willis, Connie (Constance E. Willis) *author*
Woody, William Douglas *social sciences educator, researcher*
Worley, Lloyd Douglas *English language educator*

Greenwood Village
Appel, Joel *household cleaner manufacturing executive*
Arvizu, Dan Eliab *mechanical engineer*
Aspinwall, David Charles *lawyer, insurance company executive*
Bain, James William *lawyer*
Battista, Guy *information technology executive*
Benson, Robert Craig, III, *business consultant*
Chesser, Al H. *union official*
Cooper, Ronald *broadcast executive*
Davidson, John Robert (Jay) *bank executive*
Dymond, Lewis Wandell *lawyer, mediator, educator*
Grainger, John R. *medical association administrator*
Hendrick, Hal Wilmans *human factors educator*
Lazarus, Jeremy A. *psychiatrist*
Liniger, Dave *real estate company executive*
Lynn, Patricia Anne *student services representative*
Magoun, Harold Ives, Jr., *osteopath*
McVey, Larry *household cleaner manufacturing executive*
Poe, Robert Alan *lawyer*
Ramsey, John Arthur *lawyer*
Sims, Douglas D. *bank executive*

Guffey
Ward, Larry Thomas *social program administrator*

Henderson
Sauceda, Augustina Jo *pre-school educator*

Highlands Ranch
Brierley, Corale L. *geological engineer*
Brierley, James Alan *biohydrometallurgy consultant*
Bublitz, Deborah Keirstead *pediatrician*
Fiess, Stephen Charles Edward *musician, music educator*
Harris, Douglas Clay *retired newspaper executive*
Hastey, Joe *engineering executive*
Hoover, Gary Lynn *banker*
Krinsky, Fredda S. *clinical chemist, consultant*
Margolis, Bette Shula *writer, educator*

Hotchkiss
Blackstock, Virginia Harriett *artist*
Ela, William MacHarg *judge, mediator, arbitrator*

Idledale
Brown, Gerri Ann *physical therapist*

Ignacio
Craig, Roy Phillip *writer, educator, rancher*

Jefferson
Maatsch, Deborah Joan *manufacturing executive*

Kersey
Guttersen, Michael *rancher, investor*

La Jara
Portnoy, Darin Arthur *medical association administrator*

La Veta
Zehring, Peggy Johnson *artist*

Lafayette
Conrad, Kelley Allen *industrial and organizational psychologist*
Hollaran, Carolyn Rada *writer, small business owner*
Manka, Ronald Eugene *lawyer*
McNeill, William *environmental scientist*
Middlebrooks, Eddie Joe *environmental engineer*
Short, Ray Everett *minister, sociology educator emeritus, author, lecturer*

Lake George
Norman, John Barstow, Jr., *designer, educator*

Lakewood
Bailey, Zelda Chapman *hydrologist*
Barber, Larry Eugene *financial planner*
Barger, Louise Baldwin *religious organization administrator*
Barrett, Michael Henry *civil engineer*
Bettinghaus, Erwin Paul *research scientist*
Buckelew, Larry C. *lab administrator*
Burkholder, Steve *mayor*
Corboy, James McNally *investment banker*
Fugate, Ivan Dee *banker, lawyer*
Goldman, L. Barton *physician*
Guyton, Samuel Percy *retired lawyer*
Hanna, Deanna *state senator*
Hansen, Richard Olaf *geophysicist, educator*
Hickman, Ruth Virginia *Bible educator*
Hummel, Carol Lucille *education educator, writer*
Humphrey, Charles Edward, Jr., *lawyer*
Isely, Henry Philip *association executive, integrative engineer, writer, educator*
Johnson, Ramey Kayes *community health nurse*
Joy, Carla Marie *history educator*
Keller, Shirley Inez *accountant*
Knott, William Alan *library director, management and building consultant*
Kulkarni, Kishore Ganesh *economics educator, consultant*
Martinen, John A. *travel company executive*
McBride, Guy Thornton, Jr., *college president emeritus*
McElwee, Dennis John *lawyer, former pharmaceutical company executive*
Mellstig, Sören *lab administrator*
Meyer, Lynn Nix *lawyer*
Nichols, Vicki Anne *financial consultant, librarian*
Quinn, John Michael *physicist, geophysicist*
Rosa, Fredric David *construction company executive*
Siska, Robert John *software engineer*
Walton, Roger Alan *public relations executive, mediator, writer*
Weskamp, Kelley S. *loan account manager, real estate company executive*
Woodruff, Kathryn Elaine *English language educator*

Laporte
Riba, Shirley *artist*

Leadville
Watson, Jack Crozier *retired state supreme court justice*

Littleton
Alykova, Valentina *musician, music educator*
Annandale, George William *engineer*
Battilega, John A. *research and development company executive*
Bennett, Janice Lynn *publisher, educator*
Brega, Kerry Elizabeth *physician, researcher*
Cabell, Elizabeth Arlisse *psychologist*
Dixon, Terry *automotive executive*
Dugan, Michael T. *communications executive*
Ergen, Charles *communications professional*
Fisher, Louis McLane, Jr., *management consultant*
Forstot, Stephan Lance *ophthalmologist*
Fryt, Monte Stanislaus *petroleum company executive, speaker, advisor*
Graf, Joseph Charles *retired foundation executive*
Grant, Newell M. *real estate investment manager*
Greenberg, Elinor Miller *university official, consultant*
Hadley, Marlin LeRoy *direct sales financial consultant*
Harney, Patricia Rae *environmental scientist, nuclear energy industry executive*
Hickman, Marjorie Anderson *small business owner*
Inzano, Karen Lee *advertising agency executive*
Johansson, Alicia Barbara *musician*
Keats, Donald Howard *composer, educator*
Kennedy, Jack *secondary education journalism educator*
Keogh, Heidi Helen Dake *advocate*
Kielmeyer, William Henry *ceramics engineer, researcher*
Kleinknecht, Kenneth Samuel *retired aerospace company executive, former federal space agency official*
Kullas, Albert John *management and systems engineering consultant*
Lesh-Laurie, Georgia Elizabeth *university administrator, biology educator, researcher*
Lohman, Loretta Cecelia *social scientist, consultant*
Marion, John Martin *information technology educator*
McDonnell, Michael R. *communications executive*
Meyer, Milton Edward, Jr., *lawyer, artist*
Paull, Richard Allen *geologist, educator*
Perlman, B. Arthur *lawyer*
Reinker, Mary Stefanich *musician, music educator*
Riley, Mary Jane *computer scientist*
Rothenberg, Harvey David *educational administrator*
Schomp, Lisa Juliana *automotive industry executive*
Shepherd, Donna Lou *interior designer*
Tucker, James Raymond *primary education educator*

Udevitz, Norman *publishing executive*
Vail, Charles Daniel *veterinarian, consultant*
VanderLinden, Camilla Denice Dunn *telecommunications industry executive*
Zwilling, Mark C. *music director*

Lone Tree
Bauer, Randy Mark *management training firm executive*
Spelts, Richard John *lawyer*
Washington, Reginald Louis *pediatric cardiologist*

Longmont
Breuer, Werner Alfred *retired plastics company executive*
Dierks, Richard Ernest *veterinarian, educational administrator*
Jones, Beverly Ann Miller *nursing administrator, retired patient services administrator*
Marcy, Charles Frederick *food company executive*
Pattyn, Sue *publishing executive*
Woollen, Evans *retired architectural firm executive*

Louisville
Adams, Eula L. *data storage executive*
Jonsen, Richard Wiliam *retired educational administrator*
Kenney, Alan Adams *lawyer*
Kocol, Robert S. *information technology executive*
Maddock, Jerome Torrence *information services specialist*
Martin, Patrick J. *technology company executive*
Schonbrun, Michael K. *senior housing developer and operator*
Shively, Merrick Lee *pharmaceutical scientist, consultant*
Sontag, Peter Michael *travel management company executive*

Loveland
Ahmann, John Stanley *retired psychologist*
Balsiger, David Wayne *television-video director, researcher, producer, writer*
Bierbaum, J. Armin *petroleum company executive, consultant*
Bierbaum, Janith Marie *artist*
Fleischer, Gerald Albert *industrial engineer, educator*
Goldberg, Laurie Lane *editor*
Hach-Darrow, Kathryn *water testing company executive*
Harrison, Craig Donald *water rights broker, real estate and land use planner*
King, Joan Caluda *medical educator, neuroscientist*
Lee, Evelyn Marie *elementary school educator, secondary school educator*
Rodman, Alpine C. *arts and crafts company executive, photographer*
Rodman, Sue A. *wholesale company executive, artist, writer*
Rosa, Linda *advocate*
Stewart, James Michael *engineer*
Walker, Laurie Shannon *psychologist, counselor*
Weresh, Thelma Faye *sculptor, artist*

Lyons
Spring, Kathleen *writer*

Mancos
Brown, Joy Alice *social services administrator*

Meeker
Omer, Robert Wendell *hospital administrator*

Montrose
Boice, Judith Lynette *physician, writer, educator*
Gates, Viola R. *writer*
Kontny, Vincent L. *rancher, engineering executive*
Yocum, Brian Lee *paramedic, educator*

Monument
Boggs, Steven Eugene *real estate broker, lawyer*
Breckner, William John, Jr., *retired military officer*
De Francesco, John Blaze, Jr., *public relations consultant, artist, writer*
Karasa, Norman Lukas *home builder, developer, geologist*
Miele, Alfonse Ralph *former government official*

Morrison
Bowen, Peter Geoffrey *arbitrator, business educator*
DeMiro, Diane Mollie *parochial school educator*
Myers, Harry J., Jr., *retired publisher*
Pettee, Daniel Starr *retired neurologist*

Nederland
Gibson, Lena S. *secondary school educator*
Lutz, Frank Wenzel *education administration educator*
Morrison, K. Jaydene *education counseling firm executive*
Sutton, Philip D. (Philip Dietrich Sutton) *psychologist, educator*

Niwot
Buss, Kathleen E. *music educator*
Farrington, Helen Agnes *personnel director*

Northglenn
Peters, LeRoy Richard *materials management consulting company executive*
Winter, William Paul, Jr., *ministry director*

Norwood
Hollinbeck, Ethel Lindell *sculptor*

Pagosa Springs
Howard, Carole Margaret Munroe *retired public relations executive*
Kelly, Reid Browne *lawyer*

Palisade
Barnewall, Marilyn MacGruder *banker, writer*
Fay, Abbott Eastman *history educator*

Palmer Lake
Dixon, Robert Clyde *systems engineer, consultant*

Paonia
Noonan, Robert Harry *art and music educator*

Parker
Greenberg, Morton Paul *lawyer, consultant, life settlement broker*
Jankura, Donald Eugene *hotel executive, educator*
Lark-Noonan, M. Ann *management consultant, strategic planner, naturalist*

Peterson AFB
Dekok, Roger Gregory *career officer*
Rees, Raymond F. *military officer*

Peyton
Dunn, Doris *retired critical care nurse, artist, rancher*

Pine
Jones, David Milton *economist, educator*

Placerville
Reagan, Harry Edwin, III, *lawyer*
Treat, John Elting *entrepreneur*

Pritchett
Hall, Carol Ann *music educator*

Pueblo
Avery, Julia May *speech pathologist, organizational volunteer*
Cress, Cecile Colleen *retired librarian*
Farley, Thomas T. *lawyer*
Farwell, Hermon Waldo, Jr., *parliamentarian, educator, former speech communication educator*
Giffin, Walter Charles *retired industrial engineer, educator, consultant*
Gregory, Leonard *publishing executive*
Hawkins, Robert Lee *health facility administrator*
Humes, James Calhoun *lawyer, communications consultant, writer, educator*
Keller, Robert L. *criminologist, educator*
Kogovsek, Daniel Charles *lawyer*
Levy, Patricia Anne *psychotherapist, educator*
Lewallen, William Marvin, Jr., *ophthalmologist*
Mo, Suchoon *psychology educator*
O'Callaghan, R.J. Patrick *lawyer*
Occhiato, Michael Anthony *city official*
Shomaker, Gordon Alexander, Jr., *poet, writer*
Sisson, Ray L. *retired dean, author*
Stevens, Jill Winifred *project expediter*
Vega, Jose Guadalupe *neuropsychologist, clinical professional*

Ridgway
Lathrop, Kaye Don *nuclear scientist, educator*

Rocky Ford
Mendenhall, Harry Barton *lawyer*

Sedalia
Ewing, Robert Craig *lawyer, educator*
McKee, John Morrison *broadcast executive*

Snowmass Village
Bancroft, Paul, III, *investment company executive*
Casebeer, Douglas Kelley *artist, ceramist, consultant*
DiBiaggio, John A. *university president*
Mattis, Louis Price *pharmaceutical and consumer products company executive*
Strand, Curt Robert *hotel executive*

Springfield
Wessler, Melvin Dean *farmer, rancher*

Steamboat Springs
Taylor, Jack *state senator*

Sterling
Jones, Laurie Ganong *sales and marketing executive*

Superior
Forshee, Gladys Marie *writer, insurance agent*

Telluride
Kuehler, Jack Dwyer *engineering consultant*

Thornton
Kane, Sean Patrick *computer engineer, consultant*
Thompson, Robert Frank, Jr., *career officer*

Trinidad
Potter, William Bartlett *business executive*
Veltri, Sandra Kay *finance educator*

Twin Lakes
Homan, Ralph William *finance company executive*

U S A F Academy
DeBerry, Fisher *college football coach*
Krise, Thomas Warren *military officer, English language educator*
Neiberg, Michael Scott *history professor*

Vail
Kelton, Arthur Marvin, Jr., *real estate developer*
Knight, Constance Bracken *writer, realtor, corporate executive*
McGee, Michael Jay *protective services official, educator*
Vosbeck, Robert Randall *architect*

Walsenburg
Mellott, George Kenneth *retired music educator*

Westcliffe
Merfeld, Gerald Lydon *artist*

Westminster
Bocock, Scott Gregory *historian*
Callier, Maria Cecile *writer, actress*
Eaves, Stephen Douglas *high school and vocational administrator, educator, consultant*
Freytag, J. Williams *medical company executive*
Gaither, John Francis, Jr., *lawyer*
Hartman, Susan P(atrice) *adult education administrator*
Hoffman, Stephen J. *pharmaceutical executive*
Lingle, JoLynn Fleishman *writer, educator*
Michael, Hart E. *pharmaceutical executive*
Shirai, Scott *communications executive*

Wheat Ridge
Brown, Steven Brien *radiologist*
Fleischaker, Gordon Henry, Jr., *pediatrician*
Gerlick, Helen J. *tax practitioner, accountant*
Hashimoto, Christine L. *physician*
Leino, Deanna Rose *business educator*
Morriss, Frank *writer, educator*
Parrish, Peter Trasel *retired civil engineer*
Scherich, Erwin Thomas *civil engineer, consultant*
Wells, Karen Kay *medical librarian*

Wolcott
Flacke, Joan Wareham *physician, anesthesiology educator*

Woodland Park
Cockrille, Stephen *art director, business owner*
Mason, David James *English language educator*
Olson, Warren Kinley *operations research analyst, engineer, physicist*
Stewart, Robert Lee *retired career officer, astronaut*
Trench, William Frederick *mathematician, educator*

Woody Creek
Jenkins, Robert Berryman *real estate developer*

Yuma
Hertneky, Randy Lee *optometrist*

CONNECTICUT

Ansonia
Kerpa, Gary J. *computer science consultant*

Avon
Dahl, Andrew Wilbur *health services executive*
Drapeau, Suzanne Eva *art educator*
Godbout, Arthur Richard, Jr., *lawyer*
Hinz, Carl Frederick, Jr., *immunologist, educator*
Kling, Phradie (Phradie Kling Gold) *small business owner, educator*
Mazur, Edward John, Jr., *financial planner*
Weiss, Robert Michael *dentist*

Barkhamsted
Stokes, Susan *political science educator*

Berlin
Grise, Cheryl *electric power industry executive*
Pulito, Francis N. *artist*
Shivery, Charles W. *utilities executive*

Bethel
Cheh, Huk Yuk *electrochemist, battery company executive*
DeLugo, Ernest Mario, Jr., *electrical engineer*
Kurfehs, Harold Charles *real estate executive*
Medvecky, Thomas Edward *lawyer*
Schetky, Laurence McDonald *metallurgist, researcher*
Shepard, Jean Heck *retired publishing consultant*

Bloomfield
Coburn, Richard Joseph *company executive, electrical engineer*
Cornell, Robert Witherspoon *engineering consultant*
De Maria, Anthony John *electrical engineer*
Foster, Benjamin, Jr., *educational administrator*
Garneau, Robert M. *aerospace and industrial products manufacturer*
Handel, Morton Emanuel *management consultation executive*
Ivey, Elizabeth S. *retired physicist, educator*
Kaman, Charles Huron *diversified technologies corporation executive*
Kissa, Karl Martin *electrical engineer*
Messemer, Glenn Matthew *lawyer*
Scheuch, Richard *economist, educator*
Shimelman, Susan Fromm *state policy administrator*
Thorpe, James *humanities researcher*

Bolton
Banas, Conrad Martin *mechanical engineer, chief scientist*

Branford
Begley, Richard F. *medical products executive*
Blake, Peter Jost *architect*
Carroll, Deirdre Holden *psychiatric nurse practitioner, clinical researcher, educator*
Charlot, Joseph Leonce, Jr., *preventive medicine physician*
Cronin, Michael Thomas Ignatius *pathologist, educator*
Gejdenson, Sam *former congressman*
Gordon, John Charles *forestry educator*
LeVasseur, Lee Allan *artist*
Milgram, Richard Myron *music school administrator*
Rothberg, Jonathan M. *medical products executive*
Sipprell, George Sidney *engineering professional*
Smith, Richard Emerson (Dick Smith) *make-up artist*
Tchernev, Velizar Tzvetanov *physician and biomedical scientist*
Vietzke, Wesley Maunder *internist, educator*
Wegener, Peter Paul *engineering educator, author*
Wright, Nancy Howell *interior designer*

Bridgeport
Black, Hillel Moses *publisher*
Bowen, Patrick Harvey *lawyer, consultant*
Chih, Chung-Ying *physicist, consultant*
Dexter, Gregory Warren *real estate and financial investor*
Eginton, Warren William *federal judge*
Garcia, Edna I. *state legislator, secondary education educator*
Graham, Kenneth Albert *lawyer*
Hendricks, Edward David *education director, consultant, speaker, trainer*
Huo, Yangchung Paul *business educator*
Lanci, Janet Mead *academic administrator, educator*
Lobdell, David Hill *pathologist*
Lori, William E. *bishop*
Macdonald, Karen Crane *occupational therapist, geriatric counselor*
Maloney, Maureen Murphy *social sciences educator*
Nijensohn, Daniel Edgardo *neurosurgeon*
Reed, Charles Eli *retired chemist, chemical engineer*
Schrandt, Curtis Leon *lawyer, securities analyst, financial advisor*
Schwartz, James Peter *real estate broker*
Semple, Cecil Snowdon *retired manufacturing company executive*
Simoneau, Cynthia Lambert *newspaper editor, journalism educator*
Trefry, Robert J. *healthcare administrator*
Twist-Rudolph, Donna Joy *neurophysiology and neuropsychology researcher*
Williams, Yotisse R. *music educator*

Bridgewater
Crooke, Robert Andrew *media consultant, writer, educator*

Bristol
Barnes, Carlyle Fuller *manufacturing executive*
Barnes, Wallace *manufacturing executive*
Bodenheimer, George *broadcast executive*
Copeland, Karin A. *training director*
Driessen, Christine F. *broadcast executive*
Eisen, Rich *reporter*
LaGanga, Donna Brandeis *sales and marketing executive, management/educational administrator*
Melrose, Barry James *sportscaster, former professional hockey team coach*
Morales, Mary E. *social worker*
Morgan, Joe Leonard *investment company executive, retired professional baseball player, commentator*
Patrick, Dan *sportscaster*
Reynolds, Harold Craig *professional baseball player*
Roberts, Robin *sportscaster*

Broad Brook
Johnston, Robert Everett *information management executive*

Brookfield
Cohen, Mark Steven *dentist*
Foncello, Martin John, Jr., *municipal official*
Lewis, Edwin Leonard, III, *lawyer*
Reynolds, Jean Edwards *publishing executive*
Secola, Joseph Paul *lawyer*
Stern, Michael Lawrence *psychologist, educator*

Brooklyn
Dune, Steve Charles *retired lawyer*

Burlington
Ghiglia, Oscar Alberto *classical guitarist*

Canaan
Kettenhofen, Gretchen Maria *development executive*

Canton
Jordan, Evora Ruth *writer, researcher, publishing executive*
Richardson, Dana Roland *technology consultant*

Canton Center
Humphrey, Samuel Stockwell *town official, physicist*

Centerbrook
Harper, Robert Leslie *architect, educator*

Chaplin
Wood, Wendy Deborah *filmmaker*

Cheshire
Bell, Leonard *pharmaceutical executive*
Bozzuto, Michael Adam *wholesale grocery company executive*
Keiser, David Wharton *biotechnology executive*
McKee, Margaret Jean *federal agency administrator*
Rowland, Ralph Thomas *retired architect*
Tufte, Edward Rolf *writer, publisher, statistics educator*
Walter, Kenneth Gaines *library director*

Chester
Harwood, Eleanor Cash *librarian*
Hilsman, Roger *government educator*
Stark, Evelyn Brill *poet, musician*

Clinton
Gilman, Frances M. *genealogist, librarian*
Panayotov, Christo Angelov *research scientist, consultant*

Cobalt
Stevens, Robert Edwin *bank executive, former insurance company executive*

Colchester
Winter, John Dawson, III, *blues guitarist, singer*

Colebrook
Ash, Hiram Newton *graphic designer*
McNeill, William Hardy *retired history educator, writer*

Collinsville
Whitney, Carol Marie *securities sales professional*

Cos Cob
Barnard, Charles Nelson *editorial consultant, author*
Duncalf, Deryck *retired anesthesiologist*
Halvorsen, Ole Andreas *financier*
Hauptman, Michael *broadcasting company executive*
Kane, Jay Brassler *banker*
Kane, Margaret Brassler *sculptor*
Leamy, Nancy M. *professional athletics coach*
Murphy, Robert Blair *management consulting company executive*
Neal, Irene Collins *artist, educator*

Coventry
Ferguson, Ronald Max *chemistry educator, researcher*

Cromwell
Günther-Stirn, Dagmar Dorothea *retired social sciences educator*

Danbury
Annesi, Adele Mary *editor, writer*
Baker, Leonard Morton *manufacturing executive*
Balmaseda, Ricardo Antonio *stockbroker*
Finkelstein, Annette Anuhid *nurse*
Fuller, Cassandra Miller *applications specialist*
Geoghan, Joseph Edward *former lawyer, chemical company executive*
Gezurian, Dorothy Ellen *accounting executive*
Hawkes, Carol Ann *academic administrator*
Jennings, Alfred Higson, Jr., *music educator, actor, singer*
Jensen-Ruopp, Helga Spitko *school program administrator, consultant*
Johns, William David *nuclear medicine physician, internist*
Layton, Howard Manton *electrical engineer*
Lichtenberger, H(orst) William *chemical company executive*
Mann, Richard O. *public relations consulting company executive*
Meyers, Abbey S. *foundation administrator*
Moskowitz, Stanley Alan *financial executive*
Nelson, Willie Hugh *musician, songwriter*
Proctor, Richard Jerome, Jr., *business educator, accountant, expert witness*
Reilley, Dennis H. *chemicals executive*
Roach, James Richard *university president*
Saghir, Adel Jamil *artist, painter, sculptor*
Sawyer, James S. *manufacturing executive*
Soviero, Joseph C. *chemical company executive*
Stichnoth, John A. *corporate lawyer*
Tolor, Alexander *psychologist, educator*
Williamson, Brian David *information systems executive, consultant*
Yamin, Dianne Elizabeth *judge*

Darien
Brooke, Avery Rogers *publisher, writer*
Brown, James Shelly *lawyer*
Chyung, Chi Han *management consultant*
Cronk, Leonard *management consultant*
Dale, Erwin Randolph *lawyer, author*
Dordelman, William Forsyth *food company executive*
Forman, J(oseph) Charles *chemical engineer, consultant, writer*
Hailey, Arthur *author*
Himmelreich, David Baker *lawyer*
Kobak, James Benedict *management consultant*
Koontz, Carl Lennis, II, *investment counselor*
Lim, Ralph Wei Hsiong *finance educator*
Mapel, William Marlen Raines *retired banking executive*
McIntire, William Tredick, II, *municipal official, investment banker*
Moltz, James Edward *investment brokerage company executive*
Morano, Gerard John *marketing executive*
Nava, Eloy Luis *financial planner, financial consultant*
Ossi, James Matthew *artist*
Penrose, Charles, Jr., *professional society administrator*
Prince, Kenneth Stephen *lawyer*
Schell, James Munson *financial executive*
Smith, Elwin Earl *mining and oil company executive*
Sprole, Frank Arnott *retired pharmaceutical executive, lawyer*
Welsh, John Francis *retired advertising executive*
Ziegler, William, III, *diversified industry executive*

Deep River
Cobb, Hubbard Hanford *magazine editor, writer*

Derby
Jekel, James Franklin *physician, public health educator*
McEvoy, Sharlene Ann *law educator*

East Glastonbury
Smith, David Clark *research scientist*

East Granby
Kozlowski, Michael *state agency administrator*
Scanlon, Lawrence Eugene *English language educator*

East Haddam
Borton, John Carter, Jr., (Terry Borton) *theatrical producer*
Clarke, Cordelia Kay Knight Mazuy *management consultant, artist*
Clarke, Logan, Jr., *management consultant*

East Hampton
Tucceri, Clive Knowles *science writer and educator, consultant*

East Hartford
Barredo, Rita M. *auditor*
Cassidy, John Francis, Jr., *industrial technology executive*
Pfeifer, Howard Melford *mechanical engineer*
Scholsky, Martin Joseph *priest*
Vacher, Clive Graham *aerospace executive*
Young, Albert Frederick Antonio *grants coordinator*

Easton
Constantinople, Alexandra *communications executive*
Enos, Randall *cartoonist, illustrator*
Lorenz, Lee Sharp *cartoonist*
Maloney, John Joseph *writer*
Meyer, Alice Virginia *state official*

Ellington
Adams, Timothy Gene *music educator*

Enfield
Folmsbee, Patricia Hurley *reading and language arts consultant*
Oliver, Bruce Lawrence *retired information systems specialist, educator*

Essex
Burris, Harriet Louise *emergency physician*
Goff, Christopher Wallick *pediatrician*
Hieatt, Allen Kent *language professional, educator*
Hieatt, Constance Bartlett *English language educator*
Miller, Elliott Cairns *retired bank executive, lawyer*
Miller, Walter Neal *insurance company consultant*
Thompson, George Lee *consulting and retailing company executive*

Fairfield
Barone, Rose Marie Pace *writer, retired educator, entertainer*
Beccalli, Ferdinando *manufacturing executive*
Booth, George Keefer *financial service executive*
Brett, Arthur Cushman, Jr., *banker*
Bryan, Barbara Day *retired librarian*
Bullard, Roger Perrin *artist*
Burd, Robert Meyer *hematologist, oncologist, educator*
Calhoun, David L. *manufacturing executive*
Campbell, James P. *utilities executive*
Caruso, Daniel F. *lawyer, judge, former state legislator*
Cernera, Anthony Joseph *academic administrator*
Comstock, Elizabeth J. *marketing executive*
Conaty, William J. *electric power industry executive*
Daley, Pamela *diversified services, technology and manufacturing company executive*
Eigel, Edwin George, Jr., *mathematics educator, retired university president*
Evans, Margaret A. *volunteer*
Fash, Victoria R. *healthcare company executive*
Ford, Maureen Morrissey *civic worker*
Futterman, Jack *retail executive*
Harris, Wiley Lee *financial services executive*
Heineman, Benjamin Walter, Jr., *lawyer*
Hergenhan, Joyce *public relations executive*
Hodgkinson, William James *publishing executive*
Howell, Karen Jane *private school educator*
Immelt, Jeffrey R. *diversified technology and services company executive*
Ingis, Gail *interior designer, educator, photographer, artist, writer*
Jeffe, Robert Allan *diversities technology and services company executive*
Johnsen, Walter Craig *security firm executive*
Kaff, Albert Ernest *reporter, writer*
Kelley, Aloysius Paul *university administrator, priest*
Kleine, Herman *economist*
Krenicki, John, Jr., *manufacturing executive*
Levine, Stanley Walter *chemical company executive*
Levinson, Stephen Ronald *retired otolaryngologist*
Levitt, Jesse *retired foreign language educator*
Luther, David Byron *management consultant*
Mascia, Mark Joseph *language educator*
McLaughlin, John Richardson *electric motor company executive*
Mead, Philomena *mental health nurse*
Miles, Leland Weber *university president*
Murphy, Eugene F. *retired aerospace, communications and electronics executive*
Newton, Lisa Haenlein *philosopher, educator*
Orris-Modugno, Michele Marie *public relations, marketing and advertising consultant*
Paolini, Claire Jacqueline *dean, educator*
Pinto, Edward Ralph *internist, cardiologist*
Reeves, Edmund Hoffman, III, *food products executive*
Reiner, Gary M. *diversified technology and services company executive*
Rice, John G. *diversified technology and services executive*
Shaffer, Dorothy Browne *retired mathematician, educator*
Sherin, Keith S. *electrical manufacturing company executive*
Spence, Barbara E. *publishing company executive*
Sutphen, Harold Amerman, Jr., *retired paper company executive*
Timmermann, Sandra *educational gerontologist, communication specialist*
Weissman, Robert Evan *information services company executive*
Wexler, Herbert Ira *retail company executive*
Woodburn, William A. *utilities executive*
Wright, Robert C. *broadcast executive*

Falls Village
Cronin, Robert Lawrence *painter*
Purcell, Dale *college president, consultant*
Purcell, Mary Louise Gerlinger *retired adult education educator*
Toomey, Jeanne Elizabeth *animal activist*

Farmington
Arnold, Andrew *medical researcher, physician*
Blechner, Barbara B. *law educator, consultant, lawyer*
Bronner, Felix *physiologist, biophysicist, educator, painter*
Burki, Nausherwan *pulmonologist*
Cone, Robert Edward *immunologist, educator*
Cooperstein, Sherwin Jerome *medical educator*
Cutler, Leslie Stuart *academic administrator, educator*
Deckers, Peter John *dean*
DiCicco, Tony *soccer coach*
DiFrancesco, John *design engineering services company executive*
Donaldson, James Oswell, III, *neurologist, educator*
Estes, George L., III, *investment company executive*
Goodson, Richard Carle, Jr., *chemist*
Grafstein, Joel M. *lawyer*
Halligan, Howard Ansel *investment management company executive*
Herzog, Brigitte *lawyer*
Higgins-Biddle, John Charles *humanities educator, consultant*
Houchin, John Frederick, Sr., *human services administrator*
Keiler, Richard W. *advertising executive*
Klobutcher, Lawrence Anthony *biologist, educator*
Koulos, John *medical association administrator, medical educator*
Liebowitz, Neil Robert *psychiatrist*
McCawley, Austin *psychiatrist, educator*
Metersky, Mark L. *physician*
Osborn, Mary Jane Merten *biochemist, educator*
Owens, Guy *retired neurosurgeon*
Reeves, John Drummond *English language professional, writer*
Robinson, Peter J. *dean, periodontal educator, pathologist*
Rothfield, Lawrence I. *microbiology educator*
Rothfield, Naomi Fox *physician*
Schenkman, John Boris *pharmacologist, educator*
Spencer, Richard Paul *biochemist, educator, physician*
Wiechmann, Eric Watt *lawyer*

Jewett City
Pucel, Robert Albin *electronics research engineer*

Kent
Friedman, Frances *public relations executive*
Peck, Darryl *software company executive*

Killingworth
Buchanan, J(ohn) Robert *physician, educator*
Christy, Nicholas Pierson *physician*
Kilby, Peter *economics educator*

Lakeville
Cook, Charles David *international lawyer, arbitrator, consultant*
Estabrook, Robert Harley *journalist*
Jones, Ronald David *lawyer*
Levy, Ira Howard *marketing professional, real estate developer*

Ledyard
Chiang, Albert Chinfa *polymer chemist*
Hammond, Russell Paul *music educator*

Litchfield
Booth, John Thomas *investment banker*
Ellison, William Theodore *marine engineer*
Fiederowicz, Walter Michael *lawyer*
Kenagy, Robert Coffman *planning consulting company executive*
Privitera, Joseph F. *retired foreign service officer, writer-researcher*
Sherva, Dennis G. *retired investment company executive*

Lyme
Bessie, Simon Michael *publisher*
Bloom, Barry Malcolm *pharmaceutical consultant*
Hoyt, Charles King *architect, editor*

Madison
Atkinson, Neil Norman *mechanical engineer*
Clendenen, William Herbert, Jr., *lawyer*
Egbert, Emerson Charles *retired publisher*
Evans, Evan *petroleum executive*
Golembeski, Jerome John *wire and cable company executive*
Houghton, Alan Nourse *association executive, educator, consultant*
James, John Whitaker, Sr., *financial services executive*
Kay, Herbert *retired natural resources company executive*
Kilbourne, Edwin Dennis *virologist, educator*
Nebel, Sara Drought *artist, poet*
Purcell, Bradford Moore *publishing company executive*
Scully, Roger Tehan, II, *lawyer*
Snell, Richard Saxon *anatomist*
Stevenson, Robert Edwin *microbiologist, consultant*

Manchester
Galasso, Francis Salvatore *materials scientist*
Jacobs, Ronald *prosecutor*
Sears, Sandra Lee *computer consultant*

Mansfield Center
Petrus, Robert Thomas *internet business owner, real estate investor*

Mashantucket
Yale, John Paul *computer systems developer*

Meriden
Bertolli, Eugene Emil *sculptor, goldsmith, designer, consultant*
Chiarenza, Frank John *English language educator*
Frederick, Paul G. *financial services systems company executive*
Horton, Paul Chester *psychiatrist*
Licata, Ronald Charles *insurance company executive*
Luby, Thomas Stewart *lawyer*
Molder, Sybil Ailene *retired occupational health nurse*
Perricone, Nicholas V. *dermatologist*
Shemchuk, Mary Elizabeth *occupational therapist*

Middlebury
Arnold, William Parsons, Jr., *retired internist*
Calarco, Vincent Anthony *specialty chemicals company executive*
Fickenscher, Gerald H. *chemicals company executive*
Galie, Louis Michael *electronics company executive*
Phillips, Walter Mills, III, *psychologist, educator*
Scarpetti, Angelina (Lee Scarpetti) *state legislator*
Turcotte, Glenn W. *electrical products company executive*
Wood, R. L. (Bob Wood) *chemicals executive*

Middletown
Balay, Robert Elmore *editor, reference librarian*
Barber, William Joseph *educator, economist*
Bennet, Douglas Joseph, Jr., *university president*
Blume, Ginger (Elaine Blume) *psychologist*
Brown, Judith *academic administrator*
Buel, Richard Van Wyck, Jr., *history educator, writer, editor*
Comfort, William Wistar *mathematics professor*
Craig, Barbara Kinkson *academic administrator*
Crenshaw, Martha *political science educator*
Crites, Stephen Decatur *religion educator*
De Rocco, Andrew Gabriel *physicist, educator*
Ettre, Leslie Stephen *chemist*
Fry, Albert Joseph *chemistry professor*
Gillmor, Charles Stewart *history and science educator, researcher*
Grothendieck, Alexandre *retired mathematician*
Harris, Dale Benner *psychologist, educator*
Heimann-Hast, Sybil Dorothea *language arts and literature educator*
Hoffmann, Leonard A *church administrator, director*
Kordonskiy, Yuriy *performing arts educator, actor, director*
Malkin, Moses Montefiore *employee benefits administration company executive*
Meyer, Priscilla Ann *Russian language and literature educator*
Miel, Jan *humanities educator*
Miller, Richard Alan *economist, educator*
Narad, Joan Stern *psychiatrist*
Pomper, Philip *history educator*
Reed, Joseph Wayne *American studies educator, artist*
Rockwood, Irving E., Jr., *publisher*
Scheibe, Karl Edward *psychology educator*
Shapiro, Norman Richard *Romance languages and literatures educator*
Shields, David Brandon *historian, educator*
Swain, James Barrett *pastor, education educator*
Torop, Paul *psychiatrist*
Wasch, William Karl *gerontologist, consultant*
Wensinger, Arthur Stevens *language and literature educator, writer, translator*
Winston, Krishna *foreign language professional*
Zito, Christopher Richard *molecular biologist, biochemist*

Milford
Basso, Jason Michael *film producer, actor*
Benedosso, Anthony Nechols *lawyer*
Berchem, Robert Lee, Sr., *lawyer*
Broughel, Andrew Joseph *lawyer*
Curt, Denise Morris *artist, limner, photographer*
Ferguson, Richard A. *communications executive*
Haigh, Charles *criminal justice educator*
Henderson, Albert Kossack *publishing company executive, dairy executive, consultant*
Muth, Eric Peter *ophthalmic optician*
Sagarin, J. Daniel *lawyer*
Schwartz, Richard Edward Derecktor *retired sociologist, educator*
Upson, Thomas Fisher *judge, former state senator, lawyer*

Monroe
Davis, Bobby J. *pastor, family therapist*
Hyman, Andrew Theodore *patent lawyer, physicist*
Kranyik, Elizabeth Ann *secondary school educator*
Paniccia, Mario Domenic *architect*

Moodus
Cumming, Robert Emil *editor, writer*

Mystic
Ballard, Robert Duane *marine geologist*
Bobruff, Carole Marks *radio producer, radio personality*
Burrow, Gerard Noel *internist, educator*
Chace, William Murdough *former university administrator*
Lincoln, Walter Butler, Jr., *marine engineer, educator*
Nolf, David M. *financial consultant*
Palmer, Richard Crist *lawyer*
Rogers, Brian Deane *librarian*
Rooney, Maria Dewing *photographer*
Thompson, Robert Allan *aerospace engineer*

Naugatuck
Flannery, Joseph Patrick *manufacturing executive, director*
Mannweiler, Mary-Elizabeth *painter*
Suscovich, David J. *neuropsychologist, marriage and family therapist*

New Britain
Baker, Patricia *health foundation administrator*
Baskerville, Charles Alexander *geologist, educator*
Chavarro, Adolfo *psychology professor, researcher*
Czajkowski, Eva Anna *aerospace engineer, educator*
Darius, Franklin Alexander, Jr., (Chip Darius) *safety consultant, educator*
Dimmick, Charles William *geology educator*
Emeagwali, Gloria Thomas *humanities educator*
Foster, Patrick *technologist, educator, writer, educational consultant*
Fothergill, William Corey *counselor, therapist*
Heitner, John A. (Jack Heitner) *English language educator, writer*
Hogan, John W., Jr., *lawyer*
Leeds, Barry Howard *English language educator*
Loree, James M. *consumer products company executive*
Lundgren, John F. *consumer products company executive, bank executive*
Lunn, Charles Paul *secondary school educator*
Martin, Vivian Bonita *journalist, educator*
Meskill, Thomas J. *federal judge*
O'Connell, Brian Michael *computer scientist, educator*
Opie, John D. *retired electric power industry executive*
Parikh, Nimmi Chandra *Physics educator*
Sohn, Jeanne *librarian*
Tedford, Deborah J. *lawyer*

New Canaan
Ackerman, Sigurd Howard *psychiatrist*
Babcock, Warner King *entrepreneur, venture capitalist, investment advisor*
Bartlett, Dede Thompson *association executive*
Bisbee, Gerald Elftman, Jr., *investment company executive*
Brakeley, George Archibald, Jr., *fundraising consultant*
Burns, Ivan Alfred *grocery products and industrial company executive*
Christensen, Donna Radovich *needlecraft designer, consultant, educator*
Cohen, Richard Norman *insurance executive*
Coughlin, Francis Raymond, Jr., *surgeon, educator, lawyer*
Dean, Robert Bruce *architect*
Fredericks, Jeanne Maria Judson *literary agent*
Gilbert, Steven Jeffrey *venture capitalist, screenwriter*
Giusti, Kathy *foundation administrator*
Grace, Julianne Alice *retired investor relations firm executive*
Jakacki, Diane Katherine *multimedia entertainment company executive*
Johnston, Douglas Frederick *industrial holding company executive*
Kamerschen, Robert Jerome *consumer products executive, investor*
Kovatch, Jak Gene *artist*
MacEwan, Nigel Savage *merchant banker*
McCreight, John A. *management consultant*
McIvor, Donald Kenneth *retired petroleum company executive*
Mc Mennamin, George Barry *advertising agency executive*
McNamara, Francis Joseph, Jr., *retired foundation executive, lawyer*
Means, David Hammond *retired advertising executive*
Mountcastle, Kenneth Franklin, Jr., *retired stockbroker*
Pifer, Alan (Jay Parrish) *former foundation executive*
Pike, William Edward *business executive*
Richards, Walter DuBois *artist, illustrator*
Risom, Jens *furniture designer, manufacturing executive*
Sachs, John Peter *carbon company executive*
Steinmetz, Richard Bird, Jr., *lawyer*
Stewart, James Montgomery *retired bank executive*
Ward, Richard Vance, Jr., *management executive*
White, Richard Booth *management consultant*

New Fairfield
Lambrech, Régine M. *college program administrator, language educator*

New Haven
Abdelsayed, Wafeek Hakim *accounting educator*
Abramson, Arthur Seymour *linguistics educator, researcher*
Adair, Robert Kemp *physicist, educator*
Aghajanian, George Kevork *medical educator*
Alexander, Bruce Donald *real estate executive, educator*
Alpern, Robert J. *dean, medical educator*
Altman, Sidney *biology professor*
Anderson, Carl Albert *association executive, lawyer, dean*
Anderson, John Fredric *science administrator, entomologist, researcher*
Armbruster, Paula *child mental health educator, university director*
Arons, Marvin Shield *plastic and hand surgeon*
Aronson, Peter Samuel *physiologist, researcher*
Arterton, Janet Bond *federal judge*
Ayres, Ian *law educator*
Bailey, William Harrison *artist, educator*
Baker, Robert Stevens *organist, educator*
Baltay, Charles *physicist, educator*
Baltayan, Ara M. *engineering executive*
Barash, Paul George *anesthesiologist, educator*
Bartoshuk, Linda J. *otolaryngologist, educator*
Behrman, Harold Richard *endocrinologist, physiologist, educator*
Bell, Wendell *sociologist, educator, futurist*
Belt, David Levin *lawyer*
Benfer, David William *hospital administrator*
Berdon, Robert Irwin *judge trial referee, retired state supreme court justice*
Berson, Jerome Abraham *chemistry professor*
Birnbaum, Irwin Morton *lawyer*
Blatt, Sidney Jules *psychology educator and investigator, psychoanalyst*
Bloom, Harold *humanities educator, writer*
Blum, John Morton *historian, educator*
Borroff, Marie *English language educator*
Boyer, James Lorenzen *physician, educator*
Brainard, William Crittenden *economist, educator, university official*
Brantl, Sister Charlesmarie *economics professor*
Braverman, Irwin Merton *dermatologist, educator*
Brisman, Leslie *English language educator*
Bromley, David Allan *physicist, engineer, educator*
Brown, Thomas Huntington *neuroscientist*
Brownell, Kelly David *psychologist, educator*
Brunson, Kenneth Wayne *cancer biologist*
Buck, Donald Tirrell *retired finance educator*
Buckley, Richard Bennett *asset management company executive*
Bunney, Benjamin Stephenson *psychiatrist, educator*
Burger, Richard L. *museum director*
Burns, Ellen Bree *federal judge*
Bynum, Terrell Ward *humanities educator, consultant*
Cabranes, José Alberto *judge*
Calabresi, Guido *federal judge, law educator*
Carty, Paul Vernon *lawyer*
Casten, Richard Francis *physicist*
Chandler, William Knox *physiologist*
Chilton, William David *architect*
Chupka, William Andrew *chemical physicist, educator*
Ciuparu, Dragos Mihael *research scientist, educator*
Clarie, Thomas Cashin, II, *librarian*
Clark, Elias *law educator*
Clarke, Fred W., III, *architect, architectural firm executive*
Coe, Michael Douglas *anthropologist, educator*
Cohen, Lawrence Baruch *neurobiologist, educator*
Cohen, Lawrence Sorel *internist, educator*
Cohen, Morris Leo *retired law librarian and educator*
Coifman, Ronald R. *mathematician, educator*
Collins, William F., Jr., *neurosurgery educator*
Comer, James Pierpont *psychiatrist, educator*
Conklin, Harold Colyer *anthropologist, educator*
Cooper, Dennis Lawrence *oncologist, educator*
Cooper, Jack Ross *pharmacology educator, researcher*
Crakes, Gary Michael *economics professor*
Cresswell, Peter *immunobiologist, educator*
Cullen, Mark Richard *medical educator*
Danaher, John Anthony, III, *prosecutor*
Davey, Lycurgus Michael *neurosurgeon*
Days, Drew S., III, *lawyer, law educator*
Deamer, Peggy *architecture educator*
De Lio, Anthony Peter *lawyer*
DePino, Chris Anthoney *state legislator*
De Rose, Sandra Michele *psychotherapist, educator, supervisor, administrator*
Diers, Donna Kaye *nursing educator*
Dolan, Thomas Francis, Jr., *pediatrician, educator*
Donnelly, Robert L. *lawyer, corporation executive*
Donohue, John Joseph *law educator*
Dorsey, Peter Collins *federal judge*
DuBois, Arthur Brooks *physiologist, educator*
Duke, Steven Barry *law educator*
Dunkle, Lisa Marie *pharmaceutical research executive*
Dyson, William R. *state legislator, educator*
Ehrenkranz, Richard Allan *pediatrician*
Ellickson, Robert Chester *law educator*
Ember, Carol R. *anthropology educator, author*
Ember, Melvin Lawrence *anthropologist, educator*
Erikson, Kai *sociologist, educator*
Erlich, Victor *Slavic languages educator*
Errington, James Joseph *anthropology educator*
Evenson, Robert Eugene *economist, educator*
Fang, Hanming *economist, educator*
Fei, Yijian *ophthalmologist, biomedical researcher*
Feinstein, Rochelle *artist, educator*
Ferholt, J. Deborah Lott *pediatrician*
Fikrig, Erol *rheumatologist, medical educator*
Fischer, Michael John *computer science educator*
Flavell, Richard *science educator, department chairman*
Forster, Susan H. *ophthalmologist, educator*
Frank, Roberta *English language educator*
Freed, Daniel Josef *law educator*
Freedman, Gerald Stanley *radiologist, healthcare administrator, educator*
Freedman, Paul Harris *historian, educator*
Fried, Charles A. *retired accountant, financial executive*
Galston, Arthur William *biology professor*
Garten, Jeffrey E. *college dean, educator, marketing professional*
Gastwirth, Donald Edward *lawyer, literary agent*
Gaudiani, Claire Lynn *retired academic administrator*
Geisler, Thomas Milton, Jr., *lawyer*
Genel, Myron *pediatrician, educator*
Gewirtz, Paul D. *lawyer, legal educator*
Gilbert, Creighton Eddy *art historian*
Gildea, Brian Michael *lawyer*
Gilliss, Catherine Lynch *nursing educator*
Glaser, Gilbert Herbert *neuroscientist, physician, educator*
Glier, Ingeborg Johanna *German language and literature educator*
Goffart, Walter André *history professor*
Goldstein, Abraham Samuel *lawyer, educator*
Goodrich, Isaac *neurosurgeon, educator*
Graedel, Thomas Eldon *industrial ecology educator, researcher*
Grausman, Philip *sculptor*
Green, Donald Philip *political scientist, educator*
Greene, Liliane *French language and literature educator, editor*
Greenfield, James Robert *lawyer*
Gross, Ian *academic pediatrician, neonatologist*
Hallo, William Wolfgang *literature and language professor, writer*
Hansmann, Henry Baethke *law educator*
Harries, Karsten *philosophy educator, researcher*
Harrison, Henry Starin *real estate educator, entrepreneur*
Hartman, Geoffrey H. *language professional, educator*
Hayden, Dolores *author, architect, educator*
Hennah, Vivian Lisa *school system administrator*
Hersey, George Leonard *retired art history educator*
Herzenberg, Arvid *physicist, researcher*
Hickey, Leo J(oseph) *museum curator, educator*
Hines, Roberta Leigh *medical educator*
Hollander, John *humanities educator, poet*
Holquist, James Michael *Russian and comparative literature educator*
Horwich, Arthur L. *medical educator*
Hostetter, Margaret K. *pediatrician, medical educator*
Howe, Roger Evans *mathematician, educator*
Hyman, Paula E(llen) *history professor*
Insler, Stanley *philologist, educator*
Jackson, Shirley Ann *sociology educator*
Jacobson, John D. *architecture educator*
Jacoby, Robert Ottinger *comparative medicine educator*
Jatlow, Peter I. *pathologist, medical educator, researcher*
Johnson, Lester Fredrick *artist*
Johnstone, Quintin *law educator*
Kagan, Donald *historian, educator*
Kashgarian, Michael *pathologist, educator*
Katz, Jay *psychiatry and law educator*
Kauffman, Stephen Blair *law librarian, educator*
Kazdin, Alan E. *psychology educator*
Kennedy, Paul Michael *history professor*
Kevles, Daniel Jerome *history educator, writer*
Klein, Martin Jesse *physicist, educator, science historian*
Knag, Paul Everett *lawyer*
Krasner, David *education educator*
Krauss, Judith Belliveau *nursing educator*
Kronman, Anthony Townsend *law educator, dean*
Kushlan, Samuel Daniel *physician, educator, hospital administrator*
Lamar, Howard Roberts *educational administrator, historian*
Langbein, John Harriss *lawyer, educator*
Langer, Lawrence Lee *English educator, writer*
Lannin, Donald Rowe *oncologist, surgeon*
LaPalombara, Joseph *political science and industrial management educator*
Lee, Sin Hang *pathologist, educator*
Leeney, Robert Joseph *newspaper editor*
Leffell, David Joel *dermatologist, surgeon, health facility administrator, educator, writer*
Lentz, Thomas Lawrence *biomedical educator, dean, researcher*
Levin, Richard Charles *academic administrator, economist*
Levine, Robert John *physician, educator*
Lewis, Melvin *psychiatrist, pediatrician, psychoanalyst*
Lindroth, Linda (Linda Hammer) *artist, curator, writer*
Lord, George deForest *English educator*
Lorimer, Linda Koch *university educator*
Lytton, Bernard *urology educator*
Macey, Jonathan R. *law educator*
MacMullen, Ramsay *retired history educator*
Malherbe, Abraham Johannes, VI, *religion educator, writer*
Mandelbrot, Benoit B. *mathematician, scientist, educator*
Marchesi, Vincent T. *biochemist, educator*
Marcus, Ruth Barcan *philosopher, educator, writer, lecturer*
Margulis, Gregory A. *mathematics educator, researcher*
Marks, Lawrence Edward *psychologist, educator*
Marmor, Theodore Richard *political science and public management educator*
Martinsson, Per-Gunnar Johan *mathematician, mechanical engineer*
Massey, William S. *mathematician, educator*
Mayhew, David Raymond *political science educator*
McClatchy, J. D. *editor, writer, educator*
McCorkle, Ruth *oncological nurse, educator*
McGlashan, Thomas Hamel *psychiatry educator*
McGuire, William James *social psychology educator*

Southington
Byeff, Peter David *hematologist, oncologist*
Rudolph, Kathleen Ann *insurance company executive*

Southport
Damson, Barrie Morton *oil and gas exploration company executive*
Gryka, George Edwin *chemical company executive*
Hill, David Lawrence *research corporation executive*
Sanetti, Stephen Louis *lawyer*
Savage, Robert Heath *advertising executive*
Sheppard, William Stevens *investment banker*
Walker, Charles Dodsley *conductor, organist*
Wheeler, Wilmot Fitch, Jr., *diversified manufacturing company executive*
Wilbur, E. Packer *investment company executive*

Stafford Springs
Guglielmo, Anthony *state legislator, insurance agency executive*

Stamford
Allocca, Antoinette *computer company executive*
Amen, Robert M. *paper company executive*
Anderson, Susan Leigh *philosophy educator*
Anderson, Susan Stuebing *business equipment company executive*
Apfelbaum, Marc *lawyer*
Babson, Jane Frances *artist, writer*
Balduino, Michael J. *paper company executive*
Barker, James Rex *water transportation executive, director*
Barreca, Christopher Anthony *lawyer*
Beck, Angel C. *columnist, screenwriter, educator, film director*
Bijur, Peter I. *retired petroleum company executive*
Block, Ruth *retired insurance company executive*
Bostin, Marvin Jay *hospital and health services consultant*
Brandon, Joseph P. *reinsurance company executive*
Brannigan, Michael D. *sales executive*
Britt, Glenn Alan *media company executive*
Buehler, William Frank *manufacturing executive*
Burgess, Lynne A *lawyer*
Burke, Alexander James, Jr., *publishing company executive, scripture scholar*
Burns, Ursula *printing company executive*
Burston, Richard Mervin *business executive*
Buzzard, James A. *manufacturing executive*
Cacace, Michael Joseph *lawyer*
Caldwell, Philip *retired automobile manufacturing company executive, retired financial services company executive*
Callahan, Robert Jeremiah *retired judge, mediator*
Candland, Catherine C. *human resources executive*
Chang, Ted T. *chemist*
Chickering, Howard Allen *insurance company executive, lawyer*
Chisholm, Andrea Lynne *business association administrator, foundation administrator*
Christophe, Cleveland Aleridge *investment company executive*
Cohen, Steven A. *investment company executive*
Collins, Joseph Jameson *communications executive*
Colthup, Norman Bertram *retired spectroscopist*
Cook, Colin Burford *psychiatrist*
Critelli, Michael J. *lawyer, manufacturing executive*
Daleo, Robert *communications executive*
Dammerman, Dennis Dean *diversified technology and services company executive*
Dell, Warren Frank, II, *management consultant*
Dennies, Sandra Lee *city official*
Dillon, John T. *retired paper company executive*
Di Maria, Valerie Theresa *public relations executive*
Dolan, Thomas J. *consumer products company executive*
Dupont, Ralph Paul *lawyer, educator*
Eagan, Sherman G. *producer, communications executive*
Evans, Robert Sheldon *manufacturing executive, director*
Evans, Thomas R. *magazine publisher*
Everhart, Judd *public relations executive*
Fein, Ronnie *writer, journalist*
Ferguson, Ronald Eugene *reinsurance company executive*
Fernandez, Manual A. *information technology consulting executive*
Filter, E. Margie *business equipment manufacturing executive*
Firestone, James A. *consumer products company executive*
Fleisher, Michael D. *information technology consulting executive*
Forster, Paul H. *executive recruiter*
Fraizer, Michael D. *insurance company executive*
Frank, Laura Jean *computer scientist*
Frese, Alan D.R. *publishing executive*
Friedman, Michael *pharmaceutical executive*
Frishkorn, David Loy *finance company executive*
Gallaire, Hervé Jean *executive*
Gantos, LeRoy Douglas *retail clothing executive*
Gilman, Kenneth B. *retail executive*
Godfrey, Robert R. *financial services executive*
Gold, Steven Michael *lawyer*
Goldsmith, Donna *sports association executive*
Gonnelli, Patrick M. *finance company executive*
Goodhue, Peter Ames *obstetrician and gynecologist, educator*
Gross, Ronald Martin *forest products executive*
Grossman, Sanford Jay *economics professor*
Harper, Arthur H. *manufacturing executive*
Harrington, Richard J. *information business executive*
Hatch, Gilbert J. *consumer products company executive*
Hawley, Frank Jordan, Jr., *venture capital executive*
Hicks, Wayland R. *electronic business equipment executive*
Hogan, Frank W., III, *manufacturing executive*
Hollander, Milton Bernard *corporate executive*
Hollinger, Morton *small business owner, artist*
Horrigan, D. Gregory *packaging products executive*
Hubschman, Henry A. *lawyer*
Hudson, Harold Jordon, Jr., *retired insurance executive*
Jacobson, Ishier *retired utility executive*
Johnson, Dwayne Douglas (The Rock) *professional wrestler, actor*
Karp, Steve *producing director*
Kerr, Ian *public relations executive*
Kingsley, John McCall, Jr., *manufacturing executive*
Kisseberth, Paul Barto *retired publishing executive*
Klein, Neil Charles *physician*
Klenk, Rosemary Ellen *pediatrician*
Koproski, Alexander Robert *real estate company executive*
Lane, Hana Umlauf *editor*
Lennard, Gerald *metal products executive*
Lesko, Newland A. *paper company executive*
Lessin, Andrew Richard *accounting executive*
Lewis, Perry Joshua *investment banker*
Liddell, Chris R. *paper company executive*
Light, (Marvin) Lawrence *advertising agency executive*
Livolsi, Frank William, Jr., *lawyer*
Loh, Arthur Tsung Yuan *finance company executive*
Maarbjerg, Mary Penzold *office equipment company executive*
MacDonald, Michael C. *consumer products company executive*
Mactas, Mark V. *diversified financial services company executive*
Mahony, Edward B. *corporate financial executive*
Malloy, Dannel Patrick *mayor*
Margolis, Emanuel *lawyer, educator*
Masino, Frank A. *radiologist*
Mayes, Michele Coleman *lawyer*
McClave, Wilkes, III, *lawyer, business executive*
McGarry, Diane E. *marketing professional*
McKean, Thomas B. *company executive*
Mc Kinley, John Key *retired oil company executive*
McMahon, Linda E. *sports association executive*
Merritt, William Alfred, Jr., *retired lawyer, real estate company executive*
Mersereau, Stephen Crocker *electronic commerce executive*
Miller, Wilbur Hobart *management consultant*
Morgan, William J. *accounting company executive*
Motroni, Hector John *manufacturing executive*
Mulcahy, Anne Marie *printing company executive*
Munera, Gerard Emmanuel *manufacturing executive*
Neal, A. Michael *utilities executive*
Nevans, Roy Norman *food products executive, producer*
Nichols, Ralph Arthur *lawyer*
Nissen, David R. *utilities executive*
Olson, Richard E. *paper company executive*
Pansini, Michael Samuel *tax and financial consultant*
Paolillo, Regina M. *information technology consulting executive*
Papp, Laszlo George *architect*
Pardue, Bill *publishing executive*
Parke, James A. *corporate financial executive*
Parker, Jack Steele *retired manufacturing company executive*
Pascual, Carlos *marketing professional*
Perle, Eugene Gabriel *lawyer*
Peterson, Karen L. *information technology manager*
Phillips, Richard B. *paper company executive*
Pollock, M. Duncan *advertising executive*
Rand, A. Barry *financial services executive*
Reichenstein, Murray L. *electronics executive*
Rizzuto, Leandro Peter *consumer products company executive*
Roberts, Victoria Lynn P. *antique expert*
Robins, Robert Sidwar *political science educator, administrator*
Rogan, Stephen Joseph *software implementation consultant*
Romeril, Barry D. *office equipment company executive*
Rose, Richard Loomis *lawyer*
Rowe, William John *retired newspaper publishing executive*
Rudman, Joan Eleanor *artist, educator*
Sahota, Gurcharn Singh *mechanical engineer*
Scott, Gregory Alan *pharmacist, writer*
Shanman, James Alan *lawyer*
Sharp, Daniel Asher *foundation executive*
Sherman, Michael *lawyer*
Silver, Charles Morton *communications company executive*
Silver, R. Philip *metal products executive*
Skidd, Thomas Patrick, Jr., *lawyer*
Smith, J. Gordon *automotive executive*
Speziale, John Albert *lawyer*
Staab, Diane D. *lawyer*
Stapleton, James Francis *lawyer*
Steenburgh, Frank D. *consumer products company executive*
Stern, Arlene Helen *human resources specialist*
Stern, Brian E. *consumer products company executive*
Stevenson, Alexandra *professional tennis player*
Stillings, Irene Ella Grace Cordiner *foundation executive*
Stoveken, James E., Jr., *paper packaging and chemical company executive*
Teeters, Nancy Hays *economist, director*
Teitell, Conrad Laurence *lawyer, author*
Thomas, Dennis *paper company executive, former government official*
Tierney, Patrick John *information services executive*
Tregurtha, Paul Richard *marine transportation company executive*
Tully, Daniel Patrick *financial services executive*
Udell, Howard R. *pharmaceutical executive*
Valentine, Robert John (Bobby Valentine) *former professional baseball manager*
Walsh, David James *lawyer*
Walsh, Thomas Joseph *neuro-ophthalmologist*
Wilensky, Julius M. *publishing company executive*
Williamson, Keith Harvey *lawyer*
Willkie, Wendell Lewis, II, *lawyer*
Wilson, Mark *corporate financial executive*
Wunsch, Bonnie Rubenstein *fraternal organization executive*
Zimmerman, Lawrence A. *corporate financial executive*

Stonington
Elliott, Inger McCabe *designer, textile company executive, design consultant*
Elliott, Osborn *journalist, educator, urban activist, former dean*
Gilliland-McEnerney, Tressa Mae *performing arts educator*
Mantz, Arlan W. *physics educator*
Rees, Charles H. G. *retired finance company executive, investor, consultant*
Stoddard, Alexandra *designer, writer, lecturer*
Van Rees, Cornelius S. *lawyer*

Storrs
Cirakoglu, Menderes *researcher*
Lee, Hanho *educator, researcher*
Miceli, Thomas Joseph *economist, educator*
Piao, Daqing *biomedical researcher*
Siegle, Del *education educator*

Storrs Mansfield
Abikoff, William *mathematician, educator*
Auriemma, Geno *women's college basketball coach*
Austin, Philip Edward *university president*
Bartram, Ralph Herbert *physicist*
Brown, Richard David *history educator*
Bzymek, Zbigniew Marian *engineering educator*
Calhoun, Jim *college basketball coach*
Censky, Ellen Joan *curator, biologist*
Chinn, Peggy Lois *nursing educator, editor*
Coons, Ronald Edward *historian, educator*
Croteau, Maureen Elizabeth *journalism educator*
Crow, Laura Jean *design educator, costume designer*
Devereux, Owen Francis *retired metallurgy educator*
Gross, Robert Alan *history professor*
Jensen, Robert Gordon *nutritionist, consultant*
Jones, Clyde Adam *art educator, artist*
Kerr, Kirklyn M. *university administrator, veterinary pathologist, researcher*
Klemens, Paul Gustav *physicist, researcher*
Laufer, Hans *developmental biologist, educator*
MacDonald, John Thomas *educational administrator*
Maier, Romulus *journalist*
Marcus, Harris Leon *materials science educator*
Marcus, Philip Irving *virology educator, researcher*
Maryanski, Fred *academic administrator*
Merrill, Denise *state legislator*
Pitkin, Edward Thaddeus *aerospace engineer, consultant*
Price, Glenda Delores *university dean*
Reed, Howard Alexander *historian, educator*
Reifsnider, Kenneth Leonard *metallurgist, educator*
Shaw, Montgomery Throop *chemical engineering educator*
Skauen, Donald Matthew *retired pharmaceutical educator*
Slater, James Alexander *entomologist, educator*
Stephens, Jack Edward *civil engineer, consultant*
Troyer, John Gordon *philosopher, educator*
Tucker, Edwin Wallace *law educator*
Xu, Yu *nursing educator*

Stratford
Cox, Richard Joseph *former broadcasting executive*
DiCicco, Margaret C. *lawyer*
Feinberg, Dennis Lowell *dermatologist*
O'Rourke, James Louis *lawyer*

Suffield
Bianchi, Maria *critical care specialist, adult and acute care nurse practitioner, nursing administrator*
Hanzalek, Astrid Teicher *public information officer, consultant*
Sullivan, Edmund Bertram *writer*

Thomaston
Mühlanger, Erich *ski manufacturing company executive*

Thompson
Fisher, William Thomas *business administration educator*

Tolland
Feller, Winthrop Bruce *physycist, executive*
Wyman, Nancy S. *state legislator*

Torrington
Drobena, Thomas John *minister, educator*
McKenzie, Kathleen Julianna *artist*

Trumbull
Allen, Richard Stanley (Dick Allen) *English language educator, author*
Berg, Charles G. *insurance company executive*
Czajkowski, Frank Henry *lawyer*
Kole, Marc M. *healthcare provider executive*
Lang, James Richard *education consultant*
Madigan, Rita Duffy *career education coordinator*
Nevins, Lyn (Carolyn A. Nevins) *educational supervisor, trainer, consultant*
Norcel, Jacqueline Joyce Casale *educational administrator*
Potter, Andrew Harold *secondary school educator*
Schneider, Charles M. *healthcare provider company executive*
Thompson, Kurt B. *healthcare provider executive*
Watson, Donald Ralph *architect, artist, educator, author*
Williams, Ronald Doherty *lawyer*

Uncasville
Lobo, Rebecca *professional basketball player*

Vernon
Collins, Shawn Thomas *mechanical engineer*

Vernon Rockville
Brooks, Neil H. *physician*
Marmer, Ellen Lucille *pediatric cardiologist, mayor*
Orr, Jim (James D. Orr) *editor, writer*
Purnell, Oliver James, III, *judge*
Putnam, Richard *dentist, educator*
Roden, Jon-Paul *retired educator, labor union organizer, educational consultant*
Williams, Julius Penson *composer, conductor*
Wolff, Gregory Steven *insurance company executive*

Voluntown
Caddell, Foster *artist*
Thevenet, Patricia Confrey *social studies educator*

Wallingford
Cline, John Carroll *clinical psychologist*
Fritz, Mary G. *state legislator*
Jia, Weitao *dental products executive, researcher*
Lacourciere, William J. *pharmaceutical executive*
Lauttenbach, Carol *artist*
Romine, Jeffrey Lee *chemist*
Spero, Barry Melvin *health facility administrator*

Washington
Fishman, Mitchell Steven *lawyer*
Grimes, Margaret Whitehurst *artist, educator*
Leab, Daniel Joseph *history professor*
Nussbaum, Paul A. *retired hospitality executive*
Renouf, Edda *artist*

Washington Depot
Pendleton, Moses Robert Andrew *dancer, choreographer*
Tracy, Michael Cameron *choreographer, performer, educator*
Wolken, Jonathan *performing company executive*

Waterbury
Brown, Lillian Hill *retired academic administrator*
DeFrancesco, Mark Stephen *physician*
Dost, Mark W. *lawyer*
Dreisbach, Mary Elizabeth *manufacturing engineer*
Dudrick, Stanley John *surgeon, scientist, educator*
Eisen, Steven Leslie *neurologist*
Fischbein, Charles Alan *pediatrician*
Garsten, Joel Jay *gastroenterologist*
Goettel, Gerard Louis *federal judge*
Harper, Barbara Clara *counselor, educational program administrator, counselor*
Luedke, Frederick Lee *manufacturing executive*
McDonald, Francis Michael *judge trial referee, retired state supreme court justice*
Pape, William James, II, *newspaper publisher*
Rosa, Domenico *mathematics professor*
Shetty, Jayakara *surgeon*
Vignola, Andrew Michael, Sr., *systems management executive*
Wu, Zheng Y. *hydroinformatics engineer, hydrologist, consultant*

Waterford
Commire, Anne *playwright, writer, editor*
Hinkle, Janet *project leader*
Hinkle, Muriel Ruth Nelson *naval warfare analysis company executive*
Johnson, Gary William *environmental scientist, consultant*
Pavetti, Francis James *lawyer*
Pierson, Anne Bingham *physician*
Walsh, Peter Joseph *marketing professional*
White, George Cooke *theater director, foundation executive*

Watertown
Sherwood, James Alan *physician, scientist, educator*

West Hartford
Anderson, Michael *education educator*
Bigler, Harold Edwin, Jr., *retired investment company executive*
Calip, Roger *writer, educator*
Collins, Alma Jones *English educator, writer*
DeLibero, Mary Smellie *insurance company professional, pianist, soprano*
Doran, James Martin *retired food products company executive*
Dowling, Vincent John *retired lawyer*
Echols, Ivor Tatum *retired educator, assistant dean*
Elliot, Ralph Gregory *lawyer*
Farnen, Russell Francis *political scientist, educator*
Faude, Wilson Hinsdale *museum director, consultant*
Gaumond, Lynn E. *elementary school educator*
Gerjuoy, Herbert George *educator, psychologist, consultant, poet*
Gitterman, Alex *social work educator*
Glasser, Joseph *manufacturing and marketing executive*
Harrison, Walter Lee *university president*
Hugg, Geraldine Bertha Novotny *retired gerontology specialist, journalist*
Karotkin, Rose A. *marketing professional*
Lynch, Karen Renzulli *lawyer*
Malone, Thomas Francis *academic administrator, meteorologist*
Markham, Claire Agnes (M. Clare Markham) *retired chemistry educator, consultant*
Pressman, Thane A. *consumer products executive*
Raffay, Stephen Joseph *manufacturing executive, director*
Schweitzer, N. Tina *fiction writer, photojournalist, television producer, director, international consultant public relations, media relations, government relations*
Stavola, John Joseph *retired obstetrician-gynecologist*
Tonkin, Humphrey Richard *academic administrator, educator*
Whitman, Mara Arden *publishing executive*
Wilder, Michael Stephen *former insurance company executive*

West Haven
DeNardis, Lawrence J. *academic administrator*
Druss, Benjamin George *health services researcher, psychiatrist*
Ellis, Lynn Webster *retired finance educator, retired media consultant*
Ezekowitz, Michael David *physician*
Farquharson, Patrice Ellen *primary school educator*
Haley, Usha C.V. *international business educator*
Hatch, Annia *gymnast*
Kyriakides, Tassos Constantino *biostatistician*
Onton, Ann Louise Reuther *chemist*
Singh, Parbudyal *dean, educator*
Suster, Zeljan *business educator, dean*

West Mystic
Hoagland, Porter, Jr., *electrical and mechanical engineer, consultant*

West Simsbury
Morest, Donald Kent *neuroscientist, educator*
Ross, Coleman DeVane *accountant, insurance company executive*

Weston
Aibel, Howard J. *arbitrator, mediator*
Bleifeld, Stanley *sculptor*
Cohen, Fred Howard *lawyer, investment company executive*
Daniel, James *curator, writer*
Diforio, Robert George *literary agent*
Fredrik, Burry *theatrical producer, director*
Gerber, Frances Joyce *retired early childhood educator*
Harmon, James Allen *bank executive*
Kilty, Jerome Timothy *playwright, stage director, actor*
Murray, Stephen James *lawyer*
Murray, Thomas J. *advertising executive*

Oliver, Sandra *art dealer, painter*
Tavrow, Richard Lawrence *lawyer, corporate executive*
Thompson, N(orman) David *insurance company executive*
Wiseman, Carter Sterling *writer, educator*
Zimmerman, Bernard *investment banker*

Westport

Aasen, Lawrence Obert *public relations executive*
Altman, Lawrence Gene *biologist, educator*
Amschler, James Ralph *lawyer, relocation company executive, consultant*
Baliban, Jeffrey Lee *accountant, economist*
Barton, James Miller *lawyer, international business consultant*
Blau, Barry *marketing professional, financial consultant*
Burns, John Joseph *pharmacology educator*
Carr, Cynthia *lawyer*
Carvalko, Debora G. *editor, writer*
Chernow, Ann Levy *artist, art educator*
Clausman, Gilbert Joseph *retired medical librarian*
Crumer, Allan P. *lawyer*
Daw, Harold John *lawyer, director*
Defeo, Ronald M. *machinery manufacturing executive*
Donaldson, James Neill *banker*
Feliciano, José *entertainer*
Ferris, Roger Patrick *architect*
Fisher, Leonard Everett *artist, writer, educator*
Freedman, Judith Greenberg *state legislator, importer*
Frese, Edward Scheer, Jr., (Ted Frese) *information technology executive, consultant*
Frey, Dale Franklin *financial investment company executive, manufacturing company executive*
Gallagher, Michael Robert *consumer products company executive*
Grodd, Leslie Eric *lawyer*
Hedge, Arthur Joseph, Jr., *corporate executive*
Hotchner, Aaron Edward *author*
Kelly, Paul Knox *investment banker*
Kramer, Sidney B. *publisher, lawyer, literary agent*
Kurz, Mitchell Howard *marketing communications executive*
Levien, Roger Eli *strategy and innovation consultant*
McCormack, Donald Paul *newspaper consultant*
McFarland, Richard M. *executive recruiting consultant*
McKane, David Bennett *business executive*
Murphy, Thomas John *publishing executive*
Nedom, H. Arthur *petroleum consultant*
Newman, Paul *actor, professional race-car driver, food company executive*
O'Keefe, John David *investment specialist*
Paul, Roland Arthur *lawyer*
Razzano, Pasquale Angelo *lawyer*
Ready, Robert James *financial company executive*
Reilly, Nancy (Anne Caulfield Reilly) *painter*
Rudd, Nicholas *investor, consultant*
Sacks, Herbert Simeon *psychiatrist, educator, consultant*
Santoro, Charles William *investment banker*
Schriever, Fred Martin *management consultant, financial investor*
Sheiman, Ronald Lee *lawyer*
Siff, Marlene Ida *artist, designer*
Smith, Peter Wolfgang *physicist, artist*
Solum, John Henry *flutist, educator, author*
Spitzer, Vlad Gerard *lawyer*
Stern, Robert D. *publishing executive*
Stolz, Alan Jay *youth camp executive*
Walton, Alan George *venture capitalist*
Weyher, Harry Frederick, III, *merchant banker*
Widman, Phillip C. *machinery manufacturing executive*

Wethersfield

Bussiere, Bruce Emile *protective services official*
Jenks, Dennis *publishing executive*
Osborne, Louise *publishing executive*
Rioux, Scott Paul *music educator*
Terk, Glenn Thomas *lawyer*

Willimantic

Carter, David George, Sr., *university administrator*
Danforth, Jeffrey Scott *psychologist, educator*
Lacey, James Francis *American studies educator*
Meznar, Joan Ellen *historian, educator*
Wilson, Margaret Sullivan *retired executive dean, consultant*

Wilton

Adams, Thomas Tilley *lawyer*
Bair, Tom *publishing executive*
Binder, Steven F. *publishing executive*
Bishop, William Wade *advertising executive*
Brown, James Thompson, Jr., *computer information scientist, logistics specialist*
Caravatt, Paul Joseph, Jr., *communications company executive*
Danvers, David Bell *equity broker*
Davis, Joel *publisher*
Duke, Robert Dominick *lawyer*
Farley, James Parker *retired advertising agency executive*
Forger, Robert Durkin *retired professional association administrator*
Fox, Mitchell B. *magazine publisher*
Frank, Robert Allen *advertising executive*
Grunewald, Donald *former college president, educator*
Harty, Thomas H. *publishing executive*
Healy, James Casey *lawyer*
Hersh, Ira Paul *tax specialist, financial consultant*
Hughes, Joan Mottola *education association representative*
Juran, Joseph Moses *engineer, consultant*
Kangas, Edward A. *former diversified financial services company executive*
Kenton, James Alan *healthcare products executive*
Kriss, Patricia Anne *health services executive*
McCracken, Douglas M. *consultant company executive*
Mitchell, Richard Boyle *security consultant*
Nickel, Albert George *advertising agency executive*
Nugent, Gordon Walker *writer*
Poundstone, Sally Hill *library director*
Seitz, Nicholas Joseph *magazine editor, journalist*
Slater, Ralph Evan *lawyer*
Steinfeld, Thomas Albert *retired publisher*
Tarde, Gerard (Jerry) *magazine executive*

Weiland, Juliette Marie *public relations executive, freelance writer and photographer, freelance photographer, writer*
Winger, Dennis L. *health products executive*

Windsor

Auten, Arthur Herbert *history educator*
Ferraro, John Francis *investment banker*
Morelli, Carmen *lawyer*
Stone, William Charles *software executive, consultant*
Woodard, Peter Clark *music educator, musician*

Windsor Locks

Coelho, Sandra Signorelli *secondary school educator, consultant*

Winsted

Baccus, R. Eileen Turner *academic administrator*
Finch, Frank Herschel, Jr., *lawyer*

Woodbridge

Alvine, Robert *industrialist, entrepreneur, philanthropist*
Bondy, Philip Kramer *physician, educator*
Dupré, Louis *retired philosopher, educator*
Just, Jennifer Ramsay *television and video producer, writer*
Kleiner, Diana Elizabeth Edelman *art history educator, administrator*
Menchaca, Frank *editorial director*

Woodbury

McHale-Hendricks, Cynthia *writer*
Peck, Carole *food service executive*
Skinner, Brian John *geologist, educator*

Woodstock

Boote, Alfred Shepard *marketing researcher, educator*
Susla, Jeffrey Jonathan *English language educator*

DELAWARE

Bear

Hersi, Dorothy Talbert *education educator*
McLain, William Tome *principal, educator*
Stewart, Shirley Anne *educational administrator*

Camden Wyoming

Pfeuffer, Robert John *musician*

Dover

Adams, Thurman G., Jr., *state legislator*
Amick, Steven Hammond *state legislator, lawyer*
Boardman, Iva J. *nursing association administrator*
Braverman, Ray Howard *secondary school educator*
Britt, Maisha Dorrah *protective services official*
Broderick, Cyril Emery, Sr., *plant physiologist, educator*
Carney, John C., Jr., *lieutenant governor*
Cloutier, Catherine A. *state legislator*
Connor, Dorinda A. *state legislator*
Cook, Nancy W. *state legislator*
Delauder, William B. *academic administrator*
Denn, Matthew P. *lawyer*
Ennis, Bruce Clifford *retired lawyer*
Fallon, Tina K. *state legislator*
Ferrari, Mercedes V *secondary school educator*
Glen, Robert Alexander *state agency administrator*
Gorum, Jacquelyne W. *dean, social work educator*
Hoff, Samuel Boyer *political scientist, educator*
Lewis, Larry *communications educator, video producer*
McCabe, Margaret Clark *family nurse practitioner*
Minner, Ruth Ann *governor*
Peiffer, Randel Aaron *agricultural sciences educator, researcher*
Schroeder, John R. *state legislator, banker*
Sessoms, Allen Lee *academic administrator, former diplomat, physicist*
Smith, Charles Nathaniel *academic administrator*
Smyth, Joel Douglas *newspaper executive*
Sorenson, Liane Beth McDowell *women's affairs director, state legislator*
Spence, Terry R. *state legislator*
Steele, Myron Thomas *state supreme court chief justice*
Still, John C., III, *insurance agent, state legislator*
Stone, F. L. Peter *lawyer*
Taylor, Suzonne Berry Stewart *real estate broker*
Twilley, Joshua Marion *lawyer*
Wagner, Nancy Hughes *secondary school educator, state legislator*
Wasfi, Sadiq Hassan *chemistry professor*
Wetherall, Robert Shaw *librarian*
Williams, Donna Lee H. *state agency administrator*
Wilson, Samuel Mayhew *surgeon*
Windsor, Harriet Smith *state official*
Woodruff, Valerie *secretary of education*

Georgetown

Holland, Randy James *state supreme court justice*

Greenville

Cooch, Nancy duPont (Mrs. Edward W. Cooch Jr.) *sculptor*
DeWees, Donald Charles *securities company executive*
Long, Linda Ann *lawyer*
Schroeder, Herman Elbert *scientific consultant*

Hockessin

Croyle, Barbara Ann *health care management executive*
Dombeck, Harold Arthur *insurance company executive*

Laurel

Kile, Kenda Jones *educational consultant*

Lewes

Carriker, Melbourne Romaine *retired marine biologist*
Chapman, Janet Carter Goodrich (Mrs. John William Chapman) *economist, educator*
Costigan, Constance Frances *artist, educator*
Fried, Jeffrey Michael *health care administrator*
Spence, Sandra *retired professional society administrator*

Warden, Richard Dana *government labor union official*

Milford

Bergmann, William J. *personnel director*
Konowitz, Herbert Henry *textile company executive*

Millsboro

Carter, William Allen *sales executive, insurance company executive*
Gallite-McGinnis, Anne Rita *elementary school educator*
Kettinger, David John *broadcast executive*
Lasher, Hiram Nelson *international biological consultant, entrepreneur*

Millville

Zinman, David Joel *conductor*

Milton

Provost, Thomas Taylor *dermatology educator, researcher*
Scott, Phyllis Wright *coach, music educator*

Montchanin

Freytag, Richard Arthur *banker*
Olney, Robert C. *diversified products manufacturing executive*

New Castle

Almquist, Don *illustrator, artist*
Bellenger, George Collier, Jr., *physics educator*
Brownson, Kenneth C. *university dean*
Cansler, Leslie Ervin *retired newspaper editor*
Doberstein, Audrey K. *college president*
Henley, Deborah S. *newspaper editor*
Hill, J. Nathan *trust company executive*
von Hoelle, John Jacob Lewis *publisher, commercial developer*

Newark

Abrams, Burton A. *economics professor*
Allen, Herbert Ellis *environmental chemistry educator*
Barteau, Mark Alan *chemical engineering and chemistry educator*
Bilinsky, Yaroslav *political scientist*
Brams, Marvin Robert *economist, mental health counselor, interfaith minister*
Brown, Hilton *visual arts educator, artist, writer*
Brown, Robert Fath *philosopher, educator*
Bunkše, Edmunds Valdemārs *geographer, educator, consultant*
Burmeister, John Luther *chemistry professor, consultant*
Byrne, John Michael *energy and environmental policy educator, researcher*
Campbell, Linzy Leon *molecular biology researcher, educator*
Carroll, Charles E. *electronics executive*
Carter, Mae Riedy *retired academic official, consultant*
Christy, Charles Wesley, III, *industrial engineering educator*
Clayton, John Middleton, Jr., *development officer*
Colton, David Lem *mathematician, educator*
Connelly, Donald Preston *retired electric and gas utility company executive*
Coulet du Gard, Donna M. *language educator*
Dadmarz, Kewmars Ebrahim *physician, educator*
Davis, Darwin Jacob *operations management educator*
Day, Robert Androus *English language educator, former library director, editor, publisher*
DeLorme, Michael *toxicologist, researcher*
DiRenzo, Gordon James *sociologist, psychologist, educator*
Elson, Charles Myer *law educator*
Fattah, Abbas *research scientist*
Freel, Edward J. *former state official*
Gantzer, Mary Lou *research chemist*
Garland, Howard *psychology educator*
Gehrlein, William Vincent *business education educator*
Giacco, Alexander Fortunatus *chemical industry executive*
Godwin, Ralph Edward *retired computer operator*
Gore, Genevieve Walton *manufacturing executive*
Gore, Robert W. *electronics executive*
Graham, Frances Keesler (Mrs. David Tredway Graham) *psychologist, educator*
Halio, Jay Leon *language professional, educator*
Harik, Vasyl Michael *research scientist*
Hockersmith, Charles Edwin *information technology educator*
Homer, William Innes *art history educator, art expert, author*
Huang, Chin-pao *education educator*
Hutton, David Glenn *environmental scientist, consultant, chemical engineer*
Isaacs, Diane Scharfeld *English educator*
Jackson, M.(arvin) Dennis *journalism educator, writer*
Kaler, Eric William *chemical engineer, educator*
Kim, Hee June *engineer*
Kobayashi, Nobuhisa *civil and coastal engineer, educator*
Lathrop, Thomas Albert *language educator*
Lemay, J(oseph) A(lberic) Leo *American literature educator*
Le Min, Thomas Francis *protective services official, educator*
Lemole, Gerald Michael *surgeon*
Mangone, Gerard J. *international and maritime law educator*
McCann, Richard Stephen *lawyer*
Molz, Robert Joseph *manufacturing executive*
Murray, Richard Bennett *physics educator*
Neal, James Preston *state senator, project engineer*
Ness, Norman Frederick *astrophysicist, educator, administrator*
Raffel, Jeffrey Allen *urban affairs educator*
Rich, Daniel *provost*
Ritter, William Frederick *civil and agricultural engineering educator*
Roselle, David Paul *university president, mathematics educator*
Rowe, Charles Alfred *artist, designer, educator*
Sandler, Stanley Irving *chemical engineering educator*
Sawyer, John Edward *management educator*
Schiavelli, Melvyn David *academic administrator, science educator, researcher*
Silva, Luis M. *marketing professional*

Snair, Roger Clifford *writer, comedian*
Stark, Robert Martin *mathematician, civil engineer, educator*
Steiner, Roger Jacob *linguistics educator, writer, researcher*
Stick, Thomas Howard Fitchett *corporate architect, construction litigation consultant*
Talbert, Dorothy Georgie Burkett *social worker*
Tannian, Francis Xavier *economist, educator*
Theopold, Klaus Hellmut *chemistry professor*
Tolles, Bryant Franklin, Jr., *history and art history educator*
Townsend, Brenda S. *educational association administrator*
Venezky, Richard Lawrence *English language educator*
Weintraub, Stanley *arts and humanities educator, writer*
Welsh, Paul Patrick *retired lawyer*
Wilson, Deborrah *physical education educator*
Wolters, Raymond *historian, educator*
Woo, S. B. (Shien-Biau Woo) *former lieutenant governor, physics educator*

Rehoboth Beach

Bischoff, Kenneth Bruce *chemical engineer, educator*
Little, R. Donald *real estate entrepreneur*

Rockland

Harvey, Andre *sculptor*
Levinson, John Milton *obstetrician, gynecologist*
Rubin, Alan A. *pharmaceutical and biotechnology consultant*

Seaford

Campbell, Eugene Paul *retired public health administrator*

Smyrna

Hutchison, James Arthur, Jr., *architectural and engineering company executive*

Washington

Comey, James B., Jr., *federal agency administrator*
Diaz-Balart, Mario *congressman*
Hutchinson, Tim *former senator*

Wilmington

Amado, David *conductor*
Ambro, Thomas L. *federal judge*
Bader, John Merwin *lawyer*
Battaglia, Basil Richard *former political party official, company executive*
Baumann, Julian Henry, Jr., *lawyer*
Benes, Solomon *biomedical scientist, physician*
Berger, Carolyn *state supreme court justice*
Biondi, O. Francis *lawyer*
Blankenship, Roy *conservator, artist, writer*
Blevins, Patricia M. *state legislator*
Blumenfeld, Jack Barry *lawyer*
Boardman, William Penniman *lawyer, banker*
Borel, James Calvin *chemical company executive*
Bounds-Seemans, Pamella J. *artist*
Brady, M. Jane *state attorney general*
Brown Leatherberry, Thomas Henry *gospel music company executive, clergy member*
Butterfield, Margaret Anne Davis *music educator, vocalist*
Carpenter, Edmund Nelson, II, *retired lawyer*
Cason, June Macnabb *musician, educator, arts administrator, fundraiser*
Cason, Roger Lee *retired chemical company executive, educator, consultant*
Chagnon, Lucille Tessier *workforce development and literacy specialist*
Cochran, John R. *bank executive*
Connelly, Thomas M., Jr., *pharmaceutical executive*
Connolly, Colm F. *prosecutor*
Copeland, Tatiana Brandt *accountant*
Corbo, Vincent J. *textiles executive*
Cornelison, Floyd Shovington, Jr., *retired psychiatrist, former educator*
Cosgrove, Howard Edward, Jr., *utilities executive*
Crittenden, Eugene Dwight, Jr., *chemical company executive*
Dalziel, Sean Mark *pharmaceuticals researcher*
Dao, Thuy Dinh *personal care industry executive*
Darko, Denis F. *research scientist, educator, physician*
Devine, Donn *lawyer, genealogist, former city official*
Donnelly, Edward J., Jr., *pharmaceutical executive*
Emmert, Richard Eugene *retired industrial and professional association executive*
Erisman, James A. *lawyer*
Fenton, Wendell *lawyer*
Finkelstein, Jesse Adam *lawyer*
Floyd, Israel J. *chemicals executive*
Freeh, Louis Joseph *lawyer*
Frelick, Robert Westcott *physician, consultant*
Frywald, J. Erik *agricultural products executive*
Gamble, Donald Geoffrey Bidmead *lawyer*
Gibson, Joseph Whitton, Jr., *retired chemical company executive*
Goldberg, Morton Edward *pharmacologist*
Goldstein, Jack Charles *lawyer*
Gonzalez, Ricardo *surgeon, educator*
Goodmanson, Richard R. *chemicals executive*
Graham, Barbara S. *electric power industry executive*
Green, James Samuel *lawyer*
Griffin, Jo Ann Thomas *retired financial planner, tax specialist*
Gulyas, Diane H. *manufacturing executive*
Gupta, Rakesh Kumar *internist*
Hammonds, Bruce L. *bank executive*
Hannigan, Patricia C. *prosecutor*
Harley, Robison Dooling *ophthalmologist, educator*
Hartwick, Paul S., Jr., *bank executive, writer*
Hartzell, Charles R. *research administrator, biochemist, cell biologist*
Herdeg, John Andrew *lawyer*
Higgins, Roxanne Snelling *educational consultant*
Hodgson, John C. *manufacturing executive*
Holliday, Charles O., Jr., *chemical company executive*
Holtzman, Arnold Harold *chemical company executive*
Ianni, Francis Alphonse *state official, former army officer*
Ikeda, Satoshi *thoracic and cardiovascular surgeon*
Inselman, Laura Sue *pediatrician, educator*
Jacobs, Jack Bernard *judge*

Jewell, George Benson *lawyer, educator, minister*
Jezl, Barbara Ann *retired chemist, automation consultant*
Johnson, W. Donald *research and development company executive*
Johnston, William David *lawyer*
Julian, J. R. *lawyer*
Kalil, James, Sr., *investment executive*
Kelleher, Daniel Francis *lawyer*
Kirk, Richard Dillon *lawyer*
Kirkpatrick, Andrew Booth, Jr., *lawyer*
Kissa, Erik *retired chemist, consultant*
Klayman, Barry Martin *lawyer*
Kneavel, Ann Callanan *humanities educator, communications consultant*
Kneavel, Thomas Charles, Jr., *psychologist, educator*
Kristol, Daniel Marvin *lawyer*
Krol, John A. *retired diversified chemicals executive*
Krulak, Charles Chandler *marine officer*
Kullman, Ellen J. *manufacturing executive*
Kwolek, Stephanie Louise *chemist, researcher*
Landgraf, Kurt M. *chemicals executive*
Lanyon, E. Jean *artist, poet*
Lassen, John Kai *development company executive*
Latchum, James Levin *federal judge*
Lerner, Randolph D. *finance company executive*
Lewis, George Withrow *business executive*
Lewis, Mary Therese *publisher*
Lukach, Carl Andrew *retired chemicals executive*
MacCormack, George F. *pharmaceutical executive*
Magee, Thomas Hugh *lawyer*
Maley, Patricia Ann *preservation planner*
Mand, Martin G. *financial executive*
Marcali, Jean Gregory *retired chemist*
Martin, Patricia Carmella *counselor, entrepreneur*
Mathieu, Henri-Pierre *physician*
McCoy, Verl Eugene, Jr., *physical chemist, consultant*
McDowell, Charles S. *lawyer*
McLeer, Laureen Dorothy *drug development and pharmaceutical professional*
Memeger, Wesley, Jr., *retired chemist, painter*
Mobley, Stacey J. *consumer products company executive*
Moore, Brian Clive *actuary*
Murphy, Arthur Thomas *systems engineer*
Naylor, Craig G. *engineering company executive*
Nottingham, Robinson Kendall *insurance company executive*
Olson, Leroy Calvin *retired educational administration educator*
Pahnke, Greg Randolph *surgeon*
Parshall, George William *chemist, researcher*
Parsons, Donald Francis *lawyer*
Pazuniak, George *lawyer*
Pell, Sidney *epidemiologist*
Peterson, Russell Wilbur *former association executive, former state governor*
Pfeiffer, Gary M. *chemical company executive*
Robinson, Sue L(ewis) *federal judge*
Rodgers, Stephen John *lawyer, physician, consultant*
Rogerson, Craig Allan *manufacturing executive*
Rogoski, Patricia Diana *financial executive*
Rose, Selwyn H. *chemical company executive*
Roth, Jane Richards *federal judge*
Rothschild, Steven James *lawyer*
Rudge, Howard J. *corporate lawyer*
Sager, Philip Travis *research physician, cardiologist, cardiac electrophysiologist*
St. Clair, Jesse Walton, Jr., *retired savings and loan executive*
Saltarelli, Michael A. *priest*
Saye, JoAnne M. *research scientist, pharmacologist*
Schmerling, Erwin Robert *counselor, retired physicist*
Schwartz, Murray Merle *federal judge*
Semple, James William *lawyer*
Sheridan, John Robert *lawyer*
Shevchuck, Harry *retired image systems consultant*
Shipley, Samuel Lynn *advertising and public relations executive*
Sleet, Gregory M. *lawyer, judge*
Smeck, William H. *computer scientist*
Smith, Craig Bennett *lawyer*
Smith, S(tewart) Gregory *ophthalmologist, inventor, product developer, consultant, author*
Smook, Malcolm Andrew *chemist, chemical company executive*
Spence, Janet Blake Conley (Mrs. Alexander Pyott Spence) *civic worker*
Stapleton, Walter King *federal judge*
Stein, Robert Benjamin *biomedical researcher, physician*
Sullivan, Lawrence Matthew *lawyer*
Sutton, Ernest Shaw *chemical engineer*
Syer, Fontaine *theater director*
Tigani, Bruce William *lawyer*
Townsend, P(reston) Coleman *agricultural business executive*
Uffner, Michael S. *automotive executive*
Van Dyk, Tina Kangas *microbiologist, researcher*
Vattilana, Joseph William *retired chief state safety inspector*
Wachtel, Howard K. *mathematician, educator*
Waisanen, Christine M. *lawyer, writer*
Wallace, Jesse Wyatt *pharmaceutical scientist*
Ward, Rodman, Jr., *lawyer, director*
Waritz, Richard Stefan *toxicologist, researcher*
Wells, James Robert *pharmaceutical company executive*
Wesler, Ken *performing arts company executive*
Whitney, Douglas Edgar, Sr., *lawyer*
Wier, Richard Royal, Jr., *lawyer*
Williams, Richmond Dean *library appraiser, consultant*
Wong, Pancras C. *biomedical researcher, educator*
Wright, Vernon Hugh Carroll *bank executive*
Ziolkowska-Boehm, Aleksandra *writer*

Wyoming
Bailey, Kay Wood *management consultant*

DISTRICT OF COLUMBIA

Bolling AFB
Dendinger, William J. *career officer, chaplain*

Fort Mcnair
Chilcoat, Richard Allen *army officer, university president*
Miller, David Allen *air force officer*

Pentagon
Adams, Ronald Emerson *army officer, federal agency administrator*

Washington
Aall, Pamela R. *foundation administrator*
Aaron, Henry J. *economist*
Aaron, Henry Jacob *economics professor*
Aaronson, David Ernest *law educator, lawyer*
Abbott, Alden Francis *lawyer, government official, educator*
Abeles, Charles Calvert *retired lawyer*
Abercrombie, Neil *congressman*
Abernathy, Kathleen Q. *government agency administrator*
Able, Edward H. *association executive*
Abler, Ronald Francis *geography educator*
Aboul-Enein, Youssef H. *military officer*
Abraham, Katharine Gail *economics professor*
Abraham, Spencer *secretary of energy*
Abrams, Elliott *governmental official*
Abramson, Patty *investment company executive*
Abshire, David Manker *diplomat, research executive*
Acevedo-Vila, Anibal *congressional representative, state legislator, lawyer*
Acheson, David Campion *lawyer, author, policy analyst*
Ackerman, Gary Leonard *congressman*
Ackerson, Nels J(ohn) *lawyer*
Acord, Bobby *health science association administrator*
Adams, A. John Bertrand *public affairs consultant*
Adams, Lorraine *reporter*
Adams, Robert Edward *journalist*
Adams, Roger C. *lawyer*
Adams-Campbell, Lucille L. *health facility administrator*
Adamson, Terrence Burdett *lawyer*
Aderholt, Robert B. *congressman, attorney*
Adler, Howard, Jr., *lawyer*
Adler, Howard Bruce *lawyer*
Affronti, Lewis Francis, Sr., *microbiologist, educator*
Agrast, Mark David *lawyer*
Aguirre, Eduardo, Jr., *federal agency administrator*
Aguirre-Baca, Francisco *publisher, consultant*
Aguirre-Sacasa, Francisco Xavier *international banker, diplomat*
Aguirre-Sacasa, Rafael Eugenio *international consultant*
Aisenberg, Irwin Morton *lawyer*
Akaka, Daniel Kahikina *senator*
Akerson, Daniel F. *investment company executive*
Akey, Steven John *public relations executive*
Akin, W. Todd *congressman, former state legislator*
Akunwafor, Daniel Dominic *librarian, educator*
Alatis, James Efstathios *university dean emeritus*
Albanese, Jay Samuel *criminologist, educator*
Albernathy, Kathleen Q. *federal agency administrator*
Alberts, Bruce Michael *President National Academy of Sciences, biochemist*
Albrecht, Kathe Hicks *art historian, visual resources manager*
Albright, Joseph William *army officer*
Albright, Penrose Carballo *federal agency administrator*
Aldonas, Grant D. *federal agency administrator*
Aleinikoff, Thomas Alexander *dean, law educator*
Alexander, Clifford Joseph *lawyer*
Alexander, Clifford L., Jr., *management consultant, lawyer, former secretary of army*
Alexander, Donald Crichton *lawyer*
Alexander, Joseph Kunkle, Jr., *physicist*
Alexander, Lamar (Andrew Lamar Alexander) *senator, former secretary of education, former governor, lawyer*
Alexander, Richard C. *association administrator*
Alexander, Rodney M. *congressman*
Allan, Ronald Gage *university research coordinator*
Allard, Nicholas W. *lawyer*
Allard, Wayne (A. Wayne Allard) *senator, veterinarian*
Allard, William Albert *photographer*
Allen, Beverly E. *medical librarian*
Allen, Charles E. *federal agency administrator*
Allen, Claude Alexander *federal agency administrator*
Allen, George Felix *senator, former governor*
Allen, Richard Vincent *international business consultant, policy advisor*
Allen, Thomas H. *congressman, lawyer*
Allen, William Hayes *lawyer, educator*
Allen, William Jere *minister*
Allen, William L. *editor*
Alleyne, George A.O. *public health administrator, educator*
Allgeier, Peter F. *federal agency administrator*
Allman, William G. *curator*
Allnutt, Robert Frederick *management consultant, corporate director*
Alloway, Robert Malcombe *computer consulting executive*
Alperovitz, Gar *author, educator*
Altenhofen, Jane Ellen *federal agency administrator, auditor*
Altschul, Alfred Samuel *airline executive*
Alvarez, Scott G. *lawyer*
Alvarez de DeClaris, María Clemencia *writer, educator*
Alvillar-Speake, Theresa *federal agency administrator*
Alward, Ruth Rosendall *nursing consultant*
Ames, Frank Anthony *percussionist, film producer*
Ampy, Franklin Roosevelt *zoologist, educator*
Amron, Cory M. *lawyer*
Amyx, Terry Don *corporate financial executive*
Andersen, Margo K. *federal agency administrator*
Andersen, Robert Allen *retired government official*
Andersen, Robert Michael *lawyer*
Anderson, David Wayne *federal agency administrator*
Anderson, Donald Morgan *entomologist, researcher*
Anderson, Frederick Randolph, Jr., *lawyer, law educator*
Anderson, Mary Ann Grasso *theater association executive*
Andreadis, Tim D. *physicist, researcher*
Andrew, Joseph Jerald *lawyer*
Andrews, John Frank *editor, author, educator*
Andrews, Laureen E. *foundation administrator*
Andrews, Lewis Davis, Jr., *trade association executive*
Andrews, Mark Joseph *lawyer*
Andrews, Robert E. *congressman*
Anfinson, Thomas Elmer *government financial administrator*
Angell, Lois Louise *writer, comedienne, poet*
Angier, Natalie Marie *science journalist*
Angotti, Catherine Marie *occupational health director*
Aninat, Eduardo *international banking official*
Anjaria, Shailendra J. *international finance official*
Anlian, Steven James *urban planner, consultant*
Ansary, Cyrus A. *investment company executive, lawyer*
Anthony, Donald Barrett *engineering executive*
Anthony, Sheila Foster *government official*
Anthony, Stephen Pierce *lawyer*
Anthony, Virginia Quinn Bausch *medical association executive*
Antonelli, Angela Maria *federal agency administrator*
Apostolos-Cappadona, Diane Pan *religion and art educator*
Apple, Daina Dravnieks *government agency official*
Apple, James Glenn *lawyer, educator*
Apple, Martin Allen *science executive, scientist, educator*
Apple, Raymond Walter, Jr., *journalist*
Applebaum, Anne *journalist, writer*
Arana, Marie *editor, writer*
Archambault, JoAllyn *museum administrator, anthropologist*
Archer, Glenn LeRoy, Jr., *federal judge*
Archer, William Reynolds, Jr., (Bill Archer) *lobbyist, former congressman*
Archibald, George *reporter*
Arena, Kelli *news correspondent*
Arend, Anthony Clark *international relations educator*
Argrett, Loretta Collins *assistant attorney general, educator*
Argyros, George L. *ambassador, former development company executive, former professional sports team owner*
Aring, Monika Kosmahl *education economist, consultant, researcher*
Arkilic, Galip Mehmet *mechanical engineer, educator*
Arling, Bryan Jeremy *internist*
Arling, Donna Dickson *social worker*
Arlook, Ira Arthur *non-profit association executive, communications firm administrator*
Armacost, Michael Hayden *research institution executive, ambassador*
Armendariz, Tony *federal agency administrator*
Armitage, Richard Lee *federal agency administrator*
Armstrong, Alexandra *financial advisor*
Armstrong, Spence M. *aerospace technology administrator*
Arndt, Richard Tallmadge *writer, consultant, cultural organization administrator*
Arnez, Nancy Levi *educational leadership educator*
Arnold, G. Dewey, Jr., *accountant*
Arnold, Gary Howard *film critic*
Arnold, William Edwin *health advocate, consultant*
Arnovitz, Benton Mayer *editor*
Aron, Mark G. *lawyer, transportation executive*
Arundel, John Howard *financial consultant*
Ascensão, João Luis Afonso *physician, researcher*
Aschheim, Joseph *economist, educator*
Ashcroft, John David *attorney general*
Ashton, Richard M. *federal lawyer*
Asker, James Robert *magazine editor*
Åslund, Anders *economist*
Assad, George John *investment banker*
Atcheson, Richard *editor*
Atherton, Charles Henry *federal commission administrator*
Atkins, Paul S. *commissioner*
Atkinson, Lawrence Rush, IV, (Rick Atkinson) *journalist*
Atlas, Liane Wiener *writer*
Atlas, Terry *journalist*
Attkisson, Sharyl T. *newscaster, correspondent, writer*
Atwood, James R. *lawyer*
Auerbach, Judith Diane *public health service officer*
Auerbach, Stuart Charles *development loan fund administrator, journalist*
Aufhauser, David D. *lawyer, former federal agency administrator*
Augustyn, Noel James *lawyer*
Austin, Roy L. *ambassador*
Avery, Byllye Yvonne *health association administrator*
Avery, Gordon Bennett *medical educator, neonatologist*
Avil, Richard Daniel, Jr., *lawyer*
Axelrod, Jonathan Gans *lawyer*
Ayer, Donald Belton *lawyer*
Ayres, Judith Elizabeth *federal agency administrator*
Ayres, Mary Ellen *government official*
Azar, Alex Michael, II, *federal agency administrator*
Baasan, Ragchaa *diplomat*
Babbitt, Bruce Edward *former federal official, lawyer*
Babby, Ellen Reisman *education administrator*
Babby, Lon S. *lawyer*
Baca, Joe *congressman*
Bachman, Kenneth Leroy, Jr., *lawyer*
Bachus, Spencer T., III, *congressman, lawyer*
Bacon, Kenneth H. *federal agency administrator, editor, journalist*
Bacon, Sylvia *judge, law educator*
Bader, William Banks *historian, foundation executive, former corporate executive*
Badger, Doug *federal agency administrator*
Baer, Michael Alan *political scientist, educator*
Baer, William J. *lawyer*
Baginski, Maureen A. *federal agency administrator*
Bahr, Morton *labor union administrator*
Baigis, Judith Ann *nursing educator, academic administrator*
Bailar, John Christian, III, *retired public health educator, physician, statistician*
Bailey, Charles Waldo, II, *journalist, author*
Bailey, Sue *federal agency administrator, osteopath*
Bailey, Vicky A. *federal agency administrator*
Bainum, Peter Montgomery *aerospace engineer, consultant*
Bair, Sheila Colleen *federal agency administrator*
Baird, Brian N. *congressman*
Baker, D. James *oceanographic and atmospheric administrator*
Baker, Howard Henry, Jr., *ambassador, former senator, lawyer*
Baker, Richard Hugh *congressman*
Baldwin, Tammy *congresswoman*
Baldyga, Leonard J. *retired diplomat, international consultant*
Ballenger, Thomas Cass (Thomas Ballenger) *congressman*
Balz, Daniel John *newspaper editor, journalist*
Bandar, Prince bin Sultan bin Abd al-Aziz Al Saud *Saudi Arabian ambassador to United States*
Bandler, Donald Keith *diplomat*
Bandow, Douglas Leighton *editor, columnist, policy consultant*
Banfield, Marian D. *federal agency administrator*
Banks, Richard Charles *ornithologist*
Banzhaf, John F., III, *legal association administrator, lawyer*
Baran, Jan Witold *lawyer, educator*
Barber, Ben Bernard Andrew *journalist*
Barbosa, Rubens Antonio *Brazilian ambassador*
Bardin, David J. *lawyer*
Barnes, Donald Michael *lawyer*
Barnes, Mark James *lawyer*
Barnes, Michael Darr *lawyer, think tank executive*
Barnet, Richard Jackson *author, educator*
Barnett, Robert Bruce *lawyer, educator*
Barr, Michael Blanton *lawyer*
Barreto, Hector V. *federal agency administrator*
Barrett, James Gresham *congressman*
Barrett, Laurence Irwin *public relations executive, writer*
Barrett, Richard David *university director, consultant, bank executive*
Barrie, John Paul *lawyer, educator*
Barr-Kumar, Raj *architect*
Barron, Jerome Aure *law educator*
Barron, Myra Hymovich *lawyer*
Barry, John J. *labor union leader*
Barry, John L. *military officer*
Barshefsky, Charlene *lawyer, former diplomat*
Barthwell, Andrea G. *federal agency administrator*
Bartlett, Bruce Reeves *economist, columnist*
Bartlett, Charles Leffingwell *foundation executive, former newspaperman*
Bartlett, Roscoe G. *congressman*
Bartnoff, Judith *judge*
Barton, Jean Marie *psychologist, educator*
Bartuska, Ann *government official, biologist*
Barusch, Ronald Charles *lawyer*
Basch, Richard Vennard *photographer, producer, writer, director*
Baskir, Lawrence M. *chief judge*
Bass, Charles F. *congressman*
Bass, Gary D. *advocate, director*
Basseches, Robert Treinis *lawyer*
Bassin, Jules *foreign service officer*
Batdorf, Lynn Robert *horticulturist*
Bateman, Paul William *government official, business executive*
Bath, Ronald J. *military officer*
Batla, Raymond John, Jr., *lawyer*
Batiss, Emery John *actor*
Battle, Vincent M. *ambassador*
Baucus, Max S. *senator*
Baughman, J. Ross *photographer, writer, educator*
Baum, Ingeborg Ruth *librarian*
Baxter, Nathan Dwight *dean*
Baxter, Nevins Dennis *bank consultant*
Baxter, Sandra L *government agency administrator*
Bayh, Evan *senator, former governor*
Bayly, John Henry, Jr., *judge*
Beach, Walter Eggert *retired publishing organization executive*
Beale, Betty (Mrs. George K. Graeber) *columnist, writer*
Beale, Susan Yates *social worker*
Beall, James Howard *physicist, educator*
Beato, Cristina V. *government agency administrator*
Beauprez, Bob *congressman*
Bebchick, Leonard Norman *lawyer*
Becerra, Xavier *congressman, lawyer*
Beck, Richard Thomas *government agency administrator*
Becker, Brenda L. *federal agency administrator*
Becker, Grace Chung *lawyer*
Becker, Mary Louise *political scientist*
Beckham, Edgar Frederick *educational consultant*
Beckner, Everet Hess *federal agency administrator*
Beckwith, Edward Jay *lawyer*
Becraft, Carolyn Howland *communications executive*
Bedard, Emil R. *career officer*
Bedini, Silvio A. *historian, author*
Bednash, Geraldine Polly *educational association administrator*
Beers, Donald Osborne *lawyer*
Begala, Paul Edward *television personality, political scientist, consultant*
Beghe, Renato *federal judge*
Behney, Clyde Joseph *health policy researcher*
Behrman, Greg *writer, health policy coordinator*
Beisner, Robert Lee *historian*
Beizer, Robert A. *lawyer*
Bell, Jeanne Viner *public relations counselor*
Bell, Jerry Alan *science education association administrator*
Bell, Robert Christopher (Chris Bell) *congressman*
Bell, Stephen Robert *lawyer*
Bellanti, Joseph A. *microbiologist, educator*
Beller, Herbert N. *lawyer*
Bellinger, Edgar Thomson *lawyer*
Bello, Judith Hippler *lawyer, trade association administrator*
Bellows, Michael Donald *foreign service officer*
Belman, A. Barry *pediatric urologist*
Belman, Murray Joel *lawyer*
Belson, James Anthony *judge*
Bender, David Ray *library association executive*
Benitez, Juan Carlos *federal agency administrator*
Benjamin, Georges Curtis *emergency physician, consultant*
Bennett, Alexander Elliot *lawyer*
Bennett, Betty T. *English literature educator, university dean, writer*
Bennett, Robert F. *senator*
Bennett, Robert Stephen *lawyer*
Benoit, Marilyn B. *psychiatrist, medical association administrator*
Benson, Miles Richard *journalist*
Bentsen, Kenneth E., Jr., *congressman*
Berendzen, Richard *astronomer, educator, author*
Beresford, Douglas Lincoln *lawyer*
Bereuter, Douglas Kent *congressman*
Berg, Patricia Elene *molecular biologist*

Graham, Daniel Robert (Bob Graham) *senator, former governor*
Graham, Donald Edward *publishing company executive*
Graham, John David *federal agency administrator*
Graham, Lindsey O. *senator*
Graham, Thomas, Jr., *lawyer*
Graham, Thomas Richard *lawyer*
Graham, William Pierson *investment banker, entrepreneur*
Gramlich, Edward Martin *public policy, economics educator, federal agency administrator*
Granados, Francisco D. *retired physician*
Grandmaison, J. Joseph *federal agency administrator*
Grant, Carl N. *communications and sales executive*
Grapin, Jacqueline G. *economist*
Grassley, Charles Ernest *senator*
Graves, Samuel B. *congressman, former state legislator*
Graves-Roman, Patricia Ann *educator, researcher, writer*
Gravitz, Melvin A *psychologist, consultant*
Gray, Bradford Hitch *health policy researcher*
Gray, Clayland Boyden *lawyer*
Gray, Mary Wheat *statistician, lawyer*
Gray, Sheila Hafter *psychiatrist, psychoanalyst*
Gray, Todd *food service executive*
Grealy, Mary R. *medical association administrator*
Grebow, Edward *media specialist, finance company executive*
Green, Donald Hugh *lawyer*
Green, Gene *congressman*
Green, Grant S., Jr., *federal agency administrator*
Green, Joyce Hens *federal judge*
Green, Mark Andrew *congressman, lawyer*
Green, Thomas Charles *lawyer*
Greenberg, Milton *political scientist, educator*
Greenberger, I. Michael *lawyer*
Greene, Thomas Hardy *architect*
Greenert, Jonathan W. *career officer*
Greenfield, Michael A. *federal agency administrator*
Greenhouse, Linda Joyce *journalist*
Greenspan, Alan *bank executive, economist*
Greenwald, John Doyle *lawyer*
Greenwood, James Charles *congressman*
Greenwood, William Warren *journalist*
Gregg, Judd *senator, former governor*
Gregorian, Raffi *diplomat*
Gregory, Bettina Louise *journalist*
Gregory, John Forrest *information technology specialist, librarian*
Grenier, Edward Joseph, Jr., *lawyer*
Gribbon, Daniel McNamara *lawyer*
Grier, Phillip Michael *lawyer, former association executive*
Griffenhagen, George Bernard *trade association executive*
Griffin, Janice *political organization professional*
Griffin, Kelly Ann *public relations executive, consultant*
Griffin, Richard J. *federal agency administrator*
Griffin, Robert Thomas *automotive company executive*
Grijalva, Raul *congressman*
Griles, James Steven *federal agency administrator*
Grob, George Frederick *health, social services association administrator*
Gross, Patrick Walter *management consultant*
Gross, Roberta Lee *inspector general*
Grossi, Ralph Edward *agricultural conservation organization executive, farmer, rancher*
Grossman, Joanne Barbara *lawyer*
Grosvenor, Gilbert Melville *journalist, educator, business executive*
Grove, Brandon Hambright, Jr., *diplomat*
Grucci, Felix J., Jr., *former congressman*
Guard, Patricia J. *federal agency administrator*
Guenther, Jack Donald *banker*
Gulland, Eugene D. *lawyer*
Gumpert, Gunther *artist*
Gurulé, Jimmy *legal educator, federal agency administrator*
Gutierrez, Luis V. *congressman, elementary education educator*
Gutknecht, Gilbert William, Jr., *congressman, former state legislator*
Gutman, Harry Largman *lawyer, educator*
Gutman, Roy William *reporter*
Guttman, Egon *law educator*
Guzda, Henry Peter *industrial relations specialist*
Guzy, Carol *photojournalist*
Gwaltney, Corbin *editor, publishing executive*
Haaga, John Gregory *demographer*
Hackbarth, Glenn M. *human services administrator*
Hagan, Philip Edward, Jr., *academic administrator*
Hagee, Michael W. *commandant of the US Marine Corps*
Hagel, Charles *senator*
Hager, Mary Hastings *nutritionist, educator, consultant*
Hager, Susan Kulka *public relations executive*
Hahn, Lorna *political organization executive, author*
Haines, Terry L. *lawyer, consultant*
Hale, Janet *federal agency administrator*
Haley, John *risk management consultant*
Haley, Roger Kendall *librarian*
Hall, Betty Jean *public interest group executive, lawyer*
Hall, George Robert *economist*
Hall, Kathryn Walt *ambassador*
Hall, Michael Lee *federal government agency grants administrator*
Hall, Ralph Moody *congressman*
Hall, Thomas Forrest *federal agency administrator, naval officer*
Hallett, Carol Boyd *air transportation executive*
Hallgren, Richard Edwin *meteorologist*
Halperin, Jerome Arthur *pharmaceutical executive*
Halperin, Morton H. *political scientist*
Halperin, Samuel *education and training policy analyst*
Halpern, Cheryl F. *federal agency administrator*
Halsey, Ashley, III, *newspaper editor*
Halstead, Edward Allen (Ted Halstead) *think-tank executive*
Halvorson, Newman Thorbus, Jr., *lawyer*
Hamburg, Margaret Ann (Peggy Hamburg) *public health administrator*
Hamilton, Lee Herbert *educational organization administrator, former congressman*
Hamilton, Richard Clay *professional basketball player*
Hamlisch, Marvin *composer, conductor, pianist, entertainer*
Hammerschmidt, John Arthur *federal agency administrator*
Hammond, Anthony *commissioner*
Hammond, William Michael *historian, educator*
Hammonds, Timothy Merrill *association executive, economist*
Hamre, John J. *think-tank executive*
Hand, John Oliver *museum curator*
Handman, Bobbie (Barbara Handman) *foundation executive*
Hanford, John V., III, *federal agency administrator*
Hanley, Frank *labor union official*
Hanlon, Glen *professional athletics coach*
Hannaford, Peter Dor *public relations executive, writer*
Hannett, Frederick James *healthcare consulting company executive*
Hansen, Charles Martin, III, *lobbyist*
Hansen, James Vear *former congressman*
Hansen, Joseph T. *labor union administrator*
Hansen, Mark Charles *lawyer*
Harbour, Pamela Jones *lawyer*
Harding, Fann *health scientist, administrator*
Hargrove, Linda *professional basketball coach*
Harkin, Thomas Richard *senator*
Harlem, Susan Lynn *librarian*
Harman, Jane *congresswoman*
Harman, William Boys, Jr., *lawyer*
Harness, Gregory C. *Senate librarian*
Harpham, Virginia Ruth *violinist*
Harrington, Anthony Stephen *lawyer, diplomat*
Harrington, Kathleen M. *federal agency administrator*
Harris, Don Victor, Jr., *lawyer*
Harris, Jeffrey *lawyer*
Harris, Katherine *congresswoman*
Harris, Scott Blake *lawyer*
Harris, Steven Brown *lawyer*
Harrison, Donald *lawyer*
Harrison, Earl David *lawyer, real estate company officer*
Harrison, Marion Edwyn *lawyer*
Harrison, Patricia de Stacy *federal agency administrator*
Harrison, Ronald O. *association administrator*
Harrop, William Caldwell *retired ambassador, foreign service officer*
Hart, Christopher Alvin *lawyer*
Hart, Clyde J., Jr., *federal agency administrator*
Hart, Melissa Anne *congresswoman*
Hart, Sarah V. *federal agency administrator*
Harter, Donald Harry *neurologist, medical educator*
Hartman, Carl (Howard Carl Hartman) *reporter*
Hartman, Gary E. *pediatric surgeon*
Hartman, George Eitel *architect*
Hartmann, Heidi Irmgard Victoria *economist, research organization executive*
Hartmann, Robert Sankey *hospital administrator, communications and fundraising executive*
Hartwell, Stephen *investment company executive*
Harty, Maura *federal agency administrator, former ambassador*
Harvey, Edith M. *federal agency administrator*
Harvey, Eleanor Jones *museum curator*
Harvey, Jane Hull *church administrator*
Harvey, John Collins *physician, educator*
Harwit, Martin Otto *astrophysicist, writer, educator, museum director*
Hassan, Aftab Syed *education specialist, author, editor*
Hasselmo, Ann Hayes Die *executive recruiter, consultant, psychologist, educator, retired academic administrator*
Hassett, Joseph Mark *lawyer*
Hastert, Dennis (J. Dennis Hastert) *congressman*
Hastings, Alcee Lamar *congressman, former federal judge*
Hastings, Richard Doc *congressman*
Hattan, Susan K. *legislative staff member*
Hauser, Richard Alan *Federal Agency Administrator, Lawyer*
Hausfeld, Michael D. *lawyer*
Havens, Arnold I. *federal agency administrator*
Havlicek, Franklin J. *communications executive*
Hawke, John Daniel, Jr., *United States Comptroller of the Currency*
Hawke, Paul Henry *historian*
Hawkins, Philip Linton *real estate executive*
Hawks, William T. *federal agency administrator*
Hayes, Allene Valerie Farmer *government executive*
Hayes, Kevin Gregory *university administrator*
Hayes, Paula Freda *governmental official*
Hayes, Robert (Robin Hayes) *congressman*
Haynes, R. Michael *lawyer*
Haynes, William J(ames), II, *lawyer*
Haythe, Winston McDonald *lawyer, educator, consultant, real estate investor*
Hayworth, J(ohn) D(avid), Jr., *congressman, former sportscaster*
Hazard, Roberta Louise *career officer*
Headden, Susan M. *editor*
Hebert, Jay Howell *lawyer*
Hecht, Anthony Evan *poet*
Hecht, Marjorie Mazel *editor*
Hecklinger, Richard E. *ambassador*
Heckman, Jerome Harold *lawyer*
Heddell, Gordon S. *federal agency administrator*
Hedges, Harry George *retired computer scientist, educator*
Hedges, Kamla King *library director*
Hedlund, Charles John *oil company executive, conservationist*
Heelan, Patrick Aidan *philosophy educator*
Heenan, Michael Terence *lawyer*
Heffernan, James Vincent *lawyer*
Hefley, Joel M. *congressman*
Hefter, Laurence Roy *lawyer*
Height, Dorothy I. *association executive*
Heineman, Heinz *chemist*
Heinemann, Heinz *chemist, educator, researcher, consultant*
Heinz Kerry, Teresa F. *foundation administrator*
Heiss, Harry Glen *archivist*
Helfer, Ricki Tigert *banking consultant*
Helgerson, John Leonard *federal agency administrator*
Heller, (Douglas) Brian *human services administrator*
Heller, Jack Isaac *lawyer*
Heller, John Roderick, III, *lawyer, business executive*
Hellmuth, George William *architect*
Hellwig, Monika Konrad *organization executive, theology educator*
Helmly, James R. *military officer*
Helms, Robert Brake *economist, research director*
Helms, W. David *health research and policy organization administrator*
Henderson, Douglas Boyd *lawyer*
Henderson, Karen LeCraft *federal judge*
Henderson, Thomas Henry, Jr., *lawyer, legal association executive*
Henke, Michael John *lawyer, educator*
Henkin, Robert Irwin *neurobiologist, internal medicine, nutrition and neurology educator, scientific products company executive, taste and smell disease physician*
Hennessy, Ellen Anne *lawyer, benefits compensation analyst, educator*
Henningsen, Jacqueline Vincent *civilian military official*
Henry, John Cooper *journalist*
Henry, Thomas Joseph *research entomologist*
Hensarling, Jeb *congressman*
Hense, Donald Langford *educational association administrator*
Henshaw, John Lester *federal agency administrator*
Hentges, Harriet *not-for-profit developer*
Herbert, James Charles *academic administrator*
Herbst, John Edward *ambassador*
Herdman, Roger C. *physician, policy analyst*
Herger, Wally W. *congressman*
Herman, Andrea Maxine *newspaper editor*
Herman, George Edward *radio and television correspondent*
Hernreich, Nancy *federal official*
Herraiz, Domingo S. *federal agency administrator*
Herrera, Jessica Rae *lawyer, educator*
Herrett, Richard Allison *agricultural research institute administrator*
Herseth, Stephanie *congresswoman*
Hershey, Robert Lewis *mechanical engineer, management consultant*
Herson, Michael Harry *lobbyist, consultant*
Herzstein, Robert Erwin *lawyer*
Hess, Stephen *political scientist, author*
Heumann, Judith *bank executive*
Hevel, Gary Francis *public information officer, consultant*
Hewitt, Emily Clark *judge, minister*
Hewitt, Paul Buck *lawyer*
Hezir, Joseph S. *energy and environmental company executive*
Hiatt, Fred *editorial editor*
Hiatt, Johnathan P. *lawyer, labor union administrator*
Hickey, Bruce William *lawyer*
Hickey, James Aloysius Cardinal *emeritus archbishop*
Hiebert, Ray Eldon *educator, author, consultant*
Hiestand, O.S., Jr., *lawyer*
Higgins, James Henry, III, *marketing executive*
Higgins, Kathryn O'Leary *consulting firm executive*
Higgins, Robin L. *federal agency administrator*
Higham, Scott *reporter*
Higuchi, Shirley A. *lawyer*
Hill, Baron P. *congressman*
Hill, Christopher R. *ambassador*
Hill, Edwin D. *trade association administrator*
Hill, Eleanor Jean *lawyer*
Hill, Jefferson Borden *regulatory oversight officer, lawyer*
Hill, Kent Richmond *federal agency administrator*
Hillman, Devlin *entrepreneur, researcher*
Hillman, Jennifer Anne *commissioner, ambassador, trade negotiator*
Hills, Carla Anderson *lawyer, former federal official*
Hills, John Merrill *educational administrator, consultant, former public policy research center executive*
Hills, Roderick M. *lawyer, former government official*
Hinchey, Maurice D. *congressman*
Hinden, Stanley Jay *newspaper editor*
Hinojosa, Ruben *congressman*
Hinson, David Russell *airline company executive, federal agency administrator*
Hirschhorn, Eric Leonard *lawyer*
Hoagland, Jimmie Lee *newspaper editor*
Hobbins, William T. *career officer*
Hobbs, Ira *federal agency administrator*
Hobbs, J. Timothy, Sr., *lawyer*
Hobelman, Carl Donald *lawyer*
Hobson, David Lee *congressman, lawyer*
Hobson, James Richmond *lawyer*
Hocker, John Robert *technical operations executive*
Hoeffel, Joseph M. *congressman, lawyer*
Hoehn, Richard Albert *association executive, clergyman*
Hoekstra, Peter *congressman, manufacturing executive*
Hoffa, James P. *labor union administrator*
Hoffinger, Adam Steven *lawyer*
Hoffman, Joel Elihu *lawyer*
Hoffmann, Melane Kinney *marketing and public relations executive, writer*
Hoffmann, Robert Shaw *museum administrator, educator*
Hoglander, Harry R. *legislative staff member*
Ho-Gonzalez, William *lawyer*
Holcomb, Lee *federal agency administrator*
Holdaway, Ronald M. *retired federal judge*
Holden, Raymond Thomas *physician, educator*
Holden, Tim *congressman, protective official*
Holdsclaw, Chamique Shaunta *professional basketball player*
Holladay, Wilhelmina Cole *interior design and museum executive*
Holland, Joy *health care facility executive*
Hollings, Ernest Frederick *senator*
Hollis, Sheila Slocum *lawyer*
Holloway, John Thomas *physicist, consultant*
Holmer, Alan Freeman *trade association executive, lawyer*
Holmstead, Jeffrey Ralph *federal agency administrator*
Holt, Rush Dew *congressman, physics educator, researcher, consultant*
Honda, Michael M. *congressman*
Hooks, Aubrey *ambassador*
Hooley, Darlene *congresswoman*
Hooper, John David *coast guard officer*
Hope, William Duane *zoologist, curator*
Hopper, V. Linda *communications educator, writer*
Hopson, Mark D. *lawyer*
Horahan, Edward Bernard, III, *lawyer*
Horinko, Marianne Lamant *former federal agency administrator*
Horlick, Gary Norman *lawyer, legal educator*
Horn, Charles M. *lawyer*
Horn, Donald Herbert *lawyer*
Horn, Marian Blank *federal judge*
Horn, Sharon K. *government agency administrator*
Horn, Wade Frederick *federal agency administrator*
Horne, Michael Stewart *lawyer*
Horner, Constance Joan *federal agency administrator*
Horowitz, Herbert Eugene *retired diplomat*
Horwitz, Sari *reporter*
Hostettler, John N. *congressman*
Houghton, Amory, Jr., (Amo Houghton) *congressman*
House, W(illiam) Michael *lawyer*
Houseman, Alan William *lawyer*
Hove, Andrew Christian *federal agency administrator*
Howard, Barbara Viventi *research foundation executive*
Howard, Glen Scott *foundation executive, lawyer*
Howard, J. Timothy *finance company executive*
Howard, Jack *labor relations consultant*
Howard, John *federal agency administrator*
Howard, Roscoe Conklin, Jr., *lawyer, educator*
Howe, Fisher *management consultant, former government official*
Howell, Deborah *editor*
Howell, Deborah S. *career officer*
Howell, Mary L. *diversified company executive*
Howland, Nina Davis *historian*
Howland, Richard Hubbard *architectural historian*
Hoyer, Steny Hamilton *congressman*
Hoyes, Louis W. *mortgage company executive*
Hoyt, Clark Freeland *journalist, newspaper editor*
Hoyt, John Arthur *cultural organization administrator, minister*
Hrung, Warren *economist*
Huang, Yiau-Min *entomologist, researcher*
Huband, Frank Louis *educational association executive*
Huberman, Benjamin *technology consultant*
Huberman, Richard Lee *lawyer*
Huddleson, Edwin Emmett, III, *lawyer*
Hudnut, William Herbert, III, *senior resident fellow, political scientist*
Hudson, Melinda B. *foundation administrator*
Hudson, Michael Craig *political science educator*
Hudson, Timothy Leon *nursing educator*
Hufbauer, Gary Clyde *economist, lawyer, educator*
Hug, James Edwin *religious organization executive*
Huge, Harry *lawyer*
Huggins, James Bernard *corporate executive*
Hughes, Kent Higgon *economist*
Hughes, Marija Matich *law librarian*
Hughes, Sharon Mary *trade association executive*
Hughes, Thomas Lowe *foundation executive*
Hugler, Edward Charles *lawyer, federal and state government*
Hull, Edmund J. *ambassador*
Hulshof, Kenny *congressman*
Hume, Brit (Alexander Britton Hume) *journalist*
Hundt, Reed Eric *information industry advisor, lawyer*
Hungate, Joseph Irvin, III, *information technology executive*
Hunnicutt, Charles Alvin *lawyer*
Hunt, Albert R. *newspaper executive*
Hunt, Earl Stephen *federal agency administrator*
Hunt, Lynne *federal agency administrator*
Hunter, Michael James *state government official, lawyer, educator*
Hunter, Ronald V. *administrator*
Hunter, Stephen *film critic, writer*
Huntress, Wesley Theodore, Jr., *scientist*
Huntsman, Jon Meade, Jr., *federal agency administrator*
Husband, Phillip Lyle *lawyer*
Hussain, Syed Taseer *biomedical educator, researcher*
Huston, John Wilson *air force officer, historian*
Hutchinson, Asa *federal agency administrator*
Hutchison, Claude B., Jr., *federal agency administrator*
Hutt, Peter Barton *lawyer*
Hyde, Henry John *congressman*
Hyman, Lester Samuel *lawyer*
Iglesias, Enrique V. *bank executive, former government minister*
Ignagni, Karen *healthcare association executive*
Ihrie, John Richard, III, *art educator*
Iklé, Fred Charles *former federal agency administrator, policy advisor, defense expert*
Indyk, Martin S. *diplomat*
Ingram, Richard Thomas *educational association executive*
Inhofe, James M. *senator*
Inman, Harry Ansel *lawyer*
Innis, Pauline *writer, publishing company executive*
Inouye, Daniel Ken *senator*
Inslee, Jay R. *congressman*
Ireland, Oliver *lawyer*
Ireland, Patricia *not-for-profit developer*
Irvin, Necole S *government relations director*
Irvine, Reed John *media critic, corporation executive*
Irwin, Paul Garfield *minister, social services executive*
Isaacs, Amy Fay *political organization executive*
Isaacson, Walter Seff *think-tank executive*
Isakson, Johnny *congressman*
Isbell, David Bradford *lawyer, educator*
Ishak, Kamal George *pathologist, consultant, educator, researcher*
Israelite, David M. *prosecutor*
Issa, Darrell E. *congressman*
Istook, Ernest James, Jr., (Jim Istook) *congressman, lawyer*
Itoh, William H. *former ambassador*
Ivers, Donald Louis *judge*
Iverson, Kristine Ann *federal agency administrator*
Ives, Stephen Bradshaw, Jr., *retired lawyer*
Ivey, William James *foundation executive, writer, producer*
Ivry, David *diplomat*
Jackson, Alphonso R. *secretary of housing and urban development*
Jackson, Beverly Roberson *state agency administrator, consultant*
Jackson, Brian D. *diversified financial services company executive*
Jackson, Jacquelyn C. *federal agency administrator*
Jackson, James Kinsey *lawyer*

Leonard, Will Ernest, Jr., *lawyer*
Leshner, Alan Irvin *science administrator*
Leskes, Andrea *educational association administrator, educator*
Leslie, Donald S. *information technology manager*
Lessenco, Gilbert Barry *lawyer*
Lessin, Lawrence Stephen *hematologist, oncologist, educator*
Lettow, Charles Frederick *lawyer*
Leubsdorf, Carl Philipp *publishing executive*
Levey, Robert Frank *newspaper columnist, fundraiser*
Levin, Carl *senator*
Levin, Edward M. *law consultant*
Levin, Edward Ross *lawyer*
Levin, George Martin *association and organization administrator, aeronautical engineer*
Levin, Robert J. *mortgage company executive*
Levin, Sander M. *congressman*
Levine, Felice *educational association administrator*
Levine, Henry David *lawyer*
Levinson, Daniel Ronald *federal agency administrator, lawyer*
Levinson, Lawrence Edward *lawyer, corporation executive*
Levinson, Nanette Segal *international relations educator, administrator*
Levy, David Corcos *museum director*
Levy, Leah Garrigan *federal official*
Levy, Mark Irving *lawyer*
Levy, Michael B. *business educator*
Lewis, Ann Frank *former government official*
Lewis, Anne McCutcheon *architect*
Lewis, Benjamin Pershing, Jr., *pharmacist, public health service officer*
Lewis, Charles Jeremy (Jerry Lewis) *congressman*
Lewis, Charles Joseph *journalist*
Lewis, David John *lawyer*
Lewis, Eleanor Roberts *lawyer*
Lewis, Glenn C. *lawyer*
Lewis, Guy A. *prosecutor*
Lewis, John R. *congressman*
Lewis, Jordan David *charity organization director, author, international speaker, educator*
Lewis, Lorraine *general counsel*
Lewis, Robert David Gilmore *retired editor*
Lewis, Ron *congressman*
Lewis, Stephen Joseph *television producer*
Lewis, William Henry, Jr., *lawyer*
Lewis, Wilma Antoinette *lawyer, former prosecutor and federal agency admin*
Li, Theodore C.M. *medical educator*
Liberty, Arthur Andrew *judge*
Libutti, Frank *federal agency administrator*
Lichtenbaum, Peter *federal agency administrator*
Lichtenstein, Elissa Charlene *legal association executive*
Lichtman, Allan Jay *historian, educator, consultant*
Lichtman, Judith L. *lawyer, organization administrator*
Lieber, Robert James *political science educator, writer*
Lieberman, Evelyn S. *diplomat*
Lieberman, Joseph I. *senator*
Liebman, Ronald Stanley *lawyer*
Liebman, Wilma B. *government agency administrator*
Liedquist, Robert Eric *lawyer*
Lief, Beth *educational association administrator*
Lietzau, William Kendall *career officer, lawyer*
Lifschitz, Judah *lawyer*
Lightfoot, David William *linguistics educator*
Lilly, William Eldridge *government official*
Lim, Jeanette J. *federal agency administrator*
Limon, Lavinia *social services administrator*
Lincoln, Blanche Lambert *senator*
Lindberg, Tod Marshall *editor, writer*
Linder, John E. *congressman, dentist*
Lindsay, Joseph, Jr., *cardiologist, educator*
Lindsey, Seth Mark *lawyer, federal agency administrator*
Linn, Johannes *bank executive*
Linowitz, Sol Myron *lawyer*
Lipinski, William Oliver *congressman*
Lipnic, Victoria A. *federal agency administrator*
Lippman, Marc Estes *pharmacology educator*
Lipstein, Robert A. *lawyer*
Lisboa-Farrow, Elizabeth Oliver *public and government relations consultant*
Littig, Lawrence William *psychologist, educator*
Little, John William *plastic surgeon, educator*
Liu, Michael Minoru Fawn *federal agency administrator*
Liu, Xiao *physicist, researcher*
Livingood, Wilson S. *law enforcement official*
Livingston, Bob (Robert Linlithgow Livingston Jr.) *lawyer, former congressman*
Livingston, Robert Gerald *historian, journalist*
Lloyd, James D. *federal agency administrator*
Llubién, Joseph Herman *psychotherapist, counselor*
LoBiondo, Frank A. *congressman*
Lockhart, James Bicknell, III, *federal agency administrator*
Lofgren, Zoe *congresswoman*
Loftis, Robert G. *ambassador*
Logan, Ann D. *financial company executive*
Logsdon, John Mortimer, III, *aerospace analyst, physics professor*
Loker, Elizabeth St. John *newspaper executive*
Lombardo, Fredric Alan *pharmacist, educator*
Long, Pamela Olivia *historian*
Longstreth, Richard Washington *education educator, consultant*
Loosbrock, Carol Marie *information management professional*
Loots, James Mason *lawyer*
Lopatin, Alan G. *lawyer*
Lord, Jerome Edmund *education administrator, writer*
Lorsung, Thomas Nicholas *news service editor*
Lott, Cindy M. *lawyer*
Lott, Trent *senator*
Lourie, Alan David *federal judge*
Lovell, Malcolm Read, Jr., *public policy institute executive, educator, former government official, former trade association executive*
Lovett, Clara Maria *university administrator, historian*
Low, Stephen *foundation executive, educator, former diplomat*
Lowe, Mary Frances *federal government official*
Lowe, Randall Brian *lawyer*
Lowenstein, James Gordon *former diplomat, international consultant*
Lowery, W. Wilson, Jr., *federal agency administrator*
Lowey, Nita M. *congresswoman*
Lowrey, Barbara R. *federal official*
Loy, James Milton *federal agency administrator, retired coast guard officer*
Loyevsky, Mark Michael *biochemist, researcher*
Loyless, Betsy Seymour *political organization worker*
Lozada, Jacob *federal agency administrator*
Lozansky, Edward Dmitry *physicist, consultant, writer*
Lubar, Jeffrey Stuart *journalist, trade association executive*
Lubic, Benita Joan Alk *travel executive*
Lubic, Robert Bennett *lawyer, arbitrator, law educator*
Lucas, C. Payne *development organization executive*
Lucas, Frank D. *congressman*
Lucas, James Walter *federal government official*
Lucas, Ken *congressman*
Luce, Gregory M. *lawyer*
Ludwig, Eugene Allan *financial consultant, former US Comptroller of the Currency, lawyer*
Luessenhop, Alfred John *neurosurgeon, educator*
Lugar, Richard Green *senator*
Lukken, Walt *commissioner*
Lupo, Raphael V. *lawyer*
Lurton, Horace VanDeventer *brokerage house executive*
Luther, Michael R. *federal agency administrator*
Lutterodt, Clement H. *mathematician, educator*
Luttwak, Edward Nicolae *academic administrator, educator, policy and business consultant*
Lybecker, Martin Earl *lawyer*
Lynch, John Joseph *health facility administrator*
Lynch, Robert L. *art association administrator*
Lynch, Stephen F. *congressman*
Lynker, John Paul *newscaster*
Lynn, D. Joanne *physician, ethicist, health services researcher*
Lyons, Dennis Gerald *lawyer*
MacBeth, Angus *lawyer*
Macdonald, David Robert *lawyer, fund administrator*
MacDonald, Purificacion O. *statistician, researcher*
MacDougall, Gordon Pier *lawyer*
Mack, Connie, III, (Cornelius Mack) *former senator*
Mack, Julia Cooper *retired judge*
MacKay, Kenneth Hood, Jr., (Buddy MacKay) *federal official*
Mackay, Leo Sidney, Jr., *federal agency administrator*
MacLaury, Bruce King *financial institution executive*
MacLeish, Roderick *novelist, screenwriter, television producer*
Macleod, John Amend *lawyer*
Maco, Paul Stephen *securities and exchange administrator*
Macomber, John D. *investment company executive*
Maddaloni, Martin J. *labor union administrator*
Madden, Murdaugh Stuart *lawyer*
Madden, Thomas James *lawyer, educator*
Madian, Alan Leonard *economist, management consultant*
Maechling, Charles, Jr., *lawyer, diplomat, educator, writer*
Magaw, John W. *former federal agency administrator*
Magee, Charles Thomas *international consultant, retired diplomat*
Magielnicki, Robert L. *lawyer*
Maginnis, John C., III, *lawyer*
Magnee, Tom *federal agency administrator*
Magrath, C. Peter *educational association executive*
Magwood, William D. *federal agency administrator*
Mahaffey, Kathryn Rose *risk assessor*
Mahar, Ellen Patricia *law librarian*
Mahone, Glenn *federal agency administrator*
Mainella, Frances P. *federal agency administrator*
Maisto, John F. *ambassador*
Maizel, Roy *federal agency administrator*
Majak, Roger *administration executive*
Majette, Denise *congresswoman*
Majev, Howard Rudolph *lawyer*
Makalou, Oumar *economic advisor*
Makins, Christopher James *foreign policy institute administrator*
Makris, Andreas *composer*
Maldonado, F. César *priest, educator*
Malek, Frederic Vincent *finance company executive*
Maletsky, Alfred F. *sculptor, engraver*
Malinowski, Michael E. *ambassador*
Malone, William Robert *lawyer*
Maloney, Carolyn Bosher *congresswoman*
Malott, Frank Stephen *foreign service officer*
Malveaux, Floyd Joseph *dean*
Manatos, Andrew E. *public relations executive*
Manatt, Charles Taylor *lawyer*
Manchester, Paul Brunson *economist*
Mandel, H(arold) George *pharmacologist, educator*
Mandula, Jeffrey Ellis *physicist*
Mangano, Michael F. *federal official*
Mani, Inderjeet *computer scientist, educator*
Mankiewicz, Frank F. *journalist, writer*
Manley, Audrey Forbes *retired academic administrator, pediatrician, military officer*
Manley, James P. *congressional press secretary*
Mann, Charles Roy *statistician*
Mann, Donegan *lawyer*
Mann, Lawrence Moses *lawyer*
Mann, Marion *pathologist, educator*
Mann, Oscar *retired physician, internist, educator*
Mann, Thomas Edward *political scientist*
Manning, Michael J. *lawyer*
Mansfield, Edward Patrick, Jr., *advertising executive*
Mansfield, Gordon Hall *federal agency administrator*
Manson, Harold Craig *federal agency administrator*
Manson, Joseph Lloyd, III, *lawyer*
Manwell, John Parker, II, *lawyer*
Manzullo, Donald A *congressman, lawyer*
Mao, Ho-kwang *geophysicist, educator*
Mapes, William Rodgers, Jr., *lawyer*
Marans, J. Eugene *lawyer*
Marburger, Darla A. *federal agency administrator*
Marburger, John Harmen, III, *federal agency administrator*
Marchand, Michael J. *military officer*
Marcin, Peter R. *lawyer, real estate broker*
Marcotte, Michael Steven *municipal administrator*
Marcoullis, Erato Kozakou *ambassador*
Marcum, Deanna Bowling *library administrator*
Marcus, Devra Joy Cohen *internist*
Marcuss, Rosemary Daly *economist*
Marcuss, Stanley Joseph *lawyer*
Margeton, Stephen George *law librarian*
Margolis, Doris May Rosenberg *editor, writer*
Margolis, Lawrence Stanley *federal judge*
Marimow, William Kalmon *editor*
Marinaccio, Charles Lindbergh *lawyer, consultant*
Markey, Edward John *congressman*
Marks, Andrew H. *lawyer*
Marks, Herbert Edward *lawyer*
Marks, Jonathan Bowles *mediator, arbitrator*
Marks, Leonard Harold *lawyer*
Marks, Susan Collin *foundation administrator*
Marlay, Robert Charles *physicist, engineer*
Marquez, Joaquin Alfredo *lawyer*
Marr, Phebe Ann *retired historian, educator*
Marrett, Michael McFarlene *chaplain*
Marriott, John Willard, Jr., *lodging and senior living executive*
Marriott, Richard Edwin *hotel and contract services executive*
Marshall, Brian Laurence *trade association executive*
Marshall, James Creel *congressman*
Marshall, John *federal agency administrator*
Marshall, Susanne T. *government agency administrator*
Marshall, William, III, *think-tank executive*
Martin, David O'Brien *congressman*
Martin, Guy *lawyer*
Martin, Jack *federal agency administrator*
Martin, Jerry Lee *organization executive, educator*
Martin, Julie A. *retired insurance company executive*
Martin, Kate Abbott *lawyer*
Martin, Kathleen *medical center administrator*
Martin, Kevin J. *federal agency administrator*
Martin, Ralph Drury *lawyer, columnist*
Martin, Robert Sidney *federal agency administrator*
Martinez, Carmen M. *ambassador*
Martinez, Herminia S. *economist, banker*
Martinez, Rose Marie *health science association administrator*
Marumoto, William Hideo *management consultant*
Marvel, L. Paige *judge*
Marvin, Charles Rodney, Jr., *lawyer*
Marx, Paul Louis *economist*
Marzol, Adolfo *mortgage company executive*
Masi, Dale A. *research company executive, social work educator*
Mason, Eileen B. *federal administrator*
Massaro, Donald John *medical educator, medical researcher*
Massey, Jeanne Kelly *music festival producer*
Masters, Edward E. *association executive, former foreign service officer*
Matheson, Jim *congressman*
Mathews, Jessica Tuchman *executive, foreign policy expert*
Mathias, Edward Joseph *merchant banker*
Mathis, John Prentiss *lawyer*
Matsui, Robert Takeo *congressman*
Matthews, Barbara Caridad *lawyer*
Matthiesen, Lance *publishing executive*
Mattingly, J. Virgil, Jr., *federal lawyer*
Mattsson, Ake *psychiatrist, physician*
Maudlin, Robert V. *economics and government affairs consultant*
Maul, Kevin Jay *financial consultant*
Maxey, Randall W. *medical researcher, health science association administrator*
Maxwell, David Ogden *former government official and financial executive*
May, Clifford Daniel *director of communications, newspaper editor, journalist*
May, Stephen *writer, former government official*
May, Timothy James *lawyer*
Mayer, Haldane Robert *federal chief judge*
Mayer, Neal Michael *lawyer*
Mayer, Susan *telecommunications company executive*
Mayers, Daniel Kriegsman *lawyer*
Maynes, Charles William *foundation executive*
Mayo, George Washington, Jr., *lawyer*
Mayo, John W. *dean, educator, researcher*
Mays, Janice Ann *lawyer*
Mazo, Mark Elliott *lawyer*
Mazzaferri, Katherine Aquino *lawyer, bar association executive*
Mc Afee, William *government official*
McAleavey, David *English educator*
McAuliffe, Jane Dammen *religious studies and Islamic studies educator*
McAuliffe, Terry (Terence Richard McAuliffe) *political organization administrator*
McBee, Susanna Barnes *retired journalist*
McBride, Jonathan Evans *executive search consultant*
McBride, Michael Flynn *lawyer*
McCain, John Sidney, III, *senator*
McCaleb, Margaret Anne Sheehan *application developer*
McCallum, Robert D., Jr., *federal agency administrator*
McCargar, James Goodrich *diplomat, writer*
McCarrick, Theodore Edgar Cardinal *archbishop*
McCarron, Douglas J. *labor union administrator*
McCarter, Katherine Sauter *association executive*
McCarthy, Carolyn *congresswoman*
McCarthy, John F. *healthcare administrator*
McCarthy, Karen P. *congresswoman, former state legislator*
McCartin, Joseph Anthony *historian, educator*
McCaul, Elizabeth *investment advisor, former state agency administrator*
McClain, Tim S. *federal agency administrator*
McClellan, Mark B. *federal agency administrator*
McClure, William Pendleton *lawyer*
McCluskey, Susan D. *lawyer*
McCollam, William, Jr., *utility company executive*
McCollum, Betty *congresswoman*
McConnell, Bruce William *information technology executive*
McConnell, Mitchell, Jr., (Mitch McConnell Jr., Addison Mitchell McConnell Jr.) *senator, lawyer*
McConnell, Nicholas Stillwell *lawyer*
McCormally, Kevin Jay *editor*
McCotter, Thaddeus G. *congressman*
McCrabb, Donald Raymond *pastoral field educator*
McCracken, Ursula E. *museum director*
McCray, Nikki Kesangame *professional basketball player*
McCrery, James (Jim McCrery) *congressman*
McCrum, Robert Timothy *lawyer*
McCune, Greg E. *communications media executive*
McCutchen, Tammy Dee *federal agency administrator*
McDaniels, William E. *lawyer*
McDavid, Janet Louise *lawyer*
McDermott, James A. *congressman, psychiatrist*
McDiarmid, Robert Campbell *lawyer*
McDonald, Frances D. *government official, editor, lawyer*
McDonald, Jackson *ambassador*
McDonald, Patricia Ann *legislative administrator*
McDonough, William J. *banker*
McElroy, Edward J. *labor union administrator*
McElveen, Junius Carlisle, Jr., *lawyer*
McElveen-Hunter, Bonnie *ambassador*
McEntee, Gerald W. *labor union official*
McEwen, Gerald Noah, Jr., *bio-scientist executive*
McFarland, Patrick E. *federal agency administrator*
McFarland, Robert N. *federal agency administrator*
McFeatters, Ann Carey *journalist*
McGarry, W. David *real estate company executive*
McGee, Robert Merrill *oil company executive*
Mc Giffert, David Eliot *lawyer, former government official*
McGill, Willis Alexander *anesthesiologist*
McGinn, Dennis Vincent *career officer*
McGinnies, Elliott Morse *psychologist, educator*
McGinnis, Patricia Gwaltney *nonprofit organization executive*
McGovern, James P. *congressman*
McGovern, Michael Barbot *lawyer*
McGranery, Regina C. *judge*
McGrath, Kathryn Bradley *lawyer*
McGraw, Lavinia Morgan *retired retail executive*
McGuire, Carole Baker *legislative staff member*
McGuire, Patricia A. *lawyer, academic administrator*
McGuirl, Marlene Dana Callis *law librarian, educator*
McHale, Paul F., Jr., *federal official, former congressman*
McHugh, James Lenahan, Jr., *lawyer*
McHugh, John Michael *congressman, former state senator*
McIlwain, John Knox *housing policy fellow*
McInerney, Joseph Aloysius *hotel executive*
McInnis, Scott Steve *congressman, lawyer*
McIntyre, Bernice Kay *lawyer, management consultant*
McIntyre, Douglas Carmichael, II, (Mike McIntyre) *congressman*
Mc Kay, Emily Gantz *civil rights professional*
McKeever, Joseph Francis, III, *lawyer*
McKelvey, Virginia Maude *language educator*
McKeon, Howard P. (Buck McKeon) *congressman, former mayor*
McLarty, Thomas F., III, (Mack McLarty) *former governement advisor, business executive*
McLaughlin, David *foundation administrator*
McLaughlin, John E. *federal agency administrator*
McLaughlin, John J. *broadcast executive, television producer, journalist, political commentator*
McLean, Christopher Anthony *lawyer, former government official*
McLean, R. Bruce *lawyer*
McLeod, David G. *urologist, educator*
McMahon, Joseph Einar *lawyer, consultant*
McMichael, Guy H., III, *federal official*
McNamara, Robert M., Jr., *federal agency administrator, lawyer*
McNamara, Robert Strange *former banking executive, former Secretary of Defense*
McNicholas, Edward *lawyer*
McNulty, Michael Robert *congressman*
McPhee, George *professional sports team executive*
Mc Phee, Henry Roemer *lawyer*
McPherson, Alan L. *history professor*
McPherson, Edward Russell *federal agency administrator*
Mc Pherson, Harry Cummings, Jr., *lawyer*
McQueary, Charles E. *federal official*
McReynolds, Mary Armilda *lawyer*
McSlarrow, Kyle E. *federal agency administrator*
Mead, Christina Dykstra *church administrator*
Mead, Kenneth Minor *federal agency administrator*
Meadows, Vickers B. *federal agency administrator*
Means, Marianne *political columnist*
Means, Thomas Cornell *lawyer*
Medalie, Richard James *lawyer*
Medalie, Susan Diane *lawyer, management consultant*
Mederos, Carolina Luisa *public policy consultant*
Meece, Roger A. *ambassador*
Meehan, Martin Thomas *congressman, lawyer*
Meek, Kendrick B. *congressman*
Meeks, Gregory Weldon *congressman*
Meggers, Betty Jane *anthropologist, researcher*
Mehan, George Tracey, III, *federal agency administrator*
Mehlman, Bruce P. *federal agency administrator*
Meijer, Paul Herman Ernst *educator, physicist*
Melamed, Arthur Douglas *lawyer*
Melamed, Carol Drescher *lawyer*
Melanson, Richard Allen *political science educator*
Melendez, Rodrigo Cuauhtemoc *dentist, read admiral US Navy*
Melendy, David Russell *broadcast journalist*
Mellor, John Williams *economist, policy consultant firm executive*
Meloy, Sybil Piskur *retired lawyer*
Mencer, C. Suzanne *federal agency administrator*
Mencher, Bruce Stephan *judge*
Mendelowitz, Allan Irwin *federal agency administrator*
Mendelsohn, Martin *lawyer*
Menendez, Robert *congressman, lawyer*
Menkel-Meadow, Carrie Joan *law educator*
Mercanti, John M. *sculptor, engraver*
Merow, James F. *federal judge*
Merrell, Jesse Howard *writer*
Merrifield, Dudley Bruce *business educator, former government official*
Merritt, Carolyn *government agency administrator*
Mery, Robert William *publishing executive*
Metcalf, Howard *military officer*
Metzger, James W. *military officer*
Meyer, Alden Merrill *environmental association executive*
Meyer, Armin Henry *retired diplomat, author, educator*
Meyer, Dennis Irwin *lawyer*
Meyer, Laurence Harvey *former federal official*
Meyers, Linda Dee *federal agency administrator*
Meyers, Tedson Jay *lawyer*
Meyers, Wayne Marvin *microbiologist*

Pendleton, Miles Stevens, Jr., *diplomat*
Penner, Rudolph Gerhard *economist, educator*
Pensky, Carol *political organization administrator*
Peoples, Carolyn Y. *federal agency administrator*
Perez, Lucille C. Norville *medical association administrator, pediatrician*
Perez-Gelabert, Daniel Ernesto *biologist*
Perito, Robert Michael *political scientist*
Perkins, Joseph S. *medical association administrator*
Perkins, Lucian *photographer*
Perkins, Nancy Leeds *lawyer*
Perle, Richard Norman *former government official*
Perlik, William R. *lawyer*
Perlman, Matthew Saul *lawyer*
Perper, Michael Joseph *federal agency administrator*
Perry, George Lewis *research economist, consultant*
Persinger, Del Louis *pharmaceutical company executive*
Peters, Charles Given, Jr., *editor*
Peters, F. Whitten *lawyer, former federal official*
Peters, Frederick Whitten *lawyer*
Peters, Mary E. *federal agency administrator*
Peterson, Charles Hayes *lawyer*
Peterson, Collin C. *congressman*
Peterson, E. Anne *federal agency administrator*
Peterson, John E. *congressman*
Peterson, Katherine H. *federal agency administrator, former ambassador*
Petito, Margaret L. *foundation administrator*
Petrash, Jeffrey Michael *lawyer*
Petri, Thomas Evert *congressman*
Petrou, David Michael *marketing and communications executive*
Petty, Rachel *academic administrator*
Pfeiffer, Leonard, IV, *executive recruiter, consultant*
Pfeiffer, Margaret Kolodny *lawyer*
Pfeiffer, Steven Bernard *lawyer*
Phillips, Carter Glasgow *lawyer*
Phillips, James D. *retired diplomat*
Phillips, Jeanne L. *ambassador*
Phillips, Karen Borlaug *economist, railroad industry executive*
Phillips, Michael M. *gastroenterologist*
Phillips, Susan Meredith *financial economist, university administrator*
Pibulsonggram, Nitya *diplomat*
Piccininno, Anthony Ray *government administrative executive*
Picciotto, Robert *bank executive*
Pickenpaugh, Thomas Edward *archaeologist, anthropologist*
Pickering, Charles W., Jr., *congressman*
Pickering, John Harold *lawyer*
Pickholtz, Raymond Lee *electrical engineering educator, consultant*
Piemme, Thomas Euegene *medical educator*
Pierce, David R. *educational administrator*
Pierce, Margaret Hunter *government official*
Pincus, Ann Terry *federal agency administrator, editor, writer*
Pincus, Jonathan Henry *neurologist, educator*
Pincus, Stephanie Hoyer *dermatologist*
Pincus, Walter Haskell *editor*
Pines, Wayne Lloyd *public relations executive*
Pionk, Jerome Lee *government official, association administrator*
Pirchner, Herman, Jr., *foreign policy specialist*
Pittman, Lisa *lawyer*
Pittman, Steuart Lansing *lawyer*
Pitts, Joseph R. *congressman*
Pitts, Tyrone S. *reverend*
Pizzella, Patrick *federal agency administrator*
Placke, James A(nthony) *foreign service officer, international affairs consultant*
Plager, S. Jay *judge*
Plaine, Daniel J. *lawyer*
Plaine, Lloyd Leva *lawyer*
Plaisted, Joan M. *diplomat*
Platts, Howard Gregory *scientific, educational organization executive*
Platts, Todd Russell *congressman, state legislator*
Player, Thelma B. *librarian*
Pleasure, Robert Jonathan *association director, lawyer*
Plewes, Thomas Jeffrey *military officer*
Plusquellec, Herve Louis *irrigation and agricultural engineering consultant*
Podberesky, Samuel *lawyer*
Poe, Luke Harvey, Jr., *lawyer*
Pojeta, John, Jr., *geologist, researcher*
Polito, Robert J. *federal agency administrator*
Pollack, Ronald F(rank) *healthcare organization executive, lawyer*
Pollard, Michael Ross *lawyer, health policy researcher and consultant*
Pollin, Abe *professional basketball team executive, builder*
Pollock, Alexander John *retired banker*
Polon, Ira H. *lawyer*
Pombo, Richard *congressman, rancher, farmer*
Pomeroy, Earl R. *congressman, former state insurance commissioner*
Poneman, Daniel Bruce *lawyer*
Pope, Andrew *health science association administrator*
Pope, Anne B. *agency head, business executive, lawyer*
Pope, Michael Thor *chemistry professor*
Pope, Nancy *historian, curator*
Popkin, Joel *economist, consultant*
Poppleton, Janet Waters *legislative staff member*
Porter, Barbara *anchorwoman, writer, educator*
Porter, John Edward *former congressman*
Porter, John Weston *counselor, consultant, hospital administrator*
Porter, Jon Christopher *congressman*
Portman, Rob *congressman*
Portney, Paul Rogers *research and educational organization executive*
Posner, Paul Leonard *government official*
Postol, Lawrence Philip *lawyer*
Potenza, Joseph Michael *lawyer*
Potok, Nancy Ann Fagenson *federal agency administrator*
Potter, Deborah Ann *news correspondent, educator*
Potter, John E. *postal service executive*
Potter, John Francis *surgical oncologist, educator*
Potter, Lorraine K. *career military officer*
Potter, Trevor Alexander McClurg *lawyer*
Potts, Ramsay Douglas *lawyer, aviator*
Potts, Stephen Deaderick *lawyer*
Pouillon, Nora Emanuela *food service executive*
Povich, David *lawyer*
Powell, Colin Luther *secretary of state, retired military officer, author, public speaker*
Powell, Donald E. *federal agency administrator*
Powell, Michael Kevin *federal agency administrator*
Powers, Richard Edward, Jr., *lawyer*
Poxon, Stephanie Lyn *music specialist, accompanist*
Pratt, Carin *television executive*
Preer, James Randolph *science educator*
Preer, Jean Lyon *information science educator*
Press, Frank *geophysicist*
Preston, Stephen W. *lawyer*
Prestowitz, Clyde Vincent *economist, researcher*
Prettyman, Elijah Barrett, Jr., *lawyer*
Price, Daniel Martin *lawyer*
Price, David Eugene *congressman, educator*
Price, Griffith Baley, Jr., *lawyer*
Price, Joseph Hubbard *lawyer*
Prina, L(ouis) Edgar *journalist*
Principi, Anthony Joseph *secretary of veterans affairs*
Prosper, Pierre-Richard *federal agency administrator*
Prost, Sharon *federal judge*
Prouty, Charles S. *federal agency administrator*
Pryce, Deborah D. *congresswoman*
Pryor, Mark Lunsford *senator*
Puchalski, Christina M. *physician, medical educator*
Pucie, Charles R., Jr., *public affairs executive*
Puryear, Martin *artist, educator*
Pusey, William Anderson *lawyer*
Putnam, Adam Hughes *congressman, farmer, rancher*
Putzel, Michael *journalist, editor*
Pyke, Thomas Nicholas, Jr., *government science and engineering administrator*
Pyle, Robert Noble *government relations executive*
Quainton, Anthony Cecil Eden *diplomat*
Quale, John Carter *lawyer*
Quarles, James Linwood, III, *lawyer*
Quarles, Randal Keith *lawyer, federal official*
Quarterman, Cynthia Louise *lawyer*
Queen, Evelyn E. Crawford *retired judge*
Quello, James Henry *government official*
Quinn, Jack *congressman, English language educator, coach*
Quinn, Maureen E. *ambassador*
Quinn, Pat Maloy *engineering company executive*
Quint, Arnold Harris *lawyer*
Quintanilla-Villanueva, Rosalinda *economist*
Quintiere, Gary Gandolfo *lawyer*
Quivers, Eric Stanley *physician*
Rabecs, Robert Nicholas *lawyer*
Racicot, Marc F. *lawyer, former governor*
Radanovich, George P. *congressman*
Rademaker, Stephen Geoffrey *federal agency administrator, lawyer*
Rader, Randall Ray *federal judge*
Radin, Alex *former association executive, consultant*
Rafferty, James Gerard *lawyer*
Rahall, Nick Joe, II, (Nick Rahall) *congressman*
Railton, William Scott *federal agency administrator*
Rainey, Jean Osgood *public relations executive*
Raizen, Senta Amon *educational administrator, researcher*
Rales, Mitchell P. *automotive parts company executive*
Rales, Steven M. *automotive parts company executive*
Raley, Bennett W. *federal agency administrator*
Ramberg, Walter Dodd *architect*
Ramos, Flavia Sales *education educator, consultant*
Ramphele, Mamphela A. *medical educator*
Ramsey, Charles H. *police chief*
Ramsey, Robert Leslie *oncologist*
Ramstad, James *congressman, lawyer*
Ranck, Edna Runnels *academic administrator, researcher*
Rand, Harry Zvi *art historian, poet*
Randall, Robert L(ee) *ecological economist*
Randolph, A(rthur) Raymond *federal judge*
Randt, Clark Thorp, Jr., *ambassador, lawyer*
Rangel, Charles Bernard *congressman*
Rankin, Robert Arthur *journalist*
Rao, Vijayendra *economist*
Raphael, Louise Arakelian *mathematician, educator*
Raphel, Robin *ambassador*
Raslear, Thomas Gregory *psychologist*
Rasmus, John Charles *trade association executive, lawyer*
Ratner, Ellen Faith *radio talk show host, writer*
Rato Figaredo, Rodrigo *international official*
Rauh, Carl Stephen *lawyer*
Raul, Alan Charles *lawyer*
Rausch, Howard *information service executive*
Ravenal, Earl Cedric *international relations educator, author*
Rayner, Victoria Leigh *medical educator, estheticist, consultant*
Razavi, Hossein *bank executive*
Reade, Claire Elizabeth *lawyer*
Reagon, Bernice Johnson *cultural historian, educator, curator, singer, composer*
Reaman, Gregory Harold *pediatric hematologist, oncologist*
Reback, Joyce Ellen *lawyer*
Reddel, Carl Walter *educational administrator*
Redman, Robert Shelton *pathologist, dentist*
Reed, Anne F. Thomson *government official*
Reed, John Francis (Jack Reed) *senator*
Reed, John Hathaway *former ambassador*
Reed, Travis Dean *public relations executive*
Reef, Grace *government official*
Rees, Nina Shokraii *federal official, writer*
Reese, George W. *federal agency administrator*
Reger, Lawrence Lee *trade association administrator*
Regula, Ralph *congressman, lawyer*
Rehberg, Dennis R. *congressman*
Rehnquist, William Hubbs *United States supreme court chief justice*
Reich, Alan Anderson *foundation administrator*
Reid, Harry *senator*
Reid, Inez Smith *lawyer, educator*
Rein, Bert Walter *lawyer*
Reining, Priscilla Copeland *anthropologist*
Reinsch, William Alan *association executive, educator*
Reischauer, Robert D. *research organization executive*
Relch, John *banker, federal agency administrator*
Relyea, Harold Clarence *political scientist*
Remez, Shereen G. *government executive*
Rennert, Wolfgang Peter *pediatrician, educator*
Renninger, Mary Karen *librarian*
Renzi, Rick *congressman*
Replogle, Michael A. *civil engineer, urban planner, environmentalist*
Resor, Stanley Rogers *lawyer*
Ressel, Teresa Mullett *federal agency administrator*
Rey, Mark E. *federal agency administrator*
Reyes Heroles, Jesus *former Mexican government official*
Reyna, Benigno G. *federal agency administrator*
Reynolds, Gerald *federal agency administrator*
Reynolds, Thomas M. *congressman*
Rezneck, Daniel Albert *lawyer*
Rheintgen, Laura Dale *research center official*
Rhoades, Margaret *health care association executive*
Rhyne, Sidney White *lawyer*
Riccards, Michael Patrick *academic administrator*
Ricciardone, Francis J. *ambassador*
Rice, Condoleezza *national security advisor*
Rice, Lois Dickson *former computer company executive*
Rice, Paul Jackson *lawyer, educator*
Rich, Dorothy Kovitz *writer, educational administrator*
Rich, Laurie M. *federal official, educator*
Richards, Femi Soyinka *lawyer*
Richards, Suzanne V. *lawyer*
Richardson, Ann Bishop *foundation executive, lawyer*
Richert, John Rolin *neuroimmunologist, educator*
Richeson, James G., Jr., *dentist*
Richman, Joseph Herbert *retired public health services official*
Richman, Phyllis Chasanow *newspaper critic*
Richmond, David Walker *lawyer*
Richmond, Marilyn Susan *lawyer*
Ridenour, Amy Moritz *research center administrator*
Rider, James Lincoln *lawyer*
Ridge, Thomas Joseph (Tom Ridge) *secretary of homeland security*
Ridgeway, James Fowler *journalist*
Ridgway, Delissa Anne *lawyer*
Ridings, Dorothy Sattes *association executive*
Ridley, Keith Alexander, IV, *funeral director*
Ridley, Stanley Eugene *clinical psychologist, consultant*
Riedel, Bunnie *not-for-profit organization executive*
Riegler, Guenter *federal agency administrator*
Riehle, B. Hudson *trade association executive*
Rieser, Joseph A., Jr., *lawyer*
Riffee, Stephen *corporate financial executive*
Riley, Daniel Joseph *lawyer, educator*
Rill, James Franklin *lawyer*
Ring, James Edward Patrick *mortgage banking consulting executive*
Ris, William Krakow, Jr., *lawyer*
Rissetto, Harry A. *lawyer*
Ritchie, Donald A. *historian*
Ritter, Donald Lawrence *environmental policy institute executive*
Ritter, Jeffrey Blake *lawyer, consultant*
Rivers, Richard Robinson *lawyer*
Rives, Jack L. *military officer*
Rivlin, Alice Mitchell *federal agency administrator, economist*
Robb, James Willis *Romance languages educator*
Robb, Lynda Johnson *writer*
Robbins, Ira Paul *law educator*
Robbins, Robert B. *lawyer*
Roberson, Jessie Hill *federal agency administrator*
Roberts, Charles Patrick (Pat Roberts) *senator*
Roberts, James Harold, III, *lawyer*
Roberts, Jeanne Addison *retired literature educator*
Roberts, John Glover, Jr., *federal judge*
Roberts, Markley *economist, educator*
Roberts, Walter Ronald *political science educator, former government official*
Robertson, James *judge*
Robinson, Davis Rowland *lawyer, arbitrator*
Robinson, Leonard Harrison, Jr., *international government consultant, business executive*
Robinson, Sharon Porter *professional society administrator*
Robison, Victor James, Jr., *retired military officer*
Roby, Cheryl J. *deputy assistant secretary*
Rocca, Christina B. *federal agency administrator*
Roche, James G. *civilian military employee*
Rockefeller, Edwin Shaffer *lawyer*
Rockefeller, John Davison, IV, (Jay Rockefeller) *senator, former governor*
Rocque, Vincent Joseph *lawyer*
Rodemeyer, Michael Leonard, Jr., *lawyer*
Rodman, Peter Warren *government official*
Rodriguez, Ciro Davis *congressman*
Rodriguez, Rita Maria *economist*
Roemer, Timothy J. *think-tank executive, former congressman*
Roessel, Faith *Indian arts and crafts administrator*
Roett, Riordan *political science educator, consultant*
Rogan, James E. *federal agency administrator, former congressman*
Rogers, Harold Dallas (Hal Rogers) *congressman*
Rogers, Judith W. *federal judge*
Rogers, Julie *foundation administrator*
Rogers, Mike *congressman*
Rogers, Thomasina Venese *federal commissioner*
Rogers, William Dill *lawyer*
Rogovin, John A. *lawyer*
Rogowsky, Robert Arthur *trade commission operations director, educator*
Rohner, Ralph John *lawyer, educator, university dean*
Rohrabacher, Dana *congressman*
Roll, David Lee *lawyer*
Romani, Paul Nicholas *government official*
Romeo, Peter John *lawyer*
Romig, Edgar Dutcher *clergyman*
Romig, Thomas J. *military officer*
Rooney, Kevin Davitt *lawyer*
Roque, Francis Xavier *auxiliary bishop*
Roscher, Nina Matheny *chemistry professor*
Rose, George Andrew *software developer, information systems specialist*
Rose, Jonathan Chapman *lawyer*
Roseboro, Brian Carlton *federal agency administrator*
Rosebush, James Scott *marketing professional, international management and public affairs consultant, former government official*
Rosen, Carol *editor*
Rosen, Gerald Robert *editor*
Rosen, Jeffrey Adam *federal agency administrator, lawyer*
Rosenau, James Nathan *political scientist, author*
Rosenberg, Jerome David *physicist*
Rosenberg, Joel Barry *government economist*
Rosenblatt, Jason Philip *English language educator*
Rosenblatt, Peter Ronald *lawyer, former ambassador*
Rosenbloom, David Harry *political science and law educator*
Rosenbloom, H. David *lawyer*
Rosendhal, Jeffrey David *federal science agency administrator, astronomer*
Rosenfeld, Arthur F. *federal agency administrator*
Rosenfeld, Ronald A. *federal agency administrator*
Rosenker, Mark Victor *federal agency administrator*
Rosenkrantz, Steven Jay *lawyer*
Rosenstein, Peter D. *educational association administrator, consultant*
Rosenstock, Linda *federal agency administrator, medical educator*
Rosenthal, Douglas Eurico *lawyer, author*
Rosenthal, Steven Siegmund *lawyer*
Ros-Lehtinen, Ileana *congresswoman*
Ross, Douglas *lawyer*
Ross, Malcolm *minerals consultant*
Ross, Mike *congressman*
Ross, Robinette Davis *publisher*
Ross, Stanford G. *lawyer, government official*
Rossides, Eugene Telemachus *lawyer, writer*
Rossin, Lawrence G. *ambassador*
Rossotti, Barbara Jill Margulies *lawyer*
Roswell, Robert H. *federal agency administrator*
Rotberg, Eugene Harvey *investment banker, lawyer*
Rotenberg, Marc Steven *public interest advocate, lawyer*
Roth, Stanley Owen *federal agency administrator*
Rother, John Charles *association executive, lawyer*
Rothman, Steven R. *congressman*
Rothstein, Barbara Jacobs *federal judge*
Rottman, Ellis *public information officer*
Rotunda, Donald Theodore *public relations consultant*
Rouse, James J. *oil industry executive*
Rouse, Leo E. *dean, dental educator*
Rove, Karl Christian *government advisor, consultant*
Rovelstad, Mathilde V(erner) *library science educator*
Rowden, Marcus Aubrey *lawyer, former government official*
Rowe, Richard Holmes *lawyer*
Rowson, Richard Cavanagh *publisher*
Roybal-Allard, Lucille *congresswoman*
Royce, Edward R. (Ed Royce) *congressman*
Royle, David Brian Layton *television producer, journalist*
Rubin, Blake Douglas *lawyer*
Rubin, Kenneth Allen *lawyer*
Ruckman, Roger Norris *pediatric cardiologist*
Ruddy, Frank *lawyer, former ambassador*
Rudman, Warren Bruce *former senator, lawyer, think tank executive*
Ruehle, Charles Joseph *pathologist, military officer*
Ruiz, Vanessa *federal judge*
Rule, Charles Frederick (Rick Rule) *lawyer*
Rumsfeld, Donald Henry *secretary of defense*
Runge, Jeffrey William *federal agency administrator*
Ruppersberger, Charles Albert, III, *congressman*
Rush, Bobby L. *congressman*
Rush, Jeffrey, Jr., *federal agency administrator*
Ruskin, Robert Sterling *association executive*
Russell, Judy C. *government agency administrator*
Russell, Mark *comedian*
Russell, Michael James *lawyer*
Russell, Richard M. *federal agency administrator*
Russell, William Joseph *educational association administrator*
Russert, Timothy John *broadcast journalist, executive*
Russin, Jonathan *lawyer, consultant*
Russo, Roy R. *lawyer*
Rust, William David, Jr., *retired structural engineer*
Rutledge, Peter J. *federal agency administrator*
Ruttenberg, Charles Byron *lawyer*
Rutter, Alan *federal agency administrator*
Ruttinger, George David *lawyer*
Ruwe, Robert P. *federal judge*
Ryan, David Alan *computer specialist*
Ryan, Mary A. *diplomat*
Ryan, Paul *congressman*
Ryan, Timothy *congressman*
Ryerson, Paul Sommer *lawyer*
Ryn, Claes Gösta *political science educator, author, research institute administrator*
Ryun, James Ronald *congressman*
Sabelhaus, Melanie R. *government agency administrator*
Sabo, Martin Olav *congressman*
Sabol, Carolyn A. *lawyer, government official*
Sabshin, Melvin *psychiatrist, educator, medical association administrator*
Sacher, Steven Jay *lawyer*
Sackler, Arthur Brian *lawyer*
Sacksteder, Frederick Henry *former foreign service officer*
Saffuri, Khaled Ahmad *cultural organization executive*
Safire, William *journalist, writer*
St. Amand, Janet G. *government relations lawyer*
St. John, Julie *mortgage company executive*
Sakoda, Robin (Sak Sakoda) *government official*
Salamon, Linda Bradley *English literature educator*
Saleeba, David A. *federal agency administrator*
Saleh, Ali-Abdullah *state official*
Salem, George Richard *lawyer*
Saliba, George *Maltese government official*
Salisbury, Dallas L. *research institute executive*
Salsbury, Michael H. *lawyer*
Saltzburg, Stephen Allan *law educator, consultant*
Sambur, Marvin *federal agency administrator*
Samet, Kenneth Alan *hospital administrator*
Sampson, David Allan *federal agency administrator*
Samsot, Robert Louis *newspaper editor, consultant*
Samuelson, Kenneth Lee *lawyer*
Sanchez, Linda T. *congresswoman*
Sanchez, Loretta *congresswoman*
Sanchez-Way, Ruth Dolores *health services administrator*
Sanders, Bernard (Bernie Sanders) *congressman*
Sanders, Charles F. *dean*
Sandler, Bernice Resnick *women's rights specialist*
Sandlin, Max Allen, Jr., *congressman*
Sandman, James Joseph *lawyer*
Sanford, Bruce William *lawyer*
Sansonetti, Thomas L. *federal agency administrator*
Santoro, Miléna *education educator*

Sullivan, Michael J. *labor union administrator*
Sullivan, Thomas M. *federal agency administrator*
Sullivan, Timothy *lawyer*
Summerford, Ben Long *retired artist, educator*
Sunderlin, Charles Eugene *consultant*
Sundermeyer, Michael S. *lawyer*
Sunley, Emil McKee *economist*
Sununu, John E. *senator*
Sussman, Monica Hilton *lawyer*
Sutter, Eleanor Bly *retired diplomat*
Swain, Susan Marie *communications executive*
Swankin, David Arnold *lawyer, consumer advocate*
Swarthworth, Sharon T. *military officer*
Sweeney, John E. *congressman*
Sweeney, John Joseph *labor union administrator*
Sweeney, Richard James *economics educator*
Sweet, Lynn D. *journalist*
Sweeting, Sharon Howe *school librarian, editor*
Swenson, Sue *foundation administrator, former health and education administrator*
Swift, Stephen Jensen *federal judge*
Swygert, Haywood Patrick *academic administrator*
Sypolt, Diane Gilbert *federal judge*
Tabackman, Steven Carl *lawyer*
Tacha, Athena *sculptor, artist, educator*
Taft, William Howard, IV, *federal agency administrator*
Talbott, Strobe *think-tank executive*
Talent, James M. *senator, former congressman, lawyer*
Tallent, Stephen Edison *lawyer*
Tamargo, Mauricio J. *federal agency administrator*
Taminiaux, Pierre Simon *writer, educator*
Tancredo, Thomas G. *congressman*
Tanham, George Kilpatrick *retired research company executive*
Tannen, Deborah Frances *writer*
Tannenwald, Peter *lawyer*
Tanner, John S. *congressman, lawyer*
Tanous, Peter Joseph *investment advisor*
Tarrants, William Eugene *federal official*
Tate, Sheila Burke *public relations executive*
Tatel, David Stephen *federal judge*
Tauber, Mark J. *lawyer*
Taurman, John David *lawyer*
Tauzin, W. J. Billy, II, (Wilbert J. Tauzin) *congressman*
Taylor, Charles H. *congressman*
Taylor, David Kerr *international business educator, consultant*
Taylor, Estelle Wormley *English educator, dean*
Taylor, Gene *congressman*
Taylor, Henry Splawn *literature educator, poet, writer*
Taylor, James, Jr., *lawyer*
Taylor, John Brian *federal agency administrator*
Taylor, Ralph Arthur, Jr., *lawyer*
Taylor, Richard Powell *lawyer*
Taylor, Sandra E. *public relations executive*
Taylor, William B., Jr., *ambassador*
Teague, Randal Cornell, Sr., *lawyer*
Teare, Richard Wallace *retired foreign service officer*
Tedeschi, George *labor union administrator*
Teets, Peter B. *federal agency administrator*
Tefft, John *ambassador*
Teich, Albert Harris *professional society administrator*
Temko, Stanley Leonard *lawyer*
Teng, Bing-Sheng *finance educator, researcher*
Tenorio, Pedro A. *resident representative*
Terpeluk, Peter, Jr., *ambassador*
Terry, John Alfred *state supreme court judge*
Terry, Lee R. *congressman, lawyer*
Terzian, Philip Henry *journalist*
Tetelman, Alice Fran *small business owner*
Tether, Anthony J. *government agency administrator*
Tetzlaff, Charles Robert *lawyer*
Thaler, Paul Sanders *lawyer, arbitrator, mediator*
Thawley, Michael *diplomat*
Theiss, Patricia Kelley *public health researcher, educator*
Theodore, Eustace D. *educational advancement consultant, management consultant*
Thomas, Clarence *United States supreme court justice*
Thomas, Craig *senator*
Thomas, Gerald E. *ambassador*
Thomas, Harry K., Jr., *ambassador*
Thomas, Mary Augusta *library administrator*
Thomas, Ralph Charles, III, *federal official*
Thomas, Ritchie Tucker *lawyer*
Thomas, Scott E. *federal government executive, lawyer*
Thomas, Tracey Williams *researcher*
Thomas, William Marshall (Bill Thomas) *congressman*
Thompson, Bennie G. *congressman*
Thompson, Bernida Lamerle *principal, consultant, educator*
Thompson, C. Michael *congressman*
Thompson, Diane E. *lawyer*
Thompson, Lawrence Hyde *federal agency official*
Thompson, Richard Leon *pharmaceutical company executive, lawyer*
Thompson, Sally Engstrom *state official*
Thompson, Tommy George *secretary of health and human services*
Thompson, William Reid *public utility executive, lawyer*
Thornberry, Mac *congressman*
Thornburgh, Dick (Richard L. Thornburgh) *lawyer, former United Nations official, former United States attorney general, former governor*
Thornton, Michael B. *federal judge*
Thurber, James A. *political scientist, educator*
Tiahrt, W. Todd *congressman, former state senator*
Tiberi, Patrick J. *congressman, former state legislator*
Tidball, M. Elizabeth Peters *physiologist, educator*
Tiede, Tom Robert *journalist*
Tierney, John F. *congressman, lawyer*
Tigar, Michael Edward *law educator*
Tilley, Jack L. *military officer*
Timmer, Charles Peter *agricultural and development economist*
Timmons, William Evan *corporate executive*
Timpane, Philip Michael *education educator, policy analyst*
Tingus, Steven James *physiologist researcher, educator, policymaker*
Tinsley, Nikki Lee *federal agency administrator*
Tipton, E. Linwood *trade association executive*
Tirana, Bardyl Rifat *lawyer*
Titus-Dillon, Pauline Yvonne *associate dean academic affairs, medical educator*
Tobias, Randall Lee *ambassador, retired pharmaceutical executive*
Tobias, Robert Max *labor leader, lawyer*
Todhunter, John Anthony *toxicologist, consultant*
Toedtman, James Smith *newspaper editor, journalist*
Tolchin, Martin *retired newspaper reporter, author*
Toledano, Ralph de *columnist, author, poet*
Toles, Thomas Gregory *editorial cartoonist*
Tolu, Tolu *foundation administrator*
Tomb, Diane Lenegan *federal agency administrator*
Tomich, Paul *medical association administrator, obstetrician, gynecologist*
Tomita, Kazuo (Joe) *automotive executive*
Tomlinson, Alexander Cooper *investment banker, consultant*
Tompkins, Joseph Buford, Jr., *lawyer*
Toner, Michael E. *commissioner*
Tonkin, Leo Sampson *educational foundation administrator*
Toomey, Patrick J. *congressman*
Topelius, Kathleen Ellis *lawyer*
Torkelson, Jodie Rae *charitable organization executive*
Tornblom, Claudia L. *civilian military employee*
Torrey, Barbara Boyle *research council administrator*
Tosi, Gloria C. *labor union administrator*
Totenberg, Nina *journalist*
Towey, Carroll Francis *senior education specialist*
Towle, Alexis Charles (Lex Towle) *education advocate*
Towns, Edolphus *congressman*
Townsend, Ann Van Devanter *foundation administrator, art historian*
Townsend, Brian Douglas *paralegal*
Townsend, Frances Fragos *federal agency administrator*
Townsend, John Michael *lawyer*
Townsend, Marjorie Rhodes *aerospace engineer, engineering executive*
Tracey, Patricia A. *career officer*
Trachtenberg, Stephen Joel *university president*
Tracy, Alan Thomas *trade association administrator*
Trafford, Abigail *columnist, editor, writer*
Train, Russell Errol *environmentalist*
Tranyham, David Francis *United States Government administrator*
Trencher, William Mannes *lawyer*
Trimble, Kathleen Louise *library director*
Trimble, Sandra Ellingson *lawyer*
Trisco, Robert Frederick *church historian, educator*
Trowbridge, Alexander Buel, Jr., *business consultant*
Troyer, Thomas Alfred *lawyer*
Truitt, Anne Dean *artist*
Truman, Edwin Malcolm *federal official*
Trumka, Richard Louis *labor leader, lawyer*
Truscott, Carl J. *federal agency administrator*
Tse, Man-Chun Marina *educational association administrator*
Tuck, John Chatfield *former federal agency administrator, public policy advisor*
Tucker, Marc Stephen *education policy analyst, author*
Tufaro, Richard Chase *lawyer*
Tung, Ko-Yung *lawyer*
Tuohey, Mark Henry, III, *lawyer*
Turner, Douglas Laird *writer, editor, columnist*
Turner, James *congressman*
Turner, James Thomas *judge*
Turner, John Andrew *economist*
Turner, John Freeland *federal agency administrator*
Turner, Michael *congressman*
Turner, Ted (Robert Edward Turner) *former television executive, philanthropist*
Turtell, Neal Timothy *librarian*
Tuttle, Marv *finance association executive*
Tychan, Terrence J. *grants and acquisitions administrator*
Tyner, Lee Reichelderfer *lawyer*
Uberall, Herbert Michael Stefan *physicist, researcher*
Ucko, David Alan *museum consultant*
Udall, Mark *congressman*
Udall, Thomas (Tom Udall) *congressman*
Uehlein, E(dward) Carl, Jr., *lawyer*
Umpleby, Stuart Anspach *management consultant, educator*
Underwood, Robert Anacletus *former congressman, university official*
Unger, Laura Simone *lawyer, commissioner*
Unsell, Lloyd Neal *energy organization executive, former journalist*
Upshaw, Gene *sports association executive*
Upton, Frederick Stephen *congressman*
Urbina, Ricardo Manuel *judge*
Ushakov, Yuri Viktorovich *diplomat*
Utley, Jon Basil *think-tank executive, journalist*
Vacketta, Carl Lee *lawyer, educator*
Vakerics, Thomas Vincent *lawyer*
Valachovic, Richard W. *medical association administrator*
Valentine, Debra A. *lawyer*
Valentine, Nancy Marie *nursing administrator, educator*
Valentine, Steven Richards *lawyer*
Van Allen, Barbara Martz *marketing professional*
VandenBos, Gary Roger *psychologist, publisher*
Vanderryn, Jack *philanthropic foundation administrator*
Vanderver, Timothy Arthur, Jr., *lawyer*
Van de Water, Mark E. *investment company executive*
Van Hollen, Christopher, Jr., *congressman*
Van Metre, Lauren *foundation administrator*
Van Tine, Kirk Kelso *federal agency administrator*
Van Ummersen, Claire A(nn) *academic administrator, biologist, educator*
Van Winkle, Hans A. *military officer*
Vaslef, Irene *historian, librarian*
Vasques, Victoria L. *federal agency administrator*
Vasquez, Gaddi *federal agency administrator*
Vaughan, Kenneth Edward *application developer*
Vaughn, Robert Gene *law educator*
Vazirani-Fales, Heea *legislative staff member, lawyer*
Veatch, Elizabeth Wilson *educational administrator*
Veatch, Robert Marlin *philosophy educator, medical ethics researcher*
Velazquez, Nydia M. *congresswoman*
Veneman, Ann M. *secretary of agriculture*
Venneri, Samuel L. *federal agency administrator*
Verner, James Melton *lawyer*
Verrill, Charles Owen, Jr., *lawyer*
Verstandig, Toni Grant *federal agency administrator*
Verville, Elizabeth Giavani *federal official*
Vickery, Raymond Ezekiel, Jr., *international business consultant, lawyer*
Victory, Nancy *federal agency administrator*
Viehe, Karl William *mathematics educator, lawyer, investment banker*
Vieth, Gifford Duane *lawyer*
Villa, John Kazar *lawyer*
Villarreal, June Patricia *sales consultant*
Vining, Margaret Simmons *historian, curator*
Vinyard, Walter Darnall *lawyer*
Visclosky, Peter John *congressman, lawyer*
Vitter, David *congressman*
Voinovich, George V. *senator, former governor*
Voll, John Obert *history professor*
Vondracek, M. Jon *communications executive*
von Kann, Clifton Ferdinand *aviation and space executive, software executive*
Vos, Joris Michael *diplomat*
Vose, Kathryn Kahler *marketing and communication executive*
Wagner, Annice McBryde *judge*
Wagner, Curtis Lee, Jr., *judge*
Wagstaff, Grayson *musicologist, educator*
Wahba, Marcelle M. *ambassador*
Waits, John A. *lawyer*
Walcott, John L. *communications executive*
Wald, Patricia McGowan *retired federal judge*
Walden, Greg *congressman*
Walder, Debby Jean *program director, quality manager, nursing service administrator, nurse, educator*
Wali, Sima *foundation administrator*
Walker, Barbara Dodson *cultural organization administrator, consultant, lecturer, researcher*
Walker, David A(lan) *finance educator*
Walker, David Michael *US government officer*
Walker, Edward S., Jr., *diplomat*
Walker, Mary L. *federal agency administrator, lawyer*
Walker, Robert Smith *former congressman*
Walker, Savannah T. *retired executive assistant, legislative assistant*
Wallace, Don, Jr., *law educator*
Wallace Douglas, Jean *conservationist*
Walsh, Dennis P. *government agency administrator*
Walsh, James Thomas *congressman*
Walsh, John *television show host*
Walsh, John F. *government agency administrator*
Walsh, Michael J. *lawyer*
Walsh, Raymond John *medical educator*
Walston, Roderick Eugene *federal official*
Walter, Sheryl Lynn *lawyer*
Walters, John P. *federal official*
Walton, Reggie Barnett *judge*
Walton, Tracy Matthew, Jr., *radiologist*
Wamp, Zach *congressman*
Wand, Patricia Ann *librarian*
Wang, John Cheng Hwai *communications engineer, researcher*
Wang, Kim *real estate broker, librarian*
Ward, David *academic administrator, educator*
Warner, John William *senator*
Warnick, Walter Lee *mechanical engineer*
Warren, Albert *publishing executive*
Warren, Clay *communications educator*
Warren, David Liles *educational association executive*
Warren, Steven F. *psychologist, educator*
Warrington, George D. *rail transportation executive*
Warshawsky, Mark Joel *federal agency administrator, economist*
Washburn, Kathryn Hazel *government agency executive*
Washington, Eric T. *state supreme court justice*
Wasshausen, Dieter Carl *systematic botanist*
Waters, Jennifer Nash *lawyer*
Waters, Mary Brice Kirtley *federal agency administrator*
Waters, Maxine *congresswoman*
Watkins, Shirley Robinson *agriculture department administrator*
Watson, Arthur Dennis *federal official*
Watson, Diane Edith *congresswoman*
Watson, Harlan L(eroy) *federal official, physicist, economist*
Watson, Peter S. *federal agency administrator*
Watson, Rebecca Wunder *federal agency administrator, lawyer*
Watson, Thomas C. *lawyer*
Watson, William Hughes *news service publisher, network executive*
Watt, Melvin L. *congressman, lawyer*
Wattenmaker, Richard Joel *archive director, art scholar*
Watters, Susan J. *communications executive*
Watts, Glenn Ellis *union official*
Waxman, Henry Arnold *congressman*
Wayne, Earl Anthony *federal agency administrator*
Wayne, Stephen J. *government educator, writer*
Waz, Joseph Walter, Jr., *government relations consultant, author*
Weaver, Christopher E. *naval officer*
Weaver, Donna L. *engraver*
Weaver, Reg *National Education Association president*
Webber, Richard John *lawyer*
Webre, Septime *ballet company artistic director, choreographer*
Webster, William Hedgcock *lawyer*
Wedgwood, Ruth *law educator, international affairs expert*
Weems, Kerry N. *federal agency administrator*
Wegener, Mark Douglas *lawyer*
Weicher, John Charles *federal agency administrator*
Weidenfeld, Edward Lee *lawyer*
Weidenfeld, Sheila Rabb *television producer, author*
Weil, Stephen Edward *retired museum official*
Weiler, Edward J. *federal agency administrator*
Weinberg, Larry *lawyer, labor union administrator*
Weinberg, Myrl *medical association administrator*
Weinberger, Caspar Willard *publishing executive, former secretary of defense*
Weinberger, Mark *federal agency administrator*
Weiner, Edward *civil engineer, federal agency administrator*
Weiner, Kenneth Brian *lawyer*
Weiner, Robert Stephen *federal agency administrator*
Weingold, Allan Byrne *obstetrician, gynecologist, educator*
Weinhold, Linda Lillian *psychologist, researcher*
Weinman, Howard Mark *lawyer*
Weinmann, Eric *retired lawyer*
Weinstein, Allen *educator, historian, non-profit administrator*
Weinstein, Harris *lawyer*
Weintraub, Ellen L. *commissioner*
Weintraub, Sidney *economist, educator*
Weisgall, Jonathan Michael *lawyer*
Weiss, Arnold Hans *lawyer*
Weiss, Charles, Jr., *educator*
Weiss, Gail Ellen *legislative staff director*
Weiss, Mark Anschel *lawyer*
Weissman, William R. *lawyer*
Weldon, David Joseph, Jr., *congressman, physician*
Weldon, W(ayne) Curtis (Curt Weldon) *congressman*
Wellen, Robert Howard *lawyer*
Weller, Gerald C. *congressman*
Wells, Samuel Fogle, Jr., *research center administrator*
Wells, Thomas B. *federal judge*
Wenner, Charles Roderick *lawyer*
Wenzel, Bob *federal agency administrator*
Werkman, Sidney Lee *psychiatry educator*
Werner, Mary Ann *lawyer*
Werronen, Betsy Warren *political organization administrator*
Wertheim, Mitzi Mallina *technology company executive*
Wertheimer, Fredric Michael *public policy advocate*
Wesberry, James Pickett, Jr., *financial management consultant, auditor, international organization executive*
Wesley, LaTonya Rashawn *legislative assistant*
West, Douglas M. *automotive executive*
West, Gail Berry *lawyer*
West, Jake *labor union administrator*
West, Robert MacLellan *science educator, consultant*
West, Togo Dennis, Jr., *lawyer, former cabinet member, former aerospace executive*
West, W. Richard *museum director*
Westmoreland, Timothy M. *education educator*
Wexler, Anne *government relations and public affairs consultant*
Wexler, Robert *congressman*
Weyrich, Paul Michael *political organizations executive*
Whalen, Thomas J. *lawyer*
Wheatley, Katherine Holbrook *federal official*
Wheeler, Douglas Paul *conservationist, government official, lawyer*
Wheeler, Thomas Edgar *former telecommunications executive*
Whitaker, Scott *federal agency administrator*
White, Evelyn *human resources administrator*
White, George Malcolm *architect*
White, John Kenneth *politics educator*
White, Robert Mayer *meteorologist*
White, Robert Roy *retired chemical engineer*
White, Roger Stuart *economist*
Whitehead, Alfred K. *labor union administrator*
Whitehurst, Grover Jay *federal official, psychologist and educator*
Whitfield, Edward (Wayne Whitfield) *congressman*
Whiting, Meredith Armstrong *public affairs executive*
Whiting, Richard Albert *lawyer*
Whitley, Joe Dally *lawyer*
Whittlesey, Judith Holloway *public relations executive*
Whitworth, Horace Algernon *mechanical engineer*
Wicker, Roger F. *congressman, lawyer*
Wiener, Leonard *journalist*
Wiesel, Sam W. *medical educator, academic administrator*
Wilchins, Howard Martin *lawyer*
Wilder, James Edward *resident manager*
Wilder, Roland Percival, Jr., *lawyer*
Wilderotter, James Arthur *lawyer*
Wilensky, Gail Roggin *economist, researcher*
Wilensky, Robert J. *plastic surgeon, historian*
Wiley, Richard Emerson *lawyer*
Wilf, Peter Daniel *paleobiologist*
Wilhelm, John W. *labor union administrator*
Wilkie, Edith B. *foundation administrator*
Wilkinson, Sharon P. *department of state official, former ambassador*
Will, George Frederick *editor, political columnist, news commentator*
Willard, Matthew Ashe *materials scientist, researcher*
Willeford, Pamela P. *ambassador*
Williams, Andrew W. *energy executive*
Williams, Anthony A. *mayor*
Williams, David C. *federal agency administrator*
Williams, Eddie Nathan *research institution executive*
Williams, Jackie L. *public administrator*
Williams, James A. *labor union administrator*
Williams, Jody *political organization administrator*
Williams, John Franklin *anesthesiologist educator and administrator*
Williams, Julie Lloyd *lawyer*
Williams, Karen Hastie *lawyer*
Williams, Leaford Clemetson *writer, political scientist*
Williams, Lori Anne *foundation administrator, vocalist*
Williams, Mary Ellen Coster *judge*
Williams, Maurice Jacoutot *development organization executive*
Williams, Stephen Fain *federal judge*
Williams, Steven A., Jr., *federal agency administrator*
Williams, Thomas Raymond *lawyer*
Williams, Wesley Samuel, Jr., *lawyer*
Williamson, Carl Augustus *engineering executive*
Williamson, John *economist*
Williamson, Michael *photographer*
Willis, Kevin *airport administrator*
Willner, Ann Ruth *political scientist, educator*
Willner, Dorothy *anthropologist, educator*
Wills, E. Ashley *ambassador*
Wilner, Thomas Bernard *lawyer*
Wilson, Addison Graves (Joe Wilson) *congressman, former senator, lawyer*
Wilson, Charles *former congressman*
Wilson, Ewen Maclellan *economist*
Wilson, Heather Ann *congresswoman*
Wilson, Joanne *federal agency administrator*
Wilson, Joseph Charles, IV, *former ambassador*
Wilson, Michael Moureau *lawyer, physician*
Wine, L. Mark *lawyer*
Winfrey, Carey Wells *journalist, magazine editor*

Winkenwerder, William, Jr., *federal agency administrator*
Winn, Morris X. *federal agency administrator*
Winnie, Glenna Barbara *pediatric pulmonologist*
Winston, Judith Ann *lawyer*
Winter, Douglas E. *lawyer, writer*
Winter, Michael Alex *federal agency administrator*
Winter, Roger Paul *federal agency administrator*
Winter, Thomas Swanson *editor, newspaper executive*
Wintrol, John Patrick *lawyer*
Wippel, John Francis *philosophy educator*
Wise, William Harvey, IV, *human service executive*
Wiseman, Alan M(itchell) *lawyer*
Wiseman, Laurence Donald *foundation executive*
Wiss, Marcia A. *lawyer*
Witcover, Jules Joseph *newspaper columnist, author*
Witek, John W. *history professor*
Withrow, Mary Ellen *federal agency administrator*
Withuhn, William Lawrence *museum director, railroad economics and management consultant*
Witorsch, Philip *internist, educator*
Wofford, Harris *former senator, national service executive*
Wogaman, John Philip *retired minister and educator*
Woicke, Peter *corporate financial executive*
Wolanin, Barbara Ann Boese *art curator, art historian*
Wolanin, Thomas Richard *educator, researcher*
Wolf, Alfred Clarence *retired economist*
Wolf, Frank R. *congressman, lawyer*
Wolf, John S. *ambassador, federal agency administrator*
Wolf, William B., Jr., *lawyer*
Wolfe, Leslie R. *think-tank executive*
Wolfe, Sidney Manuel *physician*
Wolfensohn, James David *government agency administrator*
Wolff, Elroy Harris *lawyer*
Wolff, Otto *federal agency administrator*
Wolff, Paul Martin *lawyer*
Wolfowitz, Paul Dundes *federal official, former ambassador to Indonesia*
Won, Delmond Jack Hing *commissioner*
Wood, Bernard Anthony *anthropology educator*
Wood, Mary Louise *humanities educator*
Wood, Patrick Henry, III, *federal agency administrator*
Woodall, Samuel Roy, Jr., *lawyer*
Woodruff, Judy Carline *broadcast journalist*
Woods, Stephanie *television producer, reporter*
Woodward, Robert Upshur *newspaper reporter, writer*
Woodworth, Ramsey Lloyd *lawyer*
Woolley, John Edward *trade association executive*
Woolsey, Lynn *congresswoman*
Work, Charles Robert *lawyer*
Worsley, James Randolph, Jr., *lawyer*
Worthy, K(enneth) Martin *retired lawyer*
Wortley, George Cornelius *government affairs consultant, investor*
Woteki, Catherine Ellen *nutritionist*
Wouk, Herman *writer*
Wraase, Dennis Richard *utilities company executive, accountant*
Wray, Robert *lawyer*
Wright, Sylvia *government agency administrator*
Wu, David *congressman*
Wulf, Norman *federal official*
Wulf, William Allan *computer information scientist, educator, federal agency administrator*
Wurtzel, Alan Leon *retail company executive*
Wyden, Ron *senator*
Wynn, Albert Russell *congressman*
Wyss, John Benedict *lawyer*
Yablon, Jeffery Lee *lawyer*
Yaklin, Lori Stillwagon *government agency administrator*
Yambrusic, Edward Slavko *lawyer, consultant*
Yanai, Shunji *former diplomat*
Yang, John *lawyer*
Yannucci, Thomas David *lawyer*
Yardley, Jonathan *journalist*
Yarrow, Andrew Louis *writer, journalist, educator, international relations consultant*
Yates, Mary Carlin *ambassador*
Yerkes, David Norton *architect*
Yochelson, Ellis L(eon) *paleontologist*
Yoder, Ronnie A. *judge*
Yonts-Shepard, Susan *forest service administrator*
Yoo, Grace *legal association administrator*
Yost, Paul Alexander, Jr., *foundation executive, retired coast guard officer*
Young, C. W. (Bill Young) *congressman*
Young, Donald Alan *physician*
Young, Donald E. *congressman*
Young, Jennifer B. *federal agency administrator*
Young, Marlene Annette *lawyer*
Young, Peter Robert *librarian*
Young, William H. *labor union administrator*
Youtcheff, John Sheldon *physicist*
Yrizarry, Magda N. *communications executive*
Yulish, Charles Barry *public relations executive*
Yurko, Michiko Kathleen *music educator, writer*
Yzaguirre, Raul Humberto *civil rights leader*
Zahn, Paula *newscaster*
Zane, Phillip Craig *lawyer*
Zaragoza, Lawrence Jay *government manager*
Zax, Leonard A. *lawyer*
Zechman, Edwin Kerper, Jr., *medical facility administrator*
Zeidman, Fred S. *corporate financial executive*
Zenker, Wendy *financial executive*
Zhang, Shengman *corporate financial executive*
Zhao, Quansheng *university administrator, educator*
Zielinski, Paul Bernard *grant program administrator, civil engineer*
Zietz, Karyl Lynn Kopelman *writer, opera critic, television correspondent, producer, documentary filmmaker*
Ziglar, James W. *federal agency administrator, investment banker, lawyer, educator*
Zimmer, Richard Alan *educational association administrator, lawyer, former congressman*
Zimmerman, Carole Lee *public relations professional*
Zimmerman, Edwin Morton *lawyer*
Zipp, Joel Frederick *lawyer*
Zoeller, Jack Carl *financial executive*
Zook, Bernard Charles *pathology educator, administrator, researcher*
Zuckman, Harvey Lyle *law educator*
Zwadiuk, Oleh *radio executive*

FLORIDA

Alachua
Gaines, Weaver Henderson *lawyer*
Neubauer, Hugo Duane, Jr., *computer network engineer*
Schneider, Richard T(heodore) *optics research executive, engineer*

Altamonte Springs
Frankel, Andrew Joel *management and information technology consultant*
Heindl, Phares Matthews *lawyer*
LeBlanc, Janet M. *addictions and relationship counselor*
Linberger, Lara Jane *marriage and family therapist, music educator*
Sepulveda, Nicasio *hydrologist, researcher*

Alva
Darlow, George Anthony Gratton *investor*

Amelia Island
Adelman, Robert Paul *retired construction company executive, lawyer*
Ash, Frederick Melvin *retired manufacturing company executive*
Britt, David Van Buren *retired educational communications executive*
Jesser, Benn Wainwright *retired chemical engineering and construction company executive*
Schiebler, Gerold Ludwig *pediatrician, educator*

Anna Maria
Hall, Edwin Huddleston, Jr., *retired investment company executive*
Kaiser, Albert Farr *diversified corporation executive*

Apopka
Lobinske, Richard John *entomologist*
Rath, Maurice Monroe *retired physician*
Reinecke, William T. *conductor, educator*

Arcadia
White, Will Walter, III, *public relations consultant, writer*

Atlantic Beach
Gartland, Alice Johnson *artist*
Walker, Richard Harold *pathologist, educator*

Atlantis
Louie, Steven J. *allergist, immunologist*

Auburndale
Mercer, Earnest Brant *retired finance educator*

Aventura
Alisetti, Edwin Luis *engineer, financial executive*
Babson, Irving K. *publishing company executive*
Burton, Richard Jay *lawyer*
Cantor, Norman Frank *history educator, writer*
Fishel, Peter Livingston *accounting business executive*
Goodman, Neal Robert *international management consultant and educator*
Kliger, Milton Richard *financial services executive*
Krop, Lois Pulver *psychologist*
McKenna, Peter Dennis *lawyer*
Perkel, Robert Simon *photojournalist, educator*

Avon Park
Cranfill, Virginia May *retired nursing administrator*

Babson Park
Morrison, Kenneth Douglas *author, columnist*
Warner, Steven S. *dean*

Bal Harbour
Bernay, Betti *artist*
Bond, Alma Halbert *psychoanalyst, author*
Horton, Jeanette *municipal government official*
Katz, Shmuel *surgeon*
Spiegel, Siegmund *architect*

Bartow
Cury, Bruce Paul *lawyer, magistrate, law educator*
Jackson, Elijah, Jr., *communication executive*

Bascom
Brooten, Kenneth Edward, Jr., *retired lawyer*
Hart, James Whitfield, Jr., *retired corporate public affairs executive, lawyer*

Bay Harbor Islands
Rosenbluth, Morton *periodontist, educator*

Bay Pines
Law, David Hillis *physician*
Stewart, Jonathan Taylor *psychiatrist, educator*

Bayonet Point
Errington, Norman *television producer, photographer*

Belle Glade
Oeffner, Barbara Dunning *writer, educator, scriptwriter*

Belleair
Dexter, Helen Louise *dermatologist, consultant*
Goldenfarb, Paul Bennett *internist, oncologist*
Szep, Paul Michael *editorial cartoonist*

Belleair Beach
Ayers, Richard Wayne *electric power industry executive, writer, journalist*
Fuentes, Martha Ayers *playwright*

Belleview
Bellis, Arthur Albert *financial executive, government official*

Beverly Hills
Larsen, Erik *art history educator*

Boca Grande
de Saint Phalle, Thibaut *investment banker, educator, lawyer, financial consultant*
Heffernan, John William *retired journalist*
Maguire, John Patrick *investment company executive*
Winterer, Victoria Thompson *hospitality executive*

Boca Raton
Agler, Richard Dean *rabbi*
Arden, Eugene *retired university provost*
Arent, Albert Ezra *retired lawyer*
Armstrong, Edward Bradford, Jr., *oral and maxillofacial surgeon, educator*
Balter, Murray *interior designer*
Barwell, Cindy Ann *lawyer*
Batmasian, Marta Tersakian *investment company owner*
Baumgarten, Diana Virginia *gerontological nurse*
Beber, Robert H. *lawyer, financial services executive*
Beck, Louis S. *hotel executive*
Bell, Marc H. *investment company executive*
Bernstein, Edwin S. *judge*
Boggess, Jerry Reid *protective services official*
Borman, Frank *former astronaut, laser patent company executive*
Boykin, Anne J. *dean*
Breakstone, Robert Albert *consumer products, e-commerce, information technology and consulting executive*
Brogan, Frank T. *former lieutenant governor*
Camilleri, Michael *lawyer, educator*
Cannon, Herbert Seth *investment banker*
Capps, David Edward, Jr., *assistant dean*
Castillo, William John *music educator*
Chestnov, Richard Franklin *private investor*
Collins, Robert Arnold *English language educator*
Connor, Frances Partridge *retired education educator*
Connor, Leo Edward *special education administrator*
David, Ronald Albert *lawyer*
Decker, Larry E. *education educator*
Dembowski, Frederick Lester *educational administrator, educator, consultant*
Dorfman, Allen Bernard *international management consultant*
Dower Gold, Catherine Anne *music history educator*
Dunhill, Robert *advertising direct mail executive*
Erdman, Joseph *lawyer*
Feld, Joseph *construction executive*
Fengler, John Peter *television producer, director, advertising executive*
Ferrari, Roberto C. *librarian*
Fier, Elihu *lawyer, educator*
Finegold, Ronald *computer services executive*
Fournet, Ronald A. *electronics executive*
Frank, William Edward, Jr., *executive recruitment company executive*
Frazer, Heather Turner *historian, educator*
Friedland, Michael Lawrence *medical educator*
Friend, Harold Charles *neurologist*
Furman, Mark Evan *neuroscientist*
Gagliardi, Raymond Alfred *physician*
Galin, Tad, Sr., *home business owner*
Garelick, Martin *retired transportation executive*
Garland, Joan Bruder *social worker, psychologist*
Godofsky, Stanley *lawyer*
Goldberger, Melvin Tobias *executive investment banker*
Goldman, Stuart Miles *podiatrist*
Goodstone, Erica Mae *sex therapist, psychotherapist*
Goray, Gerald Allen *real estate company executive, lawyer*
Gralla, Eugene *natural gas company executive*
Hoppenstein, Abraham Solomon *investment and merchant banker, consultant*
Innes-Brown, Georgette Meyer *real estate broker, insurance broker*
Jacobs, Joseph James *lawyer, communications company executive*
Jamkus, Tom *wholesale distribution executive*
Jessup, Jan Amis *arts volunteer, writer*
Jessup, Joe Lee *business educator, management consultant*
Judovits, Martin *textiles executive*
Karmelin, Michael Allen *financial executive*
Kassner, Herbert Seymore *lawyer*
Katz, Richard Jon *marketing and advertising company executive*
Kauffman, Alan Charles *lawyer*
Kaye, Barry *insurance company executive*
Kaye, Carole *museum director and curator*
Kephart, Larry Robert *architect*
Keyes, Daniel *author*
Kitzes, William Fredric *lawyer, safety analyst, consultant*
Kleinberg, Brian *financial services executive*
Koch, Robert Charles *lawyer, community activist*
Kotheimer, William Conrad *consulting engineer*
Kramer, Cecile E. *retired medical librarian*
Laine, Iris Ruth *minister, public relations/advertising executive*
Langbort, Polly *retired advertising executive*
Lazar, Charna L. *retired protective services official, private investigator, consultant*
Leary, William James *educational administrator*
Lerner, Theodore Raphael *dentist*
Levin, Marlene *human resources executive, educator*
Levine, Irving R. *commentator, dean, writer, educator*
Lin, Yukweng M. *engineer, educator*
Lowe, Benno Powers, II, *History professor*
McNair, Russell Arthur, Jr., *lawyer*
McQueen, Scott Robert *broadcasting company executive*
Miles, Jesse Mc Lane *retired accounting company executive*
Miller, Eugene *university official, business executive*
Miller, Tonya Alicia *training and development specialist, management consultant*
Monroe, William Lewis *human resources executive*
Myers, Michelle *publishing executive*
O'Donnell, Joseph Michael *electronics executive*
Ohlman, Douglas Ronald *commodities and securities trader, investment consultant, lawyer*
Ortiz, Jaime *business educator*
Ortlip, Paul Daniel *artist*
Owen, Daniel Bruce *financial consultant*
Peterson, Mark F. *business educator*
Pradere, Sonia *accounting administrator*
Resnick, Robert *physicist, researcher*
Reynolds, George Anthony, Jr., *engineering executive*
Ricciardi, Salvatore *wholesale distribution executive*
Richardson, R(oss) Fred(erick) *insurance executive*
Robbins, Norman Nelson *lawyer*
Rosenkranz, Herbert S. *public health educator*
Rosner, M. Norton *business systems and financial services company executive*
Ross, Donald Edward *university administrator*
Ross, Fred Michael *organic chemist*
Rothberg-Blackman, June Simmonds *retired nursing educator, psychotherapist, psychoanalyst*
Rutner, Alan *wholesale grocery executive*
Samuels, William Mason *physiology association executive*
Schechterman, Lawrence *private chef, business consultant*
Siegel, Ned Lawrence *real estate developer*
Sigel, Marshall Elliot *financial consultant*
Singer, Merle Elliot *rabbi*
Snyder, Mark Steven *theater educator*
Tanner, Travis *travel executive*
Tata, Robert Joseph *retired geographer, educator*
Tennies, Robert Hunter *headmaster*
Tescher, Donald R. *lawyer*
Turner, Lisa Phillips *human resources executive*
Wallach, Steven Ernst *lawyer, pilot*
Warshaw, Carole Klein *education educator, consultant*
Waxman, Donald *composer*
Weiner, Howard Marc *physician*
Weissbach, Herbert *biochemist, researcher*
Wertheimer, Esther *sculptor*
Wiesenfeld, John Richard *chemistry professor*
Wyatt, James Luther *drapery hardware company executive*
Yelin, Robert Bruce *musician, recording artist, composer, lyricist*
Yoder, Patricia Doherty *public relations executive*
Zuckerman, Sidney *retired allergist, immunologist*

Bokeelia
Adams, Alfred Hugh *retired college president*

Bonita Springs
Becker, Richard Charles *retired college president*
Brown, Theodore Lawrence *chemistry professor*
Dignan, Thomas Gregory, Jr., *lawyer*
Dougherty, James *orthopedic surgeon, educator, author*
Dunning, Herbert Neal *government industry official, physical chemist*
Hauserman, Jacquita Knight *management consultant*
Johnson, Franklyn Arthur *academic administrator*
Katzen, Raphael *consulting chemical engineer*
McManigal, Shirley Ann *university educator, dean emerita*
McNamara-Ringewald, Mary Ann Thérèse *artist, educator*
Mehuron, William Otto *retired government official, consultant*
Olander, Ray Gunnar *retired lawyer*
Powell, Robert Ellis *mathematics educator, college dean*
Sargent, Charles Lee *manufacturing executive*
Trudnak, Stephen Joseph *landscape architect*

Boynton Beach
Bartholomew, Arthur Peck, Jr., *accountant*
Bryant, Donald Loyd *insurance company executive*
Caras, Joseph Sheldon *life insurance company executive*
Davant, James Waring *investment banker*
Glickman, Franklin Sheldon *dermatologist, educator*
Hermann, Philip J. *lawyer*
Hill, Patricia Jo *workforce development specialist*
Jacobs, Wendy *editor, writer, translator*
Jensen, Reuben Rolland *former automotive company executive*
Klein, Bernard *publishing company executive*
Kronman, Joseph Henry *orthodontist, educator*
Lemanski, Larry Fredrick *medical educator, university administrator*
Machtiger, Harriet Gordon *retired psychoanalyst*
Mittel, John J. *economist, corporate executive*
Oppler, Ralph Leo *retired publishing executive, advertising executive*
Pataky, Paul Eric *ophthalmologist*
Polinsky, Janet Naboicheck *retired state official, former state legislator*
Rogers, John S. *retired union official*
Sanderson, Jerome Alan *retired statistician, accountant*
Srinath, Latha *physician*
Stubbins, Hugh A(sher), Jr., *architect*
Sutter, William Paul *lawyer*
Vella, Fred John *social studies educator*
Waterman, Daniel *mathematician, educator*

Braden River
Wilkerson, Janet Stafford *publishing executive, educator*

Bradenton
Anderson, Herbert G. *marine biologist, researcher*
Bateman, John Jay *classics educator*
Beall, Robert Matthews, II, *retail chain executive*
Bjorklund, Nancy Margarette Watts *music educator*
Blanchard, Leonard Albert *educator, consultant, writer*
Brenner, Frank *lawyer*
Compton, Charles Daniel *chemistry professor*
Crouthamel, Thomas Grover, Sr., *editor, consultant*
Diana, John Nicholas *physiologist*
Dickie, George Thomas *philosopher, educator*
Driscoll, Constance Fitzgerald *education educator, writer, consultant*
Engelman, Melvin Alkon *retired dentist, dental products executive*
French, Richard Paul *artist*
Groseclose, Lynn Hunter *lawyer*
Houston, Stanley Dunsmore *retired public relations executive*
Howe, Carroll Victor *construction equipment company executive*
Kournikova, Anna *professional tennis player*
LaForest, Lana Jean *lawyer*
Lister, Thomas Mosie *composer, lyricist, publishing company executive, minister*
McFarland, Richard Macklin *retired journalist*
Melcher, Sandra J. *artist*
Merrick, Janna Carol *political scientist, educator*
Nelson, Ralph Erwin *investment company executive, coin dealer*
Padgett, Gail Blanchard *lawyer*
Pillot, Gene Merrill *retired school system administrator*

Price, Edgar Hilleary, Jr., *business consultant*
Rechcigl, Jack Edward *soil and environmental sciences educator*
Robinson, Hugh R. *retired marketing executive*
Rutstein, Stanley Harold *apparel retailing company executive*
St. Paul, Alexandra De La Vergne *lawyer*
Stewart, Priscilla Ann Mabie *art historian, educator*
Thomas, Ella Cooper *lawyer*
Voorhees, Stephanie Robin Faught *retired art educator*
Watkins, William, Jr., *electric power industry executive*
White, Dale Andrew *journalist*
Wolf, John Michael *adult education seminar consultant*
Woodson-Howard, Marlene Erdley *former state legislator*

Brandon
Cartlidge, Edward Sutterley *mechanical engineer*
Curry, Clifton Conrad, Jr., *lawyer*
Halse, Frank Adams, Jr., *retired minister*
Jurch, George R., Jr., *retired science educator*
Landry, Richard *publishing executive*
Mack, Arthur Neal *emergency medicine and family practice physician*
Mussenden, Gerald *psychologist*

Brooksville
Anderson, Richard Edmund *city manager, management consultant*
Brown, James Milton *law educator*
Lauer, Harry Curtis *retired civil engineer*
Pylipow, Stanley Ross *retired manufacturing company executive*

Cape Canaveral
Hess, Terry Lee *writer, educator, logistician*

Cape Coral
Graham, Minnie Dorothy *elementary school educator*
Longo, Paul Albert *retired industrial engineer, consultant*
Martin, Benjamin Gaufman *ophthalmologist*
McKinley, James Frank, Jr., *retired manufacturing executive*
Milaski, John Joseph *business transformation industry consultant*
Parrett, Sherman O. *lawyer*
Shuman, Carolyn Rae (Thorburn) *psychologist, columnist, writer, nurse*
Stuart, Robert *container manufacturing executive*
Wendel, Joan Audrey *music educator*
West, John Merle *retired physicist, nuclear consultant*

Carrollwood
O'Keefe, Fredrick Rea *bishop, consultant, educator, writer*

Casselberry
Pantuso, Vincent Joseph *food service consultant*

Cedar Key
Starnes, Earl Maxwell *urban and regional planner, architect*

Celebration
O'Neal, Kathleen Len *communications executive, writer, management speaker, financial consultant*
Schroeder, James White *retired lawyer*
Whelden, Craig B. *retired army officer*
Wilson, George Peter *international organization executive*

Christmas
Fowler, Ronald James *journalist*

Citra
Parisi, Marita *artist, art gallery director*

Clearwater
Barry, Joyce Alice *dietician, consultant*
Bazzone, Theresa (Terry) A. *sales executive*
Benavente, Javier Edgar *venture technology executive*
Blumencranz, Peter William *surgeon*
Borja, Mary Ellen Murphy *lawyer*
Brady, Sheila Ann *manufacturing executive*
Brown, Richard Christopher *retired epidemiologist*
Campolettano, Thomas Alfred *international contract manager*
Cano, Néstor *computer company executive*
Chisholm, William DeWayne *retired contract manager*
Coleman, Jeffrey Peters *lawyer*
Crites, Richard Ray *financial planner, investment advisor, financial services company executive*
Dannewitz, Charles V. *information technology executive*
Dodge, Adriana *real estate investor, educator*
Dougall-Sides, Leslie K. *lawyer*
Duerst, Andreas *information technology executive*
Fine, A(rthur) Kenneth *lawyer*
Gass, Andy *information technology executive*
Glymph, Dianne Tyler *librarian*
Grala, Jane M. *securities firm executive*
Graves, Robert Lee *health facility administrator*
Hallam, Arlita Warrick *quality of life administrator*
Hamilton, Lawrence White *human resources executive*
Heid, Michael Patrick *surgeon*
Henderson, Janet Lynn *small business owner*
Hibbard, Frank V. *diversified financial services company executive*
Hogan, Elwood *lawyer*
Hoornstra, Edward H. *retail company executive*
Howells, Jeffrey P. *computer company executive*
Hunter, William J. *information technology executive*
Jacobs, Marilyn Arlene Potoker *gifted education educator, consultant, author*
Kiehl, E. Robert *manufacturing executive, consultant*
Lansky, Zena *surgeon*
Levy, Elio *marketing professional*
Loos, Randolph Meade *financial planner*
Maxwell, Richard Anthony *retail executive*
McCormack, John Robert *lawyer*
Osbourn, Joseph A. *information technology executive*
Peterson, James Robert *engineering psychologist*
Pope, Fred Wallace, Jr., *lawyer*
Raymund, Steven A. *computer company executive*
Sandefer, G(eorge) Larry *lawyer*
Saydun, Yuda *information technology executive*
Scarne, John *game company executive*
Slade, Roy *artist, college president, museum director*
Smith, Marion Pafford *avionics company executive, retired*
Thomas, Patrick Robert Maxwell *oncology educator, academic administrator*
Todd, William K., Jr., *information technology executive*
Tragos, George Euripedes *lawyer*
Trepani, Joseph B. *information technology executive*
Turley, Stewart *retired retail company executive*
VanMeer, Mary Ann *publisher, writer, researcher, webmaster*
Weidemeyer, Carleton Lloyd *lawyer*
Whedon, George Donald *medical administrator, researcher*
Youna, Gerard *information technology executive*
Zschau, Julius James *lawyer*

Clearwater Beach
Strenski, James B. *retired communications executive*

Clermont
Jolley, Franklin David, Jr., *journalist, writer*

Cocoa
Block, David L. *solar engineering executive*
Fountain, Edwin Byrd *minister, educator, librarian, poet*
Gamble, Thomas Ellsworth *academic administrator*
McLendon, Dorothy *school psychologist*

Cocoa Beach
Kennedy, Thomas Patrick *financial executive*
Wirtschafter, Irene Nerove *tax specialist, consultant*

Coconut Creek
Brenner, Egon *university official, education consultant*
Casey, Thomas Warren *graphic design company executive, architect*
Marshak, Arthur *artist, sculptor*
Rogge, James Alan *education educator*
Sheehy, Frances Diane *lawyer*

Coconut Grove
Martinez-Carbonell, Karelia *not-for-profit fundraiser*
Nahmad, Albert H. *manufacturing executive, United States federal commissioner*
Soto, Patricia McFarlane *elementary school educator*
Taylor, J(ames) Bennett *management consultant*
Turkel, Bruce *advertising executive*

Cooper City
Maugere, Dannis Paul *historian, educator*

Coral Gables
Aitken, Anne E. *computer company executive*
Aljifri, Hassan *engineering educator, consultant*
Anthony, Andrew John *lawyer*
Blumberg, Philip Flayderman *real estate developer*
Bolton, David *lawyer, educator*
Brandt, Frederic Sheldon *dermatologist*
Buchsbaum, Karen Fuson *public relations executive, consultant*
Burini, Sonia Montes de Oca *apparel manufacturing and public relations executive*
Cole, Todd Godwin *management consultant transportation*
Crespo, Fernando Calderon *retired civil engineer*
Criss, Cecil M. *chemistry professor*
Dady, Robert Edward *lawyer*
David, George A. *lawyer*
Einspruch, Norman Gerald *physicist, engineering educator*
Fitzgerald, John Thomas, Jr., *religious studies educator*
Fournaris, Theodore James *lawyer*
Glaser, Luis *biochemistry educator*
Gonzalez, Ervin Amado *lawyer*
Hall, Miles Lewis, Jr., *lawyer*
Herald, Sara Barli *bank executive*
Hertz, Arthur Herman *communications executive*
Hirschhorn, Joel *lawyer*
Hoffman, Carl H. *lawyer*
Horner, Diane L. *dean*
Howard, Bernard Eufinger *mathematics and computer science educator*
Keeley, Brian E. *hospital administrator*
Landon, Robert Kirkwood *philanthropist, retired insurance company executive*
Leblanc, Roger Maurice *chemistry professor*
Lomonosoff, James Marc *marketing professional*
Lucà-Moretti, Maurizio *research scientist, nutrition researcher*
Mantell, Murray I. *engineering educator*
McGrane, Miles A., III, *lawyer*
Miller, Bruce J. *performing arts educator, director*
Modestino, James William *electrical engineering educator*
Moreno, Fernando *lawyer, educator*
Moss, Ambler Holmes, Jr., *lawyer, former ambassador*
Mundy, Peter *psychology educator*
Murfin, Ross C *university dean, English educator*
Nunez-Portuondo, Ricardo *investment company executive*
Olazabal, Ann Morales *business law educator*
Paul, Robert *lawyer*
Perez, Josephine *psychiatrist, educator*
Pitcher, Jonathan Michael *language educator, researcher*
Potamkin, Alan *automotive company executive*
Quillian, Warren Wilson, II, *pediatrician, educator*
Roberts, Samuel Smith *television news executive*
Rodriguez, Nestor Joaquin *insurance broker*
Saffir, Herbert Seymour *structural engineer, consultant*
Scandura, Teresa Anne *management educator*
Schaiberger, George Elmer *microbiologist educator*
Schwartztol, Holly Wechsler *psychologist*
Shalala, Donna E. *university administrator, former federal official, political scientist, educator*
Simpson, Russell Gordon *lawyer, former mayor, not-for-profit developer, consultant*
Steinberg, Alan Wolfe *investment company executive*
Suarez, George Michael *urologist*
Sumanth, David Jonnakoty *industrial engineer, educator*
Van Aken, Norman *chef*
Van Vliet, Carolyne Marina *physicist, researcher*
Weiner, Morton David *banker, insurance agent*
Weiner, Ruth Eileen Blower Kassewitz *retired public relations executive*
Young, Tzay Y. *electrical and computer engineering educator*
Yusko, Dave *automotive executive*
Zand, Lloyd Craig *radiologist*

Coral Springs
Becker, Allienne R. *education educator, writer*
Bolene, Rosalie Steele (Margaret Bolene) *bacteriologist, volunteer*
Burg, Ralph *art association executive*
Hoffman, Avi *performing company executive*
Medina-Salinas, Elizabeth *publishing executive, writer*
Ritter, Stacy Joy *state legislator, lawyer*
Singh, Vijay *professional golfer*
Wechsler, Arnold *osteopathic obstetrician, gynecologist*

Crawfordville
Brumby, James Remley, III, (Knox Brumby) *retired priest*

Crestview
Scott, George Gallmann *accountant*

Crystal River
Stone, Fred Lyndon *retired human resources administrator*

Dade City
Brennan, Thomas Emmett *lawyer*
Burdick, Glenn Arthur *physicist, engineering educator*

Dania
Dodge, Richard Eugene *oceanographer, educator, marine life administrator*
Fernander, Karen Geneine *secondary school educator*
Satin, Claire Jeanine *sculptor, book artist*

Davenport
Vaughn, Rosalyn Mae *educational association administrator*

Davie
Boston, David *professional football player*
Ganson, Barbara Anne *history professor*
Jackson, Lisa Keisha *educational consultant*
Madison, Sam A., Jr., *professional football player*
Mare, Olindo Franco *professional football player*
Martin, Tony Derrick *professional football player*
McDuffie, Otis James (O.J. McDuffie) *professional football player*
Morris, Joseph Raymond *business and economics educator*
Seau, Junior (Tiana Seau Jr.) *professional football player*
Silva, Yvonne N. *registrar*
Thomas, Thurman Lee *professional football player*
Thomas, Zach Michael *professional football player*
Upadhiaya, Umesh Chandra *engineer, consultant*
Wannstedt, David Raymond *professional football coach*

Daytona Beach
Adams, John Carter, Jr., *insurance executive*
Alvarez, Marianne *artist, photographer, educator*
Andrews, Donna L. *professional golfer*
Barker, Robert Osborne (Bob Barker) *educator, mediator*
Barrett, Tina *professional golfer*
Betancourt, Ralph Ernest *mayor*
Bodine, Brett *race car driver*
Bodine, Geoff *race car driver*
Brady, Tim *dean*
Bronson, Oswald Perry, Sr., *religious organization administrator, clergyman*
Brown, Benjamin Thomas *urologist, educator*
Buckelew, Richard Allan *historian, educator*
Cardwell, Harold Douglas, Sr., *retired rehabilitation specialist*
Carmona, José Antonio *Spanish language educator, English language educator*
Chabrian, Peggy *air transportation executive*
Chesnut, Nondis Lorine *screenwriter, consultant, reading and language arts educator, instructor, counselor*
Davidson, Herbert M., Jr., (Tippen Davidson) *newspaper owner*
Davies, Laura *professional golfer*
DeLuca, Annette *professional golfer*
Di Nicolo, Roberto *allergist*
Duma, Richard Joseph *microbiologist, educator, pathologist, researcher, physician*
Dumm, Robert Wayne *musician, educator, writer*
Ebbs, George Heberling, Jr., *university executive*
Figg-Currier, Cindy *professional golfer*
France, William Clifton, Jr., *professional sports team executive*
Frederick-Recascino, Christina Marie *psychologist, educator*
Fuqua, Muriel *education educator*
Furstman, Shirley Elise Daddow *retired executive secretary*
Gordon, Jeff *race car driver*
Harris, Christy Franklin *lawyer*
Harrison, William D. *humanities educator*
Hartsell, Horace Ed *college president*
Helton, Mike *professional sports team executive*
Inkster, Juli *professional golfer*
Jones, Rose *professional golfer*
Kane, Lorie *professional golfer*
King, Betsy *professional golfer*
Klein, Emilee *professional golfer*
Kuehne, Kelli *professional golfer*
Libbey, James K. *education educator*
Libby, Gary Russell *museum director emeritus, writer*
Mallon, Meg *professional golfer*
Mc Collister, John Charles *writer, clergyman, educator, executive producer*
Miller, Sanford *car rental company executive*
Moodie, Janice *professional golfer*
Neitzke, Eric Karl *lawyer*
Neumann, Liselotte *professional golfer*
Pagan Ortiz, Alex Omar *computer systems analyst, educator*
Pak, Se Ri *professional golfer*
Palmer, William D. *judge*
Patterson, Roger Lewis *psychologist*
Pepper, Dottie *professional golfer*
Richards, Virginia (Ginnie) *social worker*
Robbins, Kelly *professional golfer*
Rudd, Ricky *race car driver*
Schrader, Ken *race car driver*
Scott, John Brooks *retired research institute executive*
Seenith, Sivasundaram *mathematician, educator*
Sharples, D. Kent *college administrator*
Sheehan, Patty *professional golfer*
Sigerson, Marjorie Lorraine *librarian*
Sloane, James Robert *chemical engineer*
Sorenstam, Annika *professional golfer*
Steinhauer, Sherri *professional golfer*
Tiblier, Fernand Joseph, Jr., *municipal engineering administrator*
Tschetter, Kris *professional golfer*
Votaw, Ty M. *golf association commissioner*
Wallace, Rusty *race car driver*
Wanjohi, Elsie Wairimu *communications educator*
Webb, Karrie *professional golfer*
Whitworth, Kathrynne Ann *professional golfer*
Wie, Michelle Sung *amateur golfer*
Xepapas, Anargyros *architect*
Yarborough, William Caleb *retired race car driver*

Daytona Beach Shores
Dalia, Vesta Mayo *artist*

Debary
Pelosi, Haydee *sculptor*

Deerfield Beach
Allaire, Gaston George *music educator, researcher*
Brown, Colin *automotive executive*
Caso, Dawn Marie *lawyer, consultant, law educator*
Foster, James R. *former wholesale distribution auto executive*
Gambino, S(alvatore) Raymond *medical laboratory executive, educator*
Hoppenstedt, Elbert M. *retired school system administrator*
King, Don *boxing promoter*
Laser, Charles, Jr., *oil company executive*
Moran, James M. *automotive sales executive*
Moran, Patricia Genevieve *corporate financial executive*
Siegel, Steven L. *finance company executive, consultant*
Solomon, Barry Jason *healthcare administrator*

Deland
Brakeman, Louis Freeman *retired university official*
Caccamise, Genevra Louise Ball (Mrs. Alfred E. Caccamise) *retired librarian*
Dascher, Paul Edward *university dean, accounting educator*
Dinkins, Debora E. *librarian*
Gill, Donald George *retired education educator*
Goldberg, Paul Bernard *gastroenterologist, clinical researcher*
Gross, Mitchell Neal *ceramics engineer*
Hodges, Brian W. *consumer products company executive*
Langston, Paul T. *music educator, university dean, composer*
Lee, Howard Douglas *academic administrator*
McCann, Greg *law educator, consultant*
Morland, Richard Boyd *retired educator*
Musco, Lynn Ann *music educator*
Rattman, William John *electronics and electro-optic engineer*
Robinson, Stephen A. *music educator, musician*
Sanders, Edwin Perry Bartley *judge*
Tedros, Theodore Zaki *real estate broker, appraiser, educator*
Wittich, John Jacob *retired academic administrator, business executive*
Wood, Richard Harvey, Jr., *economics professor*

Delray Beach
Armstrong, Jack Gilliland *lawyer*
Baine, Stuart Allan *cardiologist*
Beckman, Frank Samuel *computer science educator, researcher*
Brown, Charles E. *retail executive*
Campbell, Cynthia *retail executive*
Carter-Miller, Jocelyn *retail executive*
Case, Manning Eugene, Jr., *retired food products executive*
Charyk, Joseph Vincent *retired satellite telecommunications executive*
Chavin, Walter *biological science educator and researcher*
Colley, Gerald (Jerry) E. *retail executive*
Crosson, Jay *retail executive*
DeMueller, Lucia *investment consultant*
Ehrlich, Geraldine Elizabeth *management consultant*
Ehrlich, S(aul) Paul, Jr., *physician, consultant, former government official*
Ellsweig, Phyllis Leah *retired psychotherapist*
Fannin, David Cecil *lawyer*
Fitzpatrick, David J. *electronics executive*
Friend, Miriam Ruth *personnel company executive*
Goldenberg, George *retired pharmaceutical company executive*
Goldstein, Barry J. *former home improvement center manufacturing executive*
Hegstrom, William Jean *retired mathematics professor*
Heit, Ivan *packaging equipment company executive*
Himmelright, Robert John, Jr., *rubber company executive*
Holifield, Mark *retail executive*
Horowitz, Fedora Cohen *music educator, pianist*
Jacobson, Herbert Leonard *licensing executive*
Larry, R. Heath *lawyer, director*
Luechtefeld, Monica *retail executive*
Mavrides, Gregory *computer scientist, psychoanalyst, computer engineer, computer company executive*
Mayer, Marilyn Gooder *steel company executive*
Mills, Agnes Eunice Karlin *artist, printmaker, sculptor*
Morrison, Patricia B. *retail executive*
Nelson, Bruce *consumer products company executive*
Randall, Priscilla Richmond *retired travel company executive*

Reichart, Stuart Richard *lawyer*
Rippeteau, Darrel Downing *retired architect*
Robinson, Richard Francis *genealogist, personal historian, writer*
Rosenfeld, Steven Ira *ophthalmologist*
Ross, Beatrice Brook *artist*
Saffer, Alfred *retired chemical company executive*
Salsberg, Arthur Philip *publishing company executive*
Schaffer, Marvin W. *investor*
Schenkel, Suzanne Chance *retired natural resource specialist*
Schwarz, Rose Oberman *artist*
Sherwood, Louis Maier *physician, scientist, pharmaceutical company executive*
Siegel, Ira T. *publishing executive*
Silberman, Charlotte Schatzberg *retired lawyer, artist*
Smith, Charles Oliver *engineer*
Solon, Leonard R(aymond) *retired physicist, educator, consultant*
Spyker, Harry A., III, *music educator*
Stewart, Patricia Carry *foundation administrator*
Teisch, Morton *management consultant*
van Kaldekerken, Rolf *retail executive*
Warshaw, Stanley Irving *federal official, consultant*
Weiner, Anne Lee *social worker*
Wells, Mary Elizabeth Thompson *minister*
Zarwyn, Berthold *physical scientist*
Zepnick, Seymour *civil engineer, consultant*

Deltona
Bondinell, Stephanie *counselor, academic administrator*
Zagnoli, Roland Candiano *management and marketing consultant, pharmacist*

Destin
Asher, Betty Turner *academic administrator*
Clary, Charles William, III, *state legislator, architect, consultant*
Deel, Frances Quinn *retired librarian*
De Revere, David Wilsen *retired professional society administrator*
Giadrosich, Donald Louis *research scientist, retired electrical engineer*
Harmuth, Henning F. *electrical engineer, educator*
Linn, James Eldon, II, *insurance company executive*
Robinson, Wilkes Coleman *retired federal judge*
Schuster, Julia Horst *writer, publishing executive*
Stansberry, James Wesley *air force officer*

Doral
Feito, Jose *architect*

Dover
Pearson, Walter Donald *editor, columnist*

Dunedin
Allison, Brooke Hastings *artist, educator*
Goodale, Arthur Worthington *civil engineer, researcher*
Klingbiel, Paul Herman *retired information scientist*
Krone, Norman Bernard *commercial real estate developer, lawyer*
Metcalf, Robert John Elmer *industrial consultant*
O'Dea, J. David *psychologist, educator*
Rosa, Raymond Ulric *retired banker*
Tweedy, Robert Hugh *retired equipment company executive*
Whiting, Susan D. *marketing professional*

Dunnellon
Fonseca, Julio *retired secondary school educator*
Martell, Thomas Stewart *accountant*
Sawick, Karen Ann *real estate agent*

Eagle Lake
McNeil, Edward Warren *real estate company executive*

Edgewater
Collard, Eugene Robert *writer*
Schubert, Jeanne *artist*

Eglin AFB
Head, William Christopher *military officer, health care administrator*

Ellenton
Edson, Herbert Robbins *retired foundation and hospital executive*

Englewood
Brainard, Paul Henry *musicologist, retired music educator*
Clark, Carolyn Chambers *nurse, educator, publishing executive*
Sanders, W(illiam) Eugene, Jr., *internist, educator*
Simis, Theodore Luckey *investment banker, information technology executive*

Estero
Brown, William Robert *association executive, consultant*
Brush, George W. *college president*
Routh, Donald K(ent) *psychology educator*

Eustis
Chorosinski, Eugene Conrad *writer, poet, author*
Welch, Jerry *oil company executive*

Fernandina Beach
Barlow, Anne Louise *pediatrician, medical research administrator*
Kurtz, Myers Richard *hospital administrator*
Lilly, Wesley Cooper *marine engineer, surveyor*
Rogers, Robert Burnett *naval officer*
Smeeton, Thomas Rooney *governmental affairs consultant*

Fisher Island
Rogers, Mark Charles *anesthesiologist, pediatrician, entrepreneur, educator*

Flagler Beach
Stockton, Anderson Berrian *electronics company executive, consultant, genealogist*

Fort Lauderdale
Alpert, Martin Jeffrey *chiropractic physician*
Ambrose, Judith Ann *designer*
Austin, John Norman *classics educator*
Azrin, Nathan Harold *psychologist, educator*
Bartelstone, Rona Sue *gerontologist*
Baruch, Eduard *management consultant*
Beatty, Robert Clinton *religious studies educator*
Benjamin, James Scott *lawyer*
Berrard, S.R. *automotive executive, waste management administrator*
Bogenschutz, J. David *lawyer*
Boire, Ron *retail executive*
Bolanos, Michael Templeton *new media executive*
Boles, Eric Paul *staffing company executive*
Bowen, Judith Reina *fundraising executive*
Brawer, Marc Harris *lawyer*
Bunnell, George Eli *lawyer*
Burleigh, A. Peter *ambassador*
Bustamante, Nestor *lawyer*
Cane, Marilyn Blumberg *lawyer, educator*
Cannon, Robert Eugene *library director*
Cantwell, John Walsh *advertising executive*
Castillo, Carmen *staffing company executive*
Cavendish, Kim L. Maher *museum administrator*
Chapman, Erie, III, *hospital administrator*
Chernow, Bart *critical care physician*
Clubb, Bruce Edwin *retired lawyer*
Cobb, David Keith *accountant*
Cole, James Otis *lawyer*
Collins, Ronald William *psychologist, educator*
Cordesman, Michael J. *waste management administrator*
Costa, Robin Leueen *psychologist, counselor*
Costello, John H., III, *business and marketing executive*
Cox, Linda Susan *allergist, immunologist*
Craib, Kenneth Bryden *resource development executive, physicist, economist*
Crikelair, George Francis *retired plastic surgeon, educator, researcher*
Danzig, William Harold *marketing executive*
Dawson, Muriel Amanda (Mandy Dawson) *state legislator*
Donaway, Carl D. *messenger service executive*
Donoho, Tim Mark *not-for-profit developer*
Dörken, Uwe R. *finance company executive*
Dressler, Robert A. *lawyer*
Drury, John R. *retail executive*
Duke, James T *art educator, consumer products company executive*
Dwors, Robert F. *retail executive*
Edmund, Norman Wilson *educational researcher*
Eisner, Will *publishing company executive*
Evans, James D., Jr., *retail executive*
Fanizza, Joanne *lawyer*
Feldman, Les J. *finance educator*
Ferrando, Jonathan P. *retail executive*
Fine, Howard Alan *management consultant*
Fischler, Abraham Saul *retired academic administrator, educator*
Fitzpatrick, George E. *research scientist, educator*
Gardner, Russell Menese *lawyer*
Geronemus, Diann Fox *social work consultant*
Ginn, Vera Walker *director*
Glantz, Wendy Newman *lawyer*
Goldberg, Alan Joel *lawyer*
Gonzalez, Jose Alejandro, Jr., *federal judge*
Gordon, Marc *retail executive*
Gore, George Henry *lawyer*
Greenberger, Sheldon Lee *newspaper advertising executive*
Gremillion, Robert *publishing executive*
Gunzburger, Suzanne Nathan *municipal official, social worker*
Haliczer, James Solomon *lawyer*
Hallman, Cinda A. *management consultant*
Hanbury, George Lafayette, II, *academic administrator*
Harbaugh, Joseph Delbert *legal educator, consultant*
Hargrove, John Russell *lawyer*
Hartz, Deborah Sophia *editor, writer*
Hershenson, Miriam Hannah Ratner *librarian*
Hess, George Franklin, II, *lawyer*
Hester, Julia A. *lawyer*
Hirsch, Jeffrey Allan *lawyer*
Hudson, Harris W. *automobile dealership executive*
Huizenga, H. Wayne *entrepreneur, professional sports team executive*
Hull, Richard Franklin *insurance brokerage executive*
Jackson, Michael J. *automotive retail company executive*
Jarvis, Robert Mark *law educator*
Jean, Alain *protective services official*
Joseph, Paul R *law educator*
Jotcham, Thomas Denis *marketing communications consultant*
Karsner, Michael S. *industrial company executive*
Kelly, John Patrick *lawyer*
Kendall, James Robert *air transportation executive, consultant*
Kjellmark, Eric W., Jr., *management consultant, opera company director*
Klein, Stacy Lynn *educational consultant*
Knight, Kenneth Vincent *leisure company executive, entrepreneur, venture capitalist*
Koch, Katherine Rose *communications executive*
Kornblau, Barbara L. *physical therapist*
Krause, Roy G. *management consultant*
Kreizinger, Loreen I. *lawyer*
Kubler, Frank Lawrence *lawyer*
Lampert, Wayne Morris *corporate financier*
Lassiter, Roy *professional soccer player*
Lataif, Lawrence P. *lawyer*
Leach, Ralph F. *banker*
Leighton, James H. *law educator, department chairman*
LeRoy, Miss Joy *model, apparel designer*
Levy, Michael *electronic manufacturing company executive*
Littman, Marlyn Kemper *information scientist, educator*
Lodwick, Gwilym Savage *radiologist, educator*
London, Michael *retail executive*
Loos, John Thompson *business owner*
MacInnes, Donald A. *automotive executive*
Marcy, Raymond *staffing and consulting company executive*
Marine, Michael R. *healthcare company executive*
Markos, Chris *retired real estate company executive*
Markus, Robert Michael *retired journalist*
Maroone, Michael E. *car and truck sales executive*
Maucker, Earl Robert *newspaper editor, newspaper executive*
Maxwell, Sara Elizabeth *psychologist, educator, speech pathologist, director*
McCan, James Lawton *education educator*
Meeks, William Herman, III, *lawyer*
Melo, Welton *professional soccer player*
Miller, Stephen Warren *dean*
Mintz, Joel Alan *law educator*
Monaghan, Craig Thomas *automotive executive*
Moorhead, Rolande Annette Reverdy *artist, educator*
Morse, Edward J. *automotive executive*
Nyce, John Daniel *lawyer*
O'Connor, James E. *waste management executive*
Olen, Milton William, Jr., *marketing executive*
Oliet, Seymour *endodontics educator, dean, dentist*
Oltman, John Harold *patent lawyer*
Parrish, Lori Nance *commissioner*
Peltzer, Douglas Lea *semiconductor device manufacturing company executive*
Pohlman, Randolph A. *business administration educator, dean*
Randi, James (Randall James Hamilton Zwinge) *magician, writer, educator*
Ray, Raymond B. *federal judge*
Reisinger, Sandra Sue *columnist*
Rentoumis, Ann Mastroianni *psychotherapist*
Richmond, Gail Levin *law educator*
Riggs, Donald Eugene *librarian, university official*
Robb, James Arthur *pathologist*
Rubinson, Howard Alan *physician*
Russell, Terrence Joseph *lawyer*
Sale, David Todd *lawyer*
Sanders, Dale R. *lawyer*
Sanderson, Rita Marye *history educator*
Schear, Betty Z. *engineering executive, consultant*
Schoonover, Philip *retail executive*
Schreiber, Alan Hickman *lawyer*
Schulte, Frederick James *newspaper editor*
Searcy, Leon, Jr., *professional football player*
Seltzer, Barry S. *federal judge*
Sherman, Richard Allen, Sr., *lawyer*
Sherry, William F. *airport executive*
Shoemaker, William Edward *financial executive*
Siegel, Michael Alan *dental educator*
Silvagni, Anthony Joseph *dean, osteopath*
Simon, Robert Stephen *artist*
Skellings, Edmund *communications educator, poet*
Sklar, Alexander *electric company executive*
Smith, Mark W. *management consultant*
Spangler, David Sheridan *composer, director, creative arts educator, writer*
Spungin, Charlotte Isabelle *retired secondary education educator, writer*
Stephan, John *finance educator*
Stern, Edith Lois *counselor, hypno-therapist*
Stewart, John Murray *retired bank executive*
Strickland, Wilton L. *lawyer*
Sundel, Sandra Stone *social worker*
Tacher, Robert Frederick *lawyer*
Taylor, Ralph Orien, Jr., *real estate developer, investor*
Thayer, Charles J. *investment banker*
Thomas, John Melvin *retired surgeon*
Tolchin, Karen Rebecca *adult education educator*
Torchetti, John *professional athletics coach*
Trubey, Lillian Priscilla *secondary education educator, retired*
Turner, Hugh Joseph, Jr., *lawyer*
Uchin, Robert Allen *dean, endodontist*
van der Veur, Paul W. *humanities educator*
Walden, John *retail executive*
Walker, Barabara J. *interior designer, writer*
Washington, Alice Hester *human services professional*
Whitmore, Douglas Michael *physician*
Wich, Donald Anthony, Jr., *lawyer*
Williamson, William Paul, Jr., *journalist*
Wojcik, Cass *decorative supply company executive, former city official*
Zimmerman, Jordan *marketing professional*
Zloch, William J. *federal judge*
Zumbano, Anthony Ralph *risk, claims management executive*

Fort Myers
Antonic, James Paul *international marketing consultant*
Barbour, William Rinehart, Jr., *retired book publisher*
Blomquist, Robert Oscar *retired insurance company executive*
Canham, Pruella Cromartie Niver *retired educator*
Colasurd, Richard Michael *lawyer*
Colgate, Doris Eleanor *sailing school owner and administrator*
Consilio, Barbara Ann *legal administrator, management consultant*
Courtney, James Edmond *real estate developer*
Dean, Jean Beverly *artist*
Diers, Hank H. *drama educator, playwright, director*
Dockins, George Joel *retired insurance and securities company executive*
Fite, Gilbert Courtland *historian, educator, retired*
Fromm, Winfield Eric *retired corporate executive, engineering consultant and investor*
Fulker, Edmund Norman *management consultant*
Goyak, Elizabeth Fairbairn *retired public relations executive*
Harman, Joyce Elizabeth *humanities educator*
Horecker, Bernard Leonard *retired biochemistry educator*
Johnson, Sally A. *nurse, educator*
Kiernan, Edwin A., Jr., *lawyer, corporation executive*
Kleman, Charles J. *finance company executive*
Laboda, Gerald *oral and maxillofacial surgeon*
Mair, Bruce Logan *interior designer, company executive*
Mc Queen, Robert Charles *retired insurance executive*
Medvecky, Robert Stephen *lawyer*
Mergler, Harry Winston *retired engineering educator*
Miller, William Charles *lawyer*
Missimer, Thomas Michael *geologist*
Moeschl, Stanley Francis *electrical engineer, management consultant*
Monear, Edwin Everett *writer*
Moore, Spencer Roneal *retired business owner, accounts receivable funder*
Nugent, Timothy Scott *alcohol/drug abuse services professional*
O'Dell, William Francis *retired business executive, writer*
O'Donnell, Bernard Joseph, Jr., *lawyer*
Oligario, Max *retired accountant*
Peterson, Rodney Delos *retired mediator, economist*
Pouliot, Assunta Gallucci *retired business school owner and director, consultant*
Renfroe, W. Douglas *musician, conductor, music educator*
Rubinstein, Alan Jay *lawyer*
Schoonover, Jack Ronald *retired judge*
Schultz, Gerald Alfred (Jerry Schultz) *retired chemicals executive*
Schwartz, Carl Edward *artist, printmaker*
Scott, Kenneth Elsner *mechanical engineering educator*
Shafer, Robert Tinsley, Jr., *judge*
Sheline, Raymond K. *nuclear chemistry educator*
Simmons, Vaughan Pippen *medical consultant*
Smith, Paul Frederick *economist, former educator*
Sprinkel, Beryl Wayne *economist, consultant*
Steier, Michael Edward *cardiac surgeon*
Thurman, Cynthia Denise *human services administrator*
Vera, Enrique *psychiatrist*
Waites, William Ernest *advertising executive*
Wall, Robert J. *author, researcher*
Wendeborn, Richard Donald *retired manufacturing company executive*
Woodbridge, Norma Jean *registered nurse, writer*

Fort Pierce
Belcher, Dorothy S. *state correctional department administrator*
Conklin, Howard Lawrence *lawyer*
Garment, Robert James *clergyman*
Hurley, William Joseph *retired information technology executive*
Massey, Edwin R. *college president*
Moore, Jo Ella *construction executive*
Norton, Robert Howard *entertainer, musical arranger, author*
Partenheimer, Robert Chapin *emergency physician*
Rice, Mary Esther *biologist*
Sneed, Richard Durwood, Jr., *lawyer*
Starner, Don Edward *radiographer, educator*
Thoma, Richard William *chemical safety and waste management consultant*

Fort Walton Beach
Bolt, Lynda Elaine *alcohol/drug abuse services professional*
Hill, Carol Koelling *library director*
Lindegren, Cecile Keyser *music educator*
Sanders, Jimmy Devon *public administration and health services educator*

Frostproof
Alia, Stephen Louis *music educator*

Gainesville
Albarracín, Dolores *psychologist, educator*
Anderson, Timothy J. *chemical engineering educator*
Barber, Charles Edward *newspaper executive, journalist*
Behnke, Marylou *pediatrician, educator*
Bernard, H. Russell *anthropologist, educator, editor*
Berns, Kenneth Ira *physician*
Besch, Emerson Louis *physiology educator, past academic administrator*
Bona, Miklos *mathematician, educator*
Bonzongo, Jean-Claude Justin *science educator*
Boothroyd, Herbert J. *insurance company executive*
Boyes, Patrice Flinchbaugh *lawyer*
Brodeur, Michael Stephen *dean*
Brown, Myra Suzanne *university librarian*
Brown, William Samuel, Jr., *communication sciences and disorders educator*
Brushwood, David Benson *pharmacy educator, lawyer*
Bryan, Robert Armistead *university administrator, educator*
Burns, Theodore Weber *gastroenterologist*
Burridge, Michael John *veterinarian, educator, research director*
Bzoch, Kenneth Rudolph *speech and language educator, department chairman*
Cabrera-Trujillo, Remigio *research scientist, physicist*
Calin, William *literature educator*
Cance, William George *surgery educator*
Cantliffe, Daniel James *horticulture educator*
Capehart, Barney Lee *industrial and systems engineer*
Cassisi, Nicholas John *otolaryngologist, dean*
Catalanotto, Frank A. *dentist, association executive*
Cenzer, Douglas Alfred *mathematician, educator*
Cha, Seunghee *molecular biologist, dentist*
Challoner, David Reynolds *academic administrator, endocrinologist*
Chan, Edward K.L. *biology professor, researcher*
Chaovalitwongse, Wanpracha *mathematician, researcher*
Cheek, Jimmy Geary *university administrator, agricultural education and communications educator*
Chestnut, Cynthia Moore *state legislator*
Chmielewski, Terese Lynn *physical therapist, educator*
Colburn, David R. *academic administrator*
Conrad, Joseph Henry *animal nutrition educator*
Copeland, Edward Meadors, III, *surgery educator*
Cousins, Robert John *nutritional biochemist, educator*
Criser, Marshall M. *lawyer, retired university president*
Cristescu, Nicolaie Dan *engineering educator*
Cuda, James Paul *entomologist, educator*
Dasta, Anthony J. *architecture educator*
Davis, George Kelso *nutrition biochemist, educator*
Delfino, Joseph John *environmental engineering sciences educator*
Der-Houssikian, Haig *linguistics educator*
Dewsbury, Donald Allen *psychology historian, comparative psychologist*
Dickinson, Joshua Clifton, Jr., *museum director, educator*
Dilcher, David Leonard *paleobotany educator, research scholar*
Dinculeanu, Nicolae *mathematician, educator*
DiPietro, Joseph A. *dean, educator*
Doering, Paul Louis *pharmacist, educator*
Dolan, Teresa A. *dean, educator, researcher*
Donnelly, William Henry *pathology educator*
Donovan, Billy *university basketball coach*
Doty, Leilani *geriatric neuropsychologist, administrator*
Drummond, Willa Hendricks *physiology and medical educator*

Drury, Kenneth Clayton *biological scientist*
Dunn, William A., Jr., *cell biologist, educator*
Emch, Gerard Gustav *mathematics and physics educator*
Emery, Kitty Frances *curator, educator*
Estrin, Mitchell Stewart *musician*
Fan, Z. Hugh *chemist, biomedical engineer*
Fossum, Jerry George *electrical engineering educator*
Freund, Gerhard *medical educator*
Gaintner, Richard J. *health facility administrator*
Gets, Lispbeth Ella *educational administrator*
Ginway, Mary Elizabeth *language educator*
Gold, Mark Stephen *psychopharmacologist, physician*
Gordon, Michael Wallace *law educator*
Greer, Melvin *medical educator*
Grobman, Arnold Brams *retired biology educator and academic administrator*
Grobman, Hulda Gross (Mrs. Arnold B. Grobman) *retired health sciences educator*
Gutekunst, Richard Ralph *microbiology educator*
Hall, David Walter *botanist, consultant*
Hanrahan, Robert Joseph *chemist, educator*
Hanson, Harold Palmer *physicist, government official, editor, academic administrator*
Hartigan, Karelisa Dorothy *classics educator*
Hasell, Mary Joyce (Jo) *architecture educator*
Hay-Roe, Mirian Medina *education educator, researcher*
Heflin, Martin Ganier *foreign service officer, international political economist*
Heo, Young-Woo *research scientist*
Himes, James Albert *retired veterinary medicine educator*
Hochmuth, George J. *horticultural educator*
Holbrook, Karen Ann *biology educator, researcher, dean*
Holland, Norman Norwood *literary critic*
Hollien, Harry Francis *speech and communications scientist, educator*
Hollien, Patricia Ann *small business owner, researcher*
Hoy, Marjorie Ann *entomology educator*
Huang, Jinhua *mechanical engineer, researcher*
Isaacs, Gerald William *retired agricultural engineering educator, consultant*
Israel, Jerold Harvey *law educator*
Jones, Elizabeth Nordwall *county government official*
Jones, Richard Lamar *entomology educator*
Kaid, Lynda Lee *communications educator*
Kaplan, John *photojournalist, educator, consultant*
Katritzky, Alan Roy *chemistry professor*
Kersey, Talana S. *mental health counselor*
Kohen, Martha *architecture educator*
Kurzweg, Ulrich Hermann *engineering science educator*
Kushner, David Zakeri *musicologist*
Lane, Jodi *education educator*
Law, Mark Edward *electrical engineer, educator*
Leahy, Thomas Melvin, Jr., *writer*
Leavitt, David Adam *writer, English educator*
LeVeen, Robert Frederick *radiologist*
Li, Qin-Bao *biological scientist, laboratory manager*
Limacher, Marian Cecile *cardiologist*
Lin, Steve T. *technology executive*
Lindholm, Fredrik Arthur *electrical engineering educator*
Long, Kathleen Ann *nursing educator, dean, consultant*
Lowenstein, Ralph Lynn *university dean emeritus*
Machen, James Bernard *academic administrator*
Mahla, Michael E. *anesthesiologist, educator*
Malasanos, Lois Julanne Fosse *nursing educator*
Maple, Marilyn Jean *educational media coordinator*
Mareci, Thomas Harold *biophysicist, educator*
Mariani, Christopher Leonard *veterinarian, educator*
Maurer, Virginia Gallaher *law educator*
Mazzaferri, Ernest Louis *endocrinologist, educator*
McClellan, Richard Augustus *retired small business owner*
McConn, William Everett *music educator*
McMahon, Martin James, Jr., *law educator, consultant*
Mead, Frank Waldreth *taxonomic entomologist*
Meakin, Faith Anne *medical library director*
Micha, David Allan *chemistry and physics educator*
Milanich, Jerald Thomas *archaeologist, museum curator*
Milbrath, Robert Henry *retired petroleum executive*
Mills, Jon *dean, law educator*
Mills, Teheran L. (Terry Mills) *sociology educator*
Mitselmakher, Guenakh *physics educator, researcher*
Modell, Jerome Herbert *anesthesiologist, educator*
Moore, John Hartwell *anthropology educator, consultant*
Morgan, Anne Margaret Barclay *artist, author, psychologist*
Mukherjee, Bhramar *statistician, educator*
Needell, Jeffrey David *historian, educator*
Neims, Allen Howard *pediatrician, educator, dean, researcher*
Nguyen, Ru *entomologist*
Nicoletti, Paul Lee *retired veterinarian, educator*
Oberlander, Herbert *retired physiologist*
Opdyke, Neil Donald *geology educator*
Peebles, Peyton Zimmermann, Jr., *electrical engineer, educator*
Pfaff, William Wallace *medical educator*
Pham, Andrea Hoa *educator, writer*
Phillips, Winfred Marshall *university administrator, biomedical research executive, mechanical engineer, educator*
Phoenix, Joaquin Raphael *actor*
Polasek, Edward John *retired electrical engineer, consultant*
Pop, Emil *research chemist*
Popenoe, Hugh Llywelyn *soils educator*
Proctor, Samuel *history educator*
Puckett, Ruby Parker *nutritionist, hospital food service administrator, consultant, author*
Purcifull, Dan Elwood *plant virologist, educator*
Quesenberry, Kenneth Hays *agronomy educator*
Randall, Malcom *health care administrator*
Ray, Timothy Britt *social worker, lawyer, administrator*
Reynolds, Richard Clyde *internist, educator*
Rhoton, Albert Loren, Jr., *neurological surgery educator*
Rosenberger, Margaret Adaline *retired elementary school educator, writer*

Ross, Melanie Fridl *journalist, writer*
Rowe, Bobby Louise *art educator*
Rubin, Melvin Lynne *ophthalmologist, educator*
Ruth, Byron Edward *civil engineering educator*
Sabin, John Rogers *physics educator*
Sah, Chih-Tang *electrical and computer engineering educator*
Schelske, Claire L. *limnologist, educator*
Schlenker, Barry Richard *psychologist, educator, researcher*
Schmeling, Gareth *classics educator*
Schmertmann, John Henry *civil engineer, educator, consultant*
Schmidt-Nielsen, Bodil Mimi (Mrs. Roger G. Chagnon) *physiologist, educator*
Schmitz, Andrew *agricultural studies educator*
Schneider, Markus *computer scientist, researcher*
Seale, James Lawrence, Jr., *agricultural economics educator, international trade researcher*
Sherif, S. A. *engineering educator*
Shih, Chuan-kang *anthropologist*
Shyy, Wei *aerospace and mechanical engineering researcher, educator*
Siegel, Robert James *communications executive*
Silas, Nancy *small business owner*
Singley, John Edward, Jr., *retired environmental scientist, consultant*
Sisler, Harry Hall *retired chemistry professor*
Small, Natalie Settimelli *pediatric mental health counselor*
Small, Parker Adams, Jr., *pediatrician, educator*
Smith, Jo Anne *writer, retired educator*
Suzuki, Howard Kazuro *retired anatomist, educator*
Swait, Joffre Dan, Jr., *marketing professional, educator*
Talbert, James Lewis *pediatric surgeon, educator*
Taylor, William Jape *physician*
Teixeira, Arthur Alves *food engineer, educator, consultant*
Thiele, Leslie Paul *political science educator*
Thompson, Neal Philip *food science and nutrition educator*
Tia, Mang *civil engineering educator*
Tiep, Pham Huu *mathematician, educator*
Tisher, C. Craig *nephrologist, educator, dean*
Toskes, Phillip Paul *gastroenterologist, educator, clinical researcher*
Trickey, Samuel Baldwin *physics educator, researcher, university administrator*
Van Alstyne, W. Scott, Jr., *lawyer, educator*
Verink, Ellis Daniel, Jr., *metallurgical engineering educator, consultant*
Vierck, Charles John, Jr., *neuroscience educator, scientist*
Viessman, Warren, Jr., *civil engineering educator emeritus, researcher*
von Mering, Otto Oswald *anthropology educator*
Wagner, Eric Armin *sociology educator*
Wass, Hannelore Lina *educational psychology educator*
Watson, Robert Joe *health facility administrator, retired career officer*
Weinrich, Brian Erwin *mathematician, computer scientist*
Wethington, John Abner, Jr., *retired nuclear engineering educator*
Weyrauch, Walter Otto *law educator*
Wilcox, Charles Julian *geneticist, educator*
Willocks, Robert Max *retired librarian*
Willumson, Glenn Gardner *curator, art historian*
Wing, Elizabeth Schwarz *museum curator, educator*
Xie, Huikai *electrical engineer, educator*
Yamamoto, Janet Kazuko *science educator*
York, E. Travis *academic administrator, former university chancellor, consultant*
York, Vermelle Cardwell *real estate broker and developer*
Yost, Richard Alan *chemistry professor*
Zieger, Robert Harman *history educator, historian*

Gonzalez
Plischke, Le Moyne Wilfred *research chemist*

Goulds
Taylor, Millicent Ruth *elementary school educator*

Graceville
Kinchen, Thomas Alexander *college president*

Green Cove Springs
Davidson, Joy Elaine *mezzo-soprano*

Greenacres
Goldfarb, Arthur A. *allergist, immunologist, educator*
Valliere, Flora Lee *law firm official*

Groveland
Miles, Doris Cooper *bank executive*

Gulf Breeze
Burr, Timothy Fuller *lawyer*
DeBardeleben, John Thomas, Jr., *retired insurance company executive*
French, Jere Stuart *landscape architect*
Menzer, Robert Everett *toxicologist, educator*
Pettyjohn, Frank Schmermund *cardiology and emergency medicine educator*
Rainwater, Freddie Barrett *volunteer worker*
Walker, Peggy Jean *retired social work agency administrator*
Wickramasekera, Ian Edward *psychophysiologist, psychology educator*
Williams, Betty *peace activist*

Gulf Stream
Nalen, Craig Anthony *government official*

Gulfport
Allen, John Thomas, Jr., *lawyer*
Athanson, Mary Catheryne *school system administrator*
Bourke, Thomas Anthony *librarian, writer*
Cox, Nicholas Bernard *law educator*
Jackson, Nicholas Miller *lawyer, researcher*

Haines City
Clement, Robert William *retired air force officer*
Kirk, Sherwood *librarian*
Mc Dougall, Dugald Stewart *retired lawyer*

Hallandale
Engel, Tala *lawyer*

Glaubinger, Lawrence David *retired manufacturing company executive*
Schatken, Nancy Leah *medical editor*
Tasker, John Baker *veterinary medical educator, college dean*
Vaserstein, Ludmila *music educator*
Yigit, Nuyan *journalist*

Hallandale Beach
Geller, Bunny Zelda *poet, author, publisher, sculptor, artist, photographer*

Heathrow
Argirion, Michael *editor*
Darbelnet, Robert Louis *automobile association executive*

Hernando
Park, Chung Il *retired librarian*

Hialeah
Agrawal, Piyush C. *school system administrator*
Economides, Christopher George *pathologist*
Engler, Eva Kay *dental and veterinary products company executive*
Gil de Gibaja, Susana *artist, small business owner*
Gross, Richard Wilson *lawyer*
Hernandez, Roland *broadcast executive*
Palacios, Olga *director*
Perez, Leyanee C. *nutritionist, consultant*
Rhee, Sorah *biomedical engineer*

Hialeah Gardens
Tuninskaya, Galina M. *chemist, consultant*

Highland Beach
Frager, Albert S. *retired retail food company executive*
Lane, James McConkey *retired investment executive*
Schor, Stanley Sidney *mathematical sciences educator*
Settler, Eugene Brian *recording industry executive*
Tolf, Robert Walter *writer*
Zagoria, Sam D(avid) *reporter, government official, educator*

Hillsboro Beach
Gibbons, Celia Victoria Townsend (Mrs. John Sheldon) *editor, publisher*
Marshall, Jo Taylor *social worker*

Hobe Sound
Casey, Edward Paul *manufacturing executive*
Caspersen, Finn Michael Westby *diversified financial services company executive*
Craig, David Jeoffrey *retired manufacturing company executive*
Gold, Kenneth R. *computer software consulting executive*
Graham, Bruce John *architect*
Hand, Peter James *neurobiologist, educator*
Houser, Jim (James Cowing Houser Jr., Jim Houser) *painter, art educator*
Markoe, Frank, Jr., *lawyer, business and hospital executive*
McChristian, Joseph Alexander *international business executive*
Parker, H. Lawrence *investor, rancher, retired investment banker*
Snook, Stover Hoffman *social sciences educator, researcher*

Holiday
Peterson, George F. *retired insurance company executive, writer*

Hollywood
Angstrom, Wayne Raymond *communications executive*
Blakley, John Clyde *telecommunications consultant*
Constantinescu, Alex R. *pediatrician, nephrologist*
Cowan, Irving *real estate owner, developer*
Duffner, Lee R. *ophthalmologist*
Foreman, Edwin Francis *economist, real estate broker*
Giulianti, Mara Selena *mayor, civic worker*
Harkin, Daniel John *controller*
Harringer, Olaf Carl *architect, museum consultant*
King, Alma Jean *retired physical education educator, healthcare educator*
Korthals, Candace Durbin *lawyer*
Ladin, Eugene *communications company executive*
Martinez, Carlos *insurance adjuster, company manager*
Matasa, Claude George *researcher, science administrator, educator*
Mendelson, Laurans Adam *accountant*
Poirier, Robert J. *floral company executive*
Rogovin, Lawrence H. *lawyer*
Russell, Antonette Patrice *lawyer*
Sadowski, Carol Johnson *artist*
Schwartz, Joseph *retired container company executive*
Spencer, Richard Thomas, III, *healthcare industry executive*
Sundel, Martin *psychologist, educator, management consultant*
Tannen, Ricki Lewis *lawyer, psychologist, educator*
Tucker, Nina Angella *hospital administrator*
Valdes, Jacqueline Chehebar *psychologist, consultant, researcher*

Holmes Beach
Dunne, Nancy Anne *retired social services administrator*
McCartney, James Harold *newspaper columnist, journalist, educator*
Rose, Dennis Norman *manufacturing executive*

Homestead
Davis, Scott Michael *director, music educator*
Dong, Quan *ecologist, educator*
Horton, Thelma White *educational administrator, author*
Roberts, Larry Spurgeon *biological science educator, zoologist*
Willner, Eugene Burton *food and liquor company executive*

Homosassa
Acton, Norman *international organization executive*
Carmichael, Roberta Kay *writer*

Homosassa Springs
Burch, Annetta Jane *writer*

Hutchinson Island
Wegman, Harold Hugh *management consultant*

Indialantic
Pavlakos, Ellen Tsatiri *sculptor*

Indian Harbor Beach
Phelan, John Densmore *insurance executive, consultant*
Rains, Baxter Smith *sculptor, consultant*
Tasker, Molly Jean *lawyer*
Traylor, Angelika *stained glass artist*

Indian River Shores
Ahrens, William Henry *architect*
Wiegner, Edward Alex *multi-industry executive*

Indian Rocks Beach
DeLucia, Gene Anthony *government administrator, computer company executive*
Sullivan, Paul William *communications specialist*

Inverness
Dowdell, Michael Francis *critical care nurse, forensic and anesthesia nurse practitioner*
Esquibel, Edward V. *psychiatrist, clinical medical program developer*

Islamorada
Gates, Richard Daniel *retired manufacturing company executive*
Hawkins, Frank Nelson, Jr., *investor relations consultant, writer*
Papy, Frank Marin, III, *writer, editor*
Sieber, Dawn *food service executive*

Jacksonville
Adams, Scott Leslie *accountant*
Aftoora, Patricia Joan *transportation executive*
Aleschus, Justine Lawrence *retired real estate broker*
Anderson, John Quentin *retired rail transportation executive*
Ansbacher, Barry Barnett *lawyer*
Appel, Laurence B. *lawyer, retail executive*
Arbogast, Gordon Wade *systems engineer, educator, consultant, retired military officer*
Barrow, Sally Settle *media specialist, librarian*
Bartley, George B. *ophthalmologist, surgeon*
Beattie, Donald A. *energy scientist, consultant*
Bedell, Elizabeth Snyder (Betty Bedell) *editor-in-chief, marketing professional*
Beytagh, Francis Xavier, Jr., *law educator*
Black, Susan Harrell *federal judge*
Bodkin, Lawrence Edward *essayist, research development company executive, gemologist, inventor, writer*
Bodkin, Ruby Pate *corporate executive, real estate broker, educator*
Boyer, Tyrie Alvis *lawyer*
Boylan, Kevin Bernard *neurologist*
Braddock, Donald Layton *lawyer, accountant, real estate broker, investor*
Bradford, Dana Gibson, II, *lawyer*
Brady, Kyle James *professional football player*
Broughton, Carolyn Miles *multimedia executive, public relations executive*
Brown, Lloyd Harcourt, Jr., *newspaper editor*
Bryan, Joseph Shepard, Jr., *lawyer*
Bullock, Bruce Stanley *lawyer*
Callender, John Francis *lawyer*
Cannon, Carl *publishing executive*
Carlson, Raymond Howard *retired military officer, prosecutor*
Carpenter, Alvin Rauso *transportation executive*
Cason, Fred Lee *political scientist, educator*
Chambers, Jack Allen *educator*
Clarkson, Charles Andrew *real estate investment executive*
Coker, Howard Coleman *lawyer*
Cole, Linda Sue *grant and program planner, computer software professional*
Commander, Charles Edward *lawyer, real estate consultant*
Constantini, JoAnn M. *small business owner, systems administrator, consultant*
Cornelius, Jacquelyn H. *high school principal, educator*
Corse, John Doggett *university official, lawyer*
Costin, Rea-Silvia *civil engineer*
Courtwright, David Todd *history educator, author*
Crawford, John Richard *lawyer*
Crowe, Jeffrey C. *transportation executive, federal agency administrator*
Davis, A. Dano *grocery store chain executive*
Davis, Fred *journalist, educator*
Delaney, John Adrian *academic administrator*
Delaney, Kevin Francis *retired naval officer, consulting firm executive*
Del Rio, Jack *professional football coach, former professional football player*
DeOrio, James Keith *orthopedic surgeon*
Dewan, Derek E. *staffing services executive*
Dorsher, Peter T. *physician*
Dumbleton, Duane Dean *college president, educator*
Duncan, Shirley A. *portfolio manager*
Dundon, Margo Elaine *museum director*
Duvall, Janet Ann *volunteer*
Earle, J.D. *physician*
Eden, F. Brown *artist*
Edwards, Marvin Raymond *investment counselor, economic consultant*
Ejimofor, Cornelius Ogu *political scientist, educator*
Fahner, Harold Thomas *marketing executive*
Farmer, Guy Otto, II, *lawyer*
Fawbush, Andrew Jackson *lawyer*
Feinglass, Neil Gordon *anesthesiologist*
Ferguson, Thomas Crooks *lawyer*
Fine, Cory R. *education educator, consultant*
Fracis, Sohrab Homi *writer, education educator*
Francis, James Delbert *oil company executive*
Fulton-Quindoza, Debra Ann *emergency nurse practitioner*
Gabel, George DeSaussure, Jr., *lawyer*
Gerkens, Henry H. *trucking executive*
Getman, Willard Etheridge *lawyer, arbitrator, mediator*
Glover, Nathaniel, Jr., *sheriff*

Goldhagen, Jeffrey Lee city health department administrator
Gonwa, Thomas Arthur nephrologist, educator, transplant physician
Gooding, David Michael judge
Halverson, Steven Thomas lawyer, construction executive
Hartmann, Frederick William newspaper editor
Hecht, Frederick pediatrician, educator, medical geneticist, researcher, consultant, writer
Hered, Robert W. ophthalmologist
Hill, Debra S. lawyer
Hill, James Clinkscales federal judge
Holliday, Patricia Ruth McKenzie evangelist
Homsley, Denise Louise music educator
Houser, John Edward lawyer
Huber, Mary Susan music educator
Jackson, Julian Ellis food company executive
Jamrich, John Xavier retired university administrator
Jenkins, Jimmy Raymond university president
Johnson, Douglas William radiation oncologist, educator
Jones, Herman Otto, Jr., corporate professional
Kaunitz, Karen Rose Koppel retired lawyer
Kelso, Linda Yayoi lawyer
Kent, John Bradford lawyer
Kimmich, Haydee Javier orthopedist, consultant
Kinne, Frances Bartlett academic administrator
Klain, David Richard naval officer
Koeppel, Mary Sue communications educator, writer
Kress, Mary Elizabeth retired newspaper editor
Lane, Edward Wood, Jr., retired banker
Langford, Cecilia Motes nursing educator
LaRose, Robert C. trucking executive
Lazaran, Frank retail executive
Lee, Lewis Swift lawyer
Leftwich, Byron Antron professional football player
Legler, Mitchell Wooten lawyer
Lehmbeck, John Pierce journalist
Leonard, Thomas Michael university program director, educator
Lestage, Daniel Barfield retired military officer, physician
Libby, Ronald Theodore political science educator, consultant, researcher
Liles, Rutledge Richardson lawyer
Lovett, Radford Dow marine terminal real estate and investment company executive
Lyon, Wilford Charles, Jr., insurance executive
Magill, Sherry foundation administrator
Mahaffy, Telfair safety scientist
Main, Edna Dewey (Juno Main) education educator
Mason, William Cordell, III, hospital administrator
Maxwell, W(ilbur) Richard retired management consultant
McBurney, Charles Walker, Jr., lawyer
McCook, Richard Paul grocery chain financial executive
McKinney, James Clayton electronics executive, electrical engineer
McWilliams, John Lawrence, III, lawyer
Melton, Howell Webster, Sr., federal judge
Milton, Joseph Payne lawyer
Mizrahi, Edward Alan allergist
Monsky, John Bertrand investment banking executive
Morehead, Charles Richard insurance company executive
Morgan, William Newton architect, educator
Moseley, James Francis lawyer
Mueller, Cherone religious organization administrator, writer, minister
Mueller, Edward Albert retired transportation engineer executive
Munoz, Oscar corporate financial executive
Murphy, Nickie Latrice writer, insurance adjuster
Narayan, Vaduvur Srinivasan preventive medicine physician
Nutter, Wallace Lee paper manufacturing executive
O'Connor, R. D. retired health care executive
Oldenburg, Warner Andrew vascular surgeon
Olin, Marilyn secondary school educator
Osborn, Marvin Griffing, Jr., educational consultant
Patel, Vinod Motibhai accountant
Pavlick, Pamela Kay nurse, consultant
Prussin, Jeffrey A. management consultant
Rader, David insurance company executive
Raynor, Eileen Margolies otolaryngologist, educator
Reagan, James Raymond safety and ergonomics consultant
Rice, Charles Edward bank executive
Rinaman, James Curtis, Jr., lawyer
Robinson, Christine Marie mathematics educator
Rodney, Roxanne Audrey cardiologist, consultant
Rowland, Allen R. grocery company executive
Russell, David Emerson mechanical engineer, consultant, writer
Salem, Karen E. information technology executive
Sandercox, Robert Allen college official, clergyman
Sanders, Marion Yvonne retired geriatrics nurse
Schlageter, Robert William museum administrator
Schlesinger, Harvey Erwin judge
Schramm, Bernard Charles, Jr., retired advertising agency executive
Schultz, Frederick Henry investor, former government official
Schultz, Nancy Reilly artist
Schupp, Robert Warren law educator
Sederbaum, William
Sheehan, John R. food products executive
Siegel, Edward lawyer
Siegel, Steven Douglas oncologist
Simms, Jacqueline Kamp secondary school educator
Smith, David A. medical services executive
Smith, Jimmy, Jr., professional football player
Smith, Stephen Mark music educator
Soud, Ginger city councilwoman
Stanley, Helen Camille composer, musician
Stanton, Robert John, Jr., English language educator
Stein, Jay retail executive
Stein, Martin (Hap), Jr., real estate company executive
Stephenson, Samuel Edward, Jr., retired physician
Stern, Steven Alan sports development owner
Stewart, Sandra Kay music educator
Stiehl, Ruth Rasco nursing educator
Surrency, Gary Lawrence military officer, counselor, writer
Taylor, Fred professional football player
Taylor, Gavin Hall music educator
Taylor, Robert M. minister
Thomas, Archibald Johns, III, lawyer
Thorsteinsson, Gudni physiatrist
Thrasher, John lawyer, former state legislator
Threlkel, Robert Hays pediatrician
Tjoflat, Gerald Bard federal judge
Tolford, Frank Stefan bookstore executive
Tomlinson, William Holmes management educator, retired army officer
Urbina, Susana Patricia psychology educator, consultant
Vadnal, John Louis dean, mathematician, educator
Van Cleve, Robert Baldwin cardiologist
Vane, Terence G., Jr., finance company executive, lawyer
Vincent, Norman Fuller broadcast executive
Wallace, Steven R. college president
Wallis, Donald Wills lawyer
Walters, John Sherwood retired newspaperman
Ward, Michael J. rail transportation executive
Weaver, Dianne Jay lawyer
Weikle, Paul Eugene, Jr., music educator, musician
Welch, Philip Burland electronics and office products company executive
White, Edward Alfred lawyer
Williams, Leola Wilkerson social worker, writer
Wilson, C. Nick health educator, consultant, researcher, lecturer
Wirtz, Gregg Lee lawyer
Zahra, Ellis E. lawyer

Jacksonville Beach
Mahorner, James M. lawyer
Morris, Max King foundation executive, former naval officer
Saltzman, Irene Cameron consumer products company executive
Tempelman, Jerry Henry investment funds trader, financial analyst

Jasper
McCormick, John Hoyle lawyer

Jensen Beach
Carney, Robert Arthur restaurant executive
Gamble, Raymond Wesley marriage and family therapist, clergyman
Gruppe, Charles Camille artist
Peterson, David Frederick government agency executive
Skrupky, Elaine Charlotte art educator
Stuart, Harold Cutliff lawyer, business executive
Traines, Rose Wunderbaum sculptor, educator

Juno Beach
Broadhead, James Lowell electrical power industry executive
Dewhurst, Moray P. energy executive
Holmes, Melvin Almont insurance company executive
Zuckerman, Stuart psychiatrist, forensic examiner, educator

Jupiter
Brophy, Gilbert Thomas lawyer
Click, David Forrest lawyer, investment advisor
De George, Lawrence Joseph diversified company executive
del Russo, Alessandra Luini retired law educator
Ernst, Calvin Bradley vascular surgeon, surgery educator
Feinberg, Herbert apparel, real estate, video and beverage executive
Garfinkel, Harmon Mark retired specialty chemicals company executive
Gerson, Irwin Conrad advertising executive
Jacobson, Jerry Irving biophysicist, theoretical physicist
Kulok, William Allan entrepreneur, venture capitalist
Malm, Rita H. securities executive
Migliaro, Marco William electrical engineer
Mock, Robert Claude architect
Nessmith, H(erbert) Alva dentist
Welch, Martha Lynn environmentalist, educator
Wolff, Edward Alvin electronics engineer
Zelnick, Ronald Stuart surgeon

Kennedy Space Center
Banks, Lisa Jean government official
Feldman, Stephen academic administrator
Malone, Lisa A. federal agency administrator

Key Biscayne
Aleniewski, Monica Irene retired anesthesiologist
Duffy, Earl Gavin hotel executive
Evans, Peter Kenneth advertising executive
Palmer, Roger Farley pharmacology educator
Pearson, John Edward lawyer
Pope, John Edwin, III, newspaper sports editor, columnist
Ross, Marilyn J. English and communications educator
Smith, Harrison Harvey journalism consultant
Stephens, William Theodore lawyer, business executive
Wilson, Robert Gordon investment banker

Key Largo
Benestante, Vincenzo writer
Chevins, Anthony Charles retired advertising agency executive
Daenzer, Bernard John insurance company executive, legal consultant
Davidson, Thomas Noel metal products executive
Kennedy, Mary Sussock artist
Lynn, James Thomas insurance company executive, government executive, lawyer, investment banker
Mattson, James Stewart lawyer, environmental scientist, educator

Key West
Buffett, Jimmy (James William Buffett) singer, songwriter, writer
Eden, Nathan E. lawyer
Evans, John Derby telecommunications company executive
MacDougall, Peter lawyer
McIntosh, Jon Charles illustrator, graphics designer, painter
Mitchell, John Dietrich theatre arts institute executive
Murphy, S(usan) (Jane Murphy) small business owner
Taylor, Victoria sculptor
Trammell, Herbert Eugene physicist, laboratory executive

Keystone Heights
Ohanian, Mihran Jacob nuclear engineering educator, research dean

Kissimmee
Cody, Aldus Morrill journalist, retired editor, typographer
Gagne, Antoine F. retired mechanical engineer, writer
Haynes, Ulric St. Clair, Jr., retired dean
McCann, Jean Friedrichs artist, educator
McEnaney, Sherrie Jeanine writer, marketing professional, advertising executive
Rajyaguru, Vrajlal Laljibhai anesthesiologist
Rattie, Margaret Elizabeth (Beth Rattie) elementary school educator
Saha, Asis Kumar cardiologist
Toothe, Karen Lee elementary and secondary school educator

Lady Lake
Akins, Zane Vernon association executive
Dore, Stephen Edward, Jr., retired civil engineer
Granger, Robert Alan mechanical and aerospace engineering educator
Hartzler, Genevieve Lucille physical education educator
Langevin, Thomas Harvey higher education consultant
Morse, Gary H. construction executive

Lake Alfred
Kender, Walter John horticulturist, educator

Lake Buena Vista
Bill, Theodore Theoron technology consultant
Rasulo, James A. parks director
Sereno, Keala musician

Lake City
McMahon, Sean Howard social studies educator
Montgomery, June C. musician, composer
Norman, Alline L. health facility administrator

Lake Forest
Ross, Jimmy Douglas retired military officer

Lake Helen
Finn, Stephen Martin producer

Lake Mary
Bachmann, Bill photographer
Bodden, M. David computer professional, consultant

Lake Park
Heaton, Janet Nichols artist, art gallery director

Lake Placid
Brightwell, Dennis Richard psychiatrist
Rew, William Edmund civil engineer
Roberts, William B. lawyer, business executive

Lake Suzy
Ogan, Russell Griffith business executive, retired air force officer

Lake Wales
Adams, Paul Winfrey lawyer, business executive
Luing, Gary Alan financial management educator
Wales, Gwynne Huntington retired lawyer
Walton, Madalyn Carol music educator

Lake Worth
Asher, Kathleen May communications educator
Cohen, Edward civil engineer
Dembicer, Edwin Herbert retired lawyer
Gallon, Dennis P. college president
Goldstein, Jerome Charles retired professional association executive, surgeon, otolaryngologist
Gorman, Marcie Sothern personal care industry executive
Pecker, David J. magazine publishing company executive
Saffir, Leonard public relations executive
Stone, Ross Gluck orthopedic surgeon
Taylor, Clifford Otis retired principal
Wilson, William J. English language educator

Lakeland
Cassell, Robert Holland internist, oncologist
Cooper, James Russell retired law educator
Griffiths, James Thompson, Jr., agricultural products supplier
Hatten, William Seward manufacturing executive
Herron, Robert Wilburn, Jr., academic administrator, educator
Hixon, Andrea Kaye healthcare quality specialist
Jay, James Albert retired insurance company executive
Jelsovsky, Daniel Douglas mathematician, educator
Jenkins, Howard M. supermarket executive
Kittleson, Henry Marshall lawyer
Koren, Edward Franz lawyer
Luther, George Albert truck brokerage executive
Mahr, Aaron Lee retired government executive
McFarlin, Richard Francis retired industrial chemist, researcher
McKeel, Seth Douglas real estate manager, commissioner
Meads, Walter Frederick communications executive, consultant, writer
Mooney, Burton Lee retired secondary school educator, editor
Mutz, Oscar Ulysses manufacturing and distribution executive
Phillips, David P. grocery company executive
Pospichal, Marcie W. neuroscientist, psychologist, educator
Ratliff, Charles Edward, Jr., economics professor
Reich, David Lee library director
Rhodes, Jim human resources professional
Rogers, James Gordon, Jr., art educator
Siedle, Robert Douglas management consultant
Spencer, Mary Miller civic worker
Stark, Bruce Gunsten artist
Tate, Robert Hale academic administrator
Tripi, Vincent James physician
Wade, Ben Frank college administrator
Waugaman, Richard William sales executive
Wendel, John Fredric lawyer, professional sports consultant

Lakeland,
Washington, Gloria Dunn secondary school educator

Land O Lakes
O'Connell, Carmela Digristina appraisal executive, consultant

Lantana
Balis, Moses Earl biochemist, educator
Barrett, Robert James, III, investment banker
Schmaus, Siegfried H. A. engineering executive, consultant
Weeks, Charles, Jr., real estate executive, retired publishing company executive
Wetherby, Ivor Lois librarian

Largo
Bush, Debra W. occupational health nurse
Camara, Vincent Antonin Reginald mathematician, educator, statistician, researcher
Dolan, John E. consultant, retired utility executive
Eisele, William David insurance agency executive
Ellis, Susan Gottenberg psychologist
Fedor, Allan John lawyer
Grove, Jeffrey Scott family practice physician
Hamlin, Robert Henry public health educator, management consultant
Hasen-Sinz, Susan Katherine state agency administrator, actress
Loader, Jay Gordon retired utility company executive
Mandelker, Lester veterinarian
May, Andrew technology company executive
Ray, Roger Buchanan retired communications executive, lawyer
Shillinglaw, Gordon accounting educator, consultant
Simmons, Deborah Jo pharmacy executive
Trevena, John Harry lawyer
Wheat, Myron William, Jr., cardiothoracic surgeon

Lauderdale By The Sea
Wynne, Brian James former association executive, consultant
Yonkman, Fredrick Albers lawyer, management consultant

Lauderhill
Bathurst, Debra Lynnette physical therapist assistant
Swisher, Charles Francis electrical engineer, consultant

Lecanto
Corsi, Philip Donald lawyer
Gessner, Donald Robert healthcare consultant
Goss, Richard Henry lawyer
Mathia, Mary Loyola parochial school educator, nun
Max, Buddy (Boris Max Pastuch) musician
Moyer-Staker, Denise Elane music educator

Leesburg
Austin, Robert Eugene, Jr., lawyer
Fechtel, Vincent John legal administrator
Moore, Wistar cardiovascular surgeon
Talley, William Giles, Jr., manufacturing executive

Lighthouse Point
Shein, Jay Lesing financial planner

Longboat Key
Dorsey, Eugene Carroll former foundation and communications executive
Frankel, Jack pediatrician, allergist
Freeman, Richard Merrell lawyer, corporate director
Gilbert, Hamlin Miller, Jr., publishing executive
Goldsmith, Jack Landman former retail company executive
Hazan, Marcella Maddalena writer, educator, consultant
Kabara, Jon Joseph biochemical pharmacology educator
Morse, Marvin Henry retired judge
Schoenberg, Lawrence Joseph computer services company executive
Stapleton, Harvey James physics educator
Van Dyke-Cooper, Anny Marion retired financial company executive
Winfree, Charles Van management consultant
Workman, George Henry structural engineering consultant

Longwood
Bernabei, Raymond management consultant
Cirello, John utility and engineering company executive
Cooper, Brian Reginald insurance company executive
Cordes, Alexander Charles lawyer
Dicks, Jack William lawyer, magazine publisher, investment advisor
Faller, Donald E. marketing and operations executive
Gasperoni, Ellen Jean Lias interior designer
Gasperoni, Emil, Sr., realtor, developer
Goddard, Edward Dean stockbroker, accountant
Hernandez, H(ermes) Manuel lawyer
Johnson, Nancy Plattner secondary school educator
O'Keefe, Maurice Timothy editor, writer, photographer, educator
St. John, John food company executive
Smyth, Joseph Patrick retired naval officer, physician
Tomasulo, Virginia Merrills retired lawyer
Walters, Philip Raymond foundation executive
Zahn, Richard Gregory construction executive

Lutz
Bedke, Ernest Alford retired air force officer
Cualing, Hernani Del Mundo physician, researcher
Currey, Cecil Barr history professor
Fritzsche, R(obert) Wayne corporate executive
Hacker, Michelle Wendy auditor, researcher, finance educator
Koff, Fred William retired research chemist
Miller, Bonnie Sewell marketing professional, writer

MacDill AFB
Barno, David W. *career military officer*
Cofer, Jonathan H. *career officer*

Madison
Shaw, Roderick Kirkpatrick, III, *dentist*

Maitland
Blackburn, John Oliver *economist, consultant*
Kaplan, Judith Helene *company executive*
Rajtar, Steven Allen *lawyer*
Sharett, Alan Richard *lawyer, environmental and disability litigator, mediator and arbitrator, law educator*
Vallee, Judith Delaney *environmentalist, writer, fundraiser*
Von Hilsheimer, George Edwin, III, *neuropsychologist*

Manalapan
Gatewood, Robert Payne *retired financial planning executive*
Phipard, Nancy Midwood *retired special education educator, poet*

Marathon
Wiecha, Joseph Augustine *linguist, educator*

Marco Island
Ballou, Mildred Oralee *elementary school educator, pre-school educator*
Blackwell, John Wesley *securities industry executive, consultant*
Boardman, Harold Frederick, Jr., *lawyer, retired corporate executive*
Cooper, Thomas Astley *bank executive*
Guerrant, David Edward *retired food company executive*
Henry, Sally *assistant principal*
Hollenbeck, Karen Fern *foundation consultant*
Krause, Charles Joseph *otolaryngologist*
Meyer, Jon Howard *utility executive, consultant*
Pettersen, Kjell Will *stockbroker, consultant*

Margate
Franks, Allen P. *research institute executive, educator*
Ory, Steven Jay *physician, educator*

Marianna
Standland, Jamie *director, music educator*

Mary Esther
McTyeire, Robert Adams *sound company executive*

Medley
Delgado, Orlando *import company executive*

Melbourne
Agarwal, Ravi P. *mathematician, educator*
Allington, Maynard *writer*
Babich, Michael Wayne *chemistry educator, educational administrator*
Bailey, J. Ronald *dean, engineering educator*
Ballantyne, Richard Lee *lawyer*
Brown, Seymour R. *lawyer*
Buescher, Howard *construction executive*
Buescher, Keith *construction executive*
Bush, Norman *research and development executive*
Cacciatore, S. Sammy *lawyer*
Catanese, Anthony James *academic administrator*
Elder, Stewart Taylor *dentist, retired naval officer*
Farmer, Phillip W. *communications executive*
Fiore, Carmen Anthony *writer*
Fox, Thomas George *health science educator*
Glindeman, Henry Peter, Jr., *real estate developer*
Greenblatt, Hellen Chaya *immunologist, microbiologist*
Helmstetter, Charles Edward *microbiologist*
Hodges, Carroll Broadus *retired army officer*
Hollingsworth, Abner Thomas *university dean*
Hughes, A. N. *psychotherapist*
Hughes, Edwin Lawson *retired information technology executive*
James-McKinney, Jodi Kaye *drug policy reformer, political organization worker*
Jones, Elaine Hancock *humanities educator*
Koenig, Harold Paul *management consultant, ecologist, evangelist, writer*
Kreines, Joseph Melvin *conductor*
Krieger, Robert Edward *publisher*
Lakshmikantham, Vangipuram *mathematics professor*
Lance, Howard L. *communications executive, industrial engineer*
Laposata, Joseph Samuel *army officer*
Lederer, William Julius *author*
Maloratsky, Leo G. *electrical engineer*
Michalski, Thomas Joseph *city planner, developer*
Minor, Mark William *allergist*
Nelson, Gordon Leigh *chemist, educator*
Pocoski, David John *cardiologist*
Regis, Nina *librarian, educator*
Rose, Peter Edward *former professional baseball player and manager*
Roub, Bryan R(oger) *financial executive*
Shaikh, Muzaffar Abid *management science educator*
Simokaitis, Frank Joseph *air force officer, lawyer*
Stack, Charles Rickman *lawyer*
Stark, Norman *secondary school educator*
Stone, Elaine Murray *author, composer, television producer*
Storrs, Eleanor Emerett *research institute consultant*
Weaver, Lynn Edward *academic administrator, consultant, editor*

Melbourne Beach
Harrington, Peter Tyrus *emergency management company executive, public relations consultant, author, photographer*
Harris, Jack Howard, II, *consulting firm executive*
Scanlon, Charles Francis *retired army officer, defense consultant, writer, publisher*

Melrose
Harley, Ruth *artist, educator*

Merritt Island
Deardoff, R. Bruce *automotive executive*
Johnson, Clarence Traylor, Jr., *state judge*
Klass, Philip Julian *technical journalist, electrical engineer*
McClanahan, Leland *university director*
Morgan, Ronald Brian *retired aerospace engineer, advocate, writer*
Ollie, Pearl Lynn *artist, singer, scriptwriter*
Smith, David Edward *small business owner, aerospace engineer, aerospace scientist*
Thompson, Hugh Lee *academic administrator*
Walter, George Anthony *elementary school educator*

Miami
Abraham, William Michael *physiologist, educator*
Abril, Marcia (Ela I. Cardinas) *writer*
Allen, Charles Norman *television, film and video producer*
Alperin, Stanley I. *publisher, writer, editor, consultant*
Alschuler, Al *freelance/self-employed writer, marketing professional*
Alvarez, Cesar L. *lawyer*
Amarilios, John Alexander *lawyer, real estate consultant*
Amos, Betty Giles *restaurant company executive, accountant*
Anbarci, Nejat Mehmet *economist, educator*
Anderson, Douglas Richard *ophthalmologist, educator, researcher*
Anderson, Terence James *law educator*
Arango, Jorge Sanin *architect*
Arbuz, Joseph Robert *lawyer*
Arison, Micky *cruise line company executive, sports team executive*
Aronovitz, Tod *lawyer*
Astigarraga, Jose I(gnacio) *lawyer*
Bachmeyer, Steven Allan *secondary school educator*
Baena, Scott Louis *lawyer*
Baker, Thomas Eugene *law educator*
Balmaseda, Liz *columnist*
Banas, Suzanne *middle school educator*
Bancalari, Eduardo *pediatrician, educator*
Bannard, Walter Darby *artist, art critic*
Barkett, Rosemary *federal judge*
Barragan, Hugo *retail executive*
Barry, Dave *columnist, author*
Bartelstone, Ted Henry *lawyer*
Barthel, William Frederick, Jr., *electrical engineer*
Batcheller, Joe Ann *entrepreneur*
Batson, Dawn Kirsten *music educator, cultural consultant*
Baumberger, Charles Henry *lawyer*
Becerra, Robert John *lawyer*
Beck, Morris *allergist*
Beckham, Walter Hull, Jr., *lawyer, educator*
Benitez, Armando German *professional baseball player*
Berger, Steven R. *lawyer, state official*
Berley, David Richard *lawyer*
Berman, Bruce Judson *lawyer*
Berman, Mona S. *actress, playwright, theater director, theater producer*
Bessette, Diane J. *homebuilding company executive*
Birsh, Arthur Thomas *publishing executive*
Bishopric, Karl *investment banker, real estate executive, advertising executive*
Black, Creed Carter *newspaper executive*
Black, Roy *lawyer*
Blake, Stanford *judge*
Blanco, Josefa Joan-Juana (Jossie Blanco) *social services administrator*
Blanton, Jerry Cain *literature educator, writer, editor*
Block, Norman Louis *physician, medical educator*
Blumberg, Edward Robert *lawyer*
Bolooki, Hooshang *cardiac surgeon*
Border, James Robert *lawyer, accountant*
Borkan, William Noah *retired biomedical electronics company executive, entrepreneur, inventor*
Bouri, Michael *civil servant*
Braman, Norman *automotive executive, sports team executive*
Bravo, Irene Maria *psychologist, educator*
Bregman, Michael Evan *urban planner*
Brenneman, Gregory D. *food service executive*
Brondello, Sandy *professional basketball player*
Bronis, Stephen Jay *lawyer*
Brooten, Dorothy *nursing educator, former dean*
Brownell, Edwin Rowland *banker, land surveyor, civil engineer*
Buchwald, Peter Sandor *science association director*
Buehler, Martin *hotel executive*
Bullard, Larcenia J. *state legislator*
Burnett, Henry *lawyer*
Burnett, Keitha Denise *social studies educator*
Butterworth, Robert A. *dean, former state attorney general*
Camner, Howard *author, poet*
Campos-Orrego, Nora Patricia *lawyer, consultant*
Capraro, Franz *accountant*
Cardenas, Alberto R. *lawyer*
Carey-Shuler, Barbara *county commissioner*
Carnesoltas, Ana-Maria *lawyer*
Casariego, Jorge Isaac *psychiatrist, psychoanalyst, educator*
Cassel, John Michael *plastic surgeon*
Cassileth, Peter Anthony *internist*
Castillo, Angel, Jr., *lawyer*
Catanzaro, Tony *dancer*
Cefaratti, Anthony Joseph *retired diplomat*
Cekauskas, Cynthia Danute *social worker*
Chakko, Simon C. *cardiologist, educator*
Chambers, Elenora Strasel *artist*
Chang-Mota, Roberto *electrical engineer*
Chaplin, Harvey *wine and liquor wholesale executive*
Chapman, Alvah Herman, Jr., *newspaper executive*
Chen, Shu-Ching *computer science educator*
Cherniack, Evan Paul *geriatrician*
Chisholm, Martha Maria *dietitian*
Ciancio, Gaetano *transplant surgeon, urologist*
Civantos, Francisco *pathologist, educator*
Clark, Ira C. *hospital association administrator, educator*
Clarke, Mercer Kaye *lawyer*
Clarkson, John G. *academic administrator, ophthalmologist*
Clem, Ralph S. *career officer, educator*
Coffey, Kendall Brindley *lawyer*
Cohen, Jeffrey Michael *lawyer*
Cohn, Don Stephen *lawyer*
Conde, Cesar Augusto *cardiologist, educator*
Connor, Terence Gregory *lawyer*
Conover, Pamela C. *cruise line executive*
Corbi, Lana *communications executive*
Cosgrove, John Francis *lawyer, state legislator*
Coton, Carlos David *finance manager*
Critchlow, Richard H. *lawyer*
Cubas, Jose M(anuel) *advertising agency executive*
Cullom, William Otis *trade association executive*
Culmer, Leome Frances *volunteer*
Dahlburg, John-Thor Theodore *newspaper correspondent*
Dann, Oliver Townsend *psychoanalyst, psychiatrist, educator*
Darmody, Stephen Jerome *lawyer*
Dasburg, John Harold *restaurant executive*
Davis, Edward Bertrand *retired federal judge, lawyer*
Davis, Richard Edmund *facial plastic surgeon*
de la Guardia, Mario Francisco *electrical engineer*
de Leon, Lidia Maria *magazine editor*
Dellapa, Gary J. *aviation consultant*
DeMaria, Joseph Angelo *lawyer*
Diaz, Alan *photojournalist*
Diaz, Manuel A. *mayor*
Dickason, John Hamilton *retired foundation executive*
Dickey, Arden *newspaper publishing executive*
Dimitriou, Dolores Ennis *computer consultant*
Doane, Harold Everett *recording executive*
Dominik, Jack Edward *lawyer*
Dorion, Robert Charles *entrepreneur, investor*
Dorn, Gordon Joseph *artist, art educator*
Duany, Andres *architectural firm executive*
DuFresne, Elizabeth Jamison *lawyer*
Dye, H. Michael *marketing professional*
Eaton, Joel Douglas *lawyer*
Edward, Julian Kevin *mathematician, educator*
Eftekhari, Nasser *physiatrist*
Ehrlich, Morton *international finance executive*
Eisdorfer, Carl *psychiatrist, health care executive*
Eisenberg, David H. *telecommunications executive*
Elliot, Cameron Robert *lawyer*
Ellis, Ryan Deane *conductor, musician*
Embden, Dawn Terris *cardiovascular nurse, writer*
Engle, Mary Allen English *retired physician*
Enriquez, Cristino Catud *radiologist, internist, cardiologist*
Escotet, Miguel-Angel *psychologist, educator*
Esteves, Vernon Xavier *financial consultant, investment advisor*
Evans, Thomas William *lawyer*
Fain, Richard David *cruise line executive*
Farcus, Joseph Jay *architect, interior designer*
Feinberg, Wendie *producer*
Ferrari, Leonardo *small business owner*
Ferré, Maurice A. *entrepreneur*
Ferrell, Milton Morgan, Jr., *lawyer*
Fichtner, Margaria *journalist*
Fiedler, Jay *professional football player*
Fiedler, Tom *editor-in-chief*
Fine, Jeffrey Louis *psychologist, writer, researcher, lecturer*
Fine, Rana Arnold *chemical and physical oceanographer*
Finley, Gordon Ellis *psychology educator*
Fleit, Martin *lawyer*
Fleming, Joseph Z. *lawyer*
Flinn, David Lynnfield *financial consultant*
Foote, Edward Thaddeus, II, *university president, lawyer*
Forgione, Dana Anthony *healthcare accounting educator*
Fort-Brescia, Bernardo *architect*
Franklin, Phyllis *retired professional society administrator*
Freire, Jose A. *physicist, writer*
Freshwater, Michael Felix *plastic surgeon, educator*
Friedman, Richard Nathan *lawyer*
Friedman, Ronald Michael *judge*
Frigo, James Peter Paul *industrial hardware company executive*
Fromkin, Ava Lynda *management consultant, healthcare risk management services*
Frost, Philip *pharmaceutical executive, dermatologist*
Furst, Alex Julian *thoracic and cardiovascular surgeon*
Gabor, Frank *insurance company executive*
Garrett, Richard G. *lawyer*
Garvin, Glenn *journalist, writer*
Gelband, Henry *pediatric cardiologist*
Getz, Morton Ernest *medical facility director, gastroenterologist*
Ginsberg, Myron David *neurologist*
Gittens, Angela *airport executive*
Glickman, Fred Elliott *lawyer*
Glogower, Michael Howard *public housing senior functional specialist*
Goin-Harding, Cecilia Margaret *poet*
Goldberg, Lee Dresden *endocrinologist, medical educator*
Gong, Edmond Joseph *lawyer*
Goodwin, W. Jarrard *otolaryngologist, educator*
Gragg, Karl Lawrence *lawyer*
Graham, Donald Lynn *federal judge*
Greenberg, Stewart Gary *lawyer*
Greenleaf, Walter Franklin *lawyer*
Greer, Alan Graham *lawyer*
Greer, Raymond B. *transportation executive*
Griffith, Daniel Alva *geography educator*
Grist, John *retired government official, engineering executive*
Grossman, Robert Louis *lawyer*
Gudorf, Christine Ekhart *religious studies educator*
Guerra, Charles Albert *financial consultant, real estate investor*
Haar, Ana Maria Fernández *advertising and public relations executive*
Halberg, F. David *principal*
Hall, Adam Stuart *lawyer*
Hall, Andrew Clifford *lawyer*
Halsey, Douglas Martin *lawyer*
Hampton, John Lewis *retired newspaper editor*
Hampton, Mark Garrison *architect*
Hardy, Michael C. *performing arts administrator*
Harmon, Monica Renee *music educator*
Harper, Kenneth Charles *clergyman*
Hartz, Steven Edward Marshall *lawyer, educator*
Hector, Louis Julius *lawyer*
Heggen, Arthur William *insurance company executive*
Henderson, Gene M. *marketing professional*
Herbits, Stephen Edward *management consultant*
Heros, Roberto Cosme *neurosurgeon*
Herron, James Michael *retired lawyer*
Herz, Marvin Ira *psychiatrist, researcher*
Heuer, Robert Maynard, II, *opera company executive*
Hicks, Dorothy Jane *obstetrician and gynecologist, educator*
Higginbottom, Samuel Logan *retired aerospace company executive*
Highsmith, Shelby *federal judge*
Higley, Bruce Wadsworth *orthodontist*
Himburg, Susan Phillips *dietician, educator*
Hirschberg, Joseph Gustav *educator, physicist*
Hoffman, Larry J. *lawyer*
Hogg, Jesse Stephen *lawyer*
Houlihan, Gerald John *lawyer*
Howell, Ralph Rodney *pediatrician, educator, geneticist*
Hrinak, Donna Jean *lawyer, former ambassador*
Hudson, Robert Franklin, Jr., *lawyer*
Humphries, Joan Ropes *psychologist, educator*
Hunter, Leland Clair, Jr., *management consultant*
Huysman, Arlene Weiss *psychologist, educator, writer*
Huysman, James David *healthcare executive, consultant*
Ibarguen, Alberto *newspaper executive*
Ibler, Gerold *finance company executive, consultant*
Imperato, Joseph John *lawyer, composer*
Iver, Robert Drew *dentist*
Jackson, Wilfried *banker*
Jacobson, Bernard *lawyer*
Jimenez, Marcos Daniel *lawyer*
Johnson, Channey *elementary school educator*
Johnston, Philip Connelly *lawyer*
Jones, Janice Cox *elementary school educator, writer*
Jones, William Kinzy *materials engineering educator*
Jones-Wills, Eunice Stephanie *mental health nurse, researcher*
Kahn, Jack Merrill *television producer*
Kaiser, Gerard A. *hospital administrator*
Kanet, Roger Edward *political science educator*
Kaplan, Betsy Hess *school board member*
Katz, Lawrence Sheldon *lawyer*
King, James Lawrence *federal judge*
Kislak, Jean Hart *art director*
Klock, Joseph Peter, Jr., *lawyer*
Kohen, Elil *science educator*
Koller, William Carl *neurology educator*
Koncsol, Stephen Wayne *psychologist, educator*
Kooima, Linda Kay *neonatal and pediatrics nurse*
Korchin, Judith Miriam *lawyer*
Kregg, Judith Lynne *accountant*
Kuczynski, Pedro-Pablo *investor*
Kuker, Alan Michael *lawyer*
Kwiat, David Mark *educator, actor*
Laje, Zilia L. *writer, publisher, translator*
Lam, Byron L. *ophthalmologist*
Lampen, Richard Jay *lawyer, investment banker, securities trader*
Landy, Burton Aaron *lawyer*
Lasseter, Kenneth Carlyle *pharmacologist*
Lawrence, David, Jr., *journalist*
LeBow, Bennett S. *communications executive*
Lee, J. Patrick *academic administrator*
Lefton, Donald E. *hotel executive*
Leinbach, Tracy A. *transportation executive*
Lemberg, Louis *cardiologist, educator*
Levine, Robert Jeffrey *lawyer*
Lew, Salvador *radio station executive*
Lewis, John Milton *cable television company executive*
Li, Qi *research scientist, consultant*
Lifshitz, Felice *historian, educator*
Ling, Jian *research scientist, consultant*
Lipcon, Charles Roy *lawyer*
Lipoff, Norman Harold *lawyer*
Long, Maxine Master *lawyer*
Lorenzo, Guadalupe *language educator, department chairman*
Loria, Jeffrey H. *sports team executive*
Louis, Paul Adolph *lawyer*
Love, Mildred Allison *retired secondary school educator, historian, writer, volunteer*
Lynch, Catherine Gores *social work administrator*
Maddern, David *artist*
Madurga, Gonzalo F. *artistic director, actor, singer*
Maher, Stephen Trivett *lawyer, educator*
Maidique, Modesto Alex *academic administrator*
Marcus, Stanley *federal judge*
Mares-Guia, Marcos Luiz *biochemist, consultant*
Margolis, Gwen *county commissioner*
Martin, Jacques *professional hockey coach*
Martínez, Luís Osvaldo *radiologist, educator*
Matthews, Douglas Eugene *lawyer, educator, consultant*
McCabe, Robert Howard *college president*
Mc Kenzie, John Maxwell *physician*
McKeon, John Aloysius (Jack McKeon) *professional baseball manager*
McSwan, Angus *news agency executive*
Meadors, Marynell *former professional basketball coach, sports team executive*
Medina, Luis Santiago *radiologist, researcher*
Mehta, Eileen Rose *lawyer*
Mendez, Luis Eduardo *medical educator, researcher*
Mendieta, Raquelín Maria de la Concepción *artist*
Mendoza De Arce, Daniel Leonel *retired humanities educator*
Miller, Gene Edward *newspaper reporter and editor*
Miller, James M. *lawyer*
Miller, Stuart A. *real estate executive, lawyer*
Miller Udell, Bronwyn *lawyer*
Milstein, Richard Craig *lawyer*
Mintz, Daniel Harvey *endocrinologist, educator, academic administrator*
Miyazaki, Anthony D. *marketing educator, consultant*
Mizel, Mark Stuart *orthopedic surgeon*
Mooers, Christopher Northrup Kennard *physical oceanographer, educator*
Moran, Kate *sculptor, photographer*
Morgan, Charles Oxford, Jr., *lawyer*
Morgan, Dahlia *museum director, art educator*
Morgan, Marabel *writer*
Morrison, Glenn *neurosurgeon*
Morton, Richard *lawyer, financial consultant*
Mouly, Eileen Louise *financial planner*
Mudd, John Philip *lawyer*
Muench, Karl Hugo *clinical geneticist*
Muir, Helen *journalist*
Munn, Janet Teresa *lawyer*
Murphy, Timothy James *lawyer*
Murray, Timothy Garrett *ophthalmologist*
Mustelier, Alina Olga *travel consultant, music educator*
Nachwalter, Michael *lawyer*

North Bay Village
Levine, Jane Sheila *nurse, health insurance consultant*

North Fort Myers
Bayuk Sr., Thomas M. *restaurant owner, writer*
Callanan, Kathleen Joan *internet consultant and marketer, retired electrical engineer*
Gray, Carlos Gibson *restaurateur, agricultural products supplier, entertainer, producer*

North Lauderdale
Altman, Miriam Elizabeth *director, music educator*

North Miami
Dellagloria, John Castle *city attorney, educator*
Pierre-louis, Rosaire *elementary school educator, educator*
Roslow, Sydney *marketing educator*
Stills, Stephen *musician, vocalist, composer*
Tate, Stanley G. *diversified business executive, expert witness*

North Miami Beach
Katzman, Chaim *real estate company executive, investment company executive*
Roif, Henry Irving *aeronautical engineer, electronic engineer, air transportation executive*
Sipzner, Howard M. *real estate executive*
Sorosky, Jeri Ruth *academic administrator*
Su, Hui Fang Huang *mathematician, educator*
Valero, Doron *real estate executive*

North Palm Beach
Coyle, Dennis Patrick *lawyer*
Crawford, Roberta *association administrator*
Edwards, William James *broadcast executive*
Fierer, Joshua Allan *pathology educator*
Frevert, James Wilmot *financial planner, investment advisor*
Hay, Lewis, III, *utilities company executive*
Hayman, Richard Warren Joseph *conductor*
Higgins, Jay F. *financial executive*
Hood, Edward Exum, Jr., *retired electrical manufacturing company executive*
Hushing, William Collins *retired corporate executive*
Jaffe, Melvin *securities company executive*
Lavine, Alan *columnist, writer*
Lynch, William Walker *banker*
Nicklaus, Jack William *professional golfer*
Siegendorf, Arden M. *judge*
Sooy, William Ray *information technology executive*
Stein, Mark Rodger *allergist*

North Port
Coe, Laurie Lynne Barker *photojournalist, artist*
Hill, Wallace Harry *sports television consultant*
Lazich, Daniel *aerospace engineer*
Seiler, Charlotte Woody *retired educator*

Oakland Park
Kilpatrick, Clifton Wayne *book dealer*
Rosenthal, Susan Barbara *retired librarian*

Ocala
Alexis, Noel Richard *mathematician, educator*
Altenburger, Karl Marion *allergist*
Booth, Jane Schuele *real estate company executive, real estate broker*
Boston, Bruce David *writer, book designer*
Delozier, Doris M. *retired secondary school educator*
DeSilva, Ann Marie *writer*
Fredericks, William John *chemistry professor*
Frow, Richard G. *retired librarian*
Gatison, Karen Ann *private school educator*
Grissom, Robert Jesse, Sr., *criminal justice educator*
Hunter, Oregon K., Jr., *physiatrist*
Massa, Conrad Harry *religious studies educator*
Niblock, Lee *recreation director*
Ovrebo, Judith *retired physical education educator*
Renda, Rosa A. *special education educator*
Roberts, Mary Belle *clinical social worker*
Sostilio, Robert Francis *office equipment marketing consultant*
Stock, Stephen Michael *broadcast journalist*
Sundstrom, Harold Walter *public relations executive*
Tesmer, Nancy Ann Stutler *retired librarian*
Vazquez, Debra Allen *literature educator*
Woods, Mae *minister*

Ocean Ridge
Bates, Edward Brill *retired insurance company executive*
Grabner, George John *manufacturing executive*
Mueller, Gerry *realtor, investor, former internet executive*

Ocoee
Smith, Stephen F. *food service executive*

Okeechobee
Bishop, Sid Glenwood *union official*
Egolf, James Edward *history educator, secondary school educator*
Mercer, Frances deCourcy *artist, educator*

Oldsmar
Brunner, George Matthew *management consultant, former business executive*
Caronis, George John *insurance executive*
Dyer, Allan M. *medical association administrator*
Thompson, Mack Eugene *history educator*

Opa Locka
Beckett, Joshua Patrick *professional baseball player*
Castillo, Luis Antonio Donato *professional baseball player*
Kotsay, Mark Steven *professional baseball player*
Lee, Derrek Leon *professional baseball player*
Perez, Tony *former baseball player*
Smith, Albert E. *college president*
Wilson, Isabel Gomez *elementary school educator, consultant*

Orange City
Schaeffer, Barbara Hamilton *retired rental leasing company executive, writer*

Orange Park
Bartholomew, John Niles *retired church administrator*
Fetchero, John Anthony, Jr., *otorhinolaryngologist*
Goss, William Allan *author, speaker*
Miller, Martin Eugene *school system consultant, negotiator, lobbyist*
Rice, Ronald James *hospital administrator*

Orlando
Abbott, Charles Warren *lawyer*
Ahlers, Glen-Peter, Sr., *law library director, educator, consultant*
Allison, Anne Marie *retired librarian*
Andrew, Brian J. *information technology company executive*
Armacost, Robert Leo *management educator, former coast guard officer*
Avery, Kay Beth *secondary school educator*
Baker, Peter Mitchell *laser scientist, educator*
Bauer, Maria Casanova *computer engineer*
Bearman, David *corporate financial executive*
Bigum, Randall K. *retired military officer*
Blackford, Robert Newton *lawyer, director*
Blaher, Neal Jonathan *lawyer*
Blue, Joseph Edward *physicist*
Bond, William L. *career officer*
Boyar, Jay Mitchell *film critic*
Bredin, Brenda Ann *communications educator*
Brownlee, Thomas Marshall *manufacturing executive*
Byrnes, John Francis, Jr., *physician assistant*
Caldero-Fiqueroa, Ana Jhanilca *language educator*
Camoes, Norma Arcamo *school nurse*
Capouano, Albert D. *lawyer*
Carson, Thomas P. *pediatric cardiologist*
Cates, Harold Thomas *aircraft and electronics company executive*
Cawthon, Frank H. *retired construction company executive*
Christiansen, Patrick T. *lawyer*
Clinton, Stephen Michael *academic administrator*
Colbourn, Trevor *retired university president, historian*
Connolly, Joseph Francis, II, *educational executive, government consultant*
Conway, Anne Callaghan *federal judge*
Davis, H. Alan *retired airline captain, consultant*
Davis, Johnny Reginald *professional basketball coach*
Dawson, Leslie Naryne *quality assurance professional*
deBeaubien, Hugo H. *lawyer*
Deli, Steven Frank *business investment and development executive*
Deo, Narsingh *computer scientist, educator*
De Vos, Daniel G. *sports team executive, marketing professional*
Dimopoulos, Linda J. *food service executive*
Dubey, Vinod Shanker *microbiologist, biochemist, researcher*
Duda, Richard Frank *architect, engineering executive*
Dunn, William Bruna, III, *journalist*
Eagan, William Leon *lawyer*
Eastmond-Robinson, June Patricia *public health nurse*
Efthimiou, Costas John *physicist, educator, physicist, researcher*
Elliott, E.J. *manufacturing executive*
Fawsett, Patricia Combs *federal judge*
Figner, William James *instructional systems designer*
Fottler, Myron David *health services educator*
Francis, Steve *professional basketball player*
Frey, Louis, Jr., *lawyer, federal and state government official*
Gallagher, Shaun Andrew *philosophy educator, writer*
Gianini, Paul C., Jr., *academic administrator*
Glazebrook, James Grinstead *judge*
Glynn, Gerard Francis *not-for-profit developer*
Gray, Anthony Rollin *retired finance company executive*
Green, Joal Fekete Stafford *library media specialist*
Guzman, Marie Elvira *school guidance counselor*
Ha, Yonggang *optical engineer*
Handley, Leon Hunter *lawyer*
Haxton, David *filmmaker, photographer*
Healy, Jane Elizabeth *newspaper editor*
Henry, Christopher Joel *software consultant*
Henry, William Oscar Eugene *lawyer*
Hill, Grant *professional basketball player*
Hitt, John Charles *academic administrator*
Hoepner, Theodore John *banker*
Hornick, Richard Bernard *physician*
Ismail, Mourad El-Houssieny *mathematician, educator, researcher*
Jacinto, George Anthony *social worker, counselor, educator, consultant*
Janzen, Lee *professional golfer*
Jennemann, Karen Sue *judge*
Jerome, Christian Joseph *psychologist, researcher*
Jontz, Jeffry Robert *lawyer*
Kelaher, James Peirce *lawyer*
Kellison, Stephen George *actuarial consultant*
Kennedy, Robert Samuel *experimental psychologist, consultant*
Kilbourne, Krystal Hewett *retired rail transportation executive*
Landaeta, Rafael Ernesto *industrial engineer, researcher*
Langton, Bryan D. *hotel executive*
Layish, Daniel T. *internist*
Lee, Joe R. *food service executive*
Lefkowitz, Ivan Martin *lawyer*
Leonhardt, Frederick Wayne *lawyer*
Limpus, Charles Everett, III, *non-commissioned officer*
Lisetti, Christine Laetitia *computer scientist, educator*
Llewellyn, Ralph Alvin *physics educator*
Losey, Ralph Colby *lawyer*
Lowndes, John Foy *lawyer*
Lucariello, Georgann *engineer*
Mahoney, Mary *hotel executive*
Maldonado, Graziano *management consultant, educator*
Marinescu, Dan Cristian *computer sciences educator, consultant*
Marsh, Ella Jean *pediatrician*
Marsh, Malcolm Roy, Jr., *electronics engineer*
Maupin, Elizabeth Thatcher *theater critic*
Mock, Frank Mackenzie *lawyer*
Mooney, Thomas Robert *lawyer*
Morgan, Thomas I. *retail executive*
Moriarty, Michael Eugene *retired humanities educator*
Morini, Angelo Sylvester *food company executive*
Morrisey, Marena Grant *art museum administrator*
Motes, Carl Dalton *lawyer*
Murphrey, Elizabeth Hobgood *history educator, librarian*
Murrah, Ann Ralls Freeman *historical association executive*
Murrell, Robert George *lawyer*
Nadeau, Robert Bertrand, Jr., *lawyer*
Neal, Thomas Frederick *lawyer*
Neff, A. Guy *lawyer*
Norris, Franklin Gray *thoracic and cardiovascular surgeon*
O'Farrell, Mark Theodore *religious organization administrator*
Okun, Neil Jeffrey *vitreoretinal surgeon*
Pauley, Bruce Frederick *history professor*
Pearlman, Louis Jay *aviation and entertainment company executive*
Peck, Carolyn *professional basketball coach*
Pierce, Jerry Earl *business executive*
Pierce, John Gerald (Jerry Pierce) *lawyer*
Pollack, Robert William *psychiatrist*
Potter, Ronald Neal, Jr., *newspaper distribution specialist*
Raffa, Jean Benedict *author, educator*
Ragland, Robert Allen *lawyer*
Reed, John Alton *lawyer*
Reinhart, Richard Paul *lawyer*
Renk, Kimberly Dawn *social sciences educator*
Reyes, Jose Antonio, Sr., *minister*
Rosenbach, Leopold *engineer, consultant*
Sheaffer, William Jay *lawyer*
Shirek, John Richard *retired savings and loan executive*
Shives, Paula J *lawyer*
Sims, Roger W. *lawyer*
Skambis, Christopher Charles, Jr., *lawyer*
Smetheram, Herbert Edwin *management consultant*
Smyth, Joseph Vincent *manufacturing executive*
Snively, Stephen Wayne *lawyer*
Steward, Sherry Ann *information technology executive, educator*
Subin, Eli Harold *lawyer*
Taitt, Earl Paul *psychiatrist, army officer*
Thorpe, Janet Claire *judge*
Ting, Robert Yen-ying *physicist*
Van den Berg, Egerton *airport executive*
Vander Weide, Cheri DeVos *sports team executive, marketing professional*
Vanryckeghem, Martine *speech pathology/audiology services professional, educator*
Velez, Diana *historian, educator*
Waltz, Kathleen M. *publishing executive*
Waltz, Kathy *publishing executive*
Warren, Dean Stuart *artist*
Weisbrod, John *professional sports team executive*
Weiss, Al *hotel executive*
Weiss, Christopher John *lawyer*
Wenski, Thomas Gerard *bishop*
Whitehouse, Gary *industrial engineer, educator*
Whitworth, Hall Baker *forest products company executive*
Williamson, Paul Richard *medical educator, surgeon*
Wu, Thomas Xinzhang *engineering educator*
Yates, Leighton Delevan, Jr., *lawyer*
Yesawich, Peter Charles *advertising executive*
Yonetani, Ayako *music educator, entertainer*
Young, George Cressler *federal judge*

Ormond Beach
Buonamano, Anthony F. *real estate agent, engineering company executive*
Burke, Marguerite Jodi Larcombe *application developer, consultant*
Burt, Wallace Joseph, Jr., *insurance company executive*
Burton, Alan Harvey *city official*
Cowley, Gerald Dean *architect*
Cromartie, Robert Samuel, III, *thoracic surgeon*
Cunsolo, Ronald S. *historian, educator*
Franchini, Roxanne *bank executive*
Hodkinson, Sydney Phillip *composer, educator*
Kaufer, Julian Norman *biochemist, educator*
Lively, Carol A. *retired professional society administrator*
Lynn, Evelyn Joan *state senator, consultant*
Moore, Frederick Appel *administrator*
Truitt, Richard byron *landscape architect*
Wendelstedt, Harry Hunter, Jr., *umpire*

Osprey
Boldt, Heinz *aerospace engineer*
Cochran, David MacDuffie *management consultant*
Gross, James Dehnert *pathologist*
Gross, Marilyn Agnes *artist, business owner, speech audiologist*
Harrington, Nancy O'Connor *volunteer*
Jones, George Steven *civil engineer*
Petrik, Gerd *pharmaceutical executive*

Oviedo
Brethauer, William Russell, Jr., *claim investigator*
Drummer, Donald Raymond *financial services executive*
MacKenzie, Charles Sherrard *academic administrator*
Millstein, Herbert Sydney *management consultant*
Parker, Harry Lee *retired army officer, counselor*

Palatka
Baldwin, Allen Adail *lawyer, writer*
Embree, Mary Evelyn *retired secondary school educator*
Svetlik, Robert Wayne *contractor, writer*

Palm Bay
Colman, Charles Kingsbury *academic administrator, criminologist*
Seifer, Ronald Leslie *psychologist*
Sheets, Fredrick Sidney *retired military officer, auditor*

Palm Bch Gdns
Wadkins, Lanny Lanston *professional golfer*

Palm Beach
Adler, Frederick Richard *lawyer, financier*
Amling, Frederick *economist, educator, investment advisor*
Bagby, Joseph Rigsby *financial investor*
Bagby, Martha L. Green *real estate holding company executive, writer, publishing executive*
Banks, Russell *financial planner, consultant*
Black, Leonard Julius *retail store consultant*
Callahan, Edward William *chemical engineer, retired manufacturing executive*
Canary, Nancy Halliday *lawyer*
Cole, Carol Alma Tomlinson *classical musician*
Coudert, Dale Hokin *real estate executive, marketing consultant*
Crawford, Sandra Kay *lawyer*
Devins, Robert Sylvester *retired lawyer*
Dillard, Rodney Jefferson *real estate executive*
Donnell, John Randolph *retired petroleum executive*
Elson, Suzanne Goodman *community activist*
Fitilis, Theodore Nicholas *portfolio manager, retired financial analyst*
Flanagan, Joseph Patrick *advertising executive*
Floyd, Raymond Loran *professional golfer*
Gaudieri, Alexander V. J. *art historian, consultant, museum director*
Gundlach, Heinz Ludwig *investment banker, lawyer*
Habicht, Frank Henry *retired industrial executive*
Halmos, Peter *entrepreneur*
Harper, Mary Sadler *financial advisor*
Hope, Margaret Lauten *civic worker*
Johnson, Theodore Mebane *investment executive*
Karp, Richard M. *advertising and communication executive*
Klotsche, Charles Martin *real estate development company executive, photographer, writer, financial columnist*
Lee, Robert Earl *retired physician*
Leone, Paul N. *hotel executive*
Levine, Laurence Brandt *investment banker*
Loring, Arthur *lawyer, diversified financial services company executive*
McCarter, Thomas Nesbitt, III, *investment counseling company executive*
Moloney, Thomas Walter *consulting firm executive*
Monath, Norman *publishing company executive*
Ness, Evaline (Mrs. Arnold A. Bayard) *illustrator, writer*
Parker, Ellis Jackson, III, *lawyer, broadcaster*
Pryor, Hubert *editor, writer*
Rauch, George Washington *lawyer, director*
Rinker, Ruby Stewart *foundation administrator*
Rumbough, Stanley Maddox, Jr., *industrialist*
Seggev, Meir *radiologist, educator*
Simon, Harold *radiologist*
Tiefel, William Reginald *hotel company executive*
Willis, Clayton *broadcaster, author, former government offical, educator, arts consultant*
Wirtz, Willem Kindler *garden and lighting designer, public relations consultant*

Palm Beach Gardens
Auerbach, Paul Ira *lawyer*
Awtrey, Jim L. *sports association executive*
Bragdon, Clifford Richardson *city planner, educator*
Brosemer, Jim P *education educator*
Colussy, Dan Alfred *aviation executive*
Couples, Frederick Steven *professional golfer*
Daly, John Patrick *professional golfer*
Deppe, Henry A. *insurance company executive*
Druck, Kalman Breschel *public relations counselor*
Duval, David Robert *professional golfer*
Falk, Bernard Henry *trade association executive*
Furda, Ivan *chemist, consultant*
Gillette, Frank C., Jr., *retired mechanical engineer*
Giordano, Andrew Anthony *retired naval officer*
Hamilton, Todd *professional golfer*
Hannon, John Robert *investment company executive*
Harnett, Joseph Durham *oil company executive*
Henninger, Brian Hatfield *professional golfer*
Holloway, Edward Olin *human services manager*
Howard, Melvin *financial executive*
Kahn, David Miller *lawyer, educator*
Keppler, William Edmund *multinational company executive*
Kleinberg, Lawrence H. *investor, consultant*
Leonard, Justin (Justin Charles Garret Leonard) *professional golfer*
Levitt, George *retired chemist*
Love, Davis Milton, III, *professional golfer*
Maggert, Jeffrey Allan *professional golfer*
McCall, Duke Kimbrough *clergyman*
Mendelson, Richard Donald *former communications company executive*
Mergler, H. Kent *investment counselor*
Mickelson, Phil *professional golfer*
Miller, John Laurence *professional golfer*
Nielsen, Steven E. *telecommunications company executive*
O'Meara, Mark *professional golfer*
Orr, Joseph Alexander *educational administrator*
Rigby, Paul Crispin *artist, cartoonist*
Samuels, Fern Jacqueline *artist, educator*
Seaman, William Bernard *physician, radiology educator*
Shapiro, Steven David *dermatologist*
Skinner, Margaret Sheppard *pathologist*
Small, Melvin D. *physician, educator*
Stankowski, Paul Francis *professional golfer*
Staub, W. Arthur *health care products executive*
Strange, Curtis Northrop *professional golfer*
Van Allen, Veronica Elaine *marketing and public relations professional*
Verplank, Scott Rachal *professional golfer*
Werner, Joanne Loucille *financial executive*
Westwood, Lee *professional golfer*
Woods, Tiger (Eldrick Woods) *professional golfer*
Yackira, Michael William *power company executive*

Palm City
Boss, Manley Leon *plant physiologist*
Conklin, George Melville *retired food products executive*
Derrickson, William Borden *manufacturing executive*
Henry, David Howe, II, *retired diplomat*
Mc Hale, John Joseph *baseball club executive*
Wishart, Ronald Sinclair *retired chemical company executive*

Palm Coast
Barnes, Judith Ann *real estate executive*
Bullard, Ervin Trowbridge *horticulturist*
Cook, Gloria Houston *civic leader*
Duncan, Donald William *lawyer*
Farrell, Joseph Christopher *retired mining executive, services executive*
Franco, Annemarie Woletz *editor*
Patz, Edward Frank *retired lawyer*

Palm Harbor
Barker, Larry Lee *communications educator*
Bennett, John Joseph *professional services company executive*
Jones, Winona Nigels *retired library media specialist*
Katzen-Guthrie, Joy *performance artist, engineering services executive*
Krawczynski, Tony Edward *music educator*
Morgan, Albert George Leonard *retired airline pilot, writer*
O'Neal, Michael L. *physician*
Padberg, Daniel Ivan *agricultural economics educator, researcher*
Rezanka, Thomas W. *lawyer*
Summers-Powell, Alan *lawyer*
Warfield, John Nelson *retired engineering educator, consultant*
Williams, Thomas Arthur *biomedical computing consultant, psychiatrist*

Palm Springs
Abou-Sayed, Hatem *plastic surgeon*

Palmetto
Angulo, Charles Bonin *foreign service officer, lawyer*
Carter, Elizabeth Wackerman *retired mental health nurse*
Dielman, Ray Walter *radiologic scientist, natural hygienist, medical herbalist*
Patton, Ray Baker *financial consultant, real estate broker*
Turlo, George Jerzy *architect, city planner, artist*

Palmetto Bay
Nakashima, Tadayoshi *retired biochemist, researcher*

Panama City
Anderson, Ruth Nathan *syndicated columnist, TV news host, writer, recording artist, lyricist*
Bankhead, Sheila Walsh *librarian*
Caiazzo, Tom A *political scientist, educator*
Campbell, Regan Helen *engineer*
Cox, Ron Dean *non-commissioned officer, educator, psychologist*
Dang, Hai *geographic information system specialist*
D'Arcy, Gerald Paul *engineering executive, consultant*
Fejer, T. William *pianist, composer, architect, furniture designer*
Fensom, James B. *lawyer*
McWhorter, Susan Carol *English language educator*
Navon, Robert *real estate investor, former book publisher*
Reedy-Dewey, Madeline Anne *retired occupational therapist*
Robbins, Dorothy Ann *librarian*
Roberts, Paul Craig, III, *economics educator, author, columnist*
Schafer, John Stephen *poet*
Walters, George John *oral and maxillofacial surgeon*

Panama City Beach
Nelson, Edith Ellen *dietitian*
Patterson, Christopher Nida *lawyer*

Parkland
Janice, Barbara *illustrator*

Parrish
Corey, Kay Janis *business owner, designer, nurse*
Wood, Rev. Dr. Benton *retired editor, priest*

Patrick AFB
Beauregard, Adam *aerospace engineer*

Pembroke Pines
Embergher, Mary Louise *elementary school educator*
Grahm, Charles Morton *retired sales executive*
Granata, Linda M. *lawyer*
Hudson, Brenda Louise *soprano, opera singer, vocal coach*

Penney Farms
Muilenburg, John Powell *minister*

Pensacola
Appleyard, Diane Paige *human service administrator*
Arnold, Barry Raynor *philosophy educator, medical ethicist, clergyman, counselor*
Bowden, Jesse Earle *newspaper editor, author, cartoonist, journalism educator*
Bozeman, Frank Carmack *lawyer*
Bradshaw, Bascom Kyle *surgeon, science educator*
Broxton, Randall *historian, educator*
Bullock, Ellis Way, Jr., *architect*
Bumgardner, Kathryn H. *retired librarian*
Canady, Alexa Irene *pediatric neurosurgeon*
Clare, George *safety engineer, systems safety consultant*
Davis, Wesley D. *psychologist, educator*
Demars, Bonnie Macon *librarian*
Dillard, Robert Perkins *pediatrician, educator*
Furlong, George Morgan, Jr., *museum foundation consultant, retired naval officer*
Gamblin, William Basil, Jr., *application developer, writer, photographer*
Geeker, Nicholas Peter *lawyer, judge*
Gill, Becky Lorette *retired psychiatrist*
Hutto, Earl *retired congressman*
Ivey, Denise H. *publishing executive*
Jaffe, Alberto P. *musician, educator*
Jones, Harry Gordon *electronics company executive*
Kernstock, Elwyn Nicholas *political science educator, author*
Killian, Lewis Martin *sociology educator*
Kimball, Bob *education educator, writer*
Lanier, Gregory Warren *theater educator*
Levin, Fredric Gerson *lawyer*
Loesch, Mabel Lorraine *social worker*
Lovoy, Joseph T. *investment advisor*
Maddock, Lawrence Hill *retired language educator*
Maygarden, Jerry Louis *health care foundation executive*
Mazzeo, Daniel Patrick *aerospace engineer, aviation consultant*
McKenzie, James Franklin *lawyer*
Moulton, Wilbur Wright, Jr., *lawyer*
Mountcastle, William Wallace, Jr., *philosophy and religion educator*
Odell, M. Carol *music educator*
Olsen, Richard Galen *biomedical engineer, consultant*
Raisler, Mary E. *nurse*
Rawlins, Joseph T. *music educator*
Redmond, Michael R. *ophthalmologist*
Ricard, John H. *bishop, educator*
Ricketson, George Manning, III, *retired surgeon*
Rubardt, Peter Craig *conductor, educator*
Shimmin, Margaret Ann *women's health nurse*
Sims, Pam *writer, minister*
Soloway, Daniel Mark *lawyer*
Sprouse, James Richardson *literature educator*
Steinhoff, Raymond O(akley) *consulting geologist*
Taggart, Linda Diane *women's health nurse*
Vuksta, Michael Joseph *surgeon*
Windham, John Franklin *lawyer, educator*
Woolf, Kenneth Howard *architect*

Pensacola Beach
Jenkins, Louis (Woody) *television executive, state legislator*

Pineland
Donlon, William James *retired lawyer*

Pinellas Park
Benedict, Gail Cleveland *music educator*
Brennan, Mary M. *state legislator*
Cramer, Kenneth Lee *protective services official, consultant*
Frantzis, Theodosios George *periodontist*
Mente, Ronald F. *consulting company executive*

Plant City
Buchman, Kenneth William *lawyer*
Henry, J. Myrle *pharmacist*
Sparkman, Steven Leonard *lawyer*

Plantation
Appel, Antoinette Ruth *neuropsychologist*
Ballantyne, Maree Anne Canine *artist*
Chou, Chung-Kwang *bio-engineer*
Fellows, John *delivery service executive*
Gay, John Marion *federal agency administrator, organization-personnel analyst*
Gewirtzman, Garry Bruce *dermatologist*
Gonshak, Isabelle Lee *nurse, civic worker*
Morris, James Bruce *internist*
Nickelson, Kim René *internist*
Sperry, Martin Jay *lawyer*
Stone, Marc J. *lawyer*
Weiss, David I. *land developer, business executive, lawyer*
Wick, Mitchell A. *physician*
Young, William Benjamin *retired special education educator*

Polk City
Closen, Michael Lee *retired law educator*

Pompano Beach
Bethel, Marilyn Joyce *librarian*
Bookbinder, Robert Max *superintendent of schools*
Bowsher, Dennis James *internist, cardiologist, pharmacologist*
Brands, Robert Franciscus *business executive*
Calatchi, Ralph Franklin *investment banker, writer*
Calevas, Harry Powell *management consultant*
Corsello, Lily Joann *minister, counselor, educator*
Ephraim, Charles *lawyer*
Gilchrist, William Risque, Jr., *economist*
Goldberg, Lois D. *health facility administrator, disability analyst*
Gude, Nancy Carlson *lawyer*
Gui, James Edmund *architect*
Hasenauer, Judith Anne *lawyer*
Hellwege, Nancy Carol *special education educator*
Johnson, Dorothy Curfman *elementary school educator*
Kester, Stewart Randolph *banker*
Kory, Marianne Greene *lawyer*
Liakos, James Christ *business manager*
McPherson, Michael *entertainer, theater producer*
Rifenburgh, Richard Philip *investment company executive*
Roen, Sheldon R. *publisher, psychologist*
Searle, Bernard G. *pharmacologist, dental educator*
Service, John Gregory *law educator*
Shulmister, M(orris) Ross *lawyer*
Szilassy, Sandor *retired lawyer, library director, educator*
Vasquez, William Leroy *business educator, consultant*

Ponte Vedra Beach
Agassi, Andre Kirk *professional tennis player*
Berry, Clare Gebert *real estate broker*
Church, Barbara Ryan *organizational psychologist*
de Selding, Edward Bertrand *retired bank executive*
Elston, William Steger *food products company executive*
Faxon, Brad *professional golfer*
Finchem, Tim *sports association executive*
Fiorentino, Thomas Martin *transportation executive, lawyer*
Gold, Keith Dean *advertising and design executive*
Green, Norman Kenneth *retired oil industry executive, former naval officer*
Hamilton, William Berry, Jr., *retired shipping company executive*
Hartzell, Karl Drew *retired university dean, historian*
Keeler, Ross Vincent *securities company executive*
Kuhn, Bowie K. *lawyer, former professional baseball commissioner, consultant*
Langford, Dean Ted *lighting and precision materials company executive*
Leek, Jay Wilbur *management consultant*
Linnen, Thomas Francis *international strategic management consulting firm executive*
MacKowski, John Joseph *retired insurance company executive*
Moore, David Graham *sociologist, educator*
O'Brien, Raymond Vincent, Jr., *banker*
Patterson, Oscar, III, *university program administrator*
Pavin, Corey Allen *professional golfer*
ReMine, William Hervey, Jr., *retired surgeon*
Roland, Melissa Montgomery *accountant*
Saltmarsh, Sara Elizabeth *lawyer*
Slayton, Gus *foundation administrator*
Sluman, Jeff (Jeffrey George Sluman) *professional golfer*
Spence, Richard Dee *retired rail transportation executive*
Stricker, Steve *professional golfer*
Toker, Karen Harkavy *physician*
Triplett, Kirk Allen *professional golfer*
Tyler, Diane Lazzelle *elementary school educator*
Watson, John Lawrence, III, *former trade association executive*
Wood, Quentin Eugene *oil company executive*
Wu, Hsiu Kwang *economist, educator*
Yessin, Gerson *musician, educator*

Port Charlotte
Al-Khatib, Tareq *surgeon*
Donovan, William Alan *retired librarian*
Hill, Richard Earl *academic administrator*
Hollinshead, Ariel Cahill *research oncologist, educator*
Kidd, A. Paul *hospital administrator, government official*
Kok, Hans Gebhard *consulting engineer*
McMullen, G. Arthur *physician, cardiologist*
Reynolds, Helen Elizabeth *management services consultant*
Von Holden, Martin Harvey *psychologist*
Winters, Stanley B. *history educator, writer, civic activist*
Wolff, Diane Patricia *writer, film producer*

Port Orange
Millar, Gordon Halstead *mechanical engineer, agricultural machinery manufacturing executive*

Port Richey
Fry, Ronald Sylvan *music educator, director*
Long, Michael Eldon *government and history educator*
Mueller, Lois M. *psychologist*

Port Saint Lucie
Augelli, John Pat *geographer, educator, writer, consultant, rancher*
Austin, Philip *research scientist*
Beatrice, Ruth Hadfield *hypnotherapist, retired educator, financial administrator*
Diltz, Jerry Dwaine *computer science educator, consultant*
Guglielmino, Lucy Margaret Madsen *education educator, researcher, consultant*
Lambert, George Robert *lawyer, realtor*
Sommers, Robert Thomas *editor, publisher, author*
Verfaillie, Roland Bruce *mental health professional*

Punta Gorda
Beever, James William, III, *biologist*
Clinton, Mariann Hancock *educational association administrator*
Eliason, Nancy Carol *education consultant*
Faerber, Abigail Hobbs *physician*
Fullman, Robert Louis *metallurgy consultant*
Haswell, Carleton Radley *banker*
Kampa, William *retired elementary school educator, writer*
Klarik, Bela William James Clark *retired school system administrator*
Koll, Richard Leroy *retired chemical company executive*
Ling, Chung-Mei *retired pharmaceutical company executive*
McDaniel, Norwood Allan *insurance broker*
Miles, Frank Charles *retired newspaper executive*
Montano, Arthur *lawyer*
Presley, Brian *investment company executive*
Smith, Charles Edwin *computer science educator*
Smith-Mooney, Marilyn Patricia *city government official, management consultant and facilitator*
Spaulding, Mar *retired special education educator, therapist*

Ramrod Key
Clark, John Russell *marine biologist*

Reddick
Corwin, Joyce Elizabeth Stedman *construction company executive*

Redington Beach
Alpert, Barry Mark *insurance company and banking executive*

Riviera Beach
Berliner, Hans Jack *retired computer science educator*
Sonnier, Joseph A. *lab administrator, physician*

Rockledge
Means, Michael David *hospital administrator*
Sutton, Betty Sheriff *elementary school educator*

Royal Palm Beach
Perez, Jorge Luis *retired manufacturing executive*
Zucker, Leonard Charles *trucking executive, rabbi*

Ruskin
Briscoe, Anne M. *retired scientist, educator*

Safety Harbor
Banks, Allan Richard *artist, art historian, researcher*
Crafton-Masterson, Adrienne *real estate company executive*

Saint Augustine
Ansbacher, Sidney Franklyn *lawyer*
Bishop, Claire DeArment *small business owner, former librarian*
Bourne, John David *retired city finance executive*
Brady, James Joseph *labor arbitrator*
Connaway, Robert Wallace *artist, computer programmer*
DeLaughter, Thomas Glenn *business administration educator, consultant*
Flemister, Launcelot Johnson *physiologist, educator*
Gilmer, Jeriel Marcus *music educator*
Gilmore, H. James *film producer, educator*
Henderson, Hazel *economist, writer, lecturer*
Jurgens, Julie Graham *mathematics professor*
Kiehlbauch, John B *psychologist*
Lund, Frederick Henry *aerospace and electrical engineer*
McCarty, Doran Chester *religious organization administrator*
Nolan, David Joseph *author, historian*
Nolan, Joseph Thomas *journalism educator, communications consultant*
Oliver, Elizabeth Kimball *writer*
Parker, Susan Richbourg *historian, consultant*
Preysz, Louis Robert Fonss, III, *management consultant, educator*
Proctor, William Lee *college chancellor*
Quirke, Lillian Mary *retired art educator*
Rahner, Jean A. *performing company executive, educator*
Rice, David Preston *minister*
Sappington, Sharon Anne *retired school librarian*
Walker, Robert Dixon, III, *retired surgeon, urologist, educator*
Wilkes, Delano Angus *architect*
Xue, Rui-De *entomologist*

Saint Cloud
Everett, Woodrow Wilson *electrical engineer, educator*
Haines, Jr., Robert L. *air transportation management, consultant*
Ortiz, Anthony *hotel executive*

Saint Leo
Astolfi, Douglas M. *history professor*

Saint Petersburg
Allshouse, Merle Frederick *educational organization administrator*
Alvarez, Wilson Eduardo *professional baseball player*
Armacost, Peter Hayden *academic administrator*
Armstrong, Kenneth *lawyer*
Bairstow, Frances Kanevsky *arbitrator, mediator, educator*
Baker, Victoria Jean *anthropology educator*
Barnes, Andrew Earl *newspaper executive*
Battaglia, Anthony Sylvester *lawyer*
Belich, John Patrick, Sr., *journalist*
Bercu, Barry Bernard *pediatric endocrinologist*
Berg, Lee R. *computer consultant*
Betzer, Susan Elizabeth Beers *physician, geriatrician*
Bolhofner, Brett Robinson *orthopedist*
Brightbill, Timothy R. *music educator*
Bryant, Timothy Clark *investment brokerage executive*
Burnette, Charles Galyon *protective services official*
Butcher-Towzey, David *public relations executive*
Byrd, Isaac Burlin *retired biologist*
Carlson, Jeannie Ann *writer*
Carrere, Charles Scott *law educator, judge*
Carroll, Charles Michael *music educator*
Castilla, Vinivio Soria *professional baseball player*
Collins, Carl Russell, Jr., *industrial engineer*
Collins, Paul Steven *vascular surgeon*
Connelly, David O'Brien *art museum administrator, journalist*
Corty, Andrew P. *publishing executive*
Craybas, Jill *professional tennis player*
Davenport, Jeffrey Paton *financial planner, investment advisor*
D'Elia, Christopher Francis *marine biologist, educator*
DeLorenzo, David Joseph *retired public relations executive*
Dimas, Marilyn J. *health resources executive*
Donovan, Denis Miller *psychiatrist, author, lecturer*
Dunlap, Karen F. Brown *academic administrator*
Emerson, William Allen *retired investment company executive*
Erman, Aila *small business owner*
Escarraz, Enrique, III, *lawyer*
Favre, Gregory *publishing executive*
Fishman, Mark Brian *computer scientist, educator*
Fleming, William Sloan *energy executive, computer company executive*
Franke, Thomas *investment company executive*
Freeman, Corinne *financial services, former mayor*
Geiger, Scott William *finance educator*
Georges, Richard Martin *lawyer, educator*
Glass, Roy Leonard *lawyer*
Godbold, Francis Stanley *investment banker, securities firm executive*
Godwin, Benjamin Braxton *finance company executive*
Gooden, Dwight Eugene *professional baseball player*
Granville, Laura *professional tennis player*
Greer, Tommy D. *marketing professional*
Griffin, Dennis Joseph *middle school principal*
Gross, Geoffrey Fries *systems architect*
Grube, Karl Bertram *judge*
Haiman, Robert James *newspaper editor, journalism educator, media consultant, media critic, expert witness*
Hallock-Muller, Pamela *oceanography educator, biogeologist, researcher*
Hamilton, John McFarland *plastic surgeon, real estate developer*
Harkleroad, Ashley *professional tennis player*
Harrell, Roy G., Jr., *lawyer*
Henniger, David Thomas *lawyer*
Hooker, Robert Wright *journalist*
Hsu, Tsong Han *chemist, researcher*
Hudkins, John W. *lawyer*
Hungate, Mark Edward *lawyer*
Hurley, John Kenneth *real estate and merchant banking executive*
Jacob, Bruce Robert *law educator*
James, Thomas A. *investment company executive*
Johnson, Edna Ruth *editor*
Joyce, Walter Joseph *retired electronics company executive*
Julien, Jeffrey P. *investment company executive*
Keane, Michael J. *lawyer*
Keistler, Betty Lou *accountant, tax consultant*
Keller, Natasha Matrina Leonidow *nursing administrator*
Kent, Allen *library and information sciences educator*
Kerlin, Max L. *academic administrator*
Kiefner, John Robert, Jr., *lawyer, educator*
Korpan, Richard *energy executive*
Kubiet, Leo Lawrence *newspaper advertising and marketing executive*
Kuttler, Carl Martin, Jr., *academic administrator*
Lacson, Atilano G. *pathologist*
Lamar, William Fred *chaplain, educator*
Lang, Joseph Hagedorn *lawyer*
Larach, Fernando C. *rheumatologist, researcher*

Leavell, William A. *publisher, editor*
Lewis, Chris A. *manufacturing executive*
Linhart, Joseph Wayland *retired cardiologist, educational administrator*
Main, Timothy L. *electronics executive*
Mann, Sam Henry, Jr., *lawyer*
Martin, Susan Taylor *newspaper editor*
Martinez, Tino *professional baseball player*
McGriff, Fred (Frederick Stanley McGriff) *professional baseball player*
McKeown, H. Mary *lawyer, law educator*
McNeill, Felita Gale *nurse, military officer*
Meyer, Robert Allen *human resource management educator*
Mills, William Harold, Jr., *construction company executive*
Mondello, Mark T. *manufacturing executive*
Moody, Lizabeth Ann *lawyer, educator*
Morean, William D. *manufacturing executive*
Mueller, O. Thomas *molecular geneticist, pediatrics educator*
Naimoli, Vincent Joseph *diversified operating and holding company executive*
Naughton, James Martin *journalist*
Nichols, Katie *investment company executive*
Nunn, Margaret Baker *owner boutique*
Nussbaum, Leo Lester *retired college president, consultant*
Pardoll, Peter Michael *gastroenterologist*
Patterson, Eugene Corbett *retired editor, publisher*
Petty, Marty *publishing executive*
Pflum, William John *physician*
Piniella, Louis Victor *professional baseball team manager*
Pittman, Robert Turner *retired newspaper editor*
Price-Smith, Andrew Thomas *social sciences educator, consultant*
Putnam, J. Stephen *financial executive*
Quiroga, Alicia Espinosa *physiatrist*
Reeves, Samantha *professional tennis player*
Rigg, Carol Margaret Elizabeth Ruth *calligrapher, graphics designer, art educator*
Roney, Paul H(itch) *federal judge*
Root, Allen William *pediatrician, educator*
Rosenblum, Martin Jerome *ophthalmologist*
Ross, Howard Philip *lawyer*
Rummel, Harold Edwin *real estate development and retail sales executive*
Rydstrom, Carlton Lionel *chemist, chemicals consultant*
Schmidt, Paul Joseph *physician, educator*
Schrader, Daryl Lynn *mathematician, educator*
Scott, Lee Hansen *retired holding company executive*
Sebastien, Anya Celita *academic administrator, consultant*
Sharapova, Maria *professional tennis player*
Shaughnessy, Meghann *professional tennis player*
Shuck, Robert F. *financial executive*
Simpson, Lisa Ann *physician, educator*
Southworth, William Dixon *retired education educator*
Stedman, R VanGorden *artist, art historian radio and television personality*
Tash, Paul Clifford *editor, publishing executive*
Vaughn, Gregory Lamont *professional baseball player*
Walker, Brigitte Maria *translator, linguistic consultant*
Wasserman, Susan Valesky *accountant, artist, yoga instructor*
Wedding, Charles Randolph *architect*
Wetzel, Laura Reiser *educator*
White, June Miller *mathematics professor, educational consultant*
Williams, Yvonne G. *corporate trainer*
Wilson, Paul *professional baseball player*
Woodard, Joseph Lamar *law librarian, law educator*
Zimmer, Donald William *professional baseball coach, former professional baseball manager*

Saint Petersburg Beach
Bradshaw, John Robert Covington, III, *internet service company executive*
Garnett, Stanley Iredale, II, *lawyer, utility company executive*
Hurley, Frank Thomas, Jr., *realtor*
Milham, Julee Lynn *lawyer, arbitrator, mediator*

Sanford
Dickison, Alexander Kane *physical science educator*
Oostwouder, Peter Henry *family physician*
Scott, Mellouise Jacqueline *retired media specialist*
Tossi, Alice Louise *special education educator*

Sanibel
Ball, Armand Baer *former association executive, consultant*
Brodbeck, William Jan *marketing consultant, speaker*
Crown, David Allan *criminologist, educator*
Davie, Joseph Myrten *physician, pathology and immunology educator, science administrator*
Hasselman, Richard B. *retired transportation company executive*
Ray, Charles Albert *photojournalist*
Rothschild, Donald Phillip *retired lawyer, arbitrator*

Santa Rosa Beach
Rees, Lane Charles *industrial relations consultant*

Sarasota
Allen, George Howard *publishing management consultant*
Altabe, Joan Augusta Berg *artist, writer, art and architecture critic*
Arreola, John Bradley *financial planner*
Atwell, Robert Herron *higher education executive*
Bailey, Robert Elliott *financial executive*
Balliett, John William *entrepreneur, real estate executive*
Bausch, James John *foundation executive*
Beck, Robert Alfred *hotel administration educator*
Benowitz, June Melby *historian, educator*
Berkoff, Charles Edward *pharmaceutical executive*
Berman, Lewis Paul *financial executive*
Best, Jerry Lavon *insurance consultant*
Blomgren, Bruce Holmes *real estate developer, marina developer, consultant*
Boersma, Lawrence Allan (Larry Allan) *animal welfare administrator, photographer*
Bowers, Charles Richard *surgeon*
Brandhorst, Wesley Theodore *retired information scientist*
Bushey, Alan Scott *retired insurance holding company executive*
Carr, Patricia Ann *community health nurse*
Cavanagh, Denis *gynecologist, obstetrician, educator, gynecological oncologist*
Christ-Janer, Arland Frederick *college president*
Christopher, William Garth *lawyer*
Clark, Eugenie *zoologist, educator*
Clarke, Garvey Elliott *lawyer*
Cleland, Sherrill *college president*
Close, Michael John *property manager, lawyer*
Cooper, William Ewing, Jr., *retired army officer*
Coufoudakis, Van *political science educator*
Cramer, Stanley Howard *psychology educator, author*
Culkin, Charles Walker, Jr., *retired trade association administrator*
Cummings, Martin Marc *retired medical educator, physician, scientific administrator*
Daoust, Donald Roger *pharmaceutical and toiletries company executive, microbiologist*
De Gennaro, Richard *retired library director, library advisor*
Deutsch, Sid *bioengineer, educator*
Dobosz, Mark Joseph *fundraiser*
Drake, Diana Ashley *retired financial planner*
Dungy, Kathryn R. *humanities educator*
Ehrlich, Bernard Herbert *lawyer, association executive*
El Shahawy, Mahfouz *internist, cardiologist, educator*
Feder, Allan Appel *management executive, consultant*
Fendrick, Alan Burton *retired advertising executive*
Garland, Richard Roger *lawyer*
Gauch, Eugene William, Jr., *retired air force officer*
Geithner, Paul Herman, Jr., *retired banker*
Giordano, David Alfred *retired internist, gastroenterologist*
Gittelson, Bernard *public relations consultant, author, lecturer*
Gladding, Nicholas C. *lawyer*
Goodman, Tracy Annette *financial consultant*
Gordon, Sanford Daniel *economics professor*
Graham, Douglass of Montrose *museum curator, banker, artist, poet*
Green, Karen Danielle *psychotherapist*
Greenfield, Bruce Harold *lawyer, merchant banker*
Greenfield, Robert Kauffman *retired lawyer*
Halladay, Laurie Ann *public relations consultant, former franchise executive*
Hamberg, Daniel *economist, educator*
Harmon, Foster (Loren Foster Harmon) *arts consultant*
Harris, Judith Ann White *health occupations vocational educator, nurse*
Hartman, Karen Marie *municipal official*
Harvey, Donald Phillips *retired naval officer*
Heiser, Rolland Valentine *former army officer, foundation executive*
Hilt, Thomas Harry *minister*
Hoffman, Oscar Allen *retired forest products company executive*
Huff, Russell Joseph *public relations and publishing executive*
Hughes, Allen *music critic*
Hull, J(ames) Richard *retired lawyer, business executive*
Hummel, Dana D. Mallett *librarian*
Iverson, Robert Louis, Jr., *internist, physician*
Jacobson, Jeanne McKee *humanities educator, writer*
James, C. Shelton *electronics company executive*
Janney, Oliver James *lawyer, plastics and semiconductor company executive*
Jelks, Mary Larson *retired pediatrician*
Jones, Sally Daviess Pickrell *writer*
Jones, Tracey Kirk, Jr., *retired minister, educator*
Kane, Stanley Bruce *food products executive*
Kelly, John Love *public relations executive*
Kerker, Milton *chemistry professor*
Kimbrough, Robert Averyt *lawyer*
Landis, Edgar David *business consultant*
Larsen, Lawrence Bernard, Jr., *priest, pastoral psychotherapist*
Lee, Nancy Ranck *management consultant*
Lengyel, Alfonz *art history, archeology and museology educator*
Levitt, Jaren *real estate corporation officer*
Levy, Gerhard *pharmacologist*
Long, Robert Radcliffe *fluid mechanics educator*
Magenheim, Mark Joseph *physician, epidemiologist, educator*
Mahadevan, Kumar *marine laboratory administrator, researcher*
Makau, John *artist*
Marino, Eugene Louis *publishing company executive*
Marks, Charles *surgeon, educator*
Martia, Dominic Francis *academic administrator*
Masters, John Christopher *psychologist, educator, writer*
Mattran, Donald Albert *management consultant, educator*
McCollum, John Morris *tenor*
McDonald, Peggy Ann Stimmel *retired automobile company official*
McFarlin, Diane Hooten *publisher*
Metzger, Sidney *retired communications engineer*
Meyer, B. Fred *small business executive, home designer and builder, product designer*
Michejda, Oskar *civil engineer, structural engineer, consultant*
Middleton, Norman Graham *social worker, psychotherapist*
Miles, Arthur J. *financial planner, consultant*
Miranda, Carlos Sa *food products company executive*
Mitchell, John Noyes, Jr., *retired electrical engineer*
Mizer, Joyce Taylor *music educator*
Morris, Gordon James *financial company executive, consultant*
Morrow, William Earl *retired government official*
Mullane, John Francis *pharmaceutical company executive*
Neeley, Delmar George *mediator, pastoral counselor*
North, Marjorie Mary *columnist*
O'Connor, Sylvia Cannon *association legislative liaison, analyst, retired*
O'Malley, Thomas Anthony *gastroenterologist, internist*
Partoyan, Garo Arakel *lawyer*
Pender, Michael Roger *engineering consultant*
Phillips, Howard William *investment banker*
Pierce, Richard Harry *oceanographer*
Plunket, Dolores *art and archaeology educator*
Proffitt, Waldo, Jr., *newspaper editor*
Raimi, Burton Louis *lawyer*
Ramsier, Paul *composer, psychotherapist*
Retzer, Mary Elizabeth Helm *retired librarian*
Ross, Gerald Fred *engineering executive, researcher*
Roth, James Frank *manufacturing company executive, chemist*
Ruva, Christine Lorraine *psychologist, educator*
Salomone, William Gerald *lawyer*
Sarakatsannis, Leonidas Nicholas *musician, concert pianist, music educator, composer, conductor*
Schlegel, John Frederick *management consultant, speaker*
Schoenhals, Katherine Viola *social worker*
Schwartz, Francis *music educator, composer*
Scott, Charles Francis *health facility administrator*
Seibert, Russell Jacob *botanist, research associate*
Serrie, Hendrick *retired anthropology and international business educator*
Shulman, Arthur *communications executive*
Simon, Joseph Patrick *food services executive*
Slocum, Donald Hillman *product development executive*
Smith, Mark Hallard *architect*
Snyder, Lee Daniel *historian, educator*
Spencer, Lonabelle (Kappie Spencer) *political agency administrator, lobbyist*
Stevens, Elisabeth Goss (Mrs. Robert Schleussner Jr.) *writer, journalist, graphic artist*
Stevens, Leonard Berry *educational consultant*
Stickler, Daniel Lee *health care management consultant*
Straight, Elsie Hosking *retired art librarian, sculptor*
Sturtevant, Ruthann Patterson *anatomy educator*
Taplin, Winn Lowell *historian, retired senior intelligence operations officer*
Tennant, Diane P. *editor*
Thompson, Annie Figueroa *retired academic director, educator*
Torrey, Richard Frank *utility executive*
Tucci, Steven Michael *health facility administrator, physician, recording industry executive*
Venit, William Bennett *electrical products company executive, consultant*
Wadsworth, Dyer Seymour *retired lawyer*
Weeks, Albert Loren *author, educator, journalist*
Welch, John Dana *retired urologist*
West, Bob *pharmaceutical executive*
Wetenhall, John *museum director*
Wetstone, Janet Meyerson *designer, journalist*
Whitbeck, Roger James *scriptwriter, lyricist*
Wilson, Kenneth Jay *writer*
Zavon, Mitchell Ralph *occupational medicine physician*

Satellite Beach
Clark, John F. *aerospace research and engineering educator*
Covault, Craig *editor*
Loney, Mary Rose *former airport administrator, aviation industry consultant*
Van Arsdall, Robert Armes *engineer, retired air force officer*

Sebastian
Mauke, Otto Russell *retired college president*
Pieper, Patricia Rita *artist*

Sebring
DeWitt, Carol A. *publishing executive, writer*
Ibrahim, George W. *physician, health facility administrator*
McCollum, James Fountain *lawyer*
Sherrick, Daniel Noah *real estate broker*
Weimer, Peter Dwight *retired mediator, lawyer, corporate executive*

Seffner
Seaman, Jeffrey *consumer products company executive*

Seminole
Evans, Thomas Passmore *management consultant*
Wolf, Elizabeth Ann *writer, storyteller, visual arts*

Shalimar
Chesser, David Michael *lawyer*

Singer Island
Tremain, Alan *hotel executive*

Sneads
Scott, Brenda D. *writer*

South Florida
Hoffman, Randy Michael *automotive executive*

South Miami
Bauman, Sandra Spiegel *nurse practitioner, mental health counselor*
Keedy, Christian David *lawyer*

Sparr
Tovi, Murray *futurist, research scientist*

Spring Hill
Burnim, Kalman Aaron *theatre educator emeritus*
Hopkins, Thomas Charles *behavior specialist*
Martin, Gary J. *retired business executive, mayor*
Rojas, Victor Hugo Macedo *retired vocational education educator*
Vanderburg, Paul Stacey *insurance executive, consultant*
Wood, Shelton Eugene *education educator, consultant, minister*

Stuart
Ankrom, Charles Franklin *golf course architect, consultant*
Bygate, Wayne Ian *controller*
Cocoves, Anita Petzold *psychotherapist*
Delagi, Edward Francis *physician, retired educator*
Dimbath, Merle F. *economic consultant, business educator*
Donohue, Edith M. *human resources specialist, educator*
Gary, Willie E. *lawyer*
Geng, Lisa Fernandez *artist*
Jaffe, Jeff Hugh *retired food products executive*
Laska, Paul Robert *protective services official, writer, educator*
Leibson, Irving *retired industrial executive*
Logan, Henry Vincent *transportation executive, consultant*
Maktouf, Samir *education company executive*
Maldonado, Carlos Manuel *surgeon*
McKenna, Sidney F. *retired technical company executive*
Patterson, Robert Arthur *physician, health care consultant, retired health care company executive, retired air force officer*
Perron, Brandon Alan *private investigator, director*
Riordan, James Quentin *retired company executive*
Robinson, Michael Hill *retired zoological park director, biologist*

Summerfield
McNulty, Carrell Stewart, Jr., *retired manufacturing company executive, architect*
Shaw, Danny Wayne *educational consultant, musician*

Summerland Key
Dallas, Joseph Anthony, Jr., *music educator*
Muth, John Fraser *economics professor*

Sun City Center
Ballard, Mildred Louise *retired adult nurse practitioner*
Crow, Harold Eugene *physician, family medicine educator*
Edwards, Paul Beverly *retired science and engineering educator*
Fuller, Samuel Ashby *retired lawyer, mining company executive*
Gummere, Walter Cooper *educator, consultant*
Hall, John Fry *retired psychologist*
Jeffries, Robert Joseph *retired engineer, educator, business executive*
Leonard, William Norris *economist, educator*
McGrath, John Francis *retired utilities executive*
Rubin, Robert Jay *toxicologist*
Ward, Jacqueline Ann Beas *nurse, healthcare administrator*

Sunny Isles Beach
Brunetto, Frank *electrical engineer*
Edelcup, Norman Scott *management and financial consultant*

Sunrise
Bainton, Donald J. *diversified manufacturing company executive*
Keenan, Michael E. *professional hockey team executive*
Larionov, Igor *professional hockey player*
Luongo, Roberto *professional hockey player*
Ozolinsh, Sandis *professional hockey player*
Sorensen, Allan Chresten *service company executive*
Stalker, Jacqueline D'Aoust *academic administrator, educator*
Torrey, William Arthur *professional hockey team executive*
Worrell, Peter *professional hockey player*

Tallahassee
AbdelRazig, Yassir A. *engineering educator*
Abele, Lawrence Gordon *biology professor, dean, academic administrator*
Alderman, Silvia Morell *lawyer*
Anstead, Harry Lee *state supreme court justice*
Argenziano, Nancy *state legislator*
Ash, Jim C. *news service executive*
Ashler, Philip Frederic *international trade and development advisor*
Aurell, John Karl *lawyer*
Bagley, James Robert *freelance writer*
Bailey, Theresa L. *director, consultant*
Barnett, Martha Walters *lawyer*
Bartlett, Richard Adams *retired history professor*
Bell, Kenneth B. *judge*
Betancourt, Annie *state legislator*
Bird, Mark Douglas *magnet designer, engineering researcher*
Blanton, Faye Wester *legislative official*
Bloom, Elaine *state legislator*
Bowden, Bobby *college football coach*
Boyd, Janegale *state legislator*
Boyd, Joseph Arthur, Jr., *lawyer*
Brady, Terrie *political organization executive*
Bucuvalas, Tina *folklorist*
Buford, Barbara Fest *retired state agency employee*
Burkman, Ernest, Jr., *education educator*
Burnette, Ada M. Puryear *retired educational administrator*
Burt, Locke *state legislator, insurance company executive*
Bush, John Ellis (Jeb Bush) *governor*
Butler, Robert Olen *writer, educator*
Byrd, Johnnie, Jr., *state legislator*
Campbell, Frances Harvell *educational association administrator*
Cantero, Raoul G., III, *judge*
Carlton, Lisa *state legislator*
Carson, Leonard Allen *lawyer*
Choppin, Gregory Robert *chemistry professor*
Cobbe, James Hamilton *economics professor*
Coloney, Wayne Herndon *civil engineer*
Conaway, Charles William *information scientist, educator*
Conti, Lisa Ann *epidemiologist, veterinarian*
Cowin, Anna P. *state legislator, educator*
Crist, Charles (Charlie Crist) *state attorney general*
Cronin, Jerome Joseph, Jr., *marketing educator, consultant*
Cummings, Frederic Alan *lawyer*
Curtin, Lawrence N. *lawyer*
Dadisman, Joseph Carrol *newspaper executive*
D'Alemberte, Talbot (Sandy D'Alemberte) *academic administrator, lawyer*
Dariotis, Terrence Theodore *lawyer*
Davis, Bertram Hylton *retired English educator*
Davis, Larry Michael *air force officer, healthcare manager, consultant*
Deal, Charles Raymond *anesthesiologist*
DeFoor, J. Allison, II, *lawyer*
De Forest, Sherwood Searle *agricultural engineer, agribusiness services executive*
Dinnen, Maureen *educational association administrator, educator*
Dockery, Paula *state legislator*
Dorn, Charles Meeker *art education educator*

Studer, William Allen *county official*
Sullebarger, John Thompson *internist, cardiologist, educator*
Sullivan, Joseph Peter *risk and insurance management consultant*
Szonntagh, Eugene L. *chemical engineer, chemist, hygienist, educator, archaeometrist, musicologist, organist, historian*
Tanzer, Jed Samuel *lawyer, financial consultant*
Taylor, Thomas S. *diversified financial services company executive*
Thelen, Gil *newspaper publisher*
Thomas, Gregg Darrow *lawyer*
Thomas, Wayne Lee *lawyer*
Tortorella, John *professional athletics coach*
Tully, Darrow *newspaper publisher*
Turner, Stephen Park *philosopher, sociologist, educator*
VanButsel, Michael R. *real estate broker, builder and developer*
Vanden, Harry Edwin *political science educator*
Vogt, Martha Diane *lawyer*
Wade, Thomas Edward *electrical engineering educator, university research administrator*
Wagner, Frederick William (Bill Wagner) *lawyer*
Waller, Edward Martin, Jr., *lawyer*
Walling, Arthur Knight *orthopedist*
Watkins, Joan Marie *osteopath, occupational medicine physician*
Weaver, Janet S. *newspaper editor*
Weaver, Steven M. *publishing executive*
Weiner, Irving Bernard *psychologist*
West, Benjamin B. *advertising executive*
Westcott, Joan Clark *poet*
Whatley, Jacqueline Beltram *lawyer*
Wilson, Charles Reginald *federal judge*
Witwer, Bruce *former newspaper editor*
Wyman, Richard Thomas *information services consultant*
Yerrid, C. Steven *lawyer*
Young, Gwynne A. *lawyer*
Zell, Samuel *transportation leasing company executive*
Zhu, Yiliang *research scientist, educator*
Ziegler, Robert Oliver *retired music and special education educator*

Tarpon Springs
Byrne, Richard Hill *counselor, educator*
Crismond, Linda Fry *public relations executive*
Georgiou, Ruth Schwab *retired social worker*
Johnson, Randall Clyde *mortgage banker*
Leisner, Anthony Baker *publishing company executive*
Mueller, Willys Francis, Jr., *retired pathologist*
Pittman, Roy Clinton, Jr., *neurosurgeon, lawyer, theologian, philospher*

Tavares
Gross, Paul Allan *health service executive*
Kaiser, Robert Lee *retired engineering executive*

Tavernier
Fundora, Thomas *artist, journalist, composer*

Temple Terrace
Kashdin, Gladys Shafran *painter, educator*
Rink, Wesley Winfred *retired bank executive*

Tequesta
Larson, Edythe K. *science educator*
Peterson, James Robert *retired writing instrument manufacturing executive*
Ragno, Nancy Nickell *educational writer*
Seal, John S., Jr., *manufacturing executive, consultant*
Swets, John Arthur *psychologist, researcher*
Turrell, Richard Horton, Sr., *banker*

The Villages
Oetjen, David L. (Jon David Douglas) *writer, film producer*
Phillips, Patricia Jeanne *retired school system administrator*

Tierra Verde
Gaffney, Thomas Francis *private investor*
Schmitz, Dolores Jean *primary education educator*

Titusville
Arnold, Arthur Joseph *writer, journalist*
Arnold, Betty Bunnell *secondary school educator*
Jackson, Philip Irving *literature educator, writer*
Morton, Craig Richard *real estate investor*
Stewart, David Witherington *aerospace engineer*
VanBrode, Derrick Brent, IV, *trade association administrator*

Treasure Island
Dunn, Craig Andrew *entertainer, conductor, composer, writer, educator*
Hemadeh, Ossama Sharif *surgeon*

Trenton
Ivey, James Frederick, Jr., *physician, health facility administrator*

Trinity
Donataccio, Dean Michael *music educator, secondary school educator*

Tyndall AFB
Arnold, Larry Keith *major general United States Air Force*

Umatilla
Balandran, Stella Varona *interpreter, lyricist, composer, writer*

University Park
Compain, Rita *librarian*
Wurlitzer, Fred Pabst *surgeon*

Valrico
Melconian, Jerry Ohanes *engineering executive*
Straub, Susan Monica *special education educator*

Venice
Barnhart, Charles Elmer *animal sciences educator*
Barritt, Evelyn Ruth Berryman *nurse, educator, dean*
Brott, Irving Deerin, Jr., *lawyer, judge*
Corrigan, William Thomas *retired broadcast news executive*
Delaney, Robert Finley *columnist, political sociologist, lecturer*
Feldmann, Edward George *pharmaceutical chemist, pharmacologist*
Finlay, Susan Sparling *education educator*
Gabriele, Charles *composer, educator*
Girman, Dee-Marie *iconographer, artist*
Gooding, Charles Thomas *psychology educator, retired college provost*
Hackett, Edward Vincent *investment research company executive*
Harrington, John Vincent *retired communications company executive, engineer, educator*
Hrachovina, Frederick Vincent *osteopathic physician and surgeon*
Kater, Victor Ricardo *marketing professional, writer, economist*
Kleinlein, Kathy Lynn *training and development executive*
Lanford, Luke Dean *retired electronics company executive*
Miller, Allan John *lawyer*
Nevins, John J. *bishop*
Peterson, Francis *physicist, educator*
Przemieniecki, Janusz Stanislaw *engineering executive, former government senior executive and college dean*
Slate, Floyd Owen *retired engineering educator*
Tafel, Edgar *architect*
Tausan, Carol A. *music educator*

Vero Beach
Ahrensfeld, Thomas Frederick *retired lawyer*
Allik, Michael *diversified industry executive*
Bennett, Jack Franklin *oil company executive*
Beran, Denis Carl *publisher*
Billeci, Andre George *art educator, sculptor*
Binney, Jan Jarrell *publishing executive*
Burton, Arthur Henry, Jr., *insurance company executive*
Cartwright, Alton Stuart *electrical manufacturing company executive*
Case, Douglas Manning *lawyer*
Christopher, Robert Paul *retired physical medicine and rehabilitation physician, educator*
Clawson, John Addison *financier, investor*
Cochrane, William Henry *former city official*
Conway, Earl Cranston *business educator, retired manufacturing company executive*
Danforth, Arthur Edwards *finance executive*
Feagles, Robert West *retired insurance company executive*
Fetter, Robert Barclay *retired administrative sciences educator*
Fisher, Andrew *management consultant*
Fitzgeorge, Harold James *former oil and gas company executive*
Freeman, Donald Wilford *real estate developer, horse breeder*
Gedeon, Lucinda Heyel *museum director*
Gibson, James Elliot *architect*
Glassmeyer, Edward *investment banker*
Gordon, William Stout *lawyer*
Ingwersen, Martin Lewis *water transportation executive*
Janicki, Robert Stephen *retired pharmaceutical executive*
Kenrich, John Lewis *retired lawyer*
Koontz, Alfred Joseph, Jr., *financial and operating management executive, consultant*
Kornicks, Margot Susan *nursing administrator*
Lagin, Neil *landscape designer, consultant*
Lamoureux, William Albert *poet*
Leonsis, Ted *media executive*
Massey, Howard Clayland *writer*
McNamara, John J(oseph) *advertising executive, writer*
Menk, Carl William *executive search company executive*
Nesbit, Robert Grover *management consultant*
Nichols, Carl Wheeler *retired advertising agency executive*
Parkyn, John William *editor, writer, columnist*
Proctor, William Gilbert, Jr., *writer*
Reed, Sherman Kennedy *chemical consultant*
Riefler, Donald Brown *financial consultant*
Satuloff, Barth *accounting executive, dispute resolution professional, investment strategist, publisher*
Schwarz, Berthold Eric *psychiatrist*
Simon, Donald John *employee benefits administrator, insurance and investment broker*
Spivak, Alvin A. *retired public relations executive*
Sprout, Francis *artist, educator*
Standish, John Spencer *textile manufacturing company executive*
Wilcox, Harry Wilbur, Jr., *retired corporate executive*

Viera
Rainwater, Tonya B. *judge*

Village Of Golf
Boer, F. Peter *chemical company executive*

Weeki Wachee
Finney, Roy Pelham, Jr., *urologist, surgeon, inventor*
Jernstrom, Joan *retired secondary school educator*
Luffsey, Walter Stith *air transportation executive, consultant*

Wellington
Beck, Jan Scott *lawyer*
Fitch, Mary Killeen *human resources specialist*
Guillama-Alvarez, Noel Jesus *merchant banker, healthcare executive*
Lane, Brian M. *management executive*
Smith, Robert Clinton *former senator*

Wesley Chapel
Mendelsohn, Louis Benjamin *financial analyst*
Revelle, Donald Gene *manufacturing and health care company executive, consultant*

West Melbourne
Grenevicki, Lance Francis *surgeon*
Vance, Jimie A. *dentist*

West Palm Beach
Aaron, M. Robert *electrical engineer*
Addison, Ferguson Lofton Lightbourne *retired bank executive*
Arzoumanidis, Gregory G. *chemist*
Beall, Kenneth Sutter, Jr., *lawyer*
Beasley, James W., Jr., *lawyer*
Bergmann, Arthur M. *writer, former county official, former newspaperman*
Bernhardt, Marcia Brenda *mental health counselor*
Bezerra, Márcio *musician, educator*
Bohn, Barbara Ann *retired laboratory director*
Brams, Jeffrey Brent *lawyer*
Brown, Paul A. *physician, business executive*
Brumback, Clarence Landen *physician*
Chopin, L. Frank *lawyer*
Chopin, Susan Gardiner *lawyer*
Clark, David William *lawyer, councilman*
Coloso, Victor Francisco *pediatrician*
Conrad, Bette Anne Kester *lawyer, writer, minister*
Coppock, Mark Stephen *not-for-profit fundraiser*
Corts, Paul Richard *college president*
Craft, Jerome Walter *plastic surgeon, health facility administrator*
Damsel, Charles H., Jr., *lawyer*
Darter, Jeffrey Allen *data processing professional*
Davis, Paul B. *retired mechanical engineer, civil engineer*
Diasio, Richard Leonard *power transmission executive, sports facility executive, race car manufacturer executive*
Doto, Paul Jerome *retired accountant*
Dye, Thomas Roy *political science educator*
Eppley, Roland Raymond, Jr., *retired financial services executive*
Escalante, Juan *performing company executive*
Farina, John *lawyer*
Fisher, Fenimore *business development consultant*
Goetz, Cecelia Helen *lawyer, retired judge*
Gold, Bela *economist, educator*
Grogan, Robert Harris *lawyer*
Gronlund, Robert B. *art collector, fund raising consultant*
Hale, Marie Stoner *artistic director*
Henry, Rene Arthur *author, consultant*
Herrick, John Dennis *financial consultant, former law firm executive, retired food products executive*
Hill, Thomas William, Jr., *lawyer, educator*
Jenkins, Ruben Lee *retired chemical company executive, lawyer*
Johnson, Martin Allen *publisher, artist*
Johnson, Samira El-Chehabi *marketing professional*
Kamen, Michael Andrew *lawyer*
Kapnick, S. Jason *oncologist*
Kiely, Dan Ray *telecommunications and banking consultant*
King, Robert Howard *marketing professional*
Koch, William I. *energy company executive*
Lacey, John William Charles *management consultant*
Laing, Robert Scott *lawyer*
Layman, David Michael *lawyer*
Lichtstein, Daniel M. *medical educator*
Livingstone, John Leslie *accountant, management consultant, business economist, educator*
Longhofer, Gordan Allen *art educator, performance artist*
Lozito, Gilda Lelia *artist, painter*
Marshall-Beasley, Elizabeth *landscape architect*
McCluskey, Neil Gerard *gerontologist, educator, literary agent*
Mims, Lloyd Lee *dean, conductor, vocalist*
Montgomery, Robert Morel, Jr., *lawyer*
Moore, George Crawford Jackson *lawyer*
Mrachek, Lorin Louis *lawyer*
Newmark, Emanuel *ophthalmologist*
Nolan, Richard Thomas *clergyman, educator*
Orlovsky, Donald Albert *lawyer*
Orr-Cahall, Christina *art museum director, art historian*
Passy, Charles *arts critic*
Pedersen, Paul Mark *sportswriter, educator, columnist*
Phillips, Kenneth Wayne *music educator*
Pottash, A. Carter *psychiatrist, hospital executive*
Robinson, Raymond Edwin *conductor, music educator, writer*
Ronan, William John *management consultant*
Rosen, Marvin Shelby *lawyer*
Ross, Edward Joseph *architect*
Royce, Raymond Watson *lawyer, rancher, citrus grower, invester*
Rukeyser, M. S., Jr., *television consultant, writer*
Ryskamp, Kenneth Lee *federal judge*
Sander, Dorothy E. *manufacturing executive*
Scarola, John *lawyer*
Sears, Edward Milner, Jr., *newspaper editor*
Smith, David Shiverick *lawyer, former ambassador*
Stambaugh, Reginald Jack *ophthalmologist*
Stauderman, Bruce Ford *writer, advertising executive*
Terwillegar, Jane Cusack *librarian, educator*
Thomashow, Steven Roy *military officer, intelligence officer*
Uzan, Bernard *artistic director*
Vecellio, Leo Arthur, Jr., *construction company executive*
Vilchez, Victoria Anne *lawyer*
Westman, Steven Ronald *rabbi*
Whitfield, Graham Frank *orthopedic surgeon*
Wisnicki, Jeffrey Leonard *plastic surgeon*
Wroble, Arthur Gerard *judge*

Weston
Barnes, William Douglas *advertising executive*
Cornell, G(eorge) Ware, Jr., *lawyer*
Galvez-Jimenez, Nestor *neurologist*
Gonzalez, Juan Guillermo *electrical engineer*
Holtzman, Gary Yale *retired administrative and financial executive*
Kniskern, Joseph Warren *lawyer*
Malave, Andres *pharmacologist, educator*
McAuliffe, John Anthony *hand surgeon*
Messa, Charles Angelo, III, *plastic surgeon*
Napp, Gudrun F. *artist*
Nogueras, Juan Jose *surgeon*
Staneart, Larry William *technology company marketing executive*
Weiss, Eric Glenn *physician*
Zlatkin, Michael Brian *physician*

Wewahitchka
Stryker, Terence Wayne *secondary school educator*

Wilton Manors
Kaufmann, Vicki Marie *social services administrator*

Wimauma
Palmer, Louis Thomas *pathologist*

Windermere
Garner, Jay Montgomery *former career officer*
Russell, Robert Leonard *professional association executive*

Winter Garden
Gillet, Pamela Kipping *special education educator*

Winter Haven
Benton, Obie Folsom *publishing executive, writer*
Burns, Arthur Lee *architect*
Cover, Norman Bernard *retired electronic data processing administrator*
Grierson, William *retired agricultural educator*
Honer, Richard Joseph *surgeon*
Johnson, Gordon Selby *consulting electrical engineer*
Peck, Maryly VanLeer *retired academic administrator, chemical engineer*
Porter, Howard Leonard, III, *health and education policy consultant*
Warner, Nelson Alfred *dermatologist*

Winter Park
Acierno, Louis Joseph *medical educator*
Alon, Ilan *international business educator*
Baker, James L., Jr., *plastic surgeon*
Benedict, Dorothy Jones *genealogist, researcher*
Bornstein, Rita *academic administrator*
Builder, J. Lindsay, Jr., *lawyer*
Farris, Michael R. *pharmaceutical executive*
Fluno, John Arthur *entomologist, consultant*
Godbold, Gene Hamilton *lawyer*
Graham, Bruce Joseph *retired judge*
Granberry, Edwin Phillips, Jr., *safety engineer, consultant*
Hadley, Ralph Vincent, III, *lawyer*
Heinle, Richard Alan *lawyer*
Helms, Roger D. *lawyer*
Hughes, David Henry *manufacturing executive*
Jernigan, Donald *hospital administrator*
Johnson, Kraig Nelson *lawyer, arbitrator, mediator*
Kerr, James Wilson *engineer*
Kincaid, Rodney Lyle *construction company executive*
Kindlund, Newton Carlton *retail executive*
Kost, Wayne L. *manufacturing executive*
Kraft, Kenneth Houston, Jr., *insurance agency executive*
Mason, Aimee Hunnicutt Romberger *retired philosophy and humanities educator*
Matulich, Serge *accounting educator, author*
McKean, Thomas Wayne *dentist, retired military officer*
Myers, Norman Lewis *fund development consultant*
Olsson, Nils William *former association executive*
Pearson, R. Scott *investment advisor, editor*
Pineless, Hal Steven *neurologist*
Powers, Ronald George *management consultant*
Rawa, Mannee Jean *writer*
Rogers, Rutherford David *librarian*
Safian, Shelley Carole *advertising executive*
Seymour, Thaddeus *English educator*
Sinclair, Gail D. *education educator*
Spake, Ned Bernarr *energy company executive*
Strawn, Frances Freeland *real estate executive*
Swan, Richard Gordon *retired mathematics educator*
Therrien, Francois Xavier, Jr., *business and tax consultant*
Wagner, Lynn Edward *lawyer*
Werner, Thomas Lee *hospital administrator*
Wilson, Cecil Bruce *internist*
Wilson, Robley Conant, Jr., *English educator, editor, author*

Winter Springs
McKinney, Frank *music educator*
San Miguel, Manuel *painter, historian, composer, poet, art collector*
San Miguel, Sandra Bonilla *social worker*

Yalaha
Searcy, Dorothy James *missionary*

Zephyrhills
Barron, Ilona Eleanor *reading educator, consultant*

GEORGIA

Acworth
Perry, Randall A. *business executive*

Albany
Coats-Hardy, Janice Ellen *counseling administrator, educator*
Ellis, Mark E. *school librarian*
Erhardt, Walter L., Jr., *medical association administrator*
Keith, Carolyn Austin *secondary school counselor*
Marbury, Ritchey McGuire, III, *engineering executive, surveyor*
Revills, Isaiah *minister*
Robinson, J. Mack *communications executive*
Rodriguez, Sergio Raul *music educator, conductor*
Shields, Portia Holmes *academic administrator*
Stallworth, Charles Derotha, Jr., *psychologist*
Stanley-Chavis, Sandra Ornecia *special education educator, consultant*

Alpharetta
Balows, Albert *microbiologist, educator*
Bettis, Barry Phillip *lawyer*
Bickell, Cliff O. *financial company executive*
Bolton, Robin Jean *artist, painter*
Brands, James Edwin *medical products executive*
Braxton, Jerry W. *communications executive*
Charania, Barkat *real estate consultant*
Chatlen, Stanley Lee *logistics executive*
Cline, Stewart M. *real estate executive*
Cook, Richard C. *application developer*
Curling, Douglas *insurance company executive*
Deitrich, Wayne H. *manufacturing executive*
Desai, Hiren D. *software engineer*
Esher, Brian Richard *chief executive officer*

GEOGRAPHIC INDEX 5269 GEORGIA

Fowler, Vivian Delores *insurance company executive*
Greene, Melinda Jean *retail maintenance analyst*
Harris, James Herman *pathologist, neuropathologist, consultant, educator*
Heyman, John H. *energy executive*
Lademacher, Hartmut *computer software and services company executive*
Le Hetet, Jean-Pierre *paper company executive*
Malloy, William G. *entertainment company executive*
Marsella, Anthony Joseph *psychologist, educator*
McCormick, James K. *application developer*
McCullar, Michael D. *pastor*
McCullough, Ross A., Jr., *delivery service executive*
Minner, Thomas O. *marketing executive*
Mock, Melinda Smith *orthopedic nurse specialist, consultant*
Rettig, Terry *veterinarian, wildlife consultant, construction contractor*
Roberts, Paul C. *paper company executive*
Smith, Derek V. *risk management consultant*
Thomas, Robert L. *retired manufacturing company executive*
Thompson, Peter J. *manufacturing executive*
Travers, James M. *application developer*
Troop, Paul Melvin *public relations executive, journalist*
Watts, William David *corporate executive, business owner*
Weitz, John Jerome, Jr., *city planner*
White, Carl Edward, Jr., *pharmaceutical administrator*

Americus
Capitan, William Harry *university president emeritus*
Fuller, Millard Dean *charitable organization executive, lawyer*
Gonzalez, George G. *pastor*
Hooks, George Bardin *state legislator, insurance and real estate company executive*
Isaacs, Harold *history professor*
Nichols, Harold James *university dean*
Stanford, Henry King *college president*
Williams, David Anthony *not-for-profit executive*
Yemelyanov, Alexander M. *mathematician, educator*

Andersonville
Boyles, Frederick Holdren *historian*

Appling
Jones, Nancy Steed *small business owner*

Ashburn
Swygert, Leslie Ann *epidemiologist, consultant*

Athens
Adams, Michael Fred *university president, political communications specialist*
Agee, Warren Kendall *journalism educator*
Albersheim, Peter *biology professor*
Algeo, John Thomas *retired educator, association executive*
Allsbrook, Ogden Olmstead, Jr., *retired economics educator*
Andrews, Grover Jene *adult education educator, administrator*
Avise, John Charles *geneticist, educator*
Balashov, Yuri V. *philosophy educator*
Bargmann, Rolf Erwin *computer scientist, educator*
Beaird, James Ralph *law educator, dean*
Benson, P. George *dean, finance educator*
Bertsch, Gary Kenneth *political scientist, educator*
Black, Clanton Candler, Jr., *biochemistry educator, researcher*
Black, Marsha C. *environmental scientist*
Bowen, John Metcalf *pharmacologist, toxicologist, educator*
Carey, Katherine M. *theater educator*
Carlson, Ronald Lee *lawyer, educator*
Carnes, Jill Andrea *artist*
Carroll, Archie Benjamin, III, *finance educator*
Chaffin, Verner Franklin *lawyer, educator*
Chu, Chung Kwang *medicinal chemistry educator*
Clements, Robert Donald *sculptor*
Clute, Robert Eugene *political and social science educator*
Coley, Linda Marie *retired secondary school educator*
Criste, Mirla *theater educator, director, choreographer*
Crowley, John Francis, III, *university dean*
Darvill, Alan G. *biochemist, plant biologist, educator*
DeZurko, Edward Robert *retired art educator*
Dickerson, Harry Wilson, Jr., *veterinary microbiologist, educator*
Dishman, Rodney King *physical education educator*
Donovan, James M. *librarian, anthropologist*
Dunn, Delmer Delano *political science educator*
Eberhart, William Coile *apparel repair specialist, writer*
Ellington, Charles Ronald *lawyer, educator*
Feldman, Daniel Charles *adult education educator*
Feldman, Edmund Burke *art critic*
Fincher, Cameron Lane *psychology professor*
Garbin, Albeno Patrick *sociology educator*
Giles, Norman Henry *geneticist, science educator*
Golembiewski, Robert Thomas *educator, management consultant*
Gómez-Martinez, José Luis *Spanish language professional, researcher*
Gray, Elmer William *entomologist, consultant*
Greenman, John Frederick *newspaper executive*
Habiger, Eugene E. *retired career officer*
Hellerstein, Walter *lawyer*
Herbert, James Arthur *artist, filmmaker*
Herrman, Margaret Susan *university official, sociologist*
Houser, Ronald Edward *lawyer, arbitrator, mediator*
Huszagh, Fredrick Wickett *lawyer, educator, information management company executive*
Johnson, Michael Kenneth *chemistry professor*
Jurat-Fuentes, Juan Luis *entomologist, researcher*
Kamerschen, David Roy *economist, educator*
Kaufman, Glen Frank *art educator*
Kretzschmar, William Addison, Jr., *English language educator*
Kurtz, Paul Michael *law educator*
Larson, Edward John *law educator, lawyer, historian*
Longman, Stanley Vincent *retired performing arts educator*
Loux, Nicholas Thomas *chemist, researcher*
Lupis, Giuseppe *musician*
Lynch, James Walter *mathematician, educator*
Mace, Arnett Clay, Jr., *university administrator*
Maier, Robert J. *microbiologist, educator*
Mamatey, Victor Samuel *history educator*
Manoguerra, Paul Andrew *curator*
Marable, Robert Blane *secondary school educator, agricultural studies educator*
Marlar, John Thomas *environmental engineer*
Masters, Orlan Vincent Wade *gynecologist*
McCutcheon, Steven Clifton *environmental and ecological engineer, hydrologist*
Melton, Wayne Charles *real estate executive*
Meyer, Judy L. *science educator, director*
Meyers, Joseph Michael *biologist, researcher*
Miller, Herbert Elmer *accountant*
Miller, Ronald Baxter *English language educator, writer*
Moore, Rayburn Sabatzky *American literature educator*
Mustard, David Brendan MacDougal *economist, educator*
Nelson, Stuart Owen *agricultural engineer, researcher, educator*
Nichols, William Curtis *psychologist, family therapist, consultant*
Olsen, Richard James *artist, educator*
O'Toole, Laurence Joseph *public administration and policy educator, researcher*
Paul, William Dewitt, Jr., *artist, educator, photographer, videographer, museum director*
Plummer, Gayther L(ynn) *ecologist, climatologist, researcher*
Pollack, Robert Harvey *psychology educator*
Prasse, Keith W. *dean*
Puckett, Elizabeth Ann *law librarian, law educator*
Reid, Leonard N. *academic administrator*
Sachs, Margaret V. *law educator*
Schaefer, Henry Frederick, III, *chemistry professor*
Shipley, David Elliott *dean, lawyer*
Shockley, Floyd Wayne *research scientist*
Shotts, Emmett Booker, Jr., *microbiology educator, researcher*
Slater, Thomas Bowie *minister, educator*
Smagorinsky, Peter *education educator*
Spears, Louise Elizabeth *minister, secondary school educator*
Spence, Sarah *comparatist educator*
Staub, August William *drama educator, theatrical producer, director*
Stipe, Michael *musician*
Tesser, Abraham *social psychologist*
Thomas, Emory M. *history professor*
Thomas, Howard Lamar *chef, consultant, writer*
Tolley, Edward Donald *lawyer*
Troutt Powell, Eve *historian, educator*
Tyler, David Earl *veterinary medical educator*
Wang, Shuzhou *mathematician, educator, research scientist*
Wraga, William Gerard *educator*

Atlanta
50 Cent, (Curtis Jackson) *rap artist*
Aaberg, Thomas Marshall, Sr., *academic administrator*
Aaron, Hank (Henry L. Aaron) *professional baseball team executive*
Abbott, Herschel Lee, Jr., *lawyer*
Abdel-Khalik, Said Ibrahim *nuclear and mechanical engineering educator*
Abernathy, Thomas Edwards, IV, *lawyer*
Abney, David *delivery service executive*
Abrams, Edward Marvin *construction company executive*
Achiron, Leonard R. *ophthalmologist, educator*
Ackerman, Arlene Alice *accountant, business consultant, artist, writer*
Ackerman, F. Duane *telecommunication industry executive*
Adams, David Porterfield, III, *real estate appraiser*
Adams, Rex M. *telecommunications executive*
Adams, Valencia I. *telecommunications industry executive*
Affonso, Dyanne D. *dean*
Albert, Ross Alan *lawyer*
Alexander, Cecil Abraham *college official, architect, consultant*
Alexander, Kent B. *lawyer*
Alexander, Miles Jordan *lawyer*
Alexander, Robert Wayne *medical educator*
Allan, Alexander R.C. (Sandy Allan) *food products executive*
Allen, Douglas C. *architecture educator*
Allen, Natalie *cable news anchor*
Allison, Stuart Anthony *chemistry educator, researcher*
Allred, Jeffrey A. *communications executive*
Altman, Robert *lawyer*
Ambrose, Samuel Sheridan, Jr., *retired urologist educator*
Ames, William Francis *mathematician, educator*
Amin, Mahul B. *physician, researcher, educator, consultant*
Anderson, Al H., Jr., *communications executive*
Anderson, Maxwell L. *former museum director*
Anderson, Peter Joseph *lawyer*
Anderson, Ray C. *carpet company executive*
Anderson, Richard A. *telecommunications industry executive*
Anstrom, Decker *broadcast executive*
Appeadu, Charles Edward *finance educator, researcher*
Arani, Ardy A. *professional sports marketing executive, lawyer*
Argenbright, Frank A., Jr., *diversified financial services company executive*
Arroyo, F. Thaddeus *telecommunications industry executive*
Arthur, Thomas Carlton *law educator*
Ashley, John Bryan *software executive, management consultant*
Averitt, Richard Garland, III, *financial services company executive*
Babcock, Peter Heartz *professional sports executive*
Bacon, Louis Albert *retired consulting civil engineer*
Baechler, Constance Elaine *writer, educator*
Bahl, Roy Winford *economist, educator, consultant*
Bailey, Joy Hafner *counselor educator*
Bailey, Michael Stewart *political science educator*
Bainbridge, Frederick Freeman, III, *architect*
Baird, Marianne Saunorus *critical care clinical nurse specialist, administrator*
Baker, Jerry Herbert *executive search consultant*
Baker, Thurbert E. *state attorney general*
Bales, Virginia Shankle *health administrator*
Bankoff, Joseph R. *lawyer*
Banks, Marvin R., Jr., *investment company executive*
Barker, Clayton Robert, III, *lawyer*
Barker, William Daniel *hospital administrator*
Barkoff, Rupert Mitchell *lawyer*
Barksdale, Richard Dillon *civil engineer, educator*
Barnard, Patricia A. *human resources specialist*
Barnett, Crawford Fannin, Jr., *internist, educator, cardiologist, travel medicine specialist*
Barnett, Preston B. *lawyer, communications executive*
Barr, Robert Laurence, Jr., *lawyer*
Barron, Patrick Kenneth *bank executive*
Barwick, William D. *lawyer*
Beasley, Ernest William, Jr., *endocrinologist*
Beaton, Rebecca Andrea *psychotherapist*
Beckham, Walter Hull, III, *lawyer*
Beik, William H. *education educator, writer*
Bekkers, John *food products company executive*
Bell, Griffin B. *lawyer, former attorney general*
Bell, Thomas D., Jr., *real estate company executive*
Bellamy, Walter *retired basketball player*
Bellanca, Joseph Paul *engineering construction executive*
Benario, Herbert William *classicist, educator*
Benham, Robert *state supreme court justice*
Benian, Guy M. *medical educator*
Benjamin, Andre Lauren (André 3000) *vocalist*
Bennett, Dick *advertising executive*
Beres, Mary Elizabeth *management educator, religious leader*
Berkelhamer, Jay Ellis *pediatrician*
Bernstein, Deena Robin *lawyer*
Berry, Dennis *newspaper publishing executive*
Betty, Charles Garry (Garry Betty) *Internet company executive*
Bevins, Karl Alten *retired engineer, musician, educator*
Beystehner, John J. *transportation executive*
Bibb, Daniel Roland *antique painting restorer and conservator*
Biggins, J. Veronica *bank executive*
Bihary, Joyce *federal judge*
Billington, Barry E. *lawyer*
Birch, Stanley Francis, Jr., *federal judge*
Bird, Wendell Raleigh *lawyer*
Birdsong, Alta Marie *volunteer*
Bisher, James Furman *journalist, writer*
Black, Kenneth, Jr., *retired insurance executive and educator, author*
Blackburn, William Stanley *lawyer*
Blackstock, Jerry B. *lawyer*
Blackwell, Michael Sidney *broker, financial services executive*
Blake, Francis Stanton *retail executive, lawyer*
Blank, A(ndrew) Russell *lawyer*
Blitch, Peg *state legislator*
Bloodworth, Albert William Franklin *lawyer*
Blount, Ben B., Jr., *administration and finance executive*
Blum, Terry C. *dean*
Bolch, Carl Edward, Jr., *petroleum company executive, lawyer*
Bondurant, Emmet Jopling, II, *lawyer*
Boniface, Barry *telecommunications industry executive*
Booth, Gordon Dean, Jr., *lawyer*
Booth, Susan Virginia *theater director*
Bostic, James E., Jr., *paper company executive*
Bostwick, John, III, *plastic surgeon, department chairman, medical educator*
Bowers, Michael Joseph *former state attorney general*
Bowling, Daniel S., III, *lawyer*
Bradley, Phillip Alden *lawyer*
Bradley, Rickford D. *telecommunications industry executive*
Bradshaw, Rod Eric *personnel consultant*
Branch, Thomas Broughton, III, *lawyer*
Branch, William Thomas, Jr., *medical educator*
Brandenburg, David Saul *gastroenterologist, educator*
Brantley, L. Wayne *apparel executive*
Braswell, Cruse C., Jr., *public relations executive*
Bratton, James Henry, Jr., *lawyer*
Bremner, James Douglas *psychiatrist, researcher, education educator*
Brewer, Charles M. *communications executive*
Bright, David Forbes *academic administrator, classicist, educator*
Broadnax, Walter D. *public policy educator*
Brody, Harold Joseph *dermatologist*
Bromley, Marcus E. *investment company executive*
Broome, Claire Veronica *epidemiologist, researcher*
Brothers, June Esternaux Scott *forest products company vice president*
Brown, Lorene B(yron) *retired library educator, educational administrator*
Brown, Sarah M. *artist, gallery owner, educator, publisher*
Brown, Terry Steven *accountant*
Brown-Olmstead, Amanda *public relations executive*
Bruckman, Amy Susan *computer scientist, educator*
Bruner, Michael Lane *communications educator*
Buckner, Gail *state legislator*
Bull, Frank James *retired architect*
Bunn, Barbara Jean *state legislator*
Buoch, William Thomas *corporate executive*
Burandt, Michael Charles *lumber company executive, paper company executive, chemicals executive, consumer products company executive*
Burge, William Lee *retired business information executive*
Burns, M. Michele *energy executive, former air transportation executive*
Burns, Richard *telecommunications industry executive*
Burns, Thomas Samuel *history professor*
Butler, Gloria Singleton *state legislator*
Byrne, Granville Bland, III, *lawyer*
Cable, Susan W. *state legislator*
Cadenhead, Alfred Paul *lawyer*
Camp, Jack Tarpley, Jr., *judge*
Campbell, Colin McLeod *journalist*
Cantley, Kevin Rilous *architectural firm executive*
Capron, John M. *lawyer*
Carbonell, Joaquin R., III, *telecommunications industry executive*
Carley, George H. *judge*
Carnes, Julie Elizabeth *judge*
Carson, Christopher Leonard *lawyer*
Carter, Jimmy (James Earl Carter Jr.) *39th President of the United States*
Casarella, William Joseph *physician*
Caseman, Austin Bert *civil engineering educator*
Casey, John M. *metal products executive*
Cavin, Kristine Smith *lawyer*
Chafee, Ingrid Roberta Hoover Coleman *retired language educator*
Chai, Xin-Sheng, Sr., *research scientist*
Chambers, Anne Cox *newspaper executive, former diplomat*
Chambers, Robert William *business broker*
Chameau, Jean-Lou *academic administrator*
Chandler, Robert Charles *healthcare consultant*
Chapman, Hugh McMaster *banker*
Chapman, Thomas F. *communications executive*
Charles, Cory Anne *television guest booking director*
Chartier, Kirk Lee Freund *business services executive*
Chasen, Sylvan Herbert *computer applications consultant, investment advisor*
Chau, Pin Pin *bank executive*
Chen, Joie *cable news anchor*
Chestnut, James E. *beverage company executive*
Chilivis, Nickolas Peter *lawyer*
Chilton, Horace Thomas *pipeline company executive*
Chisholm, Tommy *lawyer, utilities executive*
Chow, Rey *literature educator*
Churchwell, Andre *health science association administrator*
Circeo, Louis Joseph, Jr., *research scientist, civil engineer*
Clark, C. Jordan *investment company executive*
Clark, Faye Louise *retired drama and speech educator*
Clark, Gary *newspaper editor*
Clarke, Thomas Hal *lawyer*
Clayton, Xernona *media executive*
Clement, William A., Jr., *computer company executive*
Clift, W.E. *telecommunications industry executive*
Clifton, David Samuel, Jr., *research executive, economist*
Clough, Gerald Wayne *academic administrator*
Coady, William Francis *information technology executive, consultant*
Cobb, Charles Kenche, Jr., *lawyer, real estate broker*
Cochi, Stephen L. *federal agency administrator*
Cogburn, Richmond *architect*
Cohen, Ezra Harry *lawyer*
Cohen, George Leon *lawyer*
Cohen, N. Jerold *lawyer*
Cohn, Bob *public relations executive*
Cole, Thomas Winston, Jr., *chancellor, college president, chemist*
Coleman, Terry Lewis *state legislator*
Coley, Barbara Yvonne *computer software consultant*
Collins, Donnell Jawan *lawyer*
Collins, Douglas C. *hotel executive*
Collins, Steven M. *lawyer*
Colman, Robert L. *airline company executive*
Compans, Richard W. *microbiology educator*
Comstock, Robert Donald, Jr., *real estate executive*
Connelly, Terrence John, Sr., *television and cable station executive*
Cook, Don Lloyd *marketing educator, lawyer, consultant*
Cook, John M. *finance company executive*
Cooper, Gerald Rice *clinical pathologist*
Cooper, Jerome Maurice *architect*
Cooper, Simon F. *hotel executive*
Cooper, Thomas Luther *retired printing company executive*
Cordero, Jose Fernando *pediatrician, federal agency administrator, USPHS officer*
Cornelius, Charles H. *insurance company executive*
Correll, Alston Dayton, Jr., (Pete Correll) *forest products company executive*
Cousins, Thomas G. *real estate company executive*
Cowan, Keith O. *telecommunications industry executive*
Cox, Bobby (Robert Joe Cox) *professional baseball manager*
Cox, Cathy *state official*
Cox, Kathy *education commissioner*
Crackett, Delores *womens bureau administrator*
Craig, Anna Maynard *financial educator, consultant*
Cramer, Howard Ross *geologist, environmental consultant*
Crews, William Edwin *lawyer*
Crimmins, Timothy James *history professor*
Crockett, Delores *federal agency administrator*
Croft, Terrence Lee *lawyer*
Cummings, Alexander B., Jr., *food products executive*
Cupp, Robert Erhard *land use planner, golf course architect*
Curran, James W. *epidemiologist, educator, academic administrator*
Curry, Toni Griffin *counseling center executive, consultant*
Curtis, Philip Kerry *lawyer*
Cutshaw, Kenneth Andrew *lawyer*
Daft, Douglas N. *food products executive*
Dahl, Alan C. *health facility administrator*
Dahlberg, Alfred William *electric company executive*
Dalia, Thomas A. *architectural firm executive*
Dallas, H. James *textiles executive*
Dallas, Robert F. *state agency administrator*
Danielson, Gilbert Lawrence *consumer products company executive*
Darden, Calvin *delivery service executive*
Darden, Claibourne Henry, Jr., *marketing research professional*
Davis, Amanda *newscaster*
Davis, D. Scott *corporate financial executive*
Davis, E(dward) Marcus *lawyer*
Davis, Eleanor Kay *museum administrator*
Davis, Frank Tradewell, Jr., *lawyer*
Davis, Grace W. *state legislator*
Davis, Grover L. *risk management consultant*
Davis, Jay M. *wholesale distribution executive*
Davis, Lawrence William *radiation oncologist*
Davis, Marvin Arnold *manufacturing executive*
Davis, Sterling Evan *television executive*
Dayton, Harry F. *manufacturing executive*
Deane, Richard Hunter, Jr., *lawyer, former federal judge*
DeConcini, Barbara *association executive, religious studies educator*

Decosta, Benjamin *airport executive*
Dees, Lafon Carabo *brokerage house executive*
DeLong, Mahlon R. *neurologist, educator*
DeMoura, Brian L. *textile manufacturing company executive*
Denmark, Darron B. *compliance specialist*
Dennison, Daniel Bassel *chemist*
Denny, Richard Alden, Jr., *retired lawyer*
DeRodes, Robert P. *manufacturing executive*
Despriet, John G. *lawyer*
Dickinson, Robert Earl *atmospheric scientist, educator*
Diedrich, Richard Joseph *architect*
Dietz, William Harry *pediatrician*
Dobes, William Lamar, Jr., *dermatologist, educator*
Dobranski, Stephen Bitonti *literature educator*
Dobson, Bridget McColl Hursley *television executive, writer*
Dodson, Daniel, Jr., *advertising executive*
Donald, James E. *retired career officer, government agency executive*
Donoghue, John Francis *archbishop*
Donovan, Dennis *manufacturing executive*
Dortch, Carole A. *federal agency administrator*
Dowda, William F. *internist*
Dowdle, Walter Reid *microbiologist, medical center administrator*
Dowling, Kathy *telecommunications industry executive*
Dowling, Roderick Anthony *investment banker*
Downs, John H., Jr., *food products executive*
Doyle, Michael A. *lawyer*
Drake, Miriam Anna *librarian, educator, writer*
Dramis, Francis A., Jr., *communications company executive*
Draper, Stephen Elliot *lawyer, engineer*
Driver, Walter W., Jr., *lawyer*
Droege, Mark E. *telecommunications industry executive*
Drummond, Jere A. *telecommunications company executive*
Duffey, Lee *communications company executive*
Duffey, William Simon, Jr., *federal judge, lawyer*
Duncan, Dale Scott *music educator*
Dunn, Jeffrey T. *food products executive*
Dunn, Rebecca M. *telecommunications industry executive*
Dunston-Thomas, Frances Johnson *pediatrician, public health official*
Dupri, Jermaine *music company executive, music producer*
Durrett, James Frazer, Jr., *retired lawyer*
Dutt, Kamla *medical educator*
Dykes, Ronald Mitchell *telecommunications executive*
Dykstra, Gary James *administrator*
Dzvonik, Michael D. *advertising executive*
Easterly, David Eugene *communications executive*
Eastman, Charles (Chuck) M. *architecture educator*
Eaton, J. Stephen *healthcare company executive*
Eckl, William Wray *lawyer*
Edelhauser, Henry F. *ophthalmologic researcher, educator, physiologist*
Edmondson, James Larry *federal judge*
Edson, Margaret *playwright*
Edwards, Stephen Allen *lawyer*
Egan, Michael Joseph *retired lawyer, state legislator*
Ehrlich, Jeffrey *data processing company executive*
Eidson, James Anthony *lawyer*
Eisner, Rebecca Suzanne *lawyer*
Ellingwood, Bruce Russell *structural engineering researcher, educator*
Ellis, Elmo Israel *broadcast executive, consultant, columnist*
Ellis, U. Bertram, Jr., *internet services company executive*
Ellison, Earl Otto *computer scientist*
Elsas, Louis Jacob, II, *medical educator*
Endicott, John Edgar *international relations educator*
Epstein, David Gustav *lawyer*
Ergas, Jean-Pierre Maurice *packaging company executive*
Eriksen, Michael *medical educator*
Escarra, Vicki B. *airline company executive*
Eskew, Michael L. *package distribution company executive*
Etheridge, Jack Paul *arbitrator, mediator, former judge*
Evans, Gail Hirschorn *television news executive*
Evans, Orinda D. *federal judge*
Facklam, Richard R. *microbiologist, director scientific organization*
Falk, Henry *pediatrician, epidemiologist, researcher*
Farley, Charles P. *public relations executive*
Farnham, Clayton Henson *lawyer*
Fash, William Leonard *retired architecture educator, college dean*
Fayard, Gary P. *food products executive*
Feldman, Joel Martin *magistrate judge*
Felton, Dorothy *state legislator*
Felton, Jule Wimberly, Jr., *lawyer*
Fermanis, Ernest George *urologic surgeon*
Fernandez, Frank L. *lawyer, retail executive*
Ferraro, Ray *professional hockey player*
Ficke, Bruce William *real estate executive*
Findley, Norman P. *food products executive*
Fine, Frederick L. *computer company executive, health products executive*
Finkelstein, David Ritz *physicist, educator, consultant*
Finley, Michael Valton *foundation executive*
Flagg Davis, Vivian Annette *librarian, researcher, public policy consultant*
Flannery, James William *performing arts educator, vocalist, theater director*
Flannery, M. Raymond *physicist, researcher*
Fleming, Julian Denver, Jr., *lawyer*
Fletcher, Andy *marketing professional*
Fletcher, Norman S. *state supreme court justice*
Foege, William Herbert *public health administrator, educator*
Foley, James David *computer science educator, consultant*
Forbes, Theodore McCoy, Jr., *arbitrator, mediator, retired lawyer*
Ford-Roegner, Patricia A. *health services professional*
Foreman, Edward Rawson *retired lawyer*
Forney, Larry J. *chemical engineer, educator*
Forrestal, Robert Patrick *banker, lawyer*
Forrester, J. Owen *federal judge*
Fortin, Judy *cable news anchor*
Fortin, Raymond D. *lawyer*
Fosha, Kent C., Sr., *healthcare management company executive*
Fote, Charles T. *computer company executive*
Fowler, Bruce Andrew *toxicologist, researcher, public health service officer*
Fox, John T. *health facility administrator*
Fox, Ronald Forrest *physics educator*
Franch, Harold August *nephrologist, researcher*
Frank, Erica *preventive medicine physician*
Franklin, Charles Scothern *lawyer*
Franklin, Shirley Clarke *mayor*
Fredo, Peter W. *public relations executive*
Freedman, Louis Martin *dentist*
Fricks, Larry *mental health services professional*
Frieson, Ronald E. *telecommunications industry executive*
Frost, Norman Cooper *retired telephone company executive*
Fuller, Lonnie *medical educator*
Fuller, S(heri) Marce *energy executive*
Funderburg, Jan *telecommunications industry executive*
Fuqua, John Brooks *retired consumer products and services company executive*
Furnad, V. Robert (Bob Furnad) *television news executive*
Gagne, Jeffrey P. *policy analyst*
Gailey, Thomas Chandler (Chan), Jr., *college football coach*
Galambos, John Thomas *medical educator, internist*
Gallagher, Thomas C. *diversified manufacturing executive*
Galloway, Thomas D. *dean*
Gambrell, David Henry *lawyer*
Ganaway, George Kenneth *psychiatrist, psychoanalyst*
Ganzarain, Ramon Cajiao *psychoanalyst*
Garland, LaRetta Matthews *psychologist, educator, nursing educator*
Garrow, David Jeffries *historian, author*
Gay, Robert Derril *behavioral health consultant*
Gayles, Joseph Nathan, Jr., *administrator, fund raising consultant*
Geigerman, Clarice Furchgott *writer, consultant*
Geil, Mark D. *education educator*
Gelardi, Robert Charles *trade association executive, consultant*
Genberg, Ira *lawyer*
Gerberding, Julie Louise *federal agency administrator*
Gergel, Mark A. *communications executive*
Gibson, Michael *artist*
Gibson, Michael Allen *music educator*
Gibson, Wayne *retail executive*
Giddens, Don Peyton *engineering educator, researcher*
Gimmestad, Gary Gene *physicist, researcher*
Girth, Marjorie Louisa *lawyer, educator*
Glaser, Arthur Henry *lawyer, mediator*
Glass, Roger I. *virologist*
Glover, John Trapnell *real estate executive*
Godwin, John Thomas *pathologist, nuclear medicine specialist*
Goldfarb, Eric Daniel *information technology executive, computer industry analyst*
Goldman, John Abner *rheumatologist, immunologist, educator*
Goldstein, Burton Benjamin, Jr., *communications executive*
Goldstein, Elliott *lawyer, director*
Goldston, Nathaniel R., III, *food services company executive*
González, Carlos A. *lawyer*
Gonzalez-Pita, J. Alberto *lawyer*
Goodman, Seymour Evan *computer science and international studies educator, researcher, consultant*
Goodwin, George Evans *public relations executive*
Gordon, Frank Jeffrey *medical educator*
Graham, Matt Patrick *minister, librarian*
Grant, Walter Matthews *lawyer, corporate executive*
Gray, Robert F. *food products executive*
Green, Holcombe Tucker, Jr., *investment company executive*
Greenblatt, Edward Lande *lawyer*
Greene, Margaret H. *telecommunications industry executive*
Greene, Warren *advertising executive*
Greer, Bernard Lewis, Jr., *lawyer*
Gregory (Greg), Henry D., Jr., *real estate company executive*
Gregory, Mel Hyatt, Jr., *retired insurance company executive*
Griffin, Clayton Houstoun *retired power company engineer, lecturer*
Griffin, Ron *retail executive*
Grinstein, Gerald *transportation executive*
Grogan, Paula Cataldi *newspaper editor*
Gross, Stephen Randolph *accountant*
Groton, James Purnell *lawyer, arbitrator*
Grubic, Adrianne *journalist*
Grzedzinski, Edward *data processing executive*
Gude, Albert Valdemar *retired anesthesiologist*
Guest, Rita Carson *interior designer*
Gundersen, Mary Lisa Kranitzky *finance company executive*
Gunn, Robert Burns *physiology educator*
Hakes, Jay Edward *federal agency administrator*
Hale, Jack K. *mathematics educator, research center administrator*
Hall, Beverly L. *school system administrator*
Hallacy, Don *telecommunications industry executive*
Hallen, Barry *philosopher, educator*
Halloran, M. Elizabeth *statistician, educator*
Hamm, Stan(ley) (Charles Hamm) *former telecommunications company executive*
Hammill, Dick *advertising and marketing executive*
Hanna, Frank Joseph, Jr., *credit company executive*
Hanthorn, Dennis Wayne *performing arts association administrator*
Hardman, John B. *psychiatrist, director*
Harkey, Robert Shelton *retired lawyer*
Harness, William Walter *lawyer*
Harris, Eon Nigel *dean, rheumatologist, internist*
Harris, Isiah, Jr., *telecommunications industry executive*
Harrison, Clifford *chef, small business owner*
Harrison, George Brooks *research engineer, retired career officer*
Hartle, Robert Wyman *retired foreign language and literature educator*
Hartley, Bob *professional hockey coach*
Harvard, Beverly Joyce Bailey *protective service official*
Hasson, James Keith, Jr., *lawyer, law educator*
Hatcher, Charles Ross, Jr., *surgeon, health facility administrator*
Hatchett, Glenda A. *municipal judge*
Hawks, Barrett Kingsbury *lawyer*
Hay, Peter Heinrich *law educator*
Hayes, Jimmy W. *telecommunications company executive*
Hayford, Warren J. *metal products executive*
Hays, William Grady, Jr., *corporate financial and bank consultant*
Hayworth, Andrea Elizabeth *lawyer*
He, Hongyu *mathematician, educator*
Heady, Eugene Joseph *lawyer*
Healy, Maureen *marketing executive*
Heatley, Dany *professional hockey player*
Hegstrom, June *state legislator*
Heimburger, Elizabeth Morgan *psychiatrist*
Heller, John Gaylord *orthopaedic surgery educator*
Hendrick, David Richard *lawyer*
Hendricks, Nathan VanMeter, III, *lawyer*
Hendrix, Daniel T. *textile manufacturing company executive*
Henry, John Dunklin, Sr., *hospital executive*
Henry, Ronald James Whyte *academic administrator, physicist, educator*
Henson, Howard Kirk *lawyer*
Herrin, Barry Scott *lawyer, writer*
Hess, Dennis William *chemical engineering educator*
Hewitt, Paul Harrington *basketball coach*
Heyer, Steven J. *food products executive*
Hiett, Joe *publishing executive, writer, editor*
Hill, Allen E. *transportation services executive*
Hinchey, John William *lawyer*
Hines, Preston Harris *state supreme court justice*
Hodges, Dewey Harper *aerospace engineer, educator*
Hoff, Gerhardt Michael *lawyer, insurance company executive*
Hoffman, Fred L. *human resources specialist*
Hoffman, Michael William *lawyer, accountant*
Hogan, John Donald *retired college dean, finance educator*
Hogan, William Jephtha, Jr., *financial consultant*
Hollis, Timothy Martin *bank executive*
Holloway, Barbara R. *health science association administrator*
Holloway, Kelvin J. *allergist, immunologist, pediatrician*
Holsendolph, Ernest *newspaper editor*
Honaman, J. Craig *health facility administrator*
Hopkins, Donald Roswell *public health physician*
Hopkins, John David *lawyer*
Horsburgh, Charles Robert *allergist*
Houry, Debra *emergency physician, educator*
Howard, Harry Clay *lawyer*
Howard, Pierre *former state official*
Howell, Arthur *lawyer*
Howell, Hilton Hatchett, Jr., *business executive*
Hubbell, Fred Shelton *insurance company executive*
Hudson, Dean *tax accountant*
Huff, Danny W. *paper products executive*
Hug, Carl Casimir, Jr., *anesthesiology and pharmacology educator*
Hughes, James Mitchell *epidemiologist*
Hull, Frank Mays *federal judge*
Humann, L. Phillip *bank executive*
Hunstein, Carol *state supreme court justice*
Hunter, Forrest Walker *lawyer*
Hunter, Howard Owen *academic administrator, law educator*
Hutcheson, John K. *real estate company executive*
Iacobucci, Guillermo Arturo *chemist*
Ide, Roy William, III, *lawyer*
Ignatonis, Sandra Carole Autry *special education educator*
Isaf, Fred Thomas *lawyer*
Isdell, Edward Neville *food products executive*
Israili, Zafar Hasan *scientist, clinical pharmacologist, educator*
Izard, John *lawyer*
Jackson, Carol *state legislator*
Jaffe, Harold W. *federal agency administrator*
James, Donzella *state legislator*
Jamieson, Mary Jeanette *state legislator*
Janney, Donald Wayne *lawyer*
Jastrow, Robert *physicist, educator*
Jeffery, Geoffrey Marron *medical parasitologist*
Jenkins, Albert Felton, Jr., *lawyer*
Jeter, Howard F. *former ambassador*
Jiang, Baoming *scientist*
Jin, Zhenrong *electrical engineer, researcher*
Johns, Michael Marieb Edward *otolaryngologist, academic administrator*
Johnson, Carl Frederick *marriage and family therapist*
Johnson, Jeff *marketing professional*
Johnson, Phillip Murray *treasurer, lumber company executive, paper company executive, chemicals executive, consumer products company executive*
Johnson, Richard Clayton *engineer, physicist*
Johnson, Ronald Carl *chemistry professor*
Johnson, W. Thomas, Jr., *media executive*
Johnston, Summerfield K., Jr., *food products executive*
Johnston, Summerfield K., III, *food products executive*
Jolley, Samuel Delanor, Jr., *academic administrator*
Jones, Andruw Rudolf *professional baseball player*
Jones, Boland T. *communications executive*
Jones, Chipper (Larry Wayne Jones Jr.) *professional baseball player*
Jones, Frank Cater *retired lawyer*
Jones, Glower Whitehead *lawyer*
Jones, Herbert Cornelius, III, *otolaryngologist*
Jones, Ingrid Saunders *food products executive*
Jones, J. Kenley *journalist*
Judovitz, Dalia *literature educator*
Jurkiewicz, Maurice John *surgeon, educator*
Kahn, Bernd *radiochemist, educator*
Kalafut, George Wendell *distribution company executive, retired naval officer*
Karp, Herbert Rubin *neurologist, educator*
Katz, Joel Abraham *lawyer, music consultant*
Kaufman, Monica *newscaster*
Keiller, James Bruce *college dean, clergyman*
Kellermann, Arthur L. *medical educator*
Kelley, James Francis *lawyer*
Kelly, Carol White *company executive*
Kelly, James P. *delivery service executive*
Kelly, William Watkins *educational association executive*
Kemp, Rene D. *state legislator*
Kennedy, James C. *publishing and media executive*
Kent, Philip *communications executive*
Keough, Donald Raymond *investment company executive, director*
Kerley, William J. *real estate corporation executive*
Kerr, Nancy Helen *psychology educator*
Kessler, Richard Paul, Jr., *lawyer*
Khoury, Kenneth F. *lawyer*
Khuri, Fadlo Raja *oncologist, educator*
Kilgore, Cada T., III, *lawyer*
Killingsworth, Vernon Scott *technology lawyer*
Killorin, Robert Ware *lawyer*
Kimani, Grace Alexandra *internist*
King, Barbara Lewis *minister, lecturer*
King, Coretta Scott (Mrs. Martin Luther King Jr.) *educational association administrator, lecturer, writer, concert singer*
King, Dexter Scott *foundation administrator*
King, K(imberly) N(elson) *computer science educator*
King, Linda Orr *museum director, consultant*
Kingsbury, Michael Bryant *organist, retired elementary and secondary education educator*
Kintzel, Roger S. *publishing executive*
Kinzer, William Luther *lawyer*
Kirberger, Michael Patrick *application developer, researcher*
Kitchens, William H. *lawyer*
Klamon, Lawrence Paine *lawyer*
Klein, Luella Voogd *obstetrics-gynecology educator*
Kline, J. Peter *hotel executive*
Kline, Lowry F. *food products executive, lawyer*
Klinger, Steven J. *paper company executive*
Klippel, John H. *physician, association executive*
Kloer, Philip Baldwin *popular culture critic*
Knapp, Charles Boynton *economist, educator, former university president*
Knowles, Marjorie Fine *lawyer, educator, dean*
Kochengin, Sergey Alexandrovich *information technology consultant*
Kokko, Juha Pekka *physician, educator*
Koplan, Jeffrey Powell *physician*
Koros, William John *chemical engineering educator*
Kovalchuk, Ilya *professional hockey player*
Kozlov, Vyacheslav *professional hockey player*
Kravitch, Phyllis A. *federal judge*
Kringelis, Kurt *portfolio manager*
Kruger, Lon *coach*
Ku, David Nelson *medical educator*
Kuhn, Brent *advertising executive*
Kuntz, Marion Lucile Leathers *classicist, educator, historian*
Kushner, Howard I. *public health and history of medicine educator*
Lamon, Harry Vincent, Jr., *lawyer, director*
Landau, Michael B. *law educator, musician, writer*
Landess, Mike (Malcolm Lee Landess III) *television news anchorman*
Landon, James Henry *lawyer*
Lane, Brian David *accountant*
Lanier, George H. *lawyer*
Latham, Deborah L. *energy marketing and services company executive*
Lawley, Thomas Joseph *dean, medical educator*
Lee, Donna A. *telecommunications industry executive*
Lee, Hamilton H. *education educator*
Lee, John Everett *physician*
Lee, Robert *hotel executive*
Lefar, Marc *telecommunications industry executive*
Lennie, Bill *retail executive*
Leonard, David Morse *lawyer*
Lester, Charles Turner, Jr., *lawyer*
Letton, Alva Hamblin *surgeon, educator*
Levey, Allan I. *neurologist, educator, pharmacologist*
Levy, Rich *advertising executive*
Lewcock, Ronald Bentley *architect, educator*
Lewis, Earl *academic administrator*
Liebmann, Seymour W. *construction executive, consultant*
Lin, Ming-Chang *physical chemistry educator, researcher*
Lindner, Richard G. *telecommunications industry executive*
Lindsay, Michael Kenneth *obstetrics and gynecology educator*
Linkous, William Joseph, Jr., *lawyer*
Lipshutz, Robert Jerome *lawyer, former government official*
Litt, Brian *neurologist, educator, biomedical engineer*
Littrell, Jill *social sciences educator*
Lnenicka, Wade Sheridan *purchasing official, councilman*
Lobb, William Atkinson *financial services executive*
Locklin, Paul G. *executive*
Loewy, Robert Gustav *aeronautical engineering executive, engineering educator*
Logsdon, James M. *information systems executive*
Long, Leland Timothy *geophysicist educator, seismologist*
Long, Robert Richard *banker*
Louard, Rita Jean *endocrinologist, educator*
Love, Dennis M. *consumer products company executive*
Love, Gay McLawhorn *manufacturing executive*
Loven, Andrew Witherspoon *environmental engineering company executive*
Lovewell, Marjorie Klingensmith *secondary school educator*
Lower, Robert Cassel *lawyer, educator*
Lubin, Michael Frederick *physician, educator, researcher*
Lucas-Tauchar, M. Frances *university administrator*
Ludovice, Peter John *chemical engineer*
Lui, Victor King Shing *pediatrician*
Lund, Victor L. *healthcare company executive*
Lustig, Michael A. *finance company executive*
Lybarger, Jeffrey Allen *epidemiology research administrator*
Maddox-Adams, Sherry *secondary school educator*
Mahan, James S. *communications company executive*
Majmudar, Bhagirath *medical educator*
Malhotra, Naresh Kumar *management educator*
Malone, James Hiram *graphic artist, painter, writer*
Mamrack, William H. *tax specialist*
Mandel, Jack Sheldon *epidemiologist, educator*
Manley, Frank *retired English language educator, writer*
Mannelly, Patrick J. *food products executive*
Manning, Clarence Bond *lawyer*
Manning, Judith Hubert *state legislator, real estate executive*
Mansour, Kamal A. *cardiothoracic surgeon*

Williams, James Bryan *banker*
Williams, Neil, Jr., *lawyer*
Williams, Ralph Watson, Jr., *retired securities company executive*
Willis, Isaac *dermatologist, educator*
Wilson, Alexandra M. *communications executive*
Wilson, Debora J. *broadcast executive*
Wilson, Faye *retail executive*
Wilson, James Hargrove, Jr., *lawyer*
Winer, Ward Otis *mechanical engineer, educator*
Winkle, C. Christian *health facility administrator*
Winograd, Audrey Lesser *retired advertising executive*
Wittner-Neiman, Sloane Phyllis Ann *realtor, writer, artist*
Wolbrink, James Francis *real estate investor*
Wolf, Charles A. *retail camera and photographic supplies executive*
Womack, Mary Pauline *lawyer*
Wong, Ching-Ping *chemist, materials scientist, engineer, educator*
Wood, L. Lin, Jr., *lawyer*
Woody, Mary Florence *nursing educator, university administrator*
Worley, David *lawyer*
Wright, Frederick Lewis, II, *lawyer*
Wright, Peter Meldrim *lawyer*
Wulkan, Mark Lewis *pediatrician, surgeon*
Wurtz, George W., III, *paper company executive*
Wussler, Robert Joseph *broadcasting executive, media consultant*
Wylly, Barbara Bentley *performing arts association administrator*
Xu, Shucheng *chemistry educator, research scientist*
Yancey, Asa Greenwood, Sr., *physician*
Yancey, Carolyn Dunbar *educational policy maker*
Yates, Ella Gaines *library consultant*
Yeargin-Allsopp, Marshalyn *medical epidemiologist, pediatrician*
Yoganathan, Ajit Prithiviraj *biomedical engineer, educator*
Young, James E. *banker*
Z, Chris *internist, medical educator*
Zell, Glenn *lawyer*
Zeng, Wei *environmental engineer*
Zhao, Yichuan *education educator*
Zink, Charles Talbott *lawyer*
Zinn, Ben T. *engineer, educator, consultant*

Augusta

Baker, Carleton Harold *physiology educator*
Booth, Edmund A., Jr., *prosecutor*
Bowen, Dudley Hollingsworth, Jr., *federal judge*
Chandler, Arthur Bleakley *pathologist, educator*
Cheng, Wu C. *retired patent examiner*
Christensen, David William *mathematician, engineer*
Colton, Zanne Beaufort *performing company executive*
Craig, Cynthia Mae *mathematics professor*
Cundey, Paul Edward, Jr., *cardiologist*
Davis, Catherine Lucy *psychologist, diabetes researcher*
Dolen, William Kennedy *allergist, immunologist, pediatrician, educator*
Drisko, Connie Lee Hastings *dental educator, dean*
Dyer, James Harold, Jr., *language educator*
Ellison, Lois Taylor *physician, medical educator and administrator*
Feldman, Elaine Bossak *medical nutritionist, educator*
Fincher, Ruth Marie Edla *medical educator, dean*
Gadacz, Thomas Roman *surgery educator*
Gambrell, Richard Donald, Jr., *endocrinologist, educator*
Gillespie, Edward Malcolm *hospital administrator*
Given, Kenna Sidney *surgeon, educator*
Griswold, Sara Y. *language educator*
Hand, Maryanne Kelly *artist, educator*
Hayes, John Thompson *biology professor, academic administrator*
Hooks, Vendie Hudson, III, *surgeon*
Horuzsko, Anatolij *medical research scientist*
House, Fredrick Crisler *allergist*
Imig, John David *medical educator*
Inscho, Edward William *physiology educator*
Jones, Vernon Keith *minister, educator*
Kutlar, Ferdane *genetics educator, researcher*
Lee, Lansing Burrows, Jr., *lawyer, corporate executive*
Lewis, Shirley Ann Redd *college president*
Luxenberg, Malcolm Neuwahl *ophthalmologist, educator, retired*
MacLeod, James L. *minister, finance company executive, art gallery owner*
Mahesh, Virendra Bhushan *endocrinologist*
Manganiello, Louis Otto Joseph *retired neurosurgeon*
McDaniel, George M. *pediatrician*
McDonough, Paul Gerard *obstetrician-gynecologist, educator*
Miller, Alfred Montague *lawyer*
Miller, Jerry Allan, Jr., *pediatrician*
Morris, William Shivers, III, *newspaper executive*
Muntz, Ernest Gordon *historian, educator*
Nesbit, Robert Raymond, Jr., *surgeon*
Ownby, Dennis Randall *pediatrician, educator, allergist, researcher*
Potter, Brad J. *dean, researcher, educator*
Prisant, L(ouis) Michael *cardiologist*
Puryear, Joan Copeland *academic administrator*
Rippert, Eric Theodore *oral and maxillofacial surgeon*
Rogers, Michael Bruce *orthodontist*
Rowland, Arthur Ray *librarian*
Ryan, James Walter *physician, medical researcher*
Smith, Randolph Relihan *plastic surgeon*
Stern, David Mark *dean, educator*
Talledo, Oscar Eduardo *medical educator*
Tedesco, Francis Joseph *retired academic administrator, medical educator*
Thiruvaiyaru, Dharma S. *mathematics and statistics educator, consultant, researcher*
Whittemore, Ronald Paul *hospital administrator, retired army officer, nursing educator*
Woodhurst, Robert Stanford, Jr., *architect*
Wray, Betty Beasley *allergist, immunologist, pediatrician*
Xenakis, Stephen Nicholas *psychiatrist, army officer*
Yu, Robert Kuan-jen *biochemistry educator*

Austell

Fuller, Carol S. *theater educator, writer*
Halwig, J. Michael *allergist*
Orr, Zellie *entrepreneur, educator, writer, researcher*

Robinson, Russell M. *manufacturing executive*

Avondale Estates

Fowler, Andrea *teachers academy administrator*

Ball Ground

Tucker, Robert Dennard *health care products executive*

Barnesville

Horn, Jason G. *English educator*
Terry, Pamela Mays *psychology educator*
Wilcox, Rhonda V. *media studies educator*

Baxley

Reddy, Yenamala Ramachandra *metal processing executive*

Big Canoe

Bendelius, Arthur George *engineering firm executive*

Bishop

Bower, Douglas William *pastoral counselor, psychotherapist, clergyman*

Blackshear

Walker, Thomas Michael *school psychologist*

Blairsville

Dittman, Robert Allan *retired music educator*

Bogart

Hill, Ronald L. *automotive company executive*

Bowden

Sulzer, Alexander Jackson *retired research microbiologist, educator*

Braselton

Copper, James Robert *manufacturing executive*

Brunswick

Alaimo, Anthony A. *federal judge*
Hanson, Carol Hall *elementary school educator*
Herndon, Alice Patterson Latham *public health nurse*
Iannicelli, Joseph *chemical company executive, consultant*
Mihal, Sandra Powell *systems analyst*
Mohr, Janet Ann *psychiatrist*
Perniciaro, Charles Vincent *dermatologist, educator, entrepreneur*
Pittman, Catherine Sylvia *secondary school educator*
Spencer, Shirley Ann *secondary school educator, speech educator, literature educator*

Buford

Byrd, Larry Donald *behavioral pharmacologist*
Greene, William L. *marketing professional, consultant*

Calhoun

Bernstein, Phillip *crafts company executive*
Kilbride, William B. *textiles executive*
Kolb, David L. *carpet company executive*
Lorberbaum, Jeffrey S. *textiles executive*
Procopid, Frank A. *manufacturing executive*
Swift, John D. *manufacturing executive*
Thornton, H Monte *textiles executive*

Canton

Hasty, William Grady, Jr., *lawyer*

Carrollton

Aanstoos, Christopher Michael *psychology educator*
Brewer, A. Bruce *university administrator*
Cao, Li *social studies educator, educator*
Clark, Janet Eileen *political scientist, educator*
Cochran, J. Guyton, Jr., *corporate financial executive*
Doxey, Wiliam Sanford, Jr., *retired language educator, writer*
Goodson, Carol Faye *librarian*
Hibbard, Kevin Robert *music educator*
Morgan, Harry New *education educator*
Richards, Roy, Jr., *wire and cable manufacturing company executive*
Sethna, Beheruz Nariman *university president, marketing, management educator*
Steely, Melvin T. *language educator*
Swamy-Mruthinti, Satyanarayana *biochemist, developmental biologist*
Thorn, Stuart Wallace *marketing and financial executive*
Tisinger, David Harvey *lawyer*

Cartersville

Harris, Joe Frank *former governor*
Wang, Pinghua *education educator*

Cedartown

Garner, Robby Glen *software research executive, roboticist*

Chatsworth

Beasley, Troy Daniel *secondary education educator*

Chickamauga

Chill, Leonard *chemicals executive*
Dana, Joseph F. *manufacturing executive*
Sinicropi, Joseph *manufacturing executive*

Clarkesville

Dowden, Thomas Clark *telecommunication executive*

Cleveland

Edwards, John Carver *retired archivist*

Cochran

Ricks, John Addison, III, *history professor*

College Park

Ferguson, Wendell *private school educator*
Payne, Harry Charles *historian, educator*
Stokes, Arch *lawyer, writer*

Colquitt

San Jose, Angel Molina *surgeon*

Columbus

Amos, Daniel Paul *insurance company executive*
Amos, Paul Shelby *insurance company executive*
Anthony, Richard E. *bank executive*
Bailey, Herta Luise *real estate broker*
Blanchard, James Hubert *finance company executive*
Brinkley, Jack Thomas *lawyer, former congressman*
Brown, Frank Douglas *academic administrator*
Chan, Philip *retired dermatologist, retired military officer*
Cloninger, Kriss, III, *insurance company executive*
Cummins, James Donald *retired electrical engineer*
Diaz-Verson, Salvador, Jr., *investment advisor*
Feldner, Ronald A. *automotive executive*
Gibbons, Dona Alden Coe *electrical engineer*
Harbison, Ed *state legislator, broadcast journalist, motivational speaker*
Heard, William T. *automotive executive*
James, Elizabeth R. *bank executive*
Johnson, Walter Frank, Jr., *lawyer*
Kerr, Allen Stewart *retired psychologist*
Laney, John Thomas, III, *federal judge*
Leebern, Donald M., Jr., *distilled beverage executive*
Loudermilk, Joey M. *insurance company executive, lawyer*
McFarland, Samuel P., Jr., *psychologist*
McGlamry, Max Reginald *lawyer*
Montgomery, Anna Frances *elementary school educator*
Murray, James J. *textiles executive*
Nix, Jeffrey Alan *photographer*
Ogle, D. Clark *textiles executive*
Page, William Marion *lawyer*
Patrick, James Duvall, Jr., *lawyer*
Poydasheff, Robert Stephen *lawyer*
Prescott, Thomas W. *bank executive*
Riggsby, Dutchie Sellers *education educator*
Riggsby, Ernest Duward *science educator, educational consultant*
Ripple, Rochelle Poyourow *educational administrator, educator*
Siddall, Pam *publishing executive*
Simpson, Minnie Peach *interior designer*
Spencer, Kathelen V. *insurance company executive*
Sweeney, Robert David *communications engineer*
Wooten, Joel Orba, Jr., *lawyer*
Yancey, James D. *bank executive*

Conyers

Bouchillon, John Ray *education coordinator*
Bugg, Owen Bruce *state agency administrator*
Burman, Marsha Linkwald *lighting manufacturing executive, manpower development professional*
Kelly, John Hubert *diplomat, business executive*
Kilkelly, Brian Holten *lighting company executive*
King, Lori Ann *performing company executive*
Mc Clung, Jim Hill *light manufacturing company executive*
Waters, Roger Allen *music educator*

Cordele

Helms, Bobby Gillespie *music educator, consultant*

Covington

Litkea, Carole Lynn *paramedic*

Cumming

Benson, Betty Jones *retired school system administrator*
Drew, Paul S. *entrepreneur*
French, James Thomas *real estate broker*
Willadsen, Michael Chris *marketing professional, sales executive*

Dacula

Murphree, Harold T. *retired minister*

Dahlonega

Brown, Hugh Keith *medical researcher, educator*
Faulkner, James A. *financial executive*
Hansford, Nathaniel *academic administrator, lawyer*
Miller, Carol Ann *physical therapist, educator*
Newman, Thomas Daniel *minister, school administrator, archaeologist*

Dalton

Hollingsworth, Bayard *manufacturing executive*
Hutcheson, John Ambrose, Jr., *history professor*
McKay, William Paul *oncologist, health facility administrator*
Saul, Julian *retail executive*
Shaheen, Shaheen Azeez *textile executive*
Shaw, Robert E. *carpeting company executive*
Swanson, Larry *manufacturing executive*
Turner, Jackson Parks *financial company executive*
Winter, Larry Eugene *accountant*

Darien

Davis, Ann Richardson *artist, sculptor, book dealer, writer*

Dawsonville

Jorgensen, Alfred H. *retired data processing executive, retired telecommunications industry executive*

Decatur

Bain, James Arthur *pharmacologist, educator*
Baker, Stephen Monroe *school system administrator*
Beran, Michael James *research psychologist, primatologist*
Brown, William Virgil *internal medicine educator*
Bullock, Mary Brown *college president*
Cartman, Shirley Eleise *retired music educator*
Cavallaro, Joseph John *retired microbiologist*
Dillingham, William Byron *literature educator, author*
Downs, Jon Franklin *drama educator, director, writer*
Dreyer, Susan *orthopedist, educator*
Gann, Joyce Ann *obstetrician-gynecologist*
Gregory, Sharon E. *neonatal clinical nurse specialist, nurse practitioner*
Hagood, Thomas Richard, Jr., *minister, publisher*
Hale, Cynthia Lynette *religious organization administrator*
Hamilton, Frank Strawn *jazz musician, folksinger, composer and arranger, educator*
Harris, Maurice Daniel *internist*
Henderson, Ralph Hale *physician*
Hinman, Alan Richard *public health administrator, epidemiologist*

Holtzman, Mary *engineering company executive*
Knight, Walker Leigh *editor, publisher, clergyman*
Lucius, Randall H. *psychologist*
Mc Intosh, James Eugene, Jr., *interior designer*
Murphy, Deborah Jane *lawyer*
Murray, Raymond Lee *retired clothing designer, writer*
Myers, Clark Everett *retired business administration educator*
Rausher, David Benjamin *internist, gastroenterologist*
Rosenberg, Mark L. *health agency administrator*
Rutland, Robert J. *transportation executive*
Shaw, Jeanne Osborne *editor, poet*
Solomon, Hilda Pearl *wholesale executive*
Tan, Li-Zhe *engineering educator, researcher*

Demorest

Rogers, Elizabeth (Betty) Carlisle *education educator, consultant*

Doraville

Dean, Andrew Griswold *epidemiologist, consultant, medical educator*
Wempner, Gerald Arthur *engineering educator*

Douglas

Hayes, Dewey *lawyer*
Hayes, Dewey Norman, Jr., *lawyer*
Tucker, Maureen Ann *musician*

Dublin

Claxton, Harriett Maroy Jones *language educator*
Greene, Jule Blounte *lawyer*
McCord, James Richard, III, *chemical engineer, mathematician*
Nellis, Noel *thoracic surgeon, educator*
Watt, Dwight, Jr., (Arthur Dwight Watt Jr.) *computer programming and microcomputer specialist*

Duluth

Beck, Andrew H. *farm equipment manufacturing executive*
Brasher, Earlene D. *music educator, church organist*
Bridges, Alan Lynn *physicist, computer scientist, systems software engineer*
Brody, Aaron Leo *food and packaging consultant*
Burns, Carroll Dean *insurance company executive*
Colwell, Gene Thomas *engineering educator*
Evans, Paul *osteopath*
Hillstead, Richard Averill *product development executive*
Hunter, Douglas Lee *ministry executive, former elevator executive*
Johnston, William David *biotechnology executive*
Kramer, Edward E. *screenwriter, editor*
Luger, Donald R. *engineering company executive*
McClung, Samuel Brenton *music educator, consultant*
McCullough, Robert *management consultant, information technology executive*
O'Dell, Richard *trucking executive*
Pickett, Christa Langford *elementary school counselor*
Ratliff, Robert J. *farm equipment manufacturing executive*
Reed, Ralph Eugene, Jr., *political party official*
Sloan, Donnie Robert, Jr., *lawyer*
Street, David Hargett *investment company executive*
Tewes, R. Scott *lawyer*
Weldon, Thomas David *medical products manufacturer*

Dunwoody

Callison, James W. *retired lawyer, consultant, airline executive*
Duvall, Marjorie L. *English and foreign language educator*
La Motte, Louis Cossitt, Jr., *medical scientist, consultant*
Maddox, Jerry Aven *retired catalog management executive*

East Point

Bridgewater, Herbert Jeremiah, Jr., *radio host*
Johnson, Hardwick Smith, Jr., *school psychologist*
Rattray, James Bailey *lawyer*

Ellabell

Lee, Frederick Drexel *lawyer*

Ellaville

Frontz, Howard Clinton, III, *music educator*

Ellenwood

Bauman, Mark Keith *historian, educator*

Evans

Fischer, Paul M. *physician, educator*
Fournier, Joseph Andre Alphonse *nurse, social worker, psychotherapist*
Karangu, David M. *automobile company executive*
Welsh, Michael Louis *business executive*
Zachert, Virginia *psychologist, educator*

Experiment

Reeves, Alan M. *automotive company executive*

Fairburn

Hughes, Cheryl Peck *elementary school educator, director*

Fayetteville

Brown, L(arry) Eddie *tax practitioner, business accountant, real estate broker, financial planner*
Cokuslu, Lynda Elizabeth McCord *medical assistant*
Hood, Barbara W. *musician, educator*
Neal, Joan Burkes *librarian*
Turnipseed, Barnwell Rhett, III, *journalist, public relations consultant*

Flovilla

Lamb, Deryle Jean *preservationist*

Flowery Branch

Blank, Arthur M. *professional sports team executive, retired home and lumber retail chain executive*
Congdon, Jon Harvey *music educator*
Monroe, Melrose *retired bank executive*
Vick, Michael *professional football player*

Folkston
Crumbley, Esther Helen Kendrick *retired real estate agent, retired secondary school educator, councilman*
Knowles, Julie Nall *secondary school educator*
Wangsness, Genna Stead *hotel executive, innkeeper*

Forest Park
Fisher, George Alexander, Jr., *lieutenant general United States Army*
Lambert, Ethel Gibson Clark *secondary school educator*
Riggs, John M. *army officer*

Forsyth
Coleman, Steven Andrew *surveyor*

Fort Mcpherson
Edwards, Warren Chappelle *military career officer*
Hendrix, John Walter *lieutenant general United States Army*
Piacentini, Nicholas A., Jr., *military officer*
Williamson, Kenneth N. *civilian military employee*

Fort Stewart
Webster, William G., Jr., *army officer*

Fort Valley
Archer, Lloyd Daniel *communications educator*
Maddox, Richard *manufacturing executive*
Swartwout, Joseph Rodolph *obstetrics and gynecology educator, administrator*

Fortson
Schmitt, Ralph George *manufacturing executive*

Franklin Springs
Pettyjohn, Emma Kennedy *fine arts educator*

Gainesville
Burd, John Stephen *retired academic administrator, music educator*
Clary, Ronald Gordon *insurance agency executive*
Davis, Connie Waters *public relations executive, marketing professional*
Ferriss, Abbott Lamoyne *sociology educator emeritus*
Givogre, John Lee *anesthesiologist*
Hester, Francis Bartow, III, (Frank Hester) *lawyer*
Jones, David Leland *music educator*
Jones, William Benjamin, Jr., *electrical engineering educator*
Leet, Richard Hale *oil company executive*
Mills, Hugh Milton, Jr., *retired college president*
Schuder, Raymond Francis *lawyer*
Turner, John Sidney, Jr., *retired otolaryngologist, educator*
Vaughn, Betty Jean *obstetrician/gynecologist*

Gainesville Georgia
Teem, Clayton L(aVerne), II, *education educator, psychologist*

Georgetown
Briggs, Niwana Page *editor, writer*

Grayson
Nease, Judith Allgood *marriage and family therapist*

Greensboro
Watts, Ronald Lester *retired military officer*

Griffin
Beuchat, Larry R. *food scientist, educator*
Doyle, Michael Patrick *microbiologist, educator, director*
Marshall, Allen Wright, III, *communications executive, financial consultant*
Shuman, Larry Myers *soil chemist*

Hamilton
Byrd, Gary Ellis *lawyer*

Hartwell
Rushing, Tonnie Austin Page *musician, educator*

Hawkinsville
Whipple, Woodrow Thomas *artist, educator*

Hazlehurst
Reed, John Cash *music educator, researcher*

Hephzibah
Golphin, Elouise *writer, educator*

Hiawassee
Bayless, Carolyn Cotton *nurse*

High Shoals
Bracewell, Gaynor Lee *hydro electric plant owner, developer*

Hinesville
Wise, Carl Stamps *accounting educator*

Hoschton
Campbell, Leslie Caine (Caine Campbell) *writer, historian*

Hull
Melton, Charles Estel *retired physicist, educator*

Jasper
Marger, Edwin *lawyer*
Sutter, Jean *sculptor*

Jeffersonville
Fitzpatrick, Duross *federal judge*

Jekyll Island
Bentley, James Luther *former journalist*
McKinley, Douglas Webster (Webb McKinley) *consultant*

Jonesboro
Blevins, Andrea Elizabeth *secondary school educator*
Colburn, Donald Eugene *protective services official*
Demster, Dawna Kay *orchestra director*
Finley, Sarah Maude Merritt *social worker*
Galvin, John Rogers *retired army officer, law educator*

Kennesaw
Adams, Dean (Lewis Adams) *theater director*
Anderson, Steven Goodwin *medical products executive*
Barnett, Benjamin Lewis, Jr., *retired physician, educator*
Hetrick, Joan Willette *critical care nurse, administrator*
Jenkins, Joyce Ann *information technology manager, educator*
Karcher, Barbara Correnti *sociologist, educator*
Kruger, Harry *retired conductor, retired music educator*
Leahey, Thomas P. *retail floor covering company executive*
Li, Chien-pin *political scientist, educator*
McSwain, Ron *textiles executive*
Moses, Oral *music educator*
Nassar, A.J. *retail executive*
Paterson, Paul Charles *retired private investigator, security consultant*
Ribeiro, Lucia C. *language educator*
Robinson, Kenneth Charles *management educator*
Roebuck, Deborah Mae Britt *management consultant, educator*
Siegel, Betty Lentz *university president*
Whittingham, Harry Edward, Jr., *retired banker*

Kingston
Dugger, Wanda Howard *music educator*

Lagrange
Ault, Ethyl Lorita *special education educator, consultant*
Cook, John Granger *religious studies educator, philosopher, educator*
Copeland, Robert Bodine *internist, cardiologist*
Davidson, Joeline Dillard *laboratory services administrator*
Gresham, James Thomas *foundation executive*
Hudson, Charles Daugherty *insurance executive*
Malone, Thomas J. *textile company executive*
Wilkes, George Gardner, Jr., *landscape architect*

Lake Park
Blanton, Vallye J. *elementary school educator*

Lawrenceville
Crain, Mary Ann *elementary school educator*
Elleby, Gail *management consultant*
Fetner, Robert Henry *radiation biologist*
Gericke, Paul William *minister, educator*
Henson, Gene Ethridge *retired legal administrator, interior designer*
Iannazzone, Joseph Charles *judge*
Lynn, Thomas Edward *retired government agency administrator*
McClure, David H. *utilities company analyst*
Meehan, Patrick John *public health officer*
Neaton, Marcia Lynne *accountant, financial analyst*
Reeves, Gene *judge*
Reuter, Helen Hyde *psychologist*
Wall, Clarence Vinson *state legislator*

Leesburg
Myers, David Wayne *legal assistant*

Lilburn
Baranco, Gregory T. *automobile dealership executive*

Lithia Springs
Jackson, Mitchell Alexander *artist, writer*

Lithonia
Baxter, Gene Francis *chemical researcher, consultant*
Smith, Shaunte Renee *secondary school educator, poet*

Loganville
Daly, Joe Ann Godown *publishing company executive*

Louisville
Hoover, John Elwood *former military officer, consultant, author, speaker on US military history*

Lovejoy
Onukwuli, Francis Osita *computer scientist, secondary education educator, mathematician*

Mableton
Rowe, Bonnie Gordon *music company executive*

Macon
Aldridge, Melvin Dayne *engineering educator*
Anderson, Robert Lanier, III, *federal judge*
Bagley, Cathy Lorraine *obstetrician, gynecologist*
Bell, Andrew C. *music educator*
Brown, Nancy Childs *marriage and family therapist*
Brown, Stephen Phillip *judge*
Camp, Shirley A. *nursing consultant, lawyer*
Craig, Kern William *political science educator*
Davis, Anita Yvonne *small business owner, writer*
Drysdale, Joyce A *substance abuse counselor*
Dunwody, Eugene Cox *architect*
Ennis, Edgar William, Jr., *lawyer*
Fickling, William Arthur, Jr., *health care manager*
Franklin, Roosevelt *minister*
Godsey, R(aleigh) Kirby *university president*
Hails, Robert Emmet *aerospace consultant, business executive, former air force officer*
Hall, David L. *finance company executive*
Hatcher, Robert F. *financial executive*
Hershner, Robert Franklin, Jr., *judge*
Huffman, Joan Brewer *history professor*
Jobe, Ann Connor *dean, educator*
Jones, John Ellis *real estate broker*
Leonard, Michael Steven *industrial engineering educator*
Lewis, Sandra Combs *research psychologist, writer*
McCook, Thomas H. *savings and loan association executive*
McQueen, Michael Anthony *journalism educator*
Molloy, George A. *finance company executive*
Murdoch, Bernard Constantine *psychology educator*
Oliver, Katherine C. *museum director*
Owens, Wilbur Dawson, Jr., *federal judge*
Phillips, J(ohn) Taylor *judge*
Robinson, Joe Sam *neurosurgeon, educator*
Robinson, W. Lee *lawyer*
Savage, Randall Ernest *journalist*
Snow, Cubbedge, Jr., *lawyer*
Staton, Cecil Pope, Jr., *religious and academic publisher, educator, broadcast executive*
Steeples, Douglas Wayne *retired university dean, consultant, researcher*
Stewart, Jeffrey Vincent, III, *information technology educator*
Volpe, Erminio Peter *biologist, educator*
Waddy, Calista Anne *music educator, musician*
Walton, DeWitt Talmage, Jr., *dentist*
Weaver, Jacquelyn Kunkel Ivey *artist, educator*
White, John Joseph *surgery and pediatrics educator*
Wiggins, James L. *lawyer*
Wood, Frank Maxwell *lawyer*
Woody, Thomas Clifton, II, *assistant district attorney*
Young, Henry E. *tissue engineering medical educator*
Young-Zook, Monica M. *language educator*

Madison
Aldridge, John Watson *English language educator, author*
DuBose, Charles Wilson *lawyer*
Neidlinger, Sheri Kim *music educator*

Marietta
Bentley, Fred Douglas, Sr., *lawyer*
Berryhill, Henry Lee, Jr., *geologist, researcher*
Blount, Daniel J. *lumber company executive*
Bond, Barbara J. *bank executive*
Burnett, Christopher H. *bank executive*
Chastain, Mark Alan *dermatologist, otolaryngologist, educator*
Clay, Charles Commander (Chuck Clay) *lawyer, former state senator*
Dalziel, Charles Meredith, Jr., *lawyer*
Dudley, Gary Edward *clinical psychologist*
Dunwoody, Kenneth Reed *magazine and book editor*
Edwards, Charle Mundy, III, *financial consultant*
Fitzgerald, John Edmund *civil engineering educator*
Gannon, Tom *paper company executive*
Hagood, Murl Felton *surgeon*
Hays, Robert William *communications consultant, educator, writer*
Hines, P. Harris *bank executive*
Houston, Dorothy Middleton *elementary school educator*
Humphrey, Stephen M. *paperboard company executive*
Kiger, Ronald Lee *contract negotiator*
Laframboise, Joan Carol *middle school educator*
Lee, Raymond William, III, *institutional stockbroker*
Lewis, William Headley, Jr., *manufacturing executive*
Martin, Sherlonda S. *personnel director*
McAuley, Thomas H. *real estate executive*
McEntire, Betty *health facility administrator*
McGahan, Martin J. *health products executive*
Meyer, Roger Albert *surgeon*
Miles, Thomas Caswell *aerospace engineer*
Milligan, Edward C. *bank executive*
Morisco, Jerid Simon *music educator, conductor*
Moulthrop, Edward Allen *architect, artist*
Murray, Barry Wayne *economics educator*
Neff, Marilyn Lee *nursing consultant*
Nowland, James Ferrell *lawyer*
Oliver, Ann Breeding *secondary school educator*
Opre, Thomas Edward *retired editor, retired film company executive*
Petit, Parker Holmes *health care corporation executive*
Poor, Andrew Ford *music educator*
Rainey, Kenneth Tyler *English language educator*
Ranu, Harcharan Singh *biomedical scientist, administrator, orthopaedic biomechanics educator*
Rivers, Alma Faye *secondary school educator*
Rogers, Gail Elizabeth *library director*
Rossbacher, Lisa Ann *university president, geology educator, writer*
Sauder, Randy James *state legislator, lawyer*
Segerhammar, Sharon K. *special education administrator*
Short-Mayfield, Patricia Ahlene *business owner*
Simmons, Stephen Gregory *accountant*
Smith, Baker Armstrong *management executive, lawyer*
Smith, Beverly Ann Evans *management consultant, small business owner*
Smith, George Thornewell *retired state supreme court justice*
Spann, George William *management consultant*
Taylor, Frederick Jerome *music educator, consultant*
Thomas, Pamella Delores *medical director, physician, educator*
Wells, Palmer Donald *performing arts executive*
Wheatley, Joseph Kevin *physician, urologist*
Wheelock, Argil J. *urologist, medical company executive*
Wimberly, Linda Roberts *music educator, artist*

Martinez
Chaudhary, Shaukat Ali *ecologist, plant taxonomist*
Colborn, Gene Louis *anatomy educator, researcher*
Nesbitt, Robert Edward Lee, Jr., *physician, educator, scientific researcher, writer, poet*

Mcdonough
Dunlap, Donald Kelder *rental company executive*

Metter
Doremus, Ogden *lawyer*
Farmer, DeWayne Mark *director, photographer*
Guido, Michael Anthony *evangelist*

Milledgeville
Deal, Therry Nash *college dean*
DeVries, David John *mathematician, educator*
Engerrand, Doris Dieskow *business educator*
Harshbarger, D. Bruce, Sr., *director, educator*
Leland, Dorothy *academic administrator*
McGinnis, Michael Boyd *chemistry professor*
Reed, Harold Wayne *university program coordinator*

Millen
Bray, Phillip Wayne *minister, writer*

Monroe
Altherr, Jack Richard, Jr., *accountant*
Sewell, Joan Marshall *retired elementary school educator*

Morrow
Smith-Jones, Mary Emily *elementary school physical education educator*

Moultrie
Collum, Rick Daniel *lawyer*
Johnson, Edith Scott *English educator, writing consultant*
McCall, John Clark, Jr., *interior designer*
McLendon, Richard Charles *music educator*
Vereen, William Jerome *uniform manufacturing company executive*

Mount Berry
Davis, John Edward *music educator, musician*
Dhir, Krishna Swaroop *business administration educator*
Mew, Thomas Joseph, III, (Tommy Mew) *artist, educator*
Shiffman, Daniel Steven *literature educator*

Mount Vernon
Fernisse, Glenn P. *music educator*
Jossey, Laurie A. *education educator*
Smith, David Robert *higher education administrator, minister, writer*

Murrayville
Morris, Donald G. *engineering company executive*

Newnan
Barron, Thomas Willis *real estate broker*
Drake, W. Homer, Jr., *federal judge*
Franklin, Bruce Walter *lawyer*
McBroom, Thomas William, Sr., *aviation consultant*

Newton
Blood, Elizabeth R. *research scientist*

Norcross
Adams, Kenneth Francis *automobile maufacturing company executive*
Anderson, Albert Sydney, III, *lawyer*
Atkinson, A. Kelley *insurance company executive*
Balkcom, James R., Jr., *manufacturing executive*
Ballard, Robert Clifford *automation engineer, failure analysis consultant*
Barrow, Pamela H. *health services administrator*
Bowman, Jerry W. *recruiting company executive*
Caldwell, Claud Reid *lawyer*
Cramer, James Perry *management strategist, architectural author, educator*
Dibb, David Walter *research association administrator*
Dobson, Terry *medical services company executive*
Dumont, William K. *business communications management executive*
Galfas, Timothy, II, *franchising and turnaround administrator*
Granger, Philip Richard *minister*
Hahn, Stanley Robert, Jr., *lawyer, financial executive*
Harrison, Gordon Ray *engineering executive, consultant, research scientist*
Kight, Peter J. *financial services company executive*
Koscik, Ella M. *management and technology company executive*
LaFramboise, Patrick Joseph *trade association administrator*
Massey, Lewis *finance company executive*
Moore, Christopher Barry *industrial engineer*
Moreno, Veronica *food products executive*
Nabors, David *health facility executive*
Penninger, Samuel A., Jr., *consumer products company executive*
Plumb, Russell H. *business company executive*
Plummer, Michael Kenneth *financial consultant*
Puente, Jose Garza *safety engineer*
Rubright, James Alfred *paperboard and packaging company executive*
Sellers, Mark S. *retail executive*
Sharon, Thomas E. *science company executive*
Shulman, Allen L. *financial services company executive*
Sinisgalli, Peter F. *financial company executive*
Strange, J. Leland *computer company executive*
Sutherland, Mitchell Alsobrook, Jr., *mechanical engineer, consultant*
Szlam, Aleksander *manufacturing executive*
Tenoso, Harold J. *consumer products company executive*
Thompson, Keith J. *medical services company executive*
Tito, James P. *software company executive*
Tufano, Charles C. *paper company executive*
Wagner, Robert Earl *retired agronomist*

Oakwood
Jondahl, Terri Elise *importing and distribution company executive*
Martin, Johnny Benjamin *accountant*

Oxford
Cody, William Bermond *political science educator*
Sitton, Claude Fox *newspaper editor*
Stamps, George Moreland *communications consultant, facsimile pioneer*

Peachtree City
Barnes, Marylou Riddleberger *retired academic administrator, educator*
Barrell, Dawn Holman *marketing specialist*
Clark, James Kermit, Jr., *real estate executive*
Day, Annette J. *music educator*
Dillard, George Stewart, III, *minister*
Ebneter, Stewart Dwight *utility industry management consultant*
Green, Franklin Pasco *music educator*
Liang, Yue *engineer*
Marsh, Carole *author, photographer, publisher*
Roobol, Norman Richard *industrial coatings consultant, educator*
Snyder, Franklin Farison *hydrologic engineering consultant*
Wilde, Mary *secondary school educator*
Yother, Michele *publisher*

Perry
Geiger, James Norman *lawyer*

Pine Mountain
Bishop, Michael *writer*
Callaway, Howard Hollis *business executive*

Port Wentworth
Ivie, Shirley Bridges *nurse anesthetist*

Quitman
Baum, Joseph Herman *retired biomedical educator*
Carter, Roger Alan *music educator, director*

Redan
Bennett-Williams, Sharon K. *mental health services professional, writer*

Reidsville
Saad, Fathy Zaki *medical association administrator, physician*

Richmond Hill
Budde, Neil Frederick *publishing company executive, editor, publisher*

Rincon
Carter, Charles Henry, III, *music educator*

Riverdale
Waters, John W. *minister, educator*

Roberta
Clark, Donald *music educator*

Robins AFB
Batbie, John J., Jr., *military officer*
Haines, Dennis G. *military officer*
Whaley, Wallace W. *military officer*

Rome
Black, Suzanne Watkins DuPuy *psychology educator*
Carper, N. Gordon *historian, educator*
Granrose, Cherlyn Sue *psychologist, educator, medical researcher*
Janowski, Thaddeus Marian *architect*
Johnson, Alberta Clark *psychology educator*
Kines, Joan Elaine *human services administrator, consultant*
Lewis, Wayne Walton *industrial engineer*
Massing, Virginia Reeves *surgical nurse and administrator*
Murphy, Harold Loyd *federal judge*
Pethel, Stanley Robert *composer, music educator*
Potts, Glenda Rue *music educator*
Sellers, Jimmie *construction executive*
Sheeley, Steven M. *academic administrator, minister, education educator*
Stephens, Michael Thoryne *librarian*
Sumner, Melanie *writer, educator*
Tapia, Martha Luisa *mathematics professor*

Roswell
Baker, Anita Diane *lawyer*
Barnett, Florence Carsley *neurosurgeon*
Burgess, John Frank *retired utilities executive*
Christopher, Lin *artist*
Diercks, Chester William, Jr., *capital goods manufacturing company executive*
Dolan, Dennis Joseph *airline pilot, lawyer*
England, John Melvin *lawyer, clergyman*
Forbes, John Ripley *museum executive, educator, naturalist*
Hill, Donald Dee *management consultant, lecturer, writer*
Klein, John Jacob *retired economist*
Krobot, Thomas C. *construction executive*
Lawler-Johnson, Dian L. *singer, instructor of voice, vocal technician*
McCloud, Melody Theresa *obstetrician-gynecologist, surgeon*
Peterson, Donald Robert *magazine editor, vintage automobile consultant*
Rogers, Richard Hilton *hotel consultant, broker*
Roland, Raymond William *lawyer, mediator*
Siepi, Cesare *opera singer*
Thibaudeau, Mary Frances *cultural organization administrator*

Saint Marys
Hall, Lois Bremer *retired educator, volunteer*
Smith, Charles Courtland, Jr., *lawyer, state legislator*

Saint Simons
Douglas, William Ernest *retired government official*
Spivey, Ted Ray *English educator*

Saint Simons Island
Bell, Ronald Mack *university foundation administrator, consultant*
Mathis, Luster Doyle *college administrator, political scientist*
Sullivan, Barbara Boyle *management consultant*
Turbidy, John Berry *investor, management consultant*
Webb, Lamar Thaxter *architect*

Savannah
Aja-Herrera, Marie *fashion designer, educator*
Aquadro, Jeana Lauren *graphic designer, educator*
Baker, Brinda Elizabeth Garrison *infectious disease nurse*
Ball, Ardella Patricia *library media educator*
Beals, L(oren) Alan *association executive*
Boland, John Kevin *bishop*
Bowman, Catherine McKenzie *lawyer*
Brown, Carlton E. *college president*
Cartledge, Raymond Eugene *retired paper company executive*
Clemmons, John B. *bank executive, director, retired mathematics educator*
Coffey, Thomas Francis, Jr., *writer*
Dickerson, Lon Richard *library administrator*
Dickey, David Herschel *lawyer, accountant*
DiClaudio, Janet Alberta *health information administrator*
Dirlam, David Kirk *education educator*
Dixon, Harry D., Jr., (Donnie Dixon) *former prosecutor*
Dodge, William Douglas *insurance company consultant*
Eaves, George Newton *lecturer, consultant, research administrator*
Edeawo, Gale Sky *publishing company executive, writer*
Edenfield, Berry Avant *federal judge*
Ferro, Alejandro F. *obstetrician, gynecologist*
Foley, Marilyn Lorna *artist*
Forbes, Morton Gerald *lawyer*
Friedman, Julian Richard *lawyer*
Gilbert, John B. *retired electric and power company official*
Gillespie, Daniel Curtis, Sr., *retired non-profit company executive, consultant*
Goodwyn, George Waverly, Jr., *corporate financial executive, educator*
Graham, Patrick Samuel *air transportation executive*
Granger, Harvey, Jr., *retired manufacturing company executive*
Greenberg, Philip B. *symphony orchestra conductor and music director*
Gusby, Kim *newscaster*
Hammond, C.F. *automotive executive*
Hemphill, John Michael *neurologist*
Horan, Tom *automotive executive*
Hoskins, William John *obstetrician, gynecologist, educator*
Howard, Constance Adair *banker*
Hsu, Ming-Yu *engineering educator*
John, Selena Latricia *systems analyst*
Johnson, Eric B. *state legislator*
Kitchings, Alton Dwith *lawyer*
Krahl, Enzo *retired surgeon*
Leighton, Richard Frederick *retired dean*
McCracken, Eugene Luke *lawyer*
Moore, William Theodore, Jr., *judge*
O'Brien, George Aloysius, Jr., *paper company executive*
Otter, John Martin, III, *retired television advertising consultant*
Palanca, Terilyn *software industry analyst*
Parker, Sheila *newscaster*
Peer, George Joseph *metals company executive*
Phillips, Robert L., Jr., *application developer, consultant*
Polite, Evelyn C. *retired middle school educator, counselor, evangelist*
Ramsay, Linda *architect*
Rawson, William Robert *lawyer, retired manufacturing company executive*
Rozantine, Gayle Stubbs *clinical psychologist*
Sanders, James Grady *biogeochemist*
Searcy, William Nelson *lawyer, director*
Sheehy, Barry Maurice *management consultant*
Shron, Marina *playwright, scriptwriter*
Simmonds, Jimmie Neil *theater educator*
Simonaitis, Richard Ambrose *chemist*
Skelton, William Douglas *physician*
Spitz, Seymour James, Jr., *retired fragrance company executive*
Sprague, William Wallace, Jr., *retired food company executive*
Stinn, Bradley J. *jewelry retailer*
Taggart, Helen M. *adult education educator, nurse*
Taylor, Roslyn Donny *family physician*
Thomas, Dwight Rembert *writer*
Thomas, Regina D. *state legislator*
Thompson, Larry James *retired gifted and social studies education educator*
Thompson, Richard S. *lawyer*
Thorne, Kristan *newscaster*
Tyus-Shaw, Tina *newscaster*
Wallace, Paula S. *academic administrator*
Walter, Paul Hermann Lawrence *chemistry professor*
Wilder, Ginger *newscaster*
Windom, Herbert Lynn *oceanographer, environmental scientist*
Wirth, Fremont Philip, Jr., *neurosurgeon, educator*
Zoller, Michael *otolaryngologist, head and neck surgeon, educator*

Scottdale
Borochoff, Ida Sloan *artist*

Sea Island
LaWare, John Patrick *retired bank executive, federal agency administrator*
Mc Swiney, James Wilmer *retired pulp and paper manufacturing company executive*
Revoile, Charles Patrick *lawyer*

Sky Valley
Wilkinson, Albert Mims, Jr., *lawyer*

Smyrna
Atkins, William Austin, Sr., (Bill Atkins) *former state legislator*
Bean, Susan Montgomery *secondary school educator*
Buck, Lee Albert *retired insurance company executive, evangelist*
Davenport, Glenn A. *management executive*
Dumbacher, Robert J. *gas company executive*
Hawkins, Edna Bramlett *writer*
Kell, Michael Jon *physician, researcher*
Michels, Frances G. *management company executive*
Michelson, Robert C. *engineering educator, researcher*
Passantino, Richard J. *architect*
Rife, Elizabeth *musician, music educator*
Seigler, Michael Edward *lawyer, librarian*
Tabron, Wendy *paper company executive*

Snellville
Cleland, Max *former senator*
Magill, Dodie Burns *early childhood education educator*

Social Circle
Penland, John Thomas *retired import and export and development companies executive*

Statesboro
Bartels, Jean Ellen *nursing educator*
Beasley, John Julius *child and family development educator*
Bryan, Carolyn J. *music educator, saxophonist*
Classens, Michael John *lawyer*
Damelin, Steven Benjamin *mathematician, educator*
Franklin, James Burke *lawyer*
Freeman, Robert Noble *psychology educator*
Henry, Nicholas Llewellyn *public administration educator*
Humphrey, Patricia Buslee *statistician, researcher*
Kaymakcalan, Billur *mathematician, educator*
Lloyd, Margaret Ann *psychologist, educator*
Murkison, Eugene Cox *finance educator*
Ngai, Sze-Man *education educator*
Pino, Nathan Willett *criminologist, educator, sociologist*
Stone, Ralph Kenny *lawyer*
Whitaker, Mical Rozier *theater director, educator*
Wood, George Ambos *city manager*

Stockbridge
Friedman, Robert Barry *neurosurgeon*
Grimes, Richard Allen *economics professor*

Stone Mountain
Allen (Irvin M.N.), Georgianne Lydia Christian *writer, poet*
Branscome, Curtis *parks and recreation director*
Dearfield, Rock *minister, parochial school administrator*
Dees, Julian Worth *retired academic/research administrator*
Gary, C. Ceci *primary school educator*
Gotlieb, Jaquelin Smith *pediatrician*
Le, Chi-Dinh *law educator, writer*
Malone, Embry *property manager, advocate*
McNair, Nimrod, Jr., *foundation executive, consultant*
Reichert, Leo Edmund, Jr., *biochemist, endocrinologist*
Roth, Edie Cowan *rehabilitation services professional*

Summerville
Connelly, Lewis Branch Sutton *lawyer*

Suwanee
Anderson, Jamal Sharif *professional football player*
Colgan, George Phillips *real estate developer, real estate analyst*
Frey, Glenn *songwriter, vocalist, guitarist*
Harriman, John *music educator*
Swanson, David H(enry) *consultant, retired economist, educator*

Swainsboro
Cadle, Jerry Neal *lawyer*
Edenfield, Cynthia Smith *pre-school educator*

Sylvania
Harper, Michael Christopher *music educator*

Thomaston
Mauney, James Thomas, Jr., *music educator, musician*

Thomasville
Flowers, Langdon Strong *foods company executive*
Mc Mullian, Amos Ryals *food company executive*
Turner, Marta Jones *public affairs professional*

Tifton
Burton, Glenn Willard *geneticist*
Dorminey, Henry Clayton, Jr., *allergist*
Reinhardt, George Robert *lawyer*
Roberts, Curtis Creed *minister, writer*
Ruberson, John Russell *entomology educator*

Toccoa
Maypole, John Floyd *real estate holding company executive*

Toccoa Falls
Alford, Paul Legare *college and religious foundation administrator*
Allison, Norman Ernest, Jr., *anthropologist, educator*
Gardner, Donna Rae (Diehl) *education educator*

Townsend
Hicks, Harold Eugene *chemical engineer*

Tucker
Broucek, William Samuel *printing plant executive*
Brown, Betsy S. *hotel executive*
Diamond, Gerald *holding company executive*
Franklin, Carol D. *electronics company executive*
Guimbellot, Bobby E. *hotel executive*
Osborne, Thomas Eugene *oral and maxillofacial surgeon*
Risner, Ray D. *computer company executive*
Roberts, Thomas Heym *city and regional planner, consultant*
Sturges, Lynn H. *lawyer, sociologist*

Tunnel Hill
McNelley, Judy Anne *small business owner*

Union City
Jones, Emanuel D. *transportation company executive*

Valdosta
Aronson-Friedman, Amy Ilene *education educator*
Bailey, Hugh Coleman *university president*
Copeland, Roy Wilson *lawyer*
Dodd, Roger J. *lawyer*
Edwards, Edith Martha *lawyer*
Farwell, Doug George *music educator*
Phillips, Taurence Lamar *music educator*
Santas, Aristotelis *philosophy educator, massage therapist*
Sinnott, John Patrick *lawyer, educator*

Villa Rica
Hutto, John Robert, Jr., *pastor*

Waleska
Robertson, Eddie B. *biologist, educator*

Warner Robins
Beck, Rhonda Joann *paramedic, educator, writer*
DePriest, C(harles) David *engineering executive, retired military officer*
Nugteren, Cornelius *air force officer*

Watkinsville
Morrison, Darrel Gene *landscape architecture educator*
Williams, Vivian (Vinnie) Marie *publishing executive, editor, writer*
Wright, Robert Joseph *lawyer*

West Point
Andrews, Gerald Bruce, Sr., *retired textile executive*
Barnwell, Madge Owen *volunteer*
Glover, Clifford Clarke *retired construction company executive*

Wildwood
Dombrowski, Bob *artist, publisher*

Winder
McLemore, Michael Kerr *lawyer, minister*

Winterville
Anderson, David Prewitt *retired university dean*

Woodstock
Austin, John David *retired financial executive*
Collins, David Browning *religious institution administrator*

Zebulon
Bizzell Yarbrough, Cindy Lee *school counselor*

HAWAII

Aiea
Suyenaga, Elsie Sakae *secondary school educator*

Camp H M Smith
Hailston, Earl B. *career officer*
Surface, Stephen Walter *water treatment chemist, environmental protection specialist*

Ewa Beach
Chock, Alvin Keali'i *retired botanist*

Hanalei
Snyder, Francine *psychotherapist, registered nurse, writer*

Hawaii National Park
Camp, Richard J. *ecologist, statistician, researcher*
Swanson, Donald Alan *geologist*

Hickam AFB
Polk, Steven R. *military officer*

Hilo
Binder, Philippe-Michel *physicist, educator*
Buyers, John William Amerman *agribusiness and specialty foods company executive*
Chong, Clayton Elliott *lawyer*
Clark, Janet *retired health services executive*
Dinges, Richard Allen *entrepreneur*
Dixon, Paul William *psychology educator*
Fisher, Robert Scott *astronomer*
Gersting, Judith Lee *computer scientist, educator, researcher*
Kinney, Jeanne Kawelolani *English studies educator, writer*
Li, Shuguang *mathematics professor, researcher*
Merk, Elizabeth Thole *investment company executive*
Skorikov, Vladimir B. *researcher, educator*
Tseng, Rose *academic administrator*

Holualoa
Scarr, Sandra Wood *retired psychology educator, researcher*
Stoddard, Sandol *freelance/self-employed writer*

Honolulu
Abe, Gregg Koyei *music educator*
Acoba, Simeon Rivera, Jr., *state supreme court justice, educator*
Adachi, Athan Ken *civil engineer*
Adams, Jo-Ann Marie *lawyer, actress*
Adcock, Betty-Lee *real estate company officer*
Aduja, Melodie Williams *state senator*
Agrusa, Jerome *tourism studies educator, consultant*
Ahmed, Iqbal *psychiatrist, consultant*
Aiona, James R., Jr., *lieutenant governor*
Akiba, Lorraine Hiroko *lawyer*
Arakaki, Dennis A. *state representative*
Archer, Richard Joseph *lawyer*
Asai-Sato, Carol Yuki *lawyer*
Aung-Thwin, Michael Arthur *history educator*
Baker, Rosalyn Hester *state senator*
Bauman, Kay A. *physician*
Bender, Byron Wilbur *linguistics educator*
Bennett, Mark J. *state attorney general*
Betts, Barbara Stoke *artist, educator*
Billings, Kathy *national monument administrator*
Bitterman, Morton Edward *psychologist, educator*
Black, Cobey *journalist*
Bloede, Victor Carl *lawyer, academic executive*
Boas, Frank *retired lawyer*
Bossert, Philip Joseph *information systems executive*
Botsai, Elmer Eugene *architect, architecture educator, retired dean*
Brady, Stephen R.P.K. *physician*
Bronster, Margery S *state attorney general*
Buen, Jan Yagi *state legislator*
Bukoski, Kika G. *state representative*
Bunda, Robert *state legislator*
Cachola, Romy Munoz *state legislator*
Cadman, Edwin Clarence *dean, health facility administrator, medical educator*
Caldwell, Kirk *state representative*
Callies, David Lee *lawyer, educator*
Carson, Hampton Lawrence *geneticist, educator*
Cassiday, Benjamin Buckles, III, *lawyer*
Chang, Rodney Eiu Joon *artist, dentist*
Char, Vernon Fook Leong *lawyer*
Chee, Gloria Y.M. *secondary school educator*
Chee, Percival Hon Yin *ophthalmologist*
Chen, Wai-Fah *civil engineering educator*
Ching, Chauncey Tai Kin *agricultural economics educator*
Ching, Wesley H. H. *lawyer*
Cho, Lee-Jay *social scientist, demographer*
Chock, Clifford Yet-Chong *family practice physician*
Chock, Raelene *school system administrator*
Choi, Song K. *mechanical engineer, educator*
Chuck, Walter G(oonsun) *lawyer, director*
Chun-Hoon, Lowell Koon Ying *lawyer*
Clarke, Robert F. *utilities company executive*
Clifton, Richard Randall *federal judge*

Eastland, Larry L. *entertainment and theme park development executive*
Eismann, Daniel T. *state supreme court justice*
Elg, Annette *food products executive*
Ellis-Vant, Karen McGee *elementary and special education educator, consultant*
Ellsworth, Julie *state representative*
Erickson, Robert Stanley *lawyer*
Field, Debbie *state representative*
Field, Frances *state representative*
Foster, S. Thomas, Jr., *department chairman, quality management educator, consultant, writer*
Gabriel, Clarence J. *retail executive*
Geddes, Robert L. *state legislator*
Gee, Gavin M. *state agency administrator*
Gellert, Edward Bradford *advertising agency executive*
Geston, Mark Symington *lawyer*
Goedde, John W. *state senator*
Griffin, Sylvia Gail *reading specialist*
Hanks, Stephen Grant *lawyer, construction executive*
Harad, George Jay *manufacturing executive*
Hegg, David Alan *real estate analyst*
Hendren, Merlyn Churchill *investment company executive*
Herbert, Kathy *retail executive*
Hlobik, Lawrence S. *agricultural products executive*
Hoffman, William Kenneth *retired obstetrician, gynecologist*
Holleran, John W. *lawyer*
Holt, Isabel Rae *radio program producer*
Houle, Arthur Joseph *music educator*
Howard, Marilyn *school system administrator*
Hunsucker, Wayne (Carl Wayne Hunsucker) *architectural firm executive, educator*
Ilett, Frank, Jr., *trucking company executive, educator*
Ingram, Cecil D. *accountant, state legislator*
Jaquet, Wendy S. *state representative*
Johnston, Lawrence R. *food products executive*
Jones, Donna Marilyn *state agency administrator, former legislator*
Juetten, George H. *company executive*
Kaupins, Gundars Egons *education educator*
Kellogg, Hilde *state representative*
Kempthorne, Dirk Arthur *governor*
Kent, E(verett) Allen *performing arts administrator, theatrical producer*
Keough, Shawn *state legislator*
Kidwell, Wayne L. *state supreme court justice*
Lance, Alan George *former state attorney general*
Leroy, David Henry *lawyer, state and federal official*
Lodge, Edward James *federal judge*
Lodge, Patti Anne *state senator*
Long, William D. *grocery store executive*
Longeteig, Iver J. *lawyer*
Luthy, John Frederick *management consultant*
Lynch, Peter L. *supermarket/drug store executive*
Maloof, Giles Wilson *academic administrator, educator, author*
Markuson, Richard K. *former pharmaceutical association executive*
McDevitt, Charles Francis *retired state supreme court justice, lawyer*
McGown, John, Jr., *lawyer*
McKague, Shirley *state representative*
McLaughlin, Marguerite P. *state legislator, logging company executive*
Meyer, Christopher Hawkins *lawyer*
Minnich, Diane Kay *legal association administrator*
Mogensen, Dennis *agricultural products company executive*
Moss, Thomas E. *prosecutor*
Myers, William Gerry Gerry, III, *lawyer*
Nelson, Thomas G. *federal judge*
Newcomb, Bruce *state legislator, farmer, rancher*
Olson, A. Craig *foundation administrator, former retail executive, retail executive*
Overgaard, Willard Michele *retired political scientist, jurisprudent*
Park, William Anthony (Tony Park) *lawyer*
Parkinson, Del R. *music educator, pianist*
Parks, Roger *food products executive*
Parry, Atwell J., Jr., *state legislator, retail executive*
Pimble, Toni *artistic director, choreographer, educator*
Piva, Gary *retail grocery executive*
Punnoose, Alex *physics educator*
Redshaw, James Douglas *neurologist*
Ringo, Shirley G. *state representative*
Risch, James E. *lieutenant governor, former state legislator, lawyer*
Ruch, Charles P. *academic administrator*
Sandy, John A. *political organization administrator, state legislator*
Schild, Raymond Douglas *lawyer*
Shepherd, Mary Lou *state representative*
Shurtliff, Marvin Karl *lawyer*
Silak, Cathy R. *lawyer, former state supreme court justice*
Simplot, John R. *agribusiness executive*
Simplot, Scott R. *diversified food products company executive*
Sims, John R. *lawyer*
Skurzynski, Gloria Joan *writer*
Slaughter, Richard Arthur *political scientist, economist, educator*
Smith, Marsha H. *state agency administrator, lawyer*
Stablein, Lawrence A. *retail executive*
Steiner, Stanley F. *literature educator*
Stover, Wilbur G., Jr., *manufacturing executive*
Sullivan, James Kirk *management consultant*
Szerbiak, Robert Bruce *geophysicist, researcher*
Thomas, Eugene C. *lawyer*
Thornton, Felicia *food service executive, corporate financial executive*
Tripp, Kevin *retail executive*
Trott, Stephen Spangler *federal judge, musician*
Uranga, Jean R. *lawyer*
VanHole, William Remi *lawyer*
Wainwright Henbest, Margaret A. *state representative*
Walters, Jesse Raymond, Jr., *state supreme court justice*
Wasden, Lawrence *state attorney general*
Washington, Dennis R. *contracting company executive*
Wetherell, Michael E. *lawyer*
Wilson, Jack Fredrick *retired federal government official*
Winmill, B. Lynn *judge*
Wood, JoAn E. *state representative*
Ysursa, Ben T. *state official*
Zarges, Thomas H. *engineering executive*

Buhl
Blaszkiewicz, David Albin *theater educator, performing company executive*

Caldwell
Hendren, Robert Lee, Jr., *academic administrator*
Hoover, Robert Allan *university president*
Kerrick, David Ellsworth *lawyer*
Rember, John V. *literature educator*

Coeur D Alene
Dahlgren, Dorothy *museum director*
Gumprecht, Jane Caroline Doering *retired physician*
Wheeler, Dennis Earl *mining company executive, lawyer*

Eagle
Richardson, Betty H. *lawyer, former prosecutor*

Glenns Ferry
King-Barrutia, Robbie L. *state senator*

Hagerman
Lipskoch, Christy Michelle *music educator*

Hailey
Dolas, Evelyn Ann *poet, musician*
Hogue, Terry Glynn *lawyer*
Youngblood, Deborah Sue *lawyer, speech pathology/audiology services professional*

Harrison
Carlson, George Arthur *artist*

Hayden Lake
Wogsland, James Willard *retired heavy machinery manufacturing executive*

Heyburn
Barson, Ross J. *music educator, assistant principal*

Hope
Meyers, Marlene O. *retired health facility administrator*

Idaho Falls
Barbe, Betty Catherine *marketing professional, retired financial analyst*
Boring, Ronald Laurids *research scientist*
Gregory, Nelson Bruce *retired motel owner, retired naval officer*
Harris, Darryl Wayne *publishing executive*
Hart, Stephen Strong *lawyer*
Jacobsen, Richard T. *mechanical engineering educator*
King, Ronald Amos *federal official, communications professional, retired*
Lee, Glenn Richard *medical administrator, educator*
Miller, Gregory Kent *structural engineer*
Newman, Stanley Ray *oil industry executive*
Ohman, John Michael *lawyer*
Parkinson, Howard Evans *insurance company executive*
Planchon, Harry Peter, Jr., *research development manager*
Riddoch, Hilda Johnson *accountant*
Riemke, Richard Allan *mechanical engineer*
Rydalch, Ann *federal agency administrator*
Shindurling, Jon J. *judge*
Thorsen, James Hugh *retired aviation director, retired airport manager*
Thorsen, Nancy Dain *real estate broker*

Inkom
Ambrose, Tommy W. *chemical engineer, executive*
Jackson, Allen Keith *retired museum administrator*

Jerome
Akers, Sharron Loella *language educator*
Bell, Maxine Toolson *state legislator, librarian*
Ricketts, Virginia Lee *historian, researcher*

Kamiah
Mills, Carol Margaret *business consultant, public relations consultant*
Mills, Lawrence *lawyer, business and transportation consultant*

Ketchum
Holland, Robert James *retired lawyer*
McElhinny, Wilson Dunbar *banker*
Ziebarth, Robert Charles *management consultant*

Kooskia
Brandt, R. Skipper *state senator*

Lewiston
Aherin, Darrel William *lawyer*
Duley, Charlotte Dudley *vocational counselor*
Esparsen, Ray Pat *art educator*
Tait, John Reid *lawyer*
Thomas, Dene *academic administrator, educator*

McCall
Romano, Michael *publishing executive, consultant*

Meridian
Shaffer, Mary Louise *art educator*
Thorsted, V. Darleene *neonatal and community health nurse*

Moscow
Anderson, Clifton Einar *writer, communications consultant*
Clanton, Orval Gene *historian, educator*
DeShazer, James Arthur *biological engineer, educator, administrator*
Force, Ronald Wayne *librarian*
Goetschel, Roy Hartzell, Jr., *mathematician, researcher*
Greene, Timothy Geddes *lawyer*
Greever, Janet Groff *history educator*
Harris, Robert Dalton *history educator, researcher, writer*
Hendee, John Clare *university research educator*
Jackson, Melbourne Leslie *chemical engineering educator and administrator, consultant*
Johnson, Brian Keith *electrical engineering educator*
Lecompte, Janet *historian, writer*
Machleidt, Ruprecht *physicist*
Miller, Maynard Malcolm *geologist, educator, research institute director, explorer, legislator*
Patankar, Sunil Narayan *research scientist*
Renfrew, Malcolm MacKenzie *chemist, educator*
Roberts, Lorin Watson *botanist, educator*
St. Germain, Fernand Joseph *retired congressman*
Shafii, Bahman *statistician, educator, researcher*
Shreeve, Jean'ne Marie *chemist, educator*

Nampa
Bowers, Curtis Ray, Jr., *chaplain*
Hagood, Richard A. *academic administrator, educator*

Naples
Soss, Daniel Lee *social work educator*

Ola
Farr, Reeta Rae *special education administrator*

Osburn
Bardelli, Frederick Ketchell *artist, art educator*
Calabretta, Marti Ann *senator*

Pocatello
Bowen, Richard Lee *academic administrator, political science educator*
Eichman, Charles Melvin *school counselor, career assessment educator*
Gesell, Thomas Frederick *physicist, educator*
Lawson, Jonathan Nevin *academic administrator*
Nickisch, Craig Wendell *language professional, educator*
Nye, W. Marcus W. *lawyer*
Ronk, Jay H. *music educator, department chairman*
Smith, Elaine E. *school system administrator*
Smith, Evelyn Elaine *language educator*
Stanek, Alan Edward *retired music educator, performer, administrator*
Valentine, Ralph Schuyler *chemical engineer, research director*

Pollock
Rubbert, Paul Edward *engineering executive*

Post Falls
Grassi, James Edward *Christian ministry executive director*
Riggs, Jack Timothy *emergency physician, former state lieutenant governor*
Wheeler, Theodore K., Jr., *small business owner*

Rexburg
Harris, Ann Marie *mathematician, educator*
North, Danny L. *music educator*
Wayne, Barbara Ann *music educator, classical guitar performer*

Rigby
Peterson, Erle Vidaillet *retired metallurgical engineer*

Salmon
Snook, Quinton *construction company executive*

Sandpoint
Bowne, Martha Hoke *publishing consultant*
Glock, Charles Young *sociologist, writer*

Sun Valley
Bryant, Woodrow Wesley *architect*
Cassell, William Comyn *retired college president*
McLaughlin, James Daniel *architect*
Ring, Terry William *company executive, environmentalist*
Stewart, John Todd *economist, consultant*

Terreton
Burtenshaw, Don M. *state senator*

Troy
Hepler, Merlin Judson, Jr., *real estate broker*

Twin Falls
Berry, L. Clyel *lawyer*
Burton, Lawrence DeVere *agriculturist, educator*
Hohnhorst, John Charles *judge*
McGregor, Wendolyn Suzanne *elementary school educator, mathematician*
Sudweeks, Jay Dean *lawyer*

Wendell
Anderson, Marilyn Nelle *elementary education educator, librarian, counselor*

ILLINOIS

AMF Ohare
Guyette, James M. *airline executive*

Abbott Park
Amundson, Joy A. *pharmaceutical and health products executive*
Aruffo, Alejandro *pharmaceutical executive*
Begley, Christopher B. *pharmaceutical executive*
Brown, Thomas D. *pharmaceutical executive*
Dempsey, William G. *pharmaceutical executive*
Flynn, Gary L. *pharmaceutical executive*
Freyman, Thomas C. *pharmaceutical executive*
Gonzalez, Richard A. *pharmaceutical executive*
Leiden, Jeffrey Marc M. *pharmaceutical executive, molecular biologist*
Lussen, John Frederick *pharmaceutical laboratory executive*
Nemmers, Joseph M., Jr., *pharmaceutical executive*
Wascoe, Thomas M. *pharmaceutical executive*
White, Miles D. *pharmaceutical company executive*
Wyatt, Lance B. *pharmaceutical executive*

Addison
Christopher, Doris K. *consumer products company executive*
McDonald, David Eugene *transportation operator*

Aledo
Prosser, Wesley Lewis *advertising and public relations executive*

Algonquin
Carter, Jeanie *performing company executive*

Alton
Boyle, Ann M. *dental educator, dean*
Burgess, Robert Ronald *human resources executive*
Cellini, William F. *hotel executive*
Fortado, Robert Joseph *librarian, educator*
Greenwood, John E. *stock brokerage executive*
Kessler, William Eugene *health care executive*
Plummer, Laura A. *music educator*
Struif, L. James *lawyer*
Talbert, Hugh Mathis *lawyer*

Argonne
Ahmad, Irshad *physicist, nuclear chemist*
Allain, Jean Paul *research scientist*
Ban, Stephen Dennis *gas industry executive*
Chang, Yoon Il *nuclear engineer*
Crabtree, George *physicist*
Derrick, Malcolm *physicist*
Goldman, Arthur Joseph *retired research and development company executive*
Grunder, Hermann A. *science administrator*
Jody, Bassam Jamil *energy engineer, researcher*
Katz, Joseph Jacob *retired chemist, educator*
Koetzle, Thomas Frederick *chemist, researcher*
Kukhtin, Alexander V. *chemist*
Kumar, Romesh *chemical engineer*
Lawson, Robert Davis *theoretical nuclear physicist*
Marshall, Christopher L. *research scientist, chemist*
Mattas, Richard Frank *nuclear energy industry executive*
Miller, Shelby Alexander *chemical engineer, educator*
Perlow, Gilbert J(erome) *physicist, editor*
Peshkin, Murray *physicist*
Plaskacz, Edward John *computational scientist, engineer*
Sabau, Carmen Sybile *chemist*
Schriesheim, Alan *research administrator*
Vivio, Frank Michael *education educator, researcher*

Arlington Heights
Baptist, Allwyn J. *healthcare consultant*
Baumann, Daniel E. *publishing executive*
Biestek, John Paul *lawyer*
Church, Herbert Stephen, Jr., *retired construction company executive*
Ehrenpreis, Eli Daniel *physician, educator, biomedical researcher*
Fields, Sara A. *travel company executive*
Giampietro, Wayne Bruce *lawyer*
Griffin, Jean Latz *political strategist, writer*
Holtz, Michael P. *hotel executive*
Hudson, Ronald Morgan *aviation planner*
Jensen, Lynn Edward *retired medical association executive, economist*
Johnson, Margaret H. *welding company executive*
Kroll, Steven L. *lawyer*
Lampinen, John A. *newspaper editor*
Lemke, Sherry Ellen *therapist*
Leon, Edward *investor*
Lewin, Seymour Zalman *chemistry professor, consultant*
Li, Norman N. *chemicals executive*
Lim, Cheryl Cheon-Ae *music educator*
Morrow, George Lester *retired oil and gas executive*
Moser, Richard Peter *neurosurgeon*
Nerlinger, John William *retired trade association administrator*
Payne, Thomas H. *market research company executive*
Placek-Zimmerman, Ellyn Clare *school system administrator, educator, consultant*
Pochyly, Donald Frederick *physician, hospital administrator*
Ray, Douglas Kent *newspaper executive*
Smith, Norman Obed *physical chemist, educator*
Telleen, Judy *counselor*
Tongue, William Walter *economics and business consultant, educator*
Tucker, Bowen Hayward *lawyer*

Ashmore
Bagwell, Kim Diane *accountant*

Aurora
Butler, Patricia E. *mathematician, educator*
Christiansen, Raymond Stephan *librarian, educator*
Fisher, Thomas Lee *gas company executive*
Koopman, Richard Nelson *engineer, consultant*
Lowe, Ralph Edward *lawyer*
McCarthy, Mary Elizabeth (Beth) Constance *conductor, educator, music educator*
Mir, Ronen *museum director*
Noglows, William P. *electronics executive*
Stephens, Steve Arnold *real estate broker*

Barrington
Bash, Philip Edwin *publishing executive*
Chung, Joseph Sang-hoon *economics professor*
Furst, Warren Arthur *retired holding company executive*
Lee, Catherine M. *business owner, educator*
Lee, William Marshall *lawyer*
Mathis, Jack David *advertising executive, consultant*
Murphy, Robert *executive search consultant*
Nadig, Gerald George *manufacturing executive*
Quigg, Catherine Thiel *writer*
Ross, Frank Howard, III, *management consultant*
Schwan, Howard W. *manufacturing executive*
Stephens, Norval Blair, Jr., *marketing consultant*
Stoutenburg, Jane Sue Williamson *nurse practitioner, fund raiser, actress*
Sweet, Charles Wheeler *retired executive recruiter*
Wyatt, James Frank, Jr., *lawyer*
Wynn, Thomas Joseph *judge, educator*

Barrington Hills
Perry, I. Chet *petroleum company executive*
Wood, Andrée Robitaille *archaeologist, researcher*

Bartlett
Markle, Sandra *publishing company executive*
Robinson, Jack Fay *clergyman*
Robinson, Lois Hart *retired public relations executive*

Bartonville
Garrione, Robert Michael *clergy member*

Batavia
Balbekov, Valeri I. physicist, researcher
Bardeen, William Allan research physicist
Brown, Gerald Curtis retired army officer, engineering executive
Chrisman, Bruce Lowell physicist, administrator
Jonckheere, Alan Mathew physicist
Raja, Rajendran physicist
Tollestrup, Alvin Virgil physicist
Witherell, Michael S. physicist, educator
Yeh, Gong Ping (G.P.) physicist

Bedford Park
Cascino, Anthony Elmo, Jr., lawyer, insurance executive
Courtney, David W. chemical company executive

Belleville
Bauman, John Duane lawyer
Berkley, Gary Lee newspaper publisher
Connors, Jimmy (James Scott Connors) former professional tennis player
Couch, Jeffry editor
Franks, David Bryan internist, emergency physician
Gossage, Roza lawyer, educator
Gregory, Wilton D. bishop
Hanna, Phyllis Ann elementary school educator
Hedges, Patrick Armand information technology, communications and computer systems security specialist
Heiligenstein, Christian Enric lawyer
Hess, Frederick J. lawyer
Richmond, Richard Thomas journalist
Ripplinger, George Raymond, Jr., lawyer
Shim, Sang Koo mental health services professional
Studer, Louis priest, religious organization administrator
Tebbe, Jay publishing executive
Thien-Stasko, Vicki Lynn civil engineer
Wittenbrink, Boniface Leo priest

Bellwood
Miller, Denyce Karlina tax specialist

Belvidere
Luhman, William Simon community development administrator
Mc Nelly, Frederick Wright, Jr., psychologist

Bement
Kepley, Douglas Neil music educator

Bensenville
Leach, Donald Paul small business owner

Benton
Foreman, James Louis retired judge
Gilbert, J. Phil federal judge

Berwyn
Forst, Edmund Charles, Jr., communications educator, administrator, consultant
Hudik, Martin Francis hospital administrator, educator, consultant, writer
Misurec, Rudolf physician, surgeon
Parker, Alan John veterinary neurologist, educator, researcher

Bloomingdale
Flaherty, John Joseph quality assurance company executive
Kovanda, Gary computer wholesale distributing executive
Wolande, Charles Sanford former computer company executive

Bloomington
Axley, Dixie L. insurance company executive
Bragg, Michael Ellis lawyer, insurance company executive
Brakebill, Tina Stewart historian, writer
Bridges, Roger Dean historical agency administrator
Brown, Jared theater director, educator, writer
Brunner, Kim M. insurance company executive
Curry, Alan Chester insurance company executive
Deneen, Daniel Guy lawyer
Dietz, William Ronald management executive
Eckols, Thomas Aud lawyer, educator
Friedman, Joan M. accounting educator
Hining, Michael Lynn music educator, conductor
Johnson, Earle Bertrand insurance executive
Joslin, Roger Scott insurance company executive
Kindle, Otis T. secondary school educator
McHugh, Donald P. lawyer
Merwin, Davis Underwood newspaper executive
Milligan, Michael Lee dentist
Niles, Kevin Bryan music educator
Rodman, Raymond G. insurance company executive
Rust, Edward Barry, Jr., insurance company executive, lawyer
Setchell, Charles Marshall retired music educator
Streeter, Thomas Wayne music educator
Sullivan, Laura Patricia lawyer, insurance company executive
Switzer, Jon Rex architect
Tipsord, Michael L. insurance company executive
Trefzger, Richard Charles surgeon
Trosino, Vincent Joseph, Sr., insurance company executive
Vayo, David Joseph composer, music educator
Wilson, Richard F. academic administrator

Blue Island
Yager, Vincent Cook bank executive

Bolingbrook
Caddy, Edmund H.H., Jr., architect
Day, Mary Ann medical/surgical nurse
Madori, Jan art gallery director
Price, Theodora Hadzisteliou individual, child and family therapist
Sheehan, James Patrick printing company executive, former media company executive
Stoelting, Curtis W. consumer products company executive
Tot, Zvonimir musician, composer, music educator

Bourbonnais
Ball, Karen Michele music educator, musician, composer
McClure, Thomas Edward lawyer
Wilkey, Elmira Smith illustrator, artist, publisher, writer, educator

Bridgeview
Marcello, Frank F. lawyer, educator, writer
Parmer, Dan Gerald veterinarian

Broadview
Lazar, Jill Sue home healthcare company executive
Pang, Joshua Keun-Uk trade company executive

Brookfield
Rabb, George Bernard zoologist, conservationist

Buffalo Grove
Kuennen, Thomas Gerard journalist
Leonetti, Michael Edward financial planner
McConville, Rita Jean finance executive
Rai, Rajat health facility administrator
Robins, Martin B. lawyer
Ward, Michael W. lawyer
Yacktman, Donald Arthur financial executive, investment counselor
Yacktman, Stephen investment company executive

Bunker Hill
Kramer, Barbara K. musician, educator

Burr Ridge
Bottom, Dale Coyle management consultant
Brennan, James Joseph lawyer, banking and financial services executive
Clarke, Philip Ream, Jr., retired investment banker
Daly-Gawenda, Debra health facility administrator, nursing educator
Jones, Shirley Joyce small business owner, fashion designer
McCormack, Robert Cornelius investment banker
Rosenberg, Robert Brinkmann technology organization executive
Vasiliauskas, Edmund retired chemistry professor
Zaccone, Suzanne Maria sales executive

Cahokia
Healy, Steven Michael accountant, city official

Calumet City
Kovach, Joseph William management consultant, psychologist, educator
Muñoz, Romeo Solano audio visual curator
Parks, Corrine Frances insurance company executive
Scullion, Annette Murphy lawyer, educator

Carbondale
Achenbach, Laurie A. science educator
Alghazo, Jaafar M. computer engineer, educator
Barrette, Linda Jones dean
Bauner, Ruth Elizabeth library administrator, reference librarian
Benford, Robert Dee sociology educator, editor
Burr, Brooks Milo zoology educator
Clemons, John Robert lawyer
Cole, Brad mayor
Covington, Patricia Ann university administrator
Dixon, Billy Gene academic administrator, educator
Gilbert, Glenn Gordon linguistics educator
Griffiths, Brett Megan English educator, writer
Hahn, Lewis Edwin philosopher, retired educator
Hahn, Robert Alan philosophy educator
Hammond, Charles E education educator
Jugenheimer, Donald Wayne advertising and communications educator, university administrator
Karau, Steven James social psychologist, researcher
Kawewe, Saliwe Moyo social work educator, researcher
Koch, Loretta Peterson librarian, educator
Lanigan, Richard Leo, Jr., humanities educator, writer, editor
Lawson, Richard Alan literature educator, photographer
Lee, Mark Richard lawyer, educator
Mead, John Stanley university administrator
Mohanty, Manoj K. mineral engineer, educator
Neuman, Edward George mathematician, educator
Poshard, Glenn W. former congressman
Quisenberry, Nancy Lou university administrator, educator
Renzaglia, Karen A. biologist, educator
Sarvela, Paul D. health facility administrator, educator
Schroeder, William Arthur law educator
Snyder, Carolyn Ann education educator, librarian
Townsend, Gregory Williams music educator
Trescott, Paul Barton economics professor
Whitlock, John Joseph museum director
Wiesen, S. Jonathan historian, educator

Carlinville
Bellm, Joan civic worker
Pride, Miriam R. college president

Carol Stream
Franzen, Janice Marguerite Gosnell magazine editor
Gale, Neil Jan Internet company executive, computer scientist, consultant
O'Dell, Lynn Marie Luegge (Mrs. Norman D. O'Dell) librarian
Schmerold, Wilfried Lothar dermatologist
Taylor, Kenneth Nathaniel publishing executive, writer

Carrollton
McAdams, H. T. statistician, researcher
Strickland, Hugh Alfred lawyer

Carterville
Hale, Stan J. humanities educator
Montaño, Edgar J. language educator

Carthage
Ward, Roger Allen music educator, musician

Cary
Blevins, Steven W. chiropractor

Centralia
Sharp, Elaine Cecile obstetrician, gynecologist
Whitten, Mary Lou nursing educator

Champaign
Adawi, Omar mathematician, physicist, educator
Andrejasich, Michael J. architecture educator
Arnould, Richard Julius economist, educator, consultant, dean
Baker, Jack Sherman architect, educator
Balbach, Harold Edward environmental scientist
Batzli, George Oliver ecology educator
Boubekri, Mohamed architecture educator
Boyle, Francis Anthony law educator
Brighton, Gerald David accounting educator
Buschbach, Thomas Charles geologist, consultant
Cartwright, Keros hydrogeologist, researcher
Chang, Kathy Kuhl computer programmer, analyst
Cho, In-Koo economist, educator
Cohen, Dov Joseph education educator, researcher
Cribbet, John Edward law educator, former university chancellor
Crnekovic, Victoria Estefania biologist, educator
Davis, James Henry retired psychology educator
Davisson, Melvin Thomas consulting engineer
Douglas, George Halsey literature educator, educator
Due, John Fitzgerald economist, educator emeritus
Dulany, Donelson Edwin, Jr., psychology educator
Dulany, Elizabeth Gjelsness university press administrator
Eriksen, Charles Walter psychologist, educator
Farmer, Helen Sweeney psychology educator
Fredrickson, L(awrence) Thomas composer
Freedman, Philip physician, educator
Gajda, Amy columnist, educator, writer
Ganguly, Ananda Roop business management educator
Garvey, John Charles violist, conductor, retired music educator
Ghosh, Avijit dean
Gold, Paul Ernest psychology and behavioral neuroscience educator
Gomez, Terrine school director
Gross, David Lee geologist
Gunsalus, Carolyn Kristina law educator, consultant
Guttenberg, Albert Ziskind planning educator
Hager, Lowell Paul biochemistry educator
Hansen, Kathryn Gertrude editor, former state official
Harris, Zelema M. academic administrator
Herman, Richard H. academic administrator
Herzog, Beverly Leah hydrogeologist
Hopkins, Lewis Dean architecture educator
Hurd, Heidi M. law educator, humanities educator, dean
Ikenberry, Stanley Oliver education educator, former university president
Jackson, Billy Morrow artist, retired art educator
Kanfer, Frederick H. psychologist, educator
Kim, Sung O. electrical engineer, researcher
Kindt, John Warren lawyer, educator, consultant
Koenker, Diane P. history professor
Korst, Helmut Hans mechanical engineer, educator
Krause, Harry Dieter law educator
Kroner, Fred L. journalist
Krug, Edward Charles environmental scientist
Levin, Geoffrey Arthur botanist
Maggs, Peter Blount lawyer, educator
Mamer, Stuart Mies lawyer
Mc Cord, John Harrison lawyer, educator
McCulloh, Judith Marie editor
McGlathery, James Melville foreign language educator
Meyer, August Christopher, Jr., broadcasting company executive, lawyer
Miller, Gregory Allen psychology educator
Miller, Harold Arthur lawyer
Moore, Jerry Jay sales executive, retired archaeologist
Nowak, John E. law educator
Painter, Richard William law educator
Philipp, Walter Viktor mathematician, educator
Pierce, Walter J. publishing executive
Pillay, Anand education educator, researcher
Ratner, Lorman Alfred history professor
Rayward, Warden Boyd librarian, educator
Ridlen, Samuel Franklin agriculture educator
Riley, Robert Bartlett landscape architect
Risken, Jared Cleveland physician
Rosenblatt, Karin Ann cancer epidemiologist
Ruan, Lian Jin library director
Schiller, Daniel Toby communications educator
Schiro-Geist, Chrisann rehabilitation counselor
Scott, Anna Marie Porter Wall sociology educator
Semonin, Richard Gerard retired state official
Slichter, Charles Pence physicist, researcher
Smith, Ralph Alexander cultural and educational policy educator
Sohn, Chang Wook energy systems researcher, educator
Spodek, Bernard early childhood educator
Turquette, Atwell Rufus logician
Turquette, Frances Bond editor
Veasey, Byron Keith information systems consultant
Wasserman, Stanley statistician, educator
Watson, Jessica Lewis writer
Watts, Robert Allan publisher, lawyer
Wheeler, Richard Paul English educator, dean
Wolfram, Stephen physicist, computer company executive
Yannelis, Nicholas C. economist, educator
Yates, Ronald Eugene newspaper editor, journalist, educator, author

Charleston
Gano, Kenneth Redman, Jr., lawyer
Gordon, Yevgeniy I. mathematician, educator
Havey, J. Michael psychologist, educator
Hencken, Louis V. academic administrator
Moler, Donald Lewis educational psychology educator
NeSmith, Richard A. education educator, consultant
Rives, Stanley Gene university president emeritus
Surles, Carol D. academic administrator
Szabó, István music educator
Thornburgh, Daniel Eston retired university administrator, journalism educator

Chatham
Chew, Keith Elvin healthcare services administrator

Chester
Felthous, Alan Robert psychiatrist
Welge, Donald Edward food manufacturing executive

Chicago
Abcarian, Herand surgeon, educator
Abell, David Robert lawyer
Abelson, Herbert Traub pediatrician, educator
Abrams, Lee Norman lawyer
Acker, Frederick George lawyer
Adams, Austin A. bank executive
Adams, John S. insurance company executive
Adams, Rosemary Kathleen publishing executive
Adducci, James Dominick lawyer
Adelman, Pamela Bernice Kozoll education educator
Adelman, Stanley Joseph lawyer
Adelman, Steven Herbert lawyer
Adelman, Susan Hershberg surgeon
Adelson, Lawrence Seth electronics executive, lawyer
Adomavicius, Jonas gastroenterologist, writer
Agema, Gerald Walton publishing executive
Agoos, Jeff professional soccer player
Aguilera, Richard Warren (Rick Aguilera) professional baseball player
Ahern, Joseph James, Jr., television station executive
Ahern, Mary Ann reporter
Aitay, Victor concert violinist, music educator
Akers, Michelle Anne professional soccer player
Akins, Cindy S. human resources professional
Akos, Francis violinist, conductor
Alberts, Barry S. lawyer
Albrecht, Ronald Frank anesthesiologist
Alcantara, Anita Luisa artist
al-Chalabi, Suhail Abdul-Jabbar transportation executive
Alesia, James H(enry) judge
Alexander, Michael Charles historian, educator
Aliber, Robert Z. economist, educator
Allampallam, Krishnan biotechnology consultant
Allen, Belle management consulting firm executive, communications executive
Allen, Danielle political scientist, educator
Allen, Henry Sermones, Jr., lawyer
Allen, Julie O'Donnell lawyer
Allen, Richard Blose legal editor, lawyer
Allen, Ronald Jay law educator
Allen, Thomas Draper lawyer
Almen, Lowell Gordon church official
Alomar, Roberto Velazquez professional baseball player
Alou, Moises professional baseball player
Alschuler, Albert W. law educator
Altman, Edith G. sculptor
Altman, Edward G. retired psychologist, educator
Amato, Isabella Antonia real estate executive
Amberg, Thomas L. public relations executive
Amboian, John P., Jr., investment company executive
Amend, James Michael lawyer
Amstadter, Laurence retired architect
Andersen, Burton Robert immunologist, educator
Anderson, Craig Allen retired art educator, artist
Anderson, J. Trent lawyer
Anderson, Jon Stephen newswriter
Anderson, Karl Stephen editor
Anderson, Kimball Richard lawyer
Andreoli, Kathleen Gainor nurse, educator, dean
Andrica, John Dean management consultant
Angelo, Jim construction company executive
Angst, Gerald L. lawyer
Anthony, Michael Francis lawyer
Antonio, Douglas John lawyer
Anvaripour, M. A. lawyer
Apelbaum, Phyllis L. delivery messenger service executive
Appel, Nina Schick law educator, dean, academic administrator
Arena, Bruce professional soccer coach
Armstrong, Edwin Richard lawyer, publisher, editor
Aronson, Howard Isaac linguist, educator
Aronson, Virginia L. L. lawyer
Arpino, Gerald Peter performing company executive
Artest, Ron professional basketball player
Ash, J. Marshall mathematician, educator
Ashman, Martin C. federal judge
Aspen, Marvin Edward federal judge
Ast, Bruno architecture educator
Astrachan, Boris Morton psychiatry educator, consultant
Athas, Gus James lawyer
Aubin, Barbara Jean artist
Aubriot, Eric chef
Auerbach, Marshall Jay lawyer
Avery, Robert Dean lawyer
Ayman, Iraj educational consultant
Babcock, Lyndon Ross, Jr., environmental engineer, educator
Baca, Stacey newscaster
Bacevicius, John Anthony, V, (John Bace) research executive
Badel, Julie lawyer
Baer, John Richard Frederick lawyer
Bailey, Robert, Jr., advertising executive
Bailey, Robert Short lawyer
Bain, Douglas G. lawyer, air transportation executive
Baird, Douglas Gordon law educator, dean
Bakay, Roy Arpad Earle neurosurgeon, educator
Baker, Bruce Jay lawyer
Baker, Dusty (Johnnie B. Baker Jr.) professional baseball team manager
Baker, James Edward Sproul retired lawyer
Baker, Mark food service executive
Baker, Pamela lawyer
Bakris, George nephrologist, educator
Bakwin, Edward Morris banker
Balasi, Mark Geoffrey architect
Baldwin, DeWitt Clair, Jr., physician, educator
Baldwin, Shaun McParland lawyer
Balk, Robert A. medical educator
Balzekas, Stanley, Jr., museum director
Banerjee, Prashant industrial engineer, educator, computer scientist
Banoff, Sheldon Irwin lawyer
Barbour, Claude Marie minister, educator
Bardgett, John E. lawyer
Barker, Walter Lee thoracic surgeon
Barker, William Thomas lawyer
Barnes, Brenda C. food and apparel executive
Barnett, William A. lawyer
Barney, Carol Ross architect
Baron, Joseph Mandel hematologist
Barr, Emily L. television station executive
Barr, John Robert retired lawyer

Barr, John W. *investment banking executive, foundation administrator*
Barriger, John Walker, IV, *transportation executive*
Barron, Harold Sheldon *lawyer*
Barron, Howard Robert *lawyer*
Barron, John *publishing executive*
Barry, Richard A. *public relations executive*
Bart, Susan T. *lawyer*
Bartholomay, William C. *insurance brokerage company executive, professional baseball team executive*
Bartlit, Fred Holcomb, Jr., *lawyer, educator*
Barton, John Joseph *obstetrician, gynecologist, educator, health facility administrator, researcher*
Bartter, Brit Jeffrey *investment banker*
Baruch, Hurd *lawyer*
Basden, Cameron *ballet mistress, dancer*
Bashwiner, Steven Lacelle *lawyer*
Bassiouny, Hisham Sallah *surgeon, educator*
Bauer, William Joseph *federal judge*
Baugher, Peter V. *lawyer*
Baum, Bernard Helmut *sociologist, educator*
Bauman, Jerry L. *pharmacy researcher, educator*
Baumgardt, Justi Michelle *professional soccer player*
Baumhart, Raymond Charles *Roman Catholic church administrator*
Bayless, Rick *chef*
Baylor, Don Edward *former professional baseball manager*
Beane, Marjorie Noterman *academic administrator*
Beattie, Ted Arthur *zoological gardens and aquarium administrator*
Beck, Robert N. *nuclear medicine educator*
Becker, Gary Stanley *economist, educator*
Becker, Michael Allen *internist, rheumatologist, educator*
Becker, Theodore Michaelson *lawyer*
Beckers, Jacques Maurice *astrophysicist*
Beeby, Thomas H. *architect*
Beem, Jack Darrel *lawyer*
Beemster, Joseph Robert *risk management consultant*
Begel, Thomas M. *manufacturing executive*
Beigl, William *physician, hypnotist, acupuncturist, consultant*
Beitler, Stephen *private equity and venture capital executive*
Bell, Carl Compton *psychiatrist, researcher*
Bell, Dean Phillip *dean*
Bell, James A. *aerospace transportation executive*
Bell, Kevin J. *zoological park administrator*
Bellows, Laurel Gordon *lawyer*
Belluschi, Anthony C. *architect*
Benak, James Donald *lawyer*
Ben-Arie, Jezekiel *electrical engineer, computer scientist, educator*
Bendok, Bernard R. *neurosurgeon, researcher*
Benedict, Kennette Mari *foundation executive, researcher*
Bennett, Robert William *law educator*
Bensinger, Peter Benjamin *consulting firm executive*
Benson, Al Bowen, III, *oncologist, educator*
Benzon, Honorio Tabal *anesthesiologist*
Berardino, Joseph Francis *accounting company executive*
Berens, Mark Harry *lawyer*
Berenzweig, Jack Charles *lawyer*
Berger, Miles Lee *land economist*
Berger, Robert Michael *lawyer*
Bergonia, Raymond David *venture capitalist*
Berk, Harlan Joseph *numismatist, writer, antiquarian*
Berkoff, Mark Andrew *lawyer*
Berkson, Sadie *volunteer*
Berman, Arthur Leonard *retired state senator*
Berman, Cheryl R. *advertising company executive*
Berman, Laura *sex therapist*
Bernardini, Charles *lawyer, former alderman*
Bernatowicz, Frank Allen *management consultant, expert witness*
Berner, Robert Lee, Jr., *lawyer*
Bernick, David M. *lawyer*
Berning, Larry D. *lawyer*
Bernstein, Charles Bernard *lawyer*
Berolzheimer, Karl *lawyer*
Berryman, Diana (Kapnas) *radio personality*
Bertagnolli, Leslie A. *lawyer*
Bertenthal, Bennett Ira *psychologist, educator*
Be Sant, Craig *marketing executive*
Bess, Ronald W. *advertising executive*
Betz, Hans Dieter *theology educator*
Beugen, Joan Beth *communications company executive*
Bevington, David Martin *English literature educator*
Beyer, Eric C. *pediatrician, researcher*
Bidwell, Charles Edward *sociologist, educator*
Biebel, Paul Philip, Jr., *lawyer*
Bierig, Jack R. *lawyer, educator*
Biggs, Robert Dale *Near Eastern studies educator*
Bindenagel, James Dale *foundation executive*
Birnbaum, Barry William *special education educator*
Bishop, Mary Oltman *retired advertising executive*
Bitner, John Howard *lawyer*
Bixby, Frank Lyman *lawyer*
Black, Henry Richard *physician*
Black, Robert Durward *television producer*
Blackwell, Robert, Jr., *consulting firm executive*
Blackwell, Robert D., Sr., *consulting firm executive*
Blair, Edward McCormick *investment banker*
Blankenship, Edward G. *architect*
Blatt, Richard Lee *lawyer*
Bloch, Ralph Jay *professional association executive, marketing consultant*
Block, Neal Jay *lawyer*
Block, Philip Dee, III, *investment counselor*
Block, Richard L. *sociologist, criminologist, educator*
Blount, Michael Eugene *lawyer*
Bluefarb, Samuel Mitchell *retired physician*
Blumberg, Avrom Aaron *physical chemistry educator*
Blume, Paul Chiappe *lawyer*
Bobins, Norman R. *banker*
Bobrinskoy, Charles Kellogg *investment banker*
Boddie, Arthur Walker, Jr., *surgeon, cancer researcher*
Bodi, Sonia Ellen *library director, educator*
Boehnen, Daniel A. *lawyer*
Boggs, Catherine J. *lawyer*
Boggs, Joseph Dodridge *pediatric pathologist, educator*
Bogolub, David Louis *physician*
Bohn, Charlotte Galitz *retired real estate executive*
Boies, Wilber H. *lawyer*
Bolger, David P. *insurance company executive*
Bomchill, Fern Cheryl *lawyer*
Bona, Jerry Lloyd *mathematician, educator*
Bonaparte, William *communications company executive*
Bongolan-Walsh, Vena Pearl *research scientist*
Bonow, Robert Ogden *medical educator*
Boocock, Stephen William *lawyer*
Booth, Wayne Clayson *English literature and rhetoric educator, author*
Borenstine, Alvin Jerome *search company executive*
Borg, Frank *hotel executive*
Borges, Dain *education educator*
Borzutzky, Daniel J. *writer, educator*
Bosma, Jennifer *nursing association administrator*
Bourdon, Cathleen Jane *professional society administrator*
Bouton, Marshall Melvin *academic administrator*
Bowe, William J(ohn) *lawyer*
Bowen, Stephen Stewart *lawyer*
Bowman, James Edward *physician, educator*
Bowman, Leah *fashion designer, consultant, photographer, educator*
Boyda, Debora *advertising executive*
Boyer, John William *history educator, dean*
Bozic, Michael C. *retail company executive*
Bracken, Kathleen Ann *nurse*
Bradley, Bob *professional soccer coach*
Brake, Cecil Clifford *retired diversified manufacturing executive*
Bramnik, Robert Paul *lawyer*
Bramson, James B. *dentist, dental association administrator*
Branch, Ronald L. *real estate company executive*
Brandman, James Franklin *internist, oncologist*
Brandt, Gene Stuart *fundraising consultant*
Brandt, William Arthur, Jr., *consulting executive*
Bransfield, James Joseph *surgeon*
Bratcher, Juanita *journalist*
Brauer, Sasha Gerritson *church musician, music educator*
Breen, Neil Thomas *publishing executive*
Bregoli-Russo, Mauda Rita *language educator*
Brekus, Catherine Anne *historian*
Brendler, Charles Burgess *urologist, educator*
Brennan, Michael *real estate company executive*
Brice, Roger Thomas *lawyer*
Bridgman, Thomas Francis *retired lawyer*
Brinkman, John Anthony *historian, educator*
Bristo, Marca *human services administrator*
Brizzolara, Charles Anthony *lawyer, director*
Bro, Ruth Hill *lawyer*
Brock, Kathy *newscaster*
Brodsky, William J. *options exchange executive*
Brogan, Lisa S. *lawyer*
Brooker, Thomas Kimball *oil company executive*
Brooks, Marion *newscaster*
Brooksher, K. Dane *accounting, management company executive*
Brotman, Barbara Louise *columnist, writer*
Brown, Alan Crawford *lawyer*
Brown, Charles Eric *health facility administrator, biochemist*
Brown, Donald James, Jr., *lawyer*
Brown, Gregory K. *lawyer*
Brown, Jeremy Earle *advertising executive*
Brown, Richard Holbrook *library director, historian, researcher*
Brown, Rosellen *writer*
Browning, Don Spencer *religious educator*
Brumback, Charles Tiedtke *retired newspaper executive*
Brummel, Mark Joseph *religious organization administrator*
Bryan, John Henry *food and consumer products company executive*
Buckley, Joseph Paul, III, *polygraph specialist*
Bucklo, Elaine Edwards *United States district court judge*
Bucksbaum, John *real estate development company executive*
Bucksbaum, Matthew *real estate investment trust company executive*
Bueche, Wendell Francis *agricultural products company executive*
Buehrle, Mark *professional baseball player*
Bugielski, Robert Joseph *state legislator*
Bulger, Brian Wegg *lawyer*
Bumbaugh, David Edward *religious studies educator, minister*
Bunge, Jonathan Gunn *lawyer*
Buniak, Raymond *educational professional*
Bunn, William Bernice, III, *occupational health and environmental medicine executive, epidemiologist, lawyer*
Burack, Elmer Howard *management educator*
Burck, Joseph Russell *medical educator, consultant, minister*
Burdiss, James E. *paper company executive*
Burgdoerfer, Jerry *lawyer*
Burke, John Michael *lawyer*
Burke, Michelle C. *lawyer*
Burke, Thomas Joseph, Jr., *lawyer*
Burke, William Joseph *lawyer*
Burkhardt, Edward Arnold *railway executive*
Burns, Diann *newscaster*
Burns, Terrence Michael *lawyer*
Burt, Richard K. *physician, educator*
Burton, Cheryl *newscaster*
Busey, Roxane C. *lawyer*
Butler, John William *lawyer*
Cain, Harry P. *health science association administrator*
Calenoff, Leonid *radiologist*
Callahan, Timothy T. *real estate company executive*
Callaway, Karen A(lice) *journalist*
Calvin, James Eldon, Jr., *cardiologist, educator, researcher*
Campbell, Gavin Elliott *real estate investor and developer*
Camper, John Jacob *speech writer*
Campos-Pons, Maria Magdalena *artist*
Cappo, Joseph C. *journalist, writer*
Cardoso, Aldo *marketing professional*
Carlin, Dennis J. *lawyer*
Carlson, LeRoy Theodore, Jr., *telecommunications industry executive*
Carlson, Richard Gregory *accountant*
Carlson, Walter Carl *lawyer*
Caro, William Allan *physician, educator*
Carr, Anne Elizabeth *theology educator*
Carr, Jeffrey W. *manufacturing executive*
Carr, Walter Stanley *lawyer*
Carren, Jeffrey P. *lawyer*
Carroll, William Kenneth *law educator, psychologist, theologian*
Cary, Arlene D. *retired hotel company sales executive*
Case, Donni Marie *investment company executive*
Cass, Edward Roberts (Peter Cass) *hotel and travel marketing professional*
Cassel, Douglass Watts, Jr., *lawyer, educator, journalist*
Castillo, Mario Enrique *artist, educator*
Castorino, Sue *communications executive*
Cavallino, Robert P. *radiologist*
Celesia, Gastone Guglielmo *neurologist, neurophysiologist, researcher*
Chacko, Samuel *association official*
Chaden, Lee A. *food products executive*
Chakrabarty, Ananda Mohan *microbiologist*
Chaleff, Carl Thomas *brokerage house executive*
Chambers, Donald Arthur *biochemistry and molecular medicine educator*
Champagne, Ronald Oscar *medical association administrator*
Chan, Lawrence Siu-Yung *dermatologist, educator*
Chandler, John D. *dentist*
Chandler, Kent, Jr., *lawyer*
Chang, Yi-Cheng *insurance agent*
Chapman, Alger Baldwin *finance company executive, lawyer*
Chapman, Robert J. *real estate company executive*
Charles, Allan G. *physician, educator*
Charrow, Joel *pediatrician, educator, geneticist, director*
Chatterton, Robert Treat, Jr., *reproductive endocrinology educator*
Chauhan, Neelima B. *neuroscientist, researcher*
Cheely, Daniel Joseph *lawyer*
Chefitz, Joel Gerald *lawyer*
Chemers, Robert Marc *lawyer*
Chen, David *rehabilitation services professional*
Cheng, Paul Hung-Chiao *civil engineer*
Cherney, James Alan *lawyer*
Cherry, Daniel Ronald *lawyer*
Chester, Mark Vincent *lawyer*
Chestnut, John William *lawyer*
Chiappetta, Robert A. *manufacturing executive*
Childers, Mary Ann *newscaster*
Chiles, Stephen Michael *lawyer*
Chipparoni, Guy *communications company executive*
Choldin, Marianna Tax *librarian, educator*
Chookaszian, Dennis Haig *retired financial executive*
Chorengel, Bernd *international hotel corporation executive*
Christianson, Stanley David *finance company executive*
Christoffel, Katherine Kaufer *pediatrician, epidemiologist, educator*
Chromizky, William Rudolph *accountant*
Chung, Paul Myungha *mechanical engineer, educator*
Claiborne, William *journalist*
Clark, Frank M. *utilities executive*
Clark, Raymond S. *architectural firm executive*
Clarke, Richard Stewart *security company executive*
Clayton, Robert Norman *chemist, educator*
Clemens, Richard Glenn *lawyer*
Clevenger, Penelope *food products executive*
Cline, Philip J. *protective services official*
Cline, William Chambers *automotive executive*
Cloonan, James Brian *investment executive*
Coase, Ronald Harry *economist, educator*
Coble, Yank David, Jr., *internist, endocrinologist*
Coe, Fredric L. *physician, educator, researcher*
Coffey, Susanna Jean *art educator*
Cohen, Edward Philip *microbiology and immunology educator, physician*
Cohen, Ira *legislative staff member*
Cohen, Melanie Rovner *lawyer*
Cohen, Melvin R. *physician, educator*
Cohen, Stephen Bruce *lawyer*
Cohen, Ted *philosopher, educator*
Cohler, Bertram Joseph *social sciences educator, clinical psychologist*
Colker, David *stock exchange executive*
Collen, John *lawyer, educator*
Collen, Sheldon Orrin *lawyer*
Collens, Lewis Morton *university president, legal educator*
Colleran, Michael *real estate company executive*
Colley, Karen J. *medical educator, medical researcher*
Colom, Vilma *alderman*
Conant, Howard Rosset *steel company executive*
Conidi, Daniel Joseph *private investigation agency executive*
Conklin, Thomas William *lawyer*
Conlon, Suzanne B. *federal judge*
Connelly, John Dooley *social service organization executive*
Connelly, P. Kevin *lawyer*
Connors, Dorsey *television and radio commentator, newspaper columnist*
Conrad, John R. *retired electric power industry executive*
Conte, Lou *artistic director, choreographer*
Conway, James Joseph *radiologist, educator*
Conway, Michael Maurice *lawyer*
Cook, Richard Borreson *architect*
Cook, Robin Nathaniel *organizational development consultant*
Cook, Sandy *dean*
Cooke, Michael *editor-in-chief*
Cooley, John Wayne *lawyer*
Cooper, Charles Gilbert *toiletries and cosmetics company executive*
Cooper, Ilene Linda *magazine editor, author*
Cooper, Jo Marie *elementary school principal*
Copeland, Edward Jerome *lawyer*
Corbett, Frank Joseph *advertising executive*
Corlin, Richard F. *gastroenterologist*
Cornell, Rob *hotel executive*
Corriere, Jules *playwright, theater director*
Corwin, Sherman Phillip *lawyer*
Costa, Erminio *pharmacologist, cell biologist, educator*
Costello, James Paul *lawyer*
Costin, J(oseph) Laurence, Jr., *information services executive*
Cotter, Daniel A. *diversified company executive*
Covalt, Robert Byron *chemicals executive*
Cox, Allan James *management consultant*
Cox, Clifford Ernest *information systems consulting executive, former academic administrator*
Cox, Julia Diamond *lawyer*
Cox-Hayley, Deon Melayne *geriatrics services professional*
Coy, Patricia Ann *special education director, consultant*
Craine, Thomas Knowlton *non-profit administrator*
Crane, Barbara Bachmann *photographer, educator*
Crane, Charlotte *law educator*
Craven, George W. *lawyer*
Crawford, Dewey Byers *lawyer*
Crawford, Jean Andre *clinical therapist*
Cremin, Susan Elizabeth *lawyer*
Crenshaw, Carol *charitable organization administrator*
Cressey, Bryan Charles *venture capitalist*
Crockett, George Ephriam *secondary school educator*
Cromwell, Amanda Caryl *former soccer player, coach*
Cronin, James Watson *physicist, researcher*
Cropsey, Joseph *political science educator*
Cross, Dolores Evelyn *former university administrator, educator*
Cross, Robert Clark *journalist*
Crossan, John Robert *lawyer*
Crown, James Schine *investment executive*
Crown, Lester *manufacturing executive*
Crown, Susan M. *social services administrator*
Crown, William H. *manufacturing executive*
Cruickshank, John Douglas *publishing executive*
Crull, Jan, Jr., *lawyer*
Cruthird, Robert Lee *sociology educator*
Csar, Michael F. *lawyer*
Cudahy, Richard D. *judge*
Cullen, Charles Thomas *historian, librarian*
Culp, Kristine Ann *dean, theology educator*
Cummings, Andrea J. *lawyer*
Cunningham, Robert James *lawyer*
Curran, Barbara Adell *retired law foundation administrator, lawyer, writer*
Curran, Raymond M. *paper-based packaging company executive*
Curry, Raymond Howard *physician*
Curtis, Arthur William *otolaryngologist*
Curwen, Randall William *journalist, editor*
Cusack, John Thomas *lawyer*
Custer, Charles Francis *lawyer*
Dabrowski, Edward John *television technical director*
Daley, Richard Michael *mayor*
Daley, Susan Jean *lawyer*
Daley, Vincent Raymond, Jr., *real estate company executive, consultant*
Daly, Patrick F. *real estate executive, architect*
Dam, Kenneth W. *law educator, former fedral agency administrator*
Dammeyer, Rodney Foster *distribution company executive*
Dan, Bernard W. *trade association administrator*
Daniel, Elnora D. *academic administrator*
Darby, Edwin Wheeler *retired newspaper financial columnist*
Darchun, Lino Auksutis *real estate professional*
Dardai, Shahid Moinuddin *computer science educator*
Davidson, Richard Laurence *geneticist, educator*
Davis, Danny K. *congressman*
Davis, DeForest P. *architectural engineer*
Davis, Mary Ellen K. *library director*
Davis, Michael Stuart *philosopher, educator*
Davis, Muller *lawyer*
Davis, Scott Jonathan *lawyer*
Davison, Richard *internist, educator*
Daze, Eric *professional hockey player*
De, Devasmita *research aquarist*
De Armas, Frederick Alfred *foreign language educator*
Debus, Allen George *history educator*
Dechene, James Charles *lawyer*
Decker, Richard Knore *lawyer*
Dee, Ivan Richard *book publisher*
de Hoyos, Debora M. *lawyer*
Deitrick, William Edgar *lawyer*
deKool, L.M. (Theo) *food products executive*
Delaney, Timothy Quinn *lawyer, engineer*
De Leon, Rudy *aerospace transportation executive*
Deli, Anne Tynion *marketing executive*
DeLong, Ray *editor*
Delp, Wilbur Charles, Jr., *lawyer*
Dembowski, Peter Florian *foreign language educator*
DeMoss, Jon W. *insurance company executive, lawyer*
Dempsey, Mary A. *library commissioner, lawyer*
Derlacki, Eugene L(ubin) *retired otolaryngologist*
Desjardins, Claude *physiologist, dean*
Desouza, Kevin Clyde *application developer*
D'Esposito, Julian C., Jr., *lawyer*
Despres, Leon Mathis *lawyer, former city official*
DeVine, Richard A. (Dick DeVine) *lawyer*
DeVries, James Howard *lawyer*
DeWolfe, John Chauncey, Jr., *lawyer*
Deziel, Daniel J. *surgeon*
Diamond, Seymour *physician*
Diamond, Shari Seidman *law educator, psychology educator*
Dickman, Martin J. *federal agency administrator*
Dickstein, Beth J. *lawyer, accountant*
Diederichs, Janet Wood *public relations executive*
Digangi, Al *marketing executive*
Di Prima, Stephanie Marie *educational administrator*
DiStasio, Richard P. *manufacturing executive*
Dix, Rollin C(umming) *mechanical engineering educator, consultant*
Dixon, Stewart Strawn *lawyer, consultant*
Dockterman, Michael *lawyer*
Doetsch, Virginia Lamb *former advertising executive, writer*
Doherty, Sister Barbara *religious institution administrator*
Doherty, Brian Gerard *alderman*
Dolan, Thomas Christopher *professional society administrator*
Dold, Robert Bruce *journalist*
Domanskis, Alexander Rimas *lawyer*
Doniger, Wendy *history of religions educator*
Donlevy, John Dearden *lawyer*
Donnelley, James Russell *printing company executive*
Donohoe, Jerome Francis *lawyer*
Donohue, Craig S. *trade association administrator*
Dooley, Sharon L. *obstetrician, gynecologist*
Dowling, Doris Anderson *business owner, educator, consultant*

Downing, Robert Allan *lawyer*
Doyle, John Robert *lawyer*
Draft, Howard Craig *advertising executive*
Drake, Francis LeBaron *law librarian*
Draut, Eric J. *insurance company executive*
Drewry, June E. *information technology executive*
Drexler, Richard Allan *manufacturing executive*
Drinfeld, Vladimir Gershonovich *mathematician, educator*
Driskell, Claude Evans *college director, educator, dentist*
Drymalski, Raymond Hibner *lawyer, banker*
DuCanto, Joseph Nunzio *lawyer, educator*
Ducar, Tracy *former soccer player*
Duell, Daniel Paul *artistic director, choreographer, lecturer*
Duffy, Terrence A. *brokerage house executive*
Dukic, Vanja *mathematician, educator*
Dunaif, Andrea Elizabeth *endocrinologist*
Duncan, Bruce W. *real estate company executive*
Duncan, John Patrick Cavanaugh *lawyer*
Dunea, George *nephrologist, educator*
Dunlop, Karen Owen *lawyer*
Dunn, Christopher Joseph *telecommunications industry executive*
Dunn, Edwin Rydell *lawyer*
Dupont, Todd F. *mathematics and computer science educator*
Durchslag, Stephen P. *lawyer*
Dust, Margaret Cecile *psychology educator*
Dutta, Mitra *physicist, educator*
Dutta, Rono J. *air transportation executive*
Dwyer, Dennis D. *information technology executive*
Dykstra, Paul Hopkins *lawyer*
Easley, Cheryl Eileen *nursing educator, department chairman*
Eastabrook, Dianne *news correspondent*
Easterbrook, Frank Hoover Hoover *federal judge*
Eastman, Dean Eric *physicist, researcher*
Easton, Lory Barsdate Barsdate *lawyer*
Eaton, J(ames) Timothy *lawyer*
Eaton, John C. *composer, educator*
Eaton, Maja Campbell *lawyer*
Ebert, Roger Joseph *film critic*
Edelman, Alvin *lawyer*
Edelman, Daniel Joseph *public relations executive*
Edelman, Ruth Rozumoff *volunteer*
Edelstein, Teri J. *art history educator, art administrator, small business owner*
Egan, Kevin James *lawyer*
Eggert, Russell Raymond *lawyer*
Eibl, Clement *management consulting firm executive*
Eimer, Nathan Philip *lawyer*
Einoder, Camille Elizabeth *retired secondary school educator*
Ekdahl, Jon Nels *lawyer, association executive*
Elden, Gary Michael *lawyer*
Elias, Sherman *obstetrician, gynecologist, educator, clinical geneticist*
Ellis, Christopher L. *manufacturing executive*
Ellis, Randall Spencer *diversified company director*
Ellwood, Scott *lawyer*
Elshtain, Jean Bethke *social and political ethics educator*
Elson, Alex *lawyer, educator, arbitrator*
Emad, Parvis *philosophy educator*
Emmons Jr., Charles N. *music educator*
Enenbach, Mark Henry *community action agency executive, educator*
Engel, Philip L. *retired insurance company executive*
English, John Dwight *lawyer*
Enquist, Philip *architectural firm executive*
Epstein, Leon G. *neurologist*
Epstein, Raymond *engineering and architectural executive*
Epstein, Richard A. *law educator*
Epstein, Sidney *architect, civil engineer*
Erber, Thomas *physics educator*
Erens, Jay Allan *lawyer*
Erricolo, Danilo *engineering educator*
Eslinger, Ellen Therese *historian*
Essex, Joseph Michael *visual communication planner*
Eubanks-Pope, Sharon G. *real estate company executive, entrepreneur*
Evanich, Kevin R. *lawyer*
Evans, Mariwyn *periodical editor*
Evans, Thelma Jean Mathis *internist*
Even, Francis Alphonse *lawyer*
Fabisch, Gale Warren *environmental engineer*
Fahey, Hallie Joan Miller *lawyer*
Fahner, Tyrone C. *lawyer, former state attorney general*
Fairchild, Thomas E. *federal judge*
Falkowski, Patricia Ann *investment counsel*
Falls, Robert Arthur *artistic director*
Farber, Bernard John *lawyer*
Farhadi, Ashkan *physician, researcher*
Farrakhan, Louis *religious leader*
Fasolt, Constantin *history professor*
Fawcett, Joy Lynn *professional soccer player*
Faxon, David Parker *cardiologist*
Fazio, Peter Victor, Jr., *lawyer*
Feder, Robert *television and radio columnist*
Feingold, Daniel Leon *anesthesiologist, consultant*
Feinstein, Fred Ira *lawyer*
Feinstein, Paul Louis *lawyer*
Feldman, Scott Milton *lawyer*
Feldman, Ted *cardiologist*
Fellows, Jerry Kenneth *lawyer*
Felsenthal, Steven Altus *lawyer, educator*
Felton, Cynthia *educational administrator*
Feng, Yinshan *mechanical engineer, researcher*
Fennessy, John James *radiologist, educator*
Fensin, Daniel *diversified financial service company executive*
Ferencz, Robert Arnold *lawyer*
Ferguson, Diana S. *food products executive*
Ferguson, Donald John *surgeon, educator*
Ferguson, Mark Kendric *physician, educator, researcher*
Ferguson, Renee *news correspondent, reporter*
Ferguson, Stanley Lewis *lawyer*
Fernandez, James *anthropology educator*
Ferrini, James Thomas *lawyer*
Fetridge, Clark Worthington *publishing executive*
Field, Karen Ann (Karen Ann Schaffner) *real estate broker*
Field, Marshall *retail executive*
Field, Robert Edward *lawyer*
Filpi, Robert Alan *lawyer*
Fina, Paul Joseph *lawyer*
Finke, Robert Forge *lawyer*
Finley, Yvonne Smith *social worker*
Fioretti, Robert William *lawyer*
Fischbach, Charles Peter *railway executive consultant, lawyer, arbitrator, mediator*
Fischer, Paul *corporate financial executive*
Fish, Stanley Eugene *university dean, English educator*
Fisher, Eugene *marketing professional*
Fisher, Lawrence Edgar *market research executive, anthropologist*
Fisher, Lester Emil *zoo administrator*
Fitzgerald, Patrick J. *prosecutor*
Fitzgerald, Robert Maurice *financial executive*
Fitzgerald, Thomas Robert *judge*
Fitzpatrick, Christine Morris *legal administrator, former television executive*
Fitzpatrick, Robert John *museum director*
FitzSimons, Dennis Joseph *broadcasting and publishing executive*
Flaherty, Emalee Gottbrath *pediatrician*
Flaherty, Timothy Thomas *radiologist*
Flanagan, Sylvia *editor*
Flaum, Joel Martin *chief judge*
Fleming, Richard H. *finance executive*
Flock, Jeffrey Charles *news bureau chief*
Flynn, John J. *museum curator*
Fogel, Robert William *economist, educator, historian*
Fontanarosa, Phil Bernard *emergency physician*
Forbes, John Edward *financial consultant*
Forchand, Joseph W. *finance company executive*
Fort, Jeffrey C. *lawyer*
Fortuna, William Frank *architectural engineer, architect*
Foster, James Reuben *travel company executive*
Fotopoulos, Danielle *former soccer player*
Foudree, Bruce William *lawyer*
Foudy, Julia Maurine *professional soccer player, Olympic athlete*
Fox, David Wayne *banker*
Fox, Elaine Saphier *lawyer*
Fox, Leslie B. *real estate company executive*
Fox, Paul T. *lawyer*
Fox, Suzy *management consultant, educator*
Fragen, Robert Joseph *physician, anesthesiologist*
Franch, Richard Thomas *lawyer*
Franco, Carlo Diaz *surgeon, anatomist, anesthesiologist*
Francuch, Paul Charles *broadcast journalist*
Franczek, James Clement, Jr., *lawyer*
Franke, Richard James *arts advocate, former investment banker*
Frankel, Bernard *advertising executive*
Franklin, Richard Mark *lawyer*
Frazier, Anthony Vincent Earl *addictions, small business, and technology specialist*
Frederiksen, Marilynn C. *physician*
Freeborn, Michael D. *lawyer*
Freed, Karl Frederick *chemistry professor*
Freehling, Paul Edward *lawyer*
Freeman, Lee Allen, Jr., *lawyer*
Freeman, Leslie Gordon *anthropologist, educator*
Freeman, Louis S. *lawyer*
Freeman, Susan Tax *anthropologist, educator, culinary historian*
Freibaum, Bernard *real estate development company executive*
Freidheim, Cyrus F., Jr., *fruit company executive*
Freidheim, Ladonna *dance company director*
Freitag, Frederick Gerald *osteopathic physician*
Friedli, Helen Russell *lawyer*
Friedman, Daniel S. *architecture educator*
Friedman, Lawrence Milton *lawyer*
Friedman, Marla Lee *human resources specialist, marketing professional*
Friedrich, Paul *anthropologist, linguist, poet*
Froetscher, Janet *social services administrator*
Fross, Roger Raymond *lawyer*
Fuchs, Robert F. *lawyer*
Fukui, Yoshio *biology professor*
Fuller, Jack William *writer, publishing executive*
Fuller, Perry Lucian *lawyer*
Funderburk, Raymond *judge*
Funk, Carla Jean *library association executive*
Furcon, John Edward *management and organizational consultant*
Furlane, Mark Elliott *lawyer*
Furth, Yvonne *advertising executive*
Futterman, Ronald L. *lawyer*
Gabarra, Carin Leslie *professional soccer player, professional soccer coach*
Gaines, Barbara *theater director*
Galante, Jorge Osvaldo *orthopedic surgeon, educator*
Gall, Betty Bluebaum *retired office services company executive*
Galowich, Ronald Howard *real estate investment executive, venture capitalist*
Gamoran, Reuben *candy company executive*
Gand, Gayle *chef*
Gannon, Sister Ann Ida *retired philosophy educator, former college administrator*
Gapstur, Susan Mary *cancer epidemiologist, educator, researcher*
Garanzini, Michael J. *academic administrator*
Garber, Samuel B. *lawyer, business/turnaround management consultant*
Garciaparra, Nomar (Anthony Nomar Garciaparra) *professional baseball player*
Gardiner, Judith Kegan *English language and women's studies educator*
Gardner, Howard Alan *travel company executive, writer, editor*
Gardunio, Joseph *landscaping company executive*
Garofalo, Douglas *architectural firm executive, educator*
Garrigan, Richard Thomas *finance educator, consultant, editor*
Garth, Bryant Geoffrey *law educator, foundation executive*
Gassman, Merrill Loren *biologist, educator*
Gaynes, Bruce Ira *optometrist, pharmacist, educator*
Gecht, Martin Louis *physician, bank executive*
Geha, Alexander Salim *cardiothoracic surgeon, educator*
Gelber, Brian *commodities trader*
Genetski, Robert James *economist*
Geoga, Douglas Gerard *real estate developer, lawyer*
George, Francis *archbishop*
George, John Martin, Jr., *lawyer*
Geraldson, Raymond I., Jr., *lawyer*
Gerber, John J. *real estate executive*
Gerber, Lawrence *lawyer*
Gerber, Phillip *advertising executive*
Gerbie, Albert Bernard *obstetrician, gynecologist, educator*
Gerdes, Neil Wayne *library director, educator*
Gerstner, Robert William *structural engineering educator, consultant*
Getz, Bettina *lawyer*
Getz, Godfrey Shalom *dean, pathologist, educator*
Gewertz, Bruce Labe *surgeon, educator*
Gewurz, Anita Tartell *medical association administrator*
Geyer, Michael *history professor*
Gibbons, John *mortgage company executive*
Gibbons, Robert D. *biostatistics educator*
Gibbons, William John *lawyer*
Gibson, McGuire *archaeologist, educator*
Gibson, Roger *air transportation executive*
Gidwitz, Gerald *retired hair care company executive*
Giesen, Richard Allyn *manufacturing executive*
Giger, Maryellen Lissak *medical physicist*
Gilbert, Bentley Brinkerhoff *retired history professor, retired historian*
Gilbert, David R. *public relations executive*
Gilbert, Debbie Rose *entrepreneur*
Gilbert, Howard N(orman) *lawyer, director*
Gilford, Steven Ross *lawyer*
Gillet, Henri Antoine Denis Ciaran *mathematician, educator*
Gillis, Ruth Ann M. *electric company executive*
Gilson, Jerome *lawyer, writer*
Gin, Sue Ling *retail executive*
Ginsberg, Norman Arthur *physician, educator*
Ginsburg, Norton Sydney *retired geographer*
Giovacchini, Peter Louis *psychoanalyst*
Girardi, Joseph Elliott *professional baseball player*
Gislason, Eric Arni *chemistry professor*
Gittins, Anthony J. *anthropologist, theology studies educator*
Gladden, James Walter, Jr., *lawyer*
Glassenberg, Myron *neurologist*
Glasser, James J. *leasing company executive, retired*
Glaze, Robert Howe *real estate executive*
Glenner, Richard Allen *dentist, dental historian*
Glickman, Robert Jeffrey *bank executive*
Glieberman, Herbert Allen *lawyer*
Gluth, Robert C. *management company executive*
Godfrey, Donal Charles *priest*
Goetschel, Arthur W. *industrial manufacturing executive*
Golan, Stephen Leonard *lawyer*
Golb, Norman *historian, writer*
Gold, Allan Harold *architect, structural engineer, educator*
Gold, Carol R. *dean, nursing educator*
Goldblatt, Stanford Jay *lawyer*
Golden, Bruce Paul *lawyer*
Goldfein, Iris *financial company executive*
Goldring, Norman Max *advertising executive*
Goldsmith, Ethel Frank *medical social worker*
Goldstein, William A. *investment counsel*
Golin, Alvin *public relations company executive*
Golomb, Harvey Morris *hematologist, oncologist, educator*
Gomer, Robert *chemistry professor*
Gomez, Sylvia *newscaster*
Good, Sheldon Fred *realtor*
Good, Steven Loren *real estate consultant*
Goodman, Gary Alan *lawyer*
Goodman, Larry J. *health facility administrator*
Goodman, Robert Stanley *management educator*
Gorbien, Martin John *medical educator, geriatrician*
Gorchow, Bruce D. *investment company executive*
Gordon, Ellen Rubin *candy company executive*
Gordon, James S. *lawyer, director*
Gordon, Leo I. *hematologist, oncologist, educator*
Gorman, Maureen J. *lawyer*
Gossett, Philip *musicologist*
Gottlieb, Gidon Alain Guy *law educator*
Gottschall, Joan B. *judge*
Gould, John Philip *economist, educator*
Gould, Samuel Halpert *pediatrics educator*
Graber, Thomas M. *orthodontist, researcher*
Graddy, Julia Harder *music educator, researcher*
Grady, John F. *federal judge*
Graham, Bruce S. *dean, educator*
Gralen, Donald John *lawyer*
Grammer, Leslie Carroll *allergist*
Graner, Evan *academic administrator*
Grant, Dennis *newspaper publishing executive*
Grant, Robert McQueen *humanities educator*
Grant, Robert Nathan *lawyer*
Gratz, Jay M. *steel company executive*
Gray, Dawn Plambeck *work-family consultant*
Gray, Hanna Holborn *history educator*
Gray, Richard *art dealer, consultant, holding company executive*
Grayhack, John Thomas *urologist, educator*
Green, David *hematologist*
Green, RuthAnn *marketing and management consultant*
Greenberg, Bernard *entomologist, educator*
Greenberg, Steve *brokerage house executive*
Greenberger, Paul Allen *allergist, immunologist, educator, medical researcher*
Greenspan, Jeffrey Dov *lawyer*
Gregg, Lauren *women's soccer coach*
Gregory, Stephanie Ann *hematologist, educator*
Griffin, Kenneth C. *investment company executive*
Griffith, Donald Kendall *lawyer*
Gross, Hanns *history professor*
Gross, Theodore Lawrence *university administrator, author*
Grossman, Robert Mayer *lawyer*
Grumman, Cornelia *newswriter*
Grunsfeld, Ernest Alton, III, *architect*
Guggenheimer, Joan *law administrator*
Guillen, Alita (Alita Haytayan) *newscaster*
Guillen, Oswaldo Jose Barrios (Ozzie Guillen) *professional baseball team manager*
Gulbrandsen, Norman Ralph *retired music educator*
Gunning, Tom *art educator*
Gupta, Krishna Chandra *mechanical engineering educator*
Guralnick, Sidney Aaron *civil engineering educator*
Guthman, Jack *lawyer*
Gutstein, Solomon *lawyer*
Hackett, Karen L. *medical association administrator*
Hackl, Donald John *architect*
Haffner, Charles Christian, III, *retired printing company executive*
Hahn, Frederic Louis *lawyer*
Haley, George *Romance languages educator*
Hall, Joan M. *lawyer*
Hallinan, Joseph Thomas *journalist, reporter*
Halloran, Michael John *lawyer*
Halpern, Jack *chemist, educator*
Ham, Eldon *lawyer*
Hamada, Robert S(eiji) *dean, educator, economist, entrepreneur*
Hamarstrom, Patricia Ann *director, animation/multimedia specialist*
Hambrick, Ernestine *retired colon and rectal surgeon*
Hamm, Mia (Mariel Margaret Hamm) *professional soccer player*
Hammesfahr, Robert Winter *lawyer*
Hand, Roger *physician, educator*
Hannah, Wayne Robertson, Jr., *lawyer*
Hannay, William Mouat, III, *lawyer*
Hano, Randy *publishing executive*
Hanrath, Linda Carol *librarian, archivist*
Hansen, Carl R. *management consultant*
Hansen, Claire V. *financial executive*
Hanson, Floyd Bliss *mathematician*
Hanson, Mark S. *bishop*
Hanson, Ronald William *lawyer*
Hardaway, Ernest, II, *oral and maxillofacial surgeon, public health service officer*
Hardgrove, James Alan *lawyer*
Harkna, Eric *advertising executive*
Harmon, Teresa Wilton *lawyer*
Harrington, Carol A. *lawyer*
Harrington, James Timothy *lawyer*
Harris, Donald Ray *lawyer*
Harris, Gregory Scott *municipal official*
Harris, Irving Brooks *investor, director*
Harris, Jules Eli *medical educator, physician, clinical scientist, administrator*
Harris, Mildred Clopton *clergy member, educator*
Harris, Neil *historian, educator*
Harris, Shirley *elementary, secondary and adult education educator*
Harris, Susan V. *lawyer*
Harris, Thomas Liston *art educator*
Harrison, Holly A. *lawyer*
Harrold, Bernard *lawyer*
Harrow, Martin *psychologist, educator*
Hart, Katherine Miller *college dean*
Hart, Pamela Heim *banker*
Hart, William Thomas *federal judge*
Hartman, Laura Beth Pincus *management consultant, writer, academic administrator*
Hartnett, James Patrick *engineering educator*
Harvey, Katherine Abler *civic worker*
Harvey, Paul *news commentator, author, columnist*
Harvey, Ronald Gilbert *research chemist*
Haskins, Charles Gregory, Jr., *lawyer*
Hasnain, Memoona *medical educator, medical researcher*
Hast, Adele *editor, historian*
Hast, Malcolm Howard *biomedical scientist, medical educator*
Haupt, Roger A. *advertising executive*
Havala, Michael J. *real estate company executive*
Hawkins, Loretta Ann *retired secondary school educator, playwright*
Hayden, Harrold Harrison *information company executive*
Haydock, Walter James *banker*
Hayes, Alice Bourke *academic administrator, biologist, researcher*
Hayes, Charles *religious organization executive, clergyman*
Hayes, David John Arthur, Jr., *legal association executive*
Hayes, John Daniel *lawyer*
Hayes, Richard Donald *architect*
Hayward, Thomas Zander, Jr., *lawyer*
Head, Louis Rollin *surgeon*
Head, Patrick James *lawyer*
Heagy, Thomas Charles *banker*
Healy, Sondra Anita *consumer products company executive*
Heatwole, Mark M. *lawyer*
Hebel, Doris A. *astrologer*
Heckman, James Joseph *economist, econometrician, educator*
Hefner, Christie Ann *multi-media entertainment executive*
Heineman, Ben Walter *corporation executive*
Heinrichs, April *coach*
Heinz, William Denby *lawyer*
Heisler, Quentin George, Jr., *lawyer*
Heisley, Michael E., Sr., *manufacturing executive*
Hellie, Richard *Russian history educator, researcher*
Hellman, Samuel *radiologist, educator*
Helman, Robert Alan *lawyer*
Helmholz, R(ichard) H(enry) *law educator*
Helpingstine, Daniel Wallace *organization official, freelance writer*
Heltne, Paul Gregory *research scholar*
Henderson, Janet E. E. *lawyer*
Henderson, William J. *former postmaster general*
Heneghan, Thomas P. *real estate company executive*
Henikoff, Leo M., Jr., *academic administrator, educator, medical educator*
Henning, Joel Frank *lawyer, author, publisher, consultant*
Henry, Brian C. *telephone company executive*
Henry, Frederick Edward *lawyer*
Henry, Robert John *lawyer*
Herbert, William Carlisle *lawyer*
Herbst, Arthur Lee *obstetrician, gynecologist*
Herman, Sidney N. *lawyer*
Herpe, David A. *lawyer*
Herron, David A. *brokerage house executive*
Herting, Claireen LaVern *financial planner*
Herzog, Fred F. *law educator*
Hess, Sidney J., Jr., *lawyer*
Hibbard, Judith Usher *obstetrician*
Hickey, Jerome Edward *investment company executive*
Hickey, John Thomas, Jr., *lawyer*
Hickman, Frederic W. *retired lawyer*
Hicks, James Thomas *lawyer, physician*
Higgins, Ruth Ellen *theatre producer*
Hildebrand, Roger Henry *astrophysicist, physicist*
Hill, Barbara Benton *healthcare executive*
Hill, Carlotta H. *physician*
Hill, Darlene *newscaster*
Hilliard, David Craig *lawyer, educator*
Hillocks, George, Jr., *English educator, researcher, consultant*
Himmelfarb, John David *artist*
Hindman, Leslie Susan *auctioneer*
Hirsch, Martin *dentist*
Hlavacek, Roy George *publishing executive, magazine editor, association executive*

Hobson, Mellody *investment company executive*
Hodes, Scott *lawyer*
Hofer, Roy Ellis *lawyer*
Hoffman, Richard Bruce *lawyer*
Hoffman, Valerie Jane *lawyer*
Hofrichter, David Alan *management consultant*
Holabird, John Augur, Jr., *retired architect*
Holland, Eugene, Jr., *lumber company executive*
Holleb, Marshall Maynard *lawyer*
Holli, Melvin George *history educator*
Holliday, Patricia A. *elementary school educator*
Hollis, Donald Roger *management consultant*
Hollis-Sawyer, Lisa Ann *psychologist, gerontologist, researcher*
Holtschneider, Dennis H. *university official, priest*
Homburger, Thomas Charles *lawyer*
Honig, George Raymond *pediatrician*
Hooton, James G. *finance company executive*
Hoover, Paul *poet*
Horgan, Santiago *surgeon*
Horwich, Allan *lawyer*
Hoseman, Daniel *lawyer*
Hoskins, Richard Jerold *lawyer*
Houk, James Charles *physiologist, educator*
Housley, Phil F. *professional hockey player*
Howe, Jonathan Thomas *lawyer*
Howell, R(obert) Thomas, Jr., *lawyer, former food company executive*
Howley, Thomas A. *dentist*
Howser, Richard Glen *lawyer*
Hoye, Donald J. *hardware distribution company executive*
Hsu, Judy *newscaster*
Hsueh, Wei *pathologist, educator*
Hubbard, Elizabeth Louise *lawyer*
Huckman, Michael Saul *neuroradiologist, educator*
Hucles, Angela Khalia *professional soccer player*
Hughes, John Russell *neurologist, educator*
Hughes, Martin P. *insurance company executive*
Hullin, Tod Robert *aerospace transportation executive*
Hunt, Craig A. *paper company executive*
Hunt, Holly *small business owner*
Hunt, Lawrence Halley, Jr., *lawyer*
Hunter, James Galbraith, Jr., *lawyer*
Huntley, Robert Stephen *newspaper editor*
Hussey, Michael Jude *obstetrician, educator*
Husting, Peter Marden *advertising consultant*
Huston, DeVerille Anne *lawyer*
Hutchinson, Dennis James *law educator*
Hyman, Michael Bruce *lawyer*
Ibbotson, Roger G. *financial educator*
Idol, Anna Catherine *magazine editor*
Iglauer, Bruce *record company executive*
Ingham, Norman William *Russian literature educator, genealogist*
Iqbal, Zafar Mohd *cancer researcher, biochemist, pharmacologist, toxicologist, consultant, molecular biologist*
Istock, Verne George *retired bank executive*
Ivankovich, Anthony D. *anesthesiologist, educator*
Jackson, Jane F. *writer*
Jacobson, Marian Slutz *lawyer*
Jacobson, Richard Joseph *lawyer*
Jacobson, Ronald H. *lawyer*
Jaconetty, Thomas Anthony *lawyer*
Jaffe, Howard Allen *financial company executive*
Jahn, Helmut *architect*
Jahns, Jeffrey *lawyer*
James, Marie Moody *clergywoman, musician, vocal music educator*
Jamieson, James M. *manufacturing executive*
Janecek, Lenore Elaine *insurance specialist, consultant*
Jaramillo, Carlos Alberto *civil engineer*
Jarrett, Valerie Bowman *property management executive, stock exchange executive*
Jeevanandam, Valluvan *surgeon, educator*
Jegen, Sister Carol Frances *religion educator*
Jensen, Harold Leroy *medical liability insurance administrator, physician*
Jerome, Jerrold V. *retired insurance company executive*
Jezuit, Leslie James *manufacturing executive*
Jilhewar, Ashok *gastroenterologist*
Joern, Charles Edward, Jr., *lawyer*
John, Nancy R. *librarian, writer*
Johnson, Barbara Elaine Spears *retired education educator*
Johnson, Donald Harry, Jr., *government official, educator*
Johnson, Gary Thomas *lawyer*
Johnson, Glenn Thompson *retired judge*
Johnson, Janet Helen *Egyptology educator*
Johnson, Jeffrey L. *investment company executive*
Johnson, Lael Frederic *lawyer*
Johnson, Mary Ann *vocational school owner*
Johnson, Richard Fred *lawyer*
Johnson, Timothy Patrick *health and social researcher*
Jonasson, Olga *surgeon, educator*
Jones, Christopher N. *journalist, educator*
Jones, Cobi *professional soccer player*
Jones, Dorothy F. *judge*
Jones, Emil, Jr., *state legislator*
Jones, Linda *communications educator*
Jones, Mary Laura *developer, fundraiser*
Jones, Richard Jeffery *internist, educator*
Jones, Stephanie J. *federal agency administrator*
Jordan, Karen *newscaster*
Jordan, V. Craig *endocrine pharmacologist, educator*
Joseph, Robert Thomas *lawyer*
Judge, Bernard Martin *editor, publisher*
Julmy, Camille P. *real estate company executive*
Junewicz, James J. *lawyer*
Kaegi, Walter Emil *Byzantine history education educator*
Kahrilas, Peter James *medical educator, researcher*
Kalina, John *auto parts company executive*
Kallick, David A. *lawyer*
Kalver, Gail Ellen *dance company executive, musician*
Kamin, Chester Thomas *lawyer*
Kaminsky, Richard Alan *lawyer*
Kampouris, Emmanuel Andrew *retired corporate executive*
Kamyszew, Christopher D. *museum curator, executive educator, art consultant*
Kaplan, Howard Gordon *lawyer*
Kaplan, Jared *lawyer*
Kaplan, Jonathan H B *healthcare business transformation and information technology specialist*
Kaplan, Morton A. *political science and philosophy educator*
Kaplan, Sidney Mountbatten *lawyer*
Karanikas, Alexander *English language educator, author, actor*
Karon, Sheldon *lawyer*
Katsman, Zinaida *musician, music educator*
Katz, Adrian Izhack *physician, educator*
Katz, Avrum Sidney *lawyer*
Katz, Harold Ambrose *lawyer, former state legislator*
Katz, Robert Stephen *rheumatologist, educator*
Katz, Stuart Charles *lawyer, jazz musician*
Kaufman, Andrew Michael *lawyer*
Kearney, John Walter *sculptor, painter*
Kearney, Michael John *banker*
Keenan, James George *classics educator*
Keiderling, Timothy Allen *chemistry educator, researcher*
Keller, Deborah Kim *former soccer player*
Kelly, Arthur Lloyd *management and investment company executive*
Kelly, Charles Arthur *lawyer*
Kelly, Curtis Hartt *retired publishing executive*
Kelly, Jerry Bob *social services administrator*
Kelly, Maura Anne *reporter*
Kennedy, Eugene Cullen *psychology educator, writer*
Kennedy, Lawrence Allan *mechanical engineering educator*
Kenney, Colleen M. *lawyer*
Kenney, Crane H. *lawyer*
Kenney, Estelle Koval *artist, educator*
Kenney, Frank Deming *lawyer*
Kerbis, Gertrude Lempp *architect*
Kerth, Jack D. *otolaryngologist*
Kiani, Reza *endocrinology and internal medicine educator*
Kikoler, Stephen Philip *lawyer*
Kim, Daniel J. *publishing executive, editor*
Kim, Mi Ja *dean, academic administrator*
Kim, Michael Charles *lawyer*
Kincaid, Richard D. *bank executive*
King, Andre Richardson *architectural graphic designer*
King, Jennifer Elizabeth *editor*
King, Michael Howard *lawyer*
King, Sharon Louise *lawyer*
Kinslow, Monica M. *forensic scientist*
Kipperman, Lawrence I. *lawyer*
Kirkegaard, R. Lawrence *architectural acoustician*
Kirkpatrick, Anne Saunders *systems analyst*
Kirkpatrick, John Everett *lawyer*
Kirschner, Barbara Starrels *pediatric gastroenterologist*
Kirsner, Joseph Barnett *physician, educator*
Kisor, Henry Du Bois *newspaper editor, critic, columnist, writer*
Kissel, Richard John *lawyer*
Kittle, Charles Frederick *surgeon*
Klatt, Wayne Roy *editor, writer*
Klauck, Hans-Josef *theology educator*
Klaviter, Helen Lothrop *magazine editor*
Klebba, Raymond Allen *property manager*
Klein, Melvyn Norman *lawyer, investment executive*
Klenk, James Andrew *lawyer*
Kleppa, Ole J. *chemistry professor*
Kloss, Linda L. *medical association administrator*
Kloster, Carol Good *book and magazine distribution company*
Klues, Jack *communications executive*
Knapp, Paul Raymond *think-tank executive*
Knappenberger, Paul Henry, Jr., *science museum director*
Kneen, John W. *venture capitalist*
Knote, John A. *diagnostic radiologist*
Knox, James Marshall *lawyer*
Knuepfer, Robert Claude, Jr., *lawyer*
Kobler, John F. *priest, researcher*
Kobs, James Fred *direct marketing consultant*
Koch, Steven *lawyer, investment banker, finance company executive*
Kocka, Frank Edward *retired microbiologist*
Koeliner, Laurette *manufacturing executive, human resources specialist*
Koelliner, Laurette T. *aerospace transportation executive*
Koernig, Stephen K. *marketing professional, educator*
Kohn, Shalom L. *lawyer*
Kohn, William Irwin *lawyer*
Kolb, Gwin Jackson *language professional, educator*
Kolek, Robert Edward *lawyer*
Koltin, Allan David *accountant*
Konerko, Paul *professional baseball player*
Kopec, John William *research scientist*
Koppes, Steven Nelson *science writer, editor*
Kopriva, Robert S. *food products executive*
Kopytko, Edwin Edward *nursing administrator*
Kornick, Michael *chef*
Kotulak, Ronald *newspaper science writer*
Kouvel, James Spyros *physicist, researcher*
Kowal-Vern, Areta *pathology and pediatrics educator*
Kozak, John W. *lawyer*
Krakowski, Richard John *lawyer, public relations executive*
Kramer, Andrea S. *lawyer*
Kramer, Weezie Crawford *former broadcast executive*
Krasny, Paula J. *lawyer*
Kravitt, Jason Harris Paperno *lawyer*
Krawczyk, Eva *information systems analyst, educator*
Krawetz, Arthur Altshuler *chemist, science administrator*
Kriss, Robert J. *lawyer*
Krivkovich, Peter George *advertising executive*
Kroll, Barry Lewis *lawyer*
Krueger, Bonnie Lee *editor, writer*
Krueger, Herbert William *lawyer*
Kubida, Judith Ann *museum administrator*
Kubistal, Patricia Bernice *educational consultant*
Kubo, Gary Michael *advertising executive*
Kuczwara, Thomas Paul *postal inspector, lawyer*
Kudish, David J. *financial executive*
Kudo, Irma Setsuko *not-for-profit executive director*
Kullberg, Duane Reuben *accounting firm executive*
Kunkle, William Joseph *lawyer*
Kwan, Nesita *newscaster*
Kwembe, Tor Anthony *mathematical educator, researcher*
Lach, Alma Elizabeth *food and cooking writer, consultant*
Ladd, Jeffrey Raymond *lawyer*
Lagarde, Christine *lawyer*
Laidlaw, Andrew R. *lawyer*
Landan, Henry Sinclair *business consultant, financial consultant*
Landes, William M. *law educator*
Landow-Esser, Janine Marise *lawyer*
Landsberg, Lewis *dean, endocrinologist, medical researcher*
Landsman, Stephan *law educator*
Laner, Richard Warren *lawyer*
Lang, Gordon, Jr., *retired lawyer*
Langman, Craig Bradford *nephrologist*
Lapidus, Dennis *real estate developer*
Larson, Allan Louis *political scientist, educator, lay church worker*
Larson, Nancy Celeste *computer systems manager*
Lassar, Scott R. *lawyer*
Lathon, Sheraine *clergyman*
Latimer, Kenneth Alan *lawyer*
Laumann, Edward Otto *sociology educator*
Lauth, William Brian *emergency physician, internist, educator*
LaVelle, Avis *consulting firm executive*
Lavey, Martha *theater director*
Lavin, Terrence J. *lawyer*
Lawler, James Ronald *French language educator*
Lazarus, Steven *technology company executive*
Leckey, Andrew A. *financial columnist*
Lee, Michael *leasing company executive, real estate company executive*
Lee, Raphael Carl *plastic surgeon, biomedical engineer*
Leff, Alan Richard *medical educator, researcher*
Lefkow, Michael Francis *lawyer*
Legge Kemp, Diane *architect, landscape architect*
Leifer, Lyon A. *musician, educator*
Leigh, Sherren *communications executive, editor, publisher*
Leighton, George Neves *retired federal judge*
Leinenweber, Harry D. *federal judge*
Lenehan, Michael Daniel *editor, writer*
Lenti Ponsetto, Jean *athletic director*
Leonard, Laura L. L. *lawyer*
Leone, Gustavo *composer*
Lerner, Alexander Robert *insurance company executive*
Lerner, Barbara *think-tank executive, researcher*
Lerner, Wayne M. *health care executive*
Leszinske, William O. *bank executive*
Levenfeld, Milton Arthur *lawyer*
Leventhal, Bennett Lee *psychiatry and pediatrics educator, administrator*
Levi, John G. *lawyer*
Levin, Arnold Murray *social worker, psychotherapist*
Levin, Charles Edward *lawyer*
Levin, Jack S. *lawyer*
Levin, Michael David *lawyer*
Levine, Keith F. *marketing executive*
Levmore, Saul *law educator, dean*
Levy, David Henry *lawyer*
Levy, Deborah *security company executive*
Levy, Donald Harris *chemistry professor*
Lewis, Charles A. *investment company executive*
Lewis, Evelyn *management consultant*
Lewis, Russell Lamar *historian, museum administrator*
Leyhane, Francis John, III, *lawyer*
Li, Wen-Hsiung *geneticist*
Liao, Shutsung *biochemist, molecular oncologist*
Liebenow, Franklin Eastburn, Jr., *English literature educator*
Lieberman, Pamela Forbes *consumer products company executive*
Lieberman, Richard Elliot *lawyer*
Lilly, Kristine Marie *professional soccer player*
Lim, Len Gui Remolona (Mark Lim) *critical care and emergency nurse*
Lin, James Chih-I *biomedical and electrical engineer, educator*
Lincoln, Bruce Kenneth *anthropology, classics and history of religions educator*
Linden, Henry Robert *chemical engineer, researcher*
Lindquist, Susan Lee *biology and microbiology educator*
Linklater, William Joseph *lawyer*
Lipinski, Ann Marie *newspaper editor*
Lipson, Charles Henry *political scientist, educator*
Lipton, Lois Jean *lawyer*
Little, William G. *manufacturing executive*
Little, William Grady (Grady Little) *professional baseball coach*
Litwin, Burton Howard *lawyer*
Liu, Ben-chieh *economist*
Livingston, Homer J., Jr., *stock exchange executive*
Lloyd, Robert Allen *lawyer*
Lochbihler, Frederick Vincent *lawyer*
Lockwood, Frank James *manufacturing executive*
Lockwood, Gary Lee *lawyer*
Loesch, Katharine Taylor (Mrs. John George Loesch) *communication and theatre educator*
Logemann, Jerilyn Ann *speech pathologist, educator*
London, Justin Joshua *portfolio manager, consultant*
Longworth, Richard Cole *journalist*
Look, Dona Jean *artist*
Looman, James R. *lawyer*
Lopez, Carolyn Catherine *physician*
Lorch, Kenneth F. *lawyer*
Lorch, Robert K. *corporate financial executive*
Lorenz, Hugo Albert *retired insurance executive, consultant*
Lotocky, Innocent Hilarius *bishop*
Lowery, Timothy J. *lawyer*
Lowry, James Hamilton *management consultant*
Lubin, Donald G. *lawyer*
Lucas, Gregory *market researcher*
Lucas, Robert Emerson, Jr., *economist, educator*
Luchins, Daniel Jonathan *psychiatrist*
Lund, Bruce Donald *small business executive*
Lundergan, Barbara Keough *lawyer*
Lund-Molfese, Nicholas C. *academic administrator*
Lurain, John Robert, III, *gynecologic oncologist*
Luscombe, George A. II *lawyer*
Lustrea, Anita *radio personality*
Luthringshausen, Wayne *brokerage house executive*
Lutter, Paul Allen *lawyer*
Lyerla, Bradford Peter *lawyer*
Lynch, John Peter *lawyer*
Lythcott, Marcia A. *newspaper editor*
MacCarthy, Terence Francis *lawyer*
MacDougal, Gary Edward *corporate director, foundation trustee*
Mack, Jim *advertising executive*
Mackiewicz, Laura *advertising agency executive*
MacMillan, Shannon Ann *professional soccer player*
MacWilliams, Diane *communications executive*
Maczulski, Margaret Louise *event marketing professional, meeting manager*
Madansky, Albert *statistics educator*
Madara, James Lee *dean, pathologist, educator, epitheliologist*
Maddux, Gregory (Gregory Alan Maddux) *professional baseball player*
Madigan, John William *publishing executive*
Madigan, Lisa *state attorney general*
Madsen, Dorothy Louise (Meg Madsen) *writer*
Maduros, John *real estate company executive*
Mahaffey, John Christopher *professional society administrator*
Maher, David Willard *lawyer*
Maher, Francesca Marciniak *lawyer, former air transportation executive*
Mahood, William H. *gastroenterologist*
Majers, Elizabeth Louise *lawyer*
Makinen, Marvin William *biophysicist, educator*
Malcolm, Christine Anne *university hospital administrator*
Malham, Joseph Mario *artist, writer*
Malinowski, Arthur Anthony *lawyer, labor arbitrator*
Malkin, Cary Jay *lawyer*
Malkinson, Frederick David *dermatologist, educator*
Mallory, Robert Mark *controller, finance executive*
Maloy, Frances *librarian*
Manelli, Donald Dean *screenwriter, film producer*
Manganello, Timothy M. *auto parts company executive*
Manning, Blanche M. *federal judge*
Manning, Sylvia *English studies educator*
Mansfield, Karen Lee *lawyer*
Manzo, Edward David *patent lawyer*
Mao, Jeremy J *orthodontist, educator*
Markey, Howard Thomas *retired law educator, former federal judge*
Marroquin-Merino, Victor Miguel *lawyer*
Marshall, Cody *bishop*
Marshall, John David *lawyer*
Martin, Alan Joseph *lawyer*
Martin, Arthur Mead *lawyer*
Martin, Gary Joseph *medical educator*
Martinez, Josemaria Espino *computer services administrator*
Martinez, Natalie *newscaster*
Martin-Liamazares, Carlos *academic administrator*
Marwedel, Warren John *lawyer*
Mason, Gregory Wesley, Jr., *secondary school educator, educator*
Mason, Richard J. *lawyer*
Mason, William *general director of opera company*
Massura, Eileen Kathleen *family therapist*
Matanky, James E. *real estate developer*
Matasar, Ann B. *former dean, business and political science educator*
Mateles, Richard Isaac *biotechnologist*
Matthei, Edward Hodge *architect*
Mattson, Stephen Joseph *lawyer*
Maves, Michael Donald *medical association executive*
May, Aviva Rabinowitz *music educator, linguist, musician*
Mayer, Frank D., Jr., *lawyer*
Mayer, Raymond Richard *business administration educator*
McBreen, Maura Ann *lawyer*
McCaleb, Malcolm, Jr., *lawyer*
McCallister, Richard Anthony *business consulting company executive*
McCann, Renetta *advertising executive*
Mc Carter, John Wilbur, Jr., *museum executive*
McCaskey, Raymond F. *insurance company executive*
McClintock, Martha K. *biologist, educator*
McCloy, Elizabeth K. *lawyer*
McClure, James Julius, Jr., *lawyer, former city official*
McConahey, Stephen George *retired securities company executive*
McConnell, E. Hoy, II, *advertising/public policy executive*
McCracken, Thomas James, Jr., *lawyer*
McCray, Curtis Lee *academic administrator*
McCue, Judith W. *lawyer*
McCullough, Richard Lawrence *advertising agency executive*
McCurry, Margaret Irene *architect, educator, furniture designer, interior designer*
McDermott, John H(enry) *lawyer*
McDermott, Mary Ann *nursing educator*
McDermott, Raymond, Jr., *physician*
McDermott, Robert B. *lawyer*
McDonald, Larry William *neuropathologist educator*
McDonald, Theresa Beatrice Pierce (Mrs. Ollie McDonald) *church official, minister*
McDonald, Thomas Alexander *lawyer*
McDonald, William Brice *educational association administrator*
McDonnell, David Croft *diversified financial services company executive*
McDonough, John Michael *lawyer*
McGinn, Bernard John *religious educator*
McGovern, Peter John *law educator*
McGrail, Jeane Kathryn *artist, educator, poet, curator*
McGrath, Michael G. *finance company executive*
McKay, Neil *banker*
McKee, Keith Earl *manufacturing technology executive*
McKinney, William T. *psychiatrist, educator*
McLaren, Richard Wellington, Jr., *lawyer*
McLaughlin, T. Mark *lawyer*
McLawhon, Ronald William *pathology educator, biochemist*
McLees, John Alan *lawyer*
McMahon, Thomas Michael *lawyer*
McMillan, C. Steven *consumer packaged goods company executive*
McMillan, Cary D. *food products executive*
McMorrow, Mary Ann G. *state supreme court chief justice*
McNally, Alan G. *bank executive*
McNally, Andrew, IV, *publishing executive, director*
McNeill, G. David *psycholinguist, educator*
McPherson, Michael Steven *former academic administrator, economist*
McQuillen, James Francis *electronics executive*
McVisk, William Kilburn *lawyer*

Meadow, William Lee *medical educator*
Mecklenburg, Gary Alan *hospital executive*
Mehlman, David Joel *cardiologist, educator*
Mehlman, Mark Franklin *lawyer*
Mehrberg, Randall Eric *lawyer*
Meisels, Marlene *literacy and special education educator, editor*
Melamed, Leo *global consulting firm executive*
Mell, Patricia *dean*
Melnick, Jane Fisher *journalist, educator, photographer, literature educator*
Melton, David Reuben *lawyer*
Meltzer, Bernard David *law educator*
Meltzer, Robert Craig *lawyer, educator*
Menchetti, David Barry *lawyer*
Mendelson, Ellen B. *radiologist, educator*
Mendenhall, Candice *former finance company executive*
Menendez, Marcelino Eulogio (Marc Menendez) *marketing professional*
Mercer, Ron *professional basketball player*
Merk, Bradley Robert *orthopedic surgeon*
Metz, Charles Edgar *radiology educator*
Metzger, Paul Thomas *lawyer*
Meyer, John Albert *lawyer*
Meyer, Paul Reims, Jr., *orthopedic surgeon*
Miceli, William Cyril, Sr., *director*
Michaels, Richard Edward *lawyer*
Michaels, Robert A. *real estate development company executive*
Michalak, Edward Francis *lawyer*
Migala, Lucyna J. *journalist, arts administrator, radio station executive*
Miglin, Marilyn *cosmetics executive*
Mihelic, Tracey L. *lawyer*
Mikesell, Marvin Wray *geography educator*
Mikva, Abner Joseph *lawyer, retired federal judge*
Milbrett, Tiffeny Carleen *professional soccer player*
Miletich, Ivo *library and information scientist, bibliographer, educator, linguist, literature research specialist*
Milissis, Nicholas George *lawyer*
Miller, Albert J. *cardiologist, internist*
Miller, Benjamin K. *retired state supreme court justice*
Miller, Bernard Joseph, Jr., *advertising executive*
Miller, Douglas Andrew *lawyer, educator*
Miller, Ellen *advertising executive*
Miller, Heidi G. *diversified financial company executive*
Miller, Irving Franklin *chemical engineer, educator, biomedical engineer, educator, academic administrator*
Miller, John Leed *lawyer*
Miller, Oscar *economics professor*
Miller, Paul J. *lawyer*
Miller, Richard J. *pharmacologist, educator*
Miller, Stephen Ralph *lawyer*
Miller, Verne William *computer engineer, consultant*
Millichap, Joseph Gordon *neurologist, educator*
Millner, Robert B. *lawyer*
Mims, Joyce Elaine *lawyer*
Mindes, Gayle Dean *education educator*
Miner, Thomas Hawley *international entrepreneur*
Minichello, Dennis *lawyer*
Minkowycz, W.J. *mechanical engineering educator*
Minneste, Viktor, Jr., *retired engineering executive*
Minogue, John P. *academic administrator, educator, priest*
Minow, Josephine Baskin *civic volunteer*
Minow, Newton Norman *lawyer, educator*
Mintzer, David *physics educator*
Mirkin, Bernard Leo *clinical pharmacologist, pediatrician*
Mirza, Leona Lousin *elementary school educator, director*
Mitchell, Lee Mark *communications executive, investment fund manager, lawyer*
Moawad, Atef *obstetrician, gynecologist, educator*
Moen, Ronald S. *medical association administrator*
Moffatt, Joyce Anne *performing company executive*
Mohammadian, Abolfazl *civil engineer, educator*
Molins, Marcel J. *lawyer*
Montgomery, Charles Howard *retired bank executive*
Montgomery, Gary B. *manufacturing executive*
Montgomery, Julie-April *lawyer*
Montgomery, William Adam *lawyer*
Moore, Patrick J. *paper company executive*
Moore, Vernon John, Jr., *pediatrician, consultant, lawyer*
Moran, James Byron *federal judge*
Morency, Paula J. *lawyer*
Moretti, Robert James *psychologist, educator*
Morewitz, Stephen John *behavioral scientist, consultant, educator*
Morgan, Betsy Stelle *lawyer*
Morgan, Donna Evensen *lawyer*
Morgan, William Adams *lawyer*
Morley, Michael B. *public relations executive*
Morrill, R. Layne *real estate broker, executive, professional association administrator*
Morris, Ashley *information scientist, educator*
Morris, Naomi Carolyn Minner *clinical pediatrician, medical researcher, educator, health facility administrator*
Morrison, Portia Owen *lawyer*
Morris-Rogers, Cheryl-Ann *daycare provider, director, educator*
Morrow, Richard Martin *retired oil company executive*
Morsch, Thomas Harvey *lawyer*
Mosena, David R. *museum administrator*
Moskow, Michael H. *federal official*
Moss, Gerald S. *dean, medical educator*
Moster, Mary Clare *public relations executive*
Muchin, Allan B. *lawyer*
Mugnaini, Enrico *neuroscience educator*
Mullen, J. Thomas *lawyer*
Mullen, Michael T. *lawyer*
Mullins, Obera *retired microbiologist*
Mullner, Ross Michael *healthcare educator*
Munger, Benson Scott *former professional society administrator*
Murad, Sohail *engineer educator*
Murata, Tadao *engineering and computer science educator*
Murdock, Charles William *lawyer, educator*
Murphy, Ellis *association management executive*
Murphy, Michael Emmett *retired food company executive*
Murray, Daniel Richard *lawyer*
Murtaugh, Christopher David *lawyer*
Musacchio, Robert A. *medical association administrator*
Myernick, Glenn *professional soccer coach*
Myers, Lonn William *lawyer*
Myerson, Roger Bruce *economist, game theorist, educator*
Myers-Rami, Masequa *theatrical company executive, theater producer*
Naclerio, Robert Michael *otolaryngologist, educator*
Nadler, Robert B. *medical educator*
Naegele, Elizabeth Marie *musician, educator*
Nagel, Sidney Robert *physics educator*
Nahrwold, David Lange *surgeon, educator*
Najita, Tetsuo *history educator*
Nakajima, Yasuko *medical educator*
Nakamura, Kimiko *language educator*
Nambu, Yoichiro *physics educator*
Narahashi, Toshio *pharmacology educator*
Nash, Donald Gene *commodity investigator*
Nash, Gordon Bernard, Jr., *lawyer*
Nashat, Guity *historian, education educator, researcher*
Nassos, George P. *chemical engineer, educator*
Natarus, Burton F. *lawyer, municipal legislator*
Nault, William Henry *publishing executive*
Nava, Roxanne *state agency administrator*
Nechin, Herbert Benjamin *lawyer*
Needleman, Barbara *newspaper executive*
Neis, James Michael *lawyer*
Neithercut, David J. *real estate executive*
Nelson, Harry Donald *telecommunications executive*
Nelson, Richard Lawrence *surgeon, educator*
Netherland, Joseph H. *manufacturing executive*
Neubauer, Charles Frederick *investigative reporter*
Neubauer, Nickolas J. *brokerage house executive*
Neumeier, Matthew Michael *lawyer, educator*
Newman, Dennis Nathan *lawyer*
Nguyen, Tuan Manh *internist, perinatologist, obstetrician, gynecologist*
Nicastro, Tracey A. *lawyer*
Nichol, Norman J. *manufacturing executive*
Nicholas, Ralph Wallace W. *anthropologist, educator*
Nichols, John Doane *diversified manufacturing corporation executive*
Nickel, Melvin Edwin *metallurgical engineer*
Nicolaides, Mary *lawyer*
Niehaus, Mary C. C. *lawyer*
Nielsen, Nancy H. *health organization executive*
Niro, Cheryl *lawyer*
Nitikman, Franklin W. *lawyer*
Noonan, Jack *application developer*
Nora, Gerald Ernest *lawyer*
Nord, Henry J. *transportation executive*
Nord, Robert Eamor *lawyer*
Nordberg, John Albert *federal judge*
Nordland, Gerald *art museum administrator, historian, consultant*
Norgle, Charles Ronald, Sr., *federal judge*
Norton, Jerry E. *law educator*
Notz, John Kranz, Jr., *arbitrator and mediator, retired lawyer*
Novak, Mark *lawyer*
Novich, Neil S. *metals distribution company executive*
Nowacki, James Nelson *lawyer*
Nühn, Adriaan *food products executive*
Nussbaum, Martha Craven *philosophy and classics educator*
Nyhus, Lloyd Milton *surgeon, educator*
Oakes, Fred D. *editor*
O'Brien, Gregory Michael St. Lawrence *academic administrator*
O'Brien, James Phillip *lawyer*
O'Brien, Patrick William *lawyer*
O'Dell, James E. *newspaper publishing executive*
Odishoo, Sarah A. *English language educator*
O'Donnell, Michael James *computer scientist*
Odorizzi, Michele L. *lawyer*
Oehme, Reinhard *physicist, researcher*
Oesterle, Eric Adam *lawyer*
O'Hagan, James Joseph *lawyer*
Oka, Takeshi *physicist, chemist, astronomer, educator*
O'Leary, Daniel Vincent, Jr., *lawyer*
Olian, Robert Martin *lawyer*
Olin, Margaret *art educator*
Oliver, Harry Maynard, Jr., *retired brokerage house executive*
Oliver, Roseann *lawyer*
Olk, Frederick James *county official, paralegal*
Olopade, Olufunmilayo Falusi *oncologist, geneticist, educator*
Olsen, Edward John *geologist, educator, curator*
Olsen, Rex Norman *trade association executive*
Olson, Jack Conrad, Jr., *geriatrician*
Olson, Sandra Forbes *neurologist*
O'Malley, John Daniel *law educator, banker*
O'Meara, Anna M. *lawyer*
O'Meara, John Francis *lawyer*
Omosheyin, Rotimi *electronics specialist, real estate company executive*
O'Neill, Bridget R. *lawyer*
Ong, Michael King *mathematician, educator, bank executive*
Onsager, David Ralph *cardiothoracic surgeon, educator*
Orden, Alex *management science educator emeritus*
O'Reilly, Charles Terrance *university dean*
O'Reilly, Heather Ann *Olympic athlete*
Orin, Stuart I. *lawyer*
Osborn, William A. *investment company executive*
Osby, Iris *education educator*
O'Shea, James *managing editor*
O'Shea, Lynne Edeen *management consultant, educator*
O'Toole, William George *lawyer*
Overbeck, Carla Werden *soccer player, coach*
Overgaard, Mitchell Jersild *lawyer*
Owen, Clarence B. *construction materials manufacturing executive*
Owens, Charles A. *cardiovascular and interventional radiologist*
Pacher, Nancy A. *real estate company executive*
Padberg, Helen Swan *violinist*
Page, Ernest *medical educator*
Palermo, James W. *artistic director*
Pallasch, B. Michael *lawyer, director*
Pallmeyer, Rebecca Ruth *judge*
Palmer, John Bernard, III, *lawyer*
Palmer, Patrick Edward *radio astronomer, educator*
Palmer, Robert Towne *lawyer, bank executive*
Palmisano, Donald J. *surgeon, medical educator*
Palmore, Roderick Alan *lawyer*
Panich, Danuta Bembenista *lawyer*
Pappas, David Wayne *guidance counselor, consultant*
Pappas, George Demetrios *anatomy and cell biology educator, scientist*
Pappas, Philip James *real estate company executive*
Park, Thomas Joseph *biology researcher, educator*
Parkhurst, Todd Sheldon *lawyer*
Parks, Joan H. *research scientist, educator*
Parlow, Cynthia Maria *professional soccer player*
Parr, Virginia Helen *retired librarian*
Parrish, Overton Burgin, Jr., *pharmaceutical corporation executive*
Partridge, Mark Van Buren *lawyer, educator, writer*
Pascal, Roger *lawyer*
Pasche, Boris Claude Roger *physician*
Patel, Homi Burjor *apparel company executive*
Patinkin, Hugh M. *retail executive*
Patner, Marshall *lawyer*
Patterson, Jeffrey A. *real estate company executive*
Paul, Ronald Neale *management consultant*
Paup, Thomas *retail department store executive*
Pavalon, Eugene Irving *lawyer*
Pavelich, Daniel L. *retired account, tax management consulting executive*
Pearce, Christie Patricia *professional soccer player*
Peerman, Dean Gordon *magazine editor*
Pelton, Russell Meredith, Jr., *lawyer*
Peltzman, Sam *economics professor*
Pender, Nancy *newscaster*
Pendley, Kevin *communication media executive*
Pengra, R. Rene *lawyer*
Peres, Judith May *journalist*
Perez, Sylvia *newscaster, reporter*
Perlberg, Jules Martin *lawyer*
Perlmutter, Norman *finance company executive*
Pero, Perry R. *investment company executive*
Perrin, James Kirk *lawyer*
Pesch, Ellen P. *lawyer*
Peter, Bernard George *lawyer*
Peters, Elizabeth Anne *nutrition educator*
Petersen, Donald Sondergaard *lawyer*
Petersen, William Otto *lawyer*
Peterson, Randall Theodore *law educator, law librarian*
Peterson, Ronald Roger *lawyer*
Petitan, Debra Ann Burke *elementary school educator, counselor, design engineer, writer*
Petrillo, Nancy *public relations executive*
Phillips, Don *investment research company executive*
Phillips, Frederick Falley *architect*
Piderit, John J. *university educator*
Pilchen, Ira A. *editor*
Pimentel, Julio Gumeresindo *lawyer, accountant*
Pincus, Theodore Henry *public relations executive*
Pitt, George *lawyer, investment banker*
Pitt, Judson Hamilton *publisher, author*
Pizer, Howard Charles *sports and entertainment executive*
Plank, Betsy (Mrs. Sherman V. Rosenfield) *public relations counsel*
Platzman, George William *geophysicist, educator*
Plested, William G., III, *surgeon*
Plotkin, Manuel D. *management consultant, educator, former corporate executive and government official*
Plotnick, Harvey Barry *publishing executive*
Plotnik, Arthur *author, columnist*
Poethig, Eunice Blanchard *clergywoman*
Pollock, Earl Edward *lawyer*
Ponné, Nanci Teresa *entertainment promoter, writer*
Pope, Kerig Rodgers *magazine executive*
Pope, Lena Elizabeth *human resources specialist*
Posner, Kathy Robin *communications executive*
Posner, Richard Allen *judge*
Power, Joseph Aloysius, Jr., *lawyer*
Poznanski, Andrew Karol *pediatric radiologist*
Prather, Susan Lynn *public relations executive*
Preble, Robert Curtis, Jr., *insurance executive*
Preece, Lynn Sylvia *lawyer*
Presser, Stephen Bruce *lawyer, educator*
Price, Charles T. *lawyer*
Price, Henry Escoe *broadcast executive*
Primm, Earl Russell, III, *publishing executive*
Primo, Quintin E., III, *real estate company executive*
Prinz, Richard Allen *surgeon*
Prior, Gary L. *lawyer*
Pritzker, Nicholas J. *diversified services corporation executive*
Pritzker, Penny *investor*
Pritzker, Thomas Jay *hotel business executive*
Prochnow, Douglas Lee *lawyer*
Prochnow, Herbert Victor, Jr., *retired lawyer*
Prokopy, Jennifer Grover *writer, consultant*
Provus, Barbara Lee *executive search consultant*
Pugh, Roderick Wellington *retired psychologist*
Puican, Michael *small business owner, poet*
Pulido, Jose S. *physician*
Pump, Bernard John *finance company executive, consultant*
Quazzo, Stephen R. *investment company executive*
Quinn, Patrick *lieutenant governor*
Rabin, Joseph Harry *marketing research company executive*
Rami, Pemon *theatrical company executive, theater producer*
Ramsey-Goldman, Rosalind *physician*
Ran, Shulamit *composer*
Randel, Don Michael *academic administrator, musicologist*
Rankin, James Winton *lawyer*
Raphaelson, Joel *retired advertising agency executive*
Rapoport, David E. *lawyer*
Rappaport, Anna M. *actuary*
Rasin, Rudolph Stephen *corporate financial executive*
Ratner, Carl Joseph *theater director*
Ratner, Gerald *lawyer*
Rawal, Viresh *education educator*
Rea, Anne E. *lawyer*
Read, Sarah J. *lawyer*
Reardon, Patrick Thomas *reporter*
Reardon, Thomas R. *physician, medical association administrator*
Reategui, Lisa J. *lawyer*
Reddick, Catherine Anne (Cat Reddick) *Olympic athlete*
Reddy, Janardan K. *medical educator*
Redman, Clarence Owen *lawyer*
Reed, John Shedd *former railway executive*
Reed, Keith Allen *lawyer*
Reed, M. Scott *accounting company executive*
Reed, Vastina Kathryn (Tina Reed) *child and adolescent psychotherapist, family development specialist*
Reich, Allan J. *lawyer*
Reicin, Ronald Ian *lawyer*
Reid, Daniel James *public relations executive*
Reiffel, Leonard *physicist, medical physicist, scientific consultant*
Reilly, Robert Frederick *valuation consultant*
Reindl, James *newspaper editor*
Reinsdorf, Jerry Michael *professional sports teams executive, real estate executive, lawyer, accountant*
Reiter, Michael A. *lawyer, educator*
Reitman, Jerry Irving *advertising agency executive*
Relias, John Alexis *lawyer*
Remini, Robert Vincent *historian*
Rempfer, Dietmar *research scientist, consultant*
Renslow, Charles George *entrepreneur*
Replogle, Robert Lee *cardiovascular and thoracic surgeon*
Reum, James Michael *lawyer*
Reum, W. Robert *manufacturing executive*
Reyna, Claudio *professional soccer player*
Reynolds, James, Jr., *finance company executive*
Rhind, James Thomas *lawyer*
Rhone, Douglas Pierce *pathologist, educator*
Rice, Charles Lane *surgical educator*
Rice, Linda Johnson *publishing executive*
Rice, William Edward *journalist*
Richman, Harold Alan *social welfare policy educator*
Richman, Joan M. *lawyer*
Richmond, James Glidden *lawyer*
Richter, Julia Maureen *music educator, musician*
Rico, Maria L. *publishing executive*
Ridenour, Joey *medical association administrator, operations research specialist*
Rieger, Mitchell Sheridan *lawyer*
Rielly, John Edward *educational association administrator*
Riess, Steven Allan *historian, educator*
Rikoski, Richard Anthony *engineering executive, electrical engineer*
Riordan, Michael C. *hospital administrator*
Rizowy, Carlos Guillermo *lawyer, educator, political analyst*
Rizzo, Ronald Stephen *lawyer*
Roach, Kathleen Lynn *lawyer*
Robbins, Audrey *county official*
Roberts, Jo Ann Wooden *school system administrator*
Roberts, John Charles *law educator*
Roberts, Theodore Harris *banker*
Roberts, Tiffany Marie *former soccer player*
Robertson, Donna Virginia *architect, educator, dean*
Robertson, William Wright, Jr., *orthopedist, educator*
Robins, Joel *import/export company executive*
Robinson, June Kerswell *dermatologist, educator*
Robinson, Robin *newscaster*
Robinson, Sidney K. *architecture educator*
Rode, Glenn G. *music educator, secondary school educator*
Rodgers, James Foster *association executive, economist*
Roeser, Thomas Francis *columnist, commentator*
Rogers, Desiree Glapion *utilities executive*
Rogowski, Walter S. *lawyer*
Rohrman, Douglass Frederick *lawyer*
Roizen, Michael F. *dean, medical educator, internist*
Roizen, Nancy J. *physician, educator*
Roizman, Bernard *virologist, educator*
Rojek, Kenneth John *health facility administrator, hospital*
Romano-Magner, Patricia R. *English studies educator, researcher*
Rooney, Matthew A. *lawyer*
Rooney, Phillip Bernard *service company executive*
Roper, Harry Joseph *lawyer*
Ropski, Gary Melchior *lawyer*
Rosati, Allison *newscaster*
Rose, Jalen *professional basketball player*
Rosen, Ellen Freda *psychologist, educator*
Rosen, George *economist, educator*
Rosen, Steven Terry *oncologist, hematologist*
Rosenbaum, Michael A. *investor relations consultant*
Rosenberg, Gary Aron *real estate development executive, lawyer*
Rosenberg, Sheli Z. *investment company executive*
Rosenbloom, Lewis Stanley *lawyer*
Rosenheim, Edward Weil *English educator*
Rosenheim, Margaret Keeney *social welfare policy educator*
Rosenthal, Albert Jay *advertising agency executive*
Rosenthal, Ira Maurice *pediatrician, educator*
Rosner, Jonathan Lincoln *physicist, researcher*
Rosner, Robert *astrophysicist, educator*
Ross, Curtis Bennett *lawyer*
Roth, Robert A. *newspaper executive*
Rothschild, Steven K. *physician, medical educator, researcher*
Roubik, Susanne Eileen *architect*
Rovell, Michael Jay *lawyer*
Rovner, Ilana Kara Diamond *federal judge*
Rowe, Diane Elizabeth *law clerk*
Rowe, John William *utilities executive*
Rowley, Janet Davison *physician*
Roy, David Tod *Chinese literature educator*
Rozenblat, Anatoly Isaacovich *manufacturing engineer, inventor*
Rubin, E(rwin) Leonard *lawyer*
Rubin, Stephen D. *food products executive*
Rugo, Steven Alfred *architect*
Rundio, Louis Michael, Jr., *lawyer*
Rupert, Donald William *lawyer*
Russell, Thomas R. *medical association administrator*
Rutkoff, Alan Stuart *lawyer*
Ruxin, Paul Theodore *lawyer*
Ryan, Priscilla E. *lawyer*
Rynkiewicz, Stephen Michael *journalist*
Sachs, Greg Alan *preventive medicine physician*
Sager, William Frederick *retired chemistry educator*
Salem, Riad *radiologist, consultant*
Saller, Richard Paul *classics educator*
Sanderman, Maurice *construction company executive*
Sanders, Jacquelyn Seevak *psychologist, educator*
Sanders, Richard Henry *lawyer*
Sandler, Richard H. *lab administrator, gastroenterologist*
Sandlow, Leslie Jordan *gastroenterologist, educator*
Santangelo, Mario Vincent *dentist*
Sarwark, John Francis *orthopaedic surgeon, educator*
Sato, Junichi Steven *musician, music educator*

Saunders, George Lawton, Jr., *lawyer*
Saunders, Terry Rose *lawyer*
Savage, Terry *television personality, journalist, stockbroker*
Savard, Denis Joseph *former professional hockey player, coach*
Scanlan, Thomas Cleary *publishing executive, editor*
Scarse, Olivia Marie *cardiologist, consultant*
Schade, Stanley Greinert, Jr., *hematologist, educator*
Schafer, Michael Frederick *orthopedic surgeon*
Schar, Stephen L. *lawyer*
Scharf, Charles W. *bank executive*
Scherer, Karla *foundation executive, venture capitalist*
Schieser, Hans Alois *education educator*
Schiller, Donald Charles *lawyer*
Schilsky, Richard Lewis *oncologist, researcher*
Schimberg, A(rmand) Bruce *retired lawyer*
Schimberg, Barbara *organizational development consultant*
Schink, James Harvey *lawyer*
Schmeltzer, John C. *financial writer*
Schmetterer, Jack Baer *federal judge*
Schmidt, Paul Jeffrey *federal government official*
Schmitt, Natalie Crohn *theater educator*
Schneider, Dan W. *lawyer, consultant*
Schneider, Wesley Clair *marketing communications company executive*
Schneidman, Barbara Sue *psychiatrist*
Schoenfield, Rick Merrill *lawyer*
Schoonhoven, Ray James *retired lawyer*
Schornack, John James *accountant*
Schoumacher, Bruce Herbert *lawyer*
Schreck, Robert A., Jr., *lawyer*
Schroeder, Charles Edgar *investment management executive*
Schroeder, Douglas Fredrick *architect*
Schubert, William Henry *curriculum studies educator*
Schueppert, George Louis *financial executive*
Schuler, James Joseph *vascular surgeon*
Schulman, Sidney *neurologist, educator*
Schulte, David Michael *investment banker*
Schulte, Stephen Charles *lawyer*
Schultz, John L. *writer, educator*
Schulz, Keith Donald *corporate lawyer, writer*
Schuman, William Paul *lawyer*
Schumann, William Henry, III, *financial executive*
Schwartz, Alan Gifford *sport company executive*
Schwartz, Donald Lee *lawyer*
Schwartz, John Norman *human services administrator*
Schwertfeger, Timothy B. *investment company executive*
Schwoy, Laurie Annette *professional soccer player*
Sciarra, John J. *obstetrician, gynecologist, educator*
Sclove, Stanley Louis *statistics educator*
Scogland, William Lee *lawyer*
Scommegna, Antonio *obstetrician, gynecologist, educator*
Scott, Bruce A. *otolaryngologist*
Scott, Nancy L. *health facility administrator, consultant*
Scott, Stephen Brinsley *theater producer*
Scribner, Margaret Ellen *educational consultant, consultant*
Scrimshaw, Susan Crosby *dean*
Scully, John Edward, Jr., *banker*
Scurry, Briana Collette *professional soccer player*
Seaman, Irving, Jr., *banker*
Sedelmaier, John Josef *filmmaker*
Seegers, Lori C. *lawyer*
Seeler, Ruth Andrea *pediatrician, educator*
Segal, Mindy *chef*
Sen, Ashish Kumar *government administrator, urban planner, educator, statistician*
Senior, Richard John Lane *textile rental service executive*
Serota, Scott *medical association administrator*
Serritella, James Anthony *lawyer*
Serritella, William David *lawyer*
Serwer, Alan Michael *lawyer*
Sexton, Brenda *film agency director*
Sfikas, Peter Michael *lawyer, educator*
Shadur, Milton Irving *judge*
Shafer, Eric Christopher *minister*
Shaffer, Jack *real estate company executive*
Shahidehpour, Mohammad *dean, academic administrator, engineering educator*
Shank, Suzanne Adams *lawyer*
Shannon, Iris Reed *health consultant*
Shapiro, Harold David *lawyer, educator*
Shapiro, Richard Alan *surgeon*
Shapiro, Stephen Michael *lawyer*
Shapo, Marshall Schambelan *lawyer, educator*
Shaughnessy, Edward Louis *Chinese language educator*
Shaver, Joan Louise Fowler *dean*
Sheagren, John Newcomb *physician, educator*
Shedlock, James *library director, consultant*
Shen, Virginia Shiang-lan *Spanish and Chinese language educator*
Sherman, Ian Matthew *lawyer*
Shidler, Jay H. *real estate company executive*
Shields, Thomas Charles *lawyer*
Shields, Thomas William *surgeon, educator*
Shiflett, Shawn Allen *writer, educator*
Shimokubo, Janice Teruko *marketing professional*
Shindler, Donald A. *lawyer*
Shirley, Virginia Lee *advertising executive*
Shoenberger, Allen Edward *law educator*
Short, Marion Priscilla *neurogenetics educator*
Siegel, Howard Jerome *lawyer*
Siegel, Laurence B. *investment research company executive, consultant*
Siegler, Mark *internist, educator*
Sigler, Hollis *artist, educator, author*
Sigmon, Joyce Elizabeth *professional society administrator*
Silberman, Alan Harvey *lawyer*
Silets, Harvey Marvin *lawyer*
Silich, Greg *advertising executive*
Silverstein, Jonathan Charles *surgeon, researcher*
Simmons, Adele Smith *foundation executive, former educator*
Simon, Bernece Kern *retired social work educator*
Simon, John Bern *lawyer*
Simon, Mordecai *religious association administrator, clergyman*
Simon, Seymour *lawyer, former state supreme court justice*
Simoni, Christopher *dean, law educator*
Simons, Helen *school psychologist, psychotherapist, educator*
Singer, Emel *staffing industry executive*
Singer, Martin H. *Internet company executive*
Singleton, Gregory Holmes *historian, educator*
Sinha, Raj P. *education educator, researcher*
Sippey, Roger Boyd *corporate executive*
Siske, Roger Charles *lawyer*
Sistla, Aravinda Prasad *computer scientist, educator*
Sivananthan, Sivalingam *science educator*
Sive, Rebecca Anne *public affairs company executive*
Sjogren, Bengt B *corporate financial executive*
Skala, Gary Dennis *management consultant*
Skiles, Scott Allen *professional basketball coach*
Skinner, Mary "Honey" Jacobs *lawyer*
Skinner, Thomas V. *government agency administrator*
Sklarsky, Charles B. *lawyer*
Skyes, Gregory *food products executive*
Slaton, Danielle Victoria *professional soccer player*
Slavin, Konstantin Vladimirovich *neurosurgeon*
Sljivic-Simsic, Biljana B. *Slavic and Baltic languages educator*
Sloan, James Park *novelist, biographer, educator, investment adviser*
Smart, Allen Rich, II, *retired lawyer*
Smeekes, Frank *executive recruiter, consultant*
Smietana, Robert E. *real estate company executive*
Smith, Adrian Devaun *architect*
Smith, Adrian J.R. *management company executive*
Smith, Arthur B., Jr., *lawyer*
Smith, Daniel Scott *history educator, historian*
Smith, Earl Charles *nephrologist, educator*
Smith, Gordon Howell *lawyer*
Smith, Harry Buchanan, Jr., *graphic designer, painter, photographer, writer*
Smith, Kent Ernest *non-profit organization executive*
Smith, Marcia Jean *accountant, tax specialist, financial consultant*
Smith, Raymond Thomas *anthropology educator*
Smith, Sam *columnist, author*
Smith, Scott Clybourn *media company executive*
Smith, Stan Vladimir *economist, financial service company executive*
Smith, Tefft Weldon *lawyer*
Smith, Tom W. *surveyor, researcher*
Sneed, Michael (Michele Sneed) *columnist*
Snider, Lawrence K. *lawyer*
Snyder, Edward Adams *dean, economics professor*
Snyder, Graydon F. *religion educator*
Sobrero, Kate (Kathryn Michele Sobrero) *professional soccer player*
Sochen, June *history professor*
Socol, Michael Lee *obstetrician, gynecologist, educator*
Solaro, Ross John *physiologist, biophysicist*
Solovy, Jerold Sherwin *lawyer*
Sonderby, Susan Pierson *federal judge*
Sookik, Bonnie W. *air transportation executive*
Soper, Nathaniel Jolas *surgeon*
Sorensen, Leif Boge *physician, retired educator*
Sosa, Samuel (Sammy Sosa) *professional baseball player*
Sotelino, Gabino *chef*
Soto, Ramona *training specialist*
Southgate, Marie Therese *physician, editor*
Southwell, Donald G. *insurance company executive*
Spain, Richard Colby *lawyer*
Sparberg, Marshall Stuart *gastroenterologist, educator*
Spargo, Benjamin H. *educator, renal pathologist*
Spector, David M. *lawyer*
Spellmire, George W. *lawyer*
Spergel, Irving Abraham *social worker, researcher*
Spindler, George S. *lawyer, retired oil industry executive*
Spiotto, James Ernest *lawyer*
Sprieser, Judith A. *food products company executive*
Springer, Denis E. *former railroad executive*
Sproger, Charles Edmund *retired lawyer*
Sprowl, Charles Riggs *lawyer*
Squires, John Henry *judge*
Stacey, James Henry *writer, columnist*
Stack, Paul Francis *lawyer*
Stack, Stephen S. *manufacturing executive*
Stanhaus, James Steven *lawyer*
Staples, Thori Yvette *former soccer player*
Stark, Henry *technology educator*
Starkman, Gary Lee *lawyer*
Stassen, John Henry *lawyer*
Stead, James Joseph, Jr., *securities company executive*
Stearns, Neele Edward, Jr., *investment executive*
Stein, Robert Allen *legal association executive, law educator*
Steinberg, Morton M. *lawyer*
Steinberg, Salme Elizabeth Harju *academic administrator, historian*
Steiner, Donald Frederick *biochemist, physician, educator*
Steinfeld, Manfred *furniture manufacturing executive*
Steinman, Joan Ellen *law educator*
Stenger, Sarah *chef*
Sterling, John *consulting firm executive*
Stern, Carl William, Jr., *management consultant*
Stern, Grace Mary *former state legislator*
Stern, Richard Gustave *writer*
Sternstein, Allan J. *lawyer*
Stetler, David J. *lawyer*
Stevens, Mark *banker*
Stevens, Paul G., Jr., *brokerage house executive*
Stevenson, Adlai Ewing, III, *lawyer, former senator*
Stick, Michael Alan *lawyer*
Stiegel, Michael A. *lawyer*
Stifler, Venetia Chakos *dancer, educator, choreographer*
Stigler, Stephen Mack *statistician, educator*
Stillman, Nina Gidden *lawyer*
Stirling, D. Leslie *corporate financial executive*
Stirling, James Paulman *investment banker*
Stith, Mary Beth (Rae) *marketing professional for graphic design*
Stocking, George Ward, Jr., *anthropology educator*
Stoklosa, Gregory A. *paper company executive*
Stolzenberg, Ross Mark *sociology educator*
Stone, Alan *container company executive*
Stone, Geoffrey Richard *law educator, lawyer*
Stone, Susan A. *lawyer*
Stonecipher, Harry Curtis *aerospace transportation executive*
Storb, Ursula Beate *molecular genetics and cell biology educator*
Stotler, Edith Ann *retired grain company executive, financial planner*
Stovall-Brooks, Patricia *elementary school educator, writer*
Stover, Leon (Eugene Stover) *anthropology educator, writer, critic*
Stowell, Joseph, III, *academic administrator*
Strassner, Howard Taft, Jr., *obstetrician, educator*
Stratman, Deborah *filmmaker, film and video educator*
Straus, Francis Howe *pathologist, educator*
Straus, Lorna Puttkammer *biology professor*
Streff, William Albert, Jr., *lawyer*
Streiffer, Jenny *former soccer player*
Strobel, Pamela B. *energy executive*
Strohm, Bruce C. *real estate company executive*
Stroscio, Michael Anthony *physicist, researcher*
Strubel, Ella Doyle *advertising executive, public relations executive*
Struggles, John Edward *management consultant*
Studdert, Andrew Paul *air transportation executive*
Sulkin, Howard Allen *college president*
Sullivan, Barry *lawyer*
Sullivan, Marcia Waite *lawyer*
Sullivan, Peggy (Peggy Anne Sullivan) *librarian, consultant*
Sullivan, Thomas Patrick *lawyer*
Sumners, Pamela Lauren *lawyer*
Sundvall, Sheila A. *lawyer*
Sunstein, Cass Robert *law educator*
Suskin, Howard Steven *lawyer*
Susman, Louis *investment banker*
Sussman, Arthur Melvin *law educator, foundation administrator*
Swanson, Don Richard *university dean*
Swanson, Patricia Klick *foundation administrator*
Sweeney, James Raymond *lawyer*
Sweet, Allan Jay *lawyer*
Sweis Mussa, Rafiq *consular general, activist*
Swerdlow, Martin Abraham *pathologist, educator*
Swibel, Steven Warren *lawyer*
Swift, Edward Foster, III, *investment banker*
Swiger, Elinor Porter *lawyer*
Sykes, Alan O'Neil *lawyer, educator*
Sykes, Diane S. *federal judge, former state supreme court justice*
Sykes, Gregory *food products executive*
Szerlag, Chester Theodore *health facility administrator*
Szypulski, Wayne R. *controller, food products executive*
Tabin, Julius *patent lawyer, physicist*
Talbot, Pamela *public relations executive*
Tallchief, Maria *ballerina*
Tallman, Martin Stuart *hematologist, oncologist*
Tang, Chenxi *literature educator*
Tangora, Martin Charles *mathematician, educator*
Tardy, Medney Eugene, Jr., *retired otolaryngologist, facial plastic surgeon*
Taren, Jeffrey Lynn *lawyer*
Tarun, Robert Walter *lawyer*
Tatar, Arnold Marshall *internal medicine physician, educator*
Taub, Richard Paul *social sciences educator*
Taylor, Collette *public relations executive*
Taylor, Koko *singer*
Taylor-Williams, Bonnie Jean *cosmetics executive*
Techar, Frank J. *bank executive*
Teichner, Lester *management consulting executive*
Telfer, Margaret Clare *internist, hematologist, oncologist*
Telser, Lester Greenspan *educator, economist*
Terkel, Studs (Louis Terkel) *writer, interviewer*
Terry, Richard Edward *public utility holding company executive*
Tessing, Louise Scire *graphic designer*
Tetzlaff, Theodore R. *lawyer*
Thaden, Edward Carl *history professor*
Thall, Robert *photographer, educator*
Theis, William Harold *lawyer, educator*
Theobald, Edward Robert *lawyer*
Theobald, Thomas Charles *banker*
Thisted, Ronald Aaron *statistician, educator, consultant*
Thomas, Cherryl T. *former federal agency administrator*
Thomas, Frank Edward *professional baseball player*
Thomas, Frederick Bradley *lawyer*
Thomas, J. Mikesell *bank executive*
Thomas, Joseph Erumappettical *psychologist*
Thomas, Leona Marlene *health information educator*
Thomas, Richard Lee *banker*
Thomas, Stephen Paul *lawyer*
Thompson, James Robert, Jr., *lawyer, former governor*
Thompson, Jayne Carr *public relations and communications executive, lawyer*
Thompson, John H. *social science research executive*
Thompson, Michael *lawyer*
Thompson, Steven *zoological park administrator*
Thomson, George Ronald *lawyer, educator*
Thurner, Arthur W. *historian, educator*
Thurston, Stephen John *pastor*
Tigerman, Stanley *architect, educator*
Tilton, Glenn F. *air transportation executive*
Tinaglia, Michael Lee *lawyer*
Tinerella, Vincent P. *librarian, protective services official*
Tipton, Margaret Ann *religious organization administrator, writer*
Toback, Paul A. *recreational facility executive*
Tobin, Craig Daniel *lawyer*
Tobin, Thomas F. *lawyer*
Tomaino, Joseph Carmine *former retail executive, former postal inspector*
Tomar, Russell Herman *pathologist, educator, researcher*
Toohey, James Kevin *lawyer*
Topinka, Judy Baar *state official, political organization worker*
Toriumi, Dean Michael *facial, plastic and reconstructive surgery, educator*
Totlis, Gust John *retired title insurance company executive*
Towers, Kenneth Dale *journalism educator*
Tramonto, Rick *chef*
Trapp, James McCreery *lawyer*
Traudt, Mary B. *elementary school educator*
Travis, Dempsey Jerome *real estate company executive*
Tribbett, Charles *executive recruiter*
Trienens, Howard Joseph *lawyer*
Tripp, Marian Barlow Loofe *retired public relations executive*
Trogani, Monica *ballet dancer*
Trost, Eileen Bannon *lawyer*
Trotter, Charlie *chef*
True, Alison Cochran *newspaper editor*
Trumpener, Katie *literature educator*
Truran, James Wellington, Jr., *astrophysicist, educator*
Truskowski, John Budd *lawyer*
Tryban, Esther Elizabeth *lawyer*
Tryloff, Robin S. *food products executive*
Tsai, Jingpha (Jeffrey Tsai) *computer scientist, educator*
Tukes, Jamu Wayne *educational consultant*
Turner, Michael Stanley *astrophysics educator, researcher*
Turow, Scott F. *lawyer, writer*
Tyner, Howard A. *publishing executive, newspaper editor, journalist*
Tyree, James C. *insurance company executive*
Tyson, Kirk W. M. *management consultant*
Tyson, Terri Lynn *television programming producer, consultant*
Underwood, Robert Leigh *venture capitalist*
Ungaretti, Richard Anthony *lawyer*
Upshaw, Harry Stephan *psychology educator*
Valerio, Joseph Mastro *architectural firm executive, educator*
Valle, Rafael F. *obstetrician-gynecologist*
Valvassori, Galdino E. *physician*
Valyi-Nagy, Tibor G. *neuropathologist, virologist*
Van Demark, Ruth Elaine *lawyer*
Van Den Hende, Fred J(oseph) *human resources executive*
VanderBeke, Patricia K. *architect*
Van Pelt, Robert Irving *retired firefighter*
Van Tine, Matthew Eric *lawyer*
Van Zandt, David E. *dean*
Varma, Arup *finance educator, consultant*
Vazquez, Richard Michael *surgeon*
Velasquez, Arthur *food products executive*
Venturini, Tisha Lea *professional soccer player*
Veres, Bob *editor*
Verschoor, Curtis Carl *business educator, consultant*
Vertreace-Doody, Martha Modena *English educator, poet*
Veverka, Donald John *lawyer*
Vie, Richard Carl *insurance company executive*
Vilim, Nancy Catherine *advertising agency executive*
Vincent, Jim *performing company executive*
Vinci, John Nicholas *architect, educator*
Vitale, Gerald Lee *financial services executive*
Vojcanin, Sava Alexander *lawyer*
von Rhein, John Richard *music critic, editor*
Vrablik, Edward Robert *import/export company executive*
Vranicar, Michael Gregory *lawyer*
Vree, Roger Allen *lawyer*
Vukas, Ronald *publishing executive*
Wade, Edwin Lee *author, lawyer*
Wade, Nigel *former editor in chief*
Wagner, Alyson Kay (Aly Wagner) *professional soccer player*
Wahlen, Edwin Alfred *lawyer*
Waintroob, Andrea Ruth *lawyer*
Waite, Dennis Vernon *investor relations consultant*
Walberg, Herbert John *psychologist, educator, consultant*
Walker, Thomas Ray *city aviation commissioner*
Walker, Viola *writer, educator*
Wallingford, Anne *writer, editor, project developer*
Walsh, Mathew M. M. *construction executive*
Walter, Charles Sebastian *Roman Catholic priest*
Walters, Lawrence Charles *advertising executive*
Walton, Carmelita Noreen *retired nursing administrator*
Walton, Robert Lee, Jr., *plastic surgeon*
Wambach, Abby (Mary Abigail Wambach) *Olympic athlete*
Wander, Herbert Stanton *lawyer*
Wang, Albert James *violinist, educator*
Wanke, Ronald Lee *lawyer*
Warren, Glenn James *environmental scientist*
Wasan, Darsh Tilakchand *university official, chemical engineer educator*
Wasiolek, Edward *literary critic, language and literature educator*
Wasson, Jeffrey *music educator*
Wastawy, Sohair F. *library dean, consultant*
Waters, Ronald V., III, *candy company executive*
Waxler, Beverly Jean *anesthesiologist, physician*
Weaver, Timothy Allan *lawyer*
Webb, Dan K. *lawyer*
Webb, Emily *retired plant morphologist*
Weber, Hanno *architect*
Weber, Susan A. *lawyer*
Webster, David Macpherson *lawyer*
Webster, James Randolph, Jr., *physician*
Weese, Benjamin Horace *architect*
Weichselbaum, Ralph R. *oncologist chairman*
Weigel, Thomas J. *pediatrician, cardiologist*
Weigle, Maurice S. *lawyer*
Weil, Andrew Lawrence *lawyer*
Weinberg, David B. *investor*
Weinberg, Lila Shaffer *writer, editor*
Weiner, Gerald Arne *retired stockbroker*
Weinfurter, Daniel Joseph *business services executive*
Weinkopf, Friedrich J. *lawyer*
Weintraub, Joseph Barton *publishing executive*
Weis, Mervyn J. *physician, gastroenterologist*
Weisberg, Lois *arts administrator, city official*
Weisenberg, Elliot *pathologist, educator*
Weiss, Robert Alan *surgeon*
Weissman, Michael Lewis *lawyer*
Weitzman, Robert Harold *investment company executive*
Weldon-Linne, C. Michael *pathologist, microbiologist*
Weldon-Linne, Madeleine Marie *lawyer*
Wellington, Robert Hall *manufacturing executive, director*
Welsh, Kelly Raymond *lawyer, former telecommunications company executive*
Wesley, William Matthew *lawyer*
Weston, Roger Lance *banker*
Wexler, Richard Lewis *lawyer*
Wexman, Virginia Wright *English language educator*
Whalen, Sarah Eve *professional soccer player*
Whalen, Wayne W. *lawyer*
Wham, David Buffington *secondary school educator*

Bienen, Henry Samuel *academic administrator, political science educator*
Blair, Virginia Ann *public relations executive*
Bloomer, William David *radiation oncologist, educator*
Bobco, William David, Jr., *consulting engineering company executive*
Borcover, Alfred Seymour *journalist*
Boye, Roger Carl *academic administrator, journalism educator, writer*
Braeutigam, Ronald Ray *economics professor*
Buck, Tom *journalist*
Canes-Wrone, Brandice *political scientist, educator*
Carr, Stephen Howard *materials engineer, educator*
Cates, Jo Ann *library administrator, writer*
Chang, R. P. H. *materials science educator*
Chen, Gui-Qiang *mathematician, educator, researcher*
Christian, Richard Carlton *university dean, former advertising agency executive*
Conger, William Frame *artist, educator*
Connie, Leslie Lynn *secondary school educator*
Corey, Gordon Richard *financial advisor, former utilities executive*
Crawford, James Weldon *psychiatrist, educator, administrator*
Crawford, Susan *library director, writer*
Creamer, Robert Allan *lawyer*
Dallos, Peter John *neurobiologist, educator*
Daskin, Mark Stephen *engineering educator*
Davis, Stephen Howard *applied mathematics educator*
Deming, Thomas Edward *publishing executive*
Devinatz, Allen *retired mathematician, mathematics educator*
Downing, Joan Forman *editor, writer*
Dumas, Lawrence B. *academic administrator*
Eberley, Helen-Kay *opera singer, classical record company executive, poet*
Enroth-Cugell, Christina Alma Elisabeth *neurophysiologist, educator*
Felknor, Bruce Lester *editorial consultant, writer*
Fessler, Raymond R. *metallurgical engineering consultant*
Fine, Gary Alan *sociology educator*
Fine, Morris Eugene *materials engineer, educator*
Fischer Monastero, Elizabeth *voice educator*
Fourer, Robert Harold *industrial engineering educator, consultant*
Frey, Donald Nelson *industrial engineer, educator, retired manufacturing executive*
Friedman, Hans Adolf *architect*
Gaiha, Vishnu Das *cardiologist*
Galvin, Kathleen Malone *communications educator*
Gibbons, William Reginald, Jr., *poet, novelist, translator, editor*
Golbus, Joseph *rheumatologist*
Goldstick, Thomas Karl *biomedical engineering educator*
Gordon, Julie Peyton *foundation administrator*
Gordon, Robert James *economics professor*
Heitsch, James Lawrence *mathematician, educator*
Hemke, Frederick L. *music educator, university administrator*
Hirshfield, Pearl *artist*
Horowitz, Joel Lawrence *economics educator, consultant*
Hughes, Edward F. X. *preventive medicine physician, educator*
Hurter, Arthur Patrick *economist, educator*
Ibers, James Arthur *chemist, educator*
Ionescu Tulcea, Cassius *research mathematician, educator*
Irons, William George *anthropology educator*
Jacobs, Donald P. *dean emeritus, banking and finance educator*
Jacobs, Norman Joseph *publishing company executive*
Jain, Dipak Chand *dean, marketing educator, consultant*
Jennings, Hamlin Manson *materials consultant*
Jerome, Joseph Walter *mathematics professor*
Jones, Robert Russell *magazine editor*
Kalai, Ehud *finance educator, economist, researcher*
Kalantzis, George *historian, educator*
Keer, Leon Morris *engineering educator*
Kentor, Paul Martin *allergist*
Khandekar, Janardan Dinkar *oncologist, educator*
Korn, Jenny *social activist*
Kotler, Philip *marketing educator, consultant, writer*
Krizek, Raymond John *civil engineering educator, consultant*
Kuenster, John Joseph *editor*
Kujala, Walfrid Eugene *musician, educator*
Lambert, Joseph Buckley *chemistry professor*
Langsley, Donald Gene *psychiatrist, medical board executive*
Langsley, Pauline Royal *psychiatrist*
Larson, Paul William *public relations executive*
Lewis, Dan Albert *education educator*
Lloyd-Still, John Dashwood *pediatrician, educator*
Locker, Gershon Yehuda *oncologist, educator*
Macsai, John *architect*
Margoliash, Emanuel *biochemist, educator*
Mason, Thomas Oliver *materials science and engineering educator, researcher*
Matkowsky, Bernard Judah *applied mathematician, educator*
McCarron, John Francis *editor*
McCurry, Stephanie *historian, educator*
McDonough, Bridget Ann *music theatre company director*
Mc Nerney, Walter James *health policy educator, consultant*
Menke, Allen Carl *industrial corporation executive*
Meshii, Masahiro *materials science educator*
Mills, Edwin Smith *economics professor*
Mineka, Susan *psychology educator*
Mirkin, Chad A. *chemistry professor*
Moore, C. Bradley *chemistry professor*
Morrison, John Horton *lawyer*
Moskos, Charles C. *sociology educator*
Murphy, Gordon John *electrical engineer, educator*
Musa, Samuel Albert *university executive*
Mustoe, Thomas Anthony *physician, plastic surgeon*
Neaman, Mark Robert *hospital administrator*
Novales, Ronald Richards *zoologist, educator*
Oakes, Robert James *physics educator*
Olmstead, William Edward *mathematics professor*
Oranove, David *business educator, consultant, economist*
Ottino, Julio Mario *engineering educator*
Otwell, Ralph Maurice *retired newspaper editor*
Packman, Aaron Ian *environmental engineer, educator*
Paden, William D. *French literature educator*
Peck, Abraham *editor, writer, educator, media consultant*
Peponis, Harold Arthur *insurance agent, broker*
Persons, Fern *actress*
Peters, Gordon Benes *retired musician*
Plaut, Eric Alfred *retired psychiatrist, educator*
Powers, Marian *accounting educator*
Prince, Thomas Richard *accountant, educator*
Reimer, Bennett *music educator, writer*
Reiss, Lenore Ann *language educator, retired secondary school educator*
Robbins, Henry Zane *public relations and marketing executive*
Rosenzweig, Amy *biochemist, educator*
Rosic, George Steve *lawyer*
Rubenstein, Albert Harold *industrial engineering and management sciences educator*
Sachtler, Wolfgang Max Hugo *chemistry professor*
Salem, Richard Allen *mediator*
Salzman, Arthur George *architect*
Schank, Roger Carl *computer science and psychology educator*
Schluter, Robert Arvel *physicist*
Schulte, Bruce John *lawyer*
Schwartz, Neena Betty *endocrinologist, educator*
Scott, Walter Dill *management educator*
Seaman, Jerome Francis *actuary*
Seidman, David N(athaniel) *materials science and engineering educator*
Severini, Thomas Alan *statistician and educator*
Shah, Surendra Poonamchand *engineering educator*
Shanas, Ethel *sociology educator*
Sheridan, James Edward *history professor*
Silverman, Richard Bruce *chemist, educator, biochemist*
Smith, Spencer Bailey *engineering and business educator*
Sobel, Alan *electrical engineer, physicist*
Sprang, Milton LeRoy *obstetrician, gynecologist, educator*
Stern, Louis William *marketing educator, consultant*
Stumpf, David Allen *pediatric neurologist*
Sundquist, Eric John *American studies educator*
Sweet, Jerry James *clinical psychologist*
Taflove, Allen *electrical engineer, educator, researcher, consultant*
Tanner, Martin Abba *statistics and human oncology educator*
Thrash, Patricia Ann *educational association administrator*
Tornabene, Russell C. *communications executive*
Traisman, Howard Sevin *pediatrician*
Ulmer, Melville Paul *physics and astronomy educator*
Van Ness, James Edward *electrical engineering educator*
Ver Steeg, Clarence Lester *historian, educator*
Vick, Nicholas A. *neurologist*
Vladem, Steven Allen *writer, motivational speaker, film producer*
Wachs, Alan L *quality assurance engineer*
Walter, Robert Irving *chemistry professor*
Weber, Arnold Robert *academic administrator*
Weertman, Johannes *materials science educator*
Weertman, Julia Randall *materials science and engineering educator*
Wefler, Wilson Daniel *management consultant*
Weisbrod, Burton Allen *economist, educator*
Well, Irwin *language educator*
Wessels, Bruce W. *materials scientist, educator*
Wilhelm, Frank Leo *publisher, writer*
Wills, Garry *historian*
Witwer, Samuel Weiler, Jr., *lawyer*
Wright, John *classics educator*
Wu, Tai Te *biological sciences and engineering educator*
Zeman, Gregory Oswald *physician*
Zimmerman, Mary Alice *performing arts educator*
Ziomek, Jonathan S. *journalist, educator*

Evergreen Park
Hong, Kuhn *nuclear medicine physician*
Zumerchik, John *urologist*

Fairfield
Thomason, Nola Faye *critical care-emergency supervisor*

Fairview Heights
Tenpas, Ronald J. *federal agency administrator, lawyer*

Flossmoor
Barnas, Raymond Scott *music educator*
Crum, James Francis *waste recycling company executive*
Day, Gregory Lynn *music educator*
Pierce, Shelby Crawford *management and oil industry consultant*

Forest Park
Thomas, Alan *candy company executive*

Fox River Grove
Abboud, Alfred Robert *banker, consultant, investor*

Frankfort
Burhoe, Brian Walter *automotive service executive*
Sandlin, Dorothy *artist*

Franklin Park
Blanchard, Eric Alan *lawyer*
Caruso, Fred *plastics manufacturing company executive*
Dean, Howard M., Jr., *food company executive*
Greisinger, James *food products executive*
Simpson, Michael *metals service center executive*

Freeport
Galli, Joseph, Jr., *consumer products company executive*
McDonough, John J. *household products company executive*
Sovey, William Pierre *manufacturing executive*
Weaver, Michael Glenn *pharmacist*

Galena
Alexander, Barbara Leah Shapiro *clinical social worker*
Crandall, John Lynn *insurance consultant, retired insurance company executive*
Fullmer, Paul *public relations counselor*

Galesburg
Breitborde, Lawrence Bart *anthropologist, educator*
Gupta, Madan Lal *cardiologist*
Haywood, Bruce *retired academic administrator*
Kowalski, Richard Sheldon *hospital administrator*
Mathew, James *cardiologist*
Metz, Robin O. *writer, educator, poet*
Mustain, Douglas Dee *lawyer*
Pahel, Tim Allen *music educator*
Polay, Bruce *music educator, conductor*
Taylor, Roger Lee *academic administrator, lawyer*
Tourlentes, Thomas Theodore *psychiatrist*

Galva
Swatos, William Henry, Jr., *priest, sociologist*

Geneseo
Brown, Mabel Welton *lawyer*
Crisp, Sandra Sue *procurement analyst*

Geneva
Gallagher, Kent Grey *theater arts educator*
Kallstrom, Charles Clark *dentist*
Klenke, Deborah Ann *band director, choral director, department chairman*
Landmeier, Allen Lee *lawyer*
Lazzara, Dennis Joseph *orthodontist*
Montgomery, Joel Robert *communications executive, consultant*
Tyler, Lloyd John *retired lawyer*
Xagas, Steven George James *diversified employment services firm executive*
Young, Jack Allison *financial executive*

Genoa
Cromley, Jon Lowell *lawyer*

Gilberts
Barilich, Thomas Anthony *loss control specialist*

Gillespie
Verticchio, Rick *lawyer*

Gilman
Ireland, Herbert Orin *retired engineering educator*

Glen Carbon
Lazerson, Earl Edwin *academic administrator emeritus*
Ottwein, Merrill William George *real estate company executive, veterinarian*

Glen Ellyn
Agruss, Neil Stuart *cardiologist*
Baloun, John Charles *wholesale grocery company executive, retired*
Beers, V(ictor) Gilbert *publishing executive*
Bollendorf, Robert Fredrick *retired education educator, psychologist*
Conti, Lee Ann *lawyer*
Cvengros, Joseph Michael *manufacturing company executive*
Dieter, Raymond Andrew, Jr., *physician, thoracic and vascular surgeon*
Fox, Jeffrey Harrison *language educator*
Frateschi, Lawrence Jan *economist, statistician, educator*
Gage, Nancy Elizabeth *college administrator, accountant, educator*
Hudson, Dennis Lee *lawyer, retired government official, arbitrator, educator*
Mooring, F. Paul *physics editor*
Parkhurst, Edwin Wallace, Jr., *healthcare management consultant*
Patten, Ronald James *university dean*
Rogers, Teri Ellen *mathematician, educator*
Sandrok, Richard William *lawyer*
Schmidt, Karen Lee *marketing professional, sales executive*
Ulrich, Werner *patent lawyer*

Glencoe
Boyell, Gloria *musician, music educator*
Cole, Kathleen Ann *advertising executive, retired social worker*
Dean, H. Clark *retired civil engineer, professional genealogist*
Isaacs, Roger David *public relations executive*
Milloy, Frank Joseph, Jr., *surgeon*
Nebenzahl, Kenneth *rare book and map dealer, author*
Niefeld, Jaye Sutter *advertising executive*
Silver, Ralph David *financial consultant and arbitrator*
Warren, Elizabeth Curran *retired political science educator*

Glendale Heights
Cook, Doris Marie *retired accountant, educator*
Pimental, Patricia Ann *neuropsychologist, consulting company executive, author*
Rawal, Darshan Lal *civil engineer, structural engineer, consultant*

Glenview
Berkman, Michael G. *lawyer, chemical consultant*
Blase, Anthony Idomeneus *retired electronics executive, writer, poet*
Bradtke, Philip Joseph *architect*
Braun, Eunice Hockspeier *religious order executive, author, lecturer*
Casas, Laurie Ann *plastic surgeon*
Corley, Jenny Lynd Wertheim *elementary school educator*
Coulson, Elizabeth Anne *physical therapy educator, state representative*
Farrell, W. James *metal products manufacturing company executive*
Franklin, Lynne *business communications consultant, writer*
Gillis, Marvin Bob *retired chemical executive, consultant*
Graff, Jeffrey G. *emergency physician*
Grubbs, Robert W. *computer services company executive*
Hickey, John Thomas *retired electronics company executive*
Hudnut, Stewart Skinner *manufacturing executive, lawyer*
Kaplan, Steven M. *advertising executive*
King, Billie Jean Moffitt *former professional tennis player*
Kinigakis, Panagiotis *research scientist, engineer, inventor, author*
Kinney, Jon C. *metal products executive*
Knox, James Edwin *lawyer*
Letham, Dennis J. *wholesale company executive*
Levin, Donald Robert *business and finance executive, motion picture producer, professional sports team owner*
Mabley, Jack *newspaper columnist, communications consultant*
Marmet, Gottlieb John *lawyer*
Martin, James Frederick *media consultant*
Mc Nitt, Willard Charles *business executive*
Miller, Edward Boone *lawyer*
Mukoyama, James Hidefumi, Jr., *securities executive*
Olson, Roy Arthur *retired government official*
Panarese, William C. *civil engineer*
Ptak, Frank Stanley *manufacturing executive*
Ringler, James M. *cookware company executive*
Rorig, Kurt Joachim *chemist, research director*
Rubin, Susan M. *neurologist*
Russell, Henry George *structural engineer*
Salamoun, Peter V. *retired manufacturing executive*
Smith, Harold B. *manufacturing executive*
Speer, David Blakeney *industrial executive*
Tristano, Sandra *circuit court judge*
Turner, Lee *travel company executive*
Van Zelst, Theodore William *civil engineer, engineering company executive*

Glenwood
Latta, Brent *consumer products company executive*

Godfrey
King, Ordie Herbert, Jr., *oral pathologist*
McDaniels, John Louis *retired mathematics educator*
Zilm, Karl Miller *education educator*

Golf
Fellingham, Warren Luther, Jr., *retired banker*

Granite City
Eftimoff, Anita Kendall *educational consultant*
Humphrey, Owen Everett *retired education administrator*

Grayslake
Barrington, Leonard Barry *chemist, educator, writer*
Jacobson, Earl James *lawyer, investment banker*

Greenville
Flowers, Creole Duane *publishing executive*
Junod, Daniel August *podiatrist*

Gurnee
Myren, Allen W(illiam) *retired music educator*
Reinhoudt, Johannes Feike *pharmaceutical industry executive*
Schoenfeld, Howard Allen *management consultant, lawyer*
Sommerlad, Robert Edward *environmental research engineer*
Weber, James Stuart *management educator*

Hampshire
Hirn, Doris Dreyer *health service administrator*

Hanover
Bleveans, John *lawyer*

Hanover Park
Manton, William Jeffrey *operating engineer, fleet consultant*

Harrisburg
Rushing, Philip Dale *retired social worker*

Hartford
Shelton, Michael Patrick *principal*

Harvey
Heilicser, Bernard Jay *emergency physician*

Hazel Crest
Freed, Melvyn Norris *retired higher education administrator and educator, writer*

Hickory Hills
Haustein, Janis M. *musician, music educator*

Highland
Orthwein, William Coe *mechanical engineer*

Highland Park
Afterman, Allan B. *accountant, educator, researcher, consultant*
Axelrod, Leah Joy *tour company executive*
Bakalar, John Stephen *printing and publishing company executive*
Cohen, Burton David *franchising executive, lawyer*
Dubin, Arthur Detmers *architect*
Einisman, Myron Sachar *publisher*
Eldridge, Amy Helene *clinical social worker, academic dean*
Epstein, Randy J. *physician, ophthalmologist*
Gash, Lauren Beth *lawyer, state legislator*
Greenblatt, Miriam *writer, editor, educator*
Harris, Thomas L. *public relations executive*
Hattis, Albert Daniel *business executive, journalist*
Johnson, Curtis Lee *publisher, editor, writer*
Kaplan, Mark E. *allergist*
Karol, Nathaniel H. *lawyer, consultant*
Lippe, Melvin Karl *lawyer*
Nelson, Richard David *lawyer*
Pattis, Mark R. *publishing company executive*
Pattis, S. William *publishing executive*
Rabin, David Neal *radiologist*
Ruder, David Sturtevant *lawyer, educator, government official*
Rudo, Milton *retired manufacturing company executive, consultant*
Rutenberg-Rosenberg, Sharon Leslie *retired journalist*
Saltzberg, Eugene Ernest *emergency physician, educator*
Schindel, Donald Marvin *retired lawyer*
Slavick, Ann Lillian *retired art educator*
Tobin, Calvin Jay *architect*
Uhlmann, Frederick Godfrey *commodity and securities broker*
Weinstein, Barry Alan *architect*

Marshall
Freeman, Charles E. *writer, musician*
Mitchell, George Trice *physician*

Maryville
Stark, Patricia Ann *psychologist*

Matteson
Johnson, Eric G. *food products company executive*
van der Hoek, Sherry A. *counselor*

Mattoon
Corn, Stephen Leslie *lawyer*
Horsley, Jack Everett *lawyer, writer*
Maris, Charles Robert *surgeon, otolaryngologist*
Phipps, John Randolph *retired army officer*

Maywood
Albain, Kathy S. *oncologist*
Barbato, Anthony *educational association administrator, medical educator*
Barron, William M. *physician, educator*
Berman, James H. *pediatrician, gastroenterologist, educator*
Bermes, Edward William, Jr., *biochemist, educator*
Cera, Lee Marie *veterinarian*
Dado, Diane Valentina *plastic and reconstructive surgeon, pediatric plastic surgeon*
Eidem, Benjamin Walter *cardiologist*
Freeark, Robert James *surgeon, educator, health facility administrator*
Gamelli, Richard Louis *surgeon, educator*
Gaynor, Ellen Rose *hematologist*
Gianopoulos, John George *obstetrician*
Godwin, John E. *hematologist*
Hanin, Israel *pharmacologist, educator*
Higgs, Rosa Lee *special education educator, writer*
Light, Terry Richard *orthopedic hand surgeon*
Mittendorf, Robert *physician, epidemiologist*
Moran, John Francis *cardiologist*
Nand, Sucha *medical educator*
Newman, Barry Marc *pediatric surgeon*
O'Keefe, James Paul *epidemiologist*
Pickleman, Jack R. *surgeon*
Schultz, Richard Michael *biochemistry educator, researcher*
Slogoff, Stephen *dean, anesthesiologist, educator*
Stiff, Patrick Joseph *internist, hematologist, oncologist, educator*
Tobin, Martin John *pulmonary and critical care physician*
Wilber, David James *cardiologist*
Zelby, Andrew S. *neurosurgeon*
Zlobin, Andrew *molecular biologist, virologist*

Mc Gaw Park
Feather, William L. *corporate lawyer*
Kesman, Anthony K. *medical products executive*

Mchenry
Chisu, Ioan *artist*
Duel, Ward Calvin *retired health care consultant*
Koehl, Camille Joan *accountant*

Melrose Park
Bernick, Carol Lavin *consumer products company executive*
Bernick, Howard Barry *manufacturing executive*
Cernugel, William John *consumer products and special retail executive*
Douglas, Kenneth Jay *food products executive*
Hillert, Richard Walter *composer, educator, author*
Klein, Lloyd William *cardiologist, researcher*
Lavin, Bernice E. *cosmetics executive*
Umans, Alvin Robert *manufacturing executive*
Van Helden, Pete *food products executive*
Wechter, Clari Ann *manufacturing executive*

Mokena
Sangmeister, George Edward *lawyer, consultant, former congressman*

Moline
Arnell, Richard Anthony *radiologist*
Becherer, Hans Walter *retired agricultural equipment executive*
Cottrell, Frank Stewart *former lawyer, manufacturing executive*
Harrington, Roy Edwards *agricultural engineer, author*
Jenkins, James Robert *lawyer, chemicals executive*
Johnson, Mary Lou *lay worker, educator*
Jones, Nathan Jerome *farm machinery manufacturing company executive*
Lane, Robert W. *farm equipment manufacturing executive*
Norris, William Robert *engineer, researcher*
Schwiebert, Deborah Johnson *marketing executive*
Schwiebert, Mark William *lawyer, mayor*
Varela, Fernando *anesthesiologist*

Monmouth
Bruce, Mary Hanford *academic administrator, educator, writer*
Hiveley, Kelly Marie *music educator*

Mooseheart
Ross, Donald Hugh *fraternal organization executive*

Morton
Corey, Judith Ann *retired elementary school educator*

Morton Grove
Goldsmith, Barbara Cecile *sculptor, curator*
Labunski, Alma Joel *nursing educator*
McKenna, Andrew James *paper distribution and printing company executive, baseball club executive*
Smolyansky, Julie *consumer products company executive*
Vega, Steve *poet*

Mount Carmel
Fornoff, Frank J(unior) *retired chemistry educator, consultant*
Rhine, John E. *lawyer*

Mount Carroll
Rogers, Ward Junior *retired industrial designer*

Mount Prospect
Rueggeberg, Erna M. *nursing consultant, nursing administrator, researcher*
Sayers, Gale *computer company executive, retired professional football player*
Thulin, Adelaide Ann *design company executive, interior designer*

Mount Sterling
Tracy, Patrick F. *food products executive*

Mount Vernon
Hall, Sharon Gay *retired language educator, artist*
Harvey, Morris Lane *lawyer*
Nicholson, Gerald Lee *airport administrator*
Withers, W. Russell, Jr., *broadcast executive*

Mundelein
Abington, William K *corporate financial executive*
McLeskey, Charles Hamilton *anesthesiologist, educator, pharmaceutical executive*
Meehan, Jean Marie Ross *human resources, occupational health and safety management consultant*
Mills, James Stephen *medical supply company executive*
Raviv, Gabriel *medical products executive*

Naperville
Bell, Bradley J. *water treatment company executive*
Birck, Michael John *telecommunications industry executive*
Bleck, Phyllis Claire *surgeon, musician*
Briseno, Kathleen *education educator*
Bufalino, Vincent John *medical association administrator, cardiologist*
Calamos, John Peter, Sr., *financial executive*
Calamos, Nick P. *diversified financial services company executive*
Cowlishaw, Mary Lou *government educator*
Crawford, Raymond Maxwell, Jr., *nuclear engineer*
Desch, Theodore Edward *retired health insurance company executive, lawyer*
Dhar, Promila *researcher*
Dunning, Richard L. *health products executive*
Fawell, Harris W. *lawyer, former congressman*
Fenech, Joseph Charles *lawyer*
Fleming, Norman Patrick *information scientist*
Florence, Ernest Estell, Jr., *special education educator*
Ford, Ralph A. *moving and relocation company executive*
Fritz, Roger Jay *management consultant*
Fuhrer, Larry *management consultant, management educator, finance company executive*
Gannon, Jeffrey P. *trucking/relocation services executive*
Gracey, Paul C., Jr., *utilities executive*
Grimley, Jeffrey Michael *dentist*
Hawley, Richard L. *utilities executive*
Heuer, Michael Alexander *dean, endodonist educator*
Joyce, William H. *chemist*
Katai, Andrew Andras *chemical company executive*
Kelley, Karl Neal *psychology educator*
Koch, William Joseph *public relations executive*
Lake, Robert D. *transportation executive*
L'Allier, James Joseph *educational multimedia company executive, instructional designer*
Larson, Mark Edward, Jr., *lawyer, educator, financial advisor*
McCaul, Joseph Patrick *chemical engineer*
Modery, Richard Gillman *marketing and sales executive*
Nortell, Bruce *lawyer*
Penisten, Gary Dean *entrepreneur*
Prabhu, Krish Anant *telecommunications company executive, educator*
Raccah, Dominique Marcelle *publisher*
Rao, Prasad *electronics executive*
Rosenthal, Edward Leonard *secondary school educator*
Ryan, Joan *food company executive*
Schwab, Paul Josiah *psychiatrist, educator*
Sellers, Gregory Jude *physicist*
Sherren, Anne Terry *chemistry professor*
Shoemaker, Robert Willoughby *historian, educator*
Smetana, Mark *food products executive*
Snyder, Anthony Edward *communications executive*
Spiotta, Raymond Herman *editor*
Strobel, Russ M. *lawyer*
Tan, Li-Su Lin *accountant, insurance executive, investment consultant*
Tibble, Douglas Clair *lawyer*
Vanagas, Rimantas Andrius (Ray Vanagas) *entrepreneur*
Vora, Manu Kishandas *chemical engineer, quality consultant*
Wake, Richard W. *food products executive*
Wake, Thomas G. *food products executive*
Wilde, Harold Richard *college president*
Worden, William Patrick *deacon*

Nashville
Cude, Thomas Bret *real estate broker*

New Baden
Franke, Louise Anna *early childhood educator, farmland manager*

Niles
Abinion, Emir C. *automotive executive*
Beton, John Allen *communications company executive*
Grace, John Joseph *retired priest*
Herb, Marvin J. *food products executive*
Kaden, Bruce Richard *hematologist, oncologist*
Kelly, John *advertising executive*
Kessell, Charles Arthur *music educator, musician*
Martinez, Euri Anthony *music educator, small business owner*
Sassan, Dennis Donald *lawyer*
Weisbach, Lou *advertising executive*

Normal
Bender, Paul Edward *lawyer*
Bowman, C. Alvin *academic administrator*
Brown, Lauren Evans *zoologist, researcher, educator*
Cooley, William Emory, Jr., *radiologist*
Devinatz, Victor Gary *industrial relations educator*
Hesse, Douglas Dean *English educator*
Hickrod, George Alan Karnes Wallis *educational administration educator*
Joyce, Larry Wayne *physician*
Kethineni, Sesha Rajani *criminal justice professor*
Mau, Benjamin *artist*
Miller, Wilma Hildruth *education educator*
Parette, Howard P. *school system administrator, special education educator*
Presley, John Woodrow *academic administrator*
Rochelle, Victor Cleanthus *lawyer*
Shields, John Charles *American studies and African American studies and literature educator*
Temple, Mark Allen *adult education educator, consultant*
Vanden Eynden, Charles Lawrence *mathematician, educator*

North Aurora
Cole, Sarah *law enforcement librarian*
Hoover, Lola Mae *retired communications company executive*

North Chicago
Albach, Richard Allen *microbiology educator*
Barsano, Charles Paul *medical educator, dean*
Bush, Eugene Nyle *pharmacologist, research scientist*
Chedid, Antonio *pathologist, educator, researcher*
de Lasa, José M. *lawyer*
Gall, Eric Papineau *physician, educator*
Hawkins, Richard Albert *medical educator, administrator*
Kim, Yoon Berm *immunologist, educator*
Loga, Sanda *physicist, researcher*
Nair, Velayudhan *pharmacologist, medical educator, academic administrator*
Rogers, Eugene Jack *medical educator*
Rudy, David Robert *physician, educator*
Sierles, Frederick Stephen *psychiatrist, educator*
Yoon, Ji-Won *virology, immunology and diabetes educator, research administrator*

Northbrook
Adler, Robert *electronics engineer*
Ben-Arie, Ronit Peleg *elementary school educator*
Betz, Ronald Philip *pharmacist*
Boettcher, Robert Walter *civil engineer*
Bohlender, Hugh Darrow *lawyer*
Clarey, John Robert *executive search consultant*
Colburn, David Dunton *investment manager*
Crockett, Joan M. *human resources executive*
Cruikshank, John W., III, *insurance agent*
Cucco, Ulisse P. *retired obstetrician, gynecologist*
Di Spigno, Guy Joseph *international management consultant, industrial psychologist*
Edelson, Ira J. *venture banker, trade finance executive*
Ehrenberg, Maureen *management consultant*
Feibel, Frederick Arthur *financial consultant*
Gratalo, John, Jr., *banker, small business owner*
Green, David *manufacturing executive*
Hale, Danny Lyman *financial executive*
Hicks, Judith Eileen *nursing administrator*
Hindo, Walid Afram *radiology educator, researcher*
Hirsch, Lawrence Leonard *physician, retired educator*
Hughes, William Franklin, Jr., *ophthalmologist, emeritus educator*
Kahn, Sandra S. *psychotherapist*
Keehn, Silas *retired bank executive*
King, Robert Charles *biologist, educator*
Lane, William Noble, III, *financial executive*
Lapin, Harvey I. *lawyer*
Lever, Alvin *health science association administrator*
Levy, Arnold S(tuart) *real estate company executive*
Liddy, Edward M. *insurance company executive*
Mandel, Karyl Lynn *accountant*
McCabe, Michael J. *insurance executive*
Metz, Adam S. *real estate executive*
Newman, Lawrence William *financial executive*
Noeth, Carolyn Frances *speech and language pathologist*
Parker, Kathleen Kappel *state legislator*
Pertz, Douglas A. *engineering executive*
Pesmen, Sandra (Mrs. Harold William Pesmen) *editor*
Pike, Robert William *insurance company executive, lawyer*
Pilch, Samuel H. *controller, corporate financial executive*
Rosemarin, Carey Stephen *lawyer*
Ross, Debra Benita *jewelry designer, marketing executive*
Sernett, Richard Patrick *lawyer*
Siegal, Judy A. *social services administrator*
Slattery, James Joseph (Joe Slattery) *actor*
Snader, Jack Ross *publishing company executive*
Stamper, James M. *retired English language educator*
Stewart, Charles Leslie *lawyer*
Storhoff, James Justin *scientist*
Sudbrink, Jane Marie *sales and marketing executive*
Teichner, Bruce A. *lawyer*
Wajer, Ronald Edward *management consultant*
Wallace, Harry Leland *lawyer*
Wilson, Rita P. *insurance company executive*
Wilson, Thomas Joseph *insurance company executive*
Young, R. James *insurance company executive*
Young, Susan Jean *music specialist*

Northfield
Brown, A. Demetrius *metal products executive*
Bruns, Nicolaus, Jr., *retired agricultural chemicals company executive, lawyer*
Carlin, Donald Walter *retired food products executive, consultant*
Hadley, Stanton Thomas *manufacturing and marketing company executive, lawyer*
Holden, Betsy D. *food products company executive*
Hotze, Charles Wayne *publisher, printer*
Knight, James Atwood *manufacturing executive*
Lubawski, James Lawrence *healthcare consultant*
Pratt, Murray Lester *collaborative commerce specialist*
Quaal, Ward Louis *broadcast executive*
Schneider-Criezis, Susan Marie *architect*
Shabica, Charles Wright *geologist, earth science educator*
Shillestad, John Gardner *financial services company executive*
Smeds, Edward William *retired food company executive*
Sneed, Paula Ann *food products executive*
Stepan, Frank Quinn *chemical company executive*

Northlake
Haack, Richard Wilson *retired police officer*

O Fallon
Bjerkaas, Carlton Lee *technology services company executive*
Voellger, Gary A. *business consulting executive, retired air force officer*
Wilhelm, Phillip Eugene *church administrator, music educator*

Oak Brook
Alvarez, Ralph *food service executive*
Armario, Jose *restaurant executive*
Babrowski, Claire Harbeck *fast food chain executive*
Baker, Robert J(ohn) *hospital administrator*
Barnes, Karen Kay *lawyer*
Barnholt, Brandon K. *gas station/convenience store executive*
Bell, Charles H. *food service executive*
Bennett, Margaret Airola *lawyer*
Biedron, Theodore John *newspaper advertising executive*
Bossmann, Laurie *controller, hardware company executive*
Bower, Barbara Jean *nurse, consultant*
Bryan, R. Nick *medical association administrator*
Christian, Joseph Ralph *physician*
Congalton, Susan Tichenor *lawyer*
Conley, Michael L. *food products executive*
Crump-Caine, Lynn *food service executive*
Curt, Carol Lynn *psychologist, consultant*
Degerstrom, James Marvin *retired engineering executive*
DeLorey, John Alfred *printing company executive*
Ding, Jianchi *embryologist, researcher*
Duerinck, Louis T. *retired railroad executive, attorney*
Fenton, Tim *food service executive*
Fields, Janice L. *food service executive*
Fisher, Paul S. *real estate company executive*
Gates, John S., Jr., *real estate company executive*
Glenn, J. Thomas *consumer products company executive*
Goodwin, Daniel L. *real estate company executive*
Harless, Katherine J. *telecommunications company executive*
Hodnik, David F. *retail company executive*
Hollins, Mitchell Leslie *lawyer*
John, Richard C. *enterprise development organization executive*
Jones, Jeffrey W. *retail executive*
Kanzler, Michael W. *manufacturing executive*
Kelly, Donald Philip *entrepreneur*
Khoshabe, Steven Y. *mortgage company executive*
Kirshnan, Raama *electronics executive*
Koufis, John Theodore *accountant*
Loughead, Jeffrey Lee *physician*
Mullen, Michael M. *real estate company executive*
Nelson, Robert Eddinger *retired management consultant*
Onstead, R. Randall, Jr., *food products executive*
Paull, Matthew H. *food service executive*
Quinlan, Michael Robert *fast food franchise company executive*
Risk, Richard Robert *health care executive*
Roberts, Michael J. *food products executive*
Santona, Gloria *lawyer*
Skinner, Jim *food products executive*
Skogsbergh, James H. *health facility administrator*
Smyth, Russell P. *food products executive*
Thompson, Don *food products executive*
Turner, Fred L. *retired fast food company executive*
Veno, Ronald James, Jr., *travel industry executive*
Whaley, Marvin *food products executive*
Wigginton, Adam *marketing professional*

Oak Forest
Kogut, Kenneth Joseph *consulting engineer*
Lee, David Chang *physician*

Oak Lawn
Byrnes, Michael Francis *podiatrist*
Jachna, Joseph David *photographer, educator*
Jandes, Kenneth Michael *superintendent of schools*
Laird, Jean Elouise Rydeski (Mrs. Jack E. Laird) *author, adult education educator*

Oak Park
Adelman, William John *university labor and industrial relations educator*
Ankrum, Dennis R. *industrial ergonomist, consultant*
Bedrossian, Ursula Kay Kennedy *editor*
Cannon, Patrick Francis *public relations executive*
Cary, William Sterling *retired church executive*
Clark, John Peter, III, *engineering consultant*
Devereux, Timothy Edward *advertising executive*
Dong, Hanmin *forest products executive*
Fanta, Paul Edward *chemist, educator*
Gerson, Gary Stanford *rabbi*
Heitzman, Frank Edward *architect*
Kinzie, Raymond Wyant *banker, lawyer*
Leitch, Stuart *music educator, musician*
Matsuda, Takayoshi *surgeon, educator, biomedical researcher*
Schubert, Blake H. *lawyer*
Sengpiehl, Paul Marvin *lawyer, former state official*
Varchmin, Thomas Edward *environmental health administrator*
Venerable, Shirley Marie *gifted education educator*

Oakbrook Terrace
Becker, Robert Jerome *allergist, health care consultant*
Catalano, Gerald *accountant*
Hegenderfer, Jonita Susan *public relations executive*
Levine, Norman M. *academic administrator*
Savage, Murray *engineering executive*
Singhal, Vivek Kumar *management consultant*
Weiland, Mark Bradley *corporate lawyer*

Oglesby
Charry, Stephen Walter *historian, educator*

Olympia Fields
Delano, Jimmy Gboyega *business executive, accountant*
MacMaster, Daniel Miller *retired museum official*
Means-Willis, Emily W. *secondary school educator, writer*
Nuding, Doris Leona *law librarian, legal assistant, researcher*

Strong, Dorothy Swearengen *school system administrator*

Oregon
Cates, Jeffrey R. *chiropractor*
Hayes, Randy Alan *family therapist*
Haynes, Gary Allen *photographer, journalist, newspaper editor*

Orland Park
Kahn, Jan Edward *manufacturing executive*
Russell, Edward Francis *humanities educator, social sciences educator*

Oswego
Eberhardt, Robert Michael *diversified financial services company executive, sales executive*
May, Frank Brendan, Jr., *lawyer*

Ottawa
Benning, Joseph Raymond *principal*
Breipohl, Walter Eugene *real estate broker*
Thornton, Edmund B. *philanthropist*

Palatine
Bender, Virginia Best *computer scientist, educator*
Butler, John Musgrave *financial consultant*
Carranza, Cesar Augusto *surgeon*
Cesario, Robert Charles *franchise executive, consultant*
Fitzgerald, Gerald Francis *retired banker*
Harbeck, William James *real estate executive, lawyer, international consultant*
Hellyer, Timothy Michael *protective services officer*
Hershenhorn, Robert Gene *bank executive*
Keres, Karen Lynne *English language educator*
Kieft, Gerald Nelson *mechanical engineer*
Medin, Lowell Ansgard *management executive*
Pinderski, Jerome Wilbert, Jr., *lawyer*
Pohl, Frederik *freelance/self-employed writer*
Ramunno, Thomas Paul *management consultant*
Spinner, Lee Louis *accountant*
Victor, Michael Gary *lawyer, physician*
Wardell, John Watson *lawyer*
Zamarin, Ronald George *lawyer*

Palos Hills
Crawley, Vernon Obadiah *academic administrator*
Healy, Judith Ann *social worker*
McInerney, Noreen Linda *lawyer*
Zickus, Anne *state legislator*

Palos Park
Nelson, Lawrence Evan *business consultant*

Park Forest
Goodrich, John Bernard *lawyer, consultant*
Orr, Marcia *child development researcher, child care consultant*
Steinmetz, Jon David *mental health executive, psychologist*
Williams, Jack Raymond *civil engineer*

Park Ridge
Albert, Elizabeth Franz (Mrs. Henry B. Albert) *investor, artist, conservationist*
Barnett, Patrick Shawn *music educator*
Bitran, Jacob David *internist*
Boe, Gerard Patrick *health science association administrator, educator*
Campbell, Bruce Crichton *hospital administrator*
Campbell, Dorothy May *management consultant*
Carr, Gilbert Randle *retired railroad executive*
Catizone, Carmen A. *health science association administrator, secretary*
Charewicz, David Michael *photographer*
Ewald, Robert Frederick *insurance company executive, consultant*
Greenspahn, Bruce Robert *cardiologist*
Hegarty, Mary Frances *lawyer*
Johnson, Glenn W. *medical association administrator*
Kenney, John Patrick *dentist*
LaRue, Paul Hubert *retired lawyer*
Pielet, Bruce William *obstetrician*
Russell, William Steven *finance executive*
Schmidt, Wayne Walter *law association executive*
Sersen, Howard Harry *retired interior designer, cabinetry consultant*
Wasko, Steven E. *lawyer*
White, John Vincent *surgeon, consultant*
Williams, Sandra Lynn *management consultant*

Pekin
Dancey, Charles Lohman *newspaper executive*

Peoria
Allen, Lyle Wallace *lawyer*
Baumgartner, Vito H. *manufacturing executive*
Buda, James B. *lawyer, manufacturing executive*
Bussone, Frank Joseph *bank executive, television broadcaster, director*
Chamberlain, Joseph Miles *astronomer, educator*
Coletta, Ralph John *retired lawyer*
DuBois, Mark Benjamin *former utilities executive, educator*
Fanta, George Frederick *chemist, researcher*
George, Carl R. *accounting company executie*
Harkrader, Alan Dale, Jr., *retired photojournalist*
Heiple, James Dee *retired state supreme court justice*
Jibben, Laura Ann *state agency administrator*
Kelly, Grace Dentino *secondary school educator*
Kroll, Dennis Edwards *industrial engineering educator*
Kurtzman, Cletus Paul *microbiologist, researcher*
Lanzino, Giuseppe *physician*
Lorenz, Rodney Alan *physician, educator*
May, Janet Sue *playwright, lyricist*
McCollum, Jean Hubble *medical assistant*
McConnell, John Thomas *newspaper executive, publisher*
McPheeters, F. Lynn *manufacturing executive*
Meriden, Terry *physician*
Michael, Jonathan Edward *insurance company executive*
Mihm, Michael Martin *federal judge*
Murphy, Sharon Margaret *communications educator*
Nielsen, Harald Christian *retired chemist, researcher*
Oberhelman, Douglas R. *tractor company executive*
Owens, James W. *manufacturing executive*
Parsons, Donald James *retired bishop*
Parsons, Richard Hugo *lawyer*
Pollak, Raymond *general and transplant surgeon*
Reith, Maarten Edward A. *neurochemist*
Saxon, Randall Lee *pastor, author, educator*
Shaheen, Gerald L. *manufacturing executive*
Smith, Barbara Roderick *health and social services administrator, nursing consultant*
Szeto, George *mathematician, educator*
Thompson, Richard L. *manufacturing executive*
Thorstenson, Terry N. *construction equipment company executive*
Tomlin, James Milton *lawyer*
Vaughan, David John *corporate financial executive*
Walker, Philip Chamberlain, II, *health care executive*
Wiltse, Mark Edward *academic administrator, director*

Peoria Heights
Bergia, Roger Merle *school system administrator*
Taylor, Kathy Deanne *marketing executive, consultant*

Peru
Carus, Andre Wolfgang *educational publishing firm executive*
Carus, Milton Blouke *publisher children's periodicals*
Kurtz, James Eugene *freelance writer, minister*

Petersburg
Wood, Harlington, Jr., *federal judge*

Pinckneyville
Cawvey, Clarence Eugene *retired physician*

Plainfield
Bennett-Hammerberg, Janie Marie *small business owner, writer, consultant, administrative assistant*
Chakrabarti, Subrata Kumar *marine research engineer*
Cook, Bruce Lawrence *editor*
Diercks, Eileen Kay *educational media coordinator, elementary school educator*
Hofer, Thomas W. *landscape company executive*
Schinderle, Robert Frank *retired hospital administrator*

Pleasant Plains
Thomas, Evelyn B. *agricultural products supplier*

Pontiac
Ewing, Thomas William *former congressman, lawyer*
Glennon, Charles Edward *retired judge, lawyer*

Prarie Grove
Kruper, John Gerald (Jack Kruper) *sales and marketing executive*

Princeton
Tillman, June Torrison *musician*

Prophetstown
Williamsen, Dannye Sue *personal development educator, health facility administrator*

Prospect Heights
Aldinger, William F., III, *diversified financial services company executive*
Byrne, Michael Joseph *manufacturing executive*
Harvey, Kenneth M *corporate financial executive*
Leopold, Mark F. *lawyer*
Lynch, William Thomas, Jr., *advertising agency executive*
McDonald, Steven L. *controller*
Robinson, Martin (Marty Robinson) *television and radio broadcaster, media consultant*
Schoenholz, David A. *diversified financial services company executive*

Quincy
Barnes, Walter C., Jr., *physician*
Bohn, Donna May *music educator*
Centanni, Ross J. *engineering executive*
Cornell, Helen W. *manufacturing executive*
Donahue, Laura Kent *former state senator*
Finlay, Timothy *agricultural products supplier*
Foster, Michael *agricultural products supplier*
Mallory, Troy L. *accountant*
Points, Roy Wilson *municipal official*
Tyer, Travis Earl *library consultant*

Richton Park
Burt, Gwen Behrens *elementary school administrator*

River Forest
Bush, Gail *library educator, librarian*
Carroll, Donna M. *academic administrator*
Coe, Donald Kirk *retired university official*
Eisel, Jean Ellen *university educational administrator*
Hamper, Robert Joseph *marketing executive*
Harvey, Lynne Cooper *broadcasting executive, civic worker*
Li, Tze-chung *lawyer, educator*
O'Meara, Thomas Franklin *priest, educator*
Wirsching, Charles Philipp, Jr., *retired brokerage house executive, private investor*

River Grove
Gardner, Sandi B. *biology professor*
Hillert, Gloria Bonnin *anatomist, educator*
Litzsinger, Richard Mark *retail executive*
Nestor, Larry *songwriter, musician*
Rodriguez, Ileana P. *academic administrator, director*
Stanton, Kathryn *retail bookstores/educational products and services executive*
Stein, Thomas Henry *social science educator*
Traut, Christopher D. *educational materials distribution executive*

Riverdale
Hoekwater, James Warren *treasurer*
Kruszynski, Timothy Edward *retired corrections officer, poet*

Riverside
Chmell, Samuel Jay *orthopedic surgeon*
Dengler, Robert Anthony *professional association executive, educator*
Marty, Martin Emil *religion educator, editor*
Perkins, William H., Jr., *retired finance company executive*
Van Cura, Joyce Bennett *librarian*

Riverwoods
Del Tiempo, Sandra Kay *sales executive*
Douglas, Bruce Lee *oral and maxillofacial surgeon, public health educator, gerontology and workplace health consultant*
Ford, Michael W. *lawyer*
Yarrington, Hugh *corporate lawyer, communications company executive*

Rochester
Petterchak, Janice A. *researcher, writer, editor*

Rock Island
Anderson, Richard Charles *geology educator*
Bahls, Steven Carl *academic administrator, educator*
Brandenburg, Sister M. Luka *nun, educator*
Cheney, Thomas Ward *retired insurance company executive*
Ciaccio, Karin McLaughlin *lawyer*
Griffin-Brown, Dianna Lynn *entrepreneur, educator*
Hammer, William Roy *paleontologist, educator*
Horstmann, James Douglas *retired academic administrator*
Lardner, Henry Petersen (Peter Lardner) *insurance company executive*
Sundelius, Harold W. *geology educator*
Tredway, Thomas *college president*
Wallace, Franklin Sherwood *lawyer, director*

Rockford
Albert, Janyce Louise *human resources specialist, retired business educator, banker, consultant*
Baptist, Errol Christopher *pediatrician, educator*
Berry, Wes *literature educator*
Bippus, David Paul *manufacturing executive*
Borling, John Lorin *military officer*
Bradley, Charles MacArthur *retired architect*
Clodius, Robert LeRoy *retired economist*
Doran, Thomas George *bishop*
Duck, Vaughn Michael *software company executive*
Eliason, Jon Tate *electrical engineer*
Fleming, Thomas J. *editor, publishing executive*
Heerens, Robert Edward *physician*
Hoshaw, Lloyd *retired historian, educator*
Howard, John Addison *former college president, institute executive*
Jacobi, Fredrick Thomas *newspaper publisher*
Johnson, Thomas Stuart *lawyer*
Lien, Hsien-Lian *music educator, conductor*
McClelland, Patricia G. *minister*
Morrissey, Mary F. (Fran) *human resource consulting company executive*
O'Donnell, William David *retired construction firm executive*
Pribbenow, Paul C. *higher education administrator, consultant*
Reinhard, Philip G. *federal judge*
Reno, Roger *lawyer*
Robinson, Donald Peter *musician, retired electrical engineer*
Schauer, Jeffrey Edward *surgeon*
Shepler, John Edward *engineering executive*
Steele, Carl Lavern *academic administrator*
Walhout, Justine Simon *chemistry professor*
Wallem, Paul Sigurd *financial planner*

Rockton
Pennell, Danny Joe *social worker*

Rolling Meadows
Cain, R. Wayne *sales, finance and leasing company executive*
Cash, Alan Sherwin *electronics assembly specialist*
Eckel, James J. *flight test engineer*
Giese, Robert James *minister*
Hill, David K., Jr., *construction executive*
Roti, Thomas David *judge*
Strongin, Bonnie Lynn *English language educator*
Theis, Steven Thomas *safety engineer*

Romeoville
Lifka, Mary Lauranne *history professor*

Roselle
Marshall, James Andrew *civil engineer, real estate developer*

Rosemont
Blake, Norman Perkins, Jr., *computer company executive*
Good, William Allen *professional society executive*
Grosso, James Alan *information technology executive*
Isenberg, Howard Lee *manufacturing executive*
Macioch, James Edward *investment consultant, financial planner*
Meinert, John Raymond *investment banker, clothing manufacturing and retailing executive*
Nichols, Robert Hastings *lawyer*
Small, Richard Donald *travel company executive*

Round Lake
Abdullah, Bashar Y. *pharmacist, researcher*
Laskowski, Richard E. *retail hardware company executive*

Rushville
Zingher, Harry Lee *chemical engineer*

Saint Anne
Holtzman, Michael *alcohol abuse professional*

Saint Charles
Benjamin, Lawrence *food service executive*
Fishbune, Robert *food products executive*
Griffin, Sheila MB *strategic marketing excutive*
LaHood, Julie Ann *small business owner*
Liska, Margaret Naylor *retired small business owner*
Osowiec, Darlene Ann *clinical psychologist, educator, consultant*
Stone, John McWilliams, Jr., *electronics executive*
Stovall, April Leanne *music educator*
Urhausen, James Nicholas *real estate developer, construction executive*
Wolski, L.G. *heavy manufacturing executive*

Saint Francisville
Harezi, Ilonka Jo *medical technology research executive*

Saint Jacob
Carter, Dennis R. *music educator, band director, musician*

Saint Joseph
Valencia, Rogelio Pasco *electronics engineer*

Savoy
Gauger, Randy Jay *minister*
Sinclair, James Burton *retired plant pathology educator, consultant*

Scales Mound
Lieberman, Archie *photographer, writer*

Schaumburg
Adrianopoli, Barbara Catherine *librarian*
Anderson, Scott A. *electronics executive*
Bhatia, Viresh *computer company executive*
Brown, Greg *electronics executive*
Canavan, Patrick J. *electronics executive*
Delaney, Gene *electronics executive*
De Lerno, Manuel Joseph *electrical engineer*
Desai, Samir T. *electronics executive*
Devonshire, David W. *financial executive*
Galvin, Robert W. *electronics executive*
Growney, Robert L. *communications company professional*
Guimond, Richard Joseph *communications executive*
Hambley, Douglas Frederick *geological and environmental engineer*
Hanna, Nessim *marketing educator*
Hill, Raymond Joseph *packaging company executive*
Kornowski, Robert Richard *engineer, science educator*
Lawson, A. Peter *lawyer*
Little, Bruce Washington *professional society administrator*
Lynch, Thomas J. *telecommunications industry executive*
Metty, Theresa M. *communications executive*
Moloney, Daniel M. *electronics executive*
Muhich, Brian William *insurance broker*
Narkiewicz-Laine, Christian K. Gf. *museum director, painter, poet*
Nemcek, Adrian R. *electronics executive*
Richter, Glenn *manufacturing executive*
Sandler, Norman *communications executive*
Shlapak, Fred *electronics executive*
Sikora, Sheryl L. *application developer*
Soderberg, Leif G. *electronics company executive*
Soon-Shiong, Patrick *pharmaceutical executive*
Stabej, Rudolph John *computer consultant*
Talukdar, Anup Kumar *computer engineer, researcher*
Tompson, Marian Leonard *professional society administrator*
Turlik, Iwona *communication executive*
Uhrik, Steven Brian *clinical social worker, psychotherapist, employee assistance professional, behavioral science consultant*
Warrior, Padmasree *communications executive*
Westlund, Maribeth *secondary school educator*
Zafirovski, Mike S. *communications executive*
Zander, Edward *electronics executive*

Schiller Park
Congalton, Christopher William *lawyer*

Scott Air Force Base
Fox, Leonard Dean *civil engineer, air force officer*
Welser, William, III, *military officer*

Seymour
Carringer, Robert *English language and film educator*

Silvis
Bobb, Harold Daniel *chiropractor, consultant*

Skokie
Alter, Michael *real estate company executive*
Bell, Rosonald Renae *toxicologist*
Corley, William Gene *engineering research executive*
Feinberg, Henry J. *publishing executive*
Ginn, Martin E. *writer, consultant*
Gleason, John Patrick, Jr., *trade association executive*
Guillermo, Linda Sue *clinical social worker*
Hamer, Martin *retired chemist*
Hedien, Wayne Evans *retired insurance company executive*
Hoopis, Harry Peter *insurance executive, entrepreneur*
Karp, Gary *marketing and public relations executive*
Langguth, Margaret Witty *health facility administrator*
Levy, Mark Hirsch *internist, medical educator, researcher*
Mamet, David Alan *playwright, director, essayist*
Manos, John *editor-in-chief*
McCarthy, Michael Shawn *health care company executive, lawyer*
Siegal, Burton Lee *product designer, consultant, inventor*
Siegal, Rita Goran *engineering company executive*
Sloan, Judi C. *former physical education educator*
Sperzel, George E., Jr., *former personal care industry executive*
Van Gelder, Marc Christiaan *retail executive*
Wallace, Rick *marketing professional*
Wasik, John Francis *editor, writer, publisher*
Weber, Randy *publishing executive*
Weidmann, K. Timothy *not-for-profit fundraiser, writer*

South Holland
Perry, Joseph N. *bishop*
Wolf, Wayne Lowell *criminal justice educator, researcher*

Spring Grove
York, Karen Kay *accountant, farmer*

Springfield
Abbott, Randall (Lee Abbott) *lawyer*

Ballenger, Hurley René *electrical engineer*
Bannister, Dan Wesley *retired historian*
Beaubien, Mark H., Jr., *state representative*
Beckwith, Peter Hess *bishop*
Bell, John Perry *minister, religious organization administrator*
Blagojevich, Rod R. *governor, former congressman*
Bowles, Evelyn Margaret *state legislator*
Bradley, Richard T. *state representative*
Brady, Daniel P. *state representative*
Burns, James B. *prosecutor*
Collins, Annazette R. *state representative*
Collins, Jacqueline Y *state senator*
Crotty, M. Maggie *state senator*
Cullen, Mark Kenneth *lawyer*
Cultra, Shane *state representative*
Currie, Barbara Flynn *state legislator*
Daniels, Lee Albert *state legislator*
Darr, William A. *commissioner*
Deal, Karen Lynne *conductor*
Dodge, Edward John *retired insurance company executive*
Dodge, James William *lawyer, educator*
Dorsey, John Kevin *dean*
Doyle, Rebecca Carlisle *state agency administrator*
Duggan, Timothy E. *lawyer*
Dunn, Joe *state representative*
Eddy, Roger L. *state representative*
Erwin, Judy *state legislator*
Evans, Charles H. *federal judge*
Ferguson, Mark Harmon *banker, lawyer*
Forby, Gary F. *state representative*
Frank, Stuart *cardiologist*
Fritchey, John A. *state representative*
Gamble, Douglas Irvin *state official, educator*
Garrett, Susan *state senator*
Graham, Donald R. *epidemiologist*
Gramlich, Charles J. *judge*
Gregg, Phillip Martin *political scientist, educator*
Haine, William R. *state senator*
Hallmark, Donald Parker *museum director, lecturer*
Hamos, Julie E. *state representative*
Hannig, Gary L. *state representative*
Hasara, Karen A. *mayor*
Herriford, Robert Levi, Sr., *army officer*
Holland, John Madison *retired family practice physician*
Howard, Constance A. *state representative*
Hundley, Elaine E. *retired nursing education administrator*
Jakobsson, Naomi D. *state representative*
Jefferson, Charles E. *state representative*
Jones, Shirley M. *state legislator*
Karpiel, Doris Catherine *state legislator*
Kelly, Robin L. *state representative*
Kerr, Gary Enrico *lawyer, educator*
Klingler, Gwendolyn Walbolt *state representative*
Kosel, Renée *state representative*
Kuhn, Kathleen Jo *accountant*
Kurtz, Rosemary *state representative*
Lightford, Kimberly A. *state legislator*
Lindley, Maralee Irwin *county official, consultant, speaker*
Lyons, Joseph M. *state representative*
Malany, Le Grand Lynn *lawyer, engineer, bank executive*
Martinez, Iris *state senator*
Mathewson, Mark Stuart *lawyer, editor*
Mathias, Sidney H. *state representative*
McCarthy, Kevin A. *state representative*
McKeon, Larry J. *state representative*
Mc Millan, R(obert) Bruce *museum executive, anthropologist*
Meeks, James T. *state senator*
Mikell, Frank Leonard *cardiologist*
Miller, David E. *state representative*
Miller, Jan Paul *lawyer*
Mills, Richard Henry *federal judge*
Mogerman, Susan *state agency administrator*
Moore, Andrea S. *state legislator*
Morford, Lynn Ellen *state official*
Morse, Saul Julian *lawyer*
Munyer, Edward A. *zoologist*
Myers, Phillip Ward *otolaryngologist*
Nekritz, Elaine *state representative*
Obama, Barack H. *state legislator*
O'Brien, Dennis Sean *lawyer*
O'Shea, Helene Claire *bookkeeper*
Pankau, Carole *state legislator*
Parke, Terry Richard *state legislator*
Patton, Mary Knox *mathematician, educator*
Phelps, David Dwain *state agency administrator, former congressman*
Phillips, John Robert *political scientist, educator*
Pihos, Sandra M *state representative*
Poorman, Robert Lewis *education consultant, former college president*
Rabinovich, Sergio *physician, educator*
Rarick, Philip Joseph *judge*
Reitz, Dan *state representative*
Reyman, Jonathan Eric *archaeologist, anthropologist, researcher*
Righter, Dale A. *state senator*
Ryan, Daniel Leo *bishop*
Sacia, Jim *state representative*
Schaffer, Jack *former state senator*
Schroeder, Joyce Katherine *state agency administrator, research analyst*
Simpson, William Arthur *insurance company executive*
Slone, Ricca C *state representative*
Smith, Margaret *state legislator*
Steiner, Janet *educational association administrator*
Stroh, Raymond Eugene *retired personnel executive*
Sumner, David Spurgeon *surgery educator*
Swartz, Conrad Melton *psychiatrist*
Temple, Wayne Calhoun *historian, writer*
Travis, Lawrence Allan *accountant*
Van Meter, Abram DeBois *lawyer, retired banker*
Voycheck, Gerald Louis *nursing home administrator, social worker*
Walbaum, Robert C. *lawyer*
Washington, Eddie *state representative*
Wehrle, Leroy Snyder *economist, educator*
Whitaker, Victoria Manuela Katz *publisher, public relations executive, educator, consultant*
White, Jesse *state official*
Woodson, Gayle Ellen *otolaryngologist*
Wynn, Nan L. *historic site administrator*
Yaffe, Stuart Allen *physician*
Yarbrough, Karen A. *state representative*
Zaricznyj, Basilius *orthopedic surgeon*
Zook, Elvin Glenn *plastic surgeon, educator*

Sterling
Donahue, Shirley Ohnstad *elementary school educator*

Stoy
Rhoten, Kenneth D. *writer*

Streator
Cassady, Zoe Anne *theater educator, director*

Sugar Grove
Carella, J(oseph) Dino *printing company executive*
Debartolo, Hansel Marion, Jr., *otolaryngologist, plastic surgeon*
Durrenberger, William John *retired army general, educator, investor*

Sycamore
Burzynski, James Bradley *state legislator*
Fanning, Gary Lee *anesthesiologist*
Johnson, Yvonne Amalia *elementary education educator, science consultant*
Stone, Van Courtright *not-for-profit developer*
Vance Siebrasse, Kathy Ann *legislative staff member*
Young, Arthur Price *librarian, educator*

Table Grove
Thomson, Helen Louise *artist*

Taylor Ridge
Potthast, David Raymond *retired military officer, secondary school educator*

Taylorville
Austin, Daniel William *lawyer*
Garner, John Lee *protective services official, educator*
Spears, Ronald Dean *judge*

Techny
Vanderstappen, Harrie Albert *Far Eastern art educator*

Tinley Park
Baker, Betty Louise *retired secondary school educator*
Basit, Abdul *mental health services professional*
Daniels, Kurt R. *speech and language pathologist*
Data, Linda Laski *music educator*
Flanagan, John F. *publishing executive*
Keenan, Robert Arthur *bank executive, consultant*
Kostka, Elmer Bohumil *secondary school educator*
Leeson, Janet Caroline Tollefson *cake specialties company executive*
West, David Wayne *mechanical engineer*

Toledo
Prather, William C., III, *lawyer, writer*

Tuscola
Henderson, E. Suzanne *elementary school educator*

University Park
Hakala, Reino William *mathematician, educator*
Keys, Paul Ross *university provost/academic affairs official*
McMaster, Michele *communications educator*
Patton, June Odessa *writer, consultant, educator, researcher*
Peterson, Kenneth Allen, Sr., *retired superintendent*

Urbana
Accad, Evelyne *language educator*
Addy, Alva Leroy *mechanical engineer*
Aldridge, Alfred Owen *English language educator*
Arends-Kuenning, Mary Paula *economics professor, consultant*
Arnstein, Walter Leonard *historian, educator*
Axford, Roy Arthur *nuclear engineering educator*
Baker, David Hiram *nutritionist, nutrition educator*
Balbach, Stanley Byron *lawyer*
Banwart, Wayne Lee *agronomy, environmental science educator*
Baym, Nina *English educator*
Beak, Peter Andrew *chemistry professor*
Bennett, Scott Boyce *retired librarian*
Bentley, Orville George *retired agricultural educator, dean emeritus*
Berenbaum, May Roberta *entomology educator*
Bergeron, Clifton George *ceramics engineer, educator*
Bérubé, Michael *literature educator*
Birnbaum, Howard Kent *materials science educator*
Blahut, Richard Edward *electrical and computer engineering educator*
Braatz, Richard Dean *chemical engineer*
Brichford, Maynard Jay *archivist*
Brozak, George A. *music educator*
Bruner, Edward M. *anthropology educator*
Bullo, Francesco *science educator*
Carmen, Ira Harris *political scientist, educator*
Carroll, Robert Wayne *mathematics professor*
Chao, Bei Tse *mechanical engineering educator*
Chato, John Clark *mechanical and bioengineering educator*
Chow, Poo *wood technologist, scientist*
Christians, Clifford Glenn *communications educator*
Coleman, James J. *electrical engineer, educator*
Conry, Thomas Francis *mechanical engineering educator, consultant*
Crang, Richard Francis Earl *plant and cell biologist, research center administrator*
Crofts, Antony Richard *biochemistry and biophysics educator*
Cronan, Jr., John Emerson *microbiologist*
Cusano, Cristino *mechanical engineer, educator*
D'Angelo, John Philip *mathematician*
Daniel, David Edwin *civil engineer, educator*
Dash, Leon DeCosta, Jr., *journalist*
Davis, Ollie Watts *musician, educator*
Dick, William Allen *engineering educator*
Dovring, Karin Elsa Ingeborg *writer, poet, playwright, media specialist*
Dziuk, Philip John *animal scientist educator*
Eden, James Gary *electrical engineer, educator, physicist, researcher*
Edgar, Jim *former governor*
Ehrlich, Gert *science educator, researcher*
Endress, Anton G. *horticulturist, educator*
Erdman, John W. *nutritionist, educator*
Ferber, Marianne Abeles *economics professor*
Fitz-Gerald, Roger Miller *lawyer*
Forbes, Richard Mather *biochemistry educator*
Fossum, Robert Merle *mathematician, educator*
Frazzetta, Thomas Henry *evolutionary biologist, functional morphologist, educator*
Gabriel, Michael *psychology educator*
Gaddy, Oscar Lee *electrical engineering educator*
Giles, Eugene *anthropology educator*
Ginsberg, Donald Maurice *physicist, researcher*
Glick, Karen Lynne *college administrator*
Goldwasser, Edwin Leo *physicist*
Gove, Samuel Kimball *political science educator*
Govindjee, *biophysics, biochemistry, and biology educator*
Greene, Laura Helen *physicist*
Gruebele, Martin *chemistry, physics, and biophysics educator*
Haile, H. G. *German language and literature educator*
Hall, William Joel *civil engineer, educator*
Hannon, Bruce Michael *engineering educator*
Heath, James Edward *retired physiology educator*
Hedlund, Ronald *baritone*
Heichel, Gary Harold *agronomist, educator*
Henderson, Stanley Elwood *academic administrator, consultant*
Hendrick, George *retired English language educator*
Henson, C. Ward *mathematician, educator*
Hess, Karl *electrical and computer engineering educator*
Hill, Lowell Dean *agricultural marketing educator*
Hitchins, Keith Arnold *historian, educator*
Hoeft, Robert Gene *agriculture educator*
Holonyak, Nick, Jr., *electrical engineering educator*
Holt, Donald A. *agronomist, consultant, researcher, retired academic administrator*
Hou, Xiaoqiang *mineralogist*
Hoxie, Frederick Eugene *history professor*
Huang, Thomas Shi-Tao *electrical engineering educator, researcher*
Iben, Icko, Jr., *astrophysicist, educator*
Jackson, Edwin Atlee *physicist, educator*
Jockusch, Carl Groos, Jr., *mathematics professor*
Johnson, Duane D. *education educator, researcher*
Jonas, Jiri *chemist, educator*
Kaufman, Jerome Benzion *neurosurgeon*
Kieffer, Susan Werner *geologist, educator, media consultant*
Kim, Chin-Woo *linguist, educator*
Kirkpatrick, R(obert) James *geology educator*
Klein, Miles Vincent *physics educator*
Knight, Frank Bardsley *mathematics professor*
Kotynek, Jan George *surgeon*
Krier, Herman *mechanical and industrial engineering educator*
Krock, Curtis Josselyn *pulmonologist*
Kumar, Panganamala Ramana *electrical and computer engineering educator*
Lauterbur, Paul C(hristian) *chemistry professor*
Leggett, Anthony J. *education educator*
Lieberman, Laurence *poet, educator*
Liebman, Judith Rae Stenzel *operations research educator*
Love, Joseph L. *history educator, former cultural studies center administrator*
Lüschen, Günther Rudolf Friedo *sociology educator*
Makri, Nancy *chemistry educator*
Mapother, Dillon Edward *physicist, academic administrator*
Mayes, Paul Eugene *engineering educator, consultant*
Mc Glamery, Marshal Dean *crop scientist, weed science educator*
McKay, John Patrick *history educator*
Meyer, Richard Charles *microbiologist, educator*
Miley, George Hunter *nuclear and electrical engineering educator*
Miller, Robert Earl *engineering educator*
Nanney, David Ledbetter *geneticist, educator*
Nelson, Ralph Alfred *physician*
Nettl, Bruno *anthropology and musicology educator*
O'Brien, Nancy Patricia *librarian, educator*
Oliphant, Uretz John *physician, surgeon*
O'Morchoe, Charles Christopher Creagh *anatomical sciences educator, science administrator*
Portis, Archie Ray, Jr., *plant physiologist, agronomy educator*
Powers, Elizabeth T. *economist*
Prussing, Laurel Lunt *public interest lobbyist, economist, auditor*
Rao, Nannapaneni Narayana *electrical engineer*
Ravaioli, Umberto *electrical engineer, educator*
Rebeiz, Constantin A. *plant biochemist, educator, lab administrator*
Resek, Robert William *economist*
Rich, Robert F. *law and political science educator*
Ridgway, Marcella Davies *veterinarian*
Robinson, Gene Ezia *biologist, educator*
Salamon, Myron Ben *physicist, educator, dean*
Satterthwaite, Cameron B. *physics educator*
Sauer, Peter William *electrical engineer, educator*
Schleis, Thomas Henry *music educator, organist*
Schupp, Paul Eugene *mathematician, educator*
Seigler, David Stanley *botanist, educator, chemist*
Shtohryn, Dmytro Michael *librarian, educator*
Simon, Jack Aaron *geologist, former state official*
Snoeyink, Vernon L. *civil engineer, educator*
Snyder, Lewis Emil *astrophysicist, educator*
Solberg, Winton Udell *history educator*
Sousa, Ronald Wayne *foreign language educator*
Splittstoesser, Walter Emil *plant physiologist*
Sprague, Robert L. *retired psychologist*
Stukel, James Joseph *academic administrator, mechanical engineer, educator*
Sullivan, John Matthew *mathematician, educator*
Suslick, Kenneth Sanders *chemistry professor*
Switzer, Robert Lee *biochemistry educator*
Talbot, Emile Joseph *French language educator*
Temperley, Nicholas *music educator, writer*
Thies, Richard Leon *lawyer, director*
Thompson, Robert Lee *agricultural economist, educator*
Toby, Ronald Paul *historian*
Tondeur, Philippe Maurice *mathematician, educator*
Tripp, April *special education services professional*
Visek, Willard James *nutritionist, animal scientist, physician, educator*
Von Gunden, Heidi *music educator*
Walker, William Hamilton *civil engineer, educator*
Watson, Paula D. *library administrator*
Watts, Emily Stipes *English language educator*
Weaver, John H *research scientist, educator*
Webber, Carl Maddra *lawyer*
Weidner, Robert Wright *musician, music educator, musicologist*
Whiteley, H. E. *dean*
Whitt, Gregory Sidney *evolution educator*
Williams, Martha Ethelyn *information science educator*
Wong, Martin D.F. *computer scientist, educator*
Woodard, Beth Stuckey *librarian, educator*
Yu, George Tzuchiao *political science educator*

Vandalia
Low, Louise O. *volunteer*

Vernon Hills
Cho, Yong Hyo *public administrator, educator*
Claassen, W(alter) Marshall *employment company executive*
Curns, Eileen Bohan *counselor, author, speaker*
Edwardson, John Albert *security firm executive*
Halitsky, Steve *application developer, researcher*
Kaplan, Edward L. *electronics executive*
Klein, Barbara A. *information technology executive*
Krasny, Michael P. *computer company executive*
Leahy, Christine A. *information technology executive*
Richards, Alan Edward *lawyer*

Villa Park
Antonelli, Joseph K. *musician, educator*
Camp, Jeffery Mark *Web specialist, military officer*
Pittelko, Roger Dean *clergyman, religious educator*

Walnut
Meisenheimer, Sharon Lee *nurse*

Warrenville
Boardman, Robert A. *lawyer*
Grote, Byron *gas industry executive*
Horne, John R. *farm equipment company executive*
Johnson, Douglas Wells *lawyer*
Lannert, Robert Cornelius *manufacturing executive*
Lennes, Gregory *manufacturing and financing company executive*
Slavin, Thomas John *industrial hygienist, director*
Ustian, Daniel C. *trucking executive*

Washington
Hallinan, John Cornelius *mechanical engineering consultant*
Stine, Robert Howard *retired pediatrician, allergist*

Watseka
Tungate, James Lester *lawyer*

Wauconda
Kramer, Pamela Kostenko *librarian*
Malik, Thomas Warren *lawyer*

Waukegan
Brady, Terrence Joseph *judge*
Cherry, Peter Ballard *electrical products corporation executive*
Drapalik, Betty R. *volunteer, artist, educator*
Hall, Albert L. *retired lawyer*
Henrick, Michael Francis *lawyer*
Keller, Richard Loran *physician*
Leibowitz, David Perry *lawyer*
Martis, Leo *healthcare researcher*

Wayne City
Blank, Stanley Bruce *secondary school educator*

West Brooklyn
Mays, K. J. *writer, musician*

West Chicago
Paulissen, James Peter *retired pediatrician, county official*

West Frankfort
Williams, Joseph Scott *energy and natural resources company executive, city commissioner*

West Peoria
McBride, Sharon Louise *counselor, technical communication educator*

Westchester
Anderson, Carol Lee *communications executive*
Calder, Robert Austin *preventive medicine physician, administrator*
Clarke, Richard Lewis *health science association administrator*
Faulkner, Robert Lloyd *advertising executive, graphics designer*
Masterson, John Patrick *retired English language educator*
Pavelka, Elaine Blanche *mathematics professor*
Shaffer, Susan E. *nutrition specialist*
Tutins, Antons *electrical and audio engineer*

Western Springs
Frommelt, Jeffrey James *management consulting firm executive*
Hanson, Heidi Elizabeth *lawyer*
Reggio, Vito Anthony *management consultant*
Rhoads, Paul Kelly *lawyer*
Shannon, Peter Michael, Jr., *lawyer*
Tiefenthal, Marguerite Aurand *school social worker*
Walsh, Robert Joseph *psychotherapist*
Zamora, Marjorie Dixon *retired political science educator*

Westmont
DuBose, Michael T. *manufacturing executive*
Hansen, Donald Marty *journalist, retired accountant*
Harten, Ann M. *relocation services executive*
Kelley, Brian P. *transportation executive*
Kuhn, Robert Mitchell *retired rubber company executive*
Moor, Roy Edward *finance educator*
Rogers, James W. *trucking executive*
Tricase, Elizabeth *gymnast*

Wheaton
Allen, Henry Lee *sociology educator, consultant*
Astrup, Jens Leo *retired civil engineer*
Back, Robert Wyatt *investment company executive, pharmaceutical executive, consultant*
Bogdonoff, Maurice Lambert *physician*
Cunningham, William Francis *lawyer*
DaRosa, Ronald Anthony *lawyer*
Didzerekis, Paul Patrick *lawyer*

Gill, Kenneth Duane *minister, director*
Hamilton, Robert Appleby, Jr., *insurance company executive*
Harris, Eleanor Lynne *religious studies educator, literature educator, minister, writer*
Hollingsworth, Pierce *publishing executive*
Holman, James Lewis *financial and management consultant*
Kaenel, Rosemary Therese *community health nurse, educator*
Leston, Patrick John *judge*
Litfin, A. Duane *academic administrator*
Long, Charles Franklin *retired corporate communications executive*
Lowrie, Pamela Burt *educator, artist*
McCartney, Charles Price *retired obstetrician-gynecologist*
Mellott, Robert Vernon *retired advertising executive*
Oesterle, Carolyn Scherer *pediatric ophthalmologist*
Page, L. Kristen *biologist, educator*
Pape, Patricia Ann *social worker, consultant*
Pappas, Barbara Estelle *Biblical studies educator, author*
Payne, Mary Louise *music educator, musician*
Stein, Lawrence A. *lawyer*
Taylor, Mark Douglas *publishing executive*
Thomas, Robert R. *state supreme court justice*
Thompson, Bert Allen *retired librarian*
Tucker, Beverly Sowers *information specialist*
Votaw, John Frederick *educational foundation executive, educator*

Wheeling
Kenny, James Casey *ambassador, construction company executive*
Long, Sarah Ann *librarian*
Ochsner, Othon Henry, II, *importer, restaurant critic*
Rogers, Richard F. *construction company executive, architect, engineer*
Schulman, Alan Michael *small business owner*

Willow Springs
Jashel, Larry Steven (L. Steven Rose) *entrepreneur, media consultant*

Willowbrook
Burrows, Donald Albert *artist, painter, photographer, dean*
Foley, Joseph Lawrence *sales executive*
Mathisen-Reid, Rhoda Sharon *international communications consultant*
Walton, Stanley Anthony, III, *lawyer*

Wilmette
Albright, Townsend Shaul *investment banker, government benefits consultant*
Atkinson, Jeff John Frederick *law educator, lawyer, writer*
Blake, Douglas Munro *music educator*
Brink, Marion Francis *trade association administrator*
Browder, William Bayard *corporation executive, lawyer*
Chiaro, A. William *management consultant*
Coughlan, Gary Patrick *pharmaceutical company executive*
Ellis, Helene Rita *social worker*
Erickson, James Clifford, III, *anesthesiologist, educator*
Frick, Robert Hathaway *retired lawyer*
Geller, William Alan *criminal justice researcher, police and public safety consultant*
Hansen, Andrew Marius *retired library association executive*
Hier, Daniel Barnet *neurologist*
Jampole, Michael *music educator, composer*
Klotz, Irving Myron *chemist, educator*
Lieberman, Eugene *lawyer*
McNeill, Thomas B. *director, retired lawyer*
Merrier, Helen *actress, writer*
Miller, Frederick Staten *retired music educator, academic administrator*
Montgomery Tobias, Karen Twerdahl *music educator*
Muhlenbruch, Carl W. *civil engineer*
Pearlman, Jerry Kent *electronics company executive*
Rocek, Jan *chemist, educator*
Schloss, Nathan *retired economist*
Smutny, Joan Franklin *academic director, educator*
Wadden, Richard Albert *environmental engineer, educator, science administrator, consultant*
Walker, Ronald Edward *psychologist, educator*
Wishner, Maynard Ira *retired finance company executive, lawyer*

Winfield
Young, Quentin Hayse *family counselor*

Winnetka
Bro, William Price *communications executive*
Bundy, Blakely Fetridge *early childhood educator, advocate*
Burke, John Edward *communications editor*
Burt, Robert Norcross *retired diversified manufacturing company executive*
Carrow, Leon Albert *physician*
Crowe, Robert William *lawyer, mediator*
Fawcett, Dwight Winter *retired lawyer*
Fenton, Clifton Lucien *investment banker*
Gavin, James John, Jr., *diversified company executive*
Greenblatt, Ray Harris *lawyer*
Hales, Daniel B. *lawyer*
Hartman, Robert S. *retired paper company executive*
Hausfeld, James Frank *executive director*
Hermann, Edward Robert *health engineer, educator, writer, consultant, hygieologist*
Huggins, Charlotte Susan Harrison *secondary school educator, author, travel specialist*
Kahn, Paul Frederick *executive search company executive*
Kennedy, George Danner *chemical company executive*
Klapperich, Frank Lawrence, Jr., *investment banker*
Krucks, William Norman *lawyer*
Krueger, Deborah A. Blake *school psychologist, consultant*
McWhirter, Bruce J. *retired lawyer*
Piper, Robert Johnston *retired architect, urban planner*
Plowden, David *photographer*
Puth, John Wells *consulting company executive*
Rossi, Ennio C. *physician, educator*
Rubnitz, Myron Ethan *pathologist, educator*
Schlossman, John Isaac *architect*
Sick, William Norman, Jr., *venture capital company executive*
Thomas, John Thieme *management consultant*
Weber, John Bertram *architect*
Weldon, Theodore Tefft, Jr., *manufacturing executive*

Wood Dale
Bullen, Daniel Bernard *mechanical engineering educator*
Goodwin, James E. *retired air transportation executive*
Storch, David *manufacturing executive*
Yumoto, Futoshi *statistician, researcher*

Woodridge
O'Connor, William Michael *search company executive*
Puthenpurakal, Joseph Mathew *information technology executive*
Stall, Alan David *packaging company executive*

Woodstock
Ackley, Robert O. *lawyer*
Levandowski, Barbara Sue *educational administrator*

Worden
Dole, Thomas Brader *retired secondary school educator, musician*

Yorkville
McEachern, Joan *medical association administrator*

Zion
Birdsall, Timothy Carroll *naturopathic physician*

INDIANA

Akron
Allen, Elizabeth Ann *writer*

Albany
White, William Richard *manufacturing engineer, consultant*

Alexandria
Irwin, Gerald Port *physician*

Anderson
Carrell, Terry Eugene *manufacturing executive*
Conrad, Harold August *retired religious pension board executive*
Harris, Ronald *state agency administrator*
King, Charles Ross *physician*
Kufeldt, George *biblical educator*
Lambert, Lloyd Laverne *minister*
Long, Brian Thomas *music educator*
Neidert, David Lynn *administrator*
Olson, Carol Lea *lithographer, educator*
Snyder, Thomas J. *automotive company executive*

Angola
Lin, Ping-Wha *engineering educator, consultant*
Meeks, Kenneth W. *civil engineer, educator*
Reynolds, R. John *academic administrator, educator*
Zimmerman, James Allen *historian, educator*

Auburn
Kempf, Jane Elmira *marketing executive*

Batesville
Hillenbrand, Daniel A. *manufacturing executive*
Rockwood, Frederick Whitney *insurance company executive*
Sorenson, Scott K. *manufacturing executive*
Volk, Cecilia Ann *elementary school educator*

Bedford
Hunter, Harlen Charles *orthopedic surgeon*

Beech Grove
Brown, Richard Lawrence *lawyer*
Byrkett, Gary Lee *hospital engineer*
Hughes, Charles E., III, *plastic surgeon*

Berne
Habegger, Cynthia A. *medical/surgical nurse*

Beverly Shores
Collins, Moira Ann *graphics and communications company executive, calligrapher*

Bicknell
Risley, Gregory Byron *furniture company executive, interior designer*

Bloomington
Alex-Assensoh, Yvette Marie *political scientist*
Aman, Alfred Charles, Jr., *law educator*
Anderson, Judith Helena *English language educator*
Arnove, Robert Frederick *education educator*
Assensoh, Akwasi Bretuo *historian, educator*
Atwood, Christopher Pratt *social studies professor*
Austin, Joan Kessner *mental health nurse*
Barnes, A. James *academic dean*
Bartleson, Amy Aileen *psychotherapist*
Baye, Michael Roy *economics professor*
Becker, Robert Allen *economist, educator*
Belth, Joseph Morton *retired business educator*
Bernhardt-Kabisch, Ernest Karl-Heinz *English and comparative literature educator*
Bishop, Michael D. *emergency physician*
Biss, Paul Martin *music educator*
Bornholdt, Laura Anna *university administrator*
Brehm, Sharon Stephens *psychology educator, university administrator*
Brinkman, Paul Del(bert) *foundation executive, university administrator*
Brown, Keith *musician, educator*
Buelow, George John *musicologist, educator*
Caldwell, Lynton Keith *social scientist, educator*
Calinescu, Adriana Gabriela *museum curator, art historian*
Cameron, John M. *nuclear scientist, educator, science administrator*
Chafel, Judith Ann *education educator*
Chitwood, Julius Richard *retired librarian*
Choksy, Jamsheed Kairshasp *historian, religious scholar, language professional, humanities educator*
Clevenger, Sarah *botanist, computer consultant*
Collins, Dorothy Craig *retired educational administrator*
Connally, Sandra Jane Oppy *retired art educator, artist*
Conrad, Geoffrey Wentworth *archaeologist, educator*
Cookman, Claude *journalist, educator*
Dalton, Dan R. *finance educator, former dean*
Day, Harry Gilbert *nutritional biochemist, consultant*
DeHayes, Daniel Wesley *management executive, educator*
DeVoe, Robert Donald *visual physiologist*
Dunn, Jon Michael *informatics educator, dean*
Dunning, Jeremy David *application developer, dean, educator*
Easton, Susan Dawn *biochemist, educator*
Edgerton, William B. *foreign language educator*
Edmondson, Frank Kelley *retired astronomer*
Eisenberg, Paul David *philosophy educator*
Estes, William Kaye *psychologist, educator*
Finkelstein, David Barry *geologist, researcher*
Franks, Steven Laurence *linguist, educator*
Gest, Howard *microbiologist, educator*
Goldstone, Robert L. *psychologist, educator*
Gordon, Paul John *management educator*
Gough, Pauline Bjerke *magazine editor*
Guth, Sherman Leon (S. Lee Guth) *psychologist, educator*
Hammel, Harold Theodore *physiology and biophysics educator, researcher*
Hanks, Lawrence Julius, Sr., *management consultant, researcher*
Hanson, Karen *philosopher, educator*
Hara, Noriko *information scientist, educator*
Hattin, Donald Edward *geologist, educator*
Heiser, Charles Bixler, Jr., *botany educator*
Hendry, Archibald Wagstaff *physics educator*
Herbert, Adam William, Jr., *academic administrator, educator*
Hites, Ronald Atlee *environmental science educator, chemist*
Hofstadter, Douglas Richard *cognitive scientist, educator, writer*
Hogan, Jeremy Robert *photojournalist*
Housworth, Elizabeth Ann *mathematics professor*
Hustad, Thomas Pegg *marketing educator*
Ingersoll, Gary Michael *educational psychologist*
Jacobi, Peter Paul *journalism educator, author*
Johnson, Kevin LaMont *educator*
Johnson, Owen Verne *historian, educator*
Johnson, Rodney *writer*
Johnson-D'Alessio, Anna *writer, poet*
Juergens, George Ivar *history professor*
Kauffman, Erle Galen *geologist, paleontologist*
Ketterson, Ellen D. *biologist, educator*
Kibbey, Hal Stephen *science writer*
Knudsen, Laura Georgia *linguist*
Kunkler, Arnold William *retired surgeon, educator*
Lebano, Edoardo Antonio *foreign language educator*
Lee, Don Yoon *publisher, academic researcher and writer*
Legler, April Arington *librarian, educator*
Letsinger, Robert Lewis *chemistry professor*
Lloyd, Rosemary *language educator*
Louis, Kenneth R.R. Gross *academic administrator*
Maccaby, Rivkah *writer, interpreter*
MacKay, David B. *finance educator*
Mac Watters, Virginia Elizabeth *singer, music educator, actress*
Mallor, Andrew C. *lawyer*
Markman, Ronald *artist, educator*
Martins, Heitor Miranda *foreign language educator*
McCluskey, John Asberry, Jr., *literature educator, writer*
McGibbon, Murray Lewis James *theater educator, theater director*
McRobbie, Michael Alexander *computer scientist, researcher, academic administrator*
Mehlinger, Howard Dean *education educator*
Mickel, Emanuel John *foreign language educator*
Mikesell, John L. *economics professor*
Mobley, Tony Allen *foundation administrator, former dean, recreation educator*
Moore, Ward Wilfred *medical educator*
Moran, Emilio Federico *anthropology and ecology educator*
Mostafa, Javed *information scientist, educator*
Nolan, Val, Jr., *biologist, lawyer*
Nordloh, David Joseph *English language educator*
Nosofsky, Robert M. *psychology educator*
O'Hearn, Robert Raymond *stage designer*
Ostrom, Elinor *political science educator, researcher*
Ostrom, Vincent A(lfred) *political science educator*
Palmer, Judith Grace *university administrator*
Patrick, John Joseph *social sciences educator*
Patterson, James Milton *marketing specialist, educator*
Peebles, Christopher Spalding *anthropologist, educator, dean, academic administrator*
Peters, Dennis Gail *chemist*
Phillips, Harvey G. *musician, soloist, music educator, arts consultant*
Pollock, Robert Elwood *nuclear scientist*
Prosser, Franklin Pierce *computer scientist*
Purdom, Paul Walton, Jr., *computer scientist*
Puri, Madan Lal *mathematics professor*
Ransel, David Lorimer *history professor*
Reingold, David Ami *sociologist, educator*
Rink, Lawrence Donald *cardiologist*
Risinger, C. Frederick *social studies educator*
Robel, Lauren *law educator*
Rosenberg, Samuel Nathan *French and Italian language educator*
Rudolph, Lavere Christian *library director*
Ruesink, Albert William *biologist, plant sciences educator*
Ryan, John William *academic administrator*
Ryan, Marianne Elizabeth *lawyer*
St. John, Edward P. *social sciences educator*
Saunders, W(arren) Phillip, Jr., *economics educator, consultant, author*
Schaich, William L. *physics educator*
Schurz, Scott Clark *journalist, publisher*
Senchuk, Dennis M. *philosopher, educator*
Shreve, Gene Russell *law educator*
Sinor, Denis *Orientalist, educator*
Smith, Daniel C. *finance educator*
Smith, Ronald Thomas *environmental scientist*
Spera, Dominic Gregorio *music educator, writer*
Steinmetz, Joseph Edward *neuroscience and psychology educator*
Stephens, Jay Martin *business owner*
Stines, Betty Irene *artist*
Studwell, William Emmett *librarian, writer*
Svetlova, Marina *ballerina, choreographer, educator*
Temam, Roger M. *mathematician, educator*
Timberlake, William David *psychology educator*
Valdman, Albert *language and linguistics educator*
von Furstenberg, George Michael *economics educator, researcher*
Walbridge, John *foreign language educator*
Walling, Donovan Robert *educational book editor*
Ward-Steinman, Patrice Madura *music educator*
Weaver, David Hugh *journalism educator, communications researcher*
Webb, Charles Haizlip, Jr., *retired university dean*
Weinberg, Eugene David *microbiologist, educator*
Wells, Kimberly K. *not-for-profit organization executive*
Wentworth, Jack Roberts *business educator, consultant*
Williams, Camilla *soprano, voice educator*

Bluffton
Brockmann, William Frank *medical facility administrator*
Elliott, Barbara Jean *librarian*
Lawson, William Hogan, III, *electrical motor manufacturing executive*
Pitts, Neal Chase *rheumatologist*

Boonville
Campbell, Edward Adolph *judge, electrical engineer*

Brownstown
Robertson, Joseph Edmond *grain processing company executive*
Robertson, Richard Robert *grain milling executive*

Cambridge City
Slonaker, Mary Joanna King *columnist*

Carmel
Capehart, Craig Earl *lawyer*
Chokel, Charles B. *insurance company executive*
Cohen, Marlene Lois *pharmacologist*
Cuneo, Ngaire E. *corporate development executive*
Dick, Rollin Merle *insurance company executive*
Eden, Barbara Janiece *commercial and residential interior designer*
Fadely, James Philip *writer, educator*
Hagerty, Thomas M. *insurance executive*
Hilbert, Stephen C. *former insurance company executive*
Husman, Catherine Bigot *retired insurance company executive, actuary*
Kalwara, Joseph John *engineer*
Kilian, Thomas J. *insurance company executive*
Mahoney, Margaret Ellis *accountant*
McLaughlin, Harry Roll *architect*
Rand, Leon *academic administrator*
Rott, Stephen Ross *biologist, educator*
Rychlak, Joseph Frank *psychology educator, theoretician*
Shea, William J. *insurance company executive*
Shoup, Charles Samuel, Jr., *chemicals and materials executive*
Sukapdjo, Wilma Irene *language educator*
Thomas, John David *musician, composer, arranger, graphic designer, recording engineer, producer, photographer*
Walsh, John Charles *metallurgical company executive*
Wendt, Gary Carl *finance company executive*

Chesterton
Crewe, Albert Victor *physicist, artist, business executive*
Nelson, Paul James *educator*
Petrakis, Harry Mark *author*
Wiemann, Marion Russell, Jr., (Baron of Camster) *biologist*

Columbus
Able, Warren Walter *natural resource company executive, physician*
Abts, Henry William *retired banker*
Binkley, John Frey, Jr., *financial consultant, writer*
Brunner, Ellen Margaret *not-for-profit fundraiser*
Carter, Pamela Lynn *former state attorney general*
Crump, Francis Jefferson, III, *lawyer*
Engelking, Ellen Melinda *textiles executive, manufacturing executive, real estate broker*
Garton, Robert Dean *state legislator*
Harrison, Patrick Woods *lawyer*
Henderson, James Alan *former engine company executive*
Kuehl, Jeffry Steven (Jeff Keel) *performing arts association administrator, actor*
Loughrey, F. Joseph *manufacturing executive*
Matthews, Drexel Gene *quality control executive*
Miller, Joseph Irwin *automotive manufacturing company executive*
Miller, William Irwin *finance company executive*
Shannon, Carolyn Jean *real estate company executive*
Tucker, Thomas Randall *public relations executive*
Williams, Robert Joseph *behavioral health services executive, psychologist*

Corydon
Kelty, Paul David *obstetrician, educator*
Speth, Camille *engineer*
Walker, James Harper *retired security firm executive, writer*

Crawfordsville
Barnes, James John *history educator*
Ford, Andrew Thomas *academic administrator*

Crown Point
Back, Michael Wayne *lawyer*
Dywan, Jeffery Joseph *judge*
Harder, Heather Anne *education educator*
Palmeri, Sharon Elizabeth *freelance writer, community educator*

Danville
Baldwin, Jeffrey Kenton *lawyer, educator*

Baldwin, Patricia Ann *lawyer*

Decatur
Fitzgerald, Robert Hannon, Jr., *orthopedic surgeon*

Demotte
Huff, John David *church administrator*
Mitchell, Timmy J. *principal*

Dune Acres
Martino, Robert Salvatore *orthopedic surgeon*

Dyer
Van Bokkelen, Joseph Scott *prosecutor*

East Chicago
Fortenberry, Delores B. *dean*
Psaltis, Helen *medical and surgical nurse*
Ramos, John C., Jr., *protective services official, educator*
Riddle, Jared Matthew *English educator, actor*
Valia, Hardarshan S. *research scientist*

Elkhart
Drexler, Rudy Matthew, Jr., *professional law enforcement dog trainer*
Eddy, Darlene Mathis *poet, educator*
Free, Helen Murray *chemist, consultant*
Holtz, Glenn Edward *band instrument manufacturing executive*
Kloska, Ronald Frank *manufacturing executive*
Martin, Rex *manufacturing executive*
Mathias, Margaret Grossman *manufacturing company executive, leasing company executive*
Mischke, Frederick Charles *retired manufacturing executive*
Treckelo, Richard M. *lawyer*
Vite, Frank Anthony *realtor*

Elwood
Barnett, Marilyn Doan *secondary education business educator*

Evansville
Baker, Gloria Marie *visual artist, art educator*
Blandford, Dick *electrical engineering and communications educator*
Bodkin, Robert Thomas *lawyer*
Brill, Alan Richard *entrepreneur*
Capshaw, Tommie Dean *judge*
Clouse, John Daniel *lawyer*
Dean, K. Matthew *elementary school educator*
Frary, Charles O., III, (Chuck Frary) *venture capitalist*
Fritz, Edward Lane *dentist*
Gaither, John Francis *accountant, consultant*
Giancola, James J. *bank executive*
Hampel, Robert Edward *advertising executive*
Harrison, Joseph Heavrin *lawyer*
Hoy, George Philip *clergyman, county official*
Jennings, Stephen Grant *academic administrator*
Kimberling, Clark Hershall *mathematics educator, small business owner*
Koch, Robert Louis, II, *manufacturing company executive, mechanical engineer*
McGuire, Brian Lyle *educator, consultant*
Miller, Daniel Raymond *prosecutor*
Muehlbauer, James Herman *manufacturing executive*
Pate, Jack D. *publishing executive*
Penkava, Robert Ray *radiologist, educator*
Price, Charles Lee *science educator*
Raibley, Parvin Rudolph *dentist*
Reed, Helen Skuggedal *law librarian, musician*
Roth, Carolyn Louise *art educator*
Savia, Alfred *conductor*
Shaffer, Michael L. *transportation company executive*
Stamps, Douglas *mechanical engineer, educator*
Streetman, John William, III, *museum official*

Fishers
Baach, Michael L. *internist*
Christenson, Le Roy Howard *missions consultant*
Gatto, Louis Constantine *educational association administrator*

Fort Wayne
Andorfer, Donald Joseph *university president*
Balthaser, Linda Irene *retired academic administrator*
Beineke, Lowell Wayne *mathematics professor*
Bunkowske, Eugene Walter *religious studies educator*
Burns, Thagrus Asher *manufacturing company executive, former life insurance company executive*
Cain, Tim J. *lawyer*
Cast, Anita Hursh *small business owner*
Colvin, Sherrill William *lawyer*
Cummings, William Robert, Jr., *business executive*
Curtis, Douglas Homer *small business owner*
Cutshall-Hayes, Diane Marion *elementary school educator*
Dragnev, Peter D. *mathematician, educator*
Dunsire, P(eter) Kenneth *insurance company executive*
Frost, Helen Marie *writer*
Hannigan, John Dennis *logistics engineer*
Heger, James Joseph *internist, cardiologist*
Helmke, Paul (Walter Paul Helmke Jr.) *mayor, lawyer*
Hirschy, Gordon Harold *real estate broker, auctioneer*
Inskeep, Richard Glenn *publishing executive*
Klugman, Stephan Craig *newspaper editor*
Krull, Jeffrey Robert *library director*
Lebamoff, Ivan Argire *lawyer*
Lee, Shuishih Sage *pathologist*
Lee, Timothy Earl *international agency executive, paralegal*
Lee, William Charles *judge*
Lutz, James Michael *political scientist, educator, writer*
Lyons, Jerry Lee *mechanical engineer*
Mann, David William *minister*
Marine, Clyde Lockwood *agricultural business consultant*
Mather, George Ross *clergy member*
Miller, Dawn L. *literature educator*
Moses, Winfield Carroll, Jr., *state legislator, construction company executive*
Owen, Dave A. *finance executive*
Oxley, Ann *television executive*
Pellegrene, Thomas James, Jr., *editor, researcher*
Pope, Mark Andrew *lawyer, university administrator*
Rhoad, Richard E. *healthcare executive*
Richardson, Joseph Hill *physician, medical educator*
Ridderheim, Mary Margaret *psychotherapist*
Rifkin, Leonard *metals company executive*
Robertson, Richard Stuart *insurance holding company executive*
Robinson, Wendy Y. *school system administrator*
Roby, Daniel Arthur *lawyer*
Romary, Thomas Gerald *mathematician, educator, writer*
Sack, James McDonald, Jr., *radio and television producer, marketing executive*
Sasko, Nancy Ann *insurance agent*
Scheetz, Sister Mary JoEllen *English language educator*
Schmidt, Donald J. *councilman, educator*
Schweickart, Jim *advertising executive, broadcast executive, consultant*
Shaffer, Paul E. *retired banker*
Shannon, Angela Lynn *minister*
Shoaff, Thomas Mitchell *lawyer*
Smith, Maxwell Paul *retired lawyer*
Steiner, Paul Andrew *retired insurance executive*
Stevenson, Kenneth Lee *chemist, educator*
Stolba, K. Marie *music educator*
Streeter, Robert Davenport *electrical engineer, consultant*
Tourkow, Joshua Isaac *lawyer*
Ushenko, Audrey Andreyevna *painter, art historian, educator*
Vachon, Marilyn Ann *retired insurance company executive*
Wartell, Michael Alan *academic administrator*
Watkinson, Patricia Grieve *museum director*
Weatherford, George Edward *civil engineer*

Fortville
VanArsdel, Thomas Paul *architect, engineering consultant*

Frankfort
Borland, Kathryn Kilby *author*
Stonehill, Lloyd Herschel *gas industry executive, mechanical engineer*

Franklin
Hamner, Lance Dalton *prosecutor*
Launey, George Volney, III, *economics professor*
Nuwer, Henry Joseph (Hank Nuwer) *journalist, educator*

Gary
Bennett, Richard Carl *social worker*
Hall, James Rayford, III, *political science educator*
Hall, John Henry *lawyer, historian, educator*
Hozo, Iztok *mathematician, educator*
Iatridis, Panayotis George *medical educator*
Isla, Exu Reidemer Quero *corrections professional, lawyer, author*
Johnson, Jerome *engineer*
Kern, Paul Bentley *historian, educator*
King, Marcia *library director*
Poulard, Jean Victor *political scientist, educator*
Prettyman, Wendy Pettit *management company executive*
Smith, Vernon G. *education educator, state representative*
Stephens, Paul Alfred *dentist*
Woodson, Porsha Marie *speech pathology/audiology services professional*

Goshen
Davis, Cole (Coleman Davis III) *recreational vehicle manufacturing executive*
Meyer, Albert James *educational researcher*
Roberts, Mary Lois *music educator*
Stoltzfus, Victor Ezra *retired university president*
Whitcraft, James Richard, Jr., *accountant*

Granger
Craypo, Charles *labor economics educator*
Miller, Callix Edwin *manufacturing executive, consultant*
Morgan, Ardys Nord *school improvement consultant*
Thomas, Debi (Debra J. Thomas) *ice skater*

Greencastle
Anderson, John Robert *retired mathematics educator*
Bottoms, Robert Garvin *academic administrator*
Dittmer, John Avery *history professor*
Hall, David *newspaper editor*
Ross, Scott R. *psychologist, educator*
Spicer, Harold Otis *retired English language educator, communications educator*
Weiss, Robert Orr *speech educator*

Greenfield
Powdrill, Gary Leo *production operations manager*
Wolff, Ronald Keith *toxicologist, researcher*

Greensburg
Black, Marsha Jean *art educator, writer*

Greenwood
Broscoe, Peter A. *mortgage company executive, consultant*
Grube, Elizabeth *investment company executive*
Saint-Pierre, Michael Robert *funeral director, consultant*
Tomlin, Jeanne Brannon *real estate broker, small business owner*
Van Valer, Joe Ned *lawyer, land developer*
Waldkoetter, Raymond Oliver *psychologist, consultant*

Griffith
Luetschwager, Mary Susan *transportation company professional*

Hagerstown
Bex, Brian William Louis *educational administrator*

Hammond
Ashbach, David Laurence *internist, nephrologist*
Chandler, Melanie Lynn *surgical technologist, paralegal*
Curiel, Carolyn *ambassador*
Diamond, Eugene Christopher *lawyer, hospital administrator*
Fehring, Mary Ann *secondary school educator*
Gealt, Michael A. *environmental microbiologist, educator*
Hansen, Jack Winsor *musician, educator*
Kamalipour, Yahya R. *communications educator*
Kopischke, Chris David *mechanical engineer*
Pierson, Edward Samuel *engineering educator, consultant*
Ruman, Saul I. *lawyer*
Schroer, Edmund Armin *retired utility company executive*
Smokvina, Gloria Jacqueline *nursing educator*
Weber, Elsa Koenig *pre-school educator*
Woodson, Adrianne Marie *secondary school educator and coordinator*

Hanover
Batchvarova, Madlen Todorova *music educator, conductor*
Calkins, Ralph Nelson *economics professor*
Heck, Richard T. *tree farmer*
Nickels, Ruth Elizabeth *band director*

Highland
DeVaney, Cynthia Ann *retired elementary school educator, real estate instructor*
Forsythe, Randall Newman *paralegal, educator*
Sedia, John Michael *lawyer*
Steen, Lowell Harrison *retired physician*

Hobart
Hanley, Roberta Lynn *alternative education coordinator, educator*
Seeley, Mark *agronomist*

Howe
Bowerman, Ann Louise *writer, genealogist, educator*

Huntertown
Becker, Cheri A(nn) *marketing professional, business consultant*

Huntington
Brown, Robert Clark, Jr., *county official*
Eggleton, Patrick J. *mathematician, educator*
Fairchild, Mark Robin *theology studies educator*
Michelson, Paul E. *historian, educator*

Indianapolis
Abdul-Jabbar, Karim *retired professional football player*
Adamak, M. Jeanelle *broadcast executive*
Afshar, Nader *application developer*
Albright, Terrill D. *lawyer*
Aliev, Eldar *artistic director, choreographer, educator*
Allen, David James *lawyer*
Allen, Stephen D(ean) *pathologist, microbiologist*
Alvarez, Thomas *foundation administrator, writer, consultant*
Antich-Carr, Rose Ann *state legislator*
Aprison, Morris Herman *retired biochemist, experimental and theoretical neurobiologist, emeritus educator*
Armitage, Robert Allen *lawyer*
Atkins, Clayton H. *family physician, epidemiologist, educator*
Atkins, Steven *construction executive, contractor*
Austin, Terri Jo *state representative*
Badger, David Harry *lawyer*
Baetzhold, Howard George *English language educator*
Baker, Jerry L. *protective services official*
Barcus, Robert Gene *retired educational association administrator*
Barker, Sarah Evans *judge*
Bates, Gerald Earl *bishop emeritus*
Batten, Kimberly Jane *Olympic athlete*
Becker, Karla Lynn *systems analyst*
Becker, Vaneta G. *state representative*
Beckwith, Lewis Daniel *lawyer*
Beltz, Homer Ferguson *radiologist, healthcare executive*
Bepko, Gerald Lewis *university administrator, law educator, lecturer, consultant, lawyer*
Bergstein, Jerry Michael *nephrologist*
Beyer, Werner William *retired English educator*
Biller, Jose *neurologist*
Bindley, William Edward *pharmaceutical executive*
Bird, Larry Joe *professional athletics manager, former professional basketball coach*
Blaydes, June Louise *volunteer*
Bloch, Richard *physician*
Blythe, James David, II, *lawyer*
Boehm, Peggy *state agency administrator*
Boehm, Theodore Reed *judge*
Boldt, Michael Herbert *lawyer*
Bolin, Daniel Paul *music educator*
Bonaventura, Leo Mark *gynecologist, educator*
Booth, Nancy Davis *voice educator*
Born, Samuel Roydon, II, *lawyer*
Borns, Robert Aaron *real estate developer*
Bowser, Anita Olga *state legislator, education educator*
Braham, Delphine Doris *accountant, government official*
Brand, Myles *academic administrator*
Brandt, Ira Kive *pediatrician, medical geneticist*
Brash, Susan Kay *principal*
Brater, Donald Craig *dean, educator*
Brauer, Keith E. *medical products executive*
Braun, Robert Clare *retired association and advertising executive*
Breier, Alan *pharmaceutical executive*
Brenner, Mark Lee *academic administrator, physiologist, educator*
Brickley, Richard Agar *retired surgeon*
Brizzi, Carl *prosecutor*
Broadie, Thomas Allen *surgeon, educator*
Broden, John E. *state legislator*
Brooks, Susan W. *prosecutor*
Broome, Marion *dean*
Brown, Edwin Wilson, Jr., *preventive medicine physician, educator*
Broxmeyer, Hal Edward *medical educator*
Budak, Mary Kay *state legislator*
Buechlein, Daniel Mark *archbishop*
Buford-Bailey, Tonja Yevette *Olympic athlete*
Buhner, Byron Bevis *health science facility administrator*
Burks, Keith W. *pharmaceutical executive*
Burr, David Bentley *anatomy educator*
Caine, Virginia A. *city health department administrator*
Caperton, Albert Franklin *retired newspaper editor*
Carey, Edward Marshel, Jr., *accountant*
Carlisle, Rick *professional basketball coach*
Carney, Joseph Buckingham *lawyer*
Carter, Steve *state attorney general*
Catchings, Tamika Devonne *professional basketball player*
Chase, Alyssa Ann *editor*
Cheng, Liang *pathologist*
Choplin, John M., II, *lawyer*
Christen, Arden Gale *dental educator, researcher, consultant*
Chuang, Tsu-Yi *dermatologist, epidemiologist, educator*
Cilella, Salvatore George, Jr., *museum director*
Clanin, Douglas Edward *editor, researcher*
Clark, Charles M., Jr., *medical school administrator*
Clary, Keith Uhl *retired employee relations executive*
Cleary, Robert Emmet *gynecologist, infertility specialist*
Cliff, Johnnie Marie *mathematics and chemistry educator*
Coffey, Charles Moore *communication research professional, writer*
Cohen, Gabriel Murrel *editor, publisher*
Cohen, Morton A. *venture capitalist*
Cohoat, Matthew A. *real estate company executive*
Colander-Richardson, LaTasha *Olympic athlete*
Coleman, John Joseph, III, *surgery educator*
Comiskey, Nancy *newspaper editor*
Conour, William Frederick *lawyer*
Coomer, Steven Robert *music educator, musician*
Corkins, Mark R. *physician, pediatric gastroenterologist*
Corley, William Edward *hospital administrator*
Cortopassi, Ray *newscaster*
Cox, Archibald, Jr., *investment company executive*
Cramer, Betty F. *life insurance company executive*
Crosser, Richard H. *real estate company executive*
Crow, Paul Abernathy, Jr., *retired minister*
Culp, Charles William *lawyer*
Daly, Walter Joseph *medical educator*
D'Amico, Carol *educational administrator*
Dumush, Teresa Marie *research scientist*
Davis, Edgar Glenn *science and health policy executive*
Davis, Katherine Lyon *lieutenant governor*
Davis, Kenneth Wayne *English language educator, business communication consultant*
Dawes, Dominique *Olympic athlete*
Dembrowski, Nancy J. *state senator*
Dempsey, Cedric W. *former sports association administrator*
Dere, Willard Honglen *internist, educator*
Dickenson-Hazard, Nancy Ann *pediatric nurse practitioner, consultant*
Dickinson, Mae *state legislator*
Dickinson, Richard Donald Nye *clergyman, educator, theological seminary administrator*
Dickson, Brent E(llis) *state supreme court justice*
Dillin, S. Hugh *federal judge*
Dimas, Trent *Olympic athlete, gymnast*
Dollens, Ronald W. *pharmaceuticals company executive*
Donovan, Anne *professional basketball coach, coach*
Downs, Thomas K. *lawyer*
Drummond, Jon *Olympic athlete*
Dungy, Tony *professional football coach*
Dutton, Clarence Benjamin *retired lawyer*
Dutton, Stephen James *lawyer*
Dyken, Mark Lewis, Jr., *neurologist, educator*
Dykstra, Clifford Elliot *chemistry educator, researcher*
Eble, John Nelson *pathologist, oncology researcher*
Eigen, Howard *pediatrician, educator*
Einhorn, Lawrence Henry *medical educator*
Eisenberg, Paul Richard *cardiologist, consultant, educator*
Elberger, Ronald Edward *lawyer*
Emhardt, Charles David *lawyer*
Everly, Jack *conductor*
Ewbank, Thomas Peters *lawyer, retired banker*
Ewick, Ray (Charles Ray Ewick) *librarian*
Fastenau, Philip S. *neuropsychologist, educator*
Favor-Hamilton, Suzanne Marie *track and field athlete, Olympian*
Featherstonaugh, Henry Gordon *psychologist, health facility administrator*
Feng, Gen-sheng *medical educator, researcher*
Fibiger, Hans Christian *science administrator*
Fife, Wilmer Krafft *chemistry professor*
Fine, Pamela B. *newspaper editor*
Finley, Katherine Mandusic *professional society administrator*
Fischer, A. Charles *pharmaceutical executive*
Fischler, Barbara Brand *librarian*
Fisher, Gene Lawrence *financial executive*
FitzGibbon, Daniel Harvey *lawyer*
Fleming, Marcella *journalist*
Fletcher, Brady Jones *vocational education career specialist*
Florestano, Dana Joseph *architect*
Fortner, Nell *professional athletics coach*
Foster, Kennard P. *magistrate judge*
Franson, Timothy Raymond *pharmaceutical executive, epidemiologist*
French, Tarence Wade, Sr., *minister*
Frick, David Rhoads *lawyer*
Frisch, Fred I. *real estate executive*
Fruehwald, Kristin G. *lawyer*
Funk, David Albert *retired law educator*
Funk, James William, Jr., *insurance agency administrator, business owner*
Furlow, Mack Vernon, Jr., *retired financial executive, treasurer*
Ganassi, Chip *professional race car executive, owner*
Ganote, Angela *newscaster*
Gantz, Richard Alan *museum administrator*
Gard, Beverly J. *state legislator*
Garmel, Marion Bess Simon *retired arts journalist*
Gaunce, Michael Paul *insurance company executive*
Gerdes, Ralph Donald *fire safety consultant*
Ghetti, Bernardino Francesco *neuropathologist, neurobiology researcher*
Gilliland, John Campbell, II, *lawyer*
Gilman, Alan B. *restaurant company executive*
Givan, Richard Martin *retired judge*
Glasscock, Larry Claborn *insurance company executive*

Gnat, Raymond Earl *librarian*
Goldblatt, Lawrence I. *dean, educator, researcher*
Golden, Charles Edward *pharmaceutical company executive*
Goldstein, Paul Robert *management company executive, consultant*
Goodman, Dwight *manufacturing executive*
Goodwin, William Maxwell *financial executive*
Gooldy, Patricia Alice *retired elementary education educator*
Green, Morris *pediatrician, educator*
Greene, Maurice *Olympic athlete, track and field athlete*
Gregory, Valiska *writer*
Greist, Mary Coffey *dermatologist*
Griffith, Roy Lloyd *design engineer*
Grosfeld, Jay Lazar *surgeon, educator*
Hamilton, David F. *judge*
Hamilton, Sharon J. *literature educator, dean, writer*
Hamm, Richard L. *church administrator*
Hancock, Joan Herrin *retired executive search company executive*
Handel, David Jonathan *healthcare administrator*
Hansell, Richard Stanley *obstetrician, educator, gynecologist, educator*
Harden, Anita Joyce *nurse*
Harrison, Alvin *Olympic athlete*
Harrison, Calvin *Olympic athlete*
Harrison, Marvin *professional football player*
Hartsfield, James Kennedy, Jr., *orthodontist, geneticist*
Hefner, Thomas L. *real estate company executive*
Hegel, Carolyn Marie *farm bureau executive*
Heger, Martin L. *bank executive*
Helveston, Eugene McGillis *pediatric ophthalmologist, educator*
Hennagan, Monique *Olympic athlete*
Henry, Barbara A. *publishing executive*
Hershman, Brandt *state legislator*
Hitchens, William Randolph (Randy Hitchens) *health care executive*
Holden, Robert Watson *radiologist, educator, university dean*
Holt, John Manly *retired corporate lawyer*
Horn, Brenda Sue *lawyer*
Houser, Nathan *philosopher, educator*
Hovde, F. Boyd *lawyer*
Huffman, Rosemary Adams *lawyer, corporate executive*
Humphreys, Katie *health agency administrator*
Hunt, Robert Chester *construction company executive*
Hunt, Robert G. *construction company executive*
Ilgen, Dorothy L. *arts foundation executive*
Inui, Thomas Spencer *physician, educator*
Irsay, James Steven *professional football team owner*
Irwin, Glenn Ward, Jr., *medical educator, physician, university official*
Israelov, Rhoda *financial planner, writer, entrepreneur*
Jackson, Valerie Pascuzzi *radiologist, educator*
James, Edgerrin *professional football player*
Jarvis, Debra Jean *fire chief, consultant*
Jegen, Lawrence A., III, *law educator*
Jewett, John Rhodes *real estate executive*
Johnson, David Allen *vocalist, minister, lyricist, investment advisor*
Johnson, James P. *religious organization executive*
Johnson, Michael *former international athlete*
Johnston, Cyrus Conrad, Jr., *medical educator*
Johnstone, Robert Philip *lawyer*
Jones, Marion *track and field athlete*
Jones, Robert Brooke *microbiologist, educator, associate dean*
Kahlenbeck, Howard, Jr., *lawyer*
Kalsi, Swadesh Singh *lawyer, educator*
Kappes, Philip Spangler *lawyer*
Kashani, Hamid Reza *lawyer, computer consultant*
Kaufman, Barton Lowell *financial services company executive*
Kautzman, John Fredrick *lawyer*
Kaye, Gordon Israel *pathologist, anatomist, educator*
Kendall, Rebecca O. *lawyer, pharmaceutical company executive*
Kenley, Luke *state legislator*
Kennedy, Russell Edward *academic administrator*
Kernan, Joseph E., III, *governor*
Kerr, William Andrew *lawyer, educator*
Khurana, Poonam *neonatologist*
King, J. B. *medical device company executive, lawyer*
Kirk, Carol *lawyer*
Kirkham, James Alvin *manufacturing executive*
Kirkpatrick, Robert Hugh *communications executive*
Kittle, Jim, Jr., *state representative, political party administrator*
Kleiman, David Harold *lawyer*
Klika, Cristine M. *state official*
Klinker, Sheila Ann J. *state legislator, middle school educator*
Knebel, Donald Earl *lawyer*
Knoebel, Suzanne Buckner *cardiologist, educator*
Koeller, Robert Marion *lawyer, director*
Krasean, Thomas Karl *historian*
Krauss, John Landers *public policy, urban affairs consultant, mediator, arbitrator*
Krueger, Betty Jane *telecommunications company executive*
Labsvirs, Janis *economist, educator*
LaCrosse, James *retail executive*
Lacy, Andre Balz *industrial executive*
Lamkin, Martha Dampf *lawyer*
Landis, Larry Seabrook *state agency administrator*
Landske, Dorothy Suzanne (Sue Landske) *state legislator*
Lau, Pauline Young *chemist*
Lawson, Connie *state legislator*
Lawson, Linda *state senator*
Lee, Kristi *broadcast executive, reporter*
Lemberger, Louis *pharmacologist, physician*
Leuck, Claire M. *state legislator*
Lewis, Brian *Olympic athlete*
Lewis, Jeff *construction company executive*
Lipshaw, Jeffrey Marc *lawyer, chemicals executive*
Lisher, John Leonard *lawyer*
Livers, Catherine McGhee *writer*
Lofton, Thomas Milton *lawyer*
Long, Clarence William *accountant*
Long, William Allan *retired forest products company executive*
Lorell, Beverly H. *medical products executive*
Loveday, William John *hospital administrator*
Lowe, Louis Robert, Jr., *lawyer*
Lowe, Mary Katherine *technology company executive, writer*
Lubbers, Teresa S. *state legislator, public relations executive*
Luerssen, Thomas George *pediatric neurosurgeon, educator*
Lumeng, Lawrence *physician, educator*
Lyst, John Henry *former newspaper editor*
Lytle, L(arry) Ben *insurance company executive, lawyer*
MacDougall, John Duncan *surgeon*
Madura, James Anthony *surgical educator*
Mahomed, Yousuf *physician, cardiothoracic surgeon*
Maine, Michael Roland *lawyer*
Malik, David Joseph *chemist, educator*
Manders, Karl Lee *neurosurgeon*
Manning, Peyton *professional football player*
Marendt, Candace L. *state legislator*
Marsh, Michael Lawrence *track and field athlete*
Marshall, Carolyn Ann M. *church official*
Mason, Thomas Alexander *historian, educator, author*
Maxwell, Florence Hinshaw *civic worker*
Mays, Carolene *state representative*
Mays, William G. *chemical company executive*
McCarthy, Harold Charles *retired insurance company executive*
McCarthy, Kevin Bart *lawyer*
McConnell, William F., Jr., *medical products executive*
Mc Farland, H. Richard *food company executive*
McIntyre, Lola Mazza *music educator*
McKeand, Patrick Joseph *newspaper publisher, educator*
McKinney, E. Kirk, Jr., *retired insurance company executive*
McKinney, Larry J. *federal judge*
McLaughlin, Sherry *association administrator*
McTurnan, Lee Bowes *lawyer*
Merrill, William H., Jr., *lawyer, corporate professional*
Merritt, James W., Jr., *state legislator, real estate developer*
Metz, Anthony J., III, *federal judge*
Metzner, Barbara Stone *university counselor*
Meyer, Fred William, Jr., *memorial parks executive*
Mikelsons, J. George *air aerospace transportation executive*
Miles-Clark, Jearl *olympic athlete, track and field*
Miller, David W. *lawyer*
Miller, Reginald Wayne *professional basketball player*
Miniear, J. Dederick *software company executive, consultant*
Mirsky, Arthur *geologist, department chairman*
Miyamoto, Richard Takashi *otolaryngologist*
Moelhman, Amy Jo *social worker*
Molitoris, Bruce Albert *nephrologist, educator*
Mosbaugh, Phillip George *urologist, educator*
Nass, Connie Kay *state auditor*
Neff, Robert Matthew *lawyer, financial services executive*
Niederberger, Jane *information technology executive*
Noe, Cindy J. *state representative*
Norins, Arthur Leonard *physician, educator*
Norman, LaLander Stadig *retired insurance company executive*
Norwalk, Kelli Curran *retail executive, entrepreneur*
Nugent, Johnny Wesley *state legislator, tractor company executive*
Nurnberger, John I., Jr., *psychiatrist, educator*
Nyhart, Eldon Howard *employee benefits consultant, lawyer*
Ochs, Sidney *neurophysiology educator*
Oklak, Dennis D. *real estate company executive*
Padgett, Gregory Lee *lawyer*
Page, Curtis Matthewson *minister*
Palmer, Robert P. *professional association executive*
Paul, Stephen Howard *lawyer*
Peribere, Jerome A. *agricultural products executive*
Pesut, Daniel J. *nursing educator*
Petersen, James L. *lawyer*
Peterson, Bart *mayor*
Peterson, Erling Winston *religion educator*
Pettigrew, Antonio *Olympic athlete*
Phelps, Jaycie *gymnast, Olympic athlete*
Phillips, Charles W. *state agency administrator*
Plater, William Marmaduke *English language educator, academic administrator*
Poel, Robert Walter *air force officer, physician*
Poinsette, Donald Eugene *business executive, value management consultant*
Pursley, Julie *newscaster*
Pyle, R. Michael *wholesale distribution executive, educator*
Quarles, Beth *civil rights administrator*
Ramadan, Nabih M. *pharmaceutical company official, educator*
Ramos, Jose A. *engineering educator*
Rati, Robert Dean *data processing executive*
Raughter, John B. *editor*
Recker, Thomas Edward *fraternal organization executive*
Reed, Suellen Kinder *school system administrator*
Reuben, Lawrence Mark *lawyer*
Reynolds, Robert Hugh *lawyer*
Rhoades, Rodney Allen *physiologist, educator*
Richardson, Kathy Kreag *state legislator*
Richter, Judith Anne *pharmacology educator*
Riegsecker, Marvin Dean *pharmacist, state senator*
Risdon, Michael Paul *manufacturing executive*
Roberts, David *airport executive*
Roberts, Wilbur Eugene *dental educator, research scientist, wine importer*
Roberts, William Everett *lawyer*
Robinson, Keith *newspaper editor*
Rogers, Earline S. *state legislator*
Rogers, Robert Ernest *medical educator*
Rokita, Todd *secretary of state*
Ross, Edward *cardiologist*
Roth, Lawrence Max *pathologist, educator*
Rucker, Robert D. *state supreme court justice*
Russell, David Williams *lawyer*
Russell, Frank Eli *retired newspaper publishing executive*
Rusthoven, Peter James *lawyer*
Rutledge, Joanne *artist, consultant*
Ryder, Henry C(lay) *lawyer*
Ryder, Kenneth William *pathologist, educator*
Ryerson, Dennis *editor*
Sachs, Stephen Mark *political scientist, consultant*
Salentine, Thomas James *pharmaceutical company executive*
Santini, Gino *marketing professional*
Santos, Richard J. *association administrator*
Scaletta, Phillip Ralph, III, *lawyer*
Schamberger, Marcus S. *pediatric cardiologist*
Scheumann, John B. *construction executive*
Schlegel, Fred Eugene *lawyer*
Schmetzer, Alan David *psychiatrist*
Scholer, Sue Wyant *state legislator*
Scism, Daniel Reed *lawyer*
Scott, Thomas Clifford *lawyer, writer*
SerVaas, Beurt Richard *manufacturing executive*
SerVaas, Cory *health sciences association administrator*
Shaffer, Alfred Garfield (Terry Shaffer) *retired service organization executive*
Shepard, Randall Terry *state supreme court chief justice*
Sherman, Stuart *internist, gastroenterologist*
Shi, Lizheng *health economist*
Shideler, Shirley Ann Williams *lawyer*
Shields, V. Sue *federal magistrate judge*
Shula, Robert Joseph *lawyer*
Silver, Gregory K. *lawyer*
Simmons, Roberta Johnson *public relations firm executive*
Simon, David *real estate company officer*
Simon, Melvon *real estate company officer*
Simpson, Vi *state senator*
Sipes, Connie W. *state legislator, educator*
Skillman, Becky Sue *state legislator*
Slaughter Andrew, Anne *lawyer*
Slaymaker, Gene Arthur *public relations executive*
Smith, Carson Clay *business executive*
Smith, Donald Archie *religion business executive, consultant*
Smith, Donald Eugene *healthcare facility management administrator owner*
Smith, James Warren *pathologist, educator, microbiologist, parasitologist*
Smith, Keith *protective services official*
Sokolov, Richard Saul *real estate company executive*
Solomon, Marilyn Kay *educator, consultant*
Sommer, James Koch *lawyer*
Sowers, Jodi Louise *music educator*
Sparks, Donald Eugene *interscholastic activities association executive*
Speth, Gerald Lennus *education and business consultant*
Stayton, Thomas George *lawyer*
Steger, Evan Evans, III, *retired lawyer*
Stehman, Frederick Bates *gynecologic oncologist, educator*
Stern, Phyllis Noerager *nursing educator*
Sterrett, Steven E. *real estate company officer*
Storhoff, Diana Carmack *research scientist*
Storm, Janet S. *psychiatric social worker*
Strain, James Arthur *lawyer*
Sullivan, Frank, Jr., *state supreme court justice*
Summers, Vanessa *state legislator*
Surawicz, Borys *physician, educator*
Sutherland, Donald Gray *retired lawyer*
Sutton, Gregory Paul *obstetrician, gynecologist*
Suzuki, Hidetaro *violinist*
Svirsky, Mario Alfredo *biomedical engineer*
Sweezy, John William *political party official*
Tabler, Susan Beidler *lawyer*
Taurel, Sidney *pharmaceutical executive*
Taylor, Angelo *Olympic athlete*
Tedesco, Kristi *newscaster*
Todd, Zane Grey *retired utilities executive*
Torrence, Gwen *Olympic athlete*
Torres, Judith *lab administrator*
Towne, Edgar Arthur *theologian, educator*
Townsend, Earl C., Jr., *lawyer, writer*
Tracy, Paul Anthony *race car driver*
Trahan, Grace *newscaster*
Tuchman, Steven Leslie *lawyer, consul*
Turner, Barbara A. *former dance company executive*
Turner, James Lee *lawyer*
Vasser, Jimmy *professional race car driver*
Venzago, Mario *conductor*
Vereen, Robert Charles *retired trade association executive*
Walker, Frank Dilling *market research executive*
Wallace, Edna Marie *paralegal*
Walther, Joseph Edward *health facility administrator, retired physician*
Wampler, Lloyd Charles *retired lawyer*
Ware, J(oe) Anthony *cardiologist*
Watanabe, August Masaru *physician, medical educator*
Watkins, Harold Robert *minister*
Watkins, Sherry Lynne *elementary school educator*
Waymire, Bonnie Gladine *nursing administrator*
Weaver, Martha *newscaster*
Weber, George *oncology and pharmacology researcher, educator*
Weeks, A. Ray *real estate company executive*
Weinberger, Myron Hilmar *medical educator*
Weisfeld, Eric *newscaster*
Welch, Peggy *state representative*
Wensits, David L. *aerospace executive*
Whale, Arthur Richard *retired lawyer*
Wheeler, Daniel Scott *management executive, editor*
Wheeler, Harold H. *state legislator, utility contractor*
White, James Patrick *law educator*
Wilkinson, Laura *Olympic athlete*
Williams, Bernard *Olympic athlete*
Williams, Gregory Keith *accountant*
Willing, Katherine *former state legislator*
Wilson, Fred M., II, *ophthalmologist, educator*
Winters, Peter Lee *dermatologist*
Wise, Rita J. *writer*
Wishard, Gordon Davis *lawyer*
Wolf, Katie Louise *state legislator*
Wolfe, Elaine Claire Daughetee *junior high school educator*
Woodring, DeWayne Stanley *religious organization administrator*
Woody, John Frederick *retired secondary education educator*
Woolling, Kenneth Rau *vascular internist*
Wright, David Burton *retired newspaper publishing company executive*
Wu, Min *cell biologist, researcher, educator*
Yeager, Joseph Heizer, Jr., *lawyer*
Yee, Robert Donald *ophthalmologist*
Yip-Schneider, Michele Terrell *researcher*
Young, Philip Howard *library director*
Young, Richard D. *state legislator*
Yovits, Marshall Clinton *computer and information science educator, university dean*
Zheng, Qi-Huang *chemist, educator*
Zipes, Douglas Peter *cardiologist, researcher*
Zurick, John *consultant, former dance company director*

Jasper
Brenner, Raymond Anthony *priest*
Newman, Leonard Jay *retail jewel merchant, gemologist*
Schneider, Robert F. *treasurer*
Thyen, James C. *furniture company executive*

Jeffersonville
Hagan, Michael Charles *transporation executive*
Hoehn, Elmer Louis *lawyer, state and federal agency administrator, educator, consultant*
Reisert, Charles Edward, Jr., *real estate executive*
Walburn, John Clifford *mental health services professional*

Kendallville
Martin, Daniel Francis *small business owner*

Knightstown
Richardson, Shirley Maxine *editor*

Knox
Gudeman, Leroy Dennis *lawyer*
Weiss, Randall A. *television and radio producer, supermarket executive*

Kokomo
Cameron, Ann M. *language educator*
Coppock, Janet Elaine *mental health nurse*
Highlen, Larry Wade *music educator, piano rebuilder, tuner*
Hockney, Dean Wesley *editor, writer*
Maugans, John Conrad *lawyer*
Person, Ruth Janssen *academic administrator*
Ranney, Sandra Kay *artist, fine arts and humanities educator*
Stein, Eleanor Bankoff *judge*
Wysong, Earl Edward *sociologist, educator*

Kouts
Miller, Sarabeth *secondary school educator*

La Porte
Johnson, Bruce Ross *elementary school educator*
Morris, Leigh Edward *mayor, retired hospital executive officer*

Lafayette
Achgill, Ralph Kenneth *retired research scientist*
Bodine, Gerald Bradley *composer, educator*
Brewster, James Henry *retired chemistry educator*
Brown, Herbert Charles *chemistry professor*
Buckles, Judith Ann *dental educator, program administrator*
Caldwell, Barrett Scott *industrial engineering educator*
Chen, Qingyan *educator*
de Branges de Bourcia, Louis *mathematics professor*
Drazin, Michael Peter *mathematician, researcher*
Etzel, James Edward *environmental engineering educator*
Feuer, Henry *retired chemist*
Finch, Robert Jonathan *communications engineer, consultant*
Geddes, LaNelle Evelyn *nurse, physiologist*
Geddes, Leslie Alexander *engineering educator, forensic engineer, physiologist*
Gordon, Irene Marlow *radiology educator*
Gustafson, Winthrop Adolph *aeronautical and astronautical engineering educator*
Hardin, Lowell Stewart *retired economics educator*
Harris, Donald Wayne *research scientist*
Hart, Russell Holiday *retired lawyer*
Hasegawa, Paul M. *horticulturist, educator*
Helmuth, Ned D. *certified financial planner*
Huynh, Victor C. *process engineer*
Kanne, Michael Stephen *federal judge*
Langston, Edward Lee *physician, pharmacist*
Liley, Peter Edward *retired mechanical engineering educator*
Lindenlaub, John Charles *electrical engineer, educator*
Loeffler, Frank Joseph *physicist, educator*
Maickel, Roger Philip *pharmacologist, educator*
McBride, Angela Barron *nursing educator*
McKowen, Dorothy Keeton *librarian, educator, consultant*
Meyer, Brud Richard *retired pharmaceutical company executive*
Mobley, Emily Ruth *library dean, educator*
Nicholson, Ralph Lester *botanist, educator*
Osborn, John Robert *retired mechanical engineer*
Ott, Karl Otto *nuclear engineer, consultant*
Porile, Norbert Thomas *chemistry professor*
Schönemann, Peter Hans *psychology educator*
Schweickert, Richard Justus *psychologist, educator*
Shook, James Creighton *real estate executive*
Smith, Kenneth Dale *civil engineer, consultant*
Troutner, Joanne Johnson *director, consultant, secondary school educator*
Whistler, Roy Lester *chemist, educator, industrialist*

Lagrange
Brown, George E. *judge, educator*
Glick, Cynthia Susan *lawyer*
Schultess, LeRoy Kenneth *lawyer, consultant*

Lagro
Lynn, Richard Jo *freelance/self-employed illustrator, journalist, cartoonist*

Lanesville
Cleveland, Peggy Rose Richey *cytotechnologist*

Lawrenceburg
Dautel, Charles Shreve *retired mining company executive*
Edwards, Marie D. *social services administrator*

Leavenworth
Kreisle, William Eckman *civil engineer, surveyor, research cartographer, writer*

Leo
Wright, Marsha Jane *pastor*

Liberty
Pringle, Lewis Gordon *marketing professional, educator*

Logansport
Brewer, Robert Allen *physician*

Lowell
Elkins, Jeni L. McIntosh *webmaster*

Madison
Helms, Rebecca J. *finance educator*
Rawson, Harve E. *psychologist, writer*
Tatera, James Frank *chemist, process analysis specialist*

Marion
Barnes, James Byron *university president*
Brannon, Ronald Roy *retired minister*
DeMichael, Mark Joseph *physical education educator, baseball coach*
Fisher, Pierre James, Jr., *physician*
Goff, Albert Michael *entomologist, educator*
Lau, Patrick Hing-Leung *radiologist, educator*
Walker, Corean Jones *evangelist*

Markle
Strait, Nick Edward *elementary school educator*

Martinsville
Fritsche, Volitta *county detective*
Kendall, Robert Stanton *newspaper editor, journalist, automotive executive*
Smith, Peg L. *foundation administrator*

Merrillville
Brenman, Stephen Morris *lawyer*
Doumanian, Heratch Ohannes *radiologist*
Gioia, Daniel August *lawyer*
Manous, Peter J. *lawyer*
Neale, Gary Lee *utilities executive*
Nguyen, Thach Ngoc *cardiologist*
Reitmeister, Noel William *financial planner, investment advisor, insurance agent, writer*
White, Dean *advertising executive*

Michigan City
Brockway, Lee J. *architect*
Brown, Arnold *physical therapy consultant*
Glossinger, Donald Leo *library director*
Manny, Carter Hugh, Jr., *architect, foundation administrator*
Moldenhauer, Nancy A. *social worker, educator*
Mothkur, Sridhar Rao *radiologist*

Middlebury
Corson, Thomas Harold *manufacturing executive*
Guequierre, John Phillip *manufacturing executive*

Mishawaka
Altman, Arnold David *manufacturing executive*
Erdel, Sally Elizabeth *nurse*
Harmon, David Edward *education educator, artist*
Kapson, Jordan *automotive executive*
Merryman, George *automotive executive*
Ponko, William Reuben *architect*
Rubenstein, Pamela Silver *manufacturing executive*
Silver, Neil Marvin *manufacturing executive*
Troyer, LeRoy Seth *architect*

Monroeville
Ray, Annette D. *executive secretary*
Sorgen, Elizabeth Ann *retired educator*

Morgantown
Callon, Margaret Joann *writer, minister*

Mount Vernon
Bach, Steve Crawford *lawyer*
Moll, Joseph Eugene *chemical engineer, chemical company executive*
Robinson, Pamela Gayle *writer*

Muncie
Ali, Mir Masoom *statistician, educator*
Amschler, Denise H. *health science educator*
Anderson, Stefan Stolen *banker*
Bakken, Douglas Adair *foundation executive*
Barber, Earl Eugene *management consultant*
Bell, Stephen Scott (Steve Bell) *journalist, educator*
Bogg, Richard Allan *sociologist, educator*
Cheng, Chu Yuan *economics professor*
Dennis, Ralph Emerson, Jr., *lawyer*
Ernstberger, Eric *landplanning architectural company executive*
Fisher, John Wesley *manufacturing executive, director*
Gora, JoAnn M. *academic administrator*
Goswami, Ajanta *psychiatrist*
Harris, Joseph McAllister *retired chemist*
Hayashi, Tetsumaro *retired literature educator, writer, editor*
Hendrix, Jon Richard *biology professor*
Henzlik, Raymond Eugene *zoophysiologist, educator*
Hoffman, Mary Catherine *retired nurse, anesthetist*
Hozeski, Bruce William *English language and literature educator*
Irvine, Phyllis Eleanor *nursing educator, administrator*
Kelly, Eric Damian *lawyer, educator*
Kitchens, Frederick Lynton, III, *education educator, researcher*
Kuratko, Donald F. *entrepreneur, educator, consultant*
Lawhead, Victor Bernard *education educator*
McIntosh, David M. *former congressman*
Mertens, Thomas Robert *biology professor*
Meyer, Fred Albert, Jr., *political science educator*
Norris, Tracy Hopkins *retired public relations executive*
Reed, Samuel Lee *lawyer*
Roch, Lewis Marshall, II, *ophthalmic surgeon, medical entrepreneur*
Schaefer, Patricia *librarian*
Scheib, John W. *music educator, conductor*
Seymour, Richard Deming *technology educator*
Shoemaker, Helen E. Martin Achor *civic worker*
Simmons, Carl Kenneth *cooperative executive*
Smith, Van P. *holding company executive*
Stewart, Rita Joan *academic administrator*
Swartz, B(enjamin) K(insell), Jr., *archaeologist, educator*
Thornbro, William Graden *writer*
Wise, Charles Davidson *science educator*
Yeamans, George Thomas *librarian, educator*
Zemtsov, Alexander *dermatology and biochemistry educator, inventor*

Munster
Amber, Douglas George *lawyer*
Colander, Patricia Marie *newspaper editor*
Corsiglia, Robert Joseph *electrical construction company executive*
Neff, Bonita Dostal *communication development facilitator*
Potempa, Philip Matthew *journalist, columnist, communications educator*
Shields, Robert Francis *stockbroker*
Singh, Manmohan *orthopedic surgeon, educator*

Nappanee
Borger, Michael Hinton Ivers *osteopathic physician, educator*
Shea, James F. *manufacturing executive*

Nashville
Kriner, Sally Gladys Pearl *artist*
Wills, Katherine V. Tsiopos *English language educator*

New Albany
Bourne, James E. *lawyer*
Chowhan, Naveed Mahfooz *oncologist*
Crump, Claudia *geography educator*
Rhodes, Betty Fleming *rehabilitation services professional, nurse*
Riehl, Jane Ellen *education educator*

New Harmony
Rice, David Lee *university president emeritus*

Newburgh
Belleau, Leisa A. *English educator*
Haley, David Alan *healthcare executive*
Reese, Jerry Wayne *music educator, band director*
Tierney, Gordon Paul *real estate broker, genealogist*

Noblesville
Evans, Richard James *mechanical engineer*
Monical, Robert Duane *engineering company executive*
Wilson, Norman Glenn *church administrator, writer*

North Manchester
Mason, Stephen Olin *academic administrator*
Myers, Anne M. *developer*
Strode, Scott K. *communications educator*
Switzer, Jo Young *academic administrator, dean*

Notre Dame
Appleby, R(obert) Scott *history educator*
Arnold, Peri Ethan *political scientist*
Bartell, Ernest *economist, educator, priest*
Bass, Steven Craig *computer science educator*
Bederman, Gail *education educator, historian*
Blantz, Thomas Edward *Roman Catholic priest, educator*
Burke, Leo *dean, director*
Burns, Peter C. *science educator, engineering educator*
Burns, Peter Carman *geologist, educator*
Conlon, Edward J. *management educator*
Crosson, Frederick James *retired dean, humanities educator*
Despres, Leo Arthur *sociology and anthropology educator, academic administrator*
Doody, Margaret Anne *English language educator*
Dowty, Alan Kent *political scientist, educator*
Dubreil, Sebastien *language educator*
Faybusovich, Leonid *mathematician, educator*
Feigl, Dorothy Marie *chemistry educator, university official*
Gernes, Sonia Grace *literature educator, writer*
Ghilarducci, M. Teresa *economist, educator*
Goulet, Denis André *development ethicist, writer*
Gray, William Guerin *civil engineering educator*
Gunn, Alan *law educator*
Haenggi, Martin *education educator, researcher*
Hallinan, Maureen Theresa *sociologist, educator*
Hatch, Nathan Orr *university administrator*
Hayes, Stephen Matthew *librarian*
Hesburgh, Theodore Martin *clergyman, former university president*
Huber, Paul William *biochemistry educator, researcher*
Hyder, Anthony K. *academic administrator, science educator*
Iapalucci, Philip Joseph, Jr., *accountant*
Incropera, Frank Paul *mechanical engineering educator*
Jensen, Richard Jorg *biologist, educator*
Jerger, Edward William *engineering educator, dean*
Kselman, Thomas *education educator*
Lanzinger, Klaus *language educator*
Mainwaring, Scott Patterson *political scientist, educator*
Malloy, Edward Aloysius *academic administrator*
Marsden, George *writer*
Matthias, John Edward *English literature educator*
McElroy, Jerome Lathrop *economics professor*
McInerny, Ralph Matthew *philosopher, educator, writer*
Meisel, Dan *chemist*
Merz, James Logan *electrical engineering and materials educator, researcher*
Michel, Anthony Nikolaus *electrical engineering educator, researcher*
Mirowski, Philip Edward *economics professor*
Mobashery, Shahriar *chemist*
Moore, Kenneth E. *anthropologist, educator, writer*
Mueller, Thomas James *engineering educator, researcher*
O'Hara, Patricia A. *dean, law educator*
O'Meara, Onorato Timothy *academic administrator, mathematician*
Ovaert, Timothy Christopher *mechanical engineering educator*
Pollak, Barth *mathematics professor*
Pollard, Morris *microbiologist, educator*
Quinn, Philip Lawrence *philosophy educator*
Reilly, Frank Kelly *business educator*
Rosenberg, Charles Michael *art historian, educator*
Scheidt, W. Robert *chemistry educator, researcher*
Schmitz, Roger Anthony *chemical engineer, educator, academic administrator*
Schuler, Robert Hugo *chemist, educator*
Shannon, William Norman, III, *marketing and international business educator, food service executive*
Shephard, William Danks *physicist, educator*
Sommese, Andrew John *mathematics professor*
Stadtherr, Mark A. *chemical engineer, educator*
Stoll, Wilhelm *mathematics professor*
Swartz, Thomas R. *economist, educator*
Trozzolo, Anthony Marion *chemistry professor*
Valenzuela, Julio Samuel *sociologist, educator*
Vecchio, Robert Peter *business management educator*
Weigert, Andrew Joseph *sociology educator*
Welch, Michael R. *sociologist, educator*
Williams, Oliver Franklin *priest, educator*
Woo, Carolyn Yauyan *dean*

Oakland City
Johnson, Ora J. *clergyman*

Pendleton
Corby, Francis Michael, Jr., *financial executive*
Kischuk, Richard Karl *insurance company executive*
Phenis-Bourke, Nancy Sue *educational administrator*

Plainfield
Bryant, John Howard *writer*
Harkness, Maurice Stephen *utility company executive*
Lucas, Georgetta Marie Snell *retired educator, artist*

Plymouth
Fager, Everett Dean *minister*
Stiver, James Frederick *pharmacist, health physicist, administrator, scientist*

Portage
Popp, Joseph Bruce *manufacturing executive*

Princeton
Okamoto, Seizo *transportation executive*

Purdue University
Ramkrishna, Doraiswami *chemical engineering educator, researcher*

Remington
Legler, Christine Kay *music educator*

Richmond
Bennett, Douglas Carleton *academic administrator*
Bordo, Guy Victor *conductor*
Kirk, Thomas Garrett, Jr., *librarian*
MacAdams, William *writer*
Rains, Joanne Warner *nursing educator*
Veramallay, Ashton Isardatt *economist, educator*

Ridgeville
Church, Jay Kay *psychologist, educator*

Rochester
Willard, Shirley Ann Ogle *museum director, editor, historian*

Rockport
Davis, Karen Sue *hospital nursing supervisor*

Rosemont
Reyes, J. Christopher *food products distribution executive*

Royal Center
Blume, Craig Lee *music educator*

Rushville
Zwickey, Sheila Kaye *lawyer*

Saint Meinrad
Daly, Simeon *retired librarian*

Sandborn
Gregg, John Richard *lawyer*

Santa Claus
Edwards, James Dallas, III, *consulting company executive*

Schererville
Opacich, Milan *protective services official, musician*
Platis, Chris Steven *educator*

Scottsburg
Dockery-Schillig, Linda *writer*
Kho, Eusebio *surgeon*

Sellersburg
MacEva, Carol Ann *accountant*

Seymour
Lake, Nancy Jean *nursing educator, medical/surgical nurse*
Pardieck, Roger L. *lawyer*
Rust, Lois *food company executive*

Shelbyville
Lisher, James Richard *lawyer*
McNeely, James Lee *lawyer*

Shoals
Boyd, Earl E., Jr., *councilman*

South Bend
Agbetsiafa, Douglas Kofi *financial consultant, management consultant*
Anderson, Kenneth Paul *nephrologist, administrator*
Bauer, Burnett Patrick *state legislator*
Beker, Bernardo Enrique *anesthesiologist*
Bella, Dantina Carmen Quartaroli *human services consultant*
Blacharski, Dan W. *writer*
Carey, John Leo *lawyer*
Carrington, Michael Davis *criminal justice administrator, educator, consultant*
Casey, Robert Fitzgerald *lawyer, educator*
Cerny, William *retired education educator, musician*
Cohen, Ronald S. *accountant*
Cook, Pamela Margaret *French educator*
Creps, Philip Lloyd *child psychiatrist*
Guyberson, Randy Alan *writer*
Harriman, Gerald Eugene *retired business administrator, economics educator*
Horsbrugh, Patrick *architect, educator, environologist*
House, Harold Von *education educator, consultant*
Karns, Elizabeth (Libby) A. *retired daycare administrator*
Manion, Daniel Anthony *federal judge*
Norton, Sally Pauline *lawyer*
Phillipoff, Mark James *lawyer*
Reamer, Shirley Jean *minister*
Redmond, Mark Leroy *secondary school educator*
Reed, Robert Frederick *physician*
Reinke, William John *lawyer*
Ripple, Kenneth Francis *federal judge*
Rodibaugh, Robert Kurtz *retired judge*
Schreiber, Roy Edward *education educator, writer*
Seall, Stephen Albert *lawyer*
Shaffer, Thomas Lindsay *lawyer, educator*
Sharp, Allen *federal judge*
Smith, E. Berry *television and radio consultant*
Smith, Thomas Gordon *architect*
Storin, Matthew Victor *academic administrator, educator, retired editor*
van Inwagen, Peter Jan *philosophy educator*
Vasta, Edward *humanities educator*
Vogel, Nelson J., Jr., *lawyer*
Walters, Isaac Clayton *theater educator, director*
White, Robert Dennis *pediatrician, director*
Wrenn, Walter Bruce *marketing educator, consultant*

Spencer
Young, Frederic Hisgin *information systems executive, data processing consultant*

Sullivan
Chavez, Mary Ann *osteopathic family physician*

Syracuse
Blakesley, Wayne Lavere, Jr., *retired production engineer*

Tangier
Bates, Allan Charles *playwright, educator*

Tell City
Rutherford, Michael Francis *retired music educator*

Terre Haute
Aldridge, Sandra *civic volunteer*
Anderson, Louise A. *public health service officer*
Baker, Ronald Lee *English educator*
Bopp, James, Jr., *lawyer*
Britton, Louis Franklin *lawyer*
Carmony, Marvin Dale *retired linguist, educator*
Chambers, Curtis Allen *clergyman, church communications executive*
Chesebro, James William *communications educator*
Conway, Lucian Gideon, III, *social sciences educator*
De Marr, Mary Jean *English language educator*
Guthrie, Frank Albert *chemistry professor*
Hulbert, Samuel Foster *college president*
Hunt, Effie Neva *former college dean, former English language educator*
Kondras, Holly Witten *publishing executive*
Kukral, Michael Andrew *geographer, educator*
Lamis, Leroy *artist, retired educator*
Landini, Richard George *university president emeritus, English educator*
Leach, Ronald George *education educator, librarian*
Malooley, David Joseph *electronics and computer technology educator*
Miller, Maurice Dean *special education educator*
Olsen, Christopher John *education educator*
Perry, Eston Lee *real estate and equipment leasing company executive*
Pickett, William Beatty *history educator*
Roshel, John Albert, Jr., *orthodontist*
Sawyer, Thomas Harrison *health, physical education and recreation director*
Siebenmorgen, Paul *retired family physician, lay church worker*
Tomey, Ann Louise Marriner *nursing educator*
Van Til, William *education educator, writer*
Wheelock, Larry Arthur *retired engineer, consultant*

Trafalgar
Montgomery, Steven Charles *psychologist, minister*

Upland
Kesler, Jay Lewis *retired academic administrator*
Parker, Richard Allan *music educator*

Valparaiso
Becker, Matthew Lee *religious studies educator, minister*
Blaschke, Lawrence Raymond *electronic security services professional*
Bognar, Joseph Andrew *music educator, musician*
Collie, John, Jr., *insurance agent*
Harre, Alan Frederick *academic administrator*
Kobak, Alfred Julian, Jr., *obstetrician, gynecologist*
Mundinger, Donald Charles *retired college president*
Olson, Lynn *sculptor, painter, writer*
Peters, Howard Nevin *foreign language educator*
Poracky, Bernard Francis *radiologist*
Scales, Freda S. *dean, nursing educator*
Schlender, William Elmer *management sciences educator*
Schnabel, Robert Victor *retired academic administrator*

Vincennes
Emison, Ewing Rabb, Jr., *lawyer*
Rogers, John Headley *literature and language professor*

Wabash
Whitehead, Wendy Lee *special education educator*

Walton
Chu, Johnson Chin Sheng *retired physician*

Washington
Graham, David Bolden *food products executive*

West Lafayette
Abhyankar, Shreeram S. *mathematics and industrial engineering educator*
Adelman, Steven Allen *theoretical physical chemist, chemistry educator*
Albright, Jack Lawrence *animal science and veterinary educator*
Albright, Lyle Frederick *chemical engineering educator*

Altschaeffl, Adolph George *civil engineering educator, retired*
Amstutz, Harold Emerson *veterinarian, educator*
Andres, Ronald Paul *chemical engineer, educator*
Andrews, Theodora Anne *retired librarian, educator*
Asher, J. William *education educator, psychology professor*
Barany, James Walter *industrial engineering educator*
Barnes, Virgil Everett, II, *physics educator*
Baumgardt, Billy Ray *professional society administrator, agriculturist*
Beering, Steven Claus *academic administrator, medical educator*
Belcastro, Patrick Frank *pharmaceutical scientist*
Bergstrom, Donald E. *medical educator*
Bertolet, Rodney Jay *philosophy educator*
Borch, Richard Frederic *pharmacology and chemistry educator*
Borowitz, Joseph Leo *pharmacologist, educator*
Brey, Eric Trent *hospitality and tourism educator*
Carney, Thomas Quentin *academic administrator, educator, pilot*
Cassens, Daniel Lee *forester, educator*
Chao, Kwang-Chu *chemical engineer, educator*
Christian, John Edward *health science educator*
Cicirelli, Victor George *psychologist*
Cohen, Raymond *mechanical engineer, educator*
Connor, John Murray *agricultural economics educator*
Contreni, John Joseph, Jr., *humanities educator, educator*
Cooks, R(obert) Graham *chemist, educator*
Cooper, Arnold Cook *management educator, researcher*
Cosier, Richard A. *dean, business educator, consultant*
Cramer, William Anthony *biochemistry and biophysics researcher, educator*
Delleur, Jacques William *civil engineering educator*
Diekman, Mark A. *animal science educator*
Duerstock, Bradley S. *neurobiologist, researcher*
Farris, Paul Leonard *agricultural economist*
Feld, Scott Lauren *sociologist, political scientist*
Feng, Zhilan J *mathematician, educator*
Fosmire, Michael *librarian, educator*
Frey, Harley Harrison, Jr., *retired anesthesiologist*
Frick, Gene Armin *university administrator*
Gappa, Judith M. *university administrator*
Gennett, Timothy *academic administrator*
Greene, John Oscar *communications educator*
Greenkorn, Robert Albert *chemical engineering educator*
Gruen, Gerald Elmer *psychologist, educator*
Hanks, Alan R. *chemistry professor*
Horwich, George *economist, educator*
Hoxie, Robert Prynne *retired entomologist*
Hunt, Michael O'Leary *wood science and engineering educator*
Ichiyama, Dennis Yoshihide *design educator, consultant, administrator*
Jackson, Mark James *engineering educator*
Janick, Jules *horticultural scientist, educator*
Jischke, Martin C. *academic administrator*
Judd, William Robert *engineering geologist, educator*
Kadiyala, Koteswara Rao *econometrics educator*
Kirksey, Avanelle *nutrition educator*
Knudsen, Dean DeWayne *sociology educator*
Kovenock, Daniel J. *economist, educator*
Ladisch, Michael R. *engineering educator*
Landgrebe, David Allen *electrical engineer*
Laskowski, Michael, Jr., *chemist, educator*
Lechtenberg, Victor L. *agricultural studies educator*
Le Master, Dennis Clyde *natural resource economics and policy educator*
Lewellen, Wilbur Garrett *management educator, consultant*
Lin, Pen-Min *electrical engineer, educator*
Lipschutz, Michael Elazar *chemistry educator, consultant, researcher*
Markee, Katherine Madigan *librarian, educator*
Marshall, Francis Joseph *aerospace engineer*
Mason, Sally Kay Frost *biology professor, provost, dean*
Mc Bride, William Leon *philosopher, educator*
McFee, William Warren *soil scientist*
Mc Laughlin, John Francis *civil engineer, educator*
McMillin, David Robert *chemistry professor*
Mohtar, Rabi H. *hydrologist*
Mork, Gordon Robert *historian, educator*
Morrison, Harry *chemistry professor*
Moskowitz, Herbert *management educator*
Moyars-Johnson, Mary Annis *university official*
Mullins, James Lee *library administrator*
Negishi, Ei-ichi *chemistry professor*
Nixon, Judith May *librarian*
Oakley, James Louis *marketing educator, researcher*
Ohm, Herbert Willis *agronomy educator*
Ong, Chee-Mun *engineering educator*
Ortman, Eldon E. *entomologist, educator*
Overhauser, Albert Warner *physicist*
Peck, Garnet Edward *pharmacist, educator*
Peeta, Srinivas *civil engineering educator, consultant*
Perrucci, Robert *sociologist, educator*
Phillips, Terry LeMoine *investment advisor*
Pittendrigh, Barry Robert *entomology professor*
Plante, Robert Donald *dean*
Poulos, James Thomas *endocrinologist, educator*
Rebar, Alan H. *dean*
Ringel, Robert Lewis *university administrator*
Robinson, Farrel Richard *pathologist, toxicologist*
Rossmann, Michael George *biochemist, educator*
Rutledge, Charles Ozwin *pharmacologist, educator*
Salvendy, Gavriel *industrial engineer, educator*
Saunders, Elmo Stewart *librarian, historian*
Saunders, James Robert *English educator*
Scaletta, Phillip Jasper *lawyer, educator*
Schendel, Dan Eldon *management consultant, business educator*
Schwartz, Richard John *electrical engineering educator, researcher*
Shaw, Stanley Miner *nuclear pharmacy scientist*
Sherman, Louis Allen *biology professor, department chairman*
Shertzer, Bruce Eldon *education educator*
Sims-Curry, Kristy *women's college basketball coach*
Solberg, James Joseph *industrial engineering educator*
Stob, Martin *physiology educator*
Sweet, Arnold Lawrence *industrial engineering educator*

Swensen, Clifford Henrik, Jr., *psychologist, educator*
Taber, Margaret Ruth *engineering educator*
Thomas, Marlin Uluess *industrial engineer, educator, academic administrator*
Tomovic, Mileta Milos *mechanical engineer, educator*
Varma, Arvind *chemical engineering educator, researcher*
Viskanta, Raymond *mechanical engineering educator*
Wankat, Phillip Charles *chemical engineering educator*
Weidenaar, Dennis Jay *economics professor*
Weinstein, Michael Alan *political science educator*
White, Joe Lloyd *soil scientist, educator*
Williams, Theodore Joseph *engineering educator*
Woodman, Harold David *historian, educator*
Wright, Alfred George James *band symphony orchestra conductor, educator*
Yao, Bin *mechanical engineering educator*

Westfield
Tanov, Romil Raykov *mechanical engineer, researcher*

Whiting
Finnegan, Eugene G. *religious studies educator*

Winamac
Ligocki, Gordon Michael *artist, educator*

Winona Lake
Ashman, Charles H. *retired minister*
Davis, John James *religion educator*
Dilling, Richard A. *mathematician, educator*
Henry, Ronald O. *academic administrator*
Julien, Thomas Theodore *religious denomination administrator*

Yorktown
Bryja, Frank Joseph *food distribution executive*

Zionsville
Garfunkel, Art *singer, actor*
Grimm, Kay L. *agricultural products executive*

IOWA

Adel
Hougham, Norman Russell *diversified financial services company executive*

Akron
Hultgren, Dennis Eugene *farmer, management consultant*

Albia
Pabst, Alfred Mark *lawyer*

Algona
Andreasen, James Hallis *retired state supreme court judge*

Ames
Abbott, David L. *agricultural products executive*
Adams, Andrew David *music educator*
Allen, Benjamin J. *academic administrator*
Alumbaugh, JoAnn McCalla *magazine editor*
Anderson, Lloyd Lee *animal science educator*
Anderson, Robert Morris, Jr., *electrical engineer*
Armstrong, Daniel Wayne *chemist, educator*
Avalos, Hector Ignacio *language educator*
Barton, Thomas Jackson *chemistry professor, researcher*
Baum, Robert M. *religious studies educator, researcher*
Baumann, Edward Robert *environmental engineering educator*
Beran, George Wesley *veterinary microbiology educator*
Bibi, Tauqir *mathematician, educator, researcher*
Black, James Robert *industrial engineer*
Bolin, Steven Robert *veterinarian researcher*
Bonomi, Ferne Gater *public relations executive*
Bowen, George Hamilton, Jr., *astrophysicist, educator*
Brown, Frederick Gramm *psychology educator*
Brown, Robert Grover *engineering educator*
Cheville, Norman Frederick *veterinary pathologist, dean*
Clem, John Richard *physicist, educator*
Colvin, Thomas Stuart *agricultural engineer, farmer*
Crabtree, Beverly June *retired dean*
Cravens, Hamilton *history educator*
Dahiya, Rajbir Singh *mathematics educator, researcher*
David, Herbert Aron *statistician, educator*
Ebbers, Larry Harold *education educator*
Fennelly, William *basketball coach*
Fleming, Jon Lee *gastroenterologist*
Fox, Karl August *economist, eco-behavioral scientist*
Freeman, Albert E. *agricultural science educator, dairy cattle geneticist*
Fuller, Wayne Arthur *statistics educator*
Geoffroy, Gregory L. *academic administrator, educator*
Gordon, Mark S. *chemist, educator*
Greve, John Henry *veterinary parasitologist, educator*
Hallauer, Arnel Roy *geneticist*
Hatfield, Jerry Lee *plant physiologist, biometeorologist*
Horowitz, Jack *biochemistry educator*
Hunger, J(ohn) David *business educator*
Isaacson, Dean Leroy *statistician*
Jacobson, Norman L. *retired agricultural educator, researcher*
Jacobson, Robert Andrew *chemistry professor*
Johnson, Howard Paul *agricultural engineering educator*
Johnson, Lawrence Alan *cereal technologist, educator, administrator*
Jones, Edwin Channing, Jr., *electrical and computer engineering educator*
Kanwar, Rameshwar Singh *agricultural engineer, researcher, educator*
Kaplan, Murray Lee *nutritionist, educator*
Karlen, Douglas Lawrence *soil scientist*
Kaufmann, Jeffrey Baer *business educator, lawyer*
Larsen, William Lawrence *engineering educator*

Lee, Seong-Jae *research scientist*
Lo, Chester C.H. *research scientist*
Manatt, Richard *retired education educator*
Mattila, Mary Jo Kalsem *elementary and art educator*
Maxwell-Dial, Eleanore *foreign language educator*
Melvin, Stewart Wayne *engineering educator*
Mengeling, William Lloyd *retired veterinarian, virologist*
Mertins, James Walter *entomologist*
Mitchell, Jacqueline Keaton *English language educator*
Moon, Harley William *veterinarian*
Moore, Kenneth James *agronomy educator, scientist*
Mullen, Russell Edward *agricultural studies educator*
Nostwich, Theodore Daniel *literature educator, researcher*
O'Berry, Phillip Aaron *veterinarian*
Okiishi, Theodore Hisao *mechanical engineering educator*
Orazem, Peter Francis *economics professor*
Pearce, Robert Brent *agricultural studies educator*
Quirmbach, Herman Charles *economics professor*
Reilly, Peter John *chemical engineer, educator*
Rosenberg, Ralph *former state senator, lawyer, consultant, educator, foundation administrator*
Roskey, Carol Boyd *social studies educator, dean, director*
Ross, Richard Francis *veterinarian, microbiologist, educator, dean*
Sanders, Wallace Wolfred, Jr., *civil engineer*
Schuh, John Howard *higher education educator, academic administrator*
Seaton, Vaughn Allen *retired veterinary pathology educator*
Smith, John Francis *materials science educator*
Stalheim, Ole Henry V. *veterinarian, educator*
Tabatabai, M. Ali *chemist, biochemist*
Tesfatsion, Leigh S. *economics educator, consultant*
Thompson, Louis Milton *agronomy educator, scientist*
Topel, David Glen *agricultural studies educator*
Ugurlu, Ozan *research scientist*
Voss, Regis Dale *agronomist, educator*
Weber, Eric Scott *mathematician, educator*
Wilder, David Randolph *materials engineer, consultant*
Willham, Richard Lewis *animal science educator*
Willis, Jerry Weldon *computer systems educator, writer*
Work, George Paul *cellist*
Yeung, Edward Szeshing *chemist*
Zimmerman, Zora Devrnja *comparative literature and folklore educator*

Anita
Everhart, Robert Phillip (Bobby Williams) *entertainer, songwriter, recording artist*

Ankeny
Lamb, Ronald M. *convenience stores executive*
Lamberti, Donald *convenience store executive*
Lynn, Robert William *strategic planning consultant*
Scott, Beverly Jeanne *contractor, writer*
Stahr, Curtis Brent *photographer, art association administrator, educator*
Weigel, Ollie J. *dentist, former mayor*
Wirtz, Eli J. *convenience stores executive*

Avoca
Hardisty, William Lee *English language educator*

Belle Plaine
Danker, Thomas Nathan *agronomist*

Bettendorf
Hanzelka, Richard Louis *education educator*
Heyderman, Arthur Jerome *engineer, civilian military employee*

Boone
Beckwith, F. William *food products executive*
Cramer, Robert *retail executive*
Danilson, David Ray *lawyer*

Britt
Castillo, Leanne Marlow *artist, geriatrics nurse*

Burlington
Hoth, Steven Sergey *lawyer, educator*
Hutchins, Timothy Paul *military officer*
Lundy, Sherman Perry *secondary school educator*
Paragas, Rolando G. *physician*

Camanche
Stearns, Roxann Lynn *social worker*

Cedar Falls
Clohesy, William Warren *philosopher, educator*
DeSoto, M. Catherine *biological psychologist*
Echeverria, Frje *art educator, artist*
Fanelli, Michael Paul *music educator*
Gilgen, Albert Rudolph *psychologist, educator*
Jedlicka, Allen Dean *finance educator, consultant*
Koob, Robert Duane *chemistry educator, educational administrator*
Lettow, Lucille Jane *school librarian, education educator*
Lindberg, Duane R. *bishop, historian*
Mitra, Atul *management consultant, educator*
Olsen-Dunbar, Jessica Ida *sign language educator*
Price, Nancy *education educator, writer*
Rao, Posinasetti Nageswara *manufacturing engineering educator*
Sells, Larry Joe *writer*
Shimp, Karen Ann *accountant, municipal financial executive*
Wirth, David Eugene *software designer, consultant*

Cedar Rapids
Armitage, Thomas Edward *library director*
Arnold-Olson, Helen B. *nonprofit consultant*
Baermann, Donna Lee Roth *real estate property executive, retired insurance analyst*
Bahadur, Birendra *display specialist, liquid crystal researcher*
Baldwin, George Koehler *retired retail executive*
Brooks, Debra L. *healthcare executive, neuromuscular therapist*
Collins, Kevin Heath *lawyer*
Condon, Sherri Kay *secondary school educator*

Erickson, Lawrence A. (Larry Erickson) *electronics executive*
Hall, Kathy L. *orchestra executive*
Hansen, David Rasmussen *federal judge*
Houmes, Blaine V. *emergency physician, county medical examiner*
Huber, Rita Norma *civic worker*
Jones, Clayton M. *computer and electronics company executive*
Keller, Eliot Aaron *broadcast executive*
Knepper, Eugene Arthur *realtor*
Krivit, Jeffrey Scot *surgeon*
Larson, Charles W. *prosecutor*
Lemos, John Paul *philosopher, educator*
Maikon, Marc Steven *podiatrist*
Mc Manus, Edward Joseph *federal judge*
Melloy, Michael J. *federal judge*
Nassif, Gary Tannus *singer and entertainer, art and special education educator, sculptor*
Nebergall, Donald Charles *management consultant*
Norris, Albert Stanley *psychiatrist, educator*
Novetzke, Sally Johnson *former ambassador*
O'Brien, David A. *lawyer*
Pundt, Richard Arthur *lawyer*
Renter, Lois Irene Hutson *librarian*
Reppert, Nancy Lue *retired municipal official, legal consultant*
Riley, Tom Joseph *lawyer*
Rosberg, Merilee Ann *education educator*
Stephens, Ralph Renne *massage therapy educator*
Stepp, Waylon Gene *management consultant, retired municipal official*
Stolte, Larry Gene *marketing executive, former computer and publishing company executive*
Stone, Herbert Marshall *architect*
Tiemeyer, Christian *conductor*
Vanderpool, Ward Melvin *management and marketing consultant*
Wax, Nadine Virginia *retired bank executive*
Weber, Frederick Edwin *management recruiter*
Whipple, William Perry *foundation administrator*
Wiese, Daniel Edward *marketing and communications researcher*
Willey, Wythe *lawyer, cattleman, trade association executive*
Wilson, Robert Foster *lawyer*
Ziese, Nancylee Hanson *social worker*

Chariton
McKinley, Paul *state legislator*
Stuart, William Corwin *judge*

Charles City
Mc Cartney, Ralph Farnham *lawyer*

Cherokee
Clark, Larry Dalton *civil engineer*

Clear Lake
Broshar, Robert Clare *architect*

Clinton
Vidal, Ronald Anthony *otolaryngology*
Warner, Jean Lollich *poet*
Woodman, Grey Musgrave *psychiatrist*

Clive
Miller, Kenneth Edward *sociologist, educator*
Neis, Arthur Veral *healthcare and development company executive*

Coggon
Hammer, Robert Eugene *psychologist*

Coralville
Allen, (Edwin) Lee *artist*

Council Bluffs
Kurt, Johnny Thomas *music educator*
Moeller, James Charles *writer*
Peterson, Richard William *retired judge, lawyer*

Davenport
Bannick, Janice Carol *automotive dealerships executive*
Beguhn, Sandra E. *poet, writer*
Brocka, Bruce *editor, educator, application developer*
Chowdhury, Ali Asraf *electrical engineer, researcher*
Dcamp, Charles Barton *educator, musician*
Dettmann, David Allen *lawyer*
Edgerton, Winfield Dow *retired gynecologist*
Foster, James Franklin *professional sports management executive*
Gottlieb, Richard Douglas *media executive*
Goudy, Josephine Gray *social worker*
Hudson, Celeste Nutting *education educator, reading clinic administrator, consultant*
Juckem, Wilfred Philip *manufacturing executive*
Lane, Gary Matthew *lawyer*
Le Grand, Clay *lawyer, former state justice*
Monty, Mitchell *landscape company executive*
Pedersen, Karen Sue *electrical engineer*
Phelps, Robert J. *lawyer*
Rogalski, Edward J. *university administrator*
Rotherham, Thomas G. *diversified financial services company executive*
Scally, Mark *diversified financial services company executive*
Schleicher, Donald *music director*
Shammas, Nicolas Wahib *internist, cardiologist*
Sievert, Mary Elizabeth *small business owner, retired secondary school educator*
Skora, Susan Sundman *lawyer*
Tinsman, Margaret Neir *state legislator*
Willett, Lance *orchestra executive*

Decorah
Christianson, John Robert *historian, educator*
Farwell, Elwin D. *minister, educational consultant*

Denison
Bekkerus, Perry Charles *music educator*

Des Moines
Abbott, Aloris Jean *retired medical/surgical nurse, retired nursing administrator*
Abel, Gregory E. *utility company executive*
Anderson, Eric Anthony *city manager*
Bair, Gerald D. *state government official*
Bartschat, Klaus Richard Wilhelm *physics educator*
Begleiter, Martin David *law educator, consultant*

Begleiter, Ronni Frankel *lawyer*
Bennett, Edward James *lawyer*
Bergman, Bruce E. *municipal official*
Berry, Deborah *state representative*
Blank, Myron Nathan *theater executive*
Boal, Carmine *state official*
Boettger, Nancy J. *state legislator*
Boyle, Bruce James *publisher*
Branstad, Christine Ellen *lawyer*
Bremer, Celeste F. *judge*
Brickman, Kenneth Alan *state lottery executive*
Brooks, Roger Kay *insurance company executive*
Brown, Paul Edmondson *lawyer*
Buhr, Florence D. *county official*
Bukta, Polly *state representative*
Burns, Bernard John, III, *public defender*
Byal, Nancy Louise *food editor*
Calkins, Richard M. *lawyer*
Carroll, Frank James *lawyer, educator*
Carter, James H. *judge*
Charron, Joseph L. *bishop*
Claypool, David L. *lawyer*
Colloton, Steven M. *federal judge*
Conlin, Roxanne Barton *lawyer*
Corning, Joy Cole *retired state official*
Cortese, Joseph Samuel, II, *lawyer*
Culver, Chester J. *state official, educator*
Dandekar, Swati *state representative*
DeBoef, Betty *state representative*
Deluhery, Patrick John *state official*
Demorest, Allan Frederick *retired psychologist*
DeWulf Nickell, Karol *editor*
Doyle, Richard Henry, IV, *lawyer*
Drake, Richard Francis *state legislator*
Dukes, Vanessa Johnson *dietician*
Eaton, Jay *lawyer*
Ellis, Mary Louise Helgeson *retired insurance company executive, business consultant*
Elmets, Harry Barnard *retired osteopath, dermatologist*
Erickson, Elaine Mae *composer, poet*
Fagg, George Gardner *federal judge*
Finley, Kerry A. *lawyer*
Fisher, Thomas George *lawyer, retired media company executive*
Fisher, Thomas George, Jr., *lawyer*
Flynn, Scott D. *lawyer*
Foxhoven, Jerry Ray *lawyer*
Frederici, C. Carleton *lawyer*
Freeman, Mary Louise *state legislator*
Gaines, Ruth Ann *secondary school educator*
Garman, Teresa Agnes *state legislator*
Gartner, Michael Gay *editor, television executive, baseball executive*
Gaskill, Mary *state official*
Gersie, Michael H. *insurance company executive*
Giunta, Joseph *conductor, music director*
Graham, Diane E. *newspaper editor*
Granzow, Polly *state representative, language educator*
Graziano, Craig Frank *lawyer*
Greimann, Jane *state representative, elementary school educator*
Griswell, J. Barry *insurance company executive*
Gronstal, Tom *commissioner, bank executive*
Grundberg, Betty *state legislator, property manager*
Hansell, Edgar Frank *lawyer*
Harris, Charles Elmer *lawyer*
Harris, K. David *senior state supreme court justice*
Heddens, Lisa *state official*
Henry, Phylliss Jeanette *marshal*
Hill, Luther Lyons, Jr., *lawyer*
Hockenberg, Harlan David *lawyer*
Hoffmann, Michael Richard *lawyer*
Holveck, Jack *state legislator*
Hosch, Julie *state senator*
Huser, Geri D. *state official*
Inman, Lorinda K. *nursing administrator*
Isenstein, Laura *library director*
Jacobs, Libby Swanson *state official*
Jensen, Dick Leroy *lawyer*
Jessen, Lloyd K. *pharmacist, lawyer*
Jochum, Pam *state representative*
Kandris, Michael *trucking executive*
Kelley, Bruce Gunn *insurance company executive, lawyer*
Kerr, William T. *publishing and broadcasting executive*
Koehn, William James *lawyer*
Kramer, Mary Elizabeth *state legislator, health services executive*
Kruidenier, David *retired newspaper executive*
Lacy, Stephen M. *broadcast and publishing executive*
Larson, Chuck, Jr., *state representative, political organization administrator*
Larson, Jerry Leroy *state supreme court justice*
Lavorato, Louis A. *state supreme court chief justice*
Leach, Dave Francis *editor, musician*
Lensing, Vicki *state representative, funeral home business owner*
Lewis, Calvin Fred *architect, educator*
Martens, Harvey Arthur *retired government worker, academic administrator*
Maxwell, David E. *academic executive, educator*
McGiverin, Arthur A. *former state supreme court chief justice*
McGuire-Riggs, Sheila *chairman Democratic party*
Mertz, Dolores Mary *farmer, state legislator*
Mill, Jeth *performing company executive*
Miller, Helen *state representative, lawyer*
Miller, Thomas J. *state attorney general*
Munson, Jay Donald *statistician*
Myers, Mary Kathleen *publishing executive*
Neiman, Donald Flint *lawyer*
Nelson, Charlotte Bowers *public administrator*
Norris, Glenn L. *lawyer*
Olds, John Ward *internist*
Oldson, Jo *state representative, lawyer*
Paterik, Frances Sue *secondary school educator, actress*
Peddicord, Roland Dale *lawyer*
Pederson, Sally *lieutenant governor*
Petersen, Janet *state representative*
Power, Joseph Edward *lawyer*
Ragan, Amanda *state senator*
Rants, Christopher C. *state representative*
Reece, Maynard Fred *artist, writer*
Rehberg, Kitty *state legislator*
Rhein, Dave *newspaper editor*
Rodgers, Louis Dean *retired surgeon*
Rosen, Matthew Stephen *botanist, consultant*
Runge, Kay Kretschmar *library director*
Schneider, William George *former life insurance company executive*
Scholten, Gary P. *finance company executive*
Shaff, Karen E. *lawyer, insurance company executive*
Sheehan, Carol Sama *magazine editor*
Shors, John D. *lawyer*
Simpson, Lyle Lee *lawyer*
Smith, Diana Marie *business educator*
Smith, Neal Edward *congressman*
Sokol, David L. *energy services provider company executive*
Song, Joseph *pathologist, educator*
Soukup, Betty A. *state legislator*
Stier, Mary P. *publishing executive*
Streit, Michael J. *state supreme court justice*
Szymoniak, Elaine Eisfelder *retired state senator*
Teitelbaum, Howard S. *academic administrator*
Ternus, Marsha K. *state supreme court justice*
Tipton, Sheila Kay *lawyer*
Tymeson, Jodi *state official*
Upmeyer, Linda *state official*
Van Zante, Shirley M(ae) *magazine editor*
Vaughan, Therese Michele *insurance commissioner*
Vietor, Harold Duane *federal judge*
Vilsack, Thomas *governor*
Wallace, Samuel Taylor *health system administrator*
Walters, Ross A. *federal judge*
Wattleworth, Roberta Ann *physician, medical educator*
Webb, Mary Christine *reading recovery educator, in-class reading specialist*
Whitaker, Matthew George *prosecutor*
Wilcox, Gregory B. *lawyer*
Williams, Carl Chanson *insurance company executive*
Williamson, Rose Ann *insurance agent*
Winckler, Cindy *state representative*
Witke, David Rodney *retired newspaper editor, consultant*
Wolle, Charles Robert *judge*
Zieser, John S. *lawyer, publishing executive*
Zumbach, Steven Elmer *lawyer*

Dubuque
Barker, Barbara Yvonne *nursing home administrator*
Barta, James Omer *priest, psychology educator, church administrator*
Beck, Robert Raymond *priest*
Burkhart, John Ernest *minister, theology studies educator*
Collins, Barbara Louise *retired elementary school educator*
Crahan, Jack Bertsch *retired manufacturing company executive*
Dunn, Frank M. (Francis Michael Dunn) *banker*
Dunn, M. Catherine *college administrator, educator*
Ernst, Daniel Pearson *lawyer*
Gansen, Ronald E. *lumber company executive*
Hammer, David Lindley *lawyer, writer*
Hanus, Jerome George *archbishop*
Hemmer, Paul Edward *musician, composer, broadcasting executive*
Hughes, Brian Lee *music educator*
Jorgensen, Gerald Thomas *psychologist, educator, lawyer*
Keller, Robert Scott *education educator*
Kerrigan, John E. *academic administrator*
McDonald, Robert Delos *manufacturing executive*
Nessan, Craig Lee *minister, educator*
Perry, E. Eugene *communication educator*
Tigges, John Thomas *writer, musician, lecturer*
Toale, Thomas Edward *school system administrator, priest*
Tully, Thomas Alois *building materials executive, consultant, educator*

Epworth
Wozniak, John S. *dean*

Fairfield
Aubrey, Bryan *educator, writer, editor*
Hawthorne, Timothy Robert *direct response advertising and communications company executive*
Johnson, Robert Michael *controller, educator*
Kelly, Thomas *advertising executive*

Fayette
Barker, Richard Alexander *organizational psychologist*

Fort Dodge
Cady, Mark S. *state supreme court justice*
Cassady, Daniel Bennet *music educator*
Pratt, Diane Adele *talented and gifted education educator*
Smith, William G. *transportation executive*

Fort Madison
Chapman, Allen D. *music educator*

Garner
Hovda, Theodore James *lawyer*

George
Symens, Maxine Brinkert Tanner *retired marketing professional*

Glenwood
Campbell, William Edward *mental hospital administrator*

Grinnell
Adelberg, Arnold Melvin *mathematics educator, researcher*
Campbell, David George *ecologist, researcher, author*
Carl, Janet A. *writing instructor, consultant*
Kintner, Philip L. *history professor*
Knight, Rita Cecilia *school librarian*
McKee, Christopher Fulton *librarian, historian, educator*
Michaels, Jennifer Tonks *foreign language educator*
Mitchell, Orlan E. *clergyman, former college president*
Moyer, H. Wayne *political science educator*
Osgood, Russell King *academic administrator*
Smith, Don Alan *history professor*
Swartz, James Edward *chemistry educator, dean, university administrator*
Walker, Waldo Sylvester *biologist, educator, academic administrator*

Grundy Center
Kliebenstein, Don *lawyer*

Hiawatha
Pate, Paul Danny *mayor*

Humboldt
Dodgen, John N. *manufacturing executive*
Sandblom, Steven Kirk *lawyer*

Ida Grove
Snell, Bruce M., Jr., *retired judge*

Indianola
Duke, Michael Liston *music educator, musician*
Larsen, Robert LeRoy *artistic director*
Mace, Jerilee Marie *opera company executive*
Poulsen, James Viggo, III, *music educator, composer*

Iowa City
Abboud, Francois Mitry *physician, educator*
Addis, Laird Clark, Jr., *philosopher, educator, musician*
Afifi, Adel Kassim *physician*
Albrecht, William Price *economist, educator, government official*
Alford, Steve *college basketball coach*
Andreasen, Nancy Coover *psychiatrist, educator, neuroscientist*
Apicella, Michael Allen *physician, educator*
Aspel, Paulene Violette *retired language educator*
Baker, Richard Graves *geology educator, palynologist*
Banker, Gilbert Stephen *industrial and physical pharmacy educator, administrator*
Bar, Robert S. *endocrinologist, educator*
Barkan, Joel David *political science educator, consultant*
Bedell, George Noble *physician, educator*
Bell, Marvin Hartley *poet, English language educator*
Bentz, Dale Monroe *librarian*
Berg, Mary Jaylene *pharmacy educator, researcher*
Bishara, Samir Edward *orthodontist*
Bjorndal, Arne Magne *endodontist*
Bonfield, Arthur Earl *lawyer, educator*
Bowlsby, Bob *athletic director*
Boyd, Willard Lee *academic administrator, educator, lawyer, museum director*
Bozeman, Theodore D. *religion educator*
Brennan, Robert Lawrence *educational director, psychometrician*
Broffitt, James Drake *statistics and actuarial science educator*
Buckwalter, Joseph Addison *orthopedic surgeon, educator*
Buckwalter, Kathleen C. *academic administrator, educator*
Burns, C(harles) Patrick *hematologist, oncologist*
Burton, Donald Joseph *chemistry professor*
Butler, John Edward *biomedical sciences educator, consultant*
Campbell, Kevin Peter *physiology and biophysics educator, researcher*
Clark, Dianne Elizabeth *religious studies and reading educator*
Clifton, James Albert *physician, educator*
Collins, Daniel W. *accountant, educator*
Colloton, John William *university health care executive*
Conway, Thomas William *biochemist, educator*
Coolidge, Archibald Cary, Jr., *English language educator, literature researcher*
Cooper, Reginald Rudyard *orthopedic surgeon, educator*
Craft-Rosenberg, Martha Jane *nursing educator, researcher*
Cruden, Robert William *botany educator*
Cyphert, Stacey Todd *health facilities administrator*
Damasio, Antonio R. *physician, neurologist*
Dettmer, Helena R. *classics educator*
DiPardo, Anne *English language and education educator*
Donelson, John Everett *biochemistry educator, molecular biologist*
Downer, Robert Nelson *lawyer*
Dreher, Melanie Creagan *dean, nursing educator*
Duffy, William Edward, Jr., *retired education educator*
Eckstein, John William *internist, educator, retired dean*
Erkonen, William E. *radiologist, medical educator*
Ertl, Wolfgang *German language and literature educator*
Feldt, Leonard Samuel *university educator and administrator*
Fellows, Robert Ellis *medical educator, medical scientist*
Fethke, Gary C. *dean*
Folk, James Calvin *ophthalmologist, researcher*
Folsom, Lowell Edwin *language educator*
Forell, George Wolfgang *religion educator*
Forsythe, Robert Elliott *economics professor*
Fumerton, Richard Anthony *philosopher, educator*
Galask, Rudolph Peter *obstetrician and gynecologist*
Gantz, Bruce Jay *otolaryngologist, educator*
Gelfand, Lawrence Emerson *historian, educator*
Gergis, Samir Danial *anesthesiologist, educator*
Geweke, John Frederick *economics professor*
Gibson, David Thomas *microbiology educator*
Gittler, Josephine *law educator*
Goldstein, Jonathan Amos *retired ancient history and classics educator*
Gray, George Trumon *test development professional*
Green, Peter Morris *classics educator, writer, translator*
Grose, Charles Frederick *pediatrician, infectious disease specialist*
Hammond, Harold Logan *oral and maxillofacial pathologist, educator*
Hartz, Arthur J. *medical researcher*
Hausler, William John, Jr., *microbiologist, educator, public health service officer*
Hawley, Ellis Wayne *historian, educator*
Heistad, Donald Dean *cardiologist*
Hell, Johannes Wilhelm *neuroscientist, researcher*
Helms, Charles Milton *medical educator, consultant*
Hethcote, Herbert Wayne *mathematician, educator*
Hettmansperger, Sue *artist*
Hines, N. William *dean, law educator, administrator*
Hogan, Michael *academic administrator*
Hogg, Robert Vincent, Jr., *mathematical statistician, educator*
Holland, Charles Joseph *lawyer*
Hovland, Jody *theater director*
Hudson, John Boswell *sociologist, educator*
Hussey, David Holbert *physician*
Husted, Russell Forest *research scientist*
Huttner, Sidney Frederick *librarian*
Johnsen, David C. *dean, dentistry educator*
Johnson, Eugene Walter *mathematician, educator*
Johnson, Nicholas *writer, lawyer, lecturer*
Jorgensen, Palle E.T. *mathematician, educator*
Katen-Bahensky, Donna *health facility administrator*
Kerber, Richard E. *cardiologist*
Kessel, Richard Glen *zoology educator*
Kim, Chong Lim *political science educator*
King, Jeri Ripley *academic administrator*
Kisker, Carl Thomas *pediatrician, educator*
Koontz, Frank P. *microbiology educator, research administrator*
Kottick, Edward Leon *music educator, harpsichord maker*
Kurtz, Sheldon Francis *lawyer, educator*
Lamping, Kathryn G. *medical educator, medical researcher*
Lariviere, Gene Robert *surgeon*
Lauer, Ronald Martin *pediatric cardiologist, researcher*
LeBlond, Richard Foard *internist, educator*
Lee, Angie *basketball coach*
Lee, John D. *science educator*
Lim, Ramon (Khe-Siong Lim) *neuroscience educator, researcher*
Linhardt, Robert John J *medicinal chemistry educator*
Loewenberg, Gerhard *political science educator*
Long, John Paul *pharmacologist, educator*
Lynch, Richard Gregory *medical educator*
Markham, Sanford Max *obstetrician-gynecologist, educator*
Marshall, Jeffrey Scott *mechanical engineer, educator*
Mason, Edward Eaton *surgeon*
Mather, Roger Frederick *music educator, writer*
Maxson, Linda Ellen *biologist, educator*
McGovern, Jennifer Anne *education educator*
Medh, Jheem D. *medical educator, biochemist, researcher*
Mentzer, Raymond Albert *religious history educator*
Merchant, James A. *medical educator*
Miller, Dwight Merrick *archivist, historian*
Mills, Margaret H. *language educator*
Montgomery, Rex *biochemist, educator*
Morriss, Frank Howard, Jr., *pediatrics educator*
Muir, Ruth Brooks *counselor, substance abuse service coordinator*
Muller, Barbara Ann *allergist*
Myers, Virginia Anne *art educator*
Nash, Jan R. Olive *historian, consultant*
Nathan, Peter E. *psychologist, educator*
Nesbitt, John Arthur *recreational therapist, writer, educator, researcher*
Neumann, Roy Covert *architect*
Niebyl, Jennifer Robinson *obstetrician, gynecologist, educator*
Noyes, Russell, Jr., *psychiatrist*
Olin, William Harold *orthodontist, educator*
Packer, ZZ (Zuwena) *writer, literature educator*
Paredes, Robert Wesley *music educator*
Park, Joon Bu *biomedical engineer, researcher, educator*
Patel, Virendra Chaturbhai *mechanical engineer, educator*
Peloso, Paul Michael *medical educator*
Pessin, Jeffrey E. *physiology educator*
Plapp, Bryce Vernon *biochemistry educator*
Raeburn, John Hay *English language educator*
Richerson, Hal Bates *physician, internist, allergist, immunologist, educator*
Riesz, Peter Charles *marketing educator, consultant*
Robertson, Timothy Joel *statistician, educator*
Robillard, Jean Eugene *dean, educator*
Robinson, Robert George *psychiatry educator*
Roe, Gerald Bruce *director, writer*
Schmidt, Julius *sculptor*
Scullion, Rosemarie *literature educator*
Shannon, Lyle William *sociology educator*
Siebert, Calvin D. *economist, educator*
Skorton, David Jan *academic administrator*
Smoker, Wendy Rue Kartinos *neuroradiologist, consultant, educator*
Smothers, Ann Elizabeth *museum director*
Snyder, Peter M. *medical educator, medical researcher*
Solbrig, Ingeborg Hildegard *literature educator, writer*
Spriestersbach, Duane Caryl *academic administrator, speech pathology/audiology services professional, educator*
Stay, Barbara *zoologist, educator*
Stein, Robert A. *writer, educator*
Strauss, John Steinert *dermatologist, educator*
Suls, Jerry M. *psychologist, educator*
Sun, Lizhi *engineering educator, researcher*
Sutphin, John E. *ophthalmologist, educator*
Tephly, Thomas Robert *pharmacologist, educator, toxicologist*
Thompson, Basil F. *ballet master*
Thompson, Herbert Stanley *neuro-ophthalmologist*
Trank, Douglas Monty *rhetoric and speech communications educator*
Tsalikian, Eva *physician, educator*
Van Allen, James Alfred *physicist, researcher*
Van Gilder, John Corley *neurosurgeon, educator*
Wallace, Robert B. *medical educator*
Wasserman, Edward Arnold *psychology educator*
Weinberger, Miles M. *pediatrician, educator*
Weiner, George Jay *internist*
Weingeist, Thomas Alan *ophthalmology educator*
Weinstock, Joel Vincent *immunologist*
Weintraub, Neal L. *medical educator, cardiologist*
Welsh, Michael James *medical educator, biophysicist, educator*
Williams, Richard Dwayne *physician, educator, urologist*
Wing, Adrien Katherine *law educator*
Wunder, Charles C(ooper) *physiology and biophysics educator, gravitational biologist*
Wurster, Dale Eric *pharmacy educator*
Wurster, Dale Erwin *pharmacist, educator, retired dean*
Ziegler, Ekhard Erich *pediatrics educator*

Johnston
Duvick, Donald Nelson *plant breeder*
Thoman, Mark Edward *pediatrician*

Kellogg
Anderson, Dale C. *state agency professional, travel consultant*

Keokuk
Hardy, Julia Irene *elementary school educator*
Hoffman, James Paul *lawyer, hypnotist*

Keota
Greiner, Sandra *state legislator*

Lamoni
Kirkpatrick, Sharon Minton *nursing educator, college administrator*

Le Mars
Cottrell, David Milton *sound recording engineer*
Murphy, Patrick Neil *lawyer*
Rebstock, Theodore Lynn *chemist, educator, retired research scientist*

Leon
Miller, Eleanora Genevieve *freelance/self-employed poet*
Swisher, Robert Keim, Jr., *writer*

Madrid
Handy, Richard Lincoln *civil engineer, educator*

Mallard
Heldt, Kristin R. *conductor*

Maquoketa
Tubbs, Edward Lane *banker*

Marshalltown
Brennecke, Allen Eugene *lawyer*
Cassidy, Eugene Patrick *pathologist*
Packer, Karen Gilliland *cancer patient educator, researcher*
Thomas, David Llewellyn *physician*

Mason City
Backlin, William Wayne *music educator, composer*
Collison, Jim *publishing executive*
Duffy, John Leonard *lawyer*
Kinsey, Robert Stanleigh, III, *lawyer*
Rodamaker, Marti Tomson *bank executive*
Winston, Harold Ronald *lawyer*

Milford
Fontaine, Sue (Jeane Fontaine) *public relations professional*

Mount Ayr
Smith, Howard Alan *editor, publishing executive*

Mount Pleasant
Vance, Michael Charles *lawyer*

Mount Vernon
Molleur, Joseph *religious studies educator*
Ruppel, Howard James, Jr., *sociologist, sexologist, educator*

Moville
Baker, Kent Alfred *broadcasting, publishing company executive*

Muscatine
Coulter, Charles Roy *lawyer*
Michaels, Jack D. *office furniture manufacturing executive*
Stanley, Richard Holt *consulting engineer*
Thomopulos, Gregs G. *consulting engineering company executive*

Nevada
Bivens, Gordon Ellsworth *economist, educator*
Countryman, Dayton Wendell *lawyer*

Newton
Moore, George C. *manufacturing executive*
Ponder, Marian Ruth *retired mathematics educator*
Ward, Lloyd D. *appliance company executive*

North Liberty
Crowner, Dee Kay *library administrator*
Glenister, Brian Frederick *geologist, educator*

Oelwein
McFarlane, Beth Lucetta Troester *former mayor*

Okoboji
Pearson, Gerald Leon *food company executive*

Orange City
Hancock, Albert Sidney, Jr., *engineering executive*
Scorza, Sylvio Joseph *religion educator*

Osceola
Reynoldson, Walter Ward *retired judge, lawyer*

Oskaloosa
Burrow, Paul Irving *secondary school educator*
Clovis, Samuel Harvey *academic administrator*
Mangold, Archie Wayne, II, *insurance agent*
Porter, David Lindsey *history and political science educator, author*

Ottumwa
Downing, Darrell W. *aviation educator*
Krafka, Mary Baird *lawyer*

Pacific Junction
Krogstad, Jack Lynn *associate dean, accounting educator*

Pella
Bouler, Steven William *theater educator*
Chia, Ning *history educator*
Den Adel, Raymond Lee *classics educator*
Muether, Charles Alexander *writer, educator*

Pleasant Valley
Myatt, William Howard *theater educator, director, actor*

Prairie City
Buckingham, Betty Jo *library media consultant*

Red Oak
Stoner, Leonard D. *automotive parts company executive*

Saint Ansgar
Kleinworth, Edward J. *agricultural company executive*

Sheldon
Gifford, Carla J. *education educator*

Sioux City
Andersen, Leonard Christian *former state legislator, real estate investor*
Ayi, Bertha Serwa *epidemiologist, internist*
Deeds, William Charles *university dean, executive*
Doyle, Donald Vincent *retired state senator, lawyer*
Dykstra, Daniel D. *lawyer*
Fredregill, Alan *lawyer*
Giles, William Jefferson, III, *lawyer*
Hamilton, Ruth Milton Green *retired college administrator, consultant*
Hassenger, James Michael *writer, retired small business owner*
Mack, Thomas Russell *foundation administrator, management consultant*
Madsen, George Frank *lawyer*
Mayne, Wiley Edward *lawyer*
Nichols, Roger Sabin *genealogist, retired school counselor*
O'Brien, Donald Eugene *federal judge*
Peterson, Delaine Charles *lawyer, bank executive*
Rants, Carolyn Jean *college official*
Silverberg, David Stanley *financial consultant*
Waller, Ephraim Everett *retired association executive*
Wick, Sister Margaret *former college administrator*

Solon
Healey, Edward Hopkins *retired architect*

Spencer
Lemke, Alan James *environmental specialist*
Maranell, Debra Jean *human resources specialist, quality assurance professional, insurance agent*

Spirit Lake
Brett, George Wendell *former geologist, philatelist*
Hedberg, Paul Clifford *broadcast executive*

Springville
Nyquist, John Davis *retired radio manufacturing company executive*

Storm Lake
Larson, Bethany Ann *theater educator, actress*
Richey, Scott H *language educator*

Stuart
Bump, Wilbur Neil *retired lawyer*

Sumner
Wright, James Timothy *music educator, composer*

Tipton
Farwell, Walter Maurice *vocalist, educator*

Toddville
Hazeltine, Gerald Lester *food products executive*

Treynor
Guttau, Michael K. *state agency administrator, banker*

Wapello
Hicklin, Edwin Anderson *lawyer*

Waterloo
Eilers, Bruce Dean *music educator*
Hasek, Jane Ellen *academic administrator*
Kober, Arletta Refshauge (Mrs. Kay L. Kober) *supervisor*
Lueders, Sara Jeanne *music educator, director*
Newcomer, James Henry *retired federal agency administrator*
Waters, Ronald W. *theology studies educator, church executive, pastor*

Waverly
Brunkhorst, Robert John *computer programmer, analyst*
Koob, Kathryn Loraine *religious studies educator*
Rose, Mary Mabel *elementary school educator*

West Bend
Wuebker, Colleen Marie *retired librarian*

West Branch
Forsythe, Patricia Hays *development professional*
Mather, Mildred Eunice *retired archivist*
Walch, Timothy George *library administrator*

West Des Moines
Alberts, Marion Edward *physician*
Briggs, John C. *food products executive*
Burnett, Robert A. *retired publisher*
Churchill, Steven Wayne *former state legislator, marketing professional*
Goldsmith, Janet Jane *pediatric nurse practitioner*
Holderness, Susan Rutherford *at-risk educator*
Johnson, John Paul *lawyer, administrative law judge*
Lynch, David William *physicist, retired educator*
Marshall, Russell Frank *consulting company executive*
McEnroe, Michael Louis *lawyer*
McNamara, David Joseph *financial and tax planning executive*
Pearson, Ronald Dale *retail food stores corporation executive*
Pomerantz, Marvin Alvin *manufacturing executive*
Wheeler, Mike *retail food store corporate executive*
Zimmerman, Jo Ann *health services and educational consultant, former lieutenant governor*

West Union
Rivera, Shawna Colleen *small business owner*

Windsor Heights
Beadel, Stephen Jay *author*

Winfield
Carty, John Wesley *lawyer*

Winterset
Feirer, Alan David *music educator, organizational development consultant*

Zearing
Britten, William Harry *editor, publisher*

KANSAS

Abilene
Britt, Ronald leroy *retired manufacturing company executive*

Arkansas City
Bachman, Neal Kenyon *librarian*
Bruton, Rebecca Ann *mayor, commissioner*
Nichols, Gregory A. *mathematician, educator*
Rowen, Sharon Marie *journalist, photographer*

Atchison
Donaldson, Penny LeeAnne *library director*
Fellin, Jo Ann *mathematics professor*
Lane, Elizabeth Ann *genealogist, researcher*
Lowry, Patrick Emmet *journalist*
McDonald, Joseph Andrew *information services director, consultant, writer*
Seago, Diana Marie *college administrator*

Baldwin City
Lambert, Daniel Michael *academic administrator*

Baxter Springs
Whiteley, Henry Howard *religious studies educator, minister*

Brookville
Bohata, Emil Anton *rancher*

Bucyrus
Hoffman, John Raymond *lawyer*

Caldwell
Robinson, Alice Jean McDonnell *retired drama and speech educator*

Carbondale
McCollum, Susan *elementary school educator*

Chanute
Dillard, Dean Innes *English language educator, academic administrator*

Claflin
Burmeister, Paul Frederick *farmer*

Clay Center
Braden, James Dale *former state legislator*
Churchill, Thomas John *broadcast meteorologist*

Clearwater
Taverner, Pamela Johnson *secondary school educator*

Clifton
Taddiken, Mark *state legislator*

Coffeyville
Garner, Jim D. *state official, lawyer*
Hawley, Raymond Glen *pathologist*

Colby
Baldwin, Irene S. *corporate executive, real estate investor*
Morrison, James Frank *optometrist, state legislator*

Coldwater
Adams, Elizabeth Herrington *banker*

Concordia
Fowler, Wayne Lewis, Sr., *internist*
Freeborn, Joann Lee *state legislator, farmer, former educator*
Kalthoff, Theodore Joseph *academic administrator*

Copeland
Birney, Walter Leroy *religious administrator*

Courtland
Johnson, Dorothy Phyllis *retired counselor, art therapist*

De Soto
Strubbe, Thomas R. *insurance industry executive*

Dighton
Stanley, Ellen May *historian, consultant*

Dodge City
Rosel, Carol Ann *artist*
Ross, Connie L. *music educator*

El Dorado
Jenkinson, John Stephen *literature educator*
Mack, Valerie Lippoldt *music educator, performing arts educator, freelance/self-employed choreographer*
Stone, Duane Snyder *school psychologist, clergyman*

Emporia
Barham, Terry J. *music educator*
DeBauge, Janice B. *musician*
Frogge, Beverly Ann *nurse, consultant*
Hashmi, Sajjad Ahmad *business educator, university dean*
Helbert, Michael Clinton *lawyer*
Mehring, Teresa Ann *dean, education educator*
Meierhoff, Gayle Patrice *lawyer, accountant*
Schallenkamp, Kay *academic administrator*
Sundberg, Marshall David *biology professor*

Enterprise
Wickman, John Edward *librarian, historian*

Eskridge
Taylor, Russell Benton *mining executive*

Eudora
Miller, David Groff *insurance agent*

Fort Leavenworth
Alvarez, Jeffrey L. *psychologist, researcher*
Oliver, Thornal Goodloe *health care executive*
Rafuse, Ethan Sepp *historian, educator*
Riley, James Clifford *military career officer*

Fort Riley
Spurrier-Bright, Patricia Ann *professional society administrator*

Fort Scott
Hudson, Leigh Carleton *lawyer*
Mann, Henry Dean *accountant*

Garden City
Buchele, Wesley Fisher *retired agricultural engineering educator*
Loyd, Ward Eugene *lawyer, state legislator*
Pierce, Ricklin Ray *lawyer*
Reeve, Lee M. *farmer*
Thomas, Gregory Hall *psychology professor*

Garden Plain
Stovall, Carla Jo *former state attorney general*

Gardner
Webb, William Duncan *lawyer, mediator*

Girard
Beezley, Sara S. *lawyer*

Great Bend
Rittenhouse, Nancy Carol *elementary school educator*

Haddam
Hardenburger, Janice *state legislator*

Haven
Schlickau, George Hans *cattle breeder, professional association executive*
Schlickau, Lois Marie *farmer*

Hays
Bustos, Rudolph R. *health facility administrator*
Coyne, Patrick Ivan *physiological ecologist*
Duffy, Cheryl Hofstetter *language educator*
Hammond, Edward H. *university president*
Harbin, Calvin Edward *retired educator*
Hassett, Mary Ruth *nursing educator*
Levy, Patricia Anne *social sciences educator*
Vesely, Suzanne Araas *school librarian, educator*

Herington
Weber, Shari *state legislator*

Hillsboro
Miller, Douglas B. *theology studies educator*

Humboldt
Finney, Paul David *acupuncturist, Chinese herbologist, entrepreneur*

Hutchinson
Baumer, Beverly Belle *journalist*
Buzbee, Richard Edgar *retired newspaper editor*
Crater, Timothy Andrews *internist*
Davis, Mary Elizabeth *speech pathologist, educator, counselor*
Dick, Harold Latham *manufacturing executive*
Hayes, John Francis *lawyer*
Kerr, Dave *state official, marketing professional*
O'Neal, Michael Ralph *state legislator, lawyer*
Rosenblad, Helen Viola *social services coordinator*
Swearer, William Brooks *lawyer*
Wendelburg, Norma Ruth *composer, pianist, educator*

Independence
Ellenstein, Peter *theater director, theater producer*

Iola
Lynn, Emerson Elwood, Jr., *retired newspaper editor/publisher*
Strickler, Ivan K. *dairy farmer*
Toland, John Robert *lawyer*

Junction City
Craft, Barbara J. *state representative*
Davis, Victor Allen, Jr., *executive magistrate*
Werts, Merrill Harmon *retired management consultant*

Kansas City
Anderson, Harrison Clarke *pathologist, educator, biomedical researcher*
Arakawa, Kasumi *physician, educator*
Atkinson, Barbara F. *dean, medical educator, academic administrator*
Ator, Gregory A. *otolaryngologist, consultant*
Baker, Clarence Albert, Sr., *structural steel construction company executive*
Baska, James Louis *wholesale grocery company executive*
Brown, Norman Jack *lawyer*
Carolan, Douglas *wholesale company executive*
Cheney, Paul D. *physiologist, educator*
Damjanov, Ivan *pathologist, educator*
Doull, John *toxicologist, pharmacologist*
Dunn, Marvin Irvin *physician*
Godwin, Harold Norman *pharmacist, educator*
Grantham, Jared James *nephrologist, educator*
Greenwald, Gilbert Saul *physiologist*
Gulliford, James B. *government agency administrator*
Hagen, Donald Floyd *university administrator, former military officer*
Hite, Pamela Rene *emergency medicine physician*
Hudson, Robert Paul *medical educator*
Jerome, Norge Winifred *nutritionist, anthropologist*
Johnson, Joy Ann *diagnostic radiologist*
Jones, Charles W. *labor union executive*
Keleher, James P. *bishop*
Krantz, Kermit Edward *physician, educator*
Lawrence, Walter Thomas *plastic surgeon*
Lee, Kyo Rak *radiology educator*

Lungstrum, John W. *federal judge*
Mathewson, Hugh Spalding *anesthesiologist, educator*
McCallum, Richard Warwick *medical researcher, clinician, educator*
Meyers, David George *internist, cardiologist, educator*
Miller, Karen L. *dean, nursing educator*
Mohn, Melvin Paul *anatomist, educator*
Nastri, Wayne *government agency administrator*
Neuberger, John Stephen *preventive medicine and epidemiology educator*
Noelken, Milton Edward *biochemistry educator, researcher*
Olofson, Tom William *computer executive*
Pehlivanov, Nonko Dimitrov *gastroenterologist, researcher*
Penick, Elizabeth C. *psychologist*
Rawitch, Allen Barry *medical educator, academic administrator*
Sanders-Hall, Patricia E. *health facility administrator*
Schloerb, Paul Richard *surgeon, educator*
Sciolaro, Charles Michael *cardiac surgeon*
Starling, Carol King *nursing educator*
Steineger, Chris *state legislator*
Steineger, Margaret Leisy *non-profit organization officer*
Suzuki, Tsuneo *molecular immunologist*
Twillman, Robert Keith *psychologist*
VanBebber, George Thomas *federal judge*
Voogt, James Leonard *medical educator*
Vratil, Kathryn Hoefer *federal judge*
Warne, Alan M. *adult education educator, consultant*
Waxman, David *internist, consultant, academic administrator*
Wendel, Shirley Anne *college dean*
Ziegler, Dewey Kiper *neurologist, educator*

Lansing
Rawlings, Gregory Owen *science educator, consultant*

Larned
Linderer, Steve *historic site executive*

Lawrence
Ammar, Raymond George *physicist, researcher*
Angino, Ernest Edward *retired geology and engineering educator*
Armitage, Kenneth Barclay *biology and ecology professor*
Ballard, Barbara W. *state legislator*
Barnett, William Arnold *economics professor*
Baron, Frank *language educator*
Benjamin, Bezaleel Solomon *architectural engineer, educator*
Berry, James Lee *retired educator*
Bovee, Eugene Cleveland *protozoologist, emeritus educator*
Bowman, Laird Price *retired foundation administrator*
Brady, Lawrence Lee *geologist*
Briscoe, Mary Beck *federal judge*
Brundage, James Arthur *historian, educator*
Buck, Henry William, Jr., *obstetrician-gynecologist*
Burke, Paul E., Jr., *governmental relations consultant*
Byers, George William *retired entomology educator*
Canda, Edward R. *social work educator*
Capps, Jason Scott *education educator, researcher*
Castle, Joyce *mezzo soprano*
Conard, John Joseph *financial official*
Crowe, William Joseph *librarian*
Darwin, David *civil engineering educator, researcher, consultant*
Debicki, Andrew Peter *foreign language educator*
Dick, Ernst S. *retired German language educator*
Dickinson, William Boyd, Jr., *editorial consultant*
Dooley, Patrick John *graphic designer, design educator*
Downing, David *science administrator*
Dreschhoff, Gisela Auguste Marie *physicist, researcher*
Duerksen, George Louis *music educator, music therapist*
Eldredge, Charles Child, III, *art history educator*
Enos, Paul *geologist, educator*
Farmer, Frank *language educator*
Frederickson, Horace George *former college president, public administration educator*
Gerhard, Lee Clarence *geologist, educator*
Grabow, Stephen Harris *architecture educator*
Green, Don Wesley *chemical and petroleum engineering educator*
Grzymala-Busse, Jerzy Witold *engineering educator*
Gunn, James E. *English language educator*
Hale, Richard Lee *magazine editor*
Harmony, Marlin Dale *chemistry professor*
Harvey, Douglas Scott *historian, educator*
Harvey, Mark Austin *political scientist, educator, political scientist, consultant*
Heller, Francis H(oward) *law and political science educator emeritus*
Hemenway, Robert E. *academic administrator, language educator*
Hilding, Jerel Lee *music and dance educator, former dancer*
Hilt, Betty Marie *special education educator*
Himmelberg, Charles John, III, *mathematics educator, researcher*
Johnston, Richard Fourness *biologist, educator*
Karcz, Andrzej *literature educator*
Kuznesof, Elizabeth Anne *history educator*
Landgrebe, John Allan *chemistry professor*
Lane, Meredith Anne *botany educator, museum curator*
Levin, Murray Scott *law educator, arbitrator, mediator*
Li, Chu-Tsing *art history educator*
Lichtwardt, Robert William *mycologist*
Locke, Carl Edwin, Jr., *academic administrator, engineer, educator*
Mackenzie, Kenneth Donald *management consultant, educator*
McCabe, John Lee *engineer, educator*
McCabe, Steven Lee *structural engineer*
Mc Coin, John Mack *social worker*
Merriam, Daniel F(rancis) *geologist*
Mitscher, Lester Allen *chemist, educator*
Moore, Richard Kerr *electrical engineering educator*
Muirhead, Vincent Uriel *retired aerospace engineer*
Nordling, Bernard Erick *lawyer*
Pasco, Allan Humphrey *literature educator*
Penny, Paul Baldwin *landscape artist*
Peterson, Nancy *special education educator*
Pickett, Calder Marcus *retired journalism educator*
Pozdro, John Walter *music educator, composer*
Rosenbloom, Joshua Levi *economist, educator*
Roskam, Jan *aerospace engineer*
Rowland, James Richard *electrical engineering educator*
Rury, John Leslie *education educator*
Saul, Norman Eugene *history educator*
Schoeck, Richard J(oseph) *English and humanities scholar, poet*
Schroeder, Stephen Robert *psychology researcher*
Shaffer, Harry George *economics professor*
Shankel, Delbert Merrill *microbiologist, biologist, educator*
Sheridan, Rick D. *educator*
Shulenburger, David Edwin *economics educator, university official*
Siemsen, Susan Anne *physician assistant*
Simons, Dolph Collins, Jr., *newspaper executive and editor*
Six, Fred N. *retired state supreme court justice*
Smith, Glee Sidney, Jr., *lawyer*
Spires, Robert Cecil *foreign language educator*
Springer, Byron Eugene *lawyer*
Tsubaki, Andrew Takahisa *theater director, educator*
Turnbull, Ann Patterson *special educator, consultant, research director*
Turnbull, H. Rutherford, III, *law educator, lawyer*
Tuttle, William McCullough, Jr., *history professor*
Van Vleck, Fred Scott *mathematician, educator, researcher*
Wallace, Victor Lew *computer science educator*
Washington, Marian *women's college basketball coach*
Wiechert, Allen LeRoy *educational planning consultant, architect*
Winter, Winton Allen, Jr., *lawyer, state senator*
Woelfel, James Warren *philosophy and humanities educator*
Worth, George John *English literature educator*

Leavenworth
Arneson, George Stephen *manufacturing executive, management consultant*
Crow, Martha Ellen *lawyer*
Heim, Dixie Sharp *family practice nurse practitioner*

Leawood
Dykes, Archie Reece *financial services executive*
Garwood, Julie *writer*
Joslin, Janine Elizabeth *preservation consultant*
Karmeier, Delbert Fred *engineer, consultant, realtor*
Kordash, Dorothy Mae *artist*
White, Shanon Kathleen *accountant, consultant*

Lenexa
Ascher, James John *pharmaceutical executive*
Barr, William Crawford *manufacturing executive*
Grant, W. Thomas, II, *insurance company executive*
Hewitt, William Harley *investment and marketing executive*

Lewis
Cross, David Rusk *farmer, livestock raiser*

Lincoln
Crangle, Robert D. *lawyer, manufacturing executive, management consultant, entrepreneur*

Lindsborg
Humphrey, Karen Ann *college director*

Lyons
Hodgson, Arthur Clay *lawyer*

Madison
Clark, Doris Ellen *music educator*

Manhattan
Amtoft, Torben *adult education educator, researcher*
Babcock, Michael Ward *economics professor*
Ball, Louis Alvin *insurance company executive*
Cai, Liang-Wu *engineering educator*
Chakrabarti, Seemanti *entomologist, researcher*
Chung, Do Sup *agricultural engineering educator*
Coffman, James Richard *academic administrator, veterinarian, educator*
Durkee, William Robert *retired internist*
Erickson, Howard Hugh *veterinarian, physiology educator*
Fateley, William Gene *chemist, educator, inventor, administrator*
Foerster, Bernd *architecture educator*
Gillispie, Harold Leon *minister*
Glasscock, Kenton *state legislator*
Hagen, Lawrence Jacob *agricultural engineer*
Haub, Mark D. *exercise physiologist*
Higgins, James Jacob *statistics educator*
Higham, Robin *historian, editor, publisher*
Hoyt, Kenneth Boyd *educational psychology educator*
Jiang, Hongxing *physics educator, researcher*
Johnson, William Howard *agricultural engineer, educator*
Kirkham, M. B. *plant physiologist, educator*
Lee, E(ugene) Stanley *engineering educator*
Machor, James Lawrence *language educator*
Mengel, David Bruce *agronomy and soil science educator*
Miller, Anne Burke *lawyer*
Mortenson, Kristin Oppenheim *violinist*
Muir, William Lloyd, III, *academic administrator*
Murray, John Patrick *psychologist, educator, researcher*
Nellis, M. Duane *dean*
Oehme, Frederick Wolfgang *medical researcher, educator*
Patterson, Deb *women's college basketball coach*
Pei, Zj *engineer, educator, researcher*
Posler, Gerry Lynn *agronomist, educator*
Richardson, Ralph C. *dean*
Roper, Donna C. *archaeologist*
Russell, Eugene Robert, Sr., *engineering educator, administrator*
Seaton, Edward Lee *editor, publishing executive*
Shanklin, Carol W. *dietician*
Shanklin, Carol Williams *academic administrator, researcher*
Sheu, Chwen *finance educator*
Simons, Gale Gene *nuclear and electrical engineer, educator*
Spears, Marian Caddy *dietetics and institutional management educator*
Stolzer, Leo William *bank executive*
Streeter, John Willis *information systems manager*
Swanson, Diane L. *business management and economics educator, researcher*
Thomas, Lloyd Brewster *economics professor*
Wallis, Robert Ray *psychologist*
Wefald, Jon *university president*

Marion
Meyer, Bill *publishing executive, editor*

Mcpherson
Entz, Gary R. *historian, educator*
Hull, Robert Glenn *retired financial administrator*
Stevens, Leota Mae *retired elementary education educator*

Meade
Brannan, Cleo Estella *retired elementary education educator*

Mission
Sheets, Cynthia Ann *elementary school educator, gifted and talented educator*
Trevino, Lee Buck *professional golfer*
Watson, Thomas Sturges *professional golfer*

Neodesha
Chronister, Rochelle Beach *former state legislator*
Depew, Harry Luther *lawyer*
James, Charles (Chuck) Edward *small business owner, writer*

Neosho Falls
Bader, Robert Smith *biology, zoology educator and researcher*

New Century
Huber, Dennis G. *communications executive*

Newton
Sprunger, Keith L. *history educator*

North Newton
Ediger, Marlow *education educator*
Snider, Marie Anna *syndicated columnist*

Offerle
Herrmann, Lorena Joyce *retired music educator*

Olathe
Borel, Steven James *lawyer*
Dodd, James B. *internet executive*
Fraser, David Charles *investment banker*
Goodwin, Becky K. *educational technology resource educator*
Graham, James C. *food service executive*
O'Connor, Kay F. *state legislator*
Prestley, Mark Douglas *video director*
Smith, Katheryn Jeanette *music educator*
Stevens, Diana Lynn *elementary school educator*
Taylor, L(ynn) Franklin *lawyer*

Oskaloosa
Flower, Joann *nurse, former state legislator*

Ottawa
Brady, Gordon Leonard, Jr., *economist*
Davidson, Medora Lea *dance educator*
DeShazer, Ruth Shomler *health facility administrator, consultant*
Howe, William Hugh *artist*

Overland Park
Appelbaum, Elizabeth Berman (Elizabeth Berman) *mathematician*
Ayers, Jeffrey David *lawyer*
Betts, Gene M. *telecommunications industry executive*
Burger, Henry G. *vocabulary scientist, anthropologist, publisher*
Callahan, Michael Thomas *arbitrator, consultant, construction executive*
Campbell, Harry *communications executive*
Conrad, William Merrill *architect*
Daniel, Karen *engineering and design company executive*
Dockhorn, Robert John *physician, educator*
FitzGerald, Thomas Joe *psychologist*
Forsee, Gary D. *telecommunications industry executive*
Fuller, Michael B. *communications executive*
Garcia, John A. *telecommunications industry executive*
Gerke, Thomas A. *communications executive*
Goetz, Kenneth Lee *cardiovascular physiologist, research consultant, writer*
Griswold, Thomas L. *lawyer*
Guckenheimer, Daniel Paul *financial advisor*
Hansen, Jim *telecommunications industry executive*
Hawthorne, Bruce N. *lawyer, telecommunications industry executive*
Hodge, Ralph J. *communications executive*
Javadi, Yousef B. *communications executive*
Keplinger, Bruce (Donald Keplinger) *lawyer*
Kissinger, Jim *communications executive*
Klamann, John Michael *lawyer*
Kuppuswamy, Carthy *news analyst*
Lamb, Gordon Howard *music educator*
Landry, Mark Edward *podiatrist, researcher*
Lauer, Len J. *telecommunications industry executive*
Leonard, Markus Dayle *software systems engineer*
Lucas, James Raymond *business executive, leadership consultant, author, speaker*
McCann, Vonya B. *federal agency administrator, telecommunications industry executive*
McChesney, Samuel Parker, III, *real estate executive*
McCready, Matt *music educator*
McEvoy, Thomas J. *communications executive*
Meyer, John P. *communications executive*
Miller, Mark William *investment advisor, writer*
Molz, Philip Jack *management consultant*
Murphy, Thomas E. *communications executive*
Murray, Thomas Veatch *lawyer*
Ostby, Frederick Paul, Jr., *meteorologist, retired government official, science administrator*
Pretzel, Mark William *musician*
Prout, William C. *telecommunications industry executive*
Short, Joel Bradley *lawyer, software publisher*
Smith, Daniel Lynn *lawyer*
Spaeth, Nicholas John *lawyer, former state attorney general*
Stem, Carl Herbert *business educator*
Stout, Michael W. *communications executive*
Strandjord, M. Jeannine *telecommunications industry executive*
Surbaugh, Dolores Sayas *accounting and professional development educator*
Thomas, David P. *telecommunications industry executive*
Tubbs, David Eugene *mechanical engineer, marketing professional*
Vaughan, Brad *engineering and design company executive*
Voeller, John George *engineer*
Voska, Kathryn Caples *consultant, facilitator*
Vratil, John Logan *state legislator, lawyer*
Walker, Kathryn A. *telecommunications industry executive*
Westerhaus, Douglas Bernard *lawyer*
Whelan, Richard J. *retired academic administrator*
Whitaker, Freda N. *trust company executive*
Woods, Richard Dale *lawyer*
Zinke, Michael Duane *finance and accountancy manager*
Zollars, William D. *freight company executive*

Paola
Krum, Jack Kern *food products executive*

Parsons
Lomas, Lyle Wayne *agricultural research administrator, educator*

Pittsburg
Beer, Pamela Jill Porr *writer, retired vocational school educator*
Berger, Reena *musician, music educator*
Darling, John Rothburn, Jr., *business educator*
Jayawardhana, Ananda Amarasekara *statistician, educator*
Lee, Earl Wayne *library science educator*
Nettels, George Edward, Jr., *retired mining executive*
Runyan, Charles Kent *education educator*
Sullivan, William John *osteopath*
Trent, Darrell M. *academic and corporate executive*
Viney, Donald Wayne *philosophy educator*

Pomona
Gentry, Alberta Elizabeth *elementary school educator*

Prairie Village
Fairchild, Robert Charles *pediatrician*
Goheen, Ellen Rozanne *art historian*
Langworthy, Audrey Hansen *state legislator*
Stanton, Roger D. *lawyer*
Vogel, Arthur Anton *clergyman*

Pratt
Hart, Don Lee *academic administrator, writer*
Loomis, Howard Krey *banker, director*
Westerhaus, Catherine K. *social worker*

Rossville
Budden, Frederick Richard *music educator*

Saint John
Robinson, Alexander Jacob *clinical psychologist*

Saint Marys
Byers, Walter *athletic association executive*

Salina
Cosco, John Anthony *health care executive, educator, consultant, author*
Entriken, Robert Kersey, Jr., *editor, writer*
Fitzsimons, George Kinzie *bishop*
Horst, Deena Louise *state legislator*
Owens, William Dean *lawyer*
Selm, Robert Prickett *engineer, consultant*
Sigai, A. Gary *engineer*

Scott City
Duff, Craig *agricultural products executive*

Shawnee Mission
Badgerow, John Nicholas *lawyer*
Barger, Donald Gordon, Jr., *automotive products company executive*
Bartlett, Roger Danforth *engineering executive*
Barton, Betty Louise *school system administrator*
Bell, Deloris Wiley *physician*
Billings, Patricia Jean *inventor*
Braude, Michael *retired commodity exchange executive*
Breen, Katherine Anne *speech and language pathologist*
Crooks, Lisa Zahn *elementary school educator*
Fleming, Michael O. *physician*
Flora, Jairus Dale, Jr., *statistician*
Gaar, Marilyn Audrey Wiegraffe *political scientist, educator, property manager*
Gaar, Norman Edward *lawyer, former state senator*
Gaboury, David *engineering company executive*
Gamet, Donald Max *appliance company executive*
Green, John Lafayette, Jr., *education executive*
Hartzler, Geoffrey Oliver *retired cardiologist*
Helder, Jan Pleasant, Jr., *lawyer*
Hill, Lloyd L. *food service executive*
Hoffman, Alfred John *retired mutual fund executive*
Johntz, John Hoffman, Jr., *lawyer*
Mandl, Herbert Jay *rabbi*
Martin, Donna Lee *retired publishing company executive*
McEachen, Richard Edward *banker, lawyer*
Mealman, Glenn *corporate marketing executive*
Miller, Stanford *retired reinsurance executive, lawyer*
Moeller, Laura Lee *former retail executive, library consultant*
Morford, John A. *investment company executive*
Nulton, William Clements *retired lawyer*
Picciano, R.J. *renal technician*
Pressman, Ronald R. *utilities executive*
Price, James Gordon *physician, educator*
Putman, Dale Cornelius *management consultant, lawyer*

Sader, Carol Hope former state legislator
Slater, William Adcock retired social services organization executive
Smith, Michael L. transportation company executive
Snyder, Willard Breidenthal lawyer
Sparks, Billy Schley lawyer
Starrett, Frederick Kent lawyer
Talley, Douglas Eric music educator
Thomas, Christopher Yancey, III, surgeon, educator
Tucker, Keith A. investment company executive
Van Tuyl, Cecil L. investment company executive

Stockton
Kollman, Chris L. bank executive

Sublette
Swinney, Carol Joyce secondary school educator

Topeka
Allegrucci, Donald Lee state supreme court justice
Averill, Thomas Fox writer, educator
Barbieri-Lightner, Patricia state representative
Barnett, Mary Lorene real estate manager
Barton, Janice Sweeny chemistry educator
Bauman-Bork, Marceil health services administrator
Bleeker, Laurie state legislator
Bunten, William Daniel retired banker
Bunten, William Wallace state senator
Burroughs, Tom L. state representative
Campbell, Larry L. state representative
Cann, Steven J. political science educator
Cantrell, Duane L. retail executive
Carlin, Sydney state representative
Carter, Eric state representative
Concannon, James M. law educator, university dean
Cox, Joseph Lawrence judge
Crow, Sam Alfred judge
Dahl, Donald L. state representative
Dan, Johnson state representative
Davis, Robert Edward state supreme court justice
Dicus, John Carmack savings bank executive
Dillmore, Nile state representative
Douglass, Steven J. retail executive
Dreher, Stanley E., Jr., state representative
Elwood, H. Philip lawyer
Etzel, Timothy manufacturing executive
Faber, John M. state representative
Findley, Troy Ray former state legislator, bank officer
Flaharty, Geraldine state representative
Frahm, Sheila association executive, former government official, academic administrator
Franklin, Benjamin Barnum dinner club executive
Freden, Sharon Elsie Christman state education official
Fyler, Carl John dentist
Gatewood, Doug state representative
Gernon, Robert L. judge
Gilmore, Phyllis state legislator
Glashausser, Alex law educator
Glasscock, Joyce H. state official
Goetz, Roger Melvin minister
Goodwin, Greta Hall state legislator
Gordon, Lana G. state representative
Grant, Robert state representative
Haney, Thomas Dwight lawyer, educator
Hedrick, Lois Jean retired investment company executive, state official
Hill, Don state representative
Horttor, Donald J. lawyer
Jackson, David D. state legislator
Jenkins, Lynn M. state official, former state legislator
Jennings, Nancy Ann retired elementary education educator
Johnson, Duane Fadinand librarian
Johnson, Patsy nursing association administrator
Karst, Gary Gene retired architect
Kirk, Nancy A. state legislator, nursing home administrator
Kline, Phillip D. state attorney general
Krehbiel, Carl state representative
Kuether, Annie state representative
Larson, Edward retired state supreme court justice
Lee, Janis K. state legislator
Lee, Karen art appraiser
Light, Bill state representative
Long-Mast, Peggy state representative
Luckert, Marla Jo state supreme court justice
Mara, John Lawrence retired veterinarian, consultant
Marquardt, Christel Elisabeth judge
Mays, M. Douglas state legislator, financial consultant
McClure, Laura state legislator
McCreary, Bill state representative
McFarland, Kay Eleanor state supreme court chief justice
Menninger, William Walter psychiatrist
Merrick, Raymond F. state representative
Moler, Donald Lewis, Jr., lawyer
Moore, John Eddy lieutenant governor
Nason, Barry Mark systems engineer, mathematician, educator
Navone, Edward William artist, educator
Nelson, Franklin W. commissioner, retired banker
Newton, Dean state representative
Nuss, Lawton R. judge
Oleen, Lana state legislator
Owens, Thomas C. state representative
Parks, Blanche Cecile public administrator
Patterson, Doug state representative
Pauls, Janice Long state legislator
Peters, Barb Waterman artist, educator
Petty, Marge D. state senator
Porzig, Ullrich E. retail executive
Praeger, Sandy state legislator
Reardon, William J. state representative
Rehorn, Rick state representative
Reitz, Roger state representative
Rivers, Julie Elaine concert pianist, composer, recording industry executive
Robinson, Julie Ann judge
Rogers, Richard Dean federal judge
Roy, William Robert physician, lawyer, former congressman
Ruff, L. Candy state legislator
Salisbury, Alicia Laing state senator
Schmidt, Derek state legislator
Schodorf, Jean state legislator
Schroer, Gene Eldon lawyer
Schultz, LeAnne violinist, performer, music educator
Schultz, Richard Allen lawyer, farmer
Schwartz, Sharon J. state representative
Sebelius, Kathleen Gilligan governor
Sheffel, Irving Eugene psychiatric institution executive
Showalter, Judy state representative
Sipes, Karen Kay communications executive
Slemmons, Robert Sheldon architect
Smith, Loran Bradford education educator
Snyder, Brock Robert lawyer
Spencer, William Edwin telephone company executive, engineer
Storm, Suzanne state representative
Stroud, Herschel Leon retired dentist
Stroud, Jacqueline Lucille medical supply company executive
Sutherland, John Bennett chemical engineer
Tafanelli, Lee state representative
Thornburgh, Ron E. secretary of state
Thull, Tom state representative
Toelkes, Dixie E. state legislator
Varner, Charleen LaVerne McClanahan nutritionist, educator, administrator, dietitian
Varner, Robert Bernard counselor, educator
Vidricksen, Ben Eugene food service executive, state legislator
Ward, Jim state representative
Welshimer, Gwen R. state legislator, real estate broker, appraiser
Williams, Daniel A. state representative
Wilson, R. J. state representative
Winn, Valdenia C. state representative
Wittig, David C. energy executive

Viola
Sanderson, Kimberly Lea dancer, educator, small business owner

Wellington
Ferguson, William McDonald rancher, writer, banker, retired lawyer, former state official

Westwood
Dellinger, Robert J. corporate financial executive
Hart, Paul Vincent, Jr., emergency and acute care physician, inventor

Wichita
Acker, Andrew French, III, mathematics educator, researcher
Andrew, Kenneth L. research physicist, physics educator
Ayres, Ted Dean lawyer, academic counsel
Badger, Ronald Kay lawyer
Bagai, Rajiv computer science educator
Beggs, Donald Lee academic administrator
Bell, Baillis F. airport terminal executive
Berman, Mitchell A. orchestra executive
Brada, Donald Robert psychiatrist
Brown, Wesley Ernest federal judge
Burket, George Edward, Jr., retired family physician
Byers, Stephen Wesley music educator
Cadman, Wilson Kennedy retired utility company executive
Chopra, Dharam Vir statistician, educator
Clark, Susan Matthews psychologist
Cummings, Richard J. retired otologist
Da'Luz Vieira-Jones, Lorraine Christine C. acupuncturist, researcher
Depew, Spencer Long lawyer
Dill, Sheri publishing executive
Docking, Thomas Robert lawyer, former state lieutenant governor
Dorr, Stephanie Tilden psychotherapist
Ericson, David Frank political scientist, educator
Etter, Gregg Wayne, Sr., police officer, educator
Feilmeier, Steve energy executive
Foulston, Nola Tedesco lawyer
Frazier, Linda M. medical educator
French, James Edward surgeon
Gates, Walter Edward small business owner
Guthrie, Diana Fern nursing educator
Guthrie, Richard Alan physician
Hatteberg, Larry Merle photojournalist
Herr, Peter Helmut Friederich sales executive
Hicks, M. Elizabeth (Liz Hicks) pharmacist
Hull, Spring Sasha researcher
Hund, Edward Joseph lawyer
Jennison, Robin L. former state legislator, lobbyist
Johnson, C. Nicholas dance company executive
Johnson, George Taylor training and manufacturing executive
Johnson, Steven M. food service executive
Kahn, Melvin A. political science educator
Kellogg, Darrell Dean lawyer
Kennedy, Joseph Winston lawyer
Knight, Robert G. mayor, investment banker
Koch, Charles de Ganahl engineering company executive
Korf, Clifford Dean physician assistant
Landwehr, Brenda state legislator, corporate financial executive
McCrary, Larry Dale minister, religious studies educator
McKee, George Moffitt, Jr., civil engineer, consultant
McKenzie, Harry James cardiothoracic surgeon, surgical researcher
Melgren, Eric Franklin lawyer
Menefee, Frederick Lewis advertising executive
Meyer, Russell William, Jr., aircraft company executive
Mitchell, Linda Marlene education educator
Moeller, Joseph (Joe) W. energy executive
Nienke, Steven A. construction company executive
Oxley, Dwight K(ahala) pathologist
Palmer, Ada Margaret systems analyst, consultant
Park, Chan Hyung cell biologist, physician
Pett, Timothy finance educator, management consultant
Platt, George Milo university administrator
Pottorff, Jo Ann state legislator
Rogers, Rita Doris Luck family nurse practitioner
Rosendale, George William aircraft company executive
Rueb, Sheree A. social services administrator
Schuster, James Edward aircraft manufacturing executive
Sevart, Daniel Joseph lawyer
Sewell, Andrew music director
Sherwood, Joan Karolyn Sargent retired career counselor
Siginer, Dennis A. mechanical engineering educator, university dean
Stephenson, Richard Ismert lawyer
Sullivan, Mitzi accountant
Trombold, Walter Stevenson supply company executive
Van Milligen, James M. health care administrator
Varner, Sterling Verl retired oil company executive
Wagle, Susan state legislator, small business owner
Wilhelm, William Jean civil engineering educator
Williams, Jackie N. law educator, former prosecutor
Winkler, Dana John lawyer

Winfield
Dolsen, David Horton mortician
Gray, Ina Turner fraternal organization administrator
Hall, Lydia Jane geriatrics nurse
Schul, Bill Dean psychological administrator, author
Yau, Oi Yan Eugenia music educator

KENTUCKY

Albany
Smith, Eugenia Sewell funeral home executive

Ashland
Carter, David Edward communications executive, director
Luellen, Charles J. retired oil company executive
Roth, Oliver Ralph radiologist
Scharp, Robert Charles mining engineer, energy company executive
Tepper, Scott M. mining executive
Weaver, Carlton Davis retired oil industry executive
Yancey, Robert Earl, Jr., retired oil company executive

Beaver Dam
Morris, Theresa Janette (TJ Morris) vocalist, writer, composer, publishing executive

Bellevue
Carpenter, Woodrow Wilson enamel company executive, ceramic engineer
Lemlich, Robert chemical engineer, educator

Berea
Krug, John Carleton (Tony Krug) college administrator, library consultant
Lamb, Irene Hendricks medical researcher

Boston
Rosenbaum, Stanley Ned theology educator

Bowling Green
Ahmed, S. Basheer research company executive, educator
Atwell, Nedra Wheeler education educator, consultant
Berry, Mark Sean music educator
Burch, Barbara G. academic administrator
Cangemi, Joseph Peter psychologist, consultant, educator
Catron, Stephen Barnard lawyer, real estate developer, director
Cooper, Davis A. city official
Cravens, Raymond Lewis retired political science educator
Garrison, Geneva retired administrative assistant
Gipson, Jim wholesale distribution executive
Holland, John Ben clothing manufacturing company executive
Huddleston, Joseph Russell judge
Jhamb, Indar Mohan physician
Minton, John Dean historian, educator
Rahim, M. Afzalur management educator, editor
Rudloff, William Joseph lawyer
Slocum, Donald Warren chemist
Stewart, Harold Sanford real estate investment and supply executive
Tutino, Thomas James theater educator, set designer
Wells, Jerry Wayne protective services official
Wilcher, Larry K. lawyer

Calvert City
Butler, Sheila Morris occupational health nurse

Campbellsville
Burch, John Russell, Jr., library director
Chowning, John E. political scientist, educator, minister
Gaddis, John Robert music educator
McArthur, Lisa R music educator, musician
Roberts, M. Wesley musician, educator

Caneyville
Embry, C B, Jr., state representative

Carlisle
Wolf, John Howell retired publisher

Cecilia
Thompson, Kathy Self secondary school educator

Central City
McMurray, Jamie race car driver

Corbin
Barton-Collings, Nelda Ann political activist, newspaper, bank and nursing home executive
Doby, John Thomas social psychologist

Covington
Brothers, John Alfred retired oil company executive
Cimprich, John Vincent history educator
D'Antoni, David J. chemicals executive
Davidson, David Edgar lawyer
Fleischer-Rieveschl, Ellen Lee real estate agent
Gemunder, Joel Frank healthcare company executive
Giesbrecht, Martin Gerhard retired economics educator, clarinetist
Hausrath, David L. lawyer
Hughes, William Anthony retired bishop
Kerr, Thomas Robert lawyer
McQueen, Regenia writer
O'Brien, James J. manufacturing executive
Quin, Joseph Marvin chemicals executive
Stepner, Donald Leon lawyer
Surber, David Francis public relations executive, consultant, television producer, journalist

Crescent Springs
Chellgren, Paul Wilbur industrial company executive
Ott, James Daniel journalist, educator

Crestview Hills
Cory, Edward William, Jr., underwriting executive
Harper, Kenneth Franklin retired state legislator, real estate broker

Crestwood
Ray, Ronald Dudley lawyer
Roy, Elmon Harold minister
Snow, Edwin Fawcett management consultant

Cynthiana
Bandurski, Bruce Lord retired ecological and environmental scientist

Danville
Breeze, William Hancock college administrator
Haigh, Anthony R. performing arts educator, actor
Kennan, Elizabeth Topham academic administrator, retired historian
Morris, Alvin Leonard retired dentist, educational administrator
Nickens, Harry Carl medical association administrator
Pappas, Marjorie L. library studies educator
Roush, John A. academic administrator

East Point
Whitaker, Herbert Loyd retired special education educator

Edgewood
Gross, Joseph Wallace hospital administrator
Martin, Kevin Douglas surgeon

Elizabethtown
Cooper, William S. state supreme court justice
Phelps, Dennis Lane minister, educator, author
Rahman, Rafiq Ur oncologist, educator

Elsmere
Miller, Jackie Dean, I, genealogist, historian

Erlanger
Cuneo, Dennis Clifford automotive company executive
Niimi, Atsushi automotive executive

Flemingsburg
McCartney, Frank Howard, III, lawyer

Florence
Lawson, Harry Wilbur chemist, consultant, writer
Monohan, Edward Sheehan, IV, lawyer

Fort Campbell
Clark, Robert T. career officer

Fort Knox
Barnes, Larry Glen journalist, editor, educator

Fort Mitchell
Drees, David G. construction executive
Drees, Ralph construction executive
Silvers, Gerald Thomas retired publishing executive
Weiskittel, Ralph Joseph retired real estate broker

Fort Thomas
Besier, James Louis pharmacist, educator

Fort Wright
Sullivan, Connie Castleberry artist

Frankfort
Adams, John W. state representative
Arnold, Adrian King state representative
Barrows, Joseph Howard state representative
Bather, Paul state representative
Belcher, Carolyn R. state representative
Burch, Thomas Joseph state representative
Carroll, Julian Morton lawyer, former governor
Casebier, Lindy state legislator
Cherry, Mike E. state legislator
Clark, Lawrence D. state representative
Collins, Hubert real estate broker, state representative
Comer, James R., Jr., state representative
Cornett, Howard state representative
Crimm, Ronald E. state representative
Damron, Robert R. state representative
DeWeese, Bob M. state representative
Draud, Jon E. state representative
Embry, Michael Dale writer, editor
Feeley, Timothy E. state representative
Fleming, Juanita Wilson nursing educator, academic administrator
Fletcher, Ernie (Ernest L. Fletcher) governor, former congressman
Fletcher, Winona Lee theater educator
Ford, Danny R. state representative
Graham, Derrick W. state representative, educator
Gray, J. R. state representative
Greyson, Trey (C.M. Grayson) state official
Griffith, Patricia Barnes music educator, pianist
Hamilton, John Kennedy former state treasurer
Hatchett, Edward Bryan, Jr., lawyer
Haydon, Joseph A. (Jodie) state representative
Holsinger, James Wilson, Jr., physician
Jenkins, Joni Lynn state legislator
Johns, Susan D. state senator
Johnson, Jerry D. legislative staff member
Johnstone, Martin E. state supreme court justice
Lambert, Joseph Earl state supreme court chief justice
Lanham, Sallie Clay artist, educator
Liler, Charles L. state representative
Marcotte, Paul Henry state representative
McKee, Thomas M. state representative
Miller, Charles W. state representative
Mone, Michael A. social welfare administrator
Nowland-Curry, Betsy state official
Nunn, Stephen R. state representative
Palmore, Carol M. state official
Palmore, John Stanley, Jr., retired lawyer
Palumbo, Ruth Ann state legislator

Patton, Nicki *former political organization executive*
Pence, Stephen Beville *lieutenant governor*
Pullin, Tanya *state representative*
Richards, Jody *state legislator, journalism educator, small business owner*
Robinson, Ella D. *state agency administrator*
Shabazz, David Lorenzo *vocational school educator*
Sias, Mary *university executive*
Sonego, Ian G. *assistant attorney general*
Stein, Kathy W. *state representative*
Stine, Katie Kratz *state legislator*
Stumbo, Gregory D. *state attorney general*
Tapp, Gary L. *state senator*
Wayne, Jim *state representative*
Williams, David Lewis *state senator*
Williams, Ellen C. *political party official*
Williamson, Deborah McKibben *social services administrator, educator*
Wintersheimer, Donald Carl *state supreme court justice*

Franklin
Baldock, Brian F. *corporate financial executive*
Clark, James Benton *railroad industry consultant, former executive*
David, Phillip J. *biotechnology company executive*

Georgetown
Allison, James Claybrooke, II, *broadcasting executive*
Chi, Keon Soo *editor, educator, researcher*
Convis, Gary L. *automotive executive*
Klotter, James C. *historian, educator*

Glasgow
Baker, Walter Arnold *lawyer*
Knicely, Carroll Franklin *publishing executive*

Goshen
Strode, William Hall, III, *photojournalist, publisher*

Greenville
Walters, Sue Fox *business executive, accountant*
Yonts, Larry Brent *lawyer*

Hardin
Morrow, Bruce William *educational administrator, business executive, consultant, author*

Harlan
Ford, Mark L. *lawyer*
Greene, James S., III, *school administrator*

Harrods Creek
Keeney, Steven Harris *lawyer*

Harrodsburg
Bradshaw, Phyllis Bowman *historian, historic site staff member*
Semones, Charles W. *retired elementary school educator, writer*

Hazard
Roark, Jimmy Lee *lawyer*

Hebron
Howell, Joseph Toy *company owner*

Henderson
Logan, John A., III, *hospital administrator*

Highland Heights
Donnelly, Sharlotte K. B. Neely *anthropology educator, author*
Forman, Sandra H. *theater educator*
Hagner, Carolyn Zepf *music educator*
Moss, Nancy Evans *nurse midwife, women's health nurse*
Pennington, Randy Keith *music educator*
Staneck, Joseph L. *microbiologist, science administrator*

Hindman
Bailey, Benny Ray *health care administrator, state senator*

Hopkinsville
Neville, Thomas Lee *food service company executive*
Satterwhite, Robert Lee *library director*

Horse Cave
Brock, Robert F. *performing company executive, educator*

Independence
Hopgood, James F. *anthropologist, educator*

Inez
Duncan, Robert Michael *banker, lawyer, Republican national committeeman*

Kings Mountain
Gill, Allen (Dale Gill) *health facility administrator*

Lebanon
Higdon, Jimmy *state representative*

Lexington
Anderson, James Wingo *physician*
Assael, Leon A. *dean, educator*
Avant, Robert Frank *physician, educator*
Baker, Merl *engineering educator*
Beshear, Steven Lynn *lawyer*
Blanchard, Richard Emile, Sr., *retired management services executive, consultant*
Boyd, James Robert *energy company executive*
Brock, Carolyn Pratt *chemist, educator*
Brock, Louis Milton, Jr., *engineering educator, researcher*
Calvert, C(lyde) Emmett *former state agency administrator*
Caroland, William Bourne *structural engineer*
Chance, Kenneth Bernard *endodontist, educator, university official*
Chen, Zhi *electrical engineering educator*
Chowdhury, Dipak K. *pharmaceutical executive, researcher*
Clawson, David Kay *orthopedic surgeon*
Coffman, Edward McKenzie *retired history professor*
Coffman, Jennifer Burcham *judge*
Cole, Henry Philip *educational psychology educator*
Cole, Vincent J. *lawyer*
Cross, Alvin Miller (Al Cross) *journalist*
Cui, Chengwu *imaging scientist, researcher*
Curlander, Paul Joseph *computer company executive*
Curtz, Chauncey S.R. *lawyer, real estate company executive*
Daniel, Marilyn S. *lawyer*
Davey, Diane Davis *pathologist, educator*
Davis, George A. *pharmacologist, medical researcher*
Deener, Larry Colby *lawyer*
DeLong, Lance Eric *physics educator, researcher*
DeLuca, Patrick Phillip *pharmaceutical scientist, educator, administrator*
Dewees, Kathy Paxton *music educator*
Donohew, Robert Lewis, Sr., *communications educator*
Drake, Vaughn Paris, Jr., *electrical engineer, retired telephone company executive*
Ehmann, William Donald *chemistry professor*
Ettensohn, Frank Robert *geologist, educator*
Farrar, Donna Beatrice *hospital official*
Forester, Karl S. *chief district court judge*
Frye, Wilbur Wayne *retired soil science educator, researcher, administrator*
Fryman, Virgil Thomas, Jr., *lawyer*
Gable, Robert Elledy *real estate investment company executive*
Gallagher, Eugene Bennett *sociologist, medical educator*
Garmer, William Robert *lawyer*
Gill, Karen V. *secondary school educator, consultant*
Gilliam, M(elvin) Randolph *retired urologist, educator*
Glenn, James Francis *urologist, educator*
Goodman, Norman Loyal *microbiologist, educator*
Gornik, Kathy *electronics executive*
Gray, Lois Howard *construction company executive*
Grubbs, Misty D. *music educator*
Hagen, Michael Dale *family physician educator*
Hall, Harry H. *agricultural economics educator*
Halley, Samuel Hampton, III, *architect, architectural firm executive*
Hamilton-Kemp, Thomas Rogers *organic chemist, educator*
Haney, Donald Clay *geologist*
Henry, Kevin Gudgel *lawyer*
Hill, John Sylvester *allergist*
Hochstrasser, Donald Lee *cultural anthropologist, community health and public administrator*
Holland, Robert, Jr., *food products executive*
Hood, Gregory A. *internal medicine physician*
Hopper, Kevin R. *biologist*
Hultman, Charles William *economics professor*
Humphries, Asa Alan, Jr., *biologist, educator, dean*
Irtz, Frederick G., II, *lawyer*
Jones, Bonnie Quantrell *automobile dealer*
Kang, Bann C. *immunologist*
Kaplan, Martin P. *allergist, immunologist, pediatrician*
Karpf, Michael *medical administrator*
Keeling, Larry Dale *journalist*
Keller, James *state supreme court justice*
Kelly, Timothy Michael *newspaper publisher*
Kern, Bernard Donald *retired educator, physicist*
Kerr, Alice Forgy *state legislator*
Kibler, William Benjamin *orthopedist, surgeon*
Kissling, Fred Ralph, Jr., *publishing executive, insurance agency executive*
Leukefeld, Carl George *researcher, educator*
Lewis, Robert Kay, Jr., *fundraising executive*
Lodder, Robert A. *science educator*
Male, Alan Thomas *engineering educator, association executive*
Manivannan, Dakshnamoorthy *computer scientist, educator*
Markesbery, William R. *neurology and pathology educator, physician*
Mason, Ellsworth Goodwin *librarian*
Matl Prewitt, Lois Tudor *lawyer*
Mayer, Lloyd Dewald *allergist, immunologist, physician, medical educator*
McEllistrem, Marcus T. *physics professor, nuclear researcher*
Means, Robert Taylor, Jr., *hematologist, educator*
Mentzer, Robert Melvin, Jr., *surgeon*
Millard, James Kemper *marketing executive*
Miller, Pamela Gundersen *mayor*
Mitchell, George Ernest, Jr., *animal scientist, educator*
Monsen, Ronald Peter *musician, music educator, artist*
Nikolova - Karakashian, Mariana *biomedical researcher*
Noonan, Jacqueline Anne *pediatrics educator*
Reed, Michael Robert *agricultural economist*
Robinson, Thomas Christopher *academic administrator, educator*
Romanowitz, Byron Foster *architect, engineer*
Rowe, Melinda Grace *public health service officer*
Rowland, Randall G. *urologist*
Salisbury, Holly Buckner *university arts director*
Sandoval, Arturo Alonzo *art educator*
Sawyer, Donald T. *retired chemistry professor*
Scharlatt, Harold *management company executive*
Sekulic, Dusan P. *science educator, researcher*
Sexton, Robert Fenimore *educational organization executive*
Sharkey, Michael Joseph *education educator, researcher*
Sherman, Steven S.J. *architectural firm executive*
Sineath, Timothy Wayne *library educator, university dean*
Snowden, Ruth O'Dell Gillespie *artist*
Steensland, Ronald Paul *librarian*
Stempel, John Dallas *international studies educator*
Stilwell, William Earle, III, *psychology educator, retired military officer*
Straus, Robert *behavioral sciences educator*
Teegavarapu, Ramesh Satya *engineering educator, researcher*
Terry, Joseph H. *lawyer*
Thelin, John Robert *academic administrator, education educator, historian*
Timoney, Peter Joseph *veterinarian, virologist, educator, consultant*
Todd, Lee Trover, Jr., *electrical engineer*
Tollison, Joseph W. *family practice physician*
Turner, Sharon P. *dean, dental educator, dentist*
Van Meter, Woodford Spears *ophthalmologist, surgeon*
Van Tatenhove, Gregory F. *prosecutor*
Varellas, Sandra Motte *judge*
Vestal, Allan W. *dean, law educator*
Vimont, Richard Elgin *lawyer*
Warth, Robert Douglas *history educator*
Weitzel, William David *psychiatrist*
Wekstein, David Robert *physiology educator, researcher*
Wethington, Charles T., Jr., *academic administrator*
Whayne, Thomas French, Jr., *cardiologist, educator*
Whitmer, Leslie Gay *federal official*
Wildasin, David E(arl) *economics educator*
Williams, Carolyn Antonides *university dean*
Wilson, Emery Allen *university dean, obstetrician-gynecologist, educator*
Woodring, John Howell *radiologist*
Worell, Judith P. *psychologist, educator*
Young, Paul Ray *medical board executive, physician*
Zack, George J. *conductor, music director*
Zentall, Thomas R. *psychologist, educator*
Zinser, Elisabeth Ann *academic administrator*

Liberty
Wright, Rodney H. *architect*

London
Giles, William Elmer *retired newspaper editor*
Jensen, Thomas Lee *lawyer*
Keller, John Warren *lawyer*
Siler, Eugene Edward, Jr., *federal judge*

Louisville
Adams, Robert Waugh *state agency administrator, economics educator*
Amin, Mohammad *urology educator*
Anderson, Linda Jean *critical care nurse, psychiatric nurse practitioner*
Andrews, Adam Gregory *lobbyist, political scientist, educator*
Andrews, Billy Franklin *pediatrician, educator*
Appleberry, James Bruce *higher education consultant*
Ardery, Philip Pendleton *lawyer*
Aronoff, George Rodger *medicine and pharmacology educator*
Atz, Sarah J. *music educator*
Ballantine, John Tilden *lawyer*
Barnett, Joyce Lyndel *freelance/self-employed writer*
Barr, James Houston, III, *lawyer*
Becker, Gail Roselyn *museum director*
Belanger, William Joseph *chemist, polymer applications consultant*
Benfield, Ann Kolb *lawyer*
Bentley, James Robert *association curator, historian, genealogist*
Bertolone, Salvatore J. *pediatric medicine educator*
Bloem, James H. *managed health care executive*
Boggs, Danny Julian *federal judge*
Boykin, Gladys *retired religious organization administrator*
Brantley, William Albert *information architect, consultant*
Bratton, Ida Frank *retired secondary school educator*
Bridgeman, Ulysses, Jr., *food service executive*
Brittian, Kenneth Ray *research scientist*
Brown, Bonnie Maryetta *lawyer*
Brown, Owsley, II, *diversified consumer products company executive*
Brugioni, David Michael *graphic designer, illustrator, artist*
Buckaway, William Allen, Jr., *lawyer*
Bujake, John Edward, Jr., *beverage company executive*
Callen, Jeffrey Phillip *dermatologist, educator*
Campbell, Christian L. *restaurant company executive*
Carlisle, Douglas R. *managed health care company executive*
Carranza, Jovita *delivery service executive*
Carroll, Wayne Jackson *lawyer*
Cecil, Bonnie Susan *elementary school educator*
Chauvin, Leonard Stanley, Jr., *lawyer*
Chien, Sufan *surgeon, educator*
Christopher, Ray Louis *pilot, journalist, author*
Cohn, David V(alor) *biochemist, educator*
Columbus, Shanna S. *advertising executive*
Conner, Stewart Edmund *lawyer*
Cook, Larry Norman *pediatrician, neonatologist, educator*
Cooper, Richard Earl *lawyer*
Cornelius, Wayne Anderson *electrical and computer engineering consultant*
Cowan, Frederic Joseph *lawyer*
Crum, Denny (Denzel Edwin Crum) *retired collegiate basketball coach*
Crum, John Evan *physician, executive*
Crutcher, Michael Bayard *lawyer*
Dale, Judy Ries *religious organization administrator, consultant*
Danzl, Daniel Frank *emergency physician*
Davidson, Gordon Byron *lawyer*
Decker, Jack Neal *production executive*
Deering, Ronald Franklin *librarian, minister*
DeKay, Barbara Ann *social worker*
DeLong, James Clifford *air transportation executive*
DeMunbrun-Harmon, Donne O'Donnell *retired family physician*
Deno, David *restaurant executive*
DeVitis, Joseph L. *education educator*
Diaz, Paul J. *service industry executive*
Doran, Vincent Francis *economic development executive*
Doyle, Michael Joseph *neurosurgeon*
Drazin, Avrum I. *manufacturing executive*
Dreher, Donald Dean *furniture manufacturing executive*
Dudley, George Ellsworth *lawyer*
Duffy, Martin Patrick *lawyer*
Early, Jack Jones *foundation executive*
Edgell, Stephen Edward *psychology educator, statistical consultant*
Egilmez, Nejat K. *science educator*
Eighmey, Douglas Joseph, Jr., *hospital administrator*
Elin, Ronald John *pathologist, educator*
Eschels, Philip C. *lawyer*
Ethridge, Larry Clayton *lawyer*
Faller, Rhoda *lawyer*
Farman, Allan George *radiologist, oral pathologist, educator*
Fassett, Frances Nicholas (Kitty Fassett) *pianist, record producer*
Fassler, Charles *lawyer*
Ferguson, Jo McCown *lawyer*
Force, Jill L. *health facility executive*
Ford, Gordon Buell, Jr., *literature educator, writer*
Foster, Teresa E. *choral director, piano teacher*
French, Michael Bruce *marketing executive*
Fuchs, Olivia Anne Morris *lawyer*
Galandiuk, Susan *colon and rectal surgeon, educator*
Gall, Stanley Adolph *physician, immunology researcher*
Garcia, Rafael Jorge *retired chemical engineer*
Garretson, Henry David *neurosurgeon*
Garver, David L. *psychiatrist*
Gillenwater, James H. *health facility administrator*
Gilman, Sheldon Glenn *lawyer*
Gist, William Claude, Jr., *retired dentist*
Godsey, H. Carleton, Jr., *architectural firm executive*
Goodman, Bruce *managed health care company executive*
Gorman, Chris *lawyer*
Gray, Laman A., Jr., *thoracic surgeon, educator*
Greaver, Joanne Hutchins *mathematics educator, author*
Grissom, J. David *private investor, bank executive*
Guethlein, William O. *lawyer*
Guillaume, Raymond Kendrick *banker*
Haddaway, James David *retired insurance company official*
Haddy, Richard Ian *family physician, educator*
Hale, Roger W. *utilities company executive*
Hanson, Dennis Michael *medical imaging executive*
Harris, Patrick Donald *physiology educator*
Hawpe, David Vaughn *newspaper editor, journalist*
Hayes, William Meredith *pilot, retired career officer*
Haynes, Douglas Martin *obstetrician, gynecologist, educator*
Heiden, Charles Kenneth *metal products executive, consultant, retired military officer*
Hernandez, John E. *musician, music educator*
Heyburn, John Gilpin, II, *federal judge*
Hipwell, Art *managed health care company executive*
Hoffer, Debra Humes *educational association administrator*
Holt, Homer Anthony, Jr., *urologist, educator*
Hoye, Robert Earl *systems science educator*
Ivory, Bennie *editor*
Johnson, Alan Arthur *physicist, educator, consultant*
Johnson, Charlie W. *transportation executive*
Jones, David Allen *health benefits company executive*
Juber, David L. *prosecutor*
Kaplan, Henry Jerrold *ophthalmologist, educator*
Kaplan, Joel A. *academic administrator*
Kee, Brenda Eltrine *music educator, concert pianist*
Kelly, Thomas Cajetan *archbishop*
King, Tim *orchestra executive*
Klotter, John Charles *retired legal educator*
Kmetz, Donald R. *retired academic administrator*
Kuntz, Edward Lawrence *healthcare executive*
Kutz, Joseph Edward *hand surgeon, educator*
Lanier, Philip M. *lawyer*
Lavelle, Charles Joseph *lawyer*
Lay, Norvie Lee *law educator*
Lechleiter, Richard A. *service industry executive*
Lego, Paul Edward *retired corporation executive*
Lei, Zhenmin *endocrinologist, reproductive biologist, researcher*
Lewis, Aylwin B. *food service executive*
Lewis, Ronald Chapman *record company executive*
Lilly, Charles G. *protective services official, consultant*
Lloyd, Kimcherie *performing company executive*
Lofton, Kevin Eugene *medical facility administrator*
Lominadze, David *physiologist, researcher*
Longuet, Gregory Arthur *automation engineer, consultant*
Lord, Jonathan T. (Jack Lord) *medical association administrator*
Lunsford, W. Bruce *health facility administrator, health and medical products executive*
Lyndrup, Peggy B. *lawyer*
Maggiolo, Allison Joseph *lawyer*
Manassah, Edward E. *publishing executive*
Margulis, Heidi *managed health care company executive*
Marsh, Donald Louis *investment banker*
Martin, Boyce Ficklen, Jr., *federal judge*
Mather, Elizabeth Vivian *healthcare executive*
Matuschka, Paul R. *pharmacist*
McCallister, Michael B. *managed health care executive*
McCormick, Steven Thomas *insurance company executive*
McKim, Ruth Ann *financial planner*
Mellen, Francis Joseph, Jr., *lawyer*
Miller, Marilee Hebert *arts administrator, producer, director, consultant*
Mohler, Richard Albert, Jr., *academic administrator, theologian*
Mountz, Wade *retired health service management executive*
Mowery, Ward Franklin *retired music educator*
Moya, Steve *managed health care company executive*
Murray, James E. *managed health care company executive*
Northern, Richard *lawyer*
Novak, David C. *restaurant company executive*
Oates, Thomas R. *university executive*
Oglesby, Joseph Woodson (Mike English) *writer, publishing executive*
Oh, Christopher J. *advertising executive*
Oliphant, Naomi Joyce *music educator, performer*
Olson, William Henry *neurology educator, administrator*
Osborn, John Simcoe, Jr., *lawyer*
Palmer, Larry Isaac *lawyer, educator*
Parker, Joseph Corbin, Jr., *pathologist, educator*
Parkins, Frederick Milton *dental educator, university dean*
Partin, C. Fred *lawyer*
Pearson, Andrall Edwin *food service executive*
Pedley, Lawrence Lindsay *lawyer*
Pelfrey, D. Patton *lawyer*
Pence, Hobert Lee *physician*
Pitino, Richard *collegiate basketball coach, former professional basketball coach*
Polk, Hiram Carey, Jr., *surgeon, educator*
Popp, Shaun Raymond *secondary school educator, music educator*
Porter, Henry Homes, Jr., *investor*
Power, David M. *advertising executive*

Power, Michael L. *advertising executive*
Powers, Larry K. *lighting fixtures manufacturing executive*
Prough, Russell Allen *biochemistry educator, academic administrator*
Raff, Martin Jay *internist, infectious diseases educator, lawyer*
Rawley, Charles E., III, *food service executive*
Reed, D. Gary *lawyer*
Reed, David Benson *bishop*
Reed, John Squires, II, *lawyer*
Renau, Donald Irwin *lawyer*
Richardson, James David *surgeon*
Rockey, Eugene A., Jr., *vocational school educator, scriptwriter*
Ronald, Peter *utilities executive*
Rose, Charles Alexander *lawyer*
Rosky, Theodore Samuel *insurance company executive*
Rothstein, Mark Alan *health law and bioethics educator*
Royer, Robert Lewis *retired utility company executive*
Runyon, Keith Leslie *lawyer, newspaper editor*
Sandler, Deborah *performing company executive*
Saunders, Robert Samuel *venture capital executive*
Schwab, John Joseph *psychiatrist, educator*
Scott, Ralph Mason *physician, radiation oncology educator*
Segal, Uriel *music director*
Shaver, Kathryn *retired performing company executive, design educator*
Sherman, Mildred Mozelle *music educator, vocalist, actress, opera director*
Shield, Gene *managed health care company executive*
Siewert, Robin Noelle *planning engineer*
Silverthorn, Robert Sterner, Jr., *lawyer*
Simpson, Charles R., III, *judge*
Skees, William Leonard, Jr., *lawyer*
Smith, J. Lea *education educator, researcher*
Spalding, Catherine *lawyer*
Staats, Howard E. *newspaper editor*
Staffieri, Victor A. *energy company executive*
Stanton, M(orris) Duncan *psychologist, researcher, dean*
Strause, Randall Scott *judge*
Street, William May *beverage company executive*
Swain, Donald Christie *retired university president, history educator*
Syed, Ibrahim Bijli *medical educator and physicist, author, philosopher, theologist, public speaker, writer*
Talbott, Ben Johnson, Jr., *lawyer*
Tanguay, Peter Eugene *child and adolescent psychiatry educator*
Tasman, Allan *psychiatry educator*
Taylor, Robert Lewis *management educator*
Theiss, Gena Lee *genealogist, researcher*
Thomas, Riedel *education educator*
Thompson, Kathy C. *bank executive*
Thongboonkerd, Visith *nephrologist, researcher*
Towles, Donald Blackburn *retired publishing executive*
Tran, Long Trieu *industrial engineer*
Trotter, Lloyd G. *electric power industry executive*
Troutman, J. Gregory *lawyer*
Vish, Donald H. *lawyer, pension fund administrator*
Vogel, Werner Paul *retired machine company executive*
Waddell, William Joseph *pharmacologist, toxicologist*
Wagner, James Miller *funeral director*
Wagoner, Ruth R *education coach*
Wang, Chung-Hsiao *industrial engineer*
Watts, Beverly L. *civil rights executive*
Weisenbeck, Sharon M. *healthcare regulatory administrator*
Weisskopf, Bernard *pediatrician, child behavior, development and genetics specialist, educator*
Welsh, Sir Alfred John *lawyer, international advisor*
Welsh, Douglas Lee *psychologist, researcher*
Wesley, Stephen Burton *training professional*
Whitelaw, Christine Cappelle *pediatrician, aesthetic medicine educator*
Willenbrink, Rose Ann *lawyer*
Williams, John N. *dean, dental educator*
Wood, Phoebe A. *food products executive*
Wright, Jesse Hartzell *psychiatrist, educator*
Ziegler, Charles Edward *political science educator, department chairman*
Zimmerman, Gideon K. *minister*

Madisonville
Baldwin, Kathryn Leigh *psychologist, educator, consultant*
May, Richard Warren *writer, consultant, inventor*
Spain, Thomas B. *retired state supreme court justice*

Masonic Home
Coryell, Glynn Heath *financial services executive*

Mayfield
Viles, Henry *pathologist*

Middlesboro
Daniel, Barbara Ann *realtor, advertising executive*
Marcum, Joseph Susong *education educator*

Morehead
Besant, Larry Xon *librarian, administrator, consultant*
Detweiler, Greg Jeffrey *music educator*
Huber, John Michael *lumber executive*
Miller, Green Russell *economist, educator*

Mount Olivet
Dorton, Truda Lou *medical/surgical nurse, geriatrics nurse*

Munfordville
Craddock, John Durrett, III, *lawyer*
Lang, George Edward *lawyer*

Murray
Boston, Betty Lee *investment company executive, financial consultant, financial planner*
Brown, Jonathon Andrew *healthcare executive*
Buckingham, David Cowan *judge*
Glass, Mary Jean *quality assurance professional*
Masthay, Mark Buell *chemist, educator, research scientist*
Pearson, Kelly Jeanne *education educator*
Steffa, John Amon *music educator, composer*
Whisenhunt, Donald Wayne *history educator*

Newport
Clinkenbeard, James Howard *principal*
Siverd, Robert Joseph *lawyer*
Trauth, David E. *dairy company executive*
Wehr, William James *judge*

Nicholasville
Jones, Coletta Marie *music educator, composer*

Owensboro
McRaith, John Jeremiah *bishop*
Mowers, Kathy A. *mathematics professor*
Roberts, Brian Wayne *middle school educator, minister*
Ruckdeschel, David Claude *music educator*
Stevenson, John W. *lawyer*
West, William Robert *history educator*

Paducah
Graves, John William *state supreme court justice*
King, W. David *magistrate judge*
Starkey, Russell Bruce, Jr., *energy executive*
Stice, Dwayne Lee *broadcasting company executive*

Paint Lick
Burton, Charles Lawrence *priest, small business owner*

Paris
Steffer, Robert Wesley *clergyman*

Pewee Valley
Gill, George Norman *newspaper publishing company executive*

Pikeville
Cade, Nancy Jean *history and political science educator*
Johnson, Amy M. *elementary school educator*
Smith, Harold Hasken *university administrator*
Strosnider, John *dean*

Pineville
Lucas, Roy Edward, Jr., *minister*
Whittaker, Bill Douglas *minister*

Prestonsburg
Mc Aninch, Robert Danford *philosophy and government affairs educator*
Pridham, Thomas Grenville *retired research microbiologist*
Stumbo, Janet Lynn *state supreme court justice*
Wells, Zella Faye *school system administrator*

Prospect
Kehlbeck, Joseph H. *software developer and consultant*
Shipley, Alden Peverly *broadcaster, broadcasting executive*

Radcliff
Flores, George H. *obstetrician-gynecologist*
Jarvis, John Michael *logistical engineer, writer*

Richmond
Blanchard, Paul *academic administrator, educator*
Branson, Branley Allan *biology professor*
Chenault, James Stouffer *judge*
Engle, Fred Allen, Jr., *economics professor, writer*
Hall, Kathy *nursing official*
Huch, Ronald Kind *historian, educator*
Inman, Larry Joe *basketball coach*

Russellville
Arshad, Abrar Mehmood *physician*
Harper, Shirley Fay *nutritionist, educator, consultant, lecturer*

Saint Catharine
Collins, Martha Layne *college president, former governor*

Scottsville
Secrest, James Seaton, Sr., *lawyer*

Shelbyville
Hedrick, William David *secondary school educator, musician, educator*
Igleheart, Ted Lewis *lawyer*
Miller, Mary Helen *retired public administrator*

Shepherdsville
Pike, Burlyn *retired bank director, lawyer*

Somerset
Prather, John Gideon *lawyer*

Southgate
Glenn, Jerry Hosmer, Jr., *retired language educator*

Stanford
Baughman, James Carson *minister, sports official*

Sturgis
Thornsberry, Willis Lee, Jr., *chemist*

Utica
Mountjoy, Helen W. *educational association administrator*

Vancleve
Murphree, Quincy Carl *physicist, educator*

Versailles
Farish, William S. *former United States ambassador to United Kingdom, horse breeder*
Taylor, Elizabeth *elementary school educator*

Whitley City
Stephens, Robert Ernest *retired educator*

Wickliffe
Shadoan, William Lewis *judge*

Williamsburg
Smoak, Jeff C., Jr., *music educator*
Trickett, Paula J. *assistant principal*

Wilmore
Kinlaw, Dennis Franklin *clergyman, society executive*
Kuhn, Anne Naomi Wicker (Mrs. Harold B. Kuhn) *foreign language educator*
Pohl, Gunther Erich *retired library administrator*
Rader, Paul Alexander *minister, religious organization administrator*
Savage, William Earl *savings and loan executive, religious educator*

Winchester
Book, John Kenneth (Kenny Book) *retail store owner*
Hall, Bennett Freeman *minister*
Studebaker, John Milton *utilities engineer, consultant, educator*

LOUISIANA

Alexandria
Bradford, Louise Mathilde *social work administrator*
Burns, Ronald C. *music educator*
DeWitt, Charles Woodrow *state legislator*
Gist, Howard Battle, Jr., *lawyer*
Hanley, Henry Gorman *cardiologist*
Rogers, James Edwin *geology and hydrology consultant*
Sampson, Jerome Mark *pulmonologist*
Smith, Joe Dorsey, Jr., *retired newspaper executive*
Thevenot, Maude Travis *retired home economist*

Arcadia
Cummings, Kenneth Ila *coroner, medical examiner*

Arnaudville
Matas, Myra Dorothea *interior architect, designer, consultant*

Baker
Cross, James Edward *electrical engineering educator*
Roberson, Patt Foster *mass communications educator*
Steward, Alfred *education educator, researcher*

Baton Rouge
Adams, Sharon Butler *minister, philosopher, researcher*
Anderson, Lawrence Robert, Jr., *lawyer*
Arceneaux, William *historian, educator, educational association administrator*
Arman, Ara *civil engineering educator*
Avent, Raymond Richard, Jr., *civil engineering educator*
Barfield, Tim *manufacturing executive*
Bayard, Alton Ernest, III, *lawyer*
Beard, Thomas Rex *economics professor*
Bedeian, Arthur George *business educator*
Belk, Robert L. *manufacturing executive*
Bellinger, Michael Craig *education educator, musician*
Bengtson, Richard Lee *agricultural engineer, educator*
Bensman, Stephen J. *school librarian, researcher*
Bernhard, James M., Jr., *engineering executive*
Besch, Everett Dickman *veterinarian, university dean and educator emeritus*
Blackman, John Calhoun, IV, *lawyer*
Blanco, Kathleen Babineaux *governor*
Bohlinger, Lewis Hall *state government official*
Bray, George August *internist, researcher, educator*
Brister, Pat *political party executive*
Buchmann, Molly O'Banion *choreographer, ballet educator*
Burns, Paul Yoder *forester, educator*
Caffey, H(orace) Rouse *academic administrator, agricultural company executive*
Chapman, Russell Leonard *botany educator*
Chen, Jianhua *computer science educator, researcher*
Chen, Peter Pin-Shan *electrical engineering, computer science and internet/web educator, data processing executive*
Cherry, William Ashley *surgeon, state health officer, educator*
Cole, Luther Francis *former state supreme court associate justice*
Constantinides, Dinos Demetrios (Constantine Constantinides) *music educator, composer, conductor*
Cooper, William James, Jr., *history professor*
Corripio, Armando Benito *chemical engineering educator*
Cramer, Gail Latimer *economist*
Crumbley, Donald Larry *accounting educator, writer, consultant*
Culbert, David Holbrook *historian, educator, editor, writer*
Daniel, Ross Preston, III, *economist, educator*
Davidge, Robert Cunninghame, Jr., *hospital administrator*
Davis, Carol *educational association administrator, educator*
de Queiroz, Marcio S. *engineering educator*
Desmond, John Jacob *retired architect*
DeVille, Donald Charles *accountant*
DiBenedetto, Robert Lawrence *retired obstetrician, gynecologist, insurance company executive*
Doty, Gresdna Ann *theatre historian, educator*
Dugas, David Roy *lawyer*
Durresi, Arjan *computer science educator*
Finan, John Joseph *hospital administrator*
Finney, Clifton Donald *publishing executive*
Foti, Charles C., Jr., *state attorney general*
Gammon, Malcolm Ernest, Sr., *surveying and engineering executive*
Gettys, Thomas Wigington *medical researcher*
Giger, Andreas *education educator*
Gikas, Carol Sommerfeldt *museum director*
Gill, Richard F. *manufacturing executive*
Gilmore, Clarence Percy *writer, magazine editor*
Groves, Michael G. *dean*
Hainkel, John J., Jr., *state senator*
Hansel, William *biology professor*
Hardy, John Edward *English language educator, author*
Harrelson, Clyde Lee *retired secondary school educator*
Hartzog, Elizabeth Windham *music educator*
Hayward, Olga Loretta Hines (Mrs. Samuel Ellsworth Hayward) *retired librarian*
Head, Jonathan Frederick *cell biologist*
Hewitt, Maureen Gilgore *scholarly book publishing executive*
Hymel, L(ezin) J(oseph) *lawyer, former prosecutor*
Jaques, Thomas Francis *librarian*
Jeffers, Ben *political organization executive*
Johnson, Joseph Clayton, Jr., *lawyer*
Jones, Mary Elizabeth *school counselor*
Kastin, Abba Jeremiah *endocrinologist, researcher*
Khonsari, Michael M. *mechanical engineering educator*
Kidd, James Marion, III, *allergist, immunologist, educator*
Kisner, Wendell Howard, Jr., *plastic surgeon*
Koehler, Robert Brien *priest*
Kovacs, Mihaly *mathematician, researcher*
Landrieu, Mitchell Joseph *lieutenant governor*
Lane, Margaret Beynon Taylor *librarian*
Lee, Betty Redding *architect*
Leonard, Paul Haralson *retired lawyer*
Le Vine, Jerome Edward *retired ophthalmologist*
Lima, Marybeth *engineering educator*
Lovejoy, Jennifer Carole *medical educator*
Lusk, Glenna Rae Knight (Mrs. Edwin Bruce Lusk) *librarian*
Madden, David *author*
Martin, Freddie Anthony *agronomist, educator*
Mathews, Sharon Walker *artistic director, secondary school educator*
Maxcy, Spencer John *education educator*
Mc Cameron, Fritz Allen *retired university administrator*
McCoy, Wesley Lawrence *musician, conductor, educator*
Mc Glynn, Sean Patrick *physical chemist, educator*
McKeithen, Walter Fox *secretary of state*
Mohan, Brij *social work educator*
Moody, Gene Byron *engineering executive, small business owner, minister*
Mueller, Lisel *writer, poet*
Ngandu, Pius Nkashama *education educator*
Noland, Christine A. *magistrate judge*
Norem, Richard Frederick, Sr., *musician, music educator*
O'Connell, Robert Francis *physics educator*
Olney, James *English language educator*
Owen, Sue Ann *poet*
Oxley, James Grieve *mathematics professor*
Palmer, Curtis Dwayne *cardiopulmonary practitioner, microbiologist, researcher, builder*
Parker, John Victor *federal judge*
Parks, James William, II, *public facilities executive, lawyer*
Patrick, William Hardy, Jr., *wetland biogeochemist, educator, laboratory director*
Patterson, Charles Darold *librarian, educator*
Perkins, Huel Davis *academic administrator*
Phillabaum, Leslie Ervin *publisher*
Pike, Ralph Webster *chemical engineer, educator, university administrator*
Pollock, David Daniel *biologist, educator, research scientist*
Polozola, Frank Joseph *federal judge*
Prestage, James Jordan *university chancellor*
Pugh, George Willard *law educator*
Puyau, Francis Albert *retired physician, radiology educator*
Rami, Janet Simmons *university dean, nursing educator*
Ramirez, Arnulfo Gonzalez *language educator, linguist*
Reible, Danny David *environmental chemical engineer, educator*
Reich, Robert Sigmund *landscape architect*
Ricapito, Joseph Virgil (Giuseppe Ricapito) *Spanish, Italian and comparative literature educator*
Richards, Marta Alison *lawyer*
Riddick, Winston Wade, Sr., *lawyer*
Riedlinger, Stephen C. *federal judge*
Riopelle, Arthur Jean *psychologist*
Rubin, Michael Harry *lawyer, educator*
Sanders, Mary Elizabeth *author, historian*
Sasek, Gloria Burns *English language and literature educator*
Seaver, Jeffrey Mark, Sr., *lawyer*
Sen Gupta, Barun Kumar *geology educator, researcher*
Sinclair, Glenn Bruce *mechanical engineering educator, researcher*
Skillman, Ernest Edward, Jr., *real estate sales and management executive*
Smith, David Jeddie *American literature educator*
Smith, Michael *college president*
Smith, Richard James *retired music educator*
Stockbauer, Roger Lewis *physicist, researcher*
Sutherland, Wade Alan *music educator, director*
Taylor, John McKowen *lawyer*
Thomas, Jeffrey Cone *financial executive, consultant*
Tipton, Kenneth Warren *agricultural administrator, researcher*
Travis, John D. *bank commission official*
Traynham, James Gibson *chemist, educator*
Tumay, Mehmet Taner *geotechnical consultant, educator, research administrator*
Turner, Bert S. *construction executive*
Unglesby, Lewis O. *lawyer*
Vaidyanathan, Ramachandran *computer engineer, educator*
Voyiadjis, George Zino *civil engineer, educator*
Wallyn, Joan M. *social worker, writer*
Wheeler, Otis Bullard *retired English educator and university official*
Willett, Anna Hart *composer, painter*
Witcher, Robert Campbell, Sr., *bishop*
Wittenbrink, Jeffrey Scott *lawyer*
Wu, H. Denis *communications educator*
Yarbrough, Martha Cornelia *music educator*

Belle Chasse
Arimura, Akira *biomedical research laboratory administrator, educator*
Yandle, Sylvester Elwood, II, *sales executive*

Benton
Hudson, Marguerite W. *secondary school educator*

Bogalusa
Gallaspy, Dixie *interior designer, innkeeper*

Bossier City
French, Holly Lynn *education educator*

Boyce
Lewis, Patsy Joanne *religious studies educator, writer*

Cecilia
Girouard, Tina *artist, curator*

Chalmette
Bayham, Michael Robert, Jr., *political consultant*
Williamson, Ramona Diane *special education educator*

Chauvin
Sammarco, Paul William *ecologist, researcher*

Cheneyville
Ewin, Gordon Overton *retired lawyer, farmer*

Choudrant
Ford, John Charles *artist*

Columbia
McGee, Bruce D. *evangelist*

Convent
Deroche, Kathleen Samrow *elementary educator, mathematics consultant, assistant principal*

Coushatta
Wiggins, Mary Ann Wise *small business owner, educator*

Covington
Blossman, Alfred Rhody, Jr., *banker*
Bourgeois, Priscilla Elzey *educational administrator*
Darr, Kevin F. *orthopedic surgeon*
Files, Mark Willard *business and financial consultant*
Gerone, Peter John *microbiologist, research institute administrator*
Looney, James Holland *lawyer*
Maurin, James E. *real estate executive*
Napier, William James, Jr., *marine oil and gas construction consultant*
Rice, Winston Edward *lawyer*
Vercellotti, John Raymond *research chemist*

Crowley
Foreman, Alfred G. *theologian, philosopher*

Delhi
House, Ann *home health nurse, administrator*

Denham Springs
Cowart, Keith Bertrand *minister, educator*
May, Kenneth Nathaniel *food industry consultant*
Perkins, Arthur Lee, Sr., *retired principal, real estate broker, insurance agent*

Deridder
Iles, Kay C. *state representative*

Destrehan
Griffith, Steven Franklin, Sr., *lawyer, real estate title insurance agent and investor*
Toups, Byron Joseph *musician, educator*

Dubach
Straughan, William Thomas *engineering educator*

Elm Grove
Livingston, John H. *retired engineer, retired military officer*

Eunice
Attole, Mary Bertha *writer*
Randall Joubert, Lorrie Boullion *science educator*

Franklin
Fairchild, Phyllis Elaine *school counselor*
McClelland, James Ray *lawyer*

Franklinton
Payne, Eric Alan *physician*
Von Kanel, Danny Renard *minister, writer*

Gonzales
Young, David Nelson *media and communications consultant*

Grambling
Favors, Steve Alexander *academic administrator*
Judson, Horace Augustus *academic administrator, chemistry educator*
Porter, Wilma Jean *educational consultant*
Robinson, Eddie Gay *college football coach*
Stentiford, Barry Maxfield *education educator, military officer*
Warner, Neari Francois *university president*
Wilkerson, Pinkie Carolyn *state legislator, lawyer*

Gretna
Calhoun, Milburn *publishing executive, rare book dealer, physician*
Weekley, Judy Liddington *special education educator*

Hammond
Brown, Robert Carl *mathematician, educator*
Johansen, David Alan *musician, educator*
Kulkin, Heidi Sharon *education educator*
LaFargue, Melba Faye Fulmer *credit manager, realtor*
Nauman, Ann Keith *education educator, department chairman*
Parish, Richard Lee *engineer, consultant*
Parker, Clea Edward *retired university president*
Richardson, Thaddeus Maurice *funeral director*
Thorburn, James Alexander *retired humanities educator*

Harahan
Bowler, Shirley *state legislator*

Harvey
Lamid, Sofjan *physician, educator*
Pete, Eric E. *claims representative, writer*
Simon, Keith R. *safety engineer, petroleum engineer, professional disc jockey*

Houma
Ferguson, Thomas Glen *internist*
Walker, Craig M. *cardiologist, medical association administrator*

Jefferson
Conino, Joseph Aloysius *lawyer*

Jennings
Moniruzzaman, Mohammed *chemical engineer*

Kaplan
LeMoine, Frank Eugene *lawyer, judge*

Kenner
Hallila, Bruce Allan *welding engineer*
McShan, Clyde Griffin, II, *financial executive*
Scherich, Edward Baptiste *retired diversified company executive*
Siebel, Mathias Paul *mechanical engineer, consultant*
Valvo, Barbara-Ann *lawyer, surgeon*
Williams, Roy *airport terminal executive*

La Place
Cicet, Donald James *lawyer*
Fiffie Proctor, JoAnn *media and technology specialist*
Lodwick, Judith Lynne *nursing educator*

Lacombe
Hendricks, Donald Duane *retired school librarian*

Lafayette
Angers, Winston Thomas *lawyer*
Authement, Ray P. *college president*
Cain, Judith Sharp *mathematics educator and consultant*
Carstens, Jane Ellen *retired library science educator*
Ceballos, Jacqui Michot *feminist activist, organizer, administrator*
Colbert-Cormier, Patricia A. *secondary school educator*
Darwish, Tarek *computer engineer*
Davidson, James Joseph, III, *lawyer*
Davis, William Eugene *judge*
Domingue, Emery *retired consulting engineering company executive*
Duhe, John Malcolm, Jr., *federal judge*
Dur, Philip Francis *political scientist, educator, retired foreign service officer*
Fang, Cheng-Shen *chemical engineering educator*
Goforth, William H. *lawyer*
Henderson, Mary Stanley *museum director, writer*
Judice, Marc Wayne *lawyer*
Marshak, Alan Howard *electrical engineer, educator*
Pate, James Lavert *lawyer*
Petry, Ruth Vidrine *principal*
Raffel, Burton Nathan *retired educator, poet, writer, translator*
Redding, Evelyn A. *dean*
Rickey, Horace B., Jr., *retired engineer*
Rieck, William Albert *education educator, academic administrator*
Saloom, Kaliste Joseph, Jr., *lawyer, retired judge*
Salters, Richard Stewart *engineering company executive*
Sides, Larry Eugene *advertising executive*
Stuart, Walter Bynum, III, *banker*
Taylor, Brian Stevon *music educator*
Tearpock, Daniel J. *geologist*
Theall, Susan Lorna *lawyer*
Turner, I. Bruce *archivist*

Lake Arthur
Dronet, Judy Lynn *elementary school educator, librarian*

Lake Charles
Beam, James Carroll (Jim Beam) *retired newspaper editor*
Buckles, Michael Kim *music educator, musician*
Clement, Richard Joseph *obstetrician-gynecologist*
Drez, David Jacob, Jr., *orthopedic surgeon, educator*
Fields-Gold, Anita *retired dean*
Gunderson, Clark Alan *orthopedic surgeon*
Hebert, Robert D. *academic administrator*
Levingston, Ernest Lee *engineering company executive*
McLeod, William Lasater, Jr., *lawyer, former judge and state legislator*
Middleton, George, Jr., *clinical child psychologist*
Mount, Willie Landry *state legislator*
Premeaux, Shane Richard *marketing educator*
Roy, Donald *artist, poet*
Sanchez, Walter Marshall *lawyer*
Stacey, Truman *journalist, consultant*
Trimble, James T., Jr., *federal judge*
Veron, J. Michael *lawyer, writer*
Weeber, Stan C. *sociologist, educator*

Leesville
Gutman, Lucy Toni *school social worker, educator, counselor*
Norman, Paralee Frances *English language educator, researcher*
Smith, Simeon Christie, III, *lawyer, judge*
Thompson, Darlene Bennett *realtor, musician*
Wimberly, Beadie Reneau (Leigh Wimberly) *financial services executive*

Mandeville
Christian, John Catlett, Jr., *lawyer*
Cressy, David Sarrat *lawyer*
Klein, Bernard Joseph *management specialist*
Landry, Joseph L., Jr., *retired affirmative action specialist*
Pittman, Jacquelyn *retired mental health nurse, nursing educator*
Treuting, Edna Gannon *retired nursing administrator, retired nursing educator*
Young, Lucy Cleaver *physician*

Many
Dutton, Frank Elroy *data processing executive, writer*

Marksville
Riddle, Charles Addison, III, *district attorney, former state legislator*

Marrero
Brown, Courtney Allison *composer, writer, singer*
Kushner, Frederick Gary *cardiologist, medical educator*

Metairie
Album, Jerald Lewis *lawyer*
Arthur, Jett Clinton *retired chemist*
Banton, Kathleen Ariatti *artist, educator*
Brooks, Aaron Lafette *professional football player*
Chambers, Thomas Edward *college president, psychologist*
Crosby, Deborah Berry *artist*
Dean, Bruce Campbell *lawyer*
deMoruelle, Charmaine *music educator*
Doody, Barbara Pettett *computer specialist*
Doody, Louis Clarence, Jr., *accountant*
Dugan, Fortune Anthony *cardiologist, consultant*
Edisen, Clayton Byron *physician*
Evans, Carol Rockwell *nursing administrator*
Falco, Maria Josephine *political scientist, academic administrator*
Feran, Russell G. *sales executive*
Friedman, Lynn Joseph *counselor*
Gereighty, Andrea Saunders *polling company executive, poet*
Grau, Shirley Ann (Mrs. James Kern Feibleman) *writer*
Grimm, John Lloyd *marketing professional*
Hardy, Ashton Richard *lawyer*
Hartman, James Austin *retired geologist*
Haslett, Jim *professional football coach*
Johnson, Beth Michael *school administrator*
Johnston, William J., Jr., *neurosurgeon*
Lake, Wesley Wayne, Jr., *internist, allergist, educator*
McAllister, Deuce *professional football player*
McMahon, Robert Albert, Jr., *lawyer*
Morcos, Ann Conti *writing and editing company executive*
Morvant, Barbara L. *nursing administrator*
Nix, Linda Anne Bean *public relations executive*
Ochsner, Seymour Fiske *radiologist, editor*
Reed, Jake *professional football player*
St. John, Bridgette Alayne *secondary school educator*
Schwartz, Charles, Jr., *federal judge*
Schwegmann, Melinda *supermarket executive, former state official*
Spruiell, Vann *psychoanalyst, educator, editor, researcher*
Wood, Jonathan Stuart *economist, educator*

Minden
Kemmerly, James Robert *obstetrician, gynecologist*

Monroe
Bulot, James John *gerontologist, educator*
Cooksey, John Charles *former congressman, ophthalmic surgeon*
Corder, Jan Busby *nursing educator, university dean*
Ewing, R. Stewart *telecommunications company executive*
Foreman, Teresa *educational consultant, educator*
Fouts, Elizabeth Browne *psychologist, metals company executive*
Fouts, James Fremont *mining company executive*
Guy, William Achilles, Jr., (Rod Guy Jr.) *urban planner, economic development consultant*
Post, Glen Fleming, III, *telecommunications executive*
Sartor, Daniel Ryan, Jr., *lawyer*
Smith, Donald Raymond *librarian*
Thompson, Myrrah McCully Terzolas *music educator, director*
Zander, Arlen Ray *retired physics educator*

Natchitoches
Egan, Shirley Anne *retired nursing educator*
Keller, Nadya Clark *retired biochemistry educator, researcher*
Kuroda, Masahito *music educator*
Ludu, Andrei *physicist, educator*
Nagel, Paul B. *geography and social studies educator*
Smith, Jeffrey Robert *historian, educator*
Wells, Carol McConnell *genealogist, retired archivist*
Wolfe, George Cropper *retired private school educator, artist, writer*

New Iberia
Henton, Willis Ryan *retired bishop*
Subra, Wilma Alpha *chemist, environmentalist*

New Orleans
Abaunza, Donald Richard *lawyer*
Abbott, Hirschel Theron, Jr., *lawyer*
Acomb, Robert Bailey, Jr., *lawyer, educator*
Adkerson, Richard C. *mining executive*
Agrawal, Krishna Chandra *pharmacology educator*
Allen, Frank Clinton, Jr., *lawyer, chemical engineer*
Allen, Gary Curtiss *geology educator*
Allerton, William, III, *public relations executive*
Alsobrook, Henry Bernis, Jr., *lawyer*
Amoss, W. James, Jr., *shipping company executive*
Amoss, Walter James (Jim), III, *editor*
Andrews, E. Wyllys *archaeologist, educator*
Arshad, M. Kaleem *psychiatrist*
Ates, J. Robert *lawyer*
Babst, James A. *lawyer*
Bachmann, Richard Arthur *oil company executive*
Bailey, Barry Stone *sculptor, educator*
Bajoie, Diana E. *state legislator*
Balée, William L. *anthropology educator*
Ball, Millie (Mildred Porteous Ball) *editor, journalist*
Barham, Mack Elwin *lawyer, educator*
Barreiro, Elias *music educator, researcher*
Barroso, Luis Q. *actor, educator, theater director*
Barry, Francis Julian, Jr., *lawyer*
Barton, Fredrick Preston *English language educator, administrator*
Beahm, Franklin D. *lawyer*
Beard, Elizabeth Letitia *physiologist, educator*
Beck, David Edward *surgeon*
Beck, Guy Leon *music educator*
Beck, William Harold, Jr., *lawyer*
Beckerman, Robert Cy *pediatrician, educator*
Beer, Peter Hill *federal judge*
Bell, Bryan *real estate and oil investment executive, educator*
Benerito, Ruth Rogan (Mrs. Frank H. Benerito) *chemist*
Benjamin, Adelaide Wisdom *community volunteer and activist, retired lawyer*
Benjamin, Edward Bernard, Jr., *lawyer*
Bennett-Johnson, Earnestine Rose *education educator, consultant*
Berrigan, Helen Ginger *federal judge*
Bertoniere, Noelie Rita *research chemist*
Bertrand, William Ellis *public health educator, academic administrator*
Best, Susan Marie *artist, educator*
Bieck, Robert Barton, Jr., *lawyer*
Birtel, Frank Thomas *mathematician, philosopher, educator*
Bischof, Günter Josef *history professor*
Blitch, Ronald Buchanan *architect*
Boggs, Corinne Claiborne (Lindy Boggs) *retired congresswoman*
Boh, Robert Henry *civil engineer, construction company executive*
Bookhardt, Fred Barringer, Jr., *architect*
Boswell, Stephanie *newscaster*
Boudreaux, Kenneth Justin *economics and finance educator, consultant*
Brazda, Frederick Wicks *pathologist, educator*
Brennan, Lally *food service executive*
Bricker, Harvey Miller *anthropology educator*
Bricker, Victoria Reifler *anthropology educator*
Bronfin, Fred *lawyer*
Brown, Jerry A. *federal bankruptcy judge*
Brown, Mary Willoughby *health facilities administrator*
Brumfield, William Craft *Slavic studies educator, photographer, writer*
Buddington, Steve Apalong *social worker, educator*
Bullard, Edgar John, III, *museum director*
Caldwell, Delmar Ray *ophthalmologist, educator*
Calogero, Pascal Frank, Jr., *judge*
Campeau, Richard John, Jr., *internal medicine and radiology educator*
Carey, Michael Emmett *neurosurgeon, educator*
Cargille, Charles M. *emergency physician, educator*
Carter, James Clarence *pastor, educator*
Casellas, Joachim *art gallery executive*
Cazayoux, Charles *airport executive*
Cefalu, Charles A. *medical educator*
Chan, Albert W. *cardiologist*
Cheatwood, Roy Clifton *lawyer*
Ciolino, Dane Stephen *law educator*
Claverie, Philip deVilliers *lawyer*
Clement, Edith Brown *federal judge*
Cody, Wilmer St. Clair *retired educational administrator, educational policy consultant*
Cohen, Rosalie *civic worker*
Cohn, Isidore, Jr., *surgeon, educator*
Coleman, James Julian *lawyer*
Coleman, James Julian, Jr., *lawyer, industrialist, real estate executive*
Collins, Harry David *forensic engineer, mechanical engineer, nuclear engineer, claims consultant*
Combe, John Clifford, Jr., *lawyer*
Connolly, Edward S. *neurological surgeon*
Cook, Bernard Anthony *historian, educator*
Cook, Victor Joseph, Jr., *marketing educator, consultant*
Corey, Orlin Russell *publisher, editor*
Correro, Anthony James, III, *lawyer*
Cospolich, James Donald *electrical engineering executive, consultant*
Cotton, John G. *career military officer*
Cowen, Scott S. *academic administrator*
Crumley, David Oliver *publishing executive, writer, corporate executive*
Crumley, Martha Ann *company executive*
Crusto, Mitchell Ferdinand *lawyer, educator, consultant*
Culbertson, Richard Allen *healthcare educator, health system director*
Dahlberg, Carl Fredrick, Jr., *entrepreneur*
Daniels, Robert Sanford *psychiatrist, administrator*
Dauns, John *mathematician, educator*
Denegre, George *lawyer*
Dennis, James Leon *federal judge*
Dittman, Stevan Craig *lawyer*
Doley, Harold Emanuel, Jr., *securities company executive*
Domingue, Gerald James *medical scientist, microbiology, immunology and urology educator, researcher, clinical bacteriologist, artist*
Dunbar, Prescott Nelson *investment company executive*
Duncan, Margaret Caroline *physician*
Duplantier, Adrian Guy *federal judge*
Duval, Stanwood Richardson, Jr., *judge*
Easson, William McAlpine *psychiatrist, educator*
Eckstein, Michael Lehman *lawyer*
Ensenat, Louis Albert *surgeon*
Epstein, Arthur William *physician, educator*
Eskew, R. Allen *architect, director*
Espinoza, Luis Rolan *rheumatologist, researcher*
Ewin, Dabney Minor *surgeon*
Fagaly, William Arthur *curator*
Fairbairn, Kriss *newscaster*
Falgoust, Dean Thomas *lawyer, accountant*
Farris, Charles, Jr., *obstetrician, gynecologist*
Feldman, Martin L. C. *federal judge*
Fendler, Sherman Gene *lawyer*
Ferguson, Charles Austin *retired newspaper editor*
Filson, Ronald Coulter *architect, educator, college dean*
Fingerman, Milton *biologist, educator*
Fisch, Bruce Jeffrey *physician, educator*
Fisher, James William *pharmacologist, medical educator*
Fisk, Raymond Paul *marketing educator*
Florman, Sander Scott *transplant surgeon*
Flower, Walter Chew, III, *investment counselor*
Folse, Henry Joseph, Jr. *education educator*
Fonseca, Vivian Andrew *physician*
Force, Robert *law educator*
Forman, William Harper, Jr., *lawyer*
Foundas, Anne Leigh *psychiatrist*
Francis, Norman C. *academic administrator*
Frantz, Phares Albert *architect*
Freudenberger, Herman *retired economics educator*
Friedman, Joel William *law educator*
Friedmann, Patricia Ann *writer*
Frohlich, Edward David *medical educator*
Fuselier, Harold Anthony, Jr., *urologist, director, educator*
Gates, Audrey Castine *city government administrator*
Gay, Esmond Phelps *lawyer*
Gensler, Philip, Jr., *investment counselor*
Gertler, Meyer H. *lawyer*

Gery, John Roy Octavius secondary school educator, poet
Getten, Thomas Frank lawyer
Gitlin, Melvin Charles anesthesiologist, educator
Goins, Richard Anthony lawyer, educator
Gokcen, Ibrahim computer science researcher
Gordon, Joseph Elwell university official, educator
Grau, Jean Elizabeth retired insurance agent
Griffin, Jeffrey Farrow surgeon
Guidry, Susan Gail lawyer
Hansel, Stephen Arthur holding company executive
Hartz, Renee Semo cardiothoracic surgeon
Harvey, John Grover mathematics professor, information scientist
Hasselbach, Karlheinz literature educator
Hassenboehler, Donalyn principal
Healy, George William, III, lawyer, mediator
Hearn, Sharon Sklamba lawyer
Hebert, Thomas Joseph university educator
Henault, Richard A. healthcare hospital administrator
Hence, Jane Knight designer
Henderson, Helena Naughton legal association administrator
Hicks, Terrell Cohlman surgeon, educator, health facility administrator, academic administrator
Hintz, Donald C. energy executive
Hoffman, Donald Alfred lawyer
Holditch, William Kenneth American literature educator
Hollier, Larry Harold vascular surgeon, hospital administrator
Hovland, Eric Jeffrey dean, endodontics educator
Howard, Richard Ralston, II, medical health advisor, financial consultant
Hughes, Alfred Clifton archbishop
Humphrey, Elizabeth Ann women's health nurse
Hyman, Albert Lewis cardiologist, educator
Hyslop, Newton Everett, Jr., infectious disease specialist
Incaprera, Frank Philip internist
Irons, Paulette Riley state legislator, lawyer
Ivens, Mary Sue microbiologist, mycologist
Jacobsen, Thomas Warren retired archaeologist, educator, freelance journalist
Jaffe, Bernard Michael surgeon, department chairman
Jazwinski, Barbara Marie composer, educator
Johnson, Arnold Ray public relations executive
Johnson, Bernette J. state supreme court justice
Johnson, Mark J. mining executive
Johnson, Peter Forbes transportation executive, business owner
Jones, Glenn Earle property management executive
Jones, Philip Kirkpatrick, Jr., lawyer
Jordan, Eddie J. lawyer, former prosecutor
Judell, Harold Benn lawyer
Kadowtiz, Philip J. social sciences educator
Katz, Morton Howard lawyer
Kearney, Anne chef
Kelly, Eamon Michael university president emeritus
Kemp, James Bradley, Jr., lawyer
Kemp, John Randolph journalist, writer
Kern, Clifford Harold, Jr., retired lawyer
Kewalramani, Laxman Sunderdas surgeon, consultant
Khaton, Sabrina Roslyn librarian, accountant
Kilroy, James Francis humanities educator
Kimball, Catherine D. state supreme court justice
King, Rebecca J. lawyer, consultant
Kline, David Gellinger neurosurgery educator
Knoll, Jeannette Theriot state supreme court justice
Kolinsky, Michael Allen emergency physician
Krementz, Edward Thomas surgeon
Langston, Thomas Samuel political science educator
Lannes, William Joseph, III, electrical engineer
LaRosa, John Charles internist, educator, researcher
Latorre, Robert George naval architecture and engineering educator
Layman, Kim Florinda Marie pharmacist, writer
Le Blanc, Alice Isabelle academic administrator
Ledbetter, Linda Carol professional society administrator
Lee, Wayne J. lawyer
Lemann, Thomas Berthelot lawyer
Lennox, Edward Newman holding company executive
Leonard, J. Wayne energy company executive
Letten, James prosecutor
Levitzky, Michael Gordon physiology educator, researcher
Lewy, John Edwin pediatric nephrologist
Lind, Thomas Otto barge transportation company executive
Lingle, Sarah Elizabeth research scientist
Lintinger, Gregory John electrical engineer, educator
Litwin, Sharon orchestra executive
Livaudais, Marcel, Jr., federal judge
Locke, William retired endocrinologist
Longstreet, Wilma S. curriculum and instruction educator
Lopez, Manuel immunology and allergy educator
Lovett, William Anthony law and economics educator
Lowe, Robert Charles lawyer
Luft, Robert energy executive
Lundy, Larry food franchise company executive
Lupberger, Edwin Adolph retired utility executive
Lupo, Robert Edward Smith real estate developer and investor
Luza, Radomir Vaclav historian, educator
Maloney, Marilyn C. lawyer
Marcus, Bernard lawyer, consultant
Marier, Robert L. dean, hospital administrator
Marks, Charles Dennery insurance consultant
Markuly, Mark Steven religious studies educator
Martin, David Hubert internist, epidemiologist, educator
Martin, Louis Frank surgery and healthcare outcomes analyst
Martinez, Judy Perry lawyer
Mathes, Edward Conrad architect
Matthews, Brenda J. human resources specialist
McCall, John Patrick college president, educator
McCarthy, Dennis M. military officer
McCorquodale, J. Alexander civil and environmental engineer, educator
McFarland, James W. dean, finance educator
McGlone, Michael Anthony lawyer
McKinnon, William Mitchell Patrick surgeon
McMillan, Lee Richards, II, lawyer
McReynolds, Rosalee librarian
Meekers, Dominique Armand health and demographics researcher
Mentz, Henry Alvan, Jr., federal judge
Menutis, Jamie training services executive, writer
Michaelides, Efstathios Emmanuel mechanical engineer
Miller, Gary H. lawyer
Millikan, Larry Edward dermatologist
Mintz, Albert lawyer
Mitchell, Kenneth D. physiologist, educator
Moely, Barbara E. psychology researcher, educator
Moffett, James Robert oil and gas company executive
Molony, Michael Janssens, Jr., lawyer, arbitrator, mediator
Morales-Ramos, Juan Alfredo entomologist, researcher
Moreno, Helena newscaster
Mosier, John education educator, writer
Murrish, Charles Howard oil and gas exploration company executive, geologist
Nagin, C. Ray mayor
Navar, Luis Gabriel physiology educator, researcher
Neff, Carole Cukell lawyer
Nehrbass, Seth Martin patent lawyer
Nelson, James Smith pathologist, educator
Nelson, Waldemar Stanley civil engineer, consultant
Nichols, Ronald Lee surgeon, educator
Novakov, George John, Jr., gifted and talented educator, consultant, administrative assistant
Ochsner, John Lockwood thoracic-cardiovascular surgeon
Oliver, Ronald retired medical technologist
Olson, Richard David psychology educator
O'Neal, Edgar Carl psychology educator
O'Quinn, April Gale obstetrician, gynecologist, educator
Orihel, Thomas Charles parasitology educator, research scientist
Orr, Margaret newscaster
Ortique, Revius Oliver, Jr., city official, retired state supreme court justice
Osakwe, Christopher lawyer, educator
Ostendorf, Lance Stephen lawyer, educator, financial consultant
Palmer, Vernon Valentine law educator
Pankey, George Atkinson internist, educator, researcher
Paolini, Gilberto literature and science educator
Paradise, Louis Vincent educational psychology educator, university official
Pastorek, Marcia Jambu language educator, writer
Pearce, John Y. lawyer
Pedersen, Pedie physiology educator
Perdew, John Paul physics educator, condensed matter and density functional theorist
Perez, August, III, architectural firm executive
Phelps, Ashton, Jr., newspaper publisher
Pickering, Charles W., Sr., federal judge
Pindle, Arthur Jackson, Jr., philosopher, researcher
Plavsic, Branko Milenko radiology educator
Poesch, Jessie Jean art historian
Pope, John M. journalist
Porteous, G. Thomas, Jr., judge
Pratt, Renee Gill state legislator
Prockop, Darwin Johnson biochemist, physician
Prudhomme, Paul chef, restaurant owner
Pugh, William Whitmell Hill, III, lawyer
Puri, Pratap educator, researcher
Purvis, George Frank, Jr., life insurance company executive
Puschett, Jules B. medical educator, nephrologist, researcher
Quirk, Kathleen L. mining executive
Quirk, Peter Richard engineering company executive
Rajasekaran, Kanniah agricultural biotechnologist, researcher
Rathke, Dale Lawrence retired aerospace executive, management consultant
Re, Richard Noel endocrinologist
Reck, Andrew Joseph philosopher, retired educator
Redmann, John William lawyer, consultant
Reisin, Efrain nephrologist, researcher, educator
Remley, Theodore Phant, Jr., counseling educator, lawyer
Reyes, Raul Gregorio surgeon
Reza, Ali Hajmohammad cardiologist
Riddick, Frank Adams, Jr., physician, health care administrator
Rigby, Perry Gardner medical center administrator, educator, former university dean, physician
Roberts, Louise Nisbet philosopher, educator
Roberts, Shauna S. editor, writer
Rock, John Aubrey gynecologist and obstetrician, educator
Rodriguez, Antonio Jose lawyer
Roesler, Robert Harry media consultant
Rosen, Charles, II, lawyer
Rosen, William Warren lawyer
Rosensteel, George Thomas physics educator, nuclear physicist
Roskoski, Robert, Jr., biochemist, educator, author
Ryan, Timothy P. academic administrator
St. Julien, Thais Mary soprano, musician
Sanders, Melanie newscaster
Scelfo, Chris university football coach
Schally, Andrew Victor endocrine oncologist, researcher
Schalow, Frank Hickey philosopher, educator
Schulte, Francis B. retired archbishop
Scott, Byron Alton professional basketball coach, former professional basketball player
Sear, Morey Leonard federal judge, educator
Seibel, Klauspeter conductor
Sessions, Cicero Columbus retired lawyer
Setlow, Valerie Petit health science association director
Sherman, Edward Francis dean, law educator
Simakajornboon, Narong physician
Simmons, Norbert A. entertainment company executive
Simon, H(uey) Paul lawyer
Sinor, Howard Earl, Jr., lawyer
Skinner, Robert Earle librarian, writer
Sloan, Robert D. energy executive
Smith, Geraldine historic site administrator
Snyder, Charles Aubrey lawyer
Somers, Sally West librarian
Spicer, Susan food service executive
Stansbury, Harry Case state commissioner
Stanton, Vivian Brennan (Mrs. Ernest Stanton) retired guidance counselor
Stapp, Dan Ernest retired lawyer, utilities executive
Steinmetz, Robert Charles architect
Stewart, Gregory Wallace physician
Strong, Jack Perry pathologist, educator
Sullivan, Jerry Warner educator, physician
Superneau, Duane William geneticist, physician
Sutterfield, James Ray lawyer
Szepeshazi, Karoly Istvan pathologist
Tahir, Mary Elizabeth (Liz Tahir) marketing professional, consultant, speaker, writer
Taylor, Ian Logan dean
Thomas, Joseph Winand lawyer
Thompson, Annie Laura (Anne) foreign language educator
Thompson, Martyn Philip political and literary studies educator, translator
Thomson, Jessica Lee biostatistician, educator, consultant, researcher
Thornell, Jack Randolph photographer
Timmcke, Alan Edward colon and rectal surgeon
Title, Peter Stephen lawyer
Tracy, Richard E. medical educator
Trapolin, Frank Winter retired insurance executive
Traylor, Chet D. state supreme court justice
Udall, John Nicholas, Jr., pediatric gastroenterologist
Usdin, Gene Leonard psychiatrist
Vance, Robert Patrick lawyer
Vaudry, J. William, Jr., lawyer
Victory, Jeffrey Paul state supreme court justice
Villia, Morris Sabastian music producer, publishing executive, writer
Wafer, Douglas Drew environmental engineer
Wallace, Julian Craig psychology educator, researcher
Walsh, James Paton composer
Wang, Ting mechanical engineering educator
Waring, William Winburn pediatric pulmonologist, educator
Watson, James Raymond education educator
Wax, George Louis lawyer
Webb, Watts Rankin surgeon
Wegmann, Cynthia Anne lawyer
Wegmann, Mary Katherine art director
Weimer, John L. state supreme court justice
Weinmann, John Giffen lawyer, diplomat
Weiss, Kenneth Andrew lawyer, law educator
Welden, Arthur Luna biology professor
Werner, Robin A. humanities educator
Wheat, Robert E. museum director
Whidden, Stanley John physiologist, physician
Wiener, Jacques Loeb, Jr., judge
Willems, Constance Charles lawyer
Williams, Ronald David telecommunications executive
Willis, Gladden Williams pathologist, scientific photographer, tree farmer
Winstead, Daniel Keith psychiatrist
Wisznia, Walter architectural firm executive
Wolfe, Richard Peel lawyer
Wright, William Everard, Jr., lawyer
Yang, DaGang mathematician, educator

Newllano
Boren, Lynda Sue gifted education educator

Oakdale
Bellah, Lisa Danielle psychologist, educator

Opelousas
Lafleur, Kenneth Charles ophthalmologist
Pinac, André Louis, III, obstetrician, gynecologist

Parks
Durand, Sydnie Mae M. state legislator

Patterson
Wilkinson III, Elwyn Nathaniel music educator

Pineville
Conway, Evelyn Atkinson accountant, financial analyst
Cummings, Karen Sue retired corrections classification administrator
Howell, Thomas history professor
Jones, Syble Thornhill retired dietitian
Nesbitt, Gregory Leon utility executive, mechanical engineer
Thrasher, Fay C. clinical psychologist

Ponchatoula
Kuhn, James E. judge

Ruston
Barker, Jon Albert music educator
Bourgeois, Patricia McLin women's health and pediatrics nurse, educator
Deasy, William John construction, marine dredging, engineering and mining company executive
Dodge Robbins, Dorothy Ellin English educator
Freasier, Aileen W. special education educator
Hale, Paul Nolen, Jr., engineering administrator, educator
Halliburton, Lloyd Romance philology educator
Hudnall, Jarrett, Jr., management and marketing educator
Marbury, Virginia Lomax insurance and investment executive
Maxfield, John Edward retired university dean
Mesak, Hani Ibrahim finance educator
Reneau, Daniel D. academic administrator
Sabin, Paul Edgar not-for-profit developer
Sale, Tom S., III, financial economist
Selmic, Rastko R. engineering educator
Sterling, Raymond Leslie civil engineering educator, researcher, consultant
Taylor, Foster Jay retired university president
Thompson, Ronald H. chemical engineer, educator
White, James C. science educator, consultant

Schriever
Shaffer, Margaret Minor retired library director

Scott
Bergeron, Wilton Lee physician

Shreveport
Achee, Roland Joseph lawyer
Albores-Saavedra, Jorge pathologist, educator
Beaird, Charles T. former publishing executive
Birchfield, Karol Yarbrough writer, speaker
Blondin, Joan nephrologist educator
Bogue, Ernest Grady academic administrator, educator
Brandl, Mary-Katherine mathematics professor
Brannon, Guy Emilio physician
Bryant, J(ames) Bruce lawyer
Burton, Jr, George Aubrey accountant
Carmody, Arthur Roderick, Jr., lawyer, director
Carter, Louvenia McGee nursing educator
Chastain, Merritt Banning, Jr., lawyer
Conrad, Steven Allen critical care and emergency physician, biomedical engineer, educator
Cox, John Thomas, Jr., lawyer
DeRousse, Cathy Lynn composer, music educator
Dhanireddy, Ramasubbareddy neonatologist, researcher
Dickson, Markham Allen wholesale company executive
Feldman, Larry, Jr., lawyer
Fort, Arthur Tomlinson, III, physician, educator
Fowler, Marjorie Ellen Rees pathologist
Freeman, Arthur Merrimon, III, psychiatry educator, dean
Friend, William Benedict bishop
Gallagher, Patrick Timothy emergency physician
Goodman, Robert Uhle lawyer
Goodman, Sylvia Klumok volunteer
Goorley, John Theodore consulting chemist
Griffith, Robert Charles allergist, educator, planter
Halliburton, John Robert lawyer
Harbuck, Edwin Charles insurance agent
Hardtner, Quintin Theodore, III, lawyer
Heacock, Donald Dee social worker
Hetherwick, Gilbert Lewis lawyer
Hughes, Mary Sorrows artist
Hummel, Kay Jean physical therapist
Jamison, Richard Melvin virologist, educator
Jarzabek, Mary G. language educator
Johnson, Kristen A. public relations executive, not-for-profit fundraiser
Joiner, Gary Dillard cartographer, history educator, author
Jones, Kenneth B., Jr., surgeon
Joshua, Percy English educator
Lazarus, Allan Matthew retired newspaper editor
Lenard, Lloyd Edgar financial consultant
Levine, Steven Neil endocrinologist
Lewis, William D. writer, educator
Lloyd, Cecil Rhodes pediatric dentist
London, Steve Norman obstetrician-gynecologist, educator
Makishi, Yasuko securities trader, writer
Misra, Raghunath Prasad physician, educator
Nelson, George Dalman, Jr., banker
Nelson, Ralph Stanley lawyer
Payne, Roy Steven judge
Pederson, William David political scientist, educator
Pelton, James Rodger librarian
Perlman, Jerald Lee lawyer
Robinson, Edna Earle real estate company executive
Robinson, Garry Lewin television news executive
St. Aubyn, Ronald Anthony pediatrics nurse
Sandifer, Kevin Wayne archival services executive
Shelby, James Stanford cardiovascular surgeon
Shemwell, Mary Anne adapted physical education specialist
Simons, Dennis performing company executive
Smith, Brian David lawyer, educator
Staats, Thomas Elwyn neuropsychologist
Stagg, Tom federal judge
Stewart, Carl E. federal judge
Stone, Thomas D. music educator, composer
Sutton, Hal Evan professional golfer
Thurmon, Theodore Francis medical educator
Washington, Donald W. prosecutor
Watts, Jessica Milan director
Webb, Donald Arthur minister
Wolf, Robert Edward physician, educator
Wood, Julienne Louise librarian, historian
Woodman, Walter James lawyer
Wray, Geraldine Smitherman (Jerry Wray) artist
Wright, Marie Beulah Battey retired advertising executive

Slidell
Dearing, Reinhard Josef city official
Faust, Marilyn B. middle school principal
Fishman, Louis physicist, researcher
Lovell, Emily Kalled retired journalist
McBurney, Elizabeth Innes dermatologist, physician, educator
Muller, Robert Joseph gynecologist
Neale, Zahidi Sahaj artist, educator
Schedler, John Thomas, Jr., state legislator, bank executive
SSingletary, Alvin D. lawyer
Stroud, Robert Arlen medical equipment company executive
Tewell, Joseph Robert, Jr., electrical engineer

Sorrento
Welch, Joe Ben academic administrator

Springfield
Annable, Charles Roy pathologist

Springhill
Morgan, Larry Ronald minister
Thomas, Faye Evelyn J. elementary and secondary school educator

Sulphur
Fuller, Betty Stamps music educator

Thibodaux
Bryant, Thomas A. management educator
Fairchild, Joseph Virgil, Jr., accounting educator
Hulbert, Stephen Thompson academic administrator

Tioga
Brandow, Stephen Jon priest
Tenney, Tom Fred bishop

Zachary
Rogillio, Kathy June musician, piano rebuilder, educator

MAINE

Allagash
Hafford, Faye O'Leary writer

Andover
Ellis, George Hathaway retired bank executive, utilities executive

Kaltsos, Angelo John *electronics executive, educator, photographer*

Ashland
Morrow, David Andrew *secondary school educator*

Auburn
Clifford, Robert William *state supreme court justice*
Douglass, Neria Gay *state legislator, lawyer*
Umpierre, Luz María *women studies educator, foreign language educator*

Augusta
Amero, Jane Adams *state senator*
Baldacci, John Elias *governor, former congressman*
Barstow, Christopher R. *state representative*
Bennett, Richard A. *state senator*
Bromley, Lynn *state legislator*
Calkins, Susan W. *state supreme court justice*
Caron, Jean C. *nursing association administrator*
Cathcart, Mary R. *state legislator*
Cheng, Hsueh Ching *physician*
Daggett, Beverly Clark *state legislator*
Dana, Howard H., Jr., *state supreme court justice*
Dunlap, Matthew Gordon *legislator*
Edmonds, Beth A. *state legislator*
Gendron, Susan Ann *commissioner, educator*
Gervais, Paul Nelson *foundation administrator, psychotherapist, public relations executive, author*
Gray, Howard R., Jr., *former commissioner*
Gwadosky, Dan A. *secretary of state*
Hatch, Pamela H. *state legislator*
Hussey, John Francis *physician, geriatrician*
Jacobson, James Lamma, Jr., *data processing company executive*
Jenkins, Pamela Lynn *music educator*
Ketterer, Andrew *state commissioner, former state attorney general*
Kontos, Carol A. *state senator, educator*
Ledwin, Mary Ellen *state legislator*
Libby, James Delmas *state senator, educator, marketing consultant*
Lyons, Charles M. *academic administrator*
Martin, John Lewis *state legislator*
McCormick, Dale *state treasurer*
Melanson, Dorothy *political organization administrator*
Mitchell, Betty Lou *state legislator, retired operations director*
Nickerson, John Mitchell *political science educator*
Norman, Melora Ranney *library director, educator*
Paradis, Judy *state legislator*
Pendleton, Peggy A. *state legislator, nurse education consultant*
Raths, Barbara *political organization worker*
Roberts, Donald Albert *advertising, public relations, marketing and media consultant*
Rotundo, Margaret R. *state legislator*
Rowe, G. Steven *state attorney general*
Savage, Christine R. *state legislator*
Saxl, Jane Wilhelm *state legislator*
Small, Mary E. *state legislator*
Townsend, Elizabeth *state legislator*
Waldron, Janet E. *state commissioner*
Weil, Gordon Lee *energy executive, publishing executive*
Wilkinson, Lester F., Jr., *lawyer*

Bangor
Albrecht, Ronald Lewis *financial services executive*
Austin, Linda S. *psychiatrist*
Beaupain, Elaine Shapiro *psychiatric social worker*
Bullock, William Clapp, Jr., *banker*
Coffman, Michael S. *international organization official, ecologist*
Donnelly, James Owen *state legislator, bank executive*
Foster, Walter Herbert, Jr., *real estate company executive*
Hsu, Yu Kao *aerospace scientist, mathematician, educator*
Hupp, Rebecca *airport terminal executive*
Kelley, Barbara Bannin *physical education educator*
King, Stephen Edwin *novelist, scriptwriter*
King, Tabitha *author*
MacTaggart, Terrence Joseph *professor, former university chancellor*
McKinnon, Carolyn Ann *child care center director*
Rea, Ann W. *librarian*
Read, William B. *business educator*
Rosen, Clifford James *internist*
Rudman, Paul Lewis *judge*
Swanson, Lisa Tucker *human services manager, consultant*
Warren, Richard Jordan *newspaper publisher*
Warren, Richard Kearney *newspaper publisher*
Westphal, Joseph W. *academic administrator*

Bar Harbor
Carpenter, William Morton *English educator, writer*
Goldthwait, Jill Murdoch *state legislator*
Krevans, Julius Richard *academic administrator, internist*
Leiter, Edward Henry *cell biologist, researcher*
Nass, Meryl J. *physician, writer, research scientist*
Paigen, Kenneth *geneticist, science administrator*
Swazey, Judith Pound *academic administrator, sociomedical science educator*

Bath
Stoudt, Howard Webster *biological anthropologist, human factors specialist, consultant*

Belfast
Griffith, Patricia King *journalist*
Porter, Bernard Harden *consulting physicist, author, publisher*
Worth, Mary Page *mayor*

Belgrade Lakes
Kany, Judy C(asperson) *health policy analyst, former state senator*

Bethel
Farrar, Susan Clement *choreographer, performing company executive, writer*

Biddeford
Bolle, Kees Willem *history professor*
Featherman, Sandra *academic administrator, political science educator*
Ford, Charles Willard *health science educator*

Riley, Pamela Janerico *artist*
Rothermel, Dan *humanities educator*
Shannon, Stephen Curtis *dean, occupational health physician*

Blue Hill
Papert, Seymour Aubrey *mathematician, educator, writer*
Young, David Michael *biochemistry and molecular biology educator, physician*

Bremen
Wilson, Linda Smith *academic administrator*

Bridgton
Normann, Margaret Ella *deacon, educator*

Bristol
Sabin, William Albert *writer*

Brooklin
Meserve, Mollie Ann *publisher*
Schmidt, Klaus Dieter *management consultant, university administrator, marketing and management educator*
Schmidt, Lynda Wheelwright *psychotherapist*

Brooksville
Sutherland, Malcolm Read, Jr., *clergyman, educator*

Brownfield
Kloskowski, Vincent John, Jr., *educational consultant, writer, educator*

Brunswick
Ault, James Mase *bishop*
Crandall, Elizabeth Walbert *home economics educator*
Fiori, Michael J. *pharmacist*
Fitzgerald, John Michael *economist, educator*
Fuchs, Alfred Herman *psychologist, educator*
Geoghegan, William Davidson *religion educator, minister*
Greason, Arthur LeRoy, Jr., *retired university administrator*
Hodge, James Lee *German language educator*
King, Angus S., Jr., *former governor*
Martin, Harold Clark *humanities educator*
McEwen, Craig A. *dean*
Morgan, Richard Ernest *political scientist, educator*
Nagle, Jeffrey Karl *chemist, educator*
Owen, H. Martyn *retired lawyer*
Pfeiffer, Sophia Douglass *state legislator, lawyer*
Riley, Matilda White (Mrs. John W. Riley Jr.) *sociologist*
Rosser, Richard Franklin *higher education consultant*
Schwartz, Elliott Shelling *composer, author, music educator*
Tautz, Birgit *education educator, researcher*

Bryant Pond
Conary, David Arlan *investment company executive*

Bucksport
Ives, Edward Dawson *folklore educator*

Camden
Cagle, William Rea *librarian*
Dyer, Barbara F. *retired accountant, writer*
Fisher, Craig Becker *film and television executive*
Moran, Elizabeth Ames *library director*
Russo, Richard *writer*
Sanford, John Joseph *lawyer, director*

Cape Elizabeth
Cotter, Joseph Francis *retired hotel and bank executive*
Gelzer, Lois Auge *foundation administrator*
Simonds, Stephen Paige *former state legislator*

Cape Neddick
Ksypka, Helen *organizational consultant*

Caribou
Swanson, Shirley June *emergency room nurse, travel nurse, adult education educator*

Cary Plt
Geishecker, Rueline Taylor *music educator*

Castine
Berleant, Arnold *philosopher*
Bernstein, Lester *editorial consultant*
Davis, Peter Frank *filmmaker, author*
Hall, David *sound archivist, writer*
Wiswall, Frank Lawrence, Jr., *lawyer, educator*

Center Lovell
Adams, Herbert Ryan *management consultant, retired minister*

Chebeague Island
Traina, Albert Salvatore *publishing executive*

Corea
Harward, Donald West *retired academic administrator*

Cumberland Center
Thomas, Charles Carroll *retired investment management executive*

Cumberland Foreside
Dill, William Rankin *college president*

Cushing
Magee, Alan *artist*

Damariscotta
Blake, Bud (Julian Watson) *cartoonist*
Fuller, Melvin Stuart *botany educator*

Deer Isle
Smith, Gardner Watkins *physician*

Dover Foxcroft
Young-Coombs, Esther Elizabeth (Betsey Eveleth, Betsey L. Eveleth) *poet*

Dresden
Turco, Lewis Putnam *English educator*

East Blue Hill
Stroud, Patricia Tyson *writer*

East Boothbay
Eldred, Kenneth McKechnie *acoustical consultant*
Ford, Richard *writer*
Turndorf, Herman *anesthesiologist, educator*

East Millinocket
Michaud, Michael Herman *congressman*

Edgecomb
Carlson, Suzanne Olive *architect*
Wait, Lea *writer, small business owner*

Eliot
Lawrence, Mark W. *former state legislator, lawyer*
Tillinghast, John Avery *utilities executive*

Ellsworth
Becker, Ray Everett *management consultant*

Falmouth
Cabot, Lewis Pickering *manufacturing company executive, art consultant*
Gulliver, Jean K. *educational association administrator*
Hathaway, Lynn McDonald *education advocate, administrator*
Kendrick, Peter Murray *communications executive, investor*
Pierce, Philip Sargent *clinical psychologist*
Rohsenow, Warren Max *retired mechanical engineer, educator*
Winton, Linda *international trainer and consultant*

Farmington
Downs, Gary M. *bank executive*
Kalikow, Theodora June *university president*
Melcher, James Patrick *political scientist, educator*
Reid, Jennifer Irene McPherran *religious studies educator*
Szybist, Mary *poet*

Fort Fairfield
Shapiro, Joan Isabelle *lab administrator, medical/surgical nurse*

Freeport
Cushman, Margaret Jane *herbalist, nurse*
Gorman, Leon A. *mail order company executive*
Lewis, Jessica Helen (Mrs. Jack D. Myers) *physician, educator*
Sidar, Thomas Wilson *retail executive*

Friendship
MacIlvaine, Chalmers Acheson *retired financial executive, former association executive*

Gardiner
Dunbar, Robert Everett *writer, educator*
Gosline, Norman Abbot *real estate appraiser, consultant*
Treat, Sharon Anglin *state legislator*

Georgetown
Chapin, Maryan Fox *civic worker*
Chapin, Richard *arbitrator, consultant*
Ludgin, Donald Hugh *editor*

Glenburn
Rauch, Charles Frederick, Jr., *retired university official and business educator*

Gorham
Bearce, Jeana Dale *artist, educator*
Canniff, Julie G. *education educator, researcher*

Hancock
Silvestro, Clement Mario *museum director, historian*

Hollis
Milardo, Margaret Powers *language educator*

Hollis Center
Kaake, Norman Bradford *quality assurance professional*

Houlton
Levien, David Harold *surgeon*

Islesboro
Caplow, Theodore *sociologist, educator*
Maes, John Leopold *theologian, psychologist, educator*

Jackman
Thomas, Paulette Suzanne *holistic health practitioner, physician assistant*

Kennebunk
Damon, Edmund Holcombe *retired plastics company executive*
Escalet, Frank Diaz *art gallery owner, artist, educator*
Sholl, John Gurney, III, *physician*
Ward, Nina Gillson *jewelry store executive*

Kennebunkport
Featherman, Bernard *steel company executive*
Mulvihill, James Edward *periodontist, educator*
Ray, Virginia H. S. *columnist, writer*

Kingfield
Collins, H(erschel) Douglas *retired physician*

Kittery
McNally, James Henry *physicist, defense consultant*

Kittery Point
Howells, William White *anthropology educator*

Lewiston
Christie, Donald Melvin, Jr., *physician*
Dennison, Gerard Francis *economic analyst*
Hansen, Elaine Tuttle *academic administrator*
Kessler, Mark Allen *political scientist, educator*

Payne, Jean L. *writer*
Reich, Jill *dean*
Semon, Mark David *physicist, researcher*

Lincoln
Kneeland, Douglas Eugene *retired newspaper editor*

Lincolnville
Williams, Robert Luther *city planning consultant*

Lisbon Falls
Raskin, Michael Neil *psychologist, writer*

Lubec
Hayes, Ernest M. *podiatrist*
Hudson, Miles *retired special education educator*

Manchester
Clark, Beth *minister*
Moody, Stanley Alton *entrepreneur, financial consultant*

Milbridge
Enslin, Theodore Vernon *poet*

Morrill
Hitt, Robert Willaim *actor*

Mount Desert
Crawford, Richard Bradway *biologist, biochemist, educator*
Singleton, Francis Seth *international educator*

New Gloucester
Jaccaci, August Thayer, Jr., *social architect, educator*

New Harbor
Lyford, Cabot *sculptor*

New Vineyard
Smith, Frederick Orville, II, *wood products manufacturer, retired naval officer*

Newcastle
Waterman, Charles Albert *actor, director, retired sales executive*

Nobleboro
Fisher, Allan Campbell *retired railway executive*

North Haven
Pingree, Rochelle M. *state legislator*

North Yarmouth
Fecteau, Rosemary Louise *educational administrator, educator, consultant*

Northeast Harbor
Hafkenschiel, Joseph Henry, Jr., *cardiologist, educator*

Oakland
Rutherford, Robert Barry *vascular surgeon*

Ogunquit
Carpenter, George Robert *artist*
West, Norman Ellsworth *artist*

Old Town
Alex, Joanne DeFilipp *elementary school educator*
Nelligan, Annette Frances *clinical coordinator*
Scribner, Princess Rose-Marie *not-for-profit developer*

Orono
Allen, Anne Elliott *academic administrator*
Borns, Harold William, Jr., *geologist, educator*
Bradley, David Michael *mathematician, educator*
Chute, Harold LeRoy *veterinary pathologist, former chemical company executive*
Cohn, Steven Frederick *sociology educator, consultant*
Devino, William Stanley *economist, educator*
Ellis, William Grenville, Jr., *marine biologist, educator*
Estler, Suzanne E. *education educator*
Goldstone, Sanford *psychology educator*
Hoff, Peter Sloat *academic administrator*
MacDonald, Elizabeth Helen *bassoonist, educator*
Marston-Scott, Mary Vesta *nurse, educator*
Martindale, Colin Eugene *psychology educator, author*
Matthews, Larryl Kent *mechanical engineering educator*
Rice, Edward Perry *secondary school educator*
Risberg, Erica Lynn *archivist, film producer*
See, Scott William *history professor*
Segal, Howard Paul *history educator*
Weiss, Robert Jerome *psychiatrist, educator*
Wiersma, G. Bruce *dean, forest resources educator*

Orrington
Snyder, Arnold Lee, Jr., *retired air force officer, research director*

Orrs Island
Nelson, Robert Louis *lawyer*

Palermo
Anderson, Alfred Oliver *mathematician, consultant*

Pembroke
Moody, Michael Dorn *playwright, entertainer*

Port Clyde
Duarte, Patricia M. *real estate and insurance broker*

Portland
Alexander, Donald G. *state supreme court justice*
Anderson, Stephen Mills *investment broker*
Berry, Henry Newhall, III, *lawyer*
Bohan, Thomas Lynch *physicist, lawyer*
Boris, James R. *investment company executive*
Boyle, John Edward Whiteford *cultural organization administrator*
Boyson, Michael Andrew *investment consultant*
Bradford, Carl O. *judge*
Bride, John W. *communications executive, entrepreneur*

Bucci, Thomas Vincent *music educator, pianist, composer*
Burgess, Meredith Nancy Strang *advertising agency executive*
Burns, George F. *lawyer*
Bushell, Agnes *art educator, writer*
Candage, Howard Everett *insurance management consultant, agent, broker*
Carter, Gene *judge*
Chandler, Patricia Ann *retired special education educator*
Chow, Amy *gymnast, Olympic athlete*
Clark, Gordon Hostetter, Jr., *physician*
Coffin, Frank Morey *judge*
Courtney, Ann M. *lawyer*
Farrington, Hugh G. *wholesale food and retail drug company executive*
Gerry, Joseph John *bishop*
Gilmore, Roger *college consultant*
Glassman, Caroline Duby *state supreme court justice*
Graffam, Ward Irving *lawyer*
Harvey, Charles Albert, Jr., *lawyer*
Henshaw, Nathaniel Venable *venture capitalist*
Hornby, David Brock *federal judge*
Hotelling, David Rawson *endocrinologist, medical educator*
Hunt, David Evans *lawyer*
Ingalls, Everett Palmer, III, *lawyer*
Ives, Samuel Clifton *minister*
Khoury, Colleen A. *dean*
Konkel, Harry Wagner *civic volunteer, retired career officer*
Lancaster, Ralph Ivan, Jr., *lawyer*
Lipez, Kermit V. *federal judge, former state supreme court justice*
Louden, Robert Burton *philosopher, educator*
Massaua, John Roger *retail executive*
McDowell, Donald L. *hospital administrator*
McKusick, Vincent Lee *former state supreme court chief justice, lawyer, arbitrator, mediator*
Miller, Buffy *dancer*
Morgan, Robin Evonne *poet, author, journalist, activist, editor*
Neavoll, George Franklin *writer*
O'Brien, John Matthew *psychologist, educator*
Pattenaude, Richard Louis *university administrator*
Powers, Ross *Olympic athlete*
Reid, Rosemary Anne *insurance agent*
Rhinehardt, Peter Kevin *elementary school educator, writer, artist*
Robinson, John Beinecke *writer*
Rockefeller, Richard Gilder *medical association administrator*
Rogers, Richard Mead *food service executive*
Rundlett, Ellsworth Turner, III, *lawyer*
Russell, Robert Jackson *music educator, conductor*
Saufley, Leigh Ingalls *judge*
Saufley, William Edward *banker, lawyer*
Schwanauer, Francis *philosopher, educator*
Silsby, Paula *prosecutor*
Smith, William Charles *lawyer*
Stanley, Eliot Hungerford *small business owner, writer, lawyer*
Stauffer, Eric P. *lawyer*
Thompson, Peter L. *lawyer*
Tooker, John Phillip *internist, educator*
Wathen, Daniel Everett *former state supreme court chief justice*
Weir, Anne *writer*
Whedon, Ralph Gibbs *manufacturing executive*
White, Jeffrey Munroe *lawyer*
Zarr, Melvyn *lawyer, law educator*

Presque Isle
Hensel, Nancy H. *academic administrator*

Rangeley
Gallant, Roy Arthur *writer, education educator*

Raymond
Coughlan, Patrick Campbell *lawyer, mediator*

Rockland
Collins, Samuel W., Jr., *judge*
Platt, David Day *journalist, editor*
Ziegelaar, Bob W. *transportation executive*

Rockport
Goodwin, Doris Helen Kearns *historian*
Hinrichs, Stephen *design educator, consultant*

Saco
Mason, Nancy Tolman *retired state agency director*
Prescott, Dana E. *lawyer*

Sanford
Allan, Jonathan David *autograph dealer, pop culture historian*
Collins, Thomas Michael *surgeon*
Will, Jerrie Ann *psychologist*

Sangerville
Harris, Norman Edwin *food scientist, consultant*

Scarborough
Connolly, Elaine Alexander Paterson *nurse*
Devlin, John Tobey *physician, educator*
Hayden, Lisa C. *interpreter, translator, language educator, writer*
Raisbeck, Gordon *systems engineer, consultant*
Sadik, Marvin Sherwood *art consultant, former museum director*
Shire, Donald Thomas *retired air products and chemicals executive, lawyer*
Shulman, Richard *musician, composer, recording label owner*

Seal Harbor
Forbes, Peter *architect*

Sebago Lake
Murray, Wallace Shordon *publisher, educator*

Sedgwick
Donnell, William Ray *small business owner, communications executive*
Schroth, Thomas Nolan *editor*

Sidney
Tietenberg, Thomas *economist, department chairman*

Skowhegan
Ross, James Owen *education educator, researcher*
Youney, John William *lawyer*

South Bristol
Wells, Arthur Stanton *retired manufacturing company executive*

South Paris
Hamilton, Kenneth Hawley *surgeon, consultant*

South Portland
Baker, Arlene Ann *speech pathology/audiology services professional, consultant*
Fetteroll, Eugene Carl, Jr., *human resources professional*
Harris, Penny Smith *fundraising consultant*
Huntoon, Abby Elizabeth *artist, educator*
Lovett, E. J., III, *cytometrist, immunologist*
Martin, Joseph Robert *corporate financial executive*
Wheeler, Hewitt Brownell *surgeon, educator*

Starks
Medeiros, M. Joyce *community health educator*

Stonington
Pitts, Edgar Thurlow *writer, retired educator*

Sumner
Rudd, David William *management consultant, chemical engineer, consultant*

Sunset
Knowlton, Leslie Brooks *journalist*

Surry
Kilgore, John Edward, Jr., *former petroleum company executive*
Sopkin, George *cellist, music educator*

Tenants Harbor
Bates, John Cecil, Jr., *lawyer*

Topsham
Palesky, Carol East *tax accountant*

Trevett
Mathias, Cordula *art dealer*

Veazie
Kennedy, Robert Alan *educational administrator*

Waterford
Stockwell, William F. *fundraiser, management consultant*

Waterville
Adams, William D. *academic administrator*
Armstrong, Darlene L. *elementary school educator*
Bassett, Charles Walker *English language educator*
Box, Laura Diane Chakravarty *theater educator*
Cook, Susan Farwell *associate director planned giving*
Fleming, James Rodger *science historian, educator*
Gemery, Henry Albert *economics professor*
Gilkes, Cheryl Louise Townsend *sociologist, educator, minister*
Laurence, Robert Lionel *chemical engineering educator*
Massarski, Leonid *physicist*
Moroni, Mario *humanities educator*
Muehlner, Suanne Wilson *library director*
Sandy, Robert Edward, Jr., *lawyer*
Yeterian, Edward Harry *psychologist, educator, administrator*

Wells
Carleton, Joseph George, Jr., *lawyer, state legislator*

West Baldwin
Pierce, Elizabeth Gay *civic worker*
Simmonds, Rae Nichols *musician, composer, educator*

West Boothbay Harbor
Marshall, Howard Lowen *musicologist, retired music educator*

West Southport
Barker, Walter William, Jr., *artist, writer*

Westbrook
Lee, Shepard *automobile dealership owner*
O'Gara, William B. *state legislator, real estate agent*
Parks, George Richard *retired librarian*

Whitefield
Marden, Kenneth Allen *advertising executive*

Winthrop
Saunders, Joseph Arthur *office products manufacturing company executive*

Yarmouth
Bischoff, David Canby *retired university dean*
Clark, Gail Theroux *artist*
Grover, Mark Donald *computer scientist*
Hart, Loring Edward *academic administrator*
Haynes, Peter Lancaster *retired utility executive*
Mansmann, Paris Taylor *medical educator*
Northrup, Christiane *gynecologist-obstetrician*
Webster, Peter Bridgman *lawyer*

York
Berlew, Frank Kingston *lawyer*
Haley, Priscilla Jane *printmaker*
Hallam, Beverly (Beverly Linney) *artist*
Lyman, William Welles, Jr., *retired architect*
Smart, Mary-Leigh Call (Mrs. J. Scott Smart) *civic worker*

York Harbor
Rust, Libby Karen *fundraising and public relations counsel*

MARYLAND

Aberdeen Proving Ground
Berry, Patrick Lowell *chemical engineer*
Carrieri, Arthur Helmut *physicist, researcher*
Cavallaro, Nicholas John *environmental scientist*
Cozby, Richard Scott *electronics engineer, military officer*
Doesburg, John C. *military career officer*
Gupta, Aaron Das *mechanical engineer*
Miziolek, Andrzej Wladyslaw *research physicist*
Sliney, David Hammond *medical physicist*
Steger, Ralph James *chemist*
Stuebing, Edward Willis *research scientist*
Tobin, Aileen Webb *educational administrator*
Waugh, John Douglas *engineer, researcher*

Abingdon
Wolf, Martin Eugene *lawyer, educator*

Accokeek
Beddow, Richard Harold *retired judge*

Adamstown
Church, Martha Eleanor *retired academic administrator, scholar*
Munson, John Christian *acoustician*
Tidball, Charles Stanley *computer scientist, educator*

Adelphi
Bayne, Stephen B. *electronics engineer, researcher*
Brandt, Howard Edward *physicist*
Chang, Sam Shifeng *meteorologist*
Gaunaurd, Guillermo C. *physicist, engineer, researcher*
Heeger, Gerald Arthur *university president*
Kendrick, Kerry *military officer*
Kirwan, William English, II, *mathematics educator, university official, academic administrator*
Mait, Joseph N. *electrical engineer, educator*
Sutherland, Alan Roy *business educator*
Torrieri, Don Joseph *electronics engineer, mathematician, researcher*
Whalin, Robert W. *physicist*
Whitford, Dennis J. *military officer*

Andrews Air Force Base
Hall, Molly J. *psychiatrist, educator*

Annapolis
Alderdice, Cynthia Lou *artist*
ames, Steven Reede *financial planner*
Andrews, Archie Moulton *government official*
Aumann, R. Karl *state official, lawyer*
Battaglia, Lynne Ann *judge*
Benson, Joanne C. *state legislator*
Bontoyan, Warren Roberts *chemist, state laboratories administrator*
Bowen, Linnell R. *director*
Branand, Claire Diane *advertising executive, writer*
Brann, Eva Toni Helene *archaeology educator*
Brunk, William Edward *astronomer*
Burnett, Calvin Wilks *academic administrator*
Busch, Michael *state legislator*
Cadden, Joan *state legislator*
Casey, Edward Dennis *newspaper editor*
Cathell, Dale Roberts *judge*
Chambers, Ronald D. *book publishing executive*
Clagett, Virginia Parker *county official*
Clotworthy, John Harris *oceanographic consultant*
Connolly, Janet Elizabeth *retired sociologist and criminal justice educator*
Conroy, Mary A. *state legislator*
Conway, Joan Carter *state legislator*
Coulter, James Bennett *state official*
Crawford, Carol Gloria *mathematician, educator*
Crosby, Ralph Wolf *communications executive*
DiAiso, Robert Joseph *civil engineer*
DiPentima, Renato Anthony *systems executive*
Ehrlich, Robert L., Jr., *governor, former congressman*
Eldridge, John Cole *judge*
Essandoh, Louis Kofi *cardiologist*
Farmer, Martha Louise *retired college administrator*
Ferris, William Michael *lawyer*
Finerty, Martin Joseph, Jr., *military officer, researcher, association management executive*
Forehand, Jennie Meador *state senator*
Fry, Virginia Milne *artist, poet*
Galvin, Michael Francis *state agency administrator, arborist*
Gavian, Peter Wood *venture capitalist*
Goldwater, Marilyn R(ubin) *medical/surgical nurse, state legislator*
Halpern, Joseph Alan *physician*
Hammer, Jacob Myer *physicist, consultant*
Harrison, Hattie N. *state senator*
Healey, Anne *state legislator*
Hill, Kennard F. *computing systems company executive*
Hixson, Sheila Ellis *state legislator*
Hoffman, Barbara A. *state legislator*
Hollinger, Paula Colodny *state legislator*
Holston, A. Frank *retired broadcaster, communications educator*
Holtgrewe, Henry Logan *urologist*
Howard, Carolyn J. B. *state legislator*
Hoyer, Leon William *physician, educator*
Hunkele, Lester Martin, III, *retired federal agency administrator*
Hyde, Lawrence Henry, Jr., *industrial company executive*
Jacobs, Linda Joan *secondary school educator*
Jacobs, Nancy *state legislator*
Jansson, John Phillip *architect, consultant*
Jefferson, Ralph Harvey *international affairs consultant*
Johnson, Bruce *engineering educator*
Josephson, Diana Hayward *not-for-profit company executive*
Kane, John *political organization administrator*
Katz, Douglas Jeffrey *retired naval officer, consultant*
Kelley, Delores Goodwin *state legislator*
Kirk, Ruth M. *state legislator*
Klein, Robert Dale *lawyer*
Klima, Martha Scanlan *state legislator*
Kopp, Nancy Kornblith *state official*
Krysiak, Carolyn *state legislator*
Kushner, Jack *retired physician executive*
Levin, Gilbert Victor *health services administrator*
Levitan, Laurence *lawyer, former state senator*
Lillard, John Franklin, III, *lawyer*
Lucas, George Ramsdell, Jr., *philosophy educator*
Lucas, Steven Mitchell *lawyer*
Madden, Martin Gerard *former state legislator*
Manos, Pete Lazaros *supermarket executive*
Marienthal, George *telecommunications company executive*
Martino, Peter Dominic *financial software company executive, real estate developer, real estate broker, federal agency administrator, consultant*
McGuirk, Ronald Charles *retired bank executive, economic advisor*
McIntosh, Maggie *state legislator*
Michaelson, Benjamin, Jr., *lawyer, director*
Miller, John Grider *writer*
Miller, Patricia A. *training services executive*
Miller, Richards Thorn *naval architect, engineer*
Miller, Thomas V. Mike, Jr., *state legislator*
Nelson, Charles Arthur *publishing executive, writer*
Papenfuse, Edward Carl, Jr., *archivist, state official*
Parham, Carol Sheffey *school system administrator*
Perkins, Roger Allan *lawyer*
Reich, Merrill Drury *intelligence consultant, writer*
Rogers, David Freeman *aerospace engineering educator*
Rogers, Wayne L. *political organization administrator*
Ruben, Ida Gass *state senator*
Sheppard, John Wilbur *computer research scientist*
Smith, Robert Myron *investment company executive*
Snodgrass, Louise Virginia *state legislator, dental assistant*
Snyder, Kathleen Theresa *state agency administrator*
Steele, Michael *lieutenant governor*
Stern, Margaret Bassett *retired special education educator, author*
Teitelbaum, Leonard H. *state legislator*
Thoms, Josephine Bowers *artist*
Trost, Carlisle Albert Herman *retired naval officer*
Welch, Robert Bond *ophthalmologist, educator*
Werking, Richard Hume *librarian, historian, academic administrator*
Williams, J. Linda *librarian*
Wolf, Alfred A. *physicist, educator*
Wright, David Lawrence *realtor, real estate broker*
Yee, Cordell D.K. *liberal arts educator, historian*

Arbutus
Maloney, Charles Wayne *gunsmith*

Arnold
Green, John Cawley *lawyer*
Harris, Roger Clark *psychiatrist, consultant*
Smith, Martha A. *academic administrator*
Teklu, Dawit *researcher*
Williams, James Arthur *retired army officer, information systems company executive*

Ashton
Whelan, Roger Michael *lawyer, educator*

Baldwin
Decker, James Ludlow *management consultant*

Baltimore
Abeloff, Martin David *medical administrator, educator, researcher*
Achinstein, Peter Jacob *philosopher, educator*
Adams, Clara I. *academic administrator*
Adams, Harold Lynn *architect*
Agnew, William S. *physiology educator*
Agre, Peter Courtland *medical educator*
Albuquerque, Edson Xavier *pharmacology educator*
Allan, Janet D. *dean*
Allen, Norma Ann *librarian, educator*
Allen, Ronald John *astrophysics educator, researcher*
Amos, Helen *hospital administrator*
Anderson, Brady Kevin *professional baseball player*
Anderson, Gerard Fenton *economist, university program administrator*
Anderson, Jean R. *women's health physician*
Angelos, Peter G. *professional sports team executive, lawyer*
Anthony, James Christopher *mental hygiene educator*
Applebaum, Gary E. *medical director, executive*
Applefeld, Laurie S. *lawyer*
Archibald, James Kenway *lawyer*
Arnick, John Stephen *lawyer, legislator*
Arsham, Hossein *operations research analyst*
Askew, Laurin Barker, Jr., *architect*
August, Joseph Thomas *pharmacology educator*
Ayres, Jeffrey Peabody *lawyer*
Bachur, Nicholas Robert, Sr., *research physician*
Baines, Henry T., Sr., *supermarkets executive*
Bair, Robert Rippel *lawyer*
Baker, Nadine Lois *cardiovascular technician*
Baker, R. Robinson *surgeon*
Baker, Timothy Danforth *physician, educator*
Baker, William Parr *lawyer*
Baldwin, Henry Furlong *banker*
Baldwin, John Wesley *history professor*
Ball, Gregory Francis *biological psychology educator*
Ball, Marion Jokl *academic administrator*
Baramki, Theodore Atallah *gynecologist, reproductive endocrinologist*
Barnes, Kathleen Carole *medical educator*
Barnhart, Jo Anne B. *federal agency administrator*
Barnhill, Gregory Hurd *investment banker*
Barnow, Burt S. *economist*
Barth, John Simmons *writer, educator*
Bartlett, James Wilson, III, *lawyer*
Bartlett, John Gill *infectious disease physician*
Baumgartner, William Anthony *cardiac surgeon*
Bausell, R. Barker, Jr., *research methodology educator*
Bayless, Theodore M(orris) *gastroenterologist, educator, researcher*
Beachy, Philip Arden *molecular biology educator*
Beckwith, Steven Van Walter *astronomy educator*
Beer, Michael *biophysicist, educator, environmentalist*
Behm, Mark Edward *university administrator, consultant*
Beilenson, Peter Lowell *public health official*
Bell, Robert M. *state supreme court justice*
Belle, Albert Jojuan *professional baseball player*
Berghuis, Brian *investment company executive*
Berlage, Jan Ingham *lawyer*
Bero, Joseph Martin *manufacturing engineer*
Bhardwaj, Anish *neuroscientist, medical educator*
Bigelow, George E. *psychology and pharmacology scientist*
Black, Walter Evan, Jr., *federal judge*
Blake, Catherine C. *judge*

Blakemore, Karin Jane *obstetrician, geneticist*
Blakeslee, Wesley Daniel *lawyer, consultant*
Blanton, Edward Lee, Jr., *lawyer*
Blattner, William Albert *physician, epidemiology researcher*
Block, James A. *hospital administrator, pediatrician*
Boardman, John Michael *mathematician, educator*
Bochner, Bruce Scott *immunologist, educator*
Bogen, David Skillen *law educator*
Bolger, Doreen *museum director*
Boston, Wallace Ellsworth, Jr., *healthcare executive, financial consultant*
Boughman, Joann Ashley *dean*
Bowen, Lowell Reed *lawyer*
Bowman, Donald Eugene *investment advisor*
Bradley, Wanda Louise *librarian*
Brady, Joseph Vincent *behavioral biologist, educator*
Bramble, Frank P. *bank executive*
Bredar, James Kelleher *judge*
Breitner, John C. S. *psychiatrist, educator, academic administrator*
Brem, Henry *neurosurgeon, educator, researcher*
Brewster, Gerry Leiper *educator, lawyer*
Brieger, Gert Henry *medical historian, educator*
Bright, Margaret *sociologist*
Brinkley, James Wellons *investment company executive*
Brock, Roslyn McCallister *association executive*
Broda-Hydorn, Susan *entomologist*
Brodie, M. J. (Jay Brodie) *architect, city planner, government executive*
Brody, Eugene Bloor *psychiatrist, educator*
Brody, William Ralph *academic administrator, radiologist, educator*
Broening, Walter Stephens, Jr., *journalist, history educator*
Brookmeyer, Ronald *medical educator*
Brotman, Phyllis Block *advertising and public relations executive*
Brown, Donald David *biology professor*
Brown, Eddie C. *investment company executive*
Brown, Patricia Mary Clare *health facility administrator*
Browne, Lovetie W. *special education educator, small business owner*
Brushart, Thomas Marshall *hand surgeon, neuroscience researcher*
Bryn-Julson, Phyllis *soprano, music educator*
Burch, Francis Boucher, Jr., *lawyer*
Burke, Colin Bradley *retired historian*
Buser, Carolyn Elizabeth *correctional education administrator*
Byron, William James *author, management educator, researcher, former university president*
Cacossa, Anthony Alexander *Romance languages educator*
Cain, Marcena Jean Beesley *retail executive*
Cameron, Duke Edward *cardiac surgeon, educator*
Campbell, Jacquelyn C. *community health nurse*
Carbine, James Edmond *lawyer*
Carey, Anthony Morris *lawyer*
Carlin, Paul Victor *legal association executive*
Carper, Gertrude Esther *artist, marina owner*
Carrier, France *medical educator*
Carson, Benjamin Solomon *neurosurgeon*
Catania, A(nthony) Charles *psychology educator*
Chagnoni, Kathleen *energy executive*
Chapelle, Suzanne Ellery Greene *history professor*
Chaplin, Peggy Louie *lawyer*
Chen, Yu *acupuncturist, Chinese herbologist*
Chernow, Jeffrey Scott *lawyer, educator, writer*
Childs, Barton *retired physician, educator*
Chiu, Hungdah *lawyer, legal educator*
Christ, Carl Finley *economist, educator*
Civiletti, Benjamin R. *lawyer, former United States attorney general*
Clark, Kevin P. *police commissioner*
Clements, Janice *science educator*
Clements, Mary Lou *epidemiologist, educator*
Cohen, Eric *optometrist*
Cohen, Warren I. *history professor*
Cole, Emried Dargan, Jr., *lawyer*
Coleman, Carolyn Quilloin *association executive*
Colomer, Veronica *medical educator, researcher*
Cook, Bryson Leitch *lawyer*
Cooper, Jerrold Stephen *historian, educator*
Cooper, Joseph *political scientist, educator*
Coppel, Lawrence David *lawyer*
Cornett, Stanley Orin *music educator*
Cosner, David Dale, Sr., *plastics industry executive, marketing executive*
Cotter, Robert *pharmacology and science educator*
Crawford, Fred Lee *public affairs officer*
Cripps, Richard E. *diversified financial services company executive*
Crowe, Thomas Leonard *lawyer*
Crowel, Raymond L. *medical educator*
Culurciello, Eugenio *research engineer, educator*
Cummings, Charles William *physician, educator*
Curl, Leigh Ann *orthopedist, surgeon*
Curley, John Francis, Jr., *mutual fund executive*
Curran, J. Joseph, Jr., *state attorney general*
Curran, Robert Bruce *lawyer*
Dang, Chi Van *hematology and oncology educator*
Daniels, Susan M. *commissioner*
Dannenberg, Arthur Milton, Jr., *experimental pathologist, immunologist, educator*
Davidson, Roger, Jr., *historian, educator*
Davis, Andre Maurice *judge, educator*
Davis, Carole Joan *psychologist, consultant*
Davis, Linda L. *social welfare executive director*
Dawson, Valina L. *science educator*
DeAngelis, Catherine D. *pediatrics educator*
Deffenbaugh, Ralston H., Jr., *immigration agency executive, lawyer*
DeLateur, Barbara Jane *medical educator*
D'Erasmo, Martha Jean *health company executive*
Derby, Ernest Stephen *federal judge*
De Shields-Minnis, Tarra Ramit *lawyer*
Desiderio, Stephen *molecular biology educator*
Desoto, Clinton Burgel *psychologist, educator*
DeTolla, Louis James *research scientist and veterinarian*
Deutsch, Robert William *physicist*
Devan, Deborah Hunt *lawyer*
DeVito, Mathias Joseph *retired real estate executive*
DeVries, Donald Lawson, Jr., *lawyer*
DiBiagio, Thomas M. *prosecutor*
Dicello, John Francis, Jr., *physicist, researcher*
Dickey, George Edward *water resources consultant, economics educator*
Dickinson, Jane W. *social services administrator*
Dietze, Gottfried *political science educator*
Digges, Edward S(imms) *business management consultant*
Dilsizian, Vasken *cardiologist, nuclear medicine physician*
Djordjevic, Borislav Boro *materials scientist, researcher*
Dodge, Calvert Renaul *education and training executive, author, educator*
Donaldson, Sue Karen *nursing educator, researcher*
Donkervoet, Richard Cornelius *architect*
Donovan, Dianne Francys *journalist*
Doory, Ann Marie *lawyer, legislator*
Dorsey, Donna Morgan *state agency administrator*
Dorsey, John Russell *journalist*
Drachman, Daniel Bruce *neurologist, educator*
Duncan, Lionel Sebastian *artist, educator*
Dunn, Edward K., Jr., *banker*
Durbin, Dean B. *corporate financial executive*
Eaton, William W. *mental hygiene educator*
Eichhorn, Gunther Louis *chemist, researcher*
Eisenberg, Howard Michael *neurosurgeon*
Eisner, Henry Wolfgang *advertising agency executive*
Ellin, Marvin *lawyer*
Ellis, Brother Patrick (H. J. Ellis) *academic administrator*
Emerick, Norman Cooper *consulting engineer*
Entwisle, Doris Roberts *sociology educator*
Ephross, Paul Hullman *social work educator*
Epstein, Daniel Mark *poet, dramatist, biographer*
Erwin, H. Robert *lawyer*
Evans, Nolly Seymour *lawyer*
Eveleth, Janet Stidman *law association administrator*
Faden, Ruth R. *medical educator, ethicist, researcher*
Fassel, Jim (James E. Fassel) *professional football coach*
Fax, Charles Samuel *lawyer*
Feder, David L. *lawyer*
Feldman, Gordon *physics educator*
Felsenthal, Gerald *physiatrist, educator*
Fenton, Charles E. *lawyer*
Ferencz, Charlotte *pediatrician, epidemiology and preventive medicine educator*
Ferentz, Kevin Scott *physician*
Ferro, Elizabeth Krams *lawyer*
Fiori, Dennis A. *museum director*
Fisher, Alan Hall *guidebook writer*
Fisher, Morton Poe, Jr., *lawyer*
Fitzgerald, Robert Schaefer *physiologist, educator*
Fleisher, Lee Alan *anesthesiologist, medical educator*
Fleisher, Leon *concert pianist, conductor*
Fontanazza, Franklin Joseph *accountant, business executive*
Ford, John Gilmore *interior designer*
Foster, Lester Anderson, Jr., *retired steel company executive*
Fox, Claude Earl *former federal health official*
Fox, Harold Edward *obstetrician, gynecologist, educator, researcher*
Franklin, Timothy A. *editor*
Freedman, Janet Whittle *retired academic administrator, writer*
Freeman, John Mark *pediatric neurologist*
Freischlag, Julie Ann *surgeon*
Frey, Ruth Lazetta *historian, educator*
Fried, Linda P. *medical educator*
Friedman, Maria Andre *public relations executive*
Fuentealba, Victor William *professional society administrator*
Fulton, Thomas *theoretical physicist, educator*
Gall, Joseph Grafton *biologist, researcher, educator*
Gallant, Joel Emanuel *physician*
Gallo, Robert Charles *research scientist*
Gambert, Steven Ross *geriatrician, internist*
Garbis, Marvin Joseph *judge*
Gary, Tiffany L. *healthcare educator*
Gately, Mark Donohue *lawyer*
Gifford, Donald George *legal educator*
Gimenez, Luis Fernando *physician, educator*
Ginsberg, Benjamin *political science educator*
Girovich, Mark Jacob *mechanical engineer*
Giuliano, Michael Philip *arts journalist, educator*
Glassgold, Israel Leon *construction company executive, engineer, consultant*
Glassman, Jon David *research and development company executive*
Gleichmann, Frances Evangeline *retired elementary educator*
Godenne, Ghislaine Dudley *physician, psychoanalyst, educator*
Goldberg, Alan Marvin *toxicologist, educator*
Goldberg, Morton Falk *ophthalmologist, educator*
Goldman, Brian Arthur *lawyer, accountant*
Goldman, Lynn Rose *medical educator*
Gooden, Eric *government agency administrator, real estate agent*
Goodman, William Richard *insurance adjusting company executive*
Gordis, Leon *physician*
Grasmick, Nancy S. *school system administrator*
Gray, Frank Truan *lawyer*
Gray, Oscar Shalom *lawyer*
Green, Bert Franklin, Jr., *psychologist*
Green, Robert Edward, Jr., *physicist, researcher*
Greenough, William Bates, III, *medical educator*
Greider, Carol Widney *molecular biology educator*
Grieb, Elizabeth *lawyer*
Griffin, Diane Edmund *research physician, virologist, educator*
Griffith, Lawrence Stacey Cameron *cardiologist, educator*
Groenheim, Henri Arnold *psychologist, consultant*
Grossman, Stuart Alan *oncologist, medical educator*
Guilarte, Tomas R. *medical educator*
Gustafson, Thomas *medical association administrator*
Habermann, Helen Margaret *plant physiologist, educator*
Hackerman, Willard *construction services executive*
Hafets, Richard Jay *lawyer*
Hahn Waranch, Helene *educational association administrator*
Haig, Frank Rawle *physics educator, clergyman*
Haines, Thomas W. W. *lawyer*
Hansen, Barbara Caleen *physiologist, science educator*
Hansen, Christopher Agnew *lawyer*
Haq, Rizwan *oncologist, researcher*
Hardiman, Joseph Raymond *securities industry executive*
Harris, James Carol Overton, Jr., *psychiatrist, pediatrician*
Harris, Reginald Mervyn, Jr., *librarian, writer*
Harrison, Michael *opera company executive*
Hart, Robert Gordon *federal agency administrator*
Harvey, Alexander, II, *federal judge*
Hauser, Michael George *astrophysicist*
Hayden, Carla Diane *library director, educator*
Hecht, Alan Dannenberg *insurance executive*
Helfman, Carolyn Rae *middle school educator*
Heller, Barbara R. *former dean, nursing educator*
Hellmann, David Bruce *medical educator*
Helm, Donald Cairney *hydrogeologist, engineer, educator*
Henderson, Donald Ainslie *public health educator*
Herschman, Jeffrey D. *lawyer*
Hicks, Sherman Gregory *pastor*
Higginbotham, Eve Juliet *ophthalmologist, educator*
Hildreth, James E.K. *pharmacology and molecular science educator, dean*
Himelfarb, Richard Jay *investment firm executive*
Hirsh, Allan T., III, *book publisher*
Hirsh, Allan Thurman, Jr., *publishing executive*
Hirsh, Theodore William *lawyer*
Hochberg, Bayard Zabdial *lawyer*
Hoffman, Elmer *surgeon*
Hofkin, Gerald Alan *gastroenterologist*
Holder, Lawrence Edward *radiologist, educator*
Hollwitz, John Charles *educational administrator, consultant*
Holt-Stone, C. Yvonne *judge*
Honemann, Daniel Henry *lawyer*
Hopkins, Samuel *retired investment banker*
Hopps, Raymond, Jr., *lawyer, film producer*
Howard, J. Woodford, Jr., *political science educator*
Howard, John Vincent, Jr., *lawyer*
Howell, Harley Thomas *lawyer*
Howes, James Guerdon *communications company executive*
Hrabowski, Freeman Alphonsa, III, *university president*
Hsu, Cornelia Wang Mei-Chih *education educator*
Hug, Richard Ernest *environmental company executive*
Huganir, Richard Lewis *neuroscientist, educator, researcher*
Huggins, Amy Branum *music educator*
Hughes, Brenda Bethea *state legislator*
Hughes, Catherine L. (Cathy Hughes) *radio personality, broadcast executive*
Hungerford, David Samuel *orthopedic surgeon, educator*
Huntoon, Ann Kristen *performing arts association administrator, music educator*
Huse, James G. *federal agency administrator*
Hwang, Wenke *health services researcher*
Ihrie, Robert *oil, gas and real estate company executive*
Irish, Charles *construction executive*
Irwin, John Thomas *humanities educator*
Isable, Alisha *elementary school educator*
Jackson, Stanley Edward *retired special education educator*
Jacobs, Richard James *banker, educator*
Jacobson, Katherine Louise *musician, music educator*
Jamison, Kay *psychologist*
Jeffcoat, Cathleen Merle *musician, educator*
Jeffries, John Worthington *historian, educator*
Jelinek, Frederick *electrical engineer, educator*
Jenniches, F. Suzanne *engineering executive*
Johns, Richard James *physician, educator*
Johns, Roger *anesthesiologist, educator*
Johnson, Harry Sterling *lawyer*
Johnson, Michael Paul *history educator*
Johnson, Richard Tidball *neurology, microbiology and neuroscience educator, research virologist*
Johnston, Edward Allan *lawyer*
Johnston, George W. *lawyer*
Jones, Dan L. *academic administrator*
Jones, John Martin, Jr., *lawyer*
Jones, Raymond Moylan *strategy and public policy educator*
Joseph, Kevin Mark *financial services executive*
Judd, Brian Raymond *physicist*
Kandel, Nelson Robert *lawyer*
Kaplan, Abner J. *social worker, public relations executive*
Karni, Edi *economics professor*
Karp, Judith Esther *oncologist, science administrator*
Karwacki, Robert Lee *former judge*
Kastor, John Alfred *cardiologist, educator*
Kattel, Bheem Prakash *engineering educator, consultant*
Katz, Joseph Louis *chemical engineer, educator*
Katz, Laurence M. *legal educator*
Kellam, Sheppard G. *medical educator*
Keller, George Charles *higher education consultant, writer*
Kesselring, Linda J. *medical editor, writer*
Kessler, Herbert Leon *art historian, educator, university administrator*
Kessler, Irving Isar *epidemiologist, consultant*
Kim, Lillian G. Lee *retired administrative assistant*
Kinzler, Kenneth *medical educator, director*
Kirsch, Thorsten *cell biologist, educator*
Klitzke, Theodore Elmer *former college dean, arts consultant*
Knapp, David Allan *pharmaceutical educator, researcher*
Knapp, Steven *provost*
Knoedler, Elmer L. *retired chemical engineer*
Kosaraju, S. Rao *computer science educator, researcher*
Kotter, Laurie Marie *small business owner, music educator*
Kowarski, Allen Avinoam *endocrinologist, educator*
Kramer, Paul R. *lawyer*
Krolik, Julian Henry *astrophysicist, educator*
Krueger, Arlin James *physicist*
Krumholz, Allan *medical educator*
Kues, Irvin William *health care financial executive*
Kumin, Libby Barbara *speech language pathologist, educator*
Kuppusamy, Periannan *medical educator, medical researcher*
Kurth, Lieselotte *foreign language educator*
Kwon, Chul Soo *psychiatrist*
Lane, Malcolm Daniel *biological chemistry educator*
Langmead, Joseph Michael *accountant, consultant, educator*
Larch, Sara Margaret *chief operating officer*
Laric, Michael Victor *marketing professional, management consultant*
Lawrence, Robert Swan *physician, educator*
Lawson, Edward Earle *neonatologist*
Lazarus, Fred, IV, *college president*
Lazarus, Gerald Sylvan *dermatologist, educator, dean*
Leary, Michael Warren *journalist*
Lee, Yung-Keun *physicist, researcher*
Legg, Benson Everett *federal judge*
Legum, Jeffrey Alfred *holding company executive*
Lemer, Andrew Charles *engineer, economist*
Lesser, Ronald Peter *neurologist*
Levin, Edward Jesse *lawyer*
Levine, Audrey Pearlstein *foundation administrator*
Levine, Richard E. *lawyer*
Lewis, Jamal *professional football player*
Lewis, Ray *professional football player*
Lewison, Edward Frederick *surgeon*
Liang, Kung-Yee *medical educator*
Liberto, Joseph Salvatore *retired bank executive*
Lichtenstein, Lawrence Mark *immunologist, allergist, educator*
Lidtke, Doris Keefe *retired computer science educator*
Lidtke, Vernon LeRoy *history educator*
Liebmann, George W(illiam) *lawyer*
Lion, John René *psychiatrist, educator*
Litrenta, Frances Marie *psychiatrist*
Littlefield, John Walley *geneticist, cell biologist, pediatrician*
Liu, Dong *researcher*
Longo, Dan Louis *internist, researcher, oncologist*
Lowenthal, Henry *retired greeting card company executive*
Lucas, Barbara B. *electrical equipment manufacturing executive*
Lundy, Audie Lee, Jr., *lawyer*
Lungaro Cid, Lisa *educational association administrator*
Maccini, Louis John *economic educator*
Magnuson, Nancy *librarian*
Mansfield, Carl Major *radiation oncology educator*
Manson, Paul Nellis *plastic surgeon*
Margon, Bruce Henry *astrophysicist, educator*
Marsh, Bruce David *geologist, educator*
Marshall, Fray Francis *urology educator*
Mason, Raymond Adams *brokerage company executive*
Massof, Robert William *neuroscientist, educator*
Masson, Gerald M. *computer science educator*
Matheson, Nina W. *medical researcher*
Mathison, Theodore E. *retired air transportation executive*
Matjasko, M. Jane *anesthesiologist, educator*
Maultsby, Marilyn D. *health science association administrator*
Maumenee, Irene H. *ophthalmology educator*
Mazzilli, Lee *professional baseball coach*
McAdam, Paul Edward *retired library administrator*
Mc Cabe, Gerard Benedict *retired library administrator*
McClung, A(lexander) Keith, Jr., *retired lawyer*
McDonnell, Peter *ophthalmologist, health facility administrator, medical educator, researcher*
McHugh, Paul R. *psychiatrist, neurologist, educator*
McKhann, Guy Mead *pediatrician, educator*
McKusick, Victor Almon *geneticist, educator, physician*
McMillan, Julia A. *pediatrician*
McNally, David D. *federal agency administrator*
McPartland, James Michael *university official*
McPherson, Donald Paxton, III, *lawyer*
McWilliams, John Michael *lawyer*
Mears, Frances R. *communications media executive*
Melick, Clifford Francis *sociologist, researcher*
Melvin, Norman Cecil *lawyer*
Messina, Bonnie Lynn *lawyer*
Metzger, Delores Virginia *social services professional*
Mfume, Kweisi *civil rights advocate, former congressman*
Michitsch, John F. *career officer*
Migeon, Barbara Ruben *pediatrician, geneticist*
Milio, Louis Romolo *retired law educator, social worker*
Miller, Decatur Howard *lawyer*
Miller, Edward Doring *anesthesiologist*
Miller, Michael *physician, educator*
Miller, Stuart D. *surgeon*
Mocko, George Paul *minister*
Modell, Arthur B. *professional football team executive*
Mogol, Alan Jay *lawyer*
Molmenti, Ernesto P. *surgeon*
Moloney, Herbert W., III, *advertising executive*
Money, John William *retired psychologist, educator*
Moos, H. Warren *physicist, astronomer, educator, administrator*
Moran, John Gregory *musician*
Morford, Thomas *administrator*
Morrel, William Griffin, Jr., *banker*
Moser, Hugo Wolfgang *physician*
Moser, M(artin) Peter *lawyer*
Mosley, Wiley Henry *medical educator*
Motz, Diana Gribbon *judge*
Motz, John Frederick *federal judge*
Mower, Morton Maimon *cardiologist*
Murray, Eddie Clarence *baseball batting coach*
Murray, Joseph William *banker*
Mysko, William Kiefer *emergency physician, educator*
Myslinski, Norbert Raymond *medical educator*
Nathanson, Harvey Charles *electrical engineer*
Nichols, David Gregory *anesthesiologist, pediatrician, educator*
Nickon, Alex *chemist, educator*
Niemeyer, Paul Victor *federal judge*
Noar, Mark David *internist, gastroenterologist, therapeutic endoscopist, consultant, inventor*
Noga, Stephen Joseph *oncologist, researcher*
Norman, Colin Arthur *astrophysics educator*
Norman, Philip Sidney *physician*
Ogden, Jonathan *professional football player*
O'Malley, Martin Joseph *mayor, former councilman, lawyer*
O'Melia, Charles Richard *environmental engineer, educator*
Orman, Leonard Arnold *lawyer*
Owsley, Thomas L. *oil industry executive*
Palley, Howard A. *social work educator*
Palmeiro, Rafael Corrales *professional baseball player*
Palmer, Denise *publishing executive*
Pappas, George Frank *lawyer*
Park, Mary Woodfill *information consultant*
Pass, Carolyn Joan *dermatologist*
Patz, Arnall *ophthalmologist*

Hodgdon, Harry Edward *association executive, wildlife biologist*
Holland, Robert Carl *economist*
Hoyer, Mary Louise *social worker, educator*
Hrynkow, Sharon Hemond *federal agency administrator, neuroscientist, researcher*
Hsu, S. Dana *biologist*
Huebner, Emily Zug *judicial administrator*
Huebner, John Stephen *geologist*
Humphreys, Betsy L. *librarian*
Hutton, John Evans, Jr., *surgery educator, retired military officer*
Ikle, Doris Margret *energy executive*
Insel, Thomas R. *federal agency administrator, psychiatrist*
Ito, Yoichiro *pathologist*
Jackson, Michael John *retired physiologist, association executive*
Jameson, Sanford Chandler *education educator*
Jamieson, Graham A. *biochemist, researcher, retired organization official*
Jamison, Dean Tecumseh *economist*
Javitt, Jonathan C. *physician, ophthalmologist, health information technologist*
Johnson, Eugene Clare *data processing company executive*
Johnson, Joyce Marie *psychiatrist, epidemiologist, public health officer*
Johnson, Thomas Dale *management consultant*
Jonas, Gary Fred *healthcare executive*
Joy, Robert John Thomas *medical history educator*
Joyce, Bernita Anne *former federal government agency administrator*
Kallioniemi, Olli Pekka *geneticist, researcher*
Kaplan, Marjorie *broadcast executive*
Karson, Emile *international business executive*
Katz, Stephen Ira *federal agency administrator, dermatologist, immunologist*
Kawazoe, Robin Inada *federal official*
Keiser, Harry Robert *retired physician*
Kem, Richard Samuel *retired army officer*
Kemelhor, Robert E(lias) *mechanical engineer*
Kesaris, Paul *publishing executive*
Kibbe, James William *real estate broker*
Kington, Raynard S. *federal agency administrator*
Kirby, Harmon E. *retired ambassador*
Kirschstein, Ruth Lillian *physician*
Klatzkin, Terri *real estate company executive*
Klee, Claude Blenc *medical researcher*
Knachel, Philip Atherton *librarian*
Kochanski, Lois Whidden *foundation administrator*
Koenig, Elizabeth Barbara *sculptor*
Koonce, Calvin Scott *brokerage firm executive, physicist*
Korn, Edward David *biochemist*
Koslow, Stephen Hugh *science administrator, pharmacologist*
Kramer, Barnett Sheldon *oncologist*
Krantz, David S. *medical psychology educator, researcher*
Krause, Richard Michael *medical scientist, government official, educator, senior researcher*
Kruger, Gustav Otto, Jr., *oral surgeon, educator, department chairman*
Krumsiek, Barbara J. *investment company executive*
Kubasik, Christopher E. *aerospace transportation executive*
Kupfer, Carl *ophthalmologist, educator, science administrator*
Kutemeyer, Peter Martin *industrial engineering executive*
Lai, Zhennan *research scientist*
Laingen, Lowell Bruce *diplomat*
Lamb, Michael E. *psychology researcher*
Landis, Story C. *federal agency administrator, neurobiologist*
Larrabee, Barbara Princelau *retired intelligence officer*
Larrabee, Donald Richard *publishing company executive*
Laughlin, Larry W. *academic administrator, military officer*
Leon-Sarmiento, Fidias E. *neurologist, researcher*
Leppert, Phyllis Carolyn *obstetrician, gynecologist*
Less, Anthony Albert *retired naval officer*
Li, Ting-Kai *federal agency administrator, biologist*
Lillard, Mark Hill, III, *computer consulting executive, former air force officer*
Lindberg, Donald Allan Bror *library administrator, pathologist, educator*
Liotta, Lance Allen *pathologist*
Lipman, David J. *medical association administrator, researcher*
Longfellow, David *administrator*
Lorber, Mortimer *retired physiology educator*
Lowry, Douglas R. *internist, dermatologist*
Lowy, Douglas Ronald *oncologist*
Lystad, Mary Hanemann (Mrs. Robert Lystad) *sociologist, writer*
MacKay, Charles Robert *federal official, consultant*
MacLean, Paul Donald *government institute medical research official*
Malone, Winfred Francis *health scientist*
Manolio, Teri A *physician*
Marini, Ann Marie *medical researcher, educator*
Marsh, G. Thomas *aerospace transportation executive*
Martin, Kathleen L. *military officer, hospital administrator*
Martin, Malcolm A. *health facility administrator*
Masoni, Patricia M. *writer*
Masur, Henry *internist*
Mattison, Donald Roger *gynecologist, toxicologist, educator, medical association administrator, public health service officer*
McClure, Brooks *management consultant*
McCray, Alexa T. *health science association administrator, director*
McCurdy, Harry Ward *otolaryngologist*
McDonough, Thomas P. *health facility administrator*
Mc Gurn, Barrett *communications executive, writer*
McHale, Judith A. (Judith Ottalloran) *broadcast executive, lawyer*
McMurphy, Michael Allen *energy company executive, lawyer*
Meakem, Carolyn Soliday *investment executive, financial planner, money manager, consultant*
Menaker, Frank H., Jr., *lawyer*
Merchant, P. Glenn *military officer, physician*
Metcalfe, Dean Darrel *medical research physician*
Metzenbaum, Howard Morton *former senator, consumer organization official*
Metzger, Henry *federal research institution administrator*
Miller, Judith Wolfe Cohen *consultant*
Millstein, Richard Allen *federal agency administrator*
Mirsky, Allan Franklin *psychologist, researcher*
Mishkin, Mortimer *neuropsychologist*
Monjan, Andrew Arthur *health science association administrator, educator*
Montgomery, Dan T. *construction company executive*
Morgan, John Davis *consultant*
Moriyama, Iwao Milton *statistician, consultant*
Morrison, Bruce Andrew *government executive, public affairs consultant*
Moshman, Jack *statistical consultant*
Moss, Bernard *virologist, researcher*
Mukunda, Ram *communications executive*
Mullan, Fitzhugh *public health physician*
Muraro, Paolo A. *immunologist, neurologist*
Murayama, Makio *biochemist*
Murphy, Dennis L. *psychiatrist*
Nabel, Elizabeth G. *medical researcher, cardiologist*
Nakamura, Richard *mental health research professional*
Nash, Howard Allen *geneticist, researcher*
Nason, Charles Tuckey *diversified financial services company executive*
Nassetta, Christopher J. *hotel facility executive*
Naylor, Phyllis Reynolds *writer*
Nee, Linda Elizabeth *social science analyst*
Neill, Denis Michael *international consultant*
Nejelski, Paul Arthur *retired judge, freelance writer*
Nelson, John Howard (Jack Howard Nelson) *journalist*
Nelson, William Eugene *lawyer*
Neumann, Ronald Daniel *nuclear medicine physician, educator*
North, A. Frederick *physician*
North, William Haven *foreign service officer*
Nussdorf, Lawrence C. *real estate/construction executive*
Nyirjesy, Istvan *obstetrician, gynecologist*
O'Callaghan, Jerry Alexander *government official*
Ochej, Helen Wanda *biologist, researcher, information scientist*
Oddis, Joseph Anthony *associations executive*
Ogbureke, Kalu Ugwa Emmanuel *oral surgeon, oral and maxillofacial pathologist, molecular biologist*
Ognibene, Frederick Peter *internist*
Oldfield, Edward Hudson *neurosurgeon, researcher*
Olmsted, Jerauld Lockwood *telephone company executive*
Olson, Lynn *editor*
Ommaya, Ayub Khan *neurosurgeon, educator*
O'Neill, Malcolm R. *aerospace executive*
Optican, Lance Michael *research scientist*
Owen, Thomas Barron *retired naval officer, space company executive*
Pakaluk, Debra Lorraine Behm *science educator, community service coordinator*
Palmer, James Alvin *baseball commentator*
Parrish, Edgar Lee *financial services executive*
Paul, William Erwin *immunologist, researcher*
Peck, Edward Lionel *retired foreign service officer, corporate executive*
Penn, Audrey S. *federal agency administrator*
Perlin, Seymour *psychiatrist, educator*
Perlmutter, Jack *artist, lithographer*
Peterson, Charles Marquis *medical educator*
Petralia, Ronald Sebastian *entomologist, neurobiologist*
Pettigrew, Roderic I. *federal agency administrator, radiologist, researcher*
Petty, John Robert *financier*
Pickerell, James Howard *photojournalist*
Pinn, Vivian W. *federal agency administrator, pathologist*
Pipkin, James Harold, Jr., *lawyer*
Pollard, Harvey B. *medical educator, neuroscientist*
Polsby, Gail K. *psychotherapist*
Popescu, Daniel *interior designer*
Potter, Michael *genetics researcher, medical researcher*
Pratt, Dana Joseph *publishing consultant*
Puck, Jennifer M. *physician, scientist*
Purcell, Robert Harry *virologist, researcher*
Quinnan, Gerald Vincent, Jr., *medical educator*
Quon, Michael James *medical researcher, internist*
Rabson, Alan Saul *federal agency administrator, physician, educator*
Rall, Joseph Edward *physician*
Ramm, Louise *administrator*
Rapoport, Judith *psychiatrist*
Reed, Berenice Anne *art historian, artist, government official*
Reed, Miriam Bell *legislative staff member*
Reiser, Brian Sydney *economist, statistician*
Rennert, Owen Murray *pediatrician, geneticist, educator*
Revesz, Akos George *physicist*
Reynolds, Herbert Young *physician, internist*
Reynolds, Robert Joel *economist, consultant*
Rhim, Johng Sik *physician, educator, medical researcher*
Rice, Jerry Mercer *biochemist, consultant, pathologist*
Rice, Kenner Cralle *medicinal chemist*
Richardson, John *retired international relations executive*
Robbins, John Bennett *medical researcher*
Roberts, Doris Emma *epidemiologist, consultant, public health nurse*
Robinson, David Mason *cell physiologist*
Robinson, Sharon Beth *health science association administrator*
Rosenbaum, Greg Alan *merchant banker, consultant*
Rosenberg, Mark Louis *lawyer*
Rosenberg, Steven Aaron *surgeon, medical researcher*
Rosengren, Paul Gregory *lawyer*
Ross, William Warfield *lawyer*
Rowell, Edward Morgan *retired foreign service officer, lecturer*
Rubin, Gerald Mayer *molecular biologist, biochemistry educator*
Ruffin, John *federal agency administrator, researcher*
Ruttenberg, Ruth A. *economist*
Ryan, Joseph *lawyer*
Ryan, Kevin William *virologist, researcher, science educator, clinical research administrator*
Rymarcsuk, Jim Arthur *aerospace industry executive, consultant*
Saffiotti, Umberto *pathologist*
Salisbury, Tamara Paula *foundation executive*
Salmoiraghi, Gian Carlo *physiologist, educator*
Saloschin, Robert L. *lawyer*
Sams, James Farid *real estate development company executive*
SanGiovanni, John Paul *ophthalmic epidemiologist, eye and vision researcher*
Sanoff, Alvin Paul *education consultant, writer*
Sarnoff, Lili-Charlotte (Lolo Sarnoff) *artist*
Saul, B. Francis, II, *bank executive, director*
Saunders, Charles Baskerville, Jr., *retired association executive*
Saville, Thorndike, Jr., *coastal engineer*
Schaeffer, Charles Perry *newswriter, editor*
Schifter, Richard *lawyer*
Schimel, Richard E. *lawyer*
Schlom, Jeffrey Bert *research scientist*
Schmidt, Raymond Paul *military officer, historian, diplomat*
Schneerson, Rachel *immunologist*
Schoem, Alan Howard *lawyer*
Sewell, Rodney milton *biologist*
Shapeero, Lorraine G. *physician, researcher, educator*
Shekar, Sam *health facility administrator*
Shellow, Robert *management service company executive, consultant*
Sher, Alan *health science association administrator, immunologist*
Shulman, Lawrence Edward *biomedical research administrator, rheumatologist*
Sieving, Paul A. *federal agency administrator, ophthalmologist, educator*
Silver, David *lawyer*
Singer, Dinah S. *federal agency administrator, immunologist, researcher*
Sizemore, R. Tom, III, *military officer, hospital administrator*
Skirboll, Lana R. *federal health policy director*
Smith, Albert E. *areonautics company professional*
Smith, Kent Ashton *scientific and technical information executive*
Smoller, Bruce Melvyn *psychiatrist*
Sobel, Mark Esar *pathologist, researcher*
Sokoloff, Louis *physiologist, neuroscientist*
Solomon, Robert *economist*
Southwick, Paul *retired public relations executive*
Sowell, R. Douglas *medical association administrator, podiatrist*
Spector, Eleanor Ruth *corporation executive*
Spector, Melbourne Louis *retired foreign service officer*
Spiegel, Allen *federal agency administrator, internist*
Spong, Catherine Yvonne *obstetrician, gynecologist, researcher*
Sprott, Richard Lawrence *foundation administrator, researcher*
Stadtman, Earl Reece *biochemist, researcher*
Stanfield, Brent B. *federal agency administrator*
Stearman, William Lloyd *military association executive, author*
Sternberg, Esther May *neuroendocrinologist, immunologist, rheumatologist*
Stetler-Stevenson, William George *pathologist*
Stith, Kenneth *federal agency administrator*
Stoddard, Philip Hendrick *foreign affairs analyst, consultant, writer*
Stone, Jeremy Judah *public interest activist*
Stover, Ellen L. *health scientist, psychologist*
Straus, Stephen Ezra *biomedical researcher*
Strausberg, Robert L. *federal agency administrator*
Striner, Herbert Edward *economics educator*
Sturtz, Donald Lee *physician, educator, naval officer*
Swartz, Gordon *management consultant*
Tabak, Lawrence *federal agency administrator, dentist*
Tabor, Herbert *biochemist*
Talbot, Bernard *government medical research facility official, physician*
Tape, Gerald Frederick *former association executive*
Tavel, Jorge Alberto *internist, researcher*
Taylor, Lindsay David, Jr., *health care executive*
Taylor, William Jesse, Jr., *international studies educator, research corporation president*
Tellep, Daniel Michael *aerospace executive, mechanical engineer*
Terragno, Paul James *information industry executive*
Tilley, Carolyn Bittner *technical information specialist*
Tourino, Ralph Gene *aerospace transportation executive*
Tracy, Thomas Miles *international health organization official*
Ungerleider, Leslie G. *neuroscientist*
Ursano, Robert Joseph *psychiatrist*
van der Linden, Frank Morris *historian*
Vaughan, Martha *biochemist, educator*
Vest, George Southall *retired diplomat*
Volkow, Nora Dolores *medical research center director*
von Eschenbach, Andrew C. *director National Cancer Institute, oncologist*
Wagner, Cynthia Gail *editor, writer*
Waldmann, Thomas Alexander *medical researcher, physician*
Walsh, Thomas John *infectious disease physician, oncologist, researcher, educator*
Walter, W. Edward *hotel executive, corporate financial executive*
Walters, Judith Richmond *neuropharmacologist*
Wardinski, Bruce David *hotel chain executive*
Webster, Henry de Forest *neuroscientist*
Wechsler, Andrew Robert *international economic consultant*
Weinberger, Alan David *lawyer*
Weinberger, Daniel R. *psychiatrist, neurologist*
Weiss, George Herbert *mathematician, consultant*
Wente, Van Arthur *retired aerospace scientist*
Whaley, Storm Hammond *retired government official, consultant*
White, Jeannette Lee *information technology executive*
Whitescarver, Jack Edward *federal agency administrator*
Wiese, Wolfgang Lothar *physicist, researcher*
Willoughby, Anne *health facility administrator, researcher, educator*
Wise, Allen F. *health care administrator*
Witkop, Bernhard *chemist*
Wolf, Dale B. *corporate financial executive, health facility administrator*
Wolfe, William J. *management consultant*
Wolman, Sandra R. *health science association administrator, pathologist, geneticist*
Wolpert-DeFilippes, Mary K. *science administrator*
Work, Henry Harcus *psychiatrist, educator*
Worth, Melvin H. *surgeon, educator*
Wurtz, Robert Henry *neuroscientist*
Yamada, Kenneth Manao *cell biologist*
Yang, Key Paik *librarian, archivist*
Zerhouni, Elias Adam *Director National Institutes of Health*
Zheng, Gang *mathematician, statistician, researcher*
Zierdt, Charles Henry *microbiologist*
Zimble, James Allen *military officer, obstetrician, gynecologist, educator*
Zoon, Kathryn Christine *biochemist*
Zurkowski, Paul George *publisher*

Betterton
Kohl, Benjamin Gibbs *historian, educator*

Bowie
Alvarez, Aida *former federal agency administrator*
Angebranndt, Betsy Jo *music educator, composer*
Bushnell, David Sherman *psychologist, consultant*
Dawodu, Segun Toyin *pain medicine and sports medicine physician, physiatrist*
Francois, Francis Bernard *retired professional society administrator, lawyer, transportation consultant*
Gottlieb, Sylma R. *music educator, performing arts educator*
Perkins, Dana Stela *pharmacologist, research scientist*
Silva, Lawrence Kehinde *physical education educator*
Speller-Brown, Barbara Jean *pediatric nurse practitioner*
Sterling, Richard Leroy *English and foreign language educator*
Stone, Edward Harris, II, *landscape architect*
Yager, Joseph Arthur, Jr., *economist*

Boyds
Kammer, Raymond Gerard, Jr., *government official*
Love, Dana Francis Ignatius *telecommunications industry executive*

Bozman
Wyatt, Wilson Watkins, Jr., *management and public affairs executive, writer*

Brandywine
Briggs, John H., Sr., *music educator*

Brentwood
Kaskey, Raymond John *sculptor*

Burtonsville
Hudson, McKinley *army officer, retired zoo deputy director*

Cabin John
Capo, Rafael V. *lawyer*
Ingraham, Edward Clarke, Jr., *retired foreign service officer*
Oertel, Goetz Kuno Heinrich *physicist, professional science administrator*
Shropshire, Walter, Jr., *biophysicist emeritus, pastor*
Townsend, John William, Jr., *physicist, retired federal aerospace agency executive*

California
Avram, Henriette Davidson *librarian, government official*

Cambridge
Ames, George Robert, Jr., *judge*
Burke, Gerard Patrick *business executive, lawyer*
Eckardt, Adelaide Campbell *state legislator, psychiatric nurse*
Jenkins, Robert Rowe *lawyer*
Miller, Robert Edvin *environmental education specialist, researcher, industrial hygienist*
Spahr, Elizabeth *environmental services administrator*

Camp Springs
Nalli, Nicholas Rocco *physical scientist*

Catonsville
Hubbard, Herbert Hendrix *lawyer*
Loerke, William Carl *art history educator*
Woolley, Alma Schelle *nursing educator*
Wynn, John Charles *clergyman, retired religion educator*
Zumbrun, Alvin John Thomas *law and criminology educator*

Centreville
Amos, James Lysle *photographer*

Charlotte Hall
Brown, Ira Hugo *psychologist, educator*

Chester
Dabich, Eli, Jr., *insurance company executive*

Chestertown
Clarke, Garry Evans *composer, educator, musician, administrator*
Docksteader, Karen Kemp *marketing professional*
Kellogg-Smith, Peter *sculptor, educator*
Littlefield, Lauren Montenegro *psychologist, educator*
Rather, Lucia Porcher Johnson *library administrator*
Schreiber, Harry, Jr., *management consultant*
Tipson, Lynn Baird (Baird Tipson) *academic administrator, religion educator*
Wendel, Richard Frederick *economist, educator, consultant*

Cheverly
Miller, Mark Karl *journalist*

Chevy Chase
Adler, James Barron *publishing executive*
Albright, Raymond Jacob *government official*
Alexander, Arthur Jacob *economist*
Alpert, Seymour *anesthesiologist, educator*
Ashe, Aaron Matthew *sales professional*
Auerbach, Seymour *architect*
Bacon, Donald Conrad *author, editor*
Baruch, Jordan Jay *management consultant*
Basa, Enikö Molnár *librarian*

Binder, Mildred Katherine *retired public welfare agency executive*
Bissinger, Frederick Lewis *retired manufacturing executive, consultant*
Broide, Mace Irwin *retired public affairs consultant*
Bruder, George Frederick *lawyer*
Bruno, Harold Robinson, Jr., *retired journalist, writer*
Bush, Frederick Morris *federal official*
Cech, Thomas Robert *chemistry and biochemistry educator*
Cheng, David Keun *engineering educator*
Choppin, Purnell Whittington *research administrator, virology researcher, educator*
Cline, Ruth Eleanor Harwood *translator*
Cody, Peter Malcolm *economist, development, management consultant*
Cooley, William Crockett *mechanical engineer, retired educator*
Cron, Theodore Oscar *writer, editor, educator*
Curris, Constantine William *university president*
Duvall, Bernice Bettum *artist, exhibit coordinator, jewelry designer*
Emery, Robert Firestone *economist, educator*
Epstein, Sidney *retired editor*
Ewing, Frank Marion *lumber company executive, industrial land developer*
Farrell, Joseph Michael *steamship company executive*
Feldman, Bruce Allen *otolaryngologist*
Fern, Alan Maxwell *art historian, retired museum director*
Freeman, Harry Louis *investment executive*
Gaasterland, Douglas E. *physician, ophthalmologist*
Gaines, Michael Johnston *parole commissioner*
Gavin, James Raphael, III, *biochemist*
Gildenhorn, Joseph Bernard *lawyer, businessman, former diplomat*
Greene, Kay C. *psychologist, author*
Guenther, Kenneth Allen *economist, consultant*
Hani, Antoine George *psychiatrist, psychoanalyst*
Harlan, William Robert, Jr., *internist, educator, researcher*
Hersh, Stephen Peter *psychiatrist, psycho-oncologist, educator*
Hirschhorn, Joel Stephen *engineer*
Hudson, Ralph P. *physicist*
Hunt, Frederick Talley Drum, Jr., *association executive*
Jones, Philip Howard *broadcast journalist*
Kandel, Eric Richard *neuroscience educator*
Ketcham, Orman Weston *lawyer, former judge*
Kingsley, Nathan *journalist, consultant, educator*
Klain, Ronald Alan *lawyer*
Kranking, Margaret Graham *artist, educator*
Kriegsman, Alan M. *retired critic*
Lebow, Irwin Leon *communications engineering consultant*
Lee, Edward Brooke, Jr., *real estate executive, fund raiser*
Linowes, David Francis *political economist, educator, corporate executive*
Lukens, Alan Wood *retired ambassador and foreign service officer*
Mackall, Laidler Bowie *lawyer*
Mathis, Laurelle Sheedy *academic administrator, volunteer*
Meyerson, Christopher Cortlandt *lawyer*
Michaelis, Michael *management and technical consultant*
Mielke, James Edward *geochemist*
Morgan, Elizabeth *plastic surgeon*
Norwood, Bernard *economist*
Norwood, Janet Lippe *economist*
Opper, Barbara Negri *financial economist*
Ostar, Allan William *academic administrator, higher education consultant*
Oudens, Gerald Francis *architect, architectural firm executive*
Pierson, W. DeVier *lawyer*
Pilkerton, Arthur Raymond, Jr., *surgeon, educator*
Pitofsky, Robert *federal agency administrator, law educator*
Pogue, John Marshall *physician*
Prince, Julius S. (Bud Prince) *retired foreign service reserve officer*
Promisel, Nathan E. *materials scientist, metallurgical engineer*
Rockwell, Theodore *nuclear engineer*
Romansky, Monroe James *physician, educator*
Rose, John Charles *internist, educator*
Sagawa, Shirley Sachi *lawyer*
Sanz, Luis E. *gynecologist, educator*
Sapin, Burton Malcolm *political science educator, foreign policy analyst*
Shipler, David Karr *journalist, correspondent, author*
Shogan, Robert *news correspondent*
Short, Steve Eugene *engineer*
Silver, George Albert *preventive medicine physician, educator*
Sinclair, Rolf Malcolm *retired physicist*
Smith, Peter Leonard *diversified financial services company executive*
Tacket, Hall Sanford *retired internist*
Teitel, Simon *economist, educator*
Toth, Robert Charles *retired polling consultant, journalist, writer*
Towsner, Cynthia Merle *vocational school educator*
Toy, Charles David *lawyer*
Van Akkeren, Lorraine Sue *research assistant*
Williams, Charles Laval, Jr., *physician, international organization official*
Wright, Frank *artist, educator*
Wright, Helen Patton *professional society administrator*

Chillum
Malbon, Louise *nursing educator, hypnotherapist*

Clarksville
Hung, Mei-Jong Chow *social worker*
Peirce, James Walter *secondary school educator, historian*
Zhu, Kangmin *epidemiologist*

Clinton
Brooks, Pauline C. *computer and networking services company executive*
Davis, Mark Cameron *radiologist*
Whittington, Ralph Edward *curator, librarian*

Cockeysville
Barnes, Peter *federal official*
Dye, Robert Harris *retired manufacturing company executive*

Cockeysville Hunt Valley
Barr, Irwin Robert *retired aeronautical engineer*
Roeder Vaughan, Mimi *small business owner*
Whitehurst, William Wilfred, Jr., *management consultant*

College Park
Aggour, Mohamed Sherif *civil engineer, educator*
Amershek, Kathleen *education educator*
Anderson, John David, Jr., *aerospace engineer*
Antman, Stuart Sheldon *mathematician, educator*
Ayyub, Bilal M. *civil engineering educator, researcher, executive*
Barbe, David Franklin *electrical engineer, educator*
Beasley, Maurine Hoffman *journalism educator, historian*
Benedick, Richard Elliot *diplomat*
Brazile, Donna *advocate*
Brush, Stephen George *historian, educator*
Coffey, Timothy *physicist*
Collins, Merle *English and comparative literature educator*
Cooper, Chester Lawrence *research administrator*
Datta, Madhumita *electrical engineer, researcher*
DeLio, Thomas *music educator, composer*
De Lorenzo, William E. *foreign language educator*
DeSilva, Alan W. *physics educator, researcher*
Destler, William W. *academic administrator*
Diachenko, Gregory William *chemist, researcher, federal agency administrator*
Diener, Theodor Otto *plant pathologist, researcher*
Dieter, George Elwood, Jr., *university official*
Dill, Bonnie Thornton *sociology educator*
Dopp, Bonnie Jo *musicologist, school librarian*
Dusold, Laurence Richard *chemist, computer specialist*
Edgeman, Rick Lee *statistics educator, consultant*
Einstein, Theodore Lee *physics educator*
Ernstein, Julie H. *archaeologist, educator, researcher*
Fanning, Delvin Seymour *soil science educator*
Farquhar, James *geochemist, researcher*
Feinstein, Frederick Lee *lawyer*
Fenselau, Catherine Clarke *chemistry professor*
Finkelstein, Barbara *education educator*
Fisher, Michael Ellis *mathematical physicist, chemist*
Frank, Howard *dean, educator, systems company executive*
Fretz, Thomas A. *agricultural studies educator*
Fu, Michael C. *management science educator*
Gantt, Elisabeth *plant biology educator, researcher*
Gaylin, Ned L. *psychology educator*
Gluckstern, Robert Leonard *physics educator*
Gomery, Douglas *communications educator, writer*
Goode, B. Erich *sociologist, educator, retired criminologist*
Gordon, Lawrence Allan *accountant, educator*
Granatstein, Victor Lawrence *electrical engineer, educator*
Griem, Hans Rudolf *physicist, researcher*
Griffin, James Joseph *physics educator*
Grim, Samuel Oram *chemistry professor*
Grunig, James Elmer *communications educator, researcher, public relations consultant*
Gupta, Ashwani Kumar *mechanical engineering educator*
Hallett, Judith Peller *classical studies educator*
Helz, George Rudolph *chemistry educator, research center director*
Hendler, James Alexander *computer science educator, consultant*
Hey, Nancy Henson *educational administrator*
Hill, Clara Edith *psychology educator*
Izaurralde, Roberto César *science educator, researcher*
Jeffery, William Richard *developmental biology educator, researcher*
Johnson, Haynes Bonner *author, journalist, television commentator*
Just, Richard Eugene *agricultural and resource economics educator consultant*
Katz, Ronald Alan *dermatologist*
(Thompson) Knill, April Michele *historian, educator*
Kundu, Mukul Ranjan *physics and astronomy educator*
Lamone, Rudolph Philip *business educator*
Langenberg, Donald Newton *retired academic administrator, physicist*
Lathan, Corinna Elisabeth *aerospace engineer*
Leitenberg, Milton *political scientist, researcher*
Levine, William Silver *electrical engineer, educator*
Levinson, Jerrold *humanities educator*
Li, Zhanqing *meteorologist, educator*
Lichtenberg, Erik Russell *economics professor*
Lin, Hung C. *electrical engineer educator*
Lowell, Howard Parsons *archivist, federal agency administrator*
Lubkin, Gloria Becker *physicist*
Lucas, Henry Cameron, Jr., *information systems educator, writer, consultant*
Malen, Betty *education policy and leadership educator*
Marcus, Steven Irl *electrical engineering educator*
Marshall, Monty Glenn *political research scientist, consultant*
Martin, L(eslie) John *retired journalism educator and dean*
Mc Donald, Frank Bethune *physicist*
McIlrath, Thomas *physicist, researcher*
McNaughton, Kenneth John *publisher*
Miller, Raymond Edward *computer science educator*
Miller, Raymond Jarvis *agronomy educator*
Minker, Jack *computer scientist, educator*
Misner, Charles William *physics educator*
Modarres, Mohammad *education educator*
Morris, Joseph Anthony *retired health science association administrator*
Mote, Clayton Daniel, Jr., *university president, mechanical engineer, educator*
Nerlove, Marc Leon *economics professor*
Newcomb, Robert Wayne *electrical engineer educator*
O'Connor, John Dennis *biology professor*
Olson, Charles Eric *economist*
Olson, Keith Waldemar *history educator*
Olver, Frank William John *research mathematician*
Oster, Rose Marie Gunhild *foreign language professional, educator*
Pasch, Alan *philosopher, educator*
Piper, Don Courtney *political scientist, educator*
Popper, Arthur N. *biology professor*
Prentice, Ann Ethelynd *university dean*
Presser, Harriet Betty *sociology educator*
Presser, Stanley *sociology educator*
Qi, Jianwei *mechanical engineer, researcher*
Qu, Gang *education educator, researcher*
Quester, George Herman *political science educator*
Quick, Edward Raymond *museum director, educator, curator*
Rabin, Herbert *physicist, university official*
Ramsey, S. Robert *education educator*
Rao, Jaganmohan Boppana Lakshimi *electrical engineer*
Redish, Edward Frederick *physicist, researcher*
Resnik, Harvey Lewis Paul *psychiatrist*
Rosenberg, Norman Jack *agricultural meteorologist, educator*
Rosenfeld, Azriel *computer science educator, consultant*
Sacks, Charles Bernard *physician, educator*
Schelling, Thomas Crombie *economist, educator*
Schwab, Susan Carroll *dean*
Sedlacek, William *education educator*
Segal, David Robert *sociology educator*
Shen, Qing *urban planning educator, researcher*
Shneiderman, Ben Abraham *computer science educator, writer*
Sigall, Harold Fred *psychology educator*
Silverman, Joseph *chemistry educator, scientist*
Sims, Henry P., Jr., *management educator*
Sorenson, Georgia Lynn Jones *political scientist, educator*
Souza, Gilvan Castro *operations and management educator*
Spear, Richard Edmund *art history educator*
Stover, Carl Frederick *foundation executive*
Struna, Nancy L. *social historian and American studies educator*
Stumpff, Robert Thomas *academic administrator*
Szymanski, Edna Mora *dean*
Taylor, Leonard Stuart *engineering educator, consultant*
Tismaneanu, Vladimir *political science educator, researcher*
Toll, John Sampson *university president, physics educator*
Vanderveen, John E. *nutritionist, federal agency administrator*
Vankatesan, Thirumalai *engineering educator*
Walters, William Ben *chemistry professor*
Wasserman, Paul *library and information science educator*
Weart, Spencer Richard *historian*
Weiner, Ronald Martin *microbiology and cell biology educator, research scientist*
White, Marilyn Domas *information science educator*
Whittemore, Edward Reed, II, *poet, retired educator*
Winik, Jay B. *writer, political scientist, consultant*
Yoho, Billy Lee *lawyer*
Yorke, James Alan *chaos mathematician*
Youssef, Moustafa Amin *computer scientist, researcher*
Zelkowitz, Marvin Victor *computer science educator*
Zen, E-an *research geologist, educator*

Colora
Borland, Raymond M. *researcher*

Columbia
Bailey, John Martin *retired transportation planner, educator*
Bareis, Donna Lynn *biochemist, pharmacologist*
Bell, James Edward *psychologist, educator*
Bruley, Duane Frederick *academic administrator, consultant, engineer*
Cargo, William Ira *retired ambassador*
Davis, Benjamin George *theologian, educator*
Davis, Guy Donald *research scientist*
Deering, Anthony Wayne Marion *real estate developer*
DeRosa, Thomas J. *investment banker, investment company executive*
Doi, Yutaka *electrical engineer*
Dreir, R. Chad *real estate executive*
Drier, R. Chad *construction executive*
Drummond, LaCreda Renee *journalist*
Fisher, Dale John *retired chemist*
Folkenberg, Lois Waxter *principal, educator, psychologist*
Fritz, Steven L. *physicist*
Gottfeld, Gunther Max *retired urban mass transit official, consultant*
Gray, Kirk Lamond *social investment firm executive, anthropologist*
Gregorie, Corazon Arzalem *operations supervisor*
Gruhl, Andrea Morris *librarian*
Harbin, Henry T. *health facility administrator*
Harrison, Elza Stanley *medical association executive*
Hartman, Lee Ann Walraff *secondary school educator, consultant*
Hyman, Lawrence Robert *psychiatrist*
Jacobs, William Michael *lawyer*
Jones-Wilson, Faustine Clarisse *retired education educator*
Keeton, Morris Teuton *research scholar*
Kendrick, John Lawrence *software engineer*
Khare, Mohan *chemist, researcher*
Kurlander, Neale *accounting and law educator, lawyer*
Latkin, Carl *healthcare educator*
Lorton, Lewis *researcher, computer executive, dentist*
Madison, Anne Conway *public relations and marketing professional*
Marshall, Linda Murphy *linguist, government official*
Maseritz, Guy B. *lawyer*
May, John Raymond *clinical psychologist*
McCuan, William Patrick *real estate company executive*
McGregor, Douglas A. *real estate company executive*
Messina, Daniel S. *insurance company executive*
Miller, James L. *food products executive*
Millspaugh, Martin Laurence *real estate developer, urban development consultant*
Morice, William Daniel *business and tax counselor*
Moulton, Paul Douglas (Pete Moulton) *information technology consultant*
Pacifico, Joseph Carl *counselor*
Palumbo, James Fredrick *financial services company executive*
Purcell, James Nelson, Jr., *international organization administrator*
Rogers, Thomas Francis *foundation administrator*
Rovelstad, Gordon H. *dentist, researcher*
Scates, Alice Yeomans *former government official, consultant*
Siegel, David Burton *lawyer*
Singerman, Phillip A. *corporate executive*
Spicknall, Joan *music educator*
Starks, Doris N. *nursing educator, administrator*
Stolley, Paul David *medical educator, researcher*
Strain, Lucille Brewton *education educator, researcher*
Straja, Sorin Radu *chemical engineer, mathematician, computer programmer*
Ulman, Louis Jay *lawyer*
Van Buiten, Robert D. *aerospace engineer*
Weems, Helen Rachel *piano teacher, accompanist*
Whiting, Albert Nathaniel *former university chancellor*
Wilson, Imogene R. *counselor*
Zhu, Jian Zhong *research scientist*

Comus
Choukas-Bradley, James Richard *lawyer*

Crofton
Boland, Gerald Lee *health facility administrator*
Kniffen, Donald Avery *astrophysicist, educator, researcher*
Laurenson, Robert Mark *mechanical engineer*
Ross, E(dwin) Clarke *association executive, educator*

Crownsville
Hanna, James Curtis *state official*
Irish, Leon Eugene *lawyer, educator, non-profit organization executive*

Cumberland
Heckert, Paul Charles *sociologist, educator*
Jancuk, Kathleen Frances *educational administrator*

Damascus
Nelligan, William David, III, *professional association executive*

Darnestown
Cohen, Sanford Irwin *physician, educator*
Gottlieb, Julius Judah *podiatrist*
Lightner, Gene Cleek *investment banker*

Davidsonville
Blaxall, Martha Ossoff *economist*

Dayton
Fischell, Robert Ellentuch *physicist*

Denton
Doster, Rose Eleanor Wilhelm *artist*

Derwood
Blank, Leta Sondra *health and long term care insurance specialist*
Kusterer, Thomas *project administrator*
Mylonakis, Stamatios Gregory *patent agent, polymer science consultant*
Stadtman, Thressa Campbell *biochemist*
Vaughn, Steven D. *veterinary administrator*
Wong, Richard Lee *lawyer*

Easton
Ikenberry, Henry Cephas, Jr., *lawyer*
Maffitt, James Strawbridge *lawyer*
Peterson, James Kenneth *manufacturing executive*
Potter, Blair Burns *editor*
Snow, James Byron, Jr., *otolaryngologist, research administrator, educator*
U'Ren, Marie Rita *travel company executive, pre-school educator*

Edgewater
Kushlan, James A. *biologist, research administrator, author, educator*
Simons, Ross B. *environmental center director*

Eldersburg
Spohn, William Gideon, Jr., *mathematician, retired musician*

Elkridge
Byrd, Alicia D. *minister, sociologist*
Culton, Sandra Jeane *accountant*
Zheng, Wenxin *fiber optic communication specialist*

Elkton
Chen, Oliver Tsung-Yu *chemical engineer, researcher*
Harrington, Benjamin Franklin, III, *retired business consultant*
Jasinski-Caldwell, Mary L. *company executive*
Scott, Doris Petersen *lawyer*
Xu, Ping *chemist*

Ellicott City
Benjamin, Thomas Edward *music educator, composer, conductor*
Galinsky, Deborah Jean *county official*
Pairo, Preston Abercrombie, Jr., *lawyer*
Powell, Lillian Marie *retired music educator*
Robison, Susan Miller *psychologist, speaker, consultant*
Thompson, Richard *writer*
Wann, Michael Stephen *music educator*
Webster, Sharon B. *economist*

Emmitsburg
Howes, Theodore Clark *claims examiner*
Paulison, R. David *federal agency administrator*

Essex
Bunn, Wm. Jeffrey *secondary school educator, director*

Finksburg
Konigsberg, Robert Lee *electrical engineer*

Forest Hill
Klein, Shirley Snyderman *retail executive*
McIntosh, L(orne) William *marketing executive*

Fort Detrick
Maher, Cornelius Creedon, III, *neurologist, toxicologist, army officer*

Fort George G Meade
Black, William B., Jr., *government agency administrator*
Hayden, Michael V. *career officer, federal agency administrator*
Kera, Tiiu *career officer*
Schmitt, Robert Lee *computer scientist*

Fort Washington
Alexander, Gary R. *lawyer, state legislator, lobbyist*
Bradley, Melvin LeRoy *communications company executive*
Cameron, Rita Giovannetti *writer, publisher*
Canlas, Luzano Pancho, Sr., *writer, researcher*
Caveny, Leonard Hugh *mechanical engineer, aerospace scientist, consultant*
Coffey, Matthew B. *trade association executive*
McCafferty, James Arthur *sociologist*
Miller, John Richard *interior designer*
Satterthwaite, George, II, *security firm executive*
Simpson, Raven C. *administrative assistant*
Smoot, Burgess Howard *federal official*
Wooten, Ralph G. *career officer*

Frederick
Aaslestad, Halvor Gunerius *retired dean*
Anderson, Arthur Osmund *pathologist, immunologist, army officer*
Baker, Joanne Evelyn *retired government official*
Berger, John Morris, Sr., *construction executive*
Borison, Scott Craig *lawyer*
Boyd, Joseph Aubrey *communications company executive*
Bryan, John Leland *retired engineering educator*
Byron, Beverly Butcher *retired congresswoman*
Cannon, Faye E. *bank executive*
Carlson, David Emil *physicist, researcher*
Copeland, Neal G. *biochemist*
Delaplaine, George Birely, Jr., *newspaper editor, cable television executive*
Devineni, Mohan *pharmacist*
Duncan, Stephen Mack *lawyer*
Garver, Robert Vernon *retired research physicist*
Hamilton, Rhoda Lillian Rosén *guidance counselor, language educator, consultant*
Hanna, Michael George, Jr., *immunologist, pharmaceutical executive*
Henderson, Madeline Mary (Berry Henderson) *chemist, researcher, consultant*
Hogan, Ilona Modly *lawyer*
Jenkins, Nancy A. *research scientist*
Kelsey, Ronald Grant *retired environmental engineer*
Klein, Elaine Charlotte *school system administrator*
Knisely, Ralph Franklin *retired microbiologist*
Kung, Hsiang-fu *health facility administrator*
Malone, Robert Wallace *surgeon*
McKewen Amato, Mary Patricia *musician*
Smith, Sharron Williams *chemistry professor*
Swanson, Norma Frances *federal agency administrator*
Weincek, Craig James *communications educator, writer*
Whelihan, Alan Stuart *real estate developer, automotive executive*
Wickizer, Stephen Wesley *pharmacist*
Wolf, Donald Joseph *industrial engineer, consultant*

Frostburg
Childs, William Parker *education educator*
Clulee, Nicholas Harkins *history professor*
Gira, Catherine Russell *university president*
Root, Edward Lakin *education educator, academic administrator*

Fruitland
Woods, William Ellis *lawyer, pharmacist, association executive*

Gaithersburg
Adams, James Michael *nuclear physicist*
Aiuto, Russell *science education consultant*
Baum, Howard Richard *research scientist*
Bernstein, Steven *librarian, writer*
Boddiger, George Cyrus *insurance corporate executive, consultant*
Booth, Melvin D. *pharmaceutical company execuive*
Bowen, Rafael Lee *dental materials researcher*
Cahn, John Werner *metallurgist, educator*
Caplin, Jerrold Leon *health physicist*
Carasso, Alfred Sam *mathematician*
Carey, John Edward *information services executive*
Caswell, Randall Smith *physicist*
Celotta, Robert James *physicist*
Chang, Ren Fang *physicist, researcher*
Cookson, Alan Howard *electrical engineer, researcher*
Currie, Lloyd Arthur *nuclear scientist, educator*
Delgado, Dwighd D(ubied) *company executive*
Dermody, William Christian *biomedical consultant*
Dowd, Carolyn Lay *social worker*
Ehrlich, Clifford John *Internet company executive*
Esposito, V. M. *research and development company executive*
Ferrell, Charles Madison *retired nuclear engineer, health physicist*
Fratantoni, Joseph Charles *medical researcher, hematologist, biotechnology executive*
French, Judson Cull *government official*
Gebbie, Katharine Blodgett *physicist*
George, Kathryn Elaine *economist, financial writer*
Gottlieb, H. David *podiatrist*
Gu, Xiaohong *polymer engineer, chemist*
Hall, Arthur Raymond, Jr., *retired minister*
Hamer, Walter Jay *chemical consultant, science writer*
Harman, George Gibson *physicist, consultant*
Hertz, Harry Steven *government official*
Hockmeyer, Wayne T. *pharmaceutical company executive*
Hoferek, Mary Judith *information systems specialist, educator*
Hsu, Stephen Ming *materials scientist, chemical engineer*
Hubbell, John Howard *radiation physicist*
Hultquist, Micki M. *biostatistician*
Jacox, Marilyn Esther *chemist*
Jahanmir, Said *materials scientist, mechanical engineer*
Jevtic, Milomir *artist, sculptor*
Johnson, George H. *financial services company executive*
Keith, Stephen N. *research and development company executive*
Kress, Jill Clancy *human resources professional, consultant*
Landel, Michel *food service and management company executive*
Lenfant, Claude Jean-Marie *physician*
Levine, Robert Sidney *chemical engineer, consultant*
Lynn, Jeffrey Whidden *research physicist, educator*
Marin, Cynthia Myers (Cheryl Marin) *systems engineer*
McCann, Joseph Leo *lawyer, former government official*
McDowell, Donna Schultz *lawyer, educator*
Peele, Roger *hospital administrator*
Phillips, William Daniel *physicist*
Pierce, Daniel Thornton *physicist*
Powell, Lura J. *science association administrator*
Presser, Cary *research engineer*
Quraishi, Mohammed Sayeed *retired health scientist, administrator*
Reader, Joseph *physicist*
Reynolds, Frank Miller *retired government administrator*
Rosenblatt, Joan Raup *mathematical statistician*
Ross, Sherman *psychologist, educator*
Rupert, Hoover (Lynn Hoover Rupert) *minister, writer*
Ruth, James Perry *financial planning executive*
Scharf, Mark Edward *playwright*
Schwartzberg, Allan Zelig *psychiatrist, educator*
Sengers, Johanna M. H. Levelt *thermophysicist*
Sherer, Samuel Ayers *lawyer, urban planning consultant*
Taylor, Barry Norman *physicist*
Tesk, John Aloysius *materials scientist*
Ulbrecht, Jaromir Josef *chemical engineer*
Wang, Josephine Jung-Shan *language educator, translator*
Watson, Royce Andrew *retired federal official*
Weber, Alfons *physicist*
Werner, Samuel Alfred *physics and astronomy educator*
Wicklein, John Frederick *journalist, educator*
Wiederhorn, Sheldon M. *materials engineer*
Wohl, Ronald H. *management consultant, writing and editorial expert*
Wright, Richard Newport, III, *retired engineering executive, engineering educator*
Yuan, Jian *network technician, researcher, engineering educator*

Galena
Hunsperger, Elizabeth Jane *art and design consultant, educator*
Jolly, Charles Nelson *lawyer, pharmaceutical company executive*

Gambrills
Messner, Howard Myron *professional association executive*
White, Elizabeth G. *music educator*

Garrett Park
Baldwin, Calvin Benham, Jr., *retired medical research administrator*
Franklin, Benjamin A. *editor, reporter*
Kornberg, Warren Stanley *science journalist*
Melville, Robert Seaman *chemist*

Germantown
Bhonsle, Jayendra *chemist, researcher, computer scientist, educator*
Bu, Rulei *artist, educator*
Hartley, James R. *musician, writer*
Iqbal, Zafar *biochemist, neurochemist*
Isaacson, Elaine Marie *sales and training agent*
Isbister, James David *pharmaceutical business executive*
Lewis, Robert John Cornelius Koons *retired library director*
Norcross, Marvin Augustus *veterinarian, retired government agency official*
Taylor, Douglas Howard *translator*
Weiner, Claire Muriel *freelance writer*

Gibson Island
Forster, William Hull *aerospace executive, management consultant*

Glen Arm
Jackson, Theodore Marshall *retired oil company executive*
Lotz, George Michael *retired computer graphics executive, graphic designer, photographer*

Glen Burnie
Barteet, Barbara Boyter *retired social worker*
Merinoff, Spencer *food products executive*
Rubin, Amy Rochelle *speech-language pathologist*
Ruth, Shiela Grant *music educator*
Smith, John Stanley *lawyer, arbitrator, mediator*
Wityk, Joseph John *radiologist*

Glen Echo
Stevenson, A. Brockie *retired artist*

Glenelg
Williams, Donald John *physicist, researcher*

Glenwood
Billig, Frederick Stucky *mechanical engineer*

Glyndon
Renbaum, Barry Jeffrey *lawyer*

Greenbelt
Acker, James G. *oceanographer, archivist*
Amato, Deborah Douglass *aerospace engineer*
Billingsley, Lance W. *lawyer*
Brugger, George Albert *lawyer*
Bryant, Paul T. *electronics engineering manager*
Chasanow, Deborah K. *federal judge*
Chasanow, Howard Stuart *retired judge, mediator*
Cohen, Steven Charles *geophysicist*
Comiso, Josefino Cacas *research scientist*
Fontaine, Kathleen Sturey *policy analyst*
Greenwald, Andrew Eric *lawyer*
Harris, Marion Hopkins *former government official*
Healey, John Joseph *engineering executive, civil engineer*
Hogensen, Margaret Hiner *librarian, consultant*
Jackley, Michael Dano *lawyer*
Jascourt, Hugh D. *lawyer, arbitrator, mediator*
Kalnay, Eugenia *university administrator, meteorologist*
Kessel, Mona *space physicist*
Levitt, Gerald Steven *engineering executive*
Linn, Terry Ann Noffsinger *secondary school educator*
Maran, Stephen Paul *astronomer*
Mather, John Cromwell *astrophysicist*
Messitte, Peter Jo *judge*
Middleton, Elizabeth McPhee *research scientist*
Miller, Alwin Vermar *educational advisor, consultant*
Moore, Virginia Bradley *librarian*
Mumma, Michael Jon *physicist, researcher*
Obamogie, Mercy A. *physician*
Ormes, Jonathan Fairfield *astrophysicist, science administrator, researcher*
Scott-Childress, Reynolds Johnson *historian, educator*
Simpson, Joanne Malkus *meteorologist*
Suid, Lawrence H. *historian, writer*
Tao, Wei-Kuo *meteorologist, researcher*
Tate, Antoinette Cooper *marriage and family therapist*
Thomas, Lindsey Kay, Jr., *research ecology biologist, educator, consultant*
Titus, Roger Warren *judge*
Vranish, John Michael *electrical engineer, researcher*

Hagerstown
Baer, John Metz *entrepreneur*
Berkson, Jacob Benjamin *lawyer, writer*
Coffen, Richard Wayne *minister, editor*
Conte, Joseph John, II, *meteorologist, management consultant*
Harrison, Lois Smith *hospital executive, educator*
Noia, Alan James *utility company executive*
Serkes, Jeffrey D. *energy executive*
Strauss, Albert John, Jr., *pediatrician*
Ward, Spring Tina *history and political science educator*
Warner, Charles David, III, *academic administrator*

Hanover
Chiarella, Donald Joseph Gray *information systems specialist, educator*
Feng, Lan *health analyst*
Rochdi, Myriam *pharmacist, researcher*
Roenigk, Martin Allen *insurance company executive*

Highland
Varga, Deborah Trigg *music educator, entertainment company owner*

Hollywood
Powledge, Fred Arlius *freelance writer*
Shah, Nayan *internist*

Hughesville
Hilwig, Joseph Michael *electric company director*
Tudor, Thomas Rae *electric power industry executive*

Hunt Valley
Carney, Stephen Patrick *insurance company executive*
Collier, Stephen N *educational consultant*
Deieso, Donald Allan *environmental goods and services executive*
Igusa, Jun-Ichi *mathematician, educator*
Kinstlinger, Jack *engineering executive, consultant*
Mussina, Michael Cole *professional baseball player*
Plaks, Albert I. *electrical engineer, educator*

Huntingtown
Faust, William Roscoe *physicist*
Wilson-Dawes, Judy Ann *music educator*

Hyattsville
Asongu, Januarius Jingwa *information technology executive*
Bender, Howard Jeffrey *software engineering consultant*
Bloomfield, Maxwell Herron, III, *retired history and law educator*
Clifford, Maurice Cecil *physician, former college president, foundation executive*
Embody, Daniel Robert *biometrician*
Fortson-Rivers, Tina E. (Thomasena Elizabeth Fortson-Rivers) *information technology specialist*
Golden, Marita *English language educator, foundation executive*
Gonzalez, Joe Fred, Jr., *mathematical statistician, educator*
Kirk, James Allen *mechanical engineering educator*
Lovick, Norman *accountant*
Rodgers, Mary Columbro *literature educator, writer, academic administrator*
Rose, Deborah *epidemiologist*
Rummel, Edgar Ferrand *retired lawyer*
Shestack, Alan *museum administrator*
Shimizu, Iris M. *statistician, consultant*
Sondik, Edward J. *health science administrator*

Indian Head
Latimer, Paul Jerry *non-destructive testing engineer*
Price, Teresa Annette *elementary school educator*

Jefferson
Beall, James Robert *toxicologist, consultant*

Jessup
Fox, Dawne Marie *safety scientist*
Hsiao, Chao-Tsung *engineer*

Joppa
Bates, Charles Benjamin *elementary school administrator*

Kennedyville
Schiff, Gary Stuart *academic administrator, educator, consultant*

Kensington
Dauster, William Gary *lawyer, economist*
Holloway, William Jimmerson *retired educator*
Hum, Vance York *technology consulting executive*
Hurt, Frank *labor union administrator*
Jackson, William David *research executive*
Mathias, Joseph Marshall *lawyer, judge*
Mintz, Suzanne *association executive*
Mirkin, Gabe Baron *allergist, pediatrician, medical educator, writer, radio personality*
Rosenthal, Alan Sayre *government official*
Suraci, Charles Xavier, Jr., *retired federal agency administrator, aerospace education consultant*
Szára, Stephen István *pharmacologist, consultant*

La Plata
Bishop, Rex L. *finance educator, department chairman*
Core, Mary Carolyn W. Parsons *health facility administrator*
Fisher, Gail Feimster *epidemiologist, researcher, government agency administrator*
Mariya, Deborah Luethje *minister*

Landover
DeCesaris, Geaton A., Jr., *construction executive*
Grasselli, Margaret Morgan *curator*
Green, R. Keith *automotive executive*
Maduka, Chikezie *journalist*

Lanham
Degnan, John James, III, *physicist*
Godwin, Mary Jo *editor, librarian consultant*
Heiserman, Alice E. *publishing executive, editor*
Lyons, James Edward *publishing executive*
McClain, George Nelson *economist, lawyer*
Rodgers, Johnathan *broadcast executive*

Lanham Seabrook
Cooper, Robert Alfred *electrical engineer*
Hill, Ben *broadcast executive*
Klein, Stephen *recreational fee-based club executive*
Liggins, Alfred C., III, *broadcasting company executive*
Littlefield, Roy Everett, III, *association executive, law educator*
Ojinnaka, Becky *publishing executive*
Parker, William H., Jr., *telecommunications industry executive*
Pleasant-Jackson, Tonya *therapist, consultant*
Plotnick, Stanley D. *recreational fee-based club executive*

Largo
Mahaffey, Redge Allan *movie producer, director, writer, actor, scientist*

Laurel
Babin, Steven Michael *atmospheric scientist, researcher*
Cheng, Andrew Francis *physicist*
Chrismer, Ronald Michael *federal agency administrator*
Dallman, Paul Jerald *engineer, writer*
Darrell, Charles G. *engineer*
Dorsey, John Wesley, Jr., *university administrator, economist*
Eaton, Alvin Ralph *aeronautical and systems engineer, research and development administrator*
Kossiakoff, Alexander *chemist, researcher*
Krimigis, Stamatios Mike *physicist, researcher, engineering executive, consultant*
Landis, Donna Marie *nursing administrator, women's health nurse*
Lui, Anthony Tat Yin *physicist*
Maurer, Richard Hornsby *physicist*
McConnaughey, James Walter *economist*
Rorie, Conrad Jonathan *scientist, naval officer*
Westhaver, Lawrence Albert *electronics engineer, consultant*

Leominster
Markham, John Thomas *social worker, educator*

Leonardtown
Donely, George Anthony Thomas, III, *economist, consultant*
Smalley, Robert Manning *government official*

Lexington Park
Jackameit, Kevin Charles *information scientist*
Morgan, Dennis Alan *retired federal official, education educator*
White, Donna C *music educator, director*

Linthicum
Burns, Michael William *lawyer former state legislator*
Metzel, Alan Barry *manufacturing engineer*

Linthicum Heights
Skillman, William Alfred *consulting engineering executive*
Stein, David Eric *physicist, defense analyst*
Tietz, Dietmar Juergen *website engineer, scientist*

Lusby
Eshelman, Ralph Ellsworth *maritime historian, vertebrate paleontologist, cultural resource consultant*
Hutchins, Edith Elizabeth *accountant*
Ladd, Culver Sprogle *secondary school educator*
Sprague, Edward Auchincloss *retired association executive, economist*

Lutherville
Eisenberg, Joseph Martin *psychologist, consultant*
Elma, Bayani Borja *physician*
Freeland, Charles *lawyer, accountant*
Kissel, William Thorn, Jr., *sculptor*
Meyer, Jon Keith *psychiatrist, psychoanalyst, educator*
Morison, Warwick Lindsay *dermatologist, educator, consultant*
Moyer, Bernadette Ann *writer, small business owner*

Lutherville Timonium
Bevis, Robert E. *retired oil company executive*
Cappiello, Frank Anthony, Jr., *investment advisor*
Cedrone, Louis Robert, Jr., *critic*
Muuss, Rolf Eduard *retired psychologist, author*
Park, Lee Crandall *psychiatrist*
Pierpont, Ross Z. *retired surgeon*
Sagerholm, James Alvin *retired naval officer*
Sternberger, Ludwig Amadeus *neurologist, educator*

Madison
Hoffman, Kenneth Myron *mathematician, educator*

Mardela Springs
Harcum, Louise Mary Davis *retired elementary education educator*

Marion Station
Handy, Mary Thomas *retired elementary school educator*

Marlow Heights
Ourisman, Mandell J. *automotives executive*

Marriottsville
Strange, Donald Ernest *health care company executive*

Marydel
LaBarge, Christopher W. *priest*
Neil, Fred Applestein *public relations executive*

Mc Henry
Kelly, Robert William *economist*

Mechanicsville
Rands, Robert Lawrence *archaeologist*

Mitchellville
Akridge, Paul Bai *business consultant*
Ball, Robert M. *social security and health insurance specialist*
Ball, Robert M(yers) *social security, welfare and health policy specialist, writer, lecturer*
Blasier, Cole *political scientist, educator*
Brubaker, Lauren Edgar *minister, educator*
Chilman, Catherine Earles Street *social welfare educator, author*
Embree, Ainslie Thomas *history educator*
Heald, Morrell *humanities educator*
Henle, Peter *retired economic consultant, arbitrator*
Kendall, Katherine Anne *social worker*
Marsh, Caryl Amsterdam *museum exhibitions curator, psychologist, advisor*
Sober, Sidney *retired diplomat, educator*

Monkton
Mountcastle, Vernon Benjamin *neurophysiologist*

Montgomery Village
Kushner, Lawrence Maurice *physical chemist, consultant*
Molloy, Angela Margaret *advertising, marketing, and public relations executive*
Murray, Peter *metallurgist, manufacturing company executive*
Robinson, Henry Ward *meteorologist*
Zabrek, Albert Samuel *architect*

Morningside
McClain, Edward Fifer, Jr., *retired physicist*

Myersville
Patrick, Georgia O'Brien Lakaytis *communications executive*

Newburg
Mason, Christine Chapman *psychotherapist*

North Bethesda
Shapiro, Maurice Mandel *nuclear astrophysicist*
Sherman, Deane Murray *culture organization administrator*
Siegel, Jacob Stuart *writer, consultant, demographer, researcher, genentologist, statistician*
Szabo, Daniel *government official*

North East
Goldbach, Jennifer D. *bank executive*

North Potomac
Geller, Ronald Gene *biomedical researcher, consultant*
Lehman, Leonard *retired lawyer, consultant*
Lide, David Reynolds *handbook and database editor*

Oakland
Cavarocchi, Nicholas Guy *public relations executive*

Ocean City
O'Hanlon, Richard Thomas *counseling educator*
Phillips, Shirley Flowers *food service executive*

Ocean Pines
Crawford, Norman Crane, Jr., *academic administrator, consultant*

Odenton
Aho, Brien *photojournalist*

Olney
Baker, Carl Gwin *research administrator*
Delmar, Eugene Anthony *architect*
Michael, Jerrold Mark *public health specialist, former university dean, educator*
Northrop, Edward Skottowe *federal judge*
Schneider, William Charles *aerospace consultant*
Westerman, Rosemary Matzzie *nurse, administrator*

Owings
Oring, Stuart August *visual information specialist, writer, photographer, researcher*

Owings Mills
Billick, Brian *professional football coach*
Coates, Ben Terrence *professional football player*
Disharoon, Leslie Benjamin *retired insurance executive*
Heck, Albert Frank *retired neurologist*
Holdridge, Barbara *book publisher*
Nes, David Gulick *retired diplomat*
Newsome, Ozzie *manager professional athletics*
Sanner, George Bradley *bank executive*
Tapp, Mamie Pearl *educational association administration*
Uleau, Thomas F. *corporate executive*

Oxford
Radcliffe, George Grove *retired life insurance company executive*
Shepard, William Seth *government official, diplomat, writer*

Parkton
Cummins, Paul Zach, II, *insurance company executive*
Fitzgerald, Edwin Roger *physicist, researcher*

Parkville
Hill, Milton King, Jr., *retired lawyer*
Jensen, Arthur Seigfried *consulting engineering physicist*

Pasadena
Bueltmann, Kenneth W. *periodontist*
Douglass, Gordon L. *periodontist, educator*
Murphy, Alma Shirley *political organization worker*
Young, Russell Dawson *physics consultant*

Patuxent River
Adams, Richard Eugene *aerospace engineer, project manager*
Conway, Frank P. *military officer, educator*
Fitzhugh, David Michael *lawyer*

Phoenix
Hairston, Walter Albert *school system administrator*

Pikesville
Lanzkron, Rolf Wolfgang *manufacturing executive*
Whitaker, Marsha Jones *author, educator*

Port Republic
Sugarman, Jule Meyer *children's services consultant, former public administrator*

Potomac
Benton, Kay Myers *sales executive*
Bremenstuhl, David P. *elementary school educator*
Brewer, Nathan Ronald *veterinarian, consultant*
Broderick, John Caruthers *retired librarian, educator*
Bush, Mark Robert *physician*
Carper, Fern Gayle *small business owner, writer*
Casella, Russell Carl *physicist*
Chandler, James Phillip *law educator*
Chang, Ya-Ting *pianist, music educator*
Christian, John Kenton *organization executive, publisher, writer, marketing consultant*
Coligan, John Ernest *biochemist*
Cotton, William Robert *retired dentist*
Crowson, Henry Lawrence *mathematician, educator*
Eaves, Maria Perry *realtor*
Epstein, Mark Robert *electronics manufacturing executive*
Feldman, Myer *lawyer*
Fink, Daniel Julien *management consultant*
Foley, Joseph Patrick *public relations executive*
Foord, Robert LaVerne *intelligence executive, consultant*
Fox, Arthur Joseph, Jr., *editor*
Frieder, Gideon *computer science and engineering educator*
Hall, William Darlington *lawyer*
Heller, Peggy Osna *psychotherapist, poetry therapist*
Johnson, Anne Hale *educational association administrator, director*
Jones, Sidney Lewis *economist, researcher, educator*
Jones, Warren H. *physician, educator*
Karch, Karen Brooke *principal*
Karnow, Stanley *journalist, writer*
Keefe, Arthur Thomas, III, *non-profit fund raising executive*
Keil, Marilyn Martin *artist*
Kernan, Barbara Desind *senior government executive*
Kessler, Ronald *author*
Khachaturian, Zaven Setrak *neuroscientist*
Kling, William *economist, retired foreign service officer*
Kuykendall, Crystal Arlene *educational consultant, lawyer*
Lawrence, Robert Edward *electrical engineer*
Leva, Neil Irwin *psychotherapist, hypnotherapist*
Marincola, Elizabeth Mark *scientific society executive*
Medin, A. Louis *computer company executive*
Medin, Julia Adele *mathematics educator, researcher*
Meyer, Lawrence George *lawyer*
Navarro, Joseph Anthony *statistician, consultant*
Noonan, Patrick Francis *conservation executive*
Oh, John Kie-Chiang *political science educator, university official*
Orski, C. Kenneth *consulting company executive, lawyer, publisher*
Owen, Harrison Hollingsworth *management consultant*
Pastan, Linda Olenik *poet*
Peter, Phillips Smith *lawyer*
Peters, Frank Albert *retired chemical engineer*
Redding, Robert Ellsworth *lawyer*
Rehns, Marsha Lee *magazine editor, writer*
Reichley, A. James *political scientist*
Rhode, Alfred Shimon *business consultant, finance educator*
Rosenberg, Sarah Zacher *retired cultural organization administrator*
Rotberg, Iris Comens *social scientist*
Schonholtz, Joan Sondra Hirsch *banker, civic worker*
Schuessler, Isabelle Sweeny *school administrator*
Shapiro, Richard Gerald *retired department store executive, consultant*
Shirvinski, Adam John *management consultant*
Sundick, Sherry Small *author, journalist, poet*
Troffkin, Howard Julian *lawyer, diversified company executive*
Vadus, Gloria A. *scientific document examiner*
Walker, Charls Edward *economist, consultant*
Waugaman, Richard Merle *psychiatrist, psychoanalyst, educator*
Williams, Peter MacLellan *nuclear engineer*
Wolman, Eric *health care consultant*
Wonnacott, Paul *retired economics professor*
Young, Lih Ying H. *economist, consultant, advocate*
Yufik, Yan Mark *director research development*

Preston
Suggs, Leo H. *transportation executive*

Prince Frederick
Reynolds, Christopher John *lawyer*

Princess Anne
Acquah, Sarah Nipah *agricultural educator*
du Nord, Jeanne *writer, publishing executive*
Nnadi, Eucharia E. *academic administrator*

Queenstown
Corn, Morton *environmental engineer, educator*

Randallstown
McDowell, Elizabeth Mary *retired pathology educator*

Reisterstown
Bart, Polly Turner *real estate developer*
Bond, Nelson Leighton, Jr., *health care executive*
Broadbent, J. Streett *engineering executive*
Donaho, John Albert *consultant*
Tannenbaum, Harvey *defense technology consultant*
Tirone, Barbara Jean *health insurance administrator*

Riva
Barto, Bradley Edward *small business owner, educator*

Riverdale
Bernard, Cathy S. *management corporation executive*
Gonzalez Arias, Victor Hugo *management executive*
Guetzkow, Daniel *technology company entrepreneur*
Kumar, Shailendra *urologist, educator*

Rock Hall
Cowperthwait, Lindley Murray *lawyer*
Lang, Lillian Owen *retired accountant*

Rockville
Aamodt, Roger Louis *federal agency administrator*
Bainum, Stewart William, Jr., *health care and lodging company executive*
Balbier, Thomas E., Jr., *health facility administrator*
Barbera, Thomas P. *health care company executive*
Barkley, Brian Evan *lawyer, political consultant*
Barnette, Doris *public health services professional*
Barr, Solomon Efrem *allergist, educator*
Beer, Janusz Zygmunt *radiation and photo biologist, scientist*
Berryman, Richard Byron *lawyer*
Birns, Mark Theodore *physician*
Boetticher, Helene *lawyer*
Boice, John Dunning, Jr., *epidemiologist, science administrator*
Bolle, Robert L. *lawyer, administrator*
Brasoveanu, Dan *systems analyst*
Buchanan, John Donald *retired health physicist, radiochemist*
Burdick, William MacDonald *biomedical engineer*
Burt, Marvin Roger *financial advisor, investment manager*
Cantelon, Philip Louis *historian*
Carmona, Richard Henry *Surgeon General of the US*
Carter, Kenneth Charles *geneticist*
Cheston, Sheila Carol *lawyer*
Chiogioji, Melvin Hiroaki *retired federal official, entrepreneur*
Chretien, Paul Bernard *oncologist, medical researcher*
Clancy, Carolyn M. *social services administrator, former science foundation director*
Clark, H. Westley *health facility administrator*
Corley, Rose Ann McAfee *government official*
Couig, Mary Patricia *federal agency administrator*
Crawford, Lester Mills, Jr., *veterinarian*
Croyle, Robert T. *federal agency administrator, psychologist, educator*
Culliton, Barbara J. *medical association administrator*
Curie, Charles G. *federal agency administrator*
Cyr, Karen D. *lawyer*
Daisley, William Prescott *lawyer*
Davis, Beverly Watts *federal agency administrator*
De Jong, David Samuel *lawyer, educator*
Donnally, Robert Andrew *lawyer*
Duke, Elizabeth M. *health facility administrator*
DuPont, Robert Louis *psychiatrist, physician*
Edinger, Stanley Evan *clinical chemist*
Edwards, Bert Tvedt *accountant*
Eisen, Jonathan A. *research scientist*
Epstein, Jay Stuart *federal regulator*
Ermolaeva, Maria D. *biophysicist, researcher*
Finlayson, John Sylvester *biochemist*
Fleischmann, Robert D. *research scientist*
Foss, Robert E. *health care company executive*
Fraser, Claire M. *research scientist, science administrator*
Frazier, Walter Ronald *real estate investment company executive*
Friedman, Greg Stuart *lawyer, investment advisor*
Frye, Roland Mushat, Jr., *lawyer*
Fthenakis, Emanuel John *diversified aerospace company executive*
Funches, Jesse L. *financial administrator*
Futrovsky, Cheryl Jean *foundation administrator, performing company executive*
Gail, Mitchell H. *science foundation executive*
Gibson, William M. *technology company executive*
Gluckstein, Fritz Paul *veterinarian, biomedical information specialist*
Gonzalez-Licea, Augustin *pathologist, public health service officer*
Goodman, Jesse *health facility administrator*
Gordon, Joan Irma *lawyer*
Gordon, Michael Robert *lawyer, state legislator*
Gougé, Susan Cornelia Jones *microbiologist*
Graham, Robert *medical association executive*
Grandy, Fred *foundation administrator, former congressman, former actor*
Greenberg, Jerrold Selig *health education educator*
Griffith, Jerry Dice *energy and management consultant*
Grim, Charles W. *federal agency administrator*
Groban, Mark D. *health care company executive*
Grozbean, Stuart Harvey *lawyer*
Gulya, Aina Julianna *neurotologist, surgeon, educator*
Henderson, Harriet *librarian*
Henricson, Beth Ellen *microbiologist*
Hewlett, Richard Greening *historian*
Hisada, Michie *physician, epidemiologist*
Hoar, William Patrick *editor, author*
Howard, Lee Milton *international health consultant*
Kadish, Richard L. *lawyer*
Kalton, Graham *survey statistician*
Kamerow, Martin Laurence *accountant*
Kaplan, Lawrence Samuel *historian, educator*
Karp, Ronald Alvin *lawyer*
Katz, Steven Martin *lawyer, accountant*
Kerxton, Alan Smith *lawyer*
Kiger, F. Louise *nursing administrator*
Kinnane, Adrian *historian*
Kirkness, Ewen F. *research scientist*
Kline, Raymond Adam *professional organization executive*
Kohlhorst, Gail Lewis *librarian*
Kohlmeier, Louis Martin, Jr., *newspaper reporter*
Kopf, Randi *family and oncology nurse practitioner, lawyer*
Kruger, Jerome *materials science educator, consultant*
Kurkul, Wenyi Wang *musician, educator, administrator*
Kurzman, Harold Philip *transportation economist, consultant*
Landon, John Campbell *research and development company executive*
Lee, Jhong Sam *electronics company executive*
Lee, Norman H. *research scientist*
Leef, James Lewis *biology professor, immunology research executive, immunologist, director*
Leventhal, Carl M. *neurologist, consultant, retired government agency administrator*
Leventhal, George L. *councilman, consultant*
Lincoln, Michael E. *administrator*
Littman, Burt A. *obstetrician-gynecologist*
Long, Cedric William *health research executive*
Lumpkin, Murray M. *federal agency administrator*
MacArthur, Diana Taylor *advanced technology executive*
Madle, Robert Albert *writer*
Manasse, Henri Richard, Jr., *pharmaceutical executive*
Manderscheid, Ronald William *federal program administrator*
Marcuccio, Phyllis Rose *retired association executive, editor*
McCormick, Kathleen Ann Krym *geriatrics nurse, computer information specialist, federal agency administrator*
McDonald, Capers Walter *biomedical engineer, manufacturing executive, educator*
Megan, Thomas Ignatius *retired judge*
Menendez, Adolfo *engineering company executive*
Mertz, Walter *retired government research executive*
Meyer, F. Weller *bank executive*
Miller, Claire Ellen *children's writer, editor, educator*
Miller, Kenneth Michael *electronics executive, director*
Mofenson, Lynne Meryl *pediatrician*
Moore, Melinda *public health physician*
Morgan, William Bruce *naval architect*
Moritsugu, Kenneth Paul *physician, government official*
Mummaneni, Padmaja *research scientist, educator*
Nene, Vishvanath *research scientist*
Nevin, Joseph Francis *computer systems engineer*
Nierman, William C. *research scientist*
Niewiaroski, Trudi Osmers (Gertrude Niewiaroski) *social studies educator*
O'Donnell, James Francis *retired health science administrator*
Parham-Hopson, Deborah *health administrator*
Pennello, Gene Anthony *statistician*
Pensinger, John Lynn *lawyer*
Petzold, Carol Stoker *state legislator*
Poljak, Roberto J(uan) *research director, biotechnology educator*
Pospisil, George Curtis *human research educator*
Power, A. Kathryn *social services administrator*
Proffitt, John Richard *business executive, educator*
Rachanow, Gerald Marvin *lawyer, pharmacist*
Raker, Irma *judge*
Rankin, Rachel Ann *retired media specialist*
Rao, Potarazu Krishna *environmental consultant*
Rashid, Mushfiqur M *statistician*
Rasmussen, Caren Nancy *hospital executive*
Reddy, Thikkavarapu Ramachandra *electrical engineer*
Robinowitz, Max *pathologist, consultant*
Rodriguez, William Julio *physician*
Rosen, Saul Woolf *research scientist, health facility administrator*
Rourke, Bradley Kevin *public affairs executive*
Salzberg, Steven *research scientist*
Sansalone, William Robert *biochemist, educator, biomedical researcher*
Scardelletti, Robert A. *labor union officer*
Schindler, Albert Isadore *physicist, researcher*
Schneider, Steven L. *information company executive*
Scully, Martha Seebach *speech and language pathologist*
Seagle, Edgar Franklin *environmental engineer, consultant*
Smith, Mark Alan *management consultant*
Sorensen, John Noble *retired mechanical and nuclear engineer*
Spahr, Frederick Thomas *association executive*
Sparks, David Stanley *university administrator*
Standing, Kimberly Anna *educational researcher*
Stangel, Ivan *biomaterials scientist, educator*
Sumberg, Alfred Donald *professional association executive*
Sundlof, Stephen Frederick *veterinary administrator*
Temple, Robert *physician, federal agency administrator*
Thompson, James Lee *lawyer*
Tracy, LaRee Ann *statistician, medical researcher*
Tripp, Frederick Gerald *investment advisor*
van Dyck, Peter Cuyler *health services administrator, pediatrics educator*
Van Grack, Steven *lawyer*
Veech, Richard Lewis *medical researcher, physician*
Venter, J. Craig *science foundation director, geneticist*
Viertel, George Joseph *lawyer, arbitrator, mediator, consulting engineer*
Waksberg, Joseph *statistical company executive, researcher*
Wallenmeyer, William Anton *retired physicist*
Wang, Chung Shan *physicist*
Wang, Kung-Lee *economics consultant*

Watson, Jerome Roland *marketing professional, researcher*
Weiss, Joel Alexander *environmental and manufacturing executive*
Welsch, Federico *cancer researcher*
White, Owen *research scientist*
Wilson, James J. *public administration consultant*
Woodcock, Janet *federal official*
Yu, Mei-ying Wong *chemist, researcher*
Zaphiriou, George Aristotle *lawyer, educator*

Royal Oak
Israel, Lesley Lowe *retired political consultant*

Saint Marys City
Clifton, Lucille Thelma *author*

Saint Michaels
Brown, Omer Forrest, II, *lawyer*
Feisel, Lyle Dean *retired dean, electrical engineer, educator*
Jones, Raymond Edward, Jr., *brewing executive*
Meendsen, Fred Charles *retired food company executive*
Peck, Charles Edward *retired construction and mortgage executive*
Shipley, L. Parks, Jr., *banker*

Salisbury
Booker, Betty Mae *poet*
Clarke, Wm. A. Lee, III, *lawyer*
Cooper, Michael *food products executive*
DiGiovanna, Augustine Gaspar *biologist, educator*
Ezell-Grim, Annette Schram *business management educator, academic administrator*
House, Charletta *librarian*
Jennings, Louis Brown *retired humanities educator*
Kleiman, Gary Howard *broadcast, advertising and cellular communications consultant*
Leonard, Joseph Howard *association organization executive*
Losonczy, Marta Elizabeth *psychologist, educator*
Moultrie, Fred *geneticist, researcher*
Mulligan, Joseph Francis *physicist, science historian, educator*
Nutter, David George *urban planner*
Oldland, Kevin Bradley *architect*
Parente, Ronaldo *business educator, consultant*
Perdue, James A. *food products executive*
Wolter, John Amadeus *librarian, government official*
Wu, Ying *economics educator, researcher*

Severn
Freeman, Joel Arthur *author, organizational cultural change facilitator*

Severna Park
Allison, John Langsdale *naval architect, marine engineer*
Chatelaine, Kenneth Leo *education educator, psychoanalyst*
Daly, Charles Arthur *health services administrator*
Davis, Clayton *writer, pilot, photographer*
Ebersberger, Arthur Darryl *insurance company executive, consultant*
Hall, Marcia Joy *non-profit organization administrator*
Humphreys Troy, Patricia *communications executive*
Meima, Ralph Chester, Jr., *retired diplomat, real estate company executive*
Moore, John Leo, Jr., *journalist, writer, editor*
Rheinstein, Peter Howard *healthcare company executive, consultant, physician, lawyer*
Schick, Edgar Brehob *German literature educator*
Simonds, Valerie Deverse *healthcare educator*
Sundeen, Sandra Joan *mental health nurse*
Windsor, Patricia (Katonah Summertree, Perrin Winters, Anna Seeling) *author, educator, lecturer*

Shady Side
Devine, Donald J. *management and political consultant*

Silver Spring
Adams, Diane Loretta *physician*
Ahmad, Mirza Muzaffar *economic advisor*
Alexander, Herbert E. *political scientist*
Altschul, B J *public relations counselor*
Anderson, Richard McDonald *hydrologist, engineer*
Beach, Bert Beverly *clergyman*
Beard, Lillian B. McLean *pediatrician, consultant*
Bennett, Carol(ine) Elise *retired reporter, actress*
Bernard, Hugh Y(ancey), Jr., *law educator, librarian*
Biberman, Lucien Morton *physicist, researcher*
Blankenheimer, Bernard *economics consultant*
Borkovec, Vera Z. *Russian studies educator*
Brandt, Carl David *research virologist*
Briese, Michael W. *writer*
Brog, David *consultant, former air force officer*
Burcroff, Richard Tomkinson, II, *economist*
Burgos-Sasscer, Ruth *chancellor emeritus*
Calinger, Ronald Steve *historian*
Camphor, James Winky, Jr., *educational administrator*
Carson, Steven Lee *newspaper publisher*
Cathey, Mary Ellen Jackson *religious studies educator*
Chacko, George Kuttickal *systems science educator, consultant*
Chery, Reginald *minister*
Coates, Robert Jay *retired electronic scientist, consultant*
Cole, Wayne Stanley *historian, educator*
Coles, Anna Louise Bailey *retired dean, nurse*
Compton, Mary Beatrice Brown (Mrs. Ralph Theodore Compton) *public relations executive, writer*
Corwin, Jeff *biologist, anthropologist, television host*
Craig, Paul Max, Jr., *retired lawyer*
Cruze, Kenneth *retired surgeon*
Cunningham, Keith Allen *corporate executive, accountant, lawyer, engineer*
Cunningham, Keith Allen, II, *computer services company executive*
Darvish, John *automotive executive*
Davis, Richmond T.P. *lawyer*
Ehrlich, Charles David *physicist*
Eiserer, Leonard Albert Carl *publishing executive*
Erk, Frank Chris *biologist, educator*
Ewing, Blair Gordon *federal official*
Fields, Daisy Bresley *human resources specialist, writer*
Fockler, Herbert Hill *foundation executive*
Fustero, Robert Raymond *retired political organization worker*
Gandy, Kim Allison *feminist organization executive, lawyer*
Gaydos, Joel Carl *physician*
Gilbert, Charles Richard Alsop *obstetrician, gynecologist, surgeon, educator*
Glickman, Albert Seymour *psychologist, educator*
Goodall, Jane *ethologist*
Goott, Daniel *government official, consultant*
Hayman, Harry *association executive, electrical engineer*
Heppner, Donald Gray, Jr., *immunology research physician, army officer*
Herbers, Tod Arthur *publisher*
Hermach, Francis Lewis *consulting engineer*
Hermanson Ogilvie, Judith *foundation executive*
Holcomb, Minnie Irby *elementary school educator, educator*
Hsueh, Chun-tu *political scientist, historian, foundation executive*
Hubbell, Katherine Jean *retired marketing professional*
Jackson, Mary Jane McHale Flickinger *principal*
Jacobs, George *broadcast engineering consulting company executive*
Jaskot, John Joseph *retired insurance company executive*
Junemann, Gregory J. *labor union administrator*
Kant, Gloria Jean *retired neuroscientist, researcher*
Katz, Pearl *anthropoligist, public health analyst*
Keating, Susan C. *credit foundation executive*
Kelley, Patrick W. *health science association administrator, preventive medicine physician*
Kellner, Mark Allen *writer*
Kelly, John Joseph, Jr., *government executive*
Kenner, Mary Ellen *marketing and communications executive*
Kline, Jerry Robert *government official, ecologist*
Koltnow, Peter Gregory *engineering consultant*
Korth, Thomas A. *musician, educator*
Kramer, Gerson Balfour *lawyer*
Kriegel, Robin *medical association administrator*
Kuratu, Phillip Cedomir *journalist*
Landry, Donald J. *hotel executive*
Latson, Richard Charles *retired audio-visual specialist*
Laughlin, Naomi Myers *realtor*
Ledsinger, Charles A. *hotel executive*
luDoherty, William Thomas, Jr., *historian, retired educator*
Maas, Joe (Melvin Joseph Maas) *retired federal agency administrator*
Mahoney, James R. *federal agency administrator*
Mashin, Jacqueline Ann Cook *medical sciences administrator, nursing administrator*
McCray, Lora *real estate developer*
McGinn, Cherie M. *secondary school educator*
Mohr, Christina *retired economist*
Mok, Carson Kwok-Chi *structural engineer*
Moon, Marilyn Lee *economist*
Neumann, Alfred John *music director*
Nevans, Laurel S. *rehabilitation counselor*
Null, Elisabeth Higgins *librarian, writer*
Oberst, Richard B. *military officer, hospital administrator*
Okigbo, Franklin C. *engineering company executive*
O'Meara, Noel P. *priest, religious organization administrator*
Oswald, Rudolph A. *economist*
Pacuska, Alison Brandi *Russian studies professional*
Papas, Irene Kalandros *English language educator, poet, writer*
Paulsen, Jan *clergyman, church administrator*
Peiperl, Adam *kinetic sculptor, photographer*
Perlmutter, Jerome Herbert *communications specialist*
Raphael, Coleman *business consultant*
Rayburn, Carole Ann (Mary Aida Rayburn) *psychologist, researcher, writer, consultant*
Sammet, Jean E. *computer scientist*
Saunders, George Wendell *management consultant, retired government official*
Schick, Irvin Henry *academic administrator, educator*
Scipio, L(ouis) Albert, II, *retired aerospace science engineering educator, architect, military historian*
Secular, Sidney *writer, weather forecaster, actor, model, fundraiser, consultant*
Shalowitz, Erwin Emmanuel *civil engineer*
Shih-Carducci, Joan Chia-mo *cooking educator, biochemist, medical technologist, author, writer*
Sirken, Monroe Gilbert *statistician*
Smedley, Lawrence Thomas *retired organization executive*
Speights, Michael David *newsletter editor*
Sterling, Eric Edward *lawyer, legal policy advocate*
Telesetsky, Walter *government official*
Thompson, George Ralph *church administrator*
Vanzant, Iyanla *writer*
Vernon, Weston, III, (Wes Vernon) *broadcaster, writer, actor*
Ware, Thaddeus Van *government official*
Weiss, Leonard *mathematician, consultant*
Whalen, John Philip *retired educational administrator, clergyman, lawyer*
Whitmore, Frank Clifford, Jr., *geologist*
Whitten, Leslie Hunter, Jr., *author, newspaper reporter, poet*
Williams, Barbara Ivory *educational researcher*
Williams, James Thomas *physician, educator*
Williams, Paul *retired federal agency administrator*
Wilson, William Stanley *oceanographer*
Winston, Michael Russell *foundation executive, historian*
Woolard, Connie Ward *artist, retired art gallery manager*
Yanushevsky, Rafael Tovie *electromechanical engineer, scientist, consultant, educator*
Yasher, Michael *retired accountant*
Young, Jay Alfred *chemical safety and health consultant, writer, editor*
Zakheim, Barbara Jane *development professional*
Ziegler, Gwendolyn Woods *minister, consultant*

Simpsonville
Altschuler, Bruce Robert *research dentist*
Bluher, Gregory *computer scientist, mathematician*

Solomons
Dorsey, James Francis, Jr., *naval officer*

Sparks
Lawless, Robert J. *food products executive*
Rallo, James Gilbert *management company executive*
Suarez-Murias, Marguerite C. *retired language educator, retired literature educator*

Sparks Glencoe
Contino, Francis A. *food products executive*
Swackhamer, Gene L. *bank executive*

Stevenson
Hendler, Nelson Howard *physician, medical clinic director*
Hilgenberg, John Christian *corporate financial executive, consultant*
Hyman, Mary Bloom *science education programs coordinator*
Manning, Kevin James *academic administrator*
Margalit, Shlomo *educator*
Middendorf, Alice Carter *volunteer*
North, Percy *art historian, educator*

Stevensville
Barrett, John Anthony *publishing and printing company financial executive*
Lain, David Cornelius *health scientist, researcher*

Street
Spangler, Ronald Leroy *retired television executive, aircraft executive, automobile collector*

Sudlersville
Covington, Donald Kingsley, Jr., *plywood sales executive*

Suitland
Basinger, William Daniel *computer programmer*
Brooks, Richard C. *electrical engineer, federal government executive*
Cheng, Jian-Yu *mechanical engineer, researcher, application developer*
Scofield, Roderick Arthur *meteorologist, researcher, educator*
Smith, Lois Ann (L.A. Smith) *foundation administrator, consultant*

Sunderland
Franklin, Jon Daniel *writer, journalist, educator*

Swanton
Cummins, Delmer Duane *academic administrator, historian*

Sykesville
O'Connor, William Thomas *retired surgeon*
Vreeland, Russell Glenn *accountant, consultant*

Takoma Park
Conroy, Sarah Booth *columnist, writer, educator*
Fatiadi, Alexander John *retired chemist*
Lott, Alfred Davis *assistant city manager*
Meijer, Miriam Claude *information technology executive, historian*
Rice, Rick Blackburn *computer programmer, systems analyst*
Richie, Robert Douglas *not-for-profit executive*
Silverman, Charlotte *epidemiologist, educator*
Stephenson, Patricia Ann *public health researcher, educator*
Urciolo, John Raphael, II, *real estate developer, real estate and finance educator*
von Hake, Margaret Joan *librarian*

Temple Hills
Curry, Emma Beatrice *elementary school educator*
Day, Mary Jane Thomas *cartographer*
Lawlah, Gloria Gary *state legislator, educator*
Smith, Irving *gerontologist*
Strauss, Simon Wolf *chemist, materials scientist*

Thurmont
Dexter, Frederick Jay *dentist*

Timonium
Deise, Martin Van *management consultant*
Forrester, Alfred Whitfield *psychiatrist, educator*
Reinhart, Walter Josef *finance educator*

Towson
Baker, Jean Harvey *history professor*
Caret, Robert Laurent *academic administrator*
Carney, Bradford George Yost *lawyer, educator*
Coughlin, James Patrick *mathematician, educator*
Evangeliou, Christos C. *researcher, educator*
Ferrer, Roberto O. *surgeon*
Fish, James Henry *library director*
Harriss, Clarinda *language educator, poet*
Hirschmann, Edwin A. *historian, educator*
Hoch, David Allen *athletic director*
Huang, Joseph Chen-Huan *civil engineer*
Lazar, Jonathan Kumin *computer scientist, educator*
Linz, James G. *health facility administrator*
Lund, Mark Fifield *secondary school educator*
Lutz, Randall Matthew *lawyer*
McIntire, T. Bryan *lawyer, councilman*
McManus, Walter Leonard *investment executive*
Meny, Robert George *former medical research administrator, physician*
Passano, E. Magruder, Jr., *strategic planning consultant*
Pineo, Ronn *historian, educator*
Proctor, Kenneth Donald *lawyer*
Propst, M. Teresa Carson *historian*
Putzel, Constance Kellner *lawyer*
Serpick, Arthur Allen *health facility administrator, physician*
Shah, Shirish Kalyanbhai *computer science, chemistry and environmental science educator*
Shriver, Pamela H. *retired professional tennis player, sports analyst*
Spodak, Michael Kenneth *forensic psychiatrist*
Thompson, John Tilynn *ophthalmologist, medical educator*
Tull, Willis Clayton, Jr., *librarian*
Wilkinson, Charles P. *ophthalmologist*
Wilner, Alan M. *judge*
Young, William Sherban *investment broker*
Zweback, Stanley *psychologist, educator*

Tracys Landing
Smith, Elbert Benjamin *historian, educator*

Trappe
Anderson, Andrew Herbert *retired army officer*
Blades, G(ene) Granville *accountant*

University Park
Beckenstein, Myron *journalist*

Upper Marlboro
Buffenbarger, Robert Thomas *labor union administrator*
Freeman, Ernest Robert *engineering executive*
Harrell, Glenn T., Jr., *judge*
Hewlett, Elizabeth M. *county official*
Morrison, Anne Deinlein *law librarian*
Platt, Steven Irving *lawyer, judge*
Symlar, Jesse Lee *executive*

Waldorf
Hastings, Lee L. *secondary school educator*
Wiggins, Stephen Edward *physician, medical association administrator*

Walkersville
Huiberts, Pieter J. *development chemist*

Washington
Bevan, William Charles *systems analyst*

West Bethesda
Sevik, Maurice *acoustical engineer, researcher*
Vogelgesang, Sandra Louise *business executive, writer, consultant*

West River
Pratt, Katherine Merrick *environmental consulting company executive*

Westminster
Dulany, William Bevard *lawyer*
Dundes, Lauren *education educator*
Erb, Betty Jane *retired real estate agent, activist*
Medina, Janet Gail *school psychologist, educator*
Pappalardo, Faye *academic administrator*
Rogers, Jeffery Paul *music educator*
Rosenthal, Michael Ross *academic administrator, consultant*
Staples, Lyle Newton *lawyer*
Wheatley, Charles Henry, III, *education and technology company executive, lawyer*

Wheaton
Ghosh, Arun Kumar *economics, social sciences and accounting educator*
Kirchman, Eric Hans *lawyer*
Ma, Qingli *environmental hydrologist*
White, Martha Vetter *allergy and immunology physician, researcher*

White Hall
Buhite, Thomas Jesse, Sr., *employee benefits consultant*
Radigan, Frank Xavier *pharmaceutical company executive*

White Plains
Robinson, Scharn *lawyer, author, researcher*

Whitehaven
Scott, David Winfield *artist, museum consultant*

Woodbine
Mc Indoe, Darrell Winfred *retired nuclear medicine physician*
Nuss, Barbara Gough *artist*

Woodstock
Price, John Roy, Jr., *financial executive*

Wye Mills
Schnaitman, William Kenneth *finance company executive*

MASSACHUSETTS

Abington
Margolis, Jay M. *clothing executive*

Acton
Boghani, Ashok Balvantrai *entrepreneur, management consultant*
Buck-Moore, Joanne Rose *nursing administrator, educator*
Conoby, Joseph Francis *chemist*
Coughlin, Cornelius Edward *accounting company executive*
Evans, Robert, Jr., *economics professor*
Gilpin, Deborah J. *museum administrator*
Hicks, Walter Joseph *electrical engineer*
Kittross, John Michael *retired communications educator*
Munson, Lawrence Shipley *management consultant*
Smith, Raoul Normand *computer science educator*

Agawam
Kantor, Simon William *chemistry professor*
Potts, Harold Francis, Jr., *elevator company executive*
Sylvester, John Andrew *social studies educator*

Allston
Becton, Henry Prentiss, Jr., *broadcasting company executive*
Burton, Gary *musician*
Mills, Daniel Quinn *business educator, consultant, author*
Spencer, Lara *television personality, journalist*

Amesbury
Heyman, Joseph Martin *obstetrician, gynecologist*
Labaree, Benjamin Woods *history professor*
Parker, William H., III, *federal official*

Amherst
Aizen, Icek *psychology professor, consultant*
Alexander, Alison F. *communication educator*
Alfange, Dean, Jr., *political science educator*
Anderson, Ronald Trent *artist, educator*
Archer, Ronald Dean *chemist, educator*
Averill, James Reed *psychology educator*
Baker, Lynne Rudder *philosophy educator*
Benson, Lucy Wilson *political and diplomatic consultant*

Bentley, Richard Norcross *regional planner, writer, educator*
Berger, Seymour Maurice *social psychologist*
Bezucha, Robert Joseph *history educator*
Bickford, John H. *psychologist, educator*
Blass, Elliott M. *psychologist, educator*
Bobba, Kumar Manoj *engineer, researcher*
Breslin, Eileen Theresa *women's health nurse*
Bridegam, Willis Edward, Jr., *retired librarian*
Byron, Frederick William, Jr., *physicist, educator, university vice chancellor*
Call, Gregory S. *academic administrator*
Clark, Carol Canda *art historian, educator*
Cohen, Alvin P. *language educator*
Cornish, Geoffrey St. John *golf course architect*
Dabrowski, Thaddeus E. *art educator, art consultant, painter*
Dolan, Michael Francis *science educator*
Donoghue, John *physics professor*
Donohue, Therese Brady *artistic director, choreographer, designer*
Elman, Naomi Geist *artist, producer*
Feldman, Allan *education educator*
Fink, Richard David *chemist, educator*
Fleischman, Paul Robert *psychiatrist, writer*
Folbre, Nancy *economics professor*
Franks, Lewis E. *electrical and computer engineering educator, researcher*
Gettier, Edmund Lee, III, *retired humanities educator*
Gibson, Walker *retired English language educator, poet, writer*
Glazier, Lyle *writer, educator*
Goldstein, Joseph Irwin *materials scientist, educator*
Greene, Theodore Phinney *historian, educator*
Hallock, Robert Bruce *physics educator*
Hayes, David Ryan *mathematics professor*
Hepler, Peter K. *biologist, educator*
Holland, Noy *writer, educator*
Howland, Richard Moulton *retired lawyer*
Immerman, Neil *academic administrator, computer science educator*
Jeneralczuk, Joanna Maria *mathematician, educator*
Kimball, Justin *photographer, educator*
Kinney, Arthur Frederick *literary history educator, writer, editor*
Klare, Michael Thomas *social science educator, program director*
Klement, Kevin Charles *humanities educator*
Koren, Israel *electrical and computer engineering educator*
Larson, Joseph Stanley *environmentalist, educator*
Lasch, Pat *artist, educator*
Liebling, Jerome *photographer, educator*
Litsky, Bertha Yanis *microbiologist, artist*
Lombardi, John V. *university administrator, historian*
MacKnight, William John *chemist, educator*
Manz, Charles C. *management educator*
Margulis, Lynn (Lynn Alexander) *evolutionist, educator*
Marx, Anthony W. *academic administrator*
May, Ernest Dewey *university administrator, musician, executive*
Mc Donagh, Edward Charles *sociologist, university administrator*
Nash, William Arthur *civil engineer, educator*
Oates, Stephen Baery *retired history educator*
Palmer, John Derry *physiology educator*
Palser, Barbara F. *botany researcher, retired educator*
Partee, Barbara Hall *linguist, educator*
Peterson, Gerald Alvin *physics educator*
Prince, Gregory Smith, Jr., *academic administrator*
Roberts, Chris *strategy and finance educator, researcher*
Romer, Robert Horton *physicist, researcher*
Sandweiss, Martha A. *author, American studies and history educator*
Schaubert, Daniel Harold *electrical engineering educator*
Scott, David Knight *physicist, university administrator*
Seymour, Charlena *academic administrator*
Sinha, Manisha *historian, educator*
Strickland, Bonnie Ruth *psychologist, educator*
Swift, Calvin Thomas *electrical and computer engineering educator*
Taubman, Jane Andelman *Russian literature educator*
Taubman, William Chase *political science educator, writer*
Taylor, Robert Edward *foreign language educator*
Terpenny, Janis P. *engineering educator, researcher*
Velleman, Daniel Jon *mathematics professor*
Vogl, Otto *polymer science and engineering educator*
Webley, Wilmore Christopher *microbiologist, researcher*
Wideman, John Edgar *English literature educator, novelist*
Wier, Dara *poet, English language educator*
Wills, David Wood *minister, educator*
Winter, Horst Henning *chemical engineer, educator*
Wolff, Robert Paul *philosophy educator*
Woodbury, Richard Benjamin *anthropologist, educator*
Wyman, David Sword *historian, educator*
Xing, Baoshan *science educator*
Yarde, Richard Foster *art educator*
Zimmermann, Robert A. *molecular biologist, science educator*

Andover
Appleby, David *biotechnologist*
Arce, Pedro L. *economic development executive, banker*
Hasegawa, Tomohiro *marketing manager*
Jakes, William Chester *electrical engineer*
Keleher, David *electronics executive*
Marsh, Robert Buford *chemical engineer, consultant*
Murray, Sabina *writer*
Regan, James P. *technology services executive*
Simone, Joseph *clergyman, educator*

Arlington
Berkoben, John Perri *physician*
Birk, Lee (Carl Lee Birk) *psychiatrist, educator*
Brooke, John L. *history professor*
Fulmer, Vincent Anthony *retired college president*
Hamilton, Malcolm Cowan *retired librarian, editor, indexer, personnel professional*
Keshian, Richard *lawyer*
Samuelson, Joan Benoit *professional runner*
Thomas, Patricia Joanne *journalist, writer*
Vaughn, Thomas Joseph *earth science educator, administrator*

Ashburnham
Von Deck, Joseph Francis *secondary school educator, researcher*

Ashfield
Gabriel, Peter Paul *finance educator*
Klein, Stacy A. *theater director*
Pepyne, Edward Walter *lawyer, psychologist, former educator*

Ashland
Jost, David Nelson *art educator*
Pettinella, Nicholas Anthony *financial executive*

Attleboro
Bischoff, Marilyn Brett *clinical social worker, personal life coach*
Brodeur, Russell P. *design engineer*
Hammerle, Fredric Joseph *technical manufacturing executive*

Attleboro Falls
Kulwicki, Bernard Michael *ceramics engineer, researcher*

Auburn
Bachelder, Robert Stephen *minister*
Baker, David Arthur *small business owner, manufacturer*
Berg, G. Vivian *artist*

Auburndale
Bernard, Michael Mark *lawyer, city planning consultant*
Doran, Kathleen Brewer *dean, consultant*
Gulbrandsen, Natalie Webber *religious association administrator*
Kibrick, Anne *retired nursing educator and university dean*
Lindgren, Charlotte Holt *English language educator*

Ayer
Bloom, Edwin John, Jr., *retired human resources consultant*
Desper, Clyde Richard *retired polymer scientist*
Holmes, Jean Louise *real estate investor, Holocaust scholar, educator*

Babson Park
Palmerio, Elvira Castano *art gallery director, art historian*
Rufin, Carlos *finance educator, consultant*
Zacharakis, Andrew *business educator*

Barnstable
Lummus, Carol Travers *artist, printmaker*
Perry, Blair Lane *lawyer*

Barre
Sullivan, James Edward *poet*

Bedford
Abbott, John Cope *forensic research administrator*
An, Hong *engineer*
Daltas, Arthur John *management consultant, software services manager*
Driscoll, Kimberlee Marie *lawyer*
Ellenbogen, S. David *electronics company executive*
Fante, Ronald Louis *engineering scientist*
Goodman, William Beehler *editor, literary agent*
Herlihy, Maura Ann *psychology technician*
Jelalian, Albert V. *electrical engineer*
Johansen, Jack T. *engineering company executive*
Klyosov, Anatole Alex *biochemist, researcher*
Labudovic, Marko *research scientist, consultant*
Payne, Harry Morse, Jr., *architect*
Shepley, Hugh *architect*
Steinberg, James Jonah *physician, medical administrator, educator*
Taylor, Cora Hodge *social worker*
Wasson, Lila Elizabeth *educational consultant*
Webber, Howard Rodney *computer company executive*
Wieand, Jeffrey Scott *lawyer*
Winter, David Louis *systems engineer, human factors scientist, retired*
Zadel, C. William *business executive*

Belchertown
Burstein, Michael Clifford *management consultant*
Lester, Julius B. *author*
Marsh, Brian Richard *management executive, playwright, educator, clergyman*

Belmont
Bingham, George Walter Chandler *retired sales executive*
Cavarnos, Constantine Peter *philosopher, writer*
Cohen, Bruce Michael *psychiatrist, educator, scientist, health facility administrator*
Coyle, Joseph Thomas *psychiatrist*
de Marneffe, Francis *psychiatrist, hospital administrator*
Dohanian, Diran Kavork *art historian, educator*
Feldstein, Kathleen Foley *economist, consultant*
Fuller, Stephen Herbert *business administration educator*
Gabrieli, Anna *voice educator*
Greer, Gordon Bruce *retired lawyer, writer*
Haralampu, George Stelios *electric power engineer, former engineering executive electric utility company*
Harris, William Wolpert *foundation administrator*
Hauser, George *biochemist, educator*
Heyman, Gene Morris *research psychologist, educator*
Hilt, Mary Louise *artist*
Junger, Miguel Chapero *acoustics researcher*
Kargman (Witkin), Marie *marriage counselor, consultant*
Ke, Yong *medical educator, researcher*
Killgore, William Dale (Scott), Jr., *neuropsychologist*
Klein, Martin Samuel *management consulting executive*
Levendusky, Philip George *psychologist, education administrator*
Lloyd, Boardman *investment executive*
McGaw, Bridger E. *management consultant*
Merrill, Edward Wilson *chemical engineering educator*
Neumeyer, John Leopold *research company administrator, chemistry educator*
Onesti, Silvio Joseph *psychiatrist*
Pope, Harrison Graham, Jr., *psychiatrist, educator*
Rand, Peter *writer, editor, educator*
Reynolds, William Francis *mathematics professor*
Ruocchio, Patricia Jeanne *writer*
Sifneos, Peter Emanuel *psychiatrist, educator*
Simpson, Russell Avington *retired law firm administrator*
Todtenkopf, Mark Steven *neuroscientist*
Zhang, Kehong *neuropharmacologist, educator*

Berkley
Murtagh, Michael Paul *psychologist*

Berlin
Lohr, Harold Russell *retired bishop*

Beverly
Barger, Richard Wilson *hotel executive*
Chitre, Sharadchandra Raghunandan *physician*
Daya, Jackie *publishing company executive*
DeVore, Dale Paul *scientific research organization executive*
Eastman, W. Dean *secondary school educator*
Manning, William Frederick *retired wire service photographer*
Ozzie, Ray *Internet company executive*
Pierard, Richard Victor *history educator*
Roberts, Richard John *molecular biologist, consultant, research director*
Roy, Robert William *artist, educator*
Smith, Derek Armand *information technology executive*

Billerica
Akhavan, Farhad *electrical engineer*
Furlong, Patrick David *educator, researcher*
Kinsman, Robert Preston *biomedical plastics engineer*
Luong, Nam Thoai *biochemist, researcher*
Wacker-Brawley, Margaret *communications executive*

Bolton
Keane, Karen M. *auction house executive*
Leighton, Charles Milton *retired specialty consumer products executive*

Boston
Abbott, William Saunders *lawyer*
Aber, John William *finance educator*
Ablow, Joseph *artist, educator*
Ablow, Roz Karol (Roselyn Karol Ablow) *painter, curator*
Aborn, Foster Litchfield *insurance company executive*
Abraham, Nicholas Albert *lawyer, real estate developer*
Abrahm, Janet Lee *hematologist, oncologist, palliative care specialist, educator*
Abrams, Roger Ian *law educator, arbitrator*
Abu-moustafa, Adel H. *medical educator, dean*
Ackroyd, Peter Warwick *publishing company executive*
Adamis, Mary K. *medical educator*
Adams, Phoebe-Lou *journalist*
Adelstein, S(tanley) James *pathologist, educator*
Adler, Sidney W. *lawyer*
Ahlbeck, Laura A. *musician, educator*
Aikman, William Francis *venture capitalist*
Akins, Cary Willard *surgeon, educator*
Albert, Martin Lawrence *behavioral neurologist*
Alden, Vernon Roger *corporate director, trustee*
Alexander, James Garth *architect*
Alpert, Joel Jacobs *medical educator, pediatrician*
Alt, Frederick W. *geneticist, pediatrician*
Ampola, Mary G. *pediatrician, geneticist*
Anderson, Jewelle Lucille *musician, educator*
Anderson, Kenneth Carl *physician, educator*
Andrews, Kenneth Richmond *business administration educator*
Angell, Marcia *pathologist, editor-in-chief*
Angelou, Maya (Marguerite Johnson) *writer, playwright, actress, activist*
Anis, Wagdy A.Y. *architect*
Anselme, Jean-Pierre Louis Marie *chemist*
Anthony, Ethan *architect*
Appley, Mortimer Herbert *psychologist, university president emeritus*
Aquilino, Daniel *banker*
Aresty, Jeffrey M. *lawyer*
Argyropoulos, Stylianos *food service executive*
Arky, Ronald Alfred *medical educator*
Armstrong, Rodney *librarian*
Arnold, David John *marketing educator, consultant*
Atkins, Cory *state legislator, writer*
Attar, Eyal *physician assistant*
Auchincloss, Hugh, Jr., *transplant surgeon*
Auerbach, Arnold Jacob (Red Auerbach) *professional basketball team executive*
Auerbach, John M. *city health department administrator*
Auerbach, Joseph *former lawyer, law educator*
Austen, K(arl) Frank *internist, educator*
Austen, W(illiam) Gerald *surgeon, educator*
Avery, Mary Ellen *pediatrician, educator*
Axelrod, Lloyd *endocrinologist, diabetologist, educator*
Bacon, A. Smoki *television host*
Bae, Frank S. H. *law educator, law library administrator*
Bailey, Peter Arthur *real estate executive*
Bailey, Richard Briggs *investment company executive*
Baillieul, John Brouard *aerospace engineering and applied mathematics educator*
Baker, Charles Duane *business administration educator, former management executive*
Baker, Vincent Lamont *professional basketball player*
Baldassano, Corinne Leslie *radio executive*
Balser, Ruth B. *state legislator, psychologist*
Bangs, Will Johnston *lawyer*
Banks, Henry H. *orthopedic surgeon, educator, dean*
Barker, Edwin Bogue *musician*
Barnett, Guy Octo *physician, educator*
Barouch, Dan Hung *physician, scientist*
Bates, David Westfall *internist, educator, medical researcher*
Baughman, James Carroll *information and communication educator*
Baughman, Kenneth Lee *cardiologist, educator*
Bavaria, Joan *finance company executive*
Beal, Robert Lawrence *real estate executive*
Beardslee, William Rigby *psychiatrist*
Beatty, Carl *music educator*
Bebo, Joseph Anthony *counselor, educator*
Becker, James Murdoch *surgeon, educator*
Beinfeld, Margery Cohen *neurobiology educator*
Bell, Michael A. *investment company executive*
Benacerraf, Baruj *pathologist, educator*
Bennett, Clay *cartoonist*
Bennett, George Frederick *investment manager*
Benson, James M. *investment company executive*
Benz, Edward John, Jr., *internist, hematologist, educator, health facility executive*
Berger, Harvey Robert *psychologist*
Berger, Jerome Morris *communications executive*
Berk, Lee Eliot *academic administrator*
Berkey, Dennis D. *mathematics professor*
Berkman, Lisa F. *public health educator*
Berliner, Harvey P. *sales executive*
Berman, Lisa *advertising executive*
Berman, Mark Niles *lawyer*
Bern, Murray Morris *hematologist, oncologist*
Bernhard, Alexander Alfred *lawyer*
Bernhard, William Francis *thoracic and cardiovascular surgeon*
Berry, Janis Marie *lawyer*
Berson, Eliot Lawrence *ophthalmologist, medical educator*
Bertino, Fred *advertising executive*
Berwick, Donald M. *administrator*
Beyerl, Scott Alan *investment company executive*
Bieber, Frederick Robert *medical geneticist*
Bigby, JudyAnn *medical educator*
Bines, Harvey Ernest *lawyer, educator, writer*
Bistrian, Bruce Ryan *internist, educator*
Black, Paul Henry *medical educator, researcher*
Black, Peter *surgeon, educator*
Blakely, Allison *history professor*
Blakeney, Barbara A. *public health service officer*
Blendon, Robert Jay *health policy educator*
Bliss, Charles Michael *gastroenterologist*
Bloch, Donald Martin *lawyer*
Bloch, Kurt Julius *physician*
Bloom, Barry R. *dean*
Bloom, Edward (Ted) *research and development company executive*
Blumenthal, David *health policy expert*
Blumer, Deborah *state legislator*
Boden, Mark Emmanual *investment company executive, investment advisor*
Bodoff, Joseph Samuel Uberman *lawyer*
Bohnen, Michael J. *lawyer*
Bok, John Fairfield *retired lawyer*
Bonanno, Theresa M. *nursing administrator*
Bonifaz, John Cristopher *lawyer*
Boodram, Mohan David *academic administrator*
Bornheimer, Allen Millard *lawyer*
Boudin, Michael *federal judge*
Bougas, James Andrew *physician, educator, surgeon*
Bourne, Katherine Day *journalist, educator*
Bousvaros, Athos *pediatric gastroenterologist*
Bowler, Marianne Bianca *federal judge*
Boyd, David Preston *business educator*
Brain, Joseph David *biomedical scientist*
Braunwald, Eugene *physician, educator*
Brazelton, Thomas Berry *pediatrician, educator*
Brecher, Kenneth *astrophysicist, educator*
Breitbart, Roger Eric *pediatrician*
Breitman, Leo R. *banker*
Brenner, Barry Morton *physician*
Brenner, Michael Barry *rheumatologist, educator*
Briggs, Susan Miller *surgeon*
Brodeur, John *public relations executive*
Brody, Richard Eric *lawyer*
Broitman, Selwyn Arthur *microbiologist, educator*
Bromsen, Maury Austin *historian, bibliographer, antiquarian bookseller*
Bronner, Michael *advertising executive, education assistance company executive*
Brountas, Paul Peter *lawyer*
Brown, Michael Robert *lawyer*
Brown, Stephen Lee *retired insurance company executive*
Brown, William L. *banker*
Brugge, Joan S. *medical educator*
Bruns, William John, Jr., *business administration educator*
Buchanan, Robert McLeod *lawyer*
Buchanan, Walter Woolwine *electrical engineer, educator, academic administrator*
Buchin, Stanley Ira *management consultant, finance educator*
Buckley, Mortimer Joseph *physician*
Budd, Wayne A. *U.S. attorney*
Bunker, Beryl H. *retired insurance company executive, volunteer*
Burleigh, Lewis Albert *lawyer*
Burns, Thomas David *lawyer*
Burr, Francis Hardon *lawyer*
Buxbaum, Robert C(ourtney) *internist*
Cabot, Louis Wellington *foundation trustee*
Caldwell, Ann Wickins *academic administrator*
Caldwell, Gail *book critic*
Calkins, David Ross *physician, medical educator*
Callahan, Jennifer *state legislator, education educator*
Callow, Allan Dana *surgeon*
Campbell, Levin Hicks *federal judge*
Canavan, Christine Estelle *state legislator*
Candaras, Gale D. *state legislator, lawyer*
Canellos, George Peter *physician educator*
Cantella, Vincent Michele *stockbroker*
Caplan, Louis Robert *neurologist, educator*
Cardona, Rodolfo *Spanish language and literature educator*
Carey, John Andrew *investment company executive*
Carey, Martin Conrad *gastroenterologist, molecular biophysicist, educator, medical geneticist*
Carpenter, Robert Brent *lawyer*
Carr, Daniel Barry *anesthesiologist, endocrinologist, medical researcher*
Carr, Stephen W. *lawyer*
Carradini, Lawrence *comparative biologist, science administrator*
Carroll, James *author*
Carter, Marshall Nichols *retired banker*
Carter, Peyton Franklin, III, *accountant*
Carter, T(homas) Barton *law educator*
Carvalho, John Joseph, IV, *molecular geneticist, philosopher of science*
Chakrabarti, Supriya *space astrophysicist*

Chakravarti, Arnab *physician, researcher*
Chamillard, George W. *electronics company executive*
Chapman, Paul H. *pediatric neurosurgeon*
Chattopadhyay, Naibedya *physiologist, educator, researcher*
Chen, Chih-Fan *electrical engineer*
Chen, Ching-chih *information science educator, consultant*
Chesky, Evelyn G. *state legislator*
Chilvers, Derek *insurance company executive*
Chobanian, Aram *medical school dean, cardiologist*
Choo, Arthur C.S. *structural engineer, consultant*
Chou, Laisheng *education educator*
Christenson, Charles John *retired business educator*
Chung, Jennifer M. *not-for-profit executive*
Ciraulo, Domenic Anthony *psychiatrist, educator*
Clark, Kim Bryce *dean, business educator*
Clarke, John Terrel *astrophysicist*
Clarke, Terence Michael *public relations and advertising executive*
Cleary, Paul David *sociomedical educator*
Clouse, Melvin E. *radiologist*
Coady, Nicole *food service executive*
Cody, Alan Morrow *financial consultant*
Coffman, Jay Denton *physician, educator*
Cogan, John Francis, Jr., *lawyer*
Cohen, Alan Barry *researcher, educator*
Cohen, Alan Seymour *internist*
Cohen, Rachelle Sharon *journalist*
Cohen, Robert Sonné *physicist, philosopher, educator*
Cohn, Andrew Howard *lawyer*
Cohn, Lawrence H. *cardiothoracic surgeon*
Collatos, William Peter *venture capitalist*
Collier, R(obert) John *biomedical researcher, dean*
Collings, Robert Biddlecombe *judge*
Collins, James H., Jr., *architectural firm executive*
Collins, Monica Ann *journalist*
Comeau, Susan *bank executive*
Condrin, J. Paul *insurance company executive*
Cone, Carol Lynn *public relations executive*
Conley, Daniel F. *prosecutor*
Conner, Terry L *insurance company executive*
Connolly, James Leo *physician, pathologist*
Connolly, Thomas Edward *judge*
Connor, Walter Downing *political scientist, educator, researcher*
Connors, Jack, Jr., *advertising executive*
Connors, John Michael, Jr., *advertising agency executive*
Convey, Kevin R. *editor*
Copithorne, David A. *public relations executive*
Cordy, Robert J. *judge*
Cornwall, Deborah Joyce *consulting firm executive, management consultant*
Cosimi, A. Benedict *surgeon*
Costa, Daniel Lawrence *architect*
Costa, Mark E. *medical director, educator*
Costello, Andrew F. *newspaper editor*
Cotran, Ramzi S. *pathologist, educator*
Cotter, William Reckling *foundation president*
Coutermarsh, Eva Marina *personnel executive*
Coville, Andrea *public relations executive*
Cowin, Judith Arnold *state supreme court judge*
Cox, Malcolm *academic administrator, medical educator*
Crate, Darrell *political organization administrator*
Craver, James Bernard *lawyer*
Creedon, Geraldine *state legislator*
Creem, Cynthia Stone *state legislator, lawyer*
Crimlisk, Jane Therese *probation officer*
Crocker, Allen Carrol *pediatrician*
Cronin, Bonnie Kathryn Lamb *museum director*
Cronin, Philip Mark *lawyer*
Crowley, William Francis, Jr., *medical researcher and educator*
Curley, Robert Ambrose, Jr., *lawyer*
Curran, Emily Katherine *museum director*
Curran, Michael J. *finance company executive*
Cursiefen, Claus *ophthalmologist, researcher*
Cutter, Curtis Carly *consulting company executive*
Dafoe, Byron Jaromir *professional hockey player*
D'Agostino, Ralph Benedict *mathematician, statistician, educator, consultant*
D'Alessandro, David Francis *insurance company executive*
Daley, Paul Patrick *lawyer*
Dallek, Robert *history educator*
D'Allesandro, David F. *insurance company executive*
Daly, Benedict Dudley Thomas, Jr., *cardiothoracic surgeon*
Dando, A. Jeffrey *lawyer, consultant*
Daniels, Norman *philosopher, educator*
Darehshori, Nader Farhang *publishing sales executive*
David, John R. *internist, educator*
Davies, Don *education educator*
Davis, Christopher C. *diversified financial services company executive*
Davison, Peter Hubert *editor, poet*
D'Avolio, Gerald Donald *religious organization administrator, lawyer*
Dawson-Hughes, Bess *scientist*
Daynard, Richard Alan *law educator*
DeAmicis, Susan McNair *small business owner*
de Burlo, Comegys Russell, Jr., *investment advisor, educator*
DeCiccio, John M. *investment company executive*
DeGraan, Edward F. *consumer products company executive*
Deissler, Mary Alice *foundation executive*
Delaney, John White *lawyer*
Delbanco, Thomas Lewis *medical educator, researcher*
Del Sesto, Janice Mancini *opera company executive*
De Luca, Carlo John *biomedical engineer, educator*
DeLuca, Norman J. *finance company executive*
Dentler, Robert Arnold *sociologist, educator*
DePaola, Dominick Philip *academic administrator*
de Rham, Casimir, Jr., *lawyer*
DeSanctis, Roman William *cardiologist, educator*
Deshpandé, Rohit *business educator*
Desnoyers, Megan Floyd *archivist, educator*
Deutsch, Stephen B. *lawyer*
DiCara, Lawrence S. *lawyer*
Dillon, James Joseph *lawyer*
Dineen, John K. *lawyer*
Dluhy, Deborah Haigh *college dean*
Dluhy, Robert George *physician*
Doherty, Robert Francis, Jr., *aerospace and defense industry professional*
Dolin, Raphael *medical educator*
Domini, Amy Lee *trustee*
Donahoe, Patricia Kilroy *surgeon*
Donahue, Charlotte Mary *lawyer*
Donovan, Carol Ann *state legislator*
Donovan, Helen W. *newspaper editor*
Dowd, Peter Jerome *public relations executive*
Doyle, Mathias Francis *academic administrator, political scientist, educator*
Drazen, Jeffrey Mark *medical educator*
Dreben, Raya Spiegel *judge*
Driscoll, James S. *entrepreneurial strategist*
Drought, James Henry *healthcare business owner, exercise physiologist*
Duffy, James Francis, III, *lawyer*
Duncan, Lyn M. *pathology educator*
Dvorak, Harold Fisher *pathologist, educator, scientist*
Dwyer, Johanna Todd *nutrition research scientist, clinical nutritionist, educator*
Dzau, Victor Joseph *cardiologist, educator, researcher*
Ebsworth, William Robert *investment company executive*
Eddleston, Kimberly Ann *finance educator*
Edelin, Kenneth Carlton *physician*
Eder, Richard Gray *newspaper critic*
Edmonds, Dean Stockett, Jr., *physicist, educator, director*
Egdahl, Richard Harrison *surgeon, medical educator, health science administrator*
Ehrlich, M. Gordon *lawyer*
Eisenberg, Leon *psychiatrist, educator*
Eisner, Sister Janet Margaret *college president*
El-Baz, Farouk *science administrator, educator*
Elfman, Eric Michael *lawyer*
Elfner, Albert Henry, III, *retired mutual fund management company executive*
Elkus, Howard Felix *architect*
Ellis, Douglass N., Jr., *lawyer*
Ellis, F. Henry, Jr., *surgeon, educator*
Ellis, Fredric Lee *lawyer*
Ellis, Randall Poor *economist, educator*
Emerson, Anne Devereux *museum administrator*
Engel, David Lewis *lawyer*
Epler, Gary Robert *physician, author, educator*
Epstein, Arnold M. *medical educator*
Epstein, Elaine May *lawyer*
Epstein, Franklin Harold *physician, educator*
Epstein, Theo N. *professional sports team executive*
Ericson, Elizabeth (Zibby) *architect*
Eskandarian, Edward *advertising agency executive*
Essex, Max *epidemiology educator*
Essex, Myron Elmer *microbiology and virology educator*
Estin, Hans Howard *investment executive*
Eurich, Richard Rex *lawyer*
Evgenov, Oleg V. *medical scientist*
Falb, Peter Lawrence *mathematician, educator, investment company executive*
Fallon, John Golden *banker*
Fargo, Susan C. *state legislator*
Farmer, Paul Edward *medical anthropologist*
Farnam, Walter Edward *insurance company executive*
Farris, R. Wesley, II, *neurologist*
Feder, Donald Albert *syndicated columnist*
Federman, Daniel David *medical educator, academic administrator, endocrinologist*
Feeney, Joan N. *judge*
Fein, Rashi *health sciences educator*
Feisel, Lyle Dean *lawyer*
Felter, John Kenneth *lawyer*
Fennell, Robert F. *state legislator, small business owner*
Ferencik, Maros *medical researcher*
Finegold, Barry R. *state legislator, banker, lawyer*
Finegold, Maurice Nathan *architect*
Fink, Aaron *artist*
Finn, Terrence M. *lawyer*
Finnegan, Neal Francis *banker*
Finneran, Thomas M. *state legislator, lawyer*
Finucane, Anne M. *communications and marketing executive*
Fischer, Eric Robert *lawyer, educator*
Fishman, Len *state commissioner*
FitzGerald, Maura *public relations executive*
Fitzmaurice, Garrett Martin *education educator, researcher*
Flaherty, Lois Talbot *editor, psychiatrist, educator*
Flanders, Jefferson *publishing executive*
Flansburgh, Earl Robert *architect*
Flavin, Nancy Ann *state legislator*
Fleming, Jonathan J. *venture capitalist*
Fletcher, Cathy Ann *auditor*
Fletcher, Robert Hillman *medical educator*
Flier, Jeffrey S. *endocrinologist*
Floor, Richard Earl *lawyer*
Florescu, Radu Radu *East European history educator*
Folkman, Moses Judah *surgeon, educator*
Foote, Warren Edgar *neuroscientist, psychologist, educator*
Ford, Maureen R. *insurance company executive*
Foreman, Judy *journalist*
Fortier, Albert Mark, Jr., *lawyer*
Foulke, Keith Charles *professional baseball player*
Fowler, Floyd Jackson, Jr., *researcher*
Fox, Francis Haney *lawyer*
Fox, Gloria L. *state representative, state legislator*
Franco, Ramon Arturo *medical educator*
Francona, Terry Jon *professional baseball manager*
Frank, Richard G. *health educator*
Frank-Kamenetskii, Maxim D. *biomedical engineer*
Frankl, Spencer Nelson *dentist, dean*
Fraser, Robert Burchmore *lawyer*
Frazier, Howard Stanley *physician*
Frederick, Albert R., Jr., *ophthalmologist, surgeon*
Freed, Rita Evelyn *curator, Egyptologist, educator*
Freedberg, A. Stone *physician*
Freeland, Richard Middleton *academic affairs administrator, historian*
Frei, Emil, III, *physician, medical researcher, medical educator*
Friedman, David Samuel *lawyer*
Friedman, Paula Konowitch *dentist, academic administrator*
Gadiesh, Orit *management consulting executive*
Gagnon, Paul A. *historian, researcher*
Gallagher, Ellen *artist*
Galvin, Robert J. *lawyer*
Galvin, William Francis *state official*
Gamst, Frederick Charles *social anthropologist*
Garcia, Adolfo Ramon *lawyer*
Garcia, Frieda *community foundation executive*
Gargiulo, Andrea W. *lawyer*
Gargiulo, Antonio Rosario *reproductive endocrinologist, researcher, clinician*
Garrett, Gerald R. *sociology educator, criminologist, consultant*
Garry, Colleen M. *state legislator*
Gasson, David S. *communications executive*
Gaudreau, Russell A., Jr., *lawyer, educator*
Gelb, Richard Mark *lawyer*
Gelber, Matthew Brian *securities trader*
Gelfand, Jeffrey Alan *physician, educator*
Gendron, George *magazine editor*
Gertner, Nancy *federal judge, educator*
Gevirtz, Leslie *communications media executive*
Gewirtz, Henry *health facility administrator, medical educator*
Ghabbour, Elham A. *research scientist, educator*
Ghirardi, James *communications executive*
Gibran, Kahlil *sculptor*
Gibson, Barry Joseph *magazine editor*
Gifford, Charles Kilvert *banker*
Gifford, Nelson Sage *financial company executive*
Gilchrest, Barbara Ann *dermatologist*
Gilman, Richard H. *newspaper publishing executive*
Gilmore, Maurice Eugene *mathematics professor*
Gimbrone, Michael Anthony, Jr., *research scientist, pathologist, educator*
Giso, Frank, III, *lawyer*
Glass, Milton Louis *retired manufacturing company executive*
Glass, Renée *educational health foundation executive*
Gleason, Jean Berko *psychology educator*
Glimcher, Melvin Jacob *orthopedic surgeon*
Glosband, Daniel Martin *lawyer*
Gobi, Anne *state legislator, lawyer*
Goldberg, Irving Hyman *molecular pharmacology and biochemistry educator*
Goldberg, Marcia B. *medical educator*
Golder, Herbert Alan *classics educator*
Goldhaber, Paul *dental educator*
Goldman, Peter *nutrition and clinical pharmacology educator*
Gomes, Shirley *state legislator*
Gonchar, Sergei *professional hockey player*
Gonson, S. Donald *lawyer*
Gonyeau, Michael J. *pharmacy professor, internal medicine clinical pharmacist*
Goodman, Louis Allan *lawyer*
Goody, Joan Edelman *architect*
Gormley, Pamela D. *controller*
Gorton, Nathaniel M. *federal judge*
Gossels, Claus Peter Rolf *lawyer*
Gottlieb, Leonard Solomon *pathology educator*
Grant, Barbara Hurwitz *educator*
Gray, Carla *marketing professional*
Greaney, John M. *state supreme court justice*
Greco, Michael S. *lawyer*
Green, Howard *biologist, educator*
Greenberg, Michael *neuroscientist, educator*
Greenberger, Norton Jerald *physician*
Greenblatt, David J. *pharmacologist*
Greene, Michael F. *obstetrician*
Greenes, Robert A. *medical educator*
Greenwood, Joen Elizabeth *economist, consultant*
Greiner, Jack Volker *ophthalmologist, physician, surgeon, scientist*
Grillo, Hermes Conrad *surgeon*
Grimes, Calvin M., Jr., *oil industry executive*
Grimes, Heilan Yvette *publishing executive*
Groopman, Jerome *medical educator*
Grossfeld, Stan *newspaper photography executive, author*
Grossman, Frances Kaplan *psychologist*
Grousbeck, Wyc *professional sports team executive*
Grundfast, Kenneth Martin *otolaryngologist*
Guertin, Robert Powell *physics educator, university dean*
Habener, Joel Francis *medical educator, researcher*
Haddad, Ernest Mudarri *lawyer*
Haddad, Patricia A. *state legislator*
Hahn, Celia Ferner *state representative, broadcaster*
Haley, Paul Richard *lawyer, state legislator*
Hall, David *law educator, dean, department chairman*
Hall, Henry Lyon, Jr., *lawyer*
Hall, John Emmett *orthopedic surgeon, educator*
Hallagan, Robert E. *management consultant*
Halström, Frederic Norman *lawyer*
Hamersley, Gordon *food service executive*
Hammond, Norman David Curle *archaeology educator, researcher*
Hardy, Victoria Elizabeth *management educator*
Harkins, Lida E. *state legislator, educator*
Harkness, John Cheesman *architect*
Harlow, Edward E., Jr., *oncologist*
Harrington, John Michael, Jr., *lawyer*
Harris, Andrew Michael *director*
Harris, Barbara C(lementine) *bishop*
Harris, Jay Robert *radiation oncologist, educator*
Harris, Roy Jay, Jr., *editor, business journalist*
Harris, Virginia *religious organization administrator, publisher*
Harvey, Mark Sumner *composer, minister, educator, musician*
Haseltine, William Alan *virology educator*
Hawkey, G. Michael *lawyer, real estate investor and developer*
Hawley, Anne *museum director*
Hayes, Andrew Wallace, II, *consumer products company executive*
Hayes, Robert Francis *lawyer*
Hayes, Robert Herrick *technology management educator*
Hayes, Samuel Linton, III, *business educator*
Healey, Kerry Murphy *lieutenant governor*
Healy, Gerald Burke *otolaryngologist*
Hedley-Whyte, Elizabeth Tessa *neuropathologist*
Hedley-Whyte, John *anesthesiologist, educator*
Hedlund, Ronald David *academic administrator, researcher, educator*
Henderson, Jeffrey J. *dean, educator*
Henry, DeWitt Pawling, II, *creative writing educator, writer, arts administrator*
Henry, John W. *professional sports team executive*
Herndon, James Henry *orthopedic surgeon, educator*
Hiatt, Howard H. *physician*
Hickey, Paul Robert *anesthesiologist, educator*
Hieken, Charles *lawyer*
Higgins, Robert Joseph *bank executive*
Hill, Richard Devereux *retired banker*
Hillenbrand, Shea Matthew *professional baseball player*
Hills, Patricia Gorton Schulze *curator*
Hinchey, Edward Thomas *lawyer*
Hintikka, Jaakko *philosopher, educator*
Hochschild, Ann *molecular biologist*
Hoffman, Stanley Marc *editor, composer*
Holland, James R. *real estate company officer*
Hoskins, William Keller *pharmaceutical executive, lawyer, mediator, arbitrator*
Hostetter, Amos Barr, Jr., *cable television executive*
Howlett, D(onald) Roger *art gallery executive, art historian*
Howley, Peter Maxwell *pathology educator*
Hrones, Stephen Baylis *lawyer, educator*
Hu, Jianming *virologist, molecular biologist*
Huang, Thomas Weishing *lawyer*
Hubel, David Hunter *physiologist, science educator*
Hudson, Bradford Taylor *management educator*
Hunter, Durant Adams *executive search company executive*
Hunter, Floyd Dore *lawyer*
Hurd, J. Nicholas *executive recruiting consultant, former banker*
Hutchinson, Bernard Thomas *ophthalmologist*
Hutter, Adolph Matthew, Jr., *cardiologist, educator*
Huvos, Andrew *internist, cardiologist, educator*
Hyland, Barbara Claire *state legislator*
Iezzoni, Lisa I. *medical educator, healthcare educator, researcher*
Infante, Isa Maria *political scientist, educator*
Inman, Jean A. *political party official*
Ireland, Roderick L. *state supreme court justice*
Ives, J. Atwood *financial executive*
Jackson, Ralph T. *architect*
Jacques, Cheryl Ann *state legislator*
Jain, Rakesh K. *chemical engineer, tumor biology educator*
Januzzi, James *cardiologist*
Jehlen, Patricia D. *state legislator*
Jellinek, Michael Steven *psychiatrist, pediatrician*
Jennings, Jon Paul *nonprofit foundation executive*
Jochum, Veronica *pianist*
Johansen, Erling *retired dental educator and dean*
Johnson, Abigail Pierrepont *investment company executive*
Johnson, Edward Crosby, III, (Ned Johnson) *financial company executive*
Johnson, Michael Lewis *psychiatrist*
Jolesz, Ferenc A. *medical association administrator*
Jonas, Richard Andrew *medical educator*
Jonas, Stephen P. *investment company executive*
Jones, Robert Emmet *French language educator, novelist*
Jones, Sheldon Atwell *lawyer*
Jordan, Alexander Joseph, Jr., *lawyer*
Joseph, J. Jonathan *interior designer*
Joyce-Brady, Martin Francis *medical educator, physician, researcher*
Judson, Arnold Sidney *management consultant*
Juusela, Kari Henrik *dean*
Kafker, Frank A. *historian, educator*
Kahn, C. Ronald *research laboratory administrator*
Kalkstein, Joshua Adam *lawyer*
Kalogeras, Alexandros *composer, music educator*
Kamer, Joel Victor *insurance company executive, actuary*
Kaminer, Benjamin *physician, educator*
Kandarian, Susan Christine *medical educator*
Kanin, Dennis Roy *lawyer*
Kanter, Rosabeth Moss *management educator, consultant, writer*
Kaplan, Marshall Myles *medical educator, researcher, gastroenterologist*
Kaplan, Robert Samuel *finance educator*
Kaplan, Steven F. *business management executive*
Kaprielian, Rachel *state legislator*
Karman, James B. *real estate company executive*
Karnovsky, Morris John *pathologist, biologist*
Kasper, Dennis Lee *health facility administrator, educator*
Kasser, James R. *medical educator*
Kassirer, Jerome Paul *medical educator, editor-in-chief*
Kassler, Haskell A. *lawyer*
Katzmann, Gary Stephen *lawyer*
Kauffman, Godfrey *former newspaper publishing executive*
Kavanaugh, James Francis, Jr., *lawyer*
Kazemi, Homayoun *internist, educator*
Kearns, Thomas D. *architect*
Keating, Michael Burns *lawyer, educator*
Keeton, Robert Ernest *federal judge*
Kehoe, William Francis *lawyer*
Keller, Stanley *lawyer*
Kelley, Kevin H. *insurance company executive*
Kelly, Edmund Francis *insurance company executive*
Kelly, Francis J., III, *global marketing company president and COO*
Kelsey, Karl Timothy *medical educator*
Kennedy, Joseph Patrick, II, *utilities executive, former congressman*
Kenny, David *internet professional services executive*
Kessler, Diane Cooksey *religious organization administrator, minister*
Keusch, Gerald Tilden *academic administrator*
Khazanov, Marina Boris *academic administrator, educator*
Kiang, Nelson Yuan-sheng *medical educator*
Kidder, George Howell *lawyer*
Kieff, Elliott Dan *medical educator*
Kilts, James M. *consumer products company executive*
Kimball, George Edward, III, *sports columnist*
Kindregan, Charles Peter *law educator*
King, William Bruce *retired lawyer*
Kirchick, William Dean *lawyer*
Kirkpatrick, Edward Thomson *academic administrator, mechanical engineer*
Kitz, Richard John *anesthesiologist, educator*
Klarfeld, Jonathan Michael *journalism educator*
Kleiner, Fred Scott *art historian, archaeologist, educator, editor*
Klema, Donald David *architect*
Klipp, Todd Lamont Causey *lawyer*
Klotz, Charles Rodger *shipping company and investment company executive*
Knight, Norman *philanthropist, former broadcast executive*
Kocher, Mininder Singh *pediaric orthopaedic surgeon, epidemiologist*
Kominis, Katherine Elizabeth *librarian*
Kopelman, Leonard *lawyer*
Korff, Y. A. *grand rabbi*
Kornberg, Sir Hans Leo *biochemist, educator*
Korsmeyer, Stanley Joel *pathologist, educator*
Koutoujian, Peter John *lawyer*

Smith, Philip Jones *lawyer*
Snydman, David Richard *infectious diseases specialist, educator*
Soden, Richard Allan *lawyer*
Sodroski, Joseph G. *medical educator*
Solet, Maxwell David *lawyer*
Solomon, Caren Grossbard *internist*
Sonenshein, Abraham Lincoln *microbiology educator*
Sonnenschein, Adam *lawyer*
Sonnenschein, David *music educator, composer*
Sosman, Martha B. *state supreme court justice*
Southard, William G. *lawyer*
Southgate, Richard W. *lawyer, director*
Southworth, William Walter *lawyer, title insurance company executive*
Speizer, Frank E. *physician, researcher*
Spelfogel, Scott David *lawyer*
Spellman, Mitchell Wright *surgeon, academic administrator, educator*
Spiess, Gary A. *lawyer*
Spiliotis, Joyce A. *state legislator*
Spilka, Karen *state legislator, lawyer*
Spina, Francis X. *state supreme court judge*
Spooner, John D. *financial planner, writer*
Sprague, Jo Ann *state legislator*
Stachel, John Jay *physicist, researcher*
Stahl, Norman H. *judge*
Stair, Thomas Osborne *physician, educator*
Stallman, Richard Matthew *software developer*
Standard, John Robert *academic administrator*
Stanley, Harriett Lari *state legislator*
Stanley, Harry Eugene *physicist, researcher*
Stearns, Richard Gaylore *judge*
Stefanos, Asgedet *educational consultant*
Steinberg, Laura *lawyer*
Stern, Donald Kenneth *lawyer*
Stevens, Joyce West *social worker, educator, researcher*
Stevens, Marilyn Ruth *editor*
Stevenson, Howard Higginbotham *business educator*
Stobaugh, Robert Blair *business educator, business executive*
Stollar, Bernard David *biochemist, educator*
Storey, James Moorfield *lawyer*
Story, Ellen *state legislator*
Stossel, Thomas Peter *medical educator, medical researcher, director*
Strominger, Jack Leonard *biochemist*
Strothman, Wendy Jo *book publisher*
Sugarman, Paul Ronald *lawyer, educator, academic administrator*
Suit, Herman Day *physician, medical educator*
Sullivan, James Leo *organization executive*
Sullivan, Michael J. *prosecutor*
Sullivan, Mike *professional sports team executive*
Surkin, Elliot Mark *lawyer*
Surman, Owen Stanley *psychiatrist*
Swaim, C. Hall *lawyer*
Swartz, Morton Norman *medical educator*
Swaysland, Janet *advertising executive*
Swope, Jeffrey Peyton *lawyer*
Szostak, Jack William *molecular biologist, educator*
Tabin, Clifford S. *geneticist, educator*
Tang, Yi *radiologist, researcher*
Tappé, Albert Anthony *architect*
Tarantino, Louis Gerald *business executive, consultant, lawyer*
Tashjian, Armen H., Jr., *medical educator*
Tate, Randall J. (Randy Tate) *former congressman*
Taubman, Martin Arnold *immunologist, educator*
Tauro, Joseph Louis *federal judge*
Taylor, Edward Michael *insurance, enterprise risk management consultant*
Taylor, Stephen Emlyn *publishing executive*
Taylor, Thomas William *lawyer*
Taylor, William C. *physician, medical educator*
Taylor, William Osgood *newspaper executive*
Teahan, Kathleen M. *state legislator, educator*
Teich, Jonathan Marc *emergency medicine physician, internist, medical informatics specialist*
Teich, Malvin Carl *electrical engineering educator*
Tempel, Jean Curtin *venture capitalist*
Terrill, Ross Gladwin *writer, educator*
Theoharides, Theoharis Constantin *pharmacologist, physician, educator*
Thibault, George Edwin *medical educator, non-profit healthcare organization administrator*
Thibeault, George Walter *lawyer*
Thomas, Carol Louise Joseph *community planning company executive*
Thornton, Joe *professional hockey player*
Tilney, Nicholas Lechmere *surgery educator*
Tischler, Arthur Steven *pathologist, researcher*
Tocco, Stephen *former airport administrator*
Todaro, Elisabeth M. *lawyer*
Tompkins, Ronald Gary *surgeon, educator, biomedical investigator*
Torkildsen, Peter G. *state agency administrator*
Torruella, Juan R. *federal judge*
Tosteson, Daniel Charles *physiologist, medical school dean emeritus*
Totenberg, Roman *violinist, music educator*
Touster, Saul *law educator*
Towers, John R. *manufacturing executive, lawyer*
Towles, Stokley Porter *commercial and investment banking executive*
Travaglini, Robert E. *state legislator*
Trier, Jerry Steven *gastroenterologist, educator*
Trinkaus-Randall, Gregor *librarian, archivist, preservation administrator*
Trumbull, David Lewis Kitchen *trade association executive*
Tuchmann, Robert *lawyer*
Tucker, Susan Carol *state legislator*
Turner, Raymond Edward *science educator, researcher, administrator*
Twomey, Timothy *architect*
Tyszkowski, Robert *business executive*
Ullian, Elaine S. *health facility administrator*
Upton Puccinelli, Nancy Marie *education educator, researcher*
Urion, David Kimball *pediatric neurologist, researcher, educator*
Vacanti, Joseph Philip *pediatric surgeon, transplant surgeon*
Vachon, Louis *psychiatrist, educator*
Van, Peter *lawyer*
Van Allsburg, Chris *author, artist*
Vance, Verne Widney, Jr., *retired lawyer*
Van Domelen, John Francis *academic administrator*
Van Faasen, William C. *health insurance company executive*
Varney, Robert W. *government agency administrator*
Vatter, Paul August *business administration educator, dean*
Vaughan, Herbert Wiley *retired lawyer*
Vermeule, Cornelius Clarkson, III, *museum curator*
Vermilye, Peter Hoagland *banker*
Vernon, Heidi *international business educator*
Vila, Robert Joseph *television host, designer, real estate developer*
Volpe, Joseph John *pediatric neurologist, educator*
von Fettweis, Yvonne Caché *archivist, historian*
Voss, Peter S. *investment company executive*
Wagle, Udaya *educator*
Waite, Charles Prescott *entrepreneur*
Waksler, Frances Chaput *sociologist, educator*
Walker, Antoine Devon *professional basketball player*
Walrath, Patricia A. *state legislator*
Walsh, Christopher Thomas *biochemist, department chairman*
Walsh, Marian C. *state legislator*
Walsh, Peter L. *arts administrator, writer, consultant, researcher, art critic*
Walters, Robert F. *diversified financial services company executive*
Wang, Jian *physical chemist, researcher*
Warner, Bradford H. *finance company executive*
Warren, Rosanna *poet*
Warshaw, Andrew Louis *surgeon, researcher*
Warth, James Arthur *physician, researcher*
Washburn, Bradford (Henry B. Washburn Jr.) *museum administrator, cartographer, photographer*
Watanabe, Paul Yashihiko *political scientist, educator*
Weaver, Paul David *lawyer*
Weber, Larry *public relations executive*
Wedge, Carole C. *architectural firm executive*
Weinbaum, Paul Owen *historian*
Weinberg, Arnold N. *physician, educator*
Weiner, Stephen Mark *lawyer*
Weinstein, Milton Charles *health policy educator, decision scientist*
Weinstein, Robert *hematologist, researcher*
Weiss, Earle Burton *physician*
Weiss, Phillip Marion *philosopher, educator, head of religious order*
Weitzel, John Patterson *lawyer*
Wellington, Carol Strong *law librarian*
Weltman, David Lee *lawyer*
Wendorf, Richard Harold *library director, scholar*
Wermuth, Paul Charles *retired English educator*
Westling, Jon *university administrator*
Weygand, Bob A. *former congressman*
Wheatland, Richard, II, *fiduciary services executive, museum executive*
Wheeler, W(illiam) Scott *composer, conductor, music educator*
White, George Edward *pedodontist, educator*
White, Jan Tuttle (Mrs. Benjamin Winthrop White) *information technology executive*
White, Morris Francis *biochemistry educator*
Whitlock, John L. *lawyer*
Whittemore, Anthony Dunster *vascular surgeon, chief medical officer*
Whitters, James Payton, III, *lawyer, university administrator*
Whitworth, William A. *magazine editor*
Wiegner, Allen Walter *biomedical engineering educator, researcher*
Wiesel, Elie *writer, educator*
Wiesner, David *illustrator, children's writer*
Wiggleworth, Margaret *property manager*
Wild, Victor Allyn *prosecutor, educator*
Wilkerson, Dianne *state legislator*
Willard, Richard Kennon *lawyer*
Willett, Walter Churchill *epidemiologist, educator*
Williams, David J. *diversified financial services company executive*
Williams Gifford, Susan *state legislator*
Winn, Joseph Lampher *financial officer*
Wiseman, James Richard *classicist, archaeologist, educator*
Woerner, Frederick Frank *international relations educator*
Wolf, Alice K. *state legislator, former mayor*
Wolf, Mark Lawrence *federal judge*
Wood, Peter Wyatt *education educator, writer*
Woodard, Jr., Fredrick James *music educator, musician*
Woodburn, Ralph Robert, Jr., *lawyer*
Woodlock, Douglas Preston *judge*
Woods, Cathi L. *human services administrator*
Wright, Russell D. *electrical utility executive*
Wu, Guofa Felix *computer company executive*
Wu, Tung *curator, art historian, art educator, artist*
Wyszynski, Diego Federico *epidemiologist, educator*
Xi, Hongwei *computer scientist, educator*
Xu, Xiping *adult education educator, director*
Yeager, Peter Cleary *sociologist, educator*
Yerxa, Donald A. *historian, educator, editor*
Young, Anne B. *neurologist, educator*
Young, David William *management educator*
Young, Laura *dance educator, choreographer*
Young, Lucy H.Y. *physician, retina surgeon*
Young, Raymond Henry *lawyer*
Young, William Glover *federal judge*
Yuan, Junying *medical educator, researcher*
Zack, Arnold Marshall *lawyer, mediator, arbitrator*
Zaldastani, Othar *structural engineer*
Zaleznik, Abraham *psychoanalyst, management specialist, educator*
Zambrano, Eduardo Vicente *pathologist, researcher*
Zander, Benjamin *conductor, educator*
Zannieri, Nina *museum director*
Zapol, Warren Myron *anesthesiologist*
Zarins, Bertram *orthopaedic surgeon*
Zawaideh, Samer K. *orthodontist*
Zelen, Marvin *statistics educator*
Zelnick, Carl Robert Robert *writer, educator*
Zervas, Nicholas Themistocles *neurosurgeon*
Zimmerman, George Ogurek *physicist, researcher*
Zinner, Michael Jeffrey *surgeon, educator*
Zobel, Rya Weickert *federal judge*
Zuckerman, Barry *medical educator*
Zungolo, Eileen H. *dean*

Bourne
Fantozzi, Peggy Ryone *geologist, environmental planner*

Boxboro
Berry, Robert John *architect*

Boxford
Yates, John Robert, Jr., *engineer, educator*

Boylston
Hanshaw, James Barry *physician, educator*
Larson, Roland Elmer *healthcare executive*

Braintree
Riccio, Frank Joseph *lawyer, educator*
Robertson, Michael Swing *minister*

Brewster
Adam, John, Jr., *insurance company executive emeritus*
Johnson, Jill Ann *lyricist, actress*

Bridgewater
Cavanaugh, Deborah Jean *mental health services professional*
Heffernan, Peter John *state official*
Jeffries, Frances Moore *academic administrator*
Tinsley, Adrian *college president*

Brighton
Fischer, Irene Kaminka *geodesist, researcher, retired mathematician*
Garber, Paul William *lawyer*
Murphy, William F. *priest, monsignor, religion educator*
O'Malley, Sean Patrick *archbishop*

Brimfield
Curtis, William Edgar *conductor, composer*

Brockton
Carlson, Desiree Anice *pathologist*
Compton, William Thomas *real estate investor*
Holland, David Vernon *minister*
Jellows, Tracy Patrick *application developer*
Lawrence, Janice Elaine *psychiatric and mental health nurse*
Lightford, Melvin *minister*
O'Brien, John Steininger *clinical psychologist*
O'Farrell, Timothy James *psychologist, educator*
Sullivan, Brendan Paul *state official, communications educator*

Brookfield
Anderson, Theodore Robert *physicist, small business owner*
Couture, Ronald David *art administrator, design consultant*

Brookline
Alarcon, Rogelio Alfonso *physician, researcher*
Barron, Ros *artist*
Basu, Soumendra Nath *materials scientist, educator*
Cromwell, Adelaide M. *sociology educator*
Eden, Murray *electrical engineer, emeritus educator*
Ellis, Sharon Henderson *arbitrator, mediator*
Epstein, Alvin *actor, mime, theater director, make-up artist*
Felsen, Leopold B. *engineering educator*
Frankel, Ernst Gabriel *shipping and aviation business executive, educator*
Golden, Herbert Hershel *retired Romance languages educator*
Gurian, Bennett Sheppe *psychiatrist*
Jakab, Irene *psychiatrist*
Jordan, Ruth Ann *physician*
Kay, Reed *artist, educator*
Kliman, Sylvia May Stern *film executive, editor, realtor*
Koretsky, Sidney *internist, educator, paper historian*
Lerman, Herbert S. *lawyer*
Lown, Bernard *cardiologist, educator*
Martel, Lisa *food service executive*
Michopoulos, Aristotle V. *humanities educator, researcher*
Moon, John Ellis van Courtland *retired historian*
Qualls, Roxanne *mayor*
Reedy, Harry Lee *financial services executive*
Rubin-Katz, Barbara *sculptor, human services administrator*
Ruthchild, Rochelle Goldberg *education educator*
Samra, Nicholas James *bishop*
Schwartz, Bernard *physician*
Sho, Jennifer Yu-Fei *music educator, musician*
Skeete, Helen Watkins *minister, counselor*
Swirnoff, Lois *artist, color theorist*
Tyler, H. Richard *physician, educator*
Workman, Jerome James, Jr., *chemist*
Zhang, Xin *science educator*

Brookline Village
Frankenthaler, Stan *food service executive*

Burlington
Barrett, David M. *urologist*
Choi, In-Sup *radiologist*
Coffin, George Jarvis, III, *advertising executive*
DeCrosta, Susan Elyse *graphic designer*
Dyer, Joseph Wendell *retired naval officer*
Freidberg, Stephen Roy *neurosurgeon*
Halvorson, Peter Chase *social studies educator*
Hurd, Joseph Kindall, Jr., *obstetrician, gynecologist*
Jones, Harvey Royden, Jr., *neurologist*
McLellan, Robert *gynecologist, oncologist, educator*
Moschella, Samuel L. *dermatology educator*
Nananukul, Soracha *electrical engineer*
Oberfield, Richard Alan *oncologist*
Reeve, Pamela *communications executive*
Schoetz, David John, Jr., *colon and rectal surgeon, educator*
Sproull, Robert Fletcher *research and development company executive*

Byfield
Kozol, Jonathan *writer*
Yesair, David Wayne *biochemist*

Cambridge
Abelson, Harold *electrical engineer, educator*
Abernathy, Frederick Henry *mechanical engineering educator*
Abrams, Ruth Ida *retired state supreme court justice*
Ackerman, James Sloss *fine arts educator*
Adams, Jody *chef, restaurant owner*
Aitken, Ellen Bradshaw *religious studies educator*
Alberty, Robert Arnold *chemistry professor*
Alcalay, Albert S. *artist, design educator*
Alevizos, Susan Bamberger *lawyer, santouri player, author*
Alevizos, Theodore G. *lawyer, singer, author*
Alt, James Edward *political science educator*
Altshuler, David T. *software company executive*
Amon, Angelika *medical researcher*
Anderson, James Gilbert *chemistry professor*
Anderson, Stanford Owen *architect, architectural historian, educator*
Anderson, William Henry *psychobiologist, educator*
Andrews, William Dorey *law educator, lawyer*
Argon, Ali Suphi *mechanical engineering educator*
Arkani-Hamed, Nima *physicist*
Arkhipova, Irina R. *biologist*
Aronson, Michael Andrew *editor*
Axelrod, Emily H. *urban planner*
Baggeroer, Arthur Bernard *electrical engineering educator*
Bailyn, Bernard *historian, educator*
Bailyn, Lotte *psychology and management educator*
Baird, George *architecture educator*
Bakanowsky, Louis Joseph *visual arts educator, architect, artist*
Bane, Mary Jo *political science educator*
Barger, James Edwin *physicist*
Barnes, Edward Larrabee *architect*
Barnett, David Philip *horticulturist*
Bartee, Thomas Creson *computer scientist, educator*
Bartholet, Elizabeth *law educator*
Bathe, Klaus-Jurgen *mechanical engineering educator, science association director*
Bator, Francis Michel *economist, educator*
Battin, Richard Horace *astronautical engineer*
Batycky, Richard *pharmaceutical executive*
Bazzaz, Fakhri A. *plant biology educator, administrator*
Beckwith, Jonathan Roger *geneticist*
Bedrosian, Edward Robert *investment management company executive*
Beér, János Miklós *engineering educator*
Bellamy, Werten F. W., Jr., *lawyer*
Ben-Akiva, Moshe Emanuel *civil engineering educator*
Benedek, George Bernard *physicist, researcher*
Benedict, Manson *chemical engineer, educator*
Beranek, Leo Leroy *acoustical consultant*
Bercaw, Roy *freelance/self-employed writer*
Berger, Harvey James *pharmaceutical company executive, physician, educator*
Berlowitz, Leslie *cultural organization administrator*
Berndt, Ernst Rudolf *economist, educator*
Berners-Lee, Tim *web inventor*
Biagioli, Mario *history of science educator*
Biemann, Klaus *chemistry professor*
Blackmer, Donald Laurence Morton *political scientist*
Blair, Ann *historian*
Blake, Patricia *writer*
Bloch, Herbert *classicist, medievalist, historian, educator*
Bloomfield, Steven B. *think-tank executive*
Blout, Elkan Rogers *biological chemistry educator, university dean*
Bok, Derek *law educator, former university president*
Bolster, Arthur Stanley, Jr., *history professor*
Boorstein, Beverly Weinger *judge*
Borjas, George J(esus) *economics professor*
Botkin, James W. *leadership and life coach*
Bott, Raoul *mathematician, educator*
Bourneuf, Henri Joseph, Jr., *librarian*
Bradt, Hale Van Dorn *physicist, x-ray astronomer, educator*
Branscomb, Lewis McAdory *physicist, researcher*
Branton, Daniel *biology professor*
Bras, Rafael Luis *engineering educator*
Brenner, Howard *chemical engineering educator*
Broecker, David A. *pharmaceutical executive*
Brown, Robert Arthur *chemical engineering educator*
Bruck, Phoebe Ann Mason *landscape architect*
Brusch, John Lynch *physician, educator, hospital administrator*
Brustein, Robert Sanford *English language educator, theatre director, author*
Buchwald, Jed Zachary *environmental health researcher, science history educator*
Burchfiel, Burrell Clark *geology educator*
Burke, Bernard Flood *physicist, researcher*
Burns, Virginia *social worker*
Bush, Michael *architectural firm executive*
Campbell, Robert *architect, writer*
Canizares, Claude Roger *astrophysicist, educator*
Caramazza, Alfonso *psychology educator*
Carmichael, Alexander Douglas *engineering educator*
Caves, Richard Earl *economist, educator*
Ceyer, Sylvia T. *chemistry professor*
Champion, Hale (Charles Hale Champion) *political science educator, former public official*
Chandler, Fay Martin *artist*
Chandra, Satish *psychologist*
Chen, Lincoln Chin-ho *former medical educator*
Chen, Sow-Hsin *nuclear engineering educator, researcher*
Chiles, Carol S. *architectural firm executive*
Chin, Wayman *musician, educator*
Chisholm, Sallie Watson *biological oceanography educator, researcher*
Chomsky, (Avram) Noam (Avram Chomsky) *linguistics and philosophy educator*
Chow, Shein-Chung *statistician, researcher*
Clark, George Whipple *physics educator*
Clark, Steven Charles *pharmaceutical executive*
Clausen, Wendell Vernon *classics educator*
Clay, Phillip L. *academic administrator*
Cleary, David Michael *composer, critic, library assistant*
Clement McKinley, Sandi *performing arts association administrator, not-for-profit fundraiser*
Clifford, Richard John *religious studies educator*
Clifton, Anne Rutenber *psychotherapist, educator*
Coglianese, Cary *lawyer, educator*
Cohen, Morris *engineering educator*
Cohen, Preston Scott *architecture educator*
Cohen, Robert Edward *chemical engineering educator, consultant*
Cohn, Daniel Ross *physicist*
Cohn, Marjorie Benedict *curator, art historian, educator*
Cole, Heather Ellen *librarian*
Coleman, Sidney Richard *physicist, researcher*
Coles, Robert *child psychiatrist, educator, writer*

Colton, Clark Kenneth chemical engineering educator
Connick, Harry, Jr., musician, actor, vocalist, composer, lyricist
Cooper, Richard Newell economist, educator
Corey, Elias James chemistry professor
Covert, Eugene Edzards aerospace engineer, physics educator
Crandall, Stephen Harry engineering educator
Crawford, Linda Sibery lawyer, educator
Croson, David Carroll finance educator
Cross, Frank Moore, Jr., foreign language educator
Cuomo, Andrew former federal agency administrator
Cutler, David M. finance educator
Dalgarno, Alexander astronomy educator
D'Arbeloff, Alexander V. former electronics company executive
de Marneffe, Barbara Rowe historic preservationist
de Monteiro, Nadsa chef
de Neufville, Richard Lawrence engineering educator
Dennis, Jack Bonnell computer scientist, educator
Dershowitz, Alan Morton lawyer, educator
Deutch, John M. former federal agency administrator, chemistry educator
de Varon, Lorna Cooke choral conductor
Dewart, Christopher architectural educator, furniture maker
Dewey, Clarence Forbes, Jr., engineering educator
DiCamillo, Kate writer
DiGiustini, Antonetta Anna educational association administrator, educator
Dominguez, Jorge Ignacio government educator
Donahue, John David public official, educator
Doty, Paul Mead biochemist, educator, arms control specialist
Dowling, John Elliott biology professor
Downes, Gregory architectural organization executive
Downey, Richard Ralph lawyer, accountant, management consultant
Drake, Elisabeth Mertz chemical engineer, consultant
Dresselhaus, Mildred Spiewak physics and engineering educator
Dudley, Richard Mansfield mathematician, educator
Duffy, Robert Aloysius aeronautical engineer
Dugundji, John aeronautical engineer
Dyck, Martin literary theorist, German literature theorist, mathematics historian
Eagar, Thomas Waddy metallurgist, educator
Eagleson, Peter Sturges civil engineer, environmental engineer, educator
Eckaus, Richard Samuel economist, educator
Edgerly, William Skelton banker
Edley, Christopher F., Jr., law educator
Effron, Seth Alan editor, journalist
Eisen, Herman Nathaniel immunology researcher, medical educator
Eisenberg, Carola psychiatry educator
Ellwood, David Tabor public policy educator
Emanuel, Kerry Andrew academic administrator, meteorologist, oceanographer, educator
Emsley, Sarah Louise Baxter critic, educator
Engell, James Theodore English educator
Epstein, Henry David electronics company executive
Erdely, Stephen Lajos music educator
Erikson, Raymond Leo biology professor
Eurich, Nell P. education educator
Evans, David A(lbert) chemistry educator
Evans, James Brian geophysics educator
Ewing, Scott Edwin physician, psychiatrist, educator, researcher
Fantone, Stephen Dennis electrical engineer
Faust, Drew Gilpin historian, educator
Fay, James Alan mechanical engineering educator
Feininger, Theodore Lux artist
Feld, Michael Stephen physics educator
Feldstein, Martin Stuart economist, educator
Field, George Brooks theoretical astrophysicist
Field, Robert Warren chemistry professor
Fiorenza, Francis P. religion educator
Fischer, Kurt Walter education educator
Fisher, Franklin Marvin economist
Fisher, Roger Dummer lawyer, educator, negotiation expert
Flannery, Susan Marie library administrator
Flaschen, David Jenkin Steward venture capitalist
Fleming, Ronald Lee urban designer, arts administrator, preservation planner, environmental educator
Flemings, Merton Corson engineering educator, materials scientist
Flier, Michael Stephen Slavic languages educator
Fogelson, Robert Michael history educator, writer, consultant
Foner, Simon research physicist
Ford, Patrick Kildea Celtic studies educator
Forman, Richard T. T. ecology educator
Forney, G(eorge) David, Jr., retired electronics company executive
Fox, John Bayley, Jr., university dean
Fox, Maurice Sanford molecular biologist, educator
French, Anthony Philip physicist, educator
French, Kenneth Ronald finance educator
Frey, Frederick August geochemistry researcher, educator
Friedman, Benjamin Morton economics professor
Friedman, Jerome Isaac physics educator, researcher
Friend, Cynthia M. chemist, educator
Frisch, Rose Epstein population sciences researcher
Frug, Gerald E. law educator
Fujimoto, James G. electrical engineering educator
Furman, Thomas D., Jr., engineering company executive
Gagliardi, Ugo Oscar systems software architect, educator
Galbraith, John Kenneth retired economist
Gallager, Robert Gray electrical engineering educator
Gardner, Howard Earl psychologist, educator, writer
Garrelick, Joel Marc acoustical scientist, consultant
Gaskell, Ivan George Alexander De Wend art museum curator
Gatos, Harry Constantine engineering educator
Geller, Margaret Joan astrophysicist, educator
George, Kenneth Martin anthropology educator
Georgi, Howard physics educator
Gerratt, Bradley Scott public administrator
Gibbs, Brian J. behavioral scientist, educator, consultant
Gilbert, Walter molecular biologist, educator
Giles, Robert Hartmann journalist, educator
Gilligan, Carol psychologist, writer
Gingerich, Owen Jay astronomer, educator
Glaser, Victoria Merrylees retired music educator
Gleason, Andrew Mattei retired mathematician, educator
Glendon, Mary Ann law educator
Goell, James Emanuel electronics company executive
Goldberg, Ray Allan agriculturist, educator
Goldin, Claudia Dale economics educator
Goldman, Marshall Irwin economist, educator
Goldstone, Jeffrey physicist, educator
Gomes, Peter John clergyman, educator
Goodman, Ellen Holtz journalist
Graham, Jorie writer, educator
Graham, Loren Raymond historian, educator
Graham, Patricia Albjerg education educator
Gray, Paul Edward academic official
Graybiel, Ann M. medical educator
Green, Richard John architect
Greenberg, Jerry A. information technology executive
Greenblatt, Stephen J. English language educator
Greene, Frederick D., II, chemistry professor
Greenspan, Harvey Philip applied mathematician, educator
Greitzer, Edward Marc aeronautical engineering educator, consultant
Greyser, Linda Lorraine education educator
Grindlay, Jonathan Ellis astrophysics educator
Grosz, Barbara Jean computer science educator
Grove, Timothy Lynn geology educator
Guth, Alan Harvey physicist, researcher
Guthke, Karl Siegfried foreign language educator
Gyftopoulos, Elias Panayiotis mechanical and nuclear engineering educator
Hall, Peter Dobkin historian, educator
Halperin, Bertrand Israel physics educator
Hamner, W. Easley architect
Handford, Martin John illustrator, author
Hansen, Kent Forrest nuclear engineering educator
Hansman, Robert John, Jr., aeronautics and astronautics educator
Harbison, John composer
Harris, Joseph C. education educator
Harris, Wesley L. aeronautical engineer, educator
Hartl, Daniel Lee genetics educator
Hass, Michael Shepherdson architect
Hastings, John Woodland biologist, educator
Hau, Lene physicist, optics scientist
Hauser, John Richard marketing and management science educator
Hausman, Jerry Allen economics educator, consultant
Havens, Leston Laycock psychiatrist, educator
Hax, Arnoldo Cubillos management educator, industrial engineer
Hays, K. Michael architecture educator
Helgason, Sigurdur mathematician, educator
Henrichs, Albert Maximinus classicist, educator
Hersch, Joni economist, educator
Herschbach, Dudley Robert chemistry professor
Herzlinger, Regina economist, educator
Hewitt, Jacqueline N. astronomy educator
Heywood, John Benjamin mechanical engineering educator
Hirsch, Martin Stanley internist, educator, infectious disease physician, reseacher
Hockfield, Susan academic administrator, medical educator
Hoffman, Paul Felix geologist, educator
Hoffmann, Inge Schneier psychologist, educator
Holdren, John Paul energy and resource educator, researcher, author, consultant
Holm, Richard Hadley chemist, educator
Holton, Gerald physicist, science historian
Holtzman, Steven H. pharmaceutical executive
Hopkins, Nancy H. biology professor
Horn, Berthold Klaus Paul computer scientist, engineering educator
Horn, Henry Eyster retired minister
Horvitz, Howard Robert biology professor, researcher
Hostage, John Brayne Arthur law librarian
Houtchens, Robert Austin, Jr., biochemist
How, Hoton electrical engineer
Hoyt, Herbert Austin Aikins television producer
Hu, Haijun atmospheric scientist, electrical engineer
Huang, Cheng-Teh James linguistics educator
Huang, Kerson physics educator
Hubbard, Ruth biology professor
Huchra, John Peter astronomer, educator
Hunt, Swanee G. public policy educator, former ambassador
Hutchison, William Edward, Jr., military officer, aerospace engineer, aerospace scientist
Hynes, Richard Olding biology researcher, educator
Ippen, Erich Peter electrical engineer, educator, physicist
Iriye, Akira historian, educator
Jackiw, Roman physicist, researcher
Jacoby, Henry Donnan economist, educator
Jaenisch, Rudolf biologist, educator
Jaffe, Arthur Michael physicist, mathematician, educator
Jencks, Christopher Sandys public policy educator
John, Richard Rodda transportation executive
Johnson, Howard Wesley former university president, business executive
Johnson, Steve chef, restaurant owner
Johnson, Willard Raymond political science educator, consultant
Jones, Alex S. journalist, writer, broadcaster
Jones, Christopher Prestige classicist, historian
Jones, Mary M. landscape architect
Jorgenson, Dale Weldeau economist, educator
Joskow, Paul Lewis economist, educator
Joss, Paul Christopher astrophysicist, atmospheric physicist, educator
Juma, Calestous international development educator
Kac, Victor G. mathematician, educator
Kagan, Elena law educator
Kagan, Jerome psychologist, educator
Kamentsky, Louis Aaron biophysicist
Kanwisher, Nancy G. neuroscientist
Kaplan, Benjamin judge
Kaplan, Justin author
Kaplow, Louis law educator
Katz, Lawrence Francis economics professor
Kaufman, Andrew Lee law educator
Kaufman, Gordon Dester theology educator
Kaysen, Carl economics professor
Kazhdan, David mathematician, educator
Kazimi, Mujid Suliman nuclear engineer, educator
Keck, James Collyer physicist, researcher
Kellogg, Peter Newman biotechnology company executive
Kelly, John Francis company executive
Kelman, Herbert Chanoch psychology educator
Kelman, Steven Jay management educator
Keniston, Kenneth psychologist, educator
Kennedy, Roger George museum director, park service executive
Kennedy, Stephen Dandridge economist, researcher
Ketchian, Sonia I(sabel) literature educator, researcher
Ketterle, Wolfgang physics educator
Keyfitz, Nathan sociologist, demographer, educator
Keyser, Samuel Jay linguistics educator, university official
Keyssar, Alexander historian, educator
Khakifirooz, Ali information technology researcher
Khorana, Har Gobind chemist, educator
Khoury, Philip S. academic administrator
Kilpatrick, Maureen food service executive
King, Ronold Wyeth Percival physics educator
Kistiakowsky, Vera physics researcher, educator
Kleinman, Arthur Michael medical anthropologist, psychiatrist, educator
Klemperer, William chemistry professor
Knickrehm, Glenn Allen management executive
Knoll, Andrew Herbert T. biology professor
Knowles, Jeremy Randall chemist, educator
Kobus, Richard Lawrence architect, designer, executive, photographer
Kochan, Thomas A. business educator
Koester, Helmut Heinrich history professor
Kosslyn, Stephen M. psychologist educator
Kremer, Michael economist, educator
Krieger, Alex architecture and design educator
Kruger, Kenneth architect
Kurtz, Michael Julian astronomer, computer scientist
Ladd, Charles Cushing, III, civil engineer, educator
Lagace, Paul Alfred college educator
Laiou, Angeliki Evangelos history professor
Lamberg-Karlovsky, Clifford Charles anthropologist, archaeologist
Lanciano, Peter L. pharmaceutical executive
Lander, Eric Steven geneticist, molecular biologist, mathematician, director
Langer, Ellen Jane psychologist, educator, writer, artist
Langer, Robert Samuel chemical, biomedical engineering educator
Langermann, John W. R. financial services company executive
Langmuir, Charles Herbert geology educator
Latanision, Ronald Michael materials science and engineering consultant
Lauzier, Marijean public relations executive
Lenger, John Richard journalism educator
Leonard, Herman Beukema (Dutch Leonard) public finance and management educator
Leonard, James Patrick writer, editor, communications consultant, instructor
Leveson, Nancy G. aeronautical engineer
Levi, Herbert Walter biologist, educator
LeVine, Robert Alan anthropology educator, researcher
Lewis, Henry Rafalsky manufacturing executive
Liau, Gene medical educator
Lieberson, Stanley sociologist, educator
Light, Richard Jay statistician, educator
Lim, Jae Soo engineering educator, information systems
Lindzen, Richard Siegmund meteorologist, educator
Linsky, Marty public policy educator, consultant
Lippard, Stephen James chemist, educator
Lipscomb, William Nunn, Jr., physical chemistry educator
Lipsitt, Don Richard psychiatrist, educator
Lipson, Pamela information scientist
Little, John Dutton Conant management scientist, educator
Livingston, James Duane physicist, researcher
Lomon, Earle Leonard physicist, educator, consultant
London, Irving Myer physician, educator
Low, Francis Eugene physics educator
Lunt, Horace Gray linguist, educator
Lydon, Amanda chef
Lynch, Nancy Ann computer scientist, educator
Lyon, Richard Harold physicist, educator
Maass, Arthur political science and environmental studies educator
Mackey, George Whitelaw mathematician, educator
MacMaster, Robert Ellsworth historian, educator
Magasanik, Boris microbiology educator
Magee, Christopher L. systems engineer
Magnanti, Thomas L. management educator, engineering educator
Maher, Brendan Arnold psychology educator, editor
Maier, Pauline history educator
Malmstad, John Earl Slavic languages and literatures educator
Maniatis, Thomas Peter molecular biology educator
Mankiw, Nicholas Gregory economics professor, federal agency administrator
Mann, Robert Wellesley biomedical engineer, educator
Manzi, Jim P. computer software company executive
Marcus, Richard Sargon research scientist
Marder, William David health economist
Marini, Robert Charles environmental engineering executive
Markey, Winston Roscoe aeronautical engineering educator
Marks, David Hunter civil engineering educator
Marsden, Brian Geoffrey astronomer
Martin, Harry S., III, law educator, law librarian
Martin, Lynn Morley former secretary of labor
Martin, Paul Cecil physicist, researcher
Martino, Donald James composer, clarinetist, educator
Mathews, Joan Helene pediatrician
Matsui, Connie L. pharmaceutical executive
Maxwell, Kenneth Robert historian
Mayr, Ernst retired zoologist, philosopher
Mazur, Barry Charles mathematician
Mazur, Michael artist
McBride, Robert Albert training services executive
McDonald, Christie Anne Romance languages and literature educator, writer
McKenna, Margaret Anne university president
Mc Kie, Todd Stoddard artist
McMullen, Curtis T. mathematics professor
Melton, Douglas A. molecular and cell biology educator
Meng, Xiao-Li statistician
Meselson, Matthew Stanley biochemist, educator
Meyer, John Robert economist, educator
Mickelson, Claudia Ann biosafety officer, scientist
Milgram, Jerome H. marine and ocean engineer, educator
Miller, Arthur Raphael law educator
Miller, Earl K. neuroscientist, educator
Milner, Richard Gerard physicist
Mitchell, William J. academic administrator, architecture educator
Mitten, David Gordon classical archaeologist
Mohamed, Mustafa A. management educator
Molina, Mario Jose physical chemist, educator
Monath, Thomas Patrick physician
Moneo, José Rafael architecture educator
Montana, Enrico Sakai research scientist
Moore, J. Stuart information technology executive
Moore, Mark Harrison criminal justice and public policy educator
Moore, Sally Falk anthropology educator
Moran, James Michael, Jr., astronomer, educator
Mori, Toshiko architecture educator
Moscicki, Richard A. health products executive
Moses, Joel computer scientist, educator
Mosteller, Frederick mathematical statistician, educator
Muldowney, Michael Patrick finance executive
Mullainathan, Sendhil education educator, researcher
Narayan, Ramesh astronomy educator
Narayanamurti, Venkatesh research administrator
Nathanson, Larry medical educator, physician
Nelson, David Robert physics educator
Newell, Reginald Edward physics educator
Nightingale, Deborah Seifert systems engineer, consultant
Nordell, Hans Roderick journalist, retired editor
Nye, Joseph Samuel, Jr., dean, political science educator
Nykrog, Per French literature educator
Obiechina, Emmanuel Nwanonye humanities educator
Oettinger, Anthony Gervin mathematician, educator
Olbert, Stanislaw physicist
O'Neil, Wayne linguist, educator
Oppenheim, Irwin chemical physicist, educator
Orchard, Robert John theater producer, educator
Orlin, James Berger mathematician, management scientist, educator
Oupree, Anderson Hunter historian, educator
Owens, David M. architect
Paicopolos, Ernest Michael public opinion research company executive
Pak, Igor mathematician, educator
Pardue, Mary-Lou biology professor
Patterson, Orlando sociologist
Patton, Bruce M. law educator, management consultant
Paul, William physicist, researcher
Penfield, Paul Livingstone, Jr., electrical engineering educator
Perkins, Dwight Heald economics professor
Pesetsky, David Michael linguist
Petersen, Ulrich geology educator
Pettengill, Gordon H(emenway) physicist, researcher
Pfaltzgraff, Robert Louis, Jr., political scientist, educator
Pfister, Donald Henry biology professor
Pian, Rulan Chao musicologist, scholar
Pian, Theodore Hsueh-Huang engineering educator, consultant
Picardi, Gerard A. publisher
Pierce, Naomi Ellen biology professor, researcher
Pinker, Steven A. cognitive scientist, educator
Pinkham, Daniel composer
Pipes, Richard historian, educator
Pollock, Wilson F. architectural firm executive
Porter, Roger Blaine government official, educator
Porter, William Lyman architect, educator
Poterba, James Michael economist, educator
Pounds, William Frank management educator
Power, Samantha academic administrator, writer
Prinn, Ronald G. atmospheric science educator
Pritchard, David Edward physics educator
Probstein, Ronald Filmore mechanical engineering educator
Quane, James human services administrator
Ramsey, Norman F. physicist, researcher
Rathjens, George William political scientist, educator
Raymo, Maureen Elizabeth geologist, researcher
Redwine, Robert Page physicist, researcher
Reid, Robert Clark chemical engineering educator
Rhoda, Janice Tucker writer, educator, musician
Rice, James Robert engineering scientist, geophysicist
Rich, Alexander molecular biologist, educator
Roazen, Paul writer
Roberts, Edward Baer technology management educator
Roberts, Nancy computer educator
Rockart, John Fralick information systems researcher
Rogers, Peter Phillips environmental engineering educator, city planner
Rogers, Stephen G. biotechnologist
Rogoff, Kenneth Saul economics professor
Roos, Daniel engineering educator
Rose, Robert Michael materials science and engineering educator
Rosenberg, Charles Ernest historian, educator
Rosenbloom, Richard Selig business administration educator
Rosenkrantz, Barbara Gutmann historian of science and medicine
Rosovsky, Henry economist, educator
Rotberg, Robert Irwin historian, political economist, educator, editor
Rowe, Mary P. organizational ombudsman, management educator
Rowe, Peter Grimmond architecture educator, researcher
Rowley, Geoffrey Herbert management consultant
Rubin, Donald Bruce statistician, educator, research company executive
Rubin, Lawrence Gilbert physicist, laboratory manager
Ruggie, John Gerard political science educator, diplomat
Ruina, Jack Philip electrical engineer, educator

Russell, George Allen *composer, theoritician, author, conductor*
Russell, Kenneth Calvin *metallurgical engineer, educator*
Sallee, Marguerite *association executive*
Samson, Leona D. *biological engineering educator, research center director, researcher*
Samuelson, Paul Anthony *economist, educator*
Sander, Frank Ernest Arnold *law educator*
Sapienza, Tony *public relations executive*
Sapolsky, Harvey Morton *political scientist, educator*
Satterfield, Charles Nelson *chemical engineer, educator*
Schauer, Frederick Franklin *law educator*
Schechter, Paul *physicist, educator*
Schlesinger, Chris *food service executive*
Schmalensee, Richard Lee *dean, economist, former government official, educator*
Schodek, Daniel L. *architecture educator*
Schrock, Richard Royce *chemistry educator*
Schuessler Fiorenza, Elisabeth *theology educator*
Sen, Amartya Kumar *economist, educator*
Sevcenko, Ihor *history and literature educator*
Seyferth, Dietmar *chemist, educator*
Shapiro, Irwin Ira *physicist, researcher*
Shieber, Stuart Merrill *natural sciences educator*
Shinagel, Michael *dean, English literature educator*
Shine, Daniel Joseph, Jr., *management consultant*
Shore, Miles Frederick *psychiatrist, educator*
Shubart, Dorothy Louise Tepfer *artist, educator*
Siegel, Abraham J. *economics educator, academic administrator*
Silbey, Robert James *chemistry educator, researcher, consultant*
Simon, Eckehard (Peter) *foreign language educator*
Simons, Thomas W., Jr., *history professor*
Sims, Ezra *composer*
Singer, Irving *philosophy educator*
Singer, Isadore Manuel *mathematician, educator*
Skocpol, Theda Ruth *sociology and political science educator*
Skolnikoff, Eugene B. *political science educator*
Slive, Seymour *museum director, fine arts educator*
Slosburg-Ackerman, Jill Rose *artist, educator*
Smith, Kenneth Alan *chemical engineer, educator*
Smith, Merritt Roe *history professor*
Sollors, Werner *English language, literature and American studies educator*
Solomon, Arthur Kaskel *biophysics educator*
Solow, Robert Merton *economist, educator*
Sortun, Ana *food service executive*
Spaepen, Frans August *applied physics researcher, educator*
Spunt, Shepard Armin *real estate company executive, management and financial consultant*
Staelin, David Hudson *electrical engineering educator, consultant*
Stager, Lawrence E. *archaeologist, educator*
Stanley, Richard P. *mathematics professor*
Stauffer, John William *cultural historian*
Steadman, Stephen Geoffrey *physicist*
Steiner, Henry Jacob *law and human rights educator*
Steinfeld, Jeffrey Irwin *chemistry educator, consultant, writer*
Sterbenz, James Philip Guenther *computer network scientist*
Stevens, Kenneth Noble *electrical engineer, educator*
Stoddard, Roger Eliot *librarian*
Stone, Alan Abraham *law and psychiatry educator, psychiatrist*
Strandberg, Malcom Woodrow Pershing *physicist*
Stubbe, JoAnne *chemistry professor*
Suh, Nam Pyo *mechanical engineering educator*
Summers, Lawrence H. *academic administrator, former government official*
Susskind, Lawrence Elliott *urban and environmental planner, educator, public dispute mediator*
Ta, Tai Van *lawyer, researcher*
Tannenbaum, Steven Robert *toxicologist, chemist*
Tarrant, R(ichard) J(ohn) *classicist, educator*
Temin, Peter *economist, educator*
Termeer, Henricus Adrianus *biotechnology company executive*
Thaddeus, Patrick *physicist, researcher*
Thernstrom, Stephan *historian, educator*
Thiemann, Ronald Frank *dean, religion educator*
Thompson, Doreen *public relations executive*
Thompson, Robert L., Jr., *pharmaceutical executive, lawyer*
Thompson, Samuel G. *artist*
Thompson, William Irwin *educational consultant, writer*
Ting, Samuel Chao Chung *physicist, researcher*
Tinkham, Michael *physicist, researcher*
Tocio, Mary Ann *association executive*
Todreas, Neil Emmanuel *nuclear engineering educator*
Tonegawa, Susumu *biology professor*
Toomre, Alar *applied mathematician, theoretical astronomer*
Torriani-Gorini, Annamaria *microbiologist, educator*
Treitel, Corinna *social studies educator*
Triantafyllou, Michael Stefanos *ocean engineering educator*
Tribe, Laurence Henry *lawyer, educator*
Trilling, Leon *aeronautical engineering educator*
Trumpbour, John *historian, researcher, director*
Tsoi, Edward Tze Ming *architect, interior designer, urban planner*
Tu, Wei-Ming *historian, philosopher, writer*
Tucker, Louis Leonard *retired historical society administrator*
Tuller, Harry Louis *materials science and engineering educator*
Ulrich, Laurel Thatcher *historian, educator*
Ungar, Eric Edward *mechanical engineer*
Urban, Glen L. *management educator*
Urbanowski, Frank *publishing company executive*
Vadhan, Salil Pravin *computer scientist, educator*
Vafa, Cumrun *education educator*
Vagts, Detlev Frederick *law educator*
Valiant, Leslie Gabriel *computer scientist, educator*
Vander Velde, Wallace Earl *aeronautical and astronautical educator*
Vanger, Milton Isadore *history educator*
Vendler, Helen Hennessy *literature educator, poetry critic*
Verba, Sidney *political scientist, educator*
Verdine, Gregory Lawrence *chemist, educator*
Vessot, Robert Frederick Charles *physicist, researcher*
Vigier, François Claude Denis *city planning educator*
Villa-Komaroff, Lydia *molecular biologist, educator, university official*
Vogel, Ezra F. *sociology educator*
von Hippel, Eric Arthur *innovation educator*
von Mehren, Arthur Taylor *lawyer, educator*
Wacker, Warren Ernest Clyde *physician, educator*
Wang, James Chuo *biochemistry and molecular biology educator*
Ware, Susan W. *historian*
Warren, Alvin Clifford, Jr., *lawyer*
Warren, Elizabeth *law educator*
Watson, Rubie *museum director*
Waugh, John Stewart *chemist, educator*
Weiler, Paul Cronin *law educator*
Weinberg, Robert Allan *biochemist, educator*
Weiner, Charles *historian, educator*
Weitzman, Arthur Joshua *English educator*
Westfall, David *lawyer, educator*
Westheimer, Frank Henry *chemist, educator*
White, Alan Frederick *academic administrator*
White, David Calvin *electrical engineer, energy educator, consultant*
White, Jasper *food service executive*
White, John P *federal agency administrator*
Whitesides, George McClelland *chemistry professor*
Whitlock, Charles Preston *former university dean*
Whitman, Robert Van Duyne *civil engineer, educator*
Widnall, Sheila Evans *aeronautical educator, former secretary of the airforce, former university official*
Wilcox, Maud *editor*
Wilczek, Frank Anthony *physics educator*
Williams, James Henry, Jr., *mechanical engineer, educator, consultant*
Williams, Preston Noah *theology educator*
Willie, Charles Vert *sociology educator*
Wilson, Edward Osborne *biologist, educator, writer*
Wilson, Robert Woodrow *radio astronomer*
Wilson, William Julius *sociology educator*
Wodiczko, Krzysztof *artist, architect, educator*
Wood, John Armstead *planetary scientist, geological sciences educator*
Wood, Richard Robinson *real estate company executive*
Wuensch, Bernhardt John *ceramic engineering educator*
Wurtman, Richard Jay *physician, educator, inventor*
Wygza, Michael S. *health care products and services executive*
Xie, Xiaoliang Sunney *chemist, educator*
Yannas, Ioannis Vassilios *polymer scientist, educator*
Yau, Shing-Tung *mathematics professor*
Yergin, Daniel Howard *writer, consultant*
Yip, Winnie *health economics educator*
Young, Laurence R. *biomedical researcher, biomedical engineer, aeronautical engineer, aerospace engineer*
Young, Richard Allen *molecular biologist, educator*
Zeckhauser, Richard Jay *economist, educator*
Zeidenstein, George *population educator*
Zinberg, Dorothy Shore *science policy educator*
Ziolkowski, Jan Michael *medievalist educator*
Zittrain, Jonathan L. *law educator*
Zollar, Alfred *computer company executive*

Canton
Bentas, Lily Haseotes *retail executive*
Bihldorff, John Pearson *hospital director*
Brenner, Harry J. *retail executive*
Costa, Pat Vincent *automation sciences executive*
Fireman, Paul B. *footwear and apparel company executive*
Fuchs, Lawrence Howard *government official, educator*
Kurzman, Stephen Alan *accountant, educator*
Palihnich, Nicholas Joseph, Jr., *retail executive*
Parker, Virginia Marie *English language educator*
Pitts, Virginia M. *human resources executive*
Rankin, James *financial services company executive*
Reichman, Joel H. *retail executive*
Sawtelle, Carl S. *psychiatric social worker*
Watchmaker, Kenneth *retail executive*

Carlisle
Drew, Philip Garfield *retired engineering company executive, consultant*
Fohl, Timothy *consulting and investment company executive*
Hedden, Heather Behn *information specialist*

Carver
Neubauer, Richard A. *library science educator, consultant*

Centerville
Anderson, Gerald Edwin *utilities executive*
Kiernan, Owen Burns *educational consultant*
Scherer, Harold Nicholas, Jr., *electric utility company executive, engineer*
Shapiro, Harvey *journalist, writer, lyricist*

Charlestown
Ackerman, Jerome Leonard *radiology educator*
Brown, Robert Horatio *physician, neuromuscular research scientist*
Bush, Ashley Ian *neuroscientist, psychiatrist*
Cheng, Leo Ling *biophysicist, researcher*
Faustman, Denise L. *immunologist*
Gross, Jerome *physician, biologist, educator*
Hyman, Bradley T. *neurologist, educator*
Isselbacher, Kurt Julius *internist, educator*
Lamont-Havers, Ronald William *physician, research administrator*
Lasko, Natasha B. *psychologist*
Leaf, Alexander *preventive medicine physician, epidemiologist*
Moskowitz, Michael Arthur *neuroscientist, neurologist*
Potts, John Thomas, Jr., *physician, educator*
Tansey, Robert Paul, Sr., *pharmaceutical chemist*
Valera, Eve Marie *neuroscientist*
Wetherell, David S. *communications executive*
Zamecnik, Paul Charles *oncologist, medical research scientist*

Chatham
Bohman, Raynard Frederick, Jr., *transportation consultant, professional association administrator*
Escalante, Judson Robert *business consultant*
Popkin, Alice Brandeis *lawyer*

Chelmsford
Barlas, Julie Sandall *computer scientist, former librarian*
Bright, Willard Mead *manufacturing executive, director*
Fulks, Robert Grady *computer company executive*

Chelsea
Jenkins, Alexander, III, *business executive*
Kaneb, Gary R. *oil industry executive*
Kaneb, John A. *food products executive*
Kuhne, Alice *oil industry executive*

Chestnut Hill
Altbach, Philip *director, educator*
Auld, David Stuart *biochemist, educator*
Ayas, Karen *management consultant, educator*
Bando, Patricia Alice *director*
Barth, John Robert *English educator, priest*
Bartunek, Jean Marie *management educator*
Batchelder, Samuel Lawrence, Jr., *retired corporate lawyer*
Blanchette, Oliva *philosophy educator*
Bresnahan, James Francis *retired medical educator*
Burgess, Ann Wolbert *nursing educator*
Carfora, John Michael *economics educator, academic administrator*
Cohen, David Joel *medical educator*
Dahlben, Salin Abraham *neuropsychiatrist*
Edward, G. Gail *investment company executive, theater operator*
Flax, Martin Howard *pathologist, retired educator*
Fourkas, John T. *chemistry educator*
Gaiser, Ted Joseph *academic administrator, minister*
Goizueta, Roberto Segundo *theology studies educator*
Grossman, Jerome Harvey *medical educator, medical association administrator*
Hawkins, Joellen Margaret Beck *nursing educator*
Helmick, Raymond Glen *priest, educator*
Keating, Patrick J. *academic administrator*
Kosasky, Harold Jack *fertility researcher*
Leahy, William P. *academic administrator, historian, educator*
Mc Innes, William Charles *priest, academic administrator*
Monan, James Donald *university chancellor*
Munro, Barbara Hazard *nursing educator, dean, researcher*
Nemerowicz, Gloria *academic administrator*
O'Block, Robert Paul *management consultant*
Reed, James Eldin *consultant, historian*
Reyes-Cubides, William *language educator, researcher, writer*
Rosensaft, Lester Jay *management consultant, lawyer, consultant*
Safizadeh, M. Hossein *finance educator*
Schildkraut, Joseph Jacob *psychiatrist, educator*
Smith, David Horton *retired social sciences educator*
Stanbury, John Bruton *retired pharmacologist, educator*
Taylor, E. Dennis *English language educator, editor*
Thier, Samuel Osiah *physician, educator*
Ting, Yu-chen *science educator, researcher*
Valette, Jean Paul *writer*
Valette, Rebecca Marianne *Romance languages educator*
Waddock, Sandra *finance educator*
Williamson, John Butler *sociology educator*
Wolfe, Alan *political science educator, writer*
Yavarkovsky, Jerome Harold *library director*

Chicopee
Dame, Catherine Elaine *acupuncturist*
Elleman, Barbara *editor*
Pace, Eston A. *systems administrator*
Stevens, Joyce Ann *author, publisher, writer, speaker*

Chilmark
Lazarus, David *physicist, researcher*
Low, Joseph *artist*

Cohasset
Dickstein, Harvey Leonard *pharmaceutical executive, researcher*
Rabstejnek, George John *photomics executive*
Replogle, David Robert *publishing company executive*

Concord
Andrews, Joseph Lyon, Jr., *medical practitioner, educator, writer*
Bander, Edward Julius *law librarian emeritus, lawyer*
Boger, William Pierce, III, *ophthalmologist*
Codere, Helen Frances *anthropologist, educator, university dean*
Davidson, Frank Paul *retired macroengineer, retired lawyer*
Davies, Michael A. M. *management consultant*
Domar, Carola Rosenthal *social worker*
Emerson, Richard B. *marketing company executive*
Ghosh, Partha S. *management consultant*
Gomberg, Sydelle *dancer educator*
Ihara, Michio *sculptor*
Meistas, Mary Therese *endocrinologist, diabetes researcher*
Melia, Kevin *manufacturing executive*
Olsen, Kenneth Harry *manufacturing executive*
Plummer, William Torsch *optical physicist*
Rathore, Naeem Gul *retired United Nations official*
Schiller, Pieter Jon *venture capital executive*
Smith, Eric Parkman *retired railroad executive*
Smith, Peter Walker *finance executive*
Villers, Philippe *mechanical engineer*
Wang, Arthur Woods *retired publisher*
Weiss, James Michael *financial analyst, portfolio manager*
Wickfield, Eric Nelson *investment company executive*
Woll, Harry J. *electrical engineer*

Cotuit
Ballou, Kenneth Walter *retired business executive, university dean*
Miller, Robert Charles *retired physicist*

Cummington
Bannister, Geoffrey *academic administrator, geographer*
Smith, William Jay *author*

Wilbur, Richard Purdy *writer, educator*

Danvers
Clark, Sharon Jackson *private school administrator*
Dolan, John Ralph *retired corporation executive*
Dunn, Norman Samuel *plastics and textiles company executive*
Lombard, George *electronics company executive*
Shenai, Deodatta Vinayak *chemical engineer*
Waite, Charles Morrison *food company executive*
Wilkes, Brent Ames *management consultant*

Dartmouth
Frothingham, Thomas Eliot *pediatrician*
Notaros, Branislav M. *electrical engineer, educator*

Dedham
Balsamo, Salvatore Anthony *technical and temporary employment companies executive*
DiCamillo, Gary Thomas *manufacturing executive*
Firth, Everett Joseph *timpanist*
Janson, Barbara Jean *publisher*
Magner, Jerome Allen *entertainment company executive*
Redstone, Sumner Murray *entertainment company executive, lawyer*
Spoolstra, Linda Carol *minister, educator, religious organization administrator*

Dennis Port
Singer, Myer R(ichard) *lawyer*

Dighton
Buote, Rosemarie Boschen *retired special education educator*

Dorchester
Baron, Martin *editor*
Berg, John Conrad *political science educator*
Boles, John P. *bishop*
Brelis, Matthew Dean Burns *journalist*
Daniels, Richard J. *communications executive*
Garrison, Althea *government official*

Dover
Aldrich, Frank Nathan *banker*
Bonis, Laszlo Joseph *business executive, scientist*
Buyse, Marylou *pediatrician, geneticist, medical association administrator*
Edwards, Carl Norman *lawyer*
Kim, Ducksoo *radiologist, inventor and educator*
Mehta, Narinder Kumar *marketing executive*
Rankine, V.V. *sculptor, painter*
Salhany, Lucille S. *broadcast executive*

Duxbury
Albritton, William Hoyle *training and consulting executive, lecturer, writer*
Erickson, Phyllis Traver *marketing executive*
Safe, Kenneth Shaw, Jr., *fiduciary firm executive*
Thrasher, Dianne Elizabeth *mathematics educator, computer consultant*
Wangler, William Clarence *retired insurance company executive*
Zachmann, William Francis *computer and communications industry market research company executive*

East Boston
Coy, Craig P. *airport terminal executive*
Patinkin, Terry Allan *physician*

East Bridgewater
Farrell, Sharon Elaine *retired real estate broker*
Heywood, Anne *artist, educator, author*

East Dennis
Ely, David (David E. Lilienthal Jr.) *writer*

East Falmouth
Howard, Louis Norberg *former mathematics educator*

East Orleans
Burkert, Robert Randall *artist*
Romey, William Dowden *geologist, educator*

Easthampton
Perkins, Homer Guy *manufacturing executive*

Easton
Chichetto, James William *editor, educator*

Edgartown
Rosenfeld, Walter David, Jr., *architect, writer*

Fairhaven
Hotchkiss, Henry Washington *real estate broker and financial consultant*
Merolla, Michele Edward *chiropractor, broadcaster*
Rose, Anita Carroll *retired educator*

Fall River
Alam, Akm A. *ceramics engineer*
Liebenow, Larry Albert *federal agency administrator, textile company executive*
Sullivan, Ruth Anne *librarian*
Washburn, Stewart Putnam *management consultant*

Falmouth
Adelman, William J., Jr., *biophysicist*
Funkhouser, John Jeremiah *urologist*
Goody, Richard Mead *geophysicist*
Heisler, Kenneth Avery *surgeon*
Litschgi, Richard John *computer manufacturing company executive*
McInnes, Donald Gordon *railroad executive*
Milkman, Roger Dawson *genetics educator, molecular evolution researcher*
Nolan, Edmund Francis *management consultant*
Sato, Kazuyoshi *pathologist*

Fitchburg
Jareckie, Stephen Barlow *museum curator*
Kemp, Deborah K. *primary school educator*
Lee, Robert Dorwin *retired public affairs educator, administrator*
Mara, Vincent Joseph *college president*
Schilling, Thomas Harold *education educator*

Florence
Park, Beverly Goodman *lawyer*

Platt, Rutherford Hayes *lawyer, educator, geographer, consultant*

Forestdale
Bissell, Phil (Charles P. Bissell) *cartoonist*

Foxboro
Belichick, Bill *professional football coach*
Brady, Tom *professional football player*
Bush, Raymond T. *accountant, architectural firm executive*
Cai, Hongzhi *electrical engineer, researcher*
Dillon, Corey *professional football player*
Harkes, John *professional soccer player*
Imbault, James Joseph *manufacturing executive*
Karelitz, Richard Alan *financial executive, lawyer*
Kennedy, Susan Marie *music educator*
Kraft, Robert K. *professional sports team executive*
Martin, Peter Gerard *marketing infosystems specialist, consultant, secondary school educator*
Pierce, Francis Casimir *civil engineer*
Vinatieri, Adam Matthew *professional football player*

Framingham
Anderson, Basil L. *retail executive*
Aronson, Benjamin *artist*
Austin, Sandra Ikenberry *nursing educator, consultant*
Bilsky, Edward Gerald *clinical social worker*
Bloom, Ted *communications executive*
Bogard, Carole Christine *lyric soprano*
Bose, Amar Gopal *electrical engineering educator*
Campbell, Donald *apparel executive*
Capobianco, Anthony G. *physician*
Carrigan, Robert *technology media company executive*
Crossley, Frank Alphonso *retired metallurgical engineer*
Curry, Thomas Francis *lawyer*
Donovan, R. Michael *management consultant*
Doody, Joseph G. *retail executive*
English, Edmond *retail company executive*
Eykman, Christoph W. *language educator*
Feldberg, Sumner Lee *retired retail company executive*
Feldman, Susan Eleanor *technology analyst*
Goldman, Ralph Frederick *research physiologist, educator*
Harrington, Joseph Francis *educational company executive, history educator*
Heineman, Helen L. *provost*
Hillman, Carol Barbara *communications executive, consultant*
Horn, Bernard *English language educator, writer, translator*
Hoyt, Susan *retail stores executive*
Johnson, Maryfran *editor*
Kendall, Julius *consulting engineer*
Kenealy, Patrick *publishing company executive*
Kennedy, Samantha Ann *special education educator*
Kriegsman, Edward Michael *lawyer*
Lavin, Philip Todd *medical educator, lab administrator*
Lesser, Richard G. *retail apparel company executive*
Levy, Joseph Louis *publishing company executive*
Lindsay, Leslie *packaging engineer*
Lipton, Leah *art historian, educator, museum curator*
Mahoney, John J. *office supply company executive*
McCarthy, Desmond Fergus *English literature educator*
Meltzer, Jay H. *lawyer, retail executive*
Oleskiewicz, Francis Stanley *lawyer, retired insurance executive*
Ostrow, Robert *publishing executive*
Parneros, Demos *retail executive*
Sargent, Ronald L. *retail office and business products executive*
Struyk, Pieter M. *music educator*
Twombly, Stephen Doane *magazine publisher*
Valakis, M. Lois *retired elementary school educator*
VanWoerkom, Jack *retail executive, lawyer*
Vassalluzzo, Joseph S. *retail company executive*
Vermette, Raymond Edward *clinical laboratories administrator*
Vrabel, Joseph P. *lawyer*
Welte, A. Theodore *chamber of commerce executive*
West, Doe *bioethicist, social justice activist, researcher*
Wulf, Sharon Ann *management consultant*
Yonda, Alfred William *mathematician*

Franklin
Maril, David C. *editor*
Rafal, Keith W.L. *physician*

Gardner
Du Buske, Lawrence Michael *immunologist, allergist, rheumatologist*
Hawke, Robert Douglas *retired state legislator*
Koller, John Dryden *media educator, scriptwriter*
Yablonski, Michael Edward *application developer*

Georgetown
Ramseur, T. Michael *social worker*

Gloucester
Baxter, Larry K. *electrical engineer, consultant*
Birchfield, John Kermit, Jr., *lawyer*
Fioravanti, Nancy Eleanor *retired banker*
Hausman, William Ray *fund raising and management consultant*
Knupp, Ralph *information technology executive*
Marolda, Anthony Joseph *management consulting company executive*
McCarl, Henry Newton *economics and geology consultant, venture capitalist*
Means, Rosaline *business executive, business educator*
Sallah, Majeed (Jim Sallah) *retired real estate developer*
Socolow, Arthur Abraham *geologist*
White, Harold Jack *pathologist*

Granville
Fields, Margaret Mary *elementary school educator, paralegal*

Great Barrington
Curtin, Phyllis *music educator, dean, vocalist*
Gilmour, Robert Arthur *foundation executive, educator*
Yanoff, Arthur Samuel *artist, art therapist educator*

Greenfield
Curtiss, Carol Perry *healthcare consultant*
Hutcheson, Thomas Worthington *trade association administrator*
Nix, Michael Charles *musician, educator*

Groton
Anthony, Sylvia *social welfare organization executive*

Groveland
deNapoli, Paul Frederick *investment manager*

Hanover
Garrett, Matthew Langley *music educator*
Lonborg, James Reynold *dentist, former professional baseball player*

Hanscom AFB
Johnson, Charles L., II, *military officer*
Mailloux, Robert Joseph *physicist*
Schmitt, Stephen Richard *electronics engineer*

Hanson
Norris, John Anthony *health products executive, lawyer, educator*

Harwich
Geberth, Frances White *painter*
Steward, Aleta Joanna *fine artist, digital artist*

Harwich Port
Smith, Ralph Wesley, Jr., *retired federal judge*
Staszesky, Francis Myron *independent energy consultant*

Hatfield
Yolen, Jane *author*

Hathorne
McCarthy, Thomas Stephen *manufacturing executive*

Haverhill
Bigelow, Peter *electronics executive*
Korinow, Ira Lee *rabbi*
Walker, Robert Ross *social worker*

Haydenville
Connolly, John Matthew *philosophy educator, administrator*
Shallcross, Doris Jane *creative behavioral educator*

Hingham
Calnan, Arthur Francis *ophthalmologist*
Hart, Richard Nevel, Jr., *financial exective, consultant*
Hedlund, Robert L. *state legislator, automobile executive*
Llewellyn, John Schofield, Jr., *former food company executive*
Macchia, David Alan *management consultant*
Mackiewicz, Theresa Ann *special education educator*

Hinsdale
Rutiger, Paul *lawyer, educator*

Holbrook
Crandlemere, Robert Wayne *engineering executive*

Holden
O'Neil, William Francis *academic administrator*
Price, Robert DeMille *lawyer*

Holland
McGrory, Mary Kathleen *retired academic administrator, humanities educator*

Holliston
Prosser, Robert Arthur *retired research scientist*

Holyoke
Crampton Kamukala, Rebekah Jean *judge, educator*
Radner, Sidney Hollis *retired rug company executive*

Hopkinton
DiDomenico, Angela Terese *industrial engineer, researcher*
Gielo-Perczak, Krystyna *research scientist*
Ruettgers, Michael Cadet *electronics executive*
Teuber, William J, Jr., *corporate financial executive*
Tucci, Joseph M. *computer software and services executive*
Tueber, William *electronics executive*

Housatonic
Charpentier, Gail Wigutow *private school executive director*
Gilder, George Franklin *communications executive, writer*

Hubbardston
Marceau, Judith Marie *retired elementary school educator, small business owner*

Hudson
Osoff, Jeffrey Arlin *media executive*

Hull
Anderson, Timothy Christopher *educational association administrator*

Humarock
Murphy, Ann Marguerite *artist*

Hyannis
Chiotellis, Philip Nicos *cardiologist*
Makkay, Albert *broadcast executive*
Makkay, Maureen Ann *broadcast executive*
Nicholson, Ellen Ellis *clinical social worker*
Segersten, Robert Hagy *lawyer, investment banker*

Hyde Park
Harris, Emily Louise *special education educator*

Indian Orchard
Daley, Veta Adassa *educational administrator*

Ipswich
Barth, Elmer Ernest *wire and cable company executive*
Getchell, Charles Willard, Jr., *lawyer, publisher*
Herrmann, Robert Lawrence *biochemist, educator*
Jennings, Frederic Beach, Jr., *economist, saltwater flyfishing guide*
Munro, Donald William, Jr., *non-profit organization executive*
Wilson, Doris H. *volunteer*

Jamaica Plain
Florio, Christopher John *multimedia producer*
Howland, Llewellyn, III, *publishing executive, writer*
Parris, Thomas Martin *research scientist, consultant*
Pierce, Chester Middlebrook *retired psychiatrist, educator*
Shapiro, Ascher Herman *mechanical engineer, educator, consultant*
Tsuang, Ming Tso *psychiatrist, educator*
Zahn, Carl Frederick *museum publications director, designer, photographer*

Lakeville
Barry, Marilyn White *retired special education educator, dean*

Lawrence
Barbagallo, Joseph C. *small business owner*
Devaney, Robert James, Jr., *environmental engineer*

Leeds
Deane, James Garner *magazine editor, conservationist*
Grenz, Linda L. *Episcopal priest*

Lenox
Coffin, Louis Fussell, Jr., *mechanical engineer*
Newton, Frank George *bank executive*
Pirani, Conrad Levi *pathologist, educator*

Leominster
Cucchiara, Sandra Chiavaras *special education educator*

Lexington
Abeles, James David *manufacturing executive*
Aldrich, Nancy Cook *engineer, administrator*
Aronin, Lewis Richard *metallurgical engineer*
Bailey, Fred Coolidge *retired engineering consulting company executive*
Baron, Sheldon *research and development company executive*
Bernardi, John Lawrence, Jr., *economic historian, educator, consultant*
Berstein, Irving Aaron *biotechnology and medical technology executive*
Beusch, John Ulrich *engineer, researcher*
Bombardieri, Merle Ann *psychotherapist*
Brick, Donald Bernard *software company executive*
Brookner, Eli *electrical engineer*
Buchanan, John Machlin *biochemistry educator*
Burkett, Bradford Charles *lawyer*
Burnham, Daniel Patrick *aerospace transportation executive*
Burwen, Barbara R. *painter*
Bussgang, Julian Jakub *electronics engineer*
Cardwell, Guy Adams *retired language educator*
Champion, Kenneth Stanley Warner *physicist*
Collins, Allan Meakin *cognitive scientist, psychologist, educator*
Davis, Barbara M(ae) *librarian*
Densmore, Ann *speech pathology/audiology services professional, audiologist, writer*
Dietrich, Melinda *visual arts administrator*
Dinneen, Gerald Paul *electrical engineer, former government official*
Dionne, Gerald Francis *research physicist, educator, consultant*
Drouilhet, Paul Raymond, Jr., *science laboratory director, electrical engineer*
Fillios, Louis Charles *retired science educator*
Fray, Lionel Louis *management consultant*
Freed, Charles *engineering consultant, researcher*
Freitag, Wolfgang Martin *librarian, educator*
Frey, John Ward *landscape architect*
Frieden, Bernard Joel *urban studies educator*
Garing, Ione Davis *civic worker*
Gelb, Arthur *electrical and systems engineering executive*
Gibbs, Martin *biologist, educator*
Glaser, Peter Edward *mechanical engineer, consultant, educator*
Goglia, Richard A. *corporate financial executive*
Gutheim, Allen Herman *economist*
Haldeman, Charles Waldo, III, *aeronautical engineer*
Harris, John D., II, *electronics executive*
Hines, Edward Francis, Jr., *lawyer*
Horowitz, Morris A. *retired economics educator*
Hurd, Philip Justin *executive search consultant*
Jordan, Judith Victoria *clinical psychologist, educator*
Kapples, John W. *electronics executive*
Keicher, William Eugene *electrical engineer*
Kelly, Kevin A. *mathematician, educator*
Kennedy, X. J. (Joseph Kennedy) *writer*
Klein, Lawrence Allen *accounting educator*
Lacson, Eduardo K., Jr., *nephrologist*
Li, Tongchuan *pharmacologist, researcher*
Manganello, James Angelo *psychologist*
Marchilena, Frank S. *engineering company executive*
Martinez, David R. *electrical engineer, science educator*
McFarland, Philip James *educator, writer*
McGirr, David William John *pharmaceutical executive*
Morrow, Walter Edwin, Jr., *electrical engineer, university laboratory administrator*
Nash, Leonard Kollender *retired chemistry professor*
Noether, Emiliana Pasca *historian, educator*
O'Connell, Brian Morgan *music educator*
Ott, John Harlow *museum administrator*
Otten, Jeffrey *former hospital administrator*
Paul, Norman Leo *psychiatrist, educator*
Peden, Keith J. *human resources specialist*
Piano, Phyllis J. *communications executive*
Pliner, Edward S. *corporate financial executive*
Rhoads, Rebecca R. *electronics executive*
Ronchi, Donald M. *psychologist, educator*
Schafer, Alice Turner *retired mathematics educator*
Shelton, Gregory S. *electronics executive*
Silverman, Sam Mendel *physicist, lawyer*
Smith, Robert Louis *construction company executive*
Spero, Rand Kevin *management consultant*
Steiner, John William *retired biophysicist*
Swanson, William Henry *equipment manufacturing company executive*
Topalian, Naomi Getsoyan *writer*
Trainor, Bernard Edmund *retired military officer*
Wang, Chi Hua *chemist, education educator*
Washburn, Barbara Polk *cartographer, researcher, explorer*
Williamson, Richard Cardinal *physicist*

Lincoln
Baum, Laura *secondary school educator*
Brandt, John Henry *physician*
Donald, David Herbert *author, history educator*
Elias, Daniel *art gallery owner*
Giles, Allen *pianist, composer, music educator*
Gnichtel, William Van Orden *lawyer*
Green, David Henry *manufacturing executive*
Holberton, Philip Vaughan *entrepreneur, educator, professional speaker*
Kerrebrock, Jack Leo *aeronautics and astronautics engineering educator*
Kusik, Charles Lembit *chemical engineer*
LeGates, John Crews Boulton *information scientist*
Lufkin, Martha B.G. *lawyer, legal writer*
Nenneman, Richard Arthur *retired publishing executive*
Payne, Roger Searle *zoology researcher and administrator, conservationist*
Schwartz, Edward Arthur *lawyer*
Searle, Andrew Barton *fund raising consultant*

Longmeadow
Katz, Barbara Stein *special education educator*
Keady, George Cregan, Jr., *judge*
Leary, Carol Ann *academic administrator*
Lemnios, Andrew Zachery *aerospace engineer, educator, researcher*
Lo Bello, Joseph David *bank executive*
Locklin, Wilbert Edwin *management consultant*
Quinn, Andrew Peter, Jr., *lawyer, insurance executive retired*

Lowell
Aste, Mario Andrea *foreign language educator*
Burke, William Joseph *law educator, lawyer*
Curtis, James Theodore *lawyer*
Donoghue, Eileen M. *former mayor*
Kannenberg, Lloyd Chambers *physicist, researcher*
Karr, Ronald Dale *librarian, historian*
Maille, Brenda Patricia *lawyer*
Martin, William Francis, Jr., *lawyer*
Mercier, Rita *mayor*
Natsios, Nicholas Andrew *retired foreign service officer*
Pike, Jonathan Hamilton *writer*
Pyle, Jean L. *economist, consultant, educator*
Suplinskas, Raymond Joseph *materials scientist*
Sweed, Art *social worker, adult education educator*
Wegman, David Howe *health science educator, consultant*

Ludlow
Budnick, Thomas Peter *social worker*
Szlosek, Elaine Marie (Saloio) *music educator*

Lynn
Astuccio, Sheila Margaret *educational administrator*
Chow, Humphrey Wai *mechanical engineer*
D'Entremont, Edward Joseph *infosystems engineer, educator*
Donovan, Elaine F. *social worker*
Farris, Robert Harold, Jr., *artist, educator*
McManus, Patrick J. *mayor, lawyer, accountant*
Ryder, Edward Francis *secondary school educator*

Lynnfield
Hodgkins, Douglas Wendell *music educator*
Kerrigan, Nancy *professional figure skater, former Olympic athlete*
McGivney, John Joseph *lawyer*

Malden
Guild, Richard Samuel *trade association management company executive*
Jiang, Yong Ping *research scientist*
Kemp, Loretta Christine *human services administrator*

Manchester
Arntsen, Arnt Peter *engineer, consultant*

Marblehead
Heins, Esther *botanical artist, painter*
Page, George Alfred, Jr., *lawyer*
Phillips, Peter Lawrence *communications executive*
Quigley, Stephen Howard *executive editor*
Snow, George Bartlett *city official, accountant*
Speller, Kerstin G. Rinta *psychologist*
Tamaren, Michele Carol *coach, educational consultant, writer, retired special education educator*

Marion
Latham, Christopher Robert *alumni and development director*
McPartland, Patricia Ann *health educator and administrator*
Walsh, William Egan, Jr., *electronics executive*
Worley, Robert William, Jr., *retired lawyer*

Marlborough
Bennett, C. Leonard *electrical engineer*
Birstein, Seymour Joseph *aerospace company executive*
Carter, James W. *electronics executive*
Hunt, Philip Charles *engineer, consultant*
Illson, James Elias *management consultant*
Matera, Richard Ernest *retired minister*
Miotto, Mary Elizabeth G. *pediatrician*
Wheeler, Diana D. *educational consultant*
Wolkovich-Valkavicius, William Lawrence *priest*

Marshfield
Arapoff, John Richard *artist*

Marshfield Hills
Krause, Dorothy Simpson *fine artist*

Marstons Mills
Martin, David Standish *education educator*
Martin, Susan Katherine *librarian*

Mashpee
Payne, Paula Marie *minister*
Porter, John Stephen *retired television executive*

Mattapoisett
Andersen, Laird Bryce *retired university administrator*
Rosenfield, M(anuel) C(harles) *retired history educator, retired coastguard officer*

Maynard
Holway, Ellen Twombly Hay *primary education educator*

Medfield
McQuillen, Jeremiah Joseph *distribution executive*
Phillips, Marion Grumman *writer, civic worker*
Woolston-Catlin, Marian *psychiatrist*

Medford
Abriola, Linda M. *civil engineer, environmental engineer*
Ambady, Nalini *social psychologist, educator, researcher*
Anderson, Thomas Jefferson, Jr., *composer, educator*
Bacow, Lawrence Seldon *academic administrator, environmental educator*
Bedau, Hugo Adam *philosophy educator*
Berman, David *lawyer, poet*
Bernstein, Jane Agar *music educator, writer*
Bosworth, Stephen Warren *dean, former ambassador*
Cavallaro, Mary Caroline *retired physics educator*
Chaturvedi, Pravin R. *pharmaceutical executive*
Ch'en, Li-li *writer, Chinese language, literature and comparative literature educator*
Conklin, John Evan *sociology educator*
DeBold, Joseph Francis *psychology educator*
Dubus, Andre, III, *writer*
Elkind, David *psychology educator*
Fyler, John Morgan *English language educator*
Gasarian, Gerard S. *language educator, writer*
Gittleman, Sol *university official, humanities educator*
Goldberg, Pamela Winer *business professor, director*
Goodwin, Neva R. *economist*
Granott, Nira *psychology researcher*
Greif, Robert *mechanical engineering educator*
Gunther, Leon *physicist, educator*
Howell, Alvin Harold *engineering executive, educator*
Jacob, Robert Joseph Kassel *computer scientist, educator*
Jamshed, Bharucha *academic administrator*
Logan, Bernard J. *obstetrician*
Luria, Zella Hurwitz *psychology educator*
Marcopoulos, George John *history educator*
Miczek, Klaus Alexander *psychology educator*
Nelson, Frederick Carl *mechanical engineering educator*
O'Connell, Brian *community organizer, public administrator, writer, educator*
O'Leary, David *priest, theologian, educator*
Salacuse, Jeswald William *lawyer, educator*
Schneps, Jack *physics educator*
Sloane, Marshall M. *banker*
SSarno, Christopher Ed *writer*
Thompson, David *economist, researcher*
Ueda, Reed Takashi *historian, educator*
Uhlir, Arthur, Jr., *electrical engineer, university administrator*

Medway
Arthur, Wallace *physicist, educator*
Hoag, David Garratt *aerospace engineer*
Saenger, Bruce Walter *consulting firm executive*

Melrose
Brown, Ronald Osborne *telecommunications and computer systems consultant*
Desforges, Jane Fay *retired internist, hematologist, educator*
Hamburger, Ronald Daniel *dermatologist*
McLennan, Bernice Claire *human resources professional*

Methuen
DiFruscia, Anthony R. *lawyer, real estate executive*
McNaughton, William John *retired bishop*
Stanley, (Malchan) Craig *school superintendent, psychologist*

Middleboro
Cacciatore, Sharen Wendy *educational administrator*

Milford
Carson, Charles Henry *microwave engineer*

Milton
Randall, Lilian Maria Charlotte *museum curator*
Warren, John Coolidge *private school administrator, history educator*
Wengler, Marguerite Marie *educational therapist*

Milton Village
Canton, Mamie Ruth *humanities educator*

Monson
Krach, Mitchell Peter *retired financial services executive*

Montague
Kohler, Heinz *economics professor*

Monterey
Frye-Moquin, Marsha Marie *social worker*

Monument Beach
Sullivan, Philip G. *retired obstetrician-gynecologist*

Nantucket
Bartlett, Cheryl Ann *public health service administrator*
Carr, James Revell *museum executive, curator*
Kales, Paul Albert *engineering educator, cartoonist*
Louderback, Peter Darragh *accountant, consultant*
Rorem, Ned *composer, author*
Sangree, Walter Hinchman *social anthropologist, educator*
Schultz, Franklin M. *retired law educator*

Natick
Abele, John E. *medical products executive*
Best, Lawrence C. *medical products executive, manufacturing executive*
Forward, Frank *wholesale distribution executive*
Geller, Esther (Bailey Geller) *artist*
Goglia, Charles A., Jr., *lawyer*
Gottlieb, Michael Norman *internist, educator, health facility administrator*
Grassia, Thomas Charles *lawyer, writer*
Lachica, R(eynato) Victor *microbiologist*
Lebowitz, Charlotte Meyersohn *social worker*
Marr, David E. *lawyer*
Miller, George David *retired military officer, not-for-profit executive*
Myers, Timothy James *chemical engineer, consultant*
Nicholas, Peter M. *medical products executive*
Rendell, Kenneth William *rare and historical documents dealer, consultant*
Sahatjian, Ronald Alexander *science foundation executive*
Sandman, Paul William *lawyer*
Sen, Laura J. *wholesale distribution executive*
Strauss, Harlee Sue *environmental consultant*
Tobin, James Robert *biomedical device manufacturing company executive*
Wedge, Michael T. *wholesale distribution executive*
Zarkin, Herbert J. *retail company executive*

Needham
Bottiglia, William Filbert *humanities educator*
Boulding, Elise Marie *sociologist, educator*
Carr, Iris Constantine *artist, writer*
Cogswell, John Heyland *retired telecommunications industry executive, financial consultant*
Cohen, Lewis Cobrain *security products firm executive*
Cox, Gilbert W., Jr., *lawyer*
Di Domenica, Robert Anthony *musician, composer*
Glaser, Daniel *sociologist, educator*
Grasso, James Anthony *public relations executive, educator*
Greenway, Hugh Davids Scott *journalist*
Holt, Stephen S. *astrophysicist*
Kardon, Brian *music company executive*
Meisner, Mary Jo *editor*
Reed, David Patrick *infosystems specialist*
Rodman, Sumner *insurance company executive*
Ryan, Una Scully *health sciences professional, medical educator*
Walworth, Arthur *author*
Weller, Thomas Huckle *physician, former educator*
Zambone, Alana Maria *special education educator, consultant*

Needham Heights
Hubbell, John Platt *pediatrician, educator*

New Bedford
Buff, Eugene *geneticist, researcher*
Bullard, John Kilburn *educational association administrator*
Cordeiro, Elizabeth Dalein *law enforcement training educator*
Hurwitz, Barrett Alan *lawyer*
Kellaway, Richard Allen *minister, art association administrator*
LaPorte, Adrienne Aroxie *nursing administrator*
Smietana, Walter *educational research director*
Soares, Carl Lionel *quality assurance professional, metrologist*

New Town
Carton, Lonnie Caming *educational psychologist*

Newbury
Ablow, Keith Russell *psychiatrist, journalist, author*

Newburyport
Connolly, James Thomas *lawyer*

Newton
Appleman, Lawrence Joel *lawyer, engineer*
Aronow, Saul *radiological physicist, consultant*
Baron, Charles Hillel *lawyer, educator*
Bassuk, Ellen Linda *psychiatrist*
Benner, Mary Wright *event planner*
Blacher, Richard Stanley *psychiatrist*
Brown, Michael Robert *communications educator, poet*
Chubb, Stephen Darrow *medical corporation executive*
Coquillette, Daniel Robert *lawyer, educator*
Dunlap, William Crawford *physicist*
Fragala, Guy Andrew *safety engineer, educator*
Frankenheim, Samuel *retired lawyer*
Gerrity, J(ames) Frank, II, *building materials company executive*
Glazer, Donald Wayne *lawyer, business executive, educator*
Glick-Weil, Kathy *library director*
Goldweitz, Julie *lawyer*
Gryska, Paul Von Ryll *surgeon*
Harrington, John Leo *former baseball company executive*
Holbik, Karel *economics professor*
Horbaczewski, Henry Zygmunt *lawyer, publishing executive*
Huber, Richard Gregory *lawyer, educator*
Hume, Ellen Hunsberger *media analyst, journalist*
Jeanloz, Roger William *biochemist, educator*
Kenny, Kevin *historian, educator*
Khan, Kay *state legislator*
Knez, Brian J. *publishing executive*
Kosowsky, David I. *retired biotechnical company executive*
Lane, Newton Alexander *retired lawyer*
Li, Fan *pianist, music educator*
Lichtin, Norman Nahum *chemistry professor*
Marshall, Robert Lewis *musicologist, educator*
Matteson, Carol J. *academic administrator*
Meador, Charles Lawrence *management and systems consultant, educator*
Metzer, Patricia Ann *lawyer*
Monaco, Anthony Peter *surgery educator, medical institute administrator*
Nahigian, Robert John *real estate development broker*
Peterson, Osler Leopold *lawyer*
Pill, Cynthia Joan *social worker*
Saffran, Kalman *entrepreneur, venture capitalist*
Sasahara, Arthur Asao *cardiologist, educator, researcher*
Scheffler, Israel *philosopher, educator, education educator*
Sheridan, Thomas Brown *mechanical engineering and applied psychology educator, researcher, consultant*
Tannenwald, Leslie Keiter *rabbi, justice of peace, educational administrator, chaplain*
Teig, Marlowe Gilman *investment banker*
Temkin, Robert Harvey *accountant*
Walker, Paul Howard *retired lawyer*

Newton Center
Cousineau, Madeleine *sociologist, educator*
Garvey, John Hugh *dean, law educator*
Mark, Melvin *consulting mechanical engineer, educator*
Schuller, Gunther Alexander *composer*
Snyder, John Gorvers *lawyer*
Soifer, Aviam *law educator, dean*
Williamson, Susan *mathematician, educator*

Newtonville
Polonsky, Arthur *artist, educator*

North Adams
Cavicchio, Daniel Joseph, Jr., *investment executive*
Cruse, Howard *writer, illustrator*
Howe, Candace Jo-Lynn *writer*
Rodrigues, Raymond Joseph *academic administrator*
Sabot, Richard Henry *economics educator, researcher, investor, entrepreneur*
Thurston, Donald Allen *broadcast executive*

North Amherst
Plaček, Roman *cellist, music educator*

North Andover
Goldstein, Charles Henry *architect, consultant*
Jannini, Ralph Humbert, III, *electronics executive*
Kurzweil, Raymond C. *computer scientist, entrepreneur*
Scully, Stephen J. *plastic surgeon*
Shenai-Khatkhate, Deodatta Vinayak *chemical researcher*
Volpe, Ellen Marie *secondary school educator*
Wessel, Harry *political scientist, educator, director*
Wessler, Stanford *physician, educator*

North Attleboro
Koussa, Harold Alan *insurance account executive*
Reed, Douglas H. *editor, publishing executive*
Zani, Frederick Caesar *retired corporate consultant*

North Billerica
Chu, Jeffrey Chuan *business executive, consultant*
Mellon, Timothy *transportation executive*
Panditi, Surya *electronics executive*

North Chatham
O'Brien, Robert Emmet *insurance company executive*
Wilson, E. B. *business executive, consultant, writer*

North Chelmsford
Erkkila-Ricker, Barbara Howell *writer, photographer*

North Dartmouth
Barrow, Clyde Wayne *political scientist, educator*
Dowd, John Peter *physics educator*
Hegedus, Stephen John *mathematician, educator, researcher*
Khanna, Gaurav *education educator, researcher*
Magrass, Yale Robert *sociology educator, writer*
Noel, Barbara Hughes McMurtry *retired music educator*
Twomey, John Humphrey, Jr., *language educator*
Werly, John McIntyre *retired historian, educator*
Yoken, Mel B(arton) *French language educator, radio commentator, writer*

North Dighton
Silvia, David Alan *insurance broker*

North Easton
Keogh, Martin Jay *dancer, educator*
Paul, Donald W. *audiologist*
Varella, Hazel L. *education educator, historian*
Wolf-Devine, Celia Curtis *philosophy educator*

North Grafton
Kosch, Philip Cobe *dean, veterinary medicine educator*
Schwartz, Anthony *veterinary surgeon, educator*

North Oxford
Carney, Roger Francis Xavier *retired army officer*

North Reading
Day, Ronald Elwin *consulting executive*

Northampton
Bartók-Baratta, Edward *poet, artist*
Christ, Carol Tecla *academic administrator*
Derr, Thomas Sieger *religion educator*
Donfried, Karl Paul *minister, theology educator*
Elkins, Stanley Maurice *historian, educator*
Ellis, Frank Hale *English literature educator*
Fabing, Suzannah *museum director*
Garvey, Richard Conrad *journalist*
Hastings, Wilmot Reed *lawyer, writer*
Knapp, Lucretia A *artist, educator, filmmaker*
Lehmann, Phyllis Williams *archaeologist, educator*
Levy, Ralph Jacob, Jr., *retired theater educator*
Lightburn, Anita Louise *dean, social work educator*
Mahoney, Maureen A. *academic administrator*
Miles, Harry Lehman *lawyer, educator*
Naegele, Philipp Otto *violinist, violist, music educator*
Piccinino, Rocco Michael *librarian*
Rayevsky, Robert *illustrator*
Robinson, John Alan *logic and computer science educator*
Rose, Peter Isaac *sociologist, writer*
Rupp, Sheron Adeline *photographer, educator*
Skarda, Patricia Lyn *English language educator*
Smith, Malcolm Barry Estes *philosophy educator, lawyer*
Snedeker, James Peter *music educator*
Vaget, Hans Rudolf *language professional, educator*
von Klemperer, Klemens *historian, educator*
Wheelock, Donald F. *music educator, composer*
Zimbalist, Andrew S. *economist, educator*

Northborough
Fulmer, Hugh Scott *physician, educator*
Jeas, William C. *aerospace engineering executive, consultant*
Licht, Robert H. *ceramics engineer*

Norton
Crutcher, Ronald Andrew *academic administrator, music educator, musician*
Holden, William *food service executive*
Marshall, Dale Rogers *academic administrator, political scientist, educator*
Nicolas, John Scott (Jack Nicolas) *benefits company executive*
Woods, Susanne *academic administrator, educator*
Worthley, Harold Field *retired minister, educator*

Norwell
Brett, Jan Churchill *illustrator, author*
Case, David Knowlton *management consultant*
Mullare, T(homas) Kenwood, Jr., *lawyer*

Norwood
Berliner, Allen Irwin *dermatologist*
Fishman, Jerald G. *semiconductor executive*
Fuller, Samuel Henry, III, *computer engineer*
Pence, Robert Dudley *biomedical research administrator, hospital administrator*
Reilley, Margaret Randall *secondary school educator*
Sheingold, Daniel H. *electrical engineer*
Singer, Paula Noyes *lawyer, software company executive*

Oak Bluffs
Harris, Margaret T. *school system administrator*
Lamb, Robert *industrial executive*
Schott, John William *psychiatrist*

Onset
Barrs, James Thomas *linguistics educator*

Orange
Rivers, Robert Alfred *microwave company executive*

Orleans
Baird, Julian Thompson, Jr., *art dealer*
Bast, James Louis *retired trade association executive*
Putnam, Allan Ray *association executive*
Rappaport, Margaret M.W.E. *psychologist, physician, writer, pilot, consultant*

Osterville
El-Fayoumy, J. P. Quinn *writer, poet, teacher*
Faris, Stacey Elise *music educator*
Kennedy, Michele Lyn *artist*
Schwarztrauber, Sayre Archie *former naval officer, maritime consultant*
Silk, Alvin John *business educator, management consultant*

Oxford
Schur, Walter Robert *physician*

Palmer
Ferriss, John Alden, III, *medical educator*

Paxton
Clarke, Edward Nielsen *engineering science educator*
Hellman, Daniel Stuart *music educator*

Peabody
Bakrow, William John *college president emeritus*
Bierman, George William *technical consulting executive, food technologist*
Finch, Rogers Burton *association management consultant*
Gordon, Bernard M. *computer company executive*
Lipman, Richard Paul *pediatrician*
Peters, Leo Francis *environmental engineer*

Petersham
Chivian, Eric Seth *psychiatrist, environmental scientist, educator*

Pittsfield
Cornelio, Albert Carmen *insurance executive*
Doyle, Anthony Peter *lawyer*
Fanelli, Robert D. *surgeon*
Fawcett, Gayle P. *bank executive*
Feigenbaum, Armand Vallin *systems engineer, systems equipment executive*
Feldman, Robert J. *retail executive*
Glazer, Michael L. *consumer products company executive*
Green, Nathaniel Kimball *lawyer*
Malkani, Prakash *medical educator, neuroradiologist*
Rich, Philip Dewey *publishing executive*
Shammas, Nazih Kheirallah *environmental engineer, consultant, engineering educator*
Watts, Dennis Lester *retired military officer*
Wenner, Gene Charles *arts management executive*
Wheelock, Kenneth Steven *chemist*

Plymouth
Flood, H(ulda) Gay *editor, consultant*
Freyermuth, Virginia Karen *art educator*
Gregory, Dick *comedian, civil rights activist*
Madonna, Jon C. *accounting firm executive*
Merrill, Vincent Nichols *retired landscape architect*
Paul, Carol Ann *retired academic administrator, biology educator*
Pieters, Richard Sawyer, Jr., *radiation oncologist, educator*

Plympton
Smith, Robert Rutherford *university dean, communication educator*

Provincetown
Cook, Molly Malone *literary agent*

Hutchinson, Peter Arthur *artist*
Oliver, Mary *poet*
Wolfman, Brunetta Reid *education educator*

Quincy
Adams, Ronald G. *middle school educator*
Britt, Margaret Mary *finance educator*
Chisholm, Maureen *academic administrator*
Colgan, Sumner *manufacturing engineer, chemical engineer*
Conley, Olga L. *retail executive*
Cooke, Gordon R. *retail executive*
Cooke, Gordon Richard *retail executive*
Hall, John Raymond, Jr., *fire protection executive*
Hayes, Mary Dianne Wixted *lawyer*
Henck, Anita Fitzgerald *academic administrator, educator*
Holway, David *labor union administrator*
Johnson, Norine Goode *psychologist, educator*
Levin, Robert Joseph *retail grocery chain store executive*
Lippincott, Joseph P. *photojournalist, educator*
Luo, Hong Yuan *biomedical scientist, educator*
McClung, J(ames) David *corporate executive, lawyer, academic administrator*
Moran, James Joseph, Jr., *insurance executive*
Somers, Susan Eileen *business educator*
Spangler, Arthur Stephenson, Jr., *psychologist*
Wilson, Blenda Jacqueline *foundation administrator*
Young, Richard William *corporate director*

Randolph
Boers, Celia Ann *public relations executive*
Cammarata, Richard John *financial advisor*
Huntington, Robert Howard *business management executive*
Johnson, Laurence Michael *lawyer*
Morrissey, Edmond Joseph *classical philologist*
Whitaker, Arthur Luther *retired minister, psychologist*

Reading
Burbank, Nelson Stone *investment banker*
Frey, Joanne Alice Tupper *art educator*
Hambartsoumian, Edouard *obstetrician, researcher, embryologist*
Nordstrand, Nathalie Elizabeth Johnson *artist*
Terilli, Joseph Anthony *secondary school educator*

Rehoboth
Spooner, Russell Edward *retired printing company executive*

Revere
Paananen, Victor Niles *English educator*
Recupero-Faiella, Anna Antonietta *poet*

Rockland
Blethen, Sandra Lee *pediatric endocrinologist*
LaFerney, Michael C. *mental health nurse, mental health counselor*

Rockport
Ambrogi, Robert James *arbitrator*
Calabro, Joanna Joan Sondra *artist*
Gavelis, Jonas Rimvydas *dentist, educator*
Harries, James Theodore *psychologist*
Johnson, Janet Lou *real estate company executive, writer*
Mosher, Donald Allen *artist*
Walen, Harry Leonard *historian, lecturer, author*
Wiberg, Lars-Erik *occupational compatibility consultant*

Roslindale
Driscoll, Kathleen J. *writer*
Sullivan, Dorothy Rona *state official*

Roxbury
Berman, Marlene Oscar *neuropsychologist, educator*
Martinborough, Samuel Neil *music educator, conductor, musician*
Peters, Alan *anatomy educator*
Simons, Elizabeth R(eiman) *biochemist, educator*

Salem
Brown, Walter Redvers John *physicist*
Everitt, Amy Lynn *healthcare educator*
Griffin, Thomas McLean *retired lawyer*
Harrington, Nancy D. *college president*
Hayes, John Charles *lawyer*
Higgins, Gina O'Connell *psychologist, writer*
McLaughlin, Michael Angelo *mortgage consultant, author*
Melby, John B. *composer, educator*
Mendoza, Laurie Parker *social worker*
Moran, Philip David *lawyer*
Reich, Michael Ira *obstetrician/gynecologist*

Salisbury
Berggren, Dick *editor*

Saugus
Austill, Allen *dean emeritus*
Maillet, Martin Joseph, Sr., *retired police captain*

Scituate
Ekstrom, John Edward *mathematician, educator*
Reynolds, Paul Davidson *social sciences educator*
Spangler, Stanley Eugene *international relations educator*

Seekonk
Backes, Joan *artist, educator*

Sharon
Blaszkowsky, David M. *publishing executive*
Reilley, Dennen *research agency administrator, educator*
Wisotsky, Serge Sidorovich *engineering executive*

Sheffield
Baritz, Loren *history professor*
Schmehl Morley, Susan Linda *fine arts educator, artist*
Velmans, Loet Abraham *retired public relations executive*
Young, Susan Babson *retired library director*

Shelburne Falls
Bagg, Robert Ely *poet, educator, translator*
Collard, Roberta R. *emeritus educator, researcher*
Merrill, Deane Whitney, Jr., *secondary school educator, consultant*
Torras, Joseph Hill *pulp and paper company executive*

Sherborn
Cushing, Steven *linguist, educator, writer, researcher, consultant*
Hancock, William Frank, Jr., *management consultant*
Kennedy, Chester Ralph, Jr., *former state official, art director*
Pickhardt, Carl Emile, Jr., *artist*

Shrewsbury
Baguisi, Alexander *embryologist*
Charney, Evan *pediatrician, educator*
Falter, Robert Gary *long-term care administrator, educator*
Fondurulia, Julie A. *computer scientist*
Lucas, Sandra J. *psychologist*
McCluskey, James Francis *music educator, musician*
Nixon, Eugene Ray *chemist, educator*
Onorato, Nicholas Louis *retired program director, economist*

Shutesbury
Abbott, Douglas Eugene *engineering educator*
Creed, Robert Payson, Sr., *retired literature educator*

Siasconset
Albani, Thomas J. *investor*
Emerson, Alice Frey *political scientist, educator emerita*

Somerset
Bower, John *retired fluid mechanics engineer, commissioner*
Manchester, Steven Herbert *writer, educator*

Somerville
Auspitz, Josiah Lee *writer, consultant*
Chambers, Herbert G. *automotive company executive*
Halevi, Marcus *photographer*
Romanoff, Richard Arthur *music educator, musician*
Safdie, Moshe *architect*
Yu, Shan *artist*

South Boston
Burnstein, Daniel *lawyer*

South Dartmouth
Greene, William Caswell *investment company executive*
Ward, Richard Joseph *university dean, educator, author*

South Deerfield
Bete, Channing Lindquist, Jr., *publishing company executive*
Fritz, Nancy H. *educational researcher, administrator*
Waluk, Stanley Peter *corporate engineering official*

South Hadley
Berek, Peter *English educator*
Bergen, Robert Ludlum, Jr., *retired materials scientist*
Bledzki, Leszek Andrzej *limnologist, researcher*
Bowie, Lee *academic administrator, philosopher, educator*
Burns, Michael Thornton *historian, educator, farmer*
Campbell, Mary Kathryn *chemistry professor*
Colino, Richard Ralph *communications consultant*
Creighton, Joanne Vanish *academic administrator*
Farnham, Anthony Edward *English language educator*
Johnson, Richard August *English language educator*
Kaltenbach, Jane Couffer *biology educator*
Leal, Joseph Rogers *chemist*
Mazzocco, Angelo *language educator, cultural historian, linguist*
Shaw, Robert Burns *poet, educator*
Tatum, Beverly Daniel *psychology and education educator*
Townsend, Jane Kaltenbach *biologist, educator*
Viereck, Peter *poet, historian, educator*
Williamson, Kenneth Lee *chemistry professor*

South Hamilton
Ciampa, Roy Emilius *religious studies educator*
Kroeger, Catherine C. *writer, educator, editor*

South Orleans
Hale, Margaret Smith *insurance company executive, educator*

South Wellfleet
Blau, Monte *retired radiology educator*

South Weymouth
Young, Michael Chung-En *allergist, immunologist, pediatrician*

Southampton
Slater, Jess Everett *artist*

Southborough
Madras, Bertha Kalifon *neuroscientist, educator, consultant*
Mylotte, John Arnold *writer, educator*
Noble, Richard Edwards *historian, educator*

Southbridge
Mangion, Richard Michael *health care executive*
Rutanen, Roy Stewart *producer, television personality*

Southfield
Melvin, Ronald McKnight *retired museum director*

Spencer
Goldman, Ethan Harris *finance executive*

Springfield
Agonafer, Mulugeta Gabriel *political scientist, educator*
Baick, John S. *historian, educator*
Burkett, Lawrence V. *insurance company executive, lawyer*
Burkman, Ronald Thomas, Jr., *physician administrator, medical educator*
Caprio, Anthony S. *academic administrator*
Carvalho, Joseph, III, *museum and library executive*
Cohen, Andrew Jay *lawyer*
Cook, Kathryn Anne *secondary school educator*
D'Amour, Donald H. *supermarket chain executive*
Dibble, Francis Daniel, Jr., *lawyer*
Engebretson, Douglas Kenneth *architect, interior designer*
Ervin, Billy Maxwell *management consultant*
Farkas, Paul Stephen *gastroenterologist*
Fein, Sherman Edward *lawyer, psychologist*
Frankel, Kenneth Mark *thoracic surgeon*
Frey, Mary Elizabeth *artist*
Friedmann, Paul *surgeon, educator*
Gallup, John Gardiner *retired paper company executive*
Garabedian-Urbanowski, Martha Ann *foreign language educator*
Goldstein, Anne Brenda *law educator*
Gonzalez De Leon, Fernando *historian, educator*
Gordon, Ronni Anne *journalist*
Gunton, Howard E. *insurance company executive*
Habermehl, Lawrence LeRoy *philosophy educator*
Haggerty, Thomas Francis *newspaper editor*
Johnson, Robert Allison *life insurance company executive*
Kirkwood, John Robert *neuroradiologist*
Kottamasu, Mohan Rao (K.V.R. Mohan Rao) *physician, health facility administrator*
Liptzin, Benjamin *psychiatrist*
Lynn, Morton Daniel *orthopedist*
Maidman, Stephen Paul *lawyer*
Mantoni, Philip Joseph *principal*
Mariani, Marita C. *secondary school educator*
Mazza Moriarty, Rosemarie *municipal official*
McDermott, Larry Arnold *newspaper publisher, newspaper editor*
McDonnell, Timothy Anthony *bishop*
McGee, William Tobin *intensive care physician*
Miller, J(ohn) Wesley, III, *lawyer*
Miller, Leroy Paul, Jr., *secondary English educator*
Modie, Christine M. *insurance company executive*
Morse, John M. *book publishing executive*
Muhlberger, Richard Charles *former museum administrator, writer, educator*
Neiman, Kenneth Paul *judge*
Nicolai, Paul Peter *lawyer*
O'Connell, Robert John *diversified financial services company executive*
Oldershaw, Louis Frederick *retired lawyer*
Petrone, William Francis *pediatrician, microbiologist, corporate executive*
Ponsor, Michael Adrian *federal judge*
Santopietro, Albert Robert *lawyer*
Smist, Julianne Marie *chemist, educator*
Smolowitz, Ira Ephraim *finance educator, academic dean*
Starr, David *newspaper editor, publisher*
Susse, Sandra Slone *lawyer*
Sweeney, Kevin Michael *lawyer*
Utley, F. Knowlton *library director, educator*
Vincensi, Avis A. *sales executive, medical educator*
Weiss, Ronald Phillip *lawyer*

Sterling
Garafalo, Lynne Mary *audiologist, speech and language pathologist*

Stockbridge
Fitzpatrick, Jane *entrepreneur*
Shapiro, Edward Robert *psychiatrist, administrator educator psychoanalyst*
Silverstein, Joseph Harry *conductor, musician*

Stoneham
Adamson, Joyce Roberts *physician*
Igou, Raymond Alvin, Jr., *orthopedic surgeon*
Mc Donald, Andrew Jewett *securities firm executive*

Stonehill College
Conboy, Katie (Sheila C. Conboy) *academic administrator*

Stoughton
Gabovitch, Steven Alan *lawyer, accountant*
Gallant, George William *political scientist*
George, Arthur Charles *lawyer*
Graber, Samuel David *environmental and water resources engineer, consultant*
Schepps, Victoria Hayward *lawyer*
Ural, Erdem A. *engineering executive, educator*

Stow
Golder, Leonard Howard *lawyer, writer*
Langenwalter, Gary Allan *manufacturing and management consulting company executive*
Shrader, William Whitney *radar consulting scientist*

Sturbridge
Belforte, David Arthur *business executive*

Sudbury
Aronson, David *artist, retired art educator*
Deutsch, Marshall E(manuel) *medical products company executive, inventor*
Fowler, Charles Albert *electronics engineer*
Henderson, Ernest, III, *health care executive*
Hillery, Mary Jane Larato *columnist, television personality, television producer, writer, military officer*
McCree, Paul William, Jr., *systems design and engineering company executive*
Meltzer, Donald Richard *treasurer*
Thompson, Mary Lou *elementary school educator*

Swampscott
Kaufman, William Morris *engineer consultant*
Smith, Carl Dean, Jr., *rehabilitation services professional, young adult advocate*
Wolff, Richard Carl *financial planner, insurance agency and pension planning company executive*

Swansea
Curry, Thomas John *academic administrator*
Deston, Albert, III, *musician, educator*
Hjerpe, Edward Alfred, III, *finance and banking executive*

Taunton
Anderson, Peter D. *pharmacist, forensic scientist*
Bornstein, Myer Sidney *gynecologist*
McMullen, John Henry, Jr., *manufacturing company executive, educator*

Tewksbury
Black, Richard Bruce *business executive, consultant*
DeMoulas, Telemachus A. *retail grocery company executive*
Foley, Sylvester Robert, III, *human resources specialist, retired military officer*
Lacourse, Julien *food products executive*
Mulligan, Donald *retail grocery company executive*
Smith, Daniel L. *electronics executive*
Sullivan, D. Harold *retail grocery company executive*

Tiverton
Brock, Dawn Marie *counselor*

Townsend
Thorpe, Samuel Stanley, Jr., *artist*

Truro
Chaplin, Ansel Burt *lawyer*
Friedman, Edward David *lawyer, arbitrator*
Woolley, Catherine (Jane Thayer) *writer*

Vineyard Haven
Jacobs, Gretchen Huntley *psychiatrist*

Waban
Christian, John Thomas *civil engineer*
Hewlett-Kierstead, Nancy Carrick *psychologist, educator*
Portuondo, Jose Francisco *management consultant*
Rogoff, Jerome Howard *psychiatrist, psychoanalyst, forensic expert*
Rossolimo, Alexander Nicholas *management consultant, business executive, corporate director*
Tofias, Allan *accountant*

Wakefield
Brady, Patrick *advertising executive*
Courtenay, Lisa A. *paralegal, foundation administrator*
Fioravanti, Jeff *artist*
Greeno, John Ladd *chemicals executive*
Prabhala, Rao H. *pharmaceutical executive*

Walpole
Coleman, John Joseph *telephone company executive*

Waltham
Ackerman, Robert Wallace *venture management company executive*
Adamian, Gregory Harry *academic administrator*
Altman, Stuart Harold *economist, educator*
Arena, Albert A. *museum director*
Bernstein, Stanley Joseph *manufacturing executive*
Boykan, Martin *composer, music educator*
Brooker, Richard I. *architect*
Brown, Edgar Henry, Jr., *mathematician, educator*
Buchholz, William James *communications executive, educator*
Cantarella, Paolo *former automotive executive*
Chasalow, Eric David *composer, educator*
Cox, Howard Ellis, Jr., *venture capitalist*
Davis, Robert J. *internet company executive*
Dekkers, Marijn E. *electronics executive*
Delaney, Mary Anne *retired theology studies educator*
Deser, Stanley *physicist, researcher*
Dickie, Robert Benjamin *lawyer, consultant, educator*
Domar, Alice Diane *psychologist, educator*
Dulchinos, Peter *lawyer*
Elfers, William *retired investment company director*
Epstein, Irving Robert *chemistry professor*
Farb, Thomas Forest *financial executive*
Floyd, John Taylor *electronics executive*
Foxman, Bruce Mayer *chemist, educator*
Galinat, Walton Clarence *research scientist*
Gittell, Jody Hoffer *finance educator, writer*
Goodheart, Eugene *English language educator*
Guerra, John Michael *optical engineer*
Gumpertz, Werner Herbert *structural engineering company executive*
Hahn, Bessie King *library administrator, lecturer*
Hale, Jane Alison *French and comparative literature educator*
Hansen, Karen Vyonne *sociology educator*
Hayes, Ailish Maire *pediatrician*
Hennessey, Robert John *pharmaceutical company executive*
Hester, Patrick Joseph *lawyer*
Hoogasian, Seth H. *electronics executive, lawyer*
Jackendoff, Ray Saul *linguistics educator*
Jaffe, Adam Benjamin *education educator*
Jones, Jacqueline *historian*
Kasputys, Joseph Edward *finance company executive, economist*
Krauss, Marty Wyngaarden *academic administrator*
Lackner, James Robert *aerospace medicine educator*
Leach, Robert Ellis *orthopedic surgeon, educator, department chair*
Lees, Marjorie Berman *biochemist, neuroscientist*
Lenzen, Glenn Howard, Jr., *lawyer*
Lichtenstein, Stephen David *law educator*
Liu, Huamin Patrick *industrial engineer, researcher*
Mangano, Salvatore Nicholas *surgeon*
McClary, Loretta Mary *accountant*
McCulloch, Rachel *economics researcher, educator*
McManmon, Thomas Arthur, Jr., *oil industry executive*
Mc Menimen, Kathleen Brennan *secondary school educator, consultant*
Melas-Kyriazi, Theo *electronics executive*
Messman, Jack L. *oil executive*
Mitchell, Janet Brew *health services researcher*
Nelson, Arthur Hunt *real estate company executive*
Neumann, Ed *human resource executive*
Notkin, Leonard Sheldon *architect*
O'Connell, Jeanne *financial planner, insurance broker*
Petsko, Gregory Anthony *chemistry and biochemistry scientist educator*
Pocock, J. Michael *consumer products company executive*
Preve, Roberta Jean *librarian, researcher*
Reilly, Philip Raymond *medical research administrator*
Reinharz, Jehuda *academic administrator, history educator*

Roosevelt, James, Jr., *health plan executive, lawyer*
Sarna, Jonathan Daniel *history professor*
Schwartz, Paula Mae *communications company executive*
Schwartz, Steven Mark *marketing executive*
Sekuler, Robert William *psychologist, educator*
Shepard, Donald Sloane *public policy research educator*
Shonkoff, Jack P. *dean, educator*
Slifka, Alfred A. *oil corporation executive*
Snider, Barry B. *organic chemist*
Spoon, Alan Gary *venture capital company executive*
Staves, Susan *English educator*
Stephens, Jay B. *lawyer, manufacturing executive*
Symosek, Peter Frank *research scientist*
Tchaicha, Jane Davagian *education educator, consultant*
Thamhain, Hans Jurgen *management educator*
Turillo, Michael Joseph, Jr., *management consultant*
Wallack, Stanley S. *healthcare administrator*
Wyner, Yehudi *composer, pianist, conductor, educator*
Zebrowitz, Leslie Ann *psychology educator*
Zhabotinsky, Anatol Markovitch *biophysicist, educator*

Watertown
Berk, Harold *dentist, consultant, educator*
Fairbanks, Jonathan Leo *museum curator*
Karaian, Norma Maksoodian *lawyer*
Langstaff, John Meredith *musician*
Lin, Juchui Ray (Ju-Chui Lin) *polymer scientist*
Pellegrom, Daniel Earl *international health and development executive*
Pirolli, John Paul *poet, writer, building materials company executive*
Rivers, Wilga Marie *foreign language educator*
Stoddard, Anne Maher *biostatistician, researcher, educator*

Wayland
Anderson, Monica Luffman *school librarian, educator, real estate broker*
Blair, John *consultant*
Brynjolfsson, Ari *nuclear physicist*
Clark, Melville, Jr., *physicist, electrical engineer*
Dergalis, George *artist, educator*
Huff, William Braid *retired publishing company executive*
Humphrey, Diana Young *fund raiser*
Huygens, Remmert William *architect*
Norris, Melvin *lawyer*
Prabakaran, Daniel *biochemist, researcher*
Puorro, Gerard E. *pharmaceutical executive*

Wellesley
Auerbach, Jerold S. *university educator*
Baker, Charles D. *health insurance company executive*
Bishop, Robert Lyle *economist, educator*
Charpie, Robert Alan *physicist, researcher*
Copplestone, David Wesley *artist, business owner*
Cuba, Lee *dean*
Eilts, Hermann Frederick *international relations educator, former diplomat*
Fuccillo, Ralph *foundation administrator, consultant*
Gailius, Gilbert Keistutis *manufacturing executive*
Giddon, Donald B(ernard) *psychologist, educator*
Heartt, Charlotte Beebe *university official*
Heisler, Elwood Douglas *hotel executive*
Henderson, Mary Louise *civic worker*
Hobbs, Edward Craig *religious studies educator*
Jacobs, Ruth Harriet *poet, playwright, sociologist, gerontologist*
Kato, Walter Yoneo *physicist*
Krieg, Arthur M. *pharmaceutical company executive, internist*
Landaw, Stephen Arthur *physician, educator*
Lloyd-Jones, Sir (Peter) Hugh (Jefferd) *Greek scholar*
Martin, Tony *humanities educator*
Maxwell, J. B. *financial consultant, marketing professional, consultant*
McGibbon, Phyllis Isabel *art educator, artist*
Merguerian, Arshag *architect*
Miller, Linda B. *political scientist*
Mistacco, Vicki E. *foreign language educator*
Mitchell, Donald Wayne *management consultant, investment manager, lawyer, writer*
Montague, Joel Gedney *public health officer*
Morant, Ricardo Bernardino *psychology educator*
Murray, Joseph Edward *retired plastic surgeon*
Myers, Arthur B. *journalist*
Pierce, Donald Shelton *retired orthopedic surgeon, educator*
Piper, Adrian Margaret Smith *philosopher, artist, educator*
Putnam, Ruth Anna *philosopher, educator*
Ragone, David Vincent *former university president*
Sexton, John Joseph *oral and maxillofacial surgeon, educator*
Shea, Megan Carroll *lawyer, law educator*
Silberman, Robert A. S. *lawyer*
Small, Parker Adams, III, *investment banker*
Snitzer, Elias *physicist*
Stettner, Edward A. *political science educator*
Thayer, Gaylord Bertram, Jr., *retired electronics executive*
Tierney, Thomas J. *social entrepreneur*
Twitchell, Thomas Evans *neurologist, educator*
Walsh, Diana Chapman *academic administrator, sociologist, educator*
Weil, Thomas Alexander *electronics engineer, retired*
Wong, Bella Toy Funnd *lawyer*

Wellesley Hills
Clarkson, Cheryl Lee *healthcare executive*
Coco, Samuel Barbin *venture consultant*
Marcus, William Michael *rubber and vinyl products manufacturing company executive*

Wellfleet
Limpitlaw, John Donald *retired publishing executive, clergyman*
Mashberg, Arthur *medical educator*
Mc Feely, William Shield *historian, writer*
Piercy, Marge *poet, writer*

Wenham
Baker, Ruth Holmes *retired secondary education educator*
Beauregard, John *college librarian, consultant*
Johnson, Alan B. *advertising executive*

West Brookfield
Higgins, Brian Alton *art gallery owner, pastel artist*

West Chatham
Rhinesmith, Stephen Headley *management consultant*
Rowley, Glenn Harry *lawyer*

West Falmouth
Bass, Norman Herbert *neurologist, educator, research scientist, hospital adminstrator, healthcare executive, academic administrator*
Carlson, David Bret *lawyer*
Holz, George G., IV, *medical educator, research scientist*
King, Richard Hood *newspaper executive*
Vaccaro, Ralph Francis *marine biologist*

West Hyannisport
Gingold, George Norman *insurance company executive, lawyer*

West Newbury
Dooley, Ann Elizabeth *freelance writers cooperative executive, editor*
Taylor, Bruce Stevenson *architect, planner*

West Newton
Angiolillo, Paul F. *retired language educator*
Porter, Jack Nusan *writer, sociologist, educator, political activist*
Stahl, Marilyn Brown *interior designer*

West Roxbury
Cohen, Carolyn Alta *healthcare educator*
Ellenbogen, George *poet, educator*
Mandell, Marvin *retired humanities educator*
Roach, Maureen S. *primary school educator*
Seltzer, Richard Warren, Jr., *writer, editor, consultant*

West Springfield
Desai, Veena Balvantrai *obstetrician, gynecologist, educator*
Eaton, Danny *theater producer, director*
Ely, John P. *lawyer*
Martorell, Claudia *infectious diseases physician*

Westborough
Antalek, Eileen Elizabeth *educational consultant*
Bok, Joan Toland *utilities executive*
Crosby, Thomas W. *computer scientist*
Gionfriddo, Maurice Paul *aeronautical engineer, research and development company executive*
Horwitz, Eleanor Catherine *information and education official*
Kodenkandath, Thomas A. *research scientist*
Nichols, Guy Warren *retired institute executive, utilities executive*
Rappaport, Jonathan C. *composer, educator, conductor*
Staffier, Pamela Moorman *psychologist*
Tobias, Lester Lee *psychological consultant*
Young, Roger Austin *natural gas distribution company executive*

Westfield
Buckmore, Alvah Clarence, Jr., *computer scientist, ballistician*
Gardner, Thomas Neville *communications educator*
Niles, DeBorah Olive *veteran benefits coordinator*

Westford
Decker, Michael B. *utilities executive*
Endyke, Debra Joan *data communications marketing professional*
Salah, Joseph Elias *research scientist, educator*
Selesky, Donald Bryant *software developer*

Weston
Alcock, George Lewis, Jr., (Peter Alcock) *investor, business strategist*
Barry, William Anthony *priest, writer*
Bateman, Thomas Robert *lawyer*
Berwick, Robert Cregar *computer science educator*
Daly, Charles Ulick *foundation executive*
Fish, David Earl *insurance company executive*
Goldstein, Arthur Louis *retired water purification company executive*
Higgins, Sister Therese *English educator, former college president*
Katz, William Emanuel *retired chemical engineer*
Kim, Young Ho *orthodontist*
Kraft, Gerald *economist*
Lashman, L. Edward *arbitrator, mediator, consultant*
Lin, Alice Lee Lan *physicist, researcher, educator*
Marshall, Jean McElroy *physiologist*
Oates, Mary Josephine *historian, educator*
Oelgeschlager, Guenther Karl *publisher*
Rearick, Anne *photographer, educator*
Sanzone, Donna S. *publishing executive*
Smick, Susan Schnee *manufacturing executive, tile designer, marketing professional*
Stambaugh, Armstrong A., Jr., *restaurant and hotel executive*
Tenney, Sarah G. *music educator*
Thomas, Roger Meriwether *lawyer*
Valente, Louis Patrick (Dan Valente) *business and financial executive*
Wang, Chia Ping *physicist, researcher*
Wood, Jeremy Scott *architect, urban designer*

Westport
Gormley, Robert John *publishing executive*
Nichols, C. Walter, III, *retired trust company executive*
Norcross, Alvin Watt *retired personnel administrator, consultant*

Westport Point
Fanning, William Henry, Jr., *computer specialist*

Westwood
Bier, Louis Henry Gustav *minister*
Bloomingdale, Lewis Morgan *retired psychiatrist*
Borgman, George Allan *journalist*
Daley, Charles Mike *consumer products company executive*
Gillette, Hyde *retired investment banker*
Kushner, Jeffrey L. *manufacturing executive*
Plimpton, Calvin Hastings *physician, university president*
Riley, Henry Charles *banker*

Weymouth
Fitzsimmons, B. Joseph, Jr., *lawyer*
Parks, Kristin M. *pediatrics health nurse, educator and practitioner*

Whitinsville
O'Connell, Roberta M. *realtor*

Wilbraham
Woloshchuk, Candace Dixon *secondary school educator, artist, consultant*

Williamsburg
Healy, Robert Danforth *manufacturing executive*

Williamstown
Blair, Phyllis E. *artist*
Bleezarde, Thomas Warren *retired magazine editor*
Bolton, Roger Edwin *economist, educator*
Chandler, John Wesley *educational consultant*
Conforti, Michael Peter *museum director, art historian*
Crider, Andrew Blake *psychologist*
Dalzell, Robert Fenton, Jr., *historian, educator*
Dew, Charles Burgess *historian, educator*
Driscoll, Genevieve Bosson (Jeanne Bosson Driscoll) *management and organization development consultant*
Eusden, John Dykstra *theology educator, minister*
Fuller, Renee Nuni *psychologist, educational publisher*
Fuqua, Charles John *retired classics educator*
Graver, Lawrence Stanley *English language professional*
Graver, Suzanne Levy *English literature educator*
Hill, Catharine B. *economics professor, provost*
Kassin, Saul *psychology educator*
Lee, Arthur Virgil, III, *biotechnology company executive*
Markgraf, J(ohn) Hodge *chemist, educator*
McGill, Robert Ernest, III, *retired manufacturing company executive*
Oakley, Francis Christopher *history educator, former college president*
Park, David Allen *physicist, researcher*
Pasachoff, Jay Myron *astronomer, educator*
Rudolph, Frederick *history educator*
Schapiro, Morton Owen *university administrator*
Shainman, Irwin *music educator, musician*
Sheahan, John Bernard *economist, educator*
Solomon, Paul Robert *neuropsychologist, educator*
Sprague, John Louis *management consultant*
Stamelman, Richard Howard *French and humanities educator*
Stuebner, Erwin August, Jr., *internist*
Wilkins, Earle Wayne, Jr., *surgery educator emeritus*
Wobus, Reinhard Arthur *geologist, educator*

Wilmington
D'Alene, Alixandria Frances *human resources professional*
Eldada, Louay A. *fiber optic engineer*

Winchendon
Holohan, Jane Patricia *shop owner, writer*

Winchester
Bigelow, Robert P. *lawyer, arbitrator, mediator, journalist*
Blackham, Ann Rosemary (Mrs. J. W. Blackham) *realtor*
Brennan, Francis Patrick *banker*
Dalton, Robert Edgar *retired mathematician, computer scientist*
Ericson, William B. *orthopedic hand surgeon*
Ferrara, Lee *graphics designer, artist, educator*
Ferrera, Arthur Rocco *food distribution company executive*
Hansen, Robert Joseph *civil engineer*
Jackson, Francis Joseph *research and development company executive*
Koppel, Lowell B. *chemical engineer*
Milburn, Richard Henry *physics educator*
Neuman, Robert Sterling *art educator, artist*
Ockerbloom, Richard C. *newspaper executive*
Reno, John F. *foundation administrator*

Windsor
Leaf, Martin Norman *lawyer*

Winthrop
Brown, Patricia Irene *retired law librarian, lawyer*

Woburn
Cox, Terrence Guy *manufacturing automation executive*
Gerson, Samuel J. *apparel executive*
Hill, Stephen A. *research and development company executive*
Lundquist, Eric *editor-in-chief*
Mehra, Raman Kumar *aerospace and defense technology executive, automation and control engineering researcher*
Offermann, Peter *financial executive*
Paul, Lois *public relations company executive*
Potter, Douglas R. *pharmaceutical executive*
Sherwood, Charles H. *pharmaceutical executive*
Zabriskie, John L. *healthcare and agricultural products manufacturing company executive*

Woods Hole
Berggren, William Alfred *geologist, research micropaleontologist, educator*
Cohen, Seymour Stanley *biochemist, educator*
Farrington, John William *academic administrator, dean, research scientist*
Fenwick, Judith L. *oceanographer, researcher*
Gagosian, Robert B. *chemist, educator*
Hart, Stanley Robert *geochemist, educator*
Laster, Leonard *internist, gastroenterologist, academic administrator, educator, writer*
Loewenstein, Werner Randolph *physiologist, biophysicist, educator*
Newman, John Nicholas *naval architect educator*
Prendergast, Robert Anthony *pathologist educator*
Raskin, Fred Charles *transportation and utility holding company executive*
Speck, William T. *former physician, health facility administrator*
Steele, John Hyslop *marine scientist, oceanographic institute administrator*
Uchupi, Elazar *geologist, researcher*
Woodwell, George Masters *ecology research director, lecturer*

Worcester
Ainlay, Stephen Charles *academic administrator*
Angel, David *academic administrator*
Angelini, Michael P. *insurance company executive*
Appelbaum, Paul Stuart *psychiatrist, medical educator, department chairman*
Bagshaw, Joseph Charles *molecular biologist, educator*
Baldiga, Joseph Hilding *lawyer*
Banks, McRae Cave, II, *management educator, consultant*
Bassett, John E. *academic administrator, English educator*
Bennett, Bruce S. *publishing executive*
Bernhard, Jeffrey David *dermatologist, educator*
Bernstein, William Elliott *lawyer*
Billias, George Athan *history educator*
Brooks, John Edward *college president emeritus*
Camougis, George *health, safety and environmental consultant*
Candib, Murray A. *business executive, retail management consultant*
Carney, John F., III, *academic administrator*
Catto, Bonnie A. *classicist, educator*
Clark, William Anthony *religious studies educator*
Clifford, Jay *artist*
Coonan, Cathleen A. *controller, accountant*
Corbin, Frank Wayne *music educator*
Cowan, Fairman Chaffee *lawyer*
Daly, Jennifer *physician*
Davis, Roger J. *medical educator*
Delorey, John Francis *music educator*
Donnelly, James Corcoran, Jr., *lawyer*
Drachman, David Alexander *neurologist*
Dunlap, Ellen S. *library administrator*
Engle, Linda Jane *molecular biologist*
Eppinger, Frederick H., Jr., *finance company executive*
Falco, Richard Gerard *music educator*
Fanale, James E. *geriatrician, educator*
Feener, Donald Edward *lawyer*
Fehribach, Joseph David *mathematician, educator*
Fox, Douglas Lee *lawyer*
Gandhi, Pritesh *medical educator*
Geller, Jeffrey L. *psychiatrist, educator*
Goss, Thomas Pixton *orthopaedic surgeon*
Greenberg, Nathan *accountant*
Hagar, Richard Joseph *music educator, musician*
Harnois, Marion C. *toxicologist, consultant*
Hunt, John David *retired bank executive*
Hunter, Richard Edward *retired physician*
Johnson, Nancy Ann *education educator*
Joshi, Harihar S. *medical laboratory executive*
Katz, Robert Nathan *ceramic engineer, educator*
Kempskie, Jeffrey T. *music educator*
Kennedy, Linda Mann *neuroscience educator, researcher*
Klooster, Willem Wubbo *historian*
Lamothe, Donat Romeo *music educator*
Lanza, Robert Paul *medical scientist*
Lazare, Aaron *dean, psychiatrist*
Ledbetter, Steven *musicologist*
Leonard, Thomas J. *biologist, department chairman*
Levine, Peter Hughes *physician, health facility administrator*
Lidz, Charles Wilmanns *sociologist*
Loew, Franklin Martin *college president, biologist, consultant*
Lougee, David Louis *lawyer*
Malone, Joseph James *mathematics educator, researcher*
Mardilovich, Ivan P *education educator, researcher*
Mathisen, Howard *psychologist, minister*
McCorison, Marcus Allen *librarian, cultural organization administrator*
McFarland, Michael C. *academic administrator*
Mello, Craig C. *molecular medicine educator, researcher*
Mendenhall, Harlan Vincent *research surgeon*
Morse, Leonard J. *epidemiologist, public health service officer*
Moschos, Michael Christos *lawyer*
Murray, Timothy P. *mayor*
Nelson, John Martin *corporate executive*
Palmer, John Anthony, III, *secondary school educator, music educator*
Parham, Valerie deForest Byron *artist*
Parrish, Edward Alton, Jr., *electrical and computer engineering educator, academic administrator*
Parry, Edward Jones, III, *insurance company executive*
Parsons, Edwin Spencer *clergyman, educator*
Pavlik, James William *chemistry professor*
Ravnikar, Veronika A. *reproductive endocrinologist, educator*
Rong, Yiming *manufacturing engineering educator*
Ropp, Paul Stanley *historian*
Ross, Robert Jon Sanford *sociology educator*
Rothschild, Anthony Joseph *psychiatrist*
Santamarina, Rodrigo *surgeon, researcher*
Scanlon, Peter Joseph *priest*
Schmalz, Mathew Nelson *academic administrator*
Selin, Lisa K. *physician*
Shannon, Thomas A. *religious studies educator*
Silver, Marvin S. *lawyer*
Smith, Thomas William *neuropathologist*
Smyrnios, Nicholas A. *physician, educator*
Snyder, L. Michael *hospital administrator*
Spencer, Harry Irving, Jr., *retired bank executive*
Stoff, Jeffrey S. *physician, educator*
Tonkonogy, Joseph Moses *physician, neuropsychiatrist, researcher*
Townes, Philip Leonard *pediatrician, educator*
Turner, Billie Lee, II, *geography educator*
Upshur, Carole Christofk *psychologist, educator*
Van Nostrand, Richard Charles *lawyer*
Vaughan, Alden True *history professor*
Vellaccio, Frank *academic administrator*
Vick, Susan *playwright, educator, director, actress*
Vinciguerra, Salvatore Joseph *scientific instrument company executive*
Welu, James A. *art museum director*
Wilkes, John M. *sociologist*
Zeng, Amy Z. *finance educator, engineering educator*
Zeugner, John Finn *history educator, writer*

Zurier, Robert Burton medical educator, clinical investigator

Worthington
De Mott, Benjamin Haile literature educator, writer
Schrade, Rolande Maxwell Young composer, pianist, educator

Wrentham
Bittenbender, Brad James safety and health engineer
Cohen, Donna Lynn music educator

Yarmouth Port
Darby, Joseph Branch, Jr., retired metallurgist, retired federal agency administrator
Gordon, Benjamin Dichter pediatrician, educator, health facility administrator
LeBaron, Francis Newton biochemistry educator
Mitchell, Garry management consultant, writer
Nichols, Robert Lyman retired foreign service officer, lecturer
Paquin, Thomas Christopher lawyer
Phelps, Judson Hewett health facility administrator, marketing professional
Terrill, Robert Carl hospital administrator

MICHIGAN

Ada
Brenner, David H. marketing executive
Lyall, Lynn consumer products company executive
Mc Callum, Charles Edward lawyer
Van Andel, Jay direct selling company executive
Van Andel, Steve Alan consumer products company executive

Adrian
Caine, Stanley Paul college administrator
Coleman, John Wesley fluid mechanics engineer, heat transfer engineer
Lamprecht, Elizabeth Ann educator
Weathers, Milledge Wright retired economics educator

Albion
Cocks, Geoffrey Campbell history professor
Green, David William chemist, educator
Horstman, Allen law educator
Moore, David Gregory lawyer
Taylor, Lawrence Dow geologist, educator

Algonac
Majewski, Anthony brokerage house executive
Paquet, Gary Lee elementary school educator

Allegan
Drozd, Phyllis Ann agricultural products supplier
Kupstas, Corrine Lynn manufacturing executive

Allen Park
Howard, Desmond Kevin professional football player
Jauron, Dick (Richard M. Jauron) former professional football coach
Kirby, Dorothy Manville social worker
Mariucci, Steve professional football coach, former college coach

Allendale
Baker-Clark, Charles Allen food scientist, educator
Beasecker, Robert Francis librarian, archivist
Blumreich, Kathleen Marie humanities educator
Bullock, Kurt Evan humanities educator
Campbell, Arthur J. music educator
De La Barrera, Carlos Eduardo music educator
Hong, Ran-E literature educator
Jellema, Jon state legislator, educator
Kindschi, P. Douglas dean, educator
Murray, Diane Elizabeth librarian
Osborn, William Palmer writer, English language educator
Reichert, Aviram concert pianist, educator
Vanden Wyngaard, Julianne Marguerite music educator

Alma
Sanders, Jack Ford physician
Swanson, Robert Draper college president
Tracy, Saundra J. academic administrator

Ann Arbor
Abrams, Gerald David physician, educator
Adamson, Thomas Charles, Jr., aerospace engineering educator, consultant
Agno, John G. management consultant
Agranoff, Bernard William biochemist, educator
Aikman, James Whitton composer, music educator
Akerlof, Carl William physics educator
Akil, Huda neuroscientist, educator, researcher
Alfred, Richard Lincoln education educator, educational association administrator, consultant, researcher
Allen, Layman Edward law educator, research scientist
Ansbacher, Rudi physician
Apperson, Jean psychologist
Arlinghaus, Sandra Judith Lach mathematical geographer, educator
Arneson, Wallace Aggergaard, Jr., surgeon
Arvan, Peter endocrinologist, educator
Ash, Major McKinley, Jr., dentist, educator
Ashe, Arthur James, III, chemistry professor
Atreya, Sushil Kumar planetary-space science educator, astrophysicist
Bachelder, Cheryl Anne marketing professional
Bacon, George Edgar pediatrician
Bagian, James Philip former astronaut, public health service officer, medical educator
Bailey, Reeve Maclaren museum curator
Bailey, Richard Weld English language educator
Baker, Laurence Howard oncology educator
Ball, Deborah Loewenberg education educator
Barr, Michael S. law educator
Barsan, William George emergency physician
Bartell, Lawrence Sims chemist, educator
Bartlett, Robert Hawes surgeon
Bashshur, Rashid L. health facility administrator, educator
Beaubien, Anne Kathleen librarian
Beaver, Frank Eugene communication educator, film critic and historian
Becher, William Don retired electrical engineer, engineering educator, writer
Becker, Mark Paul Paul statistics and sociology educator, consultant
Beckley, Robert Mark architect, educator
Bedard, Patrick Joseph editor, writer, consultant
Beeton, Alfred Merle laboratory director, limnologist, biologist, educator, environmentalist
Belcher, Louis David marketing and operations executive, former mayor
Benford, Harry Bell naval architect
Bengtsson, Erling Blöndal classical cellist, educator
Berent, Stanley psychologist, educator, researcher, consultant
Bergstrom, Terry Joseph medical educator, physician
Beutler, Frederick Joseph information scientist
Beutler, Suzanne A. retired secondary school educator, artist
Bilello, John Charles engineering educator, director
Bilyeau, Amy Marie law librarian
Bishop, Elizabeth Shreve psychologist
Bitondo, Domenic engineering executive
Bloom, Jane Maginnis emergency physician
Blouin, Francis Xavier, Jr., history professor
Bodmer, Rolf A. medical educator
Bolcom, William Elden musician, composer, educator, pianist
Bole, Giles G. physician, researcher, medical educator
Borer, Katarina T. exercise endocrinologist
Bornstein, George Jay literary educator
Bowdler, Anthony John physician, educator
Brandon, David A. food service executive/restaurant manager
Britton, Clarold Lawrence lawyer, consultant
Brouhard, Gary John research scientist, web site designer
Browder, Olin Lorraine legal educator
Brown, Donald Robert psychology educator
Brown, William Ernest dentist
Bryant, Barbara Everitt academic researcher, market research consultant, former federal agency administrator
Buesser, Anthony Carpenter lawyer
Burdi, Alphonse Rocco anatomist
Burke, Robert Harry surgeon, educator
Cameron, Oliver Gene psychiatrist, educator, psychobiology researcher
Campbell, John Creighton political science educator
Carlson, Bruce Martin anatomist
Carnahan, Brice chemical engineer, educator
Casey, Kenneth Lyman neurologist
Caveney, William John former pharmaceutical company executive, lawyer
Cerny, Joseph Charles urologist, educator
Chaffin, Don Brian industrial engineering educator, research director
Chang, Chun-Shu historian, educator, writer
Chin, Chen Ooi dean
Cho, Kyung Jae physician, radiologist, educator
Christiansen, Richard Louis orthodontics educator, research director, former dean
Clague, Mark Allan musicologist, bassoonist
Clark, Noreen Morrison behavioral science educator, researcher
Clark, Thomas B., Sr., real estate broker
Clewell, Don B. microbial geneticist, educator
Cochran, Kenneth William toxicologist
Cohen, Malcolm Stuart economist, business executive
Cole, David Edward automotive executive, educator
Converse, Philip Ernest social science educator
Conway, Lynn computer scientist, electrical engineer, educator
Cooper, Edward Hayes lawyer, educator
Copeland, Carolyn Abigail retired dean
Coran, Arnold Gerald pediatrician, surgeon
Coward, James Kenderdine chemist
Cowen, Roy Chadwell, Jr., language educator
Craig, Clifford Lindley orthopaedic pediatric surgery educator
Csere, Csaba magazine editor
Curley, Edwin Munson philosophy educator
Dann, John Christie historian, library director
Davis, Wayne Kay medical educator
Dawson, William Ryan zoology educator
Decaire, John electronics executive, aerospace engineer
Decker, Raymond Frank technology transfer executive, metal products executive, scientist
Dekker, Eugene Earl biochemistry educator
DeVine, Edmond Francis lawyer
Dew, Thomas Edward lawyer
Diana, Joseph A. retired foundation executive
Director, Stephen William electrical and computer engineering educator, academic administrator
Dobranski, Bernard law educator
Dolan, Robert J. dean
Donabedian, Avedis physician, educator
Donahue, Thomas Michael physics educator
Dougherty, Richard Martin library and information science educator
Doyle, Constance Talcott Johnston physician, educator, medical association administrator
Drach, John Charles research scientist, educator
Drake, John Warren aviation consultant
Duderstadt, James Johnson academic administrator, engineering educator
Duff, Michael James physicist
Dumas, Rhetaugh Etheldra Graves university official
Dunlap, Connie librarian
Dunnigan, Brian Leigh military historian, curator
Duquette, Donald Norman law educator
Eagle, Kim Allen cardiologist
Easter, Stephen Sherman, Jr., biology professor
Eberbach, Steven John retired electronics company executive
Eccles, Jacquelynne S. psychology educator
Edwards, Paul N. science educator
Eggertsen, John Hale lawyer
Eisenberg, Marvin Julius art history educator
Eisendrath, Charles Rice journalism educator, farmer, consultant
Eisenstein, Elizabeth Lewisohn historian, educator
Ekotto, Frieda French language and literature professor
Elger, William Robert, Jr., accountant
El-Kattan, Ayman Fawzi pharmacist, researcher
Ellis, Charles Norman professor, researcher
Ellmann, Douglas Stanley lawyer
England, Anthony Wayne engineering educator, dean, educator, science educator
Faeth, Gerard Michael aerospace and mechanical engineering educator, researcher
Fajans, Stefan Stanislaus retired internist
Farrand, William Richard geology educator
Faulkner, John Arthur physiologist, educator
Featherman, David Lee social science research executive
Fekety, Robert physician, educator
Feldman, Eva Lucille neurology educator
Ferrara, James Lawrence Michael medical educator, physician, scientist
Ferrell, Robert Hugh historian, educator
Feuerwerker, Albert history educator
Filisko, Frank Edward physicist, researcher
Fishback, Robert Lawrence retired secondary education educator
Fisk, Lennard Ayres physicist, researcher
Fitzsimmons, Joseph John publishing executive
Fleming, Suzanne Marie academic administrator, freelance/self-employed writer
Flint, H. Howard, II, printing company executive
Forsyth, Ilene Haering art historian
Foster, Alan Herbert financial consultant, educator
Frankena, Karl R. lawyer
Freedman, Ronald sociology educator
Freese, Katherine physicist, researcher
Frey, William H. demographer, educator
Friedmann, Peretz Peter aerospace engineer, educator
Frueh, Bartley Richard surgeon
Fry, Richard E. architectural firm executive
Funk, Sherman Maxwell former government official, writer, consultant
Fusfeld, Daniel Roland economist
Gannon, Michael J. printing company executive
Garbaty, Thomas Jay retired English language educator
Gebarski, Stephen S. neuroradiologist, educator
Gehring, Frederick William mathematician, educator
Gelehrter, Thomas David medical and genetics educator, physician
Gerlitz, Frank Edward engineer
Gibala, Ronald metallurgical engineering educator
Gikas, Paul William medical educator
Gilbert, Elmer Grant aerospace engineering educator, control theorist
Gillespie, R. Brent engineering educator
Gilman, Sid neurologist
Ginsburg, David human genetics educator, researcher
Goldstein, Irwin Joseph medical research executive
Goldstein, Steven Alan medical and engineering educator
Gomberg, Edith S. psychologist, educator
Gomez, Luis Oscar Asian and religious studies educator, clinical psychology educator
Goodenough, Elizabeth Noble literature educator, child advocate
Gordon, Anitra librarian
Greden, John Francis psychiatrist, educator
Greenfield, Lazar John surgeon, educator
Gregerson, Linda Karen poet, language educator, critic
Griffin, Henry Claude chemistry professor
Griffith, John Randall health services administrator, educator
Gruppen, Larry Dale psychologist, educational researcher
Guardo, Carol J. association executive
Gutmann, Myron Peter history educator
Guy, Ralph B., Jr., federal judge
Haddock, Fred(erick) T(heodore), Jr., retired astronomer
Haefner, Don Paul retired psychology educator
Hagel, William Carl metallurgical consultant
Hagen, John William psychology educator
Halter, Jeffrey Brian internal medicine educator, geriatrician
Hartung, Rolf environmental toxicology educator, researcher, consultant
Hawkins, Joseph Elmer, Jr., retired acoustic physiologist, medical educator
Hawthorne, Victor Morrison epidemiologist, educator
Hayes, John Patrick electrical engineering and computer science educator, consultant
Hensinger, Robert Neil orthopedist
Hertz, Dawn Leslie lawyer
Herzig, David Jacob retired pharmaceutical company executive, consultant
Hessler, David William information and multimedia systems educator
Heydon, Peter Northrup farmer, educator, philanthropist
Hill, Bruce Marvin statistician, scientist, educator
Hinshaw, Ada Sue dean, nursing educator
Hiss, Roland Graham internist, educator
Hoff, Julian Theodore neurosurgeon, educator
Hollenberg, Paul Frederick pharmacology educator
Horowitz, Samuel Boris biomedical researcher, educational consultant
House, James Stephen sociological social psychologist, educator
Howrey, Eugene Philip economics educator, consultant
Humes, H(arvey) David nephrologist, educator
Inglehart, Ronald Franklin political science educator
Izzo, Herbert John language and linguistics educator, researcher
Jackson, James Sidney psychology educator
Janko, Richard Charles Murray humanities educator
Jiang, Wenhui materials scientist
Johnson, Neil Monroe test engineer
Johnson, Timothy R. B. obstetrician, gynecologist, educator
Johnston, Lloyd Douglas social scientist
Jones, Lawrence William retired educator, physicist
Joscelyn, Kent B(uckley) lawyer
Josefowicz, Gregory P. retail executive
Julius, Stevo internist, physiologist, educator
Kahn, Douglas Allen legal educator
Kahn, Robert L(ouis) psychologist, educator
Kalbfleisch, John David statistics educator
Kamisar, Yale lawyer, educator
Kaplan, George A. medical educator
Kaufman, Peter Bishop biological sciences educator
Kelch, Robert Paul former dean, pediatric endocrinologist
Kendall, Kay Lynn interior designer, consultant
Kennedy, David Boyd foundation executive, lawyer
Kenyon, George Lommel pharmaceutical educator, dean
Kesler, Stephen Edward economic geology educator
Ketefian, Shaké nursing educator
Killeen, Timothy L. aerospace scientist, research administrator
Kim, E. Han finance and business administration educator
Kingdon, John Wells political science educator
Kmenta, Jan economics professor
Knott, John Ray, Jr., language professional, educator
Koc, Muammer engineering educator, researcher
Korsyn, Kevin Ernest music educator
Kostyo, Jack Lawrence physiology educator
Kothary, Piyush C. research scientist
Kozma, Adam electrical engineer
Krier, James Edward law educator, writer
Krisch, Alan David physics educator
Kuhl, David Edmund physician, nuclear medicine educator
Kunkel, Steven pathologist, educator
La Du, Bert Nichols, Jr., pharmacology educator, physician
La Fountain-Stokes, Lawrence M. education educator
Lawrence, Merle medical educator
Leabo, Dick A. retired statistics educator
Leary, Margaret law librarian, library director
Leith, Emmett Norman electrical engineer, educator
Lempert, Richard Owen lawyer, educator
Lewis, Robert Enzer lexicographer, educator
Lichter, Allen S. oncology educator, university dean
Lichter, Paul Richard ophthalmology educator
Lightfoot, Albert J. clergyman
Linderman, Gerald Floyd retired historian
Lindsay, June Campbell McKee communications executive
Ling, Song research scientist
Lockwood, Dean H. physician, pharmaceutical executive
Lomax, Margaret Irene molecular biologist
Lopatin, Dennis Edward immunologist, educator
Lowe, John Burton molecular biologist, educator, pathologist
Lowenstein, Joan Holly lawyer
Ludwig, Martha biochemist, educator
Lupia, Arthur W. political science educator
Lusk, Sally L. medical educator
Lyons, Harvey Isaac mechanical engineering educator
MacDonald, Michael Patrick humanities educator
MacKinnon, Catharine Alice lawyer, law educator, legal scholar, writer
Manis, Melvin psychologist, educator
Margolis, Philip Marcus psychiatrist, educator
Markel, Howard medical educator
Markman, Jon business journalist
Markovits, Andrei Steven political science educator
Martin, Bruce James newspaper editor
Martin, Claude Raymond, Jr., marketing consultant, educator
Martin, William Russell nuclear engineering educator
Mártonyi, Csaba Lászlo ophthalmic photographer, imager
Massey, Vincent biochemist, educator
Matjias, Christian music educator, musician
Mayes, Ila Laverne minister
Mazumder, Jyotirmoy mechanical and materials engineering educator
Mazzeo, Anthony R. chemist
Mc Cracken, Paul Winston retired economist, business educator
McGinn, Terence James business consultant, minister
McKeachie, Wilbert James psychologist, educator
McLaughlin, Catherine G. healthcare educator
Meezan, William Alan social work educator, consultant
Mehta, Rajendra H cardiologist, researcher
Meitzler, Allen Henry electrical engineering educator, automotive scientist
Mersereau, John, Jr., Slavic languages and literatures educator
Meyer, John Frederick engineering educator
Midgley, A(lvin) Rees, Jr., reproductive endocrinology educator, researcher
Miller, Josef M. otolaryngologist, educator
Mitchell, Edward John economist, retired educator
Mizruchi, Mark Sheldon sociology and business administration educator
Modell, Stephen Mark medical researcher, educator
Moholy-Nagy, Hattula archaeologist
Monto, Arnold Simon epidemiology educator
Moore, Thomas Edwin biologist, educator, museum director
Morgenstern, Lewis B. medical educator
Morris, Michael David chemistry professor
Mosberg, Henry I. pharmacist, educator, medicinal chemist
Motoyama, Keiichi mechanical engineer, consultant
Mourou, Gerard A. research administrator
Mueggler, Erik anthropologist, educator
Munro, Donald Jacques
Murnane, Margaret Mary engineering and physics educator
Musch, David C. epidemiologist
Musich, Shirley Ann research and development company executive
Nabel, Gary J. internal medicine and biological chemistry educator
Neal, Homer Alfred physics educator, researcher, university administrator
Neidhardt, Frederick Carl microbiologist, educator
Nelson, Jason Craig company executive
Nelson, Virginia Simson pediatrician, educator, physiatrist
Nikoui, Hossein Reza quality assurance professional
Nordman, Christer Eric chemistry professor
Nriagu, Jerome Okon environmental geochemist
Oliver, Marguerite Bertoni food service executive
Oliver, William John pediatrician, educator
Omenn, Gilbert Stanley academic administrator, internist
Ono, Hiromi sociologist, researcher
Orlin, Louis Lawrence literature and history educator
Orringer, Mark Burton surgeon, educator
Owyang, Chung gastroenterologist, researcher
Paige, Jeffery Mayland sociologist, educator
Parkinson, William Charles physicist, researcher
Parsons, Jeffrey Robinson anthropologist, educator
Paul, Ara Garo university dean
Pedley, John Griffiths archaeologist, educator
Penske, Roger S. manufacturing and transportation executive

Perkins, Bradford *history educator*
Perkins, George *educator, writer*
Petrick, Ernest Nicholas *mechanical engineer, researcher*
Petty, Elizabeth Marie *geneticist*
Pitt, Bertram *cardiologist, educator, consultant*
Pollack, Henry Nathan *geophysics educator*
Pollock, Stephen Michael *operations research engineer, educator, consultant*
Polverini, Peter J. *dean, dental educator*
Powsner, Edward Raphael *physician*
Pradhan, Sandeep *engineering educator*
Prins, Johanna *literature educator*
Pulgram, Ernst *linguist, philologist, Romance and classical linguistics educator, writer*
Quint, Douglas Joseph *neuroradiology educator*
Quintyn, Conrad Bezekiah *anthropologist, educator*
Radock, Michael *foundation executive*
Railton, Peter Albert *philosophy educator*
Ramírez-Betances, Beatriz Eugenia *student activist*
Raoof, Ameed Mohammed Saeed *anatomist*
Ray, Elise *gymnast*
Reame, Nancy *nursing educator*
Reddy, Venkat Narsimha *ophthalmologist, researcher*
Reed, John Wesley *lawyer, educator*
Reeves, Daniel Martin *computer scientist*
Richardson, Rudy James *toxicology and neurosciences educator*
Robertson, Richard Earl *physical chemist, educator*
Roe, Byron Paul *physics educator*
Rogers, Bryan Leigh *artist, art educator*
Romani, John Henry *health administration educator*
Root, William Lucas *electrical engineering educator*
Rosenthal, Amnon *pediatric cardiologist*
Ross, Theresa Mae *secondary school educator*
Roush, William R. *chemistry educator*
Rowley, Larry Lee *education educator*
Rupp, Ralph Russell *audiologist, educator, author*
Russell, James William *neurologist, neuroscientist, electrophysiologist*
St. Antoine, Theodore Joseph *retired law educator, arbitrator*
Samons, Sandra Lea *psychotherapist*
Sarabandi, Kamal *science administrator*
Savari, Serap Ayse *engineering educator, researcher*
Scavarda, Donald Robert *composer, artist*
Schacht, Jochen Heinrich *biochemistry educator*
Scharp-Radovic, Carol Ann *choreographer, classical ballet educator, artistic director*
Schneider, Carl Edward *law educator*
Schottenfeld, David *epidemiologist, educator*
Schteingart, David Eduardo *internist*
Scodel, Ruth *humanities educator*
Seibold, James Richard *physician, educator*
Senior, Thomas Bryan A. *electrical engineering educator, researcher, consultant*
Shapiro, Brahm *nuclear medicine physician, endocrinologist*
Shapiro, Matthew David *economist, educator*
Shappirio, David Gordon *biologist, educator*
Sheldon, Ingrid Kristina *former mayor, bookkeeper*
Siedel, George John, III, *law educator*
Silverman, Harry J. *pizza delivery company executive*
Sloan, Herbert Elias *physician, surgeon*
Sloat, Barbara Furin *cell biologist, educator*
Smith, Donald Cameron *preventive medicine physician, educator*
Smith, Sidonie *literature educator*
Stafford, Frank P. *economist, educator*
Stafford, Frank Peter, Jr., *economics educator, consultant*
Stein, Howard *economics professor*
Steiner, Peter Otto *economics educator, dean*
Stevenson, Harold William *psychology educator*
Stevenson, Robert Bruce *lawyer*
Stoermer, Eugene Filmore *biologist, educator*
Strang, Ruth Hancock *pediatric educator, pediatric cardiologist, priest*
Stross, Jeoffrey Knight *internist, educator*
Sullivan, Thomas Patrick *academic administrator*
Sun, Kai *materials scientist, research scientist*
Surovell, Edward David *real estate company executive*
Tandon, Rajiv *psychiatrist, educator*
Tharney, Leonard John *education educator, consultant*
Thompson, Norman Winslow *surgeon, educator*
Thornton, Arland *sociologist, educator*
Tice, Carol Hoff *intergenerational specialist, consultant*
Todd, Robert Franklin, III, *oncologist, educator*
Tran, Tuan Diep *pediatrician, educator*
Trautmann, Thomas Roger *history and anthropology educator*
Tsimhoni, Omer *engineering educator*
Turner, James A. *architecture educator*
Van der Voo, Rob *geophysicist*
Veltman, Martinus J.G. *retired physics educator*
Verrett, Shirley *soprano*
Vining, Joseph (George Joseph Vining) *law educator*
Voorhees, John James *dermatologist, department chairman*
Waggoner, Lawrence William *law educator*
Walsh, James Joseph *lawyer*
Walter, Lynn M. *geologist, educator*
Waltz, Susan *international relations educator*
Ward, Peter Allan *pathologist, educator*
Ware, Richard Anderson *foundation executive*
Warner, Kenneth E. *public health educator, consultant*
Warner, Robert Mark *university dean, archivist, historian,*
Weg, John Gerard *physician*
Weiss, Stephen J. *medical educator, researcher, oncologist*
White, B. Joseph *former dean, business educator*
White, James Boyd *law educator*
Whitehouse, Frank, Jr., *microbiologist, educator*
Whitman, Marina Von Neumann *economist, educator*
Wicha, Max S. *oncologist, educator*
Wiggins, Roger C. *internist, educator, researcher*
Wilhelm, Edward W. *corporate financial executive*
Williams, David R. *sociologist, educator, senior research scientist*
Williams, DeWayne Arthur, Jr., *artist*
Williams, John Andrew *physiology educator, consultant*
Williams, Melvin Donald *anthropologist, educator*
Wilson, Richard Christian *engineering firm executive*
Wineman, Jean D. *architecture educator*
Woods, James H. *research scientist, consultant*
Woronoff, Israel *former psychology educator*
Xie, Yu *adult education educator*
Yagle, Andrew Emil *engineering educator*
Yamada, Tadataka *internist*
Yamashina, Tadashi (George) *transportation executive*
Young, Edwin Harold *chemical and metallurgical engineering educator*
Yu, Mei-yu *medical researcher*
Zhang, Youxue *geology educator*
Zucker, Robert A(lpert) *psychologist*
Zurier, Rebecca *art history educator*

Armada
Kummerow, Arnold A. *superintendent of schools*

Au Gres
Dhawan, Vikas *plastic surgeon*

Auburn Hills
Bahman, Mujibur *engineer*
Billups, Chauncey *professional basketball player*
Brown, Lawrence Harvey (Larry Brown) *professional basketball coach*
Davidson, William M. *manufacturing executive, professional sports team executive*
De Martin, Colleen Dianne *college official, interior designer, consultant*
Dumars, Joe, III, *retired professional basketball player*
Etefia, Florence Victoria *school psychologist*
Farrar, Stephen Prescott *glass products manufacturing executive*
Gerson, Ralph Joseph *corporate executive*
Knight, Jeffrey Alan *finance executive*
Kulesza, Chester Stephen (Bud Kulesza) *finance executive*
LaSorda, Thomas W. *automotive executive*
MacDonald, John *marketing executive*
McDyess, Antonio *professional basketball player*
Neumann, Charles Henry *mathematician, educator*
O'Brien, William J., III, *lawyer*
Palmer, Wendy *professional basketball player*
Sidlik, Thomas W. *automotive executive*
Trebing, David Martin *automotive executive*
Valade, Gary C. *automobile company executive*
Wallace, Ben *professional basketball player*
Wallace, Rasheed *professional basketball player, marketing professional*

Bad Axe
Sullivan, James Gerald *small business owner*

Battle Creek
Baldwin, Susan Olin *commissioner, management consultant*
Bryant, John A. *food products executive*
Cline, Charles William *poet, pianist, rhetoric and literature educator*
Davis, Laura Arlene *retired foundation administrator*
Gutierrez, Carlos M. *grocery manufacturing company executive*
Kelly, Janet Langford *lawyer*
Mackay, A.D. David *food products executive*
Markey, James Kevin *lawyer*
Mawby, Russell George *retired foundation executive*
Pilnick, Gary H. *food products executive*
Risukhin, Vladimir Nikolayevich *aeronautical engineer, educator*
Shei, H. Ray *food products executive*

Bay City
Greve, Guy Robert *lawyer*
Van Dyke, Clifford Craig *retired bank executive*
Zuraw, Kathleen Ann *special education and physical education educator*

Belleville
Wilson, David James *chemistry researcher, educator*

Bellevue
Hamel, Louis Reginald *systems analysis consultant*

Benton Harbor
Brown, Mark E. *manufacturing executive*
Fettig, Jeff M. *manufacturing executive*
Periquito, Paulo F.M.O. *manufacturing executive*
Thieneman, Michael D. *manufacturing executive*
Todman, Michael A. *manufacturing executive*

Benzonia
Acker, Nathaniel Hull *retired educational administrator*

Berrien Springs
Caceres, Hernan Marcelo *composer, educator*
Cotro, Hugo Antonio *education educator, researcher*
Lesher, William Richard *retired academic administrator*
Lundgren, Dennis D. *elementary school educator*

Beulah
Auch, Walter Edward *securities company executive*
Edwards, Wallace Winfield *retired automotive executive*
Tanner, Helen Hornbeck *historian, consultant*

Beverly Hills
Dalka-Prysby, Sandra Sue *news correspondent*
Hertzberg, David Gordon *retired lawyer*

Big Rapids
Haneline, Douglas Latham *literature educator*
Kantar, Andrew *literature educator*
Mathison, Ian William *chemistry professor, dean, consultant*
Roy, Donald H. *political scientist, educator*
Siddikov, Bakhodirzhon *mathematician, educator*
Thapa, Khagendra *survey engineering educator*
Tymes, Nathaniel, Jr., *statistician, educator*

Bingham Farms
Banas, C(hristine) Leslie *lawyer*
Baumkel, Mark S. *lawyer*
Berman, Leonard Keith *lawyer*
Burstein, Richard Joel *lawyer*
Giles, Conrad Leslie *ophthalmic surgeon*
Gratch, Serge *mechanical engineering educator*
Katz, Sidney Franklin *obstetrician, gynecologist*
Larky, Sheldon Glen *lawyer*
Shaevsky, Mark *lawyer*

Birch Run
Thompson-Christie, Heather Marie *adult education educator*

Birmingham
Ashleigh, Caroline *art and antiques appraiser*
Berman, Laura *journalist, writer*
Cohen, Adam J. *plastic surgeon*
Edwards, Michael Gerard *physician*
Elsman, James Leonard, Jr., *lawyer*
Foxen, Richard William *manufacturing executive*
Glassman, Eric I. *retail executive*
Harms, Steven Alan *lawyer*
Helppie, Charles Everett, III, *financial consultant*
Kaufman, Ira Gladstone *judge*
Kienbaum, Thomas Gerd *lawyer*
Lesser, Margo Rogers *legal consultant*
McCuen, John Joachim *finance company executive, columnist, educator*
Moss, Charles Joseph, III, (Chuck Moss) *writer, broadcaster*
Reeves, Kathleen Walker *English and French language educator*
Robinson, Marietta S. *lawyer*
Smith, George Wolfram *physicist, researcher*
Sweeney, Thomas Frederick *lawyer*
VanDeusen, Bruce Dudley *educational association administrator*
Wagner, Bruce Stanley *marketing professional*
Wells, Steven Wayne *lawyer*

Bloomfield
Gabriel, Martin George *engineering consultant*
Kanter, Alan Michael *lawyer*

Bloomfield Hills
Abel Horowitz, Michelle Susan *advertising executive*
Adams, Charles Francis *advertising executive, real estate company executive*
Allen, Maurice Bartelle, Jr., *architect*
Baker, Robert Edward *lawyer, retired financial corporation executive*
Ball, Patricia Ann *physician*
Berline, James H. *advertising executive, public relations executive*
Birkerts, Gunnar *architect*
Birnkrant, Sherwin Maurice *lawyer*
Bithell, Thomas Charles *human resources specialist, insurance consultant*
Brown, Jack Wyman *architect*
Burnett, Patricia Hill *portrait artist, author, sculptor, lecturer*
Callow, Thomas Edward *lawyer*
Charla, Leonard Francis *lawyer*
Clippert, Charles Frederick *lawyer*
Cuffe, Stafford Sigesmund *engineering company executive, consultant in E-business, E-commerce, technology, manufacturing & management*
Cunningham, Gary H. *lawyer*
Czarnecki, Walter P. *truck rental company executive*
Dawson, Stephen Everette *lawyer*
DiFeo, Samuel X. *automotive executive*
Dugas, Richard J., Jr., *construction executive*
Frey, Stuart Macklin *automobile manufacturing company executive*
Googasian, George Ara *lawyer*
Gornbein, Henry Seidel *lawyer*
Greenwood, Frank *information scientist, educator*
Grosfeld, James *real estate development company executive*
Hagenlocker, Edward E. *retired automobile company executive*
Haidostian, Alice Berberian *concert pianist, volunteer, not-for-profit fundraiser*
Halso, Robert *real estate company executive*
Hertz, Howard *lawyer*
James, William Ramsay *broadcast executive*
Janover, Robert H. *lawyer*
Kasischke, Louis Walter *lawyer*
Kirk, John MacGregor *lawyer*
Ledwidge, Patrick Joseph *lawyer*
Lehman, Richard Leroy *lawyer*
LoPrete, James Hugh *lawyer*
Martin, J(oseph) Patrick *lawyer, judge*
Mathog, Robert Henry *otolaryngologist, educator*
McCuen, John Francis, Jr., *lawyer*
McGarry, Alexander Banting *lawyer*
McQueen, Patrick M. *bank executive*
Meyer, George Herbert *lawyer*
Miller, Dorothy Anne Smith *retired cytogenetics educator*
Miller, Eugene Albert *retired bank executive*
Morganroth, Fred *lawyer*
Mullens, Delbert W. *automotive executive*
Nern, Christopher Carl *lawyer*
Norris, John Hart *lawyer, director*
O'Brien, Mark J. *real estate/residential construction executive*
Poth, Stefan Michael *retired sales financing company executive*
Prasad, Niru *physician, television personality*
Pulte, William J. *construction executive*
Putchakayala, Hari Babu *engineering company executive*
Rader, Ralph Terrance *lawyer*
Robinson, Jack Albert *retail executive*
Rom, Martin (Melvyn Rom) *investor*
Sandy, William Haskell *training and communication systems executive*
Simon, Evelyn *lawyer*
Snyder, George Edward *lawyer*
Solomon, Mark Raymond *lawyer, educator*
Stepp, James Michael *business executive*
Stewart, Michael B. *lawyer, mechanical and aerospace engineer*
Stivender, Donald Lewis *mechanical engineering consultant*
Stoller, John R. *lawyer*
Stunz, John Henry, Jr., *retired physician*
Sugrue, Dennis Patrick *clinical psychologist*
Swift, Jonathan *educator, television personality*
Syme, Daniel Bailey *rabbi, institution executive*
Taubman, Robert S. *real estate developer*
Thompson, Richard Thomas *academic administrator*
Van Dine, Harold Forster, Jr., *architect, artist*
Weil, John William *technology management consultant*
Williams, Walter Joseph *lawyer*
Yamin, Joseph Francis *lawyer, counselor*

Bloomfield Township
Brown, Lynette Ralya *journalist, publicist*
Dempsey, Donald Chandler *stockbroker, financial planner*

Bloomfield Village
Maxwell, Jack Erwin *manufacturing executive*

Brighton
Gardella, Robert Christopher *lawyer*
Jensen, Baiba *principal*

Brooklyn
Vischer, Harold Harry *manufacturing executive*

Buckley
Gingerich, Martin Ellsworth *literature educator*

Burt
Wolverton, Thomas Frank *automotive company supervisor*

Burton
Breczinski, Michael Joseph *lawyer*

Cadillac
Walker, Dale Maxwell *city official*

Caledonia
Antonini, Richard Lee *insurance executive*

Camden
Falls, Kathleene Joyce *photographer*

Canadian Lake
Cawthorne, Kenneth Clifford *retired financial planner*

Canton
Csaszar, Peter *software engineer*
Schulz, Karen Alice *psychologist, medical psychotherapist, medical and vocational case manager*
Wickus, James D. *food service executive*
Wiloch, Thomas *writer, editor*

Capac
Wagner, Dorothy Marie *retired senior creative designer, artist*

Caro
Wright, Stephen Nathan *religious organization administrator*

Cass City
Althaver, Lambert Ewing *manufacturing executive*

Charlevoix
Telgenhof, Allen Ray *lawyer*

Charlotte
Herrick, Kathleen Magara *social worker*
Young, Everett J. *management consultant, agricultural economist*

Chassell
Spain, James Dorris, Jr., *biochemist, educator*

Chelsea
Crane, Horace Richard *physicist, researcher*
Kitchens, Frederick Lynton, Jr., *retired insurance company executive*
Paulsen, Serenus Glen *architect, educator*
Sawyer, Charles Henry *art educator, art museum director emeritus*
Yarows, Steven Allen *internist*

Clarkston
Keough, James Gillman, Jr., *minister*
Pieknik, Rebecca Anne *technologist, educator*
Wydra, Frank Thomas *healthcare executive*

Clinton Township
Jarmolowicz, C. Renee *artist, art educator*

Comstock Park
Harris, R(ichard) Steven *data processing executive, consultant, educator*

Coopersville
Menning, Daleene Yvonne *artist, art educator, sculptor*

Dearborn
Ardisana, Beth *communications company executive*
Bannister, Michael E. *corporate financial executive*
Barnhart, Mary C. *health facility administrator*
Barton, Robert H., III, *automotive executive*
Beauford, Sandra *registered nurse, data processing executive*
Booker, W. Wayne *former automotive executive*
Boulanger, Rodney Edmund *energy company executive*
Brown, James Ward *mathematician, educator, author*
Brown, Thomas K. *automotive executive*
Buckingham, Lorie *automotive executive*
Byars, Leisa *marketing professional, automotive executive*
Cairns, James Robert *mechanical engineering educator*
Chatterjee, Anjan *automotive executive*
Coburn, Ronald Murray *ophthalmic surgeon, researcher*
Corlett, Ed *automotive executive*
D'Alessio, Gina Maria *music educator*
David, Daniel *musician, social studies educator*
Dziuba, Henry Frank *retired university official*
Fair, Jean Everhard *retired education educator*
Fields, Mark *automotive executive*
Ford, William Clay *automotive company executive, professional sports team executive*
Ford, William Clay, Jr., (Bill Ford) *automotive executive*
Fox, Stacy *automotive executive*
Gandhi, Haren S. *chemical engineer*
Gu, Jianmin *mechanical engineer, researcher*
Haskara, Ibrahim *electronics engineer, researcher*
Hess, Margaret Johnston *religious writer, educator*
Hogan, Brian Joseph *editor*
Irick, Brett D *manufacturing engineer*

Ballbach, Philip Thornton *political consultant, investor*
Bandes, Susan Jane *museum director, educator*
Beck, James V. *mechanical engineering educator*
Beckmeyer, Henry Ernest *anesthesiologist, pain management specialist, medical educator*
Benenson, Walter *nuclear physics educator*
Blosser, Henry Gabriel *physicist*
Brody, Howard *medical educator*
Brody, Theodore Meyer *pharmacologist, educator*
Bromley, Stephen C. *zoology educator*
Brophy, Jere Edward *education educator, researcher*
Bukovac, Martin John *horticulturist, educator*
Burnett, Jean Bullard (Mrs. James R. Burnett) *biochemist, educator*
Busch, Lawrence Michael *sociologist, researcher*
Byerrum, Richard Uglow *college dean*
Case, Eldon Darrel *materials science educator*
Chapin, Richard Earl *retired librarian*
Chen, Kun-Mu *electrical engineering educator*
Crewe, Nancy Moe *psychologist and educator*
Cross, Aureal Theophilus *geology and botany educator*
Cutts, Charles Eugene *civil engineering educator*
Davis, Glenn Craig *psychiatrist*
Dennis, Frank George, Jr., *retired horticulture educator*
Dewhurst, Charles Kurt *museum director, cultural administrator, curator, folklorist, English language educator*
Dow, Steven Benjamin *social studies educator*
Dye, James Louis *chemistry professor*
Essa, Daniel F. *lawyer*
Finifter, Ada Weintraub *political scientist, educator*
Fisher, Alan Washburn *historian, educator*
Fluck, Michele M(arguerite) *biology professor*
Foss, John Frank *mechanical engineering educator*
Freedman, Eric *journalist, educator, writer*
Gass, Gertrude Zemon *psychologist, researcher*
Gelbke, Claus-Konrad *nuclear physics educator*
Gerhardt, Philipp *microbiologist, educator*
Gift, David Ayres *academic administrator*
Goodman, Erik David *engineering educator*
Gottschalk, Alexander *radiologist, diagnostic radiology educator*
Greenberg, Bradley Sander *communications educator*
Hackel, Emanuel *science educator*
Harrison, Jeremy Thomas *dean, law educator*
Harrison, Michael Jay *physicist, researcher*
Hilbert, Virginia Lois *computer consultant and training executive*
Honhart, Frederick Lewis, III, *academic director*
Ilgen, Daniel Richard *psychology educator*
Izzo, Thomas *college basketball coach*
Jackson-Elmoore, Cynthia *director, educator*
Johnson, Clark Cumings *lawyer, educator, department chairman*
Kende, Hans Janos *plant physiology educator*
King, Lonnie J. *dean*
Kirk, Edgar Lee *musician, educator*
Koo, Anthony Ying Chang *economist, educator*
Kreinin, Mordecha Eliahu *economics professor*
Kronegger, Maria Elisabeth *French and comparative literature educator*
Kumar, Ashir *pediatrician, medical educator*
Ladenson, Mark Lawrence *economist, educator*
La Ferle, Carrie *advertising executive, educator*
Lashbrooke, Elvin Carroll, Jr., *law educator, consultant*
Li, Shu-Guang *science educator*
Li, Tien-Yien *mathematics professor*
Liedholm, Carl Edward *economics professor*
Lloyd, John Raymond *mechanical engineering educator*
Magen, Myron Shimin *osteopathic physician, educator, university dean*
Manderscheid, Lester Vincent *agricultural economics educator*
Mansour, George P. *Spanish language and literature educator*
McCarthy, John David *mathematician, educator*
McMeekin, Dorothy *botany, plant pathology educator*
Mead, Carl David *retired educator*
Menchik, Paul Leonard *economist, educator*
Miracle, Gordon Eldon *advertising educator*
Mitstifer, Dorothy Irwin *honor society administrator*
Moore, Kenneth Edwin *pharmacology educator*
Natoli, Joseph *English language educator*
Nelson, James Lindemann *philosophy educator, bioethicist*
Nelson, Ronald Harvey *animal science educator, researcher*
Pathak, Dorothy Rybaczyk *epidemiologist, biostatistician*
Perrin, Robert *editorial consultant, writer*
Petrides, George Athan *ecologist, educator*
Petropoulos, Evangelos *former health institute director, educator, researcher*
Pierre, Percy Anthony *engineering educator*
Pollack, Gerald Leslie *physicist, researcher*
Preiss, Jack *biochemistry educator*
Press, Charles *retired political science educator*
Ralph, David Clinton *communications educator*
Raper, Kellie Curry *education educator, researcher*
Rechtien, James Joseph *osteopath, educator*
Reinhart, Mary Ann *medical board executive*
Revelos, Constantine Nicholas *law educator, writer*
Root-Bernstein, Robert Scott *biologist, educator*
Rosenman, Kenneth D. *medical educator*
Rothert, Marilyn L. *dean, nursing educator*
Sato, Paul Hisashi *pharmacologist*
Saul, William Edward *civil engineering educator*
Schemmel, Rachel Anne *food science and human nutrition educator, researcher*
Schoenl, William James *history professor*
Schwille, John Robert *education educator, researcher*
Segerlind, Larry J. *agricultural engineering educator*
Simon, Lou Anna Kimsey *academic administrator*
Snoddy, James Ernest *education educator*
Sowards, Steven Wesley *librarian*
Spence, Robert Dean *physics educator*
Stapleton, James Hall *statistician, educator*
Stein, Robert Foster *astrophysicist, educator*
Strampel, William Derkey *dean, medical educator*
Strassmann, W. Paul *economics professor*
Strauss, Eric James *urban planning educator, lawyer, consultant*
Thomashow, Michael F. *microbiologist, educator*
Tiedje, James Michael *microbiologist, educator, ecologist*
Torto, Christopher *communications executive*
Tzitsikas, Helene *retired Hispanic literature educator*
Velicer, Janet Schafbuch *retired elementary school educator*
von Bernuth, Robert Dean *agricultural engineering educator, consultant*
Von Tersch, Lawrence Wayne *engineering educator, dean*
Waite, Donald Eugene *medical educator, consultant*
Wakoski, Diane *poet, educator*
Walker, Bruce Edward *anatomy educator*
Wang, Donna Hui *investigative medicine director*
Watson, Ralph Edward *physician, educator*
Weng, Juyang John *computer science educator, researcher*
Werner, Arnold *psychiatrist*
Whallon, William *humanities educator*
White, James Alfred *lawyer*
Whiting Dobson, Lisa Lorraine *video production educator, producer, director*
Wilkinson, William Sherwood *lawyer*
Wilson, R. Dale *marketing educator, consultant*
Winder, Clarence Leland *psychologist, educator*
Woodbury, Stephen Abbott *economics educator*
Zeikus, J. Gregory *microbiologist, educator*

Eastport
Tomlinson, James Lawrence *mechanical engineer*

Edwardsburg
Floyd, Alton David *cell biologist, consultant*

Escanaba
Karweick, June Klees *education educator*

Farmington
Badawy, Aly Ahmed *automotive parts manufacturing company executive*
Burns, Sister Elizabeth Mary *hospital administrator*
Chou, Clifford Chi Fong *research engineering executive*
Dixson, J. B. *communications executive*
Ellens, J(ay) Harold *philosopher, educator, psychotherapist, pastor*
Fleming, Jill Louise *education educator*
Ginsberg, Myron *computer scientist*
Gordon, Arnold Mark *lawyer*
Gordon, Craig Jeffrey *oncologist, educator*
McFarland, Robert Edwin *lawyer*
Neyer, Jerome Charles *consulting civil engineer*
Penberthy, Stanley Josiah, Jr., *publisher*
Wine, Sherwin Theodore *rabbi*

Farmington Hills
Barry, Essie Marilyn *elementary school educator, writer*
Bassett, Tina *communications executive*
Bauser, Nancy *social worker*
Benedict, Elise *moving company executive*
Brodhead, William McNulty *lawyer, former congressman*
Bryfonski, Dedria Anne *publishing company executive*
Chapman, Gilbert Bryant *physicist*
Dobritt, Dennis William *physician, researcher, pain management specialist*
Ellmann, Sheila Frenkel *investment company executive*
Faxon, Jack *headmaster*
Fenton, Robert Leonard *lawyer, literary agent, movie producer, writer*
Goslin, Gerald Hugh *concert pianist, educator*
Hurd, Mary K. *civil engineer, writer*
Kalib, Sholom (Sylvan Kalib) *conductor, educator*
McQuiggan, Mark C. *urologist*
Meyer, Philip Gilbert *lawyer*
Olendorf, Donna *editor*
Papai, Beverly Daffern *library director*
Plaut, Jonathan Victor *rabbi*
Reddig, Walter Eduard *architect, master cabinet maker*
Rinker, Marianne Marie *rehabilitation nurse*
Sargent, Eric Winslow *otolaryngologist, surgeon*
Simpson, David Allen *osteopath*
Smith, Isabel Francis *financial planner*
Theodore, Ares Nicholas *research chemist*
Yagahashi, Takashi *chef*

Fennville
Kamman, Curtis Warren *retired ambassador*

Ferndale
Dodd, Geralda *metal products executive*

Fife Lake
Knecht, Richard Arden *family practitioner*

Flint
Belcher, Max *social services administrator, college dean*
Bever, Timothy Michael *systems software engineer*
Bonner, Darlene E. *minister, writer*
Davidek, Stefan *artist*
Echempati, Raghu *mechanical engineering educator, consultant*
Farrehi, Cyrus *cardiologist, educator*
Gernstein, Stanley B. *lawyer*
Johnson, Gary Keith *pediatrician*
Lorenz, John Douglas *college official*
Maynard, Olivia P. *foundation administrator*
McCartin, Brian James *mathematician, educator*
Munerlyn, Lorraine *administrative secretary, writer*
Novak, Jo-Ann Stout *chemical engineer*
Samuel, Roger D. *newspaper publishing executive*
Stone, Pamela Ann *accountant*
Tomblinson, James Edmond *architect*
White, William Samuel *foundation executive*
Wigston, David Lawrence *biologist, dean*
Williams, Veronica Myres *psychotherapist, social worker*

Flushing
Bain, William David *electronics systems technician, writer*

Fort Gratiot
Zimmer, Lawrence Joseph *psychiatrist, internist*

Frankenmuth
Shetlar, James Francis *physician*

Frankfort
Foster, Robert Carmichael *banker*
Gerberding, Miles Carston *lawyer*
Storrer, William Allin *consultant*

Franklin
Reinhart, Anne Christine *special education educator, consultant*
Sax, Mary Randolph *speech and language pathologist*

Fraser
Butler, James E. *automotive executive*
Winget, Larry J., Sr., *automotive industry executive*

Garden City
Elmouchi, Joan Leslie *library director*
Polin, Colleen Marie *special education educator*

Gaylord
Cooney, Patrick Ronald *bishop*

Glen Arbor
Newblatt, Stewart Albert *federal judge*

Grand Blanc
Byerly, Carl Wesley *music educator, academic administrator*
Riley, Ronald Jim *industrial engineer, consultant*
Serra, Joe *investment company executive*

Grand Haven
Disbrow, Sidney Arden, Jr., *chiropractor*
Sabolcik, Gene *manufacturing executive*

Grand Ledge
Evert, Sandra Florence (Sandra Wheeler) *medical/surgical nurse*

Grand Rapids
Anderson, Roger Gordon *minister*
Auwers, Stanley John *motor carrier executive*
Bair, Joel Evan *lawyer*
Baker, Frank C. (Buzz Baker) *advertising executive*
Baker, Hollis MacLure *furniture manufacturing company executive*
Baker, Richard Lee *book publishing company executive*
Bander, Thomas Samuel *retired dentist*
Barnes, Thomas John *lawyer*
Bartek, Gordon Luke *radiologist*
Beals, Paul Archer *religious studies educator*
Becker, Robert Joseph *database consultant, computer science specialist, database software developer and educator*
Bell, Robert Holmes *district judge*
Birkbeck, A.J. Koerts *lawyer*
Bolinder, Scott W. *publishing company executive*
Bolt, Eunice Mildred DeVries *artist*
Bradshaw, Conrad Allan *lawyer*
Brenneman, Hugh Warren, Jr., *judge*
Brent, Helen Teressa *school nurse*
Brinkmeyer, Scott S. *lawyer*
Bruyn, Kimberly Ann *public relations executive, consultant*
Canepa, John Charles *banking consultant*
Carlotti, Ronald John *food scientist*
Chase, Sandra Lee *clinical pharmacist, consultant*
Chiara, Margaret-Mary *United States attorney*
Curtin, Timothy John *lawyer*
Davis, Henry Barnard, Jr., *lawyer*
DeLapa, Judith Anne *business owner*
DeVries, Robert K. *religious book publisher*
Dickerson, Allen Bruce *interior designer, consultant*
Diekema, Anthony J. *college president, educational consultant*
Drew, Stephen Richard *lawyer*
Dykstra, William Dwight *business executive, consultant*
Fortner, Robert Steven *media educator, researcher*
Frankforter, Weldon DeLoss *retired museum administrator*
Frye, Della Mae *portrait artist*
Garver, Frederick Merrill *industrial engineering executive*
Glinski, Timothy P. *computer company executive*
Gordon, Dan *food service executive*
Hackett, James P. *manufacturing executive*
Harris, Richard W. *law educator, lawyer, accountant*
Henry, Karen Lee *writer, lecturer*
Hermann, William M. *finance company executive*
Hofman, Leonard John *minister*
Horn, Joyce Elaine *music educator*
Jackoboice, Sandra Kay *artist*
Kaczmarczyk, Jeffrey Allen *journalist, classical music critic*
Keane, James P. *manufacturing executive*
Kolk, Fritz D. *retail executive*
Kooistra, William Henry *clinical psychologist*
Kregel, James R. *publishing executive*
Lockington, David *conductor*
Logie, John Hoult *former mayor, lawyer*
Lubbers, Arend Donselaar *retired academic administrator*
Marshall, J. Stephen *lawyer*
Mavima, Paul *finance educator*
Mayo, David Wayne *sportswriter*
Mbah, Chris H.N. *business educator*
Mears, Patrick Edward *lawyer*
Meijer, Douglas *retail company executive*
Meijer, Hank *retail company executive*
Meijer, Mark *retail executive*
Messner, James W. *advertising executive*
Miles, Wendell A. *federal judge*
Mitchell, James Albee *lawyer*
Monsma, Stephen Vos *political scientist, educator*
Neckers, Bruce Warren *lawyer*
Pasquale, Michael David *linguist, educator, linguist, consultant*
Pew, Robert Cunningham, II, *office equipment manufacturing company executive*
Plakmeyer, Steve *food service executive*
Portelli, Vincent George *business executive, consultant*
Posthumus, Richard Earl *former lieutenant governor, farmer*
Purchase-Owens, Francena *human resources specialist, educator*
Quist, Gordon Jay *federal judge*
Rougier-Chapman, Alwyn Spencer Douglas *furniture manufacturing company executive*
Ryskamp, Bruce E. *publishing executive*
Sadler, David G(ary) *management executive*
Schmidt, Gordon Peirce *artistic director*
Schwanda, Tom *religious studies educator*
Seyferth, Virginia M. *public relations executive*
Sieger, Diana R. *foundation administrator*
Smith, Bill *advertising and marketing executive*
Smith, David I. *German language educator*
Spaulding, Dan *public relations executive*
Staples, David M. *corporate financial executive*
Stevenson, Jo Ann C. *federal bankruptcy judge*
Sturken, Craig *retail executive*
Swanson, Alfred Bertil *orthopaedic and hand surgeon, inventor, educator*
Taylor, Mark Lyman *music educator*
Tiemstra, John Peter *economics professor*
Titley, Larry J. *lawyer*
Vande Woude, George Franklin *molecular biologist, cancer researcher*
Van Haren, W(illiam) Michael *lawyer*
Van Oostenburg, Paul Gary *lawyer*
Verdier, David D'Ooge *ophthalmologist, educator*
Walsh, James *retail supermarket executive*
West, Terence Douglas *furniture company design executive*
Williams, Glenn Carl *music educator, secondary school educator*
Wilt, Jeffrey Lynn *pulmonary and critical care physician, educator*
Woodrick, Robert *food products executive*
Yamazaki, Makoto *economics professor*
Yarington, David Jon *retired educator*
Zimmerman, John *public relations executive*

Greenbush
Paulson, James Marvin *engineering educator*

Greenville
Mullendore, James Myers *lawyer*
Palmer, Richard Douglas *lawyer*

Grosse Ile
Smith, Veronica Latta *real estate corporation officer*
Stump, M. Pamela *sculptor*

Grosse Pointe
Barrows, Ronald Thomas *lawyer*
Behringer, Samuel Joseph, Jr., *lawyer*
Beltz, Charles Robert *retired engineering executive*
Blevins, William Edward *management consultant*
Casey, Genevieve M(ary) *librarian, educator*
Dzul, Paul J. *physician, medical journal editor*
Goss, James William *lawyer*
Hill, Draper *editorial cartoonist*
Marshall, Douglas William *medical administrator, educator*
Mengden, Joseph Michael *retired investment banker*
Pytell, Robert Henry *retired lawyer, former judge*
Ruffner, Frederick G., Jr., *book publisher*
Sphire, Raymond Daniel *anesthesiologist, educator*
Whittaker, Jeanne Evans *former newspaper columnist*
Wilkinson, Warren Scripps *manufacturing executive*

Grosse Pointe Farms
Allen, Lee Harrison *industrial consultant, wholesale company executive*
Axe, John Randolph *lawyer, finance company executive*
Christian, Edward Kieren *broadcasting station executive*
Fromm, Joseph L. *financial consultant*
Obolensky, Marilyn Wall (Mrs. Serge Obolensky) *metals company executive*
Surdam, Robert McClellan *retired banker*
Valk, Robert Earl *corporate executive*

Grosse Pointe Park
Centner, Charles William *lawyer, educator*
Elsila, David August *editor*
Knapp, Mildred Florence *retired social worker*
Krebs, William Hoyt *industrial hygienist, health science association administrator*
Mogk, John Edward *law educator, association executive, consultant*

Grosse Pointe Shores
Caldwell, John Thomas, Jr., *communications executive*
LaHood, Mary Anne *real estate investor*

Grosse Pointe Woods
Cusmano, J. Joyce *public relations executive*
McWhirter, Glenna Suzanne (Nickie McWhirter) *retired newspaper columnist*
Prather, Kenneth Earl *lawyer*
Robie, Joan *elementary school principal*
Simonds, Richard Kimball *investment executive*
Sul, Yi Chul *neurologist*

Gwinn
Lasich, Vivian Esther Layne *secondary school educator*

Hancock
Puotinen, Arthur Edwin *college president, clergyman*

Harbor Springs
Cappel, Constance *educational consultant, writer*
Lampert, Charles E. *lawyer*
Smith, Wayne Richard *lawyer*

Harper Woods
Havrilcsak, Gregory Michael *history professor*

Harrison Township
Rivard, Jerome G. *engineering executive*

Haslett
Hotaling, Robert Bachman *community planner, educator*
Warrington, Willard Glade *former university official*

Hastings
Adrounie, V. Harry *public health administrator, scientist, educator, environmentalist*
Jones, Kensinger *advertising executive*

Hazel Park
Renforth, D. Joyce *art educator, artist*

Hickory Corners
Lauff, George Howard *biologist*

Highland
Brown, Ray Kent *biochemist, physician, educator*

Bullard, Willis Clare, Jr., *lawyer*

Highland Park
Crittenden, Mary Lynne *science educator*

Hillsdale
Grassl, Wolfgang *adult education educator*
Knecht, Melissa *music educator, musician*

Holland
Franken, Darrell *counselor, writer, publisher*
Haworth, Gerrard Wendell *office furniture manufacturing company executive*
Haworth, Richard G. *office furniture manufacturer*
Holmes, Jack Edward *political science educator*
Krasa, Robert *manufacturing executive*
Kreuze, Calvin *office products company executive*
Mc Gurk, James Henry *consultant company executive*
Muyres, David Allen *industrial designer*
Nieuwsma, Milton John *writer, journalist*
Nyenhuis, Jacob Eugene *college official*
Schieringa, Paul Kenneth *special education educator, entertainer*
Stynes, Stanley Kenneth *retired chemical engineer, educator*
Swierenga, Robert *humanities educator, researcher*
Van Noord, Diane C. *artist, educator*
Van Voorst, Robert E. *theology educator, minister*
Van Wylen, Gordon John *former college president*
Zuidema, George Dale *surgeon, educator*

Holly
Stolpin, William Roger *artist, printmaker, retired engineer*

Holt
Legere Jr, Henry J. *lawyer*
Smith, Betty W. *librarian*

Houghton
Crittenden, John Charles *engineering educator*
Fink, William Orman *federal agency administrator, management consultant*
Heckel, Richard Wayne *metallurgical engineering educator*
Huang, Eugene Yuching *civil engineer, educator*
Mroz, Glenn D. *academic administrator*
Pelc, Karol Ignacy *engineering and technology management educator, researcher*
Pennington, Wayne D. *science educator*
Utt, Glenn S., Jr., *medical products executive*
White, Calvin Lamont *engineer*
Wray, Kent *academic administrator*
Wright, Debra Denise *education educator*

Howell
Cotton, Larry *ranching executive*
Parker, Robert Ernser *lawyer*
Rohrabacher, Janet Hammond *geneologist, archivist*
Watkins, Curtis WinthroP *artist*
Yanga, Ismael Duran *surgeon*

Hudsonville
DeHoop, Troy Timothy *small business owner*

Inkster
Bullock, Steven Carl *lawyer*
Hall, Andrea Jenella *special education educator*

Ionia
Palmer, Charles A. *lawyer, educator*
Ulmer, Evonne Gail *health science facility executive*

Ishpeming
Steward, James Brian *lawyer, pharmacist*

Jackson
Fryling, Victor J. *energy company executive*
Kelly, Robert Vincent, Jr., *metal company executive*
Kleiner, Elaine Laura *English literature educator*
McCormick, William Thomas, Jr., *electric and gas company executive*
Mills, P. Gerald *retail executive*
Popp, Nathaniel *archbishop*
Reid, Mona Gay *education educator*
Smith, Stanton Kinnie, Jr., *lawyer*
Webb, Thomas J. *utilities executive*
Whipple, Kenneth *utilities executive*

Jerome
Dillon, Merton Lynn *historian, educator*

Kalamazoo
Ahmad, Shah Mahmood *chemical engineer, consultant*
Badra, Robert George *theology studies educator, humanities educator*
Bailey, Judith Irene *university official, consultant*
Bauhof, James Francis *lawyer*
Bennett, Arlie Joyce *clinical social worker emeritus*
Bergy, Dean H. *health products executive*
Breisach, Ernst A. *historian, educator*
Brown, John Wilford *health products executive*
Bus, Roger Jay *lawyer*
Carver, Norman Francis, Jr., *architect, photographer*
Chateauneuf, John Edward *chemistry educator, researcher*
Cody, Frank Joseph *secondary school educator*
Curry, John Patrick *insurance company executive, management consultant*
Dybek, Stuart *English educator, writer*
Enslen, Pamela Chapman *lawyer*
Enslen, Richard Alan *federal judge*
Fang, Yichuan *aeronautical engineer, researcher*
Fredericks, Sharon Kay *nurse's aide*
Gilchrist, James A. *communication educator*
Gladstone, William Sheldon, Jr., *radiologist*
Gordon, Edgar George *retired lawyer*
Greenfield, John Charles *bio-organic chemist*
Greydanus, Donald Everett *pediatrician, consultant*
Grotzinger, Laurel Ann *librarian, educator*
Haenicke, Diether Hans *academic administrator emeritus, educator*
Hilboldt, James Sonnemann *lawyer, investment advisor*
Hubbard, William Neill, Jr., *retired pharmaceutical executive*
Hudson, Roy Davage *retired pharmaceutical executive*
Jamison, Frank Raymond *independent video producer, retired communications educator*
Jones, Eugene Gordon *pharmaceutical company executive*
Jones, James Fleming, Jr., *academic administrator, Roman language and literature educator*
Jones, Leander Corbin *educator, media specialist*
Joyce, Margaret *chemical engineer, educator*
Julien, Catherine *history professor*
Kujawski, Daniel *science educator*
Lander, Joyce Ann *nursing educator, medical/surgical nurse*
Lavery, J. Patrick *perinatologist*
Lawrence, William Joseph, Jr., *retired corporate executive*
Lawson, Gary D. *audiology educator*
Light, Christopher Upjohn *writer, computer musician, photographer*
Light, John Richard *sculptor*
Litynski, Daniel Mitchell *engineering educator, retired military officer*
Markin, David Robert *motor company executive*
Marshall, Vincent de Paul *industrial microbiologist, researcher*
Mc Allister, Lester Belden *economics professor*
Meisenhelder, Robert John, II, *pharmaceutical company executive*
Moe, James Burton *pharmaceutical company executive*
Morris, Christopher David *lawyer*
Norris, Richard Patrick *museum director, historian, educator*
Ortiz-Button, Olga *social worker*
Palchick, Bernard S. *academic administrator, art educator*
Palmitessa, James R. *historian, educator*
Parfet, Donald Reid *pharmaceutical executive*
Petersen, Anne C.(Cheryl) *foundation administrator, educator*
Pratt, Helen Diann *clinical psychologist, educator*
Ruoff, Cynthia Osowiec *foreign language educator*
Saber, Alan A. *surgeon*
Showalter, Shirley H. *academic administrator*
Skipper, Jason Edward *writer, educator*
Spradling, Robert Ledford *music educator, conductor*
Stufflebeam, Daniel LeRoy *education educator*
Tang, Roger Yin Wu *accounting educator*
Toledo-Pereyra, Luis Horacio *transplant surgeon, researcher, historian educator*
Yang, Li *computer scientist, educator*

Kalkaska
Batsakis, John George *pathology educator*

Keego Harbor
Gee, Sharon Lynn *funeral director, educator*

Kentwood
Yovich, Daniel John *education educator*

Laingsburg
Zabriskie, Sherry LaFollette *filmmaker, author, actress*

Lake Angelus
Kresge, Bruce Anderson *retired physician*

Lanse
Berggren-Moilanen, Bonnie Lee *education educator*

Lansing
Arends, Herman Joseph *insurance company executive*
Baker, Frederick Milton, Jr., *lawyer*
Barcia, James A. *state senator, former congressman*
Brater, Elizabeth *state legislator*
Brewer, Mark Courtland *lawyer*
Brown, Nancy Field *editor*
Byrum, Dianne *state legislator, small business owner*
Cannon, Patrick D. *federal official, broadcaster*
Cavanagh, Michael Francis *state supreme court justice*
Cherry, John D., Jr., *lieutenant governor*
Christian, Sandra Svec *retired state official*
Coey, David Conrad *lawyer*
Cox, Mike *state attorney general*
DeHart, Eileen *state legislator*
Devaney, Dennis Martin *lawyer, educator*
Emmons, Joanne *state legislator*
Ewert, Quentin Albert *lawyer, consultant*
Fisher, John W. *insurance company executive*
Fitzgerald, Frank Moore *commissioner*
Fitzgerald, John Warner *law educator*
Foster, Joe C., Jr., *lawyer*
Gomoll, Matilde I. *multi-media specialist*
Granholm, Jennifer Mulhern *governor*
Hammerstrom, Beverly Swoish *state legislator*
Hills, Rusty *state official*
Johnson, Rick *state official*
Johnson, Veronica Ann Wilkerson *library director*
Kelley, Frank Joseph *lawyer, former state attorney general*
Kelly, Marilyn *state supreme court justice*
Kepros, John Paul *trauma surgeon*
Kissling, Paul Joseph *academic administrator, religious studies educator, minister*
Kluge, Len H. *director, actor, theater educator*
LaHaine, Gilbert Eugene *retail lumber company executive*
Land, Terri Lynn *state official*
Linder, Iris Kay *lawyer*
Lobenherz, William Ernest *container company/association executive, lawyer*
Markman, Stephen J. *state supreme court justice*
Marvin, David Edward Shreve *lawyer*
McKeague, David William *judge*
McKeague, Nancy Palmer *trade association executive*
Nguyen, Hoa Thai *academic administrator*
Nsofor, Leslie Monagolum *food scientist, researcher*
Rasmusson, Thomas Elmo *lawyer*
Rogers, Mike *congressman*
Rooney, John Philip *law educator*
Sauer, Harold John *physician, educator*
Schwarz, John J.H. *state legislator, surgeon*
Scott, Martha G. *state legislator*
Severin, Blaine Frank *environmental engineer*
Shirtum, Earl Edward *retired civil engineer*
Stockmeyer, Norman Otto *law educator, consultant*
Stowers, Mark David *chemicals executive*
Straus, Kathleen Nagler *education administrator, consultant*
Suhrheinrich, Richard Fred *federal judge*
Taylor, Clifford Woodworth *state supreme court justice*
Umfleet, Randy Gene *minister, music educator*
Van Regenmorter, William *state legislator*
Vincent, Frederick Michael, Sr., *neurologist, educator*
Warren, Joseph Addison, III, *law and history educator*
Wilbur, Kathleen *state agency administrator*
Young, Robert P., Jr., *state supreme court justice*

Leland
Hamelin, Paul Robert *pharmacist, pharmaceutical executive, consultant*
Small, Hamish *chemist*
Soutas-Little, Robert William *mechanical engineer, educator*

Lincoln Park
Kissel, Kevin Karl *warehouse manager, freelance/self-employed writer*
Russell, Harriet Shaw *social worker*
Zelenak, Edward Michael *lawyer, musician*

Livonia
Barfield, Jon E. *employment company executive*
Bialosky, David L. *lawyer, automotive executive*
Cantie, Joseph S. *automotive executive*
Chowdhury, Subir *business executive, author, researcher*
Drouin, Joe *automotive executive*
Gepford, Barbara Beebe *retired nutrition educator*
Haggard, Joan Claire *church musician, piano instructor, accompanist, adjudicator*
Hoffman, Barry Paul *lawyer*
Holtzman, Roberta Lee *French and Spanish language educator*
Kujawa, Sister Rose Marie *academic administrator*
Lunn, Steve *automotive executive*
Maibach, Ben C., Jr., *service executive*
McHard, James Lorin *corporate financial executive*
Plant, John Charles *automotive equipment company executive*
Rhoades Dumler, Kelly J. *medical educator*
Schwartz, Randy Ken *mathematician, educator*
Sobel, Howard Bernard *osteopath, educator*
Stamelos, Electra Georgia *artist*
Uicker, Joseph Bernard *retired engineering company executive*
Valerio, Michael Anthony *diversified financial services company executive*
Van de Vyver, Sister Mary Francilene *academic administrator*

Ludington
Puffer, Richard Judson *retired college chancellor*

Lupton
Scott, George Alfred *advertising executive, writer*

Mackinac Island
Mc Cabe, John Charles, III, *writer*

Macomb
Farmakis, George Leonard *education educator*

Madison Heights
Janke, Kenneth *investment consultant*
Kafarski, Mitchell I. *chemical processing company executive*
Woodruff, Jane *sales executive*
Xia, Jiding *chemical engineering educator*

Mancelona
Whelan, Joseph L. *neurologist*

Manistee
Behring, Daniel William *educational and business professional, consultant*
Trussell, Charles Tait *columnist*

Maple City
Duff, James George *retired autotobile industry and financial services executive*
Morris, Donald Arthur Adams *college president*

Marine City
Brown, Ronald Delano *endocrinologist*

Marquette
Burt, John Harris *bishop*
Camerius, James Walter *marketing educator, corporate researcher*
Donovan, David William *physics professor, researcher*
Kendall, Keith Harold *history professor*
Manning, Robert Hendrick *media consultant*
Osstyn, Randolph Beier *lawyer*
Pesola, William Ernest *restaurant management executive*
Roy, Michael Joseph *higher education administrator*
Saville, Kathleen Jo *instructional technologist*
Sherony, Cheryl Anne *dietician*
Stulz, Karin M. *educator*

Mason
Myers, William *food container manufacturing executive*
Thayer, Bruce Allen *automotive executive, artist*
Yoakam, Lynn Kelly *harpist, educator*

Mears
Binder, L. James *retired magazine editor, journalist*

Midland
Adams, Thomas Walton *corrections official*
Allemang, Arnold A. *chemicals executive*
Bader, Kathleen M. *chemicals executive*
Barker, Nancy Lepard *university official*
Brodeur, Julie Celine *marine biologist*
Bus, James Stanley *toxicologist*
Carbone, Anthony J. *chemicals executive*
Chao, Marshall *chemist*
Clulo, Paul Jacques *judge*
Davidson, John Hunter *agriculturist*
Diehl, Ann *radio personality*
Dorman, Linneaus Cuthbert *retired chemist*
Duncan, Christopher *information technology executive*
Gross, Richard M. *chemicals executive*
Grzesiak, Katherine Ann *primary educator*
Hampton, Leroy *retired chemical company executive*
Hazleton, Richard A. *chemicals executive*
Kepler, David E., II, *chemicals executive*
Kreinberg, Romeo *chemicals executive*
Leng, Douglas Ellis *chemical engineer, scientist*
Liveris, Andrew N. *chemicals executive*
Ludington, Thomas Lamson *judge*
Maneri, Remo R. *management consultant*
Manetta, Richard *chemicals executive*
McMaster, Lee P. *chemicals executive*
Meister, Bernard John *chemical engineer*
Morgan, Frank T. *business educator, consultant*
Reinhard, Joao Pedro *chemicals company executive*
Schmidt, William C. *retired chemicals executive*
Scriven, John G. *retired lawyer, chemical company executive*
Sosville, Dick *sales and marketing executive*
Stavropoulos, William S. *chemical executive*
Walthie, I. H. *chemicals executive*
Washington, Lawrence J., Jr., *chemicals executive*
Wood, Robert L. *chemicals executive*

Milford
McGhie, Michael *real estate company executive*
Oliveri, Eugene Alfred *gastroenterologist*

Monroe
Darrow, Kurt L.
DeVries, James E. *historian, educator*
Kiser, Gerald L. *furniture company executive*
Lipford, Rocque Edward *lawyer, corporate executive*
Mlocek, Sister Frances Angeline *financial executive*
Nuechterlain, James Howard *music educator*
Siciliano, Elizabeth Marie *secondary school educator*

Mount Clemens
Brumbaugh, George Edwin, Jr., *lawyer*
Kolakowski, Diana Jean *county commissioner*
Rocca, Sue *state legislator*
Vosburg, Kathy D *tax specialist, consultant*

Mount Pleasant
Browne, William P. *political science educator*
Dietrich, Richard Vincent *geologist, educator*
Kirchner, Richard Jay *retired physical education educator*
Kopp, Stephen James *academic administrator*
Lee, Carl *statistician, educator*
Lynch, John Joseph *lawyer*
Orlik, Christina Bear *music educator*
Petrick, Michael Joseph *journalism educator*
Smallwood, Carol *writer*
Thayer, Frederick Clifton *public policy educator*

Muskegon
Blystone, John B. *manufacturing executive*
DeLong, Donald R. *accountant*
Kara, Paul Mark *corporate executive*
Kolenic, Anthony James, Jr., *lawyer, educator*
McKendry, John H., Jr., *lawyer, educator*
Nehra, Gerald Peter *lawyer*
Turner, Peter Merrick *retired manufacturing company executive*

Naubinway
Beaudoin, Robert Lawrence *small business owner*
Smith, Richard Ernest *retired insurance company executive*

New Haven
Shaw, Charles Rusanda *retired government investigator*

Niles
Chmiel, Chester T. *chemist, consultant*
Gibbs, Denis Laurel *radiologist*
Kim, Choong-Man Joseph *radiologist*
Marshall, Gerald Francis *optical engineer, consultant, physicist*
Pasula, Angela Marie *lawyer*

North Branch
Sorensen, Shawn Richard *secondary school educator*
Stevenson, James Laraway *communications engineer, consultant*

North Muskegon
Lynch, Robert Emmett *mathematics educator*

Northport
Schultz, Richard Carlton *plastic surgeon*
Scripps, Douglas Jerry *music educator, conductor*
Thomas, Philip Stanley *economist, educator*

Northville
Bohm, Henry Victor *physicist*
Carhuapoma, Juan Ricardo *critical care neurologist, researcher*
Clawson, Curtis J. *manufacturing executive*
Clemens, Michael Terrence *furniture manufacturing representative*
Davis, Lawrence Edward *church official*
Leavitt, Martin Jack *lawyer*
Yost, James A. *manufacturing executive*

Novi
Barr, David John *retired art educator*
Chow, Chi-Ming *retired mathematics educator*
Kinsey, Charles John *industrial auctioneer, consultant, cattle breeder, farmer*
Ligocki, Kathleen A. *auto parts company executive*
Mallak, James A. *auto parts company executive*
Maniscalco, Joseph *artist, educator*
Pelham, Judith *health system administrator*
Sobczak, Judy Marie *clinical psychologist*

Oak Park
Agboruche, William *accountant, educator, toxicologist, philosopher*
Dill, Ellen Renée *minister, educator, writer*
Novick, Marvin *investment company executive*
Piper, Annette Cleone *social services administrator, researcher*

Okemos
Berkman, Claire Fleet *psychologist*
Dowley, Joel Edward *manufacturing executive, lawyer*

Giacoletto, Lawrence Joseph *electronics engineering educator, researcher, consultant*
Klunzinger, Thomas Edward *writer, actor, director*
Monson, Carol Lynn *osteopath, psychotherapist*
Ristow, George Edward *neurologist, educator*
Solo, Robert Alexander *economist, educator*

Onsted
Freeman, Fred Wesley *forester, educator*

Ontonagon
Clark, Raymond John *academic administrator*

Owosso
Guthrie, Carlton L. *automotive manufacturing company executive*
Uptigrove, Kenneth R. *library administrator*

Oxford
Smith, Jay Lawrence *planning company executive*

Pentwater
Noffke, Frank Edward *educational planner, writer, educator*

Petoskey
Baird, Gregory Ross *residence life/student activities director, theater educator*
Beierwaltes, William Henry *physician, educator*
Ketcham, Warren Andrew *psychologist, educator*
Meengs, William Lloyd *cardiologist*
Nicholson, William Noel *clinical neuropsychologist*
Winter, Kenneth Michael *editor, publishing executive, educator*

Pinckney
Davis, Robert Leach *retired government official, consultant*
McNamara, Ann Dowd *medical technologist*

Pleasant Ridge
Bertin, Leonard Gerard *graphics designer, artist*
Krabbenhoft, Kenneth Lester *radiologist, educator*
Sneed, Marie Eleanor Wilkey *retired secondary school educator*

Plymouth
Berry, Charlene Helen *librarian, musician*
deBear, Richard Stephen *library planning consultant*
Leuliette, Timothy D. *automotive executive*
Longhofer, Ronald Stephen *lawyer*
Massey, Donald E. *automotive executive*
Moore-Viculin, Charlotte Anne *artist, musician*
Stafeil, Jeff *corporate financial executive*
Vlcek, Donald Joseph, Jr., *food distribution company executive, consultant, business author, executive coach*

Pontiac
Bowman, Kone J *small business owner, financial analyst*
Brychtova, Jaroslava *sculptor*
Decker, Peter William *academic administrator*
Hampton, Philip Michael *consulting engineering company executive*
James, Reese Joseph *physician*
Love, Sharon Irene *elementary school educator*
Moss, Edward R. *publishing executive*

Port Huron
Keyes, Allen E. *judge*
Miller, Theresa L. *library director*
Moss, Carl Arthur *psychologist*
Rowark, Maureen *fine arts photographer*
Wu, Harry Pao-Tung *retired librarian*

Port Sanilac
Birdsall, Arthur Anthony *management consultant*

Portage
Chodos, Dale David Jerome *physician, consumer advocate*
Gardner-Bonneau, Daryle Jean *human factors engineering scientist, consultant*
Lee, Edward L. *retired bishop*
MacMillan, Stephen P. *health products executive*
Zhang, Charles C. *financial planner*

Portland
Rich, Joseph John *accountant*

Presque Isle
Kinney, Mark Baldwin *cultural organization administrator, educator*

Rapid City
Ring, Ronald Herman *lawyer*

Redford
Aubertin, Madeline Katherine *retired nursing educator, medical/surgical nurse, mental health services professional*
Barnaby, Alan *retail executive*
Hu, Weilong *engineer*
Karpinski, Huberta Elaine *library trustee*

Republic
Wixtrom, Donald Joseph *translator*

Riverdale
Kirby, Kent Bruce *artist, educator*

Rochester
Alston, Lettie Beckon *music educator, musician*
Appleton, Sheldon Lee *education educator*
Arrathoon, Leigh Adelaide *medievalist, editor, writer, educator*
Burke, Richard John *education educator*
Conaway, Charles C. *former retail company executive*
Crissman, Penny M. *state legislator*
Gallagher, Edward Arthur *retired academic administrator, real estate developer*
Loh, Robert N. K. *engineering educator*
Ovshinsky, Stanford Robert *physicist, inventor, energy executive, information company executive*
Packard, Sandra Podolin *education educator, consultant*
Russi, Gary D. *academic administrator*
Varani, Flavio *musician, music educator*
Xia, Yang *physicist, educator*

Yang, Lianxiang *optical engineer, educator*
Zeppelin, Mary Frances *special education educator, elementary school educator, consultant*

Rochester Hills
Akeel, Hadi Abu *robotics executive*
Badalament, Robert Anthony *urologist, oncologist*
Bovee, David R. *automotive executive*
Denton, Lawrence A. *automotive executive*
Eisenhower, Laurie *performing company executive*
Fritzsche, Hellmut *physics educator*
Mills, Helene Audrey *education educator*
Minton, Henry Lee *psychology educator*
Pfister, Karl Anton *industrial company executive*
Romero, Josefino Tabernilla *nurse anesthetist*
Thoma, August John *music educator*
Unakar, Nalin Jayantilal *biological sciences educator*

Rockford
Irish, Diana Maria *wildlife rehabilitation agent*
Knape, Herbert Fritz *business executive*

Romeo
Clark, Mark Lee *lawyer*
Stryker, James William *retired automotive executive, former military officer*

Romulus
Yussouff, Mohammed *retired physicist, educator*

Roscommon
Carton, Gary L. *performing arts association administrator*
Gagnier, Joseph C. *artist*
Mainprize, Donald Charles *minister, writer*

Rose Township
Fleming, Kathryn Alice *retired automotive executive*

Royal Oak
Al-Sarraf, Muhyi *internist, oncologist*
Bohy, Ric *magazine editor, consultant, broadcast commentator*
Cook, Noel Robert *manufacturing executive*
Dworkin, Howard Jerry *nuclear medicine physician, educator*
Farhy, Rodolfo David *internist, cardiologist*
Kagan, Ron *zoological park administrator*
LaBan, Myron Miles *physician, administrator*
Malik, Ghaus Muhammad *neurosurgeon*
Matzick, Kenneth John *hospital administrator*
McCarroll, Kathleen Ann *radiologist, educator*
Monnich, John Robert *lawyer*
O'Neill, William Walter *physician, educator*
Proctor, Conrad Arnold *physician*
Stanalajczo, Greg Charles *computer and technology company executive*

Saginaw
Chaffee, Paul Charles *newspaper editor*
Cline, Thomas William *real estate leasing company executive, management consultant*
Evans, Harold Edward *banker*
Ferlinz, Jack *cardiologist, medical educator*
Houshiar, Bobbie Kay *language arts educator*
Leppert-Largent, Anna M. *church musician*
Manning, John Warren, III, *retired surgeon, medical educator*
Martin, Walter *retired lawyer*
Remenar, Robert J. *automotive executive*
Scharffe, William Granville *academic administrator, educator*

Saint Clair Shores
Field, Stephen Ira *dermatologist, educator*
Glancy, Alfred Robinson, III, *retired public utility company executive*
Hausner, John Herman *retired judge*
Joslyn, Robert Bruce *lawyer*
Kachman, Frances Guiducci *artist*
Ryan, Harold Martin *judge*
Shine, Neal James *journalism educator, former newspaper editor, publisher*
Skoney, Sophie Essa *educational administrator*
Smith, Frank Earl *retired association executive*
Stevens, Clark Valentine *lawyer*
Vogel, Sally Thomas *psychologist, social worker, educator*
Woodford, Arthur MacKinnon *library director, historian*

Saint Ignace
Dodson, Bruce J. *funeral director*

Saint Joseph
King, George Raleigh *retired manufacturing executive*
Wood, Dirk Gregory *surgeon, physician, forensic consultant*

Saline
Anderson, Austin Gothard *lawyer, consultant, academic administrator*
Cornell, Richard Garth *biostatistics educator*
Frank, Richard Calhoun *architect*
Hansen, Janice Elizabeth *psychologist*
Harbour, Nancy Caine *lawyer*
Macher, Frank E. *automotive executive*

Saranac
Herbrucks, Stephen *food products executive*

Saugatuck
Blair, John Raymond *educational psychology educator*

Sault Sainte Marie
Fields, Polly Stevens *humanities educator, researcher, writer*
Johnson, Gary Robert *political scientist*
Youngblood, Betty J. *academic administrator*

Scottville
Meyers, Daniel Michael *music educator, researcher*

Sears
McCullough, Willard G. *retired biochemist*

Shelby
Burrows, Jay Edward *lawyer*

Shelby Township
Fillbrook, Thomas George *telephone company executive*
Heremans, Joseph Pierre *physicist*
Nagy, Louis Leonard *engineering executive, researcher*
Schultz, Arthur Joseph, Jr., *retired trade association executive*

Sodus
Handy, Virginia Mae *writer*

South Haven
LaRocque, Linda Lou *interior designer, educator, playwright*
Waxman, Sheldon Robert *lawyer*

South Lyon
Palmer, Kimberly Anne *director*

Southfield
Adelman, Martin Jerome *law educator*
Amladi, Prasad Ganesh *management consulting executive, health care consultant, researcher*
Bindschadler, David E. *mathematician, department chairman, application developer*
Birdsong, Emil Ardell *clinical psychologist*
Bledsoe, Laurita *small business owner, publisher*
Boyce, Daniel Hobbs *finance company executive*
Caponigro, Jeffrey Ralph *public relations counselor*
Catallo, Heather *newscaster*
Chambers, Charles MacKay *academic administrator, lawyer, consultant*
Dawson, Dennis Ray *lawyer, manufacturing executive*
DelGrosso, Douglas G. *manufacturing executive*
DeLong, Donald Alan *lawyer*
Dickerson, Brian *columnist*
Fieger, Geoffrey Nels *lawyer*
Fleming, Mac Arthur *labor union administrator*
Gayle, Monica *broadcast journalist*
Gleichman, John Alan *safety and loss control executive*
Gouldey, Glenn Charles *manufacturing executive*
Graves, Ray Reynolds *retired judge*
Gregory, Karl Dwight *economist, educator, consultant*
Hanisko, John-Cyril Patrick *electronics engineer, physicist*
Hanket, Mark John *lawyer*
Hotelling, Harold *law and economics educator*
Hudson, Cheryl L. *communications executive*
Ibrahim, Ibrahim N. *bishop*
Jackson, Michael B. *service company executive*
Jackson, William Gene *computer company executive*
Jacobs, John E. *lawyer*
Kalter, Alan *advertising agency executive*
Koch, Albert Acheson *management consultant*
Lee, James Edward, Jr., *educational consultant*
Leib, Jeffrey M. *lawyer*
Lynch, George Michael *auto parts manufacturing executive*
Maibach, Ben C., III, *construction company executive*
Makupson, Amyre Porter *television station executive*
Margolis, Sherry *newscaster*
Martin, Marcella Edric *retired community health nurse*
McClow, Roger James *labor lawyer*
McClure, Charles G. *automotive executive*
McKeen, Alexander C. *retired engineering executive, foundation administrator*
Miller, Robert Stevens, Jr., *finance professional*
Newman, Steven E. *neurologist*
O'Hara, John Paul, III, *orthopedic surgeon*
Perez-Cruet, Mick Jorge *neurological surgeon, educator*
Ponka, Lawrence John *automotive executive*
Primo, Joan Erwina *retail and real estate consulting business owner*
Rawden, David *financial services company executive*
Riley, Rochelle Rosalind *writer*
Ritchie, Alexander Buchan *lawyer*
Ross, Dale Garand *therapist, programming consultant, speaker, writer*
Rossiter, Robert E. *interior auto parts manufacturing executive*
Sedler, Rozanne Friedlander *social worker, educator*
Selis, Stuart L. *financial consultant, underwriter*
Shields, Robert Emmet *merchant banker, lawyer*
Shilts, Nancy S. *automotive executive, lawyer*
Snell, Richard A. *equipment manufacturing company executive*
Soo, Teck Mun *neurosurgeon*
Stebbins, Donald J. *car parts manufacturing company executive*
Stinger, Fanchon *newscaster*
Sullivan, Robert Emmet, Jr., *lawyer*
Targan, Holli Hart *lawyer*
Thimotheose, Kadakampallil George *psychologist*
Thomas, Judy Janet *reporter, health services professional*
Thurswell, Gerald Elliott *lawyer*
Toll, Sheldon Samuel *lawyer*
Tripp, James E. *psychotherapist, educator*
Tupper, Leon F. *manufacturing executive*
Turner, Lee Irwin *lawyer*
Wajsgras, David C. *manufacturing executive*
Way, Kenneth L. *motor vehicle seat manufacturing company executive*
Weiner, Karen Colby (Karen Lynn Colby) *psychologist, lawyer*
Willingham, Edward Bacon, Jr., *ecumenical minister, administrator*
Winzenreid, James Ernest *lawyer, entrepreneur*
Wisne, Lawrence A. *metal products executive*
Zubroff, Leonard Saul *surgeon*

Southgate
Kohn, Julieanne *travel agent*
Torok, Margaret Louise *insurance company executive*

Sparta
McDonald, Lois Alice *elementary school educator*

Spring Arbor
Moore-Jumonville, Kimberly *literature educator*
Thompson, Stanley B. *church administrator*

Spring Lake
Bussard, Janice Wingeier *retired educator, inventor*

Stanton
Winchell, George William *curriculum and technology educator*

Sterling Heights
Abbasi, Tariq Afzal *psychiatrist, educator*
Burke, Thomas Joseph *civil engineer*
Novak, Joseph Anthony *law librarian*

Sturgis
Hair, Robert Eugene *editor, writer, historian*
Reiff, James Stanley *osteopathic physician, addictions and psychiatric physician, surgeon*

Swartz Creek
Russell, Charles Harry *music educator, restaurant manager*

Taylor
Barry, Alan H. *consumer products company executive*
Fleshman, James W. *medical association administrator*
Lavery, Ian C. *colon and rectal surgeon, medical association administrator*
Leekley, John Robert *lawyer*
Manoogian, Richard Alexander *manufacturing executive*
Rosowski, Robert Bernard *manufacturing executive*
Wadhams, Timothy *consumer products company executive*

Tecumseh
Herrick, Kenneth Gilbert *manufacturing executive*
Herrick, Todd W. *manufacturing executive*

Three Rivers
Truesdell, Timothy L. *private investor*
Warnock, William Reid *lawyer*

Traverse City
Bagley, Colleen *marketing executive*
Burton, Betty June *retired pastor*
Dettmer, Michael Hayes *lawyer, former prosecutor*
Faulmann, Roger Ray *retired music educator*
Gillman, Michael Joseph *lawyer*
Parsons, John Thoren *manufacturing executive*
Quandt, Joseph Edward *lawyer, educator*
Quick, Albert Thomas *lawyer, educator*
Supanich, Barbara Ann *family practice physician*
Tobin, Patrick John *dermatologist*
VanderKolk, Mary DeDecker *nursing educator*
Weaver, Elizabeth A. *state supreme court justice*
Zimmerman, Paul Albert *retired college president, minister*

Trenton
Go, Benedict Anthony *internist*
Wukovits, John Francis *secondary school educator, writer*

Troy
Acton, David L(awrence) *automobile company executive*
Adderley, Terence E. *personnel director*
Alterman, Irwin Michael *lawyer*
Arking, Lucille Musser *nurse, epidemiologist*
Arle, John P. *electronics executive*
Austin, Karen *retail executive*
Baker, Ernest Waldo, Jr., *advertising executive*
Baker, Vernon G., II, *lawyer*
Barth, Volker J. *electronics executive*
Barton, Stanley L. *ophthalmologist, consultant*
Battenberg, J. T., III, *automotive company executive*
Bertrand, James A. *electronics executive*
Bickmeyer, Robert A. *retired automotive executive*
Blahnik, John G. *electronics executive*
Buschmann, Siegfried *manufacturing executive*
Butler, Kevin M. *electronics executive*
Cantor, Bernard Jack *lawyer*
Corace, Joseph Russell *automotive executive*
Criancamilli, Andrew A. *retail executive*
Crowley, William C. *retail executive*
Dawes, Alan S. *automotive company executive*
Day, Julian C. *retail executive*
Elder, Irma *retail automotive executive*
Gelder, John William *lawyer*
Given, Kerry Wade *plastics industry executive*
Golusin, Millard R. *obstetrician and gynecologist*
Hachey, Guy C. *electronics executive*
Handleman, David *audio products company executive*
Haron, David Lawrence *lawyer*
Harrison, Christine Delane *company executive*
Healy, Karen *automotive executive*
Hill, Richard A. *advertising executive*
Hsi, Morris Yu *mechanical engineer, educator*
Janak, Peter Harold *automotive company executive*
Kelly, Janet G. *retail executive*
Kruse, John Alphonse *lawyer*
LaDuke, Nancie *lawyer, corporate executive*
Lan, Xuekui *engineer*
Lorencz, Mary *public relations executive*
Lorenz, Mark C. *automotive executive*
Lueken, Harold W. *retail executive*
Marshall, John Elbert, III, *foundation executive*
Martin, Raymond Bruce *plumbing equipment manufacturing company executive*
May, Alan Alfred *lawyer*
McLaren, Karen Lynn *advertising executive*
Meerschaert, Joseph Richard *physician*
Meyers, Christine Laine *marketing and media executive, consultant*
Misra, Dwijen Cristobal *surgeon*
Moore, Oliver Semon, III, *publishing executive, consultant*
Morgan, Michael Vincent *lawyer*
Nelson, R. David *electronics executive*
Nolte, Henry R., Jr., *lawyer, former automobile company executive*
Okun, Maury *dance company executive*
O'Neal, Rodney *automotive executive*
Ordonez, Francisco A. (Frank) *automotive executive*
Owens, Jeffrey J. *electronics executive*
Pasricha, Atul *automotive executive*
Potts, Anthony Vincent *optometrist, orthokeratologist*
Robinson, Logan Gilmore *lawyer*
Runkle, Donald L. *electronics executive*
Schmidt, Michael Francis *lawyer*
Sharf, Stephan *automotive company executive*
Sheehan, John D. *automotive executive*
Sloan, Hugh Walter, Jr., *automotive executive*

Strome, Stephen *distribution company executive*
Thurber, John Alexander *lawyer*
Walker, Bette *automotive executive*
Weber, Mark R. *electronics executive*
Webster, Robert Byron *lawyer*
White, James, Jr., *psychiatric, mental health nurse, consultant*
White, Tommi A. *human resources firm executive*
Whitson, James P. *automotive executive*
Williams, David Perry *manufacturing executive*
Wohleen, David B. *electronics executive*
Yost, Larry D. *automotive executive*

University Center
Boyse, Peter Dent *academic administrator*
Dykhuizen, C. Jeffrey *child development psychologist, educator*
Gilbertson, Eric Raymond *academic administrator, lawyer*
Hill, Alan Gordon *sociologist, educator*
Hoerneman, Calvin A., Jr., *economics professor*
Jezierski, John Vincent *historian, educator*
Puia, George M. *writer, educator*

Walled Lake
Gillespie, J. Martin *sales and distribution company executive*
Williams, Sam B. *engineering executive*

Warren
Ableson, Donald William *automobile industry executive*
Akmakjian, Alan Paul *English language, literature and creative writing educator*
Bridenstine, Louis Henry, Jr., *lawyer*
Cheng, Yang-Tse *research scientist, materials scientist, physicist*
Deak, Charles Karol *chemist*
Gaarenstroom, Stephen William *chemist*
Gervason, Robert J *advertising executive*
Gilbert, Suzanne Harris *advertising executive*
Herbst, Jan Francis *physicist, researcher*
Hopp, Anthony James *advertising agency executive*
Johnson, Leonard Gustave *research mathematician, consultant*
Lett, Philip W. *engineering executive*
Lorenzo, Albert L. *academic administrator*
Mahone, Barbara Jean *automotive company executive*
Nefske, Donald Joseph *engineer*
Zoubareff, Kathy Olga *administrative assistant*

Washington
Chatterley, James Philip *retired automotive development engineer*
Gothard, Donald Lee *retired auto company executive*

Waterford
Anderson, Francile Mary *secondary school educator*
Hall, Terrence Lyon *lawyer*
Hallemann, James Raymond *media specialist, educator*
Houston, E. James, Jr., *banker, consultant*
Laing, James Thomas *retired not-for-profit developer*
Morgan, Paul William *engineer, researcher*
Randall, Karl W. *aviation executive, lawyer*

Wayne
Carpenter, Arthur Lloyd *education educator*

Wellston
Spain, Frederick William *retired secondary school educator, writer*

West Bloomfield
Barr, Martin *health care and higher education administrator*
Brin, David *writer, astronomer*
Darke, Richard Francis *lawyer*
Gullen, Christopher Roy *lawyer*
Harwood, Julius J. *metallurgist, educator*
Jones, Lewis Arnold, Jr., *physician, radiologist, consultant*
Joseph, Ramon Rafael *physician, educator*
Lewis, Harold Allen *childcare company executive*
Mamut, Mary Catherine *retired entrepreneur*
Meyers, Gerald Carl *finance educator, writer, expert witness, consultant*
Miller, Nancy Ellen *computer consultant*
Myers, Kenneth Ellis *hospital administrator*
Rauwerdink, William Jay *accountant*
Sarwer-Foner, Gerald Jacob *psychiatrist, educator*
Sawyer, Howard Jerome *physician*
Simpson, Robert Lee *university official, biology educator*
Smith, Nancy Hohendorf *retired sales and marketing executive*
Starr, Monica *company executive*
Stern, Guy *German language and literature educator, writer*
Williamson, Marilyn Lammert *English educator, university administrator*

Westland
Coates, Dianne Kay *social worker*

White Cloud
De Haan-Puls, Joyce Elaine *sales account representative, educator*

White Lake
Boyle, Patricia Jean *retired state supreme court justice*
Clyburn, Luther Linn *real estate broker, appraiser, ship captain*

Whitehall
Sirotko, Theodore Francis *priest, retired military officer*
Squier, David Louis *manufacturing executive*
Weber, Alban *association executive, lawyer*

Williamston
Johnson, Tom Milroy *academic dean, medical educator, physician*

Woodhaven
Kim, Hyo Sook *anesthesiologist*

Wyandotte
Kaurin, Douglas Edward *protective services official*

Ypsilanti
Barnes, James Milton *physics and astronomy educator*
Barr, John Monte *lawyer*
Boone, Morell Douglas *information and communications technology educator*
Brown-Chappell, Betty L. *social worker, educator*
Caswell, Herbert Hall, Jr., *retired biology educator*
Cere, Ronald Carl *languages educator, consultant, researcher*
Edwards, Gerald *plastics company executive*
Evans, Gary Lee *communications educator and consultant*
Farah, Badie Naiem *computer information systems educator, consultant*
Friedman, Monroe *psychologist, educator*
Gwaltney, Thomas Marion *education educator, writer*
Holoka, James Paul *classicist, educator, historian*
Lottie, Adrian Jerome *public policy educator, consultant*
McLain, Dennis O. *lawyer*
Okafor, Victor O. *journalist, educator*
Robbins, Jerry Hal *educational administration educator*
Sealy, Vernol St. Clair *scientist*
Weinstein, Jay A. *social science educator, researcher*

Zeeland
Bauer, Fred T. *technology products executive*
Nickels, Elizabeth Anne *office furniture manufacturing executive*
Volkema, Michael A. *office furniture manufacturer*

MINNESOTA

Ada
Sillerud, Arlen Roger *retired educator*

Alexandria
DeGier, Gregory Alan *music educator*
Hultstrand, Donald Maynard *bishop*

Andover
Peterson, Jill Susan *elementary school educator*
Rudzitis, Roland Talis *music educator*

Anoka
Goodell, Robert D. *lawyer, educator*
Quinn, R. Joseph *district judge*

Apple Valley
Brown, Francis William *chemist, consultant*
Knutson, David Lee *state legislator, lawyer*

Austin
Alcorn, Wallace Arthur *minister, writer*
Budd, Jim *communications manager*
Johnson, Joel W. *food products executive*
McCoy, Michael J. *food products company executive*
Rioux, Pierre August *psychiatrist*
Schmid, Harald Heinrich Otto *biochemistry educator, academic director*
Schneider, Mahlon C. *lawyer*

Bayport
Garofalo, Donald R. *window manufacturing executive*
Humphrey, James E. *manufacturing executive*
Johnson, Michael O. *window manufacturing executive*

Belle Plaine
Townsend, C. Edward *publishing executive*

Bemidji
Bridston, Paul Joseph *strategic consultant*
Christenson, Eileen Esther *geriatrics nurse*
Kief, Paul Allan *lawyer*
Martinson, Ida Marie *nursing educator, physiologist, medical/surgical nurse*
Nohner, Allen M. *corporate communications specialist*
Rogers, Patricia Louise *education educator, consultant*
Wettstein, Shannon Leigh *music educator*

Big Lake
Fillafer, Richard *music educator*

Blaine
Yecke, Cheri Pierson *education policy fellow, columnist, author*

Bloomington
Bekrenev, Anatoliy *physicist*
Boedigheimer, Robert David *lawyer*
Broeker, John Milton *lawyer*
Brokke, Catherine Juliet *mission executive*
Carpel, Emmett Franklin *ophthalmologist, consultant*
Grinnell, Joseph Fox *lawyer*
Jeffries, Mary *public relations executive*
Jensen, Richard Allen *mathematician, educator*
Kuntz, Lila Elaine *secondary business education educator*
Larson, Michael Len *newspaper editor, hospital administrator, publishing executive*
Matlon, David Michael *insurance agent, treasurer*
Miller, Kevin Robert *employee benefit consultant*
Mooty, John William *lawyer*
Nichols, Donna Mardell *nurse anesthetist*
Norris, William C. *retired computer systems executive*
Sherman, Patsy O'Connell *retired technical development administrator, chemist*
Smith, Henry Charles, III, *symphony orchestra conductor*
Thomas, Margaret Jean *clergywoman, religious research consultant*
Tsu, I-Fei *materials engineer*

Brainerd
O'Hara, William Desmond, Jr., *lawyer*
Samuelson, Donald B. *former state legislator*
Wannamaker, Mary Ruth *music educator*

Brandon
Bettermann, Hilda *state legislator*

Brooklyn Park
Rogers, David *apparel executive*

Burnsville
Lai, Juey Hong *chemical engineer*
Lakin, James Dennis *allergist, immunologist, director*
O'Brien, Gerald James *utilities executive*

Canby
Larson, Gary Arthur *farmer, financial consultant*

Champlin
Lyons, Steven Gerard *music educator*

Chanhassen
Prince, (Prince Rogers Nelson) *musician, actor*
Severson, Roger Allan *bank executive*
Shanahan, Eugene Miles *flow measurement instrumentation company executive*

Chaska
Burke, Steven Francis *organization executive*
Knapp, Peggy Durda *international company administrator*
Kwak, Seung Koon *research scientist*
Spargo, Carolyn Marie *language educator, music educator*

Chatfield
Opat, Matthew John *lawyer*

Chisago City
Miller, Robert Carl *retired library director*

Chisholm
Peterson, Marjorie *former mayor*

Circle Pines
Barott, Pat Robert *broadcast technician*
Davis, Richard Carlton *rehabilitation services administrator*

Clarissa
Titrud, Oliver George *retired medical educator*

Coleraine
Ersayin, Salih *engineering educator, researcher*
Iwasaki, Iwao *engineering educator*

Collegeville
Joyce, Robert E. *philosopher, educator*
Reinhart, Dietrich Thomas *academic administrator, social studies educator*
Rolfson, Helen C. *theology studies educator, translator*

Coon Rapids
Bordner, Patricia Anne *insurance agent, writer*
Wilson, Sylvia Alyce *musician, educator*

Cottage Grove
Hudnut, Robert Kilborne *clergyman, author*

Crookston
Balke, Victor H. *bishop*

Crosby
Barnum, Charles Earl, III, *lawyer*

Dellwood
Ventura, Jesse (James Janos) *former governor*

Detroit Lakes
Eginton, Charles Theodore *surgeon, educator*
Johansson, John Thomas *retired science educator*
Remmen, Lawrence P. *city planner*

Duluth
Aufderheide, Arthur Carl *pathologist*
Bakk-Hansen, Heidi K. *writer, researcher*
Balmer, James Walter *lawyer*
Bower, John Richard Fenn *archaeologist, educator*
Bowman, Roger Manwaring *real estate executive*
Burns, Richard Ramsey *lawyer*
Chee, Cheng-Khee *artist, educator*
Craig, Robert H. *theology studies educator*
Feroz, Ehsan Habib *accounting educator, researcher, writer*
Fields, Allen *artistic director*
Gruver, Nancy *publishing executive*
Heaney, Gerald William *federal judge*
Heller, Lois Jane *physiologist, educator, researcher*
Johnson, Arthur Gilbert *microbiology educator*
Latto, Lewis M. *broadcasting company executive*
Martin, Kathryn A. *academic administrator*
McKee, David Charles *physician, neurologist*
Mehrotra, Chandra *psychology professor, dean*
Nelson, Dennis Lee *finance educator*
Pearce, Donald Joslin *retired librarian*
Rapp, George Robert (Rip Rapp) *geology and archeology educator*
Salmela, David Daniel *architect*
Salmela, Lynn Marie *clinical nurse specialist*
Schroeder, Fred Erich Harald *humanities educator*
Tezla, Albert *English educator*
Whiteman, Richard Frank *architect*
Zhdankin, Viktor Vladimirovich *chemistry professor*
Ziegler, Richard J. *dean, educator*
Zinn, Gesa *education educator*

Eagan
Clemens, T. Pat *manufacturing executive*
Collier, Ken O. *editor*
Felix, Cheryl A. *air transportation executive*
Han, Bernard L. *air transportation executive*
Steenland, Douglas *air transportation executive*
Todd, John Joseph *lawyer*
Wendler, M. Cecilia *nursing educator*

Eden Prairie
Arthur, Lindsay Grier *retired judge, author, editor*
Borlik, Robert W. *information technology executive*
Carlson, Jeffrey *lawyer*
Cervilla, Constance Marlene *marketing consultant*
Culpepper, Daunte *professional football player*
Emison, James Wade *petroleum company executive*
Engel, Susan E. *retail executive*
Erickson, Kim *consumer products company executive*
Friederichs, Norman Paul *lawyer*
Hanson, Dale S. *retired bank executive*
Harmel, Paul *photography company executive*
Harmon, Robert Gerald *health company executive, educator*
Henningsen, Peter, Jr., *diversified industry executive*
Higgins, Robert Arthur *electrical engineer, educator, consultant*
Jackson, Darren Richard *retail company executive*
Johnson, Howard Arthur, Jr., *corporate executive, operations analyst, financial officer*
Knous, Pamela K. *wholesale distribution executive*
Lindbloom, Chad M. *transportation executive*
McCombs, Billy Joe (Red McCombs) *professional football team executive*
McCombs, Charline *professional sports team executive*
Moss, Randy *professional football player*
Nilles, John Michael *lawyer*
Noddle, Jeffrey *retail and food distribution executive*
Petersen, Maureen Jeanette Miller *management information consultant, former nurse*
Radunz, Paul A. *transportation executive*
Thompson, Sally Ann *editor*
Verdoorn, D.R. (Sid) *food service executive*
Wiehoff, John P. *trucking executive*
Woods, Gary V. *professional football team executive, former professional basketball team executive, automotive executive*
Wright, Michael William *wholesale distribution and retail executive*

Edina
Bisping, Bruce Henry *photojournalist*
Brown, Charles Eugene *retired electronics company executive*
Brown, Laurence David *retired bishop*
Burdick, Lou Brum *public relations executive*
Burk, Robert S. *lawyer*
Campbell, James Robert *retired bank executive*
Christensen, Nadia Margaret *writer, translator, editor, educator*
Emmerich, Karol Denise *foundation executive, daylily hybridizer, former retail executive*
Froemming, Herbert Dean *retired retail executive*
Frys, Russell N. *obstetrician-gynecologist*
Gottesman, Irving Isadore *psychology educator*
Justman, Richard Allen *pediatrician*
Neff, Fred Leonard *lawyer*
Putnam, Frederick Warren, Jr., *bishop*
Sampson, John Eugene *consulting company executive*
Sandy, Lewis Gordon *physician, healthcare executive*
Schroeder, Albert John *retired pediatrician*
Schwarzrock, Shirley Pratt *writer, educator*
Steinberg, Michael *music critic, educator*
Tagatz, George Elmo *retired obstetrician, gynecologist, educator*
Taylor, Scott Maxfield *business educator*
Van Beek, Allen Lester *plastic surgeon*
Wilder, Walter Llewellyn *allergist, immunologist, pediatrician*

Elk River
Goss, Cynthia Lee *tax accountant*

Elysian
Thayer, Edna Louise *medical facility and nursing administrator*

Erskine
Moe, Roger Deane *former state legislator, secondary education educator*
Rongen, Renee Wall *entrepreneur, consultant, writer*

Excelsior
Beeler, Donald Daryl *retired retail executive*
Fazio, Anthony Lee *investment company executive*
Fenske, Jerald Allan *minister*
Parker, Robert Chauncey Humphrey *clergyman, publishing executive, psychic*

Fairmont
Fowler, Chuck *former state legislator*
Rosen, Thomas J. *food and agricultural products executive*

Falcon Heights
Kreuter, Gretchen V. *academic administrator*

Farmington
Wurdeman, Lew Edward *Internet company executive, consultant*

Fergus Falls
Bigwood, Robert William *lawyer*
MacFarlane, John Charles *utility company executive*
Overgaard, Robert Milton *retired religious organization administrator*

Forest Lake
Broecker, Sherry *state legislator*
Marchese, Ronald Thomas *ancient history and archaeology educator*
Rachie, Cyrus *retired lawyer*

Fort Ripley
Scott, Ivan Carl *historian, educator*

Fridley
Larson, Marilyn J. *retired elementary music educator*
Savelkoul, Donald Charles *retired lawyer*

Golden Valley
Dahl, Gerald LuVern *psychotherapist, educator*
Harrison, David D. *corporate financial executive*
Hogan, Randall J. *manufacturing executive, electronics executive*
Leppik, Margaret White *municipal official*
Lester, Susan E. *bank executive*
Schlichting, William Henry *lawyer, writer*

Grand Marais
Napadensky, Hyla Sarane *engineering consultant*

Grand Rapids
King, Sheryl Jayne *secondary education educator, counselor*

Merrill, Arthur Lewis *retired theology educator*

Hallock
Malm, Roger Charles *lawyer*

Hamel
Tiller, Thomas C. *manufacturing executive*

Harmony
Webster, Jeffrey Leon *graphic designer*

Hastings
Avent, Sharon L. Hoffman *manufacturing company executive*

Hawley
Baer, Zenas *lawyer*

Hopkins
Hunter, Donald Forrest *lawyer*
Ramberg, Patricia Lynn *college president*
Rappaport, Gary Burton *defense equipment executive*

Inver Grove Heights
Johnson, John D. *grain company executive*
Koenig, Robert August *minister, educator*
Schmitz, John *grain company executive*

Kenyon
Peterson, Franklin Delano *lawyer*

Lake Crystal
Pawlitschek, Donald Paul *business consultant*

Lake Elmo
Schultz, Clarence John *minister*
Tomljanovich, Esther M. *retired judge*
Vivona, Daniel Nicholas *chemist*

Lakeland
Larsen, Peg *state legislator*

Lakeville
Phinney, William Charles *retired geologist*
Setterholm, Jeffrey Miles *systems engineer*

Lauderdale
Resch, Joseph Anthony *neurologist*

Lindstrom
Messin, Marlene Ann *plastics company executive*

Little Canada
Hardman, James Charles *lawyer, motor carrier executive*

Long Lake
Hofkin, Ann Ginsburgh *photographer, poet*
Lowthian, Petrena *academic administrator*

Loretto
Veit, Gae *construction executive*

Madelia
Lucek, Donald Walter *surgeon*

Madison
Husby, Donald Evans *engineering company executive*

Mahtomedi
Brainerd, Richard Charles *human resources executive, consultant, educator*
Holmen, Reynold Algott Emanuel *chemist*

Mankato
Bell, Sue Ellen *research analyst, administrator, nursing educator*
Dumke, Melvin Philip *dentist*
Friend, Donald Agar *geographer, geomorphologist, educator*
Hopkins, Layne Victor *computer science educator*
Huot, Rachel Irene *biomedical educator, research scientist, physician*
Janc, John J. *language educator*
Moldstad, Joslyn M. *pre-school educator, writer*
Nickerson, James Findley *retired educator*
Orvick, George Myron *church denomination executive, minister*
Preska, Margaret Louise Robinson *education historian, administrator*
Purscell, Keith William *minister*
Rahman, Mezbahur *statistics educator*
Schreier, Bradley *sales executive, marketing executive*
Taylor, Glen A. *printing, direct mail and technology company executive, professional sports team executive*
Widner, Robert Lee, Jr., *psychologist, educator*

Maple Grove
Kirpes, Anne Irene *elementary school educator*
Limmer, Warren E. *state legislator, real estate broker*

Mapleton
John, Hugo Herman *natural resources educator*

Marcell
Aldrich, Richard John *agronomist, educator*

Marine On Saint Croix
Gavin, Robert Michael, Jr., *education consultant*
Haynsworth, Harry Jay, IV, *lawyer, educator*

Marshall
Beadle, John M. *food products executive*
Burr, Tracy L. *food products executive*
Danahar, David C. *academic administrator, historian, educator*
Herrmann, Dan *food products executive*
Joo, Hee-Jong *criminology educator*
Miller, Donald *food products executive*
Paskach, David M. *lawyer, food products executive*
Pippin, M. Lenny *food products executive*

Medford
Paschke, Jerry Bryan *lawyer*

Melrose
Hammarsten, James Francis *internist, educator*

Mendota Heights
Frechette, Peter Loren *dental products executive*

Milaca
Wig, Robert Curtis *retired music educator, conductor*

Minneapolis
Aanerud, Melvin Bernard *federal agency administrator*
Abi-Ghanem, Georges Victor *engineer, scientist*
Ackerman, Eugene *biophysics educator*
Adams, John Stephen *geography educator*
Agyenkwah, Kennedy Seth *communications executive*
Ahlers, Linda L. *retail executive*
Al, Marc Andre *lawyer*
Allers, Marlene Elaine *legal administrator*
Alton, Ann Leslie *judge, lawyer, educator*
Amdahl, Douglas Kenneth *retired state supreme court justice*
Anderson, Alan Marshall *lawyer*
Anderson, Eric Scott *lawyer*
Anderson, John Edward *mechanical engineering educator*
Anderson, Tim *airport terminal executive*
Appel, John C. *investment company executive*
Arnold, Douglas Norman *mathematician*
Asp, William George *librarian*
Atwood, John Brian *dean*
Avella, Joseph Ralph *university educator*
Ayling, Corey John *lawyer*
Bache, Robert James *physician, medical educator*
Bae, Seongtae *electrical engineer*
Baillie, James Leonard *lawyer*
Baker, John Stevenson (Michael Dyregrov) *writer*
Bakken, Earl Elmer *electrical engineer, bioengineering company executive*
Bancroft, Ann E. *polar explorer*
Barnhill, Howard Eugene *insurance company executive*
Bashiri, Iraj *Central Asian studies educator*
Bastiaens, F. Guillaume *food products executive*
Beardsley, John Ray *public relations firm executive*
Bearmon, Lee *lawyer*
Bell, Constance Conklin *child care association administrator*
Benson, Donald Erick *holding company executive*
Benveniste, Lawrence *dean*
Berens, William Joseph *lawyer*
Berg, Stanton Oneal *firearms and ballistics consultant*
Berg, Thomas Kenneth *lawyer*
Bergerson, David Raymond *lawyer*
Bergeson, James *advertising executive*
Bernhardson, Ivy Schutz *lawyer*
Berry, David J. *former financial services company executive*
Berryman, Robert Glen *accounting educator, consultant*
Berscheid, Ellen S. *psychology educator, writer, researcher*
Bingham, Christopher *statistics educator*
Bird, Dick *sign painter*
Blackburn, Henry Webster, Jr., *retired epidemiologist*
Bland, J(ohn) Richard *lawyer*
Bly, Robert *poet*
Boelter, Philip Floyd *real estate company officer, mortgage company executive*
Bolan, Richard Stuart *urban planner, educator, researcher*
Bonner, Brigid Ann *marketing professional*
Bonneville, Katherine Ann *human resources specialist, consultant*
Bonsignore, Michael Robert *former electronics and computer company executive*
Borger, John Philip *lawyer*
Boudreau, Robert James *nuclear medicine physician, researcher*
Bowie, Norman Ernest *university official, educator*
Boylan, Brian Richard *author, historian, educator, photographer, literary agent*
Brasket, Curt Justin *systems analyst, chess player*
Breimayer, Joseph Frederick *patent lawyer*
Bress, Michael E. *retired lawyer*
Brink, David Ryrie *lawyer*
Brown, David Mitchell *pediatrician, educator, dean*
Bruininks, Robert H. *academic administrator, psychologist, educator*
Bruner, Philip Lane *lawyer*
Brunetti, Wayne Henry *utilities executive*
Buchwald, Henry *surgeon, educator, researcher*
Buckley, John William *financial company executive*
Buhrmaster, Robert C. *manufacturing executive*
Buoen, Roger *newspaper editor*
Buratti, Dennis P. *lawyer*
Burchell, Howard Bertram *retired physician, educator*
Burns, Robert Arthur *lawyer*
Burton, Charles Victor *neurosurgeon, inventor*
Busdicker, Gordon G. *retired lawyer*
Cameron, Patricia *advertising executive*
Campbell, Karlyn Kohrs *speech and communication educator*
Carlson, Arne Helge *former governor*
Carlson, Jennie Peaslack *bank executive*
Carlson, Thomas David *lawyer*
Carr, Peter William *chemistry professor*
Casey, Lynn M. *public relations executive*
Cecere, Andrew *bank executive*
Cerra, Frank Bernard *dean*
Charnas, Lawrence *neurologist*
Chavers, Blanche Marie *pediatrician, educator, researcher*
Chemberlin, Peg *clergy, religious organization administrator*
Chipman, John Somerset *economist, educator*
Ciresi, Michael Vincent *lawyer*
Clary, Bradley G. *lawyer, educator*
Clayton, Thomas Swoverland *English educator*
Clemence, Roger Davidson *landscape architect, educator*
Cline, Richard Ryan *education educator*
Cohn, Jay N. *cardiologist, educator*
Cole, Phillip Allen *lawyer*
Collins, Arthur D., Jr., *medical products executive*
Comstock, Rebecca Ann *lawyer*
Conn, Gordon Brainard, Jr., *lawyer*
Conway, William F. *architect, architecture educator*
Cooper, William Allen *bank executive*
Cope, Lewis *journalist*
Courtney, Eugene Whitmal *computer company executive*
Cowles, John, Jr., *publisher, women's sports promoter*
Cowles, John Jay, III, *investment company executive, entrepreneur*
Cracchiolo, James M. *diversified financial services company executive*
Craig, James Lynn *physician*
Crosby, Jacqueline Garton *newspaper editor, journalist*
Curler, Jeffrey H. *packaging manufacturing executive*
Cussler, Edward Lansing, Jr., *chemical engineer, educator*
Dale, John Sorensen *investment company executive, portfolio manager*
Davis, Howard Ted *engineering educator*
Davis, Michael J. *judge*
Davis, Richard K. *corporate financial executive*
Demeritt, Stephen R. *food products executive*
DeNavaez, Denny *health facility administrator*
Diemand, Kim Eugene *human resources executive*
DiGangi, Frank Edward *academic administrator*
Dimond, Robert B. *food products executive*
DiPietro, Mark Joseph *lawyer*
Doherty, Valerie *employment services professional, lawyer*
Domino, Constance Mae *genetics researcher*
Doroschak, John Z. *dentist, consultant*
Doty, David Singleton *federal judge*
Douglas, William *dental educator, biomedical research administrator*
Doyle, Michael J. *corporate financial executive*
Duff, Andrew S. *corporate financial executive*
Dunlap, William DeWayne, Jr., *advertising agency executive*
Durkin, G. Michael *food products executive*
Dworkin, Martin *microbiologist, educator*
Dykstra, Dennis Dale *physiatrist*
Dyrud, Amos Oliver *minister, educator*
Eck, George Gregory *lawyer*
Eckberg, E. Daniel *secondary school educator*
Edwardson, Sandra *dean, nursing educator*
Eich, Susan *public relations executive*
Eickhoff, John R. *information services company executive*
Elm, Dawn Rae *management educator*
Erickson, Gerald Meyer *classical studies educator*
Ernst, James Allan *safety engineer*
Erstad, Leon Robert *lawyer*
Falker, John Richard *investment advisor*
Fallon, Patrick R. *advertising executive*
Farah, Caesar Elie *Middle Eastern and Islamic studies educator*
Faricy, John Hartnett, Jr., *lawyer*
Faricy, Richard Thomas *architect*
Farr, Leonard Alfred *hospital administrator*
Fauth, John J. *venture capitalist*
Fawcett, Marie Ann Formanek (Mrs. Roscoe Kent Fawcett) *civic leader*
Feldman, Nancy Jane *health organization executive*
Fergus, Patricia Marguerita *English language educator, writer, editor*
Ferrari, Giannantonio *electronics executive*
Fetler, Paul *retired composer*
Feuss, Linda Anne Upsall *lawyer*
Filloon, Karen *radio personality*
Findorff, Robert Lewis *retired air filtration equipment company executive*
Finzen, Bruce Arthur *lawyer*
Firchow, Evelyn Scherabon *German language and literature educator, writer*
Firchow, Peter Edgerly *language professional, educator, author*
Fisch, Robert Otto *medical educator*
Fisher, Tom *architecture educator*
Flanagan, Barbara *journalist*
Fletcher, Edward Abraham *engineering educator*
Flom, Gerald Trossen *lawyer*
Forneris, Jeanne M. *lawyer*
Fowke, Benjamin G.S., III, *energy executive*
Francis, Michael R. *retail executive*
Frank, Kerry Dean *psychology educator, consultant*
Fraser, Arvonne Skelton *former United Nations ambassador*
Freese, Andrew *neurosurgeon, educator, scientist*
French, Catherine E. Wolfgram *engineering educator, researcher*
French, John Dwyer *lawyer*
Fruen, Lois *secondary school educator*
Fulop, Laszlo G. *architect*
Gage, Edwin C., III, (Skip Gage) *travel and marketing services executive*
Gajl-Peczalska, Kazimiera J. *retired surgical pathologist, pathology educator*
Galambos, Theodore Victor *civil engineer, educator*
Gallagher, Gerald Raphael *venture capitalist*
Gardebring, Sandra S. *academic administrator*
Gardenhire, Ronald Clyde *professional athletics manager*
Garfield, Joan Barbara *statistics educator*
Garner, Shirley Nelson *English language educator*
Garnett, Kevin *professional basketball player*
Garon, Philip Stephen *lawyer*
Garton, Thomas William *lawyer*
Gavin, Sara *public relations executive*
Gerberich, Susan Goodwin *epidemiologist, educator, medical researcher*
Gerdner, Linda Ann *nursing researcher, educator*
Gill, Richard Lawrence *lawyer*
Goldberg, Luella Gross *corporation executive*
Goldberger, Robert D. *food products company executive*
Goldman, Allen Marshall *physics educator*
Gordon, Corey Lee *lawyer*
Gordon, John Bennett *lawyer*
Gorham, Eville *ecologist, biogeochemist, educator*
Gorlin, Robert James *medical educator*
Gottschalk, Stephen Elmer *lawyer*
Grant, David James William *pharmacy educator*
Greener, Ralph Bertram *lawyer*
Greenfield, Lee *state legislator*
Griffith, G. Larry *lawyer*
Griffith, Sima Lynn *investment banker, consultant*
Grodsky, Jamie Anne *law educator*
Grundhofer, Jerry A. *bank executive*
Grundhofer, John F. *bank executive*
Gudmundson, Barbara Rohrke *ecologist*
Gullickson, Glenn, Jr., *physician, educator*
Gulliver, John Stephen *civil engineering educator, consultant*
Guo, Meiwen *structural engineer*
Gyllenhaal, Anders *publishing executive, editor*
Haase, Ashley Thomson *microbiology educator, researcher*
Hagglund, Clarance Edward *lawyer, publishing company owner*
Haines, Stephen John *neurological surgeon*
Hale, James Thomas *retail executive, lawyer*
Hale, Roger Loucks *manufacturing executive, director*
Halley, James Woods *physics educator*
Hallman, Gary L. *photographer, educator*
Hamel, William John *church administrator, minister*
Hamiel, Jeff *airport executive*
Hansen, Jo-Ida Charlotte *psychology educator, researcher*
Hanson, Arthur Stuart *physician, consultant*
Hanson, Bruce Eugene *lawyer*
Hanson, Kent Bryan *lawyer*
Harper, Donald Victor *retired transportation and logistics educator*
Hart, Buster Clarence *lawyer*
Hasten, Joseph E. *corporate financial executive*
Haverkamp, Judson *editor*
Hawkins, Paul E. *real estate company executive*
Hays, Thomas S. *medical educator, medical researcher*
Hayward, Edward Joseph *lawyer*
He, Bin *biomedical engineer, educator*
Heffelfinger, Thomas Backer *lawyer*
Heiberg, Robert Alan *lawyer*
Hektner, Candice Elaine *lawyer*
Heller, Kenneth Jeffrey *physicist*
Hendra, Tony *writer, comedian, actor*
Hendrixson, Peter S. *lawyer*
Henson, Robert Frank *lawyer*
Herbison, Priscilla Joan *public policy and law educator, consultant*
Hibbs, John Stanley *lawyer*
Hill, Tessa *president non profit environmental group*
Hillstrom, Thomas Peter *engineering executive*
Hippee, William H., *lawyer*
Hobbins, Robert Leo *lawyer*
Hoffmann, Thomas Russell *business management educator*
Hogenkamp, Henricus Petrus Cornelis *biochemistry researcher, biochemistry educator*
Holen, Norman Dean *retired art educator, artist*
Hollencamp, Greg *architectural firm executive*
Hollis, Martha *director, researcher*
Holt, Robert Theodore *political scientist, dean, educator*
Hom, David Brian *surgeon*
Homolka, Daniel Michael *lawyer*
Horsager, Kent *brokerage house executive*
Houe, Poul *language educator, literature educator, writer*
Houlton, Lise *performing company executive*
Howland, Joan Sidney *law librarian, educator*
Humar, Abhinav *transplant surgeon, clinical researcher*
Hurwicz, Leonid *economist, educator*
Isaak, Larry A. *educational association administrator*
Jackson, Donna Cardamone *music educator*
Jackson, Renee Leone *lawyer*
Jacob, Bernard Michel *architect*
Jacobs, Irwin Lawrence *diversified corporate executive*
Jarboe, Mark Alan *lawyer*
Jeffrey-Smith, Lilli Ann *biofeedback specialist, educator, administrator*
Jeffries, Kim *radio personality*
Johannsen, Marc Alan *lawyer*
Johnson, Alex Moore *lawyer, educator*
Johnson, Carol R. *school system administrator*
Johnson, David Chester *university chancellor, sociology educator*
Johnson, David Wolcott *psychologist, educator*
Johnson, Donald Clay *librarian, curator*
Johnson, Gary L. *publishing executive*
Johnson, Gary M. *lawyer*
Johnson, John Warren *retired association executive*
Johnson, Kenneth Harvey *veterinary pathologist*
Johnson, Lola Norine *retired advertising and public relations executive, educator*
Johnson, Margaret Ann (Peggy) *library administrator*
Johnson, Walter Kline *civil engineer*
Jones, B. Todd *lawyer, former prosecutor*
Jones, Susie *radio personality*
Jones, Will(iam) (William Arnold Jones) *writer, former newspaper columnist*
Joseph, Daniel Donald *aeronautical engineer, educator*
Joseph, Marilyn Susan *gynecologist*
Kaess, John Philip *music educator, choir director*
Kane, Robert Lewis *public health educator*
Kantor, David *lawyer*
Kapelac, Samuel James *writer, sales executive*
Kaplan, Sheldon *lawyer, director*
Keane, William Francis *nephrology educator, research foundation executive*
Keets, John David, Jr., *insurance company executive*
Keiser, Kenneth E. *food products executive*
Keller, Kenneth Harrison *engineering educator*
Kelly, A. David *lawyer*
Kelly, Tom (Jay Thomas Kelly) *retired professional sports team manager*
Keppel, William James *lawyer, educator, writer*
King, Lyndel Irene Saunders *art museum director*
King, Reatha Clark *community foundation executive*
Kinney, Earl Robert *mutual funds company executive*
Kirtley, Jane Elizabeth *law educator*
Klaas, Paul Barry *lawyer*
Klemp, Harold *minister, writer*
Knoke, David Harmon *sociology educator*
Kohlstedt, Sally Gregory *history educator*
Koneck, John Michael *lawyer*
Kopf, David *history professor*
Korotkin, Fred *writer, philatelist*
Koutsky, Dean Roger *advertising executive*
Kralewski, John Edward *health service research educator*
Kramer, Joel Roy *journalist, newspaper executive*
Krause, Timothy Gilbert *web site manager*
Kreiser, Frank David *real estate executive*
Kudrle, Robert Thomas *economist, educator*
Kuhi, Leonard Vello *astronomer, university administrator*
Kukla, Edward Richard *rare books & special collections librarian*
Kulacki, Francis Alfred *engineer, educator*
Kump, Warren Lee *retired diagnostic radiologist*
Kuplic, David Michael *portfolio manager*

McDonald, Malcolm Willis *retired real estate company executive*

Northfield
Appleyard, David Frank *mathematics and computer science educator*
Benkowski, Ann Marie *writer*
Boardman, Shelby J. *academic administrator*
Casper, Barry Michael *physics educator*
Cederberg, James *physics educator*
Clark, Clifford Edward, Jr., *history professor*
Clark, William Hartley *political science educator*
Edwards, Mark U., Jr., *academic administrator, history educator, author*
Fick, Herbert J. *chemist, consultant*
Flaten, Robert Arnold *former ambassador*
Gao, Hong *music educator*
Henrickson, Eiler Leonard *retired geologist, educator*
Kutulas, Judy A. *historian, educator*
Levin, Burton *diplomat*
Oden, Robert A., Jr., *academic administrator*
Priore, Jr., Charles Frank *school librarian*
Soule, George Alan *literature educator, writer*
Sovik, Edward Anders *architect, consultant*
Steen, Lynn Arthur *mathematician, educator*
Swanson, Stephen Olney *minister, retired English educator*
Talen, William Claire *bank executive, financial consultant*
Wickramasekara, Sujeev *physicist, educator*
Yandell, Cathy Marleen *language educator*
Zelliot, Eleanor Mae *history educator*

Oakdale
Cederburg, Barbara M. *printing company executive*
Maekawa, Koji Ogura *technology company administrator*
Monahan, William T. *computer company executive*
Tran, Nang Tri *engineering executive, electrical engineer*

Olivia
Cosgriff, James Arthur *physician*

Ortonville
Schrom, Elizabeth Ann *retired writer*

Ottertail
Anderson, Bob *state legislator, business executive*

Owatonna
Aune, Debra Bjurquist *lawyer*
Groff, Stanley Allen *social services administrator, educator*

Palisade
Kilde, Sandra Jean *nurse, anesthetist, educator, consultant*

Pequot Lakes
Gray, Allen (Ernest Bungaard) *radio executive*
Weaver, Arthur Lawrence *rheumatologist, consultant*

Pipestone
Scott, William Paul *lawyer*

Plymouth
Hauser, Elloyd *finance company executive*
Kahler, Herbert Frederick *diversified business executive*
Peterson, Donn Neal *forensic engineer*
Redgrave, Martyn Robert *hotel, food service executive*
Saville, Derric James *lawyer*
Shadley, Robert D. *retired army officer*

Preston
Hokenson, David Leonard *secondary school educator*
Schommer, Trudy Marie *pastoral minister, religion education*

Proctor
Scheibe, Margaret Helen *elementary school educator, librarian*

Red Wing
Fritz, Henry Eugene *historian, educator*

Richfield
Anderson, Bradbury H. *retail executive*
Devlin, Barbara Jo *school district administrator*
Linton, Michael Alan *retail company executive*
Reilly, Jill Marlene *school system administrator*
Schuett, Carol Ann *travel industry business analyst*
Thompson, Steve Allan *writer*

Robbinsdale
Anderson, Scott Robbins *hospital administrator*

Rochester
Archibald, Reginald Mac Gregor *pediatrician, endocrinologist, chemist, educator*
Bartholomew, Lloyd Gibson *physician*
Beahrs, Oliver Howard *surgeon, educator*
Beckman, Thomas J. *physician*
Berry, Daniel John *orthopedist, surgeon*
Bowie, E(dward) J(ohn) Walter *hematologist, researcher*
Brimijoin, William Stephen *pharmacologist, educator, neuroscientist, researcher*
Brown, Arnold Lanehart, Jr., *pathologist, educator, university dean*
Charboneau, Joseph William *radiologist, medical educator*
Cofield, Robert Hahn *orthopedic surgeon, educator*
Cortese, Denis A. *medical educator, healthcare executive*
Czaja, Albert Joseph *physician, educator*
Danielson, Gordon Kenneth, Jr., *cardiovascular surgeon, educator*
DeRemee, Richard Arthur *physician, educator, researcher*
Dickson, Edgar Rolland *gastroenterologist*
Douglas, William W. *physician, consultant*
Douglass, Bruce E. *physician*
Du Shane, James William *physician, educator*
Engel, Andrew George *neurologist*
Fervenza, Fernando C. *nephrologist, educator*
Foote, Robert Leonard *oncologist, educator, researcher*
Frusti, Doreen Kaye *nursing administrator*
Fye, W. Bruce, III, *cardiologist*
Geda, Yonas Endale *neuropsychiatrist, researcher*
Gervais, Sister Generose *hospital consultant*
Gharib, Hossein *medical educator*
Gomez, Manuel Rodriguez *physician*
Goodman, Julie *nurse midwife*
Gorman, Colum Alphonsus *retired endocrinologist*
Gracey, Douglas Robert *physician, physiologist, educator*
Haddy, Francis John *physician, educator*
Hiniker, LuAnn *management consultant, educator, researcher, grants consultant*
Hodgson, Jane Elizabeth *obstetrician, gynecologist, consultant*
Huffine, Coy Lee *retired chemical engineer*
Hunder, Gene Gerald *physician, educator*
Jaffe, Allan S. *cardiologist, educator, medical researcher*
Jankowski, Christopher James *anesthesiologist, educator*
Kelemen, Linda Elizabeth *epidemiologist, dietician*
Key, Jack Dayton *librarian*
Knopman, David S. *neurologist*
Kyle, Robert Arthur *medical educator, oncologist*
Lanier, William Lovel, Jr., *anesthesiologist, educator*
Lantz, William Charles *lawyer*
LaRusso, Nicholas F. *gastroenterologist, educator, scientist*
Lofgren, Karl Adolph *surgeon, educator*
Loftus, Edward Vincent, Jr., *gastroenterologist, writer*
Lucas, Alexander Ralph *child psychiatrist, educator, writer*
Mackenzie, Ronald Alexander *anesthesiologist*
Maher, L. James, III, *molecular biologist*
Malek, Reza Said *urological surgeon*
Malkasian, George Durand, Jr., *physician, educator*
Mayr, James Jerome *fertilizer company executive*
McConnell, Joseph Paul *lab administrator, researcher, biochemist, consultant*
Morlock, Carl Grismore *physician, medical educator*
Mrazek, David Allen *pediatric psychiatrist*
Mulder, Donald William *physician, educator*
Neel, Harry Bryan, III, *surgeon, scientist, educator*
Nelson, Audrey May *physician*
Nevling, Harry Reed *human resources consultant*
O'Driscoll, Shawn William *surgeon, researcher*
O'Hare, Daniel John *electrical engineer*
Orwoll, Gregg S.K. *lawyer*
Pairolero, Peter Charles *surgeon, educator*
Perry, Harold Otto *dermatologist*
Phillips, Sidney Frederick *gastroenterologist, educator*
Piepgras, David G. *neurosurgeon, educator*
Pisansky, Thomas Michael *physician*
Pittelkow, Mark Robert *physician, dermatology educator, researcher*
Platt, Jeffrey Louis *surgeon, immunologist, educator, pediatric nephrologist*
Podratz, Karl C. *gynecologic surgeon, oncologist, educator*
Prakash, Udaya B.S. *internist, educator*
Prendergast, Franklyn G. *health facility administrator, medical educator*
Reitemeier, Richard Joseph *physician*
Riggs, Jeanette Templeton *civic worker*
Rinden, David Lee *clergyman*
Robbins, Thomas Landau *humanities researcher*
Rogers, Roy Steele, III, *dermatologist, educator, dean*
Rosenow, Edward Carl, III, *medical educator*
Scanlon, Paul David *pulmonologist, educator*
Scott, John Paul *medical educator*
Shampo, Marc Anthony *retired medical editor, writer*
Shepherd, John Thompson *physiologist*
Shulman, Carole Karen *professional society administrator*
Siekert, Robert George *neurologist*
Sim, Franklin H. *orthopedic surgery educator*
Smith, Hugh Cadham *cardiovascular diseases physician*
Somers, Virend Kristen *physician, researcher*
Somsen, Henry Northrop *retired lawyer*
Stegall, Mark D. *surgeon, medical educator*
Stickler, Gunnar Brynolf *pediatrician*
Talley, Nicholas Joseph *educator, physician, scientist*
Tarvestad, Anthony M. *psychiatrist*
Varkey, Prathibha *preventive medicine physician, medical educator*
Ward, Louis Emmerson *retired physician*
Weinshilboum, Richard M. *pharmacologist, educator, biomedical researcher*
Wells, Lloyd Allan *psychiatrist, educator*
Whisnant, Jack Page *neurologist*
Williams, Arthur Ross *health service and public administrator*
Windebank, Anthony J. *dean*
Wood, Michael B. *chief executive officer, president*
Wood, Michael Bruce *orthopaedic surgeon, researcher, educator*
Woods, John Elmer *plastic surgeon*

Rosemount
Aadland, Thomas Vernon *minister*
Morrison, James R. *retired banker*

Roseville
Gross, Alan Gerald *rhetoric educator*
Marten, Gordon Cornelius *research agronomist, educator, federal agency administrator*
McMillan, Mary Bigelow *retired minister, volunteer*
Miller, Suzanne Marie *state librarian*
Ucko, Franz *research scientist, consultant, writer*

Rush City
Jennings, Loren G. *state legislator, business owner*

Rushford
Curmano, Billy X. *art director*
Stras, Penny Lynn *director*

Saginaw
Stauber, Marilyn Jean *retired secondary school educator, retired elementary school educator*

Saint Charles
Van Norman, Willis Roger *retired computer systems researcher, consultant*

Saint Cloud
Carpenter, Kevin Starr *lawyer*
Falk, Armand Elroy *retired English educator, writer*
Frank, Jan L. H. *education educator, consultant*
Frank, Stephen Ira *political science educator*
Gangopadhyay, Partha *management consultant*
Hofsommer, Donovan Lowell *history professor*
Leppman, Elizabeth Jane *geographer, educator*
Mullins, Jeffrey Alan *historian, educator*
Olagunju, Amos Omotayo *computer science educator, consultant*
Olson, Barbara Ford *physician*
Porter, Laurinda Wright *communications educator, consultant*
Prout, Robert Stephen *higher education consultant, law enforcement consultant*
Reha, Rose Krivisky *retired finance educator*
Supanvanij, Janikan *finance educator*
Verrilli, Catherine Jean *music educator, soprano*
Ward, Edward Anthony *economist, educator*
Wertz, John Alan *retired secondary school educator*

Saint Joseph
Kirick, Daniel John *agronomist*
Rowland, Howard Ray *mass communications educator*

Saint Louis Park
Croll, Jillian Kathleen *dietician, researcher*
Frestedt, Joy Louise *science administrator*
Harstad, Carl Leslie *consultant, writer*
Kalman, Marc *radio station executive*
Wikman, Michael Raymond *advertising executive*

Saint Paul
Abrams, Laura Sue *social worker, educator*
Allison, John Robert *lawyer*
Alsop, Donald Douglas *federal judge*
Amidon, Paul Charles *publishing executive*
Anderson, Ellen Ruth *state legislator*
Anderson, Gordon Louis *foundation administrator*
Anderson, Paul Holden *state supreme court justice*
Anderson, Richard H. *air transportation executive*
Anderson, Russell A. *state supreme court justice*
Archabal, Nina M(archetti) *historical society director*
Archer, Joan M. *trade association administrator*
Axelrod, Leonard *management consultant*
Bachmann, Michele *state legislator*
Baker, Douglas M., Jr., *service industry executive*
Barnwell, Franklin Hershel *zoology educator*
Barry, Anne M. *public health officer*
Bastian, Gary Warren *judge*
Baukol, Ronald Oliver *retired finance company executive*
Beers, Anne *protective services official*
Berglin, Linda *state legislator*
Bernstein, James C. *commissioner*
Bessette, Andy F. *diversified financial services company executive*
Blanchard, J. A., III, *publishing executive*
Blatz, Kathleen Anne *judge, state agency administrator, state legislator*
Boehnen, David Leo *food service executive, lawyer*
Bombardir, Brad *professional hockey player*
Boudreau, Lynda L. *state legislator*
Bradley, Thomas A. *insurance company executive*
Braun, Richard J. *lab administrator*
Bree, Marlin Duane *publisher, author*
Brooks, Phillip *advertising executive*
Brudvig, Glenn Lowell *retired library director*
Brushaber, George Karl *academic administrator, minister*
Busch, Robert Henry *geneticist, researcher*
Calkins, Mark R. *tenor, educator*
Campbell, Patrick D. *manufacturing executive*
Caneday, Ardel Bruce *religious studies educator, writer*
Carruthers, Philip Charles *lawyer, public official*
Cavert, Henry Mead *physician, retired educator*
Chaudhary, Satveer *state senator*
Cheng, H(wei) H(sien) *soil scientist, agronomic and environmental science educator*
Clark, Karen *state legislator*
Close, Elizabeth Scheu *retired architect*
Connly, Michael R. *insurance company executive*
Coppock, Bruce *orchestra executive*
Crabb, Kenneth Wayne *obstetrician, gynecologist*
Crittenden, Bruce A. *finance company executive*
Critzer, Susan L. *health products company executive*
Dahl, Reynold Paul *applied economics educator*
Dahlberg, Eric Ross *music educator*
Daly, Joseph Leo *law educator*
Davis, Margaret Bryan *paleoecology researcher, educator*
Dennis, Clarence *surgeon, educator*
DeSimone, Livio Diego *retired diversified manufacturing company executive*
Diesch, Stanley La Verne *veterinarian, educator*
Dordell, Timothy Paul *lawyer*
Dutcher, Judi *state auditor*
Dykstra, Robert *retired education educator*
Edwards, Jesse Efrem *pathologist, educator*
Ehlke, Nancy Jo *agronomist*
Eibensteiner, Ron *political organization administrator, venture capitalist*
Ek, Alan Ryan *forester, educator*
Estenson, Noel K. *refining and fertilizer company executive*
Fairweather, Scott James *music educator*
Feeney, Daniel Arthur *veterinary radiologist*
Feinberg, David Erwin *publishing company executive*
Finley, Joseph Michael *lawyer*
Fischbach, Michelle L. *state legislator*
Fisk, Martin H. *lawyer*
Flynn, Carol *state legislator*
Flynn, Harry Joseph *bishop*
Fogerty, James Edward *archivist, state official*
Forshay, Steven R. *marketing professional, consultant*
Fritze, Steven L. *service industry executive*
Fruehling, Rosemary Therese *publishing executive, author*
Galvin, Michael John, Jr., *lawyer*
Gehan, Mark William *lawyer*
Geis, Jerome Arthur *lawyer, legal educator*
Geisser, Seymour *statistics educator*
Gherty, John E. *food products and agricultural products company executive*
Gilbert, James H. *judge*
Gilgun, Jane Frances *social work educator*
Glancy, Helen Diane *literature educator*
Gleason, Bruce Philip *education educator, writer*
Graham, Charles John *university educator, former university president*
Greiling, Mindy *state legislator*
Griffin, Michael Scott *communications educator, writer*
Haemig, Mary Jane *religious studies educator*
Hansen, Eric Peter *lawyer*
Hansen, Robyn L. *lawyer*
Hanson, Paula E. *state legislator*
Hanson, Samuel Lee *judge*
Harder, Elaine Rene *state legislator*
Harvey, Patricia A. *school system administrator*
Hatch, Mike *state attorney general*
Heyman, William Herbert *financial services executive*
Higgins, Linda I. *state legislator*
Hill, James Stanley *computer consulting company executive*
Hobbie, Russell Klyver *physics educator*
Hollister, Clifton David *social work educator*
Holter, Arlen Rolf *cardiothoracic surgeon*
Hopper, David Henry *religion educator*
Hornbach, Daniel J. *academic administrator, biologist, educator*
Hubbard, Stanley Stub *broadcast executive*
Huber, Sister Alberta *college president*
Ihlenfeld, Jay V. *manufacturing executive*
Jessup, Paul Frederick *financial economist, educator*
Johnson, Alice M. *state legislator*
Johnson, Badri Nahvi *sociology educator, real estate company officer*
Johnson, James Erling *insurance executive*
Johnson, Lynn *liquor company wholesaler*
Johnson, Paul Oren *lawyer*
Johnston, Manley Roderick *research and development company executive, chemist*
Jones, C. Paul *lawyer, educator*
Kahn, Phyllis *state legislator*
Kane, Stanley Phillip *insurance company executive*
Keillor, Garrison Edward *writer, radio host*
Kiffmeyer, Mary *state official*
Kirwin, Kenneth Francis *law educator*
Kiscaden, Sheila M. *state legislator*
Klausner, Jeffrey *dean*
Kling, William Hugh *broadcast executive*
Knudson, Mark Bradley *medical corporation executive, venture capitalist*
Kommedahl, Thor *plant pathology educator*
Krentz, Jane *state legislator, elementary school educator*
Kurtz, Harold Paul *foundation executive*
Kurzer, Mindy Susan *educator*
Kyle, Richard House *federal judge*
Labuza, Theodore Peter *food science educator*
Landwehr, Steven J. *manufacturing executive*
Laptewicz, Joseph E., Jr., *medical products executive*
Larkin, John Edward, Jr., *orthopedic surgeon*
Larson, David Allen *law educator*
Lay, Donald Pomeroy *federal judge*
Lebedoff, Randy Miller *lawyer*
Lee, Andrea Jane *academic administrator, nun*
Leighton, Robert Joseph *lawyer*
Lemaire, Jacques *professional hockey coach*
Leonard, Kurt John *plant pathologist, retired university program director*
Lesewski, Arlene *state legislator, insurance agent*
Lessard, Robert Bernard *state legislator, recreational facility executive*
Mabry, Paul Davis *psychobiologist, educator, researcher*
Mahan, James T. *manufacturing executive*
Maitland, Margaret Todd *editor*
Malecki, Edward Stanley, Jr., *political science educator*
Mather, Richard Burroughs *retired Chinese language and literature educator*
Matteson, Clarice Chris *artist, educator*
May, Georgiana *biologist, educator*
McCormick, James Harold *academic administrator*
McDonough, Paul H. *corporate financial executive*
McDougal, Stuart Yeatman *comparative literature educator, author*
McGuire, Mary Jo *state legislator*
McKinnell, Robert Gilmore *retired zoology, genetics and cell biology educator*
McNeely, John J. *lawyer*
McNerney, Walter James (Jim McNerney) *manufacturing executive*
Meyer, Helen M. *judge*
Micallef, Joseph Stephen *retired lawyer*
Michael, Alfred Frederick, Jr., *pediatric nephrology educator*
Minge, David *former congressman, lawyer, law educator*
Molnau, Carol *lieutenant governor*
Monson, Dianne Lynn *literacy educator*
Mullin, James Albert *executive*
Murphy, Mary C. *state legislator*
Nash, Nicholas David *retail executive*
Newmark, Richard Alan *chemist*
Nielsen, Suzanne Ruth *literature educator, writer*
Nozari, Moe S. *manufacturing executive*
O'Brien, Odessa Louise *protective services official*
O'Leary, Daniel Brian *lawyer, educator*
Oliver, Marlys Mae *retired editor, writer*
Olson, Gen *state legislator*
Ortega, Rafael Enrique *county official, educator*
Osnes, Larry G. *academic administrator*
Owens, B. Mitchell *lab administrator*
Page, Alan C. *state supreme court justice*
Palensky, Frederick J. *manufacturing executive*
Pampusch, Anita Marie *foundation administrator*
Pappas, Sandra Lee *state senator*
Pariseau, Patricia *state legislator*
Pawlenty, Timothy J. *governor*
Perry, James Alfred *environmental scientist, consultant, science educator, department chairman*
Peterson, James Lincoln *museum executive*
Phillips, Ronald Lewis *plant geneticist, educator*
Powell, David W. *manufacturing executive*
Prager, Stephen *chemistry professor*
Ranum, Jane Barnhardt *state senator, lawyer*
Reich, Charles *manufacturing executive, research scientist*
Renner, Robert George *federal judge*
Rest, Ann H. *state legislator*
Ring, Twyla L. *state legislator, newspaper editor*
Robertson, Jerry Earl *retired manufacturing company executive*
Robertson, Martha Rappaport *state legislator, consultant*
Robling, Claire A. *state legislator*
Rosenberg, Brian C *academic administrator*

Malloy, James Matthew *health management executive, healthcare consultant*
Marks, Michael *association administrator*
Marshall, Gailen Daugherty, Jr., *physician, scientist, educator*
Martinson, Rita R. *state legislator*
McElvaine, Robert Stuart *writer, educator*
McLemore-Wheeler, Linda M. *literature educator*
McLeod, Stephen Glenn *education educator, language educator*
McRae, Charles R. (Chuck McCrae) *state supreme court justice*
Mettetal, H. Nolan *state legislator, pharmacist*
Moize, Jerry Dee *lawyer, government official*
Moll, George William *pediatrician, educator*
Molpus, Dick H. *management company executive*
Moore, Mike *former state attorney general*
Mosley, Jessie Bryant *retired science educator*
Munera, Pedro Antonio *child and adolescent psychiatrist*
O'Mara, James Wright *lawyer*
Otieno, Tabitha Nyaboke *social sciences educator, researcher*
Patterson, Chan *food service executive*
Peden, James Alton, Jr., *lawyer*
Peranich, Diane C. *state legislator*
Petty, David *newspaper editor*
Pittman, Edwin Lloyd *state supreme court chief justice*
Poole, Galen Vincent *surgeon, educator, researcher*
Purdy, William Richard *lawyer*
Raila, Frank Arthur *radiologist*
Rawson, John Elton *neonatologist, educator*
Ray, H. M. *lawyer*
Read, John O. *state legislator, pharmacist*
Rhodes, Linda L. *medical transcriptionist, medical assistant*
Risley, Rod Alan *education association executive*
Roberts, Kristie *researcher*
Roberts, Richard C., III, *lawyer*
Robertson, Valeria Brower *state legislator, land developer*
Rogers, Oscar Allan, Jr., *college president*
Ross, Ian Beaudoin *neurosurgeon, educator*
Sawyer, Donald E. *urologist*
Scanlon, Pat H. *lawyer*
Scott, Eloise Hale *state legislator*
Scott, Omeria McDonald *state legislator*
Segal, Jane *newscaster*
Shinn, Clinton Wesley *lawyer*
Shirley, Aaron *pediatrician*
Smith, (Floyd) Clayton *state legislator, business owner*
Smith, Edgar Eugene *biochemist, university administrator*
Smith, James W., Jr., *state supreme court chief justice*
Smith, Sharman Bridges *state librarian*
Sneed, Raphael Corcoran *physiatrist, pediatrician*
Srinivasan, Seetha *publishing company executive*
Stevens, Mary Ann *state legislator*
Stubblefield, J(oseph) Stephen *lawyer*
Suess, James Francis *retired psychiatry educator*
Sugg, Robert Perkins *former state supreme court justice*
Sullivan, Bettye Yarborough *foundation administrator*
Tchounwou, Paul Bernard *environmental health specialist, toxicologist, educator*
Thaw, Andrew Kurt *psychologist, educator, research scientist*
Thigpen, James Tate *physician, oncology educator*
Thomas, Sara R. *state legislator*
Thompson, Marsha *newscaster*
Thornton, Larry Lee *psychotherapist, author, educator, minister*
Travis, Jay A., III, *lawyer*
Tuck, Amy *lieutenant governor*
Vance, Ralph Brooks, Sr., *oncologist, educator*
Wade, Maggie *newscaster*
Waites, Robert Guinn *utilities executive*
Walker, Earl *food service executive*
Walker, John Leonard *lawyer*
Waller, William Lowe, Jr., *state supreme court justice*
West, Carol Catherine *law educator*
Winter, William Forrest *former governor, lawyer*

Keesler AFB
Harrell, Elizabeth Ann *career officer*
Locker, Dan Lewis *career officer*

Kosciusko
Shoemaker, William C. *journalist*

Laurel
Lacey, Peeler Grayson *diagnostic radiologist*
Lindstrom, Eric Everett *ophthalmologist*
Ruth, Edward Keith *information systems specialist, management consultant*

Long Beach
Easton, Jill Johanna *state official*
Kanagy, Steven Albert *foundation administrator*
Miller, James Edward *computer scientist, educator*
Williams, James Orrin *university administrator, educator*

Lorman
Hylander, Walter Raymond, Jr., *retired civil engineer*
Panicker, Girish Kumar *agricultural scientist, consultant*

Madison
Dean, Jack Pearce *retired insurance company executive*
Obert, Keith David *lawyer*
Priest, Melville Stanton *retired consulting hydraulic engineer*

Magnolia
Coney, Elaine Marie *English and foreign languages educator*

Mantachie
Marcy, William L. *physician, consultant*

Mendenhall
Cockrell, Jean D. *elementary school educator*

Meridian
Church, George Millord *retired real estate company executive*
Thomas, Kenneth Eugene *auditor*

Minter City
Mitchell, Patsy Malier *religious school founder and administrator*

Mississippi State
Cliett, Charles Buren *aeronautical engineer, educator, academic administrator*
Clynch, Edward John *political science educator, researcher*
Cosby, Arthur G. *social sciences educator*
Croom, Sylvester *football coach*
Jenkins, Johnie Norton *research geneticist, research administrator*
Mabry, Donald Joseph *university administrator, history educator*
Martin, Edward Curtis, Jr., *landscape architect, educator*
Or, Ka Lun *research assistant*
Qian, Chuanxi *mathematics professor*
Rabideau, Peter Wayne *university administrator, chemistry educator*
Reddy, Kambham Raja *plant physiology educator*
Rent, Clyda Stokes *academic administrator*
Taylor, Clayborne Dudley *engineering educator*
Thompson, Joe Floyd *aerospace engineer, researcher*
Thomson, John U. *veterinarian, dean*
Truax, Dennis Dale *civil engineer, educator, consultant*

Natchez
Bramlette, David C., III, *federal judge*
Marion, Ann *school psychologist, educator*

New Albany
Sumners, Lester Furr *lawyer*

Ocean Springs
Austin, Claude Lidell *retired surgeon*
Foster, William Silas, Jr., *retired minister*
Furlow, William Lawrence *manufacturing and financial consultant*
Lee, Kathleen Mary *administration and nursing executive*
Luckey, Alwyn Hall *lawyer*

Olive Branch
Carnall, George Hursey, II, *lawyer, business executive*
Farr, Walter Evans *chemist, chemical engineer*
Frischenmeyer, Michael Leo *sales executive*

Oxford
Costner, Charles Lynn *retired civil engineer*
Duke, Stephen Oscar *physiologist, research scientist, educator*
Greenlee, Jim Ming *prosecutor*
Horton, Thomas Edward, Jr., *mechanical engineering educator*
Mills, Michael Paul *judge*
Moorhead, Sylvester Andrew *retired education educator*
Neal, Mary Darlin' *writer, education educator*
Rayburn, S. T. *lawyer*
Rego, Cesar *science educator, researcher*

Pascagoula
Chapel, Theron Theodore *retired quality assurance engineer*
Dur, Philip Alphonse *defense aerospace executive, retired naval officer*
Smith, Donald Vaughan *artist, educator*

Pass Christian
Clark, John Walter, Jr., *shipping company executive*
Dawkins, Deborah Jeanne *state legislator*
McCardell, James Elton *retired naval officer*

Perkinston
Douglas, Sam Lister *musician, writer*
Mellinger, Barry Lee *community college president, vocational educator*

Philadelphia
Williamson, Gloria *state legislator*

Ridgeland
Lewis, Larry Lisle *human resources specialist company executive*
Long, Roger Leonard *artist*
O'Neill, Paul John *retired psychology educator*

Senatobia
Banham, Sandra Rodgers *language educator*

Southaven
Johnson, Joyce Thedford *state agency administrator*
Taylor, Ronald Louis *lawyer*
White, Marguerite *writer*

Starkville
Ford, Robert MacDonald, III, *architect, educator*
George, Ernest Thornton, III, *financial consultant*
Gregg, Billy Ray *seed industry executive, consultant*
Jacob, Paul Bernard, Jr., *electrical engineering educator*
Martin, Theodore Krinn *former university administrator*
Thomas, Garnett Jett *accountant*
Yoste, Charles Todd *lawyer*

Stennis Space Center
Chin-Bing, Stanley Arthur *physicist, educator*
Fleischer, Peter *research geologist, oceanographer, educator*

Stoneville
Hamel, Paul Bernard *ornithologist, researcher*
Meadows, James Steven *forester*
Ranney, Carleton David *retired plant pathology researcher, administrator*

Sumrall
Downey, James Cecil *retired music and humanities educator*
Hudson, Mary Kay *business executive*

Thaxton
Dillard, Faye Graham *education educator*

Tougaloo
Whittington, Felicia Trenise *social services administrator, educator*

Tupelo
Bush, Fred Marshall, Jr., *lawyer*
Clayton, Claude F., Jr., *lawyer*
Hill, J. Edward *physician, educator*
Moffett, T(errill) K(ay) *lawyer*
Nash, Henry Warren *marketing educator*
Patterson, Aubrey Burns, Jr., *banker*
Ramage, Martis Donald, Jr., *banker*
Witty, Thomas Ezekiel, III, *psychologist, researcher*
Zurawski, Jeanette *rehabilitation services professional*

Tylertown
Barrett, Dawn Dillon *counseling administrator, journalist, editor*
Mord, Irving Conrad, II, *lawyer*

University
Breazeale, Mack Alfred *physics educator*
Cheng, Alexander Hung-Darh *engineering educator, consultant*
Flesher, Dale Lee *accounting educator, dean*
Fox, Garey A. *civil engineer, educator*
Frink, Dwight David *management educator*
Hall, J(ames) R(obert) *English educator*
Jordan, Winthrop Donaldson *historian, educator*
Keiser, Edmund Davis, Jr., *biologist, educator*
Khayat, Robert Conrad *academic administrator*
Kiger, Joseph Charles *history professor*
Landon, Michael de Laval *historian, educator*
Martin, Jeanette St. Clair *adult education educator*
Miller, Brian Craig *historian, educator*
Potts, Marjorie *executive secretary, systems support specialist*
Smith, Allie Maitland *engineering educator*
Steel, David Warren *music history educator, organist, harpsichordist*
Tschumper, Gregory Scott *chemist, educator*
Wang, Sam Shu-Yi *mechanical engineer, educator*

Vaiden
Murphy, Ben Carroll *engineering company executive*

Vicksburg
Hopson, William Briggs, Jr., *surgeon*
Joyner, Elizabeth *curator*
Keulegan, Emma Pauline *special education educator*
Masterson, Chester W. *otolaryngologist, state representative*
Mazzeo-Merkle, Linda Lou *legal administrator*
McRae, John Leonidas *civil engineer, consultant*

Washington
Branyan, Cheryl Munyer *museum administrator, consultant*

Yazoo City
Hawthorne, Minnie *elementary school educator*

MISSOURI

Arcadia
Davis, Jo *nurse, writer, professional speaker, small business owner, photographer*

Arrow Rock
Bollinger, Michael *artistic director*

Ballwin
Ackerson, Charles Stanley *minister, social worker*
Bond, Dennis Earl *auditor*
Cornell, William Daniel *mechanical engineer*
Guinther, Christine Louise *special education educator*
Haller, Karen Sue *writer*
Macauley, Edward C. *retired company executive*
Pallozola, Christine *non-profit administrator*
Winning, John Patrick *lawyer*

Belton
Blim, Richard Don *retired pediatrician, health facility administrator*

Benton
Heckemeyer, Anthony Joseph *circuit court judge*

Bethel
Coonrod, Delberta Hollaway (Debbie Coonrod) *retired elementary education educator, consultant, freelance writer*

Bloomfield
Ferrell, Paul Cleveland *writer*

Blue Eye
Anderson, Ruth G. *retired education educator, educational consultant*

Blue Springs
McElroy, Michelle Marie *physician*
Sugarbaker, Stephen Philip *surgeon, educator*

Bolivar
Brown, Autry *psychology educator, clergyman*
Harrison, Carol L. *music educator*
Hood, Michael Lee *psychologist, clinical researcher, educator*
Hooper, William Loyd *music educator, university administrator*
Padgett, Thomas Eugene *language educator*
Thaller, Gregg P. *music educator*

Bonne Terre
Mitchell, Bart Allen *secondary school educator*

Bourbon
Heitsch, Leona Mason *artist, writer*

Bowling Green
Bruce, Judith Esther *retired music educator, elementary education educator*

Branson
Bradley, Leon Charles *musician, educator, consultant*
Ownby, Jerry Steve *landscape architect, educator*

Bridgeton
Asma, Lawrence Francis *priest*
Faulk, Marshall William *professional football player*
Kenison, Raymond Robert *fraternal organization administrator, director*

Burlington Junction
Mathers, Bradley L. *music educator*

Butler
Cochran, Beth *gifted and talented educator*

California
Lewis, Philip Henry *music educator*

Cameron
Rose-Heim, William Bentley *minister, mediator, business owner, entrepreneur*

Canton
Howe, Sandra Jo *library director*
McSpadden, David Larry *music educator*

Cape Girardeau
Blanton, Lewis M. *federal judge*
Bruening, James Theodore *mathematician, educator*
Eom, Sean Bock *education educator, researcher*
Haugland, Jerry Lee *accounting educator*
McManaman, Kenneth Charles *lawyer*
MohdZain, A. Zaidy *counselor, educator*
Potter, Richard Kevin *accountant, controller, consultant*
Rhodes, Joel Paul *social studies educator*
Smallwood, Glenn Walter, Jr., *utility marketing management executive*

Carrollton
Evans, James Hays *photographer*

Carthage
Flanigan, Matthew C. *manufacturing executive*
Potter, Jacqueline Jean *writer*
Workman, Leatta Ardyce *management consultant*
Wright, Felix E. *manufacturing executive*

Caruthersville
Puangsuvan, Somporn *surgeon, consultant*

Cassville
Melton, Emory Leon *lawyer, state legislator, publisher*

Centralia
Everhart, James Gray *retired manufacturing executive*

Charleston
Cassell, Lucille Richardson *small business owner*
Wallhausen, Mildred Carolyn *publisher*

Chesterfield
Armstrong, Theodore Morelock *financial executive*
Ashworth, Ronald Broughton *health facility executive, accountant*
Carpenter, Will Dockery *chemical company executive*
Crock, Winifred Woodard *director, music educator, conductor, musician*
Denneen, John Paul *lawyer*
Fagerberg, Roger Richard *lawyer*
Fowler, Marti *fine arts consultant*
Fujiwara, Hideji *chemist, researcher*
Graham, Donald James *food technologist*
Henderson, William J. *association executive*
Henry, Roy Monroe *financial planner*
Hier, Marshall David *lawyer*
Higgins, Edward Aloysius *retired newspaper editor*
Hinrichs, Charles A. *commercial banker*
Hunter, Buddy D. *holding company executive*
Lala, Deepak S. *research scientist*
Landram, Christina Louella *librarian*
Malvern, Donald *retired aircraft manufacturing company executive*
McLain, Donald J. *retired academic administrator, educational consultant*
Metzler, Paul Raymond *electrical engineer, consultant*
Morley, Harry Thomas, Jr., *real estate executive*
Morse, Stacey Ann *art studio owner*
Qazi, Mujtaba A. *ophthalmologist*
Reid, Lorene Frances *middle school educator*
Ross, E. Earl *small business owner*
Selfridge, George Dever *retired dentist, retired naval officer*
Sikorski, James Alan *research chemist*
Williams, Luther Steward *research scientist*
Willis, Frank Edward *retired air force officer*

Clayton
Bartmann, William R. *financial services company executive*
Christner, Theodore Carroll *architect*
Costas, Bob (Robert Quinlan Costas) *sportscaster*
Davenport, Dennis Lynn *protective services official*
Davis, William Albert *theme park director*
Farragut-Hemphill, Sandra *judge*
Kemper, David Woods, II, *banker*
Komen, Leonard *lawyer*
Mach, Ruth *principal*
Mohrman, Henry J(oe), Jr., *lawyer, investment manager*
Novelly, Paul Anthony *petrochemical and refining company executive*
O'Donnell, Edward Joseph *bishop, former editor*
Post, Stephen Lightner *psychiatrist, psychoanalyst, educator*
Tremayne, Eric Flory *lawyer*
Vecchiotti, Robert Anthony *management and organizational consultant*

Cleveland
Dunham, Michael D. *design engineer*

Clinton
Kelsay, David Roland *chemist*
Wentz, Wendell Franklin *columnist, writer*

Columbia
Aggarwal, Kul *internist, cardiologist, educator*

Butler, Merlin Gene *physician, medical geneticist, educator*
Byers-Pevitts, Beverley *college administrator, educator*
Cahill, Patricia Deal *radio station executive*
Campbell, Terry M. *food products executive*
Canfield, Robert Cleo *lawyer*
Caulfield, Joan *director, educator*
Cheng, Kuang Lu *chemist, educator*
Ching, Wai Yim *physics educator, researcher*
Churchman, Michael Steele Bright *educational consultant, educator*
Clark, Charles Edward *arbitrator*
Clarke, Milton Charles *lawyer*
Clegg, Karen Kohler *lawyer*
Courson, Marna B.P. *public relations executive*
Crawford, Howard Allen *lawyer*
Creighton, Neal *retired army officer*
Cross, William Dennis *lawyer*
Cunningham, Gunther *professional football coach*
Cunningham, Paul George *minister*
Danner, Kathleen Frances Steele *federal official*
Davis, F(rancis) Keith *civil engineer*
Davis, James Robert *cartoonist*
Davis, John Charles *lawyer*
Davis, Richard Francis *city government official*
Deacy, Thomas Edward, Jr., *lawyer*
Dees, Stephen Phillip *agricultural finance executive, lawyer*
Delaware, Richard Raymond *mathematician, educator*
DeParle, Nancy-Ann Min *former federal agency administrator, lawyer*
Devanny, E.H. (Trace) III *healthcare informatics executive*
Dicus, Stephen Howard *lawyer*
Diehl, James Harvey *church administrator*
Dillingham, John Allen *marketing professional*
Dimond, Edmunds Grey *medical educator*
Diuguid, Lewis Walter *newspaper executive, columnist*
Doan, Kirk Hugh *lawyer*
Dobson, Rick *energy executive*
Drees, Betty *dean, educator*
Druten, Robert S. *greeting card company executive*
Dumovich, Loretta *real estate and transportation company executive*
Dunn, Terrence P. *manufacturing executive*
Durig, James Robert *chemistry professor*
Dye, Jermaine *professional baseball player*
Eddy, Charles Alan *chiropractor*
Eddy, William Bahret *psychology educator, university dean*
Egan, Charles Joseph, Jr., *lawyer, consumer products company executive*
Eldridge, Truman Kermit, Jr., *lawyer*
English, R(obert) Bradford *marshal*
Ernst, Mark A. *diversified financial services company executive*
Esrey, Robert E. *real estate company executive*
Finn, Robert W. *bishop*
Fiorella, Russell Michael *pathologist*
Foster, Mark Stephen *lawyer*
Frantze, David Wayne *lawyer*
Friedlander, Edward Robert *pathologist*
Gaitan, Fernando J., Jr., *federal judge*
Gansler, Robert *professional soccer coach*
Gibson, John Robert *federal judge*
Godfrey, William Ashley *ophthalmologist*
Gonzalez, Tony *professional football player*
Gorman, Gerald Warner *lawyer*
Graham, Charles *research psychologist*
Graves, Todd Peterson *prosecutor*
Gray, Helen Theresa Gott *religion editor*
Green, Frank Earl *civil engineer*
Green, Jerry Howard *investment banker*
Green, Robert K. *energy executive*
Green, Trent Jason *professional football player*
Grossman, Jerome Barnett *retired service firm executive*
Guilliland, Martha W. *academic administrator*
Guisewite, Cathy Lee *cartoonist*
Gusewelle, Charles Wesley *journalist, writer, documentary maker*
Hagan, John Charles, III, *ophthalmologist*
Hagsten, Ib *animal scientist, livestock consultant*
Hall, Donald Joyce, Sr., *greeting card company executive*
Hall, Donald Joyce, Jr., *consumer products company executive*
Hall, Wayne F. *engineering company executive*
Hamilton, Richard Alfred *university administrator, marketing educator*
Harris, R. Lee *real estate company executive*
Hebenstreit, Jean Estill Stark *religion educator, practitioner*
Hernandez, Roberto *professional baseball player*
Heymach, George John, III, *physician, educator, health facility administrator, consultant*
Hill, Stephen L., Jr., *lawyer, former prosecutor*
Hindman, Larrie C. *lawyer*
Hoenig, Thomas M. *bank executive*
Hoffer, Sharon Marie *secondary school educator*
Hoffmann, Donald *architectural historian*
Holmes, Priest *professional football player*
Hoyland, Janet Louise *clergywoman*
Hubbell, Ernest *lawyer*
Hunt, Lamar *professional football team executive*
Huston, Kent Allen *rheumatologist*
Ingraham, James H. *diversified financial services company executive*
Johnson, Mark Eugene *lawyer*
Johnson, Richard Dean *pharmaceutical consultant, educator*
Johnson, Sondra Lea *accountant*
Jonas, Harry S. *medical education consultant*
Jones, Charles Calhoun *estate and business planning consultant*
Kafoure, Michael D. *food products executive*
Kagan, Stuart Michael *pediatrician*
Kaplan, Harvey L. *lawyer*
Kemper, Jonathan McBride *banker*
Kilroy, John Muir *lawyer*
King, Richard Allen *lawyer*
Knight, John Allan *clergyman, philosophy and religion educator*
Kovac, F. Peter *advertising executive*
Krumlauf, Robert Eugene *neuroscientist, educator*
Kuenn, Marjorie Asp *music educator*
Kuhn, Whitey *advertising executive*
Lakin, Scott Bradley *insurance agent*
Langworthy, Robert Burton *lawyer*
Lannigan, James William *voluntary service officer*
Latshaw, John *entrepreneur, director*
Laughrey, Nanette Kay *judge, federal*
Lee, Margaret Norma *artist*
Leigh, Cheri J. *engineering consulting executive*
Levings, Theresa Lawrence *lawyer*
Lindenbaum, Sharon *publishing executive*
Lindsey, David Hosford *lawyer*
Litan, Robert Eli *lawyer, economist*
Lofland, Gary Kenneth *cardiac surgeon*
Lolli, Don R(ay) *lawyer*
Lombardi, Cornelius Ennis, Jr., *lawyer*
Londré, Felicia Mae Hardison *theater educator*
Long, Edwin Tutt *surgeon*
Lotuaco, Luisa Go *pathologist*
Louis, William Joseph (Jonn Garvie Monks) *theater educator, actor, director, artist, poet*
Lubin, Bernard *psychologist, educator*
Lyon, Bob *state legislator*
Ma, O. John *emergency physician, editor*
Mancusi, Roberto Francesco Costantino *vocalist, educator*
Manimtim, Winston Mendoza *pediatrician, neonatologist*
Manson, Anne *music director*
Margolin, Abraham Eugene *lawyer, director*
Martin-Bowen, Lindsey *freelance writer*
Mast, Kande White *artist*
Mazza-Deblauwe, Tania Sue *software engineer, technology educator*
McCollum, Clifford Glenn *college dean emeritus*
McCoy, Frederick John *retired plastic surgeon*
McDermott, Alan *newspaper editor*
McElwreath, Sally Chin *corporate communications executive*
Mc Gee, Joseph John, Jr., *former insurance company executive*
McGregor, Douglas Hugh *pathologist, educator*
McKelvey, John Clifford *mental health services professional*
McKenna, George LaVerne *art museum curator*
McKinsey, David Stephen *infectious diseases specialist*
McManus, James William *lawyer*
Mc Meel, John Paul *newspaper syndicate and publishing executive*
McPhee, Mark Steven *medical educator, physician, gastroenterologist*
McSweeney, William Lincoln, Jr., *retired publishing executive*
Mebust, Winston Keith *surgeon, educator*
Meola, Tony *professional soccer player, actor*
Miller, William Charles *theological librarian, educator*
Milton, Chad Earl *lawyer*
Minnick, David Michael *lawyer*
Mobberley, James *music educator, composer*
Molteni, Agostino *pathology educator*
Monello, Joseph D. *financial asset management company executive*
Moore, Stephen James *lawyer*
Mordy, James Calvin *lawyer*
Morgison, F. Edward *investment broker*
Muser, Tony *former manager professional athletics*
Mutti, Albert Frederick *retired minister*
Nagle, Jean Susan Karabacz *sociologist, psychologist*
Newsom, James Thomas *lawyer*
Noe, James Kirby *computer consultant*
Northrip, Robert Earl *lawyer*
O'Dell, Jane *automotive company executive*
Oliphant, Patrick *cartoonist*
O'Shields, Charlie *marketing professional*
Owens, Dennis James Campbell *lawyer*
Paden, John Bruce *community resource executive*
Palmer, Cruise *newspaper editor*
Parcell, John Cleo *music educator*
Parizek, Eldon Joseph *geologist, educator, dean*
Parker, Dennis Gene *former sheriff, martial arts instructor*
Parker, Marietta *prosecutor*
Patterson, Neal L. *information systems company executive*
Pelofsky, Joel *lawyer*
Pemberton, Bradley Powell *lawyer*
Pena, Antonio Francisco (Tony Pena) *professional athletics coach*
Peters, Ralph Irwin, Jr., *biology professor, researcher*
Petersen, Robert R. *brokerage house executive*
Petosa, Jason Joseph *publisher*
Piepho, Robert Walter *pharmacy educator, researcher*
Plax, Karen Ann *lawyer*
Popper, Robert *law educator, former dean*
Poston, Walker Seward, II, *medical educator, researcher*
Potter, George William, Jr., *mining executive*
Price, Charles H., II, *former ambassador*
Price, James Tucker *lawyer*
Pruitt, Stephen Wallace *finance educator*
Reed, Michael John *dentist, dean, oral biology educator*
Reichard, Larry A. *biologist, educator*
Reiter, Robert Edward *banker*
Rich, Ruthanne *musician, educator*
Roaf, William Layton *professional football player*
Robb, Gary Charles *lawyer*
Robertson, Kenneth Carl *music educator*
Robertson, Leon H. *management consultant, educator*
Rocha, Catherine Tomasa *municipal official*
Rodman, Leonard C. *civil and communication engineering executive*
Roosa, Jan Bertorotta *clinical psychologist*
Rost, William Joseph *chemist*
Roush, Sue *newspaper editor*
Rowland, Landon Hill *diversified holding company executive*
Sachs, Howard F(rederic) *federal judge*
Salizzoni, Frank L. *finance company executive*
Sampson, William Roth *lawyer*
Sanchez, Beatrice Rivas *art institute executive, artist*
Sauer, Brian *molecular geneticist, researcher*
Sauer, Gordon Chenoweth *retired dermatologist, educator*
Scarritt, Richard Winn *lawyer*
Schrum, Janice Lynn *social sciences educator*
Schuchman, Philip Melchor *education educator*
Schulkin, Carl Roger *secondary school educator*
Schuster, Fred *federal agency administrator*
Scott, Deborah Emont *curator*
Seligson, Theodore H. *architect, art appraiser, interior designer*
Setzler, Edward Allan *lawyer*
Shaw, John W. *lawyer*
Shaw, Richard David *marketing and management educator*
Sheldon, Ted Preston *library dean*
Shindler, Dorman Truett, Jr., *writer, journalist, critic, photographer, cartoonist*
Shughart, Donald Louis *retired lawyer*
Shutz, Byron Christopher *real estate executive*
Siro, Rik Neal *lawyer*
Sizemore, William Christian *retired academic administrator, county official*
Slaughter, Rochelle Denise *elementary school educator*
Small, Stephen Bradley *lawyer*
Smiley, David Bruce *administrative director*
Smith, Louis *sports association administrator*
Smithson, Lowell Lee *lawyer*
Spalding, Helen H. *library director*
Spalty, Edward Robert *lawyer*
Spencer, Richard Henry *lawyer*
Spigarelli, James L. *science administrator*
Stamm, Keith G. *energy executive*
Stelmach, Walter Jack *physician, medical education administrator*
Stevens, James Hervey, Jr., *retired financial advisor*
Stevens, Jane *advertising executive*
Stevens, Paul *newspaper editor*
Stoup, Arthur Harry *lawyer*
Stowers, James Evans, Jr., *investment company executive*
Stowers, James W., III, *data processing executive*
Streek, Dan *corporate financial executive*
Stroup, Kala Mays *educational alliance administrator, former state higher education commissioner*
Stueck, William Noble *small business owner*
Sullivan, Charles A. *food products executive*
Sweeney, Mike *professional baseball player*
Tammeus, William David *journalist, columnist*
Terry, Robert Brooks *food products executive, lawyer*
Thornton, Thomas Noel *publishing executive*
Toll, Perry Mark *lawyer, educator*
Treffer, Kevin Duane *physician, educator*
Truog, William Edward, III, *pediatrician, educator, researcher*
Tyler, John Edward, III, *lawyer*
Valliere, Roland Edward *performing company executive*
Vandever, William Dirk *lawyer*
Vando, Gloria *poet, publishing executive*
Van Dyke, Thomas Wesley *lawyer*
Van Way, Charles Ward, III, *surgery educator, research scientist*
Vering, John Albert *lawyer*
Vermeil, Dick *professional football coach*
Viani, James Laurence *lawyer*
Vleisides, Gregory William *lawyer*
Wade, Robert Glenn *engineering executive*
Waeckerle, Joseph *emergency physician, educator*
Warakomski, Alphonse Walter Joseph, Jr., *sales executive, marketing professional*
Whipple, Dean *federal judge*
Whitener, William Garnett *dancer, choreographer*
Whittaker, Judith Ann Cameron *lawyer*
Widmar, Russell C. *airport executive*
Wilder, Terry L. *religious studies educator*
Wilkins, Arthur Norman *retired academic administrator*
Wilkinson, Ralph Russell *biochemistry educator, toxicologist*
Willsie, Sandra K. *dean, internist, educator*
Willy, Thomas Ralph *lawyer*
Wirken, James Charles *lawyer*
Wittenborn, Dale *advertising executive*
Wolf, Dale Joseph *utilities company executive*
Wolf, Jerome Thomas *lawyer*
Woodson, Stephen William *collection agency executive*
Wright, Scott Olin *federal judge*
Wrobley, Ralph Gene *lawyer*
Wyrsch, James Robert *lawyer, educator, writer*
Yabuki, Jeffrey W. *diversified financial services company executive*
Yarick, Paul E. *food products executive*
Yarmo, Fanny F. *not-for-profit fundraiser*
Zieman, Mark *newspaper editor*

Kearney
Waltz, James Richard *physician*

Kimberling City
Stovall, Richard L. *retired academic administrator*

Kingsville
Stimac, John Anthony *small business owner, poet, cartoonist, inventor*

Kirbyville
Burch, Lori Ann *obstetrics nurse*

Kirksville
Engber, Cheryl Ann *language educator, linguist*
Festa, Roger Reginald *chemist, educator*
French, Michael Francis *non-profit education agency administrator*
Hanley, Mark Young *historian, educator, researcher*
McDuff, Elaine Marie *sociologist, educator*
Osborn, Gerald Guy *dean, psychiatrist, educator*
Peterson, Donald Fred *physiologist, educator*
Schwend, Michael T. *hospital administrator*

Kirkwood
Holsen, James Noble, Jr., *retired chemical engineer*

Lake Lotawana
Zobrist, Benedict Karl *library director, historian*

Lake Saint Louis
Callahan, Robert John, Jr., *lawyer, arbitrator*
Dommermuth, William Peter *marketing consultant, educator*
Royal, William Henry *retired real estate developer, architect*

Lambert Airport
Griggs, Leonard LeRoy, Jr., *airport executive*

Lebanon
Beavers, Roy Lackey *retired utility executive, essayist, activist*
Louderback, Kevin Wayne *business owner*

Lees Summit
Carter, William Gerald *non-profit corporation executive*
Foudree, Charles M. *financial consultant*
Henley, Joseph Oliver *manufacturing executive*
Himes, Brian David *reading educator*
Hubbard, Harold Mead *energy and environmental scientist, consultant*
Korschot, Benjamin Calvin *retired investment executive*
Linder, Beverly L. *elementary school educator*
Mosley, Glenn Richard *religious organization administrator, minister*
Parker, Deborah A. *language educator, translator*
Plantz, Jerry Anthony *writer, consultant, consumer products company executive*

Lewistown
Terpening, Virginia Ann *artist*

Lexington
Giorza, John C. *lawyer*

Liberty
Harriman, Richard Lee *performing arts association administrator, educator*
Kersten, Joanne Wilkerson *nursing educator*
McCaslin, W.C. *products and packaging executive*
Samuel, Robert Thompson *optometrist*
Sayles, Cathy A. *lawyer*
Seward, Nancy H. *retired band director, composer*
Tanner, Jimmie Eugene *retired dean*

Licking
Katz, Aya *jurist, linguist, writer*

Louisiana
Warner, Eleanore Joyce *nurse, educator*

Macon
Maddox, Wilma *health facility administrator*

Manchester
Forsman, Alpheus Edwin *retired lawyer*

Marshall
Wildt, Katherine Ann *literature educator, writer, educator*

Maryland Heights
Cacchione, Patrick Joseph *health association executive*
Cooper, Richard Alan *lawyer*
Lowenberg, David A. *pharmaceutical executive*
Marcus, John *wholesale distribution executive*
Ramanuja, Teralandur Krishnaswamy *retired structural engineer*
Steward, David L. *technology company executive*
Tenholder, Edward J. *pharmaceutical executive*
Toan, Barrett A. *health products executive*

Maryville
Clayton, John Andrew *director, coroner*
Hubbard, Dean Leon *academic administrator*
Kharadia, Virabhai Chelabhai *economist, educator, researcher*
Kramer, Ernest Joachim *music educator, composer*
McLaughlin, James Patrick *lawyer, educator*
Schultz, Patricia Bowers *vocal music educator, performer*
Sergel, Alfred E., III, (Al Sergel) *music educator*
Strating, Sharon L. *elementary school educator, professional staff developer, educational consultant*

Mexico
Teague, Deborah Gant *elementary school educator*
Tillman, Charles Herbert, Jr., *cardiologist*

Miller
Spencer, Jane Rene *music educator*

Moline Acres
Hinton, Velecia Ann *social welfare administrator*

Monett
Henry, Michael E. *computer company executive*

Mount Vernon
Stemmons, Randee Smith *lawyer*

Mountain Grove
Allmon, Sandra J. *writer*
Waldstein, Daniel Eric *science educator*

Naylor
Seratt, Rodger Calvin *manufacturing executive*

Neosho
Allman, Margaret Ann Lowrance *counseling administrator*

Nevada
Goldberger, Stephen Henry *otolaryngologist*

Nixa
Kreider, Jim *farmer, former state legislator*

North Kansas City
Davis, Michael Leonard *private investigator, consultant*
Hellman, Richard *endocrinologist*
Staloff, Arnold Fred *financial executive*

O Fallon
Gross, Stanley Merhl *chiropractor*
Jamison, Darlene *geriatrics nurse, artist*
Ractliffe, Robert Edward George *management executive*
Raeuchle, John Steven *application developer*
Wood, Leslie Ann *retail administrator*

Oak Grove
Davis, Jo *naturopath, hypnotherapist*

Overland
Clark, Maxine *retail executive*

Ozark
Thornton, Andrew John *minister*

Kieschnick, Gerald B. *religious organization administrator*
Killenberg, George Andrew *newspaper consultant, former newspaper editor*
Kimmey, James Richard, Jr., *foundation administrator*
Kincaid, Marilyn Coburn *medical educator*
King, Joseph, Jr., *government administrator, educator, consultant*
Kinsella, Ralph Aloysius, Jr., *physician*
Kipnis, David Morris *physician, educator*
Klahr, Saulo *nephrologist, educator*
Kling, Merle *political scientist, university official*
Klobasa, John Anthony *lawyer*
Knight, Charles Field *electrical equipment manufacturing company executive*
Knutsen, Alan Paul *pediatrician, immunologist, allergist*
Kodner, Martin *art dealer, consultant*
Kolker, Allan Erwin *ophthalmologist*
Korando, Donna Kay *journalist*
Kornfeld, Stuart A. *hematology educator*
Kortenhof, Joseph Michael *lawyer, educator*
Kouchoukos, Nicholas Thomas *surgeon*
Kuhlmann, Fred Mark *lawyer, business executive*
Kummer, Fred S. *construction company executive*
Lackey, Kayle Diann *elementary school educator*
Lacy, Paul Eston *pathologist*
Lalime, Patrick *professional hockey player*
Lambright, Stephen Kirk *brewing company executive, lawyer*
Landau, William Milton *neurologist, department chairman*
Lane, Frank Joseph, Jr., *lawyer*
Lang, Danny Robert *planning consultant*
La Russa, Tony, Jr., (Anthony La Russa Jr.) *professional baseball manager*
Laskowski, Leonard Francis, Jr., *microbiologist*
Lauenstein, Ann Gail *librarian*
Laurie, William *sports team executive*
Lause, Michael Francis *lawyer*
Lebowitz, Albert *lawyer, writer*
Leguey-Feilleux, Jean-Robert *political scientist, educator*
Lents, Peggy Iglauer *marketing professional*
Leonard, Judith Price *educational advisor*
Leven, Charles Louis *economics professor*
Le Vine, Victor Theodore *political science educator*
Lewis, Robert David *ophthalmologist, educator*
Li, Ping *pharmacologist, educator, researcher*
Liapis, Helen *pathologist, researcher, medical educator*
Liddy, Richard A. *insurance company executive*
Lieberman, Edward Jay *lawyer*
Liggett, Hiram Shaw, Jr., *retired diversified industry financial executive*
Limbaugh, Stephen Nathaniel *federal judge*
Lindsey, Linda Lee *sociology educator*
Lock, Albert Larry, Jr., *financial services company executive*
Loeb, Jerome Thomas *retail executive*
Loeb, Virgil, Jr., *oncologist, hematologist*
Lovelace, Eldridge Hirst *retired landscape architect, city planner*
Lovin, Keith Harold *academic administrator, philosophy educator*
Lowenhaupt, Charles Abraham *lawyer*
Loynd, Richard Birkett *consumer products company executive*
Lubbock, James Edward *retired writer, photographer, publicity consultant*
Luberda, George Joseph *lawyer, educator*
Lucchesi, Lionel Louis *lawyer*
Lucy, Robert Meredith *lawyer*
Ludbrook, Philip Albert *cardiologist, clinical researcher, educator*
Luebbert, Karen Merritt *academic administrator*
Lutz, John Thomas *author*
Lyons, Gordon *marketing executive*
Macias, Edward S. *chemistry educator, university official and dean*
MacInnis, Al *professional hockey player*
MacKeith, Peter *architecture educator*
Madden, Thomas F. *medieval history eductor, author*
Mahan, David James *retired university official*
Mahsman, David Lawrence *religious publications editor*
Majerus, Philip Warren *physician*
Mandelstamm, Jerome Robert *lawyer*
Mangelsdorf, Thomas Kelly *psychiatrist, consultant*
Manske, Paul Robert *orthopedic hand surgeon, educator*
Mantovani, John F. *pediatric neurologist*
Marking, T(heodore) Joseph, Jr., *transportation and urban planner*
Martin, Kevin John *nephrologist, educator*
Martínez-Solís, Luis Fernando *journalist, writer, historian*
Martz, Mike *professional football coach*
Massey, Raymond Lee *lawyer*
Maurer, Frederic George, III, *banker*
McCarter, Charles Chase *lawyer*
McCarter, James Philip *biotechnology company executive, researcher*
McCarthy, Michael M. *construction executive*
McClain, Curtis Keith, Jr., *religious studies educator, minister*
McCoole, Robert F. *construction company executive*
McDaniel, James Edwin *lawyer*
McDonnell, Sanford Noyes *aircraft company executive*
McFadden, James Frederick, Jr., *surgeon*
McGinnis, W. Patrick *diversified company executive*
McKelvey, James Morgan *chemical engineering educator*
McKenna, William John *textile products executive*
McKinnis, Michael B. *lawyer*
McMahon, Robert M. *physician, lawyer*
McMillian, Theodore *federal judge*
McNamara, William P. *retail executive*
Mc Namee, Maurice Basil *English language educator*
Medler, Mary Ann L. *federal judge*
Meisel, George Vincent *lawyer*
Meissner, Edwin Benjamin, Jr., *retired real estate broker*
Mendel, Mark J. *venture capitalist*
Merrell, James Lee *religious editor, clergyman*
Merrill, Charles Eugene *lawyer*
Metcalfe, Walter Lee, Jr., *lawyer*
Michaelides, Constantine Evangelos *architect, educator*
Michenfelder, Albert A. *lawyer*
Middelkamp, John Neal *pediatrician, educator*
Miller, Gary J. *political economist*
Miller, James Gegan *research scientist, physics educator*
Miller, Judith Braffman *writer*
Mohan, John J. *lawyer*
Molloff, Florence Jeanine *speech and language therapist*
Monroe, Thomas Edward *industrial corporation executive*
Monser, Edward L. *electric power industry executive*
Monteleone, Patricia *dean*
Montgomery, Alice Elizabeth *vocalist, speech pathologist*
Mooradian, Arshag Dertad *internist, educator*
Moore, McPherson Dorsett *lawyer*
Morley, John Edward *physician*
Mueller, Charles William *electric utility executive*
Mullens, William Reese *retired insurance company executive*
Mulligan, Michael Dennis *lawyer*
Mumm, Steven Robert *geneticist, educator*
Murray, Patrick Robert *microbiologist, educator*
Murray, Robert Wallace *chemistry professor*
Musial, Stan(ley) (Frank Musial) *hotel and restaurant executive, former baseball team executive, former baseball player*
Myerson, Robert J. *radiation oncologist, educator*
Naumann, Joseph F. *bishop*
Navarre, Richard A. *mining executive*
Nedwek, Brian *academic administrator*
Needham, Carol Ann *lawyer, educator*
Needleman, Philip *cardiologist, pharmacologist*
Neely, John Gail *otolaryngologist*
Nelly, (Cornell Haynes Jr.) *rap artist*
Nelson, Ronald Erwin *not-for-profit fundraiser*
Neville, James Morton *retired lawyer, consumer products company executive*
Newman, Andrew Edison *restaurant executive*
Newman, Charles A. *lawyer*
Newman, Joan Meskiel *lawyer*
Nickolai, Beatrice Rose *education educator*
Noel, Edwin Lawrence *lawyer*
North, Douglass Cecil *economist, educator*
Novak, Camille *small business owner, consultant*
Novik, Steve *finance company executive*
Nygard, Paul David *social sciences educator*
Obata, Gyo *architect*
O'Connell, Daniel Craig *psychology educator*
O'Keefe, Martin D. *priest, philosopher, educator, classicist*
O'Keefe, Michael Daniel *lawyer*
Olney, John William *psychiatry educator*
Olsen, Tava Maryanne Lennon *industrial and operations engineering educator*
Olson, Robert Grant *lawyer*
O'Malley, Kevin Francis *lawyer, writer, educator*
O'Malley, Thomas D. *petroleum industry executive*
O'Neill, Eugene Milton *retired investor*
O'Neill, Sheila *principal*
Onovwerosuoke, Fred *music educator, musicologist*
Ortbals, Gerald Ray *lawyer*
Orton, George Frederick *aerospace engineer*
Osborn, Mark Eliot *dentist*
Ott, David T. *insurance company executive*
Ottinger, Maurice Armand *software engineer, educator*
Owens, William Don *anesthesiology educator*
Ozawa, Martha Naoko *social work educator*
Pace, Orlando Lamar *professional football player*
Palans, Lloyd Alex *lawyer*
Pautrot, Jean-Louis Jacques *literature and language professor*
Payne, Meredith Jorstad *physician*
Paz, George *accountant*
Peck, William Arno *internist, educator, dean, academic administrator*
Peper, Christian Baird *lawyer*
Perkins, Norris Lynwood, III, (Terry Perkins) *columnist and writer*
Perotti, Rose Norma *lawyer*
Perry, Catherine D. *judge*
Perry, Lewis Curtis *historian, educator*
Peters, Charles A *electronics executive*
Peters, David Allen *mechanical engineering educator, consultant*
Petersen, Steven E. *neuroscientist, educator, health facility administrator*
Phoenix, G. Keith *lawyer*
Pickle, Robert Douglas *lawyer, apparel executive*
Place, Michael D. *health association administrator*
Pollack, Joe *retired newspaper critic and columnist, writer*
Pollack, Seymour Victor *computer science educator*
Poole, William *bank executive*
Pope, Robert E(ugene) *fraternal organization administrator*
Poscover, Maury B. *lawyer*
Posgay, Betty Marie *medical equipment company executive, artist*
Powers, William John *neurologist*
Prensky, Arthur Lawrence *pediatric neurologist, educator*
Provost, Cheryl Louise Winters *account executive*
Pryor, David Bram *health science association administrator*
Pujols, Albert *professional baseball player*
Purkerson, Mabel Louise *physician, physiologist, educator*
Purnell, John H. *beverage company executive*
Quenon, Robert Hagerty *retired mining consultant and holding company executive*
Rabbitt, Daniel Thomas, Jr., *lawyer*
Rainwater, Gary L. *corporate financial executive*
Ramming, Michael Alexander *retired school system administrator*
Randolph, Jennings, Jr., (Jay Randolph) *sportscaster*
Rao, Dabeeru C. *epidemiologist, educator*
Rasche, Robert Harold *banker, retired economics educator*
Ratner, Lee *medical educator*
Raven, Peter Hamilton *botanical garden director, botany educator*
Redd, Charles Appleton *lawyer*
Reese, Martha Grace *minister, lawyer*
Reh, Thomas Edward *radiologist, educator*
Reynolds, Robert A., Jr., *electric distributor executive*
Rice, Patricia Jane *journalist*
Rich, Harry Earl *corporate financial executive*
Richardson, Thomas Hampton *design consulting engineer*
Ricks, David Artel *business educator, editor*
Riddle, Veryl Lee *lawyer*
Riew, K. Daniel *cervical spine surgeon*
Riggio, Nicholas Jospeh, Sr., *lawyer*
Riley, Michael Robert *marketing and business development executive*
Riner, Ronald Nathan *cardiologist, business consultant*
Ringkamp, Stephen H. *lawyer, educator*
Ritter, Robert Forcier *lawyer*
Ritterskamp, Douglas Dolvin *lawyer*
Robins, Lee Nelken *medical educator*
Robins, Marjorie McCarthy (Mrs. George Kenneth Robins) *civic worker*
Rolen, Scott Bruce *professional baseball player*
Rose, Albert Schoenburg *lawyer, educator*
Rosen, Adrienne *artist, educator*
Rosen, Fred *travel company executive*
Rosenblum, Barry Norton *physician*
Rosenzweig, Saul *psychologist, educator, administrator*
Ross, Donald *transportation executive*
Ross, Monte *electrical engineer, researcher*
Royal, Henry Duval *nuclear medicine physician*
Rubenstein, Jerome Max *lawyer*
Ruland, Richard Eugene *English and American literature educator, critic, literary historian*
Ryall, Jo-Ellyn M. *psychiatrist*
Ryan, Sister Mary Jean *health facility executive*
Sale, Llewellyn, III, *lawyer*
Sale, Merritt *classicist, comparatist, educator*
Saleem, Kadharbatcha S *neurobiologist, research scientist*
Salisbury, Robert Holt *political science educator*
Sant, John Talbot *lawyer*
Schaal, Barbara Anna *evolutionary biologist, educator*
Scheffing, Dianne Elizabeth *special education educator*
Scherer, George F. *construction executive*
Schilling, James Stanford *physicist, educator*
Schindler, Laura Ann *piano teacher, accompanist*
Schlafly, Phyllis Stewart *writer*
Schlesinger, Milton J. *virology educator, researcher*
Schmid, Frank Andreas *economist*
Schmidt, Robert Charles, Jr., *finance executive*
Schnuck, Craig D. *grocery store company executive*
Schnuck, Scott C. *grocery store executive*
Schnuck, Todd Robert *grocery store company executive*
Schoene, Kathleen Snyder *lawyer*
Schoenhard, William Charles, Jr., *health care executive*
Schonfeld, Gustav *medical educator, researcher, administrator*
Schreiber, James Ralph *obstetrician, researcher*
Schumm, Steven A *corporate financial executive*
Schwartz, Alan Leigh *pediatrician, educator*
Schwarz, Egon *humanities and German language educator, writer, literary critic*
Sehorn, Jason *professional football player*
Seiler, James Elmer *judge*
Seligman, Joel *dean*
Sestric, Anthony James *lawyer*
Shanahan, Michael Francis *retired manufacturing executive, former hockey team executive*
Shapiro, Larry J. *pediatrician, scientist, educator*
Shapiro, Robert B. *former food products manufacturing executive*
Shaw, Charles Alexander *judge*
Shaw, Curt *lawyer, communications executive*
Shaw, Curtis S *lawyer*
Shea, Daniel Bartholomew, Jr., *English language educator, actor*
Sheffield, DeBorah Lagreta *poet, writer*
Shepperd, Thomas Eugene *accountant*
Sherby, Kathleen Reilly *lawyer*
Shevitz, Mark H. *sales promotion and marketing executive*
Shrauner, Barbara Wayne Abraham *electrical engineer, educator*
Shreckhise, Robert Lynn *minister, theology studies educator*
Sibbald, John Ristow *management consultant*
Siegel, Barry Alan *nuclear radiologist*
Sigala, Stephanie Childs *art historian, librarian*
Singh, Inderjit *nephrologist, internist, medical educator*
Skinner, Robert C., Jr., *retail executive*
Slatopolsky, Eduardo *nephrologist, educator*
Slavin, Raymond Granam *allergist, immunologist*
Slay, Francis G. *mayor*
Sly, William S. *biochemist, educator*
Smith, Arthur Lee *lawyer*
Smith, C. Grant *scriptwriter, film producer*
Smith, Gladys Ann *counselor, military medic*
Smith, Morton Edward *ophthalmology educator, dean*
Smith, Ozzie (Osborne Earl Smith) *retired professional baseball player*
Smith, Richard Jay *anthropologist, orthodontist, educator*
Sneeringer, Stephen Geddes *lawyer*
Snyder, William W. *corporate financial executive*
Sobol, Lawrence Raymond *lawyer*
Soeteber, Ellen *journalist, editor*
Sortwell, Christopher T. *food products executive*
Spector, Gershon Jerry *otolaryngologist, educator, researcher*
Stann, John Anthony *investment banker*
Stanton, Frank Lawrence, Jr., *graphic designer, illustrator, educator*
States, David Johnson *biomedical scientist, physician*
Stencer, Mark Joseph *healthcare administrator, consultant*
Stenson, William Frederick *gastroenterologist*
Stewart, Allan Forbes *lawyer*
Stewart, John Harger *music educator*
Stoecker, David Thomas *banker*
Stohr, Donald J. *federal judge*
Stokes, Patrick T. *brewery company executive*
Stoneman, William, III, *physician, educator*
Storandt, Martha *psychologist*
Stork, Donald Arthur *advertising executive*
Stretch, John Joseph *social work educator, management and evaluation consultant*
Strevey, Tracy Elmer, Jr., *army officer, surgeon, physician executive*
Suhre, Walter Anthony, Jr., *retired lawyer, brewery executive*
Suter, Albert Edward *manufacturing executive*
Sutera, Salvatore Philip *mechanical engineer, educator*
Sutter, Jane Elizabeth *science educator, writer, lecturer, conservationist*
Swain, David O. *manufacturing executive*
Swank, Darryl *agricultural products executive*
Sweet, Stuart C. *pediatrician*
Szabo, Barna Aladar *engineering educator*
Taylor, Andrew C. *rental and leasing company executive*
Taylor, Jack C. *rental and leasing company executive*
Teasdale, Kenneth Fulbright *lawyer*
Tei, Takuri *accountant*
Teitelbaum, Steven Lazarus *pathology educator*
Templeton, Alan Robert *biology professor*
Ternberg, Jessie Lamoin *pediatric surgeon*
Thach, William Thomas, Jr., *neurobiology and neurology educator*
Thalden, Barry R. *architect*
Thompson, Vetta Lynn Sanders *psychologist, educator*
Tiefenbrunn, Alan James *medical educator*
Tierney, Michael Edward *lawyer*
Tkachuk, Keith *professional hockey player*
Trevathan, Edwin *neurologist, educator*
Turcotte, John Arthur, Jr., *lawyer*
Tyler, William Howard, Jr., *advertising executive, educator*
Tyree, Donald Andrew *financial educator*
Unanue, Emil Raphael *immunopathologist*
Upbin, Hal J. *consumer products executive*
van den Berg, Sara Jane *English educator*
Vandiver, Donna *public relations executive*
Van Luven, William Robert *management consultant*
Van Trease, Sandra Ann *insurance company executive*
Virgo, John Michael *economist, researcher, educator*
Virtel, James John *lawyer*
Vogel, Carl E. *telecommunications industry executive*
Voss, K. Dirk *social sciences educator, researcher*
Walsh, Thomas Charles *lawyer*
Ward-Brown, Denise *sculptor, educator*
Ware, Judith Boyd *education educator*
Warner, Susan *federal agency administrator*
Waterbury, Jackson DeWitt *retired marketing executive*
Waters, Richard *retired publishing company executive*
Waterston, Robert Hugh *medical educator, researcher, medical geneticist, department chairman*
Watson, Patty Jo *anthropology educator*
Webb Anderson, JoAnn Marie *lawyer, community advocate*
Weber, Mark F. *medical executive*
Weck, Margaret A. *science educator*
Wedner, H. James *physician, researcher*
Weese, Cynthia Rogers *architect, educator*
Weidenbaum, Murray Lew *economist, educator*
Weight, Doug *professional hockey player*
Weir, Thomas Albert *education educator*
Weiss, Charles Andrew *lawyer*
Weiss, Robert Francis *former academic administrator, religious organization administrator, consultant*
Weixlmann, Joseph Norman, Jr., *English educator, provost*
Welch, Michael John *chemistry educator, researcher*
Welch, Patrick James *economics educator, author, consultant*
Weldon, Virginia V. *retired corporate executive, pediatrician*
Wellman, Carl Pierce *philosophy educator*
Werner, Burton Kready *insurance company executive*
Wickline, Samuel Alan *cardiologist, educator*
Wildhaber, Michael Rene *accountant*
Wiley, Gregory Robert *publisher*
Wilke, LeRoy *church administrator*
Williams, Mary Alice Baldwin *retired home economist, volunteer consultant*
Williams, Nellie James Batt *secondary school educator, minister*
Williamson, Marilyn *retired secondary school educator*
Willman, Vallee Louis *physician, surgery educator*
Willmore, Luther James, Jr., *neurologist, academic administrator, educator*
Wilson, Edward Nathan *mathematician, educator*
Wilson, Margaret Bush *lawyer*
Wilson, Margaret Mary Georgiana *geriatrician, researcher, physician*
Wilson, Martin D. *pharmaceutical executive*
Wiltenburg, Robert Edward *university dean*
Winer, Warren James *insurance executive*
Winter, David Ferdinand *electrical engineering educator, consultant*
Winter, Mildred M. *educational administrator*
Winter, Richard Lawrence *financial and health care company executive*
Winter, William Earl *retired beverage company executive*
Withers, W. Wayne *lawyer*
Witherspoon, William *investment economist*
Witt, Michael John *history educator, priest*
Wold, William Sydney *molecular biology educator*
Woodruff, Bruce Emery *lawyer*
Woolf, Steven Michael *artistic director*
Woolsey, Thomas Allen *neurobiologist*
Wrighton, Mark Stephen *chemistry professor*
Yeckel, Anita T. *state legislator*
Young, Leroy *plastic surgeon*
Young, Marvin Oscar *lawyer*
Young, Paul Andrew *anatomist*
Zhu, Xin Liang *molecular biologist, researcher*
Zurheide, Charles Henry *consulting electrical engineer*
Zwikelmaier, Kurt E. *pharmaceutical executive*

Saint Peters

Brandes, Gary Wayne *music educator*
Pring, Robert Bradford *financial consultant*
Van Lokeren, Mary Ann Krey *beer wholesaler executive*

Salem

Hall, Glenn Allen *lawyer, state representative*
Wood, Thomas Wesley *humanities educator, editor*

Sedalia

Gingerich, Naomi R. *emergency room nurse*
Hazen, Elizabeth Frances *retired special education educator*

Sibley

Morrow, Elizabeth Hostetter *sculptress, museum administrator, farmer, educator*

Stevensville
Derrick, William Dennis *retired physical plant administrator, consultant*

Trout Creek
Elliott, Jim *state senator*

Troy
Sherman, Signe Lidfeldt *portfolio manager, former research chemist*

Victor
Davenport, Anne Marilyn *dietician*

Whitefish
DeFranco, Boniface Ferdinand Leonard (Buddy DeFranco) *clarinetist, bandleader*
James, Marion Ray *magazine founder, editor*
Miller, Ronald Alfred *family physician*

Whitehall
Bernard, Donald Ray *law educator, international business counselor*

Winifred
Butcher, Edward Bernie *state senator*

NEBRASKA

Alliance
Haefele, Edwin Theodore *political theorist, consultant*
Riemenschneider, Albert Louis *retired engineering educator*

Atkinson
Sutherland, John Campbell *pathologist, educator*

Bellevue
Jackson, Alan William *consulting company executive, educator*
Kayne, Jon Barry *industrial psychologist*
Muller, John Bartlett *university president*
Schroeder, Van Ace *lawyer*
Wydeven, Joseph Jude *university dean, educator*

Benkelman
Whiteley, Rose Marie *city clerk, treasurer*

Blair
Christopherson, Myrvin Frederick *college president*

Boys Town
Lynch, Thomas Joseph *museum and historic house manager*

Chadron
Buschkopf, Debora J. *court reporter*
Schaefer, George W. Sandy *musician, educator*

Clay Center
Hahn, George LeRoy *agricultural engineer*

Columbus
Schumacher, Paul Maynard *lawyer*

Crete
Monson, Larry Lee *music educator*
Panec, William Joseph *lawyer*

Fremont
Dunklau, Rupert Louis *personal investments consultant*
Keasling, Gerald Frank *obstetrician-gynecologist, educator*
Line, William Gunderson *lawyer*
Roesch, Robert Eugene *dentist*

Friend
De Bevoise, Lee Raymond *editor, writer*

Grand Island
Ahlschwede, Earl David *lawyer*
Buettner, Anne Yu Ramona Wing-mui *psychologist*
Maupin, Larry D. *retired music educator, musician*
Mc Namara, Lawrence J. *bishop*
Weseman, Vicki Lynne *elementary school educator*
Zichek, Melvin Eddie *retired minister*
Zichek, Shannon Elaine *retired secondary school educator*

Gretna
Druliner, Marcia Marie *education educator*

Harrison
Coffee, Virginia Claire *civic worker, former mayor*
Knudson, Ruthann *environmental consultant*

Hastings
Bohlke, Ardyce *state legislator*
Bush, Marjorie Evelynn Tower-Tooker *educator, media specialist, librarian*
Creigh, Thomas, Jr., *utilities executive*
Dungan, John Russell, Jr., (12th Viscount Dungan of Clane, Hereditary Prince of Fermoy and Arra) *anesthesiologist, health facility administrator*
Kort, Betty *secondary school educator*
Pankratz, Todd Alan *obstetrician, gynecologist*
Yost, Dee Renee *librarian, educator*

Holdrege
Hendrickson, Bruce Carl *life insurance company executive*

Kearney
Buckner, Nathan Andrew *music educator, musician*
Fendt, Gene J. *poet, philosopher, educator*
Fredrickson, Scott Alfred *instructional technology educator, consultant*
Harrold, Francis Bernard, Jr., *anthropology educator*
Johnston, Gladys Styles *university official*
Schnoor, Neal Henry *music educator*
Wubbels, Gene Gerald *chemistry professor*
Young, Ann Elizabeth O'Quinn *historian, educator*

Lincoln
Alexis, Carl Odman *lawyer, earth scientist*
Anderson, John Edwin *economics professor, consultant*
Angle, John Charles *retired life insurance company executive*
Arth, Lawrence Joseph *insurance executive*
Atwood, Raymond Percival, Jr., *lawyer*
Baird, Samuel P. *state finance director*
Beam, Clarence Arlen *judge*
Beermann, Allen J. *former state official*
Bernthal, John E. *medical association administrator*
Blanke, Henry H., Jr., *retired theater educator*
Bodvarsson, Orn Bodvar *economist, educator*
Boyle, Anne C. *state commissioner*
Bradley, Richard Edwin *retired academic administrator*
Bromm, Curt *state legislator*
Brown, Pam *state legislator*
Bruning, Jon Cumberland *state attorney general*
Bruskewitz, Fabian W. *bishop*
Burnham, Stephen John *civil engineer*
Byrd, Lorelee *state treasurer*
Callahan, Bill *college football coach*
Collier, Nathan Morris *musician, music educator*
Connolly, William M. *state supreme court justice*
Connor, Carol J. *library director*
Crosby, LaVon Kehoe Stuart *state legislator, civic leader*
Deegan, Mary Jo *sociology educator*
Digman, Lester Aloysius *management educator*
Dixon, Wheeler Winston *film and video studies educator, writer*
Drullinger, Leona Pearl Blair *obstetrics nurse*
Dyer, William Earl, Jr., *retired newspaper editor*
Edison, Allen Ray *electrical engineer, educator*
Edwards, Donald Mervin *systems engineer, educator, dean*
Elias, Samy E. G. *engineering executive*
Erdman, Philip *state legislator, farmer*
Exon, J(ohn) James *former senator*
Fisher, Calvin David *food manufacturing company executive*
Fleharty, Mary Sue *state government staff member*
Francis, Charles Andrew *agronomy educator, consultant*
Frobom, LeAnn Larson *lawyer*
Gale, John A. *secretary of state*
Genoways, Hugh Howard *systematic biologist, educator*
Gerrard, John M. *state supreme court justice*
Gitelson, Anatoly Avraam *engineering educator*
Goddard, Steve *computer engineer, educator*
Gray, Joni Nadine *state agency administrator*
Grew, Priscilla Croswell *university official, geology educator*
Guthery, John M. *lawyer*
Handa, Rumiko *architect, educator*
Hanna, Milford A. *agricultural engineering educator*
Hanway, Donald Grant *retired agronomist, educator*
Hardin, Clifford Morris *retired academic administrator*
Hardin, Martha Love Wood *civic leader*
Harnsberger, Richard Stephen *law educator*
Harris, Bernard *statistician, mathematician, educator*
Hastings, William Charles *retired state supreme court chief justice*
Hayes, Jason William *lawyer, law educator*
Hays, Michael D. *research company executive*
Heineman, David *lieutenant governor*
Hendry, John *state supreme court justice*
Hewitt, James Watt *retired lawyer*
Hill, Ronald Clair *anesthesiologist*
Iyengar, Srikanth B *mathematician, educator*
Janzow, Walter Theophilus *retired college administrator*
Johanns, Michael O. *governor*
Johnson, Douglas Blaikie *lawyer*
Jones, Lee Bennett *chemist, educator, university official*
Kamil, Alan C. *biology professor*
Knox, Arthur Lloyd *investor*
Kopf, Richard G. *federal judge*
Koszewski, Bohdan Julius *retired internist, medical educator*
Koubek, Ekaterina N. *education educator*
Kramer, David J. *state representative, lawyer*
Kraus, Joseph C. *education educator*
Kristensen, Douglas Allan *former state legislator*
Krogh, Rodney S. *legislative staff member*
Landis, David Morrison *state legislator*
Laphen, James A. *investment company executive*
Lee, Sang M. *management educator*
Leinieks, Valdis *classicist, educator*
Leiter, Richard Allen *law librarian, law educator*
Lichty, Warren Dewey, Jr., *lawyer*
Lienemann, Delmar Arthur, Sr., *accountant, real estate developer*
Lundstrom, Gilbert Gene *banker, lawyer*
Lyons, William Harry *law educator*
MacPhee, Craig Robert *economist, educator*
Magorian, James *poet, writer*
Massengale, Martin Andrew *agronomist, university president*
Maxwell, Chip *state legislator*
McCormack, Michael *state supreme court justice*
McCutcheon, Allan Lee *sociology educator*
Miller-Lerman, Lindsey *state supreme court justice*
Milligan, Cynthia Hardin *university dean, lawyer*
Mohebbi, Esmail *industrial engineer*
Moul, Maxine Burnett *state official*
Mulvaney, Mary Jean *physical education educator, department chairman*
Mutunayagam, N. Brito *architecture and planning educator*
Nelson, Darrell Wayne *university administrator, scientist*
Novoa, Yanira *diplomat*
Ogle, Robbin Sue *criminal justice educator*
Ottoson, Howard Warren *economist, retired academic administrator*
Perlman, Harvey Stuart *lawyer, educator*
Peterson, Wallace Carroll, Sr., *economics professor*
Piester, David L(ee) *magistrate judge*
Preister, Donald George *state legislator, greeting card manufacturer*
Price, Marian L. *state legislator*
Rawley, James Albert *history professor*
Raz, Hilda *editor-in-chief, educator, English educator*
Redfield, Pamela A. *state legislator*
Reinhardt, John W. *dean, dental educator*
Rembolt, James Earl *lawyer*
Robak, Jennie *state legislator*
Robak, Kim M. *academic administrator, lawyer*
Rohren, Brenda Marie Anderson *therapist, educator*
Rosenow, John Edward *foundation executive*
Rowe, David Winfield *lawyer*
Royster, Paul Barnett *publishing executive*
Sawyer, Robert McLaran *history educator*
Schimek, DiAnna Ruth Rebman *state legislator*
Schizas, Jennifer Anne *law association administrator*
Seng, Coleen Joy *mayor*
Smith, Adrian M. *state legislator, real estate agent*
Smith, L. Dennis *former academic administrator*
Smith, Richard Wendell *lawyer*
Splinter, William Eldon *agricultural engineering educator*
Spreitzer, Robert Joseph *biochemist, educator*
Stange, James Henry *architect*
Steffan, Judy Mae *medical/surgical nurse*
Stephan, Kenneth C. *judge*
Steward, Weldon Cecil *architecture educator, architect, consultant*
Stoddard, Robert H. *geography educator*
Stover, John Ford *railroad historian, educator*
Stuhr, Elaine Ruth *state legislator*
Sullivan, Robert Emmett *pediatric dentist, educator*
Suttle, Deborah S. *state legislator*
Taylor, Stephen Lloyd *food toxicologist, educator, food scientist*
Thompson, Nancy P. *state legislator*
Tinstman, Dale Clinton *food products company consultant*
Tonack, DeLoris *elementary school educator*
Urbom, Warren Keith *federal judge*
Van Etten, James *plant pathologist, educator*
Vidaver, Anne Marie *plant pathology educator*
Wagner, Rod *library director*
Wallis, Deborah *curator*
Wiegand, Sylvia Margaret *mathematician, educator*
Wiersbe, Warren Wendell *clergyman, author, lecturer*
Wilson, Charles Stephen *cardiologist, educator*
Witek, Kate *state senator, trucking company executive*
Withem, Ronald E. *state senator, trade association executive*
Woollam, John Arthur *electrical engineering educator*
Wright, John F. *judge*
Yoder, Bruce Alan *chemist*
Young, Dale Lee *banker*
Zink, Walter Earl, II, *lawyer*

Lindsay
Parker, Gary Dean *manufacturing executive*

Lyons
Hassebrook, Chuck *not-for-profit developer*
Rose, Dwight Dean *music educator*

Mc Cook
Blank, Don Sargent *dentist*

Norfolk
Huse, Eugene Franklin *newspaper publisher*
Mortensen-Say, Marlys *school system administrator*
Nielsen, Daniel C. *poet*
Timmer, Margaret Louise (Peg Timmer) *art educator*
Wehrer, Charles Siecke *business and education educator*

North Platte
Kay, Stephen William *lawyer*
Mueller, Wayne Dennis *music educator*
Wohler, Ruth *humanities educator*

Offutt A F B
Cartwright, James E. *career military officer*
Goslin, Thomas B. *career officer*
Hinson, Robert C. *career officer*
Mies, Richard W. *career officer*

Ogallala
Bourque, Richard Michael *foundation administrator*

Omaha
Achelpohl, Steven Edward *lawyer, political organization worker*
Allen, Robert Francis *economist, educator*
Armitage, James O. *medical educator*
Badeer, Henry Sarkis *physiology educator*
Balaji, K.C. *urologist, researcher*
Baldwin, Jeffrey Nathan *pharmacy educator*
Barber, Roger L. *grain marketing company executive*
Barkmeier, Wayne W. *academic administrator*
Barrett, Frank Joseph *lawyer, former insurance company executive*
Bartle, John R. *social sciences educator*
Batchelder, Anne Stuart *retired publishing executive, political organization worker*
Belck, Nancy Garrison *dean, educator*
Belian, Julia *law educator*
Bell, C(lyde) R(oberts) (Bob Bell) *foundation administrator*
Benson, John Alexander, Jr., *internist, educator*
Bergt, Gregory Paul *chemist, consultant*
Bolding, Jay D. *food products executive*
Bowen, Brent *aviation educator*
Bradbury, Doug *construction company executive*
Bragg, Russell J. *food products executive*
Brailey, Susan Louise *quality analyst, educator*
Brock, Stephen L. *supervisor international languages, consultant*
Brownrigg, John Clinton *lawyer*
Bruckner, Martha *academic administrator*
Brumback, Roger Alan *neuropathologist, researcher*
Buffett, Warren Edward *entrepreneur, investment company executive*
Burris, Janice Elaine *educational administrator*
Caggiano, Joseph *advertising executive*
Caporale, D. Nick *lawyer*
Carson, Steven Douglas *science educator, biomedical researcher*
Casale, Thomas Bruce *medical educator*
Casey, Murray Joseph *physician, educator*
Chan, Wing-Chung *pathologist, educator*
Chen, Zhengxin *computer scientist*
Clark, Terry Dee *political scientist, educator*
Cleary, Pamela Ann *symphony executive*
Clifton, James K. *market research company executive*
Conley, Eugene Allen *retired insurance company executive*
Corbin, David E. *health education and public health educator*
Crouse, Jerry K. *energy company executive*
Curtiss, Elden F. *bishop*
Danielson, Mary Ann *communications educator, department chairman*
Daub, Hal *former mayor, former congressman*
Davidson, Richard K. *railroad company executive*
Diamond, Arthur Mansfield, Jr., *economics professor*
Dolan, James Vincent *lawyer*
Durham, Charles William *civil engineer, director*
Dvornyk, Volodymyr *research geneticist*
Eggers, James Wesley *executive search consultant*
Eisenhardt, James William *performing arts educator, department chairman*
Evans, Ivor J. (Ike) *railroad executive*
Fahey, Mike *mayor*
Fairbanks, Charles F. *law educator*
Fairfield, Bill L. *finance company executive*
Ferlic, Randolph *medical educator*
Fitzgerald, James Patrick *lawyer*
Fitzgerald, William Allingham *savings and loan association executive, director*
Forbes, Franklin Sim *lawyer, educator*
Frazier, Chet June *advertising agency executive*
Fusaro, Ramon Michael *dermatologist, researcher*
Gerhardt, Kenneth W. *retired agricultural products executive*
Gershovich, Moshe *historian, educator*
Gleason, James Mullaney *lawyer, insurance executive*
Golden, Dona Lee *artist*
Gollan, John Lachlan *dean, educator*
Goslee, Dwight J. *agricultural products executive*
Gottschalk, John E. *newspaper publishing executive*
Grant, John P. *lawyer*
Grant, John Thomas *retired state supreme court justice*
Graves, Maureen Ann *self esteem and spirituality consultant*
Grewcock, Bruce E. *mining executive*
Gupta, Vinod *business lists company executive*
Hachten, Richard Arthur, II, *health system executive*
Hamburg, Marc D. *insurance company executive*
Hansen, James Allen *state agency administrator*
Harmless, J. William *theologian, educator*
Harned, Roger Kent *radiology educator*
Hartman, Herbert Arthur, Jr., *oncologist*
Harvey, Jack K. *holding company executive*
Haselwood, Eldon LaVerne *retired education educator*
Hawks, Howard L. *energy executive*
Heavican, Michael G. *prosecutor*
Hinder, Ronald Albert *surgeon, researcher*
Hodgson, Paul Edmund *surgeon, department chairman*
Horning, Ross Charles, Jr., *historian, educator*
Howard, Thomas Clement *surgeon*
Howard, Walter Burke *chemical engineer*
Huurman, Walter William *pediatric orthopaedic surgeon, educator*
Imray, Thomas John *radiologist, educator*
Jacobs, Danny O. *surgeon, medical educator*
Jansen, James Steven *lawyer*
Jantz, Kenneth M. *construction executive*
Jenkins, Melvin Lemuel *lawyer*
Jetter, Arthur Carl, Jr., *insurance company executive*
Jiang, Hong *information scientist*
Johnson, James David *concert pianist, organist, educator*
Johnson, Owen C. *food products executive*
Justice, Bob Joe *corporate development executive*
Kelly, Robert Quaine *retired law librarian, educator*
Kessinger, Margaret Anne *medical educator*
King, Larry *editor*
Kobayashi, Roger Hideo *allergy and immunology educator*
Korbitz, Bernard Carl *retired oncologist, hematologist, educator, consultant*
Kostecki, Martin Paul *industrial engineer*
Krutter, Forrest Nathan *lawyer*
Kuhlman, Thomas Ashford *American studies educator, writer*
Lamson, William Maxwell, Jr., *lawyer*
Lauritzen, Bruce Ronnow *banker*
Lechowicz, Lisa Marie *retired insurance company executive*
Leininger, Madeleine Monica *nursing educator, consultant, anthropologist, theorist, editor, writer*
Lindsey, Ada Marie *dean, nursing educator*
Linville, Randal L. *agricultural company executive*
Liu, Mingsheng *engineering educator*
Longo, Amy L. *lawyer*
Louisa, Angelo Joseph *social studies educator, researcher*
Lynch, Benjamin Leo *oral surgeon, educator*
Lynch, Henry Thomson *medical educator*
Lynch, Thomas Gerald *surgeon, educator*
Maher, Susan Marguerite *language educator*
Mardis, Hal Kennedy *urological surgeon, educator, researcher*
Maurer, Harold Maurice *pediatrician*
McCusker, Thomas J. *lawyer, insurance company executive*
Miller, Larry Thomas *accountant*
Mohiuddin, Syed Maqdoom *cardiologist, educator*
Monaghan, Thomas Justin *former prosecutor*
Moore, Scott *former state official*
Mukherjee, Sandeep *gastroenterologist, educator*
Munger, Charles T. *diversified company executive*
Nairn, Roderick *immunologist, educator, biochemist*
Neary, Daniel *insurance company executive*
Newton, John Milton *academic administrator, psychologist, educator*
Nicol, Brian *publishing executive*
Nielsen, Fredrick Henry *historian, educator*
Nogg, Donald Irwin *retired paper distribution executive, population researcher*
North, Terry Claire *clinical psychologist*
Norton, Robert R., Jr., *former food products executive*
O'Brien, Richard L(ee) *medical educator, academic administrator, physician, cell biologist*
O'Connor, Robert Edward, Jr., *lawyer*
O'Donnell, James P. *food service executive*
Okhamafe, Imafedia *English literature and philosophy educator*
Patrick, Erline M. *federal agency administrator*
Pearson, Paul Hammond *physician*
Phares, Lynn Levisay *public relations communications executive*
Pirsch, Carol McBride *county official, former state senator, community relations manager*
Pitts, Robert Eugene, Jr., *marketing educator, consultant*

Polsky, Donald Perry *architect*
Quigley, Herbert Joseph, Jr., *pathologist, educator*
Regan, Timothy James *grain company executive*
Riley, William Jay *federal judge*
Rogan, Eleanor Groeniger *cancer researcher, educator*
Rohde, Bruce C. *food company executive, lawyer*
Roskens, Ronald William *international business consultant*
Ross, Donald Roe *federal judge*
Ross, Larry *education educator, researcher*
Ryan, Mark Anthony *architect, lawyer*
Ryan, Sheila A. *nursing educator, former dean*
Sample, Lisa L. *education educator*
Sands, Deanna *editor*
Schlegel, John P. *academic administrator*
Schropp, Tobin *lawyer*
Scott, Walter, Jr., *construction company executive*
Shanahan, Thomas M. *judge*
Shaw, Raymond Arthur *retail manager*
Shilling, Kay Marlene *psychiatrist*
Sigerson, Charles Willard, Jr., *insurance agency executive*
Simmons, Lee Guyton, Jr., *zoological park director*
Simon, Paul H. *newspaper editor*
Skau, Michael W. *English educator*
Skoog, Donald Paul *retired pathologist, educator*
Smith, Philip W. *epidemiologist*
Smithey, Donald Leon *airport authority director*
Sooriyaarachchi, Gamini Sarathchandra *oncologist, hematologist, educator, researcher*
Stenberg, Donald B. *lawyer*
Stinson, Kenneth E. *construction and mining company executive*
Strawhecker, Paul Joseph *fundraising consultant*
Strom, Lyle Elmer *judge*
Stubblefield, Robert F. *travel agency executive*
Sturgeon, John Ashley *insurance company executive*
Tinker, John Heath *anesthesiologist, educator*
Tunnicliff, David George *civil engineer, consultant*
von Bernuth, Carl W. *lawyer, diversified corporation executive*
Vosburg, Bruce David *lawyer*
Waggener, Ronald Edgar *radiologist*
Walter, Michael D. *food products executive*
Ward, Vernon Graves *internist*
Weekly, John William *insurance company executive*
Welch, James Douglas *lawyer, engineer*
Wells, Roger W. *lawyer, food products executive*
Wild, Stephen Kent *securities broker, dealer*
Wilhelmi, Cynthia Joy *information technology professional, consultant*
Yampolsky, Victor *conductor*
Young, James R. *railroad transportation executive*
Zaiman, K(oichi) Robert *dentist*
Zardetto-Smith, Andrea *medical educator*
Zepf, Thomas Herman *physics educator, researcher*
Zerbs, Stephen Taylor *communications engineer*

Oneill
Hedren, Paul Leslie *national park administrator, historian*

Papillion
Dvorak, Allen Dale *radiologist*
James, Geneva Behrens *secondary school educator*
Zuerlein, Damian Joseph *priest*

Schuyler
Johnson, Dolores DeBower *consultant*

Scottsbluff
DiBacco, T. Jay *financial services planner, retired military officer*
Kabalin, John Nicholas *urologist*
Rogers, Cindy L. *music educator*

South Sioux City
Conley, Randy Joe *city official, private investigator*

Valentine
O'Kief, W. Gerald *lawyer*

Waterloo
O'Brien, Nancy Lynn *bank executive*

Wayne
Burge, Steven Donald *city administrator*

York
Givens, Randal Jack *communications educator*

NEVADA

Baker
Mills, Rebecca *national park administrator*

Boulder City
Fisher, Paul Cary *writing supplies company executive*
Kidd, Hillery Gene *educational publisher*
Schultheis, Adam John *music educator, consultant*
Wyman, Richard Vaughn *engineering educator, exploration company executive*

Cambridge
Jonson, Sondra Lenore *sculptor, educator*

Carson City
Agosti, Deborah Ann *state supreme court justice*
Amodei, Mark E. *state legislator, lawyer*
Ayres, Janice Ruth *social services administrator*
Brant, James William *educational consultant, mathematician, educator*
Bugli, David *conductor, arranger, composer*
Burns, Dan W. *manufacturing executive*
Chanos, Adriana Escobar *state agency administrator*
Convis, Charles Lester *publisher*
Crawford, John Edward *geologist, scientist*
Deterding, Paul E. *pastor*
Empey, Gene F. *real estate executive*
Evangelatos, Gregory Gerasimos *city planner*
Gibbons, Mark *judge*
Guinn, Kenny C. *governor*
Heller, Dean *state official*
Hull, Dennis Jacques *counselor*
Hunt, Lorraine T. *lieutenant governor*
Jones, Sara Sue Fisher *librarian*
Klippert, Richard Hobdell, Jr., *engineering executive*
Krolicki, Brian Keith *state official*

Maupin, A. William *state supreme court justice*
O'Connell, Mary Ann *state legislator, small business owner*
Peterson, Mary L. *state agency official*
Reid, Belmont Mervyn *brokerage house executive*
Rocha, Guy Louis *archivist, historian*
Rose, Robert Edgar *state supreme court justice*
Springer, Charles Edward *retired judge*
Titus, Alice Costandina (Dina Titus) *state legislator*
Traylor, William Robert *publisher*
Wadman, William Wood, III, *educational director, technical research executive, consulting company executive*
Walshaw, L. Scott *commissioner*
wSandoval, Brian *state attorney general*

Cold Springs
Turner VanLydegraf, Claudia Beth *writer, researcher*

Dayton
Clements, Linda L. *materials engineer, educator, journalist*

Elko
Lovell, Walter Benjamin *secondary education educator, radio broadcaster*
Seymour, Lisa *museum director*

Ely
Alderman, Minnis Amelia *psychologist, educator, small business owner*

Gardnerville
Smith, Roderick Joel *behavioral consultant, researcher, educator*

Genoa
Goode, John Martin *manufacturing executive*

Glenbrook
Goldsmith, Harry Sawyer *surgeon, educator*

Hawthorne
Chenoweth-Hage, Helen P. *former congresswoman*
Pierce, Mildred Louise *librarian*

Henderson
Bruno, Cathy Eileen *management consultant, former state official, social sciences educator*
Chairsell, Christine *academic administrator*
Cohan, George Sheldon *advertising and public relations executive*
DeVol, Luana *vocalist, consultant*
Fehr, Gregory Paris *marketing and distribution company executive*
Fiore, Nicholas Francis *special components and materials company executive*
Freyd, William Pattinson *fund raising executive, consultant*
Gibson, James B. *mayor*
Goldstein, Morris *retired entertainment company executive*
Holloway, Robert Wester *radiochemist*
Kelley, Michael John *newspaper editor*
Klink, Karin Elizabeth *medical communications company executive, writer*
McKinney, Sally Vitkus *state official*
Moon, David A. *manufacturing executive*
Moore, Richard *former academic administrator, educator*
Pellock, John David *chemist, educator*
Perkins, Richard D(ale) *police official, state legislator*
Riske, William Kenneth *producer, cultural services consultant*
Roll, Irwin Clifford (Win Roll) *advertising, marketing and publishing executive*
Roth, Jeffrey Joseph *plastic surgeon*
Thomas, James Patrick *special education educator*
Tiffany, Sandra L. *state legislator*
Trimble, Thomas James *retired utility company executive, lawyer*
Trivelpiece, Alvin William *physicist, educator, consultant*
Van Noy, Terry Willard *health care executive*
Wennerstrom, Arthur John *aeronautical engineer*
Wills, Robert Hamilton *retired newspaper executive*

Hendersonville
Niemeyer, Erin Janice *pharmaceutical sales consultant, journalist, editor*

Incline Village
Bixby, Robert Eugene *computer, mathematics educator*
Diederich, J(ohn) William *internet publisher*
Ealy, Cynthia Pike *artist, real estate agent*
Johnson, James Arnold *business consultant, venture capitalist*
Johnston, Bernard Fox *foundation executive, writer*
Jones, Robert Alonzo *economist*
Merdinger, Charles John *civil engineer, naval officer, academic administrator*
Moore, Patricia Ann *medical technology investor, consultant*
O'Connor, Thomas Patrick *screenwriter*
Strack, Harold Arthur *retired electronics company executive, retired air force officer, planner, analyst, author, musician*
Tagayev, Lev C. *art director*
Tedford, Jack Nowlan, III, *construction executive, small business owner*
Thompson, David Alfred *industrial engineer*
Timinsky, Dale *academic administrator*
Yount, George Stuart *paper company executive*

Lake Tahoe
Sprague, Billy Michael *aerospace transportation executive*

Las Vegas
Adelson, Sheldon G. *hotel executive*
Albanese, Thomas *food industry executive, consultant*
Alexander, John Bradfield *scientist, retired army officer*
Ananias, José *retired school system administrator*
Arce, Phillip William *hotel and casino executive*
Arend, Richard J *finance educator, consultant*
Arum, Robert *lawyer, sports events promoter*
Ashbaugh, Nancy Gould *writer, performing arts educator*

Atwood, Charles L. *recreational facility executive*
Bandt, Paul Douglas *physician, neurologist*
Barr, Wallace R. *electronics executive*
Basile, Richard Emanuel *retired management consultant, educator*
Beagles, Dorothy Boetticher *office administrator, homeopathic consultant*
Becker, Nancy Anne *state supreme court justice*
Berghel, Hal L. *computer science educator, columnist, author, consultant*
Bersi, Ann *lawyer*
Bishop, Leo Kenneth *clergyman, educator*
Blattner, Meera McCuaig *computer science educator*
Blau, Elizabeth Anne *restaurant executive*
Bogden, Daniel G. *prosecutor*
Bolt, J. *communications executive*
Borovicka, Marsha Lorraine *music educator*
Bowers, Michael Wayne *political science educator, writer*
Boyle, Carolyn Moore *public relations executive, marketing communications manager*
Bridges, B. Ried *lawyer*
Broca, Laurent Antoine *aerospace scientist*
Brown, Joseph Wentling *lawyer*
Brown, Lori Lipman *secondary school educator*
Bryan, Richard H. *lawyer, educator, former senator*
Buzard, Kurt Andre *ophthalmologist*
Canada, William H. *plastic surgeon*
Canarelli, Lawrence D. *real estate developer*
Capanna, Albert Howard *neurosurgeon, neuroscientist, lawyer*
Care, Terry *state legislator, lawyer*
Carlton, Maggie *state legislator*
Carroll, Rossye O'Neal *college administrator*
Carter, Paul Richard *physician*
Castro, Joseph Armand *music director, pianist, composer, orchestrator*
Chance, Patti Lynn *school leadership educator*
Chesnut, Carol Fitting *lawyer*
Close, Jack Dean, Sr., *physical therapist*
Coffin, James Robert *state legislator, small business owner*
Cole, Ann Harriet *psychologist, consultant*
Collis, Kay Lynn *sales executive*
Connolly, Owen Robert *sales and business consultant*
Cooper, Matthew Marc *cardiothoracic surgeon*
Crevelt, Dwight Eugene *computer company executive*
Culp, Gordon Louis *consulting engineer*
Curran, William P. *lawyer*
Dastin, Samuel J. *aerospace engineer, consultant*
Davies, Alma (Alma Rosita) *producer, playwright, lyricist, composer, designer, sculptor*
Deasy, Jacqueline Hildegard *management consultant*
DeLury, Bernard Edward, Jr., *lawyer*
de Rocher, Denise D. *social sciences educator, language educator*
Di Palma, Joseph Alphonse *investment company executive, lawyer*
Donaghy, Henry James *English literature educator, academic administrator*
Duncombe, Patricia Warburton *retired social worker*
Duva-Mikhail, Donna Marie *financial executive*
Edler, Lisa Ann *middle school educator*
Eich, Jerry L. *architectural firm executive*
Ensign, Michael S. *resort company executive*
Eskin, Jeffrey Laurence *lawyer*
Faiss, Robert Dean *lawyer*
Ferrillo, Patrick J., Jr., *dean, endodontist*
Francis, Timothy Duane *chiropractor*
Frederick, Sherman *publishing executive*
Gaffga, Timothy Frederick *elementary school educator*
Gallagher, Thomas Edmund *hotel executive, lawyer*
Gaspar, Anna Louise *retired elementary school educator, consultant*
George, Lloyd D. *federal judge*
Gideon-Hawke, Pamela Lawrence *fine arts small business owner*
Gilchrist, Ann Roundey *hospice nurse*
Gillespie, Marilyn *museum administrator*
Gjurich, Michael John *music educator*
Goldberg, Aubrey *lawyer*
Goldblatt, Hal Michael *photographer, accountant*
Goldin, Martin Bruce *financial executive, consultant*
Goldstein, Steven Edward *psychologist*
Goodall, Leonard Edwin *public administration educator*
Goodman, Oscar Baylin *mayor, lawyer*
Goodwin, John Robert *lawyer, law educator, author*
Goodwin, Nancy Lee *corporate executive*
Goulet, Robert Gerard *singer, actor*
Grace, John William *electrical company executive*
Gray, Phyllis Anne *librarian*
Gremse, David Albert *pediatrician, educator*
Griesche, Robert Price *hospital purchasing executive*
Gross, Marvin Samuel *lawyer*
Grosshans, Merilyn La Vonne *retired librarian*
Gubler, John Gray *lawyer*
Haas, Robert John *aerospace engineer*
Hammargren, Lonnie L. *former lieutenant governor*
Hanson, Gerald Eugene *oral and maxillofacial surgeon*
Hardie, George Graham *casino executive*
Harter, Carol Clancey *university president, English language educator*
Healy, Mary (Mrs. Peter Lind Hayes) *singer, actress*
Herzlich, Harold J. *chemical engineer*
Hickey, David C. *art historian*
Hilbrecht, Norman Ty *lawyer*
Hill, Judith Deegan *retired lawyer*
Hobbs, Guy Stephen *financial executive*
Holmes, BarbaraAnn Krajkoski *secondary school educator*
Holmes, David Leo *recreation and leisure educator*
Honsa, Vlasta *retired librarian*
Hughes, Nicholas Melvin *mining company executive*
Jabara, Michael Dean *technology and business development entrepreneur*
Jacobs, Gary N. *hotel executive, lawyer*
Jaffe, Herb *retired newspaper editor, columnist*
Jakopec, Carl Thomas *pharmaceutical company executive*
Jelen, Ted G. *political scientist*
Johnston, Robert Jake *federal magistrate judge*
Jones, Fletcher, Jr., *automotive company executive*
Kalb, Benjamin Stuart *television producer, director*
Kam, James Ting *engineer, consultant, scientist*
Kastle, Kenneth Dimitrius *interior designer, educator, writer*

Kirsch, Lynn *lawyer*
Knight, Gladys (Gladys Maria Knight) *singer*
Kobberoe, Birthe *corporate financial executive, accountant*
Komm, Kermit Matthew *software engineer*
Kurlinski, John Parker *physician*
Lally, Norma Ross *retired federal agency administrator*
Landau, Ellis *gaming company executive*
Landreth, Kathryn E. *lawyer*
Lanni, J(oseph) Terrence *hotel corporation executive*
Latimer, Heather *writer*
Laub, William Murray *retired utility executive*
Le Blanc, Suzanne *museum director*
Lee, Theodore Bo *real estate developer*
Leleu, Jonathan Paul *lawyer*
Lewis, Jerry (Joseph Levitch) *comedian*
Lewis, Oli Parepa *curator*
Lima, Donald Roger *retired computer programmer*
Litman, Brian David *communications executive*
Lovell, Carl Erwin, Jr., *lawyer*
Loveman, Gary W. *gaming company executive*
Lovern, Terrance Lee *production manager*
Lukens, John Patrick *lawyer*
MacDonald, Erin E. *healthcare company executive*
Mahan, James Cameron *judge*
Mancl, Dustin Bernard *elementary school educator, language educator*
Manley, Edward Harry, Jr., *food products executive*
Mansfield, Lorraine J. *lawyer*
Marcella, Joseph *information system administrator*
Marcovitz, Leonard Edward *retail executive*
Marlon, Anthony M. *healthcare company executive, cardiologist*
Marmann, Sigrid *software development company executive*
Marnell, Anthony Austin, II, *architect*
Martin, Myron Gregory *foundation administrator*
Martinez, Adriana *political organization worker, photographer*
Massier, Paul Ferdinand *mechanical engineer*
Mataseje, Veronica Julia *sales executive*
Mc Elroy, John Harley *electrical and industrial engineering educator*
McNeal, Betty Jean *librarian, writer*
Merkin, Albert Charles *pediatrician, allergist*
Messenger, George Clement *engineering executive, consultant*
Michel, Mary Ann Kedzuf *nursing educator*
Miller, Robert Joseph *lawyer, former governor*
Miller, Valerie Carol *journalist*
Mizer, Richard Anthony *technology company executive*
Moritz, Timothy Bovie *psychiatrist*
Mortillaro, Louis Francis *psychologist*
Mulvihill, Peter James *fire protection engineer*
Murren, James Joseph *recreational facility executive, hotel executive*
Nasky, H(arold) Gregory *lawyer*
Neilsen, Craig H. *hotel executive*
Neumann, Edward Schreiber *transportation engineering educator*
Nicholson, R. Stephen *organization administrator*
Noback, Richardson Kilbourne *medical educator*
Norman, Jean Reid *journalist*
Opfer, Neil David *construction educator, consultant*
Paine (Williams), Alan (Al) K. *recording industry executive*
Palmer, Lynne *writer, astrologer*
Palmer, William Berry, II, *lawyer*
Patterson, William T. *writer*
Philips, John Chase *retired process engineer*
Pierce, Thresia Korte (Tish Pierce) *primary school educator*
Pollak, Norman Lee *accountant*
Pro, Philip Martin *judge*
Pulliam, Francine Sarno *real estate broker, real estate developer*
Ramos, Albert A. *electrical engineer*
Ramsey, Inez Linn *librarian, educator*
Rawlinson, Johnnie Blakeney *federal judge*
Rawson, Raymond D. *dentist, state legislator*
Reed, Ellen Beth *librarian*
Regazzi, John Henry *retired electronic distributor executive*
Reid, Rory *former political organization administrator*
Roberts, Lia *investor, political organization worker*
Rodgers, Steven Edward *tax practitioner, educator*
Rogers, David Hughes *finance executive*
Root, Alan Charles *diversified manufacturing company executive*
Rowe, Carl Osborn *business consultant*
Satre, Philip Glen *casino entertainment executive, lawyer*
Schaeffer, Glenn William *casino corporate financial executive*
Scherf, Dietmar *publishing executive, artist, minister*
Schneiter, George Malan *golfer, development company executive*
Schreiber, David M. *lawyer, judge*
Segerblom, Sharon B. *social services administrator*
Shires, George Thomas *surgeon, educator*
Shively, Judith Carolyn (Judy Shively) *contract administrator*
Shuman, R. Baird *academic program director, writer, English language educator, educational consultant*
Singer, Kathryn J. *assistant principal*
Sklar, Alan Curtis *lawyer*
Solomon, Jack Avrum, Jr., *lawyer, automotive distributor, art dealer*
Sopko, Andrew S.J. *musician, educator*
Sorrell, Michael E. *consulting company executive, hospitality executive*
Speck, Eugene Lewis *internist*
Springer, Christine Gibbs *management consultant, business owner, educator*
Stanley, Tim *recreational facility executive*
Stark, S. Daniel, Jr., *gaming industry executive*
Steckler, Larry *publisher, editor, writer*
Steffen, Thomas Lee *retired judge, lawyer*
Stoberski, Michael Edward *lawyer*
Sturman, Glorida J. *lawyer*
Swanson, Kurt *metal fabricating company executive*
Tan, Keah-Choon *finance educator*
Tanenhaus, David Spinoza *historian, educator*
Thill, John Val *communications professional, writer, consultant*
Trigiano, Lucien Lewis *physician*
Vandever, Judith Ann *county official*
Wade, Daniel M. *recreational facility executive, hotel executive*

Walker, Randall H. *air transportation executive*
Warren, Susan Carol *legal assistant, clerk, writer*
Wax, Arnold *physician*
Weeks, Gerald *psychology educator*
Weiss, Robert Michael *dermatologist*
Welter, William Michael *marketing and advertising executive*
Wiemer, Robert Ernest *film and television producer, writer, director*
Wiener, Valerie *state senator, writer, positioning strategist, communications executive*
Wieting, Gary Lee *federal agency executive*
Wilmott, Timothy J. *recreational facility executive*
Wilson, Joseph Morris, III, *lawyer*
Wooten, Glen Donovan *media consultant*
Wynn, Stephen A. *hotel, entertainment facility executive*
Zobell, Charles W. *newspaper managing editor*
Zuspan, Frederick Paul *obstetrician, gynecologist, educator*

Logandale
Smiley, Robert William, Jr., *investment banker*

Minden
Bently, Donald Emery *electrical engineer*
Petchenev, Alex *scientist*
Tyndall, Gaye Lynn *secondary school educator*
Yu, John Junyao *mechanical engineer, researcher*

North Las Vegas
Blizard, Susan Kennedy *biology professor*
Folden, Norman C. (Skip Folden) *information systems executive, consultant*
Jones, Terri Ann *hotel management educator*
Kelly, Christopher Pat *dean, educator*
Kennedy-Talley, Brenda S. *performing arts center executive, theatrical light designer*
Marchand, Russell David, II, *retired protective services official*
Miller, Eleanor *English language and literature educator*

Panaca
Soderborg, Martin Todd *elementary school educator*

Reno
Adams, Kenneth Robert *gaming analyst, writer, consultant, historian*
Apassa, Cyril Omo-Osagie *clergyman, educator*
Augustine, Kathy Marie *state controller, state legislator, secondary education educator*
Barnet, Robert Joseph *cardiologist, ethicist*
Binns, James Edward *retired banker*
Bohmont, Dale Wendell *agricultural consultant*
Bramwell, Marvel Lynnette *mental health nurse, social worker*
Brennan, Susan Mallick *utilities executive*
Brunetti, Melvin T. *federal judge*
Busig, Rick Harold *mining executive*
Byrd, Ronald Dallas *civil engineer*
Cargill, Thomas Frank *economist, educator*
Cathey-Gibson, Sharon Sue Rinn *school principal, college administrator*
Chapman, Samuel Greeley *political science educator, criminologist*
Chase, Shelley Lynne *management consultant*
Chrystal, William George *minister*
Coleman, James Scott *environmental research executive*
Crowley, Joseph Neil *university president, political science educator*
Cummings, Nicholas Andrew *psychologist*
Cunning, Tonia *newspaper managing editor*
Dale, Debra Eileen *elementary school educator*
Danko, George *engineering educator*
Dietrich, Dean Forbes *academic administrator*
Feinhandler, Edward Sanford *writer, photographer, art dealer, sports mentor, consultant, educator*
Flanagan, Norman Patrick *lawyer*
Fletcher, Douglas Charles *lawyer*
Forbes, Kenneth Albert Faucher *urological surgeon*
Ford, Victoria *retired public relations executive, writer, oral historian*
Fruzzetti, Alan E. *psychologist, educator*
Fuerstenau, M(aurice) C(lark) *metallurgical engineer*
Gifford, Gerald Frederic *retired science educator*
Gillies, John Angus *education educator*
Goin, Peter Jackson *art educator*
Grady, Sean Michael *writer*
Graham, Denis David *marriage and family therapist, educational consultant*
Griffin, Jeff *federal agency administrator, mayor*
Guild, Clark Joseph, Jr., *lawyer*
Gundersen, Wayne Campbell *management consultant, oil and gas consultant*
Hagen, David Warner *judge*
Harder, Kelsie T. *artist, educator*
Haupt, Randy Larry *electrical engineering educator*
Haynes, Gary Anthony *archaeologist*
Hengstler, Gary Ardell *publisher, editor, lawyer*
Hibbs, Loyal Robert *lawyer*
Higgins, Walter M., III, *electric power industry executive*
Hill, Earl McColl *lawyer*
Holder, Anna Maria *holding company executive*
Huckle, Norman Matthew *school librarian*
Hug, Procter Ralph, Jr., *federal judge*
Humphrey, Neil Darwin *retired academic administrator*
Hunterton, C. Stanley *lawyer*
Jacobson, Raymond Earl *electronics company entrepreneur and executive*
Johnson, David D. *lawyer, game company executive*
Kent, Stephen Smiley *lawyer*
Kleinfeld, Erwin *mathematician, educator*
Kleppe, John Arthur *electrical engineering educator, business executive*
Klinefelter, Gary V. *transportation executive, insurance company executive*
Krenkel, Peter Ashton *engineer, educator*
Lee, H. Helen *music educator*
Leland, Joy Hanson *retired anthropologist, alcohol research specialist*
Lemire, David Stephen *school psychologist, educator*
Lilley, John Mark *academic administrator*
MacKintosh, Frederick Roy *oncologist*
Marshall, Robert William *lawyer, rancher*
Mathews, Bernice Martin *state legislator, small business owner*
Matthews, Thomas J. *game company executive*
McFarlane, Stephen C. *dean, researcher*
McKibben, Howard D. *federal judge*
Middlebrooks, Deloris Jeanette *nurse, educator*
Miller, Newton Edd, Jr., *communications educator*
Mullarkey, Maureen T. *game company executive*
Munro, Roderick Anthony *business improvement coach*
Neidert, Kalo Edward *accountant, educator*
Newberg, Dorothy Beck (Mrs. William C. Newberg) *portrait artist*
Pagni, Albert Frank *lawyer*
Perry, Anthony Frank *entertainment company executive, printing company executive, graphic designer*
Perry, Jean Louise *dean*
Pinson, Larry Lee *pharmacist*
Price, Jonathan G. *geologist*
Ragavan, Anpalaki Jeyabalasinkham *software developer, researcher*
Raggio, William John *state legislator*
Raja, Krishnan Selva *materials engineer*
Redmond, Kelly Thomas *climatologist*
Reed, Edward Cornelius, Jr., *federal judge*
Robison, Kent Richard *lawyer*
Ross, Robert Donald *library director*
Savoy, Douglas Eugene *bishop, religious studies educator, explorer, writer*
Scrimgeour, Gary James *writer, educator*
Shoen, Edward Joseph *transportation and insurance companies executive*
Sklar, Louise Margaret *computer company executive*
Sladek, Ronald John *physics educator*
Small, Elisabeth Chan *psychiatrist, educator*
Smith, Aaron *retired research director, clinical psychologist*
Straling, Phillip Francis *bishop*
Stumpf, Felix Franklin *law educator*
Svahn, John Alfred *government official*
Taranik, James Vladimir *geologist, educator*
Walrath, Harry Rienzi *retired minister*
Walther, Steven T. *lawyer*
Waltz, Marcus Ernest *retired prosthodontist*
Weber, Michael Mathew *small business owner*
Webster, Michael Anderson *experimental psychologist*
Weld, Roger Bowen *retired religious organization administrator*
Weniger-Phelps, Nancy Ann *media specialist, photographer*
White, Robert C. *air transportation executive*
Zadra, Sharon Kay *business development professional*
Zager, Bernard Solomon *physician, consultant*

Smith
Weaver, William Merritt, Jr., *investment banker*

Sparks
Bonham, Harold Florian *research geologist, consultant*
Boyer, Patricia W. *publishing executive, editor*
Holder, Harold Douglas, Sr., *investor, hotel executive*
Kramer, Gordon Edward *manufacturing executive*
Lagasse, Bruce Kenneth *retired structural engineer*
McKenzie, Wesley Melvin, Jr., *music educator, composer*
Pryor, Eric Jon *minister, writer*
Tran, Can Ngoc *educator, researcher*

Sun Valley
Mumm, Christopher Eric *lawyer, county government official*

Winnemucca
Hesse, Martha O. *gas industry executive*

Yerington
Burrowes, Robert Arthur *transportation consultant, travel-tour operator*
Scatena, Lorraine Borba *retired rancher, women's rights advocate*

Zephyr Cove
Camille, Pamela *writer, educator*
Hudzinski, Leonard Gerard *social sciences educator, researcher*
Peters, Raymond Robert *bank executive*

NEW HAMPSHIRE

Alstead
Holloway, Robert Charles *orchestrator, arranger, composer*

Alton Bay
Scott, Susan Shattuck *retired secondary school educator*

Amherst
Atwater, Verne Stafford *finance educator*
Buff, Margaret Anne *psychiatric nurse practitioner*

Barrington
DeChane, Marlene M. *state legislator*

Bartlett
Chandler, Gene G. *state legislator*

Bath
Page, Patti (Clara Ann Fowler) *vocalist*

Bedford
Collins, Diana Josephine *psychologist*
Demers, Nancy Kae *nursing educator*
Hall, Pamela S. *environmental consulting firm executive*
Steadman, David Rosslyn Ayton *business executive, corporate director*
Twarjan, Colleen Ann *dental hygienist*

Bennington
Verney, Richard Greville *paper company executive*

Berlin
Doherty, Katherine Mann *librarian, writer*
May, William Francis *ethicist, educator*

Boscawen
Clarke, Claire Diggs *academic counselor*

Bow
Emery, Paul Emile *psychiatrist*
Sytek, Donna P. *former state legislator*

Brentwood
Bunker, Dusty *writer*

Bristol
Peirce, Neal R. *journalist*

Campton
Scrimshaw, Nevin Stewart *physician, nutrition and health educator*

Canaan
Taussig, Margaret C. *artist*

Center Harbor
Patten, Betsey Leland *state legislator*
Shaw, Robert William, Jr., *management consultant, venture capitalist*
Smith, William Hulse *forestry and environmental studies educator*

Center Sandwich
Booty, John Everitt *emeritus educator*
Kilbourn, William Douglas, Jr., *law educator*

Concord
Arnold, Thomas Ivan, Jr., *state legislator*
Ayotte, Kelly A. *state attorney general*
Bagan, Merwyn *neurological surgeon*
Barbadoro, Paul James *federal judge*
Benson, Craig Robert *governor*
Boisseau, Paul G. *pharmacist, executive secretary*
Brock, David Allen *state supreme court chief justice*
Broderick, John T., Jr., *state supreme court chief justice*
Brown, Tom Christian *newspaper publisher*
Chamberlain, Douglas Reginald *lawyer*
Chapman, William Lansing *lawyer*
Clark, Martha Fuller *state legislator, architectural historian, preservation consultant*
Clemons, Jane Andrea *state legislator*
Colantuono, Thomas Paul *state legislator*
Cote, David Edward *state legislator*
Cote, Patricia L. *state legislator*
Crosby, Toni M. *state legislator*
Crosier, John David *trade association administrator*
Dalianis, Linda Stewart *judge*
Day, Russell Clover *state agency administrator*
DiClerico, Joseph Anthony, Jr., *federal judge*
Drabinowicz, A. Theresa *state legislator*
Duggan, James E., Jr., *state supreme court justice*
Dunlap, Patricia C. *state legislator*
Eaton, Thomas R. *state legislator*
Ferland, Brenda L. *state representative*
Flanagan, Natalie Smith *state representative*
Flora, Kathleen M. *state representative*
Folch-Pi, Willa Babcock *romance language educator*
Foster, Linda Timberlake *state legislator*
Francoeur, Sheila T. *state representative*
Fraser, Marilyn Anne *state legislator*
Gardner, William Michael *state official*
Ginsburg, Ruth *state representative*
Griffin, Mary E. *state representative*
Hager, Elizabeth Sears *state legislator, social services organization administrator*
Hall, Betty B. *state legislator, manufacturing executive*
Hartman, Sally P. *toxicologist*
Hildreth, Peter C. *state agency administrator*
Hill, Donald S. *commissioner, state*
Hilliard, Russell F. *lawyer*
Hodes, Paul William *lawyer, recording industry executive*
Howard, Jeffrey R. *federal judge*
Hutchinson, Rebecca *state representative*
Kaen, Naida *state representative*
Kane, Cecelia Drapeau *state legislator, registered nurse*
Katsakiores, Phyllis May *small business owner, city councilor*
Keans, Sandra B. *state legislator*
Larsen, Sylvia B. *state legislator*
Laughlin, Larry *communications media executive*
Lohmann, Keith Henry *police department official, consultant*
Lozeau, Donnalee M. *state legislator*
Lynch, Margaret A. *state legislator*
Lynott, Margaret *state legislator*
MacKay, James Robert *psychiatric social worker, mayor, educator, state legislator*
Martin, Mary Ellen *state legislator, human development specialist*
McAuliffe, Steven James *federal judge*
McCarley, Caroline *state legislator*
McLaughlin, Philip T. *lawyer, former state attorney general*
McRae, Karen K. *state legislator*
Merritt, Deborah Foote *state legislator, vocational coordinator*
Messier, Irene M. *state legislator*
Mevers, Frank Clement *state archivist, historian*
Millerick, Jayne Marcucci *Republican party chairman*
Moore, Carol *state legislator*
Muirhead, James Russell *federal judge*
Nadeau, Joseph P. *state supreme court justice*
Nichols, Avis B. *state legislator*
Nordgren, Sharon L. *state legislator*
Norelli, Terie Thompson *state legislator*
Nowe, Ronald John *state legislator, small business owner*
O'Hearn, Jane E. *state legislator*
O'Keefe, Patricia M. *state legislator*
Packard, Bonnie Bennett *former state legislator*
Pilliod, James P. *state legislator, physician*
Potter, Fred Leon *lawyer, insurance company executive, consultant*
Pratt, Irene Agnes *state legislator*
Rath, Thomas David *lawyer, former state attorney general*
Reardon, Tara G. *state legislator*
Richardson, Barbara Hull *state legislator, social worker*
Rines, Robert Harvey *lawyer, educator, composer*
Roberge, M. Sheila *state legislator*
Roberts, George Bernard, Jr., *management and government relations consultant, former state legislator*
Robinson, V. Gene (The Right Reverend V. Gene Robinson) *bishop*
Rogers, Katherine Diane *political consultant, commissioner*
Seldin, Gloria *state legislator*
Slusser, Eugene Alvin *electronics manufacturing executive*
Smith, Marjorie K. *state legislator*
Snyder, Clair A. *state legislator*
Stickney, Nancy Carver *state legislator*
Taylor, Stephen H. *state commissioner*
Thomas, Georgie A. *state official*
Twomey, Elizabeth Ann Molloy *education educator*
Unger, Gere Nathan *emergency physician, lawyer*
Wall, Janet G. *state legislator*
Wallin, Jean R. *state legislator*
Wallner, Mary Jane *state legislator, director child care organization*
Weatherspoon, Jackie K. *state legislator*
White, Jeffrey George *healthcare consultant*
Wiggins, Celestine K. *state legislator*
Williams, Carol Ann *state legislator*
Winterling, Ann *artist*

Conway
Blodgett, Julian Robert *small business owner*

Cornish
Atkinson, James Blakely *writer, editor*

Deering
Spitzer, Morton Edward *management consultant*

Derry
Holmes, Richard Dale *history consultant*
Katsakiores, George Nicholas *state legislator, retired restaurateur*
Sapareto, Frank Vincent, II, *investment advisor, state legislator*

Dover
Catalfo, Alfred, Jr., (Alfio Catalfo) *lawyer*
Mitchell, William Clark *printmaker, graphic artist*
Nelson, Michael Underhill *association executive*
Parks, Joe Benjamin *entrepreneur, former state legislator*
Pelletier, Arthur Joseph *state legislator, data processing executive, educator*
Pelletier, Marsha Lynn *secondary school educator, poet*

Dublin
Carlton, Michael *magazine editor*
Hale, Judson Drake, Sr., *publishing executive, editor, writer*

Durham
Berona, David A. *computer systems librarian, educator*
Boy, Angelo V. *psychologist, educator*
DeMitchell, Todd Allan *education educator*
Estabrook, Iris W. *state representative*
Farrell, William Joseph *university chancellor*
Ford, Daniel (Daniel Francis Ford) *writer*
Gold, Janet Nowakowski *Spanish language educator*
Golinski, Jan Victor *history of science educator*
Greenberg, Arthur *dean, chemistry professor*
Gumprecht, Blake *geographer, educator*
Hapgood, Robert Derry *English educator*
Hart, Ann Weaver *academic administrator*
Kempster, William Geoffrey *conductor, music educator*
Kendall-Tackett, Kathleen Ann *researcher, health psychologist*
Mallory, Bruce *academic administrator*
Miller, Joseph Morton *internist*
Palmer, Stuart Hunter *sociology educator*
Pistole, Thomas Gordon *microbiology educator, researcher*
Scharff, Robert Caesar *social sciences educator, writer, humanities educator*
Simic, Charles *English language educator, poet*
Stubbs, Jeffrey Matthew *research scientist*
Wheeler, Douglas Lanphier *history educator, writer*
Wheeler, Katherine Wells *retired state legislator*
Woodward, Robert Simpson, IV, *economics professor*

East Sullivan
Hoffman, John Ernest, Jr., *retired lawyer*

Etna
Ferm, Vergil Harkness *anatomist, embryologist*
Rous, Stephen Norman *urologist, educator*

Exeter
Beeson, Paul Bruce *physician*
Cole, Donald Barnard *education educator*
Richardson, Artemas P(artridge) *retired landscape architect*
Thomas, Jacquelyn May *librarian*

Farmington
Meyers, James B. *secondary school educator*
Panek, William Dominick *systems engineer executive*

Fitzwilliam
Schott, John Robert *international consultant, educator*
Welcher, Rosalind *artist, author*

Francestown
Foster, Margery Somers *economics professor*

Franconia
Schaffer, David Edwin *retired management systems executive*

Freedom
Kucera, Henry *linguistics educator*

Gilmanton
Osler, Howard Lloyd *retired controller*

Glen
Zager, Ronald I. *chemist, consultant*

Goffstown
Gillmore, Robert *landscape designer, author, editor, publisher*

Oktavec, Eileen M. *anthropologist, artist*
Wajenberg, Arnold Sherman *retired librarian, educator*

Gorham
Guay, Lawrence J. *state legislator, business owner*

Grantham
Feldman, Roger Bruce *government official*
Figley, Melvin Morgan *radiologist, physician, educator*
Grimley, Robert Thomas *chemistry professor*

Hampstead
Moore, Raymond Edward *retired physician*

Hampton
Clark, Kevin P. *medical products executive*
Della Penta, David T. *medical products executive*
DuChene, Todd Michael *lawyer*
Meister, Paul M. *medical products executive*
Montrone, Paul Michael *scientific instruments company executive*
Morton, Donald John *librarian*
Russell, Richard R. *industrial executive*

Hancock
Baddour, Anne Bridge *pilot*
Pollaro, Paul Philip *artist*

Hanover
Anthony, Robert Newton *management educator emeritus*
Baldwin, John Charles *surgeon, researcher*
Baldwin, William Lee *retired economics professor*
Baumgartner, James Earl *mathematics educator*
Bien, Peter Adolph *English language educator, author*
Boghosian, Varujan Yegan *sculptor, educator*
Bower, Richard Stuart *economist, educator*
Brooks, H. Allen *architectural educator, author, lecturer*
Burgess, Robert Sargent *retired human services consultant*
Chapman, Robert James *psychiatrist, educator*
Cook, William Wilbert *English language educator*
Copenhaver, Marion Lamson *former state legislator*
Crory, Elizabeth L. *former state legislator*
Curphey, Thomas John *chemist, researcher*
Daniell, Jere Rogers, II, *retired history educator, consultant, public lecturer*
Danos, Paul *dean, accounting educator*
Demko, George Joseph *geographer*
Dietrich, Allen J. *medical educator*
Dmitrovsky, Ethan *oncologist, medical educator, researcher*
Doney, Willis Frederick *philosophy educator*
Dong, Kui *music educator, composer*
Ehrlich, David Gordon *film director, educator*
Endicott, Kirk Michael *anthropologist, educator*
Fiering, Steven *medical educator*
Fischel, William Alan *economics professor*
Freedman, James Oliver *former university president, lawyer*
Gardner, Peter Jaglom *lawyer, publishing executive*
Garmire, Elsa Meints *electrical engineering educator, consultant*
Garthwaite, Gene Ralph *historian, educator*
Gert, Bernard *philosopher, educator*
Gilbert, John Jouett *aquatic ecologist, educator*
Graves, Robert John *industrial engineering educator*
Green, Ronald Michael *ethics and religious studies educator*
Hall, Raymond *sociology educator*
Haselton, Mary Michelson *retired foreign service officer, artist*
Hemphill, Margaret Ayars *priest, artist*
Hennessey, John William, Jr., *academic administrator, educator*
Higgins, Lynn Anthony *humanities educator, writer*
Hutchinson, Charles Edgar *engineering educator*
Kantrowitz, Arthur *physicist, researcher, educator*
Kemp, Karl Thomas *insurance company executive*
Kennedy, Francis Edward *engineering educator*
Kleck, Robert Eldon *psychology educator*
Koop, Charles Everett *surgeon, educator, former surgeon general*
Kremer, Richard Lynn *historian, educator*
Kurtz, Thomas Eugene *mathematics professor*
Likosky, Donald *epidemiologist, consultant*
Long, Carl Ferdinand *retired engineering educator*
Lundquist, Weyman Ivan *lawyer*
Lyons, Gene Martin *political scientist, educator*
Mansell, Darrel Lee, Jr., *English educator*
Masters, Roger Davis *government and neurotoxicology educator*
Montgomery, David Campbell *physicist, researcher*
Moss, Ben Frank, III, *art educator, painter*
Otto, Margaret Amelia *librarian*
Oxenhandler, Neal *language educator, writer*
Petitto, Laura-Ann *cognitive neuroscience educator*
Platt, James David *academic administrator, educator*
Prager, Susan Westerberg *law educator, provost*
Queneau, Paul Etienne *metallurgical engineer, educator*
Rawnsley, Howard Melody *pathologist, educator*
Riggs, Lorrin Andrews *psychologist, educator*
Rolett, Ellis Lawrence *medical educator, cardiologist*
Rueckert, Frederic *retired plastic, reconstructive and hand surgeon*
Russell, Robert Hilton *Romance languages and literature educator*
Rutter, Jeremy Bentham *archaeologist, educator*
Scher, Steven Paul *literature educator*
Scherr, Barry Paul *foreign language educator*
Sheldon, Richard Robert *Russian language and literature educator*
Shewmaker, Kenneth Earl *history professor*
Spiegel, Evelyn Sclufer *biology professor*
Spiegel, Melvin *retired biology educator*
Spielberg, Stephen Paul *dean, educator*
Sporn, Michael Benjamin *cancer researcher*
Starzinger, Vincent Evans *political scientist, educator*
Stockmayer, Walter H(ugo) *chemistry professor*
Wegner, Gary Alan *astronomer*
Welsch, Robert Louis *anthropologist, curator*
Wennberg, John E. *epidemiologist*
Wood, Charles Tuttle *history educator*
Wright, James Edward *academic administrator, historian, educator*
Zubkoff, Michael *medical educator*

Henniker
Braiterman, Thea Gilda *economics educator, state legislator, selectman*
French, Barbara C. *state representative*

Hillsboro
Pearson, William Rowland *retired nuclear engineer*

Hinsdale
Smith, Edwin O. *real estate executive, state legislator*

Hollis
Durham, Susan B. *state legislator*
Lumbard, Eliot Howland *lawyer, educator*
Nolin, John Charles *product specialist, engineering consultant*

Hooksett
Clamp, Christina A. *sociology educator*
Denaco, Parker Alden *state official, lawyer, arbitrator*

Hopkinton
Mekeel, Robert K. *lawyer*

Hudson
Dumond, Robert Wilfred *clinical mental health consultant, lay pastoral worker*

Jaffrey
Foster, Walter Herbert, III, *mechanical and manufacturing engineer, executive*
Press, Fred *artist*
Van Ness, Patricia Wood *religious studies educator, consultant, author*
Walling, Cheves Thomson *chemistry professor*

Keene
Alvarez, Kristin Jones *geographer, educator*
Baldwin, Peter Arthur *psychologist, educator, author, minister*
Bell, Ernest Lorne, III, *retired lawyer*
Crocker, Matthew Hallowell *historian, educator, writer, researcher*
Hackett, John Thomas *retired economist*
Lichtenstein, Sally (Ali) Tucker *small business owner, writer, educator*
Perkins, Richard P. *pilot*
Robertson, Timothy N. *state legislator, retired real estate agent*

Kingston
Saunders, Janet McGee *small business owner, healthcare administrator*

Laconia
Brody, Spencer John *pediatrician*
Martin, Willard Gordon, Jr., *lawyer*
Mitchell, Walter Louis, III, *lawyer*

Lancaster
Horton, Lynn C. *state legislator*
Pratt, Leighton Calvin *state legislator*

Lebanon
Baker, William Arnold *lawyer*
Bernat, James Lawrence *neurologist, educator*
Clendenning, William Edmund *dermatologist*
Cohen, Jeffrey Allen *neurologist, educator*
Cronenwett, Jack LeMoyne *vascular surgeon educator*
Emery, Virginia Olga Beattie *psychologist, researcher*
Fanger, Michael W. *medical educator*
Fillinger, Mark F. *vascular surgeon, researcher*
Fromm, Hans *gastroenterologist, educator, researcher, hepatologist*
Glass, Donald David *anesthesiologist*
Gosselin, Benoit Jean *otolaryngologist, facial plastic surgeon, head and neck and reconstructive surgeon*
Greenberg, E. Robert *medical research administrator*
Guest, Robert Henry *former state legislator, management educator*
Kelley, Maurice Leslie, Jr., *gastroenterologist, educator*
Linnell, Robert Hartley *editor-in-chief*
McCollum, Robert Wayne *physician, educator*
Moeschler, John Boyer *physician, educator*
Munck, Allan Ulf *physiologist, educator*
Ou, Lo-Chang *physiology educator*
Schoolwerth, Anton C. *nephrologist, educator*
Silberfarb, Peter Michael *psychiatrist, educator*
Thompson, Pamela A. *nurse administrator*
Trunzo, Thomas Harold, Jr., *lawyer*
Varnum, James William *hospital administrator*
von Reyn, C. Fordham *infectious disease physician*
Waugh, Theodore Rogers *orthopedic surgeon*

Lee
Blidberg, D. Richard *marine engineer*
Young, James Morningstar *internist, military officer*

Lempster
Jillette, Arthur George, Jr., *school system administrator, educator*

Lincoln
Seletz, Jules Mortimer *surgeon*

Lisbon
Trelfa, Richard Thomas *paper company executive*

Litchfield
Darlington, David William *management consultant*

Littleton
Eaton, Stephanie *state legislator*
Merritt, Thomas Butler *lawyer*

Londonderry
Dunham, Vivian L. *state legislator*
McKinney, Betsy *state legislator*
Osen, Gregory Alan *water conditioning company executive*

Loudon
Moore, Beatrice *religious organization administrator*

Lyme
Carmichael, Donald Scott *lawyer, business executive*
Cornwell, Gibbons Gray, III, *retired internist, educator*
Dwight, Donald Rathbun *newspaper publisher, corporate communications executive*
McIntyre, Oswald Ross *physician*
Swan, Henry *forester, consultant*

Manchester
Angoff, Gerald Harvey *cardiologist*
Arnold, Barbara Eileen *state legislator*
Bolduc, Diane Eileen Mary Buchholz *psychotherapist*
Bramante, Fredrick J., Jr., *retail executive*
Buckley, Raymond Carl, II, *state legislator, business consultant*
Bussiere, Emile R. *lawyer*
Christian, Francis Joseph *bishop*
Colby, George Vincent, III, *logistics executive*
Cusson-Cail, Kathleen *consulting company executive*
DesRochers, Gerard Camille *surgeon*
Desrosiers, Aprylle Lynn *director, consultant*
Groulx, Aimé René *artist, photographer*
Harvell, Michael Cleland *lawyer*
Holden, Carol H. *county official*
Hower, Philip Leland *semiconductor device engineer*
Hutchins, Peter Edward *lawyer*
Kamen, Dean *biomedical engineer*
Krueger, Patricia *state representative*
Maloney, Simone *accountant*
McCormack, John Brendan *bishop*
Merideth, Susan Carol *business administration educator*
Middleton, Jack Baer *lawyer*
Monson, John Rudolph *lawyer*
Nixon, David L. *lawyer*
Paradis, Wilfrid H. *retired historian*
Perkins, Charles, III, *newspaper editor*
Poloian, Lynda Gamans *retailing educator*
Richards, Thomas H. *lawyer, arbitrator*
Ronalter, Chelsea Maria *artist, graphic designer*
Stebbins, Henry Blanchard *lawyer*
Stimpson, Patricia *software company executive*
Sullivan, Kathleen N. *political organization administrator, lawyer*
Zachos, Kimon Stephen *lawyer*

Mason
Jones, Elizabeth Orton *artist, author*

Melvin Village
Allison, Dwight Leonard, Jr., *investor*

Meredith
Hatch, Frederick Tasker *chemicals consultant*
Heald, Bruce Day *English and music educator, historian*
Lovett, Miller Currier *management educator, clergyman*

Merrimack
Gallup, Patricia *computer company executive*
Kotelly, George Vincent *editor, writer, electrical engineer*
Milligan, Robert H. *state legislator, air traffic controller*

Milford
Dokmo, Cynthia J. *state legislator*
Morison, John Hopkins *casting manufacturing company executive*
Nolan-Piteri, Dawn C. *state legislator*

Mount Sunapee
Marashio, Paul William *humanities educator*

Munsonville
Lyon, Ronald Edward *management consultant, computer consultant*

Nashua
An, Ning *computer scientist, researcher*
Descoteaux, Carol J. *health facility administrator*
Egan, John Frederick *retired electronics executive*
Flynn, William Berchman, Jr., *psychology educator, clinical psychologist*
Franks, Suzan L. R. *state legislator*
Garbacz, Gerald George *information services company executive*
Gregg, Hugh *former cabinet manufacturing company executive, former governor New Hampshire*
Hanson, Arnold Philip *retired lawyer*
Hargreaves, David William *communications company executive*
Hemming, Walter William *business financial consultant*
Jette, Ernest Arthur *lawyer*
Johnson, Arthur V., II, *secondary school educator*
Knights, Edwin Munroe *pathologist*
Mitsakos, Charles Leonidas *education educator, consultant*
Phelps, Bonnie Noreen *language educator, secondary school educator*
Pignatelli, Debora Becker *state legislator*
Piper, Linda Ammann *staffing services executive*
Seidel, Carl William *business executive, consultant*
Seifer, Arnold David *systems engineer*
Siroty, William Charles *physician*
Smith, Thomas Raymond, III, *software engineer*
Woodruff, Thomas Ellis *electronics consulting executive*

New Castle
Baker, Robert I. *manufacturing executive*
Friese, George Ralph *retail executive*
Levin, Harvey Jay *financial institution design and construction specialist, developer, auctioneer*
Rauh, John David *manufacturing executive*

New Durham
Herman, William George *municipal government executive*
Uttal, Susan *legal administrator*

New Hampton
Taylor, Kenneth Richard *information technology executive, consultant*

New London
Baldwin, William Howard *lawyer, retired foundation executive*
Condict, Edgar Rhodes *medical electronics, aviation instrument manufacturing and medical health care executive, inventor, mediator, pastor*
Crane, Robert Kendall *engineering educator, researcher, consultant*
Gepfert, Alan Harry *management consultant, business educator, author*
Merwin, John David *retired lawyer, former governor*
Sheerr, Deirdre McCrystal *architectural firm executive*
Thoma, Kurt Michael *business owner*
Twombly, Jean Sawyer *musician, educator*
Vulgamore, Melvin L. *retired college president*
Zuehlke, Richard William *technical communications consultant, writer*

Newmarket
Ellis, David Wertz *retired museum director*

Newport
Gayvoronsky, Ludmila *artist, educator*
Stamatakis, Carol Marie *lawyer, former state legislator*

North Hampton
Osenton, Thomas George *publisher*
Taylor, Donald *retired manufacturing company executive*
White, Ralph Paul *automotive executive, consultant*

North Salem
Stone, Robert Eldred *small business owner, museum director*

North Woodstock
Ham, Bonnie Davis *state legislator*

Northwood
Lynne-O'Brien, Vincent *stage manager, director, actor*

Nottingham
Case, Margaret A. *state legislator*

Orford
Karol, John J., Jr., *producer, filmmaker*
Martin, Allen *retired lawyer*

Peterborough
Day, John Sidney *management sciences educator*
Eppes, William David *arts/humanities supporter*
Farnham, Sherman Brett *retired electrical engineer*
Thomas, Elizabeth Marshall *writer*

Pike
Teschner, Douglass Paul *project administrator*

Plainfield
Brown, Judith Olans *lawyer, educator*

Plaistow
Goddu, Kevin Albert *secondary school educator*
Wilder, Dwight Safford *academic administrator*

Plymouth
Bourgelais, Paul *music educator*
Gorin, Stephen H. *social worker, educator*
Graff, Carleen *music educator*
Rolph, Matthew G. J. *literature and language professor, consultant*
Sawyer, Leonard Sylvester *retired lawyer*

Portsmouth
Abelson, Elias *lawyer*
Akridge, William David *hotel management company executive*
Baumann, Hans D. *engineering executive*
Breen, Edward D. *manufacturing executive*
Cole-McCrea, Candace *social sciences educator*
Doleac, Charles Bartholomew *lawyer*
Greene, Douglas Edward *hotel executive*
Harter, Hugh Anthony *foreign language educator*
Hopkins, Jeannette Ethel *book publisher, editor*
Kozlowski, L. Dennis (Dennis Kozlowski) *manufacturing executive*
Lytton, William Bryan *lawyer*
Mason, J. William L. *lawyer*
Michelsen, W(olfgang) Jost *neurosurgeon, educator, retired*
Nylander, Jane Louise *museum director, lecturer, writer*
Pantelakos, Laura C. *state legislator*
Powers, Henry Martin, Jr., *oil industry executive*
Sinaisky, Nicholas Alekseevich *mechanical engineer, researcher, consultant*
Tober, Stephen Lloyd *lawyer*
Volk, Kenneth Hohne *lawyer*
Waterhouse, Trenton Dean *marketing director*
Watson, Thomas Roger *lawyer*

Randolph
Bradley, Paula E. *former state legislator*
Bradley, William Lee *retired foundation executive, educator*

Rindge
Dangelantonio, Sarah Teresa *academic administrator, educator*
Lupinin, Nickolas *history educator, editor, publisher*

Rochester
Brown, George F. *state legislator, retired sales executive*
Brown, Julie M. *state legislator*
Coviello, Robert Frank *retail executive*
Dworkin, Gary Steven *insurance company executive*
Grassie, Anne C. *state legislator*
Jones, Franklin Charles *judge*
Kramer, Sherri Marcelle *gemologist, jeweler*
Patel, Piyush Hirjibhai *communications executive*
Rogers, Rose Marie *state legislator*
Shean, Timothy Joseph *manufacturing executive*

Rye
MacRury, King *management counselor*

Rye Beach
Langley, Jane S. *state legislator*

Salem
Bitter, Frank Gordon *manufacturing executive*
Jones, Michael Earl *lawyer*
Simmons, Marvin Gene *geophysics educator*
Spero, Nora Mancini *realtor, writer*

Sanbornton
Weiant, Elizabeth Abbott *retired biology educator*

Sanbornville
Berg, Warren Stanley *retired bank executive*

Sandown
Densen, Paul Maximillian *former health administrator, educator*

Silver Lake
Pallone, Adrian Joseph *research scientist*
Tregenza, Norman Hughson *investment banker*

Somersworth
Gow, Linda Yvonne Carignan Cherwin *travel executive*
Tully, Hugh Michael *music educator*

Stratham
Green, Catherine Cooper *artist*
Terry, Elizabeth Hays *needlepoint designer*

Sunapee
Springer, John Kelley *hospital administrator*

Tamworth
Colten, Harvey Radin *pediatrician, educator*

Walpole
Burns, Kenneth Lauren *filmmaker, historian*
Fargnoli, Patricia B. *poet, educator*
Gooding, Judson *writer*
Hunter, Barbara Way *public relations consultant*

Waterville Valley
Grimes, Howard Ray *management consultant*

Weare
White, Karen Ruth Jones *information systems executive*

West Chesterfield
Garinger, Louis Daniel *religion educator*

West Lebanon
Day, Emerson *physician*
Halperin, George Bennett *education educator, retired naval officer*
Isaacs, Robert Charles *retired lawyer*
Lawton, Jacqueline Agnes *retired communications company executive, management consultant*

Wilton
Ritchie-Dunham, James Loomis *academic administrator, researcher*

Winchester
MacKay, Neil Duncan *plastics company executive*

Windham
Arndt, Janet S. *former state legislator, educator*
Delahunty, Joseph Lawrence *state senator, business investor*
George, Kimberly Ann *lawyer*
Levin, Murray Newman *retired surgeon*
Nease, Stephen Wesley *college president*

Wolfeboro
Hutchins, Carleen Maley *acoustical engineer, consultant*

NEW JERSEY

Adelphia
Carter, Harry Robert *fire protection consultant*

Allendale
Bisanzo, Mark Thomas *sales executive*
DiBlasi, Dianne Clark *editor*
Morris, Edward William, Jr., *lawyer*
Petersen, Martin Ross *public affairs executive*
Ruth, Rodney *musician, music consultant, contractor, educator*

Allenhurst
Hinson, Robert William *advertising executive, consultant*
Tognoli, Era M. *performing company executive, artistic director*

Allentown
Huang, Wenlin *scientist, researcher*
Sulyok, Paul David *music educator, composer*

Annandale
Gorbaty, Martin Leo *chemist, researcher*

Asbury Park
Avella, John Thomas *educational administrator*
Rosenbloom, Norma Frisch *lawyer*
Sandberg-Morgan, Barbara *retired communication and women's studies educator*

Atco
Beard, Richard Burnham *engineering educator emeritus, researcher*

Atlantic City
Jacobson, Carole Renee *lawyer, educator*
Jamieson, John Edward, Jr., *social services administrator, minister*
Knight, Edward R. *judge, lawyer, educator, psychologist*
McMaster, Art *beauty pageant organization executive*
Mora, Kathleen Rita *state judicial administrator*
Oswell, Audrey S. *casino executive*
Zlotnick, Norman Lee *lawyer*

Atlantic Highlands
Hawley, Joseph B. *property management executive, educator*
Royce, Paul Chadwick *medical administrator*
Tice, George A(ndrew) *photographer*

Augusta
Martin, Richard L. *retired insurance executive*

Avenel
Berg, Louis Leslie *investment executive*
Sansone, Paul J. *automotive executive*
Segal, Barry *company executive*

Avon By The Sea
Bruno, Grace Angelia *accountant, retired educator*
Potter, Emma Josephine Hill *language educator*

Barnegat
Bronkowski, Mark John *textiles executive, real estate agent*

Barnegat Light
Gibbs, Frederick Winfield *lawyer, communications company executive*

Basking Ridge
Besch, Lorraine W. *special education educator*
Buist, Richardson *retired corporate executive, retired banker*
Collis, Sidney Robert *retired telephone company executive*
Conklin, Donald Ransford *retired pharmaceutical company executive*
Drewry, Don Neal *fire protection engineer*
Fotiades, George L. *pharmaceutical executive*
Matthews, Craig Gerard *energy company executive*
McGuire, Garry K., Sr., *communications executive*
McNamee, James M. *lab administrator*
Morgan, Samuel P(ope) *physicist, applied mathematician*
Munch, Douglas Francis *pharmaceutical and health industry consultant*
Peterson, Donald K. *telecommunications executive*
Probert, Edward Whitford *foundation executive, volunteer*
Riesenberger, John Richard *science administrator*
Samuelson, Cynthia *information technology executive*
Tamarelli, Alan Wayne *venture captial executive*
Whelan, Mary Kathleen *marketing professional, consultant*

Bay Head
O'Brien, Robert Brownell, Jr., *investment banker, consultant, yacht broker, opera company executive*

Bayonne
Doria, Joseph V., Jr., *state legislator*
Gorman, William David *artist, graphic artist*
Lo Re, Vincent, Jr., *retired academic administrator, municipal official*
McMahon, Eileen Marie *artist agent*
Olsen, Mary Ann *lawyer*
Pelosi, Marco Antonio *obstetrician and gynecologist*
Zuckerman, Nancy Carol *learning disabilities specialist, consultant*

Beach Haven
Houlihan, Gail Lanier *child advocate, educator*

Bedminster
David, Edward Emil, Jr., *electrical engineer, business executive*
Delehanty, Martha *human services administrator*
Dorman, David W. *telecommunications industry executive*
Eslambolchi, Hossein *communications executive*
Hannigan, William J. *telecommunications industry executive*
Hart, Terry Jonathan *communications executive*
Horton, Thomas W. *telecommunications executive*
Hudacsko, Dennis Wayne *urban planner*
Kean, John *utility company executive*
Polumbo, John *communications executive*
Strigl, Dennis F. *telecommunications industry executive*
Weaver, Constance *communications executive*
Zeglis, John D. *communications executive, lawyer*

Belle Mead
Brown, Elizabeth Schmeck *fashion historian*
Gladstone, Robert Albert *lawyer*
Goodnick, Paul Joel *psychiatrist*
Moevs, Maria Teresa Marabini *archaeologist*
Sarle, Charles Richard *health facility executive*

Belleville
Berenfeld, Mark M. *chemist*

Bellmawr
Wilke, Constance Regina *elementary school educator*

Belmar
De Santo, Donald James *psychologist, educational administrator*
Landeck, Carl *cable company executive*
Paetzold, Mary E. *agricultural products supplier*
Rasmussen, Mark William *restaurant owner and chef*
Swett, Stephen Frederick, Jr., *artist, educator*

Belvidere
Walsh, John Alfred *retired social worker*

Bergenfield
Clark, Fred *legal writer, editor*

Berkeley Heights
Connell, Grover *food company executive*
Geusic, Joseph Edward Edward *physicist*
Mac Rae, Alfred Urquhart *physicist, electrical engineer*
Rabiner, Lawrence Richard *electrical engineer, educator*
Rabinovich, Eliezer M. *retired ceramics engineer*
Shaffer, Gail Dorothy *secondary school educator*
Webster, John Kimball *investment executive*

Bernardsville
Cooperman, Saul *educational administrator*
Dixon, Richard Wayne *retired communications company executive*
Dixon, Rosina Berry *physician, pharmaceutical development consultant*
Robinson, Maureen Loretta *retired elementary school educator*
Salinger, Anthony Wilshire *educator, organization consultant*
Spofford, Sally (Sally Hyslop) *artist*

Beverly
Taylor, Lyn Ann *principal*

Blackwood
Cloyd, Thomas Earl *broadcast designer, consultant*

Bloomfield
Conta, Richard Vincent *actuary*
Hutcheon, Forbes Clifford Robert *engineer, company executive*
Kreie, Richard James *retired advertising executive*
Lordi, Katherine Mary *lawyer*
McCulloch, George McQuillan *retired foundation executive, fundraiser*
Shogen, Kuslima *pharmaceutical executive*
Weisert, Kent Albert Frederick *lawyer*

Bloomsbury
Rohloff, Claire Marie *interior designer, educator*

Bogota
Condon, Francis Edward *retired chemistry educator*

Boonton
Bona, Frederick Emil *public relations executive*
Bridges, Beryl Clarke *marketing executive*
Cappeline, Gary Anthoney *chemical company executive*
Lin, Ping *mechanical engineer*
Massler, Howard Arnold *lawyer*

Bordentown
Lowery, William Odell *personnel services executive*

Bound Brook
Chandler, Marguerite Nella *real estate corporation executive*
Gould, Donald Everett *retired chemical company executive, consultant*
Shive, Richard Byron *architect*

Bradley Beach
Senkiw-Rudowsky, Patricia Joan *artist, writer, educator*

Branchburg
Hulse, Robert Douglas *high technology executive*

Branchville
Johanson, Gregory John *psychotherapy trainer, minister*

Brick
Abel, Mark *dermatologist*
Roache, Patrick Michael, Jr., *management consultant*

Bridgeton
Fisher, Douglas Howard *state legislator*
Howell, James Burt, III, *retired agricultural products company sales consultant*

Bridgewater
Albrethsen, Adrian Edysel *metallurgist, consultant*
Ball, Owen Keith, Jr., *lawyer*
Bernson, Marcella S. *psychiatrist*
Dahling, Gerald Vernon *lawyer*
Faruqi, Abdul Rab *physician, consultant*
Feingold, Mark Howard *lawyer*
Feldman, Margit *volunteer*
Glesmann, Sylvia-Maria *artist*
Hirsch, Paul J. *orthopedist, surgeon, medical executive, educator, editor*
Kennedy, James Andrew *chemical company executive*
Linett, David *lawyer*
Lowman, Tyrone David *entrepreneur*
Maynard, Kenneth Irwin *medical educator, researcher*
Mc Cormick, Richard Patrick *history professor*
Patton, Diana Lee Wilkoc *artist, educator*
Sethi, Shyam Sunder *management consultant*
Skidmore, James Albert, Jr., *management, computer technology and engineering services company executive*
Taylor, Duncan Paul *research neuropharmacologist*
Weingast, Marvin *laboratory executive*

Brielle
McIntyre, Elizabeth Jones *retired multi-media specialist, educator*

Brigantine
Holl, James Andrew *prehospital care administrator*
Kickish, Margaret Elizabeth *elementary school educator*

Brookside
Fairchild, Samuel Wilson *professional services company executive, former federal agency administrator*

Browns Mills
Cha, Se Do *internist*
Di Nunzio, Dominick *educational administrator*
Moore, Roger Addison *pediatrician, anesthesiologist*

Budd Lake
Davis-Kalugin, Dorinne Sue *audiologist*
Hilbert, Rita L. *librarian*
Webb, John Gibbon, III, *lawyer*

Buena
Monastra, Richard J. *secondary school educator*
Woitach, Paul *health products executive*

Burlington
Domzalski, Kenneth Stanley *lawyer*
Kennedy, Christopher Robin *ceramic engineer, director*
Matlack, Maria Theresa *elementary school educator*
Nesci, Mark A. *retail executive*
Rowlette, Henry Allen, Jr., *social worker, counseling psychologist*
Tang, Paul C. *lawyer*

Butler
Ward, Robert Allen, Jr., *advertising executive*

Caldwell
Campbell, Sister Maura *theology and philosophy educator*
Castano, Gregory Joseph *lawyer*
Chatlos, William Edward *management consultant*
Choi, Sook Chong Yoo *physiologist, educator*
Mann, Robert Christopher *communications educator, television host, producer*
Ott, Walter Richard *academic administrator*
Palombo, Lisa *artist*
Randall, Lynn Ellen *librarian*
Surmatis, Joseph D. *retired chemist*
Werner, Patrice (Patricia Ann Werner) *academic administrator*

Califon
Alvarez, Jaime *language educator, poet*
Clarke, Frank Henderson *retired chemical company executive, scientist*
Fouillade, Jean-Paul Eric *management consultant*
Rosen, Carol Mendes *artist*

Camden
Ances, I. G(eorge) *obstetrician, gynecologist, educator*
Beck, David Paul *biochemist*
Bodofsky, Elliot Bruce *physician, researcher*
Brotman, Stanley Seymour *federal judge*
Conant, Douglas R. *food products executive*
Daniels, Albertina Diana *secondary school educator*
Feinman, Jay Murray *law educator*
Furey, John J. *lawyer*
Gans, Samuel Myer *temporary employment service executive*
Gordon, Walter Kelly *retired provost, English language educator*
Harrison, Russell Sage *political science educator, consultant*
Irenas, Joseph Eron *judge, director*
Johnson, David Willis *former food products executive*
Jones, Larry Darnell *tax specialist*
Kaden, Ellen Oran *lawyer, consumer products company executive*
Laskin, Lee B. *judge, lawyer, state senator*
Lawrence, Francis Leo *former university president, language educator*
Madan, Deepak S. *engineering executive*
Maxymuk, John Michael *librarian, writer*
Morrison, Dale F. *food company executive*
Parrillo, Joseph Edison, Jr., *allergist, immunologist, cardiologist*
Pello, Mark Joel *surgeon, educator*
Pomorski, Stanislaw *lawyer, educator*
Showalter, English, Jr., *French language educator*
Simandle, Jerome B. *federal judge*
Stahl, Gary Edward *neonatologist*
Uhler, Walter Charles *government official, writer*
Van Til, Jon *sociology educator*
Worrall, John Dennis *economics educator, consultant, writer*
Yamada, Tetsuji *health economist, educator*

Cape May
Fox, Matthew Ignatius *publishing company executive*
Lassner, Franz George *retired history professor, archivist*
Turner, Almon Richard *retired art historian, educator*

Cape May Court House
Altman, Brian David *pediatric ophthalmologist*
Cohen, Daniel Edward *writer*
Cohen, Susan Lois *writer*
Fineberg, Robert Alan *lawyer*
Pierson, Jeffrey Lynn *protective services officer*
Weber, Lesley Elizabeth *music educator*

Cape May Point
Fraser, Malcolm Cavanagh *mayor*
Jordan, Joe J. *architect*

Carlstadt
Cooke, Edward Francis, Jr., *accountant*
Levy, Stuart S. *apparel company executive*

Carteret
Donald, James L. *supermarket executive*
Neff, Richard B. *consumer products company executive*
Scott, Eileen Rose *retail executive*
Strassler, Marc A. *corporate lawyer*
Vitrano, Frank *supermarket executive*
Volla, Steven L. *food products executive*

Cedar Grove
Carlozzi, Catherine L. *corporate communications consultant, writer*
O'Keefe, Paul *editor*

Chatham
Earle, Jean Buist *financial officer*
Glover, Janet Briggs *artist*
Hurley, Allyson Kingsley *dentist*
Jacobs, Andrew Robert *lawyer*
Lax, Philip *land developer, space planner*
Leonett, Anthony Arthur *banker*
Marconi, Dominic Anthony *retired bishop*
Meagher, James Proctor *editor*
Murphy, Joseph James *chiropractic physician*
Sundberg, Carl-Erik Wilhelm *telecommunications executive, researcher*
Warm, Elliot L. *lawyer*
White, Benjamin Steven *mathematician, researcher*
Zegas, Alan Lee *lawyer*

Cherry Hill
Adler, John Herbert *lawyer, state legislator*
Barton, Diane *physician*
Batterman, Steven Charles *engineering mechanics and bioengineering educator, forensic engineering and biomechanics consultant*
Berman, Steven Eric *audiologist*
Betchen, Stephen Jay *marital, family and sex therapist*

Brachfeld, Jonas *cardiologist, educator*
Bryan, Henry Collier *clergyman, retired secondary school educator*
Camardo, Michael F. *engineering company executive*
Clauser, Donald Roberdeau *musician*
Copsetta, Norman George *real estate executive*
Erving, Julius (Julius Winfield Erving II) *retired professional basketball player, business executive*
Fuentevilla, Manuel Edward *chemical engineer*
Gardner, Joel Robert *writer, historian*
Garrigle, William Aloysius *lawyer*
Grado-Wolynies, Evelyn (Evelyn Wolynies) *clinical nurse specialist, educator*
Hill, Vernon W., II, *bank executive*
Israelsky, Roberta Schwartz *speech pathologist, audiologist*
Jozwiak, Steven Jay *lawyer*
Kahn, Marc Leslie *orthopedic surgeon*
Kapel, David Edward *retired academic administrator, education educator*
Kole, Janet Stephanie *lawyer, writer, photographer*
Korin, Joel Benjamin *lawyer, educator*
Levin, Joshua Zev *computer scientist, consultant, transportation engineer*
Liebman, Emmanuel *lawyer*
Margolis, Gerald Joseph *psychiatrist, psychoanalyst*
Matthiessen, Robert E. *business executive*
Myers, Daniel William, II, *lawyer*
Newell, Eric James *financial planner, tax consultant, former insurance executive*
Olearchyk, Andrew *cardiothoracic surgeon, educator*
Proper, Michael Charles *cardiologist, educator*
Rabil, Mitchell Joseph *lawyer*
Rose, Joel Alan *legal consultant*
Rudman, Solomon Kal *magazine publisher*
Sax, Robert Edward *food service equipment company executive*
Schelm, Roger Leonard *information systems specialist*
Swibinski, Edward Thomas *internist, endocrinologist, educator*
Tomar, William *lawyer*
Werbitt, Warren *gastroenterologist, educator*

Chester
Di Battista, Anthony Paul *secondary school educator*
Pfaffenroth, Peter Albert *lawyer*

Cinnaminson
Johnson, Victor Lawrence *banker, director*

Clark
Barr, Jon-Henry *lawyer*
Hasselman, San D *secondary school educator*

Clayton
Bertenshaw, William Howard, III, *radio and television producer*

Cliffside Park
Chryssanthou, Chryssanthos *pathologist, educator*
De Pol, John *artist*
Ginos, James Zissis *retired research chemist*
Goldstein, Howard Bernard *investment banker*
Perhacs, Marylouise Helen *musician, educator*
Pushkarev, Boris S. *research foundation director, writer*
Swann, Barbara *lawyer*
Zucker, Howard Alan *pediatric cardiologist, intensivist, anesthesiologist, government agency administrator*

Clifton
Anzaldi, James Anthony *mayor*
Axelrod, Norman *retail company executive*
Bronkesh, Annette Cylia *public relations executive*
Feinstein, Miles Roger *lawyer*
Giles, William (Bill) T. *retail executive*
Goldberger, Alan Steven *lawyer*
Klein, Hubert *accountant*
Lieb, L. Robert *lawyer*
Malamud, Alexander *lawyer, consultant*
Minkoff, John *applied mathematics, signal processing, and engineering educator*
Palma, Nicholas James *lawyer*
Pineda, Albert Anthony *obstetrician, gynecologist, educator*
Silber, Judy G. *dermatologist*

Clinton
Hansen, Arthur Magne *engineering and manufacturing executive*
Milchovich, Raymond J. *engineering executive*
Moore, Alma Donst *writer, lyricist*

Collingswood
Martin, Burchard V. *lawyer*

Colonia
Wiesenfeld, Bess G. *interior designer*

Colts Neck
Borisov, George P. *music educator*
Mauro, Anthony Peter *small business owner*
Ridoux, Denise C. *director, educator*

Columbia
Timcenko, Lydia Teodora *biochemist, chemist*

Columbus
Litman, Bernard *electrical engineer, consultant*

Cranbury
Hawver, Dennis A. *psychological consultant*
Iatesta, John Michael *lawyer*
Kemmerer, Peter Ream *financial executive*
Yoseloff, Julien David *publishing company executive*
Yoseloff, Thomas *publisher*

Cranford
Halleck, George Thomas *marketing professional*
Hersh, Mitchell E. *real estate company executive, director*
Herz, Sylvia Beatrice *clinical and community psychologist*
Jenssen, Warren Donald *microbiologist, consultant*
Jones, Timothy M. *real estate company executive*
Lefkowitz, Barry *real estate company executive*
McCreedy, Edwin James *lawyer*
Messing, Sara Virginia Drick *lawyer*
Mullen, Edward K. *paper company executive*
Petryshyn, Wolodymyr V. *retired mathematician*
Russell, John Joseph *English educator*
Von Zuben, Fred G. *corporate executive*

Cresskill
Cardinale, Gerald *state legislator*
Smyth, Craig Hugh *fine arts educator*

Deal
Becker, Richard Stanley *music publisher*

Deal Park
Meisels, Judith A. *piano instructor, classical pianist*

Deepwater
Baillie, Joan M. *chemical company official, biology educator*

Delanco
Muhlschlegel, Harry J. *transportation company executive*

Delran
Conaway, Herb(ert) C., Jr., *assemblyman*
Gilbert, Harry Ephraim, Jr., *retired hotel executive*
Parker, Michael J. *editor, writer, researcher*

Demarest
Brody, Saul Nathaniel *retired English literature educator*
Dornfest, Burton Saul *anatomy educator*
Ruderman, Warren *chemist*

Denville
Breed, Ria *anthropologist*
Fisher, Sharon Mary *musician*
Husar, Walter Gene *neurologist, neuroscientist, educator*
Minter, Jerry Burnett *electronic component company executive, engineer*
O'Keefe, Robert James *retired bank executive*
Tartaglia, Richard V. *priest*
Veech, Lynda Anne *musician, educator*

Deptford
Johns, Michael Douglas *health care corporate executive, writer, former federal government offical*

Dover
Kassell, Paula Sally *editor, publisher*
Seadler, Stephen Edward *social scientist, philosopher, writer*

Dumont
Sadock, Karen *editor, writer*

East Brunswick
Applebaum, Charles *lawyer*
Burns, Barbara *lawyer*
Dombrowski, Anne Wesseling *retired microbiologist, researcher*
Goldberg, Bertram J. *social agency administrator*
Grundman, Thomas K. *energy executive*
Hurst, Gregory Squire *director, producer, investment executive*
Kupchynsky, Jerry Markian *orchestra conductor, educator*
Meningall, Evelyn L. *educational media specialist*
Savio, Frances Margaret Cammarotta *music educator*
Wagman, Gerald Howard *retired biochemist*
Yahya, Muhammad Javaid *financial consultant, economist*
Yttrehus, Rolv Berger *composer, educator*

East Hanover
Bess, Alan L. *pharmaceutical executive, physician*
Davidson, Anne Stowell *lawyer*
Dodsworth, Roy W. *pharmaceutical company executive*
Edelson, Edward Harold *research chemist*
Harshman, Richard R. *manufacturing executive*
Iovel, Alla *music educator, writer, pianist*
Nemecek, Georgina Marie *molecular pharmacologist*
Purkayastha, Das D. *biostatistician*
Raymond, Pawlicki *pharmaceutical executive*
Tamburro, Peter James, Jr., *secondary school educator*

East Orange
Banks, Anna Delceina *financial planner*
Brown, Rosa Elizabeth *social worker, writer*
Brundage, Gertrude Barnes *pediatrician*
Caldwell, Toni Lucille *not-for-profit developer*
Fellus, Jonathan L. *neurologist*
Fielo, Muriel Bryant *interior designer*
Hudson-Zonn, Eliza *nurse, psychologist*
Ilogienboh, Caroline O. *protective services official, publishing executive*
Jones-Gregory, Patricia *secondary art educator*
Masucci, Nicholas J. *engineering company executive*
Teetsell, Janice Marie Newman *business owner, lawyer*
Wolff, Derish Michael *economist, company executive*

East Rutherford
Accorsi, Ernest William, Jr., *professional football team executive*
Blate, Alissa *advertising executive*
Brodeur, Martin *professional hockey player*
Burns, Pat *professional hockey coach*
Coughlin, Tom *professional football coach*
DiEleuterio, James A. *state official*
Frank, Lawrence *professional basketball coach*
Glassell, Claes *health products executive*
Holyfield, Evander *professional boxer*
Jefferson, Richard *professional basketball player*
Kempner, Michael W. *public relations executive*
Kidd, Jason *professional basketball player*
Lamoriello, Louis Anthony *professional hockey team executive*
Langenbrunner, Jamie *professional hockey player*
Mack, James A. *health products executive*
Manning, Eli (Elisha Nelson Manning) *professional football player*
Mara, Wellington T. (Duke Mara) *professional football team executive*
Maresca, Robert A. *broadcasting and advertising executive*
Moorer, Michael *professional boxer*
Ratner, Bruce *professional sports team executive*
Shockey, Jeremy Charles *professional football player*
Stevens, Scott *professional hockey player*
Strahan, Michael *professional football player*
Warner, Kurt (Kurtis Warner) *professional football player*
Whitaker, Pernell (Sweet Pea Whitaker) *professional boxer*

East Windsor
Adams, Stephen M. *publishing company executive*

Eastampton
Haws, Elizabeth Anne *education administrator, school psychologist*

Eatontown
DeGiglio, Michael A. *food products executive*
Hollander, Kenneth S. *food products executive*
Priesand, Sally Jane *rabbi*
Ryan, David J. *food products executive*

Edgewater
Virelli, Louis James, Jr., *lawyer*

Edison
Alexander, John Charles *pharmaceutical company executive, physician*
Angelakos, Evangelos Theodorou *physician, physiologist, pharmacologist, educator*
Barnes, Peter J., Jr., *assemblyman*
Behr, Omri M. *lawyer*
Blumengold, Jeffrey Gene *health facility administrator*
Calder, John Mackenzie *publisher, theatre director, writer*
Cangemi, Michael Paul *accountant, finance company executive, writer*
Citron, Jeffrey A. *telecommunications industry executive*
Currence, Anna *publishing executive*
Currie, Robert *communications executive*
Dore, James Francis *financial services executive*
Fan, Shirley Tsui-Yu *music educator*
Gizzi, Martin Sherman *neurologist, neurophysiologist*
Hecht, William David *accountant*
Hunter, Michael *publishing executive*
Islam, Naushad S. *pharmacist, government agency administrator*
Kraut, William *financial executive*
Kushinsky, Jeanne Alice *humanities educator*
Lunt, Alan Nicholas *psychiatric rehabilitation counselor*
Maeroff, Gene I. *academic administrator, journalist*
Menoutis, James Vassillios *research scientist*
Miniere, Michael Anthony *mathematician, educator*
Moussouttas, Michael M. *medical educator*
Nessel, Edward Harry *swimming coach*
Robinson, Donald Warren *retired art educator, artist*
Roskoski, John *religious studies educator, coach*
Salvati, Eugene Philip *retired surgeon*
Samek, Edward Lasker *service company executive*
Selvakumar, Ariamalar *environmental engineer*
Strax, Thomas E. *physiatrist*
Vercammen, Kenneth Albert *lawyer, prosecutor*
Zhao, Jiwei *lawyer*

Egg Harbor City
Farris, Vera King *former college president*

Egg Harbor Township
Lashman, Shelley Bortin *retired judge*
Raftner, Thomas *airport terminal executive*

Elizabeth
Berger, Harold Richard *physician*
Bollwage, J. Christian *mayor*
Cinberg, James Zubow *otolaryngologist, educator*
Gellert, George Geza *food importing company executive*
Karlberg, John *transportation company executive*
Lucco, James Perry *writer*
Mogensen, Charles Ray, Jr., *food service administrator*
Rosenstein, Neil *surgeon, genealogical researcher*
Sananman, Michael Lawrence *neurologist*
Wilchins, Sidney A. *gynecologist*

Elmwood Park
Grodman, Marc D. *lab administrator, physician, medical educator*
Nadzick, Judith Ann *accountant*
Wygod, Martin J. *pharmaceuticals executive*

Emerson
Hannon, Patricia Ann *library director*

Englewood
Albee, Gloria *playwright*
Anuszkiewicz, Richard Joseph *artist*
Beltran, Elio F. *writer, painter*
Butler, David George *obstetrician, gynecologist*
Dardik, Herbert *vascular surgeon, general surgeon*
Deresiewicz, Herbert *mechanical engineering educator*
Fay, Toni Georgette *communications executive*
Frieden, Faith Joy *obstetrician*
Goldweit, Richard Scott *cardiologist*
Harish, Ziv *allergist, immunologist*
Herman, Steven Douglas *cardiothoracic surgeon, educator*
Hoexter, Corinne Rosenfelder Katz *author, editor*
Hurst, Wendy R(obin) *obstetrician*
Rubin, Kenneth Phillip *gastroenterologist*
Saliba, Philip E. *archbishop*
Schmidt, Ronald Hans *architect*
Svezia, Vera Tisheff *concert pianist*
Tobias, Geoffrey *otolaryngologist, plastic surgeon*
Volk, Austin N. *insurance company executive*
Willner, Joseph H. *neurologist*
Wuhl, Charles Michael *psychiatrist*
Zwilich, Ellen Taaffe *composer*

Englewood Cliffs
Books, Roberta Paula *real estate finance executive*
Cohen, Philip Gary *lawyer*
Dash, Barry Harold *pharmaceutical company executive*
Dobrzynski, Judith Helen *journalist, commentator*
Faber, David *broadcast business news network correspondent*
Farrell, Patricia Ann *psychologist, educator, writer*
Feuerstein, Herbert *food company executive*
Fisher, Andrew, IV, *newswriter, television producer*
Haltiwanger, Robert Sidney, Jr., *book publishing executive*
Heller, Hanes Ayres *lawyer*
Henderson, Mary R. (Nina) *food/consumer products executive*
Kastory, Bernard H. *food products executive*
Kernen, Joe *broadcast business news network correspondent*
Kim, Jae Taik *educator*
Kim, Soo-Ryong *investment banker*
Murray, Brian Victor *investment banker*
Nels, Arnold Hayward *pharmaceutical company executive*
Saible, Stephanie Irene *magazine editor*
Shoemate, Charles R. *former food company executive*
Vane, Dena *magazine editor-in-chief*
Van Gelder, Rudolph *sound recording engineer*
Yu, Fei *internist*

Englishtown
Dorfman, Dan *news correspondent*

Erial
Browna, Jo McIntyre *nurse*

Essex Fells
Thummel, Rosa *artist*

Ewing
Brunda, Daniel Donald *retired aerospace engineer, consultant, inventor, writer*
Gitenstein, Donna M. *academic administrator*
Hamm, Claire Rose *development information services administrator*
McCarty, John Albert *advertising and marketing educator, consultant*
Meola, Marc *librarian*
Sirbaugh, Nora B. *performing arts educator, vocalist*

Fair Haven
Derchin, Dary Bret Ingham *writer*
Di Turi, Christopher *dentist, maxillofacial prosthodontist, educator, researcher*
Wyndrum, Ralph William, Jr., *communications executive consultant*

Fair Lawn
Ahearn, Matthew J. *assemblyman*
Aitchison, Suann *elementary school educator*
Dadurian, Medina Diana *pediatric dentist, educator*
Mazel, Joseph Lucas *publishing executive, consultant*
Namerow, David Mark *pediatrician*

Fairfield
Byer, Theodore Scott *accountant*
Connell, William Terrence *lawyer, judge*
Govic, Rudolf *structural engineer*
Grant, Daniel Gordon *information services company executive*
Petrocelli, A. F. *hotel executive*
Purcell, Fenton Peter *engineering consultant*
Stein, Robert Alan *electronics company executive*

Fairview
Anton, Harvey *textile company executive*
Park, Chung *painter, educator, computer software developer*

Fanwood
Berger, Ivan Bennett *magazine editor, writer*
Whitaker, Joel *publisher, editor, elected public official*

Far Hills
Alexandre, Kristin Kuhns *public relations executive, writer*

Farmingdale
Schluter, Peter Mueller *electronics company executive*

Flanders
Huang, Jacob Chen-ya *physician, educator, city health official*

Flemington
Buchsbaum, Peter A. *lawyer*
Jackson, Ryno Marshall *forensic psychologist, consultant*
Kettler, Carl Frederick *airline executive*
Lance, Leonard *state legislator*
Lenagh, Thomas Hugh *lawyer, financial advisor*
Miller, Louis H. *lawyer*
Post, Richard Henry *pharmaceuticals executive*
Rushton, Alan R. *physician, medical historian*
Salamon, Renay *real estate broker*
Sozansky, Michael William, Jr., *lawyer*
Thomas, Anne Moreau *former newspaper owner*
Zulker, Charles Bates *broadcasting company executive*

Florham Park
Abramson, Clarence Allen *pharmaceutical company executive, lawyer*
Begeja, Lee *inventive researcher*
Bossen, Wendell John *retired financial consultant*
Brodkin, Adele Ruth Meyer *psychologist*
Calabrese, Arnold J. *lawyer*
Chase, Eric Lewis *lawyer*
Darr, John *finance company executive*
Duquette, David Joseph, Jr., *lawyer, investor*
Fischer, Pamela Shadel *public relations executive*
Gale, Stan *real estate company executive*
Hardin, William Downer *retired lawyer*
Kandravy, John *lawyer*
Laulicht, Murray Jack *lawyer*
MacMillan, David Paul *retired oil company executive*
Naimark, George Modell *marketing and management consultant*
Negi, Devendra S. *communications services company administrator*

Nittoly, Paul Gerard *lawyer*
O'Connell, Daniel F. *lawyer*
Oths, Richard Philip *health systems administrator*
Reid, Charles Adams, III, *lawyer*
Russell, Jesse E. *communications executive*
Shor, Peter W. *mathematician, researcher*
Weisberg, Lynne Willing *psychiatrist, consultant*
Witman, Leonard Joel *lawyer*
Yeager, Mark *real estate company executive*

Fords
Blond, Stuart Richard *newsletter editor*
Brown, James *singer, broadcasting executive*

Forked River
Novak, Dennis E. *physician*

Fort Lee
Adler, Earl *insurance executive*
Altomara, Rita Ecke *library director, writer*
Amara, Lucine *opera and concert singer*
Armellino, Michael Ralph *retired asset management executive*
Baiul, Oksana *clothing designer, former figure skater*
Bohner, Kate *correspondent*
Bolster, William Lawrence *broadcast executive*
Chessler, Richard Kenneth *gastroenterologist, endoscopist*
Cox, Melvin Monroe *lawyer*
Epperson, Sharon *television correspondent*
Goldfarb, Joel Peter *internist, gastroenterologist*
Herera, Sue *television host*
Insana, Ronald Gerard *newscaster*
Kiriakopoulos, George Constantine *dentist*
Kofman, Mikhail *economist, engineering executive*
Kramer, Orin Stuart *investment services company executive*
Li, Tien-Shun *obstetrician, gynecologist, educator*
Lippman, William Jennings *investment company executive*
MacCallum, Martha *correspondent*
Nadeine, Vladimir *journalist, editor*
Nemser, Robert Solomon *visual communications consultant, art director, creative director, designer, writer, educator*
Orman, Suze *news correspondent, writer*
Schiessler, Robert Walter *retired chemical and oil company executive*
Screpetis, Dennis *retired nuclear engineer, consultant*
Sherry, Paul Henry *minister, religious organization administrator*
Smith, Jeffrey E. *pharmaceutical executive*
Stuart, Carole *publishing executive*
Stuart, Lyle *publishing company executive*
Sugarman, Alan William *educational consultant, national speaker*
Thomopoulos, Michael *music educator*
Treskov, Yakov Maks *engineer*
Yoo, Choon Wang *financial consultant*
Young, Vera Lee Hall *educational administrator, association executive*

Fort Monmouth
Perlman, Barry Stuart *electrical engineering executive, researcher*
Schwering, Felix Karl *electronics engineer, researcher*
Su, Wei *electrical engineer*
Thornton, Clarence Gould *electronics engineering executive*

Franklin Lakes
Albright, Judith Anne *writer, educator*
Baker, Cornelia Draves *artist*
Castellini, Clateo *retired medical technology company executive*
Considine, John *pharmaceutical company executive*
Friedman, Martin Burton *chemical company executive*
Ginsberg, Barry Howard *physician, researcher*
Ludwig, Edward J. *medical technology company executive*
Mattie, Jeanne Marie *public relations and communications consultant*
Williams, Edward David *consulting executive*

Franklin Park
Jones, Frank A., Jr., *psychiatrist, educator*

Freehold
Christ, Duane Marland *retired computer systems engineer*
Foster, Eric Harold, Jr., *retail executive*
Greenstein, Gary *periodontist, dental educator*
Jawidzik, Edward Mark *priest*
Karcher, Ellen M. *state senator*
Kwon, Joon Taek *retired chemistry researcher*
Lijoi, Peter Bruno *lawyer*
Saker, Joseph J. *supermarket company executive*
Schwartz, Perry Lester *information systems engineer, consultant*
Shapiro, Michael *supermarket corporate officer*
Soto-Fernandez, Liliana *education educator*
Stirrat, William Albert *electronics engineer*

Frenchtown
Fogelson, Brian David *educational administrator*

Garfield
Herpst, Robert Dix *lawyer, optics and materials technology executive*
Rosenberg, Raymond David *special education educator, consultant*

Gillette
Nathanson, Linda Sue *publisher, author, technical writer*

Gladstone
Close, Donald Pembroke *management consultant*
O'Connor, Karen Lende *Olympic athlete*
Standish, Robert C. *professional sports team executive*

Glassboro
Davis, Ronald P. *secondary school administrator*
Detofsky, Louis Bennett *secondary school educator*
Gephardt, Donald Louis *university official*
James, Herman Delano *former college administrator*
Jiao, Allan Y. *law educator*

Martin, Marilyn Joan *library director*
Mosto, Patricia *environmental scientist, educator*
Robinette, Joseph Allen *theater educator, playwright*
Wang, Q. Edward *history professor*

Glen Gardner
Epstein, Edward Joseph *textile company executive*

Glen Ridge
Agnew, Peter Tomlin *employee benefit consultant*
Connolly, Joseph Thomas *lawyer, judge*
Pendley, Donald Lee *association executive*
Rubin, Roberta Gail *pathologist*
Zbar, Lloyd Irwin Stanley *otolaryngologist, educator*

Glen Rock
Britcher, E. Drew *lawyer*
D'Angelo, Thomas J. *not-for-profit developer, financial consultant*
Davis, Alison B. *management consultant executive*
Mc Elrath, Richard Elsworth *retired insurance company executive*
Sirower, Bonnie Fox *fundraising executive*

Glenwood
Donald, William Robert, Jr., *performing arts educator, theater director, consultant*

Green Brook
Balsamello, Melissa (Marley) *elementary school educator*
Bohanan, David John *management consultant*
Bokhari, Sabahat *cardiologist*
Hertzberg, Henry *retired radiologist*
Spoeri, Randall Keith *healthcare company executive*

Green Village
Castenschiold, René *engineering executive, consultant, writer*

Greenwich
Lane, Mark *lawyer, educator, writer*

Guttenberg
Wright, Jane Cooke *oncologist, educator, consultant*

Hackensack
Ahearn, James *newspaper columnist*
Barry, Jan *journalist, poet*
Borg, Malcolm Austin *publishing executive*
Bronson, Meridith J. *lawyer*
Caminiti, Donald Angelo *lawyer*
Davies, Richard John *surgical oncologist*
De Groote, Robert David *general and vascular surgeon*
Dent, Thompson S. *health care organization executive*
Dexheimer, Larry William *advertising agency executive*
Fatemi, Saeid *language educator, writer, researcher*
Ferguson, John Patrick *health facility administrator*
Greenberg, Steven Morey *lawyer*
Gross, Peter Alan *epidemiologist, researcher*
Haines, Kathleen Ann *pediatrician, educator*
Harris, Michael Bertram *pediatrician, educator*
Heilborn, George Heinz *investor*
Imus, Deirdre *health facility administrator*
Kestin, Howard H. *judge*
Margulies, James Howard *editorial cartoonist*
Masullo, Alfredo Salvatore *dermatologist*
Mavrovic, Ivo *chemical engineer*
Mehta, Jay *financial executive*
Mullin, Patrick Allen *lawyer*
Navatta, Anna Paula *lawyer*
Parisi, Cheryl Lynn *elementary school educator*
Pascal, Mark S. *oncologist*
Pecora, Andrew Louis *hematologist*
Perl, Harold *pediatrician*
Peterson, Linda Ellen *lawyer*
Pollinger, William Joshua *lawyer*
Schwartz, Mildred Anne *retired sociologist*
Spiegel, Linda F. *lawyer*
Stein, Gary S. *retired judge, lawyer*
Strull, James Richard *lawyer*
Vort, Robert A. *lawyer*
Waixel, Vivian *journalist*
Yagoda, Harry Nathan *system engineering executive*
Zimmerman, Marlin U., Jr., *chemical engineer*

Hackettstown
Alper, Michael F. *lawyer, political consultant*
Boody, Kathleen Marie *dean*
Fremon, Richard C. *retired infosystems specialist*
Grigsby, Bryon Lee *dean*
Kobert, Joel A. *lawyer*
Mulligan, Elinor Patterson *lawyer*
Scalza, Margaret T. *publishing executive*
Van Campen, Stephen Bernard *executive recruiter, consultant*
Wiedemann, Charles Louis *dentist*

Haddon Heights
Gwiazda, Stanley John *retired university dean*

Haddonfield
Bauer, Raymond Gale *sales professional*
Capelli, John Placido *nephrologist, educator*
Carter, Joan Pauline *investment company executive*
Chu, Horn Dean *chemical engineer*
Ewan, David E. *lawyer*
Gatti, Eugene Anthony *immunologist, pediatrician*
Halscheid, Therese Anne *poet*
Harris, Stuart Innes *construction equipment engineer, marketing professional*
Iavicoli, Mario Anthony *lawyer*
Newell, Russell Anderson *financial planner*
Siskin, Edward Joseph *engineering and construction company executive*

Hainesport
Sylk, Leonard Allen *housing company executive, real estate developer*

Haledon
Dougherty, June Eileen *librarian*

Hamburg
Buist, Jean Mackerley *veterinarian*

Hamilton
Blohm, Robert *investment banker, economist, statistician*

Gideon, Richard Walter *broadcasting management consultant*
Lacy, John Russell *retired state government administrator, public affairs counselor*
Pucciatti, Sandra Milstein *opera company director*
Sipski, Mary Leonide *physician, healthcare administrator*
Sporn, Aaron Adolph *physician, educator*

Hamilton Square
Ridolfi, Dorothy Porter Boulden *nurse, real estate broker*

Hampton
Yates, Michael Francis *management consultant*

Harrington Park
Manafette, Michael *writer*

Hasbrouck Heights
Perham, Roy Gates, III, *industrial psychologist*

Haworth
Biesel, David Barrie *publishing executive*
Biesel, Diane Jane *editor, publishing executive*
Posner, Roy Edward *retired finance executive*
Strum, Brian J. *real estate executive*

Hazlet
Shea, James Bryan *writer*

Helmetta
Gabay, Eleonora V. *mechanical engineer, educator*

Hewitt
Mollenkott, Virginia Ramey *English literature and language educator, author, guest lecturer*
Selwyn, Donald *engineering administrator, researcher, inventor, educator*

Highland Lakes
Kiraly, Bèla Kàlmàn *retired history educator, Hungarian army officer*

Highland Park
Brudner, Harvey Jerome *physicist*
Chamberlin-Davis, Ann Elizabeth *artist, writer*
Cheiten, Marvin Harold *playwright, manufacturing executive*
Feuerwerker, Elie *biologist, educator*
Glasgold, Alvin Irwin *physician*
Grady, Joyce (Marian Joyce Grady) *psychotherapist, consultant*
Spencer, Herbert Harry *structural engineering researcher, computer analyst*

Highlands
Dann, Emily *mathematics professor*
Hansen, Christian Andreas, Jr., *plastics and chemical company executive*
Psuty, Norbert Phillip *marine sciences educator*

Hightstown
Finn, Gerald C. *real estate company executive*
Finn, Jeffrey M. *real estate company executive*
Howard, Barbara Sue Mesner *artist*
Hull, Gretchen Gaebelein *lay worker, writer, lecturer*
Johnson, Ernest Frederick *chemical engineer, educator*
Johnson, Walter Curtis *electrical engineering educator*
Martin, David George *historian, Latin educator, author*
Shoemaker, Frank Crawford *retired physicist*
Wham, George Sims *retired publishing executive*

Hillsborough
Kenyhercz, Thomas Michael *pharmaceutical company executive*
Nahass, Ronald G(eorge) *internist, educator*
Weinman, Steven Alan *emergency nurse, researcher, writer, educator, consultant*
Yuster-Freeman, Leigh Carol *broadcast executive*

Hillsdale
Copeland, Lois Jacqueline *physician*

Hillside
Franks, Robert D. (Bob Franks) *former congressman*

Ho Ho Kus
Bryan, Thomas Lynn *lawyer, educator*
Ciannella, Joeen Moore *museum director*
Deupree, Marvin Mattox *accountant, business consultant*
Van Slooten, Ronald Henry Joseph *dentist*

Hoboken
Abel, Robert Berger *science administrator*
Besser, Ronald *information technology educator*
Boesch, Francis Theodore *electrical engineer, educator*
Bose, Ajay Kumar *chemistry professor*
Bostwick, Randell A. *retired retail food company executive*
Eide, Hans A. *physicist, educator*
Fassoulis, Satiris Galahad *communications company executive*
Fernandez, Fernando Lawrence *aeronautical engineer, research and development company executive*
Griskey, Richard George *chemical engineering educator*
Moeller, Joseph John, Jr., *university official*
Paradise, Paul Richard *writer, editor*
Pochiraju, Kishore *mechanical engineer, educator*
Raveché, Harold Joseph *university administrator, physical chemist*
Rose, Roslyn *artist*
Savitsky, Daniel *engineer, educator*
Schmidt, George *physicist, educator*
Schultz, Kenneth Carl *antiques dealer*
Sisto, Fernando *mechanical engineering educator*
Sniffen, Michael Joseph *hospital administrator*
Sommers, George R. *lawyer*
Spring, Michael *editor, writer*
Tardiff, Jill Alexandria *publishing executive*
Ubell, Robert Neil *editor, publisher, educator, consultant*
Widdicombe, Richard Palmer *librarian*
Yevick, George Johannus *scientist*

Holmdel
Catanese, Vincent Joseph *internist*
Gordon, James Power *optics scientist*
Hudson, Wendy Joy *software manager*
Kaminow, Ivan Paul *physicist*
Kogelnik, Herwig Werner *electronics company executive*
Lang, Howard Lawrence *electrical engineer*
Meyer, Robert Alan *consultant*
Mollenauer, Linn Frederick *retired physicist*
Papadias, Constantinos Basil *electrical engineer*
Polinsky, Joseph Thomas *recruiting and training consultant*
Ross, Ian Munro *electrical engineer*
Slovik, Sandra Lee *retired art educator*
Smith, Sibley Judson, Jr., *historic site administrator, educator*
Zhang, Xuemei *reliability scientist*

Hopatcong
Ferderber-Hersonski, Boris Constantin *process engineer*
Oken, Robert *neuroscientist, researcher, consultant*
Reese, Harry Edwin, Jr., *electronics executive*

Hope
McDonald, John Joseph *electronics executive*

Hopewell
Baeckler, Virginia Van Wynen *librarian*
VanMarcke, Erik Hector *civil engineer, educator*

Irvington
Akinsanmi, Lawrence Akintunde *medical researcher*
Paden, Harry *municipal official*
Stanley, Craig A. *state legislator*
Treadwell, Kenneth, Jr., *obstetrician/gynecologist*

Iselin
Barre, Steven Craig *lawyer*
Clarke, David H. *industrial products executive*
De Rose, Louis John *financial services executive*
Dornbusch, Arthur A., II, *lawyer*
Goodwin, Billy W. *manufacturing executive*
Perry, Barry W. *manufacturing executive*
Smith, Orin Robert *chemical company executive*
Sperduto, Michael A. *corporate financial executive*

Jackson
Arminas, Scott Arnold *chemist, poet, writer*
Carney, Rita J. *educational administrator*
Cohen, Walter Stanley *accountant, financial consultant*
Dancer, Ronald S. *assemblyman*
Hagberg, Carl Thomas *financial executive*
Leveson, Irving Frederick *economist*
McCormick, Harold J. *music educator*
Rickabaugh, Vicki *horse farm owner, mayor*
Turner, Pamela *psychologist*
Vacchiano, Julie Catherine *special education educator*
Wagner, Edward Kurt *publishing company executive*

Jamesburg
Olmsted, David John *capital management company executive*

Jersey City
Ascolese, Michael J. *corporate communications executive*
Ashley, Willard Walden C., Sr., *minister*
Balsamo, Stephen *brokerage house executive*
Balter, Leslie Marvin *business communications educator*
Breuer, Ronald Karl, Sr., *investment banking executive*
Bruso, Arthur *artist*
Connolly, Theodore Daniel *protective services official, councilman*
Coreil, Raymond Clyde *English educator*
Coyne, Frank J. *insurance industry executive*
D'Ambra, Eve *art historian*
Dupey, Michele Mary *communications specialist*
Ezrati, Milton Joseph *investment manager, economist, writer*
Fan, Chonglun *materials scientist, researcher*
Farrior, Evan Bell *special education educator, writer*
Fletcher, Anthony C. *artist, graphics designer*
Goldberg, Arthur Abba *merchant banker, financial advisor*
Gopikrishnan, Parameswaran *investment company executive*
Gurevich, Grigory *visual artist, educator, mime*
Hayes, Isaac *rhythm and blues singer, composer*
Hitchcock, John C. *communications media executive*
Hordon, Harris Eugene *economics professor*
Ingrassia, Paul Joseph *publishing executive*
Jennings, Sister Vivien *English language educator*
Katz, Colleen *publisher*
Klyatis, Lev Matusovich *test and reliability scientist*
Kontos, Arthur *investment company executive*
Koster, Emlyn Howard *geologist, educator*
Levine, Richard James *publishing executive*
Lipschutz, Neal *editor*
Liu, Kejian *biostatistician*
McFadden, Rosemary Theresa *lawyer, financial services executive*
Miller, Adele Engelbrecht *educational administrator*
Nevins, Arthur Gerard, Jr., *lawyer*
O'Dea, William Patrick *research and development company executive*
Pasternak, Kenneth D. *trading company executive*
Patterson, Grace Limerick *library director*
Perhach, James Lawrence *pharmaceutical company executive*
Pietrini, Andrew Gabriel *automotive aftermarket executive*
Poiani, Eileen Louise *mathematics educator, college administrator, higher education planner*
Pratt, Minnie Bruce *writer, educator*
Queen Latifah, (Dana Owens) *recording artist, actress*
Raffelson, Michael *financial executive*
Scharfstein, Sol *publishing executive*
Schundler, Bret Davis *former mayor*
Signorile, Vincent Anthony *lawyer*
Singer, Howard Jack *biology professor, researcher*
Smith, James Frederick *securities executive*
Steinman, Steven L. *financial company executive*
Stinchcomb, Albert Monroe *producer, designer/realtor*

Eager, George Sidney, Jr., *electrical engineer, engineering executive*
Gill, Nia H. *state legislator*
Gollob, Herman Cohen *retired publishing company, editor*
Gutman, Richard Martin *lawyer*
Harvey, Richard Dudley *marketing consultant*
Jacoby, Tamar *journalist*
Kaiser, Richard Alan *surgeon*
Koeller, Andreas *computer scientist, educator*
Luftglass, Murray Arnold *corporate financial executive*
Lynde, Richard A. *academic administrator*
Murphy, Betty Jagoda *small business owner*
Nance, Tony Max-Perry *designer, illustrator*
Pastor, Peter *history professor*
Rosen, Allen David *plastic surgeon*
Stertz, Stephen Allen *historian, educator*
Tintle, Carmel Joseph *public relations executive*
Walker, George Theophilus, Jr., *composer, pianist, music educator*
Ward, Roger Coursen *lawyer*
Williamson, Philemona *artist*

Montvale
Baba, Thomas Frank *corporate economist, economics educator*
Cervantez, Michelle *marketing professional*
Corrado, Fred *food company executive*
Olson, Frank Albert *car rental company executive*
Politi, Beth Kukkonen *publishing services company executive*
Roob, Richard *manufacturing executive*
Scullion, Tony *pharmaceutical executive*
Showalter, David Scott *accounting executive*
Ulrich, Robert Gardner *retail food chain executive, lawyer*
Unterbeck, Axel Joachim *pharmaceutical executive, director*
Wood, James *supermarket executive*

Montville
Coleman, Earl Maxwell *publishing company executive*
Keefe, Deborah Lynn *cardiologist, educator*
Klapper, Byron D. *financial company executive*
Leeson, Lewis Joseph *pharmacist, researcher*
Teubner, Ferdinand Cary, Jr., *retired publishing company executive*

Moorestown
Apperson, Jack Alfonso *retired army officer, business executive*
Atilgan, Timur Faik *structural engineer*
Cervantes, Luis Augusto *neurosurgeon*
Delano-Condax, Kate (Kate Delano-Condax Decker) *marketing and public relations executive*
Kalidindi, Surya Raju *science educator*
McDaniel, Joanava B. *medical/surgical nurse*
Springer, Douglas Hyde *retired food company executive, lawyer*
Weeks, Maurice Richard, Jr., *educational consultant, academic administrator*

Morganville
Lechtanski, Cheryl Lee *chiropractor*
Sternfeld, Marc Howard *finance educator*

Morris Plains
Bennett, John Charles *former engineering and construction executive*
Capellos, Chris Spiridon *chemist*
Elias, Salwa Emil Ghabrial *allergist, immunologist, pediatrician*
Fielding, Stuart *psychopharmacologist*
Goldenberg, David Milton *experimental pathologist, oncologist*
Goodes, Melvin Russell *retired manufacturing company executive*
Gulfo, Adele Madelyn *pharmaceutical marketing executive*
Inez, Donna Lee *hospital administrator*
Johnson, Gregory L. *lawyer*
Kagan, Val Alexander *engineer, researcher, educator*
Larini, Ernest J. *former pharmaceuticals company executive*
Mellinger, Louis Philip *lawyer*
O'Neill, Robert Edward *business journal editor*
Otani, Mike *optical company executive*
Pluciennik, Thomas Casimir *lawyer, former assistant county prosecutor*
Spong, John Shelby *retired bishop*

Morristown
Adler, Kenneth R. *oncologist*
Anderson, David J. *corporate financial executive*
Aspero, Benedict Vincent *lawyer*
Bailye, John E. *software company executive*
Barba, Julius William *lawyer*
Baughman, Ray Henry *materials scientist*
Berkley, Peter Lee *lawyer*
Bernstein, Jan Lenore *lawyer*
Bockian, James Bernard *computer systems executive, writer*
Bromberg, Myron James *lawyer*
Cameron, Nicholas Allen *diversified corporation executive*
Carroll, Michael Patrick *assemblyman*
Clemente, Mark Andrew *lawyer*
Cote, David M. *diversified technology and manufacturing company executive*
De Rosa, William Thomas *internist, hematologist, oncologist*
Desch, Matthew J. *telecommunications industry executive*
Finkel, Marion Judith *internist, pharmaceutical administrator*
Flynn, Marie Cosgrove *portfolio manager, corporate financial executive*
Fredericks, Robert Joseph *language company executive*
Galeotti, Steven *insurance executive*
Gillen, James Robert *lawyer, insurance company executive*
Gillette, Rob *corporate financial executive*
Gilligan, Kevin *manufacturing executive*
Gorrell, Nancy S. *English language educator*
Hafer, Frederick Douglass *utilities executive*
Handler, Lauren E. *lawyer*
Haselmann, John Philip *management consultant*
Hedley, David Van Houten *retired investment banker*
Herman, Robert Lewis *cork company executive*
Herzberg, Peter Jay *lawyer*
Huettner, Richard Alfred *lawyer*
Humick, Thomas Charles Campbell *lawyer*
Hyland, William Francis *lawyer*
Jolles, Ira Hervey *lawyer*
Kearns, William Michael, Jr., *investment banker*
Kirby, Fred Morgan, II, *corporation executive*
Kittelberger, Larry E. *engineering executive*
Korf, Gene Robert *lawyer*
Kreindler, Peter Michael *lawyer*
LaVecchia, Jaynee *state supreme court justice*
Lieberman, Lester Zane *engineering company executive*
Lieblich, Frederich *real estate consultant*
MacKinnis, Ann Phelps *municipal government and land use management executive*
McConnell, John Howard *personnel management consultant, writer*
Miller, Steven H. *museum director*
Moore, Milo Anderson *banker*
Musa, John Davis *computer and infosystems executive, software reliability engineering researcher and expert, independent consultant, educator*
Nadaskay, Raymond *architect*
Newhouse, Robert J., Jr., *insurance executive*
Newman, John Merle *lawyer*
O'Grady, Dennis Joseph *lawyer*
Olcott, John Whiting *aviation executive*
Papish, Steven William *internist*
Parr, Grant Van Siclen *surgeon*
Pavlovich, John Stephen *civil engineer*
Pawelec, William John *retired electronics company executive*
Pellecchia, John Michael *lawyer*
Pokelwaldt, Robert N. *former manufacturing company executive*
Pollock, Stewart Glasson *lawyer, former state supreme court justice*
Porter, James T. *computer company executive*
Prince, Leah Fanchon *art educator and research institute administrator*
Rainal, Attilio Joseph *retired electronics engineer, researcher*
Raska, Karel *internist, cardiologist*
Robson, George T., Sr., *computer company executive*
Rose, Robert Gordon *lawyer*
Savage, R. Bruce *computer company executive*
Scott, Richard Thomas, Jr., *reproductive endocrinologist*
Sherman, Sandra Brown *lawyer*
Sperber, Martin *pharmaceutical company executive, pharmacist*
Sperling, Joy Harmon *lawyer*
Stanton, Patrick Michael *lawyer*
Starkman, Harold S. *physician, researcher*
Trien, Jay William *accountant*
Venezia, William Thomas *school system administrator, counseling consultant*
Weidenkopf, Thomas W. *human resources specialist*
WilliamS, Joseph Dalton *pharmaceutical company executive*

Mount Arlington
Cohen, Irving David *science administrator*

Mount Holly
Denniston, Marjorie McGeorge *retired elementary school educator*

Mount Laurel
Buchan, Alan Bradley *rail transportation executive, consultant*
Burnham, Lem *psychologist, think-tank executive*
Chatzidakis, Larry *assemblyman*
Hayken, Gerald Dreux *orthopedic surgeon*
Huttner, Louise Ann *mathematician, educator*
Laubach, Roger Alvin *accountant*
Li, Pearl Nei-Chien Chu *technology company executive*
Sapega, Alexander A. *sports medicine physician, orthopedic surgeon*
Topiel, Martin Stanley *epidemiologist*
Vidas, Vincent George *engineering executive*

Mountain Lakes
Daniel, Royal Thomas, III, *lawyer, engineer, accountant*
Loomis, Rebecca C. *psychology educator*
O'Gara, Barbara Ann *soap company executive*

Mountainside
Helander, Robert Charles *lawyer*
Holton, Carlotta *editor-in-chief, writer*
Horner, Shirley Jaye *columnist, writing and publishing consultant*
Lipton, Bronna Jane *marketing communications executive*
Nielsen, Gwyn English *writer, illustrator, publishing executive*
Weigele, Richard Sayre *police officer*

Mullica Hill
Bahal, Vishal *cardiologist*
Rose, Carol Ann *retired air transportation executive*

Murray Hill
Brewington, James *telecommunications industry executive*
Bruch, Ruth E. *information technology executive*
Case, Christopher *technologist*
Christy, Cindy *telecommunications industry executive*
D'Amelio, Frank Anthony *communications company executive*
Davidson, Janet G. *telecommunications industry executive*
Fleming, James William *ceramics engineer*
Mejia, Jose A. *telecommunications industry executive*
Ng, Hock Min *research scientist*
Ritchie, Dennis M. *software engineer*

Neptune
Aguiar, Adam Martin *chemist, educator*
Ahmed, Nasim *surgeon*
Alston, Goldie Venessa *early childhood educator*
Breen, Stephen P. *editorial cartoonist*
Collins, Robert T. *publisher*
Harran, Susan R. *small business owner, writer*
Hersh, Steven Lance *clinical hypnotherapist, hypnocounselor, author*
Mann, William Joseph, Jr., *gynecologic oncologist*
Manuel, Sandra Lorraine *minister*
Rice, Stephen Gary *medical educator, pediatrician, sports medicine physician*
Siegel, Harris G. *managing editor*

Neptune City
Axelrod, Glen Scott *publishing company executive, pet product company executive*

Neshanic Station
Muckenhoupt, Benjamin *retired mathematics educator*

New Brunswick
Aisenberg, Javier E. *endocrinologist, pediatrician*
Alexander, Robert Jackson *economist, educator*
Amorosa, Louis F. *endocrinologist*
August, David Allen *surgeon*
Bachmann, Gloria Ann *obstetrician, gynecologist, educator*
Bahri, Abbas *mathematician, educator*
Bahun, Sanja *literature educator, researcher*
Bancila, Edita *pathologist, educator*
Barone, Dean *physician assistant, small business owner*
Bertino, Joseph Rocco *physician, educator*
Biribauer, Richard Frank *lawyer*
Borah, Gregory Louis *plastic and reconstructive surgeon*
Bowden, Henry Warner *religion educator*
Boyarsky, Andrew Harold *surgeon*
Brilliant, Eleanor Luria *social work educator*
Bunch, Charlotte *advocate*
Burke, James Edward *consumer products company executive*
Carson, Jeffrey L. *internist*
Castello, Frank V. *pediatrician*
Chambers, John Whiteclay, II, *history professor*
Chandler, James John *surgeon, educator*
Chikindas, Michael L. *science educator*
Choi, Young K. *anesthesiologist*
Corbett, Siobhan Aiden *surgeon*
Darretta, Robert J. *pharmaceutical executive*
Das, Kiron M. *gastroenterologist*
Datta, Prasun *molecular biologist*
Day-Salvatore, Debra Lynn *medical geneticist*
DiPaola, Robert *internist*
Doorley, John *public relations executive, educator*
Dougherty, Neil Joseph *physical education educator, safety consultant*
Drachtman, Richard A. *pediatrician, educator*
Durnin, Richard Gerry *education educator*
Dutta, Manoranjan *economics professor*
Ehrenfeld, David William *biology professor, writer*
Ettinger, Lawrence Jay *pediatric hematologist and oncologist, educator*
Fine, Roger Seth *pharmaceutical executive, lawyer*
Fishbein, Leslie Ellen *humanities educator*
Funk, Cyril Reed, Jr., *agronomist, educator*
Garner, Charles William *educational administration educator, consultant*
Gillette, William *historian, educator*
Glasser, Paul Harold *sociologist, educator, social worker, university administrator*
Glickman, Norman Jay *economist, urban policy analyst*
Goffen, Rona *art historian, educator*
Golbe, Lawrence Ingram *neurologist*
Goldberg, Michael Ira *obstetrician, gynecologist*
Gorski, David Henry *surgeon, biomedical researcher*
Gottlieb, Alice B. *dermatologist*
Greenberg, Michael Richard *urban studies and community health educator*
Greenwald, Alfred Emanuel *retired cosmetic surgeon*
Grimes, Julia Patrice *physician, researcher*
Grob, Gerald N. *historian, educator*
Gussin, Robert Zalmon *retired healthcare company executive*
Haines, William Joseph *retired pharmaceutical executive*
Hait, William Neil *oncologist*
Hartman, Mary S. *historian, educator*
Harwood, David A. *orthopedist, surgeon*
Hassett, Afton Luevano *psychologist, educator*
Hegyi, Thomas *pediatrician*
Heisen, JoAnn Heffernan *health care company executive*
Hiatt, I. Mark *pediatrician*
Holmes, Nathaniel J. *surgeon*
Horowitz, Irving Louis *publisher, educator*
Jaluria, Yogesh *mechanical engineering educator*
Jenkins, Alyce Mitchem *writer, educator*
Jenkins, Reese V. *historian, educator*
John, Joseph F., Jr., *internist*
Johnson, James Turner *theology studies educator*
Kahn, Jeffry *mathematics professor*
Kairys, Steven W. *pediatrician, hospital administrator*
Kansfield, Norman J. *seminary president*
Kantor, Paul *information scientist, educator*
Karp, George Isaac *hematologist, oncologist*
Katz, James E. *communications educator*
Kaufman, Kenneth Roland *psychiatrist, educator*
Kelley, Donald Reed *historian*
Kemmann, Eckhard *obstetrician, gynecologist*
Kesarwala, Hermant H. *pediatrician, educator*
Khachadurian, Avedis *physician*
Killingsworth, Mark R. *economics educator, consultant*
Knapp, J. Barclay *entrepreneur*
Knuppel, Robert Alan *obstetrics-gynecology educator, healthcare consultant*
Koniaris, Soula G. *pediatrician, educator*
Kostis, John Basil *cardiologist*
Kountz, David S. *physician, educator*
Krasna, Irwin H. *pediatric surgeon, educator*
Kruskal, Martin David *mathematical physicist, astrophysicist*
Kugler, Steven L. *pediatrician, educator*
Kulikowski, Casimir Alexander *computer science and engineering educator*
Kurer, Cheryl C. *pediatric cardiologist*
Kushins, Lawrence G. *anesthesiologist, educator*
Lachance, Paul Albert *food science educator, clergyman*
Lacy, Clifton R. *internist, commissioner*
Laraya-Cuasay, Lourdes Redublo *pediatric pulmonologist, educator*
Larsen, Ralph S(tanley) *retired pharmaceutical executive*
Leddy, Joseph Patrick *orthopedist*
Lenehan, James T. *pharmaceutical executive*
Lepore, Frederick Everett *neurologist, educator*
Leventhal, Elaine A. *internist*
Leventhal, Howard *health psychology educator, researcher*
Levine, George Lewis *English language educator, literature critic*
Liao, Mei-June *biopharmaceutical company executive*
Livingston, Lee Franklin *real estate and finance consultant*
Lowry, Stephen Frederick *surgeon, educator*
Mainelis, Gediminas *research scientist, educator*
Mandel, Ruth Blumenstock *politics educator, educational association administrator, researcher*
Mann, Richard Alan *physician, educator*
Manoukian, Aram V. *gastroenterologist*
Maramorosch, Karl *virologist, educator*
Marder, Tod A. *art historian, educator*
McCormick, Richard Levis *academic administrator*
Mechanic, David *social sciences educator*
Mehta, Rajeev *neonatologist, researcher*
Midlarsky, Manus Issachar *political scientist, educator*
Mills, George Marshall *insurance consultant*
Momah, Ethel Chukwuekwe *women's health nurse*
Moreyra, Abel E. *physician, medical educator*
Morrow, Lesley Mandel *literacy and elementary education educator*
Nelson, Jack Lee *education educator*
Nissenblatt, Michael Jeffrey *medical oncologist*
Nordstrom, Karl Fredrik *geographer, educator*
Nosher, John Louis *radiologist*
Notterman, Daniel A. *pediatrician, educator, scientist*
O'Neill, William Lawrence *history professor*
Onwuchekwa, Michael O. *accountant, educator*
Ortiz, Raphael Montañez *performance artist, educator*
Ostriker, Alicia Suskin *poet*
Pallone, Nathaniel John *psychologist, educator*
Palmeri, Sebastian T. *cardiologist, educator*
Pandey, Ramesh Chandra *chemist, chemicals executive*
Paz, Harold Louis *dean, educator, internist*
Pinals, Robert Stanton *physician*
Pitchumoni, Capecomorin Sankar *gastroenterologist, educator*
Poon, Christine A. *pharmaceutical executive*
Pramer, David *microbiologist, educator, research administrator*
Price, Mitchell R. *pediatric surgeon*
Raska, Karel Frantisek Julian, Jr., *pathologist, virologist, educator*
Raskin, Ilya *biology professor*
Reed, James Wesley *social historian, educator*
Reock, Ernest C., Jr., *retired government services educator, academic director*
Rhodes, Edward Joseph *national security specialist, political scientist*
Robock, Alan *meteorology educator*
Rockoff, Hugh Touff *economist, educator*
Rodgers, Denise V. *medical educator*
Rosen, Robert Thomas *analytical and food chemist*
Rosenberg, Seymour *psychologist, educator*
Rosenthal, Susan R. *pediatrician, educator*
Russell, Louise Bennett *economist, educator*
Sachdeo, Rajesh C. *neurologist, educator*
Sage, Jacob I. *neurologist, educator*
Saidi, Parvin *hematologist, medical educator*
Salas, Max *pediatrician, educator*
Saracevic, Tefko *information science educator*
Scanlon, Jane Cronin *mathematics professor*
Schneider, Stephen Harley *medical educator*
Scholz, Peter M. *surgeon*
Scott, David Rodick *lawyer, legal educator*
Scully, John Thomas *obstetrician, gynecologist, educator*
Sisler, Glen E. *surgeon, educator*
Smith, Bonnie Gene *historian, educator*
Snyder, Barbara K. *pediatrician, educator*
Sommer, Warren K. *anesthesiologist, educator*
Sonnenberg, Frank A. *internist*
Spotnitz, Alan Jeffrey *cardiothoracic surgeon*
Stich, Stephen Peter *philosophy educator*
Strair, Roger K. *oncologist*
Strauss, Ulrich Paul *chemist, educator*
Strawderman, William E. *statistics educator*
Strickland, Dorothy *education educator*
Swee, David Ethan *physician*
Tanner, Daniel *curriculum theory educator*
Tedrow, John Charles Fremont *soils educator*
Tiger, Lionel *social scientist, anthropology consultant*
Toby, Jackson *sociologist, educator*
Totten, Lisa Ann *science educator*
Treiman, David Murray *neurology educator*
Trelstad, Robert Laurence *pathology educator, cell biologist*
Tu, Ching-I *humanities educator, researcher*
Turock, Betty Jane *library and information science educator*
Vayda, Andrew P. *human ecology and anthropology educator*
Vintzileos, Anthony Mark *obstetrician-gynecologist*
Wang, Yanxin *research scientist*
Weibel, Charles Alexander *mathematician*
Weinstein, Melvin Phillip *physician educator*
Weiss, Lynne S. *pediatrician, educator*
Weiss, Robert Edward *urologist, educator*
Weldon, William C. *pharmaceutical executive*
Weng, George Jueng-Cious *engineering educator*
Willett, Laura R. *internist*
Wilson, Donald Malcolm *publishing executive*
Wilson, Robert Nathan *health care company executive*
Yorke, Marianne *lawyer, real estate executive*
Zatlin, Phyllis *Spanish language educator, translator*

New Bruswick
Kjer, Karl Morgan *biologist*

New Milford
Nesoff, Robert (Bob Nesoff) *newspaper publisher*
Rosato, Melissa Anne *educator*
Walsh, Joseph Michael *magazine distribution executive*

New Monmouth
Santos, Sharon Lee *parochial school educator*

New Providence
Bernstein, Nadia J. *lawyer*
Chatterji, Debajyoti *retired manufacturing company executive, educator*

Perth Amboy
Richardson-Melech, Joyce Suzanne *music educator, singer*

Phillipsburg
Drago, Joseph Rosario *urologist, educator*
Johnson, Laurie Lynn *history educator*
Richards, Jay Claude *commercial photographer, news service executive, historian*

Pilesgrove
Mohrfeld, Richard Gentel *marketing professional*

Piscataway
Balaguru, Perumalsamy *civil engineering educator*
Browning, Edward Tracy *neurobiologist, pharmacologist*
Cohen, Morrel Herman *physicist, biologist, educator*
Colaizzi, John Louis *dean*
Conney, Allan Howard *pharmacologist, researcher*
D'Aloia, G(iambattista) Peter *corporate executive*
Denhardt, David Tilton *molecular and cell biology educator*
Devlin, Thomas Joseph *physicist*
Dill, Ellis Harold *university dean*
Douglas, Michael Ronald *science educator*
Elsayed, Elsayed Abdelrazik *industrial engineer, educator*
Escobar, Javier Ignacio *psychiatrist*
Essien, Francine B. *biologist, educator*
Fecko, Mariusz Andrzej *research scientist*
Flanagan, James Loton *electrical engineer, researcher, engineering educator*
Fogiel, Max *publishing executive*
Freeman, Herbert *computer engineering educator*
Frenkiel, Richard Henry *retired systems engineer, consultant*
Gessner, Myron S. *psychiatrist, educator*
Goetz, George Edward *adult education educator*
Goldin, Gerald Alan *physicist, educator*
Hsiao, Michael S. *electrical engineer, educator*
Idol, James Daniel, Jr., *chemist, educator, inventor, consultant*
Kear, Bernard Henry *materials scientist, consultant*
Kenney, Mary R. *software engineer*
Kiddie, Thomas James *application developer, educator*
Kipen, Howard Matthew *environmental and occupational health educator*
Kivetz, Michael Adam *artist, sculptor*
Klein, Lisa Carol *materials scientist, educator*
Klein, Michael Tully *university dean, chemical engineer, consultant*
Kotliar, B. Gabriel *physics educator*
Lambert, George H. *pediatrician, educator*
Leath, Paul Larry *physicist, educator, former university official*
Lebowitz, Joel Louis *mathematical physicist, educator*
Lee, Barbara Anne *law educator, dean*
Leibowitz, Michael Jonathan *medical educator*
Lepowsky, James *mathematician, educator*
Lewis, Peter A. *energy consultant*
Lindenfeld, Peter *physics educator*
Liu, Alice Y. C. *biology professor*
Mammone, Richard James *engineering educator*
Manowitz, Paul *biochemist, researcher, educator*
McCrady, Barbara Sachs *psychologist, educator*
Menza, Matthew A. *psychiatrist*
Messing, Joachim Wilhelm *molecular biology educator*
Peterson, Donald Robert *psychologist, educator, university administrator*
Polefka, Thomas Gregory *biochemist*
Poses, Frederic M. *engineering company executive*
Quinn, Christopher Cardinal *neurobiologist, educator*
Reiley, T. Phillip *systems analyst, consultant*
Reinberg, Danny *biochemist, educator*
Rhoads, George Grant *medical epidemiologist*
Riley, David Joseph *medical educator*
Riss, Richard Michael *research economist, church history educator*
Robbins, Allen Bishop *physics educator*
Roberts, Fred Stephen *mathematician, educator*
Rosalsky, Barbara Ellen *artist, home health aide*
Sahota, Amrik *medical researcher, educator, lab administrator*
Scher, Karen Maria *illustrator, multimedia specialist, systems engineer*
Schwartz, Arthur Harold *psychiatry educator*
Schwartz, Stuart R. *psychiatrist*
Schwebel, Milton *psychologist, educator*
Seiden, David *anatomist, academic administrator*
Shanefield, Daniel Jay *ceramics engineering educator*
Sincoskie, W. David *computer engineer*
Smith, Bob *lawyer, state senator, educator*
Taft, Earl Jay *mathematics professor*
Trontell, Marie Celestine *dean*
Upton, Arthur Canfield *experimental pathologist, educator*
Wang, Tsuey Tang *science educator, venture capitalist*
Wasserman, Marlie P(arker) *publisher*
Waxman, Chaim I. *sociology educator, researcher*
Welkowitz, Walter *biomedical engineer, educator*
West, Mark Otto *psychology educator*
White, Helene R. *sociologist, educator*
Wing, Michael James *telecommunications executive*
Yacowitz, Harold *biochemist, nutritionist*
You, Aleta *education educator*
Yuen, Wing Ho *electrical engineer, researcher*
Zhang, Li *engineer, researcher*
Zimmermann, Frank Martin *physicist, surface scientist, educator*

Pitman
Carpenter, Hoyle Dameron *music educator emeritus*
Cloues, Edward Blanchard, II, *lawyer*

Plainfield
Allen, Stuart (Stuart Allen Sup) *film and television company executive*
Bober, Joanne L. *lawyer*
Cox, Robert C. *insurance company executive*
DeFreitas, Douglas Davis *small business owner*
Frost, David *former biology educator, medical editor, consultant*
Green, Gerald B. *state legislator*
Holdorf, Harry Hulbert *health services administrator*
Ireland, Christopher P. *music educator*
Johnson, Lonnie L., Jr., *information specialist*
Krump, Paul J. *insurance company executive*
Limpert, John H., Jr., *fund raising executive*
Mattson, Joy Louise *oncological nurse*
O'Reilly, Michael *corporate financial executive*
Reeder, Hubert *elementary school educator*
Thomas, William Joseph *secondary school educator, administrator*

Plainsboro
Devine, Hugh James, Jr., *marketing executive, consultant*
Dezii, Christopher Michael *medical researcher, organ transplant nurse*
Lansing, Martha Hempel *internist*
Schreyer, William Allen *retired investment firm executive*
Spiegel, Phyllis *public relations consultant, journalist*
Tenner, Edward *publishing executive, writer*

Pleasantville
Applewhite, Kim *music company executive, educator*
Etim, Terris *geriatrics nurse*
London, Charlotte Isabella *secondary education educator, reading specialist*
Sinderbrand, David I. *lawyer*

Point Pleasant
Albano, Pasquale Charles *management educator, management and organization development consultant*
Marjanczyk, Joseph Anicetus *priest*

Point Pleasant Beach
Herr, Philip Michael *lawyer, accountant*

Pomona
Colijn, Geert Jan *academic administrator, political scientist*
Constantelos, Demetrios John *priest, educator*
Mench, Fred Charles *classics educator*
Paul, Edward *chemistry professor*
Poorman, Ronald James *music educator*
Sharon, Yitzhak Yaakov *physicist, researcher*
Sutman, Francis Xavier *university dean*

Pompton Plains
Meyer, Chester F. *language educator, writer*
Shrem, Charles Joseph *metals corporation executive*

Port Elizabeth
Ficcaglia, Leslie M. *psychologist, portrait artist*
Gross, Robert Floyd *music educator, composer*

Port Murray
Kunzler, John Eugene *physicist*

Port Norris
Canzonier, Walter Jude *shellfish aquaculturist*

Princeton
Aarsleff, Hans *linguistics educator*
Ackourey, Peter Paul *lawyer*
Adler, Stephen Louis *physicist*
Alexe, Gabriela *research scientist*
Allen, Diogenes *clergyman, philosophy educator*
Allen, Stanley T. *architect, dean, educator*
Altmann, Jeanne *zoologist, educator*
Altmann, Stuart Allen *biologist, educator*
Anderson, Ellis Bernard *retired lawyer, pharmaceutical company executive*
Anderson, Philip W. *physicist*
Armstrong, Richard Stoll *minister, educator, writer, poet*
Arunasalam, Vickramasingam (Willie) *retired physicist*
Bahcall, John Norris *astrophysicist*
Balch, Stephen Howard *professional society administrator*
Ballou, Janice Donelon *research director*
Barlow, Walter Greenwood *public opinion analyst, management consultant*
Bartolini, Robert Alfred *electrical engineer, researcher*
Basáñez, Miguel Ebergenyi *opinion pollster, political science educator*
Bassler, Bonnie *molecular biologist*
Beidler, Marsha Wolf *lawyer*
Belshaw, George Phelps Mellick *bishop*
Bergman, Edward Jonathan *lawyer, educator*
Bergman, Richard Isaac *health information company executive*
Bergman, Victoria Besterman *small business owner, consultant*
Bermann, Sandra Lekas *English language educator*
Berridge, Mary Lloyd *photographer*
Billington, David Perkins *civil engineering educator*
Blackman, Sue Anne Batey *economics researcher*
Blair, David William *mechanical engineer*
Blinder, Alan Stuart *economist, educator*
Bogan, Elizabeth Chapin *economist, educator*
Bogucki, Peter Ignatius *archaeologist*
Bombieri, Enrico *mathematician, educator*
Bonini, William Emory *geophysics educator*
Boretz, Naomi Messinger *artist, educator*
Bourgain, Jean *mathematician*
Bowersock, Glen Warren *historian, educator*
Boyer, M. Christine *architecture educator*
Brinkman, William Frank *physicist, research executive*
Broad, Barbara Prentice *retired real estate agent*
Brombert, Victor Henri *literature educator, author*
Browder, William *mathematician, educator*
Brown, Leon Carl *history educator*
Bryan, Kirk, Jr., *research meteorologist, research oceanographer*
Bunnell, Peter Curtis *photography and art educator, museum curator*
Campbell, Mildred Corum *business owner, nurse*
Campbell, Robert Emmett *retired health products executive, medical association administrator*
Carver, David Harold *physician, educator*
Cavanaugh, James Henry *medical corporate executive, former government official*
Chamberlin, John Stephen *investor, former cosmetics company executive*
Chang, Sun-Yung Alice *mathematics professor*
Chazelle, Bernard *computer science educator*
Chow, Gregory Chi-Chong *economist, educator*
Christman, Edward Arthur *physicist*
Coffey, Joseph Irving *international affairs educator*
Connelly, John F. *communications executive*
Cook, Michael Allan *social sciences educator*
Cooper, Joel *psychology educator*
Cooper, John Madison *philosophy educator*
Cooper, Michael R. *dean*
Corngold, Stanley Alan *German and comparative literature educator, writer*
Cox, Douglas Lynn *financial corporation executive*
Craigie, James R. *consumer products company executive, former sports equipment apparel company executive*
Crawford, Franklin David *publishing company executive*
Curschmann, Michael Johann Hendrik *retired German language and literature educator*
Davidson, Ronald Crosby *physicist, researcher*
Debenedetti, Pablo Gaston *chemical engineering educator*
Deligne, Pierre René *mathematician*
De Lung, Jane Solberger *independent sector executive*
Diller, Elizabeth E. *architect, educator, artist*
Doig, Jameson Wallace *political science educator*
Dovey, Brian Hugh *health care products company executive, venture capitalist*
Drakeman, Donald Lee *biotechnology company executive, lawyer*
Drakeman, Lisa N. *biotechnology company executive*
Durst, Robert Joseph, II, *lawyer*
Dyson, Freeman John *physicist, educator*
Ermolaev, Herman Sergei *Slavic languages educator*
Evslin, Tom *internet telephone service executive*
Farley, Edward Raymond, Jr., *mining and manufacturing company executive*
Feeney, John Robert *banker*
Fefferman, Charles Louis *mathematics professor*
Fernholz, Erhard Robert *investment executive*
File, Joseph *research physics engineer*
Fisch, Nathaniel Joseph *physicist*
Fitch, Val Logsdon *physics educator*
Flanagan, Theresa *quality assurance professional*
Florey, Klaus Georg *chemist, pharmaceutical consultant*
Ford, Jeremiah, III, *architect*
Forester, Gary P. *gastroenterologist*
Fox, Mary Ann Williams *librarian*
Freeman, Bruce George *fundraising consultant*
Fried, Eleanor Reingold *psychologist, educator*
Friedberg, Aaron Louis *political science educator*
Gallo, Ruben *Latin American literature educator, art critic*
Galloway, Patricia Denese *civil engineer*
Ganoe, Charles Stratford *banker, consultant*
Geertz, Clifford James *anthropology educator*
George, Mary Wiedenbeck *reference librarian, educator*
George, Thomas *artist*
Gillespie, Thomas William *theological seminary administrator, religion educator*
Gillham, John Kinsey *chemical engineering educator*
Gillispie, Charles Coulston *history of science educator*
Gilpin, Robert George, Jr., *political science educator*
Girgus, Joan Stern *psychologist, university administrator*
Glassman, Irvin *mechanical and aeronautical engineering educator, consultant*
Glucksberg, Sam *psychology educator*
Goddard, Peter *academic administrator, mathematical physicist*
Goheen, Robert Francis *classicist, educator, former ambassador*
Goldblatt, Barry Lance *manufacturing executive*
Goldfarb, Irene Dale *retired financial planner*
Gordenker, Leon *political sciences educator*
Gould, Elizabeth *neuroscientist, educator*
Grabar, Oleg *retired art educator*
Grafton, Anthony Thomas *history professor*
Graham, Nancy Love *music educator*
Grant, Peter Raymond *biologist, researcher, educator*
Graves, Michael *architect, educator*
Greenman, Jane Friedlieb *lawyer, human resources executive*
Greenstein, Fred Irwin *political science educator*
Griffith, Ruth Marie *religious studies educator*
Grigger, Jane Elizabeth *earth science educator, photographer*
Grisham, Larry Richard *physicist*
Gross, Charles Gordon *psychology educator, neuroscientist*
Grossman, Allen Neil *lawyer*
Groves, John Taylor, III, *chemist, educator*
Gu, Henry Hongsheng *pharmacist, researcher*
Gund, Gordon *venture capitalist, professional sports team executive*
Gunning, Robert Clifford *mathematician, educator*
Haberman, Shelby Joel *statistician, educator*
Habicht, Christian Herbert *history professor*
Harford, James Joseph *writer*
Harman, Gilbert Helms *philosophy educator*
Harvey, Norman Ronald *retired finance company executive*
Haxby, James Van Loan *psychologist, educator*
Haynes, William Forby, Jr., *retired internist, cardiologist, educator*
Hearn, Ruby Puryear *foundation executive*
Henkel, William *financial services executive*
Hill, James Scott *lawyer*
Hillier, James *technology management executive, researcher*
Hillier, J(ames) Robert *architect*
Hirschman, Albert Otto *political economist, educator*
Hitz, Frederick Porter *public and international affairs educator*
Hochschwender, Karl Albert *international trade and government relations consultant*
Hoebel, Bartley Gore *psychology educator*
Hollander, Lawrence Jay *marketing executive*
Hollander, Robert B., Jr., *Romance languages educator*
Holt, Philetus Havens, III, *architect*
Hough, Robert Alan *civil engineer*
Howarth, William (Louis Howarth) *education educator, writer*
Hulse, Russell Alan *physicist*
Huse, David A. *physicist, educator*
Hut, Piet *astrophysics educator*
Hynes, Samuel *English language educator, author*
Jackson, Roy *chemical engineering educator*
Jacobs, William Paul *botanist, educator*
Jenkins, Edward Beynon *research astronomer*
Johnson, Barbara Piasecka *philanthropist, art historian and collector, business investor*
Johnston, Robert Fowler *venture capitalist*
Jordan, William Chester *history educator*
Kahneman, Daniel *psychology educator*
Karpoff, Michael Steven *lawyer*
Kassof, Allen H. *foundation administrator*
Kateb, George Anthony *political science educator*
Katzenbach, Nicholas deBelleville *lawyer*
Kauzmann, Walter Joseph *chemistry professor*
Kawarsky, Jay A. *music educator, conductor, composer*
Kehrt, Allan William *architect*
Kelly, Paul J. *lab administrator, physician, researcher*
Kenen, Peter Bain *economist, educator*
Kenny, Robert *lawyer*
Kenyon, Regan Clair *educational research executive*
Khutoryansky, Naum M. *mathematician, educator*
King, Alfred Meehan *financial executive*
Knoepflmacher, Ulrich Camillus *literature educator*
Kobayashi, Hisashi *computer scientist, dean*
Kohn, Joseph John *mathematician, educator*
Kornhauser, Henry *advertising executive*
Krugman, Paul Robin *economics professor*
Kuebler, Christopher Allen *pharmaceutical executive*
Kuenne, Robert Eugene *economics professor*
Langlands, Robert Phelan *mathematician, educator*
Lavizzo-Mourey, Risa Juanita *medical foundation administrator, academic administrator*
Lazarus, Arnold Allan *psychologist, educator*
Lechner, Bernard Joseph *consulting electrical engineer*
Lehmann, Kevin *chemist, educator*
Lerner, Ralph *architect, university dean*
Levy, Kenneth *music educator*
Lewis, Bernard *Near Eastern studies educator*
Lieb, Elliott Hershel *physicist, mathematician, educator*
Lincoln, Anna *publishing executive, language educator*
Linke, Richard A. *systems engineer, researcher*
Lippincott, Walter Heulings, Jr., *publishing executive*
Liu, Bede *electrical engineering educator*
Lo, Arthur Wu-nien *electrical engineering educator*
Logue, Judith Felton *psychoanalyst, educator, professional coach*
Long, Frank Wesley, Jr., *chemist*
Lustig, Graham *artistic director*
Mackey, Louis Henry *philosophy educator*
Makadok, Stanley *management consultant*
Malkiel, Burton Gordon *economist, educator*
Malkiel, Nancy Weiss *dean, historian, educator*
Manabe, Syukuro *climatologist*
Manning, Winton Howard *psychologist, educational administrator*
Mario, Ernest *pharmaceutical company executive*
Marks, John Henry *Near Eastern studies educator*
Maskin, Eric Stark *economics professor*
Matlock, Jack Foust, Jr., *diplomat*
McClelland, Richard Lee *dentist*
McCullough, John Price *retired oil company executive*
McGinnis, James Michael *physician*
Mc Pherson, James Munro *history professor*
Metzger, Bruce Manning *clergyman, educator*
Mihram, George Arthur *mathematician*
Miles, Richard Bryant *mechanical and aerospace engineering educator*
Miller, George Armitage *psychologist, educator*
Miller, Patrick Dwight, Jr., *religion educator, minister*
Miller, Richard Mark *lawyer*
Mills, Michael James *architect*
Minton, Dwight Church *manufacturing executive*
Mollica, Joseph A. *pharmaceutical executive*
Moote, A. Lloyd *history professor*
Morgan, William Jason *geophysics educator*
Morris, Mac Glenn *advertising bureau executive*
Morrison, Toni (Chloe Anthony Morrison) *novelist*
Moynahan, Julian Lane *English language educator, author*
Muldoon, Paul *creative writing educator, poet*
Mulhauser, Craig H. *energy executive*
Narayanan, Vadake K. *management educator, consultant*
Nash, John Forbes, Jr., *research mathematician*
Nehamas, Alexander *philosophy educator*
Newlin, George Christian *writer*
Nichols, Karen *architect*
Nied, Thomas H. *media company executive*
O'Donnell, Laurence Gerard *editorial consultant, former managing editor The Wall Street Journal*
Olsen, Gregory H. *fiber optic manufacturing executive, researcher*
Ondetti, Miguel Angel *chemist, consultant*
O'Neill, Harry William *survey research company executive*
Oppenheimer, Michael *physicist*
Orphanides, Nora Charlotte *ballet educator*
Orrill, Robert Thomas *foundation executive, former history educator*
Ostriker, Jeremiah Paul *astrophysicist, educator*
Painter, Nell Irvin *historian, educator, writer*
Paret, Peter *historian*
Parry, Scott Brink *psychologist*
Pechura, Constance Mary *foundation official*
Petrin, Jurij *pharmaceutical company executive*
Plaks, Livia Basch *foundation executive*
Plevy, Arthur L. *lawyer*
Poor, Harold Vincent *electrical engineering educator*
Rabb, Theodore K. *historian, educator*
Ramaprasad, Kackadasam Raghavachar *physical chemist*
Reinhardt, Uwe Ernst *economist, educator*
Rigolot, François *French literature educator, literary critic*
Robertson, David Allan, Jr., *English educator*
Rogula, James Leroy *consumer products company executive*
Rose, Edith Sprung *retired lawyer*
Rosen, Marvin Abraham *music educator*
Rosenthal, Howard Lewis *political science educator*
Royce, Barrie Saunders Hart *physicist, researcher*
Rozman, Gilbert Friedell *sociologist, educator*
Russel, William Bailey *engineering educator*
Rutherford, Paul Harding *physicist*
Sabb, Annmarie Louise *chemist, researcher*
Salkind, Alvin J. *electrochemical engineer, biomedical engineer, educator, dean*

Sandman, Peter M. *risk communication consultant, speaker*
Sandoval, Amada *education program director*
Sapoff, Meyer *retired electronics executive*
Saville, Dudley Albert *chemical engineering educator*
Scasta, David Lynn *forensic psychiatrist*
Schafer, Carl Walter *investment executive*
Schofield, Robert E(dwin) *history educator, academic administrator*
Schorske, Carl Emil *historian, educator*
Seawright, James L., Jr., *sculptor, educator*
Seiberg, Nathan *physics educator*
Selberg, Atle *retired mathematician*
Semrod, T. Joseph *banker*
Seymour, Paul Douglas *mathematician, educator*
Shapiro, Harold Tafler *former academic administrator, economist*
Shaver, Philip Alcott *lawyer*
Shear, Ione Mylonas *archaeologist*
Shear, Theodore Leslie, Jr., *archaeologist, educator*
Shenk, Thomas Eugene *molecular biology educator, academic administrator*
Shimizu, Yoshiaki *art historian, department chairman*
Shimura, Goro *mathematician, educator*
Showalter, Elaine *humanities educator*
Sierocki, John Stanley *oncologist*
Silbergeld, Jerome Leslie *art historian, educator*
Silverman, Jane Aresty *not-for-profit organizational consultant*
Sinharay, Sandip *statistician, researcher*
Spence, Donald Pond *psychologist, psychoanalyst*
Spicer, Michael E. *lab administrator*
Stackhouse, Max Lynn *religious studies educator*
Starr, Paul Elliot *sociologist, writer, editor, educator*
Stengel, Robert Frank *engineering and applied science educator*
Stern, Bruce H. *lawyer*
Stern, Gail Frieda *historical association director*
Sterzer, Fred *research physicist*
Stillinger, Frank Henry *chemist, educator*
Sugerman, Abraham Arthur *psychiatrist, educator*
Szaban, Marilyn C. *small business owner*
Szwalbenest, Benedykt Jan *lawyer*
Taylor, Edward Curtis *chemistry professor*
Taylor, Joseph Hooton, Jr., *radio astronomer*
Theroux, William Gerard *lawyer*
Tienda, Marta *demographer, educator*
Tierney, Bill *university athletic coach*
Tilghman, Shirley Marie *academic administrator, biology professor*
Tomson, Jon Scott *business professional*
Torquato, Salvatore *materials science and chemistry educator*
Tremaine, Scott Duncan *astrophysicist*
Treu, Jesse Isaiah *venture capitalist*
Trussell, James *economist, educator, dean*
Tsui, Daniel C. *electrical engineer, physicist*
Tucker, Joshua Aaron *political scientist*
Ufford, Charles Wilbur, Jr., *lawyer*
Unruh, Howard K., Jr., *military officer, university administrator*
Vahaviolos, Sotirios John *electrical engineer, researcher, engineering executive*
Van Houten, Franklyn Bosworth *geologist, educator*
Verdu, Sergio *engineering educator*
Villafranca, Joseph J. *pharmaceutical executive, chemistry educator*
Voevodsky, Vladimir *mathematician*
von der Schmidt, Edward, III, *neurosurgeon, veterinarian*
Wei, Fong *nephrologist*
Wei, James *chemical engineering educator, academic dean*
Weiss, Renée Karol *editor, musician*
West, Charles Converse *retired theologian*
West, Cornel *humanities educator, writer*
Westoff, Charles Francis *demographer, educator*
Wheeler, John Archibald *physicist, educator*
Whipple, William, Jr., *government policy consultant, writer*
White, Morton Gabriel *philosopher, historian*
Wieschaus, Eric F. *molecular biologist, educator*
Wightman, Arthur Strong *physicist, researcher*
Wightman, Ludmilla G. Popova *language educator, foreign educator, translator*
Wildnauer, Richard Harry *pharmaceutical executive*
Wiles, Andrew J. *mathematician, educator*
Williams, Brown F *media services company executive*
Williams, C(harles) K(enneth) *poet, literature and writing educator*
Willig, Robert Daniel *economics professor*
Willingham, Warren Willcox *psychologist, testing service executive*
Wilmerding, John *art history educator, museum curator*
Winn, Paul T. *electronics executive*
Witkin, Evelyn Maisel *retired geneticist*
Witten, Edward *mathematical physicist*
Zatz, Irving J. *structural engineer*
Zhao, Wenyi *systems analyst*
Ziolkowski, Theodore Joseph *comparative literature educator*

Princeton Junction
Amenta, Peter Sebastian *pathologist*
Bair, William Alois *engineer*
Butorac, Frank George *librarian, educator*
Cohen, Florence Emery *retired financial services executive*
Denlinger, Edgar Jacob *electronics engineering research executive*
DiSciullo, Alan Michael *lawyer*
Haddad, James Henry *chemical engineer, consultant*
Lull, William Paul *engineering consultant*
Norback, Craig Thomas *writer*
Wu, Huan-ter *statistician*

Rahway
Garcia, Maria Luisa *biochemist, researcher*
Kaczorowski, Gregory John *biochemist, researcher, science administrator*
Reldan, Robert Ronald *law educator, psychological consultant, poet*
Reynolds, Glenn Franklin *medicinal research scientist*

Ramsey
Underwood, Steven Clark *publishing executive*
Weber, Walter Winfield, Jr., *lawyer, director*

Rancocas
Rowan, Henry M. *electrical engineer*

Randolph
Charm, Joel Barry *management consultant*
Chen, Kevin S. *corporate executive, consultant, educator*
Rathore, Uma Pandey *utilities executive*
Scheneck, Carol Ann *lawyer, educator*
Zulauf, Sander (William) *poet, educator, editor*

Raritan
Alatzas, George *delivery service company executive*
Bower, David Norman *music educator, researcher*

Red Bank
Anderson, James Francis *lawyer*
Arnone, Michael John *dentist, former state legislator*
Auerbach, Philip Gary *lawyer*
Braddom, Randall Lee *physiatrist, educator*
Brown, Valerie Anne *psychiatric social worker, educator*
Calabro, Joseph John, III, *physician*
Chynoweth, Alan Gerald *retired telecommunications research executive, consultant*
Dreman, David Nasaniel *investment counselor, security analyst*
Fred, Rogers Murray, III, *veterinary oncologist*
Gutentag, Patricia Richmond *social worker, family counselor, occupational therapist*
Hempstead, George H., III, *lawyer, diversified company executive*
Hertz, Daniel Leroy, Jr., *entrepreneur*
Hovnanian, Ara K. *real estate developer*
Hovnanian, Kevork S. *real estate developer*
Hughes, Barnard *actor*
Lucky, Robert Wendell *electrical engineer*
Macdonald, Donald Arthur, Jr., *physician, surgeon*
McWhinney, Madeline H. (Mrs. John Denny Dale) *economist, director*
Michaelson, Peter Lee *lawyer*
Neff, Robert Carey *lawyer*
O'Hern, Daniel Joseph *retired state supreme court justice*
Reinhart, Peter Sargent *corporate executive, lawyer*
Schneider, Sol *electronic engineer, consultant, researcher*
Sorsby, James Larry *home building company executive*
Sullivan, Timothy Patrick *telecommunications company executive*
Terris, Albert *metal sculptor*
Waldman, Daniel M. *lawyer*
Warshaw, Michael Thomas *lawyer*

Ridgefield
Riggs, Rory B. *pharmaceutical executive*
Tracey, Matthew Sean *music educator, musician*

Ridgefield Park
D'Avella, Bernard Johnson, Jr., *publishing company executive, lawyer*
Litwinowicz, Anthony *information specialist, researcher*

Ridgewood
Arnt, Georgia Lee *psychiatric social worker*
Baddoura, Rashid Joseph *emergency medicine physician*
Clements, Lynne Fleming *marriage and family therapist, application developer*
Ege, Hans Alsnes *securities company executive*
Harris, Micalyn Shafer *lawyer, educator, arbitrator, consultant, mediator*
Healey, Frank Henry *retired research executive*
Hinckley, Deborah Clark *language services professional*
Holt, Natalie Frances *physician*
Kiernan, Richard Francis *publisher*
Lucca, John James *retired dentist*
Mitgang, Lee David *journalist, writer, educator, foundation administrator*
O'Leary, Paul Gerard *investment executive*
Seigel, Jan Kearney *lawyer*
Sommer, Robert George *public relations executive*
Sumers, Anne Ricks *ophthalmologist, museum director*
Tohme, Jack Fouad *endocrinologist*
Trocano, Russell Peter *lawyer*
Tuthill, Jay Dean, II, *investment executive*
Warner, John Edward *advertising executive*

River Edge
Gass, Manus M. *accountant, business executive*
Jones, Thomas Owen *computer industry executive*

River Vale
Clemen, John Douglas *lawyer*

Rivervale
LaGreca, Thomas Richard *flooring company executive, lawyer*
Moderacki, Edmund Anthony *music educator, conductor*
Posamentier, Alfred Steven *mathematics educator, university administrator*

Rochelle Park
Olzerowicz, Sharon *information technology executive*
Schapiro, Jerome Bentley *chemicals executive*

Rockaway
Allen, Dorothea *secondary school educator*
Bruno, Anthony D. *lawyer*
Catlin, Robert Thomas *city planning consultant*
Gebauer, Kurt Manfred *management executive*
Kelsey, Ann Lee *library administrator*
Laine, Cleo (Clementina Dinah Dankworth) *singer*

Rockleigh
Siracusano, Louis H. *communications company executive*

Roseland
Bennett, John K. *lawyer*
Besser, Albert Gordon *lawyer*
Butler, Gary C. *computer company executive*
Clemente, Celestino *physician, surgeon*
Danzis, Colin Michael *lawyer*
Eakeley, Douglas Scott *lawyer*
Eichler, Burton Lawrence *lawyer*
Foster, M. Joan *lawyer*
Golden, Robert Charles *finance company executive*
Graham, Patricia *information technology executive*
Haviland, Richard John *data processing company executive*
Hayden, Joseph A., Jr., *lawyer*
Levithan, Allen B. *lawyer*
Lowenstein, Alan Victor *lawyer*
Malafronte, Donald *health executive*
McMahon, Edward Richard *lawyer*
Panagides, John *pharmacologist*
Ploscowe, Stephen Allen *lawyer*
Positan, Wayne John *lawyer*
Schenkler, Bernard *lawyer*
Smith, Wendy Hope *lawyer*
Stern, Herbert Jay *lawyer*
Sugahara, Byron Masahiko *transportation company executive*
Tarino, Gary Edward *lawyer*
Taub, Henry *retired computer services company executive*
Vanderbilt, Arthur T., II, *lawyer*
Weinbach, Arthur Frederic *computer company executive*
Wells, Theodore V., Jr., *lawyer*
Wovsaniker, Alan *lawyer, educator*

Roselle
Budanitsky, Sander *lawyer*
Di Marco, Barbaranne Yanus *principal*
Meister, Karen Olivia *secondary school educator*

Roselle Park
Scarpelli, Vito *adult education educator, administrator*

Rosemont
Torricelli, Robert G. *former senator*

Rumson
Brenner, Theodore Engelbert *retired trade association executive*
Creamer, William Henry, III, *retired insurance company executive*
Rowe, Harrison Edward *electrical engineer*
Strong, George Hotham *private investor, consultant*
Swartz, Renee Becker *civic volunteer*
Topham, Sally Jane *ballet educator*

Rutherford
Baker, Don L. *band director*
Bealmear, Michael William *financial service executive, technology consultant*
Gerety, Peter Leo *archbishop*
Petrie, Ferdinand Ralph *illustrator, artist*
Tortorello, Nicholas John *public opinion and market research company executive*

Saddle Brook
Clifton, Nelida *social worker*
Kelsey, David *manufacturing executive*
Pearlman, Peter Steven *lawyer*
Roth, Steven *realty company executive*

Saddle River
Goodman, Jerome David *psychiatrist*
Lasser, Gail Maria *psychologist, educator*
McClelland, William Craig *paper company executive*
Noyes, Robert Edwin *publisher, writer*
Roes, Nicholas A. *communications executive*
Weissmann, Heidi Seitelblum *radiologist, educator*

Salem
Carpenter, Margaret S. (Molly Carpenter) *artist*
Seabrook, John Martin *retired food products executive, chemical engineer*

Sayreville
Corman, Randy *lawyer*

Scotch Plains
Hallard, Wayne Bruce *retired economist*
Johnsen, Karen Kennedy *marketing professional*
Kalischer, Alan Lester *cardiologist*
Klock, John Henry *lawyer*
Kraus, Robert H. *lawyer*
Margiotta, Joseph M. *printing company executive*
Marlowe, Chris Sean *safety engineer*
Plumeri, Joseph James, II, *financial executive*
Shaw, Alan *lawyer, corporate executive*

Sea Girt
Cleary, Martin Joseph *real estate company executive*

Sea Isle City
Tull, Theresa Anne *retired diplomat*

Seaside Heights
Cone, Michael McKay *venture capitalist*

Secaucus
Bailey, Steven Frederick *publishing executive*
Blackman, Brenda *newscaster*
Cho, Alina *anchor*
Fitzpatrick, Harold Francis *lawyer*
Goldstein, Ira J. *lawyer*
Liao, Paul Foo-Hung *electronics executive*
Lynch, Joseph Michael *engineer, consultant*
Pinsker, Penny Collias (Pangeota Pinsker) *television producer*
Sakiewicz, Nick *professional sports team executive*
Silver, Adam *sports association executive*
Stern, Emanuel *real estate developer*
Syms, Marcy *retail executive*
Williams, Brian *news anchor, correspondent*

Sewell
Wright, William Cook *archivist, historian, researcher*

Shiloh
Dickson, Robert W., III, *internist*
Garrison, John Raymond *organization executive*

Ship Bottom
Shackleton, Richard James *lawyer, director*

Short Hills
Benn, Theodore Alexander (Alec Benn) *writer*
Chaiken, Bernard Henry *internist, gastroenterologist*
Fast, Kenneth H. *lawyer*
Gibson, William Lee *financial consultant*
Hazlehurst, Robert Purviance, Jr., *lawyer*
Howe, James Everett *investment company executive*
Hurlbut, Terry Allison *pathologist*
Lohse, Austin Webb *banker*
Loren, Allan Z. *business information company executive*
MacKinnon, Malcolm D(avid) *retired insurance company executive*
Marshall, John Patrick *lawyer*
Mebane, William Black *controller, financial consultant*
Ogden, Maureen Black *retired state legislator*
Price, Michael F. *money management executive*
Robbins-Wilf, Marcia *educational consultant*
Schaefer, Charles James, III, *advertising agency executive, consultant*
Schirmeister, Charles F. *retired lawyer*
Siegfried, David Charles *retired lawyer*
Soderlind, Sterling Eugene *newspaper industry consultant*
Spector, Shelly *company executive*
Wharton, Lennard *engineering company executive*
Winter, Ruth Grosman (Mrs. Arthur Winter) *journalist*
Yorinks, Adrienne Berg *artist, illustrator*

Shrewsbury
Hopkins, Charles Peter, II, *lawyer*
Jones, Charles Hill, Jr., *banker*
Westerman, Liane Marie *research scientist executive*

Sicklerville
Miller, Audrey Thornton *retired educational administrator*

Skillman
Brill, Yvonne Claeys *engineer, consultant*
Eiger, Richard William *retired publisher*
Gauff, Susan Tyrrell *marketing and human resources executive*
Hackel, Adam William *music educator*
Liro, Joseph R. *diversified financial services company executive*
Rhett, Haskell Emery Smith *educator*
Wheelock, Keith Ward *retired consulting company executive, educator*

Smithville
Bergeron, Robert Francis, Jr., (Terry Bergeron) *software engineer*

Somers Point
Beakley, Robert Paul *lawyer*
Berenato, Anthony Francis *financial executive*
Hughes, David Robert *gaming company executive*
Hunter, Kevin Edward *neurologist*

Somerset
Aronson, Louis Vincent, II, *manufacturing executive*
Becker, Phyllis *systems analyst*
Bess, Leon *application developer, consultant, systems analyst*
Brophy, Joseph Thomas *information company executive*
Chivukula, Upendra J. *assemblyman, electrical engineer*
Dahbany, Avivah *psychologist, educator*
De Salva, Salvatore Joseph *retired pharmacologist, toxicologist*
Eggleton, Benjamin John *physics researcher*
Ilogu, Noel Obiajulu *physician*
Jones, Andrew William *pharmaceutical executive*
Lee, Thai Theresa *information technology executive*
Lichtig, Leo Kenneth *health economist*
Sell, Noel Bruce *music educator*
Sofia, R. D. *pharmacologist*
Wallfesh, Henry Maurice *business communications company executive, editor, writer*
Young, James Earl *ceramics educator, educational administrator*

Somerville
Alfred, Siham A. *mathematician, educator*
Biondi, Peter J. *assemblyman*
Dobrinsky, Susan Elizabeth *human resources director*
Dreier, William Alan *lawyer*
Dunbar, Holly Jean *communications and public relations executive*
Fox, James Allen *allergist, pediatrician, immunologist*
Herman, David J. *epidemiologist*
Hutcheon, Peter David *lawyer*
Ligorano, Michael Kenneth *lawyer*
O'Brian, Harold Samuel *lawyer*
Sponzilli, Edward George *lawyer*
Thompson, William *director*
Weisblatt, Barbara Ann *secondary school educator*
Yurasko, Frank Noel *judge*

South Amboy
Moskal, Anthony John *former dean, professor, management and education consultant*
Panagis, Pete *writer*

South Bound Brook
Weir, Sonja Ann *artist*

South Hackensack
Cohen, Brett I. *health products executive*
Jacobs, George Braun *neurosurgeon*
Stier, Roger Edwin *chemist, researcher*
Wille, Rosanne Louise *higher education administrator*

South Orange
Amar, A. D. *business educator, management consultant*
Bao, Xue-Ming *librarian, educator*
Collins, John W., Jr., *retired military officer, technologist, educator*
Delo, Ellen Sanderson *lawyer*
DeVaris, Panayotis Eric *architect*
Deyrup, Marta Mestrovic *academic librarian, writer*
Hackett, Mims, Jr., *state legislator*
Hanbury, Kevin M. *dean, priest*
Hansell, Phyllis Shanley *nursing educator, administrator, researcher, consultant*
Hecht, Marion B. *mental health counselor, mental health therapist*
Long, Philip Lee *information systems executive*
Nowik, John David *music educator, musician*
Sheeran, Robert *academic administrator*
Stringile, Marie Elizabeth *educational administrator*

Thonet, John A. *environmental planning and engineering consultant*
Wright, Barbara Wincklhofer *nursing educator*

South Plainfield
Barone, Joseph G. *surgeon, urologist, pediatrician*
Choi, Soon Chae *orthopaedic surgeon*
Hunsinger, Doyle J. *electronics executive*
Kennedy, John William *engineering company executive*
Santoro, Frank Anthony *lawyer*

South River
Jackiewicz, Frederick Waclaw *priest*

Southampton
Callaway, Ben Anderson *journalist*
Knortz, Walter Robert *accountant, former insurance company executive*

Sparta
Guida, Pat *information broker, literature chemist*
McHose, Alison Littell *assemblywoman*
McMeen, Elmer Ellsworth, III, *retired lawyer, guitarist*
Rosser, Alvin Raymon *artist*
Spence, Robert Leroy *publishing executive*
Truran, William Richard *electrical engineer*

Spring Lake
Bonhag, Thomas Edward *insurance company executive, financial planner, financial consultant*
D'Luhy, John James *investment banker*
Ernst, John Louis *management consultant*
Harrigan, John Thomas, Jr., *physician, obstetrician-gynecologist*
O'Connor, Francis X. *financial executive*
Pandolfe, John Thomas, Jr., *lawyer*

Springfield
Baker, Alden *artist*
Kerner, Michael Bernard *gastroenterologist*
Kwartler, Jed Aryeh *otolaryngologist*
Marino, Natalie Marie *artist*
Mytelka, Arnold Krieger *lawyer*
Newler, Jerome Marc *accountant*
Panish, Morton B. *retired physical chemist*
Reeve, Christopher *actor*
Shilling, A. Gary *economic consultant, investment advisor*
Toresco, Donald *automotive executive*
Wosnitzer, Morey *urologist*

Stanton
Kille, John William, Jr., *toxicology and biomedical product consultant*

Stewartsville
Busch, Beverly Gail *English language educator, literature educator, instructional resource center administrator*

Stirling
Walsh, Peter Joseph *physics educator*

Stockholm
dePaolo, Ronald Francis *editor, writer*

Stockton
Mahon, Robert *photographer*
Schoenherr, John (Carl) *artist, illustrator*
Taylor, Rosemary *artist*

Stone Harbor
Koss, Rosabel Steinhauer *retired health and physical education educator*

Stratford
Gallagher, R. Michael *academic administrator*
Li, David Wan-Cheng *cell biologist*
Stein, T. Peter *medical educator*
Vitale, Patty A. *pediatrician, consultant, medical educator*

Succasunna
Romance, Mary C. *library director*

Summit
Burbank, Robinson Derry *crystallographer*
Caming, H. W. William *lawyer, consultant*
Carniol, Paul J. *plastic and reconstructive surgeon, otolaryngologist*
Cooper, John Weeks *lawyer*
Fuess, Billings Sibley, Jr., *advertising executive*
Fukui, Hatsuaki *electrical engineer, art historian*
Gerathy, E. Carroll *former insurance executive, real estate developer*
Good, Joan Duffey *artist*
Halpern, Steven Lon *physician*
Hickman, J. Kenneth *accounting company executive*
Hodosh, Richard M. *neurosurgeon*
Keith, Garnett Lee, Jr., *investment executive*
Kenyon, Edward Tipton *lawyer*
Lewis, Donald Emerson *banker*
Lindars, Laurence Edward *retired health care products executive*
Longfield, William Herman *health care company executive*
Macioce, Frank Michael *lawyer, financial services company executive*
Malin, Robert Abernethy *investment management executive*
Mueller, Paul Henry *retired bank executive*
Pace, Leonard *retired management consultant*
Pfaltz, Hugo Menzel, Jr., *lawyer*
Phillips, James Charles *physicist, researcher*
Rosensweig, Ronald Ellis *scientist consultant*
Rossey, Paul William *school superintendent, university president*
Rousseau, Irene Victoria *artist*
Saffer, Judith Mack *lawyer*
Singleterry, Gary Lee *investment banker*
Starks, Florence Elizabeth *retired special education educator*
Stone, Frank Bush *lawyer*
Vandenberg, Joka Maria *physicist, researcher*
Weinstein, Stephen Brant *communications executive, researcher, writer*
Wissbrun, Kurt Falke *chemist, consultant*
Woller, James Alan *lawyer*
Young, Diane Caroline *pharmaceutical executive*
Zachary, Louis George *chemical company consultant*

Sussex
MacMurren, Harold Henry, Jr., *psychologist, lawyer*

Swedesboro
Lovell, Theodore *electrical engineer, consultant*

Teaneck
Allen, Brenda Joyce *management consultant, editor-in-chief*
Alperin, Richard Martin *social worker, psychoanalyst*
Baldwin, Dorothy Leila *secondary school educator*
Brudner, Helen Gross *social sciences educator*
Bullough, John Frank *organist, music educator*
Cassimatis, Peter John *economics professor*
Coburn, Gordon *Internet company executive*
Connola, Donald Pascal, Jr., *management consultant*
Daddario, Richard *chief financial officer, accountant*
Dewey, Ralph Jay *school system administrator*
Donato, Jeanne Gilam *musician*
Ehrlich, Ira Robert *mechanical engineering consultant*
Fajans, Jack *physics educator*
Feinberg, Robert S. *plastics company executive, marketing professional*
Fjordbotten, Alf Lee *language educator*
Goldman, Eric A. *film company executive*
Gordon, Lois G. *English language educator*
Halper, June *medical center director*
Indick, Janet *sculptor*
Jackson, Millie *vocalist, songwriter, playwright, producer*
Kaplan, Howard M(ark) *lawyer*
Ladenheim, Jules Calvin *neurosurgeon*
Lafer, Fred Seymour *data processing company executive*
Lewis, Karen Ann *director*
Mahadeva, Kumar *information technology executive*
McGrath, Robert Edward *psychology educator*
Meno, John Peter *chorepiscopus*
Mirza, Muhammad Zubair *medical products executive, engineering consultant, inventor, product development company executive, researcher*
Pfeffer, Robert *chemical engineer, academic administrator, educator*
Pischl, Adolph John *school administrator*
Rudy, Willis *historian*
Scotti, Dennis Joseph *educator, researcher, consultant*
Shen, Michael *lawyer*
Smith, Susan Elizabeth *guidance director*
Solá, Victoria M. *announcer, writer*
Walker, Lucy Doris *secondary school educator, writer*
Wallmann, Jeffrey Miner *author*
Weinberg, Loretta *state legislator*
Wiener, Joel Howard *historian, educator*
Zwass, Vladimir *computer science and information systems educator*

Tenafly
Blank, Marion Sue *psychologist, educator*
Golomb, Frederick Martin *surgeon, educator*
Grieco, Michael Henry *allergy and infectious diseases physician*
Gritsman, Andrey *pathologist, poet*
Koons, Irvin Louis *design and marketing executive, graphic artist, consultant*
Levy, Norman Jay *investment banker, financial consultant*
Spike, Michele Kahn *lawyer*

Teterboro
Adams, James Mills *retired chemicals executive*
Freeman, Kenneth W. *laboratory executive*
Hagemann, Robert A. *health facility administrator*
Mohapatra, Surya N. *laboratory executive*
Prevoznik, Michael E. *health facility administrator*
Schwartz, Joyce Gensberg *pathologist*

Three Bridges
Lawrence, Gerald Graham *management consultant*

Tinton Falls
Schink, Frank Edward *electrical engineer*
Tague, Charles Francis *retired engineering, construction and real estate development company executive*
Van Winkle, William *financial planner*

Titusville
Bhattacharjya, Ashoke Sanjoy *economist, researcher*
Bridge, T(homas) Peter *psychiatrist, researcher*
Cooper, Paul *retired mechanical engineer, research director*

Toms River
Berman, Michael Barry *lawyer*
Boisseau, Jerry Philip *financial services company executive*
Bosley, Karen Lee *English and journalism educator*
Chopyk, Dan Bohdan *language educator, poet*
Donaldson, Marcia Jean *lay worker*
Fanuele, Michael Anthony *retired electronics engineer, research engineer*
Finale, Frank Louis *retired elementary school educator, writer*
Garcia, Jesus I. *medical association administrator, surgeon*
Kanarkowski, Edward Joseph *data processing company executive*
Kudryasheva, Aleksandra A. *scientist, researcher, educator*
Luzky, Leonard *law enforcement official, national guard officer, educator*
Marchese, Michael James, Jr., *radiation oncologist*
Schockaert, Barbara Ann *marketing professional*
Unger, Howard Albert *artist, photographer, educator*

Towaco
Stern, Richard Henry *advertising executive*

Trenton
Albin, Barry Todd *state supreme court justice*
Bakke, Holly C. *bank commission official*
Barclay, Warren M. *human resources specialist, researcher*
Ben-Asher, Daniel Lawrence *legislative researcher, writer*
Bigham, William J. *lawyer*
Binder, Elaine Kotell *associations consultant*
Caldwell, Dale Gilbert *state official*
Caldwell, Wesley Stuart, III, *lawyer, lobbyist*
Caspersen, Sidney J. *state agency administrator*
Castro, Ida L. *state official, former federal official*
Christopherson, Elizabeth Good *broadcast executive*
Codey, Richard James *state legislator*
Coleman, Bonnie Watson *assemblywoman*
Collins, Jack *retired state legislator*
Cooper, Mary Little *federal judge, former banking commissioner*
Cowen, Robert E. *federal judge*
Dahme, Maud *educational association administrator*
DeCotiis, Michael R. *lawyer*
Doherty, Robert Christopher *lawyer*
Farmer, John J. *state commissioner, former state attorney general*
George, Emery Edward *foreign language and studies educator, writer*
Gomez, William *orthopedist*
Greenberg, Morton Ira *federal judge*
Gupta, Rajendra Prasad *physician*
Gusciora, Reed *assemblyman*
Harvey, Peter C. *state attorney general*
Iszard, Calvin Oscar, Jr., *television production executive, public relations manager, former county freeholder*
Jelenic, Robert M. *newspaper publishing executive*
Jones, Dale Edwin *public defender*
Jones, Sarah Lucille *supervisor, consultant, principal*
Kaminski, Isabelle *pre-school educator, music educator*
Kyrillos, Joseph M., Jr., *state legislator, political organization worker*
Leipzig, Melvin *art educator*
Lockhart, Tina Marie *librarian*
Long, Virginia *state supreme court justice*
McCann, Colleen Mary *public affairs specialist, lobbyist*
McGowan, Joan Yuhas *development researcher*
McGreevey, James Edward *governor*
Miller, Velvet G. *healthcare administrator*
Mittelstadt, Mark *news service executive*
Old, Hughes Oliphant *research theologian, clergyman*
Palmer, Douglas Harold *mayor*
Poritz, Deborah T. *state supreme court chief justice, former attorney general*
Pruitt, George Albert *college president*
Rahman, Mohammed Siddiqur *environmental engineer, researcher*
Robinson, Susan Mittleman *data processing executive*
Roshon, George Kenneth *manufacturing executive*
Russell, Joyce Anne Rogers *librarian*
Samuel, Steven A. *cardiologist*
Scheiring, Michael James *college official*
Smallwood, Robert Albian, Jr., *secondary education educator*
Sterns, Joel Henry *lawyer*
Suter, Karen L. *former state banking department administrator*
Taboada, Javier Gustavo *neurologist*
Terrill, Thomas Edward *health facility administrator*
Thatsneyakul, Yaovares *physician, consultant*
Thomas, Regena L. *secretary of state*
Thompson, Anne Elise *federal judge*
Tolan, Robert Warren *pediatric infectious disease specialist*
Tucci, Mark A. *state agency administrator*
Wallace, John E. *judge*
Zanna, Martin Thomas *physician*
Zazzali, James R. *state supreme court associate justice*

Tuckerton
Foley, Eugene Arthur *accountant, consultant*

Turnersville
DePace, Nicholas Louis *physician*

Union
Applbaum, Ronald Lee *academic administrator*
Bassano, C. Louis *state legislator, fuel oil company executive*
Black, Jappie King *education educator, artist*
Bottitta, Joseph Anthony *lawyer*
Cryan, Joseph P. *assemblyman*
Darden, Barbara S. *library director*
Darden, Joseph Samuel, Jr., *health educator*
David, Ivo *artist, poet, real estate broker*
Eisenberg, Warren *retail executive*
Emanouilidis, Emanuel Vasilios *computer scientist, educator*
Feinstein, Leonard *retail executive*
Franklin, William George *manufacturing executive*
Jacobs-Carey, Sheila L. *immunologist*
Kim, Youn-Suk Ernest *economist, educator*
Lederman, Susan Sturc *public administration educator*
Lewandowski, Andrew Anthony *utilities executive, consultant*
Mark, Michael David *lawyer*
Nesoff, Irwin *social work educator, management consultant*
Newman, Stephen Alexander *chemical engineer, thermodynamicist*
Pasvolsky, Richard Lloyd *parks, recreation, and environment educator*
Samer, Bill Fred Carl *illustrator, writer, multimedia designer*
Sigmon, Scott B. *psychologist*
Suplee, Katherine Ann *lawyer*
Temares, Steven H. *retail executive*
White, Robert Leslie Gordon, Jr., *aerospace company executive*
Yoskowitz, Marlene *lawyer, educator*
Zois, Constantine Nicholas Athanasios *meteorology educator*

Union Beach
Gilmartin, Clara T. *volunteer*

Union City
Bull, Inez Stewart *pianist, editor, author, music educator, curator, coloratura soprano*
Erbe, Gary Thomas *artist*
Sheehy, Janice Ann *education technology coordinator*
Stier, Edwin H. *lawyer*
Younan, Joseph *bishop*

Upper Montclair
Adarkar, Aditya *humanities educator*
Bergen, Christopher Brooke *opera company administrator, translator, editor*
Bluestein, Sanfurd G. *radiologist*
Valdez del Alamo, Elizabeth *art historian, educator*
Vega, Carlos B. *language educator, writer*

Upper Saddle River
Cappitella, Mauro John *architect*
Jovanovich, Peter William *publishing executive*
Marron, Darlene Lorraine *real estate company executive*
Oolie, Sam *manufacturing and investment company executive*
Smith, Miranda Constance *writer, educator*
Wallace, William, III, *engineering executive*

Ventnor City
Bolton, Kenneth Albert *management consultant*
Campbell, Thomas Douglas *lawyer, consultant*
Robbins, Hulda Dornblatt *artist, printmaker*

Vernon
Megna, Steve Allan *secondary school educator*

Verona
Aronow, Edward *psychologist, educator*
Ayaso, Manuel *artist*
Brightman, Robert Lloyd *importer, textile company executive, consultant*
Greenwald, Robert *public relations executive*

Vincentown
Foster, David Ramsey *soap company executive*
Trainor, Lillian (Midge Trainor) *elections official, campaign consultant*

Vineland
Bracken, Thomas *bank executive*
Clinton, Lawrence Paul *psychiatrist*
DeVivo, Sal J. *newspaper executive*
O'Neill, Joseph Dean *lawyer*

Voorhees
Glasofer, Eric David *allergist, immunologist, pediatrician, educator*
Piermatti, Jack *dentist*
Rowello, Robert John *communications executive*
Suflas, Steven William *lawyer*

Waldwick
Lynch, Carol *director special services, psychologist*

Wall
Leupold, Herbert August *physicist*
Monaco, Robert Anthony *radiologist*
Nucciarone, A. Patrick *lawyer*
O'Neill, James Paul *psychiatrist*
Petrovich, Dorothy *elementary school educator*
Tanno, Janice Poland *financial consultant, investment advisor*

Warren
Blass, Walter Paul *consultant, management educator*
Chubb, Percy, III, *insurance company executive*
Degnan, John J. *diversified financial company executive*
DiFrancesco, Donald T. *lawyer*
DiPietro, Ralph Anthony *marketing and management consultant, educator*
Finnegan, John D. *insurance company executive*
Hartman, David G. *actuary*
Hennings, Dorothy Grant (Mrs. George Hennings) *education educator*
Jackson, John Wyant *medical products executive*
Jacobson, Gary Steven *lawyer*
Kelso, David Blair *insurance company executive*
Kozberg, Donna Walters *rehabilitation administration executive*
Kozberg, Ronald Paul *health and human services administrator*
Maull, George Marriner *music director, conductor*
Motamed, Thomas Firouz *insurance company executive*
Wildrick, Kenyon Jones *minister*

Washington
De Sanctis, Vincent *college president*

Watchung
Cohen, Melvin Irwin *retired communications systems and technology executive*
Grey, Ruthann E. *communications specialist, management consultant*
Michaelis, Paul Charles *engineering physicist executive*
Miller, John Ronald *minister*
Tornqvist, Erik Gustav Markus *chemical engineer, research scientist, consultant*

Wayne
Arthur, Ray *retail executive*
Arthur, Raymond L. *retail toy and game company executive*
Barbour, John *retail executive*
Bebele, John *manufacturing executive*
Boronico, Jess Stephen *management science educator, academic dean*
Brockett, Francesca L. *retail executive*
Bronstein, Jagoda Ewa *pediatrician*
Cetrulo, Jerry *artist, sculptor*
Cheo, Li-hsiang S. *education educator*
Derby, Deborah *retail executive*
Edelstein, Melvin *education educator*
Feldt, James E. *retail executive*
Fiedler, Laurie W. *lawyer*
Garcia, Ofelia *dean*
Gelman, Jon Leonard *lawyer*
Gollance, Robert Barnett *ophthalmologist*
Harrington, Kevin Paul *lawyer*
Heyman, Samuel J. *building materials manufacturing company executive*
Holohan, John *retail executive*
Jeffrey, Robert George, Jr., *industrial company executive*
Kardan, Mahmoud *chemist, educator*
Katz, Leandro *artist, filmmaker*
Kay, Christopher K. *retail executive*
Khoury, Hani *surgeon, educator*
Kornblum, Warren *retail executive*
Kresky, Jeffrey *music educator, writer, composer*
Li, Fuan *marketing educator, researcher*
Markee, Richard L. *retail executive*

Meeldijk, Victor Anthony *engineering professional*
Nalle, Sara Tilghman *historian, educator*
Pardo, Janette M. *archivist, librarian*
Principe, Michael Luis *political science educator*
Rogoff, Paula Drimmer *English and foreign language educator*
Salny, Abbie Feinstein *psychologist*
Schmidt, Barnet Michael *communications and electronic engineer*
Sheffield, Carole Jean *political science educator*
Speert, Arnold *academic administrator, chemistry educator*
Sullivan, Glenn D. *music educator*
Wahle, Elliott *retail executive*

Weehawken
Hobson, Burton Harold *publishing company executive*
Kelleher, Kathleen *financial services marketing specialist*
Metallo, Frances Rosebell *mathematics professor*

West Caldwell
Dixon, Jo-Ann Conte *management consultant*
Giblin, Thomas Patrick *labor union administrator, political organization administrator*
Piel, Emil J. *retired science and engineering educator*
Schiff, Robert *healthcare consulting company executive*
Sze, Melanie Chia-Yu *librarian*

West Long Branch
Dvoichenko-Markov, Demetrius *history educator*
Gaffney, Paul Golden, II, *academic administrator, military officer*
Kovacs, Aimee *conference speaker, minister*
Lutz, Francis Charles *university dean, civil engineering educator*

West Milford
Ferguson, Harley Robert *service company executive*
Stelpstra, William John *minister*

West New York
Avello, Alfredo J. *retired secondary school educator*
Gruenberg, Elliot Lewis *electronics engineer and company executive*
Kelly, Lucie Stirm Young *nursing educator*
Knopf, Claire *editor, writer*
Schmidt, Nancy Anne *psychotherapist*
Sires, Albio *legislative staff member, business owner*
Steinberg, Louis Marshall *dentist, researcher*

West Orange
Atkins, Richard Bart *film, television producer*
Bogstahl, Deborah Marcelle *marketing professional, consultant*
Bornstein, Lester Milton *retired health facility administrator*
Brodkin, Roger Harrison *dermatologist, educator*
Casella, Anthony John *cardiologist*
Cuozzi, William Francis, Jr., *lawyer*
De Lisa, Joel Alan *rehabilitation physician, rehabilitation research executive*
Dispaltro, Franklin L. *plastic surgeon*
Dohr, Donald R. *metallurgical engineer, researcher*
Eisenberg, R. Neal *restoration company executive*
Gans, Bruce Merrill *physiatrist, educator, health facility administrator*
Ghali, Anwar Youssef *psychiatrist, educator*
Goldberg, Leonard Marvin *lawyer*
Gordon, Michael *lawyer*
Hill, George James *physician, educator*
Jordan, Leo John *lawyer*
Katz, Jeffrey Ivan *urologist*
Ko, Chia-Wen *biostatistician, researcher*
Kyle, Corinne Silverman *management consultant*
Langsner, Alan Michael *pediatric cardiologist*
Laves, Benjamin Samuel *lawyer*
Lieberman, Rob *performing company executive*
Linsenmeyer, Todd Alan *medical educator, physician*
Martin, Boston Faust *neurosurgeon*
McKinney, John Adams, Jr., *lawyer*
McMullen, John J. *former professional hockey team executive, management consultant*
Petrokubi, Marilyn *film company executive, researcher, film producer, writer*
Pollara, Joanne *learning disabilities educator consultant*
Richmond, Harold Nicholas *lawyer*
Rinsky, Judith Sue Lynn *foundation administrator, educator consultant*
Roseff, Scott *reproductive endocrinologist*
Wu, Nan Faion *pediatrician*
Zimmerman, David Carl *controller, corporate financial executive*

West Paterson
DeLouise, Tia Caputi *university executive*
Miller, Gail Wood *literature educator, consultant*
Pataki, Andrew *bishop*

West Trenton
Tessler, Steven *ecologist, data processing executive*

Westampton
Patel, Anjana *education educator, consultant*

Westfield
Bhagat, Phiroz Maneck *mechanical engineer*
Blum, Richard H. *obstetrician-gynecologist, educator*
Bobis, Daniel Harold *lawyer*
Feret, Adam Edward, Jr., *dentist*
Hull, Kathleen Ann *humanities educator*
Jannotti, Gene Patrick *business consultant, telecommunications professional*
Mazzarese, Michael Louis *executive coach, consultant*
McDevitt, Brian Peter *history professor, educational consultant*
McLean, Vincent Ronald *former manufacturing company financial executive*
Schlosberg, Theodore K. *music educator*
Simon, Martin Stanley *commodity marketing company executive, economist*

Westmont
Martin, Burchard Samuel *lawyer*

Westwood
Badalamenti, Anthony Francis *mathematician, researcher*
Black, Theodore Halsey *retired manufacturing company executive*
Diernisse, Hans Vilhelm (Villy Diernisse) *writer, mechanical engineer*
Fabrikant, Craig Steven *psychologist*
French, Phyllis Olivia *artistic director, dance instructor*
Roesch, Roberta *writer*

Wharton
Krosser, Howard S. *aerospace company executive*

Whippany
Curwin, Ronald *home equipment stores executive*
Meola, Janice Grace *lawyer*

Whitehouse
Shelton, Craig *food service executive*

Whitehouse Station
Anstice, David W. *pharmaceutical executive*
Avedon, Marcia J. *pharmaceutical executive*
Bell, Paul R. *pharmaceutical executive*
Bossidy, Lawrence Arthur *former industrial manufacturing executive*
Clark, Richard T. *pharmaceutical executive*
Fiscus, Philip Wayne *underwriter*
Frazier, Kenneth C. *pharmaceutical executive*
Gilmartin, Raymond V. *pharmaceutical company executive*
Hunsche, Elke Greta Irma *economist*
Kelley, Bernard J. *pharmaceutical executive*
Lewent, Judy Carol *pharmaceutical executive*
Mahmoud, Adel A. *infectious disease and tropical medicine physician, educator, pharmaceutical executive*
McGlynn, Margaret G. *pharmaceutical executive*
McGuire, John Lawrence *pharmaceutical executive*
Wold Olsen, Per *pharmaceutical executive*
Yarno, Wendy *pharmaceutical executive*

Whiting
Kelsey, George E. *language educator*
Parker, John Osmyn *management consultant*
Willis, Ben *writer, artist*

Wilkesboro
Jennings, Perry G. *retail executive*
Kasberger, John L. *retail executive*

Willingboro
Bass, Joseph Oscar *minister*
Denslow, Deborah Pierson *primary education educator*
Green, Riva Lee *social worker, minister*
Ingerman, Peter Zilahy *systems analyst, consultant*
Tarver, Margaret Leggett *retired lawyer, forensic scientist*

Woodbridge
Ayub, Yacub *financial consultant*
Barcan, Stephen Emanuel *lawyer*
Estis, Dennis Arnold *lawyer*
Friscia, Arline M. *assemblywoman*
Galkin, Samuel Bernard *orthodontist*
Qiu, Li-Hui *music educator, actress*
Santulli, Richard T. *air transportation executive*

Woodbury
Doughty, A. Glenn *minister*
Duffield-Myers, Arlene Anna *elementary school educator*
Nace, Donald M. *retired chemist*
Stambaugh, John Edgar *oncologist, hematologist, pharmacologist, educator*

Woodcliff Lake
Bablin, Mark Edward *security administrator, mortgage consultant*
Falcon, Raymond Jesus, Jr., *lawyer*
Henkel, Herbert Ludwig *manufacturing executive*
Jacobs, Charles Nathan *editor, writer*
Nachtigal, Patricia *lawyer*
Perrella, James Elbert *former manufacturing company executive*
Phillips, John C. *lawyer*

Wyckoff
Bauer, Theodore James *physician*
Brown, James Joseph *manufacturing executive*
Cropper, Susan Peggy *veterinarian*
Lavery, Daniel P. *management consultant*
Marcus, Linda Susan *dermatologist*
Munson, William Leslie *insurance company executive*

Yardville
Zweig, Steven Frederick *statistician*

NEW MEXICO

Alamogordo
Ashdown, Franklin Donald *physician, composer*
Lindley, Norman Dale *physician*
McFadin, Helen Lozetta *retired elementary education educator*

Albuquerque
Abraham, Karen A. *university administrator*
Anaya, Rudolfo *educator, writer*
Anderson, Lawrence Keith *electrical engineer, consultant*
Antreasian, Garo Zareh *artist, lithographer, art educator*
Arthur, Michelle Marie *education educator*
Baack, Bret Rolyn *plastic surgeon*
Baker, Arnold Barry *economist*
Baker, Chester Bird *agricultural economics educator*
Ballard, David Eugene *anesthesiologist*
Bardacke, Paul Gregory *lawyer, former attorney general*
Barker, Lynn M. *business executive*
Barry, Steve *sculptor, educator*
Basso, Keith Hamilton *cultural anthropologist, linguist, educator*
Beach, Arthur O'Neal *lawyer*
Bear, David George *cell biologist, educator*
Beckel, Charles Leroy *physicist, educator*
Bell, Stoughton *computer scientist, mathematician, educator*
Berman, Stanley Zissman *allergist, immunologist, internist, educator*
Black, Bruce D. *judge*
Blake, Renée *broadcast executive*
Blewett, Kenneth K. *business executive*
Borden, Thomas Allen *urologist, educator*
Bova, Vincent Arthur, Jr., *lawyer, consultant, photographer*
Bradshaw, Elaine A. *pediatrician*
Burris, Beverly Hudeck *sociology educator*
Burrows, Kathy S. *health facility administrator*
Caldera, Louis Edward *academic administrator, former federal official*
Caplan, Edwin Harvey *university dean, accounting educator*
Cargo, David Francis *lawyer*
Chang, Barbara Karen *medical educator*
Chávez, Carmela Bernadette *lawyer, consultant*
Chavez, Martin Joseph *lawyer, mayor*
Cheng, Yung Sung *research scientist*
Chilton, Lance Alix *pediatrician*
Cliff, Norman *psychology educator, consultant, writer*
Cobb, John Candler *medical educator*
Cole, Terri Lynn *organization administrator*
Coleman, Barbara McReynolds *artist*
Collins, Julie *healthcare organization executive*
Condie, Carol Joy *anthropologist, research facility administrator*
Conway, John E. *federal judge*
Danziger, Jerry *broadcast executive*
Davidge, K. Genevieve *clinical social worker*
Davis, Betty Bourbonia *real estate company executive*
Davis, Jon L. *logistics consultant*
Day, David Minot *mathematician, researcher*
Dendahl, John *political organization administrator*
Dorato, Peter *electrical and computer engineering educator*
Duke, Rachele Marongiu *language educator*
Duncan, Irma Wagner *retired biochemist, museum educator*
Dunlap, Sam Bathurst *personnel consulting firm executive*
Eichenberg, Peter Thompson *retired state agency administrator*
Eldredge, Jonathan DeForest *medical librarian, educator*
Elliott, Charles Harold *clinical psychologist*
Evans, Bill (James William Evans) *dancer, choreographer, educator, arts administrator*
Everitt, Elizabeth M. *school system administrator*
Farmer, Terry D(wayne) *lawyer*
Feinberg, Elen Amy *artist, educator*
Feldman, Dede *state legislator*
Fish, Paul Mathew *lawyer*
Flournoy, John Charles, Sr., *retired civilian military employee, retired military officer*
Freeman, Patricia Elizabeth *multi-media specialist, educational consultant*
Friberg, George Joseph *electronics company executive, entrepreneur*
Fry, Donald Edmund *surgeon*
Gander, John Edward *biochemistry educator*
Garcia, F. Chris *academic administrator, political science educator, public opinion researcher*
Gardner, Lenann McGookey *management consultant*
Garland, James Wilson, Jr., *retired physics educator*
Giller, Edward Bonfoy *retired government official, retired air force officer*
Gish, Robert Franklin *English language educator, writer*
Godfrey, Richard George *real estate appraiser, consultant*
Gordon, Larry Jean *environmental health educator*
Graff, Pat Stuever *secondary school educator*
Graham, Timothy Charles *historian, director*
Green, Mae Maera *artist*
Gupchup, Gireesh Vijay *pharmacist, educator*
Gutierrez, Gabriella *architecture educator*
Gutierrez, Joni Marie *landscape architect, political organization worker*
Gutierrez, Sidney M. *federal agency administrator*
Hadas, Elizabeth Chamberlayne *editor*
Haddad, Edward Raouf *civil engineer, consultant*
Hahn, Betty *artist, photographer, educator*
Haley, Richard Edward, Jr., *computer scientist*
Hall, Jerome William *research engineering educator*
Hancock, Don Ray *researcher*
Hansen, Curtis LeRoy *federal judge*
Hansen, Harold B., Jr., *elementary school educator*
Harbert, Kenneth Ray *physician assistant*
Harris, Fred R. *political scientist, educator, retired senator*
Harrison, Charles Wagner, Jr., *applied physicist*
Hart, Frederick Michael *law educator*
Hartz, Harris L *federal judge*
Hayo, George Edward *management consultant*
Heady, Ferrel *retired political science educator*
Heffron, Warren A. *physician, educator*
Henderson, Rogene Faulkner *toxicologist, researcher*
Herrera, Gilbert Victor *engineering executive*
Hovel, Esther Harrison *art educator*
Hsi, David Ching Heng *plant pathologist and geneticist, educator*
Hudson, Patrick A. *plastic surgeon*
Hulsbos, Cornie Leonard *civil engineering educator*
Hutton, Paul Andrew *history educator, writer*
Iglesias, David Claudio *prosecutor*
Ihde, Mary Katherine *retired mathematics educator*
Jaramillo, Mari-Luci *retired federal agency administrator*
Jones, Rondall Eugene *mathematician*
Kaehele, Bettie Louise *accountant*
Keating, David *photographer*
Keep, Marcus Floyd *neurosurgeon*
Keleher, Michael Lawrence *lawyer*
King, Lowell Restell *pediatric urologist*
Knospe, William Herbert *medical educator*
Koch, Jamie *political party official*
Kohn, Emil *real estate broker*
Korman, Nathaniel Irving *research and development company executive*
Kotchian, Sarah Bruff *municipal official*
Lang, Thompson Hughes *publishing company executive*
Lattman, Laurence Harold *retired academic administrator*
Lawit, John Walter *lawyer*
Leach, Richard Maxwell, Jr., (Max Leach Jr.) *corporate professional*
Lederer, John Martin *retired aeronautical engineer*
Lee, David Ol *engineer*
Leeper, Ramon Joe *physicist*
Lee-Smith, Hughie *artist, educator*
Lind, Levi Robert *classics educator, writer*
Lipka, Ronald C. *music educator, musician*
Liss, Norman Richard *insurance executive*
Loftfield, Robert Berner *biochemistry educator*
Lohrding, Ronald K. *business executive*
Long, Robert Leroy *retired utilities executive, consultant*
Long, Stephen Carrel Mike *lawyer*
Lopez, Linda M. *state legislator*
Loubet, Jeffrey W. *lawyer*
Lowrance, Muriel Edwards *program specialist*
Masefield, Oliver Leslie Peter *aerospace transportation executive, aerospace engineer*
Mason, William vanHorn *dermatologist*
Matros, Richard K. *insurance company executive*
Mauderly, Joe Lloyd *pulmonary toxicologist*
May, Philip Alan *sociology educator*
McBride, Teresa *information systems specialist*
McGuire, Susan Grayson *legislative staff member*
Miera, Lucille Catherine Miera *artist, retired art educator*
Mock, Joan Bodet *music educator*
Montoya, Patricia T. *federal agency administrator*
Moore, Charles Loyd *lawyer*
Mora, Federico *neurosurgeon*
Moses, Karen *editor*
Moskos, Harry *writer, former newspaper editor*
Moughan, Peter Richard, Jr., *lawyer*
Moulds, William J. *retired aeronautical engineer*
Muggenburg, Bruce Al *veterinary physiologist*
Multhaup, Merrel Keyes *artist*
Myers, Carol McClary *retired sales administrator, editor*
Nelson, Mary Carroll *artist, writer*
Nevin, Jean Shaw *artist*
O'Brien, Daniel J. *lawyer*
Ofte, Donald *business executive*
Omer, George Elbert, Jr., *orthopaedic surgeon, educator*
Oppedahl, Phillip Edward *computer company executive*
Orona, Ernest Joseph *real estate and construction company executive*
O'Toole, Robert John, II, *telemarketing consultant*
Papyrin, Anatolii Nikiforovich *physicist, researcher*
Parker, James Aubrey *federal judge*
Paster, Janice Dubinsky *lawyer, former state legislator*
Peck, Ralph Brazelton *civil engineering educator, consultant*
Peña, Juan José *interpreter*
Pendergest, Kevin W. *insurance company executive*
Pohl, Elizabeth *contracting company executive*
Pressman, Andy *architecture educator*
Qualley, Charles Albert *art educator*
Raish, Carol Brooks *anthropologist, archaeologist*
Ramo, Roberta Cooper *lawyer*
Raybourn, Elaine Marie *research scientist*
Renschler, Clifford L. *chemist*
Rhetts, Paul Fisher *publishing executive*
Richter, Harvena *retired english literature and creative writing teacher, writer*
Rivera, Rhonda Rae *law professor, legal scholary lawyer, artibrator*
Roberts, Dennis William *association executive*
Robinson, Charles Paul *nuclear physicist, diplomat, business executive*
Roehl, Jerrald J. *lawyer*
Romero, Richard M. *state legislator, educator*
Romig, Alton Dale, Jr., *materials scientist, educator*
Roseman, Steven A. *insurance company executive*
Roth, Paul Barry *dean, educator, emergency medicine physician*
Rutherford, Thomas Truxtun, II, *county commissioner, former state senator*
Sabatini, William Quinn *architect*
Saland, Linda Carol *anatomy educator, neuroscience researcher*
Salazar, John Paul *lawyer*
Sanchez, Raymond G. *former state legislator*
Sanderlin, Terry Keith *counselor*
Schluntz, Roger *architecture educator*
Schuler, Alison Kay *lawyer*
Schwerin, Karl Henry *anthropology educator, researcher*
Sena, Kathleen F. *academic administrator*
Sinnott, Linda Johnette *educational association administrator*
Sisk, Daniel Arthur *lawyer*
Smith, Edgar Benton *dermatologist*
Snell, Patricia Poldervaart *librarian, consultant*
Solomon, Arthur Charles *pharmacist*
Stahl, Jack Leland *real estate company executive*
Steider, Doris *artist*
Steinbach, Falko *musician, music educator*
Stevenson, James Richard *radiologist, lawyer*
Stewart, Mimi (Miriam) (Kay) (Mimi Stewart) *state legislator, educator*
Strasburger, Victor C. *pediatrician*
Stuart, Cynthia Morgan *university administrator*
Stuart, David Edward *anthropologist, writer, educator*
Studer, James Edward *geological engineer*
Summers, William Koopmans *neuropsychiatrist, researcher*
Szasz, Ferenc M. *historian, educator*
Taylor, Douglas John *materials scientist, researcher, materials engineer*
Thornton, J. Duke *lawyer*
Tinnin, Robert Priest, Jr., *lawyer*
Travelstead, Chester Coleman *former educational administrator*
Turner, Andrew L. *healthcare management company executive*
Twigg, Nancy L. *nursing association administrator*
Uhlenhuth, Eberhard Henry *psychiatrist, educator*
Van Devender, J. Pace *physical scientist, management consultant*
Waitzkin, Howard Bruce *internist, sociologist, educator*
Walch, Peter Sanborn *museum director, publisher*
Walz, Kent *publishing executive*
Weagel, Deborah Fillerup *writer, composer*
Weeth, George Wright *lawyer*
Weh, Allen Edward *aviation executive*
Wellborn, Charles Ivey *science and technology business consultant*
Westwood, Albert Ronald Clifton *management consultant, researcher*

White, Jennifer Phelps *counselor*
Williams, Marion Lester *government official*
Wilson, Sue *state legislator*
Wimer, Mark G. *healthcare management company executive*
Winslow, Walter William *psychiatrist, educator*
Witkin, Joel-Peter *photographer, poet*
Woltil, Robert D. *healthcare management company executive*
Wong, Phillip Allen *osteopathic physician*
Worrell, Audrey Martiny *geriatric psychiatrist*
Wynne, Louis *psychologist*
Zink, Lee Berkey *retired academic administrator, economist, educator*

Alto
Thrasher, Jack Dwayne *toxicologist, researcher, consultant*
Zeitelhack, Gloria Jeanne *artist*

Bayard
Foy, Thomas Paul *lawyer, retired state legislator, retired bank executive*
Lopez, Linda Carol *social sciences educator*

Belen
Chicago, Judy *artist*
Toliver, Lee *mechanical engineer*

Carlsbad
Byers, Matthew T(odd) *lawyer, educator*
Paviet-Hartmann, Patricia *chemist, researcher*
Piper, Lloyd Llewellyn, II, *engineer, government and service industry executive*
Queen, Dorothy *distribution company executive*
Regan Gossage, Muriel *librarian*

Cerrillos
Lutz, Raymond Price *retired industrial engineer, educator*

Chama
McElhaney, James Willson *lawyer, educator, author, trial consultant*

Cloudcroft
Hadfield, Michael James *electrical engineer*

Clovis
Rehorn, Lois M(arie) (Lois Marie Smith) *nursing administrator*
Skarda, Lynell Griffith *lawyer, banker*

Corrales
Adams, James Frederick *psychologist, educational administrator*
Eaton, Pauline *artist, educator*
Foryst, Carole *computer electronics executive*
Radcliffe, Glena Eloise *lyricist, poet, composer*
Sageser, Kendall Wayne *mineral exploration executive*

Deming
Becker-Klicker, Margaret Chan *library director*
Rogers, Alice Louise *retired bank executive, writer, researcher*

Dona Ana
Garcia, Mary Jane Madrid *state legislator*

Edgewood
Hamilton, Jerald *musician*

El Prado
Young, Jon Nathan *archaeologist*

Embudo
Rogers, Benjamin Talbot *former consulting engineer, solar energy consultant*

Estancia
Swenka, Arthur John *retired food products executive*

Farmington
Graham, Warren Kirkland *dentist*
Lewis, Homer Dick *retired nuclear engineer*
Mathers, Margaret *reference librarian, archivist*
Moeller, Floyd Douglas *lawyer*
Morgan, Jack M. *lawyer*
Neidhart, James Allen *oncologist, educator*
Thompson, Joseph T., Jr., *health facility administrator*
Titus, Victor Allen *lawyer*

Fort Wingate
Neff, Patrick Lee (Pat Neff) *music educator*

Galisteo
Lippard, Lucy Rowland *writer, lecturer*

Gallup
Cattaneo, Jacquelyn Annette Kammerer *artist, educator*
Lundstrom, Patricia *state government administrator*
Zongolowicz, Helen Michaeline *education and psychology educator*

Hobbs
Dill, Gary A. *academic administrator*
DiUlus, Frederick Alfonso-Edward *business educator*
Garey, Donald Lee *pipeline and oil company executive*
Garey, Patricia Martin *artist*
Payton-Robinson, Constance Marian *educational consultant, writer*
Reagan, Gary Don *state legislator, lawyer*
Ritchie, Fran A. *interior designer, small business owner*

Holloman Afb
Minto, David W. *aeronautical engineer*

Jemez Springs
Brandon, John Boyd *artist*

Kirtland Afb
Alejandro, Steven B. *physicist*
Anderson, Christine Marlene *software engineer*
Baum, Carl Edward *electromagnetic theorist*
Degnan, James Henry *physicist*
Gideon, Francis C., Jr., *career officer*
Huybrechts, Steven Marc *space system technologist*
Tritten, James John *national security educator*

La Plata
Kent, Mollie *writer, publishing executive, editor*

Laguna
Reichmann, Péter Iván *mathematics professor*

Las Cruces
Adaime, Hamed Nazin *counselor*
Bell, M. Joy Miller *financial planner, real estate broker*
Cochrun, John Wesley *financial consultant*
Conroy, William B. *retired university administrator*
Cooch, F. Graham *ecologist, educator, ecologist, researcher*
Dasenbrock, Reed Way *literature educator*
Egginton, Everett *educational administrator*
Flores, William Vincent *Latin American studies educator*
Ford, Clarence Quentin *mechanical engineer, educator*
Gale, Thomas Martin *university dean*
Heger, Herbert Krueger *education educator*
Holechek, Jerry *agricultural studies educator*
Jacobs, Kent Frederick *dermatologist*
Kilmer, Neal Harold *application developer*
Lindley, Jearl Ray *lawyer*
Lutz, William Lan *lawyer*
McElyea, Ulysses, Jr., *veterinarian*
Medoff, Mark Howard *playwright, screenwriter, novelist*
Murphy, Michael Terrence *lawyer*
Nelson, Antonya *writer*
Neumann, Rita Nunez *lawyer*
Parsley, Steven Dwayne *title company executive*
Peterson, Robin Tucker *marketing educator*
Richardson, Albert Edward *chemistry educator, consultant, researcher*
Roscoe, Stanley Nelson *psychologist, aeronautical engineer*
Schemnitz, Sanford David *wildlife biology educator*
Selden, Annie *mathematics professor*
Sengupta-Gopalan, Champa *research scientist, educator*
Smith, Tom *playwright, theater arts educator*
Strickland, Jennifer Laura *engineer*
Tonn, Robert James *retired entomologist*
Welsh, Mary McAnaw *family mediator, educator*
Winfree, Latham Thomas *law educator*

Las Vegas
Casey, Barbara A. Perea *state legislator, school superintendent*
Riley, Carroll Lavern *anthropology educator*
Simpson, Dorothy Audrey *retired speech educator*

Los Alamos
Brown, Lowell Severt *physicist, researcher*
Canavan, Gregory H. *science educator*
Clausen, Bjørn *materials scientist, researcher*
Dudziak, Donald John *nuclear engineer, educator*
Engelhardt, Albert George *physicist*
Gibson, Benjamin Franklin *physicist*
Gonzales, Stephanie *state official*
Gregg, Charles Thornton *research company executive*
Grilly, Edward Rogers *physicist*
Jackson, James F. *nuclear engineer, educator*
Judd, O'Dean P. *physicist*
Keepin, George Robert, Jr., *physicist*
King, Jerry Wayne *research chemist*
Kloepper, David Alan *retired management consultant*
Lu, Ningping *environmental chemist*
Lyman, John L. *chemist, researcher*
Makaruk, Hanna Ewa *theoretical physicist*
Maloy, Stuart *materials scientist, engineer*
Masse, William Bruce *archaeologist*
Masunov, Artem *theoretical chemist, researcher*
McDonald, Thomas Edwin, Jr., *retired electrical engineer*
Mead, William Charles *physicist*
Mendius, Patricia Dodd Winter *editor, educator, writer*
Michaudon, André Francisque *physicist*
Mihalas, Dimitri Manuel *astrophysicist, educator*
Mitchell, Terence Edward *materials scientist*
Morales, Reynaldo *physicist*
Nanos, George Peter, Jr., *science administrator, military officer, physicist*
Nieto, Michael Martin *theoretical physicist*
Nix, James Rayford *nuclear physicist, consultant*
Nunz, Gregory Joseph *aerospace engineer, program manager, educator, entrepreneur*
Petrini, Fabrizio *computer science researcher*
Press, William Henry *astrophysicist, computer scientist*
Ramirez, Arthur P. *physicist*
Redmond, Bill *former congressman, minister*
Rosen, Louis *physicist*
Sayre, Edward Charles *librarian, consultant*
Selden, Robert Wentworth *physicist, science advisor*
Sharp, David Howland *physicist*
Smith, Fredrica Emrich *rheumatologist, internist*
Smith, James Lawrence *research physicist*
Snell, Charles Murrell *physicist, astrophysicist*
Stoddard, Stephen Davidson *ceramic engineer, former state senator*
Stoopes, Gary Robert *technical consultant, geoscientist*
Thompson, Joe D. *physicist*
Thompson, Lois Jean Heidke Ore *psychologist*
Van Tuyle, Gregory Jay *nuclear engineer*
Venhaus, Thomas J. *physicist*
Wahl, Arthur Charles *retired chemistry educator*
Wallace, Jeannette Owens *state legislator*
Wallace, Terry Charles, Sr., *retired technical administrator, researcher*
Wallstrom, Timothy C. *physicist*
Wingo, Robert Matthew *chemist, chemical engineer*
WoldeGabriel, Giday *research geologist*
Zhang, Dongxiao *research scientist*

Los Lunas
Robinson, Mary Reid *mathematics professor*
Seiler, Fritz Arnold *physicist*

Mayhill
Pastor, Stephen Daniel *chemistry educator, researcher, consultant*

Mesilla
Lewis, Delano Eugene *ambassador, retired broadcast executive*

Montezuma
Geier, Philip Otto, III, *academic administrator*

Mora
Hanks, Eugene Ralph *real estate developer, rancher, forester, retired military officer, investor*

Moriarty
Costello, Judith Marie *writer, artist*
Haver, Jurgen F. *marketing consultant*
Moonwalker, Tu *minister, counselor, artist*

Mountainair
Woodruff, Joan Leslie *occupational therapist, counselor*

Nogal
Moeller, Susan Elaine *artist*

Pinos Altos
Rogers, Linda Lee *artist*

Placitas
Dunmire, William Werden *writer, photographer, naturalist*
Golleher, George *food company executive*
Hidy, George Martel *chemical engineer, executive*
Long, Timothy Scott *chemist, consultant*
Pirkl, James Joseph *industrial designer, educator, writer*
Reade, Lewis Pollock *business executive, retired diplomat, engineer*
Schoen, Stevan Jay *lawyer*
Smith, Richard Bowen *retired national park superintendent*

Pomona
Lubenow, William Cornelius *historian, educator*

Portales
Cobb, Jeanne Beck *education educator, researcher, consultant*
Dal Porto, Mark Daniel *music educator*
Goodwin, Martin Brune *radiologist*
Howard, Carolyn F. *elementary school educator*
Overton, Edwin Dean *campus minister, educator*
Seifert, Dustin David *conductor, music educator*
Williamson, Jack (John Stewart) *writer*
Wozencraft-Ornellas, (Betty) Jean *singer, music educator*

Ranchos De Taos
Marx, Nicki Diane *sculptor, painter*

Raton
Carroll, William *publishing company executive*

Rio Rancho
Bencke, Ronald Lee *finance company executive*
Brown-Grayson, Ron *foundation administrator, writer*
Delahanty, Carlos Anthony *industrial engineer*
Goss, Jerome Eldon *cardiologist*
Isenberg, Abraham Charles *shoe manufacturing company executive*
Sei, Ibrahim *process engineer*
Stevens, Roger Templeton *writer*
Weber, Alois Hughes *principal*

Rodeo
Scholes, Robert Thornton *physician, research administrator*

Roswell
Anderson, Donald Bernard *oil company executive*
Anderson, Sally Midgette *social services administrator, linguist*
Armstrong, Billie Bert *retired highway contractor*
Choudhary, Adil Mushtaq *gastroenterologist*
Franzoni, Delaina Day *special education educator, department chairman*
Haines, Thomas David, Jr., *lawyer*
Hedin, Edna Jenks *musician, educator*
Kraft, Richard Lee *lawyer*
Nibert, Gregory James *lawyer*
Robinson, Mark Leighton *oil company executive, petroleum geologist, horse farm owner*
Tabrez, Shams S.M. *gastroenterologist*
Wiggins, Kim Douglas *artist, art appraiser, art dealer*

Rowe
Cowles, William Sheffield, III, *rancher*

Ruidoso
McIntosh, Cathleen Anne *small business owner, educator*
Pittman, Kathleen M. *education educator, consultant*

Sandia Park
Greenwell, Ronald Everett *communications executive*
Weitz, Jeanne Stewart *artist, educator*
Wilczynski, Janusz S. *packaging technology executive, retired physicist*

Santa Fe
Abeles, Richard Alan *lawyer*
Alfidi, Ralph Joseph *retired radiologist*
Allen, Page Randolph *artist*
Amtmann, Hans Henry *retired aeronautical engineer, architect*
Anderson, Darrell Edward *psychologist, educator*
Arnold-Jones, Janice E. *state representative*
Ballard, Louis Wayne *composer*
Beam, Gail C. *state representative*
Bergé, Carol *writer*
Bosson, Richard Campbell *state supreme court justice*
Bowman, Jon Robert *magazine editor, film critic*
Bradley, Walter D. *lieutenant governor, real estate broker*
Brandt, Richard Paul *communications and entertainment company executive*
Brannen, Jeffrey Richard *lawyer*
Brown, Norman Wesley *retired advertising agency executive*
Burke, Lawrence J. *editor-in-chief*
Burton, John Paul (Jack Burton) *lawyer*
Carpenter, Richard Norris *retired lawyer*
Casey, Patrick Anthony *lawyer*
Cerny, Charlene Ann *director*
Chambers, Letitia Pearl Caroline *state agency administrator*
Charles, Cheryl *non-profit and business executive*
Chavez, Edward L. *judge*
Clyde, Larry Forbes *banker*
Coffield, Conrad Eugene *lawyer*
Cohen, Saul *lawyer*
Colvin, Greta Wilmoth *entrepreneur*
Cowan, George Arthur *chemist, bank executive, director*
Cravens, Kent L. *state senator*
Culbert, Peter V. *lawyer*
Culp, Marguerite Buckman *writer*
Davis, Shelby Moore Cullom *investment executive, consultant*
Denish, Diane D. *lieutenant governor*
Dirks, Lee Edward *newspaper executive*
Dodds, Robert James, III, *lawyer*
Dreisbach, John Gustave *investment banker*
Enyeart, James L. *museum director*
Feist-Fite, Bernadette *international health education consultant*
Ferguson, Glenn Walker *lecturer, author*
Field, Harold *state finance administrator*
Fisher, Nora Caldwell *retired curator, photographer, researcher, writer*
Fisher, Robert Alan *laser physicist*
Gaddes, Richard *performing arts administrator*
Garcia, Mary Helen *state representative*
Gaustad, Edwin Scott *historian, educator*
Gell-Mann, Murray *theoretical physicist, educator*
Gilbert, Alan *conductor*
Gilmour, Edward Ellis *retired psychiatrist*
Giovanielli, Damon Vincent *physicist, consulting company executive*
Goorley, John Timothy *nuclear engineer*
Groseclose, Everett Harrison *retired editor*
Guthrie, Catherine S. (Catherine S. Nicholson-Guthrie) *retired research scientist*
Hanson, Linda N. *academic administrator, educator*
Harcourt, Robert Neff *educational administrator, journalist, genealogist*
Harding, Marie *ecological executive, artist*
Harris, David W. *state agency administrator*
Harroun, Dorothy Sumner *painter, educator*
Hickey, John Miller *lawyer*
Hoffmann, Louis Gerhard *immunologist, educator*
Howes, Gloria *state legislator*
Huffaker, Gregory Dorian, Jr., *lawyer*
Hurt, Allen V. *state senator*
Hyde, Pamela Suzon *housing and human services administrator*
Jones, Walter Harrison *chemist, educator*
Justice, Jack Burton *retired lawyer, writer*
Kellner, Richard George *mathematician, computer scientist*
Kelly, Paul Joseph, Jr., *judge*
Kinderwater, Diane *state official*
Kingman, Elizabeth Yelm *anthropologist*
Komadina, Steve *state senator*
Kotin, Paul *pathologist*
Kropschot, Richard Henry *retired physicist, science laboratory administrator*
Lehmberg, Stanford Eugene *historian, educator*
Leibowitz, Jack Richard *physicist, educator*
Leon, Bruno *architect, architecture educator*
Lichtenberg, Margaret Klee *publishing company executive*
Lovejoy, Lynda M. *state agency administrator*
Lujan, Ben *state representative*
Lukac, George Joseph *not-for-profit fundraiser*
Lynn, John Eric *nuclear physics research consultant*
Madrid, Patricia A. *state attorney general*
Maehl, William Henry *historian, university administrator, educational consultant*
Maes, Petra Jimenez *state supreme court justice*
Malone, Roxanne Enyeart *artist, educator*
Martinez, Richard C. *state senator*
McClaugherty, Joe L. *lawyer, educator*
McIntosh, Kathleen Ann *music educator*
Melnick, Alice Jean (AJ Melnick) *counselor*
Mercer, James Lee *management consultant*
Merrin, Seymour *computer marketing company executive*
Miller, Dwight Richard *professional hair care industry executive, cosmetologist, consultant*
Minzner, Pamela Burgy *state supreme court justice*
Moll, Deborah Adelaide *lawyer*
Montoya, Michael A. *state official, accountant*
Morrissey, Michael Joseph *investment banker*
Myers, R. David *library director, dean*
Nava, Cynthia L. *state legislator*
Noble, Merrill Emmett *retired psychology educator, psychologist*
Odell, John H. *construction executive*
Otten, Robin Dozier *state agency administrator*
Papen, Mary Kay *state senator*
Peat, Randall Dean *defense analysis company executive, retired air force officer*
Perry, Nancy Estelle *psychologist*
Pickrell, Thomas Richard *retired oil company executive*
Pound, John Bennett *lawyer*
Powdrell-Culbert, Jane E. *state representative*
Pulitzer, Roslyn Kitty *social worker, psychotherapist*
Rainaldi, Lidio G. *state senator*
Randolph, Somers *sculptor*
Richardson, William Blaine *governor*
Robinson, Richard Gary *management consultant, accountant*
Rodello, Debbie A. *state representative*
Rodriguez, Nancy *state legislator*
Romanowski, Thomas Andrew *physics educator*
Rubenstein, Bernard *orchestra conductor*
Ruybalid, Louis Arthur *social worker, community development consultant*
Sanchez, Bernadette M. *state senator*
Sandoval, Isabelle Medina *education educator*
Sayre, William O. *geologist, educator*
Schiller, William Richard *surgeon*
Schuyler, Robert Len *investment company executive*
Schwartz, George R. *physician, researcher*
Schwarz, Michael *lawyer*
Serna, Patricio *state supreme court justice*
Sharer, William E. *state senator*
Sloan, Jeanette Pasin *artist*
Smith, Philip Meek *science policy consultant, writer*
Snyder, Helen Diane *state senator*

Stalker, James Raghi meteorologist, environmental services administrator
Stapleton, Sheryl Williams state representative
Stieber, Tamar journalist
Stocking, Valerie playwright
Sumner, Gordon, Jr., retired military officer
Swartz, William John retired transportation resources company executive
Tarn, Nathaniel poet, translator, educator
Thompson, Waite investment company executive, researcher
Townsend, Sandra L. state representative
Vaughn, Gloria C. state representative
Vazquez, Martha Alicia judge
Verant, William J. state agency administrator
Vigil-Giron, Rebecca state official
Villela, Khristaan David art educator
Wakashige, Benjamin Taka librarian
Watkins, Stephen Edward accountant, newspaper executive
White, David Hywel physics educator
Williams, Ralph Chester, Jr., physician, educator
Williams, Stephen anthropologist, educator
Wilson, Avon W. state representative
Wilson, Thomas museum director
Wolford, Richard Howard lawyer
Yalman, Ann judge, lawyer
Zanetti, Teresa A. state representative
Zlatoff-Mirsky, Everett Igor violinist

Santa Rosa
Alcott, Colin C. prosecutor

Santa Teresa
McDonald, Charles Edward lawyer

Seneca
Monroe, Kendyl Kurth retired lawyer

Shiprock
Atcitty, Fannie L. elementary school educator, education educator
Austin-Garrison, Martha A. educator, researcher

Silver City
Bettison, Cynthia Ann museum director, archaeologist
Charland, William A., Jr., writer, educator, consultant
Cox, Robert Gene management consultant
Fryxell, David Allen publishing executive
Hall, Jean Quintero communications and history educator
Hamlin, Don Auer financial executive
Hodges, Norman retired district judge
McCray, Dorothy Westaby artist, printmaker, educator
Snedeker, John Haggner university president

Socorro
Cardenas, Meinhard Bayani Ramos hydrologist
Scholle, Peter Allen geologist, researcher

Sunspot
Keil, Stephen Lesley astrophysicist

Taos
Becker, Elisabeth Maria artist, educator
Bell, Larry Stuart artist
Boles, David LaVelle lawyer
Bolls, Imogene Lamb English language educator, poet
Brown, David Warfield management educator
Farnsworth, John Edward artist, educator
Garcia, Christine academic administrator, educator, researcher
Harmon, Barbara Sayre artist
Martin, Agnes artist
Tisdale, Shelby Jo-Anne museum director, consultant
Witt, David L. curator, writer

Tesuque
MacGraw, Ali actress
Novak, Joe artist

Tijeras
Sholtis, Joseph Arnold, Jr., business owner, nuclear and aerospace engineer, consultant

Tome
Koopmans, Lambert Herman retired mathematician

Truth Or Consequences
Rush, Domenica Marie health facilities administrator

Tucumcari
Woodard, Dorothy Marie insurance broker

Tularosa
Duran, Dianna J. state legislator

Valdez
Jacobs, Roland William psychiatrist

White Sands Missile Range
Arthur, Paul Keith electronic engineer
Linzey, James Franklin minister, military officer, vocalist

NEW YORK

Adams Center
Hood, Thomas Gregory minister

Afton
Schwartz, Aubrey Earl artist, educator

Akron
Hoover, Eddie Lee cardiothoracic surgeon, educator

Albany
Aceto, Vincent John librarian, educator
Alba, Richard Denis sociologist, educator
Alessi, Robert Joseph lawyer, real estate developer, pharmacist
Arroyo, Carmen Elsie state legislator
Arseneau, James Charles physician
Barker-Benfield, Graham John historian
Baum, Joseph Thomas lawyer
Bellizzi, John J. law enforcement association administrator, educator, pharmacist
Berman, Carol commissioner
Berman, Jeffrey language educator
Blount, Stanley Freeman marketing educator
Bowen, Mary Lu ecumenical administrator
Brademas, John retired university president, former congressman
Bradley, Edward James state official, computer programmer and analyst
Bradley, Wesley Holmes physician
Brewer, Aida M. treasurer
Bruno, Joseph L. state legislator, senate majority leader
Burger, Harold Alan virologist
Burian, Jarka Marsano performing arts educator
Canestrari, Ronald state legislator
Capaldi, Elizabeth Ann Deutsch psychological sciences educator
Casey, Glen P. state official
Castro, Bernadette state official
Catalano, Jane Donna lawyer
Christensen, Joan K. state legislator
Clarey, Donald Alexander government affairs consultant
Clark, David Albert pediatrician, consultant
Cole, John Adam insurance executive
Colombí-Monguió, Alicia de foreign language educator, poet
Conway de Macario, Everly immunologist, molecular biologist
Croce, Alan J. government agency executive
Cross, Robert Francis commissioner
Cruz, José Edgardo political science educator
Dal Col, Richard Herbert cardiothoracic surgeon
D'Ambra, Thomas E. pharmaceutical executive
Daniels, Randy A. secretary of state
Davis, Paul Joseph endocrinologist
DeBuono, Barbara Ann physician, state official
DeNuzzo, Rinaldo Vincent pharmacy educator
Destito, RoAnn M. state legislator
Devine, Eugene Peter lawyer
Doherty, Glen Patrick lawyer
Donohue, Mary lieutenant governor
Donovan, Robert Alan English educator
Dulin, Thomas N. lawyer
Edwin-Trotman, Michelle R. legislative staff member
Elwell, Rowland John pharmacist, researcher
Fakundiny, Robert Harry geologist, educator, consultant
Fanuele, Frank John engineering executive
Fein, Scott Norris lawyer
Ferrara, Donna state legislator
Gaddy, Sheila Mae application developer, geriatrics nurse, writer, volunteer
Gilliam, Marsha Sampson state agency administrator
Glazer, Joseph A. medical association administrator
Glick, Deborah J. state legislator
Graffeo, Victoria A. state appeals court judge
Greene, Aurelia state legislator
Hancox, David R(obert) audit administrator, educator
Happ, Harvey Heinz electrical engineer, educator
Hassell-Thompson, Ruth state legislator
Heshmat, Hooshang manufacturing executive
Hitchcock, Karen Ruth biology professor, dean, academic administrator
Hoffmeister, Jana Marie cardiologist
Hooper, Earlene state legislator
Howard, Lyn Jennifer medical educator
Howell, Robert Charles philosopher, educator
Hubbard, Howard James bishop
Huxley, Carole Frances Corcoran educational adminstrator
Iyer, Seema chemist
Jacobs, Rhoda S. state legislator
Jasinski, Kenneth M. energy executive
Jennings, Gerald D. (Jerry Jennings) mayor
Jiha, Jacques economist
Joyce, William George, Jr., transportation executive
Kaye, Judith Smith state appeals court chief judge
Kecskes, Istvan linguist, educator
Kekes, John philosopher, educator
Kelley, Sister Helen health facility executive
Kennedy, William Joseph novelist, educator
Kermani, Peter Rustam recording industry executive
Kim, Jai Soo retired physicist
Koff, Howard Michael lawyer
Kristofferson, Kris singer, songwriter, actor
Krueger, Liz state legislator
Kuhla, Donald E. chemicals executive
Laird, Edward DeHart, Jr., lawyer
Langer, Judith Ann literacy educator
Lawton, Nancy artist
Lenart, Cristian Paul mathematician, educator
Lepow, Martha Lipson pediatric educator
Lessner, Lawrence education educator
Lustenader, Barbara Diane human resources specialist
Macario, Alberto Juan Lorenzo physician
MacDowell, Richard T. surgeon, educator
Mancinelli-Cahill, Maggie theater director
Martland, T(homas) R(odolphe) philosophy educator
Mayersohn, Nettie state legislator
Meader, John Daniel judge
Mendez, Olga A. state legislator
Meo, Diane Sue artist, writer
Merbler, Candace Anne librarian
Meyer, Dale Robert ophthalmologist
Miles, Christine Marie museum director
Mills, Richard Paul school system administrator
Miner, Roger Jeffrey judge
Morga Bellizzi, Celeste editor
Mueller, I. Lynn strategic planning and communications consultant
Mumpower, Jeryl L. academic administrator
Naumann, Hans J. manufacturing executive
Nolan, Catherine T. state legislator
Novello, Antonia Coello state health commissioner, former surgeon general, pediatric nephrologist, educator, retired federal agency administrator
Olmstead, Lucinda Sue English professor
Pataki, George E. governor
Paulson, Peter John librarian, publishing company executive
Pheffer, Audrey Iris state legislator
Platkin, Richard M. lawyer
Powers, John Kieran lawyer
Provorny, Frederick Alan lawyer, educator
Qi, Zhigang materials scientist, chemist
Quackenbush, Roger E. retired secondary school educator
Read, Susan Phillips state appeals court judge
Reaulo, Arthur Robert mental health specialist, advocate
Reese, William Lewis philosophy educator
Refai, Shahid history professor
Rej, Robert biochemist
Rieder, Conly LeRoy cell biologist, consultant
Robbins, Cornelius (Cornelius Van Vorse) educational administration educator
Rosenfeld, Harry Morris editor
Rosenkrantz, Daniel J. computer science educator
Rosenthal, Irene L. education educator, consultant
Salins, Peter D. academic administrator
Schalit, Robert Edward advertising executive
Schell, Lawrence M. education educator, biologist
Schneider, Allan Stanford biochemistry, neuroscience and pharmacology educator, biomedical research scientist
Schneider, Duane Bernard English literature educator
Scott, William Proctor, III, lawyer
Sherman, Sandra Lynn auditor
Shubert, Joseph Francis librarian
Smith, Ada L. state legislator
Smith, Michael Ernest archaeologist, educator
Snitkoff, Gail Goodman immunologist, educator
Spitzer, Eliot Laurence state attorney general
Staley, Harry Charles retired literature educator, poet
Standard, Kenneth G. lawyer
Stavisky, Toby Ann state legislator
Stenson, Brian T. academic administrator
Stevens, Roy W. microbiologist, researcher
Stewart, Margaret McBride biology professor, researcher
Sullivan, Frances Taylor state legislator
Swartz, Donald Percy physician
Tepper, Clifford allergist, immunologist, educator
Thompson, Frank Joseph political science educator
Travers, W. Lawrence healthcare executive
Treadwell, Alexander F. former state official, political party chairman & leader
Tyksinski, Eugene Kory broadcast executive
Veille, Jean-Claude maternal-fetal medicine physician, educator
Verdile, Vincent Paul dean, emergency physician
Volker, Dale Martin state legislator, lawyer
von Schack, Wesley W. energy services company executive
Waldek, David P. pharmaceutical executive
Wallender, Michael Todd lawyer
Weinstein, Helene E. state legislator
Wilber, Roger Alan library supervisor, writer
Wildemann, Gregg Nylund writer
Williman, Pauline shorthand reporter, farm foundation administrator
Yu, Jiang W. research scientist
Zimmerman, Earl Abram physician, scientist, educator, neuroendocrinology researcher
Zimmerman, Joseph Francis political scientist, educator
Zonder, Adam Steven theater educator, production manager

Alfred
Coll, Edward Girard, Jr., university president
Greil, Arthur Lawrence sociology educator
Higby, Wayne (Donald Higby) artist, educator
Pye, Lenwood David materials science educator, researcher, consultant
Scheer, Joseph H. artist, education educator
Spriggs, Richard Moore ceramic engineer, research center administrator
Wang, Xingwu physics educator

Alfred Station
Condrate, Robert Adam, Sr., spectroscopy educator

Altamont
Armstrong, Agnes Rose Fingerlin musicologist

Amagansett
Fleetwood, M. Freile psychiatrist, educator
Frankl, Jeanne Silver association executive, lawyer
Frankl, Kenneth Richard retired lawyer
Zychick, Joel David lawyer

Amenia
Hale, Nathan Cabot sculptor, artist, poet

Amherst
Anisman, Martin Jay academic administrator
Aurbach, Herbert Alexander sociology educator
Bobinski, Mary Form library director
Brown, Murray economist, educator
Clark, Donald Malin professional association executive
Cohen, Herman Nathan private investigator
Edsberg, Laura E. research scientist, consultant
Goldhaber, Gerald Martin communication educator, author, consultant
Hu, Yun Hang chemical engineer
Ismail, Abu Zafar Mohamed physics educator, researcher, consultant
Kang, Cong X. mathematician, educator
Kurtz, Paul philosopher, educator, writer, publisher
Kutsin, Leonid engineering educator, researcher
Nickell, Joe paranormal expert
Pajak, David Joseph lawyer, consultant
Roehmholdt, John Michael urologist, educator
Wiesenberg, Jacqueline Leonardi social sciences educator

Amityville
Imbert, Richard Conrad insurance company executive, real estate developer
Palumbo, Anthony education educator
Soloway, Richard Lewis electronic manufacturing company executive
Upadhyay, Yogendra Nath physician, educator
Wright, Nannie Bell retired secondary school educator

Ancram
Blechman, R. O. artist, filmmaker

Ancramdale
Weinstein, Joyce artist

Angola
Green, Gerard Leo priest, educator

Annandale
Cutler, Robert W. biologist, educator

Annandale On Hudson
Achebe, Chinua writer, humanities educator
Botstein, Leon academic administrator, conductor, historian
Darrow, Emily M. public relations executive, writer
Manea, Norman writer, educator
Miyagawa, Chiori theater educator, playwright
Papadimitriou, Dimitri Basil economist, educator, academic administrator
Sourian, Peter writer, English educator

Appleton
Singer, Thomas Kenyon international business consultant, fruit grower

Ardsley
Dogaty, Lewis writer, publisher, lawyer, educator
Mohl, Allan S. social worker
Utermohlen, Herbert Georg dermatologist

Ardsley On Hudson
Stein, Milton Michael lawyer

Arkville
Downing, Darlene L. non-for-profit organization executive

Armonk
Boies, David lawyer
Bolduc, Ernest Joseph association management consultant, not-for-profit developer, consultant
Donofrio, Nicholas M. computer engineer
Dunton, Gary C. insurance company executive
Engel, Joel Stanley telecommunications executive
Gerstner, Louis Vincent, Jr., retired information technology executive
Harreld, James Bruce information technology executive
Iwata, Jon C. computer company executive
Joyce, John R. computer company executive
Kohnstamm, Abby E. marketing executive
Levere, Richard David internist, educator
Lineen, Edward M. lawyer, information technology executive
Loughridge, Mark computer company executive
Lowell, Stanley Herbert retired lawyer
Maine, Douglas L. computer company executive
Mellors, Robert Charles physician, scientist, educator
Quinn, James W. lawyer
Scotto, Renata soprano
Sharpe, Myron Emanuel publisher, editor, writer
Tantillo Elton, Nina artist, graphics designer, educator
Ward, Stephen M., Jr., computer company executive
Wolff, Kurt Jakob lawyer, director

Astonia
Carroll, David Joseph stage manager

Astoria
Aquino, Robert Joseph health care executive, consultant
Ghosal, Dino lawyer, educator, social worker
Griffin, Daniel Bernard, Jr., writer, scriptwriter, lyricist
Matheson, Linda retired social worker
Raymond, Barbara writer, educator
Salzberg, Russ sportscaster
Sirignano, Monica Ann performing company executive, playwright

Atlantic Beach
Lore, Martin Maxwell lawyer

Auburn
Mochel, Myron George mechanical engineer, educator

Aurora
Ryerson, Lisa M. academic administrator
Shilepsky, Arnold Charles mathematics educator, computer consultant
Thoburn, Crawford Randall music educator, composer

Averill Park
Haines, Walter Wells retired economics educator
Nevai, Lucia writer
Traver, Robert William, Sr., management consultant, writer, engineer

Babylon
Brackett, Ronald E. investment company executive, lawyer
Collis, Charles aircraft company executive
Hennelly, Edmund Paul lawyer, oil company executive
Kroll, Brian Walter Thomas music educator

Bainbridge
Compton, John Robinson retired rake company executive
Goerlich, Shirley Alice Boyce publishing executive, educator, media consultant

Baldwin
Lister, Bruce Alcott food scientist, consultant

Baldwin Place
Kurian, George Thomas publisher

Baldwinsville
Wilson, Harold Batting treasurer

Ballston Lake
McCann, Chris (Christian David McCann) application developer, educator

Ballston Spa
Barba, Harry author, educator, publisher
Brown, Ifigenia Theodore lawyer

Bangall
Swanson, David Heath agricultural company executive

Batavia
Bidlack, Jerald Dean manufacturing executive

Grieger, Donald L. *artist*
Steiner, Stuart *college president*

Bay Shore
Bloom, William Herman *neurosurgeon, author*
Goldstein, Leonard Barry
Kirsch, Scott Douglas *family practice physician*
Lindner, Deborah *writer, illustrator, photographer*
Williams, Tonda *entrepreneur, consultant*

Bayport
Mohanty, Christine Ann *retired language educator, actress*

Bayside
Adoquei, Sam *art educator, artist*
Ausubel, Hillel *librarian*
Bernstein, Barry S. *lawyer*
Carrozza, Ann-Margaret E. *state legislator, lawyer*
Low, Frederick Emerson *English educator*
Madden, Joseph Daniel *trade association executive*
Roth, Joshua S. *obstetrician/gynecologist, educator*
Zinn, William *musician, composer*

Bayville
Arenberg, Irving Kaufman Karchmer *otolaryngologist*

Beacon
Mc Keown, William Taylor *magazine editor, author*
Metz, Ferdinand *chef, educator, academic administrator*

Bearsville
Ruellan, Andree *artist*

Bedford
Atkins, Ronald Raymond *lawyer*
Bowman, James Kinsey *publishing company executive, rare book specialist*
Chase, Chevy (Cornelius Crane Chase) *comedian, actor, author*
Husted, William Armstrong *sales executive*
Kluge, Steve *secondary school educator*
Margolin, Carl M. *psychotherapist*
Philip, Peter Van Ness *former trust company executive*
Tischler, Gary Lowell *psychiatrist, educator*
Tognino, John Nicholas *financial services executive*

Bedford Corners
Greene, Jesse J., Jr., *former computer company executive*
Singer, Craig *entrepreneur, inventor, investor, consultant*

Bedford Hills
Fierstein, Harvey Forbes *playwright, actor*
Lustbader, Eric Van *writer*

Beechhurst
Wingate, Constance Blandy *librarian*

Bellerose
Dornagon, Mandy M. *lawyer*

Bellmore
Andrews, Charles Rolland *library administrator*
Bregman, Davis *physician, pain management specialist*
Brown, Earle Palmer *advertising agency executive*
Evers, Gene *writer*
Feldman, Harriet Ruth *dean*
Rosenstein, Elyse S. *secondary school educator*

Bellport
Hendrie, Elaine *public relations executive*
Moeller, Mary Ella *retired home economist, educator, radio commentator*
Regalmuto, Nancy Marie *small business owner, psychic consultant, therapist*
Schultheis, Edwin Milford *dean, business educator*
Townsend, Terry *publishing executive*

Bemus Point
Ross, Roderic Henry *insurance company executive*

Berlin
Pelz, Caroline Duncombe *retired educational administrator*

Bethpage
Albergo, Margaret *broadcast executive*
Conti, James Joseph *retired chemical engineer, educator*
Dolan, Charles Francis *media and entertainment company executive*
Dolan, James L *communications executive*
Janczak, Andrew Anthony *executive*
Mahony, Sheila Anne *broadcast executive*
Martin, Darryl James *audio-visual specialist*
McEnroe, Kate *broadcast executive*
Ratner, Hank J. *broadcast executive*
Sanna, Richard Jeffrey *lawyer*
Schwartz, Jonathan *broadcast executive*

Big Flats
Keck, Donald Bruce *physicist*
Orsillo, James Edward *computer systems engineer, company executive*

Binghamton
Anderson, Warren Mattice *lawyer*
Axtell, Clayton Morgan, Jr., *lawyer*
Bearsch, Lee Palmer *architect, city planner*
Best, Robert Mulvane *insurance company executive*
Bethje, Robert *retired general surgeon*
Bochnovich, John Andrew *small business owner*
Carrigg, James A. *retired utility company executive*
Clark, Clifford Dale *university president*
Coates, Donald Robert *geology educator, scientist*
Coffey, Margaret Tobin *education educator, county official*
Collins, Mary Shaffer *community nursing educator*
Crocker, Margaret Suydam Smith *art association executive director, art historian*
DeFleur, Lois B. *university president, sociology educator*
Eisch, John Joseph *chemist, educator, writer, consultant*
Gaddis Rose, Marilyn *literature educator, translator*
Gates, Gregory Ansel *lawyer*
Geer, James Francis *mathematics professor*
Gerhart, Eugene Clifton *lawyer*
Gouldin, David Millen *lawyer*
Hilton, Peter John *mathematician, educator*
Isaacson, Robert Lee *psychology educator, researcher*
James, Gary Douglas *biological anthropologist, educator, researcher*
Klir, George Jiri *systems science educator*
Levis, Donald James *psychologist, educator*
Marella, Philip Daniel *broadcasting company executive*
Meador, John Milward, Jr., *university dean*
Naslund, Howard Richard *geological science educator*
Nelson, Charles A. *physicist, educator*
Peckham, Eugene Eliot *judge, lawyer*
Peterson, Alfred Edward *family physician*
Polachek, Solomon William *economist, educator*
Sklar, Kathryn Kish *historian, educator*
Smales, Joel Robert *music educator*
Stein, George Henry *historian, educator, administrator*
Swain, Mary Ann Price *university official*
Taylor, Kenneth Douglas *stockbroker, finance and computer consultant, educator*
Thompson, Carlton Frederick *lawyer*
Villecco, Anthony Charles *tenor, travel company executive, consultant*
Whittingham, M(ichael) Stanley *chemist*
Yammarino, Francis Joseph *management consultant, educator*
Zaslavsky, Thomas *mathematics professor*
Ziemski, Connie Marie *social studies educator*

Bloomfield
Hansen, Widmer Case *retired weapons systems engineer, analyst*

Bloomington
Culver, Michael Patrick *music educator, composer*

Blue Mountain Lake
Day, Jacqueline Frances *museum director*

Blue Point
Owen, Thomas Llewellyn *investment executive*

Bohemia
Hausman, Howard *electronics executive*
Rudolph, Scott *pharmaceutical executive*

Bolton Landing
Crosby, John Griffith *investment banker*

Brainard
Isaksen, Robert L. *retired bishop*

Brewster
Bates, Barbara J. Neuner *retired municipal official*
Blyakhman, Yefim Moisei *chemist, researcher*
Nadel, Norman Allen *civil engineer*
Simon, Andrew L. *educational publishing executive*

Briarcliff Manor
Driver, Sharon Humphreys *marketing executive*
Hopkins, Lee Bennett *writer, educator*
Kennell, Richard Wayne *recording artist, business manager*
Lew, Leslie *artist*
Pousada, Lidia *physician*
Read, John Conyers *non-profit management*
Windham, Revish *poet*

Briarwood
Benedict, Joseph Harold, Jr., *academic administrator, management consultant*
Takacs, Michael Joseph *secondary school educator*

Bridgehampton
Coy, Christopher James *architect*
Cummings, Richard M. *law educator, consultant, writer*
Enstine, Raymond Wilton, Jr., *propane gas company executive*
Phillips, Warren Henry *publishing executive*

Bridgeport
Sheldon, Thomas Donald *academic administrator*

Brightwaters
Kavanagh, Eileen J. *librarian*
North, E(dward) Lee *retired writer, former aerospace company professional*
Zayas, Elinor Abrams *music educator*

Brockport
Dabbagh, Mahmoud *language educator, researcher*
Gemmett, Robert J. *university dean, English language educator*
Keiser, John Dougherty *business educator*
Leslie, William Bruce *history professor*
Owen, Karen Ann *historian, educator*
Prioleau, Darwin E. *dance educator, choreographer*
Stier, William Frederick, Jr., *academic administrator, educator*

Bronx
Adams, Alice *sculptor*
Adinolfi, Marion Darlyne *research scientist*
Adinolfi, Vincent John *realtor, product designer*
Afterman, Jean *professional sports team executive*
Ahmose, Nefertari A. *journalism educator*
Albrecht, Roberta J. *writer*
Aronowitz, Julian *management consultant*
Balka, Sigmund Ronell *lawyer*
Bamberger, Phylis Skloot *judge*
Bauman, Laurie Julia *sociologist, researcher*
Behnken, William Joseph *art educator, artist*
Bella, Jonathan Noriega *cardiologist*
Bennett, Michael Vander Laan *neuroscience educator*
Bhalodkar, Narendra Chandrakant *cardiologist*
Bigal, Marcelo E *physician, researcher*
Billett, Henny Heisler *hematologist*
Bingham, June *writer, playwright*
Blaufox, Morton Donald *hypertension specialist, educator, nuclear medicine physician*
Bowers, Francis Robert *literature educator*
Brandt, Lawrence Jay *internist, gastroenterologist, educator*
Brosius, Scott David *professional baseball player*
Bullaro, Grace Russo *literature, film and foreign language educator, speaker, book reviewer*
Burde, Ronald Marshall *neuro-ophthalmologist*
Burgio, Michael *medical researcher*
Burton, Leslie Anne *psychologist*
Buschke, Herman *neurologist*
Busch-Rossnagel, Nancy Ann *psychology educator, university dean*
Cammarata, Joan Frances *Spanish language and literature educator*
Canavan, Francis *priest, educator*
Capodilupo, Jeanne Hatton *public relations executive*
Casiano, Américo, Jr., *grants administrator, poet*
Clary, Roy *hospital administration executive*
Cohen, Herbert Jesse *physician, educator*
Cohen, Michael I. *pediatrician*
Cone, David Brian *professional baseball player*
Conway, William Gaylord *zoologist, zoo director, conservationist*
Cornfield, Melvin *lawyer, university institute director*
Correa, Nereida *women's health physician*
Coupey, Susan McGuire *pediatrician, educator*
Cubeñas, José Antonio *social worker, consultant*
Currie, Joseph Aloysius *campus ministry director, theology studies educator*
Das, Ashoke Kumar *internist, consultant*
Dimler, George Richard *German language educator, editor*
Dong, Feng *molecular biologist*
Drepaul, Loris Omesh *internist, infectious diseases physician*
Dulles, Avery *cardinal, theologian*
Dutcher, Janice Jean Phillips *oncologist*
Elenko, Stuart S. *historian, educator*
Eliasoph, Joan *radiologist, educator*
Elkins, Alfred David *insurance company executive*
Ellentuck, Elmer *journal editor*
Fahey, Charles Joseph *priest, gerontology educator*
Fernandez, Ricardo R. *university administrator*
Fishman, Joshua Aaron *sociolinguist, educator*
Foreman, Spencer *pulmonary specialist, hospital executive*
Freeman, Leonard Murray *radiologist, nuclear medicine physician, educator*
Friedman, Joel M. *biophysicist, educator*
Fulop, Milford *physician*
Gerst, Paul Howard *physician*
Giambi, Jason Gilbert *professional baseball player*
Gillison, David Andrew *artist, educator*
Gillman, Arthur Emanuel *psychiatrist*
Goldberg, Gary L. *oncologist, medical educator*
Goldman, Israel David *hematologist, director, oncologist, educator*
Goldstein, Eugene Bernard *comedian, educator*
Gonzalez, Rose A-Navarro *artist*
Goodrich, James Tait *neuroscientist, neurosurgeon*
Gurland, Judith E. *ophthalmologist, education educator*
Hallett, Charles Arthur, Jr., *English and humanities educator*
Hamerman, David Jay *gerontologist, educator*
Hauser, Bernice Worman *director*
Heagarty, Margaret Caroline *retired pediatrician*
Hennessy, Thomas Christopher *clergyman, educator, retired university dean*
Hermalyn, Gary Douglas *historian, educator*
Hilaris, Basil S. *radiologist, educator*
Hirano, Asao *neuropathologist*
Hodgson, W(alter) John (Barry Hodgson) *surgeon*
Hooker, Olivia J. *psychologist, educator*
Horan, Gary S. *healthcare executive*
Horwitz, Susan Band *molecular pharmacologist*
Hudson, Frederick Bernard *management consultant*
Humphry, James, III, *librarian, publishing executive*
Hunt, George William *priest, magazine editor*
Iezza, Anita Kay *physician assistant*
Jaffé, Ernst Richard *medical educator and administrator*
Jeter, Derek Sanderson *professional baseball player*
Juszczyk, James Joseph *artist*
Kahn, Thomas *medical educator*
Kanofsky, Jacob Daniel *psychiatrist, educator*
Karkanias, George B. *neurologist, educator*
Kassoy, Hortense (Honey Kassoy) *artist, sculptor, painter*
Keen, Linda *mathematician, educator*
Kelly, George Anthony *clergyman, author, educator*
Kelly, Roberto Conrado (Bobby Kelly) *professional baseball player*
Kitt, Olga *artist*
Koranyi, Adam *mathematics professor*
Kornfeld, Robert Jonathan *playwright, photographer*
Koss, Leopold G. *physician, pathologist, educator*
Kramer, Eleanor *retired real estate broker, tax practitioner, financial consultant*
Kuhn, Leslie Alvin *cardiologist*
Lee, Dong Hwan *business administration educator*
Leighton, Anne Renita *writer, educator*
Lerner, Laurence M. *college administrator*
Lewis, Darin John *music educator, composer*
Lieber, Charles Saul *physician, educator*
Lienert, Christoph *physical education educator*
Lofton, Kenneth *professional baseball player*
Lomke, Evander *publishing executive*
Long, Gregory R. *botanic garden administrator*
Lopez-Fitzsimmons, Bernadette Maria *librarian*
Lyons, Maxine Evadney *small business owner, poet*
Macklin, Ruth *bioethics educator*
Margolin, Leon *physician*
Marún, Gioconda *Spanish language educator*
McShane, Joseph Michael *academic administrator, priest*
Mendez, Hermann Armando *pediatrician, educator*
Mendez, Ruben Policarpio *diplomat, educator, economist*
Mercurio, Mia Lynn *education educator*
Mittler, Diana (Diana Mittler-Battipaglia) *music educator, administrator, pianist*
Mobasher, Maher Attia *academic administrator*
Mukherjee, Asit Baran *geneticist, educator*
Nagler, Arnold Leon *pathologist, research scientist, educator*
Nitowsky, Harold Martin *physician, educator*
Ofodile, Ferdinand *plastic surgeon*
Okpalanma, Chika *psychiatrist*
Olerud, John Garrett *professional baseball player*
Osborne, Claudina Rosetta *financial analyst*
Parker, Everett Carlton *clergyman*
Posada, Jorge Rafael *professional baseball player*
Purpura, Dominick P. *dean, neuroscientist*
Radel, Eva *pediatrician, hematologist*
Rapin, Isabelle *physician*
Regan, Richard Joseph *political science professor, writer*
Reynolds, Benedict Michael *surgeon*
Reynolds, Joseph Patrick *chemical engineering educator, consultant*
Reznik, Sandra Eve *physician, consultant*
Rivera, Mariano *professional baseball player*
Robinson, Bernard Pahl *retired thoracic surgeon, educator*
Robinson, Nadine Caroline *artist*
Rodriguez, Alexander Emmanuel *professional baseball player*
Romney, Seymour Leonard *physician, educator*
Rose, Israel Harold *mathematics professor*
Rothstein, Anne Louise *education educator, college official*
Ruben, Robert Joel *pediatric otorhinolaryngolist, educator*
Ryan, James Daniel *history professor*
Sable, Robert Allen *gastroenterologist*
Safyer, Steven Michael *medical administrator, educator*
Samuels, Leslie Eugene *marketing and management consultant*
Satir, Birgit H. *medical educator, medical researcher*
Scanlan, Thomas Joseph *college president, educator*
Schaller, George Beals *zoologist*
Scharff, Matthew Daniel *immunologist, cell biologist, educator*
Schaumburg, Herbert Howard *neurology educator*
Schwam, Marvin Albert *graphic design company executive*
Sedacca, Angelo Anthony *police investigator, educator, notary public*
Seltzer, William *statistician, social researcher, former international organization director*
Senturia, Yvonne Dreyfus *pediatrician, epidemiologist*
Shafritz, David Andrew *physician, research scientist*
Shapiro, Nella Irene *surgeon*
Sheffield, Gary Antonian *professional baseball player*
Sherman, Judith Dorothy *producer, recording company owner, recording engineer*
Shinnar, Shlomo *child neurologist, educator*
Spatt, Hartley Steven *humanities educator*
Spitzer, Adrian *pediatrician, educator*
Stein, Bernard L. *journalist*
Stein, Ruth Elizabeth Klein *physician*
Steinbrenner, George Michael, III, *professional baseball team executive, shipbuilding company executive*
Strate, Lance Adam *communications educator*
Strauch, Berish *plastic surgeon, hand and cosmetic surgeon*
Stuhr, David Paul *business educator, consultant*
Susso, Alhaji Papa *musician*
Sy, Stanley Peter Sison *internist*
Todd, Thomas Alexander *secondary school educator*
Torre, Joseph Paul (Joe Torre) *professional baseball team manager*
Ultan, Lloyd *historian, educator*
Valgemae, Mardi *English educator*
Vassel, Lee Hylton *urbanist, social services administrator, writer*
Ventura, Robin Mark *professional baseball player*
Waelsch, Salome Glueckssohn *geneticist, educator*
Walsh, Christine Ann *cardiologist*
Wertenbaker, Christian T. *neuro-ophthalmologist, writer*
Wertheim, Mary Danielle *elementary education coordinator*
Widger, Chris *professional baseball player*
Wiernik, Peter Harris *oncologist, educator*
Williams, Bernie (Bernabe Figueroa Williams) *professional baseball player*
Wosk, Julie *humanities educator*
Yadeka, Theophilus Adeniyi *hospital administrator*
Yalow, Rosalyn Sussman *nobel laureate, biophysicist*
Zalaznick, Sheldon *editor, journalist*

Bronxville
Bertles, John Francis *physician, educator*
Biscardi, Chester *composer, educator*
Bottino, Clement Gino *surgeon*
Brunale, Vito John *aerospace engineer*
Civiello, Mary *correspondent*
Cutler, Kenneth Burnett *lawyer, investment company executive*
DeMartino, Anthony Gabriel *cardiologist, internist*
Edleson, Michael Edward *economist, finance educator, consultant, writer*
Ellinghaus, William Maurice *communications executive*
Falvey, Patrick Joseph *lawyer*
Frost, A. Corwin *architect, consultant*
Fuller, David Otis, Jr., *lawyer*
Hagendorn, William H. *lawyer*
Hutchison, Dorris Jeannette *retired microbiologist, educator*
Levitt, Miriam *pediatrician*
L'Huillier, Peter *archbishop*
Lombardo, Philip Joseph *broadcasting company executive*
Mills, Nicolaus *American studies educator, writer*
Morton, Brian *writer, editor*
Myers, Michele Tolela *academic administrator*
Peters, Sarah Whitaker *art historian, writer, lecturer*
Pollin, Burton Ralph *English educator*
Rosenthal, Lucy Gabrielle *writer, educator, editor*

Brookhaven
Grucci Butler, Donna *fireworks company executive*
Kouts, Herbert John Cecil *retired physicist*

Brooklyn
Abott, Michael Larry *physician*
Abraham, Teena *pharmacist, educator*
Ackerman, Jacob Lewis *ophthalmologist*
Adler, Lee *artist, educator, marketing executive*
Afshinnia, Farsad *endocrinologist, researcher*
Al-Hafeez, Humza *minister, editor*
Allison, Mary Ann *consulting company executive, author, speaker*
Altura, Burton Myron *physiologist, educator*
Amendola, Sal John *artist, educator, writer*
Amon, Carol Bagley *federal judge*
Aquino, Humberto *painter, artist*
Arcuri, Leonard Philip *elementary school educator*
Argie, Jenny Lynn *artist*
Armenakas, Anthony Emmanuel *aerospace educator*

Avram, Morrell M. nephrologist, educator, consultant
Baehr, Sonya Kay theater educator, theater director
Baker, Kristina Marie adult nurse practitioner
Baker, Richard Joseph artist
Bandler, Martin physician
Barabash, Claire lawyer, special education administrator, psychologist
Barran, Thomas Paul language educator
Barth, Robert Henry nephrologist, educator
Beaufait, Frederick W(illiam) civil engineering educator
Bedrick, Anthony Edward oral surgeon, educator
Berger, David history professor
Berliner, Eve writer, editor, publishing executive
Bhattacharya, Bhaswati preventive medicine physician
Bianco, Anthony Joseph, III, newswriter
Birenbaum, Leo retired engineering educator
Birenbaum, William M. former university president
Biro, Laszlo dermatologist
Blasi, Alberto Romance languages educator, writer
Bloom, Howard Kenneth paleopsychologist, writer
Blue, Rose writer, educator
Bové, Robert Charles writer, editor, poet
Bramwell, Henry federal judge
Brenner, Beryl H. arts therapist
Brody-Lederman, Stephanie artist
Brooks, Peter computer company executive, application developer
Brown, Lawrence Stewart, Jr., physician
Browne, Ruth health science association administrator
Bugliarello, George academic administrator, educator
Burlacu, Constantin journalist, educator
Burrows, Edwin G. education educator
Buttaro, Lucia language educator, consultant
Cammarata, Jerry Frank hospital administrator, speech pathology/audiology services professional
Carswell, Lois Malakoff botanical gardens executive, consultant
Castleman, Louis Samuel metallurgist, educator
Catanello, Ignatius Anthony bishop
Catell, Robert Barry gas utility executive
Chambers, William Edmond telephone techician, writer
Chandan, Jit S. management consultant, educator
Chao, Tsai Chung physician, residency program director
Charchaflieh, Jean physician, educator
Charton, Marvin chemist, educator
Chernow, Ron writer, columnist
Cheung, Chi Pui internist
Choudhury, Deo Chand physicist, researcher
Chung, Ping Tsai education educator
Clark, James O. sculptor, art educator
Clayton, Julia B. academic administrator, musician
Cohen, Alan investment banker
Cohen, Carl I. psychiatry educator, researcher
Collier, Sadikisha Saundra artist, educator
Collins, Ronald Leslie Leopold physician, neurosurgeon
Cottrell, James E. anesthesiologist, medical educator
Cracco, Roger Quinlan medical educator, neurologist
Crânganu, Constantin engineer
Crum, Albert Byrd psychiatrist, consultant
Cummings, Josephine Anna writer, consultant, advertising executive
Cunningham, Joseph Newton, Jr., cardiothoracic and vascular surgeon
Dantzic, Cynthia Maris artist, educator
Das, Nirod K. engineering educator
Davis, Lawrence James editor, writer
Davis, William Terry software engineer, technology manager
D'Elia, Nicholas secondary school educator
Diamond, Jessica artist
Diamond, Murray J. lawyer
Dimant, Jacob internist
DiMarzio, Nicholas Anthony bishop
Dinnerstein, Harvey artist
Dinnerstein, Simon Abraham artist, educator
Donovan, Rita R. nurse anesthetist, trauma and critical care nurse, educator
Doucette, David Robert computer systems company executive
Douglass, Melvin Isadore middle school administrator, educator, clergyman
Duberstein, Conrad B. federal judge
Eirich, Frederick Roland chemist, educator
Eisenberg, Karen Sue Byer nurse
Eliasi, Jennifer Rebecca dietician, consultant
El Kodsi, Baroukh gastroenterologist, educator
Enseki, Carol museum director
Ensminger, John J. publishing executive, lawyer
Erber, William Franklin gastroenterologist
Evans, John T. finance educator, consultant, social sciences educator, researcher
Everdell, William Romeyn humanities educator, historian
Faison, Seth Shepard retired insurance broker
Feigelson, Eugene B. dean
Ferber, Linda S. museum curator
Fernandes, David Richard physician
Finger, Stephen otolaryngologist
Fischer, R. M. sculptor
Fischman, Myrna Leah accountant, educator
Flam, Jack Donald art historian, educator
Fleyshman, Bentsion physicist, researcher, retired mathematician
Forsberg, Suzanne humanities educator, humanities speaker
Fowler, John Dale, Jr., biotechnology management consultant, private equity investor
Franco, Victor theoretical physics educator
Friedman, Eli A. nephrologist, educator
Friedman, Gerald Manfred geologist, educator
Fuller, Marney Cecelia painter, graphics designer
Furchgott, Robert Francis pharmacologist, educator
Gabriel, Mordecai Lionel biologist, educator
Galgan, Gerald Joseph philosopher, educator
Garaufis, Nicholas G. district court judge
Garrett, Nancy Fales playwright, educator
Garrison, Maurice Allen Martin missionary, minister
Gershon, Nina federal judge
Gianlorenzi, Nona Elena painter, art dealer, educator
Gilmore, Jennifer A.W. computer specialist, educator
Gioseffi, Daniela (Dorothy Daniela Gioseffi) poet, novelist, critic, playwright
Gisolfi, Diana (Diana Gisolfi Pechukas) art history educator
Giuliano, Steven filmmaker
Giusti, Karin F. artist, educator
Glasser, Israel Leo federal judge
Goodman, Alvin S. engineering educator, consultant
Gootman, Phyllis Myrna physiology, neuroscience and biophysics educator
Gordon, Diane state legislator
Gotta, Alexander Walter anesthesiologist, educator
Graham, RosaLind Carlies nursing educator
Greene, Gladstone Fitzpatrick educator, consultant
Greenwood, Monique innkeeper, writer, restaurant owner
Gross, Stephen Mark pharmacist, academic dean
Gustin, Mark Douglas health facility administrator
Haber, Ira Joel artist, art educator
Ham, Karen musician, music educator
Hamarman, Stephanie psychiatrist, educator
Haque, Dewan Nazimul physician, anesthesiologist
Harpham, Heather Elise performing arts educator
Harris, Fred prosthetist
Hausman, Jill Susan rabbi, cantor, vocalist, lyricist, poet, composer
Hechtman, Howard financial analyst
Heisler, Norma Boodman psychotherapist
Helly, Walter Sigmund engineering educator
Hill, Elizabeth Anne academic administrator, lawyer
Hood, Ernest Alva, Sr., pharmaceutical company executive
Hopkins, Karen Brooks performing arts executive
Horowitz, Sara labor organizer
Ierardi, Eric Joseph school system administrator
Imperato, Pascal James physician, healthcare administrator, writer, historian
Isaacson, Arline Levine food association administrator
Isacoff, Mark psychologist
Iskander, Magued engineering educator, consultant
Ivens, Rosalind artist
Izmailov, Alexander F. physicist, mathematician, researcher
Jacobowitz, Israel Jacob cardiothoracic surgeon
Jaffe, Eric Allen physician, educator, researcher
Jaffe, Louise English language educator, creative writer
James, Milton Garnet economist
Jean-Louis, Girardin psychologist, educator, researcher
Jemisin, Noah artist, educator
Jivetin, Alexander geophysicist, educator
Jones, Lawrence Worth poet, editor, performance art producer, songwriter
Jones, Susan Emily fashion educator, administrator, educator emeritus
Kamins, Barry Michael lawyer
Karan, Hiroko Ito organic chemistry educator
Karmel, Roberta Segal lawyer, educator
Katavolos, William architecture educator, furniture designer
Kay, Arthur David neurologist
Kemp, James William graphic artist
Kempner, Joseph aerospace engineering educator
Kimmich, Christoph Martin academic administrator, educator
King, Margaret Leah history professor
Kirshenbaum, Richard Irving retired public health physician
Kjok, Sol artist, art historian, linguist, translator
Korman, Edward R. federal judge
Korolev, Anatoly Y. management consultant
LaFont, Suzanne anthropologist, educator
Lash, James radiologist
Lee, Spike (Shelton Jackson Lee) filmmaker
Lehman, Arnold Lester museum official, art historian
Lehner-Quam, Alison Lynn library administrator
Lentini, Francine physical education educator
Leonard, James Kevin mechanical engineer
Levy, Norman B. psychiatrist, educator
Lichter, Stephen Marc oncologist
Lindo, J. Trevor psychiatrist, consultant
Lipson, Steven Mark applied virologist, microbiologist, educator
List, Bobye Goodman science foundation director
Lobron, Barbara L. speech educator, writer, editor, photographer
Logan, Janet Artisam mental health nurse
Logan, Paula M. entertainment company executive, accountant
Lovett, Edward Richardson not-for-profit developer, writer
Lowery, Robert Chesley thoracic surgeon, educator
Luterman, Gerald electronics company executive
Lutwak, Erwin mathematician, educator
Ma, Tsu Sheng chemist, educator, consultant
Magliocco, John wholesale distribution executive
Mahler, Howard Samuel psychiatrist
Mannheimer, Zachary R. performing company executive
Mark, Richard Kushakow internist
Marlow, Shelley F. writer
Martinez-Pons, Manuel psychologist, educator
Mashkevich, Stefan Vladimirovich physicist, researcher, computer scientist
Maslow, Aaron D. lawyer
Maslow, Jeffrey R. not-for-profit fundraiser
Mauskopf, Roslynn R. prosecutor
Mayer, Ira Edward gastroenterologist
Mc Clenney, Byron Nelson community college administrator
McLean, William Ronald retired electrical engineer, consultant
Menil, Violeta Cruz mathematician, educator, consultant
Mezey, Andrew Peter pediatrician, educator
Millman, Joan state legislator
Mirra, Suzanne Samuels neuropathologist, researcher
Montgomery, Velmanette state senator
Mook, Sarah retired chemist
Moore, Jane Ross librarian, educator
Moosazadeh, Kioomars orthopedist, educator, physiatrist, researcher
Morales, Jose psychotherapist, writer
Morgan, Mary Louise Fitzsimmons fund raising executive, lobbyist
Morris, Mark William choreographer
Murillo-Rohde, Ildaura Maria marriage and family therapist, consultant, educator, dean
Nadel, Monroe Stanley retired architect, landscape architect
Nakanishi, Yuko Julie engineering educator, consultant
Neu, Jim A playwright
Newbauer, John Arthur editor
Niesen, James Louis theater director
Nozzolillo, Anthony utilities executive
Nurhussein, Mohammed Alamin internist, geriatrician, educator
Nussbaum, Arnold pediatrician
Nye, William Roger psychologist
Ocasio, Wilfred writer
O'Connor, Sister George Aquin (Margaret M. O'Connor) academic administrator, sociology educator
Onken, George Marcellus retired lawyer
Ortega, Maria A. security firm executive, educator
Ortiz, Lori J. painter, writer
Ortner, Everett Howard magazine editor, writer
Otterness, Tom artist
Oussani, James John stapling company executive
Palermo, Robert James architect, consultant, inventor
Parlamis, Michael Frank civil engineer, construction company executive
Pasciuto, Joseph Doria priest
Paton, Bob theater director, writer
Pearlstein, Seymour artist
Peker, Elya Abel artist
Pennisten, John William computer scientist, actuary, linguist
Pertschuk, Louis Philip pathologist, consultant
Peruggi, Regina S. academic administrator
Peters, Mercedes psychoanalyst
Petersen, Richard John small business owner, educator
Phillips, Gretchen social worker
Phillips, William Charles T'ai Chi instructor
Pine, Bessie Miriam social worker, editor, columnist
Pitynski, Andrzej Piotr sculptor
Ponnambalam, Ananthasekar pediatrician, gastroenterologist
Price, Ely dermatologist
Purdy, James writer
Quick, Walter Curtis music company executive
Quinones, Jose Ramon, Jr., obstetrician-gynecologist, educator
Rachko, Maurice cardiologist
Raggi, Reena circuit judge
Raskind, Leo Joseph law educator
Rauschenbusch, Stephanie artist, educator, poet
Ravitz, Leonard J., Jr., physician, scientist, consultant
Reich, Nathaniel Edwin internist, educator, poet, artist
Reichbach, Gustin Lewis state supreme court justice
Reichel, Walter Emil advertising executive
Reinisch, June Machover psychologist, educator
Reisler, Helen Barbara public relations executive
Reynolds, Nancy Remick writer, researcher, editor
Rezkalla, Laurence internist
Rice, John Thomas architecture educator
Richmond, Eero composer, music librarian
Roach, Kevin Joseph set designer
Robinson, Annette councilwoman
Roche, John Edward educator, human resources consultant
Rogers, Michael Alan writer
Rokhvarger, Anatoly Efim materials science and ceramic technology scientist
Rosario-Olmedo, Carmen Gloria principal
Ross, Randolph Ernest investor
Rumohr, Floyd performing company executive, educator
Rutsky, Lester retired textiles executive, writer
Ryan, Leonard Eames judge
Saint-Fort, Raymond Paul writer
Salwen, Martin J. pathologist, educator
Salzman, Eric composer, writer
Samuel, Carren C. hospital administrator
Sanford, David Boyer writer, editor
Savits, Barry Sorrel surgeon
Schaefer, Marilyn Louise artist, writer, educator
Schiffman, Gerald microbiologist, educator
Schneider, Adele Goldberg librarian, educator
Schoutens, Hans mathematician, educator
Schussler, Theodore lawyer, physician, educator, consultant
Schutte, Thomas Frederick academic administrator
Schwarz, Richard Howard obstetrician, gynecologist, educator
Schweikert, Edgar Oskar dentist
Segelnick, Stuart Lawrence periodontist
Shalita, Alan Remi dermatologist
Sharify, Nasser educator, author, librarian
Shaw, Kendall (George Shaw) artist, educator
Shaw, Leonard Glazer retired electrical engineering educator, consultant
Shcherbakova, Estella chemist, mathematician, educator
Shedrinsky, Alexander Mikchail chemistry professor, conservator, consultant
Shelov, Steven Patrick pediatrician, educator
Shubert, Gabrielle S. museum executive director
Shulman, Abraham otolaryngology educator, hospital administrator
Sifton, Charles Proctor federal judge
Silverstein, Louis art director, designer, editor
Singer, Eric T. investment banker
Skrobela, Katherine Creelman music producer
Smith, Bernadine M. radio announcer, filmmaker, writer, producer, director
Smith, John W(esley), Jr., data processing executive, consultant
Sonenberg, Jack artist
Sorscher, Marvin Loeb religious studies educator, rabbi
Spector, Robert Donald language professional, educator
Staggers, Mary E. minister
Stellman, Jeanne Mager public health educator
Stuckey, James P. real estate company executive
Sun, Wei Yue internist
Swirsky, Judith Perlman arts administrator, consultant, writer
Szenberg, Michael economics educator, editor, consultant
Tamir, Theodor electrophysics researcher, educator
Taylor, Shannon lawyer, not-for-profit developer
Thacher, Barbara Auchincloss history educator
Thoering, Robert Charles elementary school educator
Thomson, David dancer, vocalist
Tomaselli, Fred artist
Torras, Mariano economist, educator
Trager, David G. federal judge
Tunuguntla, Hari Siva Gurunadha Rao urologist
Turtz, Marilyn Joan artist, painter, educator
Twining, Lynne Dianne clinical psychologist and psychoanalyst, professional society administrator, educator, writer
Varma, Ranbir economics professor
Vassalle, Mario physiologist
Vidal, Maureen Eris theater educator, actress
Vinegrad, Alan prosecutor
Viswanathan, Ramaswamy physician, educator
Von Essen, Thomas protective services official
von Rydingsvard, Ursula Karoliszyn sculptor
Walsh, George William publishing company executive, editor, author
Weil, Edward David chemistry researcher, consultant, educator
Weill, Georges Gustave mathematics educator
Weiner, Anthony David congressman
Weinstein, Jack Bertrand federal judge
Weinstock, Judith obstetrician/gynecologist
Weston, I. Donald architect
Wiener, Hesh (Harold Frederic Wiener) publisher, editor, consultant
Williams, Alun artist, curator, art gallery director
Williams, Edward Frank poet, entertainment company executive
Wilson, Arthur Theodore education consultant
Wilson, Robert Warne philanthropist, investor
Witherspoon, Maria Bernarda Pena bilingual educator
Wolfe, Ethyle Renee (Mrs. Coleman Hamilton Benedict) college administrator
Wolintz, Arthur Harry neurologist, ophthalmologist
Woodham, Joseph Ed artist, art educator
Wrotten, Marylean medical coordinator, counselor
Yogeswaran, Pararajasingam physician
Zakanitch, Robert Rahway artist
Zelin, Jerome retired retail executive
Zisser, Martin Shepherd fur apparel manufacturer, investor, trader
Zollar, Jawole Willa Jo artist, choreographer
Zuk, Judith botanic garden administrator
Zweig, Janet artist

Brookville

Kusukawa, Akira demographer, educator
Maillet, Lucienne humanities educator

Buffalo

Albert, Michael Salvatore pathologist, medical laboratory executive
Amborski, Leonard Edward retired chemist
Ambrus, Clara Maria physician
Ambrus, Julian L. physician, medical educator
Anbar, Michael biophysics educator
Anderson, Wayne Arthur electrical engineering educator
Armfield, Felix L. education educator, consultant
Axlerod, Harvey Steven application developer
Baier, Robert Edward chemist, educator
Ballow, Mark physician, educator
Barber, Janice Ann lawyer
Bardos, Thomas Joseph chemist, educator
Battle, Michael A. lawyer
Bayles, Jennifer Lucene museum program director, educator
Bernardino, Michael E. academic administrator, physician, educator
Blane, Howard Thomas research institute administrator
Bobinski, George Sylvan librarian, educator
Boot, John C.G. economist, educator
Boyar, Benjamin music educator
Brody, Harold neuroanatomist, gerontologist
Brydges, Thomas Eugene lawyer
Buchanan, Richard N. dean, dental educator
Bucki, Carl Leo judge
Butsch, John Lord surgeon, educator
Cañedo, Marion school system administrator
Carlson, Bruce William diversified holding company executive
Catalano, James Anthony social worker, consultant
Cathey, Patrice Antoinette secondary school educator, director
Chang, Ching Ming (Carl Chang) engineering executive, mechanical engineer, educator
Chiewanichakorn, Methee research scientist
Chu, Tsann Ming immunochemist, educator
Clarkson, Elisabeth Ann Hudnut volunteer
Coburn, Lewis Alan mathematics professor
Coles, Robert Traynham architect
Coppens, Philip chemist
Creaven, Patrick Joseph physician, clinical pharmacologist
Cryan, Richard James, Jr., academic administrator
Day, Donald Sheldon lawyer
Delaney, Tim sociologist, educator
Dennis, Carl poet
De Veaux, Alexis writer, educator
DiFranco, Ani music executive, musician
Doren, Robert Alan lawyer
Doyno, Victor Anthony literature educator
Drury, Chris professional hockey player
Duax, William Leo biological researcher
Dumitru, Magdalena Lucia linguist, educator
Ehrlich, Isaac economist, educator, department chairman
Elfvin, John Thomas federal judge
Enhorning, Goran obstetrician, gynecologist, educator
Epstein, Jonathan Daniel journalist
Fallavollita, James A. cardiologist, educator, cardiologist, researcher
Feldman, Irving poet
Fernbach, John diverified financial services executive
Floss, Frederick George economics and finance educator, consultant
Freedman, Maryann Saccomando lawyer
Frone, Michael R. psychologist, researcher
Fryer, Appleton publisher, sales executive, lecturer, diplomat
Fuda, Siri Narayan K.K. (Elaine T. Barber) director
Gardner, Arnold Burton lawyer
Genco, Robert Joseph immunologist, periodontist, educator, scientist
Gentile, Carmen James lawyer
Giambra, Joel Anthony county executive
Gisel, Bill food products executive
Glanville, Robert Edward lawyer
Goldberg, Neil A. lawyer
Goralski, Donald John public relations executive, counselor
Gort, Michael economics professor

Grasser, George Robert *lawyer, real estate consultant*
Greene, Robert Michael *lawyer*
Greiner, William Robert *university administrator, educator, lawyer*
Gress, Edward J(ules) *educator, consultant*
Grol, Regina *literature educator, translator*
Gruen, David Henry *financial executive, consultant*
Hahn, Theresa *epidemiologist, researcher*
Halbreich, Uriel Morav *psychiatrist, educator*
Halpern, Ralph Lawrence *lawyer*
Halt, James George *advertising executive, graphic designer*
Hare, Peter Hewitt *philosophy educator*
Hauptman, Herbert Aaron *mathematician, educator, researcher*
Hayes, David Ralph *lawyer*
Hayes, J. Michael *lawyer*
Headrick, Thomas Edward *lawyer, educator*
Heckman, Carol E. *lawyer*
Herdzik, Arthur Alan *lawyer*
Hetzner, Donald Raymund *social studies educator, forensic social scientist*
Hoffman, Faith Louise *social worker*
Hohn, David *physician*
Holm, Bruce Allen *academic administrator, researcher*
Holmes, James M. *social studies educator, economist*
Houseknecht, Stephen *artist, educator*
Howard, Muriel A. *academic administrator*
Hudson, Raymond Anthony *physician*
Iggers, Georg Gerson *history professor*
Irwin, Robert James Armstrong *investment company executive*
Jacobs, Jeremy M. *diversified financial services company executive, professional sports team executive*
Jain, Piyare Lal *physics educator*
Jasen, Matthew Joseph *lawyer, state justice*
Jusko, William Joseph *pharmaceutical scientist, educator*
Karwan, Mark Henry *engineering educator, dean*
Kelly, Jim (James Edward Kelly) *former professional football player*
Kipping, Hans F. *dermatologist, educator*
Knopf, Robert Michael *theater educator, theater director*
Kristoff, Karl W. *lawyer*
Krzyzanski, Wojciech *pharmacokineticist, consultant, mathematician*
Kurlan, Marvin Zeft *retired surgeon*
LaHood, Marvin John *English educator*
Lamb, Charles Moody *political scientist, educator*
Landi, Dale Michael *industrial engineer, academic administrator*
Layton, Rodney Eugene *financial executive, newspaper executive*
Leist, Susan Mondschein *communications educator, consultant*
Lele, Amol Shashikant *obstetrician and gynecologist*
Levy, Harold James *physician, psychiatrist*
Lipke, Brian J. *metal products executive*
Littlewood, Douglas Burden *business brokerage executive*
Manes, Stephen Gabriel *concert pianist, educator*
Manning, Kenneth Alan *lawyer*
Masiello, Anthony M. (Tony Masiello) *mayor*
Mattar, Lawrence Joseph *lawyer*
McClary, Glen David *education educator*
McGuire, William Dennis *health facility administrator*
McKibbin, William Alex *artist*
Meredith, Dale Dean *civil engineering educator*
Merini, Rafika *foreign language, cultures and literatures educator*
Metzger, Erika Alma *education educator*
Metzger, Ernest Hugh *aerospace engineer, research scientist*
Milgrom, Felix *immunologist, educator*
Milligan, John Drane *historian, educator*
Mindell, Eugene Robert *surgeon, educator*
Mitchell, Mike L. *academic administrator*
Moran, Charles *consumer products company executive*
Mucci, Gary Louis *lawyer*
Naughton, John Patrick *cardiologist, medical educator*
Naylon, Betsy Zimmermann *artist*
Neuner, Jerome Lawrence *academic administrator, educator*
Newman, Stephen Michael *lawyer*
Nolan, James Paul *internist, educator, medical researcher*
O'Donnell, Denise Ellen *lawyer*
Odza, Randall M. *lawyer*
O'Loughlin, Sandra S. *lawyer*
Patel, Mulchand Shambhubhai *biochemist, researcher*
Payne, Frances Anne *literature educator, researcher*
Pearson, Paul David *lawyer, arbitrator, mediator*
Penniman, W. David *information scientist, educator, consultant*
Peoples, Crystal D. *state legislator*
Peradotto, John Joseph *classics educator, editor*
Perry, J. Warren *health sciences educator, administrator*
Pett, John Lyman *banker*
Piazza, Kris A. *writer, editor*
Piech, Margaret Ann *mathematics professor*
Pietruszka, Michael F. *judge*
Piver, M. Steven *gynecologic oncologist*
Priore, Roger L. *biostatistics educator, consultant*
Rachlin, Lauren David *lawyer*
Reed, Janet *dance educator, choreographer*
Regier, Darcy John *professional hockey team coach*
Reinhorn, Andrei M. *civil structural engineering educator, consultant*
Reismann, Herbert *engineer, educator*
Reitan, Paul Hartman *geologist, educator*
Rich, Robert E., Sr., *frozen foods company executive*
Riepe, Dale Maurice *philosopher, writer, illustrator, educator, Asian art dealer*
Robinson, David Clinton *reporter*
Robinson, Zan Dale *language educator, writer*
Rogovin, Milton *documentary photographer, retired optometrist*
Ruckenstein, Eli *chemical engineering educator*
Ruff, Lindy *professional hockey coach*
Runfola, Ross Thomas *lawyer, educator, writer, journalist, poet*
Salisbury, Eugene W. *lawyer, justice*
Satan, Miroslav *professional hockey player*
Schentag, Jerome John *pharmacy educator*
Schmidli, Keith William *vocational education administrator, educator, researcher*
Schroeder, Harold Kenneth, Jr., *US magistrate judge*
Schultz, Douglas George *art museum director*
Segalla, Thomas Francis *lawyer*
Seitz, Mary Lee *mathematics professor*
Seller, Robert Herman *cardiologist, physician*
Shapiro, Stuart Charles *computer scientist, educator*
Shaw, David Tai-Ko *electrical and computer engineering educator, university administrator*
Shedd, Donald Pomroy *surgeon*
Sherris, David Allan *surgeon, medical researcher, educator*
Sherwood, Arthur Morley *lawyer*
Shick, Richard Arlon *finance educator*
Siedlecki, Peter Anthony *English language and literature educator*
Simpson, George True *surgeon, educator*
Simpson, John Barclay *academic administrator*
Skretny, William Marion *federal judge*
Small, William C. *religious organization administrator*
Sobolewski, Timothy Richard *marketing executive*
Spengler, Paul Albert *grants and foundation administrator*
Starks, Fred William *chemicals executive*
Stoll, Howard Lester, Jr., *dermatologist*
Stoss, Frederick Warren *librarian, educator*
Sullivan, Margaret M. *editor*
Swihart, Mark Thomas *chemical engineer, educator*
Tedlock, Barbara Helen *anthropologist, educator, academic administrator*
Tomasi, Thomas B. *cell biologist, administrator*
Toohey, Philip S. *lawyer*
Treanor, Charles Edward *scientist*
Trego, Charles R., Jr., *food products company executive*
Trevisan, Maurizio *epidemiologist*
Triggle, David John *dean, pharmacist, consultant*
Tritsch, George Leopold *biochemist, educator, retired biomedical researcher*
Trotter, Herman Eager, Jr., (Herman Trotter) *retired music critic*
Tsai, Christina W. *civil engineer, educator*
Tucker, Melvin Jay *education educator, researcher*
Twagilimana, Aimable *English educator, writer*
Urban, Henry Zeller *newspaperman*
Vladutiu, Adrian O. *physician, educator*
Vogel, Michael N. *journalist, writer, historian*
Wang, Jui Hsin *biochemistry educator*
Weber, Thomas William *chemical engineering educator*
Weekes, Rey *theater educator*
Weller, Sol William *chemical engineering educator*
Wiesenberg, Russel John *statistician*
Wilbur, Barbara Marie *elementary school educator*
Williams, Lillian Serece *historian, social studies educator*
Williams, Stephen Lawrence *writer, consultant*
Wilmers, Robert George *banker*
Wisbaum, Wayne David *lawyer*
Wise, Roland *retired art educator, artist*
Wright, John Robert *pathologist, educator*
Yu, Jiyuan *philosopher, educator*
Zhang, Jie *education educator, researcher*
Zhitnik, Alexei *professional hockey player*

Burke
Crippen, Juanita Witherell *elementary school educator*

Burnt Hills
DeVries, Robert Charles *scientist, researcher, consultant*

Buskirk
Johanson, Patricia Maureen *artist, architect, park designer*

Cairo
Ludwig, Laura Lonshein *poet*

Callicoon
Kurtz, Joel *construction company executive*

Cambridge
Kriss, Gary W(ayne) *Episcopal priest*
Tougias, Mark A. *artist*

Camillus
Alvaro, Anthony Joseph *music educator*
Caryl, William R., Jr., *orthodontist*
Davis, Lynn Harry *secondary school educator*

Campbell Hall
Austin, Danforth Whitley *newspaper executive*
Greenly, Colin *artist*
Ottaway, James Haller, Jr., *newspaper publisher*

Canaan
Belknap, Michael H. P. *real estate developer*
Knebel, Constance *potter, ceramist*
Pennell, William Brooke *lawyer*
Rothenberg, Albert *psychiatrist, educator*
Walker, William Bond *painter, retired librarian*

Canandaigua
Barden, George V. *county official, watershed specialist*
Chappelle, Lou Jo *physical therapist assistant*
Love, Robert Lyman *educational consulting company executive*
Lowther, Frank Eugene *research physicist*
Sands, Richard E. *food products executive*
Wormer, Thomas Andrew *surgeon*

Canton
Goldberg, Rita Maria *foreign language educator*
O'Connor, Daniel William *retired religious studies and classical languages educator*
Pollard, Fred Don *finance company executive, director*
Shuman, James C. *education educator*
Sullivan, Daniel F. *academic administrator, sociologist, educator*
Swinwood, Laurie A. *writer, educator*

Carle Place
Mulhern, Edwin Joseph *lawyer*

Carmel
Calegari, Maria *ballerina*
Iglehart, Patricia Ann *business development and communications executive*
Laporte, Cloyd, Jr., *lawyer, retired manufacturing executive*
Shen, Chia Theng *former steamship company executive, religious institute official*

Carthage
Ebbels, Bruce Jeffery *retired physician, health facility administrator*

Castile
Krolikowski, Gary E. *social sciences educator*

Castleton On Hudson
Kienzle, John Fred *history educator*
Lanford, Oscar Erasmus, Jr., *retired university vice chancellor*

Cato
Sheckler, Ross David *engineering executive*

Catskill
Green, Francis Eugene *artist, educator*
Wolfe, Geraldine *academic administrator*

Cazenovia
Carlson, William Clifford *retired defense company executive, retired naval officer*
Shattuck, George Clement *retired lawyer*

Cedarhurst
Cohen, Harris L. *diagnostic radiologist, consultant*
Cohen, Philip Herman *accountant*
Lipsky, Linda Ethel *health facility administrator*
Milk, Jared Marc *real estate company executive, writer*
Taubenfeld, Harry Samuel *lawyer*
Van Raalte, Polly Ann *reading and writing specialist, photojournalist*

Centereach
Chassman, Karen Moss *educational administrator*
Greene, Marc Elliot *educational association administrator*

Centerport
Fischel, Edward Elliot *physician, educator*
McQueeney, Henry Martin, Sr., *publisher*
Rogers, Ailene Kane *retired secondary school educator*
Stevens, Martin Brian *publisher*
Trotta, Ric Charles *aerospace company executive, consultant*
Tunick, Laraine Donisi *publishing executive*

Central Islip
Bernstein, Stan *federal bankruptcy judge*
Boyle, E. Thomas *federal magistrate judge*
Cyganowski, Melanie L. *bankruptcy judge*
Eisenberg, Dorothy *federal judge*
Loughlin, Timothy Arthur *mathematics professor*
McCrain, Michael William *accountant, financial advisor*
McGowan, Harold *real estate developer, investor, scientist, author, philanthropist*
Platt, Thomas Collier, Jr., *federal judge*
Seybert, Joanna *federal judge*
Spatt, Arthur Donald *federal judge*

Central Square
BuMann, Sharon Ann *sculptor*

Chappaqua
Boal, Lyndall Elizabeth *social worker*
Caranicas, Peter *editor*
George, Jean Craighead *author, illustrator*
Glazer, Richard Basil *university program director*
Laun, Louis Frederick *government official*
Melvin, Russell Johnston (Jay Melvin) *magazine publishing consultant*
O'Neill, Robert Charles *inventor, consultant*
Pomerene, James Herbert *retired computer engineer*
Ujifusa, Grant Masashi *editor*

Chatham
Kherdian, David *writer*
Squier, Rita Ann Holmberg *graphic designer*

Chautauqua
Campbell, Joan Brown *religious organization executive*

Chazy
Ratner, Gayle *special education educator*

Cheektowaga
Keem, Michael Dennis *veterinarian*
Mruk, Eugene Robert *retired marketing professional, urban planner*
Woldman, Sherman *pediatrician*
Wozniak, Richard Anthony *computer engineer*

Cherry Valley
Humes, Graham *investment banker*
Sapinsky, Joseph Charles *magazine executive, photographer*

Chester
Amelar, Richard Daniel *urologist, andrologist*
Karen, Linda Tricarico *interior designer*
Mackerodt, Fred *public relations specialist*

Chestnut Ridge
Burns, Richard Owen *lawyer*
Day, Stacey Biswas *physician, medical educator*
Huntoon, Robert Brian *chemist, food industry consultant*

Chittenango
Cassell, William Walter *retired accounting operations consultant*

Churchville
Balch, Glenn McClain, Jr., *academic administrator, minister, writer*
Clarke, Stephan Paul *retired language educator, retired writer*

Cicero
Pink, (Alecia Moore) *singer*

Clarence
Greatbatch, Wilson *biomedical engineer*
Johnston, Joan Lawler *director, consultant*

Claverack
Barrett, William Gary *advertising and marketing executive*

Clayton
Blassingame, Ronald Jay *social worker*
Schmidt, Karl M., Jr., *political science educator*

Clifton Park
Blais, Bernard Raymond *ophthalmologist, occupational health physician, educator*
Elken, Alar E. *publishing executive*
Healy, Joseph Robert *lawyer*
Hilts, Earl T. *lawyer, government official, educator*
Monguió, Luis *Spanish language educator*
Scher, Robert Sander *instrument design company executive*

Clinton
Behrens, John (Jack) *editor, writer, columnist, educator*
Pagani, Albert Louis *aerospace system engineer*
Paris, David C. *academic administrator, political scientist, educator*
Rabinowitz, Peter J. *literature educator, music critic*
Raybeck, Douglas *anthropologist, educator*
Redfield, Robert Horace *mathematician, educator*
Ring, James Walter *physics educator*

Clinton Corners
McDermott, Patricia Ann *nursing administrator*

Clymer
Hasbrouck, Kem L. *controller*

Cobleskill
Ingels, Jack Edward *horticulture educator*

Cohocton
Sarfaty, Wayne Allen *insurance agent, financial planner*

Cold Spring
Battersby, Katherine Sue *elementary school educator*
Milner, Debbi Elissa *computer company executive*
Milner, John *computer company executive*
Pugh, Emerson William *electrical engineer*

Cold Spring Harbor
Honey, Sangeet *molecular biologist*
Kidner, Catherine Anne *biologist*
MacKay, Robert Battin *museum director*
Wallin, James Peter *lawyer*
Watson, James Dewey *molecular biologist, educator*

Commack
Cohen, Judith W. *retired academic administrator*
Kurtz, Joel Barry *finance executive*
Ohman, Franklin Eric *ballet educator, choreographer*
Price, Amelia Ruth *not-for-profit foundation president, artist, small business owner*
Rakower, Joel A. *business appraiser, litigation consultant*
Steindler, Walter G. *retired lawyer*

Conesus
Dadrian, Vahakn Norair *sociology educator*

Cooperstown
Bordley, James, IV, *surgeon*
Cossa, Joanne *performing company executive*
Fenton, William Nelson *anthropologist, anthropology educator emeritus*
Franck, Walter Alfred *rheumatologist, medical administrator, educator*
Gavey, James Edward *investment company executive*
Harman, Willard Nelson *malacologist, educator*
Mays, Willie Howard, Jr., (Say Hey Kid) *former professional baseball player*
Robertson, Stewart *conductor*
Tilton, Webster, Jr., *contractor*
Yount, Robin *retired professional baseball player*

Copake
Johnson, Paul Edward *poet, writer*

Coram
Fialkow, Steven *accountant*
Uh, David Keun *civil engineer*

Corinth
Winslow, Norma Mae *elementary school educator*

Corning
Beall, George Halsey *ceramics engineer*
Becraft, Charles D., Jr., *lawyer*
Behm, Forrest Edwin *glass manufacturing company executive*
Bonomo, Timothy Paul *education educator, consultant*
Buechner, Thomas Scharman *artist, retired glass manufacturing company executive, museum director*
Cicerchi, Eleanor Ann Tomb *fundraising executive*
Davis, Francis Raymond *priest*
Ecklin, Robert Luther *materials company executive*
Flaws, James B. *technology executive*
Houghton, James Richardson *glass manufacturing company executive*
Loose, John W. *sales company executive*
Miller, Joseph A. *chemicals executive*
Miller, Roger Allen *physicist*
Peters, Linda S. *musician, music educator*
Pindel, David Lee *biologist, educator*
Sala, Martin Andrew *biophysicist, inventor*
Spillman, Jane Shadel *curator, researcher, writer*
Stookey, Stanley Donald *chemist*
Ughetta, William Casper *lawyer, manufacturing executive, director*
Visovsky, Nick John *research scientist*
Weeks, Wendell P. *opto-electronics executive*
Whitehouse, David Bryn *museum director*

Cornwall On Hudson
Abrams-Collens, Vivien *artist*
Rosenof, Theodore Dimon *historian, educator*

Corona
Jackson, Andrew Preston *library director*
Maruca, Rita *real estate company executive, real estate broker*

Cortland
Anderson, Donna Kay *musicologist, educator*
Gauss, Karl Frederik *internist, educator, geriatrician*
Nagel, Mechthild Euphrosyne *philosopher, educator, sociologist*
Taylor, Leland Baridon *lawyer*
Valentine, Gordon Carlton *retired secondary school educator*

Cortlandt Manor
Frischmuth, Robert Alfred *landscape planner, filmmaker*
Rosenberg, Marilyn Rosenthal *artist, visual poet*

Coxsackie
Moyna, John Lawrence *priest*

Cranberry Lake
Glavin, James Edward *landscape architect*

Cross River
Lang, Robert Mays, Jr., *manufacturing executive*
Thorn, Susan Howe *interior designer*

Croton On Hudson
Eswein, Bruce James, II, *human resources specialist*
Hoffman, Paul Shafer *lawyer*
Johann, Anne Dorothy *visual artist, painter, printmaker, graphic artist*
Kazim, Victor *accountant*
Lewins, Steven *security analyst, investment advisor, corporate executive, diplomatic, military, and airline safety advisor*
Plotch, Walter *management consultant, fund raising counselor*
Rubinfien, Leo H. *photographer, filmmaker*
Straka, Laszlo Richard *publishing consultant*
Turner, David Reuben *publisher, author*

Crugers
Norman, Jessye *soprano*

Cutchogue
Cottrell, Thomas Sylvester *pathology educator, university dean*
Dank, Leonard Dewey *medical illustrator, audio-visual consultant*
Gibson, Pamela *business development consultant, audio director*
Strimban, Robert *graphic designer*

De Witt
Belden, Sanford Adams *banker*
Pearl, Harvey *rehabilitation psychologist*

Deer Park
Amend, Stephen J. *guitarist*
D'Amore, Victor *director, choreographer, dance educator*

Delhi
Becker, Carl Frederick *judge*
Duncan, Mary Ellen *academic administrator*
Hartmann, James M. *lawyer*
Van Brunt, Arthur Hoffman (Peter) *economist, educator*

Delmar
Button, Rena Pritsker *public affairs executive*
Campas, Anna Penelope *civil engineer, architect*
Eldridge, Douglas Alan *lawyer*
Everett, James W., Jr., *lawyer*
Houghton, Raymond Carl, Jr., *education educator*
Matuszek, John Michael, Jr., *environmental scientist, educator, consultant*
Schwarz, Louise A. *band director*
Shen, Thomas To *environmental engineer*
Yeara, James Carroll *secondary school educator, writer*

Depew
Saleh, David John *lawyer*

Derby
Goodell, Joseph Edward *manufacturing executive*
Pordum, Francis J. *former state legislator, educator, marketing professional*

Dix Hills
Braun, Ludwig *educational technology consultant*
Fouladvand, Hengameh *artist*
Guram, Gurpal Singh *mathematician, educator*
Lin, Ching-Shen *pathologist*
Mastrogiannis, Dimitrios S. *obstetrician/gynecologist, perinatologist*
Mymit, Chuck W. *music educator, musician*

Dobbs Ferry
Anbinder, Paul *publishing company executive*
Briskin, Efrem *music educator*
Cassella, William Nathan, Jr., *retired organization executive*
Culhane, Hind Rassam *psychologist, educator, film historian*
Guggenheimer, Tobias Immanuel Simon *architect*
Kalvin-Stiefel, Judy *public relations executive*
Kraetzer, Mary C. *sociologist, educator, consultant*
Kravath, Richard Elliot *retired pediatrician, educator*
Lavinder, Gale June *medical educator, physical therapist, clinician*
Medoff, Richard Brad *speech educator*
Miss, Robert Edward *fundraiser*
Perelle, Ira B. *psychologist, educator*
Poian, Edward Licio *historian*
Scudder, Charles Seelye Kellgren *lawyer*
Simon, Lothar *publishing company executive*
Sutton, Francis Xavier *social scientist, consultant*

Dolgeville
Riedman, James Robert *insurance company executive*

Douglaston
Balbi, Kenneth Emilio *environmental specialist, researcher*
Palatnick, Frank Sidney *educational consultant*
Salvo, Joseph Aldo *lawyer*
Valero, René Arnold *clergyman*

Downsville
Hornick, Susan Florence Stegmuller *secondary education educator, fine arts educator, curriculum specialist, artist*

Dryden
Baxter, Robert Banning *insurance company executive*
Slocum, Robert Bigney *retired librarian*

Dundee
Miller, Ronald K. *real estate broker, educator*
Pfendt, Henry George *retired information systems executive, management consultant*

Dunkirk
Levan, Kimberly Ann *music educator*
Woodbury, Robert Charles *lawyer*

East Amherst
Llop, Tobey Hooker *information technology executive*
Soong, Tsu-Teh *engineering science educator*
Watson, Stewart Charles *construction company executive*

East Aurora
Carfagna, Vincent O. *physician*
Hawk, George Wayne *retired electronics company executive*
Sand, Seaward Alwyn *geneticist, researcher*
Weidemann, Julia Clark *retired principal, educator*
Woodard, Carol Jane *educational consultant*

East Garden City
Bákér, J. A., II, *executive management advisor and consultant, architect, financial engineer*

East Greenbush
McConville, Edward Patrick *lawyer*
Pruett, Joyce H. *writer*

East Hampton
Bromley, Bruce Ditmas *language educator, writer*
Dello Joio, Norman *composer*
Delson, Elizabeth *artist*
Delson, Sidney Leon *architect*
Ehren, Charles Alexander, Jr., *lawyer, educator*
Garrett, Charles Geoffrey Blythe *physicist, consultant*
Gladstone, Josh Adam *theater director, actor*
Hope, Judith H. *former political organization administrator*
Jaudon, Valerie *artist*
Karp, Harvey Lawrence *metal products manufacturing company executive*
Kelley, Christopher Donald *lawyer*
Mencher, Stuart Alan *sales and marketing executive*
Metz, Robert Roy *publisher, editor*
Osterweil, Adam Matthew *elementary school educator, writer*
Paton, David *ophthalmologist, educator*
Schetlin, Eleanor M. *retired university official*
Scott, Rosa Mae *art educator, artist*
Twomey, Thomas A., Jr., *lawyer, educator*

East Islip
Donohue, Claire P. *retired school librarian*
Harrington, Carolyn Marie *accountant, artist, jewelry designer*

East Meadow
Adler, Ira Jay *lawyer*
Albert, Gerald *clinical psychologist*
Bergman, Bruce J. *lawyer*
Bleidner, Clifford W. *pharmacologist, chemist*
Cymbler, Murray Joel *corporate professional*
Fuchs, Jerome Herbert *management consultant*
Hyman, Montague Allan *lawyer, educator*
Price, Marilyn *lawyer*

East Northport
Ambrosio, Joseph Michael *secondary school educator, composer*
Juliano, John Louis *lawyer*
Kehoe, Thomas J. *food products executive*

East Norwich
Rosen, Meyer Robert *chemical engineer*

East Quogue
Setlow, Neva Delihas *artist, research biologist*
Weiss, Elaine Landsberg *community development management official*

East Rochester
Murray, James Doyle *accountant, educator*

East Setauket
Badalamenti, Fred Leopoldo *artist, educator*
Maffia, Christina *elementary school educator, consultant*
Malbon, Craig Curtis *pharmacology educator, university official*
Simons, James *technology company executive*

East Syracuse
Duffy, Nancy Keogh *television broadcast professional*
Mohan, Sankar Krishnan *mechanical engineer*
Nivarthi, Raju Naga *anesthesiology educator*

Eastchester
Giuliano, Robert Paul *pharmacist*
Gottschall, Edward Maurice *graphic arts company executive*
Katz, Kenneth Arthur *lawyer, accountant*
Weinberg, Dale Glaser *technical writer, consultant, trainer*

Eden
Thomas, Jimmy Lynn *financial executive*

Edmeston
Blackman, Dorothy F. *library director*

Elba
Kauffman, William Joseph *writer, editor*

Elizabethtown
Houseal, Brian L. *conservationist*
Sayward, Teresa R. *state representative*

Elizaville
Koeppel, Harry Saul *interior designer, educator*

Elma
Virkler, Mark William *religious educator*
Wirth, Sandra Lee *real estate company owner*

Elmhurst
Cush, John Patrick *priest, theology studies educator*
Masci, Joseph Richard *medical educator, physician*
Matsa, Loula Zacharoula *social services administrator, educator*

Elmira
Abderhalden, Robert Thomas *internist*
Graham, David Richard *orthopedic surgeon*
Laux, Edward J. *advertising executive*
Meier, Thomas Keith *college president, English educator*
Nast, Edward Paul *cardiac surgeon*
Shephard, Robert Parrish *historian, educator*
Van den Blink, Nelson Mooers *light industrial manufacturing executive*
Wright, Linda Ellen *nursing educator*

Elmont
Butera, Ann Michele *consulting company executive*
Cusack, Thomas Joseph *retired banker*

Elmsford
Fachnie, H(ugh) Douglas *film manufacturing company official*
Miranda, Robert Nicholas *publishing company executive*
Parker, James K. *corporate lawyer*
Raymond, George Marc *city planner, educator*

Endicott
Leonard, James Edward *accountant*
Szabo, Andras *internist*

Fairport
Carlton, Charles Merritt *linguistics educator*
Graham, Susette Ryan *retired English educator*
Holtzclaw, Diane Smith *elementary school educator*
Rueckert, William Howe *literature educator, writer*
Ryan, Frank J. *construction executive*
Sands, Robert *food products executive*
Stewart, Barbara Dean *writer, musician, educational consultant*
Summer, Thomas S. *food products executive*
Talty, Lorraine Caguioa *accountant*

Falconer
Benke, Paul Arthur *academic administrator*
Ruhlman, Herman C(loyd), Jr., *manufacturing executive*

Fallsburg
Sperber, Marilyn Janice *special education educator*

Far Rockaway
Epstein, Samuel Abraham *sales executive*
Madhusoodanan, Subramoniam *psychiatrist, educator*
Sussman, Laureen Glicklin *junior high school educator*
Titus, Michele R. *state legislator*

Farmingdale
Baglio, Vincent Paul *manufacturing executive*
Bandyopadhyay, Amitabha *engineering educator*
Blum, Melvin *chemical company executive, researcher*
Chrysafi, Loucas Andrew *mathematician, educator*
Lieberman, Michael Jay *ophthalmologist*
Lobel, Sharon *retail executive*
Madeska, Valerie Gay *research scientist*
Nolan, Peter John *physics educator*
O'Brien, Joan Susan *lawyer, educator*
Vainder, Melanie *speech pathology/audiology services professional, educator*

Farmingville
Olson, Gary Robert *banker*

Fayetteville
Baker, Mark Allen *author, historian, consultant, graphologist*
Chevli, Renate Naren *obstetrician, gynecologist*
Dosanjh, Darshan S(ingh) *aeronautical engineer, educator*
Hadyk-Wepf, Sonia Margaret *artist, real estate manager*
Pachter, Irwin Jacob *pharmaceutical consultant*
Pirodsky, Donald Max *psychiatrist, educator*
Serafin, John Alfred *art educator*
Stewart, William A. *medical educator, neurosurgeon*

Feura Bush
Byrne, Donn Erwin *psychologist, educator*

Fillmore
Barry, Lynn Sharon *writer, small business owner*

Findley Lake
Gundersen, Allison Maureen *management consultant*

Fishers Island
Baue, Arthur Edward *surgeon, educator, retired health facility administrator*

Fishkill
Brocks, Eric *ophthalmologist, surgeon*

Floral Park
Chatoff, Michael Alan *lawyer*
Corbett, William John *government and public relations consultant, lawyer*
Deerson, Adele Shapiro *lawyer, arbitrator, educator*
Mazlen, Roger Geoffrey *physician, clinical pharmacologist, nutritionist*

Flushing
Andrews, Phillip *public relations executive*
Baik-Han, Won H. *pediatrician, educator, consultant*
Bell, Derek *professional baseball player*
Bird, Thomas Edward *foreign language and literature educator*
Chook, Paul Howard *publishing executive*
Commoner, Barry *biologist, educator*
Duquette, Jim *professional sports team executive*
Electra, Carmen *actress*
Engel, Robert *chemist, educator, dean*
Erickson, Raymond *music historian, musician*
Farago, John Michael *law educator, hearing officer, consultant*
Fichtel, Rudolph Robert *retired association executive*
Finks, Robert Melvin *paleontologist, educator*
Flechner, Roberta Fay *graphic designer*
Galdamez, Ricardo *internist*
Georghiou, Michael *construction and development executive*
Ghazarbekian, Sahak *retired civil servant, consultant*
Glavine, Tom (Thomas Michael Glavine) *professional baseball player*
Goh, David Shuh-Jen *psychology educator*
Goldenshteyn, Vladimir Lev *civil engineer*
Goldman, Norman Lewis *chemistry professor*
Goldsmith, Howard *writer, consultant*
Hacker, Andrew *political science educator*
Henshel, Harry Bulova *watch manufacturer*
Hon, John Wingsun *physician*
Horowitz, Gayle Lynn *physical education educator*
Howe, Art (Arthur Henry Howe Jr.) *professional baseball manager*
Hsu, Charles Jui-cheng *manufacturing company executive, advertising agent*
Kopp, Ilya Zinovij *energy and environmental researcher*
Kroeppel, Warren *airport terminal executive*
Lakah, Jacqueline Rabbat *political scientist, consultant*
Leiter, Alois Terry (Al) *professional baseball player*
Li, Hongzhi *Falun Dafa founder, author*
Li, Qin *television anchor, reporter, director, producer*
Lin, Pi-Tang *physician*
Lonigan, Paul Raymond *language professional, educator*
Mendelson, Elliott *mathematician, educator*
Morales, Michael Angelo *physician*
Nesbeth-Tong, Serena Bridget *finance educator, consultant*
Nussbaum, Michel Ernest *physician*
Pellitteri, John Steven *psychologist, therapist, educator*
Person, Philip *biomedical consultant, biochemist, dentist*
Piazza, Mike (Michael Joseph Piazza) *professional baseball player*
Rabassa, Gregory *Romance languages educator, translator, poet*
Ranald, Margaret Loftus *English literature educator, author*
Roberts, Kathleen Joy Doty *secondary school educator*
Rusu, Sir Andrew Peter (Sir Andrew Rusu Baron Rochefort) *ambassador, lawyer*
Sanborn, Anna Lucille *pension and insurance consultant*
Schwartz, Estar Alma *lawyer*
Smaldone, Edward Michael *composer*
Speidel, David Harold *geology educator*
Stahl, Frank Ludwig *civil engineer*
Totakura, Satyanarayana Raju *secondary school educator*
Tytell, John *humanities educator, writer*
Vaughn, Mo (Maurice Samuel Vaughn) *professional baseball player*
Yeo, Kim Eng *artist*
Yoshida, Roland Kiyoshi *academic dean, special education educator*
Zeile, Todd Edward *professional baseball player*

Fly Creek
Dusenbery, Walter Condit *sculptor*

Forest Hills
Addabbo, Dominic Lucian *lawyer*
Ashvil-Bibi, Sigalit *musician, artist*
Bertolini, Joseph Clifford *political scientist, educator*
Dybman, Nick Nison (Nick China) *poet*
Eden, Alvin Noam *pediatrician, writer*
Fernandez, Amy *artist, illustrator, writer, educator*
Grant, Susan Irene *lawyer*
Henley, Arthur *author, editor, television consultant*
Koslowitz, Karen *councilwoman*
Kra, Pauline Skornicki *French language educator*
Narasimhan, Parthasarathy *physician*
Neeleman, David *air transportation executive*
Polakoff, Abe *baritone*
Povman, Morton *lawyer*
Prager, Alice Heinecke *music company executive*
Reis, Don *publishing executive*
Rosenhaus, Steven L. *composer, conductor, music educator*
Sekler-Katz, Rudolfine *internist, psychiatrist*
Torrence-Thompson, Juanita Lee *public relations executive*
Tvildiani, Dimitry *cardiologist*
Ustayev, Rakhim *psychologist*
Van Westering, James Francis *management consultant, educator*

Forestburgh
Orisek, Ivan *financial executive*

Forestville
Adams, Lee Towne *lawyer*

Fort Drum
Hilferty, Bryan Carey *public relations specialist*
Miller, Thomas G. *career officer*

Frankfort
Conigilaro, Phyllis Ann *retired elementary education educator*

Franklin Square
Cantilli, Edmund Joseph *safety engineering educator, translator, writer, consultant*

Indiviglia, Salvatore Joseph *artist, retired naval officer*
Vanora, Jerome Patrick *lawyer*

Fredonia
Benton, Allen Haydon *biology professor*
Berkley, John L. *geology educator, meteoriticist*
Brown, William Douglas *biology professor*
Conradi, Janet K. *art educator*
Goetz, Thomas Henry Paul *French literature educator*
Klonsky, Bruce Gary *psychology professor*
Krohn, Franklin Bernard *marketing specialist, educator*
Reiff, Daniel D. *art history educator*
Vassoler-Froeligh, Ivani *education educator, journalist*

Freeport
Berg, Alan *lawyer, arbitrator*
Burstein, Stephen David *neurosurgeon*
Martorana, Barbara Joan *secondary school educator*
Pullman, Maynard Edward *biochemist*
Walker, Lula Noriega *secondary administrator*

Fresh Meadows
Castellano, Joseph P. *assistant principal*
Cohen, Robert L. *editor*
Duckett, Lila Wheeler *retired language educator, writer*
Godfrey, Philip M. *plastic surgeon*
Jackson, Rhonda *telecommunications professional, poet*
Kaplan, Barry Hubert *physician*

Fulton
Long, Robert Emmet *author*

Garden City
Balkan, Kenneth J. *lawyer*
Berka, Marianne Guthrie *health and physical education educator*
Calamari, Joseph August *law librarian*
Campbell, James R. *transportation executive*
Carnesi, Kenneth Brian *lawyer*
Cohen, Harvey *lawyer*
Conlon, Thomas James *marketing executive*
Cook, George Valentine *lawyer, consultant*
Crom, James Oliver *professional training company executive*
DaSilva, Willard H. *lawyer, educator*
Deane, Leland Marc *plastic surgeon*
Demuth, Nina Lewis *engineering company executive*
Dent, Thomas Augustine *lawyer*
DiGregorio, Vincent R. *plastic surgeon*
DiMascio, John Philip *lawyer*
Doucette, Mary-Alyce *computer company executive*
Egan, Frank T. *writer, editor*
Fanelli, Sean A. *college president*
Fishberg, Gerard *lawyer*
Garner, Richard Keith *classicist, educator*
Ginsberg, Eugene Stanley *lawyer, arbitrator, mediator*
Good, Larry Irwin *gastroenterologist, educator*
Gorin, Robert Murray, Jr., *history educator*
Harwood, Stanley *retired judge, lawyer*
Haskel, Jules J. *lawyer*
Hinerfeld, Norman Martin *manufacturing executive*
Jenkins, Kenneth Vincent *literature educator, writer*
Jones, Lawrence Tunnicliffe *lawyer*
Kaplan, Joel Stuart *lawyer*
Klein, Arnold Spencer *lawyer*
Kline, Eileen Mary *secondary school educator*
Koenig, Louis William *political science educator, author*
Korshak, Yvonne *art historian*
Laureano, Mari *government agency administrator, writer*
Lederer, Susan Hendler *speech/language pathologist, educator*
Lilly, Thomas Joseph *lawyer*
Lovely, Thomas Dixon *banker*
Minicucci, Richard Francis *lawyer, former hospital administrator*
Moravec, Paul *composer*
Nicklin, George Leslie, Jr., *psychoanalyst, educator, physician, author*
O'Connell, Marueen C. *state legislator, lawyer*
Ohrenstein, Roman Abraham *economics educator, economist, rabbi*
Ostrow, Michael Jay *lawyer*
Podwall, Kathryn Stanley *biology professor*
Posch, Robert John, Jr., *lawyer*
Rhein, John Hancock Willing, III, *publishing executive*
Sawyer, James *lawyer*
Scollard, Patrick John *hospital executive*
Scott, Robert Allyn *academic administrator*
Seyfried, Vincent F. *historian*
Shneidman, J. Lee *historian, educator*
Shuart, James Martin *retired academic administrator*
Webb, Igor Michael *academic administrator*

Gardiner
Mabee, Carleton *historian, educator*

Garrison
Callahan, Daniel John *biomedical researcher*
Egan, Daniel Francis *priest*
Goggin, Dan Charles *playwright, composer, theater director*
Murray, Thomas Henry *bioethics educator, writer*

Geneseo
Battersby, Harold Ronald *retired anthropologist, archaeologist, linguist*
Edgar, William John *philosophy educator*
Gouvernet, Gerard Raoul *language educator*
Lin, Rong *computer scientist, educator*
Olczak, Paul Vincent *psychology educator*
Strong, Michael Corrin *publishing executive, writer*

Geneva
Brind, David Hutchison *lawyer, judge*
Dickson, James Edwin, II, *obstetrician, gynecologist*
Lurie, Daphne *clinical psychologist, lecturer, educator*
Nault, Brian A. *entomologist, researcher, education educator*
Roelofs, Wendell Lee *biochemistry educator, consultant*
Siebert, Karl Joseph *food science educator, consultant*
Stranahan, Patricia *dean*

Germantown
Farberman, Harold *conductor, composer*
Linney, Romulus *author, educator*
Rollins, Sonny (Theodore Rollins) *composer, musician*

Getzville
Clare, Roy Wallace *music educator, musician, bookseller*
Saveth, Edward Norman *history educator*

Ghent
Rich, Donna L. *school system administrator*

Gilbertsville
Greefkes, Roland Cornelis *artist*
Roos, Casper *actor*

Glen Cove
Burnham, Harold Arthur *pharmaceutical company executive, physician*
Carbuto, Nicholas *music educator*
Compton, Roger H. *dean, engineering educator*
Costa, Thomas Charles *priest*
Fajors, Nique *computer company executive, application developer*
Joel, Billy (William Martin Joel) *musician*
Makris, Constantine John *computer engineer*
Mills, Charles Gardner *lawyer*
Pettersen, Kevin Will *investment company executive*
Sheehy, John Paul *pediatrician*

Glen Head
Conway, David Antony *management executive, marketing professional*
Fairman, Joel Martin *broadcasting consultant*
Huber, Don Lawrence *publisher*

Glen Oaks
Miller, Rachel L. *social worker, consultant*
Siris, Samuel Gidding *psychiatrist*

Glen Wild
Kaszas, William Joseph *technology educator*

Glendale
Maltese, Serphin Ralph *state legislator, lawyer*

Glens Falls
Bartlett, Richard James *lawyer*
Little, Elizabeth O'Connor *state legislator*
McMillen, Robert Stewart *lawyer*
Mitscherlich Reynolds, A. Christine *conservator*
Pontiff, Paul E. *lawyer*
Trombley, Joseph Edward *insurance company executive, underwriter*
Vitvitsky, Jack *physician assistant*

Glenville
Anderson, Roy Everett *retired electrical engineer*

Goshen
Roncal, Rogelio *psychiatrist*
Ward, William Francis, Jr., *real estate investment banker*

Gouverneur
Leader, Robert John *lawyer*
Scozzafava, Dede *state representative*

Grand Central
Freedman, Mollie Cecille *researcher*

Grand Island
Hennigar, William Grant, Jr., *dentist*
Mendell, Mark *architect*

GrandView-on-Hudson
Meriwether, Heath J. *newspaper consultant, retired newspaper publisher*

Granville
Ranney, Daniel Anthony *minister, language educator*

Great Neck
Abraham, Carl Joel *corporate executive, safety specialist, inventor, consultant*
Appel, Gerald *investment advisor*
Arams, Frank Robert *electronics company executive*
Blanda, Sandi *artist*
Blumberg, Barbara Salmanson (Mrs. Arnold G. Blumberg) *retired state housing official, housing consultant*
Breidbart, Rory Steven *endocrinologist*
Brill, Steven Charles *financial advisor, lawyer*
Dines, David Michael *surgeon, educator*
Elkowitz, Lloyd Kent *dental anesthesiologist, dentist, pharmacist*
Feldman, Gary Marc *nutritionist, consultant*
Fiel, Maxine Lucille *journalist, behavior analyst, educator*
Fried, Belle Warshavsky *education educator*
Friedland, Louis N. *retired communications executive*
Gallagher, John S. T. (Jack Gallagher) *health facility executive*
Gold, Alan H. *plastic surgeon*
Goldman, Ira Steven *gastroenterologist*
Gross, Beatrice Schaap *writer*
Gross, Lillian *psychiatrist, educator*
Hampton, Benjamin Bertram *brokerage house executive*
Hecht, Marie Bergenfeld *retired educator, author*
Hurwitz, Johanna (Johanna Frank) *writer*
Joskow, Jules *economic research company executive*
Kahn, David *editor, author*
Katz, Edward Morris *banker*
Kechijian, Paul *dermatologist, educator*
Kimm, Michael S. *lawyer*
Lieber, Constance E. *medical association administrator*
Mayer, Susan Lee *nurse, educator*
Minkoff, Jack *retired economics educator*
Packer, Samuel *ophthalmologist*
Panes, Jack Samuel *publishing company executive*
Peterson, Jon A. *education educator*
Pollack, Paul Robert *airline service company executive*
Puttlitz, Donald Herbert *medical microbiologist*
Rockowitz, Noah Ezra *lawyer*
Rosenberg, Richard F. *physician, radiologist*
Rosenthal, Irving *journalism educator*
Roth, Harvey Paul *publishing executive*
Rothbaum, David *obstetrician-gynecologist*
Samuel, Paul *retired cardiologist, educator*
Schlesinger, Irwin D. *neurologist*
Schwartz, Alan Paul *corporate executive*
Seidler, Doris *artist*
Shons, Alan Rance *plastic surgeon, surgical oncologist, educator*
Simon, Arthur *pharmacologist, research laboratory executive*
Tosheff, Julij Gospodinoff *psychiatrist*

Great River
Hayman, Martin Arthur *psychiatrist, educator*

Greenfield Center
Conant, Robert Scott *harpsichordist, music educator*
Templin, John Leon, Jr., *healthcare consulting executive*

Greenlawn
Bachman, Henry Lee *electrical engineer, engineering company executive*

Greenport
Cowley, Joseph Gilbert *writer*
Jackson, Richard Montgomery *former airline executive*
Loomis, Earl Alfred, Jr., *psychiatrist*
Monsell, Thomas Oliver *secondary English educator, writer*
Watts, Harold Wesley *economist, educator*

Greenvale
Brier, Robert M *Egyptologist, educator, documentary presenter*
Cordaro, Matthew Charles *energy and utility executive, educator*
Dircks, Phyllis Toal *English language educator*
Halper, Emanuel B(arry) *real estate lawyer, developer, consultant, author*
Kebbede, Hanna Maryam *writer, poet*
Megay-Nespoli, Karen Patricia *elementary school educator*
Pall, David B. *manufacturing company executive, chemist*
Senft, Mason George *musician*
Shenker, Joseph *academic administrator*
Steinberg, David Joel *academic administrator, historian, educator*
Westermann-Cicio, Mary Louise *academic administrator, library studies educator*
Zwicker, Charles *economist, educator, accountant, consultant*

Greenwich
Fung, Paul, Jr., *cartoonist, illustrator*
Smethurst, E(dward) William, Jr., *investment manager*

Groton
Henry, James Richard *lawyer*

Guilderland
Berger, Morris Isaiah *humanities educator*
Escobar, Deborah Ann *gifted and talented education educator*

Hamburg
Calkins, Evan *physician, educator*
Markulis, Henryk John *career military officer*
O'Day, John Ignatius *retired computer science educator*
Wiltse, Peter Christian *lawyer*

Hamilton
Berlind, Bruce Peter *poet, educator*
Blum, Lester *economics professor*
Busch, Briton Cooper *historian, educator*
Chopp, Rebecca S. *university president*
Dovidio, John Francis *psychology educator*
Edmonston, William Edward, Jr., *publisher, educator*
Godwin, Joscelyn *humanities educator, writer*
Haines, Michael Robert *economist, educator*
Jones, Howard Langworthy *retired educational administrator, consultant*
Knuth, Deborah Jane *English and women's studies educator*
Moynihan, William J. *museum executive*
Pinchin, Jane *literature educator*
Shen, Quang *science educator*
Soderberg, Dale LeRoy *English language educator, drama director, producer*
Staley, Lynn *English educator*
Tucker, Thomas William *mathematics professor*

Hampton Bays
Baker, Donald Gene *social sciences educator*
Komoski, Paul Kenneth *community activist, educational research executive*

Hancock
DeLuca, Ronald *former advertising agency executive, consultant*

Hannacroix
Schwebler, Stephen *retired chemist*

Harpursville
Sweeney, Phillip Peter *poet*

Harrison
Nardone, Dennis M. *protective services official, radio personality*
Northcutt, Marie Rose *elementary, secondary, & special education educator*
Schulz, Helmut Wilhelm *chemical engineer, environmental executive*
Strone, Michael Jonathan *lawyer*
Wadsworth, Frank Whittemore *foundation executive, literature educator*
Wilson, William James *marketing professional*

Hartsdale
Aker, Susan K. *elementary school educator*
Chait, Maxwell Mani *physician*
Feigenbaum, Eric Seth *display designer, educator*
Goodman, Stanley Leonard *advertising executive*
Greenawalt, Peggy Freed Tomarkin *advertising executive*
Katz, David *gastroenterologist, educator*
Katz, John *investment banker*
Kroll, Arthur Herbert *educator, consultant*
Martin, Daniel Richard *pharmaceutical company executive*
McMann, Edith Brozak *dancer, artist*
Pell, Arthur Robert *human resources specialist, consultant, author*
Stein, Michael David *psychologist*

Hastings On Hudson
Barolini, Helen *writer, translator, educator*
Considine, Russel A. *publisher, real estate consultant*
Cooney, Patrick Louis *writer*
Cooper, Doris Jean *market research executive*
Cornwell, Anne Chritake *neuropsychologist, scientist, educator, researcher*
D'Antoni, Philip *producer*
Del Colle, Paul Lawrence *communications administrator, educator*
Del Duca, Rita *language educator*
Landau, Peter Edward *editor*
Reich, Herb *editor*
Rosch, Paul John *internist, educator*
Sharpe, Robert Kent *writer, director, producer, photographer*
Stillman, Jeanne Betsock *public health administrator, consultant*
Thornlow, Carolyn *law firm administrator, consultant*
Weinstein, Edward Michael *architect, consultant*
Wolfe, Stanley *composer, educator*

Hauppauge
Buckley, Robert Matthew *electrical engineer*

Hawthorne
Cantor, Arnold *labor relations official*
Dan, Asit *computer scientist, research scientist*
Darzynkiewicz, Zbigniew D. *research scientist*
Jacobs, Jeffrey Lee *lawyer, education network company executive*
Kiamie, Don Albert Najeeb *accountant*
Lavenberg, Stephen S. *electrical engineer, researcher*
Nandedkar, Sanjeev Dattatraya *medical researcher, educator*
Panitz, Lawrence *physician*
Scheffler, Eckart Arthur *publisher*
Traub, Richard Kenneth *lawyer*

Hempstead
Aaron, Merik Roy *financial executive, educator, lawyer*
Ades, Janet *social worker*
Beasley, Aaron Bruce *professional football player*
Berliner, Herman Albert *university provost and officer, economics educator*
Block, Jules Richard *retired psychologist, educator, university official*
Bradway, Terry *professional sports team executive*
Carter, Quincy *professional football player*
Cassidy, David C. *science educator, historian*
Chapman, Ronald Thomas *musician, educator*
Chrebet, Wayne *professional football player*
Couser, G(riffith) Thomas *literature educator*
Edwards, Herman *professional football coach*
Evans, Joel Raymond *marketing educator, consultant*
Glassman, Paul *library administrator, architecture educator*
Goldstein, Stanley Philip *engineering educator*
Graffeo, Mary Thérèse *music educator, performer*
Greenwell, Raymond N. *mathematician, educator, writer*
Hastings, Harold Morris *science educator*
Johnson, Robert Wood, IV, *sports team executive, philanthropist*
Kaplan, Janet E. *poet*
Kruh, Louis *advertising executive, lawyer*
Lazarus, Harold *management educator*
Lee, Keun Sok *business educator, consultant*
Mahon, Malachy Thomas, Sr., *lawyer, educator*
Martin, Curtis *professional football player*
Masheck, Joseph Daniel *art critic, educator*
McPhee, Martha *literature educator*
Pennington, Chad *professional football player*
Roble, Carole Marcia *accountant*
Salten, David George *academic administrator*
Salzinger, Kurt *psychology educator*
Wattel, Harold Louis *economics professor*
Wolff, Manfred Paul (Fred Paul Wolff) *geologist, educator, environmental scientist, consultant*
Yashin, Alexei *professional hockey player*
Zagano, Phyllis *religious studies educator*
Zajac, Alfred *physicist, researcher*

Henrietta
Byfield, Bert A. *conservative humanitarian novelist*

Hensonville
Newman, Oscar *architect, city planner, sculptor*

Herkimer
Kirk, Patrick Laine *lawyer*

Hewlett
Cirker, Blanche *retired publishing executive*
Cohen, David Leon *physician*
Haralick, Robert Martin *electrical engineering educator*
Salamon, Michael Jacob *psychologist, health care and psychology educator, media consultant*
Steinfeld, Philip Sheldon *pediatrician*
Wolff, Eleanor Blunk *actress*

Hicksville
Ballweg, Sallyanne K. *finance company executive*
Batule, Robert John *priest, writer*
Estrin, Morton *pianist, music educator*
Giuffré, John Joseph *lawyer*
Goldman, Donald Howard *lawyer*
Horowitz, Barry Allan *music company executive*
Korn, Bernard *corporation executive, accountant, real estate broker, insurance broker*
Mund, Lorraine G. *English studies educator, writer*
Notaro, Anthony *application developer*
Stein, Melvin A. *accountant*

Tucci, Gerald Frank *manufacturing executive*
Whitlock, Prentice Earle *retired mathematics educator, clergyman*
Yen, Henry Chin-Yuan *computer systems programmer, software engineer, consulting company executive*

Hillsdale
Lunde, Asbjørn Rudolph *lawyer*
Parmet, Herbert Samuel *historian, writer*
Richards, Joseph Edward *artist*

Holbrook
Galijan-Simovic, Kamelija *music educator*

Holland
Loockerman, William Delmer *retired educational administrator*

Hollis
Stephens, B. Consuela *minister, consultant*

Hollis Hills
Malis, Leonard Irving *neurosurgeon*

Holliswood
Greenblatt, Fred Harold *data processing consultant*

Holmes
Conyers, Claude Brunson *publishing consultant, editor, dance historian*

Homer
Bull, Beverly Jane *piano and voice educator*
Gustafson, John Alfred *biology professor*

Honeoye
Stone, Alan John *manufacturing company executive, real estate executive*

Honeoye Falls
Hillabrandt, Larry Lee *service industry executive*
VanAuken, Alan Bradley *management consultant*

Hoosick Falls
Dodge, Cleveland Earl, Jr., *manufacturing executive, director*

Hopewell Junction
Novak, Robert Dennis *contractor, real estate developer*
Park, Byeongju *engineer*
Sikka, Kamal K. *engineering executive*

Horseheads
Andrake, Nancy Carolyn *secondary school educator*

Houghton
Chamberlain, Daniel Robert *college president*
Hijleh, Mark *composer, educator*
Luckey, Robert Reuel Raphael *retired academic administrator*

Howard Beach
Krein, Catherine Cecilia *broadcast and journalism educator*

Hudson
Agata, Burton C. *law educator, lawyer*
Artschwager, Richard Ernst *artist*
Lyons, Rosemary *language educator*
Miner, Jacqueline *political consultant*
Mustapha, Tamton *gastroenterologist*

Hudson Falls
Leary, Daniel *artist*

Huletts Landing
Kapusinski, Albert Thomas *economist, educator*

Hunter
Khanzadian, Vahan *tenor*

Huntington
Alsop, Reese Fell *medical educator*
Brettschneider, Rita Roberta Fischman *lawyer*
Chmelev, Vsevolod *engineer, consultant*
Christiansen, Donald David *electrical engineer, editor, publishing consultant*
Connor, Joseph Robert *editor*
D'Addario, Alice Marie *school administrator*
Dircks, Richard Joseph *English language educator, writer*
Engstrand, Beatrice C. *neurologist, educator*
German, June Resnick *lawyer*
Glickstein, Howard Alan *law educator*
Hochberg, Ronald Mark *lawyer*
Houslanger, Todd Eric *lawyer*
Israel, Steve *congressman*
Jones, Farrell *retired judge*
LaTourrette, James Thomas *retired electrophysics, electrical engineering and computer science educator*
Levitan, Katherine D. *lawyer*
Liput, Andrew Lawrence *lawyer, educator*
Masear, Claude *music educator, musician*
Moglia, Greg *education educator*
Morris, Jeffrey Brandon *law educator*
Munson, Nancy K. *lawyer*
Robinson, Kenneth Patrick *lawyer, electronics company executive*
Salcedo-Dovi, Hector Eduardo *anatomist, educator, surgeon*
Seidman, Glenn Elliott *sales executive, marketing professional*
Sforza, Alfred Vincent *dentist, educator, writer*
Sparacino, Philip William *psychotherapist, consultant*
Tar, Laszlo *artist*
Trager, Gary Alan *endocrinologist, diabetologist*
Tucker, William P. *lawyer, writer*
Twardowicz, Stanley Jan *artist, photographer*
Vale, Margo Rose *physician*

Huntington Station
Agosta, Vito *mechanical and aerospace engineering educator*
Williams, Una Joyce *psychiatric social worker*

Hurley
O'Boyle, Maureen *television show host*
Opdahl, Viola Elizabeth *secondary school educator*
Petruski, Jennifer Andrea *speech and language pathologist*
Smith, Lewis Motter, Jr., *retired advertising and direct marketing executive*

Hurleyville
Hilfstein, Erna *science historian, educator*

Hyde Park
Eastwood, Dana Alan *author, publisher, consultant*
Hunt, Mark Alan *museum director*
Pragman, Kurt Daniel *media specialist*
Rider, Kathleen Mary *dietician*
Ryan, L. Timothy *chef, educator, academic administrator*

Ilion
Gay, Douglas MacKenzie *pharmacologist*
Nemyier, Margaret Gertrude *sales executive*

Interlaken
Bleiler, Everett Franklin *writer, publishing company executive*

Irvington
Bendixen, Henrik Holt *physician, educator, dean*
Carey, Edward John *utilities executive*
Yablon, Leonard Harold *publishing company executive*

Islandia
Clarke, Jeff *computer company executive*
Cron, Kenneth D. *information technology executive*
Gupta, Yogesh *computer company executive*
Pruzansky, Joshua Murdock *lawyer*
Robinson, Douglas *computer company executive*

Ithaca
Abrams, Meyer Howard *English language educator*
Aiosa, Vincent Nestor *music educator*
Alexander, Gregory Stewart *law educator, educator*
Alexander, Martin *microbiologist, educator*
Arquit, Nora Harris *retired music educator, writer*
Ascher, Robert *anthropologist, educator, archaeologist, film producer*
Assie-Lumumba, N'Dri T. *Africana studies educator*
Bailey, Lee Worth *philosophy and religion educator*
Barcelo, John James, III, *law educator*
Bassett, William Akers *geologist, educator, retired*
Bauer, Simon Harvey *chemistry professor*
Bauman, Dale Elton *nutritional biochemistry educator*
Ben Daniel, David Jacob *entrepreneurship educator, consultant*
Beneria, Lourdes *economist, educator*
Bensel, Richard Franklin *political science educator*
Benson, Frances Goldsmith *publishing executive*
Berger, Toby *electrical engineer, educator*
Berkelman, Karl *physics educator*
Bethe, Hans Albrecht *physicist, researcher*
Billera, Louis J(oseph) *mathematics professor*
Borden, David *composer, educator*
Bourne, Russell *publisher, author*
Bramble, James Henry *mathematician, educator*
Briggs, Vernon Mason, Jr., *economics professor*
Burns, Joseph Arthur *planetary science educator*
Carlin, Herbert J. *electrical engineering educator, researcher*
Carpenter, Barry Keith *chemistry educator, researcher*
Cawley, John Horan *health policy educator*
Chapman, Lewis Duane *economist*
Chiang, Huai Chang *entomologist, educator*
Clermont, Kevin Michael *law educator*
Colbert, Robert Reed, Jr., *real estate developer*
Colby-Hall, Alice Mary *Romance studies educator*
Craighead, Harold G. *physics educator*
Cramton, Roger Conant *law educator, lawyer*
Darlington, Richard Benjamin *psychology educator*
Davies, Peter John *plant physiology educator, researcher*
De Boer, Pieter Cornelis Tobias *mechanical and aerospace engineering educator*
Dick, Richard Irwin *environmental engineer, educator*
Dietert, Rodney Reynolds *immunology and toxicology educator*
Dyckman, Thomas Richard *accountant, educator*
Dynkin, Eugene B. *mathematics professor*
Earle, Clifford John, Jr., *mathematician*
Earle, Elizabeth Deutsch *biology professor*
Easley, David *economics professor*
Eastman, Lester Fuess *electrical engineer, educator*
Eddy, Donald Davis *English language educator*
Ehrenberg, Ronald Gordon *economist, educator*
Eisenberg, Theodore *law educator*
Eisner, Thomas *biologist, educator*
Fick, Gary Warren *agronomy educator, forage crops researcher*
Finch, C. Herbert *retired archivist, library administrator, historian*
Firebaugh, Francille Maloch *university official*
Fireside, Harvey Francis *political scientist, educator*
Foote, Robert Hutchinson *animal physiology educator*
Freed, Jack Herschel *chemist, educator*
Garrison, Elizabeth Jane *artist*
Gearhart, Pamela Caum *conductor, educator*
Germain, Claire Madeleine *law librarian, educator, lawyer*
Ghiorse, William Cushing *microbiology educator, editor*
Gierasch, Peter Jay *astronomy educator*
Gillett, James Warren *ecotoxicology educator*
Gillis, Andrew J. *photographer*
Ginsparg, Paul *physicist*
Gold, Michael Evan *law educator*
Goldsmith, Paul Felix *physics and astronomy educator*
Gottfried, Kurt *physicist, researcher*
Grady, James Michael, Jr., *art educator, theater director*
Green, Edward Thomas, Jr., *education educator*
Grippi, Salvatore William *artist*
Groos, Arthur Bernhard, Jr., *German studies educator, music educator*
Habicht, Jean Pierre *public health educator*
Hairston, Nelson George, Jr., *ecologist, educator*
Halpern, Bruce Peter *academic administrator, researcher, educator*
Hammond, Jane Laura *retired law librarian, lawyer*
Hardy, Jane Elizabeth *communications educator*
Harriott, Peter *chemical engineering educator*
Harris, Robert Lee, Jr., *history professor*
Hart, Edward Walter *physicist*
Hartmanis, Juris *computer scientist, educator*
Hay, George Alan *law and economics educator*
Heckathorn, Douglas D. *sociologist, educator, epidemiologist*
Henry, Susan Armstrong *biology professor, dean*
Hess, George Paul *biochemist, educator*
Hillman, Robert Andrew *law educator, former academic dean*
Hoffmann, Roald *chemist, educator*
Hohendahl, Peter Uwe *German language and literature educator*
Hojnowski, Jules Austin *entrepreneur*
Holcomb, Donald Frank *physicist, academic administrator*
Hopcroft, John Edward *computer scientist*
Hudler, George *plant pathologist, educator*
Husa, Karel *composer, conductor, educator*
Hutcheson, Richard Ervin *philosophy educator, academic administrator*
Isakovic, Abdel *physicist, researcher*
Jagendorf, André Tridon *plant physiologist*
Jarrow, Robert Alan *economics and finance educator, consultant*
Kahn, Alfred Edward *economist, educator, government official*
Kallfelz, Francis A. *veterinary medicine educator*
Kammen, Michael *historian, educator*
Kendler, Bernhard *editor*
Kennedy, Kenneth Adrian Raine *biological anthropologist, forensic anthropologist*
Kennedy, Wilbert Keith, Sr., *agronomy educator, retired university official*
Kingsbury, John Merriam *botanist, educator*
Kinoshita, Toichiro *physicist*
Korf, Richard Paul *mycology educator*
Koschmann, J. Victor *history educator, academic program director*
Kramer, John Paul *entomologist, educator*
Kronik, John William *Romance studies educator*
LaCapra, Dominick Charles *historian, educator*
LaDue, Eddy Lorain *economist, educator*
LaFeber, Walter Frederick *history educator, author*
Lee, David Morris *physics educator*
Lee, Stephen *chemist, educator*
Lehman, Jeffrey Sean *academic administrator, educator*
Leibovich, Sidney *engineering educator*
Lengemann, Frederick William *physiology educator, scientist*
Leopold, A. Carl *plant physiologist*
Lesser, William Henri *marketing educator*
Liboff, Richard Lawrence *physicist, researcher*
Lifton, Barbara *state legislator, secondary school educator*
Linke, Simpson *electrical engineering educator*
Loucks, Daniel Peter *environmental systems engineer*
Lovelace, Richard Van Evera *education educator, research scientist*
Lowi, Theodore J(ay) *political science educator*
Lumley, John Leask *physicist, researcher*
Lurie, Alison *writer*
Lyons, Thomas Patrick *economics professor*
Mackin, Jeanne Ann *journalist, educator*
Mai, William Frederick *plant nematologist, educator*
Martin, Carolyn A. (Biddy Martin) *provost*
Martin, Peter William *lawyer, educator*
Maxwell, William Laughlin *retired industrial engineering educator*
McClary, Patricia Ann *lawyer*
McConkey, James Rodney *English educator, writer*
McCue, Arthur Harry *artist, educator*
McGuire, William *civil engineer, educator*
McKinney, Cynthia Ann *former congresswoman*
McMillin, Scott *language educator*
McMurry, John Edward *chemistry professor*
Mermin, N. David *physicist, researcher, writer*
Meyburg, Arnim Hans *transportation engineer, educator, consultant*
Mikus, Eleanore Ann *artist*
Morgan, Robert *writer, educator*
Morgenstern, Matthew *computer scientist*
Mortlock, Robert Paul *microbiologist, educator*
Mueller, Betty Jeanne *social work educator*
Nasrallah, June *plant pathologist, department chairman*
Nerode, Anil *mathematician, educator*
Nesheim, Malden C. *academic administrator, nutrition educator*
Norton, Mary Beth *history educator, writer*
Novak, Joseph Donald *science educator, knowledge studies specialist*
Oliver, Jack Ertle *geophysicist, educator*
Olpadwala, Porus *architecture educator, dean*
O'Rourke, Thomas Denis *civil engineer, educator*
Park, Roy Hampton, Jr., *advertising executive*
Pelto, Gretel H. *nutritional anthropologist, educator*
Perry, Margaret *librarian, writer*
Phelan, Richard Magruder *mechanical engineer*
Pimentel, David *entomologist, educator*
Pinch, Trevor J. *education educator*
Pinstrup-Andersen, Per *economist, educator*
Pohl, Robert Otto *physics educator*
Poleskie, Stephen Francis *artist, retired educator, writer*
Poppensiek, George Charles *veterinary scientist, educator*
Porte, Joel Miles *English educator*
Rader, Nancy Louise de Villiers *psychology educator, consultant*
Radice, Mark A. *musicologist*
Radzinowicz, Mary Ann *language educator*
Rhodes, Frank Harold Trevor *academic administrator, geologist*
Richardson, Robert Coleman *physics educator, researcher*
Roberts, E. F. *lawyer, educator*
Rodríguez, Ferdinand *chemical engineer, educator*
Rosen, Bernard Carl *sociologist, social psychologist, educator*
Rossi, Faust F. *lawyer, educator*
Salpeter, Edwin Ernest *physical sciences educator*
Sass, Stephen Louis *education educator*
Scheraga, Harold Abraham *physical chemistry educator*
Schlafer, Donald Hughes *veterinary pathologist*
Schwab, Stewart Jon *dean*
Schwartz, Donald Franklin *communication scientist*
Schwarz, Daniel Roger *English and American literature educator*
Scott, Norman Roy *academic administrator, agricultural engineering educator*
Seeley, John George *horticulture educator*
Seraji-Bozorgzad, Nasrine *architecture educator*
Shell, Karl *economist*
Shore, Richard Arnold *mathematics professor*
Simson, Gary Joseph *law educator*
Smith, Donald F. *dean*
Smith, Julian Cleveland, Jr., *chemical engineering educator*
Smith, Robert John *anthropology educator*
Smith, Robert Samuel *banker, former agricultural finance educator*
Squier, Jack Leslie *sculptor, educator*
Squyres, Steven Weldon *astronomy educator, planetary geology researcher*
Stedinger, Jery Russell *civil and environmental engineer, researcher*
Streett, William Bernard *retired university dean, engineering educator*
Stycos, Joseph Mayone *retired demographer, educator*
Summers, Robert Samuel *lawyer, author, educator*
Swieringa, Robert Jay *dean, accountant, educator*
Terzian, Yervant *astronomy and astrophysics educator*
Teukolsky, Saul *physicist, educator*
Thorbecke, Erik *economics professor*
Thoron, Gray *lawyer, educator*
Tomek, William Goodrich *agricultural economist*
Trotter, Leslie Earl *operations research educator, consultant*
Tucker, Scott Arthur *music educator*
Ullrich, Robert Albert *academic administrator*
Walcott, Charles *neurobiology and behavior educator*
Waldman, Michael *economist, educator*
Wasserman, Robert Harold *biology professor*
Welch, Ross Maynard *plant physiologist, researcher, educator*
Whitaker, Susanne Kanis *veterinary medical librarian*
Widom, Benjamin *chemistry professor*
Williams, Peggy Ryan *academic administrator*
Wootton, John Francis *physiology educator*
Yale-Loehr, Stephen William *lawyer, editor*
York, James Wesley, Jr., *theoretical physicist, educator*

Jackson Heights
Cayón, José C. *editor-in-chief, artist, sculptor*
Chang, Lydia Liang-Hwa *social worker, educator*
Dacey, Paul *artist*
Lippman, Susan E. *social worker, psychotherapist, educator*
Macia, Nanette *social worker, secondary school educator*
Morrow, Nana Kwasi Scott Douglas *choreographer, director, writer, filmmaker, educator*
Parascos, Edward Themistocles *engineering consultant*
Stevenson, Amanda (Sandy Stevens) *librettist, composer, document examiner*

Jamaica
Angione, Howard Francis *lawyer, editor*
Bakshi, Sanjiv *internist*
Brown, Kenneth Lloyd *lawyer*
Cade, Walter, III, *artist, actor, musician, vocalist*
Chropufka, Mark A. *information management specialist, poet*
Cline, Janice Claire *education educator*
Coppa, Frank John *historian, educator*
Davis-Jerome, Eileen George *educational consultant, principal*
Delener, Nejdet *college dean, marketing and international business educator*
Drobnicki, John Arthur *librarian, educator*
Duffoo, Frantz Michel *nephrologist, medical director*
Ekbatani, Glayol *language educator, director, writer*
Faust, Naomi Flowe *education educator*
Feldman, Arlene Butler *aviation industry executive*
Flake, Floyd Harold *former congressman*
Fogel, Jacqueline *artist*
Garner, Steven C. *radiologist, emergency physician*
Gati, William Eugene *architect, designer and planner*
Gesualdi, Louis J. *social sciences educator*
Gillespie, Marc E. *molecular biologist, educator*
Graser, Alfred J. *airport terminal executive, director*
Greenberg, Jacob *biochemist, educator, consultant*
Grünwald, Hans Wolfgang *internist, hematologist, oncologist*
Harmond, Richard Peter *historian, educator*
Harrington, Donald James *university president*
Heckstall, Robyn Amina *performing arts educator, choreographer*
Jawin, Ann Juliano *human resource specialist*
Kinkley, Jeffrey C. *historian*
Lee, Joseph *musician, educator*
Lees, Francis *economics professor*
Lengyel, István *chemist, educator*
Malewitz, Joan *elementary school educator, multi-media specialist*
Mc Kinnon, Clinton Dan *aerospace transportation executive*
Mentz, Steven Roger *language educator*
Morrill, Joyce Marie *social worker, educator*
Parmet, Robert David *historian, educator*
Ramos, Alice M *education educator*
Retzel, Frank *music educator, composer*
Sciame, Joseph *university administrator*
Skirde, Edward George *academic administrator, consultant*
Sun, Siao Fang *chemistry professor*
Tschinkel, Andrew Joseph, Jr., *law librarian*
Washington, William Thomas *technical manager, educator*

Jamestown
Beckstrom, Charles G. *lawyer*
DJang, Arthur H.K. *physician, scientist*
Idzik, Martin Francis *lawyer*
Walker, Timothy Craig *transportation executive*
Wellman, Barclay Ormes *furniture company executive*
White, Rae Alison *artist, writer*

Jamesville
DeCrow, Karen *lawyer, writer, educator*

Jamiaca
Kemeny, M. Margaret *oncologist, hospital administrator, surgeon*

Jefferson Valley
Huyghe, Patrick Antoine *writer, editor*

Jeffersonville
Harms, Elizabeth Louise *artist*

Jericho
Astuto, Philip Louis *retired Spanish educator*
Auster, Ellen *finance company executive*
Blau, Harvey Ronald *lawyer*
Dore, Kathleen A. *broadcast executive*
Fitteron, John Joseph *gas industry executive, real estate company executive*
Liebowitz, Leo *oil company executive*
Rosen, Robert Arnold *management company executive, real estate investor*
Schell, Norman Barnett *preventive medicine physician, consultant*
Shinners, Stanley Marvin *electrical engineer*
Shulman, Madelyn R. Spatt *lawyer*
Spatafore, Anthony R. *financial executive*

Johnson City
Bernardo, Aldo Sisto *retired foreign language educator*
Goddard, Bryan Lance *physician, director*
McGovern, Thomas Boardman *physician, pediatrician*

Johnstown
DiNitto, Andrew Joseph *political scientist, educator*
Gibson, Jahnn Hansen Swanker *mental health nurse*
Prestopnik, Richard John *electronics and computer educator*

Jordanville
Durham, Jeanette Randall *artist, educator*

Katonah
Baker, John Milnes *architect*
Bashkow, Theodore Robert *electrical engineering consultant, former educator*
Brownlee, Delphine *actress, musician*
Fry, John *magazine editor*
Grunebaum, Ernest Michael *investment banker*
Levine, Pamela Gail *business owner*
McCauley, Gerard Francis *literary agent*
Simpson, William Kelly *curator, Egyptologist, educator*
Wenglowski, Gary Martin *economist*

Kendall
Rak, Linda Marie *elementary education educator, consultant*

Kenmore
Auerbach, Rita Argen *artist, educator*
Elibol, Tarik *gastroenterologist, educator*
Kenny, John Edward *computer analyst*

Kew Gardens
Adler, David Neil *lawyer*
Aldea, Patricia *architect*
Breslin, Jimmy *columnist, author*
Chipkin, Frederick *textile designer, consultant*
Schechter, Donald Robert *lawyer*
Schnakenberg, Donald G. *financial administrator*

King Ferry
Cottrell, G. Walton *manufacturing executive*

Kings Park
Fay, Thomas A. *philosopher, educator*
Greene, Robert William *journalism educator, media consultant*

Kings Point
Billy, George John *library director*
Greenwald, Richard Alan *history professor*

Kingston
Abrams, Bruce D. *music educator*
Bradley, Vincent Gerard *judge*
Johnson, Marie-Louise Tully *dermatologist, educator*
McGuire, Thomas Peter *show boat captain, secondary school educator*
Shaffer, Sheila Weekes *mathematics educator*
Tsirpanlis, Constantine N. *theology, philosophy, classics and history educator*

Krumville
Nagi, Catherine Raseh *retired educational administrator, financial planner*
Schuckman, Nancy Lee *retired principal*

Lake George
Gordon, H. William *media specialist*

Lake Katrine
Dolamore, Michael John *physician*

Lake Luzerne
Goldstein, Manfred *retired consultant*

Lake Placid
Bakken, Jill *Olympic athlete*
Gale, Tristan *Olympic athlete*
Grimmette, Mark *Olympic athlete*
Lussi, Caroline Frances Draper *resort executive*
Martin, Brian *Olympic athlete*
Reiss, Paul Jacob *academic administrator*
Rossi, Ronald Aldo *sports association administrator, Olympic athlete*

Lake Ronkonkoma
Spahr, Clinton S., Jr., *retired elementary education educator*

Lake Success
Jaffe, Richard S. *lawyer*
Lee, Brian Edward *lawyer*
Rickin, Sheila Anne *personnel professional*
Uchida, Kinya *consumer products company executive*

Lakemont
Brothers, Fletcher Arnold *minister, religious organization founder, director*

Lakewood
Anderson, Raymond Quintus *diversified company executive*

Lancaster
Batt, Ronald Elmer *gynecologist, scientist, historian*
Neumaier, Gerhard John *environment consulting company executive*

Lansing
Dalman, Gisli Conrad *electrical engineering educator*
Gage, George Henry *retired high technology company executive*

Larchmont
Berridge, George Bradford *retired lawyer*
Bloom, Lee Hurley *lawyer, public affairs consultant, retired household products manufacturing executive*
Cavanna, Dino Francesco *chemicals executive*
Davis, Wendell, Jr., *lawyer*
Folter, Roland *book historian, rare books company executive, bibliographer*
Gaffney, Mark William *lawyer*
Greenwald, Carol Schiro *professional services marketing research executive*
Hinerfeld, Ruth G. *civic organization executive*
Kaufmann, Henry Mark *mortgage banker*
Levi, James Harry *real estate executive, investment banker*
McSherry, William John, Jr., *lawyer, consultant*
Moody, Kathryn Currier *communications executive, educator*
Pelton, Russell Gilbert *retired lawyer*
Plumez, Jean Paul *advertising agency executive, consultant*
Quigley, Martin Schofield *writer, educator*
Rainier, Robert Paul *publisher, consultant*
Rockland, Lawrence Howard *psychiatrist, educator*
Siegel, Nathaniel Harold *sociology educator*
Sklarew, Robert Jay *biomedical research educator, consultant*
White, Thomas Edward *lawyer*
Wielgus, Charles Joseph *information services company executive*
Wit, David Edmund *software company executive*

Latham
Condon, Joseph Dennis *broadcasting executive*
Conway, Robert George, Jr., *lawyer*
Couch, Mark Woodworth *lawyer*
Irwin, Heather May *writer, interior designer*
Lvovsky, Yuri *physicist, engineer*
Piedmont, Richard Stuart *lawyer*
Schwartz, Robert William *management consultant*
Silverman, Warren *physician*
Stallman, Donald Lee *corporate executive*

Lawrence
Press, Marlyn Rothman *special education and literacy educator*

Le Roy
Sovocool, Mary Anne Elizabeth Cranston *secondary school educator*

Levittown
Elliott, Franklyn *psychologist*
Juszczak, Nicholas Mauro *psychology educator*
Massie, Clifford Michael *music company executive*
Romano, Joseph Scott *music educator*
Stalter, Richard B. *biology professor, researcher*

Lewiston
Askins, Nancy Ellen Paulsen *training and organizational development professional*
Dexter, Theodore Henry *chemist*
Kelly, Sean Q *education educator*
LoTempio, Julia Matild *retired accountant*
Newlin, Lyman Wilbur *bookseller, consultant*

Liberty
Green, Harold Martin *social science writer*

Lido Beach
Shear, Richard Gary *education administrator*

Lincolndale
Joerger, Jay Herman *psychologist, entrepreneur*
Morton, Mary Madeline *family nurse practitioner*

Lindenhurst
Farrell Logan, Vivian *actress*
Hungerford, Gary A. *insurance company executive, columnist, writer, editor*

Little Neck
Overton, Rosilyn Gay Hoffman *financial services executive*

Liverpool
Allen, David Charles *computer science educator*
Cady, Duane Maynard *surgeon*
Egan, Marsha Christine *school psychologist*
Hamlett, James Gordon *electronics engineer, management consultant, educator*

Lockport
Carr, Edward Albert, Jr., *medical educator, physician*
Penney, Charles Rand *lawyer, civic worker, world traveler*
Pirtle, Ronald M. *automotive executive*
Spero, Joseph J. *secondary school educator*
Steinagle, Martin Gene *contractor, paralegal, poet, writer*

Locust Valley
Bentel, Carol Rusche *architect*
Bentel, Frederick Richard *architect, educator*
Bentel, Paul Louis *architect, educator*
DeRegibus, William *artist*
Mathews, Walter Michael *educational consultant*
Peek, William DeWitt, Jr., *music educator*
Schor, Joseph Martin *pharmaceutical executive, biochemist*
Zulch, Joan Carolyn *retired medical publishing company executive*

Long Beach
Levine, Samuel Milton *lawyer, retired judge, mediator, arbitrator*
Robbins, Jeffrey Howard *media consultant, research writer, educator*
Solomon, Robert H. *lawyer*
Thompson, Dorothy Barnard *elementary school educator*

Long Eddy
Hoiby, Lee *composer, concert pianist*

Long Island
Berry, Andrew Jonathan *mathematician, educator*

Long Island City
Barbanel, Sidney William *engineering consulting firm executive*
Blythe, Catherine L. *writer, consultant*
Della-Giustina, Jo-Ann Subotin *lawyer*
DiGiovanni, Eleanor Elma *scaffold installation company executive*
Donneson, Seena Sand *artist*
Falk, Charles H. (Harry Falk) *stock exchange executive*
Heiss, Alanna *museum director*
Hoffman, Merle Holly *political activist, social psychologist, author*
Lieberman, Janet Elaine *academic administrator*
Lutz, Karen *finance company executive*
Markus, Maura *bank executive*
Mathers, Allen Stanley *judge, arbitrator, consultant*
Moran, Kevin J. *book publisher*
Sadao, Shoji *architect*
Wanderman, Susan Mae *lawyer*

Loudonville
Boisvert, Raymond Donat *philosopher, educator*
Burstein, Sharon Ann *corporate communications specialist, designer*
Fiore, Peter Amadeus *English educator, clergy*
LaRow, Edward J. *biologist, educator*
Toal, James Francis *academic administrator*

Lowville
Becker, Robert Otto *orthopedic surgery educator*
Herrman, John Clinton *surgeon*

Lynbrook
O'Malley, Edward Joseph, Jr., *financial services administrator*

Mahopac
Gonzalez-Tornero, Sergio *artist*
McCluskey, Frank Bryce *director*
Sequeira, Manuel Alexandre, Jr., *lawyer*

Mahopac Falls
Travis, Alice Dimery *journalist*

Malverne
Benigno, Thomas Daniel *lawyer*
Freund, Richard L. *communications company executive, consultant, lawyer*
Knight, John Francis *retired insurance company executive*
Pollio, Ralph Thomas *managing editor, writer, magazine publishing consultant*

Mamaroneck
Coleman, Marshall Donald *psychiatrist, psychoanalyst*
Du Boff, Michael H(arold) *lawyer*
Feigin, Nancy J. *guidance counselor*
Halpern, Abraham Leon *psychiatrist*
Hoffert, Paul Washington *surgeon*
Katz, Babette *artist*
McEnroe, Patrick *former professional tennis player, sports commentator*
Mizrahi, Abraham Mordechay *retired cosmetics and health care company executive, physician*
Scheidlinger, Saul *psychologist*
Smith, Douglas LaRue *marketing executive*

Manhasset
Benewitz, Maurice Charles *labor arbitrator, educator*
Boal, Bernard Harvey *cardiologist, educator, author*
Bosworth, Jay L. *radiation oncologist*
Bradley, Thomas Paul *internist*
Brand, Oscar *folksinger, writer, educator*
Calvin, Donald Lee *business executive, stock exchange consultant*
Chaudhry, Saima *physician, educator*
D'Olimpio, James Thomas *oncologist*
Evans, Robert (Bob) *publishing executive*
Foerst, John George, Jr., *retired fundraising executive*
Fountain, Karen Schueler *physician*
Friedenberg, Mike *publishing executive*
Gardner, Robert *financial services executive*
Grossi, Olindo *architect, educator*
Milhorat, Thomas Herrick *neurosurgeon*
Nelson, Roy Leslie *cardiac surgeon, researcher, educator*
Pitti, Donald Robert *financial services consultant*
Pogo, Gustave Javier *cardiothoracic surgeon*
Scherr, Lawrence *internist, educator*
Schiller, Arthur A. *architect, educator*
Vizard, Michael *periodical editor*
Wachtler, Sol *law educator, retired judge, arbitration corporation executive, writer*
Wallace, Richard *editor, writer*
Wecksell, Alan *radiologist*

Manhattan
Khalil, Mounir A. *librarian, educator*

Manlius
Brophy, Mary O'Reilly *environmental scientist*
Cotter, William Donald *former state commissioner, former newspaper editor*
Harriff, Suzanna Elizabeth (Bahner) *advertising consultant*
Jefferies, Michael John *retired electrical engineer*
Martonosi, Anthony Nicholas *biochemistry educator, researcher*
Prior, John Thompson *pathology educator*

Marcellus
Baker, Bruce Roy *retired art educator, artist*
Taylor, Robert Wilson *military officer, publishing executive*

Marlboro
Cash, Sydney *sculptor, jewelry designer*

Maspeth
Heppa, Douglas Van *computer specialist*

Massapequa
De Micoli, Salvatore *metals commodity executive*
Kappenberg, Marilyn Kascius *library director*
Turk, Elizabeth Ann *music educator*
Van Gorder, John Frederic *lawyer*
Zwanger, Jerome *physician*

Massena
Edwards, Keith B. *airport administrator*
Schroll, Edwin John *retired secondary educator, stage director*

Mattituck
Kanas, John Adam *banker*

Mechanicville
Rhodes, Alan Charles *minister*

Medford
Brower, Robert Charles *rehabilitation counselor, small business owner*
Saunders, Audrey Jayne *federal official*
Snyder, Mark Jeffrey *financial consultant, actuary*

Melville
Bergman, Stanley M. *health products executive*
Blechschmidt, Edward Allan *data processing executive*
Bongiorno, Joseph John, Jr., *electrical engineering educator*
Bultan, Aykut *communications systems engineer*
Campofranco, Salvatore *real estate company executive*
Carter, Sylvia *journalist*
Collura, John J. *health care services company executive*
Copperman, Stuart Morton *pediatrician, educator*
Cummings, Anthony William *lawyer, educator, banker*
Damadian, Raymond Vahan *biophysicist*
Davidson, Justin *music critic*
Dooley, James C. *newspaper editor, director of photography*
Forsyth, Stephen A. *lab administrator, venture capitalist*
Gothard, Paul *lab administrator*
Hildebrand, John Frederick *newspaper columnist*
Horton, Theodore G. *industrial engineer*
Jansen, Raymond A., Jr., *former newspaper publishing executive*
Kaufman, Stephen P. *former electronics company executive, business educator*
Kissinger, Walter Bernhard *retired automotive test and service equipment manufacturing executive*
Kitman, Marvin *journalist*
Klatell, Robert Edward *lawyer, electronics company executive*
Klein, Steven Douglas *financial planner, securities broker*
Knight, Timothy P. *publishing executive*
Komaroff, Stanley *lawyer*
Kornberg, Fred *electronics executive*
Krenek, Debby *newspaper editor*
Krusos, Denis Angelo *communications company executive*
Lane, Arthur Alan *lawyer*
Leno, Sam R. *retail executive*
Lieberman, Carol *healthcare marketing communications consultant*
Marro, Anthony James *newspaper editor*
Maturo, J. Michael *real estate company executive, corporate financial executive*
McKeon, John C. *publishing executive*
Mitchell, William Edmund *electronics executive*
Moran, Paul James *journalist, columnist*
Newman, Samuel *retired trust company executive*
Ostertag, Ronald A. *manufacturing company executive*
Payne, Leslie (Les Payne) *newspaper editor, columnist, author, journalist*
Ponzi Kay, Marylou *human resources specialist*
Provenzano, Dominic *information specialist*
Rechler, Scott *real estate company executive*
Reilly, Paul J. *finance company executive*
Richards, Carol Ann Rubright *editor, columnist*
Saul, Stephanie *journalist*
Schmid, Charles Ernest *acoustical engineer, administrator*
Schneider, Howard Stewart *newspaper editor, educator*
Schoenfeld, Michael P. *lawyer*
Scricco, Francis M. *electronics company executive*
Settle, Mark *information technology executive*
Sobol, Elise Schwarcz *music educator*
Sullivan, Kenneth Wayne *engineer*
Taub, Jesse J. *electrical engineering researcher*
Waddell, John Comer *electronics distribution company executive*
Webber, Pamela D. *information technology executive*
Weiner, Alan E. *accountant, lawyer*

Merrick
Baron, Theodore *retired public relations executive*
Cariola, Robert Joseph *artist*
Cherry, Harold *insurance company executive*
Garfinkel, Lawrence Saul *academic administrator, educator, television producer*
Gutnik, Zhanna *physician, gastroenterology consultant*
Poppel, Seth Raphael *entrepreneur*
Sardo, Sanford *music educator*

Mexico
Sade, Donald Stone *anthropology educator*

Middle Island
Andrews, Gaylen *measurable response public relations expert*
Crowder, Lillie Mae Brown *retired architectural engineer*
Linick, Andrew S. *direct marketing expert*
Sanfilippo, Stephen Nicholas *retired secondary school educator*

Middle Village
Kolatch, Alfred Jacob *publisher*
Schiffman, Jacquelyn Linda *psychologist, consultant, artist*

Aronsson, Jeffry Michael *apparel executive*
Aronstam, Neil Lee *media marketing firm executive*
Arouh, Jeffrey Alan *lawyer*
Arquit, Kevin James *lawyer*
Arther, Richard Oberlin *polygraphist, educator*
Arvio, Sarah *poet*
Arvystas, Michael Geciauskas *orthodontist, educator*
Arystanbekova, Akmaral Khaidarovna *diplomat*
Asadorian, Diana C. *electrical engineer, educator*
Asakawa, Takako *dancer, dance teacher, director, choreographer*
Aschoff, Lawrence Michael (Mick Aschoff) *computer information scientist*
Ash, Jennifer Gertrude *writer, editor*
Ashanti, Baron James *poet, educator*
Ashbery, John Lawrence *language educator, poet, playwright, art critic*
Ashdown, Marie Matranga (Mrs. Cecil Spanton Ashdown Jr.) *writer, educator, lecturer, cultural organization administrator*
Asher, Aaron *editor, publisher*
Ashkin, Michael *artist*
Ashkinazy, Larry Robert *dentist*
Ashley, Elizabeth *actress*
Ashton, Dore *writer, educator*
Assael, Henry *marketing educator*
Aston, Sherrell Jerone *plastic surgeon, educator*
Astor, David Warren *journalist*
Atkins, John *concert pianist, voice teacher, model*
Atkins, Peter Allan *lawyer*
Atkinson, Holly Gail *physician, journalist, business executive, author, lecturer, human rights activist*
Atlas, James Robert *editor, writer*
Atsada, Chaiyanam *diplomat*
Atwood, Margaret Eleanor *writer*
Auchincloss, Louis Stanton *writer*
Audet, Paul L. *diversified financial services company executive*
Auer, Manfred Stefan *structural biologist, biochemist*
Aufses, Arthur H(arold), Jr., *surgeon, medical educator*
Augustine, Cynthia H. *lawyer*
Auletta, Ken *writer, columnist*
Auletta, Robert Anthony *playwright, educator*
Auster, Paul *writer*
Austin, John H.M. *radiologist*
Avedon, Richard *photographer*
Avery, Patricia I. *lawyer*
Avgerakis, George Harris *film director*
Aviv, Jonathan Enoch *otolaryngologist, educator*
Ax, Emanuel *pianist*
Axel, Richard *pathology and biochemistry educator*
Axelrod, Norman N(athan) *optical technical planning and technology application consultant*
Axelson, Linda Rae *event planning specialist*
Axinn, Stephen Mark *lawyer*
Axthelm, Nancy *advertising executive*
Ayafor, Martin Chungong *ambassador*
Azrielant, Aya *jewelry manufacturing executive*
Azzoli, Val *music company executive*
Babbio, Lawrence T. *telecommunications industry executive*
Bacall, Lauren (Betty Joan Perske) *actress*
Bach, Thomas Handford *lawyer, investor*
Bachelder, Joseph Elmer, III, *lawyer*
Bacher, Judith St. George *executive search consultant*
Bachner, Barbara LaVerdiere *artist*
Bachrach, Nancy *advertising executive*
Backman, Gerald Stephen *lawyer*
Bacon, Chantal *retail executive*
Bader, Ian *architectural firm executive*
Baderinwa, Sade *newscaster*
Badertscher, David Glen *law librarian, consultant*
Badu, Erykah *singer, songwriter*
Baechtold, Robert Louis *lawyer*
Baer, Harold, Jr., *judge*
Bagatelle, Warren Denis *investment banker*
Bagger, Richard Hartvig *lawyer*
Bahash, Robert J. *publishing executive*
Bahler, Gary M. *lawyer*
Bahlke, Conrad George *lawyer*
Bahr, Lauren S. *publishing executive*
Bailey, Darlyne *social worker, educator*
Bailey, Janet Dee *publishing company executive*
Bailey, Xenobia (Sherilyn Bailey) *artist, educator*
Bains, Harrison MacKellar, Jr., *financial executive*
Bains, Leslie Elizabeth *banker*
Bainton, J(ohn) Joseph *lawyer*
Baird, Douglas James *investment banker*
Baird, Penny Drue *interior designer*
Baird, Zoë *foundation president, lawyer*
Baity, John Cooley *lawyer*
Baker, Daniel C. *plastic surgeon, educator*
Baker, Elizabeth Calhoun *magazine editor*
Baker, George R. *insurance industry executive*
Baker, Mark M. *lawyer, law educator*
Baker, Paul Raymond *history educator*
Baker, Stephen *advertising executive, author*
Baker, Stuart David *lawyer*
Baker, William Franklin *public broadcasting company executive*
Baker, William Oliver *retired research chemist*
Baker, William W. *nonprofit company executive*
Bakinowski, Carol Ann *journalist*
Bakker, Ron *architect*
Balaz, Beverly Ann *publishing executive*
Baldwin, C. Stephen *human resources specialist*
Baldwin, David Allen *political science educator*
Baldwin, David Shepard *physician*
Baldwin, William *editor*
Ball, John Paul *publishing company executive*
Ballard, Charles Alan *investment banker*
Balogh, Mary *writer*
Balter, Bernice *religious organization administrator*
Bamberger, Michael Albert *lawyer*
Bana, Eric *actor*
Bancroft, Alexander Clerihew *lawyer*
Bancroft, Margaret Armstrong *lawyer*
Banerjee, (Bimal Banerjee) *artist, educator*
Banfield, Ashleigh Dennistoun *news correspondent*
Banks, Helen Augusta *singer, actress*
Banks, Tyra *model, actress*
Baquero, Lynda *newscaster, reporter*
Baragwanath, Albert Kingsmill *curator, writer*
Barakat, Richard *oncologist, gynecological surgeon*
Barandes, Robert *lawyer*
Baranski, Joan Sullivan *publisher*
Barasch, Clarence Sylvan *lawyer*
Barasch, Mal Livingston *lawyer*
Barash, Susan Shapiro *writer, humanities educator*
Barber, Russell Brooks Butler *television producer*
Barbour, Catherine Jean *actress, director, mime, set designer*
Barbour, Celia *editor*
Barchas, Jack D. *psychiatrist, medical researcher, educator, behavioral molecular neurobiologist*
Barclay, Dolores *editor, writer*
Bardach, Joan Lucile *clinical psychologist*
Bardin, Mary Beth *telecommunications company executive*
Bardos, Karoly *television and film educator, writer, director*
Barenholtz, Celia Goldwag *lawyer*
Barie, Philip Steven *surgeon, educator*
Barino, Fantasia *singer*
Barist, Jeffrey *lawyer*
Barker, Barbara Ann *ophthalmologist*
Barlow, Barbara Ann *surgeon*
Barnard, Robert N. *lawyer*
Barnes, Arthur Roosevelt *advertising executive*
Barnes, Jhane Elizabeth *fashion design company executive, designer*
Barnet, Will *artist, educator*
Barnett, Amy DuBois *editor-in-chief*
Barnett, Bernard *accountant*
Barnett, Vivian Endicott *curator*
Barnum, Barbara Stevens *writer, retired nursing educator*
Barolini, Teodolinda *literary critic*
Baron, Sheri *advertising agency executive*
Barondess, Jeremiah Abraham *physician*
Barquero, Pedro B. *mathematician, researcher*
Barr, Thomas D. *lawyer*
Barr, William Pelham *lawyer, former attorney general of United States*
Barrett, Edward Mitchell *lawyer*
Barrett, Elizabeth Ann Manhart *nursing educator, psychotherapist, consultant*
Barrett, Herbert *artists management executive*
Barrett, William Joel *investment banker*
Barrio, Soledad *dancer*
Barrios, Richard (John) *freelance/self-employed writer, film historian*
Barron, Susan *clinical psychologist*
Barry, David Earl *lawyer*
Barry, Desmond Thomas, Jr., *lawyer*
Barry, Nancy Marie *bank executive*
Barry, Thomas Corcoran *investment counselor*
Barsalona, Frank Samuel *theatrical agent*
Barse, David M. *financial services executive*
Barstow, David *journalist*
Bart, Roger *actor*
Barth, Mark Harold *lawyer*
Barth, Richard *pharmaceutical executive*
Bartlett, Joseph Warren *lawyer*
Bartlett, Peter B. *investment company executive*
Bartlett, Thomas A. *telecommunications industry executive*
Bartlett, Thomas Foster *management consultant*
Bartoli, Cecilia *soprano*
Bartolini, Leonardo *economist*
Barton, Lewis *consultant*
Barton, Richard N. *computer company executive*
Barton, Thomas Heisler *management consultant*
Bartow, Diane Grace *marketing and sales executive*
Baruch, Ralph M. *communications executive*
Baryshnikov, Mikhail *ballet dancer, actor*
Barzilay, Judith Morgenstern *federal judge*
Bashkow, Jack Simon *musician*
Bason, George R., Jr., *lawyer*
Basquin, Mary Smyth (Kit Basquin) *museum administrator*
Bassen, Ned Henry *lawyer*
Basta, Paul M. *lawyer*
Bastianich, Lidia Matticchio *chef, food service executive*
Bastidas, Hugo Xavier *painter*
Batali, Mario *chef*
Batavia, Mitchell *physical therapist, educator*
Battista, Richard *entertainment company executive*
Battle, Pat *reporter*
Batts, Deborah A. *judge*
Bauer, Marion Dane *writer*
Bauer, Peter *publishing executive*
Baum, Richard Theodore *engineering executive*
Bauman, Susan *communications executive*
Baumann, Karl-Hermann *health and medical products executive*
Baumgardner, John Ellwood, Jr., *lawyer*
Baumgardner, Matthew Clay *artist*
Baumgarten, Paul Anthony *retired lawyer*
Baumgarten, Sidney *lawyer, company executive*
Baumrin, Bernard Stefan Herbert *lawyer, educator*
Bawden, Nina (Mary Bawden) *author*
Bazell, Robert Joseph *science correspondent*
Beal, Jack *artist*
Bear, Stephen E. *pharmaceutical executive*
Beardsley, Theodore S(terling), Jr., *professional society administrator*
Beattie, Ann *writer*
Beattie, Richard Irwin *lawyer*
Beauford, Carter *musician*
Beausoleil, Doris Mae *federal agency housing specialist*
Beck, Andrew James *lawyer*
Beck, Jill *dance educator, director*
Becker, Barbara Lynn *lawyer*
Becker, Isidore A. *business executive*
Becker, Norbert *finance company executive*
Becker, Susan Kaplan *management and marketing communication consultant, educator*
Beckerman, Michael Brim *music educator, writer, television personality*
Beckman, Michael *lawyer*
Beckman, Richard David *publishing executive, advertising executive*
Beckmann, John *architect, designer, writer*
Beckwith, Rodney Fisk *management consulting firm executive*
Bederson, Benjamin *physicist, researcher*
Bednar, Rudy *television producer, director*
Bee, Samantha *comedian, actress*
Beecher, William Manuel *management consultant*
Beekman, William Bedloe *lawyer*
Beer, David Wells *architect*
Beerbower, Cynthia Gibson *lawyer*
Beerman, Joseph *health educator*
Beeson, Jack Hamilton *composer, educator, writer*
Begell, William *publisher*
Begley, Louis *writer, lawyer*
Begley, Sharon Lynn *journalist*
Behar, Joy *television personality*
Behrendt, John Thomas *lawyer*
Behrens, Myles Michael *neuro-ophthalmologist*
Beim, David Odell *investment banker, educator*
Beim, Norman *playwright, actor, theater director, writer*
Beinecke, Candace Krugman *lawyer*
Beinecke, Frederick William *investment company executive*
Beinecke, William Sperry *corporate executive*
Bekaert, Geert *finance educator*
Belden, David Leigh *professional association executive, engineering educator*
Belfer, Robert Alexander *oil and gas company executive*
Bel Geddes, Joan *writer*
Belknap, Norton *foundation administrator*
Bell, David Arthur *advertising agency executive*
Bell, Derrick Albert *law educator, author, lecturer*
Bell, James Brugler *historian, writer*
Bell, Jonathan Robert *lawyer*
Bell, Martin Allen *investment company executive*
Bell, Theodore Augustus *writer, former advertising executive*
Bell, Thomas Devereaux, Jr., *communications company executive*
Bellamy, Carol *international organization executive*
Bellando, John W. *accountant*
Bellanger, Florian *food service executive, educator*
Bellanger, Serge René *bank executive*
Bellas, Albert Constantine *investment banker, advisor*
Beller, Gary A. *lawyer, finance company executive, insurance company executive*
Belliveau, Gerard Joseph, Jr., *librarian*
Bellows, Howard Arthur, Jr., *marketing research executive*
Belotserkovsky, Maxim *dancer*
Beltzer, Howard Stewart *lawyer*
Benchley, Peter Bradford *author*
Bendelac, Roger E. *investment executive, financial consultant*
Bender, Bruce F. *book publishing executive*
Bender, John Charles *lawyer*
Bender, Thomas *history and humanities educator, writer*
Bendor, Susan Julia *social worker, educator*
Benedek, Melinda *television executive*
Benedict, James Nelson *lawyer*
Benenson, Edward Hartley *realty company executive*
Benenson, Mark Keith *lawyer*
Benglis, Lynda *artist, sculptor*
Benhabib, Jess *adult education educator*
Ben-Haim, Zigi *artist*
Benjamin, Jeff *lawyer, pharmaceutical executive*
Benjamin, Ruth *writer*
Benkard, James W. B. *lawyer*
Benmosche, Robert H. *insurance company executive*
Bennett, Dave W. *talent agent, consultant*
Bennett, Douglas Marshall *construction and marketing executive*
Bennett, Joel Herbert *construction company executive*
Bennett, Paul B. *stock exchange executive*
Bennett, Tony (Anthony Dominick Benedetto) *entertainer*
Benshoof, Janet Lee *lawyer, association executive*
Benson, David H. *telecommunications industry executive*
Benson, Thomas Luther *academic administrator*
Bentley, Anthony Miles *lawyer*
Benton, Donald Stewart *publishing company executive, lawyer*
Benton, Nicholas *theater producer*
Berc, Kenneth Myles *psychiatrist*
Berdick, Leonard Stanley *insurance broker*
Berendt, John Lawrence *writer, editor*
Berenson, Robert Leonard *advertising agency executive*
Berg, A(ndrew) Scott *author, biographer*
Bergan, Edmund Paul, Jr., *lawyer*
Bergen, John Donald *communications, public affairs executive*
Berger, Frank Milan *biomedical researcher, scientist, former pharmaceutical company executive*
Berger, Marvin *medical educator*
Berger, Pearl *library director*
Berger, Stephen *financial services company executive*
Berger, Thomas Louis *author*
Berghahn, Volker Rolf *history professor*
Bergman, Charles Cabe *foundation executive*
Bergman, Donald Arthur *endocrinologist*
Bergman, Lowell *television news producer*
Bergreen, Bernard D. *investment company executive*
Bergstrom, Elaine *novelist*
Berk, Paul David *physician, scientist, educator*
Berkery, Rosemary T. *lawyer, investment company executive*
Berkley, Seth Franklin *epidemiologist, international health specialist*
Berkow, Ira Harvey *author, journalist*
Berkowitz, Brad Alan *stock analyst*
Berkowitz, Richard Lee *obstetrician/gynecologist*
Berkowitz, Susan J. *investment banking executive*
Berlin, Andrew Mark *advertising agency executive*
Berlind, Robert Elliot *artist, educator*
Berman, Ariane R. *artist*
Berman, Keith *solicitor, lawyer*
Berman, Michael Allen *hospital administrator, pediatric cardiologist*
Berman, Rachel *dancer*
Berman, Richard Miles *judge*
Berman, Walter S. *treasurer*
Bermudez, Jorge Alberto *bank executive*
Bernard, André Philippe *publishing executive, writer*
Bernard, David George *retired management consultant*
Bernard, Richard Phillip *lawyer*
Bernardi, Mario *conductor*
Bernardin, Thomas L. *advertising executive*
Bernbach, John Lincoln *corporate strategies and investment executive*
Berne, Bruce J. *chemistry professor*
Berner, Andrew Jay *library director, writer*
Berner, Mary *publisher*
Bernfield, Susan *playwright, performing company executive*
Bernstein, Bonnie *sportscaster*
Bernstein, Carl *jewelry designer, artist*
Bernstein, Daniel Lewis *lawyer*
Bernstein, David William *lawyer*
Bernstein, Donald Scott *lawyer*
Bernstein, Douglas Lon *writer, composer, actor*
Bernstein, Phyllis J. *financial consultant*
Bernstein, Richard Allen *food products executive*
Bernstein, Robert Jay *lawyer*
Bernstein, Robert M. *plastic surgeon*
Berresford, Susan Vail *philanthropic foundation executive*
Berris, Brian A. *investment company executive*
Berruga-Filloy, Enrique *ambassador*
Berry, John Nichols, III, *publishing executive, editor*
Berson, Anthony M. *oncologist*
Berthot, Jake *artist, educator*
Bertini, Catherine Ann *international organization official*
Bertram, Paul Benjamin *English language educator*
Beshar, Christine *lawyer*
Beshar, Robert Peter *lawyer*
Besman, Pascal Michel *diversified financial services company executive*
Bessey, Palmer Quintard *surgeon*
Besterman, Douglas *composer, orchestrator*
Bettman, Gary Bruce *National Hockey League Commissioner*
Betts, Richard Kevin *political science educator*
Betts, Roland W. *real estate developer*
Beverley, Cordia Luvonne *gastroenterologist*
Bewkes, Eugene Garrett, Jr., *investment company executive, consultant*
Bewkes, Jeffrey L. *television broadcasting company executive*
Beyer, John H. *architectural firm executive*
Beyer, Lisa *journalist*
Beyoncé, (Beyoncé Giselle Knowles) *singer*
Bezanson, Thomas Edward *lawyer*
Bhattacharya, Satyajit *research scientist*
Bhavsar, Natvar Prahladji *artist*
Bialkin, Kenneth Jules *lawyer, director*
Bialo, Kenneth Marc *lawyer*
Bianco, S. Anthony *lawyer*
Bibliowicz, Jessica M. *financial analyst*
Bickers, David Rinsey *physician, educator*
Bicks, David Peter *lawyer*
Biddle, Flora Miller *writer*
Bidwell, James Truman, Jr., *lawyer*
Biedel, Alexis *actress*
Biederman, Barron Zachary (Barry Biederman) *advertising agency executive*
Biel, Leonard, Jr., *urologist*
Bigelow, Robert Wilson *trial lawyer*
Biggs, Barton Michael *investment company executive*
Biggs, John Herron *retired insurance company executive*
Biglari, Hamid *investment banker*
Bikel, Theodore *actor, singer*
Billig, Robert Emanuel *psychiatric social worker*
Binder, Susan A. *chemical company executive*
Birch, Ian *editor-in-chief*
Bird, Mary Lynne Miller *professional society administrator*
Birkelund, John Peter *investment banking executive*
Birkenhead, Thomas Bruce *theatrical producer and manager, educator*
Birman, Joseph Leon *physics educator*
Birnbaum, Bernard A *radiology educator*
Birnbaum, Edward Lester *lawyer*
Birnbaum, Sheila L. *lawyer, educator*
Birns, Nicholas Boe *literature educator, editor*
Birstein, Ann *writer, educator*
Bisbee, Joyce Evelyn *retired utility company executive*
Bischoff, Theresa A. *not-for-profit association administrator, former medical center executive*
Bishop, Frances Blackburn *civic worker*
Bishop, Susan Katharine *executive search company executive*
Bishop, Thomas Walter *French language and literature educator*
Bishopric, Susan Ehrlich *public relations executive*
Bisignano, Frank *diversified financial services company executive*
Bisson, Terry Ballantine *author, editor*
Black, Barbara Aronstein *legal history educator*
Black, Carole *broadcast executive*
Black, Cathleen Prunty *publishing executive*
Black, Jack *actor*
Black, James Isaac, III, *lawyer*
Black, Louis Engleman *lawyer*
Black, Shawn Morgado *dancer*
Blackford, John *magazine editor*
Blackman, Cindy *musician, composer*
Blackman, Kenneth Robert *lawyer*
Blair, William Granger *retired newspaperman*
Blake, Grace *cultural organization administrator*
Blakemore, Michael Howell *theatre and film director*
Blalock, Sherrill *investment advisor*
Blamer, Steven W. *advertising executive*
Blanchard, Kimberly Staggers *lawyer, educator*
Bland, Frederick Aves *architect*
Bland, Teresa P. *policy analyst, consultant*
Blank, Matthew C. *broadcast company executive*
Blankfein, Lloyd C. *investment banker*
Blaser, Martin Jack *medical educator*
Blasi, Vincent A. *lawyer, educator*
Blatner, Barbara Ann *literature educator*
Blau, John *retired social worker*
Blazejowski, Carol A. *professional sports team executive, retired professional basketball player*
Blechner, Mark Jacob *psychologist, educator*
Blige, Mary Jane *recording artist*
Blinder, Abe Lionel *management consultant*
Blinder, Albert Allan *judge*
Blinken, Donald *ambassador, investment banker, brokerage house executive*
Blinken, Robert James *manufacturing and communications company executive*
Blitzer, Andrew *otolaryngologist, educator, research scientist, writer*
Blix, Hans Martin *retired international atomic energy official*
Blobel, Günter *cell biologist, educator*
Bloch, Peter *editor*
Block, Francesca Lia *writer*
Block, William Kenneth *lawyer*
Bloom, Jack Sandler *investment banker*
Bloomberg, Michael Rubens *mayor*
Bloomgarden, Kathy Finn *public relations executive*
Bluestone, Andrew Lavoott *lawyer*
Bluh, Bonnie *writer, playwright, performer*
Blum, Barbara B. *foundation administrator*
Blum, Diane S. *human services manager*
Blumberg, Gerald *lawyer*
Blume, Judy *author*
Blume, Lawrence Dayton *lawyer*
Blumenfeld, Joan *architect*

Chajet, Clive *brand and corporate image consultant*
Chamberlain, Neil Cornelius Wolverton *economist, emeritus educator*
Chamberlin, Ward Bryan, Jr., *public broadcasting executive*
Champion, Sara Stewart *lawyer*
Chan, Janet *publishing executive*
Chan, Lo-Yi Cheung Yuen *architect*
Chan, Siu-Wai *materials science educator*
Chandler, Robert Leslie *public relations executive*
Chandrasekhar, Sujana S. *surgeon, otologist/neurotologist*
Chaney, Gerald M. *retail executive*
Chaney, Verne Edward, Jr., *surgeon, foundation executive, educator*
Chang, Jeannette *publishing executive*
Chang, Ling Wei *consulting services executive*
Chang, Marian S. *filmmaker, composer*
Channing, Stockard (Susan Stockard) *actress*
Chao, James S. C. *maritime executive*
Chapin, Samuel R. *investment company executive*
Chapin, Schuyler Garrison *cultural affairs executive, university dean*
Chapman, Paul B. *oncologist*
Chapman, Peter Herbert *investment company executive*
Chapman, Shelley C. *lawyer*
Chapnick, David B. *lawyer*
Chappell, John Charles *lawyer*
Chappell, Wallace *performing company executive*
Chappelle, David (Dave Chappelle) *actor, comedian*
Charash, Bruce D. *cardiologist, educator*
Charbonnet, Gabrielle *writer*
Charles, Michael Harrison *architectural interior designer*
Charney, Craig Russell *pollster, political scientist*
Charnin, Martin *theatrical director, lyricist, producer*
Charon, Rita *medical educator*
Charron, Paul Richard *apparel company executive*
Chase, Oscar G(ottfried) *law educator, consultant, author*
Chasey, Jacqueline *lawyer*
Chast, Roz *cartoonist*
Chatfield-Taylor, Adele *historic preservationist*
Chaves, Jose Maria *diplomat, foundation administrator, lawyer, educator*
Chazen, Hartley James *lawyer*
Checkman, Neil Bruce *lawyer*
Chell, Beverly C. *lawyer, media company executive*
Chelstrom, Marilyn Ann *political education consultant*
Chen, James Tsing-fang *artist, educator, cultural center administrator*
Chen, Julie *newscaster*
Chen, Lu *figure skater*
Chen, Qiang *medical researcher*
Chen, Tak-Ming *civil engineer, consultant*
Chen, Wesley *lawyer*
Chenault, Kenneth Irvine *financial services company executive*
Cheney, Richard Eugene *public relations executive, psychoanalyst*
Cheng, Chuen Yan *biochemist, educator*
Chenoweth, Kristin *actress*
Chermayeff, Ivan *graphic designer*
Chernoff, Allan *correspondent*
Chesler, Gail *arts organization development executive*
Chesnutt, Jane *publishing executive*
Chess, William *public relations executive*
Chevray, Rene *physics educator*
Chi, Dennis S. *oncologist, researcher*
Chianese, Dominic *actor*
Chiang, Yung Frank *law educator*
Chiarchiaro, Frank John *lawyer*
Chichilnisky, Graciela *mathematician, educator, economist, writer*
Childs, David *architectural firm executive*
Childs, John Farnsworth *consultant, retired investment banker*
Chilstrom, Robert Meade *lawyer*
Chin, Sylvia Fung *lawyer*
Chira, Susan *editor*
Chiu, David Tak Wai *surgeon*
Chodorow, Jeffrey *restaurant owner*
Choi, Jay Lee *women's apparel executive*
Chopey, Nicholas P. *editor*
Chou, Ting-Chao *pharmacology educator*
Chowdhury, Shoaib *engineer*
Christ, Lily Esther Shih *mathematics educator*
Christensen, Dieter *ethnomusicologist*
Christensen, Henry, III, *lawyer*
Christensen, Kathleen Elizabeth *foundation administrator*
Christian, Darrell L. *journalist*
Christoforous, Alexis *reporter*
Christopher, Maurine Brooks *foundation administrator, writer, editor*
Christopher, Nicholas *poet, novelist*
Christy, Arthur Hill *lawyer*
Chromow, Sheri P. *lawyer*
Chu, Benjamin K. *hospital administrator*
Chu, Mary Lynn *pediatric neurologist*
Chua, Nam-Hai *plant molecular biologist, educator*
Chung, Chia Mou (Charles Chung) *former Oriental art business owner*
Church, Charlotte *vocalist*
Church, Frank Forrester *minister, author, columnist*
Chwast, Seymour *graphic artist*
Chwat, Anne *recording industry executive*
Chwatsky, Ann *photographer, educator*
Ciarrocchi, Maya *dancer*
Cioppa, Robert *architectural firm executive*
Ciparick, Carmen Beauchamp *judge*
Cisneros, Sandra *poet, short story writer, essayist*
Clamar, Aphrodite J. *psychologist*
Clapman, Peter Carlyle *lawyer, insurance company executive*
Clark, Carolyn Cochran *lawyer*
Clark, Celia Rue *lawyer*
Clark, Howard Longstreth, Jr., *finance company executive, director*
Clark, Joan Hardy *retired journalist*
Clark, Jonathan Montgomery *lawyer*
Clark, Merrell Edward, Jr., *lawyer*
Clark, Nancy Ellen *podiatrist*
Clark, Ric *real estate company executive*
Clark, Robert Henry, Jr., *holding company executive*
Clarke, Frank William *communication executive*
Clarke, Kenneth Kingsley *retired electronics executive*
Clarke, Lewis Ryland *history educator*
Clarkson, Kelly Brianne *singer*
Clarkson, Patricia *actress*
Clary, Richard Wayland *lawyer*
Claster, Jill Nadell *university administrator, history educator*
Clay, John Peter *investment company executive*
Clayton, Jonathan Alan *banker*
Cleary, Beverly Atlee (Mrs. Clarence T. Cleary) *writer*
Clement, Gregory *architect*
Clemente, Lilia Calderon *capital company executive*
Cliff, Walter Conway *lawyer*
Clifford, Stewart Burnett *banker, director*
Clinkscales, Keith *media company executive*
Clinton, William Jefferson (Bill Clinton) *42d President of the United States*
Close, Lanny Garth *otolaryngologist, educator*
Clutz, William (Hartman Clutz) *artist, educator*
Cobb, Henry Nichols *architect*
Cobb, Peter Z. *lawyer*
Cochran, Raymond Martin *university auditor*
Cochrane, James Louis *economist*
Cockrell, Sanford Alonza, III, *accountant*
Coffee, John Collins, Jr., *legal educator*
Coffin, Anne Gagnebin *art association administrator, editor*
Cogliano, Dan *tax accountant*
Cohane, Heather Christina *magazine publisher, editor*
Cohen, Abby Joseph *investment strategist*
Cohen, Alan M. *investment company executive*
Cohen, Brian S. *public relations executive*
Cohen, Burton A. *radiologist*
Cohen, Carmel *oncologist*
Cohen, Claire Gorham *investors service company executive*
Cohen, Claudia *journalist, television personality*
Cohen, Cora *artist*
Cohen, David Harris *neurobiology educator, university official*
Cohen, Edmund Stephen *lawyer*
Cohen, Ezechiel Godert David *physicist, researcher*
Cohen, Henry Rodgin *lawyer*
Cohen, Irving Elias *real estate executive*
Cohen, Jesse *editor*
Cohen, Joel Ephraim *biologist, educator, demographer*
Cohen, Jonathan Little *investment banker*
Cohen, Joseph M. *investment company executive*
Cohen, Joshua Robert *lawyer*
Cohen, Lyor *recording industry executive*
Cohen, Michael *psychologist*
Cohen, Michael T. *real estate company executive*
Cohen, Mildred Thaler *art gallery director*
Cohen, Morton Norton *English educator, writer*
Cohen, Noel Lee *otolaryngologist, educator*
Cohen, Richard Martin *journalist*
Cohen, Robert Stephan *lawyer*
Cohen, Selma *reference librarian, researcher*
Cohen, Seymour Martin *oncologist, hematologist, educator*
Cohen, Stephen Frand *political scientist, historian, educator, author, broadcaster*
Cohen, Steven Alan *program director*
Cohen, Steven Paul *anesthesiologist, researcher*
Cohn, Ian J. *architect*
Colbert, Stephen *comedian, actor*
Cole, Carolyn Jo *brokerage company executive*
Cole, Charles Dewey, Jr., *lawyer*
Cole, Harriett *writer, media consultant*
Cole, Kenneth D. *footwear and accessories company executive*
Cole, Kirsten *reporter*
Cole, Lewis George *lawyer*
Cole, Willie *artist*
Coleman, Cy *pianist, composer, producer*
Coleman, D. Jackson *ophthalmologist, educator*
Coleman, George Edward *tenor, alto and soprano saxophonist*
Coleman, Jerome P. *lawyer*
Coleman, John William *urologist*
Coleman, Lester Laudy *otolaryngologist*
Coleman, Morton *oncologist, hematologist*
Colen, Helen Sass *plastic surgeon*
Colen, Stephen R. *plastic and reconstructive surgeon*
Coll, John Peter, Jr., *lawyer*
Colletti, Roseanne *reporter*
Colligan, John Aloysius *music director, composer*
Collins, Adriana Delia *banker*
Collins, Gail *editor*
Collins, J. Barclay, II, *lawyer, oil industry executive*
Collins, Jackie *writer*
Collins, Judy Marjorie *singer, songwriter*
Collins, Phil (Philip David Charles Collins) *singer, songwriter, drummer, record producer*
Collins, Timothy Clark *holding company executive*
Collins, Wayne Dale *lawyer*
Colp, Norman Barry *photographic artist, curator*
Colvin, Geoffrey *editor*
Colvin, Shawn *recording artist, songwriter*
Combs, Sean (P. Diddy) *record company executive, producer*
Comfort, William Twyman, Jr., *banker*
Comissiona, Sergiu *conductor*
Comitas, Lambros *anthropologist, educator*
Compagnon, Antoine Marcel *French language educator*
Compte, Maria Emilia *physician, educator, administrator*
Cona, Louis *publishing executive*
Conarroe, Joel Osborne *foundation administrator, educator, editor*
Conboy, Kenneth *lawyer, former federal judge*
Conde, Yvonne M. *freelance journalist*
Condron, Christopher (Kip Condron) *investment company executive*
Cone, James Hal *theologian, educator, author*
Conlin, Kelly P. *communications executive*
Conlon, Peggy Eileen *publisher*
Connelly, Joan Breton *archaeologist*
Connolly, John Joseph *healthcare company executive*
Connolly, Judith *financial consultant*
Connolly, Kevin Jude *lawyer*
Connors, Peter J. *lawyer*
Conrad, Winthrop Brown, Jr., *lawyer*
Conroy, Frances *actress*
Conroy, Pat (Donald Patrick Conroy) *writer*
Consagra, Sophie Chandler *academic administrator*
Considine, Jill *banker*
Consolo, Faith Hope *real estate broker*
Constantine, Jan Friedman *lawyer*
Constantinides, Minas Spiros *otolaryngologist, plastic surgeon*
Constantino, Yamila *journalist, media executive*
Conston, Henry Siegismund *lawyer*
Conway, E. Virgil *financial consultant, banker, lawyer*
Conway, Gordon Richard *foundation executive*
Conway, Kevin *actor, director*
Conway, Richard Francis *investment company executive*
Cook, Blanche Wiesen *history educator, journalist*
Cook, Ian M. *consumer products company executive*
Cook, John Wesley *foundation administrator*
Cook, Michael Lewis *lawyer*
Cook, Traci *sports association executive*
Cooke, Alfred Alistair *correspondent, writer, broadcaster*
Cooley, Lisa *television news anchor*
Cooley, Thomas F. *dean, economist, educator*
Cooney, Joan Ganz *broadcast executive, director*
Cooney, John Patrick, Jr., *lawyer*
Cooper, Gloria *editor, press critic*
Cooper, Kenneth *harpsicordist, pianist, music educator, conductor, musicologist*
Cooper, Louis Zucker *pediatrician, educator*
Cooper, Michael Anthony *lawyer*
Cooper, Stephen Herbert *lawyer*
Cooperman, Alvin *television and theatrical producer*
Cooperman, Leon G. *investment company executive*
Copeland, Michelle *plastic surgeon, dentist*
Copeland, Stewart *composer, musician*
Coppola, Sofia Carmina *film director, scriptwriter, actress*
Coraggio, Linus *sculptor, consultant*
Corbet, Kathleen A. *financial information company executive*
Corbin, Herbert Leonard *public relations executive, director*
Corbin, Patrick *dancer*
Corbin, Sol Neil *lawyer*
Corcoran, Barbara *real estate company executive*
Corcoran, David *newspaper editor*
Corcoran, Joseph P. *health facility administrator*
Corddry, Rob *comedian, actor*
Corman, Judith *corporate communications specialist*
Cornell, John Robert *lawyer*
Cornish, Kelley A. *lawyer*
Cornwell, Patricia Daniels *writer*
Corporon, John Robert *broadcast executive*
Corr, Peter B. *pharmaceutical executive*
Corrigan, E(dward) Gerald *investment banker*
Corsaro, Frank Andrew *theater, musical and opera director*
Cortez, Ricardo Lee *investment management executive*
Cortina, Betty *magazine editor*
Corujo, Marlene *urologic surgeon*
Corwin, Steven *hospital administrator*
Cory, Christopher Thayer *communications executive*
Cosbey, Ted *water transportation executive*
Cosgriff, Stuart Worcester *internist, consultant, medical educator*
Costa, Max *health facility administrator, pharmacology educator, environmental medicine educator*
Costello, Elvis (Declan Patrick McManus) *musician, songwriter*
Coster, Peter *management consulting firm executive*
Costikyan, Edward N. *lawyer*
Cote, Denise Louise *federal judge*
Cotter, James Michael *lawyer*
Cotton, Richard *lawyer*
Couchman, Jeffrey G. *literature educator, writer*
Coughlin, Christopher J. *financial executive*
Coulter, David A. *investment banker*
Courant, Ernest David *physicist, educator*
Couric, Katie (Katherine Anne Couric) *broadcast journalist*
Court, Kathryn Diana *editor*
Cowan, Wallace Edgar *lawyer*
Cowen, Edward S. *lawyer, consultant*
Cowen, Robert Nathan *lawyer*
Cowin, Stephen Corteen *biomedical engineering educator, consultant*
Cowles, Charles *art dealer*
Cox, Carole Beth *social worker, educator*
Coyne, Judith *editor*
Coyne, Nancy Carol *advertising executive*
Cracauer, Cynthia Phifer *architectural firm executive*
Cracraft, Joel *curator*
Craft, Randal Robert, Jr., *lawyer*
Craig, Charles Samuel *marketing educator*
Craig, Edward Vincent *orthopaedic surgeon, educator*
Cramer, Edward Morton *lawyer, music company executive*
Cramer, Jim *online financial information executive*
Crandell, Susan *magazine editor*
Crane, Benjamin Field *lawyer*
Crane, Charles Grant *securities analyst*
Crane, Roger Ryan, Jr., *lawyer*
Cranefield, Paul Frederic *physiology educator, physician, scientist*
Cranney, Marilyn Kanrek *lawyer*
Crary, Miner Dunham, Jr., *lawyer*
Craven, Frank John *actor, playwright, poet*
Craven, Wes *film director*
Crawford, Bruce Edgar *performing company executive*
Crawford, R. George *investment manager, educator, filmmaker*
Crawford, Stephen S. *financial services executive*
Crawley, John Boevey *former publisher*
Creamer, German Gonzalo *bank executive, educator*
Crean, Peter Thomas *lawyer*
Creech, Sharon *children's author*
Creel, Thomas Leonard *lawyer*
Creenan, Katherine Heras *lawyer*
Creshevsky, Noah Ephraim *composer, music educator*
Crews, Harry Eugene *author*
Crist, Judith *film and drama critic*
Cristea, Ruxandra Maria *corporate financial executive*
Critchlow, Charles Howard *lawyer*
Critchlow, Paul *communication and public affairs executive*
Crittenden, Danielle Ann *writer, journalist*
Crittenden, Gary Lewis *diversified financial services company executive*
Croce, Arlene Louise *critic*
Crockett, Andrew Duncan *bank executive*
Cromwell, Oliver Dean *investment banker*
Crone, Penny *reporter*
Cronin, Doreen *writer, former lawyer*
Cronkite, Walter *radio and television news correspondent*
Cronson, Caroline Mary *financial executive*
Cross, George Alan Martin *biochemistry educator, researcher*
Cross, Theodore Lamont *publisher, author*
Crough, Maureen M. *lawyer*
Crowdus, Gary Alan *film company executive*
Crowell, Kenneth E. *lawyer, chemical engineer*
Croyden, Margaret *writer, educator*
Cruz, Nilo *playwright*
Cruz, Zoe *investment company executive*
Cryer, Gretchen *playwright, lyricist, actress*
Crystal, J. Scott *publishing executive*
Crystal, James William *insurance company executive*
Cubitto, Robert J. *lawyer*
Cucin, Robert Louis *plastic surgeon, lawyer*
Cuiffo, Frank Wayne *lawyer*
Culhane, John William *journalist, author, film historian*
Culligan, John William *retired corporate executive*
Cullman, Edgar M., Jr., *tobacco products company executive*
Cumming, Ian M. *holding company executive*
Cummings, John W. *diversified financial services company executive*
Cuneo, Donald Lane *lawyer, educator*
Cunha, Mark Geoffrey *lawyer*
Cunningham, Merce *dancer*
Cunningham, Michael *author, educator*
Cuomo, Mario Matthew *lawyer, former governor*
Cuozzo, Steven David *newspaper editor*
Curci-Gonzalez, Lucy *law librarian*
Curley, Thomas *newspaper executive*
Curley, Walter Joseph Patrick *diplomat, investment banker*
Curran, Leigh *actress, playwright*
Currie, Russell *composer, educator*
Curry, Ann *correspondent, anchor*
Curry, Jane Louise *writer*
Curtin, Jane Therese *actress, writer*
Curtin, John Paul, Jr., *investment banker*
Curtis, Frank R. *lawyer*
Curtis, Paul James *mime director*
Curtis, Susan Grace *lawyer*
Curtis, Susan M. *lawyer*
Curtis, Tony (Bernard Schwartz) *actor*
Cushman, Karen Lipski *writer*
Cuti, Anthony J. *consumer products company executive*
Cutler, Laurel *advertising agency executive*
Cutler, Laurence Stephan *architect, urban designer, museum founder, advertising executive, educator*
Cutler, Ronnie *artist*
Cuttner, Janet *hematologist, educator*
Czajka, James Vincent *architect*
Czepiel, Lori Anne *lawyer*
Czerwinski, Edward Joseph *foreign language educator*
D'Abruzzo, Stephanie *actress*
D'Addario, Edith *performing company executive*
Daidone, Lewis Eugene *financial services company executive*
Daines, Richard *health services executive*
Dajani, Virginia *arts association administrator*
Dakin, Christine Whitney *dancer, educator*
Dales, Samuel *microbiologist, virologist, educator*
D'Alessio, Frederick D. *telecommunications company executive*
Dallas, William Moffit, Jr., *lawyer*
Dallen, Russell Morris, Jr., *investment company executive, lawyer, publishing company executive*
Dalton, Dennis Gilmore *political science educator*
Daltrey, Roger *musician*
Daly, Cheryl *broadcast executive*
Daly, George Garman *college dean, educator*
Daly, John Neal *investment company executive*
Damashek, Philip Michael *lawyer*
D'Amato, Alfonse M. *lawyer, former senator*
Dana, F(rank) Mitchell *theatrical lighting designer*
Danaher, Frank Erwin *transportation technologist*
Dandashi, S. Alexander-Levy *operations research scientist, consultant, corporate and government advisor*
Danforth, John Claggett *ambassador, former senator*
D'Angelo, Joseph Francis *publishing company executive*
Dangue Rewaka, Denis *diplomat*
Daniel, Charles Timothy *transportation engineer, consultant*
Daniel, David Ronald *management consultant*
Daniel, Richard H. *trust company executive*
Daniel, Samuel J. *hospital administrator, medical educator*
Danielides, Joannie C. *public relations executive*
Daniels, J. Yolande *architectural firm executive, educator*
Danikas, Dimitrios *plastic surgeon*
Danishefsky, Samuel J. *chemistry professor*
Danisi, John J. *philosopher, educator*
Danitz, Marilynn Patricia *choreographer, videographer*
Dankin, Peter Alfred *lawyer*
Danner, Mark David *writer*
Dannhauser, Stephen J. *lawyer*
Dansky, Ira M. *lawyer*
Danto, Arthur Coleman *author, philosopher, art critic*
D'Antuono, Eleanor *ballet director, teacher, coach*
Dantzker, David Roy *venture capitalist*
Danziger, Lucy *editor*
Daphnis, Nassos *artist*
Darlington, Henry, Jr., *investment broker*
Darnell, James Edwin, Jr., *molecular biologist, educator*
Darrell, Norris, Jr., *lawyer*
Darrow, Jill E(llen) *lawyer*
Darst, David Martin *investment company executive, educator, writer*
Dash, Damon *broadcast executive, recording industry executive*
Datema, Jessica Venning *humanities educator*
Dauer, Sheila A. *human rights program director*
Davenport, John J. *philosopher, educator*
David, Hal *lyricist*
David, Reuben *lawyer*
David, Theoharis Lambros *architect, educator*
Davidovsky, Mario *composer*
Davidson, Anthony R. *education educator, consultant*
Davidson, Donald William *advertising executive*
Davidson, George Allan *lawyer*
Davidson, Jack *actor*

Feder, Saul E. *lawyer*
Federle, Michael *publishing executive*
Fedunok, Suzanne *librarian*
Feeley, Michael John *investment counselor*
Feerick, John David *law educator*
Feigen, Richard L. *art dealer, collector, writer*
Feigin, Barbara Sommer *marketing consultant*
Feiman, Ronald Mark *lawyer*
Feinberg, Wilfred *judge*
Feintuch, Henry Philip *public relations executive*
Feintuch, Richard David *lawyer*
Feit, Barberi Paull *composer, lyricist, psychotherapist, author, speaker*
Feit, Glenn M. *lawyer*
Feld, Eliot *dancer, choreographer*
Feldberg, Meyer *university dean*
Feldberg, Michael Svetkey *lawyer*
Felder, Myrna *lawyer*
Felder, Raoul Lionel *lawyer*
Feldman, Franklin *lawyer, printmaker*
Feldman, Mark *lawyer*
Feldman, Noah *law educator*
Feldman, Robert C. *public relations executive*
Feldman, Ronald Arthur *social work educator, researcher*
Feldman, Samuel Mitchell *neuroscientist, educator*
Feldschuh, Jonathan Adam *artist*
Feldstein, Eric A. *finance company executive*
Feldt, Gloria A. *social service administrator*
Felgran, Steven David *economist, educator*
Felicitas, C.S. *foundation director, library director*
Felious, Odetta *vocalist*
Felix, Ted Mark *accountant*
Feltenstein, Martha *lawyer*
Fenchel, Gerd Herman *psychoanalyst*
Feniger, Jerome Roland, Jr., *broadcast executive*
Fennell, Thomas Edward, Jr., *engineering educator*
Fennell Robbins, Sally *writer*
Fenster, Marvin *lawyer, department store executive*
Fensterstock, Blair Courtney *lawyer*
Fenton, Thomas Trail *journalist*
Fenwick, Lex *communications executive*
Ferguson, Sarah *The Duchess of York*
Ferguson, Tim Wayne *editor, journalist*
Ferm, David G. *magazine publisher*
Fernandes, Jeanne Mary *human resource administrator*
Fernandez, James *retail products executive*
Ferrante, Joan Marguerite *language educator, literature educator, writer*
Ferri, David *lighting designer*
Ferry, Martha Morton *nonprofit executive*
Fertig, Howard *publisher, editor*
Feskoe, Gaffney Jon *management consultant*
Feuer, Cy *motion picture and theatrical producer, director*
Feuerman, Carole A. *sculptor, artist*
Feurey, Claudia Packer *not-for-profit executive*
Fey, Tina *actress*
Field, Patricia *apparel designer*
Field, Steven Philip *medical educator*
Filarski Hasselbeck, Elizabeth *television host/personality*
Fili-Krushel, Patricia *media company executive*
Filimonov, Mikhail Anatolyevitch *investment company executive*
Filler, Ronald Howard *lawyer*
Finauri, Graciela Maria *foreign service professional*
Finberg, Barbara Denning *not-for-profit developer*
Finch, Edward Ridley, Jr., *lawyer, diplomat, writer, educator*
Finch, Peter *editor-in-chief*
Findlay, Michael Alistair *art dealer, poet*
Fine, Deborah *publishing executive*
Fine, Jo Renée *management executive*
Fine, Michael Joseph *publishing company executive*
Finegold, Amy Beth *elementary school educator, consultant*
Finger, Seymour Maxwell *political science educator, former ambassador*
Fink, Laurence D. *diversified financial services company executive*
Fink, Matthew E. *health facility executive, educator*
Fink, Raymond *medical educator*
Fink, Robert Steven *lawyer, writer, educator*
Finkel, Robert *finance company executive*
Finkelstein, Allen Lewis *lawyer*
Finkelstein, Bernard *lawyer*
Finkelstein, Edward Sydney *department store executive*
Finkelstein, Ira Allen *lawyer*
Finkelstein, James A. *media executive*
Finkelstein, Nancy R. *lawyer*
Finkelstein, Stuart M. *lawyer*
Finley, Skip *media and communications executive*
Finn, Brian D. *financial services executive*
Finn, David *public relations company executive, artist*
Finn, Edwin A., Jr., *publishing executive*
Finn, Peter *public relations executive*
Finn, Peter Michael *television production executive*
Finnerty, Joseph Gregory, III, *lawyer*
Fins, Joseph Jack *internist*
Fiorato, Hugo *conductor*
Fiore, Joseph Albert *artist*
Fiori, Pamela *publishing executive, magazine editor, writer*
Fiorilla, John Leopoldo *lawyer, investment company executive*
First, Harry *law educator*
Fischbach, Gerald D. *dean, neurobiology educator*
Fischer, Carl *graphic designer, photographer, actor*
Fishbein, Peter Melvin *lawyer*
Fisher, Ann Bailen *lawyer*
Fisher, Arthur *magazine editor*
Fisher, Edward Abraham *cardiologist, educator*
Fisher, Gary Alan *marketing professional*
Fisher, Laura Lani *physician, medical educator*
Fisher, Peter R. *investment company executive*
Fisher, Richard B. *investment banker*
Fisher, Robert I. *lawyer*
Fishman, Ellen Beth *lawyer*
Fishman, Fred Norman *lawyer*
Fishman, Jay Steven *financial services executive*
Fiske, Robert Bishop, Jr., *lawyer*
Fitch, Janet *writer*
Fitzpatrick, Joseph Mark *lawyer*
Flach, Frederic Francis *psychiatrist*
Flack, Roberta *singer*
Flaherty, Pamela Potter *bank executive*
Flaherty, Stephen *composer, orchestrator*
Flaherty, Tina Santi *corporate communications executive, writer*
Flanagan, Deborah Mary *lawyer*
Flanagan, Dennis *journalist*
Flanagan, Sean Patrick *publishing executive*
Flannelly, Kevin J. *psychologist, research analyst*
Flannelly, Laura T. *mental health nurse, nursing educator, researcher*
Flaum, Sander Allen *advertising and marketing executive*
Flax, Herschel *surgeon*
Flay, Bobby *food service executive*
Fleischer, Arthur, Jr., *lawyer*
Fleischer, Joseph Linden *architect*
Fleischman, Albert Sidney (Sid Fleischman) *writer*
Fleischman, Barbara Greenberg *public relations consultant*
Fleischman, Edward Hirsh *lawyer, consultant*
Fleischman, Keith Martin *lawyer*
Fleischman, Paul *children's author*
Fleming, Alice Carew Mulcahey *writer*
Fleming, Gregory J. *finance company executive*
Fleming, Renée L. *opera singer*
Fleming, Thomas James *writer*
Flesh, Henry, Jr., *writer, editor*
Fletcher, Anthony L. *lawyer*
Fletcher, Harry George, III, *library director*
Fletcher, Mary Lee *retired marketing professional*
Flicker, John *foundation executive*
Flinn, Michael de Vlaming *investment banker, former state legislator*
Flint, George Squire *lawyer*
Flom, Joseph Harold *lawyer, director*
Flores, Clemente, Jr., *counselor, educator*
Florio, Steven T. *magazine executive*
Florio, Thomas A. *magazine publisher*
Fluhr, Howard *consulting firm executive*
Flynn, Elizabeth E. *bank executive*
Flynn, Laurie M. *social worker*
Flynn, Michael D. *architectural firm executive*
Fodor, Susanna Serena *lawyer*
Fogel, Henry *orchestra administrator*
Fogel, Irving Martin *consulting engineer*
Fogelman, Martin *lawyer, law educator*
Foley, Ann *broadcast executive*
Foley, Duncan Karl *economist, educator*
Foley, Kathleen M. *neurologist, educator, researcher*
Foley, Maura *picture editor*
Folkenflik, Max *lawyer*
Folta, Carl D. *communications executive*
Foncillas, Ignacio *lawyer*
Foner, Eric *historian, educator*
Fong, Yuman *surgeon, researcher*
Fontana, Thomas Michael *producer, scriptwriter*
Forbes, Christopher (Kip Forbes) *publisher*
Forbes, Steve (Malcolm Stevenson Forbes Jr.) *publishing executive*
Forbes, Timothy Carter *publishing executive*
Ford, Eileen Otte (Mrs. Gerard W. Ford) *modeling agency executive*
Ford, John Charles *communications executive*
Foreman, Richard *theater director, playwright*
Forger, Alexander Darrow *lawyer*
Forman, Leonard P. *media company executive*
Formenti, Silvia C. *radiation oncologist*
Formento, Daniel *radio company executive, writer*
Forrest, David Vickers *psychiatrist, educator*
Forst, Edward C. *investment company executive*
Forstadt, Joseph Lawrence *lawyer*
Forstmann, Theodore J. *investment firm executive*
Fort, Randall Martin *investment banking executive*
Fortenbaugh, Samuel Byrod, III, *lawyer*
Fortner, Joseph Gerald *surgeon, educator*
Foster, Craig Allen *plastic surgeon*
Foster, David Lee *lawyer*
Foster, Gary *publishing executive, information technology executive*
Foster, Sutton *actress*
Foti, Samuel J. *insurance company executive*
Fournier, Nicole D *graphics designer, photographer*
Fowler, Beth *actress*
Fowler, John M. *financial services executive*
Fowler, Karen Joy *writer*
Fowler, Robert Ramsay *former Canadian government official*
Fowler, William A. *accounting firm executive*
Fox, Arthur Charles *physician, educator*
Fox, Daniel Michael *foundation executive, writer*
Fox, Donald Thomas *lawyer*
Fox, Paula (Mrs. Martin Greenberg) *writer*
Fox, Richard Gabriel *anthropologist, educator*
Fox, Richard Paul *medical association administrator*
Fox, Sylvan *journalist, educator*
Fox-Freund, Barbara Susan *real estate company executive*
Foxman, Abraham Henry *advocacy organization administrator*
Foxworth, Jo *advertising agency executive*
Fraenkel, George Kessler *chemistry professor*
Fragos, Emily *poet, educator*
Fraguela, James *publishing executive*
France, Joseph David *securities analyst*
Francis, James Clark, IV, *judge*
Franck, Thomas Martin *law educator*
Frank, Elizabeth *literature educator, writer*
Frank, Lloyd *lawyer, retired chemical company executive*
Frank, Peter Bruce *management consultant, accountant*
Frankel, Alice Kross *physician, director*
Frankel, Gene *theater director, writer, producer, educator*
Frankel, Martin Richard *statistician, educator, consultant*
Frankel, Max *retired journalist*
Frankel, Sandor *lawyer, author*
Frankenthaler, Helen *artist*
Franklin, Aretha *singer*
Franklin, Blake Timothy *lawyer*
Franklin, Edward Ward *international investment consultant, lawyer, actor*
Franklin, Julian Harold *political science educator*
Franks, Andrew George *dermatologist*
Franks, Lucinda Laura *journalist*
Franks, Martin Davis *broadcast executive*
Frantz, Andrew Gibson *endocrinologist, educator, dean*
Franzen, Jonathan *writer*
Franzen, Ulrich J. *architect*
Frazier, Charles Robinson *writer*
Frazza, George S. *lawyer, business executive*
Fredericks, Wesley Charles, Jr., *lawyer*
Fredericks, William Curtis *lawyer*
Freed, James Ingo *architect*
Freed, Stanley Arthur *retired museum curator*
Freedberg, David Adrian *art educator, historian*
Freedberg, Irwin Mark *dermatologist*
Freedman, Aaron David *medical educator, former university dean*
Freedman, Albert Z. *publishing company executive*
Freedman, Alfred Mordecai *psychiatrist, educator*
Freedman, Gerald M. *lawyer*
Freedman, Helen E. *justice*
Freedman, (Moses) Maurice *historian, researcher*
Freedman, Michael Leonard *geriatrician, educator*
Freedman, Robert L. *real estate company executive*
Freeman, David John *lawyer*
Freeman, Harold Paul *oncologist, educator, medical center director*
Freeman, James Beaumont *philosophy educator*
Freeman, Michael J. *inventor, professor, author, corporate executive*
Freeman, Morgan *actor*
Freeman, Peter Sunderlin *textile executive*
Freiberg, Lowell Carl *insurance company executive*
Freiberg, Steven J. *diversified financial services company executive*
Freidenbergs, Ingrid *psychologist*
Freidheim, Lynn *not-for-profit fundraiser*
Freidheim, Stephen C. *investment company executive*
Freilich, Joan Sherman *utilities executive*
Freilicher, Morton *lawyer, educator*
Freiman, Alvin Henry *cardiologist, educator*
Freiman, Charles Visvald *engineering foundation administrator*
Freizer, Louis A. *radio news producer*
French, John, III, *lawyer, director*
Frenkel, Jacob Aharon *insurance company executive*
Freston, Thomas E. *broadcast executive*
Freudenheim, Milton B. *journalist*
Freund, Fred A. *retired lawyer*
Freund, William Curt *economist, educator*
Frey, Andrew Lewis *lawyer*
Frey, Julia Bloch *French language educator, art historian educator*
Freyer, Dana Hartman *lawyer*
Freyre, Fabio *publishing executive*
Fribourg, Paul J. *grain company executive*
Fricklas, Michael David *lawyer*
Fridson, Martin Steven *finance executive*
Fried, Albert, Jr., *investment banker*
Fried, Arthur *lawyer*
Fried, Burton Theodore *lawyer*
Fried, Donald David *lawyer*
Friedberg, Barry Sewell *investment banker*
Frieden, Thomas R. *public health physician*
Friedenberg, Daniel Meyer *financial investor, writer*
Friedlander, Jeffrey D. *lawyer*
Friedman, Alan Herbert *ophthalmologist*
Friedman, Alan Roy *lawyer*
Friedman, Alvin Edward *investment executive*
Friedman, Bart *lawyer*
Friedman, B(ernard) H(arper) *writer*
Friedman, Emanuel A. *medical educator*
Friedman, Eugene Warren *surgeon*
Friedman, Herbert A. *rabbi, educator, fund raising executive*
Friedman, Ira Hugh *surgeon*
Friedman, J. Roger *publisher*
Friedman, Jane *publishing executive*
Friedman, Rachelle *music retail executive*
Friedman, Robert Laurence *investment professional*
Friedman, Samuel Selig *lawyer*
Friedman, Sanford *literature educator, writer*
Friedman, Steven M. *investment company executive*
Friedman, Victor Stanley *lawyer*
Friedman, W. Robert, Jr., *investment banker*
Friedman, Wilbur Harvey *lawyer*
Friedrich, Dennis H. *real estate company executive*
Friend, David *publishing executive*
Frisch, Harry David *lawyer, consultant, investment company executive*
Frisell-Schröder, Sonja Bettie *opera producer, stage director*
Froimitz, Ray *construction executive, contractor*
Frommer, William S. *lawyer*
Frost, Ellen Elizabeth *psychologist*
Frost, William Lee *lawyer*
Froum, Stuart Jay *periodontist, educator*
Fruitman, Frederick Howard *investment banker*
Fry, Morton Harrison, II, *lawyer*
Frye, Clayton Wesley, Jr., *finance executive*
Fuchs, Elaine V. *molecular biologist, educator*
Fuchs, Lillian *classical musician, educator, composer*
Fudge, Ann Marie *advertising executive*
Fugate-Wilcox, Tery *artist*
Fuld, Richard Severin, Jr., *investment banking executive*
Fulweiler, Patricia Platt *civic worker*
Furlaud, Richard Mortimer *pharmaceutical company executive*
Furman, Roy Lance *investment banker*
Furmanski, Philip *cancer research scientist*
Furnary, Stephen J. *real estate company executive*
Fuster, Valentin *cardiologist, educator*
Futter, Ellen Victoria *museum administrator*
Fuzesi, Stephen, Jr., *lawyer, communications executive*
Gabaldon, Diana *writer*
Gabay, Donald *lawyer*
Gables, Shon *newscaster*
Gabrielson, Charles *publishing executive*
Gabrilove, Jacques Lester *physician*
Gage, Beau *artist*
Gage, Robert Clifford *minister*
Gaines, Boyd *actor*
Gainsburg, Roy Ellis *publishing executive*
Galan, Leonidez Vindollo *architect*
Galant, Herbert Lewis *lawyer*
Galanter, Eugene *psychologist, educator*
Galanter, Marc *psychiatrist, educator*
Galassi, Jonathan White *book publishing company executive*
Gallagher, Brian John *lawyer*
Gallagher, Edward Peter *foundation executive*
Galletti, Scott M. *finance company executive*
Gallo, William Victor *cartoonist*
Galway, James *flutist*
Gambari, Ibrahim Agboola *diplomat, international organization official*
Gamble, Theodore Robert, Jr., *investment banker*
Gamboni, Ciro Anthony *lawyer*
Gambro, Michael S. *lawyer*
Gammill, Lee Morgan, Jr., *retired insurance company executive*
Gamper, Albert R., Jr., *insurance executive*
Gans, Herbert J. *sociologist, educator*
Gans, Walter Gideon *lawyer*
Gant, Donald Ross *investment banker*
Ganz, Axel *publishing executive*
Ganz, David L. *lawyer*
Ganz, Howard Laurence *lawyer*
Ganzi, Victor Frederick *publishing executive*
Garabedian, Paul Roesel *mathematics professor*
Garcia, Andy *actor*
Garcia, Angela G. *lawyer*
Gardella, Francis John *mathematics professor*
Gardiner, E. Nicholas P. *executive search executive*
Gardino, Vincent Anthony *broadcast executive*
Gardner, H. McIntrye *diversified financial services company executive*
Gardner, James Richard *pharmaceutical company executive*
Gardner, Janet Paxton *journalist, film/video producer*
Gardner, Ralph David *advertising executive*
Gardner, Richard Newton *diplomat, lawyer, educator*
Garfield, Leslie Jerome *real estate executive*
Garfinkel, Barry Herbert *lawyer*
Garfinkel, Lee *advertising agency executive*
Garfunkel, Alan J. *lawyer*
Garland, Sylvia Dillof *lawyer*
Garlin, Jeff *actor*
Garner, Albert Headden *investment banker*
Garrett, Laurie *journalist, global health scholar*
Garrett, Robert *financial advisory executive*
Garrett, Wendell *antiques appraiser, auctioneer, editor*
Garson, Gary Wayne *lawyer*
Garvey, Richard Anthony *retired lawyer*
Garvin, Andrew Paul *information company executive, author, consultant*
Gassel, Philip Michael *lawyer*
Gastil, Raymond Wesley *urban designer*
Gath, Jean Marie *architectural firm executive*
Gatje, Robert Frederick *architect, writer*
Gatto, Carolyn Michele *editor-in-chief*
Gatto, John Taylor *educational consultant, writer, speaker*
Gaughan, Eugene Francis *retired accountant, lawyer*
Gaveras, Harry *architect*
Gavin, Paula Lance *investment company executive*
Gay, Faith E. *lawyer, educator*
Gay, Peter *history educator, author*
Gayle, King *editor*
Ge, Yulin *radiologist, educator*
Geary, Hilary R. *society editor*
Gebbie, Kristine Moore *health science educator, health official*
Geckle, Robert Alan *manufacturing executive*
Geer, John Farr *retired religious organization administrator*
Geier, Philip Henry, Jr., *advertising executive*
Geiger, H. Jack *medical educator*
Geiser, Elizabeth Able *publishing company executive*
Geismar, Thomas H. *graphic designer*
Geissbuhler, Stephan *graphics designer*
Geithner, Timothy F. *bank executive*
Gelb, Bruce Stuart *city commissioner, consultant*
Gelb, Judith Anne *lawyer*
Gelb, Leslie Howard *organization president, lecturer*
Gelfand, Neal *oil company executive*
Gelfman, Peter Trustman *lawyer*
Geller, Jeffrey Lawrence *financier*
Geller, Robert James *advertising agency executive*
Gellert, Michael Erwin *investment banker*
Gellhorn, Alfred *physician, educator*
Geltzer, Robert Lawrence *lawyer, former retail executive, arbitrator, mediator*
Gemorah, Solomon *education educator, historian*
Gendler, Ellen *dermatologist*
Genkins, Gabriel *physician*
Genova, Diane Melisano *lawyer*
Georges, Paul Gordon *artist, educator*
Gerard, Ian *performing arts association administrator*
Gerard, Whitney Ian *lawyer*
Gerard-Sharp, Monica Fleur *communications executive*
Gerber, Robert Evan *judge*
Gerdts, William Henry *art history educator*
Gerety, Tom *academic administrator, lawyer, educator, philosopher*
Germano, William Paul *publisher*
Gero, Anthony George *securities and commodities trader*
Geronemus, Roy G. *dermatologist*
Gershon, Bernard *broadcast executive*
Gerson, Donald Franklin *pharmaceutical executive*
Gersony, Welton Mark *physician, pediatric cardiologist, educator*
Gerstein, Mordicai *illustrator*
Gertjejansen, Doyle *artist, educator*
Gertler, Menard M. *physician, educator*
Getnick, Neil Victor *lawyer*
Gewirtz-Friedman, Gerry *editor*
Geyer, Thomas Powick *newspaper publisher*
Gharib, Susie *television newscaster*
Giampietro, Philip Francis *clinical geneticist, pediatrics educator*
Gianaris, Nicholas Vasil *economics professor*
Giancotti, Filippo Giusto *cell and molecular biologist*
Giannetti, Stephen P. *publishing executive*
Giannini, A. Christina *costume designer, set designer*
Giardina, Elsa Grace Vonna *cardiologist, educator*
Gibbons, Kaye *writer*
Gibbs, Lippman Martin *lawyer*
Gibbs, Richard L. *insurance company executive*
Giblin, James Cross *author, editor*
Gibson, Charles DeWolf *broadcast journalist*
Gibson, John *news anchor, correspondent*
Gibson, Jon Charles *composer, musician, artist*
Gibson, Ralph H(olmes) *photographer*
Gibson, William S. *lawyer*
Giddens-Jones, Emily Jane *architectural and interior designer, consultant*
Gifford, William C. *lawyer, educator*
Gigot, Paul Anthony *editor*
Gilbert, Rose Bennett *communications company executive*
Gilburne, Miles R. *communications executive*
Gill, E. Ann *lawyer*
Gillers, Stephen *law educator, university official*
Gillespie, George Joseph, III, *lawyer*
Gillespie, John Thomas *university administrator*
Gilligan, Edward P. *diversified financial services company executive*
Giniger, Kenneth Seeman *publisher*
Ginsberg, David Lawrence *architect*

Harris, Patricia E. *deputy mayor*
Harris, William Vernon *history educator*
Harrison, Gilbert Warner *investment banker*
Harrison, S. David *lawyer*
Harrison, Theodore Joel *otolaryngologist, facial plastic surgeon*
Harrison, Warren *finance company executive*
Harrow, Nancy (Mrs. Jan Krukowski) *jazz singer, songwriter, editor*
Hart, Gurnee Fellows *investment counselor*
Hart, Joseph Thomas Campbell *lawyer*
Hart, Karen Ann *advertising executive*
Hart, Kitty Carlisle *arts administrator*
Hart, Robert M. *lawyer*
Harter, Theo C. *music educator, composer*
Hartley, Hal *film director*
Hartman, Bruce L. *apparel executive*
Hartman, Joan Edna *English educator*
Hartmann, Carl Joseph *lawyer, consultant*
Hartnick, Alan Jay *lawyer, law educator*
Hartwick, Gary Glenn *entertainment company executive*
Hartzell, Andrew Cornelius, Jr., *retired lawyer*
Harvey, Donald Joseph *historian, educator*
Harvey, Steven Patrick (Steve Harvey) *comedian, actor*
Harvey, O.S.F.S., John F *priest, theologian, educator*
Haseley, Dennis *psychoanalyst, writer*
Hashimoto, Kyosuke *investment company executive*
Haskell, Barbara *curator*
Haskell, John Henry Farrell, Jr., *investment banking company executive*
Hassan, Ibne *lawyer, diplomat, political philosopher, international strategist*
Hatfield, Juliana *vocalist*
Hatheway, John Harris *advertising agency executive*
Haubegger, Christy *media consultant, publishing executive*
Hauck, Marguerite Hall *broadcast executive*
Hauptman, William *playwright*
Hauser, Gustave M. *cable television and electronic communications company executive*
Hauser, Rita Eleanore Abrams *lawyer*
Hauser, Sarah B. *artist*
Hausman, Marvin S. *research and development company executive*
Havens, John P *investment company executive*
Hawke, Ethan *actor*
Hawke, Roger Jewett *lawyer*
Hawkins, Katherine Ann *hematologist, lawyer*
Hayden, Donald J., Jr., *pharmaceutical executive*
Hayden, Raymond Paul *lawyer*
Hayden, Richard Seth *architectural firm executive*
Hayes, Constance J. *pediatric cardiologist*
Hayes, Gerald Joseph *lawyer*
Hayes, John D. *diversified financial services company executive*
Hayman, Linda C. *lawyer*
Hays, Kathleen *news correspondent*
Hazzard, Shirley *author*
Head, Elizabeth *lawyer*
Head, Glenn Oakes *investment company executive*
Heal, Geoffrey Martin *economics and business educator*
Healey, Thomas J. *former government official, brokerage house executive*
Healy, Harold Harris, Jr., *lawyer*
Healy, James P. *securities trader*
Healy, Nicholas Joseph *lawyer, educator*
Hearn, David *advertising executive*
Hearn, George Henry *lawyer, steamship corporate executive*
Hearst, George Randolph, Jr., *publishing executive, diversified ranching and real estate executive*
Heasley, Philip *financial services company executive*
Hebert, Bliss Edmund *opera director*
Hedbring, Charles *computer consultant, writer*
Hedstrom, Mitchell Warren *banker*
Heekin, James Robson, III, *advertising executive*
Heekin-Canedy, Scott *publishing executive*
Heffner, Richard Douglas *historian, educator, communications consultant, television producer*
Heftler, Thomas E. *lawyer*
Heidenry, John M. *editor*
Heilbroner, Robert Louis *economist, writer*
Heilbrun, James *economist, educator*
Heimann, John Gaines *investment banker*
Heineman, Andrew David *retired lawyer*
Heinsen, Hans H. *packaging/containers executive*
Heintz, Joseph E. *financial services company executive*
Heinzerling, Larry Edward *communications executive*
Heisler, Stanley Dean *lawyer*
Heitmann, William F. *telecommunications industry executive*
Heitner, Kenneth Howard *lawyer*
Heleniak, David William *lawyer, educator*
Hellenbrand, Samuel Henry *lawyer*
Hellenbrand, William E. *physician, pediatric cardiologist*
Helliker, Kevin *journalist*
Helmreich, William Benno *sociology educator, consultant*
Helmsley, Leona Mindy *hotel executive*
Helpern, David Moses *shoe corporation executive*
Helsby, Keith R. *stock exchange executive*
Hemmerdinger, H. Dale *real estate executive*
Hemsing, Josephine Claudia *public relations executive*
Henderson, Donald Bernard, Jr., *lawyer*
Hendin, Josephine Gattuso *language educator, writer*
Hendrickson, Wayne A(rthur) *biochemist, educator*
Hendry, Andrew Delaney *lawyer, consumer products company executive*
Henkel, David Seabury *retired lawyer*
Henkin, Louis *lawyer, law educator*
Hennessy, John Francis, III, *engineering executive, mechanical engineer*
Hennessy, John M. *brokerage house executive*
Henriques, Diana Blackmon *journalist*
Henry, Sally McDonald *lawyer*
Hensel, Katherine Ruth *portfolio manager, investment strategist, securities analyst*
Henselmann, Caspar Gustav Fidelis *sculptor*
Herald, George William *news correspondent*
Herbert, Bob *newspaper columnist*
Herbert, Marilynne *public relations executive, freelance photographer*
Herbst, Edward Ian *brokerage firm executive*
Herbst, Todd L. *lawyer*
Herlihy, Edward D. *lawyer*
Herman, Kenneth Beaumont *lawyer*
Herman, Mindy *broadcast executive*
Herman, R(obert) Thomas *journalist*
Herndon, Russell H. *research and development company executive*
Hernstadt, Judith Filenbaum *city planner, real estate executive, broadcasting executive*
Herold, Karl Guenter *lawyer*
Herregat, Guy-Georges Jacques *banker*
Herrera, Arturo *artist*
Herrera, Carolina *fashion designer*
Herrera, Paloma *dancer*
Herrikson, C. Robert *insurance company executive*
Herring, Oliver *artist*
Herrmann, Lacy Bunnell *investment company executive, entrepreneur, venture capitalist*
Herron, Cindy *actress, vocalist*
Hersh, Robert Michael *lawyer, insurance company executive*
Hersh, Seymour Myron *journalist, writer*
Hershcopf, Gerald Thea *lawyer*
Hertog, Roger *investment company executive*
Hertz, Leon *publishing executive*
Hertzberg, Arthur *rabbi, educator*
Hertzig, Margaret E. *psychiatrist*
Herz, Andrew Lee *lawyer*
Herzeca, Lois Friedman *lawyer*
Herzog, John E. *commodities trader*
Hess, John B. *oil industry executive*
Hesse, Karen (Karen Sue Hesse) *writer, educator*
Hesselbein, Frances Richards *foundation administrator, consultant, editor*
Hessinger, Greg *trade association administrator*
Hewitt, Don S. *television news producer*
Hewitt, Vivian Ann Davidson (Mrs. John Hamilton Hewitt Jr.) *retired librarian*
Heyde, Martha Bennett (Mrs. Ernest R. Heyde) *psychologist*
Heydebrand, Wolf Von *sociology educator*
Heymann, C(lemens) David *author*
Heyward, Andrew John *television producer*
Heyzer, Noeleen *international organization official*
Hiaasen, Carl *writer, reporter*
Hickey, Catherine Josephine *school system administrator*
Hicks, Tyler Gregory *publishing company executive, writer*
Hidalgo, David Arthur *plastic surgeon*
Hiden, Robert Battaile, Jr., *lawyer*
Hieber, William George, Jr., *stockbroker*
Higgins, E. Tory *psychology educator, research scientist*
Higgs, John H. *lawyer*
Highstein, Jene Abel *sculptor*
Hildebrand, Phillip J. *insurance company executive*
Hilfiger, Tommy *fashion designer*
Hilgartner, Margaret Wehr *retired pediatric hematologist, educator*
Hill, Alfred *lawyer, educator*
Hill, J(ames) Tomilson *investment banker*
Hill, Lauryn *vocalist, actress*
Hill, May Brawley *art historian*
Hillel, Zaharia *anesthesiologist*
Hillenbrand, Laura *writer*
Hilliard, Landon *banker*
Hillman, Howard Budrow *author, editor, publisher, consultant*
Hillman, Rita *investor*
Hills, Frederic Wheeler *editor, publishing company executive*
Hilse, Walter Bruno *music educator, organist*
Hilton, Andrew Carson *investor, management consultant, former manufacturing company executive*
Himmel, Leslie Wohlman *real estate manager*
Hines, Walter James *stock exchange executive*
Hinojosa, Maria L. *news correspondent*
Hintz, Charles B. *finance company executive*
Hinz, Theodore Vincent *architect*
Hippeau, Eric *book publishing executive*
Hirsch, Barry *lawyer*
Hirsch, Charles Flynn *writer, editor*
Hirsch, Charles S. *city health department administrator*
Hirsch, Edward Mark *poet, English language educator, foundation administrator*
Hirsch, Harvey Stuart *psychiatrist*
Hirsch, Jerome S. *lawyer*
Hirsch, Jules *clinical investigator*
Hirsch, Roseann Conte *publisher*
Hirschberg, D. Jeffrey *former financial company executive*
Hirschfeld, Michael *lawyer*
Hirschhorn, Kurt *pediatrics educator*
Hirschhorn, Rochelle *genetics educator*
Hirshfield, Stuart *lawyer*
Hirshowitz, Melvin Stephen *lawyer*
Hjortsberg, William Reinhold *writer*
Ho, David D. *research physician, virologist*
Hoag, Tami *writer*
Hoagland, Edward *author*
Hochlerin, Diane *pediatrician, educator*
Hochschild, Roger C *investment company executive*
Hochster, Howard S. *oncologist*
Hock, Morton *entertainment advertising executive*
Hodes, Robert Bernard *lawyer*
Hodges, Deborah *investment company executive*
Hoeflin, Ronald Kent *philosopher, writer*
Hofer, Myron A. (Myron Arms Hofer) *psychiatrist, researcher*
Hoffert, Martin Irving *applied science educator*
Hoffman, Alice *writer*
Hoffman, David Nathaniel *lawyer*
Hoffman, Linda M. *chemist, educator*
Hoffman, Linda R. *social services administrator*
Hoffman, Lloyd Alan *plastic surgeon*
Hoffman, Martin Leon *psychology educator*
Hoffman, Mathew *lawyer*
Hoffman, Michael Eugene *editor, publisher, museum curator*
Hoffman, Nancy *art gallery director*
Hoffman, Ronald L. *manufacturing executive*
Hoffman, William M(oses) *playwright, editor*
Hoffmann, Brian *lawyer*
Hoffmann, Elinor R. *lawyer*
Hoffner, Marilyn *university administrator*
Hoge, Warren M. *newspaper and magazine correspondent, editor*
Hohauser, Marilyn *artist*
Hohn, Harry George *retired insurance company executive, lawyer*
Holbrooke, Richard Charles Albert *ambassador, investment banker, writer*
Holch, Gregory John *editor, writer*
Holder, Donald *lighting designer*
Holder, Geoffrey Lamont *dancer, actor, choreographer, director*
Holik, Bobby *professional hockey player*
Holl, Steven Myron *architect, educator*
Holland, Jimmie C. *psychiatrist, educator*
Holland, Michael Francis *investment company executive*
Holley, Steven Lyon *lawyer*
Holliday, Guy D. "Doc" *publishing executive*
Holloway, Ralph Leslie *anthropology educator*
Hollyer, A(rthur) Rene *lawyer*
Holman, Bud George *lawyer*
Holmes, Anna-Marie *ballerina, ballet mistress*
Holmes, Miriam H. *publisher*
Holroyd, Michael *author*
Holsenbeck, G(eorge) Penn *lawyer*
Holt, Lester *commentator*
Holt, Peter Rolf *physician, educator*
Holt, Sidney Clark *journalist*
Holt, Thelma *theatrical producer*
Holton, William *artist*
Holtzman, Elizabeth *lawyer*
Holtzman, Ellen A. *foundation executive*
Holtzmann, Howard Marshall *lawyer, judge*
Holub, Martin *architect*
Holzer, Harold *public affairs officer, historian, writer*
Homayun, Tahira *obstetrician/gynecologist*
Honan, William Holmes *journalist, writer*
Hood, Donald Charles *university administrator, psychology educator*
Hoog, Marjorie *architect*
Hoog, Thomas W. *public relations executive*
Hooker, Wade Stuart, Jr., *lawyer*
Hooper, Ian (John Derek Glass) *marketing communications executive*
Hoover, Thomas E. *writer*
Hopkins, C.J. (Christopher Jaynes) *playwright*
Hopkins, Deborah C. *diversified financial services company executive*
Hopkins, Jan *journalist, newscaster*
Hoppensteadt, Frank Charles *educator, mathematician, university administrator*
Hopple, Richard Van Tromp, Jr., *internet media executive*
Hormats, Robert David *economist, investment banker*
Horn, Shirley *vocalist, pianist*
Hornbacher, Sara S. *visual artist, educator, video producer*
Hornbostel, Paula Rand *art historian*
Horne, Marilyn Berneice *mezzo-soprano*
Hornstein, Mark *financial executive*
Horowitz, Frances Degen *academic administrator, psychology educator*
Horowitz, Gedale Bob *investment banker*
Horowitz, Mitch *editor, writer*
Horowitz, Raymond J. *lawyer, director*
Horvath, Polly *writer*
Horwitz, Ethan *lawyer*
Hoskins, Carol Noll *nursing educator, researcher*
Hoskins, Donald W. *medical association administrator*
Host, Stig *real estate company executive, oil company executive*
Hotchner, Holly *curator, museum director, conservator*
Hotz, Robert Lee *science writer, editor*
Houghtelling, Ayres *artist, architect, engineer*
Houghton, James *performing company executive*
House, David C. *diversified financial services company executive*
House, Karen Elliott *company executive, former editor, reporter*
Houston, Allan Wade *professional basketball player*
Hoving, Thomas *museum and cultural affairs consultant, author*
Howard, David *educational administrator*
Howard, Mildred *sculptor*
Howard, Nathan Southard *investment banker, lawyer*
Howat, John Keith *retired museum executive*
Howat, Kevin John *publishing executive*
Howe, Florence *English educator, writer*
Howe, Richard Rives *lawyer*
Howe, Tina *playwright*
Howell, William Page *real estate company executive*
Howson, Tamar D. *pharmaceutical executive*
Hoxter, Curtis Joseph *international economic advisor, public relations executive*
Hricik, Lorraine E. *bank executive*
Hritz, George F. *lawyer*
Hruska, Alan J. *lawyer*
Hsu, Cindy Kwang-Mei *news correspondent, anchor*
Hu, Chuan *cell biologist*
Huang, Limin *chemist, researcher*
Huck, L. Francis *lawyer*
Hudes, Nana Brenda *marketing professional*
Hudspeth, Albert James *biomedical researcher, educator*
Hudspeth, Stephen Mason *lawyer*
Huey, John Wesley, Jr., *editor*
Huff, Janice *newscaster, meteorologist*
Huffman, Richard Lee *lawyer*
Hughes, Brigid *editor*
Hughes, Kevin Peter *lawyer*
Hughes, Norah Ann O'Brien *bank securities executive*
Hugo, Norman Eliot *plastic surgeon, medical educator*
Huhs, John I. *international lawyer*
Hulbert, Richard Woodward *lawyer*
Hull, Cathy *artist, illustrator*
Hull, Philip Glasgow *lawyer*
Humphreys, Josephine *novelist*
Hundley, James W., III, *think-tank executive, consultant, researcher*
Hunsinger, Peter *publishing executive*
Hunter, John Gerard *plastic surgeon*
Hupper, John Roscoe *retired lawyer*
Hurd, Ruth *publishing executive*
Hurley, Cheryl Joyce *book publishing executive*
Hurley, Dean C. *bank executive, lawyer*
Hurlin, Dan *actor, theater director*
Hurlock, James Bickford *retired lawyer*
Hurst, Robert Jay *securities company executive*
Hussey, Mark Francis *English language educator*
Hussey, Mary-Theresa *editor*
Hutchings, Peter Lounsbery *retird insurance company executive, director*
Hutchins, Traver *publishing executive*
Hutchinson, Lynda Ronette *vocalist, musician, comedian, actress*
Hutsaliuk, Yarema *public relations executive, military officer*
Huttner, Constance S. *lawyer*
Huxtable, Ada Louise *architecture critic*
Hwang, David Henry *playwright, screenwriter*
Hwu, Wen-Jen *physician, oncologist, educator*
Hyde, David Rowley *lawyer*
Hyman, Bruce Malcolm *ophthalmologist*
Hyman, Jerome Elliot *lawyer*
Hyman, Morton Peter *shipping company executive*
Hynde, Chrissie *musician*
Hynes, Patricia Mary *lawyer*
Iannuzzi, John Nicholas *lawyer, author, educator*
Ichikawa, Akiko *artist, editor*
Idol, John D. *apparel company executive*
Ienner, Don *music company executive*
Ilacqua, Rosario Salvatore *securities analyst*
Ilchman, Alice Stone *foundation administrator, former college president, former government official*
Ilchman, Warren Frederick *university administrator, foundation director, educator*
Iler, Robert *actor*
Ilse-Neuman, Ursula *curator*
Ilson, Bernard *public relations executive*
Imber, Gerald *plastic surgeon*
Immergut, Mel M. *lawyer*
Imparato, Anthony Michael *vascular surgeon, medical educator, researcher*
Imperato, Joseph Edward *otolaryngologist*
Imperato-McGinley, Julianne Leonore *endocrinologist, educator*
Imus, Don (John Donald Imus Jr.) *radio host*
Inabnet, William Barlow, III, *surgeon*
Incandela, Gerald Jean-Marie *artist*
Ingram, Samuel William, Jr., *lawyer*
Ingrassia, Lawrence *editor*
Innis, Roy Emile Alfredo *organization executive*
Insel, Michael S. *lawyer*
Intilli, Sharon Marie *television director, small business owner*
Intriligator, Marc Steven *lawyer*
Ireland, Patrick *artist*
Isaacs, Jeremy M. *finance company executive*
Isaacs, Richard B. *investigative and protective services professional*
Isaacs, Robert *conductor, tenor*
Isaacson, Allen Ira *lawyer*
Isaacson, Steven Robert *surgeon*
Isay, Jane Franzblau *publisher*
Isay, Richard Alexander *psychiatrist*
Isbin, Sharon *classical guitarist, guitar educator*
Iselin, John Jay *foundation president*
Iseman, Joseph Seeman *lawyer*
Isenberg, Steven Lawrence *retired publishing executive*
Isogai, Masaharu *international business consultant, former women's apparel executive*
Isquith, Fred Taylor *lawyer*
Issler, Harry *lawyer*
Istomin, Marta Casals *performing arts administrator, former educator*
Itzkoff, Norman Jay *lawyer*
Ivanick, Carol W. Trencher *lawyer*
Ivanovitch, Michael S. *economist*
Ives, Colta Feller *museum curator, educator*
Ivory, James Francis *film director*
Ivy, Robert Adams, Jr., *architect, editor-in-chief*
Izzo, Francesco *musicologist*
Jabbur, Ramzi J. *management consultant*
Jablonsky, Stephen *music educator, composer, artist, writer*
Jack, Bradley H. *investment banker*
Jacker, Corinne Litvin *playwright, writer*
Jackson, Anne (Anne Jackson Wallach) *actress*
Jackson, James Lewis Perdue, II, *entertainment company executive*
Jackson, Kenneth Terry *historian, administrator*
Jackson, Kristin *choreographer, educator*
Jackson, Reggie (Reginald Martinez Jackson) *former professional baseball player*
Jackson, Thomas Gene *lawyer*
Jackson, Yvonne *pharmaceutical executive*
Jackson McCabe, Jewell *not-for-profit developer*
Jacob, Edwin J. *lawyer*
Jacobs, Arnold Stephen *lawyer*
Jacobs, Dennis *federal judge*
Jacobs, Harry Allan, Jr., *investment firm executive*
Jacobs, Jane *author*
Jacobs, Jim *actor, playwright, composer, lyricist*
Jacobs, Mark Neil *financial services corporation executive, lawyer*
Jacobs, Paul *lawyer*
Jacobs, Robert Alan *lawyer*
Jacobs, Thomas Price *internist, educator*
Jacobsen, Sally *communications executive*
Jacobsen, Theodore H. (Ted H. Jacobsen) *labor union administrator, secondary school educator*
Jacobson, Jerold Dennis *lawyer*
Jacobson, Lawrence Seymour *television executive producer*
Jacobson, Sibyl C. *insurance company executive*
Jacoby, Coleman *scriptwriter*
Jacoby, Jacob *consumer psychology educator*
Jacoby, Robert Harold *management consulting executive*
Jacquette, Yvonne Helene *artist*
Jaffe, Alan Steven *lawyer*
Jaffe, Fredrick F. *surgeon*
Jaffe, Mark M. *lawyer*
Jaffe, Susan *ballerina*
Jagr, Jaromir *professional hockey player*
Jakes, John *author*
James, Belinda Sue *choreographer*
James, Cheryl *vocalist*
James, Hamilton Evans (Tony James) *investment banking firm executive*
James, Marc Stephen *brokerage house executive*
James, Robert Gregory *investment company executive*
James, Robert Leo *advertising agency executive*
James, Warren A. *architect*
Jamison, Douglas W. *venture capitalist*
Jamison, Jayne *publishing executive*
Jamison, Judith *dancer*
Jamison, Sheila Ann English *stockbroker, retirement planning specialist*
Janiak, Anthony Richard, Jr., *investment banker*
Janklow, Morton Lloyd *lawyer, literary agent*
Janney, Stuart Symington, III, *investment company executive*
Jannot, Mark Allen *magazine publishing executive*
Jannuzzi, Luigi *playwright, educator*
Janowitz, James Arnold *lawyer*
Jarecki, Henry George *physician, financial executive*

Jaroff, Leon Morton *magazine editor*
Jasper, Seymour *lawyer*
Jasperse, John *performing company executive*
Jasso, Guillermina *sociologist, educator*
Jassy, Everett Lewis *lawyer*
Javitt, Norman B. *medical educator, researcher*
Jay, Harvey H. *dermatologist, educator, researcher*
Jean-Baptiste, Tricia *public relations executive*
Jeanson, Cedric *film company executive*
Jefferson, Denise *dance school director*
Jefferson, Margo L. *journalist*
Jelinek, Vera *university director*
Jelks, Glenn William *plastic surgeon*
Jellinek, George *broadcast executive, music educator, writer*
Jenkins, Anthony Charles *correspondent*
Jenkins, Paul *artist*
Jennings, Peter Charles *television anchorman*
Jepson, Hans Godfrey *investment company executive, director*
Jerome, John James *lawyer*
Jervis, Robert *political science educator*
Jessell, Thomas M. *medical educator*
Jett, Joan (Joan Larkin) *musician*
Jetter, Frances S. *illustrator, educator, artist*
Jewel, (Jewel Kilcher) *folk singer, songwriter*
Jeydel, Richard K. *lawyer*
Jeynes, Mary Kay *college dean*
Jhabvala, Ruth Prawer *writer*
Jiménez, Emilio *corporate lawyer*
Jinnett, Robert Jefferson *lawyer*
Joachim, Brigitta Golden *writer, advertising agency executive, media consultant*
Jock, Paul F., II, *lawyer*
Joel, Richard Marc *academic administrator, law educator, dean*
Joffe, Robert David *lawyer*
Johnsen, Niels Winchester *ocean shipping company executive*
Johnson, Angela *children's book author*
Johnson, Betsey Lee *fashion designer*
Johnson, Brooke Bailey *consultant, former television executive*
Johnson, Clarke Courtney *financial consultant, educator*
Johnson, Erik Ludwig *editor*
Johnson, Horton Anton *pathologist*
Johnson, J. Chester *financial executive, poet*
Johnson, Jeh Charles *lawyer*
Johnson, John H. *publisher, consumer products executive*
Johnson, John William, Jr., *executive recruiter*
Johnson, Larry Demetric *professional basketball player*
Johnson, Scott Stuart *merchant banker*
Johnson, Thomas Stephen *banker*
Johnson, Verdia E. *marketing professional*
Johnson, Vickie *professional basketball player*
Johnson, Warren Douglas *infectious diseases physician, researcher*
Johnston, Lynn Beverley *animator*
Johnston, Ruth D. *English literature educator, women's studies educator, film studies educator*
Jonas, Gilbert *public relations and fund raising executive*
Jonas, Saran *neurologist, educator*
Jones, Abbott C. *investment banking executive*
Jones, Bill T. *dancer, choreographer*
Jones, Diana Wynne *writer*
Jones, Douglas Wiley *lawyer*
Jones, Frank Joseph *insurance company executive*
Jones, Kristin Andrea *artist*
Jones, Laurie Lynn *magazine editor*
Jones, Maxine *vocalist*
Jones, Ronald Arthur *physician, composer*
Jones, Star (Starlet Marie Jones) *television host*
Jones, Thomas E. *bank executive*
Jones, Thomas Wade *financial services executive*
Jones, Tom *publishing executive*
Jong, Erica Mann *writer*
Joo, Michael *artist, educator*
Jordan, Richard Thomas *environmental organizations consultant*
Jordan, Theresa Joan *psychologist, educator*
Jordan, Vernon Eulion, Jr., *lawyer, former association official*
Josell, Jessica (Jessica Wechsler) *public relations executive*
Joseph, Donald W. *health care products executive*
Joseph, Ellen R. *lawyer*
Joseph, Frederick Harold *investment banker*
Joseph, Gregory Paul *lawyer*
Joseph, Leonard *lawyer*
Joseph, Wendy Evans *architect*
Josephs, Ray *public relations and advertising executive, writer, international relations consultant*
Josephson, Marvin *talent and literary agency executive*
Josephson, William Howard *lawyer*
Juceam, Robert E. *lawyer*
Judge, Jerry *business executive*
Juliber, Lois D. *manufacturing executive*
Jung, Andrea *cosmetics executive*
Jung, Doris *dramatic soprano*
Juran, Sylvia Louise *editor*
Jurka, Edith Mila *psychiatrist, researcher*
Jurow, George *judge*
Just, Gemma Rivoli *retired advertising executive*
Kadar, Avraham *immunologist*
Kaden, Lewis B. *law educator, lawyer*
Kaess, Ken *advertising executive*
Kafin, Robert Joseph *lawyer*
Kagan, Ilse Echt *research librarian, village historian*
Kaggen, Lois Sheila *non-profit organization executive*
Kahan, Marlene *professional association executive*
Kahane, Jeffrey *conductor, pianist*
Kahn, Alan Edwin *lawyer*
Kahn, Alan J. *book distribution executive*
Kahn, Alfred Joseph *social worker and policy scholar, educator*
Kahn, Alfred Robert *toy manufacturing company executive*
Kahn, Anthony F. *lawyer*
Kahn, Charlotte *psychotherapist, marriage and family therapist*
Kahn, Norman *pharmacology and dentistry educator*
Kahn, Robert Theodore *author, photographer*
Kailas, Leo George *lawyer*
Kaiser, Walter *English language educator*
Kaish, Luise Clayborn *sculptor, former educator*
Kaish, Morton *artist, educator*
Kaku, Michio *theoretical nuclear physicist, educator*
Kakutani, Michiko *critic*
Kalajian-Lagani, Donna *publishing executive*
Kalayjian, Anie *psychotherapist, nurse, educator, consultant*
Kalech, Marc *newspaper editor*
Kalfin, Robert Z. *theater director*
Kalikow, Peter Stephen *real estate developer, former newspaper owner, publisher*
Kalikow, Richard R. *lawyer*
Kalish, Arthur *lawyer*
Kalish, Myron *lawyer*
Kallen, Laurel Lynn *prosecutor*
Kallir, Jane Katherine *art gallery director, author*
Kalmanoff, Martin *composer*
Kalsner, Stanley *pharmacologist, physiologist, educator*
Kamali, Norma *fashion designer*
Kambour, Annaliese Spofford *lawyer, media company executive*
Kamerman, Sheila Brody *educator, social worker*
Kamiel, Jerald *apparel executive*
Kamin, Sherwin *lawyer*
Kaminsky, Arthur Charles *lawyer*
Kamlot, Robert *performing arts executive*
Kan, Diana Artemis Mann Shu *painter, art educator, writer*
Kanai, Yoshikuni *manufacturing executive*
Kanak, Donald Perry, Jr., *insurance company executive, lawyer, diversified financial services company executive*
Kandel, Denise Bystryn *sociologist*
Kandel, Myron *newscaster, columnist*
Kandel, William Lloyd *lawyer, mediator, arbitrator, educator, writer*
Kane, Alice Theresa *lawyer*
Kane, William Jeffrey *investment firm executive*
Kang, Eliot *advertising executive*
Kanick, Virginia *retired radiologist*
Kann, Peter Robert *publishing executive, journalist*
Kanner, Bernice *columnist*
Kanof, Norman B. *dermatologist*
Kanrek, Victoria Jane *lawyer*
Kanter, Carl Irwin *retired lawyer*
Kanter, Stacy J. *lawyer*
Kantor, Jodi M. *editor*
Kapito, Robert S. *diversified financial services company executive*
Kaplan, Carl Eliot *lawyer*
Kaplan, Ira *import/export company executive*
Kaplan, Keith Eugene *insurance company executive, lawyer*
Kaplan, Lawrence Jay *economist, educator*
Kaplan, Lewis A. *judge*
Kaplan, Mark Norman *lawyer*
Kaplan, Robert S. *investment banker*
Kaplan, Susan *lawyer*
Kaplen, Michael V. *lawyer*
Kaplitt, Michael Gordon *neurosurgeon, medical educator*
Kapner, Lori *marketing professional*
Kapoor, Neera *optometrist, vision scientist*
Kappas, Attallah *physician*
Karalekas, George Steven *advertising agency executive, political consultant*
Karan, Donna (Donna Faske) *fashion designer*
Karasz, Peter *lawyer*
Karatz, William Warren *lawyer*
Karcher, John Drake *textile and apparel company executive*
Karchin, Louis Samuel *composer, educator*
Kardon, Dennis *artist, educator*
Kardon, Janet *museum director, curator, educator*
Kardon, Robert *mortgage company executive*
Karl, Kurt Erskine *economist*
Karlgaard, Rich *publishing executive*
Karlin, Susan *design company executive*
Karls, John Spencer *lawyer, accountant*
Karmazin, Mel *broadcast executive*
Karp, Martin Everett *management consultant*
Karp, Nolan S. *plastic surgeon*
Karpel, Craig S. *journalist, editor*
Karpen, Marian Joan *financial executive*
Karr, Kathleen *writer*
Karr, Robert A. *financier*
Karsen, Sonja Petra *retired American-Hispanic literature educator*
Kartiganer, Joseph *retired lawyer*
Kartsev, Vladimir Petrovich *publisher*
Kasakove, Susan *interior designer*
Kase, Nathan Ginden *dean*
Kasinec, Edward Joseph *library administrator*
Kaskell, Peter Howard *association executive, lawyer*
Kaslick, Ralph Sidney *dentist, educator*
Kasowitz, Marc Elliot *lawyer*
Kassebaum, John Philip *lawyer*
Kassel, Catherine M. *community, maternal, and women's health nurse, consultant*
Kassel, Virginia Weltmer *television producer, writer*
Kastan, David Scott *literature educator, writer*
Katen, Karen L. *pharmaceutical executive*
Kates, Brian C. *newspaper editor*
Katsh, Salem Michael *lawyer*
Katsoris, Constantine Nicholas *lawyer, consultant*
Katsoyannis, Panayotis George *biochemist, educator*
Katz, Abraham *retired foreign service officer*
Katz, Alex *artist*
Katz, Bruce Elliot *dermatologist*
Katz, Jane *swimming educator*
Katz, Jerome Charles *lawyer*
Katz, Jose *cardiologist, theoretical physicist, educator*
Katz, Lois Anne *internist, nephrologist*
Katz, Marc D *apparel executive*
Katz, Marcia *public relations company executive*
Katz, Robert James *lawyer*
Katz, Ronald Scott *lawyer*
Katz, Thomas J. *chemistry educator*
Katzmann, Robert Allen *federal judge*
Katzowitz Shenfield, Lauren *philanthropic consultant, foundation executive*
Kauffmann, Stanley Jules *author*
Kaufman, Amy *film company executive, film producer*
Kaufman, Arthur Stephen *lawyer*
Kaufman, Bel *author, educator*
Kaufman, David Marc *pediatric neurologist*
Kaufman, Henry *financial services executive*
Kaufman, Robert Max *lawyer, director*
Kaufman, Victor A. *entertainment executive, former film company executive*
Kaufmann, Charles Arthur *psychiatrist, neuroscientist, educator*
Kaufmann, Mark David *dermatologist*
Kaufmann, Mark Steiner *banker, director*
Kaur, Harminder *language educator*
Kavaler, Rebecca *writer*
Kavaler, Thomas J. *lawyer*
Kavaler-Adler, Susan *clinical psychologist, psychoanalyst*
Kavalerchik, Boris Yakovlevich *information technology developer, researcher*
Kavesh, Robert A. *economist, educator*
Kavoukjian, Michael Edward *lawyer*
Kavovit, Barbara *entrepreneur*
Kaye, Stephen Rackow *lawyer*
Kaye, Walter *financial executive*
Kayse, Kathleen *publishing executive*
Kazemi, Farhad *political scientist, educator*
Keagy, Dorothy (Dotti Keagy) *copy director*
Kean, Hamilton Fish *lawyer*
Keane, Bil *cartoonist*
Keany, Sutton *lawyer*
Kearns, Richard P. *diversified financial services company executive*
Kearse, Amalya Lyle *federal judge*
Keating, Isabel *actress*
Keefe, Diane Marie *portfolio manager*
Keegan, Peter W. *diversified financial services company executive*
Keenan, John Fontaine *judge*
Keenan, Michael Edgar *marketing professional*
Keenan, Terry *anchor, correspondent*
Keene, Donald *writer, translator, language educator*
Keene, Lonnie Stuart *lawyer*
Kehoe, John P. *investor relations and corporate development consultant*
Kehret, Peg *writer*
Keilin, Eugene Jacob *investment banker, lawyer*
Keller, Bill *editor*
Kellerman, Jonathan Seth *writer, pediatric psychologist*
Kellner, George *securities executive*
Kellogg, Paul *performing company executive*
Kelly, Alfred F., Jr., *diversified financial services company executive*
Kelly, Christina *editor*
Kelly, J. Michael *communications executive*
Kelly, Patrick Joseph *neurosurgeon, educator*
Kelly, Peter *communications executive*
Kelly, Raymond W. *police commissioner*
Kelly, Thomas Jesse, Jr., *molecular biologist*
Kelly, Thomas Michael *lawyer*
Kelly, William Michael *investment executive*
Kelman, Edward Michael *lawyer*
Kelmenson, Leo-Arthur *advertising executive*
Kelson, Richard B. *metal products executive*
Kempa, Gerald *manufacturing executive*
Kempf, Donald G., Jr., *lawyer*
Kendall Levine, Judy *real estate broker, interior designer, writer*
Kende, Christopher Burgess *lawyer*
Keneally, Kathryn Marie *lawyer*
Kennan, Christopher James *investment executive, not-for-profit fundraiser*
Kenneally, Michael E. *diversified financial services company executive*
Kennedy, Adrienne Lita *playwright*
Kennedy, James M. *editor*
Kennedy, Kevin W. *finance company executive*
Kennedy, Michael John *lawyer*
Kennedy, Patrick F. *federal official*
Kenney, John Joseph *lawyer*
Kenny, Jane Marie *government agency administrator*
Kenny, Roger Michael *executive search consultant, writer*
Keno, Leigh R. *antiques dealer, appraiser*
Keno, Leslie B. *antiques dealer, appraiser*
Kent, Deborah Warren *hypnotherapist, consultant, lecturer*
Kent, Julie *ballet dancer, actress, model*
Kent, Linda Gail *dancer*
Kent, Susan *library director, consultant*
Kent, Jr., Thomas Jefferson, Jr., *corporate financial executive*
Keogh, Kevin *lawyer*
Keppler, Herbert *publishing company executive*
Kern, George Calvin, Jr., *lawyer*
Kern, Heath Thayer *producer*
Kern, William Bliem, Jr., *minister*
Kernis, Aaron Jay *composer*
Kernochan, John Marshall *lawyer, educator*
Kerrey, Bob (J. Robert Kerrey) *academic administrator, former senator*
Kersels, Martin *artist*
Kerz, Louise *historian*
Kessel, Mark *lawyer*
Kessler, Jeffrey L. *lawyer*
Kessler, Michael George *forensic accountant*
Kessler, Stuart *accountant, financial planner*
Ketchum, Richard G. *stock exchange executive, lawyer*
Ketels, Gerhard H. *lawyer*
Kettaneh, Anthony C. *small business owner, consultant*
Keys, Alicia *vocalist, musician, songwriter*
Khan, Sura *film company executive*
Khedoori, Toba *artist*
Kheel, Theodore Woodrow *lawyer, arbitrator and mediator*
Khuri, Nicola Najib *physicist, researcher*
Kiechel, Walter, III, *editor*
Kieren, Thomas Henry *management consultant*
Kiernan, Pat *news correspondent*
Kies, David M. *lawyer*
Kilbourn, Joseph A. *lawyer*
Kilburn, H(enry) T(homas), Jr., *investment banker*
Kill, Lawrence *lawyer*
Killip, Thomas *cardiologist*
Kim, Dow *finance company executive*
Kim, Michael S. *lawyer*
Kim, Se Jung *civil engineer*
Kimball, Robert Eric *author*
Kimball, Roger *editor, writer*
Kimsey, William L. *diversified financial services company executive*
Kinberg, Judy *television producer, director*
Kind, Phyllis *art gallery owner*
Kinder, Lawrence E. *manufacturing executive*
Kindler, Jeffrey B. *lawyer*
King, B. B. (Riley B. King) *singer, guitarist*
King, Henry Lawrence *lawyer*
King, Marcia Gygli *artist*
Kinnally, William Lee, Jr., *lawyer*
Kinnell, Galway *poet, translator*
Kinney, Catherine R. *stock exchange executive*
Kinney, Stephen Hoyt, Jr., *lawyer*
Kinser, Richard Edward *management consultant*
Kinsolving, Charles McIlvaine, Jr., *marketing executive*
Kinstler, Everett Raymond *artist*
Kinzler, Thomas Benjamin *lawyer*
Kirby, John Joseph, Jr., *lawyer*
Kirdar, Nemir Amin *banker*
Kirk, Susanne Smith *editor*
Kirkland, Richard Ide (Rik), Jr., *magazine editor*
Kirkwood, John *medical association administrator*
Kirsch, Arthur William *financial consultant*
Kirsch, Donald *financial consultant, writer*
Kirschbaum, Laurence J. *publishing executive*
Kirschbaum, Myron *lawyer*
Kirschenbaum, Lisa L. *portfolio manager, financial advisor*
Kirshbaum, Laurence J. *book publishing executive*
Kiser, Molly *musician*
Kislik, Richard William *publishing executive*
Kissel, Howard William *drama critic*
Kitagawa, Audrey Emiko *retired lawyer*
Kitahata-Sporn, Amy *movement educator*
Kitatani, Kenji *electronics executive*
Kitt, Eartha Mae *actress, singer*
Kiwanuka, Semakula Mathias Mulumba *United Nations ambassador*
Kizer, Jorge R. *cardiologist, epidemiologist*
Klamm de Betas, Ullrich *investment banker*
Klapper, Molly *lawyer, educator*
Klausmeyer, David Michael *scientific instruments manufacturing company executive*
Klawans, Stuart *film critic, writer*
Kleber, Herbert David *psychiatrist, educator*
Kleckner, Robert George, Jr., *retired lawyer*
Kleckner, Simone Marie *law librarian*
Kleeblatt, Norman L. *museum curator*
Klein, Calvin Richard *fashion designer*
Klein, Donald Franklin *psychiatrist, director, research scientist, educator*
Klein, Harvey *physician, educator*
Klein, Jason Evan *magazine publishing executive*
Klein, Jeffrey Peter *investor*
Klein, Joel Irwin *school system administrator*
Klein, Laura *publishing executive*
Klein, Martin I. *lawyer*
Klein, Michael *investment banker*
Klein, T(heodore) E(ibon) D(onald) *writer*
Kleinbard, Edward D. *lawyer*
Kleinman, Charles Stephan *physician, medical educator*
Klemann, Gilbert Lacy, II, *lawyer*
Klenikov, Vlad *investment banker*
Kliment, Robert Michael *architect*
Kliment, Stephen Alexander *architect, editor, journalist*
Kline, Eugene Monroe *lawyer*
Kline, Kevin Delaney *actor*
Klingensmith, Michael *publishing executive*
Klinger, Harvey *publishing executive*
Klingsberg, David *lawyer*
Klink, Fredric J. *lawyer*
Klipper, Mitchell S. *book publishing executive*
Klotz, Florence *costume designer*
Kmiotek-Welsh, Jacqueline *lawyer*
Knapp, Albert Bruce *gastroenterologist*
Knapp, Amy K. *insurance company executive*
Knapp, Ellen M. *financial company executive*
Knapp, Robert Charles *retired obstetrics and gynecology educator*
Kneale, Dennis Randall *publishing executive*
Knepper, Ronald Alan *sculptor, educator*
Knerr, Anthony David *strategic consultant*
Knight, Robert Huntington *lawyer, bank executive*
Knight, Shirley *actress*
Knight, Townsend Jones *lawyer*
Knightley, Keira *actress*
Knobler, Alfred Everett *ceramic engineer, manufacturing company executive, publisher*
Knopf, Alfred, Jr., *retired publisher*
Kobak, James Benedict, Jr., *lawyer, educator*
Kober, Jane *lawyer*
Koblenz, Michael Robert *lawyer*
Kobrin, Lawrence Alan *lawyer*
Koch, David Hamilton *chemical company executive*
Koch, Edward I. *former mayor, lawyer*
Koch, Kenneth *poet, playwright*
Koegel, William Fisher *lawyer*
Koeltl, John George *judge*
Koenig, Jerome *newspaper advertising executive, actor, poet*
Koenig, Marvin *heavy manufacturing executive*
Koeppel, Noel Immanuel *financial planner, securities and real estate broker*
Kohn, A. Eugene *architect*
Kohn, Immanuel *lawyer*
Kohut, John Walter *corporate executive*
Kojevnikov, Boris Oleg *lawyer, foreign legal consultant*
Koke, Richard Joseph *author, exhibit designer, museum curator*
Kolatch, Myron *magazine editor*
Kolbe, Karl William, Jr., *lawyer*
Kolesar, Peter John *business and engineering educator, entrepreneur*
Kolker, Lawrence Paul *lawyer*
Kolm, Petter N. *investment advisor, mathematician*
Kolodny, Edwin Hillel *neurologist, geneticist, director*
Komisar, Arnold *otolaryngologist, educator*
Komisarjevsky, Christopher P.A. *public relations executive*
Konner, Joan Weiner *academic administrator, educator, television producer, writer*
Kono, Toshihiko *cellist*
Konopko, Deborah *federal agency administrator*
Koob, Charles Edward *lawyer*
Koontz, Dean Ray *writer*
Kopelman, Richard Eric *management educator*
Koplewicz, Harold Samuel *child and adolescent psychiatrist*
Koplik, Michael R. *durable goods company executive*
Kopp, Wendy *teaching program administrator*
Koppelman, Chaim *artist, educator*
Koppelman, Charles A. *record company executive*
Koppelman, Dorothy Myers *artist, consultant*
Koral, Alan Max *lawyer*
Korelitz, Burton I. *gastroenterologist, educator*
Korff, Phyllis G. *lawyer*
Korman, Lewis J. *entertainment/media company executive, entrepreneur*
Kornberg, Alan William *lawyer*
Kornreich, Edward Scott *lawyer*
Korot, Beryl *artist*
Korotkin, Michael Paul *lawyer*
Korvin, Catherine Madeleine *editor*

Kostelanetz, Boris *lawyer*
Kostelanetz, Richard *writer, media and visual artist*
Koster, Elaine Landis *publishing executive*
Kotcher, Raymond Lowell *public relations executive*
Koteff, Ellen *periodical editor*
Koten, John *editor-in-chief*
Kothbauer, Karl F. *neurosurgeon, researcher*
Kotlowitz, Robert *writer, editor*
Kotuk, Andrea Mikotajuk *public relations executive, writer*
Kotzwinkle, William *author*
Kourides, Ione Anne *endocrinologist, researcher, educator*
Kourides, Peter Theologos *lawyer*
Kovacs, James *brokerage house executive*
Kovner, Bruce *investment company executive*
Kovner, Victor A. *lawyer*
Kowalski, Michael J. *retail executive*
Kowroski, Maria *dancer*
Kozik, Susan S. *information technology executive*
Kozlowski, Cheryl M. *principal*
Kozodoy, Neal *magazine editor*
Kraemer, David C. *theology educator*
Kraemer, Lillian Elizabeth *lawyer*
Kram, Shirley Wohl *federal judge*
Kramer, Alan Sharfsin *lawyer*
Kramer, George P. *lawyer*
Kramer, Jane *writer*
Kramer, Linda Konheim *curator, art historian*
Kramer, Marc Z. *publishing executive*
Kramer, Michelle *reporter*
Krane, Steven Charles *lawyer*
Krantz, Judith Tarcher *novelist*
Krasna, Alvin Isaac *biochemist, educator*
Krasner, Daniel Walter *lawyer*
Krasnow, Norman *cardiologist*
Kraus, Norma Jean *human resources executive*
Kraushar, Jonathan Pollack *communications and media consultant*
Krauss, Herbert Harris *psychologist*
Krauss, Judith Scheer *art dealer*
Kraut, Harry John *music producer, consultant*
Kravis, Henry R. *venture capitalist*
Kravitz, Lee *publishing executive*
Krawcheck, Sallie L. *investment company executive*
Kraynak, Michael, Jr., *investment company executive*
Krebs, Carl F. *architectural firm executive*
Kreek, Mary Jeanne *physician*
Kreisberg, Neil Ivan *advertising executive*
Kreitman, James E. *securities trader*
Kreitzman, Ralph J. *lawyer*
Krementz, Jill *photographer, author*
Krens, Thomas *museum director*
Kress, Nancy *writer*
Kressel, Henry *venture capitalist*
Kreston, Martin Howard *advertising, marketing, public relations, and publishing executive*
Kriegel, Jay L. *Olympic organizing committee executive, public relations executive*
Krieger, Sanford *lawyer*
Krim, Mathilde *medical educator*
Krimendahl, Herbert Frederick, II, *investment banker*
Krinsky, Carol Herselle *art history educator*
Krinsky, Robert Daniel *consulting firm executive*
Kristof, Nicholas Donabet *journalist*
Krizer, Jodi *performing arts executive*
Kroeber, Karl *English language educator*
Kroeger, Brooke W. *journalist, writer*
Kroft, Steve *news correspondent, editor*
Krol, Marina *computer scientist, researcher*
Kroll, Sol *lawyer*
Krominga, Lynn *cosmetic and health care company executive, lawyer*
Kronzon, Itzhak *physician, educator*
Kropf, Susan J. *cosmetics company executive*
Krosnick, Joel *cellist*
Krouse, George Raymond, Jr., *lawyer*
Krukowski, Jan *communications executive*
Krulwich, Robert *broadcast news correspondent*
Krupman, William Allan *lawyer*
Krupp, Fred D. *lawyer, environmental agency executive*
Kruse, Douglas Charles *financial industry consultant, educator*
Kuby, Ronald Lawrence *lawyer*
Kuchta, Ronald Andrew *art museum director, magazine editor, curator*
Kucic, Joseph *management consultant, industrial engineer, network engineer, information security specialist*
Kuck, Lea Haber *lawyer*
Kugelman, Stephanie *advertising executive*
Kuh, Richard Henry *lawyer*
Kuhbach, Robert Gerdes *lawyer*
Kuhl, William Bernard *landscape architect*
Kuhn, James D. *real estate company executive*
Kujawski, Elizabeth Szancer *art curator, consultant*
Kuklin, Anthony Bennett *lawyer*
Kumble, Steven Jay *lawyer*
Kunes, Ellen *magazine executive*
Kunes, Richard W. *cosmetics executive*
Kunitz, Stanley Jasspon *poet, editor, educator*
Kuntz, Lee Allan *lawyer*
Kuntz, William Francis, II, *lawyer, educator*
Kuo, John Tsungfen *geophysicist, educator, researcher*
Kuperman, Robert Ian *advertising agency executive*
Kupper, William P., Jr., *publishing executive*
Kurian, Marian *surgeon*
Kurland, Paul Carl *lawyer, educator*
Kurnow, Ernest *statistician, educator*
Kurtz, Jerome *lawyer, educator*
Kurzweil, Edith *sociology educator, editor*
Kurzweil, Harvey *lawyer*
Kushner, Robert Ellis *artist*
Kushnir, Andrei *artist, consultant*
Kutosh, Sue *artist*
Kuttner, Neil *investment company executive*
Kuwayama, Teru *photographer*
Kuyper, Joan Carolyn *foundation administrator*
Kyriakou, Linda Grace *communications executive*
LaBelle, Patti (Patricia Louise Holt) *singer, entertainer*
Labovitz, Deborah Rose Rubin *occupational therapist, educator*
Labunski, Stephen Bronislaw *professional society administrator*
LaChapelle, David *photographer*
Lachmann, Elisabeth Amanda *physician*
Lack, Andrew R. *music company executive*
Lacovara, Philip Allen *lawyer*
Lacy, Robinson Burrell *lawyer*
Lader, Lawrence *writer*
Ladjevardi, Hamid *fund manager*
Lagani, Daniel *publishing executive*
Lagomasino, Maria Elena *bank executive*
Laibman, David *economist, educator*
Lakatos, Susan Carol *investment banker, artist*
Lake, Ricki *talk show host, actress*
Lalas, Alexi *retired professional soccer player*
Laliberte, Antonio M. *financial company executive*
Lalwani, Anil Kumar *otolaryngologist*
Lamb, Robert Boyden *finance and management educator*
Lamb, Wally *writer*
Lamberg, Carol *housing fund executive*
Lamia, Thomas Roger *lawyer*
Lamm, Donald Stephen *publishing company executive*
Lamm, Norman *academic administrator, rabbi*
Lammie, James Louis *engineering executive, retired military officer*
Lamont, Lansing *journalist, public affairs executive, author*
Lamont, Lee *music management executive*
Lamont, Rosette Clementine *Romance languages educator, theatre journalist, translator*
Lampert, Zohra *actress*
Lamport, Anthony Matthew *investments and venture capitalist*
Lamster, Ira Barry *academic administrator*
Lanchner, Bertrand Martin *lawyer, advertising executive*
Land, Irene Stokvis *marketing executive*
Landa, Howard Martin *lawyer, business executive*
Landau, Sidney Ivan *lexicographer*
Landau, Walter Loeber *lawyer*
Landegger, Carl Clement *machinery and pulp manufacturing executive*
Landrigan, Philip John *epidemiologist, educator*
Landro, Laura *editor*
Lane, Alvin S. *lawyer*
Lane, Jeffrey Bruce *financial services company executive*
Lane, Joseph M. *orthopedic surgeon, educator, oncologist*
Lane, Kenneth Robert *producer, distributor*
Lane, Louis *musician, conductor*
Lane, Nancy *editor, human rights activist*
Lane, Robin *lawyer*
Lang, Everett Francis, Jr., *brokerage house executive*
Lang, George *restaurateur*
Lang, Pearl *dancer, choreographer*
Langan, Marie-Noelle Suzanne *cardiologist, educator*
Langbert, Mitchell Berke *business educator*
Lange, Liz Steinberg *apparel designer and executive*
Lange, Phil C. *retired education educator*
Langhammer, Fred H. *cosmetics company executive*
Langone, Kenneth *investment company executive*
Langton, Cleve Swanson *advertising executive*
LaNicca Albanese, Ellen *public relations executive*
Lanier, Richard Sanders *foundation administrator*
Lans, Deborah Eisner *lawyer*
Lansbury, Edgar George *theatrical producer*
Lanza, Frank C. *electronics executive*
Lao, Joseph R. *education educator, researcher*
Lapham, Lewis Henry *editor, author, television host*
Lapierre, Dominique *writer, historian, philanthropist*
Lapine, James Elliot *playwright, director*
Lappin, Joan E. *financial executive*
Laragh, John Henry *physician, scientist, educator*
Larberg, John Frederick *wine consultant, educator*
Larmore, Jennifer *mezzo-soprano*
Larose, Lawrence Alfred *lawyer*
La Rossa, James M(ichael) *lawyer*
Larsen, Jonathan Zerbe *journalist*
LaRue, Jan (Pieters) (Adrian LaRue) *musicologist, educator, writer*
Lascher, Alan Alfred *lawyer*
Lash, Stephen Sycle *auction company executive*
Lasker, Jonathan Lewis *artist*
Laskin, Richard Sheldon *orthopedic surgeon*
Lasser, Joseph Robert *investment company executive*
Last, Ruth Edith *actress*
Lategno-Nicholas, Cristyne *travel company executive*
Lattin, Albert Floyd *banker*
Lau, Harry Hung-Kwan *acoustical and interior designer, consultant*
Lauder, Aerin *cosmetics executive*
Lauder, Evelyn H. *cosmetics executive*
Lauder, Leonard Alan *cosmetic and fragrance company executive*
Lauder, Ronald Stephen *investor*
Lauder, William P. *cosmetics executive*
Laue, Bruce Antonio *financial consultant, writer*
Lauer, Matt *broadcast journalist*
Laufer, Mark Vladimir *retired engineering educator*
Laufman, Harold *surgeon, consultant*
Laumont, Philippe Emile *communications executive*
Lauper, Cyndi *musician*
Lauren, Ralph *fashion designer*
Laurence, Jeffrey Conrad *immunologist, educator*
Laurents, Arthur *playwright*
Laurie, Craig *real estate company executive*
Laurus, (Laurus Skurla) *archbishop*
Laventhol, David Abram *newspaper editor*
Lavine, Lawrence Neal *investment banker*
Lavori, Nora *real estate executive, lawyer*
Lawhon, Charla *editor*
Lawrence, Bryan Hunt *investment banking executive*
Lawrence, Lauren *author, dreams expert, psychoanalytical theorist, psychoanalyst*
Lawrence, Robert Cutting, III, *lawyer*
Lawson, William *otolaryngologist, educator*
Lawson-Johnston, Peter Orman *foundation executive*
Lax, Peter David *mathematician, educator*
Laybourne, Geraldine B. *broadcast executive*
Layton, Donald Harvey *banker*
Layton, Robert *lawyer*
Lazarcik, Gregor *educator, financial research company executive, economist*
Lazarus, Rochelle Braff (Shelly Lazarus) *advertising executive*
Leach, Richard *food service executive*
Leach, Robin *producer, writer, television host*
Leaf, Clinton *publishing executive*
Leahey, Lynn *editor-in-chief*
Leahy, Michael Joseph *newspaper editor*
Leaman, Leonard S., Jr., *science educator*
Leavitt, David Livingstone *architect*
Lebenthal, Alexandra *investment firm executive*
LeBlond, Richard Knight, II, *banker*
Lebow, Mark Denis *lawyer*
Lebwohl, Mark Gabriel *dermatologist, educator*
le Carré, John (David John Moore Cornwell) *author*
LeClerc, Paul *library director*
LeCompte, Elizabeth *theater director*
Le Count, Virginia G. *communications company executive*
Lederberg, Joshua *geneticist, educator*
Lederman, Lawrence *lawyer, writer, educator*
Ledger, William Joe *physician, educator*
LeDoux, Harold Anthony *cartoonist, painter*
Lee, Amy *singer*
Lee, Bruce *editor, writer*
Lee, Catherine *sculptor, painter*
Lee, Charles Robert *telecommunications company executive*
Lee, Clement William Khan *trade association administrator*
Lee, Dai-Keong *composer*
Lee, David Hee-Don *trade association administrator, educator*
Lee, Frances Helen *editor*
Lee, In-Young *lawyer*
Lee, Jerome G. *lawyer*
Lee, Mathew Hung Mun *physiatrist, educator, health facility administrator*
Lee, Paul Lawrence *lawyer*
Lee, Sally A. *editor-in-chief*
Lee, Tay Bong *surgeon, otolaryngologist*
Lee, Thomas F. *art association administrator*
Lee, Tsung-Dao *physicist, researcher*
Leebron, David Wayne *dean, law educator*
Leeds, Norman E. *medical educator, radiologist*
Lees, Alfred William *writer, former magazine editor*
Leet, Mildred Robbins *corporate executive, consultant*
LeFevre, David E. *lawyer, former professional sports team executive*
Leff, Ilene J(afnel) *management consultant, corporate and government executive*
Lefferts, Gillet, Jr., *architect*
Lefkovits, Albert Meyer *dermatologist*
Lefkowitz, Howard N. *lawyer*
Lefkowitz, Joel M. *psychologist, educator*
Legato, Marianne *internist, medical educator*
LeGrady, George *photographer, educator*
Legrand, Michel Jean *composer*
Lehane, Dennis *writer*
Lehman, Edward William *sociology educator, researcher*
Lehman, Orin *retired state official*
Lehmann-Haupt, Christopher Charles Herbert *book reviewer*
Lehodey, John Francois *hotel company executive*
Leibel, Steven Arnold *radiologist*
Leibovitz, Annie *photographer*
Leibowitz, Herbert Akiba *English language educator, author*
Leibowitz, Martin L. *investment company executive*
Leich-Galland, Claire *film and theatre indexer*
Leichtling, Michael Alfred *lawyer*
Leifer, Edgar *physician, retired medical educator*
Leigh, Stephen *industrial designer*
Leighton, Lawrence Ward *investment banker*
Leiman, Joan Maisel *university administrator, hospital administrator*
Leisure, Peter Keeton *federal judge*
Leive, Cindi *editor-in-chief*
Leland, Jack *cosmetics executive*
Leland, Richard G(uy) *lawyer*
Lelyveld, Joseph Salem *writer, retired newspaper editor, correspondent*
Lemann, Nicholas B. *journalist, writer*
Lencek, Rado Ludovik *Slavic languages educator*
L'Engle, Madeleine (Mrs. Hugh Franklin) *writer*
Lentner, Howard Henry *political scientist*
Lenzner, Robert L. *journalist*
Leonard, Arthur Sherman *law educator, journalist*
Leonard, Edwin Deane *lawyer*
Leonard, Elmore John *novelist, screenwriter*
Leonard, Richard Davis *minister*
Leonard, Zoe *artist*
Leone, Rose Marie *psychotherapist*
Leppard, Raymond John *conductor, harpsichordist*
Lerangis, Peter D. *writer*
Leritz, Lawrence R. *choreographer, singer, actor, dancer, producer*
Lerner, Jill *architect*
Lerner, Martin *museum curator*
Lesch, Michael Oscar *lawyer*
Lesk, Ann Berger *lawyer*
Leslie, John Webster, Jr., (Jack Leslie) *communications company executive*
Leslie, Seymour Marvin *communications executive, director*
Lessard, Stefan *musician*
Lesser, Gerson Theodore *medical educator, researcher*
Lesser, Seth Richard *lawyer*
Lessing, Brian Reid *actuary*
Lessing, Stephen M. *finance company executive*
Lester, Pamela Robin *lawyer*
Letterman, David *television personality, producer, comedian, writer*
Leubert, Alfred Otto Paul *international business consultant, investor*
Leung, Firman *investment bank executive*
Levai, Pierre Alexandre *art gallery executive*
Leval, Pierre Nelson *federal judge*
Leven, Ann Ruth *museum financial officer*
Levie, Joseph Henry *lawyer, banker*
Levin, Alan M. *television journalist*
Levin, Ezra Gurion *lawyer*
Levin, Gail *author, photographer, educator*
Levin, Herbert *retired diplomat, retired foundation executive*
Levin, Ira *author, playwright*
Levin, Kim *writer, curator*
Levin, Michael Joseph *lawyer*
Levin, Michael Stuart *steel company executive*
Levin, Roger Michael *lawyer*
Levine, Alan *lawyer*
Levine, Arthur Elliott *academic administrator, educator*
Levine, David *artist*
Levine, Ellen R. *editor-in-chief*
Levine, Gail Carson *writer*
Levine, James *conductor, pianist, artistic director*
Levine, Lawrence Steven *lawyer*
Levine, Louis D. *museum director, archaeologist*
Levine, Melvin Charles *lawyer*
Levine, Naomi Bronheim *academic administrator*
Levine, Robert Jay *lawyer*
Levine, Ronald Jay *lawyer*
Levinson, Paul Howard *lawyer*
Levinson, Robert Alan *textiles executive*
Levinson, Warren Mitchell *broadcast journalist*
Levitan, David M(aurice) *lawyer, educator*
Levitan, James A. *lawyer*
Levitan, Max Fishel *geneticist, anatomy educator*
Levitt, Harry *speech and hearing scientist*
Levitz, Paul Elliot *publishing executive*
Levoy, Myron *author*
Levy, Alan Joseph *editor, journalist, writer*
Levy, Albert *family physician*
Levy, Clifford J. *reporter*
Levy, Daniel H. *apparel executive*
Levy, Herbert Monte *lawyer*
Levy, Mark Allan *lawyer*
Levy, Matthew Degen *investment banking technology and operations company executive, consumer products business development and planning executive, management consultant*
Levy, Matthys Paul *structural engineer*
Levy, Stanley Herbert *lawyer*
Lew, Jacob *public administration educator*
Lewin, Betsy R. *illustrator*
Lewis, Alfred Baker *psychiatrist*
Lewis, George Ralph *consumer goods company executive*
Lewis, Jonathan Joseph *surgical oncologist, molecular biologist, educator*
Lewis, Loida Nicolas *food products holding company executive*
Lewis, Marcia *actress*
Lewis, Paul *architecture educator*
Lewis, Richard Warren *advertising agency executive*
Lewis, Russell T. *publishing executive*
Lewis, W. Walker *strategic and financial advisory company executive*
Lewis, William *bank executive*
LeWitt, Sol *artist*
Lewyn, Ann Salfeld *retired English as a second language educator*
Libby, John Kelway *financial services company executive*
Libeskind, Daniel *architect*
Libin, Laurence Elliot *museum official*
Libin, Paul *theatre executive, producer*
LiBretto, John Charles *television director*
Lichtblau, John H. *economist*
Lichtenstein, Seymour *clothing manufacturing company executive*
Lieberman, James S. *physiatrist, neurologist*
Lieberman, Nancy Ann *lawyer*
Lieberman, Robert C(harles) *political scientist*
Liebermann, Lowell *composer, pianist, conductor*
Liebman, Lance Malcolm *law educator, lawyer*
Liebman, Theodore *architect*
Liebmann, Ruth *writer*
Lief, Eugene Paul *medical physicist*
Lifland, William Thomas *lawyer*
Liftin, Joan R. *photojournalist, educator*
Lifton, Robert Kenneth *diversified companies executive*
Lightfoot, Gordon Meredith *singer, songwriter*
Lightman, Harold Allen *marketing executive*
Lilien, Robert Jarrett *diversified financial services company executive*
Limbaugh, Rush Hudson *radio and talk show host*
Lin, Hamilton *investment banker, education educator*
Lin, Maria C. H. *lawyer*
Lin, Yiling Ellen *investment advisor*
Lincoln, Edmond Lynch *investment banker*
Lindegren, Lennart S. *diversified financial services company executive*
Lindenbaum, Samuel Harvey *lawyer*
Lindros, Eric Bryan *professional hockey player*
Lindsay, George Peter *lawyer*
Linen, Jonathan S. *diversified financial services company executive*
Lingeman, Richard Roberts *editor, writer*
Link, Robert O., Jr., *lawyer*
Linsenmeyer, John Michael *lawyer*
Linz, Werner Mark *international publishing executive*
Lipan, Howard Kenneth *information and technology consultant*
Lipin, Joan Carol *healthcare executive, consultant*
Lipkin, Martin *physician, scientist*
Lipper, Kenneth *investment banker, film producer, writer*
Lipscomb, James Chapman *film producer*
Lipscomb, Thomas Heber, III, *media executive*
Lipsey, Robert Edward *economist, educator*
Lipsky, Burton G. *lawyer*
Lipsky, Pat *artist*
Lipton, Charles *public relations executive*
Lipton, Charles Jules *lawyer*
Lipton, James *television personality*
Lipton, Joan Elaine *advertising executive*
Lipton, Lester *ophthalmologist, entrepreneur*
Lipton, Martin *lawyer*
Lipton, Robert Steven *lawyer*
Lipton, William James *accountant, lawyer*
Lisovicz, Susan *anchor, correspondent*
Liss, Norman *lawyer*
Little, Robert David *library science educator*
Lituchy, Gregg *dentist*
Liu, Charles *astrophysicist*
Liu, Hung-Ching *medical educator*
Liu, Si-kwang *veterinary pathologist*
Liu, Xinyu *securities trader, financial analyst*
Livingston, Julie *publicist*
Ljungqvist, Alexander *finance educator*
Llinás, Rodolfo Riascos *neuroscientist, researcher*
Lloyd, Jean *retired early childhood educator*
Lo, Shaw-Hwa *statistician, educator*
Lobo, Rogerio A. *obstetrician, gynecologist*
LoCascio, Robert P. *computer company executive*
Lockshin, Michael Dan *rheumatologist*
Lockwood, Helshi *advertising executive*
Lodge, Henry Sears *physician*
Lodge, Kirsten *language educator*
Loeb, John Langeloth, Jr., *investment counselor*
Loeb, John Nichols *physician, educator*
Loeb, Larry Morris *communications company executive*
Loeb, Lisa *singer, songwriter*
Loeb, Marshall Robert *journalist*
Loeb, Peter Kenneth *money manager*
Loengard, John Borg *photographer, editor*
Loengard, Richard Otto, Jr., *lawyer*
Logan, Don *publishing executive*
Logan, Douglas George *sports commissioner*
Logan, J. Murray *investment manager*

Meisel, Martin English and comparative literature educator
Meisel, Perry English educator
Melancon, Barry C. professional society adminstrator
Mellencamp, John (John Cougar) singer, songwriter
Mellins, Robert B. pediatrician, educator
Mello, Dawn retail executive
Melloan, George Richard editor, columnist, writer
Melone, Joseph James retired insurance company executive
Melsheimer, Mel P(owell) venture capital and consumer products executive
Meltzer, Harold performing company executive, composer
Meltzer, Milton author
Menaker, Daniel publishing executive
Menand, Louis literature educator
Mencher, Melvin journalist, retired educator
Mendelson, Haim artist, educator, art gallery director
Mendez, Albert Orlando industrialist, financier
Mendini, Douglas A. publishing company executive, writer
Mendoza, Roberto G., Jr., banker
Menken, Alan composer
Menschel, Richard Lee investment banker
Menschel, Robert Benjamin investment banker
Menton, Tanya Lia lawyer, educator
Mentz, Barbara Antonello lawyer
Mentz, Lawrence lawyer
Menza, Claudia Marcella literary agent
Menzel, Idina actress, singer
Mercado, Nancy writer, educator
Mercado-Valdes, Frank broadcast executive
Merchant, Ismail Noormohamed film producer, film director
Merchant, Natalie Anne musician, singer
Merin, Mitchell M corporate financial executive
Merlo, Michael J. investment banker
Meron, Theodor judge, law educator, researcher
Merow, John lawyer
Merrifield, Robert Bruce biochemist, educator
Merrill, George Vanderneth lawyer, investment executive
Merrill, Thomas Wendell lawyer, educator
Merriss, Philip Ramsay, Jr., banker
Merritt, Jean consulting firm executive, psychotherapist
Mertens, Joan R. museum curator, art historian
Mesa, Nilda artist
Mesia, Augusto Fajardo pathologist
Mesnikoff, Alvin Murray psychiatry educator
Messer, Thomas Maria museum director
Messier, Mark Douglas professional hockey player
Messner, Thomas G. advertising executive, copywriter
Mestres, Ricardo Angelo, Jr., lawyer
Metz, Emmanuel Michael investment company executive, lawyer
Metzl, Jordan D sports medicine physician, director
Meunier, Monique dancer
Mew, Calvin Marshall advertising executive
Meyer, Edgar musician, composer
Meyer, Edward Henry advertising agency executive
Meyer, Fred Josef financial executive
Meyer, Karl Ernest journalist
Meyer, Mike management consultant
Meyer, Pearl executive compensation consultant
Meyer, Scott D. public relations firm executive
Meyer, Sheldon publisher
Meyer-Bahlburg, Heino F.L. psychology educator
Meyerhoff, Erich librarian, administrator
Meyers, John Allen magazine publisher
Meyers, Michael E. venture capitalist
Mezei, Mihaly chemist
Miano, Louis Stephen arts advisor
Michaels, Alan Richard sports commentator
Michaels, Lorne television writer, producer
Michaelson, Arthur M. lawyer
Michelis, Michael Frank nephrologist
Michels, Robert psychiatrist, educator
Michelsen, Christopher Bruce Hermann surgeon
Michelson, Gertrude Geraldine retired retail company executive
Michenfelder, Joseph Francis public relations executive
Michielli, Frank V. architectural firm executive
Middendorf, John Harlan English literature educator
Middlebrook, Diane Wood English language educator, writer
Middleton, David physicist, applied mathematician, educator
Mikita, Joseph Karl broadcast executive
Mikumo, Akiko lawyer
Milbank, Jeremiah foundation executive
Mildvan, Donna infectious diseases physician
Milgrim, Roger Michael lawyer
Miller, Arthur Madden lawyer, investment banker, brokerage house executive
Miller, Barbara Kenton retired librarian
Miller, Bebe choreographer
Miller, Beth McCarthy television director
Miller, Charles Hampton lawyer
Miller, Corbin Russell investment company executive
Miller, Edward Daniel financial services executive
Miller, Erika on-air business news reporter
Miller, Ernest Charles management consultant
Miller, George H. architectural firm executive
Miller, Harry Brill scenic designer, actor, director, acting instructor, lyricist, interior designer
Miller, Harvey R. lawyer, bankruptcy reorganization specialist
Miller, Harvey S. Shipley foundation trustee, private investor
Miller, John R. accountant
Miller, Michael Jeffrey editor, columnist
Miller, Morgan Lincoln textile manufacturing company executive
Miller, Nancy K. literature educator
Miller, Neil Stuart advertising executive
Miller, Nicole Jacqueline fashion designer
Miller, Paul S(amuel) lawyer
Miller, Richard Kidwell artist, actor, educator
Miller, Richard McDermott sculptor
Miller, Richard Steven lawyer
Miller, Robert advertising executive
Miller, Sanford Marvin anesthesiology educator
Miller, Steven Scott lawyer
Miller, Walter James English and humanities educator, writer
Miller, William Harlowe, Jr., lawyer
Miller, Yvette lawyer, publishing executive
Millman, Bruce Russell lawyer
Mills, Barry academic administrator, lawyer
Mills, Stephanie Ellen writer
Millstein, Ira M. lawyer, lecturer
Millstein, Lincoln digital media company executive
Milman, Doris Hope retired pediatrics educator, psychiatrist
Milnes, Sherrill E. baritone
Milonas, Minos artist, designer, poet
Milton, Christian Michel insurance executive
Minarik, Else Holmelund (Bigart Minarik) author
Mincer, Jacob economics educator
Minick, Michael publishing executive
Minicucci, Robert A. business executive
Minkel, Herbert Philip, Jr., lawyer
Minkowitz, Martin lawyer, former state government official
Minotti, Mark Anthony assistant principal
Minsky, Bruce William lawyer
Mintz, Norman Nelson investment banker, educator
Mintz, Samuel Isaiah English language educator, writer
Mintz, Shlomo conductor, violist
Mintz, Walter investment company executive
Mirante, Arthur J., II, real estate company executive
Mironovich, Alex publisher
Mirrer, Louise language educator, consultant
Mitchard, Jacquelyn writer
Mitchell, Arthur dancer, choreographer, educator
Mitchell, John W. pharmaceutical executive
Mitterand, Henri C. education educator, writer
Mittl, Rainer N. ophthalmologist
Mockler, Robert Joseph management educator
Moden, Joleen communications executive
Modlin, Howard S. lawyer
Moerdler, Charles Gerard lawyer
Mohler, Mary Gail magazine editor
Moldow, Susan publishing executive
Molho, Emanuel publisher
Moline, Jacqueline occupational physician
Molino, Virginia Louise lawyer
Mollica, Santo percussionist, songwriter, performer
Molnar, Lawrence lawyer
Moloney, Thomas Joseph lawyer
Molz, Redmond Kathleen public administration educator
Mombaerts, Peter biology professor
Mondlin, Marvin retail executive, antiquarian book dealer
Monk, Meredith Jane artistic director, composer, choreographer, filmmaker, director
Monk Kidd, Sue writer
Monrad, Elizabeth A. corporate financial executive
Monson, Robert Joseph education educator
Montorio, John Angelo magazine editor
Mooney, James F. telecommunications industry executive
Mooney, Richard Emerson writer
Moonves, Leslie broadcast executive
Moor, Kristian P. insurance company executive
Moore, Ann S. magazine executive
Moore, Anne physician
Moore, Charles Hewes, Jr., industrial and engineered products executive
Moore, David J. media company executive
Moore, Donald Francis lawyer
Moore, Harold food service executive
Moore, John P. microbiologist, immunologist, medical educator
Moore, Leroi musician
Moore, Mandy (Amanda Leigh Moore) singer, actress
Moore, Michael Watson musician, educator
Moore, Rachel Suzanne performing company executive, dancer
Moore, Thomas A. lawyer
Moore, Thomas Ronald (Lord Bridestowe) lawyer
Moore, William H., III, investment company executive
Moran, Juliette M. retired chemicals executive
Moran, Martin Joseph fundraising company executive
Moran, Patricia lawyer
Morano, Kevin R. mining company executive
Morath, Max Edward entertainer, composer, writer
Morawetz, Cathleen Synge mathematician
Morehouse, Ward, III, theater critic, writer, playwright
Moreira, Marcio Martins advertising executive
Moreno, Barry historian, writer
Morfopoulos, V. metallurgical engineer, materials engineer
Morgan, Arlene Notoro university administrator
Morgan, Frank Edward, II, lawyer
Morgan, Jacqui illustrator, painter, educator, writer
Morgan, Mary E. publishing executive
Morgenson, Gretchen C. reporter
Morgenthau, Robert Morris prosecutor
Mori, Mariko artist
Morial, Marc Haydel former mayor, association executive
Moroz, Pavel Emanuel research scientist
Morphy, James Calvin lawyer
Morreale, Joseph Constantino higher education administrator, public administration educator, economic and financial consultant
Morris, Clayton Leslie priest
Morris, David publishing executive
Morris, Douglas Peter recording company executive
Morris, Eugene Jerome retired lawyer
Morris, James Peppler bass
Morris, John composer, conductor, arranger
Morris, Stephen Burritt marketing information executive
Morris, Valerie news correspondent
Morris, William Charles investor
Morrison, Patricia Kennealy author
Morrison, Stacy Lynne magazine editor
Morse, Edward Lewis petroleum industry executive
Morse, Robert Parker investment company executive
Morse, Stephen Scott virologist, epidemiologist, immunologist, educator
Morton, Joëlle musician, editor
Morvillo, Robert Guy lawyer
Mosellie, Anthony architect
Moses, Jeffrey Warren cardiologist, educator
Moshkin, Nickolay V. financial consultant, litigation consultant
Moskin, John Robert historian, editor, writer
Moskin, Morton lawyer, director
Moskovitz, Jim radio, television and film producer, writer
Moskowitz, Arnold X. economist, strategist, educator
Mosler, Bruce E. real estate company executive
Mosley, Walter writer
Moss, Adam Wender editor
Moss, Charles advertising agency executive
Moss, Douglas architectural firm executive
Moss, Melvin Lionel anatomist, educator
Mossavar-Rahmani, Bijan oil and gas company executive
Mossberg, Walter columnist
Mosse, Peter John Charles financial services executive
Moss-Salentijn, Letty (Aleida Moss-Salentijn) anatomist, educator
Most, Jack Lawrence lawyer, consultant
Motley, Constance Baker (Mrs. Joel Wilson Motley) federal judge, former city official
Motzer, Robert John oncologist, educator
Moulton, Sara chef, magazine editor
Mow, Van C. engineering educator, researcher
Moy, Mary Anastasia lawyer
Moy, Richard L. virologist
Moyer, David S. executive search consultant
Moyers, Bill D. journalist
Moyers, Judith Davidson television producer
Moylan, Steve publishing executive
Moyles, Philip Vincent, Jr., financial services company executive
Moyne, John Abel computer scientist, linguist, educator
Mroz, John Edwin political scientist
Muccia, Joseph William lawyer
Muchnick, Richard Stuart ophthalmologist, educator
Mueller, Shirley Anne lawyer, real estate broker
Mui, Jimmy Kun architect
Mukasey, Michael B. federal judge
Mulhern, Patrick J. lawyer, banker
Mullaney, Thomas Joseph lawyer
Mullen, Peter P. lawyer
Muller, Charlotte Feldman economist, educator
Muller, Henry James journalist, magazine editor
Muller, Jennifer choreographer, dancer
Mulligan, Jeremiah T. lawyer
Mullman, Michael S. lawyer
Mulvihill, William J. former health science association administrator
Mundell, Robert Alexander economist, educator
Mundheim, Robert Harry law educator
Mundinger, Mary O'Neil nursing educator
Munro, Alice author
Munroe, George Barber retired mining and manufacturing company executive
Munzer, Cynthia Brown mezzo-soprano
Munzer, Stephen Ira lawyer
Muradian, Vazgen violist, composer
Murase, Jiro lawyer
Murdoch, Lachlan Keith publishing executive
Murdoch, (Keith) Rupert publisher
Murdock, Robert Mead curator
Murphy, Arthur William lawyer, educator
Murphy, Austin de la Salle economist, educator, banker
Murphy, Brian Stuart internist, consultant
Murphy, Carolyn model
Murphy, Charles Joseph investment banker
Murphy, Donald B. investment company executive
Murphy, Donna actress
Murphy, Helen recording industry executive
Murphy, James Edward public relations and marketing executive
Murphy, John Arthur tobacco, food and brewing company executive
Murphy, John B. investment advisor
Murphy, John Joseph, Jr., investment company executive
Murphy, Kenneth F. human resources specialist
Murphy, Mark Joseph enterprise sales executive
Murphy, Patrice Ann (Pat Murphy) writer
Murphy, Ramon Jeremiah Castroviejo physician, pediatrician
Murphy, Richard William retired foreign service officer, Middle East specialist, consultant
Murphy, Rosemary actress
Murphy, Stacia health service association executive
Murray, Brian publishing executive
Murray, Eileen K. investment company executive
Murray, Elizabeth artist
Murray, Richard Maximilian insurance executive
Muscato, Andrew lawyer
Musgrave, R. Kenton federal judge
Musham, Bettye Martin consumer products executive
Muskin, Victor Philip lawyer
Myerberg, Marcia investment banker
Myers, Gerald E. humanities educator
Myers, Roberta editor-in-chief
Nabi, Stanley Andrew investment executive
Nachman, Ralph Louis physician, educator
Nachum, Lilach international business educator
Nadelberg, Eric Paul brokerage house executive
Nadich, Judah rabbi
Nadiri, M. Ishaq economics educator, researcher, lecturer, consultant
Nadler-Hurvich, Hedda Carol public relations executive
Naegle, Madeline Anne mental health nurse, educator
Nafisi, Azar humanities educator
Naftalis, Gary Philip lawyer, educator
Nagano, Kent George conductor
Nagler, Harris M. urologic surgeon
Nagler, Stewart Gordon insurance company executive
Nagourney, Herbert publishing company executive
Nahas, Gabriel Georges pharmacologist, educator, writer
Naidich, Thomas Paul neuroradiologist, educator
Naito, Akemi composer
Naka, Yoshifumi surgeon, researcher
Nakamura, James I. economics educator
Nakanishi, Koji chemistry educator, research institute administrator
Nally, Dennis Mathew accountant, finance company executive
Nance, Allan Taylor retired lawyer
Nash, Edward L. advertising agency executive
Nash, Graham William singer, composer
Nash, Paul LeNoir lawyer
Nasr, George Elias electrical engineer, consultant, computer engineer, educator
Nassau, Michael Jay lawyer
Nathan, Frederic Solis lawyer
Nathan, Paul S. editor, writer
Natori, Josie Cruz apparel executive
Navarra, Tova writer
Navasky, Victor Saul magazine editor, publisher
Nazem, Fereydoun F. venture capitalist
Nearing, Vivienne W. lawyer
Necarsulmer, Henry investment banker
Nederlander, James Morton theater executive
Nederlander, Robert E. entertainment and television executive, lawyer
Needham, Ed editor
Needham, George Austin investment banker
Neewoor, Anund Priyay ambassador
Neff, Michael Alan lawyer
Neff, Thomas Joseph executive search firm executive
Neiman, LeRoy artist
Nelson, Barry actor
Nelson, Edwin Stafford actor, educator
Nelson, Iris Dorothy retired guidance and rehabilitation counselor
Nelson, Lester lawyer
Nelson, Merlin Edward international business consultant, company director, lawyer
Nelson, Richard John playwright, film director, screenwriter
Nelson, Stanley film director, writer, film producer
Nelson, Wayne K. advertising executive
Neman, Eileen not-for-profit organization executive
Nemser, Earl Harold lawyer
Nesbit, Lynn literary agent
Nesbitt, Lois Ellen personal trainer, writer
Netzer, Dick economics professor
Neubauer, Peter Bela psychoanalyst
Neuberg, Hans W. internist, educator
Neufeld, Peter lawyer
Neugeboren, Jay author
Neuger, Win J. insurance company executive
Neuner, Robert lawyer
Neustein, Robin investment company executive
Neuwirth, Alan James lawyer
Neuwirth, Gloria S. lawyer
Neuwirth, Robert Samuel obstetrician, gynecologist
Neveloff, Jay A. lawyer
New, Maria Iandolo pediatrician, educator
Newberg, Esther literary agent
Newbold, John Lowe retired banker, financial consultant
Newcomb, Jonathan publishing executive
Newell, Norman Dennis paleontologist, geologist, museum curator, educator
Newhouse, Nancy Riley newspaper editor
Newhouse, Stephan F. securities company executive
Newman, Arnold photographer
Newman, Frank Neil retired bank executive
Newman, Fredric Samuel lawyer, business executive
Newman, Geraldine Anne advertising executive
Newman, Joyce A. obstetrician/gynecologist
Newman, Lawrence Walker lawyer
Newman, Nancy publishing executive
Newman, Phyllis adult education educator, psychologist
Newman, Robert Gabriel physician
Newman, William real estate executive
Newsome, James E. commodity futures exchange executive
Ney, Alexander artist, sculptor
Ney, Edward N. ambassador, advertising and public relations company executive
Niblack, John F. pharmaceutical company executive
Nibley, Andrew Mathews editorial executive
Niccolini, Dianora photographer
Nicholas, James A. surgeon, consultant, educator
Nicholls, Richard H. lawyer
Nichols, Edie Diane executive recruiter
Nickell, Frank (Nick) T. diversified financial services company executive
Nickoloff, Edward Lee radiology physicist
Nicol, Dominik writer, photographer
Nicoll, Edward J. internet financial company executive
Nides, Thomas Richard diversified financial services company executive
Nielsen, John A. investment company executive
Nielsen, Nancy publishing executive
Niemiec, David Wallace investment management executive
Nieporent, Drew restaurant group executive
Niles, Thomas Michael Tolliver business association executive
Nimer, Stephen physician, leukemia researcher
Nimkin, Bernard William retired lawyer
Nirenberg, Louis mathematician, educator
Nisce, Lourdes radiologist
Nischan, Michel food service executive
Nisenholtz, Martin Abram telecommunications executive, educator
Nish, Wayne Paul chef, restaurant owner
Nissim, Shai special education educator, consultant
Nixon, Agnes Eckhardt television writer, producer
Nixon, Daniel Walker oncologist, researcher
Nocera, Joseph editor, writer
Nolan, Christopher Aloysius, III, real estate developer, architect
Nolan, William Joseph, III, banker
Nonna, John Michael lawyer
Noonan, Peggy writer
Noonan, Susan Abert public relations executive
Norell, Mark Allen paleontology educator
Norfolk, William Ray lawyer
Norman, Christina broadcast executive
Norman, Stephen Peckham financial services company executive
Norris, Floyd Hamilton financial journalist
North, Steven Edward lawyer, educator
Norton, Larry oncologist
Norville, Deborah Anne news correspondent
Norwitz, Trevor S. lawyer
Noski, Charles H. telecommunications executive
Notarbartolo, Albert artist
Novick, Nelson Lee dermatologist, internist, writer, consultant, dermatological surgeon
Novick, Stephen Alan cardiologist
Novikoff, Harold Stephen lawyer
Novitz, Charles Richard television executive
Novogrod, Nancy Gerstein editor
Nugent, Jeffrey M. cosmetics executive
Nugent, Nelle theater, film and television producer
Nurnberg, Charles Gordon publishing company marketing executive
Nurse, Sir Paul M. academic administrator
Nusbacher, Gloria Weinberg lawyer
Nusim, Stanley Herbert chemical engineer, consultant
Nussbaum, Jeffrey Joseph musician
Nyren, Neil Sebastian publisher, editor
Oates, Joyce Carol author
Obaid, Thoraya Ahmed international organization official
Oberfield, Sharon Elefant pediatric endocrinologist

Quest, Donald O. *neurological surgeon*
Quick, Peter *former brokerage firm executive*
Quick, Thomas Clarkson *brokerage house executive*
Quicke, John J. *aerospace company executive*
Quigley, James H. *finance company executive*
Quigley, James R. *investment company executive*
Quimby, Fred William *pathology educator, veterinarian*
Quindlen, Anna *journalist*
Quinlan, Guy Christian *lawyer*
Quinlan, Mary Lou *advertising executive*
Quinn, Alice Freeman *literature educator*
Quinn, Francis F. *lawyer*
Quinn, James E. *retail products executive*
Quinn, Jane Bryant *journalist, writer*
Quinn, Yvonne Susan *lawyer*
Quiñones Keber, Eloise *art historian, educator*
Quinson, Bruno Andre *publishing executive*
Quint, Ira *retail executive*
Quintero, Ronald Gary *management consultant*
Quirk, John James *investment company executive*
Quittner, Josh *editor-in-chief*
Quivers, Robin *radio personality*
Quraishi, Nisar Ali *internist*
Raab, Jennifer J. *city commissioner*
Raab, Sheldon *lawyer*
Rabassa, Clementine Christos *humanities educator, translator*
Rabb, Bruce *lawyer*
Rabb, Harriet Schaffer *academic administrator, educator, lawyer, government official*
Rabbani, Farhang *urologic oncologist*
Rabinowitz, Dorothy *television critic*
Rabinowitz, Jack Grant *radiologist, educator*
Rabinowitz, Wilbur Melvin *manufacturing executive, consultant*
Rabiu, Badru I.O. *federal official*
Rachlin, Alan Sanders *lawyer*
Rachow, Louis A(ugust) *librarian*
Rackow, Eric C. *health facility administrator*
Radice, Frank J. *communications executive*
Radin, Sam *lawyer, estate planner*
Radner, Roy *economist, educator, researcher*
Rado, Peter Thomas *lawyer*
Radon, Jenik Richard *lawyer*
Radway, Robert J. *lawyer, consultant, law educator*
Radwin, Jerome *public health service officer*
Rafaloff, Gary B. *financial company executive*
Ragusa, Olga Maria *retired Italian language educator*
Rahl, Leslie *risk advisor, entrepreneur*
Rahm, David Alan *lawyer*
Rahm, Susan Berkman *lawyer*
Rainess, Alan Edward *psychiatrist, neurologist, educator*
Rainis, Eugene Charles *bank executive*
Raisler, Kenneth Mark *lawyer*
Rakoff, Jed Saul *federal judge, author*
Ralli, Constantine Pandia *lawyer*
Ramat, Charles S. *apparel executive*
Ramey, Samuel Edward *bass soloist*
Ramirez, Tina *artistic director*
Rampe, Kevin M. *real estate developer*
Rampino, Michael Robert *earth and environmental science educator*
Ramsay, David Leslie *physician, dermatologist, medical educator*
Ramsay, Gustavus Remak *actor*
Ranald, Ralph Arthur *former government official, educator*
Rand, Deborah *lawyer*
Rand, Harry Israel *lawyer*
Rand, Lawrence Anthony *investor, financial relations executive*
Rand, William *lawyer, former state justice*
Randall, Francis Ballard *historian, educator, writer*
Randolph, David *conductor*
Rankin, Clyde Evan, III, *lawyer*
Ranney-Marinelli, Alesia *lawyer*
Rao, Sethuramiah Lakshminarayana *demographer, United Nations official*
Raphael, Sally Jessy *talk-show host*
Rapoport, Bernard Robert *lawyer*
Rapoport, Miles S. *former state offical*
Rappaport, Linda Ellen *lawyer*
Raskin, Joshua R. *financial analyst, researcher*
Raskin, Keith B. *surgeon*
Rather, Dan *broadcast journalist*
Rathmann, Peggy *writer, illustrator*
Ratzman, Zachary M. *lawyer, consultant*
Rauch, Arthur Irving *management consultant*
Rauch, Michael H. *lawyer*
Rauch, Paul David *television producer*
Rauch, Rudolph Stewart, III, *periodical editor, arts education executive*
Rauschenberg, Robert *artist*
Rausen, Aaron Reuben *pediatric hematologist, oncologist*
Raven, Abbe *broadcast executive*
Ravitch, Diane Silvers *historian, educator, author, government official*
Rawson, Eleanor S. *publishing company executive*
Ray, Rachael *chef*
Raylesberg, Alan Ira *lawyer*
Raymond, Dorothy Sarnoff *communications consultant, former actress and singer*
Raymond, Jack *journalist, public relations executive, foundation executive*
Raynor, Bruce S. *labor union administrator*
Raynor, Richard Benjamin *neurosurgeon, educator*
Reader, George G. *retired internal-public health medicine educator*
Rebell, Arthur L. *corporate financial executive*
Recanati, Dina *artist*
Reda, James Francis *business consultant*
Redd, J. Diane *professional fundraiser and grants management executive*
Reddy, Krishna Narayana *artist, educator*
Redlich, Norman *lawyer, educator*
Redo, S(averio) Frank *surgeon*
Reece, Thomas L. *manufacturing executive*
Reed, Ishmael Scott (Emmett Coleman) *writer*
Reed, John Shepard *stock exchange executive*
Reed, Lou *musician*
Reed, Susan K *editor-in-chief*
Reed, W. Allen *automotive executive*
Regan, Judith Terrance *publishing executive*
Regazzi, John James, III, *publishing executive*
Reges, Marianna Alice *marketing executive*
Reiback, Earl Martin *artist*
Reice, Sylvie *columnist, editor, author*
Reich, Steve *composer*
Reichl, Ruth Molly *editor*
Reid, Antonio (L.A. Reid) *music company executive*
Reid, Edward Snover, III, *lawyer*
Reid, John Phillip *law educator*
Reidenberg, Marcus Milton *physician, educator*
Reidy, Carolyn Kroll *publisher*
Reiffel, James *cardiologist, educator*
Reifler, Stewart *lawyer*
Reig, June Wilson *scriptwriter, television director, television producer*
Reilly, Edward Arthur *lawyer*
Reilly, Edward T., Jr., *advertising executive*
Reilly, William Francis *media company executive*
Reiman, Donald Henry *English language educator*
Rein, Catherine Amelia *insurance company executive, lawyer*
Reiner, Mark Allen *surgeon, educator*
Reinganum, Marc Richard *finance educator*
Reinhard, Keith Leon *advertising executive*
Reinhart, Charles Lawrence *performing company executive*
Reinhold, Richard Lawrence *lawyer*
Reininghaus, Ruth *retired artist*
Reinking, Ann H. *dancer, actress*
Reinthaler, Richard Walter *lawyer*
Reisberg, Barry *geropsychiatrist, neuropsychopharmacologist*
Reisner, Lorin L. *lawyer*
Reisner, Milton *psychiatrist, psychoanalyst*
Reiss, Dale Anne *accounting executive, investment company executive*
Reiss, Robert Francis *physician*
Reiss, Steven Alan *lawyer, law educator*
Remington, Deborah Williams *artist*
Remnick, David J. *journalist, editor*
Remshard, John W. *insurance company executive*
Renick, Kyle *artistic director*
Renna, Cathy *communications executive, activist*
Rennert, Ira Leon *manufacturing executive*
Renney, Tom *professional hockey coach*
Rennie, Milbrey Tower *television news producer*
Rescigno, Richard Joseph *editor*
Resika, Paul *artist*
Resnick, Rhoda Brodowsky *psychotherapist*
Resnick, Rosalind *multimedia executive*
Restani, Jane A. *federal judge*
Reuben, Gloria *actress*
Reuter, Victor E. *pathologist, educator*
Reuther, David Louis *retired children's book publisher, writer*
Reutter, Eberhard Edmund, Jr., *education and law educator*
Reverdin, Bernard J. *lawyer*
Revesz, Richard Luis *law educator*
Reynolds, Donald Martin *art historian, foundation administrator, educator*
Reynolds, Fredric G. *broadcasting company executive*
Reynolds, James *management consultant*
Reynolds, John R. *hospital executive*
Rheins, Carl Jeffrey *historian, director*
Rhoads, Geraldine Emeline *editor, consultant*
Rhodes, David J. *academic administrator*
Rhodes, Dorothy Lee *public health service officer*
Rhodes, Richard (Lee) *writer*
Rhodes, Samuel *violist, educator*
Rhodes, William Reginald *banker*
Rhodes, Yorke E(dward) *organic chemist, educator*
Ribary, Urs *neuroscientist, researcher, educator*
Rice, Anne *writer*
Rice, Charles M. *virologist, educator*
Rice, Donald Sands *lawyer, entrepreneur*
Rice, Luanne *writer*
Rich, Adrienne *writer*
Rich, Frank Hart *newscaster*
Rich, Frederic Carl *lawyer*
Rich, R(obert) Bruce *lawyer*
Richard, Ellen *theater executive*
Richards, David Alan *lawyer*
Richards, Keith *musician*
Richards, Lloyd George *theatrical director, university administrator*
Richards, Martin *theatrical producer*
Richardson, Grace Elizabeth *consumer products company executive*
Richardson, Paul *publishing executive*
Richman, Martin Franklin *lawyer*
Richtman, Jack *French language educator*
Ridell, Carol Anne *reporter*
Rifkind, Arleen B. *pharmacologist, researcher, educator*
Rifkind, Robert S. *lawyer*
Rigg, Dame Diana *actress*
Riggin, Donald L. *health science association administrator*
Riggio, Leonard *book publishing executive*
Riggio, Stephen *book store chain executive*
Rigney, James Oliver, Jr., (Robert Jordan, Chang Lung, Reagan O'Neal, Jackson O'Reilly) *writer*
Rigney, Jane *copy editor, writer*
Rigolosi, Elaine La Monica *lawyer, educator, consultant*
Rikon, Michael *lawyer*
Riley, William *corporate executive, writer, conservationist*
Rinaldini, Luis Emilio *investment banker*
Rines, John Randolph *investment banker*
Ringel, Dean *lawyer*
Ringer, James Milton *lawyer*
Ringer, Jennifer *dancer*
Ringgold, Faith *artist*
Riordan, John Thomas *trade association executive*
Ripa, Kelly Maria *television personality*
Riss, Eric *psychologist*
Ristich, Miodrag *psychiatrist*
Ritch, Kathleen *diversified company executive*
Ritch, Robert Harry *ophthalmologist, educator*
Ritchie, Richard Lee *media company executive*
Ritter, Ann L. *lawyer*
Ritterseiser, Robert *investment company executive*
Rivera, Chita (Conchita del Rivero) *actress, singer, dancer*
Rivera, Geraldo *television personality, journalist*
Rivera-Valdés, Sonia *humanities educator*
Rivlin, Benjamin *political science educator*
Rizer, Maggie *model*
Rizzuto, Richard Peter *entrepreneur*
Roach, John Hendee, Jr., *bank executive, investment banker, financial service executive*
Roach, Margaret *editor-in-chief*
Robbins, Carrie F(ishbein) *costume designer, educator*
Robbins, John Clapp *management consultant*
Robbins, Rachel F. *lawyer*
Robbins, Timothy (Francis) *director, actor*
Roberts, Burton Bennett *lawyer, retired judge*
Roberts, Denise (Denise Roberts Hurlin) *dancer*
Roberts, Donald Munier *retired banker, trust company executive*
Roberts, Dorothy Hyman *accessory company executive*
Roberts, Francis Stone *advertising executive*
Roberts, John *news anchor*
Roberts, John J. *accounting firm executive*
Roberts, Kevin *advertising executive*
Roberts, Kevin John *ideas company executive*
Roberts, Nancy Cohen *art dealer, marketing professional*
Roberts, Nora *writer*
Robertson, Andrew *dancer*
Robertson, Andrew *advertising executive*
Robertson, Andrew Whitmore *historian*
Robertson, Edwin David *lawyer*
Robertson, Hugh Dunbar *biomedical researcher, consultant*
Robertson, Mark Allen *lawyer*
Robin, Kenneth Howard *lawyer*
Robinson, Barbara Paul *lawyer*
Robinson, Barry E. *financial company executive*
Robinson, Daniel N. *psychology and philosophy educator*
Robinson, Enders Anthony *geophysicist, educator, writer*
Robinson, Irwin Jay *lawyer*
Robinson, James D., III, *finance company executive, investor*
Robinson, James LeRoy *architect, educator, developer*
Robinson, Janet L. *publishing executive*
Robinson, Joyce McPeake *administrator*
Robinson, Kim Stanley *science fiction author*
Robinson, Maurice Richard, Jr., *publishing executive*
Robinson, Nan Senior *not-for-profit organization consultant*
Robinson, Richard *publishing company executive*
Robinson, Russell F. *foundation administrator*
Robles-Roman, Carol A. *municipal official*
Roche, Gerard Raymond *management consultant*
Roche, Joyce M. *marketing executive*
Rock, Allan Michael *ambassador, former Canadian government official*
Rockas, Anastasia T. *lawyer*
Rockefeller, David *banker*
Rocklen, Kathy Hellenbrand *lawyer*
Rodeo, Scott A. *surgeon, sports medicine specialist*
Rodin, Rita A. *lawyer*
Rodman, Leroy Eli *lawyer*
Rodriguez, Darlene *newscaster*
Rodriguez, Freddy *actor*
Rodriguez, Geno (Eugene Rodriguez) *artist, arts administrator*
Rodriguez, Julio *information technology executive*
Rodriguez, Vincent Angel *lawyer, director*
Rodriguez-Sains, Rene S. *physician, surgeon, educator*
Rodzianko, Paul *energy and environmental company executive*
Roeder, Robert Gayle *biochemist, molecular biologist, educator*
Roen, Philip Ruben *urologist, surgeon, medical educator*
Roethenmund, Otto Emil *financial and banking executive*
Rogers, James Beeland, Jr., *investment company executive*
Rogers, Theodore Courtney *investment company executive*
Rogers, Theodore Otto, Jr., *lawyer*
Rogers, Thomas Sydney *communications executive*
Rogin, Gilbert Leslie *editor, author*
Roglieri, John Louis *health facility administrator*
Rohrbach, Heidi A. *lawyer*
Roker, Al *broadcast journalist*
Roland, John *newscaster*
Rolfe, Ronald Stuart *lawyer*
Rollin, Betty *writer, television journalist, lecturer*
Romano, John Francis *dermatologist*
Romano, Michael *chef, restaurant owner*
Romans, John Niebrugge *lawyer*
Romas, Nicholas Achilles *urologist, educator*
Romero, Anthony D. *legal association administrator*
Romita, Mauro Charles *plastic surgeon*
Romney, Richard Bruce *lawyer*
Ronde, John Herman *author, translator*
Ronstadt, Linda Marie *singer*
Rooney, Andrew Aitken *writer, columnist*
Roorda, Peter *lawyer*
Roos, Jane Mayo *art history educator*
Roosevelt, Phil *periodical editor*
Roosevelt, Theodore, IV, *investment banker*
Root, Nina J. *librarian, writer*
Root, William Pitt *poet, educator*
Rosado, Rossana *publishing executive, editor-in-chief*
Rosand, David *art history educator*
Rose, Aaron *artist*
Rose, Charles *television journalist*
Rose, Daniel *real estate company executive, consultant*
Rose, Elihu *real estate executive*
Rose, Joanna Semel *cultural activist*
Rose, Joanne W. *rating service executive*
Rose, Merrill *public relations counselor*
Rose, Robert Neal *investment banker*
Rosen, Nathaniel Kent *cellist*
Rosen, Richard Lewis *lawyer, real estate developer*
Rosen, Scott Alan *corporate financial executive, financial analyst*
Rosenbaum, Joan Hannah *museum director*
Rosenberg, Alan David *accountant*
Rosenberg, Alan Stewart *lawyer*
Rosenberg, Alex Jacob *art dealer, curator, fine arts appraiser, educator*
Rosenberg, David *lawyer*
Rosenberg, Ellen Y. *religious association administrator*
Rosenberg, Harold Nmi *preventive medicine physician, consultant*
Rosenberg, John David *English educator, literary critic*
Rosenberg, Michael Joseph *financial executive*
Rosenberg, Robert Charles *housing corporation executive*
Rosenberg, Tina *international relations educator, writer*
Rosenberg, Victor I. *plastic surgeon, educator*
Rosenblatt, Arthur Isaac *architect, former museum director*
Rosenbloom, Daniel *investment banker, lawyer*
Rosenblum, Robert *art historian, educator*
Rosenblum, William F., Jr., *lawyer*
Rosenfeld, Arthur Herbert *lawyer, publisher*
Rosenfeld, Steven B. *lawyer*
Rosenfield, Allan *physician*
Rosengarten, Frank *retired language educator, retired literature educator, writer*
Rosensaft, Menachem Zwi *lawyer, writer, foundation administrator, advocate*
Rosenshine, Allen Gilbert *advertising agency executive*
Rosenstein, Brad *cultural organization administrator, playwright*
Rosenthal, Charles Michael *financial executive*
Rosenthal, Donna Myra *social worker*
Rosenthal, Faigi *librarian*
Rosenthal, Gert *economist*
Rosenthal, Jacob (Jack Rosenthal) *foundation executive*
Rosenthal, Jane *film company executive*
Rosenthal, Joel Howard *think-tank executive*
Rosenthal, Larry *cosmetic dentist*
Rosenthal, Milton Frederick *chemical and minerals company executive*
Rosenthal, Shirley Lord *cosmetics magazine executive, novelist*
Rosenwasser, Donna *management consulting company executive*
Rosenzweig, Charles Leonard *lawyer*
Roskin, William A. *communications executive*
Rosner, David *history educator*
Rosow, Stuart L. *lawyer*
Ross, Charles *artist*
Ross, Diana Ernestine Earle *singer, actress, entertainer, fashion designer*
Ross, Donald Keith *retired insurance company executive*
Ross, Jeffrey Allan *political scientist, educator*
Ross, Karen *information technology executive*
Ross, Matthew *lawyer*
Ross, Michael Aaron *lawyer*
Ross, Norman Alan *publisher*
Ross, Rhoda *artist*
Ross, Thomas Bernard *communications company executive*
Rossellini, Isabella *actress, model*
Rossen, Jordan *lawyer*
Rosset, Barnet Lee, Jr., *publishing executive*
Rossettos, Nicholas J. *research and development company executive*
Rostow, Charles Nicholas *lawyer, educator*
Rostropovich, Mstislav Leopoldovich *conductor, music director, musician*
Roth, Daryl *theater producer*
Roth, Eric M. *lawyer*
Roth, Judith Shulman *lawyer*
Roth, Kenneth *human rights advocate*
Roth, Michael I. *lawyer, corporate financial executive*
Roth, Sol *rabbi*
Rothberg, Gerald *editor, publisher, editor-in-chief*
Rothberg, Glenda Fay Morris *lawyer*
Rothe, Desider J. *gynecologist-obstetrician*
Rothenberg, Jerome *author, visual arts and literary educator*
Rothenberg, Robert Philip *public relations counselor*
Rothfeld, Michael B. *theatrical productions executive, investor*
Rothman, Bernard *lawyer*
Rothman, Carol *theater director*
Rothman, David J. *history and medical educator*
Rothman, Henry Isaac *lawyer*
Rothman, James Edward *cell biologist, educator*
Rothschild, Amalie Randolph *filmmaker, producer, director, digital artist, photographer*
Rothstein, Gerald Alan *retired investment company executive*
Rotman, Marvin *radiation oncologist, radiologist, educator*
Rotner, Philip *lawyer*
Rouse, Christopher Chapman, III, *composer, educator*
Rover, Edward Frank *foundation administrator, lawyer*
Rovine, Arthur William *lawyer*
Rovit, Richard Lee *neurological surgeon*
Rowe, David Lee *financial advisor*
Rowe, Elizabeth Webb *community volunteer*
Rowen, Ruth Halle *musicologist, educator*
Rowland, Esther E(delman) *retired dean*
Rowland, Lewis Phillip *neurology educator, editor, clinical investigator*
Roy, Arundhati *writer*
Rozen, Jerome George, Jr., *research entomologist, museum curator and research administrator*
Rozenberg, Lana *cosmetic dentist*
Roznovschi, Mirela *law librarian, writer*
Ruben, Lawrence *real estate developer, building company executive, lawyer*
Rubenstein, Atoosa Behnegar *editor-in-chief*
Rubenstein, Howard Joseph *public relations executive*
Rubenstein, Joshua Seth *lawyer*
Rubenstein, Leonard *engineering company executive*
Rubin, Albert Louis *internist, nephrologist, educator*
Rubin, Harry Meyer *entertainment and software industry executive*
Rubin, Harvey *publishing executive*
Rubin, Herbert *lawyer*
Rubin, Joel Edward *consulting company executive*
Rubin, Richard Allan *lawyer*
Rubin, Robert Samuel *investment banker*
Rubin, Stephen Edward *publishing executive, editor, journalist*
Rubin, Theodore Isaac *psychiatrist, writer*
Rubino, Victor Joseph *academic administrator, lawyer*
Rubinstein, Ellis Marc *science association director*
Rubinstein, Ernest *librarian, educator*
Rubinstein, Frederic Armand *lawyer*
Rubinstein, Ruth P. *medical educator, researcher*
Ruda, Howard *lawyer, finance company executive*
Rudel, Julius *conductor*
Rudenstine, Neil Leon *former academic administrator, educator*
Ruder, Usha C. *pathologist*
Ruder, William *public relations executive*
Rudick, A. Joseph *research and development company executive*
Rudin, Scott *film and theatre producer*
Rudoff, Sheldon *lawyer*
Rudolph, Maya *actress, comedienne*
Ruebhausen, Oscar Melick *retired lawyer*

Shinkle, John Thomas *lawyer*
Shinnar, Reuel *chemical engineering educator, industrial consultant*
Shipley, Walter Vincent *retired bank executive*
Shnayerson, Robert Beahan *editor, consultant*
Shocked, Michelle *vocalist, songwriter*
Shohen, Saundra Anne *health care communications and public relations executive*
Short, Thomas C. *theatre union executive*
Shorter, James Russell, Jr., *lawyer*
Shortliffe, Edward Hance *internist, medical educator, computer scientist*
Shortz, Will *puzzle editor*
Shoss, Cynthia Renée *lawyer*
Shreve, Elizabeth Steward *publishing executive*
Shriver, Donald Woods, Jr., *theology educator*
Shulevitz, Uri *author, illustrator*
Shull, Mikki *media consultant*
Shuman, Earl Stanley *songwriter, music publisher*
Shuman, Stanley S. *investment banker*
Shungu, Dikoma Cyrille *radiology educator*
Shurdut, Jeffrey Hayden *artist*
Shyer, John D. *lawyer*
Sidamon-Eristoff, Anne Phipps *community trust executive*
Sidamon-Eristoff, Constantine *lawyer*
Siderow, Neil *real estate company executive*
Sidran, Miriam *retired physics educator, researcher*
Sidwell, David H. *bank executive*
Siebert, Muriel (Mickie) *brokerage house executive, former state banking official*
Siegal, Allan Marshall *newspaper editor*
Siegal, Peggy *public relations executive*
Siegel, Arthur Herbert *finance company executive*
Siegel, Herbert Jay *communications executive, director*
Siegel, Jeffrey Norton *lawyer*
Siegel, Joel Steven *television news correspondent*
Siegel, Lucy Boswell *public relations executive*
Siegel, Marc Monroe *television and film producer, writer, director*
Siegel, Marvin *newspaper editor*
Siegel, Max Laurence *recording industry executive*
Siegel, Morton Kallos *religious organization administrator, educational administrator*
Siegel, Randy *publishing executive*
Siegel, Stanley *lawyer, educator*
Siegel, Stephen *real estate company executive*
Sievert, Frederick *insurance company executive*
Siffert, John Sand *lawyer, educator, writer*
Sifton, Elisabeth *book publisher*
Sigal-Ibsen, Rose *artist*
Sigety, Cornelius Edward *family office manager*
Sigmond, Carol Ann *lawyer*
Siguler, George William *financial services executive*
Sikander, Shahzia *artist*
Silber, Steven A. *lab administrator, physician*
Silberberg, Richard Howard *lawyer*
Silkenat, James Robert *lawyer*
Siller, Stephen I. *lawyer*
Sills, Beverly (Mrs. Peter B. Greenough) *performing arts organization executive, coloratura soprano*
Silver, Joan Micklin *film director, screenwriter*
Silver, John L. *artist, educator, poet*
Silver, Morris *economist, educator*
Silver, Richard Tobias *physician, educator*
Silver, Sheldon *state legislator, lawyer*
Silverberg, Michael Joel *lawyer*
Silverman, Al *editor*
Silverman, Arthur Charles *lawyer*
Silverman, Burton Philip *artist*
Silverman, Henry Richard *diversified business executive, lawyer*
Silverman, Leon *lawyer*
Silverman, Martin Morris Bernard *secondary school educator*
Silverman, Moses *lawyer*
Silvers, Robert B. *editor*
Silvers, Sally *choreographer, performing company executive*
Silverstein, Larry A. *real estate developer*
Simmons, Gene *musician*
Simmons, John Derek *retired financial consultant*
Simmons, Peter Lawrence *lawyer*
Simmons, Richard Milton Teagle *physical fitness specialist, television personality*
Simmons, Robert J. *treasurer*
Simmons, Sue *newscaster*
Simon, Abbey *pianist*
Simon, Bob *news correspondent, anchor*
Simon, Carly *singer, composer, author*
Simon, Eric Jacob *neurochemist, educator*
Simon, Jacqueline Albert *political scientist, journalist*
Simon, Neil *playwright, screenwriter, television writer*
Simon, Peter J. *editor*
Simon, Ronald Charles *curator*
Simonds, Charles Frederick *artist*
Simone, Joseph R. *lawyer*
Simons, Albert, III, *lawyer*
Simons, Eric Ward *financial executive*
Simons, James *publishing executive*
Simpson, Jessica Ann *vocalist*
Simpson, Mary Michael *priest, psychotherapist*
Sinagra, Jack G. *air transportation executive*
Sinclair, Daisy *casting executive*
Singer, Barbara Helen *photographer*
Singer, Ezra D. *telecommunications industry executive*
Singer, Niki *media consultant*
Singh, Jyoti Shankar *international organization executive*
Singleton, Donald Edward *journalist*
Sinsheimer, Warren Jack *lawyer*
Sirico, Genaro *actor*
Siris, Ethel Silverman *endocrinologist*
Sis, Peter *illustrator, children's book author, artist, filmmaker*
Sischy, Ingrid Barbara *editor, art critic*
Siskind, Arthur *lawyer, director*
Siskind, Donald Henry *lawyer*
Sisti, Michael Brian *neurosurgeon*
Sitarz, Anneliese Lotte *pediatrics educator, physician*
Sitomer, Sheila Marie *television producer, director*
Siv, Sichan Aun *ambassador*
Sivakumaran, Kumaraswamy *civil engineer, consultant, lawyer*
Sivy, Michael *journalist*
Size, Dennis Michael *lighting and scenery designer*
Skigen, Patricia Sue *lawyer*
Skinner, Elliott Percival *anthropology educator*
Skinner, Peter Graeme *publishing executive, lawyer*
Skirnick, Robert Andrew *lawyer*
Sklar, Stanley Lawrence *judge*
Skol, Michael *anti-corruption and counter-money laundering consultant*
Skolnick, Jerome H. *law educator*
Skolnik, Richard Alan *plastic surgeon*
Skule, John L. *pharmaceutical company executive*
Skupinski, Bogdan Kazimierz *artist*
Skwiersky, Paul *accountant*
Sladkus, Harvey Ira *lawyer*
Slavin, Arlene *artist*
Slawsky, Donna Susan *librarian, singer*
Slazberg, Barry *accounting firm executive*
Sleed, Joel *columnist*
Sleigh, Sylvia *artist, educator*
Sloan, Allan Herbert *journalist*
Slomanson, Lloyd Howard *architect, musician, photographer*
Slone, Sandi *artist*
Slosberg, Mike *advertising executive*
Sloss, Merle *shoe company executive*
Slotkin, Todd *holding company executive*
Slotnick, Barry Ivan *lawyer*
Slusser, William Peter *investment banker*
Slutsky, Lorie A(nn) *foundation executive*
Small, George LeRoy *geographer, educator*
Small, Jonathan Andrew *lawyer*
Smalley, David Vincent *lawyer*
Smigel, Irwin *dentist*
Smiley, Jane Graves *author, educator*
Smith, Andrew Alfred, Jr., *urban planner*
Smith, Anna Nicole (Vickie Lynn Hogan) *television personality, model*
Smith, Barbara *food service executive, model*
Smith, Barry Hamilton *foundation administrator, physician*
Smith, Betty *writer, nonprofit foundation executive*
Smith, Bradley Youle *lawyer*
Smith, Corlies Morgan *publishing executive*
Smith, Craig Richey *thoracic surgeon*
Smith, Daniel *oncologist, gynecologist*
Smith, Dennis (Edward Smith) *author, publisher*
Smith, Edward Paul, Jr., *lawyer*
Smith, George Bundy *state appeals court judge*
Smith, Gordon H. *civil engineer, consultant, forensic engineer consultant*
Smith, Harry *newscaster*
Smith, Hilary Cranwell Bowen *investment banker*
Smith, Howard I. *insurance company executive*
Smith, James Walker *lawyer*
Smith, Joseph Phelan *film company executive*
Smith, Kiki *artist*
Smith, Liz (Mary Elizabeth Smith) *newspaper columnist, broadcast journalist*
Smith, Malcolm Bernard *investment company executive*
Smith, Malcolm Sommerville *bass*
Smith, Martin Jay *advertising and marketing executive*
Smith, Mimi *artist*
Smith, Patrick John *editor, writer*
Smith, Raymond W. *investment banking executive*
Smith, Richard Mills *editor-in-chief*
Smith, Robert Everett *lawyer*
Smith, Robert Sherlock *judge*
Smith, Shirley *artist*
Smith, Thomas A. *lawyer, investment company executive*
Smith, Thomas Ramsaur, Jr., *lawyer*
Smith, Vincent Milton *lawyer, designer, Feng Shui lecturer, consultant, writer*
Smith, Warren Allen *writer*
Smith, Zadie *writer*
Smithson, Charles Wayne *economist, consultant*
Smits, Helen Lida *physician, medical administrator, educator*
Smoak, Evan L. *lawyer*
Smotrich, David Isadore *architect*
Snow, Charles *lawyer*
Snyder, Arlen Dean *actor*
Snyder, Donald Ivandale *music educator, musician*
Snyder, Jack L. *international relations educator*
Soave, Rosemary *internist*
Sobel, Howard D. *dermatologist*
Sobell, Nina R. *artist*
Socol, Sheldon Eleazer *university official*
Sodano, Salvatore F. *stock exchange executive*
Soejima, Daisuke *international trade engineer, economist*
Soering, Jens *writer*
Softness, Donald Gabriel *marketing and manufacturing executive*
Sohl, Joyce Darlene *religious organization administrator*
Sohmer, Bernard *mathematics educator, administrator*
Sokoloff, Audrey L. *lawyer*
Solecki, R. Stefan *anthropologist, educator*
Soley, David Benjamin *composer*
Solnit, Rebecca *writer, art critic*
Solomon, Gail Ellen *physician*
Solomon, Howard *pharmaceutical company executive*
Solomon, Libertina *pharmacist, educator*
Solomon, Maynard Elliott *music historian, former recording company executive*
Solomon, Stephen L. *lawyer*
Solomons, Gus, Jr., (Gustave Martinez) *choreographer, dancer, writer*
Solov, Zachary *choreographer, ballet artist*
Somers, John Arthur *insurance company executive*
Somogyi, Jennie *dancer*
Sonders, Elizabeth Ann *diversified financial services company executive*
Sonneman, Eve *artist*
Sontag, Susan *writer*
Sopanen, Jeri Rainer *photography director*
Sorell, Kitty Julia *public relations executive*
Sorensen, Gillian Martin *United Nations official*
Soriano, Nancy Mernit *editor-in-chief*
Sorkin, Ira Lee *lawyer*
Sorkin, Laurence Truman *lawyer*
Soros, George *fund management executive*
Soros, Susan Weber *educational administrator*
Sorte, John Follett *investment firm executive*
Sorter, George Hans *accounting and law educator, consultant*
Soter, George Nicholas *advertising executive*
Soter, Steven *research scientist*
Soto, Jock *dancer*
Sotomayor, Sonia *federal judge*
Souham, Gérard *communications executive*
Southworth, Linda Jean *artist, critic, educator, poet*
Sovern, Michael Ira *law educator*
Soyer, David *cellist, music educator*
Soyster, Margaret Blair *lawyer*
Spacey, Kevin *actor*
Spade, Kate (Katherine Noel Spade) *apparel designer*
Spanbock, Maurice Samuel *lawyer*
Spanfeller, James John, Jr., *publishing executive*
Spangler, Arnold Eugene *investment banker*
Sparks, Nicholas *writer*
Spatt, Robert Edward *lawyer*
Spear, Harvey M. *lawyer*
Spears, Britney *singer*
Speciale, Richard *investment company executive*
Spector, Warren J. *investment banker*
Spelfogel, Evan J. *lawyer, educator*
Speller, Robert Ernest Blakefield, Jr., *choreographer*
Speller, Robert Ernest Blakefield *publishing executive*
Spence, James Robert, Jr., *television sports executive, educator*
Spence, Sique (Mary Stewart Spence) *art dealer*
Spencer, Frank Cole *medical educator*
Spencer, Jameel Haasan *marketing professional*
Sperakis, Nicholas George *artist*
Sperling, Allan George *lawyer*
Spero, Joan Edelman *foundation president*
Speyer, James L. *oncologist*
Speyer, Jerry I. *real estate company executive*
Spiegel, Elwyn *advertising agency executive, creative director*
Spiegel, Herbert *psychiatrist, educator*
Spiegel, Jerrold Bruce *lawyer*
Spielman, Andrew Ian *biochemist*
Spielvogel, Sidney Meyer *investment banker*
Spillane, Dennis Kevin *lawyer*
Spillane, Mickey (Frank Morrison Spillane) *author*
Spindler, James Andrew *not-for-profit executive*
Spinetta, Jean-Cyril *airline executive*
Spira, Robert Alan *securities company executive*
Spivak, Stuart *retail executive*
Sporn, Kalman Chaim *banker*
Sprague, Peter Julian *software company executive, lecturer*
Springsteen, Bruce *singer, songwriter, guitarist*
Sprizzo, John Emilio *judge*
Sproule, Michael E. *insurance company executive*
Squire, Walter Charles *lawyer*
Squires, John *publishing executive*
Srivastava, Shekhar *research scientist*
Stack, Edward William *business management and foundation executive*
Stacom, Darcy A. *real estate company executive*
Stade, George Gustav *humanities educator*
Staffaroni, Robert J. *lawyer*
Stahl, Lesley R. *news correspondent*
Stainrook, Harry Richard *retired bank executive*
Stakias, G. Michael *merchant banker*
Stamm, Charles H. *lawyer*
Stang, Arnold *actor, director, writer*
Stang, Rolf Kristian *vocalist, actor, educator, writer, advertising executive*
Stanger, Ila *writer, editor*
Stanton, Alex *public relations executive*
Stanton, Ronald P. *export company executive*
Starbuck, William Haynes *business management educator*
Starer, Brian Douglas *lawyer*
Stark, Richard Boies *surgeon, artist*
Stark, Robert J. *lawyer*
Stark, Robin Caryl *psychotherapist, consultant*
Starr, Steven Dawson *photographer*
Starren, Justin Bruce *medical educator*
Stathis, Nicholas John *lawyer*
Stead, Jerre L. *investment company executive*
Steadman, E. Thomas *gynecologist*
Stecher, Esta E. *lawyer, investment company executive*
Steck, Jodi *photojournalist*
Steedman, Doria Lynne Silberberg *organization executive*
Steel, Danielle Fernande *author*
Steel, Robert K. *finance company executive*
Steere, William Campbell, Jr., *pharmaceutical executive*
Steffens, John Laundon *brokerage house executive*
Steigbigel, Neal H. *medical educator*
Steiger, Paul Ernest *newspaper editor, journalist*
Stein, David Fred *investment executive*
Stein, Ellen Gail *executive manager*
Stein, Elliot, Jr., *business executive*
Stein, Howard S. *banker*
Stein, Joseph *playwright*
Stein, Marcia *not-for-profit executive*
Stein, Marvin *psychiatrist, historian*
Stein, Richard Alan *cardiologist, educator*
Stein, Stephen William *lawyer*
Stein, Zena A. *health facility administrator, psychiatry educator*
Steinberg, Howard Eli *lawyer, diversified financial services company executive*
Steinberg, Leo *art historian, educator*
Steinberg, Nancy *healthcare public relations executive*
Steinberg, Saul Phillip *holding company executive*
Steiner, Richard C. *semitic linguist, educator*
Steinfeld, Allan *sports association administrator*
Steinman, Ralph M. *medical educator*
Stelzer, Paul *cardiac surgeon, educator*
Stepanek, Daniel P. *public relations executive*
Stephanopoulos, George Robert *political reporter*
Stephens, Gary Ralph *American literature and journalism educator*
Stephenson, Alan Clements *lawyer*
Sterling, Robert Lee, Jr., *investment company executive*
Stern, Claudio Daniel *medical educator, embryological researcher*
Stern, David Joel *National Basketball Association Commissioner*
Stern, Fritz Richard *historian, educator*
Stern, Howard Allan *radio personality, television show host*
Stern, James Andrew *investment banker*
Stern, Leonard Norman *real estate developer, former pet supply manufacturing company executive*
Stern, Madeleine Bettina *rare books dealer, author*
Stern, Mitchell *broadcast executive*
Stern, Peter R. *lawyer*
Stern, Robert Arthur Morton *architect, educator, writer*
Stern, Roslyne Paige *magazine publisher*
Stern, Walter Phillips *investment executive*
Sternberg, Seymour *insurance company executive*
Stern-Larosa, Caryl M. *advocate, educational association administrator*
Sternman, Joel W. *lawyer*
Stetler, Russell Dearnley, Jr., *private investigator*
Steuer, Gary Paul *art association administrator*
Steuer, Richard Marc *lawyer*
Stevens, Art *public relations executive*
Stevens, Jerome Hebert *entrepreneur*
Stevens, Risë *performing arts company administrator*
Stever, Donald Winfred *lawyer*
Steves, Gale C. *marketing professional, writer, editor-in-chief, publishing executive*
Stewart, E(dward) Nicholson *investment management executive*
Stewart, Jack *artist, educator, writer*
Stewart, Richard Burleson *law educator*
Stiassny, Melanie L.J. *curator*
Stich, June Jeacoma *psychotherapist*
Stiefel, Ethan *dancer*
Stiglitz, Joseph Eugene *economist, educator*
Stimmel, Barry *cardiologist, internist, educator, university dean*
Stimpson, Catharine Rosalind *English language educator, writer*
Sting, (Gordon Matthew Sumner) *musician, songwriter, actor*
Stirling, Alexandra Lucero *science administrator, writer*
Stocker, Michael Aubrey *health insurance company executive*
Stoddard, George Earl *investment company financial executive*
Stokes, Lori *newscaster*
Stolfi, Thomas Edward *advertising executive*
Stoll, Neal Richard *lawyer*
Stolper, Pinchas Aryeh *religious organization executive, rabbi*
Stoltzman, Richard Leslie *clarinetist*
Stone, Amy *reporter*
Stone, Caroline Fleming *artist*
Stone, David Philip *lawyer*
Stone, Matt *animator*
Stone, Merrill Brent *lawyer*
Stone, Robert Anthony *author*
Stoney, George Cashel *film educator*
Stoopler, Mark Benjamin *physician*
Storch, Arthur *theater director*
Stork, Gilbert *chemistry educator, investigator*
Storm, Hannah *newscaster*
Storm, Jackie *nutritionist, health education specialist*
Störmer, Horst Ludwig *physicist*
Storper, David H. *bank executive*
Storr, Robert *curator, art educator*
Storrs, Immi Casagrande *sculptor*
Stotzky, Guenther *microbiologist, educator*
Strasfogel, Ian *stage director, playwright*
Strasser, Robert *architectural firm executive*
Stratakis, Christ *lawyer*
Stratas, Teresa (Anastasia Strataki) *opera singer, soprano*
Stratigos, William Narge *computer company executive*
Straton, John Charles, Jr., *investment banker*
Straub, Chester John *judge*
Straus, Oscar S., II, *foundation executive*
Strauss, Gary Joseph *lawyer*
Strauss, Peter L(estr) *law educator*
Strear, Joseph D. *public relations executive*
Streator, Edward *retired diplomat, management consultant*
Streicker, John H. *real estate company executive*
Strickon, Harvey Alan *lawyer*
Stringer, Howard *media executive*
Stroke, Hinko Henry *physicist, researcher*
Strom, Milton Gary *lawyer*
Stroman, Susan *choreographer, theater director*
Stroock, Mark Edwin, II, *public relations company executive*
Strossen, Nadine *legal association administrator, law educator*
Strubel, Deborah Weaver *think-tank associate*
Strum, Jay Gerson *lawyer*
Struve, Guy Miller *lawyer*
Stuart, Alice Melissa *lawyer*
Stuart, Lori Ames *public relations executive*
Stuart, Ned *film producer*
Stuart, Tara *international business intelligence advisor*
Stubbs, John Howell *architectural educator, preservationist*
Stübgen, Joerg-Patrick *neurologist*
Studdard, Ruben (Christopher Ruben Studdard) *singer*
Studin, Jan *publishing executive*
Stumer, Mark Bradley *lawyer, business consultant, restaurateur*
Sturman, Deborah Muscha *lawyer, columnist*
Sturtevant, Peter Mann, Jr., *television news executive*
Stutman, Leonard Jay *research scientist, cardiologist*
Subak-Sharpe, Gerald Emil *electrical engineer, educator*
Subirats, Eduardo *language educator*
Subramanian, Valavanur A. *surgeon, director, thoracic surgeon*
Suero, José Agustin *company executive*
Sugarman, Irwin J. *lawyer*
Sugarman, Robert Gary *lawyer*
Sugihara, Kenzi *publishing executive*
Sulimirski, Witold Stanislaw *banker*
Sullivan, Frank L., Jr., *real estate company executive*
Sullivan, Irene A. *lawyer*
Sullivan, Kathryn Ann *performing arts educator*
Sullivan, Larry Edward *librarian*
Sullivan, Martin J. *insurance company executive*
Sullivan, Mary Brosnahan *advocate, social services administrator*
Sultan, Mark R. *plastic surgeon*
Sultzer, Barnet Martin *microbiology and immunology researcher*
Sulzberger, Arthur Ochs *newspaper executive*
Sulzberger, Arthur Ochs, Jr., *newspaper publisher*
Summer, Sharon *marketing professional, former publisher*
Sun, Jeffrey C. *legal educator*
Sun, Tung-Tien *medical science educator*
Suraci, Patrick Joseph *clinical psychologist*
Suskind, Dennis A. *investment banker*
Susman, Sally *cosmetics executive*
Susser, Ezra Saul *psychiatry educator*
Susser, Mervyn Wilfred *epidemiologist, educator*
Susskind, Emily H. *broadcast executive*
Sussman, Alexander Ralph *lawyer*

Sussman, Gerald *publishing company executive*
Sussman, Jeffrey Bruce *public relations and marketing executive*
Sussman, Leonard Richard *foundation executive*
Sutherland, Dame Joan *retired soprano*
Sutherland, Susan J. *lawyer*
Sutton, Karen E. *administrator*
Sutton, Mark B. *diversified financial services company executive*
Suzuki, Kenji (Ken) *automotive executive*
Suzuki, Wendy A. *neural science educator*
Svenson, Charles Oscar *investment banker*
Sverdlik, Samuel Simon *physiatrist, physician*
Swain, Robert *artist*
Swan, Philip George *librarian, educator, artist*
Swan, William *actor*
Swardenski, Jay Gordon *lawyer*
Swartz, Steven R. *publishing executive*
Sweed, Phyllis *publishing executive*
Sweeney, Thomas Joseph, Jr., *lawyer*
Swid, Stephen Claar *business executive*
Swift, John Francis *retired health care advertising company executive*
Swing, William Lacy *ambassador*
Swire, James Bennett *lawyer*
Sykes, John *communications company executive*
Syler, Rene *newscaster*
Sylla, Richard Eugene *economics professor*
Symonette, Lys *foundation executive, musician, writer*
Szeto, Yvonne *architectural firm executive*
Szymanczyk, Michael *tobacco products executive*
Taaffe, Paul *utilities company executive*
Tabatsky, David *theater educator, director*
Tabbal, Nicolas G. *plastic surgeon*
Tada, Hiroshi *manufacturing executive*
Tafoya, Michele *sports reporter*
Tagliabue, Paul John *national football league commissioner*
Tagliaferri, Lee Gene *investment banker*
Tagliarino, Salvatore *set designer, educator*
Taha, Assad M. *surgeon*
Takamura, Jeanette Chiyoko *dean*
Takatsu, Ko *automotive executive*
Talbot, Phillips *Asian affairs specialist*
Talese, Gay *writer*
Talese, Nan Ahearn *publishing company executive*
Talley, Truman Macdonald *publisher*
Tallmer, Margot Sallop *psychologist, psychoanalyst, gerontologist*
Talmi, Yoav *conductor, composer*
Tamaro, George John *consulting engineer*
Tamboli, Akbar Rasul *consulting engineer*
Tamony, Katie *editor-in-chief*
Tan, Amy Ruth *writer*
Tanaka, Patrice Aiko *public relations executive*
Tancredi, Laurence Richard *law and psychiatry educator, physician*
Tanenhaus, Sam *editor*
Tannenbaum, Bernice Salpeter *national religious organization executive*
Tanner, Harold *investment banker*
Tanner, Lois *magazine editor*
Tanselle, George Thomas *English language educator, foundation executive*
Tapella, Gary Louis *manufacturing executive*
Tapia, Mario Eduardo *cultural organization administrator*
Taran, Leonardo *classicist, educator*
Tarnoff, Jerome *lawyer*
Tarnofsky-Ostroff, Dawn *broadcast executive*
Tarnopol, Michael Lazar *bank executive*
Tarr, Robert Joseph, Jr., *publishing executive, retail executive*
Tarter, Fred Barry *advertising executive*
Tauke, Thomas Joseph *telecommunications company executive, former congressman*
Tavares, Jos(é) Antonio *finance executive*
Tavel, Mark Kivey *money management company executive, economist*
Taylor, Barbara Alden *public relations executive*
Taylor, Diana Lancaster *school system administrator*
Taylor, Felicia *newscaster*
Taylor, Humphrey John Fausitt *information services executive*
Taylor, Lance Jerome *economics professor*
Taylor, Marilyn Jordan *architectural firm executive*
Taylor, Mildred D. *author*
Taylor, Paul B. *choreographer*
Taylor, Richard William *investment banker, securities broker*
Taylor, Sherril Wightman *broadcasting company executive*
Taylor, Terry R. *editor, educator*
Taylor, Willard B. *lawyer*
Taymor, Julie *theater, film and opera director and designer*
tBreslow, Esther May Greenberg *biochemistry educator, researcher*
Tehan, John Bashir *lawyer*
Teich, Howard Bernard *lawyer, activist, public affairs specialist*
Teiman, Richard B. *lawyer*
Telsey, Suzanne Lisa *lawyer*
Temin, Davia B. *marketing executive*
Temple, Donald Edward *medical association administrator*
Tendler, David *international trade company executive*
Tennant, William J. *consumer products company executive*
Teplen, Philip H. *lawyer*
Tepper, Lynn Marsha *gerontology educator*
Teren, Marc *publishing executive*
Terrell, J. Anthony *lawyer*
Terris, Lillian Dick *psychologist, association executive*
Terry, Frederick Arthur, Jr., *lawyer*
Terry, James Joseph, Jr., *lawyer*
Tesori, Jeanine *composer*
Testa, Michael Harold *lawyer*
Tester, Leonard Wayne *psychology educator*
Tetzeli, Rick *editor*
Thackeray, Jonathan E. *lawyer*
Thain, John A. *stock exchange executive*
Thalacker, Arbie Robert *lawyer, director*
Thaler, Linda Kaplan *communications executive*
Thayer, Russell, III, *airlines executive*
Thierry, Lauren *anchor*
Thoman, G. Richard *corporate and financial executive*
Thomas, Brooks *publishing company executive*
Thomas, Helen A. (Mrs. Douglas B. Cornell) *columnist, former White House correspondent*
Thomas, Isiah Lord, III, *professional sports team executive, former professional basketball coach,*
Thomas, Jeremiah Lindsay, III, *lawyer*
Thomas, Richard *actor*
Thomas, Robert Morton, Jr., *lawyer*
Thomas, Stephen Jay *anesthesiologist*
Thomas, Violeta de los Angeles *real estate broker*
Thomason, Dustin *writer*
Thomasos, Denyse *artist*
Thompson, Gary W. *public relations executive*
Thompson, Loran Tyson *lawyer*
Thompson, Martin Christian *news service executive*
Thomson, Gerald Edmund *physician, educator*
Thomson, Todd Stuart *corporate finance executive*
Thorn, Rod *professional basketball executive*
Thornburgh, Richard Edward *bank executive*
Thorne, Francis *composer*
Thornton, Yvonne Shirley *physician, author, musician*
Thoyer, Judith Reinhardt *lawyer*
Thurman, Robert *philosophy, religious studies educator*
Thurston, Sally A. *lawyer*
Tiano, Linda V. *lawyer*
Tierno, Philip Mario, Jr., *microbiologist, educator, researcher*
Tighe, Mary Ann *real estate company executive*
Tilewick, Robert *lawyer*
Tillinghast, David Rollhaus *lawyer*
Tillman, Lynne (Merrill) *writer*
Tillman, Vickie A. *diversified financial services company executive*
Tilson Thomas, Michael *symphony conductor*
Timberlake, Justin *vocalist*
Tinsley, Boyd Calvin *musician*
Tisch, Andrew Herbert *corporate executive*
Tisch, James Solomon *diversified holding company executive*
Tisch, Jonathan Mark *hotel company executive*
Tisch, Preston Robert *finance and sports executive*
Tischler, Judith Blanche *retired music publishing executive, educator*
Tishman, Danel R *entrepreneur*
Tishman, John L. *realty and construction company executive*
Titone, Vito Joseph *former state court justice*
Tizzio, Thomas Ralph *brokerage executive*
Tkacz, Virlana Maria *theater director, writer, translator*
Tobach, Ethel *retired curator*
Toben, Doreen A. *corporate financial executive*
Tober, Barbara D. (Mrs. Donald Gibbs Tober) *editor*
Tobey, Peter C. *art dealer, conservator, consultant*
Tobin, Eugene Marc *foundation administrator, retired academic administrator*
Todaro, Michael Paul *economics educator, consultant*
Todd, Andrew Christian *research scientist, consultant*
Todd, Ronald Gary *lawyer*
Toepfer, Susan Jill *editor*
Tofel, Richard Jeffrey *communication executive*
Toff, Nancy Ellen *book editor*
Toffolon, John, Jr., *investment company executive*
Tolchin, Joan Gubin *psychiatrist, educator*
Toldalagi, Marianne *foundation administrator*
Toll, Barbara Elizabeth *art gallery director*
Tom, Howard S. *company executive*
Tomkins, Calvin *writer*
Tomlinson, James Francis *retired news agency executive*
Tong, Kaity *anchor*
Toobin, Jeffrey Ross *writer, legal analyst*
Toohey, Edward Joseph *financial services company executive, retired*
Tooker, George *artist*
Toote, Gloria E. A. *real estate developer, lawyer, columnist*
Toppeta, William John *insurance company executive, lawyer*
Torchin, Mimi *periodical editor*
Torn, Rip (Elmore Rual Torn Jr.) *actor, director*
Torrenzano, Richard *public affairs executive*
Torres, Dalys E. *music educator, consultant*
Torres, Jacques *food service executive*
Tortolani, Anthony John *surgeon, educator*
Tortora, Leslie C. *finance company executive*
Toulantis, Marie *retail executive*
Toumey, Donald Joseph *lawyer*
Tourlitsas, John Constantine *radiologist*
Toussaint, Allen Richard *recording studio executive, composer, pianist*
Tovey, Joseph *investment banker*
Towbin, A(braham) Robert *investment banker*
Townsend, Alair Ane *publisher, municipal official*
Townsend, Charles H. *publishing executive*
Townsend, Kathleen Kennedy *former lieutenant governor*
Toy, Stephen J. *corporate financial executive*
Tozer, Elizabeth Farran *interior and floral designer*
Tozer, W. James, Jr., *investment company executive*
Trachtenberg, Matthew J. *bank executive*
Tract, Marc Mitchell *lawyer*
Trager, William *biology professor*
Train, John *investment counselor, writer, government official*
Trammell, Joseph Emanuel *small business owner, media consultant*
Tramontine, John Orlando *retired lawyer*
Trapp, Peter Jarl Rudolf *portfolio manager, farmer*
Traub, J(oseph) F(rederick) *computer scientist, educator*
Trauthwein, Christina *editor-in-chief*
Traverso, Anthony A. *lawyer*
Travis, Jeremy *academic administrator*
Treadway, James Curran Erik Corbett *lawyer, investment company executive, former government official*
Tree, Michael *violinist, violist, educator*
Treitel, David Henry *financial consultant*
Trent, Charles H., Jr., *social work educator*
Trillin, Calvin *writer, journalist*
Trinkaus, John William *management educator*
Trippi, Peter *museum director*
Tritter, Daniel F. *lawyer, writer*
Trivisonno, Nicholas Louis *communications company executive, accountant*
Trueblood, Emily Herrick *artist, librarian*
Truesdell, Walter George *minister, librarian*
Trujillo, Robert *musician*
Trump, Martha Lindley Blaine Beard *philanthropist*
Tsai, Cynthia Ekberg *entertainment executive*
Tsai, James C. *ophthalmologist, researcher*
Tsao, Vivian J. *artist, educator*
Tscherny, George *graphic designer*
Tschumi, Bernard *architect*
Tse, Charles Yung Chang *pharmaceutical executive, lawyer*
Tsividis, Yannis P. *electrical engineering educator*
Tsoucalas, Nicholas *federal judge*
Tucker, Alan David *publisher*
Tucker, Allan Marc *mastering engineer*
Tucker, Diane Straus *publishing executive*
Tucker, Lawrence C. *investment company executive*
Tuckwell, Barry Emmanuel *musician, music educator*
Tudryn, Joyce Marie *professional society administrator*
Tulchin, David Bruce *lawyer*
Turino, Gerard Michael *physician, medical scientist, educator*
Turley, James S. *corporate financial executive*
Turner, Alice Kennedy *editor*
Turner, E. Deane *lawyer*
Turner, Megan Whalen *author*
Turner, Patrick Noel Waddington *fund manager*
Turro, Nicholas John *chemistry professor*
Turso, Vito Anthony *government and public affairs executive*
Turturro, Aida *actress*
Turturro, John *actor*
Tusiani, Joseph *foreign language educator, author*
Tuttle, Ashley *dancer*
Tutwiler, Margaret DeBardeleben *stock exchange executive, former federal agency administrator*
Twiname, John Dean *minister, human services administrator*
Tyler, Dana *anchor*
Tyson, Neil DeGrasse *museum director*
Tzimas, Nicholas Achilles *orthopedic surgeon, educator*
Uchitelle, Louis *journalist*
Uggams, Leslie *entertainer*
Uhry, Alfred Fox *playwright*
Ule, Guy Maxwell, Jr., *stockbroker*
Ulrich, Lars *drummer*
Umansky, Diane *publishing executive*
Umeh, Marie Arlene *English language educator*
Underberg, Mark Alan *lawyer*
Underhill, Jacob Berry, III, *retired insurance company executive*
Ungaro, Susan Kelliher *magazine editor*
Unger, Irwin *historian, educator*
Unger, Peter Kenneth *philosophy educator*
Unruh, Richard Greenwood, III, *artist*
Updike, Helen Hill *investment manager, financial advisor*
Uppman, Theodor *concert and opera singer, voice educator*
Upright, Diane Warner *art dealer*
Upson, Stuart Barnard *advertising agency executive*
Uram, Gerald Robert *lawyer*
Urban, Amanda (Binky Urban) *literary agent*
Urdang, Alexandra *book publishing executive*
Urena, Alex *chef*
Urkowitz, Michael *bank executive*
Urowsky, Richard J. *lawyer*
Urroz-Rapold, Patricia Julia S. *retired diplomat, writer*
Urstadt, Charles Deane *real estate executive*
Vachss, Andrew Henry *lawyer, writer, juvenile justice and child abuse consultant*
Valbuena, Vivian *brokerage house executive*
Valenstein, Suzanne Gebhart *art historian*
Valente, Peter Charles *lawyer*
Valletta, Amber *model*
Van Bellinghen III, Julian *composer, writer, actor, film company executive*
Van de Bovenkamp, Sue Erpf *charitable organization executive*
Vanden Heuvel, Katrina *magazine editor*
Vanderbeek, Jeffrey *diversified financial services company executive*
Van Dine, Vance *investment banker*
Vandross, Luther *singer*
Van Etten, Peter Walbridge *foundation executive*
Van Halen, Eddie *guitarist, rock musician*
van Hengel, Maarten *banker*
Vanni, Robert John *lawyer*
Van Saun, Bruce *bank executive*
Varet, Michael A. *lawyer*
Vargas, Martha *government liaison*
Varmus, Harold Eliot *former health science association administrator, research scientist, health facility executive, educator*
Varney, Carleton Bates, Jr., *interior designer, columnist, educator*
Vass, Joan *apparel designer*
Vassallo, Edward E. *lawyer*
Vassil, John Charles *lawyer*
Vaughan, Edwin Darracott, Jr., *urologist, surgeon*
Vaughan, Linda *publishing executive*
Veasey, Eugene Norman *lawyer, retired state supreme court chief justice*
Vedder, Eddie *singer*
Vega, Matias Alfonso *lawyer*
Velayo, Richard Soriano *psychologist, educator, researcher*
Velshi, Ali *news correspondent*
Vendela, *model*
Verdol, Joseph Arthur *chemist*
Verme, Alberto J. *investment banker*
Vermeer, Maureen Dorothy *sales executive*
Vernon, Darryl Mitchell *lawyer*
Versfelt, David Scott *lawyer*
Vick, Edward Hoge, Jr., *advertising executive*
Vick, James Albert *publishing executive, consultant*
Vickers, Marcia *journalist*
Victor, A. Paul *lawyer*
Victor, Jack *former health association executive, consultant*
Vidal, David Jonathan *insurance company executive, journalist*
Vidal, Gore *writer*
Vidler, Anthony *architecture educator, dean*
Vieira, Meredith *television personality*
Viener, John D. *lawyer*
Vig, Vernon Edward *lawyer*
Viktora, Richard Emil *lawyer*
Vilcek, Jan Tomas *immunologist, medical educator*
Vilchez, Ricardo S. *library supervisor*
Villela, Daniel Antunes Maciel *electrical engineer, researcher*
Viniar, David *investment banker*
Virtue, Ted *investment company executive*
Vitkowsky, Vincent Joseph *lawyer*
Vittor, Kenneth Mark *lawyer*
Vitz, Paul Clayton *psychologist, educator*
Vladeck, Bruce Charney *health services administrator, policy educator*
Vladeck, Judith Pomarlen *lawyer*
Vlamis, Susan (Suzanne) Anne *editor, photographer*
Vogel, Howard Stanley *lawyer*
Vogelman, Joseph Herbert *scientific engineering company executive*
Vogelstein, John L. *venture capitalist*
Volk, Kristin *advertising agency executive*
Volk, Norman Hans *financial executive*
Volk, Stephen Richard *diversified financial services company executive, investment banker, lawyer*
Volpe, Joseph *opera company general manager*
von Baillou, Astrid *executive search consultant*
Von Betzen, Valerie *artist*
von Fraunhofer-Kosinski, Katherina *bank executive*
Vongerichten, Jean-Georges *food service executive*
von Knorring, Henrik Johan *publisher*
von Mehren, Robert Brandt *retired lawyer*
Vonnegut, Kurt, Jr., *writer*
Von Stade, Frederica *mezzo-soprano*
Voorsanger, Bartholomew *architect*
Vrancik, Barbara A. *lawyer*
Vural, Volkan *Turkish representative to UN*
Wachsman, Harvey Frederick *lawyer, neurosurgeon*
Wachtel, Norman Jay *lawyer*
Wackermann, William *publishing executive*
Wadsworth, Oliver *actor, playwright*
Wages, Robert Coleman *equity investor*
Wagner, Alan Cyril *television and film producer, consultant, performing arts educator*
Wagner, Barry J. *lawyer*
Wailand, George *lawyer*
Wainwright, Carroll Livingston, Jr., *lawyer*
Waite, David Allen *software development executive*
Waks, Jay Warren *lawyer*
Waksman, Byron Halsted *neuroimmunologist, experimental pathologist, educator, medical association administrator*
Wald, Bernard Joseph *lawyer*
Wald, Richard Charles *broadcasting executive*
Wald, Sylvia *artist*
Walden, Janet C. *lawyer*
Walden, Shelton Harrison *radio personality, educator*
Waldhorn, Arthur *literature educator, researcher, scriptwriter*
Waldman, Seymour Morton *lawyer*
Walke, David Michael *business advisory, consulting and research executive*
Walker, Alice *writer*
Walker, Jeffrey Clemens *venture capitalist*
Walker, Jennie Louise *not-for-profit fundraiser, consultant*
Walker, Kara *artist*
Walker, Mort *cartoonist*
Walker, Robert Harris *historian, writer, editor*
Walker, Sally Barbara *retired glass company executive*
Walkowitz, Daniel Jay *historian, filmmaker, educator*
Wall, Charles R. *lawyer*
Wall, Duane *lawyer*
Wallace, Carol *editor at large*
Wallace, Daniel *writer*
Wallace, Joyce Irene Malakoff *internist*
Wallace, Ken *magazine publisher*
Wallace, Michele *media company executive*
Wallace, Mike *television interviewer and reporter*
Wallace, Nora Ann *lawyer*
Wallace, Thomas C(hristopher) *editor, literary agent*
Wallace, Walter C. *lawyer, government official*
Wallach, Eli *actor*
Wallach, Eric Jean *lawyer*
Wallach, Robert Charles *obstetrician, gynecologist, educator*
Wallance, Gregory J. *lawyer*
Waller, Robert James *writer*
Walpin, Gerald *lawyer*
Walsh, Annmarie Hauck *research firm executive*
Walter, Ingo *economics professor*
Walters, Barbara Ann *television journalist*
Walters, Milton James *investment banker*
Walton, Anthony John (Tony Walton) *theater and film designer, book illustrator*
Walton, R. Keith *academic administrator, lawyer*
Waltuck, David *chef, restaurant owner*
Walzer, Judith Borodovko *academic administrator, educator*
Wanek, William Charles *public relations executive*
Wang, Albert Huai-En *lawyer*
Wang, Frederick Mark *pediatric ophthalmologist, medical educator*
Wang, John *not-for-profit company executive*
Wang, Lu-Hai *medical educator, scientist, researcher*
Wang, Vera *fashion designer*
Wank, Gerald Sidney *periodontist, educator*
Wanner, Eric *foundation executive*
Ward, Geoffrey Champion *author, editor*
Ward, Sarah M. *lawyer*
Warden, John L. *lawyer*
Wardropper, Ian Bruce *museum curator, educator*
Ware, Alberta *minister, educator*
Wareham, Raymond Noble *investment professional*
Waren, Stanley Arnold *university administrator, theatre and arts center administrator, director*
Waricha, Joan *publishing executive*
Warner, Douglas Alexander, III, *banker*
Warner, Miner Hill *investment banker*
Warner, Peter David *publishing executive*
Warner, Rawleigh, Jr., *oil company executive*
Warren, David P. *stock exchange executive*
Warren, Peter *advertising executive*
Warren, William Bradford *lawyer*
Warrick, Ruth *actress*
Warshauer, Irene C. *lawyer*
Warshawsky, Stanford Seymour *investment banker*
Warwick, Dionne *singer*
Washburn, David Thacher *lawyer*
Washburn, Joan Thomas *business owner, art gallery director*
Washington, Clarence Edward, Jr., *insurance company executive*
Wasow, Omar *reporter*
Wasser, Henry *retired American literature and sociology educator*
Wasserman, Albert *film producer, writer, director*
Wasserstein, Bruce *investment banker*
Wasserstein, Wendy *playwright*
Wastberg, Olle M. *diplomat*
Watanabe, Roy Noboru *lawyer*
Waterhouse, Stephen Lee *management consultant*
Waters, Crystal *vocalist, songwriter*

Waters, Donald Joseph information services administrator
Waters, Sylvia dance company artistic director
Watkins, Charles Booker, Jr., mechanical engineering educator
Watson, Anthony L. health facility executive
Watson, Marlan reporter
Watson, Richard Allen lawyer
Watson, Solomon Brown, IV, lawyer, business executive
Watt, Douglas (Benjamin Watt) writer, critic
Wattleton, Faye (Alyce Faye Wattleton) research and education institute administrator, advocate
Watts, André concert pianist
Watts, David Eide lawyer
Wauford, J. Ben. architect
Wax, David Louis corporate financial executive
Waxman, Anita producer
Wayne, Andrew Mark diversified financial services company executive
Wearne, Susan L mathematical biology research scientist
Weaver, John Borland organist, composer
Webb, William H. consumer products company executive
Weber, Alan J. insurance company executive
Weber, Lisa M. insurance company executive
Weber, Mark clothing company executive
Weber, Robert Maxwell cartoonist
Webster, Lesley Daniels bank executive
Wechsler, Gil lighting designer
Wedgeworth, Ann actress
Weeks, Brigitte publishing executive
Weems, Carrie Mae photographer
Weese, Miranda dancer
Weg, Kenneth E. pharmaceutical executive
Wegleitner, Mark A. telecommunications industry executive
Weida, Lewis Dixon marketing analyst, consultant
Weiksner, Sandra S. lawyer
Weil, Frank A. investment banker, lawyer
Weiland, Andrew J. orthopaedic surgeon
Weiland, Scott Richard singer
Weiler, Joseph law educator
Weil-Garris Brandt, Kathleen (Kathleen Brandt) art historian
Weill, Sanford I. bank executive
Wein, George Theodore music festivals producer, pianist, singer
Weinbaum, Sheldon biomedical engineer
Weinberg, Adam D. museum director
Weinberg, H. Barbara art historian, educator, curator
Weinberg, Herschel Mayer lawyer
Weinberg, Jeffrey Mitchell dermatologist, researcher
Weinberg, John Livingston investment banker
Weinberger, Harold Paul lawyer
Weiner, Andrew Jay lawyer
Weiner, Earl David lawyer
Weiner, Edward G. export company executive
Weiner, Lawrence Charles artist
Weiner, Ronald Gary accounting firm executive
Weiner, Stephen Arthur lawyer
Weiner, Walter Herman banker, lawyer
Weingarten, Rhonda lawyer
Weingrow, Howard L. financial executive, investor
Weinreb, Tzvi Hersh religious organization administrator, rabbi
Weinrich, Johnathan Edward lawyer
Weinschel, Alan Jay lawyer
Weinshenker, Naomi Joyce clinical psychiatrist, educator, researcher
Weinstein, Ellen performing company executive
Weinstein, George William retired ophthalmology educator
Weinstein, Harvey film company executive, film producer
Weinstein, Herbert chemical engineer, educator
Weinstein, I. Bernard oncologist, director, geneticist, educator
Weinstein, Martin aerospace manufacturing executive, materials scientist
Weinstein, Robert film company executive
Weinstein, Sidney retired university program director
Weinstein, Todd Jay photographer
Weinstock, David Marc bone marrow transplantation and infectious diseases physician, researcher
Weinstock, Leonard lawyer
Weintz, Jacob Frederick, Jr., retired investment banker
Weisbrod, Carl lawyer, public official
Weisenburger, Randall J. retired company executive
Weisl, Edwin Louis, Jr., foundation executive, lawyer
Weiss, Barry recording industry executive
Weiss, Donald S. real estate developer
Weiss, Jonathan Arthur lawyer
Weiss, Lawrence N. lawyer
Weiss, Mark public relations executive
Weiss, Melvyn I. lawyer
Weiss, Myrna Grace management consultant
Weiss, Paul Richard plastic surgeon
Weiss, Phillip W. social worker, writer
Weiss, Samuel Abraham psychologist, psychoanalyst
Weissler, Fran theatrical producer
Weissman, Morris printing company executive
Weissman, Myrna M. epidemiologist, researcher, medical educator
Weissmann, Gerald internist, medical educator, researcher, writer, editor
Weitz, Harvey lawyer, educator
Welch, Martha Grace physician, researcher
Weld, Jonathan Minot lawyer
Wellin, Keith Sears investment banker
Wellington, Harry Hillel lawyer, educator
Wellington, Sheila Wacks foundation administrator, psychiatry educator
Wellisz, Stanislaw economics professor
Wells, Linda Ann editor-in-chief
Wells, Peter Scoville retired marketing executive
Welsh, Donald Emory publisher
Wen, George Walter Sun editor
Wender, Ira Tensard lawyer
Wender, Phyllis Bellows literary agent
Wendlandt, Gary E. insurance company executive
Wenegrat, Saul S. arts administrator, art educator, consultant
Wenner, Jann Simon editor, publisher
Werfelman, William Herman, Jr., public relations executive
Werman, David Sanford psychiatrist, psychoanalyst, educator
Werner, Robert L. lawyer, consultant
Werthamer, Nathan Richard physicist
Wesely, Edwin Joseph lawyer
Wesley, John Mercer artist
Wesley, Richard C. federal judge
West, Alexander Brian pathologist
West, Betsy broadcast executive
West, Blair investment banker, consultant
West, James Reyenard dance educator, health educator
West, Paul Noden author, playwright
West, Stephen Kingsbury lawyer, director
Westheimer, Ruth Siegel (Karola Westheimer) psychologist, television personality
Wetschler, Ed editor
Wexelbaum, Michael lawyer
Wexler, Allan architect, art educator
Wexler, Nancy Sabin clinical neuropsychology educator
Wexler, Patricia Susan dermatologist, surgeon
Wharton, Danny Carroll zoo biologist
Wharton, Ralph Nathaniel psychiatrist, educator
Wheatley, Steven Charles educational association administrator
Whitaker, Mark Theis magazine editor
Whitcomb, James Howard, Jr., investment banker
White, Harry Edward, Jr., lawyer
White, John Patrick lawyer
White, Kate editor-in-chief
White, Lawrence J. economics professor
White, Lillias actress
White, Roger L., Jr., graphic designer, art director
White, Russell publishing executive
Whitehead, Colson writer
Whitehead, Edgar Douglas urology educator
Whitehead, John Cunningham bank executive, diplomat, philanthropist
Whitehead, William J. advertising executive
Whitehouse, Anne Cherner writer
Whiteman, Douglas E. publisher
Whiting, Anthony executive search consultant
Whiting, Gordon James investment banker
Whitman, Martin J. portfolio manager
Whitmer, Frederick Lee lawyer
Whitney, Craig Richard journalist
Whitney, Phyllis Ayame author
Whittemore, Laurence Frederick private banker
Whittingham, Charles Arthur publisher, library administrator
Whitty, Jeff playwright, actor
Whoriskey, Robert Donald lawyer
Wibisono, Makarim diplomat
Wick, Tamara photographer, artist, writer
Widlund, Olof Bertil computer science educator
Wiegley, Roger Douglas lawyer
Wiener, Arthur C. textiles executive
Wiener, Marvin S. rabbi, editor, executive
Wiener, Solomon writer, consultant, former city official
Wiesel, Torsten Nils neurobiologist, educator
Wiesenthal, Robert S. corporate financial executive
Wiggers, Charlotte Suzanne Ward magazine editor
Wigley, Mark Antony architecture educator
Wigmore, Barrie Atherton investment banker
Wijnberg, Sandra S. professional services company executive
Wilcox, John Caven lawyer, corporate consultant
Wilcox, T.J. filmmaker
Wildes, Leon lawyer, educator
Wilds, Bonnie author, community volunteer
Wile, Joan composer, lyricist, singer
Wilford, John Noble, Jr., science news correspondent
Wilhjelm, Christian conductor, artist
Wilkens, Leonard Randolph, Jr., (Lenny Wilkens) professional basketball coach
Wilkins, Amy P. publishing executive
Wilkinson, John Hart lawyer
Will, Alfred Joseph lawyer
Willett, Roslyn Leonore public relations executive, food service consultant, writer
Willett Bird, Susan public and motivational speaker
Williams, Christopher investment company executive
Williams, Dave Harrell investment executive
Williams, Lena sportswriter
Williams, Lucinda country musician
Williams, Michael G. publishing executive
Williams, Milton Lawrence judge, educator
Williams, Montel television talk show host
Williams, Pharrell music producer, arranger, vocalist
Williams, Simon diversified financial services company executive
Williams, Sue artist
Williams, Terrie Michelle publicity agency executive
Williams, Vanessa recording artist, actress
Williamson, Douglas Franklin, Jr., lawyer
Williamson, Richard Salisbury ambassador
Willis, Beverly Ann architect
Willis, Carol museum director
Willis, Gerri news correspondent
Willis, John Alvin editor
Willis, Thornton Wilson painter
Willis, William Ervin lawyer
Willumstad, Robert B. bank executive
Wils, Madelyn film company executive
Wilson, August playwright
Wilson, Cassandra singer
Wilson, Edwin theater critic, educator
Wilson, Fred retail executive
Wilson, Marie C. foundation administrator
Wilson, Pamela K. corporate financial executive
Wilson, Paul Holliday, Jr., lawyer
Wilson, Robert Frank graphics designer, property manager
Wilson, Stephen R. financial infromation executive
Winawer, Sidney J. physician, clinical investigator, educator
Windels, Paul, Jr., lawyer
Windhager, Erich Ernst physiologist, educator
Winfield, Richard Neill lawyer
Wing, John Russell lawyer
Winick, Myron educator, physician
Winkler, Matthew Adam editor-in-chief, reporter, editor
Winn, H. Richard surgeon
Winship, Frederick Moery journalist
Winslade, Thomas Edwin lawyer
Winston, Mary A. publishing executive
Winterer, Philip Steele lawyer
Winters, Robert Wayne medical educator, pediatrician, healthcare executive
Winters, Terry artist
Wintour, Anna editor
Wintrob, Jay S. insurance company executive
Wise, Aaron Noah lawyer
Wisner, Frank George insurance company executive, former ambassador
Wit, Harold Maurice investment banker, lawyer, investor
Witherell, Mary editor
Witkin, Eric Douglas lawyer
Witmer, Richard H. investment company executive
Witmeyer, John Jacob, III, lawyer
Wittes, Robert E. physician, science foundation director
Wittstein, Edwin Frank stage and film production designer
Witzel, Steven M. lawyer
Wixom, Max Valentine artist
Wixom, William David art historian, museum administrator, educator
Wogan, Robert broadcasting company executive
Wohl, Frank Harold lawyer
Wolf, Abe hotel executive
Wolf, Carl F.W. physician, biomedical engineer
Wolf, James Anthony insurance company executive
Wolf, Peter Michael investment manager, writer
Wolfe, George C. theater director, producer, playwright
Wolfe, James Ronald lawyer
Wolfe, Melinda Beth human resources executive
Wolfe, Scott W. orthopedic hand surgeon
Wolfe, Thomas Kennerly, Jr., writer, journalist
Wolff, Edward Nathan economist, educator
Wolff, Jesse David lawyer
Wolff, Margaret Louise lawyer
Wolff, Richard Joseph public relations executive, consultant, historian
Wolff, Virginia Euwer writer
Wolff, William F., III, investment banker
Wolff, William I. surgeon, educator
Wolkoff, Eugene Arnold lawyer
Wollan, Eugene lawyer
Wollman, Eric lawyer
Wolman, William economist, journalist, broadcaster
Wolnek, Stephen S. religious organization administrator
Wolper, Allan journalist, educator
Wolson, Craig Alan lawyer
Wong, B.D. actor
Wong, Y. S. diversified financial services company executive
Wood, David Clarence lawyer
Wood, Jerry investment company executive
Wood, Joshua Warren, III, lawyer, alternative dispute resolution executive
Wood, Kimba M. judge
Wood, Ronald musician
Woodruff, Jay Noel editor, writer
Woodruff, Mark Reed magazine editor
Woods, Dan information technology manager, consultant
Woods, Emily apparel executive
Woods, Robert Evans, Jr., banker
Woods, Ward Wilson, Jr., investment company executive
Wood-Smith, Donald plastic surgeon
Woodward, Joanne Gignilliat actress
Worenklein, Jacob Joshua lawyer
Worman, Howard Jay internist, educator
Worsham, Hal Glenn marketing professional
Wortman, Richard S. historian, educator
Wössner, Mark Matthias retired publishing company executive
Wray, Cecil, Jr., lawyer
Wren, Gayden playwright, theater director
Wren, John D. advertising executive
Wright, Douglas playwright
Wright, Faith-dorian artist
Wright, Gwendolyn art center director, writer, educator
Wright, Jason H. communications executive
Wright, Joseph Robert, Jr., corporate executive
Wright, Margaret Taylor marketing consultant, publisher
Wright, Sarah Elizabeth writer, poet
Wright, Steven comedian
Wriston, Walter Bigelow bank executive, director
Wrobel, Bruce J. energy and utilities company executive
Wrubel, Barbara lawyer, educator, former editor
Wu, Robin Chi Ching lawyer
Wu, Sarah Zheng investment banker
WuDunn, Sheryl journalist, correspondent
Wulf, Melvin Lawrence lawyer
Wunderman, Jan Darcourt artist
Wuorinen, Charles Peter composer
Wurmfeld, Sanford artist, educator
Wyckoff, E. Lisk, Jr., lawyer
Wyeth, James Browning artist
Wylde, Kathryn S. business organization executive
Wylie, James Malcolm adult education educator
Wyn-Jones, Alun (William Wyn-Jones) software developer, mathematician
Wyschogrod, Edith philosophy educator
Wyse, Lois advertising executive
Wyss, David Alen financial service executive
Wyzner, Eugeniusz diplomat
Xia, Lulin private equity investor
Yaffe, James writer
Yahalom, Joachim radiologist, educator, oncologist, researcher
Yalen, Gary N. retired insurance company executive
Yamaguchi, Masaya musician, educator
Yamin, Michael Geoffrey lawyer
Yancey, Richard Charles investment banker
Yao, David Da-Wei engineering educator
Yapijakis, Constantine environmental engineer, educator, consultant
Yastine, Barbara A. diversified financial services company executive
Yegulalp, Tuncel M. mining engineer, educator
Yeh, Hsu-Chong radiology educator
Yeh, Ming-Neng obstetrician, gynecologist
Yelenick, Mary Therese lawyer
Yellin, Victor Fell composer, music educator
Yerman, Fredric Warren lawyer
Yerushalmi, Yosef Hayim historian, educator
Yetman, Gary investment company executive
Yetman, Leith Eleanor academic administrator
Yeung, Wei-Jun Jean research scientist
Yglesias, Helen Bassine author, educator
Yodowitz, Edward Jay lawyer
Yoffie, Erich H. religious organization administrator
Yohay, Steven Jacob healthcare company executive, consultant
Yorinks, Arthur children's author, writer, director
Young, Alice lawyer
Young, Bruce K. obstetrician, gynecologist, educator
Young, Estelle Irene dermatologist, educator
Young, Genevieve Leman publishing executive, editor
Young, George Haywood, III, investment banker
Young, John Edward lawyer
Young, Michael Warren geneticist, educator
Young, Robert Craig banker
Young, Steve correspondent, anchor
Young, William F. legal educator
Younger, Stephen P. lawyer
Youngwood, Alfred Donald lawyer
Yu, Andrew minister
Yu, Pauline Ruth former dean, educational association administrator
Yu, Yi-Hao endocrinologist, educator, physician, research scientist
Yurchenco, Henrietta Weiss ethnomusicologist, writer
Yurt, Roger William surgeon, educator
Zachem, Tyler investment company executive
Zackheim, Adrian Walter editor
Zagat, Nina publishing executive
Zagat, Tim publishing executive
Zahnd, Richard H. professional sports executive, lawyer
Zaitzeff, Roger Michael lawyer
Zamarra, Galen chef
Zammit, Joseph Paul lawyer
Zand, Dale Ezra business management educator
Zanetti, Richard Joseph publisher
Zarghami, Cyma broadcast executive
Zatlin, Gabriel Stanley physician
Zauderer, Mark Carl lawyer
Zawistowski, Stephen Louis psychologist, educator
Zedrosser, Joseph John lawyer
Zeitlin, Jide James investment banker
Zeldin, Richard Packer publisher
Zelin, Madeleine think-tank executive
Zelnick, Strauss entertainment company executive
Zerin, Steven David lawyer
Zerman, Melvyn Bernard publishing company executive, author
Zeuschner, Erwin Arnold investment advisory company executive
Zevon, Susan Jane editor
Zha, Jianying writer, educator
Ziegler, Henry Steinway lawyer
Ziegler, John Augustus, Jr., lawyer
Zifchak, William C. lawyer
Zimand, Harvey Folks lawyer
Zimmerman, Kathleen Marie artist
Zimmerman, Michael agricultural products, grain company executive
Zimmerman, Sol Shea pediatrician
Zimmerman, William Edwin newspaper editor, publisher, writer
Zimmett, Mark Paul lawyer, educator
Zinczenko, David publishing executive
Zinder, Norton David genetics educator, university dean
Zinn, Keith Marshall ophthalmologist, educator
Zirinsky, Susan television producer
Zissu, Michael Jerome lawyer
Zissu, Roger L. lawyer
Zitrin, Arthur physician
Zivin, Norman H. lawyer
Zoogman, Nicholas Jay lawyer
Zornow, David M. lawyer
Zotos, Frederic P. research and development company executive
Zuccotti, John Eugene real estate company executive
Zuck, Alfred Christian consulting mechanical engineer
Zucker, Stefan tenor, writer, editor, radio broadcaster
Zucker-Franklin, Dorothea internist, educator
Zuckerman, Mortimer Benjamin publisher, editor, real estate developer
Zuckerman, Paul Herbert lawyer
Zugazagoitia, Julian museum director
Zukerman, Michael lawyer
Zukerman, Pinchas concert violinist, violist, conductor
Zwickler, Allen investment advisor, educator
Zwillenberg, Paul management consultant

Newark

Hemmings, Madeleine Blanchet management consultant, not-for-profit administrator, media consultant
Reid, James Edward lawyer

Newburgh

Adams, Barbara English language educator, poet, writer
Begley, Vincent Joseph writer, educator
Conner, Susan elementary school educator
Grossman, Stanley Lawrence surgeon
Joyce, Mary Ann principal
Liberth, Richard Francis lawyer
Ochs, Richard Wayne artist, gallery owner
Sakac, Sister Ann academic administrator
Seliga, Charles G. airport administrator
Severo, Richard writer
Weintraub, Arthur E. health service association executive
Zarutskie, Andrew John town official
Zeisel, Laura lawyer, educator, environmental council

Newcomb

Chatzky, Herbert music educator

Newfield

Rawlings, Hunter Ripley, III, academic administrator, classicist

Newport

Wilson, Eldon Ray minister

Newtonville

Conroy-LaCivita, Diane Catherine city administrator

Niagara Falls

Anton, Ronald David lawyer
Askins, Arthur James accountant, finance management and auditing executive

Zhang, Tianxi *research scientist, researcher*

Poughkeepsie
Bari, Paola *application developer*
Bartlett, Lynn Conant *English literature educator*
Beck, Curt Werner *chemist, educator*
Berlin, Doris Ada *psychiatrist*
Bjork, Christopher Brian *education educator*
Bodack, Mark Peter *physician, medical educator*
Brakas, Nora Jachym *education educator*
Carino, Aurora Lao *psychiatrist, hospital administrator*
Chu, Richard Chao-Fan *mechanical engineer*
Conklin, Donald David *academic administrator*
Daniels, Elizabeth Adams *English language educator*
Deiters, Sister Joan Adele *psychoanalyst, nun, chemistry educator*
Dolan, Thomas Joseph *judge*
Fergusson, Frances Daly *college president, educator*
Glasse, John Howell *retired philosophy and theology educator*
Gold, Burton *real estate developer*
Griffen, Clyde Chesterman *retired history educator*
Hadaller, David Lawrence *dean*
Hansraj, Kenneth Karamchand *surgeon, research scientist*
Harmelink, Herman, III, *minister, writer, religious studies educator*
Heller, Mary Bernita *psychotherapist*
Henley, Richard James *health facility administrator*
Hytier, Adrienne Doris *French language educator*
Jackson, Judy Faye *academic administrator*
Johnson, M(aurice) Glen *political science educator*
Katopis, George A. *electrical engineer*
Kelley, David Christopher *philosopher*
Kim, David Sang Chul *publishing executive, evangelist, retired academic administrator*
Lang, William Warner *physicist*
Logue, Joseph Carl *electronics engineer, consultant*
Mack, John Edward, III, *utility company executive*
McCormack, Dan *photographer, educator*
Merrell, James Hart *history educator*
Millett, Kate (Katherine Murray Millett) *political activist, sculptor, artist, writer*
Moon, Seungsook *sociologist, educator*
Opdycke, Leonard Emerson *retired elementary, secondary and college-level educator, publisher*
Ostertag, Robert Louis *lawyer*
Peck, H. Daniel *literature educator*
Pliskin, William Aaron *physicist*
Rashid, Ismail O. D. *historian, educator*
Rosenblatt, Albert Martin *state appeals court judge*
Sharp, Ronald Alan *English literature educator, dean, author*
Shatz, Phillip *lawyer*
Sherman, Ethan *contractor, publisher*
Simons, Robert Edward *mechanical engineer, consultant*
Slade, Bernard Newton *electronics company executive*
Taphorn, Joseph Bernard *lawyer*
Teal, Arabella W. *lawyer, former state attorney general*
Trumbetta, Susan L. *psychology educator*
Turgeon, Paul R. *computer program manager*
VanBuren, Denise Doring *corporate communications executive*
Van Zanten, Frank Veldhuyzen *retired library system director*
Willard, Nancy Margaret *writer, educator*
Wilson, Richard Edward *composer, pianist, music educator*

Poughquag
LaRussa, Joseph Anthony *optical company executive*

Pound Ridge
Bennett, Edward Henry *reinsurance executive*
Darcy, Keith Thomas *finance company executive, educator*
Ferro, Walter *artist*
Sacco, John Michael *accountant*
Schwebel, Renata Manasse *sculptor*
Webb, Richard Gilbert *financial executive, antique selling service executive*

Purchase
Akers, John Fellows *retired information processing company executive*
Andrews, David Ralph *lawyer*
Bannon, Nancy *performing arts educator*
Black, Leon David *private investment firm executive*
Bridgman, Peter Alwyn *beverage company executive*
Carey, Albert P. *retail sales professional*
DeMond, Jeffrey Stuart *cable television and telecommunications executive*
Ehrman, Lee *geneticist, educator*
Eisenstein, Joshua J. *paper company executive*
Enrico, Roger A. *soft drink company executive*
Faraci, John Vincent, Jr., *paper company executive*
Finnerty, Louise Hoppe *beverage and food company executive*
Frost, Elizabeth Ann McArthur *physician*
Gioffre, Bruno Joseph *lawyer*
Hanft, Noah Jonathan *lawyer*
Kelly, Edmund Joseph *lawyer, bank executive, investment banker*
Lacy, Bill *academic administrator, architect*
Magaziner, Elliot Albert *musician, conductor, educator*
McKenna, Matthew Morgan *lawyer*
Mizelle, Dary John *composer, educator*
Moore, Margaret D. *human resources specialist*
Newton, Esther Mary *anthropologist, educator*
Noonan, Frank Russell *business executive*
Nooyi, Indra K. *food products company executive*
Nowell, Lionel L. *food products executive*
Parrs, Marianne M. *paper and lumber company executive*
Phillips, Carly *writer*
Reinemund, Steven S. *food products executive*
Rodkin, Gary M. *beverage company executive*
Ryan, Edward W. *economics professor*
Thompson, Peter M. *retired food products executive*
Vardin, Patricia Anne *education educator*
Wallach, Ira David *lawyer, business executive*
Wepner, Shelley Beth *education educator, software developer*
White, Michael Dennis *food manufacturing company executive*
Wright, David L. *food and beverage company executive*
Xiao, Shuyi *finance company executive*

Putnam Valley
Amram, David Werner *composer, conductor, musician*

Queens
Geffner, Donna Sue *speech pathology/audiology services professional, audiologist, educator*
Kreisler, Rochelle *psychologist*
Singh, Ronald *social sciences educator, researcher*

Queens Village
Chowdhury, Mohammed Shamsul *economics professor*
Clark, Barbara Marlene *state legislator*
Cook, Michael Anthony *financial services executive*
Maroney-Davoren, Danette Edna *pharmacist, writer, publishing executive*

Queensbury
Bitner, William Lawrence, III, *retired banker, educator*
Cavaluzzi, Anthony David *English studies educator*
De Pan, Harry McCarthy *retired surgeon*

Quogue
Hines, William Eugene *banker*

Red Hook
Altshuler, Miriam R. *literary agent*
Fitzpatrick, John *poet*
Pfeiffer, Werner Bernhard *artist, educator*

Rego Park
Cortese, Edward *marketing and public relations executive*
Manton, Thomas Joseph *former congressman*
Thomas, James Edward *accountant*
Weinstein, Gerald *former housing and building corporation executive*
Winter, Darius Gerjon *internist*

Remsenburg
Billman, Irwin Edward *publishing company executive*

Rensselaer
Hull, Raymond Whitford *public relations executive*
Nack, Claire Durani *artist, author*
Robinson, John Bowers, Jr., *retired bank holding company executive*

Rensselaerville
Dudley, George Austin *architect, planning consultant, educator*
Fletcher, Raymond Russwald, Jr., *lawyer*

Rexford
Habetler, George Joseph *retired mathematics educator*
Nitecki, Joseph Zbigniew *librarian*
Schmitt, Roland Walter *retired academic administrator*

Rhinebeck
McGuire, John Francis, Jr., *construction company executive*
Melley, Steven Michael *lawyer*
Scherr, Allan Lee *computer scientist, executive, consultant*

Richmondville
Bartholomew, Debra Lee *publishing executive*

Ridge
Blume, Martin *physicist*

Ridgewood
Jones, Harold Antony *banker*

Riverdale
Bencsáth, Katalin A. *mathematician*
Chimsky-Lustig, Mark Evan *publishing consultant*
Diaz, Marlene Carmen *language educator*

Riverhead
Acampora, Patricia L. *state legislator*
Banfelder, Robert Joseph *novelist, lecturer*
Buck, Leslie Elizabeth *mathematics educator, poet*
Kent, Robert John *marine biologist*
Maggipinto, V. Anthony *lawyer*
Mehling, Robert R. *artist*
Roland, David Leonard *retired broadcast production educator*

Rochester
Affronti, Francis Christopher *lawyer*
Agrawal, Govind Prasad *optics educator*
Akiyama, Toshio *cardiologist, educator, researcher*
Aldersley, Stephanie Polowe *language educator*
Anderson, Porter Warren, Jr., *retired pediatrics educator*
Angel, Allen Robert *mathematics educator, author, consultant*
Atkin, Louis Phillip *recycling business executive*
Atkins, Carl J. *conductor, educator*
Aydelotte, Myrtle Kitchell *retired nursing administrator*
Bannon, Anthony Leo *museum director*
Basavappa, Ravi *biophysical scientist, educator*
Baum, John *physician*
Bauman, M. Garrett *English educator*
Berg, Robert Lewis *physician, educator*
Bidlack, Jean Marie *pharmacologist, educator, medical researcher*
Bigelow, Nicholas Pierre *physicist, researcher*
Billings, Ronald J. *dental research administrator*
Bluhm, William Theodore *political scientist, educator*
Boeckman, Robert Kenneth, Jr., *chemistry educator, organic chemistry researcher*
Boehly, Thomas *forensic specialist*
Bonfiglio, Thomas Albert *pathologist, educator*
Bouyoucos, John Vinton *research and development company executive*
Braley, Oleta Pearl *home health care provider*
Briggs, James T. *marketing executive*
Brody, Bernard B. *internist, educator*
Brooks, Walter S. *dermatologist*
Brovitz, Richard Stuart *lawyer*
Brust, Robert H. *film processing company executive*
Buckingham, Barbara Rae *social studies educator*
Buckley, Michael Francis *lawyer*
Buff, Frank Paul *chemist, educator*
Buff, Iva Moore *librarian, musicologist*
Burton, Richard Irving *orthopedist, educator*
Cain, B(urton) Edward *chemistry professor*
Cameros, Alan Lee *financial services executive*
Carp, Daniel A. *manufacturing executive*
Carstensen, Edwin Lorenz *biomedical engineer, biophysicist*
Chang, Chawnshang *science educator, laboratory administrator*
Chey, William Yoon *physician*
Chiarenza, Carl *art historian, critic, artist, educator*
Chiverton, Patricia Ann *nursing educator, dean*
Ciccone, J. Richard *psychiatrist, educator*
Ciolek, Nancy A. *information technology educator*
Clark, Matthew Harvey *bishop*
Clarkson, Thomas William *toxicologist, educator*
Clement, Thomas Earl *retired lawyer*
Clifford, Eugene Thomas *lawyer*
Cohen, Jules *physician, educator, former academic dean*
Cohen, Nicholas *immunologist, educator*
Colby, William Michael *lawyer*
Collins, Christopher Carl *manufacturing executive*
Conwell, Esther Marly *physicist, researcher*
Corio, Mark Andrew *electronics executive*
Danforth-Morningstar, Elizabeth *obstetrician, gynecologist*
Deci, Edward Lewis *psychologist, educator*
De Mattia, Marlene J. *psychotherapist*
Demers, Elizabeth Anne *education educator*
DeWeese, James Arville *surgeon, educator*
Diamond, David Leo *composer*
Dolin, Lonny H. *lawyer*
Doty, Robert William *neurophysiologist, educator*
Drummond, Malcolm McAllister *electronics engineer*
Duarte, Francisco Javier *physicist, researcher*
DuBrin, Andrew John *behavioral sciences, management educator, writer*
Dye, Timothy De Ver *epidemiologist, anthropologist, educator*
Elliot, Andrew J. *psychology professor*
Elliott, Ralph H. *educator*
Evans, Eric Alan *lawyer*
Everett, Claudia Kellam *retired special education educator*
Farmer, Richard Gilbert *physician, foundation administrator, medical advisor, healthcare consultant*
Fenno, Richard Francis, Jr., *political scientist, educator*
Ferbel, Thomas *physics educator, physicist*
Fielding, Ronald Herbert *investment company executive*
Fisher, George Myles Cordell *retired photographic imaging company executive, mathematician, engineer*
Flynn, R. Thomas *academic administrator*
Ford, Marcia Marie *financial consultant*
Fox, Bruce R. *food company executive*
Frazer, John Paul *surgeon*
Freeman, Leslie Jean *neuropsychologist, researcher*
Friedman, Susan Marie *geriatrician, educator, medical researcher*
Frisina, Robert Dana *sensory neuroscientist, educator*
Galaria, Noreen Ahmad *physician, medical researcher, consultant*
Garg, Devendra *financial executive*
Gates, Marshall DeMotte, Jr., *chemistry educator*
Geiger, Alexander *lawyer*
Georges, John Peter *information technology consultant*
Giebel, Douglas Richard *art educator, artist*
Glazer, Jane *consumer products company executive*
Goldberg-Schaible, Jocelyn Hope Schnier *market research professional*
Golden, Reynold Stephen *geriatrician, educator*
Goldfarb, Barry Joseph *education educator*
Goldman, Joel J. *retired lawyer*
Goldstein, Marvin Norman *physician*
Golisano, B. Thomas *finance company director, human resources director*
Goodell, Gary Lloyd *minister, educator*
Gootnick, Margery Fischbein *lawyer*
Gordon, Dane Rex *philosophy educator, minister*
Gorlick, Dennis Lester *marketing professional*
Griggs, Robert Charles *physician*
Gripe, Alan Gordon *minister*
Gulling, Mark V. *consumer products company executive*
Gustin, Carl E., Jr., *manufacturing executive*
Guzick, David S. *dean, educator*
Hakim, Fares Samih *physician*
Hallenbeck, Alfred M. *lawyer*
Hanford, M. Shae *lawyer*
Harris, Diane Carol *merger and acquisition consulting firm executive*
Harris, Wayne Manley *lawyer*
Harter, Ralph Millard Peter *lawyer, educator*
Harvey, Douglass Coate *retired photographic company executive*
Hauser, William Barry *history educator, historian*
Herminghouse, Patricia Anne *foreign language educator*
Hetnarski, Richard Bozyslaw *mechanical engineering educator*
Hoch, Edward Dentinger *writer*
Hoffman, Nancy Yanes *medical author, patient educator, writer, pharmaceutical editor, health care consultant, lecturer*
Holcomb, Grant, III, *museum director*
Hollis, Susan Tower *history professor*
Hopkins, Thomas Duvall *economics professor*
Huddleston, Vicki Jean *diplomat*
Hurlbut, Robert Harold *health care services executive*
Huston, Samuel Richard *health facility executive*
Jackson, Thomas Humphrey *academic administrator, lawyer*
Johnson, Bruce Marvin *English language educator*
Jones, Ronald Winthrop *economics professor*
Joos, Felipe Miguel *mechanical engineer, researcher*
Joynt, Robert James *academic administrator, physician*
Kaidy, Mitchell *journalist, writer, legislative staff member*
Kampmeier, Jack August Carlos *chemist, educator*
Kehoe, L. Paul *state judge*
Kende, Andrew Steven *chemist, educator*
King, Kathleen Bernadette *nursing educator*
Kirschenbaum, Howard *education educator*
Klein, Jonathan David *physician, researcher*
Klinke, Louise Hoyt *volunteer*
Knauer, James Philip *physicist*
Knox, Robert Seiple *physicist, researcher*
Kurland, Harold Arthur *lawyer*
La Celle, Paul Louis *biophysics educator*
Lacey, Dorothy Ellen *theology studies educator, religious organization administrator*
Larimer, David George *federal judge*
Laties, Victor Gregory *psychology educator*
Lawton, Kathy G. *biology professor*
Lebman, Robert Richard *social services administrator*
Leo, James J. *food service executive*
Lever, O. William, Jr., *chemist*
Levy, Harold David *psycholinguist*
Li, James Chen Min *materials science educator*
Lichtman, Marshall Albert *internist, educator, medical researcher*
Loewen, Erwin G. *precision engineer, educator, consultant*
Long, John Broaddus, Jr., *economist, educator*
Lotta, Tom (Anthony Tom Lotta) *artist*
Lundback, Staffan Bengt Gunnar *lawyer*
Lyman, Gary Herbert *epidemiologist, cancer researcher, educator*
Magnuson, Karen M. *editor*
Mahar, Jason *education educator*
Makous, Walter Leon *visual scientist, educator*
Marriott, Marcia Ann *business and economics educator, health facility administrator*
Mars, John Eugene *protective services official, artist*
Mayka, Stephen Paul *lawyer*
McAnarney, Elizabeth R. *pediatrician, educator*
McClurg, Robert James *emergency nurse practitioner, educator*
McCrory, John Brooks *retired lawyer*
McCurdy, Gilbert Geier *retired retailer*
McDonald, Joseph Valentine *neurosurgeon*
Mc Kenzie, Lionel Wilfred *economist, educator*
McKenzie, Stanley Don *academic administrator, English educator*
McMeekin, Thomas Owen *dermatologist*
McQuillen, Michael Paul *neurologist, educator, clinical ethicist*
Melissinos, Adrian Constantin *physicist, researcher*
Merritt, Howard Sutermeister *retired art educator*
Messing, Edward M. *urologic surgeon*
Miller, Richard Bruce *electronics company executive*
Moore, Duncan Thomas *optics educator*
Moore, James Conklin *lawyer*
Moore, Matthew Scott *publisher, deaf advocate, author*
Morgan, William Lionel, Jr., *physician, educator*
Morley, Michael P. *research and development company executive*
Morphy, John *manufacturing executive*
Morris, James E. *lawyer, judge, educator*
Morrison, Patrice B. *lawyer*
Mosmann, Tim *microbiologist, educator, immunologist*
Moss, Arthur Jay *physician*
Munson, Harold Lewis *education educator*
Nace, Morton Oliver, Jr., *human resources professional, performance consultant*
Nasr, Nabil Zaki *national center executive*
Nazarian, Lawrence Fred *pediatrician*
Niznik, Carol Ann *electrical engineer, educator, consultant*
Oldshue, James Y. *chemical engineering consultant*
Ornt, Jeanine Arden *lawyer*
Pacala, Leon *retired association executive*
Palermo, Anthony Robert *lawyer*
Paley, Gerald Larry *lawyer*
Palmer, Harvey John *dean*
Panner, Bernard J. *pathologist, educator*
Parker, Kevin James *electrical engineer, educator*
Parrinello, Kathleen Ann Mulholland *nursing administrator, educator*
Payment, Kenneth Arnold *lawyer*
Pearson, Thomas Arthur *epidemiologist, educator*
Perez, Antonio M. *consumer products company executive*
Pettinella, Edward *real estate company executive*
Phelps, Charles Elliott *economics professor, director*
Pitoniak, Scott Michael *sportswriter*
Plosser, Charles Irving *economist, educator*
Portanova, Carolyn Amick *religious organization administrator*
Powers, James Matthew *neuropathologist*
Raimi, Ralph Alexis *mathematics professor*
Regenstreif, S(amuel) Peter *political scientist, educator*
Robbins, Nancy Slinker *volunteer*
Robfogel, Susan Salitan *lawyer*
Rodgers, Suzanne Hooker *ergonomics consultant, physiologist*
Rosenbaum, Richard Merrill *lawyer*
Rosenhouse, Michael Allan *lawyer, editorial consultant*
Rothberg, Abraham *author, educator, editor*
Rowley, Peter Templeton *pediatrician, educator*
Rulison, Joseph Richard *investment advisor*
Salamone, Joseph Charles *polymer chemistry educator*
Saunders, William Hundley, Jr., *retired chemist, educator*
Schrock, Robert D., Jr., *orthopaedic surgeon, educator*
Schumacher, Jon Lee *lawyer*
Schwantner, Joseph *composer, educator*
Schwartz, Seymour Ira *surgeon, educator*
Schwert, G(eorge) William, III, *finance educator*
Shah, Ramesh Keshavlal *researcher, engineering educator*
Sheller, G. A. *artist, educator*
Sherman, Fred *biochemist, educator*
Shirley, Bonnie J. *secondary school educator*
Sieg, Albert Louis *photographic company executive*
Simmons, Russell *recording industry executive*
Simon, William *biomathematician, educator*
Simone, Albert Joseph *academic administrator*
Singer, Alan Daniel *artist*
Siragusa, Charles J. *judge*
Smith, Julia Ladd *medical oncologist, hospice physician*
Smoral, Vincent J. *electrical engineer*
Sodervick, Bruce Werner *sculptor, art educator*
Sparks, Charles Edward *pathologist, educator*
Sparks, Janet Lindsay Dehoff *pathology educator*
Steamer, Robert Julius *political science educator*

Stewart, Sue S. *lawyer*
Stratton, John Alfred *electrical engineer, educator*
Sutter, Jane E. *editor*
Swanton, Susan Irene *retired library director*
Swett, Albert Hersey *retired lawyer, business executive, consultant*
Telesca, Michael Anthony *federal judge*
Thomas, John Howard *astrophysicist, engineer, educator*
Thorndike, Edward Harmon *physicist*
Trevett, Thomas Neil *lawyer*
Utell, Mark Jeffrey *medical educator*
Van Graafeiland, Ellsworth Alfred *federal judge*
Van Graafeiland, Gary P. *lawyer*
Vernarelli, Michael Joseph *economics educator, consultant*
Vick, Paul Ashton *lawyer*
Vigdor, Justin Leonard *lawyer*
Waite, Stephen Holden *lawyer*
Walker, Michael Charles, Sr., *retirement services executive*
Watts, Ross Leslie *accounting educator, consultant*
Wax, Paul Matthew *emergency medicine physician, educator, medical toxicologist*
Wayland-Smith, Robert Dean *retired banker*
Webster, Gordon Visscher, Jr., *minister*
Wegman, Daniel R. *retail executive*
Wegman, Robert B. *food service executive*
Weiss, Bernard *toxicology educator*
Wheeless, Leon Lum *pathology educator*
Wild, Robert Warren *lawyer*
Wiley, Jason LaRue, Jr., *neurosurgeon*
Williams, Thomas Franklin *physician, educator*
Witmer, G. Robert *retired state supreme court justice*
Witmer, George Robert, Jr., *lawyer*
Young, Deborah Schwind *lawyer*
Zagorin, Perez *historian, educator*
Zax, Melvin *psychologist, educator*
Zhao, Hongwei *biostatistician*
Zupan, Mark A. *dean, business professor*

Rock Hill
Lombardi, Kent Bailey *insurance company administrator*

Rockville Centre
Beyer, Suzanne *advertising agency executive*
Erland, Shirley May *nurse*
Fitzgerald, Janet Anne *philosophy educator, academic administrator*
Lewittes, Don Jordan *clinical psychologist*
Meredith, Gary S. *physician*
Schwartz, Arthur *playwright, poet*
Teyan, Frederick Gene *pediatrician*

Rocky Point
Knapp, Craig Brian *music educator, musician*
Stever, Edward W. *writer, English language educator*

Rome
Ferens, Daniel Vincent *civilian military employee*
Sanders, Robin Renee *diplomat*
Simons, Richard Duncan *lawyer, retired judge*
Waters, George Bausch *newspaper publisher*

Romulus
Ostrander, Robert Edwin *retired United Nations interregional advisor, petroleum company executive*

Ronkonkoma
Mishoe, Thomas M. *dairy products executive*
Nussdorf, Glenn *distribution executive*
Wolff, Paul D. *weight management products executive*

Roosevelt
Adams, Mary A. *retired assistant principal*

Rosedale
Affleck, Gilbert Leslie *editor, journalist*

Rosendale
Goldpaugh Brown, Bethany J. *theater educator, writer, costume designer*

Roslyn
Gulotta, Stephen J. *cardiologist*
Hartman, Nancy Lee *physician*
Lidonnici, Leslie *surgeon*
Rosegarten, Rory *personal manager, television producer, theater producer*
Siahpoosh, Farideh Tamaddon *librarian*
Stein, Theodore Anthony *biochemist, educator*
Stracher, Dorothy Altman *education educator, consultant*
Ulanoff, Stanley M. *communications executive*

Roslyn Heights
Guthart, Leo A. *electronics executive*
Jordan, Patricia James *secondary school educator*
Malekoff, Andrew *social services administrator, writer*
Newmark, Marilyn *sculptor*
Rogatz, Peter *retired physician*
Rubrum, Erica Courtney *family therapist, school counselor*

Rotterdam Junction
Cox, Paulyn Mae *retired elementary school educator*

Rouses Point
Weierstall, Richard Paul *retired pharmaceutical chemist*

Rush
Smith, Katherine Teresa *history educator*

Rye
Anderson, Allan *architectural firm executive*
Barker, Harold Grant *surgeon, educator*
Casson Madden, Chris *entrepreneur, interior designer*
Curtin, Brian Joseph *ophthalmologist*
Davis, Samuel *hospital administrator, educator, consultant*
Dixon, Paul Edward *lawyer, metal products and manufacturing company executive*
Feinberg, Norman Maurice *real estate company executive*
Francis, Charles Gordon *business executive, writer*
Fumasoli, John *music educator*
Gabelli, Mario J. *diversified financial services company executive*
Gambee, Robert Rankin *investment banker*
Hurwitz, Sol *writer, consultant*
Kaulakis, Arnold Francis *management consultant*
Ketchum, William Clarence *author, educator*
Lawi, David Steven *utilities executive, merchant banker*
Lehman, Lawrence Herbert *consulting engineering executive*
Lehman, Myra Harriet *sculptor, dental hygienist*
Lobl, Herbert Max *lawyer, writer*
Mahoney, Thomas Henry, IV, *finance executive*
Nelson, Vita Joy *editor, publisher*
Newburger, Howard Martin *psychoanalyst*
Norcia, Stephen William *advertising and internet advertising executive, consultant*
Roberts, Thomas Alba *lawyer*
Schmitz, Robert Allen *publishing executive, investor*
Troller, Fred *graphic designer, painter, visual consultant, educator*
Vernon, Lillian *mail order company executive*
Waltz, Joseph McKendree *neurosurgeon, educator*
Wilmot, Irvin Gorsage *former hospital administrator, educator, consultant*

Rye Brook
Aquino, Joseph Mario *clinical psychologist*
Ghazey, Kenneth A. *data processing executive*
Kuntzman, Ronald *pharmacology research executive*
Landegger, George F. *engineering executive*
Levy, Howard Alan *music educator*
Lo Russo, Diane *radiologist*
Masson, Robert Henry *paper company executive*
McKenna, John A., Jr., *data processing executive*

Sag Harbor
Blanc, Peter (William Peters Blanc) *sculptor, painter*
Brody, Eugene David *investment company executive*
Brody, Jacqueline *editor*
de Cordova, Hector Armando *artist, consultant, art educator*
Epstein, Jason *publishing company executive*
Pashman, Susan Ellen *writer*
Pierce, Lawrence Warren *retired federal judge*

Sagaponack
Cedering, Siv *poet, writer*

Saint Albans
Bess, Olean *educator, counselor*
Xu, Ying-Pei *artist*

Saint Bonaventure
Godet-Calogeras, JeanFrançois *historian, educator*

Saint James
Bigeleisen, Jacob *chemist, educator*
Kelly, Michael Joseph *academic administrator, consultant*

Saint Johnsville
Dillenbeck, Marianne Frances *elementary school educator*

Salamanca
Brady, Thomas Carl *lawyer*

Sanborn
Gerbasi, Kathleen Carrese *psychologist, educator*
Hill, Rosemary Louise *artist*
Michalak, Janet Carol *childhood education educator, coordinator*

Sands Point
Busner, Philip H. *retired lawyer, judge*
Cullinan, Bernice E(llinger) *education educator*
Lear, Erwin *anesthesiologist, educator*
Olian, JoAnne Constance *curator, art historian*
Wurzel, Leonard *retired candy manufacturing company executive*

Saranac
Smith, J. Kellum, Jr., *foundation executive, lawyer*

Saranac Lake
Caguiat, Carlos Jose *health facility administrator, priest*
Hixson, Edward George *general surgeon*

Saratoga Springs
Auriemmo, Frank Joseph, Jr., *financial holding company executive*
Carey, Margot Beckmann *fundraiser*
Dickinson, Richard Henry *accountant*
Fenton, Michael I. *artist, educator*
Ford, Dexter *retired insurance company executive*
Glotzbach, Philip A. *academic administrator*
Masie, Elliott *training executive*
McKnight, Joyce Sheldon *adult educator, community organizer, mediator*
McNairy, Kate *humanities educator*
Millhauser, Steven *writer*
O'Baire, Marika *nurse, writer*
Porter, David Hugh *pianist, classicist, academic administrator, liberal arts educator*
Richardson, Elaina *foundation administrator, former magazine editor*
Sainer, Arthur *writer, theater educator*
Stanley, Karen Francine Mary Lesniewski *human resources professional*
Upton, Richard Thomas *artist*
Wait, Charles Valentine *banker*
Winne, Elizabeth (Lise) *lyricist*

Saugerties
de Mare, George *author*

Sayville
Leuzzi, Linda *writer*
Lippman, Sharon Rochelle *art historian, art therapist, filmmaker*
Wurtz, Margaret Johnston *artist, calligrapher*

Scarborough
Byrne, Robert Eugene *chess columnist*
Parks, Robert Henry *consulting economist, educator*
Stigall, Phyllis Graham *retired librarian*
Wittcoff, Harold Aaron *chemist*

Scarsdale
Abbe, Colman *investment banker*
Angel, Dennis *lawyer*
Bayar, Julia Beryl *interior designer*
Beuchert, Edward William *lawyer*
Blitman, Howard Norton *construction company executive*
Bloomfield, Keith Martin *management executive*
Borg, Robert Frederic *civil engineer*
Bruck Lieb Port, Lilly *retired consumer advisor, broadcaster, columnist*
Byers, John Raoul, III, *cocoa grader, conservationist*
Carnase, Thomas Paul *graphic designer, typographic consultant*
Citrin, Yale *light industry executive*
Clark, Merrell Mays *management consultant*
Cohen, Irwin *economist*
Decaminada, Joseph Pio *retired insurance company executive*
Dulit, Everett Paul *psychiatrist, educator*
Edis, Gloria Toby *pediatrician*
Ellis, James Henry *lawyer, management consultant*
Erbsen, Claude Ernest *retired journalist*
Fishbach, Mitchell Harvey *cardiologist*
Florman, Samuel Charles *civil engineer*
Gelb, Harold Seymour *manufacturing executive, consultant, entrepreneur*
Gollin, Stuart Allen *accountant*
Goodman, Jordan Elliot *journalist*
Graff, Henry Franklin *historian, educator*
Heese, William John *music publishing company executive*
Hemley, Eugene Adams *trade association executive*
Hoffman, Richard M. *lawyer*
Jacobs, Theodore Joseph *psychiatrist, educator*
Johnson, Boine Theodore *instruments company executive, mayor*
Johnson, William Alexander *clergyman, philosophy educator*
Kaufman, Robert Jules *communications consultant, lawyer*
Liston, Mary Frances *retired nursing educator*
Macchia, Vincent Michael *lawyer*
Moser, Marvin *physician, educator, writer*
Naughton, Ann Elsie *primary school educator*
Newman, Stacey Clarfield *artist, curator*
O'Brien, Edward Ignatius *private investor, corporation director*
O'Neill, Michael James *editor, author*
Paige, Susanne Lynn *financial consultant*
Paulin, Amy Ruth *civic activist, consultant*
Perez, Louis Anthony *radiologist*
Pope, Leavitt Joseph *broadcast company executive*
Porosoff, Harold *chemist, research and development director*
Rivlin, Richard Saul *physiologist, educator*
Rogalski, Lois Ann *speech and language pathologist*
Rothschild, Eric *editor, consultant*
Rubenstein, Jacob Samuel *rabbi*
Sabadie, Francisca Alejandra *lawyer, interpreter, translator*
Schultz, Harley *consulting company executive*
Shaw, Grace Goodfriend (Mrs. Herbert Franklin Shaw) *publisher, editor*
Tolliver, Lisa Marie *management consultant*
Topping, Audrey Ronning *photojournalist*
Topping, Seymour *author, educator*
Van Gundy, Gregory Frank *retired lawyer*

Schenectady
Banjamin, Martin E. *photographer, art educator*
Board, Joseph Breckinridge, Jr., *political scientist, educator*
Cullen, Kathleen Joy *lawyer*
DeLuke, Dean M. *oral surgeon*
Donnelly, Scott C. *manufacturing executive*
Endres, John J. *supermarket company executive*
Fell, Samuel Kennedy (Ken Fell) *infosystems executive*
Fischer, Michael David *civil engineer*
Frost, Robert Edwin *chemistry professor*
Golub, Lewis *supermarket company executive*
Golub, Neil *supermarket chain executive*
Greskovich, Charles D. *retired materials engineer*
Hermance, Jr., Myron E. *conductor, educator*
Hull, Roger Harold *academic administrator*
Levine, Howard Arnold *judge*
Levine, Sanford Harold *lawyer*
Mikata, Yozo *mechanical engineer, application developer*
Morris, John Selwyn *philosophy educator, college president emeritus*
Murray, Edward Rock *insurance broker*
Oliker, David William *healthcare management administrator*
Pearson, Timothy Alfred *newspaper circulation executive*
Philip, A. G. Davis *astronomer, editor, educator*
Ringlee, Robert James *consulting engineering executive*
Robb, Walter Lee *retired electric company executive, management company executive*
Schenck, John Frederic *physician*
Sharlet, Robert *political science educator, researcher*
Sternlicht, Beno *research and development company executive*
Sutherland, Peter Edward *electrical engineer*
Szokody, Aniko *pianist, educator*
Weiner, Clare Frances *social worker, psychotherapist*
Zhu, Yudong *medical imaging researcher*

Schoharie
Duncombe, Raynor Bailey *lawyer*

Schroon Lake
Williams, Wayne M. *music educator*

Scotia
de la Rocha, Carlos A. *retired physician*
Schulman, Ruth Meryl Aronson *development director*

Scottsville
Williams, Henry Ward, Jr., *lawyer, writer*

Sea Cliff
Hassani, Mojdeh *special education educator*
Martin, David S. *retired secondary school educator, administrator*
Mourashkin, Boris V. *composer, sound therapist, poet, performer, producer*
Popova, Nina *dancer, choreographer, director*

Seaford
Moore, Sister Mary Francis *parochial school educator*
Setzler, William Edward *chemical company executive*
Spencer, Jean *food products executive*
Tuzil, Teresa Jordan *clinical social worker, psychotherapist*

Selden
Connors, William Francis, Jr., *academic administrator*

Selkirk
Christoph, Peter Richard *historical editor, archivist*

Seneca Falls
Norman, Mary Marshall *alcohol/drug abuse services professional*

Setauket
Card, Richard Abbott *religious institute executive, educator*
Doering, Charles Henry *research scientist, educator, editor, publisher*
Dunaief, Leah S. *newspaper editor, publisher, writer*
Levine, Sumner Norton *industrial engineer, educator, editor, author, financial consultant*
McClean, Lenora James *nursing educator, dean*
Palmedo, Philip Franklin *management consulting company executive*
Robinson, Richard M. *technical communication specialist*
Simpson, Louis Aston Marantz *English educator, author*

Setaukey
Venkateswaran, Pramila *literature educator*

Shady
Malkine-Falvey, Fern Sylvie *writer, journalist, painter*

Shelter Island
Dowd, David Joseph *banker, builder, construction executive*
Mayer, Martin Prager *writer*

Shelter Island Heights
Culbertson, Janet Lynn *artist*

Sherburne
Dodd, Jack Gordon, Jr., *physicist, researcher*
Smith, William Edward *sales executive, telecommunications executive*

Shirley
Harper, Catherine B. *primary school educator*
Kruk, Barbara Guarino *entrepreneur, public relations executive*

Shushan
Witten, Anita *artist, editor*

Sidney
Rivers Baker, Dawn *writer, publisher, consultant*
Werner, David A. *paper company executive*

Skaneateles
Huxford, J. David *retired sales representative*

Sleepy Hollow
Chia, David Thien-Shing *internist, gastroenterologist*
Ferguson, Douglas Edward *finance company executive*
Flynn-Connors, Elizabeth Kathryn *editor*
Resnick, Adrienne Jo *psychotherapist*
Schmidt, Klaus Franz *advertising executive*
Zegarelli, Edward Victor *retired dental educator, researcher*

Slingerlands
Bragle, George W. *criminal justice educator*
Herman, Robert S. *former state official, economist, author, educator*
Jacobs, Karen Louise *medical technologist*
Zacek, Joseph Frederick *history educator, international studies consultant, Central and East European culture and affairs specialist*

Smallwood
Golden, Elliott *judge*

Smithtown
Dowis, Lenore *lawyer*
Goodman, Richard Shalem *lawyer, orthopedic surgeon*
Rockensies, John William *mechanical engineer*
Spellman, Thomas Joseph, Jr., *lawyer*

Snyder
Breverman, Harvey *artist*
Levine, George Richard *English language educator*

Somers
Anderson, John Erling *chemical engineer*
Bauman, William Allen *pediatrician, educator, health systems consultant*
Bensen, Annette Wolf *graphic art company consultant*
Cahill, John T. *consumer products company executive*
Cohn, Howard *retired magazine editor*
Drewes, Alfred H. *consumer products company executive*
Lane, David Oliver *retired librarian*
Lemke, Judith A. *lawyer*
Reznick, Steven Michael *orthopedic surgeon, educator*
Rubin, Samuel Harold *internist, consultant*
Sora, Sebastian Antony *business machines manufacturing executive, educator*
Trzasko, Joseph Anthony *psychologist, educator*
Wladawsky-Berger, Irving *communications executive*

South Dayton
Jones, Richard Allen *horse breeder, educator*

South Ozone Park
Cook, Vivian *state legislator*

South Richmond Hill
Goldsmith, Michael Lawrence *lawyer*

South Salem
Cowles, Frederick Oliver *lawyer*
Knijff, Jan-Piet *musician, educator*
Tafrate, Polly Hare *retired elementary school educator*

South Setauket
Berger, H. Jean *retired physical education educator*
Friedlander, Gerhart *nuclear chemist*
Poli, Kenneth Joseph *editor, writer, photographer*

Southampton
Atkins, Victor Kennicott, Jr., *investment banker*
Brokaw, Clifford Vail, III, *investment banker, business executive*
Culp, Michael Bronston *investor, writer, publisher*
Dublis, Raymond Anthony *insurance executive*
Graham, Howard Barrett *publishing company executive*
Kanovitz, Howard *artist, educator*
Lerner, Abram *retired museum director, artist*
Lopez, David *lawyer*
Needham, James Joseph *retired financial services executive, consultant*
Rodas, Daniel *academic administrator, management educator*

Southold
Bachrach, Howard L. *biochemist*
Callis, Jerry Jackson *veterinarian*
Small, Bertrice W. *writer*

Sparkill
Dahl, Arlene *actress, writer, apparel designer, cosmetics executive*
Lauture, Denize Lucien *language educator, writer*
Myers, Adele Anna *artist, educator, nun*

Sparrow Bush
Murray, William Bruce *opera singer*

Spencer
Grunberg, Slawomir *film and television producer and director, director of photography*

Spencerport
Sawyer, William Curtis *pest control company executive*
Vizy, Kalman Nicholas *research physicist, educator*

Spencertown
Hawkins, Robert Garvin *management educator*
Lieber, Charles Donald *publisher*

Spring Valley
Barr, Harvey Stephen *lawyer*
Cacciola, Patrick Barry *art association administrator*
Stedge-Fowler, Joyce *retired clergywoman*
Steinberg, Milton *civilian military employee*

Springfield Gardens
Moore, Deborah Chantay *protective services official, psychotherapist*

Staatsburg
Reagan, Paul Terrence *retired social worker*

Stamford
Bergleitner, George Charles, Jr., *investment banker*

Stanfordville
Tetor, David R. *agriculturist, consultant*

Staten Island
Auh, Yang John *librarian, educational administrator*
Banner, Burton *pediatrician*
Black, Lawrence *librarian*
Brady, Christine Ellen *education coordinator*
Bruckstein, Alex Harry *internist, gastroenterologist, geriatrician*
Choo, Kristin E. *journalist*
Clark, Sylvia Dolores *business educator*
Cooper, Sandi E. *history educator*
Cross, Ronald *musicologist, educator*
De Luca, Anthony James *psychoanalyst, theologian*
Doherty, Harry Patrick *bank executive*
Fafian, Joseph, Jr., *management consultant*
Ferzli, George Salem *surgeon*
Foster, Paul *playwright*
Gavrity, John Decker *insurance company executive*
Gelbein, Jay Joel *accountant*
Gennari, Flint *photographer*
Gonzalez, Richard *maritime safety officer*
Grodman, Richard Stephen *internist, cardiologist*
Holder, Calvin Beresford *history professor*
Howard, Davis Jonathan *lawyer, educator, writer*
Humphries, Edward Francis *lawyer*
Jarrett, Mark Paul *rheumatologist, medical administrator*
Kahn, Jim *former magazine publisher*
Khan, Tariq *marketing professional*
Landron, Michel John *lawyer*
Lutkenhouse, Anne *non-profit executive*
Maiman, Mitchell *oncologist, gynecologist*
Manister, Craig Alan *artist, educator*
Meltzer, Yale Leon *economist, educator*
Miller, Wayne *actor, designer, producer, impresario*
Nadler, Nona Jean *social worker*
Newhouse, Donald E. *newspaper publishing executive*
Newhouse, Samuel I., Jr., *publishing executive*
Pillari, Vincent Thomas *obstetrician-gynecologist, educator*
Popler, Kenneth *behavioral health services administrator, psychologist*
Popp, Lilian Mustaki *writer, educator*
Porter, Darwin Fred *writer*
Prince, Danforth *publishing executive, journalist*
Robison, Paula Judith *flutist*
Silverberg, Michael Barry *anesthesiologist*
Silverstein, Arthur *publishing executive*
Spada, Dominick *pharmacist*
Springer, Marlene *university administrator, educator*
Stathopoulos, Peter *internist*
Thomas, Charles Columbus *dance educator, artist*
Wilson, Alice McAteer *secondary school educator*
Winter, Steven *internist, cardiologist*
Yang, Song-Yu *research biochemist*

Stillwater
O'Connor, Abigail Elizabeth *mathematician, educator, science educator*

Stone Ridge
Terpening, Donald Lester *science educator, medical technologist*

Stony Brook
Ahn, Hongshik *statistician, educator*
Akella, Umasundari Srivenkata *research scholar*
Alexander, John Macmillan, Jr., *chemistry professor*
Anderson, Michael Thomas *mathematics researcher, educator*
Asryan, Levon V. *physicist, electrical engineer, researcher*
Bennett, Tyrone LaMont *engineer, director*
Bokuniewicz, Henry Joseph *oceanography educator*
Bonner, Francis Truesdale *chemist, educator, university dean*
Booth, George *cartoonist*
Brandwein, Ruth Ann *social welfare educator, administrator, author*
Brown, Gerald Edward *physicist, researcher*
Carr, Edward Gary *psychology educator*
Chandran, Latha *pediatrician, educator*
Chen, JiuHua *physicist, geophysicist, educator*
Cochran, James Kirk *dean, oceanographer, geochemist, educator*
Cook, Jeannine Salvo *librarian, consultant*
Corman, Marvin Leonard *surgeon, educator*
Dinkins, Stephanie A. *artist, educator*
Friedman, Harold Leo *chemistry professor*
Fritts, Harry Washington, Jr., *physician, educator*
Gambino, Richard Joseph *materials science engineering*
Geller, Marvin Alan *meteorology educator, researcher*
Glimm, James Gilbert *mathematician, educator*
Goldberg, Homer Beryl *English language educator*
Goodman, Norman *sociologist, researcher*
Grim, Patrick Neal *philosopher, logician, educator*
Grudens, Richard William *retail executive, writer*
Harris, Alice Carmichael *linguist, educator*
Harvey, Christine Lynn *publishing executive*
Ihde, Don *philosophy educator, university administrator*
Jonas, Steven *public health physician, health policy analyst, writer*
Judex, Stefan *biomedical engineer, educator*
Kenny, Shirley Strum *academic administrator*
Koppelman, Lee Edward *regional planner, educator*
Kuchner, Eugene Frederick *neurosurgeon, educator, neuroscientist*
Kuspit, Donald Burton *art historian, art critic, educator*
Lane, Dorothy Spiegel *preventive medicine physician*
Laspina, Peter Joseph *computer resource educator*
Lawson, H(erbert) Blaine, Jr., *mathematician, educator*
Leakey, Richard Erskine *paleoanthropologist, museum director*
Lennarz, William Joseph *research biologist, educator*
Leske, M. Cristina *medical educator, medical researcher*
Levin, Richard Louis *language educator*
Liang, Jerome Zhengrong *radiology educator*
McGrath, Robert L. *academic administrator*
Meyers, Morton Allen *physician, radiology educator*
Michelsohn, Marie-Louise *mathematician, educator*
Mignone, Mario B. *Italian studies educator*
Milnor, John Willard *mathematician*
Mirza, Humair *cardiologist, educator*
Neuberger, Egon *economics professor*
Ojima, Iwao *chemistry educator*
Pindell, Howardena Doreen *artist*
Priebe, Cedric Joseph, Jr., *pediatric surgeon*
Ricotta, John Joseph *vascular surgeon, educator*
Rifkin, Barry R. *dean, dental educator, researcher*
Rohlf, F. James *biometrician, educator*
Roth, Susan Austin *author, photographer*
Schneider, Mark *political science educator*
Semmel, Bernard *historian, educator*
Semyonov, Oleg G. *research scientist*
Shamash, Yacov *dean, electrical engineering educator*
Shrock, Robert E. *physicist, educator, research scientist*
Sokoloff, Leon *pathology educator*
Sreebny, Leo M. *oral biology and pathology educator*
Steigbigel, Roy Theodore *epidemiologist, educator, research scientist*
Stolzberg, Mark Elliott *psychologist*
Stone, Elizabeth Cecilia *anthropology educator*
Suchoff, Benjamin *music educator*
Swanson, Robert Lawrence *oceanographer, academic program administrator*
Tanur, Judith Mark *sociologist, educator*
Tewarson, Reginald Prabhakar *retired mathematics educator, consultant*
Travis, Martin Bice *political scientist, educator*
Tucker, Alan Curtiss *mathematics professor*
Videbaek, Bente A. *humanities educator*
Wurster, Charles Frederick *environmental scientist, educator*
Yang, Chen Ning *physicist, educator*
Zemanian, Armen Humpartsoum *electrical engineer, mathematician*

Stony Point
Carter, Richard *publisher, writer*
Diederich, Michael David, Jr., *lawyer*

Stuyvesant
Tripp, Susan Gerwe *museum director*

Suffern
Codispoti, Andre John *allergist, immunologist*
Hawver, Carolyn Dunn *pharmaceutical production executive*
Jaffe, Elliot Stanley *retail executive*
Oppenheim, Jeffrey Sable *neurosurgeon, educator*
Raven, Luisa Antonia *nurse, psychotherapist*
Stack, Daniel *lawyer, financial consultant*
Sutherland, George Leslie *retired chemical company executive*

Sunnyside
Gil Orrios, Angel *theater director, lighting designer, translator*
Privo, Alexander *finance educator, department chairman*

Syosset
Barry, Richard Francis *retired life insurance company executive*
Bermas, Stephen *lawyer*
Donoghue, John *communications executive*
Heller, Al *marketing consultant, business journalist*
Irving, Jeffrey Alan *management consultant, educator, lawyer*
Kniffin, Paula Sichel *insurance sales executive*
Theodosius, *retired leader of the Orthodox Church in America*
Vermylen, Paul Anthony, Jr., *oil company executive*

Syracuse
Abbott, George Lindell *librarian*
Ackerman, Kenneth Edward *lawyer, educator*
Albino, Joseph Xavier *writer, educator, photographer*
Alston, William Payne *philosophy educator*
Ashutosh, Kumar *pulmonologist, educator*
Baker, Bruce Edward *orthopedic surgeon, consultant*
Baker, Sandra Lynn *county official, minister*
Baldwin, John Edwin *chemistry educator*
Barclay, H(ugh) Douglas *ambassador, lawyer*
Becker, Lorne Arthur *family physician*
Berinstein, William Paul *business executive*
Birge, Robert Richards *chemistry professor*
Birkhead, Guthrie Sweeney, Jr., *political scientist, university dean*
Bodow, Wayne R. *lawyer*
Boeheim, Jim *college basketball coach*
Bornhurst, Robert Allan *radiologist*
Braungart, Margaret Mitchell *psychology and bioethics educator*
Braungart, Richard Gottfried *sociology and international relations educator*
Brickwedde, Richard James *lawyer*
Bullock, Stephen C. *lawyer*
Bunn, Timothy David *newspaper editor*
Burstyn, Joan Netta *education educator*
Butler, John Edward *lawyer*
Cantor, Nancy *academic administrator*
Charters, Alexander Nathaniel *retired adult education educator*
Chickadonz, Grace Harlow *dean*
Church, Philip Throop *retired mathematics professor*
Cohen, William Nathan *radiologist*
Cooper, John Ambrose *management consultant, marketing professional*
Costello, Thomas Joseph *bishop*
Daly, Robert W. *psychiatrist, medical educator*
Davis, William E. *utilities executive*
Day, Christian C. *lawyer, educator, department chairman*
DeFrancisco, John Anthony *state legislator, lawyer*
De Long, Jacob Edward *real estate broker*
Denise, Theodore Cullom *philosophy educator*
DiLorenzo, Louis Patrick *lawyer*
Driscoll, Matthew J. *mayor, real estate developer, small business owner*
Drucker, Alan Steven *mechanical engineer*
Duerr, Dianne Marie *sports medicine consultant, educator*
Dunham, Philip Bigelow *biology professor, physiologist*
Eastwood, Gregory Lindsay *academic administrator*
Elms, Ben *actor, director*
Engel, Richard Lee *lawyer, educator*
Everett, Charles Roosevelt, Jr., *airport executive*
Farah, Fuad Salim *dermatologist, educator*
Federman Stein, Ruth *educational consultant*
Field, Daniel *history educator*
Fiske, Jordan Jay *lawyer, retired prosecutor*
Fiske, Sandra Rappaport *psychologist, educator*
Fitzgerald, Harold Kenneth *social work educator, consultant*
Fitzpatrick, James David *lawyer*
Fluck, Robert R., Jr., *respiratory therapist, educator*
Freund, Deborah A. *academic administrator*
Frohock, Fred Manuel *political science educator*
Furze, Edward William *fundraising consultant*
Gaal, John *lawyer*
Gerber, Edward F. *retired lawyer*
Gold, Joseph *medical researcher*
Grant, William Davis *medical educator, dean*
Graver, Jack Edward *mathematics professor*
Gray, Charles Augustus *banker*
Guharoy, Roy Sudip *pharmacist*
Hale, Karen Suzanne *mathematics professor*
Hancock, Stewart F., Jr., *law educator, judge*
Hansen, Per Brinch *computer scientist, researcher*
Harrison, Frank J. *retired bishop*
Hayes, David Michael *lawyer*
Henry, John Bernard *pathologist, educator, academic administrator*
Herzog, Peter Emilius *retired legal educator*
Hildebrandt, George Frederick *lawyer*
Hole, Richard Douglas *lawyer*
Honig, Arnold *physics professor, researcher*
Horst, Pamela Sue *medical educator, family physician*
Hsu, Lifang *statistician, department chairman*
Jankiewicz, Henry John *writer, educator, musician*
Jensen, Robert Granville *geography educator, university dean*
Kane, Peter Bayard *physician*
Kaplan, Eugene Alken *psychiatry educator, department chairman*
Kerr, Darlene Dixon *electric power company executive*
King, Bernard T. *lawyer*
King, Marcia Jones *potter, physicist, photographer*
Konski, James Louis *civil engineer*
Krathwohl, David Reading *retired education educator*
Kriesberg, Louis *sociologist, educator*
Lang, James Patrick *priest*
Levitsky, Melvyn *former ambassador, professor*
Levy, Alan Joseph *mechanical engineer, educator*
Levy, H. Richard *biochemistry educator*
Luft, Eric v.d. *librarian, educator, publisher*
Malhotra, Yogesh *former computer scientist, management educator, corporate and national consultant, entrepreneur, former computer engineer*
Marcoccia, Louis Gary *accountant, university administrator*
Mazur, Allan Carl *sociologist, engineer, educator*
McCurn, Neal Peters *federal judge*
McGuire, George R. *lawyer, educator*
Meguid, Michael M. *medical educator, researcher*
Meinig, Donald William *geography educator*
Miles, Kenneth Ontario *academic program director*
Monmonier, Mark *geographer, graphics educator, essayist*
Moynihan, James M. *bishop*
Muller, Ernest H. *geology educator*
Munson, Howard G. *federal judge*
Murphy, Cornelius B., Jr., (Neil Murphy) *academic administrator*
Muters, Michael C. *printmaker*
Numann, Patricia Joy *surgeon, educator*
O'Connor, Michael E. *lawyer*
Ortiz, Fernando, Jr., *commissioner*
Pardee, Otway O'Meara *computer scientist, educator*
Pennock, Donald William *retired mechanical engineer*
Phillips, Larry Arthur *artist*
Phillips, Paul Everard *physician, medical educator*
Pinchuk, Nicholas Thomas *manufacturing executive*
Pinsky, Roy David *lawyer*
Pirozzi, Mildred Jean *nursing administrator*
Powell, James Matthew *history professor*
Prucha, John James *geologist, educator*
Rabuzzi, Daniel D. *medical administrator*
Rivette, Francis Robert *lawyer*
Rogers, Sherry Anne *physician*
Rosenthal, Alan *lawyer*
Rubin, David M. *dean, educator*
Russo, Joseph Maria *public affairs executive*
Sage, Martin Lee *chemistry professor*
Sagerman, Robert Howard *radiation oncologist*
Sargent, Robert George *engineering educator*
Scheinman, Steven Jay *medical educator*
Scullin, Frederick James, Jr., *judge*
Shaw, Kenneth Alan *university president*
Sheehan, Michael Gerard *allergist*
Shires, Linda M. *English educator, writer*
Shulman, Barry Martin *lawyer*
Skoler, Celia Rebecca *retired art gallery director*
Skoler, Louis *architect, educator*
Smardon, Richard Clay *landscape architecture and environmental studies educator*
Smith, Kenneth Judson, Jr., *chemist, theoretician, educator*
Smith, Robert L. *medical research administrator*
Soyars, M. Douglas *academic administrator, music educator*
Sprafkin, Robert Peter *psychologist, educator*
Stam, David Harry *librarian*
Steigerwald, Louis John, III, *corporate executive*
Sternlicht, Sanford *English and theater arts educator, writer*
Streeten, Barbara Wiard *ophthalmologist, medical educator*
Suddaby, Glenn T. *lawyer*
Szasz, Thomas Stephen *psychiatrist, educator, writer*
Tatham, David Frederic *art historian, educator*
Thomas, Sidney *fine arts educator, researcher*
Threatte, Gregory Allen *pathology educator, academic director*
Traylor, Robert Arthur *lawyer*
Trop, Sandra *museum administrator*
Tully, William P. *civil engineer, academic administrator*
Turner, Christopher Edward *cell biology educator*
Vardan, Suman *medical educator*
Verrillo, Ronald Thomas *neuroscience educator, researcher*
Vitharana, Padmal M. *management educator*
Waddy, Patricia A. *architectural history educator*
Ware, Bennie *university administrator*
Weiss, Volker *university administrator, educator*
Welch, Thomas Robert *pediatrician, educator*
Wells, Peter Nathaniel *judge, lawyer*
Whaley, Ross Samuel *environmentalist, educator*
Wiggins, James Bryan *religion educator*
Wilkinson, Louise Cherry *psychology educator, dean*
Williams, Samuel Robert *lawyer*
Williams, William Joseph *physician, educator*
Witkin, Jerome *education educator, painter*
Wolff, Catherine Elizabeth *opera company executive*
Wolff, L. Thomas *physician, educator*
Zimmerman, Golda *lawyer, educator*
Zito, George Vincent *sociologist, sociology educator*

Tallman
Strasser, Joel A. *public relations executive, engineer, executive producer*

Tappan
Dell, Robert Christopher *geothermal sculptor, educator*
Fox, Muriel *retired public relations executive*

Tarrytown
Andreen, Aviva Louise *dentist, researcher, academic administrator, educator*
Bergson, Henry Paul *professional society administrator*
Bowen, Christopher Edward *library director*
Bunton, Phil *editor-in-chief*
Farrell, Gregory Alan *biomedical engineer*
Fazzino, Adis Louise *language educator*
Ferrari, Robert Joseph *business educator, former banker*
Field, Barry Elliot *internist, gastroenterologist*
Gutheil, Irene A. *social work educator, researcher*
Harrison, Michael *lawyer*
Hyman, Leonard Stephen *financial consultant, economist, writer*
Kaplan, Richard *magazine editor*
Kenney, Dion Patrick *information technology executive, entrepreneur*
Kenney, John Michel *architect*
Kirsch, Abigail *culinary productions executive*
Lawry, John D. *psychologist, educator*
LeGrice, Stephen *magazine editor*
Loxley, Alice Anne *writer, educator*
Marcus, Sheldon *adult education educator*
Maun, Mary Ellen *computer consultant*
Neill, Richard Robert *retired publishing company executive*
Safian, Keith Franklin *hospital administrator*
Singh, Brahma Nand *pharmaceutical scientist*
Stein, Sol *publisher, writer, editor in chief*
Sullivan, Janet Nelson *dermatologist, department chairman, health facility administrator*

Vagelos, Pindaros Roy *pharmaceutical executive, researcher*
Weiner, Max *educational psychology educator*
Yancopoulos, George *health facility administrator*

Thornwood
Bassett, Lawrence C *management consultant*

Tonawanda
Drozdziel, Marion John *aeronautical engineer*
Glickman, Marlene *non-profit organization administrator*
Haller, Calvin John *banker*

Troy
Ahlers, Rolf Willi *philosopher, theologian*
Ajayan, Pulickel M. *materials engineering educator*
Arcak, Murat *engineering educator, consultant*
Baecker, David Alan *humanities educator*
Balfour, Alan *architecture educator*
Belfort, Georges *chemical engineering educator, consultant*
Berg, Daniel *science and technology educator*
Bergles, Arthur Edward *mechanical engineering educator*
Block, Robert Charles *nuclear engineering educator, engineering physics educator*
Boyina, Ramana Prasad Venkata *civil engineering educator, researcher*
Brazil, Harold Edmund *political science educator*
Canier, Caren R. *painter, educator*
Carovano, John Martin *not-for-profit administrator, conservationist*
De, Suvranu *education educator*
Demertzoglou, Pindaro Epaminonda *systems administrator, education educator*
Duquette, David Joseph *materials science and engineering educator*
Dvorak, George J. *mechanics and materials engineering educator*
Ehrlich, Henry Lutz *biology professor*
Feeser, Larry James *civil engineering educator, researcher*
Ferris, James Peter *chemist, educator*
Finkel, Sanford Norman *lawyer*
Friedman, Sue Tyler *technical publications executive*
Frost, Jerome Kenneth *lawyer*
Fusfeld, Herbert Irving *research management and public policy executive*
Gerhardt, Lester A. *engineering educator, dean*
Giaever, Ivar *physicist*
Gill, William Nelson *chemical engineering educator*
Glicksman, Martin Eden *materials engineering educator*
Haviland, David Sands *architectural educator, researcher, administrator*
Hsu, Cheng *decision sciences and engineering systems educator*
Jackson, Shirley Ann *academic administrator, physicist*
Jones, E. Stewart, Jr., *lawyer*
Judd, Gary *university administrator*
Kahl, William Frederick *retired college president*
Krause, Sonja *chemistry professor*
Lahey, Richard Thomas, Jr., *nuclear engineer, fluid mechanics engineer*
Layne, Linda Louise *cultural anthropologist, educator*
Levinger, Joseph Solomon *physicist, researcher*
Linton, Jonathan D *management researcher, educator*
Littman, Howard *chemical engineer, educator*
Lvov, Yuri Victorovich *science educator*
McDonald, John Francis Patrick *electrical engineering educator*
Medicus, Heinrich Adolf *physicist, researcher*
Messac, Achille *mechanical engineer, aerospace engineer*
Murtagh, James Patrick *finance educator, consultant*
Nagy, George *education educator*
Neff, Jeanne Henry *academic administrator*
Nelson, John Keith *electrical engineer, educator*
Oatman, Michael James *artist, art educator*
Peterson, G. P. "Bud" *academic administrator*
Phelan, Thomas *clergyman, academic administrator, educator*
Rumyantsev, Sergey L. *research scientist, educator*
Sanderson, Arthur Clark *engineering educator*
Saridis, George Nicholas *electrical, computers and system engineering educator, robotics and automation researcher*
Schechter, Stephen L. *political scientist*
Shephard, Mark Scott *civil and mechanical engineering educator*
Shuey, Richard Lyman *engineering educator, consultant*
Snyder, Patricia Di Benedetto *theater director and administrator*
Sperber, Daniel *physicist*
Szymanski, Boleslaw Karol *computer scientist, educator, entrepreneur*
Wait, Samuel Charles, Jr., *academic administrator, educator*
Willis, John Patrick *chemist*
Woods, John William *electrical, computer and systems engineering educator, consultant*
Xu, Xie George *engineering educator*
Zimmie, Thomas Frank *civil engineer, educator*

Truxton
Schultz, Helen Welkley *marriage and family therapist, minister*

Tuckahoe
Brecher, Bernd *management consultant*

Tupper Lake
Welsh, Peter Corbett *museum consultant, historian*

Tuxedo Park
Domjan, Joseph *artist*
Friedman, Rodger *antiquarian bookseller, consultant*
Regan, Ellen Frances (Mrs. Walston Shepard Brown) *ophthalmologist, educator*

Uniondale
Cassidy, David Michael *lawyer*
Gracin, Hank *lawyer*
Hamrlik, Roman *professional hockey player*
Lemle, Robert Spencer *lawyer*
Meng, M. Kathryn *lawyer*
Milbury, Mike *professional hockey coach*
Osgood, Chris *professional hockey player*
Pratt, George Cheney *law educator, retired federal judge*
Tulchin, Stanley *banker, lecturer, author, business reorganization consultant, credit manager*
Wang, Charles B. *professional sports team executive*

Unionville
Kemnitz, Myrna Kay *publishing executive*
Kemnitz, Thomas Milton *publisher*

Upton
Ben-Zvi, Ilan *physicist, educator*
Bond, Peter Danford *physicist*
Carsten, Arland Leon *radiobiologist, researcher, educator, consultant*
Chaudhari, Praveen *science administrator, materials physicist*
Foerster, Conrad Louis *project engineer*
Fowler, Joanna S. *chemist*
Fthenakis, Vasilis *chemical engineer, consultant, educator*
Goldhaber, Maurice *physicist, researcher*
Hamilton, Leonard Derwent *physician, molecular biologist*
Hendrie, Joseph Mallam *physicist, nuclear engineer, government official*
Lindenbaum, S(eymour) J(oseph) *physicist*
Lowenstein, Derek Irving *physicist*
Mu, Yeming *statistician, medical researcher*
Meinhold, Charles Boyd *health physicist*
Melucci, Richard Charles *research institute administrator*
Ozaki, Satoshi *physicist*
Paul, Peter *science administrator*
Ruggiero, Alessandro G. *physicist, researcher*
Samios, Nicholas Peter *physicist*
Setlow, Jane Kellock *biophysicist*
Setlow, Richard Burton *biophysicist, researcher*
Steinberg, Meyer *chemical engineer*
Susskind, Herbert *biomedical engineer, educator*
Sutin, Norman *chemistry educator, scientist*
Tannenbaum, Michael J(ay) *physicist*

Utica
Antzelevitch, Charles *research center executive*
Austin, Michael Charles *insurance company executive*
Boyle, William Leo, Jr., *educational consultant, retired college president*
Cardamone, Richard J. *judge*
Fiori-Blanchfield, Joan *artist, art historian*
Millet, John Bradford *retired surgeon*
Min, Balshik *pathologist*
Mortenson, Thomas Theodore *medical products executive, management consultant*
Schrauth, William Lawrence *banker, lawyer*
Schweizer, Paul Douglas *museum director*
Wagner, Frederick Reese *retired language educator*

Valatie
Smith, Albert Aloysius, Jr., *electrical engineer, consultant*

Valhalla
Aronow, Wilbert Solomon *physician, educator*
Balazy, Michael *pharmacologist, educator*
Christesen, John Denis *business educator*
Chung, Fung-Lung *cancer research scientist*
Cimino, Joseph Anthony *preventive medicine physician, educator*
Czarnecki, Anthony J. *correction administrator, educator*
Del Guercio, Louis Richard Maurice *surgeon, educator*
De Nicola, Peter Francis *photographic distributor*
Duan, Jiandong *neurologist, researcher*
Frishman, William Howard *cardiology educator, cardiovascular pharmacologist, gerontologist*
Goodman, Alvin Irwin *internist, nephrologist, educator*
Hankin, Joseph Nathan *college president*
Kline, Susan Anderson *medical school official and dean, internist*
Madden, Robert Edward *surgeon, educator*
Marks, Stephen J. *neurologist, educator*
McGoldrick, Kathryn Elizabeth *anesthesiologist, educator, writer*
O'Connell, Ralph Anthony *dean, psychiatrist, educator*
Peterson, Stephen Joseph *internist*
Reed, George Elliott *surgeon, educator, dean*
Safai, Bijan *physician, investigator*
Slim, Michel S. *surgeon, educator, health facility administrator*
Stringel, Gustavo *pediatric surgeon*
Weinberg, Hubert *plastic surgeon*
Weisburger, John Hans *medical researcher*
Williams, Gary Murray *medical researcher, pathology educator*

Valley Cottage
Lazecko, David John *broadcast executive*
Tombros, Peter George *pharmaceutical company executive*

Valley Stream
De Mita, Francis Anthony *mathematics professor*
Isaacs, Leonard Bernard *lawyer*
Lehner, Remy D. *publishing executive*
Levine, Marilyn Markovich *lawyer, arbitrator*
Rachlin, Harvey Brant *writer*
Robbins, Harvey Arnold *textile company executive*
Rodgers, John Joseph, III, *educational administration consultant, educator*
Viegas, Louis Paul *real estate salesperson, retired postmaster*

Van Hornesville
Durham, Ormonde George, III, *manufacturing executive*

Vestal
Cohen, Marvin A. *writer*
Day, Stephen Fred *school system administrator, writer*
McGuire, John Thomas *lawyer, educator*
Piaker, Philip Martin *accountant, educator*
Wagar, (Walter) Warren (Walter Wagar) *historian, educator*

Victor
Van Bortel, Mary Catherine *sales executive*

Waccabuc
Krefting, Robert J(ohn) *publishing company executive*

Wading River
Marlow, Audrey Swanson *artist, designer*

Wainscott
Henderson, William Charles *editor*
Herzog, Arthur, III, *author*
Russo, Alexander Peter *artist, educator*

Wallkill
Leopold, Richard William *middle school educator*
Strauser, Susan Parkyn *performing arts educator, singer*

Walton
Bartlett, Raymond L. *music educator*

Wantagh
Galvan, Max *humanities educator*
Glaser, David *painter, sculptor*
Marcatante, John Joseph *educational administrator*
Ross, Sheldon Jules *dentist*
Smits, Edward John *museum consultant*
Zinder, Newton Donald *stock market analyst, consultant*

Wappingers Falls
Aguero-Rosenfeld, Maria E. *pathologist, medical microbiologist*
Haynes, Paul R. *lawyer*
Hogan, Edward Robert *financial services executive*
Johnson, Jeh Vincent *architect*
Kells, Albert John *financial consultant*
Nolan, John Thomas, Jr., *retired oil industry administrator*

Warsaw
Cook, Charlotte Smallwood *lawyer*

Warwick
Franck, Frederick Sigfred *artist, author, dental surgeon*
Gould, Keely Ann *music educator, conductor*
Greenwood, John Edward Douglas *investment banker, lawyer*
Kaminsky, Anatol *educator, writer*
Linnéa, Sharon *writer, playwright*
Simon, Dolores Daly *copy editor*
Tinney, Diane Linda *publishing executive*

Water Mill
Hagstrom, Jack Walter Carl Kling *retired pathology educator*
Kreimer, Michael Walter *financial planner, investment company executive*

Waterford
Glavin, A. Rita Chandellier (Mrs. James Henry Glavin III) *lawyer*
Glavin, James Henry, III, *lawyer*
Gold, James Paul *museum director*
Novotny, F. Douglas *lawyer*

Waterloo
Schreck, Richard Thomas *accountant*

Watertown
Brett, James Clarence *retired journalism educator*
Coe, Benjamin Plaisted *retired state official*
Faunce, Russ *educator, musician*
Ingalsbe, Marie Esther *artist*
Machuga, Thomas Richard *music educator*
Militello, Samuel Philip *lawyer*

Webster
Duke, Charles Bryan *electronics executive, physicist, educator*
McCormack, Stanley Eugene *financial consultant*
McWilliams, C. Paul, Jr., *engineering executive*
Nicastro, Kathleen Wanda *artist, educator*
Nicholson, Douglas Robert *accountant*
Southard, Paul Raymond *financial executive*
Zhang, Shengliang *materials scientist, physicist*

Weedsport
Cichello, Samuel Joseph *architect*
English, Richard Paul *music educator*
Kinch, Christopher Peter *priest*

Wellsville
Fuller, Bruce E. *mechanical engineer*
Tezak, Edward George *mechanics educator*
Van Tyne, Arthur Morris *geologist*

West Chazy
Slosson, Constance Sweet *retired music educator*

West Harrison
Johnson, Craig Edward *lawyer*
Verano, Anthony Frank *retired banker*

West Haverstraw
Cavaliere, Rossella *neurologist*

West Hempstead
Conway-Gervais, Kathleen Marie *reading specialist, educational consultant*
DeGroff, Dale *food service executive*
Dillmon, Robert Otho *music educator, editor*
Guggenheimer, Heinrich Walter *mathematician, educator*

West Hurley
Martucci, Vincent James *composer, pianist*

West Islip
Doganay, Kazim Levent *physician*
Elkowitz, Sheryl Sue *radiologist*
Keller, Joyce *television and radio host, counselor, writer*

West Kill
Dwon, Larry *retired electrical engineer, educator, consultant*

West Nyack
Coffey, Kimberly E. *secondary school educator*
Hilpert, Dale W. *retail shoe company executive*
Oppenheim, Robert *beauty industry executive*
Pringle, Laurence Patrick *writer*

West Point
Boettner, Daisie Dawson *military officer, mechanical engineering educator*
Bozeman, Laura Beth *military officer, educator*
Keith, Bruce Edward *sociologist*
Ross, Robert Joseph (Bobby Ross) *college football coach*
Stock, Margaret Deborah *lawyer*
Watson, Georgianna *librarian*

Westbury
Boes, Lawrence William *lawyer*
De Pauw, Gommar Albert *priest, educator*
Lorber, Howard Mark *investments executive*
McCann, James F. *consumer products company executive*
Ross-Lee, Barbara *dean, educator*
Sandler, Gerald Howard *computer science educator, company executive*
Sherbell, Rhoda *artist, sculptor*

Westchester
Kepcher, Carolyn *real estate company executive*

Westhampton Beach
Flood, Angela *interior designer, artist*
Maas, Jane Brown *advertising executive*

White Plains
Adkins, Rodney *computer company executive*
Alin, Robert David *lawyer*
Allen, Ralph Dean *diversified company corporate executive*
Araskog, Rand Vincent *former diversified telecommunications multinational company executive*
Barland, Peter *rheumatologist, medical educator*
Beldock, Donald Travis *corporate financial executive*
Berlin, Alan Daniel *lawyer, international energy and legal consultant*
Bernard, Robert William *plastic surgeon*
Biers, Martin Henry *physician*
Blass, John Paul *psychiatrist, neurologist, geriatrician, educator*
Bloom, Adam I. *psychologist*
Bober, Lawrence Harold *retired banker*
Bodnar, Peter O. *lawyer*
Brieant, Charles La Monte *federal judge*
Brown, Ronald C. *hotel executive*
Bushkin, Merle Jerome *investment banker*
Carey, John *judge*
Carlisle, Jay Charles, II, *lawyer, educator*
Carlucci, Joseph P. *lawyer*
Chen, Shuang *computer science professional*
Cohn, John L. *merchant banker*
Colwell, Howard Otis *advertising executive*
Conner, William Curtis *judge*
Cotter, Robert F. *hotel executive*
D'Aloise, Lawrence T., Jr., *lawyer*
Davenport, Lindsay *professional tennis player*
David, Miles *association and marketing executive*
Davies, Matt *cartoonist*
Dee, William *engineering executive*
Denham, Paul *technology sales and marketing executive*
Donofrio, Nick *information technology executive*
Doyle, Dennis T. *lawyer*
Doyle, John McCormick *actuary, pension plan consultant*
Dvorak, Roger Gran *health facility executive*
Erla, Karen *artist, painter, collagist, printmaker*
Feder, Robert *lawyer*
Feldman, Jerome Ira *lawyer, patent development executive*
Fleming, Robert Burke *law educator, lawyer*
Foster, John Horace *consulting environmental engineer*
Fowler, James D., Jr., *leadership executive*
Fowlkes, Nancy Lanetta Pinkard *social worker*
Frazier, Amy *professional tennis player*
Freed, Arthur *civil engineer*
Friedman, Stephen J *lawyer*
Frieling, Jerry *engineering executive*
Garrison-Jackson, Zina *retired professional tennis player*
Gilbert, Bradley *professional tennis coach, former professional tennis player, former Olympic athlete*
Gimelstob, Justin *professional tennis player*
Giuliano, Louis J. *industrial manufacturing company executive*
Gjertsen, O. Gerard *lawyer*
Gottlieb, Lester M. *entrepreneur*
Greene, Leonard Michael *aerospace manufacturing executive, institute executive*
Greenspan, Leon Joseph *lawyer*
Greer, Robert E. *retired insurance executive*
Grossman, Ann (Ann Grossman-Wunderlich) *retired professional tennis player*
Haines, Daniel Webster *engineering consultant, educator*
Halpern, Philip Morgan *lawyer*
Hardin, Adlai Stevenson, Jr., *judge*
Heimerdinger, John Frederick *association executive*
Heo, Moonseong *statistician, researcher*
Horn, Paul M. *information technology executive, crystallographer*
Howse, Jennifer Louise *foundation administrator*
Howson, Christopher Paul *medical association administrator, epidemiologist*
Isaak, Robert Allen *international management and political economy educator, writer*
Jacobson, Sandra W. *lawyer*
Katz, Michael *pediatrician, educator*
Kaushik, Surendra Kumar *economist*
Kelly, John E., III, *information technology executive*
Krasne, Charles A. *food products executive*
Kroner, Arnold Friedrich *financial consultant, economist*
Kurzman, Robert Graham *lawyer, educator*
Leung, Betty Brigid *nursing administrator*
Levine, Steven Jon *lawyer*
Liebert, Peter Selig *pediatric surgeon, consultant*
Loranger, Steven R. *industrial manufacturing company executive*
Lukaszewski, James Edmund *communications executive*
MacDonald, J. Randall *information technology executive, human resources specialist*
Machover, Carl *computer graphics consultant*
Madden, M. Stuart *lawyer*

Maffeo, Vincent Anthony *lawyer, executive*
Manville, Stewart Roebling *archivist*
Marano, Anthony Joseph *cardiologist*
McAuliffe, John C. *health/medical products executive*
McCarthy, John Robert *real estate company officer*
McCulloch, James Callahan *corporate executive*
McDowell, Fletcher Hughes *physician, educator*
McNeil, Lori Michelle *professional tennis player*
Mills, Steven A. *information technology executive*
Mitchell, Robert Dale *consulting engineer*
Moffat, Robert W., Jr., *information technology executive*
Morariu, Corina *professional tennis player*
Morello, Daniel Conway *plastic surgeon*
Munneke, Gary Arthur *law educator, consultant*
Nastasi, Aldo A. *judge*
Nesci, Vincent Peter *lawyer*
Newman, Marie Stefanini *law librarian, educator*
Null, William Seth *lawyer*
Ottinger, Richard Lawrence *dean emeritus*
Palmisano, Samuel J. *information technology executive*
Parker, Barrington D., Jr., *federal judge, lawyer*
Payson, Martin F. *lawyer*
Peyton, Donald Leon *retired standards association executive*
Pfeffer, Cynthia Roberta *psychiatrist, educator*
Pitegoff, Thomas Michael *lawyer*
Pollak, Martin Marshall *lawyer, training company executive*
Prabhu, Vasant *corporate financial executive*
Rapp, Richard Tilden *economist, consultant*
Raymond, Lisa *professional tennis player*
Robinson, Nicholas Adams *lawyer, educator*
Rosenberg, Michael *lawyer*
Rosner, Jonathan Levi *lawyer*
Royle, Cynthia *editor*
Rubin, Chanda *professional tennis player*
Salameh, Samer Fadi *communications executive*
Scott-Williams, Wendy Lee *information technology specialist*
Sedelmaier, J. J. *filmmaker*
Silverberg, Steven Mark *lawyer*
Slaughter, John Brooks *professional society administrator*
Sloan, F(rank) Blaine *law educator*
Smith, Gerard Peter *neuroscientist*
Soley, Robert Lawrence *plastic surgeon*
Sternlicht, Barry Stuart *hotel executive*
Surpris, Joseph W. *research scientist*
Sussberg, Milton Joel *marketing professional*
Underweiser, Irwin Philip *mining executive, lawyer*
Urbach, Michael H. *utilities/energy executive*
Volpe, Bruce Thomas *neurologist*
Wedge, Chris *animation director, studio executive*
Westerhoff, Garret Peter *environmental engineer, executive*
Wheaton, David *professional tennis player*
Williams, Edward W. *information technology executive*
Williams, Serena *professional tennis player*
Williams, Ted Vaughnell *physical education educator*
Williams, Venus *professional tennis player*
Zuckerman, Marc Abraham *accountant, educator*

Whitesboro
Bulman, William Patrick *data processing executive*
Kwiat, Kevin Anthony *computer engineer*
O'Hara, Cynthia O'Connor *writer, columnist, food consultant*

Whitestone
Bocchino, Frances Lucia *retired oil company official*
Bodinger, William *health, medical products executive*
Caputo, Daniel Vincent *psychologist*
Lodico, Cheryl Madeline *secondary school educator*
Rahr, Stewart *health medical products executive*
Rosmarin, Leonard Alan *dermatologist*

Williamstown
Frank, Joshua M. *economist, think-tank executive*

Williamsville
Ackerman, Philip Charles *utilities executive, lawyer*
Berner, Robert Frank *managerial statistics educator, administrator*
Brown, Stephen Ira *philosophy educator*
Canfield, Cheryl Lucas *epidemiologist*
Cloudsley, Donald Hugh *library administrator*
Drew, Fraser Bragg Robert *language educator*
Garton, Charles *classics educator*
Jones, Robert Alfred *retired clergyman*
Kennedy, Bernard Joseph *retired utility executive*
Levite, Laurence A. *publishing executive*
Mack, Gregory John *financial executive and consultant*
Ogra, Pearay L. *pediatrician, educator*
Rath, Mary Lou *state legislator*
Reisman, Robert E. *physician, educator*
Rekate, Albert C. *physician*
Truell, George Foster *management consultant*
Whitcomb, James Stuart *videographer, photographer, production company executive*

Williston Park
Segel, J. Norman *garment manufacturing company executive*

Willow
Bley, Carla Borg *composer*

Willsboro
Gillilland, Thomas *art gallery director*

Windsor
Warner, Roberta Arlene *retired accountant, financial services executive*

Wolcott
Bartlett, Cody Blake *lawyer, educator*
Searle, Robert Ferguson *minister*

Woodbury
Agresti, Miriam Monell *psychologist*
Berezin, Evelyn *management consultant*
Bleicher, Sheldon Joseph *endocrinologist, medical educator*
Guttenplan, Harold Esau *retired food company executive*
Kantarci, Sibel *geneticist*
Mangia, Angelo James *lawyer*

Woodhaven
Bolster, Jacqueline Neben (Mrs. John A. Bolster) *communications consultant*
Zizi, *artist*

Woodmere
Cohen, Lawrence Alan *health facility administrator*
Raab, Ira Jerry *lawyer, judge*
Seyfert, Wayne George *secondary education educator, anatomy educator*
Winick, Bernyce Alpert *artist, photographer*

Woodside
Hofmann, Herbert C. *diversified financial services company executive*
Unsal-Tunay, Nuran *geological engineer, researcher*
VanArsdale, Diana Cort *social worker*

Woodstock
Banks, Rela *sculptor*
Currie, Bruce *artist*
Godwin, Gail Kathleen *writer*
Lieberman, Josefa Nina *psychologist, educator, writer*
Ober, Stuart Alan *investment consultant, book publisher*

Wyandanch
Hodges-Robinson, Chettina M. *nursing administrator*

Yaphank
Ahern, John James *software company executive*
Digilio, Jr., John Thomas *health care executive, consultant*

Yonkers
Baumel, Herbert *violinist, conductor*
Baumel, Joan Patricia French *educator, writer, lecturer*
Chumaceiro, Rolando Jose Mendez *family practice physician*
Colabella, George Michael *management, fund raising consultant*
Connors, James Patrick *lawyer*
Daman, Harlan Richard *allergist, educator*
Denver, Eileen Ann *retired magazine editor*
Fyle, Clifford Nelson *publishing executive, educator*
Gunner, Murray *religious organization administrator*
Halloran, Jean *advocate*
Holtz, Gilbert Joseph *steel company executive*
Johansen, Robert Joseph *consulting actuary*
Kagan, Julia Lee *magazine editor*
Karpatkin, Rhoda Hendrick *retired consumer information organization executive, lawyer*
Lawson, Beverly Elaine *nursing administrator*
Lieberman, Trudy *healthcare journalist*
Liggio, Jean Vincenza *adult education educator, artist*
Lupiani, Donald Anthony *psychologist*
Miller, Karl A. *management counselor*
Monegro, Francisco *psychology educator, alternative medicine consultant*
Neal, Leora Louise Haskett *social services administrator*
Philipps, Edward William *banker, real estate appraiser*
Roberson, Doris Jean Herold *retired social worker*
Rosch, Elliott Carl *internist*
Singer, Cecile Doris *bank executive, former state legislator*
Slade, Margot *editor*
Smith, Aldo Ralston, Jr., *brokerage house executive*
Spagnuolo, Mario *physician*
Speirs, Greg *artist*
Torrese, Dante Michael *prosthodontist, educator*
Trentanelli, John Anthony *educational administrator*
Varma, Baidya Nath *sociologist, broadcaster, poet*
Viola, Mary Jo *art history educator*
Wen, Sheree *computer company executive*
Weston, Francine Evans *secondary school educator*
Wolfson, Irwin M. *insurance company executive*

York
Coleman, David Cecil *financial executive*

Yorktown Heights
Agerwala, Tilak Krishna Mahesh *computer company executive*
Auslander, Marc Alan *computer scientist*
Avouris, Phaedon *chemical physicist*
Berk, George Ellis *cardiologist*
Bogdanoff, Stewart Ronald *physical education educator, coach*
Cai, Jin *research scientist, electrical engineer*
Delmoro, Ronald Anthony *elementary school principal*
Dennard, Robert Heath *engineering executive, scientist*
d'Heurle, François Max *research scientist, engineering educator*
Donovan, Andrew Joseph *financial consultant*
Fowler, Alan Bicksler *retired physicist*
Gerard, Mayer J. *physician*
Hoffman, Alan Jerome *mathematician, educator*
Jones, Lauretta Marie *artist, designer, computer science researcher*
Keyes, Robert W. *physicist, researcher*
Kim, Hyungjun *materials scientist, researcher*
Lang, Norton David *physicist*
Lei, Hui *computer scientist*
Lu, Yingdong *research scientist*
Neti, Chalapathy *computer scientist, researcher*
Rosenblatt, Stephen Paul *marketing and sales promotion company executive*
Saon, George A. *computer scientist, researcher*
Sorokin, Peter Pitirimovich *physicist, researcher*
Terman, Lewis Madison *electrical engineer, researcher*
Tersoff, Jerry David *physicist*
Wade, James O'Shea *editor, writer*
Winterton, Joseph Henry *computer software executive*
Witt, John J. *artist*
Wu, Chai Wah *research scientist*
Wynne, James *research scientist*

Youngstown
Alpert, Norman *chemical company executive*
Lamb, Charles F. *educator, retired minister*

NORTH CAROLINA

Aberdeen
Jacobson, Peter Lars *neurologist, educator*

Advance
Cochrane, Betsy Lane *former state senator*
Guth, Caryl Joy *retired anesthesiologist*
Herpel, George Lloyd *marketing educator*
Walser, Sandra Teresa Johnson *rehabilitation nurse, preceptor*

Andrews
Cozart, Kimberly Marie *music educator*
Fonda, Ronald Alan *epistemologist*

Angier
Carwell, Gloria Jean *writer*

Archdale
O'Hara, Karen Ann *mathematician, educator*

Arden
Baker, Kerry Allen *management consultant*
Seagle, J. Harold *lawyer*

Asheboro
Boone, Harvey Claxton *quality assurance professional, writer*
Bunch, W(alter) Edward *lawyer*
Burton, Bernard Ottway *lawyer*
Clark, Lawrence James *minister*
Croom, John Henry, III, *utility company executive*
Helsabeck, Eric H. *emergency physician*
Jones, David M. *zoological park administrator*

Asheville
Astler, Vernon Benson *surgeon*
Bissette, Winston Louis, Jr., *lawyer, mayor*
Boyce, Emily Stewart *retired library and information science educator*
Brown, David G. *academic administrator*
Bushong, Joe Gregory *finance educator, accountant*
Carver, Peter James *education educator, director*
Chapman, Gary H. *artist, educator*
Chidnese, Patrick N. *retired lawyer*
Codd, Richard Trent, Jr., *computer scientist, educator*
Cogburn, Max Oliver *lawyer*
Coli, Guido John *chemical company executive*
Davis, Roy Walton, Jr., *lawyer*
De Bruhl, A. Marshall *writer, editor, publishing consultant*
Dickens, Charles Henderson *retired social scientist, consultant*
Dillard, John Robert *lawyer*
Dunn, Shari *public relations executive*
Easterling, David Royer *climatologist*
Fobes, John Edwin *international organization official*
Frue, William Calhoun *lawyer*
Haggard, William Henry *meteorologist*
Hamilton, Jackson Douglas *lawyer*
Horwitz, Bertrand Nathan *accounting educator, finance educator*
Hyde, Herbert Lee *lawyer*
Jaslow, Howard *engineer*
Johnston, John Devereaux, Jr., *retired law educator*
Jones-Rafferty, Brenda Anne *personal growth and development company executive*
Kessler, Donald Joe *research scientist, physicist, consultant*
King, Joseph Bertram *architect*
Lavelle, Brian Francis David *lawyer*
Letzig, Betty Jean *financial consultant*
McGrotty, Carole Weaver *elementary school educator, parochial school educator*
McKeown, Peter Philip *medical center administrator, medical educator, cardiothoracic surgeon*
Meyerson, Seymour *retired chemist*
Parresol, Bernard Ross *research biometrician, statistician*
Reed, Patsy Bostick *former academic administrator*
Sarai, Darshan Singh *environmentalist, entomologist*
Schaffer, Bryan Stuart *finance educator*
Scully, Bonnie Diane *financial planner*
Sgro, Beverly Huston *day school administrator, educator, state official*
Sims, Bennett Jones *minister, educator*
Thornburg, Lacy Herman *federal judge*
Vander Voort, Dale Gilbert *textile company executive*
Voigt, Ellen *literature educator*
Weed, Maurice James *composer, retired music educator*
White, Terry Edward *physician*
Wilson, Thomas Douglas, Jr., *lawyer*

Banner Elk
Bernstein, Mark R. *retired lawyer*
Robinson, Earl James *academic administrator, information systems and statistics educator, consultant*
Tilden, Ralph Fulton *retired music educator, organist*

Beaufort
Bonaventura, Celia Jean *biochemist, researcher*
Burgard, Ralph *cultural and education planner*
Cullman, Hugh *retired tobacco company executive*
Ramus, Joseph S. *marine biologist*
Tilghman, Carl Lewis *lawyer*

Beech Mountain
Alea, Jorge Antonio *physician*

Belmont
Abernathy, Dixie Friend *elementary school educator, principal*
Baumstein, Paschal M. *priest*
Stowe, Robert Lee, III, *textile company executive*

Biltmore Forest
Sgro, Joseph Anthony *retired psychologist, educator*

Black Mountain
Cody, Hiram Sedgwick, Jr., *retired telecommunications industry executive*
Ingle, Robert P. *retail groceries company executive*
Lanning, James W. *retail executive*
Proctor, Jesse Harris, Jr., *political science educator*
Tudor, Brenda S. *retail company executive*

Blowing Rock
Barnebey, Kenneth Alan *food company executive*
Corlett, Edward Stanley, III, *retired lawyer*
Kay, Kenneth *performing company executive*
Littlejohn, Mark Hays *retired radiologist, artist*

Boiling Springs
White, Martin Christopher *academic administrator*

Boone
Bowden, Elbert Victor *banking, finance and economics educator, author*
Cole, Susan Stockbridge *theater educator*
Domer, Floyd Ray *pharmacologist, educator*
Duke, Charles Richard *academic dean*
Hay, Fred J. *education educator, librarian, editor*
Jones, Dan Lewis *psychologist*
Keefe, Susan Emley *anthropology educator*
Krug, Jeffrey Alan *international business educator*
Land, Ming Huey *college dean*
Lugo, Emil J. *retired secondary school educator*
Mackorell, James Theodore, Jr., *entrepreneur, small business owner*
McFadden, Margaret H. *education educator, writer*
Morris, Robert Darrell *reading education educator*
Oelberg, Robert Nathan *landscape architect*
Pollard, William Barlow, III, *university educator*
Stahl, Ray Emerson *freelance writer, historian, researcher*
Warren, Robert Lee *dentist, educator*
Woollcombe, Graham Douglas *dean*

Brevard
Dillon, Doris (Doris Dillon Kenofer) *artist, art historian, educator*
Effron, David Louis *conductor, music director*
Finnerty, Frances Martin *medical administrator*
Flory, Margaret Martha *retired religious organization administrator*
Glesener, Robert Richard *biologist, educator, researcher*
Phillips, Euan Hywel *publishing executive*

Buies Creek
Blalock, Mary Wright *counselor*
Davis, Ferd Leary, Jr., *law educator, lawyer, consultant*
Johnson, George Lloyd *education educator, consultant, writer*
Martin, James Ingram *education educator*
Whichard, Willis Padgett *law educator, retired state supreme court justice*
Wiggins, Norman Adrian *university administrator, legal educator*

Bullock
Stead, Eugene Anson, Jr., *physician*

Burlington
Blevins, James Ray *lawyer, insurance company claims executive*
Buckley, J. Stephen *newspaper publisher*
Elingburg, Wesley R. *health products executive*
Flagg, Raymond Osbourn *retired biology executive*
Holt, Bertha Merrill *state legislator*
Knesel, Ernest Arthur, Jr., *diagnostic company executive*
MacMahon, Thomas P. *healthcare company executive*
Malinda, Paul F. *emergency physician*
Mark, Edna Brown *health facility administrator, writer*
Novak, Richard L. *health products executive*
Powell, James Bobbitt *biomedical laboratories executive, pathologist*
Slayton, John Howard *lawyer, trust company executive*
Wilson, William Preston *psychiatrist, educator*

Burnsville
Doyle, John Lawrence *artist*

Camden
Hammond, Roy Joseph *reinsurance company executive*

Canton
Dixon, Shirley Juanita *retired restaurant owner*
Roberts, Bill Glen *retired fire chief, investor, consultant*

Cape Carteret
Mullikin, Thomas Wilson *mathematics professor*

Carthage
Lapping, Sherwood Foster *lawyer*

Cary
Alstadt, Donald Martin *business executive*
Atwood, Brent A *investment banker*
Bogdanovich, Alexander *manufacturing executive*
Bowen, Chester Edward *financial consultant, financial planner*
Briggs, Joseph Jay *communications engineer*
Buckler, Sheldon A. *technology company executive*
Conrad, Hans *materials engineering educator*
Craig, Harold Kent *mechanical contracting executive, systems analyst*
Cromer, Charles Lemuel *lawyer, state legislator*
Goodnight, James H. *software company executive*
Hagan, John Aubrey *retired financial executive*
Kimbrell, Odell Culp, Jr., *internist*
Kung, Pang-Jen *materials scientist, electrical engineer*
Martin, William Royall, Jr., *retired association executive*
Mata, Elizabeth Adams *language educator, land investor*
Montgomery, Charles Harvey *lawyer*
Odum, Jeffery Neal *mechanical engineer*
Pchelnikov, Yuriy Nikitich *microwave engineer*
Sail, John *computer company executive*
Sall, John *information technology executive*
Siporin, David *human resources specialist*
Slaattè, Howard Alexander *minister, philosophy educator*
Taylor, David Wyatt Aiken *retired clergyman*
Taylor, James Francis *marketing professional*

Vick, Columbus Edwin, Jr., *retired civil engineering design firm executive*
Wait, George William *sales executive*
Wright, Robert G. *engineering executive*

Cashiers

O'Connell, Edward James, Jr., *psychology educator, computer applications and data analysis consultant*

Chapel Hill

Aamoth, Gordon M. *medical association administrator*
Andrews, Richard Nigel Lyon *public policy educator, environmental studies administrator*
Arnold, Roland R. *dental educator and researcher*
Bailey, Donald B., Jr., *medical and special education educator*
Bailey, Herbert Smith, Jr., *retired publisher*
Baker, Christopher Cameron *surgeon*
Baker, Paul Thornell *anthropology educator*
Barbarin, Oscar Anthony *psychologist*
Baroff, George Stanley *psychologist, educator*
Bauer, Frederick Christian *motor carrier executive*
Bawden, James Wyatt *dental educator, dental scientist*
Berkey, Douglas Bryan *dental educator, researcher, gerontologist, clinician*
Black, Stanley Warren, III, *economics professor*
Bondurant, Stuart *physician, educational association administrator*
Bovarsky, Rose Fisman *psychologist*
Boyarsky, Saul *lawyer, forensic urologist, physiologist, educator*
Briggaman, Robert Alan *dermatologist, medical educator*
Broad, Margaret Corbett (Molly Broad) *academic administrator*
Brooks, Frederick Phillips, Jr., *computer scientist, educator*
Broun, Kenneth Stanley *lawyer, educator*
Brower, David John *lawyer, urban planner, educator*
Brown, Frank *social science educator*
Brown, Keith John *computer applications analyst*
Browning, Christopher R. *historian, educator*
Bursey, Maurice M. *chemistry professor*
Campbell, Bobby Jack *university official*
Campbell, William Aubrey *law educator*
Carroll, Roy *retired academic administrator*
Carson, Culley Clyde, III, *urologist, educator*
Chang, Kuk Won *theology educator, researcher, pastor*
Chapman, Robert Lee, III, *real estate developer*
Clemmons, David Robert *internist, educator*
Cole, Richard Ray *university dean*
Coles, William Henry *ophthalmologist, educator*
Collier, Albert M. *pediatric educator, child development center director*
Coulter, Elizabeth Jackson *biostatistician, educator*
Crews, Fulton Timm *pharmacology educator*
Cromartie, William James *medical educator, researcher*
Cronenwett, Linda Houk *dean*
Cunningham, James William *literacy education educator, researcher*
Dahlstrom, William Grant *psychologist, educator*
Davis, Sarah Irwin *retired English language educator*
Daye, Charles Edward *law educator*
Debreczeny, Paul *Slavic language educator, writer*
De Friese, Gordon H. *health services researcher*
De Rosa, Guy Paul *orthopedic surgery educator*
Dixon, Frederick Dail *architect*
Dixon, John Wesley, Jr., *retired religion and art educator*
Dolan, Louise Ann *physicist*
Droegemueller, William *gynecologist, obstetrician, medical educator*
Drossman, Douglas Arnold *medical investigator, educator, gastroenterologist*
Drutz, David Jules *biotechnology executive*
Eaton, Charles Edward *English language educator, author*
Edwards, Richard LeRoy *dean, social sciences educator, management consultant*
Eliel, Ernest Ludwig *chemist, educator*
Falk, Ronald J. *medical educator*
Feduccia, J. Alan *biologist, educator*
Feinberg, Lawrence Edward *language educator, researcher*
Ferrell, Joseph Stevens *law educator*
Ferris, William Reynolds *humanities organization administrator, folklore educator*
Fieleke, Norman Siegfried *economist, educator*
Fine, J(ames) Allen *insurance company executive*
Fletcher, Suzanne Wright *epidemiologist, medical educator, editor*
Flora, Joseph M(artin) *English language educator*
Fordham, Christopher Columbus, III, *dean, academic administrator, medical educator*
Forman, Donald T. *biochemist, educator*
Fowler, Wesley Caswell, Jr., *obstetrician, gynecologist*
Fox, Ronald Ernest *psychologist*
Frampton, Paul Howard *physics researcher, educator*
Freedman, Irving Melvin *lawyer*
Freund, Cynthia M. *dean*
Friedman, James Winstein *economist, educator*
Froeber, Sarah Marjorie *actress, playwright, educator*
Ganley, Oswald Harold *retired director*
Godschalk, David Robinson *architect, urban development planner, educator*
Goldsmith, Lowell Alan *medical educator*
Gottlieb, Gilbert *psychobiologist, educator*
Goyer, Robert Andrew *pathology educator*
Graham, George Adams *political scientist, emeritus educator*
Graham, John Borden *pathologist, writer, educator*
Gray, Virginia Hickman *political science educator*
Gray-Little, Bernadette *psychologist, educator*
Grayson, Mark *organization executive*
Grendler, Paul Frederick *history educator*
Gressman, Eugene *lawyer*
Hackenbrock, Charles R. *cell biologist, educator*
Hammond, David Alan *stage director, educator*
Handy, Rollo Leroy *philosopher, researcher*
Harden, T. Kendall *pharmacologist, educator*
Hardin, Paul, III, *law educator*
Hartlyn, Jonathan *political scientist, educator*
Haskell, Paul Gershon *retired law educator*
Hauser, Charles Newland McCorkle *newspaper consultant*
Hawkins, David Rollo, Sr., *psychiatrist, educator*
Heninger, Simeon Kahn, Jr., *English language educator*
Henson, O'Dell Williams, Jr., *retired anatomy educator*
Hobson, Fred Colby, Jr., *English educator, author*
Houpt, Jeffrey Lyle *psychiatrist, educator, former dean*
Howard, James Francis, Jr., *medical educator, neurologist*
Hsiao, Li-Ling *philosopher, educator*
Huber, Evelyne *political science educator*
Hulka, Barbara Sorenson *epidemiologist, educator*
Hulka, Jaroslav Fabian *obstetrician, gynecologist*
Hunt, Katrina Weisner *marketing professional*
Illiano, Antonio *language educator, researcher*
Ingram, James Carlton *economist, educator*
Irene, Eugene Arthur *physical chemistry and materials science educator, researcher*
James, Alton Everette, Jr., *radiologist*
Jerdee, Thomas Harlan *business administration educator, organization psychology researcher and consultant*
Jones, Houston Gwynne *history professor*
Jones, Lyle Vincent *psychologist, educator*
Jones, W. S. (Steve Jones) *dean*
Judd, Burke Haycock *geneticist*
Juliano, Rudolph L. *medical educator*
Keagy, Blair Allen *surgery educator*
Kenan, Thomas Stephen, III, *philanthropist*
Kilgour, Frederick Gridley *librarian, educator*
Kim, Chong Soong *aerosol science and inhalation technology researcher*
Kinnaird, Eleanor Gates *state legislator, lawyer*
Kohn, Richard H. *historian, educator*
Krasno, Richard Michael *foundation executive, educator*
Kusy, Robert Peter *biomedical engineering and orthodontics educator*
Latané, Bibb *social psychologist*
Lauder, Valarie Anne *editor, educator*
Lawrence, David Michael *lawyer, educator*
Lee, Kuo-Hsiung *medicinal chemistry educator*
Leith, David *engineering educator*
Levine, Madeline Geltman *Slavic literatures educator, translator*
Lichtman, Steven N. *pediatrician, educator*
Lieberman, Jeffrey Alan *psychiatrist, educator*
Ligett, Waldo Buford *chemist*
Lilley, Albert Frederick *retired lawyer*
Linville, Ray Pate *educational administrator, analyst, editor, writer*
Loeb, Ben Fohl, Jr., *retired law educator*
Lohr, Jacob Andrew *physician, pediatrician, educator*
Ludington, Townsend *English and American studies educator*
Lundblad, Roger Lauren *biotechnology consultant*
Macdonald, James Ross *physicist, researcher*
MacGillivray, Lois Ann *organization executive*
Magill, Samuel Hays *academic administrator, higher education consultant*
Mangum, William Goodson *artist*
Martikainen, A(une) Helen *retired health education specialist*
Marzluff, William Frank *medical educator*
McCoy, William O. *former academic administrator, retired telecommunications executive*
Mc Kean, John Rosseel Overton *university dean*
McKinney, Ross Erwin *civil engineering educator*
McMillan, Campbell White *pediatric hematologist*
Merzbacher, Eugen *physicist, researcher*
Miller, C. Arden *physician, educator*
Mitchell, Beverly Shriver *hematologist, oncologist, educator*
Mitchell, Earl Nelson *physicist, researcher*
Moellering, John Henry *aviation maintenance company executive*
Moeser, James Charles *university chancellor, musician*
Moran, Barbara Burns *librarian, educator*
Mueller, Nancy Schneider *retired biology educator*
Munson, Eric Bruce *hospital administrator*
Murray, Michael Dennis *pharmacist*
Neff, Severine *music educator*
Nelson, Philip Francis *musicology educator, consultant, choral conductor*
Neumann, Andrew Conrad *geological oceanography educator*
Nichol, Gene Ray, Jr., *dean, department chairman*
Okun, Daniel Alexander *environmental engineering educator*
Ornstein, Peter Arnold *psychologist, educator*
Pagano, Joseph Stephen *physician, researcher, educator*
Palmer, Jeffress Gary *hematologist, educator*
Parr, Robert Ghormley *chemistry professor*
Passaro, Paul Charles *business executive*
Peacock, Erle Ewart, Jr., *surgeon, lawyer, educator*
Pedersen, Lee G. *chemistry educator*
Perreault, William Daniel, Jr., *business administration educator*
Pfaff, Richard William *historian, educator*
Pfouts, Ralph William *economist, consultant*
Pillsbury, Harold Crockett, III, *otolaryngologist*
Powell, Carolyn Wilkerson *retired music educator*
Prange, Arthur Jergen, Jr., *psychiatrist, neurobiologist, educator*
Proffit, William Robert *orthodontics educator*
Rabil, Albert, Jr., *humanities educator*
Ravenel, Shannon *book publishing professional*
Redinbo, Matthew R. *science educator, researcher*
Rindfuss, Ronald Richard *sociology educator*
Roberts, Harold Ross *medical educator, hematologist*
Rogers, John James William *geology educator*
Rondinelli, Dennis A(ugust) *business administration educator, researcher*
Roper, William Lee *dean, physician*
Roth, Aleda Vender *business educator*
Salemi, Michael Kerry *economist, educator*
Sanders, Charles Addison *retired physician*
Satterfield, John Roberts, Jr., *retired college president and music educator*
Schier, Donald Stephen *language educator*
Schoonover, Brenda B. *ambassador*
Schoultz, Lars *political scientist, educator*
Senior, Brent Anthony *otolaryngologist, educator*
Sheldon, George Frank *medical educator*
Shelton, Robert Neal *physics educator, researcher*
Simmons, Michael Anthony *pediatrician*
Singer, Philip Charles *environmental engineer, educator*
Slifkin, Lawrence Myer *physics educator*
Smith, Dean Edwards *university basketball coach*
Smith, James Finley *economist, educator*
Smith, Janet Sue *systems specialist*
Smith, Sidney Rufus, Jr., *linguist, educator*
Smithies, Oliver *geneticist, educator*
Snyder, Glenn Herald *political science educator, writer*
Soltys, Florence Gray *social worker*
Sorenson, James Roger *public health educator*
Southern, Robert Allen *lawyer*
Spencer, Elizabeth *author*
Spencer, Roger Felix *psychiatrist, psychoanalyst, medical educator*
Stadter, Philip Austin *classicist, educator*
Stamm, John William Randolph *dentist, educator, academic dean*
Stenberg, Carl W., III, *public administration educator, dean*
Stephens, Laurence David, Jr., *linguist, investor, oil industry executive*
Steponaitis, Vincas Petras *archaeologist, anthropologist, educator*
Stewart, Richard Edwin *insurance consulting company executive*
Stewart, Sarah *elementary school educator*
Stidham, Shaler, Jr., *operations research educator*
Stipe, Robert Edwin *design educator*
Stockman, James Anthony, III, *pediatrician*
Straley, Joseph Ward *retired molecular spectroscopist, retired science educator*
Stumpf, Walter Erich *cell biology educator, researcher*
Sugioka, Kenneth *anesthesiologist, educator*
Sullivan, Robert S. *college dean*
Thomas, Colin Gordon, Jr., *surgeon, medical educator*
Tilson, Hugh Hanna *epidemiologist*
Tolley, Aubrey Granville *psychiatrist, health facility administrator*
Trejo, JoAnn *medical researcher*
Treml, Vladimir Guy *economist, educator*
Tsui, Frank *physicist, educator*
Tyroler, Herman Alfred *epidemiologist*
Usher, Charles Lindsey *social work educator, public policy analyst*
Vogler, Frederick Wright *French language educator*
Waller, Patricia Fossum *transportation executive, researcher, psychologist*
Ware, William Brettel *education educator*
Warren, Donald William *physiology educator, dentistry educator*
Wasik, Barbara Hanna *psychologist, educator*
Wegner, Judith Welch *law educator, former dean*
Weinstein, Sidney *neuropsychologist*
Weiss, Charles Manuel *environmental biologist*
Weiss, Shirley F. *urban and regional planner, economist, educator*
Wetzel, Robert George *botany educator*
Wheeler, Clayton Eugene, Jr., *dermatologist, educator*
White, Raymond Petrie, Jr., *dentist, educator, dean*
Whybark, David Clay *business educator, researcher*
Wilcox, Benson Reid *cardiothoracic surgeon, educator*
Wilfert, Catherine M. *medical association administrator, medical educator*
Williamson, Joel Rudolph *humanities educator*
Wilson, Glenn *economist, educator*
Winfield, John Buckner *rheumatologist, educator*
Wolfenden, Richard Vance *biochemistry educator*
Wright, Deil Spencer *political science educator*
Youngman, Paul A. *language educator*
Zeisel, Steven H. *nutritionist, scientist, educator*

Charlotte

Abels, Debbie *publishing executive*
Alexander, R. David *retail executive*
Aliaga-Buchenau, Ana-Isabel *humanities educator*
Alphin, J. Steele *bank executive*
Anderson, Gerald Leslie *financial executive*
Anderson, Paul Milton *energy executive*
Arnoult, J. Tim *bank executive*
Atwood, Robert T. *former bank executive*
Aycock, Hugh David *steel manufacturing company executive*
Ayscue, Edwin Osborne, Jr., *lawyer*
Barrows, Frank Clemence *editor*
Bates, Michael *professional football player, former Olympic athlete, track and field*
Beddow, John Warren *lawyer*
Belk, Irwin *retail executive*
Belk, John Montgomery *retired retail executive*
Belk, John R. *retail executive*
Belthoff, Richard Charles, Jr., *lawyer*
Bessant, Catherine Pombier *bank executive, marketing professional*
Boggs, Willene Graythen *property manager, oil and gas broker, consultant*
Bolick, Ryan *lobbyist, consultant*
Bonazzi, Elaine Claire *mezzo-soprano*
Bonnefoux, Jean-Pierre *artistic director, choreographer, dancer*
Bosse, Michael Joseph *orthopedic trauma surgeon*
Bowles, Erskine *former White House staff member, consultant*
Brackett, Martin Luther, Jr., *lawyer*
Bradley, Dana Burr *educational researcher, consultant*
Bragg, Ellis Meredith, Jr., *lawyer*
Brandon, William Pew, Jr., *social sciences educator*
Brinkley, Amy Woods *bank executive*
Brown, Edward J, III, *bank executive*
Browning, Peter Crane *packaging company executive*
Browning, Roy Wilson, III, *former mortgage banking executive*
Brynn, Edward Paul *former ambassador*
Buckley, Charles Robinson, III, *lawyer*
Burke, Peggy Hudgins (Margaret Hudgins Burke) *auditor*
Burke, Steven Charles *healthcare administration executive*
Burner, David L. *aerospace services company executive*
Calloway, Mark T. *lawyer, former prosecutor*
Campbell, Clair Gilliland *lawyer*
Campbell, J(ohn) Jette *corporate finance executive*
Carroll, David M. *communications professional*
Castro, Mary McDermott *language educator*
Chadwick, Gregory D. *endodontist*
Chambers, Julius LeVonne *lawyer*
Clark, Ann Blakeney *educational administrator*
Clark, Ranjana B. *bank executive*
Cleghorn, John Michael *communications executive*
Clodfelter, Daniel Gray *state legislator, lawyer*
Colavita, Paul Gerard *cardiologist, medical educator*
Colvard, Dean Wallace *emeritus university chancellor*
Combs, Cindy Culbreth *social sciences educator, consultant*
Conrad, Robert J. *prosecutor*
Cowell, Marion Aubrey, Jr., *lawyer*
Cox, Linda Smoak *real estate broker*
Cramer, Robert W. *lawyer*
Crutchfield, Edward Elliott, Jr., *retired banking executive*
Culbreth, James Harold, Jr., *lawyer*
Cummings, Stephen Emery *investment banking executive*
Curlin, William G. *bishop*
Dagenhart, Larry Jones *lawyer*
Dalton, Parks H. *investment company executive*
D'Angelo, Peter R. *electronics company executive*
Davis, Jean E. *bank executive*
Davis, Stephen *professional football player*
Davis, William Maxie, Jr., *lawyer*
Delhomme, Jake Christopher *professional football player*
Desoer, Barbara J. *bank executive*
DiMicco, Daniel R. *manufacturing executive*
Doherty, Barbara Whitehurst *chemical purchasing manager*
Dorin, Dennis Daniel *political science educator, researcher*
Dunlap, Edward *broadcast executive, transportation executive*
Dunn, Jackson Thomas, Jr., *lawyer, legal educator*
Elanayar, Sunil K. *research and development engineer*
Eppes, Thomas Evans *advertising executive, public relations executive*
Erdman, David Williams *lawyer*
Ervine, Timothy DuWayne *utilities executive*
Eski, John Robert *residential appraiser, real estate consultant*
Ethridge, Mark Foster, III, *writer, publisher, media consultant*
Evans, Robert B. *energy executive*
Eve, Robert Michael, Jr., *lawyer*
Faison, Henry *electronics executive*
Ferebee, Stephen Scott, Jr., *architect*
Finley, Glenna *writer*
Fitzpatrick, James Ward, Jr., *engineering technology educator*
Ford, Steven J. *manufacturing executive*
Fowler, Fred J. *energy executive*
Fox, John *professional football coach*
Freeman, Sidney Lee *minister*
Fretwell, Elbert K., Jr., *retired university chancellor, consultant*
Fussell, Tracey Mattox *medical/surgical nurse*
Gage, Gaston Hemphill *lawyer*
Gallagher, Thomas Joseph *banker*
Gambrell, Sarah Belk *retail executive*
Gay, David Braxton *finance company executive*
George, Paul G. *bank executive, human resources specialist*
Georgius, John R. *bank executive*
Goolkasian, Paula A. *psychologist, educator*
Graham, William Franklin (William Franklin Graham) *evangelist*
Gregory, Jeannette T. *publisher, writer*
Griffith, Dewey Maurice *mechanical engineer, investor*
Grigg, Eddie Garman *minister, educator*
Grigg, William Humphrey *utilities executive*
Grimaldi, James Thomas *investment fund executive*
Gross, Edward H. *wholesale distributing executive*
Haines, Kenneth H. *sports television broadcasting and marketing executive*
Halas, Paul Anthony, Jr., *business appraisal and valuation specialist, consultant*
Hance, James Henry, Jr., *bank executive*
Hanna, George Verner, III, *lawyer*
Harris, John W. *real estate company executive*
Harrison, J. Frank, Jr., *soft drink company executive*
Harver, Andrew Robert *psychology educator*
Hauptfuhrer, W. Barnes *bank executive*
Helton, Max Edward *minister, consultant, religious organization executive*
Hendrick, Ricky *race car driver*
Horn, Carl, III, *federal judge*
Horner, Robert (Bob) *broadcast executive*
Howard, Grazell *risk management executive*
Huberman, Jeffrey Allen *architect*
Hutcheson, J. Sterling *allergist, immunologist, physician*
Huzl, James Frank *automotive executive*
Ignozzi, Bryan K. *management consultant*
Iley, Martha Strawn *music educator*
Jenkins, Benjamin P., III, *bank executive*
Johnson, Jimmie *race car driver*
Jones, Milton H., Jr., *bank executive*
Kearney, Christopher J. *lawyer*
Kelly, R. James *retail executive*
Kelly, Stanhope A. *bank executive*
Kincaid, Steven Randall *marketing professional*
Kirkpatrick, James Alexander *education educator, writer*
Kuehnert, Deborah Anne *medical center administrator*
Lacey, Trudi *professional athletics coach*
Ladd, Robert T. *energy executive*
Lapp, Charles Warren *internal medicine physician, pediatrician*
Larsen, Marshall O. *corporate financial executive*
Latimer, Ben William *healthcare executive*
Lea, Scott Carter *retired packaging company executive*
Lehman, Alice *bank executive*
Levine, Howard R. *retail executive*
Lewis, Kenneth D. *bank executive*
Lisenby, Terry S. *waste management executive*
Little, William B. *architectural firm executive*
Locke, Elizabeth Hughes *foundation executive*
Loughridge, John Halsted, Jr., *lawyer*
Lyerly, Elaine Myrick *advertising executive*
Maclean, Rhonda *information technology executive*
Mapp, Rhonda *professional basketball player*
Marley, Brian Thomas *accountant*
Martin, James Grubbs *medical executive, former governor*
Mascavage, Joseph Peter *training executive*
May, Benjamin Tallman *securities specialist, administrator*
McBryde, Neill Gregory *lawyer*
McClure, Howard Jean, Jr., *advocate*
McCrory, Patrick *mayor*

McFayden, Shannon *bank holding company executive*
McGee, Richard K. *energy executive*
McGill, John Knox *lawyer*
McKay-Wilkinson, Julie Ann *minister, marriage and family therapist*
McKinnish, Richmond D. *manufacturing executive*
McMullen, Donald A., Jr., *bank executive*
Means, Natrone Jermaine *professional football player*
Mercer, Evelyn Lois *retired guidance counselor*
Metcalf, Eric Quinn *professional football player*
Mogg, Jimmy W. *gas industry executive*
Monge, Jay Parry *lawyer*
Montague, Edgar Burwell, III, (Monty Montague) *industrial designer*
Moore, James L., Jr., *beverage company executive*
Morgan, James H. *investment company executive*
Muhammad, Muhsin, II, *professional football player*
Mullen, Graham C. *federal judge*
Mullinax, A. R. *energy executive*
Munn, Stephen P. *manufacturing executive*
Myers, Robert Manson *English educator, author*
Myrick, Sue *congresswoman, former mayor*
Nadeau, Jerry *race car driver*
Neel, Richard Eugene *economics and business educator*
Neill, Rolfe *retired newspaper executive*
Nelson, Thomas C. *manufacturing executive*
Nichols, Debra *bank executive*
Nicholson, Freda Hyams *museum executive, medical educator*
Nicholson, Henry Hale, Jr., *surgeon*
O'Connor, Thomas C. *gas industry executive*
Ogirri, Dennis Arekpita *educator, political/business management consultant*
Okafor, Emeka *professional basketball player*
Oken, Marc *bank executive*
O'Leary, Patrick J. *manufacturing executive*
Oliver, John William Posegate *minister*
Orr, T(homas) J(erome) (Jerry Orr) *airport terminal executive*
Orsbon, Richard Anthony *lawyer*
Osborne, Richard Jay *electric utility company executive*
Osteen, Louis *chef*
Owen, Kenneth Dale *orthodontist, real estate broker*
Parmelee, William Douglas *financial executive, accountant*
Parmelle, William *light manufacturing executive*
Peacock, A(lvin) Ward *textile company executive*
Perkins, Jim C. *automotive executive*
Phambu, Nsoki *physical chemist, researcher*
Polking, Paul J. *lawyer*
Price, Charles R., Jr., *advertising executive*
Priestley, G. T. Eric *manufacturing executive*
Pruden, James Norfleet, III, *lawyer*
Pyle, Gerald Fredric *medical geographer, educator*
Ragan, Robert Allison *private investment executive, financial consultant*
Raper, William Cranford *lawyer*
Rathke, Dieter B. *construction company executive*
Reese, Annette Evelyn *music educator*
Reid, Tracy *professional basketball player*
Ridder, Peter B. *publishing executive*
Rivenbark, Jan Meredith *business consultant*
Robinson, Russell Marable, II, *lawyer*
Robinson, Shawna *race car driver*
Rodite, Robert R.R. *engineering scientist*
Rosenburgh, Stephen Aruthur *corporate financial executive*
Ruff, Edward Carr *retired investment company executive*
Ruiz, Macedonio *entomologist*
Saikevych, Irene A. *pathologist*
Schafermeyer, Robert William *emergency physician, educator*
Schneider, Stanley Scott *biology professor*
Shaw, Ruth G. *energy company executive*
Siegel, Samuel *metals company executive*
Sintz, Edward Francis *librarian*
Smith, O. Bruton *automotive company executive*
Smith, Wilburn Jackson, Jr., *retired bank executive*
Spangler, Clemmie Dixon, Jr., *construction company executive*
Sprague, Jack *race car driver*
Squires, James Ralph *development company executive*
Staley, Dawn Michelle *professional basketball player*
Stephens, Kitty Frances *academic administrator*
Stinson, Andrea Maria *professional basketball player*
Stobbe, Michael *reporter*
Sulg, Madis *corporation executive, entrepreneur*
Sutton, Cecilia (Cece Sutton) *bank executive*
Taylor, David Brooke *lawyer, banker*
Taylor, R. Eugene *bank executive*
Thames, Rick *publishing executive, editor*
Thigpen, Richard Elton, Jr., *lawyer*
Thompson, G. Kennedy (Ken Thompson) *bank executive*
Thompson, John Albert, Jr., *dermatologist*
Thompson, Sydnor, Jr., (Charles William Sydnor Thompson Jr.) *lawyer, mediator, arbitrator*
Treanor, Mark C. *lawyer, diversified financial services company executive*
Truslow, Donald *bank executive*
Twisdale, Harold Winfred *dentist*
Tyson, Cynthia Haldenby *academic administrator*
Valasquez, Joseph Louis *industrial engineer*
Van Allen, William Kent *lawyer*
Van Alstyne, Vance Brownell *arbitration management consultant*
Van Hoy, Philip Marshall *lawyer*
Vinroot, Richard Allen *lawyer, mayor*
Visser, Valya Elizabeth *physician*
Voorhees, Richard Lesley *federal judge*
Walker, Clarence Wesley *lawyer*
Walker, Jewett Lynius *clergyman, church official*
Walker, Kenneth Dale *automotive service company executive*
Walls, Wesley (Charles Wesley Walls) *professional football player*
Walton, Bill R. *retail executive*
Webster, Murray Alexander, Jr., *sociologist, educator*
Weinke, Chris *professional football player*
Welch, Jeanie Maxine *librarian*
Wiggins, Nancy Bowen *real estate broker, market research consultant*
Williams, Edwin Neel *newspaper editor*
Wilson, Constance Kramer *banker*
Wood, Donald Craig *retired marketing professional*
Wood, William McBrayer *lawyer*
Woodward, James Hoyt *academic administrator, engineer*
Woolard, William Leon *lawyer, electrical distributing company executive*
Wright, Wayne Kenneth *federal agency statistician*
Wyrsch, Martha B. *lawyer*
Yancy, Dorothy Cowser *college president*
″awczak, Janusz *mathematician, educator*

Cherokee
Martin, Harry Corpening *lawyer, retired state supreme court justice*
Parker, Joyce White *application developer, educator*

Cherryville
Barger, Linda Kale *choral director*
Huffstetler, Palmer Eugene *lawyer*
Mayhew, Kenneth Edwin, Jr., *transportation company executive*

Chocowinity
Castle, William Eugene *retired academic administrator*

Clayton
Branch, Stacy *veterinarian, educator*
Scott, Stephen Carlos *academic administrator*
Silberman, H. Lee *public relations executive, editorial consultant*

Clemmons
Church, Avery Grenfell *retired anthropology educator, poet*
Maloney, Sean Robert *physician, biomedical engineer*
Taquey, Antony *accountant*

Clinton
Faircloth, Duncan McLauchlin (Lauch Faircloth) *former senator, businessman, farmer*
Fetterman, Annabelle L. *packing company executive*
Griffin, Betty Lou *not-for-profit developer, educator*

Columbus
Blate, Michael *author, lecturer*
Brooks, Jerry Claude *safety engineer, educator*
Sauvé, Carolyn Opal *writer, journalist, poet*

Concord
Biffle, Greg *race car driver*
Busch, Kurt *race car driver*
Robinson, Harold Oscar *clergyman, educator*

Conover
Jarrett, Dale *race car driver*

Cornelius
Wortman, William Jerome, Jr., *obstetrician-gynecologist*

Corolla
Schrote, John Ellis *retired government executive*

Cove City
Hawkins, Elinor Dixon (Mrs. Carroll Woodard Hawkins) *retired librarian*

Creedmoor
Husketh, Alma Ormond *retired language educator*

Cullowhee
Bardo, John William *university administrator*
Coulter, Myron Lee *retired academic administrator*
Crowe, Thomas Rain *poet*
Reed, Alfred Douglas *retired academic administrator*
Stripling Byer, Kathryn *poet*
Willis, Ralph Houston *mathematics professor*
Wilson, LeVon Edward *law educator, lawyer*

Davidson
Barnes, Robin *historian, educator*
Brown, Douglas Ivan *law enforcement officer, educator, consultant*
Grosch, Laura Dudley *artist, educator*
Jackson, Herb *artist, educator*
Jones, Arthur Edwin, Jr., *library administrator, English and American literature educator*
Kamp, Barbara Ann *artist, poet, photographer, educator*
Park, Leland Madison *librarian*
Plyler, John Laney, Jr., *retired healthcare management professional*
Ross, Clark Grant *economics professor*
Spencer, Samuel Reid, Jr., *education consultant, former college president*
Turner, Kathleen J. *communications educator, consultant*
Vagt, Robert F. *academic administrator*

Denton
Tuttle, Bynum R., Jr., *brokerage house executive*

Denver
Eppley, Frances Fielden *retired secondary education educator, writer*
McIntosh, Anita Jane *retired administrative assistant*

Dobson
Smith, Richard Jackson *elementary school educator*

Dunn
Davis, Dolly *religious organization administrator*
Heath, Preston *clergy member, religious organization administrator*
Pope, Wiley Jackson *lawyer, small business owner*
Robison, Frederick Mason *retired financial executive*

Durham
Adams, Rex *dean*
Aldrich, John Herbert *political science educator*
Alexander, Michael Jozef *neurosurgeon, radiologist*
Althaus, David Steven *consultant*
Amaldoss, Wilfred *marketing educator*
Anderson, William Banks, Jr., *ophthalmology educator*
Anlyan, William George *surgeon, educator, academic administrator*
Armstrong, Brenda Estelle *pediatric cardiologist, educator*
Barker, Karen *restaurant owner, chef*
Bartlett, Katharine Tiffany *law educator*
Bejan, Adrian *mechanical engineering educator*
Bennett, Peter Brian *researcher, hyperbaric medicine*
Bettman, James Ross *management educator*
Bevan, William *retired foundation executive*
Blazer, Dan German, II, *psychiatrist, epidemiologist*
Blazing, Michael August *internist*
Blum, Jacob Joseph *physiologist, educator*
Blumenthal, James A. *psychologist, researcher*
Boguslavsky, George William *psychologist, educator*
Bollerslev, Tim Peter *economics professor*
Bollinger, Ralph Randal *surgeon, researcher*
Bolognesi, Dani Paul *virologist, educator*
Bradford, William Dalton *pathologist, educator*
Braibanti, Ralph John *political scientist, educator*
Brantley, Jeffrey Garland *health science facility administrator*
Breeden, Douglas Tower *financial consultant, university dean*
Brodhead, Richard H. *academic administrator*
Brodie, Harlow Keith Hammond *psychiatrist, educator, former university president*
Buchanan, Phillip Hoge *lawyer, foundation executive, educator, academic administrator*
Buckley, Charles Edward, III, *physician, educator*
Buckley, Rebecca Hatcher *allergist, immunologist, pediatrician, educator*
Budd, Louis John *English language educator*
Burks, A. Wesley *pediatrics educator*
Burmeister, Edwin *economics educator*
Caesar, Shirley *gospel singer, evangelist*
Canada, Mary Whitfield *retired librarian*
Carrington, Paul DeWitt *lawyer, educator*
Carter, James Harvey *psychiatrist, educator*
Casey, H(orace) Craig, Jr., *electrical engineering educator*
Cayne, Bernard Stanley *editor*
Chafe, William Henry *history educator*
Champagne, Mary T. *dean*
Christie, George Custis *lawyer, educator, author*
Clark, Arthur Watts *insurance company executive*
Cohen, Harvey Jay *hematologist, oncologist, educator*
Coleman, Ralph Edward *nuclear medicine physician, educator*
Colton, Joel *historian, educator*
Colvin, O. Michael *medical director, medical educator*
Conklin, George Henry *sociologist, educator*
Conner, James Leon, II, *lawyer, arbitrator, mediator*
Cook, Philip Jackson *economist, educator*
Cook-Deegan, Robert Mullan *science and health policy analyst, physician*
Coppridge, Alton James *urological surgeon*
Córdoba Montoya, Daniel Amado *psychologist, researcher, educator*
Cox, James D. *law educator*
Cullen, Bryan Richard *microbiologist, educator*
Davis, Calvin De Armond *historian, educator*
Dawson, Jeffrey Robert *immunology educator*
Dawson, Robert Edward, Sr., *ophthalmologist*
Demott, Deborah Ann *lawyer, educator*
Denlinger, Ann T. *school system administrator*
Dorn, Louis Otto *retired minister*
Edelsbrunner, Herbert *computer scientist, mathematician*
Edwards, Christopher Levon *medical association administrator*
Elliot, Jeffrey M. *political science educator, author*
Falletta, John Matthew *pediatrician, educator*
Fassett, John D. *retired utility executive, consultant*
Fiske, Edward B. *editor, journalist, educational consultant*
Flippen, Brenda Jane *psychology professor, consultant*
Foreman, John William *pediatrician, educator*
Frank, Michael M. *physician*
Franklin, John Hope *historian, educator, author*
Freemark, Michael Scott *pediatric endocrinologist, educator*
Fridovich, Irwin *biochemistry educator*
Fulkerson, William *health facility executive, pulmonologist*
George, Timothy Merrill *neurosurgeon*
Gillespie, Michael Allen *political science and philosophy educator, writer*
Gillham, Nicholas Wright *geneticist, educator*
Gillings, Dennis B. *medical products executive*
Gittler, Joseph Bertram *sociology educator*
Goestenkors, Gail *basketball coach*
Goodwin, Frank Erik *materials engineer*
Gosselin, Tracy Karen *nursing administrator*
Greenfield, Joseph Cholmondeley, Jr., *physician, educator*
Guseh, James Sawalla *public administration educator*
Hamilton, Michael A. *medical educator*
Hammes, Gordon G. *chemistry professor*
Hammond, Charles Bessellieu *obstetrician, gynecologist, educator*
Han, Moo-Young *physicist, educator*
Harman, Charles Morgan *mechanical engineer*
Harmel, Merel Hilber *anesthesiologist, educator*
Harrell, Carlton (Benjamin Carlton Harrell) *writer, retired editor*
Harris, Jerome Sylvan *pediatrician, pediatrics and biochemistry educator*
Hawkins, William E. N. *newspaper editor*
Heinz, E(dward) Ralph *neuroradiologist, educator*
Hobbs, Marcus Edwin *retired chemistry educator*
Hochmuth, Robert Milo *mechanical and biomedical engineer, educator*
Hogan, Brigid L. *molecular biologist*
Holder, Angela Roddey *lawyer, educator*
Holley, Edward Gailon *library science educator, former university dean*
Holley, Irving Brinton, Jr., *historian, educator*
Holsti, Ole Rudolf *political scientist, educator*
Holzworth, Donald A. *lab administrator*
Horowitz, Donald Leonard *lawyer, educator, researcher, political scientist, arbitrator*
Huestis, Charles Benjamin *former academic administrator*
James, Sherman Athonia *social epidemiologist, educator*
Jaszczak, Ronald Jack *physicist, researcher, consultant*
Jeffreys, Arcelia Taylor *education educator*
Jenkins, Richard Erik *patent lawyer*
Johnson, Kristina M. *technology director*
Joklik, Wolfgang Karl *biochemist, virologist, educator*
Joseph, James Alfred *retired ambassador, political scientist, educator*
Katz, Samuel Lawrence *pediatrician, researcher*
Keene, Jack Donald *molecular genetics and microbiology educator*
Keller, Thomas Franklin *business administration educator*
Kelley, Allen Charles *economist, educator*
Keohane, Robert Owen *political scientist, educator*
Kirshner, Norman *pharmacologist, researcher, educator*
Klitzman, Bruce *physiologist, plastic surgery educator, researcher*
Koepke, John Arthur *hematologist, clinical pathologist*
Krishnan, Ranga Rama *psychiatrist*
Krzyzewski, Mike *university athletic coach*
Kuniholm, Bruce Robellet *university administrator*
Kurtzberg, Joanne *pediatrics educator*
Lack, Leon *pharmacology and biochemistry educator*
Ladd, Marcia Lee *medical equipment and supplies company executive*
Land, Kenneth Carl *sociology educator, demographer, statistician, consultant*
Lange, Peter *academic administrator*
Lee, Paul P. *ophthalmologist, educator, consultant, lawyer*
Lefkowitz, Robert Joseph *physician, educator*
LeGrand, Chris *lab administrator*
Lerner, Warren *historian, educator*
Levin, Lawrence Scott *plastic surgeon*
Lieberman, Rochelle Phyllis *relocation company executive*
Lilly, James Edward *minister, entrepreneur*
Livingstone, Daniel Archibald *zoology educator*
Lockhead, Gregory Roger *psychology educator*
London, William Lord *pediatrician*
Marchuk, Douglas Alan *medical educator*
Mark, Daniel Benjamin *cardiologist*
Markert, Mary Louise *pediatrics educator*
Markham, Charles Buchanan *retired lawyer*
Massey, Ben F., Jr., *medical association administrator*
Maxwell, Richard Callender *retired lawyer, educator*
McClain, Paula Denice *political scientist, educator*
McCusker, Paul Donald *lawyer, educator*
McMahon, John Alexander *law educator*
Means, Anthony Ross *pharmacology educator*
Meyer, Horst *physics educator*
Meyers, Carol Lyons *religion, history and archaeology educator*
Meyers, Eric Mark *religion educator*
Michener, James Lloyd *medical educator*
Mickiewicz, Ellen Propper *political and social science educator*
Miller, David Edmond *physician*
Modrich, Paul L. *biochemistry educator*
Mofidi, Mahyar *dentist, researcher*
Mosteller, Robert P. *law educator*
Murphy, Barbara Anne *emergency physician, surgery educator*
Murphy, Thomas Miles *pediatrician, educator*
Mushak, Paul *toxicologist, consultant*
Nadadur, Srikanth S *molecular biologist*
Nakarai, Charles Frederick Toyozo *music educator, adjudicator*
Naylor, Aubrey Willard *botany educator*
Oates, John Francis *classics educator*
Ogede, Ode *literature educator*
Osterhout, Suydam *internist, educator*
Otterbourg, Robert Kenneth *public relations consultant, writer*
Page, Bernadette Ryan *emergency physician*
Pamula, Vamsee K. *electrical engineer, researcher*
Paolantonio, Edmund Joseph *musician, music educator*
Pearsall, George Wilbur *materials scientist, mechanical engineer, educator, consultant*
Pearsall, Samuel Haff, III, *landscape ecologist, geographer, foundation administrator*
Peele, Anne Marie *government relations administrator*
Pericak-Vance, Margaret A. *health facility administrator*
Perkins, Ronald Dee *geologist, educator*
Peterson, Max Rupert, Jr., *chemist, researcher*
Petroski, Henry *engineer educator, writer*
Pinnell, Sheldon Richard *dermatologist, researcher, retired educator*
Pizzo, Salvatore Vincent *pathologist*
Plonsey, Robert *electrical and biomedical engineer*
Poole, Robert Steven *lawyer, writer*
Preston, Richard Arthur *historian*
Prosnitz, Leonard R. *radiologist*
Purves, Dale *neurobiology research educator*
Quinn, Jarus William *physicist, former association executive*
Raetz, Christian R. H. *biochemistry educator*
Ravin, Carl Eric *radiologist, educator, department chairman*
Reller, L. Barth *medical microbiologist, infectious diseases physician, educator*
Richardson, Lawrence, Jr., *Latin language educator, archeologist*
Richardson, Stephen Giles *biotechnology company executive*
Robboy, Stanley J. *pathologist, educator*
Roberson, Nathan Russell *physicist, researcher*
Robertson, Horace Bascomb, Jr., *retired law educator*
Robins, Clive Justin *psychology educator, researcher, psychotherapist*
Roessler, Ernest Christian *bank executive*
Roland, Alex Frederick *history professor*
Rollins, Edward Tyler, Jr., *newspaper executive*
Rossiter, Alexander, Jr., *news service executive, editor*
Rouse, Doris Jane *physiologist, research administrator*
Rowe, Thomas Dudley, Jr., *law educator*
Sabiston, David Coston, Jr., *surgeon, educator*
Sanford, David Hawley *philosophy educator*
Schmalbeck, Richard Louis *university dean, lawyer*
Schmechel, Donald E. *medical educator*
Schmidt-Nielsen, Knut *physiologist, educator*
Schwarcz, Steven Lance *law educator, lawyer*
Scott, Anne Byrd Firor *history professor*
Semans, Mary Duke Biddle Trent *foundation administrator*
Serafin, Donald *plastic surgeon, educator*
Shelburne, John Daniel *pathologist*

Lawndale
Williams, Robert Leonard *publishing executive, photographer*

Leland
Barnhardt, Zeb Elonzo, Jr., *lawyer*
Karch, Jacqueline *artist*

Lenoir
Flaherty, David Thomas, Jr., *lawyer*

Lexington
Younts, Patty Lou *interior design executive,inventor, researcher*

Lillington
McClain, Gregory David *chaplin*

Lincolnton
Gamble, John Reeves, Jr., *surgeon*
Kempster, Norman Roy *journalist*

Linwood
Barnes, Melver Raymond *retired chemist*

Locust
Barbee, Bobby Harold *state legislator, insurance agency executive*

Lumberton
Jackson, Anita Louise *otolaryngologist, editor-in-chief*

Maggie Valley
Pickard, John Benedict *English language educator*

Marion
Burgin, Charles Edward *lawyer*

Mars Hill
Corley, Alton L. *music educator*
Newton, Paul George *musician, retired librarian*

Matthews
Freeman, Tyler Ira *physician*
Kocsis, Joan Bosco *elementary education educator, administrative assistant, assistant principal*
Polanis, Julie *accountant*

Mebane
Langley, Ricky Lee *occupational medicine physician*

Merritt
de Vos, Peter Jon *ambassador*

Midland
Voncannon, Brian Everett *writer, scriptwriter, radio personality*

Mill Spring
Saunders, Barry Wayne *state official*

Monroe
Kyle, John Emery *mission executive*
Rorie, Nancy Catherine *retired elementary and secondary school educator*
Taylor, Jimmy Lynn *retired family practice physician, administrator*

Montreat
Stackhouse, Eunice Wonderly *education educator, musician*
Struble, Dan *academic administrator*

Mooresville
Atwood, Casey *race car driver*
Black, Kenneth W., Jr., *retail executive*
Blaney, Dave *race car driver*
Compton, Stacy *race car driver*
Cope, Derrike *race car driver*
Earnhardt, Dale, Jr., *race car driver*
Earnhardt, Kerry *race car driver*
Earnhardt, Teresa *race team owner*
Elder, Christian *race car driver*
Foyt, Larry *race car driver*
Keller, Jason *race car driver*
LaJoie, Randy *race car driver*
Little, Charles Glen, Jr., *professional race car driver*
Marlin, Sterling *race car driver*
Martin, Mark *race car driver*
Münter, Leilani Maaja *race car driver*
Nemechek, Joe *race car driver*
Newman, Ryan *race car driver*
Park, Steve *race car driver*
Pond, Dale C. *company executive*
Riggs, Scott *race car driver*
Stewart, Patricia Canup *vocal music and performing arts educator*
Wallace, Mike *race car driver*
Waltrip, Michael *professional race car driver*

Morehead City
Drury, Bradford David *surgeon*

Morganton
Charles, Shawn Thomas *finance company executive*
Simpson, Daniel Reid *lawyer, mediator*

Morrisville
Cannon, Alice Grace *counselor*
Clancy, Thomas L., Jr., *novelist*
Wing, Vanette *sales executive, consultant*

Mount Airy
Woltz, Howard Osler, Jr., *steel and wire products company executive*

Mount Olive
Raper, William Burkette *retired college president*
Rigsbee, David E. *poet, educator*

Murfreesboro
Muller, William Albert, III, *retired library director*
Obuchowska, Wieslawa Teresa *mathematician, educator*

Murphy
Bata, Rudolph Andrew, Jr., *lawyer*
Dickey, Jeannetta Burkett *social worker*
Kerr, Walter Belnap *retired electrical engineer, English language researcher, consultant*
Pezzella, Jerry James, Jr., *investment and real estate executive*

New Bern
Baughman, Fred Hubbard *aeronautical engineer, retired military officer*
Davis, James Lee *lawyer*
Forrester, Ann *nurse*
Hawley, Nancy Ann *editor, writer*
McKee, Francis John *medical association consultant, lawyer*
Moeller, Dade William *environmental engineer, educator*
Naumann, William Carl *consumer products company executive*
Overholt, Hugh Robert *lawyer, retired army officer*
Painter, Jack Timberlake *civil engineer*
Sinning, Mark Alan *thoracic and vascular surgeon*
White, James Edward, III, *historian, educator*
White, Rhea Amelia *information scientist, consciousness researcher*
Whitehurst, Brooks Morris *chemical engineer*

Newland
Lustig, Susan Gardner *occupational therapist*

Newport
Burge, Larry Brady *artist*
Rettie, Dwight Fay *retired political science educator, writer*

Newton
Cutchin, John Franks *lawyer*

North Wilkesboro
Parsons, Irene Adelaide *management consultant*
Stone, Larry Dean *management executive*
Warden, William C. *lawyer*
Wessling, Gregory Jay *retail executive*
Whiddon, Thomas E. *retail executive*

Otto
Able, Luke William *pediatric surgeon, consultant*

Oxford
Harvey, Gloria-Stroud *physician assistant*

Pembroke
Jordan, Chester I. *communication educator, theater educator*
King, Beverly Rae *developmental psychologist*
Meadors, Allen Coats *health administrator, educator*

Pilot Mountain
Daoud, Abraham Joseph, IV, *funeral director, former police officer*

Pinehurst
Broadhurst, Judith Buck *art gallery owner*
Bussey, George Davis *psychiatrist*
Carroll, Kent Jean *retired naval officer*
Funderburk, David Britton *former congressman and ambassador, consultant*
Gilmore, Voit *travel executive*
Huizenga, John Robert *nuclear chemist, educator*
Mc Dannald, Clyde Elliott, Jr., *management consultation company executive*
O'Loughlin, John Kirby *retired insurance executive*
O'Neill, John Joseph, Jr., *business consultant, former chemical company executive*
Schneider, Donald Frederic *banker*

Pisgah Forest
Albyn, Richard Keith *retired architect*
Kempe, Ludwig George *neurological surgeon*

Pittsboro
Betts, Doris June Waugh *writer, English language educator*
Cotter, Michael William *retired ambassador, business consultant*
Doenges, Byron Frederick *economist, educator, former government official*
Hubbard, Thomas Edwin (Tim Hubbard) *lawyer*
Kachergis, Joyce W. *designer*
Richardson, Richard Judson *retired political science educator*
Schwinn-Jordan, Barbara (Barbara Schwinn) *painter*
Squire, Alexander *management consultant*

Pleasant Garden
Kennett, Lee Boone, Jr., *historian, educator*

Raeford
Abreu, Sue Hudson *physician, army officer, organizational and healthcare consultant*

Raleigh
Aiken, Clayton Holmes *singer*
Aldridge, Adrienne Yingling *accountant, financial analyst*
Allen, Barbara Kirkman *politcal organization administrator*
Allen, Steven Glen *economics and business educator*
Anderson, Jala *newscaster*
Aronson, Arthur Lawrence *retired veterinarian, toxicologist, educator, pharmacologist*
Aspnes, David Erik *physicist, researcher*
Bailey, Mary Beatrice *retired nursing information systems director*
Bakalov, Bojko *mathematician*
Baker, Stanley Beckwith *education educator*
Barefoot, Aldos Cortez, Jr., *forester, educator*
Barish, Charles Franklin *internist, gastroenterologist, researcher*
Barnhardt, Robert Alexander *college dean*
Barrett, Rolin Farrar, Jr., *mechanical engineer, consultant*
Basnight, Marc *state senator, small business owner, construction executive*
Beatty, Kenneth Orion, Jr., *chemical engineer, educator*
Belk, Leotis S. *language educator*
Bennett, Barbara Jean *mortgage company executive, writer*
Benson, D(avid) Michael *plant pathologist*
Bernholc, Jerzy *physicist, educator*
Berry, Cherie Killian *commissioner*
Berry, Joni Ingram *hospice pharmacist, educator*
Bitzer, Donald Lester *electrical engineering educator, retired research laboratory administrator*
Black, James M. *state representative, optometrist*
Blackburn, James B., III, *lawyer*
Bowie, Joanne Walker (Joni Bowie) *state legislator*
Boylan, Winnie Carleen *secondary school educator, writer*
Boyles, Harlan Edward *former state official*
Bradley, Elizabeth Clay *financial planner, educator*
Brady, Edward Thomas *judge*
Brantley, John C., III, *airport executive*
Brind'Amour, Rod Jean *professional hockey player*
Britt, W. Earl *federal judge*
Brown, James Joseph *judge*
Brown, Marilyn Shull *music educator*
Bruck, Robert Ian *education educator*
Buchanan, Ray Allen *clergyman*
Burkholder, Joann M. *botany educator*
Burris, Craven Allen *retired college administrator, educator*
Byrd, Emily *newscaster*
Carlton, Alfred Pershing, Jr., *lawyer*
Carpenter, Robert C. *state legislator, former banker*
Carrington, John H. *state legislator, law enforcement supply company executive*
Carter, Jean Gordon *lawyer*
Case, Charles Dixon *lawyer*
Cavanaugh, William, III, *electric utility company executive*
Chou, Wushow *computer scientist, educator*
Clapp, Allen Linville *electric supply and communications utility consultant, mediator/arbitrator*
Clarke, Lewis James *landscape architect*
Cobey, William Wilfred, Jr., *political organization administrator*
Colpetzer, Keith Edward *entomologist, consultant*
Cook, Maurice Gayle *soil science educator, consultant*
Cooper, Arthur Wells *ecologist, educator*
Cooper, Roy Asberry, III, *state attorney general, lawyer*
Corder, Billie Farmer *clinical psychologist, artist*
Cornish, Thelbert Bernard, Jr., *internet service provider executive*
Crawford, Jennifer Chapman *editor*
Crisp, Fred *retired publishing executive*
Cuculo, John A. *chemist, educator*
Cuomo, Jerome John *materials scientist*
Currin, Samuel Thomas *lawyer, former judge*
Daniels, Frank Arthur, Jr., *newspaper publisher*
Daniels, Frank Arthur, III, *internet publishing executive*
Dannelly, William David *lawyer*
Daubert, Erik Joseph *organization administrator*
Davey, Charles Bingham *soil science educator*
Davis, Egbert Lawrence, III, *lawyer*
Davis, Joseph Randall *engineer, ergonomist*
Dean, Christine Witcover *lawyer*
Deihl, Susan Galyen *historic preservationist*
Deja, Heidi *newscaster*
Delaney, Sharon *newscaster*
Dixon, Wright Tracy, Jr., *retired lawyer*
Doherty, Robert Cunningham *retired advertising executive*
Dolce, Carl John *education administration educator*
Dornan, John Neill *public policy center professional*
Dorsett, James K., III, *lawyer*
Drew, Nancy McLaurin Shannon *counselor, consultant*
Duncan, Allyson K. *federal judge*
Dunphy, Edward James *crop science extension specialist*
Eagles, Sidney Smith, Jr., *judge*
Easley, Michael F. *governor*
Eberly, Harry Landis *retired communications company executive*
Edmunds, Robert H., Jr., *state supreme court justice*
Edwards, Charles Archibald *lawyer*
Ellis, Lester Neal, Jr., *lawyer*
Ellis, Richard W. *lawyer*
Entman, Robert Mathew *communications educator, consultant*
Faulkner, Janice H. *state official*
Fearn, Robert Morcom *economics professor, finance educator, consultant*
Flath, David Joseph *economist, educator*
Fletcher, Oscar Jasper, Jr., *dean*
Flournoy, William Louis, Jr., *landscape architect*
Foegeding, Edward A. *food scientist, educator*
Foxx, Virginia Ann *state legislator, small business owner*
Freeman, Franklin Edward, Jr., *state governmental assistant*
Fritsch, Edward *real estate company executive*
Gardner, Robin Pierce *engineering educator*
Garrett, Leland Earl *nephrologist, educator*
Garrou, Linda *state legislator*
Geller, Janice Grace *nurse*
Genardo, Kim *newscaster*
Gibson, Ronald P. *finance company executive*
Glass, Fred Stephen *lawyer*
Godwin, James Beckham *retired landscape architect*
Goodman, Major Merlin *botanical sciences educator*
Gordon, Morris Aaron *medical mycologist, microbiologist*
Graham, William Edgar, Jr., *lawyer, retired utility company executive*
Grantham, Donald James *chemical engineer, educator, author*
Green, Richard Bertram *sculptor*
Hagan, Kay R. *state legislator, lawyer*
Hall, John Thomas *lawyer, educator*
Hansen, Patricia Sellers *personal services executive*
Harder, Glenn E. *utilities, energy company executive*
Hardin, Eugene Brooks, Jr., *bank executive*
Hardin, James W. *botanist, herbarium curator, educator*
Hargrove, Wade Hampton *lawyer*
Harris, Oscar N. *state legislator, accountant*
Harrison-Jervay, Evelyn Yvonne *publishing executive*
Hartford, Maureen A. *academic administrator*
Hauser, John Reid *electrical engineering educator*
Havlin, John Leroy *soil scientist, educator*
Havner, Kerry Shuford *civil engineering and solid mechanics educator*
Hayes, Charles Austin *economic development executive, consultant*
Heidari, Amir Homayoun *computational mechanic*
Henry, Janice K. *construction materials company executive*
Hiday, Virginia Aldigé *sociologist educator*
Hodgson, Ernest *toxicology educator*
Holding, Lewis R. *banker*
Holton, William Coffeen *electrical engineering executive*
Hoon, Peggy Ellen *lawyer, librarian*
Howard, Julia C. *state legislator*
Howell, Bruce Inman *academic administrator*
Hoyle, David W. *state legislator, real estate developer*
Huber, Steven C. *plant physiologist, educator*
Hughes, Francis P. *medical organization executive*
Hunt, James Baxter, Jr., *lawyer, former governor*
Hunt, Kemp Neal *real estate company executive*
Imade, Lucky Osagie *political scientist, educator*
Irbe, Arturs *professional hockey player*
Jarrett, Polly Hawkins *secondary education educator, retired*
Jernigan, John Lee *lawyer*
Jessen, David Wayne *accountant*
Johnson, Charles Lavon, Jr., *clinical neuropsychologist, consultant*
Johnson, Janet Gray Andrews *clinical social worker*
Johnson, William Dean *power company executive*
Jones, Janice *newscaster*
Jordan, John Richard, Jr., *lawyer*
Joyner, Lorinzo Little *commissioner*
Joyner, Walton Kitchin *lawyer*
Kang, Min *mathematician, educator*
Kapp, Michael Keith *lawyer*
Karmanos, Peter, Jr., *computer software company executive, professional sports team executive*
Katz, Steven Barry *language educator, writer*
Kauffman, Terry *broadcast and creative arts communication educator, artist*
Kimbrough, Lorelei *elementary school educator*
Kirk-Duggan, Michael Allan *retired law, economics and computer sciences educator*
Klaenhammer, Todd R. *microbiologist, educator*
Kolbas, Robert Michael *electrical engineering educator*
Kuhler, Renaldo Gillet *retired museum official, scientific illustrator*
Kuykendall, William *automotive executive*
Lake, I. Beverly, Jr., *judge*
Lambe, Catherine van de Velde *law librarian*
Lancaster, H(arold) Martin *former congressman, former presidential advisor, academic administrator*
Larsen, Ralph Irving *environmental research engineer*
Laviolette, Peter *professional hockey coach*
Leak, Robert Edwards *economic development consultant*
Lee, Howard N. *state senator, concessions company executive*
Levine, Ronald H. *physician, educator*
Lin, Changqing *chemical engineer, researcher*
Littleton, Isaac Thomas, III, *retired university library administrator, consultant*
Lolley, William Randall *minister*
Lucas, Jeanne Hopkins *state senator, retired educational administrator*
Mac Cormac, Earl Ronald *retired education educator*
Maidon, Carolyn Howser *director*
Maldonado-DeOliveira, Débora *classicist, researcher*
Malecha, Marvin John *architect, academic administrator*
Maness, Edwin Clinton, III, *highway patrol officer, video coordinator*
Marsh, Melissa *newscaster*
Marshall, Elaine Folk *state official*
Martin, John Charles *judge*
Martin, Mark D. *state supreme court justice*
Maupin, Armistead Jones *lawyer*
McClure, William F. *agricultural studies educator*
McCormick, Thomas A., Jr., *city attorney*
McDowell, Robert E. *animal science educator*
McGee, Linda Mace *judge, lawyer*
McGehee, Robert B. *energy executive*
McKinney, Carolyn *educational association administrator, educator*
McKinney, Charles Cecil *investment company executive*
McKinney, Donald Lee *magazine editor*
Meier, Wilbur Leroy, Jr., *industrial engineer, educator, former university chancellor*
Memory, Jasper Durham *academic administrator, physics educator*
Merrell, W. M. *advertising executive*
Millberg, John C. *lawyer*
Mitchell, Burley Bayard, Jr., *lawyer*
Mitchell, Gary Earl *physicist, researcher*
Mitchell, Henry Allen, Jr., *lawyer, insurance company executive*
Moore, Thomas Lloyd *librarian*
Moreland, Donald Edwin *plant physiologist*
Nation, Philip David *financial planner*
Neely, Charles B., Jr., *lawyer*
Neenan, Peter Anthony *state agency administrator*
Nelson, Larry A. *statistics educator, consultant*
Newman, Slater Edmund *psychologist, educator*
Noori, Mohammad Noori *mechanical engineering educator*
Oblinger, James L. *academic administrator*
O'Brien, Helen Margaret *healthcare educator, environmentalist*
O'Neill, Jeff *professional hockey player*
Oraefo, Johnny Ndubuisi *geologist, corporation executive, consultant*
Orr, Robert F. *judge*
Osteryoung, Janet Gretchen *chemistry professor*
Page, Anne Ruth *gifted education educator, education specialist*
Pao, Chia-Ven *mathematics professor*
Parker, John Hill *lawyer*
Parker, Joseph Mayon *retired publishing executive*
Parker, Sarah Elizabeth *state supreme court justice*
Parramore, Barbara Mitchell *education educator*
Parsons, William Jonathan *cardiologist*
Peacock, Charles H. *agricultural studies educator*
Peele, Katherine N. *architect*
Perdue, Beverly E. *lieutenant governor, geriatric consultant*
Pinnix, John Lawrence *lawyer*
Plyler, Aaron W. *state legislator, farmer, contractor*
Powell, Durwood Royce *lawyer*
Prior, William Allen *electronics company executive*
Quarles, Orage, III, *publishing executive*
Quiambao, Dalisay Lelay *dietician, consultant, surveyor*

Lister-Sink, Barabara Ann *musician, education educator*
Little, William Campbell *cardiologist, physiologist*
Livengood, Scott A. *food products executive*
Ludolf, Marilyn Marie Keaton *lay worker*
Maready, William Frank *lawyer*
Margitić, Milorad R. *language educator, researcher*
Maselli, John Anthony *food products company executive*
Matlaga, Brian Richard *physician*
Maynard, Charles Douglas *radiologist*
McNair, John Franklin, III, *banker*
Mecimore, Charles Douglas *retired accounting educator*
Medlin, John Grimes, Jr., *banker, director*
Meis, Paul Jean *obstetrics and gynecology educator*
Mendez, John *minister*
Mitchener, John Edward *music educator, musician*
Mokrasch, Lewis Carl *neurochemist, educator*
Moody, Dixon McGuire *radiologist*
Moyer, R. Charles *finance educator, consultant*
Mueller, Margaret S. *musician, educator*
Mueller-Heubach, Eberhard *medical educator*
Murphy, Frank *lawyer*
Olympio, Michael Allen *anesthesiologist, researcher*
Osborn, Malcolm Everett *lawyer*
O'Steen, Wendall Keith *neurobiology and anatomy educator*
Pandres, Dave, Jr., *science educator, researcher*
Patel, Ajay *dean*
Peeples, Mary Louise *music educator, musician*
Pera, McCall *newscaster*
Peters, Stephen Paul *medical educator*
Pitovski, Dimitri Zivko *otolaryngologist, educator*
Pittaway, Donald Edward *endocrinology educator, gynecologist*
Podgorny, George *emergency physician*
Preslar, Len Broughton, Jr., *hospital administrator*
Rauschenberg, Bradford Lee *museum researcher*
Rautaharju, Pentti Matti *research scientist, educator*
Ray, Michael Edwin *lawyer*
Rights, Graham Henry *retired minister*
Robinson, Edward Norwood *lawyer*
Rodgman, Alan *chemist, consultant*
Roemer, Henry Conrad, Jr., *lawyer*
Ross, Charles Thomas *lawyer*
Roth, Marjory Joan Jarboe *special education educator*
Runnion, Howard J., Jr., *banker*
Sandridge, William Pendleton, Jr., *lawyer*
Schexnider, Alvin J. *academic administrator*
Schindler, Andrew J. *tobacco company executive*
Schollander, Wendell Leslie, Jr., *lawyer*
Shapere, Dudley *philosophy educator*
Sharpe, Keith Yount *retired lawyer*
Sigal, Gale *literature educator*
Simon, Jimmy Louis *pediatrician, educator*
Smunt, Marsha Lynn Haeflinger *financial executive*
Soares, Joseph Arlie *sociologist, educator*
Somerville, Atwell Wilson, Jr., *medical editor, director*
Spach, Jule Christian *church executive*
Steele, Thomas McKnight *law educator*
Stein, Barry Edward *medical educator*
Sticht, J. Paul *retired food products and tobacco company executive*
Stockton, Ralph Madison, Jr., *lawyer*
Strickland, Robert Louis *former retail company executive*
Sutton, Lynn Sorensen *librarian*
Tate, John William *food products executive*
Toole, James Francis *medical educator*
Torti, Frank Michael *physician, healthcare administrator*
Trautwein, George William *conductor, educator*
Twiggs, Dennis Glenn *psychologist, writer*
Uhl, Henry Stephen Magraw *internist, educator*
Vaughn, Robert Candler, Jr., *lawyer*
Walker, George Kontz *law educator*
Wallace, Roanne *hosiery company executive*
Walsh, Robert K. *dean*
Wanders, Hans Walter *banker*
Whittington, Stephen Lunn *museum director*
Wiles, Paul Martin *hospital administration executive*
Winn, Albert Curry *clergyman*
Womble, William Fletcher *lawyer*
Woodford, Duane Hugh *aerospace equipment manufacturing company executive, electrical engineer*
Yeatts, Dorothy Elizabeth Freeman *nurse, educator, retired county official*
Zubov, Lynn *special education educator, researcher*

Winton
Williams, Sue Darden *library director*

Woodland
Wilson, Lloyd Lee *organization administrator*

Wrightsville Beach
Mc Ilwain, William Franklin *newspaper editor, writer*

Yanceyville
Wiggins, Sarah *assistant principal, secondary school educator*

Youngsville
Riggs, Susan Dunnagan *music educator, musician*

Zebulon
Ruffing, Anne Elizabeth *artist*

NORTH DAKOTA

Amidon
Bergquist, Gene Alfred *farmer, rancher, county commissioner, retired county commissioner*

Ashley
Kretschmar, William Edward *state legislator, lawyer*

Bisbee
Keller, Michelle R. *science educator, secondary education educator*

Bismarck
Clairmont, William Edward *real estate developer*
Clark, Tony *state commissioner*
Conmy, Patrick A. *federal judge*
Cramer, Kevin *foundation administrator*
Dalrymple, Jack *lieutenant governor*
Dever, Dick *state legislator*
Edin, Charles Thomas *lawyer*
Gilmore, Kathi *state treasurer*
Gulleson, Pam *state legislator*
Heigaard, William Steven *state senator*
Hoeven, John *governor*
Jaeger, Alvin A. (Al Jaeger) *secretary of state*
Joersz, Fran Woodmansee *secondary school educator*
Kapsner, Carol Ronning *state supreme court justice*
Karsky, Timothy J. *bank commission official*
Kelsch, RaeAnn *state legislator*
Kleingartner, Larry *agricultural association executive*
Klemin, Lawrence R. *lawyer*
Loble, Lester Henry, II, *lawyer, business executive*
Lundberg, Susan Ona *musical organization administrator*
Maring, Mary Muehlen *state supreme court justice*
Murry, Charles Emerson *lawyer, official*
Nelson, Carolyn *state legislator*
Neumann, William Allen *state supreme court justice*
Newborg, Gerald Gordon *state archives administrator*
Ott, Doris Ann *librarian*
Potts, Robert Leslie *academic administrator*
Price, Clara Sue *state legislator*
Robinson, Warren Lowe *utilities executive*
Sandstrom, Dale Vernon *state supreme court justice*
Sandvig, Sally *state legislator*
Sanstead, Wayne Godfrey *school system administrator*
Schwartz, Judy Ellen *cardiothoracic surgeon*
Snyder, Robert John *lawyer*
Stenehjem, Wayne Kevin *state attorney general, lawyer*
Stoller, Rose *think-tank executive*
Strutz, William A. *lawyer*
Thompson, Vern *political organization executive*
Tornow, L. William *musician*
Traynor, Daniel M. *state representative*
Urlacher, Herbert *state legislator*
VandeWalle, Gerald Wayne *state supreme court chief justice*
Van Sickle, Bruce Marion *federal judge*
Warner, John Merritt *legislative staff member*
Wefald, Susan *state commissioner*
Wellin, Thomas *music director*

Cavalier
Trenbeath, Thomas L. *state legislator, lawyer*

Dickinson
Medlar, Deborah Starkey *history and political science educator*
Vranna, Jeffrey *music educator*
Wald, Francis John *state legislator*

Edgeley
Schimke, Dennis J. *former state legislator*

Edinburg
Myrdal, Rosemarie Caryle *state official, former state legislator*

Ellendale
Schlieve, Hy C. J. *school administrator*

Fargo
Amlund, Curtis Arthur *law educator*
Anderson, Gerald Dwight *history educator*
Berg, Rick Alan *state legislator, real estate investor*
Bernstein, LeRoy George *state legislator*
Bright, Myron H. *federal judge*
Bye, Kermit Edward *judge, lawyer*
Crothers, Daniel J. *lawyer*
Danbom, David Byers *history educator*
Foss, Richard John *bishop*
Ghatta, Srinivas *pharmacist, researcher*
Helweg, Otto Jennings *civil engineer, educator*
Holman, Maureen *lawyer*
Klein, Karen K. *federal judge*
Lardy, Sister Susan Marie *academic administrator*
Li, Kam Wu *mechanical engineer, educator*
Littlefield, Robert Stephen *communications educator, training consultant*
Magill, Frank John *federal judge*
Marcil, William Christ, Sr., *publisher, broadcast executive*
Mathern, Deb *state legislator*
McWilliams, Carey Scott *small business owner, writer*
Mengedoth, Donald Roy *commercial banker*
Mitchell, James Edward *physician, educator*
Nickel, Janet Marlene Milton *geriatrics nurse*
Olson, Robert Wallace *voice educator*
Reitan, Daniel Kinseth *electrical and computer engineering educator*
Rice, Jon Richard *managed care administrator, physician*
Riley, Thomas Joseph *anthropologist, educational administrator*
Rogers, David Anthony *electrical engineer, educator, researcher*
Sanford, Glenda Levonne *educational administrator*
Schmidt, Claude Henri *retired research administrator*
Shi, Zhengzhong *finance educator*
Sullivan, James Stephen *retired bishop*
Tallman, Dennis Earl *chemistry professor, research scientist*
Tallman, Robert Hall *investment company executive*
Tharaldson, Gary Dean *hotel developer and owner*
Unhjem, Michael Bruce *lawyer*
Wagner, Alexander Johannes *physicist, educator*
Wegenast, Judy H. *elementary school educator, consultant*
Wrigley, Drew H. *lawyer*

Grafton
Tallackson, Harvey Dean *state legislator, real estate and insurance salesman*

Grand Forks
Alfonso, Peter J. *educator*
Ashe, Kathy Rae *special education educator*
Aune, Adonica Schultz *education educator, consultant*
Berger, Albert Isaac *historian, consultant*
Carlson, Edward C. *anatomy educator*
Christenson, Linda *state legislator*
Delmore, Lois M. *state legislator*
Espegard, Duaine C. *state legislator*
Gallo, Sergio Roberto *music educator, researcher*
Gjovig, Bruce Quentin *entrepreneur coach, consultant, entrepreneur*
Glassheim, Eliot Alan *editor, state legislator*
Hoffmann, Mark R. *physical chemist, educator*
Jacobs, Francis Albin *biochemist, educator*
Kupchella, Charles Edward *academic administrator, author, educator*
Lerma, Edgar Villaneuva *nephrologist*
Nielsen, Forrest Harold *research nutritionist*
Nordlie, Robert Conrad *biochemistry educator*
Page, Sally Jacquelyn *university official, management educator*
Patton, Gregory Kenneth *management educator*
Polovitz, Michael *state legislator*
Popejoy, James Richard *music educator*
Porter, Kimberly K. *education educator, consultant*
Ransom, Michael T. *counselor*
Russell, Sue Ann *clinical psychologist*
Siegel, Mark Bernard *surgeon*
Skroch, Larry Eugene *railway conductor*
Sobus, Kerstin MaryLouise *physician, physical therapist*
Tyler, John Duke *psychologist, educator*
Vitton, John Joseph *education educator*
Warnke, Amy Nicholle *state legislator*
Wilson, H. David *dean*
Wogaman, George Elsworth *insurance company executive, financial consultant*

Hazen
Harvey, Chris S. *music educator*

Lehr
Erbele, Robert S. *state legislator*

Maddock
Aadland, Kathleen A. *counselor, army intelligence officer*

Mandan
Bair, Bruce B. *lawyer*
Hodge, Ann Linton *artist*

Mayville
Karaim, Betty June *retired librarian*

Minnewaukan
Every, Michael A. *state legislator*

Minot
Armstrong, Phillip Dale *lawyer*
Ellis, Lee *social sciences educator*
Jermiason, John Lynn *elementary school educator, farmer, rancher*
Kerian, Jon Robert *retired judge*
Krebsbach, Karen K. *state legislator*
Lee, Gary *lawyer*
Shaar, H. Erik *academic administrator*
Tollefson, Ben C. *state legislator, retired utility sales manager*
Watne, Darlene Claire *state legislator*
Welstad, Kirk *small business owner*

Minot AFB
Luckett, Byron Edward, Jr., *chaplain, career officer*

Taylor
Miller, Jean Patricia Salmon *art educator*

Towner
Gunter, G. Jane *state legislator*

Wahpeton
Reubish, Gary Richard *English language educator*

Williston
Adducci, Joseph Edward *obstetrician, gynecologist*
Benson, Robert John *physical therapist, department chairman, massage therapist*
Casler, Michael M. *protective services official*
Naranja, Rogelio Darusin, Sr., *psychiatrist*
Yockim, James Craig *former state senator, foundation administrator*

OHIO

Ada
Altstaetter, Dean Edward *music educator, musician*
Baker, Kendall L. *academic administrator*
Cooper, Ken Errol *retired management educator*
Fenton, Howard Nathan, III, *lawyer, educator*
Herr, Sharon Marie *librarian*
Lomax, John Phillip *history professor*
Neeley, Vernon Dean *music educator*

Akron
Aldana, Philipp Roque *neurosurgeon*
Alexander, Anthony J. *electric power industry executive*
Allen, Marc Kevin *emergency physician, educator*
Aynes, Richard L(ee) *law educator*
Barker, Harold Kenneth *former university dean*
Bell, Samuel H. *federal judge, educator*
Bentley, Bonnie J. *retired medical and oncological nurse*
Bird, Forrest M. *retired medical inventor*
Bonsky, Jack Alan *lawyer*
Borowiec, Andrew *art educator, photographer*
Bowman-Dalton, Burdene Kathryn *education testing coordinator, computer consultant*
Brown, David Rupert *engineering executive*
Burbach, Mike *editor*
Buzzelli, Charlotte Grace *special education educator*
Cahoon, Peter Thomas *lawyer*
Capers, Cynthia Flynn *dean, nursing educator*
Castronovo, Thomas Paul *architect, consultant*
Cherpas, Christopher Theodore *lawyer*
Chrisant, Rosemarie Kathryn *law library administrator*
Chung, Benjamin T. F. *science educator*
Cochran, John R. *bank executive*
Collier, Alice Elizabeth *retired community organization executive*
Coyne, Thomas Joseph *economist, finance educator*
Crawford, Robert John *credit company executive*
Dietz, Margaret Jane *retired public information director*
Donehey, Marilyn Moss *foundation administrator*
Duan, Zhong-Hui *education educator, researcher*
Emmett, John Colin *retired inventor, consultant*
Evans, Douglas McCullough *surgeon, educator*
Fisher, James Lee *lawyer*
Franck, Ardath Amond *psychologist, educator*
Frank, John V. *foundation administrator*
Gent, Alan Neville *physicist, researcher*
Gibara, Samir G. *tire manufacturing executive*
Glomski, Edward Earl *sales executive*
Gregoire, Larry V. *labor union administrator*
Hackbirth, David William *aluminum company executive*
Harvie, Crawford Thomas *lawyer*
Hochschwender, Herman Karl *international consultant*
Hodakievic, James Joseph *retired secondary education educator*
Holloway, Donald Phillip *lawyer*
Houston, Alma Faye *psychiatrist*
Hundley, Larry Willis *aerospace company executive*
Isayev, Avraam Isayevich *polymer engineer, educator*
Jana, Sadhan C *education educator, researcher*
Jasso, William Gattis *public relations executive*
Kahan, Mitchell Douglas *art museum director*
Kaufman, Donald Leroy *building products executive*
Keegan, Robert J. *manufacturing executive*
Kennedy, Joseph Paul *chemist, researcher*
Knepper, George W. *history educator*
Lee, Brant Thomas *lawyer, federal official, educator*
Levy, Richard Philip *physician, educator*
Linberger, Peter *school librarian*
Lombardi, Frederick McKean *lawyer*
Marsh, Richard H. *utilities company executive*
Martino, Frank Dominic *union executive*
McMahon, William Edward *philosophy educator*
Meeker, David Anthony *public relations executive*
Millman, Irving *microbiologist, educator, retired inventor*
Milsted, Amy *biomedical educator*
Molinari, Marco *marketing executive*
Moriarty, John Timothy *transportation consultant, writer*
Mubashir, Bashar A. *internist, oncologist, hematologist*
O'Brien, Gayle Ann *nurse*
Peavy, Homer Louis, Jr., *real estate executive, accountant*
Pipes, Robert Byron *mechanical engineer, educator*
Plusquellic, Donald L. *mayor*
Prosnick, Kevin Paul *psychologist, researcher*
Rapp, Larry P. *financial advisor*
Ray, Roy Lee *state legislator, public finance consultant*
Rebenack, John Henry *retired librarian*
Rooney, George Willard *lawyer*
Ruebel, Marion A. *university president*
Sahoo, Sangrama Kesari *physical chemist, researcher*
Seiberling, John Frederick *former congressman, law educator, lawyer*
Seiwald, Robert J. *retired inventor*
Shea-Stonum, Marilyn *federal bankruptcy judge*
Simmons, Debra Adams *editor*
Slowiak, James *theater director, educator*
Snider, George Runyon, Jr., *franchising company executive*
Sonnecken, Edwin Herbert *management consultant*
Sterns, Harvey Leonard *psychologist, gerontologist*
Stull, Robert L. *trucking executive*
Su, Dongwei *economist, educator*
Symens, Ronald Edwin *electrical engineer, consultant*
Tieken, Robert W. *tire manufacturing company executive*
Timmons, Gerald Dean *pediatric neurologist*
Trotter, Thomas Robert *lawyer*
Tyrrell, Thomas Neil *former metal processing executive*
Vespoli, Leila L. *energy executive, lawyer*
Wang, Ya-Hui *conductor*
Weaver, Thomas Jay *music educator*
West, Michael Alan *retired hospital administrator*
Wickham, Michael W. *transportation executive*
Wilding, James *music educator, composer*
Wolfe, John Leslie *lawyer*
Wortham, James Calvin *retired mathematics educator*

Alliance
Clem, Harriet Frances *library director*
DeStefano, L. Timothy *music educator, conductor*
Kotolup, James Alexander *finance company executive, accountant*
Woods, Rose Mary *former presidential assistant, consultant*
Zwilling, Michael Louis *mathematician, educator*

Alpha
James, Francis Edward, Jr., *investment counselor*

Amelia
Hayden, John W. *real estate company executive*
Hayden, Joseph Page, Jr., *finance company executive*

Andover
Mathay, John Preston *elementary school educator*
Mole, Richard Jay *accounting company executive*

Ashland
Drushal, Mary Ellen *education educator, former academic administrator*
Ford, Lucille Garber *economist, educator*
Hawk, L. Daniel *minister, religious studies educator*
Heimann, Beverly Ann *business educator, consultant*
Jamieson, Duncan Robert *historian, educator*
Rueger, Daniel Scott *horticulture educator*
Schmidt-Rinehart, Barbara Coe *Spanish language educator*
Shelly, Ann Converse *education educator, administrator*
Suggs, Robert Chinello *academic administrator, educator*
Watson, JoAnn Ford *theology studies educator*

Athens
Ahrens, Kent *museum director, art historian*
Alexander, Charles Comer *history educator, writer*
Bond, Zinny Sans *linguistics educator*
Borchert, Donald Marvin *philosopher, educator*
Bridgewater, Erle Henry *lawyer*
Bugeja, Michael Joseph *educator, writer*

Horrell, Karen Holley *insurance company executive, lawyer*
Horseman, Nelson Douglas *molecular and cellular physiology educator*
Hoverson, Robert L. *finance company executive*
Howe, John Kingman *manufacturing, sales and marketing executive*
Howison, Joan L. *geographer, writer*
Huenefeld, Thomas Ernst *financial consultant, retired banker*
Huggins, Bob *college basketball coach*
Hutton, Edward Luke *diversified public corporation executive*
Ingle, Gary L. *performing arts association administrator*
Iroh, Jude Onwuegbu *chemistry professor*
Ivey, Tom Dexter *cardiac surgeon*
James, George Barker, II, *investment executive*
James, Jefferson Ann *performing company executive, choreographer*
Janson, Julia S. *utilities executive*
Jarvi, Paavo *conductor*
Javosky, Rudolph V. *retail executive*
Jensen, Elwood Vernon *biochemist*
Johnson, James J. *lawyer*
Jones, Daniel W. *construction executive*
Jones, Mark Allen *structural engineer*
Jones, Nathaniel Raphael *retired federal judge*
Kalagayan, Jay B. *theater producer, director*
Kaune, James Edward *ship repair company executive, former naval officer*
Kawahara, Fred Katsumi *research chemist*
Kelley, Cleophus O. *city official*
Kelley, John Joseph, Jr., *lawyer*
Kelz, Rochelle Shelle K. *academic administrator*
Kendle, Candace *pharmaceutical executive*
Kennedy, Cornelia Groefsema *federal judge*
Kereiakes, Dean James *cardiologist*
Kernan, Jerome Bernard *retired marketing educator, researcher*
Khan, Sohaib Ahmed *cancer researcher, molecular cell biology educator*
Kiel, Frederick Orin *lawyer*
Kiggen, James D. *telecommunications industry executive*
Kim, Sung Eun *statistician, educator*
Kitna, Jon *professional football player*
Klein, Charles Henle *lithographing company executive*
Klein, Jerry Emanuel *insurance and financial planning executive*
Klinedinst, Thomas John, Jr., *insurance agency executive*
Klingshirn, David *performing arts association administrator*
Knue, Paul Frederick *newspaper editor*
Koebel, Sister Celestia *health care system executive*
Kollstedt, Paula Lubke *communications executive, writer*
Kordons, Uldis *lawyer*
Kowel, Stephen Thomas *electrical engineer, educator*
Krantz, William Bernard *chemical engineering educator*
Krishnan, Hema A. *finance educator*
Krohn, Claus Dankertsen *insurance company executive*
Kronick, Susan D. *retail executive*
Kulwin, Dwight Robert *surgeon, educator*
Kuntz, Charles, IV, *neurological surgeon*
Kunzel, Erich, Jr., *conductor, arranger, educator*
Lafley, Alan G. *consumer products company executive*
Laney, Sandra Eileen *service company executive*
Lang, Jackie Ann *nursing consultant*
Larkin, Barry Louis *professional baseball player*
Lawrence, James Kaufman Lebensburger *lawyer*
Lawson, Kenneth L. *lawyer*
Lawson, Randall Clayton, II, *financial executive*
Lesick, John Richard *retired lawyer, consultant*
Levin, Debbe Ann *lawyer*
Levinson, Joseph E. *physician, emeritus educator*
Lewis, Gene Dale *historian, educator*
Leyda, James Perkins *small business consultant, retired pharmaceutical company executive*
Lichtin, Leon (Judah Leon Lichtin) *pharmacist*
Lindberg, Charles David *lawyer*
Lindell, Andrea Regina *dean, nurse*
Linder, Carl H., III, *diversified financial services company executive*
Lindner, Carl H., III, *corporate financial executive*
Lindner, Robert David *finance company executive*
Lintz, Robert Carroll *retired financial holding company executive*
Lippincott, Jonathan Ramsay *healthcare executive*
Liss, Herbert Myron *communications educator*
Lockhart, John Mallery *management consultant*
Loggie, Jennifer Mary Hildreth *medical educator, physician*
Lucas, Stanley Jerome *retired radiologist, physician*
Lucke, Robert Vito *merger and acquisition executive*
Luckner, Herman Richard, III, *interior designer*
Lucky, Anne Weissman *dermatologist*
Luse, Kimberly Ann *radiologic technologist, educator*
Lynch, Timothy Patrick *historian, educator*
Lytle, James DeVore *retired dentist*
Madson, Philip Ward *engineering executive, consultant*
Maier, Jack C. *food products company executive*
Maltz, Robert *surgeon*
Manley, Robert Edward *lawyer, economist*
Manly, Marc Edward *lawyer*
Mann, David Scott *lawyer*
Mantel, Samuel Joseph, Jr., *management educator, consultant*
Mara, Timothy Gerald *lawyer*
Marks, Edward G. *lawyer*
Martin, William Joseph, II, *dean, educator*
Martineau, Robert John *law educator*
Marx, Marjorie McCullough *service organization executive*
Maxwell, Robert Wallace, II, *lawyer*
McAusland, Randolph M. N. *arts consultant*
McClain, William Andrew *lawyer*
McDowell, John Eugene *lawyer*
McFarlan, Rebecca Collins *secondary school educator, consultant*
McGeorge, Don W. *retail executive*
McMullin, Ruth Roney *publishing executive, trustee, management fellow*
McNay, John T. *humanities educator*
Meal, Larie *chemistry educator, researcher, consultant*
Mechem, Charles Stanley, Jr., *former broadcasting executive, former golf association executive*
Meranus, Leonard Stanley *lawyer*
Merchant, Mylon Eugene *physicist, engineer*
Meyer, Daniel Joseph *machinery company executive*
Meyers, Karen Diane *lawyer, educator, corporate officer*
Meyers, Pamela Sue *lawyer*
Miles, John Bill *accountant, tax advisor*
Miley, David *professional baseball coach*
Milligan, Terence Gilbert *music educator*
Monaco, John J. *molecular genetics research educator*
Monder, Steven I. *orchestra executive*
Monroe, Erin *psychiatric nurse practitioner*
Moore, John Edward *marketing professional, freelance writer*
Morgan, John Bruce *hospital care consultant*
Morgan, Victoria *performing company executive, choreographer*
Morgan, William Richard *mechanical engineer*
Morris, Margaret Elizabeth *marketing professional*
Morrow, Ardythe Luxion *adult education educator, researcher*
Mukerjee, Debdas *environmental health scientist, educator*
Murphy, Theodore R., II, *utilities executive*
Nasrallah, Henry Ata *psychiatry researcher, educator*
Neagle, Dennis Edward (Denny Neagle) *professional baseball player*
Neale, Henry Whitehead *plastic surgery educator*
Nebert, Daniel Walter *molecular geneticist, research administrator*
Nechemias, Stephen Murray *lawyer*
Nelson, David Aldrich *judge*
Nelson, Frederick Dickson *judge*
Nester, William Raymond, Jr., *retired academic administrator and educator*
Neumark, Michael Harry *lawyer*
Newton, Frederick J., III, *utilities executive*
Nielsen, George Lee *architect*
Noonan, Sheila M. *energy consulting company executive*
O'Donnell, Robert Patrick *priest*
O'Reilly, James Thomas *lawyer, educator, author*
Orr, James Francis *marketing and information services executive*
Otto, Charlotte R. *consumer products company executive*
Paavo, Jarvi *conductor*
Painter, Mark Philip *judge*
Palmer, Paul Richard *school librarian, archivist, curator*
Panioto, Ronald Angelo *judge*
Parker, R. Joseph *lawyer*
Perlman, Burton *judge*
Petrie, Bruce Inglis *lawyer*
Petty, Priscilla Hayes *writer, columnist, producer*
Pichler, Joseph Anton *food products executive*
Pilarczyk, Daniel Edward *archbishop*
Pirtle, Laurie Lee *women's college basketball coach*
Porte, Michael Sheldon *communication educator, consultant*
Porter, Robert Carl, Jr., *lawyer*
Price, Thomas Emile *investment company executive*
Pryor, Jerry Dennis *corporate professional*
Putnam, Frank William *biochemistry and immunology educator*
Putnam, Frank William, Jr., *medical researcher*
Randman, Barry I. *real estate developer*
Randolph, Jackson Harold *utility company executive*
Rapoport, Robert Morton *medical educator*
Rashkin, Mitchell Carl *internist, pulmonary medicine specialist*
Ratliff, Thomas Asbury, Jr., *retired engineer*
Reichert, David *lawyer*
Reising, Ronald *utilities executive*
Relyea, Carl Miller *retired hydrologist*
Rexroth, Nancy Louise *photographer*
Rich, Robert Edward *lawyer*
Rigaud, Edwin Joseph *museum administrator*
Rishel, James Burton *manufacturing executive, director*
Rogers, James Eugene *electric and gas utility executive*
Rogers, John Marshall *judge, law educator*
Rogers, Millard Foster, Jr., *art museum director emeritus*
Rolls, Steven George *communications executive*
Roomann, Hugo *architect*
Rose, Donald McGregor *retired lawyer*
Rosen, Roberta *philosophy educator*
Rub, Timothy F. *museum director*
Rubin, Robert Samuel *lawyer*
Rudich, Steven Mark *surgeon*
Ruehlmann, Virginia Juergens *foundation creativity director, writer*
Runk, Fred J. *insurance company executive*
Ruthman, Thomas Robert *manufacturing executive*
Ryan, Richard J. *emergency medicine physician*
Saal, Howard Max *clinical geneticist, pediatrician, educator*
Sacher, Ronald Alan *hematologist*
Safferman, Robert Samuel *microbiologist, researcher*
Sallquist, Gary Ardin *minister, non-profit executive*
Santiago, Benito Rivera *professional baseball player*
Schaefer, Dale W. *physicist, researcher, administrator*
Schaefer, Frank William, III, *microbiologist, researcher*
Schaefer, George A., Jr., *bank executive*
Schiff, Gilbert Martin *virologist, microbiologist, medical educator*
Schiff, John Jefferson, Jr., *finance company executive*
Schlotman, J. Michael *food products executive*
Schreiner, Albert William *physician, educator*
Schrier, Arnold *historian, educator*
Schubert, William Kuenneth *hospital medical center executive*
Schuck, Thomas Robert *lawyer, farmer*
Schuler, Robert Leo *appraiser, consultant*
Schutzius, Lucy Jean *retired librarian*
Schwab, Nelson, Jr., *lawyer*
Sedgwick, Sally Belle *publishing company executive*
Sekhar, Jainagesh Akkaraja *entrepreneur, educator*
Semon, Warren Lloyd *retired computer sciences educator*
Senhauser, John Crater *architect*
Shanks, Earl *marketing professional*
Sheffield, Elizabeth Baker *special education educator, lecturer, consultant*
Shepherd, Elsbeth Weichsel *supply chain consultant*
Sherman, Kenneth Eliot *medicine educator, researcher*
Shipley, Tony L(ee) *software company executive*
Shott, Sally Richard *otolaryngologist*
Siekmann, Donald Charles *accountant*
Sierra-Amor, Rosa Isabel *health facility administrator*
Silbersack, Mark Louis *lawyer*
Silberstein, Edward Bernard *nuclear medicine educator, oncologist, researcher*
Sims, Victor Dwayne *lawyer*
Skavlem, Melissa Kline *publisher*
Smale, John Gray *diversified industry executive*
Smith, Gregory Allgire *college administrator*
Smith, Sheila Marie *lawyer*
Smittle, Nelson Dean *military analyst, artist*
Sowder, Fred Allen *foundation administrator, alphabet specialist*
Sperelakis, Nicholas, Sr., *physiology and biophysics educator, researcher*
Spiegel, S. Arthur *federal judge*
Spinnato, Joseph Anthony, II, *obstetrician*
Stanton, Jeanne Frances *retired lawyer*
Steger, Joseph A. *university president*
Steinberg, Janet Eckstein *journalist*
Stern, Joseph Smith, Jr., *former footwear manufacturing company executive*
Stinson, Mary Florence *retired nursing educator*
Stolley, Alexander *advertising executive*
Strauss, William Victor *lawyer*
Strohmaier, Thomas Edward *designer, educator, photographer*
Sullivan, James F. *physicist, researcher*
Sunagawa, Masanori *physiologist, researcher*
Sutton, Jeffrey S. *federal judge*
Swigert, James Mack *lawyer*
Teasley, John Ray Sanders, Jr., *writer*
Tenbosch, Gerald John *fundraising executive*
Tengen, Thomas L. *financial planner, finance educator*
Thiemann, Charles Lee *banker*
Thomas, Michael A. *endocrinologist, gynecologist*
Thompson, Adrienne *secondary school educator*
Thompson, Morley Punshon *textile company executive*
Timpano, Anne *museum director, art historian*
Tobias, Charles Harrison, Jr., *lawyer*
Tobias, Paul Henry *lawyer*
Tocco, James *pianist*
Toftner, Richard Orville *engineering executive*
Tomain, Joseph Patrick *dean, law educator*
Trauth, Joseph Louis, Jr., *lawyer*
Trofe, Jennifer *pharmacist, educator*
Trotta, Vincent John *transportation executive*
Turner, Joan Dale *elementary school educator*
Turpening, Patricia Eileen Keller *law librarian*
Tysoe, Ronald W. *retail executive*
Tysor, Ronald W. *retail executive*
Utegulov, Zhandos N. *research scientist*
Vander Laan, Mark Alan *lawyer*
Verhagen, Timothy *utilities executive*
Vilter, Richard William *internist, educator*
Vogel, Cedric Wakelee *lawyer*
Wachenfeld, Timothy H. *aeronautical engineering executive*
Wales, Ross Elliot *lawyer*
Warrick, Peter *professional football player*
Watts, Barbara Gayle *law academic administrator*
Weber, Herman Jacob *federal judge*
Weeks, Steven Wiley *lawyer*
Weinrich, Alan Jeffrey *occupational hygienist*
Weisman, Joel *retired engineering educator*
Welsh, George Franklin *plastic surgeon, educator, healthcare consultant*
West, Clark Darwin *pediatric nephrologist, educator*
Weston, Phyllis Jean *art gallery director*
Whipple, Harry M. *newspaper publishing executive*
White, Alfred Kenneth, Jr., *lawyer*
Whitsett, Jeffrey Allen *pediatric educator*
Williams, Daniel Bryan *obstetrician/gynecologist, educator*
Wilson, Arthur Henry *charitable institution executive*
Wilson, William Alexander *manufacturing engineer, consultant*
Winkler, Henry Ralph *retired academic administrator, historian*
Wiot, Jerome Francis *radiologist*
Wisler, David Charles *aerospace engineer*
Witten, Louis *physics educator*
Wood, Robert Emerson *pediatrics educator*
Woodside, Frank C., III, *lawyer, educator, physician*
Wozny, David *utilities executive*
Wright, Creighton Bolter *cardiovascular surgeon, educator*
Wulker, Laurence Joseph *portfolio manager, educator, financial planner*
Wygant, Foster Laurance *art educator, educator*
Zafren, Herbert Cecil *librarian, educator*
Zaring, Allen G. *homebuilding company executive*
Zimmerman, James M. *retail company executive*
Zimpher, Nancy Lusk *academic administrator*
Zola, Gary Phillip *rabbi, historian, religious educational administrator*
Zuccarello, Mario *neurosurgeon, researcher*

Circleville
Ammer, William *retired judge*
Long, Jan Michael *judge*

Clayton
Stutzman, L. Lee *pastor*

Cleveland
Abrams, Sylvia Fleck *religious studies educator*
Abughali, Nazha *pediatrician, consultant*
Acheampong, Robert Kwabena *investment consultant*
Adamo, Kenneth R. *lawyer*
Adams, H. Leslie *composer*
Agani, Faton Hilmi *anatomist, educator*
Aldrich, Ann *federal judge*
Anderson, James M. *pathologist*
Anderson, Warren *distribution company executive*
Andrews, Oakley V. *lawyer*
Angus, John Cotton *chemical engineering educator*
Ashmus, Keith Allen *lawyer*
Austin, Arthur Donald, II, *lawyer, educator*
Awais, George Musa *obstetrician, gynecologist*
Bacon, Brett Kermit *lawyer*
Badal, Daniel Walter *psychiatrist, educator*
Bahniuk, Eugene *mechanical engineering educator*
Baker, Melvin *hospital pharmacy administrator*
Baker, Saul Phillip *geriatrician, cardiologist, internist*
Bansal, Narottam Prasad *ceramic research engineer*
Barnett, Gene Henry *neurosurgeon*
Bate, Brian R. *retired psychologist*
Bates, Walter Alan *retired lawyer*
Battle, Hilary Howard *minister, educator*
Baughman, R(obert) Patrick *lawyer*
Bause, George Stephen Loneraven *anesthesiologist*
Beall, Cynthia *anthropologist, educator*
Behnke, William Alfred *retired landscape architect*
Bell, David Gus (Buddy) (Buddy Bell) *professional baseball manager*
Benseler, David Price *foreign language educator*
Berger, Melvin *allergist, immunologist*
Berger, Nathan Allen *academic administrator*
Berger, Sanford Jason *lawyer, securities dealer, real estate broker*
Bergholz, David *foundation administrator*
Berick, James Herschel *lawyer*
Bidelman, William Pendry *astronomer, educator*
Bingham, Richard Donnelly *journal editor, director, educator*
Binstock, Robert Henry *public policy educator, writer, lecturer*
Blackwell, John *science educator*
Blum, Arthur *social worker, educator*
Boboc, Marius *education educator*
Bodner, Donald Roger *urologist, medical educator*
Boland, James C. *sports association executive*
Borchert, Catherine Glennan *minister*
Bouie, Oliver D. *minister*
Bowen, Richard Lee *architect*
Bowerfind, Edgar Sihler, Jr., *retired physician, medical administrator*
Boyd, Arthur Bernette, Jr., *surgeon, clergyman, beverage company executive*
Boyd, Byron A. *labor union administrator*
Braverman, Herbert Leslie *lawyer*
Bravo, Kenneth Allan *lawyer*
Brennan, Maureen *lawyer*
Brentlinger, Paul Smith *venture capital executive*
Bridges, John Francis Patrick *healthcare educator, researcher*
Brinzo, John S. *mining executive*
Brody, Robert *dermatologist, educator*
Bronson, David Leigh *physician, educator*
Brown, Bruce Andrew *lawyer*
Brown, Robert William *physics educator, physicist*
Brucken, Robert Matthew *lawyer*
Bruner, William Evans, II, *ophthalmologist, educator, researcher*
Buck, Matthias *science educator*
Budd, John Henry *physician*
Buhrow, William Carl *religious organization administrator*
Burge, David Alan *patent lawyer, writer*
Burghart, James Henry *electrical engineer, educator*
Burke, Kathleen B. B. *lawyer*
Burke, Lillian Walker *retired judge*
Butler, Christopher David *mathematics professor*
Butler, William E. *retired manufacturing company executive*
Byrd-Bennett, Barbara *school system administrator*
Byron, Rita Ellen Cooney *travel executive, publisher, real estate agent, civic leader, photojournalist, writer*
Cairns, James Donald *lawyer*
Calfee, John Beverly *retired lawyer*
Calkins, Hugh *foundation executive*
Callahan, Thomas James *lawyer*
Campbell, Jane Louise *mayor*
Carey, Paul Richard *biophysicist*
Carlsson, Bo Axel Vilhelm *economics professor*
Carrick, Kathleen Michele *law librarian*
Carrol, Edward Nicholas *psychologist*
Carter, Daniel Paul *lawyer, educator*
Carter, John Dale *organizational development coordinator*
Cassill, Herbert Carroll *artist*
Castele, Theodore John *radiologist*
Cavanagh, Peter Robert *academic administrator, science educator, researcher*
Cerone, David *academic administrator*
Chae, Han *medical researcher*
Chamis, Christos Constantinos *aerospace scientist, educator*
Chao, Jason *family physician, educator*
Charnas, Michael (Mannie Charnas) *investment company executive*
Chema, Thomas V. *consultant, government official, lawyer, academic administrator*
Chester, Russell Gilbert, Jr., *accountant, auditor*
Cirincione, Ross Joseph *mathematician, educator*
Clark, Robert Arthur *mathematician, educator*
Clarke, Charles Fenton *lawyer*
Clifton, Douglas C. *newspaper editor*
Cola, Philip Andrew *research administrator*
Collin, Thomas James *lawyer*
Collins, Duane E. *manufacturing executive*
Collis, John Stanley *neurosurgeon*
Connor, Christopher M. *textiles executive*
Conrad, Robert David *broadcast executive, educator*
Cooper, Gregory Scott *epidemiologist, gastroenterologist, educator*
Coquillette, William Hollis *lawyer*
Cosgrove, Delos M. *health facility administrator, surgeon*
Cotleur, Mark A. *hospital administrator*
Cowan, Dale Harvey *internist, lawyer*
Crandall, Karen *government agency administrator*
Crawford, Edward E. *consumer products company executive*
Crehore, Charles Aaron *lawyer*
Crispin, Patricia Lynnette *social worker*
Crosby, Fred McClellan *retail home and office furnishings executive*
Cudak, Gail Linda *lawyer*
Curnow, Kathy *art historian, educator*
Curran, Phyllis Marie *counselor*
Currivan, John Daniel *lawyer*
Cutler, Alexander MacDonald *manufacturing executive*
Cyphert, Michael A. *lawyer*
Daberko, David A. *banker*
Dadley, Arlene Jeanne *sleep technologist*
Dampeer, John Lyell *retired lawyer*
Danco, Léon Antoine *management consultant, educator*
Dannemiller, John C. *transportation company executive*
Daroff, Robert Barry *neurologist, educator*

Dauscher, Raymond G. *lawyer*
Davis, Pamela Bowes *pediatric pulmonologist*
Deal, William Thomas *school psychologist*
Decker, John William *metal products executive*
DeGroote, Michael G. *management consulting* [illegible]
Deissler, Robert George *fluid dynamicist, researcher*
DellaCorte, Christopher *engineer*
Dell'Osso, Louis Frank *neuroscience educator*
De Marco, Thomas Joseph *periodontist, educator*
DiGirolamo, Vincent A. *retired banking services executive*
Distelhorst, Garis Fred *trade association executive*
Doershuk, Carl Frederick *pediatrician, pediatrics educator*
Domiano, Joseph Charles *lawyer*
Douglas, Janice Green *physician, educator*
Dowell, Michael Brendan *chemist*
Drake, Grace L. *retired state senator, cultural organization administrator*
Drinko, John Deaver *lawyer*
Dunbar, Mary Asmundson *communications executive, investor and public relations consultant*
Duncan, Ed Eugene *lawyer*
Dunlap, Jeffrey Scott *lawyer*
Dunn, George J. *lawyer, oil company executive*
Duvin, Robert Phillip *lawyer*
Dweik, Raed A. *physician, researcher, educator*
Eaton, Henry Felix *public relations executive*
Eberhard, William Thomas *architect*
Edwards, Michelle Denise *professional basketball player*
Eiben, Robert Michael *pediatric neurologist, educator*
Eklund, Claudia Rieth *lawyer*
Ellis, Lloyd H., Jr., *emergency physician, art historian*
Enty, Richard McDougald *rail transportation administrator*
Erb, Donald *composer*
Esselstyn, Caldwell Blakeman, Jr., *physician*
Fabens, Andrew Lawrie, III, *lawyer*
Fabris, James A. *journalist*
Falcone, Tommaso *reproductive endocrinologist*
Fallcreek, Stephanie Jean *non-profit organization executive*
Fallon, Pat *artist, educator*
Falsgraf, William Wendell *retired lawyer*
Fanaroff, Avroy A. *pediatrician, educator*
Fay, Regan Joseph *lawyer*
Fazio, Victor Warren *physician, colon and rectal surgeon*
Fei, Baowei *biomedical researcher*
Fijalkowski, Isabelle *professional basketball player*
Finley, Chuck (Charles Edward Finley) *professional baseball player*
Finn, Robert *writer, lecturer, broadcaster*
Fischer, Michelle K. *lawyer*
Fisher, Thomas Edward *lawyer*
Fitzpatrick, Joyce J. *nursing educator, former dean*
Fletcher, Robert *retired lawyer, horologist*
Flynn, James O'Donnell *statistician, educator*
Foster, Dennis James *legal recruiting services executive*
Fountain, Ronald Glenn *management consultant, finance/marketing executive, management educator*
Freimuth, Marc William *lawyer*
Friedman, Barton Robert *English educator*
Friedman, Harold Edward *lawyer*
Fryman, David Travis *professional baseball player*
Gambetti, Perluigi *pathologist*
Gardner, Richard Kent *retired librarian, educator, consultant*
Gardocki, Christopher *professional football player*
Garrison, William Lloyd *cemetery executive*
Gaughan, Patricia Anne *judge*
Gelfand, Ivan *investment advisor*
Gellert, Edward Bradford, III, *architect*
Giannetti, Louis Daniel *film critic, educator*
Gibans, James David *architect*
Gillespie, Robert Wayne *banker*
Ginn, Robert Martin *retired utility company executive*
Glaser, Robert Edward *lawyer*
Gleisser, Marcus David *writer, lawyer, journalist*
Glickman, Carl David *banker*
Goffman, William *mathematician, educator*
Goins, Frances Floriano *lawyer*
Gold, Gerald Seymour *lawyer*
Goldberg, Jerold S. *dean*
Goldfarb, Bernard Sanford *lawyer*
Goler, Michael David *lawyer*
Gorney, John *information technology executive*
Gould, Bonnie M(arincic) *realtor*
Grabow, Raymond John *mayor, lawyer*
Grabowski, John Joseph *education educator, researcher*
Graham, John W. *advertising executive*
Greer, Thomas H. *newspaper executive*
Greppin, John Aird Coutts *philologist, editor, educator*
Griffith, Mary H. *corporate communications executive*
Grossman, Theodore Martin *lawyer*
Grundy, Kenneth William *political science educator*
Guffey, Edith Ann *religious organization administrator*
Haiman, Irwin Sanford *lawyer*
Hamilton, William Milton *retired manufacturing executive*
Hammack, David Conrad *history professor*
Hancock, James Beaty *interior designer*
Hansman, Catherine Ann *adult education educator, researcher*
Hanson, Richard Winfield *biochemist, educator*
Harding, Clifford Vincent, III, *medical educator*
Hardis, Stephen Roger *retired manufacturing company executive*
Hardy, Michael Lynn *lawyer*
Hardy, Richard Allen *mechanical engineer, engineering executive*
Hargrove, Mike (Dudley Michael Hargrove, Mike Hargrove) *former professional baseball team manager*
Hart, John *professional sports team executive*
Hartley, Duncan *fundraising executive*
Hemann, Patricia A. *federal judge*
Henes, Samuel Ernst *lawyer*
Hennessy, Sean P. *retail executive*
Henry, Edward Frank *computer accounting service executive*
Hermann, Robert Ewald *retired surgeon*
Herrup, Karl *neurobiologist*
Heuer, Arthur Harold *ceramics engineer, educator*
Hiemstra, Michael J. *manufacturing executive*
Hill, Tyrone *professional basketball player*
Hochman, Kenneth George *lawyer*
[illegible]
Hokenstad, Merl Clifford, Jr., *social work educator*
Holland, Brian Joseph *corporate financial executive*
Hollington, Richard Rings, Jr., *lawyer*
Holmes, Arthur S. *manufacturing executive*
Holzbach, Raymond Thomas *gastroenterologist, educator, writer*
Horvitz, Michael John *lawyer*
Horwitz, Ralph Irving *internist, medical educator, epidemiologist*
Hundert, Edward M. *academic administrator*
Huterer, Dragon *physicist*
Irving, Lee G. *bank executive*
Ivy, Conway Gayle *paint company executive*
Jackson, Edgar B., Jr., *medical educator*
Jacobs, Leslie William *lawyer*
Jacobs, Michael Roy *microbiologist, researcher*
Jacobs, Richard E. *real estate company executive, sports team owner*
Jaffe, Donald Nolan *lawyer*
James, LeBron *professional basketball player*
Jameson, J(ames) Larry *chemical company executive*
Janke, Ronald Robert *lawyer*
Jensen, Kathryn Patricia (Kit) *public radio and television station executive*
Jenson, Jon Eberdt *association executive*
Jettke, Harry Jerome *retired government official*
Johnson, John Frank *professional recruitment executive*
Johnson, Mattiedna *medical/surgical nurse*
Johnson, Victoria Houston *elementary school educator, poet*
Johnston, Alastair J. *sports association executive*
Jorgenson, Mary Ann *lawyer*
Kahrl, Robert Conley *lawyer*
Kanzeg, David George *radio station executive*
Karp, Marvin Louis *lawyer*
Kashyap, Vikram S. *vascular surgeon, military officer*
Kass, Lawrence *hematologist, oncologist, educator, hematopathologist*
Katcher, Richard *lawyer*
Katz, Lewis Robert *law educator*
Kelly, Dennis Michael *lawyer*
Kelly, Jeffrey D. *corporate financial executive*
Kelly, John Terence *architect*
Key, Helen Elaine *accountant, educator, consulting company executive*
Kilbane, Sally Conway *economics professor*
Kilbane, Thomas Stanton *lawyer*
Klopman, Gilles *chemistry professor*
Ko, Wen-Hsiung *electrical engineering educator*
Koblenz, N(orman) Herschel *lawyer*
Koch, Charles John *credit agency executive*
Koenig, Jack L. *chemist, educator*
Kohn, Mary Louise Beatrice *nurse*
Kolb, David Allen *psychology educator*
Kovacs, Rosemary *newpaper editor*
Kovel, Ralph M. *writer, antiques expert*
Kovel, Terry Horvitz (Mrs. Ralph Kovel) *writer, antiques authority*
Kowalski, Kenneth Lawrence *physicist, researcher*
Kramer, Edward George *lawyer*
Kramer, Eugene Leo *lawyer*
Krieger, Irvin Mitchell *chemistry professor, consultant*
Krulitz, Leo Morrion *financial executive*
Kurit, Neil *lawyer*
Lafave, Arthur J., Jr., *financial executive, lawyer*
Lamm, Michael Emanuel *pathologist, immunologist, educator*
Landau, Bernard Robert *biochemistry educator, physician*
Lando, Jerome Burton *macromolecular science educator*
Lawniczak, James Michael *lawyer*
Lawrence, Estelene Yvonne *musician, transportation executive*
Lazar, Kathy Pittak *lawyer*
Lazzaro, S. Robert E. *lawyer*
Leaks, Marna Hale *utilities executive*
Lease, Robert K. *lawyer*
Leavitt, Jeffrey Stuart *lawyer*
Lebovitz, Harold Paul (Hal Lebovitz) *journalist*
Lee, Jae-won *journalism educator, political campaign consultant*
Lefferts, William Geoffrey *internist, educator*
Leiken, Earl Murray *lawyer*
Lemmo, Roberta June *financial advisor*
Lenn, Stephen Andrew *investment banker*
Lennox, Heather *lawyer*
Leukart, Barbara J. J. *lawyer*
Levin, Miriam R. *historian, educator*
Lewis, John Bruce *lawyer*
Lewis, Peter Benjamin *insurance company executive*
Little, Robert Andrews *architect, artist*
Long, Robert M. *newspaper publishing executive*
Lopez, Nancy *former professional golfer*
Lowe, James Allison *lawyer, educator*
Lowry, Joan Marie Dondrea *broadcaster*
Luce, Edward Andrew *plastic surgeon*
Luke, Randall Dan *retired tire and rubber company executive, lawyer*
Mabee, Keith V. *communications/investor relations executive*
Machaskee, Alex *newspaper publishing company executive*
Macklis, Roger Milton *physician, educator, researcher*
Mac Laren, David Sergeant *manufacturing corporation executive, inventor*
Madden, James D. *forensic engineer*
Madison, Robert Prince *architect*
Maher, Edward Joseph *lawyer*
Maier, Howard Robert *urban planner, government agency administrator*
Malangoni, Mark Alan *surgeon, educator*
Maloney, Mary D. *lawyer*
Mandel, Jack N. *manufacturing executive*
Manley, David Thomas *employee benefits plan administration executive*
Manos, John M. *federal judge*
Manos, Peter John *social studies educator, theater director, writer, actor*
Manuel, Charlie Fuqua, Jr., *professional baseball manager*
Marcus, Donald Howard *advertising executive*
Markey, Robert Guy *lawyer*
Markus, Richard M. *judge, mediator*
Marting, Michael G. *lawyer*
Mason, Thomas Albert *lawyer*
Mast, Bernadette Mihalic *lawyer*
Matia, Paul Roman *federal judge*
Mawardi, Osman Kamel *plasma physicist*
Mayland, Kenneth Theodore *economist*
Mayne, Lucille Stringer *finance educator*
Mazgalev, Todor Nikolov *health science association administrator, research scientist*
McAndrews, James Patrick *lawyer*
McArdle, Richard Joseph *retired academic administrator*
Mc Cartan, Patrick Francis *lawyer*
McCarthy, Mark Francis *lawyer*
McCrae, Keith R. *medical educator, researcher*
McCullough, Joseph *college president emeritus*
McFadden, John Volney *retired manufacturing company executive*
McHale, Vincent Edward *political science educator*
McHenry, Martin Christopher *physician, educator*
McLaughlin, Patrick Michael *lawyer*
McQuarrie, Irvine Gray *neurosurgeon, educator*
Medalie, Jack Harvey *physician*
Mehlman, Maxwell Jonathan *law educator*
Melsop, James William *architect*
Meyer, G. Christopher *lawyer*
Meziane, Moulay Ahmed *physician*
Michaels, Alex P. *film company executive*
Miller, Carl George *automotive parts manufacturing executive*
Miller, Genevieve *retired medical historian*
Miller, John Robert *oil industry executive*
Miller, Sandra A. Caramela *gerontologist, educator*
Millisor, Kenneth Ray *lawyer*
Millstone, David Jeffrey *lawyer*
Minai, Omar Ahmad *physician*
Moll, Curtis E. *manufacturing executive*
Molyneaux, David Glenn *newspaper travel editor*
Montague, Drogo K. *urologist*
Mooney, James P. *chemicals executive*
Moore, Karen Nelson *judge*
Moore, Kenneth Cameron *lawyer*
Moravec, Christine D. Schomis *medical educator*
Morgenthaler, David Turner *venture capitalist*
Morris, Thomas William *symphony orchestra administrator*
Myers, Eddie Earl *clinical psychologist*
Nahat, Dennis F. *performing company executive, choreographer*
Nemcova, Eva *professional basketball player*
Neu, Richard W. *credit agency executive*
Neuger, Sanford *orthodontics educator*
Neuhauser, Duncan vonBriesen *medical educator*
Newman, John M., Jr., *lawyer*
Noall, Roger *bank executive*
Norman, Forrest Alonzo *lawyer*
Novick, Andrew Carl *urologist*
Oakar, Mary Rose *congresswoman*
O'Donnell, Thomas Michael *former brokerage firm executive*
O'Hara, Thomas Patrick *managing editor*
Okojie, Robert Sylvester *electronics engineer, researcher, aerospace scientist*
Olivares-Cuhat, Gabriela Antonia *literature and language professor*
Oliver, Solomon, Jr., *judge*
Ollinger, W. James *lawyer*
Olness, Karen Norma *pediatrics and international health educator*
O'Malley, Kathleen M. *federal judge*
O'Neil, Thomas J. *mining company executive*
Ornt, Daniel B. *physician*
Pace, Stanley Dan *lawyer*
Papay, Francis Anthony *plastic surgeon, researcher*
Parker, Patrick Streeter *manufacturing executive*
Parker, Robert Frederic *university dean emeritus*
Pascarella, Perry James *author, editor, speaker*
Pearlman, Samuel Segel *lawyer, educator*
Perkovic, Robert Branko *retired international management consultant*
Perris, Terrence George *lawyer*
Perry, George *neuroscientist, educator*
Pierson, Marilyn Ehle *financial planner*
Pike, Kermit Jerome *cultural organization administrator*
Pilla, Anthony Michael *bishop*
Pina, Ileana *medical educator*
Podboy, Alvin Michael, Jr., *law library director, lawyer*
Pollock, R. Jeffrey *lawyer*
Potter, Susan Kuniholm *bank executive*
Pretlow, Thomas Garrett *physician, pathology educator, researcher*
Previts, Gary John *accounting educator, consultant*
Pringle, Barbara Carroll *state legislator*
Pucko, Diane Bowles *public relations executive*
Putka, Andrew Charles *lawyer*
Queen, Joyce Ellen *elementary school educator*
Quigney, Theresa Ann *special education educator*
Quinlan, Eileen *nun, literature educator*
Quinlan, Mark *credit agency executive*
Qutubuddin, Syed Abu Shams *chemical engineer, educator*
Raaf, John Hart *surgeon, health facility administrator, educator*
Raghavan, Derek *oncologist, medical researcher and educator*
Rains, M. Neal *lawyer*
Rakita, Louis *cardiologist, educator*
Ransohoff, Richard Milton *neurologist, researcher*
Rapp, Robert Neil *lawyer*
Ratcheson, Robert Allan *neurological surgeon*
Ratner, Albert B. *building products company executive, land developer*
Ratnoff, Oscar Davis *physician, educator*
Rauzi, Harold Ray *lawyer, respiratory therapist*
Raven, Hyacinthe L. *publishing executive, editor*
Rawson, Rachel L. *lawyer*
Rehm, Susan *physician*
Reid, James Sims, Jr., *former automobile parts manufacturer*
Reid, Katharine Lee *museum director*
Renwick, Glenn M. *insurance company executive*
Reppert, Richard Levi *lawyer*
Reshotko, Eli *aerospace engineer, educator*
Rich, Lawrence Vincent *manufacturing and engineering company executive*
Richardson, Allison *financial services company official*
Rickert, Jeanne Martin M. *lawyer*
Roberts, James Owen *financial planning executive, consultant*
Roberts-Mamone, Lisa A. *lawyer*
Rogers, Charles Edwin *physical chemistry educator*
Roop, James John *public relations executive*
Rose, Peter Graham *gynecologic oncologist*
Rosenbaum, Jacob I. *lawyer*
Ross, Harold Anthony *lawyer*
[illegible]
Rudy, Yoram *biomedical engineer, biophysicist, educator*
Ruf, H(arold) William, Jr., *retired lawyer, corporation executive*
Ruff, Robert Louis *neurologist, physiology researcher*
Rupert, John Edward *retired savings and loan executive, business and civic affairs consultant*
Rutledge, Virgie Marilyn *elementary school educator*
Ryder, Robert P.
Saada, Adel Selim *civil engineer, educator*
Saidel, Gerald Maxwell *biomedical engineering educator*
Salomon, Roger Blaine *English language educator*
Sande, Theodore Anton *architect, educator, foundation executive*
Savinell, Robert Francis *engineering educator*
Sawyer, Raymond Terry *lawyer, consultant, theater producer*
Scarpa, Antonio *medical educator, researcher, physiologist*
Schiller, James Joseph *lawyer*
Schlotfeldt, Rozella May *nursing educator*
Schrott, Norman *retired clinical social worker*
Schuele, Donald Edward *physics educator*
Schultz, Jeffrey Eric *optometrist*
Schwartz, Michael Alan *physician*
Seaton, Robert Finlayson *retired finance company executive*
Seifert, Shelley Jane *bank executive, human resources specialist*
Seles, Monica *professional tennis player*
Shakno, Robert Julian *hospital and social services administrator*
Shapiro, Fred David *lawyer*
Sharpe, Calvin William *law educator, arbitrator*
Shuck, Jerry Mark *surgeon, educator*
Sibley, Willis Elbridge *anthropology educator, consultant*
Sicherman, Marvin Allen *lawyer*
Siefers, Robert George *banker*
Silas, Paul *professional basketball coach*
Simmons, Clinton Craig *human resources executive*
Skulina, Thomas Raymond *lawyer*
Slinger, Michael Jeffery *law library director*
Slobozhanin, Lev Arkadievich *fluid mechanics researcher*
Smith, Barbara Jean *lawyer*
Smith, Jerome *not-for-profit developer, film producer, writer*
Sogg, Wilton Sherman *lawyer*
Solomon, Randall Lee *lawyer*
Somers, K(arl) Brent *consumer products company executive*
Spero, Keith Erwin *lawyer, educator*
Spivey, Terrence *performing company executive, educator, actor, theater director, playwright*
Stange, Kurt C. *medical educator*
Stanley, Hugh Monroe, Jr., *lawyer*
Stanton-Hicks, Michael D'Arcy *anesthesiologist, pain medicine specialist*
Stark, George Robert *health science association administrator*
Stashower, David L. *advertising executive*
Stavitsky, Abram Benjamin *immunologist, educator*
Steinmetz, Michael Patrick *physician, neurosurgeon*
Stellato, Louis Eugene *lawyer*
Stern, Robert C. *pediatrician, medical educator*
Stewart, Jack M. *management consulting firm executive*
Stone, Harry H. *retail executive*
Strang, James Dennis *editor*
Stratton-Crooke, Thomas Edward *financial consultant*
Strauch, John L. *lawyer*
Strauss, David J. *lawyer*
Striefsky, Linda A(nn) *lawyer*
Strimbu, Victor, Jr., *lawyer*
Strome, Marshall *otolaryngologist, educator*
Stuhan, Richard George *lawyer*
Stuhldreher, George William *lawyer*
Summers, William B., Jr., *brokerage house executive*
Summers, William Lawrence *lawyer*
Suri, Jasjit S. *research scientist*
Swartzbaugh, Marc L. *lawyer*
Szaller, James Francis *lawyer*
Szarek, Stanislaw Jerzy *mathematics professor*
Taft, Seth Chase *retired lawyer*
Taw, Dudley Joseph *sales executive, director*
Taylor, Harris C. *consultant endocrinologist, diabetologist*
Taylor, Margaret Wischmeyer *retired language educator*
Taylor, Nellie Ruby *artist, poet*
Taylor, Steve Henry *zoologist*
Tetzlaff, John Edwin *physician*
Thimmig, Diana M. *lawyer*
Thome, Jim *professional baseball player*
Thompson, Paul C. *labor union administrator*
Thompson, Stephen Arthur *sales consultant*
Thornton, Jerry Sue *community college president*
Toohey, Brian Frederick *lawyer*
Toomajian, William Martin *lawyer*
Torgerson, Katherine P. *diversified business media company executive*
Trapp, Bruce D. *neurologist*
Trapp, Mary Jane *lawyer*
Utian, Wulf Hessel *gynecologist, endocrinologist*
Utrata, Carl Ignatius *corporate counsel, corporate executive*
Van Aken, William J. *construction executive*
Vega, Manuel Thomas *medical/surgical nurse*
Vergon, Frederick Porter, Jr., *lawyer*
Vizquel, Omar Enrique *professional baseball player*
von Mehren, George M. *lawyer*
Walcott, Robert *health facility administrator, priest*
Waldeck, John Walter, Jr., *lawyer*
Wallach, Mark Irwin *lawyer*
Waltermire, Thomas Allen *financial executive*
Walters, Mark Douglas *obstetrician, gynecologist*
Wang, Yunzeng *finance educator*
Waren, Allan David *computer information scientist, educator*
Warren, Russell James *investment banker, consultant*
Washkewicz, Donald E. *manufacturing executive*
Watson, Richard Thomas *lawyer*
Weaver, Robin Geoffrey *lawyer, educator*
Weber, Robert Carl *lawyer*

Webster, Leslie Tillotson, Jr., *pharmacologist, educator*
Weidenthal, Maurice David (Bud Weidenthal) *educational administrator, journalist*
Weiler, Jeffry Louis *lawyer*
Weinberger, Peter Henry *lawyer*
Weir, Dame Gillian Constance *concert organist, harpsichordist*
Weiss, Jeffrey M.
Weiss, Morry *greeting card company executive*
Weiss, Zev
Wells, Lesley *federal judge*
Welser-Möst, Franz *conductor*
Werber, Stephen Jay *lawyer, educator*
Wertheim, Sally Harris *academic administrator, dean, education educator, consultant*
White, Gregory A. *lawyer*
White, Michael Reed *former mayor*
Whitney, Richard Buckner *lawyer*
Williams, Arthur Benjamin, Jr., *bishop*
Williams, Steven *investment banker, venture capitalist*
Wilson, Jack *aeronautical engineer*
Wish, Jay Barry *nephrologist, specialist*
Withers, Carl Raymond *lawyer*
Wolfman, Alan *medical educator, researcher*
Wolinsky, Emanuel *physician, educator*
Womack, John W. *pharmacist*
Woyczynski, Wojbor Andrzej *mathematician, educator*
Wykle, May L. *dean, educator, researcher*
Young, James Edward *lawyer*
Young, Jess Ray *retired internist*
Zambie, Allan John *lawyer*
Zhang, Nengli *thermophysics scientist*
Zhu, Dongming *materials scientist*
Zung, Thomas Tse-Kwai *architect*

Cleveland Heights

Byramjee, Aspi Minoo *surgeon*
Caswell Harris, Lucky Jean *community service administrator*
Sandburg, Helga *author*
Weinbaum, Batya *artist, writer*

Columbia Station

Bender, Peggy Wallace *charitable gift planning consultant*
Goll, Paulette Susan *education educator*

Columbus

Adams, John Marshall *lawyer*
Adams, Richard C. *information technology executive*
Adeli, Hojjat *engineer, educator, computer scientist*
Adelson, Edward *physicist, educator, musician*
Akers, Saundra Ruth *disability rights advocate*
Alban, Roger Charles *small business consultant*
Alexander, Carl Albert *ceramics engineer, educator*
Alger, Chadwick Fairfax *political scientist, educator*
Allen, Dixie J. *state representative*
Allen, Lois Arlene Height (Mrs. James Pierpont Allen) *musician*
Altan, Taylan *engineering educator, director*
Alutto, Joseph Anthony *dean, management educator*
Anderson, Carole Ann *nursing educator, academic administrator*
Anderson, Donald Kennedy, Jr., *English educator*
Anderson, Jon Mac *lawyer, educator*
Applegate, Ralph Asa *engineering educator*
Armes, Walter Scott *vocational school administrator*
Austria, Steve *state legislator*
Babcock, Charles Luther *classics educator*
Bachman, Sister Janice *healthcare executive, religious order administrator*
Bagby, Ross Frederick *educational consultant*
Bailey, Cecil Dewitt *aerospace engineer, educator*
Bailey, Daniel Allen *lawyer*
Bailey, Robert L. *finance company executive*
Baird, Leonard Lynn *social scientist, educator, researcher, editor*
Balcerzak, Stanley Paul *hematologist, oncologist, director, retired medical educator*
Banasik, Robert Casmer *nursing home administrator, educator*
Barnes, Galen R. *insurance company executive*
Barnes, Wallace Ray *retired lawyer*
Barrett, Catherine L. *state representative*
Barry, James P(otvin) *writer, editor*
Barsky, Constance Kay *education educator*
Barth, Rolf Frederick *pathologist, educator*
Barthelmas, Ned Kelton *investment and commercial real estate developer*
Battersby, James Lyons, Jr., *English language educator*
Beatty, Joyce *state representative*
Bechtel, Stephen E. *mechanical engineer, educator*
Beck, Paul Allen *political science educator*
Behrman, Edward Joseph *biochemistry educator*
Beja, Morris *English literature educator*
Bell, Albert Jerome *lawyer*
Benjamin, Ann Womer *former state legislator, lawyer*
Bergstrom, Stig Magnus *geology educator*
Berndt, Ellen German *lawyer*
Berntson, Gary Glen *psychiatry, psychology and pediatrics educator*
Berry, William Lee *business administration educator*
Beversdorf, David Quentin *neurologist, researcher*
Bhushan, Bharat *mechanical engineer*
Billings, Charles Edgar *physician*
Binning, J. Boyd *lawyer*
Biresi, Mark A. *retail executive*
Blackburn, John D(avid) *legal educator, lawyer*
Blackwell, J(ohn) Kenneth *state official*
Blom, Dave *healthcare industry executive*
Bloomfield, Clara Derber *oncologist, medical institute administrator*
Boerner, Ralph E. J. *forest soil ecologist, plant biology educator*
Bohm, Friedrich (Friedl) K.M. *architectural firm executive*
Bonini, James *federal court official*
Boudoulas, Harisios *physician, educator, researcher*
Boué, Daniel Robert *pediatric pathologist, neuropathologist, educator*
Bowen, John Wesley Edward, IV, *lawyer*
Bradley, Jennette *lieutenant governor*
Branscomb, Lewis Capers, Jr., *retired librarian, educator*
Bridgman, G(eorge) Ross *lawyer*
Brodkey, Robert Stanley *chemical engineering educator*
Brooks, Richard Dickinson *lawyer*
Brown, Edna *state representative*
Brown, Herbert Russell *lawyer, writer*
Brown, Rowland Chauncey Widrig *information systems, strategic planning and ethics consultant*
Brubaker, Robert Loring *lawyer*
Buchenroth, Stephen Richard *lawyer*
Buchsieb, Walter Charles *orthodontist, director*
Bullock, Joseph Daniel *pediatrician, educator*
Burchfield, James Ralph *lawyer*
Burgdoerfer, Stuart *controller, retail executive*
Burke, Kenneth Andrew *advertising executive*
Campbell, Joel Roderick *lawyer*
Capen, Charles Chabert *veterinary pathology educator*
Carnahan, John Anderson *lawyer*
Carpenter, Michael H. *lawyer*
Carter, Melinda *municipal official*
Carter, William H. *chemicals executive*
Chandrasekaran, Balakrishnan *computer and information science educator*
Charles, Bertram *radio broadcasting executive*
Charles, Gerard *performing company executive, choreographer*
Cheesman, Kerry Lee *education educator, researcher*
Chester, John Jonas *lawyer, educator*
Chisholm, Malcolm Harold *chemistry professor*
Christoforidis, A. John *radiologist, educator*
Chu, Roderick Gong-Wah *educational administrator*
Cirelli, Mary M. *state representative*
Clancy, Patricia *state representative*
Cole, Clarence Russell *college dean*
Cole, Ransey Guy, Jr., *federal judge*
Coleman, Michael B. *mayor*
Collins, Jack Adam *mechanical engineer*
Cooper, John *university football coach*
Cooper, Stuart Leonard *chemical engineering educator, researcher, consultant*
Coopersmith, Jeffrey Alan *real estate developer*
Corbato, Charles Edward *geology educator*
Cordle, Christopher T. *immunologist, race boat driver*
Cornwell, David George *biochemist, educator*
Cottingham, Richard Sumner *paper company executive*
Cox, Mitchel Neal *editor*
Cox, Paul L. *lawyer*
Cramblett, Henry Gaylord *pediatrician, virologist, educator*
Cross, Jeffrey D. *lawyer, electric power industry executive*
Crowder, Marjorie Briggs *lawyer*
Cruz, Jose Bejar, Jr., *engineering educator*
Culbertson, Jack Arthur *education educator*
Curtin, Michael Francis *printing company executive, publisher*
Cvetanovich, Dan L. *lawyer*
Daab-Krzykowski, Andre *pharmaceutical and nutritional manufacturing company administrator*
Daehn, Glenn Steven *materials scientist*
Darling, George Curtis *minister, administrator*
Davidson, Jo Ann *former state legislator*
De Maria, Paolo *policy advisor*
Di Lorenzo, John Florio, Jr., *retired lawyer (corporate)*
Disinger, John Franklin *natural resources educator*
Donovan, Dennis Dale *priest*
Douglas, Andrew *retired state supreme court justice*
Dowd, Andrew Joseph *lawyer, utility company executive*
Draper, Gerald Linden *lawyer*
Drvota, Mojmir *cinema educator, author*
Duckworth, Winston Howard *retired ceramic engineer*
Dull, Clifford John *religious groups analyst*
Dull, Pamela *physician, educator*
Duryee, Harold Taylor *insurance consultant*
Eaton, Antoinette Joan *pediatrician*
Eaton, Michael Christopher *contractor*
Eckert, Douglas *academic administrator, educator*
Ellingson, Jill Evelyn *psychologist, educator*
Elliot, David Hawksley *geologist, educator*
Ellis, Greg Evan *investment sales executive, consultant*
Ellison, Edwin Christopher *surgeon, educator*
Ensminger, Dale *mechanical engineer, electrical engineer*
Evans, Daniel E. *manufacturing and restaurant chain company executive*
Evans, Paul Dale *economist, educator*
Faber, Timothy *retail executive*
Fahey, Richard Paul *lawyer*
Fan, Liang-Shih *chemical engineering educator*
Farr, Marcia Elizabeth *English and linguistics educator*
Fass, Robert J. *epidemiologist, academic administrator*
Faure, Gunter *geology educator*
Fawcett, Sherwood Luther *research laboratory executive*
Fay, Terrence Michael *lawyer*
Fayne, Henry W. *electric power industry executive*
Federle, Katherine Hunt *lawyer*
Fedor, Teresa *state senator*
Fenton, Robert Earl *electrical engineering educator*
Ferderber, June H. *state legislator*
Ferguson, Ronald Morris *surgeon, educator*
Fessler, Diana M. *state representative*
Finkelman, Daniel P. *retail executive*
Firestone, Richard Francis *chemistry professor*
Fisher, Lloyd Edison, Jr., *lawyer*
Floyd, Gary Leon *plant cell biologist*
Foland, Kenneth A. *geological sciences educator*
Fornshell, Dave Lee *educational broadcasting executive*
Foucht, Joan Lucille *retired elementary school educator, retired counseling administrator*
Fox, Kate Templeton *editor, writer*
Franano, Susan Margaret Ketteman *arts consultant and adminstrator, musician*
Frasier, Ralph Kennedy *lawyer, investment banker*
Fried, Samuel *lawyer*
Friedman, Avner *mathematician, educator*
Fry, Donald Lewis *physiologist, educator*
Frye, Richard Arthur *lawyer*
Fu, Paul Shan *law librarian, consultant*
Furney, Linda Jeanne *state legislator*
Furste, Wesley Leonard, II, *surgeon, educator*
Gahbauer, Reinhard A. *physician*
Gasper, Joseph J. *insurance company executive*
Geary, William Lee *lawyer*
Geier, Peter E. *bank executive, health facility executive*
Gerhardstein, Samuel Edward *public utility administrator*
Gibson, Rick J. *lawyer*
Gilliom, Morris Eugene *social studies and global educator*
Gillmor, Karen Lako *state agency administrator*
Glaser, Gary A. *bank executive*
Glaser, Ronald *microbiology educator, scientist*
Glenn, John Herschel, Jr., *former senator, former astronaut*
Glimcher, Herbert *real estate company executive*
Glimcher, Michael P. *real estate company executive*
Goodridge, Alan Gardner *research biochemist, educator*
Goulder, Diane Kessler *lawyer*
Gozon, Jozsef Stephan *engineering educator*
Graff, Douglas Eric *lawyer*
Graham, James Lowell *federal judge*
Grant, Michael Peter *electrical engineer*
Gravlee, Glenn P(age) *anesthesiologist, educator*
Greek, Darold I. *lawyer*
Grendell, Diane V. *state legislator, nurse*
Gribble, Charles Edward *editor, Slavic languages educator*
Gross, James Howard *lawyer*
Grossberg, Michael Lee *theater critic, writer*
Gutfeld, Norman E. *lawyer*
Hagan, Thomas M. *electric power industry executive*
Hailey, V. Ann *retail executive*
Hansen, Thomas Nanastad *pediatrician, health facility administrator*
Haque, Malika Hakim *pediatrician*
Hardymon, David Wayne *lawyer*
Hare, Robert Yates *music history educator*
Harris, Donald *composer*
Harris, Ronald David *chemical engineer*
Hart, Daniel *orchestra executive*
Harwood, Sandra Stabile *lawyer, state representative*
Hatler, Patricia Ruth *lawyer*
Headley, Richard D. *corporate financial executive, diversified financial services company executive*
Herson, Lawrence J.R. *social sciences educator, consultant*
Hill, Terri *diversified financial services company executive*
Hilliard, Andrea Leigh *writer*
Hilliard, Kirk Loveland *osteopathic physician, educator*
Hoaglin, Thomas E. *savings and loan association executive*
Hoffmann, Charles Wesley *retired foreign language educator*
Hogan, Michael F. *state official*
Hollenbaugh, H(enry) Ritchey *lawyer*
Hollister, Nancy *state legislator*
Holman-Rao, Marie *retail executive*
Holschuh, John David *federal judge*
Holtz, Diane *retail executive*
Householder, Larry *state official, small business owner*
Houser, Donald Russell *mechanical engineering educator, consultant*
Huheey, Marilyn Jane *ophthalmologist, educator*
Hutson, Jeffrey Woodward *lawyer*
Jackson, James G. *police chief*
Jackson, Janet Elizabeth *city attorney, association executive*
Jacobs, Alexis A. *automobile company executive*
Jacox, John William *retired mechanical engineer and consulting company executive*
James, Donna A. *diversified financial services company executive*
Janik, Melinda A. *real estate company executive*
Jarvis, Gilbert Andrew *humanities educator, writer*
Johnson, Julia F. *bank executive*
Johnson, Mark Alan *lawyer*
Johnson, Neal Frederick *psychological scientist, educator*
Johnston, Jeffery W. *publishing executive*
Jolly, Daniel Ehs *dental educator*
Jurgensen, W.G. *insurance company executive*
Kagel, John Henry *economist, researcher*
Kakos, Gerard Stephen *thoracic and cardiovascular surgeon*
Kapenda, Simon Shidule *broadcast executive*
Kapral, Frank Albert *medical microbiology and immunology educator*
Kasouf, Joseph Chickery *lawyer, consultant*
Kasper, Larry John *accountant, litigation support consultant*
Kasulis, Thomas Patrick *humanities educator*
Katz, Janyce C(harlene) *lawyer*
Kaufman, Barry D. *retail executive*
Kearns, Merle Grace *state representative*
Kefauver, Weldon Addison *publishing executive*
Keller, Michael C. *diversified financial services company executive*
Kelley, William G. *retail stores executive*
Kemp, Daniel Warren *lawyer*
Kerner, Joseph Frank, Jr., *management consultant, educator*
Kerns, Allen Franklin *education educator*
Kessel, John Howard *political scientist, educator*
Ketcham, Richard Scott *lawyer*
Ketteler, Thomas R. *retail executive*
Key, Annie L. *state representative*
Kidder, C. Robert *food products executive*
Kiecolt-Glaser, Janice Kay *psychologist*
Kiefer, Gary *newspaper editor*
Killion, Theo *retail executive*
King, G. Roger *lawyer*
Kirk, Ballard Harry Thurston *architect*
Knilans, Michael Jerome *supermarkets executive*
Koblentz, Robert Alan *lawyer*
Koenigsknecht, Roy A. *education administrator*
Koeppel, Holly *electric power industry executive*
Kohrt, Carl Fredrick *research and development company executive*
Kontos, Mark *treasurer*
Kreager, Eileen Davis *administrative consultant*
Kronmiller, Jan E. *academic administrator*
Ksienski, Aharon Arthur *electrical engineer*
Kuehnle, Kenton Lee *lawyer*
Kuhn, Albert Joseph *English educator*
Kukielka, Gilbert Leon *physician*
Kurtz, Charles Jewett, III, *lawyer*
La Cour, Louis Bernard *retired lawyer*
Ladinsky, Morissa Jean *medical educator, pediatrician*
LaHowchic, Nicholas John *retail specialty company executive*
LaLonde, Bernard Joseph *finance educator*
Lander, Ruth A. *medical group and association administrator*
Larzelere, Kathy Lynn Heckler *paralegal*
Lashutka, Gregory S. *mayor, lawyer*
Laufman, Leslie Rodgers *hematologist, oncologist*
Lawrence, Joan Wipf *former state legislator*
Lazar, Theodore Aaron *retired manufacturing company executive, lawyer*
Lee, Lung-fei *economist, educator*
Lee, Robert J. *education educator, consultant*
Lefavre, Hadia *human resources executive*
Lehman, Harry Jac *lawyer*
Lehmann, Richard J. *former banker*
Lehto, Gail S. *education educator, musician*
Leier, Carl Victor *internist, cardiologist*
Leitzel, Joan Ruth *university president emerita*
Lewis, Richard Phelps *cardiologist, educator*
Ling, Ta-Yung *physicist*
Lippe, Jerry Leonard *lawyer*
Lisko (Dozer), Bonnie Lee *education educator*
Long, Sarah Elizabeth Brackney *physician*
Long, Teresa C. *city health department administrator*
Long, Thomas Leslie *lawyer*
Lowe, Clayton Kent *radio film critic, educator*
Luck, James I. *foundation executive*
Lundstedt, Sven Bertil *behavioral and social scientist, educator*
Lynn, Arthur Dellert, Jr., *economist, educator*
MacGhee, David F. *retired military officer, air transportation executive*
Madia, William Juul *chemist*
Magro, Cynthia Maria *pathologist*
Mahoney, Kimberly Lynne *event and facility executive*
Mann, William Craig *lawyer*
Marilley, Suzanne Marie *political scientist, educator*
Markus, Kent Richard *lawyer*
Mason, Raymond E., Jr., *distributing company executive*
Massey, Robert John *telecommunications executive*
Massie, Robert Joseph *publishing company executive*
Mayer, Victor James *geologist, educator*
McBride, Brian *professional soccer player*
McClain, Thomas Emerson *communications executive*
McClung, Hugo Juhling *pediatrician, educator*
McConnaughey, George Carlton, Jr., *retired lawyer*
McConnell, Donald Patrick *research institute executive*
McConnell, John Henderson *metal and plastic products manufacturing executive, professional sports team executive*
Mc Cormac, John Waverly *judge*
McCoy, John Bonnet *retired bank executive*
McCutchan, Gordon Eugene *retired lawyer, insurance company executive*
McDermott, Kevin R. *lawyer*
McInturff, Floyd M. *retired state agency administrator*
McKenna, Alvin James *lawyer*
McMahon, John Patrick *retired lawyer*
McMennamin, Michael J. *savings and loan executive, investment banker*
McNealey, J. Jeffrey *lawyer, corporate executive*
Mead, Priscilla *state legislator*
Meckler, Michael Louis *historian, journalist*
Mehta, Kamal Deep *biochemistry educator, molecular biology educator*
Meier, Samuel Arthur, III, *historian, educator*
Melling, Jack *biotechnologist, director*
Mencer, Jetta *lawyer*
Milenthal, David *advertising executive*
Milford, Frederick John *retired research company executive*
Miller, Alan D. *editor*
Miller, Don Wilson *nuclear engineering educator*
Miller, Nodine *judge*
Miller, Terry Morrow *lawyer*
Millett, Stephen Malcolm *futurist, consultant, historian*
Milligan, Glenn Wesley *business educator*
Min, David B. *chemist, educator, research scientist*
Minor, Robert Allen *lawyer*
Mirman, Joel Harvey *lawyer*
Mollenhauer, Jude *musician, music educator*
Moloney, Thomas E. *lawyer*
Mone, Robert Paul *lawyer*
Montgomery, Betty Dee *state auditor, former state attorney general, former state legislator*
Moone, Robert H. *finance company executive*
Morgan, Dennis Richard *lawyer*
Morris, Michael G. *utilities executive*
Morrison, Ashton Byrom *pathologist, medical school official*
Morrison, Craig O. *chemicals executive*
Morrow, Grant, III, *medical research director, pediatrician*
Moser, Debra Kay *medical educator*
Moul, William Charles *lawyer*
Moulton, Edward Quentin *civil engineer, educator*
Moyer, Thomas J. *state supreme court chief justice*
Mueller, Charles Frederick *radiologist, educator*
Mueller, John Ernest *political science educator, dance critic and historian*
Muller, Mervin Edgar *computer scientist, statistician, educator*
Munson, Robert Sydney *biomedical researcher*
Murden, Robert A. *medical administrator, physician*
Murphy, Andrew J. *managing news editor*
Murphy, Earl Finbar *law educator*
Namboodiri, Krishnan *sociology educator*
Nappi, James Francis *hand surgeon, educator*
Naylor, James Charles *psychologist, educator*
Newman, Diana S. *development consultant*
Newsom, Gerald Higley *astronomy educator*
Newton, Herbert Bruce *neuro-oncologist*
Newton, William Allen, Jr., *pediatric pathologist*
Norris, Alan Eugene *federal judge*
Oakley, Robert Alan *insurance executive*
Ockerman, Herbert W. *agricultural studies educator*
O'Connor, Maureen *judge*
O'Donnell, F. Scott *state agency administrator*
Oman, Richard Heer *lawyer*
Osgood, Robert T., Jr., *architect, strategic planner*
O'Shaughnessy, Christopher T. *lawyer*
Osipow, Samuel Herman *psychology educator*
Otte, Paul John *academic administrator, consultant, trainer*
Oubrerie, José R. *architecture educator*
Ozkan, Umit Sivrioglu *chemical engineering educator*
Pastore, Donna Lee *physical education educator*

Eastlake
Balester, Vivian Shelton *legal research consultant, retired lawyer*
Wheeler, Melanie Elaine *administrative assistant, realtor*

Eaton
Thomas, James William *lawyer*

Edgerton
Wu, Lawrence Mg Hla Myin *physician*

Elmore
Huizenga, Georgiana R. *public library director, storyteller*

Elyria
Bonnell-Mihalis, Pamela Gay *library director*
Mixon, Aaron Malachi, III, *medical products executive*
Patton, Thomas James *sales and marketing executive*
Spitzer, Alan *automotive executive*

Enon
Whitlock, David C. *retired military officer*

Euclid
Matthews, Eric Joddy *film director*
Obloy, Leonard Gerard *priest*

Fairborn
Conklin, Robert Eugene *electronics engineer*
Johansen, Mark Daniel *application developer*
Krane, Dan E *DNA expert, education educator*
Szucs, Andrew Eric *freelance/self-employed writer*
Workman, John Mitchell *chemist*

Fairfield
Grove, Jack Frederick *lawyer, educator*
Robertson, Oscar Palmer (Big O Robertson) *chemical company executive, former professional basketball player*
Royer, Thomas Jerry *financial planner*
Sheehan, Samantha *gymnast*
Stecher, Kenneth W. *financial corporation executive*
Tumbleson, Stephan Norman *music educator*
Walsh, Thomas James *environmental engineer, consultant*
Wilson, James Miller, IV, *cardiovascular surgeon, educator*

Fairfiled
Flick, Debra Renee *music educator*

Fairlawn
Brubaker, Karen Sue *small business owner*

Fairview Park
Flynn, Patricia M. *director, special education educator, gifted and talented educator*
Fordyce, James Stuart *non-profit organization executive*
Kothari, Purnima *obstetrician/gynecologist*

Findlay
Dattilo, Thomas A. *diversified corporation executive*
Freed, DeBow *academic administrator*
Fry, Charles George *theologian, educator*
Hackenberg, David Alan *lawyer*
Hanson, David Alan *music educator*
Kline, James Edward *lawyer*
Peters, Milton Eugene *educational psychologist*
Stephani, Nancy Jean *social worker, journalist*
Stephens, D. Richard *manufacturing executive*
Weaver, Philip G. *tire company executive*
Wilkin, Richard Edwin *clergyman, religious organization executive*
Yammine, Riad Nassif *retired oil company executive*

Fostoria
Howard, Kathleen *computer company executive*

Franklin
Ruppert, Rupert Earl *lawyer, political consultant*

Fremont
Gerlach, Murney *administrator, educator, historian*
Johnson, Laurence F. *college executive*
Recktenwald, Fred William *city financial official*
Wethington, Norbert Anthony *medieval scholar*

Gahanna
Breen, John Wakefield *personnel services company executive*

Galena
Berggren, Ronald Bernard *surgeon, retired educator*

Galion
Cobey, Ralph *industrialist*

Gallipolis
Ferguson, A. H. *poet, medical/surgical nurse*
Niehm, Bernard Frank *retired health facility administrator*
Senthil Nathan, Selvaraj *internist, geriatrician*

Galloway
Barner, Bruce Monroe *former state agency administrator, not-for-profit company chairman*

Gambier
Nugent, S. Georgia *academic administrator*
Ponder, Anne *dean*
Shutt, Timothy Baker *humanities educator, writer*
Spaid, Gregory P. *academic administrator, art educator*

Gates Mills
Abbott, James Samuel, III, *marketing executive*
Enyedy, Gustav, Jr., *chemical engineer*
Pace, Stanley Carter *retired aeronautical engineer*
Reitman, Robert Stanley *business consultant, nonprofit agency advisor*
Veale, Tinkham, II, *former chemical company executive, engineer*

Geneva on the Lake
Clement, Daniel Roy, IV, *accountant, community health nurse*

Germantown
Lansaw, Charles Ray *rendering industry executive*

Girard
Denney, James Allen *lawyer*

Glendale
Strom, Kristina Chase *writer, consultant*

Grafton
Barber, Clarence E. *music educator*

Granville
Bonar, Daniel Donald *mathematics professor*
Haubrich, Robert Rice *biology professor*
Knobel, Dale Thomas *historian, educator, academic administrator*
Kretchmar, R. Matthew *computer science educator*
Lisska, Anthony Joseph *humanities educator, philosopher*
Pollard, Jeffrey Wallace *college counseling, health services director*
Santoni, Ronald Ernest *philosophy educator*
Vogel, Steven Michael *philosopher, educator*

Greenville
Alexander, Paul Richard *illustrator*
Buchy, Jim *food products executive*

Grove City
Hosler, Elizabeth *management consultant*
Kilman, James William *surgeon, educator*
Kimethu, Susan Wanja *computer specialist, database manager*
Lok, Silmond Ray *pharmaceutical executive*

Hamilton
Cantrell, Joseph Sires *chemistry professor*
Epp, Mary Elizabeth *technologies consultant*
Fein, Linda Ann *nurse anesthetist, consultant*
Glass, Robert Edward *retired music educator*
Gruenwald, James Howard *association executive, consultant*
Kramer, Benjamin Robert *sheriff's deputy, accident reconstructionist*
Marcum, Joseph LaRue *insurance company executive*
New, Rosetta Holbrock *home economics educator, nutrition consultant*
Zahner-Krach, Anne Colette *preschool educator*

Harrison
Kocher, Juanita Fay *retired auditor*

Hebron
Slater, Wanda Marie Worth *property manager*

Hilliard
Baker, John *electronics executive*
Cooper, Almeta E. *lawyer, medical association administrator*
Cupp, David Foster *photographer, journalist*
Griffith, Gail *performing arts educator, actress*
Herta, Bryan *race car driver*
Koehler, Jim *electronics executive*
Pyles, Selma Broadway *music educator*

Hiram
Bane, James Wallace *music educator*
Oliver, G(eorge) Benjamin *educational administrator, philosophy educator*

Holgate
Oberhaus, James Edward *secondary school educator*

Holland
Conlin, Thomas *conductor*
Sacksteder, Thomas Michael *corporate executive, entrepreneur, writer*

Howard
Griffith, Jason Scott *education educator*
Lee, William Johnson *lawyer*

Hubbard
Trucksis, Theresa A. *retired library director*

Hudson
Ashcroft, Richard Carter *investment company executive*
Carducci, Judith Weeks Barker *artist, former social worker*
Duchon, Roseann Marie *small business owner, consultant*
Elliott, Frances Carano *lawyer, educator*
Goheen, Janet Moore *counseling administrator, sales executive*
Hallenbeck, Linda S. *elementary school educator*
Kempe, Robert Aron *venture management executive*
Morris, Jeffrey Selman *orthopedic surgeon*
Sorgi, Mercedes Prieto *psychologist*
Stec, John Zygmunt *real estate executive*
Wilfong, Brenda Ann *telecommunications executive*
Wooldredge, William Dunbar *health facility administrator*

Independence
Boyle, Kammer *estate planner, financial analyst*
Kola, Arthur Anthony *lawyer*
Van Kirk, Robert John *nursing case manager, educator*

Ironton
Allen, Craig Adams *lawyer, director*
Curry, Estella Roberta *education educator, consultant*
Oakes, Maria Spachner *nurse*

Jackson Center
Thompson, Wade Francis Bruce *manufacturing executive*

Jefferson
Geary, Michael Philip *lawyer*

Kent
Anderson, William John, II, *engineering and business management consultant*
Bansal, Arvind Kumar *computer scientist, educator*
Beer, Barrett Lynn *historian*
Biordi, Diana L. *healthcare educator, dean*

Bissler, Richard Thomas *mortician*
Buttlar, Rudolph Otto *retired college dean*
Cartwright, Carol Ann *university president*
Chism, Rebecca Lynn *language educator*
Cielinski-Kessler, Audrey Ann *writer, publishing executive, small business owner*
Cooperrider, Tom S. *retired botanist, educator*
Dutta, Hiran Moyee *biologist, educator*
Feinberg, Richard *anthropologist, educator*
Ference-Valenta, Mary Jean *osteopath, health facility administrator*
Gaston, Paul Lee *academic administrator, language educator*
Gosnell, Davina J. *dean, nursing educator*
Hassler, Donald Mackey, II, *English language educator, writer*
House-Soremekun, Bessie *political science educator*
Juvan, Dennis Paul *securities trader*
Kasten, Wendy Christina *literacy educator, writer, consultant*
Kinney, Daryl Wayne *music educator*
Lilly, Erica Barditch *academic librarian*
Los, Cornelis Albertus *portfolio risk manager, financial economist, finance educator*
Madden, Elisabeth Anne *theater director*
McCormick, Edgar Lindsley *language educator, writer*
Myers, R(alph) Thomas *chemist, educator*
Neal-Barnett, Angela Marie *psychology educator*
Odell-Scott, David Winfield *education educator*
Okantah, Mwatabu S. *writer, educator*
Piccirillo, Linda Ann *literature educator*
Pino, Julio Cesar *social studies educator, writer*
Reed, Beverly Marie *mathematician, educator*
Reid, S.W. *English educator*
Rick, Newton Marcus *literature and language professor, classicist*
Rollick, Mary Beth *mathematician, educator*
Schwartz, Michael *university president, sociology educator*
Tiene, Drew *communications educator, consultant*
Varga, Richard Steven *mathematics professor*

Kettering
Clark, Leland Charles, Jr., *biochemist, medical products executive*
Kankey, Roland Doyle *finance educator*
Porter, Walter Arthur *retired judge*

Kirtland
Johnston, Stanley Howard, Jr., *rare books curator, bibliographer*
Petrone, John R. *music educator, composer*

Lakeside Marblehead
Garrow, Robert Joseph, Jr., *mathematician, educator*
Haering, Edwin Raymond *chemical engineering educator, consultant*

Lakewood
Baxter, Howard H. *retired lawyer*
Cain, Madeline Ann *mayor*
Cochran, Earl Vernon *retired manufacturing company executive*
Condon, George Edward *journalist*

Lancaster
Burns, Glenn Richard *dentist*
Katlic, John Edward *management consultant*
Libert, Donald Joseph *lawyer*
Phillips, Edward John *consulting firm executive*
Varney, Richard Alan *health facility administrator*
Woodward, James Kenneth *retired pharmacologist*
Young, Paul Garlin *principal*

Lebanon
Baldwin, James Edward *lawyer, city administrator*

Lewis Center
Heinlen, Daniel Lee *alumni organization administrator*

Lexington
Maxwell, Mark *music educator*

Lima
Becker, Dwight Lowell *physician*
Meek, Violet Imhof *retired dean*
Miller, Roy Raymond *optician, oculist*
Pranses, Anthony Louis *retired electric company executive, organization executive*
Robenalt, John Alton *lawyer*
Rogers, Richard Michael *judge*
Roller, Duane Williamson *archaeologist, educator*

Lisbon
Berthoff, Frederic Warner *painter*

Little Hocking
Corbin, David P. *counselor*

Logan
Carmean, Jerry Richard *broadcast engineer*

London
Hughes, Clyde Matthew *religious denomination executive*

Lorain
Mumford, Beverly Jean *paralegal*
Pèrez-Rodríguez, Juan Esteban, II, (Esteban de Lares) *journalist, writer, historian, researcher*

Louisville
Faigley, Joseph Raymond *social studies educator*

Loveland
Grimmet, Alex J. *clergyman, school administrator, elementary and secondary education educator*
Newton, Baldwin Charles *artist, educator*
Peters, Thomas J *management consultant, writer*
Stanger, Nora Lynn *educational consultant*

Lucasville
Reno, Ottie Wayne *former judge*

Lyndhurst
Dellas, Marie C. *retired psychology educator, consultant*

Madison
Stafford, Arthur Charles *medical association administrator*

Maineville
Cook, Janice Eleanor Nolan *retired elementary school educator*

Malvern
Witosky, Gary J. *manufacturing company executive*

Mansfield
Adair, Charles Valloyd *retired physician*
Ash, Thomas Phillip *superintendent of schools*
Burke, Victor Lee *sociologist, educator*
Burnell, Elvin Wallace *industrial engineer, security specialist*
Converse, Sandra *city finance director, financial planner*
Gibson, David Mark *biochemist, educator*
Gorman, James Carvill *pump manufacturing company executive*
Granter, Sharon Savoy *restaurateur, caterer*
Gregory, Deirdre Dianne *secondary educator*
Gregory, Thomas Bradford *mathematics professor*
Houston, William Robert Montgomery *ophthalmic surgeon*
Hussain, Nayyer *economics professor*
Miller, Kenneth William, II, *research and development engineering executive*
Olinger, Angela Marie *adult education educator*
Pesec, David John *data systems executive*
Riedl, John Orth *university dean*
Shah, James M. *actuary*
Sheridan, Mark William *mechanical engineer, strategic planner*
Sturgill, Judith Lynn *education educator, lawyer*
Sturts, Donna Jean *music educator*
Whitmer, Eugene Roger *minister, retired secondary school educator*

Marietta
Evans, Robert E. *bank executive*
Fields, William Albert *lawyer*
Huck, Daniel N. *lawyer, educator*
Jache, Albert William *retired chemistry educator, scientist*
Montgomery, Jerry Lynn *retired education educator*
Putnam, Robert Ervin *chemist, consultant*
Wilbanks, Jan Joseph *retired philosopher*

Marion
Beals, Clem Kip, III, *dentist*
Fassler, Crystal G. *marketing consultant*
Frericks, Timothy Matthew *lawyer*
Nutbrown, Edwin Emanuel *safety engineer, writer*

Marysville
Baik-Kromalic, Sue S. *metallurgical engineer*
Hamilton, Robert Otte *lawyer*

Mason
Beary, John Francis, III, *rheumatologist, researcher, pharmaceutical executive*
Chesley, Ann Marie *systems analyst*
Clements, Michael Craig *health services consulting executive, retired renal dialysis technician*
Jackobs, Miriam Ann *dietitian*
Smith, C. LeMoyne *publishing company executive*
Wilson, Frederic Sandford *pharmaceutical company executive*

Massillon
Dishong, Morris William *forensic investigator, nurse*
Netzly, Dwight H. *lawyer*

Maumee
Anderson, Richard Paul *agricultural company executive*
Kimble, James A. *management consultant, accountant*
Konopinski, Virgil James *industrial hygienist, consultant*
Marsh, Benjamin Franklin *lawyer*
McBride, Beverly Jean *lawyer*
Risley, David Milo *controller*
Tuschman, James Marshall *lawyer*

Mayfield
Forrester, W. Thomas, II, *insurance company executive*
Jarrett, Charles Elwood *insurance company executive, lawyer*

Mayfield Heights
Billick, Steven M. *emergency medical technician*
Newman, Joseph Herzl *advertising consultant*
Rankin, Alfred Marshall, Jr., *manufacturing executive*
Rhein, Arthur *emergency medical technician*

Mechanicsburg
Saxbe, William Bart *lawyer, former government official*

Medina
Arnold, Alanna S. Welling *lawyer, mediator*
Balest, Victor Rudolph *sales executive*
Ballard, John Stuart *retired educator, former mayor, former lawyer*
Batchelder, Alice M. *federal judge*
Feola, David Craig *secondary school administrator*
Liauba, Danute *music educator*
Matejka, Robert *chemicals executive*
Neiman, Marcus Lawrence *educational consultant*
Rog, Joseph W. *engineering company executive*
Smith, Richey *manufacturing executive*
Sullivan, Frank C. *manufacturing executive*
Sullivan, Thomas Christopher *coatings company executive*
Williams, Paul C(hester) *consultant*

Mentor
Callsen, Christian Edward *medical device company executive*
Driggs, Charles Mulford *lawyer*
Jurewicz, Lynn *library director*
Miller, Frances Suzanne *historic site curator*
Sanford, Bill R. *medical products executive*
Schock, Trisha Kay *primary school educator*

Miamisburg

Andreozzi, Louis Joseph *lawyer*
Brewster, Charles Edward *writer, engineer*
Byrd, James Everett *lawyer*
McLaughlin, Allan D. *information technology executive*
Peppel, Michael E. *computer company executive*
Thompson, Holley Marker *lawyer, marketing professional*

Middleburg Heights

Maciuszko, Kathleen Lynn *librarian, educator*
Molnar, Bela *school administrator*

Middletown

Bailey, William Rufus *lawyer, corporation executive*
Gordon, Sandy Gale Combs *medical/surgical nurse, community health nurse*
Jenkins, Robert H. *steel company executive*
Marine, Susan Sonchik *analytical chemist, educator*
McClain, Michael H. *writer*
Newby, John Robert *metallurgical engineer*
Powell, Stephen Walter *judge*
Rathman, William Ernest *retired lawyer, minister*
Schaefer, Patricia Ann *retired librarian*
Turpin, Richard E. *sales executive*
Wainscott, James Lawrence *accountant*

Milan

Henry, Joseph Patrick *chemical company executive*

Milford

Conover, Nellie Coburn *retired retail furniture company executive*
Creath, Curtis Janssen *pediatric dentist*
Donahue, John Lawrence, Jr., *paper company executive*
Klosterman, Albert Leonard *technical development business executive, mechanical engineer*
Weyand, William J. *engineering executive*

Milford Center

McDonald, Alan Thomas *lawyer*

Montpelier

Deckrosh, Hazen Douglas *retired state agency educator and administrator*

Moreland Hills

Hardie, James Carl *college administrator, consultant*
Tolchinsky, Paul Dean *organization design psychologist*

Mount Healthy

Scheffel, Kenneth Paul *retired archivist*

Mount Vernon

Rose, Kim Matthew *lawyer, educator*
Shriver, William Russell *secondary school educator*
Tocheff, Robert Dale *music educator*
Turner, Harry Edward *lawyer*
Wallace, Geri Lynn *special education educator, landscape architect*
Wells-Maxwell, Violet *writer, artist*

Napoleon

Frame, Lawrence Milven, Jr., *inventor*
Meekison, MaryFran *writer*

Nelsonville

Davis, Mary W. Allen *medical secretary*

New Albany

Duggan, Thomas Patrick *management consultant*
Jeffries, Michael S. *apparel executive*
Page, Linda Kay *bank executive*
Riley, Susan Jean *retail executive*
Williams, James Case *metallurgist*

New Bremen

Dicke, James Frederick, II, *manufacturing executive*

New Concord

Schumann, Laura Elaine *conductor*

New Matamoras

Brown, Blanche Y. *secondary education educator, genealogy researcher*

New Philadelphia

Doughten, Mary Katherine (Molly Doughten) *retired secondary school educator*
Goforth, Mary Elaine Davey *secondary school educator*

Newark

Billy, Gerry Dee *protective services official*
Black, Boyd Carson *small business owner*
Hite, David L. *lawyer*
Mantonya, John Butcher *lawyer*
McConnell, William Thompson *commercial banker*
Meyer, Christopher Richard *lawyer*
Pacht, Eric Reed *pulmonary and critical care physician*
Tebben, Joseph Richard *ancient language educator*

Niles

Linden, Carol Marie *special education educator*

North Canton

Dettinger, Warren Walter *lawyer*
Di Simone, Robert Nicholas *radiologist, educator*
Geswein, Gregory T. *electronic company executive*
Lynham, C(harles) Richard *manufacturing executive*
Magoon, Donald W. *retired business educator*
Pollock, Rachel Rebecca *publishing executive, educator*
Vazzano, Frank Paul *historian, educator*

North Olmsted

Bluford, Guion Stewart, Jr., *engineering company executive*
Janson, Patrick *singer, actor, conductor, educator*
Lundin, Bruce Theodore *engineering and management consultant*
Werner, Wade W. *secondary school educator*

North Ridgeville

Stewart, Arden Ruth *automotive aftermarket manufacturing executive*

North Royalton

Pamin, Diana Dolhancyk (Diana Dolhancyk) *poet*

Norwalk

Germann, Richard P(aul) *consultant, pharmaceutical company chemist, executive*
Gutowicz, Matthew Francis, Jr., *radiologist*

Norwood

Jones, Hobert W. *health physics and radiochemistry consultant*

Oak Harbor

Randels, David George *retired secondary school educator*

Oberlin

Baumann, Roland M. *historian, archivist, consultant*
Brown, John Lott *psychology professor*
Carlton, Terry Scott *chemist, educator*
Cartier, Brian Evans *association executive*
Collins, Martha *English language educator, writer*
Dye, Nancy Schrom *academic administrator, historian, educator*
English, Ray *library administrator*
Faber, Sebastiaan *humanities educator*
Friedman, William John *psychology educator*
Greenberg, Eva Mueller *librarian*
Kennedy, Laurie Jean *music educator, musician*
Koppes, Clayton R. *academic administrator*
Kruks, Sonia R. *social sciences educator, researcher*
Luck, Dennis Noel *biologist, educator, researcher*
MacKay, Alfred F. *dean, philosophy educator*
Miller, Judith Beinstein *psychology professor*
Reinoehl, Richard Louis *artist, scholar, martial artist*
Rutstein, Sedmara Zakarian *piano educator, concert pianist*
Sakakeeny II, George J. *music educator, musician*
Singer, Leonard S. *chemist, research scientist, consultant*
Taylor, Richard Wirth *political science educator*
Taylor, Robert Larry *author, freelance writer*
Warner, Robert Edson *physics educator*
Weinstock, Robert *physics educator*
Young, Margaret Helen *educational association administrator, writer*

Olmsted Falls

Faller, Dorothy Anderson *international agency administrator*
Hohman, Lawrence Henry *graphics designer, publishing executive*

Oregon

Knorr, John Christian *entertainment executive, bandleader, producer*
Poad, Flora Virginia *retired librarian and educator, retired elementary school educator*

Orrville

Hennell, Robert William, III, *secondary school educator*
Kamp, Philip *food products executive*
Mackus, Eloise L. *food products company executive*
Smucker, Richard K. *food company executive*
Smucker, Timothy P. *food company executive*
Warner, Patricia Ann *secondary school educator*

Orwell

Carlson, Timothy A. *music educator*

Oxford

Baird, Jay Warren *historian, educator*
Barilleaux, Ryan J. *politcal science educator*
Bauer, Steven Albert *English educator, writer*
Becker, Stephen Bradbury *fraternal organization administrator*
Bergen, Doris *psychologist, educator*
Brown, Edward Maurice *retired lawyer, business executive*
Cox, James Allan *chemistry professor*
DeLue, Steven Muller *political scientist, educator*
Eshbaugh, W(illiam) Hardy *botanist, educator*
Ewing, Susan R. *art educator, artist*
Garland, James C. *academic administrator*
Gordon, Gilbert *chemist, educator*
Macklin, Philip Alan *physics educator*
Miller, Robert James *educational association administrator*
Pont, John *football coach, educator*
Pratt, William Crouch, Jr., *English language educator, writer*
Rejai, Mostafa *political science educator*
Rypstra, Ann *zoology educator*
Sanders, Gerald Hollie *communications educator, educator*
Shriver, Phillip Raymond *academic administrator*
Thompson, Bertha Boya *retired education educator, antique dealer and appraiser*
Ward, Roscoe Fredrick *engineering educator*
Weinrich, Barbara Diane *speech pathology/audiology services professional, educator*
Yamauchi, Edwin Masao *history professor*
Yang, Kewu *chemist*

Painesville

Aveni, Anthony Joseph *lawyer, educator*
Davis, Barbara Snell *education educator*
Dean, J. Thomas *lawyer*
McQuaid, Kim *historian, educator, writer*
Smith, William Robert *utility company executive*

Parma

Cratty, David Michael *education educator*
Laycock, Randolph Philip *music educator, conductor*
Peck, Andrea Sue *writer, educator*
Scheffel, Donna Jean *elementary school educator*
Tener, Carol Joan *retired secondary school educator*

Pataskala

Caw, Thomas William *retired publisher and editor*

Patriot

Riggle, Patricia Carol *special education educator*

Paulding

Moore, Pamela Rae *elementary school educator*

Pemberville

King, Laura Jane *librarian, genealogist*
Sterling, William Carlisle *physician assistant*

Peninsula

Shaw, Doris Beaumar *film and video producer, executive recruiter, management consultant*

Pepper Pike

Alexander-Haynes, Sandra *psychologist, educator*
Goodman, Donald Joseph *dentist*
Mc Call, Julien Lachicotte *banker*
Snell, James Blaine *music educator*
Stano, Sister Diana *academic administrator*
Vail, Thomas Van Husen *retired newspaper publisher and editor*

Perrysburg

Autry, Carolyn *artist, art history educator*
Billnitzer, Bonnie Jeanne *nurse, gerontologist*
Celeste, Ardella Hazel *retired writer*
King, John Joseph *manufacturing executive*
Kovacik, Neal Stephen *hotel and restaurant executive*
Loeffler, William Robert *quality productivity delivery specialist, engineering educator*
Schwier, Priscilla Lamb Guyton *television broadcasting company executive*
Spitzer, John Brumback *lawyer*
Weaver, Richard L., II, *writer, speaker, educator*
Williamson, John Pritchard *utilities executive*

Pettisville

Beck, Duane J. *choir director*

Pickerington

Callander, Kay Eileen Paisley *business owner, retired education educator, writer*
Collins, Arlene *secondary school educator*
Parulekar, Marc Samir *music educator*

Plain City

Karrer, Carol Converse *nursing educator, consultant*
Kinman, Gary *landscape company executive*

Plymouth

Hartman, Ruth Campbell *director, educator*

Poland

Murphy, Thomas Michael *civil engineer*

Pomeroy

Brockert, Joseph Paul *government executive, writer, editor, designer*

Portsmouth

Akhtar, Muhammad I. *neurologist, researcher*
Burns, Eugene Hugh, Jr., *biology professor*
Cain, Beverly Lynn *library director*
Gerlach, Franklin Theodore *lawyer*
Horr, William Henry *retired lawyer*
Johnson, Janice E. *education educator, writer*
Mirabello, Mark Linden *history professor*
Turner, Elvin L. *retired educational administrator*

Powell

Arnold, A. Joel *pharmaceuticals company executive*
Borin, Gerald W. *zoological park administrator*
Emanuelson, James Robert *retired insurance company executive*
Lee, Robert J. Y. *marketing professional*
Spangler, Edra Mildred *clinical psychologist*
White, George Washington *automotive consultant*

Randolph

Pecano, Donald Carl *automotive manufacturing executive*

Ravenna

Benshoff-Ludick, Dixie Lee *psychologist, educator*
Felton, Robert O'Neil, II, *secondary education educator*
Nolfi, Edward Anthony *lawyer*
Turcotte, Margaret Jane *retired nurse*

Reynoldsburg

Cochran, Shirley Ann *mediator*
Dailey, Fred L. *state agency administrator*
Fiske, Neil *retail executive*
Gunnels, Lee O. *retired finance and management educator, manufacturing/research company director, inventor*
Nichols, Grace A. *retail executive*
Serraglio, Mario *architect*
Stevens, Kenneth T. *personal care industry executive*
Woodward, Greta Charmaine *construction company executive, rental and investment property manager*

Richfield

Anthony, Leonard Morris *steel company administrator, consultant*
Fry, W. Logan *artist*
Lewis, Sylvia Davidson *foundation executive*
Mott, Rodney *metal products executive*
Pelagalli, James A. *surgeon*

Richmond

Mills, Holly Lynn *registered nurse*
Radinsky, Troy D. *assistant principal*

Richmond Heights

Friedman, Jeffrey I. *real estate company executive*

Rockford

Thompson, Robert Douglas *computer science educator, banker, consultant*

Rocky River

Hosek, John Jude *planning organization executive*
Kamm, Christian Philip *manufacturing company executive, writer, investment company executive*
Nisenson, James Howard *retired government agency administrator*
Riedthaler, William Allen *risk management professional*
Shaffer, Clarence F. *retired electronics executive*
Shively, Daniel Jerome *retired transportation executive*

Rootstown

Blacklow, Robert Stanley *internist, educator*
Brodell, Robert Thomas *internal medicine educator*
Campbell, Colin *obstetrician, gynecologist, school dean*
Nora, Lois Margaret *neurologist, educator, academic administrator, dean*

Roseville

Carney, Karen Rose *music educator, pianist*

Saint Marys

Ball, Judy Kay *minister*
Dallura, Sal Anthony *physician*
Huber, William Evan *lawyer*

Salem

Fehr, Kenneth Manbeck *retired computer systems company executive*

Sandusky

Bailey, K. Ronald *lawyer*
Rothermel, Joan Ashley *artist*
Stacey, James Allen *retired judge*

Sardinia

Evans, C(aroline) Sue *social sciences educator*

Seaman

Cartaino, Carol Ann *editor*
Young, Vernon Lewis *lawyer*

Sebring

Doty, James Edward *pastor, psychologist*
Saffell, John Edgar *retired history educator*

Seven Hills

Stanczak, Julian *artist, educator*

Shaker Heights

Donnem, Sarah Lund *financial analyst, non-profit and political organization consultant*
Eakin, Thomas Capper *sports promotion executive*
Ekelman, Daniel Louis *lawyer*
Feuer, Michael *office products superstore executive*
Killeen, Michael F. *retail executive*
Ludwig, L(owell) Mark *social science educator*
Messinger, Donald Hathaway *lawyer*
Siegel, Robert *heat transfer engineer*
Smith, Jonathan David *medical educator*
Solganik, Marvin *real estate executive*
Trefts, Joan Landenberger *retired educator, administrator*
Unger, Paul A. *packaging and international affairs specialist*
White, Eugene A. *retired physician, neuroradiologist*
Winter, John Alexander *realtor, real estate appraiser*

Shandon

Wilson, James Ray *international business educator*

Shauck

Garvick, Kenneth Ryan *broadcast engineer, announcer, educator*

Sheffield Village

Herdendorf, Charles Edward, III, *oceanographer, limnologist, consultant*

Shelby

Phelan, Martha Armstrong *realtor*

Shreve

Denman, Nicholas Werner *insurance executive*

Sidney

Evans, Eric Charles *management executive*
Laurence, Michael Marshall *magazine publisher, writer*
Leffler, Carole Elizabeth *mental health nurse, women's health nurse*
Seitz, James Eugene *retired college president, freelance writer*
Stevens, Robert Jay *magazine editor*
Thompson, James W., Jr., *state official*

Solon

Bayman, James L. *electronics executive*
Gallo, Donald Robert *retired English educator*
Rosica, Gabriel Adam *manufacturing executive, electrical engineer*
Youdelman, Robert Arthur *financial executive, lawyer*

Somerset

Green, Tammie *professional golfer*

South Charleston

Weatherby, Donald Alan *telecommunications industry executive, writer*

South Euclid

Sazima, Henry John *retired oral and maxillofacial surgery educator*

South Russell

Preston, Robert Bruce *retired lawyer*

Spencer

Snyder, Teresa Ann *medical/surgical nurse*

Spring Valley

Atkins, Laura Jane *music educator*

Springboro

Saxer, Richard Karl *metallurgical engineer, retired air force officer*
Walden, James William *accountant, educator*

Springfield

Browne, William Bitner *lawyer*
Chen, Peng-Hsin *composer, music educator*
Dominick, Charles Alva *college official*
Faber, Trudy *music educator*
Harkins, Daniel Conger *lawyer*
Henning, William Clifford *cemetery consulting company executive*
Hobbs, Horton Holcombe, III, *biology professor*

Kinnison, William Andrew *retired university president*
Kurian, Pius *nephrologist, educator*
Lagos, James Harry *lawyer*
Moore, Florian Howard *retired electronics engineer*
Ryu, Kyoo-Hai Lee *physiologist*
Sweet, Robert T. *humanities educator*

Steubenville
Reddy, Vardhan Jonnala *surgeon*
Scanlan, Michael *priest, academic administrator*
Sheldon, Gilbert Ignatius *clergyman*

Stockport
Winebrenner, William Patrick *writer*

Stow
Fatchet, Jo A. *private investigator*
Hessler, William Gerhard *tax consultant*
Jahn, Cynthia Patton *secondary school educator*
Kalkhoff, William Webster *sociologist, educator*
Kim, Kwang-Jea *research scientist, polymer engineer*

Strongsville
Berkey, Donald Frederick *counseling administrator*
Blumer, Frederick Elwin *retired philosophy educator*
Lamberton, Jacquelyn E. *psychotherapist*
Myers, Jack Fredrick *artist, educator, author*
Pinkerton, Richard LaDoyt *retired management educator*

Struthers
Noble, Robert William, Jr., *retired elementary school educator, minister*

Sylvania
Bergsmark, Edwin Martin *mortgage bank executive*
Burkhart, Craig Garrett *dermatologist*
Helmer, Robert C. *academic administrator*
Kastner, Michael James *dentist*
Ring, Herbert Everett *management executive*
Sampson, Earldine Robison *education educator*
White, Alan Edward *computer company executive*

Tallmadge
Kaul, Mohan Lal *social worker, educator*

The Plains
Klare, George Roger *psychology educator*

Tiffin
Davison, Kenneth Edwin *American studies educator, genealogist*
Einsel, David William, Jr., *retired army officer and consultant*
Galipeau, Peter Armand *city councilman*
Gridley, Mark Charles *psychologist*
Hillmer, Margaret Patricia *library director*
Moore, Vincent D. *humanities educator, writer*
Spellerberg, Elinor M. *riding instructor*

Tipp City
Taylor, Robert Homer *quality assurance professional, pilot*
Tighe-Moore, Barbara Jeanne *electronics executive*

Toledo
Alexander, Kenneth Saul *pharmaceuticals educator*
Al-Marayati, Abid A. *political science educator*
Anspach, Robert Michael *lawyer*
Baker, Richard Southworth *lawyer*
Barrett, Michael John *anesthesiologist*
Batt, Nick *property and investment executive*
Bell, Robert *orchestra executive*
Billups, Norman Fredrick *college dean, pharmacist, educator*
Block, Allan James *communications executive*
Block, John Robinson *newspaper publisher*
Block, William K., Jr., *media executive*
Brass, Alan W. *healthcare executive*
Brower, James Calvin *graphic artist, painter*
Brown, Charles Earl *lawyer*
Brown, David T. *manufacturing executive*
Cardwell, Michael Steven
Carney, Margaret Lou *historian, curator*
Carr, James Gray *judge*
Carroll, William J. *automotive executive*
Carson, Samuel Goodman *retired banker, company director*
Chakraborty, Joana *physiologist, educator, science administrator*
Comerota, Anthony James *vascular surgeon, biomedical researcher*
Condon, Elizabeth M. *education educator*
Cousino, Joe Ann *sculptor*
Dalrymple, Thomas Lawrence *retired lawyer*
Dane, Stephen Mark *lawyer*
Danko-McGhee, Katherina Elaine *art educator, consultant*
Davis, David Howard *political science educator*
DeBacker, Michael L. *automotive executive, lawyer*
Diehl, Dean R. *engineering company executive*
Doner, Gary William *lawyer*
Finkbeiner, Carlton S. (Carty Finkbeiner) *radio personality, former mayor*
Girgis-Hanna, Mary Fahim *music educator*
Glaab, Charles Nelson *historian, educator*
Goodenday, Lucy Sherman *physician, educator*
Gouttiere, John P. *lawyer*
Gutteridge, Thomas G. *academic administrator, consultant and labor arbitrator*
Hartung, James H. *airport authority executive*
Heintz, Carolinea Cabaniss *retired home economics educator*
Hilbert, John Warren, II, *lawyer*
Hills, Arthur W. *architectural firm executive*
Hiner, Glen Harold, Jr., *materials company executive*
Howard, John Malone *surgeon, educator*
Hyman, Melvin *speech-language pathologist, consultant*
Ivanov, Alexander V. *biochemist, researcher*
Jackson, Reginald Sherman, Jr., *lawyer, educator*
Jacobs, Lloyd A. *vascular surgeon*
Jan, George Pokung *political science educator*
Katz, David Allan *federal judge*
Kneen, James Russell *health care administrator*
Knotts, Frank Barry *physician, surgeon*
Koppus, Betty Jane *retired savings and loan association executive*
Kunze, Ralph Carl *retired savings and loan executive*
Lawrence, Edmund Pond, Jr., *neurosurgeon*
Lemieux, Joseph Henry *manufacturing executive*
Lessick, Mira Lee *nursing educator*
Machin, Barbara E. *lawyer*
Mahr, Joe *journalist*
Majdalani, Brenda J. *prosecutor, educator*
Martin, John Thomas *physician, author, educator*
Martin, Robert Edward *architect*
McClair, Annette *protective services official*
McGlauchlin, Tom *artist*
Medhkour, Azedine *neurosurgeon, educator*
Meier, John F. *consumer products company executive*
Metress, Seamus P. *anthropology educator, Irish studies researcher*
Meyers, Geoffrey Groman *financial executive*
Mihura, Joni L. *psychologist, educator*
Miroshnichenko, Anatoly S. *astronomer, researcher*
Mohler, Terence John *psychologist*
Mulrow, Patrick Joseph *medical educator*
Norton, Patrick H. *manufacturing executive*
O'Connell, Maurice Daniel *lawyer*
Ormond, Paul A. *healthcare company executive*
Pham, David Lan *secondary school educator, writer*
Pletz, Thomas Gregory *lawyer*
Potter, John William *federal judge*
Rabideau, Margaret Catherine *retired media center director*
Rejent, Marian Magdalen *retired pediatrician*
Richter, Robert C. *automotive executive*
Romanoff, Marjorie Reinwald *retired education educator*
Romanoff, Milford Martin *retired building contractor*
Royhab, Ronald *journalist, editor*
St. Clair, Donald David *lawyer*
Sallah, Michael D. *journalist*
Shelley, Walter Brown *physician, educator*
Simpson, John S. *former finance executive*
Smith, Robert Freeman *history educator*
Smith, Robert Nelson *former government official, anesthesiologist*
Talmage, Lance Allen *obstetrician/gynecologist, career military officer*
Thaman, Michael H. *building material systems executive*
Van Hooser, David *retired manufacturing executive*
Vicary, William Charles, Jr., *director sales and marketing*
Ward, David A. *corporate lawyer*
Webb, Thomas Irwin, Jr., *lawyer, director*
Weikel, Malcolm Keith *healthcare company executive*
Weinblatt, Charles Samuel *university administrator, employment consultant*
Weiss, Mitch *journalist*
Wicklund, David Wayne *lawyer*
Willey, John Douglas *retired newspaper executive*
Witherell, Dennis Patrick *lawyer*
Wolff, Edwin Ray *retired construction engineer, consultant*
Zrull, Joel Peter *psychiatry educator*

Troy
Savage, Joseph Scott *physician*

Uniontown
Krabill, Robert Elmer *osteopathic physician*

University Heights
Carrington, Gary *psychologist*
Cook, Alexander Burns *museum curator, artist, educator*
Eslinger, Kenneth Nelson *social sciences educator*
Glynn, Edward *college administrator*
Seaton, Shirley Smith *academic administrator, consultant*
Starcher-Dell'Aquila, Judy Lynn *special education educator*

Upper Sandusky
Baker, Harrison Scott *computer consultant*

Valley View
Miller, Susan Ann *retired school system administrator*

Vandalia
Korte, Genevieve L *music educator*

Vermilion
Vance, Elbridge Putnam *mathematics educator*

Wadsworth
Neumann, Jeffrey Jay *photographer, minister*
Pipitone, Phyllis L. *psychologist, educator, author*

Walton Hills
Elliott, Stanley B. *chemist, researcher*
Thellmann, Edward L. *mayor*

Warren
Chapman, Willie Dean *sales executive*
Corson, Joseph Martin *multimedia designer*
He, Min *mathematics professor*
Letson, William Normand *lawyer*
McGeough, Robert Saunders *lawyer*
Nader, Robert Alexander *judge, lawyer*
Robbins, Robert Marvin *accountant*
Rossi, Anthony Gerald *lawyer*
Spencer, James A. *automotive executive*
Vigorito, Philip Michael *lawyer*

Wellston
Loxley, Kathryn *retired elementary school educator*

West Carrollton
McLaughlin, Daniel R. *display designer, lighting designer*
Rabold, Barbara Ann *artist, writer, illustrator, systems analyst*

West Chester
End, William Thomas *business executive*
Mack, Mark Philip *chemical company executive*
Mital, Anil *engineering educator*
Pease, Stacey Lyn *music educator*

West Farmington
Smith, Agnes Monroe *history professor*

Westerville
Chivington, Amy Doan *education educator*
Dawdy, W. David *pediatrician*
DeVore, C. Brent *college president, educator*
Grover, Kevin Patrick *publishing executive, consultant*
Husarik, Ernest Alfred *educational administrator*
Keller, Kenneth Christen *advertising executive*
Kerr, Thomas Jefferson, IV, *academic official*
Krueger-Horn, Cheryl *apparel executive*
Schultz, Arthur LeRoy *clergyman, educator*
Swinehart, Timothy E. *music educator*
Washington, La Trice M. *social studies educator*
Westervelt, Charles Ephraim, Jr., *lawyer*
Young, Sheldon Mike *lawyer, author*

Westfield Center
Bock, Carolyn A. *writer, consultant, small business owner*
Spinelli, Anne Catherine *elementary school educator*

Westlake
Doane, Tim *travel company executive*
Donahue, Charles Bertrand, II, *lawyer*
FitzRandolph, Casey *Olympic athlete*
George, James W. *travel company executive*
Hellman, Peter Stuart *technical manufacturing executive*
Kuhn, Edwin P. *travel company executive*
Loehr, Marla *spiritual care coordinator*
Ohno, Apolo Anton *Olympic athlete*
Parra, Derek *Olympic athlete*
Whitehouse, John Harlan, Jr., *systems software consultant, diagnostician*

Whitehall
Van Camp, Diana J. *music educator*

Whitehouse
Boyle, Daniel Robert *musician, delivery service executive*

Wickliffe
Cooley, Charles P. *chemicals executive*
Dunn, Horton, Jr., *organic chemist*
Fisher, Nancy DeButts *library director*
Hambrick, James L. *chemicals executive*
Kidder, Fred Dockstater *lawyer*
Krause, Marjorie N. *biochemist*
Pevec, Anthony Edward *bishop*

Wilberforce
Anyalewechi, Patrick Okechukwu *psychology educator*
Elali, Taan *engineering and computer science educator*
Hargraves, William Frederick, II, *mathematics and computer science educator*
Omolewu, Gabriel Adebayo *business educator, researcher*

Willoughby
Abelt, Ralph William *bank executive*
Baker, Charles Stephen *music educator*
Carter, John Robert *physician*
Combs, Steven Paul *orthopedic surgeon*
Corrigan, Faith *journalist, educator, historian*
Elias, Judith Helen *music educator*
Grossman, Mary Margaret *elementary school educator*
Primavera, Fred Joseph *music educator*
Stern, Michael David *dentist*

Wilmington
Evans, Elizabeth Ann West *retired real estate agent*
Schutt, Walter Eugene *lawyer*
Townsend, June H. *foreign language educator*

Wooster
August, Robert Olin *retired journalist*
Calhoun, Daniel Fairchild *history educator*
Christopher, David L. *bank executive*
Ferree, David Curtis *horticultural researcher*
Geiser, Robert Neil *computer scientist*
Hales, Raleigh Stanton, Jr., *mathematics professor, academic administrator*
Hickey, Damon Douglas *library director*
Johnston, John Clifford, Jr., *lawyer*
Kennedy, Charles Allen *lawyer*
Linehan, Mary *historian, educator*
Madden, Laurence Vincent *plant pathology educator*
Saif, Linda J. *animal scientist*
Schmitt, Wolf Rudolf *consumer products executive*

Worthington
Bender, Bob *advertising executive*
Bernhagen, Lillian Flickinger *retired school health consultant*
Browning, Robert Lynn *educator, clergyman*
Compton, Ralph Theodore, Jr., *electrical engineering educator*
Lentz, Edward Allen *consultant, retired health administrator*
Trevor, Alexander Bruen *technology consultant*
Whitney, Ray *professional hockey player*
Winter, Chester Caldwell *physician, surgery educator, historian, writer*
Wu, Tien Hsing *civil engineering educator, consulting engineer*

Wright Patterson Afb
Amend, Joseph H., III, *military officer*
Boff, Kenneth Richard *engineering research psychologist*
Caudill, Tom Holden *governmental policy and analysis executive*
Fernelius, Nils Conard *physicist*
Garscadden, Alan *physicist*
Kelley, Joseph E. *career officer*
Paul, Richard R. *military officer*
Reston, Rocky Russell *anesthesiologist, engineer, educator*

Wyoming
Cooley, William Edward *research scientist, consultant*

Xenia
Bigelow, Daniel James *aerospace executive*
Chappars, Timothy Stephen *lawyer*
Nutter, Zoe Dell Lantis *retired public relations executive*
Wolaver, Stephen Arthur *judge*

Yellow Springs
Cawood, Albert McLaurin (Hap Cawood) *retired newspaper editor*
Fogarty, Robert Stephen *historian, educator, editor*
Graham, Jewel Freeman *social worker, lawyer, educator*
Rinehart, John McLain *composer, education educator*
Spokane, Robert Bruce *biophysical chemist*
Straumanis, Joan *academic administrator*
Trolander, Hardy Wilcox *engineering executive, consultant*
Von Gierke, Henning Edgar *biomedical science educator, former government official, researcher*
Webb, Paul *physiologist, educator, researcher, consultant*

Youngstown
Atwater, Tony *provost,dean, educator*
Binning, William Charles *political scientist, educator*
Blair, Richard Bryson *lawyer*
Bowers, Bege K. *English educator, academic administrator*
Camacci, Michael A. *commercial real estate broker, development consultant*
Carlin, Clair Myron *lawyer*
Catoline-Ackerman, Pauline Dessie *small business owner*
Cernica, John N. *engineering educator, civil engineer, consultant*
DeBartolo, Edward John, Jr., *professional football team owner, real estate developer*
Estrin, Melvyn J. *computer products company executive*
Fok, Thomas Dso Yun *civil engineer*
Gransee, Marsha L. *federal agency executive*
Iannucci, Marleen *physical therapist, educator*
Jeren, John Anthony, Jr., *lawyer*
Lacivita, Michael John *safety engineer*
Loch, John Robert *university administrator*
Majzik, William *accountant, writer*
Marks, Esther L. *metals company executive*
Matune, Frank Joseph *lawyer*
McCollum, Everett *retired school system administrator, music educator*
Mehra, Jagdish *economics professor*
Nadler, Myron Jay *lawyer, director*
Powers, Paul J. *manufacturing executive*
Ragland, Thomas Eugene *osteopath, protective services official*
Roth, Daniel Benjamin *lawyer, business executive*
Ruffer, David Gray *museum director, former college president*
Rupeka, Robert W. *court administrator*
Smotzer, Thomas David *mathematician*
Sweeney, Christopher John *psychology educator, consultant*
Usip, Ebenge Etefia *economics professor*
Walton, Ralph Gerald *psychiatrist, educator*
Zitto, Richard Joseph *physics educator*
Zorn, Robert Lynn *education educator*

Zanesville
Brown, Karen Rima *orchestra manager, Spanish language educator*
Kopf, George Michael *retired ophthalmologist*
Micheli, Frank James *lawyer*
O'Sullivan, Christine *retired executive director social service agency, consultant*
Ray, John Walker *otolaryngologist, educator, broadcast commentator*
Ray, Susanne Gettings *counselor*
Shatz, Mark Allen *psychologist, educator*
Workman, James E. *retired school psychologist*

OKLAHOMA

Ada
Anoatubby, Bill *governor of Chickawaw Nation*
Baker, Judith Ann *retired computer technician*
Daniel, Arlie Verl *speech education educator*
Davenport, Ann Adele Mayfield *retired home care agency administrator*
Frye, Linda Beth (Linda Beth Hisle) *elementary, secondary education educator*
Harris, Kim A. *elementary school educator*
Mynatt, Cecil Ferrell *psychiatrist*
Reese, Patricia Ann *retired editor, columnist*
Stafford, Donald Gene *chemistry professor*

Altus
Brown, Roger Dale *academic administrator*
Carson, S. Kirk *music educator*
Stine, Earle John, Jr., *radiologist*

Alva
Mitchell, Allan Edwin *lawyer*

Anadarko
Kidd, Lovetta Monza *music educator*

Atoka
Gabbard, Douglas, II, (James Gabbard) *judge*

Bartlesville
Allen, W. Wayne *retired oil industry executive*
Chambers, Imogene Klutts *school system administrator, financial consultant*
Cox, Glenn Andrew, Jr., *petroleum company executive*
Doty, Donald D. *retired bank executive*
Dwiggins, Claudius William, Jr., *chemist*
Hogan, John Paul *chemistry researcher, consultant*
Johnson, Marvin Merrill *chemical engineer, chemist*
Lambert, Joseph Parker *retired dentist*
Mihm, John Clifford *chemical engineer*
Mulva, James Joseph *oil company executive*
Risner, Anita Jane *vocational school educator*
Roff, Alan Lee *lawyer, consultant*
Silas, Cecil Jesse *retired petroleum company executive*
Sweem, Billy Don *minister*

Bethany
Ballweg, David Brent *music educator, conductor*
Crabtree, John Michael *college administrator, consultant*

Halpain, Sue R. *music educator, musician*
Hendrick, Howard H. *state official*
Leggett, James Daniel *bishop*
McGowan, Bernard W. *venture capitalist, writer*
Murrow, Wayne Lee *retired communications educator, dean*

Billings
Matthiesen, Robert L. *education educator, farmer, rancher*

Blanchard
Harris, Barbara Ellen *mayor*

Bristow
Primeaux, Henry, III, *automotive executive, author, speaker*

Broken Arrow
Cruzan, Clarah Catherine *dietitian*
Frieze, H(arold) Delbert *lawyer*
Paden, Larry J. *consulting electronics engineer, lawyer*
Steeley, Jill Edwards *education educator*
Stewart, Murray Baker *retired lawyer*

Calera
Young, James Oliver *dentist, communication company executive*

Chandler
Foster, Robert Lawson *retired judge, deacon*
Swanson, Robert Lee *lawyer*

Choctaw
Howard, David L. *music educator, conductor*
Uselton, Bill W. *secondary school educator*

Chouteau
Sasser, Charles Wayne *journalist, educator, writer*

Claremore
Whinery, Michael Albert *physician*

Cleveland
Anderson, Patricia Sue *writer*
Henry, Kathleen Marie *marketing executive*

Clinton
Askew, Penny Sue *choreographer, artistic director, ballet instructor*

Coalgate
Willis, Tricia Lee *special education educator*

Collinsville
Rogers, Jimmy Don *county official, writer*

Cyril
Rains, Scott Wyatt *editor, musician*

Disney
Hamilton, Carl Hulet *retired academic administrator*

Durant
Gregg, David Christopher *music educator*
Kennedy, Elizabeth Carol *psychologist, educator*
Rice, Stanley Arthur *biology professor*
Spencer, Mark Benner *education educator*

Edmond
Acers, Patsy Pierce *financial seminars company executive*
Edwards, Jon Brian *food service executive*
Harryman, Rhonda L. *education educator*
Haywood, B(etty) J(ean) *anesthesiologist*
Hopwood, Howard Hoppy Perry *military officer*
Lester, Andrew William *lawyer*
Lewis, Gladys Sherman *nursing educator*
Loman, Mary LaVerne *retired mathematics educator*
Loving, Susan Brimer *lawyer, former state official*
Miller, Shannon *Olympic athlete*
Necco, E(dna) Joanne *school psychologist*
Remy-Schumacher, Tess *music educator, musician*
Sibley, William Arthur *academic administrator, physics educator, consultant*
Smock, Donald Joe *governmental liaison, political consultant*
Wylie, Quineta G. Beagle *state political party executive*
Zabel, Vivian Ellouise *secondary school educator*

El Reno
Buendia, Imelda Bernardo *health facility administrator, physician*
Hughey, Billy *publishing executive*
Slagell-Gossen, Reonna Richele *science educator, researcher*

Enid
Abdul-Jabbar, Kareem (Lewis Ferdinand Alcindor) *professional basketball coach*
Jones, Stephen *lawyer*
McCobb, Allan Paul *not-for-profit organization executive*
Record, Donald D. *music educator, literature educator*
Ward, Llewellyn Orcutt, III, *oil company executive*

Goodwell
Duren, Brad L. *social studies educator*

Grove
Trippensee, Gary Alan *retired aerospace transportation executive*

Guthrie
Davis, Frank Wayne *lawyer*

Guymon
Lim, Jeffrey James *internist*
Wood, Donald Euriah *lawyer*

Healdton
Eck, Kenneth Frank *pharmacist*

Hodgen
Brower, Janice Kathleen *library technician*

Jennings
Nixon, Arlie James *gas and oil company executive*

Kingfisher
Buswell, Arthur Wilcox *physician, surgeon*

Lane
Edelson, Jonathan Victor *entomologist, educator*

Langston
Holloway, Ernest Leon *university president*
Mallik, Muhammad Abdul-Bari *soil microbiologist*

Lawton
Cates, Dennis Lynn *education educator*
Dishman, Bob N. *pharmacist*
Follett, M. Paul *genealogist, librarian*
Goetz, Gary D., Sr., *writer, retired chef, restaurateur*
Hooper, Roy B. *lobbyist, consultant*
McKeown, Rebecca J. *principal*
Moore, Roy Dean *retired judge*
Nalley, Elizabeth Ann *chemistry professor*
Ragan, Marilyn Kay *performing arts educator, costume designer*
Smiley, Frederick Melvin *education educator, consultant*
Webb, Orville Lynn *retired physician, pharmacologist, educator*

Lone Wolf
Cole, Burna L. *writer, retired curator*

Mangum
Bronson, William Cavolt, Jr., *counselor*

Mcalester
Cornish, Richard Pool *lawyer*
Neal, Charles D., Jr., *lawyer*

Midwest City
Gonzalez, Richard Theodore *photographer*
McDowell, Cassandra *multi-media specialist*

Monkey Island
Vanatta, Chester B. *retired business executive, educator*

Mounds
Fellows, Esther Elizabeth *musician, music educator*
Halsey, James Albert *international entertainment impresario, theatrical producer, talent manager*

Muskogee
Coburn, Tom A. *former congressman*
Edwards, Terri Lyn Wilmoth *education educator*
Ehlers, Deborah Layne *theater director*
Kent, Bartis Milton *retired physician*
Peddy, Lisa Lynn *secondary school educator*
Robinson, Adelbert Carl *lawyer, judge*
Sperling, Sheldon J. *prosecutor*
Wiles, James Steven *music educator*

Mustang
Laurent, Jerry Suzanna *technical communications specialist*
Wood, Jean Carol *poet, lyricist*

Newkirk
Newport, L. Joan *clinical social worker, retired psychotherapist*

Norman
Affleck, Marilyn *retired sociology educator*
Apanasov, Boris N. *mathematics professor, researcher*
Bell, Robert Eugene *anthropologist educator*
Bert, Charles Wesley *mechanical and aerospace engineer, educator*
Bethel, Joann D. *computer programmer, analyst*
Bluestein, Howard Bruce *meteorology educator*
Boren, David Lyle *academic administrator*
Brown, Sidney DeVere *history educator*
Campbell, John Morgan *retired chemical engineer*
Carpenter, Charles Congden *zoologist, educator*
Carroll, Frances Laverne *librarian, educator*
Casey, Rebecca Powell *apparel executive*
Chidambaram, Laku *information technology educator*
Cochran, Gloria Grimes *retired pediatrician*
Corr, Edwin Gharst *ambassador*
Cowan, John James *physicist, educator, astronomer, educator*
Croft, Janet Brennan *academic librarian*
Dalton, Deborah Whitmore *dean*
Daniel, Sean *retired voice educator, baritone, artist*
Dary, David Archie *journalism educator, author*
Dickey, Leonid Alexander *mathematician, educator*
Dille, John Robert *retired physician*
Drayton, John N. *publishing executive*
Egle, Davis Max *mechanical engineering educator*
Fairbanks, Robert Alvin *lawyer*
Fears, Jesse Rufus *historian, educator, academic dean*
Fillpot, Bob G. *architecture educator*
Gilje, Paul Arn *history educator*
Green, Ronald Simonds *historian, educator*
Haring, Kathryn Ann *special education educator, research scientist*
Henderson, Arnold Glenn *architect, educator*
Henderson, George *educational sociologist, educator*
Hengst, Herbert Randall *retired educator*
Henkle, James L. *industrial designer*
Herstand, Theodore *theatre artist, educator*
Houser, Robert P., Jr., *chemist, educator*
Hutchison, Victor Hobbs *biologist, educator*
Kemp, Betty Ruth *retired librarian*
Kessler, Edwin *meteorology educator, consultant*
Kondonassis, Alexander John *economist, educator*
Kudrna, James *architecture educator*
Lakshmivarahan, Sivaramakrishnan *computer science educator*
Lamb, Peter James *meteorology educator, researcher, consultant*
Leitch, Vincent Barry *literary and cultural studies educator*
Lester, June *library information studies educator*
Logue, Dennis Emhardt *financial economics educator, consultant, dean*
Lowitt, Richard *history professor*
MacFarland, Miriam Katherine (Mimi MacFarland) *writer*
Madden, Glenda Gail *sales professional*
Magarian, Robert Armen *medicinal chemist, researcher, educator, author, inventor*
Magrath, Jane *music educator*
Mallinson, Richard Gregory *chemical engineering educator*
Matlick, Eldon R. *music educator*
Meiller, James R. *music educator*
Mergler, Nancy L. *academic administrator*
Munteanu, Laura *mathematician, educator*
Nelson, Donna Jean *chemistry educator, researcher*
O'Rear, Edgar Allen, III, *chemical engineering educator*
Papavassiliou, Dimitrios Vassilios *chemical engineer, educator*
Pappas, James Pete *university administrator*
Perkins, Edward J. *diplomat*
Petersen, Catherine Holland *lawyer*
Pigott, John Dowling *geologist, geophysicist, geochemist, educator, consultant*
Provine, Lorraine *retired mathematics educator*
Ross, Allan Anderson *music educator, university official*
Savage, William Woodrow, Jr., *historian, consultant, social sciences educator*
Sharp, Paul Frederick *former university president, education consultant*
Sherman, Mary Angus *public library administrator*
Sorcy, Thomas Lester, Jr., *architect, educator*
Southwell, Kristina Lynn *archivist, librarian*
Striz, Alfred Gerhard *aerospace engineer, educator*
Trimble, Preston Albert *retired judge*
Winchell, Michael George *lawyer*
Zapffe, Nina Byrom *retired elementary education educator*
Zelby, Leon Wolf *electrical engineering educator, consulting engineer*

Oklahoma City
Ackerman, Raymond Basil *advertising agency executive*
Adair, Larry E. *state representative*
Alaupovic, Alexandra Vrbanic *artist, educator*
Alaupovic, Petar *biochemist, educator*
Alexander, Patrick Byron *university administrator*
Allbright, Karan Elizabeth *psychologist, consultant*
Allen, Robert Dee *lawyer*
Alley, Wayne Edward *federal judge, retired army officer*
Andrews, M. Dewayne *dean, internist, educator*
Askins, Jari *lawyer, department chairman, state representative*
Bahr, Carman Bloedow *internist*
Bailey, Burck *lawyer*
Baker, Doug W. *history and humanities educator*
Barth, J. Edward *lawyer, shareholder*
Batenic, Mark K. *manufacturing executive*
Beltran, Eusebius Joseph *archbishop*
Berg, Laura *Olympic athlete*
Binning, Bette Finese (Mrs. Gene Hedgcock Binning) *athletic association official*
Binning, Gene Barton *computer company executive*
Blackburn, Debbie *elementary school educator, state representative*
Blackwell, John Adrian, Jr., *computer company executive*
Bode, Denise Anne *petroleum association executive*
Bogardus, Carl Robert, Jr., *radiologist, educator*
Boomer, Dennis Keith *college official, clergyman*
Boston, Billie *costume designer, costume history educator*
Boston, William Clayton *lawyer*
Bowlby, Leymond Ambrose *linguist, translator*
Boyd, Betty *government official*
Bozalis, John Russell *physician*
Bradford, Dennis Doyle *real estate broker, developer*
Branch, John Curtis *biology professor, lawyer*
Brandt, Edward Newman, Jr., *physician, educator*
Brooks, Gene (Leslie Gene Brooks) *cultural association administrator*
Brooks, Norma Newton *legal assistant*
Brown, Kenneth Ray *banker*
Browne, John Robinson *banker*
Burget, Mark Edward *lawyer*
Bush, William Arden *federal agency administrator*
Bustos, Crystl *softball player*
Butkin, Robert *state treasurer*
Campbell, David Gwynne *petroleum executive, geologist*
Cantrell, Charles L. *lawyer, educator*
Carballo, Bernard A. *computer technology company executive*
Cassel, John Elden *accountant*
Cauthron, Robin J. *federal judge*
Claflin, James Robert *pediatrician, allergist*
Clayton, Lawrence Otto *minister, writer, educator, alcohol and drug counselor*
Clonts, George Gary *packaging company executive*
Coats, Andrew Montgomery *lawyer, former mayor, dean*
Coleman, Carolyn *state legislator*
Coll, Mario M *engineering company executive*
Collins, William Edward *aeromedical administrator, researcher*
Comp, Philip Cinnamon *medical researcher*
Cook, Gayle Freeman *lawyer*
Corbett, Luke R. *energy executive*
Cornett, Mick *mayor*
Couch, James Russell, Jr., *neurology educator*
Court, Leonard *lawyer, educator*
Cox, Kevin *state representative*
Craig, George Dennis *economics educator, consultant*
Crites, Carl D. *auditor*
Crow, Charles Delmar *human resources manager, consultant*
Crowder, Carolyn *educational association administrator, educator*
Cunningham, Stanley Lloyd *lawyer*
Davis, Emery Stephen *wholesale food company executive*
Daxon, Tom *state agency administrator*
Derrick, Gary Wayne *lawyer*
Douty, Sheila *softball player*
Dubowski, Kurt Max *toxicologist, educator, consultant*
Durland, Jack Raymond *retired lawyer*
Easley, Mary *retired elementary school educator, state representative*
Edmondson, William Andrew *state attorney general*
Elder, James Carl *lawyer*
England, Gary Alan *television meteorologist*
Everett, Mark Allen *dermatologist, educator*
Fallin, Mary Copeland *lieutenant governor*
Faltyn, Timothy Wayne *education educator, writer*
Felton, Warren Locker, II, *surgeon*
Fenton, Elliott Clayton *lawyer*
Fernandez, Lisa *softball player*
Filley, Warren Vernon *allergist*
Finch, Jennie *softball player*
Flowers, Tairia Mims *softball player, Olympic athlete*
Ford, Charles Reed *state legislator*
Forni, Patricia Rose *nursing educator*
Frankfurt, William W. *architectural firm executive*
Freed, Amanda Louise *Olympic athlete*
Garrett, Sandy Langley *school system administrator*
George, James Noel *hematologist, oncologist, educator*
Gilchrist, John Mark *otolaryngologist*
Gonzalez, Larry Paul *research scientist, medical educator*
Gourley, James Leland *editor, publishing executive*
Gourley, Vicki Clark *publishing executive*
Greenwood, Joan *state representative*
Grupe, Robert Charles *corporate training consultant*
Gumerson, Jean Gilderhus *health foundation executive*
Gustafson, William Gene *oil industry executive*
Hageman, Dale *alternative staffing company executive*
Hale, Sue A. *editor*
Hall, Nancy K. *college dean*
Halpin, Anna Marie *architect, writer*
Halverstadt, Donald Bruce *urologist, educator*
Hamilton, Rebecca *state representative*
Hamilton, Thomas Allen *independent insurance agent, securities representative*
Hampton, Carol McDonald *priest, educator, historian*
Hampton, James Wilburn *hematologist, medical oncologist*
Hanna, Terry Ross *lawyer, small business owner*
Hansen, Mark S. *food marketing and distribution company executive*
Hargrave, Rudolph *state supreme court chief justice*
Harlan, Ross Edgar *retired utility company executive, writer, lecturer, consultant*
Harper, Robbie Jane *critical care nurse, administrator*
Harrigan, Lori *Olympic athlete*
Harrington, Gary Burnes *retired controller*
Hefner, Jerry W. *state legislator, concrete block plant executive*
Hefner, William Johnson, Jr., (W. John Hefner Jr.) *oil and gas industry executive*
Hemry, Jerome Eldon *lawyer*
Henley, Everett Scott *health care marketing firm executive*
Henry, C. Brad *governor*
Henry, Robert Harlan *federal judge, former attorney general*
Hobson, Calvin J., III, *state legislator, real estate firm executive*
Hodges, Ralph B. *state supreme court justice*
Holeman, Lora White *music educator*
Holloway, William Judson, Jr., *federal judge*
Holt, Karen Anita Young *English educator*
Horner, Maxine Edwyna Cissel *state legislator*
Humphreys, Kirk *mayor*
Hutson, Lindel G. *newspaper editor*
Ille, Bernard Glenn *insurance company executive, director*
Jacocks, Mac Alexander *surgeon*
Jenkins, Sherry L. *state insurance program administrator*
Johnson, B(ruce) Connor *biochemist, educator, consultant*
Johnson, Mike *state legislator, automobile agency executive*
Johnson, Robert Max *lawyer*
Johnson, Thomas Harold *radiologist*
Jung, Lovieanne *Olympic athlete*
Kelley, Ed *editor*
Kenney, John Arthur *lawyer*
Kerr, Lou C. *foundation administrator*
Kirkpatrick, John Elson *retired oil company executive, retired naval reserve officer*
Kline, David Adam *lawyer, educator, writer*
Kraker, Deborah Schovanec *special education educator*
Kretschman, Kelly *Olympic athlete*
Lambird, Mona Salyer *lawyer*
LaMotte, Janet Allison *retired management specialist*
Lappin, Lauren *Olympic athlete*
Lavender, Robert Eugene *state supreme court justice*
Lawler, Daisy *state senator, elementary school educator, farmer, rancher*
Legg, William Jefferson *lawyer*
Leonard, Timothy Dwight *judge*
Levine, Joel *music director, conductor*
Ligon, Duke R *lawyer*
Lo, Patrick Punchuk *physician*
Lovallo, William Robert *psychologist, educator, researcher*
Martin, Caroline June *state senator*
Mass, Michael Don *state legislator*
Mather, Ruth Elsie *writer*
Mather, Stephanie June *lawyer*
Mathews, Louise Robison *real estate broker, writer, historian*
McCampbell, Robert Garner *prosecutor*
McClellan, Mary Ann *pediatric nurse practitioner*
McEwen, Irene Ruble *physical therapy educator*
McIntyre, Judy *social worker, state representative*
McKenzie, Clif Allen *Indian tribe official, accountant*
Mendoza, Jessica *Olympic athlete*
Mikkelson, Dean Harold *geological engineer, writer*
Mildren, Jack *bank executive, former state official*
Miles-La Grange, Vicki *judge*
Miller, Herbert Dell *petroleum engineer*
Mitrovgenis, James William, Jr., *journalist*
Moffett, Sulinda *nursing association administrator*
Moler, Edward Harold *lawyer*
Monson, Angela Zoe *state legislator*
Moore, Billy Don *video scriptwriter, producer*
Morgan, Catherine Marie *psychologist, writer*
Mustion, Alan Lee *pharmacist*
Nakagawara, Van B. *optometrist, researcher*
Nations, Bill *dentist, state representative*
Nelon, Robert Dale *lawyer*
Nesbitt, Charles Rudolph *lawyer, energy consultant*
Niccum, Larry Curt *minister, educator*
Nichols, J. Larry *energy company executive, lawyer*

Nour, Bakr M. *surgeon, health facility administrator*
Nuveman, Stacey *Olympic athlete*
Oehlert, William Herbert, Jr., *cardiologist, administrator, educator*
Opala, Marian P(eter) *state supreme court justice*
Osterman, Catherine *Olympic athlete*
O'Brien-Amico, Leah *Olympic athlete*
Pain, Betsy M. *lawyer*
Pardo, Gabriel *neuro-ophthalmologist, neurologist, researcher*
Paris, Wayne *social worker, researcher*
Parke, David Wilkin, II, *ophthalmologist, educator, healthcare executive*
Parmley, Jay *political organization administrator*
Paul, William George *lawyer*
Peace, H. W., II, *oil company executive*
Pelofsky, Stan *neurosurgeon, educator*
Perez-Cruet, Jorge *physician, psychopharmacologist, psychophysiologist, psychiatrist, educator, addictionologist, geropsychiatrist*
Pfefferbaum, Betty Jane *psychiatrist, educator*
Pilcher, Gregory F. *manufacturing executive*
Pitts, Bryan *performing company executive*
Prinzo, O. Veronika *engineering research psychologist*
Prodan, Calin Ioan *physician*
Rahhal, Donald K. *obstetrician, gynecologist*
Rainbolt, H. E. *bank executive*
Reimer, Dennis J. *retired career military officer*
Reynolds, Edwin Clinton, Jr., *engineering manager*
Richardson, Dot (Dorothy Gay) *softball player, physician*
Rider, Neal J. *food wholesale executive*
Ridley, Betty Ann *religous educator, lay worker*
Riley, Nancy C. *state legislator*
Risser, Paul Gillan *academic administrator, botanist*
Robison, Clarence, Jr., *surgeon*
Ross, William Jarboe *lawyer*
Rossavik, Ivar Kristian *obstetrician, gynecologist*
Rundell, Orvis Herman, Jr., *psychologist, educator*
Russell, David L. *federal judge*
Ryan, Patrick M. *lawyer*
Savage, Susan M. *state official, former mayor*
Schroeder, David J. Dean *psychologist*
Schroyer, Michael Kevin *critical care nurse and hospital administrator*
Schwemin, Joseph *retired pharmacist*
Shao, John Jianping *finance educator*
Shillingburg, Herbert Thompson, Jr., *dental educator*
Skuta, Gregory Louis *ophthalmologist, educator*
Sorrin, Mary Louise *artist*
Spencer, Melvin Joe *health facility administrator, lawyer*
Staggs, Barbara *state representative*
Steinhorn, Irwin Harry *lawyer, educator, corporate executive*
Strecker, Al *energy executive*
Stringer, L. E. (Dean Stringer) *retired lawyer*
Sulc, Dwight George *investment advisor*
Summers, Hardy *state supreme court justice*
Taylor, Stratton *state legislator, lawyer*
Thadani, Udho *physician, cardiologist*
Thomas, Gary Wayne *actor*
Thompson, David *publishing executive*
Thompson, Mick *state commissioner*
Thompson, Ralph Gordon *federal judge*
Tibbs, Sue *state representative*
Todd, Janet Stapleton *law librarian*
Todd, Joe Lee *historian*
Tompkins, Raymond Edgar *lawyer*
Topping, Jennifer *Olympic athlete*
Trent, Luther E. *airport executive, state agency executive*
Triplett, E. Eugene *editor*
Trost, Louis Frederick, Jr., *banker, financial planner*
Troutman, George William *geologist, petroleum geological advisor*
Turner, Eugene Andrew *manufacturing executive*
Vaughn, William T *corporate financial executive*
Voth, Douglas W. *dean, educator*
Walsh, Lawrence Edward *lawyer*
Watley, Natasha *Olympic athlete*
Watt, Joseph Michael *state supreme court chief justice*
Weedn, Trish *state legislator*
Weigel, Paul Henry *biochemistry educator, researcher, consultant*
West, Lee Roy *federal judge*
Whitener, Carolyn Raye *artist*
Wickens, Donald Lee *engineer executive, consultant, rancher*
Wilcoxson, Kathleen Louise *state legislator, educator*
Wiles, Edwin McKinley *education educator, librarian*
Wilkerson, Matha Ann *oil company executive*
Williams, Richard Donald *retired wholesale food company executive*
Williamson, Marvel *dean, nursing administrator, sexologist, educator, writer*
Winchester, James R. *state supreme court justice*
Winchester, Susan *human resources specialist, state representative*
Wisdom, Peggy Jean *neurologist*
Wohleber, Robert Michael *oil industry executive*
Wolraich, Mark Lee *pediatrician, educator*
Wood, Paula Davidson *lawyer*
Woods, Pendleton *college director, author*
Worsham, Bertrand Ray *psychiatrist*
Wynn, Brenda Reneau *trade association executive*
Young, Stephen K. *academic administrator*
Zevnik-Sawatzky, Donna Dee *retired litigation coordinator*
Zhao, Wei (Wayne) *materials scientist, researcher, transmission electron microscopist*
Zhu, Hua *biochemist, researcher*
Zuhdi, Nabil (Bill Zuhdi) *lawyer, litigator, consultant, producer*
Zuhdi, Nazih *former surgeon, administrator*

Owasso
Reed, Walter George, Jr., *osteopathic physician*

Park Hill
Mankiller, Wilma Pearl *tribal leader, retired*

Pawhuska
Strahm, Samuel Edward *veterinarian*

Pawnee
Towery, Curtis Kent *lawyer*

Perry
Gard, Michael Floyd *research engineer*

Ponca City
Collins, Walter Lloyd George *editor*
Gallagher, Gary W(ayne) *educational services executive*
Gong, Xiaoyi *engineer*
Leonard, Samuel Wallace *oil company and bank executive*
Northcutt, Clarence Dewey *lawyer*
Raley, John W., Jr., *lawyer*
Rice, Sue Ann *dean, industrial and organizational psychologist*
Surber, Joe Robert *assistant superintendent*
Wann, Laymond Doyle *retired petroleum research scientist*
Wood-Warren, Maxine *artist, art educator*

Prague
Stefansen, Peggy Ann *special education educator*

Pryor
Burdick, Larry G. *school system administrator*
Stinson, Marion Dennis *lawyer, land use planner, judge*

Sallisaw
Crowson, Watie Dee *foundation administrator*

Sand Springs
Quinn, Art Jay *veterinarian, retired educator*

Sapulpa
Gardner, Dale Ray *lawyer*
Weinstock Rad, Katheryn Louise *music educator*

Seminole
Elsener, G. Dale *lawyer*
Moran, Melvin Robert *oil industry executive*

Shawnee
Hicks, Steve L. *artist, art educator*
Hill, Bryce Dale *school administrator*
Stoddard, Allan Lee *writer, musician*
Wilks, Jacquelin Holsomback *campus ministries director*
Wilks, Thomas Milton *religious studies educator, minister*
Wilson, Robert Godfrey *radiologist*

Skiatook
Harwell, Kenneth E. *chemist, researcher, consultant*

Stillwater
Agnew, Theodore Lee, Jr., *historian, educator*
Berlin, Kenneth Darrell *chemistry educator, consultant, researcher*
Case, Kenneth Eugene *industrial engineering educator*
Chung, Jong-Moon *education educator*
Confer, Anthony Wayne *veterinary pathologist, educator*
Cooper, Donald Lee *physician*
Curl, Samuel Everett *university dean, agricultural scientist*
Darcy, Robert Emmett *political scientist, educator, statistician*
Eastman, Kenneth Karl *academic administrator*
Ewing, Sidney Alton *veterinary medical educator, parasitologist*
Fischer, LeRoy Henry *historian, educator*
Fischer, Richard Samuel *lawyer*
Gasem, Khaled A.M. *chemical engineer, educator*
Gilliland, Stanley Eugene *dairy-food microbiology educator*
Grischkowsky, Daniel Richard *research scientist, educator*
Gunzenhauser, Michael Gerard *educator, researcher*
Hoberock, Lawrence Linden *mechanical engineer, educator*
Hughes, Michael *civil engineer*
Huhnke, Raymond Leroy *engineering educator*
Langwig, John Edward *retired wood science educator*
Lorenz, Michael Duane *veterinary medicine educator, dean*
Luebke, Neil Robert *philosophy educator*
Luper, Charles C. *agricultural studies educator*
Lynch, Thomas Bernard *science educator*
Maddox, Robert Nott *chemical engineer, educator*
Melcher, Ulrich Karl *biochemistry educator*
Mize, Joe Henry *industrial engineer, educator*
Moomaw, Ronald Lee *economics professor*
Mowen, John C. *business educator*
Noyes, Ronald Tacie *agricultural engineering educator*
Pagilla, Prabhakar Reddy *science educator, consultant*
Payton, Mark Edward *statistician, educator*
Poole, Richard William *economics professor*
Pritsker, Igor *mathematics professor*
Rickman, Dan Scott *economics professor*
Royer, Tom A. *entomologist, educator*
Sherman, Robert Lee, Jr., *chemist, educator*
Steindl, Frank George *economist, educator*
te Velde, Rebecca Groom *organist, music educator, composer*
Thompson, David Russell *engineering educator, academic dean*
Vestal, Theodore Merrill *education educator*
Wicksted, James Peter *physicist, educator, research scientist*

Tahlequah
Agnew, Brad *history professor*
Alexander, Grant *education educator, consultant*
Carment, Thomas Maxwell *accounting educator, consultant, researcher*
Diamantopoulos, John C.D. *mathematician, educator*
Hare, Jerry Wayne *communications executive*
Howard, James Kenton *academic administrator, journalist*
Rozell, Herbert *state legislator, construction executive*
Williams, Larry Bill *academic administrator*

Texhoma
Jackson, Paul Howard *minister*

Tinker AFB
Livingston, Douglas Mark *lawyer*

Tulsa
Abagnale, Frank William, Jr., *document security company executive*
Abbott, William Thomas *private investigator*
Angelini, Marcello *artistic director*
Arrington, John Leslie, Jr., *lawyer*
Bailey, Keith E. *petroleum pipeline company executive*
Ball, Rex Martin *urban designer, architect*
Balman, Steven K. *lawyer*
Beck, Robert James *editor, writer, economist, consultant*
Belsky, Martin Henry *law educator, lawyer*
Bender, James J. *oil industry executive*
Bender, John Henry, Jr., (Jack Bender) *editor, cartoonist*
Berlin, Steven Ritt *oil company executive*
Biolchini, Robert Fredrick *lawyer*
Blais, Roger Nathaniel *physics educator*
Bowman, David Wesley *lawyer*
Braumiller, Allen Spooner *oil and gas exploration company executive, geologist*
Brian, Tom J. *psychologist, director*
Broach, David E. *architectural firm executive*
Brooker, Timothy Douglas *social studies educator*
Brunk, Samuel Frederick *oncologist*
Bryant, Hubert Hale *lawyer*
Busch, Daniel Adolph *geologist, educator*
Buthod, Mary Clare *school administrator*
Cadieux, Chester *gas industry executive*
Calvert, Jon Channing *physician, department chairman*
Carpenter, Nancy J. *health science association administrator*
Carter, Terry *gas industry executive*
Chappel, Donald R. *petroleum pipeline company executive*
Cherry, Andrew Lawrence, Jr., *social work educator, researcher*
Chung, I-Ping *mechanical engineer*
Clark, Gary Carl *lawyer*
Clark, Joseph Francis, Jr., *lawyer*
Cobbs, James Harold *engineer, consultant*
Cook, Harold Dale *federal judge*
Cooper, Richard Casey *lawyer*
Cottingham, Barbara J. *music educator*
Cox, William Jackson *retired bishop*
Crawford, B. *lawyer*
Crouch, Gary Clinton *financial management company executive, accountant*
Davenport, Gerald Bruce *lawyer*
Davis, Lourie Irene Bell *computer education and information systems specialist*
Deihl, Michael Allen *federal agency administrator*
de Leon, Antonio Carmelo, Jr., *retired internist, cardiologist*
Dimiceli, Vincent Edward *mathematician, educator*
Donaldson, Robert Herschel *university administrator, educator*
Dotson, George Stephen *drilling company executive*
Eagleton, Edward John *lawyer*
Earlougher, Robert Charles, Sr., *petroleum engineer*
Eaton, Leonard James, Jr., *aerospace executive*
Eldridge, Richard Mark *lawyer*
Ellerbach, Susan *editor*
Engel, David Wayne *lawyer, federal official*
Faingold, Eduardo Daniel *language and linguistics educator, researcher*
Farrell, John L., Jr., *lawyer, business executive*
Fleifil, Mahmoud Mohamed *acoustical engineer, researcher*
Fleming, Ken *publishing executive*
Frazier, Mary Ann *artist*
Frey, Martin Alan *lawyer, educator*
Friedman, Mark Joel *cardiologist, educator*
Gaberino, John Anthony, Jr., *lawyer*
Gentry, Bern Leon, Sr., *minority consulting company executive*
Goodman, Jerry L(ynn) *judge*
Gottschalk, Sister Mary Therese *nun, hospital administrator*
Gotwals, Charles Place, Jr., *lawyer*
Gray, Karen Kay *counselor*
Gregg, Lawrence J. *physician*
Guthrie, Joseph Randall *music educator*
Haring, Robert Westing *newspaper editor*
Hatfield, Jack Kenton *lawyer, accountant*
Healey, David Lee *investment company executive*
Helmerich, Walter Hugo, III, *oil company executive*
Hess, Stanley O. *retired art educator*
Hildebrand, Steven B. *automobile rental company*
Holmes, Sven Erik *federal judge, educator*
Horkey, William Richard *retired diversified oil company executive*
Howard, Gene Claude *lawyer, retired state senator*
Huffman, Robert Allen, Jr., *lawyer*
Imel, John Michael *lawyer*
Imhoff, Pamela M. *marketing educator*
Ingram, Charles Clark, Jr., *energy company executive*
Johnson, Cornelius Raymond *assistant city attorney*
Jones, Jenk, Jr., *editor, educator*
Jones, Michael Lynn *financial consultant, branch operations manager*
Kaiser, George B. *corporate financial executive*
Kalbfleisch, John McDowell *cardiologist, educator*
Kern, Terry C. *judge*
Kihle, Donald Arthur *lawyer*
Kitchen, Brent A. *airport executive*
Kneale, James C. *gas company executive*
Korstad, John Edward *biology professor*
Kronfeld, Edwin *natural gas company executive*
Kyle, David L. *gas industry executive*
LaFortune, Bill *mayor*
Lang, Andrew Stuart Ian Donald *mathematician, consultant*
Larkin, Moscelyne *retired artistic director, dancer*
Lawless, Robert William *academic administrator*
Lewis, Corinne Hemeter *psychotherapist, educator*
Liebendorfer, Richard Arthur *internist*
Liggitt, Lonnie Robert *music educator, researcher*
Lorton, Robert E., Jr., *publishing executive*
Luthey, Graydon Dean, Jr., *lawyer, educator*
Madison, Eddie Lawrence, Jr., *public relations consultant, editor, writer*
Malcolm, Steven J. *petroleum pipeline company executive*
Marlar, Donald Floyd *lawyer*
Marshall-Chapman, Paula *food products executive*
McCall, Charles Barnard *health facility administrator, educator*
McCarthy, Jack D. *oil industry executive*
McCullough, Robert Dale, II, *osteopath*
Medina, J. Michael *lawyer, educator*
Mojtabai, Ann Grace *author, educator*
Moody, George Walter *aviation executive*
Munro, Michael Donald *air transportation executive, retired military officer*
Narwold, Lewis Lammers, Jr., *paper products manufacturer*
Neas, John Theodore *investment company executive*
Nettles, John Barnwell *obstetrics and gynecology educator*
Nevinny-Stickel, Hans Boris *oncologist*
O'Meilia, David E. *lawyer*
Osborn, La Donna Carol *clergywoman*
Owens, Jana Jae *entertainer*
Plunket, Daniel Clark *pediatrician, department chairman*
Price, Alice Lindsay *writer*
Raynolds, William F., II, *lawyer*
Reed, Robert A. *performing arts executive*
Rex, Lonnie Royce *religious organization administrator*
Roberts, Oral (Granville Oral Roberts) *clergyman*
Roger, Jerry Lee *academic administrator*
Saied, James Guy *conductor, consultant*
St. George, Sheryl Lea *air transportation executive, writer*
Sanditen, Edgar Richard *investment company executive*
Say, Burhan *physician*
Seymour, Stephanie Kulp *federal judge*
Sherburn, Eric W. *neurosurgeon*
Shurley, Jay Talmadge *writer, retired psychiatrist, medical educator, administrator, behavioral scientist, polar explorer, genealogist*
Slaucitajs, Andrew Paul *videographer, video producer*
Slicker, Frederick Kent *lawyer*
Smith, Betty Gene *physical education educator*
Sneed, James Lynde *lawyer*
Sotak, John Joseph *priest, educator*
Sowell, Debra Ann Olson *mathematician, educator, academic administrator*
Sowell, Laven *retired music educator*
Steltzlen, Janelle Hicks *lawyer*
Strecker, David Eugene *lawyer*
Taylor, Joe Clinton *judge*
Thomas, Robert Eggleston *retired corporate executive*
Trennepohl, Gary Lee *university administrator, finance educator*
Upton, Howard B., Jr., *writer, lawyer*
Vetal, Bradley S. *service company executive*
Vincent, Carl G., Jr., *real estate portfolio manager*
Warren, W. K., Jr., *oil industry executive*
Watson, Eric N. *corporate executive*
Williams, John Horter *civil engineer, oil, gas, telecommunications and allied products distribution company executive*
Williams, Penny *state legislator*
Wood, Emily Churchill *special education educator, social studies educator, consultant*
Worley, Joe *editor*
Wortmann, Dorothy Woodward *physician*

Vinita
Johnston, Oscar Black, III, *lawyer*
Lollman, Matthew Tobias *music educator*
Neer, Charles Sumner, II, *orthopedic surgeon, educator*
Wright, Jo Anne *Episcopal priest*

Warr Acres
Engle, Richard Victor *publishing executive*
Phillips, Richard Carey *real estate executive*

Weatherford
Aspedon, Mary D. *education educator*
Strickler, Steve P *theater educator*
Widen, Dennis Charles *music educator*
Wolgamott, Gary Dean *medical educator*

Welling
Varner, Joyce Ehrhardt *retired librarian*

Wewoka
Rains, Mary Jo *banker*
Trimble, Vance Henry *retired newspaper editor*

Wilburton
Pate, Thomas Lowell *manufacturing executive*

Woodward
Fisher, Deena Kaye *social studies education administrator*

Yukon
Hixson, Wendell Mark *lawyer*

OREGON

Albany
Chowning, Orr-Lyda Brown *dietician*
Smart, Ann Catherine *dean*
White, Diane O'Donnell *retired librarian*
Wood, Kenneth Arthur *retired editor, writer*

Aloha
Gorea, Lucia-Iosefina *English educator, writer, poet*

Ashland
Addicott, Warren Oliver *retired geologist, educator*
Appel, Libby Eve *theater director*
Backus, John *computer scientist*
Bornet, Vaughn Davis *former social science educator, research historian*
Christianson, Roger Gordon *biology professor, department chairman*
Espinoza, Edgard O'Niel *forensic chemist*
Goddard, Kenneth William *forensic scientist, writer*
Grover, James Robb *chemist, editor*
Kostka, Robert Anton *artist, educator*
Kreisman, Arthur *higher education consultant, humanities educator emeritus*
Levy, Leonard Williams *history professor, writer*
Masters, Robert Edward Lee *psychotherapist, neural researcher, human potential educator, philosopher*
Meese, Celia Edwards *pharmaceutical company executive*
Morris, Daniel Robert *language educator*
Mularz, Theodore Leonard *architect*
Risser, James Vaulx, Jr., *journalist, educator*

Astoria
Foster, Michael William *librarian*
Haskell, Donald McMillan *lawyer*
Holcom, Floyd Everett *international business consultant*

Bandon
Lindquist, Louis William *artist, researcher, writer*
Millard, Esther Lound *foundation administrator, educator*

Beatty
Nettelbeck, Fred Arthur *poet*

Beaverton
Austin, Glenn *retired pediatrician, medical researcher*
Blair, Donald W. *shoe manufacturing company executive*
Carter, James C. *apparel executive, lawyer*
Cassidy, Richard Arthur *environmental engineer, governmental water resources specialist*
Chartier, Vernon Lee *electrical engineer*
Clarke, Thomas E. *apparel executive*
Cohen, Stuart F. *software development company executive*
Deckert, Ryan P. *state senator*
de Sá e Silva, Elizabeth Anne *secondary school educator*
Dinh, Thin Van *electronics specialist*
Edlich, Richard French *biomedical engineering educator*
Fisher, K. Kimball *human resources specialist, consultant*
Hall, Howard Pickering *engineering and mathematics educator*
Harold, Robert *apparel executive*
Knight, Philip H(ampson) *apparel executive*
Liu, Kevin H. *research scientist, software architect*
Meyer, Jerome J. *diversified technology company executive*
Pond, Patricia Brown *library science educator, university administrator*
Ray, Ruth Alice Yancey *retired rancher, real estate developer*
Stewart, Kirk T. *public relations executive*
Timmins, Timothy A. *telecommunications industry executive*
Torvalds, Linus (Benedict) *application developer*
Vancil, Bernard K. *research and development company executive, physicist*
von Linsowe, Marina Dorothy *information systems consultant*
Wang, Baoliang (Bob Wang) *applications scientist, researcher*
Wills, Richard H. *electronics manufacturing executive*

Bend
Babcock, Walter Christian, Jr., *membrane company executive*
Brundage, Bruce Howard *cardiologist*
Collins, Sally Duke *forest service manager*
Connolly, Brian Anthony *writer*
Crampton, George Harris *neuroscientist, retired military officer*
Evers-Williams, Myrlie *cultural organization administrator*
Fain, Jay Lindsey *brokerage house executive, consultant*
Gillem, Elise (Elise Michaels) *radio and television personality*
Irwin, Kerri Lynne *pharmacist, writer, small business owner*
Loewenthal, Nessa Parker *intercultural communications consultant*
Moss, Patricia L. *bank executive*
Nosler, Robert Amos *sports company executive*
Seed, Brian Bruce *music educator*
Thow, George Bruce *surgeon*
Wonser, Michael Dean *retired public affairs director, art history educator*

Brookings
Hinton, Floyd *lawyer*
Maxwell, William Stirling *retired lawyer*
Shepherd, William Michael *music educator, musician*

Burns
Timms, Eugene Dale *wholesale business owner, state senator*

Canby
Drummond, Gerard Kasper *lawyer, retired minerals company executive*
Flinn, Roberta Jeanne *management, computer applications consultant*
Jarvey, Paulette Sue *publishing executive*

Cannon Beach
Greaver, Harry *artist*
Hellyer, Constance Anne (Connie Anne Conway) *writer, musician*

Central Point
Brown, Christopher Patrick *health care administrator, educator*
Ingraham, Laura *lawyer, political commentator*
Richardson, Dennis Michael *lawyer, educator*

Cheshire
Antikajian, Sarkis Serop *artist, retired pharmacist*

Chiloquin
Harreld, Karen L. *jewelry designer, photographer*
Lane, Colette Marie *writer*
Reed, David George *entrepreneur*

Clackamas
Etulain, Richard Wayne *historian, educator*
Woods, Dennis Oliver *headmaster, market and political research analyst*

Coos Bay
Messerle, Kenneth C. *state senator*

Coquille
Lounsbury, Steven Richard *lawyer*

Corvallis
Achterman, Gail Louise *lawyer*
Arnold, Roy Gary *academic administrator*
Baird, William McKenzie *chemical carcinogenesis researcher, biochemistry educator*
Birdseye, Thomas Earl *freelance/self-employed writer*
Byrne, John Vincent *higher education consultant*
Campbell, Courtney Scott *humanities educator*
Castle, Emery Neal *agricultural and resource economist, educator*
Chambers, Kenton Lee *botany educator*
Clinton, Richard Lee *international relations educator*
Coffin, Chris *managing editor*
Conatser, Brian Keith *music educator, musician*
Dalrymple, Gary Brent *research geologist*
Davis, John Rowland *university administrator*
Dennis, John Davison *minister*
Dougherty, William G. *microbiologist, educator*
Drake, Charles Whitney *physicist*
Engelbrecht, Rudolf *electrical engineering educator*
Forbes, Leonard *engineering educator*
Frakes, Rodney Vance *plant geneticist, educator*
Gillis, John Simon *psychologist, educator*
Hall, Don Alan *editor, writer*
Harter, Lafayette George, Jr., *retired economics educator*
Healey, Deborah Lynn *education administrator*
Huyer, Adriana *oceanographer, educator*
Karplus, Paul Andrew *biochemistry educator*
Landers, Teresa Price *librarian*
Loper, Joyce E. *plant pathologist, educator*
Lubchenco, Jane *marine biologist, educator*
Mathews, Christopher King *biochemist, educator*
McCarthy, William Robert *minister*
McKee-Ryan, Frances M. *education educator*
McKinney, William Mark *retired geology educator*
Morita, Richard Yukio *microbiology and oceanography educator*
Oldfield, James Edmund *nutrition educator*
Parker, Donald Fred *college dean, human resources management educator*
Parks, Harold Raymond *mathematician, educator*
Pinkerton, John N. *plant pathologist*
Poinar, George Orlo, Jr., *insect pathologist and paleontologist, educator*
Rose, Robert William, Jr., (Robin Rose) *forest regeneration scientist, educator*
Shiue, Wen-Tsong *electrical and computer scientist, educator*
Sleight, Arthur William *chemist, educator*
Steele, Robert Edwin *orthopedic surgeon*
Temes, Gabor Charles *electrical engineering educator*
Van Holde, Kensal Edward *biochemistry educator*
Verts, Lita Jeanne *university administrator*
Westwood, Melvin Neil *horticulturist, pomologist*
Whanger, Philip Daniel *biochemistry educator and researcher, nutrition educator*
Wilkins, Caroline Hanke *consumer agency administrator, political worker*
Yeats, Robert Sheppard *geologist, educator*
Young, Roy Alton *university administrator, educator*
Yu, Shiao-ling S. *humanities educator*
Zwahlen, Fred Casper, Jr., *journalism educator*

Cove
Kerper, Meike *family violence, sex abuse and addiction educator, consultant*

Culver
Siebert, Diane Dolores *author, poet*

Dallas
Calkins, Loren Gene *religious organization administrator, pastor*
White, Donald Harvey *physics educator emeritus*

Dayton
McKaughan, Howard Paul *linguistics educator*

Depoe Bay
Blacketer, James Richard *artist*

Eugene
Acker, Martin Herbert *psychotherapist, educator*
Aldave, Barbara Bader *law educator, lawyer*
Bailey, Exine Margaret Anderson *soprano, educator*
Baker, Alton Fletcher, III, *newspaper editor, publishing executive*
Baker, Bridget Downey *publishing executive*
Bascom, Ruth F. *retired mayor*
Bergquist, Peter *music educator emeritus*
Bergquist, Timothy M. *business educator, researcher*
Biglan, Anthony *medical educator*
Camp, Delpha Jeanne *counselor*
Castenholz, Richard William *ecologist, researcher, educator*
Chambers, Carolyn Silva *communications company executive*
Chaney, James Alan *construction company executive*
Collis, Dennis K. *orthopedic surgeon*
Cone, June Elizabeth *civic worker*
Crasemann, Bernd *physicist, researcher*
Csonka, Paul L. *theoretical physicist, educator*
Davis, Richard Malone *economics professor*
Donnelly, Russell James *physicist, researcher*
DuPriest, Douglas Millhollen *lawyer*
Edwards, Ralph M. *librarian*
Flanagan, Latham, Jr., *surgeon*
Freyd, Jennifer Joy *psychology educator*
Frohnmayer, David Braden *academic administrator*
Gall, Meredith Damien (Meredith Mark Damien Gall) *education educator, writer*
Green, Paul John *critic*
Griffith, Osbie Hayes *chemistry professor*
Gwartney, Patricia Anne *sociology educator*
Hogan, Michael R(obert) *judge*
Horn, John Harold *lawyer*
Jewell, Mark Laurence *plastic surgeon*
Jiler, Linda Cerise *retired fire and aviation program support specialist, fire emergency dispatcher, consultant, researcher, writer*
Kennevan, Walter James *computer science educator*
Khang, Chulsoon *economics professor*
Kirkpatrick, Laird Clifford *law educator*
Lindholm, Richard Theodore *economics and finance educator*
Littman, Richard Anton *psychologist, educator*
Loescher, Richard Alvin *gastroenterologist*
Lowry, Robert Dudley *lawyer*
Lukacs, John Robert *anthropologist, educator*
Majdic, Michael James *film producer, director*
Matthews, Brian W. *molecular biology educator*
Mazo, Robert Marc *retired chemistry educator*
Meyer, Alan Downing *management educator*
Mikesell, Raymond French *economics professor*
Miner, John Burnham *industrial relations educator, writer*
Moseley, John Travis *university administrator, research physicist*
Mumford, William Porter, II, *retired lawyer*
Newton, Julianne H *education educator, photographer*
Pascal, C(ecil) Bennett *classics educator*
Peterson, Donna Rae *gerontologist*
Pickett, Stephen Wesley *academic administrator, consultant*
Piele, Philip Kern *education infosystems educator*
Retallack, Gregory John *geologist, educator*
Roe, Thomas Leroy Willis *pediatrician*
Sanders, Jack Thomas *religious studies educator*
Schellman, John A. *chemistry professor*
Scoles, Eugene Francis *law educator, lawyer*
Sisley, Becky Lynn *physical education educator*
Theodoropoulos, Christine O. *architecture educator*
Tobin, Tary Jeanne *educational consultant, researcher*
Torrey, James D. *mayor, communications executive, consultant*
Tykeson, Donald Erwin *broadcast executive*
Upham, Steadman *academic administrator, anthropologist, educator*
Utsey, Glenda Fravel *architecture educator*
Vacchi, Steve *music educator*
Viles, Andrew Michael *English language educator*
von Hippel, Peter Hans *chemistry educator, molecular biology researcher*
Warpinski, Terri L. *academic administrator, artist*
Wickes, George *English literature educator, writer*
Wilhelm, Kate (Katy Gertrude) *author*
Wilson, Jackman Lee *editor*
Womack, James Errol *college president*
Woolley, Donna Pearl *lumber company executive*
Youngquist, Walter Lewellyn *geologist, consultant*

Fairview
Blodgett, Forrest Clinton *economics professor*
Muller jr., Thomas G *music educator*

Florence
Ericksen, Jerald Laverne *retired engineering scientist, educator*
Marble, Duane Francis *geography educator, researcher*
Van Horn, O. Frank *retired counselor, consultant*

Forest Grove
Boersema, David Brian *philosopher, educator*
Burch-Pesses, Thomas Michael *music educator*
Carson, William Morris *manpower planning and development advisor*
Coleman, Deborah Ann *electronics company executive*

Gladstone
Beals, Herbert Kyle *community planner, historian, consultant*

Gold Hill
Barron, (Richard) Neil *librarian*

Grants Pass
Adams, Brady *bank executive, former state legislator*
Baker, Lindi L. *lawyer*
Roberts, Susan Sturgeon *art educator, writer*
Sloan, William Marshall *lawyer*
Smith, Barnard Elliot *management educator*

Gresham
Light, Betty Jensen Pritchett *former college dean*
Vela, Joel E. *college president*

Hebo
Kesey, Jimmy Marvin *counselor, writer*

Hillsboro
Abtin, Keyvan *neurosurgeon*
Barnes, Keith Lee *electronics executive*
Daim, Tugrul Unsal *technology management specialist, educator*
Dyess, Kirby A. *computer company executive*
Ferguson, James Clarke *mathematician, algorithmist*
Furse, Elizabeth *former congresswoman, small business owner*
Matlock, John Hudson *science administrator, materials engineer*
Pixley, Carl Preston *mathematician*
Sharp, Steven *information technology executive*
Venkatesan, Raguraman *computer engineer*

Jacksonville
Hennion, Reeve Lawrence *communications executive*
Langworthy, William Clayton *college official*

John Day
Tuttle, Kenneth Lewis *engineering educator, consultant*

Joseph
Gilbert, David Erwin *retired academic administrator, physicist*

Junction City
Stong, John Elliott *retail music and electronic company executive*

Keizer
Kenyon, Carleton Weller *librarian*

Klamath Falls
Dow, Martha Anne *biology professor*
Hoggarth, Karen *lumber company executive*
Klepper, Carol Herdman *mental health therapist*
Koch, Margaret Rau *writer, artist, historian*
Korson, Victoria Lynn *writer*
Novak, James F. *physician*
Taylor, Gregory Alwin *coast guard officer, engineer*
Wendt, Roderick C. *manufacturing executive*
Woodall, David Monroe *research engineer, dean*

La Grande
Woodward, Ralph Frederick, Jr., *elementary school educator, consultant, education educator*

Lake Oswego
Bruce, John Allen *foundation executive, educator*
Byczynski, Edward Frank *lawyer, financial executive*
Campbell, Colin Herald *former mayor*
Edstrom, Pam *public relations executive*
Gehrig, Edward Harry *electrical engineer, consultant*
Hutchens, Tyra Thornton *physician, educator*
Kuntz, Joel Dubois *lawyer*
Lenderman, Joanie *elementary school educator*
McPeak, Merrill Anthony *business executive, consultant, retired officer*
Miller, Barbara Stallcup *development consultant*
Mylnechuk, Larry Herbert *financial executive*
Parrick, Gerald Hathaway *communications and marketing executive*
Pearson, Conrad E. *financial services executive*
Rasmussen, Richard Robert *lawyer*
Tammen, Ronald *international politics educator*
Thong, Tran *biomedical company executive*
Tyler, Darlene Jasmer *retired dietitian*
Zorkin, Melissa Waggener *public relations executive*

Lincoln City
Arant, Eugene Wesley *lawyer*
Daves, Glenn Doyle, Jr., *science educator, chemist, researcher*
Decker, Mary Duryea *volunteer, educator, retired social worker*
Morrow, James Thomas *energy executive*

Lorane
Plēsums, Guntis *architect, retired educator*

Lyons
Acuff, L. (Lewis) Steven *nutritionist, educator*

Madras
Ramsey, Jarold William *English language educator, author*

Mcminnville
Bull, Vivian Ann *college president*
Lane, Larry K. *air industry service executive*
Naylor-Jackson, Jerry *public relations consultant, retired, entertainer, broadcaster*
Nelson, Donna Gayle *state representative*
Walker, Charles Urmston *retired university president*

Medford
Carter, William G. *lawyer*
Deatherage, William Vernon *lawyer*
De Boer, Sydney B. *auto dealership executive*
Dixon, Andrew Derart *retired academic administrator*
Drysdale, John Edwin *retired music educator, performing arts association administrator, director*
Frost, Orcutt William *historian, educator*
Heimann, M.L. "Dick" *auto dealership executive*
Hellemose, Aage *minister*
Hennion, Carolyn Laird (Lyn Hennion) *investment executive*
Horton, Lawrence Stanley *electrical engineer, apartment developer*
O'Connor, Karl William (Goodyear Johnson) *lawyer*
Rogers, Gardner Spencer *railroad company executive*
Schubert, Ruth Carol Hickok *artist, educator*
Shekhar, Stephen S. *obstetrician, gynecologist*
Skelton, Douglas H. *architect*
Smith, Robert F. (Bob Smith) *rancher, former congressman*
Sours, James Kingsley *association executive, former college president*
Straus, David A. *architectural firm executive*
Tracy, Harold Dewayne *retired secondary school educator*

Milton Freewater
Gipson, Stephen Richard *journalist, construction executive*

Milwaukie
Eichinger, Marilynne Hildegarde *museum administrator*
Orloff, Barbara-Lee Marguerite Hewitt *social worker*
Sklovsky, Robert Joel *naturopathic physician, pharmacist, educator*

Monmouth
Balke, Frank H. *language educator, director*
Dunn, Doris Marjory *retired educator, volunteer*

Myrtle Point
Walsh, Don *marine consultant, executive*

Newberg
Adams, Wayne Verdun *pediatric psychologist, educator*
Austin, Joan D. *personal care industry executive*
Campbell, Douglas G. *art educator*
Corning, Caitlin *historian, educator*
Hockett, Betty May *writer, educator*
Johnson, Thomas Floyd *former academic administrator, educator*
Keith, Pauline Mary *artist, illustrator, writer*
McMahon, Paul Francis *finance company executive*
Tsohantaridis, Timotheos *minister, religion educator*

Newport
Gilhooly, David James, III, *artist*

North Plains
Wood, James Anderson *cardiac surgeon*

Oakland
Smelt, Ronald *retired air transportation executive*

Oceanside
Wadlow, Joan Krueger *retired academic administrator, construction executive*

Odell
Garcia, David *agricultural products executive*
Girardelli, Ronald K. *food products executive*

Ontario
Tyler, Donald Earl *urologist*

Oregon City
Baratto, Stefan *mathematics professor*
Burke, William Romney *urologist*
McFarland, Carol Anne *lawyer*

Otter Rock
Eaton, Leonard Kimball *retired architecture educator*

Pendleton
Grover, Dorys C. *English educator*
Klepper, Elizabeth Lee *physiologist*
Reeder, Clinton Bruce *economist, public policy consultant, farmer*
Rew, Lawrence Boyd *lawyer*
Smiley, Richard Wayne *researcher*
Williams-Steinwender, Karin Mae *artist*

Phoenix
Dodd, Darlene Mae *retired nurse, retired military officer*

Port Orford
Drinnon, Richard *retired history educator*

Portland
Abrams, Marc *lawyer, state political party executive*
Abravanel, Allan Ray *lawyer*
Ahuja, Jagdish Chand *mathematics professor*
Ainsilie, Coln Dayle *retired music educator*
Albright, Robert James *electrical engineering educator*
Allen, Rex Whitaker *retired architect*
Anderson, Herbert Hatfield *lawyer, farmer*
Anderson, Mark Alexander *lawyer*
Arnold, Ralph Leo, III, *valuation analyst, consultant*
Arthur, Michael Elbert *lawyer, financial advisor*
Backlar, Byron *lawyer*
Bacon, Vicky Lee *lighting services executive*
Bailey, Robert C. *opera company executive*
Baker, Diane R.H. *dermatologist*
Bardana, Emil John, Jr., *allergist, immunologist, internist*
Barkhuizen, Andre *academic rheumatologist*
Barmack, Neal Herbert *neuroscientist*
Barry, John Maynard *urologist*
Bartlett, Thomas Alva *retired educational administrator*
Bartley, Murray Hill *retired dental educator*
Baughman, Pauline Clara *librarian*
Bauman, Frank Anthony *retired lawyer*
Beatty, John Cabeen, Jr., *judge*
Becker, Bruce Douglas *mechanical engineer*
Bennett, Charles Leon *vocational and graphic arts educator*
Bennett, William Michael *internist, nephrologist, educator*
Berentsen, Kurtis George *music educator, choral conductor*
Bernstine, Daniel O'Neal *law educator, university president*
Berthelsdorf, Siegfried *psychiatrist*
Bhatia, Peter K. *newspaper editor, journalist*
Birmingham, Patrick Michael *lawyer*
Blachly, Beverly Jean *retired vocational and insurance consultant*
Blank, Eugene *pediatrician, radiologist, educator*
Bloom, Joseph D. *medical educator, psychiatrist*
Blumberg, Naomi *symphony musician, educator*
Blumel, Joseph Carlton *university president*
Boly, Jeffrey Elwyn *retired lawyer*
Bosch, Samuel Henry *computer company executive*
Bottomly, Therese *editor*
Bouchard, Joan C. *nursing association administrator*
Boulot, Philippe *chef*
Bovarnick, Paul Simon *lawyer*
Boyle, Gertrude *sportswear company executive*
Braun, Stephen Baker *academic administrator*
Brenneman, Delbert Jay *lawyer*
Brewin, Michael K. *writer, publisher, musician*
Brown, James Chandler *retired education educator*
Browne, Joseph Peter *retired librarian*
Buckstein, Steve *think-tank executive*
Bunza, Linda Hathaway *editor, writer, composer, institution director*
Burris, Terry Eugene *ophthalmologist, corneal specialist*
Cable, John Franklin *lawyer*
Canaday, Richard A. *lawyer*
Canfield, James *artistic director*
Cantelon, John Edward *retired university chancellor*
Cassard, Christopher D. *lumber company executive*
Chevis, Cheryl Ann *lawyer*
Claycomb, Cecil Keith *biochemist, educator*
Clemens, Charles Joseph *retired insurance agent*
Clinton, Jack W. *dean*
Cogan, Arnold M. *planning consultant*
Collins, Maribeth Wilson *foundation president*
Conkling, Roger Linton *management consultant, business administration educator, retired utilities executive*
Connor, William Elliott *physician, educator*
Cookson, Peter Willis, Jr., *sociologist, writer*
Cooper, Ginnie *library director*
Corbett, Alice Catherine *investor*
Cox, Joseph William *former academic administrator, education educator*
Crabbs, Roger Alan *publisher, consultant, small business owner, educator, military officer*
Crawshaw, Ralph *psychiatrist*
Crowell, John B., Jr., *lawyer, former government official*
Daescu, Dacian N. *mathematics professor*
Daniels, Antonio *professional basketball player*
Davis, James Allan *gerontologist, educator*
DeChaine, Dean Dennis *lawyer*
Deering, Thomas Phillips *retired lawyer*
Denhart, Gun *direct mail order company executive*
DePreist, James Anderson *conductor*
Dinh, Hoat Khang *mechanical engineer, educator*
Diver, Colin S. *academic administrator, educator*
Dolan, William J. *media executive*
Donegan, Mark *metal products executive*
Dotten, Michael Chester *lawyer*
Dow, Mary Alexis *auditor*
Drinkward, Cecil W. *construction company executive*
Druker, Brian Jay *medical educator, researcher*
Dunleavy, Michael Joseph *professional basketball coach*
Dunn, Randall L. *federal judge*
Eakin, Margaretta Morgan *lawyer*
Edmunson, James L. *political organization administrator*
Eifler, Mark Anthony *historian, educator*
English, Stephen Francis *lawyer*
Epperson, Eric Robert *company executive, film producer*
Eshelman, William Robert *librarian, editor*
Faller, Thompson Mason *philosophy educator*
Fenner, Peter David *communications executive*
Feuerstein, Howard M. *lawyer*
Finch, Rob *photographer*
Finley, Lewis Merren *financial consultant*
Flowerree, Robert Edmund *retired forest products company executive*
Foley, Ridgway Knight, Jr., *lawyer, writer*
Forsberg, Charles Alton *computer, information systems engineer*
Franklin, Dolores Roberts *elementary school educator*
Franzke, Richard Albert *lawyer*
Frasca, Robert John *architect*
Fraunfelder, Frederick Theodore *ophthalmologist, educator*
Freeman, Sarah Elisabeth *poet, literature and language educator*
Frisbee, Don Calvin *retired utilities executive*
Fritz, Barbara Jean *occupational health nurse*
Frolick, Patricia Mary *retired elementary school educator*
Frye, Helen Jackson *federal judge*
Galbraith, John Robert *insurance company executive*
Gillette, Richard Gareth *neurophysiology educator, researcher*
Glasgow, Robert Efrom *lawyer*
Goldfarb, Timothy Moore *hospital administrator*
Gordly, Avel Louise *state legislator, community activist*
Greenlick, Merwyn Ronald *health services researcher*
Greer, Monte Arnold *endocrinologist, educator*
Griggs, Gail *former marketing executive*
Grossmann, Ronald Stanyer *lawyer*
Guderian, Ronald Howard *pathologist*
Guillen, Jerome *trucking executive*
Gunsul, Brooks R. W. *architect*
Hacker, Thomas Owen *architect*
Hagenstein, William David *forester, consultant*
Hammond, George Simms *chemist, consultant*
Hanlon, Michael Gregory *lawyer*
Hanna, Harry Mitchell *lawyer*
Harnden, Edwin A. *lawyer*
Harrell, Gary Paul *lawyer*
Harris, Charles David *music educator*
Hart, John Edward *lawyer*
Hatfield, Mark Odom *former senator*
Hedges, Jerris *medical educator, health services researcher*
Helmer, M(artha) Christie *lawyer*
Hergenhan, Kenneth William *lawyer*
Higdon, Polly Susanne *federal judge*
Hill, James Edward *insurance company executive*
Hinckley, Gregory Keith *software industry executive*
Hirshon, Robert Edward *lawyer*
Holman, Donald Reid *retired lawyer*
Holtz, Andrew *health care journalist*
Hooker, Elaine Norton *news executive*
Houser, Douglas Guy *lawyer*
Hribernick, Paul R. *lawyer*
Huffman, James Lloyd *law educator*
Hull, Samuel Logan, Jr., *theater educator*
Jacob, Stanley Wallace *surgeon, educator*
Jarvis, Peter R. *lawyer*
Jarvis, Richard S. *academic administrator*
Jenkins, Donald John *museum administrator*
Johansen, Judith A. *lawyer*
Johnson, H. Thomas *business educator*
Johnston, David Frederick *lawyer*
Johnston, Richard C. *newspaper editor*
Johnston, Virginia Evelyn *retired editor*
Jolles, Bernard *lawyer*
Jones, Robert Edward *federal judge*
Josephson, Richard Carl *lawyer*
Julien, Robert Michael *anesthesiologist, writer*
Kanter, Stephen *law educator, dean*
Karant-Nunn, Susan Catherine *history educator*
Katz, Vera *mayor, former college administrator, state legislator*
Kendall, John Walker, Jr., *medical educator, researcher, university dean*
Kennedy, Jack Leland *lawyer*
Kennedy, R(obert) Evan *engineering executive, consultant, retired structural engineer*
Kester, Randall Blair *lawyer*
Khalil, Mohammad Aslam Khan *environmental science and engineering educator, physics educator*
Kilbourn, Lee Ferris *architect, specfications writer*
King, John G. *health service administrator*
Kirschner, Marc Alan *neuroscientist*
Kitzhaber, John Albert *former governor, emergency physician, former state senator*
Kleim, E. Denise *city official*
Kleszynski, Kenneth *music educator, conductor*
Koblik, Steven S. *academic administrator*
Kocaoglu, Dundar F. *engineering management educator, industrial and civil engineer*
Kohl, Steve *pediatrician, infectious disease physician*
Kohler, Peter Ogden *internist, educator, academic administrator*
Kolmes, Steven Albert *biologist, educator*
Krahmer, Donald Leroy, Jr., *lawyer*
Kupel, Frederick John *business services executive*
Kyles-Omari, Cynthia Lee *editor, career consultant*
Lall, B. Kent *civil engineer, educator*
Lambert, Richard William *retired mathematics professor*
Lang, Philip David *former state legislator, insurance company executive*
Langrock, Karl Frederick *former academic administrator*
Larson, Wanda Z. *writer, poet*
Larsson, William Dean *manufacturing executive*
Layman, Charles Donald *plastic surgeon*
Leavy, Edward *federal judge*
Leineweber, Peter Anthony *forest products company executive*
Leupp, Edythe Peterson *retired education educator*
Lewis, Kenneth *shipping executive*
Li, Fu *electrical engineering educator, editor*
Lilly, Elizabeth Giles *small business owner*
Lincoln, Sandra Eleanor *chemistry professor*
Livingston, Louis Bayer *lawyer*
Lorenz, Nancy *artist*
Love, Edith Holmes *theater producer*
Love, William Edward *lawyer*
Lusky, John Anderson *lawyer*
MacArthur, Carol Jeanne *pediatric otolaryngology educator*
Maloney, Robert E., Jr., *lawyer*
Mapes, Jeffrey Robert *journalist*
Marker, Carl W. *diversified financial services company executive*
Marsh, Malcolm F. *federal judge*
Martin, Lucy Z. *public relations executive*
Matarazzo, Harris Starr *lawyer*
Matarazzo, Joseph Dominic *psychologist, educator*
Matarazzo, Ruth Gadbois *psychologist, educator*
Matejuk, Agata *immunologist*
Mazzola, Michael *lighting designer*
McClave, Donald Silsbee *academic administrator*
McCormick, William Charles *manufacturing executive*
Mendelson, Lottie M. *retired pediatric nurse practitioner, writer*
Miller, William Richey, Jr., *lawyer*
Milton, Catherine Higgs *social service entrepreneur*
Mittelstaedt, Janet Rugen *music educator, composer*
Mooney, Michael Joseph *college president*
Moore, Thomas Scott *lawyer*
Moorhead, John Couper *emergency physician*
Mosman, Michael W. *prosecutor*
Mowe, Gregory Robert *lawyer*
Nokes, John Richard *retired newspaper editor, writer*
Noonan, William Donald *lawyer, physician*
Olson, Kristine *prosecutor*
O'Scannlain, Diarmuid Fionntain *federal judge*
Packard, Robert Goodale, III, *urban planner*
Pamplin, Robert Boisseau, Sr., *retired textile manufacturing executive*
Pamplin, Robert Boisseau, Jr., *manufacturing company executive, minister, writer*
Panner, Owen M. *federal judge*
Patterson, Beverly Ann Gross *not-for-profit fundraiser, consultant, social services administrator*
Patterson, James Randolph *physician*
Patterson, Steve *professional basketball team executive*
Paulus, Norma Jean Petersen *lawyer*
Pearson, David Petri *chemist*
Perotto, Gregory Todd *public relations professional*
Pfeifer, Larry Alan *public health service coordinator*
Phillips, Vicki L. *school system administrator*
Pierson, Wayne George *trust company executive*
Pine, William Charles *foundation executive*
Pippen, Scottie *professional basketball player*
Pladel, John Gerald *psychiatric nurse practitioner, psychologist, psychotherapist*
Plonski, Halina Maria *retired pharmacist*
Porter, Elsa Allgood *writer, lecturer*
Potempa, Kathleen *dean*
Pratt, Scott Owen *lawyer*
Prendergast, William John *ophthalmologist*
Press, Edward *consulting physician*
Purcell, John F. *lawyer*
Quigley, Thomas *research scientist*
Ramsby, Mark Delivan *lighting designer and consultant*
Redden, James Anthony *federal judge*
Reiten, Richard G. *natural gas industry executive*
Richards, Herbert East *minister emeritus, commentator*
Richards, Robert Charles *management consultant*
Richardson, Campbell *retired lawyer*
Richens, Muriel Whittaker *marriage and family therapist, educator*
Richter, Peter Christian *lawyer*
Riddle, Matthew C(asey) *physician, educator*
Robertson, Joseph E., Jr., *ophthalmologist, educator*
Rooks, Charles S. *foundation administrator*
Rosen, Steven O. *lawyer*
Rosenberg, Kenneth David *epidemiologist*
Rosenblum, Ellen F. *judge*
Roth, Phillip Joseph *retired judge*
Rottschaefer, William Andrew *philosophy educator*
Rotzien, Frederick William, III, *marketing executive*
Rowe, Sandra Mims *editor*
Rushen, Elizabeth Rae Marshall *director*
Russell, Marjorie Rose *manufacturing executive*
Rutherford, William Drake *investment executive*
Ryan, John Duncan *lawyer*
Ryberg, William A. *orchestra executive*
Sachs, Harley Luther *writer, educator*
Sacks, David Harris *historian, humanities educator*
Sand, Thomas Charles *lawyer*
Savage, John William *lawyer*
Schmidt, Stanley Eugene *retired speech educator*
Schmidt, Waldemar Adrian *pathologist, educator*
Schumacher, Maria *biomedical researcher, educator*
Schuster, Philip Frederick, II, *lawyer, writer, law educator*
Schwartz, Martin Lerner *physician*
Scott, John D. *pharmacologist*
Seaman, Robert E., III, *lawyer*
Seil, Fredrick John *retired neuroscientist*
Sells, Clifford Wayne *pediatrician*
Service, William W. *restaurant company executive*
Shinn, Michael Robert *lawyer*
Shireman, Joan Foster *social work educator*
Simpson, Robert Glenn *lawyer*
Sims, Kathleen Marie Eichner *nursing educator*
Skopil, Otto Richard, Jr., *federal judge*
Smith, Dennis B. *neurologist, educator*
Smith, Russell Wesley *management and computer applications consultant, organizational development trainer*
Standring, James Douglas *real estate developer*
Steele, William Donald *literature educator*
Steinman, Lisa Malinowski *English literature educator, writer*
Stephens, Donald L., Jr., *lawyer*
Stevens, Curtis *consumer products company executive*
Stevens, Wendell Claire *retired anesthesiology educator*
Stewart, Janice Mae *federal judge*
Stewart, Milton Roy *lawyer*
Stickel, Frederick A. *publishing executive*
Stickel, Patrick Francis *publishing executive, newspaper*
Stone, Richard James *lawyer*
Stott, Peter Walter *forest products company executive*
Stowell, Christopher R. *artistic director, choreographer, retired dancer*
Sullivan, Donal D. *federal bankruptcy judge*
Sullivan, Edward Joseph *lawyer, educator*
Sutherland, Donald Wood *cardiologist*
Suwyn, Mark A. *building products executive*
Swan, Kenneth Carl *surgeon*
Swindells, William, Jr., *lumber and paper company executive*
Taylor, J(ocelyn) Mary *museum administrator, zoologist, educator*
Taylor, Robert Brown *medical educator, physician, writer*
Thomas, Carol F. *educational association administrator*
Thompson, Jill Lynette Long *federal agency administrator, former congresswoman*
Thompson, Terrie Lee *graphic designer*
Thurston, George R. *lumber company executive*
Timpe, Ronald Ernest *insurance company executive*
Tolle, Susan W. *internist, educator, educational administrator*
Tolon, Michael Oded *music educator, director*
Tomjack, T.J. *wholesale distribution executive*
Tuska, Jon *author, publisher*
Tyson, David T. *academic administrator*
Unger, Karen Virginia *director*
Unis, Richard L. *judge*
Van Exel, Nickey Maxwell *professional basketball player*
Van Hoomissen, George Albert *state supreme court justice*
VanSickle, Sharon Dee *public relations executive*
Van Valkenburg, Edgar Walter *lawyer*
Vernon, Jack Allen *otolaryngology educator, laboratory administrator*
Viator, John A. *biomedical physicist, military officer*
Waggoner, James Clyde *lawyer*
Watne, Donald Arthur *accountant, educator, retired*
Weaver, Delbert Allen *lawyer*
Weber, George Richard *financial and internet marketing executive, writer*
Weeks, Wilford Frank *retired geophysics educator, glaciologist*
Weleber, Richard Gordon *ophthalmologist, geneticist, medical educator, researcher*
Westwood, James Nicholson *lawyer*
White, Douglas James, Jr., *lawyer*
Whitlow, Lillian *retired elementary school educator, poet*
Whitsell, Helen Jo *lumber executive*
Wieden, Dan G. *advertising executive*
Wiens, Arthur Nicholai *psychology educator*
Wilde, Thomas Andrew *state legislator, home remodeler, writer*
Williamson, Charles Ready, III, *lawyer*
Wilson, Owen Meredith, Jr., *lawyer*
Wilson, Thomas Dale *philanthropic fundraising consultant*
Witherspoon, Sophia *professional basketball player*
Wood, Marcus Andrew *lawyer*
Woodward, Stephen Richard *newspaper reporter*
Workman, Norman Allan *accountant, graphic arts consultant*
Wyatt, Bill *airport executive*
Wyse, William Walker *lawyer, real estate executive*
Yamayee, Zia Ahmad *engineering educator, dean*
Zalutsky, Morton Herman *lawyer*
Zerbe, Kathryn Jane *psychiatrist*
Zerzan, Charles Joseph, Jr., *retired gastroenterologist*

Prineville
Wick, Philip *wholesale distribution executive*

Redmond
Clarno, Beverly Ann *state legislator, farmer*
Dey, Charlotte Jane *retired community health nurse*

Roseburg
Cook, Sybilla Avery *school library consultant*
Ford, Allyn *manufacturing executive*
Oliphant, Charles Romig *retired physician*

Salem
Anderson, Laurie Monnes *state representative*
Atkinson, Jason A. *state senator*
Atkinson, Perry *political organization administrator*
Bailey, Henry John, III, *retired lawyer, educator*
Balmer, Thomas Ancil *state supreme court justice*
Bauer, James Richard *academic administrator*
Bauer, Richard LeRoy *music educator, musician*
Benson, Steven Donald *sheet metal research and marketing executive, sheet metal mechanic, programmer, author*
Bentley, Sara *newspaper publishing executive*
Benton, Jack Mitchell *management consultant*
Berger, Vicki *state representative*
Beyer, Elizabeth Terry *state representative*
Beyer, Roger *state senator*
Bradbury, William Chapman, III, *state official*
Breen, Richard F., Jr., *law librarian, lawyer, educator*
Brown, Kate *state legislator*
Burdick, Ginny Marie *state legislator*
Butts, Edward Perry *civil engineer, environmental consultant*
Carson, Wallace Preston, Jr., *judge*
Castillo, Susan *school system administrator*
Clark, David Scott *law educator, consultant*
Close, Betsy L. *state representative*
Courtney, Peter C. *state legislator*
De Muniz, Paul J. *state supreme court justice*
Dingfelder, Jackie *state representative*
Dixon, Robert Gene *retired manufacturing engineering educator, retired mechanical engineering company executive*
Dmytryshyn, Basil *historian, educator*
Donais, Gerald Alan *manufacturing executive*
Dukes, Joan *state legislator*
Durham, Robert Donald, Jr., *state supreme court justice*
Edge, James Edward *health care administrator*
Erickson, Ray Charles *retired wildlife biologist*
Fisher, William G.E. *state legislator, rental investor, assisted living facility owner*
Flores, Linda *state representative*
Frank, Gerald Wendel *civic leader, journalist*
Gallegos, Mary *state representative*
Gillette, P. Roger *physicist, systems engineer*
Harper, Steven V. *state senator*
Haselton, Rick Thomas *lawyer*
Heine, Steven Robert *telecommunications industry executive, poet, writer*
Hoff, Reno R. *academic administrator*
Hopson, Elaine M. *state representative*
Kafoury, Deborah *state representative*

Beyer
Cornell, William Harvey *clergyman*

Blakeslee
Albano, Patrick Marino *historian, educator, archivist*

Bloomsburg
Bertelsen, Dale Alan *communications educator*
Holloway, Sybil Lymorise *psychologist, writer*
Keyser, Leslie D. *writer*
Kozloff, Jessica S. *university president*
Liu, Hsien-Tung *dean*
Perner, Darlene E. *special education educator, consultant, editor*
Tloczynski, Joseph *psychology professor, researcher*
Vann, John Daniel, III, *library consultant, historian*
Yenika-Agbaw, Vivian S. *English studies educator, researcher*

Blue Bell
Astheimer, Wesley *bank executive*
Baine, Richard Joseph *vocational rehabilitation counselor*
Brendlinger, LeRoy R. *academic administrator*
Carrow, John C. *computer company executive*
Connelly, Patrick O'Neil *financial executive*
Deschaine, Barbara Ralph *retired real estate broker*
Elliott, John Michael *lawyer*
Giordano, Nicholas Anthony *stock exchange executive*
Haugen, Janet B. *corporate financial executive*
McAdam, Will *electronics consultant*
McGrath, Joseph W. *information technology executive*
Ostroff, Nat S. *communications executive*
Rose, Kenneth L. *business executive*
Siedzikowski, Henry Francis *lawyer*
Sundheim, Nancy Straus *lawyer*
Swansen, Samuel Theodore *lawyer*
Teklits, Joseph Anthony *lawyer*
Weinbach, Lawrence Allen *computer company executive*
Wilson, H(arold) Fred(erick) *chemist, research scientist*
Young, Charles Randall *application developer, marketing professional*

Boalsburg
Gettig, Martin Winthrop *retired mechanical engineer*

Boswell
Croft, Daniel Thomas *music educator*

Bowmansville
Weinhold, Clifford Lee *photographer*

Boyertown
Jilk, Lawrence T., Jr., *banker*

Brackenridge
Bozzone, Robert P. *steel company executive*

Braddock
Lebovitz, Charles Neal *surgeon*

Bradford
Cox, J. Arthur *minister*
Rice, Lester *electronics company executive*

Brentwood
Swanson, Fred A. *retired communications designer, councilman*

Bridgeville
Fox, Debra L. *educational association administrator, business owner*
Irvine, Peter Bennington *clergyman*
Moore, Daniel Edmund *psychologist, educator, retired educational administrator*

Bristol
Boneparth, Peter *retail executive*
Kimmel, Sidney *apparel company executive*
Shenefelt, Arthur B. *transportation executive, consultant*

Broomall
Cohen, Philip D. *book publishing executive*
DiRosa, Steven Joseph *primary and secondary school educator*
Emplit, Raymond Henry *electrical engineer*
McHugh, Gerald C. *bank executive*
Saunders, Sally Love *poet, educator*

Brownsville
Martin, Richard H. *principal*
Nantus, Sheryl *writer*

Bryn Mawr
Ackoff, Russell Lincoln *systems sciences educator*
Anderson, Eric Edward *psychologist, consultant, director*
Baird, John Absalom, Jr., *retired academic administrator*
Bolger, Stephen Garrett *retired English and American studies educator*
Braha, Thomas I. *business executive*
Brunt, Manly Yates, Jr., *psychiatrist*
Cooke, M(erritt) Todd *retired bank executive*
Cooney, Patricia Ruth *civic worker*
Crawford, Maria Luisa Buse *geology educator*
Daly, Donald Francis *consultant, retired investment counsel*
Dudden, Arthur Power *historian, educator*
Fletcher, Marjorie Amos *librarian*
Frank, Edward David, II, *history educator*
Frick, Benjamin Charles *lawyer*
Gaisser, Julia Haig *classics educator*
Giese, William Herbert *tax accountant*
Hoaglund, Susan Elizabeth *music educator*
Hoffman, Howard Stanley *experimental psychologist, educator*
Huth, Edward Janavel *internist, educator, editor*
King, Willard Fahrenkamp (Mrs. Edmund Ludwig King) *Spanish language educator*
Kline, John Charles *painter, educator*
Krausz, Michael *philosopher, educator*
Kuncl, Ralph *provost*
Lane, Barbara Miller (Barbara Miller-Lane) *humanities educator*
Lang, Mabel Louise *classics educator*
Leto, Francis Joseph *lawyer, educator*
Levitt, Robert E. *gastroenterologist*
Littell, Julia Harrington *social sciences educator*
Maehl, Jane Cecilia *social worker, administrator*
McCabe, Louise Beachboard *language educator*
Mezvinsky, Edward M. *lawyer*
Moyer, F. Stanton *financial executive, advisor*
Noone, R. Barrett *plastic surgeon*
Opendak, Irene *academic administrator*
Peters, Douglas Scott *health care executive*
Phillips, Stephen S. *lawyer*
Porter, Judith Deborah Revitch *sociologist*
Price, Trevor Robert Pryce *psychiatrist, educator*
Salisbury, Helen Holland *education educator*
Stucky, Steven (Edward) *composer, conductor*
Trout, Charles Hathaway *historian, educator*
Vickers, Nancy J. *academic administrator*
Wheeler, Grace R. *retired market researcher*

Buckingham
Altier, William John *management consultant*
Hover, John Calvin, II, *banker*

Bushkill
Garretto, Leonard Anthony, Jr., *insurance company executive*

Butler
Day, Margaret Ann *research librarian, information specialist*
Hawk, Kathleen Patricia *broadcast consultant*
Kosar, John E. *architectural firm executive*
Wise, Vernon L., Jr., *publishing executive*

California
Langham, Norma E. *playwright, educator, poet, composer, inventor*
O'Donnell, William W. *theater educator, lighting designer*

Camp Hill
Anderson, Dorothy Kentner *interior designer*
Beasley, Ed *retail executive*
Brouse, John S. *medical association administrator*
Cardinale, Gerald P. *retail executive*
Crider, Rudyard Lee *psychotherapist*
Crist, Christine Myers *consulting executive*
Custer, John Charles *investment broker*
Davis, Don P. *retail executive*
deBruin, Jerry Mark *retail executive*
Drnevich, Ronald *engineering executive*
Fazzolari, Salvatore D. *mining products executive*
Gerson, Elliot S. *lawyer, retail company executive*
Hall, Christopher S. *retail executive*
Hathaway, Derek C. *mining products executive*
Johnston, Thomas McElree, Jr., *retired church administrator*
Keough, Philip J., IV, *retail executive*
Kleiman, Richard *realtor*
Learish, John *retail executive*
Lester, Wilson A., Jr., *retail executive*
Lovett, Keith W *retail executive*
Mackin, Charles Philip, Jr., *lawyer*
Mastrian, James P. *retail executive*
Mead, James Matthew *insurance company executive*
Miller, Robert G. *drug store chain company executive*
Nowak, Jacquelyn Louise *state agency administrator, artist, realtor, consultant*
Panzer, Mark *retail executive*
Parry-Solá, Cheryl Lee *critical care nurse*
Roach, Ralph Lee *human services and rehabilitation consultant*
Rowe, Michael Duane *artist*
Rugen, Karen *manufacturing executive, corporate communications specialist*
Sammons, Mary F. *retail executive*
Sari, Robert *retail executive*
Shirtliff, Bryan *retail executive*
Standley, John *drug retail company executive*
Swamidoss, Stephenson *pathologist, health facility administrator*
Todd, Murray *retail executive*
Tokuhata, George K. *retired medical educator, epidemiologist, consultant*
Twomey, Kevin *pharmaceutical executive*
Yates, James Arthur *plastic surgeon*

Canonsburg
Colaizzo, Anthony Louis *mayor, former state legislator, small business owner*
Coury, Robert J. *pharmaceutical executive*
Mascetta, Joseph Anthony *principal*
Prado, Gerald M. *investment banker*
Puskar, Milan *pharmaceuticals executive*

Carbondale
Niles, John Southworth, III, *counselor, farmer*

Carlisle
Allan, George *retired philosophy educator*
Anderson, Howard Wayne, Jr., *training company executive*
Biddle, Tami Davis *social studies educator*
Durden, William G. *academic administrator*
Fish, Chester Boardman, Jr., *retired editor*
Fox, Arturo Angel *Spanish language educator*
Jacobs, Norman G(abriel) *sociologist, educator*
Jones, Oliver Hastings *consulting economist*
Laws, Kenneth L. *physics educator, author*
Long, Howard Charles *physics educator emeritus*
Robinson, Ronald Michael *financial executive, financial consultant*
Shrader, Charles Reginald *historian*
Song, Yongyi *librarian*
Talley, Carol Lee *newspaper editor*

Carlisle Barracks
Metz, Steven Kent *federal agency administrator, writer*

Carnegie
Dybeck, Alfred Charles *labor arbitrator*
Moretti, Edward Charles *environmental engineer, consultant*

Cecil
Keddie, Roland Thomas *physician, hospital administrator, lawyer*

Center Valley
Bartolacci, Paulette Marie *middle school educator, aerobics instructor*
Turner, Brian Allen *sport management director, educator*

Central City
Brown, Robert Alan *retired construction materials company executive*

Chadds Ford
Cohen, Felix Asher *lawyer*
Duff, James Henry *museum director, environmental administrator*
Gordon, William Edmund, Jr., *lawyer*
Isakoff, Sheldon Erwin *chemical engineer*
King, M. Jean *association executive*
Lamonaca, Joseph Michael *lawyer, pilot*
Martin, David Warren *management consultant*
Milner, John D. *architectural firm executive, educator*
Moore, Bruce E. *real estate company executive*
Sanford, Richard D. *computer company executive*
Swensson, Evelyn Dickenson *conductor, composer, librettist*
Webster, Owen Wright *chemist*
Werner DeNadai, Mary *architectural firm executive*

Chalfont
Pederson, Linda Lue *epidemiologist, researcher*
Wilson, Jean L. *retired state legislator*

Chambersburg
Furr, Quint Eugene *marketing executive*
Lesher, Richard Lee *retired association executive*
Mehrmann, CraigAnn *nurse practitioner*
Neilson, Winthrop Cunningham, III, *communications executive, financial communications consultant, photographer*
O'Connor, John Morris, III, *retired humanities educator*
Reber, Calvin Henry *theological studies educator, minister*
Rumler, Robert Hoke *agricultural consultant, retired association executive*
Scarlata, Paul Anthony *oral surgeon*
Yeun, Paul Lorenzo *minister*

Cheltenham
Weinstock, Walter Wolfe *systems engineer*

Chester
Bruce, Robert James *retired academic administrator*
Buck, Lawrence Paul *academic administrator, educator*
Carnwath, Thomas Howlan *academic administrator*
Harris, James Thomas, III, *college administrator, educator*
Saad, Germaine H. *finance educator, researcher*

Chester Springs
Dallas, Noelle Marie *financial analyst*
Scheer, R. Scott *physician*

Cheswick
Nair, Bala Radhakrishnan *engineer*

Cheyney
Ellis-Scruggs, Jan *theater arts educator*

Claridge
Perich, Terry Miller *secondary school educator*

Clarion
Foreman, Thomas Alexander *dentist*
Frakes, Robert M. *humanities educator, writer*
Grejda, Gail Fulton *dean*
Miller, Andrea Lynn *library science educator*
Reinhard, Diane L. *university president*

Clarks Summit
Alperin, Irwin Ephraim *clothing company executive*
Beemer, John Barry *lawyer*

Clearfield
Krebs, Margaret Eloise *publishing executive*
Mandell, Raymond Andrew *music educator*
Singh, Shiwendra Prasad *civil engineer*

Clifton Heights
Pagano, Richard Donald *physical education educator, researcher*

Clinton
Talbot, Mary Lee *minister*

Coatesville
Ainslie, George William *psychiatrist, behavioral economist*
Bell, Robert Lloyd *retired neurosurgeon*
Burton, Mary Louise Himes *computer specialist*
Green, Norman Marston, Jr., *retired minister*
Lee, Daniel *retired physician, public health service officer*
Makous, Norman *internist, cardiologist, educator*
Rodkey, Frances Theresa *elementary school educator*
Smith, Patricia Anne *special education educator*
Zarychta, William Alex *physician assistant*

Cochranville
Sazegar, Morteza *artist*

Collegeville
Barnes, Jo Anne *investment advisor*
Graeff, David Wayne *maintenance executive, consultant*
Kun, Kenneth A. *business executive*
Neylan, John Francis, III, *nephrologist, educator, scientist*
Richter, Richard Paul *academic administrator*
Ruffolo, Robert R. *research and development company executive*
Stiles, Gary Lester *cardiologist, molecular pharmacologist, educator*
Strassburger, John Robert *academic administrator*
Zwerling, Philip *language educator, playwright*

Conshohocken
Bramson, Robert Sherman *lawyer*
Hondros, Paul J. *diversified financial services company executive*
Jacoby, Richard Allen *pathologist, dermatologist*
Johnson, Waine Cecil *dermatologist*
Lotman, Herbert *food processing executive*
Naples, Ronald James *manufacturing executive*
Nowak, Gregory Joseph *lawyer, educator*
Senturk, Ufuk *ceramics engineer, researcher*
Spaeth, Karl Henry *retired chemical company executive, lawyer*

Coopersburg
Bednar, Charles Sokol *political scientist, educator*
Bolle, Donald Martin *retired engineering educator*
Kohler, Deborah Diamond *dietitian, food service executive*
Peserik, James E. *electrical, controls and computer engineer, consultant, forensics and safety engineer, fire cause and origin investigator*
Siess, Alfred Albert, Jr., *engineering executive, management consultant*

Cooperstown
Hogg, James Henry, Jr., *retired education educator*

Coraopolis
Kay, George Paul *environmental engineer*
Koepfinger, Joseph Leo *retired utilities executive*
Shaw, Richard Leslie *engineering company executive*
Wang, Xueming *application developer, educator*

Corsica
Elza, Betty Ann *retired librarian*

Coudersport
Kysor, Daniel Francis *psychologist*
Schleyer, William T. *cable company executive*

Cranberry Township
Fitzpatrick, Robert *psychologist*
Hogberg, Carl Gustav *retired steel company executive*
Lorenz, John George *librarian, consultant*
MacDonald, Barbara Katic *secondary school educator*
Patten, Charles Anthony *management consultant, retired manufacturing company executive, author, publisher*
Tiller, Olive Marie *retired church worker*

Cresson
D'Emilio, Deanne A. *education educator, lawyer*

Dallas
Comitz, John Joseph *retired secondary school educator*
Fiegelman, Richard Paul *sales consultant, freelance writer*

Dallastown
Morton, David K. *language educator*

Danvilel
Chanaga, Jaime Gabriel *information technology manager*

Danville
Bakri, Younes Noaman *surgeon, oncologist, gynecologist*
Bower, Jack R. *music educator*
Chan, Yiumo *biochemist*
Cochran, William John *physician, pediatrician, gastroenterologist, nutritionist, consultant*
Franklin, David Perdue *vascular surgeon, educator*
Pierce, James Clarence *surgeon, educator*
Steele, Glenn Daniel, Jr., *oncologist, healthcare system executive*

Darby
Eiser, Arnold Robert *bioethicist, nephrologist, internist*
Wardell, Lindy Constance *nonprofit organization administrator*

Denver
Milner, Charles Fremont, Jr., *manufacturing executive*

Devon
Boehne, Edward George *banker*
Lamb, William H. *state supreme court justices*
Porter, Roger John *medical research executive, educator, neurologist, pharmacologist*
Wilson, Malcolm Campbell *bank executive*

Dillsburg
Bowers, Glenn Lee *retired professional society administrator*
Jackson, George Lyman *retired nuclear medicine physician*
Smith, William Raymond *farmer, horse breeder*

Dingmans Ferry
Bartle, Barrie G. *music educator*
Haas, Karen Marie *secondary school educator*

Donora
Todd, Norma Ross *retired government official*

Downingtown
Alburger, George J., Jr., *accountant, finance company executive*
Hankowsky, William P. *real estate company executive*
Hemingway, David C. *elementary school principal*
Kovach, George Daniel *writer*
Newman, Richard August *psychiatrist, educator*
Romanosky, LuAnn *elementary school educator*

Doylestown
Brink, Frank, Jr., *biophysicist, former educator*
Elliott, Richard Howard *lawyer*
Ginsberg, Barry Gavrille *psychologist, marriage and family therapist, consultant, trainer*
Kohlhepp, Edward John *financial planner*
Long, Ronald Alex *real estate and financial consultant, lawyer, educator*
Marino, Paul Michael *science education educator*
McGarvey, Joseph F. X., Sr., *cardiologist*
Meyer, Diane Christine *social worker*
Mishler, John Milton (Yochanan Menashsheh ben Shaul) *natural sciences educator, administrator, artist*
Rodenbaugh, Marcia Louise *retired elementary school educator*
Wolfinger, Audrey Jane *retired librarian*

Drexel Hill
Alexander, Lloyd Chudley author
Bay, Joann Reeder financial planner
Martino, Michael Charles entertainer, musician, actor
Schiazza, Guido Domenic (Guy Schiazza) educational association administrator
Thompson, William David minister, homiletics educator

Drums
Frask, Robin Ann Kostanesky secondary school educator

Du Bois
Blakley, Benjamin Spencer, III, lawyer
Forsythe-Adamson, Velma Brown accountant, consultant, English language educator

Duncansville
Smith, D. Brooks federal judge

Dunmore
Krogh-Jespersen, Mary-Beth academic administrator
McDonald, Nancy E. retired secondary school educator
Pencek, Carolyn Carlson treasurer, educator
Sebastianelli, Mario Joseph internist, nephrologist, health services administrator

Durham
de Limantour, Clarice Barr food scientist

Eagles Mere
Gruver, William Rolfe investment banker

East Berlin
Greer, Robert Bruce, III, retired orthopedic surgeon, educator

East Earl
Jonassen, Gaylord D. computer company executive, new products and market development

East Lansdowne
Tolliver, Elkin, Jr., judge

East Stroudsburg
Bishop, Gerald Iveson pharmaceutical executive
Boyd, Katherine Ann clinical therapist
Braithwaite, Barbara J. secondary school educator
Crotty, Patricia McGee political science educator
Dillman, Robert John academic administrator
Hoyt, Earl Edward, Jr., industrial designer
Miller, Robert W. music educator, musician
Upright, Kirby Grant lawyer

Easton
Danjczek, Michael Harvey social service administrator
DeGrandis, Ronald Wayne music educator
Delong, Ronald artist, educator
Fried, Bernard parasitologist, biology educator
Grunberg, Robert Leon Willy nephrologist, educator
Hay, Samuel Arthur theater educator, playwright
Holmes, Larry, Jr., retired professional boxer
Hughes, Michael P. principal
Kincaid, John political science educator, editor
Lear, Floyd Raymond, III, entrepreneur
Murphy, Bruce Allen government and law educator, author
Pysher, Zane Kermit counselor
Reibman, Jeanette Fichman retired state senator
Rothkopf, Arthur J. college president
Schlueter, June Mayer English educator, author
Schwab, Mark marketing executive
Stipe, Edwin, III, mechanical contracting company executive
Stitt, Dorothy Jewett journalist
Sun, Robert Zu Jei manufacturing company executive, inventor
Traldi, Lorenzo mathematician, educator

Edinboro
Cox, Clifford Laird retired academic administrator
Miller, G(erson) H(arry) research institute director, mathematician, computer scientist, chemist
Snyder, Donald Benjamin biology professor
Thomas, Paul Milton retired science educator
Travis, Grant Carner lawyer

Edwardsville
Lukas, Edward Michael retired secondary school educator

Eighty Four
Capone, Alphonse William retired industrial executive
Hardy, Joseph A., Sr., wholesale distribution executive
Magerko, Maggie Hardy lumber company executive
Wallach, Dan lumber company executive

Elizabethtown
Brown, Dale Weaver clergyman, theologian, educator
Chambers, David Lee music educator
Coren, Jonathon Silow science educator, researcher
Geder, Laszlo retired neurologist, educator
Gottfried, Paul Edward humanities educator, editor
Kitchen, Otis Dorsey music educator
Madeira, Robert Lehman professional society administrator
Sample, Frederick Palmer former college president

Elizabethville
McCartney, Chad Edward music educator
Romberger, John Albert scientist, historian

Elkins Park
Burnley, June Williams secondary school educator
Davidson, Abraham Aba art historian, educator, photographer
Erlebacher, Martha Mayer artist, educator
Hart, William C. underwriter, educator, writer
Pak, Hyung Woong community advocate
Romberg, Osvaldo artist
Shmukler, Stanford lawyer
Verma, Satya Bhushan optometrist, educator
Yun, Daniel Duwhan physician, foundation administrator

Emmaus
Adcock, Albert Eugene (Gene) night vision equipment company executive
Bowers, Klaus D(ieter) retired electronics research development company executive
Bricklin, Mark Harris magazine editor, publisher
Favorule, Denise publishing executive
Rodale, Ardath Harter publishing executive
Teufel, Robert J. publishing executive

Ephrata
Ohlinger, Kristie L music educator
Sweigart, Anne B. communications company executive

Erdenheim
Murphy, Mary Marguerite artist

Erie
Adovasio, J. M. anthropologist, archeologist, educator
Allshouse, Robert Harold history educator
Ayrault, Evelyn West psychologist, writer
Begley, Charlene electronics executive
Belfiore, Phillip Joseph education educator, researcher
Bennett, Charles Andrew economics professor, department chairman
Bracken, Charles Herbert banker
Crankshaw, John Hamilton mechanical engineer
Cullen, James Donald lawyer
Dever, Merrill Thomas academic administrator, retired police chief
Dockstader, Emmett Stanley engineer, construction executive
Duval, Albert Frank paper company executive
Earll, Jane state legislator, lawyer
Ferretti, Silvia dean
Filippi, Richard mayor, lawyer, real estate company executive
Garcia, Philip A. insurance company executive
George, Annmarie Irene music educator
Gottschalk, Frank Klaus real estate company executive
Hagen, Thomas Bailey business owner, former state official, retired insurance company executive
Hauck, Barbara Jean fund raising executive, writer, artist
Henry, Martin Daniel university president
Ludrof, Jeffrey A. insurance company executive
Lund, Edwin Harrison business accounting systems executive
Mason, Gregg Claude orthopedic surgeon, researcher
Mencer, Glenn Everell federal judge
Mercer, Christina Marie writer, artist
Michaelides, Doros Nikita internist, medical educator
Monahan, Thomas Andrew, Jr., accountant
Murphy, Michael Joseph retired bishop
Myers, Jeffrey Daniel concert pianist, music educator
Nihill, Karen Bailey nursing home executive, nurse clinician
Renkis, Alan Ilmars plastics formulating company executive
Rowley, Robert Deane, Jr., bishop
Ryan, James Thomas organizational consultant, business owner
Sensor, Mary Delores hospital official, consultant
Taylor, Margaret Uhrich educational administrator
Trautman, Donald W. bishop
Vanco, John L. art museum director
Van Gorder, Jan Reid lawyer, insurance company executive

Essington
Piasecki, Frank Nicholas aircraft corporation executive, aeronautics engineer

Etters
Garloff, Samuel John psychiatrist
Steps, Barbara Jill lawyer

Exeter
Stocker, Joyce Arlene retired secondary school educator

Export
Carter, Linda Whitehead oncology nurse, educator, consultant, researcher

Exton
Aungst, Bruce Jeffrey pharmaceutical company scientist
de Rosen, Michel pharmaceutical company executive
Dorsey, Jeremiah Edmund pharmaceutical company executive
Hedges, Donald Walton lawyer
Hidalgo, Ismael J. pharmaceutical scientist
Ma, Jinpeng economics and business educator
Mauch, Robert Carl energy executive
Stuart, John E. Internet company executive
Teti, Louis N. lawyer
Webber, Helen artist, designer

Fairless Hills
Marable, Simeon-David artist
Rosella, John Daniel clinical psychologist, educator
Scrocca, Anthony Charles bank executive

Fayetteville
Molitor, Graham Thomas Tate lawyer

Feasterville
Dickstein, Jack chemist

Feasterville Trevose
Osterhout, Richard Cadwallader lawyer
Schwartz, Theodore A. investment company executive

Felton
Shoemaker, Eleanor Boggs television production company executive

Flourtown
Christy, John Gilray financial company executive
Dressler, Mark Christopher writer
Lee, Adrian Iselin, Jr., journalist
Reneberg, Richard (Richey Reneberg) professional tennis player

Ford City
Skamai, Robert Walter music educator

Fort Washington
Bajpai, Sanjay Kumar strategic healthcare marketing, economics executive
Moulton, Hugh Geoffrey lawyer, retired business executive
Pappas, Charles Engelos plastic surgeon
Wint, Dennis Michael museum director

Forty Fort
Kopen, Dan Francis surgeon, consultant

Frackville
Domalakes, Paul George lawyer

Franklin
Sauer, Mary Julia special education educator

Fredericksburg
Daubert, Harlan Aaron music educator, director

Freeport
Chvala, Kathleen Ann customer service supervisor

Friendsville
Babb, Harold psychologist, educator

Gaines
Beller, Martin Leonard retired orthopaedic surgeon

Gap
Beiler, Anne F. food company executive

Gettysburg
Coughenour, Kavin Luther career officer, military historian
Gritsch, Ruth Christine Lisa editor
Hallberg, Budd Jaye management consulting firm executive
Hendrix, Sherman Samuel biology professor, researcher
Plischke, Elmer political science educator
Roach, James Clark government official
Schein, Virginia Ellen psychologist, editor
Smith, Emory Clark lawyer, financial advisor
Will, Katherine Haley academic administrator

Gibsonia
Cauna, Nikolajs physician, medical educator, scientist
Groves, Michael banker
Haas, Eileen Marie homecare advocate
Krause, Helen Fox otolaryngologist

Gilbertsville
Poste, George Henry pharmaceutical company executive

Gladwyne
Acton, David lawyer
Allen, Theresa Ohotnicky neurobiologist, consultant
Booth, Harold Waverly lawyer, finance and investment company executive
Cathcart, Harold Robert hospital administrator
Fenichel, Richard Lee retired biochemist
Geisel, Cameron Meade, Jr., investment professional
Harkins, Herbert Perrin otolaryngologist, educator
Kaye, Donald physician, educator
Morrison, Gail internist, nephrologist, educator
Patten, Lanny Ray industrial gas industry executive

Glassport
Coslov, I. Michael manufacturing executive

Glen Mills
Churchill, Stuart Winston chemical engineering educator
Dunion, Celeste Mogab consultant, business manager, township official
Turner, Janet Sullivan painter, sculptor

Glenshaw
Guentner, James Francis, Jr., art educator, artist

Glenside
Block, Isaac Edward professional society administrator
Doman, Janet Joy professional society administrator
Frudakis, Rosalie small business owner
Frudakis, Zenos Antonios sculptor, artist
Goldberg, Steven Selig education law educator
Landman, Bette Emeline academic administrator
McCartney, Dan G. theology studies educator, musician
Medel, Rebecca Rosalie artist
Mermelstein, Jules Joshua lawyer, township commissioner
Powlison, David A. writer
Reiss, George Russell, Jr., physician

Glenwillard
Milne, Christopher McQuiston Wilmoth photographer, journalist, educator

Gouldsboro
Nass, Leonard Ira chemist, consultant

Grantham
Kreamer, Carolyn Lee nursing educator, community health nurse

Greencastle
Horst, Carolyn Diane accountant
Scott, Leighton Reeves interior designer, artist, writer

Greensburg
Belden, H. Reginald, Jr., lawyer
Catalano, Louis William, Jr., neurologist
Duck, Patricia Mary librarian
Flórez-Estrada, Nancy B. language educator
Foreman, John Daniel financial executive
Gounley, Dennis Joseph lawyer
Heubel, William Bernard lawyer, international contract consultant
Kathuria, Nirmal Bhatia psychiatrist
Ramm, Douglas Robert psychologist
Shafer-Kenney, Jolie E. writer, columnist
Spurlock, John history professor

Greentown
Askins, Wallace Boyd manufacturing executive
Forcheskie, Carl S. former apparel company executive

Greenville
Hall, Mary Theresa literature educator
Parmiter, Karen Lynn education educator
Stuver, Francis Edward former railway car company executive

Grove City
Campbell, George Van Pelt sociology and religion educator
Groves, Edgar Stephens music educator, conductor
McBride, Milford Lawrence, Jr., lawyer

Gwynedd
Bieber, Konrad Ferdinand retired language educator
LeFevre, Perry Deyo minister, theology educator

Gwynedd Valley
Duclow, Donald Francis philosophy educator, researcher
McGarry, Lisa Coughlin language educator
Owens, Kathleen C. academic administrator
Strasburg, William Edward retired newspaper publisher

Hamburg
Schappell, Abigail Susan speech, language, hearing and massage therapist

Hanover
Conway, Samuel Anthony retired chiropractor
Kline, Donald food company executive

Hanover Township
Ginyard, Caleb Nathaniel, III, government agency administrator

Harleysville
Daller, Walter E., Jr., bank executive
Hendricks, Tim construction company executive
Smagalski, Carolyn M publishing executive, webmaster, director

Harrisburg
Antoun, Annette Agnes newspaper editor, publisher
Baehre, Edna Victoria college president
Baker Knoll, Catherine lieutenant governor
Barron, Cate editor
Bebko-Jones, Linda state legislator
Bishop, Louise Williams state legislator
Bittenbender, Robert A. state official
Boscola, Lisa M. state legislator
Breslin, Michael Joseph, III, social services administrator, educator
Brewer, Steven Gregory human services administrator
Brown, John Walter vocational education supervisor
Cadieux, Roger Joseph physician, mental health care executive
Campbell, Carl Lester banker
Chernicoff, David Paul osteopathic physician, educator
Cline, Andrew Haley lawyer
Cohen, Lita Indzel state legislator
Cooper, Jane Todd (J. C. Todd) poet, writer, educator
Cooper, Jeffrey lawyer
Cortés, Pedro secretary to commonwealth
Crahalla, Jacqueline R. state representative
Dattilo, Nicholas C. bishop
DeKok, David writer, reporter
Diehm, James Warren lawyer, educator
Dietz, John Raphael consulting engineer executive
Emerick, John L. library director
Farrington, Debra Kelli publisher, writer
Forcier, Teresa Elaine state legislator
Franco, Barbara Alice museum director
Gale, Randall Glenn lawyer
Gerlach, James William congressman
Gingrich, Mauree A. state representative
Golden, Thomas M. lawyer
Gornish, Gerald lawyer
Gover, Raymond Lewis retired newspaper executive
Greenleaf, Stewart John state legislator
Grobman, Gary M. writer
Hafer, Barbara state official
Hample, Judy G. academic administrator
Hanson, Robert DeLolle lawyer
Herman, Lynn Briggs state legislator
Houstoun, Feather O'Connor state official
Howett, John Charles, Jr., lawyer
Jubelirer, Robert C. lieutenant governor
Kane, Yvette lawyer, judge
Kelly, Robert Edward, Jr., lawyer
Khanzhina, Helen P. English educator, translator
Klein, Michael D. lawyer
Knackstedt, Mary V. interior designer
Koken, M. Diane state commissioner
Kukovich, Allen Gale state legislator, lawyer
Kury, Franklin Leo lawyer
Lappas, Spero Thomas lawyer
Laughlin, Susan state legislator
Lederer, Marie A. state legislator
Logue, James Nicholas epidemiologist
Long, Robert Howard, Jr., lawyer
Mackereth, Beverly D. state representative
Mahey, John Andrew retired museum director
Mann, Jennifer L. state representative
Margolis, David Leslie government agency administrator
Marley, James Earl former manufacturing company executive
Miller, Leslie Anne lawyer
Miller, Sheila state legislator
Moritz, Milton Edward security consultant
Nauman, Spencer Gilbert, Jr., lawyer, director
Novak, Alan P. political organization administrator
Pappert, Gerald J. (Jerry) state attorney general
Patterson, Robert Eugene insurance company executive
Perzel, John Michael state legislator
Pickett, Tina L. state representative
Pizzingrilli, Kim state official

Pringle, Rebecca *elementary school educator*
Prioleau, Sara Nelliene *dentist*
Rambo, Sylvia H. *federal judge*
Rendell, Edward Gene *governor, former mayor, lawyer*
Saylor, Thomas G. *state supreme court justice*
Schwartz, Allyson Y. *state legislator*
Sheldon, J. Michael *lawyer, educator*
Stanley, Edward Alexander *geologist, forensic scientist, technical and academic administrator*
Staub, Shalom David *cultural organization administrator*
Stwalley, Brian David *pharmacist*
Sullivan, John Cornelius, Jr., *lawyer*
Tartaglione, Christine M. *state legislator*
Taylor, Elinor Zimmerman *state legislator*
True, Katie *state legislator*
Tyler, Brian Joseph *lawyer*
Urkiel, William Stanley *diversified company executive*
Vance, Patricia H. *state legislator*
Van Zile, Philip Taylor, III, *lawyer, educator*
Warshaw, Allen Charles *lawyer*
Watson, Katharine M. *state representative*
Weber, Melissa Murphy *state representative*
Wentzel, Paul H., Jr., *state agency administrator*
West, James Joseph *lawyer*
White, Mary Jo *state legislator, lawyer*
Williams, Constance *state senator*
Wolfe, Gary Donald *library commissioner, retired state education official*

Harrison City
Langer, Alois *communications executive*
McWilliams, Samuel Robert *secondary school educator*

Harveys Lake
Wolensky, Joan *occupational therapist, interfaith minister*

Hatboro
Carroll, Lucy Ellen *choral director, music coordinator, educator*
Cuozzo, James Richard *paper converting machinery manufacturing executive*
Nicholson, Bruce Allen *lawyer*

Hatfield
Jesberg, Robert Ottis, Jr., *educational consultant, science educator*
Taylor, Alan Charles *chaplain, counselor, researcher*

Haverford
Aronson, Carl Edward *pharmacology and toxicology educator*
Brand, Charles Macy *history professor*
Brownlow, Donald Grey *private school educator*
Dawson, John David *academic administrator, religious studies educator*
de Laguna, Frederica *anthropology educator emeritus, writer, publisher*
DiBerardino, Marie Antoinette *developmental biologist, educator*
Erickson, Ralph O. *botany educator*
Glickman, Harvey *retired social sciences educator*
Goppelt, John Walter *physician, psychiatrist*
Jorden, Eleanor Harz *linguist, educator*
Kee, Howard Clark *religion educator*
Merrill, Arthur Alexander *financial analyst*
Northrup, Herbert Roof *economist, business executive*
Olson, Robert Edward *coal mining executive*
Roelofs, Lyle Dean *physicist, researcher*
Rosefsky, Jonathan Benensohn *pediatrician*
Stiller, Jennifer Anne *lawyer*
Stroud, James Stanley *retired lawyer*
Stuard, Susan Mosher *education educator*
Talucci, Samuel James *retired chemical company executive*
Tritton, Thomas Richard *academic administrator, biologist, educator*

Havertown
Brinker, Thomas Michael *finance executive*
Craley, Carol Ruth *art educator, academic administrator*
Hendrickson, Paul Joseph *journalist, author, writing educator*
Korényi-Both, András Levente *pathologist, educator*
Kostkiewicz, Krzysztof *electrical engineer, journalist*
Smith, Phillip Thurmond *historian, educator*
Somach, S. Dennis *communications executive*
Wing, Kennard Thompson *educational organization official*

Hawley
Kanzer, Larry *small business owner, food service director*
Persche, Henry-Peter *art consultant, artist*

Hazleton
Ambrose, Sherry L *principal, elementary school educator*
Colangelo, Rocco, Jr., *sales executive*
Miller, David Emanuel *physics educator, researcher*
Schiavo, Pasco Louis *lawyer*

Herman
Dittmer, Sylvester Stephen Wess *retired nursing administrator*

Herminie
Taylor, John Calvin *dentist, missionary*

Hermitage
Gurgovits, Stephen J. *trust company executive*

Hershey
Adams, David R. *dermatologist*
Ballard, James Otis, III, *medical educator, physician*
Butterfield, Andrea Christine *elementary school educator, adult education educator, psychology educator*
Cerminara, Frank *food products executive*
Christensen, Dawn Michelle *family practice nurse practitioner, consultant*
Davis, Dwight *cardiologist, educator*
Davis, George F. *food products executive*
Domen, Ronald Eugene *physician*
Eyster, Mary Elaine *hematologist, educator*
Hopper, Anita Klein *molecular genetics educator*
Hortman, David Jones *secondary school educator*
Jones, Marshall Bush *education educator, researcher*
Kees-Folts, Deborah *pediatrician, educator*
Kirch, Darrell Gene *academic administrator, dean*
Leaman, David Martin *cardiologist, educator*
Lenny, Richard Herbert *food products executive, marketing professional*
Lingle, Virginia Ann *school librarian*
Madewell, John Edward *radiologist*
Marks, James Garfield, Jr., *dermatologist*
Marshall, Wayne Keith *anesthesiology educator*
Moskowitz, Jay *health sciences administrator*
Naeye, Richard L. *pathologist, educator*
Naides, Stanley J. *physician, educator, researcher*
Norgren, Ralph *neuroscientist*
Ouyang, Ann *physician, researcher, educator*
Pierce, William Schuler *cardiac surgeon*
Reese, Robert M. *retired lawyer*
Rogowicz, Edward Joseph *industrial arts, technology educator*
Severs, Walter Bruce *pharmacology educator, researcher*
Tan, Tjiauw-Ling *psychiatrist, educator*
Uhde, Thomas Whitley *psychiatry educator, psychiatrist*
Undar, Akif *research scientist, biomedical engineer, educator*
Vesell, Elliot Saul *pharmacologist, educator*
Viviano, Joseph P. *food products executive*
Waldhausen, John Anton *retired surgeon, educator, editor*
Wassner, Steven Joel *pediatric nephrologist, educator*
Wolfe, Kenneth L. *food products manufacturing company executive*
Zelis, Robert Felix *cardiologist, educator*

Holland
Umbreit, Wayne William *bacteriologist, educator*

Hollidaysburg
Bloom, Lawrence Stephen *retired clothing company executive*
Cottle, Harold Ranson *pathologist, laboratory owner*
Deskevich, Paul *mathematics professor*

Honesdale
Algieri, Sal Edward *sportswriter*
Barbe, Walter Burke *education educator*
Brown, Kent Louis, Jr., *magazine editor*
Clark, Christine May *editor, author*

Hopwood
Syphers, James Edgar *retired social worker*

Horsham
Best, Franklin Luther, Jr., *lawyer*
Fisher, Darryl *information services company executive*
Johnson, G. Carol *financial services executive*
Perdue, Franklin P. *retired poultry/agricultural products executive*
Schopp, David L. *music educator*

Houston
Briggs, Rich *secondary school educator*

Hulmeville
Jackson, Mary L. *health services executive*

Hummelstown
Clouse, Jerry Allan *architectural historian*
Creswell, Charles Alexander *process engineering and management consultant*
Worthington, John M. *information technology executive*

Huntingdon
Durnbaugh, Donald Floyd *church history educator, researcher*
Kepple, Thomas Ray, Jr., *college administrator*
Trexler, John Peter *retired geology educator, researcher*
Tuten, James H. *educational association administrator, educator*

Huntingdon Valley
Barzilay, Zvi *real estate executive*
Cohen, Michael R. *health facility administrator, pharmacist*
Edelman, Janice *artist, educator*
Forman, Howard Irving *lawyer, former government official*
Godfrey, John Carl *medicinal chemist*
Isard, Phillip Isaac *medical nutritionist, consultant*
Kaufman, David Joseph *lawyer*
Lefton, Harvey Bennett *gastroenterologist, educator, author*
Toll, Robert Irwin *lawyer, real estate developer*
Vollum, Robert Boone *management consultant*
West, A(rnold) Sumner *chemical engineer*

Immaculata
Fadden, Sister R. Patricia *academic administrator, nun*
Rondinaro, Peter Dominick *social sciences educator, psychologist*

Indiana
Bowers, Fredalene Barletta *education educator, consultant*
Cashdollar, Charles David *history educator*
Farag, Waleed E *science educator*
Garvin, C(larence) Alexander, Jr., *economics professor*
Horner, Ronald George *music educator, musician*
Jeckavitch, David M. *music educator*
LaRoche, Lynda *artist, educator*
Masilela, Calvin Onias *land use planner, educator*
Mc Cauley, R. Paul *criminologist, educator*
Miller, Vincent Paul, Jr., *geography and regional planning educator*
Perlongo, Daniel James *composer, educator*
Pettit, Lawrence Kay *university president*
Princes, Carolyn Diane Wilbon *educational director*
Shim, Leem Seop *computer scinetist, educator, researcher*
Soule, Robert D. *safety and health educator, administrator*
Steelman, Sara Gerling *art association administrator*
Stern, T. Noel *political scientist, educator*
Thibadeau, Eugene Francis *education educator, consultant*
Tobin, Lois Moore *retired home economist, educator*
Walker, Donald Anthony *economist, educator*

Irwin
Brown, Donald Clyde *surgeon*
Kuhn, Howard Arthur *engineering executive, educator*

Ivyland
Thorne, John Watson, III, *advertising and marketing executive*

Jamison
O'Hanlon, Michael A. *finance company executive*
Touhill, C. Joseph *environmental engineer*

Jenkintown
Dickstein, Joan Borteck *arbitrator, conflict management consultant*
DiSandro, Linda Anita *counselor*
Greenspan-Margolis, June E. *psychiatrist*
Purcell, James Michael *science educator*
Reese, Francis Edward *retired chemical company executive, consultant*
Robbins, Jack Winton *lawyer*
Sadoff, Robert Leslie *psychiatrist, educator*
Worthington, Sandra Boulton *lawyer*

Jersey Shore
Flayhart, Martin Albert *lawyer*

Jessup
Karluk, Lori Jean *craft designer, copy editor*

Jim Thorpe
Umbehocker, Kenneth Sheldon *priest*

Johnstown
Alcamo, Frank Paul *retired educational administrator*
Babik, Dennis Allen *social worker, consultant*
Brice, William Riley *geology educator, planetary science educator*
Danchanko, Marilyn A. *mathematics professor*
Depra, Alan Jay *mechanical engineer*
Glosser, William Louis *lawyer*
Lindberg, Stephen *secondary school educator*
Miloro, Protopresbter Frank *church official, religious studies educator*
Nicholas, (Richard G. Smisko) *bishop*
Samples, Jerry Wayne *military officer, educator*
Sheehan, Edward James *technical consultant, former government official*
Simmons, Elroy, Jr., *retired utility executive*
Smisko, Nicholas Richard *bishop, educator*
Stevens, Terry L. *realty company executive*

Jones Mills
Fish, Paul Waring *lawyer*

Kelton
Gulick, Walter Lawrence *psychologist, former college president*

Kempton
Lenhart, Cynthia Rae *conservation organization executive*

Kennett Square
Bainbridge, John Seaman *retired law school administrator, law educator, lawyer*
Bell, Philip Wilkes *accounting and economics educator*
Brigman, Dorothea Jane Pengelly *secondary and elementary education educator*
Dwyer, Francis Gerard *chemical engineer, researcher*
Fish, Robert H. *long term care industry executive*
Fussell, Catharine Pugh *biological researcher*
Hager, George V. *health services executive*
Hennes, Robert Taft *former management consultant, investment executive*
Landstrom, Elsie Hayes *retired editor*
Lippincott, Sarah Lee *astronomer, graphologist*
Martin, George (George Whitney Martin) *writer*
May, Harold Edward *chemical company executive*
Partnoy, Ronald Allen *lawyer*
Poppenga, Robert H. *veterinary toxicology educator*
Souney, Paul Frederick *pharmacist*

Kimberton
Williams, Lawrence Soper, Jr., *photographer*

King Of Prussia
Anderson, Eric E. *healthcare services executive*
Anderson, Jerry Allen *financial analyst*
Boles, Donald Michael *lawyer*
Broido, Arnold Peace *music publishing company executive*
Clauson, Sharyn Ferne *consulting company executive, educator*
Filton, Steve G. *corporate financial executive*
Gadsden, Christopher Henry *lawyer, educator*
Gallis, John Nicholas *retired military officer, executive leadership training consultant*
Greenberg, Lon Richard *energy company executive, lawyer*
Hegedus, L. Louis *chemical engineer, research and development company executive*
Helmetag, Diana *music educator*
Lee, Robert *engineer*
Marcus, Stephen Cecil *former printing company executive*
Martini, Perry James *educational consultant*
Mendicino, Anthony J. *gas company executive*
Miller, Alan B. *hospital management executive*
Schneider, Pam Horvitz *lawyer*
Schumann, Paula M. L. *writer*
Szabo, Joseph Laszlo *management consultant*
Volpe, Ralph Pasquale *retired insurance company executive*
Wachs, David V. *retired apparel executive*
Yan, Ying *statistician, researcher*

Kingston
Denaro, Anthony Thomas *psychiatrist*
Friedman, Pauline Poplin *civic worker, consultant*
Marko, Andrew Paul *school system administrator*
Shaffer, Charles Alan *lawyer*
Weisberger, Barbara *artistic director, educator, choreographer*

Kinzers
Blake, Richard E. *sculptor, art educator*

Kittanning
Smits, Ronald Francis *English educator, poet*

Knox
Rupert, Elizabeth Anastasia *retired dean*

Kutztown
Dougherty, Percy H. *geographer, educator, politician, planner*
Laub, Mary Lou *elementary school educator*
Meyer, Susan Moon *speech language pathologist, educator*
Ogden, James Russell *marketing educator, consultant, lecturer, writer*
Pirmot, Thomas L. *mathematician, educator*
Watrous, Robert Thomas *academic director*

La Plume
Boehm, Edward Gordon, Jr., *college administrator, educator*

Lafayette Hill
Delacato, Janice Elaine *learning consultant, educator*
Duncalfe Holt, Lucinda Bromwyn *marketing executive*
Green, Raymond Ferguson St. John *marketing and advertising executive*
King, Diane Averbach *education educator*
King, Leon *financial services executive*

Lake Harmony
Polansky, Larry Paul *court administrator, consultant*

Lancaster
Ashby, Richard James, Jr., *bank executive, lawyer*
Binkley, Luther John *philosophy educator*
Brod, Roy David *ophthalmologist, educator*
Brunner, Lillian Sholtis *nurse, writer*
Buchanan, Lovell *entertainer*
Burlingame, Mark Wayne *cardiothoracic surgeon*
Carlisle, James Patton *entrepreneur*
Dodge, Arthur Byron, Jr., *business executive, marketing professional*
Drum, Alice *academic administrator, educator*
Ebersole, J. Glenn, Jr., *engineering, marketing, management and public relations executive*
Ebersole, Mark Chester *emeritus college president*
Falk, Robert Barclay, Jr., *anesthesiologist, educator*
Freeman, Clarence Calvin *financial executive*
Fry, John Anderson *academic administrator*
Glick, Garland Wayne *retired theological seminary president*
Grochowski, Jelsia *music educator*
Hall, Kimberly *language educator, consultant*
Hall, Thomas Wayne *lawyer*
Hart, LeRoy Banks *systems administrator, director*
Heil, Paul Samuel *radio program producer*
High, S. Dale *diversified company executive*
Hudak, Joseph David *forensic engineer, educator, police investigator*
Kelly, Robert Lynn *advertising agency executive*
Kendall, Leigh Wakefield *surgeon*
Kermes, Constantine John *artist, industrial designer*
Kneedler, Richard (Alvin Kneedler) *former academic administrator*
Lewis, Alvin Bower, Jr., *lawyer*
Liddell, W. Kirk *specialty contracting company executive*
Linton, Joy Smith *primary school educator*
Lockhart, Michael D. *building materials company executive*
Lorch, George A. *manufacturing executive*
Lu, Milton Ming-Deh *plastic surgeon, consultant*
Minney, Michael Jay *lawyer*
Nast, Dianne Martha *lawyer*
Pyfer, John Frederick, Jr., *lawyer*
Roda, Joseph Francis *lawyer*
Rung, George W. *physician*
Shaw, Charles Raymond *journalist*
Shenk, Lois Elaine Landis *writer*
Shenk, Willis Weidman *newspaper executive*
Smith, Thomas Clair *retired manufacturing company executive*
Steiner, Robert Lisle *retired language consultant*
Stephenson, Donald Grier, Jr., *political science professor*
Stewart, Arlene Jean Golden *designer, stylist*
Taylor, Ann *human resources specialist, educator*
Veitch, Boyer Lewis *printing company executive*
Watson, Mark S. *music educator*
Wenger, Jay Lamar *psychology educator*
Zimmerman, D(onald) Patrick *lawyer*

Langhorne
Babb, Wylie Sherrill *college president*
Hillje, Barbara Brown *lawyer*

Lansdale
Anton, Francis Matthew, Jr., *information technology manager*
Elliott, Arthur Y. *microbiologist, administrator*
Fawley, John Jones *retired banker*
Rothenberger, Jack Renninger *clergyman*
Strohecker, Leon Harry, Jr., *orthodontist*
Sultanik, Jeffrey Ted *lawyer*

Lansdowne
Larsen, Terrance A. *retired bank holding company executive*

Large
Dick, Douglas Patrick *construction company executive*

Latrobe
Tambakeras, Markos I. *machine tool manufacturer*
Torisky, Eugene Vincent, Jr., *philosopher, educator*

Laureldale
Rozzi, Christine M. *mathematician, educator*

Lebanon
Copenhaver, John Edward *music educator*
McMindes, Roy James *aggregate company executive*
Moss, Richard Spencer *communications executive*

Paul, Herman Louis, Jr., *valve manufacturing company executive*

Lederach
Hallman, H(enry) Theodore, Jr., (Ted Hallman) *artist, textile designer*

Leesport
Jackson, Eric Allen *philatelist*

Lehman
Felty, Wayne Lee *chemist, educator*

Lemoyne
Klein, Michael Elihu *physician*
Stewart, Richard Williams *lawyer*
Vickery, Jon Livingstone *neurologist*

Levittown
Halberstein, Joseph Leonard *retired associate editor*
Henshaw, Jonathan Cook *retired manufacturing executive*

Lewisberry
Smith, Bruce I. *state legislator*

Lewisburg
Aldrich, Robert Adams *agricultural engineer, consultant*
Bannon, George *retired economics educator, department chairman*
Candland, Douglas Keith *psychology professor*
Huffines, Marion Lois *academic administrator, linguist, educator, language educator*
Jump, Chester Jackson, Jr., *clergyman, church official*
Knight, Louise Osborn *lawyer*
Neuman, Nancy Adams Mosshammer *civic leader*
Orbison, James Graham *civil engineer, educator*
Payne, Michael David *English language educator*
Rote, Nelle Fairchild Hefty *management consultant*
Schlegel, Richard LaMar *advocate, writer*
Sojka, Gary Allan *biologist, educator, academic administrator*
Warner-Mills, Susan *organizational and community development consultant*

Ligonier
Mellon, Seward Prosser *investment executive*
Pilz, Alfred Norman *manufacturing executive*

Lincoln University
Nelson, Ivory Vance *academic administrator*
Nwachuku, Levi Akalazu *social sciences and behavioral studies educator*
Williams, Willie, Jr., *physicist, researcher*

Linwood
Cogan, Marshall S. *entrepreneur*

Lititz
Haines, Ronald H. *retired bishop*
Hartz, Brian David *physical therapist, educator, small business owner*
Koch, Bruce R. *diplomat*

Lock Haven
Almes, June *retired education educator, librarian*
Congdon, Howard Krebs *philosopher, clergyman, educator*
Forbes, Edward John, III, *developmental psychologist, educator*
Moyer, Anna Blackburn *retired secondary and elementary school educator*
Story, Julie Ann *English educator*
Willis, Craig Dean *academic administrator*

Loretto
Melusky, Joseph Anthony *political science professor, department chairman*

Lower Gwynedd
Pendleton, Robert Grubb *pharmacologist*

Lumberville
Fallon, Robert Thomas *English language educator*
Katsiff, Bruce *artist*

Lykens
Sultzbaugh, John Stephan *historian, educator*

Lyon Station
Breidegam, DeLight Edgar, Jr., *battery company executive*

Macungie
Farr, Lona Mae *non-profit executive, business owner*
Moore, Joyce Kristina *financial planner, director*
Nenstiel, Susan Kisthart *fundraising professional*
Rubin, Arthur Herman *retired university official, consultant*

Malvern
Bedford, Anne Marie *musician, educator, insurance agent*
Bedrosian, Gregory Ronald *investment banker*
Brighton, Ruth Louise *lay worker, educator*
Clariana, Roy Boris *education educator*
Espe, Matthew J. *manufacturing executive*
Everhart, Rodney Lee *software industry executive*
Forese, James John *business machine company executive*
Hendrix, Stephen C. *financial executive*
Herring, Raymond Mark *marketing professional, researcher*
Hilzinger, Kurt John *healthcare company executive*
James, George L. *healthcare manufacturing executive*
Prichard, Joyce S. *music educator*
Rucker, Donald W. *emergency physician, educator, consultant*
Stetson, John Batterson, IV, *construction executive*

Manheim
Soltys, Stephen Robert *mathematician, educator*

Manns Choice
Braendel, Douglas Arthur *hotel executive*

Mansfield
Dettwiler, Peggy Diane *music educator*
Guenther, Karen *history professor*

Maple Glen
Jacobson, Bonnie Brown *writer, energy executive, statistician, researcher*
Weaver-Stroh, Joanne Mateer *education educator, consultant*

Marion Center
Purdy, David Lawrence *medical products executive*

Mars
Seltzer, Mitchell Sherman *hotel executive*

Marshalls Creek
Johnson, Loren Charisse *publishing executive, writer*

Martinsburg
Keith, Tammy Leah *geriatrics nurse*
Neff, Robert Wilbur *academic administrator, educator, minister*

Mc Kees Rocks
Barczynski, John Leslie *periodontist*

Mc Keesport
Kessler, Steven Fisher *lawyer*

Mc Murray
Brzustowicz, John Cinq-Mars *lawyer*
Diamond, Daniel Lloyd *surgeon*
Langenberg, Frederick Charles *business executive*

Meadville
Adams, Earl William, Jr., *economics professor*
Barrett, Bruce Alan *lawyer*
Cable, Charles Allen *mathematician*
Cable, Mabel Elizabeth *urban planner, artist*
Dixon, Armendia Pierce *school program administrator*
Gilles, Bruce Carlson *civil engineer*
Helmreich, Jonathan Ernst *history professor*
Hoover, Lynn E. *manufacturing executive*

Mechanicsburg
Derr, William James *retired non-commissioned officer*
Eakin, J. Michael *judge*
Gibbons, Miles Joseph, Jr., *foundation administrator*
Hoffman, Diane Mae *special education educator*
Stone, Thomas Richardson *management consultant*

Media
Berman, Bernard Mayer *lawyer*
Blake, David Gordon *lawyer*
Brobeck, John Raymond *physiology educator*
Chambers, Ed *convenience store executive*
Cimbala, Stephen Joseph *political science educator*
Durham, James W. *lawyer*
Emerson, Sterling Jonathan *lawyer*
Ewing, Robert Clark *lawyer*
Garrison, Susan Kay *lawyer*
Garrison, Walter R. *engineering executive, director*
Garvin, Florence Ward *management consultant*
Ginsberg, Robert E. *philosophy educator, editor*
Gordon, Lisa Diane *psychologist*
Hemphill, James S. *investment management executive, financial advisor*
Hornet, Andrea *education educator, consultant*
Resnick, Stewart Allen *diversified company executive*
Rubin, Arnold E. *lawyer*
Sorkin, Adam J. *English educator*
Steinhardt Gutman, Bertha *artist, educator*
Turner, Letitia Rhodes *artist*
Voltz, Sterling Ernest *physical chemist, researcher*
Wood, Richard D., Jr., *retail executive*

Melrose Park
Rabinovitz, Nili *language educator, consultant*

Mendenhall
Frangopoulos, Zissimos A. *banker*
Reinert, Norbert Frederick *patent lawyer, retired chemical company executive*

Mercersburg
Tompkins, Christopher Robin *director, educator*

Merion Station
Camp, Kimberly N. *museum administrator, artist*
Coppa, Anthony Patrick *engineer, consultant*
Freeze, James Donald *administrator, clergyman*
Lewis, Paul Le Roy *pathology educator*
Littell, Marcia Sachs *Holocaust and genocide studies educator*
Mayer, Charles Arthur *management consultant, musician*

Milford
Le Guin, Ursula Kroeber *writer*
Reynolds, Edwin Wilfred, Jr., *retired secondary education educator*
Rosenblum, Jeffrey Ira *consulting economist*

Milford Square
Sewell, Gloriana *piano teacher*

Millersville
Heintzelman, Carol Ann *social work educator*
Miller, Steven Max *humanities educator*

Millville
Shoup, Michael C. *newspaper reporter, editor*

Mohnton
Bowers, Richard Philip *manufacturing executive*
Hildreth, Eugene A. *physician, educator*

Monaca
Soltes, Joann Margaret *retired music educator, realtor*

Monroeville
Cohen, Laura *lawyer*
Di Gioia, Anthony Michael, Jr., *civil engineer, business executive*
Hribar, John Anthony *civil engineer, consultant*
Jacobi, William Mallett *nuclear engineer, consultant*
Klink, Ron *former congressman, reporter, newscaster*
Mandel, Herbert Maurice *civil engineer*
Read, Robert Allen *music educator*
Skolnick, Marilyn *civic worker*

Montgomeryville
Detwiler, Christine Wendler *special education educator*
Schmidt, William Max *management consultant, business executive*

Montoursville
Morrison, Michael Christopher *advertising executive*
Woolever, Naomi Louise *retired editor-in-chief*

Moon Township
Alstadt, Lynn Jeffery *lawyer*
Lipson, Barry J. *lawyer, columnist*
Rabosky, Joseph George *engineering consulting company executive*

Morrisville
Heefner, William Frederick *lawyer*

Moscow
Shotko, Kurt Joseph *entrepreneur, music entertainer*

Mount Gretna
Warshaw, Roberta Sue *lawyer*

Mount Joy
Lodde, Gordon Maynard *health physics consultant*

Mount Pleasant
Dangelo, Eugene Michael *elementary school educator*
Domit, John *surgeon*

Mountainhome
Buttz, Charles William *outdoor advertising executive*

Mountaintop
Pendziwiatr, William J. *music educator*

Muncy
West, Thomas James *music educator*

Murrysville
Maurer, Richard Michael *investment company executive*

Nanticoke
Domzalski, Ronald Laurence *audio-visual specialist, educator*
Donohue, Patricia Carol *academic administrator*

Narberth
Chait, Arnold *retired radiologist*
Comer, Nathan Lawrence *psychiatrist, educator*
Goldstein, Martin Barne *osteopathic physician, psychiatrist*
Grenald, Raymond *architectural lighting designer*
Nathanson, Neal *virologist, epidemiologist, educator*
Strom, Brian Leslie *internist, educator*

Natrona Heights
Maleski, Cynthia Maria *lawyer*

Nazareth
Haynes, Thomas Morris *philosophy educator*
Rayner, Robert Martin *financial executive*

Nescopeck
Shultz, Jack Ellsworth *education educator*

New Bethlehem
Reefer, Russell Charles *music educator*

New Buffalo
Cramer, John McNaight *lawyer*

New Castle
Manolis, James William *lawyer*
Roux, Mildred Anna *retired secondary school educator*
Sands, Christine Louise *English educator*

New Cumberland
Loux, Jonathan Dale *business development consultant*
Peters, Ralph Edgar *architectural firm executive, engineering executive*
Scheiner, James Ira *engineering company executive*

New Freedom
Sedlak, Valerie Frances *retired English language educator, retired academic administrator*

New Holland
Fanus, Pauline Rife *librarian*
West, Daniel Charles *dentist*

New Hope
Freyer, Victoria C. *fashion and interior design executive*
John, Francis D. *energy executive*
Knight, Douglas Maitland *educational administrator, optical executive, writer*
Raabe, Gerhard Karl *epidemiologist*
Rodwell, John Dennis *biochemist*
Sergey, John Michael, Jr., *investment company executive*
Stahl, Stephen Lee *theater director, writer, producer*
Thomsen, Thomas Richard *retired communications company executive*

New Kensington
Demmler, Albert William, Jr., *retired editor, metallurgical engineer*
Jarrett, Noel *chemical engineer, researcher*
Kalavar, Jyotsna Mirle *education educator*
Wallace, Henry Jared, Jr., *lawyer*

New Kingstown
DiSipio, Rocco Thomas *writer*

New Oxford
Frock, J. Daniel *transportation executive, retired manufacturing company executive*
Rohrbaugh, Nova R *retired music educator*

New Tripoli
Hess, Darla Bakersmith *cardiologist, educator*

New Wilmington
Martin, Russell *historian, educator*
McCormick, Kimberly A *elementary school educator*
McKee, Delber L. *retired education educator*
Taylor, Gary B. *music educator*

Newfoundland
Grotta, Daniel *writer, editor*

Newtown
Booraem, Hendrik, V, *education educator, historian*
Brennan, Thomas John *city and state official, consultant, educator*
Duncan, Stephen Robert *elementary school educator*
Fiore, James Louis, Jr., *accountant, educator*
Golub, Harvey *financial services company executive*
Grubbs, Donald Shaw, Jr., *retired actuary*
Kardos, Mel D. *lawyer, educator*
Keenan, Terrance *foundation executive*
Long, Harry (On-Yuen Eng) *chemist, science and technology executive, consultant*
Nowak, Jerry (Gerald C. Nowak) *music educator, musician, writer*
Richard, James Thomas *retired psychologist, educator*
Ross, Edwin William *rubber company executive*
Schroeder, Alfred Christian *electronics research engineer*
Sheridan, John J. *musician, music educator*
Somers, Anne Ramsay *retired medical educator*
Woods, Howard James, Jr., *civil engineer*
Zicherman, David L. *lawyer, educator, financial consultant*

Newtown Square
Benenson, James, Jr., *manufacturer*
Bower, Ward Alan *management consultant, lawyer*
Cordes, Eugene Harold *pharmacy and chemistry educator*
de Rivas, Carmela Foderaro *retired psychiatrist, retired health facility administrator*
Graf, Arnold Harold *employee benefits executive, financial planner*
Lawrence, Theodore *physician*
Lewis, James Earl *investor*
Perrone, Nicholas *mechanical engineer, business executive*
Staats, Dean Roy *retired reinsurance executive*

Norristown
Aman, George Matthias, III, *lawyer*
Biondi, Anthony *municipal official*
Britt, Earl Thomas *lawyer*
Gaber, Robert *psychologist*
Garabedian, Joseph Andre *physician*
Gold-Bikin, Lynne Z. *lawyer*
Hess, Wanda Jean *health facility administrator*
Raquet, Maureen Graham *protective services official, educator*
Rees, Thomas Dynevor *lawyer*
Reilley, Gail Goodwin *soprano, music educator, musician*
Rounick, Jack A. *lawyer, company executive*
Scheffler, Stuart Jay *lawyer*
Steinberg, Arthur Irwin *periodontist, educator*
Whittington, Cathy Dee *chemist*

North Hills
Price, Nancy D. *retired banker, writer*

North Wales
Sheares, Bradley T. *pharmaceutical executive*

Nottingham
White, Richard Edmund *marketing executive*

Oakdale
Humbert, Darren Mark *music educator*
Wang, Chuan-Bao *chemist, research scientist*

Oil City
Loring, Richard William *psychotherapist*
Sabousky, Richard Anthony *adult education educator*

Olyphant
Batzel, Edward Lee *surgeon*

Orefield
Dimmich, Jeffrey Robert *lawyer*

Oxford
Palser, Beth Anne *painter*

Palmyra
Moseley, Marc Robards *sales executive*

Paoli
Blankley, Walter Elwood *manufacturing executive*
Denny, William Murdoch, Jr., *investment management executive*
Yake, Sarah Louise *poet*

Parkesburg
Zevtchin, J. Mark *financial executive, consultant*

Peach Glen
Carey, Dean Lavere *fruit canning company executive*

Pen Argyl
Martocci, Lewis Nicholas, III, *writer*

Penn Valley
Newhall, John Harrison *retired non profit company executive*

Perkasie
Ferry, Joan Evans *school counselor*
Lang, Susan Marie *minister*
White, Michael R. *secondary school educator, consultant*

Philadelphia

Abramowitz, Robert Leslie *lawyer*
Abrams, Charles S. *oncologist, hematologist, educator*
Abreu, Bobby *professional baseball player*
Adamany, David Walter *law and political science educator*
Adams, Arlin Marvin *lawyer, arbitrator, mediator, retired judge*
Adawi, Nadia Sharon *energy cooperative executive*
Adler, Martin William *neuropharmacologist*
Aiken, Linda Harman *nurse, sociologist, educator*
Ajzenberg-Selove, Fay *physicist, researcher*
Alaigh, Poonam *health facility administrator*
Albertini, William Oliver *retired telecommunications industry executive*
Alchin, John Reginald *cable company executive*
Alcock, Charles Roger *science educator*
Alexander, Elmore Rosebur, III, *business educator, dean*
Alexander, William Herbert *business educator, former construction executive*
Alsardary, Salar *mathematician, educator*
Altschuler, Steven M. *health facility executive, pediatrician, gastroenterologist*
Amsterdam, Jay D. *psychiatrist, department chairman*
Anania, Andrea *insurance company executive*
Anders, Jerrold P. *lawyer*
Anderson, Rolph Ely *finance educator*
Andrisani, Paul J. *business educator, management consultant*
Anyanwu, Chukwukre *alcohol/drug abuse services professional*
Arce, A. Anthony *psychiatrist, educator*
Armstrong, C. Michael *communications company executive*
Armstrong, Clay *physiology educator*
Arnold, Lee *library director, archivist*
Asbury, Arthur Knight *neurologist, educator*
Asher, Steven Alan *lawyer*
Assoian, Richard Kenneth *molecular biologist, educator*
Aston-Jones, Gary S. *psychiatry educator*
Auerbach, Sheryl Lynn *lawyer*
Austan, Frank Acosta *clinician, educator*
Austrian, Robert *internist, medical educator, department chairman*
Auten, David Charles *lawyer*
Aversa, Dolores Sejda *educational administrator*
Avery, William Joseph *packaging manufacturing company executive*
Azoulay, Bernard *chemicals company executive*
Babbel, David Frederick *finance and insurance educator*
Babich, George, Jr., *retail executive*
Baccini, Laurance Ellis *lawyer*
Bachman, Arthur *lawyer*
Backstrom, C. Stephen *communications executive*
Bacon, Edmund Norwood *city planner*
Ballard, Roberta A. *pediatrics educator*
Ballou, Roger H. *travel company executive*
Baltuch, Gordon Hirsh *neurosurgeon*
Banerji, Ranan Bihari *mathematics and computer science educator*
Banse, Amy L. *communications executive, lawyer*
Bantel, Linda Mae *former museum curator, consultant*
Barchi, Robert Lawrence *clinical neurologist, neuroscientist, educator*
Barker, Clyde Frederick *surgeon, educator*
Barnes, Vaughn Lamont, Jr., *social services administrator, social worker*
Barnett, Jonathan *architect, urban planner, educator*
Barnett, Samuel Treutlen *international company executive*
Barrett, James Edward, Jr., *management consultant*
Barrett, John J(ames), Jr., *lawyer*
Bartle, Harvey, III, *federal judge*
Bartlett, Allen Lyman, Jr., *retired bishop*
Bartolomeo, Paul Joseph, Jr., *lawyer*
Baserga, Renato Luigi *pathology educator*
Bass, Aaron *school system administrator*
Bates, James Earl *academic administrator*
Baum, Stanley *radiologist, educator*
Baxt, William Gordon *medical educator*
Bearn, Alexander Gordon *physician, researcher, retired pharmaceutical executive*
Beasley, James Edwin *lawyer*
Beauchamp, Gary Keith *physiologist*
Bechtle, Louis Charles *lawyer, retired federal judge*
Beck, Aaron Temkin *psychiatrist, educator*
Beck, Christine Safford *photographer, publisher, volunteer, school system administrator, academic administrator*
Beck, John Robert *pathologist, information scientist*
Becker, Edward Roy *judge*
Behrman, Jere Richard *economics professor*
Bell, Michael W. *insurance company executive*
Bennett, Amanda *editor*
Berg, Ivar Elis, Jr., *social science educator*
Bergelson, Jeffrey Michael *pediatrician, educator*
Berger, David *lawyer*
Berger, Harold *lawyer, electrical engineer*
Berger, Lawrence Howard *lawyer*
Berkley, Emily Carolan *lawyer*
Berkman, Richard Lyle *lawyer*
Berrettini, Wade H. *psychiatry educator*
Bershad, Jack R. *retired lawyer*
Bibbo, Marluce *physician, educator*
Biddle, Anthony Joseph Drexel, III, *investment banker*
Biddle, Daniel R. *editor, reporter*
Bigelow, Douglas C. *otolaryngologist*
Bilaniuk, Larissa Tetiana *neuroradiologist, educator*
Bildersee, Robert Alan *lawyer*
Binder, David Franklin *lawyer, writer*
Binswanger, David R. *business executive*
Binswanger, Frank G., Jr., *realty company executive*
Binswanger, John K. *real estate company executive*
Binzen, Peter Husted *columnist*
Bjärngard, Bengt Erik *medical educator*
Black, Allen Decatur *lawyer*
Black, Perry *neurological surgeon, educator*
Blavat, Jerry (Gerald Joseph Blavat) *radio and television personality, actor*
Bleshman, Michael Henry *radiologist*
Block, Arthur R. *communications executive*
Bluemle, Lewis William, Jr., *medical educator*
Blumberg, Baruch Samuel *academic research scientist*
Blume, Marshall Edward *finance educator*
Boden, Guenther *endocrinologist*
Bodine, James Forney *retired civic leader*
Boggia, Eugene Stephen *lawyer*
Bogis, Nana Eileen *librarian*
Bogutz, Jerome Edwin *lawyer, educator*
Bonner-Coles, Rochelle Denise *journalist, educator*
Bookspan, Michael Lloyd *musician*
Booth, Anna Belle *accountant*
Borer, Edward Turner *investment banker*
Boscia, Jon Andrew *insurance company executive*
Boss, Amelia Helen *law educator, lawyer*
Bove, Alfred Anthony *medical educator*
Bowa, Lawrence Robert (Larry Bowa) *professional baseball manager*
Bowman, Marjorie Ann *family practice physician, educator*
Boyer, Lisa *basketball coach*
Bracey, Cookie Frances Lee *minister*
Bradley, Kevin J. *publishing company executive*
Bradshaw, William Elbert *lawyer*
Brady, Luther W., Jr., *physician, radiation oncology educator*
Bressler, Barry E. *lawyer*
Brinster, Ralph Lawrence *biologist, educator*
Brodeur, Garret M. *oncologist*
Brodsky, Julian A. *broadcast executive, telecommunications industry executive*
Broennle, A. Michael *anesthesiologist*
Brooks, John Samuel Joseph *pathologist, researcher*
Brown, Betty Marie *government agency administrator*
Brown, Denise Scott *architect, urban planner*
Brown, Stephen D. *lawyer*
Brown, William Hill, III, *lawyer*
Browne, Stanhope Stryker *lawyer*
Broytman, Vladislav I. *hygenist*
Brucker, Paul C. *academic administrator, physician*
Buccino, Ernest John, Jr., *lawyer*
Buckwalter, Ronald Lawrence *federal judge*
Burbank, Stephen Bradner *law educator*
Burch, Francis Floyd *clergyman*
Burke, Sean *professional hockey player*
Burke, Stephen B. *communications executive*
Byrnes, Maureen K. *foundation administrator*
Caggiula, Samuel Matthew *publishing executive, consultant*
Calman, Robert Frederick *mining executive*
Calvert, Jay H., Jr., *lawyer*
Camp, Donald Eugene *experimental photographer, educator*
Campbell, Robert H. *retired oil company executive*
Cannon, John, III, *lawyer*
Capers, Gregg *secondary school educator, musician*
Carasik, Michael *writer, researcher*
Carey, Arthur Bernard, Jr., *editor, writer, columnist*
Carnecchia, Baldo M., Jr., *lawyer*
Carpenter, Nathaniel Dennard *resident health services director*
Carroll, Mark Thomas *lawyer*
Carson, Timothy Joseph *lawyer*
Carter, John Swain *museum administrator, consultant*
Carter, William A. *pharmaceuticals executive, medical educator*
Cashmore, Anthony *biologist, educator*
Casper, Charles B. *lawyer*
Cass, David *economist, educator*
Cassel, Christine Karen *physician*
Castille, Ronald D. *judge*
Cawley, Michael J. *medical educator, pharmacist*
Chance, Britton *biophysics and physical chemistry educator emeritus*
Charney, Natalie J. *behavioral health services administrator, researcher, educator and clinician*
Chen, Philip Minkang *investment banker, corporate executive, lawyer, engineer*
Cherken, Harry Sarkis, Jr., *lawyer*
Chertoff, Michael *federal judge*
Child, John Sowden, Jr., *lawyer*
Childress, Scott Julius *medicinal chemist*
Chimples, George *lawyer*
Christman, Jolley Bruce *educational research executive, educator*
Clark, Christopher Michael *neurologist, educator, clinic director*
Clark, John Arthur *lawyer*
Clark, John J. *economist, finance educator*
Clark, William H., Jr., *lawyer*
Clarke, Robert Earle (Bobby Clarke) *hockey executive*
Clarkin, John Francis *health care management educator*
Clearfield, Harris Reynold *physician*
Coblitz, Mark A. *communications executive*
Coché, Judith *psychologist, educator*
Cohen, Betsy Z. *bank executive*
Cohen, David Louis *lawyer*
Cohen, David Walter *academic administrator, educator, periodontist*
Cohen, Ira Myron *aeronautical and mechanical engineering educator*
Cohn, Mildred *biochemist, educator*
Coleman, Gerald Charles *judge, law educator*
Coleman, Robert J. *lawyer*
Colli, Bart Joseph *lawyer*
Collings, Robert L. *lawyer*
Colman, Robert Wolf *physician, medical educator, researcher*
Colson, Rosemary *music educator*
Comisky, Hope A. *lawyer*
Conn, Rex Boland, Jr., *physician, educator*
Connor, Bernadette Yvonne *retired writer*
Connor, Joseph Patrick, III, *lawyer*
Connor, Nancy L. *foundation executive*
Conway, John W. *manufacturing executive*
Cooney, J(ohn) Gordon, Jr., *lawyer*
Cooper, Edward Sawyer *cardiologist, internist, educator*
Cooper, Richard Lee *newspaper editor, journalist*
Cooperman, Barry S. *educational administrator, educator, scientist*
Coraza, Mary Catherine *psychologist*
Cornelius, Jeffrey Michael *music educator*
Coulson, Zoe Elizabeth *retired consumer marketing executive*
Cowles, Roger E. *computer consultant*
Cox, Robert Harold *physiology educator*
Cox, Roger Frazier *lawyer*
Coyne, Charles Cole *lawyer*
Cozen, Stephen Allen *lawyer*
Cramer, Harold *lawyer*
Crissey, Harrington E., Jr., *English as second language educator*
Croce, Pat *author, fitness trainer, former sports team executive*
Croisetiere, Jacques M. *chemicals executive*
Crumb, George Henry *composer, educator*
Cunningham, Jacqueline Lemmé *psychologist, educator, researcher*
Cunningham, Jessie Jerome *entrepreneur*
Dagit, Charles Edward, Jr., *architect, educator*
Dalinka, Murray Kenneth *radiologist, educator*
Dalton, David Robert *chemistry professor*
Daly, John M. *surgeon, educator*
Dalzell, Stewart *federal judge*
Damsgaard, Kell Marsh *lawyer*
D'Angio, Giulio John *radiologist, educator*
Danzon, Patricia M. *medical educator*
Dasgupta, Indranil *physician, educator*
Davies, Helen C. *microbiology educator*
Davis, Alan Jay *lawyer*
Davis, Allen Freeman *history educator, author*
Davis, C. VanLeer, III, *lawyer*
Davis, Paige (Mindy Paige Davis) *television host/personality*
Davis, Raymond, Jr., *physical chemistry researcher*
DeBunda, Salvatore Michael *lawyer*
de Cani, John Stapley *statistician, educator*
Delaney, Terence (Terry) P. *gas industry executive*
DeLong, David G. *architect, urban planner, educator*
Del Raso, Joseph Vincent *lawyer*
Devlin, John Gerard *lawyer, author*
d'Harnoncourt, Anne *museum director, museum administrator*
Diamond, Paul Steven *federal judge, lawyer, educator*
Diaz, Nelson *lawyer*
Di Benedetto, C. Anthony *marketing educator*
Dichter, Marc Allen *physician*
Dichter, Mark S. *lawyer*
Diebold, Francis X. *economist, educator*
Di Falco, Gerard A. *visual artist*
Dileo, Cheryl *music therapist*
Dilks, Park Bankert, Jr., *lawyer*
Dinges, David F. *psychology and psychiatry educator*
Dingus, Michael H. *gas industry executive*
Dinoso, Vicente Pescador, Jr., *physician, educator*
DiPalma, Joseph Rupert *pharmacology educator*
DiTrolio, Joseph *controller*
Djerassi, Isaac *physician, medical researcher*
Dobbs, Stanley *military officer, information quality engineer*
Doms, Robert W. *science educator*
Domzalski, John F. *city health department administrator*
Donaldson, Thomas *ethicist, educator*
Donnelly, Gloria Ferraro *university dean*
Donohue, James J. *lawyer*
Donohue, John Patrick *lawyer*
Dooner, Marlene S. *communications executive*
Doran, William Michael *lawyer*
Dordelman, William E. *communications executive*
Dorfman, John Charles *lawyer*
Dormans, John Paul *surgeon, educator*
Dougherty Buchholz, Karen *communications executive*
Douglas, Steven Daniel *immunologist, educator, director*
Dragon, Albert *lawyer*
Drake, Jayne Kribbs *university administrator, English educator*
Drake, William Frank, Jr., *lawyer*
Driver, Robert Baylor, Jr., *opera company administrator*
Drosdick, John Girard *oil company executive*
Drucker, Richard M. *educational consultant*
Dua, Kamal *communications executive*
Dubin, Leonard *lawyer*
Dubin, Stephen Victor *lawyer*
DuBois, Jan Ely *federal judge*
Dunn, Linda Kay *physician*
Dunn, Mary Maples *former university dean*
Dutton, P(eter) Leslie *biochemist, educator*
Dworetzky, Joseph Anthony *lawyer, city official*
Dymicky, Michael *retired chemist*
Eckenrode, William J. *former manufacturing executive*
Edwards, Barry R. *pharmaceutical executive*
Efstratiades, Anastasius *lawyer*
Ehrenpreis, Leon *mathematician, educator, rabbi*
Ehrlich, George Edward *rheumatologist, international pharmaceutical consultant*
Eisen, Howard Joel *internist, researcher*
Eisenberg, Burton L. *surgeon*
Eisenstein, Toby K. *microbiology educator*
Eiswerth, Barry Neil *architect, educator*
El-Deiry, Wafik S. *medical educator*
El-Sherif, Mahmoud A. *electrical engineering educator*
Erdmann, James Bernard *educational psychologist*
Eskin, Bernard Abraham *obstetrics and gynecology educator, medical researcher*
Esser, Carl Eric *lawyer*
Esterhai, John Louis, Jr., *surgeon, medical educator*
Evan, William Martin *sociologist, educator*
Ewald, William Bragg, III, *law educator, philosopher, educator*
Fader, Henry Conrad *lawyer*
Fagin, Claire Mintzer *nursing educator, nursing administrator*
Fala, Herman C. *lawyer*
Falkie, Thomas Victor *mining engineer, mining executive*
Farley, Barbara L. *lawyer*
Fegley, Kenneth Allen *systems engineering educator*
Feirson, Steven B. *lawyer*
Feldman, Arthur M. *cardiologist*
Feldman, Michael Saul *cardiologist, educator*
Feninger, Claude *industry management services company executive*
Fernandez, Happy Craven (Gladys Fernandez) *academic administrator*
Fernholz, Luisa Turrin *statistician, educator*
Ferrari, Victor Alfred *cardiologist*
Fickler, Arlene *lawyer*
Fiebach, H. Robert *lawyer*
Fielding, Allen Fred *oral and maxillofacial surgeon, educator*
Fineman, S. David *lawyer*
Finkelstein, Joseph Simon *lawyer*
Finney, Graham Stanley *management consultant*
Fischer, Bruce G. *gas industry executive*
Fisher, Aron Baer *physiology and medicine educator*
Fisher, Marshall Lee *operations management educator*
Fisher, Robert *gastroenterologist, health facility administrator*
Fisher, Wesley Andrew *museum director*
Fishman, Alfred Paul *physician*
Fitts, Donald Dennis *chemist, educator*
Fitts, Michael Andrew *law educator, dean*
FitzGerald, Garret Adare *medical educator*
Fitzpatrick, J. Michael *chemicals executive*
Flanagan, Joseph Patrick, Jr., *lawyer*
Flicker, Eric Lee *civil engineer, consultant*
Fonseca, Raymond J. *dental medicine educator*
Foti, Margaret *medical association administrator, editor, consultant*
Foulke, William Green *retired banker*
Fox, Reeder Rodman *lawyer*
Fox, Renée Claire *sociology educator*
Foxman, Stephen Mark *lawyer*
Fraker, Douglas L. *oncologist, endocrinologist, surgeon, educator*
Frank, Barbara Balis *gastroenterologist, educator*
Frank, Barry H. *lawyer*
Frank, George Andrew *lawyer*
Frank, Harvey *lawyer, author*
Frankel, Francine Ruth *political science educator*
Frankel, Sherman *physicist, educator*
Franklin, Harold Leroy *graphic artist, filmmaker*
Freedman, Robert Louis *lawyer*
Freeman, Sharon Elizabeth *psychiatric nurse practitioner*
Fretz, Deborah McDermott *oil industry executive*
Freyd, Peter John *mathematician, computer scientist, educator*
Friedman, Harvey Michael *infectious diseases educator*
Friedman, Murray *civil rights official, historian*
Friedman, Polly *public relations executive, marketing professional*
Friedman, Sidney A. *financial services executive*
Frucher, Meyer S. (Sandy Frucher) *brokerage house executive*
Fullam, John P. *federal judge*
Furstenberg, Frank F. *social studies educator*
Furth, John Jacob *molecular biologist, pathologist, educator*
Fusco, Richard *English literature educator*
Fussell, Paul *author, English literature educator*
Gadon, Steven Franklin *lawyer*
Gaiser, Robert Raymond *obstetric anesthesiologist, educator*
Garcia, Rudolph *lawyer*
Gardner, Timothy Joseph *surgeon, educator*
Garfield, Eugene *information scientist, author, publisher*
Garnier, Jean-Pierre *pharmaceutical executive*
Garonzik, Sara Ellen *stage producer*
Gartland, John Joseph *physician, writer*
Gary, Nancy Elizabeth *nephrologist, academic administrator*
Gatti, Leonard J. *communications executive*
Gefen, David *information technology educator*
Gelles, Richard James *sociology and psychology educator, academic administrator*
Genkin, Barry Howard *lawyer*
George, Paul M. *law librarian, library director*
German, Edward Cecil *lawyer*
Gerrity, Thomas P. *management educator*
Gerstenhber, Murray *law educator, mathematics professor*
Giegengack, Robert *university administrator*
Giger, Urs *veterinarian, educator*
Gilberg, Kenneth Roy *lawyer*
Giorgio, Robert *engineering executive*
Gittis, Howard *lawyer*
Glanton, Richard H. *lawyer*
Glazier, Eric James *management consultant*
Glazier, Jason S. *finance company executive*
Glick, Jane Mills *biomedical researcher, educator*
Glick, John H. *oncologist, medical educator*
Glusker, Jenny Pickworth *chemist*
Gogotsi, Yury *materials science educator*
Goldberg, Joseph *lawyer*
Goldberg, Martin *physician, educator*
Goldberg, Marvin Allen *lawyer, business consultant*
Goldberg, Richard Robert *lawyer*
Goldhamer, David J. *medical educator, researcher*
Goldstein, William Marks *lawyer*
Gonnella, Joseph Salvator *medical educator, university dean and official, consultant, researcher*
Gontarek, Leonard Andrew *editor, writer*
Gonzalez-Scarano, Francisco Antonio *neurologist, virologist*
Goodenough, Ward Hunt *anthropologist, educator*
Goodman, Stephen Murry *lawyer*
Gordesky, Morton *lawyer*
Gordon, Anne Kathleen *editor*
Gordon, George G. *lawyer*
Gordon, Susan Joan *physician, educator*
Gough, John Francis *lawyer*
Gould, Claudia *museum director*
Gowa, Andrew *investor, lawyer*
Grady, Thomas Michael *lawyer*
Graffman, Gary *pianist, music educator*
Granato, Carol Anne *writer*
Grant, M. Duncan *lawyer*
Grayson, Zachary Louis *lawyer*
Green, Clifford Scott *federal judge*
Greenberger, Alan *architectural firm executive*
Greene, Hans *facilities administrator*
Greenstein, Jeffrey Ian *neurologist*
Grove, David Lavan *lawyer*
Gruneich, Jeffrey Alan *biotechnology executive*
Grunfeld, David I. *lawyer*
Gueson, Emerita Torres *obstetrician, gynecologist*
Gulati, Gene L. *hematologist, educator, consultant*
Gupta, Rajiv Lochan *chemical company executive*
Gur, Raquel E. *academic administrator*
Gutmann, Amy *academic administrator, political science and philosophy educator*
Guyer, Hedy-Ann Klein *special education educator*
Hack, Gary Arthur *dean*
Hackney, Francis Sheldon *university president*
Hackney, Sheldon *former federal agency administrator, history educator*
Hahn, Steven *history professor, writer*
Hairston, Harold B. *protective services official*
Hale, Zan *editor, publisher*
Haley, Vincent Peter *lawyer*
Hall, Charles P(otter), Jr., *economics professor*
Hall, Marcia Brown *art historian, educator*
Hall, Robert J. *newspaper executive*
Hallock, James Anthony *pediatrician, health facility administrator*
Halpern, Eric Franklin *university publishing director*
Hameka, Hendrik Frederik *chemist, educator*
Hamme, David Codrington *architect*

Rollins, James Calvin *professional baseball player*
Romasco, Robert G. *insurance company executive*
Romer, Daniel *university official, psychologist, educator*
Root, Stanley William, Jr., *lawyer, retired*
Rorer, John Whiteley *publisher, consultant*
Rorke-Adams, Lucy Balian *pathologist, educator*
Rose, Robert Lawrence *financial services company executive*
Rosen, Arye *microwave, optoelectronics and medicine researcher*
Rosenberg, Howell K. *lawyer*
Rosenberg, Robert Allen *psychologist, educator, optometrist*
Rosenbleeth, Richard M. *lawyer*
Rosenbloom, Bert *marketing educator, consultant, writer*
Rosenstein, James Alfred *lawyer, mediator, negotiation facilitator*
Rosenthal, Edward Charles *management science educator*
Ross, Daniel R. *lawyer*
Ross, Darrin *composer*
Ross, Leonard Lester *anatomist, educator*
Ross, Murray Louis *lawyer, business executive*
Ross, Warren E. *dean*
Roth, Marilyn Dorothy *information scientist*
Rouse, Terrie S. *museum administrator*
Rovera, Giovanni Aurelio *medical educator, scientist*
Rowan, Richard Lamar *business management educator*
Rubenstein, Arthur Harold *academic administrator, educator, dean, internist*
Rubin, Benjamin Arnold *microbiologist, immunologist, medical educator, researcher*
Rubin, George *real estate executive*
Rubin, Ronald *real estate executive*
Rubin, Stephen Curtis *gynecologic oncologist, educator*
Rudczynski, Andrew B. *academic administrator, medical researcher*
Rueter, Thomas James *federal judge*
Russo, Irma Haydee Alvarez de *pathologist*
Rutherford, Alan *manufacturing executive*
Rybczynski, Witold Marian *architect, educator, writer*
Rykwert, Joseph *architecture and art history educator*
Sabili, Erlinda Asa *internist, psychiatrist, pastoral care minister*
Sabloff, Jeremy Arac *archaeologist*
Salessi, Jorge *language educator, writer*
Salva, Lawrence J. *communications executive*
Samuel, Ralph David *lawyer*
Sanchez, Sonia *English literature educator*
Sanger, Joseph William *cell biologist*
Santomero, Anthony M. *bank executive, public policymaker*
Santos, Adele Naude *architect, educator*
Sanyour, Michael Louis, Jr., *diversified financial services company executive*
Satinsky, Barnett *lawyer*
Saul, April *photographer*
Saul, Ralph Southey *financial service executive*
Saulino, Michael Francis *physiatrist*
Savage, Michael Paul *medicine educator, interventional cardiologist*
Savitz, Samuel J. *actuarial consulting firm executive*
Sawallisch, Wolfgang *conductor*
Saylor, Peter M. *architect*
Scaglione, Louis, III, *music educator, conductor*
Scandura, Joseph Michael *cognitive scientist, software engineer*
Scedrov, Andre *mathematics and computer science researcher, educator*
Schaedler, Russell William *microbiologist, physician, educator*
Schaub, Harry Carl *lawyer*
Schaubroeck, John Michael *education educator, academic administrator*
Scheff, Alice Mellors *nuclear medicine physician*
Scheib, Garry L. *hospital administrator*
Scher, Howard Dennis *lawyer*
Schiffman, Harold Fosdick *Asian language educator*
Schless, Guy Lacy *endocrinologist*
Schneider, Adele Sandra *clinical geneticist*
Schneider, Richard Graham *lawyer*
Schorling, William Harrison *lawyer*
Schotland, Donald Lewis *retired medical educator, neurologist*
Schumacher, H(arry) Ralph *internist, rheumatologist, medical educator, researcher*
Schwan, Herman Paul *electrical engineering and physical science educator, research scientist*
Schwartz, Arthur Gerald *microbiology educator*
Schwartz, Gordon Francis *surgeon, educator*
Schwartz, Marshall Zane *pediatric surgeon*
Schwartz, Robert M. *lawyer*
Scirica, Anthony Joseph *federal judge*
Sebold, Russell Perry, III, *Romance languages educator, writer*
Segal, Bernard Louis *physician, educator*
Segal, Robert Martin *lawyer*
Seidel, Arthur Harris *lawyer*
Seider, Warren D. *engineering educator*
Seligman, Martin E.P. *psychologist, educator*
Selles, Robert Hendrikus *retired actuary*
Seneca, Michael Joseph *historian*
Sevy, Roger Warren *retired pharmacology educator*
Shaffer, Hal J. *bank executive, lawyer*
Shapiro, Howard *newspaper editor*
Shapiro, Norma Sondra Levy *federal judge*
Shapiro, Raymond L. *lawyer*
Sharan, Ashwini D. *neurosurgeon, researcher*
Shatz, Stephen Sidney *mathematician, educator*
Sheaffer, Steven L. *medical association administrator, medical educator*
Sheils, Denis Francis *lawyer*
Shen, Benjamin Shih-Ping *scientist, engineer, educator*
Sherman, Lawrence William *criminologist*
Shestack, Jerome Joseph *lawyer*
Shields, Jerry Allen *ophthalmologist, educator*
Shils, Edward B. *finance educator, lawyer, arbitrator, mediator*
Shockman, Gerald David *microbiologist, educator*
Shoemaker, Innis Howe *art museum curator*
Shore, Eric Eugene *internist, consultant, lawyer*
Shuman, Robert Z. *architect*
Shure, Myrna Beth *psychologist, educator*
Sibolski, Elizabeth Hawley *higher education administrator*
Sicherman, Harvey *think-tank executive*
Siegel, Bernard Louis *lawyer*
Siegel, Jeremy James *finance educator, consultant*
Sigmond, Richard Brian *lawyer*
Sigmund, Diane Weiss *judge*
Silberberg, Donald H. *neurologist*
Silberman, Edward Kenneth *physician, educator*
Silvers, Willys Kent *geneticist*
Simkanich, John Joseph *lawyer, civil engineer*
Simon, Anita *psychologist*
Simpkins, Henry *medical educator*
Skalka, Anna Marie *molecular biologist*
Slaughter-Defoe, Diana Tresa *education educator*
Slipman, Curtis W. *rehabilitation medicine physician*
Sloan, Denise May *psychology educator*
Sloane, Richard *lawyer*
Sloviter, Dolores Korman *federal judge*
Smith, David Stuart *anesthesiology educator, physician*
Smith, John Francis, III, *lawyer*
Smith, Lawrence S. *communications executive*
Smith, Lloyd *musician*
Smith, Woollcott *statistician, educator*
Snider, Edward Malcolm *professional hockey club executive*
Sohn, Catherine Angell *pharmaceutical executive, pharmacist*
Solano, Carl Anthony *lawyer*
Solomon, Phyllis Linda *social work educator, researcher*
Soltz, Judith E. *insurance company executive, lawyer*
Sonnenfeld, Marc Jay *lawyer*
Sox, Harold Carleton, Jr., *physician, educator, editor*
Spaeth, Edmund Benjamin, Jr., *retired lawyer, retired law educator, former judge*
Spaeth, George Link *physician, ophthalmology educator, writer, educator*
Spandorfer, Merle Sue *artist, educator, author*
Spector, Martin Wolf *lawyer, business executive*
Spolan, Harmon Samuel *lawyer*
Stalberg, Zachary *newspaper editor*
Stallman, Robert *concert flutist, recording artist, editor, arranger*
Steinberg, Janet DeBerry *optometrist, educator, researcher*
Steinberg, Jonathan *historian*
Steinberg, Marvin Edward *orthopaedic surgeon, educator*
Steinberg, Robert Philip *lawyer*
Stern, Joan Naomi *lawyer*
Stevens, Rosemary A. *medicine and public health historian, artist*
Stevenson, Lawrence N. *retail executive*
Stewart, James Gathings *insurance company executive*
Stewart, Marvin Lewis *human resources professional*
Stewart, Robert Forrest, Jr., *lawyer*
Stewart, Susan *writer*
Still, David Barnes *banker, lawyer*
Stowell, Linda *communications executive*
Strasbaugh, Wayne Ralph *lawyer*
Strauss, Jerome Frank, III, *reproductive endocrinologist, educator*
Strickler, Matthew M. *lawyer*
Stuart, Marie Jean *physician, hematologist, researcher*
Stunkard, Albert James *psychiatrist, educator*
Stuntebeck, Clinton A. *lawyer*
Subak, John Thomas *lawyer*
Sudak, Howard Stanley *physician, psychiatry educator*
Sulyk, Stephen *retired archbishop*
Summers, Anita Arrow *public policy and management educator*
Summers, Clyde Wilson *law educator*
Summers, Robert *economics professor*
Sun, Hun H. *electrical engineering and biomedical engineering educator*
Sutherland, L. Frederick *food company executive*
Suzuki, Jon Byron *medical educator, periodontist, microbiologist*
Talerman, Aleksander *pathologist, educator*
Tannen, Richard Laurence *medical educator, nephrologist*
Tansy, Martin F. *dean*
Tasman, William Samuel *ophthalmologist, educator*
Tegenu, Mesfin *health services administrator, consultant*
Temin, Michael Lehman *lawyer*
Terry, John Joseph *transportation investor*
Terzian, Karnig Yervant *retired civil engineer*
Thomas, Lowell Shumway, Jr., *lawyer*
Tiger, Ira Paul *retired lawyer*
Tokar, Bette Lewis *economics professor*
Tomiyasu, Kiyo *consulting engineer*
Torg, Joseph Steven *orthopaedic surgeon, educator*
Tourtellotte, Charles Dee *internist, rheumatologist, educator*
Trojanowski, John Q. *health facility administrator*
Truant, Allan L. *medical educator, laboratory scientist, health science association administrator*
Trulear, Harold Dean *minister, theological educator, social researcher*
Tuan, Kailin *management consultant, educator*
Tucker, Cynthia Delores Nottage (Mrs. William M. Tucker) *political party official, former state official*
Turner, Evan Hopkins *retired art museum director*
Urahn, Susan K. *foundation administrator*
Vaccaro, Alexander R. *orthopedist, surgeon*
Vaira, Peter Francis *lawyer*
Van Antwerpen, Franklin Stuart *federal judge*
Van Arsdalen, Keith Norman *urologist*
Vanarsdall, Robert Lee, Jr., *orthodontist, educator*
Vanbiesbrouck, John *professional hockey player*
Van Bockstaele, Elisabeth Jeanne *neuroscientist, researcher*
Van der Spiegel, Jan *engineering educator*
Vaughan, Richard C. *insurance company executive*
Veit, Kenneth *dean, educator*
Venturi, Robert *architect*
Vergare, Michael J. *psychiatrist, department chairman*
Vitek, Vaclav *materials scientist*
Vitez, Michael *reporter*
Volgin, Denys V. *medical researcher*
Vredenburgh, Judy *youth organization executive*
Wachman, Marvin *retired academic administrator*
Wadden, Thomas Anthony *psychologist, educator*
Wade, Ed *professional sports team executive*
Waldman, Scott Arthur *medical educator, medical association administrator*
Wales, Walter D. *physicist, researcher*
Walker, Allen Lyon *engineer*
Walker, Douglas C. *banker*
Walker, Valaida Smith *university administrator*
Wallace, Anthony Francis Clarke *anthropologist, educator*
Wallace, Emily Mitchell *writer, editor, educator*
Wang, Yen *nuclear medicine physician, radiologist*
Ward, Butch *newspaper editor*
Warner, Theodore Kugler, Jr., *lawyer*
Watson, Bernard Charles *educator, foundation administrator*
Webber, John Bentley *orthopedic surgeon*
Webber, Ross Arkell *management educator*
Weil, Jeffrey George *lawyer*
Wein, Alan Jerome *urologist, educator, researcher*
Weiner, Charles R. *federal judge*
Welch, Charles Edgar, Jr., *retired English language educator, writer*
Welch, Patrick *health insurance company executive*
Weller, Elizabeth Boghossian *child and adolescent psychiatrist*
Weller, Jonathan *real estate investment company executive*
Welsh, Diane M. *federal judge*
Welsh, Donald S. *government agency administrator*
Wengert, Timothy *church history educator, clergyman*
Whelan, Daniel J. *communications company executive*
Whitaker, Linton Andin *plastic surgeon*
White, Howard D. *information science educator*
Whiteside, William Anthony, Jr., *retired lawyer*
Whitman, Jules Isidoré *lawyer*
Wiener, Ronald Martin *lawyer*
Wild, Richard P. *lawyer*
Wilde, Norman Taylor, Jr., *investment banking company executive*
Wilf, Frederic Marshal *lawyer*
Wilkinson, Signe *cartoonist*
Willet, E. Crosby (Everett Crosby Willet) *artist*
Willi, Steven Matthew *physician, educator, researcher*
Williams, Elizabeth A.W. *foundation administrator*
Williams, Francine Anita *community outreach worker*
Williams, Sankey Vaughan *health services researcher, internist*
Wilms, Anne M. *information technology executive*
Wilson, Rhonda Hill *lawyer*
Winfrey, Marion Lee *retired television critic*
Winkler, Gail Caskey *design historian, writer, educator*
Winkler, Sheldon *dentist, educator*
Winston, Flaura K. *engineering researcher*
Wittels, Barnaby Caesar *lawyer, writer*
Wivel, Nelson Auburn *physician, medical researcher, educator*
Wolf, Gregory H. *insurance company executive*
Wolf, Robert B. *lawyer*
Wolff, Deborah H(orowitz) *lawyer*
Wolitarsky, James William *securities industry executive*
Woodside, Lisa Nicole *humanities educator*
Woosnam, Richard Edward *venture capitalist, lawyer*
Wright, Minturn Tatum, III, *retired lawyer*
Wrobleski, Jeanne Pauline *lawyer*
Yanoff, Myron *ophthalmologist*
Yaros, Constance Greenberg *painter, sculptor*
Yoh, Harold L., III, *company executive*
Yohn, William H(endricks), Jr., *federal judge*
Young, Andrew Brodbeck *lawyer*
Young, Donald Stirling *clinical pathology educator*
Young, Robert Crabill *medical researcher, science facility administrator, internist*
Young, Roma Skeen *lawyer*
Young, Terri L. *ophthalmologist*
Yunginger, John W. *allergist*
Zavaliangos, Antonios *mechanical engineer, educator*
Zhamnov, Alexei *professional hockey player*
Zheng, Robert Zhiwei *educational technology educator*
Ziegler, Donald Robert *accountant*
Zimmer, Janie Louise *mathematics educator, administrator*
Zimmerman, Robert S., Jr., *federal agency administrator*
Zlowe, Florence Markowitz *artist*
Zorowitz, Richard David *physiatrics educator*
Zucker, William *retired business educator*
Zuckerman, Brian D. *lawyer*
Zuckerman, Marvin *psychologist*
Zweiman, Burton *physician, scientist, educator*

Philipsburg

Genesi, Susan Petrovich *school system administrator*

Phoenixville

Brundage, Russell Archibald *retired data processing executive*
Di Giacomo, Michael *historian, educator*

Pipersville

Erickson, Edward Leonard *biotechnology company executive, administrator*
McNutt, Richard Hunt *manufacturing executive*
Sigety, Charles Edward *lawyer, consultant, family business consultant*

Pitcairn

Rose, Robert Didier *neurophysiologist*

Pittsburgh

Agnew, Franklin Ernest, III, *former food company executive*
Allen, Thomas E. *obstetrician, gynecologist*
Ambrose, Donetta W. *federal judge*
Anderson, John Leonard *chemical engineering educator*
Andrews, George Reid *historian, educator*
Anthony, Edward Mason *linguistics educator*
Apone, Carl Anthony *journalist*
Arbutina, Petra *advertising executive*
Aronson, Mark Berne *retired lawyer, advocate*
Artz, John Curtis *lawyer*
Asher, Sanford Abraham *chemist, educator*
Balada, Leonardo *composer, educator*
Balas, Egon *applied mathematician, educator*
Barazzone, Esther Lynn *academic administrator, educator*
Bardyguine, Patricia Wilde *ballerina, ballet theatre executive*
Barry, Herbert, III, *psychologist, educator*
Bartley, Burnett Graham, Jr., *oil company and manufacturing executive*
Bashore, George Willis *retired bishop*
Basinski, Anthony Joseph *lawyer*
Becherer, Richard John *architecture educator*
Becker, George *labor union administrator*
Belda, Alain J. P. *metal products executive*
Bender, Charles Christian *retail home center executive*
Berkman, Louis *steel company executive*
Bernt, Benno Anthony *business executive, entrepreneur and investor*
Berry, Guy Curtis *polymer science educator, researcher*
Bettis, Jerome Abram *professional football player*
Bickel, Minnette Duffy *artist*
Biondi, Manfred Anthony *physicist, researcher*
Bleier, Michael E. *lawyer*
Blenko, Walter John, Jr., *lawyer*
Bloch, Alan Neil *federal judge*
Bloom, William Millard *furnace design engineer*
Blum, Eva Tansky *lawyer*
Blumstein, Alfred *urban and public affairs educator*
Bly, James Charles, Jr., *financial services executive*
Bobrow, Davis Bernard *public policy educator*
Bocea, Marian *mathematician*
Bochicchio, Vito Salvatore *lawyer*
Bonessa, Dennis R. *lawyer*
Borovetz, Harvey Selwyn *biomedical engineer, educator*
Boswell, William Paret *lawyer*
Boyce, Doreen Elizabeth *lecturer, civic development foundation executive*
Brand, Ronald Alvah *lawyer*
Braun, Thomas W. *academic administrator*
Brauner, Ronald Allan *religion educator*
Brett, Edward Tracy *historian, educator*
Brito, Maximo Oscar *epidemiologist*
Brockmann, Stephen Matthew *education educator*
Brown, Bobby R. *retired coal company executive*
Brown, David Ronald *lawyer*
Brown, James Benton *lawyer*
Brustein, William Irving *sociology educator*
Bryson, Michael A *corporate financial executive*
Buchanan, Bruce G. *computer scientist, educator*
Buchanan, James Junkin *classics educator*
Buchanan, Mary Beth *prosecutor*
Bunch, Charles E. *manufacturing executive*
Burger, Herbert Francis *advertising agency executive*
Burgess, David Lowry *artist*
Burnham, Donald Clemens *manufacturing executive*
Busquets, Miguel Antonio *ophthalmologist*
Caginalp, Gunduz *mathematician, educator, researcher*
Cagney, William Robert *psychologist*
Candris, Laura A. *lawyer*
Cappy, Ralph Joseph *judge*
Carbo, Toni (Toni Carbo Bearman) *information scientist, educator*
Cardenes, Andres Jorge *violinist, music educator*
Caritis, Steve Nick *obstetrician, gynecologist, educator*
Carr, Walter James, Jr., *research physicist, consultant*
Carter, Donald K. *architectural firm executive*
Casasent, David Paul *electrical engineering educator, data processing executive*
Cassidy, William Arthur *geology and planetary science educator*
Casturo, Don James *venture capitalist*
Cendes, Zoltan Joseph *electrical engineer, educator*
Chang, Yuan *neuropathologist, researcher, educator*
Charap, Stanley Harvey *electrical engineering educator*
Cheever, George Martin *lawyer*
Chengappa, Roy K. N. *psychiatrist, educator*
Chiu, Chao-Lin *civil engineer*
Choyke, Wolfgang Justus *physicist*
Chrysanthis, Panos Kypros *computer science educator, researcher*
Clack, Jerry *classics educator*
Classon, Rolf Allan *pharmaceutical company executive*
Cockerham, Kimberly Peele *ophthalmologist, educator*
Cohen, Bernard Leonard *physicist, researcher*
Cohen, Henry C. *lawyer*
Cohill, Maurice Blanchard, Jr., *federal judge*
Cohon, Jared L. *academic administrator*
Colen, Frederick Haas *lawyer*
Coltman, John Wesley *physicist*
Coney, Aims C., Jr., *lawyer, labor-management negotiator*
Connors, Eugene Kenneth *lawyer, educator*
Constantino-Bana, Rose Eva *nursing educator, researcher, lawyer*
Conti, Joy Flowers *judge*
Contractor, Farhad M. *diagnostic radiologist, educator*
Cooper, Rory Alan *engineering educator, researcher*
Cooper, Thomas Louis *lawyer*
Cooper, William Marion *physician*
Corbett, Thomas Wingett, Jr., *lawyer*
Corcoran, Thomas A. *metals and mining company executive*
Cowan, Barton Zalman *lawyer*
Cowher, Bill *professional football coach*
Craig, Fiona Elizabeth *pathologist*
Cravens, Gary Dean *informaticist, physician*
Cruz, Robyn Flaum *research scientist, clinician*
Culig, Michael H. *cardiologist, surgeon*
Curry, Nancy Ellen *psychologist, psychoanalyst, educator*
Cusick, Daniel Francis *lawyer*
Czuszak, Janis Marie *former credit company official, researcher*
Daniel, Robert Michael *lawyer*
Daniels, James R. *poet, English language educator*
Dato, Virginia Marie *public health physician*
Davenport, Ronald Ross, Jr., *lawyer*
Davis, Lewis U., Jr., *lawyer*
Davis, Otto Anderson *economics professor*
Dawes, Robyn Mason *psychology educator*
Dawson, Mary Ruth *curator, educator*
DeForest, Walter Pattison, III, *lawyer*
deGroat, William Chesney *pharmacology educator*
DeKosky, Steven Trent *neurologist*
Demchak, William S. *corporate financial executive*
Demmler, John Henry *retired lawyer*
Dempsey, Jerry Edward *retired service company executive*

Weidman, John Carl, II, *education and sociology educator, consultant*
Weil, Andrew L. *retired lawyer*
Weingartner, Rudolph Herbert *philosophy educator*
Weis, Joseph Francis, Jr., *federal judge*
Welch, William Charles *neurosurgeon*
Wenger, Sharon Louise *pediatrics educator, researcher, cytogeneticist*
Werner, Jane *museum administrator*
Westerberg, Arthur William *retired chemical engineering educator*
White, Robert Marshall *physicist, government official, educator*
Whitehead, Paul *lawyer, labor union administrator*
Wilde, Patricia *retired artistic director*
Wiley, S. Donald *lawyer, food products executive*
Wilkins, David George *fine arts educator*
Wilkinson, James Allan *lawyer, healthcare executive*
Willard, Louis Charles *librarian*
Williams, Stephen Edward *corporate lawyer*
Willke, Theodore Lawrence *research facility director*
Wilson, Wanda Lee Davis *casting director*
Winkleback, Arthur *food products executive*
Winter, Peter Michael *anesthesiologist, educator*
Yang, Wen-Ching *chemical engineer*
Yates, John Thomas, Jr., *chemistry educator, research director*
Yorsz, Stanley *lawyer*
Young, Hugh David *physics educator, writer, organist*
Zanardelli, John Joseph *healthcare services executive*
Zehel, Wendell Evans *surgeon*
Zeolla, Kim Anne *minister*
Ziegler, Arthur P., Jr., *foundation executive*
Ziegler, Donald Emil *federal judge*
Ziskind, Deborah Ziskind *public relations and legal marketing executive*
Zitelli, Basil J. *pediatrician, educator*
Zittrain, Lester Eugene *lawyer*

Plymouth Meeting
Black, Jeffrey P. *manufacturing executive*
Black, Lennox K. *manufacturing executive*
Carbine, Sharon *lawyer, corporation executive*
Kranzdorf, Norman M(elvin) *lawyer, real estate executive*
Marr, Christopher P. *real estate company executive*
Nichols, Anthony A., Sr., *trust company executive*
Nobel, Joel J. *biomedical researcher*
O'Neill, David A *music educator, musician*
Sickler, John J. *manufacturing executive*

Port Carbon
Boran, Robert Paul, Jr., *orthopedic surgeon*

Port Royal
Wert, Jonathan Maxwell, II, *management consultant*

Portland
Hutton, William Michael *manufacturing executive*

Pottstown
Hergert, Herbert Lawrence *consultant*
Hylton, Thomas James *author*
Mitchell, Eric Ehrman *photographer, stock broker*

Pottsville
Blossey, Maureen B. *mental health administrator*
Jones, Joseph Hayward *lawyer*

Presto
Moeller, Audrey Carolyn *retired energy company executive, corporate secretary*

Punxsutawney
Dinsmore, Roberta Joan Maier *library director*

Quakertown
Emory, Thomas Mercer, Jr., *data communications equipment manufacturing executive*

Quarryville
Armerding, Hudson Taylor *retired college president, consultant*
Bird, L. Raymond *investor*
Harris, Robert Laird *minister, theology educator emeritus*

Radnor
Buck, James Mahlon, Jr., *venture capital executive*
Castle, Joseph Lanktree, II, *energy company executive, consultant*
Cunningham, James Gerald, Jr., *transportation company executive*
Iadarola, Antoinette *college president*
Marland, Alkis Joseph *leasing company executive, computer scientist, educator, financial planner*
Nofer, George Hancock *lawyer*
Paier, Adolf Arthur *computer software and services company executive*
Pappas, Thomas Nicholas *insurance brokerage executive, consultant*
Rosnow, Ralph Leon *psychology researcher and educator*
Templeton, John Marks, Jr., *retired pediatric surgeon, foundation executive*
Thompson, Pamela Padwick *public relations executive*

Reading
Bell, Frances Louise *medical technologist*
Blessing, Tim H. *historian, educator*
Boscov, Albert *retail executive*
Bowles, Patricia Mary *secondary school educator*
Brigham, Robert Allan *surgeon, educator*
Cardy, Robert Willard *speciality steel company executive*
Cocuzza, Frank *truck leasing company executive*
Dersh, Rhoda E. *management consultant, business executive*
Devlin, Karin L *education educator*
Dietrich, Bruce Leinbach *planetarium and museum administrator, astronomer, educator*
Ehlerman, Paul Michael *motorcycle and recreational batteries manufacturing company executive*
Eshelman, David Richard *lawyer*
Kiehne, Frank Charles, Jr., *foreign affairs adviser*
Kline, Sidney DeLong, Jr., *lawyer*
Kraras, Gust C. *hotel executive*
Kremser, Harold L. *music educator*

Lacki, Allan Vincent *industrial engineer*
Linton, Jack Arthur *lawyer*
Lusch, Charles Jack *oncologist*
Miller, Marlin J., Jr., *pharmaceutical executive*
Moriarty, John Klinge *electronics engineer, consultant*
Rochowicz, John Anthony, Jr., *mathematician, mathematics and physics educator*
Roesch, Clarence Henry *banker*
Rothermel, Daniel Krott *lawyer, holding company executive*
Sauer, Elissa Swisher *nursing educator*
Scollick, Bryan Robert *music educator, market research consultant*
Sidhu, Jay S. *bank executive*
Unser, Alfred, Jr., *race car driver*
Yoder, James Dale *adult education educator*
Zug, Elizabeth E. *concert pianist, educator*

Red Lion
Hartman, Charles Henry *transportation executive, educator*

Reedsville
Garner, Douglas *music educator*

Richboro
Burtt, Larice Annadel Roseman *artist*
Higginbotham, Kenneth James *financial services executive*

Ridley Park
Walls, William Walton, Jr., *management consultant*

Robesonia
Hackett, Sean P. *music educator, conductor*

Rockledge
Blessing, Maribeth *lawyer, educator, mediator, arbitrator*

Roscoe
O'Hara, Paul Anthony, Jr., *retired art educator, artist*

Rosemount
Berliner, Ernst *retired chemistry professor*

Royersford
Bothe, Marie *automotive executive*
Chance, Steven Kent *lawyer*
Rhoads, Michael Dennis *sales executive*

Russellton
Curtis, Paula Annette *elementary and secondary education educator*

Rydal
Bacon, George Hughes, Jr., *retired systems analyst*
Black, Thomas Donald *retired religious organization administrator*
Boreen, Henry Isaac *computer company executive*
Fernberger, Marilyn Friedman *events organizer, consultant, civic leader*
Heebner, Albert Gilbert *economist, educator, bank executive*

Saint Davids
Bertsch, Frederick Charles, III, *business executive*
Denenberg, Herbert Sidney *journalist, lawyer, educator, retired state official*
Miles, Sara Joan *dean*
Sheftel, Roger Terry *merchant banker*
Smalley, Christopher Joseph *pharmaceutical company professional*

Saint Marys
Sorg, David Joseph *materials physicist*

Saint Peters
Detterline, Milton E., Jr., *minister*

Saltsburg
Pidgeon, John Anderson *headmaster*

Sayre
Gu, Jeng Yul *radiologist*
Moody, Robert Adams *neurosurgeon*

Schnecksville
Schillow, Ned William *mathematics educator*

Schuylkill Haven
Sarno, Patricia Ann *biology educator*

Scranton
Blewitt, Thomas Michael *chief federal magistrate judge*
Bourcier, Richard Joseph *French language and literature educator*
Burke, Henry Patrick *lawyer*
Cannon, J. Timothy *psychology educator, neuroscientist*
Conaboy, Richard Paul *federal judge*
De Celles, Charles Edouard *theologian, educator*
Dougherty, John Martin *bishop*
Eckersley, Richard Laurence *accountant*
Friedrichs, David O. *legal educator*
Giunta, Agatino John *economist, educator*
Haggerty, James Joseph *lawyer*
Homer, Francis Xavier James *history professor*
Janoski, Henry Valentine *investment advisor, former banker*
Lukasik, John Peter, Jr., *therapist, counselor, school psychologist*
Lynett, George Vincent *newspaper publisher*
Lynett, William Ruddy *publishing, broadcasting company executive*
Marino, Thomas A. *lawyer*
Marx, David Earl *chemistry professor, consultant*
Moyer, James Arthur *music educator, department chairman*
Nealon, William Joseph, Jr., *federal judge*
Nee, Sister Mary Coleman *college president emeritus*
O'Malley, Carlon Martin *judge*
Panuska, Joseph Allan *retired academic administrator*
Parente, William Joseph *political science educator*
Passon, Richard Henry *English language educator, former administrator*
Reap, Sister Mary Margaret *college administrator*

Rhiew, Francis Changnam *radiologist, physician*
Sebastianelli, Carl Thomas *clinical psychologist*
Timlin, James Clifford *bishop*
Turock, Jane Parsick *nutritionist*
Vanaskie, Thomas Ignatius *judge*
Yamanouchi-Rynn, Midori *social sciences educator*
Zaydon, Jemille Ann *language educator, communications educator*

Selinsgrove
Connolly, Elma Troutman *artist, contractor, designer*
Kolbert, Jack *foreign language educator, French literature educator, humanities educator*
Lemons, L. Jay *academic administrator*
Lopez, Andrea Michelle *political scientist, educator*
Powers, William Douglas *theater director, actor, educator*
Thomforde, Christopher Meredith *minister*
Whitman, Jeffrey Paul *philosophy educator*

Sellersville
Hollander, Irwin Joel *pathologist, educator*
Rilling, David Carl *surgeon*

Sewickley
Bouchard, James Paul *steel manufacturing and planning executive*
Fells, Charles Dayton *civil engineer, educator*
Hartwig, Thomas Leo *civil engineer, environmental engineer, sports association administrator*
Jehle, Michael Edward *financial executive*
Munoz, Alfredo Nectario *emergency medicine physician, pediatrician*
Newell, Byron Bruce, Jr., *pastor*
Ostern, Wilhelm Curt *retired holding company executive*
Swann, Lynn Curtis *sportscaster, former professional football player*
Thorbecke, Willem Henry *international company executive, consultant*
Woody, Carol Clayman *data processing executive*

Shady Grove
Bust, Jeffry D. *manufacturing executive*

Shamokin Dam
Matter, Harry H. *retired wholesale business executive, reflexologist*

Sharon
Berland, Kevin Joel *literature educator*

Shickshinny
Luksha, Rosemary Dorothy *art educator*

Shippensburg
Bej, Emil *economics educator, researcher, journalist*
Ceddia, Anthony Francis *university administrator*
Collier, Duaine Alden *manufacturing and distribution company executive*
France, Olin Kenneth, Jr., *psychologist*
Luhrs, H. Ric *toy manufacturing company executive*
Stone, Susan Ridgaway *marketing educator*

Shiremanstown
Nesbit, William Terry *small business owner, consultant*

Sinking Spring
Bausher, Verne C(harles) *retired bank executive*
Heffner, William Rudolph *engineer, consultant*

Slatington
Heffelfinger, Karl William *retired draftsman*

Slippery Rock
Bruya, John Robert *art educator*
Cobb, Larry Russell *ethics educator*
Fulton, Jane *health science institution administrator*
Kefeli, Valentin Ilich *biologist, botanist, educator, researcher*
Mukherjee, Pracheta *management educator, researcher, consultant*
Smith, Grant Warren, II, *university administrator, physical sciences educator*
Smith, Robert Mason *academic administrator*

Solebury
Anthonisen, George Rioch *sculptor, artist*
Cross, Robert William *lawyer, venture capital executive*
Gart, Herbert Steven *communications executive, producer*
Valentine, H. Jeffrey *legal association executive*

Somerset
Barkman, Annette Shaulis *real estate management executive*
Carroll, William Richard *lawyer*
Nair, Velupillai Krishnan *cardiologist*

Souderton
Delp, R. Lee *meat packing company executive*
Hoeflich, Charles Hitschler *banker*
Lapp, James Merrill *clergyman, marriage and family therapist*
Marden, Jack Mortimer *lawyer*
Silvestri, George J., Jr., *retired thermodynamics engineer*

South Canaan
Herman, *archbishop, head of Orthodox Church in America*

South Park
Lotze, Barbara *retired physicist*

Southampton
Bendiner, Robert *writer, editor*
Mitchell, William F. *environmental company executive*

Southeastern
Rassbach, Herbert David *marketing executive*
Zlotolow-Stambler, Ernest *real estate executive, architectural executive*

Spring City
Blanchard, Norman Harris *retired pharmaceutical executive*
Mayerson, Hy *lawyer*

Spring Grove
Butler, Raymond Archibald *cartographer*
Helberg, Shirley Adelaide Holden *artist, educator*

Spring House
Hann, William Mathis *chemist, researcher*
Payn, Clyde Francis *technology company executive, consultant*
Rosoff, William A. *lawyer, executive*
van Steenwyk, John Joseph *health care plan consultant, educator*

Spring Mills
Gillan, Garth Jackson *writer, psychotherapist, deacon, emeritus educator*

Springfield
Arsht, Edwin David *physician*
Maclay, Donald Merle *retired lawyer*
Sing, Robert Fong *physician*

State College
Barnoff, Robert Mark *civil engineering educator*
Book, Edward R. *consultant, retired association executive*
Brotzman, Harry, Jr., *minister*
Byrom, Fletcher Lauman *chemical manufacturing company executive*
Carnes, James Edward *technology executive*
Cowen, Barrett Stickney *microbiology educator*
DeVoss, James Thomas *community foundation administrator, retired*
Engle, Jill Callahan *law educator*
Foderaro, Anthony Harolde *nuclear engineering educator*
Forth, Stuart *librarian*
Garrett, Steven Lurie *physicist*
German, Randall Michael *materials engineering educator, consultant*
Ginoza, William *former biophysics educator*
Goldschmidt, Arthur Eduard, Jr., *history educator, author*
Grimes, Dale Mills *physics and electrical engineering educator*
Haas, John C. *architect*
Henshaw, Beverly Ann Harsh *women's health nurse, consultant*
Hettche, L. Raymond *research director*
Hoffa, Harlan Edward *retired university dean, art educator*
Huck, John Lloyd *pharmaceutical executive*
Link, Phoebe Forrest *secondary school educator, writer, social worker, poet*
Madjid, A. Hamid *retired science educator*
Max, Elizabeth *educator*
Mills, Rilla Dean *university administrator, consultant*
Mutmansky, Jan M. *retired engineering educator*
Myers, Barry Lee *lawyer*
Nollau, Lee Gordon *lawyer*
Olson, Donald Richard *mechanical engineering educator*
Pennock, Elizabeth H. *retired music educator*
Phillips, Janet Colleen *retired educational association executive, editor*
Redford, Donald Bruce *historian, archaeologist*
Remick, Forrest Jerome, Jr., *former university official*
Robinett, Betty Wallace *linguist, educator*
Roy, Della Martin *materials science educator, researcher*
Schaie, K(laus) Warner *human development and psychology educator*
Schmalstieg, William Riegel *retired Slavic languages educator*
Schmalz, Robert Fowler *geology educator*
Shaikh, Nazrul Islam *industrial engineer, researcher*
Sibul, Leon Henry *electrical engineer*
Sinha, Sunil K. *engineer, educator*
Strauss, Susan Gayle *linguistics educator*
Subler, Edward Pierre *advertising executive*
Wilson, Keith B. *rehabilitation educator*
Wyand, Martin Judd *economics educator, retired military officer*

Steelton
Zimmerman, Connie Ann *public administrator*

Strasburg
Lindsay, George Carroll *former museum director*

Stroudsburg
Jacobson, Gilbert H. *lawyer, director*

Sunbury
Ely, Donald J(ean) *retired clergyman, secondary school educator*
Fernsler, John Paul *lawyer*
Mills, William R. *food products executive*
Rich, Norman S. *food service executive*
Weis, Robert Freeman *supermarket company executive*

Swarthmore
Bilaniuk, Oleksa Myron *physicist, researcher*
Bloom, Alfred Howard *academic administrator, educator*
Carey, William Bacon *pediatrician, educator*
Devin, Lee (Philip Lee Devin) *dramaturg, author*
Elman, Gerry Jay *lawyer*
Freeman, James Douglas *music educator*
Frost, Jerry William *religion and history educator, library administrator*
Gelzer, David Georg *English educator, missionary*
Gilbert, Scott Frederick *biologist, educator, author*
Hollister, Robinson Gill, Jr., *economics professor*
Hopkins, Raymond Frederick *political science educator*
Hungerford, Constance Cain *art educator*
Kaufman, Antoinette D. *business services company executive*
Keith, Jennie *anthropology educator and administrator, writer*
Kelemen, Charles F. *computer science educator*
Kitao, T. Kaori *art history educator*
Krendel, Ezra Simon *systems and human factors engineering consultant*
Krizek, Edwin John *marketing professional*
Marecek, Jeanne *psychologist, educator*
Morgan, Kathryn Lawson *retired historian, educator*
North, Helen Florence *classicist, educator*
Ostwald, Martin *retired classicist*

Pasternack, Robert Francis *chemistry professor*
Pryor, Frederic L. *economist, educator*
Redden, Taylor Tilghman *musician*

Tannersville
Moore, James Alfred *ski company executive, lawyer*

Tarentum
McGuire, Timothy William *economics and management educator, dean*

Telford
Hagey, Walter Rex *retired bank executive*

Thorndale
Hodess, Arthur Bart *cardiologist*

Titusville
Campasino, Ellen Marie *elementary school educator*

Tobyhanna
Lapidus, Arnold *mathematician, educator*

Towanda
Mott, John C. *judge*

Tylersport
Raub, Donald Wilmer *minister, author*

Uniontown
Coldren, Ira Burdette, Jr., *lawyer*
Eberly, Robert Edward *foundation administrator*

Unionville
De Marino, Donald Nicholson *former federal agency administrator*
Forney, Robert Clyde *retired chemical industry executive*
Martin, Helen Elizabeth *educational consultant*

University Park
Allcock, Harry R. *chemistry professor*
Andrews, George Eyre *mathematics professor*
Antle, Charles Edward *statistics educator*
Aplan, Frank Fulton *metallurgical engineering educator*
Askov, Eunice May *adult education educator*
Austin, Leonard George *mineral engineer*
Badding, John Victor *chemistry professor*
Baisley, Robert William *music educator*
Barlow, Jesse Louis *computer scientist, educator*
Barnes, Hubert Lloyd *geochemistry educator*
Benkovic, Stephen James *chemist*
Blackadar, Alfred Kimball *meteorologist, educator*
Bollag, Jean-Marc *soil biochemistry educator, consultant*
Bose, Nirmal Kumar *electrical engineering, mathematics educator*
Brown, John Lawrence, Jr., *electrical engineering educator*
Broyles, Michael E. *music history educator, writer*
Buskirk, Elsworth Robert *physiologist, educator*
Cahir, John Joseph *meteorologist, educational administrator*
Castleman, Albert Welford, Jr., *physical chemist, educator*
Collins, John Clements *physicist, researcher*
Cook, Kim Diane *concert cellist*
Cougevan, Katie Pilgeram *psychologist*
Cross, Leslie Eric *electrical engineering educator*
Davids, Norman *engineering science and mechanics educator, researcher*
De Jong, Gordon Frederick *finance educator, consultant*
Duda, John Larry *chemical engineering educator*
Dutton, John Altnow *meteorologist, educator*
Eaton, Nancy Ruth Linton *librarian, dean*
Ebitz, David MacKinnon *art historian, educator, museum director*
Elliott, Herschel *agricultural engineer, educator*
Enis, Charles Richard *accountant, educator*
Ertekin, Turgay *petroleum engineer educator, researcher, consultant*
Fedoroff, Nina Vsevolod *research scientist, consultant, educator*
Feng, Tse-yun *computer engineer, educator*
Firebaugh, Glenn Allen *sociology educator*
Fowler, H(oratio) Seymour *retired science educator*
Friedman, Robert Sidney *political science educator*
Fuhrman, Susan H *education educator*
Garrison, Barbara Jane *chemistry professor*
Gnana Asir, Viji *plant pathologist*
Grewal, Rajdeep *marketing professional, educator*
Grimes, Craig Alan *electrical engineering educator*
Grosholz, Emily Rolfe *philosophy educator, poet*
Guo, Ruyan *engineering educator, researcher*
Guthrie, Helen A. *nutrition educator, registered dietitian*
Halsey, Martha Taliaferro *Spanish language educator*
Ham, Inyong *industrial engineering educator*
Hammond, J. D. *dean emeritus, corporate director*
Herr, Edwin Leon *educator, academic administrator*
Hogg, Richard *process engineer*
Holl, John William *engineering educator*
Holt, Frieda M. *nursing educator, former academic director*
Hood, Lamartine Frain *agriculture educator, former dean*
Hosler, Charles Luther, Jr., *meteorologist, educator*
Howell, Benjamin Franklin, Jr., *geophysicist, educator*
Humphrey, Craig Reed *social studies educator*
Irwin, Mary Jane *engineering educator*
Jackman, Lloyd Miles *chemistry professor*
Joyce, William Leonard *librarian*
Jung, Myung-Chul *researcher*
Junker, Edward P., III, *retired diversified financial services company executive*
Kabel, Robert Lynn *chemical engineering educator*
Kadir, Djelal *literature educator, writer, translator, editor*
Kasting, James Fraser *research meteorologist, physicist*
Kilduff, Martin James *finance educator*
Klein, Philip Alexander *economist*
Knott, Kenneth *engineering educator, consultant, expert witness*
Lacy, Norris J. *literature educator*
Larson, Russell Edward *university provost emeritus, consultant agriculture research and development*
Lauchle, Gerald Clyde *acoustics educator*

Lima, Robert *Hispanic studies and comparative literature educator*
Liu, Zi-Kui *materials science and engineering educator*
Lorence, Daniel *healthcare educator*
Ma, Xiaoliang *research scientist*
Mahan, Gerald Dennis *physics educator, researcher*
Manbeck, Harvey B. *agricultural and biological engineer, educator*
Mayers, Stanley Penrose, Jr., *public health educator*
McCormick, Barnes Warnock *aerospace engineering educator*
McDonnell, Archie Joseph *environmental engineer*
McKeown, James Charles *accounting educator, consultant*
Mentzer, John Raymond *electrical engineer, educator*
Mészáros, Peter Istvan *astrophysicist, researcher, astronomy educator*
Muhlert, Jan Keene *art museum director*
Murray-Kolb, Laura Elaine *nutritionist, researcher*
Muscarella, Christopher James *finance educator*
Naydan, Michael M. *foreign language educator*
Nei, Masatoshi *biology professor*
Newsome, Lee Ann *anthropologist, educator*
Nielsen, Aldon Lynn *literature educator*
Olian, Judy D. *dean*
Paterno, Joseph Vincent *college football coach*
Ramani, Raja Venkat *mining engineering educator*
Ray, William Jackson *psychologist*
Rose, Paul Lawrence *history educator*
Ross, A. Catharine *biochemist, educator*
Roy, Rustum *interdisciplinary educator, materials researcher*
Ruud, Clayton Olaf *engineering educator*
Savignon, Sandra J. *linguistics educator*
Shannon, Barbara *dean, nutrition educator*
Song, Chunshan *chemist, chemical engineer, educator*
Spanier, Graham Basil *university president*
Stern, Robert Morris *gastrointestinal psychophysiology researcher, psychology educator*
Stinson, Richard Floyd *retired horticulturist, educator*
Thompson, William, Jr., *engineering educator*
Tikalsky, Paul J. *civil engineering educator, structural engineer*
Tittmann, Bernhard Rainer *engineering science and mechanics educator*
Todd Copley, Judith A. *materials and metallurgical engineering educator*
Vannice, M. Albert *chemical engineering educator, researcher*
Vennam, Venkata Surya Prakash *engineering educator, researcher*
Vrentas, James Spiro *chemical engineering educator*
Walker, Alan C. *anthropologist, educator*
Wanner, Adrian J. *literature educator*
Waterhouse, William Charles *mathematics professor*
Wheeler, C. Herbert *architect, consultant, educator*
White, William Blaine *geochemist, researcher*
Winograd, Nicholas *chemist*
Witzig, Warren Frank *nuclear engineer, educator*
Wolfe, Douglas E. *science educator, researcher*
Wormley, David *dean*
Wysk, Richard A. *engineering educator, researcher*
Yoder, Edgar Paul *education educator*
Zatsiorsky, Vladimir Moiseevich (Michailovich) *biomechanics educator, researcher*

Upper Burrell
Coohill, Joseph *historian, educator*
Franco Gómez, María Angeles *language educator*

Upper Darby
Horwitz, Seth *information technology executive*
Hudiak, David Michael *academic administrator, lawyer*
Kahler, Nancy J. *music educator, director*
Leiby, Bruce Richard *secondary education educator, writer*
Toney, Angela M. *medical administrator and educator*

Upper Saint Clair
Dunkis, Patricia B. *school system administrator*
Raymond, Bruce Allen *medical association administrator*

Valley Forge
Bogle, John Clifton *investment company executive*
Brennan, John Joseph *mutual fund company executive*
Campman, Christopher Kuller *consulting company executive*
Dachowski, Peter Richard *manufacturing executive*
Erb, Robert Allan *physical scientist*
Guttentag, Jack Mark *economist, educator*
Harvey, Carole (Kate Harvey) *minister, church official*
Hilyard, James Emerson *manufacturing executive*
LaBoon, Lawrence Joseph *human resources consultant*
Medley, Alex Roy *executive minister*
Miller, Betty Brown *freelance writer*
Phelizon, Jean Francois *business executive*
Weaver, Peter David *bishop, religious organization administrator*
Wright-Riggins, Aidsand F., III, *religious organization executive*

Vandergrift
Bullard, Ray Elva, Jr., *retired psychiatrist, hospital administrator*

Verona
Bruno, Louis Vincent *principal*
Lauterbach, Robert Emil *steel company executive*

Villanova
Amin, Moeness Gamal *education educator, director*
Beck, Robert Edward *computer scientist, educator*
Beletz, Elaine Ethel *nurse, educator*
Bergquist, James Manning *history professor*
Bersoff, Donald Neil *lawyer, psychologist*
DeLaura, David Joseph *English language educator*
Dobbin, Edmund J. *university administrator*
Edwards, John Ralph *retired chemist, educator*
Fitzpatrick, M. Louise *dean, nursing educator*
Friend, Theodore Wood, III, *foundation executive, historian, writer*
Haynor, Patricia Manzi *nursing educator, consultant*

Hunt, John Mortimer, Jr., *classical studies educator*
Johannes, John Roland *political science educator, academic administrator*
Lesch, Ann Mosely *political scientist, educator*
Lewis, Wayne H. *investment company executive*
Maule, James Edward *law educator, lawyer*
McDiarmid, Lucy *English educator, author*
McLaughlin, Philip VanDoren, Jr., *mechanical engineering educator, researcher, consultant*
Phares, Alain Joseph *physicist, researcher*
Salmon, John Hearsey McMillan *historian, educator*
Savitz, Fred *education educator*
Scholz, Sally J. *philosopher, educator*
Scott, Robert Montgomery *museum executive, lawyer*
Smith, Standish Harshaw *not-for-profit developer*
Tomlinson, J. Richard *engineering services company executive*
Zearfoss, Herbert Keyser *retired lawyer*

Volant
Moore, Janet Marie *accountant, state official*

Wallingford
Cook, Harvey Carlisle *law enforcement official*
Medina, Harold Raymond, III, *marketing executive*
Morrison, Donald Franklin *statistician, educator*
Peabody, William Tyler, Jr., *retired paper manufacturing company executive*
Purcell, Mary Hamilton *speech educator*
Scherer, Frederic Michael *economics professor*
Severdia, Anthony George *chemistry researcher*

Walnutport
Fister, Michael J. *music educator*

Warminster
Brenner, Rena Claudy *communications executive*
Ciao, Frederick J. *school system administrator, educator*
Hull, Lewis Woodruff *manufacturing executive*
VanBuren, Michael Paul *music educator*

Warren
Bergstein, Jack Marshall *surgeon*
Johnson, Newkirk Lynn *not-for-profit developer*
Ristau, Mark Moody *lawyer, petroleum consultant*

Warrendale
Cooper, Eric *multimedia executive, consultant*
Gaetano, Joy M. *human resources executive*
Richards, John Thomas, Jr., *lawyer*
Rumbaugh, Max Elden, Jr., *professional society administrator*
Scott, Alexander Robinson *engineering association executive*

Warrington
Shaw, Milton Herbert *conglomerate executive*
Ward, Hiley Henry *journalist, educator*

Washington
Allison, Jonathan *retired lawyer*
Forrest, Robert Gilliland *mathematics professor*
Kastelic, Robert Frank *aerospace company executive*
Lerner, William C. *lawyer*
Mc Cune, Barron Patterson *retired federal judge*
Mitchell, Brian Christopher *academic administrator*
Posner, David S. *lawyer*
Richman, Stephen I. *lawyer*
Schwarz, Frederick A.O., Jr., *lawyer*

Washington Bord
Snyder, John Jacob *researcher*

Washington Crossing
Clevenger, Roy Edward *credit and collections manager*
Roche, Gail Connor *editor*
Sloca, Steven Lane *lawyer*

Wayne
Agersborg, Helmer Pareli K. *pharmaceutical company executive, researcher*
Burget, Dean Edwin, Jr., *plastic surgeon*
Carroll, Robert W. *retired business executive*
Collin, Frances W. *literary agent*
Conde, Cristobal I. *computer company executive*
Curry, Thomas James *retired manufacturers representative*
Etris, Samuel Franklin *trade association research consultant*
Fabbri, Anne R. *art critic, curator*
Frye, Roland Mushat *literary historian, theologian*
Garrison, Guy Grady *librarian, educator*
Karlson, Lawrence Carl *technological products company executive*
Kauffman, Joel Mervin *chemistry educator, researcher, consultant*
Krutsick, Robert Stanley *retired science center executive*
Lefevre, Thomas Vernon *retired utility company executive, lawyer*
Lief, Harold Isaiah *psychiatrist*
Long, Peter Avard Chipman *retired military officer*
MacNeal, Edward Arthur *economic consultant*
Mann, James L. *computer company executive*
Rolleri, Denise Marie *radiation therapist, business owner*
Rubley, Carole A. *state legislator*
Spiess, F. Harry, Jr., *lawyer*
Stayton, William Ralph *psychologist, educator*
Thelen, Edmund *research executive*
Wilson, Bruce Brighton *lawyer, retired transportation executive*
Wilson, James Lawrence *retired chemical company executive*
Yoskin, Jon William, II, *insurance company executive*
Yost, R. David *pharmaceutical executive*
Youman, Roger Jacob *editor, writer*

Waynesboro
Benchoff, James Martin *manufacturing executive*
Coles, Robert Nelson, Sr., *religious organization administrator*
Cryer, Theodore Hudson *ophthalmologist, educator*
Kirk, Daniel Lee *retired physician, consultant*
Martin, Harold G. *engineering consultant*

Waynesburg
Maguire, Mildred May *chemistry educator, magnetic resonance researcher*
Visser, Richard Edgar *minister*

Wellsboro
Driskell, Lucile G. *artist*

West Chester
Adler, Madeleine Wing *academic administrator*
Baldino, Frank *biopharmaceutical executive*
Blake, Paul *pharmaceutical executive*
Blasiotti, Robert Vincent *accountant, consultant*
Boruch, John N. *electronics company executive*
Bove, Patrice Magee *elementary school educator*
Branman, M. Jeffrey *investment fund company executive*
Briggs, Douglas D. *communications executive*
Buchi, J. Kevin *pharmaceutical executive*
Burton, John Bryan *music educator*
Cinelli, Bethann *school health educator*
Czako, Alan H. *human resources specialist, benefits compensation analyst*
Dinniman, Andrew Eric *county commissioner, history educator, academic program director, international studies educator*
Dunlop, Edward Arthur *computer company executive*
Dzury, Stephen Daniel *insurance company executive*
Ewing, Joseph Neff, Jr., *retired lawyer*
Gadsby, Robin Edward *chemical company executive*
Gallagher, Terrence Vincent *editor*
Gougher, Ronald Lee *foreign language educator and administrator*
Green, Andrew Wilson *economist, educator, lawyer*
Griffith, Edward *judge*
Hammonds, Jay A. *retired secondary education educator, administrator*
Hanna, Colin Arthur *county official, management and computer consultant*
Hanson, Diane Charske *management consultant*
Hardy, Charles Ashley, III, *historian, educator*
Heaps, Marvin Dale *retired food services company executive*
Heston, Thomas J. *historian, educator*
Hipple, Walter John *English language educator*
Kaufman, Daniel J. *lawyer*
Kim, James Joo-Jin *electronics company executive*
Knuth Fischer, Cynthia Strout *environmental consultant*
Mahoney, William Francis *editor, writer*
Meystel, Michael A. *Internet executive*
Murray, Lawrence *management consultant*
Myrsiades, Kostas Yannis *literature educator*
Pennington, Robert Edgar *music educator*
Rizzo, Joyce A. *environmental services executive*
Robertson, William L. *environmental services executive*
Schoelkopf, R. Gerald *archivist, librarian*
Taylor, Bernard J., II, *banker, director*
Zlotowski, Martin *psychologist*

West Conshohocken
Boenning, Henry Dorr, Jr., *investment banker*
Lenfest, Harold Fitz Gerald *former cable television executive, lawyer*
Mullen, Eileen Anne *human resources executive*
Newman, Sandra Schultz *state supreme court justice*
Taylor, Martha Elizabeth (Betsy Taylor) *investment company executive*
Teillon, Louis Pierre, Jr., *lawyer*

West Grove
Allman, Margo Hutz *sculptor, painter*
Allman, William Berthold *musician, engineer, consultant*
Fuller, Jack Glendon, Jr., *retired plastics engineer*
Seder, Jeffrey A. *entrepreneur*

West Lawn
Partridge, David Edward *secondary school educator*

West Mifflin
Ardash, Garin *mechanical engineer*

West Point
Buckland, Barry Christopher *chemical engineer*
Chang, Raymond S. L. *pharmacologist*
Choi, Dennis W. *pharmaceutical executive, neurologist, educator*
Dorsey, Bruce David *medical researcher, research scientist*
Farber, Leonid *materials scientist*
Hilleman, Maurice Ralph *virus research scientist*
Kim, Peter Sungbai *pharmaceutical executive, educator, research and development company executive*
Manning, Barton Harley *neuroscientist*
Schaffner, Carolyn Marie *research administrator, biologist*
Scolnick, Edward Mark *pharmaceutical executive*
Shahinfar, Shahnaz *pharmaceutical executive, nephrologist*

West Sunbury
Stewart, Mark Thomas *gas industry executive*

Westtown
Jackson, Katherine Church *elementary school educator, reading educator*

Wexford
Bossart, Paul Nathaniel, Jr., *geologist, geophysicist, consultant*
Foster, Donald Lee *manufacturing executive, consultant*
Micale, Frank Jude *lawyer*

White Oak
Pribanic, Victor Hunter *lawyer*

Wilkes Barre
Baldino, Thomas Joseph *political scientist, educator*
Casale, Alfred Stanley *thoracic and cardiovascular surgeon*
Hayes, Wilbur Frank *retired biology educator*
Hepp, John Henry, IV, *historian, lawyer*
Hill, Adam Aloysius *theater educator*
Holtzman, Marc Lawrence *catalog chain executive*
Krawczeniuk, Joseph Volodymyr *humanities educator*

Legg, Timothy James *nursing educator*
Mech, Terrence Francis *library director*
Morgan, Dennis Keith *lawyer*
O'Donnell, Catherine Rose *lawyer*
Ogren, Robert Edward *biologist, educator*
Rosenn, Max *federal judge*
Schiowitz, Mark F. *surgeon*
Stokes, Kimberly Ann *counselor*
Yarmey, Richard Andrew *investment manager*

Williamsport
Boone, Daniel Lee *retired music educator*
Douthat, James Evans *college administrator*
Ertel, Allen Edward *lawyer, former congressman*
Garner, Ron A. *vocational school educator*
Gouldin, Judith Ann *nuclear medicine physician*
Largen, Joseph *retailer, furniture manufacturer, book wholesaler*
McClure, James Focht, Jr., *federal judge*
Muir, Malcolm *federal judge*

Willow Grove
Asplundh, Christopher B. *tree service company executive*
Burtt, Anne Dampman *special education educator*
Chatterjee, Hem Chandra *electrical engineer*
Dwyer, Joseph P. *lumber executive*
Moore, Norma Jean *real estate broker*
Ohama, Gary Louis *dental ceramist*
Schiffman, Louis F. *management consultant*
Suer, Marvin David *architectural consultant*
Sundar, Veeraraghavan V. *materials scientist*

Willow Street
Wesbury, Stuart Arnold, Jr., *health administration and policy executive, educator*

Womelsdorf
Worley, Jane Ludwig *lawyer*

Worcester
Curtis, Alton Kenneth *film company executive, clergyman*

Wormleysburg
Grass, Alexander *retail company executive*

Wyncote
Schaffner, Roberta Irene *retired medical, surgical nurse*

Wyndmoor
Brown, Gary Christian *ophthalmologist, director*
Fishman, Marshall Lewis *chemist*
Marmer, William N. *chemist, researcher*
Pfeffer, Philip Elliot *biophysicist*

Wynnewood
Alter, Milton *retired neurologist*
Belinger, Harry Robert *retired business executive*
Bernfeld, Gerald E. *editor, writer, retired nursing educator*
Brady, John Paul *psychiatrist*
Clarke, John Rodney *surgeon*
Frankl, William Stewart *cardiologist, educator*
Kenton, Edgar Jackson, III, *neurologist*
Meyers, Mary Ann *foundation administrator, writer, consultant*
Phillips, Almarin *economics educator, consultant*
Prendergast, George C. *cancer biologist, researcher*
Robinson, Robert L. *former financial service company executive, lawyer*
Rosen, Gerald Harris *physicist, consultant, educator*
Rubin, Leonard Sidney *physiologist, educator, researcher*
Russell, Horace Orlando *theology studies educator*
Sider, Ronald J. *theology educator, author*
Waber, Harry Edward *insurance agency executive*
Wachs, Saul Philip *Jewish education educator*

Wyomissing
Beaver, Howard Oscar, Jr., *retired alloys manufacturing company executive*
Gebbia, Robert James *tax executive*
Kessler, Leona Hanover *interior designer*
Mohn, Richard E. *bank executive*
Moll, Lloyd Henry *banker*
Rosello, Jacqueline DeLapp *occupational therapist*
Smith, Raymond Leigh *plastic surgeon*

Yardley
Ahrens, Henry William *art educator, consultant, puppeteer*
Breitenfeld, Frederick, Jr., *retired educational consultant, former public broadcasting executive*
Brick, John *biological psychologist, educator, researcher*
Castellanos, Diego Antonio *television personality*
Du Bois, Paul Zinkhan *library consultant, book dealer*
Elliott, Frank Nelson *retired college president*
Fraser, David William *epidemiologist*
Gilmour, D(avid) James *financial analyst, systems analyst*
Hamberg, Gilbert Lee *lawyer*
Huret, Barry S. *marketing professional, consultant*
Huret, Marilynn Joyce *editor*
Minter, Philip Clayton *retired communications company executive*
Newsom, Carolyn Cardall *management consultant*
Newsom, John Harlan *family physician*
Soultoukis, Donna Zoccola *library director*
U'Prichard, David C. *pharmaceutical executive*
Weaver, William Clair, Jr., (Mike Weaver) *human resources development executive*
Yee, David *chemist*

York
Aarestad, James Harrison *retired educational administrator, army officer*
Amos, Stuart R. *corporate executive*
Bartels, Bruce Michael *health care executive*
Blair, William David *retired electrical engineer*
Caffrey, Lynn Regina *education educator*
Day, Ronald Richard *retired financial executive*
Grossman, Robert Allen *transportation executive*
Hoffmeyer, William Frederick *lawyer, educator*
Horn, Russell Eugene *engineering executive, consultant*
Horn, Russell Eugene, Jr., *business executive*
Jackson, Renée Bernadette *English language educator*
Jellison, William R. *medical supply company executive*
Keiser, Paul Harold *retired hospital administrator*
Kornblatt, David *corporate financial executive*
Kunkle, Gerald K. *medical supply company executive*
Laucks, Therese Elaine *commercial art instructor*
Livingston, Pamela A. *corporate image and marketing management consultant*
McDonough, Gerald Clyde *transportation leasing company executive*
McMillan, Wendell Marlin *economist*
Minissale, Anthony A. *hospital administrator*
Myers, C. David *manufacturing executive*
Owens, Marilyn Mae *elementary school educator, secondary school educator*
Perry, Ronald *lawyer*
Rebert, Jephrey Lee *transportation planner, musician*
Rosen, Raymond *health facility executive*
Thornton, George Whiteley *investment company executive*
White, Timothy Paul *brokerage house executive*
Wiles, William Wharton *retired federal government official*
Young, Michael R. *manufacturing executive*
Zortman, Mark Albert *secondary school educator, director*

Youngstown
Love, George H., Jr., *lawyer*
Palmer, Arnold Daniel *retired professional golfer*

Youngwood
Duvall, Hollie Jean *music educator*
Henry, Candy A. *education educator, writer*

RHODE ISLAND

Adamsville
Quick, Joan B. *state legislator*

Barrington
Carpenter, Charles Colcock Jones *internist, educator*
Deakin, James *writer, former newspaperman*
Mihaly, Eugene Bramer *corporate executive, consultant, writer, educator*
Paolino, Ronald Mario *clinical psychologist, consultant, psychopharmacologist, pharmacist*
Soutter, Thomas Douglas *retired lawyer*

Block Island
Connolly, Violette M. *small business owner*
Gasner, Walter Gilbert *retired dermatologist*

Bristol
Berman, Garrett L. *eyewitness and jury educator*
Bogus, Carl Thomas *law educator*
Danzberger, Alexander Harris *chemical engineer, consultant*
Hendrix, John Shannon *architecture educator*
Kent, Robert Brydon *law educator*
McMullen, Susan Taylor *librarian*
Parella, Mary A. *state legislator*

Charlestown
Rohm, Robert Hermann *sculptor, educator*
Ungaro, Joseph Michael *newspaper publishing executive, consultant*
Walsh, Donna M. *state legislator*

Chepachet
Jubinska, Patricia Ann *ballet instructor, choreographer, artist, anthropologist, archaeologist*

Coventry
Schweinsburg, Jane Duberg *librarian*

Cranston
Ferguson, Christine C. *lawyer, state agency administrator*
Hetherington, Nancy *state legislator*
Lanzi, Beatrice A. *state legislator*
Mansolillo, Charles Ronald *lawyer*
Mathewson, Doris May *retired medical/surgical nurse*
Mruk, Charles Karzimer *agronomist*
Perna, Marie Immaculate *retired physical education educator*
Simonian, John S. *lawyer*
Vavala, Domenic Anthony *medical scientist, retired military officer*

Cumberland
Rossi, Joseph Anthony *film and television make-up artist, educator*

East Greenwich
Carlson, Shawn Eric *physicist*
Dence, Edward William, Jr., *lawyer, banker*
Hunter, Garrett Bell *investment banker*
Jordan, Ronald P. *pharmacist, pharmaceutical executive, consultant*
Rockett, Thomas J. *retired management consultant*
Spivack, Gloria Jean *music educator*
Stark, Dennis Edwin *bank executive, director*

East Providence
Guggenheim, Frederick Gibson *psychiatry educator*
Parziale, John R. *physiatrist*
Spina, Douglas John *priest, educator*

Esmond
Seabra, James Joseph *music educator, professional musician*

Fiskeville
Mc Feeley, John Jay *chemical engineer*

Foster
Sawyer, Mildred Clementina *retired real estate agent*

Greenville
Hopkins, Catherine Lee *music educator*

Hope Valley
Walker, Howard Ernest *lawyer*

Jamestown
DiStefano, Gregory John *marketing professional*
Parks, Albert Lauriston *lawyer*
Todd, Thomas Abbott *architect, urban designer, city planner*
Worden, Katharine Cole *sculptor*
Wright, Harrison Morris *historian, educator*

Johnston
Bosman, Ruud H. *insurance company executive*
Hurley, Brian J. *insurance company executive*
Merolla, Carol Ann *writer, consultant*
Subramaniam, Shivan Sivaswamy *insurance company executive*

Kingston
Beauregard, Raymond A. *mathematician, educator*
Burkett, John Philip *economics professor*
Caldwell, Naomi Rachel *library and information scientist, educator*
Carothers, Robert Lee *academic administrator*
Collyer, Charles Edmund *psychologist, educator*
Cunnigen, Donald *sociologist, educator*
Goos, Roger Delmon *mycologist*
Harrison, Robert William *zoologist, educator*
Hufnagel, Linda Ann *biology professor, researcher*
Kim, Yong Choon *philosopher, theologian, educator*
Ladewig, James L. *music history educator, reseacher*
Lee, Kang-Won Wayne *engineer, educator*
Mahammad, Riyaz Basha *biomedical researcher*
Markin, Karen Mary *research scientist, journalist*
Mazze, Edward Mark *marketing educator, consultant*
Molloy, David Scott, Jr., *labor relations educator*
Muir, Donald M. *electronics company executive*
Newman, Barbara Miller *psychologist, educator*
Nixon, Scott West *oceanography science educator*
Prochaska, James O. *psychologist, educator*
Rathemacher, Andrée Jessica *librarian*
Sundlun, Bruce *former governor*
Turnbaugh, William Arthur *archaeologist, educator*

Lincoln
Barlow, August Ralph, Jr., *minister*
Carter, Wilfred Wilson *financial executive, controller*
Enos, David Michael *music educator, coach*
Marsden, Herci Ivana *classical ballet artistic director*

Little Compton
Bamberger, Lauren R. *writer, photojournalist*
Caron, Wilfred Rene *retired lawyer*
Middendorf, J. William, II, *investment banker*

Middletown
Demy, Timothy James *military chaplain*
Jackson, John Edward *educator, logistician, retired naval officer*
Ottaviano, Doris Baginski *librarian*

Narragansett
Bentley-Scheck, Grace Mary *artist*
Pilson, Michael Edward Quinton *oceanography educator*
Potty, Gopu Ramachandran *marine engineer, researcher*
Sammis, Anne Mimi *sculptor, artist*

Newport
Brown, David William *economist, educator, consultant*
Brown, Jane G. *sports association executive*
Burgin, William Lyle *architect*
Carpenter, Stanley Dean MacDonald *military officer, educator*
Cicilline, J. Clement *mental health services professional, state legislator*
Coxe, Trudy *museum administrator, former state official*
Ehrlich, Stanley Leonard *acoustical engineer, consultant*
Galivan, John Henry *biochemist, educator, public health officer, research administrator*
Grassey, Thomas Brandt *humanities educator*
Haas, William Paul *humanities educator, former college president*
Higgins, Harriet Pratt *investment advisor*
Koch, Robert Michael *research scientist, consultant, educator*
Malkovich, Mark Paul, III, *musician, artistic director, scientist, sports agent*
McConnell, David Kelso *lawyer*
Mullaney, Joann Barnes *nursing educator*
Nash, Karen Marsteller Myers *sculptor, designer, systems analyst*
Sands, Harold Winthrop *banker, financial adviser*
Scoll, Eulalie Elizabeth *writer, researcher*
Stone, Edward Luke *private equity investor, realtor*
Tinney, Harle Hope Hanson *museum administrator, owner*
Uhlig, Frank, Jr., *editor, writer*
Wood, Berenice Howland *retired secondary school educator*
Woods, Donald E. *healthcare executive*
Wurman, Richard Saul *architect*

North Kingstown
Benson, Melvoid J. *state legislator*
Kilguss, Elsie Schaich *artist, gallery owner*
Kullberg, Gary Walter *advertising agency executive*
Mellor, Kathy *National Teacher of the Year 2004, ESL educator*
Novich, Bruce Eric *chemicals executive*
Sharpe, Henry Dexter, Jr., *retired manufacturing company executive*

North Scituate
Dupree, Thomas Andrew *forester, state official*

Pawtucket
Belliveau, Kathrin Pagonis *lawyer*
Bifulco, Frank *toy company executive*
Charness, Wayne Samuel *public relations executive*
Chopra, Pradeep *physician, educator*
Crowley, James Patrick *hematologist, medical educator, immunologist*
Davison, Charles Hamilton *financial executive*
DeWerth, Gordon Henry *management consultant*
Friedman, Joseph Harold *neurologist*
Glicksman, Arvin S(igmund) *radiation oncologist*
Goldner, Brian *toy company executive*
Hargreaves, David R. *toy company executive*
Hassenfeld, Alan Geoffrey *consumer products company executive*
Holt, Richard B. *toy company executive*
Huebner, Chuck *toy manufacturing executive*
Kiessling, Louise Sadler *pediatrician, medical educator*
Orson, Barbara Tuschner *actress*
Ready, Christopher James *accountant*
Romanzi, Kenneth *toy manufacturing executive*
Trueb, Martin R. *toy company executive*
Verrecchia, Alfred Joseph *toy company executive*
Wilson, E. David *toy company executive*

Peace Dale
Brennan, Noel-Anne Gerson *anthropologist, educator, writer*

Portsmouth
Becken, Bradford Albert *engineering executive*
Bergstrom, Albion Andrew *retired military officer, educator*
Needham, Richard Lee *magazine editor*
Parker, Nancy Knowles (Mrs. Cortlandt Parker) *retired publishing executive*

Providence
Ackerman, Felicia *philosophy educator, writer*
Ajello, Edith H. *state legislator*
Alderman, Ken *construction company executive*
Algiere, Dennis Lee *state legislator*
Allio, Robert John *management consultant, educator*
Amaral, Joseph Ferreira *surgeon*
Anderson, James Alfred *psychology educator*
Anderson, Mabel M. *state legislator*
Anton, Thomas Julius *political science and public policy educator, consultant*
Armstrong, Paul Bradford *English language educator, dean*
Aronson, Stanley Maynard *physician, educator*
Avery, Donald Hills *metallurgist, educator, ethnographer*
Baar, James A. *public relations and corporate communications executive, author, consultant, internet publisher, software developer*
Barnhill, James Orris *theater educator*
Barnum, William Milo *architect*
Bensmaia, Reda *French studies educator, researcher*
Berkelhammer, Robert Bruce *lawyer*
Besdine, Richard William *medical educator, researcher*
Bewes, Timothy Richard Thomas *language educator*
Biron, Christine Anne *medical science educator, researcher*
Blasing, Mutlu Konuk *English language educator*
Block, Stanley Hoyt *pediatrician, allergist*
Boekelheide, Kim *pathologist*
Boisvert, Charles Miga *psychologist, educator*
Braman, Sidney Stuart *internist, educator*
Bready, Richard Lawrence *manufacturing executive*
Briant, Clyde Leonard *metallurgist, educator*
Bristow, Lonnie Robert *physician*
Brown, Matthew A. *state official*
Burns, Robert E. *bank executive*
Butler, John D. *human resources executive*
Cady, Blake *surgical oncologist*
Callahan, Christine H. *state legislator*
Cambio, Bambilyn Breece *state legislator*
Campbell, Lewis B. *aerospace technology executive*
Carcieri, Donald L. *governor*
Carlotti, Stephen Jon *lawyer*
Carpenter, Gene Blakely *crystallography and chemistry educator*
Choquette, Paul Joseph, Jr., *construction company executive*
Clifford, Sidney, Jr., *lawyer, judge*
Coderre, Elaine Ann *state representative*
Conley, Patrick T. *lawyer, writer, historian*
Cooper, Leon N. *physicist, researcher*
Courage, Thomas Roberts *lawyer*
Creeley, Robert White *author, English educator*
Curran, Joseph Patrick *lawyer*
Dafermos, Constantine Michael *applied mathematics educator*
Dahlberg, Albert Edward *biochemistry educator*
D'Andrea, Vincent Charles *postal clerk*
Davis, Philip J. *mathematician*
Davis, Robert Paul *physician, educator*
Deal, Joseph Maurice *academic administrator, art educator, photographer*
Demopulos, Harold William *lawyer*
Dempsey, Raymond Leo, Jr., *radio and television producer, moderator, writer*
Dickersin, Kay *researcher, educator*
DiGiovanni, Christopher William *orthopedic surgeon*
DiMonte, Vincent A. *lawyer*
Dobbins, Richard Andrew *engineering educator, researcher*
Donahue, John Edward *physician*
Donnelly, Kevin William *lawyer*
Donovan, Bruce Elliot *classics educator, university dean*
Dowben, Robert Morris *physiologist, researcher*
Dujardin, Richard Charles *journalist*
Duncan, David Frank *community health specialist, educator*
Easton, J(ohn) Donald *neurologist, educator*
Elbaum, Charles *physicist, educator, researcher*
Eltringham, Dana Kristin *writer*
Enteman, Willard Finley *philosophy educator*
Erikson, G(eorge) E(mil) (Erik Erikson) *anatomist, archivist, historian, educator, information specialist*
Ewing, John Harwood *mathematics professor, department chairman*
Farmer, Susan Lawson *broadcasting executive, former secretary of state*
Farrell, Margaret Dawson *lawyer*
Feldman, Allan Maurice *economist*
Fish, Lawrence Kingsbaker *banker*
Fishman, Bernard Philip *museum director*
Flaherty, Francis Xavier *judge*
Flanders, Robert G., Jr., *state supreme court justice*
Fleming, Wendell Helms *mathematician, educator*
Fogarty, Charles Joseph *lieutenant governor*
Fogarty, Edward Michael *lawyer*
Fornara, Charles William *historian, classicist, educator*
Franklin, Lawrence C. *state official*
Freiberger, Walter Frederick *mathematics professor, actuarial science consultant*
Frerichs, Ernest Sunley *religious studies educator*

Freund, Lambert Ben *engineering educator, researcher, consultant*
Gaebe, Morris J. *academic administrator*
Gale, Edwin John *judge*
Gallo, Hanna M. *state legislator*
Gasbarro, Pasco, Jr., *lawyer*
Gerbi, Susan Alexandra *biology professor*
Gerritsen, Hendrik Jurjen *physics educator, researcher*
Gibbs, June Nesbitt *state legislator*
Gilbane, Thomas F., Jr., *building company executive*
Gilchrist, James Manning *neurologist, researcher, educator*
Gill, Mary Louise Glanville *educator of classics and philosophy*
Gleason, Abbott *history professor*
Glicksman, Maurice *engineering educator, former dean and provost*
Gnepp, Douglas Robbin *pathologist*
Goldberg, Maureen McKenna *state supreme court justice*
Goldscheider, Frances K. *sociologist, educator*
Goldstein, Joshua S. *writer, educator*
Goldstein, Sidney *sociology educator, demographer*
Goodman, Elliot Raymond *political scientist, educator*
Goodwin, Maryellen *state legislator*
Gorn, Elliott Jacob *historian, educator, writer*
Goulder, Caroljean Hempstead *retired psychologist, consultant*
Green, Angel Yvonne *literature educator*
Greer, David S. *dean, educator, physician*
Grossman, Herschel I. *economics professor*
Hagopian, Jacob *federal judge*
Hall, Almon C., III, *investment company executive*
Hamerly, Michael T. *librarian, historian*
Hamolsky, Milton William *physician*
Hardymon, James Franklin *retired diversified products company executive*
Harleman, Ann *English language educator, writer*
Harris, Richard John *diversified holding company executive*
Harwood, Patricia L. *judge*
Hazeltine, Barrett *electrical engineer, educator*
Heath, Dwight Braley *anthropologist, educator*
Henseler, Suzanne Marie *state legislator, social studies educator, majority whip*
Heyman, Lawrence Murray *printmaker, painter*
Higginbotham, Richard A. *investment banker*
Hitt, Mary Frances Lyster *environmentalist, deacon*
Hittner, Barry G. *state agency administrator*
Holloway, Robert Ross *archaeologist, educator*
Howes, Lorraine de Wet *fashion designer, educator*
Hunt, Cheryl Ruth *librarian*
Iannitelli, Susan B. *state legislator*
Jackson, Benjamin Taylor *retired surgeon, educator, medical facility administrator*
Janitz, John A. *aerospace company executive*
Jenny, Carole *physician, researcher*
Jin, Ya *mathematics researcher*
Johnson, Melody *school system administrator*
Johnson, Vahe Duncan *lawyer*
Jones, Ferdinand Taylor, Jr., *psychologist, educator*
Jones, Lauren Evans *lawyer*
Joukowsky, Artemis A. W. *private investor*
Kacir, Barbara Brattin *lawyer*
Kagan, Marilyn D. *retired architect*
Kane, Agnes Brezak *pathologist, educator*
Kane, Steven Michael *psychotherapist, educator*
Kates, Robert William *geographer, educator*
Kean, John Vaughan *retired lawyer*
Khrushchev, Sergei Nikitich *engineering educator*
Killeen, Johanne *small business owner*
Kim, Jaegwon *philosophy educator*
Kimia, Benjamin B. *engineering educator*
Knopf, Paul Mark *immunoparasitologist, neuro-immunologist*
Konstan, David *classics and comparative literature educator, researcher*
Kraemer, Michael Frederick *lawyer*
Kramer, Ilse Elisabeth *rare book bibliographer*
Kushner, Harold Joseph *mathematics professor*
Lagueux, Ronald Rene *federal judge*
Lanou, Robert Eugene, Jr., *physicist, researcher*
Lemons, James Stanley *history educator*
Lesko, Leonard Henry *Egyptologist, educator, publisher*
Levin, Frank S. *physicist, researcher*
Leviten, Riva Shamray *artist*
Lewis, David Carleton *medical educator, university center director*
Licht, Richard A. *lawyer*
Lima, Charlene *state legislator*
Lipsey, Howard Irwin *law educator, justice, lawyer*
Lisi, Mary M. *federal judge*
Liu, Jianhong *sociologist, educator*
Lohrum, Frederick *bank executive*
Long, Beverly Glenn *retired lawyer*
Long, Nicholas Trott *lawyer*
Lopes, Maria J. *state legislator*
Lopez-Morillas, Frances M. *translator*
Lynch, Patrick C. *state attorney general*
Magendantz, Henry Guenther *physician*
Mandle, Earl Roger *design school president, former museum executive*
Marsh, Donald Jay *medical school dean, medical educator*
Marsh, Robert Mortimer *sociologist, educator*
McCann, Gail Elizabeth *lawyer*
Mc Donald, Charles J. *dermatologist, educator*
McElroy, Michael Robert *lawyer*
McIntyre, Jerry L. *lawyer*
McNeil, Paul Joseph, Jr., *employment security interviewer*
Mehlman, Edwin Stephen *endodontist*
Merlino, Anthony Frank *orthopedist*
Metrey, George David *social work educator, academic administrator*
Modell, John *social sciences educator*
Monaghan, John J. *managing editor*
Monteiro, Lois Ann *medical science educator*
Mulhearn, Christopher Michael *lawyer*
Mulvee, Robert Edward *bishop*
Mumford, David Bryant *mathematics professor*
Murphy, Christine *medical facility administrator*
Murphy, William J. *state legislator*
Nazarian, John *academic administrator, mathematics educator*
Needleman, Alan *mechanical engineering educator*
Nolan, Patricia Ann *public health officer*
Oh, William *physician*
Olsen, Hans Peter *lawyer*
Olyan, Saul Mitchell *religious studies educator*
Paiva-Weed, M. Teresa *state legislator*
Parris, Thomas Godfrey, Jr., *medical facility administrator*
Pieters, Carle McGetchin *geology educator, planetary scientist, researcher*
Pine, Jeffrey Barry *lawyer, former state attorney general*
Pueschel, Siegfried M. *pediatrician, educator*
Putnam, Michael Courtney Jenkins *classics educator*
Raaflaub, Kurt Arnold *classics educator*
Recupero, Patricia Ryan *hospital administrator, psychiatrist, lawyer, health facility executive*
Reed, Cynthia S. *manufacturing executive*
Richardson, Julie G. *investment company executive*
Richman, Marc Herbert *forensic engineer, educator*
Riordan, Cornelius *sociology educator, writer, consultant*
Robert, Stephen *academic administrator*
Roberts, Elizabeth H. *state legislator*
Roesler, Thomas Allen *psychiatrist, researcher*
Rohr, Donald Gerard *history professor*
Roney, John M. *lawyer*
Rosenberg, Alan Gene *newspaper editor*
Rueschemeyer, Marilyn Schattner *sociology educator*
St. Florian, Friedrich Gartler *architect, educator*
Salter, Lester Herbert *lawyer*
Sasso, Eleanor Catherine *state senator*
Savage, John Edmund *computer science educator, researcher*
Schevill, James Erwin *poet, playwright*
Schmitt, Johanna Marie *plant population biologist, educator*
Schulz, Juergen *art history educator*
Selya, Bruce Marshall *federal judge*
Shapiro, Ronald Gary *psychologist*
Sherman, Deming Eliot *lawyer*
Shetty, Taranath *neurologist, educator*
Shu, Chi-Wang *mathematics educator, researcher*
Silverman, Joseph Hillel *mathematics professor*
Simmons, Ruth J. *academic administrator*
Siqueland, Einar *psychology educator*
Smith, Philip A. *academic administrator*
Smith, Robert Ellis *lawyer, journalist*
Snibbe, Patricia Miscall *advertising executive*
Sosa, Ernest *philosopher, educator*
Sosnowski, V. Susan *state legislator*
Staples, Richard Farnsworth *lawyer*
Stein, Jerome Leon *economist, educator*
Steinbach, Meredith Lynn *writer, educator*
Stratt, Richard Mark *chemistry researcher, educator*
Stultz, Newell Maynard *retired political science educator*
Sutton, Howard G. *publishing executive*
Sweeney, Judith Kiernan *secondary school educator*
Symonds, Paul Southworth *mechanical engineering educator, researcher*
Takao, Motoharu *physiologist*
Tauc, Jan *physics educator*
Tobin, Bentley *lawyer*
Torres, Ernest C. *federal judge*
Tracy, Thomas Francis, Jr., *pediatric surgeon, resarcher, educator*
Valente, Luiz Fernando *Portuguese and Brazilian studies and comparative literature educator*
Vezeridis, Michael Panagiotis *surgeon, educator*
Vogel, Paula Anne *playwright*
Vorenberg, Michael *history educator*
Waite-Franzen, Ellen Jane *academic administrator*
Weiner, Jerome Harris *mechanical engineering educator*
Weisberger, Joseph Robert *retired judge*
Weitberg, Alan Barry *physician, researcher*
Wetle, Terrie Fox *gerontologist, educator, dean*
Whiting, Brian Christopher *hospitality consultant*
Widgoff, Mildred *physicist, researcher*
Williams, Anastasia P. *state legislator*
Williams, Frank J. *judge, historian, writer*
Wood, Craig Breckinridge *paleobiologist, natural science educator*
Wood, Gordon Stewart *historian, educator*
Wrenn, James Joseph *East Asian studies educator*
Yena, John A. *academic administrator*

Rumford
Irons, William V. *state legislator*

Saunderstown
Carter, Kenneth *state legislator, restauranteur*
Donovan, Gerald Alton *retired academic administrator, former university dean*
Knauss, John Atkinson *former federal agency administrator, oceanographer, educator, former university dean*
Leavitt, Thomas Whittlesey *retired museum director, educator*

Scituate
Gorham, Bradford *lawyer*

Smithfield
Kosowski, Mary *artist, educator*
Litoff, Judy Barrett *history professor*
Morahan-Martin, Janet May *psychologist, educator*

South Kingstown
Fredriksen, John Conrad *historian, consultant*
Pembrook, Richard Charles *internist, cardiologist*

Tiverton
Frost, John Mason *writer, educator, retired protective services official*

Wakefield
Boothroyd, Geoffrey *industrial and manufacturing engineering educator*
Doody, Agnes G. *communications educator, management and communication consultant*
Fera, Steven Raymond *internist, cardiologist, educator*
Hart, Kenneth Nelson *lawyer*
Leete, William White *artist*
Mason, Scott MacGregor *entrepreneur, inventor, consultant*
Moore, George Emerson, Jr., *geologist, educator*
Morrison, Fred Beverly *real estate consultant*
Newman, Philip Robert *psychologist*
Wyman, James Vernon *newspaper executive*

Warwick
Charette, Sharon Juliette *library administrator*
Gambardella, Mary Jo *secondary school educator, music educator*
Goldman, Steven Jason *lawyer, accountant, consultant*
Halperson, Michael Allen *publishing executive*
Horn, Donna M. *pharmacist, medical association administrator*
Izzi, John *mathematics educator, writer*
Jennings, Julianne *cultural organization administrator*
Kiley, Peter Michael *music educator*
Knowles, Charles Timothy *lawyer, state legislator, military officer, educator*
Lachapelle, Cleo Edward *retired real estate broker*
Lowe, David Alan *epidemiologist*
Morgan, Patricia *financial consultant, former Republican party chairman*
Reilly, John B. *lawyer*
Revens, John Cosgrove, Jr., *state legislator, lawyer*
Riffkin, Mitchell Sanford *lawyer*
St. Pierre, Michael A. *lawyer*

West Greenwich
Duggan, John David, Jr., *computer technician*
Turner, W. Bruce *computer company executive*

West Kingston
Dowdell, Rodger Birtwell, Sr., *electronics company executive*

West Warwick
Bottella, Tammy Ann *lawyer*
Galkin, Robert Theodore *company executive*
Lancellotta, John Jerry-Louis *foundation administrator*
Pollock, Bruce Gerald *lawyer*

Westerly
Bachmann, William Thompson *dermatologist*
Nardone, William Andrew *lawyer*
Panciera, Richard Conner *lawyer*

Woonsocket
Bodine, Chris W. *retail executive*
Eno, Paul Frederick *editor, writer*
Ferdinandi, V. Michael *retail executive*
Lankowsky, Zenon P. *lawyer*
Merlo, Larry J. *retail executive*
Rickard, David B. *food company executive*
Roszkowski, Joseph John *lawyer*
Ryan, Thomas M. *drug store chain executive*
Sgarro, Douglas A. *pharmaceutical executive, lawyer*
Solberg, Larry D. *retail executive*
Stubbs, Donald Clark *retired secondary school educator*

SOUTH CAROLINA

Abbeville
Cellura, A(ngele) Raymond *psychologist*

Aiken
Amabile, John Louis *lawyer*
Bertsch, Paul M. *ecologist, director*
Coble, Paul Ishler *advertising agency executive*
Dickson, Paul Wesley, Jr., *physicist*
Ely, Duncan Cairnes *non profit/human services executive, civic leader*
Hickey, Delina Rose *retired education educator*
Hootman, Harry Edward *retired nuclear engineer, consultant*
Isaacs-Bright, Susan Virginia Kirkpatrick *research librarian, public speaker, advocate*
Li, Rao *mathematician, computer scientist*
Moore, Edna Googe *primary school educator*
Naifeh, Steven Woodward *writer*
Pearce, Richard Lee *lawyer*
Punshon, Tracy *research scientist*
Ritchie, Charles Michael *education educator, consultant*
Rudnick, Irene Krugman *lawyer, former state legislator, educator*
Santos, Karey Michale *elementary school educator*
Smith, Gregory White *writer*
Sykes, Richard Nesbit *history professor, department chairman*
Wood, Susan *applied technology center executive*
Zirps, George Thomas *marine engineer, consultant*

Anderson
Baughman, Janet Irene *writer*
Chipman, Dennis Clarence, Jr., *psychiatrist, consultant*
Elzerman, Alan William *environmental chemistry educator*
Kline, George Louis *author, translator, retired philosophy and literature educator*
Martin, Terrell Owen *retired university administrator*
Sustar, T. David *religious organization administrator*
Urakami, Akio *manufacturing company executive*
Woodall, Hunter Earl *physician, educator*

Barnwell
Nichols, M(arian) Theresa *radio station executive*

Beaufort
Frederick, Jane Y. *architect*
Harvey, William Brantley, Jr., *lawyer, former lieutenant governor*
Pinkerton, Robert Bruce *mechanical engineer*
Raines, Karen Cornell *secondary school educator*

Bennettsville
Best, Carolyn Anne Hill *elementary school educator*
Kinney, William Light, Jr., *newspaper editor, publisher*

Bishopville
Cox, Janson L. *museum administrator*
Jennings, Jacob Hill *lawyer, director*

Blackstock
King, Robert Thomas *editor, freelance writer*

Bluffton
Brown, Dallas Coverdale, Jr., *retired army officer, retired history educator*
Cann, Sharon Lee *retired health science librarian*
Cork, Holly A. *former state legislator*
Pendley, William Tyler *naval officer, international relations educator*
Reuben, Alvin Bernard *communications and entertainment executive*

Blythewood
Daniels, James Douglas *retired academic administrator*

Camden
Buckley, Claude Langford *artist*
Chapman, Robert Foster *judge*
Craig, Joanna Burbank *historic site director*
Daniels, John Hancock *agricultural products company executive*
Jacobs, Rolly Warren *judge*
Sindler, Allan Jay *chemical engineer, sculptor, educator*

Cameron
Ulmer, Jeanne Wilde *judge*

Cayce
McElveen, William Lindsay *broadcasting executive, lecturer*
Paynter, Vesta Lucas *pharmacist*
Tucker, Kelly H. *music educator*

Central
Holcombe, Joseph Steven *academic administrator, educator*
Smith-Cox, Elizabeth Shelton *art educator*

Chapin
Branham, Mack Carison, Jr., *retired theological seminary educator, minister*
Freitag, Carol Wilma *state official, political scientist*

Charleston
Addlestone, Nathan Sidney *metals company executive*
Appleget, Terri Lynn *elementary school educator*
Austin, Charles John *health services educator*
Bailey, Dawn Marie *fund raising systems consultant*
Ballard, Mary Melinda *financial communications and marketing/advertising executive, consumer advocate*
Barrett, Michael Baker *historian, educator*
Bell, Norman Howard *physician, endocrinologist, educator*
Bolin, Edmund Mike *electrical engineer, franchise engineering consultant*
Bonds, John Bledsoe *musician, educator*
Bowman, Daniel Oliver *retired psychologist*
Branham, C. Michael *lawyer*
Brown, Ann Catherine *investment company executive*
Brown, Carroll Smith *anesthesiologist*
Buvinger, Jan *library director*
Cannon, Hugh *lawyer*
Cantwell, Don *artistic director*
Carek, Donald J(ohn) *child psychiatry educator*
Carter, James Folger *obstetrician-gynecologist, educator, consultant*
Chapin, Fred *airport executive*
Chapman, Howard Reed *city and county transportation engineer, consultant*
Chiaramida, Salvatore *cardiologist, educator, health facility administrator*
Clawson, Harry Quintard Moore *retired business executive*
Coates, Timothy Joel *historian*
Cordova, Maria Asuncion *dentist*
Daniell, Herman Burch *pharmacologist*
De Wolff, Louis *management consultant*
Dobson, Richard Lawrence *dermatologist, educator*
Donehue, John Douglas *interdenominational ministries executive*
Donnem, Roland William *retired lawyer, real estate owner, developer*
Dulles, Frederick Hendrik *lawyer*
Dupree, Nathalie *chef, television personality, writer*
Edwards, Darrell *orchestra executive*
Farr, Charles Sims *lawyer*
Ferguson, Esther B. *philanthropist*
Finn, Albert Frank, Jr., *physician*
Forsythe, Dennis M. *biology professor*
Freer, Robert Elliott, Jr., *lawyer*
Geentiens, Gaston Petrus, Jr., *former construction management consultant company executive*
Goff, R. Garey *architect*
Grinalds, John Southy *military officer, academic administrator*
Gunn, Morey Walker, Jr., *secondary education educator, choir director, organist*
Hainer, Barry L. *physician*
Harding, Enoch, Jr., *clothing executive*
Hawkins, Falcon Black, Jr., *federal judge*
Henson, Kenneth Tyrone *education educator*
Hoel, David Gerhard *statistician, scientist, educator*
Hoerter, Sam Spalding *transportation executive*
Hoffman, Brenda Joyce *gastroenterology educator*
Hogan, Edward Leo *neurologist*
Hollis, Bruce Warren *experimental nutritionist, industrial consultant*
Hughes, Blake *retired architectural institute administrator, publisher*
Hunter, Jairy C., Jr., *academic administrator*
Jaffa, Ayad A. *medical educator, medical researcher*
Jaffe, Murray Sherwood *retired surgeon*
Johnson, Dewey E(dward), Jr., *dentist*
Kahn, Ellis Irvin *lawyer*
Kalivas, Peter W. *physiologist, educator, department chairman*
Kaplan, Allen P. *immunologist, educator, allergist, researcher*
Key, Janice Dixon *physician, medical educator*
KilPatrick, Anne Osborne *health administration and policy educator*
Kimmel, Herbert David *psychology educator*
Kitner, Harold *artist, educator*
Knee, Stuart Eugene *historian, educator*
Lader, Philip *lawyer, academic administrator, diplomat*
Leath, William Jefferson, Jr., *lawyer*
Limehouse, Harry Bancroft, Jr., *real estate developer, transportation consultant*
Litvin, Stephen W. *management consultant, educator*
Mahoney, John Joseph *business executive, educator*
Maize, John Christopher *dermatologist, educator*
Margolius, Harry Stephen *pharmacologist, physician*
Maricq, Hildegard Rand *physician, researcher*

Martin, Roblee Boettcher *retired cement manufacturing executive*
Mayfield, Ronald Keith *endocrinologist, educator*
McCurdy, Layton *medical educator*
Mohr, Lawrence Charles *physician*
Moore, William Vincent *political science educator*
Morris, Valerie Bonita *performing arts administrator*
O'Bryant-Seabrook, Marlene Loretta Linton *retired educator*
Ogretmen, Besim *science educator, molecular biologist, researcher*
Oldham, John Michael *physician, psychiatrist, educator*
Osguthorpe, John David *otolaryngologist, educator*
Othersen, Henry Biemann, Jr., *surgeon, physician, educator*
Patrick, Charles William, Jr., *lawyer*
Quinn, E. Moore *linguistic anthropology educator*
Reves, Joseph Gerald *dean, anesthesiology educator*
Rivas, Fernando *composer*
Robinson, Neil Cibley, Jr., *lawyer*
Rosen, Richard S. *lawyer*
Rustin, Rudolph Byrd, III, *surgeon, educator*
Salmon, Edward Lloyd, Jr., *bishop*
Saul, J. Philip *pediatrician, educator*
Schreadley, Richard Lee *writer, retired newspaper editor*
Schuman, Stanley Harold *epidemiologist, educator*
Sharpe, Kathryn Moye *psychologist*
Siddons, Anne Rivers (Sybil Anne Rivers Siddons) *writer*
Simms, Lois Averetta *retired secondary school educator*
Simson, Jo Anne *retired anatomy and cell biology educator, biologist, educator*
Smedley, Charles Vincent *sociology educator*
Smith, W. Stuart *strategic planning director*
Spinale, Francis G. *medical educator, research cardiologist*
Stanley, Karen M. *mental health nurse, consultant*
Stine, Gordan Bernard *dentist, educator*
Stuart, Robert Kenneth *internist, oncologist, hematologist, educator*
Sutusky, John Charles *higher education educator*
Tarleton, Larry Wilson *editor*
Thompson, W(ilmer) Leigh *pharmaceutical company executive, physician, pharmacologist*
Underwood, Paul Benjamin *gynecologist, oncologist, educator*
Vela, Marcelo Fernando *gastroenterologist*
Waggoner, Robert *chef*
Waller, John Louis *anesthesiology educator*
Watts, Claudius Elmer, III, *retired military officer*
Williams, Barbara Stambaugh *editor*
Wilson, Frederick Allen *medical educator, medical center administrator, gastroenterologist*
Worthington, Ward Curtis, Jr., *university dean, anatomy educator*
Wyrick, Charles Lloyd, Jr., *publisher, writer, editor*
Yu, Shan Ping *neuroscientist, educator*

Chesnee
Saunders, J. Farrell *historic site director*

Clemson
Bailey, Beatrice Naff *researcher and educator in English*
Barker, James F. *academic administrator*
Bauerle, William L. *landscape architect, educator*
Beyerlein, Adolph Louis *retired chemist, educator*
Birrenkott, Glenn P., Jr., *poultry science educator*
Boykin, Joseph Floyd, Jr., *librarian*
Brawley, Joel Vincent *mathematician, educator*
Caldwell, Judith *horticultural educator*
Charney, Mark Jay *language educator*
Clayton, Donald Delbert *astrophysicist, nuclear physicist, educator*
Cox, Headley Morris, Jr., *lawyer, educator*
Denham, Bryan Errol *communications educator*
Felder, Frankie Ottowiess *academic administrator*
Golan, Lawrence Peter *mechanical engineering educator, energy researcher*
Grady, C.P. Leslie, Jr., *engineering educator*
Halfacre, Robert Gordon *ombudsman, landscape architect, horticulturist, educator*
Helms, Doris R. *academic administrator*
Kelly, John William, Jr., *university administrator*
Kimmel, Robert Michael *education educator, consultant*
Krause, Lois Ruth Breur *chemistry educator*
Logan, Barbara N. *nursing educator*
Melton, Gary Bentley *psychology and law educator*
Moran, Ronald Wesson *retired English educator, dean, writer*
Nielsen, Barbara Stock *state educational administrator*
Paul, Frank Waters *mechanical engineer, educator, consultant*
Petzel, Florence Eloise *textiles educator*
Pursley, Michael Bader *electrical engineering educator, communications systems research and consulting*
Riley, Helene Maria Kastinger *Germanist*
Skaar, Eric Christen *education educator, consultant*
Sluss, Dorothy Louise *education educator, researcher*
Straka, Thomas James *forester, educator*
Tamura, Robert *economics professor, consultant*
Underwood, Richard Allan *English language educator*
Vogel, Henry Elliott *retired university dean and physics educator*
Wagner, John Russell *mechanical engineering educator, researcher*
Wehrenberg, William Busse *agricultural studies educator*
Williamson, Robert Elmore *engineering educator*
Xu, Xiao-Bang *engineering educator*
Zumbrunnen, David Arnold *mechanical engineering and materials science educator, consultant*

Clinton
Cornelson, George Henry, IV, *retired textile company executive*
Griffith, John Vincent *academic official*
Skinner, James Lister, III, *English language educator*
Stokes, James Porter, II, *music educator*

Clover
Easter, Jr., Willie *artist, writer*
Montgomery, Connie Roger *writer*

Columbia
Adams, John Hurst *bishop*
Aelion, C. Marjorie *adult education educator*
Akhavi, Shahrough *political science professor*
Alexander, Thomas C. *state legislator, office supply company executive*
Allison, Merita Ann *state legislator*
Almond, Carl Herman *surgeon, physician, educator*
Amidon, Roger Lyman *retired health administration educator*
Arias-Haskins, Gloria *state representative*
Arthur, H. Thomas, II, *energy executive*
Arvay, Nancy Joan *lawyer*
Ashley, Perry Johnathan *journalism educator*
Averyt, Gayle Owen *retired insurance executive*
Barnum, William Douglas *retired communications company executive*
Baskin, C. R. *civil engineer*
Bauer, R. Andre *lieutenant governor*
Bell, Isaac, Jr., *music educator*
Bernstein, Barry Joel *lawyer*
Bjontegard, Arthur Martin, Jr., *foundation executive*
Blanton, Hoover Clarence *lawyer*
Boggs, Jack Aaron *banker, publisher, municipal government official, mayor*
Bowman, Ned David *medical administrator*
Breedin, Berryman Brent *journalist, public relations, historian, consultant*
Briggs, Ward Wright *classics educator*
Bristow, Thomas Cole, Jr., *social work educator*
Bristow, Walter James, Jr., *retired judge*
Brockelsby, Jeffrey Lind *investment executive*
Brooker, Jeff Zeigler *cardiologist*
Brown, Robert Charles *lawyer*
Bruccoli, Matthew Joseph *English educator, publisher*
Bryan, Charles Stone *internal medicine educator*
Bryant, Douglas E. *public health service official*
Buchanan, William Jennings *lawyer, judge*
Bueno, Otavio Augusto *philosopher, educator*
Burnett, E. C., III, *state supreme court justice*
Burnette, Mary Malissa *lawyer*
Ceips, Catherine C. *state representative*
Chernoff, Marvin *advertising executive*
Clyburn, Mignon L. *commissioner*
Cobb-Hunter, Gilda *state representative, social worker*
Cohn, Elchanan *economics professor*
Conrad, Paul Ernest *transportation consultant*
Cotty, William Frank (Bill Cotty) *lawyer, state legislator*
Courson, John Edward *state legislator, insurance company executive*
Cruikshank, Stephen Herrick *physician, consultant*
Crystal, Nathan Maxwell *law educator, consultant*
Cuffe, Steven Paul *psychiatrist*
Currie, Cameron McGowan *federal judge*
da Silva, Ercio Mario *physician*
Davis, Keith Eugene *psychologist, educator, consultant*
Dawson, Katon *political organization administrator*
Dawson, Wallace Douglas, Jr., *geneticist*
Day, Richard Earl *lawyer, educator*
Donald, Alexander Grant *psychiatrist, educator*
Douglas, Samuel Osler *musician, educator*
Drummond, John W. *state legislator, oil company executive*
Duffie, Virgil Whatley, Jr., *retired state agency administrator*
Duggan, Carol Cook *research director*
Duggan, Kevin *information technology professional*
Ede, Fred Okotchy *marketing educator*
Edens, Joe *investment company executive*
Edgar, Walter Bellingrath *historian, educator*
Edwards, James Benjamin *accountant, educator*
Elliott, Dick *state legislator, real estate developer*
Ettel, Zita Moak *nursing administrator, food services executive*
Fair, Michael L. *state legislator, insurance company executive*
Farber, Emmanuel *pathology and biochemistry educator*
Faulkner, Larry R. *dean, educator, researcher, writer*
Felix, Robert Louis *law educator*
Finkel, Gerald Michael *lawyer*
Fischer, Robert Andrew *computer executive*
Flanagan, Clyde Harvey, Jr., *psychiatrist, psychoanalyst, educator*
Ford, Robert *state legislator, black community developer*
Freeman, Mary Beth *state representative*
Friedman, Myles Ivan *education educator*
Fry, Catherine Howard *publishing executive*
Gaevski, Mikhail Erikovich *research scientist*
Gasque, Harrison (Allard Harrison Gasque) *security firm executive*
Geckle, George Leo, III, *retired English language educator*
Gibbes, William Holman *lawyer*
Gilham, JoAnne *state representative*
Glover, Maggie Wallace *state legislator*
Graulty, Robert Thomas *engineer, consultant*
Gray, Elizabeth Van Doren *lawyer*
Gressette, Lawrence M., Jr., *utilities executive*
Griffin, Mary Frances *retired library media consultant*
Grimball, Caroline Gordon *retail sales professional*
Grooms, Lawrence K. *state legislator, petroleum marketer*
Hamilton, Clyde Henry *judge*
Hammond, Mark *state official*
Handel, Richard Craig *lawyer*
Hansen, Harold John (Harry Hansen) *artist, educator*
Harpootlian, Richard Ara *lawyer*
Harries, Kent Alexander *engineering educator, structural engineer, consultant*
Harvey, Jonathan Matthew *lawyer*
Harvin, Charles Alexander, III, *state legislator, lawyer*
Helsley, Alexia Jones *archivist*
Hinson, Shirley Rogers *state representative*
Hollis, Charles Eugene, Jr., *finance company executive*
Holmes, Cecile Searson *religion editor*
Holtz, Louis Leo *college football coach*
Horger, Edgar Olin, III, *obstetrics and gynecology educator*
Hughes, Austin Leland *biological sciences educator*
Hull, Rodney L. *advertising executive*
Humphries, John O'Neal *physician, educator, university dean*
Hwang, Te-Long *neurologist, educator*
Inkley, Scott Russell, Jr., *state agency administrator*
Jackson, Darrell *state legislator, company executive, clergyman*
Jesselson, Robert *musician, educator*
Johnson, Lawrence Wilbur, Jr., *lawyer*
Jones, Hartwell Kelley, Jr., *lawyer*
Kay, Carol McGinnis *literature educator*
Kiker, Billy Frazier *economics professor*
Krantz, Palmer Eric, III, *parks and recreation director*
Leatherman, Hugh Kenneth, Sr., *state legislator, business executive*
Lee, Brenda *state representative*
Lett, Mark *editor*
Littlefield, Daniel Curtis *historian, educator, researcher*
Logan, Sandra Jean *retired economics and business educator*
Lolas, Anthony Joseph, Sr., *health and environmental business executive*
Long, Eugene Thomas, III, *philosophy educator, administrator*
Markovsky, Barry Neil *sociology educator*
Marsh, Kevin B. *energy executive*
Martin, Becky Rogers *state representative, realtor*
Martin, John Randolph *judge*
Martin, Larry A(nthony) *state legislator, textile company executive*
Martin, Robert William *econometrician*
Mash, Samuel David *dean*
Matthews, Steve Allen *lawyer*
McConnell, Glenn F. *state legislator, lawyer, art gallery executive*
McCulloch, Anne Merline Jacobs *college dean*
McCullough, Ralph Clayton, II, *lawyer, educator*
McGill, J. Yancey *state legislator, real estate broker, homebuilder*
McGill, Jennifer Houser *non-profit association administrator*
McLean, Jodie W. *investment company executive*
McLeod, Walton James *lawyer, state legislator*
McMaster, Henry Dargan *state attorney general*
Mescher, William Clarence *state legislator, management consultant*
Miller, Vida O. *state representative, art gallery owner*
Monahan, Thomas Paul *accountant*
Moody-Lawrence, Bessie *state representative, education educator*
Moore, Thomas L. *state legislator*
Morrison, Stephen George *lawyer*
Mott, Frederick B., Jr., *publishing executive*
Nagpal, Madan Lal *biochemist, educator, researcher*
Newton, Rhonwen Leonard *writer, microcomputer consultant, data processing executive, consultant*
Nexsen, Julian Jacobs *lawyer*
O'Dell, William H. *state legislator, manufacturing executive*
Odom, Jerome D. *academic administrator*
Olenchak, Frank Richard *music educator, musician*
Outin, Mary Louise *business, multi-cultural history and geneology educator*
Page, Randall *state official*
Palms, John Michael *academic administrator, physicist*
Parks, J. Anne *state representative, funeral director*
Petty, Donna Matthews *middle school educator*
Pleicones, Costa M. *state supreme court justice*
Pollard, William Albert *lawyer*
Powell, Burnele Venable *dean*
Powell, Donald Ashmore *clinical research psychologist*
Power, James Tracy *historian*
Pritchett, Samuel Travis *finance and insurance educator, researcher, consultant*
Profeta, Salvatore, Jr., *chemist*
Rabb, Gael Caution *mental health consultant*
Rawlinson, Helen Ann *librarian*
Rekers, George Alan *education educator, clinical psychologist*
Rhoades, Donald Scott *zoo and botanical park curator, biology professor*
Richardson, Becky D. *state representative*
Rippeteau, Bruce Estes *archaeologist, administrator*
Robbins, Emmalee Elizabeth *fine arts director, speech and theater coach, choreographer, writer*
Roberts, Pamela J. *lawyer*
Robinson, Robert Earl *chemicals executive*
Ruff, Cheryl Anderson *health facility administrator*
Ruth, Deborah Ann *music educator*
Ryberg, W. Greg *state legislator, food store executive*
Sanford, Marshall (Mark Sanford) *governor, former congressman*
Secor, Donald Terry, Jr., *geologist, educator*
Seigler, Ruth Queen *college nursing administrator, educator, consultant, nurse*
Shafer, John Milton *hydrologist, consultant, software developer*
Shearer, Ellen Marie *music educator*
Shedd, Dennis W. *federal judge*
Sheppe, Joseph Andrew *surgeon*
Shmunes, Edward *dermatologist*
Short, Linda Huffstetler *state legislator*
Silver, Rick *marketing professional*
Sinclair, Linda Drumwright *educational consultant*
Sloan, Saundra Jennings *real estate company executive*
Sorensen, Andrew Aaron *university president*
Sproat, John Gerald *historian, educator*
Starr, Harvey *political scientist, educator*
Starrett, William *dancer, artistic director*
Still, Charles Neal *neurologist, consultant*
Strom, J. Preston, Jr., *lawyer*
Sumwalt, Robert Llewellyn, Jr., *retired construction company executive*
Sutherland-Abel, Anne Elizabeth *pediatrician*
Swerling, Jack Bruce *lawyer*
Swinton, David Holmes *academic administrator*
Synnott, Marcia Graham *history professor*
Tarakji, Ahmad Houssam *research scientist, electrical engineer*
Tate, Harold Simmons, Jr., *lawyer*
Tenenbaum, Inez Moore *superintendent of education*
Thornhill, Joshua Taylor, IV, *psychiatrist, academic administrator*
Thurmond, J. Strom, Jr., *lawyer*
Timmerman, William B. *utilities executive, accountant*
Toal, Jean Hoefer *state supreme court chief justice*
Toombs, Kenneth Eldridge *librarian*
Tunstall, Dorothy Fiebrich *early childhood educator*
Turk, John Cobb *architect, educator*
Warren, Charles David *library administrator*
Watabe, Norimitsu *biology and marine science educator*
Weber, Lynn *sociology educator*
Wheeler, Hoyt Noland *finance educator*
White, Ralph Edward *chemical engineer, educator*
Wieland, Gilbert Darryl *health facility administrator, researcher*
Wilder, Ronald Parker *economics professor*
Wilkins, David Horton *state legislator*
Willis, Paul Allen *librarian*
Wood, Oliver Gillan, Jr., *economist, educator*
Wright, Harry Hercules *psychiatrist*
Yarborough, Clinton Joseph *lawyer*
Young, Annette D. *state representative*
Zelenka, Donald John *lawyer*
Zimmerman, Nancy Picciano *library science educator*

Conway
Delia, Claude William *retired physician, pathologist*
Martin, Gregory Keith *lawyer, mayor*
Nale, Robert D. *finance educator*
Squatriglia, Robert William *university dean, educator*
Stegall, Gary Miles *musician, music educator*

Darlington
Bischoff, Frederick Christopher, III, *retired accountant*

Denmark
Boyd-Scotland, Joann *college president*
Dolezal, Dale Francis *truck manufacturing company executive*

Donalds
Armstrong, Alfreda Juanita *real estate executive*

Due West
Carlock, John Bruce, Jr., *English educator*
Gettys, James Wylie, Jr., *education educator*
Koonts, Jones Calvin *retired education educator*

Duncan
Clarke, Jean Alderman *orchestra director*

Easley
Failing, George Edgar *editor, clergyman, educator*
Luo, Nianzhu *mechanical engineer*
Spearman, David Hagood *veterinarian*
Spearman, Patsy Cordle *real estate broker*

Edgefield
Blossom, Laurel *poet, writer*

Edisto Island
Cannon, David C. *mechanical engineer, consultant*
Van Metre, Margaret Cheryl *artistic director, dance educator*

Elgin
Belton, Sheila Jan *minister, writer*
Cochran, Myrtie Winchester *music educator*

Florence
Agnew, Samuel Gerard *orthopaedic traumatologist*
Carter, Luther Fredrick *university president*
Chapman, Richard Norman *historian, academic administrator*
Fitzkee, Thomas L. *education educator*
Imbeau, Stephen Alan *allergist*
Kaufman, Victor Scott *historian, educator*

Fort Jackson
Brinsfield, John Wesley *military officer, educator*

Fort Mill
Bowles, Crandall Close *textiles executive*
Cooper, Marvin D. *paper company executive*
Kutcher, Kenneth E. *manufacturing executive*
Park, John *finance, investment consultant*
Prud'homme, Albert Fredric *securities company executive, financial planner*

Fripp Island
Metcalf, David Roy *retired pediatrician*

Gaffney
Griffin, Walter Roland *college president, historian, educator*
Suttle, Helen Jayson *retired education educator*

Georgetown
Bazemore, Trudy McConnell *librarian*
Bowen, William Augustus *financial consultant*
McGrath, James Charles, III, *financial services company executive, lawyer, consultant*
Moore, Albert Cunningham *lawyer, insurance company executive*
Sprinkle, Ralph Stephen *podiatrist*
Walters, Alan Wayne *judge*

Goose Creek
Marks, Melvin Paul *entomologist, consultant*
Vogt, Kathleen Cunningham *musician, music educator*

Graniteville
Learnard, James Michael *middle school educator, former finance company executive, special education educator*

Greeleyville
Collins, Almon Winslow *retired engineer*

Green Pond
Ittleson, H(enry) Anthony *foundation executive*

Greenville
Abrams, Douglas Carl *social studies educator*
Aston, James A. *financial services company executive*
Bauknight, Clarence Brock *consultant*
Belk, F. Norman *librarian*
Bell, Robert Daniel *religious studies educator*
Benson, Theodore Lloyd *history professor*
Blackwell, Larry G. *computer company executive*
Bonner, Jack Wilbur, III, *psychiatrist, educator, administrator*
Burkhardt, J. Bland, Jr., *hospital administrator*
Callahan, Ralph Wilson, Jr., *advertising agency executive*

Cargill, Paula Marie *social worker, gerontologist*
Coates, William Alexander *lawyer*
Csontos, Alan Arthur *lawyer*
Davis, Joan Carroll *retired museum director*
Dobson, Robert Albertus, III, *lawyer, volunteer*
Dreskin, Erving Arthur *pathologist, educator*
Edwards, Harry LaFoy *lawyer*
Eskew, Rhea Taliaferro *newspaper publisher*
Estevez, C. Alex *computer company executive*
Fernandez, Miguel Angel *process safety and design engineer, energy consultant*
Fitzgerald, Eugene Francis *management consultant*
Foulke, Edwin Gerhart, Jr., *lawyer*
Hendrix, Susan Clelia Derrick *civic worker*
Herlong, Henry Michael, Jr., *federal judge*
Hill, Grace Lucile Garrison *education educator, consultant*
Hipp, William Hayne *broadcast executive*
Hogg, Judith E. *neurologist, educator*
Horton, James Wright *retired lawyer*
Hultstrand, Charles John *architect*
Hutson, Melvin Robert *lawyer*
Inglis, Robert D. (Bob Inglis) *former congressman, lawyer*
Jones, Bob, III, *academic administrator*
Kappel, Matthew Jay *lawyer*
Kilgore, Donald Gibson, Jr., *pathologist*
Klasing, John Christoph *manufacturing executive*
Lawson, Darren Patrick *academic administrator, educator*
LeBlanc, L(ouis) Christian *architect*
Lloyd, Wanda Smalls *newspaper editor*
Maffucci, David G. *paper company executive*
Manly, Sarah Letitia *retired state legislator, ophthalmic photographer, angiographer*
Mann, James Robert *former congressman*
Massey, Raymond David *lawyer*
Matzko, John Austin *historian*
Mauldin, John Inglis *public defender*
McKinney, Ronald W. *lawyer*
Neal, James Austin *architect*
Nemirow, Arnold Myles *manufacturing executive*
Newman, R. Donald *paper company executive*
Oxner, Glenn Ruckman *financial executive*
Phillips, Joseph Brantley, Jr., *lawyer*
Porter, Charles Michael (Mike Porter) *diversified financial services company executive*
Pribanic, Gerald J. *manufacturing executive*
Prochaska, Bobby J. *apparel executive*
Riley, Richard Wilson *lawyer, former federal official*
Rogers, Jon Martin *financial consultant, finance company executive*
Shi, David E. *academic administrator, historian*
Shockley, Milton M., Jr., *real estate brokerage executive*
Smoak, Lewis Tyson *lawyer*
Tchivzhel, Edvard *music director*
Todd, John Dickerson, Jr., *retired lawyer*
Townes, Bobby Joe *travel agency executive*
Traxler, William Byrd, Jr., *federal judge*
Trevillian, Wallace Dabney *retired economics professor, retired dean*
Varin, Roger Robert *textile executive*
Walters, Johnnie McKeiver *lawyer*
Wang, Ming De *engineer*
White, Daniel Bowman *lawyer*
Whittle, Mack Ira, Jr., *bank executive*
Wilkins, William Walter *federal judge*
Williams, Martha Garrison *lawyer*
Wyche, Cyril Thomas *lawyer*

Greenwood
Boxx, Rita McCord *banker*
Brennan, Patrick Joseph *history professor*
Cushing, Sara Elizabeth *English language educator, writer*
Jackson, Larry Artope *retired college president*
Moore, James E. *state supreme court justice*
Nexsen, Julian Jacobs, Jr., *lawyer*
Self, W. M. *textile company executive*
Transue, David Lowell *illustrator, writer*
Williams, Sylvester Emanual, III, *secondary school educator, consultant*

Greer
Gregg, Marie Byrd *retired farmer*
Jackson, J. Garrett *airport terminal executive*
Taylor, Carter W. *aviation educator, consultant, lecturer*
Vaught, Richard Loren *urologist*

Hanahan
Langdale, Emory Lawrence *retired physician*

Hardeeville
Flexon, Courtney Sprague *alderman*

Hartsville
Cecil, Allan *corporate communications executive*
Coker, Charles Westfield *diversified manufacturing company executive*
DeLoach, Harris E(ugene), Jr., *lawyer, manufacturing executive*
Hill, Frank Trent, Jr., *packaging company executive*
Hupfer, Charles J. *manufacturing executive*
Menius, Espie Flynn, Jr., *electrical engineer*

Hemingway
Chandler, William Henry *lawyer*

Hilton Head Island
Adams, William Hensley *ecologist, educator*
Baumgardner, Barbara Borke *publishing consultant*
Becker, Karl Martin *lawyer*
Berry, Loren Curtis *retired lawyer, consultant*
Bethea, William Lamar, Jr., *lawyer*
Birk, Robert Eugene *retired physician, educator*
Brock, Karena Diane *dancer, educator*
Brown, Adolph Dupree *real estate developer*
Brown, Arthur Edmon, Jr., *retired army officer*
Bruun, Per Moller *civil engineer, consultant*
Cunningham, William Henry *retired food products executive*
Donohoe, James Day *lawyer*
Duvall, Charles Patton *retired internist, retired oncologist*
Engelman, Karl *physician*
Esposito, John Vincent *lawyer*
Estrin, Deborah Perry *human resources executive*
Field, James Bernard *internist, educator*
Gruchacz, Robert S. *real estate executive*
Hagoort, Thomas Henry *lawyer*
Harty, James D. *former manufacturing company executive*
Hewes, Robert Charles *radiologist*
Hoppin, Thomas Edward *former transportation executive*
Huckins, Harold Aaron *chemical engineer*
Humphrey, Edward William *surgeon, educator*
Jarvis, William Robert *epidemiologist, educator*
Knox, John, Jr., *philosopher, educator*
Lauer, Clinton Dillman *automotive executive*
Lefer, Allan Mark *physiologist*
Lewis, Gene Evans *retired medical equipment company executive*
Love, Richard Emerson *retired equipment manufacturing company executive*
Male, Roy Raymond *English language educator*
Martin, Donald James *marketing professional*
McKeldin, William Evans *management consultant*
Mersereau, Hiram Stipe *wood products company consultant*
Ostergard, Paul Michael *not-for-profit executive*
Patton, Joseph Donald, Jr., *management consultant*
Ponder, Henry *educational association administrator*
Pritchard, Dalton Harold *retired electronics research engineer*
Reed, Frances Boogher *writer, actress*
Roehrig, C(harles) Burns *internist, health policy consultant*
Rulis, Raymond Joseph *manufacturing company executive, consultant*
Russell, Allen Stevenson *retired aluminum company executive*
Scarminach, Charles Anthony *lawyer*
Scott, Kerrigan Davis *private investor, philanthropist*
Shaheen, Jack George *communications educator*
Shepard, Steven Louis *graphic artist, painter*
Simpson, John Wistar *energy consultant, former manufacturing company executive*
Slachta, Gregory Andrew *urologist*
Wesselmann, Glenn Allen *retired hospital executive*
Windman, Arnold Lewis *retired mechanical engineer*
Woodrum, Robert Lee *executive search consultant*

Inman
Reese, Glenn G. *state legislator, food products executive*

Irmo
Brown, Leonard Ashleigh (Smokey), Jr., *lawyer*
Stewart, Alexander Constantine *medical technologist*

Isle Of Palms
Elliott, Larry Paul *cardiac radiologist, educator*
Wohltmann, Hulda Justine *pediatric endocrinologist, diabetologist*

Iva
Gentry, Margaret Burton *retired elementary school teacher*

Johns Island
Cameron, Thomas William Lane *investment company executive*
Carter, Mary Andrews *paralegal*
Norton, Norman James *retired exploration geologist, educator*

Jonesville
Summer-Strait, Beth *mental health services professional*

Kiawah Island
Coyle, Martin Adolphus, Jr., *lawyer, consultant*
Harrigan, Anthony Hart *author*
Warren, Russell Glen *academic administrator*

Ladson
Cannon, Major Tom *special education educator*

Lake Wylie
Buggie, Frederick Denman *management consultant*
Butler, Carol King *advertising executive*
Sanford, James Kenneth *public relations executive*

Lancaster
Bundy, Charles Alan *foundation executive*

Landrum
Bridwell, Barry Dean *music educator, director, musician*

Langley
Bell, Robert Morrall *lawyer*

Laurens
Bost, John Rowan *retired manufacturing executive, engineer*

Leesville
Crumley, James Robert, Jr., *retired clergyman*

Lexington
Floyd, Ann R. *elementary school educator*
Holland, Gene Grigsby (Scottie Holland) *artist*
Kennedy, Sandra Elaine *small business owner*
Lide, Vinton DeVane *lawyer*
Morris, Earle Elias, Jr., *retired state official, business executive*
Resch, Mary Louise *town agency administrator*
Russell, Candace Leigh *musician, educator*
Wilkins, Robert Pearce *lawyer*

Little River
Ehrlich, John Gunther *writer*
Sarvis, Elaine Magann *retired assistant principal*

Marion
Inabinet, Lawrence Elliott *retired pharmacist*
Kirkpatrick, Donald Robert *secondary school educator*
Manning, Leslie Carlton *counselor*
Waller, John Henry, Jr., *state supreme court justice*

Mauldin
Looper-Wilson, Leah Marie *human resources specialist, controller, interior designer*
Martin, Sharon D. *automotive executive*

Mc Cormick
Clayton, Verna Lewis *retired state legislator*

Mount Pleasant
Abbott-Lyon, Frances Dowdle *journalist, civic worker*
Ayres, Paul Erdman *artist*
Gilbert, James Eastham *academic administrator*
Hahn, H. Blair *lawyer*
Hill, Larkin Payne *real estate company operations administrator*
Macdonald, Robert Rigg, Jr., *retired museum director*
Thordarson, William *retired hydrogeologist*

Murrells Inlet
Justice, Franklin Pierce, Jr., *oil company executive*
Wollman, June Rose *clothing executive*

Myrtle Beach
Atkinson, Harold Witherspoon *utilities consultant, real estate broker*
Breen, David Hart *lawyer*
Fowler, Marilyn S. Atlas *social worker*
Harwell, David Walker *retired state supreme court chief justice*
Killian, Greg *mental health services professional*
Nirenstein, Jack *writer*
Pegram, J.J. *architectural firm executive*
Schwartz, Steve Wendelin *physician*

New Zion
Gibbons, Robert Butler, Jr., *retired military officer*

Newberry
Davidson, Michael Raymond *historian, educator*
Lander, James Albert *retired military officer, comptroller*
McGinnis, Barry Eugene *music educator, musician*
Partridge, William Franklin, Jr., *lawyer*
Wagner, John Waldorf *music educator, researcher*

Newry
Scott, Ronald S. *construction executive*

North Charleston
Fei, James Robert *engineering executive, consultant*
Mintzer, Jacobo E. *physician, researcher*
Reilly, David Henry *university dean*
Wigger, Jarrel L. *lawyer*
Zucker, Jerry *chemical manufacturing executive*

North Myrtle Beach
Damerst, William *English and humanities educator*
Maloney, Terry *horticulturist, educator*
Wheless, Albert Eugene *lawyer*

Okatie
Hardin, James Neal *German and comparative literature educator, publisher*

Orangeburg
Bozinovski, Stevo *computer science educator, researcher*
Byers, Keith Thomas *librarian, educator*
Caldwell, Rossie Juanita Brower *retired library service educator*
Dalton, Cheryl Renee *entrepreneur*
Dingle, Rosetta *music educator*
Finney, Ernest Adolphus, Jr., *retired state supreme court chief justice*
Graule, Raymond (Siegfried) *metallurgical engineer*
Hill, Howard Darnell *educator, university administrator*
Hong, Jae-Dong *industrial engineering educator*
James, Rodney Arthur *systems administrator, application developer, minister*
Johnson, Alex Claudius *English language educator*
Jones, Marcus Earl *humanities educator*
Kent, Harry Ross *construction executive, lay worker*
McIver, Barbara Basore *language educator*
Montgomery, Amanda E. *music educator*
Price, Johnnie Ulmer *retired music educator*
Sims, Edward Howell *editor, publisher*
Smoak, Randolph Duncan, Jr., *surgeon*
Sriskanda, Nesan Sithamparapillai *engineering educator, researcher*
Viswanath, Guttalu Ramachandra Rao *mathematics educator, consultant, researcher*

Pawleys Island
Brownlee, Robert Calvin *pediatrician, educator*
Grubb, William Francis Xavier *consumer software executive, marketing executive*
Hudson-Young, Jane Smither *investor*
Kay, Thomas Oliver *agricultural consultant*
Noble, Joseph Veach *fine arts administrator*
Proefrock, Carl Kenneth *academic medical administrator*
Tarbox, Gurdon Lucius, Jr., *retired museum executive*

Pendleton
Landreth, James Mack *elementary school music educator*
Marshall, Gerald Lee *mathematician, educator*

Pickens
White, Leeanne J. *music educator*

Piedmont
Winter-Neighbors, Gwen Carole *special education educator, art educator, consultant*

Prosperity
Hause, Edith Collins *college administrator*
Jennings, Wirt Holman, Jr., *retired marketing executive*
Long, William McMurray *physiology educator*

Richburg
Cox, Kevin Monterey *school administrator*

Rock Hill
Benson, Keith J. *healthcare management educator*
Bessinger, Raymond Carlton *nutritionist, educator*
Bristow, Robert O'Neil *writer, educator*
Cornick, Michael F(rederick) *accounting educator*
Di Giorgio, Anthony J. *college president*
Hardin, James Carlisle, III, *lawyer, educator*
Mitchell, Paula Levin *biology professor, editor*
Russell, Cynthia M. *college president*

Round O
Leonard, Guy Meyers, Jr., *international holding company executive*

Ruffin
Lambright, Marilyn *elementary school educator*

Salem
Darnell, William Headen *chemical engineer, medical/surgical nurse, nursing educator*
Everett, C(harles) Curtis *retired lawyer*

Santee
DuBose, James Daulton *dentist*

Seabrook Island
Call, Lawrence Michael *consumer products company executive*

Seneca
Byars, Betsy (Cromer) *writer*
Clausen, Hugh Joseph *retired army officer*
Sires, Norman Gruber, Jr., *lawyer*
Strong-Tidman, Virginia Adele *marketing professional*
Uden, David Elliott *cardiologist, educator*

Sheldon
Lowrie, William G. *former oil company executive*

Simpsonville
Davis, Shirley Harriet *social worker, editor*
Kanzler, George *journalist, critic*
Maguire, D. E. *electronics executive*
Pratt, Harry Davis *retired entomologist*
Selvy, Barbara *dance instructor*

Spartanburg
Allen, G. Ashley *chemicals executive*
Bolton, Calvin *music educator*
Bullard, John Moore *religion educator, church musician*
Carroll-Belenchia, Elizabeth *international corporate realtor*
Codespoti, Daniel Joseph *retired computer scientist*
Cogan, Jerry Albert, Jr., *chemical engineer, engineering executive*
Deku, Afrikadzata *international, French, English and Afrikan-centric Continental Afrikan scholar, researcher, publisher, writer, educator*
Dent, Frederick Baily *former mill executive, former ambassador, former secretary of commerce*
Dillard, Richard *director of public affairs*
Dineen, Joseph Lawrence *legal compliance professional, consultant*
Dunlap, Benjamin Bernard *academic administrator*
Feinstein, Marion Finke *artistic director, dance instructor*
Fogartie, James Eugene *retired clergyman*
Glassick, Charles Etzweiler *academic foundation administrator*
Hilton, Theodore Craig *computer scientist, Internet company executive*
Hutchinson, Ronald B. *restaurant executive*
Jones, William Osborne, II, *physician assistant*
King, Henry Spencer, III, *lawyer*
Law, Kenneth Ray *music educator, dean*
Leonard, Walter Raymond *retired biology educator*
Lucktenberg, Jerrie Cadek *music educator*
McAbee, Thomas Allen *psychologist*
McDaniel, Thomas Robb *academic administrator, educator*
McGehee, Larry Thomas *university administrator*
Milliken, Roger *textile company executive*
Parmley, Richard Turner *pediatric hematologist, oncologist*
Pate, John Gillis, Jr., *financial consultant, accounting educator*
Reid, Alliston King *psychology educator, researcher*
Richards, Marty Grover *foundation administrator, director*
Smith, William Douglas *lawyer*
Sovenyhazy, Gabor Ferenc *surgeon*
Stephens, Bobby Gene *college administrator, consultant*

Sullivans Island
Brewerton, Timothy David *psychiatrist*
Norton, Fran *recreation director*
Romaine, Henry Simmons *investment consultant*

Summerville
Capps, Phillip Lewis *music educator*
Deavers, James Frederick *optometrist*
Diamond, Michael Shawn *science and math educator, computer consultant*
Hardee-Thomas, Marva A. *lawyer*
Reisman, Rosemary Moody Canfield *writer, retired humanities educator*
Sexton, Donald Lee *retired business administration educator*
Young, Margaret Aletha McMullen (Mrs. Herbert Wilson Young) *social worker*

Sumter
Justus, Adalu *writer, designer*
Kellum, Donald Arthur *military officer*
Olsen, Thomas Richard, Sr., *air force officer*
Van Bulck, Hendrikus Eugenius *accountant*

Surfside Beach
Favaro, Mary Kaye Asperheim *pediatrician, writer*

Swansea
Inabinet, George Walker, Jr., *retired state agency administrator*

Taylors
Riddle, Thad (Tad) W., III, *music educator, webmaster*
Smith, Morton Howison *religious organization administrator, educator*
Vaughn, John Carroll *minister, educator*

Travelers Rest
Hall, Gregory Blake *music educator*

Union
Murphy, Peter Gregory *literature educator, writer*

Walterboro
Cone, George Wallis *lawyer*
Drain, Danny *museum director*
Meshach, Joseph Robert *music educator*

Wedgefield
McLaurin, Hugh McFaddin, III, *military officer, historian consultant*

West Columbia
Byars, Merlene Hutto *accountant, visual artist, writer*
Carter, Saralee Lessman *immunologist, microbiologist*
Moore, Shirley Throckmorton (Mrs. Elmer Lee Moore) *accountant*
Witherspoon, Walter Pennington, Jr., *orthodontist, philanthropist*

White Rock
Aull, James Stroud *retired bishop*

Williamston
Alewine, James William *financial executive*

Winnsboro
McCants, Clyde Taft *retired clergyman*

Woodruff
Childers, Bob Eugene *educational association executive*

Yemassee
Olendorf, William Carr, Jr., *small business owner*

York
Blackwell, Paul Eugene, Sr., *army officer*

SOUTH DAKOTA

Aberdeen
Fouberg, Glenna M. *career planning administrator*
Gruca, Pawel Piotr *neuroradiologist*
Hedges, Mark Stephen *clinical psychologist*
Hollingsworth, John Arthur *business educator*
Johnson, Edna Scott *English language educator, volunteer*
Manhart, Grant Lee *music educator*
Matta, William B. *language educator*
Stoia, Viorel G. *life underwriter*
Tebben, Sharon Lee *education educator*

Belle Fourche
Day, Michael W. *lawyer*

Black Hawk
Maicki, G. Carol *former state senator, consultant*

Brandon
Hunt, Roger *former state legislator*

Britton
Farrar, Frank Leroy *lawyer, former governor*

Brookings
Brown, Arnold M. *state legislator*
Catangui, Michael Aguilar *entomologist, researcher*
Evans, David Allan *English educator*
Funchion, Michael F. *historian, educator*
Gilbert, Howard Alden *retired economics professor*
Marquardt, Steve Robert *library director*
McClure-Bibby, Mary Anne *former state legislator*
Miller, Peggy Gordon Elliott *university president*
Moore, Raymond A. *consultant, retired agriculture educator*
Ryder, Mary Ruth *English language educator*
Tolle, Gordon J. *political science educator*

Canton
Perkinson, Robert Ronald *psychologist, consultant*

Dakota Dunes
Bond, Richard L. *food products executive*
Hagan, Sheila B. *corporate lawyer*
Leman, Eugene D. *meat industry executive*
Lochner, James V. *food products executive*
Peterson, Robert L. *meat processing executive*

Deadwood
Johns, Timothy Robert *judge*

Fort Pierre
Poches, Charles, Jr., *lawyer*

Freeman
Koller, Berneda Joleen *library administrator*

Gettysburg
Schreiber, Lola F. *former state legislator*

Gregory
Johnson, Charles Rick *lawyer*

Huron
Clatworthy, Catherine Lynn *educational trainer, graphics designer*

Keystone
Wagner, Mary Kathryn *sociology educator, former state legislator*

Kyle
White Buffalo, Charles Dean *social studies educator, consultant*

Madison
Knowlton, Douglas D. *academic administrator*
Mukhopadhyay, Indranath *communications engineer, researcher*

Miller
Morford, JoAnn (JoAnn Morford-Burg) *state senator, investment company executive*

Mitchell
Almjeld, Paul F. *conductor, music educator*
Widman, Paul Joseph *insurance agent*

Mud Butte
Ingalls, Marie Cecelie *former state legislator, retail executive*

North Sioux City
Shipley, Larry *food products executive*

Pierre
Adam, Patricia Ann *legislative aide*
Callahan, Patrick *communication media executive*
Collins-Adler, Catherine Kay *social services professional*
Daugaard, Dennis M. *lieutenant governor*
Diedtrich, Elmer *state legislator*
Duncan, Dick *state agency administrator*
Dunn, James Bernard *mining company executive, state legislator*
Everist, Barbara *state legislator*
Everson, Curt *commissioner, state*
Fiegen, Kristie K. *state legislator*
Gerdes, David Alan *lawyer*
Gilbertson, David *state supreme court justice*
Ham, Arlene H. *state legislator*
Johnson, Julie Marie *lawyer, lobbyist, judge*
Konenkamp, John K. *state supreme court justice*
Long, Larry *state attorney general*
Miller, Robert Arthur *former state supreme court chief justice*
Nelson, Chris A. *secretary of state*
Olson, Judith Mary Reedy *retired public information officer, former state senator*
Pederson, Gordon Roy *state legislator, retired military officer*
Rounds, Michael *governor*
Sabers, Richard Wayne *state supreme court justice*
Schoenfelder, Laska *commissioner, farmer*
Thompson, Charles Murray *lawyer*
Weyer, Dianne Sue *health facility administrator*
Zinter, Steven L. *state supreme court justice*

Rapid City
Clark, Lynda Kay *artist*
Corwin, Bert Clark *optometrist*
Daughenbaugh, Randall Jay *retired chemical company executive, consultant*
Eccarius, Scott *state official, eye surgeon*
Foye, Thomas Harold *lawyer*
Goodsell, G. Verne *lawyer*
Graslie, Thomas Eric *lawyer*
Hagg, Rexford A. *lawyer, former state legislatorr*
Hamilton, Douglas Warren *real estate executive*
Hughes, William Lewis *former university official, electrical engineer*
Lefevre, Donald Keith *electrical engineer*
Lien, Bruce Hawkins *minerals and oil company executive*
Pillay, Gautam *chemical engineer, chemist, academic administrator*
Ramakrishnan, Venkataswamy *civil engineer, educator*
Schleusener, Richard August *college president*
Schreier, Karen Elizabeth *judge*
Scofield, Gordon Lloyd *mechanical engineer, educator*
Smith, Paul Letton, Jr., *geophysicist*
Sykora, Harold James *military officer*

Rosebud
MacKichan, Margaret Anna *artist, art educator*

Saint Lawrence
Lockner, Vera Joanne *farmer, rancher, legislator*

Selby
Akre, Donald J. *school system administrator*

Sioux Falls
Aldern, Robert Judson *architectural, liturgical and landscape artist*
Ashworth, Julie *elementary school educator*
Balcer, Charles Louis *college president emeritus, educator*
Carlson, Robert James *bishop*
Carlson Aronson, Marilyn A. *English language and education educator*
Carpenter, Paul Lynn *cardiologist*
Christensen, David Allen *manufacturing executive*
Cowles, Ronald Eugene *church administrator*
Dunn, Rebecca Jo *state legislator*
Engen, Lee Emerson *retired savings and loan executive*
Fenton, Lawrence Jules *pediatric educator*
Garson, Arnold Hugh *publishing executive*
Haig, Susan *conductor*
Haraldson, Tena *newspaper editor*
Hayes, Robert E. *lawyer*
Herman, Charles Wendell *history educator*
Huseboe, Arthur Robert *American literature educator*
Hylland, Richard R. *utility company executive*
Jaqua, Richard Allen *pathologist*
Johnson, Richard Arlo *lawyer*
Koetzle, Gil *state legislator, fire fighter, professional association administrator*
Kuhle, Shirley Jean *real estate appraiser*
Lewis, Merle Dean *electric and gas utility executive*
Luce, Michael Leigh *lawyer*
Marshall, Mark F. *lawyer*
Masters, Lee *broadcast executive*
McDowell, Robert James *music educator, composer*
McMahon, James E. *lawyer*
McMillin, Joan Austin *social worker*
Meierhenry, Judith Knittel *judge, lawyer*
Morse, Peter Hodges *ophthalmologist, educator*
Newell, Daniel K. *utilities company executive*
Nygaard, Lance Corey *nurse, data processing consultant*
Olson, Gary Duane *history educator*
Piersol, Lawrence L. *federal judge*
Prendergast, Terry Neill *lawyer*
Reynolds, Leo Thomas *electronics company executive*
Richards, George Alvarez *psychiatrist, educator*
Richards, LaClaire Lissetta Jones (Mrs. George A. Richards) *social worker*
Rosenthal, Joel *manufacturing executive*
Rossing, David Robert *internist*
Smith, Murray Thomas *transportation company executive*
Staggers, Kermit LeMoyne, II, *history and political science educator, state legislator, municipal official*
Talley, Robert Cochran *medical school dean and administrator, cardiologist*
Thompson, Ronelle Kay Hildebrandt *library director*
Trujillo, Angelina *endocrinologist*
VanDemark, Michelle Volin *critical care, neuroscience nurse*
Viste, Arlen Ellard *chemistry professor*
Wagoner, Ralph Howard *academic administrator*
Wilkes, Jeffrey Blaine *real estate appraiser*
Williams, W. Vail *psychologist*
Wollman, Roger Leland *federal judge*
Zawada, Edward Thaddeus, Jr., *physician, educator*
Zinz, David Albert *humanities educator*

Spearfish
Erickson, Richard Ames *physicist, emeritus educator*
Wishard, Della Mae *former newspaper editor*

Vermillion
Basile, Joseph Lawrence *humanities educator*
Clem, Alan Leland *retired political scientist, educator*
Davidson, John Henry *legal educator*
Haddad, Emily Anne *literature educator*
Lio, Yuhlong *mathematician, educator*
Schou, Larry Brian *music educator*
Schweinle, Amy *psychologist, educator*
Wang, X. T. (Xiaotian Wang) *psychologist, educator*

Volga
Moldenhauer, William Calvin *soil scientist*

Watertown
Drake, Robert Alan *state legislator, animal nutritionist, mayor*

Wentworth
Kringen, Dale Eldon *state legislator, transportation executive*

Yankton
Foster, James Caldwell *academic dean, historian*
Piper, Kathleen *former political organization administrator*

TENNESSEE

Alamo
Finch, Evelyn Vorise *financial planner*

Alcoa
Dunlap, Bill *municipal administrator*

Antioch
Ely, Joe *singer, songwriter*
Huff, Jimmy Laurence *nurse*
Worthington, Melvin Leroy *minister, writer*

Arnold AFB
Davis, John William *government science and engineering executive*

Ashland City
Lindahl, Herbert Winfred *appliance manufacturing executive*

Athens
Brown, Sandra Lee *arts management consultant, watercolorist*

Bartlett
Huffman, D. C., Jr., *pharmacy association executive*
Huffman, Delton Cleon, Jr., *pharmacy association executive*
Wallace, William Brian *sales executive*

Big Sandy
Chastain, Kenneth Duane *retired foreign language educator*

Blaine
Bull, James C. *poet*

Bolivar
Cary, Charles Muse *lawyer*

Brentwood
Brown, Bobby Wayne *lawyer, educator, accountant*
Cash, W. Larry *health products executive*
Chapdelaine, Perry Anthony, Jr., *public health and preventive medicine physician, educator*
Flanagan, Van Kent *journalist*
Gray, Roland William *pediatrician*
Heiser, Arnold Melvin *astronomer*
Lodowski, Charles Alan *business association executive*
Martin, William Edwin *lawyer, business executive*
McClary, Jim Marston *accounting executive, consultant*
Mc Creary, James Franklin *lawyer, mediator*
Mitchell, Marilyn June *writer, lyricist*
Provine, John Calhoun *retired lawyer*
Rash, Martin S. *health facility administrator*
Schreiber, Kurt Gilbert *lawyer*
Smith, Wayne Thomas *healthcare company executive*
Stephens, Shirley Lynne *writer, editor*
Taylor, Nicole Renée (Niki Taylor) *model*
Tucker, Tanya Denise *singer*
Wells, Dennis J. *dentist*
White, Michael James *healthcare facilities administrator*

Brighton
Iles, Roger Dean *business educator*

Bristol
Gaines, John Strother *retired educator, writer, municipal official*
Gregory, John M. *pharmaceutical executive*
Markison, Brian *pharmaceutical executive*

Brownsville
Kalin, Robert *retired mathematics educator*
Stevenson, William Edward *chemical engineer*

Camden
Sayles, Kristi Renee *elementary school educator, writer, application developer*

Chapel Hill
Christman, Luther Parmalee *retired dean, consultant*

Chattanooga
Alvarez, Richard G. *orthopedist*
Apyan, Paul M. *orthopedist*
Bahner, Thomas Maxfield *lawyer*
Barker, William M. *state supreme court justice*
Bernhardt, Robert *music director, conductor*
Bowen, Maurice Richard, Jr., *lawyer, director*
Callahan, North *author, educator*
Campbell, Paul, III, *lawyer*
Campbell, William O'Neal *retired physician*
Carden, Zachary Frank, Jr., *dentist*
Chandra, Channappa *orthopedist*
Copeland, Floyd Dean *insurance company executive, lawyer*
Dawson, Gail Alesia *management educator*
Derthick, Alan Wendell *architect, architectural firm executive*
Duckworth, Jerrell James *electrical engineer*
Edgar, R(obert) Allan *federal judge*
Enriquez, Manuel Hipolito *physician*
Foster, Edwin Powell, Jr., *structural engineer, educator*
Foy, John N. *real estate company executive*
Franks, Herschel Pickens *judge*
Fry, William N., IV, *textiles executive*
Gearhiser, Charles Josef *lawyer*
Greving, Robert C. *insurance company executive*
Guo, Zibin *medical anthropologist*
Haden, Benjamin *minister, retired publishing executive, broadcast executive*
Harlin, Ray M. *trucking executive*
Hensley, Marble John, Sr., *civil engineer, consultant*
Hodge, Raymond Douglas *minister*
Holmberg, Albert William, Jr., *retired publishing company executive*
Jackson, Richard P. *writer, educator*
Kaplan, Hyman M. *internist, educator*
Knight, Ralph H. *consumer products company executive*
Lebovitz, Charles B. *real estate company executive*
Lebovitz, Stephen D. *property manager*
Lutgen, Robert Raymond *newspaper editor*
Martin, Chester Y. *sculptor, painter*
Mattice, Harry Sandlin, Jr., *prosecutor*
McFarland, Jane Elizabeth *librarian*
Meyer, Roger Arnold *management consultant, writer*
Mills, Olan, II, *photography company executive*
Mohney, Nell Webb *religion educator, speaker, author*
Moore, Hugh Jacob, Jr., *lawyer*
Morris, Buckner Stuart *lawyer*
Norris, Brent Lane *orthopedist*
Obear, Frederick Woods *academic administrator*
Parker, David R. *trucking executive*
Phillips, John Bomar *lawyer*
Quinn, Patrick *tranportation executive*
Rabin, Alan A. *economics professor*
Ragon, Robert Ronald *clergyman*
Royer, William A. *language educator*
Russe, Conrad Thomas Campbell *accountant*
Sachsman, David Bernard *communications educator*
St. Goar, Herbert *retired food corporation executive*
Scalice, John A. *nuclear energy executive*
Shuck, Edwin Haywood, III, *surgeon*
Stacy, Bill Wayne *academic administrator*
Swanger, Daniel Anthony-Ignatius *artist*
Turner, Brenda Kaye *state legislator*
Watjen, Thomas Ros *insurance company executive*
Wilson, Richard Lee *political science educator*

Clarksville
Chartrand, Danny Lewis *secondary school educator, coach*
Maynard, Terrell Dennis *minister*
Newby, Earl Fernando *educator*
Reaves, Barry Reco *minister*
Stoddard, Peter Hawkins *education educator, consultant*

Cleveland
Baker, Michael Lyndon *minister*
Benson, Will E. *music educator*
Breuer, William Bentley *author*
Lockhart, Madge Clements *educational organization executive*
Manley, Douglas Heath *music educator*
Preston, Forrest L. *health care executive*
Rhodes, Arthur Delano *benefits administrator*
Suttles, David Clyde *educator*
Taylor, William Al *church administrator*
Walker, Donald Murray *minister*
Watson, S. Michele *school nurse*
Ziegler, Steve *health care services/centers executive*

Clinton
Birdwell, James Edwin, Jr., *retired banker*
Coker, Stephanie Ila *school choir director*
Hutchens, Gail R. *chemist*
Seib, Billie McGhee Rushing *nursing administrator, consultant*

College Grove
Battle, William Robert (Bob Battle) *retired newspaper executive*

Collegedale
Bennett, Peggy Elizabeth *librarian, library director, educator*
Crosby, Berna *freelance/self-employed writer*
McKee, Ellsworth R. *food products executive*
McKee, Jack *food products executive*
Moore, Robert Crumley *mathematician, educator*

Collierville
Springfield, James Francis *retired lawyer, banker*

Columbia
Cantrell, Sharron Caulk *principal*
Cline, Shawn Fredrick *social worker*
Curry, Beatrice Chesrown *retired English educator*
Moore, Tom White, Jr., *lawyer*
Scheusner, Ronald L. *music educator*

Cookeville
Black, Gary William *industrial engineer*
Brinker, William John *history educator, researcher*
Campana, Phillip Joseph *German language educator*
Chowdhuri, Pritindra *electrical engineer, educator*
Elkins, Donald Marcum *dean, agronomy educator*
Hinton, Paula Katherine *historian, educator, historian, researcher*
Johnson, George *trucking executive*
Kumar, Krishna *retired physics educator*
Peters, Ralph Martin *academic administrator*
Qualls, Steven Daniel *lawyer*

Reynolds, Barbara C. *mental health educator, academic dean, retired*
Sasser, Gary *trucking executive*
Sissom, Leighton Esten *engineering educator, dean, consultant*
Velu, Yogeshwar Karunakaran *industrial engineer, researcher*
Volpe, Angelo Anthony *former university president, chemistry educator*

Cordova
Dean, Jimmy *meat processing company executive, entertainer*
Echols, James *agricultural products supplier*
Griffin, Walton W. *performing company executive*
Huang, Ken Shen *art educator*
Pugh, Dorothy Gunther *artistic director*

Crossville
Bell, Charles Eugene, Jr., *retired industrial engineer*
Elam, Leslie Albert *retired museum administrator*
Hovmand, Svend *chemical engineer, engineering executive*
Lansford, Edwin Gaines *accountant*
Lawrence, Ralph Waldo *manufacturing executive*
Moser, Michael R. *newspaper editor*
Sower, Milene A. *nursing educator*

Dandridge
Comer, Evan Philip *manufacturing executive*
Menzel, William Clarence, Jr., *nuclear quality engineer*
Weatherly-McWaters, Barbara Cannon *artist*

Dayton
Cornelius, Richard Meredith *English language educator*
Gartman, Max Dillon *language educator, educator*
Luther, Sigrid *music educator*

Dickson
Thomas, Janey Sue *elementary school principal*

Dyersburg
Wilder, James Sampson, III, *lawyer, judge*

East Ridge
Collins, Joda Lee *minister*

Elizabethton
Hardin, Gerald Larson *city planner and community developer, educator*

Etowah
Parker, Eugene LeRoy, III, *lawyer*

Fairview
Hutchison, Barbara Bailey *singer, songwriter*

Fayetteville
Dickey, John Harwell *lawyer*
Ralston, J. Fred, Jr., *internist*
Wolfhard, Hans Georg *research scientist*

Franklin
Andrews, William Frederick *manufacturing executive*
Bull, Sandy (Alexander Benjamin Bull) *musician, composer*
Duduit, Michael *editor, university administrator*
Jowdy, Jeffrey William *development executive*
Miller, Dennis Edward *health medical executive*
Moessner, Harold Frederic *allergist*
Sloan, W(ilson) Keith *actuary*
Smolenski, Lisabeth Ann *family practice physician*
Sutter, Lawrence A. *lawyer, educator*

Gainesboro
Ramsey, Catherine Louise *secondary school educator, horse trainer*

Gallatin
Bradley, Nolen Eugene, Jr., *retired personnel executive, educator*
Ellis, Joseph Newlin *retired distribution company executive*

Gatlinburg
Cave, Kent R. *national park ranger*
Flanagan, Judy *special events professional, entertainment and marketing specialist, professional public speaker*
Powell, Russell A. *lawyer*

Germantown
Allison, Beverly Gray *seminary president, evangelism educator*
Arendall, Charles Steven *management consultant, educator*
Depperschmidt, Thomas Orlando *economist, consultant*
Floyd, John David *theology educator, minister*
Lieberman, Phillip Louis *allergist, educator*
Murray, James Alan *urban and environmental consultant, investor*
Nolly, Robert J. *pharmacist, health facility administrator, educator*
Vastagh, George Frederick *physician*

Goodlettsville
Harper, Jewel Benton *pharmacist*
Shaffer, Donald S. *retail executive*
Vatandoost, Nossi Malek *art school administrator*

Gray
Combs, Stephen Paul *pediatrician, health facility administrator*
Surface, James Louis, Sr., *trust officer, lawyer*

Greenback
Weeks, Robert Andrew *materials science researcher, educator*

Greenbrier
Newell, Paul Haynes, Jr., *engineering educator, former college president*

Greeneville
Cook, Marshall Alan *theater producer, theater director, consultant*
Corey, Mark *historic site director*
Ford, Sally J. *physical education educator*
Hull, Thomas Gray *federal judge*
Parsons, Marcia Phillips *judge*
Smith, Myron John, Jr., *librarian, author*

Harriman
Hoppe, Sherry Lee *academic administrator*

Harrogate
Robertson, Edwin Oscar *banker*

Henderson
England, Richard C., Jr., *special education educator*
Hay, Thomas Franklin *music educator*

Hendersonville
Burt, Alvin Miller, III, *anatomist, cell biologist, educator, writer*
Davis, Robert Norman *hospital administrator*

Henning
Parker, Joann Maudie *freelance/self-employed writer, retired reporter*
Sadler, Dennis *supervisor*

Hermitage
Higgs, Mary Phil Egerton *editor*
Quaintance, Alice Lynn *elementary school media specialist*
Reid, Donna Joyce *small business owner*
Thompson, Fred Dalton *former senator*

Hickory Valley
Weaver, Peggy (Marguerite McKinnie Weaver) *plantation owner*

Humboldt
Boyte, George Griffin *lawyer*

Jackson
Agee, Bob R. *academic administrator, educator, minister*
Barlow, Richard Clay *nurse, consultant*
Boswell, G(eorge) Harvey *federal judge*
Dawson, C. Bryan *mathematician*
Holt, Michael Kenneth *management and finance educator, consultant, city councilman*
Johnsey, Geryl Lynn *elementary school educator, musician*
Kamso-Pratt, Jimmy Michael *physician, administrator*
McClure, Wesley C. *academic administrator*
McRoberts, Terry Allan *music educator*
Misulis, Karl Edward *physician*
Myatt, Dottie Woodard *education educator*
Roth, Georgia Middlebrooks *accounting educator*
Swaim, Mark Wendell *hepatologist, molecular biologist, gastroenterologist, educator, photographer*
Todd, James Dale *federal judge*
Woodall, Gilbert Earl, Jr., *medical administrator*

Jefferson City
Baumgardner, James Lewis *history professor*
Muncy, Estle Pershing *physician*
Trent, Wendell Campbell *business owner*

Jellico
Hausman, Keith Lynn *hospital administrator, physical therapist*

Johnson City
Adebonojo, Festus O. *medical educator*
Alfonso, Robert John *university administrator*
Bishop, Wilsie Sue *dean, nursing educator*
Coogan, Philip Shields *pathologist*
Cupp, Horace Ballard *surgeon, educator*
De Witt, Jan A. *emergency medicine physician*
Dunkelberger, Brian Herbert *physician*
Edwards, Joellen Beckett *dean, community health nurse educator*
Epps, James Haws, III, *lawyer*
Franks, Ronald Dwyer *dean, psychiatrist, educator*
Hamdy, Ronald Charles *geriatrician*
Hong, Don *mathematician, educator*
Ice, Billie Oberta *retail executive*
Jenrette, Thomas Shepard, Jr., *music educator, choral director*
Kalin, George Bruno *pathologist, educator*
Kao, Race Li-Chan *medical educator*
Kasmai, Hamid Saleh *chemistry educator, researcher, consultant*
Lewis, Jason Robert *computer technician*
Morgan, Robert George *accounting educator, researcher*
Olsen, Martin E. *obstetrician, educator*
Pumariega, JoAnne Buttacavoli *mathematics educator*
Rasch, Ellen Myrberg *cell biology educator*
Rice-See, Lynn *music educator*
Sanderbeck, Rande Paul *music educator, musician*
Schneider, Valerie Lois *speech educator*
Self, Jimmie Everette *music educator, musician*
Shurbaji, M. Salah *pathologist*
Wilkes, Clem Cabell, Jr., *stockbroker*

Jonesborough
Jenkins, Ronald Wayne *lawyer, engineer, mediator*

Kenton
Jenkins-Brady, Terri Lynn *publishing executive, journalist*

Kingsport
Bailey, William Henry *real estate appraiser*
Boyd, Lon Vernon *lawyer, alderman*
Coover, Harry Wesley *manufacturing executive*
Deavenport, Earnest W., Jr., *chemical executive*
Doty, Robert Douglas, Sr., *retired surgeon*
Everett, Michael David *economist, educator*
Ferguson, J. Brian *chemicals executive*
Grigsby, William P. *surgeon*
Hall, John Richard *surgery educator, researcher*
Head, William Iverson, Sr., *retired chemical company executive*
Lorraine, Richard *chemicals executive*
Mehta, Ashok Vallavdas *pediatric cardiologist*
Ogbonnaya, Chuks Alfred *entomologist, agronomist, environmentalist*
Shine, David Bruce *lawyer*
Siirola, Jeffrey John *chemical engineer*
Wolfe, Margaret Ripley *historian, educator, consultant*

Knoxville
Acker, Joseph Edington *retired cardiology educator*
Adaku, Chioma *non-profit organization administrator*
Aguilar, Julia Shell *publishing executive*
Alexeff, Igor *physicist, electrical engineer, educator emeritus*
Anderson, Charles, Jr., *printing/publishing company executive*
Anderson, Edward Riley *state supreme court justice*
Anderson, Ilse Janell *clinical geneticist*
Andrews, Rosalind *probation officer*
Armistead, Willis William *academic administrator, veterinarian*
Badiru, Adedeji Bodunde *industrial engineer*
Baldwin, Wesley Hale Barrick *music educator*
Barker, Keith Rene *investment banker*
Baxter, William *federal agency administrator*
Blake, Gerald Rutherford *retired banker*
Blanton, Priscilla White *social sciences educator, psychologist, researcher*
Boling, Edward Joseph *retired academic administrator*
Bose, Bimal Kumar *electrical engineering educator*
Brady, Patrick *French literature educator, writer*
Bressler, Marcus Nathan *consulting engineer*
Brown, Donald Vaughn *technical educator, engineering consultant*
Bruce, Donald James *economics educator*
Cagle, Frank *editor*
Campbell, John *printing/publishing company executive*
Campbell, Michael *entertainment industry executive*
Campbell, Robert Roe *lawyer*
Caponetti, James Dante *botany educator*
Chambers, Robert Ben *music educator, conductor*
Cliff, Steven Burris *engineering executive*
Cornish, Jeff *petroleum sales executive*
Crabtree, Loren William *chancellor, academic administrator, history educator*
Creasia, Donald Anthony *toxicologist, researcher*
Creasia, Joan Catherine *dean, nursing educator*
Creekmore, David Dickason *lawyer, educator*
Cutler, Everette Wayne *history educator*
DePersio, Richard John *otolaryngologist, plastic surgeon*
Dillard, W. Thomas *lawyer*
Draughon, Frances Ann *microbiology educator*
Drinnon, Janis Bolton *artist, poet, volunteer*
Edge, Lara *editor*
Erickson, Mary (Molly) Louise *speech pathology/audiology services professional, educator*
Faires, Ross Norbert *manufacturing executive*
Felder-Hoehne, Felicia Harris *librarian*
Filston, Howard Church *pediatric surgeon, educator*
Fisher, John Hurt *English language educator*
Ford, Harriet-Lynn *English educator*
Francisco, Dorman Edward *language educator, writer*
Froula, James DeWayne *national honor society executive, engineer*
Fulmer, Phillip *university football coach*
Galligan, Thomas C., Jr., *dean, law educator*
Garrison, Arlene Allen *engineering executive, engineering educator*
Gentry, Mack A. *lawyer*
Gentry, Robert Vance *physicist, researcher, writer*
Ghosh, Narendra Nath *research scientist*
Gilley, James Wade *university president*
Graber, Glenn C. *medical educator, educational consultant*
Grossbeck, Martin Lester *metallurgist*
Guy, Allen C. *health facility administrator*
Harris, Charles Edgar *retired wholesale distribution company executive*
Harris, Diana Koffman *sociologist, educator*
Harris, Skila *government agency administrator*
Hartmann, Bruce *publishing executive*
Hatton, Barbara R. *academic administrator*
He, Donghui *language educator*
Horne, Douglas A. *diversified companies executive*
Howard, George Turner, Jr., *retired surgeon*
Howard, Herbert Hoover *broadcasting and communications educator*
Igoe, Terence B. *airport terminal executive*
Jacobs, Kenneth A. *composer, educator*
Jarvis, James Howard, II, *judge*
Johnson, Steven Boyd *lawyer*
Jordan, Robert Leon *judge*
Kim, Hyunjoong *education educator*
Kirkpatrick, Carl Kimmel *prosecutor*
Kliefoth, A(rthur) Bernhard, III, *neurosurgeon*
Krauter, Lana Cain *retail executive*
Kress, Tyler A. *biomedical engineer*
Lammers, Laura Bea *writer, communications executive*
Lawson, Fred Raulston *banker*
Lett, James Chancey *retired surgeon*
LeVert, Francis Edward *nuclear engineer, researcher*
Levy, Robert A. *academic administrator*
Lucas, John Allen *lawyer*
Mankel, Francis Xavier *former principal, priest*
Markert, Cynthia Allin *artist*
Martin, James Robert *identification company executive*
Matteson, Karla J. *health science association administrator*
Mazur, Peter *cell physiologist, cryobiologist*
McCullough, Glenn L., Jr., *electric power industry executive*
Mc Dow, John Jett *biosystems engineering educator*
McGuire, Sandra Lynn *nursing educator*
Mc Hargue, Carl Jack *research laboratory administrator*
Midkiff, Kimberly Ann *paralegal*
Mise, Jesse Sherden *structural engineer, consultant*
Moore, Louise Hill *surgical technologist*
Moran, James D., III, *university administrator*
Morton, Mike *consumer products executive*
Murrian, Robert Phillip *retired federal judge, educator*
Nayak, Subhadarshi *research scientist*
nes, Sherman J. *academic administrator, management educator, investment executive*
Nesbit, Sandi Michelle *personnel director*
Oakes, Thomas Wyatt *environmental engineer, computer engineer*
Ownby, Jere Franklin, III, *lawyer*
Petersen, John D. *academic administrator*
Phillips, Thomas Wade *judge, lawyer*
Prados, John William *engineering educator*
Prince, Matthew Sperry *religious organization executive*
Prosser, George T. *utilities executive*
Pulliam, Walter Tillman *newspaper publisher*
Rayson, Edwin Hope *lawyer*
Reeves, Pamela *lawyer*
Renshaw, Amanda Frances *retired physicist, nuclear engineer*
Ritchie, Albert *lawyer*
Romeo, Joanne Josefa Marino *mathematics educator*
Roth, J(ohn) Reece *electrical engineer, educator, researcher, inventor*
Rukeyser, William Simon *journalist*
Sansom, William B. *consumer products executive*
Schaefer, Philip William *mathematics educator, researcher*
Schuler, Theodore Anthony
Schweitzer, George Keene *chemistry professor*
Siler, Susan Reeder *communications educator*
Smartt, John Madison *lawyer*
Snyder, William T. *university chancellor*
Song, Ping *research scientist, educator*
South, Stephen A. *academic administrator*
Speas, Bruce Orburn *theater educator*
Stephens, Otis Hammond, Jr., *political science and law educator*
Stringfield, Hezz, Jr., *contractor, financial consultant*
Sublett, Carl Cecil *artist, educator*
Teeter, Dwight Leland, Jr., *journalism educator*
Tenopir, Carol *information science educator*
Trevor, Kirk David Niell *orchestra conductor, cellist*
Trout, Monroe Eugene *hospital systems executive*
Uhrig, Robert Eugene *nuclear engineer, educator*
Verplanck, William Samuel *psychologist, educator*
Walker, W. Jack *retired small business owner*
Watson, Patricia L. *library director*
Wheeler, John Watson *lawyer*
White, David Cleaveland *microbial ecologist, environmental toxicologist*
Williams, Thomas Ffrancon *chemist, educator*
Worthington, Carole Yard Lynch *lawyer*
Wunderlich, Bernhard *physical chemistry educator*
Yeomans, Gordon Allan *retired education educator*

La Follette
Eads, Ora Wilbert *clergyman, church official*

La Vergne
Daniel, William Donnie *video game distribution executive*

Lawrenceburg
Hayes, Sylvia Richmond *music educator*

Lebanon
Blackstock, James Fielding *lawyer*
Burns, George Franklin *archivist, retired English language educator*
Daniels, Charlie *musician, songwriter*
Davis, Julie Kramer *communications executive*
Evins, Dan W. *food products executive*
King, Kevin William *secondary school educator*
Rochelle, Robert Thomas *lawyer, former state legislator*
Woodhouse, Michael A. *restaurant holdings company executive*

Lewisburg
Gonzalez, Raquel Maria *pharmacist*
Poole, Rhonda Ann *editor, reporter*

Linden
Mitchell, Elizabeth Marelle *family nurse practitioner, nursing educator, medical, surgical nurse*

Lookout Mountain
Wyeth, Andrew *artist*

Loudon
Hallstrand, Sarah Laymon *denomination executive*
Jones, Robert Gean *religion educator*
Lownsdale, Gary Richard *mechanical engineer*
Puckett, Robert Marion *clergyman*
Randall, Marilyn Mae *writer*

Lynchburg
Koss, Jacqueline Jarrell *women's health nurse practitioner, educator*

Madison
Cage, Allie M. *communications executive*
Campbell, Chester Douglas *writer*
Hadley, John Livingston, V, *management executive, writer*

Martin
Lemons, Mary A. *finance educator*
McCracken, Kenneth Donald *retired education educator*
Norton, Dorotha Oliver *speech educator*
Petty, James Alan *mathematics educator, consultant*
Wade, Reba *music teacher, pianist*

Maryville
Bradford, Tutt Sloan *retired publisher*
Clayton, Kevin T. *mobile home manufacturer*
Hall, Marion Trufant *botany educator, arboretum director*
Howard, Cecil Byron *pediatrician*
Oakes, Lester Cornelius *retired electrical engineer, consultant*
Simpson, Terry L. *education educator, department chairman*
Tabor, Curtis Harold, Jr., *librarian, minister*

Maynardville
Upton, Chris L. *publishing executive*

Mc Ewen
Williams, John Lee *lawyer*

Mc Kenzie
Blasick, James David *finance educator*

Mc Minnville
McGee, Chad Alan *historian, educator*
Potter, Clement Dale *district attorney general*

Memphis
Abston, Dunbar, Jr., management executive
Adsit, Russell Allan landscape architect
Allen, Newton Perkins lawyer
Amonette, Rex. A. physician
Anghelescu, Doralina Lucia anesthesiologist
Archbold, Michale G. transportation executive
Archer, Ward, Jr., advertising executive
Ashley, Aaron Lee psychologist, educator
Baioni, Louis textiles executive
Bargagliotti, Lillian Antoinette nursing dean
Bhattacharya, Syamal Kanti biomedical scientist, educator
Blake, Norman hotel executive
Born, Robert Heywood consulting civil engineer
Boucher, Bradley Albert pharmacist, educator
Brafford, H. Wayne paper company executive
Brandon, Elvis Denby, Jr., financial planner
Brandon, Elvis Denby, III, financial planner
Brandon, Raymond Wilson financial planner, securities principal
Brewer, Jeffery Burt music educator
Broadhurst, Jerome Anthony lawyer
Brown, Hubert Jude professional athletics coach
Burton, Fred Clifford visual artist, educator
Butts, Herbert Clell retired dentist, educator
Call, M. Douglas former university administrator
Cannon, Joe Louis retired orthodontist
Cannon, Robert Emmet consumer products manufacturing company executive
Carr, Oscar Clark, III, lawyer
Carroll, Billy Price artist
Carter, Michael Allen nursing educator
Carter, Robert B. delivery service executive
Chesney, Russell Wallace pediatrician
Chester, James A. music educator
Ching, James Michael artistic director opera company, composer, conductor
Clark, Ross Bert, II, lawyer
Clippard, Richard F. prosecutor
Cohen, Susan Perlman literary agent
Coleman, Veronica Freeman prosecutor
Cook, August Joseph lawyer, accountant
Cox, Clair Edward, II, urologist, medical educator
Cox, Larry D. airport executive
Crane, Laura Jane retired chemist
Curran, Thomas molecular biologist, educator
Currey, Thomas Arthur ophthalmologist
Czestochowski, Joseph Stephen museum administrator
Dagogo-Jack, Samuel E. medical educator, physician scientist, endocrinologist
Dann, Alexander William, Jr., lawyer
Daughdrill, James Harold, Jr., academic administrator
De Mere-Dwyer, Leona medical illustrator
Demir, Semahat Siddika engineering educator
Desiderio, Dominic Morse, Jr., chemistry and neurochemistry educator
Deupree, William W. investment company executive
deWitt, Charles Benjamin, III, lawyer, educator
Dickerson, Roland Nelson pharmacy educator, clinical consultant
Diggs, Walter Whitley health science facility administrator
Dixon, Samuel B. retired comedian, film director, film producer
Doggrell, Henry Patton lawyer
Donahue, Joan Elizabeth elementary school educator
Donald, Bernice B. judge
Drescher, Judith Altman library director
Dunathan, Harmon Craig college dean
Dunnigan, T. Kevin electrical and electronics manufacturing company executive
Edmonson, Allen S. orthopedist
Edwards, Doris Porter computer specialist
Edwards, Gary Thomas historian, educator
Edwards, Martin real estate company executive
Eichner, Samantha Foster medical educator, consultant, writer
Evans, James Mignon architect
Fain, John Nicholas biochemistry educator
Fields, W(ade) Thomas dental educator
Foote, Shelby author
Ford, Harold Eugene consultant, former congressman
Forde, David Robert social sciences educator, criminologist, researcher
Forell, David Charles financial executive
Freeman, Bob A. retired microbiology educator, retired dean
Frey, William Rayburn healthcare educator, consultant
Friedman, Robert Michael lawyer
Garrott, Thomas M. bank executive
Gerald, Barry retired radiology educator, neuroradiologist
Gestrich, Thomas E. paper company executive
Gibbons, Julia Smith federal judge
Gilman, Ronald Lee federal judge
Gilpatrick, Russell O. dental educator, dean
Gipson, Harvey Lofton lawyer
Glass, J. Kenneth bank executive
Glenn, T. Michael delivery/messenger service executive
Godsey, William Cole physician
Gourley, Dick R. college dean
Gourley, Greta Ann Kimbrough pharmaceutical sciences educator
Graf, Alan B., Jr., transportation executive
Greiner, Charles H. paper company executive
Griffin, Clement M. information technology executive
Haizlip, Henry Hardin, Jr., real estate consultant, former banker
Hancock, Jonathan Cromwell lawyer
Hardy, Joy Miller academic administrator, consultant
Harkins, John Edward social studies educator, historian
Harris, Edward Frederick orthodontics educator
Harris, Terrell Lee prosecutor
Harvey, Albert C. lawyer
Haslam, Edward T. finance company executive
Heimberg, Murray pharmacologist, biochemist, physician, educator
Herbert, Paul paper company executive
Herenton, Willie W. mayor
Herrod, Henry Grady, III, dean, allergist, immunologist
Hochstein, John Isaac mechanical engineer, educator
Hofmann, Polly A. physiologist, science educator
Holder, Janice Marie state supreme court justice
Horn, D. Ralph corporate financial executive
Horn, Ralph bank executive
Howe, Martha Morgan microbiologist, educator
Hughes, Walter Thompson physician, pediatrics educator
Hunt, James Calvin academic administrator, physician
Hunt, Sean Antone lawyer, civil engineer
Ihle, James N. health facility administrator
Isaacson, Bond R. finance company executive
Jackson, Thomas Francis, III, lawyer
Jalenak, Peggy Eichenbaum volunteer
Jallepalli, Raji food service executive
Jernigan, Howard Maxwell, Jr., biochemistry educator, researcher
Jerry, Robert Howard, II, law educator
Johnson, Johnny research psychologist, consultant
Jolly, William Thomas foreign language educator
Jones, Effie L. social sciences educator
Jones, Jerry C. special education educator, counselor
Kaplan, Claudette S. (Claudia Kaplan) volunteer
Kemme, David Michael economics professor
Kiphart, Richard P. finance company executive
Klesges, Robert C. medical educator, clinical psychology researcher
Knight, H. Stuart law enforcement official, consultant
Korones, Sheldon Bernarr pediatrician, educator
Krieger, Robert Lee, Jr., human resource/management consultant, educator, writer, travel/meeting planner, political analyst, internet marketing consultant
Kushma, David William journalist
Labry, Edward A., III, finance company executive
Lasslo, Andrew medicinal chemist, educator
Lazar, Rande Harris otolaryngologist
Ledbetter, Paul Mark lawyer, writer
Lee, Theresa K. chemicals executive
Leffler, Charles William physiology and pediatrics educator
Levy, Robert Halle apparel executive, writer
Lynch, Denis Patrick dentist, educator
Madlock, Yvonne city health department administrator
Magrill, Joe Richard, Jr., religious organization administrator, minister
Mahato, Ram Ishwar pharmacist, educator
Malmo, John advertising executive
Manire, James McDonnell lawyer
Mann, Donald Cameron record company executive
Mantey, Elmer Martin food company executive
Martin, Bob airport executive
Martin, Daniel C. surgeon, gynecologist, educator
Masterson, Kenneth Rhodes lawyer
Matthews, Paul Aaron lawyer
Mauer, Alvin Marx physician, medical educator
McKenzie, Steven L. theology studies educator, writer
McPherson, Larry E(ugene) photographer, educator
McRee, Celia composer, singer, actress, writer, producer
Mishra, Sanjay R physicist
Moffitt, Carolyn Mullins university official
Monypeny, David Murray lawyer
Morreim, E. Haavi medical ethics educator
Mowry, Robert Wilbur pathologist, educator
Mulholland, Kenneth Leo, Jr., health care facility administrator
Nesin, Jeffrey David academic administrator
Nienhuis, Arthur Wesley physician, researcher
Noel, Randall Deane lawyer
Odland, Steve retail executive
Palmer, Dan M. finance company executive
Papachristou, Patricia Towne economics professor
Park, Elizabeth Haskell librarian, educator
Patrick, Jane Austin association executive
Pendleton, Mary Catherine foreign service officer
Pezeshki, S. Reza education educator
Piazza, Marguerite opera singer, actress, entertainer
Pohlmann, Marcus D. political science educator
Pourciau, Lester John, Jr., retired librarian
Presley, Lisa Marie musician
Quinn, Amelia Turner writer
Raines, Jim Neal lawyer
Raines, Shirley Carol academic administrator
Ranta, Richard Robert university dean
Rawlins, Donald Ray lawyer
Reaves, Charles Durham investment company executive, lawyer
Reid, Karen Denise aerospace transportation executive, writer
Reynolds, Stephen Curtis hospital administrator
Riss, Murray photographer, educator
Robertson, James Thomas neurosurgeon
Rothman, Edward S. information technology executive, consultant
Rubin, Rose Mohr economics professor
Russell, James Franklin lawyer
Rutledge, Roger Keith lawyer
Schelp, Richard Herbert mathematics professor
Schuler, Walter E. lawyer
Scroggs, Larry Kenneth lawyer, state legislator
Sherman, Janann Margaret history educator, writer
Sherr, Charles J. medical educator
Shochat, Stephen Jay pediatric surgeon
Shorb, Gary Seymour hospital administrator
Sigler, Lois Oliver retired secondary school educator
Simone, Joseph Vincent physician, educator
Smith, Frederick Wallace delivery service executive
Solomon, Solomon Sidney endocrinologist, pharmacologist, scientist
Soskel, Norman Terry physician
Stagg, Louis Charles English language and literature educator
Steib, James Terry bishop
Steinhauer, Gillian lawyer
Stokes, Henry Arthur journalist
Swofford, Joel David education educator
Tate, Stonewall Shepherd lawyer
Taylor, Marilyn Horton secondary school educator
Tibbs, Martha Jane Pullen civic worker, retired social worker
Todd, Virgil Holcomb clergyman, religion educator
Tonkin, Ina Lynn Dyer cardiovascular radiologist, educator
Troutt, William Earl academic administrator
Umholtz, Clyde Allan financial analyst
Van Middlesworth, Lester physiology, biophysics and medicine educator
Vescovo, Diane Kirkland federal judge
Vetscher, Timothy John reporter, television anchorman
Walker, Randolph Meade minister
Waller, Robert Rex ophthalmologist, educator, foundation executive
Wallis, Carlton Lamar librarian
Walters, Jane state agency administrator
Webster, Robert G. virologist, educator
West, Christopher Eugene military officer
West, Jerry Alan professional basketball team executive
White, Nicholas L. legal educator
Wilcox, Harry Hammond retired medical educator
Wilcox, John P. publishing executive
Williams, David Russell retired music educator
Williams, Edward F(oster), III, environmental engineer
Williams, Jason professional basketball player
Williams, Russ marketing professional
Winchester, Richard Lee, Jr., lawyer
Wingate, Robert Lee, Jr., internist
Winters, Darcy LaFountain medical management company executive
Wright Carrier, J. T. business owner
Xiong, Xiaoping statistician, researcher
Yow, Asuka Taga music educator, researcher

Midway
Kutbay, Cihat process engineer

Millington
Fletchall, Sandra Kay occupational therapist
Weatherford, Donna P. library director, educator

Morristown
Conry, Ruth P language educator
Harmon, David Eugene optometrist, geneticist
Hopper, Peggy F. education educator
Johnson, Evelyn Bryan airport terminal executive
Murphy, Michael Cary lawyer
Rowland, Kyla Faye gospel songwriter

Munford
Harrington, Herbert H. accountant

Murfreesboro
Breault, Kevin D. sociology educator, research scientist
Doyle, Delores Marie retired principal
Ford, William F. banker
Gilbert, Linda Arms education educator, educational administrator
Heffington, Jack Grisham lawyer, banker, insurance company executive, horse breeder
Lee, John Thomas finance educator, financial planner
Littlepage, Glenn E. social psychology educator
Marshall, John David retired librarian, author
McCash, June Hall retired language educator
McDaniel, Rhonda Louise literature educator
Reed, Angelica Denise sculptor, writer, illustrator
Rupprecht, Nancy Ellen historian, educator
Walker, David Ellis, Jr., educator, minister, consultant
Walker, James E. academic administrator, educator
Zietz, Joachim economics professor

Nashville
Adams, Kenneth Stanley, Jr., (Bud Adams) energy company executive, football executive
Allbritton, Cliff personal and organizational consultant
Allen, George Sewell neurosurgery educator
Allison, Fred, Jr., internist, retired medical educator
Anderson, David C. healthcare company executive
Anderson, Lynn (Rene Anderson) singer
Andrews, Holdt investment banker
Auerbach, Stanley Irving ecologist, environmental scientist, educator
Bailey, Stephanie B.C. city health department administrator
Baldwin, Harold Scott pediatrician
Bass, James Orin, Sr., lawyer
Basu, Prodyot Kumar civil engineer, educator
Bates, George William obstetrician, gynecologist, educator, medical products executive
Bayuzick, Robert J. materials scientist, educator
Beach, Margaret Smith retired language educator
Beauchamp, John Jones mathematician, educator
Beck, Robert Beryl real estate executive
Belton, Robert law educator
Benbow, Camilla Persson psychology educator, researcher
Bender, Harvey W., Jr., cardiac and thoracic surgeon
Benson, Edwin Welburn, Jr., trade association executive
Bentley, Dierks country singer, songwriter
Bernard, Louis Joseph surgeon, educator
Bigham, Wanda Durrett religious organization administrator
Birch, Adolpho A., Jr., state supreme court justice
Bird, Caroline author
Blair, Margaret Mendenhall research economist, consultant, law educator
Bloch, Frank Samuel law educator
Blumstein, James Franklin law educator, lawyer, consultant
Bolian, George Clement health care executive, physician
Boorman, Howard Lyon history professor
Bostick, Charles Dent retired lawyer, educator
Boyd, Theophilus Bartholomew, III, publishing company executive
Boyer, James Floyd land surveyor, state legislator
Bracken, Richard M. corporate financial executive
Bradford, James C., Jr., brokerage house executive
Bransford, Helen M. writer, jewelry designer
Bredesen, Philip Norman governor
Brett, John Brendan, Jr., corporate advertising and public relations executive
Brigham, Kenneth Larry medical educator
Brill, Aaron Bertrand nuclear medicine educator
Brooks, Kix musician
Brophy, Jeremiah Joseph former financial company official, former army officer
Brown, Joe Blackburn judge
Brown, Tommie Florence social work educator
Brown, Tony Ersic record company executive
Brown, Wendy Weinstock nephrologist, educator
Buerhaus, Peter I. nursing administrator
Burch, John Christopher, Jr., investment banker
Burchett, Tim state legislator, small business owner
Burk, Raymond Franklin, Jr., physician, educator, researcher
Burks, Charlotte state legislator
Burnett, Lonnie Sheldon obstetrics and gynecology educator
Butler, William Blaine dean, dental educator
Byrd, Andrew Wayne investment company executive
Byrd, Benjamin Franklin, Jr., surgeon, educator
Byrne, Daniel William biostatistician, educator
Cadzow, James Archie engineering educator, researcher
Camp, Randy Coleman lawyer
Carlson, Robert Marshall hospital professional services official
Carroll, Frank Edward radiologist, medical researcher
Carson, Paul Eugene insurance examiner
Cawthon, William Connell operations management consultant
Cerjan, Martin dean, law educator
Chait, Andrea Melinda school psychologist
Chamberlain, David M. consumer products company executive
Chapman, John Edmon academic administrator, pharmacologist, educator
Chapman, Morris Hines denominational executive
Chappell, Charles Richard space scientist
Cheek, James Howe, III, lawyer, educator
Chesney, Kenny country singer, songwriter
Christie, William Gary finance educator, dean
Churchill, Larry Raymond ethics educator
Chytil, Frank biochemist
Clabough, William C. state legislator, small business owner
Clark, Terri country singer
Clay, John W., Jr., bank executive
Cleveland, Ashley musician
Clinton, Barbara Marie university health services director, social worker
Cobb, Stephen A. lawyer
Cohen, William Mark lawyer
Collins, Joe Lena retired secondary school educator
Collins, Joyce P. minister, librarian, educator
Compton, John Joseph philosophy educator
Coney, PonJola dean, researcher, educator
Conkin, Paul Keith history professor
Conley, John P. economist, educator
Conner, Lewis Homer, Jr., lawyer
Conway-Welch, Colleen dean, nurse midwife
Cooil, Bruce Kimo mathematical statistician, statistics educator
Cook, Ann Jennalie English language educator
Cornfield, Daniel Benjamin sociology educator
Crawford, Edwin Mac pharmaceutical executive
Crutchfield, William Ward lawyer, state legislator
Cunningham, Leon William biochemist, educator
Daane, James Dewey banker
Dalton, James Edgar, Jr., health facility administrator
Darnell, Riley Carlisle Secretary of State, lawyer
Daughtrey, Martha Craig federal judge
Day, John Arthur lawyer
DeBerry, Lois Marie state legislator
DeHart, Roy Lynch physician, educator
DeLanis, James Alfred lawyer
Demarcus, Jay (Stanley Demarcus) country musician, songwriter
Dettbarn, Wolf-Dietrich neurochemist, pharmacologist, educator
Dickerson, Dennis Clark history educator
Dixon, Carl Franklin lawyer
Dixon, Roscoe state legislator, consultant, insurance company executive
Dobbs, George Albert funeral director, embalmer
Donahey, Kenneth C. hospital management company executive
Donnelly, Edwin F. radiologist
Doyal, Linda E. clinical pharmacist
Draper, James Thomas, Jr., (Jimmy Draper) clergyman
Drowota, Frank F., III, state supreme court chief justice
Du Bois, Tim recording industry executive
Dunn, Ronnie musician
Dupont, William Dudley biostatistician, educator
Dye, Hank public relations executive
Dysart, Benjamin Clay, III, consultant, conservationist, engineer
Echols, Robert L. federal judge
Eckles, Mary Ann state legislator
Edwards, Mark E. healthcare company lawyer
Elam, Lloyd Charles psychiatrist, educator
Elsea, Gene apparel executive, state legislator
Ely, James Wallace, Jr., law educator
Epps, Anna Cherrie immunologist, educator, dean
Estrin, Kari (Karen Ruth Estrin) artist and tour manager, acoustic radio promoter
Etherington, Carol A. medical association administrator
Evans, Franklin Bachelder marketing educator emeritus
Evans, Sara country singer, songwriter
Fabian, Jane former ballet company executive
Farmer, William H. political organization worker, lawyer
Fazio, Sergio medical educator, researcher
Feldman, Leonard Cecil physicist
Fenichel, Gerald Mervin neurologist, educator
Ferguson, John D. prison management administrator
Fields, James Perry dermatologist, dermatopathologist, allergist, pharmacologist, pharmacist
Fischer, Charlotte Froese research scientist, educator
Fischer, Patrick Carl computer scientist, retired educator
Fisher, Jeff professional football coach
Fitzgerald, Edmund Bacon electronics industry executive
Fleck, Bela country musician
Fleischer, Arthur C. medical educator, radiologist
Flippo, Chet writer, editor
Fort, Tomlinson chemist, chemical engineering educator
Foster, Henry Wendell medical educator
Franks, John Julian anesthesiology educator, medical investigator
Freudenthal, Ernest Guenter technology and business educator
Fulmer, Douglas Alan political consultant, journalist
Gabbe, Steven Glenn G. dean, educator, obstetrician, gynecologist
Galloway, Kenneth Franklin engineering educator
Gannon, John Sexton lawyer, management consultant, arbitrator, mediator
Gee, Elwood Gordon academic administrator

George, Alfred L., Jr., medical educator, researcher
Giallombardo, Leslie publishing executive
Gillmor, John Edward lawyer
Girgus, Sam B. English literature educator
Gleaves, Edwin Sheffield librarian
Goetz, Dave trade association administrator
Goggin, Wendy prosecutor
Gore, Steven Lowell business development manager
Gore, Tipper (Mary Elizabeth Gore) wife of the former vice president of the United States
Graham, George J., Jr., political scientist, educator
Graham, Thomas Pegram, Jr., pediatric cardiologist
Granner, Daryl Kitley physiology and medicine educator
Grant, Amy singer, songwriter
Graves, Jo Ann state legislator
Green, Lisa Cannon online editor
Greer, Herschel Lynn, Jr., real estate executive
Griffin, Patti Elaine medical educator, consultant
Griffith, Nanci singer, songwriter
Guha, Sujata education educator
Guinsburg, Philip Fried alcohol and substance abuse counselor
Hahn, George Thomas materials engineering educator, researcher
Haines, Jonathan L. science educator
Hall, Hugh David oral and maxillofacial surgeon, educator
Hall, Richard Clyde, Jr., retired religious educational administrator
Halteman Harwell, Beth state legislator
Hamilton, Joseph Hants, Jr., physicist, researcher
Hanselman, Richard Wilson entrepreneur
Hardin, Hal D. lawyer, judge, former US attorney
Hargrove, Erwin Charles, Jr., political science educator
Harper, Thelma state legislator
Harris, Ben T. apparel manufacturing and retail executive
Harris, Emmylou singer
Harris, J(acob) George healthcare company executive
Harris, Thomas Raymond biomedical engineer, educator
Harrison, Clifford Joy, Jr., banker
Hart, Richard Banner lawyer
Harwell, Beth H. political organization worker
Hassel, Rudolph Christopher English educator
Haun, Tommy George state legislator, insurance agent
Havens, Murray Clark political scientist, educator
Hazelip, Herbert Harold academic administrator
Hazen, Samuel N corporate financial executive
Heard, Alexander retired educator and chancellor
Heard, Edwin Anthony banker
Hefner, James A. academic administrator
Henderson, Milton Arnold professional society administrator
Henry, Douglas lawyer, state legislator
Hercules, David Michael chemistry professor, consultant
Hill, Faith musician
Hillenmeyer, Henry Reiling, Jr., restaurant company executive
Hoekstra, Douglas Anthony writer, educator, musician
Hofstead, James Warner laundry machinery company executive, lawyer
Houston, Bill state commissioner
Howell, John Floyd insurance company executive
Inagami, Tadashi biochemistry educator
Ingram, John wholesale distribution executive
Ingram, Martha Rivers publishing executive
Ingram, Orrin Henry, II, transportation executive
Jacobsen, Harry R. hospital administrator, physician
James, Kay Louise management consultant, healthcare executive
Jennings, Henry Smith, III, cardiologist
Johnson, David medical administrator
Johnson, Greg professional hockey player
Johnson, Hollis Eugene, III, foundation executive
Johnson, R. Milton healthcare executive
Jonsson, Bjarni mathematician, educator
Joyner, John Wesley psychologist, educator
Judd, Naomi country music entertainer, singer, songwriter, writer
Kaas, Jon H. psychology educator
Kaine, Paul performing company executive
Kaiser, Allen Bernard health facility administrator
Keith, Toby (Toby Keith Covel) country singer, songwriter, producer
Kirshner, Howard S. neurologist, medical educator
Kmiec, Edward Urban bishop
Krauss, Alison country musician
Kuhn, Paul Hubert, Jr., investment counsel
Kurita, Rosalind state legislator
Kyle, Sara state agency administrator
Land, Richard Dale minister, religious organization administrator
Larry, Benno airport terminal executive
Lawrence, Thomas Patterson public relations executive
Lawrence, Tracey country singer, songwriter
Lawton, Alexander Robert immunologist, educator
Lazar, Irving psychologist
Leatherwood, Thomas insurance agent, state legislator
Ledyard, Robins Heard lawyer
Lee, Douglas A. music educator
Leftwich, Russell Bryant allergist, immunologist, consultant
Legwand, David professional hockey player
Leipold, Craig L. professional sports team executive
LeQuire, Alan Russell sculpting educator
LeVan, Martin Douglas chemical engineering educator
Levox, Gary (Gary Wayne Vernon Jr.) country/rock singer
Livingston, Robert A. brewing company executive
Longhurst, Robert Russell retired secondary school educator
Loper, Linda Sue special collections librarian
Lowe, Harold Gladstone, Jr., photojournalist, small business owner, farmer
Loyd, Stan music specialist
Luis, William language educator
Lukehart, Charles Martin chemistry professor
Lyle, Virginia Reavis retired archivist, genealogist
Lynch, John Brown plastic surgeon, educator
Lynn, Loretta Webb (Mrs. Oliver Lynn Jr.) singer
Lyon, Philip Kirkland lawyer
Madu, Leonard Ekwugha lawyer, human rights advocate, columnist
Maguire, Martha Elenor Erwin (Martie Maguire) musician
Maier, Harold Geistweit law educator, lawyer
Maines, Natalie Louise musician
Mandrell, Barbara Ann singer, entertainer, actress, producer, writer
Manning, Charles W. university chancellor
Marcic, Dorothy Anne education educator
Marney, Samuel Rowe, Jr., immunologist, educator
Martin, Henry Alan public defender
Martin, James Larence dentist, educator
Martin, Peter Robert psychiatrist, pharmacologist
Mason, Derrick professional football player
Mauksch, Ingeborg Grosser nursing educator
Maupin, John E., Jr., college president
Mawn, Louise Ann ophthalmologist, educator
May, James M. medical educator, medical researcher
May, Joseph Leserman (Jack May) retired lawyer
Mayden, Barbara Mendel lawyer
Mayhew, Aubrey music industry executive
McBride, Martina vocalist
McCarty, Richard Charles psychology educator, university dean
McCormick, Richard retired telecommunications company executive
McCowan, Otis Blakely mathematics professor
McDonald, Michael Eugene lawyer, educator, clergyman
McDonald, Reginald Adrian musician, educator
McKerley, Annette Elizabeth school system administrator
McMurry, Idanelle Sam educational consultant
McNair, Steve LaTreal professional football player
McNally, James Rand (Randy McNally) pharmacist, state legislator
McNeely, Mark marketing professional, journalist
Medwedeff, Fred Marshall dentist
Meredith, Owen Nichols public relations executive, genealogist
Merritt, Gilbert Stroud federal judge
Miller, Richard L. architectural executive
Mitchell, Robert W. diversified company executive
Mizell, Andrew Hooper, III, concrete company executive
Moon, Fletcher Froe college librarian, multi-media artist, minister
Moore, William Grover, Jr., management consultant, retired military officer
Morrow, Jason Drew medical and pharmacology educator
Moses, Harold L. oncologist
Moss, Carl Michael minister, religious studies educator
Naifeh, James O. (Jimmy Naifeh) state legislator, speaker of the house
Neel, C. Warren state finance department commissioner
Neilson, Eric Grant physician, educator, health facility administrator
Nelson, Edward Gage merchant banking investment company executive
Nixon, John Trice judge
Oates, John Alexander, III, medical educator
Oates, Sherry Charlene portraitist, artist, photographer
O'Day, Denis Michael ophthalmologist, educator
Orgebin-Crist, Marie-Claire biology professor, department chairman
Orth, David Nelson physician, educator, sculptor
Ossoff, Robert Henry otolaryngological surgeon
Pearson, Sela poet, speaker
Penterman, Carol A. opera company executive
Person, Curtis S., Jr., state legislator, lawyer
Petrie, William Marshall psychiatrist
Pfanner, Helmut Franz German language educator
Phillips, John A(tlas), III, geneticist, educator
Pincus, Theodore microbiologist, rheumatologist, educator
Pinson, Charles Wright transplant surgeon, healthcare administrator, educator
Policinski, Eugene Francis foundation executive, newspaper editor, radio and television host, producer
Porter, Andrew Calvin academic administrator, psychologist, educator
Ramer, Hal Reed academic administrator
Ramsaur, Allan Fields lawyer, lobbyist
Ramsey, Ronald L. state legislator, realtor
Ray, Wayne Allen epidemiologist, educator
Reschly, Daniel J. education educator, psychologist
Richey, Kimberly Kay singer, actress, composer
Richmond, Samuel Bernard management educator
Riley, Harris DeWitt, Jr., pediatrician, medical educator
Risko, Victoria J. language educator
Rivera, Maximiano Marquez academic administrator, writer
Roberts, Kenneth Lewis investor, lawyer, foundation administrator
Roberts, Sandra editor
Robertson, David physician, scientist, educator
Robison, Emily Burns musician
Roden, Dan Mark clinical pharmacologist, cardiologist, medical educator
Rogers, Barbara Jean (B.J. Rogers) writer, editor
Rooney, Joe Don country musician
Roos, Charles Edwin physicist
Ross, Joseph Comer physician, educator, academic administrator
Rowan, William Hamilton, Jr., computer science educator
Russell, Clifford Springer economics and public policy educator
Rutherford, William B. corporate financial executive
Saff, Edward Barry mathematics professor
Saltsman, John B. former political party executive, commissioner
Sanders, James F. lawyer
Saposnik, Ira Stephen physician, historian
Schall, Jeffrey D. psychology educator
Schermerhorn, Kenneth music director
Schnelle, Karl Benjamin, Jr., chemical engineering educator, consultant, researcher
Schoenfeld, Michael academic administrator, education educator
Schoggen, Phil H(oward) psychologist, educator
Schwartz, Herbert S. surgical oncology educator
Seivers, Lana C. commissioner of education
Seligson, Mitchell A. Latin American studies educator
Sergent, John S. hospital administrator, medical educator
Sevin, Dieter Hermann language and literature professional, educator
Shack, R. Bruce plastic surgeon
Shallcross, Richard corporate financial executive
Shaw, Carole editor, publisher
Shaw-Cohen, Lori Eve magazine editor
Shell, Owen G., Jr., retired bank executive
Sherborne, Robert editor
Shipley Biddy, Shelia artist management executive
Shneyder, Artyom V. science educator, researcher
Siegfried, John association officer
Silberman, Enrique physics researcher and administrator
Silver, Heidi Jaye nutritionist, educator, researcher
Sims, Wilson lawyer
Singh, Surendra P. agricultural economics professor, consultant
Sloan, Reba Faye dietitian, consultant
Smith, Agnes Evyonda writer
Smith, Bradley E. anesthesiologist
Snoddy, Chris Raymond athletic trainer
Soderquist, Larry Dean law educator, lawyer, consultant, writer
Speece, Richard Eugene civil engineer, educator
Spengler, Dan Michael orthopedic surgery educator, researcher, surgeon
Stahlman, Mildred Thornton pediatrics and pathology educator, researcher
Stewart, David Marshall librarian
Stone, Lawrence Mynatt publishing executive
Stringfield, Charles David hospital administrator
Strupp, Hans Hermann psychologist, educator
Strupp, John Allen oncologist
Sullivan, Dennis James, Jr., hospitality and music executive
Sullivan, James Nelson physician
Summers, Paul state attorney general
Surowiec, Andrew Julius biophysicist, researcher
Sutherland, Frank publishing executive, editor
Swan, Patricia Brintnall research administrator
Swensson, Earl Simcox architect
Swing, Marilyn S. metropolitan clerk
Syverud, Kent Douglas dean
Tarpley, John R. lawyer
TeSelle, Eugene Arthur, Jr., religion educator
Thomas, Hazel Beatrice state official
Thomas, Randall Stuart lawyer, educator
Thomas, Robert Paige lawyer
Thompson, Dean Allan cattleman
Thornton, Spencer P. ophthalmologist, educator
Torrey, Claudia Olivia lawyer
Trauger, Aleta Arthur judge
Trautman, Herman Louis lawyer, educator
Treible, Kirk retired academic administrator, foundation administrator
Trent, John Thomas, Jr., lawyer
Trotz, Barry professional hockey coach
Tuke, Robert Dudley lawyer, educator
Turk, Thomas Liebig cultural organization administrator
Turner, Cal, Jr., discount stores executive
Twain, Shania (Eilleen Regina Edwards) country musician
Ullestad, Merwin Allan tax services executive
Urban, Keith country singer, songwriter
Urmy, Norman B. hospital administrator
Valentine, Alan Darrell symphony orchestra executive
Van, George Paul international money management consultant
van Eys, Jan retired pediatrician, educator, administrator
Van Mol, Louis John, Jr., public relations executive
Vasterling, Paul artistic director
Vines, James lawyer
Voegeli, Victor Jacque history educator, dean
Wadley, Fredia Stovall state commissioner
Wagner, Michael Grafton investor, management consultant
Walkup, John Knox lawyer
Warner, Tokesha L health facility administrator
Wasserman, David H. medical educator, researcher
Waterman, Robert A. lawyer
Watkins, Sara musician
Weingartner, H(ans) Martin finance educator
Wert, James Junior materials scientist, educator
Westfield, Fred M. economics professor
White, Bruce David law and ethics educator, consultant
Wilder, John Shelton lieutenant governor
Williams, Marsha Rhea computer scientist, educator, researcher, consultant
Williams, Noel Brown information technology executive
Winstead, Elisabeth Weaver poet, writer, English language educator
Winstead, George Alvis law librarian, biochemist, educator, consultant
Wire, William Shidaker, II, retired apparel and footwear manufacturing company executive
Wiseman, Thomas Anderton, Jr., federal judge
Womack, David Andrew (Andy Womack) insurance agent, state legislator
Womack, Steven James education educator, writer
Wyatt, Joe Billy academic administrator
Yarbrough, Edward Meacham lawyer
Young, Boyd D. labor union administrator
Young, Tommie Morton social psychology educator, writer
Youngblood, Elaine Michele lawyer
Yuspeh, Alan Ralph lawyer, healthcare company executive
Zepos, Nicholas S. academic administrator
Zibart, Michael Alan wholesale book company executive
Zierdt, John Graham, Jr., transportation company executive
Zimmerman, Raymond retail chain executive

Newport
Ball, Travis, Jr., educational consultant, editor
Branam, Linda Gail psychologist, educator
Myers, John William lawyer
Porter, James Kenneth retired judge

Oak Ridge
Borie, Bernard Simon, Jr., retired physicist, educator
Carlsmith, Roger Snedden chemistry and energy conservation researcher
Cragle, Donna Lynne university administrator, researcher
David, Stanislaus Antony metallurgical engineer
Dickens, Justin Kirk nuclear physicist
George, Easo Pulinthitta materials scientist, educator
Hartley, Dean S., III, operations research specialist
Hartman, Frederick Cooper biochemist, researcher
Holloway, Jacqueline county commissioner
Hu, Zhiyu research scientist, educator
Hudson, Sheila Donnette waste management administrator
Jones, Virginia McClurkin retired social worker
Kosacki, Igor physicist, educator
Krause, Manfred Otto physicist
Larson, Bennett Charles solid state physicist, researcher
Maienschein, Fred retired physicist
Manly, William Donald metallurgist
McNeilly, Kathy Eden librarian, library director
Mullins, David Roy chemist, researcher
Paranthaman, Mariappan Parans research scientist
Phillips, Debra Helen soil scientist, researcher
Plasil, Franz physicist
Postma, Herman physicist, consultant
Poutsma, Marvin L. chemical research administrator
Protopopescu, Vladimir Alexandru research scientist, educator
Raridon, Richard Jay computer specialist
Regan-Stanton, Christa Maria artist
Runtsch, Clarence Frederick sculptor
Rupert, David Roy human resources manager
Shishlo, Andrei Petrovich physicist, researcher
Slusher, Kimberly Goode researcher
Spray, Paul Ellsworth retired surgeon
van Tol, Jenifer music educator, musician
Wang, Hong engineer, researcher
Watson, Evelyn Egner radiation scientist
Weinberg, Alvin Martin physicist
Xu, Ying computational biologist
Xu, Yongli research scientist
Young, Jack Phillip chemist
Zucker, Alexander physicist, administrator

Ooltewah
Badgley, Jeffrey I. transportation executive

Paris
Rose, Todd Alan lawyer

Pigeon Forge
Parton, Dolly Rebecca singer, composer, actress

Pikeville
Wright, Donald Gene accountant

Pleasant Hill
Hull, Charles William retired special education educator

Powell
Hyman, Roger David lawyer

Rockwood
Bane, Charles E insurance broker, writer

Saulsbury
Jacobs, Henry Madison, Jr., researcher, writer

Sevierville
Hicks, Deborah music educator
Koff, Shirley Irene writer
Waters, John B. lawyer

Sewanee
Alvarez, Laurence Richards education educator
Camp, Thomas Edward retired librarian
Chitty, Elizabeth Nickinson (Mary Chitty) university historian
Croom, Frederick Hailey academic administrator, mathematician, educator
Cunningham, Joel Luther university president, vice-chancellor
Dunkly, James Warren theological librarian
Gessell, John Maurice minister, educator
Hughes, Robert Davis, III, theology studies educator
Lytle, Guy Fitch, III, priest, educator, dean
Parsley, Henry Nutt, Jr., bishop, academic administrator
Patterson, William Brown dean, history professor
Watson, Gail H. retired librarian
Williamson, Samuel Ruthven, Jr., historian, emeritus university president
Winton, Calhoun literature educator
Yeatman, Harry Clay biologist, educator

Seymour
Steele, Ernest Clyde retired insurance company executive

Shelbyville
Nelson, Clara Singleton human resources consultant

Shiloh
Allen, Stacy Dale historian, parks director

Signal Mountain
Anderson, Charles Hill lawyer
Cooper, Robert Elbert state supreme court justice
Hall, Thor religion educator
Howe, Lyman Harold, III, chemist, researcher
Makansi, Munzer chemical engineer, researcher
Ragan, Charles Oliver, Jr., lawyer
Swann, Nat Henderson, Jr., physician

Smithville
Vaughn, Eulalia Cobb retired science educator, mathematician

Smyrna
Moore, Wesley Boyd occupational physician

Soddy Daisy
Leitner, Paul Revere lawyer
Randall, Kay Temple accountant, retired real estate agent

South Pittsburg
Ables, Charles Robert lawyer, judge

Sparta
Young, Olivia Knowles retired librarian

Spring Hill
Trudell, Cynthia automotive executive

Springfield
Fagan, A. Rudolph minister

Nutting, Paul John *city manager*

Telford
Mashburn, Donald Eugene *education educator*

Townsend
Sundquist, Don *former governor, former congressman, sales corporation executive*

Trenton
McCullough, Kathryn T. Baker *social worker*

Tullahoma
Gossick, Lee Van *consultant, executive, retired air force officer*
Hill, Susan Sloan *safety engineer*

Union City
Graham, Hardy Moore *lawyer*

Waverly
Peeler, William James *lawyer*

White House
Warpool, Christopher Paul *elementary school educator, freelance/self-employed musician*

Whiteville
Allen, Yvonne *principal*

Williamsport
Dysinger, Paul William *preventive medicine physician, educator*

TEXAS

Abilene
Bailey, Fred Arthur *history educator*
Bentley, Clarence Edward *savings and loan executive*
Boone, Billy Warren *lawyer, judge*
Boyll, David Lloyd *broadcasting company executive*
Bridges, Julian Curtis *sociologist educator, department head*
Christopher, Mary M. *education educator, consultant*
Dickerson, Russell Sturges *neurologist*
Marler, Charles Herbert *journalism educator, historian, consultant*
McCaleb, Gary Day *university official*
McWhiney, Grady *history educator*
Morgan, Clyde Nathaniel *dermatologist*
Owen, Dian Grave *investment corporation executive*
Puckett, Lauren Joy *music educator*
Retzer, Kenneth Albert *mathematics professor, entrepreneur*
Robinson, Vianei Lopez *lawyer*
Sartain, James Edward *lawyer*
Specht, Alice Wilson *university libraries dean*
Suttle, Stephen Hungate *lawyer*
Tolosa, Gustavo Alberto *music educator*
Tomme, Curtis Rabon *lawyer*
Tucker, John Mark *librarian, educator*
Turner, Stafford *education educator, baritone*
Walker, Beatriz Alem *language educator*
Waters, Michael Cooper *medical center and development corporation executive*
Wheeler, Floyd Larry *education educator*

Addison
Anderson, Jack Roy *health care company executive*
Cohn, Linkie Seltzer *professional speaker, author*
Cotter, Ka *real estate company executive*
Grote, Dick (Richard Charles Grote) *management consultant, educator, author, radio commentator*
Hinckley, Jim *real estate company executive*
Holl, David *cosmetics company executive*
Kimbler, Larry Bernard *real estate executive, accountant*
Kneipper, Richard Keith *lawyer*
Lawson, Gary B. *lawyer*
Murray, Patrick M. *oilfield service company executive*
Pommerening, Edwin Carlton *lawyer*
Pryor, Richard Walter *telecommunications executive, retired air force officer*
Ragusa, Elysia *real estate company executive*
Rinehart, Neil *financial consultant*
Rogers, Richard Raymond *cosmetics company executive*
Smith, Cece *venture capitalist*
Staubach, Roger Thomas *real estate executive, former professional football player*
Thomas, Philip Robinson *management consulting company executive*

Alamo
Pritchett, Thomas Ronald *retired metal and chemical company executive*

Aledo
Reilly, Michael Atlee *financial company executive, venture capital investor*
Rowe, Sheryl Ann *librarian*

Alice
Taylor, Bryce B *music educator, consultant*
Tetlie, Harold *priest*

Allen
Battat, Emile A. *management executive*
Lim, Jae Doeg *systems engineer, researcher*
Mitchell, Ralph *wholesale distribution executive*
Warren, Rita Simpson *manufacturing executive*
Williams, Bryan *dean, medical educator*

Alpine
Kittlitz, Rudolf Gottlieb, Jr., *chemical engineer, researcher*
Morgan, Raymond Victor, Jr., *university administrator, mathematics educator*
Sechrest, Larry J. *economist, educator*
Snyder, John Edward, Jr., *education educator*

Alvin
Roberson, Deborah Kay *secondary school educator*

Amarillo
Arnold, Winnie Jo *retired mental health nurse, nursing administrator*

Attebury, William Hugh *construction company executive*
Ayad, Joseph Magdy *retired psychologist*
Berry, Jacob Obadiah *not-for-profit developer, rancher*
Biggs, William Curtis *endocrinologist*
Bull, Walter Stephen *police officer*
Burgess, C(harles) Coney *bank executive*
Busch, Mildred Moorman *music educator*
Cox, Roger Stephen *lawyer*
Crain, Mary Tom *volunteer*
Cummins, Joseph M. *biotechnology company executive*
DeVaughn, Michael Richard *minister, administrator*
Elkins, Lloyd Edwin, Sr., *petroleum engineer, energy consultant*
Horton, Thomas Mark *futures and options trader, commodity consultant*
Johnson, Philip Wayne *judge*
Klein, Jerry Lee, Sr., *religion educator, minister*
Laur, Noel Paul Douglas *music educator*
Laur, William Edward *retired dermatologist*
Madden, Wales Hendrix, Jr., *lawyer*
Marmaduke, John H. *retail executive*
Marupudi, Sambasiva Rao *surgeon, educator*
Parker, Gerald M. *osteopath, researcher*
Pillai, Narayana Gopalakrishnan *internist, oncologist*
Pratt, Donald George *physician*
Rauscher, James Francis *music educator*
Robinson, Mary Lou *federal judge*
Saadeh, Constantine Khalil *internist, health facility administrator, educator*
Simpson, Chad W. *pharmacist, educator*
Smithee, John True *lawyer, state legislator*
Stubben, Dolus Jane (D. J. Stubben) *advertising executive*
Turks, Hildegard Maria (Hildegard Maria Chronis) *retired security investigator, writer*
Utterback, Will Hay, Jr., *retired labor union administrator, genealogist*
Von Eschen, Robert Leroy *electrical engineer, consultant*

Angleton
Germany, Garvin Holt, Jr., *retired judge, lawyer*

Aransas Pass
Stehn, Lorraine Strelnick *physician*

Argyle
Merritt, Joe Frank *industrial supply executive*
Pettit, John Douglas, Jr., *management educator*
Stallings, Frank, Jr., *realtor, director*

Arlington
Adams, Phyllis Curl *nursing educator*
Adams, Quentin Mark *neurologist*
Alicea, Luis Rene *professional baseball player*
Alvarez, Juan M. *professional baseball player*
Anderson, Dale Arden *aerospace engineer, educator*
Beckwitt, Richard *construction executive*
Brown, Sandra *writer*
Carey, Milburn Ernest *musician, educator*
Clark, Dayle Meritt *civil engineer*
Cole, Richard Louis *political scientist, educator*
Dillard, John James *school librarian*
Dowdy, John Vernard, Jr., *lawyer, educator, arbitrator*
English, Marlene Cabral *management consultant*
Eudaly, Olivia Coggin *not-for-profit executive, educator*
Everard, Noel J. *structural engineer, educator*
Ferrier, Richard Brooks *architecture educator, architect*
Forbes, Catherine Ann *music educator, musician*
Fouse, David Jesse *architect*
Gatzke, Donald Frank *architecture educator*
Gilder, Richard Earl *clinical information system administrator, data analyst*
Green, George N. *historian, educator*
Greenspan, Donald *mathematician, educator*
Guerin, Bill *professional hockey player*
Han, Chien-Pai *statistics educator*
Harris, Vera Evelyn *human resources specialist*
Horton, Donald R. *construction executive*
Ignagni, Joseph Anthony *humanities educator, associate dean*
Jensen, John Robert *lawyer*
Joyner, Henry Curtis *airline executive*
Kier, Carlos M. *rheumatologist*
Kirk, Wiley Price, Jr., *physics and electrical engineering educator*
Kojouharov, Hristo Venelinov *mathematician, educator, mathematician, researcher*
Lau, Irene B. *music educator*
LeMaster, Dale *construction executive*
Lewis, Frank Leroy *electrical engineer, educator, researcher*
Lingerfelt, B. Eugene, Jr., *minister*
Liu, Hanli *biomedical engineer, educator*
Mansen, Steven Robert *manufacturing executive*
Mc Keen, Chester M., Jr., *retired business executive*
Otto, Ludwig *publisher, educator, consultant, evangelist*
Pickard, Myrna Rae *dean*
Pierson, Grey *lawyer*
Pomerantz, Martin *chemistry educator, researcher*
Poster, Elizabeth C. *dean*
Rainey, Claude Gladwin *retired health care executive*
Ramsey, Charles Eugene *sociologist, educator*
Rollins, Albert Williamson *civil engineer, consultant*
Rosenberry, William Kenneth *lawyer, educator*
Sawyer, Dolores *motel chain executive*
Shanmugam, Ganapathy *geologist, researcher*
Showalter, Buck (William Nathaniel Showalter III) *major league baseball team manager*
Smith, Charles Isaac *geology educator*
Sobol, Harold *retired dean, manufacturing executive, consultant*
Soriano, Alfonso Guilleard *professional baseball player*
Spaniolo, James D. *academic administrator*
Spears, Georgann Wimbish *marketing executive*
Stevens, Gladstone Taylor, Jr., *industrial engineer*
Swanson, Peggy Eubanks *finance educator*
Thomas, Lois C. *musician, educator, religious organization administrator*
Tingley, Floyd Warren *retired internist*
Tomnitz, Donald J. *construction executive*
White, Alisa *communications educator, consultant*
Willoughby, Sarah-Margaret C. *chemist, educator, chemical engineer, consultant*

Witt, Robert E. *academic administrator*
Wright, C(arroll) Lee, Jr., *architecture educator*
Wright, James Edward *judge*

Aubrey
Pizzamiglio, Albert Theodore (Al Pierson) *conductor*

Austin
Abbott, Greg Wayne *state attorney general, former state supreme court justice*
Ables-Flatt, Jean Ann *commissioner*
Aboussie, Marilyn *retired state justice*
Abraham, Jacob A. *computer engineering educator, consultant*
Alexander, Drury Blakeley *architectural educator*
Allday, Martin Lewis *lawyer*
Al-Omari, Ra'ed M. *computer engineer, consultant, computer scientist, researcher*
Alpert, Mark Ira *marketing educator*
Alter, Kevin S. *architecture educator*
Anderson, David Arnold *law educator*
Anderson, Lynn D. *telecommunications industry executive*
Anderson, Mo *real estate company executive*
Anderson, Nadeane Walker *journalist*
Anderson, Urton Liggett *accounting educator*
Antokoletz, Elliott Maxim *music educator*
Armstrong, Lance *professional cyclist*
Armstrong, Neal Earl *civil engineering educator*
Ascher, Mark Louis *legal educator*
Ashworth, Kenneth Hayden *public affairs specialist*
Attal, Gene (Fred Eugene Attal) *hospital executive*
Aubery, Stephen Royston Edmund *film producer*
Austin, David Mayo *social work educator*
Auvenshine, Anna Lee Banks *school system administrator*
Ayres, Robert Moss, Jr., *retired university president*
Baade, Hans Wolfgang *legal educator, law expert*
Baker, Lee Edward *biomedical engineering educator*
Baker, Mark Bruce *lawyer, educator*
Banerjee, Sanjay Kumar *electrical engineer, director*
Banks, Virginia Anne (Ginger Banks) *association administrator*
Bard, Allen Joseph *chemist, educator*
Barnes, Richard Dale *college basketball coach*
Barnes, Thomas Joseph *writer*
Barrientos, Gonzalo *advertising executive, public relations executive, state legislator*
Bash, Frank Ness *astronomer, educator*
Baumgartner, Robert *consultant*
Beazley, Hamilton *writer, educator*
Belle-Isle, David Richard *organization and management consultant*
Benavides, Fortunato Pedro (Pete Benavides) *federal judge*
Bengtson, Roger Dean *physicist, department chairman*
Bernstein, Robert *retired physician, state official, former army officer*
Biesele, John Julius *biologist, educator*
Billings, Harold Wayne *library director, editor*
Black, William Earl *lawyer*
Blackstock, David T. *acoustical engineer, educator*
Blake, Robert Rogers *psychologist, behavioral science company executive*
Blodgett, Warren Terrell *public affairs educator*
Bobbitt, Philip Chase *writer, educator, public official*
Boggs, James Ernest *chemistry professor*
Boles, Billye Gayle *program administrator*
Bonjean, Charles Michael *foundation executive, sociologist, educator*
Bordie, John George *linguistics educator*
Botsford, David L. *lawyer*
Box, John Harold *architect, educator*
Branch, Brenda Sue *library director*
Brannon-Peppas, Lisa *chemical engineer, researcher*
Braybrooke, David *philosopher, educator*
Breen, John Edward *civil engineer, educator*
Brewer, Thomas Bowman *retired university president*
Brigham, Ben M. *oil industry executive*
Brock, James Rush *chemical engineering educator*
Brockett, Oscar Gross *theater educator*
Bronaugh, Edwin Lee *electromagnetic compatibility engineer, consultant*
Brown, Norman Donald *history professor*
Brown, Stephen Neal *computer engineer*
Buchanan, Bruce, II, *political science educator*
Burnham, Walter Dean *political science educator*
Burns, Ned Hamilton *civil engineering educator*
Burson, Betsy Lee *librarian*
Bush, Neil *business executive*
Buss, David Michael *psychology educator*
Caldwell, Shirley W. *commissioner*
Cannon, William Bernard *retired university educator*
Cantú, Norma V. *law educator, former federal official*
Cardozier, Virgus Ray *higher education educator*
Carleton, Don Edward *history center administrator, educator, writer*
Carlton, Donald Morrill *research, development and engineering executive*
Carmical, Phil *editor*
Carner, William John *banker*
Carona, John J. *management consultant, state legislator*
Casey, James Francis *management consultant*
Castaldi, Frank James *environmental engineer, consultant*
Causey, Robert Louis *philosopher, educator, consultant*
Churgin, Michael Jay *law educator*
Cindrich, Nick *medical products company executive*
Clark, Charles T(aliferro) *retired business statistics educator*
Clark, Pat English *lawyer*
Clark, Roy Thomas, Jr., *retired chemistry professor, academic administrator*
Clay, Lareatha H. *commissioner*
Cleaves, Peter Shurtleff *foundation official*
Combs, Susan *commissioner of agriculture*
Conine, Ernest *newspaper commentator, writer*
Connor, Geoffrey Scott *state official, lawyer*
Conradt, Jody *basketball coach*
Cook, J(ohn) Rowland *lawyer*
Cooke, Carlton Lee, Jr., *mayor*
Cooper, William Wager *business professor*
Corredor, Mary B. *language educator, consultant, translator*
Coultas, Edward Owen *lawyer*

Cox, Patrick *historian, writer*
Craparo, John S. *information technology executive*
Crenshaw, Ben *professional golfer*
Cruz, Ted *lawyer*
Culp, Joe C(arl) *electronics executive*
Cundiff, Edward William *marketing educator*
Cunningham, Judy Marie *lawyer*
Cunningham, William Hughes *former academic administrator, marketing educator*
Curle, Robin Lea *computer software industry executive*
Cywar, Adam Walter *management engineer*
Danburg, Debra *state legislator*
Danielson, Wayne Allen *journalism and computer science educator*
Davis, Donald Gordon, Jr., *librarian, educator, historian*
Davis, Donald Robert *nutritionist, researcher, consultant*
Davis, Robert Larry *lawyer*
Deal, Ernest Linwood, Jr., *banker*
Decaro, Angelo Anthony, Jr., *data processing executive*
Deisler, Paul Frederick, Jr., *retired oil company executive*
Demond, Walter Eugene *lawyer*
Denius, Franklin Wofford *lawyer*
Denny, Mary Craver *state legislator, business owner*
Dewhurst, David *lieutenant governor*
DeWitt-Morette, Cécile *physicist*
Divine, Robert Alexander *history professor*
Dodabalapur, Ananth *electrical engineer*
Doenges, Rudolph Conrad *finance educator*
Doluisio, James Thomas *pharmacy educator*
Donley, Dennis W. *lawyer*
Dorsch, Jeffrey Peter *journalist*
Dougal, Arwin Adelbert *electrical engineer, educator*
Dougherty, John Chrysostom, III, *retired lawyer*
Dougherty, Molly Ireland *organization executive*
Douglas, Lucien Zabielski *performing arts educator, theater director*
Douglas, Susan Hickok *music educator*
Drake, Stephen Douglas *psychologist, health facility administrator*
Drongowski, Steve *advertising executive*
Drummond Borg, Lesley Margaret *clinical geneticist*
DuBose, Gaylan Ray *elementary school educator, musician, writer*
Dulles, John Watson Foster *history professor*
Duncombe, Raynor Lockwood *astronomer*
Durbin, Richard Louis, Sr., *healthcare administration consultant*
Dusansky, Richard *economist, educator*
Dyer, Cromwell Adair, Jr., *lawyer, legal association administrator*
Easley, Christa Birgit *nurse, researcher*
Ehrlich, Stacy Wheeler *school fundraiser, administrator*
Ekland-Olson, Sheldon *sociology educator, dean*
Elequin, Cleto, Jr., *retired physician*
Ell, Travis Eugene *electronics engineer*
Epright, Charles John *retired aerospace engineer*
Epstein, Jeremiah Fain *anthropologist, educator*
Erengil, Mehmet Erdal *aeronautical engineer, researcher*
Ersek, Robert Allen *plastic surgeon, inventor*
Erskine, James Lorenzo *physics educator*
Evans, Walter Reed *retired engineering executive, consultant*
Fair, James Rutherford, Jr., *chemical engineering educator, consultant*
Falola, Toyin *history professor*
Farrell, Edmund James *retired English language educator, writer*
Faulkner, Larry Ray *university official, chemistry educator*
Fearing, William Kelly *art educator, artist*
Felsted, Carla Martindell *librarian, writer, editor*
Fernandes, Edward F. *lawyer*
Fink, Vella Mary *lawyer*
Firey, Walter Irving, Jr., *retired sociologist, educator*
Fisher, William Lawrence *geologist, educator*
Fisk, Doris Rosalie Scanlan *volunteer*
Fleeger, David Clark *colon and rectal surgeon*
Folk, Robert Louis *geologist, educator*
Folkers, Karl August *chemistry professor*
Fonken, Gerhard Joseph *retired chemistry educator, academic administrator*
Fonté, Richard W. *university administrator*
Franklin, G(eorge) Charles *retired academic administrator*
Franklin, Robert Drury *oil company executive, lawyer*
Fraser, Troy *development officer, state legislator*
Freeman, Benny Dean *engineering educator*
Freeman, Robert Schofield *musicologist, educator, pianist*
Friedman, Alan Warren *humanities educator*
Friis-Hansen, Dana *museum director*
Fryxell, Greta Albrecht *marine botany educator, oceanographer*
Furlong, Richard W. *structural engineer, educator*
Galinsky, Gotthard Karl *classicist, educator*
Gangstad, John Erik *lawyer*
Garner, Harvey Louis *computer scientist, consultant, electrical engineering educator*
Garwood, William Lockhart *judge*
Gates, Charles Woodley, Sr., *city official*
Gau, George W. *dean*
Gentle, Kenneth William *physicist*
George, Walter Eugene, Jr., *architect*
Gibbins, Bob *lawyer*
Gibson, Jerry Leigh *oil company executive*
Gillman, Leonard *mathematician, educator*
Gimble, Johnny *country musician*
Girling, Robert George William, III, *business owner*
Glade, William Patton, Jr., *economics professor*
Glenn, Norval Dwight *sociologist, educator*
Gloyna, Earnest Frederick *environmental engineer, educator*
Godfrey, Cullen Michael *lawyer, academic administrator*
Goines, Patrick L. *historian, educator*
Golden, Edwin Harold *insurance company executive*
Golden, Kimberly Kay *critical care nurse*
Goldstein, E. Ernest *lawyer, consultant*
Golemon, Ronald Kinnan *lawyer*
Gomes, Norman Vincent *retired industrial engineer*
Gonzalez, Raul A. *retired state supreme court justice, lawyer*
Gould, Lewis Ludlow *historian, educator*

Baker, Mary Alice *communication educator, consultant*
Black, Robert Allen *lawyer*
Brailsford, June Evelyn *musician, educator*
Brentlinger, William Brock *college dean*
Brooks, Jack Bascom *former congressman*
Burgess, Don R. *judge*
Chiou, Paul C.J. *statistician, educator*
Cobb, Howell *federal judge*
Doblin, Stephen Alan *academic administrator, mathematician, educator*
Dowell, James Dale *lawyer*
Dryden, Woodson E. *lawyer*
Gagne, Mary *academic administrator*
Hargove, William Richard *education educator, lawyer*
Hawkins, Emma B. *humanities educator*
Hopper, Jack Rudd *chemical engineering educator*
Janak, Robert Louis *foreign language educator*
Johnson, Leanne *lawyer*
Koehn, Enno *engineering educator, researcher*
Lord, Evelyn Marlin *mayor*
Lozano, Jose *nephrologist*
McCord, Michael David *anesthesiologist*
Morales, Emmitt *mechanical consultant*
Newton, John Wharton, III, *lawyer*
Nguyen, Nhung Thanh *psychologist, educator*
Orwig, Matthew Dane *lawyer*
Roth, Lane *communications educator*
Scofield, Louis M., Jr., *lawyer*
Smith, Floyd Rodenback *retired utilities executive*
Sooudi, Matthew M. *retired surgeon*

Bedford
Champney, Raymond Joseph *advertising and marketing executive, consultant*
Farhat, Georges Antoun *anesthesiologist*
Horvat, Vashti *online marketing consultant*
Owens, Merle Wayne *executive search consultant*

Bedias
Williamson, Norma Beth *adult education educator*

Beeville
Switzer, Linda Thrall *music educator*

Bellaire
Haywood, Theodore Joseph *physician, educator*
Hollrah, David *lawyer*
Jacobus, Charles Joseph *lawyer, title company executive, writer*
Lilienstern, O. Clayton *lawyer, educator*
Lundy, Victor Alfred *architect, educator*
Mayo, Clyde Calvin *psychologist, educator*
Pokorny, Alex Daniel *psychiatrist*
Soffar, William Douglas *lawyer*
Streeter, Kevin D. *management consultant*
Wisch, David John *structural engineer*

Bellville
Borgeson, Earl Charles *law librarian, educator*
Neely, Robert Allen *retired ophthalmologist*

Belton
Burrows, Jon Hanes *lawyer*
Guess, David Lynn *education educator*
Shoemaker, Robert Morin *retired army officer, county government official*
Smith, Marcia K. *government agency administrator*
Wood, Connie Garrison *music educator*

Bertram
Albert, Susan Wittig *writer, English educator*

Blanco
Dudley, Brooke Fitzhugh *educational consultant*

Boerne
Daugherty, Linda Hagaman *real estate company executive*
Goode, Bobby Claude *retired secondary education educator, writer*
Mitchelhill, James Moffat *retired civil engineer*
Morton, Michael Ray *retail company consultant*
Price, John Randolph *writer*
Richmond, James Ellis *retired restaurant company executive*
Wittmer, James Frederick *preventive medicine physician, educator*

Bogata
Marris, Roy O. *agriculturist, consultant*

Bonham
Gerner, Leonard Arthur *elementary school educator, minister*
Sarantakos, Lynell Moss *agricultural products executive*
Youree, Cheryl Ann *secondary school educator*

Borger
Edmonds, Thomas Leon *lawyer, management consultant*
Strecker, Judy Ellen *music educator*

Breckenridge
Reaugh, Orland H. *oil industry executive*

Brenham
Moorman, Richard Hal, IV, *lawyer*
Pipes, Paul Ray *county commissioner*
Rothermel, James Douglas *retired finance educator*
Zientek, Linda Reichwein *mathematician, educator*

Brooks AFB
Caldwell, John Alvis, Jr., *experimental psychologist*
Patterson, John C. *clinical psychology researcher*

Brownfield
Denison, James Dickey *retired broadcasting executive*

Brownsville
Adams, William Leigh *history professor*
Boze, Betsy Vogel *dean, marketing professional, educator*
Chamberlain, Steven Paul *special education educator*
Ferrier, Douglas M. *librarian*
Fitzpatrick, John J. *bishop*
Fleming, Tommy Wayne *lawyer*
Garcia, Juliet Villarreal *university administrator*
Gómez, Carlos Guillermo *artist, educator, curator*
Imperial, Henry L. *internist*
Pena, Raymundo Joseph *bishop*
Santa-Coloma, Bernardo *secondary school educator, counselor*
Soldan, Angelika *philosopher, political scientist, educator*
Wagner, Mary Satterwhite *education educator*
Walss, Rodolfo J. *obstetrician-gynecologist, artist*
Weisfeld, Sheldon *lawyer*
Yi, Taeil *mathematician, educator*
Zdansky, Janice Cecelia *mathematician*

Brownwood
Banks, Patricia Anne *music educator, minister*
Bell, Mary E. Beniteau *accountant*
Bell, William Woodward *lawyer*
Hopp, Glenn *literature educator*
Simmons, Marsha Thrift *science and reading educator, musician*
Weeks, Patsy Ann Landry *librarian, educator*

Bryan
Anderson, Frank Gist, Jr., *ophthalmologist, educator*
Branson, Robert Earl *marketing economist*
Brilliant, Alan Donald *publishing executive, writer*
Bryant, Keith Lynn, Jr., *history professor*
Buckley, John Joseph, Jr., *health care executive*
Dirks, Kenneth Ray *pathologist, medical educator, army officer*
Guitry, Loraine Dunn *community health nurse*
Hanks, Clay David *academic administrator*
Lusas, Edmund William *food processing research executive*
Milford, Murray Hudson *retired soil science educator*
Miller, Thomas Eugene *lawyer, writer*
Owens, Harold B. *former state agency consultant*
Parrott, Thena Elizabeth *nurse educator*
Samson, Charles Harold, Jr., (Car Samson) *retired engineering educator, consultant*
Smith, Elouise Beard *restaurant owner*
Smith, Steven Lee *judge*
Strong, Stephen Andrew *lawyer*
Valdez-Flores, Ciriaco *risk assessment consultant*

Buffalo
Standley, John Robert *city official*

Bullard
Morley, William George *retired military officer, educator*

Bulverde
Blasingim, Charlotte Oren DeShazor *counselor, consultant*

Burleson
Ballard, Barry Lynn *poet*

Burton
Knauss, Robert Lynn *international business educator, corporate executive*

Calvert
Alemán, Marthanne Payne *environmental planner, consultant*

Camp Wood
Triplett, William Carryl *physician, researcher*

Canyon
Long, Russell Charles *academic administrator*
Peddie, Ian A. *language educator*
Sheffield, Jovonna Michele *music educator*
Thoman, Roy Edward *political scientist, educator*
Welch, Reed Lynn *political scientist, educator*

Canyon Lake
Bowden, Virginia Massey *librarian*

Carrollton
Hart, Elizabeth Ann *foundation administrator*
Heath, Jinger L. *cosmetics executive*
Hill, B. Don *office interiors company executive*
Hulbert, Paul William, Jr., *paper, lumber company executive*
Johnson, James L. *telecommunications industry executive*
Kaiser, Robert A. *telecommunications industry executive*
Kelly, Ralph Whitley *emergency physician, health facility administrator*
Lieberman-Cline, Nancy *sports commentator, former professional basketball coach, former player*
Lucas, Jay R. *real estate company executive*
Parker, Terry S. *telecommunications industry executive*
Riggs, Arthur Jordy *retired lawyer*
Turner, Bruce Edward *lawyer*
Varner, Bruce H., Jr., *fire department official, educator*
Wang, Peter Zhenming *physicist*
Withrow, Lucille Monnot *nursing home administrator*

Carthage
Brumley, Larry Gene *music educator*

Castroville
Eyre, Pamela Catherine *retired career officer*

Cat Spring
Conner, Warren Wesley *lawyer*

Cedar Hill
Ebozue, Benson Obian *financial analyst*
Hickman, Traphene Parramore *retired library director, storyteller, library and library building consultant*
Shower, Robert Wesley *financial executive*
Stowers, Carlton Eugene *writer*

Cedar Park
Albin, Leslie Owens *biology professor*
Duke, Carol Michiels *personal care industry executive*
Lam, Pauline Poha *library director*
Love, Ben Howard *retired organization executive*

Celina
Willard, Jane *grain company executive*

Chandler
Wilson, Michael Paul *pharmacist*

Channelview
Gower, Bob G. *gas and oil industry executive*
Graves, Thurman B. *minister, counselor*

Chillicothe
Brock, Helen Rachel McCoy *retired mental health and community health nurse*

Chireno
Mayhar, Ardath Frances (Frank Cannon) *author*

Cibolo
Newsom, Melvin Max *retired research company executive*
Smith, Harry Leroy *securities firm executive*
Strojny, Joan Elizabeth *writer*

Cleburne
Bushor, Mark Eldon *pastor, writer, consultant*
Gorman, Charlotte A. *family and consumer sciences agent*

Cleveland
Rice, J. Andrew *management consultant, tree farmer*

Clutch City
Rice, Glen Anthony *professional basketball player*

Coldspring
Bunch, Robert Craig *librarian*

College Station
Adams, H. Richard *dean*
Adkisson, Perry Lee *university system chancellor*
Armstrong, Robert Beall *physiologist, educator*
Arnold, J(ames) Barto, III, *marine archaeologist*
Arnowitt, Richard Lewis *physics educator, researcher*
Bass, George Fletcher *retired archaeology educator*
Bazer, Fuller Warren *science educator, researcher*
Beaver, Bonnie Veryle *veterinarian, educator*
Berg, Robert Raymond *geologist, educator*
Bessler, David A *economist*
Black, Samuel Harold *microbiology and immunology educator*
Bond, Jon Roy *political science educator*
Borlaug, Norman Ernest *agricultural scientist*
Bowen, Ray Morris *academic administrator, engineering educator*
Brown, Robert Dale *wildlife science educator, department head*
Buth, Carl Eugene *civil engineer*
Button, Joe Wade *civil engineer, researcher, consultant*
Calhoun, John C., Jr., *academic administrator*
Cannon, Garland *linguist, educator*
Cantrell, Carol Whitaker *educational administrator*
Carlton, Dean *lawyer*
Carlton, Paul Kendall, Jr., *physician, retired air force officer*
Christiansen, James Edward *agricultural educator*
Clayton, Mark J. *architecture educator*
Cocanougher, Arthur Benton *academic administrator*
Cohen, Aaron *aerospace engineer*
Conole, Richard Clement *management consultant*
Conway, Dwight Colbur *chemistry professor*
Cotton, Frank Albert *chemist, educator*
Darensbourg, Marcetta York *chemistry professor*
Dees, William Leslie *veterinary medicine educator*
Dethloff, Henry Clay *historian, educator*
Dickey, Nancy Wilson *chancellor, physician*
Downing, Frances E. *architecture educator*
Drees, Bastiaan Meijer *entomologist*
Dunlap, Thomas R. *historian, educator*
Eaton, Gordon Pryor *geologist, consultant*
Edwards, George Charles, III, *political science educator, writer*
Edwards, Janine C. *educational administrator*
Ehsani, Mehrdad (Mark Ehsani) *electrical engineering educator, consultant*
El-Halwagi, Mahmoud M. *chemical engineer, educator*
Erlandson, David Alan *education administration educator*
Ewing, Richard Edward *mathematics, chemical and petroleum engineering educator*
Ezell, Margaret J. *language educator*
Fletcher, Leroy Stevenson *mechanical engineer, educator*
Furubotn, Eirik Grundtvig *economics professor*
Goodman, David Wayne *research chemist, educator*
Granger, Harris Joseph *physiologist, educator*
Greenhut, Melvin Leonard *economist, educator*
Gunn, Clare Alward *travel consultant, writer, retired educator*
Hall, Kenneth Richard *chemical engineering educator, consultant*
Hall, Timothy Couzens *biology professor, consultant*
Hann, Roy William, Jr., *civil engineer, educator*
Hardy, John Christopher *physicist, researcher*
Harner, James Lowell *English language educator*
Hesby, John Howard *agricultural educator*
Hise, Richard Todd *marketing professional, educator, consultant*
Huang, Chang-Shan *landscape architect, educator*
Ibragimov, Akif *research scientist, educator*
Isdale, Charles Edwin *chemical engineer*
Jackson, Thomas O. *real estate appraiser, urban planner*
Jansen, Dennis William *economics educator, consultant*
Jayasuriya, Suhada *mechanical engineering educator*
Kainthla, Ramesh Chand *manufacturing executive*
Kier, Ann Burnette *pathologist*
Knutson, Ronald Dale *economist, educator, academic administrator*
Kohel, Russell James *geneticist*
Kunze, Otto Robert *retired agricultural engineering educator*
Kuo, Way *industrial engineer, researcher*
Laane, Jaan *chemistry professor*
Lee, William John *petroleum engineering educator, consultant*
Lowery, Lee Leon, Jr., *civil engineer*
Lu, Mi *computer engineer, educator*
Lynn, Laurence Edwin, Jr., *university administrator, educator*
Lytton, Robert Leonard *civil engineer, educator*
Mannan, M. Sam *chemical engineer, educator, consultant*
Martin, Carol Jacquelyn *artist, educator*
Mathewson, Christopher Colville *engineering geologist, educator*
McCallum, Roderick Eugene *dean, microbiologist*
McCrady, James David *veterinarian, educator*
McIntyre, John Armin *physics educator*
Meier, Kenneth John *political scientist*
Mercer, Melvin Ray *electrical engineer, educator*
Mohamed, Ahmed A. *chemist, researcher*
Monroe, Haskell Moorman, Jr., *retired university educator*
Moroney, John Rodgers *economist, educator*
Nachman, Ronald James *research chemist*
Natowitz, Joseph B. *chemistry educator, research administrator*
Nederman, Cary Joseph *political scientist, director*
Neill, William Harold, Jr., *biological science educator, researcher*
Nobles, Maria Morgun *soil scientist, researcher*
O'Connor, Rod *chemist, consultant, inventor*
Page, Robert Henry *engineering educator, researcher*
Painter, John Hoyt *electrical engineer*
Palen, Joseph William *chemical process research company executive*
Parnell, Calvin Boyd, Jr., *agricultural engineering educator*
Patton, Alton DeWitt *electrical engineering consultant*
Prescott, John Mack *biochemist, retired university administrator*
Prior, David B. *academic administrator*
Reddy, J. N. *mechanical engineering educator*
Reed, Raymond Deryl *architect*
Regan, J. Thomas *architecture educator*
Reid, Robert Osborne *oceanographer*
Richardson, Herbert Heath *mechanical engineer, educator, institute director*
Riskowski, Gerald Lee *engineering educator*
Sadoski, Mark Christian *education educator*
Safe, Stephen H. *science educator*
Saving, Thomas Robert *economics educator, consultant*
Schunicht, Shannon Anthony *retired army officer, politician*
Scott, Alastair Ian *chemistry professor*
Seyed-Yagoobi, Jamal *mechanical engineering educator*
Shepley, Mardelle McCuskey *architect, educator*
Sikes, Paul Leon *music educator*
Slocum, Richard Copeland (R.C. Slocum) *university athletic coach*
Steffy, John Richard *nautical archaeologist, educator*
Storey, J. Benton *horticulturist, educator*
Strawser, Jerry *dean*
Sue, Hung-Jue *engineer, educator*
Tiffany-Castiglioni, Evelyn *biomedical science educator, researcher*
Turner, Nancy Delane *nutritionist, educator, researcher*
Unterberger, Betty Miller *history educator, writer*
Vandiver, Frank Everson *institute administrator, former university president, author, educator*
Vandiver, Renee Lillian Aubry *interior designer, architectural preservator*
Van Riper, Paul Pritchard *political science educator*
Weese, John Augustus *mechanical engineer, educator*
Wichern, Dean William *business educator*
Wild, James Robert *biochemistry and genetics educator*
Wilson, Don Whitman *retired archivist, historian*
Woodcock, David Geoffrey *architect, educator*
Zheng, Qi *statistician, biomathematician*

Colleyville
Bush, Holly Newsom *management consultant*
Donnelly, Barbara Schettler *retired medical technologist*
Hodgell, Murlin Ray *university dean*
Self, Mark Edward *communications consultant*
Tigue, Virginia Beth (Ginny Tigue) *volunteer*
Whittenberg, Ira Orville *lawyer*

Commerce
Avard, Stephen Lewis *finance educator*
Carraher, Shawn Michael *management educator*
Chang, Fenia I-fen *music educator, pianist*
Linck, Charles Edward, Jr., *English language educator*
Scott, Joyce Alaine *university official*

Conroe
Bowersox, Thomas H. *lawyer*
Gray, Janet Ethel *elementary school educator*
Harrison, Paula Jean *music educator*
Marsh, Sue Ann *special education educator*
Mitchell, Robert James *petroleum company executive*
Nachman, Joseph Frank *retired metallurgical consultant*
Sowers, Amelia Barnet *speech and language pathologist*

Coppell
Griffin, Jim *secondary school educator*
McCally, Charles Richard *construction company executive, consultant, mathematician, educator*
Williams, Gretchen Minyard *food store executive*

Copperas Cove
Haas, Lu Ann *counselor*

Corpus Christi
Abdelsamad, Moustafa Hassan *dean*
Alberts, Harold *lawyer*
Allison, Joan Kelly *music educator, pianist*
Angell, Ellen *interior designer*
Benner, Richard Walter *oil company executive, geologist, engineer*
Berkebile, Charles Alan *geology educator, hydrogeology researcher*
Birmingham, Patrick J. *newspaper executive*
Boyle, Dennis Joseph, III, *computer company executive*
Branscomb, Harvie, Jr., *lawyer*
Cassidy, Jack *academic administrator, educator*
Cook, Kenneth Ray *radiologist*
Coover, Ann E. *lawyer*
Cox, William Andrew *cardiovascular thoracic surgeon*

Cutlip, Randall Brower *retired psychologist, university president emeritus*
Davis, Martin Clay *lawyer, professor*
DuVall, Lorraine *recreation center owner*
Finley, George Alvin, III, *wholesale executive*
Fleischer, Daniel *minister, religious organization administrator*
Foster, Bayard Everson *writer*
Fregoso, Marco Antonio *advertising producer, director*
French, Dorris Towers Bryan *volunteer*
Haas, Paul Raymond *petroleum company executive*
Harper, Sandra Stecher *university administrator*
Head, Hayden Wilson, Jr., *judge*
Hunter, Jack E. *judge*
Jack, Janis Graham *judge*
Kane, Sam *meat company executive*
Kylstra, Johannes Arnold *physician*
Leon, Rolando Luis *lawyer*
Lim, Alexander Rufasta *neurologist, clinical investigator, clinical neurophysiologist, educator, writer*
Long, Ralph Stewart *clinical psychologist*
Norman, Wyatt Thomas, III, *landman, consultant*
Paulson, Bernard Arthur *oil company executive, consultant*
Rios, Jo Marie *political science educator*
Sisley, Nina Mae *physician, public health service officer*
Snouffer, Nancy Kendall *English and reading educator*
Stanford, Jane Herring *management consultant and educator, author*
Stowers, Russell Brent *physical therapy educator*
Stukenberg, Michael Wesley *lawyer*
Tagle, Hilda Gloria *former judge*
Van Burkleo, Bill Ben *osteopath, emergency physician*
Wojcik, John Casimir *music educator, director*
Wood, James Allen *retired lawyer*
Wooster, Robert *history professor*
Worden, Elizabeth Ann *artist, author, comedy writer, singer, musician, playwright, screenwriter*

Corsicana
Carroll, Ray Dean, Sr., *veterinarian*
Dyer, James Mason, Jr., *investment company executive*

Crockett
Gibbs, James Howard *broadcast executive*

Crowley
Sizemore, Deborah Lightfoot *writer, editor*

Cypress
Heath, Frank Bradford *retired dentist*
Hlozek, Carole Diane Quast *finance company executive*

Dallas
Aars, Rallin James *executive management, business development, marketing, communications, strategic planning, consultant*
Abney, Frederick Sherwood *lawyer*
Acker, Rodney *lawyer*
Ackerman, Deborah *lawyer*
Ajaev, Vladimir S. *mathematician, educator*
Al-Hashimi, Ibtisam *oral surgeon, educator*
Allen, Terry Devereux *retired urologist*
Alvey, David Lynn *advertising executive, artist, curator, poet*
Anderson, Barbara McComas *lawyer*
Anderson, E. Karl *lawyer*
Anderson, Ron Joe *health facility administrator, internist, educator*
Anglin, Michael Williams *lawyer*
Anim-Appiah, Kofi Dankwa *electrical engineer, researcher*
Arizaga, Nicolas Antonio *insurance company executive*
Arpey, Gerard J. *air transportation executive*
Atkinson, Bill *artistic director*
Attanasio, John Baptist *dean, law educator*
Augur, Marilyn Hussman *distribution executive*
Azcarraga, Gaston *hotel executive*
Babcock, Charles Lynde, IV, *lawyer*
Baggett, Steven Ray *lawyer*
Baggett, W. Mike *lawyer*
Bailon, Gilbert *newspaper editor*
Baker, James Edward *city planner*
Baker, James Guy *health facility administrator*
Banchereau, Jacques *health facility administrator*
Bangs, Nelson A. *lawyer*
Barnes, John R. *petroleum company executive*
Barnes, Robert Vertreese, Jr., *masonry contractor executive*
Baron, Frederick M. *lawyer*
Barr, Richard Stuart *computer science and management science educator*
Barrett, Colleen Crotty *airline executive*
Bartlett, Richard Chalkley *writer, conservationist*
Bashour, Fouad Anis *cardiology educator*
Bates, Barry Leon *biology professor*
Bayne, James Elwood *investor and financial consultant*
Beane, Jerry Lynn *lawyer*
Beck, Jay M. *gynecologist*
Beer, James A. *air transportation executive*
Berbary, Maurice Shehadeh *physician, military officer, hospital administrator, educator*
Bergstresser, Paul Richard *dermatologist, educator*
Berry, Phil Hunter *orthopedic surgeon*
Bersano, Bob *newspaper editor*
Best, Robert Wayne *gas transmission company executive, lawyer*
Betts, Dianne Connally *economist, educator*
Beuttenmuller, Rudolf William *lawyer*
Bick, Rodger Lee *hematologist, researcher, oncologist, educator*
Bickel, John W., II, *lawyer*
Birkeland, Bryan Collier *lawyer*
Bishop, Gene Herbert *financial corporate executive*
Blanchette, James Grady, Jr., *lawyer*
Blankenbaker, Zarina *adult education educator, consultant*
Blessen, Karen Alyce *freelance/self-employed journalist, artist*
Blinn, Mark A. *consumer products company executive*
Bliss, Robert Harms *lawyer*
Blomquist, Preston Howard *ophthalmologist*
Blue, J(ohn) Ronald *evangelical mission executive*
Blumenthal, Karen *newspaper executive*
Bockstruck, Lloyd DeWitt *librarian*
Bolton, Terrell *protective services official*
Bond, Myron Humphrey *investment executive*
Bonesio, Woodrow Michael *lawyer*
Bonner, Cathy *foundation administrator*
Bonte, Frederick James *radiologist, educator, physician*
Boswell, George Marion, Jr., *orthopedist, health care facility administrator*
Bowman, Kenneth Howard *sales executive, marketing professional*
Boyle, Jane J. *federal judge, lawyer*
Brachman, Malcolm K. *oil company executive*
Bracken, Frank D. *retail executive*
Bradford, William Edward *oil field equipment manufacturing company executive*
Bradley, Jean Marie *lawyer*
Bradley, John Andrew *hospital management company executive*
Brady, Jack Edgar *lawyer*
Braun, Susan J. *foundation administrator*
Brierley, Harold M. *advertising executive*
Briesch, Richard Allen *finance educator*
Bright, Harvey R. *petroleum corporation executive*
Brin, Royal Henry, Jr., *lawyer*
Brinker, Norman E. *restaurant company executive*
Bronstein, Fred *orchestra executive*
Brooks, Douglas H. *food service executive*
Brooks, Edgar R. (Dick Brooks) *utility company executive*
Brooks, James Elwood *geologist, educator*
Brown, Benjamin A. *investment advisor*
Brown, Colleen *broadcast executive*
Brown, Lonnie *utility company executive*
Brown, Michael Stuart *geneticist, educator, science administrator*
Brown, Phillip James *systems engineer*
Brown, Stephen Bryan *real estate editor*
Bruene, Warren Benz *electronic engineer*
Bryant, John Wiley *former congressman*
Bryant, L. Gerald *management consultant*
Buchholz, Donald Alden *stock brokerage company executive*
Bucy, J. Fred, Jr., *retired electronics company executive*
Bumpas, Stuart Maryman *lawyer*
Burke, William Temple, Jr., *lawyer*
Burns, Alton Jay *plastic surgeon*
Burns, Sandra *lawyer, educator*
Burns, Scott *columnist*
Burnside, John Wayne *medical educator, university official*
Busbee, Kline Daniel, Jr., *law educator, lawyer*
Buschang, Peter Heinz *dental educator*
Bushey, Marilyn *communications executive*
Byrd, Henry Stephenson *plastic surgeon, educator*
Byrne, Susan M. *investment company executive*
Byrne, Tim *real estate company executive*
Caetano, Raul *psychiatrist, educator*
Cain, Sally H. *federal agency administrator*
Calado, Miguel Maria *food company executive*
Campaigne, Linda Mary *special education educator*
Campbell, Kevin P. *oil industry executive*
Cantrell, Scott *newspaper music critic*
Carl, Robert E. *retired marketing company executive*
Carman, George Henry *retired physician*
Carnes, Joseph Sydney *clergyman*
Carpenter, Gordon Russell *retired lawyer, banker*
Carson, Jo Ann Simon *dietitian*
Carson, Virginia Hill *oil and gas executive*
Case, Thomas Louis *lawyer*
Castagna, Vanessa J. *retail executive*
Cavanagh, Harrison Dwight Dwight *ophthalmic surgeon, medical educator*
Cave, Skip *information technology executive*
Charriere, Suzanne *architectural firm executive*
Chase, J. Scott *Lawyer (corporate)*
Chawner, Lucia Martha *language educator*
Chen, Zhangxin John *mathematics professor*
Chimbel, Bob *advertising executive*
Cirilo, Amelia Medina *educational consultant, supervisor*
Clark, Robert Murel, Jr., *lawyer*
Cline, Bobby James *insurance company executive*
Clinkscale, Martha *music educator, researcher*
Cloud, Robert Royce *surgeon*
Cloutman, Edward Bradbury, III, *lawyer*
Cochran, George Calloway, III, *retired bank executive, lawyer*
Cochran, Kendall Pinney *economics professor*
Cochran, Mona Sheinfeld *economics educator, consultant*
Cockerham, Sidney Joe *professional society administrator*
Coldwell, Philip Edward *financial consultant*
Cole, James S. *dean, dental educator*
Coleman, Robert Winston *lawyer*
Comini, Alessandra *art historian, educator*
Conant, Allah B., Jr., *lawyer*
Cook, Gary Raymond *university president, clergyman*
Copley, Edward Alvin *lawyer*
Countryman, Edward Francis *historian, educator*
Cover, Kathi A. *lawyer*
Cowart, T(homas) David *lawyer*
Cox, James William *retired newspaper executive*
Cox, Rody P(owell) *medical educator, internist*
Creany, Cathleen Annette *television station executive*
Creel, Luther Edward, III, *lawyer*
Crichton, Thomas, IV, *lawyer*
Crockett, Robert, Dodee Frost *brokerage firm executive*
Crotty, Robert Bell *lawyer*
Crow, F. Trammell *real estate company executive*
Crowley, James Worthington *retired lawyer, business consultant, investor*
Cruikshank, Thomas Henry *energy services and engineering executive*
Crusemann, F(rederick) Ross *advertising agency official*
Cuban, Mark *professional sports team executive, Internet company executive*
Curran, G. Michael *lawyer*
Dalton, Harry Jirou, Jr., (Jerry Dalton) *public relations executive*
Daly, David Michael *neuroscientist, computer scientist, information technology executive*
Daly, Gail M. *law librarian, educator*
Daves, Don Michael *minister*
Davis, Clarice McDonald *lawyer*
Davis, Daisy Sidney *history professor*
Davis, John F., III, *travel company executive*
Davis, Nancy *real estate company executive*
Dawson, Edward Joseph *merger and acquisition executive*
Day, Maurice Jerome *automobile parts distributing company executive*
Dealey, Lynn Townsend *artist*
Decherd, Robert William *newspaper and broadcasting executive*
Dedman, Robert Henry *sales executive*
Dee, Ronda *poet, photographer, small business owner*
Dees, Tom Moore, II, *internist*
DelHomme, Beverly Ann *lawyer*
Demarest, Sylvia M. *lawyer*
Diaz Meyer, Cheryl *photojournalist*
Dicus, Brian George *lawyer*
Dieste, Tony *marketing professional*
Dillon, David Anthony *editor, educator*
Dillon, Donald Ward *management consultant*
Dir, Dave *professional soccer coach*
Doke, Marshall J., Jr., *lawyer*
Doran, Mark Richard *real estate financial executive*
Dozier, David Charles, Jr., *marketing public relations and advertising executive*
Dufner, Edward Joseph *editor*
Dumerer, Lorraine JoAnne Lori *social studies educator, clinician, consultant*
Dunn, Robert *food products executive*
Durham, Michael Jonathan *investment professional*
Dutton, Diana Cheryl *lawyer*
Duvall, William (Bill) C. *real estate company executive*
Dyess, Bobby Dale *lawyer*
Dykeman, Alice Marie *public relations executive*
Dykes, Virginia Chandler *occupational therapist, educator*
Early, James *education educator*
Eaton, Michael William *lawyer, educator*
Eberhart, Robert Clyde *biomedical engineering educator, researcher*
Echols, Leldon E. *construction executive*
Edmondson, James Howard *investor, former insurance executive*
Edwards, Barry *leasing company executive*
Edwards, Warren D. *computer company executive*
Eichenwald, Heinz Felix *physician*
Einspruch, Burton Cyril *psychiatrist*
Elkins-Elliott, Kay *law educator*
Eller, Timothy R. (Tim Eller) *real estate company executive, construction executive*
Ellis, Alfred Wright (Al Ellis) *lawyer*
Ellis, James Alvis, Jr., *lawyer*
Ellis, June B. *human resource consultant*
Emery, Herschell Gene *lawyer*
England, Julie Spicer *computer company executive*
Engles, Gregg L. *food company executive*
Ernest, Michael A. *real estate company executive*
Esqueda, Octavio Javier *religious studies educator*
Essary, Andrew Charles *philosophy educator, financial analyst*
Estabrook, Ronald Winfield *chemistry professor*
Etgen, Ann *ballet educator, artistic director, choreographer*
Ethridge, Joseph Alfred *manufacturing executive (heavy)*
Evans, Dvorah A. *organization executive, professional organizer*
Evans, Linda Perryman *foundation adminstrator*
Everbach, Otto George *lawyer*
Fanning, Barry Hedges *lawyer*
Farell, Dan *utilities executive*
Farquhar, Robert Michael *lawyer*
Fegan, Jeffrey P. *airport executive*
Feiner, Joel S. *psychiatrist*
Feld, Alan David *lawyer*
Feldman, H. Larry *lawyer*
Fenner, Suzan Ellen *lawyer*
Fielder, Charles Robert *oil industry executive*
Fifield, William O. *lawyer*
Figari, Ernest Emil, Jr., *lawyer, educator*
Fino, Arthur F. *food products executive*
Finston, Felicia A. *lawyer*
Fisher, Richard Welton *investor, ambassador*
Fix, Douglas Martin *electrical engineer*
Flatt, Adrian Ede *surgeon*
Flegle, Jim L. *lawyer*
Flood, Joan Moore *paralegal*
Fontana, Robert Edward *electrical engineering educator, retired air force officer*
Fordtran, John Satterfield *physician*
Forward, Gordon E. *former manufacturing executive*
Foster, Daniel Willett *medical educator*
France, Newell Edwin *former hospital administrator, consultant*
Frank, Paula Feldman *business executive*
Frank, Steven Neil *chemist*
Free, Mary Moore *biological and medical anthropologist*
French, Joseph Jordan, Jr., *lawyer*
Frenkel, Eugene Phillip *physician*
Freytag, Sharon Nelson *lawyer*
Friedberg, Errol Clive *pathology educator, researcher*
Friedheim, Jan V. *education administrator*
Friedheim, Stephen Bailey *educational consultant*
Frisbie, Curtis Lynn, Jr., *lawyer*
Fromberg, Barry A. *food products executive*
Fulsham, Rawles *manufacturing executive*
Gafford, Ronald J. *construction executive*
Galante, Joseph A. *bishop*
Galvin, Charles O'Neill *law educator*
Gant, Norman Ferrell, Jr., *obstetrician, gynecologist, educator*
Gantt, James Raiford *thoracic surgeon*
Gardner, Stephen Henry *lawyer*
Garner, Bryan Andrew *law educator, consultant, writer*
Garreans, Leonard Lansford *protective services official, criminal justice professional*
Gass, Wanda *engineering executive*
Gaut, C. Christopher *gas company executive*
Gibbs, James Alanson *geologist*
Gibbs, Jarrell H. *utilities executive*
Gibby, Mabel Enid Kunce *psychologist*
Gifford, Porter William *retired construction materials manufacturing company executive*
Giggleman, Gene Felton *academic administrator, veterinarian*
Gillett, Grover *author*
Gilman, Alfred Goodman *pharmacologist, educator*
Gilmore, Jerry Carl *lawyer*
Glancy, Walter John *lawyer*
Glatstein, David *investment company executive*
Glazer, Bennett J. *wholesale distribution executive*
Glazer, Robert S. *wholesale distribution executive*
Glendenning, Don Mark *lawyer*
Glines, Carroll Vane, Jr., *magazine editor*
Gold, Christina A. *cosmetics company executive*
Goldmann, James Allen *healthcare consultant*
Goldstein, Joseph Leonard *physician, medical educator, molecular genetics scientist*
Goodman, John C. *think-tank executive*
Goodstein, Barnett Maurice *lawyer*
Goolsby, Michelle *lawyer, food products executive*
Gores, Christopher Merrel *lawyer*
Gossen, Emmett Joseph, Jr., *motel chain executive, lawyer*
Govil, Manish Kumar *customer service administrator*
Grahmann, Charles V. *bishop*
Grammer, John Colquitte *cardiologist*
Grant, Joseph Moorman *finance executive*
Gratton, Patrick John Francis *oil company executive*
Green, Jesse Joseph *lawyer*
Griffeth, Landis King *nuclear medicine physician*
Griffin, Randall C. *art historian, educator*
Griffith, Dotty (Dorothy Griffith Stephenson) *journalist, writer*
Griffith, Rachel *neonatologist*
Grimes, David Lynn *communications company executive*
Gross, Gary Neil *allergist, physician*
Gross, Harriet P. Marcus *religious studies and writing educator*
Gruben, William Charles *economist, writer*
Guerin, Dean Patrick *executive*
Gumbiner, Anthony Joseph *investment banker, lawyer*
Guthrie, M. Philip *corporate financial executive*
Guy, L(eona) Ruth *medical educator*
Gyemant, Robert Ernest *diversified financial services company executive, merchant*
Haayen, Richard Jan *university official, insurance company executive*
Hackney, Hugh Edward *lawyer*
Haggar, J. M., III, *retail executive*
Hallam, Robert G. *wholesale distribution executive*
Halpin, James *former retail computer stores executive*
Hamilton, David Lee *sports association administrator, retired environmental company executive*
Hamilton, Wendy J. *foundation administrator*
Hammond, Herbert J. *lawyer, arbitrator, mediator*
Hansen, Eugenia S. *lawyer*
Hansen, John Paul *retired metallurgical engineer*
Hansen, William *educational consultant*
Harasta, Cathy Ann *journalist*
Harbin, John Pickens *oil well company executive*
Harmel, Warren *marketing professional*
Harrison, Frank *former university president*
Hartnett, Thomas Robert, III, *lawyer, author*
Hartnett, Will Ford *lawyer*
Hartt, Grover, III, *lawyer*
Hawkins, H. Ralph *architectural firm executive*
Haworth, Charles Ray *lawyer*
Hay, Betty Jo *civic worker*
Hay, Jess Thomas *retired finance company executive*
Hayes, James Edwin *emergency physician, educator*
Haynes, Catharina D. *judge*
Haynes, Linda C. *nursing educator*
Head, Mark Davies *human resources and employee benefits services executive, consultant*
Hegi, Frederick B., Jr., *mobile home manufacturing executive*
Helm, Phala Aniece *physiatrist*
Henkel, Kathryn Gundy *lawyer*
Hennessy, Daniel Kraft *lawyer*
Henry, Vic Houston *lawyer*
Hernandez, Christine *educational consultant*
Hester, Linda Hunt *retired dean, counseling administrator, sociology educator, physical education educator*
Heydrick, Linda Carol *consulting company executive, editor*
Hicks, Marion Lawrence, Jr., (Larry Hicks) *lawyer*
Hicks, Thomas O. *buyout firm executive, professional baseball team executive*
Higginbotham, Patrick Errol *federal judge*
Hilgemann, Donald William *medical educator*
Hill, Bill *prosecutor*
Hill, Jesse Hoyt *training specialist, economics & business educator*
Hill-Foster, Ialine *retired secondary school educator*
Hinnant, Jerry Herbert *surgeon*
Hinshaw, Chester John *lawyer*
Hirsch, Laurence Eliot *construction executive, mortgage banker*
Hitt, David Hamilton, Sr., *retired hospital executive*
Hofmeister, Kent S. *lawyer*
Hogan, Thomas Victor *insurance company executive*
Holman, James *allergist*
Holmes, Bert Otis E., Jr., *retired editor*
Holmes, James Hill, III, *lawyer*
Honea, Floyd Franklin *lawyer*
Horchow, S(amuel) Roger *marketing consultant*
Horn, Charles L. *construction supplies manufacturing executive*
Houser, Barbara J. *lawyer*
Howland, Grafton Dulany *financial counselor*
Huang, Yen Ti *civil engineer*
Hubach, Joseph F. *electronics executive*
Hudel, Chestella Alvis *athletics educator*
Hudson, C. B., Jr., *insurance company executive*
Huffman, Gregory Scott Combest *lawyer*
Hughes, Vester Thomas, Jr., *lawyer*
Humphreys, Jean Surratt *social sciences educator*
Hunt, Caroline Rose *hotel executive*
Hunt, Ray L. *petroleum company executive*
Hunter, Robert Grams *retired English language educator*
Hurd, Eric Ray *rheumatologist, internist, educator*
Ibach, Robert Daniel, Jr., *library director*
Idris, Ahamed H. *emergency medicine physician*
Jackson, Jimmy Lee *commissioner*
Jancauskas, Don *business executive*
Janzen, Howard E. *communications executive*
Jayson, Melinda Gayle *lawyer*
Jennings, James Burnett *oil company executive*
Jennings, Susan Jane *lawyer*
Jessen, Michael Erik *surgeon, educator*
Jialal, Ishwarlal *medical educator*
Jimenez, Mercy *corporate financial executive*
Jobe, Larry Alton *financial company executive*
Johnson, Jane Elaine *medical educator*
Johnson, Kevin Orlin *publishing executive, writer*
Johnson, Mary Elizabeth *music educator, pianist*

Johnson, Murray H. *optometrist, researcher, consultant, lecturer*
Johnson, Robert Lee, Jr., *physician, educator, researcher*
Jones, Everett Riley, Jr., *oil company executive*
Jones, Lindy Don *lawyer*
Joplin, Julian Mike *lawyer*
Jordan, William Davis *lawyer*
Josal, Lance K. *architectural firm executive*
Kaiser, Fran Elizabeth *endocrinologist, gerontologist*
Kalchev, George Dimitrov *research scientist*
Karandikar, Nitin J. *physician, scientist, educator*
Karayanis, Plato Steven *opera company executive*
Karns, Phyllis J. Spear *dean*
Keithley, Bradford Gene *lawyer*
Kelleher, Herbert David *air transportation executive, lawyer*
Kelley, Terry *financial executive*
Kelly, Gary C. *air transportation executive*
Kelly, Timothy E. *communications executive*
Kemper, Robert Van *anthropologist, educator, minister*
Kennedy, Marc J. *lawyer*
Kent, David Charles *lawyer*
Keown, Michael H. *food products executive*
Kern, Janet Kinnear *neuroscientist*
Kesterson, Ray Brent *college dean, retired air force officer*
Khan, Amanullah *physician*
Kilby, Jack St. Clair *electrical engineer*
Kindberg, Shirley Jane *pediatrician*
King, Mark *computer company executive*
Kinnebrew, Jackson Metcalfe *lawyer*
Kirby, James Edmund, Jr., *theology educator*
Kitner, David N. *lawyer*
Klein, Ronald H. *food products executive*
Kleisner, Frederick J. *hotel executive*
Kobdish, George Charles *lawyer*
Kohl, Kathleen Allison Barnhart *lawyer*
Kolb, Nathaniel Key, Jr., *architect*
Kolli, Sai *publishing executive*
Korba, Robert W. *manufacturing executive*
Kostas, Evans *manufacturing executive*
Kruse, Ann Gray *computer programmer*
Kuhn, Willis Evan, II, *lawyer, mediator*
Kunkle, David M. *police chief*
Kusin, Gary M. *consumer products company executive*
Kutner, Janet *art critic, book reviewer*
Lacy, John Ford *retired lawyer*
Laettner, Christian Donald *professional basketball player*
Lake, Joseph Edward *ambassador*
Lam, Chun Hung *finance educator, consultant*
Lan, Donald Paul, Jr., *lawyer*
Lancaster, Karine R. *city health department administrator*
Lane, Alvin Huey, Jr., *management consultant*
Lang, James Devore, Jr., *ministry executive*
Langdale, Mark *hotel executive*
Lang-Miers, Elizabeth Ann *judge*
LaRovere, Ralph *manufacturing executive*
Lastelick, Jerry *lawyer*
Lawrence, Annette *artist*
Leedom, John Nesbett *distribution company executive, state senator*
Lersch, DeLynden Rife *computer engineering executive*
Lesson, David *photojournalist*
Leven, Stephen H. *human resources professional*
Levenson, Stanley Richard *public relations and advertising executive*
Levin, Hervey Phillip *lawyer, director*
Levin, Richard C. *lawyer*
Lewis, Jerry M. *psychiatrist, educator*
Lichliter, Warren Eugene *surgeon, educator*
Liskow, Frederic Cullen (Ric) *printing company executive*
Lister, George *pediatrician*
Litton, Andrew *musical director*
Love, Sammie L. *administrative assistant, writer*
Lovin, Robin Warren *clergy member, educator*
Lovvorn, Holly *bottling manufacturing executive*
Lowe, Jack, Jr., *manufacturing executive*
Lowe, John Stanley *lawyer, educator*
Lumpkin, John O. *newspaper editor*
Lynch, William Wright, Jr., *investment company executive, engineer*
Lynn, Barbara Michele *judge*
Mackenzie, Nanci *gas company executive*
Maddrey, Willis Crocker *medical educator, internist, academic administrator, consultant, researcher*
Malone, Dan F. *journalist*
Malorzo, Thomas Vincent *lawyer*
Mandeville, Hubert Turner, Jr., *oil company executive*
Mankoff, Ronald Morton *retired lawyer*
March, Kevin P. *electronics executive*
Marentette, Elijah Chandler *health services executive*
Margerison, Richard Wayne *diversified industrial company executive*
Margolin, Solomon Begelfor *pharmacologist, consultant*
Maris, Stephen S. *lawyer, educator*
Maritz, Philip F. (Flip Maritz) *hotel executive*
Marlow, Patricia Bair Bond *realtor*
Marshall, John Harris, Jr., *geologist, oil company executive*
Martin, Boe Willis *lawyer*
Martin, Jack *physician*
Massman, Richard Allan *lawyer*
Matthews, Clark J(io), II, *retail executive, lawyer, retired*
Matthews, Jay Arlon, Jr., *publisher, editor*
McAtee, David Ray *lawyer*
McCartor, Sheila Smith *secondary school educator*
Mc Clelland, Robert Nelson *surgeon, educator*
McCormack, William Arthur *lawyer*
McCurley, Carl Michael *lawyer*
McCurley, Mary Johanna *lawyer*
McDougall, Ronald Alexander *restaurant executive*
Mc Elhaney, John Hess *lawyer*
McElvain, David Plowman *retired manufacturing company financial executive*
McElyea, Jacquelyn Suzanne *accountant, real estate consultant*
McGarry, Charles William *lawyer*
McGowan, Patrick Francis *lawyer*
McGuire, Robert C. *retired federal bankruptcy judge*
McKnight, Joseph Webb *law educator, historian*
McKnight, Steven Lanier *molecular biologist*
McLane, David Glenn *lawyer*
McLane, William Delano *mechanical engineer*
McLean, Lynne Marie *social worker*
McNally, Michael James *electric power industry executive*
McNamara, Anne H. *lawyer, corporate executive*
McTeer, Robert D., Jr., *banker*
McWhorter, Kathleen *orthodontist*
McWilliams, Mike C. *lawyer*
Metzner, Richard *advertising executive*
Meyer, Ferdinand Charles, Jr., *lawyer*
Miers, Harriet E. *lawyer*
Mighell, Kenneth John *lawyer*
Miller, Geraldine (Tincy) *real estate company executive, educational association administrator*
Miller, Jo Carolyn Dendy *family and marriage counselor, educator*
Miller, Laura *mayor, journalist*
Miller, Stewart Ransom *lawyer*
Mills, Jerry Woodrow *lawyer*
Mitchell, A. Joe, Jr., *telecommunications industry executive*
Mitchell, Teddy Lee *physician*
Mittelstet, Stephen *academic administrator*
Mondry, Lawrence N. *retail sales professional*
Mondul, Donald David *patent lawyer*
Moneypenny, Edward William *retail executive*
Mong, Robert William, Jr., *media executive*
Montgomery, Philip O'Bryan, Jr., *pathologist*
Moore, Christopher Robertson Kinley *energy industry consultant*
Moore, Edward Warren *lawyer*
Morgan, Gregory Paul *financial planner*
Moroney, James M., III, *publishing executive, broadcast executive*
Mow, Robert Henry, Jr., *lawyer*
Mueller, Mark Christopher *lawyer*
Mulcahy, Joan Catherine *elementary school educator*
Mullins, Charles Brown *physician, academic administrator*
Murphy, John Carter *economics professor*
Murphy, John Joseph *manufacturing executive*
Murphy, Randall Kent *management consultant*
Murray, John William, Jr., *writer, legal investigator*
Nelson, Donald Arvid (Nellie Nelson) *professional basketball coach*
Nelson, Elaine Edwards *lawyer*
Nelson, Keith Milton *lawyer*
Nevins, William J. *oil and gas brokerage executive, consultant*
New, William Neil *physician, retired naval officer*
Nichols, Henry Louis *lawyer*
Nishi, Yoshio *electronics executive, laboratory administrator*
Nolan, John Michael *lawyer*
Norman, Bobby Don *artist, writer, research scientist*
Norsworthy, Lamar *petroleum company executive*
Nye, Erle Allen *electric power industry executive, lawyer*
O'Bannion, Mindy Martha Martin *nurse*
Odom, Floyd Clark *surgeon*
Oesterreicher, James E. *former department stores executive*
Olson, Cory M. *food products executive*
Olson, Eric N. *molecular biologist, educator*
Osborne, Burl *newspaper publisher, editor*
O'Shea, Karen *public relations executive*
Owen, Daniel Thomas *entrepreneur, venture capitalist*
Pace, Carolina Jolliff *communications executive*
Pakes, Steven P. *medical school administrator*
Palmer, Christine (Clelia Rose Venditti) *operatic singer, pianist, vocal educator*
Parsons, Terry Thomas *psychotherapist, educator*
Patterson, Ronald Paul *publishing company executive, clergyman*
Pauley, Shirley Stewart *religious organization executive*
Pearce, Ronald *retired cosmetic company executive*
Pearson, Robert Lawrence *executive recruiter*
Pederson, Rena *newspaper editor*
Peiser, John George *accountant, consultant*
Pell, Jonathan Laurence *artistic administrator*
Penn, Linda *computer animator*
Perot, H. Ross, Jr., *real estate developer, former sports team executive*
Perry, George Wilson *oil and gas company executive*
Perry, Malcolm Oliver *vascular surgeon*
Peterson, Edward Adrian *lawyer*
Peterson, Eric H. *lawyer, energy executive*
Pew, John Glenn, Jr., *lawyer*
Phelan, Robin Eric *lawyer*
Philipson, Herman Louis, Jr., *investment banker*
Phillips, Betty Lou (Elizabeth Louise Phillips) *writer, interior designer*
Phillips, Margaret A. *pharmacology educator*
Pingree, Bruce Douglas *lawyer*
Pinson, William Meredith, Jr., *pastor, writer, administrator*
Pleasant, James Scott *lawyer*
Plummer, Paul James *energy executive*
Pogue, A Mack *real estate company executive*
Portman, Glenn Arthur *lawyer*
Powell, Boone, Jr., *hospital executive*
Prather, Robert Charles, Sr., *lawyer*
Price, John Aley *lawyer*
Price, Robert Eben *judge*
Prothro, Jerry Robert *lawyer*
Pruessner, David Morgan *lawyer*
Purkey, Thomas Eugene *social worker*
Purnell, Charles Giles *lawyer*
Purnell, Maurice Eugene, Jr., *lawyer*
Quinn, David W. *building company executive*
Quinn, William Francis *investment company executive, accountant*
Race, George Justice *pathology educator*
Raggio, Louise Ballerstedt *lawyer*
Rainey, William E., II, *medical educator*
Rainwater, R. Steven *systems engineer*
Ramsay, Michael Anthony *anesthesiologist*
Rasch, Stephen Christopher *lawyer*
Ray, Bradley Stephen *petroleum geologist*
Read, James Carroll *geneticist educator*
Rees, Frank William, Jr., *architect*
Reid, Langhorne, III, *merchant banker*
Reid, Rust Endicott *lawyer*
Reinert, James A. *entomology educator*
Reynolds, Annette *secondary school educator*
Rhodes, Samuel Earl *writer*
Rich, Jeffrey A. *computer company executive*
Richardi, Ralph Leonard *airline executive*
Richards, Stanford Harvey *advertising agency executive, design studio executive*
Richardson, Dennise Marie *physician assistant*
Riddle, Michael Lee *lawyer*
Ries, Edward Richard *petroleum geologist, consultant*
Ringle, Brett Adelbert *lawyer, petroleum company executive*
Rinne, Austin Dean *retired insurance company executive*
Risley, Tom *aerospace transportation executive*
Roach, John D. *building products company executive*
Roberts, Harry Morris, Jr., *lawyer*
Robertson, Beverly Carruth *retired steel company executive*
Robertson, Ted Zanderson *judge*
Robillard, Donald F., Jr., *gas and oil industry executive*
Robinson, Malcolm S. *lawyer*
Rodgers, John Hunter *lawyer*
Romero, Jorge Antonio *neurologist, educator*
Rosenberg, Roger Newman *neurologist, educator, department chair*
Ross, Elliott M. *pharmacologist, researcher, educator*
Rossel, Cary *corporate financial executive*
Rosson, Glenn Richard *building products and furniture company executive*
Rubottom, Roy Richard, Jr., *retired diplomat and educator, consultant*
Rush, Augustus John *psychiatrist, educator*
Rushton, Lynn Noelle *artist*
Sacco, David J. *neurosurgeon*
Salazar, Ramiro S. *library administrator*
Salazar, Steve *lawyer*
Salyer, Kenneth E. *surgeon*
Sammons, Elaine D. *manufacturing executive*
Samson, Duke Staples *neurosurgeon*
Sanders, Harold Barefoot, Jr., *judge*
Sanders, Rodger *construction executive*
Santos, Charles Daniel *cultural organization administrator*
Schecter, Arnold Joel *public health educator*
Schenkel, Pete *food company executive*
Schneider, Nancy Reynolds *pathologist, educator*
Schreiber, Sally Ann *lawyer*
Schulz, Sandra E. *art educator*
Schulze, Richard Hans *engineering executive, environmental engineer*
Schwartz, Irving Donn *architect*
Schweitzer, Loren Marcus *computer programmer*
Scott, John Roland *business law educator*
See, Robert Fleming, Jr., *lawyer*
Seldin, Donald Wayne *physician, educator*
Selinger, Jerry Robin *lawyer*
Sentell, Susan B. *telecommunications company executive*
Sepuldadl, Lynn *utility company executive*
Shambaugh, Irvin Calvin, Jr., *aptitude test firm executive*
Shapiro, Kenneth N. *neurosurgeon*
Sharp, William Wheeler *geologist*
Shelton, Virginia Kaye *director*
Sherman, Floyd F. *construction executive*
Sherrod, Danny Troy *writer, educator*
Shimer, Daniel Lewis *treasurer*
Shipley, Dan *architect*
Shultz, Brian Michael *diversified financial services company executive*
Sidhu, Sanjiv *information technology executive*
Sidu, Sanjiv *computer software executive*
Siegfried, Tom *newspaper editor*
Simmang, Clifford Liles *surgeon*
Simon, Theodore Ronald *physician, medical educator*
Singer, Robert W. *metallurgist, company executive officer*
Sizer, Phillip Spelman *consultant, retired oil field services executive*
Skaggs, Ronald Lloyd *architect*
Skinner, James E. *corporate financial executive*
Sklar, Frederick H. *neurosurgeon*
Slawter, John David, Jr., *oil company and manufacturing executive*
Sleeman, Donald George *construction executive, contractor*
Sloman, Marvin Sherk *lawyer*
Smerge, Raymond G. *mortgage company executive*
Smiles, Ronald *management educator*
Smith, Barry Samuel *physiatrist*
Smith, Brian *lawyer*
Smith, David Lee *newspaper editor*
Smith, Milton Clark, Jr., *lawyer*
Smith, Nancy Woolverton *journalist, real estate agent, appraiser, antiques broker*
Smith, R. J., Jr., *oil company executive*
Smith, Russell Bryan *lawyer*
Smith, Sue Frances *newspaper editor*
Smith, William Randolph (Randy Smith) *health care management executive*
Snead, Richard Thomas *restaurant company executive*
Solender, Robert Lawrence *real estate executive, retired newspaper executive*
Solomon, Risa Greenberg *clinical social worker, child and family therapist, former entertainment industry executive*
Solomon, William Tarver *general construction company executive*
Sonsteby, Charles M. *food service executive*
Sosa, Kena *primary school educator, writer*
Spears, Robert Fields *lawyer*
Spencer, Mary Helen *interior designer*
Spiegel, Lawrence Howard *advertising executive*
Sprague, Charles Cameron *medical foundation president*
Stackhouse, Jerry *professional basketball player*
Stacy, Dennis William *architect*
Stalcup, Joe Alan *lawyer, clergyman*
Steinberg, Lawrence Edward *lawyer*
Stephens, Richard H. *retired prosecutor*
Stern, Andrew Milton *public relations executive*
Stockard, James Alfred *lawyer*
Stone, Donald James *retired retail executive*
Stone, Karen *theater director*
Stone, Marvin Jules *physician, educator*
Storey, Charles Porter *lawyer*
Strauss, Robert Schwarz *lawyer, former ambassador*
Sudhof, Thomas Christian *molecular genetics educator, neuroscientist*
Sulentic, Robert E. *real estate company executive*
Sundgaard, Arnold Olaf *playwright*
Swift, Dale Matthew *neurosurgeon*
Szygenda, Stephen A. *electrical and computer engineering educator, researcher*
Taliaferro, Ellen *medical educator*
Tannebaum, Samuel Hugo *accountant*
Tansky, Burton *department store executive*
Tarnay, Thomas N. *lawyer*
Taulbee, Thomas Lester *psychotherapist, educator*
Templeton, Richard K. *electronics company executive*
Terry, Marshall Northway, Jr., *English language educator, author*
Thomas, James A. *pediatrician*
Thomas, Paul Lindsley *composer, organist, music director*
Thompson, James Nicholas *medical association administrator*
Thompson, Jesse Eldon *vascular surgeon*
Thompson, Zachary *city health department administrator*
Thomson, Basil Henry, Jr., *lawyer, university general counsel*
Thorne, Carl F. *gas industry executive*
Tinklepaugh, William C. *food products executive*
Tong, Alex Waiming *immunologist*
Trivedi, Madhukar H. *psychiatrist*
True, Roy Joe *lawyer*
Tubb, James Clarence *lawyer*
Tucker, J. Walter, Jr., *steel manufacturing executive*
Tucker, Laurey Dan *lawyer*
Turgeon, Pierre *professional hockey player*
Turknett, James C. *minister*
Turner, Jim L. *bottler manufacturing executive*
Turner, Ralph James *obstetrician, gynecologist*
Turner, Robert Gerald *university president*
Turocy, Catherine *performing company executive*
Tyson, Lisa N. *food products executive*
Uhr, Jonathan William *immunologist, educator, researcher*
Ulrich, Richard William *finance executive*
Unger, Roger Harold *physician, scientist*
Valentine, Foy Dan *clergyman*
Vanatta, John Crothers, III, *physiologist, physician, educator*
Vanderveld, John, Jr., *international business development specialist*
Van Ness, Paul C. *neurologist, educator*
Veach, Robert Raymond, Jr., *lawyer*
Vitetta, Ellen S. *microbiologist educator, immunologist*
Von Kennel, Gary Phillip *marketing company executive*
Waddell, Douglas Howard *family physician*
Walker, Gordon Beverley Moore, Jr., *business educator*
Walkowiak, Vincent Steven *lawyer*
Wallace, Anderson, Jr., *lawyer, educator*
Wang, Xiaodong *biomedical researcher, educator*
Wassenich, Linda Pilcher *retired health policy analyst, fund raiser*
Wasserman, Richard Lawrence *pediatrician, educator*
Waters, Rollie O. *management consultant*
Weakley, Clare George, Jr., *insurance executive, theologian, entrepreneur*
Weinkauf, William Carl *communications executive*
Weitzman, Herbert D. *real estate company executive*
Weprin, Bradley *neurosurgeon*
Westberry, David M. *executive search consultant*
Westfall, Constance Courtney *lawyer*
Wheeler, Edward Norwood *chemical consultant*
Wheeler, M. Cass *health science association administrator*
Whitaker, Elizabeth *lawyer*
White, James Richard *lawyer*
White, Tom Willingham *private investor*
Whitson, James Norfleet, Jr., *retired diversified company executive*
Wilber, Robert Edwin *trade association administrator*
Wildenthal, C(laud) Kern *physician, educator*
Wilder, C. John *energy industry executive*
Wiles, Charles Preston *minister*
Wilk, Stuart *publishing executive*
Williams, Charles Edward *engineer*
Williams, J. McDonald *real estate development company executive*
Williams, Sterling L. *computer software executive*
Willingham, Clark Suttles *lawyer*
Wilson, Catherine Cooper (Kitty Wilson) *communications executive, writer*
Wilson, Claude Raymond, Jr., *lawyer*
Wilson, Jean Donald *endocrinologist, educator*
Wilson, Lawrence Alexander *construction company executive*
Wilson, Richard A. *oil/gas industry support services executive*
Wilson, Trisha *interior architectural designer*
Winters, J(ohn) Otis *retired oil industry consultant*
Wiss, Marvin J. *public relations executive, consultant*
Wolfe, Jane *writer*
Woolley, Bryan (Lowell Bryan Woolley) *author, journalist*
Wrucke-Nelson, Ann C. *elementary school educator*
Wyant, Clyde W., Jr., *manufacturing executive*
Wyly, Charles Joseph, Jr., *corporate executive*
Young, Barney Thornton *lawyer*
Zeilstra, Donald J. *research and development company executive*
Zeitlin, Laurie *printing company executive*
Zhou, Desheng *petroleum engineer*
Zhou, Xin (Joseph Zhou) *medical educator*
Zimmerman, S(amuel) Morton (Mort Zimmerman) *engineering executive*
Zisman, Barry Stuart *lawyer*
Zubov, Sergei *professional hockey player*
Zumwalt, Richard Dowling *flour mill executive*

Danville
Robertson, Rose Marie *cardiologist, educator*

Deer Park
Wester, R. Glen *music educator, director*

Del Rio
Garrett, James William *computer company executive*
Prather, Gerald Luther *management consultant, retired air force officer, judge*

Denton
Belfiglio, Valentine John *political science educator, pharmacist, consultant*

Brown, John Fred *steel company executive*
Carlson, William Dwight *college president emeritus*
Chang, Yongbin *physicist*
Chilton, Bradley Stewart *law educator*
Chrisman, Ronald *publishing executive*
Cooper, John Michael *music educator*
Crawford, Gladys Pauline *microbiologist, educator*
Gabriel, Eberhard John *lawyer, bank executive*
Garcia, Oscar Nicolas *computer science educator*
Golding, Terry David *engineering educator, researcher*
Gough, Clarence Ray *retired designer, educator*
Grigorieva, Ellina *mathematics professor, researcher*
Hurley, Alfred Francis *historian, academic administrator emeritus, retired air force officer*
Kamman, William *historian, educator*
Katsinas, Stephen Gregory *academic administrator, education educator*
Kesterson, David Bert *English language educator*
Lawhon, John E., III, *lawyer, former county official*
Lawhon, Tommie Collins Montgomery *child development and family living educator*
Leung, Paul *psychologist, rehabilitation educator*
Marshall, David Douglas *science educator*
Mauldin, Richard Daniel *mathematics professor*
McCuistion, Robert Wiley *hospital administrator, management consultant, lawyer*
McDonald-West, Sandi MacLean *headmaster, consultant*
McTee, Cindy *classical musician, educator*
Nestler, Eric M. *music educator*
Newell, Charldean *public administration educator*
Nik, Ninfa *language educator*
Pinson, Joseph *education educator, entertainer*
Preston, Thomas Ronald *English language educator, researcher*
Renka, Robert Joseph *computer science educator, consultant*
Ryan, Melbagene T. *retired food and nutrition service director*
Shelton, James Keith *journalism educator*
Siefkin, William Charles *investor, marketing/sales executive, consultant*
Smith, H. Morgan *environmental scientist, educator*
Smith, Howard Wellington *education educator, dean emeritus*
Snapp, Elizabeth *librarian, educator*
Snapp, Harry Franklin *historian, educator*
Staples, Donald Edward *radio, film and television educator*
Swigger, Keith *library and information scientist, educator*
Tanner, Harold Miles *education educator, researcher*
Ver Duin, D'Arlene K. *research scientist*
Waage, Mervin Bernard *lawyer*
Wallace, William Hall *economic and financial consultant*
White, Nora Lizabeth *language educator*
Williams, Cheryl A. *secondary school educator*
Wood, Jane Roberts *writer*

Diboll
Fisher, Richard Forrest *research scientist, department chairman*
Harbordt, Charles Michael *forest products executive*
Jastrow, Kenneth M. *financial executive*

Dripping Springs
Nicholas, Nickie Lee *retired industrial hygienist*
Pellicone, William *artist, sculptor, architect, writer*

Duncanville
Fewel, John Gerrard *government agency administrator, director*
Jenkins, Tony Dean *salesman*

Dyess Afb
Chester, Linnes Lee, Jr., *healthcare association administrator*

Eagle Pass
May, Mitchell Johnson *controller*

East Bernard
Boettcher, Armin Schlick *lawyer, banker*

Edinburg
Cararas, Sandra A. *literature educator*
Grossman, Morley Keith *music educator*
Hannan, Mohammad A. *physicist, researcher*
Hinojosa, Federico Gustavo, Jr., *judge*
Kaynak, Hale *finance educator, researcher*
Nevarez, Miguel A. *academic administrator*
Wilson, Bruce Keith *men's health nurse*
Zeng, Liang *education educator*

Egypt
Wynn, John Thomas *retired academic administrator, farming executive, economic consultant, oil and gas producer*

El Paso
Allen, Anna J. *chiropractor*
Armitage, Shelley Sue *American studies educator*
Bailey, Kenneth Kyle *history educator*
Bang, John Jongchun *environmental scientist, researcher*
Beard, Jane Alida *retired accountant*
Benning, Mary Etzold *interior designer*
Briones, David *judge*
Burnham, Albert David *education educator, researcher, historian, consultant*
Cassidy, Richard Thomas *hotel executive, defense industry consultant, retired army officer*
Clement-Fouts, Shirley George *educational services executive*
Crossen, John Jacob *radiologist, educator*
Cummings, Patricia Anne (Felicitas Cruz) *writer, journalist, poet*
Dailey, Maceo Crenshaw, Jr., *humanities educator*
Deerman, Ruth Gillett *sales executive*
Deutsch, Sandra McGee *historian, educator*
Dinsmoor, Robert Davidson *lawyer, judge*
Dombrowski, Frank Paul, Jr., *pharmacist*
Edmonds, Velma McInnis *nursing educator*
Erskine, William Crawford *retired academic administrator, accountant, health facility administrator*
Fahy, Michael P. *civil and environmental engineer*
Feuille, Richard Harlan *lawyer, director*
Foged, Leslie Owen *mathematician, educator*
Fullerton, Thomas Mankin, Jr., *economist*
Gardner, Kerry Ann *librarian*
Goodman, Gertrude Amelia *civic worker*
Gordon, Norman James *lawyer*
Grieves, Robert Belanger *engineering educator*
Harlass, Frederick E. *obstetrician, gynecologist, perinatologist*
Harrison, Armin Otmar *music educator*
Hedrick, Wyatt Smith *pharmacist*
Heide, John Wesley *engineering executive*
Hernandez, Roberto Reyes *secondary school educator*
Hunt, M.L. *construction executive*
Hunt, Woody L. *real estate executive*
Juarez, Antonio *psychotherapist, consultant, counselor, educator*
Keller, Robert M. *real estate broker*
Kelley, Sylvia Johnson *financial services firm executive*
Korth, Charlotte Williams *furniture and interior design firm executive*
Leachman, Russell DeWitt *lawyer*
Lujan, Rosa Emma *bilingual specialist, trainer, consultant, assistant principal*
Lyle, James Arthur *real estate broker*
Magana, Jorge Carlos *pediatrician*
Marshall, Richard Treeger *lawyer*
Miller, Deane Guynes *salon and cosmetic studio owner*
Mitchell, Paula Rae *nursing educator, college dean*
Morton, Fred J. *lawyer*
Mrochek, Michael John *physician*
Mulla, Zuber *epidemiologist*
Muller, Gene Alan *historian, consultant*
Natalicio, Diana Siedhoff *academic administrator*
Nava, Patricia Ann *electrical engineering educator, researcher*
Patty, William Robert *secondary school educator, principal*
Penley, Julie Anne *psychologist, educator*
Peterscheck, Walter Hermann *chemical engineer*
Prendergast, Thomas A. *investments and management consultant*
Quevedo, Hector Adolf *operations research specialist, environmental scientist*
Renteria, Victor Manuel *secondary school educator*
Roberts, Ernst Edward *marketing consultant*
Shapiro, Stephen Richard *retired air force officer, physician*
Shelton, Patricia A. *gas company executive*
Simpson, Michael Homer *dermatologist*
Sipiora, Leonard Paul *retired museum director, art appraiser*
Small, Ray *university administrator*
Smith, Tad Randolph *lawyer*
Stanley, Duffy B. *architect, planner*
Taber, David O. *urological surgeon*
Tchoshanov, Mourat Ashirovich *mathematician, educator*
Treadwell, Hugh Wilson *retired publishing executive*
Tyroch, Roxanne Marie *internist, educator*
von Tungeln, George Robert *retired university administrator, economics consultant*
Wardy, Joe *mayor*
Williams, Darryl Marlowe *medical educator*
Wootten, John Robert *investor*
Zaloznik, Arlene Joyce *oncologist, retired military officer*

Elgin
Hallenbeck, Pomona Juanita *artist*
Shelby, Nina Claire *special education educator*

Elmendorf
Teague, Mary Elizabeth *small business owner*

Emory
Cates, Sue Sadler *educational diagnostician*

Ennis
Swanson, Wallace Martin *lawyer*

Euless
Leding, Anne Dixon *artist, educator*
Mabry, Philip T. *political consultant*
Paran, Mark Lloyd *retired lawyer*
Roark, Sheila B. *writer*

Farmers Branch
Armand, Susanne Marie *pharmaceutical products executive*
Walsh, Elizabeth Jameson *musician*

Farmersville
Seward, Richard Bevin *lawyer*

Farnsworth
Gramstorff, Jeanne B. *retired farmer*

Flower Mound
Cox, David Leon *telecommunications company executive*
Hunt, David Ford *lawyer*
Kolodny, Stanley Charles *oral surgeon, air force officer*
Maddocks, Robert Allen *lawyer, manufacturing executive*
Morrish, Thomas Jay *golf course architect*

Fort Bliss
Yingling, John A. *military officer*

Fort Hood
Metz, Thomas Fredric *career military officer*
Odierno, Raymond T. *career military officer*
Scott, Karen Lou *systems analyst*

Fort Mc Kavett
Stokes, Charles Eugene, Jr., *wool merchant, textile executive*

Fort Sam Houston
Bauman, Wendall Carter, Jr., *ophthalmologist, career officer*
Hewitson, William Craig *physician, career officer*
Kragh, John Frederick, Jr., *orthopedist, educator*
McFarren, Freddy E. *military career officer*
Moloff, Alan Lawrence *military officer, physician*
Nelson, James Harold *health sciences administrator*
Peake, James Benjamin *military career officer*
Robinson, Naomi Jean *educational training systems educator*

Fort Worth
Alberts, Dennis H. *real estate company executive*
Allen, William Marion, III, *retired graphic designer, artist*
Allmand, Linda F(aith) *retired library director*
Appel, Bernard Sidney *marketing consultant, former electronic company executive*
Ard, Harold Jacob *library administrator*
Arena, M. Scott *retired pharmaceutical company executive*
Armiger, Gene Gibbon *telecommunications executive, consultant*
Auping, Michael G. *curator*
Bacon, Thomas F. *air transportation executive*
Bailey, James Stephen *scientist*
Bailey, Susan Rudd *physician*
Bass, Perry Richardson *oil company executive*
Bass, Robert Muse *financier*
Bedford, David Allen *language educator*
Berenson, William Keith *lawyer*
Blackburn, Wyatt Douglas *insurance executive*
Blanck, Ronald Ray *health science university administrator, internist, military officer*
Boller, Paul Franklin, Jr., *retired American history educator, writer*
Bonderman, David *investment company executive*
Bonzelaar, Gregory Scott *accountant*
Boschetti, Philip J. *oil company executive*
Boschini, Victor John, Jr., *academic administrator*
Bowler, Peter M. *air transportation executive*
Bradley, William Texas *neurologist*
Bradshaw, James Edward (Jim Bradshaw) *consultant*
Brender, Art *lawyer*
Brennan, Edward A. *air transportation executive, former retail executive*
Brockman, Leslie Richard *social worker*
Brodale, Louise Lado *medical, post surgery and geriatrics nurse*
Brown, C. Harold *lawyer*
Brown, Richard Lee *lawyer, director*
Browning, Tyson R. *management consultant*
Buckner, John Kendrick *aerospace engineer*
Caldwell, Billy Ray *geologist*
Campbell, Jeffrey J. *rail transportation executive*
Canas, Eduardo *lawyer*
Catacosinos, William James *utility company executive*
Chalk, John Allen, Sr., *lawyer*
Clark, Emory Eugene *financial planning executive*
Cliburn, Van (Harvey Lavan Cliburn Jr.) *concert pianist*
Collins, Whitfield James *lawyer*
Collins Block, Cathy *education educator, writer, educational consultant*
Cooper, Alcie Lee, Jr., *entrepreneur, former insurance executive*
Corbusier, Drue *apparel and home furnishings executive*
Cottner, Donald *pathologist*
Cottongame, W. Brice *lawyer*
Cottrell, Gregory A. *application developer*
Cox, James Sidney *physician*
Cunningham, Atlee Marion, Jr., *aeronautical engineer*
Curry, Donald Robert *lawyer, oil company executive*
Curts, Harold Layne *construction executive*
Davis, Alan Tucker *foundation administrator, philanthropist, minister*
Davis, Carol Lyn *administrative assistant*
Dean, Beale *lawyer*
Deaver, Pete Eugene *civil and aeronautical engineer*
Dees, Sandra Kay Martin *psychologist, research scientist*
De Leon, Sergio Leon *protective services official*
Dent, Edward Dwain *lawyer*
de Sousa, Byron N.S. *educator, physician, health and medical consultant*
de Toledo, Catherine Holt *medical writer*
de Tonnancour, Paul Roger Godefroy *library administrator*
Dilley, Carol *association administrator*
Dolara, Peter J. *air transportation executive*
Dominiak, Geraldine Florence *accounting educator, retired*
Donovan, Nowell *academic administrator*
Doran, Robert Stuart *mathematician, educator*
Douglas, Carole Nelson *writer*
Dressler, Oscar H. *music educator*
Dunn, Bill *entrepreneur*
Durham, Floyd Wesley, Jr., *economist, educator*
Edmondson, David J. *retail executive*
Elliott, Frank Wallace *lawyer, educator*
Endres, Arthur P. "Skip" *rail transportation executive*
Faherty, David Miles *musical instrument repairman*
Fan, Peng *mathematician*
Floyd, Judy Louise Casburn *anesthesiologist, political scientist*
Follit, Evelyn V. *retail executive*
Ford, Monte E. *air transportation executive*
Galaganov, Misha *music educator*
Garrett, James Leo, Jr., *theology educator*
Garton, Daniel P. *air transportation executive, marketing professional*
Geren, Pete (Preston Geren) *former congressman*
Gilbert, James Cayce *minister*
Gilderhus, Mark Theodore *historian, educator*
Gillette, Paul Crawford *pediatric cardiologist*
Giroard, Marvin J. *retail executive*
Goff, John C. *real estate company executive*
Hahn, Marc B. *osteopath, academic administrator*
Hall, Randy Jarvis *lawyer*
Harcrow, E. Earl *lawyer*
Hardy, Cheril S. *judge*
Harris, Christopher J. *state legislator, lawyer*
Hart, John Clifton *lawyer*
Harth-Bedoya, Miguel *conductor*
Henderson, Stan *air transportation executive*
Hendricks, Scott *corporate budget specialist*
Hill, John David *television producer*
Hill, Mark C. *lawyer*
Hoferer, Paul R. *rail transportation executive, lawyer*
Hudson, Edward Randall, Jr., *gas and oil industry executive*
Huffman, Dan P. *air transportation executive*
Hund, Thomas N. *rail transportation executive*
Hyde, Clarence Brodie, II, *oil company executive*
Ice, Carl *transportation company executive*
Ingram, Denny Ouzts, Jr., *lawyer, educator*
Jackson, Donald Wilson *political science educator, lawyer*
Jackson, Stephen Eric *public speaker, life strategist*
Johnson, J. Mitchell *communications executive*
Karnes, Keith Dale *portfolio manager*
Kellerman, Shirley Rose *artist*
Kelly, Dee J. *lawyer*
Kelly, Raymond Boone, III, *lawyer*
Kemp, Thomas Joseph *retired electronics executive*
Kennedy, Gary F. *air transportation executive, lawyer*
Krebs, Robert Duncan *rail transportation company executive*
Lamensdorf, Hugh *urologist, educator*
Langenheim, Roger Allen *lawyer*
Lanigan, John *rail transportation executive, corporate financial executive*
Larimore, Tom L. *lawyer*
Lawson, Carole Jean *religious educator, author, poet*
Li, Richard T. *retired library director, secondary school educator*
Lichtman, David Michael *military officer, health care administrator, orthopedist, educator*
Lipkin, Seymour *pianist, conductor, educator*
Mallette, David *performing company executive*
Manning, Walter Scott, Jr., *veterinarian*
Marlett, Charles D. *air transportation executive*
McBryde, John Henry *federal judge*
McConnell, Michael Arthur *lawyer*
Means, Terry Robert *federal judge*
Meckna, Michael *musicologist, educator*
Michero, William Henderson *retired retail trade executive*
Minton, Jerry Davis *lawyer, consultant, retired banker*
Mitchell, Patrick John *financial executive*
Mitchell, Robert Joseph *insurance executive*
Moncrief, Michael Joseph *mayor, former state legislator*
Moncrief, William Alvin, Jr., *oil and gas producer*
Mowery, Anna Renshaw *state legislator*
Mullendore, Walter Edward *retired economist*
Munday, Stephen Dale *writer, artist*
Munn, Cecil Edwin *lawyer*
Myers, Thomas Everett *lawyer*
Nason, Scott D. *airline company executive*
Newman, Michael D. *retail executive*
Nichols, James Richard *civil engineer, consultant*
Oliver, Susan M. *air transportation executive*
Palmer, Jeffery Dean *systems engineering manager, consultant*
Patterson, Paige *church administrator, former seminary president*
Patteson, Charles Lynn *musician, retired music educator*
Pearce, Betty McMurray *retired manufacturing executive*
Peipert, James Raymond *journalist*
Prather, Robert Franklin *fund administrator*
Pratt, Jack E., Sr., *hotel executive*
Pray, Donald George *retired aerospace engineer*
Price, Michael Howard *journalist, critic, composer, cartoonist, theatrical operator*
Quarles, Carroll Adair, Jr., *physicist, researcher*
Quinn, Francis Xavier *arbitrator, mediator, author, lecturer*
Raessler, Kenneth Ray *music educator*
Rainwater, Richard *financial consultant, investor*
Ray, Paul Richard, Jr., *executive recruiter, consultant*
Record, Phillip Julius *journalist*
Reding, Robert W. *air transportation executive*
Reinecke, Manfred G. *chemistry professor*
Reuter, Frank Theodore *history educator*
Rickett, Carolyn Kaye Master *artist, criminologist*
Roach, John Vinson, II, *retail company executive*
Roberts, Leonard H. *retail executive*
Rogers, Charles Ray *minister, religious organization administrator*
Roland, Billy Ray *electronics company executive*
Rose, Matthew K. *rail transportation executive*
Saenz, Michael *college president*
Saenz, Nancy Elizabeth King (Mrs. Michael Saenz) *civic worker*
St. John, Evert Eugene *insurance company executive*
Schussler, Irwin *psychiatrist, educator*
Shannon, Joe, Jr., *lawyer*
Shannon, Larry Redding *public relations executive*
Sharpe, James Shelby *lawyer*
Shoemaker, Sandra Kaye *aerospace executive*
Simon, Roger Frank *law educator*
Simpson, Dennis Dwayne *psychologist, educator*
Slater, Carmen Rochelle *elementary school educator*
Stevenson, Ben *artistic director*
Suba, Steven Antonio *obstetrician, gynecologist*
Sullenberger, Ara Broocks *mathematics professor*
Sullivan, Frank W *judge*
Tanzi, David E. *military officer*
Tatum, Stephen Lyle *lawyer*
Taylor, Elizabeth R. *counselor, educator*
Teegarden, Kenneth Leroy *clergyman*
Thompson, Carson R. *retail and manufacturing company executive*
Thornton, Anthony L *aerospace engineer*
Thornton, Charles Victor *metals executive*
Tillman, Karen Sue *lawyer*
Tillman, Massie Monroe *mediator, arbitrator, art gallery owner, retired federal judge*
Tinsley, Jackson Bennett *newspaper editor*
Tubb, Larry *health facility administrator*
Tucker, William Edward *academic administrator, minister*
Turner, Wesley R. *publishing executive*
Vanhaecke, Erwin S. F. *pharmaceutical executive*
Watson, Robert Francis *lawyer*
Webb, Theodore Stratton, Jr., *aerospace scientist, consultant*
Weekley, Frederick Clay, Jr., *lawyer*
West, Robert Grady *lawyer*
Wilder, Thomas A. *county official*
Willard, Ralph Lawrence *surgery educator, physician, former college president*
Williamson, Philip *apparel executive*
Wilson, Evelyn M. *literature educator*
Wilson-Webb, Nancy Lou *education administration consultant, director*
Witt, Jim *editor*
Yacante, Maria Lucy *music educator, researcher*
Yanni, John Michael *pharmacologist*

Fredericksburg
Arnold, George Lawrence *retired advertising company executive*
Benedict, Mark J. *government analyst, marketing executive, lawyer, real estate investment consultant*
Chase, John David *retired dean, retired internist*

Malec, William Frank *utilities company executive*
Manhart, Marcia Y(ockey) *art museum director*
Scannell, William Edward *aerospace company executive, consultant, psychologist*

Freeport
Baskin, William Gresham *counselor, music educator, vocalist*

Friendswood
Kennedy, Priscilla Ann *elementary school educator*

Frisco
Bloskas, John D. *retired finance company executive*
de Veritch, Nina *cellist, music educator*
Ellison, Luther Frederick *oil company executive*
Forêt, Randy Blaise *insurance executive, consultant*
Gajraj, Noor *anesthesiologist, educator*
Hahn, Keith Worden *physiatrist*
Hawk, Phillip Michael *service corporation executive*
Larsen, David Wayne *telecommunications industry executive*
Mackenzie, John *retired oil industry executive*
Migdol, Marvin Jacob *public relations and marketing executive, consultant*
Modano, Mike (Michael Modano) *professional hockey player*

Fulshear
Grantham, Nan L. *music educator, writer*

Gainesville
Brooks, Jerry Robert *small business owner*
Broyles, Stephen Douglas *public administrator*
Stormer, Cindy Hodge *lawyer, educator*

Galveston
Bailey, Byron James *otolaryngologist, educator, medical association administrator*
Baker, Robert Ernest, Jr., *retired foundation executive*
Balaban, Alexandru T. *chemistry educator, researcher*
Banet, Charles Henry *academic administrator, clergyman*
Barratt, Ernest Stoelting *psychologist, educator*
Bello-Reuss, Elsa Noemi *physician, educator*
Bernier, George Matthew, Jr., *oncologist, educator, dean*
Brasier, Allan R. *medical educator*
Bryan, George Thomas *pediatrician, academic administrator*
Budelmann, Bernd Ulrich *zoologist, educator*
Burns, Chester Ray *medical history educator*
Caldwell, Garnett Ernest *lawyer*
Calverley, John Robert *physician, educator*
Carrier, Warren Pendleton *retired university chancellor, writer*
Clayton, William Howard *retired university president*
Dawson, Earl Bliss *obstetrics and gynecology educator*
Ernst, Randy *radiologist*
Fisher, Seymour *psychologist, educator*
Foster, William Edwin (Bill Foster) *nonprofessional basketball coach*
Frederickson, Christopher John *neuroscientist*
Gold, Daniel Howard *ophthalmologist, educator*
Goodwin, Jean McClung *psychiatrist*
Goodwin, Sharon Ann *academic administrator*
Gorenstein, David G. *chemistry and biochemistry educator*
Grant, J(ohn) Andrew, Jr., *medical educator, allergist*
Hargraves, Martha Ann *health services administrator, researcher*
Hawkins, Ida Faye *elementary school educator*
Heggers, John Paul *surgery, immunology and microbiology educator*
Horning, Markus *marine biologist, educator, researcher*
Hudnall, Stanley David *pathology and laboratory medicine educator*
James, Thomas Naum *cardiologist, educator*
Kilgore, Jeffrey Harper *lawyer*
Kurosky, Alexander *biochemist, educator*
Lemon, Stanley M. *hospital administrator*
Markides, Kyriakos Socrates *gerontology educator*
McLeod, E. Douglas *real estate developer, lawyer*
Mitch, William Evans *nephrologist*
Neugebauer, Volker Egdar *biomedical scientist, neuroscientist, physician*
Nusynowitz, Martin Lawrence *nuclear medicine physician*
Otis, John James *civil engineer*
O'Toole, Austin Martin *lawyer*
Phillips, Linda Goluch *plastic surgeon, educator, researcher*
Protas, Elizabeth J. *physical therapist, academic administrator*
Rassin, David Keith *nutrition educator, researcher*
Robertson, Paul Francis *mathematician, educator*
Sandstead, Harold Hilton *medical educator*
Santschi, Peter Hans *marine sciences educator*
Schoenbucher, Bruce *health physicist*
Schreiber, Melvyn Hirsh *radiologist*
Smith, David English *pathologist, educator*
Stobo, John David *dean, educator, physician*
Thompson, James Charles *surgeon*
Townsend, Courtney M. *surgeon*
Vedernikov, Yuri P. *pharmacologist, educator*
White, Robert Brown *medical educator*
Willis, William Darrell, Jr., *neurophysiologist, educator*
Würsig, Bernd Gerhard *marine biology educator*
Zimmerman, Roger Joseph *fishery biologist*

Garland
Basham, Lloyd Moman *manufacturing service company executive*
Brumit, Jo Ann *sheet metal manufacturing executive*
Christensen, Allan Robert *electrical engineer, enrolled agent*
Driver, Joe L. *state legislator, insurance agent*
Haynsworth, Robert Francis, Jr., *anesthesiologist*
Hinton, Charles *lawyer*
Hockett, Sheri Lynn *radiologist*
Irby, Holt *lawyer*
Keebaugh, Michael D. *electronics executive*
Lord, Jacqueline Ward *accountant, photographer, artist*
McGill, Maurice Leon *financial executive*
McGrath, James Thomas *real estate investment company executive*
Preston, Harry *writer, scriptwriter*

Georgetown
Aadnesen, Christopher *rail transportation executive, consultant*
Abegg, Martin Gerald *retired academic administrator*
Bryce, William Delf *lawyer*
Busfield, Roger Melvil, Jr., *retired trade association executive, educator*
Crowley, Weldon Samuel *retired history educator*
Gattis, Dan Moore *lawyer, state representative, rancher*
Gerding, Thomas Graham *medical products executive*
Girvin, Eb Carl *biology professor*
Graham, Charles Passmore *retired army officer*
Manning, Robert Thomas *physician, educator*
Moore, Pat Howard *engineering and construction company executive*
Neville, Gwen Kennedy *anthropology educator*
Ramsey, Margie *librarian*
Sawyer, William Dale *physician, educator, university dean, foundation administrator*
Schrum, Jake Bennett *university administrator*
Sellers, Fred Evans *accounting educator*
Smitheram, Margaret Etheridge *health facility administrator, director*
Teat, Herbert Leroy *retired music educator*
Weyrauch, Paul Turney *retired army officer, retired principal*

Glen Rose
Blankenship, Jenny Mary *museum administrator*

Granbury
Adams, Christopher Steve, Jr., *retired defense electronics corporation executive, former air force officer*
Almy, Earle Vaughn, Jr., (Buddy Almy) *real estate executive*
Garrison, Truitt B. *architect*

Grand Prairie
Fickling, Karl Frederick *church consultant, educator*
Puckett, Mary Alice *primary school educator, consultant*
Ritterhouse, Kathy Lee *librarian*
Thomas, Michael S. *software engineer*

Grapevine
Blair, Sylvia H. *computer systems project engineer, small business owner*
Franks, Jon Michael *lawyer, mediator*
Hahn, Edward Karl *dentist*
Hirsh, Cristy J. *principal*
Shue, Shyh-Pyng Jack *aerospace engineer, researcher, electrical engineer, consultant*
Stack, George Joseph *philosopher, writer*

Greenville
Brown, Harley Mitchell *retired computer company executive, writer*

Groveton
Pyle, Benjamin Malrey *investor*

Hale Center
Courtney, Carolyn Ann *school librarian*
Laney, James Earl (Pete Laney) *state representative, speaker of the house, farmer*

Hallettsville
Baber, Wilbur H., Jr., *lawyer*

Haltom City
Irwin, Richard D. *lab administrator, venture capitalist*

Harker Heights
Hughes, William Foster *career officer, surgeon, obstetrician, gynecologist*

Harlingen
Farris, Robert Gene *transportation company executive*
Johnson, Orrin Wendell *lawyer*
Klein, Garner Franklin *cardiologist, internist*
Martin, Leland Morris (Pappy Martin) *history educator*
Matz, James Richard *municipal official*
Pope, William L. *lawyer, judge*

Hawkins
Smialek, William *musicologist*

Heath
Hargrave, Robert Warren *retired hair styling salon chain executive*
Kolodey, Fred James *lawyer*

Hempstead
Propst, Catherine Lamb *biotechnology company executive*

Henderson
Knapp, Virginia Estella *retired secondary school educator*

Highland Village
Lawrence, William Clarence *business executive, lawyer, mediator, politician*

Hillsboro
McClendon, Fred Vernon *real estate professional, business consultant, equine and realty appraiser, financial consultant*

Hollywood Park
Smith, Richard Thomas *retired electrical engineer*

Hondo
Bryant, Jannie *corporate financial executive*
Swort, Arlowayne *retired nursing educator and administrator*

Horseshoe Bay
Anderson, Kenneth Ward *investor, consultant*
Jorden, James Roy *oil company engineering executive, consultant*
Simpson, H. Richard (Dick Simpson) *retailer*
Strang, Sandra Lee *airline official*

Houston
Abbey, George W. S. *space center executive*
Abbruzzese, James Lewis *medical oncologist*
Abramson, Stuart L. *pediatrics, microbiology and immunology educator*
Accardi, Larry J. *food service executive*
Acree, G. Hardy *airport executive*
Adams, W. Wade *research scientist*
Aday, Luann *social science educator*
Addison, Linda Leuchter *lawyer, writer, commentator, columnist*
Adkins, Albert G. *oil industry executive*
Adkins, Susan *health services administrator*
Agosto, Benny, Jr., *lawyer*
Aguilar-Bryan, Lydia *medical educator, medical researcher*
Aitken, Iam *health facility administrator*
Ajello, James A. *energy executive*
Alexander, Andrew M. *real estate investment company executive*
Alexander, Harold Campbell *insurance consultant*
Alexander, Leslie Lee *professional sports team owner*
Alexander, Stanford *real estate investment company executive*
Alexanian, Raymond *hematologist*
Alfini, James Joseph *dean, educator, lawyer*
Alford, Bobby Ray *otolaryngologist, educator, academic administrator*
Allen, Jon G. *psychologist*
Allen, Steven Jeffrey *anesthesiologist, educator*
Allender, John Roland *lawyer*
Allspach, Eugene R. *chemicals executive*
Altman, William Carl *health facility administrator, merger and acquisitions specialist, investment manager, consultant*
Amato, Paula *medical educator*
Amdur, Arthur R. *lawyer*
Anderson, Claire W. *gifted and talented educator*
Anderson, Eric Severin *lawyer*
Anderson, Richard Carl *geophysical exploration company executive*
Anderson, Thomas Dunaway *retired lawyer*
Anderson, William, Jr., (William Albion Anderson Jr.) *consultant*
Andrews, Sally S. *lawyer*
Antalffy, Leslie Peter *mechanical engineer*
Appel, Stanley Hersh *neurologist, educator*
Archambault, Lee Joseph *astronaut*
Arcilla, Demetrio Ballares, Jr., *health facility administrator, rehabilitation services professional, writer, genealogist*
Arcilla, Juanita R. *physical rehabilitation physician*
Arens, James F. *anesthesiologist, educator*
Arledge, David A. *energy executive*
Armstrong, Greg L. *oil company executive*
Arnold, Daniel Calmes *lawyer, former finance company executive*
Arnold, James Phillip *religious studies educator, history educator*
Ashby, Jeffrey S. *astronaut*
Asher, Jerry L. *retired government agency administrator*
Askew, William Earl *chemist, educator*
Atlas, Nancy Friedman *judge*
Atlas, Scott J. *lawyer*
Auchter, Norma Holmes *musician, music educator*
Austin, H. Brent *electric power industry executive*
Austin, Harry Guiden *engineering and construction company executive*
Ayadi, Olusegun Felix *finance educator*
Ayus, Juan Carlos *nephrologist*
Bachmann, Richard H. *lawyer*
Bagwell, Jeff (Jeffrey Robert Bagwell) *professional baseball player*
Bailey, Harold Randolph *surgeon*
Bair, Royden Stanley *retired architect*
Baker, Ellen Shulman *astronaut, physician*
Baker, James Addison, III, *ambassador, lawyer, former government official*
Baker, Michael A. *astronaut*
Baker, Stephen Denio *physics educator*
Ballard, Linda Christine *financial aid director*
Bally, Albert W. *retired petroleum geologist, geology educator*
Baranovich, Diana Lea *music educator*
Barcenas, Camilo Gustavo *physician*
Bargfrede, James Allen *lawyer*
Barlow, Jim B. *retired columnist*
Barnett, Donald Blake *corporate financial executive*
Barnett, Edward William *lawyer*
Barracano, Henry Ralph *retired oil company executive, consultant*
Barrere, Clem Adolph *business brokerage company executive*
Barrett, Bernard Morris, Jr., *plastic and reconstructive surgeon*
Barricklo, Jack Nelson *small business owner*
Barrow, Thomas Davies *oil and mining company educator*
Barry, Allan Ronald *ship pilot, corporate executive*
Bartling, Phyllis McGinness *oil company executive*
Baskin, David Stuart *neurosurgeon, educator*
Bast, Robert Clinton, Jr., *medical researcher, medical educator*
Batchelder, E. L. (Gene) *oil industry executive*
Battin, R. Ray (Rosabell Harriet Ray) *audiologist, neuropsychologist*
Baughn, Robert Elroy *microbiology educator*
Baumgartner, James Edumnd *pediatric neurosurgeon*
Bazelides, Diane *public relations executive*
Bazelides, Philip J. *utilities executive*
Beard, Dennis Alton *pastor*
Beasley, Robert Palmer *epidemiologist, dean, educator*
Beason, Jeffrey S. *gas industry executive, controller*
Beaudet, Arthur L. *medical genetics researcher*
Bech, Douglas York *lawyer, resort executive*
Becker, Frederick Fenimore *cancer center administrator, pathologist*
Behrman, Philip G. *oil industry executive*
Beirne, Martin Douglas *lawyer*
Belk, Joan Pardue *English educator*
Bellatti, Lawrence Lee *lawyer*
Beltran, Carlos *professional baseball player*
Bentsen, Kenneth Edward *architect*
Berg, David Howard *lawyer*
Bergstrom, Stephen W. *natural gas company executive*
Berner, Arthur Samuel *lawyer*
Berry, Martha Frances *counselor*
Berry, William B. *oil industry executive*
Bethea, Louise Huffman *allergist*
Bethune, Gordon *airline executive*
Bezold, Louis Irving, III, *pediatrician, pediatric cardiologist*
Bickel, Stephen Douglas *former insurance company executive*
Bier, Dennis M. *medical educator*
Biggio, Craig *professional baseball player*
Bilger, Bruce R. *lawyer*
Billick, L. Larkin *marketing executive*
Bischoff, Susan Ann *newspaper editor*
Black, David Charles *astrophysicist*
Black, Marilyn Hammer *non-profit organization executive*
Blackburn, Sadie Gwin Allen *business executive*
Blackshear, A. T., Jr., *lawyer*
Blackstone, W.C. *architectural firm executive*
Bland, John Lloyd *lawyer*
Blanton, Jack Sawtelle *oil company executive*
Bleiberg, Efrain *medical clinic executive*
Bliss, Ronald Glenn *lawyer*
Bloomfield, Michael J. *astronaut*
Bluestein, Edwin A., Jr., *lawyer*
Blurton, Jerry H. *oil industry executive*
Bodey, Gerald Paul *medical educator, physician*
Bollich, Elridge Nicholas *brokerage house executive*
Bonner, Billy Edward *physics educator*
Bonner, David Calhoun *chemical company executive*
Bonneville, Richard Briggs *retired petroleum exploration and production executive*
Bookout, John Frank, Jr., *oil company executive*
Boren, William Meredith *manufacturing executive*
Bott, Simon Gregory *chemistry educator, researcher*
Bovay, Harry Elmo, Jr., *retired engineering company executive*
Bowen, Raymond M., Jr., *corporate financial executive*
Bowen, William Jackson *retired gas company executive*
Bowersox, Kenneth D. *astronaut*
Bowron, Edgar Peters *art museum curator, administrator*
Bozeman, Ross Elliot *engineering executive*
Bradford, C.O. *protective services officer*
Brandenstein, Daniel Charles *astronaut, retired naval officer*
Brandt, I. Marvin *chemist, engineer*
Brann, Richard Roland *lawyer*
Brenner, Malcolm K. *pediatric and medical educator*
Brents, Daniel *architectural firm executive*
Bricker, John Timothy *pediatric cardiologist*
Bridges, David Manning *lawyer*
Brinkley, William R. *dean*
Brinson, Gay Creswell, Jr., *retired lawyer*
Brito, Dagobert Llanos *economics professor*
Brody, Baruch Alter *medical educator, academic center administrator*
Brooks, Philip Russell *chemistry educator, researcher*
Brosh, Rita *performing company executive*
Brotzen, Franz Richard *materials scientist, educator*
Brown, Glenda Ann Walters *ballet director*
Brown, Jack Harold Upton *physiologist, biomedical engineer, academic administrator*
Brown, Jacqueline Elaine *obstetrician-gynecologist*
Brown, Karen Kennedy *judge*
Brunson, John Soles *lawyer, investor*
Bryan, J(ames) P(erry), Jr., *energy company executive*
Bryan, Mary Ann *interior designer*
Bryant, John Bradbury *economics educator, consultant*
Buckingham, Edwin John, III, *lawyer*
Bue, Carl Olaf, Jr., *retired federal judge*
Bui, Khoi Tien *college counselor*
Buja, L. Maximilian *pathologist, academic administrator, educator*
Bulmahn, T. Paul *oil and gas company executive*
Bunch, Fred *newspaper picture editor*
Bungo, Michael William *physician, educator, science administrator*
Burbank, Daniel C. *astronaut*
Burch, Voris Reagan *mediator, arbitrator, retired lawyer*
Burdette, Walter James *surgeon, educator*
Burdine, John A. *hospital administrator, nuclear medicine educator*
Burgher, Cedric W. *oil industry executive*
Burke, Kevin Charles Antony *geologist*
Burke, Michael Donald *oil and gas company executive*
Bursch, Daniel W. *astronaut*
Burton, Joseph Randolph *lawyer*
Burzynski, Stanislaw Rajmund *internist*
Bush, George Herbert Walker *41st President of the United States*
Buster, John Edmond *gynecologist, medical researcher*
Butel, Janet Susan *research scientist, virology educator*
Butler, William Thomas *academic administrator, physician, educator*
Butters, David J. *oil industry executive*
Bux, William John *lawyer*
Byrne, John H. *neuroscientist, department chairman*
Cabana, Robert D. *astronaut*
Cabello, J. David *retired lawyer*
Caddy, Michael Douglas *lawyer*
Cagle, Yvonne Darlene *astronaut*
Calbert, Mike *retail executive*
Callahan, Gerald William *lawyer, oil company executive*
Callender, David L. *medical educator, health facility administrator, surgeon*
Callender, Norma Anne *psychology educator, counselor*
Cameron, William Duncan *plastics company executive*
Camfield, William Arnett *art educator, educator*
Campbell, Bert Louis *lawyer, mediator, arbitrator*
Campbell, Carl David *oil industry executive*
Campbell, Eileen M. *oil industry executive*
Campo, Richard J. *real estate company executive*
Capers, Dominic *professional football coach*
Capps, Ethan LeRoy *oil company executive*
Carabello, Blase Anthony *cardiology educator*
Caram, Dorothy Farrington *educational consultant*
Carameros, George Demitrius, Jr., *natural gas company executive*
Carey, Duane Gene (Digger) *astronaut*

Jones, Eli, III, *marketing/sales educator*
Jones, Florence M. *music educator*
Jones, Frank Griffith *lawyer*
Jones, Sonia Josephine *advertising executive*
Jordan, Charles Milton *lawyer*
Jordon, Robert Earl *physician*
Joyce, James Daniel *clergyman*
Juneja, Harinder Singh *hematologist*
Jurtshuk, Peter, Jr., *microbiologist, educator*
Justice, Blair (David Blair Justice) *psychology educator, writer*
Kakadiaris, Ioannis *computer science educator*
Kaminski, Vincent J. *utilities executive*
Kanellos, Nicolás *language educator, liberal studies educator*
Kapadia, Asha Seth *education educator, consultant*
Kaplan, Alan Leslie *gynecology educator, oncologist*
Kaplan, Lee Landa *lawyer*
Karff, Samuel Egal *rabbi*
Karger, Walter *mechanical engineer*
Kavanagh, John Joseph *medical educator*
Kavandi, Janet Lynn *aerospace power engineer, chemist*
Kay, Joel Phillip *lawyer*
Keating, Tim *chef*
Keiser, Robert Lee *retired gas and oil industry executive*
Keith, Susan S. *lawyer, business executive*
Kellner, Lawrence W. (Larry Kellner) *air and aerospace transportation company executive*
Kelly, Dorothy Helen *pediatrician, educator*
Kelly, Mark E. *astronaut*
Kemp, Roland Connor *lawyer*
Kendrick, Robert Warren *county official*
Kent, Jeffrey Franklin *professional baseball player*
Kerr, Baine Perkins *oil company executive*
Kershaw, Carol Jean *psychologist*
Ketchand, Robert Lee *lawyer*
Key, James Everett *ophthalmologist*
Kientz, Renee *newspaper editor*
Killion, Vida Frazier *minister, writer*
Kilrain, Susan *astronaut*
Kim, Han-Seob *pathologist*
Kim, Pyung-Soo *martial arts educator*
Kinder, Richard Dan *natural gas pipeline, oil and gas company executive*
King, Carolyn Dineen *federal judge*
King, Willis T., Jr., *insurance company executive*
Kinsey, James Lloyd *chemist, educator*
Kirk, John Robert, Jr., *lawyer*
Kirk, Rick U. *real estate company executive*
Kirkland, John David *oil and gas company executive, lawyer*
Kirkland, Lannis *architecture educator*
Kirkland, Rebecca Trent *pediatric endocrinologist*
Kit, Saul *biochemist, educator*
Kitowski, Vincent Joseph *medical consultant, former physical medicine and rehabilitation physician*
Kline, Mark Wendel *pediatric medicine educator*
Knapp, David Hebard *banker*
Knickel, Carin S. *oil industry executive*
Knight, Jennifer Lynn *psychologist, researcher*
Kobayashi, Riki *chemical engineer, educator*
Kochi, Jay Kazuo *chemist, educator*
Koenig, Rodney Curtis *lawyer, rancher*
Kolla, Venkatarathnam *geologist, consultant*
Kollaer, Jim C. *real estate executive, architect*
Kors, R. Paul *search company executive*
Kouri, Donald Jack *chemist, educator*
Kraft, Irvin Alan *psychiatrist*
Krajewski, Michael *conductor*
Kramer, Phillip D. *oil industry executive*
Kramm, Deborah Ann *information technology executive*
Krance, Robert A. *physician, educator, health facility administrator*
Kratochvil, L(ouis) Glen *lawyer*
Krebs, Arno William, Jr., *lawyer*
Kregel, Kevin R. *astronaut*
Kripke, Margaret Louise *immunologist, health facility executive*
Kruse, Layne E. *lawyer*
Kuntz, Hal Goggan *petroleum exploration company executive, rancher*
Kupiec, Suzanne L. *utilities executive*
Kurz, Thomas Patrick *lawyer*
Kutka, Nicholas *nuclear medicine physician*
LaBoon, Robert Bruce *lawyer*
Lacey, David Morgan *lawyer, school administrator*
Lachar, David *psychologist, educator*
Lackey, S. Allen *lawyer, petroleum company executive*
LaFuze, William L. *lawyer*
Lake, Kathleen Cooper *lawyer*
Lake, Sim *federal judge*
Lamb, Sydney MacDonald *linguistics and cognitive science educator*
Lamont, Gene *professional baseball coach, former professional baseball team manager*
Landrum, Brian *utilities executive*
Lane, Neal Francis *physics educator, former government official*
Langdon, Jerry J. *utilities executive*
Lanier, Bob *mayor*
Lanier, Robert C. (Bob Lanier) *real estate owner, developer, former mayor*
Lanier, W. Mark *lawyer*
Lankford, Thomas E. *food service company executive*
Lanza, Frank Leo *gastroenterologist, researcher*
Larkin, Lee Roy *retired lawyer*
Larkin, William Vincent, Jr., *corporate financial executive*
Latimer, Roy Truett *museum executive*
Latting, Jean Kantambu *social worker, educator*
Law, Ronnie *historian, educator*
Lawrence, C. Berdon *exploration company executive*
Lawrence, Wendy B. *astronaut*
Leak, Jessie Aronow *anesthesiologist*
Learned, Vincent Roy *electrical engineer, educator*
Lee, Janie C. *curator*
Lehne, Kathy Prasnicki *gas industry executive*
Lehrer, Kenneth Eugene *economic consultant*
Leiber, Justin *philosophy educator, writer*
Leichtman, Maria Luisa *mental health services professional*
Lepow, Ronald S. *podiatrist*
Lerup, Lars G. *architecture educator, college dean*
Lesar, David J. *oil industry executive*
Letbetter, R. Steve *energy company executive*
Leth, Steven A. *management consultant*
Levin, Bernard *physician*
Levin, Victor A. *neurologist, oncologist, educator*
Levit, Max *wholesale distribution executive, food service executive*
Levit, Milton *grocery supply company executive*
Levy, Eugene Howard *planetary sciences educator, researcher*
Lewis, Cleotrice O. Ney Tillis *retired elementary education educator*
Lewis, Edward Sheldon *chemistry professor*
Lewis, Lisa *psychologist, administrator*
Liang, Edison Parktak *astrophysicist, educator, researcher*
Lienhard, John Henry, IV, *mechanical engineer, educator*
Ligon-Borden, Betty Lee *academic director*
Liles, Clifton Roy *software designer*
Limbacher, Randy L. *energy executive*
Linden, William M. *lawyer*
Lindsey, John Horace *insurance agency executive*
Litvinov, Dmitri *engineering educator*
Liu, Lumei *chemistry researcher*
Long, Meredith J. *art dealer*
Lopez, David Tiburcio *lawyer, educator, arbitrator, mediator*
Lopez-Alegria, Michael Eladio *astronaut*
Loro, Antonio *artist*
Low, Morton David *neuroscientist, educator, policy consultant*
Lowe, John E. *oil industry executive, accountant*
Lowry, Montecue Judson *military historian*
Lu, Edward Tsang *astronaut*
Lucid, Shannon W. *biochemist, astronaut*
Luigs, Charles Russell *retired gas and oil drilling industry executive*
Lukens, Max L. *manufacturing company executive*
Luna, Mario Armando *pathologist, consultant*
Luss, Dan *chemical engineering educator*
Ma, Jingjing *mathematician*
MacAvery, Tristan Alexander (Tristan Black Wolf) *small business owner, writer, actor*
Mackwell, Stephen Joseph *geophysicist, educator*
Mallia-Hughes, Marianne *medical writer*
Mampre, Virginia Elizabeth *communications executive*
Mansell, Joyce Marilyn *retired special education educator*
Marchand, Wayne *architectural firm executive*
Marek, Joycelyn *publishing executive*
Mark, Rebecca P. *environmental services administrator*
Marshall, Gregory K. *food service executive*
Marshall, Jane Pretzer *newspaper editor*
Marston, Edgar Jean, III, *lawyer*
Martin, James Kirby *historian, educator*
Martin, Jay Griffith *lawyer*
Martin, Paul Edward *lawyer*
Martin, Randi Christine *psychology educator*
Martin, William C. *sociology educator, writer*
Martinez, Lori Anne Brubaker *mathematician, educator*
Martirosyan, Karen *research scientist*
Marzio, Peter Cort *museum director*
Mashburn, Joseph L. *architecture educator*
Mason, Chip *retired automotive executive*
Massad, Stephen Albert *lawyer*
Masters, Claude Bivin *lawyer*
Matheny, Kenneth L. *oil industry executive*
Mathis, James Forrest *retired petroleum company executive*
Matthews, Charles Sedwick *petroleum engineering consultant, research advisor*
Matthews, Kathleen Shive *biochemistry educator*
Mattox, Ethel Odessa *writer*
Mauck, William M., Jr., *retired executive recruiter, small business owner*
Max, Ernest *surgeon*
Mayo, Carolyn *marketing professional, public relations executive*
Mayo, Marti *museum director, curator*
Mayor, Heather Donald *medical educator, molecular biologist*
McClanahan, David M. *energy executive*
McCleary, Henry Glen *geophysicist*
McCleskey, Jerry Michael *retired chemical company executive*
McClure, Daniel M. *lawyer*
McCollam, Marion Andrus *consulting firm executive, educator*
McDaniel, Jarrel Dave *lawyer*
McDavid, George Eugene (Gene Mc David) *retired newspaper executive*
McDonald, Donald C. *lawyer*
McDonald, Rebecca Ann *natural gas company executive*
McEachern, Stephen Matthew *accountant*
McEvoy-Jamil, Patricia Ann *English language educator*
Mc Fadden, Joseph Michael *history educator*
McFall, Donald Beury *lawyer*
McGill, Stuart R. *oil industry executive*
Mc Ginty, John Milton *architect*
McGrady, Tracy *professional basketball player*
McGuyer, Frank *construction executive*
McKechnie, John Charles *gastroenterologist, educator*
McKim, Paul Arthur *management consultant, retired petroleum executive*
McLeod, Harry O'Neal, Jr., *retired petroleum engineer, consultant*
McPherson, Alice Ruth *ophthalmologist, educator*
McQuarrie, Claude Monroe, III, *lawyer*
Meara, James F. *oil industry executive*
Meek, Susan Bieber *lawyer, physician, mediator, consultant*
Melroy, Pamela Ann *astronaut*
Mendelsohn, John *oncologist, hematologist, educator, health facility executive*
Mendelson, Robert Allen *polymer scientist, rheologist*
Mendoza-Londono, Roberto *geneticist, pediatrician*
Meng, Ru-Ling *research scientist*
Menn, Stephen Edward *lawyer*
Menninger, Roy Wright *medical foundation executive, psychiatrist*
Menscher, Barnet Gary *steel company executive*
Mentz, Henry A., III, *plastic surgeon*
Merrill, Joseph Melton *medical educator*
Meyer, John Stirling *neurologist, educator*
Meyer, Marjorie Jean *real estate manager*
Miele, Angelo *engineering educator, researcher, consultant, author*
Milam, John Daniel *pathologist, educator*
Miles, Brian John *urologist*
Miller, Charles Rickie *thermal and fluid systems analyst, engineering manager*
Miller, Gary Evan *psychiatrist, mental health services professional*
Miller, Gary L. *gas company executive*
Miller, Geoffrey *child neurologist*
Miller, Harry Freeman *university administrator*
Miller, Jack *publishing company executive*
Miller, Janel Howell *psychologist*
Miller, Robert Harold *otolaryngologist, educator*
Mills, John T. *oil industry executive, corporate financial executive*
Miner, Michael E. *neurosurgery educator*
Ming, Yao *professional basketball player*
Minter, David Lee *English literature educator*
Mintz-Hittner, Helen Ann *physician, researcher*
Mire, Weldon J. *oil industry executive, human resources specialist*
Misner, Jeffrey J. *air transportation executive*
Mitcham, Carla J. *utilities executive*
Moehlman, Michael Scott *lawyer*
Moncure, John Lewis *lawyer*
Montgomery, Cleothus *minister*
Montgomery, Denise Karen *nurse*
Moody, Frank G. *surgeon*
Moore, Lois Jean *health science facility administrator*
Moorhead, Gerald Lee *architect*
Morabito, Philip A. *public relations executive*
Morgan, Richard Greer *lawyer*
Morgan, William V. *oil and gas pipeline and storage executive*
Morin, Lee Miller Emile *astronaut*
Morris, Carloss (William Morris) *lawyer, insurance company executive*
Morris, Gary *oil industry executive*
Morris, Owen Glenn *engineering corporation executive*
Muchmore, Robert Charles, Jr., *oil industry executive*
Munisteri, Joseph George *construction executive*
Munsell, Debra S. *physician assistant, educator*
Murad, Ferid *physician*
Murdy, William F. *diversified services executive*
Murphy, Ewell Edward, Jr., *lawyer*
Murphy, William Alexander, Jr., *diagnostic radiologist, educator*
Murray, Frank *former heating, air conditioning manufacturing executive*
Mutombo, DiKembe (Dikembe Mutombo Mpolondo Mukamba Jean Jacque Wamutombo) *professional basketball player*
Myers, A. Maurice *waste management executive*
Myers, James Clark *advertising and public relations executive*
Myers, Norman Allan *marketing professional*
Nacknouck, James Dominic *management executive*
Nacol, Mae *lawyer*
Naeve, Stephen W. *electric power industry executive*
Nance, Weldon Bailey *petroleum engineer*
Nanz, Robert Hamilton *petroleum consultant*
Nations, Howard Lynn *lawyer*
Nelson, David Loren *geneticist, educator*
Nelson, James *wholesale food distribution executive*
Nelson-Thorpe, Carlon Justine *engineering and operations executive*
Nemphos, Speros P. *chemist, consultant*
Neslage, John Edward *lawyer*
Netsiri, Chaiyapoj *academic administrator, researcher*
Neuhaus, Philip Ross *investment banker*
Neuhaus, William Oscar, III, *architect*
Nichols, Buford Lee, Jr., *pediatrician, physiologist*
Nichols, Michael Cooper *food products executive, lawyer*
Nicklas, Theresa Ann *nutritionist, educator, researcher*
Nielsen, Niels Christian, Jr., *theology educator*
Nokes, Jim W. *oil industry executive*
Nolen, Norman W. *financial executive*
Nolen, Roy Lemuel *retired lawyer*
Nora, Hope *healthcare consultant*
Nordgren, Ronald Paul *engineering educator, researcher*
Nordlander, Peter Jan Arne *physics educator, researcher*
Noriega, Carlos I. *astronaut*
Norman, Kenneth Glen *lawyer*
Nunnally, Knox Dillon *lawyer*
Obiora, Chris Sunny *architect*
O'Brien, Eva Fromm *lawyer*
O'Brient, David Warren *sales executive, consultant*
Ochoa, Ellen *astronaut*
O'Connor, Bryan D. *astronaut*
O'Connor, Ralph Sturges *investment company executive*
Oden, Keith D. *real estate company executive*
O'Donnell, Lawrence, III, *waste management executive*
Olajuwon, Akinola *investment company executive*
Oldham, Darius Dudley *lawyer*
Oldham, J. Thomas *lawyer, educator*
Olivares, Jaime Ramon *history professor, researcher*
Olstead, Christopher Eric *financial consultant, entertainment executive*
O'Neil, John *artist*
Oren, Bruce Clifford *newspaper editor, artist*
O'Rourke, Marylyn Kay *counseling administrator, consultant*
Orr, Carole *artist*
Osterberg, Edward Charles, Jr., *lawyer*
Oswalt, Roy E. *professional baseball player*
Owino, Meshack *history professor*
Page, David Randall *hospital administrator*
Pailes, William *astronaut*
Palmer, Chris *professional football coach*
Palmer, Willard Aldrich, III, *magician, writer, actor*
Parazynski, Scott E. *astronaut*
Parks, David R. *heating/air conditioning manufacturing executive*
Parle, Bertha Ibarra *writer*
Parsons, Edmund Morris *investment company executive*
Pate, James Leonard *oil company executive*
Patten, Robert Lowry *English language educator*
Paul, Alida Ruth *arts and crafts educator*
Pawelczyk, James A. *astronaut, educator*
Payton, Gary E. *astronaut*
Peabody, Arlene L. Howland Bayar *retired, nurse*
Pearson, James Boyd, Jr., *electrical engineering educator*
Pederson, Tony Weldon *newspaper editor*
Pefanis, Harry *manufacturing executive*
Pendergrass, Glen *construction executive*
Peng, Liang-Chuan *mechanical engineer*
Perez, Jose Rafael, Jr., *lawyer*
Perry, Robert (Bob Perry) *construction executive*
Pettitte, Andrew Eugene (Andy Pettitte) *professional baseball player*
Phung, Nguyen Dinh *medical educator*
Pickering, James Henry, III, *academic administrator, educator*
Pierson, Aeryk Allen *web site designer*
Pinchak, Ann Simcha *lawyer*
Pinson, Artie Frances *retired elementary school educator*
Plaeger, Frederick Joseph, II, *lawyer*
Plank, Raymond *investment corporation executive*
Plank, Roger B. *oil and gas production company executive*
Plunkett, Jack William *writer, publisher*
Poats, Lillian Brown *education educator*
Pognonec, Yves Maurice *steel products executive*
Poindexter, Alan *astronaut*
Poitevent, Edward Butts, II, *lawyer*
Pontes, Marcos C. *astronaut*
Poplack, David G. *pediatric oncologist*
Porter, Thomas William, III, *lawyer*
Portman, Ronald Jay *pediatric nephrologist, researcher*
Potluri, Venkateswara Rao *medical facility administrator*
Poulos, Michael James *insurance company executive*
Poulton, Beverly Ann *medical/surgical nurse*
Powell, Alan *scientist-engineer*
Powers, Hugh William *newspaper executive*
Powers, William Edward *emergency physician, educator*
Prats, Michael *petroleum engineer, educator*
Pravel, Bernarr Roe *lawyer*
Precourt, Charles J. *astronaut, retired military officer*
Prestridge, Pamela Adair *lawyer*
Pritchard, William Winther *lawyer, drilling company executive*
Pryor, William Daniel Lee *humanities educator*
Pudwill Gorie, Dominic L. *astronaut*
Pugsley, Frank Burruss *lawyer*
Pulliam, Larry G. *food products executive*
Pyne, Joseph H. *marine transportation executive*
Radoff, Leonard Irving *librarian, consultant*
Radomski, Marek Witold *science educator*
Rakel, Robert Edwin *internist, educator*
Raley, John Wesley, III, *lawyer*
Rao, P. Syamasundar *pediatric cardiologist*
Rapini, Ronald Peter *dermatology educator*
Rapoport, Nancy B. *dean, law educator*
Rasmussen, Nicholas Roberts *insurance company executive*
Rassidakis, George Z. *pathologist, researcher*
Rawlinson, Gayla *director, consultant*
Rawson, Jim Charles *business executive*
Ray, Hugh Massey, Jr., *lawyer*
Read, Michael Oscar *editor, consultant*
Reasoner, Harry Max *lawyer*
Redmon, Agile Hugh, Jr., *allergist*
Reed, Kathlyn Louise *occupational therapist, educator*
Reid, Katherine Louise *artist, educator, author*
Reiff, Patricia Hofer *space physicist, educator*
Reinbolt, Paul C. *oil industry executive*
Reso, Anthony *geologist, educator, earth resources economist*
Rhodes, Allen Franklin *engineering executive*
Ribble, John Charles *medical educator*
Rice, Lynda Lu *elementary school educator, writer*
Richards, Leonard Martin *investment executive, consultant*
Richter, Stephen C. *real estate company executive*
Ridge, Robert A. *oil industry executive*
Riedel, Alan Ellis *retired manufacturing company executive, lawyer*
Rieke, Ronald Alfred *computer company executive*
Riley, Harold John, Jr., *manufacturing executive*
Rives, Terry Edward *public health service officer, researcher, epidemiologist*
Robb, Geoffrey Lawrence *plastic surgeon*
Robb, James B. *utilities executive*
Robbins, Susan Paula *social work educator*
Roberts, Paul *chef*
Robertson, James Woolsey *lawyer*
Rock, Douglas Lawrence *manufacturing executive*
Roff, J(ohn) Hugh, Jr., *energy company executive*
Rogers, Arthur Hamilton, III, *lawyer*
Roos, Sybil Friedenthal *retired elementary school educator*
Rose, Beatrice Schroeder (Mrs. William H. Rose) *harpist, educator*
Rosenthal, Charles A., Jr., *prosecutor*
Rosenthal, Lee H. *federal judge*
Rosin, Lindsay Zweig *clinical psychologist*
Ross, Jerry L. *astronaut*
Ross, Michael Wallis *public health educator*
Ross, Patti Jayne *obstetrics and gynecology educator*
Rossler, Willis Kenneth, Jr., *petroleum company executive*
Rowland, Robert Alexander, III, *lawyer*
Rozzell, Scott Ellis *lawyer*
Rudolph, Andrew Henry *dermatologist, educator*
Ruiz, Pedro *psychiatrist*
Russell, Donald Glenn *oil company executive*
Russell, John Francis *retired librarian*
Rustay, Jennifer B. *lawyer*
Ryan, Thomas L. *environmentalist*
Ryan, Vince *lawyer*
Saizan, Paula Theresa *oil company executive*
Salam, Debera Jean *accounting company executive*
Salch, Steven Charles *lawyer, mediator, arbitrator*
Sales, James Bohus *lawyer*
Salinas, Martha F. *manufacturing executive*
Sampson, Franklin Delano *minister*
Sanders, Daniel S. *oil industry executive*
Sanderson, Mary Louise *medical association administrator*
Sapp, Walter William *lawyer, energy company executive*
Sargent, John *psychiatrist*
Sass, Ronald Lewis *biology and chemistry educator*
Satitpunwaycha, Pon *surgeon*
Saunders, Charles Albert *lawyer*
Saunders, Heather Marie *air transportation executive*
Sawaya, Raymond *neurosurgeon*
Sazama, Kathleen *pathologist, lawyer*
Scarbrough, Sara Eunice *librarian, archivist, consultant*
Schachtel, Barbara Harriet Levin *epidemiologist, educator*
Scharold, Mary Louise *psychoanalyst, educator*

Karnes City
Davis, Troy Arnol *reflexologist, hypnotherapist*

Katy
Chavez, Victor Manuel *process engineer*
Hill, Larry Mitchel *energy service company executive*
Hughes, Sandra Michelle *education administrator, educator*
Poland, Sydney Wade *software designer*
Sadowski, Chester Philip, Jr., *real estate executive*

Kaufman
Teagle, David Bryan *manufacturing executive*
Tygrett, Howard Volney, Jr., *judge, lawyer*

Keene
Adams, Lavonne Marilyn Beck *critical care nurse, nursing educator*
Doroftei, Mugur Gideon *music educator, conductor, composer, musician*
Jones, Steve *history professor*
Stembridge, Allen Frederick *management educator*

Keller
Patterson, Ronald R(oy) *management consultant*

Kelly A F B
Bielowicz, Paul L. *career officer*

Kemah
Cofran, George Lee *telecommunication consultant*
Sneider, Robert M. *petroleum exploration engineer*

Kemp
Chalk, J. Lee *secondary school educator, writer*

Kerrville
Chance, F. Earlayne *artist*
Dozier, William Everett, Jr., *newspaper editor and publisher*
Frudakis, Evangelos William *sculptor*
Jordan, Sam Latron *minister, mediator*
O'Shields, Richard Lee *retired natural gas company executive*
Parmley, Robert James *lawyer, consultant*
Shaw, Alan Bosworth *geologist, paleontologist*
Sparks, Don Bertrand *retired geophysicist*
Williams, William Henry, II, *publisher*
Zuber, Randolph Clark *urologist*

Kilgore
Rorschach, Richard Gordon *lawyer*

Killeen
Anderson, James Raymond *academic administrator*
Bryan, Arthur Lee *music educator*

Kingsville
Arnold, Mitylene B. *special education educator, consultant*
Cecil, David Rolf *mathematician, educator*
Chang, Ni-Bin *environmental pollution control educator*
Du, Qian *electrical engineer, educator*
Harun, Syed Mahbub *economist, educator, economist, researcher*
Hines, Gladys H. *academic administrator*
Ibanez, Manuel Luis *university official, biological sciences educator*
Kinkel, Doreen Heather *education educator*
Li, Shuhui *engineer, educator*
Morey, Philip Stockton, Jr., *mathematics professor*
Robins, James Dow *counselor*
Wiley, Millicent Yoder *realtor, pianist, accompanist, retired secondary school choir director*

Kingwood
Barkley, Bronson Lee *minister*
Chamoun-Nicolas, Habib *business development consultant*
Hagen, Barbara C. *music educator*
Spartz, Alice Anne Lenore *retired retail executive*

Kyle
Akins, Vaughn Edward *retired engineering company executive*
Atkinson, Valerie J. *writer, webmaster*

La Grange
Collins, George J., Jr., *surgeon*

La Porte
Fotsch, George Bernard, III, *chemical addiction counselor*
Svambera, Beatrice Alice *secondary school educator*

Lackland A F B
Dremsa, Theresa Lynn *military officer, researcher*
Dunn, William Jackson *dental educator, researcher*
Farage, Michael N. *career officer*
Mabry, Earl W. *military officer*

Lago Vista
Garcia y Carrillo, Martha Xochitl *pharmacist*
Hilton, James Gorton *pharmacologist*
Sandman, Kimberly Sue Adams *newswriter*

Lake Jackson
Elbert, James Peak *independent insurance agent, minister*
Tasa, Ken *college dean*

Lakehills
Spears, Diane Shields *artist, retired art academy administrator*

Lakeway
Boswell, Gary Taggart *investor, former electronics company executive*
Gans, Dennis Joseph *information technology manager, financial analyst*

Lamesa
Saleh, John *lawyer*

Lampasas
Stephens, Billie Lowell *information assurance manager*

Lancaster
Stanley, Rosalind Marie Caldwell *social welfare administrator, consultant, writer*

Laredo
Ali, Ashraf *psychiatrist*
Black, Clifford Merwyn *academic administrator, sociologist, educator*
Crabtree, Joseph Craig *voice educator, vocalist*
Engling, Ezra Samuel *Spanish and literature educator, researcher*
Gómez, Angela González *art educator*
Heimes, Charmaine Marie *elementary school educator, poet, writer*
Kazen, George Philip *federal judge*
Keck, Ray Marvin, III, *academic administrator*
Kohl, John Preston *management educator*
Lakshmana, Viswanath *computer and information systems executive*
Mandell, Marshall *pediatrician, allergist, consultant*
McBurnette-Arguelles, Shannon Heather *language educator*
Nixon, Dennis E. *financial company executive*
Reuthinger, Georgeanne *special education educator*
Stone, Michael John *music educator, conductor*
Watson, Helen Richter *artist, educator*
Zaffirini, Judith *state legislator, small business owner*

League City
Kanuth, James Gordan *chemical engineer*

Leander
Erickson, Ralph D. *retired physical education educator, small business owner, consultant*
Merriman, Chrisann *marketing professional*

Levelland
Job, Valerie Y'llise *language educator*

Lewisville
Ferguson, R. Neil *computer systems consultant*
Guthrie, Brian Michael *linguist*
Mebane, Barbara Margot *artistic director, choreographer*
Vacca, John Joseph, Jr., *television executive*
Willmott, Peter Sherman *retail executive*

Liberty Hill
West, Felton *retired journalist, councilman*

Lindale
Carter, Thomas Smith, Jr., *retired rail transportation executive*
Jackson, Gary Dean *lawyer*
Wilson, Leland Earl *petroleum engineering consultant*

Little Elm
Middleton, Linda Jean Greathouse *lawyer*

Livingston
Davidson, John Robert *dentist*
Hayes, Gordon Glenn *civil engineer*
Meyer, Roberta *mediator, communication consultant*

Lockhart
McCormick, Michael Jerry *retired judge*
Scudday, Roy George *lawyer*

Lometa
Thompson, Mary Koleta *sculptor, non-profit organization management consultant*

Longview
Frase, Larry Lynn *medical oncologist*
Gentry, Vernessa Diana *principal, consultant*
Harrison, Guy Newell *lawyer*
Haymes, Jerry Lynn *entertainment industry executive*
Mann, Jack Matthewson *bottling company executive*
McKinley, Jimmie Joe *business executive*
Roller, Robert H. *dean, finance educator*
Udy, Rae *columnist, writer*

Lorena
Maricle, Robyn LuAnn (Ford) *band director, choir director*

Lubbock
Adamcik, Joe Alfred *retired chemistry educator, retired attorney*
Aker, Suzanne Deverse *physical movement educator*
Allison, Jane Shawver *medical school administrator, management consultant*
Archer, James Elson *engineering educator*
Arnold, Sue *music educator*
Baiza, Mary Pesina *development management consultant*
Barnette, Chris W. *medical association administrator*
Barnhill, Robert Edwin, III, *lawyer*
Beck, George Preston *anesthesiologist, educator*
Blake, Robert Wade *retired insurance company executive*
Blevins, Stanley Nance *minister, educator*
Brock, Ralph Haney *lawyer*
Broselow, Linda Latt *medical office technician, aviculturist*
Buesseler, John Aure *ophthalmologist, management consultant*
Burns, John Mitchell *academic administrator*
Chung, Ya-Li *music educator*
Conover, William Jay *statistics educator*
Crowson, James Lawrence *lawyer, financial company executive, academic administrator*
Daniels, Bruce C *education educator*
Davis, Alvin G. *company executive*
Dersch, Charette Alyse *marriage and family therapist*
Dudek, Richard Albert *engineering educator*
Everse, Johannes *biochemist, researcher*
Fontenot, Andrea Dean *communications executive*
Gelca, Razvan *education educator*
Gilliam, John Charles *economist, educator*
Glasscock, Herlinda Martinez *dean*
Haragan, Donald Robert *university administrator, geosciences educator*
Hentges, David John *microbiology educator*
Huffman, Walter B. *retired army officer, dean, law educator*
Illner-Canizaro, Hana *physician, oral surgeon, researcher*
Irons, Brian K. *education educator, pharmacist*
Jackson, Raymond Carl *cytogeneticist*
Kaye, Alan David *anesthesiologist, researcher*
Ketner, Kenneth Laine *philosopher, educator*
Kiesling, Ernst Willie *civil engineering educator*
Knight, Bob *college basketball coach*
Kristiansen, Magne *electrical engineer, educator*
Kuethe, Allan J. *historian, educator*
Kurtzman, Neil A. *medical educator*
Laing, Malcolm Brian *geologist, consultant*
Lucas, Don John *music educator*
May, Donald Robert Lee *ophthalmologist, retina and vitreous surgeon, educator, farmer*
Mittemeyer, Bernhard Theodore *urology and surgery educator*
Neyland, Malcolm *priest*
Prien, Samuel David *medical educator, researcher*
Purdom, Thomas James *lawyer*
Schiffer, Randolph Brenton *physician*
Schmidly, David J. *university president, biology educator*
Schneider, Andreas *education educator, researcher*
Sears, Edward L. *English language educator, real estate investor*
Sears, Robert Stephen *finance educator, university dean*
Seshaiyer, Padmanabhan *mathematician, educator*
Sharif, M. Alan *interventional cardiologist*
Sharp, Marsha *basketball coach*
Sitton, Windy *mayor*
Skillern, Frank Fletcher *law educator*
Skoog, Gerald Duane *science educator*
Stuart, Frank Adell *county official*
van Appledorn, Mary Jeanne *composer, music educator, pianist*
Varma, Surendra K. *pediatrician, educator*
Verrone, Richard Burks *archivist, educator*
Viatchenko-Karpinski, Serge *biophysicist, researcher*
Wall, Betty Jane *real estate consultant*
Warren, Donald John *retired surgeon, educator*
Way, Barbara Haight *dermatologist*
Wendt, Charles William *soil physicist, educator*
Willingham, Mary Maxine *fashion retailer*
Willingham, Welborn Iefer *psychologist, educator*
Wilson, M. Roy *medical educator*
Wilson, Margaret Eileen *retired physical education educator*
Wood, Richard Courtney *library director, educator*
Woolam, Gerald Lynn *surgeon*
Yoder-Wise, Patricia Snyder *education educator*

Lufkin
Billingsley, Shirley Ann *writer, poet*
Harmon, Jacqueline Baas *librarian, infosystems specialist*
Mott, Earl *artist, poet, writer*
Smith, Douglas V. *manufacturing executive, heavy*

Mabank
Beets, Hughla Fae *retired secondary school educator*
Smith, Thelma Tina Harriette *gallery owner, artist*

Magnolia
Girard, Louis Joseph *ophthalmologist, educator*

Mansfield
Parnell, Charles L. *speechwriter*
Siméus, Dumas M. *food products executive*

Marfa
Chambers, Johnnie Lois (Tucker Chambers) *elementary school educator, rancher*
Edge, Daniel *art educator, artist, consultant*
McBride, Elizabeth Anne Wilmore *writer*

Marshall
Magrill, Rose Mary *library director*
Shaw, Dianne Elizabeth *school administrator*
Sudhivoraseth, Niphon *pediatrician, allergist, immunologist*
Tapp, Paul Wayne *music educator*

Mart
Mathews, B. J. *secondary school educator*

Mason
Johnson, Rufus Winfield *lawyer*
Wilkerson, James Neill *retired lawyer*

Maxwell
Peters, Carol Ann *secondary school educator*

Mc Camey
Farley, Gail Conley *retired librarian*

Mc Kinney
Dickinson, Richard Raymond *retired oil company executive*
Dowdy, William Clarence, Jr., *retired lawyer*
Fairman, Jarrett Sylvester *retail company executive*
Gill, David Brian *electrical engineer, educator*
Hoffmann, Manfred Walter *consulting company executive*
Perryman, Gerald F., Jr., *retired career officer, defense company executive*
Schottlaender, Colin *electronics executive*
Strickland, Jeffery *medical products executive*

Mcallen
Arredondo, Jenna Dolores *speech pathology/audiology services professional*
Casso, Ramiro Raul *retired family physician, college official*
Connors, Joseph Aloysius, III, *lawyer*
Friedman, Bruce David *academic administrator, educator, social worker*
Hinojosa, Ricardo H. *federal judge*
McGee, William Howard John *librarian, administrator*
Ramirez, Mario Efrain *physician*
Rebuelta, Avelino Luis *public administration educator*
Robalino, Benjamin David *cardiologist*
Roney, Glen E. *finance company executive*
Saenz, Velma Lisa *plant protection and quarantine officer*
Spyker, Leola Edith *writer, educator*
Sutton, William Blaylock *pastor*
Tupper, Ron *public health, policy, and management educator*

Meadowlakes
Wilcox, Mary Reba *music educator*

Mercedes
Alaniz, Theodora Villarreal *elementary school educator*

Mesquite
Davis, Vivian *English language educator*
Gant, Linda Gayle *elementary school educator*
Holt, Mildred Frances *special education educator*
Nye, Randall Wayne *music educator*
Patrick, Pamela Ann *research consultant*
Reid, Helen Veronica *dean*
Sepulvado, Joseph Michael *computer information scientist*
Vaughan, Joseph Lee, Jr., *education educator, consultant*
Wenrich, John William *college president*

Mexia
Chambers, Linda Dianne Thompson *social worker*

Mico
Shockey, Thomas Edward *real estate executive, engineer*

Midland
Berner, Leo De Witte, Jr., *retired oceanographer*
Bitting, George Capen *oil company executive*
Celia, George *composer, writer*
Craddick, Thomas Russell *speaker of state house of representatives*
Estes, Andrew Harper *lawyer*
Fredrickson, Mark Allan *health facility administrator, physician*
Grover, Rosalind Redfern *oil and gas company executive*
Helms, Micky *engineering executive*
Hord, John Alan *geological engineer*
Ienatsch, Gayleen Elizabeth *nursing educator*
MacDonald, Leland Lloyd *lawyer*
Morrow, William Clarence *judge, lawyer, mediator*
Roberts, David Glen *prospector, investor*
Sherpa, Fran Magruder *geography educator, animal scientist, small business owner*
Taylor, Nicholas C. *lawyer, state agency administrator, energy executive*
Tom, James Robert *accountant*
Van de Water, Susan D. *physiatrist*

Midlothian
Sibley, James Scarborough *career officer*

Mineral Wells
Braun, Gustav Milan *facial plastic surgeon, otolaryngologist*
Warfield, Gerald Alexander *composer, writer*

Mission
Capener, Regner Alvin *electronics engineer, minister, writer, inventor*
McClendon, Maxine Nichols *artist*

Missouri City
Chang, Jeffrey Chai *dentist, educator, researcher*
Hodges, Jot Holiver, Jr., *retired lawyer, business executive*
Tchamengo, Mathias Ngoufi *energy executive, mathematician*

Montgomery
Kelsey, Clyde Eastman, Jr., *philosophy and psychology educator*
Smith, John Brewster *library administrator*
Steed, Theresa Jean *manufacturing executive*

Mount Pleasant
Caskey, Judith Ann *educational director*
McCauley, Dan Paul *dentist*
Palmer, Robert Blunden *newspaper, printing executive*
Vaughn, William Preston *historian, educator*

Nacogdoches
Bommanna, Vasudeva M. *allergist, immunologist*
Dean, Michael *conductor, church music minister*
Jacobsen, Jeffrey Richard *music educator*

Navasota
Smith, Jo Ann Costa *retired comptroller*

New Braunfels
Barragán, Celia Silguero *elementary school educator*
Griffin-Thompson, Melanie *accounting firm executive*
Krueger, Robert Charles *former ambassador, former senator, congressman*
Oestreich, Charles Henry *retired university president*
Wilson, James Lee *retired geology educator, consultant*

New Caney
Hayes, Ann Carson *computer services executive*

Normangee
Rector, M. Eugene *community pharmacist*

North Richland Hills
Mutz, Gregory Thomas *insurance company executive*

North Zulch
Fleming, Jon Hugh *psychology educator, business executive, educational consultant*

Odessa
Boyd, Claude Collins *educational specialist, consultant*
Grubbs, Donald Ray *educational director, educator, welder*
Moseley, Clifford Wayne *writer, poet*
Phillips, Barry *artist, educator*
Pugh, Jessie Truman *minister*
Toruño, Rhina M. *Literature educator, researcher, writer*

Olney
Timmons, Gordon David *economics professor, farmer*

Olton
Carson, Harold Dean *music educator, composer*

Orange
Dugas, Louis, Jr., *lawyer*
Jackson, Cynthia Ann *entrepreneur*
Odom, Sarah Bernice *elementary school educator*

Paige
Trevino, Jerry Rosalez *retired secondary school principal*

Palestine
Sellers, Wayne Chadick *retired newspaper publisher, editor*
Williams, Franklin Cadmus, Jr., *bibliographer*

Pampa
Cain, Donald Ezell *retired judge*
Cooley, Loralee Coleman *professional storyteller*
Powell, Dan Clayton *physician*
Willingham, Jeanne Maggart *dance educator, ballet company executive*

Panhandle
Sherrod, Lloyd Bruce *nutritionist*

Paris
Proctor, Richard Owen *historian, public health administrator, army officer*

Pasadena
Blue, Monte Lynn *college president*
Chan, Chiu M. *information technology executive*
Chan, Philip S. *medical products executive*
Fogo, Peter C. *educator, novelist, poet*
Gilley, Mickey Leroy *musician*
Gross, Cynthia Sue *petrochemicals manufacturing executive*
Kenagy, Cheri Lynn *nurse*
Martinez, Fernando V. *civil engineer*
Mondich, Edward H. *protective services official*
Moon, John Henry, Sr., *banker*
Root, M. Belinda *chemist*
Scott, William Floyd *accountant*
Shapiro, Edward Muray *dermatologist*
Thompson, Marian Nell *poetry, historical, non-fiction and fiction writer, educator, poet*

Pearland
Hammond, Raymond William *pharmacotherapy specialist*
Powell, John S., III, *lawyer, writer*
Shurtleff, Malcolm C. *plant pathologist, consultant, educator, extension specialist*

Perryton
Doerrie, Bobette *secondary school educator*

Pharr
Medina, Jesse James *protective services official, educator*

Pittsburg
Cogdill, Richard A. *food products executive*
Goolsby, O. B., Jr., *food products executive*
Pilgrim, Lonnie (Bo Pilgrim) *poultry production company executive*

Plainview
Crawford, Felix Conkling *dentist*
Kelley, Timothy Shawn *music educator*
Misa, Elenæ May *physical therapist*

Plano
Adams, Barney *consumer products company executive*
Alberthal, Lester M., Jr., *retired information processing services executive*
Altabef, Peter Anthony *lawyer*
Bain, Travis Whitsett, II, *manufacturing and retail executive*
Benn, Douglas Frank *information technology and computer science executive*
Blachly, Jack Lee *lawyer*
Bode, Richard Albert *retired financial executive*
Bru, Abelardo E. *food products executive*
Carver, Rita *fundraising consultant*
Casavantes, Rita *defense electronics and engineering professional*
Cavanaugh, Robert B. *department store executive*
Collumb, Peter John *communications company executive*
Cotter-Smith, Cathleen Marie *art educator, artist*
Cronauer, Gail Ann *theater educator, actress*
Cumming, Marilee *apparel company executive*
Davis, Gary L. *human resources professional*
Davis, Robert D. *rental company executive*
Day, Kevin Thomas *retired bank executive*
Dougherty, F(rancis) Kelly *data processing executive*
Edmonds, Albert J. *career officer*
Evans, Pat *mayor*
Fadel, Mitchell E. *rental company executive*
Findley, John Sidney *dentist*
Flores, Marion Thomas *advertising executive*
Ford, H. Ross, III, *real estate company executive*
Friedlander, D. Gilbert *lawyer*
Giron Vives, Ana *language educator*
Haddock, Ronald Wayne *former oil company executive*
Hardy, Tom Charles, Jr., *medical equipment company*
Harris, Wayne *retail executive*
Hatfield, Darl P. *consumer products company executive*
Hemingway, Richard William *law educator*
Hiegel, James Edward *mechanical engineer*
Hilton, Steven J. *real estate executive*
Jensen, Ronald L. *insurance company executive*
Korst, Christopher A. *rental company executive*
Landon, John R. *real estate executive*
Layton, Mark C. *wholesale distribution executive*
Levine, Harold *lawyer*
Litwin, Ruth Ann Forbes *artist*
Lotter, Charles Robert *lawyer, retail executive*
MacAlpine, Michelle Lewis *neuroscientist*
McCraw, Michael K. *construction executive*
McKay, Donald A. *retail company executive*
Miller, Ken Leroy *religious studies educator, consultant, writer*
Naor, Daniel *food products executive*
Neppl, Walter Joseph *retired retail store executive*
Norwood, Cecilia Stubbs *communications executive*
Parsons, Michael J. *health facility administrator*
Powell, James R. *wholesale distribution executive*
Questrom, Allen I. *retail executive*
Raish, Stephen E *retail executive*
Rhodes, Doris Chaney *freelance/self-employed secondary school educator*
Satz, Jeffrey S. *telecommunications industry executive, consultant*
Schuh, Frank Joseph *drilling engineering company executive, consultant*
Scott, Terry Lee *communications company executive*
Shelton, James D. (Denny Shelton) *hospital management company executive*
Sivinski, Tina M. *human resources specialist*
Speese, Mark E. *rental company executive*
Swan, Robert H. *corporate financial executive*
Taylor, Paul Peak *pediatric dentist, educator*
Warburton, Ralph Joseph *architect, engineer, planner, educator*

Port Aransas
Lehmann, William Leonardo *electrical engineer, educator*
Schake, Lowell Martin *animal science educator*
Swetnam, Monte Newton *petroleum exploration executive*
Turner, Elizabeth Adams Noble (Betty Turner) *real estate company executive*
Van Baalen, Donna Gale *artist, retired pharmacist*

Port Arthur
Munoz, Andrea Lee *human resources specialist*
Vinecour, Oneida Agnes *nurse*

Post
Earl, Lewis Harold *economics and management consultant, lawyer*
Killian, Lawrence Harding, II, (Larry H. Killian) *sculptor*
Warren, Jennifer Elizabeth *family nurse practitioner*

Pottsboro
Hanning, Gary William *utility executive, water company executive, consultant*
Thomas, Ann Van Wynen *law educator*

Prairie View
Akujuobi, Cajetan Maduabuchukwu *systems engineer, electrical engineering educator, researcher*
French, Laurence Armand *social science educator, psychology educator*
Hines, Charles A. *academic administrator*
Prestage, Jewel Limar *political science educator*

Rancho Viejo
Garza, Roberto Jesus *retired education educator*

Randolph A F B
Lamontagne, Donald A. *career officer*
Stinson, Nancy *military officer*

Randolph Afb
Ellis, Edward R. *career officer*

Raymondville
Montgomery-Davis, Joseph *osteopathic physician*

Red Oak
Jones, Genia Kay *emergency supervising nurse, consultant*

Richardson
Andrews, Melinda Wilson *human development researcher*
Avadhut, HitendranandaAcarya *spiritual counselor, yoga teacher*
Berry, Brian Joe Lobley *geographer, political economist, urban planner*
Bray, Carolyn Scott *education educator*
Burke, Thomas William *executive benefits consulting company official*
Chlamtac, Imrich *computer company executive, educator*
Conkel, Robert Dale *lawyer, pension consultant*
Constantinescu, Tiberiu *mathematician*
DeBusk, Manuel Conrad *lawyer, business executive*
Dunn, David E. *university dean*
Easttom, Chuck *computer scientist, educator*
Ellwanger, J. David *lawyer*
Faria, Joao Ricardo *economist, educator*
Goodspeed, Linda A. *manufacturing executive*
Gray, Donald Melvin *molecular and cell biology educator*
Heath, Mary Ann *elementary school educator*
Hennessey, Audrey Kathleen *computer researcher, educator*
Holmes, Jennifer Smith *political scientist, educator*
Kelly, Rita Mae *academic administrator, researcher*
Krauss, Henry Frederick, Jr., *optometrist*
Laseter, John Luther *clinical and forensic toxicologist*
Lin, Zhiang *science educator*
Liu, Shelby *financial advisor, chemist*
Lowe, J. Allen *minister*
Manton, William Inwood *geologist, educator*
Martin, Richard Kelley *lawyer*
Merville, Lawrence Joseph *finance educator*
Odushkin, Taras *mathematician*
Olson, Dennis Oliver *lawyer*
Redman, Timothy Paul *English language educator, author, chess federation administrator*
Richards, Frederick Francis, Jr., *manufacturing executive, consultant*
Rogers, Mal David, Jr., *chemical engineer*
Rutford, Robert Hoxie *geologist, educator*
Schjerven, Robert E. *manufacturing executive*
Senderling, Jon Townsend *journalist, public affairs specialist*
Smith, Mark P. *foundation executive*
Smith, Richard A. *manufacturing executive*
Sodeman, Nancy Elizabeth *retired literature educator*
Sowers, Wesley Hoyt *lawyer, management consultant*
Sperrin, Graham Frederick *marketing professional*
Wildenthal, Bryan Hobson *university administrator*
Williams, James Francis, Jr., *religious organization administrator*
Wood, Joseph George *neurobiologist, educator*

Richmond
Barratt, Cynthia Louise *pharmaceutical company executive*
Elliott, Brady Gifford *judge*

Roanoke
Steward, Jerry Wayne *air transportation executive, consultant*

Rockport
Benningfield, Carol Ann *lawyer*
Johnson, Marilyn *retired obstetrician, gynecologist*
Minor, Joseph Edward *civil engineer, educator*
Porter, Charles Raleigh, Jr., *retired lawyer*
Stachiw, Jaroslaw (Jerry) Drahomyr *mechanical engineer, consultant*

Rockwall
Bruce, Dana Glenn *lawyer*
Bush, Larry Don *communications company administrator*
Crooks, Patricia Kay *counselor*
Fisher, Gene Jordan *retired chemical company executive*
Griffith, James William *systems engineer, consultant*
Kotas, Robert Vincent *research physician, educator*
Wallace, Mary Elaine *opera director, author*
Wiorkowski, Gabrielle Kay *database consultant*

Roma
Martinez, Adolfo Roberto *secondary school educator*

Rosenberg
Tourtellotte, Mills Charlton *mechanical and electrical engineer*
White, Gretchen Nance *education educator, writer*

Rosharon
Jenkins, Judith Alexander *bank consultant*

Round Mountain
McReynolds, Mary Maureen *small business owner*

Round Rock
Bell, Paul D. *computer company executive*
Carter, John Rice *congressman*
Crawford, Kim *computer company executive*
Dell, Michael S. *computer company executive*
Goodman, Kim *marketing professional, computer company executive*
Green, Thomas B. *lawyer, computer company executive*
Hudson, Michel Colette *management consultant*
Khalid, Humayun *computer scientist, consultant*
Ledbetter, Sharon Faye Welch *retired educational consultant*
Marengi, Joseph Alexander *computer company executive*
Mott, Randall D. *computer company executive*
O'Connor, Clint Haynie *electrical engineer*
Puri, Rajendra Kumar *business and tax specialist, consultant*
Ricklefs, Dale Lynne *library director*
Rollins, Kevin B. *computer company executive*
Ryan, Nolan *former professional baseball player*
Schneider, Dennis Ray *microbiology educator and executive*
Schneider, James M. *computer company executive*
Vanderslide, James T. *computer company executive*
Wahl, William Bryan *marketing professional, real estate officer*

Round Top
Lentz, Edwin Lamar *art historian*

Rowlett
Efrussy, Alan Maurice *urban planner*
Patterson, Edward Palmer *retired physical scientist*

Royse City
Borden, William Vickers *education educator, writer*

Rusk
McMinn, J. B. *retired philosophy educator, composer*

Sachse
Eichelberger, Charles Bell *retired career officer*

Salado
Parks, Lloyd Lee *oil company executive*
Willingham, Douglas Barton *dentist*
Wilmer, Harry Aron *psychiatrist, educator*

San Angelo
Butler, Michael Ward *economics professor*
Carter, James Alfred *lawyer*
Charlesworth, Ernest Neal *allergist, immunologist, dermatologist, educator*
Chatfield, Mary Van Abshoven *librarian*
Coe, Robert Stanford *retired management educator*
Curtin, David *music educator*
Davison, Elizabeth Jane Linton *education educator*
Fischer, Duncan Kinnear *neurosurgeon*
McLaughlin, John Mark *lawyer*
Moeller, Galen Ashley *lawyer*
Schell, Kraig Lee *psychologist, educator*
Smith, Karen B. *educational consultant*
Sutton, John Ewing *lawyer*

San Antonio
Abramson, Hyman Norman *engineering and science research executive*
Alvey, Dennis H. *government agency administrator*
Ammann, Lillian Ann Nicholson *writer, editor, small business owner*
Anderson, Brooks Doran, II, *geologist, consultant*
Anderson, Charles Edward, Jr., *research and development executive*
Armstrong, John Hulse *surgeon*
Armstrong, William Tucker, III, *lawyer*
Arthur, Gary L., Jr., *energy executive*
Atchley, Curtis Leon *mechanical engineer*
Aust, Joe Bradley *surgeon, educator*
Azzi, Jennifer L. *professional basketball player*
Bagley, William Evan *application technology specialist*
Bailey, Steven R. *cardiologist, researcher*
Baker, Floyd Wilmer *surgeon, retired army officer*
Balentine, James Scott *music educator, composer*
Baron, Robert M. *architecture educator*
Barrera, Elvira Puig *counselor, therapist, educator*
Bayern, Arthur Herbert *lawyer*
Beadle, Robert S. *energy executive*
Beckmann, Charles Henry *cardiologist, educator*
Bellows, Thomas John *political scientist, educator*
Bennett, Sister Elsa Mary *retired secondary education educator*
Bennett, Steven Alan *lawyer*
Benninger, Edward C., Jr., *retired petroleum-natural gas company executive*
Bettac, Robert Edward *lawyer*
Biery, Evelyn Hudson *lawyer*
Blank, Steven *energy executive*
Blonkvist, Tim *architectural firm executive*
Booke, Keith D. *energy executive*
Bramble, Ronald Lee *business and legal consultant*
Branton, James LaVoy *lawyer*
Brazil, John Russell *academic administrator*
Breit, William *economist, educator, writer*
Brewster, Olive Nesbitt *retired librarian*
Bromley, Ernest W. *communications executive*
Brooks, Franklin Ramon *psychologist, army officer*
Brouillard, John C. *grocery company executive*
Brouillard, John Charles *retail company executive*
Brown, Mary Rose *energy executive*
Browning, Jay D. *energy executive*
Bryan, Richard Ray *retired real estate and construction executive*
Budalur, Thyagarajan Subbanarayan *chemistry professor*
Burch, James Leo *science research institute executive*
Burton, Russell Rohan *aerospace scientist, researcher*
Butt, Charles Clarence *food service executive*
Caldwell, Royce S. *communications executive*
Campbell, Robert Murray, Jr., *surgeon, researcher*
Carr, Cassandra Colvin *communications company executive*
Case, Jeff Dean *lawyer*
Castleberry, James Newton, Jr., *retired law educator, dean*
Catto, Henry Edward *former government official, former ambassador*
Champion, Michael Edward *physician assistant, clinical perfusionist*
Chiego, William J. *museum director*
Ciskowski, Michael S. *energy executive*
Cisneros, Henry G. *homebuilding executive, broadcast executive, former federal official*
Clamann, York H. *biologist, educator*
Clark, Robert Phillips *newspaper editor, consultant*
Clarke, Mary Elizabeth *retired career officer*
Cloud, Bruce Benjamin, Sr., *construction company executive*
Colyer, Kirk Klein *insurance executive, real estate investment executive*
Condos, Barbara Seale *real estate broker, developer, investor*
Condos, J. Alexander *mortgage company executive*
Corrigan, Helen González *retired cytologist*
Crabtree, Ben C. *neuromuscular therapy clinic director*
Cragnolino, Gustavo Adolfo *research scientist*
Crichton, Flora Cameron *volunteer*
Crichton, John Hayes *investment banker*
Croft, Harry Allen *psychiatrist*
Daebert-Friese, Sharyn Varhely *social worker, evangelist*
Daley, William M. *former federal government official*
Daniel, Marian Phillips *language educator, secondary school educator*
Davis, George Edward *industrial designer*
Davis, Jolene Bryant *magazine publishing executive consultant*
Davis, Robert G. *insurance executive*
Davis, Sarah Jane *health care professional*
Davis, Steven Andrew *dermatologist*
Dean, Jack *protective services official*
de la Garza, Luis Adolfo *lawyer*
DeNice, Marcella L. *counselor*
Denny, John Bernard *biochemist, educator*
Detro, John Fitzgerald *military officer*
Dinwiddie, Cynthia L. *geologist*
Dumitru, Daniel *physiatrist*
Duncan, A. Baker *investment banker*
Duncan, Tim *professional basketball player*
Dunn, James David *language educator*
Ebrom, Charles *contracting executive*
Edelman, Asher Barry *financier*
Edwards, S. Eugene *energy executive*
Ellis, James D. *communications executive, lawyer*
Emery, Nancy Beth *lawyer*
Endresen, Lisa Castro *curator*
Espino, David V. *geriatrician, family practice physician*
Estep, Myrna Lynne *systems analyst, philosophy educator*
Evans, Richard W. *finance company executive*
Faules, Barbara Ruth *retired elementary education educator*
Fecher, Vincent John *priest*
Fehrenbach, T(heodore) R(eed) *author, businessman*
Feldman, Marc D. *cardiologist, physiologist, biomedical engineer*
Foerster, Paul A. *secondary school educator, writer*
Fonseca, Joseph Mojica, Jr., *financial analyst, educator*
Foster, Charles F. *communications executive*
Franklin, Larry Daniel *communications company executive*
Frazer, Robert Lee *landscape architect*
Frost, Thomas Clayborne *banker, director*
Furgeson, William Royal *federal judge*
Furino, Antonio *economist, educator*
Gambitta, Richard Anthony *political science educator*
Garb, Howard Neil *clinical psychologist, educator*
Garcia, Henry Frank *supply management and project management consultant and trainer*
Gardner, Raymond Alan *webmaster, writer*
Garza, Ed *mayor*
Garza, Emilio M(iller) *federal judge*
Gates, Mahlon Eugene *applied research executive, former government official, former army officer*
Gaulin, Jean *gas industry executive*
Goelz, Paul Cornelius *university dean*
Goff, Colleen Mullen *lawyer*
Gonzalez, Efren *former airport executive*
Gonzalez, Hector Hugo *nurse, educator, consultant*
Gorder, Joe *energy executive*
Graves, Kenneth Martin *architect*
Greehey, William Eugene *energy company executive*
Gribou, Julius M. *architecture educator*

Grigoryan, Artyom Mkrtichi *mathematician*
Grubb, Robert Lynn *computer system designer*
Guerra, Fernando A. *pediatrician, health facility administrator*
Gwathmey, Joe Neil, Jr., *broadcast executive*
Hall, Denise *special education educator*
Hall, Douglas Lee *computer science educator*
Hardberger, Phillip Duane *judge, lawyer, journalist*
Hardy, Harvey Louchard *retired lawyer*
Harvey, Candi *professional basketball coach*
Hatcher, Donald W. *government agency administrator*
Hausheer, Frederick Herman *medical oncologist, researcher, pharmaceutical company officer*
Hawken, Patty Lynn *retired nursing educator, dean of faculty*
Haywood, Norcell Dan *architect*
Hazuda, Helen Pauline *sociologist, educator*
Heidelberg, Paul *writer*
Heloise, *columnist, writer*
Hemminghaus, Roger Roy *energy company executive, chemical engineer*
Henderson, Connie Chorlton *city planner, artist and writer*
Henderson, Dwight Franklin *dean, educator*
Henry, Peter York *lawyer, mediator*
Herres, Robert Tralles *financial services executive*
Hogan, John *broadcast executive*
Hohnholt, John F. *energy executive*
Holl, Kristi Diane *writer, educator*
Holmes, Parris H., Jr., *information services professional*
Holt, Peter M. *sports team executive*
Honore, Gerard Marcel *reproductive endocrinologist*
Hood, Sandra Dale *librarian*
Hornsby, David McMillan *musician, music educator*
Horowitz, Rosalind *education educator, researcher*
Horton, Granville Eugene *occupational medicine physician, retired air force officer*
Hubbard, Walter Bryan *chemical engineer, consultant*
Huff, Robert Whitley *obstetrician, gynecologist, educator*
Irving, George Washington, III, *veterinarian, research director, small business executive*
Jacobson, Helen Gugenheim (Mrs. David Jacobson) *civic worker*
Jansen-Brown, Angelika Charlotte *art museum director, independent curator*
Jensen White, Teresa *financial planner*
Jerralds, Oswald Clarence *elementary school educator*
Jiménez, Leonardo *popular accordionist*
Johnson, Anne Stuckly *retired lawyer*
Johnson, Shannon *professional basketball player*
Jones, Daniel Hare *librarian, consultant*
Jones, James Richard *business administration educator*
Jones, Oscar Calvin *minister, dean*
Junek, Heather Diane *medical/surgical nurse*
Kalkwarf, Kenneth Lee *dean, dental educator*
Kamada-Cole, Mika M. *allergist, immunologist, medical educator*
Kaye, Celia Ilene *pediatrics educator*
Kehl, Randall Herman *executive, consultant, lawyer*
Keirnan, Donald E. *communications executive*
Kelling, George Horton *retired military officer*
Kickbusch, Consuelo Castillo *educational association administrator, consultant, former military officer*
Kiernan, Donald E. *telecommunications industry executive*
Killinger, Clayton *energy executive*
Kilpatrick, Charles Otis *newspaper editor, publisher*
King, Gregory C. *petroleum company executive*
King, Kandi Jaye *secondary school educator, consultant*
King, Ronald Baker *federal judge*
Kittle, Joseph S. *science administrator, consultant*
Klaerner, Curtis Maurice *gas industry executive*
Klesse, William R. *energy executive*
Kline, John William *retired air force officer, management consultant*
Kolaparthi, VenkataSubbaRao *oncologist*
Kosty, Carlita *secondary school educator*
Kozuch, Julianna Bernadette *librarian, educator*
Kreisberg, Jeffrey I. *medical educator, researcher*
Krier, Joseph Roland *chamber of commerce executive, lawyer*
Kutchins, Michael Joseph *aviation consultant, former airport executive*
Labenz-Hough, Marlene *dispute resolution professional*
Langland, Olaf Elmer *retired dental educator*
Le, Dung *mathmatics educator, researcher*
Leal, J. Terri *academic facility administrator*
Ledford, Frank Finley, Jr., *surgeon, army officer*
Leies, John Alex *theology educator, clergyman*
Leighton, Albert Chester *history professor*
Le Maistre, Charles Aubrey *retired internist, epidemiologist, educator*
Lenke, Joanne Marie *publishing executive*
Leon, Robert Leonard *psychiatrist, educator*
Lien, Da-Hsiang Donald *finance educator*
Lopez, M. Edward *small business owner*
Lowe, Douglas Howard *architect*
Lussky, Warren Alfred *librarian, educator, consultant*
Lyle, Robert Edward *chemist*
Macon, Jane Haun *lawyer*
Madrid, Olga Hilda Gonzalez *retired elementary education educator, association executive*
Maloney, Marynell *lawyer*
Maloney, Pat, Sr., *lawyer*
Marbut, Robert Gordon *communications, electronic security and broadcast executive, investor*
Marcogliese, Richard J. *energy executive*
Markwell, Dick R(obert) *retired chemist*
Marlin, Arthur Edward *pediatric neurosurgeon, educator*
Marrou, Chris René *television newscaster*
Martin, James Charles *physician*
Martinez, Joe Louis, Jr., *neurobiologist, educator*
Marvin, Catherine A. *financial consultant*
Massengale, Hope Vega *music educator*
Masters, Bettie Sue Siler *biochemist, educator*
Mathy, Pamela Ann *lawyer*
Maxwell, Diana Kathleen *early childhood education educator*
Mays, L(ester) Lowry *broadcast executive*
Mays, Mark Pitman *communication company executive*
Mays, Randall T. *broadcast executive*
Mc Allister, Gerald Nicholas *retired bishop, clergyman*
McBee, Lucy Armijo *retired elementary education educator, administrator, singer, actress, writer*
McClane, Robert Sanford *former bank holding company executive, entrepreneur*
McComas, David John *science administrator, space physicist*
McCombs, Red *automotive sales executive*
McDonald, James H. *anthropologist, educator*
McDonald, Mary Helen *special education educator*
McFee, Arthur Storer *physician*
McGill, Henry Coleman, Jr., *pathologist, educator, researcher*
McIntosh, Dennis Keith *veterinarian, consultant*
Mealey, Brian L. *periodontist, military officer*
Melson, Marvin E. *finance company executive*
Mendoza, Louis G. *literature educator, researcher*
Messina, Paul Francis *education consultant*
Michaels, Willard A. (Bill Michaels) *retired broadcasting executive*
Miller, Frank Lubbock (Char), IV, *historian, educator*
Millet, John Porath *lawyer*
Mills, Linda S. *public relations executive*
Mitchell, George Washington, Jr., *physician, educator*
Moder, John Joseph *non-profit administrator*
Montecel, Maria Robledo (Cuca Robledo Montecel) *educational association administrator*
Montemayor, Carlos Rene *advertising agency executive*
Montford, John Thomas *state legislator, academic administrator, lawyer*
Moya, Francisco Saez *consumer products company executive*
Moynihan, John Bignell *retired lawyer*
Murphy, Cathy *music educator*
Nance, Betty Love *librarian*
Nava, Carmen P. *communications executive*
Neel, Spurgeon Hart, Jr., *physician, retired army officer*
Newton, Virginia *archivist, historian, librarian*
Nowak, Nancy Stein *judge*
Odom, Marjorie Mildred Morgan *retired librarian*
Ognibene, Andre John *physician, army officer, educator*
Oppenheim, Martha Kunkel *pianist, educator*
Orange, Carolyn *education educator*
O'Rourke, Robert A. *cardiologist, educator*
Ortiz, Albert *police chief*
Palmer, Hubert Bernard *dentist, retired military officer*
Park, Myung Kun *medical educator*
Passty, Jeanette Nyda *English language educator, writer*
Peak, Howard W. *former mayor*
Pensado, Osvaldo *research scientist*
Persellin, Robert Harold *physician*
Pestana, Carlos *surgeon, retired dean, educator*
Peters, Richard Spencer *musician*
Petty, Scott, Jr., *rancher*
Pfeiffer, Philip J. *lawyer*
Phillips, William Thomas *nuclear medicine physician, researcher*
Pipkin, Marvin Grady *lawyer*
Pliego-Stout, Patricia *travel company executive*
Popovich, Gregg *professional basketball coach*
Prengle, Herman William, Jr., *chemical engineer, educator*
Pruitt, Basil Arthur, Jr., *surgeon, retired military officer*
Pysher, Alan Guy *nurse anesthetist*
Rafelson, Max Emanuel, Jr., *biochemist, medical school administrator*
Ramos, Raul *surgeon*
Rankin, John Karl *retired minister, retired theology studies educator*
Reams, Bernard Dinsmore, Jr., *lawyer, educator*
Recker, Patricia Bullion *secondary school educator*
Redfield, Carol Ann Luckhardt *engineering educator*
Reed, James C., Jr., *lawyer*
Reed, Susan D. *prosecutor*
Reid, Demetra Adams *insurance company executive*
Reuter, Stewart Ralston *retired radiologist, lawyer, educator*
Rhodes, Linda Jane *psychiatrist*
Ribble, Ronald George *retired psychologist, educator, writer*
Rich, Bradford Whitman *insurance executive*
Ridder, Linda Gayle *librarian*
Rivard, Robert *editor*
Roberts, James Lewis *medical sciences educator*
Robertson, Samuel Luther, Jr., *special education educator, therapist, researcher*
Robertson, Sterling Clifton *music educator, pianist*
Robinson, David Maurice *professional basketball player*
Robles, Josue, Jr., *insurance company executive*
Rodriguez, Roberto Ashley *language educator*
Rodriguez, Xavier *lawyer*
Rogers, William *psychologist, behavior specialist, writer, lecturer, journalist*
Rojo, Ruth M. *nutritionist, alternative medicine consultant*
Ross, James Ulric *lawyer, accountant, educator*
Rush, W. Marvin *trucking executive*
Ruttenberg, Frank Z. *lawyer*
Ryder, Gene Ed *retired United States Air Force training administrator*
Sablik, Martin John *research physicist*
Schenker, Steven *internist, educator*
Schlueter, David Arnold *law educator*
Schmitz, John Phillip *maxillofacial surgeon, researcher*
Schmutz, John Francis *lawyer*
Schneider, Frank David *family physician*
Shapard, Robert *gas industry executive*
Shearn, Michael Joseph *lawyer, arbitrator, mediator*
Shipman, Ross Lovelace *petroleum executive*
Shirley, Graham Edward *management executive*
Singh, Yesh Pal *mechanical engineering educator, consultant*
Sinkin, Fay Marie *environmentalist*
Smith, Bruce Alfred *oil industry executive*
Smith, H. Pete *retired oil industry executive*
Smith, John Marvin, III, *surgeon, educator*
Smith, Rebecca Lynn *language educator*
Smith, Reginald Brian Furness *retired anesthesiologist, educator*
Smith, Steven Delano *professional basketball player*
Sobre, Judith Berg *education educator*
Solomon, Diane Hurst *neurologist*
Spears, Sally *lawyer*
Spiro, Herbert John *political scientist, politician, educator, ambassador*
Spraggins, Johnnie David *social studies educator*
Steen, John Thomas, Jr., *lawyer*
Stephenson, Randall *communications executive*
Stevens, Dennis Max *audit director*
Sutton, Johnny K. *lawyer*
Swansburg, Russell Chester *nursing educator, consultant, health facility administrator*
Swiggett, Harold E. (Hal Swiggett) *writer, photographer*
Synek, Miroslav *physicist, chemist, world affairs independent consultant, researcher*
Thomas, John Arlen *pharmacology educator, health science administrator*
Thompson, Robert Knox *surgeon*
Tian, Qi *computer science educator*
Titzman, Donna M. *energy executive*
Torres, Arthuro G. *toy company executive*
Traylor, Donald Reginald *mathematics educator*
Truett, Lila Flory *economics professor*
Ujioka, Takeshi *endocrinologist*
Van de Putte, Leticia *pharmacist, state senator*
Vazquez, Gilbert Falcon *lawyer*
Verghese, Abraham Cheeran *internist, educator, writer*
Von Hoff, Daniel Douglas *physician, oncologist*
Von Honts, Jacqueline Jay *artist, educator*
von Raffler-Engel, Walburga (Walburga Engel) *linguist, cross-cultural communications specialist, lecturer, writer*
Walker, W. Lawrence, Jr., *newspaper publishing executive*
Wallis, Ben Alton, Jr., *lawyer*
Walsh, Nicolas Eugene *rehabilitation medicine physician, educator*
Wang, Samuel James *physician*
Wartman, Steven *dean, educator*
Webb, James Taylor *physiologist, pilot*
Weinbrenner, George Ryan *aeronautical engineer*
Weiner, Marcia Myra *judge*
Wellberg, Edward Louis, Jr., *insurance company executive*
West, Robert Van Osdell, Jr., *retired petroleum executive*
Whitacre, Edward E., Jr., *telecommunications executive*
White, Charles B. *academic administrator*
Whitesell, Stephen Ernest *parks and recreation director*
Wilkins, Christopher Putnam *conductor*
Wilkins, Ray *communications executive*
Williams, Thomas Eugene *pediatric hematologist-oncologist, pharmaceutical executive*
Williams, Tywanda Monceil *social services administrator*
Williamson, Deborah Daywood *lawyer*
Williamson, Fletcher Phillips *real estate broker*
Wilson, Janie Menchaca *nursing educator, researcher*
Wilson, Stephen Edward *academic administrator*
Winik, Joanne *broadcast executive*
Wolff, Hugh Lipman *urologist, educator*
Wood, Thomas Willard *health care industry executive*
Woodson, Linda Townley *English educator, writer*
Yerkes, Susan Gamble *newspaper columnist*
Young, James Julius *academic administrator, retired military officer*
Zachry, Henry Bartell, Jr., *construction executive*
Zesch, Hal *energy executive*
Zilveti, Carlos Benjamin *preventive medicine physician, pediatrician*
Zoghby, Jeriad Marcus *lead analytical specialist, consultant*

San Diego
Pena, Modesta Celedonia *retired principal*

San Juan
Guzmán, Belinda F. *elementary school educator*

San Marcos
Boehm, Richard Glennon *geography educator, writer*
Bullock, Jerry McKee *retired military officer, consultant, educator*
Carman, Mary Ann *retired special education educator*
Fite, Kathleen Elizabeth *education educator*
Keller, Thomas Michael *mathematician, educator*
Kyle, Henry Carper, III, *lawyer*
Laumer, Jack C. *musician, educator*
McLean, Robert James Cameron *microbiologist, educator*
Moore, Betty Jean *retired education educator*
Moore, Patsy Sites *food service consultant*
Oxford, William Todd *music educator*
Palmer, Roger Raymond *accounting educator*
Parkin-Speer, Diane *English law educator*
Randolph, Robert Morrison *literature educator*
Schmidt, John Charles *music educator*
Schuler, Nico Stephan *musicologist*
Taylor, Ruth Arleen Lesher *marketing educator*
Watkins, Ted Ross *social work educator*
Wetter-Kubeck, Daisy Fisher *dietitian, consultant*
Wilson, Vicki Lynn *executive secretary, administrative assistant*

Santa Fe
Blount, James Robert *military career officer*
Lambert, Willie Lee Bell *mobile equipment company owner, educator*

Schertz
Ringenbach, Paul Thomas *historian, consultant*

Schulenburg
Clark, I. E. *publisher*

Seabrook
Patten, Bernard Michael *neurologist, writer, educator*
Spears, James Grady *small business owner*
Young, Kenneth Alden *aerospace engineer, consultant*

Sealy
Stevens, Rhea Christina *lawyer*
Young, Milton Earl *retired petroleum company executive*

Seguin
Robinson, Ronald Alan *manufacturing executive*

Sheppard AFB
Cook, Sharla J. *career officer*

Sherman
Brown, Paul Neeley *federal judge*
Bueno, Lourdes *education educator*
Freels, Jesse Saunders, Jr., *lawyer*
Hardesty, Larry Lynn *librarian*
Jarma, Donna Marie *secondary school educator*
Page, Oscar C. *academic administrator*
Parker, Harry John *retired psychologist, educator*

Smithville
Clark, LaVerne Harrell *writer*

Snyder
Barnes, Maggie Lue Shifflett (Mrs. Lawrence Barnes) *nurse*
Hall, Sandra J. *education educator*

Southlake
Brunig, Robert Arthur *lawyer*
Cuomo, Andrew *information technology executive*
Elliott, Dennis Dawson *communications executive*
Gilliland, Michael S. *travel company executive*
Herrmann, Debra McGuire *chemist, educator*
Jackson, Jeffery M. *information technology executive*
Kelly, Carol A. *travel company executive*
Schwarte, David A. *travel company executive*
Sorge, Karen Lee *commercial printing company executive, consultant*

Spade
Davis, Thomas Pinkney *secondary school educator*

Spearman
Jarvis, Billy Britt *lawyer*

Spicewood
Carrell, Hammel Lee *jewelry designer*

Spring
Ciancimino, Joseph Andrew *data processing executive*
Cooley, Andrew Lyman *corporation executive, former army officer*
Farley, Andrew Newell *lawyer, consultant*
Hendricks, Randal Arlan *lawyer*
Hunt, T(homas) W(ebb) *retired religion educator*
Jackson, Guida Myrl *writer, magazine editor, book editor, publisher*
Maxfield, Mary Constance *management consultant*
Rose, Michael Elvin *oil and gas exploration company executive*
Szymczak, Edward Joseph *mechanical engineer*
Treasure-Terrell, Suzanne Marie *marketing and sales professional, writer, poet, lyricist*
Woodward, Clifford Edward *chemical engineer*

Spring Branch
Barban, Arnold Melvin *advertising educator*
Fasano, Anthony John *marketing consultant*

Springtown
Marrs, James F., Jr., (Jim Marrs) *author, journalist, educator*

Stafford
Krenek, Mary Louise *political scientist, researcher, historian*
Le, Duy-Loan *electrical engineer*
Odegard, Mark Erie *geophysicist, consultant*
Polinger, Iris Sandra *dermatologist*
Rosenkranz, Linda *English educator*

Stephenville
Batson, David Warren *lawyer*
Christopher, Joe Randell *English language educator*
Collier, Boyd Dean *finance educator, management consultant*
Moore, Linda Kathleen *personnel agency executive*
Swanson, Jacqueline V. *academic administrator, educator, women's health nurse practitioner*

Sugar Land
Chapko, Stephen J. *electronics executive*
Downs, Hartley H., III, *chemist*
Fedrick, Lonnie M. *construction executive*
Harribance, Sean Lalsingh *parapsychologist*
Hitchcock, Bion Earl *lawyer*
Hosley, Marguerite Cyril *civic worker*
Huston, Daniel Cliff *geophysicist*
Keefe, Carolyn Joan *tax accountant*
Lawrence, Lois Armes *retired language educator, writer*
Maurer, William C. *mining company executive*
Olson, Larry D. *electronics executive*
Preng, David Edward *management consultant*
Ramos, Rose Mary *elementary school educator*
Victor, Ann Michele *musician, educator*

Sulphur Springs
Gibson, Jannette Poe *educational consultant*
Law, Kerry W. *wholesale executive*
McKenzie, Michael K. *wholesale company executive*

Sweetwater
Woodrow, Natile Latreece *accountant, educator*

Temple
Allen, Steven R. *obstetrician, gynecologist, educator*
Beyer, Richard J. *priest, writer*
Buswell, Arthur Lee *psychiatrist*
Carroll, Irwin Dixon *engineer*
Clawson, James F., Jr., *judge, mediator, arbitrator*
Cuba, Benjamin James *lawyer, mediator*
Dyck, Walter Peter *gastroenterologist, educator, university official*
Erickson, Richard A. *health facility administrator, medical educator*
Gantt, David Scott *cardiologist, academic administrator*
Gillett, Victor William, Jr., *title insurance company executive*
Hoffer, J. Lee *health facility administrator, medical educator*
Holleman, Vernon Daughty *physician, internist*
Jones, Grant *retired state legislator, lawyer, insurance agent*

Blake, George Rowland *soil science educator, water resources research administrator*
Bott, Jay Cordell *oncologist, hematologist*
Boyter, Scott M. *academic administrator*
Bradshaw, Jerald Sherwin *chemistry educator, researcher*
Brown, Joseph William *retired patent agent*
Brown, Shauna Kirsti *music educator, researcher, composer*
Bullough, Robert Vernon, Jr., *educational studies professor*
Cannon, Christopher Black *congressman*
Cheney, Brigham Vernon *physical chemist, consultant*
Creer, Thomas Laselle *psychologist, educator*
Crookston, R. Kent *agronomy educator*
Densley, Colleen T. *principal*
DeTienne, Kristen Bell *finance educator*
Fleming, Joseph Clifton, Jr., *dean, law educator*
Forster, Merlin Henry *foreign languages educator, writer, researcher*
Fox, Frank Wayne *history professor*
Fry, Earl Howard *political scientist, educator*
Hansen, H. Reese *dean, educator*
Harding, Ray Murray, Jr., *judge*
Hart, Edward LeRoy *poet, educator*
Henderson, Douglas James *physicist, chemist, researcher*
Hill, Edward Jeffrey *family life educator*
Hill, Ned Cromar *dean, finance educator, consultant*
Hill, Richard Lee *lawyer*
Holbrook, Jay Mack *publishing company executive*
Howell, Larry L. *mechanical engineer, educator*
Hunt, H(arold) Keith *business management educator, marketing consultant*
Ivie, Evan Leon *computer science educator*
Izatt, Reed M. *chemistry researcher*
Jensen, Richard Dennis *librarian*
Konecny-Costa, Jennifer *computer company executive*
Kunz, Phillip Ray *sociologist, educator*
Latta, George Haworth, III, *neonatologist*
Lyon, James Karl *German language educator*
McArthur, Eldon Durant *geneticist, researcher*
Merritt, LaVere Barrus *engineering educator, civil engineer*
Murphy, John Joseph *English literature educator, critic, editor*
Nelson, Stewart *computer company executive*
Newitt, Jay *construction management educator*
Ogden, Bruce E. *pediatrician, neonatologist*
Peer, Larry Howard *literature educator*
Peterson, Erlend Dean *dean*
Porter, Blaine Robert Milton *sociology and psychology educator*
Powley, Edward Harrison, III, *musicology educator*
Samuelson, Cecil O. *academic administrator*
Schofield, Anthony Wayne *judge*
Skinner, Andrew Charles *history educator, religious writer*
Slife, Brent Donald *psychologist, educator, author*
Smith, H(oward) Duane *zoology educator*
Smoot, Leon Douglas *chemical engineering educator, former dean*
Snow, Karl Nelson, Jr., *public management educator, university administrator, former state senator*
Szucs, Loretto Dennis *internet publishing executive, editor*
Tata, Giovanni *publishing executive*
Valentine, John Lester *state legislator, lawyer*
Willes, Mark Hinckley *media industry executive*
Wilson, Ramon B. *retired economics professor*
Woodbury, Dixon John *physiologist, educator, research scientist*
Youd, T. Leslie *retired civil engineer*

Saint George

Atkin, Jerry C. *air transportation executive*
Chilow, Barbara Gail *social worker*
Strobell, Dan F. *bank executive, writer*
Terry, Gary A. *lawyer, former trade association executive*

Salem

Hahn, Joan Christensen *retired secondary education educator, travel agent*

Salt Lake City

Adams, John A. *lawyer*
Adams, Joseph Keith *lawyer*
Adashi, Eli Y. *obstetrician, gynecologist*
Alter, Edward T. *state treasurer*
Anderson, Arthur Salzner *publishing company executive, marketing executive*
Anderson, Charles Ross *civil engineer*
Anderson, Joseph Andrew, Jr., *retired apparel company executive, retail consultant*
Anderson, Robert Monte *lawyer*
Anderson, Ross Carl *mayor, lawyer*
Anderson, Stephen Hale *federal judge*
Anspaugh, Lynn Richard *research biophysicist*
Atkin, Gary Eugene *lawyer*
Baldwin, John *legal association administrator, lawyer*
Ballard, Melvin Russell, Jr., *investment executive, church official*
Barlow, Charles *oil company executive*
Barney, Kline Porter, Jr., *engineering company executive, consultant*
Barton, Paul J. *lawyer*
Barusch, Lawrence Roos *lawyer*
Bassis, Michael Steven *academic administrator*
Bateman, Merrill Joseph *church administrator*
Baucom, Sidney George *lawyer*
Bauer, A(ugust) Robert, Jr., *surgeon*
Beall, Burtch W., Jr., *architect*
Becker, Ralph Elihu, Jr., *lawyer, planner*
Beecham, William R. *newspaper editor*
Beless, Rosemary June *lawyer*
Benjamin, Lorna Smith *psychologist*
Bennion, John Warren *urban education educator*
Berman, Daniel Lewis *lawyer*
Betz, A. Lorris *dean, educator, pediatrician, consultant*
Bigler, Glade S. *lawyer*
Black, Richard Eugene *pediatric surgeon*
Black, Wilford Rex, Jr., *former state senator*
Boozer, Carlos Austin, Jr., *professional basketball player*
Bousfield, Kenneth Harold *civil engineer*
Bowen, Melanie *legislative staff administrator*
Brady, Rodney Howard *holding company executive, broadcast company executive, former college president, former government official*
Brems, David Paul *architect*
Brown, Carolyn Smith *communications educator, consultant*
Burke, John Patrick *internist, educator*
Bushnell, Daniel S. *lawyer*
Campbell, Tena *judge*
Cannell, Cyndy Michelle *elementary school principal*
Capecchi, Mario Renato *genetics educator*
Carey, John Clayton *pediatrician, educator, medical geneticist*
Carnahan, Orville Darrell *retired state legislator, retired college president*
Carrell, Stewart *computer company executive*
Carroll, Karen Colleen *physician, infectious disease educator, medical microbiologist*
Cash, R(oy) Don *retired gas and petroleum company executive*
Castleton, David J. *lawyer*
Cherkaev, Andrej Vsevolodovich *mathematician, educator*
Chong, Richard David *architect*
Christensen, Bruce LeRoy *former academic administrator, commercial broadcasting executive*
Christensen, Patricia Anne Watkins *lawyer*
Christensen, Ray Richards *lawyer*
Christopher, James Walker *architect, educator*
Chuaqui, Miguel Basim *composer, educator*
Chung, You Chung *electrical engineer, educator*
Clark, Deanna Dee *civic leader and volunteer*
Clark, Glen Edward *judge*
Clark, Scott H. *lawyer*
Clegg, Daniel Orme *rheumatologist, educator*
Cofield, Philip Thomas *educational association administrator*
Conner, Heather J. *music educator*
Conway, Nancy Ann *newspaper editor*
Cook, Joseph V. *physician*
Cornaby, Kay Sterling *lawyer, former state senator*
Curtis, LeGrand R., Jr., *lawyer*
Dahmen-Ray, Patricia *professional society administrator*
Davidson, Lee Howard *reporter*
Davis, Gene *public relations professional, state legislator*
Davis, Loyd Evan *defense industry marketing professional*
Davis, Roy Kim *otolaryngologist, health facility administrator*
Deamer, Michael Lynn *mayor, lawyer, accountant*
De Vries, Kenneth Lawrence *mechanical engineer, educator*
Dibaiyan, Fatemeh Mariam *artist*
Dick, Bertram Gale, Jr., *physics educator*
Dolcourt, John (Jack) Lawrence *pediatrician*
Dole, Janice Gail Arnold *literacy educator*
Dragoo, Denise Ann *lawyer*
Drew, Clifford James *university administrator, special education and educational psychology educator*
Durham, Christine Meaders *state supreme court chief justice*
Durrant, Matthew B. *state supreme court justice*
Dydek, Margo *professional basketball player*
Eccles, Spencer Fox *banker, director*
Efros, Alexei L. *physics educator, researcher*
Eklund, Carl Andrew *lawyer*
Elkins, Glen Ray *retired service company executive*
England, Daniel Eugene *trucking executive*
Esplin, J. Kimo *chemical company executive*
Evans, Beverly Ann *state legislator, school system administrator*
Ewers, Anne *opera company director*
Eyring, Henry Bennion *bishop*
Fehr, J. Will *newspaper editor*
Fields, Debbi *cookie franchise executive*
Foltz, Rodger Lowell *chemistry educator, mass spectroscopist*
Foxley, Cecelia Harrison *commissioner*
Frank, Thomas *design, construction and management executive*
Fujinami, Robert Shin *neurology educator*
Gandhi, Om Parkash *electrical engineer*
Gardiner, Lester Raymond, Jr., *lawyer*
Garn, Edwin Jacob (Jake Garn) *former senator*
George, Sarah B. *museum director*
Ghosh, Sambhunath (Sam Ghosh) *civil engineering educator, environmental engineer*
Gortatowski, Melvin Jerome *retired chemist*
Graham, John Wallace *pathologist*
Greene, John Thomas *judge*
Gregersen, R(oald) George *newspaper publishing executive*
Grosser, Bernard Irving *psychiatry educator*
Hale, Karen *state legislator*
Hatch, George Clinton *television executive*
Hatch, Wilda Gene *broadcast company executive*
Hembree, James D. *retired chemical company executive*
Hinckley, Gordon B. *religious organization administrator*
Hlede, Korie *professional basketball player*
Holbrook, Donald Benson *lawyer*
Holbrook, Meghan Zanolli *fundraiser, public relations specialist, political organization chairman*
Holding, R(obert) E(arl) *oil company executive*
Holland, Jeffrey R. *religious organization administrator*
Horan, John J. *pharmaceutical company executive*
Horn, Susan Dadakis *statistics educator*
Howell, Kevin L. *hotel executive*
Howell, Scott Newell *computer company executive, state legislator*
Huefner, Robert P. *political science educator*
Hull, Grafton Hazard, Jr., *social work educator*
Humpherys, LeGrande Rich *lawyer*
Hunter, M(ilton) Reed, Jr., *lawyer*
Huntsman, Jon Meade *chemical company executive*
Huntsman, Peter R. *chemicals executive*
Hutcherson, Christopher Alfred *marketing, recruiting and educational fundraising executive*
Jackson, Hunter *health products executive*
Jaskowski, Troy D. *immunologist, researcher*
Jenkins, Bruce Sterling *federal judge*
Jensen, Dallin W. *lawyer*
Jensen, Rodney H. *hotel executive*
Johnson, Auston Gilbert, III, *auditor*
Johnson, Jon L. *advertising executive*
Johnson, Spencer *physician, writer*
Johnson, Stephen Charles *exercise physiology and sport science educator*
Jones, Michael Frank *lawyer*
Jorgensen, Lou Ann Birkbeck *social worker*
Julander, Paula Foil *health care and political consultant, state senator*
Keefe, Maureen Ruth *dean*
Kim, Sung Wan *chemistry professor*
Kirkham, John Spencer *lawyer, director*
Kjeldsberg, Karl R. *lab administrator, physician, educator*
Knight, Joseph Adams *pathologist*
Kopecek, Jindrich *biomedical scientist, biomaterials and pharmaceutics educator*
Korbanka, Juergen Erich *psychologist, educator*
Krishna, Kishore Bellamkonda *biomedical researcher, educator*
Kumpfer, Karol Linda *research psychologist*
Layfield, Lester James *pathologist, educator*
Leary, G. Edward *state financial commisioner*
Lee, Blaine Nelson *executive consultant, educator, author*
Lee, James B. *lawyer*
Legant, Patricia *internist, oncologist*
Leiferman, Kristin Marie *physician, educator, science association director*
Lloyd, Ray Dix *health physicist*
Lochhead, Robert Bruce *lawyer*
Lu, Ning *music educator*
Mabey, Ralph R. *lawyer*
Maher, David L. *drug store company executive*
Manning, Brent V. *lawyer*
Markham, Reed B. *education educator, consultant*
Mason, James Ostermann *public health administrator*
McCleary, Lloyd E(verald) *education educator*
Mc Connell, Michael W. *judge, law educator*
McFerren, Carl Davis, II, *retired military officer, risk management consultant*
McKay, Monroe Gunn *federal judge*
McKeachnie, Gayle F. *lieutenant governor*
McMullin, Paul Wayne *structural engineer*
Meldrum, Peter Durkee *venture capitalist, biotechnology company executive*
Melich, Doris S. *public service worker*
Melton, Arthur Richard *healthcare executive*
Mendenhall, Robert W. *education technology executive*
Middleton, Anthony Wayne, Jr., *urologist, educator*
Miller, Jan Dean *metallurgy educator*
Miller, Larry H. *professional sports team executive, automobile dealer*
Miller, Lorraine *business owner*
Miller, William Charles *architect, educator*
Monson, Thomas Spencer *religious organization administrator, former publishing company executive*
Mooney, Jerome Henri *lawyer*
Moore, Annette B. *legislative staff member*
Moore, Debra *lawyer*
Moore, James R. *lawyer*
Morey, Charles Leonard, III, *theatrical director*
Moser, Royce, Jr., *preventive medicine physician, educator*
Motter, Thomas Franklin *medical products executive*
Murphy, Michael R. *federal judge*
Nehring, Ronald E. *judge*
Nelson, John C. *obstetrician/gynecologist*
Nelson, Roger Hugh *management educator, corporate consultant, business executive*
Nelson, Russell Marion *surgeon, educator*
Nicolatus, Stephen Jon *financial consultant*
Niederauer, George H. *bishop*
Norton, Delmar Lynn *candy company executive*
Nydegger, Rick D. *lawyer*
Oakes, Claudia *museum administrator*
Oaks, Dallin Harris *lawyer, church official*
Ockey, Ronald J. *lawyer*
Olson, Ferron Allred *metallurgist, educator*
Osherow, Jacqueline Sue *poet, English language educator*
Owen, Amy *library director*
Owen, Langdon Talbot, Jr., *lawyer*
Packer, Boyd K. *church official*
Parkin, James Lamar *otolaryngologist, educator*
Parrish, Jill Niederhauser *judge*
Parry, Robert Walter *chemistry professor*
Paulsen, Vivian *magazine editor*
Perry, L. Tom *religious organization administrator, merchant*
Pershing, David Walter *chemical engineering educator, researcher*
Peterson, Millie M. *state senator*
Planelles, Vicente *molecular biologist*
Poulter, Charles Dale *chemist, educator, consultant*
Purser, Donald Joseph *lawyer*
Quinn, Eugene Frederick *foreign service officer, clergyman*
Quist, Carol Bennion *editor*
Rasmussen, Thomas Val, Jr., *lawyer, small business owner*
Reeder, F. Robert *lawyer*
Renzetti, Attilio David, Jr., *retired physician*
Rigtrup, Kenneth *state judge, arbitrator, mediator*
Roens, Steven Thomas *music educator, dean*
St. John, Katherine Iva *artistic director, dance educator*
Salisbury, Frank Boyer *plant physiologist, educator, author*
Sam, David *federal judge*
Sandquist, Gary Marlin *engineering educator, researcher, consultant, writer*
Schow, Terry D. *state official*
Schwendiman, Stephen Glenn *lawyer*
Scofield, David William *lawyer*
Scott, Richard G. *religious organization administrator*
Seader, Junior DeVere (Bob Seader) *chemical engineering educator*
Shea, Patrick A. *lawyer, educator*
Shelledy, James Edwin, III, *newspaper editor*
Shepherd, Karen *retired congresswoman*
Shurtleff, Mark L. *state attorney general*
Sillars, Malcolm Osgood *communication educator*
Simmons, Roy William *banker, director*
Sine, Wesley Franklin *lawyer*
Sloan, Jerry (Gerald Eugene Sloan) *professional basketball coach*
Smith, Donald E. *broadcast engineer, manager*
Smith, Eldred Gee *church leader*
Smith, Janet Hugie *lawyer*
Snell, Ned Colwell *financial planner*
Sohn, Hong Yong *chemical engineer, educator, metallurgical engineer, educator*
Solano, Henry L. *lawyer*
Sorenson, Roger A. *international relations consultant*
Sparks, Mildred Thomas *state agency administrator, educator*
Stanford, Joseph Barney *medical educator, physician*
Stang, Peter John *organic chemist*
Steiner, Richard Russell *textile & apparel company executive*
Stephens, Martin R. *state official*
Stitley, James Walter, Jr., *food manufacturing executive*
Stock, Peggy A(nn) *college president, educator*
Straight, Richard Coleman *photobiologist, natural philosopher*
Straughn, Joanna Marzia *poet*
Stringfellow, Gerald B. *engineering educator*
Swinton, Jeffrey Cheever *lawyer*
Taylor, Philip Craig *physics educator*
Thalos, Mariam G *philosopher, educator*
Thomas, David Snow *plastic surgeon*
Thompson, Neil Daniel *legal and genealogical researcher, retired lawyer*
Varela, Vicki *state official*
Velick, Sidney Frederick *research biochemist, educator*
Verhaaren, Harold Carl *lawyer*
Walker, Carlene Martin *state senator*
Walker, Olene S. *governor*
Wallace, Matthew Walker *retired entrepreneur*
Ward, John Robert *internist, educator*
Warner, Paul M. *prosecutor*
Weigel, Richard George *psychologist, educator*
Weiss, Ronald L. *lab administrator*
Welch, Dominic *publishing consultant*
West, Stephen Allan *lawyer*
White, Constance Burnham *state official*
Wilcox, Adam Benjamin *medical researcher, educator*
Wilde, Robert *lawyer*
Wilkins, Michael Jon *state supreme court justice*
Williams, J. Richard *service executive, real estate executive*
Williams, Natalie *professional basketball player, restaurant executive*
Wirthlin, Joseph B. *religious organization administrator*
Wolf, Harold Herbert *pharmacy educator*
Young, Michael Kent *dean, lawyer, educator*
Zhdanov, Michael Semenovich *geophysicist, educator*
Zimmer, Markus Bernhard *federal court administrator*
Zimmerman, Michael David *lawyer*

Sandy

Clark, Jeffrey Raphiel *research and development company executive*
Park, William Laird *agricultural economics educator, consultant, college associate dean*
Skidmore, Joyce Thorum *public relations and communication executive*
Smith, Willard Grant *psychologist*

Santa Clara

Tolbert, Beth Willden *real estate company executive, real estate broker*

South Jordan

Larson, Bryan Alan *lawyer*
Rowley, Maxine Lewis *home economics and consumer educator, writer*
Wirthlin, Richard Bitner *research strategist*

Springville

Ashworth, Brent Ferrin *lawyer*
Bybee, Paul Joseph *zoologist, educator, paleontologist, biologist*
Francis, Rell Gardner *artist, photographer, writer*

Sundance

Grant, Raymond Thomas *arts administrator*

Tooele

Allen, Ronald Carl *state senator, computer consulting executive, visual artist*
Jansen, Lambertus *state agency administrator, retired judge, criminal justice educator*

Tremonton

Eakle, Arlene Haslam *genealogist*

Vernal

Judd, Dennis L. *lawyer*

Vineyard

Cannon, Joseph A. *steel products company executive, political party official*

West Jordan

Bland, Dorothy Ann *construction executive, real estate agent*
Shepherd, Paul H. *school system administrator*
Wyness, Steven Charles *illustrator*

Woods Cross

Blackley, Cheryl Ann *freelance/self-employed music educator, musician*
Hendriksen, Neil Evan *music educator*
Ingles, Joseph Legrand *social services administrator, political science educator*

VERMONT

Arlington

Nowicki, George Lucian *retired chemical company executive*

Barnard

Larson, John Hyde *retired utilities executive*

Barre

Black, Percy *psychology educator*
Koch, Thomas Frederick *lawyer*

Bellows Falls

Obuchowski, Michael J. *state legislator*

Bennington

Bernard, April *poet, literature educator*
Burkhardt, Frederick Henry *editor*
Coleman, Elizabeth *college president*

Killen, Carroll Gorden *electronics company executive*
Morrissey, Mary *state representative*
Perin, Donald Wise, Jr., *former association executive*
Wang, Shunzhu *humanities educator, researcher, translator*

Bomoseen
Ressler, Robert *sculptor*

Brandon
Farnsworth, Frank Albert *retired economics educator*

Brattleboro
Agallianos, Dennis Dionysios *psychiatrist*
Albertian, Edward *wholesale distribution executive*
Ames, Adelbert, III, *neurophysiologist, educator*
Brofsky, Howard *musician, music educator*
Bussino, Melinda Holden *human services administrator*
Cohen, Richard B. *grocery company executive*
Cosgrove, Bryan *emergency planner*
Gorman, Robert Saul *architect*
Gross, Mark *food products executive*
Hamlin, William *grocery company executive*
Harris, Reuben *wholesale distribution executive*
Hawkes, Mary Newgeon *retired minister, educator*
Kotkov, Benjamin *clinical psychologist*
Lappe, Frances Moore *author, lecturer*
McCarty, William Michael, Jr., *lawyer*
Murtha, J. Garvan *federal judge*
Oakes, James L. *federal judge*
Reid, David G. *lawyer*
Smiley, Carol Anne *home health administrator, sculptor*
Wright, Ron *retail executive*

Brownsville
Olderman, Gerald *retired medical device company executive*

Burlington
Aleong, John *statistician, educator*
Allard, Judith Louise *secondary school educator*
Allen, Bill *food service executive, writer*
Angell, Kenneth Anthony *bishop*
Bartlett, Richmond Jay *soil chemistry educator, researcher*
Berkowitz, Stephen David *sociologist, educator*
Bramley, Andrew John *animal science educator*
Brandenburg, Richard George *management educator*
Brown, Kenneth Andrew *cardiologist, educator*
Carlisle, Lilian Matarose Baker (Mrs. E. Grafton Carlisle Jr.) *writer, lecturer*
Clavelle, Peter *mayor*
Cooper, Sheldon Mark *medical educator, immunologist, researcher, rheumatologist*
Cram, Reginald Maurice *retired air force officer*
Cutler, Stephen Joel *sociologist, educator*
Daniels, Robert Vincent *history educator, former state senator*
Davis, John Herschel *retired surgeon, educator*
Dean, Howard *political activist, former governor*
Della Santa, Laura *principal*
Dinitz, Jeffrey H. *mathematics educator*
Dinse, John Merrell *lawyer*
Dominy, Garrett L. *business consulting company executive*
Donovan, Johannah L. *state representative, educator*
Erno, Margaret Jean *social worker, consultant*
Ferrari, Dennis M. *secondary school educator*
Fogel, Daniel Mark *university president, English language and American literature educator, author*
Frank, Joseph Elihu *lawyer*
Galbraith, Richard Anthony *physician, hospital administrator*
Gouli, Svetlana Yurievna *microbiologist, researcher*
Gouli, Vladimir Vasilievich *entomologist*
Hall, Robert William *philosophy and religion educator*
Hearon, Shelby *writer, lecturer, educator*
Hilberg, Raul *political science educator*
Kindstedt, Paul Stephen *food science educator*
Krag, Martin Hans *physician, orthopaedist, educator, researcher*
Kunin, Madeleine May *former ambassador to Switzerland, former governor*
Lafayette, Karen Moran *state legislator*
Lawson, Robert Bernard *psychology educator*
Lucey, Jerold Francis *pediatrician*
Mead, Philip Bartlett *healthcare administrator, obstetrician, educator*
Miller, Hinda *state senator, management consultant*
Mintz, Beth Ann *sociology educator*
Montroll, Andrew H. *lawyer, councilman*
Neale, Gail Lovejoy *non-profit organization management consultant*
Nyborg, Wesley Lemars *physics educator*
Outwater, John Ogden *mechanical engineering educator*
Pinder, George Francis *engineering educator, scientist*
Pizzagalli, Angelo *construction company executive*
Read, Thomas Lawrence *music educator, composer*
Rendall, Donald James, Jr., *lawyer*
Riddick, Daniel Howison *obstetrics and gynecology educator, priest*
Sampson, Samuel Franklin *sociology educator*
Sobel, Burton Elias *physician, educator*
Stout, Neil Ralph *retired history educator*
Sullivan, Mary Margaret *state legislator*
Tamarkin, Kate *conductor*
Tampas, John P. *radiologist*
Toner, Donald Thomas *music educator*
Tracy, John Patrick *state legislator*
Visser, Thomas Durant *social studies educator, writer*
Weed, Lawrence L. *biochemist*
Wick, Hilton Addison *lawyer*
Willis, Russell Edward *academic administrator*
Zhou, Xu *research scientist, educator*

Castleton
Stafford, Robert Theodore *lawyer, former senator*

Cavendish
Shapiro, David *artist, art historian*

Charlotte
Melby, Edward Carlos, Jr., *veterinarian*
Naylor, Thomas Herbert *economist, educator, consultant*
Robinson, Sally Winston *artist*
Sim, Craig Stephen *retired investment banker*

Chelsea
Kennedy, Sylvia C. *state representative*

Chester
Carey, Erron J. *merchant banker, state representative*
Coleman, John Royston *writer*

Colchester
Dakin, Maureen P. *state representative*
Edmundson, Lorna Duphiney *academic administrator*
Lawton, Lorilee Ann *fire sprinkler contractor company owner, accountant*
Salmon, Thomas Paul *lawyer, academic administrator*
Sweeney, Joyce C. *state representative*
Sweeny, Arthur, III, *realtor*
vanderHeyden, Marc A. *academic administrator*

Concord
Norsworthy, Elizabeth Krassovsky *lawyer*

Danby
Peel, Harris *art gallery owner, retired diplomat*

Dorset
Bamford, Joseph Charles, Jr., *gynecologist, obstetrician, educator, medical missionary, author*
Pember, John Scott *poet*

East Calais
Harding, John Hibbard *retired insurance company executive*

East Montpelier
Christiansen, Andrew P. *internet consulting business executive*

East Thetford
Cummings Rockwell, Patricia Guilbault *psychiatric nurse*

Enosburg Falls
Gervais, Avis L. *state representative, consumer products company executive*
Svendsen, Alf *artist, art educator*

Essex Junction
Bisson, Roger *middle school educator*
Eshun, Ebenezer E *electrical engineer*
Harame, David L *information technology manager, director*
Ishaq, Mousa Hanna *materials engineer*
Kirker, Linda *state representative, health facility administrator*
Lampert, S. Henry *retired dentist*
Myers, Linda K. *retired editor, state representative*
Pillsbury, Penelope DeLaire *library director*
Sweetser, Gene Gillman *quality assurance professional, state legislator*
Sweetser, Susan W. *lawyer, advocate, former state legislator*

Fairfield
Kittell, Sara Branon *state legislator*

Georgia
Branagan, Carolyn W. *state representative*

Greensboro
Hill, Lewis Reuben *horticulturist, nursery owner, author*

Guilford
Olle, David Arthur *writer, researcher*

Hardwick
Holtz, Laurence *artisan, photographer*

Hartland Four Corners
Brady, Upton Birnie *editor, literary agent*

Hinesburg
Snelling, Diane *state senator, artist*

Hyde Park
Bartlett, Susan J. *state legislator*
Bourdeau, Stephanie *state representative*

Jacksonville
Dell, Ralph Bishop *retired pediatrician, researcher*
Hein, Karen Kramer *pediatrician, epidemiologist*

Jericho
Bolin, Henry Robert *retired engineer*
Symington, Gaye R. *state representative*

Johnson
Whitehill, Angela Elizabeth *artistic director*

Lincoln
Kompass, Edward John *consulting editor*

Lower Waterford
Burnham, Patricia White *consultant, advocate, writer, business executive*
Burnham, Robert Alan *academic administrator, educator*

Ludlow
Mueller, Diane *hotel executive*
Nitka, Alice W. *social services administrator, state representative*

Lyndon Center
Dame, William Page, III, *bank executive, educational administrator*

Lyndonville
Dodson, Daryl Theodore *ballet administrator, arts consultant*
James, Bruce Allan *radio station owner, general manager*
Moore, Carol A. *academic administrator*
Toborg, Alfred *history professor*

Manchester
Carey, James Henry *banker*
Kouwenhoven, Gerrit Wolphertsen *retired museum director*

Manchester Center
Armstrong, Jane Botsford *sculptor*

Marlboro
Brelsford, Edmund Munger, III, *musician, educator*
Stevenson, Laura Caroline *writer, educator*

Middlebury
Benoit, Philip Grosvenor *communications executive, educator, writer*
Bergesen, Robert Nelson *transportation consultant*
Colander, David Charles *economist, educator*
Ferm, Robert Livingston *religion educator*
Ginevan, Anne V. *state representative*
Jacobs, Travis Beal *historian, educator*
Jenks-Jay, Nan *environmentalist educator*
Lamberti, Marjorie *retired social studies educator*
Liebowitz, Ronald D. *academic administrator*
MacDonald, Kenneth R., Jr., *author, artist*
McGlashan, Amy Gibans *educational association administrator, consultant*
Meakin, John David *retired university research executive, educator*
Nuovo, Betty A. *state representative*
O'Brien, George Dennis *retired academic administrator*
Pardee, Scott Edward *securities dealer*
Robison, Olin Clyde *political science educator, former college president*
Vail, Van Horn *German language educator*
Winkler, Paul Frank, Jr., *astrophysicist, educator*

Milton
Conrad Kemsley, Marilee *newswriter*
Rivero, Marilyn Elaine Keith *state legislator*

Montpelier
Backus, Jan *state legislator*
Barbieri, Christopher George *professional society administrator*
Costle, Elizabeth Rowe *commissioner*
Crowley, John P. *state legislator, lawyer, accountant*
Cummings, Ann E. *state legislator*
Diamond, M. Jerome *lawyer, former state official*
Dooley, John Augustine, III, *state supreme court justice*
Douglas, James Holley *governor*
Dubie, Brian E. *lieutenant governor*
Dumville, John P. *historic site director*
Emmons, Alice M. *state legislator*
Errecart, Joyce Hier *lawyer*
Facos, James Francis *English language educator, author*
Fitzhugh, William Wyvill, Jr., *printing company executive*
Fox, Sally G. *state legislator, lawyer*
Gibson, Ernest Willard, III, *retired state supreme court justice*
Guild, Alden *retired lawyer*
Johnson, Denise Reinka *state supreme court justice*
Klein, Tony *public relations executive, state representative*
Markowitz, Deborah Lynn *state government official*
Mazza, Richard T. *state legislator, small business owner*
Metcalf, Cindy W. *political organization administrator*
Munt, Janet S. *state legislator*
Paquin, Edward H., Jr., *former state legislator, non-profit organization executive*
Peaslee, Janice L. *state legislator, agricultural products executive*
Pelham, Tom *commissioner*
Peterson, Julie *public information officer*
Racine, Douglas A *former lieutenant governor*
Ready, Elizabeth M. *state legislator*
Riehle, Helen S. *state senator*
Rivers, Cheryl P. *state legislator*
Saxman, Anna Esther *lawyer*
Seibert, Ann *state legislator, physical therapist*
Sheltra, Nancy J. *state legislator, legal assistant, auditor*
Skoglund, Marilyn *state supreme court justice*
Sorrell, William H. *state attorney general*
Towne, Ruth H. *state legislator*
Valerio, Matthew F. *lawyer*

Moretown
Grad, Maxine J. *state representative, law educator*
Hartshorn, Brenda Bean *elementary school educator*

Morrisville
Besser, Gretchen Rous *writer, educator*
Lechevalier, Hubert Arthur *microbiology educator*
Lechevalier, Mary Pfeil *retired microbiologist, educator*
Roberts, Carolyn C. *former hospital administrator*

Moscow
Kende, Stephen James *insurance sales executive*

New Haven
Clifford, Deborah Pickman *historian*

Newark
Van Vliet, Claire *artist*

Newbury
McGarrell, James *artist, educator*

Newfane
Farber, Lillian *retired photography equipment company executive*

North Bennington
Adler, Irving *mathematician*

North Clarendon
Freed, Walter Everett *petroleum company executive, state representative*
Hays, John C. *sales executive, marketing professional*

North Pomfret
Crowl, John Allen *retired publishing company executive*
Shepherd, Gaal *artist*

Northfield
Schneider, Richard William *academic administrator*
Telford, Kenneth Alderman *philosopher, humanities educator*
Wick, William Shinn *clergyman, chaplain*

Norwich
Foster, Michael Kirk *anthropologist, linguist*
Katz, Arnold Martin *medical educator*
Lamperti, Claudia Jane McKay *editor*
Naumann, Robert Bruno Alexander *chemistry and physics educator*
Paine, Walter Cabot *journalist, consultant*
Snapper, Ernst *mathematics professor*
Stetson, Eugene William, III, *film producer*
Stevenson, Josiah, IV, *management consultant*

Pawlet
Buechner, Carl Frederick *minister, author*

Peacham
Barnes, Harry G., Jr., *human rights activist, conflict resolution specialist, retired ambassador*
Engle, James Bruce *ambassador*

Pittsfield
Wacker, Susan Regina *creative design director*

Pittsford
Flory, Margaret K. *state representative, lawyer*

Plainfield
Jervis, Jane Lise *college official, science historian*

Plymouth
Bittinger, Cynthia Douglas *foundation executive*

Poultney
Pentkowski, Raymond J. *principal*

Putney
Bass, Eric *artist, performing company executive*
White, Jeanette K. *state senator, health facility administrator*

Quechee
DeRouchey, Beverly Jean *investment company executive*
Vitty, Roderic Bemis *retired financial planner, publishing executive*
Wood, R. Stewart, Jr., *retired bishop*

Randolph
French, Patsy J. *property manager, state representative*
Sax, Daniel Saul *neurologist, educator*
Zimet, Matthew *graphic arts and science educator*

Rutland
Boyle, Francis Joseph *transportation and energy company executive*
Doyle, Patricia R. *state representative*
Duffy, Virginia *state representative, artist*
Ferraro, Betty Ann *former state senator*
Haley, John Charles *financial executive*
Mazzariello, Mary C. *state representative*
Taylor, A. Jeffry *lawyer*
Thompson, Marie Angela *computer engineer, consultant*

Saint Albans
Keenan, Kathleen *state legislator*

Shaftsbury
Sugarman, Robert Edward *writer*
Williams, Robert Joseph *museum director, educator*

Shelburne
Anderson, Richard Louis *electrical engineer*
Canfield, Andrew Trotter *lawyer, writer*
Foster, Roger Sherman, Jr., *surgeon, educator, health facility administrator*
Robert, Elisabeth B. *toy company executive*
Ryerson, William Newton *non profit organization executive*
Sawabini, Wadi Issa *retired dentist, educator*
Smallwood, Franklin *political science educator*
Weiger, John George *foreign language educator*
White, William North *chemistry professor*

South Burlington
Adams, Charles Jairus *lawyer*
Cohen, Bennett R. (Ben Cohen) *food products executive*
Hamilton, John J., Jr., *airport executive*
Head, Helen *state representative, management consultant*
Pizzagalli, James *construction executive*
Pugh, Anne D. *state legislator*
Shinozaki, Tamotsu *retired physician, anesthesiologist*

South Hero
Johnson, Mitzi *state representative*

South Londonderry
Spiers, Ronald Ian *diplomat*

South Pomfret
Oatway, Francis Carlyle *corporate executive*

South Royalton
Doria, Anthony Notarnicola *college dean, educator*
McLaughlin, Rosemary *horse trainer, state representative*
Powers, Thomas Moore *writer*
Wroth, L(awrence) Kinvin *lawyer, educator*

Springfield
Putnam, Paul Adin *retired government agency official*

Stamford
Stevens, Lauren Rogers *writer, environmentalist*

Stowe
Anderson, Rudolph J., Jr., *lawyer*
Fiddler Nichols, Barbara Dillow *sales and marketing professional*

Marron, Richard C. *hotel executive, state representative*
Whiteman, Joseph David *retired lawyer, manufacturing company executive*

Strafford
Williams, William Magavern *headmaster*

Swanton
LaVoie, Kathy L. *state representative*
Wooding, William Minor *statistics consultant*

Thetford
Hoagland, Mahlon *biochemist, educator*
Paley, Grace *author, educator*

Tinmouth
Fallar, Gail M. *state representative, town clerk*

Tunbridge
Stewart, Donald George *musician, composer, music industry executive*

Underhill
Danforth, Elliot, Jr., *medical educator*
Hummel, Margaret P. *state representative*

Vergennes
Grant, Edwin Randolph *retail executive, manufacturing executive*
Houston, Constance T. *state legislator*

Vernon
O'Donnell, Pat A. *state representative*

Waitsfield
Hiscock, Richard Carson *marine safety investigator*
Parrish, Thomas Kirkpatrick, III, *marketing consultant*

Warren
Connell, Kinny *state representative*
Raphael, Albert Ash, Jr., *retired lawyer*

Waterbury
Travis, Randall Howard *retired physiologist, retired endocrinologist*
Vincent, Val D. *state legislator*

Waterbury Center
Amestoy, Jeffrey Lee *state supreme court chief justice*

Weathersfield
Harris, Christopher *publisher, designer, editor*

West Rutland
Crowley, Judy B. *state representative*

Westford
Heath, Martha *state legislator*

Weston
Kasnowski, Chester Nelson *artist, educator*
Stettler, Stephen F. *performing company executive*

Weybridge
Ayer, Claire D. *state representative, women's health nurse*

White River Junction
Davis, Emily S. *lawyer*
Japikse, David *mechanical engineer, manufacturing executive*
Madden, Edward Harry *philosopher, retired educator*
Myers, Warren Powers Laird *physician, educator*
Rutter, Frances Tompson *publisher*
Welch, Peter F. *state legislator*

Williston
Ankeney, Jean B. *state legislator*
Foss, Jean Mitchell *school system administrator*
Lyons, Virginia *state legislator*
Peterson, Mary N. *state representative, lawyer*
Podhajski, Blanche Rita *language foundation administrator*

Wilmington
Little, Thomas Mayer *public relations executive*
Reeve, Franklin D. *writer, literature educator*

Windham
Partridge, Carolyn *farmer, state representative*

Windsor
Sweaney, Donna *state representative*

Winooski
Essman, Robert Norvel *artist, graphic designer*
Higgins, Margaret Ann *home health nurse, operating room nurse*

Wolcott
Fisher, Neal Floyd *religious organization administrator*

Woodstock
Billings, Franklin Swift, Jr., *federal judge*
Churchill, James Garton *retired international finance consultant*
Crocker, Patricia Conway *former state legislator*
Goulazian, Peter Robert *retired broadcasting executive*
Hoyt, Coleman Eilliams *postal consultant*
Killian, Edward James *retired pediatrician*
Matlins, Stuart M. *management consultant, publisher*

VIRGINIA

Abingdon
Beil, Clark Raymond *hospital executive*
Brownlee, John L. *prosecutor*
Clifton, D. Renee *writer, educator*
Graham, Howard Lee, Sr., *financial services company executive*
Hamilton, Bobby *professional race car driver*
Jones, James Parker *federal judge*
McElroy, Howard Chowning *lawyer*
Smith, Jack C. *supermarket executive*
Widener, Hiram Emory, Jr., *judge*
Williams, Glen Morgan *federal judge*

Afton
Anderson, Donald Norton, Jr., *retired electrical engineer*

Aldie
Weaver, Kitty Dunlap *author*

Alexandria
Abell, Richard Bender (Richard Lon Welch) *lawyer, federal official*
Adams, Ranald Trevor, Jr., *retired air force officer*
Adams, Thomas L. *medical association administrator*
Ancell, Robert Manning *leadership organization executive*
Ashford, John Edward *communications executive*
Bachus, Walter Otis *retired army general, former association executive*
Balch, Charles M. *surgeon, educator*
Baroody, Michael Elias *trade association executive*
Bartlett, Elizabeth Susan *audio-visual specialist*
Berger, Patricia Wilson *retired librarian*
Berkowitz, Martin A. *diversified financial services company executive*
Bezold, Clement *think tank executive*
Birely, William Cramer *investment banker*
Blair, Bryce *real estate company executive*
Bolger, Robert Joseph *retired trade association executive*
Borum, Olin Henry *realtor, former government official*
Bostetter, Martin V. B., Jr., *bankruptcy court judge*
Bowman, Richard Carl *defense consultant, retired air force officer*
Brenner, Alfred Ephraim *physicist*
Brinkema, Leonie Milhomme *federal judge*
Brooks, Philip Coolidge, Jr., *archivist, curator, historian*
Brotzman, Donald Glenn *government official, lawyer*
Brown, Frederic Joseph *army officer*
Brown, Quincalee *professional society administrator*
Brownfeld, Allan Charles *columnist*
Brownstein, Kevin Michael *information security analyst, consultant*
Bryant, Anne Lincoln *educational association executive*
Buechner, Jack W(illiam) *lawyer, government affairs consultant, educational association administrator*
Bumgarner, Robert Linville *pathologist, retired military officer*
Burch, John Thomas, Jr., *lawyer*
Burke, Kelly Howard *former air force officer, business executive, investor*
Byrne, John Edward (JEB Byrne) *writer, retired government official*
Cabral, Sam A. *protective services official, labor union administrator*
Callaghan, John William, Jr., *information technology manager, retired military officer*
Campbell, Francis James *retired chemist*
Carleson, Robert Bazil *public policy consultant*
Carter, Gene Raymond *professional association executive*
Carter, Richard Dennis *lawyer, educator*
Carter, William Harold, Sr., *physicist, researcher, electrical engineer*
Carvalho, Julie Ann *psychologist*
Cauley, Michael A. *prosecutor*
Chapman, Anthony Bradley *psychiatrist*
Chen, Fen *mathematician, educator, researcher*
Collins, Cardiss *retired congresswoman*
Collins, William L., III, *financial executive*
Connell, John Gibbs, Jr., *former government official*
Connell, Mary Ellen *diplomat*
Cook, Charles William *aerospace engineer, consultant, educator*
Cooper, David Earl Kaleoikaika *foundation executive*
Cooper, Edythe E.D. *political organization administrator*
Cooper, Roger Merlin *information technology executive, federal government official, school administrator*
Costagliola, Francesco *retired government official*
Cottrell, James Ray *lawyer*
Courtney, William Harrison *government agency administrator*
Coyne, James Kitchenman, III, *association executive, congressman, aviator*
Crane, Stephen Charles *professional society administrator*
Cromley, Raymond Avolon *syndicated columnist*
Cross, Dorothy Abigail *retired librarian*
Cross, Eason, Jr., *architect*
Crundwell, Duncan James *electronics executive*
Curtin, Gary Lee *air force officer*
Danaher, James William *retired federal government executive*
Davis, Ruth Margaret (Mrs. Benjamin Franklin Lohr) *information technology executive*
De Barbieri, Mary Ann *nonprofit management consultant*
DeLuca, Anthony J. *civilian military employee*
Dennison, Donald Lee *lawyer*
Devantier, Paul W. *communications executive, broadcaster, administrator*
Diachenko, Marge *political organization administrator*
DiMuro, Bernard Joseph *lawyer*
Dubin, Martin Steven *principal*
Duncan, Richard Ray *history professor*
Dunn, Bernard Daniel *former naval officer, consultant*
Eckhart, Myron, Jr., (Max Eckhart) *retired marine engineer*
Elkins, Dan *small business owner, educator*
Ellis, Thomas Selby, III, *federal judge*
Eluhow, Ljiljana Skoric *musician, educator*
Engler, Brian David *association executive*
Faenza, Michael M. *mental health association administrator*
Falk, Stanley Lawrence *historian, consultant*
Fedorochko, William, Jr., *retired army officer, defense policy analyst*
Fichenberg, Robert Gordon *newspaper editor, consultant*
Fisher, Colleen M. *trade association administrator*
Fisher, Donald Wayne *medical association executive*
Fitton, Harvey Nelson, Jr., *former government official*
Flater, Morris Eugene *lawyer*
Fleming, Douglas Riley *journalist, publisher, public affairs consultant*
Foster, Robert Francis *communications executive*
Francis, Samuel Todd *columnist*
Franklin, Jeanne F. *lawyer*
Freeman-Wilson, Karen *former attorney general, prosecutor, educational association administrator*
Frommer, Lawrence Julian *retired travel company executive*
Furash, Edward Elliott *investment company executive, banker, lecturer, writer, theater producer*
Gannon, Martin C. *lawyer*
Garrett, James F. *engineering company executive*
Gatanas, Harry D. *career officer*
Gaynor, Margaret Cryor *program director*
Georges, Peter John *lawyer*
Gernand, Bradley Elton *library manager, archivist*
Gil, Libia Socorro *school system administrator*
Glynn, Ernest B. *civil engineer, environmental engineer*
Goodling, William F. *former congressman*
Goodman, Sherri Wasserman *lawyer*
Goolrick, Robert Mason *lawyer*
Gormley, Dennis Michael *research scholar*
Gould, Phillip *engineer*
Graham, John H., IV, *health science association administrator*
Gray, Dorothy Louise Allman Pollet *librarian*
Greenstein, Ruth Louise *research institute executive, lawyer*
Greigg, Ronald Edwin *lawyer*
Guevara, Rogelio E. *federal agency administrator*
Gutsch, William Anthony, Jr., *astronomer*
Hallman, Linda D. *medical association administrator*
Hark, William Henry *medical executive, retired military officer*
Harris, David Ford *management consultant, retired government official*
Harris, Lillian Irene *marketing professional*
Hary, Douglas Alan *actor, educator*
Havens, Harry Stewart *former federal assistant comptroller general, government consultant*
Heil, Alan Lewis, Jr., *retired radio broadcast executive, writer*
Helman, Gerald Bernard *government official*
Henderson, Paul Bargas, Jr., *economic development consultant*
Henry, Catherine Ann *health science association administrator*
Herrera, Clarita *medical association administrator*
Higgins, Mary Celeste *lawyer, researcher*
Hinkle, Wade P. *political scientist*
Hirsch, Robert Louis *energy analyst, consultant*
Hirschkop, Philip Jay *lawyer, educator*
Hobbs, Michael Edwin *broadcasting company executive*
Hodgkins, Allen Ray, III, *cultural organization administrator, director*
Holcomb, Richard Dennis *lawyer*
Huckabee, Harlow Maxwell *lawyer, writer*
Hughes, Grace-Flores *federal agency administrator*
Hurtado, Rodrigo Claudio *allergist*
Hussey, Ward MacLean *lawyer, former government official*
Inman, Stephen Eugene *finance officer*
Jackson, Gary Lee *military analyst*
Jackson, Nancy Morrison *architect*
James, Carol Lee *communications executive*
Jenkins, John Smith *retired academic dean, lawyer*
Johnson, Edgar McCarthy *psychologist*
Johnson, JoAnn Mardelle *federal agency administrator*
Johnston, Richard M. *communications executive*
Jokl, Alois Louis *electrical engineer*
Jones-Lukács, Elizabeth Lucille *physician*
Justesen, Benjamin Ray, II, *writer*
Kalder, Frank M. *federal agency administrator*
Kaplan, Richard Alan *government official*
Kaufman, Beverly *political organization administrator*
Kaye, Ruth Lincoln *historical researcher*
Kemble, James Richard *retired engineering services executive*
Kern, Paul John *career military officer*
Kierscht, Marcia Selland *academic administrator, psychologist*
Kim, Sook Cha *artist*
Kitchens, David *architect*
Knowlton, William Allen *political and military consultant, educator*
Kolar, Mary Jane *trade and professional association executive*
Kopp, Eugene Paul *lawyer*
Kotlarchuk, Ihor O. E. *lawyer*
Krambeck, Frederick J. *chemical engineer*
Kratovil, Jane Lindley *think tank associate, developer/fundraiser*
Krebs, Martha *physicist, federal science agency administrator*
Kroesen, Frederick James *retired army officer, consultant*
Krueger, Gerald Peter *psychologist*
Lantz, Phillip Edward *security firm executive, consultant*
Larson, Charles Robert *naval officer*
Lasser, Howard Gilbert *chemical engineer, consultant*
Lathbury, Roger *English language educator*
Laurent, Lawrence Bell *communications executive, former journalist*
LeBlanc, James Leo *business executive, consultant*
Leestma, Robert *federal agency administrator, educator*
Lendsey, Jacquelyn L. *foundation administrator*
Lenz, Edward Arnold *trade association administrator, lawyer*
Leonhart, Michele Marie *government agency administrator*
Lightner, Candace Lynne *nonprofit management consultant, advocate*
Loren, Donald Patrick *naval officer*
Luna, Patricia Adele *marketing executive*
Lundeberg, Philip Karl Boraas *curator, historian*
Luttig, J. Michael *federal judge*
Lyons, James Aloysius, Jr., *naval officer*
Lytle, Michael Allen *criminologist, consultant*
Magazine, Alan Harrison *association executive, consultant*
Mallon, Francis J. *health science association administrator*
Malott, John Raymond *writer, consultant*
Mandil, I. Harry *nuclear engineer*
Masterson, Kleber Sanlin, Jr., *physicist*
Matalin, Mary *political consultant*
Mathias, Melvin Merle *nutrition scientist*
Matthews, Sir Stuart *aviation industry executive*
Matz, Deborah *federal agency administrator*
McCaffrey, Barry Richard *federal official, retired army officer*
McCulloch, William Leonard *trade association administrator*
McDowell, Charles Eager *lawyer, retired military officer*
McGuire, Edward David, Jr., *lawyer*
McGuire, Roger Alan *retired foreign service officer*
McMillan, Charles William *consulting company executive*
McNicol, David Leon *retired federal official, consultant*
McNulty, Paul J. *prosecutor*
Michael, Ann Dozier Marino *real estate broker*
Miller, Marian *professional society administrator*
Milling, Marcus Eugene, Sr., *geologist*
Mishra, Sanjay *music educator*
Montgomery, Gillespie V. (Sonny Montgomery) *former congressman*
Moran, Donald Will *consulting company executive*
Mossinghoff, Gerald Joseph *patent law expert, educator*
Muir, Warren Roger *chemist, executive*
Murray, Robert John *think-tank executive*
Murray, Russell, II, *aeronautical engineer, security consultant*
Nelson, David Leonard *process management systems company executive*
Newton, Hugh C. *public relations executive*
Nicholas, Lynn B. *medical association administrator*
Nodeen, Janey Price *company executive*
O'Brien, Patrick Michael *library administrator*
O'Connor, Charles P. *lawyer*
O'Hara, John Patrick *lawyer, accountant*
Parker, C. Danielle *government agency administrator*
Parsons, Henry McIlvaine *psychologist*
Pastin, Mark Joseph *association executive*
Patterson, Lillian Stanton *curator*
Paturis, E(mmanuel) Michael *lawyer*
Paulson, Gwen O. Gampel *government relations consultant*
Penrose, Cynthia C. *retired health care consultant*
Perchik, Benjamin Ivan *operations research analyst*
Pitzer, Jack Todd *purchasing agent, consultant, purchasing agent, educator*
Poehlein, Gary Wayne *retired chemical engineering educator*
Pringle, Robert Maxwell *diplomat*
Pugh, Jennifer Serafin *lobbyist*
Pyle, Howard *lawyer, consultant*
Rabun, John Brewton, Jr., *criminal justice agency administrator*
Rainwater, Joan Lucille Morse *investment company executive*
Rector, John Michael *association executive, lawyer*
Reiley, Mame Carrigan *political consultant*
Reinl, Harry Charles *economist*
Riel, Pauline *association executive*
Rogers, Paul A'Court *management consulting executive*
Romney, Carl F. *seismologist*
Saloom, Joseph A., III, *diplomat*
Sargeant, Thomas *real estate company executive*
Sargent, Carole Fungaroli *publishing executive*
Saunders, Steven R. *corporate communications specialist*
Schiff, Charlene *adult education educator*
Schubert, Richard Francis *consultant*
Seely, James Michael *defense consultant, retired naval officer, small business owner*
Senese, Donald Joseph *former government official, research administrator*
Shosky, John Edwin *media consultant, speechwriter*
Simmons, Edwin Howard *marine corps officer, historian*
Simmons, Richard De Lacey *mass media executive*
Simpkins, William B. *federal agency administrator*
Sitilides, John *government relations executive, policy analyst*
Smith, Heidi *political organization administrator*
Smith, Jeffrey Greenwood *industry executive, retired army officer*
Smith, Larry G. *career military officer*
Smith, Robert Luther *management educator*
Snyder, James P. *audio and digital television engineer, videographer, editor*
Stempler, Jack Leon *government and aerospace company executive*
Stevens, Alice Marie *educational consultant*
Stone, Ann Elizabeth *marketing agency executive, consultant*
Straub, Peter Thornton *lawyer*
Sturtevant, Brereton *retired lawyer, former government official*
Sulick, Joseph Edward, Sr., *information technology manager, retired military officer*
Swift, Stephen Christopher *lawyer*
Tandy, Karen P. *government agency administrator*
Tarpley, James Douglas *journalism educator, magazine editor*
Thayer, Marilyn *political organization executive, civic worker*
Thomas, Ramonia *political organization executive, civic worker*
Tichenor, Charles Beckham, III, *operations research analyst*
Toulmin, Priestley *retired geologist*
Tucker, Alvin Leroy *retired government official*
Tucker, Howard McKeldin *investment banker, consultant*
Turner, Mary Jane *educational administrator*
Van Cleve, Ruth Gill *retired lawyer, government official*
Verburg, Edwin Arnold *management consultant*
Von Drehle, Ramon Arnold *lawyer*
Vosbeck, William Frederick, Jr., *architect*
Walkup, Charlotte Lloyd *lawyer*
Walkup, Homer Allen *lawyer, writer*
Wallace, Barbara Brooks *writer*
Wasko-Flood, Sandra Jean *artist, educator*
Weinhagen, Eric John *writer, musician*
Weisberg, Leonard R. *retired engineering executive, researcher*
Welburn, Brenda Lilienthal *professional society administrator*
Wendel, Charles Allen *lawyer*

Whitson, Elizabeth Temple *graphics designer*
Widner, Ralph Randolph *retired civic executive*
Wieder, Bruce Terrill *lawyer, electrical engineer*
Wilcox, David Eric *electrical engineer, educational consultant*
Wilding, James Anthony *airport administrator*
Wilhide, Stephen D. *medical association administrator*
Williams, John Edward *lawyer*
Williams, Justin W. *government official*
Willis, Clifford Leon *geologist*
Wilson, Charles H. (Charles Harrison Wilson) *retired air force officer, financial planner, human resource development professional*
Woolley, Mary Elizabeth *research administrator*
Wright, Mary James *senior education consultant*
Wynn, Robert E. *electronics executive, retired career officer*
Yoder, Edwin Milton, Jr., *columnist, educator, editor, writer*
Zook, Theresa Fuetterer *gemologist, consultant*

Amherst
Campbell, Catherine Lynn *elementary school educator*
Copp, Cindy Pierce *education educator*
Martin, Stephen Clarke *lawyer, mediator, arbitrator*

Amissville
Coutu, Charles Arthur *deacon*
Hunter, Beverly Claire *research scientist, educator*

Annandale
Abdellah, Faye Glenn *retired public health service executive*
Armstrong, Henry Jere *retired judge*
Blodgett, Todd Alan *publisher, marketing executive*
Bohen, Dolores Boylston *retired school system administrator*
Brotton, Joyce Dupras *English language educator*
Christianson, Geryld B. *government relations consultant*
Connair, Stephen Michael *financial analyst*
Del Conte, L. Catherine *special education educator*
Di'Metrius, Simpson Kevin *elementary school educator*
Geiger, Richard Bernard *engineer, retired federal agency administrator*
Gioconda, Thomas F. *government services and construction company executive, retired military officer*
Greinke, Everett Donald *government agency administrator, educator*
Herbst, Robert LeRoy *organization executive*
Hollis, Daryl Joseph *judge*
Hollis, Linda Eardley *urban planning consultant*
Hovis, Robert Houston, III, *lawyer*
Hudson, William L. *conductor*
Hutcheon, Wallace Schoonmaker *historian, educator*
Jarvis, Elbert, II, (Jay Jarvis) *employee benefits specialist*
Jones, David Charles *international financial and management consultant*
Khim, Jay Wook *high technology systems integration executive*
Lefrak, Edward Arthur *cardiovascular and thoracic surgeon*
Matuszko, Anthony Joseph *research chemist, administrator*
Morales, Iris C. *secondary school educator*
Ochs, Walter J. *civil engineer, consultant*
Raab, Harry Frederick, Jr., *retired physicist*
Rogers, Stephen Hitchcock *former ambassador*
Samuelson, Douglas Alan *information systems company executive*
Shamburek, Roland Howard *physician*
Simonian, Simon John *surgeon, scientist, educator, administrator*
Wilhelmi, Mary Charlotte *education educator, college official*

Arlington
Adams, Hunter (Patch Adams) *internist, health facility administrator*
Adreon, Beatrice Marie Rice *pharmacist*
Adreon, Harry Barnes *architect*
Aggrey, Orison Rudolph *former ambassador, university administrator*
Alford, Paula N. *federal agency administrator*
Allard, Dean Conrad *historian, retired naval history center director*
Allen, David *systems engineer*
Allison, Graham Tillett, Jr., *federal government official*
Amman, Robert J. *telecommunications financial services company executive*
Anderson, Dean William *educational administrator*
Angell, Wayne D. *economist, banker*
Ankudinov, Vladimir Konstantinovich *naval architect*
Anthony, Robert Armstrong *lawyer, educator*
Asbell, Fred Thomas *health industry association executive*
Ashby, N. Bruce *air transportation executive*
Askey, Thelma J. *federal agency administrator*
Atkins, Walter J. *electrical engineer*
Bakke, Dennis W. *energy company executive*
Baldanza, B. Ben *air transportation executive*
Barry, Lance Leonard *judge*
Bawa, Raj *science educator, biodefense specialist, nanotechnology expert, biotechnology firm executive*
Beaty, James Thomas *retired buyer*
Beck, Buddy *systems engineer*
Becton, Julius Wesley, Jr., *retired military officer*
Beier, Anita P. *air transportation executive*
Bement, Arden Lee, Jr., *federal agency administrator*
Blum, H. Steven *military officer*
Bolster, Archie Milburn *retired foreign service officer*
Bordogna, Joseph *engineer, educator*
Bossman, David A. *trade association administrator*
Bowers, Ray Landis *writer*
Boylan, Michael A. *philosophy educator, writer*
Bradburn, Norman M. *behavioral science educator*
Brenner, Edgar H. *law administrator*
Bridgewater, Albert Louis *retired science foundation administrator*
Brighton, John A. *mechanical engineer, academic administrator*
Brown, Gardner Russell *engineering executive*
Bune, Karen Louise *criminal justice official*
Burgess, David *lawyer*
Caplan, Mitchell H. *diversified financial services company executive*
Carbaugh, John Edward, Jr., *lawyer*
Carr, Kenneth Monroe *naval officer*
Cavanaugh, Margaret Anne *chemist*
Chiames, Christopher L. *air transportation executive*
Chipman, Susan Elizabeth *psychologist, researcher*
Choksi, Mary *investment company executive*
Chubb, Talbot Albert *physicist, consultant*
Cinca, Silvia (Roberta King) *writer, producer*
Clare, Kenneth Guilford *economist, consultant*
Clarke, Frederic B., III, *risk analysis consultant*
Clayton, James Edwin *journalist*
Clump, Michael Aden *psychologist, educator*
Clutter, Mary Elizabeth *federal official*
Coady, Philip James, Jr., *retired naval officer*
Coats, Warren L., Jr., *economist*
Cobble, Steven Bruce *political consultant, strategist*
Cocolis, Peter Konstantine *business development executive*
Cohen, Jay *government agency administrator*
Cohen, Sheldon Irwin *lawyer*
Coleman, Rodney Albert *government affairs consultant*
Contis, George *medical services company executive*
Costello, John *military officer*
Cosumano, Joseph *military officer, government agency administrator*
Covington, James Edwin *government agency administrator, psychologist*
Cox, Henry *research engineer*
Cragin, Charles Langmaid *lawyer*
Cragin, Maureen Patricia *aerospace transportation executive, former federal agency administrator*
Crellin, Alan W. *air transportation executive*
Culligan, Thomas M. *electronics executive*
Danjczek, David William *manufacturing executive*
Davis, David M. *air transportation executive*
Davis, Lynn Etheridge *political scientist, educator*
Davis, Maynard Kirk *accountant*
DeBernard, Michael *architectural firm executive*
Debney, George C. *mathematical physicist*
DeFilippi, George *retired air force officer*
Dentzer, Susan *journalist*
Dietrick, Kevin M. *military officer*
Donnelly, Mary Beth *research analyst*
Dorman, Craig Emery *oceanographer, academic administrator*
Douglass, John W. *commissioner*
Doyle, Gerard Francis *lawyer*
Draeger, Susanne Yarbrough *interior designer*
Drayton, William *social entrepreneur, lawyer, management consultant*
Dubin, Henry C. *civilian military employee*
Dvorak, Josef Cermin *endocrinologist*
Edmondson, William Brockway *retired foreign service officer*
England, Robert Stowe *writer*
Ensminger, Luther Glenn *chemist, consultant*
Erb, Karl Albert *physicist, government official*
Ericsson, Sally Claire *not-for-profit organization administrator*
Erwin, Frank William *personnel research and publishing executive*
Ferraz, Francisco Marconi *neurological surgeon*
Fleischman, Phil *radio news executive*
Flowers, Robert B. *retired military officer*
Forrester, Eugene Priest *retired military officer*
Fowler, David Lucas *corporate lawyer*
French, Mary B. *editor, photographer, poet and former*
Freschi, Bruno Basilio *architect, educator*
Fuchs, Roland John *geography educator, university science official*
Fujito, Wayne Takeshi *international business company executive*
Fuller, Robert L(eander) *lawyer*
Futrell, John William *environmental agency executive, lawyer*
Gainer, Ronald Lee *lawyer*
Gallagher, Anne Porter *communications executive*
Galloway, William Jefferson *former foreign service officer*
Gangwal, Rakesh *airline executive*
Garnett, Griffin Taylor *lawyer, writer*
Gault, Jeffrey Wayne *air transportation executive*
Gelbard, Arlen W. *diversified financial services company executive*
Gergely, Tomas *astronomer*
Gianturco, Delio E. *management consultant, educator, author*
Glaser, Gerard *science administrator*
Glass, Jerrold A. *air transportation executive*
Goetze, Richard B., Jr., *association administrator*
Goldberg, Marvin *physicist*
Golladay, Mary Jean *statistician*
Goodman, Mark *journalist, educator*
Goodpasture, Bruce *retired editor, publisher, social sciences educator*
Gracey, James Steele *corporate director, retired coast guard officer, consultant*
Grady, Mark F. *dean, law educator*
Gramm, Wendy Lee *economics educator, former government official*
Graves, Ernest, Jr., *retired army officer, consultant, engineer*
Green, Richard Alan *lawyer*
Griffin, Paul, Jr., *navy officer, engineer, educator*
Guirguis, Raouf Albert *health science executive*
Gunderson, Steve Craig *consultant, former congressman*
Gunn, Joseph Ridgeway, III, *consulting economist*
Haggett, Rosemary Romanowski *academic administrator*
Hall, Carl William *agricultural and mechanical engineer*
Hamed, Martha Ellen *government administrator*
Hansen, Kenneth D. *lawyer, ophthalmologist*
Hansen, Orval *lawyer, former congressman, think tank executive*
Haq, Bilal Ul *national science foundation program director, researcher*
Harper, Michael John Kennedy *obstetrics and gynecology educator*
Harrington, George Fred *aviation consultant*
Harris, William James, Jr., *research administrator, educator*
Hassett, Valerie Jane *interior designer, architect, educator*
Hastings, Melanie (Melanie Jean Wotring) *television news anchor*
Hazelrigg, George Arthur, Jr., *systems engineer, educator*
Heineken, Frederick George *biochemical engineer*
Heivilin, Donna Mae *retired government executive*
Held, Joe Roger *retired veterinarian*
Hendrickson, Daniel C. *association administrator*
Hewitt, Thomas F. *hotel executive*
Hickman, Elizabeth Podesta *retired counselor, educator*
Hill, Donald Wain *education accreditation commission executive*
Hillis, John David *television news executive, producer, writer*
Hittle, James Donald *writer, business consultant*
Howenstine, E. Jay *housing economist*
Howlett, Clifford Theodore, Jr., (Kip Howlett) *chemicals executive*
Hunter, Jody Jean *association executive, naturalist*
Hunter, J(ohn) Robert *insurance consumer advocate*
Hurley, John Arthur *former national security advisor*
James, Daniel, III, *military officer*
Jankowski, John Edward, Jr., *government administrator*
Johnson, Charles Owen *retired lawyer*
Jones, Edward Paul *writer, editor*
Junker, Bobby Ray *research and development executive, physicist*
Kane, Annette Pieslak *religious organization executive*
Kanter, L. Erick *public relations executive*
Kappaz, Michael H. *engineering and energy executive*
Katona, Peter Geza *biomedical engineer, educator*
Katzen, Jay Kenneth *retired diplomat, state legislator, government agency administrator*
Kearney, Stephen Michael *corporate executive*
Kelley, Paul Xavier *retired military officer*
Kelly, John James *lawyer*
Kerns, Wilmer Lee *social science researcher*
Kinsey, John Allen *systems engineer, director*
Korman, James William *lawyer*
Krauss, Michael Ian *law educator*
Krusa-Dossin, Mary Ann *military officer*
Krys, Sheldon Jack *retired foreign service officer, career minister*
Kuelbs, John Thomas *lawyer*
Kumar, Srikanta Ponnathpur *electrical engineer, researcher*
Lakefield, Bruce R. *air transportation executive*
Lala, Jaynarayan Hotchand *computer engineer*
Langstaff, David Hamilton *aerospace industry executive*
Langworthy, Everett Walter *association executive, natural gas exploration company executive*
Lanier, Elizabeth K. *lawyer*
Latham, Ernest Hargreaves, Jr., *historian, educator*
Lauriski, Dave D. *federal agency administrator*
Lean, Judith *physicist, researcher*
Lehrer, James Charles *television journalist*
Leinen, Margaret Sandra *oceanographic researcher*
Leland, Marc Ernest *trust advisor, lawyer*
Lester, Barnett Benjamin *editor, retired foreign affairs officer*
Lewis, Hunter *investment advisor, publisher*
Lieberman, Robert J. *federal audit agency administrator*
Litman, Richard Curtis *lawyer*
Lundeen, William Bruce *radiologist*
Luraschi, William R. *utilities executive, lawyer*
Lurie, Nicole *former health science association administrator*
MacDougall, William Lowell *magazine editor*
MacNeil, Robert Breckenridge Ware *retired broadcast journalist, writer*
Mainwaring, Thomas Lloyd *management consultant, former motor freight company executive*
Malone, William Grady *retired lawyer*
Matthews, Allan Freeman *geologist*
May, Sterling Randolph *health association executive*
McCaslin, David E. *hotel executive*
McClelland, Harold Franklin *economics professor*
McCoart, Janice Greenberg *art educator*
McDermott, Francis Owen *retired lawyer*
McDonald, Bernard Robert *retired federal agency administrator*
Mc Donald, Gail Faber *musician, educator*
Mc Donald, John Warlick *diplomat, global strategist*
McFarland, Walter Gerard *management consultant*
McGinn, Daniel G. *public relations executive*
McKee, Thomas J. *association administrator*
McKinnon, Russel Francis Daniel *professional society administrator*
McMasters, Paul Kenneth *foundation executive*
McShane, Michael John *lobbyist*
McTique, Maurice P. *director*
McWethy, John Fleetwood *journalist*
Metz, Craig Huseman *business executive*
Milkman, Beverly L. *federal agency administrator*
Miller, Kenneth Gregory *retired air force officer*
Moore, Guy Will *retired public information officer, historian, writer*
Morse, Larry Eugene *botanist, conservationist*
Neikirk, William Robert *journalist*
Neuharth, Allen Harold *newspaper publisher*
Newburger, Beth Weinstein *historical association administrator*
Nguyen-Dinh, Thanh *internist, geriatrician, acupuncturist*
Niccolls, Wesley Oliver *retired electronics technician*
Nirschl, Robert Phillip *orthopedic surgeon*
Obermayer, Herman Joseph *newspaper publisher*
Ochmanek, David Alan *defense analyst*
Ochoa-Brillembourg, Hilda Margarita *investment banker*
O'Day, Paul Thomas *trade association executive*
O'Neill, Brian *research organization administrator*
Ordway, Frederick Ira, III, *science educator, consultant, researcher, writer*
Orkis, Lambert *musician, music educator*
Osterholz, John Louis *information administrator*
Page, Harry Robert *business administration educator*
Parker, Jeffrey Scott *law educator*
Paynter, Harry Alvin *retired trade association executive*
Perry, Walter Leo *information scientist, operations research specialist*
Petersen, John Laurens *future research and strategic planner*
Pickering, Thomas Reeve *diplomat*
Politi, John J. *association administrator*
Potvin, William Tracey *management consultant*
Prestifilippo, John *air transportation executive*
Price, Donald Ray *university official, agricultural engineer*
Price, Jack C. *association administrator*
Putnam, George W., Jr., *retired army officer*
Quinn, John Collins *publishing executive, newspaper editor*
Rabaut, Thomas W. *defense industry executive*
Rabbitt, Linda *construction executive*
Racette, Nancy Kelly *development company executive, consultant*
Rahman, Muhammad Abdur *mechanical engineer*
Ramaley, Judith Aitken *former university president, endocrinologist*
Rascon, Alfred *federal agency administrator*
Reagan, Lawrence Paul, Jr., *systems engineer*
Reed, Paul Allen *artist*
Reiss, Susan Marie *editor, writer*
Richtol, Herbert Harold *science foundation consultant*
Robb, Charles Spittal *former senator, former governor, lawyer, educator*
Rockefeller, Sharon Percy *broadcast executive*
Rogers, Alan Victor *former career officer*
Rogers, James Frederick *banker, management consultant*
Rogers, Sharon J. *education consultant*
Rosenblatt, Louise Michel *emerita educator*
Rosenthal, Robert M. *automotive sales executive*
Rotunda, Ronald Daniel *law educator, consultant*
Rubottom, George Milton *foundation administrator, chemist*
Salmon, William Cooper *mechanical engineer, engineering academy executive*
Samburg, A. Gene *security company executive*
Scafetta, Joseph, Jr., *lawyer*
Scarborough, Robert Henry, Jr., *enterpreneur*
Schmidt, Paul Wickham *lawyer*
Schneider, William, Jr., *commissioner*
Schrier-Polak, Carol *lawyer*
Schultz, Roger C. *career officer*
Schwartz, Lyle Howard *materials scientist, science administrator*
Serck-Hanssen, Eilif *air transportation executive*
Sewell, William George, III, *electronics engineer, writer*
Shaker, William Haygood *marketing professional, public policy reformer*
Shannon, Jacqueline *association executive*
Shannon, Thomas Alfred *retired educational association administrator emeritus*
Sharp, Barry J. *utilities executive*
Sheridan, Frederick *architectural firm executive*
Shine, Kenneth Irwin *cardiologist, educator*
Shortal, Terence Michael *systems company executive*
Siddayao, Corazón Morales *economist, educator, consultant*
Simonson, David C. *retired newspaper association executive*
Singstock, David John *military officer*
Smeal, Eleanor Cutri *civil rights executive*
Southern, Hugh *retired performing arts manager*
Stevens, Donald King *retired aeronautical engineer, consultant*
Stewart, Gordon Mead *architect*
Stokes, B. R. *retired transportation consultant*
Stone, Stuart Lee Morrison *librarian, language educator*
Stonner, David Moore *foundation administrator*
Stout, Mary Webb *education program specialist*
Strelau, Renate *historical researcher, artist*
Stuart, Charles Edward *electrical engineer, oceanographer*
Suh, Jinwoo *computer scientist*
Sundquist, James Lloyd *retired political scientist*
Sweeney, Randall W. *aerospace transportation executive*
Taddesse, Samuel *economist, consultant*
Tanzer, Lester *editor*
Tarpgaard, Peter Thorvald *naval architect*
Tarr-Whelan, Linda *policy center executive*
Thompson, Wayne Wray *historian*
Timperlake, Edward Thomas *writer*
Trombley, Edward Francis, III, *registrar*
Tugwell, Franklin *think-tank executive*
Tullock, Gordon *economics professor*
Tyler, Robert R. *psychologist, consultant*
Tyrrell, Robert Emmett, Jr., *periodical editor, writer*
Umminger, Bruce Lynn *government official, scientist, educator*
Uncapher, Mark Elson *lawyer, trade association administrator*
Van Horn, Hugh M. *physicist, astronomer, educator*
Walker, Robert S. *government agency administrator*
Walker, Woodrow Wilson *retired lawyer, timber farmer, real estate investor*
Watkins, Birge Swift *investment banker*
Watson, Alexander Fletcher *organization executive, former ambassador*
Weidemann, Celia Jean *social scientist, management consultant, financial consultant*
Weinberg, Robert Lester *lawyer, law educator*
Werbos, Paul John *neural net research director*
Wheeler, Barbara Monica *lawyer*
Whetsell, Paul W. *hotel executive*
Whitcomb, James Hall *geophysicist, foundation administrator*
Widener, Peri Ann *business development executive*
Wilcox, Shirley Jean Langdon *genealogist*
Winter, Harvey John *retired government official*
Wodarczyk, Francis John *chemist*
Wolf, Stephen M. *airline executive*
Wood, Heidi *commissioner*
Woods, Willie E. *information specialist*
Woollen, Edmund *electronics executive*
Zirkind, Ralph *physicist, educator*
Zorthian, Barry *communications executive*

Ashburn
Arrington, Lavarr *professional football player*
Boyne, Walter James *writer, former museum director*
Brunell, Mark Allen *professional football player*
Capellas, Michael D. *telecommunications industry executive*
Coles, Laveranues *professional football player*
Cuteri, Frank R., Jr., *automotive executive*
Gibbs, Joe Jackson *professional football coach*
Murrell, Adrian Bryan *professional football player*
Nickle, Dennis Edwin *electronics engineering consultant, deacon*
Portis, Clinton *professional football player*
Smith, Bruce *professional football player*

Snyder, Daniel *professional sports team executive, communications executive*
Trent, Grace Chen *communications executive*
Weyman, Steven Aloysius *retired military officer*
Williams, Gregg E. *professional football coach*

Ashland
Bruce, Jennifer Elaine *education educator*
Inge, Milton Thomas *American literature and culture educator, author*
Rice, Adrian Clifford *adult education educator*
Tuell, Steven Shawn *religious studies educator, minister*

Assawoman
Holley, Pamela Spencer *retired librarian*

Basye
Amolsch, Arthur Lewis *publishing executive*
Stanley, Robert Warren *association executive*

Bedford
Ramsey, Forrest Gladstone, Jr., *retired engineering company executive*

Blacksburg
Aref, Hassan *fluid mechanics educator*
Barksdale, Mary Alice *education educator*
Batra, Romesh Chander *engineering mechanics educator, researcher*
Baudoin, Antonius B. A. M. *plant pathologist, educator*
Baumgartner, Frederic Joseph *history professor*
Bliznakov, Milka Tcherneva *architect, educator*
Bosniak, Murray Eli *vocational school educator*
Brown, Gary Sandy *electrical engineering educator*
Brown, Gregory Neil *university administrator, forest physiology educator*
Bryant, Clifton Dow *sociologist, educator*
Burkhart, Harold Eugene *forestry educator*
Callison, Myrna C. *occupational therapist*
Campbell, Joan Virginia Loweke *secondary school educator, language educator*
Cowles, Joe Richard *biology professor*
Crawford, Peggy Smith *design educator*
De Datta, Surajit Kumar *soil scientist, agronomist, educator*
de Wolf, David Alter *electrical engineer, educator*
Disney, Ralph L(ynde) *retired industrial engineering educator*
Doswald, Herman Kenneth *German language educator, academic administrator*
Edwards, Patricia Klobus *former dean, architecture/urban studies educator*
Eyre, Peter *dean*
Fabrycky, Wolter Joseph *engineering educator, author, industrial and systems engineer*
Fowler, Virginia C. *literature educator*
Gablik, Suzi *art educator, writer*
Glasser, Wolfgang Gerhard *chemical engineering wood science researcher, educator*
Good, Irving John *statistics educator, mathematician, philosopher of science*
Gray, Festus Gail *electrical engineer, educator, researcher*
Graybeal, Jack Daniel *chemist, educator*
Grover, Norman LaMotte *theologian, philosopher*
Gwazdauskas, Francis Charles *animal science educator, dairy scientist*
Henrickson, Bonnie *college basketball coach*
Inman, Daniel John *mechanical engineer, educator*
Jannuzi, F. Tomasson *economics professor*
Jensen, Walter Edward *lawyer, educator*
Jones, James Beverly *retired mechanical engineering educator, consultant*
Kabir, Firoz *wood technologist, researcher*
Kelly, James Michael *plant and soil scientist*
Knox, Paul L. *architecture educator, dean*
Lee, Fred C. *electrical engineering educator*
Leonard, Robert Haigh *theater educator, stage director*
McKenna, James Richard *agronomy educator*
McNamee, Mark *academic administrator*
Meszaros, Peggy S. *academic administrator*
Mitchell, James Kenneth *civil engineer, educator*
Moore, Laurence John *business educator*
Patterson, Douglas MacLennan *finance educator*
Pearson, Ronald Earl *educator, researcher*
Pittman, Hunter *architecture educator, department chairman*
Poole, Scott *architecture educator*
Porter, Duncan MacNair *editor, educator*
Randall, Clifford Wendell *civil engineer, educator*
Rodriguez-Camilloni, Humberto Leonardo *architect, historian, educator*
Rott, Hans C. *architect, educator*
Sandu, Adrian *mathematician, computer scientist, educator*
Schetz, Joseph Alfred *aerospace engineer, educator*
Schnitzer, Martin Colby *economist, educator*
Smoot, Raymond D., Jr., *academic administrator*
Squires, Arthur Morton *chemical engineer, educator*
Steger, Charles William *university administrator*
Swiger, L. A. *agricultural studies educator*
Taylor, Charles Lewis *political science educator*
Torgersen, Paul Ernest *academic administrator, educator*
Uysal, Muzaffer Shamil *management educator*
Vikesland, Peter John *environmental engineering educator, researcher*
Walker, Richard David *civil engineer, educator*
Weaver, Pamela Ann *hospitality research professional*
Weiner, Frank H. *architect, educator*

Blackstone
Allen, Jeffrey Rodgers *lawyer*

Blue Ridge
Elmore, Walter A. *electrical engineer, consultant*

Bluemont
Kobetz, Richard William *criminologist, consultant*

Boston
Engle, Reed Laurence *landscape architect*
Fisher, John Morris *association official, business executive, educator*

Bridgewater
Barkley, Terrell Wayne *school librarian, archivist, curator*
Bittel, Muriel Albers *managing editor*
Geisert, Wayne Frederick *educational consultant, retired administrator*

Bristol
McGlothlin, James W. *wholesale distribution executive*

Bristow
Mac Donald, Margaret Clark *retired real estate agent*
Onufrock, Richard Shade *pharmacist, researcher*
Schrock, Simon *retail executive*

Broad Run
Kube, Harold Deming *retired financial executive*

Burgess
Burch, Michael Ira *public relations executive, former government official*
Towle, Leland Hill *retired government official*

Burke
Bermant, Gordon *psychologist, lawyer, consultant, writer*
Emery, Vicki Morris *school library media administrator*
Gelb, Sidney *writer*
Hipfel, Steven J. *lawyer*
Lynch, Charles Theodore, Sr., *materials science engineering researcher, consultant, educator*
Pfister, Cloyd Harry *consultant, former career officer*
Werfel, Sandra Diane *clinical social worker*
Woodruff, C(harles) Roy *consultant, retired professional association executive*

Castleton
Hahn, James Maglorie *former librarian, farmer*

Catlett
Broderick, Anthony James *air transportation executive*

Centreville
Etters, Ronald Milton *lawyer, former government official*
Kim-Yi, Sungsook *music educator, pianist*
Malouff, Frank Joseph *health care association executive*
Tobin, Robert Edwin *regional director*

Chantilly
Anderson, Maynard Carlyle *national and international security executive*
Becker, James Richard *lawyer*
Carlson, Robert Charles *financial advisor, writer*
Chrzanowski, Leye Jeannette *publisher*
deMonsabert, Winston Russel *chemist, consultant*
Helmer, Steven James *lawyer*
Priem, Richard Gregory *writer, information systems executive*
Srivastava, Kailash Chandra *microbiologist*
Sroka, John Walter *trade association executive*
Tian, Yonglai *electrical engineer*
Tobin, Robert G. *supermarket chain executive*
Watkins, Felix Scott *printing company executive*
Welles, Judith *public affairs executive*
Young, M. Dendy *finance company executive*

Charlottesville
Abbot, William Wright *history professor*
Abraham, Henry Julian *political science educator*
Alford, Neill Herbert, Jr., *retired law educator*
Allis, C. David *science educator*
Anderson, Robert Barber *architect*
Arnold, Albert James *foreign language educator*
Ayers, Edward *dean*
Barrett, Eugene Joseph *physician, educator, researcher*
Battestin, Martin Carey *retired English language educator*
Bednar, Michael John *architecture educator*
Beller, George Allan *medical educator*
Berkeley, Edmund, Jr., *retired archivist, educator*
Berkeley, Francis Lewis, Jr., *retired archivist*
Biltonen, Rodney Lincoln *biochemistry and pharmacology educator*
Bishop, Ruth Ann *coloratura soprano, voice educator*
Block, Gene David *biologist, educator, science administrator*
Bloomfield, Louis Aub *physicist, researcher*
Bly, Charles Albert *nuclear engineer, research scientist*
Bonnie, Richard Jeffrey *law educator, lawyer, consultant*
Bouchard, Ronald A. *health care administrator*
Brautigan, David L. *biomedical researcher*
Brettschneider, Cathie I. *editor*
Brewer, Philip Warren *retired civil engineer*
Brooks, Peter (Preston) *French and comparative literature educator, department chair, writer*
Brown, Holmes *public affairs executive*
Brownell, Blaine Allison *educational association administrator, former university administrator, history educator*
Bruns, David Eugene *medical educator, researcher*
Bull, George Albert *retired banker*
Cannon, Jonathan Z. *lawyer, educator*
Cano-Ballesta, Juan *Spanish language educator*
Cantrell, Robert Wendell *otolaryngologist, head and neck surgeon, educator*
Carey, Robert Munson *medical educator, physician*
Carter, William Walton *physicist, researcher*
Casey, John Dudley *writer, English language educator*
Casteen, John Thomas, III, *university president*
Chandler, Lawrence Bradford, Jr., *lawyer*
Chapel, Robert Clyde *stage director, theater educator*
Chase, Karen Susan *English literature educator*
Cherno, Melvin *humanities educator*
Chevalier, Roger Alan *astronomy educator, consultant*
Childress, James Franklin *theology and medical educator*
Clayton, Anita Louise *psychiatrist, physician*
Cohen, Edwin Samuel *lawyer, educator*
Colley, John Leonard, Jr., *educator, author, management consultant*
Crackel, Theodore Joseph *historian, consultant*
Crigler, B. Waugh *US magistrate judge*
Crosby, Ivan Keith *cardiac surgeon, educator*
Cushman, Stephen Bigelow *English educator, writer*
Daniel, Leon *journalist, newspaper columnist, editor*
Davis, Edward Wilson *business administration educator*
Doctor, Allan *physician, researcher*
Dooley, Michael P. *law educator*
Dove, Rita Frances *poet, English language educator*
Dunn, William Wyly *corporate lawyer*
Durbin, Charles G., Jr., *anesthesiologist, intensivist, educator*
Edson, Evelyn *history professor, writer*
Ellett, John Spears, II, *retired taxation educator, accountant, lawyer*
Elzinga, Kenneth Gerald *economics professor*
Epstein, Robert Marvin *anesthesiologist, educator*
Epstein, William *experimental psychologist*
Essig, Nancy Claire *publishing executive*
Feigert, Frank Brook *retired political science educator, writer*
Finley, Robert Van Eaton *minister*
Fiser, Karen B. *poet*
Flickinger, Charles John *anatomist, educator*
Foard, Susan Lee *editor*
Forbes, John Douglas *architectural and economic historian*
Fredrick, Laurence William *astronomer, educator*
Friedman, Susan Lynn Bell *economic development professional*
Gaden, Elmer Lewis, Jr., *chemical engineering educator, retired*
Gallagher, Thomas Francis *physicist*
Garrett, George Palmer, Jr., *creative writing and English language educator, writer*
Garrett, Reginald Hooker *biology professor, researcher*
Garson, Arthur, Jr., *dean, medical educator*
Gaskin, Felicia *biochemist, educator*
Gianniny, Omer Allan, Jr., *retired humanities educator*
Gillenwater, Jay Young *urologist, educator*
Good, Richard Standish *geologist*
Graebner, Norman Arthur *history educator*
Greer, Kenneth E. *dermatologist*
Grimes, Russell Newell *chemistry educator, inorganic chemist*
Groiss, Fred George *lawyer*
Guerrant, Richard Littleton *medical educator*
Gunter, Bradley Hunt *capital management executive*
Haberly, David Tristram *language educator*
Haigh, Robert William *business administration educator*
Haimes, Yacov Yosseph *systems and civil engineering educator, consultant*
Handler, Jerome Sidney *anthropology educator*
Hanft, Ruth S. Samuels *healthcare consultant, educator, economist*
Harbert, Guy Morley, Jr., *retired obstetrician, gynecologist*
Harris, Robert Shields *dean*
Hartz, Jill *museum director*
Henderson, Stanley Dale *lawyer, educator*
Hendrickson, Jerome Orland *trade association administrator, lawyer*
Henry, Laurin Luther *public affairs educator*
Hillman, Bruce Jay *radiologist, researcher, consultant, educator*
Hinnant, Clarence Henry, III, *health care executive*
Hirsch, Eric Donald, Jr., *English language educator, educational reformer*
Hodous, Robert Power *lawyer*
Hoel, Lester A. *civil engineering educator*
Hogshire, Edward Leigh *judge*
Hornberger, George Milton *environmental science educator*
Hostler, Sharon Lee *pediatrics educator, rehabilitation center executive*
Howard, Arthur Ellsworth Dick *law educator*
Howe, James Maxwell *materials scientist, educator*
Howell, Robert Edward *hospital administrator*
Hudson, John Lester *chemical engineering educator*
Humphreys, Paul William *philosophy educator, consultant*
Hunt, William B. *cardiopulmonary physician*
Hymes, Dell Hathaway *anthropologist, educator*
Inigo, Rafael Madrigal *retired electrical engineering educator*
Jagger, Janine *epidemiologist*
Jane, John Anthony *neurosurgeon, educator*
Jeffries, John Calvin, Jr., *law educator*
Jones, Rayford Scott *surgeon, educator*
Jordan, Daniel Porter, Jr., *foundation administrator, history educator*
Kadner, Robert Joseph *microbiology educator*
Kaiserlian, Penelope Jane *publishing company executive*
Kassell, Neal Frederic *neurosurgery educator*
Kattwinkel, John *physician, pediatrics educator, neonatologist*
Keats, Theodore Eliot *radiologist, educator*
Kelly, Thaddeus Elliott *medical geneticist*
Kett, Joseph Francis *historian, educator*
Kiewra, Gustave Paul *psychologist, educator*
Kitchin, James D., III, *obstetrician-gynecologist, educator*
Knaus, William A. *medical educator, researcher*
Koester, Robert James *publishing executive, emergency medical technician*
Kraehe, Enno Edward *history professor*
Krzysztofowicz, Roman *systems engineering and statistical science educator, consultant*
Kuhlmann-Wilsdorf, Doris *materials scientist, educator*
Landess, Fred Stone *lawyer*
Lane, Ann Judith *history and women's studies educator*
Lang, Cecil Yelverton *English language educator*
Langbaum, Robert Woodrow *English language educator, author*
Larner, Joseph *pharmacology educator*
Laseter, Timothy Marks *finance educator*
Laurencin, Cato Thomas *biomedical engineer, orthopaedic surgeon*
Lee, Jae Kyun *biomedical researcher, educator*
Lee, Jen-shih *biomedical engineering educator*
Leffler, Melvyn P. *history professor*
Levenson, Jacob Clavner *English language educator*
Linden, Peppy G. *museum director*
Little, W(illia)m A(lfred) *foreign language educator, researcher*
Lo, Fred Kwok Yung *astronomer*
Lo, Kwok-Yung *astronomer, educator, researcher*
Long, Charles Farrell *insurance company executive*
Loo, Beverly Jane *publishing company executive*
Lott, Eric William *literature educator*
Lupton, Mary Hosmer *retired small business owner*
MacIlwaine, Mary Jarratt *public relations executive*
Mandell, Gerald Lee *internist, educator*
Marshall, John Crook *internal medicine educator, researcher*
Martin, David Alan *law educator*
Martin, Robert Bruce *chemistry professor*
Matson, Robert Edward *public management educator, leadership consultant*
McCrimmon, Barbara Smith *writer, librarian*
McDuffie, Marcia Jensen *pediatrics educator, researcher*
McGann, Jerome John *English language educator*
McGinnis, Charles Irving *civil engineer*
McLaren, John Edward *economics professor*
Meador, Daniel John *law educator*
Meem, James Lawrence, Jr., *nuclear scientist*
Megill, Allan D. *historian*
Meiburg, Charles Owen *business administration educator*
Melcher, Margaret Louisa *editor, publishing executive*
Menaker, Michael *biology professor, department chairman*
Menefee, Samuel Pyeatt *lawyer, anthropologist*
Merrill, Richard Austin *lawyer*
Michael, James Harry, Jr., *federal judge*
Middleditch, Leigh Benjamin, Jr., *lawyer, educator*
Midelfort, Hans Christian Erik *history professor*
Mikalson, Jon Dennis *classics educator*
Miller, Margaret Alison *education educator*
Minehart, Jean Besse *tax accountant*
Monaghan, Charles *writer, editor*
Monahan, John T. *law educator, psychologist*
Moore, John Norton *lawyer, diplomat, educator*
Morgan, Raymond F. *plastic surgeon*
Muller, William Henry, Jr., *surgeon, educator*
Newsom, David Dunlop *foreign service officer, educator*
Nohrnberg, James Carson *English language educator*
Nolan, Stanton Peelle *surgeon, educator*
Norris, Pamela Marie *mechanical engineer, educator*
O'Connell, Jeffrey *law educator*
Oliver, Charles Montgomery *retired English educator*
Olsen, Edgar Oliver *economics professor*
O'Neil, Robert Marchant *university administrator, law educator*
O'Shaughnessy, Andrew Jackson *historic site research director, education educator*
Owen, John Atkinson, Jr., *internist, educator*
Pang, Maybeline Miusze (Maybeline Chan) *software testing and systems engineer, analyst*
Parrish, David Walker, Jr., *legal publishing company executive*
Pate, Brooks *chemist*
Pate, Robert Hewitt, Jr., *counselor educator*
Perdue, Charles L., Jr., *social sciences educator, language educator*
Perez-Reyes, Edward *molecular physiologist*
Perkowski, Jan Louis *language, literature and folklore educator*
Peterson, Merrill Daniel *history educator*
Phillips, Lawrence H., II, *neurologist, educator*
Platts-Mills, Thomas Alexander E. *immunologist, educator, researcher*
Priest, Hartwell Wyse *artist*
Rader, Louis T. *corporation executive, educator*
Rehm, Patrice Koch *radiologist, educator*
Rein, Michael Frank *physician, medical educator*
Reynolds, Albert Barnett *nuclear engineer, educator*
Rhoads, Steven Eric *political science educator*
Rini, Joel *language educator, linguist*
Root, James Benjamin *landscape architect*
Rorty, Richard McKay *philosophy educator*
Roseberry, Edwin Southall *retired state agency administrator*
Rosenblum, Marvin *mathematics educator*
Rovnyak, James *mathematician, educator*
Rowlingson, John Clyde *anesthesiologist, physician, educator*
Rubin, David Lee *humanities educator, publisher*
Sarazin, Craig Leigh *astronomer*
Sarembock, Ian Joseph *internist*
Scheld, William Michael *internist, educator*
Schneider, Edward Martin *retired internist, medical educator*
Scott, Charlotte H. *business educator*
Scott, Nathan Alexander, Jr., *minister, literary critic, religious educator*
Scott, Robert Edwin *dean, law educator*
Sedgwick, Alexander *historian, educator*
Shaw, Donald Leslie *Spanish language educator*
Shen, Tsung Ying *medicinal chemistry educator*
Shenkir, William Gary *business educator*
Sherman, William *architecture educator*
Sihler, William Wooding *finance educator*
Slaughter, Edward Ratliff, Jr., *lawyer*
Smith, Clyde Ray *dean*
Spacks, Patricia Meyer *English educator*
Spearing, Anthony Colin *English literature educator*
Stevenson, Ian *psychiatrist, educator*
Stocker, Arthur Frederick *classics educator*
Swofford, Donald Anthony *architect*
Sykes, Gresham M'Cready *sociologist, educator, artist*
Tang, Jinshan *computer scientist, researcher*
Teates, Charles David *radiologist, educator*
Theodoridis, George Constantin *biomedical engineering educator, researcher*
Thompson, David William *business educator*
Thompson, Kenneth W(inifred) *educational association administrator, writer, editor, social sciences educator*
Thorner, Michael Oliver *medical educator*
Thornhill, Arthur H., Jr., *retired book publisher*
Thornton, Kathryn C. *physicist, astronaut*
Tillack, Thomas Warner *pathologist, educator*
Townsend, Miles Averill *aerospace and mechanical engineering educator*
Turner, Robert Foster *law educator, writer*
Tuttle, Jeremy Ballou *neurobiologist*
Tyree, Lewis, Jr., *retired compressed gas company executive, inventor, technical consultant*
Unsworth, Richard Preston *minister, educator, school administrator*
Vanden Bout, Paul Adrian *astronomer, physicist, educator*
Villar-Palasi, Carlos *pharmacology educator*
Wadlington, Walter James *law educator*
Wagner, Roy *anthropology educator, researcher*
Wallace, Karl Kenneth, Jr., *physician, radiologist*

Wood, John Martin *lawyer*
Yoshimura, Yoshiko *librarian*

Farmville
Boyer, Calvin James *librarian*
Cormier, Patricia Picard *academic executive*
Dorrill, William Franklin *political scientist, educator*
Hevener, Fillmer, Jr., *English language educator, writer, portrait artist*
Kinzer, Charles Edward *music educator*
Rowland, Rhonda Stockton *mathematician, educator*
Terry, Wayne Gilbert *healthcare executive, hospital administrator, mediator*

Ferrum
Reilly, Kevin Patrick *psychology educator*

Flint Hill
Dietel, William Moore *former foundation executive*
Williamson, Richard Hall *association executive*

Floyd
Clemens, Donald Faull *chemistry professor*

Fort Belvoir
Barnholdt, Terry Joseph *chemical, industrial, and general engineer*
Clark, Trudy H. *career officer*
Clema, Joe Kotouc *computer scientist*
Foley, David W. *career officer*
Harms, John Kevin *lawyer*
Molholm, Kurt Nelson *federal agency administrator*
Raymond, George Edward, Jr., (Chip Raymond) *operations research analyst*
St. John, Adrian, II, *retired army officer*

Fort Eustis
Smail, Laurence Mitchell *lawyer, educator*

Fort Lee
Simmonds, Robert Maurer *education educator*
Sterling, Keir Brooks *historian, educator*

Fort Monroe
Abrams, John N. *army officer*

Fort Myer
Hart, Herbert Michael *military officer*

Franklin
Cobb, G. Elliott, Jr., *lawyer*

Franktown
Kellam, Caramine *volunteer*

Fredericksburg
Anderson, Roberta June *computer engineer*
Bailey, Amos Purnell *clergyman, syndicated columnist, author*
Brown, Harold Eugene *retired magistrate*
Crippen, Timothy Alan *sociology educator*
Dahnk, Jean Patricia *lawyer*
DeLong, Marlena Chipman *editor, researcher, historian*
DeMuro, Gerard J *information technology executive*
Dorman, John Frederick *genealogist*
Emory, Samuel Thomas *retired educator*
Eslinger-Brown, Vanessa Pauline *humanities educator*
Foster, Vonita White *museum director*
Geary, Patrick Joseph *security administrator, writer*
Goolrick, John Cole *congressional staff member, writer, consultant*
Hajek, Otomar *mathematician, educator*
Hasenfus, Harold Joseph *retired mechanical engineer, naval technical director*
Hickman, Margaret Capellini *advertising executive*
Ivey, David Lamar *trade association executive*
Jenks-Davies, Kathryn Ryburn *retired daycare provider and owner, civic worker*
Kusserow, Richard Phillip *government official, corporate financial executive*
Marler, Helen *writer, actress*
Medding, Walter Sherman *retired environmental engineer*
Pitts, Angela L. *humanities educator, researcher*
Potter, Sylvia *education educator*
Rampersad, Peggy A. Snellings *sociologist, consultant*
Schmutzhart, Berthold Josef *sculptor, educator, art and education consultant*
Sisk, Fred Dean *retired cartographer*
Unison-Pace, Wendy Jane *nursing educator*

Free Union
Horowitz, Barry Martin *systems research and engineering company executive*
LeBoutillier, Megan *writer*

Front Royal
Andes, Larry Dale *minister*
Bonzagni, Vincent Francis *lawyer, program administrator, analyst, researcher*
Douglas, J(ocelyn) Fielding *toxicologist, consultant*
Napier, Douglas William *lawyer*

Gainesville
Lee, Won Jay *radiologist*
Levell, Edward, Jr., *retired aiport executive*
Steger, Edward Herman *chemist*
Tuck, Russell R., Jr., *former college president*

Galax
Dunson, William Albert *biology professor, ecological consultant*
Kapp, John Paul *lawyer, physician, educator*

Garrisonville
Emely, Charles Harry *trade association executive, consultant*

Glasgow
Riegel, Kurt Wetherhold *environmental protection executive*

Glen Allen
Anderson, James Frederick *clergyman*
Batzli, Terrence Raymond *lawyer*
Chittum, Loretta Petty *federal agency administrator*
Fife, William Franklin *retired drug company executive*
Hinkle, Douglas Paddock *retired languages educator*
Jones, Carolyn *insurance company executive*
Minor, George Gilmer, III, *drug and hospital supply company executive*
Murphey, Robert Stafford *pharmaceutical executive*
Rogal, Andrew L. *insurance company executive*
Smith, Craig R. *medical equipment company executive*
Stokely, John E. *food distribution executive*
Weaver, Mollie Little *lawyer*

Gloucester
Hicks, C. Flippo *lawyer*

Gloucester Point
Sandridge, Donald Otis *music educator*

Great Falls
Andrews, Betty Bauserman *retired secondary school educator, property manager*
Bachner, John Philip *business consultant*
Cass, Ronald Andrew *dean*
Cowhill, William Joseph *retired naval officer, consultant*
DiBona, Charles Joseph *retired trade association executive*
Fisher, Bart Steven *lawyer, educator, investment banker*
Ganley, Betty *artist*
Garrett, Wilbur (Bill Garrett) *magazine editor*
Klimczuk, Stephen John *business executive, foundation director*
Mitchell, Roy Shaw *lawyer*
Neidich, George Arthur *lawyer*
Preston, Charles George *lawyer*
Skeen, David Ray *systems engineer, consultant, engineering executive, educator*

Grundy
Davis, W. Jeremy *dean, law educator, lawyer*

Gum Spring
Dilworth, Robert Lexow *career military officer, educator*

Halifax
Dunavant, Samuel Jackson, Jr., *civil engineer, contractor*
Greenbacker, John Everett *retired lawyer and naval officer*

Hamilton
Shoremount, Paul Erik *secondary school educator*

Hampden Sydney
Arieti, James Alexander *classics educator, writer*
Joyner, Weyland Thomas *physicist, educator, business consultant*
Porterfield, William Wendell *chemist, educator*

Hampton
Amer, Tahani R. *aerospace engineer*
Bangert, Linda S. *aeronautical engineer*
Bartels, Robert Edwin *aerospace engineer*
Bhuiyan, Mohammad Ali *university administrator, educator, consultant*
Brauer, Harrol Andrew, Jr., *broadcast executive*
Bridges, Roy Dubard, Jr., *federal agency administrator*
Brown, Loretta Ann Port *physician, geneticist*
Burgess, Gary Thomas *social studies educator, consultant*
Crawford, Tommy F. *career officer*
Daniels, Cindy Lou *space agency executive*
Davis, Bertha Lane *psychiatric nursing educator*
Drummond, James Everman *defense technology transfer consultant, former army officer*
Dwoyer, Douglas Leon *engineering executive*
Fay, Catharine C. *aerospace engineer*
Fox, Margaret Louise *retired secondary education educator*
Freeman, Delma C., Jr., *science association director*
Harris, Carl G. *music educator*
Harvey, William Robert *university president*
Hongyu, Liu *atmospheric scientist*
Jin, Zhonghai *physicist*
Joshi, Suresh Meghashyam *research engineer*
Kludze, Ave K.P., Jr., *aerospace engineer*
Mehrotra, Sudhir C. *engineering company executive*
Meyers, James Frank *electronics engineer*
Moser, Eugene Paul, Jr., *retired secondary school educator*
Nelson, Wallace Jay *patent attorney*
Rummel, Andrew Thomas *music educator, musician*
Singleterry, Robert Clay, Jr., *aerospace technologist, physicist*
Smith, Stephen Mark *lawyer*
Smith, Sr., Jackie Wayne *minister*
Sobieski, Jaroslaw *aerospace engineer*
Spearman, Morris Leroy *aeronautics and aerospace researcher*
Tripathi, Ram Kishore *physicist, researcher*
Verma, Arun K. *mathematician, educator*
Weiser, Erik Saul *materials research engineer, project manager*
White, Debra Saunders *technology executive*
Yamakov, Vesselin Ivanov *aerospace scientist, researcher*

Hardy
Harriett, Rebecca *park director*

Hardyville
White, Gordon Eliot *historian*

Harrisonburg
Alotta, Robert Ignatius *historian, educator, writer*
Arthur, Thomas Hahn *theater educator, director*
Baker, George Harold, III, *physicist*
Burkholder, Owen Eugene *religious organization administrator*
Carrier, Ronald Edwin *academic administrator, director*
Francfort, Alfred John, Jr., *economics professor*
Geary, Robert Francis, Jr., *English educator*
Gill, Gerald Lawson *librarian*
Hyser, Raymond M. *humanities educator*
Ivory, Ming Marie *political scientist*
Kluesner, James Francis *musician, educator*
McCurdy, Donna T. *food products company executive*
Pannell, Richard Anthony *religious organization administrator*
Reid, Susan L. *conductor*
Rollman, Steven Allan *communications educator*
Rosser, John Barkley, Jr., *economics professor*
Theodore, Crystal *artist, retired educator*
Wallinger, M(elvin) Bruce *lawyer*
Wang, Greg G. *education educator, consultant*

Hartfield
Johnson, Carl Randolph *chemist, educator*

Hayes
Casson, Richard Frederick *lawyer, travel bureau executive*
Martinez Fallon, Alma Urania *mechanical engineer*
Phillips, Elizabeth Jason *lawyer, state agency administrator*

Haymarket
Doolittle, Warren T. *retired federal official*
Frank, Jacob *lawyer*
Katz, Alan Charles *toxicologist*

Heathsville
Stubbs, Susan Conklin *retired statistician*
Winkel, Raymond Norman *aerospace industry consultant, avionics manufacturing executive, retired naval officer*

Herndon
Berry, Fred Clifton, Jr., *author, magazine editor, book packager*
Burns, Patrick Owen *venture capital company executive*
Childers, Charles *communications executive*
Cope, Laurence Brian *utilities company executive, energy/economic consultant*
Crossfield, Albert Scott *aeronautical science consultant, pilot*
Douglass, Robert Joseph, Jr., *computer scientist*
Frazier, Paul Ignatius *marketing professional*
Gilbert, Douglas Brainerd *management executive*
Guerreri, Carl Natale *electronic company executive*
Hermansen, John Christian *computational linguist*
Hollis, Katherine Mary *information scientist, consultant*
Jones, Reba (Becki) Pestun *elementary school educator, music educator*
Mandl, Alex J(ohann) *telecommunications company executive*
Miller, Donald Lane *publishing executive*
Montgomery, Hugh Everett, Jr., *civilian military executive*
O'Neill, James R. *aerospace transportation executive*
Ras-Work, Andenet T. *software company executive*
Rongen, Thomas *professional soccer coach*
Rump, Kendall E. *air transportation executive*
Walker, Lawrence Howard, Jr., *music educator, department chairman*
White, Matthew C. *advertising executive*
Woerth, Duane E. *labor union administrator*

Hillsville
Becker, Elizabeth Anne *secondary school educator*

Hollins College
O'Brien, Jane Margaret *academic administrator*

Hopewell
Clark, Bruce Arlington, Jr., *lawyer*
Williams, C. James, III, (Jim Williams) *lawyer*

Hot Springs
Deeds, Robert Creigh *lawyer, state legislator*

Independence
Craig, James Hicklin *fine arts consultant*

Ivy
Wilcox, Harvey John *lawyer*

Keswick
Hawkins, Edward J. *retired lawyer*
Johansen, Eivind Herbert *special education services executive, former army officer*
Kunkel, David Nelson *lawyer*
Nosanow, Barbara Shissler *art association administrator*
Pochick, Francis Edward *financial consultant*
Rafajko, Robert Richard *medical research company executive*
Rowe, William Joseph *internist*
Woods, Reginald Foster *management consulting executive*

Kilmarnock
Ibañez, Alvaro *patent design company executive, artist*
Moore, William Black, Jr., *retired aluminum company executive*

King George
Agnew, Christopher Mack *minister, historian*
Newhall, David, III, *former government official*

Lake Ridge
Ingrassia, Anthony Frank *human resource specialist*

Lansdowne
Fujishiro, Katakazu Kenneth *retired urban and regional planner, engineer*

Leesburg
Alwani, Ahmed J. *dean, consultant*
Hetzel, Alice M. *statistician, researcher*
Ink, Dwight A. *government agency administrator*
Jacob, Walter Charles *lawyer*
Johnson, Julia A. *writer*
Kelly, Lawrence Edward *lawyer, photographer*
Mahood, Ken *music educator*
McDonough, Joseph Corbett *former army officer, aviation consultant*
Mims, William Cleveland *state legislator, lawyer*
Mitchell, Russell Harry *dermatologist*
Robertson, Ruth *artist, art gallery owner*

Leon
Han, Nong *artist, sculptor, painter*

Lexington
Ball, Gordon Victor *education educator, writer, editor, filmmaker, photographer*
Brooke, George Mercer, Jr., *historian, educator*
Burish, Thomas Gerard *academic administrator*
DeSilvey, Dennis Lee *cardiologist, educator, university administrator*
Elmes, David Gordon *psychologist, educator*
Gaines, James Edwin, Jr., *retired librarian*
Jarrard, Leonard Everett *psychologist, educator*
John, Lewis George *political science educator*
Jost, Timothy Stoltzfus *law educator*
Kassens, Alice Louise *economist, educator*
Kirgis, Frederic Lee *law educator*
Krantz, Linda Law *librarian*
Leach, Maurice Derby, Jr., *librarian, educator*
Luecke, Pamela *professor, former editor*
Lynn, Michael A. *historic site director*
McCloud, Anece Faison *academic administrator*
Myers, Gerald C. *music educator*
Partlett, David F. *dean, law educator*
Peay, J.H. Binford, III, *retired army officer*
Phillips, Charles Franklin, Jr., *retired economist*
Simpson, Pamela Hemenway *art historian, educator*
Spencer, Edgar Winston *geology educator*
Squire, James C. *adult education educator, engineer, consultant*
Stuart, Dabney *poet, author, English language educator*
Tierney, Michael John *mathematics and computer science educator*
Velasquez, Eduardo A *education educator*
Wiant, Sarah Kirsten *law library administrator, educator, director*
Williams, H. Thomas (Tom) *academic administrator, physicist, educator*
Winfrey, John Crawford *economist, educator*
Young, Bruce Kenneth *film director*
Young, Kenneth Evans *educational consultant*

Lightfoot
Morris, Robert Louis *management consultant*

Locust Grove
Grante, Jullian Irving *criminal justice consultant*
Huntsman, Lawrence Darrow *lawyer, director*
Ingalls, Jane *university program director*
Walsh, Geraldine Frances *nursing administrator*

Lorton
Charlston, Jeffery Allen *historian, artist*

Louisa
Small, William Edwin, Jr., *association and recreation executive*

Lovettsville
Flannery, John Philip *lawyer*

Luray
Burzynski, Norman Stephen *editor*

Lynchburg
Barkley, Henry Brock, Jr., *research and development engineering executive*
Bowman, Kathleen Gill *academic administrator*
Brindle, Wayne Allan *religious studies educator*
Carey, Charles William, Jr., *historian, educator*
Cornett, Robert Arnold *philosophy educator*
Cunniff, Suzanne *surgical technician*
Cushman, Valerie Jean *athletic director*
Denham, Paul Raymond *construction executive*
Duff, Ernest Arthur *political scientist, educator*
Elson, James Martin *retired historic foundation director*
Falwell, Jerry L. *minister*
Gale, James Darren *nuclear energy industry executive*
Groshner, Maria Star *nuclear engineer*
Healy, Joseph Francis, Jr., *lawyer, retired air transportation executive*
Herndon, Merle Puckette *principal*
Hudson, Walter Tiree *artist*
Husted, Stewart Winthrop *dean, marketing educator, consultant*
Johnson, Robert Bruce *historic preservationist*
Lane, Richard Allan *preventive medicine physician, educator*
Marra, Anthony Tullio *audio visual specialist*
Massie, Anne Adams Robertson *artist*
McClenon, John Raymond *retired chemistry educator*
McRorie, William Edward *lawyer, retired life insurance company executive*
Moon, Norman K. *judge*
Morgan, Evan *retired chemist*
Morland, John Kenneth *sociology and anthropology educator*
Packert, G(ayla) Beth *retired lawyer*
Partie, David John *language educator*
Quillian, William Fletcher, Jr., *retired banker, former college president*
Schewel, Rosel Hoffberger *education educator*
Snead, George Murrell, Jr., *army officer, scientist, consultant*
Stephens, Bart Nelson *former foreign service officer*
Terzic, Petar *mathematician, educator*
Wetzel, Robert Charles *lawyer*
Whittemore, Linda Genevieve *clinical psychologist*
Womack, Edgar Allen, Jr., *energy executive, consultant, nuclear technology consultant*

Lyndhurst
Dieter, Melvin Easterday *retired minister, educator*

Manakin Sabot
Bayliss, John Temple *retired science educator, retired energy executive*
Bright, Craig Bartley *lawyer*
Thompson, Walter David, Jr., *systems analyst*

Manassas
Archer, Chalmers, Jr., *retired education educator*
Bahner, Sue (Florence Suzanna Bahner) *radio broadcasting executive*
Colgan, Charles Joseph *corporate professional, state legislator*
Cypess, Raymond Harold *bioscience organization executive*
Foote, John Holland *lawyer*
Geerdes, James D(ivine) *chemical company executive*

Heimendinger, Larry Martin *computer software manufacturing company executive*
Heishman, Ricci Lynn *information technology educator*
Isbister, Jenefir Diane Wilkinson *microbiologist, researcher, educator, consultant*
Jong, Shung-Chang *mycologist*
Parrish, Frank Jennings *retired food products executive*
Storing, Paul Edward *retired foreign service officer*
Van Broekhoven, Rollin Adrian *federal judge*

Marion
Armbrister, Douglas Kenley *surgeon*
Elledge, Glenna Ellen Tuell *journalist*
Grinstead, Paul Lee *materials company official*
Groseclose, Joanne Stowers *special education educator*

Martinsville
Frith, Douglas Kyle *retired lawyer*
Plonk, William McGuire *retired minister*
Shackleford, William Alton, Sr., *minister*

Mason Neck
Brittigan, Robert Lee *retired lawyer*
Mc Curdy, Patrick Pierre *editor, consultant*

Mathews
Busby, Morris D. *former ambassador*

Mc Dowell
Harkleroad, Jo-Ann Decker *special education educator*

Mc Lean
Adler, Larry *marketing professional*
Alberts, Henry Celler *real estate company executive*
Alexander, Fred Calvin, Jr., *lawyer*
Aucutt, Ronald David *lawyer*
Auerbach, Anita L. *clinical psychologist*
Barnes, R.F. *food products executive*
Baumann, Martin F. *savings and loan association executive*
Blair, Bonnie *former professional speedskater, former Olympic athlete*
Blazer, Randolph C. *diversified financial services company executive*
Boyd, Ralph F., Jr., *lawyer, former federal agency administrator*
Braddock, Joseph Vincent *physicist*
Brady, Phillip Donley *lawyer*
Bragg, Lynn Munroe *trade association administrator, former federal commissioner*
Brennan, Christine *journalist, columnist*
Brown, Thomas Cartmel, Jr., *lawyer*
Bullard, Marcia *publishing executive*
Burke, Sheila P. *federal administrator*
Byrnes, William Joseph *lawyer*
Cahill, Harry Amory *diplomat, educator*
Callahan, Vincent Francis, Jr., *state legislator, publisher*
Canes, Michael Edwin *research economist*
Cannon, Mark Wilcox *government official, business executive*
Capone, Lucien, Jr., *management consultant, former naval officer*
Cardwell, Thomas Augusta, III, *research scientist, retired career officer, executive*
Carlson, Richard Warner *journalist, broadcast executive, federal agency administrator, diplomat*
Carnicero, Jorge Emilio *aeronautical engineer, transportation executive*
Casciano, John P. *executive*
Chang, Michael *professional tennis player*
Chaplin, Stephen Michael *retired diplomat*
Chapple, Thomas Leslie *lawyer*
Checchi, Alfred A. *air transportation executive, financial consultant*
Church, Randolph Warner, Jr., *lawyer*
Condo, Joseph A. *lawyer*
Connelly, Mary Creedon *insurance company executive*
Corson, J. Jay, IV, *lawyer*
DeCell, Hal C. *federal agency administrator*
Dempsey, James Raymon *industrial executive*
Dobson, Donald Alfred *retired electrical engineer*
Doyle, Frederick Joseph *retired government research scientist*
Drew, K. *financial advisor, management consultant*
Edgar, Janelle Diane Ward *financial services executive*
Estren, Mark James *business and media consultant, TV producer, author*
Fairbank, Richard D. *diversified financial services company executive*
Falcone, Robert S. *diversified financial services company executive*
Feller, Millicent (Mimi) A. *newspaper publishing executive*
Filerman, Gary Lewis *health educator*
Francis, Karen *painter, television producer*
Fritz, Thomas Vincent *business executive*
Gallagher, Brian *editor-in-chief*
Gammon, James Alan *lawyer*
Gangemi, Gaetano Tommaso, Sr., *computer company executive*
Gifford, Franklin Andrew, Jr., *meteorologist, consultant*
Gniewek, Raymond Louis *newspaper editor*
Halagao, Avelino Garabiles *lawyer*
Hale, Robert Fargo *government consultant*
Halik, Eugene Egon *engineering consultant*
Healy, Theresa Ann *former ambassador*
Herge, J. Curtis *lawyer*
Hicks, C. Thomas, III, *lawyer*
Hill, Jimmie Dale *retired government official*
Hjort, Howard Warren *consultant, economist*
Hoffmann, Martin Richard *lawyer*
Hoogendoorn, Benno *food products executive*
Ingersoll, William Boley *lawyer, real estate developer*
Jackson, William Paul, Jr., *lawyer*
Jayne, Edward Randolph, II, *executive search consultant*
Johnson, Omotunde Evan George *economist*
Kautt, Glenn Gregory *financial planner, consultant*
Kennedy, Cornelius Bryant *retired lawyer*
Kim, Jay *former congressman*
Kimberly, William Essick *investment banker*
Klopfenstein, Rex Carter *electrical engineer*
Kohli, Harinder S. *business executive, development economist*
Kolombatovic, Vadja Vadim *retired management consulting company executive*
Kondracki, Edward John *lawyer*
Kropp, Edward H. *education educator, consultant*
Laning, Robert Comegys *retired physician, former naval officer*
Layman, Lawrence *naval officer*
Layson, William McIntyre *retired research consulting company executive*
Lee, Daniel Kuhn *economist*
LeSourd, Nancy Susan Oliver *lawyer, writer*
Lion, Linda N. *retired federal agency administrator*
Lorell, Monte *newspaper editor*
Lovaas, John L. *foreign aid executive, community activist*
Mahan, Clarence *retired govenment official, writer*
Malley, Raymond Charles *retired foreign service officer, industrial executive*
Marino, Michael Frank, III, *lawyer*
Mars, Forrest E., Jr., *candy company executive*
Mars, Jacqueline Badger *food products executive*
Mars, John Franklin *candy company executive*
Mathews, Linda McVeigh *newspaper editor*
Mazzarella, David *newspaper editor*
McCambridge, John James *civil engineer*
McCorkindale, Douglas Hamilton *lawyer, publishing executive*
McInerney, James Eugene, Jr., *trade association executive*
McLean, Robert, III, *real estate company executive*
Metters, Samuel *engineering executive*
Miller, Antoinette *publishing executive*
Miller, Donald Eugene *lawyer*
Moeller, Robert Charles (Bud Moeller) *management consultant*
Molineaux, Charles Borromeo *lawyer, arbitrator, columnist, poet*
Molino, Thomas Michael *retired military officer*
Moon, Craig *publishing executive*
Morris, James Malachy *lawyer*
Morse, Duane D(ale) *lawyer*
Mortensen, Robert Henry *landscape architect, golf course architect*
Murphy, Thomas Patrick *lawyer*
Nobil, James Howard, Jr., *real estate investor, developer, consultant, broker*
Noonan, Jean *lawyer*
Olson, Walter Justus, Jr., *management consultant*
Olson, William Jeffrey *lawyer*
Oren, John Birdsell *retired coast guard officer*
Park, Sunwoo *engineer*
Parshall, Gerald *journalist*
Paschall, Lee McQuerter *retired communications consultant*
Paul, Andrew Robert *defense and legislative consultant*
Paul, Peterson T. *savings and loan association executive*
Paulson, Kenneth Alan *editor*
Pho, Long Ambrose Ba *business educator, consultant*
Price, Ilene Rosenberg *lawyer*
Prichard, Peter S. *newspaper editor*
Quinlan, J(oseph) Michael *lawyer*
Rawls, Charles Richardson *lawyer, government official*
Ritter, Hal *newspaper editor*
Rose, Susan Porter *consultant*
Rosenbaum, David Mark *engineering executive, consultant, educator*
Russell, Theodore Emery *diplomat*
Safer, John *artist, lecturer, banker, real estate developer*
Saville, Paul C. *financial executive*
Schar, Dwight C. *construction company executive*
Schauer, Franz Peter *civil and nuclear engineer, educator*
Schools, Charles Hughlette *banker, lawyer*
Scott, Bruce K. *retired military officer*
Scribner, Sherlie Ann *language educator*
Shapiro, Nelson Hirsh *lawyer*
Shrader, Ralph W. *management consultant*
Skantze, Pat *model, consultant*
Smith, Esther Thomas *communications executive*
Smith, Russell Jack *former intelligence official*
Smith, Thomas Eugene *investment company executive, financial consultant*
Sparks, Robert Ronold, Jr., *lawyer*
Spaulding, Wallace Holmes *retired federal agency professional*
Spoehel, Ronald Ross *information technology executive*
Stackpole, Kerry Clifford *association executive*
Steiner, Jeffrey Josef *industrial manufacturing company executive*
Stevens, Richard Gordon *political scientist, educator*
Stokes, Jeanett Barrett *editor*
Stump, John Sutton *retired lawyer*
Syron, Richard Francis *finance company executive, economist*
Talbot, Lee Merriam *ecologist, educator, foundation administrator*
Talbot, Martha Hayne *conservationist, biologist*
Tansill, Frederick Joseph *lawyer*
Theon, John Speridon *meteorologist, researcher*
Townsend, Christopher Gordon *lawyer*
Trout, Margie Marie Mueller *civic worker*
Trout, Maurice Elmore *diplomat*
Ullmann, Owen *journalist*
Vandemark, Robert Goodyear *retired retail company executive*
Van Lare, Wendell John *lawyer*
Verhalen, Robert Donald *consultant*
Vesper, Carolyn F. *newspaper publishing executive*
Wall, Barbara Wartelle *lawyer*
Wallace, Robert Bruce *retired surgeon*
Waller, John Henry *author*
Walsh, Marie Leclerc *nurse*
Watson, Jerry Carroll *advertising executive*
Webber, Diana L. *management consultant executive, engineering educator*
Weiss, Susan *newspaper editor*
Welch, Jasper Arthur, Jr., *security company executive, consultant*
Whitehead, Clay Thomas *economist*
Williams, Earle Carter *retired professional services company executive*
Wright, William Evan *physician, consultant*
Yancik, Joseph John *government official*
Yarborough, William Glenn, Jr., *military officer, forest farmer, defense and international business executive*
Youngs, William Ellis *photographer, motion picture engineer, projectionist*
Zakheim, Dov Solomon *economist, government official*

Mechanicsville
Gerrish, Brian Albert *theologian, educator, minister*
Hinkle, Barton Leslie *retired electronics company executive*
Liggan, Joanne Dunkley *realtor*
Lordi, William Michael *psychiatrist, child psychiatrist*
Peterson, William Canova *architect*
Watkins, Carol A. *special education educator*

Melfa
Harmon, Patricia Marie *special education educator*

Merrifield
Earley, Mark Lawrence *not-for-profit administrator, former state attorney general*
Earner, William Anthony, Jr., *naval officer*

Middleburg
Beddall, Thomas Henry *lawyer*
Grove, Noel Randall *writer*
Langley, Rolland Ament, Jr., *retired engineering technology company executive*
McNichols, Gerald Robert *consulting company executive*
Parkinson, James Thomas, III, *investment consultant*
Sodolski, John *retired association administrator*
Tucker, John Richard *mathematician, educator, writer, researcher*

Midland
Andes, Donna M. *adult education educator, community health nurse*

Midlothian
Chapman, Gilbert Whipple, Jr., *publishing company executive*
Cruse, Robert Ridgely *retired research chemist*
Crutchfield, George Thomas *journalism educator*
Friedel, Robert Oliver *physician*
Hanes-Stevens, LaVerne E. *minister, social services administrator*
O'Shanick, Gregory John *physician, medical association administrator*
Pearson, Gregory David *publisher, media specialist*
Perkins, Raymond Lamont *retired government official*
Shands, William Ridley, Jr., *lawyer*
Stringham, Luther Winters *economist, administrator*
Tuttle, Roger Lewis *lawyer, educator*
Wadsworth, Robert David *advertising agency executive*
Wang, Buqian *materials research scientist*

Millboro
Minetree, James Lawrence, III, *retired military officer, educator*

Mineral
Donald, James Robert *federal agency official, economist, outdoors writer*
Speer, Jack Atkeson *publisher*

Moneta
Ulmer, Walter Francis, Jr., *consultant, former army officer*

Monroe
Pettus, William G. *retired nuclear scientist, research scientist*

Monterey
Tabatznik, Bernard *retired cardiologist*

Montross
Fountain, Robert Roy, Jr., *farmer, industrial executive, naval officer*
Monaco, Grace Powers *lawyer*

Morattico
Dawson, Carol Gene *former commissioner, writer, consultant*

Mount Vernon
Brownson, Anna Louise Harshman *publishing executive, editor*
Rees, James Conway, IV, *historic site administrator*

Natural Bridge
Watkins, Angela Marie *museum administrator, writer*

Nellysford
McWane, Joyce Hobbs *title company executive*
Pfaltz, Katharine *small business owner, writer*
Sims, John Rogers, Jr., *lawyer*
Wood, Maurice *medical educator*

Newport News
Abbott, Beverly Stubblefield *artist*
Banks, Charles Augustus, III, *manufacturing executive*
Behlmar, Cindy Lee *business manager, consultant, speaker*
Breese, Steven *theater director, actor, director, playwright*
Brink, Gerald R. *hospital executive*
Camp, Hazel Lee Burt *artist*
Cuthrell, Carl Edward *lawyer, educator, clergyman*
Donaldson, Coleman duPont *aeronautical engineer, consultant, aerospace engineer*
Eastman, John Robert *education educator*
Forbes, Sarah Elizabeth *gynecologist, real estate corporation officer*
Fricks, William Peavy *shipbuilding company executive*
Goldberg, Stanley Irwin *real estate company executive*
Harris, Charles George *research scientist, consultant*
Hightower, John Brantley *arts administrator*
Hubbard, Harvey Hart *aeroacoustician, noise control engineer, consultant*
Kamp, Arthur Joseph, Jr., *lawyer*
Keator, Margaret Whitley *legislative aide*
Kyte, Shannan Dyan *multimedia designer*
Le Mons, Kathleen Ann *securities company executive, branch manager, investment officer, portfolio manager*
Lenwell, John D. *music educator*
Matthews, Rondra J. *publishing executive*
Mazur, Rhoda Himmel *community volunteer*
Miller, W. Marshall, II, *insurance broker*
Noblitt, Nancy Anne *aerospace engineer*
Powell, Jouett Lynn *college dean, philosophy and religious studies educator*
Santoro, Anthony Richard *history professor*
Schievelbein, Thomas Clayton *shipyard executive, sales executive*
Smith, James Robert *airport terminal executive*
Summerville, Richard M. *mathematician, academic administrator*
Tracy, Tracy Faircloth *special education educator*
Trible, Paul Seward, Jr., *former United States senator*
Wargo, Lovetta Lynn *medical educator, occupational therapist, writer*
Warren, Daniel Churchman *health facility administrator*

Norfolk
Adam, John Anthony *mathematician, educator*
Adams, David Huntington *judge*
Addis, Kay Tucker *newspaper editor*
Albert, Alan Dale *lawyer*
Anderson, Darleen Shircliffe *hospital system administrator*
Andrews, Mason Cooke *mayor, obstetrician, gynecologist, educator*
Andrews, William Cooke *physician*
Archer, Robert Patrick *psychologist, educator*
Baird, Edward Rouzie, Jr., *retired lawyer*
Barry, Richard Francis, III, *publishing executive*
Batten, Frank *newspaper publisher, cable broadcaster*
Berent, Irwin Mark *writer, software executive*
Bernd, David LeMoine *multi-hospital system executive*
Berndt, Martin R. *career officer*
Bishop, Bruce Taylor *lawyer*
Bland, Gilbert Tyrone *food service executive*
Blount, Robert Haddock *corporate executive, retired naval officer*
Bonney, Hal James, Jr., *federal judge*
Bullington, James Richard *business educator, former ambassador*
Burnette, Thomas N. *career officer*
Byrne, William Andrew *education educator, historian*
Carpenter, Dee *publishing executive*
Clark, Morton Hutchinson *lawyer*
Colberg-Ochs, Sheri Renee *physiologist, educator*
Combs, Charles Donald *academic administrator*
Corcoran, Andrew Patrick, Jr., *lawyer*
Cox, David A. *rail transportation executive*
Davis, Russell Haden *consultant*
Davis, Terry Hunter, Jr., *lawyer*
Dennison, Stanley Scott *retired forest products company executive, consultant*
DeVenny, Lillian Nickell *trophy company executive*
Donohue, David Patrick *engineering executive, retired navy rear admiral*
Downey, Gary Neil *marine corps officer*
Drescher, John Webb *lawyer*
Epplein, Lawrence Elliott *hospitality management educator*
Evans, Rod L. *philosophy educator*
Evett, Russell Dougherty *internist, educator*
Fallon, William J. *career officer*
Farmer, Evan R. *academic administrator, dermatologist, researcher*
Faulconer, Robert Jamieson *pathologist, educator*
Goode, David Ronald *transportation company executive*
Griffin, O. Daniel, Jr., *reporter, writer, photographer, audio engineer, videographer, video specialist*
Griffith, Charles Dee, Jr., *state official*
Hartman, Deanna Mears *retired family counselor, addiction counselor*
Hirrel, Leo P. *historian, retired military officer*
Jackson, Raymond A. *federal judge*
Jenson, Hal Brockbank *physician*
Johnson, Thomas G., Jr., *lawyer*
Jones, Franklin Ross *education educator*
Jones, Leon Herbert, Jr., (Herb Jones) *artist*
Kagan, Harvey J. *pediatrician*
Kaneko, Hideaki *mathematics professor*
Kasparov, Andrey Rafailovich *composer, pianist, conductor, educator*
Kernan, William Frank *career officer*
Koch, James Verch *academic administrator, economist*
Konetzni, Albert H., Jr., *career officer*
Kreger, David Lawrence *gastroenterologist*
Kubic, Charles Richard *naval officer*
Lawrence, Joe Gray, Jr., *lawyer*
LeFever, Gretchen B. *clinical psychologist, educator*
Lester, Richard Garrison *radiologist, educator*
Maly, Kurt John *computer science educator*
Mark, Peter *director, conductor*
Mayo, Alex T., Jr., *lawyer*
McCaa, James Cureton, III, *lawyer*
McDemmond, Marie Valentine *academic administrator, consultant*
McKee, Timothy Carlton *taxation educator*
McKinnon, Arnold Borden *retired transportation company executive*
Morgan, Henry Coke, Jr., *judge*
Musgrave, Thea *composer, conductor*
Nichols, Brenda Sue *nursing educator*
Nixon, Patricia Saunders *music educator, performer*
Noginov, Mikhail A. *physicist, researcher, educator*
Nusbaum, Alan B. *real estate executive*
Oehninger, Sergio C. *endocrinologist, obstetrician, gynecologist*
Oelberg, David George *neonatologist, educator, researcher*
Opfer, Steven Earl *education educator, researcher*
Parker, Richard Wilson *lawyer, retired rail transportation executive*
Pearson, John Yeardley, Jr., *lawyer*
Poston, Anita Owings *lawyer*
Prince, William Taliaferro *retired federal judge*
Rashkind, Alan Brody *lawyer*
Reason, J. Paul *naval officer*
Rephan, Jack *lawyer*
Rohn, Reuben David *pediatric educator and administrator*
Runte, Roseann *academic administrator*
Russell, C. Edward, Jr., *lawyer*
Ryan, John M. *lawyer*
Ryan, Louis Farthing *lawyer*
Samuels, John M., Jr., *industrial engineer*
Sanders, Stephanie Kenyatta *music educator*
Schneider, Daniel Scott *pediatric cardiologist*

Scott, Kenneth R. *transportation executive*
Sears, Winsome Earle *congressman*
Sebren, Lucille Griggs *retired private school educator, public school educator*
Shannon, John Sanford *lawyer, retired railway executive*
Shaw, Michael Evan *librarian*
Shumadine, Anne Ballard *financial advisor, lawyer*
Sizemore, William Howard, Jr., *journalist*
Smith, Rebecca Beach *federal judge*
Stallings, Valerie A. *physician, state agency administrator*
Steele, James Eugene *retired school system administrator*
Taylor Claud, Andrea *educational consultant*
Terzis, Julia Kallipolitou *plastic surgeon*
Thompson, Thelma Barnaby *English educator, university dean*
Tobias, Stephen C. *rail transportation executive*
Train, Harry Depue, II, *retired naval officer*
Wei, Benjamin Min *engineering educator*
Wiltse, James Clark *civil engineer*
Wolcott, Hugh Dixon *obstetrics and gynecology educator*

North
Fang, Joong *philosopher, mathematician, educator*

North Garden
Moses, Hamilton, III, *academic neurologist, management consultant, hospital executive*

Norton
Vest, Gayle Southworth *obstetrician, gynecologist*

Oak Hill
Okay, John Louis *management consultant*
Ritter, Elza K. *music educator*

Oakton
Curry, Thomas Fortson *electronics engineer, defense industry executive*
Drummond, Carol Cramer *voice educator, singer, artist, writer*
Duesenberg, Robert H. *retired lawyer*
Entzminger, John Nelson, Jr., *federal agency administrator, electronic engineer, researcher*
Farwell, Albert Edmond *retired government official, consultant*
Frost, S. David *retired naval officer*
MacCracken, Thomas Gregg *musicologist*
Mosemann, Lloyd Kenneth, II, *business executive*
Pratsch, Lloyd Wilmer *government official*
Rees, Clifford Harcourt, Jr., (Ted Rees) *retired association executive, retired air force officer*
Strean, Bernard M. *retired naval officer*
Terzian, Grace Paine *publisher*
Vernava, Anthony Michael *lawyer*
Zhang, Ming *policy analyst*

Occoquan
Nemecek, Albert Duncan, Jr., *retail company executive, investment banker, management consultant*

Onancock
Verrill, John Howard *museum director*

Orange
Daniel, Daniele Mallison *elementary school educator*
Thomas, Franklin A., III, *lawyer*

Orlean
Kulski, Julian Eugeniusz *architect, planner, educator*

Paeonian Springs
Sloyan, Patrick Joseph *journalist*

Palmyra
Chapin, Suzanne Phillips *retired psychologist*
Sahr, Morris Gallup *financial planner*

Partlow
Papapetrou, Paula Bartello *special education educator, writer*

Pearisburg
Morse, F. D., Jr., *dentist*

Penhook
Coar, Richard John *mechanical engineer, aerospace consultant*
Hahn, John William *retired insurance company executive*

Penn Laird
Wise, Charles Conrad, Jr., *educator, past government official, author*

Petersburg
Brown, Jack D(elbert) *chemist, researcher*
Ende, Milton *internist*
Everitt, Alice Lubin *labor arbitrator*
Garrott, Carl Lee *foreign language educator*
Perdue, Diana S. *mathematician, educator*
Shell, Louis Calvin *lawyer*
Spero, Morton Bertram *retired lawyer*
Stronach, Carey Elliott *physicist, researcher*
Wilson, John Robert, Jr., *pharmaceutical and chemical company executive*
Wyatt, Bryant Nelson *education educator, writer*

Poquoson
Holloway, Paul Fayette *retired aerospace executive*
Tai, Elizabeth Shi-Jue Lee *library director*

Portsmouth
Barnes, Judith P. *nursing administrator*
Dunbar, Robert Paul, Jr., *orthopaedic surgeon, military officer*
Mapp, Alf Johnson, Jr., *writer, historian, educator*
Mintz, Susan Ashinoff *apparel manufacturing company executive*
Nolen, Crystal Me'Kelle *poet, educator*
O'Malley, Timothy Patrick *otolaryngologist*
Paquette, William Arthur *historian, educator*
Porter, J. Ridgely, III, *lawyer*
Randall, Marlene Dietrich *councilwoman, retired school system administrator*
Reaves, Karen Jamil *communications educator*
Wolf, Jeffrey Stephen *physician*

Potomac Falls
Merna, Gerald Francis *advertising executive, retired military officer*

Pulaski
McCarthy, Thomas James, Jr., *lawyer*

Purcellville
Grow, Robert Theodore *economist, association executive*
Kok, Frans Johan *investment banker*
Reaves, Richard Bruce *music educator*
Sharples, Winston Singleton *automobile importer and distributor*

Quantico
Evans, Gaye Lois *comptroller*
Harmon, Christopher C. *international relations educator, writer*
Harrington, Jeffrey Michael *military officer*
Howard, Patrick Gene *marine corps officer*
Mangan, Terence Joseph *federal agency professional, retired protective services official*
Sanftleben, Kurt Allen *career officer*

Radford
du Plessis, Eric *literature educator, language educator*
James, Clarity (Carolyne Faye James) *mezzo-soprano*
McNeil, Ramsey English *religious studies educator*
Phelps, George Graham *computer systems engineer, consultant*
Scartelli, Joseph Paul *music therapy educator, dean*
Templeton, Dennie, III, *educational administrator, consultant*
Turk, James Clinton, Jr., *lawyer*

Rapidan
Grimm, Ben Emmet *former library director and consultant*

Reston
Bredehoft, Elaine Charlson *lawyer*
Brennan, Norma Jean *professional society publications director*
Brown, James Robert *retired air force officer*
Butler, Katherine E. *lawyer*
Cerf, Vinton Gray *telecommunications company executive*
Chattman, Raymond Christopher *foundation executive*
Choi, Michael Kamwah *aerospace engineer, mechanical engineer, researcher*
Clark, Katherine Karen *software company executive*
Conway, William E., Jr., *telecommunications industry executive, venture capitalist*
Cravey, Clara *dancer, performing arts association administrator*
Crawford, Lawrence Robert *aviation and aerospace consultant*
Davy, William Allen *account executive*
Dietrich, Dawn *software company executive*
Donahue, Timothy M. *telecommunications industry executive*
Dussek, Steven P. *communications executive*
Easton, Glenn Hanson, Jr., *management and insurance consultant, federal official, naval officer*
Even, Bryan J. *electronics executive*
Ewell, Dena Lynette *administrative management executive*
Fernandez, Raul J. *data processing executive*
Finkelstein, Jay Gary *lawyer*
Fitzpatrick, Patrick C. *data processing executive*
Fitzpatrick, Thomas J. *mortgage company executive*
Foster, William Anthony *management consultant, educator*
Fox, Edward A. *finance company executive*
Gates, James David *retired association executive, consultant*
Groat, Charles George *geologist, science administrator*
Hammick, Patricia A. *utilities company executive*
Harris, Paul Lynwood *retired aerospace transportation executive*
Hepworth-Woolston, Connie Jo *choreographer*
Hirsch, Robert Maurice *hydrologist*
Hope, Samuel Howard *accreditation organization executive*
Johnson, Thea Jean *internet and intranet security service provider*
Kahn, Robert E. *electrical engineer*
Keefe, James Washburn *educational writer, researcher, consultant*
Keler, Marianne Martha *lawyer*
Kelly, Thomas N., Jr., *telecommunications industry executive*
Kennedy, Leonard J. *telecommunications industry executive, lawyer*
Kramish, Arnold *physicist, historian, author*
Kreyling, Edward George, Jr., *railroad executive*
Lister, Harry Joseph *finance company executive*
Lord, Albert L. *diversified financial services company executive*
Mahlmann, John James *music education association administrator*
Maitland, Guy Edison Clay *lawyer*
Minton, Joseph Paul *retired safety organization executive*
Mitchell, Ellen Clabaugh *investment executive*
Mogge, Harriet Morgan *educational association executive*
Mowbray, Robert Norman *natural resource management consultant, forest ecologist*
Naeser, Nancy Dearien *geologist, researcher*
Naylon, Michael Edward *retired army officer*
Ovissi, Nasser *artist*
Payne, Roger Lee *geographer*
Peck, Dallas Lynn *retired geologist*
Phillippi, Elmer Joseph, Jr., *data communications consultant*
Picard, Dennis J. *retired electronics company executive*
Platt, Leslie A. *lawyer*
Plum, Kenneth Ray *state legislator*
Polemitou, Olga Andrea *accountant*
Posey, Ada Louise *human resources specialist*
Powell, Anne Elizabeth *editor*
Rau, Lee Arthur *lawyer*
Reicin, Eric David *lawyer*
Saleh, Paul N. *telecommunications industry executive*
Salisbury, Alan Blanchard *information systems executive*
Sarreals, Sonia *data processing consultant*
Scharff, Joseph Laurent *lawyer*
Scheeler, James Arthur *architect*
Schick, Michael William *public relations executive*
Schleede, Glenn Roy *energy market and policy consultant*
Seiberlich, Carl Joseph *retired naval officer*
Smith, Ralph Lee *author, musician*
Stone, Lawrence D. *software company executive*
Toole, John Harper *lawyer*
Van Putten, Mark *environmentalist*
Walton, Edmund Lewis, Jr., *lawyer*
Wang, Jin *research scientist*
Wawrejko Cochran, Diane *performing arts association administrator*
Wetsch, John Robert *information systems specialist*
Wilkinson, Edward Anderson, Jr., *retired military officer, manufacturing executive*

Richlands
Stacy, Curtis Alan *secondary school educator*

Richmond
Agee, G. Steven *judge*
Aiken, Peter Haynes *systems engineer, educator*
Allen, Ann Salathe *social studies educator, researcher*
Appiah, Joseph Yaw *historian, educator*
Archer, Kellie Jo *education educator*
Ashe, Reid *publishing executive*
Ashworth, D. Neil *business educator*
Atkinson, Richard Lee, Jr., *internal medicine educator*
August, Albert T., III, *publishing executive*
Austin, John D. *corporate financial executive*
Austin-Stephens, Ann-Marie *retail executive*
Ayres, Stephen McClintock *physician, educator*
Bagley, Philip Joseph, III, *lawyer*
Baker, Julie Ann *language educator*
Baliles, Gerald L. *lawyer, former governor*
Balster, Robert Louis *drug abuse expert*
Bankos, Jean *educational association administrator, educator*
Barker, Thomas Carl *retired health care administration educator, executive*
Barnes, Milton Millard *musician*
Barton, Jonathan Miller *clergyman*
Bates, Hampton Robert, Jr., *pathologist*
Beales, Randolph A. *lawyer, former Attorney General*
Beaman, Mary Anina *psychiatric nurse, educator*
Belcher, Dennis Irl *lawyer*
Black, Robert Perry *retired banker, executive*
Blank, Florence Weiss *literacy educator, editor*
Blumberg, Michael Zangwill *allergist*
Blumberg, Peter Steven *manufacturing executive*
Boadle-Biber, Margaret Clare *physiology educator*
Bodurtha, Joanne Norma *genetics educator*
Bohannon, Sarah Virginia *personnel professional*
Bonfiglio, Thomas Paul *literature and linguistics educator*
Booker, Lewis Thomas *lawyer*
Bovender, Jack Oliver, Jr., *hospital management company executive*
Bowman, Dennis J. *retail computer executive*
Brackenridge, N. Lynn *not-for-profit developer*
Braeckmans, Paul *advertising executive*
Brasfield, Evans Booker *lawyer*
Brissette, Martha Blevins *lawyer*
Broaddus, John Alfred, Jr., *retired bank executive, economist*
Brooks, Robert Franklin, Sr., *lawyer*
Bryan, John Stewart, III, *newspaper publisher*
Bryson, William Hamilton *law educator*
Budd, Richard Wade *university official, communications scientist, priest*
Buford, Robert Pegram *lawyer*
Bunzl, Rudolph Hans *retired manufacturing executive*
Burke, John K(irkland), Jr., *lawyer*
Burrus, Robert Lewis, Jr., *lawyer*
Burtch, Jack Willard, Jr., *lawyer*
Campbell, Neal Franklin *music educator*
Campbell, Thomas Corwith, Jr., *economics professor*
Cannon, W. Stephen *retail executive, lawyer*
Capps, Thomas Edward *utilities company executive, lawyer*
Capps, Thos E. *diversified financial services company executive*
Carlton, Buzz (Clyde Gordon Carlton Jr.) *singer, songwriter, entertainer, recording artist*
Carrell, Daniel Allan *lawyer*
Carrico, Harry Lee *retired judge*
Carter, Joseph Carlyle, Jr., *lawyer*
Casini, Jane Sloan *wholesale distribution executive*
Catlett, Richard H., Jr., *retired lawyer*
Chalifoux, Michael T. *retail electronics company executive*
Chandler, Theodore Lindy, Jr., *lawyer*
Charlesworth, Arthur Thomas *mathematics and computer science educator*
Chewning, Thomas N. *energy executive*
Chichester, John H. *state legislator*
Clatterbuck, John David *music educator*
Clinard, Robert Noel *lawyer*
Coalter, Milton J., Jr., *library director, educator*
Cohn, David Stephen *lawyer*
Compton, Asbury Christian *state supreme court justice*
Compton, Olin Randall *consulting electrical engineer, researcher*
Coogle, Constance L. *gerontology educator, researcher*
Crittenden, Flora Davis *state legislator*
Crouch, Robert P., Jr., *state agency administrator, former prosecutor*
Cullen, Richard *lawyer, former state attorney general*
Curley, John J. *diversified media company executive*
Cutchins, Clifford Armstrong, IV, *lawyer*
Dabney, H. Slayton, Jr., *lawyer*
Dan, Michael T. *diversified services firm executive*
Darner, Leslie Karen *state legislator*
Dell, Willie Jones *social services executive, educator*
DeLorenzo, Robert John *neurologist, molecular neuroscientist*
DeMary, Jo Lynne *state official, elementary school educator*
Denny, Collins, III, *lawyer*
Devolites, Jeanne Marie Aragona *state legislator*
Dias, Fiona P. *retail executive*
Dombalis, Constantine Nicholas *minister, writer*
Drain, Cecil B. *university dean, nurse anesthetist educator, retired army officer*
Drake, Thelma Day *state legislator*
Dray, Mark S. *lawyer*
Dunn, Leo James *obstetrician, educator, gynecologist, educator*
Dunn, Philip J. *retail executive, treasurer, controller*
Durrett, Nancy Kashner *health science association administrator*
Edmonds, Thomas Andrew *legal association administrator*
Ellis, Andrew Jackson, Jr., *lawyer*
Ellis, Anthony John *education educator*
Estes, Gerald Walter *newspaper executive*
Face, E. Joseph, Jr., *state agency administrator*
Fenn, John Bennett *chemist, educator*
Fierro, Marcella Farinelli *forensic pathologist*
Flippen, Edward L. *lawyer*
Foss, Michael E. *retail executive*
Foster, Charles H. *real estate executive*
Framme, Lawrence Henry, III, *political organization administrator, lawyer*
Freed, David Clark *artist*
Freeman, George Clemon, Jr., *lawyer*
Freund, Emma Frances *technologist*
Froman, John W. *retail executive*
Gandy, Gerald Larmon *rehabilitation counseling educator, psychologist, writer*
Gary, Richard David *lawyer*
Geary, David Patrick *criminal justice educator, consultant, writer*
Gilliam, F. Roosevelt *cardiologist, surgeon*
Ginder, Gordon Dean *physician, educator*
Gipson, Jeffery *chemistry professor*
Girone, Joan Christine Cruse *realtor, former county official*
Goodpasture, Philip Henry *lawyer*
Goodykoontz, Charles Alfred *retired newspaper editor*
Gorr, Louis Frederick *investment consultant*
Gottwald, Bruce Cobb *chemical company executive*
Gottwald, Floyd Dewey, Jr., *chemical company executive*
Graves, H. Brice *retired lawyer*
Gray, C. Michael *food products executive*
Gregory, Roger Lee *federal judge*
Grey, Robert J. *lawyer*
Hackney, Virginia Howitz *lawyer*
Hager, John Henry *state official, former lieutenant governor*
Hall, James H(errick), Jr., *philosophy educator, writer*
Hall, Stephen Charles *lawyer*
Hamel, Dana Bertrand *academic administrator*
Hanley, Patrick D. *trucking executive*
Hardy, Richard Earl *rehabilitation counseling educator*
Harris, Grace E. *academic administrator*
Harris, Ruth Hortense Coles *retired accounting educator*
Harvey, Ollie Marie *small business owner, not-for-profit developer*
Hassell, Leroy Rountree, Sr., *state supreme court chief justice*
Heilman, E. Bruce *academic administrator*
Helwig, Arthur Woods *retired chemical company executive*
Henley, Vernard William *banker*
Hettrick, George Harrison *lawyer*
Hicks, Douglas A. *religious studies educator, minister*
Hong, James Ming *former industrialist, venture capitalist*
Horsley, Waller Holladay *lawyer*
Howell, Talmadge Rudolph *radiologist*
Howell, William James *state legislator*
Hunt, Ronald J. *dean, dental educator*
Huntsinger, Jerald E. *advertising executive*
Jacobs, Harry Milburn, Jr., *advertising executive*
James, Allix Bledsoe *retired university president*
Jamgochian, Victoria *interior designer*
Jewell-Sherman, Deborah *school system administrator*
Joel, William Lee, II, *interior and lighting designer*
Johnson, Johnny F. *marketing professional*
Jones, Jeanne Pitts *pre-school administrator*
Jones-Atkins, DeBorah Kaye *state official*
Joynes, Barbara Cole *marketing executive*
Kaczka, Jeff *trucking/relocation services executive*
Kaine, Timothy M. *lieutenant governor*
Kaplowitz, Lisa Glauser *physician, educator*
Kearfott, Joseph Conrad *lawyer*
Kellett, Janet *telecommunications industry executive, educator*
Kendler, Kenneth S. *medical educator*
Kenzer, Robert Charles *social studies educator*
Kevorkian, Richard *artist*
Kilgore, Jerry *state attorney general*
King, Allen B. *tobacco company executive*
King, Robert Leroy *business administration educator*
King, William H., Jr., *lawyer*
Kinser, Cynthia D. *state supreme court justice*
Kirkpatrick, Peter Steven *foreign language educator*
Kozlowski, Ronald Stephan *retired librarian*
Kunos, George *pharmacologist*
Lacy, Elizabeth Bermingham *state supreme court justice*
Landin, David Craig *lawyer*
Langston, Nancy Sue Friedrich *dean*
Laskin, Daniel M. *oral and maxillofacial surgeon, educator*
Lawrence, Walter, Jr., *surgeon, educator*
Leary, David Edward *psychologist, educator*
Ledbetter, David Oscar *lawyer*
Lee, Peter James *bishop*
Lemons, Donald W. *state supreme court justice*
Levit, Héloïse B. (Ginger Levit) *art historian, art dealer, art consultant, journalist*
Levit, Jay J(oseph) *lawyer*
Lilly, Arnys Clifton, Jr., *physicist*
Lingerfelt, Alan Thomas *civil engineer, real estate executive*
Linkonis, Suzanne Newbold *probation officer, counselor*
Lohuis, Ardyth June *musician, educator*
Luke, Roice D. *health science association administrator*
Luo, Shawn Haisheng *retail company executive*
Maguire, Kim D. *retail executive*
Maneker, Deanna Marie *advertising executive*
Mann, Stephen Ashby *financial consultant*
Mast, Rick *race car driver*

Mattauch, Robert Joseph *electrical engineering educator*
Mauck, Henry Page, Jr., *medical and pediatrics educator*
McCarthy, Charles R. *bioethicist, consultant*
McClard, Jack Edward *lawyer*
McCollough, W. Alan *electronics retail executive*
McCollum, Rudolph C., Jr., *mayor*
McCune, John Brian *broadcast engineer*
McDermid, Margaret E. *information technology executive, engineer*
McFarlane, Walter Alexander *lawyer, educator*
McGee, Henry Alexander, Jr., *university official*
McQuigg, Michele Berger *state legislator*
Merhige, Robert Reynold, Jr., *lawyer*
Merrell, Ronald Clifton *surgeon, educator*
Mezzullo, Louis Albert *lawyer*
Mierenfeld, Gary M. *retail executive*
Miller, Lewis Nelson, Jr., *banker*
Millhiser, Thomas McNally *lawyer*
Milme, Patrick Joseph *retired lawyer*
Minardi, Richard A., Jr., *lawyer*
Minor, Marian Thomas *elementary and secondary school educational consultant*
Mollen, Edward Leigh *pediatrician, allergist, clinical immunologist*
Moore, Andrew Taylor, Jr., *banker*
Moore, John Sterling, Jr., *retired minister*
Moore, Thurston Roach *lawyer*
Morkoç, Hadis *electrical engineer, educator*
Morrill, Richard Leslie *university administrator*
Morris, James Carl *architect*
Moyne, Yves M. *water treatment executive*
Mullinax, Perry Franklin *rheumatologist, allergist, immunologist*
Murdoch-Kitt, Norma Hood *clinical psychologist*
Narula, Subhash Chander *management science and statistics educator*
Neal, Stu M. *finance educator, writer*
Neufeld, Jacob A. *pediatrician, physiatrist, physical medicine and rehabilitation*
Newsome, Heber H. *academic administrator*
Northrop, Mary Ruth *retired mental health nurse*
Osgood, Nancy Jean *medical educator, writer*
Owen, Duncan Shaw, Jr., *internist, educator*
Owens, Arne Wesley *systems analyst*
Palen, J(oseph) John *sociology educator*
Palmer, Robert J. *corporate financial executive*
Parham, Iris Ann *gerontology educator*
Patterson, Robert Hobson, Jr., *lawyer*
Pauley, Stanley Frank *manufacturing executive*
Petera, Anne Pappas *state official*
Peterson, H(arry) William *chemicals executive, consultant*
Phillips, Thomas Edworth, Jr., *financial advisor, investment mangement consultant*
Pinckney, Charles Cotesworth *lawyer*
Plaisted, Harris Merrill, III, *real estate executive*
Poff, Richard Harding *retired state supreme court justice*
Pollard, Overton Price *retired state agency executive, lawyer*
Pope, Robert Dean *lawyer*
Powell, Lewis Franklin, III, *lawyer*
Puckett, Phillip P. *state legislator, insurance agency executive*
Puller, Linda Todd *state legislator*
Putney, Lacey Edward *state legislator*
Rainey, Gordon Fryer, Jr., *lawyer*
Raper, Mark Irvin *public relations executive*
Rapp, Melanie L. *state legislator, primary school educator*
Redmond, David Dudley *lawyer*
Reed, Christopher Robert *civil engineer*
Reynolds, Sheri *writer*
Rhodes, Anne Gregory (Panny Rhodes) *state legislator*
Richardson, David Walthall *cardiologist, educator, consultant*
Rigsby, Linda Flory *lawyer*
Rilling, John Robert *history professor*
Rimler, Anita A. *secretary of state*
Ritter, Robert T. *diversified company executive*
Robertson, LaVerne *minister*
Robinson, John Victor *lawyer*
Rogers, James Edward *paper company executive*
Rolfe, Robert Martin *lawyer*
Roper, Hartwell H. *tobacco company executive*
Rowe, James William, Sr., *engineer*
Rubinstein, Phyllis M. *lawyer*
Rucker, Douglas Pendleton, Jr., *lawyer*
Rudlin, David Alan *lawyer*
Ryland, Walter H. *lawyer*
Savedge, Anne Creery *artist, photographer*
Schall, Carol Marie *special education services professional*
Scott, George Cole, III, *investment advisor*
Scott, Sidney Buford *financial services company executive*
Seals, Margaret Louise Crumrine *newspaper editor*
Sennett, David *theater educator, actor*
Sharer, John Daniel *lawyer*
Sheehan, Jeremiah J. *former metal company executive*
Sirica, Alphonse Eugene *pathology educator*
Slater, Thomas Glascock, Jr., *lawyer*
Slaughter, Alexander Hoke *lawyer*
Slotnick, Robert D *food products executive*
Smith, Julious Perry, Jr., *lawyer*
Smith, R. Gordon *lawyer*
Snead, Thomas G. *healthcare executive*
Sneed, Jimmy *chef, restaurant owner*
Snellings, Eleanor Craig *retired economics educator*
Solan, Stuart Miley *physician*
Spindler, Judith Tarleton *elementary school educator*
Sprinkle, William Melvin *audio-acoustical engineer, engineering administrator*
Stallard, Hugh R. *retired telephone company executive*
Starke, Harold E., Jr., *lawyer*
Street, Walter Scott, III, *lawyer*
Strickland, William Jesse *lawyer*
Suit, Terrie L. *state representative*
Szakal, Andras Kalman *immunologist, anatomist, educator*
Talley, Charles Richmond *commercial banking executive*
Thomas, John Charles *lawyer, former state supreme court justice*
Thompson, Paul Michael *lawyer*
Thro, William Eugene *lawyer*
Thurber, Timothy Nels *historian, educator*
Tice, Douglas Oscar, Jr., *federal bankruptcy judge*
Trani, Eugene Paul *university president, educator*
Treadway, Sandra Gioia *library director*
Troy, Anthony Francis *lawyer*
Tuck, Grayson Edwin *real estate agent, former natural gas transmission executive*
Tunner, William Sams *urological surgeon*
Turner, Elaine S. *allergist, immunologist*
Ukrop, James E. *retail executive*
Vaughn, Ann Marie *art educator, artist*
Vijayaraman, Pugazhendhi *medical educator*
Wagner, Jody M. *treasurer*
Walker, Charles B. *chemicals company executive*
Walsh, William Arthur, Jr., *lawyer*
Walton, G. Clifford *family practice physician*
Ward, Harry Merrill *history professor*
Ward, John Wesley *retired pharmacologist*
Warner, Mark R. *governor*
Warthen, Harry Justice, III, *lawyer*
Washburn, John Rosser *entrepreneur*
Watkins, Hays Thomas *retired railroad executive*
Watts, Robert Glenn *retired pharmaceutical executive*
Wells, James M., III, *bank executive*
Wells, Jeffrey S. *retail executive, human resources specialist*
Wenzel, Richard Putnam *internist*
Wheelan, Belle S. *educational association administrator*
Whipple, Mary Margaret *state legislator*
White, Hugh Vernon, Jr., *lawyer*
White, Morris Fred, Jr., *physicist*
Wight, Jonathan B. *economist, educator*
Wilder, Eunice *city official*
Wilder, L(awrence) Douglas *former governor*
Wilkinson, David Stanley *pathologist, consultant, researcher, educator, physician*
Williams, Karen Johnson *federal judge*
Williams, Richard Leroy *federal judge*
Williams, Steven Robert *lawyer*
Winslett, Stoner *artistic director*
Winter, Joan Elizabeth *psychotherapist*
Witt, Walter Francis, Jr., *lawyer*
Wood, Jeanne Clarke *charitable organization executive*
Woolf, Steven H. *medical educator, researcher, preventive medicine physician*
Worden, Marny *artist, musician*
Wright, Wiley Reed, Jr., *lawyer, retired judge, mediator*
Wynne, Kenneth J. *chemical engineer, educator*

Roanoke
Al-Zubaidi, Amer Aziz *physicist, researcher*
Bates, Harold Martin *lawyer*
Beagle, Benjamin Stuart, Jr., *columnist*
Burcham, Darlene *state agency administrator*
Butler, Manley Caldwell *retired lawyer*
Cirasunda, Esther Bond *librarian*
Cole, Evelyn Marie *day care administrator*
Dagenhart, Betty Jane Mahaffey *nursing educator, administrator*
Effel, Laura *lawyer*
Fishwick, John Palmer *retired lawyer, retired railroad executive*
Fitzgerald, Mary Eileen *museum program director*
Fralino, W. Heywood *health facility administrator*
Glenn, Robert Eastwood *lawyer*
Glover, Harry Allen, Jr., *lawyer*
Goad, Danny Harlan *mechanical engineer*
Gray, Jeffrey T. *automotive executive*
Hutcheson, Jack Robert *hematologist, medical oncologist*
Hylton, Myles Talbert *lawyer*
Jennings, James Wilson, Jr., *lawyer*
Klein, Deborah Rae *health facility administrator*
Landis, John William *engineering and construction executive, government advisor*
Lemon, William Jacob *lawyer*
Litwiller, Roger W. *anesthesiologist, medical association executive*
Logan Lawson, Anna *social services administrator*
Marshall, Heman Alexander, III, *lawyer*
McGarry, Richard Lawrence *lawyer*
Osterhaus, Greg S. *artist, graphic designer*
Robertson, Thomas L. *health facility administrator*
Smith, Donald G. *metal products executive*
Stadler, Donald Arthur *management engineer*
Steele, Anita Martin (Margaret Anne Martin) *law librarian, legal educator*
Taubman, Jenny *museum program director*
Thomson, Paul Rice, Jr., *lawyer*
Turk, James Clinton *federal judge*
Wade, Jimmie L. *automotive executive*
Waldron, Karen *development, construction, and management company executive*
Warren, William Kermit *retired media company executive*
Willis, Gordon *construction executive*
Woodrum, Clifton A., III, *lawyer, former state legislator*
Zomparelli, Wendy *newspaper publisher*

Rocky Mount
Flora, Jenny Shreves *special education educator*

Roseland
Stemmler, Edward Joseph *physician, retired association executive, retired academic dean*

Rosslyn
McCarthy, Michael James *military intelligence officer*

Round Hill
Gunberg, Edwin Woodrow, Jr., *counseling psychologist, consultant, researcher*
Tice, Raphael Dean *army officer*

Rustburg
Finney, Barbara Ethel *journalist, actress*

Saint Paul
Gregory, Ann Young *editor, publisher*

Saint Thomas
Greiner, Kenneth Donald, Jr., *management consultant*

Salem
Brand, Edward Cabell *retail executive*
Fisher, Charles Harold *chemistry educator, researcher*
Griffith, H(oward) Morgan *lawyer*
Kim, Kye Young *psychiatrist*
Koontz, Lawrence L., Jr., *state supreme court justice*
Pearson, Henry Clyde *retired judge*
Ramsey, Lloyd Brinkley *retired savings and loan executive, retired army officer*
Sandborg, Marianne M. *voice educator, musician*
Shaffner, Patrick Noel *retired architectural engineering executive*
Weiss, Gregory Lee *sociology educator*

Schley
McVey, Henry Hanna, III, *retired lawyer*

Smithfield
Baxter, Raoul *meat packing company executive*
Luter, Joseph Williamson, III, *meat packing and processing company executive*

Sperryville
Armor, David J. *sociologist*

Spotsylvania
Clower, William Dewey *retired trade association executive*
Haddock, Raymond Earl *career officer*
Hardy, Dorcas Ruth *business and government relations executive*
Hoover, Christopher Paul *music educator*
Manthei, Richard Dale *retired lawyer, health care company executive*
Orsini, Eric Andrew *army official*
Pugh, Randall Scott *lawyer*

Springfield
Bartlow, Gene Steven *association executive, retired air force officer*
Basham, W. Ralph *federal agency administrator*
Bentz, Edward Joseph, Jr., *energy, environment and transportation management consulting firm executive*
Bruen, John Dermot *management consultant*
Casazza, John Andrew *electrical engineer, energy executive*
Chappell, Milton Leroy *lawyer*
Chatelier, Paul Richard *aviation psychologist*
Dake, Marcia Allene *retired nursing educator, university dean*
Doran, Doris Jeanne *librarian*
Edwards-LeBoeuf, Renee Camille *public relations professional, logistics engineer*
Englert, Roy Theodore *lawyer*
Fedewa, Lawrence John *management consulting firm executive, entrepreneur*
Franklin, Jude Eric *electronics executive*
Galvin, Cyril Jerome, Jr., *coastal engineer*
Hunt, Robert Gayle *former government official*
Larson, Reed Eugene *foundation administrator*
Leake, Charles Robert *systems analyst, educator*
Leavitt, Mary Janice Deimel *special education educator, civic worker*
Long, Clarence Dickinson, III, *lawyer*
Meikle, Philip G. *engineer, retired government agency executive*
Naegele, Tobias *editor*
Quick, Danny Richard *computer systems engineer*
Rankin, Jacqueline Annette *communications expert, educator*
Roberts, Paul Franklin, II, *financial executive*
Sonnemann, Harry *electrical engineer, consultant*
Spencer, William Courtney *foundation executive, international business executive*
Stottlemyer, David Lee *government official*
Turner, Stansfield *former government official, lecturer, writer, teacher*
Watts, Helena Roselle *military analyst*
Williams, Cecilia Lee Pursel *optometrist*

Stafford
Lambert, Linda Margaret *reading specialist*
Sedlak, James William *organization administrator*
Williams, Carlisle M., Jr., *municipal official*

Stanardsville
Anns, Philip Harold *international trading executive, former pharmaceutical company executive*
Gladstone, Arthur M. *artist, author, aerospace engineer*
Keel, Alton Gold, Jr., *ambassador*

Staunton
Balsley, Philip Elwood *entertainer*
Cochran, George Moffett *retired judge*
Cook, Clarence Edgar *research facility scientist*
Firehock, Barbara A. *interior designer*
Hammaker, Paul M. *retail executive, business educator, author*
Lossing, Wallace William *inventor, minister*
Smith, Rodney Wike *engineering executive*
Sweetman, Beverly Yarroll *physical therapist*

Stephenson
Johnson, Eva Maria *retired translator*

Sterling
Bernal-Labrada, Emilio *writer, poet, translator*
Blum, John Curtis *agricultural economist*
Chavez, Linda *civil rights organization executive*
Clegg, Roger Burton *lawyer*
Cleveland, Harlan *political scientist, public affairs executive*
Coulter, David Creswell *research engineer*
Friedheim, Jerry Warden *museum consultant*
Heberling, Timothy Alan *information scientist*
Hough, Lawrence A. *former financial organization executive*
Jaffe, Russell Merritt *pathologist, research director*
Jefferson, Sandra Traylor *choreographer*
Lacey, Aaron Michael *actor, director, screenwriter, executive producer*
Martin, Roger John *computer scientist*
McBarnette, Bruce Olvin *lawyer, corporate executive*
Munger, Paul David *company executive, educational administrator*
Oller, William Maxwell *retired energy company executive, retired naval officer*
Sanfelici, Arthur H(ugo) *editor, writer*
Schrader, William L. *communications executive*
Thompson, David Walker *astronautics company executive*
Thompson, Warren M. *food franchise executive*

Stuart
Clark, Martin F(illmore), Jr., *judge*
Sadler, Elliott *race car driver*

Suffolk
Birdsong, George Yancy *manufacturing executive*
Carroll, George Joseph *pathologist, educator*
Glasson, Linda *hospital security and safety official, healthcare*
Hines, Angus Irving, Jr., *petroleum marketing executive*
Holloway, Christopher Matthew *brokerage house executive*
Logan-Sutton, Floretta R. *elementary school educator*
Phipps, Patrick Michael *plant pathology educator*
Sorensen, Carl Edward *company executive*
Sweat, Carl Leondus, Jr., *minister, educator*
Young, Hubert Howell, Jr., *lawyer, real estate investor and developer*

Surry
Sprouse, Earlene Pentecost *special education educator*

Susan
Ambach, Dwight Russell *retired foreign service officer*

Sweet Briar
Muhlenfeld, Elisabeth S. *college president, educator, author*
Piepho, Lee (Edward Lee Piepho) *humanities educator*
Shea, Brent Mack *social sciences educator*
Wassell, Stephen Robert *mathematics educator, researcher*

Swoope
Avery, Robert Newell *sculptor*

Syria
Altaffer, Lawrence F., III, *retired physician, artist*

Tazewell
Claytor, Katherine W. Moss *secondary school educator*
Weeks, Ross Leonard, Jr., *museum executive*

The Plains
Gibbons, John Howard (Jack Gibbons) *government official, physicist*

Upperville
Powell Gebhard, Joy Lee (Bok Sin Lee) *small business owner*
Smart, Edith Merrill *civic worker*
Smart, Stephen Bruce, Jr., *business and government executive*

Urbanna
Garey, Francis Benjamin *retired merchant banker*
Salley, John Jones *retired academic administrator, oral pathologist*

Vienna
Almaguer, Frank *ambassador*
Anderson, Earl E. *retired military officer, legal association administrator*
Armistead, William Spencer *communications executive*
Beyer, Barbara Lynn *aviation consultant*
Bhide, Manohar Gopal *nuclear scientist, educator*
Brandel, Ralph Edward *management consultant*
Burr, Ronald Edwin *publisher*
Chamberlin, Edward Robert *career officer, educator*
Chandler, Hubert Thomas *former army officer*
Condo, Patrick C. *information technology executive*
de Bearn, Gaston, XIV, *pharmaceutical company executive, consultant*
DeWitt, Charles Barbour *federal government official*
Edwards, Phillip Milton *retired import-export company executive*
Gardenier, John Stark *statistician, research ethicist, lecturer, writer*
Gardenier, Turkan Kumbaraci *statistical company executive, researcher*
Gavin, Donald Glenn *lawyer, educator*
Gerson, Elliot Francis *foundation administrator*
Hagberg, Chris Eric *lawyer*
Hale, Thomas Morgan *professional services executive*
Higginbotham, Wendy Jacobson *political adviser, writer*
Jenkins, Robert Gordon *retired air force officer, technology executive, government executive*
Johnson, Richard Clark *lawyer*
Kader, Nancy Stowe *nurse, consultant, bioethicist*
Keiser, Bernhard Edward *engineering company executive, consulting telecommunications engineer*
Kinsolving, Sylvia Crockett *musician, educator*
Kitchens, Clarence Wesley, Jr., *technology administrator*
Koons, James E. *management consultant*
Maiwurm, James John *lawyer*
Marx, Gary Dean *international education consultant, association executive, futurist*
Mc Arthur, George *journalist*
McElveen, Joseph James, Jr., *journalist, author, educator, mass media executive*
Mujumdar, Vilas Sitaram *structural engineer, researcher*
Ogrean, David William *sports executive*
Olshaker, Mark Bruce *author, film maker*
Peltz, Paulette Beatrice *corporate lawyer*
Razzano, Frank Charles *lawyer*
Rogers, Raymond Jesse *retired federal railroad associate administrator*
Rossello, Pedro *former governor*
Salah, Sagid *retired nuclear engineer*
Schwartz, Richard Harvey *pediatrician*
Sheinbaum, Gilbert Harold *international management consultant*
Shelby, Ronald Van Dorn *information technology executive*
Spiro, Robert Harry, Jr., *foundation and business executive, educator*
Stearns, Frank Warren *lawyer*
Sturm, John F. *trade association administrator*
Thompson, Louis Milton, Jr., *association executive, horse breeder*
Thrasher, Warren Atticus, Jr., *telecommunications executive*
Titus, Bruce Earl *lawyer*

Townsend, Irene Fogleman *accountant, tax specialist*
Ulvila, Jacob Walter *management consultant*
Urbanas, Alban William *estate planner*
Van Stavoren, William David *consultant, retired government official*
Walker, Edward Keith, Jr., *retired management consultant, retired military officer*
Webb, William Loyd, Jr., *army officer*
Welters, Anthony *health services executive*
Whitaker, Thomas Patrick *lawyer*
Wiesnet, Donald Richard *retired hydrologist*
Woodward, Kenneth Emerson *retired mechanical engineer*
Yamaguchi, Yuriko Fujita *artist*

Virginia Beach
Alexander, William Powell *business advisor*
Aspiras, Mona Lisa Banzon *web site designer, artist*
Bell, Janet S. *product designer, interior designer*
Benson, Robert A. *photojournalist*
Bradshaw, Denis James *engineer, graphics designer*
Burgess, Marvin Franklin *human resources, management specialist, consultant*
Carlston, John A. *allergist*
Cehelska, Olga M. *music educator, flight instructor*
Christy, Larry Todd *publisher*
Denyes, James Richard *industrial engineer*
Denzler, James Wyatt *pharmacist*
Divaris, Gerald S. *real estate executive*
Dixon, John Spencer *international executive*
Drozda, Donna Jean *artist, educator, inventor*
Duke, Elizabeth (Betsy) A. *bank executive*
Dumville, S(amuel) Lawrence *lawyer*
Edmonds, William Bentley *artist, writer*
Eleuterius, Nancy Lea *health administrator*
Frantz, Thomas Richard *lawyer*
Hamilton, George Henry, Jr., *energy consultant*
Harrell, Charles Lydon, Jr., *lawyer*
Harter, John J. *economic analyst*
Hilgers, John Jack William *management and transportation consultant*
Isaacs, Frederick Wilson *management consultant*
Jones, John Lou *retired arbitrator, rail transportation executive*
Jones, Robert Clair *middle school educator*
Keenan, Barbara Milano *judge*
Kunzinger, Robert Stephen *education educator, writer*
Lowe, Cameron Anderson *dentist, endodontist, educator*
Martin, William Raymond *retired financial manager*
McDaniel, David Henry *physician*
McWaters, Jeffrey L. *healthcare executive*
Morgan, Raymond Franklin *education educator*
Oberndorf, Meyera E. *mayor*
Onsanit, Tawachai *physician*
Panoff, Stephen Edward *music educator*
Picache, Josefina Reyes *travel service company executive, marriage counselor*
Pickett, Owen B. *lawyer, former congressman*
Prescott, David L. C., Jr., *music educator*
Price, Celes E. *retired music educator*
Reece-Porter, Sharon Ann *international human rights educator*
Rodriguez-Rodriguez, Pedro Pablo *retired veterinarian*
Ruben, Leonard *retired art educator*
Savage, Toy Dixon, Jr., *lawyer*
Selig, William George *university official*
Seward, William W(ard), Jr., *writer, retired educator*
Sims, Martha J. *library director*
Smead, Kenneth William *music educator*
Smith, Ruth Hodges *city clerk*
Spitzli, Donald Hawkes, Jr., *lawyer*
Spivak, Maurice Sidney *chief project management, consultant*
Stanton, Pamela Freeman *interior designer, writer*
Tarbutton, Lloyd T. *franchise consultant*
Taylor, Lewis Jerome, Jr., *retired priest*
Wasserman, Kathryn *photographer*
Wick, Robert Thomas *retired supermarket executive*
Williams, J(ohn) Rodman *theologian, educator, clergyman*

Wachapreague
Wilkins, Guy (Ira Wilkins) *painter, art teacher*

Ware Neck
Tabb, Waller Crockett *retired allergist, retired immunologist*

Warrenton
Anthony, Joan Caton *administrative judge*
Brimelow, Peter *journalist*
Brooke, Edward William *lawyer, former senator*
Estaver, Paul Edward *writer, poet*
Fox, Raymond Graham *educational technologist*
Gullace, Marlene Frances *information engineer, systems analyst, consultant*
Malmgren, Harald Bernard *economist*
Morrison, Paul A. *lawyer*

Washington
Lynch, Reinhardt *chef, restaurant owner*

Washingtons Birthplace
Donahue, John Joseph *park and recreation director*

Waterford
Hallberg, Parker Franklin *environmental company executive*
Harper, James Weldon, III, *finance consultant*
Harris, Caspa, Jr., *lawyer, educator, association administrator*

Waynesboro
Dillon, William Henry *retired secondary school educator*
Glaser, Elisabeth *psychotherapist, historian*
Kerby, Robert Browning *media consultant*
Lane, Lawrence Jubin *retired electrical engineer, consultant*
Layman, J. Allen *communications executive*
Quarforth, James S. *communications executive*

White Stone
Ames, John Lewis *lawyer*
Duer, Ellen Ann Dagon *anesthesiologist, general practitioner*
Wroth, James Melvin *retired military officer*

Williamsburg
Aaron, Bertram Donald *engineering executive, management consultant*
Ackerman, Lennis Campbell *retired management consultant*
Aldrow-Liput, Priscilla Reese *retired elementary education educator*
Ball, Donald L. *retired English language educator*
Barausky, Kenneth P. *aerospace company executive*
Burdette, Robert Bruce *retired lawyer*
Calver, Richard Allen *retired college dean*
Campbell, Colin Goetze *foundation president*
Cauthen, Charles Edward, Jr., *retail executive, business consultant*
Chandler, Kimberley Lynn *educational administrator*
Chappell, Miles Linwood, Jr., *art history educator*
Christison, Muriel Branham *retired art museum director, fine arts educator*
Church, Dale Walker *lawyer*
Coleman, Henry Edwin *art educator*
Connell, Alastair McCrae *physician*
Crapol, Edward P. *history professor*
Davis, Richard Bradley *internal medicine, pathology educator, physician*
Dhillon, Avtar Singh *psychiatrist*
Dowling, John Clarkson *language educator*
Dunn, Keith A. *government agency administrator, consultant*
Dunn, Ronald Holland *civil engineer, management executive, consultant*
Ely, Melvin Patrick *historian, writer, educator*
Esler, Anthony James *historian, novelist, educator*
Farrar, John Thruston *health facility administrator*
Feiss, P. Geoffrey *university dean*
Flanders, Raymond Alan *dentist, governmental health agency administrator*
Geddy, Vernon Meredith, Jr., *lawyer*
Gentry, James William *retired state official*
Goodwin, Bruce Kesseli *retired geology educator, researcher*
Gordon, Baron Jack *stockbroker*
Gottfried, Mark Ellis *accountant, consultant*
Gough, Carolyn Harley *library director*
Griffith, Melvin Eugene *entomologist, public health official*
Guastaferro, Angelo *space science administrator, consultant*
Herbert, Albert Edward, Jr., *interior and industrial designer*
Herrmann, Benjamin Edward *former insurance executive*
Hight, Orian Langley *retired education educator*
Hoffman, Ronald *historical institute administrator, educator*
Holmes, David Lynn *religion educator*
Holstein, William Kurt *business administration educator*
Hornsby, Bruce Randall *composer, musician*
Hoving, John Hannes Forester *consulting firm executive*
Jacoby, William Jerome, Jr., *internist, retired military officer*
Johnston, Robert Atkinson *psychologist, educator*
Kossler, William John *physics educator*
Kottas, John Frederick *business administration educator*
Landen, Robert Geran *retired historian, educator, university administrator*
Lorenz, Hans Ernest *photographer*
Lund, Wendell Luther *retired lawyer*
Maloney, Milford Charles *retired internal medicine educator*
Marcus, Paul *law educator*
Margolin, Robert Jeremy *lawyer*
McGiffert, Michael *retired history educator, editor*
McLennan, Barbara Nancy *international tax specialist*
Messmer, Donald Joseph *business management educator, marketing consultant*
Montgomery, Joseph William *finance company executive*
Moorman, John A. *librarian*
Myers, Roger Paul *writer, playwright, actor*
Nettels, Elsa *English language educator*
Oakley, John Howard *humanities educator*
O'Connell, William Edward, Jr., *finance educator*
Reveley, Walter Taylor, III, *dean*
Roberson, Robert S. *investment company executive*
Robinson, Jay (Jay Thurston Robinson) *artist*
Rodman, Leiba *mathematician*
Roseberg, Carl Andersson *sculptor, educator*
Schwartz, Miles Joseph *cardiologist*
Sisk, Albert Fletcher, Jr., *retired insurance agent*
Smith, Roger Winston *political theorist, educator*
Smith, William Henry Preston *freelance/self-employed writer, editor, former telecommunications industry executive*
Spitzer, Cary Redford *avionics consultant, electrical engineer*
Stanley, Shirley Davis *artist*
Starnes, William Herbert, Jr., *chemist, educator*
Steinsmith, William *internist, research scientist*
Sullivan, Timothy Jackson *law educator, academic administrator*
Tortorice, Donald A. *law educator*
Wallach, Alan *art historian, educator*
Zhang, Xiaodong *computer scientist, educator, researcher*

Winchester
Adams, Nate Lavinder, III, *lawyer*
Bechamps, Gerald Joseph *surgeon*
Bonometti, Robert John *technology management and strategy executive*
Byrd, Harry Flood, Jr., *newspaper executive, former senator*
Creasy, Richard Alan *anesthesiologist*
Engelage, James Roland *management consultant*
Gaither, George Manney *marketing consultant*
Hall, Ralph C. *retired architect, mechanical engineer*
Halseth, Michael James *medical center administrator*
Helentjaris, Diane *physician, medical association administrator*
Hofstra, Warren Raymond *historian, educator*
Holland, James Tulley *retired plastic products company executive*
Hughes, Donna Jean *librarian*
Isenhower, Nelson Nolan *anesthesiologist*
Jolly, Bruce Dwight *manufacturing executive*
Ludwig, George Harry *retired physicist, electrical engineer*
Meschutt, David Randolph *historian, curator*
Tisinger, Billy Joe *lawyer*
Tisinger, Catherine Anne *history and economics educator*

Wintergreen
Omohundro, William Addison *research marketing executive*

Wise
Grable, Dillon Ross *computer scientist, educator, music educator*
Smiddy, Joseph Charles *retired academic administrator*
Wasem, Bruce William *football coach, educator*

Woodberry Forest
Campbell, Dennis Marion *academic administrator, educator, theologian*

Woodbridge
Andrews, Michael William *librarian, information specialist*
Bastas, Thomas G. *labor union administrator*
Denison, Cynthia Lee *accountant, tax specialist*
Dillaber, Philip Arthur *budget and resource analyst, consultant*
Englert, Helen Wiggs *writer*
Garon, Richard Joseph, Jr., *political organization worker*
Hollingsworth, Bobby G. *career officer*
Holman, Karen Marie Anderson *purchasing agent*
Hood, Ronald Chalmers, III, *historian, writer*
Kreipke, Merrill Vincent *civil engineer, consultant*
Locigno, Paul Robert *public affairs executive*
Messerschmidt, William Harclerode *retired army noncommissioned officer, musician*
Monaco, Anthony John *retired health facility administrator, writer*
Peck, Dianne Kawecki *architect*
Townsend, Kenneth Ross *retired priest*

Woodstock
Walton, Morgan Lauck, III, *lawyer*

Woodville
Mc Carthy, Eugene Joseph *writer, former senator*

Wytheville
Baird, Thomas Bryan, Jr., *retired lawyer*

Yorktown
Gross, Leroy *retired sugar company executive*
Ray, Charles Dean *neurosurgeon, spine surgeon, bioengineer, inventor*
Romjue, John Lawson *historian, writer*
Wood, James Edward, Jr., *religion educator, author*

Zacata
Gardiner, William Ralph *electronics engineer, consultant*

WASHINGTON

Aberdeen
Murrell, Gary *historian, educator*

Anacortes
Felger, Ralph William *education educator, retired military officer*
Higgins, Robert (Robert Walter Higgins) *career officer, physician*
Mc Cracken, Philip Trafton *sculptor*
Randolph, Carl Lowell *chemical company executive*

Arlington
Bullington, Gayle Rogers *writer, researcher*
Kell, Lyle Nicholas *retired minister, retired real estate broker*

Auburn
Nazaire, Michel Harry *physician*
Overholt, Miles Harvard *cable television consultant*
Sata, Lindbergh Saburo *psychiatrist, educator*
Whitmore, Donald Clark *retired engineer*

Bainbridge Island
Bowden, William Darsie *retired interior designer*
Fischer, Thomas Covell *law educator, consultant, writer*
Marsh, Donald Reppert *holding company executive*
Oechsli, Christopher George *foundation administrator*

Battle Ground
Hansen, James Lee *sculptor*

Belfair
Hager, Robert Worth *retired aerospace company executive*

Bellevue
Andersen, James A. *retired state supreme court justice*
Andrews, Richard Lee *lawyer*
Arnold, Ronald Henri *nonprofit organization executive, consultant*
Benveniste, Jacob *retired physicist*
Berkley, James Donald *clergyman*
Brockenbrough, Edwin Chamberlayne *surgeon*
Carlson, Curtis Eugene *orthodontist, periodontist*
Clark, Richard Walter *education consultant*
Clay, Orson C. *insurance company executive, director*
Davis, Stephen B. *Internet company executive, lawyer*
Douglas, Diane Miriam *museum director*
Graham, John Robert, Jr., *financial executive*
Groten, Barnet *energy company executive*
Hackett, Carol Ann Hedden *physician*
Hall, Eleanor Williams *public relations executive*
Hannah, Lawrence Burlison *lawyer*
Hibbard, Richard Paul *industrial ventilation consultant, educator*
Hovind, David J. *manufacturing executive*
Kocher, Cynthia *investment specialist*
Lipton, Judith Eve *psychiatrist*
Medved, Robert Allen *lawyer*
Morie, G. Glen *lawyer, manufacturing executive*
Mosher, Charles D. *mayor, real estate manager*
Myhrvold, Nathan *technology executive*
Neuzil, Dennis R. *civil engineer*
Nowik, Dorothy Adam *medical equipment company executive*
O'Byrne, Michael *management consultant*
O'Keefe, Kathleen Mary *state government official*
Olson, Robert William *writer, retired counselor*
Parks, Donald Lee *mechanical engineer, human factors engineer*
Phillips, Zaiga Alksnis *pediatrician*
Pigott, Charles McGee *transportation equipment manufacturing executive*
Pigott, Mark C. *automotive executive*
Pinney, Alesia L. *lawyer*
Pool, David *software executive*
Pritt, Frank W. *computer company executive*
Reinleitner, Katherine Mindlin *psychologist, foundation administrator*
Rundell, Arden Grabke *musician*
Scott, John Lennox *real estate company executive*
Sebris, Robert, Jr., *lawyer*
Shushkewich, Kenneth Wayne *structural engineer*
Sweeney, David Brian *lawyer*
Tembreull, Michael A. *automotive executive*
Tian, Hongqi *application developer, researcher*
Valdman, Bertrand A. *utilities executive*
Van Vactor, Myra Florendo *school librarian, director*
Wang, Xing *power systems engineer*
Warren, James Ronald *retired museum director, writer, columnist*
Wells-Henderson, Ronald John *investment counselor*
Westergaard, George Henry *secondary school educator*
Whatmore, George Bernard *physician, scientist, clinical neurophysiologist*

Bellingham
Albrecht, Albert Pearson *electronics/systems engineer, consultant*
Anderson, David Bowen *lawyer*
Brakke, Myron Kendall *retired research chemist, educator*
Burdge, Rabel James *sociology educator*
Clark-Langager, Sarah Ann *curator, director, university official*
Cole, Craig W. *grocery chain executive*
Cox, David Jackson *biochemistry educator*
Globerman, Steven *finance educator*
Haggen, Donald E. *food products executive*
Hansen, Leonard Joseph *writer, journalist, editor, communications executive*
Henley, Dale C. *grocery company executive*
Howe, Warren Billings *physician*
James, Helen Ann *plastic surgeon*
Jansen, Robert Bruce *consulting civil engineer*
Kapcsandy, Louis Endre *building construction and manufacturing executive, chemical engineering consultant*
Kennedy, Kathleen Ann *historian, educator*
Lau, Roy Esme *surgeon*
Lippman, Louis Grombacher *psychology educator*
Livesay, Thomas Andrew *museum administrator, lecturer*
Meals, Pamela F. *publishing executive*
Morse, Karen Williams *academic administrator*
Murdock, Mary-Elizabeth *history educator*
Nelson, George Driver *astronomy and education educator, former astronaut*
Packer, Mark Barry *lawyer, financial consultant, foundation official*
Raas, Daniel Alan *lawyer*
Ross, June Rosa Pitt *biologist, educator*
Ross, Steven Charles *business administration educator, consultant*
St. James, Margaret Jean *not-for-profit developer*
Terey-Smith, Mary *music educator, conductor*
Whyte, Nancy Marie *performing arts educator*

Blaine
Miller, Ronald *writer, critic*

Bonney Lake
Wang, Lin *physicist, computer science educator, computer software consultant*

Bothell
Anders, Harley Dillon, Sr., *retired federal agency administrator*
Craves, Frederick B. *health products executive*
Fell, H. Perry *biotechnology company executive*
Gerber, William G. *medical company executive*
Hawthorne, Nan Louise *Internet resources consultant, web site designer, writer*
Scannell, John R. *publishing consultant*
Stein, Michael A. *pharmaceutical executive*
Watts, Linda Susan *humanities educator*
Wilds, Daniel O. *health products executive*
Wirt, Sherwood Eliot *minister, writer*

Burien
Burgess, Charles Orville *history professor*

Camano Island
Clowes, Garth Anthony *electronics executive, consultant*
Hartley, Celia Love *nursing consultant, writer, retired nursing educator, nursing administrator*
O'Connor, Thomas Edward *petroleum geologist, management consultant*
Thayer, Thomas Manor, Jr., *artist*

Camas
Valanis, Kirk Christian *theoretical mechanics researcher, educator*

Centralia
Bates, Charles Walter *lawyer, human resources executive, politician*
Buzzard, Steven Ray *lawyer*
Gimbel, Hervey Willis *public health physician, medical administrator*
Kirk, Henry Port *academic administrator*
Meany, Philip Augustus *library director*
Miller, James McCalmont *pediatrician*
Wright, Daniel A. *lawyer*

Chattaroy
Ezelle, Robert Eugene *diplomat*

Cheney
Jordan, Stephen M. *university president*
Smith, Grant William *English language educator, civic fundraiser*
Stearns, Susan A *education educator*

Steiner, Henry-York *English language and literature educator*
Toneva, Elena T. *education educator, researcher*

Clarkston
Chinchinian, Harry *pathologist, educator*
Smith, Phyllis Mae *healthcare consultant, educator*
Torgerson, Linda Belle *music educator*

Clinton
Holtby, Kenneth Fraser *retired manufacturing executive*
Jacobs, Harold Robert *mechanical engineer, educator*

Clyde Hill
Condon, Robert Edward *surgeon, educator, consultant*

College Place
Anderson, Clarence Glen *dean*
Mariani, Evelyn Julia *music educator*

Coupeville
Lotzenhiser, George William *music educator, university administrator, composer*
Mayhew, Eric George *medical researcher, educator*
Piercy, Gordon Clayton *bank executive*
Thom, Richard David *retired aerospace executive*

Darrington
Powell, Gregory David *secondary school educator, coach, musician*

Davenport
Lonn, Suzanne Dallas *secondary school educator*

Des Moines
Andrews, William F. *minister*
Brandmeir, Christopher Lee *hotel and tourism management educator*
Ortmeyer, Carl Edward *retired demographer*
Tuell, Jack Marvin *retired bishop*

Dupont
Pettit, Ghery St. John *electronics engineer*

Eastsound
Anders, William Alison *aerospace and defense manufacturing executive*
de Boor, Carl *mathematician*
Fowles, George Richard *physicist, researcher*
Hoagland, Karl King, Jr., *lawyer*

Edmonds
Bell, Nancy Lee Hoyt *real estate investor, middle school educator, volunteer*
Bray, Ronald Eugene *obstetrician/gynecologist*
Conom, Tom Peter *lawyer*
Galster, Richard W. *engineering geologist*
Johnson, d'Elaine Ann Herard *artist, consultant*
Monroe, James Walter *retired organization executive*
Owen, John *retired newspaper editor*
Paul, Ronald Stanley *research institute executive*
Peckol, James Kenneth *consulting engineer*
Schmit, Lucien André, Jr., *structural engineer*
Terrel, Ronald Lee *civil engineer, business executive, educator*
Thyden, James Eskel *diplomat, educator, lecturer*
Yoon, Jay Myoung *oncologist, hematologist, internist*

Ellensburg
Comstock, Dale Robert *mathematics professor*
Jacobs, Robert Cooper *political scientist, consultant*
Kline, Celeste Marie *librarian*
McIntyre, Jerilyn Sue *university administrator*
Nethery, Vincent Michael *adult education educator*
Sand, John Halvdan *obstetrician, gynecologist*

Endicott
Ray, Billy John, Jr., *music educator*

Ephrata
Randolph, Kevin Howard *marketing executive*

Everett
Brown, Frederick Calvin *physicist, researcher*
Constantine, Kevin *professional hockey coach*
Fitzpatrick, Thomas Mark *lawyer*
Hundley, Ronnie *academic administrator*
Nelson, Carol Kobuke *bank executive*
Oliver, William Donald *orthodontist*
Ostergaard, Joni Hammersla *lawyer*
Rimbach, Evangeline Lois *retired music educator*
Smith, Thomas J. *surgeon, educator*
Valentine, Mark Conrad *dermatologist*
Vaughn, Kathy *municipal official*

Federal Way
Boling, Joseph Edward *numismatist, retired military officer*
Corbin, William R. *wood products executive*
Cunningham, John Randolph *project manager*
Dooley, James H. *product company executive*
Fulton, Daniel S. *corporate real estate executive*
Gates, Thomas Edward *civil engineer, researcher, waste management administrator, lawyer*
Hanson, Richard E. *paper company executive*
Hogans, Mack L. *paper company executive*
Holman, Kermit Layton *chemical engineer*
Keller, James R. *manufacturing executive*
Ketchersid, Wayne Lester, Jr., *medical technologist*
Ma, Zhenkui *remote sensing applications scientist, consultant*
Mail, Patricia Davison *public health specialist*
McDade, Sandy D. *manufacturing executive*
Muzyka-McGuire, Amy *marketing professional, nutrition consultant*
Nance, John Joseph *lawyer, writer, air safety analyst, broadcaster, consultant*
Onustock, Michael R. *manufacturing executive*
Rogel, Edward P. *corporate human resources executive*
Rogel, Steven R. *forest products company executive*
Simpson, Shawn Marie *secondary school educator*
Studebaker, Irving Glen *mining engineering consultant*
Taggart, Richard J. *corporate financial executive*
Taylor, Jack P. *lumber company executive*

Freeland
Calio, Anthony John *scientist, business executive*
Meador, Jo Guasasco *writer, retired information technology manager*

Friday Harbor
Agosta, William Carleton *chemist, educator*
Geyman, John Payne *physician, educator*
Gonser, Thomas Howard *lawyer, former bar association executive*
Hoyt, James *education educator*
MacGinitie, Walter Harold *psychologist, educator*

Gig Harbor
Cuzzetto, Charles Edward *accountant, financial analyst, educator*
Earley, Laurence Elliott *retired medical educator*
Holmberg, Branton Kieth *management consultant*
McMillan, John Howard *industrial designer, consultant*
Minnerly, Robert Ward *retired headmaster*
Thompson, Ronald Edward *lawyer*

Hansville
Blalock, Ann Bonar *evaluation researcher*

Hoquiam
Kessler, Keith Leon *lawyer*
Lamb, Isabelle Smith *manufacturing executive*

Issaquah
Barchet, Stephen *obstetrician, gynecologist, retired military officer*
Benoliel, Joel *lawyer*
Berto, Deborah Lynn *publisher*
Brotman, Jeffrey H. *variety stores executive*
Cain, Coleen W. *writer, educator*
Duncan, Elizabeth Charlotte *retired marriage and family therapist, educational therapist, educator*
Galanti, Richard A. *wholesale business executive*
Massick, James William *heavy equipment manufacturing company executive*
Moch, Robert Gaston *retired lawyer*
Oles, Stuart Gregory *lawyer*
Reid, John Mitchell (Jack Reid) *biomedical engineer, researcher, consultant*
Sinegal, James D. *wholesale distribution executive*
Wainwright, Paul Edward Blech *construction company executive*
Wright, Theodore Otis *forensic engineer*

Kelso
Janke, John Eric *secondary educator*

Kenmore
Guy, Arthur William *electrical engineering educator, researcher*
Jennerich, Edward John *university official and dean*
Patten, Richard E. *not-for-profit developer, director*
Sobolewski, John Stephen *computer scientist, consultant*

Kennewick
Cobb, William Thompson *environmental and agricultural consultant*
Cochran, James Alan *mathematics professor, department chairman*
Fann, Margaret Ann *counselor*
Hames, William Lester *lawyer*
Morris, Rusty Lee *architectural consulting firm executive*

Kent
Bangsund, Edward Lee *former aerospace company executive, consultant*
Brannen, George Elsdon *surgeon*
Cheung, John B. *research and development executive*
Goo, Abraham Meu Sen *retired aircraft company executive*
Hebeler, Henry Koester *retired aerospace and electronics executive*
McDermott, Richard Francis *judge*
O'Bara, Kenneth J. *physician*
Personette, Louise Metzger (Sister Mary Roger Metzger) *mathematics educator*
Pierce, Danny Parcel *artist, educator*
Popova, Olga K *geologist, researcher*
Raymond, Eugene Thomas *technical writer, consultant, retired aircraft engineer*

Keyport
Treacy, Gerald Bernard, Jr., *lawyer*

Kingston
Longwell, John Ploeger *chemical engineering educator*

Kirkland
Alexander, Shaun *professional football player*
Argue, Don Harvey *college president, minister*
Barto, Deborah Ann *physician*
Clarkson, Lawrence William *air transportation executive*
Cowan, Douglas Leo *lawyer*
Dilfer, Trent *professional football player*
Dundas, Dennis Franklin *plastic surgeon*
Dunn, Jeffrey Edward *neurologist*
Etcheson, Warren Wade *business administration educator*
Gerstman, Hubert Louis *retired speech and language pathologist, audiologist, otolaryngology educator, humorist*
Goldman, Ralph Morris *political science educator*
Holmgren, Mike *professional football coach*
Mitchell, Joseph Patrick *architect*
Randle, John *professional football player*
Rich, Clayton *retired academic administrator, educator*
Ryles, Gerald Fay *private investor, business executive*
Spence, Michael Allan *lawyer*
Steinmann, John Colburn *architect*
Szablya, Helen Mary *writer, language professional, lecturer*
Szablya, John Francis *electrical engineer, consultant*
Tyllia, Frank Michael *university official, educator*
Watters, Richard James *professional football player*
Witte, Peggy *metal products executive*

La Conner
Knopf, Kenyon Alfred *economist, educator*
Robbins, Thomas Eugene *writer*

Lacey
Breytspraak, John, Jr., *management consultant*
Louis, Glenn *music educator*
Price, David Harold *anthropologist, educator*

Lake Forest Park
Adams, Hazard Simeon *English educator, writer*

Lake Stevens
Durden, Rome L. *aircraft manufacturing company executive*

Lakewood
Cook, Anne Welsh *lumber company executive*
Kanarowski, Stanley Martin *chemist, government official*
Oakes, DuWayne Earl *retired principal*
Owen, Thomas Walker *banker, broker*

Langley
Le Roy, Robert Powell *retired minister, educator, writer*
Metcalf, Jack *former congressman, retired state senator*

Leavenworth
Caemmerer, Richard Rudolph *art educator*
Smith, G(odfrey) T(aylor) *retired academic administrator*
Taub, Alex A.G. *writer, educator*

Lilliwaup
McGrady, Corinne Young *design company executive*

Long Beach
McClintock, William Thomas *health care administrator*
West, Douglas Xavier *retired science educator*

Longview
Correll, Donald Albert *theater educator*
Wollenberg, Richard Peter *paper manufacturing company executive*

Lummi Island
Ewing, Benjamin Baugh *environmental engineer, educator, consultant*

Lynden
Harshman, Dale Richard *physicist*
Hibbs, Clair M. *retired pathologist*
Vigil, Eugene Leon *retired federal agency administrator, cell biologist*

Lynnwood
Bear, Gregory Dale *writer, illustrator*
Bergstedt, Anders Spencer *lawyer*
Floten, Barbara Jean *educational dean*
Jenes, Theodore George, Jr., *retired career officer*
Krause, Thomas Evans *record promotion and radio consultant*
Oharah, Jack *academic administrator*
Olsen, Kenneth Harold *geophysicist, astrophysicist*

Malaga
Nanto, Roxanna Lynn *marketing professional, management consultant*

Manchester
Fearon, Lee Charles *chemist*

Manson
Stager, Donald K. *retired construction company executive*

Maple Valley
Brown, Thomas Andrew *retired aircraft/weaponry manufacturing executive*
Willson, David Allen *retired reference librarian, writer*

Medical Lake
Barber, Devin *writer*
Grub, Phillip Donald *business educator*

Medina
Dagnon, James Bernard *human resources executive*
Meeker, Milton Shy *manufacturing executive*

Mercer Island
Bridgforth, Robert Moore, Jr., *aerospace engineer*
Coe, Robert Campbell *retired surgeon*
Davis, Tinka Guerguieva *secondary school educator*
Dawn, Clarence Ernest *history educator*
Dykstra, David Charles *management executive, consultant, accountant, author, educator*
Elgee, Neil Johnson *retired internist, educator, retired endocrinologist, educator*
Gould, Alvin R. *international business executive*
Haviland, James West *physician, educator*
Langhout-Nix, Nelleke *artist*
Noe, James Alva *retired judge*
Page, Ellis Batten *psychologist, educator*
Sanford, Kenneth Richard *small business owner*

Mill Creek
Latta, Diana Lennox *retired interior designer*
Sengupta, Mritunjoy *mining engineer, educator*
Stelzer, Gustav R. *retired automotive executive*

Monroe
Kirwan, Katharyn race (Mrs. Gerald Bourke Kirwan Jr.) *retail executive*

Montesano
Stewart, James Malcom *lawyer*

Mount Vernon
Garcia, John *psychologist, educator*
Gaston, Margaret Anne *retired business educator*
Hall, David Ramsay *architect*
Klein, Henry *architect*
Moser, C. Thomas *lawyer*
Witmer, Michael Douglas *education educator*

Mukilteo
Atal, Bishnu Saroop *retired speech research executive*
Black, Jackie John *artist*
Bohn, Dennis Allen *electrical engineer, executive*
Brown, Bruce Baden *accountant*

Naches
Assink, Nellie Grace *agricultural executive*

Newcastle
Erxleben, William Charles *lawyer, consultant*

North Bend
Brumbaugh, Harley Aaron *retired music educator, conductor, composer, poet*
Kaplan, Donna Elaine *artist, educator*
Pope, Frances Elaine *music educator*

Oak Harbor
Daugherty, Kenneth Earl *research company executive, educator*
Meaux, Alan Douglas *retired facilities technician, sculptor*
Miller, Robert Scott *mental health administrator, social worker*

Oakville
Magnus, Lennea D. *community development planner*

Ocean Park
Lee, Martha *artist, writer*

Olympia
Adkins, Ben Frank *management and engineering consultant*
Alexander, Gerry L. *state supreme court chief justice*
Bagg, Carter Davis *architect, urban planner*
Ballard, Clyde *state legislator*
Bergeson, Teresa *school system administrator*
Bloomquist, Rodney Gordon *geologist*
Bridge, Bobbe J. *state supreme court justice*
Brown, Lisa J. *state legislator, educator*
Bruce, Robert Vance *historian, educator*
Carlson, Don M. *state senator*
Chopp, Frank *state official*
Constatine, Dow *state senator*
Costa, Jeralita *state legislator*
Das, Tapas Kumar *chemical and environmental engineer*
Eide, Tracey J. *state legislator*
Fairhurst, Mary E. *judge*
Fairley, Darlene *state legislator*
Fisher, Nancy Louise *pediatrician, medical geneticist, former nurse*
Franklin, Rosa G. *state legislator, retired nurse*
Fraser, Karen *state legislator*
Gardner, Georgia Anne *state legislator*
Gilbert, Jorge *sociologist, educator, consul*
Gregoire, Christine O. *state attorney general*
Guy, Richard P. *retired state supreme court justice*
Hale, Patricia S. *state legislator*
Harmon, Lynn Astrid *broadcaster, writer*
Haseltine, James Lewis *artist, consultant*
Haugen, Mary Margaret *state legislator*
Heilenday, Frank Tod *science educator*
Hewitt, Mike *state senator*
Hong, Rani Jenelle *real estate broker*
Howell, Helen *state agency administrator*
Hutchins, Diane Elizabeth Rider *librarian*
Ireland, Faith *state supreme court justice*
Johnson, Charles William *state supreme court justice*
Kastama, Jim *state senator*
Kessler, Lynn Elizabeth *state legislator*
Locke, Gary *governor*
Long, Jeanine Hundley *retired state legislator*
Long, Marsha Tadano *state official*
Macduff, Ilone Margaret *music educator*
Madsen, Barbara A *state supreme court justice*
Marcelynas, Richard Chadwick *management consultant*
Markham, J. David *educator, writer, historical consultant*
McAuliffe, Rosemary *state legislator*
Myers, Sharon Diane *auditor*
O'Brien, Robert S. *state official*
Owen, Bradley Scott *lieutenant governor*
Owens, Susan *state supreme court justice*
Parlette, Linda Evans *state senator*
Patterson, Julia *state legislator*
Prentice, Margarita *state legislator, nurse*
Randlett, Mary Willis *photographer*
Rasmussen, Marilyn *state legislator*
Reed, Sam *secretary of state*
Regala, Debbie *state senator*
Roach, Pam *state legislator*
Roe, Charles Barnett *lawyer*
Rossi, Dino J. *state legislator, real estate broker*
Russman, Irene Karen *artist*
Sanders, Richard Browning *judge*
Senn, Deborah *insurance commissioner*
Sesonske, Alexander *nuclear and chemical engineer*
Sheldon, Betti L. *state legislator*
Shin, Paull Hobom *investment company executive, state legislator*
Showalter, Marilyn Grace *state agency administrator*
Smith, Charles Z. *retired state supreme court justice*
Smith, Sherwood Paul *plastic surgeon*
Snyder, Sid *state legislator, retail executive*
Spanel, Harriet *state legislator*
Stevens, Val *state legislator*
Stohl, Esther A. *senior citizen advocate*
Thibaudeau, Patricia *state legislator*
Walker, Francis Joseph *lawyer*
Weese, Bruce Eric *sales executive*
Welsh, John Beresford, Jr., *retired lawyer*
Williams, Wayne Leroy *lawyer*
Winsley, Shirley J. *state legislator, insurance agent*
Zussy, Nancy Louise *librarian*

Othello
Bowerly, Daniel Kent *music educator, musician*

Otis Orchards
Pfeiffer, Patricia Ruth *writer, consultant*

Pasco
Wells, Roger Stanley *software engineer*

Port Angeles
Barker, Barbara *registered nurse, medical researcher*
Brewer, John Charles *journalist*
Grier, George Edward *music educator, musician*
McCormick, Karen Louise *savings and loan association executive*

Muller, Carolyn Bue *physical therapist, volunteer*
Muller, Willard C(hester) *writer*
Osborne, Richard Hazelet *anthropology and medical genetics educator*
Sonnenfeld, Joseph *geographer, researcher*

Port Ludlow
Trzaska, Joyce Anne *publishing executive*

Port Townsend
Buhler, Jill Lorie *editor, writer*
Hiatt, Peter *retired librarian studies educator*
Jones, John Wesley *entrepreneur*
Ludlow, Nelson D. *information technology executive, researcher*
MacLean, Barbara Hutmacher *author, retired journalist*
Woolf, William Blauvelt *retired association executive*

Portland
Webster, Gerald Best *musician, music educator*

Poulsbo
Carle, Harry Lloyd *social worker*
Wayne, Kyra Petrovskaya *writer*

Prosser
Cooper, Lynn Dale *retired minister, retired navy chaplain*
Proebsting, Edward Louis, Jr., *retired research horticulturist*

Pullman
Ahn, Sung Keuk *statistician, educator*
Banas, Emil Mike *physicist, researcher*
Bates, Robert C. *academic administrator*
Baugh, Bradford Hamilton *occupational and environmental health advisor*
Bennett, Dick *college basketball coach*
Chermak, Gail D. *audiologist, educator*
Dillman, Donald Andrew *sociologist, educator, survey methodologist*
Edwards, Charles Gould *food scientist, educator, microbiologist, chemist*
Funk, William Henry *retired environmental engineering educator*
Gursoy, Dogan *hospitality and tourism educator, researcher*
Henson, James Bond *veterinary pathologist*
Hipps, Kerry Wayne *chemistry educator, research scientist*
Hosick, Howard Lawrence *cell biology educator, academic administrator*
Kallaher, Michael Joseph *mathematics professor*
Lewis, Norman G. *academic administrator, researcher, consultant*
McSweeney, Frances Kaye *psychology educator*
Rawlins, V. Lane *university president*
Robison, Linda M. *epidemiologist, medical researcher*
Rosa, Eugene Anthony *sociologist, environmental scientist, educator*
Ryan, Clarence Augustine, Jr., *biochemistry educator*
Stock, David Earl *mechanical engineering educator*
Swan, Susan Linda *history professor*
Thomashow, Linda Suzanne *microbiologist*
Walter, Scott *school librarian*
Warner, Dennis Allan *psychology educator*
Yasinitsky, Gregory Walter *music educator*
Zlatos, Christy *librarian*

Puyallup
Muchmore, Don Moncrief *retired museum, foundation, educational, financial fund raising and public opinion consulting firm administrator, banker*

Redmond
Allchin, Jim *information technology executive*
Ambrose, Adele D. *communications executive*
Arbogast, Brian *information technology executive*
Ayala, Orlando *information technology executive*
Bach, Robert J. *information technology executive*
Ballmer, Steven A. *software company executive*
Belluzzo, Rick *information technology executive*
Black, Deborah *information technology executive*
Boggs, Scott *information technology executive*
Borgs, Christian H. *mathematical physicist*
Brakken, William *home improvement retail executive*
Brass, Dick *information technology executive*
Brummel, Lisa *information technology executive*
Burgman, Doug *information technology executive*
Burgum, Doug *software company executive*
Button, Tom *information technology executive*
Caouette, David Paul *public relations executive*
Chakrin, Lewis M. *consumer products company executive*
Chayes, Jennifer Tour *mathematical physicist, educator*
Christensen, Juha *information technology executive*
Cole, David W. *information technology executive*
Connors, John G. *information technology executive*
Cutler, David N. *software engineer*
Dahan, Andre *consumer products company executive*
DelBene, Kurt *information technology executive*
DeVaan, Jon S. *information technology executive*
Devenuti, Richard R. *information technology executive*
Egner, John David *electrical engineer*
Elliot, Gerri *information technology executive*
Fade, Richard *information technology executive*
Flessner, Paul *information technology executive*
Forsen, Harold Kay *retired engineering executive*
Freedman, Michael Hartley *mathematician, educator*
Gates, Bill (William Henry Gates III) *software company executive*
George, Grant *information technology executive*
Gyani, Mohan *communications company executive*
Hague, William W. *consumer products company executive*
Hebert, Kathleen *information technology executive*
Herbold, Robert J. *software company executive*
Johnson, Robert H. *communications executive*
Judah, Norman *information technology executive*
Keith, Michael G. *consumer products company executive*
Kemp, Allan Reid *application developer*
Kimmich, Jon Bradford *computer science program executive*
Kirilova, Svetlana Nikolova *psychologist, consultant*
Koch, Mitchell *information technology executive*
Kong, Kenneth Sehkiang *software testing engineer*
Landis, Gregory P. *consumer products company executive*
Lappenbusch, Richard W. *software company official*
Lee, Bryan *information technology executive*
Levin, Lewis *information technology executive*
Lomet, David Bruce *computer scientist*
Markezich, Ron *information technology executive*
Martinez, Maria *computer software company executive*
Marvin, D. Jane *consumer products company executive*
Mathews, Mich *computer company executive*
McCabe, Joseph, Jr., *telecommunications industry executive*
Moore, Lori *information technology executive*
Muglia, Robert L. *information technology executive*
Mundie, Craig R. *information technology executive*
Nadella, Satya *information technology executive*
Nelson, Roderick D. *communications executive*
Neukom, William H. *lawyer*
Norman, Bill *information technology executive*
Pacholski, Richard Francis *retired securities company executive, financial advisor, consultant*
Pagulayan, Randy Jay *psychologist*
Parthasarathy, Sanjay *information technology executive*
Pathe, Peter *information technology executive*
Pawlosky, Mark A. *broadcast executive*
Poole, Will *information technology executive*
Raikes, Jeff *information technology executive*
Rashid, Richard F. *information technology executive*
Rawding, Michael *information technology executive*
Roderick, Jordan M. *communications executive*
Rudder, Eric *information technology executive*
Sasenick, Joseph Anthony *animal health and food safety company executive*
Shaw, Kendrick Matthew *software engineer*
Short, Robert *information technology executive*
Sievert, G. Michael *marketing professional*
Sinneck, Michael *information technology executive*
Sinofsky, Steven J. *information technology executive*
Slemons, Gregory L. *communications executive*
Smith, Bradford Lee *information technology executive*
Sobey, Edwin J. C. *museum director, oceanographer, consultant*
Somasegar, Sivarama Kichenane *information technology executive*
Sowder, Robert Robertson *architect*
Sparks, Lindsay *information technology executive*
Stockdale, Russell *information technology executive*
Stonecipher, Charles H. *information technology executive*
Toutonghi, Michael *information technology executive*
Valentine, Brian *information technology executive*
van Oppen, Peter H. *information technology executive*
Vaskevitch, David *information technology executive*
Veghte, Bill *information technology executive*
Vigil, Henry P. *information technology executive*
Waldman, Ben *information technology executive*
Wilderotter, Mary Agnes *software company executive, former cable television executive*
Willard, H(arrison) Robert *electrical engineer*
Willingham, Deborah N. *information technology executive*

Renton
Gaolach, Brad Wayne *academic administrator, director*
Greenwood, Loren *toy manufacturing executive*
Huck, Larry Ralph *manufacturing executive, sales consultant*
Kredlo, Thomas Andrew *real estate appraiser*
Majors, James Edward *electrical engineer*
Wong, Jee K *education educator, music consultant*

Republic
Ferguson, Robert Bruce *minerals company executive*

Richland
Bair, William J. *retired radiation biologist*
Bevelacqua, Joseph John *physicist, researcher*
Bian, Randy Xindi *research scientist*
Bush, Spencer Harrison *metallurgist, consultant*
Chikalla, Thomas David *retired science facility administrator*
Dunning, Thom H., Jr., *environmental molecular science executive*
Elderkin, Charles Edwin *retired meteorologist*
Hrma, Pavel *materials scientist, educator*
Jacobsen, Gerald Bernhardt *biochemist*
Lin, Yuehe *research scientist*
Miller, James Vince *university president*
Moore, Emmett Burris, Jr., *physical chemist, educator*
Mushen, Robert Linton *ophthalmologist, consultant*
Onishi, Yasuo *environmental researcher*
Powell, David Charles *music educator, meteorologist*
Ristow, Gail Ross *art educator, paralegal, children's rights advocate*
Roop, Joseph McLeod *economist*
Sinerius-Rupp-Bloor, Sharon Kay *painter, photographer, sculptor*
Sonnenfeld, David Allan *sociologist*
Trent, Donald Stephen *thermo fluids engineer*
Wright, Malcolm Sturtevant *nuclear energy industry executive, retired military officer*

Sammamish
Waitt, Robert Kenneth *lawyer*
Yocam, Eric Wayne *engineer*

Seattle
Albrecht, Richard Raymond *retired airplane manufacturing executive, lawyer*
Aldea, Gabriel S. *cardiothoracic surgeon, educator*
Alger, Glenn M. *meteorologist*
Alkire, John D. *lawyer, arbitrator, mediator*
Alsdorf, Robert Hermann *lawyer*
Anang, Amma Cecilia *dance company administrator*
Andersen, Niels Hjorth *chemistry professor, consultant, biophysicist, researcher*
Anderson, Peter MacArthur *lawyer*
Andrew, Lucius Archibald David, III, *bank executive*
Andrews, J. David *lawyer*
Ansell, Julian S. *physician, retired urology educator*
Appelbaum, Frederick Ray *oncologist*
Armstrong, Charles G. *professional baseball executive, lawyer*
Armstrong, Mary M. *insurance company executive*
Arnold, Robert Morris *banker*
Arthur, William Lynn *environmental/political program director*
Auer, Nancy Jane *emergency physician, medical association administrator*
Awasthi, Vidya Nidhi *accounting educator*
Ayer, William S. *air transportation executive*
Babb, Albert Leslie *biomedical engineer, educator*
Bailey, William Scherer *lawyer, educator*
Bain, William James, Jr., *architect*
Baker, Roland Jerald *finance educator*
Bandrowski, Paul *information technology executive*
Banks, James Albert *educational research director, educator*
Barnard, Kathryn Elaine *nursing educator, researcher*
Barnes, Susan Lewis *lawyer*
Bassingthwaighte, James Bucklin *physiologist, educator, medical researcher*
Baum, William Alvin *astronomer, educator*
Bayley, Christopher T. *public affairs consultant*
Beale, Jane Guthrie *music publisher, music educator, pianist*
Beezer, Robert Renaut *federal judge*
Behnke, Carl Gilbert *beverage franchise executive*
Beighle, Douglas Paul *retired aerospace industry executive*
Berendt, Paul *political organization worker*
Berger, Paul Eric *artist, photographer*
Bergman, Abraham *pediatrician*
Berkowitz, Bobbie *medical educator*
Berman, Steve William *lawyer, author*
Bernard, Eddie Nolan *oceanographer*
Berni, Rosemarian Rauch *rehabilitation and oncology nurse*
Beyers, William Bjorn *geography educator*
Bezos, Jeffrey P. *multimedia executive*
Bianco, James A. *research and development executive*
Bibaud, Rene *artist, performer, consultant*
Bird, Sue (Suzanne Brigit Bird) *professional basketball player*
Bishop, Virginia Wakeman *retired librarian, retired humanities educator*
Black, W. L. Rivers, III, *lawyer*
Bladen, Edwin Mark *lawyer, judge*
Blair, M. Wayne *lawyer*
Blake-Inada, Louis Michael *cardiologist, researcher*
Blase, Nancy Gross *librarian*
Blethen, Frank A. *newspaper publisher*
Bley, John L. *financial executive*
Blom, Daniel Charles *lawyer, investor, retired insurance company executive*
Blomdahl, Sonja *artist*
Blomstrand, Doreen Kathryn *retired physician assistant*
Boardman, David *newspaper editor*
Boeder, Thomas L. *lawyer*
Boersma, P. Dee *marine biologist, educator*
Boggs, Paula Elaine *lawyer*
Boguski, Mark S. *medical association administrator*
Boman, Marc Allen *lawyer*
Borden, Weston Thatcher *chemistry professor*
Borgatta, Edgar F. *social psychologist, educator*
Bornstein, Paul *medical educator, biochemist*
Bosworth, Thomas Lawrence *architect, educator*
Bowden, Douglas McHose *neuropsychiatric scientist, educator, research center administrator*
Bowen, Jewell Ray *chemical engineering educator*
Boxx, Karen Elizabeth *lawyer, educator*
Boylan, Merle Nelson *librarian, educator*
Brammer, Lawrence Martin *psychology educator*
Brandauer, Frederick Paul *Asian language educator*
Breslow, Norman Edward *biostatistics educator, researcher*
Bridge, Herbert Marvin *jewelry executive*
Bridge, Jonathan Joseph *lawyer, retail executive*
Bringman, Joseph Edward *lawyer*
Brown, Craig William *physical chemist*
Brown, Robert Alan *atmospheric science educator, research scientist*
Brownlee, Donald Eugene, II, *astronomer, educator*
Brownstein, Barbara Lavin *geneticist, educator, university official*
Bruner, Nancy J. *publishing executive*
Buck, Linda B. *physician, medical educator*
Bucklin, Mark Richard *lawyer*
Buckner, Philip Franklin *newspaper publisher*
Budigan, William Clay *lawyer, educator*
Bufano, Ralph A. *museum executive*
Buhner, Jay Campbell *former professional baseball player*
Bultmann, William Arnold *historian, educator*
Bundrant, Charles H. *food products executive*
Bunting, Kenneth Freeman *newspaper editor*
Bunting, Robert Louis *accounting firm executive, management consultant*
Burges, Stephen John *civil engineer, hydrologist*
Burke, William Thomas *law educator, lawyer*
Burns, Michael Joseph *operations and sales-marketing executive*
Burrows, Elizabeth MacDonald *religious organization executive, educator*
Butler, Octavia Estelle *free-lance writer*
Buursma, William F. *architect*
Campbell, Robert Hedgcock *investment banker, lawyer*
Card, Deborah Frances *orchestra administrator*
Carlson, Dale Arvid *university dean*
Carter, Bruce L.A. *biotechnology company executive*
Casey, M. Michael *food products executive*
Casey, Thomas W. *finance company executive*
Catterall, William A. *pharmacology, neurobiology educator*
Cavanaugh, Michael Everett *lawyer, arbitrator, mediator*
Cella, John J. *freight company executive*
Chapman, Craig J. *finance company executive*
Chapman, Fay L. *lawyer*
Chatard, Peter Ralph Noel, Jr., *aesthetic plastic surgeon*
Chihuly, Dale Patrick *artist*
Chirot, Daniel *sociology and international studies educator*
Christian, Gary Dale *chemistry professor*
Christiansen, Walter Henry *aeronautics educator*
Claflin, Arthur Cary *lawyer*
Clark, Dawn A. *architect*
Clark, Robert Newhall *electrical and aeronautical engineering educator*
Clarren, Sterling Keith *pediatrician*
Cline, Robert Stanley *retired air freight company executive*
Coburn, Robert Craig *philosopher, educator*
Cochran, Wendell Albert *science editor*
Coldewey, John Christopher *English literature educator*
Collett, Robert Lee *financial company executive*
Collier, Tom Ward *musician, educator*
Comfort, Robert Dennis *lawyer*
Cook, Jeremy Curnock *biotechnology executive*
Cottle, Gail Ann *retail executive*
Couser, William Griffith *medical educator, academic administrator, nephrologist*
Covey, Joy D. *finance and administration executive*
Cox, Frederick Moreland *retired university dean, social worker*
Creager, Joe Scott *geology and oceanography educator*
Crenshaw, Edward Lee, Sr., *aviation electronics technician*
Cross, Bruce Michael *lawyer*
Cullen, Bruce F. *anesthesiologist*
Dale, Beverly A. *biochemist, researcher*
Dale, David C. *physician, medical educator*
Dally, Lynn *choreographer, performing company executive, educator*
Dalton, Larry Raymond *chemistry educator, researcher, consultant*
Dalzell, Rick *information technology executive*
Daniel, Thomas L. *zoology educator*
David, Daryl D. *finance company executive*
Davidson, Ernest Roy *chemist, educator*
Davidson, Robert William *not-for-profit executive*
Davis, Earl James *chemical engineering educator*
Davis, Jennie Sue *aerospace engineer*
Davis, John MacDougall *lawyer*
Dawson, Patricia Lucille *surgeon*
Day, Robert Winsor *preventive medicine physician, researcher*
De Alessi, Ross Alan *lighting designer*
Dear, Ronald Bruce *social work educator*
Debro, Julius *education educator, sociologist*
de Chesnay, Mary *nursing educator*
Dederer, Michael Eugene *public relations company executive*
Dehmelt, Hans Georg *physicist, educator*
Deines, Katrina *architecture educator*
Deming, Jody Wheeler *oceanography educator*
Denke, Conrad William *motion picture producer*
Denny, Brewster Castberg *retired university dean*
de Tornyay, Rheba *nursing educator, retired dean*
DeVore, Paul Cameron *lawyer*
Dimmick, Carolyn Reaber *federal judge*
Disteche, Christine M. *geneticist*
Dively, Dwight Douglas *finance director*
Dolan, Andrew Kevin *lawyer*
Donnelly, Peter F. *art association administrator*
Donovan, Dennis Michael *psychologist, researcher*
Dorpat, Theodore Lorenz *psychoanalyst*
Dubrow, Gail Lee *architecture educator*
Duckworth, Tara Ann *insurance company executive*
Duncan, Dale A. *publishing executive*
Duncan, Steven Merle *construction company manager, philosophy educator*
Dunner, David Louis *medical educator*
Duryee, David Anthony *management consultant*
Eastham, John D. *business executive*
Ecklund, Ralph Earl *property manager*
Eigsti, Roger Harry *retired insurance company executive*
Elgin, Ron Alan *advertising executive*
Ellegood, Donald Russell *publishing executive*
Eller, Marlin *security firm executive*
Ellings, Richard James *political and economic research institution executive*
Elliott, Clifton Langsdale *lawyer*
Ellis, Georgiana Kehr *internist*
Ellis, James Reed *retired lawyer*
Ellis, Janice Rider *nursing educator, consultant*
Ellis, John W. *professional baseball team executive, utilities executive*
Ellison, Henry Phillips *military officer*
Ellison, Herbert Jay *historian, educator*
El-Moslimany, Ann Paxton *paleoecologist, educator, writer*
Elyn, Mark *retired opera singer, educator*
Emmert, Mark Allen *academic administrator, educator*
Engel, Thomas *chemistry professor*
Epple, Steven *architectural firm executive*
Erdmann, Joachim Christian *physicist*
Eschbach, Joseph Wetherill *nephrology educator*
Eskelin, John Thurston *city planner*
Evans, Bernard William *geologist, educator*
Evans, Jack R. (J. Glenn Evans) *writer, poet*
Evans, Robert Vincent *sales and marketing executive*
Eyre, David R. *orthopedics educator*
Fancher, Michael Reilly *newspaper editor, newspaper publishing executive*
Farbanish, Thomas *sculptor*
Farrell, Anne Van Ness *foundation executive*
Farrington-Hopf, Susan Kay *plumbing and heating contractor*
Farris, Jerome *federal judge*
Faulstich, James R. *retired bank executive*
Feldman, Roger Lawrence *artist, educator*
Fetters, Norman Craig, II, *banker*
Fidel, Raya *library science educator*
Fiedler, Fred Edward *organizational psychology educator, consultant*
Fine, Arthur I. *philosopher, educator*
Fine, James Stephen *physician*
Finlayson, Bruce Alan *chemical engineering educator*
Fischer, Edmond Henri *biochemistry educator*
Fischer, Fred Walter *physicist, engineer, educator*
Fisher, Jeffrey L. *lawyer*
Fix, Wilbur James *department store executive*
Fletcher, Betty Binns *federal judge*
Fluke, Lyla Schram (Mrs. John M. Fluke Sr.) *publisher*
Forbes, David Craig *musician*
Foster, Barry Alan *cultural organization researcher, educator*
Friend, Stephen H. *biotechnology company executive*
Frost, Barbara Sherry *lawyer*
Fry, John Craig, Jr., *portfolio manager*
Gardiner, John Jacob *leadership educator, writer, speaker, philosopher*
Gardiner, T(homas) Michael *artist*

Van Lierop, John Henry, Jr., *music educator*
Vestal, Josephine Burnet *lawyer*
Vitiello, Michael V. *gerontologist, educator*
Voegtlin-Anderson, Mary Margaret *secondary school educator, music educator*
Vogel, David Seth *lawyer*
von Bargen, Sally *stock image photography company executive*
Wagner, Patricia Hamm *lawyer*
Wagoner, David Everett *lawyer, arbitrator*
Wagoner, David Russell *writer, educator*
Waldhausen, John Henry Trescher *pediatric surgeon, educator*
Walker, Douglas *computer developement company executive*
Walker, Walter Frederick *professional basketball team executive*
Walsh, Kenneth Andrew *biochemist*
Warner, John D. *aerospace company executive*
Washington, James Winston, Jr., *artist, sculptor*
Wechsler, Mary Heyrman *lawyer*
Weinberg, John Lee *federal judge*
Weiss, Noel S. *epidemiologist*
Welk, Richard Andrew *plastic surgeon*
Wenk, Edward, Jr., *civil engineer, policy analyst, educator, writer*
Wesley, Virginia Anne *real estate property manager*
West, John Garrett *political scientist, educator*
Westphal, Paul *professional basketball coach*
White, Rebecca T. *lawyer*
White, Rick *lawyer, former congressman*
Whitson, Lish *lawyer*
Wilets, Lawrence *physics educator*
Williams, J. Vernon *retired lawyer*
Williams, Rebecca Lynn *lawyer, nurse*
Wilson, L. Michelle *lawyer*
Wilson, Lizabeth Anne *library director*
Wilson, Richard Randolph *lawyer*
Woodruff, Gene Lowry *nuclear engineer, university dean*
Woods, James Sterrett *toxicologist*
Woods, Nancy Fugate *dean, women's health nurse, educator*
Wott, John Arthur *arboretum and botanical garden executive, horticulture educator*
Yeh, Ying Chin *electrical engineer*
Yuan, Chun *physicist, educator*
Yue, Agnes Kau-Wah *otolaryngologist*
Zager, Richard A. *medical educator, researcher*
Ziadeh, Farhat J. *Middle Eastern studies educator*
Zilly, Thomas Samuel *federal judge*

Seaview
McNeil, Helen Jo Connolly *nursing educator, public health administrator*

Sedro-Woolley
Rochefort, Regina Marie *ecologist, botanist*

Selah
Markin, Karl Edward *obstetrician/gynecologist*
Ring, Lucile Wiley *lawyer*

Sequim
Beaton, Roy Howard *retired nuclear industry executive*
Guilmet, George Michael *cultural anthropologist, educator*
Huntley, James Robert *government official, international affairs scholar and consultant*
Jackson, Patrick Joseph *real estate company officer*
Kretschmer, Keith Hughes *investor*
Laube, Roger Gustav *retired trust officer, financial consultant*
Mc Hugh, Margaret Ann Gloe *retired psychologist*
McMahon, Terrence John *retired foreign service officer*
Meacham, Charles Harding *government official*
Pearson, Walter Howard *marine biologist, researcher*

Shelton
Maddux, Carolyn L. *writer, educator*
McNabb, David E. *business educator, writer*
Milander, Henry Martin *educational consultant*

Shoreline
Gilchrist, Garrett Alexander *psychotherapist*
Hanson, Kermit Osmond *business administration educator, university dean emeritus*
Hutton, Winfield Travis *management consultant, educator*
Merendino, K. Alvin *surgical educator*
Risse, Guenter Bernhard *physician, historian, educator*

Silverdale
Balcomb, Mary Nelson *design studio owner*
Fjelstad, Paul *lawyer, editor*
Raum, Mary Beth *ballet educator*
Tozer, William Evans *entomologist, educator*
Walske, M(ax) Carl, Jr., *physicist*

Snohomish
Guzak, Karen Jean Wahlstrom *artist*
Philpott, Larry La Fayette *horn player*

Snoqualmie
Giuliani, David *personal care products company executive*
Stull, Mike *personal care industry executive*

South Bend
Heinz, Roney Allen *civil engineering consultant*

Spanaway
Loete, Steven Donald *pilot*
McKinnon, James Buckner *real estate sales executive, writer, researcher*
Roberts-Dempsey, Patricia E. *secondary school educator*

Spokane
Anderson, Robert Edward *lawyer*
Antonietti, Joan L(ynn) *lawyer*
Baker, Sylvia Halldorson *music educator*
Bender, Betty Wion *librarian*
Burton, Robert Lyle *accounting firm executive*
Cameron, Alex Brian *accounting educator*
Carriker, Robert Charles *history professor*
Chamberlain, Barbara Kaye *small business owner, communications executive*
Clarke, Judy *lawyer*
Clements, Theodore *lawyer, law educator, dean*
Cohen, Arnold Norman *gastroenterologist*
Coker, Charlotte Noel *political activist*
Coughlin, Bernard John *university chancellor*
Cowles, William Stacey *newspaper publisher*
Crosby, Glenn Arthur *chemistry professor*
Demakas, John James *neurosurgeon*
Edwards, James Robert *minister, religious educator*
Eliassen, Jon Eric *retired utility company executive, economic development executive*
Ely, Gary G. *utilities company executive*
Fowler, Betty Janmae *dance company director, editor*
Geraghty, John Vincent *public relations consultant*
Gibson, Melvin Roy *pharmacology educator*
Greenwood, Collette P. *municipal official, finance officer*
Gunning, Patricia Ann *music educator*
Halvorson, Marjory *opera director*
Hansen, Laurel D. *elementary school educator*
Harbaugh, Daniel Paul *lawyer*
Hendershot, Carol Miller *physical therapist*
Herzer, Marian Day *not-for-profit developer, educator*
Hiller, Stanley, Jr., *manufacturing executive*
Hilst, Glenn Rudolph *environmental research administrator, research scientist*
Hirsch, Anne *dean*
Horton, Susan Pittman *bank executive*
Hosking, Neville John *educational administrator*
Hoyt, Bradley James *financial advisor*
Imbrogno, Cynthia *magistrate judge*
Kafentzis, John Charles *journalist, educator*
Koegen, Roy Jerome *lawyer*
Kolsrud, Henry Gerald *dentist*
Kovacevich, Robert Eugene *lawyer*
Krueger, Larry Eugene *import/export company executive, lawyer*
Kunkel, Richard Lester *public radio executive*
Lee, Hi Young *family physician, acupuncturist*
Lee, Richard Francis James *evangelical clergyman, media consultant, lawyer*
Leighton, Jack Richard *small business owner, former educator*
Lineberger, Peter Saalfield *lawyer*
Matters, Clyde Burns *former college president*
Matthews, Thomas M. *utilities company executive*
McDevitt, James A. *lawyer*
McManus, Patrick Francis *educator, writer*
McWilliams, Edwin Joseph *banker*
Mielke, Clarence Harold, Jr., *hematologist*
Mobley, Karen Ruth *art gallery director*
Moe, Orville Leroy *racetrack executive*
Mohrlang, Roger Lloyd *philosopher, educator*
Murphy, James Michael *retired judge, mediator, arbitrator*
Murphy, Mary Ann *human services administrator*
Novak, Terry Lee *public administration educator*
Nyman, Carl John, Jr., *university dean and official*
Phillips, John Grant (Jack Phillips) *theatre director*
Quackenbush, Justin Lowe *federal judge*
Robinson, Herbert Henry, III, *educator, psychotherapist*
Robinson, William P. *academic administrator, consultant, speaker*
Siegel, Louis Pendleton *forest products executive*
Sines, Randy Dwain *business executive*
Spitzer, Robert J. *academic administrator*
Stackelberg, John Roderick *history professor*
Steadman, Robert Kempton *oral and maxillofacial surgeon*
Steele, Karen Dorn *journalist*
Storey, Francis Harold *business consultant, retired bank executive*
Tarr, Gregory L. *health and medical products company executive*
Tsutakawa, Edward Masao *management consultant*
Ueberroth, Peter Victor *former baseball commissioner*
Van Sickle, Frederick L. *federal judge*
Weatherhead, Leslie R. *lawyer*
Whaley, Robert Hamilton *judge*
Williams, Patricia C. *federal judge*
Wirt, Michael James *library director*
Woodard, Alva Abe *business consultant*

Sumas
Hemry, Larry Harold *former federal agency official, writer, inventor*

Sumner
Wickizer, Cindy Louise *retired elementary school educator*

Tacoma
Anderson, Lynn L. *trust company executive*
Archangelsky, Dmitry A *application developer, researcher*
Arnold, J. Kelley *US magistrate judge*
Bartlett, Norma Thyra *retired administrative assistant*
Brenner, Elizabeth (Betsy Brenner) *publishing executive*
Bryan, Robert J. *federal judge*
Bunney, Shawn I. *councilman*
Burns, Robin C(arol) *mathematics theoretician, accountant*
Callan, Josi Irene *museum director*
Cuevas, Eduardo Samaniego *internist*
Ebersole, Brian *former mayor*
George, Nicholas *lawyer, entrepreneur*
Gorbman, Claudia L. *performing arts educator, researcher*
Harris, Robert Gaylen *art director, graphic designer, illustrator*
Holt, William E. *lawyer*
Hori, Kiyoaky *retired anesthesiologist*
Hudson, Edward Voyle *linen supply company executive*
Hutchings, George Henry *food company executive*
King, Gundar Julian *retired university dean*
Krueger, James A. *lawyer*
Liddle, Alan Curtis *retired architect*
Lowenberg, Timothy Joseph *lawyer*
Mack, Robert E. *lawyer*
Mersereau, Susan *information systems company executive*
Miller, Judson Frederick *lawyer, former military officer*
Mladenich, Ronald E. *publishing executive*
Mowery, Gerald Eugene *publishing executive, writer*
Mungia, Salvador Alejo *lawyer*
Neff Balch, Betty Marie *retired nursing educator*
Peterson, Thomas Charles *minister, pastoral counselor and therapist*
Porter, Karen Ann *anthropologist, educator*
Rahe, Richard Henry *psychiatrist, educator*
Rieke, William Oliver *foundation director, medical educator, former university president*
Schauss, Alexander George *psychologist, biomedical researcher*
Sloan, Daniel Kay *electrical engineer*
Sutherland, Douglass B. *former mayor, tent and awning company executive*
Taylor, Peter van Voorhees *advertising and public relations consultant*
Temple, Thomas C. *oil company executive*
Verhey, Joseph William *psychiatrist, educator*
Wagonfeld, James B. *gastroenterologist*
Waldo, James Chandler *lawyer*
West, Carolyn Marie *psychologist, educator, writer*
Weyerhaeuser, George H., Jr., *paper manufacturing company executive*
Wiegman, Eugene William *minister, former college administrator*
Wolf, Frederick George *environmental scientist, administrator*
Zeeck, David *newspaper editor*

Tahuya
Quesinberry, Bonita Mae *counselor, writer, editor*

Toppenish
Ross, Kathleen Anne *academic administrator*

Tukwila
Harnish, John J. *manufacturing executive*
Lamb, Ronald Alfred *editor*
Robinson, Howard Arthur, Jr., *minister*
Talmadge, Philip Albert *former state supreme court justice, former state senator*

Tumwater
Edmondson, Frank Kelley, Jr., *lawyer, legal administrator*

University Place
Bourgaize, Robert G. *economist*
Pliskow, Vita Sari *anesthesiologist*
Seiber, Richard Allan *retired minister*

Vancouver
Archer, Stephen Hunt *economist, educator*
Benton, Donald Mark *state legislator, political organization chairman*
Campbell, Scott *newspaper publishing company executive*
Congdon, Roger Douglass *theology educator, minister*
Craven, James Michael *economist, educator*
Crews, William Odell, Jr., *religious organization administrator*
Dodds, Michael Bruce *lawyer*
Hammann, Gregg C. *fitness equipment executive*
Harris, Robert L(ee) *judge*
Hixon, Robin Ray *food service executive, writer*
Hulburt, Lucille Hall *artist, educator*
Karpinski, John Stanley *lawyer*
Kodis, Mary Caroline *marketing consultant*
Middlewood, Martin Eugene *technical communications specialist, writer, consultant*
Ogden, Daniel Miller, Jr., *government official, educator*
Ogden, Valeria Munson *management consultant, state representative*
Regan, Elizabeth Anne *bail bond agent*
Robertson, Joel Thomas *railroad executive*
Smith, Linda A. *retired congresswoman*
Smith, Sam Corry *retired foundation executive, consultant*
Taylor, Carson William *electrical engineer*
Tripp, Thomas Murray *finance educator*
Woodward, Jonathan Morgan *mental health specialist*

Vashon
Mantle, Peter John *aerospace executive, consultant*
Vallarta, Josefina M. *retired child neurologist*

Walla Walla
Belay, Halefom *economist, educator*
Carlsen, James Caldwell *musicologist, educator*
Chaidarun, Sushela Songtanin *endocrinologist, researcher*
Cronin, Thomas Edward *academic administrator*
Hayner, Herman Henry *lawyer*
Johnson, Robert Arnold *physician, cardiologist, poet*
Martin, John Hugh *lawyer, retired*
Perry, Louis Barnes *retired insurance company executive*
Potts, Charles Aaron *management executive, writer, publishing executive*
Yaple, Henry Mack *librarian*

Wapato
Arthurs, Steven Paul *entomologist, researcher*

Washougal
Harness, William Edward *tenor*

Wenatchee
Birdsall, Brian *food products executive*
Chandler, Allen *food products executive*
Elfving, Don C. *horticulturist, educator*
Elwell, H. Terry *marketing professional, educator*
Gotthold, William Eugene *emergency physician*
Knecht, Ben Harrold *surgeon*
Schrader, Lawrence Edwin *plant physiologist, educator*
Williams, Keith Roy *museum director*

White Salmon
Verry, William Robert *retired mathematics researcher*

Woodinville
Alvarez, Bryan *newsletter editor, writer*
Lanter, Sean Keith *software engineer*
Sanders, Richard Kinard *actor*

Woodland
Hansen, Walter Eugene *insurance executive*

Yakima
Jongeward, George Ronald *retired systems analyst*
Larson, Paul Martin *lawyer*
Long, David R. *food products executive*
McDonald, Alan Angus *federal judge*
Meshke, George Lewis *drama and humanities educator*
Newland, Ruth Laura *small business owner*
Simonson, Susan Kay *hospital clinical care coordinator*
Suko, Lonny Ray *judge*
Tenney, Robert Carl *lawyer*
Ullas, Yvonne Lee *primary school educator*
Walker, Lorene *retired elementary school educator*
Wright, J(ames) Lawrence *lawyer*

WEST VIRGINIA

Ansted
Shriver, Thomas L. *park director*

Athens
Beasley, Jerry Lynn *academic administrator*
Marsh, Joseph Franklin, Jr., *emeritus college president, educational consultant*
Westbrook, Gary Wayne *music educator, consultant*

Beckley
Faber, David Alan *federal judge*
Hooper, William Dale *surgeon*
Kennedy, David Tinsley *retired lawyer, labor arbitrator*
Rehbein, Edward Andrew *minister, geologist, consultant*

Belmont
Drane, A. D. *adult education educator*

Bethany
Cooey, William Randolph *economics professor*

Bluefield
Blevins, Thomas E. *college administrator, educator*
Loundmon-Clay, Juanita L. *academic administrator, educator, dean*
Reid, William James *mining executive*

Bridgeport
Gorby, William Guy *anesthesiologist*

Buckhannon
McCormick, Rodger John *biologist, educator, minister*
Wright, David Andrew *music educator*

Bunker Hill
Marple, Thomas Franklin *columnist, reporter*

Charles Town
Jones, Jay *television producer, television director, educator*
McDonald, Angus Wheeler *farmer*
Na, Tsung Shun (Terry Na) *Chinese studies educator, writer*

Charleston
Albright, Joseph P. *state supreme court justice*
Anderson, Leonard W. *state legislator, small business owner*
Arrington, Carolyn Ruth *education consultant*
Ball, Homer K. *state senator*
Beary, Kimberly *newscaster, writer*
Bennett, Robert Menzies *retired gas pipeline company executive*
Betts, Rebecca A. *lawyer*
Bhasin, Madan Mohan *research scientist*
Bias, Sharon G. *state commissioner*
Boland, James Pius *surgeon, educator*
Bolen, Charles Paul *systems engineer*
Boley, Donna Jean *state legislator*
Bolt, John A. *newspaper editor*
Border, Larry Willis *pharmacist*
Brewer, Lewis Gordon *judge, lawyer, educator*
Brightbill, Janet M. *music educator*
Brookshire, Michael L. *forensic economist, economics educator*
Brown, James Knight *lawyer*
Callaghan, Dan O. *lawyer*
Chaney, Michael Thomas *lawyer*
Chapman, John Andrew *retired chamber of commerce executive*
Chilton, Elizabeth Easley Early *newspaper executive*
Cline, Michael Robert *lawyer*
Cooper, Grant *composer, conductor, music educator*
Copenhaver, John Thomas, Jr., *federal judge*
Dasher, George Roy *geologist*
Davis, Billie Johnston *school counselor*
Davis, Robin Jean *state supreme court justice*
Dissen, James Hardiman *lawyer*
Douglass, Gus Ruben *state agency administrator*
Galya, Thomas Andrew *geologist*
Gardner, Edward Tytus, III, *information technology executive*
Gillespie, William Harry *forestry executive, geology educator*
Gokcen, Uner *architectural firm executive*
Goodwin, Joseph Robert *judge*
Grimes, Richard Stuart *newswriter*
Haught, James Albert, Jr., *journalist, newspaper editor, author*
Heath, Mark E. *lawyer*
Hechler, Ken *former state official, former congressman, political science educator, writer*
Helfrich, Paul A. *orchestra executive*
Helmick, Walt *state legislator*
Isabella, Mark Douglas *management consultant*
King, Robert Bruce *federal judge*
Kiss, Robert *state legislator*
Lane, Charlotte *lawyer*
Leasor, Jane *religion and philosophy educator, musician*
Lewis, Charles Raymond, II, *traffic engineer, consultant*
Manchin, Joe, III, *secretary of state*
Martin, Jerry Harold *bank examiner*
Maynard, Elliott *state supreme court justice*
McCabe, Brooks Fleming, Jr., *state legislator*
McCuskey, John F. *lawyer*
Mc Graw, Darrell Vivian, Jr., *state attorney general*
McGraw, Warren Randolph *state supreme court justice*
Melton, G. Kemp *former mayor*
Michael, M. Blane *federal judge*

Minard, Joseph M. *state legislator*
Minear, Sarah M. *state legislator*
Moore, Mark Tobin *art educator, artist, retired museum curator*
Neely, Richard *lawyer*
O'Connor, Otis Leslie *lawyer, director*
Offutt, Rebecca Sue *business and sales executive*
Pfister, Alfred Karl *internist, educator*
Plymale, Robert H. *state legislator, lumber company executive*
Redd, Marie E. *state legislator, criminal justice educator*
Richardson, Sally Keadle *health care administrator*
Robinson, E. Glenn *lawyer*
Rowe, Larry Linwell *lawyer*
Scott, Olof Henderson, Jr., *priest*
Sharpe, William R. *state legislator, electrical contractor*
Snyder, Herb *state legislator*
Stanley, Mary Elizabeth *judge*
Starcher, Larry Victor *state supreme court justice*
Stark, Larry A. *commissioner*
Tomblin, Earl Ray *state legislator*
Victorson, Michael Bruce *lawyer*
Walker, Martha Yeager *state senator, businesswoman*
Warner, Karl K. *prosecutor*
Wehrle, Henry Bernard, III, *electrical supply company executive*
Welch, Edwin Hugh *academic administrator*
Wise, Robert Ellsworth, Jr., (Bob Ellsworth) *governor, former congressman*
Zak, Robert Joseph *lawyer*

Clarksburg
de la Pena, Cordell Amado *pathologist*
Keeley, Irene Patricia Murphy *federal judge*
Leuliette, Connie Jane *secondary educator*
Mollish, Jack James *retired insurance executive*
Ona-Sarino, Milagros Felix *pathologist*
Sarino, Edgardo Formantes *radiologist, physician*
Walmsley, James Naylor *hydroponic farming executive*
West, James C., Jr., *lawyer*

Craigsville
James, Gregory Clark *music educator*

Davisville
Huber, Clayton Lloyd *marketing professional, engineer, construction executive*

Dunbar
Russell, James Alvin, Jr., *college administrator*

Elkins
Maxwell, Robert Earl *federal judge*
Payne, Gloria Marquette *business educator*

Fairmont
Aloi, Michael John *lawyer*
Dudley-Eshbach, Janet *university president*
Ford, Alma Regina *union official, educator*
Fulda, Michael *political scientist, educator, space policy researcher*
Lach, Peter *humanities educator*
Stanton, George Patrick, Jr., *lawyer*
Swiger, Elizabeth Davis *chemist, educator*

Fairview
Bunner, William Keck *lawyer*

Gallipolis Ferry
Brown, Nancy Jane *human resources specialist*

Gassaway
Jones, Jeniver James *lawyer*

Given
Hamon, Janice M. *social worker, educator*

Glenville
Ellis, Mark Lee *mathematician, educator*
Schmetzer, Frances Myers *secondary school educator*
Tubesing, Richard Lee *library director*

Greenville
Warner, Kenneth Wilson, Jr., *editor, association and publications executive*

Harpers Ferry
Boucher, Wayne Irving *policy analyst*
Carlstrom, Terry R. *park administrator*
Lupoli, John *minister, photographer*

Huntington
Anderson, Lorraine Pearson *dean*
Bagley, Charles Frank, III, *lawyer*
Cocke, William Marvin, Jr., *plastic surgeon, educator*
Cole, Patricia Aluise *elementary school educator*
Darby, H. Darrel *podiatric surgeon*
Gould, Alan Brant *academic administrator*
Hayes, Robert Bruce *former college president, educator*
Henderson, Dan W. *psychiatric therapist, educator*
Kent, Calvin Albert *university administrator*
McKown, Charles Henry *dean*
Molina, Rafael Evencio *urologist*
Morabito, Rocco Anthony *urologist*
Mufson, Maurice Albert *infectious diseases physician, educator*
Nerhood, Robert Clarke *obstetrician and gynecologist*
Reynolds, Marshall Truman *printing company executive*
Ritchie, Garry Harlan *television broadcast executive*
Salyers, Larry G. *airport terminal executive*
Saunders, Martin Wesley *music educator*
Sypher, Blake *medical educator*
Underwood, Mark Forest *lawyer*
Welch, Lynne Brodie *nursing school dean*
Wenzel, Loren Alvin *accounting educator*

Institute
Richards, John Dale *social worker, educator, counselor*
Zaman, Naveed *mathematician, educator*

Inwood
Rizzetta, Carolyn Teresa *musical instrument, sound recording entrepreneur*

Kearneysville
Biggs, Alan Richard *plant pathologist, educator*
Smith, Gene Marcus *mental health services professional*

Kenova
Adkins, Garry Prentice *retired accountant*

Keyser
Falkowski, Theresa Gae *chemistry professor*

Kingwood
Moyers, Sylvia Dean *retired medical librarian*

Lewisburg
Adelman, Michael *dean*
Campbell, Thomas Wood *accountant*
Ford, Richard Edmond *lawyer*

Little Birch
Harman, Brenda Kay *writer, researcher*

Logan
Hrutkay, Lidella Wilson *lawyer, state legislator*

Mannington
Reese, Katherine Rose *music educator*

Martinsburg
Ayers, Anne Louise *small business owner, consultant, counselor*
Day, Michael Gordon *information technology executive, educator*
Hill, Philip Bonner *lawyer*
Malin, Howard Gerald *podiatrist*
Martin, Clarence Eugene, III, *lawyer*
Wilkes, Christopher Comas *judge*

Montgomery
Sathyamoorthy, Muthukrishnan *engineering researcher, educator*
Zatar, Wael Abdelhalim *civil engineer, educator*

Morgantown
Albrink, Margaret Joralemon *medical educator*
Allamong, Betty D. *retired academic administrator*
Amrine, James Wesley, Jr., *entomologist, educator*
Bajura, Richard Albert *university administrator, engineering educator*
Bang, Ki Moon *epidemiologist, educator*
Beattie, Diana Scott *biochemistry educator*
Bell, Lewis Clay *economics educator, government administrator*
Beresford, Annette Diana *researcher*
Beu, Danielle *management educator*
Biddington, William Robert *academic administrator, dental educator*
Blakeman, Robyn L. *advertising executive, educator*
Blaydes, Sophia Boyatzies *English language educator*
Brosky, John Michael *music educator, director*
Bucklew, Neil S. *former academic administrator, educator*
Butcher, Fred R. *biochemistry educator, university administrator*
Chisholm, Lionel Donald John *ophthalmologist*
Cleckley, Franklin D. *law educator*
Cochrane, Robert Lowe *biologist*
Cohen, Richard Paul *lawyer*
Colyer, Dale Keith *agricultural economics educator*
D'Alessandri, Robert M. *dean*
Dawley, David Daniel *finance educator*
Dawood, Mohamed Yusoff *obstetrician, gynecologist*
De Vore, Paul Warren *technology educator*
Doney, Brent Clifford *industrial hygienist, public health service officer*
D'Souza, Gerard Eugene *economist, educator*
Ducatman, Alan Marc *physician*
Eck, Ronald Warren *civil engineer, educator*
Emery, Sanford Emil *orthopedic surgeon*
Fisher, John Welton, II, *law educator, magistrate judge, university official*
Fleming, William Wright, Jr., *pharmacology educator*
Fusco, Andrew G. *lawyer*
Gladfelter, Wilbert Eugene *physiology educator*
Glover, Douglas Dennis *obstetrics, gynecology and pharmacology educator*
Guthrie, Hugh Delmar *chemical engineer*
Halabe, Udaya Bhatta *civil engineering educator, researcher*
Hardesty, David Carter, Jr., *university president*
Hensel, Robin Ann Morgan *mathematics and computer science educator*
Hill, Ronald Charles *surgeon, educator*
Hilloowala, Rumy A. *retired anatomist and anthropologist*
Hudson, David M. *minister*
Iammarino, Richard Michael *pathologist, student support services director*
Jabbour, Nabil Milad *ophthalmologist*
Jackson, Ruth Moore *academic administrator*
Kemp, Emory Leland *civil engineering educator*
Kim, Hong Nack *political science educator*
Kinsey, Donna Lee *music educator*
Koelbl, James J. *dean*
Lee, Keith D. *music educator*
Li, Qingdi Quentin *physician, research scientist, medical educator*
Martin, James Douglas *neurologist*
Mazaheri, Ali Reza *engineer, researcher*
Mei, Betty Muichi *director*
Morris, William Otis, Jr., *lawyer, educator, writer*
Mucino-Quintero, Victor Hugo *mechanical engineering educator, consultant*
Murray, Gordon Franklin *medical educator*
Nath, Joginder *genetics and biology educator, researcher*
O'Callaghan, James Patrick *neuroscientist*
Oliverio, Michael Angelo, II, *insurance agent, state legislator*
Peterson, Sophia *international studies educator*
Poland, Alan Paul *oncology educator*
Pyles, Rodney Allen *archivist, county official*
Reed, Eddie *pharmacologist*
Riggs, Jack Edward *neurologist, educator*
Seehra, Mohindar Singh *physics educator, researcher*
Sikora, Rosanna Dawn *emergency physician, educator*
Singer, Armand Edwards *foreign language educator*

Wilson, Mary Alice *violinist, music teacher*
Witt, Tom *economics researcher, educator*

Moundsville
McCraken, Vickie Darlene *nursing assistant*

Mount Gay
Pierce, Calisa A. *director*

Parkersburg
Brum, Brenda *state legislator, librarian*
Bush, Roberta B. *retired psychotherapist, accountant*
Fahlgren, H(erbert) Smoot *advertising executive*
Gilbert, Kenneth G. *art educator*
Gunter, Norma *artistic director*
Keltner, Robert Earl *lawyer, researcher, business executive*
Meadows, Lois Annette *elementary school educator*
Richardson, William Berkley *lawyer*
Sperati, Carleton Angelo *retired industrial scientist*
Young III, Harmon Griffith *music educator*

Parsons
Burns, Robert Alan *economic developer, educator*

Pennsboro
Poling, Kermit William *minister*

Ranson
Rudacille, Sharon Victoria *medical technologist*

Ravenswood
Hamrick, Leslie Wilford, Jr., *metallurgy supervisor*

Redmond
Hylbert, Paul *construction executive*

Reedsville
Williford, Drury Fisher, Jr., *historical researcher, writer, editor*

Romney
Saville, Royce Blair *lawyer*

Ronceverte
Hooper, Anne Dodge *pathologist, educator*

Saint Albans
Whiteley, John Frederick *education educator, consultant*

Salem
Raad, Virginia *pianist, lecturer*

Shenandoah Junction
Showen Jr., Donald Eugene *music educator*

Shepherdstown
Elliott, Jean Ann *librarian emeritus*
Snyder, Joseph John *editor, historian, author, lecturer, consultant*
Wilson, Miriam Janet Williams *publishing executive*

Shinnston
Spears, Jae *state legislator*

South Charleston
Nielsen, Kenneth Andrew *chemical engineer*
Warner, Kris *political organization administrator*

Summersville
Davis, Stephen Allen *lawyer*

Summit Point
Taylor, Harold Allen, Jr., *industrial mineral-speciality metals marketing consultant*

Teays
Lamb, Carl Vernon *writer, retired engineer*

Triadelphia
McCullough, John Phillip *management consultant, educator*

Vienna
Hamm, David B. *dean*
Terry, Ralph Bruce *education educator*

Weirton
Diniaco, Gus G. *retired real estate appraiser*
Fahey, William Thomas, II, *lawyer*

Wellsburg
Turner, Timothy Thomas *music educator, musician*

West Liberty
Forrester, James Ronald *political science professor*

Weston
Billeter, Robert James *newspaper publisher*
Oldaker, Bradley Russell *lawyer*

Wheeling
Bailey, John P. *lawyer*
Campbell, Clyde Del *academic administrator*
Gardill, James Clark *lawyer*
Good, Laurance Frederic *hospital administrator*
Gracey, Robert William *financial advisor, minister*
Heceta, Estherbelle Aguilar *anesthesiologist*
Hill, Barry Morton *lawyer*
Hofreuter, Donald H. *health facility administrator*
Hogan, Susan Cox *association executive*
Hooker, William *architectural firm executive*
Johnston, Thomas E. *prosecutor*
Phillis, Marilyn Hughey *artist*
Recht, Arthur *former state supreme court justice*
Thurston, Bonnie Bowman *religious educator, minister, poet*
Urval, Krishna Raj *health facility administrator, educator*
White, Lawrence Gilbert *state legislator, insurance company executive*

White Sulphur Springs
Kleisner, Ted. J. *hotel executive*

Williamson
Thornsbury, Michael *judge*

WISCONSIN

Altoona
James, Henry Thomas *former foundation executive, educator*

Appleton
Alger, Daniel Richard *economist*
Anderson, Ronald Gordon *insurance company executive*
Barlow, F(rank) John *mechanical contracting company executive*
Boldt, Oscar Charles *construction company executive*
Boren, Clark Henry, Jr., *general and vascular surgeon*
Chaney, William Albert *historian, educator*
Chudacoff, Bruce Michael *lawyer*
Doeringer, Franklin M. *historian, educator*
Drescher, Kathleen Ebben *lawyer*
Drescher, Park Morris *lawyer*
Eno, Woodrow E. *lawyer*
Froehlich, Harold Vernon *judge, former congressman*
Gilbert, John Oren *insurance company executive*
Goldgar, Bertrand Alvin *literary historian, educator*
Grayson, David S. *paper company executive*
Hasselbacher, Darlene M. *human resources executive*
Hinkens, Kay L. *social services association executive*
Lokensgard, Jerrold Paul *chemist, educator, organic chemist*
Lorge, Robert Gerald Augustine *lawyer, real estate broker*
Luther, Thomas William *retired dermatologist*
McManus, John Francis *association executive, writer*
Meidl, Kevin *secondary school educator*
Myers, Rex Charles *history educator, retired college dean*
Oppmann, Andrew James *newspaper editor*
Petinga, Charles Michael *transportation executive*
Rudolph, Carl J. *insurance company executive*
Spiegelberg, Harry Lester *retired paper products company executive*
Stellmacher, Jon Michael *corporate financial executive*
Underhill, Robert Alan *consumer products company executive*

Arcadia
Wanek, Todd *retail executive*

Argyle
Daley, Ron (Ronald Eugene Daley) *playwright, poet, director, producer*

Ashland
Small, Michele Geslin *English studies and modern languages educator*
Smith, Jane Schneberger *retired city administrator*

Balsam Lake
Mattson, Carol Linnette *social services administrator*

Barron
Kurschner, David L. *realtor, small business owner*

Bayside
Kaufman, Harvey Isidore *neuropsychology consultant*

Beaver Dam
Bleifuss, Karen K *technologist, educator*
Butterbrodt, John Ervin *real estate executive*

Belgium
Sullivan, Patricia W. (Terry Sullivan) *real estate trainer*

Beloit
Burris, John Edward *academic administrator, biologist, educator*
Davis, Harry Rex *political science educator*
Green, Harold Daniel *dentist*
Green, William *archaeologist*
Hendricks, Kenneth *wholesale distribution executive*
Kreider, Leonard Emil *economics professor*
Melvin, Charles Alfred, III, *superintendent of schools*
Story, Kendra *wholesale distribution executive*
Wheeler, Karla *education educator*

Black Earth
Klug, Scott Leo *former congressman*

Bowler
Bartholomaus, Brett William *small business owner*
Maas, Duane Harris *distilling company executive*

Brookfield
Bader, Ronald L. *advertising executive*
Bauer, Chris Michael *banker*
Curfman, Floyd Edwin *retired engineering educator*
Dillon, Donald F. *data processing executive*
Fibich, Howard Raymond *retired newspaper editor*
Hardman, Harold Francis *pharmacology educator*
Jensen, Kenneth R. *data processing executive*
Muma, Leslie M. *data processing executive*
Nickerson, Greg *public relations executive*
Nickolett, Chip *information technology executive, consultant*
Saam, Robert Harry *human resources specialist, consultant*
Schmitz, John J. *writer, educator*
Thomas, John *mechanical engineer*
Vitek, Richard Kenneth *retired scientific instrument company executive*
Welnetz, David Charles *human resources executive*
Zander, Gaillienne Glashow *psychologist*

Burlington
Oestmann, Mary Jane *retired senior radiation specialist*
Roeschen, Marlene Y. *retired elementary school educator*

Cameron
Joosten, Michael John *music educator*

Cascade
Baumann, Carol Edler *retired political scientist*

Casco
Richards, Steven George *lawyer*

Cedarburg
Hazelwood, John A. *lawyer*
Schaefer, Gordon Emory *food products executive*

Chippewa Falls
Schmider, Mary Ellen Heian *American studies educator, academic administrator*

Clintonville
Simpson, Vinson Raleigh *manufacturing executive, director*

Columbus
Brinkman, Michael Owen *health care consultant, educator*

Cottage Grove
Baird, Robert Dahlen *retired theology studies educator*
Lund, Daryl Bert *food science educator*
Zingaro, John Charles *minister*

Crivitz
Gerhart, Lorraine Pfeiffer *reading specialist, educator*

Cross Plains
Atterbury, Lee Richard *lawyer*

Darien
Miller, Malcolm Henry *manufacturing sales executive, real estate developer*

De Forest
O'Neil, J(ames) Peter *computer software designer, educator*

De Pere
Lasee, Alan J. *state legislator*
Manion, Thomas A. *chancellor*

Deerfield
Pappas, David Christopher *lawyer*
Shakespeare, Frank *ambassador*

Delafield
Gulgowski, Paul William *German language, social science, and history educator*
Hausman, C. Michael *lawyer, judge*
Kurth, Ronald James *university president, retired naval officer*
McClure, Thomas James *lawyer*
Walters, Ronald Ogden *mortgage banker*

Delavan
Lepke, Charma Davies *musician, educator*

Dodgeville
Boyer, Dennis Lee *lawyer, policy analyst, writer*
Dentinger, Ronald Lee *comedian, speaker, freelance writer*
Eisenberg, Lee B. *communications executive, author*

Drummond
Kingdon, Henry Shannon *retired internist, biochemist, science administrator*

Dunbar
Habing, Brett William *music educator*

Eagle River
Agre, James Courtland *physical medicine and rehabilitation*
Kulzick, Ken Stafford *retired lawyer, travel writer*

Eau Claire
Biegel, Eileen Mae *retired hospital executive*
Brill, Donald Maxim *educator, writer, researcher*
Brummer, James J. *adult education educator, writer*
Clark, Judy *newscaster*
Cohen, Maryjo R. *manufacturing executive*
Cohen, Melvin Samuel *manufacturing executive*
Cox, Christopher *librarian*
Davidson, John Kenneth, Sr., *sociologist, educator, researcher, writer, consultant*
Dick, Raymond Dale *psychology educator*
Dusk, Brooke *meteorologist*
Frank, John LeRoy
Helland, Mark Duane *small business owner*
Hugo, Miriam Jeanne *counseling psychologist, educator*
Klopfenstein-Fletcher, Kristine Sue *music educator, librarian, bassoonist*
Kozbial, Richard James *retired elementary education educator*
Kreibich, Robin G. *state legislator*
Larson, Brian Foix *architect*
Leary, Robin Janell *executive secretary, municipal official*
Mash, Donald J. *college president*
McEllistrem, Marcus T. *chemistry professor, semiconductor materials researcher*
Menard, John R., Jr., *home improvement retail executive*
Pace, Joel Frederic *language educator, researcher*
Patterson, Donald Lee *music educator*
Rasmussen, Earl R *lumber company and home improvement retail executive*
Richards, Jerry Lee *academic administrator, religious educator*
Rupnor, Jennifer *journalist*
Rusch, Gerald Allen *financial representative*
Tiefel, Virginia May *librarian*
Tuckner, Michelle *newscaster*
Weil, D(onald) Wallace *business administration educator*
Whitfield, Scott Burwick *physics educator*
Yasuda, Nobuyoshi *music educator*

Elkhart Lake
Schmidt, Lewis A. *retired music educator*

Elkhorn
Dunn, Walter Scott, Jr., *writer, former museum director, consultant*
Eberhardt, Daniel Hugo *lawyer*
Herr, Richard Joseph *sculptor, educator*
Reinke, Doris Marie *retired elementary school educator*
Sostarich, Mark Edward *lawyer*

Evansville
Decker, John Robert *lawyer*

Fall River
Barker, David Matthew *music educator*

Fennimore
Croft, Candace Ann *psychology educator, academic administrator*

Ferryville
Tedeschi, John Alfred *historian, librarian*

Fish Creek
Zvara, Christine C. *middle school education educator*

Fond Du Lac
Ingle, Sud Ranganath *management consultant*
Lambert, Eugene Kent *oncologist, hematologist*
Treffert, Darold Allen *psychiatrist, author, hospital director*

Fort Atkinson
Jones, Alan Porter, Jr., *food manufacturing executive*
Knox, Brian Victor *newspaper publisher, editor*
Knox, William David *publishing company executive*
Lorman, Barbara K. *former state senator*
Meyer, Eugene Carlton *retired editor*
Schumacher, Mabel G. *director, consultant*

Franklin
Roark, Barbara Ann *librarian*

Freedom
Moscinski, David Joseph *educational administrator, school psychologist*

Genoa
Parkyn, John Duwane *nuclear engineer*

Germantown
Dohmen, John F. *pharmaceutical executive*
Ehlinger, Ralph Jerome *lawyer*
Hargan, Charles James *retired lithographer, village official*

Glendale
Bosomworth, Paul A, *small business owner, ceramics engineer*
Foran, David John *public relations consultant*
Kadel, Lee A. *computer engineer*
Schenker, Eric *university dean, economist*

Grafton
Duback, Sally Wood *artist, educator*

Green Bay
Balsley, Robert Lown *musician, writer*
Banks, Robert J. *bishop*
Bender, Brian *consumer products executive*
Burnett, Ralph George *lawyer*
Conley, William Cleland *statistician, educator*
Daley, Arthur James *retired magazine publisher*
Duncan, Sam K. *retail executive*
Elwell, Mark W. *writer*
Eugster, Jack Wilson *retail executive*
Favre, Brett Lorenzo *professional football player*
Ferguson, Larry P. *food products executive*
Gannon, Thomas A. *trucking executive*
Geisendorfer, James Vernon *religious writer, researcher*
Green, Ahman *professional football player*
Hardy, Deborah Lewis *dean, educator, dental hygienist*
Harlan, Robert Ernest *professional football team executive*
Kelso, Carol *state legislator*
Kraft, Michael Eugene *political science educator*
Kress, William F. *manufacturing executive*
Kuehne, Carl W. *food products executive*
Liddy, Brian *food products executive*
Liegel, Craig A. *meat packing company executive*
Lofgren, Christopher B. *trucking executive*
Lynch, Matthew J. *retail executive*
Marsh, Miles L. *paper company executive*
McIntosh, Elaine Virginia *nutrition educator*
Nickerson, Hardy Otto *professional football player*
Panchalavarapu, Poornachandra Rao *industrial engineer, consultant*
Perkins, Mark L. *university chancellor*
Pukel, Clifford Stuart *physician*
Shepard, W. Bruce *academic administrator*
Sherman, Michael Francis *professional football coach*
Weidner, Edward William *university chancellor, political scientist*
Weyers, Larry Lee *energy executive*

Green Lake
Mitchell, Tawnia Juanita *elementary school educator, music educator*

Greendale
Kaiser, Ann Christine *magazine editor*
Kuhn, Roseann *sports association administrator*
Pohl, Kathleen Sharon *editor*
Reiman, Roy J. *publishing executive*
Vinent-Cantoral, Aida R. *mediator*

Greenfield
Helland, Sherman M. *writer*
McKillip, Patricia Claire *operatic soloist*

Greenville
Zhao, Rongguo *chemist*

Hales Corners
Case, Karen Ann *lawyer*
Kuwayama, S. Paul *physician, immunologist, allergist*
McNally, Vincent Joseph *historian, educator*

Hartford
Babbitt, Donald Patrick *radiologist*
Fowler, John *printing company executive*
Vandermeuse, David C. *music educator*

Hartland
Peterson, Louis Robert *retired consumer products company executive*
Stamsta, Jean F. *artist*

Hayward
Yakes, Penny Anne *advocate, writer*

Hollandale
Colescott, Warrington Wickham *artist, printmaker, educator*

Holmen
Meyer, Karl William *retired university president*

Horicon
Gasner, Donn Allan *music educator*

Howards Grove
Houston, Angela Marie *director*

Hudson
Dahle, Johannes Upton *retired academic administrator*
Johnson, James Robert *ceramic engineer, educator*

Iola
Krause, Chester Lee *publishing executive*
Mishler, Clifford Leslie *publisher*
Rosenberger, Carolyn Ann *art educator*

Ixonia
Peebles, Allene Kay *manufactured housing company executive*

Janesville
Axtell, Roger E. *writer, retired marketing professional*
Blazkowski, Phillip *community development and planning official*
Detert-Moriarty, Judith Anne *graphic designer, educator, volunteer*
Fitzgerald, James Francis *cable television executive*
Gianitsos, Anestis Nicholas *surgeon*
Roth, Sarah Eve *occupational safety professional*
Steil, George Kenneth, Sr., *lawyer*
Sturm, Christopher Douglas *neurosurgeon*

Jefferson
Lochow, H. John *computer company executive*
Morgan, Gaylin F. *public relations consultant*
Myers, Gary *public relations executive*

Johnson Creek
Quest, Kristina Kay *art educator, small business owner*

Juneau
Carpenter, David Erwin *county official, land use planner*

Kenosha
Adler, Seymour Jack *social services administrator*
Beyer, Sylvia *social psychologist*
Campbell, F(enton) Gregory *college administrator, historian*
Cyr, Arthur I. *political science and economics educator*
Emma, Edward C. *apparel executive*
Helman, Iris Barca *elementary school educator, consultant*
Higgins, John Patrick *lawyer, mediator, educator, lobbyist*
Iaquinta, Leonard Phillip *former university official, not-for-profit fundraiser*
Infusino, Achille Francis *financial and administrative support executive*
Kolb, Vera M. *chemist, educator*
Kummings, Donald Dale *English educator*
Leeds-Hurwitz, Wendy *communications educator*
Li, Zhaohui *science educator*
Manion, Michael T. *finance educator*
Potente, Eugene, Jr., *interior designer*

Kohler
Black, Natalie A. *lawyer*
Cheney, Jeffrey Paul *manufacturing executive*
Kohler, Herbert Vollrath, Jr., *diversified manufacturing company executive*
Kohler, Laura E. *human resources executive*
Sheedy, Kathleen Ann *lawyer*
Wells, Richard A. *manufacturing executive*

La Crosse
Davy, Michael Francis *civil engineer, consultant*
Drazkowski, Mark *food products executive*
Gelatt, Charles Daniel *manufacturing executive*
Grill, Joyce L. *musician, educator, composer*
Hitch, Elizabeth *academic administrator*
Hogan, Kerry F. *design educator*
Judson, John Irving *retired English educator, poet, writer, editor*
Klos, Jerome John *lawyer, director*
Lentz, Kirby Warren *academic administrator*
Maresh, Richard Joseph *mathematics professor*
Matchett, Andrew James *mathematics professor*
Medland, William James *university president*
Morehouse, Richard Edward *psychology educator*
Newcomer, Kermit Lee *retired internist, kidney specialist*
Nix, Edmund Alfred *lawyer*
Rooney, Brenda Louise *epidemiologist, researcher*
Rozelle, Lee Theodore *physical chemist, researcher*
Rude, Brian David *utilities company executive*
Sleik, Thomas Scott *lawyer*
Smith, Martin Jay *physician, biomedical research scientist*
Thomas-Williams, Pamela Rae *publishing executive, writer*
Webster, Stephen Burtis *dermatologist, educator*

Lake Geneva
Braden, Berwyn Bartow *lawyer*
Petersen, Edward Schmidt *retired physician*
Weed, Edward Reilly *marketing executive*

Lake Mills
Lazaris, Pamela Adriane *community planning and development consultant*

Laona
Sturzl, Alice A. *school library administrator*

Lodi
Smith, Michael W. *lawyer*

Madison
Albanese, Mark Alan *health sciences educator*
Albert, Daniel Myron *ophthalmologist, educator*
Aldag, Ramon John *management and organization educator*
Anderson, David R. *insurance company executive*
Anderson, Louis Wilmer, Jr., *physicist, researcher*
Andreano, Ralph Louis *economist, educator*
Ardissone, Mary Jean *art director, writer*
Askey, Richard Allen *mathematician, educator*
Bablitch, William A. *state supreme court justice*
Bajad Sunil, Uttamrao *pharmacologist, researcher*
Balantekin, Akif Baha *physicist, educator*
Baldwin, Gordon Brewster *law educator, lawyer*
Baldwin, Janice Murphy *lawyer*
Baldwin, Robert Edward *economics professor*
Banfield, Jillian *mineralogist, geomicrobiologist, educator*
Barger, Vernon Duane *physicist, educator*
Barish, Lawrence Stephen *nonpartisan legislative staff administrator*
Barnhill, Charles Joseph, Jr., *lawyer*
Barnick, Helen *retired judicial clerk*
Barr, James, III, *telecommunications company executive*
Bartell, Angela Gina Baldi *judge*
Bartell, Jeffrey Bruce *lawyer*
Bartley, Linda L. *musician, music educator*
Bauman, Susan Joan Mayer *mayor, lawyer*
Beachley, Norman Henry *mechanical engineer, educator*
Beck, Anatole *mathematician, educator*
Becker, David *artist, educator*
Bennett, Kenneth Alan *retired biological anthropologist*
Bentley, Charles Raymond *geophysics educator*
Berceau, Terese L. *state representative*
Berg, William James *French language educator, writer, translator*
Berghahn, Klaus Leo *German and Jewish studies educator*
Berthouex, Paul Mac *civil and environmental engineer, educator*
Berven, Norman Lee *counselor, psychologist, educator*
Beyer-Mears, Annette *physiologist*
Bird, Robert Byron *chemical engineering educator, author*
Bishop, Carolyn Benkert *public relations counselor*
Bloch, Peter Conrad *economist, educator*
Bochert, Linda H. *lawyer*
Bogue, Allan George *history educator*
Boller, Matthew Hubly *lawyer*
Borisy, Gary G. *molecular biology educator*
Botez, Dan *physicist*
Boutwell, Roswell Knight *oncology educator*
Boyle, William Charles *civil engineering educator*
Braden, Betty Jane *legal association administrator*
Bradley, Ann Walsh *state supreme court justice*
Brandt, Deborah *English educator*
Brann, Edward R(ommel) *editor*
Brembeck, Winston Lamont *retired speech communication educator*
Bremer, Howard Walter *lawyer, consultant*
Brennan, Patricia Flatley *nursing educator, systems engineer, educator*
Brennan, Robert Walter *association executive*
Brewster, Francis Anthony *lawyer*
Brock, Thomas Dale *microbiology educator*
Brock, William Allen, III, *economist, educator*
Brooks, Benjamin Rix *neurologist, educator*
Buchholz, Ronald Lewis *architect*
Bugge, Lawrence John *lawyer, educator*
Bühnemann, Gudrun *humanities educator*
Bunge, Charles Albert *library science educator*
Burgess, James Edward *newspaper publisher, executive*
Burgess, Richard Ray *oncology educator, molecular biology researcher, biotechnology consultant*
Burkholder, Wendell Eugene *retired entomology educator, researcher*
Burmaster, Elizabeth *school system administrator*
Burns, Elizabeth Murphy *media executive*
Burris, Robert Harza *biochemist, educator*
Busby, Edward Oliver *retired dean*
Buss, Daryl Dean *veterinarian, dean*
Butler, Louis Bennett, Jr., *state supreme court justice*
Carbon, Max William *nuclear engineering educator*
Cassinelli, Joseph Patrick *astronomy educator*
Chandler, Richard Gates *lawyer*
Chapman, Loren J. *psychology educator*
Charo, Robin Alta *law educator*
Christensen, Marguerite Alice *librarian*
Christensen, Nikolas Ivan *geophysicist, educator*
Chu, Hsien Ming *investment company executive*
Churchwell, Edward Bruce *astronomer, educator*
Ciplijauskaite, Birute *humanities educator*
Clay, Clarence Samuel *acoustical oceanographer*
Cleland, W(illiam) Wallace *biochemistry educator*
Code, Arthur Dodd *astrophysics educator*
Cohen, Bernard Cecil *political scientist, educator*
Cohen, Charles Lloyd *history and religious studies educator*
Cohen, Marcus *allergist, immunologist*
Connors, Kenneth Antonio *retired chemistry educator*
Cooper, Peggy (Mary Margaret) *artist, educator, poet, composer, choreographer*
Coppersmith, Susan Nan *physicist*
Crabb, Barbara Brandriff *federal judge*
Craddock, Campbell (John Campbell Craddock) *geologist, educator*
Cripps, Derek J. *dermatologist, educator*
Crocker, Stephen L. *federal magistrate judge*
Cronon, William *history educator*
Crooks, N(eil) Patrick *state supreme court justice*
Culbertson, Frances Mitchell *psychology educator*
Curtiss, Charles Francis *chemist, educator*
Darling, Alberta Statkus *state legislator, marketing executive, former art museum executive*
Davis, Erroll Brown, Jr., *utilities executive*
Davis, Kenneth Boone, Jr., *dean, law educator*
Deer, Ada E. *former federal agency official, social worker, educator*
De Foliart, Gene Ray *retired entomologist, researcher, educator*
De Main, John *orchestra musical director*

Blain, Peter Charles *lawyer*
Blasinski, Clare Marie *librarian*
Blau, Richard Miles (Dick Blau) *performing arts educator, photographer, film director*
Bleustein, Jeffrey L. *automotive executive*
Boese, Gil Karyle *cultural organization executive*
Bolger, T(homas) Michael *lawyer*
Bremer, John M. *lawyer*
Brideau, Leo Paul *healthcare executive*
Burch, Thaddeus Joseph, Jr., *physics educator, clergyman*
Busch, John Arthur *lawyer*
Buss, Daniel Frank *environmental scientist*
Calise, William Joseph, Jr., *lawyer*
Cannon, David Joseph *lawyer*
Carballo, Fernando Anthony *gastroenterologist, hepatologist*
Carter, Valerie *food products executive*
Casey, John Alexander *lawyer*
Casper, Richard Henry *lawyer*
Cassell, Samuel James *professional basketball player*
Chan, Carlyle Hung-lun *psychiatrist, educator*
Chandler, Edward William *communication systems engineer, electrical engineer, electrical engineering educator*
Cheatham, Wallace McClain *music educator*
Chenevich, William L. *bank executive*
Chokey, James A. *lawyer*
Christiansen, Keith Allan *lawyer*
Clark, James Richard *lawyer*
Cohen, Steven Howard *allergist, immunologist, educator*
Colbert, Virgis W. *food products executive*
Colbert, Virgis William *brewery company executive*
Connelly, Mark *writer, educator*
Conner, David Lee *secondary educator*
Connolly, Gerald Edward *lawyer*
Cooper, Richard Alan *hematologist, health policy analyst, dean*
Counsell, Paul S. *former advertising executive, counselor*
Cowley, Allen Wilson, Jr., *physiologist*
Crocker, Ray Dean *musician, musical director*
Curtain, Helena Hambuch *foreign language specialist*
Daily, Frank J(erome) *lawyer*
Dallman, Robert Edward *lawyer*
Daniels-Carter, Valerie *food franchise executive*
Davidson, Rick *staffing company executive*
Davies Cordova, Sarah P. *language educator*
Davis, Don H., Jr., *multi-industry high-technology company executive*
Davis, Susan F. *human resources specialist*
Dawson, Kim *reporter*
Delfs, Andreas *conductor, musical director*
De Lia, Julian Emilio *obstetrician, educator, gynecologist*
Demerdash, Nabeel Aly Omar *electrical engineer*
Donovan, Michael Joseph *lawyer*
Downey, John Wilham *composer, pianist, conductor, educator*
Duback, Steven Rahr *lawyer*
Dumas, Tyrone Pierre *architect, consultant*
Dunn, Michael J. *dean*
Elliot, Tammy *newscaster*
Ericson, James Donald *retired lawyer*
Esterly, Nancy Burton *physician*
Evans, Terence Thomas *federal judge*
Farris, Trueman Earl, Jr., *retired newspaper editor*
Feinsilver, Donald Lee *psychiatry educator*
Fink, Jordan Norman *physician, educator*
Florsheim, Richard Steven *lawyer*
Fluharty, George Mark *speech pathology/audiology services professional*
Foldy, Seth Leonard *physician*
Foster, Richard *journalist*
Fournelle, Raymond Albert *engineering educator*
Fradkin, Hillel Gideon *foundation official, educator*
Frank, Dennis *psychotherapist, educator*
Frank, Nancy *architecture educator*
Frauen, Kurt Herman *lawyer*
Frautschi, Timothy Clark *lawyer*
Friedman, James Dennis *lawyer*
Fromstein, Mitchell S. *retired office services company executive*
Gaggioli, Richard Arnold *mechanical engineering educator*
Gagliani, William Dennis *librarian*
Gaines, Irving David *lawyer*
Galanis, John William *lawyer*
Gallagher, Richard Sidney *lawyer*
Gallop, Jane (Jane Anne Gallop) *women's studies educator, writer*
Garbaciak-Bobber, Joyce Katherine *news anchor*
Garcia, Astrid J. *newspaper executive*
Gefke, Henry Jerome *lawyer*
Gemignani, Joseph Adolph *lawyer*
Geske, Janine Patricia *law educator, former state supreme court justice*
Ghiardi, James Domenic *lawyer, educator*
Giese, Heiner *lawyer, real estate investor*
Gonnering, Russell Stephen *ophthalmic plastic surgeon*
Goodkind, Conrad George *lawyer*
Goodstein, Aaron E. *federal magistrate judge*
Graber, Richard William *lawyer, political organization worker*
Grade, Jeffery T. *manufacturing executive*
Graef, Luther William *civil engineer*
Greenstreet, Robert Charles *architect, educator*
Grenig, Jay Edward *law educator*
Griffith, Owen Wendell *biochemistry educator*
Haberman, F. William *lawyer*
Habush, Robert Lee *lawyer*
Hanlon, Donald *architecture educator*
Hansen, John Herbert *university administrator, accountant*
Harrington, John Timothy *retired lawyer*
Harris, Christine *dance company executive*
Harris, Gerald Jay *ophthalmologist, educator*
Harvieux, Anne Marie *psychotherapist*
Hase, David John *lawyer*
Hatch, Michael Ward *lawyer*
Hatton, Janie R. Hill *principal*
Haworth, Daniel Thomas *chemistry professor*
Hegerty, Nannette H. *police chief*
Heinen, James Albin *electrical engineering educator*
Heinrichs, William C. *music educator, composer*
Hendee, William Richard *medical physics educator, university official, radiologist*
Hernandez, Jose *professional baseball player*
Hill, James Warren *university dean*
Hinkley, Gerry *newspaper editor*
Hirsch, June Schaut *chaplain*
Hoefle, Paul Ryan *lawyer*
Hoffman, Nathaniel A. *lawyer*
Hoffman, Robert Butler *ministry industry executive*
Holz, Harry George *lawyer*
Hosenpud, Jeffrey *cardiovascular physician*
Howe, G. Edwin *healthcare executive*
Hubbard, Nancy *architecture educator*
Hudson, Katherine Mary *manufacturing executive*
Hueneke, Terry A. *temporary services company executive*
Huff, Marsha Elkins *lawyer*
Hughes, T. Lee *newspaper editor*
Hunter, Victor Lee *marketing executive, consultant*
Hur, Su-Ryong *physician, anesthesiologist*
Huston, Kathleen Marie *library administrator*
Iding, Allan Earl *lawyer*
Ignacio, Reinere John Dy *research scientist*
Jacobs, Bruce E. *metal products executive*
Jallings, Jessica *reporter, newscaster*
Janda, Lubomir Miro *organic chemist*
Jenkins, Clarence William, Jr., *academic administrator*
Joerres, Jeffrey A. *staffing company executive*
Johannes, Kay L. *insurance company executive*
Johnson, James N. *lawyer*
Joseph, Jules K. *retired public relations executive*
Jost, Lawrence John *lawyer*
Joyce, Michael Stewart *foundation executive, political science educator*
Kaiser, Martin *newspaper editor*
Kampine, John P. *anesthesiology and physiology educator*
Karkheck, John Peter *physics educator, researcher*
Karst, Darren W. *food products executive*
Kasten, G. Frederick, Jr., *investment company executive*
Kelley, Lyle Ardell *insurance company executive*
Kendall, Leon Thomas *finance and real estate educator, retired insurance company executive*
Kerr, Dorothy Marie Burmeister *marketing executive, consultant*
Kessler, Joan F. *lawyer*
Keyes, James Henry *manufacturing executive*
King, Frederic *health services management executive, educator*
Kircher, John Joseph *law educator*
Klappa, Gale E. *corporate financial executive*
Kleefisch, Rebecca *reporter*
Knight, George B. *lawyer*
Kochar, Mahendr Singh *physician, educator, administrator, scientist, writer, consultant*
Koss, John Charles *consumer electronics products manufacturing company executive*
Kraut, Joanne Lenora *computer programmer, analyst*
Kringel, Jerome Howard *lawyer*
Kritzer, Paul Eric *media executive, communications lawyer*
Krueger, Raymond Robert *lawyer*
Kubale, Bernard Stephen *lawyer*
Kurtz, Harvey A. *lawyer*
LaBudde, Roy Christian *lawyer*
Landis, Fred *mechanical engineering educator*
Lange, Marilyn *social worker*
Larson, David Lee *surgeon*
Laughlin, Steven L. *advertising executive*
Lea, Filomena *English language educator, writer*
Leonard, Richard Hart *journalist, educator*
Leverett, Allen L. *energy executive*
Levine, Herbert *lawyer*
Levit, William Harold, Jr., *lawyer*
Lione, Gail Ann *lawyer*
Lobb, William K. *dean, dental educator*
Loehr, Stephanie Schmahl *social worker*
Long, Gary *former insurance company executive*
Lopes, Davey *former professional baseball manager*
Lueders, Wayne Richard *lawyer*
Lynch, Michael *lawyer, staffing company executive*
MacGregor, David Lee *lawyer*
Mancuso, Joseph Edward *medical psychotherapist*
Manning, Kenneth Paul *technologies company executive*
Marcus, Stephen Howard *hospitality and entertainment company executive*
Mariano, Robert A. *retail executive*
Marringa, Jacques Louis *manufacturing executive*
Marten, James Alan *historian, educator*
Martin, Quinn William *lawyer*
Maynard, John Ralph *lawyer*
McCann, Margaret Ann *sister, educator*
McGaffey, Jere D. *retired lawyer*
McGarity, Margaret Dee *federal judge*
McSweeney, Maurice J. (Marc McSweeney) *lawyer*
Meldman, Robert Edward *lawyer*
Melin, Robert Arthur *lawyer*
Michelstetter, Stanley Hubert *lawyer*
Miller, Edward Carl William *physician*
Moffie, H. Steven *psychiatrist*
Montgomery, Robert Renwick *medical association administrator, educator*
Murphy, Judith Chisholm *trust company executive*
Mykleby, Kathy *newscaster, reporter*
Namdari, Bahram *surgeon*
O'Brien, Kathleen Ann *academic administrator*
Oldham, Keith T. *surgeon*
Olinger, Gordon Nordell *surgeon*
O'Neill, James Martin *venture capitalist*
O'Shaughnessy, James Patrick *lawyer*
Ovitsky, Steven Alan *musician, symphony orchestra executive*
Pagel, Paul Stanley *anesthesiologist*
Parker, Charles Walter, Jr., *consultant, retired equipment company executive*
Penz, Carla Maria *biologist, researcher*
Perlman, Richard Wilfred *economist, educator*
Phillips, Thomas John *lawyer*
Pindyck, Bruce Eben *lawyer, corporate executive*
Pink, Michael *performing company executive*
Platt, Jeb Buchanan *health facility administrator*
Pollen, Raymond James *lawyer*
Port, Steven Charles *cardiologist, educator*
Porter, Terry *professional basketball coach*
Potter, Rosemary *state legislator*
Prucha, Francis Paul *historian, priest*
Quadracci, Thomas A. *printing company executive*
Quereshi, Mohammed Younus *psychology educator, consultant*
Rader, I. Andrew *foundation administrator*
Randall, William Seymour *leasing company executive*
Redlin, Bruce Michael *financial consultant*
Reynolds, Barbara E. *mathematics professor*
Rhead, William James *biochemical geneticist*
Rheams, Annie Elizabeth *education educator*
Rhoten, Juliana Theresa *retired principal*
Richman, Stephen Erik *lawyer*
Rintelman, Donald Brian *lawyer*
Roell, Stephen A. *manufacturing executive*
Rollins, Timothy Christopher *editor, policy analyst*
Ryan, Patrick Michael *lawyer*
Saldin, Dilano Kerzaman *physicist, educator*
Salustro, Larry J. *lawyer*
Samson, Allen Lawrence *investor, bank executive*
Samson, Richard Max *theater director, investment company executive*
Sankovitz, James Leo *retired development director, lobbyist*
Santelle, James Lewis *prosecutor*
Sayles, Ronald Lyle *computer executive*
Schaefer, Jame *religious studies educator*
Schneider, Mary Lea *college administrator*
Schneider, Thomas Paul *non-profit agency administrator*
Schnoll, Howard Manuel *financial consultant, investment company executive*
Schnur, Robert Arnold *lawyer*
Schroeder, John H. *university chancellor*
Schultz, Richard Otto *ophthalmologist, educator*
Schumann, Gail L. *plant pathologist, educator*
Scrivner, Thomas William *lawyer*
Selig-Prieb, Wendy *sports team executive*
Setright, Mildred Alberta *educator*
Severson, Sally *meteorologist*
Shapiro, James Edward *judge*
Shapiro, Robyn Sue *lawyer, educator*
Shetty, Kaup Rajmohan *endocrinologist, educator*
Shiely, John Stephen *manufacturing executive, lawyer*
Shriner, Thomas L., Jr., *lawyer*
Siegel, Kristi Ellen *English educator*
Siegel, Robert Harold *English literature educator, writer*
Simoneau, Daniel Robert *accountant, watercolorist, educator, application developer*
Smith, David Bruce *lawyer*
Sosnovsky, George *chemist, educator*
Spore, Keith Kent *newspaper executive*
Stadtmueller, Joseph Peter *federal judge*
Stafford, Lori *reporter*
Steinmiller, John F. *professional basketball team executive*
Sterner, Frank Maurice *industrial executive*
Stewart, Alex *finance educator*
Stubbe, Ray William *minister, writer*
Sturm, William Charles *lawyer*
Sullivan, Edward *periodical editor*
Surridge, Stephen Zehring *lawyer, writer*
Swanson, Roy Arthur *classicist, educator*
Tector, Alfred J. *cardiothoracic surgeon*
Telford, Gordon Laing *surgeon, educator*
Temmer, James Donald *museum director*
Teply, Mark Lawrence *mathematics professor*
Terschan, Frank Robert *lawyer*
Theis, Peter George *retired classics educator*
Theoharis, Athan George *history educator*
Thrall, Arthur Alvin *artist, educator*
Titley, Robert L. *lawyer*
Towne, Jonathan Baker *vascular surgeon*
Trebon, Lawrence Alan *lawyer*
Trecek, Timothy Scott *lawyer*
Trytek, David Douglas *insurance company executive*
Uecker, Bob *actor, radio announcer, former baseball player, television personality*
Valance, Marsha Jeanne *library director, story teller*
Van Grunsven, Paul Robert *lawyer*
van Handel, Michael J. *staffing company executive*
Van Horn, Keith *professional basketball player*
Viets, Hermann *college president, consultant*
Wackym, Phillip Ashley *surgeon, researcher, otolaryngologist*
Waldbaum, Jane Cohn *art history educator*
Waller, Mary Bellis *psychotherapist, education educator, consultant*
Walmer, Edwin Fitch *lawyer*
Warren, Richard M. *experimental psychologist, educator*
Weakland, Rembert G. *retired archbishop*
Webb, Sheila Menzies *art educator*
Weiner, Wendy L. *elementary school educator, writer*
Weisner, David *illustrator*
White-Winters, Jill Mary *nursing educator*
Widera, Georg Ernst Otto *mechanical engineering educator, consultant*
Wigdale, James B. *bank executive*
Wild, Robert Anthony *university president*
Wiley, Edwin Packard *retired lawyer*
Will, Trevor Jonathan *lawyer*
Williams, Clay Rule *lawyer*
Winsten, Saul Nathan *lawyer*
Wolfe, Christopher *political science educator*
Yancey, Kim Bruce *dermatology researcher*
Youker, James Edward *radiologist*
Zeidler, Frank P. *former association administrator, mayor, arbitrator, mediator, fact-finder*
Ziemer, James L. *automotive executive*
Zore, Edward John *financial services executive*

Minocqua
Jaye, David Robert, Jr., *retired health facility administrator*
Lund, John Richard *lawyer, director*

Monona
Brandes, Stuart Dean *historian, educator*

Monroe
Kittelsen, Rodney Olin *lawyer*

Montello
Wissbaum, Donna Cacic *lawyer*

Mosinee
Hartz, Luetta Bertha *legal secretary*

Mount Horeb
Barry, Jonathan B. *chemicals executive, communications executive*

Nashotah
Munday, Robert Stevenson *priest, academic administrator*
Neumann, Mark W. *former congressman, real estate developer*
Vincent, Norman L. *retired insurance company executive*

Neenah
Bergstrom, Dedric Waldemar *retired paper company executive*
Orm, Sally S. *music educator, consultant*

Nekoosa
Ramirez, Mary Catherine *retired secondary school educator*

New Berlin
Winkler, Dolores Eugenia *retired health facility administrator*

New Richmond
Schwan, LeRoy Bernard *artist, retired art educator*

Oak Creek
Giblin, Louis *lawyer*

Oconomowoc
Conrader, Constance Ruth *artist, writer, librarian*
Driscoll, Virgilyn Mae (Schaetzel) *retired art educator, artist, consultant*
Dupies, Donald Albert *retired civil engineer*
Kneiser, Richard John *accountant*
Vespa, Ned Angelo *photographer*

Oconto
Watson-Boone, Rebecca A. *library and information studies researcher, educator*

Onalaska
Pertzsch, Evelyn Maria *civic worker*
Reedy, David H. *music educator, musician*
Waite, Lawrence Wesley *osteopathic physician, educator*

Oregon
Draeger, Norman Arthur *physical chemist, surface scientist*
Uphoff, Charles Maynard *news correspondent, writer*

Oshkosh
Alderson, Jo Bartels *writer, poet*
Balzar, Tammy J. *research scientist*
Barwig, Regis Norbert James *priest*
Cooper, Janelle Lunette *neurologist, educator*
Cunningham, Paris Lynn *systems administrator, consultant*
Drebus, Richard William *pharmaceutical company executive*
Earns, Lane Robert *academic administrator, historian, educator*
Grieb, Kenneth Joseph *historian, educator*
Gruberg, Martin *political science educator*
Hu, Li *art educator*
Kelly, John Martin *lawyer*
Olejniczak, Bernard Charles *education educator*
Poberezny, Tom *federal agency administrator*
Siepmann, James Patrick *research company executive, retired physician*

Osseo
Crowell, Rebecca A. *artist*

Palmyra
Hammiller, Ruth Ellen *school official and psychologist*

Peshtigo
Gard, John *state legislator*

Pewaukee
Carlson, Kathleen *not-for-profit fundraiser, writer, journalist*
Farrow, Margaret Ann *former state official*
Kloehn, Ralph Anthony *plastic surgeon*
Lee, Jack (Jim Sanders Beasley) *broadcast executive*
Long, Robert Eugene *banker*

Phelps
Coccia, Michel Andre *retired lawyer*

Platteville
Markee, David James *university official, education educator*

Pleasant Prairie
Morrone, Frank *electronic manufacturing executive*

Port Washington
Meyer, Raymond George, II, *lawyer*

Racine
Bradley, Paul N. *special education educator*
Campbell, Edward Joseph *retired machinery company executive*
Coates, Glenn Richard *lawyer*
Du Rocher, James Howard *lawyer*
Elliott, Dale Frederick *marketing professional*
Hayward, Tamerin M. *secondary school educator*
Isenberg, Norbert *chemist, educator*
Johnson-Leipold, Helen P. *outdoor recreation company executive*
Klein, Gabriella Sonja *retired communications executive*
Konz, Gerald Keith *retired manufacturing company executive*
Ladwig, Bonnie L. *state legislator*
McCollum, W. Lee *chemical company executive*
Miller, Yolanda *publisher, writer*
Perez, William D. *chemical company executive*
Rosso, Jean-Pierre *electronics executive*
Schoening, Ruth Irene *retired music educator, musician*
Schoone, Adrian Paul *lawyer*
Sikora, Suzanne Marie *dentist*
Smith, Stephen James *lawyer, director*
Stewart, Richard Donald *internist, educator, writer*
Wambold, Richard Lawrence *manufacturing executive*
Wheaton, Douglas B. *lawyer*
Wright, Betty Ren *children's book writer*

Reedsburg
Miotke, David Roy *music educator*

Rhinelander
McEldowney, Todd Richard *lawyer*

Van Brunt-Bartholomew, Marcia Adele *retired social worker*

Rice Lake
Hubler, Mary *state legislator*

Richland Center
Heinen, John Timothy *environmental engineer*

Ripon
Prissel, Barbara Ann *paralegal, law educator*

River Falls
Harsdorf, Sheila Eloise *state legislator, farmer*
Hayden, Paul Allan *speech pathology educator, consultant, researcher*
Hedahl, Gorden Orlin *theatre educator, university dean*
Montgomery, Karen E. *library and information scientist*
Thibodeau, Gary A. *academic administrator*
Zajac, Claire Marie *lawyer*

Rudolph
Heywood, Gail Anne *music educator, musician*

Sauk City
Lins, Debra *bank executive*

Saukville
Gulan, Bonnie Marion *writer, researcher*

Schofield
Gettelman, Robin Claire *media specialist*

Shawano
Lyon, Thomas L. *agricultural organization administrator*
Mutter, John J., Jr., *writer, researcher*
Swetlik, William Philip *orthodontist*
Wilson, Douglas *genetics company executive*

Sheboygan
Fulop, Timothy *academic administrator*
Gore, Donald Ray *orthopedic surgeon*
Strysick, Michael Otto *terrestrial ecologist, physicist, microbiologist*

Sheboygan Falls
Potter, Calvin J. *retired library director*

Shorewood
Lietz, Jeremy Jon *educational administrator, writer*

Soldiers Grove
Quebe, Jerry Lee *retired architect*

Somerset
Gabrick, Robert William *educational consultant, writer*

South Milwaukee
Kitzke, Eugene David *research and development company executive*

Spencer
Herder, Paul O. *secondary school educator*

Spooner
Cosmano, Vincent James *retired music educator*

Stevens Point
Grahn, Lance R. *education educator, historian*
Holland, Patricia Christine *music educator, musician*
Huncharek, Michael Stephen *oncologist*
Shade, Linda Bunnell *university chancellor*
Teeple, Scott D. *conductor, music educator, director*
Walker, Hugh Dyson *educator, deacon*

Stone Lake
Voss, William Charles *retired oil company executive*

Stoughton
Huber, David Lawrence *physicist, researcher*
Wetzel, Volker Knoppke *law educator*

Sturgeon Bay
Greaves, Alison Ash *retired physician*
Van Duyse, Francis Donald (Fritz Van) *publisher*

Sturtevant
Bailey, Michael J. *manufacturing executive*
Lawton, Gregory E. *manufacturing executive*
Marschke, Sean M. *police commander, emergency management director*

Sun Prairie
Berkenstadt, James Allan *lawyer*
Eustice, Francis Joseph *lawyer*
Rollette, Harold Henry *insurance company executive*
Schmidt, Glenn Norbert *special education educator*
Terhune, Karen Marie *mathematician, secondary school educator*

Superior
Feldman, Egal *historian, educator*
Morden, Annette Sonja Knudson *education educator*
Robek, Mary Frances *business education educator*
Rodne, Kjell John *healthcare administrator*
Vance, Mary Lee *academic administrator*

Sussex
Losee, John Frederick, Jr., *manufacturing executive*
Stromberg, Gregory *printing ink company executive*

Thiensville
Roselle, William Charles *librarian*

Union Grove
Stern, Walter Wolf, III, *lawyer*

Walworth
Carlson, Victoria Thilda *merchant banker*

Washburn
Krutsch, Phyllis *academic administrator*
Stewart, John Miller *behavioral scientist, psychobiologist, educator*

Washington Island
Raup, David Malcolm *paleontology educator*
Schweikert, Norman Carl *retired musician*

Waterford
Karraker, Louis Rendleman *retired corporate executive*

Waterloo
Burke, Richard A. *manufacturing executive*

Waukesha
Davis, J. Mac *lawyer, state judge*
Demerath, Julie Ellen *music educator*
Falcone, Frank S. *academic administrator*
Graham, George Andrew, Jr., *psychologist, consultant*
Gustafson, Mardel Emma *secondary school educator, writer*
Hogan, Joseph M. *medical products executive*
Jastroch, Leonard Andrew *lawyer*
Kloss, Raymond *psychiatrist*
Kocharian, Armen *physicist*
Korach, Alice F. *editor, artist*
Larson, Russell George *magazine publisher*
LeBlanc, Julie A. *editor*
Popp, David A. *editor, educator*
Trebon, Thomas *academic administrator*
Wallskog, Joyce Marie *nursing educator, psychologist*

Waupun
Wendt, Thomas *finance executive*

Wausau
Builer, Dorothy Marion *business owner*
Deffner, Roger L. *lawyer, investment counselor, chef*
Drengler, William Allan John *lawyer*
Grischke, Alan Edward *lawyer*
Kammer, Robert Arthur, Jr., *lawyer*
Loftus, Stephen Edward *elementary art educator*
Molinaro, Thomas J. *lawyer*
Moore, Alfred P. *health facility administrator, benefits compensation analyst*
Orr, San Watterson, Jr., *lawyer*
Veninga, James Frank *humanities educator, editor, author*
Wadzinski, Mary Beth *administrative assistant*
Whitney, John Denison *English educator, writer*

Wauwassa
O'Dess, Mary Abigail *lawyer*

Wauwatosa
Franke, Brent Douglas *real estate/insurance executive*
Hollister, Winston Ned *pathologist*

West Allis
Fiorelli, Karen Lynn *registered nurse*

West Bend
Darrow, Russe M. *automotive executive*
Fraedrich, Royal Louis *magazine editor, publisher*
Gehl, William D. *manufacturing executive*
Rodney, Joel Morris *dean, campus executive officer*
VanBrunt-Kramer, Karen *business administration educator*

Weyauwega
Hanneman, Elaine Esther *salesperson*

Whitefish Bay
Hawkins, Brett William *political science educator*
Pustejovsky, Susan F. *mathematics educator*

Whitehall
Nordhagen, Hallie Huerth *nursing home administrator*

Whitewater
Baica, Malvina Florica *mathematician, educator*
Busse, Eileen Elaine *special education educator*
Connor, James Richard *retired foundation administrator*
Gauger, Michele Roberta *photographer, studio administrator, corporate executive*
Greenhill, H. Gaylon *retired academic administrator*
Joseph, Stacey Ann McGraw *music educator, church choir director*
Kolb, Sharon Marie *educator, cognitive disabilities director*
Kolda, Thomas Joseph *non-profit organization executive*
Laurent, Jerome King *economics professor*
Parboteeah, Kaviraj Praveen *finance educator*
Tuinstra, John S. *music educator, consultant*

Williams Bay
Hobbs, Lewis Mankin *astronomer*
Tobin, Dennis Michael *lawyer*

Wisconsin Rapids
Drew, Richard Allen *retired electrical and instrument engineer*
Engelhardt, LeRoy A. *retired paper company executive*
Gottschalk, Guy *agricultural products executive*
Knuteson, Miles Gene *advertising executive*
Olson-Hellerud, Linda Kathryn *elementary school educator*
Parker, Arnold John *minister*

Zenda
Sills, William Henry, III, *investment banker*

WYOMING

Alpine
Cittone, Henry Aron *hotel and restaurant management educator*

Big Horn
Schultz, Harry Pershing *chemistry researcher, retired educator*

Bondurant
Ellwood, Paul Murdock, Jr., *health policy analyst, consultant*

Buffalo
Fehir, Kim Michele *oncologist, hematologist*
Graham, Violet Joyce *writer*
Kirven, Timothy J. *lawyer*
Madden, Cheryl Beth *state legislator*

Casper
Bennion, Scott Desmond *physician*
Combs, W(illiam) Henry, III, *lawyer*
Constantino, Becky *political organization administrator*
Cottam, Keith M. *librarian, educator, administrator*
Davis, Lois Ann *computer specialist, educator*
Donley, Russell Lee, III, *former state legislator*
Downes, William F. *judge*
Durham, Harry Blaine, III, *lawyer*
Durham, Lynda Laurene *language educator*
Empey, Thomas Henry *theater educator*
Gierau, Mike *political organization worker, small business owner*
Gray, Jan Charles *lawyer, business owner*
Hawks, Bill *state legislator, oil company executive*
Hjelmstad, William David *lawyer*
Ibach, Kim L. *secondary school educator*
Keim, Michael Ray *dentist*
Lowe, Robert Stanley *lawyer*
Moler, Mary *secondary school educator*
Ptasynski, Harry *geologist, oil industry executive*
Reese, Thomas Frank *lawyer*
Richardson, Bruce Alan *academic administrator*
Ryan, Linda Lee *sculptor, art educator*
Stoval, Linda *political party official*
Stroock, Thomas Frank *oil and gas company executive*
Sullivan, Michael John *lawyer, former ambassador*
Tempest, Rick *state representative*
True, Jean Durland *entrepreneur, oil industry executive, gas industry executive*
Unruh, Eric W. *music educator, academic administrator*
Wold, John Schiller *geologist, former congressman*

Centennial
Russin, Robert Isaiah *sculptor, educator*

Cheyenne
Berger, Rosie M. *state representative*
Boughton, Lesley D. *library director*
Brimmer, Clarence Addison *federal judge*
Brorby, Wade *federal judge*
Carmichael, David H. *lawyer*
Catchpole, Judy *state official*
Crank, Pat *state attorney general*
Cuckow, Elizabeth Lena *librarian*
Dale, Marcia Lyn *nursing educator*
De Herrera, Juan Abran (Age) *federal judicial security official*
Devin, Irene K. *state legislator, nurse*
Erb, Richard A. *state legislator, real estate executive*
Fecht, Robert David *protective services official, educator*
Flick, William Fredrick *surgeon*
Freudenthal, David D. *governor*
Freudenthal, Steven Franklin *lawyer, political organization chairman*
Friess, Lynn *state agency administrator*
Gentile, Liz *state representative*
Golden, T. Michael *state supreme court justice*
Green, Laurie *state agency administrator*
Hanes, John Grier *lawyer, state legislator*
Hart, Joseph H. *bishop emeritus*
Hart, Kerry *college administrator, music educator*
Harvey, Elaine *state representative*
Hill, William U. *state supreme court chief justice*
Johnson, Lorna *state representative*
Kite, Marilyn S. *state supreme court justice, lawyer*
Knight, Robert Edward *bank executive, educator*
Kunz, April Brimmer *state legislator, lawyer*
Law, Carlene *state agency administrator*
Laycock, Anita Simon *psychotherapist*
Lehman, Larry L. *state supreme court justice*
Lummis, Cynthia Marie *state official, lawyer*
Mackey, Terrence Wayne *lawyer*
Mc Clintock, Archie Glenn *lawyer*
Mead, Matthew Hansen *prosecutor*
Meyer, Joseph B. *Secretary of State, former academic administrator*
Mockler, Esther Jayne *state senator*
Moore, Mary French (Muffy Moore) *potter, advocate*
Moser, Diane *state agency administrator*
Myers, Rolland Graham *investment counselor*
Nisbet, Toma A. *nursing administrator*
Noe, Guy *retired social services administrator*
O'Brien, Terrence Leo *federal judge*
Palma, Jack D. *lawyer*
Parady, Fred *state representative*
Robinson, Ann *state representative*
Rodekohr, Diane E. *state official*
Schrader, Robert Wesley *judge*
Sessions, Kathryn L. *state legislator, educator*
Simons, Lynn Osborn *educational consultant*
Southworth, Rod Brand *retired computer science educator*
Thomson, Thyra Godfrey *former state official*
Vogel, Jeffrey C. *commissioner*
Voigt, Barton R. *state supreme court justice*
Warren, Jane *state representative*
Weeks, William Rawle, Jr., *oil company executive*
Weigner, Brent James *secondary school educator*
Wilson-McKee, Marie *museum director*
Woodhouse, Gay Vanderpoel *former state attorney general, lawyer*

Cody
Coe, Henry H. R. *state legislator*
Jackson, Harry Andrew *artist*
Patrick, H. Hunter *judge*
Price, B. Byron *historian*
Riley, Victor J., Jr., *financial services company executive*
Simpson, Alan Kooi *former US senator, lawyer*

Douglas
Twiford, Jim *former state legislator*

Dubois
Glasser, Pamela Jean *musician, music educator*

Ethete
Tepper, Marcy Elizabeth *drug education director*

Evanston
Combs, William L. *lawyer*

Fe Warren Afb
Neary, Thomas H. *career officer*

Gillette
Lubnau, Thomas Edwin, II, *lawyer*

Glendo
Burton, Eva Ella Mary *primary school educator*

Glenrock
Anderson, James *senator*

Green River
Albers, Dolores M. *secondary school educator*

Jackson
Decker, Carol Arne *magazine publishing executive*
Furrer, John Rudolf *retired manufacturing executive*
Gordon, Stephen Maurice *manufacturing company executive, rancher*
Herrick, Gregory Evans *technology corporation executive*
Hirschfield, Alan James *entrepreneur*
Law, Clarene Alta *small business owner, state legislator*
Massy, William Francis *education educator, consultant*
Ninnemann, Thomas George *secondary school educator*
Schuster, Robert Parks *lawyer*
Shockey, Gary Lee *lawyer*
Spence, Gerald Leonard *lawyer, writer*

Jackson Hole
Farkas, Carol Garner *nurse, administrator*

Kelly
Harrice, Cy (Nicholas Psiharis) *commercial radio and television announcer*
Knowles, William S. *retired chemist*

Lander
Raynolds, David Robert *buffalo breeder, writer*

Laramie
Allen, John Logan *geographer, department chairman*
Bellamy, John Cary *civil engineer, meteorologist*
Boresi, Arthur Peter *writer, educator*
Chai, Winberg *political science educator*
Chisum, Emmett Dewain *historian, archeologist, researcher*
Crocker, Thomas Dunstan *economics professor*
Darnall, Roberta Morrow *association executive*
Dickman, Francois Moussiegt *former foreign service officer, educator*
Dubois, Philip Leon *university administrator, political science educator*
Frost, Carol D. *geology educator*
Fulton, Jo Ann *lawyer*
Gill, George Wilhelm *anthropologist*
Grandy, Walter Thomas, Jr., *physicist, researcher*
Hansen, Matilda *former state legislator*
Hardy, Deborah Welles *history professor*
Kelley, Robert Otis *medical science educator*
Kinney, Lisa Frances *lawyer*
Maxfield, Peter C. *state legislator, law educator, lawyer*
McBride, Judith *elementary school educator*
Meyer, Edmond Gerald *energy and natural resources educator, resources scientist, entrepreneur, former chemistry educator, university administrator*
Mingle, John Orville *engineer, educator, lawyer, consultant*
Nye, Eric W. *English language and literature educator*
Rechard, Paul Albert *retired civil engineering company executive, consultant*
Reif, David (Frank David Reif) *artist, educator*
Selig, Joel Louis *lawyer, educator*
Shader, Bryan Lynn *mathematics professor*
Shaffer, Sherrill Lynn *economist*
Spears, Diana Faye *computer scientist*
Spiegelberg, Emma Jo *business education educator, academic administrator*
Williams, Roger Lawrence *historian, educator*

Mountain View
Silva, Alana G *writer, speech professional*

Newcastle
Engle, Kathleen Faye *elementary education educator*

Powell
Brophy, Dennis Richard *psychology and philosophy educator, administrator, clergyman*
Bruscino, Leah *state agency administrator*

Riverton
Bebout, Eli Daniel *oil executive*
Girard, Nettabell *lawyer*
Hursh, John R. *lawyer*
Peck, Robert A. *newspaper publisher, state legislator*

Rock Springs
Job, Rae Lynn *state legislator*

Sheridan
Aguirre-Batty, Mercedes *Spanish and English language educator, literature educator, educator*
Lonabaugh, Ellsworth Eugene *retired lawyer*
Ryan, Michael Louis *controller*
van Houten, Janet E. *music educator*

Story
Bredehoeft, John Dallas *geologist*

Wheatland
Bunker, John Birkbeck *cattle rancher, retired sugar company executive*
Hunkins, Raymond Breedlove *lawyer, rancher*
Whitney, Ralph Royal, Jr., *financial executive*

Wilson
Breitenbach, Mary Louise McGraw *psychologist, chemical dependency counselor*
Chrystie, Thomas Ludlow *investor*
Fritz, Jack Wayne *communications and marketing company executive*

Harrell, Samuel Macy *agribusiness executive*
Lawroski, Harry *nuclear engineer*
Sage, Andrew Gregg Curtin, II, *corporate investor, manager*

Worland

Geis, Gerald E. *state legislator, trucking company executive*
Woods, Lawrence Milton *airline company executive*

Las Vegas

Luquette, Elise Roshau *recording industry executive*

Texas City

Bernard, Lora Marie *journalist*
Barrere, Jamie Newton *real estate executive*
Berger, David *surgeon*
Brown, Carroll *diplomat, association executive, consultant*
Cardarelli, Dr Diane *music educator, conductor*
Carney, Michael T. *financial services executive*
Connelly, Michael *writer*
Damjanovich, Chaslav M. (Casey Diamond) *filmmaker, television producer, writer*
Divita, James J. *retired social studies educator, writer, researcher*
Edwards, Sarah R. *state representative*
Gardner, Rulon E. *Olympic athlete*
Helser, Marilyn A. *business educator*
Kaplan, James *composer*
Lowe, Vevlyn Parks *music educator*
Muftu, Sinan *mechanical engineer, educator*
Sepnafski, Bill G. *secondary school educator, consultant*

TERRITORIES OF THE UNITED STATES

AMERICAN SAMOA

Pago Pago

Fung-Chen-Pen, Emma Talauna Solaita *librarian, program director*
Kruse, F. Michael *judge*
Mailo, Toetagata Albert *territory attorney general*
Richmond, Lyle L. *judge*
Sunia, Aitofele Toese F. *lieutenant governor*
Sunia, Muagututia Fiti *American Samoa attorney general*
Tulafono, Togiola T.A. *governor*
Weitzel, John Quinn *bishop*

FEDERATED STATES OF MICRONESIA

Chuuk

Samo, Amando *bishop*

GUAM

Adelup

Moylan, Kaleo *lieutenant governor*

Agana

San Agustin, Joe Taitano *political organization worker, educator*

Agana Heights

Apuron, Anthony Sablan *archbishop*

Barrigada

Cruz, Teofila Perez *nursing administrator*

Hagatna

Camacho, Felix Perez *governor*
Carbullido, F. Philip *judge*
Espaldon, Ernesto Mercader *plastic surgeon, former senator*
Maraman, Katherine Ann *judge*
Moylan, Douglas *state attorney general*
Sablan, David J. *marketing professional, political organization worker*
Siguenza, Peter Charles, Jr., *territory supreme court justice*
Troutman, Charles Henry, III, *lawyer*
Tydingco-Gatewood, Frances Marie *judge*
Unpingco, John Walter Sablan *federal judge*

Mangilao

Cohen, Arlene Guretzky *editor, librarian*
Duenas, Laurent Flores *health and nursing consultant*
Iverson, Thomas John *economist, educator*
Lobban, Christopher Simon *science educator*

Talofofo

Taylor, James John *academic administrator*

Tamuning

Aguigui, Ignacio Cruz *lawyer*
Landstrom, Jerone T. *surgeon*
Yingling, Gerald Phillip *business executive*

NORTHERN MARIANA ISLANDS

Saipan

Babauta, Juan Nekai *governor*
Benavente, Diego T. *lieutenant governor*
Brown, Pamela S. *attorney general*
Castro, Alexandro C. *judge*
Demapan, Miguel S. *judge*
Inos, Rita Hocog *school system administrator*
Kaufer, Connie Tenorio *retired reading specialist*
Manglona, John A. *judge*
Munson, Alex Robert *judge*
Soll, Herbert D. *lawyer*

PUERTO RICO

Aguadilla

Gómez-Jiménez, Carlos *science educator, microbiologist, geneticist*

Jaramillo, Juana Segarra *chancellor*

Angeles

Avila, Carlos Alberto *physics researcher, inventor*

Arecibo

Bravo LaLuz, Yamilete N. *pharmacist*

Bayamon

Juarbe, Charles *otolaryngologist, head and neck surgeon*
Ortiz, William *composer, music educator*
Rosa, Helen *dean*

Carolina

López-Hernández, Ledyana *substance abuse counselor*

Cayey

Acevedo-Loubriel, Suzette *adult education educator*

Dorado

Spector, Michael Joseph *agribusiness executive*

Fajardo

Millan, Alvin *speech pathology/audiology services professional, educator*

Guaynabo

de Cacho, Graciela Eleta *marketing executive*
Lambert, Christina *telecommunications executive*
Lasa-Ferrer, Armando *lawyer*

Gurabo

Kuruganty, Sastry Pratap *electrical engineering educator*

Hato Rey

Carrion, Richard *bank executive*
Cerezo, Carmen Consuelo *judge*
Ferrer, Miguel Antonio *brokerage firm and investment bank executive*
Vilches-O'Bourke, Octavio Augusto *accounting company executive*

Hormigueros

Acosta, Ursula *psychologist*

Juncos

Caraballo, Jose *pharmaceutical executive*

Mayaguez

Collins, Dennis Glenn *mathematics professor*
Meléndez, Enrique *chemist, educator*
Sahai, Hardeo *medical statistics educator*

Old San Juan

Weinstein-Bacal, Stuart Allen *lawyer, educator*

Ponce

Cummings, Luis Emilio *anesthesiologist, consultant*
Leon-Sotomayor, Jose Rafael *lawyer, engineer, educator*
López-Alvarez, Carmen A. *language educator*
Matta, Jaime L *research scientist, educator*
Moura, Jose *wine consultant*
Sala, Luis Francisco *surgeon, educator*

Ramey

Aponte, Abraham *secondary school educator*

San German

Mojica, Agnes *academic administrator*

San Juan

Acosta, Raymond Luis *federal judge*
Andréu-García, José Antonio *territory supreme court chief justice*
Andujar, Norma Burgos *former state official*
Aponte Martinez, Luis Cardinal *archbishop emeritus*
Arsuaga, Juan Arenado *banker*
Bonilla-Felix, Melvin A. *pediatrician, educator*
Calderón, Sila M. *governor*
Carreras, Francisco José *retired university president, foundation executive*
Casellas, Salvador E. *judge*
Casiano, Kimberly *publishing executive*
Castro-Blanco, James *professional society administrator*
Corrada del Rio, Baltasar *supreme court justice*
Cruz-Korchin, Norma I. *plastic surgeon*
Delgado-Colon, Aida M. *federal judge*
Dominguez, Daniel R. *judge*
Encarnación, Jose M. Izquierdo *Secretary of State Puerto Rico*
Fernández-Coll, Fred *microbiologist, food technology laboratory director*
Fusté, José Antonio *federal judge*
Fuster, Jaime B. *supreme court justice*
Garcia, Humberto Sigifredo *lawyer*
Garcia, Marc Anthony *diplomat*
Gierbolini-Ortiz, Gilberto *federal judge*
Gil, Guillermo *prosecutor*
Gonzalez, Roberto O. *bishop*
Guilermo, Figueroa *conductor*
Hernandez-Denton, Federico *supreme court justice*
Hillyer, George V. *microbiologist, educator, medical researcher*
Irizarry-Yunque, Carlos Juan *lawyer, educator*
Janwa, Heera Lal *mathematician, educator*
Joglar, Francisco *academic administrator*
Lambert, Cristina *telecommunications executive*
Lopez, Angel R. Pagan *dean, dentist*
Lugo, Ariel E. *ecologist, botanist, federal agency administrator*
Maldonado, Norman I. *physician, educator*
Martinez-Munoz, Hector *lawyer*
Marvel, Thomas Stahl *architect*
Matheu, Federico Manuel *university chancellor*
Merly, Miriam Naveira *state supreme court justice*
Negron-Garcia, Antonio S. *law educator, former territory supreme court justice*
Ocasio-Melendez, Marcial Enrique *history professor*
Padilla, Alfredo *commissioner*
Pasnicu, Cornel *mathematician, educator*
Pedreira, Mark Alan *education educator*
Picó, Fernando *historian, educator*
Pierluisi, Pedro R. *lawyer*
Pluke, Richard William Hay *entomologist, researcher*
Prats Palerm, Robert L. *political party chairman*

Rebollo-Lopez, Francisco *state supreme court justice*
Rivera Perez, Efrain E. *state supreme court justice*
Rodriguez, Annabelle *state attorney general*
Rodriguez-Diaz, Juan E. *lawyer*
Roldan, Ulises *sales and marketing executive*
Romero-Barceló, Carlos Antonio *former congressman, former governor of Puerto Rico, former mayor of San Juan*
Rosso de Irizarry, Carmen (Tutty Rosso de Irizarry) *finance executive*
San Miguel, Lolita *artistic director*
Santini, Jorge *mayor*
Sepúlveda, Sandra *communications educator*
Teleman, Silviu *mathematician, educator*
Uribe, Javier Miguel *investment executive*
Velez Silva, Xenia *Puerto Rican government official*

Vega Alta

Matos, Cruz Alfonso *environmental consultant*

York

Kay, Jack Robert *real estate company executive*

VIRGIN ISLANDS

Charlotte Amalie

Barnard, Geoffrey W. *magistrate judge*
Feuerzeig, Henry Louis *lawyer*
Garfield, Winifred L. *nursing administrator*
Stapleton, Marylyn Alecia *diplomat*
Stridiron, Iver Allison *attorney general*

Christiansted

Bland, James Theodore, Jr., *lawyer*
Finch, Raymond Lawrence *chief judge*
Grey, Samuel T. *lawyer*
James, Gerard Luz Amwur, II, *former lieutenant governor*
Mann, Lynne Marie *executive administrative assistant*
Resnick, Jeffrey Lance *federal magistrate judge*
Richards, Vargrave A. *lieutenant governor*

Kingshill

Llanos, Luis Socorro *retired public administrator, mediator, arbitrator, public affairs consultant*

Saint John

Fradley, Frederick Macdonell *retired architect*

Saint Thomas

Meyers, Stuart Irwin *real estate developer*
O'Bryan, James A. *communications specialist, political organization administrator*
Prior, Cornelius Bernard, Jr., *utilities company executive, financial consultant*
Turnbull, Charles W. *governor*

St Croix

Moore, Thomas Kail *magistrate district court judge*

St John

Walker, Ronald R. *writer, editor, educator*

St Thomas

Berry, Lorraine L. *state senator*
Carty, Amos W. *lawyer*
Clark, Jessie Dona *social worker*
Creque, Linda Ann *non-profit educational and research executive, former education commissioner*
de Jongh, John P., Jr., *real estate company executive*
Dudley, George H.T. *real estate company executive*
Finch, Gordon A. *airport terminal executive*
Kean, Orville *retired academic administrator*
Michael, Noreen *commissioner, educator*
Morse, Theodore Freeman *dean, writer*
Nissman, David M. *lawyer*
Ragster, LaVerne E. *academic administrator*
Williams, Wesley S., Jr., *real estate company executive*

MILITARY ADDRESSES OF THE UNITED STATES

AA

Apo

Brownfield, William R. *ambassador*
Danilovich, John J. *ambassador*
Jett, Dennis Coleman *foreign service officer*
Watt, Linda E. *ambassador*

Fpo

Green, Kevin Patrick *career officer*
Stavridis, James George *military officer*

AE

APO

Baptiste, Thomas L. *career officer*
Begert, William J. *lieutenant general United States Air Force*
Carson, Johnnie *ambassador*
Cejas, Paul L. *diplomat, executive*
Corley, John D. W. *military officer*
Fowler, Wyche, Jr., *ambassador*
Gnehm, Edward W., Jr., *ambassador*
Kammerer, Kelly Christian *lawyer*
Knudsen, Gene Arthur *school system administrator*
Korologos, Tom Chris *ambassador*
McGowan, Gerald S. *diplomat*
Morella, Constance Albanese *ambassador, former congresswoman*
Oberwetter, James C. *ambassador*
Ohman, Diana J. *government agency administrator, former state official*
Ralston, Joseph W. *career officer*
Romero, Edward L. *diplomat, environmental engineering executive*
Simpson, Sandra Kay *logistics management specialist*
Webster, Christopher White *foreign service officer*

Apo

Untermeyer, Charles Graves (Chase Untermeyer) *ambassador, diplomat*

FPO

Benedict, Lawrence Neal *foreign service officer*
Blazewick, Robert B. *lawyer, educator, military officer*
Gadsden, James Irvin *ambassador*
Holmes, Michael L. *career officer*
Mullen, Michael G. *career military officer*

Fpo

Klosson, Michael *foreign service officer*

AP

Apo

Dunkle, Keith Allen *military officer*
Dunn, Michael M. *military officer*
Herrin, Mark Malachi *military officer*
Hester, Paul V. *career officer*
Ray, Charles Aaron *foreign service officer*
Timmerman, Thomas J. *military planner, operations analyst*
Tsau, William Wen-Shiung *civil engineer, consultant, structural engineer*
Turner, David Lowery *system safety engineer*

Fpo

Tarpeh-Doe, Linda Diane *controller*

CANADA

ALBERTA

Calgary

Anderson, J.C. *oil and gas exploration company executive, rancher*
Auchinleck, Richard H. *exploration company executive*
Baldwin, Douglas Daniel *pipeline company executive*
Besant, Derek Michael *artist, educator*
Campbell, Finley Alexander *geologist, consultant*
Chrétien, Jean (Joseph Jacques Jean Chrétien) *lawyer, former prime minister of Canada*
Cumming, Thomas Alexander *stock exchange executive*
George, Richard Lee *oil industry executive*
Glockner, Peter G. *civil and mechanical engineering educator*
Haskayne, Richard Francis *petroleum company executive*
Heidemann, Robert Albert *chemical engineering educator, researcher*
Holman, J(ohn) Leonard *retired manufacturing corporation executive*
Horton, William Russell *retired utility company executive*
Hotchkiss, Harley N. *professional hockey team owner*
Hume, James Borden *corporate professional, foundation executive*
Jones, Geoffrey Melvill *physiology research educator*
Lam, Galen Ka-Ron *electrical engineer*
Lederis, Karolis Paul (Karl Lederis) *pharmacologist, educator, researcher*
Leung, Alexander Kwok-Chu *pediatrician*
Libin, Alvin G. *business executive*
Lougheed, Peter *lawyer, former Canadian premier*
MacDonald, Alan Hugh *librarian, university administrator*
Maier, Gerald James *corporate executive*
Malik, Om Parkash *electrical engineering educator, researcher*
Manz, Calvin Kim *technology sector entrepreneur*
McCaig, Jeffrey James *transportation company executive*
McDaniel, Roderick Rogers *petroleum engineer, consultant*
McEwen, Alexander Campbell *cadastral studies educator, former Canadian government official, land administration consultant*
McKinnon, F(rancis) A(rthur) Richard *utilities executive*
Milavsky, Harold Phillip *real estate executive*
Monk, Allan James *baritone*
Morgan, Gwyn *oil and gas executive*
Mossop, Grant Dilworth *geologist, researcher*
Neale, E(rnest) R(ichard) Ward *retired university official, consultant*
O'Brien, David Peter *gas industry executive, lawyer*
Pourbaix, Alexander *energy executive*
Raeburn, Andrew Harvey *performing arts association executive, record producer*
Seaman, Daryl Kenneth *oil company executive*
Shaw, Jim, Jr., *broadcast executive*
Sinclair, Brian Robert *psychologist, architect, educator*
Slater, Gary *retail executive*
Smith, Eldon *cardiologist, physiologist, educator*
Smith, Rowland James *educational administrator*
Southern, Nancy C. *utilities executive*
Southern, Ronald D. *diversified corporation executive*
Stebbins, Robert Alan *sociology educator*
Sutter, Darryl John *professional hockey coach*
Swartout, Hank B. *oil and gas industry executive*
Turek, Roman *professional hockey player*
Wagner, Norman Ernest *corporate education executive*
Walker, Roger Geoffrey *geology educator, consultant*
Watanabe, Mamoru *former university dean, physician, researcher*
White, Terrence Harold *academic administrator, sociologist*

Canmore

Janes, Robert Roy *museum executive, archaeologist, museum consultant, editor*

Drumheller

Currie, Philip John *research paleontologist, museum curator*

Aurora
Lanthier, Ronald Ross *retired manufacturing company executive*

Barry's Bay
Horoszewicz, Juliusz Stanislaw *oncologist, cancer researcher, laboratory administrator*

Belleville
Buckley, Edward Joseph *retired academic dean*
Vanclief, Lyle *former Canadian government official*

Bowmanville
Evans, Essi H. *research scientist*

Bracebridge
Evans, John David Daniel *judge*

Brampton
Bastian, Donald Noel *retired bishop*
Hu, Qiang *research scientist, educator, engineer*
Malhi, Gurbax Singh *legislator*
Paikeday, Thomas M. *lexicographer and linguistic consultant*
Plastina, Frank *communications executive*
Savoie, Leonard Norman *transportation company executive*

Brantford
Inns, Harry Douglas Ellis *retired optometrist*
Stewart, Jane *former Canadian government minister*

Brockville
Spalding, James Stuart *retired telecommunications company executive*

Burlington
Begum, Shaila Luxmy *environmental engineer*
Bullock, James R. *company executive*
Harris, Philip John *engineering educator*
McMulkin, Francis John *retired steel company executive*

Cambridge
Brown, Gregory Michael *psychiatrist, educator, researcher*
MacBain, William Halley *minister, theology educator, seminary chancellor*
Turnbull, Robert Scott *retired manufacturing executive*
White, Joseph Charles *manufacturing and retailing company executive*

Chatham
McKeough, William Darcy *investment company executive, director*
Shakhmundes, Lev *mathematician*

Collingwood
Morley, Lawrence Whitaker *geophysicist, remote sensing consultant*

Deep River
Davies, John Arthur *physics and engineering educator, scientist*
Milton, John Charles Douglas *nuclear physicist, researcher*
Newcombe, Howard Borden *biologist, consultant*

Don Mills
Collenette, David Michael *legislator, former Canadian government official*
French, William Harold *retired newspaper editor*
Hyde, Michael Arthur *consultant, retired chemical company executive*

Dorchester
Fanning, William James *professional baseball team executive, radio and television broadcaster*

Downsview
Eggleton, Arthur C. *former Canadian government official, member of Parliament*
Forer, Arthur H. *biology professor, researcher, editor*

Essex
Whelan, Susan *member of parliament*

Etobicoke
Howe, James Tarsicius *retired insurance company executive*
McIntyre, John George Wallace *real estate development and management consultant*
Scholefield, Peter Gordon *health agency executive*

Freelton
Sonnenberg, Hardy *data processing company research and development executive, engineer*

Gloucester
Boisvert, Laurier Joseph *communications executive*
Malouin, Jean-Louis *university educator*
Pelletier, David *Olympic athlete, ice skater*
Salé, Jamie *Olympic athlete, ice skater*

Greely
Lister, Earle Edward *retired animal science consultant*

Guelph
Beveridge, Terrance James *microbiology educator, researcher*
Bewley, John Derek *botany researcher, educator*
Dickinson, William Trevor *hydrologist, educator*
Jorgensen, Erik *forest pathologist, educator, consultant*
Karl, Gabriel *physics educator*
Kasha, Kenneth John *agriculturist, educator*
Land, Reginald Brian *library administrator*

Hamilton
Bandler, John William *electrical engineering educator, consultant*
Bienenstock, John *pathologist, educator, health facility administrator*
Brackney, William Henry *archivist, historian*
Campbell, Colin Kydd *electrical and computer engineering educator, researcher*
Crowe, Cameron Macmillan *chemical engineering educator*
Datars, William Ross *physicist, researcher*
Garland, William James *engineering physics educator*
George, Peter James *economist, educator*
Gillespie, Ronald James *chemistry educator, researcher, writer*
Hantho, Chuck *retired metal products executive*
Jonasson, Ralph George *research chemist*
McKay, Alexander Gordon *classics educator*
Robinson, Daniel Baruch *retired banker*
Roland, Charles Gordon *physician, medical historian, educator*
Ryan, Ellen Bouchard *psychology educator, gerontologist*
Spenser, Ian Daniel *chemist educator*
Sprung, Donald Whitfield Loyal *physics educator*

Harrow
Saha, Uttam Kumar *environmental scientist, researcher*

Holland Landing
Dempster, Barry (Edward) *writer, poet*

Kanata
Hasek, Dominik *professional hockey player*
Murray, Bryan Clarence *professional sports team executive*
Smith, Don *communications executive*

Kingston
Akenson, Donald Harman *historian, educator*
Batchelor, Barrington de Vere *civil engineer, educator*
Campbell, L(ouis) Lorne *mathematics professor*
Dick, Susan Marie *English language educator*
Ewan, George Thomson *physicist, researcher*
Kaliski, Stephan Felix *economics professor*
Kaufman, Nathan *retired pathologist, educator*
Leggett, William C. *biology professor, academic administrator*
Low, James A. *physician*
MacKinnon, James Gordon *economist, educator*
Meisel, John *political scientist*
Smallman, Beverley N. *retired biology professor*
Spencer, John Hedley *biochemistry educator*
Stewart, Alec Thompson *physicist, educator*
Szarek, Walter Anthony *chemist, educator*
Wyatt, Gerard Robert *biology professor, researcher*

Kitchener
Coles, Graham *conductor, composer*
Eldred, Gerald Marcus *retired performing arts association executive*
Winger, Roger Elson *retired church administrator*

London
Bancroft, George Michael *chemical physicist, educator*
Bauer, Michael Anthony *computer scientist, educator*
Borwein, David *mathematics professor*
Brian, Jackson *artistic director*
Collins, Thomas Joseph *English language educator*
Cornies, Larry Alan *journalist, educator*
Davenport, Alan Garnett *civil engineer, educator*
Davenport, Paul *academic administrator, economics educator*
Dreimanis, Aleksis *emeritus geology educator*
Fyfe, William Sefton *geochemist, educator*
Gerber, Douglas Earl *classics educator*
Groden, Michael Lewis *English literature educator*
Hooper, Wayne Nelson *clergy member*
Inculet, Ion I. *electrical engineering educator, research director, consultant*
Kang, Chil-Yong *virology, immunology educator*
Laidler, David Ernest William *economics professor*
Lala, Peeyush Kanti *research scientist, educator*
Livick, Stephen *fine art photographer*
Locke, Michael *zoology educator*
Marotta, Joseph Thomas *medical educator*
McWhinney, Ian Renwick *physician, educator*
Osbaldeston, Gordon Francis *business educator, former government official*
Poole, Nancy Geddes *art gallery curator*
Stewart, Harold Brown *biochemist*
Stillman, Martin J. *physical science research administrator, bioinorganic chemist*
William, David *director, actor*
Wonnacott, Ronald Johnston *economics professor*

Manotick
Hobson, George Donale *retired geophysicist*
Osmond, Dennis Gordon *medical educator, researcher*

Markham
Burns, H(erbert) Michael *corporate director*
Gulden, Simon *lawyer, investment/real estate development executive, business and legal consultant*
Ho, Kwok Yuen *data processing executive*

Mississauga
Al-Nachawati, Hicham Mustapha *statistician*
Bricel, Mark Leon *marketing executive*
Chen, Xi-Qing *mechanical engineer*
Colcleugh, David W. *chemical company executive*
Farrell, Craig *hotel executive*
Gelfond, Richard L. *film company executive*
Gupta, Rajesh *engineer, consultant*
John, Leonard Keith *aerospace and mechanical engineer*
Kennedy, John W. *health products executive*
Melnyk, Eugene N. *private investigator*
Palmer, Patrick Asa *former banker, lecturer*
Peterson, Oscar Emmanuel *pianist*
Rygiel, Edward K. *chemical engineer*
Thibault, J(oseph) Laurent *service company executive*

Nepean
Chudobiak, Walter James *electronics company executive, electronic engineer*
Kallmann, Helmut Max *music historian, retired music librarian*

Newmarket
Walker, Donald J. *automotive systems company executive*
Wood, Neil Roderick *real estate development company executive*

Niagara-on-the-Lake
Nielsen-Jones, Ian Richard *lottery and gaming executive, business operations consultant*
Olley, Robert Edward *economist, educator*

Nobleton
Embleton, Tony Frederick Wallace *retired Canadian government official*

North York
Adelman, Howard *philosophy educator*
Blundell, William Richard Charles *retired electric company executive*
Buzacott, John Alan *engineering educator*
Davey, Kenneth George *biologist, university official*
Denham, Frederick Ronald *management consultant*
Flock, Howard *psychology educator*
Gasparrini-Etheridge, Claudia *publishing company executive, scientist, writer*
Regan, David *brain researcher*
Thomas, Clara McCandless *retired English language educator, biographer*

Ottawa
Almakky, Ghazy Abdulwahed Makky *diplomat, geography educator*
Alper, Howard *chemistry professor*
Anderson, David Leslie *member of parliament*
Andrew, Bryan Haydn *astronomer*
Angus, W. David *Queen's Counsel*
Armstrong, Henry Conner *former Canadian government official, consultant*
Augustine, Jean Magdalene *Canadian government official, member of parliament*
Austin, Jacob (Jack Austin) *Canadian government official*
Axworthy, Lloyd *Canadian government official*
Bailey, Roy H. *member of parliament*
Baker, George S. *federal official*
Baum, Bernard Rene *research scientist*
Beare-Rogers, Joyce Louise *former research executive*
Beatty, Perrin *business association executive*
Bédard, Éric *Olympic athlete*
Bélanger, Mauril *member Canadian Parliament*
Bélisle, Paul Charles *Canadian government official*
Bevilacqua, Maurizio *member of Canadian parliament*
Boudria, Don *Canadian government official*
Bozozuk, Michael *civil engineer*
Brooks, David Barry *resource economist*
Bryden, Roderick M. *professional sports team executive*
Buchanan, John MacLennan *Canadian provincial official*
Burney, Derek *information technology executive*
Caplan, Elinor *former Canadian government official*
Carroll, M(argaret) Aileen *member of Canadian parliament*
Carty, Arthur John *science policy advisor, research administrator*
Catterall, Marlene *Canadian legislator*
Cauchon, Martin *former Canadian government official*
Cellucci, Paul (Argeo Paul Cellucci) *ambassador, former governor*
Chance, Graham Wilfrid *retired pediatrician, emeritus educator*
Clarkson, Adrienne *Governor General of Canada*
Coderre, Denis *Canadian government official*
Coleman, John Morley *transportation engineering executive*
Copps, Sheila *former Canadian government official*
Courtois, Bernard Andre *communications executive*
Csörgö, Miklós *mathematics and statistics educator*
Dagum, Camilo *economist, educator*
d'Aquino, Thomas *lawyer, entrepreneur, educator, strategist*
Davey, Clark William *newspaper publisher*
Dawson, Donald Andrew *mathematics educator, researcher*
Dawson, Mary E. *lawyer*
Day, Stockwell Burt *government official*
de Bold, Adolfo J. *pathology and physiology educator, research scientist*
de Chastelain, A(lfred) John G(ardyne) D(rummond) *Canadian army officer, diplomat*
Dhaliwal, Herb (Harbance Singh) *legislator, former Canadian government official*
Dlab, Vlastimil *mathematics educator, researcher*
Dray, William Herbert *philosophy educator*
Efford, R. John *Canadian government official*
Fairbairn, Joyce *Canadian government official*
Fellegi, Ivan Peter *statistician*
Fitzpatrick, Brian *member of parliament*
Francis, Charles MacKenzie *wildlife biologist*
Freedman, Charles *retired bank executive*
Gagnon, Marc *Olympic athlete*
Georganas, Nicolas D. *electrical engineering educator*
Gillingham, Bryan Reginald *music educator*
Gold, Lorne W. *Canadian government official*
Goodale, Ralph E. *Canadian government official*
Goodine, Isaac Thomas *development executive, educator*
Gordon, Steve *real estate executive*
Graham, B. Alasdair *government official*
Graham, William C. *Canadian government official*
Gray, Herbert Eser (The Right Honourable Herbert Gray) *former federal official*
Grey, Deborah Cleland *Canadian government official*
Griller, David *economics and technology consultant*
Guarnieri, Albina *Canadian government official, Canadian legislator*
Guilmette, Jonathan *Olympic athlete*
Hagen, Paul Beo *physician, medical scientist*
Halliday, Ian *astronomer*
Harb, Mac *Canadian government official*
Harington, Charles Richard *vertebrate paleontologist*
Hart, Jim *member of Canadian parliament*
Heald, Darrel Verner *retired Canadian federal judge*
Henault, R. R. *military officer*
Himms-Hagen, Jean Margaret *biochemist, educator*
Holmes, John Leonard *chemistry professor*
Hughes, Stanley John *mycologist*
Hurteau, Gilles David *retired obstetrician, gynecologist, educator, dean*
Ingold, Keith Usherwood *chemist, educator*
Jackson, W. Bruce *ophthalmology educator, researcher*
Jaenen, Cornelius John *history professor, consultant*
Jordan, Joseph Louis *education educator, government official*
Kates, Morris *biochemist, educator*
Keyes, Stan Kazmierczak *Canadian government official*
Kilgour, David *Canadian member of parliament*
Kingsley, Jean-Pierre *government official*
Kroeger, Arthur *former university chancellor, former government official*
Labarge, Margaret Wade *medieval history educator*
Laliberte, Rick *member of parliament*
Lavoie, Lionel A. *physician, health science association administrator*
Lemay-Doan, Catriona *Olympic speed skater*
MacAulay, Lawrence A. *Canadian government official, member of Parliament*
MacDonald, Flora Isabel *Canadian government official*
MacFarlane, John Alexander *former federal housing agency administrator*
MacKay, William Andrew *judge*
Macklem, Michael Kirkpatrick *publisher*
Maheu, Shirley *Canadian legislator*
Major, John Charles *judge*
Manley, John Paul *former Canadian government official*
Margeson, Theodore Earl *judge*
Marleau, Diane *Canadian government official*
Martin, Paul *Prime Minister of Canada*
Maxwell, Judith *think-tank executive, economist*
McAvity, John Gillis *museum director, association executive, museologist*
McDonald, John W. *internist*
McGuire, Joseph *Canadian government official*
McLachlin, Beverley *Canadian supreme court chief justice*
McLellan, A. Anne *Canadian government official*
McLure, John Douglas *federal official*
Mifflin, Fred John *Canadian government official*
Mills, Bob *member of Canadian parliament*
Minna, Maria *member of Canadian Parliament*
Mitchell, Andrew (Andy Mitchell) *Canadian government official*
Moore, William John Myles *retired electrical engineer, researcher*
Morand, Peter *investment company executive*
Murray, Larry *government agency administrator*
Murray, Lowell *Canadian senator*
Nault, Robert Daniel *legislator*
Nystrom, Lorne *member of parliament*
O'Neil, Maureen *think-tank executive*
Ouellet, André *business executive*
Pachner, Jaroslav (Frantisek) *nuclear engineer, consultant*
Pagtakhan, Rey D. *Canadian government official*
Pankiw, Jim *member of parliament*
Paradis, Denis *Canadian government official, member of parliament*
Penner, Keith *former Canadian government official*
Perry, Malcolm Blythe *biologist, researcher*
Peterson, James Scott (Jim Peterson) *Canadian government official*
Pettigrew, Pierre S. *Canadian government official*
Philogene, Bernard J. R. *academic administrator, science educator*
Plumptre, Tim *think-tank executive*
Poulin, Marie *Canadian government official*
Prevost, Roxane Lise *music theory educator*
Proctor, Dick *member of parliament*
Ramsay, Donald Allan *physical chemist*
Redhead, Paul Aveling *physicist*
Regan, Geoff *Canadian government official*
Ritz, Gerry *member of parliament*
Robillard, Lucienne *Canadian government official*
Rodger, Ginette *professional association executive, nurse*
Roland, Anne *registrar Supreme Court of Canada*
Rutt, James P. *design company executive*
Ryan, William Francis *priest*
Saada, Jacques *legislator*
Scherrer, Helene Chalifour *Canada government official*
Schneider, William George *chemist, research consultant*
Scott, Andy *Canadian government official*
Scott, Marianne Florence *retired librarian, educator*
Sells, Bruce Howard *biomedical sciences educator*
Sgro, Judy *Canadian government official*
Silverman, Ozzie *consulting strategist*
Skelton, Carol *member of parliament*
Squire, Anne Marguerite *religious leader*
Staines, David McKenzie *English educator*
Stanford, Joseph Stephen *diplomat, lawyer, educator*
Stewart, Christine Susan *Canadian government official*
St-Onge, Denis Alderic *geologist, research scientist*
Storey, Kenneth Bruce *biology professor*
Strayer, Barry Lee *federal judge*
Sylvestre, Jean Guy *former national librarian*
Tassé, Roger *lawyer, former Canadian government official*
Telegdi, Andrew *member of parliament*
Tremblay, Francois-Louis *Olympic athlete*
Turcotte, Mathieu *Olympic athlete*
Urie, John James *lawyer, retired Canadian federal judge*
Valeri, Tony *Canadian government official*
Vassilyadi, Michael *pediatric neurosurgeon*
Veizer, Ján *geology educator*
Vellacott, Maurice *member of parliament*
Volpe, Joseph *Canadian government official*
Wallot, Jean-Pierre *archivist, historian*
Whitehead, J. Rennie *science consultant*
Wilson, Ian Edwin *cultural organization administrator, archivist*
Withers, Ramsey Muir *retired federal agency administrator*
Yalden, Maxwell Freeman *Canadian diplomat*
Yelich, Lynne *member of parliament*
Yeomans, Donald Ralph *Canadian government official, consultant*

Owen Sound
Jones, Phyllis Edith *nursing educator*

Peterborough
Davis, Gordon Richard Fuerst *retired biologist, translator*
Dumas, Michael Godfrey Joseph *artist*
Hutchinson, Thomas Cuthbert *ecology and environmental educator*
Theall, Donald Francis *retired university president*

Pickering
Irwin, John Wesley *publisher*

Red Lake
Zaikow, Larry J. James *painter*

Richmond Hill
Garrison, Robert Frederick *astronomer, educator*

Saint Catharines
Bergevin, V. Réal *customer relationship management executive*
Miller, John Peter (Jack Miller) *journalist*
Picken, Harry Belfrage *aerospace engineer*
Stevenson, Garth *social sciences educator*

Sault Sainte Marie
Banerjee, Samarendranath *orthopedic surgeon*
Ferris, Ronald Curry *bishop*
Stinson, Deane Brian *financial executive, consultant*

Scarborough
Bassnett, Peter James *retired librarian*
Cetín, Anton *artist*
Huang, Wei *engineer, researcher*
Mikloshazy, Attila *bishop*
White, Calvin John *zoo executive, zoological association executive, financial manager*

Stittsville
MacLeod, Robert Angus *microbiology educator, researcher*
Tellier, Henri *retired Canadian military officer*

Thornhill
Lublinski, Michael *lawyer*

Thorold
O'Mara, John Aloysius *retired bishop*

Toronto
Antonijevic, Aleksandar *dancer*
Armstrong, Robin Louis *physics educator*
Arnell, Gordon Edwin *real estate development company executive*
Arthurs, Harry William *legal educator, former university president*
Astman, Barbara Ann *artist, educator*
Augustine, Jerome Samuel *merchant banker*
Bailey, Donovan *Olympic athlete*
Ballett, David Howard *property management executive*
Bandeen, Robert Angus *management consultant*
Barber, Aaron *professional golfer*
Barker, Bruce Crichlow *barrister, solicitor*
Bartleman, James K. *lieutenant governor*
Beckwith, John *musician, composer, educator*
Belfour, Ed *professional hockey player*
Berezin, Sergei *professional hockey player*
Berton, Pierre *journalist, author*
Bertram, Victoria Elaine *dancer*
Bird, Richard Miller *economics professor*
Black, Lord Conrad Moffat *former publishing corporate executive*
Blewett, David Lambert *English literature educator*
Bloomberg, Lawrence S. *securities executive, art collector*
Bohme, Diethard Kurt *chemistry professor*
Bohn, Jason *professional golfer*
Boland, Janet Lang *judge*
Bolley, Andrea *artist*
Bond, John Richard *astrophysicist*
Boorne, Ryan *ballet dancer*
Bradshaw, Richard James *performing company executive*
Braithwaite, J. Lorne *real estate executive*
Braswell, Paula Ann *artist*
Broder, Irvin *physician, educator*
Brook, Adrian Gibbs *chemistry professor*
Bruce, William Robert *physician, educator*
Bryant, Josephine Harriet *library executive*
Budrevics, Alexander *landscape architect*
Bugg, Jace *professional golfer*
Carder, Paul Charles *retired advertising executive*
Carlen, Peter Louis *neuroscientist, educator, science administrator, researcher*
Carr, Jack Leslie *economics educator, economic consultant*
Carrothers, Gerald Arthur Patrick *environmental and city planning educator*
Carter, Vince *professional basketball player*
Chabot, Diane *telecommunications executive*
Chester, Robert Simon George *lawyer*
Cleghorn, John Edward *business executive*
Clitheroe, Eleanor *utilities executive*
Cockwell, Jack Lynn *business executive*
Colgrass, Michael Charles *composer*
Colombo, John Robert *poet, editor, writer*
Comper, Tony *banker*
Connell, Philip Francis *food industry executive*
Cook, Stephen Arthur *mathematics and computer science educator*
Cook-Bennett, Gail *pension fund administrator*
Cunningham, Gordon Ross *financial executive*
Curlook, Walter *management consultant*
Dale, Robert Gordon *business executive*
D'Alessandro, Dominic *financial executive*
Davenport, Paul *professional golfer*
Davis, William Grenville *lawyer, former Canadian government official*
Davison, Edward Joseph *electrical engineering educator*
Dean, Geoffrey *book publisher*
Detlefsen, Michael E. *food products executive*
DeWitt, David B. *political scientist, educator, political organization worker*
Dey, Peter J. *investment company executive*
Dickens, Bernard Morris *law educator*
Dimma, William Andrew *real estate executive*
Dobson, Wendy Kathleen *economics professor*
Downing, John Henry *columnist, journalist*
Dryden, Ken *sports team executive*
Dubin, Charles Leonard *lawyer*
Dunlop, David John *geophysics educator, researcher*
Eagles, Stuart Ernest *business executive*
Egoyan, Atom *film director*
Eisenberg, Howard Edward *physician, psychotherapist, consultant, educator, author*
Eklof, Svea Christine *ballet dancer*
Elder, Richard Bruce *artist, writer*
Elliott, Roy Fraser *lawyer, holding and management company executive*
Endrenyi, Janos *research engineer, educator*
Espinosa, Carlos *professional golfer*
Evans, John Robert *academic administrator, cardiologist*
Eyton, John Trevor *senator, business executive*
Farkas, Leslie Gabriel *plastic surgeon*
Farley, Tom *real estate company executive*
Farquharson, Gordon MacKay *lawyer, director*
Fatt, William R. *hospitality company executive*
Ferguson, Kingsley George *retired psychologist*
Fierheller, George Alfred *corporate director*
Fife, Edward H. *landscape architecture educator*
Finlay, Terence Edward *retired archbishop*
Fox, Wayne C. *brokerage house executive, corporate financial executive*
Francis, Ron *professional hockey player*
Fraser, William Neil *government official, retired*
Freedman, Harry *composer*
Fregosi, James Louis *professional baseball team manager*
Friedlander, John Benjamin *mathematician, educator*
Fullerton, R. Donald *banker*
Galloway, David Alexander *publishing company executive*
Ganczarczyk, Jerzy Jozef *civil engineering educator, wastewater treatment consultant*
Gaston, Cito *former professional baseball manager*
Geiger, John Grigsby *editor, writer, reporter*
Godsoe, Peter Cowperthwaite *banker*
Goh, Chan Hon *ballerina*
Goldberg, David Meyer *biochemistry educator*
Goldfarb, Martin *sociologist, researcher*
Goodenow, Robert W. *labor union administrator*
Goold, Douglas *think-tank executive*
Gordon, Harold P. *bank executive*
Goring, David Arthur Ingham *chemical engineering educator, scientist*
Gotlieb, Allan E. *former ambassador*
Gotlieb, Calvin Carl *computer scientist, educator*
Granatstein, Jack Lawrence *history professor*
Grayson, Albert Kirk *Near Eastern studies educator*
Greenwood, Lawrence George *banker*
Gregor, Tibor Philip *retired management consultant*
Halladay, Roy *professional baseball player*
Hanna, William Brooks *literary agent*
Harris, Sydney Malcolm *retired judge*
Hayhurst, James Frederick Palmer *career and business consultant, inspirational speaker, author*
Helleiner, Gerald Karl *economics professor*
Herren, Michael Wayne *classical studies educator*
Hirst, Peter Christopher *consulting actuary*
Hodgkinson, Greta *dancer*
Hofmann, Theo *biochemist, educator*
Holyday, Douglas Charles *city councillor*
Hon Goh, Chan *dancer*
Hore, John Edward *commodity futures educator*
Hyland, Geoffrey Fyfe *energy service company executive*
Iacobucci, Frank *lawyer, educator, jurist*
Israelievitch, Jacques H. *violinist, conductor*
Jacob, Ellis *entertainment company executive*
Janischewskyj, Wasyl *electrical engineering educator*
Jaworska, Tamara *painter, tapestry maker*
Jay, Charles Douglas *religion educator, college administrator, clergyman*
Johnson, Robert Eugene *historian, academic administrator*
Kalow, Werner *pharmacologist, toxicologist*
Kerr, David Wylie *natural resource company executive*
Khristich, Dimitri *professional hockey player*
Knowlton, Thomas A. *university dean, retired food products executive*
Kooluris Dobbs, Linda Kia *artist*
Kramer, Burton *graphic designer, educator*
Kresge, Alexander Jerry *chemistry professor*
Kudelka, James *choreographer, artistic director*
Kunov, Hans *biomedical and electrical engineering educator*
Kushner, Eva *academic administrator, educator, author*
Landsberg, Michele *journalist*
Langer, Bernard *medical association administrator*
Lastman, Melvin D. *mayor*
Lawson, Jane Elizabeth *bank executive*
Leech, James William *investment company executive*
Leetch, Brian Joseph *professional hockey player*
Lennox, R. Ian *health products executive*
Lewis, Robert *journalist, media executive*
Lewitt, Wilfred G. *health products executive*
Lindsay, Roger Alexander (Baron of Craighall) *investment executive*
Lindsay, William Kerr *surgeon*
Litherland, Albert Edward *physics educator*
Liversage, Richard Albert *cell biologist, educator*
Macdonald, Donald Stovel *corporate director*
Macdonald, Hugh Ian *university president emeritus, economist, educator*
MacDougall, Hartland Molson *trust company executive, retired bank executive*
MacLaren, Roy *retired federal official*
MacLennan, David Herman *research scientist, educator*
Magford, Mary *investment company executive*
Mann, George Stanley *real estate and financial services corporation executive*
Marks, Ray *education educator, researcher*
Marrié, William *dancer*
Martin, Robert William *corporate director*
Masui, Yoshio *zoology educator*
Mc Culloch, Ernest Armstrong *internist, educator*
McKenna, Marianne *architect*
McKeown, William Philip *lawyer*
McMurtry, R. Roy *chief justice*
McWilliam, Joanne Elizabeth *retired religion educator*
Meagher, George Vincent *mechanical engineer*
Mercier, Eileen Ann *corporate financial executive*
Millgate, Jane *language professional*
Millgate, Michael (Michael Henry Millgate) *retired English educator*
Mintz, Jack Maurice *think-tank executive, economics professor*
Moens, Peter B. *biology researcher and educator*
Mogilny, Alexander *professional hockey player*
Mondesi, Raul *professional baseball player*
Moore, Carole Irene *librarian*
Moore, Christopher Hugh *writer*
Morey, Carl Reginald *musicologist*
Morneau, William *pension and benefits company executive*
Mulholland, William David, Jr., *retired bank executive*
Munk, Peter *mining executive*
Munro, John Henry Alexander *economics educator, writer*
Nan Yu, Xiao *dancer*
Neligan, Peter C. *plastic surgeon*
Nesbitt, Lloyd Ivan *podiatrist*
Nesbitt, Mark *management consultant*
Nolan, Owen *professional hockey player*
Norris, Geoffrey *geology educator, consultant*
Novak, David *Judaic studies educator, rabbi*
Ogilvie, Richard Ian *clinical pharmacologist*
Oliphant, Randall *financial executive*
Osler, Gordon Peter *retired utility company executive*
Ostry, Sylvia *academic administrator, economist*
Oundjian, Peter *conductor*
Packer, Katherine Helen *retired library educator*
Packham, Marian Aitchison *biochemistry educator*
Peacock, Molly *poet, educator*
Peterson, David Robert *lawyer, former Canadian government official*
Peterson, Robert B. *petroleum company executive*
Pinto, Maxwell Salustiano *management consultant*
Plaut, Wolf Gunther *minister, author*
Polanyi, John Charles *chemist, educator*
Polistuk, Eugene V. *electronics manufacturing services executive*
Pollock, Samuel *diversified financial services company executive*
Poprawa, Andrew *financial services executive, accountant*
Pratt, Robert Cranford *political scientist, educator*
Price, Timothy R. *accountant*
Pritchard, Huw Owen *chemist, educator*
Quinn, Pat (John Brian Patrick Quinn) *professional sports team manager*
Rapoport, Anatol *peace studies educator, mathematical biologist*
Rasky, Harry *producer, director, writer*
Reaney, James Crerar *dramatist, poet, educator*
Ricciardi, J.P. *professional sports team executive*
Roberts, William D. *broadcast executive*
Rodriguez, Sonia *dancer*
Rogers, Edward Samuel *communications company executive*
Rooney, Paul George *mathematics professor*
Rose, Jeffrey Raymond *economist, educator, negotiator*
Salama, C. Andre Tewfik *electrical engineering educator*
San, Nguyen Duy *psychiatrist, educator*
Schramek, Tomas *ballet dancer, educator*
Schwartz, Gerald Wilfred *financial executive*
Seiersen, Nicholas Steen *management consultant*
Semak, Michael William *photographer, educator*
Sessle, Barry John *adult education educator, researcher*
Sharp, Isadore *hotel facility executive*
Shearing, George Albert *pianist, composer*
Shepherd, Gordon Greeley *space physics educator, researcher*
Shirley, George Irving *tenor*
Silk, Frederick C.Z. *financial consultant*
Sirman, Robert *performing company executive*
Skvorecky, Josef Vaclav *English literature educator, novelist*
Slaight, Gary *broadcast executive*
Slawter, Mark *professional golfer*
Slemon, Gordon Richard *electrical engineering educator*
Sloan, David Edward *retired finance company executive*
Smith, Lawrence Berk *economist, educator*
Smith, Peter William Ebblewhite *electrical engineering educator, scientist, physicist*
Sole, Michael Joseph *cardiologist*
Stadelman, William Ralph *chemical institution executive*
Staines, Mavis Avril *artistic director, ballet principal*
Stavro, Steve A. *professional hockey team executive*
Steinberg, Gregg Martin *financial and management consultant, investment banker*
Stoicheff, Boris Peter *physicist, researcher*
Storey, Susan *investment banker*
Strong, Maurice Frederick *hydro-electric power company executive, former United Nations official*
Stymiest, Barbara *stock exchange executive*
Sundin, Mats Johan *professional hockey player*
Taylor, Allan Richard *retired banker*
Thall, Burnett Murray *retired newspaper executive*
Thomson, Kenneth R. (Lord Thomson of Fleet) *publishing executive*
Thomson, Richard Murray *retired bank executive*
Till, James Edgar *medical educator, researcher*
Tilley, Shermaine Ann *investment company executive*
Tobe, Stephen Solomon *zoology educator*
Tolmie, Kenneth Donald *artist, author*
Tsubouchi, David H. *Canadian provincial official*
Turnbull, John Cameron *retired pharmacist, consultant*
Turner, John Napier *former prime minister of Canada, legislator*
Turner, Robert Edward *psychiatrist, educator*
Van Der Wyst, Geon *dancer*
van Ginkel, Blanche Lemco *architect, educator*
Venetsanopoulos, Anastasios Nicolaos *electrical engineer, educator*
Viner, Peter *communications executive*
Volpé, Robert *endocrinologist, researcher, educator*
Ward, Milton Hawkins *former mining company executive*
Waugh, Richard Earl *banker*
Webb, Anthony Allan *banker, director*
Webster, Jill Rosemary *historian, educator*
Weston, W. Galen, Sr., *diversified holdings executive*
Wevers, John William *retired Semitic languages educator*
Whitfield, Simon *Olympic athlete*
Willis, Kevin Alvin *professional basketball player*
Wilson, Lynton Ronald *retired telecommunications company executive*
Wilson, Michael Holcombe *investment banker, former Canadian government official*
Winter, Frederick Elliot *fine arts educator*
Wleugel, John Peter *manufacturing executive*
Wonham, Walter Murray *electrical engineer, educator*
Yu, Xiao Nan *dancer*
Zeng, Hong *audio system architect, researcher*

Waterloo
Aczél, János Dezsö *mathematician*
Balsillie, Jim *information technology executive*
Berczi, Andrew Stephen *academic administrator, educator*
Falding, Harold Joseph *sociology educator*
Gladwell, Graham Maurice Leslie *mathematician, civil engineering educator*
Haworth, Lawrence Lindley *philosophy educator*
Hynes, Hugh Bernard Noel *biologist, educator*
Lazaridis, Mike *information technology executive*
Morgan, Alan Vivian *geologist, educator*
Nelson, J. Gordon *geography educator*
Paldus, Josef *mathematics professor*
Penlidis, Alexander *chemical engineering educator*
Sedra, Adel Shafeek *electrical engineering educator, academic administrator*
Sprott, David Arthur *statistics and psychology educator*
Suits, Bernard Herbert *philosophy educator*
Urquhart, Tony *artist, educator*
Van Seters, John *retired biblical literature educator*
Vlach, Jiri *electrical engineering educator, researcher*
Vogel-Sprott, Muriel Doris *psychology educator, researcher*
Warner, Barry Gregory *ecologist, educator*
Wen, Geyi *applied physics educator*
Wright, Douglas Tyndall *business executive, university executive emeritus*

Willowdale
Kerner, Fred *book publisher, writer*
Sze, Michael Ming-Chih *actuary, consultant*
Wolfe, Rose *former academic administrator*

Windsor
Auld, Frank *psychologist, educator*
Ferguson, John Duncan *medical research educator*
Hackam, Reuben *electrical engineering educator*
Kennedy, John Baptist *civil engineer*
La Rocque, Eugene Philippe *bishop emeritus*
Thibert, Roger Joseph *clinical chemist, educator*

PRINCE EDWARD ISLAND

Charlottetown
McCallum, John *Canadian government official*
Vigneault, Alain *professional hockey coach*

Montague
Cregier, Don Mesick *historian, educator, researcher, consultant*

QUEBEC

Beaconsfield
Harder, Rolf Peter *graphic designer, painter*

Beauharnois
Lebel, Robert *bishop*

Brossard
Allen, Harold Don *mathematics educator, science writer, monetary historian*

Chelsea
Warren, Jack Hamilton *former diplomat and trade policy adviser*

Chicoutimi
Cain, Michael Haney *lawyer*
Couture, Jean Guy *bishop*

Eastman
Emond, Lionel Joseph *management consultant*

Fossambault Sur Le Lac
Maranda, Guy *retired oral maxillofacial surgeon, Canadian health facility executive, educator*

Gatineau
Beaudoin, Gérald A(rmand) *lawyer, educator, senator*

Hull
Anderson, David *Canadian government official*
Blondin-Andrew, Ethel D. *Canadian government official*
Bradshaw, Claudette *Canadian government official*
Gagliano, Alfonso *Canadian government official*

Ile Perrot
Lalonde, Marc *lawyer, former Canadian government official*

Laval
Adrian, Donna Jean *retired librarian*
Pichette, Claude *former banking executive, university rector, research executive*
Savoie, Paul-André *information technology executive*
Talbot, Pierre Joseph *microbiologist, researcher*

Leclercville
Morin, Pierre Jean *retired management consultant, social services administrator*

Montpellier
Poirier, Louis Joseph *neurology educator*

Montreal
Aguayo, Alberto Juan *neuroscientist*
Barrette, Jean *physicist, researcher*
Beauregard, Luc *public relations executive*
Becker, Herbert Lawrence *writer, accountant*
Beugnot, Bernard Andre Henri *French literature educator*
Bissonnette, Anik *dancer*
Brecher, Irving *economics professor*
Brecher, Michael *political science educator*
Brisebois, Marcel *museum director*
Bruemmer, Fred *writer, photographer*
Burgess, John Herbert *cardiologist, educator*
Caillé, André *public service company executive*
Carroll, Robert Lynn *biology professor, vertebrate paleontologist, museum curator, paleontologist, curator*
Cedraschi, Tullio *investment management company executive*
Chang, Thomas Ming Swi *medical scientist, biotechnologist*

Charney, Melvin *artist, architect, educator*
Clermont, Yves Wilfrid *anatomy educator, researcher*
Corson, Shayne *professional hockey player*
Crowston, Wallace Bruce Stewart *management educator*
Cruess, Richard Leigh *orthopedic surgeon, dean*
Cyr, J. V. Raymond *telecommunications industry executive*
Daly, Gerald *accountant*
Dansereau, Pierre *ecologist*
Das Gupta, Subal *physics educator, researcher*
Davidson, Colin Henry *architect, educator*
Dealy, John Michael *chemical engineer, educator*
Desmarais, Paul *holding company executive*
de Takacsy, Nicholas Benedict *physicist, researcher*
Diksic, Mirko *research scientist, educator*
Dubuc, Serge *mathematics professor*
Dufour, Jean-Marie *economics researcher, educator*
Duquette, Jean-Pierre *retired French language and literature educator*
Eisenberg, Adi *chemist*
Engen, D(onald) Travis *diversified telecommunications company executive*
Feindel, William Howard *neurosurgeon, consultant*
Ferguson, Michael John *electronics and communications educator*
Freedman, Samuel Orkin *university official*
Freeman, Carolyn Ruth *radiation oncologist*
Gabbour, Iskandar *city and regional planning educator*
Gainey, Robert Michael *professional hockey coach, former player*
Genest, Jacques *nephrologist, clinical scientist, administrator*
Gibbs, Sarah Preble *biologist, educator*
Gillespie, Thomas Stuart *investment company executive*
Girard, Francois *film director*
Gold, Alan B. *former Canadian chief justice*
Gold, Phil *immunologist, educator, researcher*
Goldbloom, Victor Charles *pediatrician*
Goltzman, David *endocrinologist, educator, researcher*
Granger, Luc Andre *university dean, psychologist*
Gratton, Robert *diversified financial services company executive*
Guérard, Geneviève *dancer*
Gulkin, Harry *arts administrator, film producer*
Haccoun, David *electrical engineering educator*
Herling, Michael *steel company executive*
Hoffmann, Peter Conrad Werner *history educator*
Hopkins, Tom *artist*
Ikawa-Smith, Fumiko *anthropologist, educator*
Ivanier, Paul *steel products manufacturing company executive*
Johnstone, Rose Mamelak (Mrs. Douglas Johnstone) *biochemistry educator*
Jolicoeur, Paul *molecular biologist*
Joly, Clément *accountant*
Jones, Barbara Ellen *neuroscientist, educator*
Julien, Claude *professional athletics coach*
Kaufman, Donna S. *lawyer*
Kinsley, William Benton *literature educator, educator*
Kovalev, Alexei *professional hockey player*
Kramer, Michael Stuart *pediatric epidemiologist*
Krausz, Peter Thomas *artist, gallery director, educator*
Lacombe, Jacques *conductor, music director*
Lacoste, Paul *law educator, academic administrator*
Ladanyi, Branko *civil engineer, educator*
Lagacé, Bernard *performing company executive*
Lamarre, Bernard *engineering executive*
Large, John Andrew *library and information service educator*
Laurin, Pierre *finance company executive*
Leblond, Charles Philippe *anatomy educator, researcher*
Lemire, Andre *investment company executive*
Leroy, Claude *physics educator, researcher*
Lowy, Frederick Hans *academic administrator, psychiatrist*
Maag, Urs Richard *statistics educator*
Mac Lean, Lloyd Douglas *surgeon*
Matziorinis, Kenneth N. *economist*
Melzack, Ronald *psychology educator*
Messing, Karen *occupational health researcher*
Michaud, Georges Joseph *astrophysics educator*
Milic-Emili, Joseph *physiologist, educator*
Milner, Brenda Atkinson Langford *neuropsychologist*
Minaya, Omar *professional sports team executive*
Molson, Eric H. *brewery company executive*
Morin, Yves-Charles *linguistics educator, researcher*
Moser, William Oscar Jules *mathematics professor*
Mulder, David S. *cardiovascular surgeon*
Mulroney, Brian (Martin Brian Mulroney) *former prime minister of Canada*
Mysak, Lawrence Alexander *oceanographer, climatologist, mathematician, educator*
Nadeau, Bertin Felix *diversified financial services company executive*
Nadeau, Jacques O. *brokerage house executive*
Nadeau, Reginald Antoine *medical educator*
Nattel, Stanley *cardiologist, research scientist*
Nayar, Baldev Raj *political science educator*
Neveu, Jean *printing company executive*
Normandeau, Andre Gabriel *criminologist, educator*
Ohayon, Maurice M. *research center administrator, psychiatrist*
Ormsby, Eric Linn *educator, researcher, writer*
Paidoussis, Michael Pandeli *mechanical engineering educator*
Pankov, Gradimir Krunislav *ballet artistic director*
Pasternac, André *cardiologist, educator*
Perlin, Arthur Saul *chemistry professor*
Picard, Laurent A(ugustin) *retired management educator, administrator, consultant*
Plourde, Gerard *company executive*
Podgorsak, Ervin B. *medical physicist, educator, administrator*
Popovici, Adrian *law educator*
Pound, Richard William Duncan *lawyer, accountant*
Radacovský, Mário *dancer*
Ramachandran, Venkatanarayana Deekshit *electrical engineering educator*
Raynauld, Andre *economist, educator*
Redfern, John D. *manufacturing executive*
Robb, James Alexander *lawyer*
Rolland, Lucien Gilbert *paper company executive, director*
Romanov, Volodymyr Alexeevich *computer science educator, researcher*
Rothman, Melvin L. *judge*

Saint-Pierre, Guy *engineering executive*
Scriver, Charles Robert *medical researcher, human geneticist*
Silverthorne, Michael James *classics educator*
Sirois, Charles *communications executive*
Snell, Linda S. *physician, medical educator*
Solomon, Samuel *biochemistry educator, administrator*
Sourkes, Theodore Lionel *biochemistry educator*
Speirs, Derek James *diversified corporation financial executive*
Steinberg, Norman Michael *lawyer*
Stewart, Jane *psychology educator*
Suen, Ching Yee *computer scientist and educator, researcher*
Szabo, Denis *criminologist, educator*
Taras, Paul *physicist, researcher*
Tavares, Tony *professional hockey and baseball leagues executive*
Tellier, Paul M. *railroad transportation executive*
Theodore, Jose *professional hockey player*
Thompson, John Douglas *financier*
Torrey, David Leonard *investment banker*
Toutant, Sylvain *retail executive*
Tremblay, Andre Gabriel *lawyer*
Trigger, Bruce Graham *anthropology educator*
Vaillancourt, Jean-Guy *sociology researcher and educator*
Van Dyke, Donald Lee *systems engineer, consultant*
Waller, Harold Myron *political science educator*
Webster, Norman Eric *journalist, charitable foundation administrator*
Whitehead, Michael Anthony *chemistry professor*
Wood, Dennis *communications executive*

Mount Royal
Chauvette, Claude R. *building materials company administrator*
Couture, Armand *civil engineer*
Elie, Jean André *investment banker*

North Hatley
Jones, Douglas Gordon *retired literature educator*

Outremont
Derderian, Hovnan *church official*
Letourneau, Jean-Paul *business association executive and consultant*
Levesque, Rene Jules Albert *retired physicist*

Pointe Claire
Bolker, Henry Irving *retired chemist, research institute director, educator*

Pointe-Claire
Bachynski, Morrel Paul *physicist*
Lapointe, Lucie *Canadian government official*

Quebec City
L'Heureux-Dubé, Claire *judge*
Theodorescu, Radu Amza Serban *mathematician, educator*

Rimouski
Blanchet, Bertrand *archbishop*

Rosemere
Hopper, Carol *meeting and incentive trip administrator*

Rouyn
Hamelin, Jean-Guy *bishop*

Saint-Adele
Rousseau-Vermette, Mariette *artist*

Saint-Anne-Des-Lacs
Rochette, Louis *retired shipowner and shipbuilder*

Saint-Faustin-Lac-Carre
Des Marais, Pierre, II, *communications holding company executive*

Saint-Lambert
Terreault, Charles *engineer, management educator, researcher*

Saint-Laurent
Jundi, Bilal *principal*

Saint-Sauveur
Hanigan, Lawrence *retired railway executive*

Sainte Anne de Bellevue
Grant, William Frederick *geneticist, educator*

Sainte-Anne-de-Bellevue
Broughton, Robert Stephen *irrigation and drainage engineering educator, consultant*

Sainte-Foy
Bonnelly, Claude *library director*
LeDuy, Anh *engineering educator*
Murray, Warren James *philosophy educator*
Normand, Robert *retired lawyer*

Sherbrooke
Bourget, Edwin Robert *marine ecologist, educator*
Tremblay, André-Marie *physicist*

Sillery
Dinan, Robert Michael *lawyer*
La Rochelle, Pierre-Louis *civil engineering educator*

St Laurent
Dion, Stéphane *legislator*

Sutton
Bolduc, J. Emilien *bank executive*

Varennes
Bartnikas, Raymond *electrical engineer, educator*

Verdun
Gauthier, Serge Gaston *neurologist*
Lessard, Michel M. *finance company executive*

Westmount
Coolidge, Robert Tytus *deacon, historian, educator*
Fortier, L. Yves *barrister*

Kalaycioglu, Serdar *space robotics engineer, manager*

SASKATCHEWAN

Regina
Barber, Lloyd Ingram *retired university president*
Bayda, Edward Dmytro *judge*
Clayton, Raymond Edward *government official*
Cleveland, Ray LeRoy *history educator*
Haverstock, Lynda M. *lieutenant governor*
MacKay, Harold Hugh *lawyer*
Mollard, John Douglas *engineering and geology executive*
Phillips, Roger *retired steel company executive*
Sonntag, Bernard H. *retired agrologist, public service executive*
Spencer, Larry *member of parliament*
Symes, Lawrence Richard *computer science educator, university dean*
Vanderhooft, Rob *investment company executive*

Saskatoon
Babiuk, Lorne Alan *virologist, immunologist, research administrator*
Billinton, Roy *engineering educator*
Blakeney, Allan Emrys *Canadian government official, lawyer, educator*
Bornstein, Eli *artist, sculptor*
Deng, Shengliang *marketing educator*
Hirose, Akira *physics educator, researcher*
Huang, Pan Ming *soil science educator*
Irvine, Vernon Bruce *accounting educator, administrator*
Ish, Daniel Russell *law educator, academic administrator*
Jacobson, Sverre Theodore *retired minister*
Kartha, Kutty Krishnan *plant pathologist*
Kennedy, Marjorie Ellen *librarian*
Knott, Douglas Ronald *college dean, agricultural sciences educator, researcher*
Martell, Keith *bank executive*
Popkin, David Richard *obstetrician, health science administrator*
Shokeir, Mohamed Hassan Kamel *medical geneticist, educator*
Smith, C. D. *civil engineering educator*

Calgary
Grand-Maitre, Jean *performing company executive*

Edmonton
Ostroverkhova, Oksana *physicist*

Flamborough, Ontario
Lee, Alvin A. *literary educator, scholar, author*

Kugaaruk
Rodnunsky, Sidney *lawyer, educator*

Laval
Baroudy, Bahige Mourad *biochemist, researcher*

Mississauga
Runnalls, Oliver John Clyve (John Runnalls) *nuclear engineering educator*

Montreal
Becklake, Margaret Rigsby *epidemiologist, educator*
Bisson, Claude *retired chief justice of Quebec*
Ducharme, Francine Carole *nursing educator, researcher*
Gonthier, Charles Doherty *retired judge*
Hutchison, Andrew Sandford *archbishop*
Labadie, Bernard *performing company executive*
Lock, Edouard *performing company executive*
Moss, David *music company executive*
O'Neill, Daniel J. *brewery company executive*
Selvadurai, Antony Patrick Sinnappa *civil engineering educator, applied mathematician, consultant*
Turcotte, Jean-Claude Cardinal *archbishop*

Oakville
Jelinek, John Joseph *public relations executive*

Ottawa
Easter, Arnold Wayne *solicitor*
Owen, Stephen *Canadian government official*

Quebec City
Belanger, Gerard *economics professor*
LeMay, Jacques *lawyer*
Morin, Louis *government agency administrator*
Page, Michel *biochemist, researcher*
Potvin, Pierre *physiologist, educator*
Stavert, Alexander Bruce *bishop*
Tremblay, Marc Adélard *anthropologist, educator*
Verge, Pierre *legal educator*

Richmond
Cordoba, Mike *food service executive*

Saint Jean-Sur-Richelieu
Trudel, Marc J. *botanist, educator*

Sherbrooke
Deslongchamps, Pierre *chemistry professor*

Sillery
Dalens, Bernard Jacques *pediatric anesthesiologist*

Ville Saint Laurent
Braquet, Pierre G. *science educator, health science association administrator*

Winnipeg
Hodgkins, William F. *career officer*

MEXICO

Aguascalientes
Godinez Flores, Ramon *bishop*

Col Centro
Gil Diaz, Francisco *minister of finance for Mexico*

Col Lomas de Chapultepec
Guajardo Touché, Ricardo *bank executive*

Colonia Cuauhtemoc
Garza, Antonio O. *ambassador*

Cuernavaca
Bolivar Zapata, Francisco *biochemist*

Distrito Federal
de la Fuente Ramirez, Juan Ramon *academic administrator*

Garza Garcia
Gustafson, Eric William *real estate investor, wildlife habitat conservationist*

Guadalajara
Sandoval Iñiguez, Juan Cardinal *archbishop*

La Noria
Campos, Jorge *professional soccer player*

Mexico City
Abascal Carranza, Carlos Maria *secretary of labor and social planning for Mexico*
Barrio Terrazas, Francisco *government official of Mexico*
Bruton, John Macaulay *trade association executive, consultant*
Cerisola y Weber, Pedro *secretary of communications and transportation for Mexico*
Chavez, Julio Cesar *professional boxer*
Creel Miranda, Santiago *Mexican government official*
De La Riva, Myriam Ann *artist*
Derbez Bautista, Luis Ernesto *secretary of foreign affairs of Mexico*
Fox, Vicente (Vicente Fox Quesada) *President of Mexico*
Friedeberg, Pedro *painter, sculptor, designer*
Gonzalez-Sanchez, Enrique *economist*
Gurria Trevino, José Angel *former Mexican government official*
Herrera Tello, Maria Teresa *secretary of agrarian reform for Mexico*
Kim, Earnest Jae-Hyun *import and export company executive*
Leon-Portilla, Miguel *historian, educator*
Lichtinger, Victor *government official*
Macedo de la Concha, Rafael *attorney general of Mexico*
Navarro, Leticia *Mexican government official*
Nicholas, Ronald Wayde *business consultant*
Ortiz, Guillermo *banker*
Peyrot Gonzalez, Marco A. *secretary of the navy of Mexico*
Porraz, Mauricio Jimenez Labora *civil engineer, researcher*
Rivera Carrera, Norberto Cardinal *archbishop*
Rosenkranz, George *chemical company executive*
Soberon Kuri, Alejandro *performing company executive*
Tamez Guerra, Reyes S. *secretary of public education for Mexico*
Trevino, Guillermo Prieto *brokerage house executive*
Usabiaga Arroyo, Javier *secretary of agriculture, livestock and rural development for Mexico*
Vargas Legaspi, Juan *manufacturing executive*
Vazquez Mota, Josefina *secretary of social development for Mexico*
Vega Garcia, Gerardo Clemente R. *Mexico Secretary of Defense*

Monterrey
Amores, Jose E. *cultural director*

Patzcuaro
di Cori, Pat Miller *painter, sculptor*

Piso
Tellez Kuenzler, Luis *government official*

Puebla
Creuheras, Santiago *social scientist*

Reynosa
Asomoza, Miguel A. *researcher, educator*

San Nicolas
Suarez Rivera, Adolfo Antonio Cardinal *retired archbishop*

San Pedro Garza García
Defiore, Perry Dennis *director, small business owner*
Arroyo Marroquin, Romárico *former federal official*
Carabias Lillo, Julia *government official*
Carrasco Altamirano, Diódoro *former federal official*
Farell Cubillas, Arsenio *former Mexican government official*
Limón Rojas, Miguel *former Mexican government official*
Lorenzo Franco, José Ramón *former Mexican government official*
Martens Rebolledo, Ernesto *secretary of energy for Mexico*
Robledo Rincón, Eduardo *former federal official*

AFGHANISTAN

Kabul
Khalilzad, Zalmay *ambassador*

ARGENTINA

Buenos Aires
Berardi, Jorge Enrique *economist*
Diodato, Luis Hector *physician, researcher*
Green Macias, Rosario *ambassador*
Levy, Joseph Bruno *foundation administrator, educator*
Lopez-Murphy, Ricardo Hipolito *economist*
Montes, Leopoldo Feliciano *dermatologist, educator*

AUSTRALIA

Altona
Daniel-Dreyfus, Susan B. Russe *information technology executive*

Brisbane
Edwards, Sir Llewellyn Roy *company executive*

Camberwell
Base, Graeme Rowland *illustrator, author*
Peterson, Douglas Pete (Pete Peterson) *ambassador, retired congressman*

Cammeray
Besley, Morrish Alexander (Tim Besley) *civil engineer*

Canberra
Gani, Joseph Mark *statistics educator, administrator, researcher*
Harris, Stuart Francis *international relations educator, researcher*
Taylor, Stuart Ross *geochemist, author*

Darlinghurst
Davis, Judy *actress*

Double Bay
Peacock, Penne Korth *ambassador*

Double Bay Sydney
Guerin, Didier *magazine executive*

East Perth
Young, Deidra Jane *educational researcher*

Malanda
Cooper, William Thomas *natural history artist*

Melbourne
Batrouney, Clive M. *corporate financial executive*
Bellin, Howard *management consultant company executive*
Searby, Richard Henry *academic administrator, lawyer*

Nedlands
Oxnard, Charles Ernest *anatomist, anthropologist, human biologist, educator*

Norfolk Island
McCullough, Colleen *author*

North Sydney
Scott, Brian Walter *management consultant*

Paddington
Keneally, Thomas Michael *author*

Parkville
Azer, Samy Aziz *gastroenterologist, medical educator*
Denton, Derek Ashworth *medical researcher, medical scientist*
Metcalf, Donald *biomedical researcher*

Parkville Victoria
Chambers, Robert Hunter, III, *college president, American studies educator, consultant*

Perth
Dow, Simon *artistic director, coreographer*

Randwick
Hall, Peter Francis *physiologist*

Redfern
Campion, Jane *director, screenwriter*

Southport
Buckley, Ralf Christopher *research scientist*

Springfield
Spalvins, Janis Gunars *steamship company executive*

Sydney
Blakely, Edward James *economics professor*
Lucas, Peter Charles *investment company executive*
Selley, Michael L. *pharmaceutical company executive*

Townsville, Queensland
Ho, Yik Hong *colon and rectal surgeon*

Vic
DeWitt, Dawn E. *medical educator, dean*

Victoria Armadale
Neil, Sandra Eilleen Silverberg *psychologist*

Wembley
Koslow, Julian Anthony *oceanographer, research scientist*

Woollahra
Palmerlee, April Wahlestedt *management consultant*

AUSTRIA

Graz
Prisching, Manfred *sociology educator*
Weisstein, Ulrich Werner *English literature educator*

Kitzbuehel
Newman, Claire Poe *private investor*

Portland
Kalmar, Carlos *music director*

Vienna
al-Omair, Saleh *trade association administrator*
Brill, Kenneth C. *ambassador*
Higgins, William Woods *painter, art educator*
Liebscher, Klaus *stock exchange executive, banker*

Pohl, Adolf Leopold *clinical chemist, quality assurance consultant*
Sindelka, Josef *postal service and telecommunications administrator*

THE BAHAMAS

Nassau
Crone, John Thomas, IV, *portfolio manager, financial analyst*
Dingman, Michael David *industrial company executive, international investor*
Harrison, Johnnie Sheppard *religious organization administrator*

BAHRAIN

Manama
Sarhan, Mansoor Mohamed *library director*

BELARUS

Minsk
Sychov, Alyaksandr *diplomat*

BELGIUM

Antwerp
Snyders, Dirk Johan *electrophysiologist, biophysicist, educator*

Brussels
Barnum, John Wallace *lawyer*
Baxon, Paul Henri Maria *company executive*
Berna, Marie-Rose *international organization executive*
Burns, R. Nicholas *ambassador*
Bustin, George Leo *lawyer*
Horton, Linda Rae *lawyer*
Jadot, Jean Lambert Octave *clergyman*
Kempe, Frederick Schumann *newspaper editor, columnist, author*
Kerber, Frank John *diplomat*
Prodi, Romano *economist, educator, researcher, former prime minister of Italy, international commission executive*
Rossi, Pierre Marie *management consultant*
Schnabel, Rockwell Anthony *ambassador*

Liège
Mosora-Stan, Florentina Ioana *physics educator*

Oost-Vlaanderen
Stroobandt, Dirk Rudy *research scientist, educator*

Roeselare
Libbrecht, Gaspar Joseph *civil engineer, educator*

BELIZE

Belize City
Brown, Sir George Noel *chief justice*

BERMUDA

Hamilton
Johnston, Malcolm (Calum) *bank executive*
Kramer, Donald *insurance executive*

Tuckers Town
Heizer, Edgar Francis, Jr., *venture capitalist*

BRAZIL

Brasília
Amorim, Celso Luiz Nunes *government official*

Canoas
Sluberski, Thomas Richard *international educator, journalist, theologian*

Rio de Janeiro
Resende, Marcelo *economist, educator*
Sales, Eugenio de Araujo Cardinal *archbishop emeritus*

Sao Paolo
Leighton, Robert Bruce *investment company executive*

Sao Paulo
Kim, Kwang Wook *corporate financial executive*
Reigrod, Robert Hull *manufacturing executive*

Sorocaba
Martins, Nelson *physics educator*

BULGARIA

Sofia
Exerowa, Dotchi Russeva *chemist, researcher*

CAMEROON

Yaoundé
Provencher-Kambour, Frances *business development advisor*

CHAD

N'Djamena
Goldthwait, Christopher E. *ambassador*

CHANNEL ISLANDS

Guernsey
Schere, Jean *researcher*

CHILE

San Antonio
Beshears, Charles Daniel *insurance executive*

Santiago
Wilkey, Malcolm Richard *retired ambassador, former federal judge*

Talca
McNamee, Sister Catherine *theology studies educator*

CHINA

Beijing
Banister, Judith *demographer, educator*
Ren, Jiyu *library director*
Yizhong, Li *business executive*

Changchun Jilin
Bi, Shuwei *management information systems educator*

Hong Kong
Halperin, David Richard *lawyer*

Shanghai
Chueh, Chun Fei *import/export company executive*
Jackson, Robert Keith *retired manufacturing executive*
Langford, Roland Everett *environmental scientist, safety engineer, writer*
Yun, Liang *marine engineer, educator*

COSTA RICA

San José
Arias Sanchez, Oscar *former president of Costa Rica*
Hoffman, Irwin *orchestra conductor*

COTE D'IVOIRE

Abidjan
Obrou, Kouadio Olivier *physics professor, researcher*
Perry, Cynthia Shepard *federal agency administrator*

CROATIA

Zagreb
Štambuk, Nikola *research scientist*

CYPRUS

Nicosia
Aloneftis, Andreas *financial and investment executive*

CZECH REPUBLIC

Prague
Bubeník, Jan *cancer researcher, biology educator*
Čejka, Jiří *chemist, researcher*
Jech, Thomas J. *mathematics professor*
Kalkus, Stanley *librarian, administrator, consultant*
Kavan, Jan *member Czech Parliament, former president UN General Assembly*
Turková, Helga *library director*
Zharikov, Alexander Nikolaevich *trade union federation executive*

DENMARK

Charlottenlund
Garner, Fradley Hamilton *freelance writer, editor, narrator*

Copenhagen
Elmer, Michael Bendik *legal administrator*
Jiménez-Beltran, Domingo *executive*
Larsen, Poul Steen *library educator*
Martin, Vivian *soprano*
Mottelson, Ben R. *physicist*
Olgaard, Anders *economics professor*
Pethick, Christopher John *physicist*

Gentofte
Egsmose, Ragna Kopp *cultural sociologist, researcher*

Hoersholm
Sørensen, Erik *international company executive*

Holstebro
Schaufuss, Peter *dancer, producer, choreographer, ballet director*

Odense
Keldmann, Erik Christian Vilhelm *innovation company executive*
Lauritsen, Kaj Torben *retired lawyer, former association executive*

Thisted
Nordqvist, Erik Askbo *shipping company executive*

Vedbaek
Svensson, Sven Eilif *civil engineer, consultant*

EGYPT

Cairo
Abbas, Ali El-Sayed *oil company executive, researcher*
Elaraby, Nabil A. *Egyptian diplomat, judge*
Fahmy, Ibrahim Mounir *hotel executive*
Miller, Harry George *education educator*
Morsi, Abd el Wahab *artist*
Sullivan, Earl Le Roy *political science educator, academic administrator*
Welch, C. David *ambassador*

Garden City
Norris, James Arnold *federal agency administrator, consultant*

ENGLAND

Aldwych London
O'Brien, Patrick Karl *economic history educator*

Askett
Irons, Jeremy John *actor*

Barnston Wirral
Scragg, Thomas William *librarian, historical researcher, solicitor*

Beckenham Kent
Lader, Malcolm Harold *pharmaceutical consultant*

Bedfordshire
Gelman, Leonid Moiseevich *scientist, vibroacoustician, educator*

Beverley
Edles, Gary Joel *lawyer*

Birmingham
Browne, Roger Michael *oral pathology educator, consultant*

Brighton
Kroto, Harold Walter *chemistry researcher, educator*

Cambridge
Buckingham, Amyand David *chemistry professor*
Edwards, Sir Samuel Frederick *physicist, researcher*
Hawking, Stephen W. *astrophysicist, mathematician*
Hawthorne, Sir William (Sir William Rede Hawthorne) *aerospace and mechanical engineer, educator*
Hogwood, Christopher Jarvis Haley *music educator*
Huxley, Sir Andrew (Sir Andrew Fielding Huxley) *physiologist, educator*
Kermode, Frank (John Kermode) *literary critic, educator*
Klug, Aaron *molecular biologist*
Mirrlees, Sir James Alexander *economics professor*
Rees, Martin John *astronomy educator*
Renfrew, Andrew Colin (Lord Renfrew of Kaimsthorn) *archaeologist, academic administrator*
Richard, Alison Fettes *anthropology educator*
Sanger, Frederick *retired molecular biologist*
Steiner, George (Francis Steiner) *author, educator*

Canterbury
Holwell, Peter *management consultant*

Charlbury
Belkin, Boris David *violinist*

Cheshunt Hertfordshire
Leahy, Sir Terry *marketing professional, food products executive*

Chiswick
Adams, Norman *artist, educator*

Coulsdon
Vijayaratnam, Kanapathipillai *civil and environmental engineer, consultant, director, educator*

Coventry
Thomas, Howard *business educator*

Durham
Galloway, David Malcolm *retired education educator*
Spooner, Frank Clyffurde *economic history educator*

East Sussex
Katin, Peter Roy *pianist*

Ely Cambridgeshire
March, Lionel John *architecture educator, researcher*

Falmer
Cornforth, Sir John Warcup *chemist*

Guildford
Bulmer, Martin *sociologist, educator*

Harmondsworth
Marshall, Lord Colin (Lord Marshall of Knightsbridge) *airline executive*

Isle of Wight
Brown, John Robert *lawyer*
Stigwood, Robert Colin *theater, movie, television and record producer*

Kent Cranbrook
Hattersley-Smith, Geoffrey Francis *retired government research scientist*

Lane End Bucks
Blackton, Charles S(tuart) *history educator*

Leeds
Ichino, Yoko *ballet dancer*
Nixon, David *dancer*
Phillips, Oliver *tropical forest ecologist*

Leicester
Harijan, Ram *technology transfer researcher*

Letchworth
Everitt-Newton, Katherine Evelyn *international management consultant*

Liverpool
Sawko, Felicjan *civil engineering educator*

London
Akin, Steven Paul *financial company executive*
Albert, Robert Alan *lawyer*
Alexeev, Dmitri Konstantinovich *pianist*
Alvarez, A. (Al Alvarez) *writer*
Amis, Martin Louis *author*
Andsnes, Leif Ove *concert pianist*
Arman Gelenbe, Deniz *concert pianist*
Ashkenazy, Vladimir Davidovich *concert pianist, conductor*
Baird, Dugald Euan *automotive executive*
Barnevik, Percy Nils *electrical company executive*
Bertolucci, Bernardo *film director*
Bevan, Tim *film producer*
Binney, Robert Harry *bank executive*
Bloom, Orlando *actor*
Bono, (Paul Hewson) *singer, songwriter*
Bourne, Matthew *performing company executive, artistic director*
Chadwick, Derek James *foundation administrator*
Chevalier, Tracy Rose *writer*
Clay, Clifton Ford *motion picture producer, writer*
Cleese, John Marwood *writer, comedian*
Codron, Michael Victor *theatrical producer*
Cole, Richard A. *retired lawyer*
Collins, Paul John *banker*
Conti, Tom *actor, writer, director*
Cope, Wendy *poet*
Cuno, James *art museum director*
Dahrendorf, Lord Ralf Gustav *social scientist, educator*
Davis, Crispin *publishing company executive*
Davis, Ian *management consulting firm executive*
Day-Lewis, Daniel Michael Blake *actor*
Deighton, Len *author*
Desai, Anita *writer*
de Savorgnani, Adriane Aldrich *health care administrator, nurse*
Dohnányi, Christoph von *musician, conductor*
Douglas, Mary Tew *anthropology and humanities educator*
Drabble, Margaret *writer*
Duncan, Lindsay Vere *actress*
Edwards, Sylvia Ann *artist*
Elizabeth, Her Majesty, II, (Elizabeth Alexandra Mary) *Queen of United Kingdom of Great Britain, Northern Ireland and of her other Realms and Territories; Head of Commonwealth, Defender of Faith*
Ellis, Claud M. Buddy *diversified financial services company executive*
Elson, Sarah Lee *art historian and consultant*
Eustace, Dudley Graham *diversified financial services company executive*
Fabricant, Arthur E. *lawyer, corporate executive*
Fellner, Eric *film producer*
Fine, Anne *author*
Flint, Douglas J. *business executive*
Flor, Claus Peter *conductor*
Foldes, Lucien Paul *economics professor*
Fowles, John *author*
Fox, James *actor*
Furse, Clara *stock exchange executive*
Galloway, Janice *writer, editor*
Gelenbe, Sami Erol *engineering educator*
Gervais, Ricky *actor*
Gibson, William Ford *author*
Gillam, Sir Patrick *oil company executive, banker*
Glass, Douglas B. *lawyer*
Glazer, Barry David *lawyer*
Goosen, Retief *professional golfer*
Graubard, Stephen Richards *history educator, editor*
Gray, Simon James Holliday *writer, educator*
Greener, Anthony *telecommunications industry executive*
Gulliver, Stuart *bank executive*
Habgood, Anthony John *corporate executive*
Hall, Sir Peter Geoffrey *urban and regional planning educator*
Hanson, Lord James Edward *industrialist*
Hare, David *playwright*
Harney, Kathryn Ann *opera singer*
Harwood, Ronald *screenwriter, playwright*
Haubold, Samuel Allen *lawyer*
Hazell, Robert John Davidge *policy institute director, government educator*
Hicks, J. Portis *lawyer*
Hiller, Susan *artist*
Hornyak, Eugene Augustine *bishop*
Hudson, Manley O., Jr., *lawyer*
Hunsberger, Alice Chandler *religion educator, human rights activist, scholar*
Hunter Blair, Pauline Clarke *author*
James, P(hyllis) D(orothy) (Baroness James of Holland Park of Southwold in County of Suffolk) *author*
John, Sir Elton Hercules (Reginald Kenneth Dwight) *musician*
Jourdren, Marc Henri *investment banking company executive*
Junz, Helen B. *economist*
Kallakis, Achilleas Michalis S. *shipping and real estate company executive*
Keevil, Philip Clement *investment banker*
Koonin, Steven Elliot *physicist, educator*
Kuper, Adam Jonathan *anthropologist, educator*
Leaf, Robert Stephen *public relations executive*
Leigh, Mike *film director*
Lessing, Doris (Doris May) *writer*
Levi, Yoel *orchestra conductor*
Lowenthal, David *historian, geographer*
MacClean, Walter Lee *dentist*
Mackerras, Sir Charles (Alan Maclaurin) *conductor*
Mackintosh, Cameron *musical theater producer*
Masur, Kurt *conductor*
McCowen, Alec *actor*
McGregor, Ewan Gordon *actor*
Mendes, Sam (Samuel Alexander Mendes) *film director, theater director*
Meyer, Sir Christopher J.R. *former diplomat*
Miller, Jonathan Wolfe *theater and film director, physician*
Minton, Scott D. *lawyer*
Minton, Yvonne Fay *mezzo-soprano*
Montgomery, John Warwick (Baron of Kiltartan and Lord of Morris, Comte de St. Germain de Montgommery) *law educator, theologian*
Moody, Ron *actor, writer*
Morris, Desmond (John) *zoologist, writer, artist*
Morrison, William David *lawyer*
Moss, Kate *model*
Naipaul, Vidiadhar Surajprasad *author*
Navarrete, Jorge Eduardo *ambassador*
Nelson, Elizabeth Hawkins *public association administrator*
Nelson, Walter Henry *communications consultant, author*
Newell, Mike *film director*
Nicholson, Geoffrey William Greer *management consultant*
Nordberg, Donald *communications executive*
Oliver, Diane Frances *publisher, writer*
Oliver, Jamie *chef, television personality*
Palin, Michael Edward *actor, screenwriter, writer*
Paton Walsh, Jill *writer*
Paulus, Michael John *government official, bank executive, economist*
Peckham, Michael John *academic administrator*
Pennant-Rea, Rupert Lascelles *banker, economist*
Perkin, Harold James *retired social historian, educator*
Phillips, Caryl *writer*
Phocas, George John *international lawyer, business executive*
Plowright, Joan Anne *actress*
Portes, Richard David *economics professor*
Pryce, Jonathan *actor*
Quillen, Cecil Dyer, III, *lawyer*
Radcliffe, Daniel *actor*
Ralston, Anthony *computer scientist, mathematician, educator*
Read, Piers Paul *author*
Ricci, Ruggiero *violinist, educator*
Rice, Sir Timothy Miles Bindon *lyricist*
Richardson, Ian William *actor*
Richardson, Miranda *actress*
Rolle, Martha Collins (Martha Traudt Collins) *lawyer*
Rowling, J.K. (Joanne Kathleen Rowling) *writer*
Rubin, Patricia Lee *art historian*
Rutter, Michael Llewellyn *child psychiatry educator*
Sarkis, Ziad Joseph *private equity executive*
Scardino, Marjorie Morris *publishing company executive*
Scheinman, Stanley Bruce *international financial executive, lawyer*
Scott, Raymond Peter William *chemistry research educator, writer*
Shankar, Ravi *musician, sitar player, composer*
Shaw, Timothy Milton *political science educator*
Slatkin, Leonard Edward *conductor, music director, pianist*
Spillane, Mary Catherine *television producer*
Steele, Howard L. *psychology educator*
Stern, Stephen Jeffrey *lawyer*
Stevens, Robert Bocking *lawyer, educator*
Stoppard, Tom (Tomas Straussler) *playwright*
Studzinski, John Joseph Paul *investment banking executive*
Thomas, Allen Lloyd *lawyer, private investor*
Uchida, Mitsuko *pianist*
Vane, John Robert *pharmacologist*
Vanniasingham, Samuel Kanagasabapathy *accountant*
Vicari, Andrew *artist*
Waldegrave, Lord (Lord Waldegrave of North Hill) *financial services company executive*
Winner, Michael Robert *film director, writer, producer*
Zonana, Victor *lawyer, educator*

Manchester
Briscoe, John *classical languages educator*
Wilson, Keith Dudley *media and music educator, consultant, dean*

Milton Keynes
Throdahl, Mark Crandall *medical technology company executive*

North Wales
Hands, Terence David (Terry Hands) *theater and opera director*

Norwich
Aston, Peter George *music educator, composer, conductor*

Nottingham
Krasnov, Kirill *physicist, researcher*

Oxford
Carey, John *English language educator, literary critic*
Doyle, William Stowell *venture capitalist*
Gowans, Sir James Learmonth *science administrator, immunologist*
Halsey, Albert Henry *sociologist*
Mattli, Walter *political scientist, educator*
May, Robert McCredie *biology educator*
Nolan, James Lawry, Jr., *sociologist*
Robinson, Mary *former United Nations official*
Vaisey, David George *librarian, archivist*
Varese, Federico *political science educator*

Richmond
Armfield, Diana Maxwell *artist, educator*
Te Kanawa, Kiri *opera and concert singer*

Richmond-upon-Thames
Smith, Norman Raymond *academic administrator*

Saint Margaret's
Attenborough, Baron Richard Samuel *actor, producer, director, goodwill ambassador*

Southampton
Brebbia, Carlos Alberto *educator, engineering consultant*

Stevenage
Follett, Kenneth Martin *author*

Stokenchurch
Barratt, Eric George *accountant*

Storrington
Osborne, Stephen J. *philatelist*

Stroud
Robinson, John Beckwith *development management consultant*

Sunbury-on-Thames
Lynch, John Edward, Jr., *lawyer*

Surrey
Els, Ernie (Theodore Ernest Els) *professional golfer*
Olazabal, Jose Maria *professional golfer*
Vere Hodge, Richard Anthony *pharmaceutical executive, consultant*
Weston, Sir John (Sir Philip John Weston) *company non-executive director, retired diplomat*

Teddington
Roberts, Melville Parker *neurosurgeon, neuroanatomist, educator*

Tunbridge Wells
Howden, Frank Newton *Episcopal priest, humanities educator*
Singer, Norbert *health services professional, educational consultant*

Warwickshire
Warbeck, Stephen *composer*

Westminster
Broers, Lord Alec Nigel *engineering educator*

Whitchurch
Adams, Richard George *writer*

Wiltshire
Gabriel, Peter *vocalist, composer*
Sherwin, James Terry *lawyer*

York
Williams, Alan Harold *economics professor*
Kingsley, James Gordon *college administrator*

ESTONIA

Tallinn
Köörna, Arno *economist, educator*

FINLAND

Helsinki
Hamalainen, Pekka Kalevi *historian, educator*
Juhani, Erma *lawyer, former stock exchange executive*
Liewendahl, Bo Kristian *pathologist, nuclear medicine physician*

Tampere
Andriano, Kirk Patrick *pharmaceutical executive*
Pöntinen, Pekka Juhani *anesthesiologist, consultant*

FRANCE

APO
Carner, George *foreign service executive, economic strategist*

Arles
Clergue, Lucien Georges *photographer*

Biarritz
Friedman, Richard Everett *librarian*

Chartres
Benoit, Jean-Pierre Robert *retired pneumologist, consultant*

Collonges
Morgenstern, Sheldon Jon *symphony orchestra conductor*

Creteil
Renoux, André *physicist, researcher*

Croupieres Lethor
Salinger, Pierre Emil George *journalist*

Draguignan
Frame, Nancy Davis *lawyer*

Gif-sur-Yvette
Duplessy, Jean Claude *research scientist*

Grenoble
Dussopt, Laurent *electrical engineer*

Guyancourt
Dubar, Claude Roger *sociologist*

Indre-et-Loire
Schom, Alan Morris *historian, educator*

Lyon
Bazin, Patrick *library director*
Robertson, David *conductor*

Nanterre
Payri, Joel *pharmaceutical marketing executive*

Neoules
Masurel, Jean-Louis Antoine Nicolas *investment company executive*

Neuilly
Goldmark, Peter Carl, Jr., *publishing executive*

Neuilly-sur-Seine
Hewes, Thomas Francis *physician*

Noisy le Grand
Le Quéré, Jean François Marie *scientific instrumentation researcher*

Orsay
Fiszer-Szafarz, Berta (Berta Safars) *research scientist, researcher*
Friedel, Jacques *physics educator*

Paris
Allais, Maurice Felix *economist*
Annaud, Jean-Jacques *film director, screenwriter, producer*
Baum, Axel Helmuth *lawyer*
Bedjaoui, M. Mohammed *former judge International Court of Justice*
Boccara, Nino *physicist*
Bujon de L'Estang, Francois *bank executive*
Christensen, Helena *model*
Collomb, Bertrand Pierre *cement company executive*
Courtaud, Bernard Jean-Jacques *human resource consulting executive*
Courtois, Jean-Philippe *information technology executive*
Dausset, Jean *immunologist*
Dean, John Gunther *diplomat*
de Gennes, Pierre-Gilles *physicist, educator*
de Havilland, Olivia Mary *actress*
Deneuve, Catherine (Catherine Dorleac) *actress*
Fitoussi, Jean-Paul Samuel *economist, educator*
Flack, Ronald David *diplomat, public service educator, banker*
Gallant, Mavis *author*
Gontier, Jean Roger *medicine and physiology educator*
Horovitz, Israel Arthur *playwright*
Jacob, François *biologist, educator*
Janicot, Daniel Claude Emmanuel *foundation administrator*
Jolas, Betsy *composer, educator*
Kourilsky, François Michel *research scientist*
Kouyaté, Lansana *economist, federal official, diplomat*
Kurtz, Eugene Allen *composer, educator, consultant*
Lacroix, Christian Marie Marc *fashion designer*
Landers, Steven E. *lawyer*
Leach, Howard H. *ambassador, former health care products company executive*
Lecerf, Olivier Maurice Marie *construction company executive*
Lehn, Jean-Marie Pierre *chemistry professor*
Levy, David Alfred *immunology educator, physician, scientist*
Lucas, Georges *physicist, researcher*
Marcus, Claude *advertising executive*
Memmi, Albert *sociologist, educator*
Mestrallet, Gérard *utilities executive, professional society administrator*
Montagnier, Luc Antoine *virologist*
Myerson, Jacob Myer *retired diplomat*
Peugeot, Patrick *insurance executive*
Raharinaivo, André Léon *research executive, educator*
Raimondi, Ruggero *opera singer*
Rawlings, Boynton Mott *lawyer*
Reeves, Van Kirk *lawyer*
Reza, Yasmina *author, playwright*
Rosenberg, Pierre Max *museum director*
Rouvillois, Philippe *research and development executive*
Salans, Carl Fredric *lawyer*
Serre, Jean-Pierre *mathematician, scholar*
Teicher, Henry Earl *retired education educator*
Ungaro, Emanuel Matteotti *fashion designer*
Unwin, Geoff *consulting company executive*
Vandame, Jean-Marie Richard *diversified financial services company executive*
Yuechiming, Roger Yue Yuen Shing *mathematics professor*

Ramatuelle
Collins, Larry *author, journalist*

Roques
White, Norval Crawford *architect*

Saint Ceols
Saisselin, Remy Gilbert *fine arts educator*

Suresnes
de Pouzilhac, Alain Duplessis *advertising executive*

Toulouse
Courtés, Joseph Jean-Marie *humanities educator, writer, semiotician*

Vence
Polk, William Roe *historian*

Villefranche-sur-Mer
Legendre, Louis *oceanographer, educator, research scientist*

Villeneuve d'Ascq
Allain, Louis *literature educator, scientific advisor*

GEORGIA

Tbilisi
Bibilashvili, Tamar *physicist, educator*

GERMANY

Aachen
Pischinger, Franz Felix *engineer, researcher*

Berlin
Blankart, Charles Beat *economics professor*
Chrobog, Juergen *ambassador*
Iannone, Dorothy *visual artist, writer*
Saraste, Jukka-Pekka *conductor*
Weiss, Dieter Waldemar *economics educator, consultant*

Bochum
Folkers, Cay *economics professor*
Meyers, Albert Thomas Marie *academic counsellor*

Bonn
Albach, Horst *economist*
Krelle, Wilhelm Ernst *emeritus economics educator*
Selten, Reinhard *retired economist, educator*

Braunschweig
Fricke, Reiner *education educator*

Bremen
Fahle, Manfred *ophthalmology researcher*
Wells, Raymond O'Neil, Jr., *mathematics educator, researcher*

Cologne
Neisser, Horst *library director*

Dortmund
Freund, Eckhard *electrical engineering educator*
Vogt, Hartmut *education educator*

Dresden
Haitink, Bernard J. H. *conductor*
Schreier, Peter *tenor*

Düsseldorf
Schulz, Ekkehard *business executive*
Simson, Wilhelm *company executive*
Stuhl, Oskar Paul *scientific and regulatory consultant*

Essen
Albrecht, Theo *business executive*

Frankfurt
Ammann, Jean-Christophe *art director*
Glatzer, Wolfgang P. W. *sociology educator*
Michel, Hartmut *biochemist*
Neukirchen, Kajo *industry executive*
Simitis, Spiros *legal educator*

Frankfurt am Main
von Rosen, Rüdiger *stock exchange executive*

Garching
Fischer, Ernst Otto *chemist, educator*
Mössbauer, Rudolf Ludwig *physicist, researcher*

Greifswald
Knöppel, Hans-Armin *librarian*

Göttingen
Achtenhagen, Frank *economics professor*
Eigen, Manfred *physicist*
Sheldrick, George Michael *chemistry educator, crystallographer*
Starck, Christian Walter *jurist*

Halle
Schmoll, Hans Joachim *internal medicine, hematology, oncology educator*

Hamburg
Holler, Manfred Joseph *economics professor*
Ludwig, Walther *classical and neo-Latin studies educator*
Lüst, Reimar *foundation president*
Neumeier, John *choreographer, ballet company director*

Hannover
Schnaus, Peter *musical history educator*

Heidelburg
Sanchez, Ricardo S. *career military officer*
Wojdakowski, Walter *career military officer*
Yarvis, Jeffrey Scott *military officer, social worker*

Luebeck
Pagels, Jürgen Heinrich *balletmaster, dance educator, dancer, choreographer, writer*

Lübeck
Arnold, Hans Richard *neurosurgeon*
Fligge, Jörg *librarian, library director*

Mannheim
Henn, Fritz Albert *psychiatrist*

Mayen
Gartz, Rolf Fritz *foundation administrator*

Munich
Araiza, Francisco (José Francisco Araiza Andrade) *opera singer*
Hein, Fritz Eugen *engineer, consultant, architect*
Huber, Robert *biochemist, educator*
Miller, Gerald Milton, II, *management consultant*
Reimann, Helga Luise *sociologist*
Viermetz, Kurt F. *banker*
Whetten, Lawrence L. *international relations educator*

Münster
Spevack, Marvin *English educator*

Neu Isenburg
Hoare-Temple, Piers Howard *building maintenance executive*

Nuremberg
Doerries, Reinhard René *modern history educator*

Obertshausen
Albrecht, Karl *automotive and household plastic parts executive*

Radevormwald
Sergi, Arturo *tenor, music educator, academic administrator*

Schleusingen-Gethles
Frank, Dieter *retired chemicals executive*

Siegen
Buhr, Walter Heinrich Wilhelm *economics professor*

Stuttgart
Anderson, Reid Bryce *performing company executive*
Bettisch, Johann *linguist, researcher*
Cardona, Manuel *physics educator*

Geh, Hans-Peter *retired library director, consultant*
von Klitzing, Klaus *research facility administrator, physicist*

Tübingen
Nüsslein-Volhard, Christiane *medical researcher*

Walldorf
Agassi, Shai *application developer, director*
Williams, Richard Charles *computer programmer, consultant*

Witten
Gaengler, Peter Wolfgang *dentist, researcher*

Wuppertal
Schubert, Guenther Erich *pathologist*

Würzburg
Hölldobler, Berthold Karl *zoologist*

GREECE

Athens
Arnis, Efstathios Constantinos *mechanical engineer, space naval designer*
Kalamotousakis, George John *economist, merchant banker, educator*
Larounis, George Philip *manufacturing executive, director*
Papadakis, Panagiotis Agamemnon *financier, international business executive*

GUATEMALA

Antigua
Rodgers, Frank *librarian*

GUINEA

Hagatna
Flores, Juan P. *school system administrator*

HONG KONG

Greenvale Village
Chan, Kit Yu Evan *civil engineer*

Hong Kong
Choo, Yeow Ming *lawyer*
Hanrahan, Paul Thaddeus *marketing executive*
Kao, Charles Kuen *electrical engineer, educator*
Kee, Lee Shau *real estate developer*
Lau, Lawrence Juen-Yee *economics educator, consultant*
Laurie, James Andrew *journalist, broadcaster*
Li, Ka-Shing *international entrepreneur*
Mak, Wing Kwong Tony *life insurance executive, training consultant*
O'Brien, Timothy James *lawyer*
Pacter, Paul Allan *accounting standards researcher*
Pisanko, Henry Jonathan *command and control communications company executive*
Tse, Edmund Sze-Wing *insurance company executive*
Tsui, Lap-Chee *molecular genetics educator*

Kowloon
Kung, Shain-dow *molecular biologist, academic administrator*
Qiu, Larry Dongxiao *economics professor*
Randall, David John *physiologist, zoologist, educator*
Wu, Xiaogang *social sciences educator, researcher*

Pokfulam
McNaughton, William Frank *translator, educator*

South Horizons
Chen, Concordia Chao *mathematician*

Wanchai
Iwasawa, Isoo (Francis Iwasawa) *accountant, management consultant*

HUNGARY

Budapest
Forgó, Ferenc *economics professor*
Pentelényi, Thomas John *neurosurgeon*
Poprády, Géza *librarian*
Simai, Mihaly *economics and business educator*
Varkonyi, Anna *cultural organization administrator, management consultant, educator*

Szeged
Nyúl, László G. *mathematician, educator, researcher*

ICELAND

Reykjavik
Hallmundsson, Hallberg *editor*

INDIA

Fort Mumbai
Woodard, Nina Elizabeth *banker*

Kerala
Devi, Amritanandamayi (Sri Mata Amritanandamayi Devi) *spiritual advisor*

New Delhi
Anderson, Michael Hugh *diplomat*
Narain, Prem *agricultural scientist, educator, researcher*

Srivastava, Radhey Shyam *research scientist, researcher*
Watson, Paul *photojournalist, correspondent*

Ranchi
Srivastava, Vishnu Chandra *agronomy educator*

INDONESIA

Jakarta
Hsi, Edward Yang *lawyer, industrialist, medical venture capitalist, political advisor*

West Haven
Callison, Charles Stuart *retired foreign service officer, development economist*

IRAN

Tehran
Mardinkha, Khnania, IV, *church administrator*

IRAQ

Baghdad
Negroponte, John Dimitri *ambassador*

IRELAND

Donegal
Friel, Brian (Bernard Patrick Friel) *author*

Dublin
Calvani, Terry *lawyer*
Dooge, James Clement Ignatius *civil engineer, hydrologist, former senator*
Farrell, Colin James *actor*
Sheridan, Jim *director, screenwriter*

Galway
Hynes, Garry *theatre director*
Mullen, Marie *actress*

Mullingar
Donleavy, James Patrick *writer, artist*

ISRAEL

Arad
Hollander, Samuel *economist, educator*

Ashqelon
Hansen, Peter *international organization executive*

Beer Sheva
Brosilow, Coleman Bernard *chemical engineering educator*
Hare, A(lexander) Paul *sociology educator*

Givatayim
Kornel, Ludwig *medical educator, physician, scientist*

Herzlia
Gruder, Yaron E. *foundation administrator*

Jerusalem
Menses, Jan *artist, draftsman, etcher, lithographer, muralist*
Rosenne, Meir *lawyer, government agency administrator*
Shrensky, Don Steven *accountant, consultant*
Singer, Suzanne Fried *editor*

Karkur
Hillel, Daniel *soil physics and hydrology educator, researcher, consultant*

Metar
Lithwick, Norman Harvey *economics professor*

Ra ananna
Hayon, Elie M. *chemist, educator*

Rehovot
Sachs, Leo *geneticist, educator*
Sharon, Nathan *biochemist*
Zipori-Beckenstein, Pninit *business administration educator, researcher*

Rosh-Pina
Gophen, Moshe *research scientist*

Savyon
Bushinsky, Jay (Joseph Mason) *journalist, radio/TV correspondent, columnist*

Tel Aviv
Eliaz, Noam *materials engineer, researcher*
Gross, Joseph H. *lawyer, educator*
Jortner, Joshua *physical chemistry scientist, educator*
Kurtzer, Daniel C. *ambassador*

ITALY

Aviano AB
Moorhead, Glen W. (Wally), III, *career officer*

Bologna
Lino, Marisa Rose *retired diplomat*

Florence
Cecil, Charles Harkless *artist, educator*

Frascati
Haegi, Marcel *physicist*

Genova
Montanari, Franco *classicist, educator*

Milan
DeBenedetti, Carlo *entrepreneur*
Honegger, Federico *artist*

Naples
Tarro, Giulio *virologist*

Padova
Shea, William Rene *historian, science philosopher, educator*

Pesaro
Surian, Elvidio *music educator*

Pietrasanta
Bugliani, Ann C. *international studies educator*
Swarz, Sahl *sculptor*

Pisa
Settis, Salvatore *archaeologist, art historian*

Rome
Baum, William Wakefield Cardinal *archbishop emeritus*
Billy, Dennis Joseph *priest*
Gros-Pietro, Gian Maria *economics professor*
Hall, Tony P. *ambassador, retired congressman*
Kolvenbach, Peter Hans *priest, religious order superior*
Levi-Montalcini, Rita *neurobiologist, researcher*
McGurn, William Barrett, III, *lawyer*
Piovani, Nicola *composer*
Scognamiglio, Carlo *economics and finance educator, Italian government senator*
Sisulu, Sheila Violet Makate *diplomat*
Skodon, Emil Mark *diplomat*
Wales, Patrice *school system administrator*
Westley, John Richard *economist*

Vatican City
Foley, John Patrick *archbishop*
Stafford, James Francis *cardinal*
Szoka, Edmund Casimir Cardinal *archbishop*

Venice
Pasinetti, Pier Maria *author*

Verona
Pozzo, Riccardo *philosophy educator*

JAPAN

Abiko Chiba
Sakaguchi, Takehiro *healthcare educator, researcher*

Bunkyo
Kobayashi, Seiei *English literature educator*

Choyoda-ku
Sakoda, Futoshi *executive*

Gummaken
Okada, Ryozo *educator, clinician and researcher*

Gyoda
Shibasaki, Yoshio *chemistry educator, researcher*

Hachioji
Kojima, Takeshi *law educator, arbitrator, writer*

Higashi-Hiroshima
Suzuki, Nobutaka *chemistry professor*

Ibaraki
Kawano, Toshiaki *retired economics educator*

Ichihara
Kuma, Hisao *information systems educator*

Kanagawa
Fukatsu, Tanefusa *retired Chinese classics educator*
Hoshino, Yoshiro *industrial technology critic*
Kato, Tomiko *artist*

Kashiwara
Hori, Keiko *English literature educator*

Kumatori
Ohashi, Shoichi *business administration educator*

Kyoto
Zikmund, Barbara Brown *minister, church history educator*

Mie
Isshiki, Masayuki *sociologist, educator, dean*

Nagoya
Kajitani, Motohisa *sociology educator*
Kaneyoshi, Takahito *physicist, educator*
Maeda, Kenji *medical educator*
Sendo, Takeshi *mechanical engineering educator, researcher, author*
Takeyama, Eizo *company executive*

Okayama
Morooka, Hiroshi *neurosurgeon*
Okada, Shigeru *pathology educator*
Ubuka, Toshihiko *biochemist, educator, academic administrator*

Okazaki
Ebashi, Setsuro *scientist, educator*

Osaka
Ikeda, Kazuyosi *physicist, poet*
Ishihara, Tsuyoshi *humanities educator*

Ota-ku
Sano, Keiji *neurosurgeon, educator*

Saitama
Hozumi, Motoo *medical educator, researcher*

Sakai
Fujita, Sei *political economist, educator*

Sapporo
Asari, Eikichi *information sciences educator, researcher*
Nakagawa, Koji *endocrinologist, educator*

Shimizu
Uyeda, Seiya *geophysics educator*

Shinagawa
Ando, Kunitake *consumer products company executive*

Shinjuku
Shimada, Haruo *physical chemistry educator*

Shizuoka
Anma, So *engineer consultant*

Tochigi
Honma, Koichi *pathologist, researcher*
Hyodo, Haruo *radiologist, educator*

Tokorozawa
Nakamura, Hiroshi *urology educator*

Tokyo
Akutsu, Yoshihiro *communications educator*
Anderson, Ronald J. *insurance company executive*
Arai, Toshihiko *retired microbiology and immunology educator*
Arzouman, David *artist, composer*
Baba, Isamu *construction company executive*
Chang, Steve *internet security company executive*
Esaki, Leo *physicist, foundation executive, university president*
Eto, Hajime *information scientist, educator*
Foley, Thomas Stephen *diplomat, former speaker House of Representatives*
Fujimoto, Junichiro *pathologist*
Fuketa, Toyojiro *physicist*
Fukushima, Kiyohiko *economist*
Gyohten, Toyoo *economist*
Hakoshima, Shin-ichi *business executive*
Harada, Norio *software engineer, researcher, educator*
Hori, Yukio *engineering educator, scientific association administrator*
Iida, Shuichi *physicist, educator*
Iinuma, Hiroichi *international economics and trade educator, researcher*
Ishii, Akira *medical parasitologist, malariologist, allergologist*
Ishizuka, Nobuhisa *lawyer*
Kaneko, Hisashi *engineering executive*
Kato, Shuichi *information engineering educator*
Kobayashi, Noritake *business educator*
Kobayashi, Susumu *computer company executive*
Kondo, Masanobu *investment company executive*
Krisher, Bernard *foreign correspondent*
Lo, Fu-chen *economist, educator, ambassador*
Maki, Atsushi *economics professor*
Makihara, Minoru *diversified corporation executive*
Miura, Akio *quality assurance management professional*
Miyazaki, Koichi *economics professor*
Murray, Julia Kaoru (Mrs. Joseph E. Murray) *occupational therapist*
Nagata, Akira *publishing executive*
Nakajima, Hiroshi *education educator*
Nakamura, Hideo *law educator*
Nishimura, Masao *diversified financial services company executive*
Nishiyama, Chiaki *economist, educator*
Ogawa, Seiji *research scientist, biophysicist*
Ohga, Norio *retired electronics executive*
Ozawa, Seiji *conductor, music director*
Saba, Shoichi *manufacturing executive, director*
Saito, Shuzo *electrical engineering educator*
Sakurada, Yutaka *chemist*
Sakuta, Manabu *neurologist, educator*
Sakuta, Masaaki *engineering educator, consultant*
Shirai, Shun *law educator, lawyer*
Van Ginkel, Johannes Auguste *geographer, educator*
Wakumoto, Yoshihiko *electronics company executive, grants executive*
Yamamoto, Yoshiro *former diversified financial services company executive*
Yonezu, Takehiko *retired investment company executive*

Toyama
Ishii, Yoshinori *environmental science educator*
Sumiyoshi, Tomiki *psychiatrist, researcher*

Toyota
Toyoda, Shoichiro *automobile company executive*

Tsukuba-shi
Shimizu, Kazuhiko *education educator*

Yokohama
Ito, Noboru *electric power industry executive*
Kaneko, Yoshihiro *cardiologist, researcher*
Kuroda, Yasumasa *political science educator, researcher*
Tokutani, Masao *risk management educator*
Taketomi, Susamu *physicist, researcher*

KAZAKHSTAN

Almaty
Sadykova, Vera Philippovna *librarian, educator*

KYRGYZSTAN

Bishkek
Arne, Kenneth George *mining executive, mineral consultant*

LATVIA

Riga
Buholte, Agnese *library director*
Strautins, Vilnis *flute educator, past symphony orchestra executive*

LEBANON

Beirut
Habre, Samer S *mathematician, educator*
Khatib, Rustom Atfat *gynecologist, researcher, endocrinologist, consultant, economist*
Toufeili, Imad *science educator*

LITHUANIA

Vilnius
Butkevičiené, Birute *librarian*

LUXEMBOURG

Kirchberg
Leger, Philippe *legal administrator*

Luxembourg
Warner, Scott Dennis *investment banker*

Senningerberg
Fulci, Francesco Paolo *former diplomat*

MALAYSIA

Petaling Jaya
Wong, Kuok-Shoong Daniel *research scientist*

MALDIVES

Male
Habeeb, Habeeba Hussain *librarian*

MALTA

Valletta
Bonello, Michael C. *economist*

MONACO

Monte Carlo
Lovett, Laurence Dow *retired real estate and steamship executive*
Marton, Eva *opera singer*

MONGOLIA

Ulaanbaatar
Mandel, Leslie Ann *investment advisor, business owner, author*

NETHERLANDS

Aerdenhout
Vinken, Pierre Jacques *publishing executive*

Amsterdam
Kolko, Gabriel *historian, educator*
Liem, Edwin T.H. *lawyer*
Rizzi, Joseph Vito *banker*

Hague
Owada, Hisashi *judge*

Krimpen
Houtzager, Marianne Johanna (Marian de Boyen) *writer, artist, photographer*

Leiden
Dornbush, K. Terry *former ambassador, consulting company executive, educator*

Maastricht
Van Praag, Herman Meir *psychiatrist, educator, researcher*

The Hague
Aldrich, George Hoover *judge, arbitrator*
Allison, Richard Clark *judge*
Brower, Charles Nelson *lawyer, judge*
Buergenthal, Thomas *international judge, educator*
Higgins, Dame Rosalyn *judge of international court of justice*
Hodge, Susan *oil industry executive*
Jiuyong, Shi *judge*
Kooijmans, Pieter Hendrik *judge International Court of Justice*
Koroma, Abdul G. *judge of international court of justice*
Parra-Aranguren, Gonzalo *judge International Court of Justice*
Rezek, Francisco *judge, former supreme court justice, educator*
Shepard, Donald J. *insurance company executive*
Tomka, Peter *Slovakian diplomat, lawyer, judge, arbitrator*
van Wachem, Lodewijk Christiaan *petroleum company executive*

Utrecht
't Hooft, Gerardus *physicist, researcher*

NEW ZEALAND

Palmerston North
Krone, Cheryl A. *research scientist, consultant*

Wellington
Paquin, Anna *actress*
von Kohorn, Baron Ralph Steven *retired investment banker, author*

Wellington
Judd, James *conductor, music director*

NIGERIA

Abeokuta Ogun State
Soyinka, Wole *writer*

Ijebu Ode
Adedeji, Adebayo *economist, former government official*

Lagos
Omole, Gabriel Gbolabo *international venture capitalist*

NORTHERN IRELAND

Belfast
Corrigan-Maguire, Mairead *peace worker*

NORWAY

Kjeller
Maeland, Arnulf Julius *research scientist*

Oslo
Fitzpatrick, Whitfield Westfeldt *lawyer*
Fleischer, Carl August *law educator, consultant*
Heyerdahl, Jens P. *business executive*
Ong, John Doyle *ambassador, retired manufacturing executive*

Trondheim
Lunde, Øivind *cultural organization administrator, archaeologist*
Søvik, Nils *education educator*

OMAN

Medinat Qaboos
Craig, John Bruce *ambassador*

PAKISTAN

Faisalabad Punjab
Siddique, Muhammad *poultry pathobiologist*

Islamabad
Powell, Nancy J. *ambassador*

Lahore
Geoffrey, Iqbal (Mohammed Jawaid Iqbal Jafree) *artist, educator, lawyer*
Rai, Maqbool Ahmad *civil engineer, consultant*

PERU

Lima
Struble, James Curtis *ambassador*

PHILIPPINES

Dumaguete City
Galli, Darrell Joseph *retired management consultant*

Makati
Mabilangan, Felipe Hugo, Jr., *Philippine diplomat*
Thompson, Willard Scott (W. Scott Thompson) *social sciences educator*

Manila
Sumida, Gerald Aquinas *lawyer*
Tiuman, Erich Lim *textile company executive*

Paranaque
Mabasa, Teresa Albar *social welfare association administrator*

POLAND

Cracow
Kasper, Horst Manfred *lawyer*

Gdańsk
Mokrzecki, Lech Marian *history of education educator*

Poznan
Skrzypczak, Jozef Aleksander *education educator*

Warsaw
Abakanowicz, Magdalena *artist, sculptor*
Koscielak, Jerzy *scientist, science administrator*
Pluta, Ryszard *neuropathologist, educator*
Rotfeld, Adam Daniel *research institute administrator, government official, government agency administrator*

PORTUGAL

Algés
Horta, José Carlos de Oliveira Sousa *civil engineering consultant*

Coimbra
Holm, John Alexander *linguist, educator*

Lisbon
Palmer, John N. *communications executive*

REPUBLIC OF KOREA

An San
Lee, Dohyung *aeronautics research scientist*

Daejon
Jeong, Hawoong *science educator*

Dalseo-Ku Daegu
Park, Soong-Kook *internist, researcher*

Kwangju
Kim, Kyou Yung *economist, educator*
Lee, Jung-Koo *economist, educator*

Pusan
Ha, Chang Sik *polymer science educator*

Seoul
Ahn, Choong Yong *economics professor*
Chung, Ick-Joong *social worker, educator*
Han, Oksoo *pianist, music educator*
Hyun, Myung-Kwan *investment company executive*
Lee, Sungho H. *education educator, consultant, dean, academic administrator*
Park, Won Kuk *foundation administrator*
Zi, Goangseup *engineering educator*

Suwon
Lee, Tong Hun *economics professor*

Taegu
Kim, Doohie *retired public health educator*

Taejon
Kang, Kyungin *electronics engineer, researcher*
Park, Seok-Kyun *civil engineer, educator*

RUSSIA

Moscow
Collins, Mary *health science association administrator, retired legislator*
Ginzburg, Vitaly Lazarevich *physicist*
Goldanskii, Vitalii Iosifovich *chemist, physicist*
Kogan, Pavel *conductor*
Novikov, Sergei Petrovitch *mathematician*
Saltykov, Boris Georgievich *economist, politician*
Solzhenitsyn, Aleksandr Isayevich *writer*
Vershbow, Alexander R. *ambassador*
Zubritsky, Alexander Nickolaevich *pathologist*

Novocherkassk
Kiyanitza, Lubov Denisovna *library director*

SAUDI ARABIA

Dhahran
Allen, John Timothy *mechanical engineer*

Riyadh
Al-Saud, Alwaleed Bin Talal Bin Abdulaziz *investment company executive*
Alsubaie, Abdulaziz Mohamed *civil engineer*
Faraidy, Abdulaziz Abdullah *national public security officer*
Ismail, Nuhad *medical educator*

SCOTLAND

Cellardyke Fife
Roff, William Robert *history educator, writer*

Dundee
Black, Sir James (Sir James Whyte Black) *academic administrator, pharmacologist*
Lee, Thomas Alexander *accountant, educator*

Edinburgh
Atiyah, Sir Michael Francis *mathematician*
Carp, Benjamin Louis *historian*
Macneil, Ian Roderick *lawyer, educator*
Matheson, Ann *librarian, writer*
McMaster, Brian John *artistic director*

Melrose
Russell, Thomas *retired British government official*

Midlothian
Barnes, Joy Chappell *lawyer*

Saint Andrews
Dover, Sir Kenneth James *retired Greek scholar*

Stirling
Lenman, Bruce Philip *historian, educator*

Tighnabruaich
Reisinger, Ronald Busch (Baron of Inneryne, Baron of Culbin, Laird of Ascog Castle, Laird of Eilean Na Beithe, *bank executive*

SERBIA AND MONTENEGRO

Novi Sad
Vuksanović, Miro *library director, writer*

SIERRA LEONE

Freetown
Crane, David Michael *prosecutor, former judge advocate*

SINGAPORE

Singapore
Amelio, William J. *computer company executive*
Frank, Ronald Edward *marketing educator*

Kuznetsov, Vladimir A. *biomedical researcher, computational biologist*
McDonough, Richard Michael *philosophy educator*
Olds, John Theodore *banker*
Pelizzo, Riccardo *political scientist*
Yeo, Yee-Chia *engineering educator, consultant*
Zhou, Wei *engineer, educator*

SLOVAKIA

Bratislava
Fristacky, Norbert *computer engineering educator, researcher*

SLOVENIA

Ljubljana
Rotar, Tomaz *stock exchange executive*
Rupel, Dimitrij *diplomat*
Veselinovič, Draško *stock exchange executive*

Maribor
Strojnik, Tadej *neurosurgeon, researcher*

SOUTH AFRICA

Cape Town
Cleary, Sean Michael *risk management consultant*
Tutu, Desmond Mpilo *archbishop emeritus*

Johannesburg
Berk, Philip Woolf *journalist*
Dunn, David B. *ambassador*
Tager, Louise Arlene *high court advocate*

Parklands
Koekemoer, Carl Lodewicus *college official, business consultant*

Port Elizabeth
Botha, Maria Magdalena *education educator, researcher*

Waterkloof
Aiello, James Andrew *lawyer*

SPAIN

Adeje
Grindley, Bruce Alan *real estate agency executive*

Barcelona
de Larrocha, Alicia *concert pianist*
Vidal, Mercè *art historian, education educator*

Canary Islands
Wells, Melissa Foelsch *foreign service officer*

Castellon
Georgantzis, Nikolaos *economist*

Costa Den Blanes Mallorca
Polad, Farhang *company director*

Madrid
Almodovar, Pedro *filmmaker*
Feltenstein, Harry David, Jr., *chemical executive*
Frühbeck de Burgos, Rafael *conductor*
Herrero Rodriguez de Miñon, Miguel *former Spanish member of parliament, lawyer, international legal consultant*

Pamplona
Masdeu, Jose Cruz *neurologist, medical school administrator*

Santander
Ballesteros, Severiano *professional golfer*

Seville
Sanchez, Leonedes Monarrize Worthington (His Royal Highness Duke de Leonedes of Spain Sicily Greece) *fashion designer*

SRI LANKA

Colombo
Munasinghe, Mohan *development economist*
Spain, James William *political scientist, writer, investor*

SWEDEN

Askim
Bakhuizen, Willem Anthonie Hendrik Johannes *civil engineer*

Bjuv
Persson, Ronny Anders *accountant, historian*

Bralanda
Emilson, Henry Bertil *artist*

Göteborg
Johansson, Lennart Valdemar *Swedish industrialist*
Norrby, Klas Carl Vilhelm *pathology educator*

Lerum
Borei, Sven Hans Emil *translator*

Lidingö
Crapon de Caprona, Count Noël François Marie *lawyer, retired United Nations official, historian*

Lund
Janacek, Bedrich *organist*

Stockholm
Altéus, Åke *foundation administrator*
Ekman, Peter Erik *urologist, educator*
Gyll, John Sören *company executive*
Hallberg, Bengt O. *systems strategy director, fiber optic specialist*
Iverius, Per-Henrik *physician, biochemist, educator*
Johnson, Antonia Axson *corporate executive*
Lidman, Tomas Erik *national archivist*
Lindström, Lars Ernst Simon *education educator*
Peskov, Vladimir Dmitrievich *physicist, educator, consultant*
Soederstrom, Elisabeth Anna *opera singer*
Sohlman, Michael *foundation administrator*
Wachtmeister, Count Wilhelm H. F. *diplomat*
Westerberg, Lars *automotive safety systems company executive*

Uppsala
Carr, Andrew *zoologist*

Österskär
Bolin, Bert Richard Johannes *atmospheric physicist, research meteorologist*

SWITZERLAND

Basel
Arber, Werner *microbiologist*
Gehring, Walter Jakob *biology and genetics educator*
Martelet, Francois R. *pharmaceutical executive*

Bern
Braun, Reto *computer systems company executive*
Carlson, Dale Bick *writer*
Gonzalez, Guillermo Enrique *diplomat*
Jauslin, Jean-Frédéric *library director*
Leavey, Thomas Edward *international organization administrator*

Chateau d'Oex
Berman, Joshua Mordecai *lawyer, manufacturing executive*

Fribourg
Gurley, Franklin Louis *lawyer, military historian*

Geneva
Aaronson, Robert Jay *aviation executive*
Barenboim, Daniel *conductor, pianist*
Brown, Kent Newville *ambassador*
Capron, Alexander Morgan *lawyer, law educator, bioethicist*
Charpak, Georges *physicist, nuclear scientist*
Chow, Jack C. *international organization administrator*
Deily, Linnet Frazier *ambassador*
Evans, Timothy Grant *international organization administrator*
Farman-Farmaian, Ghaffar *investment company executive*
Jacquesson, Alain L. *librarian*
Maglacas, A. Mangay *nursing researcher, educator*
Marchi, Sergio Sisto *Canadian government official*
Moley, Kevin Edward *ambassador*
Ogata, Sadako *United Nations official*
Rossier, William *trade association administrator*
Schweitzer, Theodore Gottlieb, III, *United Nations administrator*
Sidjanski, Dusan *economist, educator*
Sommaruga, Cornelio *humanitarian services organization administrator, diplomat*
Steinberger, Jack *physicist, researcher*

Lausanne
Bloemsma, Marco Paul *investor*

Prilly
Domeniconi, Reto *business executive*

Versoix
Frenk, Julio Jose *secretary of health for Mexico, health systems researcher, consultant*
Mahler, Halfdan Theodor *physician, health organization executive*

Wollerau
Rohrer, Heinrich *physicist*

Zollikerberg
Bocker, Hans Jurgen *editor, analyst, consultant, management educator*

Zurich
Binnig, Gerd Karl *physicist, educator*
Burkert, Walter *Greek language educator, historian*
Cabiallavetta, Mathis *insurance company executive*
Ernst, Richard Robert *chemist, educator*
Eschenmoser, Albert *chemist*
Groebli, Werner Fritz *professional ice skater, realtor*
Morari, Manfred *chemical engineer, educator*
Siegenthaler, Walter Ernst *internal medicine educator*
Wüthrich, Kurt *molecular biologist, biophysical chemist, educator*
Zinkernagel, Rolf Martin *immunology educator*
Boutros-Ghali, Boutros *former United Nations secretary general*

SYRIA

Damascus
Scobey, Margaret *ambassador*

TAIWAN

Kaohsiung
Chien, Yie W. *pharmaceutical science educator, university dean, academic administrator*
Wang, Gwo Jaw *orthopaedic surgery educator*

Lung-tan
Shen, E-Chin *dentist, periodontist*

Taichung
Lu, Shih-Peng *history educator*
Ou, Yen-Chuan *urologist*
Wilson, Thomas Woodrow, III, *research scientist, consultant*
Yen, Gili *economics researcher*

Tainan
Huang, Ting-Chia *chemical engineering educator, researcher*
Lin, Jiin-Huey Chern *engineering educator*

Taipei
Chang, Parris Hsu-cheng *law-maker, political science educator, writer*
Chen, Chien-hsing *Chinese traditional health practices educator*
Chuang, Yii-Der *retired business executive amd diplomat*
Ho, Low-Tone *medical educator*
Hsieh, Rudy Ru-Pin *banker*
Lee, Yuan Tseh *chemistry professor*
Shen, Jinh-Biing *transportation engineer, educator*
Tsung, Christine Chai-yi *financial executive*
Yeh, Kuo Hsing *bank executive*

TANZANIA

Arusha
Rapp, Stephen John *international prosecutor*

Moshi
Pomfret, David B. *medical educator, internist*

THAILAND

Bangkok
Kornell, Ronald Frank *economist*
Kruck, Donna Jean *special education educator, consultant*
Sammon, William Joseph *historian, consultant*

TRINIDAD AND TOBAGO

Diego Martin
Walcott, Derek Alton *poet, playwright*

TUNISIA

Carthage
Sehili, Mahmoud *artist*

TURKEY

Ankara
Camlibel, Dizdar *marketing professional, advertising consultant*
Ilkin, Baki *former diplomat, Turkish government official*

Bilkent
Akman, Varol *computer engineer, educator*

Istanbul
Ongan, Nilgün Erdal *decorator, architect, artist*

UKRAINE

Mariupol
Vasiljev, Alexander Valerjovich *metallurgical engineer, economist*

UNITED ARAB EMIRATES

Abu Dhabi
Taylor, Frederick William, Jr., (Fritz Taylor) *lawyer*

VATICAN CITY

Vatican City
John Paul, His Holiness Pope, II, (Karol Jozef Wojtyla) *Bishop of Rome*
Stafford, J. Francis Cardinal *archbishop*

VENEZUELA

Caracas
Eljuri, Elisabeth *lawyer*
Nassar, Jafet M. *plant animal specialist, researcher*
Salas, Randall Nouel *automotive company executive*

VIETNAM

Hanoi
Burghardt, Raymond Francis, Jr., *ambassador*

WALES

Porthmadog
Owen, Walter Shepherd *materials science and engineering educator*

ZAMBIA

Nangoma
Hansen, Florence Marie Congiolosi (Mrs. James S. Hansen) *social worker*

ZIMBABWE

Harare
Salahuddin, Ahmad *civil engineer, educator*

ADDRESS UNPUBLISHED

Aalberts, Nola Jean *social worker, administrator*
Aall, Christian Bergengren *software company executive*
Aaron, Bud *systems analyst*
Abbe, Elfriede Martha *sculptor, graphic artist*
Abbey, Scott Gerson *computer information scientist*
Abbott, Edward Leroy *finance executive*
Abbott, Linda Joy *stained glass artisan, educator, photographer*
Abbott, Rebecca Phillips *museum director, art consultant, photographer*
Abbott, Regina A. *neurodiagnostic technologist, consultant, business owner*
Abdaladze, Merabi *physicist*
Abdulla, Mostafa Naguib *communications engineer*
Abdullaev, Yalchin *neuroscientist, physician, educator*
Abeles, Kim Victoria *artist*
Abeles, Sigmund M. *painter, printmaker, sculptor*
Aberlin, Betty Kay *actress*
Abernathy, Corbin Brett *music educator, theater educator*
Abernathy, Ronald Fitz *pharmacist*
Abetti, Pier Antonio *consulting electrical engineer, technology management and entrepreneurship educator*
Abildskov, J. A. *cardiologist, educator*
Able, Kenneth Paul *biology professor*
Abrahamson, Karen K. *theologian, editor*
Abrahamson, Shirley Schlanger *state supreme court chief justice*
Abramowitz, Morton I. *former ambassador*
Abrams, Roz *newscaster*
Abramson, Elliott Myron *law educator, researcher*
Abromson, Irving Joel *state legislator, financial services professional*
Accordino, Frank Joseph *architect*
Acerra, Michele (Mike Acerra) *engineering and construction company executive*
Achauer, Bruce Michael *plastic surgeon*
Achord, James Lee *retired gastroenterologist, educator*
Achorn, Robert Comey *retired newspaper publisher*
Ackerley, Barry *communications executive*
Ackerman, Daniel L. *audio engineer, writer*
Ackerman, Don Eugene *venture capital executive*
Ackerman, Jack Rossin *investment banker*
Ackerman, Melvin *investment company executive*
Ackerson, Barry James *social worker*
Adair, Stefan Rene *plastic surgeon*
Adams, Christine Beate Lieber *psychiatrist, educator*
Adams, David Parrish *historian, epidemiologist, educator*
Adams, Deanna Ruth *writer, educator*
Adams, Edwin Melville *former foreign service officer, actor, author, lecturer*
Adams, Gregory James *insurance company executive*
Adams, Hilary Shiels *theater director*
Adams, James Thomas *surgeon*
Adams, Jim Michael *foundation administrator*
Adams, Leocadia *secondary school educator, writer*
Adams, Mason *actor*
Adams, Michael John *retired air force non-commissioned officer*
Adams, Patrick O. *career officer*
Adams, Robert McCormick *anthropologist, educator*
Adams, Thomas Lawrence *lawyer*
Adams, Thomas Lynch, Jr., *lawyer*
Adams, Weston *former diplomat, lawyer*
Adams, Wilburn Clifton *communications educator*
Adams, William White *retired manufacturing company executive*
Adamson, Dan Klinglesmith *retired science association executive*
Adamson, James B. *retail executive*
Adamson, John William *hematologist*
Adams-Passey, Suellen S. *retired elementary school educator*
Adaniya, Kevin Seisho *lawyer*
Adar, Eytan *computer engineer, researcher*
Addison, Kalim J. *music company executive, consultant*
Addo, Charles Kwame *municipal official*
Addy, Frederick Seale *retired oil company executive*
Adekson, Mary Olufunmilayo *therapist, counselor, educator*
Adkins, Thomas Samuel *library director*
Adkinson, Brian Lee *manufacturing company executive*
Adler, Alexander *former federal government health service executive*
Adler, Raphael *educator emeritus, speech pathologist*
Adler, Richard Melvin *architect, planner*
Adler, Samuel Hans *retired conductor, composer*
Adzick, Nick Scott *surgeon, pediatric surgery educator*
Aehlert, Barbara June *health services executive*
Africa, Colby Tait *information technology executive, poet*
Aggarwal, Lalit K. *company executive, educator*
Aghdashloo, Shohreh *actress*
Agnew, Robert *retired psychologist, poet*
Agnihothri, Saligrama R. *mathematics professor*
Agreen, Linda Kerr *secondary school educator*
Agresto, John Thomas *former college president, education consultant*
Aguilar Zinser, Adolfo Miguel *former ambassador*
Aguinsky, Richard Daniel *electrical engineer, engineering executive*
Ahearne, John Francis *scientific research administrator, researcher*
Ahmad, Moghisuddin *chemist, researcher*
Ahmad, Salahuddin *nuclear scientist*
Ahmed, Syed Z. *anthropologist*
Ahrens, Franklin Alfred *veterinary pharmacology educator*
Ahsan, Omar Faruk *computer engineer, manager, consultant*
Aiken, Ann L. *federal judge*
Aikens, Martha Brunette *national park service administrator*
Aikman, Albert Edward *lawyer*

Aitken, Robert Baker *religious studies educator, writer*
Akutagawa, Donald *psychologist, educator*
Aladjem, Henrietta H. *writer*
Alagem, Beny *computer company executive*
Albano, Michael J. *former mayor*
Alberger, William Relph *lawyer, government official*
Albers, Charles Edgar *retired investment manager*
Albers, Sheryl Kay *state legislator*
Alberts, Renée Miller *substance abuse and mental health professional*
Albin, Barry G. *lawyer, rabbi*
Albino, Judith Elaine Newsom *university president*
Albright, Madeleine Korbel *former secretary of state*
Albritton, William Harold, III, *federal judge*
Albrizio, Eileen Marie *commentator, poet*
Alda, Alan *actor, writer, director*
Alderman, Annabel (Elsie Higgs Griner Jr.) *writer*
Aldredge, Theoni Vachliotis *costume designer*
Aldrich, Franklin Dalton *medical researcher, consultant*
Aldrich, Patricia Anne Richardson *retired magazine editor*
Aldridge, Amy N. *communications educator*
Aldridge, Donald O'Neal *military officer*
Aldridge, Edward Cleveland, Jr., *former federal agency administrator*
Aldrin, Buzz *former astronaut, science consultant*
Aleandri, Emelise Francesca *producer, director, television personality, actress*
Alexander, Amir Roi *writer*
Alexander, Barbara Toll *financial consultant*
Alexander, Doris Muriel *humanities educator, writer*
Alexander, Edward Russell *retired disease research administrator, educator*
Alexander, George L. *radiologist*
Alexander, James H. *industrial designer*
Alexander, Jasper D. *publishing executive*
Alexander, John Stone *retired radiologist*
Alexander, Marjorie Anne *artist, art consultant*
Alexander, Melvin Taylor *quality assurance engineer, statistician*
Alexander, Nancy A. *information technology manager, consultant*
Alexander, Richard Elmont *lawyer*
Alexander, Ruth Batchelder *interior decorator, environmental activist*
Alexander, S. Allan *magistrate judge*
Alexander, Thomas G. *chemist, researcher*
Alfano, Elaine *state representative*
Alfano, Robert R. *science educator, engineering educator*
Alfaro, Felix Benjamin *retired physician*
Alford, Becky Dianne *food products executive*
Alfred, Stephen Jay *retired lawyer*
Ali, Muhammad (Cassius Marcellus Clay) *retired professional boxer*
Alig, Frank Douglas Stalnaker *retired construction company executive*
Aliga, Olivia R. *music teacher, choral director*
Alinder, Mary Street *writer, lecturer*
Aliperti, Clifford J. *advertising specialist, writer*
Alipio, Gary Glynn *writer, consultant*
Aljian, James Donovan *investment company executive*
Alker, Hayward Rose *political scientist, educator*
Alkov, Robert Adolf *retired psychologist*
Allaire, Paul Arthur *former office equipment company executive*
Allan, James S. *sales professional*
Allard, Michael Alan *music educator, conductor*
Allbaugh, Joe M. *federal agency administrator*
Allbritton, Joe Lewis *diversified holding company executive*
Allen, Barry W. *research scientist, writer*
Allen, Bennie Carnel *employee relations specialist*
Allen, Bonnie Lynn *optometrist*
Allen, Bruce Templeton *retired economics professor*
Allen, Charles Eugene *university administrator, agriculturist, educator*
Allen, Charles T *entomologist*
Allen, Charlie Lee *air transportation executive*
Allen, Charlotte *secondary school educator*
Allen, Dianna *language educator*
Allen, Donald Vail *investment executive, writer, concert pianist*
Allen, Joseph H. *retired radiologist, educator*
Allen, Joseph T. *musician, educator*
Allen, Leatrice Delorice *psychologist*
Allen, Lew, Jr., *laboratory executive, former air force officer*
Allen, Marilyn Myers Pool *theater director, video producer*
Allen, Paul G. *computer company executive, professional sports team executive*
Allen, Ralph Gilmore *dramatist, producer, drama educator*
Allen, Roberta *fiction and nonfiction writer, conceptual artist, photographer*
Allen, Toni K. *lawyer*
Allen, William Sheridan *retired social sciences educator*
Allen, Woody (Allen Stewart Konigsberg) *director, actor, writer*
Allerton, John Stephen *association executive*
Alley, Kirstie *actress*
Allison, Andrew Marvin *church administrator*
Allison, Glorietta Travis *vocal educator, soprano*
Allison, John McComb *retired aeronautical engineer*
Allmendinger, David Frederick, Jr., *history educator*
Allmon, Michael W, Sr., *sales executive*
Allred, Michael Sylvester *lawyer*
Allukian, Myron, Jr., *government administrator, public health educator, dental educator*
Allums, James A. *retired surgeon*
Almeida, Richard Joseph *finance company administrator*
Almond, Lincoln *retired governor, retired lawyer*
Aloff, Mindy *writer*
Alonso-Crespo, Eduardo *composer, conductor*
Alper, Merlin Lionel *finance company executive*
Alpern, Andrew *lawyer, architect, historian*
Alpher, Ralph Asher *physicist, educator*
Alpher, Victor Seth *consultant, clinical psychologist*
Alraban, Munther Francis *education educator, consultant*
Altekruse, Joan Morrissey *retired preventive medicine educator*
Altman, Adele Rosenhain *radiologist*
Altman, Irwin *psychology educator*
Alton, N. Kirby *health facility administrator*
Altschul, David Edwin *record company executive, lawyer*
Altschuler, Samuel *retired electronics company executive*
Altshuler, Kenneth Z. *psychiatrist, educator*
Alvare, Charles Daguerre *television producer*
Alvarez, René Luis *historian, educator*
Alvarez-Galloso, Roberto C. *mental health professional*
Alves, Kyrin Jean *cultural organization administrator, educator*
Alvord, Joel Barnes *retired bank executive*
Amancio, Ruth Carson *safety engineer*
Amann, Charles Albert *mechanical engineer, researcher*
Amatangelo, Nicholas S. *retired financial printing and document management services executive, business educator*
Amato Chiaramonte Bordonaro, Baron Carlo Camillo *ambassador, consultant*
Ambach, Gordon Mac Kay *educational association executive*
Ambainis, Andris *computer scientist*
Amberg, Stanley Louis *lawyer*
Ambrozic, Aloysius Cardinal (His Eminence Aloysius Cardinal Ambrozic) *cardinal*
Amdahl, Byrdelle John *business consulting executive*
Ames, Donald Paul *retired aerospace company executive, researcher*
Amis, Edward Stephen, Jr., *physician, retired naval officer*
Amiscaray, Rowena Theresa *information technology manager*
Amlani, Islamshah *engineering scientist*
Ammon, R. Theodore *food products executive*
Amos, Linda K. *academic administrator*
Amparado, Keith D. *communications company executive*
Amstutz, Daniel Gordon *international agriculture industry consultant, government official, retired federal agency administrator*
Anand, Sanjay *training services executive, consultant, entrepreneur, educator*
Anaya, Richard Alfred, Jr., *accountant, investment banker*
Ancheta, Caesar Paul *software developer*
Ancker-Johnson, Betsy *physicist, engineer, retired automotive company executive*
Ancona, George Efrain *photographer, author*
Andela, Valentine Bisangena *medical researcher*
Anderegg, Karen Klok *business executive*
Anderer, Joseph Henry *textile company executive*
Anders, Edward *chemist, educator*
Anders, George Charles *writer, journalist*
Andersen, Roy Stuart *physicist*
Anderson, Alan Stewart *lawyer*
Anderson, Bernard E. *economist*
Anderson, Edgar Ratcliffe, Jr., *career officer, physician, health facility administrator*
Anderson, Ernest Frederick *social worker, educator*
Anderson, Gary William *physician*
Anderson, Geoffrey Allen *retired lawyer*
Anderson, George Kenneth *physician, foundation executive, retired air force officer*
Anderson, Geraldine Louise *medical researcher*
Anderson, Glen Robert *editor, publisher*
Anderson, Gregory Thomas *secondary school educator, researcher, historian*
Anderson, Herschel Vincent *retired librarian*
Anderson, Ivan Verner, Jr., *newspaper publisher*
Anderson, Jacqueline Annette *computer specialist*
Anderson, James George *sociologist, educator*
Anderson, Janice M. *freelance/self-employed photojournalist*
Anderson, Jerry Lee *pianist, music educator*
Anderson, Jerry Maynard *retired speech educator*
Anderson, John Bayard *lawyer, educator, former congressman*
Anderson, John Firth *retired religious organization administrator, retired librarian*
Anderson, John Gaston *electrical engineer, consultant*
Anderson, Joseph Norman *executive consultant, former food company executive, former college president*
Anderson, Kathryn D. *surgeon*
Anderson, Larry J. *federal agency administrator, researcher*
Anderson, Mary Jane *public library consultant*
Anderson, N. C. *writer, artist*
Anderson, Ned, Sr., *Apache tribal chairman*
Anderson, Odin Waldemar *sociologist, educator*
Anderson, PT (Paul Thomas IV) *film director*
Anderson, Rachael Keller *retired library administrator*
Anderson, Rhoda *language educator*
Anderson, Richard McLemore *internist*
Anderson, Robert Orville *oil and gas company executive*
Anderson, Ruth Lucille *interior designer, educator, artist, librarian, archivist*
Anderson, Susan Elaine Mosshamer *educational consultant, organization consultant, musician, mezzo soprano*
Anderson, Thomas Patrick *mechanical engineer, educator*
Anderson, Wayne Carl *public affairs officer, former corporate executive*
Anderson, William Carl *association executive, environmental engineer, consultant*
Anderson, William Robert *career naval officer*
Anderson-Spivy, Alexandra *writer, editor*
Andersson, Craig Remington *retired chemical company executive*
Andrade, Carolyn L. *foreign language educator*
Andrade, Edna *artist, art educator*
Andrain, Charles Franklin *political science educator*
Andras, Oscar Sidney *oil company executive*
Andrea, Mario Iacobucci *engineer, scientist, gemologist, appraiser*
Andreas, David Lowell *retired banker*
Andreas, Dwayne Orville *agricultural products executive*
Andreoli, Thomas Eugene *physician*
Andretti, Daniel *secondary school educator*
Andretti, Mario *retired race car driver*
Andreu, Helene C. *dancer, educator*
Andrews, Jean *artist*
Andrews, Dame Julie (Julia Elizabeth Wells) *actress, singer*
Andrews, Richard Vincent *physiologist, educator*
Andriole, Stephen John *information systems executive*
Andrisani, John Anthony *editor, author, golf consultant*
Andujar, Antonia *performing company executive*
Angel, Armando Carlos *rheumatologist, internist*
Angell, Richard Bradshaw *philosophy educator*
Angermeier, Patricia *occupational therapist*
Anjulis, Stanley Joseph *retired church administrator*
Ankrom, Barbara Burke *journalist*
Annunziata, Robert *fiber optics company executive*
Ansbro, John Joseph *philosopher, educator*
Anselmo, Robert Louis *writer*
Ansley, Shepard Bryan *lawyer*
Antioco, John F. *entertainment company executive*
Anton, Barbara *writer*
Antonelli, Rosemary *writer*
Antoun, Mikhail *medicinal chemistry and pharmacognosy educator*
Anzai, Earl I. *former state attorney general*
Apfel, Meri F *not-for-profit developer*
Appell, Louise Sophia *consulting company executive*
Appenzeller, Otto *neurologist, researcher*
Applebaum, Edward Leon *otolaryngologist, educator*
Applegarth, Paul Vollmer *investment and finance executive*
Applegate, Christina *actress*
Applegate, Edward C. *education educator, researcher, writer*
Apps, Jerold Willard *adult education educator, writer*
Aprilakis, Anna *mathematics professor*
Apted, Michael David *film director*
Aptekar, Sheldon I. *speech, theatre, and performing art educator*
Arbuckle, John Finley, Jr., *retired investment advisor*
Archer, Dennis Wayne *lawyer, former mayor*
Archer, Hugh Morris *consulting engineer, retired manufacturing executive*
Archibald, Nolan D. *household and industrial products company executive*
Archulata, Margie Baca *city clerk*
Arcos, Cresencio S. *ambassador*
Arcot, Prakash Kumar B *engineer, consultant*
Arden, Bruce Wesley *retired computer scientist, retired engineering educator*
Arden, Sherry W. *publishing company executive*
Arditti, Fred D. *economist, educator*
Areen, Judith Carol *law educator, dean*
Arenal, Julie (Mrs. Barry Primus) *choreographer*
Arenberg, Julius Theodore, Jr., *retired accounting company executive*
Arenson, Nathan *retired radiologist*
Aretz, Barbara Jane *reading specialist, educator*
Argers, Helen *novelist, playwright*
Argiris, Athanassios *oncologist, researcher*
Argo, Robert Wayne *electrical engineer*
Ariens, Karla Rae *library director*
Arlen, Michael J. *writer*
Arlidge, John Walter *retired utility company executive*
Armacost, Mary-Linda Sorber Merriam *former academic administrator, consultant*
Armaingaud, Franck *engineer*
Armaly, Mansour F(arid) *ophthalmologist, educator*
Armey, Richard Keith (Dick Armey) *former congressman*
Armistead, Katherine Kelly (Mrs. Thomas B. Armistead III) *interior designer, travel consultant, civic worker*
Armstrong, Anne Legendre (Mrs. Tobin Armstrong) *retired ambassador*
Armstrong, Donald *biochemistry, pathophysiology educator*
Armstrong, Douglas Dean *journalist*
Armstrong, F(redric) Michael *retired insurance company executive, consultant*
Armstrong, (Arthur) James (Arthur Armstrong) *minister, educator, consultant, writer*
Armstrong, Michael David *investment banker*
Armstrong, Thomas Newton, III, *art and garden specialist*
Armstrong-Law, Margaret *school administrator*
Armstrong Squall, Paula Estelle *executive secretary*
Arnett, Edward McCollin *chemistry educator, researcher*
Arnheim, Louise A. *communications executive*
Arnold, Henri *cartoonist*
Arnold, Jeffrey *Internet company executive*
Arnold, Jerome Gilbert *lawyer*
Arnold, P. A. *special education educator*
Arnold, W. H. (Dub Arnold) *former state supreme court chief justice*
Arnott, Howard Joseph *biology professor, dean*
Aron, Judy *music educator, composer*
Aron, Peter Arthur *charitable foundation executive, private investor*
Aronowitz, Jack Leon *biotechnology and diagnostic manufacturing company executive, consultant*
Aronson, Jason *publisher*
Aronson, Luann Marie *actress*
Aronson, Marc *artist*
Aronson, Norman Leonard *publishing executive, consultant*
Arrigo, Jan Elizabeth *photographer, writer*
Arrington, Richard, Jr., *former mayor*
Arrott, Patricia Graham *artist, art instructor*
Arthur, Beatrice *actress*
Arthur, John Morrison *retired utility executive*
Aruza, Albert Francis *consulting firm executive*
Arveson, Raymond Gerhard *retired state official*
Arvold, David Allen *music educator*
Arya, Vikram *research scientist*
Aschauer, Charles Joseph, Jr., *retired health products executive, corporate director*
Ascher, William *program and policy educator*
Aschheim, Eve Michele *artist, educator*
Asensi, Gustavo *advertising executive, cinematographer*
Ashby, Franklin Charles, Jr., *business executive, author*
Ashby, Norma Rae Beatty *journalist, beauty consultant*
Ashe, Bernard Flemming *arbitrator, educator, lawyer*
Ashkenaz, Judith *editor*
Ashkenazi, Elliott Uriel *historian, lawyer*
Ashkin, Roberta Ellen *lawyer*
Ashley, Renee *writer, creative writing educator, consultant*
Ashton, Betsy Finley *broadcast journalist, author, lecturer*
Ashton, Harris John *business executive*
Ashton, Thomas Walsh *investment banker*
Ashworth, Lawrence Nelson *retired bank executive*
Askey, William Hartman *US magistrate judge, lawyer*
Asmussen, Nils Wirenfeldt *pharmaceutical executive*
Asner, Glen R. *historian*
Asplin, Edward William *retired packaging company executive*
Assael, Michael *lawyer, accountant*
Astill, Robert Michael *office manager*
Astor, Brooke *foundation administrator, philanthropist, writer*
Astriab, Steven Michael *military officer*
Asura, John F. *paper company executive*
Ataie, Ata Jennati *oil products marketing executive*
Atcheson, Sue Hart *business educator*
Atchison, Joseph Edward *pulp and paper industry consultant*
Atchison, Richard Calvin *trade association director*
Athanasiou, Robert Byron *retired physician, psychologist*
Atherton, William *actor*
Atkin, Edith *artist, poet*
Atkin, J Myron *science educator*
Atlas, David *meteorologist, research scientist*
Attaway, Fritz Edward Edward *lawyer*
Attebery, Louie Wayne *English language educator, folklorist*
Atterbury, Robert Rennie, III, *retired lawyer*
Atwater, Phyllis Y. *municipal administrator*
Auberjonois, René Murat *actor*
Audet, Paul Andre *retired newspaper executive*
Auerbach, Jonathan Louis *securities trader*
Augustine, Hilton H., Jr., *computer company executive*
Aulbach, George Louis *retired real estate company executive*
Aurin, Robert James *entrepreneur*
Austin, Grant William *real estate appraiser*
Austin, James H(oward), Jr., *healthcare executive*
Austin, John DeLong *judge*
Austin, John H. *health care administrator*
Austin, Robert Clarke *naval officer*
Autolitano, Astrid *consumer products executive*
Avallone, Anthony Francis *retired lawyer*
Avant, Gayle *political science educator*
Aved, Barry *retail executive, consultant*
Avery, Stephen G. Brodie *marketing professional, consultant, sales executive*
Avery, Stephen Neal *playwright, writer*
Avian, Bob *choreographer, producer*
Avnet, Jonathan Michael *motion picture company executive, film director*
Axilrod, Stephen Harvey *global economic consultant, economist*
Azar, Fred S. *biomedical engineer, researcher*
Azarian, Mary *illustrator*
Azarnoff, Daniel Lester *pharmaceutical company consultant*
Aziel, Barbie-dae *writer, artist, poet*
Azman, Rosiana Lynne *psychologist, educator*
Azuma, Shoji *education educator*
Baba, Marietta Lynn *business anthropologist, university administrator*
Babailov, Igor V. *artist, educator*
Babao, Donna Marie *retired community health and psychiatric nurse, educator*
Babb, Frank Edward *lawyer, executive*
Babbitt, Samuel Fisher *retired university official*
Babitzke, Theresa Angeline *health facility administrator*
Baca, Jim *former mayor*
Baca, Joseph Francis *retired judge*
Bach, Jan Morris *composer, educator*
Bacharach, Burt *composer, conductor*
Bacharach, Melvin Lewis *retired venture capitalist*
Bache-Snyder, Kaye Elizabeth *humanities educator, journalist*
Backlar, Patricia *education educator*
Backowski-Dawson, Therese Marie *editor*
Bacon, Caroline Sharfman *investor relations consultant*
Baddour, Raymond Frederick *chemical engineer, educator, entrepreneur*
Badgley, Theodore McBride *psychiatrist, neurologist*
Baehr, Theodore *religious organization administrator, communications executive*
Baerg, Richard Henry *podiatrist, surgeon*
Baerwald, Susan Grad *television broadcasting company executive producer*
Baggett, Donnis Gene *journalist, editor*
Bagley, Dennis Joseph *lawyer*
Bagley, William Thompson *lawyer*
Bagwill, John Williams *retired pension fund company executive*
Bahbah, Bishara Assad *marketing company executive*
Bahr, Jane Marie *writer, retired English educator*
Bahret, Mary Ellen *lobbyist*
Bai, Chuanyong *nuclear scientist*
Baier, Edward John *former public health official, industrial hygiene engineer, consultant*
Bailar, Barbara Ann *retired statistician*
Bailey, Blake *writer*
Bailey, Brad Duane *lawyer*
Bailey, Charles-James Nice *linguistics educator*
Bailey, David Roy Shackleton *classics educator*
Bailey, F(rancis) Lee *lawyer*
Bailey, Joselyn Elizabeth *physician*
Bailey, Rita Maria *investment advisor, psychologist*
Bailey, William Waddell *writer, communications executive*
Baiman, Gail *real estate broker*
Bain, William Donald, Jr., *lawyer, chemical company executive*
Bainbridge, Dona Bardelli *marketing professional*
Baird, William David *retired anesthesiologist*
Baker, Augustus L., Jr., *retired surgeon*
Baker, Daniel Neil *physicist*
Baker, Donald *lawyer, director*
Baker, Edward Kevin *retail executive*
Baker, Henry S., Jr., *retired bank executive*
Baker, Jack Thomas *design engineer, environmental scientist, consultant*
Baker, James A. *lawyer, former state supreme court justice*
Baker, Joseph Roderick, III, *aviculturist*
Baker, Lucinda *writer*
Baker, Nancy Kassebaum (Nancy Kassebaum) *former senator, foundation official*
Baker, Ronald James *English language educator, university administrator*
Baker, Wendy Beth *editor, writer*
Baker, William Thompson, Jr., *lawyer*

Bers, Donald Martin *physiology educator*
Bershad, Neil Jeremy *electrical engineering educator*
Bersin, Alan Douglas *lawyer, school system administrator*
Bersin, Richard Lewis *physicist, plasma process technologist*
Bert, Clara Virginia *retired home economics educator, school system administrator*
Bertelsman, William Odis *federal judge*
Berthold, John William, III, *physicist*
Bertin, John Joseph *aeronautical engineer, educator, researcher*
Bertram, Jean DeSales *writer*
Bertram, Joan M. *school system administrator*
Bertram, Melissa C. *agricultural research scientist*
Bertram, Susan *rehabilitation counselor*
Bertrand, Frederic Howard *retired insurance company executive*
Bertucelli, Robert Edward *accountant, educator*
Beschloss, Michael *historian, writer, commentator*
Besing, Ray Gilbert *lawyer, writer, lecturer*
Beston, Rose Marie *retired academic administrator*
Bethke, Louise Virginia *music educator, writer*
Bettenhausen, Matthew Robert *lawyer*
Betti, John Anso *federal official, former automobile manufacturing company executive*
Betts, Elaine Wiswall *retired headmistress*
Betts, James William, Jr., *financial analyst, consultant*
Betts, Katherine *editor-in-chief, publisher*
Beukema, John Frederick *lawyer*
Beumer, Richard Eugene *retired engineering executive*
Beutler, Arthur Julius *manufacturing executive*
Be Vier, William A. *religious studies educator*
Bevilacqua, Cardinal Anthony Joseph *archbishop emeritus*
Bevington, Edmund Milton *electrical machinery manufacturing company executive*
Bey, Joan S. *retired public information specialist, writer*
Beyersdorf, Marguerite Mulloy *retired secondary school educator*
Beyman, Jonathan Eric *investment company executive*
Bhat, Ram J. *anesthesiologist*
Bhatia, Rajan *engineer, physicist, researcher*
Bhattramakki, Dinakar *research scientist*
Bibby, Douglas Martin *mortgage association executive*
Bibik, Jacqueline Avis *lawyer*
Bible, Geoffrey Cyril *former tobacco company executive*
Bick, Katherine Livingstone *neurobiologist, international liaison, consultant*
Biddle, Albert G. W. *trade association executive*
Bidwell, Roger Grafton Shelford *biologist, educator*
Bieber, Owen F. *labor union official*
Bieber-Roberts, Peggy Eilene *communications educator, editor, journalist, researcher*
Biebuyck, Julien Francois *medical educator, administrator*
Biederman, Edwin Williams, Jr., *retired geologist*
Biegel, David Eli *social worker, educator*
Biemuller, Martha Lydia *retired obstetrician-gynecologist*
Bierley, Paul Edmund *aeronautical engineer, musician, author, publisher*
Bierman, Sandra *artist*
Bieron, Louise T. *physician placement executive*
Bierstedt, Peter Richard *lawyer, entertainment industry consultant*
Bierwirth, John Cocks *retired manufacturing executive*
Bigelow, Charles Cross *retired biochemist, retired university administrator*
Biggers, William Joseph *retired manufacturing company executive*
Biggs, Arthur Edward *retired chemical manufacturing company executive*
Bikales, Norbert M. *chemist, science administrator*
Biklen, Stephen Clinton *retired student loan company executive*
Bilbray, Brian P. *former congressman*
Bilbray, James Hubert *former congressman, lawyer, consultant*
Biles, Gloria C. *historian, educator*
Billings, Judith A. *state education official*
Billingsley, Franny *writer*
Billion, John Joseph *orthopedic surgeon, former state representative*
Binder, Amy Finn *public relations company executive*
Binder, Madeline Dotti *retail executive*
Bing, Xu *artist*
Bingham, Jinsie Scott *broadcast company executive*
Binienda, John J. *state legislator*
Binkley, Timothy *computer graphics educator*
Binns, Jane Camille *humanities educator*
Bino, Marial Desolyn *librarian, educator*
Birch, Patricia *choreographer, director*
Birchard, Catherine Suzanne Sieh *artist*
Birk, John R. *management consultant*
Birky, John Edward *banker, financial advisor*
Birmingham, Thomas Harlan *civil engineer, writer*
Bisconti, Ann Stouffer *public opinion research company executive*
Bishop, Budd Harris *retired museum administrator, artist*
Bishop, C. Diane *state agency administrator, educator*
Bishop, Charles Edwin *university president emeritus, economist*
Bishop, Oliver Richard *retired state official*
Bishop, Paul Leslie *civil and environmental engineering educator, environmental engineering consultant*
Bishop, Sue Marquis (Ina Sue Marquis Bishop) *retired dean*
Bishop, William Peter *science administrator, management consultant, rancher, consultant*
Bissell, Allen Morris *engineer, consultant*
Bissell, James Dougal, III, *motion picture production designer*
Bitman, Clara *language educator, writer*
Bitner, John William *banker*
Bixby, Harold Glenn *manufacturing executive, director*
Biziou, Peter *cinematographer*
Bjerknes, Michael Leif *dancer*
Bjornsrud, Marlene *professional athletics manager*
Black, David *writer, educator, producer*
Black, David deLaine *retired investment consultant*
Black, Keith Lanier *neurosurgeon, educator*
Black, Kris Susan Lynn *marketing company executive, speaker, author, poet*
Black, Recca Marcele *elementary school educator*
Black, Shirley Temple (Mrs. Charles A. Black) *former ambassador, former actress*
Blackbourn, David Gordon *history professor*
Blackburn, Joy Martin *librarian*
Blackburn, Richard Wallace *lawyer*
Blackburn, Robin Ann *editor, writer*
Blacker, Harriet *public relations executive*
Blackledge, David William *retired academic administrator*
Blackson, Benjamin F(ranklin) *clinical social worker*
Blackwell, Jerry Alexander *professional golfer*
Blackwill, Robert D. *government agency administrator*
Blaine, Davis Robert *investment banker, valuation consultant executive*
Blair, Cary *insurance company executive*
Blair, Fred Edward *social services administrator*
Blair, Kathie Lynn *social services worker*
Blake, John Edward *retired car rental company executive*
Blakemore, Dwayne, II, *electrical engineer*
Blake Ramos, Debra Barbara *writer*
Blakley, Earnestine *elementary school educator*
Blancato, Louis Sebastian *anesthesiologist*
Blanchard, David Joseph *research scientist*
Blanchard, David Lawrence *aerospace executive, real estate developer, management consultant*
Blanchard, George Samuel *retired army officer*
Blanchard, MaryAnn N. *state legislator*
Blanchard, Richard Frederick *construction executive*
Blanchard, Townsend Eugene *retired service companies executive*
Blanco, Laura *film producer*
Blanco Mendoza, Herminio *Mexican government official*
Blank, Rebecca Margaret *economist*
Blankenship, J. Richard *former ambassador*
Blaszczynski, Andre Boguslaw *economist, educator*
Blatt, Harold Geller *lawyer*
Blausey, Jeanne Martha *accountant, financial systems analyst, fraud examiner*
Blazina, Janice Fay *transfusion medicine physician*
Blazzard, Norse Novar *lawyer*
Blecke, Arthur Edward *retired principal*
Bleher, Frauke Maria *mathematician, educator*
Bleicher, Samuel Abram *lawyer, government official*
Blewett, Robert Noall *lawyer*
Bliss, Kevin James *oil industry executive, lawyer*
Blissett, William Frank *English literature educator*
Bloch, Erich *retired electrical engineer, former science foundation administrator*
Bloch, Julia Chang *adult education educator*
Block, Amanda Roth *artist*
Block, Barbara Ann *biology professor*
Block, Dennis Jeffrey *lawyer*
Block, Emil Nathaniel, Jr., *retired air force officer*
Block, Lawrence *author*
Block, William *newspaper publisher*
Blodgett, David William *preventive medicine physician*
Blondin, C. J. *trade association administrator*
Blonz, Edward Robert *nutritionist, biochemist*
Blood, Archer Kent *retired foreign service officer*
Blood, Peggy A. *academic administrator*
Bloodworth, Gladys Leon *elementary school educator*
Bloom, Eugene Charles *gastroenterologist, educator*
Bloom, Frances Virginia *retired music educator*
Bloomer, Harold Franklin, Jr., *retired lawyer*
Bloomfield, David Charles *lawyer, educator, public and not-for-profit executive*
Bloomquist, Kenneth Gene *music educator, university bands director*
Blos, Joan W. *author, critic, lecturer*
Blossom, Beverly *choreographer, dance educator*
Blount, Benroe Wayne *physician*
Blount, Delores Overman *publishing executive*
Bloustein, Peter Edward *entertainment management consultant, producer*
Blow, George *lawyer*
Bluestone, Barry Alan *economics professor, educator*
Bluitt, Karen *information technology executive*
Blum, Barbara Davis *investor*
Blum, Barbara Meddock *retired association executive*
Blum, Betty Ann *footwear company executive*
Blum, Bradley D. *former food service executive*
Blum, Gerald Henry *department store executive*
Blum, Samuel *retired research scientist*
Blumberg, Mark Stuart *health services researcher*
Blumenthal, William *lawyer*
Blumstein, Susan Bender *fundraiser*
Blyth, Myrna Greenstein *publishing executive, editor, author*
Boal, Danielle K. *radiologist, educator*
Boal, Dean *retired arts center administrator, educator*
Boardman, Elizabeth Drake *computer science educator*
Boardman, Eunice *retired music educator*
Bobbitt, James Lyle *computer programmer, systems analyst*
Bobbitt, Juanita Crawford *international organization executive*
Bobel, Mary *video development company financial executive*
Bobrow, Richard S. *former diversified financial services executive*
Bock, Jerry (Jerrold Lewis) *composer*
Bockius, Ruth Bear *nursing educator*
Bodanszky, Miklos *chemist, educator*
Bodden, Jane Ellen *retired airline reservations manager*
Bodem, Beverly A. *state legislator*
Bodensieck, Ernest Justus *mechanical engineer*
Bodey, Richard Allen *minister, educator*
Bodsworth, Fred *author, naturalist*
Boe, David Stephen *musician, educator, dean*
Boehlke, William Fredrick *public relations executive, consultant*
Boesch, Diane Harriet *retired elementary education educator*
Boesel, Milton Charles, Jr., *lawyer, business executive*
Bogart, Carol Lynn *columnist, journalist, writer*
Boggs, Charles Harmon, Jr., *retired surgeon*
Bohannan, Lillian Muriel *elementary school educator*
Bohannan, Paul James *anthropologist, writer, former university administrator*
Bohland, Eugene R., Jr., *music educator*
Bohn, James Matthew *video editor, educator*
Bohn, Marsha J. *anthropologist, researcher*
Boho, Dan L. *lawyer*
Bohoskey, Bernice Fleming *actress, dancer, model*
Boise, Audrey Lorraine *retired special education educator*
Boitano, Brian *Olympic athlete*
Bok, Sissela *philosopher, writer*
Bolen, David Benjamin *ambassador*
Boles, John *professional baseball coach, manager*
Bolie, Victor Wayne *engineering consultant*
Boling, Eldon Avery *physician*
Bollenbacher, Herbert Kenneth *steel company official*
Bolling, Amy L. *federal agency administrator*
Bolsterli, Margaret Jones *English educator, farmer*
Bolt, Dawn Maria *financial coach, stock trader*
Bolton, Marie *elementary school educator, minister*
Bolton-Holifield, Alice Ruth *professional basketball player*
Bomer, Elton *former state official*
Bond, Julian *civil rights leader*
Bond, Meredith *medical educator*
Bond, Victoria Ellen *conductor, composer*
Bondi, Joseph Charles, Jr., *education educator, consultant*
Boner, Eleanor Katz *lawyer*
Bonfils, Darcy Reyne *television producer*
Bonham-Yeaman, Doria *retired law educator*
Bonin, Paul Joseph *real estate and banking executive*
Bon Jovi, Jon (John Francis Bongiovi Jr.) *musician, actor*
Bonn, Ethel May *psychiatrist, educator*
Bonnard, Raymond *theater director*
Bonnell, Victoria Eileen *sociologist, educator*
Bonner, John Tyler *biology professor*
Bonsack, Rose Mary Hatem *state legislator, physician*
Booher, Alice Ann *lawyer*
Boone, Charles W. *physician, pathologist*
Boone, Donna Clausen *physical therapist, biostatistician, researcher*
Boone, Richard Winston, Sr., *lawyer*
Boone, Robert Raymond *former professional baseball coach*
Boone, Stephen Christopher *retired neurosurgeon*
Booss, Claire *freelance/self-employed editor, literary agent*
Booth, Bonnie Nelson *human resources consultant*
Booth, Margaret A(nn) *communications company executive*
Booth, Robert Ward *lawyer*
Boothe, Leon Estel *academic administrator emeritus, consultant*
Borchert, Carol Ann *school librarian*
Borda, Richard Joseph *retired insurance company executive*
Bordick, Michael Todd *professional baseball player*
Bordner, Marjorie Rich *educator, civic worker*
Boren, Roger W. *judge*
Borenstein, Mark A. *lawyer*
Borenstein, Milton Conrad *lawyer, manufacturing executive*
Borg, Ruth I. *home nursing care provider*
Borges, William, III, *management consultant*
Borgnine, Ernest *actor*
Borgnine, Tova *cosmetics executive*
Bork, Robert Heron *lawyer, author, educator, former federal judge*
Borkowski, Francis Thomas *university chancellor*
Bornhorst, Kenneth Frank *electromagnetics and systems engineer*
Borntrager, John Sherwood *principal*
Borowitz, Albert Ira *lawyer, author*
Borst, Philip West *academic administrator*
Borum, Rodney Lee *financial business executive*
Borysewicz, Mary Louise *editor*
Boschmann, Erwin *chemistry professor*
Bosco, Anthony Gerard *bishop*
Bosco, Frederick J. *language and linguistics educator*
Bosco, Philip Michael *actor*
Bose, Anjan *electrical engineering educator, academic administrator*
Bosmajian, Haig Aram *speech communication educator*
Bosse, Margaret Fisher Ishler *education educator*
Bost, Raymond Morris *retired college president*
Bost, Thomas Glen *lawyer, educator*
Bostrom, Carl Otto *physicist, laboratory director emeritus*
Boswell, Dan Alan *health maintenance organization executive, health care consultant*
Botelho, Bruce Manuel *mayor, former state attorney general*
Bothwell, John Charles *retired archbishop*
Botkin, Monty Lane *computer company executive*
Bottone, Edward Joseph *microbiologist, educator*
Bottone, JoAnn *health services executive*
Boudreau, Daniel J. *state supreme court justice*
Boudreaux, John *public relations/internet specialist*
Boulden, Judith Ann *judge*
Boulez, Pierre *composer, conductor*
Bourguignon, Erika Eichhorn *anthropologist, educator*
Bourque, Susan Carolyn *political scientist*
Boutelle, Steven W. *army officer*
Bouvier, Marshall Andre *lawyer*
Bova, Benjamin William *author, editor, educator*
Bovaird, Brendan Peter *lawyer*
Bowe, Riddick Lamont *professional boxer*
Bowen, Jean *retired librarian, consultant*
Bowen-Forbes, Jorge Courtney *artist, author, poet*
Bowens, Gloria Furr *educational administrator*
Bower, Jean Ramsay *lawyer, writer*
Bower, Marilyn Kay *landscape artist*
Bowes, Frederick, III, *publishing executive, consultant*
Bowes, Henry Edward *retired communications executive*
Bowlby, Richard Eric *retired computer systems analyst*
Bowles, Barbara Landers *investment company executive*
Bowles, L. Thompson *retired medical association administrator*
Bowlin, Michael Ray *retired oil company executive*
Bowling, John C. *academic administrator*
Bowman, Charles Hay *retired engineering educator, petroleum company executive*
Bowman, Larry Wayne *investigator, English and criminal justice educator*
Bowne, Shirlee Pearson *finance and housing consultant*
Box, George Edward Pelham *statistics educator*
Boxer, Alan Lee *accountant*
Boyatt, Thomas David *former ambassador*
Boyce, Joseph Nelson *retired journalist, consultant, educator*
Boyd, Barbara *state legislator*
Boyd, Danny Douglass *financial counselor*
Boyd, Edward Lee *retired financial executive*
Boyd, Francis Virgil *retired accounting educator*
Boyd, John T. *engineering executive*
Boyd, Kenneth R. *application and web programmer, mathematician*
Boyd, Thomas Marshall *lawyer*
Boyer, Dale Kenneth *English educator*
Boyer, Daniel Christopher *artist, writer*
Boyer, Heidi Hild *public policy consultant*
Boyer, Herbert Wayne *retired biochemist*
Boyer, Robert Allan *business executive*
Boyette, Lisa Wynn *retired research scientist*
Boykin, Robert Heath *retired banker*
Boyle, Bryan Douglas *computer and network systems architect*
Boyle, R. Emmett *metal products executive*
Boyle, Richard James *banker*
Boyle, Tatiana Gennadievna *research scientist*
Boyle, Tim *apparel executive*
Boyles, James Kenneth *retired banker*
Boylston, Benjamin Calvin *retired steel company executive*
Boysen, Thomas Cyril *educational association administrator*
Boyson, William Albert *retired obstetrician, gynecologist*
Bozzette, Samuel Anthony *physician, researcher*
Brace, Robert P. *former electric power utility executive*
Brach, Paul Henry *artist*
Bracken, Michael Patrick *writer, editor*
Bracken, Peg *writer*
Brackett, Colquitt Prater, Jr., *judge, lawyer*
Bradbeer, Clive *biochemistry and microbiology educator, research scientist*
Braddock, Richard S. *internet company executive*
Braden, Charles Hosea *physicist, university administrator*
Braden, Thomas Wardell *news commentator*
Bradford, Peter Corey *design consultant*
Bradley, Amelia Jane *lawyer*
Bradley, Bill *former senator*
Bradley, William Bryan *cable television regulator*
Bradshaw, Peter *engineering educator*
Brady, Donna Elizabeth *performing arts company executive*
Brady, Jean Stein *retired librarian*
Brady, Sally Ryder *writer, literary agent*
Brady-Borland, Karen *retired reporter, columnist*
Brafford, William Charles *lawyer*
Bragdon, Paul Errol *educator*
Bragonier, John Robert *obstetrician-gynecologist*
Brain, George Bernard *university dean*
Brainard, Melissa *accountant*
Brakebill, Jean Newton *career officer, nurse, educator*
Bram, Leon Leonard *publishing company executive*
Bramucci, Raymond L. *employment and training executive*
Branagan, James Joseph *lawyer*
Branagh, Kenneth *actor, director*
Brancato, Leo John *manufacturing executive*
Brandl, John Edward *public affairs educator*
Brandon, Kathryn Elizabeth Beck *pediatrician*
Brandon, Liane *filmmaker, educator*
Brandt, Robert Frederic, III, *retired newspaper editor, journalist*
Brandt, Ronald Stirling *retired editor, researcher*
Brannon, Jean *education educator*
Bransdorfer, Stephen Christie *retired lawyer*
Branson, Harley Kenneth *finance executive*
Brantz, George Murray *retired lawyer*
Brassel, Robert Edward *insurance company executive, dancer*
Bratt, Nicholas *investment management and research company executive*
Braude, Edwin Simon *manufacturing executive*
Braude, Robert Michael *retired medical library administrator*
Braun, Edward Louis *engineer, writer*
Braun, Jerome Irwin *lawyer*
Braun, Mary Lucile Dekle (Lucy Braun) *therapist, consultant, counselor, educator*
Braun, Richard Freeman *legislative staff member*
Bravo, Rose Marie *retail executive*
Brawner, Lee Basil *retired librarian, consultant*
Bray, Charles William, III, *foundation executive*
Brazier, Don Roland *retired railroad executive*
Breakstone, Kay Louise *public relations executive*
Breathed, Berkeley *cartoonist*
Bredfeldt, John Creighton *economist, financial analyst, retired military officer*
Brehl, James William *lawyer*
Breitenberger, Ernst *scientist, educator*
Breitling, Julius *financial executive*
Brekke, Gail Louise *broadcasting administrator*
Bremer, Lewis Paul, III, *former diplomat*
Bremer Martino, Juan Jose *former ambassador*
Bremner, John McColl *agronomy and biochemistry educator*
Brenchley, Jean Elnora *microbiologist, researcher, science administrator*
Brennan, Ciaran Brendan *accountant, oil industry executive*
Brennan, Donna Lesley *public relations company executive*
Brennan, Lawrence Edward *retired electronics engineer*
Brent, Rebecca Kemp *product designer, writer*
Brent, Robert Leonard *radiology and pediatrics educator*
Breslin, Peg M. *judge*
Brett, Thomas Rutherford *federal judge*
Brettell, Richard Robson *art historian, museum consultant, educator*
Bretthauer, Erich Walter *chemist, educator*
Brewer, Barbara Bagdasarian *nursing administrator*
Brewer, Carey *retired academic administrator*
Brewer, Richard B. *biotechnology company executive*
Brewer, Timothy Francis, III, *retired cardiologist*
Brewer, Wesley Douglas *music educator*
Brewster, Elizabeth Winifred *English language educator, poet, novelist*
Brickell, Charles Hennessey, Jr., *marine engineer, retired military officer*

Carlo, Paula Wheeler *historian, history professor, researcher*
Carlsen, Mary Baird *clinical psychologist*
Carlson, Donald Otto *magazine publisher, editor*
Carlson, Gary R. *publishing executive*
Carlson, Gustav Gunnar *anthropology educator*
Carlson, Janet Frances *psychologist, educator*
Carlson, Kenneth George *data processing executive*
Carlson, Robert Codner *industrial engineering educator*
Carlson, Roger David *psychologist, clergyman, educator*
Carmack, Mildred Jean *retired lawyer*
Carman, Susan Hufert *nurse coordinator*
Carmichael, Judy Lea *record industry executive, concert jazz pianist*
Carnahan, Jean *former senator*
Carney, Kate *actor, director, educator, playwright, storyteller*
Carney, Nancy Ann *research scientist*
Carney, Robert Alfred *retired health care administrator*
Carpenter, Candice *writer, former media executive*
Carpenter, Derr Alvin *landscape architect*
Carpenter, Dorothy Fulton *retired state legislator*
Carpenter, Liz (Elizabeth Sutherland Carpenter) *journalist, writer, equal rights leader, lecturer*
Carpenter, Myron Arthur *manufacturing executive*
Carpenter, Susan Karen *defender*
Carpenter, William T., Jr., *psychiatry and pharmacology educator*
Carpenter-Mason, Beverly Nadine *quality assurance professional, medical/surgical nurse*
Carpentieri, Sarah C. *neuropsychologist, researcher, clinical psychologist*
Carr, Bessie *retired elementary school educator*
Carr, Harold Noflet *investment company executive*
Carr, Jesse Metteau, III, *lawyer, engineering executive*
Carr, Larry Dean *not-for-profit executive*
Carr, Paul Wallace *actor*
Carrado, Joseph Michael *painter, sculptor*
Carrigan, William Thomas, III, *writer*
Carrillo, Elisa Anna *history professor, consultant*
Carrison, Dale Mitchell *emergency medicine physician*
Carroll, Charles A. *manufacturing executive*
Carroll, E Jean *columnist, writer*
Carroll, Harvey Franklin *retired chemistry and nutrition educator*
Carroll, John *professional basketball coach*
Carroll, Joseph J(ohn) *lawyer*
Carroll, La Shun La Rue *dental surgeon*
Carroll, Mary Patricia *writer*
Carroll, Philip Joseph, Jr., *engineering company executive*
Carroll, Rosemary Frances *historian, educator, lawyer*
Carson, Mary Silvano *career counselor, educator*
Carstairs, Sharon *legislator*
Carswell, Jane Triplett *retired family physician*
Carten, Francis Noel *lawyer*
Carter, Betsy L. *magazine editor*
Carter, Cris *retired professional football player, sportscaster*
Carter, Danita M. *writer, securities trader*
Carter, David LaVere *soil scientist, researcher, consultant*
Carter, Henry Moore, Jr., *retired foundation executive*
Carter, Herbert Edmund *former university official*
Carter, Hodding, III, (William Hodding Carter) *foundation executive, former journalist, public official and educator*
Carter, Jaine M(arie) *human resources specialist, director*
Carter, James Harvey, Jr., *physician assistant*
Carter, Jeanne Wilmot *lawyer, publisher*
Carter, Mandy *professional organization administrator*
Carter, Nanette Carolyn *artist*
Carter, Richard Duane *business educator*
Carter, Rosalynn Smith *former First Lady of the United States*
Carter, Yvonne Breaux *retired librarian*
Cartnick, Edward Nathaniel *obstetrician-gynecologist*
Carton, Robert John *retired environmental scientist*
Cartwright, James William (Bill Cartwright) *former professional basketball coach*
Cartwright, Phillip August *management consultant*
Cartwright, Talula Elizabeth *education educator, consultant*
Carty, Donald J. *former airline company executive*
Carver, Juanita Ash *plastic company executive*
Carver, Kendall Lynn *insurance company executive*
Carvey, Dana *actor, stand up comedian*
Casadesus, Penelope Ann *advertising executive, film producer*
Casanova, Aldo John *sculptor*
Case, Colleen Mae *computer scientist, educator*
Case, Elizabeth Joy *special education administrator*
Case, Gerard Ramon *drafting technologist, paleontologist*
Case, Michael Lawrence *theology studies educator, minister*
Casei, Nedda *mezzo-soprano*
Caseiras, Jo Ann Striga *artist, educator*
Casella, Peter F(iore) *patent and licensing executive*
Casey, George William, Jr., *career military officer*
Casey, Michael D. *biotechnology company executive*
Casey, Micheal William *portfolio manager*
Casey, Nancy J. *women's healthcare company executive*
Casey, Robert Reisch *lawyer*
Casillas, Mark *lawyer*
Casper, Julie Ann *geographer, writer*
Cassady, James Robert *oncologist, educator*
Cassara, Frank *artist, art educator, printmaker*
Cassell, Eric Jonathan *physician*
Casselman, William E., II, *lawyer*
Cassidy, Donald L. *investment analyst*
Cassidy, Esther Christmas *retired government official*
Cassidy, James Mark *construction company executive*
Cassidy, John Harold *lawyer*
Casso, James C. *social worker, mental health services professional*
Castagna, William John *federal judge*
Castaldi, David Lawrence *healthcare company executive*
Castel, Jean Gabriel *lawyer*
Castellano, Mark Joseph *music educator*
Castellanos-Brandon, Alba G. *secondary school educator*
Castiglia, Patricia Anne Thorson *dean, nursing educator*
Castile, Rand (Jesse Randolph III) *retired museum director*
Castle, Howard Blaine *retired religious organization administrator*
Castle, James Cameron *information systems executive*
Castleman, Breaux Ballard *health management company executive*
Castor, Betty *academic administrator*
Castor, Jon Stuart *electronics company executive*
Castro, Maria Graciela *medical educator, geneticist, researcher*
Castro, Raul Hector *lawyer, former ambassador, former governor*
Caswell, Dorothy Ann Cottrell *visual artist, arts administrator*
Cates, Willard *medical association administrator*
Cathey, Catharine Mellon *investment company executive*
Cathou, Renata Egone *chemist, consultant*
Cattell, Heather Birkett *psychologist*
Catuzzi, J(erome) P(rimo), Jr., *lawyer*
Cauthen, Rebecca Ann *secondary school educator*
Cauthorne-Burnette, Tamera Dianne *family nurse practitioner, healthcare consultant*
Cavileer, Denise Marie *poet*
Cawley, Charles M. *retired bank executive*
Cawley, Joseph Douglas *retired reading educator*
Cayetano, Benjamin Jerome *former governor, former state senator and representative*
Cazalas, Mary Rebecca Williams *lawyer, nurse*
Cearley, Michael A. *communications executive, writer*
Ceci, Louis J. *former state supreme court justice*
Cecil, Alex Thomson *travel executive*
Cenarrusa, Pete T. *retired state official*
Centafont, Lucy Ann Alexander *occupational therapy consultant*
Cermak, Josef Rudolf Cenek *lawyer, director*
Cerny, Louis Thomas *civil engineer, railway engineering consultant*
Cerri, Robert Noel *photographer*
Cesnik, James Michael *union official, newspaperman, printer, consultant*
Cha, Soyoung Stephen *mechanical engineer, educator*
Chadsey, Harold A. *astronomer*
Chadwell, James Russell, Jr., *retired controller*
Chae, Heeyeop *chemical engineer, researcher*
Chafkin, Rita M. *dermatologist*
Chaikof, Elliot Lorne *vascular surgeon*
Chait, Fay Klein *health administrator*
Chalcraft, Elena Marie *actress, singer*
Chalsty, John Steele *investment banker*
Chamberlain, William Edwin, Jr., *management consultant*
Chamberlin, Michael Meade *lawyer*
Chambers, Audley C. *music historian, educator, researcher*
Chambers, Marjorie Bell *historian*
Chambers-Steinberg, Wanda *researcher*
Champa, John Joseph *telecommunications engineer, consultant, writer*
Champine, George A. *computer scientist*
Chan, Jackie *actor, director, stuntman*
Chan, Wilma *county official*
Chan, Wing-Chi *cultural organization administrator, musicologist*
Chandler, Alfred Dupont, Jr., *historian, educator*
Chandler, Alice *higher education consultant, university president*
Chandler, J. Harold *insurance company executive*
Chandra, Abhijit *engineering educator*
Chandra, Pramod *art history educator*
Chaney, Don *professional basketball coach*
Chang, Clarence Dayton *retired chemist*
Chang, Debbie I-Ju *health services director*
Chang, Gail Cathryn May (G. Gordan Chang) *music educator*
Chang, Helen Chung-Hung Hsiang *music educator*
Chang, Kevin C. *securities trader*
Chang, Lan Samantha *writer, educator*
Chao, James Min-Tzu *architect*
Chao, Ruth *psychologist, researcher*
Chapin, Miles Whitworth *writer, actor*
Chapman, Hope Horan *psychologist*
Chapman, Richard LeRoy *retired public policy researcher*
Chapman, Thomas William *hospital executive*
Chapman, William *baritone*
Chappell, Annette M. *higher education consultant, minister*
Chaput, Eugene Michael *advertising executive*
Charette, Cecile M. *music educator*
Charles, Jonathan Stephen *application developer*
Charles, Lyn Ellen *marketing executive, commercial artist, photograph*
Charles, Robert Bruce *lawyer*
Charles, Walter *actor*
Charlton, Betty Jo *retired state legislator*
Charlton, Catherine Marie *musician, composer*
Charlton, Jesse Melvin, Jr., *management educator, lawyer*
Charlton, Shirley Marie *educational consultant*
Charnin, Jade Hobson *magazine executive*
Charry, Michael R(onald) *musician, conductor*
Charwat, Andrew Franciszek *engineering educator*
Chase, J. Vincent *shopping center executive*
Chase, James Richard *retired college president*
Chase, Robert F. *educational association executive*
Chase, William Robert *television executive*
Chaseman, Joel *communications consultant*
Chassman, Leonard Fredric *retired labor union administrator*
Chatelain, Dalia de la Paz *elementary education educator, counselor*
Chatham, Rosemary Gail Moog *entrepreneur, musician, volunteer, composer*
Chatterji, Angana P. *anthropologist*
Chaudhri, Amin Qamar *film company executive*
Chave, Carolyn Margaret *arbitrator, retired lawyer*
Chaves-Carballo, Enrique *neuropediatrician*
Cheadle, Louise *concert pianist, educator*
Cheah, Keong-Chye *psychiatrist, educator*
Cheatham, Belzora *writer*
Checketts, David Wayne *sports executive*
Cheek, Michael Carroll *lawyer*
Cheesman, Frederick S. *editor*
Cheesman, John Michael *corporate financial executive*
Chelberg, Bruce Stanley *holding company executive*
Chelberg, Robert Douglas *army officer*
Chelle, Robert Frederick *entrepreneurial leadership educator*
Chemla, Daniel S. *physics educator*
Chen, Di *electro-optic company executive, consultant*
Chen, George Chi-Ming *energy company executive*
Chen, Kuen Hai *physician*
Chen, Shoei-Sheng *retired mechanical engineer*
Chen, Stephen S. F. *retired diplomat*
Chen, Tar Timothy *biostatistician*
Cheng, Baolian *physicist*
Cheng, Yue *molecular geneticist, pathologist*
Chercover, Murray *television executive*
Cherenzia, Bradley James *retired radiologist, consultant*
Cherin, Stephen J. *computer programmer, management consultant*
Chernichaw, Mark *television production, advertising and promotion executive, international media consultant*
Chernish, Lelia Margaret *fundraiser*
Chernoff, Amoz Immanuel *hematologist, consultant*
Cherovsky, Erwin Louis *lawyer, writer*
Cherry, Robert Steven, III, *municipal administrator*
Cheser, Raymond Norris, III, *healthcare company executive*
Chesler, Doris Adelle *real estate professional*
Chesney, Susan Talmadge *writer, developer*
Chesson, Michael Bedout *history professor, writer*
Chevalier, David Valentine *language educator*
Chevalier, Paul Edward *retired retail executive, lawyer*
Chewning, Richard Carter *retired religious business ethics educator*
Chiariello, Mario *surgeon*
Chihorek, John Paul *electronics company executive*
Child, Abigail *filmmaker, educator*
Childers, Charles Eugene *mining company executive*
Childs, Lucinda *choreographer*
Chill, Myrtle N. *advertising copywriter, promoter*
Chin, Janet Sau-Ying *data processing executive, consultant*
Chin, Jennifer Young *public health educator*
Chin, Kelvin Henry *business development director*
Chin, Mian *research scientist*
Chin, William Y. *law educator*
Chinni, Peter Anthony *artist, poet*
Chizmeshya, Andrew Vincent George *physicist, research scientist*
Chlebowski, John Francis, Jr., *leasing company executive*
Chmielinski, Edward Alexander *retired electronics company executive*
Choi, Man-Yeon *entomologist, researcher*
Cholewka, Patricia Anne *health services administrator*
Chorpenning, Frank Winslow *immunology educator, researcher*
Choueifati, Antoine (Tony Choueifati) *computer company executive*
Chouery, Farid Alexandre *electrical engineer, structural engineer, consultant*
Choukas-Bradley, Melanie *writer, photographer*
Chow, Jimmy Tai-Nin *chemist*
Chow, Rita Kathleen *nursing consultant*
Chow, Timothy Yi-Chung *mathematician, systems engineer*
Chow, Winston *engineering research executive*
Chowdhury, Anwarul Karim *international organization official*
Chretien, Jane Henkel *internist*
Chrisanthopoulos, Peter *advertising executive*
Christensen, Caroline "Connie" *vocational educator*
Christensen, Karen Kay *lawyer*
Christensen, Madonna Dries *writer*
Christenson, Gregg Andrew *bank executive*
Christenson, Shen *editor*
Christenson, William Newcome *retired occupational and internal medicine physician*
Christian, James Wayne *economist*
Christian, Juan Lee *elementary school educator, translator*
Christian, Lori Coffelt *marketing professional*
Christiano, Gregory John *claims representative, writer*
Christiansen, David K. *healthcare administrator*
Christiansen, Richard Dean *retired newspaper editor*
Christianson, Paul Alan *music educator*
Christianson, Philip D. *employee benefits executive*
Christie, Walter Scott *retired state official*
Christoffersen, Ralph Earl *chemist, researcher*
Christopher, Richard Scott *public relations and advertising executive, editor*
Christopher, Roy *set designer, production designer*
Christopher, Russell Lewis *baritone*
Christopher, Sharon A. Brown *bishop*
Chrysler, Richard R. *former congressman*
Chryssis, George Christopher *entrepreneur*
Chu, Jack J. (Jack J. Zhu) *electrical engineer*
Chu, James *electronics executive*
Chu, Steven *physics educator*
Chung, Caroline *foreign service officer*
Church, Bryan P. *business owner, educator*
Church, Eugene Lent *physicist, consulting scientist*
Church, Joseph *music educator, conductor, composer*
Churchill, Robert Wilson *state legislator, lawyer*
Ciavarelli, Maria Elisa *language educator*
Cibbarelli, Pamela Ruth *information executive*
Ciccarelli, Chick *marketing professional*
Ciccone, F. Richard *retired newspaper editor*
Cicero, J. Deborah *management consultant*
Cicolani, Angelo George *research and development company executive, operating engineer*
Cikovsky, Nicolai, Jr., *retired curator, art history educator*
Cimino, Ann Mary *education educator*
Cintron, Virginia *information scientist*
Cionek, Edmund *composer, educator*
Citron, Richard Ira *management consultant*
Clabaugh, Elmer Eugene, Jr., *retired lawyer*
Claes, Gayla Christine *writer, editorial consultant*
Claiborne, Liz (Elisabeth Claiborne Ortenberg) *fashion designer*
Clancy, John Patrick *real estate company executive*
Clapp, Beverly Booker *accountant*
Claridge, Elmond Lowell *retired engineering educator, consultant*
Clarizio, Josephine Delores *corporate services executive, former manufacturing and engineering company executive, foundation executive*
Clark, Alicia Garcia *political party official*
Clark, Barbara June *elementary school educator*
Clark, Beverly Ann *lawyer*
Clark, Caleb Morgan *political scientist, educator*
Clark, Darwin Edward *retired automotive executive*
Clark, Donald Otis *lawyer*
Clark, Edgar Sanderford *insurance broker, consultant*
Clark, Eve Vivienne *linguistics educator*
Clark, James Covington *journalist, historian*
Clark, James Milford *retired college president*
Clark, Jere Walton *economics educator, researcher*
Clark, Leif Michael *federal judge*
Clark, Mark David *public relations consultant*
Clark, Mary Higgins *writer, communications executive*
Clark, Matt *science writer*
Clark, Nancy Lucinda Brown *retired music teacher*
Clark, Peter Bruce *newspaper executive*
Clark, Philip Hart *retired urban and regional planner*
Clark, Philip Raymond *nuclear utility executive, engineer*
Clark, Raymond Oakes *banker*
Clark, Richard Eugene *music educator*
Clark, Robert Charles *law educator*
Clark, Stan *association executive*
Clark, Teri Lynn *actress, trading department manager*
Clark, Thomas Ryan *retired federal agency executive, business and technical consultant*
Clark, Wesley K. *retired military officer*
Clark, William, Jr., *political advisor*
Clarke, Sir Arthur Charles *author*
Clarke, Edward Owen, Jr., *lawyer*
Clarke, Henry Lee *foreign service officer, former ambassador*
Clarke, Lambuth McGeehee *retired academic administrator*
Clarke, Richard Alan *former national security specialist*
Claspill, James Louis *finance company executive*
Clausen, Jeanne Lorraine *musician*
Clausen, Jerry Lee *psychiatrist*
Claver, Robert Earl *television director, producer*
Clawson, Roxann Eloise *college administrator, computer company executive*
Clayton, David A(lvin) *biology professor*
Clayton, Eva M. *retired congresswoman, former commissioner*
Clayton, Richard Reese *retired holding company executive*
Claytor, Richard Anderson *retired federal agency executive, consultant*
Cleaveland, John Riddle *retired architect*
Cleaver, James Edward *radiologist, educator*
Clemendor, Anthony Arnold *obstetrician, gynecologist, educator*
Clement, Bob *former congressman*
Clement, Hope Elizabeth Anna *retired librarian*
Clement, John Edward Strausz *retired minister, retired religious organization administrator*
Clement, Yvonne Madeline *librarian*
Clements, Cathy J. *education educator*
Clemetson, Charles Alan Blake *physician*
Clemmensen, Larry P. *former investment company executive*
Clemmons, Evelyn Yvonne *administrative assistant*
Clendinen, Cynthia A.A. *healthcare professional, compliance specialist*
Clewett, Raymond Winfred *mechanical design engineer*
Clifford, Brian Elliott *writer, researcher*
Clifton, Russell B. *banking and mortgage lending consultant, retired mortgage company executive*
Cline, Ann *artist, designer*
Cline, Carolyn Joan *plastic and reconstructive surgeon*
Cline, Melissa Suzanne *computer scientist*
Cline, Pauline M. *educational administrator*
Clinger, William Floyd, Jr., *retired congressman*
Clogan, Paul Maurice *English language and literature educator*
Close, Thomas James *school administrator*
Closset, Gerard Paul *forest products consultant*
Cloud, Stanley Wills *journalist, editor, writer*
Clouston, Ross Neal *retired food and related products company executive*
Clymer, Wayne Kenton *bishop*
Coates, Shirley Jean *finance educator, secondary school educator*
Cobb, Edward Ray *actor*
Cobb, John Boswell, Jr., *clergyman, educator*
Cobb, John Cecil, Jr., (Jack Cobb) *communications specialist and executive*
Cobb, Miles Alan *retired lawyer*
Cobb, Ruth *artist*
Cobb, Sue McCourt *lawyer, educator*
Coble, Howard *congressman, lawyer*
Coburn, D(onald) L(ee) *playwright*
Coburn, Steven D. *composer, musicologist, educator, pianist*
Cochetti, Roger James *international communications and internet company executive*
Cochran, Carolyn *library director*
Cochran, John P. *economics professor*
Cochran, Thad *senator*
Cochrane, Shirley Graves *writer, educator*
Cochrane, Walter E. *academic administrator, music educator, conductor*
Cockerham, Lorris G. *radiation toxicologist*
Cockrum, William Monroe, III, *investment banker, consultant, educator*
Cody, Judith *composer, writer*
Coe, Rodney Michael *medical educator*
Coffee, Joseph Denis, Jr., *retired college chancellor*
Coffey, John Louis *judge*
Cogdell, Evelyn Denise *administrative assistant, writer*
Cohen, Allan Richard *broadcast executive*
Cohen, Anita Marilyn *retired lawyer*
Cohen, Cafi Fischer *writer, music educator*
Cohen, David John *cardiothoracic surgeon*
Cohen, Gloria Ernestine *elementary education educator*
Cohen, Jay Allen *lawyer, accountant*
Cohen, Jerome *psychology educator, electrophysiologist*
Cohen, Larry *film director, producer, screenwriter*
Cohen, Mark Herbert *broadcasting company executive*
Cohen, Norman Girard *retired social worker, writer*
Cohen, Philip *retired hydrogeologist*
Cohen, Roberta Jane *government executive*
Cohen, Stanley *biochemistry educator*
Cohen, Stanley Alvin *land use planner*

Dangerfield, Rodney (Jack Roy Dangerfield) *comedian, actor, author*
Dangoor, David Ezra Ramsi *consumer goods company executive*
Dangremond, David W. *fine arts educator*
Daniel, Beth *professional golfer*
Daniel, Coldwell, III, *economist, educator*
Daniels, Arlene Kaplan *sociology educator*
Daniels, Jonathan Paul *web architect*
Daniels, Mitchell Elias, Jr., *federal agency administrator*
Daniels, Ronald George *theater director*
Daniels, Sydney Robert *theater director, educator*
Daniels, William Burton *retired physicist, educator*
Danielsen, Albert Leroy *economics educator, energy and utilities consultant*
Danner, Patsy Ann (Mrs. C. M. Meyer) *former congresswoman*
Dansby, Ronnie *transportation executive*
Danse, Ilene Homnick Raisfeld *physician, educator, toxicologist*
Danzig, Frederick Paul *newspaper editor*
Danziger, Glenn Norman *former chemical sales company executive*
D'Arcy, John P. *investment company executive*
Daren, Sylvia *poet*
Dargan, Pamela Ann *electrical engineer*
Darien, Steven Martin *management consulting company executive*
Darkovich, Sharon Marie *nurse administrator*
Darling, Robert Edward *designer, stage director*
Darlington, Hilda Walker *real estate company officer*
Darrow, William Richard *retired pharmaceutical company executive, consultant*
Darsch, Nancy *former professional basketball coach*
Darvarova, Elmira *musician, concertmaster*
Dasch, Pat (Anne) *professional society administrator*
Dash, Sanford Mark *aerospace scientist*
Dasso, Jerome Joseph *real estate educator*
Date, Elaine Satomi *physiatrist, educator*
Datiles, J. Michelle *legal researcher*
Daugherty, Frederick Alvin *federal judge*
Daugherty, Paul D.A. *higher education executive director*
Daus, Victoria Lynn *nurse midwife*
Davatzes, Nickolas *broadcast executive*
Dave, Vinod C. *art educator*
Davenport, Lawrence Franklin *academic administrator*
DaVerne, Steven Richard *advertising director, artist, illustrator, behavior analyst*
Daves, Donald Rae *entertainment industry executive*
David, Marilyn Hattie *lawyer, retired military officer*
Davidson, Bonnie Jean *gymnastics educator, sports management consultant*
Davidson, Chris Clark *writer*
Davidson, David Isaac *artist, educator*
Davidson, Jeannie *costume designer*
Davidson, Mark *writer, educator*
Davidson, Mayer B. *medical educator, researcher*
Davies, Michael S. *security analyst*
D'Avignon, Roy Joseph *lawyer*
Dávila, Rafael Angel, III, *college counselor, educator*
Dávila, Susan *guidance counselor*
Davion, Ethel Johnson *school system administrator, curriculum specialist*
Davis, Anna Jane Ripley *elementary school educator*
Davis, Bertha *emergency nurse practitioner, emergency medical technician*
Davis, Carolyne Kahle *health care consultant*
Davis, Charles S. *biostatistician*
Davis, Clarence Clinton, Jr., *lawyer*
Davis, Crystal Michelle *state health administrator*
Davis, Darrell L. *automotive executive*
Davis, Dempsie Augustus *military officer, educator, financial planner*
Davis, Earon Scott *massage and bodywork consultant, lawyer*
Davis, Frederick Benjamin *retired law educator*
Davis, Geena (Virginia Davis) *actress*
Davis, Gray (Joseph Graham Davis) *former governor*
Davis, Henry Jefferson, Jr., *former naval officer*
Davis, Hiram Joe *public school administrator*
Davis, J. Michael *environmental health scientist*
Davis, Joanne Fatse *lawyer*
Davis (Jr.), John V. *newswriter, educator*
Davis, Joseph Lloyd *educational administrator, consultant*
Davis, Joseph Samuel *marketing executive, consultant*
Davis, June Fiksdal *medical facility owner, floral designer*
Davis, Karen Ann (Karen Ann Falconer) *special education educator*
Davis, Keigh Leigh *aerospace engineer*
Davis, Lowell Livingston *cardiovascular surgeon*
Davis, Luther *writer, producer*
Davis, Maggie (Marie Hill) *writer*
Davis, Mamie (Denise Davis) *writer*
Davis, Marc I. *journalist, writer*
Davis, Margaret Thacker *retired critical care, medical and surgical nurse*
Davis, Marjorie Ann *program analyst*
Davis, Mary Byrd *conservationist, researcher*
Davis, Mary Helen *psychiatrist, psychoanalyst, educator*
Davis, Michelle Denise *writer*
Davis, Patricia May *primary school educator, writer*
Davis, Roger Edwin *lawyer, retired discount chain executive*
Davis, Ruth Marie *retired writer*
Davis, Sid *journalist*
Davis, Wanda Rose *lawyer*
Davis, William L. *publishing company executive*
Davis Greivell, Judith Ann *artist*
Davison, Helen Irene *secondary education educator, counselor*
Dawes, Leslie Dawn *minister, small business owner*
Dawkins, Marva Phyllis *psychologist, educator*
Dawson, Karen Oltmanns *nursing educator*
Dawson, Peter John *pathologist, educator*
Dawson, Virginia Sue *retired editor*
Day, Anthony *book critic, journalist*
Day, Donald Lee *retired engineering educator, researcher*
Day, John Denton *retired company executive, cattle and horse rancher, breeder, trainer, wrangler, actor, educator*
Day, Richard Allen *chemistry professor*
Day, Roland Bernard *retired chief justice state supreme court*
Day, Steven Matthew *researcher, consultant*
Dayton, Sky *communications company executive*
de Abreu, Sue *elementary school educator*
Deacon, David Emmerson *business executive*
Deal, Gaye Follmer *writer*
Dean, Carole Lee *film company executive*
Dean, Edwin Becton *entrepreneur*
Dean, Edwin Robinson *economist, educator, consultant*
Dean, Michael M. *lawyer*
Dean, Thompson *diversified financial services company executive, investment banker*
De Angelis, Rosemary Eleanor *actress*
DeAngelo, Judith *artist*
De Antoni, Edward Paul *lab administrator*
DeBeers, Roger Norman *writer*
Debevoise, A. Clay *artist*
De Blasi, Tony (Anthony Armando De Blasi) *artist*
de Blasis, James Michael *artistic director, producer, stage director*
DeBock, Ronald Gene *real estate company executive*
Debreu, Gerard *economics and mathematics educator*
DeBruce, Paul *agricultural food products company executive*
Debs, Barbara Knowles *former college president, consultant*
Debus, Eleanor Viola *retired business management company executive*
Dechant, Virgil C. *retired fraternal organization administrator*
Dechar, Peter Henry *artist*
Decker, Gilbert Felton *consultant*
Decker, Walter Johns *toxicologist*
Dedman, Bill *journalist*
Deely, Maureen Cecelia *community health nurse*
Deering, Fred Arthur *retired insurance company executive*
Dees, Bowen Causey *institute executive, retired*
Dees, C. Stanley *lawyer*
DeFato, Joan *retired librarian*
De Felitta, Frank Paul *producer, writer, director*
De Ford, Douglas Atmetlla *biochemical, biomechanical and industrial engineer*
DeFrancis, Suellen Maria *interior architect*
Degann, Sona Irene *obstetrician, gynecologist, educator*
DeGeneres, Ellen *actress, comedienne*
Degenhardt, Robert Allan *architectural firm executive, engineering executive*
De Gette, Diana Louise *congresswoman, lawyer*
DeGeus, Wendell Ray *photographer*
Deisenhofer, Johann *biochemistry educator, researcher*
Deitz, Susan Rose *columnist, writer*
DeJack, Jacqueline Elvadeana *artist, educator*
De Jong, Arthur Jay *education consultant, former university president*
Dela Cruz, Jose Santos *retired state supreme court justice*
DeLaFuente, Charles *lawyer, educator, journalist*
Delahanty, Rebecca Ann *school system administrator*
Delaney, Robert Vernon *logistics and transportation executive*
de la Piedra, Jorge *orthopedic surgeon*
DeLapp, Tina Davis *retired nursing educator*
Delaty, Simone *retired language educator*
Delgado Barrio, Francisco Javier *former president supreme court of Spain*
Dellagnena, Gail Lynn *computer programmer analyst, consultant*
De Loach, Bernard Collins, Jr., *retired physicist*
De Looper, Willem Johan *artist, museum curator*
De Lorenzo, Robert Allan *emergency physician*
de Lorimier, Alfred Alexandre *retired physician, pediatric surgeon, medical educator*
Del Papa, Frankie Sue *former state attorney general*
Delucchi, Alfred Attilio *retired judge*
De Lutis, Donald Conse *investment adviser, consultant*
Dely, Steven *aerospace company executive*
DeMartini, Richard Michael *retired bank executive*
Demenchonok, Edward Vasilevich *philosopher, linguist, researcher, educator*
Demere, Robert Houstoun, Jr., *oil company executive*
Demharter, Cheryl Ann Marie *foreign language educator, former administrator*
DeMille, Dale Esther *medical/surgical nurse, educator*
DeMille, Nelson Richard *writer*
DeMint, James Warren *congressman, marketing professional*
Demissie, Yemane I. *filmmaker*
DeMita, Geraldine *librarian*
Demma, Joe *political scientist, consultant*
Dench, Judith Olivia *actress*
Denevan, William Maxfield *geographer, historical ecologist*
Denez, Deeva *publishing executive, writer, medical technician*
Denious, Sharon Marie *retired publishing executive*
Denison, Julian Rain *lighting designer, writer*
Denn, Cyril Joseph *retired financial advisor*
Dennehy, Leisa Jeanotta *pharmaceutical executive*
Denning, Karen Craft *finance educator*
Denny, Jera Cecilia Jane Elizabeth *musician, graphics designer*
Denton, Medona Bonner *research chemistry educator*
Deoul, Kathleen Boardsen *publishing executive*
DePalma, Ralph George *surgeon, educator*
de Planque, E. Gail *physicist*
DePriest, Jon *academic administrator, department chairman*
Derby, Robert Allen *acoustical engineer*
Derbyshire, William Wadleigh *language educator, translator*
Derchin, Michael Wayne *portfolio manager and financial analyst*
Dergarabedian, Paul *energy and environmental company executive*
Dermanis, Paul Raymond *architect*
Dern, Laura *actress*
Derrick, Bill *contracting company executive*
Derrickson, Denise Ann *secondary school educator*
Derrico, Georgia Santangelo *banker*
de Russy, Candace Uter *education reformer*
Deryuga, Vyacheslav O. *nuclear physicist, computer scientist, consultant*
Derzai, Matthew *retired telecommunications company executive*
DeSando, John Anthony *retired humanities educator, film critic*
Desbarats, Peter Hullett *journalist, academic administrator*
Deshefy, Gregory Scott *ecologist, environmentalist*
Desio, Delores Jean *writer, artist, retired elementary school educator*
Desjardins, Eric *professional hockey player*
Desjardins, Judith Anne *psychotherapist*
De Sofi, Oliver Julius *data processing executive*
Dessauer, Carin *journalist*
Detert, Miriam Anne *chemical analyst*
DeThomas, Joseph Michael *former ambassador*
Detweiler, David Kenneth *veterinary physiologist, educator*
Detwiler, Christina LeFevre *elementary school educator*
Deutsch, Herbert Arnold *music educator*
Deutsch, James I. *curator*
Deutsche, Kirsten Hansen *pharmaceutical company executive*
Deutschman, Louise Tolliver *curator*
Deutz, Natalie Rubinstein *actress, consultant*
DeVaris, Jeannette Mary *psychologist*
de Varona, Donna *sports reporter, former Olympic swimmer*
DeVera, Gertrude Quenano *education educator*
Devine, Donald C. *manufacturing executive*
Deviney, Marvin Lee, Jr., *research institute scientist, program manager*
de Vink, Lodewijk J. R. *healthcare consultant, former consumer pharmaceutical products company executive*
De Vita, Michael Richard *obstetrician-gynecologist*
DeVita, Vincent Theodore, Jr., *oncologist*
DeVivo, Ange *retired small business owner*
Devlin, Michael Coles *bass-baritone*
Devoe, Dorothy S. *elementary school educator*
DeVore, Kimberly K. *business executive*
DeVos, Elisabeth (Betsy) *political association executive*
DeVries, Linda Jane *music educator*
DeVries, Robert Allen *foundation administrator*
DeVylder, Edgar Paul, Jr., *lawyer*
Dewald, William Guenthner *economist*
Dewar, James McEwen *marketing, aerospace and defense executive, developing nations consultant*
Dewey, Donald Charles *writer*
Dewhurst, Peter *industrial engineer, educator*
deWilde, David Michael *management consultant, retired executive recruiter, lawyer, financial services executive*
DeWitt, Sallie Lee *realtor*
DeWolfe, Susan *elementary school educator*
Dews, P(eter) B(ooth) *medical scientist, educator*
Dhara, Venkata Ramana *physician, educator*
d'Heurle, Adma Jeha *psychology educator*
Diagana, Toka *mathematician, researcher*
Diamant, Anita *writer*
Diamant, William *lawyer*
Diamond, Richard *retired secondary education educator*
Diamond, Robert Mach *higher education administrator*
Diamond, Stuart *law educator, consultant*
Diamond, Susan Zee *management consultant*
Diao, Yixin *electrical engineer, researcher*
Dias, Kathleen R. *foreign language educator*
Diaz, Alphonso Vincent *aerospace executive*
Diaz, Linda Heidi *portfolio manager*
Diaz, Oscar, Jr., *voice educator, music institute director*
Diaz-Arce, Raul *professional soccer player*
DiBattiste, Carol A. *lawyer*
Dibner, David Robert *architect, writer*
DiCandilo, Michael D *corporate financial executive, accountant*
DiCaprio, Leonardo *actor*
Dicciani, Nance Katherine *chemical company executive, chemical engineer*
Dick, James Cordell *concert pianist*
Dickens, Alycia Thompson *nurse practitioner*
Dickens, Joyce Rebecca *addictions therapist, educator*
Dickerson, Eric Demetric *former professional football player*
Dickerson, Gary E. *former electronics executive*
Dickerson, John René *retired automotive engineer*
Dickerson, Quincy René *secondary school educator*
Dickes, Robert *psychiatrist*
Dickeson, Robert Celmer *retired university president, foundation executive, political science educator*
Dickey, Jay W., Jr., *former congressman, lawyer*
Dickey, Robert Marvin (Rick Dickey) *property manager*
Dickinson, Donald Charles *library science educator*
Dickinson, William Richard *retired geologist*
Dickman, James Bruce *photojournalist*
Dickman, James Earl *financial services executive*
Dickman, Robert S. *aerospace consultant, retired career officer*
Dickson, Eva Mae *credit manager*
Dickson, James Francis, III, *surgeon*
Dickson, Robert Lee *lawyer*
Dickstein, Michael Ethan *lawyer, arbitrator*
diCorcia, Philip-Lorca *artist, photographer*
Diddle, Albert W. *obstetrician, gynecologist*
DiDomenico, Mauro, Jr., *communication executive*
Diedrick, Geraldine Rose *retired nurse*
Diehl, Deborah Hilda *lawyer*
Diehl, Harry Alfred *chemist, genealogist*
Diehl, Louis F. *hematologist*
Diehl, Stephen Anthony *human resources consultant*
Diemer, Emma Lou *composer, educator*
Diener, Erwin *immunologist*
Diener, Royce *retired health products executive*
Dietz, Arthur Townsend *investment counseling company executive*
Dietze, Joachim *librarian*
Di Giacomo, Fran *artist*
Di Giovanni, Anthony *retired coal mining company executive*
DiGirolamo, Glen Francis *actor*
Dill, Laddie John *artist*
Dillon, Clifford Brien *retired lawyer*
Dillon, Phillip Michael *real estate developer, construction executive*
Dillon, Robert Sherwood *retired government official*
Dillon-McHugh, Cathleen Theresa *librarian, consultant, editor*
Dills, James Arlof *retired publishing company executive*
Dimancescu, Mihai D. *neurosurgeon, researcher, educator*
DiMento, Carol A.G. *lawyer*
Dimitry, Theodore George *retired lawyer*
Dimon, James (Jamie Dimon) *bank executive*
Dincecco, Jennie Elizabeth Williams Swanson *healthcare administrator, mentor, healthcare educator, volunteer*
Ding, Ai-Yue *conductor, music educator*
Ding, Chen *investment banker*
Ding, Jinwen *biomedical researcher*
Dingle, Carol A. *state agency administrator, writer*
Dinkel, John George *automotive executive, consultant*
DiPersio, John F. *oncologist*
Dipko, Thomas Earl *retired minister, national church executive*
Diprato, Jim *writer, video editor*
Dirvin, Gerald Vincent *retired consumer products company executive*
DiSalle, Michael Danny *secondary school educator*
Disch, Thomas M(ichael) *author*
Disney, Roy Edward *broadcasting company executive*
Dissen, Walter Charles *lawyer*
Di Suvero, Mark *sculptor*
Ditka, Michael Keller *former professional football coach*
Dito, William Robert *pathology educator*
Dittenhafer, Brian Douglas *banker, economist*
Dittmer, Linda Jean *photographer, computer artist, retired photojournalist*
Dix, Gary Errol *engineering executive*
Dix, Samuel Morman *industrial engineer, physical economist, appraiser*
Dixon, Diane Marie *statistician*
Dixon, Gordon Henry *biochemist, educator*
Dixon, Michael Wayne *designer, writer, researcher*
Dixon, William Robert *musician, composer, educator*
Dizer, John T., Jr., *engineering educator*
Djordjevic, Dimitrije *historian, educator*
Dmochowski, Jan Rafal *surgeon, researcher*
Doan, Mary Frances *advertising executive*
Dobbel, Rodger Francis *interior designer*
Dobbs, Lou *television executive, managing editor*
Dobelle, Evan Samuel *former academic administrator*
Doberenz, Alexander R. *nutrition educator, chemist*
Dobler, Donald William *retired dean*
Dobriansky, Lev Eugene *economist, educator, diplomat*
Dobson, Melanie Beroth *small business owner, public relations executive*
Doby, Margaret Gail *interior designer*
Dockery, J. Lee *retired medical school administrator*
Dodd, Steven Louis *systems engineer*
Dodge, R(alph) Edward, Jr., *physician*
Dodson, Daniel, Sr., *advertising executive*
Dodson, Samuel Robinette, III, *investment banker*
Doebler, Bettie Anne *language educator, researcher, writer*
Doerper, John Erwin *journal editor, publishing executive*
Dogançay, Burhan C. *artist, photographer, sculptor*
Dogoloff, Lee Israel *clinical social worker, psychotherapist, consultant*
Doherty, Charles Vincent *investment counsel executive*
Doherty, Peter Charles *immunologist*
Doherty, Shannon *actress*
Doherty, Thomas Joseph *financial services industry consultant*
Dohrmann, Russell William *manufacturing executive*
Dokurno, Anthony David *lawyer*
Dolan, Edward Francis *writer*
Dolan, Peter Brown *lawyer*
Dolan, Peter J. *corporate financial consultant*
Dolby, Tom Eric *writer*
Dole, Arthur Alexander *psychology educator*
Dolev, Jacqueline *physician, researcher*
Dolgow, Allan Bentley *management consultant*
Dolich, Andrew Bruce *sports marketing executive*
Dolman, John Phillips, Jr., (Tim Dolman) *communications company executive*
Dolph, Wilbert Emery *lawyer*
Doman, Elvira *retired science administrator*
Domenico, Anthony Wayne *conductor, music educator*
Dominguez, Eddie *artist*
Dominick, Kathleen Marilyn *small business owner, consultant*
Dompke, Norbert Frank *retired photography studio executive*
Domzella, Janet *retired library director*
Donahue, Donald Jordan *mining company executive*
Donahue, Mary Beth *human services administrator*
Donahue, Richard King *athletic apparel executive, lawyer*
Donaldson, Loraine *economics professor*
Donaldson, Myrtle Norma *music educator, musician*
Donaldson, Wilma Crankshaw *elementary school educator*
Donath, Fred Arthur *geologist, geophysicist*
Dondanville, John Wallace *lawyer*
Doniger, Jay *health information executive*
Donley, Deedra Ann *medical educator*
Donlon, James D, III, *controller, corporate financial executive*
Donnell, Harold Eugene, Jr., *retired professional society administrator*
Donnelly, PaJa Lee *nursing educator and nurse practitioner*
Donnelly, Patrick Stefan *writer, editor*
Donoff, R. Bruce *dean, oral surgeon, dental educator*
Donohue, George L. *mechanical engineer, educator*
Donohue, Marc David *chemical engineering educator*
Donovan, Brian *freelance journalist*
Donovan, Kathleen A. *water transportation executive, county official*
Dooley, Jo Ann Catherine *retired publishing executive*
Doornink, Barbara *military officer*
Doraiswamy, P(udugramam) Murali *psychiatrist, educator, researcher, neuroscientist*
Doran, Charles Edward *textile manufacturing executive*
Dorighi, Nancy S. *computer engineer*
Dorman, Arthur *optometrist, state legislator*
Dorman, Richard Frederick, Jr., *association executive, consultant*

Evans, Robert George, Jr., *retail and mail order executive*
Evans, Thomas E. *autoparts company executive*
Evarts, Charles McCollister *orthopaedic surgeon*
Evatt, Parker *former state commissioner, former state legislator*
Evdokimova, Eva *prima ballerina assoluta, choreographer, director, producer, actress*
Everdell, William *retired lawyer*
Everett, Carl Nicholas *management consulting executive*
Everett, Donna Raney *finance educator*
Everett, Elbert Kyle *marketing executive, consultant*
Everett, Robert Rivers *electrical engineer*
Everett, Tom *actor*
Everly, George Stotelmyer, Jr., *psychologist, psychophysiologist, educator, mathematician*
Evert, Chris (Christine Marie Evert) *retired professional tennis player*
Evosevich, Carey Lynn *elementary school educator, music educator*
Ewell, Miranda Juan *journalist*
Ewen, H.I. *physicist*
Ewing, Edgar Louis *artist, educator*
Ewing, Elisabeth Anne Rooney *priest*
Ewing, James E. *priest*
Ewing, Raymond Charles *retired ambassador*
Ewing, Susan M. *writer*
Ewing, Wayne Turner *coal company executive*
Exton, Peter Walker *artist, writer*
Eyler, John H., Jr., *retail toy and game company executive*
Eyngorn, Isaak Ykovlevich *electronics executive*
Ezell, Margaret Prather *information systems executive*
Faber, Michael Warren *lawyer*
Fabian, D'Arline D. *music educator*
Fadiman, Anne *former magazine editor*
Fagin, David Kyle *natural resources executive*
Fahlbeck, Douglas Alan *corporate development executive*
Fahringer, Catherine Hewson *retired savings and loan association executive*
Fahrnbruch, Dale E. *retired state supreme court justice*
Fairleigh, James Parkinson *music educator*
Faletra, Robert *technology company executive*
Falk, Marshall Allen *retired university dean, physician*
Famularo, Joseph L. *former prosecutor*
Fan, Cong *music educator*
Fanos, Kathleen Hilaire *osteopathic physician, podiatrist*
Fansler, Brian Caldwell *budget analyst*
Fantin, Arline Marie *state legislator*
Fantino, Lisa Maria *lawyer, reporter*
Fanwick, Ernest *lawyer*
Farber, Neal Mark *biotech executive, molecular biologist*
Fargo, Thomas Boulton *career military officer*
Farid, Farid O. *mathematics professor*
Faris, James Vannoy *interventional cardiologist, cardiology educator, hospital executive*
Fariss, Bruce Lindsay *endocrinologist, consultant*
Farkas, Daniel Frederick *food science and technology educator*
Farley, Benjamin Wirt *religious studies educator, writer*
Farmakides, John Basil *lawyer*
Farmer, Christopher J. *political scientist, writer*
Farmer, Cornelia Griffin *lawyer, consultant, hearings official*
Farmer, Crofton Bernard *atmospheric physicist*
Farmer, Kenneth, Jr., *military officer*
Farnsworth, Elizabeth *broadcast journalist*
Faron, Fay Cheryl *private investigator, writer*
Farquhar, Robin Hugh *former university president*
Farr, Ivanne Estelle *small business owner, consultant, artist, sculptor*
Farr, Mel *automotive sales executive, former professional football player*
Farrar, Elaine Willardson *artist*
Farrar, John Edson, II, *business executive, consultant, investment adviser*
Farrell, Edward Wagner *retired dentist, educator*
Farrell, Mike *actor*
Farrell, Suzanne *ballerina*
Farrelly, Peter John *screenwriter*
Farrington, Bertha Louise *retired nursing administrator*
Farronato, Cristina *writer, researcher*
Farthing, Aliana M. *critical care nurse, writer*
Fasick, Adele Mongan *information services consultant*
Faucette, Gloria Marie *accountant, educator*
Fawcett, Farrah Leni *actress, model*
Fawcett, John Thomas *archivist*
Faxon, Alicia Craig *art educator, department chairman*
Fay, Conner Martindale *retired business executive*
Fay, Peter Thorp *federal judge*
Fazio, Evelyn M. *publisher*
Fearrington, Ann Peyton *writer, illustrator, newspaper reporter, portraitist*
Feathers, Gail M. Wratny *social worker*
Feazell, Thomas Lee *lawyer, business executive*
Federici, William Vito *newspaper reporter*
Federing, Eric K. *congressional communications director, motion picture preservationist, educator, public policy advisor*
Fedorow, Denise Christine Garza *journalist, writer*
Feeney, Matthew Edward *linguist, educator*
Feigal, David W., Jr., *health science association administrator*
Fein, Seymour Howard *pharmaceutical executive*
Feiner, Ava Sophia *public affairs and management consultant, economist*
Feinstein, Martin *performing arts consultant, art director*
Feinstein, Robert P. *dermatologist*
Feir, Dorothy Jean *entomologist, physiologist, educator*
Feld, Carole Leslie *marketing executive*
Feldkamp, John Calvin *lawyer, educational administrator*
Feldman, David Edward *playwright*
Feldman, Jack L. *neurobiology educator*
Feldmann, Frank Neil *chemistry professor*
Feldstein, Joshua *educational administrator*
Felgar, Raymond E(ugene) *pathologist, medical educator*
Felhofer, Marylouise Katherine *nursing administrator*
Felicetti, Daniel A. *academic administrator*
Felix, Arthur Martin *chemistry educator, researcher*
Fella, Marie Ann *intelligence analyst, drug enforcement administration*
Feller, Robert William Andrew *baseball team public relations executive, retired baseball player*
Fellers, Rhonda Gay *lawyer*
Fellman, Gerry Louis *lawyer, arbitrator*
Fels, Rendigs *economist, educator*
Fenech, Daniel Thomas *cartoonist*
Feng, Chung-Chiang *music educator*
Fennebresque, Kim Samuel *investment banker*
Fenwick, James Henry *editor*
Ferguson, Bradford Lee *lawyer*
Ferguson, Earl Wilson *cardiologist, medical executive, telemedicine consultant*
Ferguson, Emmet Fewell, Jr., *surgeon*
Ferguson, Paula Irene *nursing administrator*
Ferguson, Ted *music educator, composer*
Ferguson, Whitworth, III, *pastor*
Fernald, Harold Allen *publishing executive*
Fernández, Alberto Antonio *security professional*
Fernández-Velazquez, Juan Ramon *university chancellor*
Ferraro, Geraldine Anne *lawyer, former congresswoman*
Ferre, Antonio Luis *newspaper publisher*
Ferreira, Armando Thomas *sculptor, educator*
Ferreira, Jo Ann Jeanette Chanoux *time-definite transportation industry executive*
Ferrell, David Stanley *aerospace company executive*
Ferstenfeld, Julian Erwin *internist, educator*
Fetzer, Mark Stephen *lawyer*
Feuer, Marshall Zev *import/export company executive*
Fey, John Theodore *retired insurance company executive*
Fey, Willard *global environmental researcher, educator*
Fibiger, John Andrew *life insurance company executive*
Fichandler, Zelda *director*
Fickinger, Wayne Joseph *communications executive*
Fiddick, Paul William *government official, broadcasting executive*
Fidler, Mark T. *mathematician, educator, writer*
Field, Arthur Norman *lawyer*
Field, Michael Jay *education educator*
Field, Sally *actress*
Fields, Cleo *state legislator*
Fields, Douglas Philip *building supply wholesale company executive*
Fields, Jerri Lynn *foundation administrator*
Fields, Leo *former jewelry company executive, investor*
Fiennes, Ralph Nathaniel *actor*
Fietzer, William Harold *school librarian, writer*
Fife, Jonathan Donald *education educator*
Figueroa, Roberto Andres *psychiatrist, researcher*
Filchock, Ethel *education educator*
Filer, Tom Hanford *writer, educator*
Filerman, Michael Herman *television producer*
Filler, Susan Melanie *musicologist*
Fillmore, John Dillon *artist*
Filomeno, Linda Jean Harvey *elementary school educator*
Finberg, Bonny *psychologist, writer*
Finder, Joseph Alan *writer*
Finder-Stone, Patricia Ann *nurse, health educator, volunteer*
Findling, Rhonda Barbara *psychotherapist*
Finelsen, Libbi June *lawyer*
Finestone, Sheila *former legislator*
Finger, Harold B. *consultant*
Fink, Alma *retired elementary education educator*
Fink, John Francis *retired newspaper editor, columnist, writer*
Fink, Matthew Pollack *trade association executive, lawyer*
Finkel, David *advertising executive*
Finlay, Robert Derek *food company executive*
Finn, Mary Ralphe *artist*
Finnberg, Elaine Agnes *psychologist, editor*
Finnegan, Sara Anne (Sara F. Lycett) *publisher*
Finneran, Kevin Joseph *editor*
Finnigan, Robert Emmet *retired small business owner*
Fino, Marie Georgette Keck *retired real estate broker*
Finocchiaro, Alfonso G. *bank executive*
Fiondella, Robert William *former insurance company executive*
Fiorito, Edward Gerald *lawyer*
Firestone, Bruce Michael *lawyer, educator*
Firestone, Nancy B. *federal judge*
Fischer, A(lbert) Alan *family physician*
Fischer, Angela Brown *business executive, civic volunteer*
Fischer, Carl Robert *retired health care facility administrator*
Fischer, David Charles *lawyer*
Fischer, David Seymour *internist, consultant*
Fischer, Maxim *electronics engineer*
Fischer, Michael Ludwig *environmental executive*
Fischer, Russell Leonard *public relations executive*
Fischer, William Samuel *composer, lecturer*
Fischmar, Richard Mayer *resort executive, financial consultant*
Fish, Andrew Joseph, Jr., *electrical engineering educator, researcher*
Fish, Howard Math *aerospace transportation executive*
Fish, Janet Isobel *artist*
Fishburn, Janet Forsythe *university dean*
Fishburne, Lillian E. *career officer*
Fisher, Anita Jeanne (Kit Fisher) *language educator*
Fisher, Carrie Frances *actress, writer*
Fisher, Dale Dunbar *animal scientist, dairy nutritionist*
Fisher, David Andrew *merchant banker, lawyer, venture capitalist*
Fisher, Gordon McCrea *mathematician, educator*
Fisher, Linda J. *federal agency administrator*
Fisher, Margaret *artist, researcher*
Fisher, Nancy *writer, producer, director*
Fisher, Robert Charles Haru *publishing company executive, editor*
Fisher, Stephen Todd *retired military officer, healthcare consultant*
Fisher, Steven Jay *architect*
Fisher, Thomas Scott *army officer, broadcasting network executive*
Fishman, Bernard *mechanical engineer*
Fishman, George Mayer *historian, educator*
Fishman, Glenn I. *medical educator*
Fishman, Lawrence Martin *endocrinologist*
Fisk, Merlin Edgar *judge*
Fiss, Owen M. *law educator*
Fitch, Frank Wesley *pathologist educator, immunologist, educator, administrator*
Fitts, Catherine Austin *investment advisor*
FitzAlan-Howard, Bennett-Thomas Henry Robert *public administration and policy analyst, political theorist, theologian*
Fitz-Enz, David G. *retired military officer, television producer*
Fitzmaurice, Laurence Dorset *retired bank executive*
Fitzpatrick, Nancy Hecht *editor*
Fitzsimmons, Ellen Marie *lawyer*
FitzSimons, Sharon Russell *international financial and treasury executive*
Fiumefreddo, Charles A. *investment management company executive*
Fix, John Neilson *banker*
Flanary, Donald Herbert, Jr., *lawyer*
Flanzraich, Neil William *pharmaceutical company executive, lawyer*
Fleisher, Gary Mitchell *employment industry and management consulting executive*
Fleishman, Philip Robert *internist*
Fleming, James Edward, Jr., *information scientist, educator*
Fleming, Rhonda *actress, singer*
Flemming, David Paul *biologist*
Fletcher, Denise Koen *strategic and financial consultant*
Fletcher, Louise *actress*
Fleury, Paul Aimé *university dean, physicist*
Fleury, Theoren *professional hockey player*
Flick, Arnold L. *retired physician, community activist*
Flick, Carl *electrical engineer, consultant*
Flick, John Edmond *lawyer*
Flickinger, Harry Harner *organization and business executive, management consultant*
Flickinger, Joe Arden *telecommunications educator*
Flinn, Charles Gallagher *lawyer, priest*
Flinner, Beatrice Jeffreys Allayaud *retired library and media sciences educator*
Flint, John E. *historian, educator*
Flint, Lou Jean *retired state agency administrator*
Flipse, John Edward *naval architect, mechanical engineer*
Flitcraft, Richard Kirby, II, *former chemical company executive*
Flood, James Tyrrell *broadcasting executive, public relations consultant*
Flor, Loy Lorenz *retired chemist, corrosion engineer, consultant*
Florea, Luminita Dana *musicologist, educator, translator*
Flores, Alfinio *mathematician, educator*
Flores, George Anthony *physicist, researcher*
Flores, Patrick F. *retired archbishop*
Flory, Louise Michell *actress*
Floyd, Tim *former professional basketball coach*
Fluharty, David Arthur *automotive executive, statistician, consultant*
Fluth, John Adam *educational administrator*
Flynn, George William *chemistry educator, researcher*
Flynn, Paul Bartholomew *foundation executive*
Flynn, Peter Anthony *judge*
Flynn, Robert James *electronic commerce executive*
Flynn, Sarah Chapin *editor*
Fodiman, Aaron Rosen *publishing executive*
Fogelman, Ann Florence *nutrition consultant, educator, researcher*
Fogg, Richard Lloyd *food products company executive*
Foglietta, Thomas Michael *former diplomat, former congressman*
Foldesi, Robert Stephen *education administrator, management educator*
Foldi, Andrew Harry *retired singer, educator*
Folds-Bennett, Trisha Helen *psychologist, educator*
Foley, Gary J. *research chemical engineer, computer scientist, federal agency administrator*
Foley, Mary Kathleen *theater arts educator*
Fomon, Samuel Joseph *pediatrician, educator*
Fonda, Bridget *actress*
Fonda, Peter *actor, director, producer*
Fontana, Mario H. *nuclear engineer*
Fontes, Patricia J. *educational psychologist*
Foote, Evelyn Patricia *retired military officer*
Foote, Horton *playwright, scriptwriter*
Foote, William Chapin *business executive*
Forbes, Michael Patrick *former congressman*
Forbes-Richardson, Helen Hilda *state agency administrator*
Ford, Barbara Jean *library studies educator*
Ford, Christopher Ashley *state official, lawyer*
Ford, Ford Barney *retired government official*
Ford, George Burt *retired lawyer*
Ford, Harrison *actor*
Ford, Jerry Lee *service company executive*
Ford, Judith Ann Tudor *retired natural gas distribution company executive*
Ford, Kenneth William *physicist*
Ford, Loretta C. *retired dean, educator, consultant, nurse*
Ford, Mark Lee *aerospace engineer, researcher*
Ford, Nancy Louise *composer, scriptwriter*
Foreman, George *former boxer, minister, boxing broadcaster*
Foreman, Kelly Marie *anthropologist, music educator*
Forest, Eva Brown *nursing administrator, songwriter*
Forester, Jean Martha Brouillette *innkeeper, retired librarian, educator*
Forman, Edgar Ross *mechanical engineer*
Forney, Ronald Dean *elementary school educator, consultant, educational therapist*
Forno, Karin Ida *physician, educator*
Foronda, Barbara Elaine *professional organizer, writer*
Foronda, Elena Isabel *secondary school educator*
Forrester, Jay Wright *management specialist, educator*
Forry, John Ingram *lawyer*
Forsgren, John H., Jr., *utilities company executive*
Forst, Marion Francis *bishop*
Forsyth, Ben Ralph *academic administrator, medical educator*
Forsythe, Henderson *actor*
Fort, Denise Douglas *law educator, former state official*
Fortgang, Charles *wholesale distribution executive*
Fortune, Annetta *management educator, accountant*
Foshay, Maxine Valentine Shottland *civic worker, public relations executive*
Foss, Lukas *composer, conductor, pianist*
Foster, Carol Elise *psychologist, writer*
Foster, Charles Henry Wheelwright *former foundation officer, consultant, author*
Foster, Judith Christine *lawyer, writer*
Foster, Ken *writer, educator*
Foster, Mary Christine *film producer*
Foster, Murphy James, Jr., (Mike Foster) *former governor*
Foster, Sonja Marguerite *musician, educator*
Foster, Stephen Kent *banker, director*
Fotopoulos, Sophia Stathopoulos *medical research scientist, administrator*
Fouché, Helen Strother *editorial design executive*
Fournier, Walter Frank *real estate executive*
Fout, Mary Jane *librarian, educator*
Foutris, Christine S. *secondary school educator*
Fowler, Donald Raymond *retired lawyer, educator*
Fowler, Flora Daun *retired lawyer*
Fowler, Robert Asa *diplomat, manufacturing executive*
Fowler, Robert Joseph *financial company executive, consultant*
Fowler, Stephen Eugene *retired military officer, human resources executive*
Fox, Carol Jean *librarian*
Fox, Eleanor Mae Cohen *lawyer, educator, writer*
Fox, Joan Phyllis *environmental engineer*
Fox, John David *educator, physicist*
Fox, Jon D. *former congressman*
Fox, Kelly Diane *financial advisor*
Fox, Michael Wilson *veterinarian, bioethicist, animal behaviorist*
Fox-Clarkson, Anne C. *computer company executive*
Foy, Charles Daley *retired soil scientist*
Frackman, Noel *art critic*
Fradkin, David Milton *physicist, researcher*
Fraga, Mike A. *history professor, accountant*
Fraguela, Rafael J. *assemblyman*
Fraidin, Stephen *lawyer*
Fralinger, Jack Bruce *surgeon*
Franciosa, Anthony (Anthony Papaleo) *actor*
Franciosa, Joseph Anthony *health care consultant*
Francis, Jerome Leslie *lawyer*
Francis, Philip Hamilton *management consultant*
Francisco, Wayne *automotive executive*
Francke, Gloria Niemeyer *pharmacist, editor, publisher*
Francke, Linda Bird *journalist*
Frank, Charles Raphael, Jr., *financial advisor*
Frank, Edgar Gerald *retired financial executive*
Frank, James Stuart *lawyer*
Frank, Lawrence James *library director*
Frank, Marshall *protective services official, writer*
Frank, Stanley Donald *publishing company executive*
Frank, William Fielding *computer systems design executive, consultant*
Franke, John Charles *retired human resources executive*
Franke, Wayne Thomas *retired government affairs director, consultant*
Frankel, Albert J. *registrar*
Frankel, James Burton *retired lawyer*
Franken, Al *humorist, actor, writer*
Frankenberger, Bertram, Jr., *investor, consultant*
Frank-Fitzner, Fontaine Lynne *geriatrics nurse, insurance company executive*
Frankish, Brian Edward *film producer, director*
Franklin, Billy Joe *international higher education specialist*
Franklin, Margery Bodansky *psychology educator, researcher*
Franklin, Mary Ann Wheeler *educator, higher education and management consultant*
Franklin, Michael Harold *arbitrator, lawyer, consultant*
Franklin, William Emery *international business educator*
Franklin-Griffin, Cathy Lou Hinson *nursing educator*
Franks, Tommy Ray *retired army officer*
Frankson-Kendrick, Sarah Jane *publisher*
Frantiska, Joseph John, Jr., *systems engineer, educator*
Frantz, Ray William, Jr., *retired librarian*
Franz, John E. *bio-organic chemist, researcher*
Franz, Judy R. *physics educator*
Fraser, Ailana Margaret *mathematician, educator*
Fraser, Brent DeWayne *industrial engineer, researcher*
Fraser, Donald C. *engineering executive, educator*
Fraser, Donald MacKay *former mayor, former congressman, educator*
Fraser, Kathleen Joy *poet, creative writing educator*
Fratkin, Leslie *photographer*
Frauenfelder, Hans *physicist, researcher*
Frauenhoffer, Rose Marie *visual artist, cosmetologist*
Frawley, Thomas Francis *retired internist, medical educator*
Frazee, James T. *financial associate*
Frazier, DuEwa M. *actor, educator, playwright*
Frazier, Henry Bowen, III, *retired judge, government official, lawyer*
Frazier, Thomas C. *protective services official*
Fréchette, Louise *international organization official*
Frederick, Elizabeth Eleanor Tatum *watercolor artist, retired educator*
Frederick-Mairs, T(hyra) Julie *administrative health services official*
Fredman, Mimi Ungar Coppersmith *advertising and publishing executive*
Fred-Mensah, Ben Kwame *international development educator, consultant*
Freed, Eva Praeger *investment advisor*
Freed, Richard (Donald) *music critic*
Freedman, Russell Bruce *author*
Freeman, Arthur *veterinarian, retired association administrator*
Freeman, Charles E. *state supreme court justice*
Freeman, Frank V. *manufacturing executive*
Freeman, Glenn *political organization worker, retired non-commissioned military officer*
Freeman, Meredith Norwin *former college president, education educator*
Freeman, Ralph Carter *investment banker, management consultant*
Freeman, Richard Francis *banker*
Freese, Barbara Tapp *nursing educator*
Frei, Brent R. *computer software executive*
Freilich, Morris *anthropologist, educator*
Freilicher, Jane *artist*

Goldstein, Naomi *retired psychiatrist*
Goldstein, Norman Ray *international trading company executive, consultant*
Goldstein, Tamara Beth *musician*
Goldstein, Walter Elliott *biotechnology executive*
Goldston, Stephen Eugene *community psychologist, educator, consultant*
Goll, Stephen E. *telecommuncations executive*
Gollin, Rita Kaplan *English literature educator*
Gomez, Mirta *musician, educator*
Goncharko, Evelyn Marie *writer, school librarian, educator*
Gonye, Zsuzsanna *mathematician, educator*
Gonzales, Richard Robert *counselor*
González, Ibrahim *radio producer, educator, musician*
Gonzalez-Vales, Luis Ernesto *historian, educational administrator*
Good, Walter Raymond *investment executive*
Goodale, Toni Krissel *development consultant*
Goode, Janet Weiss *elementary school educator*
Goode, Stephen Hogue *publishing company executive*
Gooden, Gregory Allen *music educator*
Goodfellow, Robin Irene *surgeon*
Goodkin, Michael Jon *publishing company executive*
Goodman, Elizabeth Ann *retired lawyer*
Goodman, Erika *dancer, actress*
Goodman, Gail Busman *small business owner*
Goodman, Lillian Rachel *retired dean, nursing educator*
Goodman, Rebecca Gruver *education educator, writer*
Goodman, Richard *writer*
Goodman, Robert Lee *nursing administrator*
Goodrich, Kenneth Paul *retired college dean*
Goodridge, Alejandrina *writer, space designer*
Goodsell, Charles True *retired educator*
Goodsell, Douglas Charles *bank executive*
Goodson, Raymond Eugene *business educator, retired automotive executive*
Goodstone, Edward Harold *retired insurance company executive*
Goodwin, Andrew Wirt, II, *radiologist*
Goodwin, Irwin *journalist, writer*
Goodwin, Phillip Hugh *hospital administrator*
Goodwin, Richard Hale *botany educator*
Gordimer, Nadine *author*
Gordis, David Moses *academic administrator, rabbi*
Gordis, Enoch *retired science administrator, internist*
Gordon, Ezra *architect, educator*
Gordon, Marjorie *lyric coloratura soprano, opera producer, teacher*
Gordon, Myles Adam *television producer, writer*
Gordon, Richard M. Erik *private investor, educator*
Gordon, Ruby Daniels *retired nursing educator, counselor*
Gordon, William Edwin *physicist, educator, electrical engineer, academic administrator*
Gore, Albert, Jr., *former Vice President of the United States*
Gore, Carolyn Williams Gardner *special education educator, reading specialist*
Gorence, Patricia Josetta *judge*
Gorenstein, Samuel *retired mathematician, educator*
Gorman, Joseph Batterton *elementary school educator*
Gorman, Joseph Tolle *automotive parts manufacturing executive*
Gorske, Robert H. *lawyer*
Gorski, Waldemar *chemist, educator*
Gorsline, Stephen Paul *security specialist*
Gorsuch, Edward Lee *former chancellor*
Gorup, Gregory James *marketing executive*
Gosciewski, Robert Louis *logistician*
Goss, Joel Francis *writer*
Gottesman, Stephen Thancy *astronomy educator, researcher*
Gottfried, Eugene Leslie *physician, educator*
Gottlander, Robert Jan Lars *dental company executive*
Gottlieb, Alan Merril *advertising, fundraising and broadcasting executive, writer*
Gottlieb, Gary L. *hospital administrator*
Gould, Martha Bernice *retired librarian*
Goulet, Charles Ryan *retired insurance company executive*
Goulet, Lorrie *sculptor*
Gouletas, Evangeline *investment executive*
Gourvitz, Elliot Howard *lawyer*
Gouse, S. William, Jr., *engineering executive, scientist*
Govan, Gladys Vernita Mosley *retired critical care and medical/surgical nurse*
Gowler, Vicki Sue *newspaper editor, journalist*
Goyan, Jere Edwin *business executive, former university dean*
Grab, Frederick Charles *lawyer*
Graber, William Raymond *former pharmaceutical executive*
Grace, Marcia Bell *advertising executive*
Grace, Walter Charles *retired prosecutor*
Grady, Lee Timothy *pharmaceutical chemist*
Graebner, James Herbert *transportation executive*
Graessley, William Walter *retired chemical engineering educator*
Graff, Arthur Steven *educational consultant*
Graham, Cynthia Armstrong *banker*
Graham, David G. *preventive medicine physician, psychiatrist*
Graham, James Herbert *retired dermatologist*
Graham, John Hamilton, II, *professional athletics manager*
Graham, K(athleen) M. (K. M. Graham) *artist*
Graham, Lanier *art historian, curator, cultural planner*
Graham, Norma Van Surdam *psychologist, educator*
Graham, Steven Anthony *writer*
Graham, Wallace Karl *chemical company executive*
Graham, Warren Kenyon *counselor*
Gralla, Lawrence *publishing company executive*
Gralla, Milton *publisher*
Grames-Lyra, Judith Ellen *artist*
Grams, Rodney D. *former senator, former congressman*
Grande, Alexander, IV, *artist*
Grandguist, Betty L. *former director elder affairs*
Grandi, Attilio *engineering consultant*
Granger, Kay *congresswoman*
Grann, Phyllis *former publisher, editor*
Grant, Alexander Marshall *retired ballet director*
Grant, Isabella Horton *retired judge*
Grant, James Colin *banker*
Grant, Lee (Lyova Haskell Rosenthal) *actress, television and film director*
Grant, Leonard Tydings *clergyman*
Grant, Linda Hess *language educator*
Grant, Merrill Theodore *producer*
Grant, Richard Earl *retired medical and legal consultant*
Grasserbauer, Doris *computer scientist, mathematician, educator*
Grasso, Richard A. *former stock exchange executive*
Graves, Denyce Antoinette *mezzo-soprano*
Graves, Lorraine Elizabeth *dancer, educator, coach*
Graves, Sid Foster, Jr., *retired library and museum director*
Graves, Wallace Billingsley *retired university executive*
Graves, William Preston *governor*
Gray, Barbara Bronson *nurse, foundation administrator, writer, public relations executive*
Gray, David Lawrence *retired air force officer*
Gray, Deborah Mary *wine importer*
Gray, Francine du Plessix *author*
Gray, Gavin Campbell, II, *computer information engineer*
Gray, Gordon L. *communications educator*
Gray, Harry Joshua *retired engineering educator*
Gray, Mary Jane *retired obstetrician, gynecologist*
Gray, Richard Alexander, Jr., *retired chemical company executive*
Gray, Richard Moss *retired college president*
Gray, Thomas Stephen *editor-in-chief, writer*
Grayson, Edward Davis *lawyer, manufacturing executive*
Graziani, Leonard Joseph *pediatric neurologist, researcher*
Greaser, Constance Udean *retired automotive industry executive*
Greathead, Roger J. *marketing professional*
Greaves, William Webster *chemist, patent analyst, community liaison*
Greber, Robert Martin *retired financial investments executive*
Grebstein, Sheldon Norman *university administrator*
Grech, David John *lawyer, writer*
Grechanik, Jeffrey *military officer*
Greco, Christopher Jon *musician, composer, educator*
Greeley, Andrew Moran *sociologist, writer*
Greeley, Jennifer Ann *military officer, educator*
Green, Bennett Donald *biotechnologist*
Green, Carol H. *lawyer, educator, journalist*
Green, Carole L. *lawyer*
Green, Howard Alan *management consultant, educator*
Green, Leon, Jr., *mechanical engineer*
Green, Louis Harry *retired surgeon*
Green, Nancy Loughridge *publishing executive*
Green, Patricia Pataky *school system administrator, consultant*
Green, Richard Calvin, Jr., *electric power and gas industry executive*
Green, Robert Bailey *insurance executive, retired*
Green, Thomas George *retired architect*
Green, Thornton George *software engineer*
Greenberg, Albert *art director*
Greenberg, Carolyn Phyllis *anesthesiologist, educator*
Greenberg, Harold *legal educator*
Greenberg, Hinda Feige *library director*
Greenberg, Ira Arthur *psychologist*
Greenberg, Jack M. *former food products executive*
Greenberg, Judith Ann *real estate developer*
Greenberg, Raymond Seth *academic administrator, educator, health facility administrator*
Greenberg, Ronald David *lawyer, law educator*
Greenburg, Dan *author*
Greene, Alan Guyer *retired radiologist*
Greene, Alvin *service company executive, management consultant*
Greene, Donald Richard *dermatologist, educator*
Greene, Frank Sullivan, Jr., *investment management executive*
Greene, John Colton *retired history educator*
Greene, Monica Lynn Banks *recreational therapist, director*
Greene, Richard Thaddeus *bank executive*
Greenebaum, Leonard Charles *retired lawyer*
Greenfield, Linda Sue *nursing educator*
Greenfield, Sanford Raymond *architect*
Greenfield, Val Shea *ophthalmologist*
Greenhaw, Judith Yvonne *health facility administrator, medical/surgical nurse*
Greenman, David Lewis *retired physiologist, toxicologist*
Greenstein, Robert *retired radiologist*
Greenwald, John Edward *newspaper and magazine writer, editor and executive, painter*
Greenway, Joan M. *dean*
Greenwood, Janet Kae Daly *psychologist, educational administrator, marketing professional*
Greer, Carl Crawford *petroleum company executive*
Greer, Germaine *author*
Greer, K. Gordon *banker*
Greer, Suzanne Michelle *music educator*
Greever, Margaret Quarles *retired mathematics educator*
Gregg, David, III, *investment banker*
Greggs, Elanora *social worker*
Gregor, Dorothy Deborah *retired librarian*
Gregory, Claire Distelhorst *television producer*
Gregory, Daniel Hayes *gastroenterologist*
Gregory, Frederick D. *career officer, space agency administrator*
Gregory, Jackie Sue *critical care nurse, family nurse practitioner*
Gregory, James Alexander *editor, writer, film producer*
Gregory, Myra May *religious organization administrator, educator*
Gregory, Theodore Nathan *performing company executive, performing arts educator*
Greigg, Cathryn O. *music educator, musician*
Grell, Lewis Adam *retired association executive*
Grelle, Bridget Anne *music educator*
Grendell, James Henry *medical educator*
Grenier, Laura Margiotta *medical/surgical nurse*
Grenitz, Robert *retired obstetrician-gynecologist*
Grey, Francis Joseph *accountant, accounting company executive, educator*
Grey, Robert Dean *academic administrator, biology educator*
Griesé, John William, III, *astronomer, educator, advocate*
Grieser, Jeanne K. *writer*
Griffen, Ward O., Jr., *surgeon, educator, medical board executive*
Griffey, Jacqueline Jett *journalist, writer*
Griffin, Campbell Arthur, Jr., *retired lawyer*
Griffin, Carleton Hadlock *accountant, educator*
Griffin, James Anthony *bishop*
Griffin, Mark W. *paper company executive*
Griffin, Robert Paul *former United States senator, state supreme court justice*
Griffith, B(ezaleel) Herold *physician, educator, plastic surgeon*
Griffith, Melanie *actress*
Griffiths, Phillip A. *mathematician, former academic administrator*
Griggs, Bobbie June *civic worker*
Grijns, Laine *investment company executive*
Grimes, James Gordon *geologist*
Grimes-Frederick, Dorothea D. *communications executive*
Griner, Paul Francis *physician*
Grinnell, Helen Dunn *musicologist, arts administrator*
Grittner, Michael Curtis *theater educator, theater director*
Groce, William Henry, III, *environmental engineer, consultant*
Grody, Donald *actor, judge, lawyer, arbitrator*
Groening, Matthew *writer, cartoonist*
Grolli, Frank Thomas *retired pharmacist*
Gromen, Richard John *historian, educator*
Grosbard, Ulu *director*
Groscost, Jeff *former state legislator, small business owner*
Groskopf, Aubrey Bud *motion picture television executive, lawyer*
Grosland, Emery Layton *retired banker*
Gross, Irena Gridzinska *humanities educator*
Gross, Laura Ann *marketing and communications professional, acupuncturist, herbalist*
Gross, Richard Benjamin *lawyer*
Gross, Rosalie-Ethelyn *secretary*
Gross, Ruth Taubenhaus *former pediatrician*
Grossman, Cissy *curator, art historian, art exhibit designer, Judaica connoisseur, appraiser*
Grossman, Edith Marian *translator, critic, editor*
Grossman, Janice *former magazine publishing company executive*
Grossman, Joyce Renee *pediatrician, internist*
Grossman, Marc *federal agency administrator*
Grossman, Robert James *retired architect*
Grotta, Sandra Brown *interior designer*
Grove, Richard Charles *retired power tool company executive*
Groves, Bernice Ann *retired elementary and secondary school coordinator, educator*
Growe, Joan Anderson *former state official*
Growick, Philip *advertising executive*
Grubb, Donald Hartman *paper industry company executive*
Gruber, Fredric Francis *financial planning and investment research executive*
Gruberg, Cy *educational administrator*
Grubich, Douglas Leo *cartoonist, writer*
Gruen, Margaret *actress*
Grunder, Fred Irwin *industrial hygienist, consultant*
Grushow, Sandy *broadcast executive*
Grutman, Jewel Humphrey *lawyer, writer*
Gruy, Henry Jones *engineering company executive, petroleum engineer*
Gschwind, Donald *management and engineering consultant*
Gubbins, Keith Edmund *chemical engineering educator*
Guccione, Robert Charles Josep *publisher*
Gudenberg, Harry Richard *arbitrator, mediator*
Gudmundsson, Finnbogi *library administrator*
Guedes, Alessandra Casanova *public health service officer*
Guerrero, Jeannie *music educator*
Guerrero, Olive Ciridon *retired educator, civic worker*
Guevarra, Manuel Robinson *artist, retired military officer*
Gugel, Craig Thomas *advertising and strategic research executive*
Guhr, Daniel Johannes *management consultant*
Guiliano, Francis James *office products manufacturing company executive*
Guinasso, Victor *delivery service executive*
Guittar, Lee John *retired newspaper executive*
Gulbrandsen, Patricia Hughes *physician*
Gulcher, Robert Harry *aircraft company executive*
Gulko, Paul Michael *insurance executive*
Gulledge, Sandra Smith *publishing executive, film producer*
Gullickson, JoAnne Lois *writer*
Gummel, Hermann Karl *retired physicist, laboratory administrator*
Gummere, John *insurance company executive, director*
Gumpel, Liselotte *retired language educator*
Gumpert, Gustav *public relations executive*
Gumppert, Karella Ann *federal government official*
Gunczler, Jeannette *economist, writer*
Gundersheimer, Werner Leonard *library director*
Gunderson, Ted Lee *security consultant*
Gunger, Richard William *lawyer*
Gunhus, Gaylord T. *military career officer*
Gunn, Lee Fredric *career officer*
Gunning, Carolyn Sue *dean, provost, nursing educator*
Gunter, William Dayle, Jr., *physicist, consultant*
Gunther, Vanessa Ann *historian, registered nurse*
Guo, Sheng Ming *retired history educator*
Guo, Xiaofeng *physicist*
Guo, ZengKui *research scientist*
Gupta, Krishan Lal *physician, medical educator*
Gupta, Narendra Kumar *physician, educator*
Gupta, Ritesh *cardiologist, researcher*
Gurian, Mal *telecommunications executive*
Gurney, Daniel Sexton *race car manufacturing company executive, racing team executive*
Gurnow, Michael Erwin *literature and film educator*
Gurspan, Mitchell Scott *technology architect, author*
Gurspan, Susan Judith *language educator*
Gurwitch, Arnold Andrew *communications executive*
Gurwitz-Hall, Barbara Ann *artist*
Guskin, Alan E. *university president*
Gustafson, Craig Thomas *theatrical director, playwright, graphic artist*
Gustafson, Richard Alrick *university president emeritus*
Guthrie, Janet *professional race car driver*
Guthrie, Tara Sonali *librarian, music educator, soprano*
Guthrie, Wallace Nessler, Jr., *naval officer*
Gutman, Richard Edward *lawyer*
Gutmann, Reinhart Bruno *clergyman, social worker*
Guttentag, Joseph Harris *lawyer, educator*
Guy, Eleanor Bryenton *writer*
Guyer, Bernard *maternal and child health educator*
Guymon, Gary LeRoy *civil engineering educator, consultant*
Guzzo, Glenn *former newspaper editor*
Gyles, Mary Francis *retired history educator*
Ha, Chong Wan *information technology executive*
Haaland, Gordon Arthur *former academic administrator*
Haas, Carolyn Buhai *elementary education educator, publisher, writer, consultant*
Haas, Charlie *screenwriter*
Haas, Edward Lee *business executive, consultant*
Haas, Frederick Carl *retired paper and chemical company executive*
Haas, Sheila Sperber *writer, consultant*
Haber, Joel Abba *lawyer*
Haber, Ralph Norman *psychology consultant, researcher, educator*
Haber, Warren H. *investment company executive*
Haberkorn, Judith R. *former manufacturing executive*
Haberman, Charles Morris *mechanical engineer, educator*
Hackel-Sims, Stella Bloomberg *lawyer, former government official*
Hackett, Robert John *lawyer*
Hackett, Wesley Phelps, Jr., *lawyer*
Haddock, Harold, Jr., *retired accounting firm executive*
Haden, Clovis Roland *retired academic administrator, engineering educator*
Hadley, William Melvin *retired dean*
Haeberle, Rosamond Pauline *retired music educator*
Haeberle, William Leroy *corporate director, business educator, entrepreneur*
Haegele, John Ernest *business executive*
Hagan, Joseph Henry *higher education consultant*
Hagel, John, III, *management consultant*
Hagel, Raymond Charles *publishing company executive, educator*
Hagelstein, Robert Philip *publisher*
Hageman, Richard Philip, Jr., *educational administrator*
Hagemier, Herman Frederick *chemist*
Haggerty, Robert Johns *pediatrician, educator*
Hahn, Frank Horace *economics professor*
Hain, Patricia A. *music educator*
Haines, Lee Mark, Jr., *religious denomination administrator*
Haining, Jeane *psychologist*
Haithcock, William Dana, Jr., *physician*
Hajek, Robert J., Sr., *lawyer, real estate broker, commodities broker, nursing home owner*
Hakala, Karen Louise *retired real estate administrator*
Hake, Ralph F. *appliance manufacturing executive*
Hakim, Besim Selim *architecture and urban design educator, researcher and consultant*
Hakimoglu, Ayhan *electronics company executive*
Halberstam, David *journalist, writer*
Halberstam, Heini *mathematics professor*
Haldeman, Joe William *novelist*
Hale, Wesley Raymond *research scientist, chemical engineer*
Haley, George Brock, Jr., *retired lawyer*
Haley, George W. *ambassador*
Haley, Sally Fulton *artist*
Halfen, David *retired publishing executive*
Halfvarson, Lucille Robertson *music educator*
Hall, Adrienne A. *international marketing executive, venture capitalist consultant*
Hall, Anthony Michael *actor*
Hall, Barry G. *evolutionary biologist*
Hall, Ella Taylor *clinical school psychologist*
Hall, Hansel Crimiel *communications executive*
Hall, James Evan *lawyer*
Hall, James Stanley *jazz guitarist, composer*
Hall, Jay *social psychologist*
Hall, Joan Torrens *lawyer*
Hall, John Hopkins *retired lawyer*
Hall, Kathryn Marie *elementary school educator*
Hall, Milton Reese *retired oil company executive*
Hall, Monty *television producer, actor*
Hall, Susan Laurel *artist, educator, writer*
Hall, Zach Winter *academic administrator*
Halle, Bruce T. *automotive products company executive*
Halleck, Charles White *lawyer, photographer, former judge*
Hallett, William Jared *retired nuclear engineer*
Halliday, William Ross *retired physician, speleologist, writer*
Halloran, Daniel Edward *personnel executive*
Halpern, Alvin Michael *retired physicist, educator, consultant*
Halpern, James Bladen *lawyer*
Halpin, Daniel William *civil engineering educator, consultant*
Hambidge, Douglas Walter *archbishop*
Hamblen, John Wesley *computer scientist, genealogist*
Hamblen, Lapsley Walker, Jr., *judge*
Hambrecht, Patricia G. *retail executive*
Hamdy, Mostafa Kamal *microbiologist, educator*
Hamelin, Marcel *historian, educator*
Hamilton, Allan Corning *retired oil company executive*
Hamilton, Ann Katherine *artist*
Hamilton, Jack Richard *former social psychologist*
Hamilton, Joe *communications company executive*
Hamilton, Judith Hall *computer company executive*
Hamilton, Shirley Siekmann *arts administrator*
Hamilton, Thomas Michael *marketing executive*
Hamister, Donald Bruce *retired electronics company executive*
Hamit, Francis Granger *freelance writer*
Hamlet, Richard Graham *education educator, researcher*
Hamlin, Sonya B. *communications specialist*
Hamm, Vernon Louis, Jr., *management and financial consultant*
Hammam, M. Shawky *electrical engineer, educator*
Hammel, Ernest Martin *medical educator, academic administrator*
Hammer, Harold Harlan *oil company financial executive*
Hammer, Joyce Mae *gifted and talented education educator*

Hickerson, Glenn Lindsey *leasing company executive*
Hickey, Gerald Vincent *writer*
Hickey, Joseph Michael *investment banker*
Hickey, Timothy Andrew *lawyer*
Hickey, Winifred E(spy) *former state legislator, social worker*
Hickman, Lucille *physical therapist*
Hickman, Patricia *artist, craftswoman*
Hicks, Ritchie B. *physical education educator*
Hickson, Ernest Charles *financial executive*
Hietala, Valerie Grace *realtor, environmentalist, educator*
Higby, Edward Julian *safety engineer*
Higginbotham, Edith Arleane *radiologist, researcher*
Higgins, Larkin Maureen *artist, poet, educator*
Hightower, Jack English *former state supreme court justice, congressman*
Hightower, Suzie *writer, health facility administrator*
Hijuelos, Oscar *novelist*
Hild, Matthias *finance educator*
Hildebrand, Verna Lee *human ecology educator*
Hildebrandt, Frederick Dean, Jr., *management consultant*
Hiler, Edward Allan *agricultural and engineering educator*
Hiler, Monica Jean *reading and sociology educator*
Hilker, Walter Robert, Jr., *lawyer*
Hill, C. Thomas, Jr., *radiologist*
Hill, Emita Brady *academic administrator, consultant*
Hill, Harold Nelson, Jr., *lawyer*
Hill, James T. *career officer*
Hill, Jerry Dean *secondary school educator*
Hill, Martha N. *community health nurse*
Hill, Maurice B., Jr., *dentist*
Hill, Norma Louise *librarian*
Hill, Patricia Francine *information services executive*
Hill, Virgil Lusk, Jr., *academic administrator, naval officer*
Hilleary, Van *former congressman, lawyer*
Hiller, Arthur *motion picture director*
Hillerman, Tony *writer, former journalism educator*
Hilliard, Sam Bowers *geography educator*
Hillman, Leon *electrical engineer*
Hillman, Sandra Schwartz *public relations executive, marketing professional*
Hills, John F. *language educator*
Hilsabeck, Larry L. *education educator*
Hilton, Nicky (Nicholai Olivia Hilton) *apparel designer*
Hilton, Paris *actress*
Himes, Diane Adele *buyer, fundraiser, actress, lobbyist*
Himes, John Harter *medical researcher, educator*
Himmelfarb, Milton *editor, educator*
Hind, Harry William *pharmaceutical company executive*
Hinderliter, Richard Glenn *electrical engineer*
Hindery, Leo Joseph, Jr., *former communications executive*
Hinds, Edward Dee *insurance and investment professional, financial planner*
Hines, Andrew Hampton, Jr., *utilities executive*
Hines, Anthony Loring *automotive executive*
Hines, JoAnn R. *professional association executive and consultant*
Hing, Barbara Lim *elementary school educator, assistant principal, data processing executive*
Hingle, Pat *actor*
Hinkley, Everett David, Jr., *physicist*
Hinshaw, Edward Banks *retired broadcasting company executive*
Hinton, Norman Wayne *retired information services executive*
Hintz, Charles Bradley *diversified financial executive*
Hintzke, Teresa Anna *illustrator*
Hirahara, Patti *public relations executive*
Hiraldo, Carlos *education educator, poet*
Hires, William Leland *psychologist, consultant*
Hirono, Mazie Keiko *former lieutenant governor*
Hirose, Teruo Terry *surgeon, educator*
Hirsch, George Aaron *publishing executive*
Hirsch, Horst Eberhard *business consultant*
Hirsch, Judd *actor*
Hirsch, Larry Joseph *retired retail executive, lawyer*
Hirschberg, Vera Hilda *writer*
Hirschhorn, Sidney *accountant, educator*
Hirsh-Pasek, Kathryn Ann *psychology educator*
Hirshtal, Edith *retired concert pianist, educator, chamber musician*
Hislop, Kare Elizabeth *music director, educator*
Hitchcock, Vernon Thomas *farmer, lawyer*
Hitchcock, Walter Anson *educational consultant, retired educational administrator*
Hites, Becky E. *financial executive*
Hixson, Marcia Jeanne *retired educational administrator*
Ho, Chih-Ming *physicist, researcher*
Ho, Teh Chung *chemical engineer, researcher*
Hoar, Frederick M. *public relations executive*
Hoart, Gladys Gallagher *English language educator*
Hoch, Ivo *former library director*
Hoch, Orion Lindel *corporate executive*
Hochfeld, William Sidney *construction executive, consultant*
Hochhalter, Gordon Ray *advertising communications executive*
Hochheimer, Frank Leo *brokerage and financial industry executive*
Hochreiter, John Allen *computer company owner, firefighter*
Hochschild, Carroll Shepherd *computer company and medical equipment executive, educator*
Hockeimer, Henry Eric *business executive*
Hodge, David R. *social science researcher*
Hodge, Verne Antonio *retired chief judge*
Hodgen, Maurice Denzil *management consultant, retired education educator*
Hodges, Ann *actress, singer, dancer*
Hodges, Ann *retired television editor, newspaper columnist*
Hodges, Sharon Green *editor, consultant, writer*
Hodgson, Dorothy L. *social studies educator*
Hodsoll, Francis Samuel Monaise *government official*
Hoeg, Donald Francis *chemist, consultant, former research and development executive*
Hoeprich, Paul Daniel *physician educator*
Hoff, Benjamin Lloyd *writer, scriptwriter*
Hoff, B.J. *writer*
Hoffleit, Ellen Dorrit *astronomer*
Hoffman, Alan Craig *lawyer, consultant*
Hoffman, Daniel (Gerard) *literature educator, poet*
Hoffman, Darnay Robert *management consultant*
Hoffman, Jerry Irwin *retired dental educator*
Hoffman, Judy Greenblatt *preschool director*
Hoffman, Neil James *academic administrator*
Hoffman, S. David *lawyer, engineer, educator, artist*
Hoffsis, Glen F. *dean*
Hofmann, Paul Bernard *healthcare consultant*
Hogan, Robert Henry *trust company executive, investment strategist*
Hogan, Thomas Francis *federal judge*
Hogen-Esch, Thieo E. *chemistry professor*
Hogg, Karen Sue *retired telecommunications industry executive*
Hoggard, Lara Guldmar *conductor, educator*
Hogness, John Rusten *internist, educator, academic administrator*
Hogue, James Larry *retired academic administrator, business executive*
Hoke, Sheila Wilder *retired librarian*
Holand, Pamela Krisida *professional organizer*
Holcomb, Mildred Geneva Comrie *elementary school educator*
Holcomb, Rita *landscaper*
Holden, William Hoyt, Jr., *lawyer*
Holder, Richard Gibson *retired metal products executive*
Holeman, Russell Kent *civil engineer*
Holford, Theodore Richard *biostatistician, educator*
Holgate, George Jackson *university president*
Holiday, Edith Elizabeth *former presidential adviser, cabinet secretary*
Holifield, Pearl Kam (Kam Holifield, Momi Kam Holifield) *poet*
Holland, Beth *actress*
Holland, Burt S. *statistics educator, consultant*
Holland, Charles R. *military officer*
Holland, David Thurston *former editor*
Holland, Joseph John *financial manager*
Holland, Michael James *computer services administrator*
Holland, Richard A. *retired statistician*
Holland, Robert Campbell *anatomist, educator*
Hollander, Anne *writer*
Holle, Reginald Henry *retired bishop*
Holleb, Doris B. *urban planner, economist*
Hollenberg, Norman Kenneth *medical educator*
Holliday, Polly Dean *actress*
Holliday, Robert Kelvin *retired state senator, former newspaper executive, educator*
Hollingworth, Beverly A. *former state legislator*
Hollis, Mary Fern Caudill *nurse educator, music educator, writer*
Hollis, Richard Shelton *retired obstetrician-gynecologist*
Holloran, Thomas Edward *business educator*
Hollow, Steven Morry *entertainer, educator, theater director*
Holloway, Charles Edward *language educator*
Holloway, James Lemuel, III, *foundation executive, retired naval officer*
Holm, Celeste *actress*
Holm, Sir Ian *actor*
Holman, Bill *composer*
Holman, Doris Anne *writer, illustrator, artist, educator*
Holman, Margaret Alice *writer*
Holman, Sandy Lynne *writer, consultant*
Holmes, Calvin Virgil *mathematician, educator*
Holmes, David Richard *computer and business forms company executive*
Holmes, Genta Hawkins *former diplomat*
Holmes, Henry Allen *government official*
Holmes, Jerry Dell *retired chemist*
Holmes, Joan *retired social welfare administrator*
Holmes, Michael Gene *lawyer*
Holmes, Paul Kinloch, III, *former prosecutor*
Holmes, Paul Luther *political scientist, educational consultant*
Holmes, Susan G. *music educator*
Holsclaw, Jason Scott *financial analyst*
Holsgrove, Gareth John *medical association administrator*
Holt, Marjorie Sewell *lawyer, retired congresswoman*
Holte, Debra Leah *investment executive, financial analyst*
Holten, John V. *former food products/retail grocery executive*
Holton, Grace Holland *accountant*
Holtzberg, Frederic *retired chemist*
Holtzman, David H. *technologist, security and privacy expert*
Holtzman, Robert Neil Nehemiah *neurosurgeon, neurologist*
Holtzschue, Karl Bressem *lawyer, author, educator*
Holzkamp, Jane Strauss *business owner*
Holzman, D. Keith *management consultant, record company executive, producer, arts consultant*
Hom, Doris Soo *consultant, investment manager*
Honea, Joyce Clayton *critical care nurse*
Honeystein, Karl *lawyer, entertainment company executive*
Honnold, John Otis *law educator*
Honse, Robert W. *agricultural company executive*
Hood, William Boyd, Jr., *cardiologist, educator*
Hook, Jerry B. *pharmaceutical consultant*
Hooker, Renée Michelle *perinatal and perianesthesia nurse*
Hooper, Henry Olcott *retired academic administrator, physicist*
Hooper, John Allen *retired banker*
Hooper, Josh *screen actor, director, media producer, writer*
Hooper, Robert Alexander *television producer, international educator*
Hooper, Roger Fellowes *retired architect*
Hoopes, Townsend Walter *retired management consultant, retired federal agency administrator*
Hopkins, George Mathews Marks *retired patent lawyer, business executive*
Hopkins, Kevin W. *education educator*
Hopkins, Philip Joseph *journalist, information technology executive*
Hopp, Phillip Edward *gifted and talented educator*
Hopping, Richard Lee *college president emeritus*
Horn, Howard M. *labor union administrator, consultant*
Horn, Lee Shawn *sports analyst*
Horn, Stephen *congressman, political science educator*
Hornacek, Jeffrey John *professional basketball player*
Hornak, Thomas *retired electronics company executive*
Hornback, Joseph Hope *mathematics professor*
Hornbeck, Carrie L. *photographer*
Hornby, Kenneth Peter *office technology executive*
Hornby-Anderson, Sara Ann *metallurgical engineer, marketing professional*
Horner, Charles Albert *retired air force officer*
Horner, George Marlin *retired obstetrician-gynecologist*
Horner, Matina Souretis *retired academic administrator, corporate financial executive*
Hornyak, Roy Robert *music educator, minister*
Horowitz, Kenneth A. *communications executive, entrepreneur*
Horsman, David A. Elliott *writer, finance company executive, educator*
Horsman, Lenore Lynde (Eleanora Lynde) *soprano, educator, actress*
Horst, Jason Matthew *director*
Horswill, C. Weir *retired obstetrician-gynecologist, photographer*
Horton, Patricia Mathews *artist, violist and violinist*
Horton, Robert Carlton *geologist*
Horwitz, Donald Paul *lawyer*
Horwitz, William J. *treasurer*
Hosang, Robert Michael *research scientist*
Hoskins, John Howard *urologist, educator*
Hosman, Sharon Lee *music educator*
Hostettler, Stephen John *naval officer*
Hough, Thomas Henry Michael *retired lawyer, educator*
Houghtaling, Pamela Ann *science and technology communications professional, writer*
Houghton, Diane Murley *actress, vocalist*
Houghton, Katharine *actress*
Houlihan, Patrick Thomas *museum director*
House, Ernest Robert *education educator, educational evaluator*
House, Sherman August *conservationist, emergency medical technician*
House, Stephen Eugene *information systems consultant*
Houseman, Ann Elizabeth Lord *educational administrator, state official*
Housewright, Wiley Lee *music educator*
Houston, Gloria *author, educator, consultant*
Houston, John R. *telecommunications industry executive*
Houston, Whitney *vocalist, recording artist*
Houtz, Duane Talbott *hospital administrator*
Houze, Herbert George *writer*
Howard, David *ballet school administrator*
Howard, Dean Denton *electrical engineer, researcher, consultant*
Howard, Diane Elizabeth *education educator, consultant*
Howard, Donald Searcy *banker*
Howard, Gary Scott *communications executive*
Howard, George, Jr., *federal judge*
Howard, James Joseph, III, *utility company executive*
Howard, James Webb *investment banker, lawyer, engineer*
Howard, Janet C. *former state legislator*
Howard, John Wayne *lawyer*
Howard, Joseph Harvey *retired librarian*
Howard, Michael Eliot *historian, educator*
Howard, Nancy E. *lawyer*
Howard, Robert Elliott *former federal official, consultant, educator*
Howard, Robert Franklin *observatory administrator, astronomer*
Howard, Terry Thomas *obstetrician, gynecologist*
Howard-Peebles, Patricia N. *clinical cytogeneticist*
Howards, Stuart S. *urologist, educator*
Howe, Gordon *former professional hockey player, sports association executive*
Howe, John Prentice, III, *health facility administrator, physician*
Howe, Virginia Hoffman *nurse administrator*
Howell, Ally Windsor *lawyer, author, editor*
Howell, Donald Lee *lawyer*
Howell, Janet D. *state legislator*
Howell, Joel DuBose *internist, educator*
Howell, Julius Ammons *retired plastic surgeon*
Howells, Michelle C. *music educator*
Hower, Frank Beard, Jr., *retired banker*
Howes, Sophia DuBose *writer*
Hoy, Harold Joseph *marketing educator, author, management consultant, retail executive, military officer*
Hoyle, William Vinton, Jr., *lawyer*
Hoyt, Mary Finch *author, editor, media consultant, former government official*
Hricak, Hedvig *radiologist*
Hsieh, Tsui-Hsia *artist, educator*
Hsu, Emilie Tien-Jung *lawyer*
Hsu, Gerald C. *electrical company executive*
Hsu, John S. *electrical engineer, researcher*
Huang, Russel Charles *surgeon, medical researcher*
Huang, Shouhua *electronics engineer*
Hubbard, Elizabeth *actress*
Hubbard, Robert Glenn *academic administrator, former federal agency administrator*
Hubbard, Thomas C. *former ambassador*
Hubbe, Henry Ernest *financial forecaster, funds manager*
Huber, David G. *theater educator, actor*
Hubley, Reginald Allen *publishing executive*
Hudak, Thomas F(rancis) *finance company executive*
Hudkins, Carol L. *state legislator*
Hudson, Alan C.H. *music educator, tropical fruit farmer*
Hudson, Carolyn Brauer *application developer, educator*
Hudson, Donald J. *retired stock exchange executive*
Hudson, Eliot R. *lawyer*
Hudson, Franklin Donald *diversified company executive, consultant*
Hudson, Kate *actress*
Hudson, Sharon Marie *communications executive*
Hudson, Stanton Harold, Jr., *public relations executive, educator, academic administrator*
Hudson, William Jeffrey, Jr., *manufacturing executive*
Huerta, Dolores Fernandez *labor union administrator*
Huey, Ward L(igon), Jr., *retired media executive*
Huffington, Anita *sculptor*
Huffington, Arianna *writer*
Huffman, Cady *actress*
Huffman, Durward Roy *college system official, electrical engineer*
Huffman, James Thomas William *oil exploration company executive*
Huffman, Janice Kay *middle school educator, curriculum coordinator*
Hufschmidt, Maynard Michael *resources planning educator*
Huggett, Monica *performing company executive*
Huggins, Charles Edward *obstetrician, gynecologist, educator*
Hughes, Ann Hightower *retired economist, international trade consultant*
Hughes, Edward T. *retired bishop*
Hughes, Karen Parfitt *former federal official*
Hughes, Keith William *banking and finance company executive*
Hughes, Kevin Dewayne *electronics engineer, educator*
Hughes, Michaela Kelly *actress*
Hughes, Paul *elementary school educator*
Hughes, Sue Margaret *retired librarian*
Hughes, Thomas Parke *history professor*
Hughes-Ayanru, Grace *retired geriatrician*
Hughey, Richard Kohlman *author, lawyer*
Hugley, Carolyn Fleming *state legislator*
Hui, Sai-Hung *emergency medical professional*
Huie, Carol P. *information systems educator*
Hulet, Ervin Kenneth *retired nuclear chemist*
Hulin, Frances C. *retired prosecutor*
Hull, Jane Dee *former governor, former state legislator*
Hull, Louise Knox *retired elementary educator, administrator*
Hull, McAllister Hobart, Jr., *retired university administrator*
Hull, Suzanne White *writer, retired administrator*
Humann, Richard *artist*
Hume, Cameron R. *former ambassador*
Hume, Frederick Raymond *electronics company executive*
Hume, Susan Rachel *finance and economics educator*
Humke, Ramon Lyle *utilities executive*
Hummel, Gene Maywood *retired bishop*
Humphrey, Kathryn Long *school psychologist, writer*
Humphreys, Robert Russell *lawyer, consultant, arbitrator*
Hung, James Chen *engineer, educator, consultant*
Hunsberger, J. N. *music educator, musician*
Hunsucker, Robert Dudley *physicist, electrical engineer, educator, researcher*
Hunt, Martin Kyle *corporate strategist*
Hunt, Murray Watson *humanities educator*
Hunt, Oliver Raymond, Jr., *thoracic and cardiovascular surgeon*
Hunt, Thomas Reed, Jr., *lawyer*
Hunt, V. William (Bill) *automotive supplier executive*
Hunt, William E., Sr., *retired state supreme court justice*
Hunte, Beryl Eleanor *mathematics educator, consultant*
Hunter, Daniel Clyde, Jr., *retired surgeon, educator*
Hunter, Duncan Lee *congressman*
Hunter, Holly *actress*
Hunter, Jack Duval *retired lawyer*
Hunter, Jack Duval, II, *lawyer*
Hunter, James Edward *chemist, consultant*
Hunter, J(ames) Paul *English language educator, literary critic, historian*
Hunter, Kenneth M. *business information systems educator*
Hunter, Sue Persons *former state official*
Hunter-Gault, Charlayne *journalist*
Huntington, Lawrence Smith *investment banker*
Huntsman, Lee L. *former academic administrator, director*
Huo, Bonnie Kwan *artist*
Huppe, Alex *public relations executive*
Huras, William David *retired bishop*
Hurd, Byron Thomas *retired publishing executive*
Hurd, Richard Nelson *pharmaceutical company executive*
Hurd, Suzanne Sheldon *retired federal agency health science director*
Hurlbut, Geraldine *retired elementary education educator*
Hurley, Francis T. *retired archbishop*
Hurley, Kevin *publishing executive*
Hurley, Mary Jo *elementary school educator, gas industry executive*
Huron, Roderick Eugene *minister, writer*
Hurst, Kenneth Thurston *publisher*
Hurst, Leland Lyle *natural gas company executive*
Hurt, John Vincent *actor*
Hurtt, Frances Scott *author*
Husain, Adil *management consultant*
Husain, Taqdir *mathematics professor*
Hushen, John Wallace *manufacturing executive*
Husney, Elliott Ronald *lawyer, financier*
Huston, Margo *journalist*
Hutcheon, Duncan Elliot *physician, educator*
Hutcheon, Linda Ann *English language educator*
Hutchins, James Leigh *quality assurance professional*
Hutchins, Mary Louise *retired library director*
Hutchins, Robert Ayer *architectural consultant*
Hutchinson, John Woodside *mechanical engineer, educator*
Hutchinson, Robert Joseph *writer*
Hutchison, Kay Bailey *senator*
Hutchison, Polly Anna *writer*
Huth, Thomas Joseph *retired surgeon*
Hutmacher, James K. *state legislator, water drilling contractor*
Huttenback, Robert Arthur *academic administrator, educator*
Hutton, Lauren (Mary Laurence Hutton) *model, actress*
Hutzler, Lisa Ann *mental health nurse, adult clinical psychologist*
Huyler, Jean Wiley *minister*
Hvass, Sheryl Ramstad *lawyer*
Hyatt-Smith, Ann Rose *non-profit organization executive, consultant*
Hybl, William Joseph *lawyer, foundation executive*
Hyde, Alan Litchfield *retired lawyer*
Hyde, James A. *service executive*
Hyman, Gary Scott *music educator*
Hyman, Trina Schart *illustrator*
Hymer, Tabitha Kim *music educator, writer, photographer*
Hyvonen, Sami Rikhard *research scientist*
Iacono, Bruce R. *painter*

Keala, Francis Ahloy *security executive*
Keane, James R. *neurologist*
Keane, John Michael *retired military officer*
Kearns, James Joseph *artist*
Keaty, Robert Burke *lawyer, business consultant*
Kebblish, John Basil *retired coal company executive, consultant*
Keebler, Lois Marie *elementary school educator*
Keech, Elowyn Ann *interior designer*
Keeler, James Leonard *food products company executive*
Keeler, William H. *archbishop*
Keeling, J(ohn) Michael *lawyer, trade association executive*
Keen, Constantine *retired manufacturing company executive*
Keenan, Anthony Lee *trucking company executive*
Keenan, Joseph Michael *military officer*
Keene-Burgess, Ruth Frances *military official*
Kehew, George Mansir *artist*
Kehlmann, Robert *artist, critic*
Keil, M. David *retired international association executive*
Keill, Stuart Langdon *psychiatrist*
Keilty, Bryan T. *government agency administrator*
Keiper, Marilyn Morrison *elementary school educator*
Keith, Brian Thomas *automobile executive*
Keith, Carl D. *retired chemist*
Keith, Jerry M. *molecular biologist*
Keith, Robert William *banker*
Kelalis, Barbara Anna Lisa *interior design company executive*
Kelehear, Carole Marchbanks Spann *legal assistant*
Kellaigh, Kathleen *conservatory artistic director*
Kelleher, Richard Cornelius *marketing and communications executive*
Keller, Ben Robert, Jr., *gynecologist*
Keller, Paul *advertising agency executive*
Kelley, A. Benjamin *author, consultant*
Kelley, Albert Joseph *global management strategy consultant*
Kelley, Edward Allen *publisher*
Kelley, Edward Watson, Jr., *former federal agency administrator*
Kelley, James *automotive sales executive*
Kelley, Larry Dale *retired army officer*
Kelley, Mary Elizabeth (Mary LaGrone) *information technology executive*
Kelley, Patricia Colleen *education educator, researcher*
Kelley, Patrick Alan *neurologist, educator*
Kelley, Sheila Seymour *public relations consultant*
Kelley, Thomas William *automotive sales executive*
Kelley, Wayne Plumbley, Jr., *retired federal official*
Kellogg, David *publisher*
Kellogg, Peter R. *securities dealer*
Kelly, Anastasia Donovan *lawyer*
Kelly, Anthony Odrian *flooring manufacturing company executive*
Kelly, Cheryl Ann *healthcare administrator*
Kelly, Sister Dorothy Ann *Ursuline Provincial college chancellor*
Kelly, John H., Jr., *epidemiologist, lifestyle and preventive medicine specialist*
Kelly, Michael Joesph, II, *publishing executive, investment company executive*
Kelly, Nancy Folden *art association administrator*
Kelsey, Donald Ross *chemist*
Kelso, John Hodgson *former government official*
Kemble, Penn *government official*
Kemper, John Dustin *mechanical engineering educator*
Kempner, Maximilian Walter *law school dean, lawyer*
Kemprecos, Paul *writer*
Kempski, Ralph Aloisius *bishop*
Kendall, Charles Terry *librarian*
Kendall, Gavin Starr *actor*
Kendall, Harry Ovid *internist*
Kendall, Harry Wesley *playwright, writer*
Kenderian, Shant *engineer, consultant*
Kendig, William Lamar *retired government official, accountant*
Kendrick, Budd Leroy *psychologist*
Kendrick, James Earl *business consultant*
Kendzior, Robert Joseph *marketing executive*
Kennedy, Charles *retired neuroscientist, retired medical educator*
Kennedy, Christopher *director*
Kennedy, Debra Joyce *marketing professional*
Kennedy, Harold Edward *lawyer*
Kennedy, Jerrie Ann Preston *public relations executive*
Kennedy, Karen Synece *advertising agency executive*
Kennedy, Kathleen *film producer*
Kennedy, Leo Raymond *engineering executive*
Kennedy, Linda Dale *music educator, pianist, organist*
Kennedy, Marla Catherine *psychologist*
Kennedy, Thomas J. *lawyer*
Kennedy, William F. *army reserve technician*
Kennedy-Minott, Rodney *international relations educator, former ambassador*
Kennel, Charles Frederick *physics educator, government official, academic administrator*
Kennelly, Joy A. *public relations specialist*
Kenny, Deborah *marketing professional, educator, finance educator*
Kenny, H. Sharie *music educator*
Kent, Gary Warner *film director, writer*
Kenworthy, William Eugene *judge*
Kenyon, Daphne Anne *economics professor*
Keohane, Nannerl Overholser *university president emerita, political scientist*
Kerber, Ronald Lee *industrial corporation executive*
Kercher, David Max *mechanical engineer*
Kern, Charles William *retired university official, chemistry educator*
Kern, Irving John *retired food company executive*
Kern, Jerome H. *lawyer*
Kerney, Yolonda V. *music historian*
Kernochan, Sarah M. *film director, scriptwriter, composer*
Kerns, Brian D. *former congressman*
Kerr, Donald MacLean, Jr., *physicist*
Kerr, Frederick Hohmann *retired health care company executive*
Kerr, Harry Davidson *emergency physician*
Kerr, Janet Spence *physiologist, pharmacologist, researcher*
Kerr, Michael D. *construction company executive*
Kerrick, Donald L. *career officer*
Kerstetter, Michael James *retired manufacturing company executive*
Kerstetter, Wayne Arthur *law educator, lawyer*
Kertz, Hubert Leonard *telephone company executive*
Kerwin, Walter Thomas, Jr., *career officer, consultant*
Keskinocak, Pinar *adult education educator*
Kesseler, Matthew John *librarian*
Kesselring, Debbie Anne *systems engineer*
Kessler, Stephen James *writer, editor*
Kessler-Harris, Alice *historian, educator*
Ketch, Tina *writer*
Ketron, Carrie Sue *secondary school educator*
Kettel, Edward Joseph *oil company executive, retired*
Kettelkamp, Donald Benjamin *retired orthopedic surgeon, eductor*
Keune, Russell Victor *retired architect*
Key, Ted *cartoonist*
Keyes, Alan L. *radio and talk show host, former federal government official*
Keyes, Joan Ross Rafter *education educator, writer*
Keyes, Margaret Naumann *home economics educator*
Keys, Jerry Malcom *lawyer, educator*
Kezer, Pauline Ryder *state government executive, management consultant*
Khan, Ahmed Mohiuddin *insurance company executive*
Khan, Arfa *radiologist, educator*
Khan, Aurangzeb *engineering educator*
Khan, Maryam *educator*
Khatib, Hamin Bey *data processing executive*
Khavari, Khalil Akhtar *psychology educator*
Khilnani, Vinod M. *manufacturing executive*
Khuong, Loc Huu *corporate financial executive*
Khvost-Vostrikova, Natalia S *art educator, consultant*
Kice, John Edward *engineer, educator, consultant*
Kidd, Debra Jean *communications executive*
Kidd, James Lambert *retired minister*
Kidder, Tracy (John Tracy Kidder) *writer*
Kiel, Shelley *state senator*
Kienitz, LaDonna Trapp *lawyer, librarian, municipal official*
Kiesel, Ilmar Otto *retired radiologist*
Kiesler, Charles Adolphus *psychologist, academic administrator*
Kietzman, Kris *music educator*
Kilbane, Catherine M. *lawyer*
Kilbride, Thomas L. *judge*
Kilcullen, Austin *playwright, educator*
Kildee, Jennifer *translator, editor*
Killeen, Michael John *lawyer*
Killgore, Le *journalist, political columnist*
Killhour, William Gherky *paper company executive*
Killian, William Paul *industrial corporate executive*
Kilmann, Ralph Herman *business educator*
Kilpatrick, James Jackson, Jr., *columnist, writer*
Kim, Charles Wesley *microbiology educator*
Kim, Jong-Hyun *music educator, conductor*
Kim, Marianne Weiss *humanities educator*
Kim, Seon-Young *microbiologist, researcher*
Kimball, Spencer Levan *lawyer, educator*
Kimbrell, Grady Ned *writer, educator, retired school system administrator*
Kimes, Beverly Rae *editor, writer*
Kim-Farley, Robert James *epidemiologist, educator*
Kimmel, Mark *author, venture capital company executive*
Kincaid, Jamaica *writer*
Kind, Kyle *computer company executive*
King, Algin Braddy *retired marketing educator*
King, Amy Cathryne Patterson *retired mathematics educator, researcher*
King, Edward William *retired transportation executive*
King, Glen (Lenard Glen King) *broadcasting educator, composer*
King, Imogene M. *retired nursing educator*
King, Jack A. *lawyer*
King, James Forrest, Jr., *lawyer*
King, Jane Cudlip Coblentz *volunteer educator*
King, John Charles Peter *newspaper editor*
King, John Ethelbert, Jr., *retired academic administrator*
King, Larry L. *playwright, actor*
King, Marielle Elisabeth *educational research association administrator, writer, mathematics educator*
King, Maxwell Clark *former academic administrator*
King, Philip Gordon *public relations counselor*
King, Robert Lucien *lawyer*
King, Rosalyn Mercita *social sciences educator, researcher*
King, Rosamond S. *poet, education educator*
King, Sheldon Selig *health facility administrator, educator*
King, Susan Bennett *retired glass company executive*
King, William Collins *oil company executive*
Kingsbery, Walton Waits, Jr., *retired accounting firm executive*
Kingsbury, Lonna Dee *writer, actress, educator*
Kingsley, David H *small business owner*
Kingston, Maxine Hong *writer, educator*
Kinley, Christine T. *certified physician assistant*
Kinnear, Greg *actor, producer*
Kinney, Michele A. *education educator, lawyer*
Kinney, Thomas J. John *adult education educator*
Kinser, Katherine Anne *lawyer*
Kinsley, Michael E. *newspaper editor, former magazine editor*
Kinslow, Margie Ann *volunteer*
Kinsman, Frank Ellwood *engineering executive*
Kinsolving, Augustus Blagden *lawyer*
Kinzie, Jeannie Jones *radiation oncologist, nuclear medicine physician*
Kipniss, Robert *artist*
Kipniss MacDonald, Betty Ann *artist, educator*
Kipper, Barbara Levy *wholesale distribution executive*
Kipper, Richard E. *retired financial services executive, association executive*
Kirby, David Stephen *music educator*
Kirby, Frank Eugene *musicology educator, author, editor*
Kirby, George R., III, *music educator*
Kirila, Carol Elizabeth *osteopathic physician, internist*
Kirk, Carmen Zetler *data processing executive*
Kirk, Donald James *accountant, consultant*
Kirk, Rea Helene (Rea Helene Glazer) *special education educator*
Kirkby, Maurice Anthony *oil company executive*
Kirkland, Geoffrey Alan *motion picture production designer*
Kirkland, Starr Melanie *librarian, writer*
Kirkland, Virgil Wayne *electrical engineer*
Kirkland-Cuffee, Rana Antoinette *art educator*
Kirkpatrick, Charles Harvey *physician, immunology researcher*
Kirkpatrick, Garland Penn *retired pediatrician*
Kirkpatrick, James Joseph *psychologist*
Kirsch, Roslyn Ruth *art educator, painter, printmaker*
Kirschenmann, Henry George, Jr., *management consultant, former government official, accountant*
Kirshbaum, Jon Alan *information systems consultant, retired educational administrator*
Kirsteuer, Ernst Karl Eberhart *biologist, curator*
Kiselik, Paul Howard *manufacturing executive*
Kiser, Nagiko Sato *retired librarian*
Kissinger, Henry Alfred *former secretary of state, international consulting company executive*
Kister, James Milton *retired mathematician, educator*
Kistler, John Michael *librarian, writer*
Kiszka, Sonia Ann *nurse practitioner, educator*
Kitchen, Paul Howard *hockey historian*
Kite, Thomas O., Jr., *professional golfer*
Kitt, Walter *psychiatrist*
Kittleson, Mark Douglas *veterinary cardiologist, veterinary medicine educator*
Kivikoski, Asko Ilmari *retired obstetrician, gynecologist*
Klaehne, Eberhard O W *pharmaceutical executive, chemist*
Klafter, Cary Ira *lawyer*
Klampe, Craig Allen *composer*
Klarich, David John *political organization executive, lawyer*
Klatt, Melvin John *library consultant*
Klauberg, William Joseph *technical services company executive*
Klaus, Charles *retired lawyer*
Klaus, William Robert *lawyer*
Kleiman, Alan Boyd *artist*
Kleiman, Bernard *lawyer*
Klein, Charlotte Conrad *public relations executive*
Klein, Chuck *private investigator*
Klein, Edward Joel *author, lecturer*
Klein, Irma Molligan *career planning administrator, consultant*
Klein, Judah Baer *retired lawyer*
Klein, Linda Ann *lawyer*
Klein, Lynn Ellen *artist*
Klein, Mary Ann *special education educator*
Klein, Paul E. *lawyer*
Klein, Stephen Thomas *performing arts executive*
Kleinsorge, William Peter *metallurgical engineer*
Klema, Ernest Donald *nuclear physicist, educator*
Klement, Vera *artist*
Klett, Gordon A. *retired savings and loan association executive*
Kliebhan, Sister M(ary) Camille *academic administrator*
Kline, James Edgar *actor*
Kline-Koenig, Barbara A. *nursing case manager*
Klink, Robert Michael *consulting engineer, management consultant, financial consultant, property developer*
Klitzman, Robert Lloyd *psychiatrist, writer*
Kloepfer, Clarence Victor *oil company executive*
Klohn, Earle Jardine *retired engineering company executive, consultant*
Klopfleisch, Stephanie Squance *social services agency administrator*
Klosk, Ira David *lawyer*
Kloves, Steven *film director, scriptwriter*
Kluge, John Werner *broadcasting and advertising executive*
Kluka, Darlene Ann *human performance educator, researcher*
Klusman, Judith Anderson *state legislator*
Klute, Allan Aloys *retired physicist, retired economist*
Knapp, Edward Alan *retired government agency administrator, scientist*
Knapp, Howard Raymond *internist, clinical pharmacologist*
Knapp, Lonnie Troy *elementary school educator*
Knauer, Virginia Harrington (Mrs. Wilhelm F. Knauer) *consumer consultant, former government official*
Knecht, Charles Lewis, III, *retired radiologist*
Kneller, John William *academic administrator, retired French language and literature educator*
Knies, Robert Carl, Jr., *critical care nurse*
Knight, Gary *lawyer, educator, publisher*
Knight, Herbert Borwell *manufacturing executive*
Knight, Patricia Marie *medical device researcher, consultant*
Knizeski, Justine Estelle *insurance company executive*
Knobloch, Ferdinand J. *psychiatrist, educator*
Knobloch, Marcia M. *writer*
Knoll, Florence Schust *architect, designer*
Knott, Claudette Yvonne Clark *religious studies educator*
Knott, Wiley Eugene *electronic engineer*
Knotts, Robert Lee *retired insurance company executive*
Knotts, Robert Spencer (Bob Knotts) *writer, playwright*
Knowles, Elizabeth Pringle *museum director*
Knox, Lance Lethbridge *venture capital executive*
Knox, Simmie Lee *artist*
Knudsen, William Claire *geophysicist, researcher*
Koch, John Howard *retired air transportation executive, transportation engineer, consultant*
Koehler, George Applegate *broadcasting company executive*
Koelmel, Lorna Lee *data processing executive*
Koenig, Allen Edward *higher education consultant*
Koerber, Dolores Jean *music educator, musician*
Kogan, Richard J. *former pharmaceutical company executive*
Kogut, John Anthony *retail/wholesale executive*
Kohan, Dennis Lynn *international trade educator, consultant*
Kohlenberg, Stanley *retired marketing executive*
KÖhler, Horst *former international official*
Kohler, Sheila M. *humanities educator, writer*
Kohlstedt, James August *lawyer*
Kohn, David Samuel *accountant, educator, banker*
Kohn, Jean Gatewood *retired health facility administrator, pediatrician*
Kohn, Robert Samuel, Jr., *real estate investment consultant*
Kohrman, Arthur Fisher *pediatrics educator*
Kojac, Jeffrey S. *military officer*
Kolasa, Kathryn Marianne *food and nutrition educator, consultant*
Kolb, Dorothy Gong *elementary school educator*
Kolb, Harold Hutchinson, Jr., *English language educator*
Kolb, James A. *science association director, writer*
Kolb, Janice Gray *writer*
Kolbe, Ronald Lynn *research engineer*
Kolbert, Kathryn *lawyer, educator*
Kolde, Richard Arthur *insurance company executive, consultant*
Kolenda, Joanne L. *elementary school educator, secondary school educator, volunteer*
Koleson, Donald Ralph *retired college dean, educator*
Kolff, Willem Johan *retired internist, medical educator*
Koller, Loren D. *veterinary medicine educator*
Kolodny, Stephen Arthur *lawyer*
Komar, Vitaly *artist*
Komisar, David Daniel *retired university provost*
Komlos, Peter *violinist*
Konigsburg, Elaine Lobl *writer*
Konnyu, Ernest Leslie *former congressman*
Kontos, Hermes Apostolou *retired academic administrator*
Koo, Shou-Eng *economics professor*
Kooij, Nina Michaela *editor*
Kooken, John Frederick *retired bank holding company executive*
Kopack, Pamela Lee (Pamela Lee MacMinn) *business services executive*
Kopec-Garnett, Linda *nurse, researcher*
Kopelson, Arnold *film producer*
Koplovitz, Kay *television network executive*
Kopp, Richard Edgar *electrical engineer*
Koranda, Peggy Jo *writer*
Koreman, Dorothy Goldstein *physician, dermatologist*
Koren, Edward Benjamin *cartoonist, educator*
Korey, John L. *political scientist, educator*
Korins, Leopold *stock exchange executive*
Korman, Jess J. *writer*
Kormondy, Edward John *retired academic administrator, retired science educator*
Korn, Jessica Susan *research scientist, educator*
Korn, Peter A. *arbitrator, mediator, educator*
Kornguth, Steven Edward *biologist*
Kornweibel, Theodore, Jr., *retired history professor*
Korobkin, Barry Jay *architect*
Korologos, Ann McLaughlin *public policy, communications executive*
Korpal, Eugene Stanley *banker, military officer*
Kortepeter, Karl Nuri *dietician*
Kosa, Jaymie Reeber *middle school educator*
Kosner, Edward A(lan) *former editor and publisher*
Kostere, Kim Martin *psychologist, consultant*
Koszarski, Richard *film historian, writer*
Kotcher, Shirley J.W. *lawyer*
Kothari, Vinay B. *education educator, consultant*
Kotler, Steven *investment banker*
Kotlowitz, Alex *writer, journalist*
Kott, Alan *state agency administrator*
Kott, Krystee N. *writer*
Koutrouvelis, Alexis Andrea *music educator*
Kovach, Andrew Louis *human resources specialist, consultant*
Kovacs, Malcolm *sociology educator, religious studies educator*
Kovin, John A. *writer*
Kozak, Alexander L. *engineer*
Kraemer, Harry M. Jansen, Jr., *medical products executive*
Kraft, Arthur *university dean*
Kraft, Karen Ann *secondary school educator*
Kraichnan, Robert Harry *physicist, consultant*
Krakower, Bernard Hyman *management consultant*
Krakower, Terri Jan *biochemist, researcher*
Kramer, Dale Vernon *retired English language educator*
Kramer, Peter Robin *computer company executive*
Krantz, Steven George *mathematics educator, writer*
Kranzow, Ronald Roy *lawyer*
Kraslow, David *retired publishing executive, writer, consultant, reporter*
Kratt, Peter George *lawyer*
Kraus, Naomi *retired biochemistry educator*
Krause, Edward Charles *priest, educator*
Krause, Werner William *plastics company executive*
Kraut, Joel Arthur *ophthalmologist*
Krauthammer, Charles *columnist, editor*
Kravitz, Ellen King *musicologist, educator*
Kravitz, Rubin *chemist*
Krehtinkoff-Yarlovsky, Nina *nursing administrator, medical-legal consulting firm owner*
Kreider, Clement Horst, Jr., *neurosurgeon*
Kreith, Frank *research engineer, consultant*
Kremer, Honor Frances (Noreen Kremer) *real estate broker, small business owner*
Krempel, Roger Ernest *public works management consultant*
Kreps, Juanita Morris *economics educator, former government official*
Kresa, Kent *retired aerospace executive*
Kretschmer, Frank Frederick, Jr., *electrical engineer, researcher, consultant*
Kretzmar, Mary Lynn *vocational education and sign language interpreter, educator*
Kribel, Robert Edward *academic administrator, consultant physicist*
Krieger, Michael Jay *writer*
Kriegsman, Sali Ann *arts executive, artistic director, writer, consultant*
Krishnamoorti, Ramanan *chemical engineer, educator*
Kriz, George James *former agricultural research administrator*
Krizan, Kelly Joe *physician, leather craftsman*
Krogius, Tristan Ernst Gunnar *international marketing consultant, lawyer*
Krohnke, Duane W. *retired lawyer*
Krol, Stanley Joseph, Jr., *electrical engineer*
Krongard, Howard J. *lawyer*
Kronschnabel, Robert James *retired manufacturing company executive*
Krop, Stephen *retired pharmacologist*
Krouse, Clyde Francis *writer*
Krueger, Eugene Rex *academic program consultant*
Kruger, Mollee Coppel *writer*
Kruger, Nancy R. *university program director, nurse*

Lewis, Martin Edward *shipping company executive, foreign government concessionary*
Lewis, Martin R. *paper company executive, consultant*
Lewis, Mary Jane *film producer, director, scriptwriter*
Lewis, Philip *educational and technical consultant*
Lewis, Richard *actor, comedian*
Lewis, Rita Hoffman *plastic products manufacturing company executive*
Lewis, Robert Turner *former psychologist*
Lewis, Samuel Winfield *retired government official, former ambassador*
Lewis, Thomas Proctor *law educator*
Lewis, Thomasine Elizabeth *magazine editor-in-chief*
Lewitt, Miles Martin *computer engineering company executive*
L'Heureux, Jeannine Marie *writer*
Li, Qing'an *scientist, researcher*
Li, Tingye *electrical engineer*
Li, Xiaojie *statistician*
Li, Yao-En *chemical engineer*
Liang, Junxiang *retired aeronautics and astronautics engineer, educator*
Libassi, Frank Peter *lawyer*
Liberman, Gail Jeanne *editor*
Lichtenberg, Byron K. *futurist, manufacturing executive, space flight consultant, pilot*
Lichtenstein, Harvey *performing arts executive*
Licke, Wallace John *lawyer*
Liddell, Jane Hawley Hawkes *civic worker*
Lidsky, Ella *retired law librarian*
Liebeler, Susan Wittenberg *lawyer*
Lieberfarb, Warren N. *former broadcast executive*
Lieberman, Gail Forman *investment company executive*
Lieberman, Louis (Karl Lieberman) *artist*
Liebler, Arthur C. *automotive executive*
Lief, Thomas Parrish *sociologist, educator*
Liew, Fah Pow *mechanical engineer*
Liffers, William Albert *retired chemical company executive*
Lifson, Kalman Alan *retired management consultant, banking executive*
Lifton, Robert Jay *psychiatrist, author*
Ligenza, Andrea Angela *nurse*
Light, April Gene *music educator*
Light, Arthur Heath *bishop*
Lightman, Alan Paige *writer, physicist, educator*
Lightstone, Ronald *lawyer*
Likins, Rose Marie *foreign service officer*
Lilley, William, III, *information visualization business executive*
Lilly, Edward Guerrant, Jr., *retired utility company executive*
Lilly, Thomas Gerald *retired lawyer*
Lim, Shun Ping *cardiologist, educator*
Liman, Ellen *painter, writer, arts advocate*
Limeberry, John Wesley *humanities educator*
Lin, Chenchy Jeffrey *research scientist*
Lin, Henry Baohua *consultant, writer*
Lin, Maya *architect, sculptor*
Lincicome, David Richard *biomedical and animal scientist*
Lincoln, Harry B. *musicologist*
Lincoln, James Henry, Sr., *writer*
Linda, Gerald *advertising and marketing executive*
Lindberg, Francis Laurence, Jr., *management consultant*
Lindboe, Berit Roberg *language educator, literature educator*
Linde, Maxine Helen *lawyer, business executive, private investor*
Linde, Ronald Keith *corporate executive, private investor*
Linden, Gordon Lowell *music educator*
Lindgren, William Dale *librarian*
Lindle, Jane Clark *educator*
Lindner, Carl Henry, Jr., *professional sports team executive, insurance company executive*
Lindquist, Michael Adrian *career military officer*
Lindsay, James Wiley *retired agricultural company executive*
Lindsey, Lawrence Benjamin *economist*
Lindsey, Roberta Lewise *music researcher, historian*
Lindsey, Ruth *retired education educator*
Lindstrom, Donald Fredrick, Jr., *priest, counselor, consultant*
Lingle, Marilyn Felkel *freelance writer, columnist, author*
Linhares, Judith Yvonne *artist, educator*
Link, David Thomas *dean, lawyer*
Link, George Hamilton *retired lawyer*
Link, William Theodore *television writer, producer*
Linn, Richard *federal judge*
Linz, Anthony James *osteopathic physician, consultant, educator*
Linz, Gerhard David *psychologist, consultant*
Lipinski, Tara Kristen *retired professional figure skater*
Lipke, William Alan *music educator, musician*
Lippert, Christopher Nelson *dentist, consultant*
Lippes, Richard James *lawyer*
Lippincott, James Andrew *biochemistry and biological sciences educator*
Lippincott, Philip Edward *retired paper products company executive*
Lipschutz, Pinchos *publishing executive, rabbi*
Lipsey, Joseph, Jr., *water bottling company executive, retail and wholesale corporation executive*
Lipsey, Richard George *economist, educator*
Lipsitt, Lewis Paeff *psychology educator*
Lipsman, Richard Marc *lawyer, educator*
Lipton, Glenn E. *orthopaedic surgeon*
Lisio, Donald John *historian, educator*
Liskamm, William Hugo *architect, urban planner, educator*
Lisoni, Gail Marie Landtbom *lawyer*
Lissakers, Karin Margareta *former federal agency administrator*
Listgarten, Max Albert *periodontics educator*
Lithgow, John Arthur *actor, director*
Litman, Harry Peter *lawyer, educator*
Little, Charlotte Louise *poet, writer*
Little, Freed Sebastian *retired petroleum equipment manufacturing company executive*
Little, Judith *cultural organization administrator*
Little, Loren Everton *musician, ophthalmologist*
Littleford, William Donaldson *retired publishing executive*
Littler, Gene Alec *professional golfer*
Littleton, Harvey Kline *artist*
Littman, Earl *advertising and public relations executive*
Liu, Jianhua *molecular biologist, researcher*
Liu, Katherine Chang *artist, art educator*
Liu, Kexi *music educator*
Liu, Margaret C. *music educator*
Liu, Ruth Xiaoru *criminologist, educator*
Liu, Weiping *materials engineer, research scientist*
Liu, Xiaoqing Frank *computer scientist, educator*
Liu, Xuan *computer engineer, researcher*
Liu, Yong *computer scientist, researcher*
Lively, John Pound *magazine editor, publisher*
Lively, Pierce *federal judge*
Livermore, Ann M. *computer company executive*
Livezey, Mark Douglas *physician*
Livingston, Margaret Gresham *civic leader*
Livingstone, Susan Morrisey *management consultant, former federal agency administrator*
Livingstone, Trudy Dorothy Zweig *dancer, educator*
Lloyd, Michael Jeffrey *recording producer*
Loach, Paul Allen *biochemist, biophysicist, educator*
Loarie, Thomas Merritt *healthcare executive*
Lobanov-Rostovsky, Oleg *management consultant*
Lober, Lionel M. *screenwriter, producer*
Locke, Edwin Allen, III, *retired psychologist, educator*
Locke, Norton *hotel management and construction company executive*
Locke Lloyd, Jennifer C. *elementary school educator, consultant*
Locklear, Heather *actress*
Lockwood, Paul Timothy *advertising executive, marketing professional, actor, film director*
Lockwood, Theodore Davidge *retired academic administrator*
Locricchio, Matthew *actor, writer*
Lodge, Arthur Scott *mechanical engineering educator*
Löe, Harald *retired dentist, educator, researcher*
Loeb, Ronald Marvin *retired lawyer*
Loeffler, James Joseph *lawyer*
Loftus, Elizabeth F. *psychology educator*
Logan, Dan *investor, writer*
Logan, David Bruce *health care administrator, nurse*
Logan, Earl Steven *artist*
Logan, James Kenneth *lawyer, former federal judge*
Lohan, Lindsay *actress*
Lohman, Gordon Russell *retired manufacturing executive*
Lohmann, George Young, Jr., *neurosurgeon, hospital executive, international business executive, artist*
Lohmuller, Martin Nicholas *retired bishop*
Lohrer, Richard Baker *investment consultant*
Loiello, John Peter *diplomat*
Loken, Barbara *marketing educator, social psychologist*
Lokmer, Stephanie Ann *international business development consultant*
Lombard, Richard Spencer *lawyer*
Lombardi, Paul V. *data processing executive*
London, Jan *food scientist, writer*
Lonegan, Thomas Lee *retired restaurant corporation executive*
Lonergan, Thomas Francis, III, *criminal justice consultant*
Long, Alfred B. *former oil company executive, consultant*
Long, Charles Thomas *lawyer, history educator*
Long, Elaine *writer, editor*
Long, John D. *retired insurance educator*
Longaberger, Tami *home decor accessories company executive*
Longenecker, Stephen Lewis *historian, educator*
Longobardo, Anna Kazanjian *engineering executive*
Longstreet, Stephen (Chauncey Longstreet) *author, painter*
Loomis, Salora Dale *psychiatrist*
Looney, Gerald Lee *medical educator, administrator*
Loop, Floyd D. *retired healthcare executive*
Looser, Donald William *academic administrator*
Loper, Carl Richard, Jr., *metallurgical engineer, educator*
Lopez, Barry Holstun *writer*
Lopez, Lily Samaniego *language educator*
Lopez Garcia, Diego *researcher*
Lopez Heredia, Hubert *artist*
Lopez Lysne, Robin *counselor, writer, artist*
Lopgue, Ronald *finance company executive*
Loppnow, Milo Alvin *clergyman, former church official*
Lord, Valerie Arlene *music educator, musician*
Lorelli, Michael Kevin *consumer products company executive*
Lorenz, Ronald Theodore *manufacturing executive*
Lorenzo, Francisco A. *airline companies executive*
Loring, Gloria Jean *vocalist*
Lorne, Simon Michael Michael *lawyer*
Lortie, John William *solar research company executive*
Los, Marinus *retired agrochemical researcher*
Loschen, Earl Lee *psychiatrist, educator*
Loser, Joseph Carlton, Jr., *dean, retired judge*
Losey, Michael Robert *retired professional society administrator*
Losi, Maxim John *medical communications executive*
Loss, John C. *architect, retired educator*
Lou, Gang *engineer, researcher*
Lou, Janet *electrical engineer, researcher*
Loube, Samuel Dennis *physician*
Loughran, James Newman *philosophy educator, college administrator*
Louise, Lynette *counselor, writer*
Lourenco, Ruy Valentim *physician, educator*
Love, Courtney *singer, actress*
Lovelace, Julianne *former library director*
Lovelace, Rose Marie Sniegon *federal space agency administrator*
Loveland, Eugene Franklin *retired petroleum executive*
Lovell, Walter Carl *engineer, inventor*
LoVetri, Jeannette Louise *voice educator*
Lovinger, Warren Conrad *emeritus university president*
Low, Emmet Francis, Jr., *mathematics educator*
Low, Harry William *judge*
Low, Paul Charles *protective services specialist*
Lowden, John L. *retired corporate executive*
Lowe, John, III, *consulting civil engineer*
Lowell, AnneMarie *writer, singer, actress*
Lowenberg, Georgina Grace *retired elementary school educator*
Lowenthal, Constance *art historian, consultant*
Lowenthal, Susan *realtor, artist*
Lowinsky, Naomi Ruth *psychoanalyst, poet*
Lowrie, Walter Olin *management consultant*
Lowry, Marilyn Jean *horticultural retail company executive*
Lowy, Peter *executive*
Loy, Frank Ernest *retired government official*
Lozano, Alfredo *language educator*
Lu, Zhiming *hydrologist*
Lubell, Ellen *writer*
Lubic, Ruth Watson *health facility administrator, nurse midwife*
Lubick, Donald Cyril *lawyer*
Lubin, Steven *concert pianist, musicologist*
Lubinsky, Menachem Yechiel *communications executive*
Lucas, Karen Williams *controller*
Lucas, Paul David Mark *lawyer*
Lucas, William Ray *aerospace consultant*
Luce, Donald Sanders *social worker*
Luce, Priscilla Mark *public relations executive*
Luchansky, Edward *obstetrician-gynecologist, educator*
Lucier, P. Jeffrey *publishing consultant*
Lucker, Jay K. *library science consultant*
Luckey, Doris Waring *civic volunteer*
Ludden, John Franklin *retired financial economist*
Luddy, Paula Scott *nursing educator*
Ludwig, Allan Ira *photographer, artist, author*
Ludwig, Christa *mezzo-soprano*
Ludwig, Stephen *pediatrics and emergency medicine educator*
Ludzik, Steve *former professional hockey coach*
Luedeke, J. Barton *academic administrator*
Luedtke, Roland Alfred *retired lawyer*
Lueptow, Lloyd Benjamin *retired sociology educator*
Luetkehoelter, Gottlieb Werner (Lee Luetkehoelter) *retired bishop, clergyman*
Lugenbeel, Edward Elmer *publisher*
Luhn, Robert Kent *writer, magazine editor*
Luhrs, Caro Elise *internal medicine physician, administrator, educator*
Lui, Eric Mun *civil engineering educator, practitioner*
Lukacs, Michael Edward *electro-optics researcher*
Lukasiewicz, Paul Manus *music educator*
Luke, David Lincoln, III, *retired paper company executive*
Lukian, Robert Hermann *professional tennis player, educator*
Lund, David Nathan *artist*
Lund, Doris Hibbs *retired dietitian*
Lund, Rita Pollard *aerospace engineer, consultant*
Lundgren, Cissi *artist, poet*
Lundgren, Leonard, III, *retired secondary education educator*
Lundin, Shirley Matcouff *pre-school administrator, adult education educator, consultant*
Lundquist, James Harold *lawyer*
Lung, Christine *health science association administrator*
Luntz, Benjamin F. *physicist, educator, writer*
Luo, Wenbin *computer engineer, educator*
Lupu, Radu *pianist*
Lurix, Paul Leslie, Jr., *chemist*
Lusztig, Peter Alfred *university dean, educator*
Luthy, Richard Godfrey *environmental engineering educator*
Luttner, Edward F. *consulting company executive*
Lutts, Ralph Herbert *scholar, educator, museum administrator*
Lutz, Lawrence Joseph *family practice physician*
Lyall, Katharine C(ulbert) *former academic administrator, economist, educator*
Lydon, Nicholas B. (Nick Lydon) *pharmaceutical executive, researcher*
Lyn, Jean *interior designer*
Lynch, Charles Andrew *chemical industry consultant*
Lynch, Charlotte Andrews *retired communications executive, consultant*
Lynch, Daniel C. *multimedia executive*
Lynch, Harry James *retired biologist*
Lynch, Jaylee Jean *principal*
Lynch, Jessica *military officer*
Lynch, John Thomas *retired science foundation administrator, physicist*
Lynch, Thomas Peter *securities executive*
Lynch, Thomas Wimp *lawyer*
Lynch-Polansky, Patricia *health services executive*
Lynd, Phyllis *artist, educator*
Lyndall, Janice Thompson *vocational counselor*
Lyne, Dorothy-Arden *secondary school educator*
Lyne, Susan Markham *former broadcast executive*
Lyngbye, Jørgen *hospital administrator, researcher*
Lynn, Naomi B. *academic administrator*
Lyon, Martha Sue *research engineer, retired military officer*
Lyons, Anthony Patrick *acoustician, acoustical engineer, researcher*
Lyons, John W(inship) *retired government official, chemist, consultant*
Lypka, Gerald L. *product designer, artist*
Maatman, Gerald Leonard *insurance company executive*
Macaskill, Bridget *finance company executive*
Macaulay, David (Alexander) *author, illustrator*
MacAvoy, Thomas Coleman *manufacturing executive, educator*
MacCarthy, Talbot Leland *civic volunteer*
MacCormack, Jean F. *academic administrator*
Macdonald, Sheila de Marillac *company executive*
MacDougall, Sir Donald (Sir George Donald Alastair MacDougall) *economist*
Mace, Stephen Alan *investment advisor*
MacGregor, James Grierson *retired civil engineering educator, structural engineering consultant*
MacIsaac, John Anthony *retired municipal official*
Mack, Charles Daniel, III, *labor union executive*
Mack, John J. *diversified financial services company executive*
MacKenzie, Donald Murray *healthcare administrator*
MacKenzie-Smith, Sydney (Lord Whitford) *marketing and financial executive*
Mackey, Jeffrey Allen *priest*
MacKinnon, John Alexander *lawyer*
MacLane, Saunders *mathematician, educator*
MacLaren, Robert Ian, II, *lawyer*
MacLean, Judith E. *writer, editor*
MacLennan, Beryce Winifred *psychologist*
Macleod, Angus *retired internist*
MacLeod, Donald William *secondary school educator*
MacLeod, Gordon C. *surgeon*
Macmillan, William Hooper *dean, educator*
MacMullen, Jean Alexandria Stewart *nurse, administrator*
MacNeill, James William *international environment management consultant*
Macon, Irene Elizabeth *interior designer, consultant*
Macoul, Michael K. *business executive, recruiter*
Madden, John J. *lawyer*
Madden, Richard Blaine *forest products executive*
Maddin, Robert *metallurgist, educator*
Madeira, Francis King Carey *conductor, educator*
Madhavan, Guruprasad *biomedical engineer*
Madison, T. Jerome *business executive*
Madix, Robert James *chemical engineer, educator*
Madrick, Jeffrey G. *writer, editor, economic consultant*
Madsen, H(enry) Stephen *retired lawyer*
Madsen, Susan Arrington *writer*
Maeda, J. A. *data processing executive, consultant*
Maehl, William Harvey *historian, educator*
Maehr, Martin Louis *psychology educator*
Maestrone, Frank Eusebio *diplomat*
Maffia, Roma *actress*
Magee, John Francis *research company executive*
Maginn, John Leo *retired insurance company executive*
Maginnis, Robert P. *bishop*
Maglich, Bogdan Castle *physicist*
Magnabosco, Louis Mario *chemical engineer, researcher, consultant*
Magnano, Salvatore Paul *retired financial executive, treasurer*
Magness-Eubank, Karen Ann *writer, educator*
Magnuson, Paul Arthur *federal judge*
Magnuson, Robert Martin *retired health facility administrator*
Magoni, Despo *artist*
Magor, Louis Roland *conductor*
Maguire, James Harvey *physician*
Maguire, Raymer F., Jr., *lawyer*
Maguire, Robert Francis, III, *real estate investor*
Magurno, Richard Peter *lawyer*
Mahanes, David James, Jr., *retired distillery executive*
Maharidge, Dale Dimitro *journalist, educator, writer*
Maher, Frank J. *former communications executive*
Maher, John A. *lawyer, law educator*
Maher, Lisa Krug *editor*
Maher, Patrick Joseph *retired utility company executive*
Mahle, Christoph Erhard *electrical engineer*
Mahmoud, Ahmed Mohamed *information technology executive*
Mahmud, Shireen Dianne *photographer*
Mahoney, Ann Dickinson *fundraiser*
Mahoney, John *actor*
Mahoney, John L. *English literature educator*
Mahoney, Michael J. *science administrator, educator*
Mahoney, Michael Robert Taylor *art historian, educator*
Mai, Chao Chen *engineer*
Mai, Harold Leverne *retired judge*
Maier, Robert Henry *real estate executive*
Mailer, Norman *author*
Main, Robert Gail *communications educator, training consultant, television and film producer, former army officer*
Maioriello, Richard Patrick *retired otolaryngologist*
Mair, Charles *social studies educator*
Major, Patrick Webb, III, *principal*
Majore, Frank *artist*
Majors, Nelda Faye *physical therapist*
Mak, Ben Bohdan *engineer*
Mala, Theodore Anthony *physician, consultant*
Malach, Monte *physician*
Malek, Marlene Anne *healthcare advocate, foundation administrator*
Malhotra, Pulin *financial infrastructure consultant*
Malin, Harold Martin, Jr., *sexologist, educator*
Maling, George Croswell, Jr., *physicist*
Malishenko, Timothy Peter *communications executive*
Malkin, Michael M. *lawyer*
Mallo, Luis *artist, art director, photographer*
Mallo-Garrido, Josephine Ann *advertising executive*
Mallory, Arthur Lee *university dean, retired state official*
Malloy, Craig Riggs *physician, educator*
Malloy, John Richard *lawyer, chemical company executive*
Malloy, Johnn Edward *media artist, writer*
Malloy, Michael Terrence *journalist, newspaper editor*
Malone, Claudine Berkeley *management consultant*
Malone, Richard P. *psychiatrist*
Maloney, James Henry *community development executive, former congressman*
Maloney, Pamela *minister*
Maloney, Therese Adele *insurance company executive*
Malott, Adele Renee *editor*
Malphurs, Roger Edward *biomedical marketing executive*
Malsack, James Thomas *retired manufacturing company executive*
Maltby, Florence Helen *library science educator*
Maltsev, Nikolai Elyseevich *research scientist*
Manahan, Joan Elsie *health and physical education educator*
Manchester, Kenneth Edward *electronics executive, consultant*
Manchevski, Milcho *film director, scriptwriter*
Mandalakis, Stratos John *director, music educator*
Mandel, Adrienne Abramson *state legislator*
Mandel, Lewis Richard *retired pharmaceutical executive, consultant*
Manganaro, Francis Ferdinand *naval officer*
Mangapit, Conrado, Jr., *manufacturing executive*
Manglona, Ramona V. *judge, former state attorney general*
Mangold, John Frederic *manufacturing company executive, former naval officer*
Mangold, Sylvia Plimack *artist*
Mangual, Jesus A. *army officer*
Manika, John Francis *computer systems educator, computer information systems analyst*
Mankiewicz, Thomas Frank *screenwriter, director, producer*
Manley, Joan A(dele) Daniels *retired publishing executive*

McGuffey, Carroll Wade, Jr., *lawyer*
McGuinn, Edwin J. *chemicals executive*
McGuire, Hunter Holmes, Jr., *retired surgeon, educator*
McGuire, John W., Sr., *advertising executive, marketing professional, writer*
McGuirk, Terrence *former broadcasting company executive*
McGunigle, Dorothy Greene *interior designer, artist*
McGwire, Mark David *retired professional baseball player*
McHenry, Robert (Dale) *editor*
McHugh, Robert Daniel *bank executive, writer*
McIntier, Russell J. *retired writer*
McIntosh, Carolyn Meade *retired educational administrator*
McIntosh, Molly *interior designer*
McIntosh, Terrie Tuckett *lawyer*
McIntyre, Anita Grace Jordan *lawyer*
McIntyre, Bruce Herbert *media and marketing consultant*
Mc Intyre, Vonda Neel *writer*
Mc Isaac, George Scott *retired management consultant, government official*
McKay, John M. *former state senator*
McKay, Renee *artist*
McKean, Erin Margaret *editor, writer*
McKean, Robert Jackson, Jr., *retired lawyer*
McKee, Adele Dieckmann *retired church music director, educator*
McKee, Janath deBin *medical researcher*
McKee, Roger Curtis *retired federal judge*
McKellen, Sir Ian *actor*
McKellips, Terral Lane *mathematics educator, university administrator*
McKelway, Alexander Jeffrey *religion studies educator*
McKenna, Terence Patrick *retired insurance company executive*
McKeown, Lorraine Laredo *travel company executive, writer*
McKey, Thomas J. *retired lawyer*
McKinley, Ellen Bacon *priest*
McKinney, Jerry Wayne *retired journalist*
Mc Kinney, Joseph Crescent *retired bishop*
McKinney, Renovia M. *music educator*
McKinnon, Daniel Wayne, Jr., *naval officer*
McKnight, Thomas Frederick *artist*
McLauchlan, Sylvia June *charity organization executive*
McLaughlin, Jean Wallace *art director, artist*
McLaughlin, Joseph *lawyer*
McLaughlin, Michael John *retired insurance company executive*
McLaughlin, William Irving *space technical manager, writer*
McLean, Craig Elliott *retired non-commissioned officer*
McLean, Hon. Walter Franklin *executive, pastor, legislator*
McLean, Julianne Drew *concert pianist, educator*
McLendon, Melburne Dekalb *lawyer, arbitrator*
McLennan, Robert Gordon *asset management company executive*
McLeod, Willis B. *academic administrator*
McLoone, Eugene P. *education educator*
McMahon, George Joseph *academic administrator*
McManus, Jason Donald *retired editor*
McManus, Richard Philip *lawyer, agricultural products company executive*
McMaster, Belle Miller *religious organization administrator*
McMaster, Juliet Sylvia *English language educator*
McMillan, Paul Jeffrey *application developer*
McMillan, Terry L. *writer, educator*
McMillen, Abbie *environmental manager*
McMillen, Elizabeth Cashin *artist*
McNair, John William, Jr., *civil engineer*
McNally, Connie Benson *magazine editor, publisher, antiques dealer*
McNamara, Tom *scientific consulting corporation executive*
McNeely, Carol J. *dentist*
McNeill, Robert Patrick *investment counselor*
McNown, Edythe S. *music educator*
McNulty, Kathleen Anne *clinical social worker, psychotherapist, business consultant*
McPeak, Allan *career services director, educator, lawyer, consultant*
McPeters, Sharon Jenise *artist, writer*
McPhee, John Angus *writer*
Mc Pheeters, Edwin Keith *architect, educator*
McPherson, Donald Scott *labor and employment arbitrator/mediator*
McPherson, James Alan *writer, educator*
Mc Pherson, Peter *academic administrator*
Mc Quade, Lawrence Carroll *lawyer, investment company executive*
McQuary, Vaughn *management company executive*
McQuigg, John Dolph *retired lawyer*
McQuilkin, John Robertson *religion educator, academic administrator, writer*
McRae, Robert Malcolm, Jr., *federal judge*
McShefferty, John *retired research company executive, consultant*
McSweeny, William Francis *petroleum company executive, author*
McTague, John Paul *materials scientist, educator, chemist, researcher*
Mc Tiernan, John *film director*
McVeigh-Pettigrew, Sharon Christine *communications consultant*
McVicker, Jesse Jay *artist, educator*
McWethy, Patricia Joan *educational association administrator*
McWilliams, Michael *writer, publisher*
Meacham, Margaret Marks *writer, educator*
Mead, Elizabeth *artist*
Meade, Kenneth Albert *retired minister*
Meadors, Howard Clarence, Jr., *electrical engineer*
Meads, Donald Edward *management services company executive*
Meaker, Marijane Agnes *author*
Meara, Anne *actress, playwright, writer*
Mears, Walter Robert *journalist*
Measelle, Richard Leland *accountant*
Mecham, Steven Ray *school system administrator*
Mecik, Z. Richard *communications executive*
Medavoy, Mike *motion picture company executive*
Medina, Kathryn Bach *book editor*
Medina, Sandra *social worker, educator*
Medinger, C. Wynn *design and branding consultant*
Medley, Donald Matthias *education educator, consultant*
Medney, Tania Levy *advertising agency executive*
Mednick, Robert *accountant*
Meehan, John Joseph, Jr., *hospital administrator*
Meek, Carrie P. *former congresswoman*
Meek, Forrest Burns *retired trading company executive*
Meek, Linda Duke (Linda Bullion Meek) *elementary school educator, writer*
Meek, Paul Derald *oil and chemical company executive*
Meeker, Guy Bentley *banker*
Meffert, Roland Matthew *periodontist, educator*
Mehiel, Dennis *paper and packaging company executive*
Mehling, Emily *artist*
Mehne, Paul Randolph *associate dean, medical educator*
Meiksin, Zvi H. *electrical engineering educator*
Meilan, Celia *food products executive*
Meilman, Edward *physician*
Meinhardt, Vicki R. *communications executive, consultant*
Meintsma, Peter Evans *history and political science educator*
Meis, Nancy Ruth *marketing executive*
Melady, Thomas Patrick *academic administrator, ambassador, author, public policy expert, educator*
Melczek, Dale J. *bishop*
Melillo, Joseph Vincent *producer, performing arts*
Melito, Thomas *music educator, musician*
Mell, William Eric *mathematician*
Mellema, Donald Eugene *retired radio news reporter and anchor*
Mellins, Harry Zachary *radiologist, educator*
Melman, Cynthia Sue *special education educator*
Melnick, Jodi *dancer*
Melody, Michael Edward *publishing company executive*
Meltzer, E. Alyne *elementary school educator, social worker, volunteer*
Melville, Marguerita W. *advertising executive*
Melvin, Billy Alfred *clergyman*
Melvin, Patricia E. *artist*
Melvin, Peter Joseph *astrophysicist, educator*
Menaker, Ronald Herbert *retired bank executive*
Menaker, Shirley Ann Lasch *psychology educator, academic administrator*
Mench, John William *retail store executive, electrical engineer*
Mende, Robert Graham *retired engineering association executive*
Mendels, Joseph *psychiatrist, educator*
Mendelsohn, Carol S. *television producer*
Mendelson, Sol *physical science educator, consultant*
Mendlin, Ronald C. *employment specialist, writer*
Mendonca De Amorim, Valdivia Vânia Siqueira *translator*
Mendoza, George *poet, author*
Meneeley, Edward Sterling *artist*
Menefee, Linnea-Norma *antique dealer*
Mengel, Charles Edmund *physician, medical educator*
Menhall, Dalton Winn *lawyer, insurance executive, professional association administrator*
Menn, Julius Joel *scientist*
Menotti, Gian Carlo *composer*
Mensah, George A. *medical association administrator, educator*
Menzel, Marybelle Proctor *volunteer*
Menzia, Kathryn Marie *educational consultant*
Menzies, Carl Stephen *agricultural research administrator, ruminant nutritionist*
Mercado, Mary Gonzales *cardiologist*
Mercado-Ramos, Ferdinand *former secretary of state*
Mercer, Edwin Wayne *lawyer*
Mercer, Richard Joseph *retired advertising executive, freelance writer*
Mercuri, Joan B. *museum administrator*
Mercurio, Renard Michael *real estate corporation executive*
Mereschak, Volmar A. *retired obstetrician-gynecologist*
Merfeld, Audra L. *language educator*
Merriam, Robert W. *engineering executive, educator*
Merrick, George Boesch *aerospace company executive*
Merrill, Abel Jay *lawyer*
Merrill, Frank Harrison *data processing executive, consultant*
Merrill, Jean Fairbanks *writer*
Merrill, Robert *baritone*
Merring, Robert Alan *lawyer, arbitrator, mediator*
Merritt, Bruce Gordon *lawyer*
Merritt, Eleanor Lynette *artist, educator*
Merritt, John Howard *secondary school educator*
Merritt, Loretta Gaetana *principal, primary education educator*
Mesa-Lago, Carmelo *economist, educator*
Meserve, Walter Joseph *drama studies writer, publisher*
Meshel, Harry *former state senator, political party official*
Meskill, Victor P. *academic administrator, educator*
Mesrobian, Arpena Sachaklian *publisher, editor, consultant*
Messenkopf, Eugene John *real estate developer and hotel executive*
Messier, Michael C. *television director, actor, writer*
Messier, Pierre *lawyer, manufacturing executive*
Messmore, David William *construction executive, former psychologist*
Messner, Terry Bonaccolta *communications consultant*
Metcalf, Karen *retired foundation executive*
Metcalf, William Edwards *educator, museum curator*
Metcalfe, Robert Davis, III, *lawyer*
Metz, Steven William *small business owner*
Metz, T(heodore) John *librarian, educator*
Metz, Werner Adam *physicist*
Metzenbaum, Shelley H. *educational consultant, government agency administrator, consultant*
Metzger, Jeffrey Paul *lawyer*
Metzler, Ruth Horton *genealogical educator*
Metzner, Charles Miller *federal judge*
Meunier, Robert Raymond *research electrical engineer, optical engineer*
Meunier, Vincent *physicist*
Meyer, Andrew W. *retired publishing executive*
Meyer, Daniel Kramer *real estate executive*
Meyer, Donald Robert *state agency administrator, banker, lawyer*
Meyer, Frances Margaret Anthony *elementary and secondary school educator, health education specialist*
Meyer, Greg Charles *psychiatrist*
Meyer, Harry Martin, Jr., *retired health science facility administrator*
Meyer, J. Theodore *lawyer*
Meyer, John Edward *nuclear engineering educator*
Meyer, Max Earl *lawyer*
Meyer, Pucci *newspaper editor*
Meyer, Rachel Abijah *foundation director, artist, theorist, poet*
Meyerink, Victoria Paige *film producer, actress*
Meyerovitz, Fayona Brenda *psychologist, consultant*
Meyers, Jan *retired congresswoman*
Meyers, Richard James *landscape architect*
Meyerson, Stanley Phillip *lawyer*
Mezacapa, Edna S. *music educator, elementary school educator*
Michael, George T. *real estate manager*
Michaelis, Elias K. *neurochemist*
Michaels, Marion Cecelia *newswriter, editor, news syndicate executive*
Michel, Bernard *civil engineering educator, consultant*
Michel, Clifford Lloyd *lawyer, investment executive*
Michel, Elizabeth Cheney *social reform consultant*
Middaugh, Robert Burton *artist*
Miele, Joel Arthur, Sr., *civil engineer*
Might, Thomas Owen *newspaper company executive*
Migue, Jean Luc *economics professor*
Mikan, Kathleen Joyce Kehrer *medical/surgical nurse, educator*
Mikel, Thomas Kelly, Jr., *laboratory administrator*
Mikiewicz, Anna Daniella *marketing and international business exporter*
Mikitka, Gerald Peter *investment banker, financial consultant*
Mikklesen, Edwin Jens *psychiatrist*
Mikulas, Dana Cameron *voice educator, music educator*
Mikulski, Barbara Ann *senator*
Milano, Alyssa *actress*
Miles, Jim *former state offical*
Miles, John Frederick *retired manufacturing company executive*
Miles, Laveda Ann *advertising executive*
Miles, Richard R. *writer, curator*
Milewski, Barbara Anne *pediatrics nurse, neonatal/perinatal nurse practitioner, critical care nurse*
Milhouse, Paul William *bishop*
Millane, Lynn *retired town official*
Millar, Jeffery Lynn *writer*
Millar, John Donald *occupational and environmental health consultant, essayist, musician*
Millard, Charles Warren, III, *museum director, writer*
Millard, Donald Rex *financial executive*
Miller, Alan Jay *rare book dealer, author*
Miller, Alice *state representative*
Miller, Allen Richard *retired mathematician*
Miller, Anthony Bernard *physician, medical researcher*
Miller, Arjay *retired university dean*
Miller, Arthur *playwright, author*
Miller, Camille *school system administrator*
Miller, Carole Ann Lyons *editor, publisher, video producer, writer, marketing specialist*
Miller, Charles Edmond *retired library administrator*
Miller, Charles T. *lawyer*
Miller, Cheryl DeAnn *former professional basketball coach, broadcaster*
Miller, Darcy M. *publishing executive*
Miller, Deanna *editor, writer*
Miller, Diane Doris *executive search consultant*
Miller, Donald LeSessne *publishing executive*
Miller, Donald Muxlow *accountant*
Miller, Ellen S. *marketing communications executive*
Miller, Emily Elizabeth *elementary school educator, editor*
Miller, Harold Edward *retired manufacturing conglomerate executive, consultant*
Miller, Howard *writer, researcher*
Miller, Jack Conway *landscape artist, art gallery director, owner*
Miller, Jacqueline Winslow *library director*
Miller, Jerry Huber *retired university chancellor*
Miller, John Eddie *lawyer*
Miller, Lenore Wolf Daniels *speech-language pathologist*
Miller, Lia Verena Reyes *management services executive*
Miller, Linda Karen *retired secondary school educator, social studies educator, law educator*
Miller, Louis Howard *biologist, researcher*
Miller, Marilyn Lea *library science educator*
Miller, Martin E. *engineer, consultant*
Miller, Mary Hotchkiss *lay worker*
Miller, Norman Charles, Jr., *editor, reporter*
Miller, Patricia Louise *state legislator, nurse*
Miller, Patrick William *research administrator, educator*
Miller, Paul David *aerospace executive*
Miller, Paul McGrath, Jr., *executive search consulting company executive*
Miller, Phillip Edward *environmental scientist*
Miller, Robert Branson, Jr., *retired newspaper publisher*
Miller, Ross Hays *retired neurosurgeon*
Miller, Ross M. *financial services company executive*
Miller, Steven *medical administrator*
Miller, Steven Jeffrey *lawyer*
Miller, Tammie R. *public relations consultant, writer*
Miller, Thomas J. *former ambassador*
Miller, Thormund Aubrey *lawyer*
Miller, Vernon Dallace *minister*
Miller, W. Kievit *writer*
Miller-Young, Corriene Calhoun *nursing educator*
Millican, Kirk *architect*
Milligan, Arthur Achille *retired banker*
Milligan, Sister Mary *theology educator, religious consultant*
Milligan, Victor *consulting engineer*
Millikan, Clark Harold *physician*
Millikan, William *labor historian*
Millimet, Erwin *lawyer*
Millman, Amy J. *government official*
Millman, Marilyn Estelle *elementary school educator*
Mills, Celeste Louise *dog breeder, hypnotherapist, professional magician*
Mills, Charles S. *healthcare supplies and products company executive*
Mills, Dale Douglas *journalist*
Mills, Elizabeth Shown *historical writer, genealogist*
Mills, Eugene Sumner *academic administrator*
Mills, Gloria Adams *energy service consultant*
Mills, Kevin Lee *information technology researcher*
Mills, Robert Lee *academic administrator emeritus*
Mills, Russell Andrew *dean*
Millsaps, Fred Ray *investor*
Millsaps, William Hobart, Jr., *newspaper editor*
Milne, James F. *former secretary of state*
Milner, Irvin Myron *lawyer*
Milnor, Hazel *nurse*
Milnor, William Robert *physician*
Milstein, Monroe Gary *retail executive*
Milsten, Robert B. *lawyer*
Milstone, Leonard Matthew *physician, educator, researcher*
Milunas, J. Robert *health care organization executive*
Minahan, Daniel Francis *lawyer, retired manufacturing executive*
Mindlin, Paula Rosalie *retired reading educator*
Mingle, James John *lawyer*
Minners, Howard Alyn *federal agency administrator, preventive medicine physician, researcher*
Minniti, Martha Jean *home healthcare company executive*
Minnix, Bruce Milton *television and theatre director*
Minor, Clara Mae *election judge*
Minshall, Greg *computer programmer*
Mintz, M. J. *lawyer*
Mintz, Morton Abner *author, former newspaper reporter*
Miquelon, Miriam F. *former prosecutor, lawyer*
Miracle, Doris Jean *retired medical/surgical nurse*
Miranda, Daniel Frank *lawyer, real estate executive*
Miranda-Levi, Jason *film producer, writer*
Mirin, Steven Martin *psychiatrist*
Misa, Thomas J. *history educator, writer*
Miscella, Maria Diana *humanities educator*
Mischke, Carl Herbert *retired religious association executive*
Mishel, Lawrence *economics research director*
Mishler, John Joseph *sculptor, art educator*
Miskus, Michael Anthony *electrical engineer*
Mislow, Kurt Martin *chemist, educator*
Misner, Lorraine *laboratory technologist*
Misrach, Richard Laurence *photographer*
Missan, Richard Sherman *lawyer, educator*
Mitcham, Bob Anderson *lawyer, judge*
Mitchell, Brian Stokes *actor*
Mitchell, Briane Nelson *lawyer*
Mitchell, Carol Ann *nursing educator*
Mitchell, Carolyn Cochran *foundation administrator's executive assistant*
Mitchell, Charles Edward *lawyer, arbitrator*
Mitchell, Geneva Brooke *hypnotherapist*
Mitchell, John Charles *marketing professional*
Mitchell, John Laurin Amos *biological science educator*
Mitchell, Marcia Jeanne *freelance/self-employed writer, events producer*
Mitchell, Pamela Ann *airline pilot*
Mitchell, Patricia Edenfield *television executive*
Mitchell, Peter Kenneth *educational consultant*
Mitchell, William D. *lawyer*
Mitchell, William Graham Champion *lawyer, business executive*
Mitchell, William Marvin *pathology educator*
Mitchem, Cheryl E. *accounting educator*
Mitelman, Bonnie Cossman *editor, writer*
Mitrany, Devora *writer, editor*
Mitzner, Kenneth Martin *electrical engineering consultant*
Miura, Irene Takei *academic administrator*
Mizuguchi, Norman *former state senator*
Mlyniec, Wallace John *law educator, lawyer, consultant*
Moazed, Khosrow L. *retired engineering educator*
Mobley, William Hodges *management educator, researcher, author, executive*
Modisett, Jeffrey A. *lawyer, state attorney general*
Modisher, Melvin Wayne *obstetrician/gynecologist, educator*
Moeck, Peter *crystallographer, materials scientist*
Moeller, James *retired state supreme court justice*
Moffat, MaryBeth *consulting company executive*
Moffatt, Hugh McCulloch, Jr., *hospital administrator, physical therapist*
Moffatt, Katy (Katherine Louella Moffatt) *musician, vocalist, songwriter*
Mogel, Leonard Henry *writer*
Mograbi, Robert *bank executive*
Mohaideen, A. Hassan *surgeon, healthcare executive*
Mohamed, Joseph, Sr., *real estate broker, farmer*
Mohebbi, Afshin *former telecommunications industry executive*
Mohler, Brian Jeffery *diplomat*
Mohler, Ronald Rutt *electrical engineering educator*
Mohns, Judith *artist, art educator*
Molbegott, Lester Philip *anesthesiologist*
Molinaro, Joseph Daniel *dentist*
Molitor, Michael A. *entrepreneur, consultant*
Moll, David Carter *civil engineer*
Mollohan, Beth M. *humanities educator*
Molloy, Sylvia *Latin American literature educator, writer*
Molnar, Donald Joseph *landscape architecture educator*
Molnar, Violet *mental health nurse*
Molpus, David Lee *reporter, journalist*
Monacelli, Gianfranco *publishing executive*
Monaco, Chris *historian, writer, documentary filmmaker*
Monaco, Letitia Adrienne *writer, photographer*
Monaghan, Thomas Stephen *retired restaurant chain executive*
Monas, Sidney *retired history educator*
Monck, Maureen F. *psychoanalyst*
Mondale, Walter Frederick *former Vice President of United States, diplomat, lawyer*
Monkman, Betty Claire *curator*
Monroe, Frederick Fales *geologist, oceanographer*

Nishimura, Joseph Yo *retired retail executive, accountant*
Nix, Patricia *artist*
Nixon, Carol Holladay *retired park and recreation director*
Nixon, Marni *singer*
Nixon, Sandra L. *retired registrar*
Nobles, Laurence Hewit *retired geology educator*
Nochlin-Soto, David *neuropathologist*
Nochman, Lois Wood Kivi (Mrs. Marvin Nochman) *retired educator*
Noddings, Nel *education educator, writer*
Noddings, Sarah Ellen *lawyer*
Nodelman, Nancy Ziegler *sculptor, designer*
Noe, Elnora (Ellie Noe) *retired chemicals executive*
Noel, Melvina *literature educator*
Nolan, Patrick Joseph *screenwriter, playwright, educator*
Noland, Kenneth Clifton *artist*
Nolen, William Giles *lawyer, accountant*
Noll, Richard Dean, Jr., *psychologist, educator, historian*
Nolte, Nick *actor*
Noolan, Julie Anne Carroll *management consultant*
Noonan, Patrick Sutton *management educator*
Noor, Ronny *language educator, writer*
Noorda, Raymond J. *computer software company executive*
Nora, James Jackson *physician, writer, educator*
Norbeck, Jane S. *retired nursing educator*
Nord, Eric Thomas *retired manufacturing executive*
Nordley, Gerald David *investor, writer*
Nordlund, Donald Elmer *manufacturing executive, lawyer*
Norgren, William Andrew *retired religious denomination administrator*
Norkin, Cynthia Clair *retired physical therapist*
Norman, Albert George, Jr., *lawyer*
Norman, Donald Arthur *cognitive scientist*
Norman, E. Gladys *retired business computer educator, consultant*
Norman, Gregory John *professional golfer*
Normand, Gilbert *government official*
Norquist, John Olaf *former mayor*
Norrid, Henry Gail *osteopathic physician and surgeon, researcher, educator, healthcare facility administrator*
Norris, Chuck (Carlos Ray) *actor*
Norris, Darell Forest *retired insurance company executive*
Norris, Robert Wheeler *lawyer, military officer*
North, Gerald David William *lawyer*
Norton, Andre Alice *author*
Norton, Gregory Alan *writer*
Norton, Karen Ann *accountant*
Norton, Robert Michael *mathematician, educator, statistician*
Norwood, B.J. Scott *business and management educator, Russian affairs educator*
Nott, Tara Lee *Olympic athlete*
Nottingham, William Jesse *retired church mission executive, minister*
Nova, Craig *writer*
Novack, Alvin John *physician*
Novack, Tevor D. *surgeon, consultant*
Novak, Alan Lee *retired pharmaceutical company executive*
Novak, Barbara *art history educator*
Novick, Julius Lerner *theater critic, educator*
Nowik, Henry Ian *marketing executive, consultant*
Nugent, Helen Jean *history educator*
Nugent, Shane Vincent *lawyer*
Nugent, Walter Terry King *historian*
Nunn, Charles Burgess *religious organization executive*
Nurenberg, David *retired oil company executive*
Nurick, Carl J. *writer, consultant, poet*
Nusim, Roberta *publisher*
Nuss, Joanne Ruth *sculptor, artist*
Nutt, Tami Lee *academic administrator*
Nuttelman, Doris Graves *nursing administrator*
Nuzzo, Anthony Gerald *services executive*
Nwokoye, Patrick Ikechukwu *priest, researcher*
Nyberg, Stanley Eric *cognitive scientist*
Nycklemoe, Glenn Winston *bishop*
Nykolyn, Irma M. *product manager*
Nyquist, Maurice Otto *federal agency administrator, scientist*
Oakley, Andrew Arthur *journalist, educator*
Oaks, Maurice David *retired pharmaceutical company executive*
Oates, Carl Everette *lawyer, director*
Ober, Doris Ann *writer, editor, consultant*
Ober, Richard Francis, Jr., *lawyer, banker*
Oberai, Assad A. *engineer, researcher*
Obermann, Richard Michael *governmental technology and policy analyst*
Obermayer, Michael Erik Max *management consultant*
O'Brien, Charles H. *lawyer, retired state supreme court chief justice*
O'Brien, Erin *auditor*
O'Brien, J. Willard *lawyer, educator*
O'Brien, James Edward *lawyer*
O'Brien, John F. *former insurance company executive*
O'Brien, John Wilfrid *economist, emeritus university president, educator*
O'Brien, Kevin *musician, radio producer*
O'Brien, Orin Ynez *musician, educator*
O'Brien, Robert John, Jr., *public relations executive, former government official, air force officer*
O'Brien, Thomas Henry *former bank holding company executive*
O'Brien-Palmer, Michelle Ann *educational writer, consultant*
O'Bryon, Maureen *lawyer*
Ochs, Michael *editor, librarian, music educator*
O'Connell, Philip Raymond *retired lawyer, paper company executive*
O'Connell, William Raymond, Jr., *educational consultant, retired academic administrator*
O'Connor, Doris Julia *non-profit fundraiser, consultant*
O'Connor, James John *retired utility company executive*
O'Connor, John Joseph *operations executive*
O'Connor, Michol *judge*
O'Connor, Varley *writer, education educator*
O'Connor Taylor, Sheryl Ann *medical services administrator*
Odar, Fuat *nuclear engineer*
O'Dell, Joan Elizabeth *lawyer, mediator, consumer products company executive, educator*
O'Dell, Kimberly Jane *historian, educator*
Odell, William Douglas *physician, educator, research scientist*
Oden, Jean P(hifer) *special education educator*
Oden, William Bryant *bishop, educator*
Odenigbo, Innocent Chukwunwike *linguist, consultant*
Odermatt, Robert Allen *architect*
Odom, Judy *software company executive*
O'Donnell, James Joseph *classicist, educational administrator*
O'Donnell, Kathleen C. *artist*
O'Donnell, Kathleen Mary *social services administrator*
O'Donnell, Kevin *retired metal products executive*
O'Donnell, Maureen Stacey *editor*
O'Dowd, Niall Oliver *publishing executive, writer*
Oelman, Robert Schantz *retired manufacturing executive*
Oerding, James Bryan *military educator*
Oerter, Cynthia Lynn *medical technologist*
Oesterling, Thomas Ovid *retired pharmaceutical executive*
Oettinger, Regina Marie *music educator*
Ofstad, Evelyn Larsen Boyl *retired primary school educator, radio personality, film producer*
Ogbar, Jeffrey Ogbonna Green *history professor*
Ogden, Benjamin *language educator*
Ogden, Maurice B. *retired minister, writer*
Ogliaruso, Michael Anthony *retired chemist, educator, actor*
O'Gorman, Maurice R.G. *medical researcher*
O'Grady, James S. *retired elementary school educator*
Ogunyemi, Omolola Ijeoma *medical educator*
Oh, Mark Edward *minister*
O'Halleran, Michael D. *insurance company executive*
O'Hara, Catherine *actress, comedienne*
O'Hara, Sabine U. *academic administrator, dean, economist, educator*
O'Hare, Dean Raymond *insurance company executive, director*
O'Hare, James Raymond *energy company executive*
O'Hare, Joseph Aloysius *academic administrator, priest*
Oinas, Felix J. *retired Slavic language educator*
O'Keefe, Gary Raymond *actor*
Okolski, Cynthia Antonia *psychotherapist, social worker*
Okoshi-Mukai, Sumiye *artist*
Olajuwon, Hakeem Abdul *former professional basketball player*
Oldenburg, Claes Thure *artist*
Oldman, Alfred Maurice *accountant, management consultant*
Olds, Jacqueline *psychiatrist, educator*
O'Leary, Denis Joseph *retired physician, insurance company executive*
O'Leary, Dennis Sophian *medical organization executive*
O'Leary, John Clarence *retired radiologist*
O'Leary, Kathleen Ann *writer*
Oles, Paul Stevenson (Steve Oles) *architect, perspectivist, educator*
Olins, Robert Abbot *communications research executive*
Olitski, Jules *artist*
Olive, David Michael *magazine writer, magazine editor*
Oliver, Jerry Alton *former police chief*
Oliver, Karen Lee *writer*
Oliver, Samuel William, Jr., *lawyer*
Olkinetzky, Sam *artist, retired museum director and educator*
Ologbenla, Adesoji Olaposi *financial advisor*
Olson, Dale C. *public relations executive*
Olson, Floyd Palmer *retired service company executive*
Olson, James Clifton *historian, university president*
Olson, Paul Richard *Spanish literature educator, editor*
Olson, Phillip Roger *naval officer*
Olson, William Clinton *anthologist, international affairs administrator*
Olsson-Hume, Irena *music educator*
Olszanski, S. Michael *college program administrator*
Olyphant, David *cultural, educational association executive*
O'Mara, Hugh *artist*
Omholt, Bruce Donald *product designer, mechanical engineer, consultant*
O'Neal, Harriet Roberts *psychologist, psycholegal consultant*
O'Neill, Donald Edmund *health science executive*
O'Neill, James F. *retired health facility administrator*
O'Neill, John T. *retired toy company executive*
O'Neill, Kevin *professional athletics coach*
O'Neill, Mary Jane *not-for-profit administrator, consultant*
O'Neill, Michael E. *former bank executive*
O'Neill, Robert William *marketing executive*
Onuigbo, Macaulay Amechi *physician, nephrologist, transplant physician*
Oort, Abraham Hans *meteorologist, researcher, educator*
Oppedahl, John Frederick *newspaper publisher, publishing executive*
Oppenheim, David Jerome *musician, retired university dean*
Oppewall, Jeannine Claudia *motion picture production designer*
Oppman, John Christopher *small business owner*
O'Quinn, Nancy Diane *nurse, educator, consultant*
Oransky, Ivan *writer, web editor*
Orban, Kurt *foreign trade company executive*
Orbit, William (William Wainwright) *record producer*
Orcutt, Christopher C. *language educator*
Ord, Linda Banks *artist*
Ordal, Caspar Reuben *business executive*
Orden, Stewart L. *lawyer*
O'Reilly, Sally *musician, educator*
O'Reilly, Wenda Brewster *writer, researcher, management consultant*
Orkin, Jenna *writer*
Orlebeke, William Ronald *retired lawyer, writer*
Ormai-Buza, Ildiko *soprano, composer, organist, music educator*
Ormasa, John *retired utilities executive*
Ornatowski, Cezar Maria *rhetoric and communication educator, consultant*
Orosz, Joel J. *philanthropist, educator*
O'Rourke, Joan B. Doty Werthman *retired school system administrator*
Orr, Frank Howard, III, *architect*
Orr, H. Allen *biologist, critic*
Orr, Kenneth Bradley *academic administrator*
Orrmont, Arthur *writer, editor*
Ortiz, Angel Vicente *church administrator*
Ortiz, Felix W. *state legislator*
Ortiz, Francis Vincent, Jr., *retired ambassador*
Ortiz Mena, Antonio *banker*
Ortolano, Ralph J. *engineering consultant*
Orttung, William Herbert *chemistry professor*
Osberg, Gregory John *publishing company executive*
Osborn, DeVerle Ross *insurance company executive*
Osborn, Kenneth Louis *financial executive*
Osborn, William George *savings and loan executive*
Osborne, Barrie M. *motion picture producer*
Osborne, James Alfred *religious organization administrator*
Osborne, John L. *academic administrator, educator*
Oscarson, Kathleen Dale *retired writing assessment coordinator, educator*
O'Shea, Catherine Large *marketing and public relations consultant*
Oshita, John Takao *musician*
Oskin, JoEllen Ross *special education educator, school librarian*
Osment, Lamar Sutton *retired dermatologist, educator*
Osmer-McQuade, Margaret *business executive, broadcast journalist*
Osmond, Marie *singer*
Ostaszewski, Alyce Vitella *religion educator*
Ostberg, Henry Dean *corporate executive*
Ostby, Ronald *retired dairy and food products company executive*
Oster, Lewis Henry *manufacturing executive, engineering consultant*
Osterhaus, William Eric *broadcast executive*
Osterhoff, James Marvin *retired telecommunications company executive*
Osterweil, Leon Joel *dean, computer science educator*
Ostlind, Dan A. *retired parasitologist*
Ostrow, Joseph W. *advertising executive*
Ostrow, Stuart *theatrical producer, educator, writer*
O'Sullivan, Lawrence Joseph *retired investment counselor*
O'Sullivan, Paul Kevin *business executive, management and instructional systems consultant*
Osvath, Ludovic Lajos *minister*
Oswald, Robert Bernard *retired science administrator, nuclear engineer*
Othman, Talat Mohamad *financial consultant, investment banker*
Otis, Jack *social work educator*
Otis, Lee Liberman *lawyer, educator*
Otstott, Charles Paddock *retired military officer, information technology executive, consultant*
Otto, Ingolf Helgi Elfried *banking institute fellow*
Otto, Jean Hammond *journalist*
Ouimette, Paige *psychologist, researcher*
Ouseley, William Norman *security services consultant*
Outten, Kristina Marie *secondary school educator*
Ovadiah, Janice *non-profit organization consultant, cultural institute executive*
Owen, Carol Thompson *artist, educator, writer*
Owen, Suzanne *retired savings and loan association executive*
Owens, Charles Vincent, Jr., *pharmaceutical executive, consultant*
Owens, Luvie Moore *association consultant*
Oxnam, Philip Linton *small business owner*
Ozick, Cynthia *writer*
Pace, Charles Robert *psychologist, educator*
Pace, George W. *food products company executive*
Pack, Allen S. *retired coal company executive*
Pack, Susan Joan *art consultant*
Packard, John Mallory *physician*
Packard, Ronald C. *former congressman*
Pacor, Victor J. *diversified financial services company executive*
Padget, John E. *management professional*
Padgett, Ron *writer*
Padilla, James Earl *lawyer*
Padilla, James Jerome *automobile executive*
Padin, Jeffry *aerospace engineer*
Paganelli, Charles Victor *physiologist, educator*
Page, Jonathan Roy *investment analyst*
Page, Willis *conductor*
Pagel, Inga Ann *accountant*
Paino, Javier E. *physician*
Painter, Borden W. *former academic administrator*
Painter, Robert Lowell *surgeon, educator*
Painton, Russell Elliott *lawyer, mechanical engineer*
Pakenham, Rosalie Muller Wright *magazine and newspaper editor*
Pal, Prabir Kumar (Sunny Pal) *law firm counselor*
Pal, Pratapaditya *curator*
Palacios, Gonzalo T. *education educator*
Palade, George Emil *research scientist, educator*
Paley, Russell Eliot *writer, small business owner*
Palileo, Hazel Valencia *videographer*
Paliwal, Dinesh Kumar *diplomat, educational administrator*
Palizzi, Anthony N. *retired lawyer, retail corporation executive*
Pall-Pallant, Teri *paleontologist, inventor, behavioral scientist, design engineer, advertising agency executive*
Palmer, Charlotte Marie *writer*
Palmer, Dave Richard *retired military officer, academic administrator*
Palmer, George Thomas *artist*
Palmer, Irene Sabelberg *university dean and educator emeritus, nurse, researcher, historian, genealogist*
Palmer, Jocelyn Beth *volunteer*
Palmer, Marilyn Joan *English composition educator*
Palmer, Robert Erwin *association executive*
Palmeri, Michael Thomas *financial analyst, equity trader*
Palmier, Darice *music educator*
Palms, Roger Curtis *educator, editor, clergyman*
Palter, Robert Monroe *humanities educator*
Palumbo, Daniel P. *former food products executive*
Palumbo, Matthew Aloysius *marketing executive*
Pan, Zhongqi *education educator, researcher*
Panagotis, David Timothy *editor*
Panetta, Michael Jon *retired state agency administrator, educator, writer, researcher*
Pang, Katherine Landey Squires *lawyer*
Pannell, Clifton Wyndham *geography educator, writer*
Panofsky, Wolfgang Kurt Hermann *physicist, researcher*
Pantoja, Susan Lee *secondary school educator, literature educator*
Pantojas-Concepcion, Carlos A. *rheumatologist*
Panzer, Mary Caroline *historian, museum curator*
Paolucci, Anne Attura *playwright, poet, English and comparative literature educator, educational consultant*
Paolucci, Massimo *application developer, researcher*
Papa, Vincent T. *insurance company executive*
Papadakos, Nicholas Peter *retired state supreme court justice*
Pappas, Michael *former congressman*
Paquet, Michael J. *academic administrator*
Paravastu, Swamy *economist, researcher*
Pardue, Dwight Edward *venture capitalist*
Parent, Rodolphe Jean *Canadian air force officer, pilot*
Paresky, David S. *travel company executive*
Parham, Ellen Speiden *nutrition educator*
Pariag, Haimwattie Ramkistodas *information management administrator*
Parins, Robert James *professional football team executive, judge*
Paris, David Andrew *dentist*
Park, John Thornton *academic administrator*
Park, Jon Keith *dentist, educator*
Parke, Marilyn Neils *writer*
Parke, Robert Leon *retired communications executive*
Parke, William H. *communications executive*
Parkel, James G. *former health association administrator*
Parker, Brent Mershon *retired medical educator, internist, cardiologist*
Parker, George *retired pen manufacturing company executive*
Parker, Gerald William *internist, health facility administrator, retired military officer*
Parker, James Francis *former air transportation executive, lawyer*
Parker, John William *retired pathology educator, investigator*
Parker, Mel *editor*
Parker, Michael D. *chemicals executive*
Parker, Susan Brooks *healthcare executive*
Parker, Warren Cameron *registrar, small business owner*
Parker, William Dale *management consultant, political and presidential adviser*
Parkhurst, William Michael *media consultant*
Parkins, Frederick Wallace Eugene *environmental services administrator, educator, coroner*
Parkison, James Max *trial court administrator, educator*
Parkman, Cynthia Ann *medical and surgical nurse, nursing educator*
Parks, Grace Susan *bank official*
Parks, Heather Jewel *music educator*
Park Spencer, Karen Lynn *architect, jewelry designer*
Parmley, Van Samuel *retired anesthesiologist*
Parode, Ann *lawyer*
Parr, Albert Clarence *physicist*
Parr, Royse Milton *retired lawyer, writer*
Parrish-Porter, Vallerie *controller*
Parrott, Wanda Sue *writer, journalist*
Parseghian, Gregory J. *former mortgage company executive*
Parsons, Harry Glenwood *retired surgeon*
Parsons, Patrick Jeremy *research scientist, science educator*
Partington, James Wood *engineering executive*
Partridge, Bruce James *lawyer, educator, writer*
Parviainen, Silve Katariina *marketing executive*
Pascale, Daniel Richard *lawyer*
Pascale, Jane Fay *pathologist*
Paschoud, François *university educator*
Pascoe, Patricia Hill *former state legislator*
Paskawicz, Jeanne Frances *pain specialist*
Pasquier, Joël *music educator*
Passailaigue, Ernest L., Jr., *state legislator, accountant*
Pasternak, Patricia A. *writer, freelance/self-employed newswriter*
Pastor, Millie A. *interior designer, consultant*
Pastorek, Norman Joseph *facial plastic surgeon*
Patchett, Arthur Allan *medicinal chemist, pharmaceutical executive*
Patchin, Rebecca J. *anesthesiologist, educator, administrator*
Pate, Virginia Frances *artist, educator*
Patel, Anil S. *biomedical engineer, researcher, medical products executive*
Paterson, Robert E. *trading stamp company executive*
Patmos, Adrian Edward *retired dean*
Patrick, Brenda Jean *educational consultant*
Patrick, Deval Laurdine *lawyer*
Patrick, Michele Mary *government official*
Patrick, Thomas H. *investment company executive*
Patrick, Victor Phillip *lawyer*
Pattanaik, Prasanta Kumar *economics professor*
Patterson, Collis Delano *secondary school educator*
Patterson, Elizabeth Johnston *retired congresswoman*
Patterson, James *former mayor*
Patterson, James E. *economist, author, speaker*
Patterson, James Willis *pathology and dermatology educator*
Patterson, Joseph Flanner, Jr., *surgeon, anesthesiologist*
Patterson, Richard North *novelist, writer, lawyer*
Patterson, Robert Hudson *research library consultant*
Patterson, Samuel C. *political science educator*
Patterson, Seth Matthew *music educator*
Pattillo, Manning Mason, Jr., *academic administrator*
Patton, James Richard, Jr., *lawyer*
Patton, Paul E. *former governor*
Pauken, Thomas Weir *venture capital executive, mediator*
Paul, Arthur *artist, graphic designer, illustrator, art and design consultant*
Paul, Eve W. *retired lawyer*
Paul, Richard Wright *lawyer*
Paul, Ron *congressman*
Paul, Vivek *information technology executive*
Pauley, Jane *television journalist*

GEOGRAPHIC INDEX 5487 ADDRESS UNPUBLISHED

Paulose, Anil Chiramel financial market data/trading systems software infrastructure consultant
Paulsen, Frank Robert college dean emeritus
Pauly, John Edward anatomist, educator
Paup, Martin Arnold real estate and securities investor
Pawlik, James David lawyer, historian
Payne, Daniel Harold (Harold Payne) real estate developer, small business owner
Payne, Ladell retired college president
Payne, Mary Libby retired judge
Payton, Thomas William corporate finance consultant executive
Peace, John T. religious studies educator
Peacock, Christopher A. former real estate company executive
Peacock, Mary Willa magazine editor
Peapples, George Alan retired automotive executive
Pear, Charles E., Jr., lawyer
Pearce, Paul Francis retired aerospace electronics company executive
Pearl, B. Michael business owner
Pearl, Laurence Dickson retired federal government executive
Pearlstein, Philip artist
Pearson, Jennie Sue retired government administrator
Pearson, Paul Holding insurance company executive
Pearson, Ralph Gottfrid chemistry professor
Pearson, Richard Joseph archaeologist, educator
Pease, Edward A former congressman
Peaslee, Margaret Mae Hermanek zoology educator
Peccarelli, Anthony Marando lawyer
Peck, Daniel Farnum chemical company executive
Peck, Mira P. lawyer
Peck, Paul Lachlan minister
Peck, Robert David educational foundation administrator
Peckham, Ellen artist, poet
Pedersen, Knud George economics educator, academic administrator
Pederson, William Christopher plastic surgeon
Pedhirney, Gayland food products company executive
Pedini, Egle Damijonaitis radiologist
Pedini, Kenneth radiologist
Peeler, Bob lieutenant governor
Peeples, Rufus Roderick, Jr., (Roddy Peeples) farm and ranch news radio broadcaster
Pefley, Norman Gordon corporate financial executive
Peiris, Suhithi Mahesica research chemist
Peixoto Neto, Jose Ulysses internist, researcher
Péladeau, Marius Beaudoin art and history consultant, retired museum director
Pelizzoni, Virginia Matko writer, editor, consultant
Pell, Claiborne former senator
Pelletier, Louis Conrad surgeon, educator, health facility administrator
Pelton, Walter Eugene information technology executive, mathematician, physicist
Peña, Federico Fabian retired federal official
Penachio, Anthony Joseph, Jr., psychotherapist, hypnotherapist, behavioral therapist
Pence, Jean Virginia (Jean Pence) retired real estate broker
Pendergrass, Henry Pancoast radiologist, nuclear medicine physician
Penrod, Marian Penuel retired school librarian
Pensis, Henri Bram music educator, conductor
Penso, Christine Arety obstetrician-gynecologist
Penzer, Mark lawyer, writer
Peoples, John Arthur, Jr., former university president, consultant
Pepelea, Kimberli Rae case manager
Pepper, J. Stanley construction company executive
Percy, Lee Edward motion picture film editor
Peretsman, Nancy B. investment banker
Pereyra-Suarez, Charles Albert lawyer
Perez, Dianne M. medical researcher
Perez, Gabriel Felan music educator
Pérez-Monforti, Jessica L. social sciences educator, researcher
Perine, Maxine Harriet retired reading educator
Perini, Jennifer Mary television producer
Perkins, Charles Theodore real estate developer, consultant
Perkins, James Wood lawyer
Perkins, Leeman Lloyd music educator, musicologist
Perkins, Nancy Jane industrial designer
Perle, George composer
Perlmutter, David H. physician, educator
Perlov, Dadie management consultant
Perlstein, William James lawyer
Permuth, Jaime artist, educator
Perosch, Tony Anthony George corporate executive, consul
Perrenod, Douglas Arthur engineer, astronaut
Perrin, Michael Warren lawyer
Perritt, Henry Hardy, Jr., law educator
Perrot, Paul Norman museum director
Perry, Chris Nicholas retired advertising executive
Perry, George Williamson lawyer
Perry, Kenneth Walter retired integrated oil company executive
Perry, Matthew actor
Perry, Mattie LaVora writer, web site designer, editor
Perry, Sir Michael (Sir Michael Sydney Perry) industrialist
Persaud, Andrea Nandini dermatologist
Persoff, Nehemiah actor, artist
Person, Andrea Meredith application developer
Pesch, LeRoy Allen physician, educator, health and hospital consultant, business executive
Pesci, Joe actor
Peshkin, Samuel David lawyer
Pesola, Gene Raymond physician, educator
Peszke, Michael Alfred psychiatrist, writer
Peter, Richard Ector zoology educator
Peters, Carol Ann Dudycha counselor
Peters, Douglas Alan medical-legal consultant, health law attorney
Peters, Douglas Cameron mining engineer, geologist
Peters, Evelyn Joan artist
Peters, Kristen Michele psychologist, researcher
Peters, Michael P. former mayor
Peters, R. Jonathan lawyer, manufacturing executive
Peters, Ralph Frew investment banker
Peters, Robert Woolsey architect
Petersen, Arne Joaquin chemist
Petersen, Jonathan William marketing professional, writer
Petersen-Frey, Roland manufacturing executive
Peterson, Ann Sullivan physician, health care consultant
Peterson, Carl Eric metals company executive, banker
Peterson, Coleman Hollis former retail store executive
Peterson, Gary J retail executive
Peterson, Kevin Bruce newspaper editor, publishing executive
Peterson, Robert Austin manufacturing company executive retired
Peterson, Walter Fritiof academic administrator
Petok, Samuel retired manufacturing company executive
Petraeus, David Howell career military officer
Petrequin, Harry Joseph, Jr., foreign service officer
Petrie, Richard Allen retired lawyer, tax consultant
Petrillo, Leonard Philip retired corporate securities executive, lawyer
Petryshyn, Walter Alexis otolaryngologist
Petterson, Margo artist
Pettigrew, L. Eudora retired academic administrator
Pettis-Roberson, Shirley McCumber retired congresswoman
Pettit, Ghery DeWitt retired veterinary medicine educator
Pettitt, Jay S. architect, consultant
Petz, Thomas Joseph internist
Pevear, Roberta Charlotte retired state legislator
Peyser, Joseph Leonard history professor, writer, translator
Peyton, John mayor
Pfaff, Judy artist
Pfanstiel Parr, Dorothea Ann interior designer
Pfeister, Raymond Lynn diversified financial services company executive
Pfister, Howard Frederick Carl retired surgeon
Pflanze, Otto Paul history professor
Pham, Duc engineering executive
Pham, Lara Bach-Vien small business owner
Phan, Long Thanh structural engineer, researcher
Phelan, Charles Scott retired lawyer
Phelan, Ellen artist
Phelps, Gerry Charlotte economist, minister
Philbrick, Rodman writer
Philip, James (Pate Philip) retired state legislator
Philippon, Marc Joseph orthopaedic surgeon
Philippus, Al A. protective services official
Philipson, Morris university press director
Phillips, Anne Linnea writer
Phillips, Charles Alan accounting firm executive
Phillips, Dorothy Kay lawyer
Phillips, Leo Harold, Jr., lawyer
Phillips, Mark editor, writer, publishing executive, musician
Phillips, Michelle Gilliam actress, writer
Phillips, Robert Derrick psychiatrist
Phillips, Ronald Edward artist, sales executive
Phillips, Thomas Royal law educator
Phillips, Winifred Patricia radio producer, composer
Phillis, John Whitfield physiologist, educator
Phinizy, Robert Burchall electronics company executive
Pianko, Theodore A. lawyer
Piazza, Jo Ann Christine sculptor
Pickrel, Paul English educator
Picower, Warren Michael editor
Pidgeon, Leslea Sharon artist, writer
Pierce, Charles Earl software engineer, entrepreneur
Pierce, David Hyde actor
Pierce, Diane Jean artist
Pierce, Dorothy Kohinke retired elementary school educator
Pierce, Hilda (Hilda Herta Harmel) painter
Pierce, Lisa Margaret telecommunications executive, product and market development manager, lecturer
Pierce, Ponchitta Ann TV host, producer, journalist, writer, consultant
Pierce, Shaheeda Laura midwife, consultant
Pierce, Susan Resneck academic administrator, literature educator
Pieretti, Michael product designer
Pierre, Natasha Unada accountant
Pies, Ronald E. retired city official
Pietrzak, Alfred Robert lawyer
Piga, Stephen Mulry retired lawyer
Pi-González, Amaury Francisco announcer, journalist
Pilgrim, Dianne Hauserman retired museum director
Pilkington, Mary Ellen stockbroker, trader
Pinkett-Smith, Jada actress
Pinkney, D. Timothy investment company executive
Pinsker, Walter retired allergist, immunologist
Pinter, Gabriel George physiology educator
Pinto, Rosalind retired educator, civic volunteer
Pipchick, Margaret Hopkins advance practice nurse, marriage and family therapist
Pipkin, Mary Margaret artist
Pippin, James Adrian, Jr., middle school educator
Pirie, Robert Burns, Jr., defense analyst
Pirkle, George Emory television and film actor, director
Pirro, Alfred Anthony, Jr., physician
Pitcher, Griffith Fontaine lawyer
Pitman, LaVern Frank librarian
Pitman, Sharon Gail middle school counselor
Pitt, Harvey Lloyd federal agency administrator
Pitts, Deborah Krueger healthcare consultant
Pizzuro, Salvatore Nicholas special education educator
Place, Janey banking consultant, former bank executive
Plangere, Jules Leon, Jr., retired media company executive
Plant, Linda R. music educator
Plants, Walter Dale retired elementary school educator, minister
Platis, James George secondary school educator
Platt, Lewis Emmett aerospace transportation executive
Pletcher, Eldon retired cartoonist
Plimpton, Peggy Lucas trustee
Plomp, Teunis (Tony Plomp) minister
Plotkin, Stanley Alan virologist
Plottel, Gloria Susanne Stone marketing professional
Plourd, David M. medical educator
Plummer, Leone Poindexter marriage and family therapist, nursing educator, nurse practitioner
Pniakowski, Andrew Frank structural engineer
Podell, Robert Mann obstetrician-gynecologist
Podhoretz, Norman magazine editor, writer
Poe, Bob political organization worker, communications company executive
Poe, Laura nursing educator, administrator
Poehner, Raymond Glenn retired bank executive
Pogue, Richard Welch lawyer
Pohorecky-Dolinsky, Larissa Alexandra pharmacologist
Poitier, Sidney actor, director
Poker, Nathan retired radiologist
Pokras, Sheila Frances retired judge
Polakoff, Murray Emanuel university dean, economics and finance educator
Poledouris, Basil K. composer
Poliakoff, Gary A. lawyer, educator
Polisar, Joseph Michael protective services official
Polisar, Lisa writer
Polistena, Joyce Carol art historian, educator
Polite, Carlene Hatcher writer, educator
Poll, Heinz choreographer, artistic director
Poll, Martin Harvey film producer
Pollack, Gerald Alexander economist, government official
Pollard, Henry mediator, arbitrator
Polley, Richard Donald microbiologist, inorganics and polymer chemist
Polliack, Adrian A. biomedical engineer, researcher
Pollock, Karen Anne computer analyst
Polonchak, Richard music educator
Pomerantz, James Robert psychology educator, academic administrator
Ponce, Arnoldo A. financial analyst, poet
Pond, Kirk electronics and computer parts company executive
Pontius, Stanley N. bank holding company executive
Ponton, Michael Kamano engineer, educator
Pool, Philip Bemis, Jr., investment banker
Poole, Eva Duraine librarian
Pop, Iggy (James Newell Osterberg) composer, singer, musician
Poppers, Paul Jules anesthesiologist, educator
Poppler, Doris Swords lawyer
Porrata, Samuel M. education director, foreign language educator
Port, Arthur Tyler retired government administrator, lawyer
Portal, Gilbert Marcel Adrien oil company executive
Porteous, Skipp private investigator, writer
Porter, Daniel Reed, III, museum director
Porter, Dixie Lee insurance company executive, consultant
Porter, Hayden Samuel computer science educator
Porter, James Morris retired judge
Porter, John Wilson education executive
Porter, Michael Pell lawyer
Porter, Philip Thomas retired electrical engineer
Porter, Victoria Jean editor, writer
Porter, Walter Thomas, Jr., retired bank executive
Portis, Alan Mark physicist, researcher
Portnoy, Harold David neurologist, surgeon
Portnoy, Sara S. lawyer
Portway, Patrick Stephen telecommunications consulting company executive, telecommunications educator
Posner, Sidney advertising executive
Poss, Jeffery Scott architect, educator
Post, Avery Denison retired church official
Post, Richard Bennett retired human resources executive
Post, Ruth-Ellen lawyer, educator
Post, Stephen Garrard theologian, philosopher, educator
Poteat, James Donald retired diaconal minister, retired military officer
Poteet, William Mark education educator, writer
Pott, James Thomas civil engineer, consultant
Potter, J. Stewart property manager
Potter, James Earl retired international hotel management company executive
Potter, Robert Daniel federal judge
Pottruck, David Steven brokerage house executive
Potts, Gerald Neal manufacturing executive
Potvin, Alfred Raoul engineering executive
Poucher, John Scott systems engineer, physicist
Poulos, Cynthia Jenks parochial school educator
Poulton, Roberta Doris nurse, consultant
Pound, Robert Vivian physics educator
Povich, Lynn journalist, magazine editor, internet executive
Powell, Alma Johnson writer, advocate, foundation administrator
Powell, Donald David religious studies educator
Powell, Earl Alexander, III, art museum director
Powell, Thomas Edward, III, biological supply company executive, physician
Power, Mary Susan political scientist, educator
Powers, Eldon Nathaniel computer mapping executive
Powers, Elizabeth Whitmel lawyer
Powers, John T., Jr., former mayor
Powers, Michael J. retired financial company executive
Powers, Ray Lloyd former state senator, dairy farmer, rancher
Pozzatti, Rudy Otto artist
Pracht, Drenda Kay psychologist
Prado, Edward Charles federal judge
Pradzynski, Andrzej Henryk chemist
Prager, David retired state supreme court chief justice
Prakapas, Eugene Joseph art gallery director
Prange, Hilmar Walter neurology educator
Prater, Elner W. elementary school educator
Prather, Lenore Loving former state supreme court chief justice
Pratt, Robert Windsor lawyer
Prausnitz, Frederik William conductor
Preddy, Raymond Randall retired newspaper publisher, educator
Preis, Mary Louise commissioner, former state legislator
Prem, F. Herbert, Jr., lawyer
Premack, David psychologist
Prentiss, Michael Vernon urban planner
Preschlack, John Edward management consultant
Prescott, Barbara Lodwich educational administrator
Prescott, Richard Chambers writer
Press, Aida Kabatznick former editor, writer, poet
Pressler, Larry former senator, lawyer
Preston, Colleen Ann lawyer
Preston, Kelly actress
Preston, Seymour Stotler, III, chemicals executive
Preudhomme, Marcia Denrique finance company executive, writer
Preus, David Walter bishop, minister
Prewitt, Kenneth political science educator, foundation executive
Price, Alfred Lee lawyer, mining company executive
Price, Barbara Gillette college administrator, artist
Price, Betty Jeanne choirchime soloist, writer
Price, Clifford Warren retired metallurgist, researcher
Price, Donna B. special education services professional
Price, James Melford retired physician, researcher
Price, Joseph Sterling retired air force officer
Price, Nelson (John Nelson Price) author, journalist
Price, Nick professional golfer
Price, Paul Buford physicist, researcher
Price, Robert Ira coast guard officer
Price, Robert Otis former mayor
Price, Ruthe Geier actress, writer, educator
Price, Thomas Frederick theatre educator
Price, Tom journalist
Pride, Benjamin David sales executive
Pridgen, Rufus Allen retired literature educator
Pridmore, Roy Davis government official
Prieto, Claudio R. academic administrator, lawyer
Primanzon, Andrea Jessica special events coordinator
Primosch, James Thomas music educator, composer, musician
Prince, Andrew Steven lawyer, former government official
Prins, Carol not-for-profit developer, consultant
Prins, Robert Jack retired academic administrator
Prinz, Kristie Dawn lawyer
Priore, Christopher Anselmo artist
Priory, Richard Baldwin former electric power industry executive
Pritchard, Claudius Hornby, Jr., retired university president
Pritchard, Kathleen Jo not-for-profit association administrator
Pritts, Elizabeth Anna medical educator
Probasco, Calvin Henry Charles clergyman, college administrator
Proctor, Barbara Gardner advertising agency executive, writer
Proctor, Richard J. geologist, consultant
Prokasy, William Frederick academic administrator
Prokopis, Emmanuel Charles computer company executive
Propp, Steven H. benefits compensation analyst
Propst, Michael Truman pathologist
Prosky, Robert Joseph actor
Prosperi, David Philip public relations executive
Prothro, Edwin Terry psychologist educator
Protigal, Stanley Nathan lawyer
Prout, Carl Wesley retired history educator
Provensen, Alice Rose Twitchell artist, author
Pruden, Ann Lorette chemical engineer, researcher, management consultant
Prudhomme, James Larry financial consultant, writer
Pruis, John J. business executive
Pruitt, Anne Loring academic administrator, education educator
Prusiner, Stanley Ben neurology and biochemistry educator, researcher
Pruter, Robert Douglas librarian
Pruzan, Irene arts administrator, music educator, flutist, marketing and public relations specialist
Pryor, Harold S. retired college president
Pryor, Tommi Thornbury marketing professional
Przybylski, Sandra Marie speech pathologist
Psillos, Susan Rose artist, educator
Puckett, Jim H. school system administrator
Puetz, Pamela Ann human resources executive
Pugliese, Karen Olsen freelance public relations counsel
Puhekker, Kristin Rose music educator
Pulitizer, Lilly (Lillian McKim Rousseau) apparel designer, writer
Pullen, Penny Lynne non-profit organization administrator, former state legislator
Pulliam, Yvonne Antoinette gifted education educator
Pulling, Thomas Leffingwell investment advisor
Pullman, Philip Nicholas author
Pun, Suzie biomedical engineer, educator
Punukollu, Gopi Krishna cardiologist
Punzo, Fred science educator
Purcell, Bill mayor
Purcell, George Richard artist, postal employee
Purcell, Karen Anne veterinarian
Puri, Ishwar Kanwar engineering educator, researcher
Puris, Martin Ford media executive
Purtle, John Ingram lawyer, former state supreme court justice
Puryear, Alvin Nelson management educator
Puryear, James Burton college administrator
Pusateri, Lawrence Xavier lawyer
Pustilnik, David Daniel lawyer
Putnam, Marlene Evans artist
Putterman, Florence Grace artist, printmaker
Puzzo, Joseph Anthony, Jr., elementary school educator
Pyle, Robert Milner, Jr., financial consultant
Pytlinski, Jerzy Teodor physicist, educator, research administrator
Pytte, Agnar physicist, retired academic administrator
Qi, Xiujuan mathematician, educator
Qiao, Guilin pharmacologist, medical researcher
Quade, Marshall Ross transportation planner
Quade, Vicki editor, writer, playwright, producer
Quaid, Randy actor
Qualls, Randall Wade music educator
Qualls, Robert L. manufacturing executive, banker, former state official, educator
Quam, Dori music educator, paralegal
Quant, Harold Edward retired financial services company executive, rancher
Quast, Pearl Elizabeth Kolb retired elementary school educator
Quattrone-Carroll, Diane Rose clinical social worker
Quay, Thomas Emery lawyer
Quayle, Jackie M. artist
Queen, Arthur Jerome glass company executive
Quehl, Gary Howard consultant
Quesnel, Gregory L. transportation company executive
Quetglas, Moll Juan plastic and maxillofacial surgeon
Quigley, Leonard Vincent lawyer

Scafuro, Lisa A. writer, journalist, poet
Scala, James health care industry consultant, writer
Scandary, E. Jane special education educator, consultant
Scanlan, John Douglas foreign service officer, former ambassador
Scanlon, Peter Redmond accountant
Scantlan, George William minister
Scarborough, Ann Barlow secondary school educator
Scarborough, Joe former congressman
Scarth, Bruce Worden music educator
Scarwid, Diana Elizabeth actress
Scavone, Edmond retired surgeon
Schacht, Ronald Stuart lawyer
Schadow, Karen E. public speaking trainer/educator
Schadt, James Phillip investment and software executive
Schaechter, Moselio microbiology educator
Schaefer, C. Barry railroad executive, lawyer, investment banker
Schaefer, Christina Kassabian writer, genealogist
Schaefer, Dan L. former congressman
Schaefer, Heinrich C. retired anesthesiologist
Schaefer, William Goerman lawyer
Schaler, Jeffrey Alfred psychologist, educator
Schallert, William Joseph actor
Scharf, William artist
Scharlemann, Robert Paul religious studies educator, clergyman
Schaudies, Jesse P., Jr., business executive
Schauf, Victoria pediatrician, educator, infectious diseases consultant
Schaut, Joseph William retired bank executive
Scheel, Nels Earl finance company executive, accountant
Scheele, Paul Drake former hospital supply corporate executive
Scheirer, Curry M metrologist
Schelar, Virginia Mae chemistry consultant
Schell, Allan Carter retired electrical engineer
Schellenberger, Robert Earl retired management educator and department chairman
Schenck, Jack Lee retired electric utility executive
Schenker, Leo retired utility company executive
Schenkkan, Robert Frederic writer, actor
Schepartz, Alanna biochemist, educator
Scher, Jordan Mayer physician, psychiatrist, drug abuse specialist
Scher, Laura Susan financial company executive
Scherch, Richard Otto minister, consultant
Scherer, James R. research scientist
Scherrer, George M. electrical engineer
Scheuerle, Angela Elizabeth geneticist
Schewe, Donald Bruce archivist, library director
Schexnayder, Brian Edward opera singer, voice educator
Schiaffino, S(ilvio) Stephen retired medical society executive, consultant
Schick, Paul K. hematologist
Schiff, Stacy writer
Schiffer, Claudia model
Schildknecht, Catherine Koch secondary school educator
Schiller, Lawrence Julian writer, motion picture producer, director
Schlagel, Richard H. philosophy educator
Schlegelmilch, Reuben Orville electrical engineer, consultant
Schlensker, Gary Chris landscaping company executive
Schlesser, Ethan Marc music educator, musician
Schlichting, Kimberly Sue psychologist, educator, health facility administrator
Schlossberg, Caroline Bouvier Kennedy (Caroline Kennedy) writer, lawyer
Schlub, Robert Louis plant pathologist, educator
Schmaler, Tracy Alice newspaper journalist, writer
Schmalz, Carl Nelson, Jr., artist, educator, printmaker
Schmandt-Besserat, Denise archaeologist, educator
Schmidt, Harvey Martin economic forecaster, educator, financial consultant
Schmidt, Martha Bubeck social sciences educator
Schmidt, Robert retired mechanics and civil engineering educator
Schmidt, Ruth Ann retired academic administrator
Schmidt, Sheila Elizabeth physician, writer
Schmidt, Sheri Lynn band director
Schmitt, Howard Stanley minister
Schmitz, Dennis Mathew English language educator
Schmoll, Harry F., Jr., lawyer, educator
Schmults, Edward Charles lawyer, corporate and philanthropic administrator, think-tank executive
Schnabel, Gary A. health facility administrator, director
Schneck, Stuart Austin retired neurologist, educator
Schneider, Calvin physician
Schneider, Carolyn Alice Brauch elementary school educator
Schneider, Jan retired obstetrics and gynecology educator
Schneider, Janet M. arts administrator, curator, painter
Schneider, Mary Louise retired elementary education educator
Schneider, Michael H. federal judge
Schneider, Phyllis Leah writer, editor
Schneider, Rita Joyce property management company executive, real estate broker, mortgage broker
Schneider, Sharon M. systems administrator, information technologist
Schnelle, Phillip David electrical engineer, consultant
Schnese, Carsten B. corporate financial executive
Schoen, Allen Harry retired aerospace engineering executive
Schoen, William Jack financier
Schoenberg, April Mindy nursing administrator
Schoenberger, James Edwin retired federal agency administrator
Schoenwald, Maurice Louis retired lawyer
Schoettler, Gail Sinton former ambassador
Schofield, Barbara Curtright retired school administrator
Scholes, Edison Earl army officer
Scholl, Yvette Marguerite elementary school educator, writer
Schollander, Wendell, III, lawyer
Schonberg, Alan Robert management recruiting executive
Schonhorn, Harold chemist, researcher
Schoof, Robert Norman music educator
Schooley, Robert T. medical educator
Schoonover, Alexandra Cheri special education educator
Schor, Laura Strumingher historian
Schorr, Daniel Louis broadcast journalist, author, lecturer
Schowalter, William Raymond college dean, educator
Schrage, Rose educational administrator
Schram, Ronald Byard lawyer
Schramm, Geoffrey Saunders webmaster
Schrand, Richard Henry broadcaster, writer
Schreckinger, Sy Edward advertising executive, consultant
Schreiber, Eileen Sher artist
Schrenko, Linda C. former state agency administrator
Schrier, Morris M. consultant
Schroeder, Gerald Frank state supreme court vice chief justice
Schubert, Barbara Schuele retired performing company executive
Schubert, Helen Celia public relations executive
Schuch, Cynthia Silleck nurse
Schuckman, Gregory A. academic administrator
Schueler, Gerald Joseph technical writer, systems analyst, counselor
Schuelke, John Paul religious organization administrator
Schuiski, Larry Leroy information scientist, consultant
Schulberg, Jay William foundation official
Schulman, Harold obstetrician, gynecologist, perinatologist
Schultz, Albert Barry engineering educator
Schultz, Eileen Hedy graphic designer
Schultz, Louis William retired judge
Schultz, William John artist, educator
Schulz, Lawrence A. lawyer
Schulz, Michael John fire and explosion analyst, consultant
Schulz, Ralph Richard publishing consultant
Schulz, Raymond Alexander medical marketing professional, consultant
Schulz, William Frederick human rights association executive
Schumacher, Cynthia Jo retired elementary and secondary education educator
Schumacher, Philip Gerard fundraising executive
Schunk, Mae Gasparac former state official
Schure, Alexander university chancellor
Schurenberg, Eric magazine editor
Schur Kaufman, Susan retired public affairs consultant
Schurmeier, Harris McIntosh aeronautical engineer
Schuster, Elaine civil rights professional
Schuster, Gary Francis public relations executive
Schutt, Allan Jackson retired medical oncologist
Schutz, Donald Frank geochemist, environmental corporate executive
Schuur, Diane Joan vocalist
Schwab, Eileen Caulfield lawyer, educator
Schwab, John Harris microbiology and immunology educator
Schwantes, Carlos Arnaldo history educator, consultant
Schwartz, Carol Ann investment company executive
Schwartz, Carol Levitt government official
Schwartz, Carolyn Lynn retail executive, musician
Schwartz, Eleanor Brantley academic administrator
Schwartz, John J. association executive, consultant
Schwartz, Lillian Feldman artist, filmmaker, art analyst, writer, nurse
Schwartz, Mark former retail excutive
Schwartz, Peter Isaac poet
Schwartz, Samuel retired chemical company executive, business consultant
Schwartz, Shirley E. chemist, researcher
Schwartz, Stephen Blair retired information industry executive
Schwartz, Stephen Lawrence composer, lyricist
Schwartz, Walter Richard obstetrician/gynecologist, retired
Schwartz, William Lewis retired veterinary pathologist
Schwary, Ronald Louis motion picture producer
Schwarz, Gerard conductor, musician
Schweiker, Richard Schultz trade association executive, former senator, former cabinet secretary
Schweitzer, Christoph Eugen liberal studies educator
Schwerdtner, Frederick Howard lawyer, retired police commander, real estate broker
Schwyn, Charles Edward retired accountant
Sciammarella, Maria Graciela internist, cardiologist
Sciolino, Elaine reporter
Sciorra, Annabella actress
Scipione, Richard Stephen insurance company executive, lawyer, retired
Scofidio, Ricardo artist
Scogin, Troy Pope publishing company executive, accounts executive
Scoles, Clyde Sheldon library director
Scordias, Margaret Ann education educator
Scott, Alice Holly retired librarian
Scott, Catherine Dorothy librarian, information consultant
Scott, Charles David chemical engineer, consultant
Scott, Daniel Lee dean
Scott, Deborah L. costume designer
Scott, Donahue energy executive
Scott, Dorothy writer
Scott, Gloria Randle college president
Scott, Harry Venghette, Jr., choreographer, educator
Scott, Isadore Meyer former energy company executive
Scott, Jacqueline Delmar Parker educational association administrator, business administrator, consultant, fundraiser, educator
Scott, Jane Madeline language educator
Scott, Jeffrey Lyle protective services official
Scott, Justine Ford counselor, educator
Scott, Karen Elizabeth information technology assistant
Scott, Mary Elizabeth administrative educator
Scott, Michael Coleman philosophy educator
Scott, Sandra J. not-for-profit executive
Scott, Sylvia Jane small business owner
Scott, T. Gordon chemistry and math educator, writer
Scruggs, Charles G. editor
Scruggs, Earl Eugene entertainer
Scully, Marlan Orvil physics educator
Sczudlo, Walter Joseph lawyer
Seaden, George civil engineer
Seale, James Millard retired religious organization administrator, clergyman
Seale, John Clement director, cinematographer
Seale, Robert L. former state treasurer
Seamans, Robert Channing, Jr., astronautical engineering educator
Seamans, William writer, commentator, former television and radio journalist
Searcy, Ashburn Pidcock, Sr., anesthesiologist
Searle, Philip Ford banker
Searle, Rodney Newell state legislator, farmer, insurance agent
Searles, Edna Lowe artist, illustrator, composer
Sears, Michael M. former aerospace transportation executive
Sease, Gene Elwood public relations company executive
Seaver, Robert Leslie retired law educator
Sebastian, Peter international affairs consultant, former ambassador
Sebba, Rosangela Yazbec pianist, music educator, theorist
Seccombe, Stephen Dana computer engineer
Sechrist, Chalmers Franklin, Jr., electrical engineering educator
Secor, Harold Edwin retired obstetrician/gynecologist
Seddon, Priscilla Tingey painter
Sedell, James parks director
Sedlacek, Richard Leo retired surgeon
Sedor, Frank A. chemist
Seeds, Sharon Lynn bank processor
Seeger, Leinaala Robinson law librarian, educator
Seelig, Gerard Leo management consultant
Seemann, Rosalie Mary international business and foreign policy association executive
Seff, Richard actor, writer
Segal, Robert S. retail executive
Segel, Karen Lynn Joseph lawyer, taxation specialist
Segesváry, Victor Gyözö retired diplomat
Seggerman, Anne Crellin foundation executive
Sehlaoui, Abdelilah Salim science educator, researcher
Seidel, Frederick Lewis poet
Seidman, Ellen Shapiro lawyer, government official
Seidman, Stephen Benjamin dean, computer science educator
Seifert, George retired professional football coach
Seigel, Stuart Evan retired lawyer
Seigenthaler, John Lawrence retired newspaper executive
Seinfeld, Jerry comedian, actor, television producer, scriptwriter
Seldman, Neil Norman cultural organization administrator
Seliger, Mark Alan photographer
Seligson, Judith artist
Selkowitz, Arthur retired advertising agency executive
Sells, Boake Anthony private investor
Sells, Kevin Dwayne marine engineer
Seltser, Raymond epidemiologist, educator
Semsekwa, Amir A.M.T. Juma management consultant
Senechal, Alice R. federal judge, lawyer
Sener, Joseph Ward, Jr., securities company executive
Sennema, David Carl museum and arts administration consultant
Serdari, Thomaï historian, librarian
Serenbetz, Robert financial planner, retired manufacturing executive
Serig, Daniel art educator, researcher
Serrano, Jorge Luis education educator, writer
Serwatka, Walter Dennis publishing executive
Seshadri, Arathi H. research scientist, educator
Sessions, Bettye Jean humanities educator
Sessions, Pete congressman
Sessums, T. Terrell lawyer
Sestini, Virgil Andrew retired biology educator
Sethi, Sandeep environmental engineer
Setser, Carole Sue retired food science educator
Settles, Jeanne Dobson librarian
Sever, John Louis medical researcher, educator
Severin-Hansen, Jeanne Anne poet
Sewell, Robert Dalton pediatrician
Sexton, Carol Burke consultant
Seymore, James W., Jr., magazine editor
Seymour, Frederick Prescott, Jr., industrial engineer, consultant
Seymour, Joseph John air transportation executive
Seymour, Sloan publishing executive
Sferrazza, Anthony Carl historian, writer
Shabot, Myron Michael surgeon, critical care educator, informaticist
Shacter, James Detmers editor, writer
Shaeffer, John Nees historian, educator
Shaffer, Bernard William mechanical and aerospace engineering educator
Shaffer, Judy Ann educator, data processing professional
Shaffer, Richard James lawyer, former manufacturing company executive
Shaffert, Kurt retired lawyer, chemical engineer
Shagan, Steve screenwriter, novelist, film producer
Shah, Arvind trade consultant, industrial designer
Shah, Nandlal Chimanlal retired physiatrist
Shahied, Ishak I. science educator
Shahon, Susan Valerie marketing director
Shakow, Alexander economist, government official
Shalhoup, Judy Lynn marketing communications executive
Shalikashvili, John Malchase retired military career officer
Shambaugh, Stephen Ward lawyer
Shanahan, Michael George police officer
Shands, Gail Maxine environmental scientist
Shane, Donea Lynne retired nursing educator
Shane, John Marder endocrinologist
Shane, Lawrence Edward music educator
Shank, Maurice Edwin aerospace engineering executive, consultant
Shankar, Gautham associate, financial services & sales trader
Shanks, Ann Zane filmmaker, producer/director, photographer, writer
Shanks, Kathryn Mary health care administrator
Shannon, Margaret T. nursing administrator, educator
Shannon, Mary Lou adult health nursing educator
Shao Collins, Jeannine magazine publisher
Shapira, David S. food products/retail grocery executive
Shapiro, David Benjamin researcher
Shapiro, Edwin Stanley lawyer, judge
Shapiro, Harvey poet
Shapiro, Leo J. social researcher
Shapiro, Mark advertising executive
Shapiro, Richard Charles publishing executive, sales executive, marketing professional
Shapiro, Sumner retired naval officer
Sharick, Merle Dayton, Jr., sales executive
Sharkey, Leonard Arthur automobile company executive
Sharman, William professional basketball team executive
Sharon, Timothy Michael physicist
Sharp, Richard L. retail company executive
Sharp, Timothy Allen editor
Sharp, William J. manufacturing executive
Sharpe, Donald Charles service manager
Sharpe, Sterling former professional football player, sports commentator
Sharpe, William Forsyth economics professor
Shartle, Stanley Musgrave engineering executive, consultant, surveyor
Shashidharan, Kalathil Kungatty emergency physician, internist
Shasteen, Donald Eugene government official
Shatin, Judith music composing educator
Shattuck, Cathie Ann lawyer, former government official
Shattuck, Mayo Adams, III, integrated utility executive
Shattuck, Roger Whitney author, educator
Shaughnessy, Marie Kaneko artist
Shavender, Marilyn Faye elementary school educator
Shaw, Artie musician, writer, lecturer
Shaw, Eleanor Jane newspaper editor
Shaw, Elizabeth Orr retired lawyer
Shaw, Harold (Francis Harold Shaw) retired performing arts administrator
Shaw, Helen Lester Anderson retired dean, nutrition educator, researcher
Shaw, Jack Allen communications company executive
Shaw, John Frederick retired naval officer
Shaw, L. Edward, Jr., retired lawyer
Shaw, Leander Jerry, Jr., retired state supreme court justice
Shaw, Robert Eugene retired minister, administrator
Shaw, Ronald Ahrend physician, educator
Shaw, Talbert O. university president
Shayman, James Alan nephrologist, educator
Shea, Bernard Charles retired pharmaceutical company executive
Shea, Christina former mayor
Shea, Gwyn former secretary of state
Sheaffer, Richard Allen electrical engineer
Sheard, Charles, III, dermatologist
Shearer, Charles Livingston academic administrator
Shearer, Harry Julius screenwriter, director, actor
Shearing, Miriam state supreme court justice
Sheble, Walter Franklin retired lawyer
Sheedy, Patrick Thomas judge
Sheehan, Michael Andrew diplomat
Sheehan, Robert James, II, management and market research consultant
Sheen, Martin (Ramon Estevez) actor
Sheets, Nelda artist
Sheffey, Ruthe Garnet English and humanities educator, speaker
Sheinin, Rose biochemist, educator
Sheldon, Kathleen Eddy historian
Sheldon, Terry Edwin lawyer, business consultant, advisor
Shelley, Lore writer, small business owner, realtor
Shellman-Lucas, Elizabeth C. special education educator, researcher
Shelton, Gail writer
Shelton, Henry H. former chairman of joint chiefs
Shelton, James Douglas banker
Shelton, Stephani broadcast journalist, consultant
Shep, Robert Lee editor, publisher, textile book researcher
Shepard, Roger Newland psychologist, educator
Shepherd, Cybill Lynne actress, singer
Shepherd, Douglas hospital administrator
Shepherd, Mark, Jr., retired electronics company executive
Shepherd, Steven Stewart auditor, consultant
Shepp, Bryan Eugene psychologist, educator
Sheppard, C. James composer, educator
Sher, Leo psychiatrist
Shere, Dennis lawyer, retired publishing executive
Sheridan, Patrick Michael finance company executive, retired
Sheridan, Sonia Landy artist, retired art educator
Sheriff, Seymour retired lawyer
Sherin, Edwin theatrical and film director, actor
Sherling, Fred W. lawyer
Sherman, Francis George Harry advertising agency executive
Sherman, John Foord biomedical consultant
Sherman, Joseph Owen pediatric surgeon
Sherman, Susan Jean writer, educator, editor
Sherrard, James E., III, retired military officer
Sherratt, Gerald Robert retired academic administrator
Sherrer, Charles David college dean, clergyman
Sherrer, Gary former state lieutenant governor, bank executive
Sherrick, Rebecca Louise academic administrator
Sherrill, H. Virgil securities company executive
Sherrill, Thomas Beck former state legislator, financial planner
Sherwin, Stephen A. health products executive
Sherwood, Gloria N. graphic and literary artist, genealogy researcher
Shetty, Mulki Radhakrishna retired oncologist, consultant
Shevlin, Michael W. retired cultural organization administrator
Shi, Xiangyang research scientist
Shick, John Earl retired radiologist
Shickley, Margaret S. librarian
Shields, Brooke Christa Camille actress, model
Shier, Gloria Bulan mathematics professor
Shikuma, Eugene Yujin travel company executive
Shillingsburg, Miriam Jones English educator, academic administrator
Shils, Maurice Edward physiologist, educator, research scientist
Shimoda, Jerry Yasutaka retired national historic park manager
Shindler, Merrill Karsh writer, radio personality
Shindler Price, Sherry A. writer, educator

Sponsler, George Curtis, III, *research administrator, lawyer*
Spoor, James Edward *human resources executive, entrepreneur*
Sprecher, David A. *university administrator, mathematician*
Sprecher, Baron William Gunther *pianist, composer, conductor, diplomat*
Sprince, Leila Joy *librarian*
Springer, Paul David *lawyer, motion picture company executive*
Springer, Robert Dale *retired air force officer, consultant, lecturer*
Sproat, Kezia Vanmeter *communications executive, writer*
Sproull, Lee S. *finance educator*
Sprow, Frank Barker *oil company executive*
Sprung, Arnold *lawyer*
Spurrier, Steve (Steven Orr Spurrier) *former professional football coach*
Squibb, Samuel Dexter *chemistry professor*
Squires, Connie Jo *special education educator*
Sreenivasan, Katepalli Raju *mechanical engineering educator*
Srinivasan, Rangaswamy *chemical physicist*
Srinivasan, Venkataraman *marketing and management educator*
Srivatsan, Tirumalai Srinivas *engineering educator*
Staber, Judy White *writer, director*
Stableford, Karen P. *library and information scientist*
Stadler, Craig Robert *professional golfer*
Stafford, Rebecca *retired academic administrator, sociologist, education consultant*
Stagliano, Vito Alexander *federal agency administrator, utilities executive, writer*
Stahl, David *orchestra and opera conductor*
Stahl, Madonna *retired judge*
Staker, Robert Jackson *judge*
Stallings, Viola Patricia Elizabeth *systems engineer, educational systems specialist, retired information technology manager*
Stallone, Sylvester Enzio *actor, writer, director*
Stallone, Thomas Michael Kearney *clinical psychologist*
Stamaty, Mark Alan *cartoonist, writer, artist*
Stamper, Malcolm Theodore *publishing company executive*
Stanard, Christopher Leon *statistician*
Stancil, Irene Mack *family counselor*
Standifer, Michael *music educator*
Standiford, Natalie Anne *writer*
Stanfill, Dennis Carothers *business executive*
Stanford, Kathleen Theresa *secondary school educator*
Stange, Mary Zeiss *writer, educator*
Stanic, Inja *music educator*
Stanley, George Joel *social services administrator, advocate*
Stanley, Margaret King *performing arts administrator*
Stanley, Marlyse Reed *horse breeder*
Stanley, Myrtle Brooks *minister, educational and religious consultant*
Stanley, Robert Anthony *artist, educator*
Stanley, Scott, Jr., *editor*
Stansell, Ronald Bruce *retired investment banker*
Stanton, John Jeffrey *editor, writer, print and broadcast journalist, government programs director, analyst, professional society administrator*
Stanton, Louis Lee *federal judge*
Stark, Diana *public relations executive*
Stark, Nellie May *forester, ecologist, educator*
Starks, Kelly George *systems engineer, consultant*
Starkweather, Frederick Thomas *retired data processing executive*
Starr, Arnold *neurologist, educator*
Starr, Leon *retired chemical research company executive*
Stash, Susan Michele *critical care nurse*
Staton, Johanna Bilbo *editor, writer*
Stauderman, Albert Philip, Jr., *media consultant*
Stauffer, Stanley Howard *retired newspaper and broadcasting executive*
Stavely, Keith Williams Fitzgerald *librarian*
Stavrev, Krassimir K. *chemist, researcher*
Stavroulakis, Anthea Merrie *biology professor*
Steadman, David Wilton *retired museum official, church deacon*
Stearns, Robert Leland *curator*
Stearns, Stewart Warren *charitable association executive*
Stecich, Rita Louise *secondary school educator*
Steck, Warren Franklin *retired chemical company executive, biochemist*
Steel, Kuniko June *retired artist*
Steele, Dale F. *women's healthcare company executive*
Steelman, Deborah Macon *pharmaceutical consultant*
Steen, Carlton Duane *private investor, retired food products executive*
Stefani, Gwen Renee *musician*
Steffen, Konrad *geography educator*
Steffensen, Dwight A. *former medical products and data processing services executive*
Steffy, Marion Nancy *state agency administrator*
Stefko, Joseph V. *government agency administrator*
Stein, Anthony C. *medical educator, researcher*
Stein, Bennett Mueller *neurosurgeon*
Stein, Paul David *cardiologist*
Stein, Stanley Richard *lawyer, food service executive*
Steinke, Greg A *music educator, administrator, composer, oboist*
Steinman, Theodore Irving *nephrologist, educator*
Stellar, Arthur Wayne *educational administrator*
Stemberg, Thomas George *retail office supply store executive*
Stempel, Robert C. *automobile manufacturing company executive*
Stendahl, Brita Kristina *humanities educator, social studies educator*
Stendahl, Krister *retired bishop*
Stengel, Ronald Francis *management consultant*
Stenitzer, George Ignatius *corporate communications executive*
Stennett, William Clinton (Clint Stennett) *television station executive, state legislator*
Stepak, Asa Martin *writer, linguist*
Stepanski, Anthony Francis, Jr., *computer software company executive*
Stephen, Michael *psychologist*
Stephens, Brooke *financial commentator, writer*
Stephens, Donald R(ichards) *investor*
Stephens, Edward Carl *communications educator, writer*
Stephens, Elton Bryson *bank executive, service and manufacturing company executive*
Stephenson, Herman Howard *retired banker*
Stephenson, Toni Edwards *publishing executive, investment management executive, communications executive*
Steptoe, Mary Lou *lawyer*
Stern, Arthur Paul *electronics company executive*
Stern, Daniel *author, executive, educator*
Stern, Marilyn *photographer, writer, picture editor*
Sternbach, Nancy Saporta *language educator, researcher*
Sternberg, Jeffrey *research manager*
Sternhagen, Frances *actress*
Stettner, Jerald W. *retail drugs stores executive*
Stevens, Berton Louis, Jr., *data processing manager*
Stevens, Connie *actress, singer*
Stevens, Kenneth Allen *retired defense department worker*
Stevens, Linda Doreen *intensive care nurse*
Stevens, May *artist*
Stevens, Robert J. *aerospace transportation executive*
Stevens, Shane *novelist*
Stevens, Sheila Maureen *retired teachers union administrator*
Stevens, Warren *actor*
Stevenson, Paul Michael *physics professor, researcher*
Stever, Horton Guyford *aerospace scientist and engineer, educator, consultant*
Stewart, Arthur Irving, III, (Art Stewart) *management consultant*
Stewart, Carleton M. *bank executive, director*
Stewart, Charles Todd, Jr., *retired economist*
Stewart, Dorothy K. *librarian*
Stewart, Dorothy Mary Hanton *literature and writing educator*
Stewart, Gordon Curran *association executive*
Stewart, Joan Hinde *academic administrator*
Stewart, John Wray Black *college dean*
Stewart, Joseph Turner, Jr., *retired pharmaceutical company executive*
Stewart, Kordell *professional football player*
Stewart, Lucille Marie *retired special education educator*
Stewart, Marsha Beach *performing arts educator*
Stewart, Peter Beaufort *retired beverage company executive*
Stewart, Richard Alfred *business executive*
Stewart, Robert Gordon *former museum curator*
Stewart, Thomas Clifford *trading and investment company executive*
Stewart, Thomas James, Jr., *baritone*
Stickle, David Walter *microbiologist*
Stickles, Bonnie Jean *retired nurse*
Stickney, Jessica *former state legislator*
Stickney, John Moore *lawyer*
Stickney, Robert Roy *fisheries educator*
Stief, Louis John *chemist*
Stiefel, Linda Shields *lawyer*
Stiff, Robert Martin *newspaper editor*
Stiffler, Jack Justin *electrical engineer*
Stiles, Thomas Beveridge, II, *retired investment banking executive*
Stiles, Virginia Ford *data processing executive, poet*
Stiller, Ben *actor, director*
Stiller, Jerry *actor*
Stillings, Dennis Otto *research association administrator, consultant*
Stillman, Richard Joseph *retired army officer, consultant, publisher, writer*
Stinchfield, John Edward *lawyer*
Stine, R(obert) L(awrence) *children's book author*
Stingley, Kristi Jo *writer*
Stinsmuehlen-Amend, Susan *artist*
Stinson, Melanie A *freelance/self-employed writer*
Stiritz, William P. *food company executive*
Stockar, Helena Marie Magdalena *artist*
Stocker, Gregg *quality assurance professional, writer*
Stockton, John Houston *retired professional basketball player*
Stoddard, M. Anita *psychiatric nurse*
Stoesen, Alexander Rudolph *retired history educator*
Stofferson, Terry Lee *financial officer*
Stoiber, Carlton Ray *nuclear law consultant, retired federal official*
Stokstad, Marilyn Jane *art history educator, curator*
Stolarik, M. Mark *history professor*
Stollerman, Gene Howard *physician, educator*
Stolley, Richard Brockway *journalist*
Stoltman, Claudia Jill *performing arts educator*
Stomfay-Stitz, Aline Maria *education educator*
Stone, Andrew Grover *lawyer*
Stone, Dee Wallace *actress*
Stone, Donald Raymond *lawyer*
Stone, Edward Herman *lawyer*
Stone, Glenda Lee *librarian, genealogist*
Stone, James Howard *management consultant*
Stone, James Robert *surgeon*
Stone, John Timothy, Jr., *writer*
Stonnington, Henry Herbert *physician, medical executive, educator*
Stookey, Noel Paul *folksinger, composer*
Stopp, Donald L. *retired educator, retired business owner*
Storey, Gregory Dean *publisher, editor*
Stott, Don S. *precious metals products executive*
Stotter, Harry Shelton *banker, lawyer, savings and loan association executive*
Stovall, Julia Connor *industrial engineer*
Stover, Kenneth Alan *sales executive*
Stoytcheva, Lilia Stefanova *concert pianist, educator*
Strain, James Ellsworth *pediatrician, retired association administrator*
Strand, Mark *poet*
Strandberg, John David *comparative pathologist*
Strasser, Gabor *management consultant*
Stratman, Joseph Lee *retired petroleum refining company executive, consultant, chemical engineer*
Stratton, Mariann *retired naval nursing administrator*
Stratton, Robert *retired electronics executive*
Straub, Linda Catherine *poet*
Straub, Peter Francis *novelist*
Straulman, Ann Therese *retired English language educator*
Straus, Laura *photographer, art association administrator*
Straus, Leon Stephan *physicist*
Strauss, Dorothy Brandfon *marriage and family therapist*
Stream, Arnold Crager *lawyer, writer*
Streb, Paul Gerard *arbitrator*
Street, John Charles *linguistics educator*
Street, John F. *mayor*
Street, Picabo *Olympic athlete*
Streicher, James Franklin *lawyer*
Strength, Janis Grace *management executive, educator*
Strider, Marjorie Virginia *artist, educator*
Strifler, Stanley *former business solutions executive*
Striker, Cecil Leopold *archaeologist, educator*
Stringer, C. Vivian *college basketball coach*
Stringer, Mary Evelyn *art historian, educator*
Stringfield, Sherry *actress*
Strock, Herbert Leonard *motion picture producer, director, editor, writer*
Strombom, David Glen *designer*
Stromquist, Kenneth James, Jr., *pilot, retired military officer*
Stronach, Belinda *former retail executive*
Strong, John David *insurance company executive*
Strong, Virginia Wilkerson *freelance writer, former educator*
Strongin, Jonathan David *physician*
Strothman, James Edward *editor*
Stroud, Betsy Dillard *artist*
Stroup, Stanley Stephenson *lawyer, educator*
Strouse, Jean *writer*
Strouth, Baron Howard Steven *geologist, mining engineer*
Struble, Susan C. *artist, volunteer art therapist*
Struhl, Stanley Frederick *real estate developer*
Strukoff, Rudolf Stephen *retired music educator*
Strutton, Larry D. *former newspaper executive*
Stuart, Gerard William, Jr., *investment company executive, city official*
Stuart, Joseph Martin *art museum administrator*
Stuart, Nancy Rubin (Nancy Zimman Stetson) *journalist, author, writer, producer*
Stubbs, Gerald *biochemist, educator*
Stubbs, Kendon Lee *retired librarian*
Stucky, Nancy L. *special education educator*
Studer, Carol A. *creative director, graphic designer, photographer, consultant*
Studer, Jeannette R. *dean*
Studness, Charles Michael *economist*
Stufano, Thomas Joseph *criminologist, author, inventor*
Stukenholtz, Larry Lee *music educator*
Stults, Walter Black *management consultant, former trade organization executive*
Stumpe, Warren Robert *county official, retired scientific, engineering and technical services company executive*
Stumpf, Heinrich J. *psychometrician, research consultant*
Sturges, John Siebrand *management consultant*
Stutz, Pearl Hewlett *retired photojournalist*
Stutzman, Sandra Louise *advanced nurse practitioner*
Styler, Anda Jasamine *artist, educator*
Styne, Marlys Marshall *retired English educator*
Styron, William *writer*
Su, Hung-Jue *mechanical engineer, educator*
Suarez, Michael Anthony *civil engineer, consultant*
Suber, Robin Hall *former medical and surgical nurse*
Sucher, Cheryl Pearl *writer*
Sudanowicz, Elaine Marie *government executive*
Sudarsky, Jerry M. *industrialist*
Suelto, Consuelo Quilao *retired nursing educator*
Sueltz, Patricia C. *computer company executive*
Suissa, David *advertising executive*
Sukopp, Karl Martin *sculptor, painter, graphic artist*
Sulc, Jean Luena (Jean L. Mestres) *lobbyist, consultant*
Sullivan, Charles *dean, educator, author*
Sullivan, Colleen Anne *anesthesiologist, educator*
Sullivan, Daniel Joseph *theater critic*
Sullivan, Eugene John Joseph *manufacturing executive, director*
Sullivan, G. Craig *household products executive*
Sullivan, George Edward *writer*
Sullivan, John Dominic *theater producer, writer*
Sullivan, John Louis, Jr., *retired search company executive*
Sullivan, Mary Ann *artist*
Sullivan, Mary Rose *English language educator*
Sullivan, Nicholas G. *science educator, speleologist*
Sultan, Cornel *research scientist, consultant*
Summerall, Pat (George Allan Summerall) *sportscaster*
Summerfield, John Robert *textile curator*
Summers, Cathleen Ann *film producer*
Summers, David Stewart *neurologist, consultant*
Summers, Lorraine Dey Schaeffer *retired librarian*
Summers, Ryan Charles *music educator*
Summitt, Patricia Head *basketball coach*
Sumner, William Marvin *anthropology and archaeology educator*
Sun, Chenghua *composer, music educator*
Sun, Zuo *research scientist, consultant*
Sund, Jeffrey Owen *retired publishing company executive*
Sundaramurthy, Chamundeswari *finance educator, educator*
Sunderman, Duane Neuman *chemist, research institute executive*
Suppa-Friedman, Janice DeStefano *secondary school educator, consultant*
Suppes, Patrick *philosophy, statistics, psychology educator*
Suprun, Harry Zvi *pathologist*
Suput, Ray Radoslav *librarian*
Suri, Roland Erwin *neuroscientist*
Surles, Richard Hurlbut, Jr., *retired law librarian*
Surplus, Robert Wilbur *retired music educator*
Suskind, Ronald Steven *journalist*
Sussman, Barry *author, public opinion analyst and pollster, journalist*
Sussman, Howard Sivin *lawyer*
Sustendal, Diane *media executive*
Sutherland, Maria T. *marketing professional, communications executive*
Suthers, Hannah Louise Bonsey *biologist, consultant*
Sutowski, Thor Brian *choreographer, educator*
Sutter, Laurence Brener *lawyer*
Sutton, Dolores *actress, writer*
Sutton, Julia *musicologist, dance historian*
Sutton-Straus, Joan M. *journalist*
Sveilich, Carol Joyce *writer*
Svensson, Lars Georg *cardiovascular and thoracic surgeon*
Swacker, Frank Warren *lawyer*
Swalm, Thomas Sterling *aerospace executive, retired military officer*
Swaner-Smoot, Paula Margetts *clinical psychologist*
Swansen, Larry *actor, playwright*
Swanson, Lauren A. *consultant, entrepreneur, educator, researcher*
Swanstrom, Thomas Evan *economist*
Swartz, Jon David *psychologist, educator*
Swartz, Julianne *artist*
Sweeney, Deidre Ann *lawyer*
Sweeney, Gerard H. *real estate company executive*
Sweet, Philip W. K., Jr., *former banker*
Sweet, Robert Workman *federal judge*
Sweetland, Loraine Fern *librarian, educator*
Swensen, Mary Jean Hamilton *graphic artist*
Swenson, James Reed *physician, educator*
Swett, Richard Nelson (Dick Swett) *diplomat, former congressman*
Swiecicki, Martin *retired neurosurgeon*
Swift, Jane Maria *former governor*
Swig, Roselyne Chroman *community consultant*
Swiger, Mark *social studies educator*
Swinburn, Charles *rail transportation executive*
Swinehart, David *music educator*
Switzer, Maurice Harold *journalist*
Switzer, Toccoa *artist*
Swoap, David Bruce *government affairs consultant*
Swope, Donald Downey *retired banker*
Sydnor, Edgar Starke *lawyer*
Sykes, Gregory Edward *insurance company executive, writer*
Sykes, Sam Jones *French educator*
Sykora, Barbara Zwach *state legislator*
Symchowicz, Samson *retired biochemist*
Symmes, Daniel Leslie *technology executive, producer, director*
Szabo, Yurika Lin *marketing executive, advertising executive*
Sze, Sarah *sculptor*
Szuch, Clyde Andrew *lawyer*
Szydlowski, Ralph *retired die maker, formability consultant*
Szyszka, Roswita Evelyn *artist*
Tabussi, Stephen John *banker*
Tacha, Deanell Reece *federal judge*
Tachi, Douglas Paul *architect, interior designer*
Tack, Theresa Rose *women's health nurse*
Tackett, Viti Lee *writer*
Taddei, Lois Annette Magowan *artist, decorator*
Taft, Nellie Leaman *artist*
Tagiuri, Consuelo Keller *child psychiatrist, educator*
Tagliente, Josephine Marlene *artist*
Tague, John P *air transportation executive*
Tainatonga, Rosie R. *former director of education*
Taishoff, Lawrence Bruce *publishing company executive*
Takanishi, Ruby N. *foundation administrator, researcher*
Talbot, Nina Isadora *artist, educator*
Talbott, John *mayor*
Taliaferro, Theresa Lynn *reporter, educator, artist*
Talkington, William Ale *retired publishing company executive*
Tall, Sonia Terry *humanities educator, researcher*
Tallerico, Delma Dolores *elementary school educator*
Tallet, Jorge Antonio *philosopher, writer*
Tallett, Elizabeth Edith *biopharmaceutical company executive*
Talley, Robert Morrell *aerospace company executive*
Talmage, David Wilson *microbiology and medical educator, physician, former university administrator*
Talty, Kathryn Melene *women's health nurse, artist*
Tambs, Lewis Arthur *diplomat, historian, educator*
Tamimi, Maher M. *language educator*
Tan, Guolong *research scientist*
Tan, Hui Qian *computer science and civil engineering educator*
Tan, Marianne Mee-Ryung *pharmacist, medical liaison, consultant*
Tanaka, J(eannie) E. *lawyer*
Tanaka, Kay *genetics educator*
Tandler, Bernard *cell biology educator*
Tane, Susan Jaffe *retired manufacturing company executive*
Tanenbaum, Jay Harvey *lawyer*
Tank, Gerhard Willi *obstetrician and gynecologist*
Tannenberg, Dieter E. A. *retired manufacturing company executive*
Tanner, Eric Benson *lawyer*
Tanner, Laurel Nan *education educator*
Tanner, Lynn *actress*
Tanner, Peggy *retired nurse*
Taplett, Lloyd Melvin *human resources specialist, consultant*
Tapley, James Leroy *retired lawyer, railway corporation executive*
Tarantino, David A., Jr., *military officer, emergency physician*
Taranto, Maria Antoinette *psychology researcher and educator*
Tarbuck, Barbara Joan *actress*
Taren, James Arthur *neurosurgeon, educator*
Tarjan, Robert Wegg *retired information services executive, part-time math teacher*
Tarr, Curtis W. *business executive*
Tarrance, Vernon Lance, Jr., *public opinion research executive*
Tarses, Jamie *television producer, former television network executive*
Tartaro, Christine *criminologist, educator*
Tassos, Alice Crowley *writer*
Tate, Fran M. *small business owner*
Tate, Sonsyrea *journalist, writer*
Tatgenhorst, Robert (Charles Tatgenhorst) *lawyer, educator*
Tatlock, Anne M. *trust company executive*
Tatum, Valorie *elementary school educator, pharmacist*
Taubman, A. Alfred *real estate developer*
Tauscher, Ellen O. *congresswoman*
Tavalin, Fern *educational consultant*
Tavares, Charleta B. *former state legislator*
Tavares, Clara *writer*
Tayler, Irene *English literature educator*
Taylor, Anthony Baldwin *civil engineer*
Taylor, Billy (William Edward Taylor) *jazz musician*
Taylor, Charles Henry *psychoanalyst, educator*

Varga, Jeanne-Marie *women's healthcare company executive*
Vargo, Merry Elizabeth *secondary school educator*
Varro, Barbara Joan *retired editor*
Vasholz, Lothar Alfred *retired insurance company executive*
Vasily, John Timothy *information systems executive, state government official*
Vasko, Peter Theodore Frederick *priest*
Vaughan, John Charles, III, *horticultural products executive*
Vaughan, Samuel Snell *editor, author, publisher*
Vecci, Raymond Joseph *airline industry consultant*
Vedder, Robert Allen *publishing executive*
Vellenga, Kathleen Osborne *retired state legislator*
Vennat, Michel *former bank executive, lawyer*
Vér, István László *acoustical engineer, consultant*
Vera Negron, Sandra *literature educator, translator*
Verbov, Lev Falkovich *metallurgical engineer, writer, translator*
Verderber, Joseph Anthony *capital equipment company executive*
Verdery, David Norwood *broadcast programming executive*
Verdier, Quentin Roosevelt *human resources consultant*
Verfaillie, Hendrik A. *food products company executive*
Vergara, Camilo José *photographer*
Verma, Devesh *pharmaceutical executive, researcher*
Vernazza, Trish Brown (Trish Eileen Brown) *visual artist, art therapist, sculptor*
Verniero, Peter G. *former state supreme court justice*
Vernon, Carl Atlee, Jr., *retired wholesale food distributor executive*
Veronis, George *geophysicist, educator*
Versch, Esther Marie *artist*
Veseth, Michael Aaron *economics professor*
Vessey, John William, Jr., *army officer*
Vest, Charles Marstiller *retired academic administrator*
Vestal, Marilyn Anita *writer, researcher, educator*
Vetter, David R. *lawyer, data processing executive*
Veyna, Adrienne Marie *exercise specialist*
Vichiola, Christopher Michael *educator, writer*
Vickers, George Ross *non-profit organization executive, sociology educator*
Vickers, Mark Stephen *business educator, travel industry executive, sculptor, painter*
Vickers, Stanley *biochemical pharmacologist*
Vickery, Byrdean Eyvonne Hughes (Mrs. Charles Everett Vickery Jr.) *retired library services administrator*
Victoria, Christa *composer, director*
Vidovich, Mark A. *paper products executive*
Viest, Ivan M(iroslav) *consulting structural engineer*
Vigil, David Charles *lawyer*
Vila, Adis Maria *lawyer, business and government exective, academic administrator, educator*
Villaire, Holly Hennen Hood *theater producer, director, actress, educator*
Villella, Edward Joseph *ballet dancer, educator, choreographer, artistic director, performing arts administrator*
Villforth, John Carl *engineer, health physicist*
Vince, April Renee *social worker*
Vincent, Charles Eagar, Jr., *sports columnist*
Vincent, Hal Wellman *marine corps officer, investor*
Vincent, James Louis *biotechnology company executive*
Vincent, John K. *prosecutor*
Vinet, Luc *physicist*
Vinson, Beth W. *systems analyst, web site designer*
Vinson, Kevin Raymond *music educator*
Violenus, Agnes A. *retired school system administrator*
Violet, Woodrow Wilson, Jr., *retired chiropractor*
Viorst, Judith Stahl *writer*
Viorst, Milton *writer*
Virkhaus, Taavo *symphony orchestra conductor*
Viscardi, Peter G. *risk management and environmental affairs executive*
Viscoli, David Anthony *music educator*
Visocki, Nancy Gayle *information services consultant*
Vita, Steven *poet*
Vitale, David J. *former banker*
Vitt, David Aaron *medical manufacturing company executive*
Vittetoe, Marie Clare *retired clinical laboratory science educator*
Vlachos, Peter George *economics professor*
Vlazny, John George *bishop*
Vo, Nghia Van *materials scientist, electrical engineer*
Voell, Richard Allen *retired private investor*
Vogel, Annette-Barbara *violinist, educator*
Vogel, Conrad David *artist*
Vogel, H. Victoria *psychotherapist, trauma, post-traumatic stress disorder and addiction recovery counselor and educator, author*
Vogel, William Dickerman *financial services executive*
Vohs, James Arthur *health care program executive*
Voight, Jon *actor*
Voigt, Cynthia *writer*
Voigt, Heidi M. *music educator*
Voketaitis, Arnold Matthew *bass-baritone, educator*
Volcker, Paul A. *economist*
Voldman, Steven Howard *electrical engineer*
Volk, Patricia Gay *fiction writer, essayist*
Volkhardt, John Malcolm *food company executive*
Volkman, Alvin *retired physician, research scientist, educator*
Volkmann, Frances Cooper *psychologist, educator*
Volpe, Edmond L(oris) *college president*
Von Brandenstein, Patrizia *production designer*
Vonderbrink, Gerald William *retired academic administrator, property manager*
von Furstenberg, Betsy *actress, writer*
Von Furstenberg, Diane Simone Michelle *fashion designer, writer, entrepreneur*
Von Gizycki, Alkistis Romanoff *research scientist, educator, scholar, writer*
von Hoffman, Nicholas *writer, former journalist*
von Kaenel, Howard J. *army officer*
von Sauers, Joseph F. *lawyer*
Vook, Frederick Ludwig *physicist, consultant*
Voorhees, James Dayton, Jr., *lawyer*
Voss, Omer Gerald *truck company executive*
Vralsted, Leann Christine *music educator*
Vu, Joseph Duong *financial educator*
Vucanovich, Barbara Farrell *retired congressman*
Vydareny, Kay Herzog *radiologist, medical educator*
Waage, Sissel *environmental services administrator*
Wachob, Tom Webb, Jr., *retired obstetrician-gynecologist*
Wachtell, Esther *non-profit management executive, consultant*
Waddle, John Frederick *former retail chain executive*
Wade, David Stuart *surgeon*
Wade, June Booth *secondary school educator*
Wadleigh, Kevin Richard *mathematician*
Wadley, M. Richard *consumer products executive*
Wadsworth, Jacqueline Dorèt *private investor*
Waggener, Theryn Lee *retired law enforcement professional*
Wagman, Robert John *journalist, writer*
Wagner, Arthur Ward, Jr., *lawyer*
Wagner, Julia A(nne) *retired editor*
Wagner, Marilyn Faith *retired elementary school educator*
Wagner, Melinda *musician, composer*
Wagner, Richard *athletics consultant, former baseball team executive*
Wagner, Thomas Joseph *lawyer, insurance company executive*
Wagoner, Geraldine Vander Pol *music educator*
Wahl, Floyd Michael *geologist*
Wahweah, Linda McNeil *insurance agent, writer*
Wain, Christopher Henry Fairfax Moresby *retired actuary, insurance and investment consultant*
Wald, Francine Joy Weintraub (Mrs. Bernard J. Wald) *physicist, academic administrator*
Walden, Joseph Lawrence *career officer*
Walden, Philip Michael *recording company executive, publishing company executive*
Waldmeir, Peter Nielsen *journalist*
Waldon, Alton Ronald, Jr., *judge*
Walken, Christopher *actor*
Walker, Clarence Eugene *psychology educator*
Walker, Craig Michael *lawyer*
Walker, Fred Elmer *broadcast executive*
Walker, George Herbert, III, *ambassador, former investment banking company executive*
Walker, Gloria Lee *training services executive*
Walker, Gordon Davies *former government official, writer, lecturer, consultant*
Walker, Henry Gilbert *health care executive, consultant*
Walker, James Steven *osteopath, emergency physician*
Walker, Juanita Moffett *retired elementary school educator*
Walker, Leroy Tashreau *university chancellor, coach*
Walker, Mark A. *lawyer*
Walker, Nathan C. *foundation administrator, minister, educator*
Walker, R. Tracy *retired personnel director*
Walker, Richard Henry *lawyer*
Walker, Roslyn Adele *retired museum director*
Walker-Williams, Hope Denise *administrator, business consultant*
Walkup, Mary Roe *state legislator*
Wall, Carolyn Raimondi *communications executive*
Wall, Frederick Theodore *retired chemistry educator*
Wall, Jeff F. *urban planner*
Wall, M. Danny *financial services company executive*
Wall, Mark Emanuel *banker, engineer, consultant*
Wallace, Arthur, Jr., *retired college dean*
Wallace, Edwin Ruthven, IV, *psychiatrist, neuropsychiatrist psychotherapist*
Wallace, F. Blake *aerospace executive, mechanical engineer*
Wallace, Guy William *management consultant*
Wallace, Jane House *retired geologist*
Wallace, Matthew Edward *actor*
Wallace, Michele *writer, educator*
Wallace, Robert Earl *geologist*
Wallace, Stewart S. *career military officer*
Wallach, Patricia *councilwoman, retired mayor*
Waller, Jim D. *former holding company executive*
Wallerstein, Judith Saretsky *psychologist, researcher*
Wallington, Patricia McDevitt *computer company executive*
Wallis, Diana Lynn *artistic director*
Wallis, John James (Jimmy Wallis) *comedian, impressionist, ventriloquist, comedy writer, Internet site designer*
Wallison, Frieda K. *lawyer*
Wallman, Richard F. *electronics company executive*
Walls, Carmage Lee, Jr., *newspaper publisher/executive, consultant*
Walner, Robert Joel *lawyer*
Walsh, Diane *pianist*
Walsh, Dolores Ann Gonczo (Lorry Walsh) *special education educator*
Walsh, Gerry O'Malley *lawyer*
Walsh, John E., Jr., *business educator, consultant*
Walsh, Juanita *theater educator, actress*
Walsh, M. Emmet *actor*
Walsh, Nan *artist, painter, sculptor, consultant*
Walsh, Roger N. *psychiatry, philosophy, anthropology and religious studies educator*
Walsh, William Albert *management consultant, former naval officer*
Walston, Lola Inge *dietitian*
Walter, J. Jackson *consultant*
Walters, Bette Jean *lawyer*
Walters, Matthew Paul *recreational facility executive, consultant*
Walters-Lucy, Jean Marie *personal growth educator, consultant*
Waltner, Beverly Ruland *artist*
Walton, Alice L. *bank executive*
Walton, Harold Vincent *former agricultural engineering educator, academic administrator*
Waltrip, Darrell Lee *race car driver*
Waltz, Alan Kent *clergyman, denominational executive*
Wambaugh, Joseph A., Jr., *author*
Wang, Allan Xu Hui *physician*
Wang, Chen-ku *retired library director*
Wang, Gaofeng *engineer, educator*
Wang, Leon Ru-Liang *civil engineer, educator*
Wang, Nancy *pathologist, educator*
Wang, Qigui *materials engineer, researcher*
Wang, Qin *computer engineer, researcher*
Wang, Qin *medical educator*
Wang, Xi Cheng (David Wang) *mechanical engineer*
Wang, Zhishun *biomedical engineer, consultant*
Wantland, William Charles *retired bishop, lawyer*
Warach, Marie *artist*
Warberg, Willetta *concert pianist, writer, piano educator*
Warch, Richard *former academic administrator*
Ward, Albert Eugene *archaeologist, ethnohistorian, research center executive*
Ward (Bailey), Daisy Dale *writer*
Ward, Jacqueline Selma Sklar *mathematician, educator*
Ward, Jeannette Poole *retired psychologist, educator*
Ward, JoAnn Boettner *convention and tourist bureau administrator*
Ward, Nari *sculptor*
Ward, Thomas *food products executive*
Warder, Richard Currey, Jr., *dean, mechanical aerospace engineering educator*
Wardrop, Richard M., Jr., *former steel holding company executive*
Ware, Robert K. *Internet company executive, researcher, web programmer*
Warheit, Peter S. *anesthesiologist*
Warne, William Robert *economist*
Warner, Emily Hanrahan Howell *retired pilot, writer*
Warner, Walter D. *corporate executive, director*
Warren, Alice Louise *artist*
Warren, John William *professional society administrator*
Warshawsky, Isidore *physicist, consultant*
Wartluft, David Jonathan *retired librarian, minister*
Washburn, Donald Arthur *transportation executive, investor*
Washington, Anthony Nathaniel *mechanical engineer*
Washington, Charles Henderson *laser systems designer, consultant*
Washington, Denzel *actor*
Washington, Donna Janel *engineer*
Wasmuth, Carl Erwin *physician, lawyer*
Wasserheit, Judith N. *social services administrator*
Wasserman, Gerald Steward *psychobiology educator*
Wasserman, Helene Waltman *art dealer, artist*
Wasserstein, Bernard Mano Julius *historian*
Wasson, James Walter *aircraft electronics manufacturing company executive*
Watanabe, Kyoichi A(loysius) *chemist, researcher, pharmacology educator*
Waters, Betty Lou *newspaper reporter, writer*
Waters, William Carter, III, *retired internist, educator*
Watkins, Ann Esther *mathematics professor*
Watkins, Dean Allen *electronics executive, educator*
Watkins, Esther Sherrod *secondary school educator, school librarian*
Watkins, James David *federal official, military officer*
Watkins, Wesley Wade *retired congressman*
Watring, Watson Glenn *retired gynecologic oncologist, educator*
Watson, Donald Charles *cardiothoracic surgeon, educator*
Watson, George Henry, Jr., *broadcaster, journalist*
Watson, George W. *energy executive*
Watson, H. Mitchell, Jr., *business software company executive*
Watson, Kathy *political organization administrator*
Wattenberg, Albert *physicist, researcher*
Watts, Ginny (Virginia C. Watts) *artist*
Watts, J. C., Jr., *former congressman, retired professional football player*
Watts, John Ransford *university administrator*
Watts, Karen Southall *management consultant*
Watts, Mary Ann *retired elementary education educator*
Waud, Roger Neil *economist, educator*
Wavle, James Edward, Jr., *pharmaceutical company executive, lawyer*
Waxman, Ronald *computer engineer*
Waxman, Seth Paul *lawyer*
Way, Jacob Edson, III, *museum director, realtor*
Wayans, Keenen Ivory *actor, producer*
Wayne, Lynn *photographer, writer*
Wearn, Wilson Cannon *retired media executive*
Weathersby, George Byron *business executive*
Weathersby, Kathryn *historian*
Weatherstone, Sir Dennis *bank executive*
Weaver, Agnes Jin Ai *medical/surgical nurse*
Weaver, Barbara Frances *librarian, consultant*
Weaver, Charles Horace *humanities educator*
Weaver, Franklin Thomas *retired newspaper executive*
Weaver, Gail Elaine *religious organization administrator, tax specialist, consultant*
Weaver, Howard C. *newspaper executive*
Weaver, Karen Lynn *writer, performing arts educator, actress, poet*
Weaver, Leah Ann *journalist, speech writer*
Weaver, William Charles *retired industrial executive*
Weaver, William Schildecker *retired electric power industry executive*
Webb, Doris McIntosh *human resources specialist*
Webb, Martha Jeanne *author, speaker, film producer*
Webb, O. Glenn *retired farm supplies company executive*
Webb, Pharron R. *counselor, secondary school educator*
Webb, Robert David *school system administrator*
Webb, Wellington Edward *political organization administrator, former mayor*
Webb, William Timothy *mobile communications professional*
Weber, Alvin Julian, III, *radiologist*
Weber, Arthur *magazine executive*
Weber, Gloria Richie *retired minister, retired state legislator*
Weber, Heidi Amelia-Anne *historian, educator*
Weber, John Walter *insurance company executive*
Weber, Kenneth J. *hotel executive*
Weber, Lavern John *retired marine science administrator, educator*
Weber, Mary Ellen Healy *economist*
Weber, Ralph Edward *history professor*
Webster, John Daniel *corporate financial executive*
Webster, Robert Kenly *lawyer*
Wechsler, Sergio *automotive executive, consultant*
Weckesser, Ernest Prosper, Jr., *publisher, educator*
Weddle, Laura Mildred Thomas *retired language educator*
Wedesweiler (Raye), Cheryl *writer*
Weekley, David *real estate developer*
Weeks, Clifford Myers *musician, educational administrator*
Wegman, William George *artist*
Wehling, Robert Louis *retired household products company executive*
Wei, John Hua-Fang *engineering executive*
Wei, Qingyi *cancer research educator*
Weiden, Paul Lincoln *cancer researcher, oncologist, educator*
Weigensberg, Irving Joseph *radiation oncologist*
Weihmuller, Patricia Ann *retired minister, artist*
Weil, Barry *theater director, entertainer*
Weil, John David *financial executive*
Weil, Peter Henry *lawyer*
Weil, Randolph Allen *engineering executive*
Weil, Richard, III, *surgeon, medical educator*
Weil, Rolf Alfred *economist, university president emeritus*
Weil, Thomas P. *health services consultant*
Weiland, Charles Hankes *lawyer*
Weimann, Robert Bruce *retired surgeon*
Weinberg, Steven *physics educator*
Weinberger, Arnold *retired electrical engineer*
Weiner, Jonathan David *writer*
Weiner, Richard *public relations executive*
Weiner, Sharon Rose *public relations executive*
Weiner-Heuschkel, Sydell *theater educator*
Weingarten, Joseph Leonard *aerospace engineer*
Weinhauer, William Gillette *retired bishop*
Weinkauf, Mary Louise Stanley *clergywoman*
Weinman, Irving *writer*
Weinmann, Richard Adrian *lawyer, arbitrator*
Weinreb, Michael Philip *physicist*
Weinstein, Marta *packaging services company executive*
Weinstein, Steven Wayne *lawyer*
Weintraub, Sam *reading educator*
Weir, Bryce Keith Alexander *neurosurgeon, neurologist, educator*
Weir, Morton Webster *retired academic administrator, educator*
Weis, Margaret Edith *writer, editor*
Weisberg, David Charles *lawyer*
Weisbuch, Robert Alan *English educator*
Weisburger, Elizabeth Kreiser *retired chemist*
Weisman, John *author*
Weisman, Lorenzo David *investment banker*
Weismantel, Gregory Nelson *management consultant and software executive*
Weiss, Alvin Harvey *chemical engineering educator, catalysis researcher and consultant*
Weiss, Daniel Edwin *minister, educator*
Weiss, Donald A. *naval officer*
Weiss, Jerry Kenneth *sales executive, consultant, marketing professional*
Weiss, Max Tibor *retired aerospace company executive*
Weiss, Michael Allen *retail executive*
Weiss, Scott Alan *commercial real estate consultant*
Weiss, Steven Gary *physician*
Weissenburger, David Allen *psychologist, educator, consultant*
Weissman, Jack (George Anderson) *retired editor*
Weiswasser, Stephen *electronics manufacturing executive*
Weisz, Paul B(urg) *physicist, researcher, chemical engineer*
Welch, Martin E., III, *investor, retail executive*
Welch, Oliver Wendell *retired pharmaceutical executive*
Weldon, Jeffrey Alan *lawyer*
Weldon, William Forrest *electrical and mechanical engineer, educator*
Weller, Milton Webster *wetland ecologist, educator*
Wellford, Harry Walker *retired federal judge*
Wells, Hugh Neal, IV, *lawyer*
Wells, Kitty (Muriel Deason Wright) *country western singer*
Wells, Victor Hugh, Jr., *retired advertising agency executive*
Welna, Cecilia *retired mathematics educator*
Welsome, Eileen *journalist*
Wendt, E. Allan *international affairs consultant*
Wendt, Elizabeth Warczak *retired insurance company executive*
Wendt, George Robert *actor*
Wendt, Marilynn Suzann *elementary school educator, principal*
Wenkert, Deborah *pediatric rheumatologist, researcher*
Wenstrup, H. Daniel *chemical company executive*
Wentz, Jeffrey Lee *information systems executive*
Wentz, Sidney Frederick *insurance company executive, foundation executive*
Wentz, William Henry, Jr., *aerospace engineer, educator*
Werman, Thomas Ehrlich *record producer*
Werner, Robert Joseph *dean, music educator*
Werner-Jacobsen, Emmy Elisabeth *developmental psychologist*
Wernet, Patricia A. *director*
Wernick, Richard Frank *composer, conductor*
Werries, E. Dean *food distribution company executive*
Wertsman, Vladimir Filip *librarian, information specialist, author, translator*
Wesely, Marissa Celeste *lawyer*
Wessling, Robert Bruce *retired lawyer*
West, Bill *writer, artist, photographer, composer*
West, Gregory Alan *physician*
West, Kenneth Irwin *automotive executive*
West, Mary Beth *federal agency administrator*
West, Nettie J.R. *music educator*
West, Rexford Leon *retired bank executive*
Westbie, Barbara Jane *retired graphics designer*
Westcarr, Linton Anthony *nurse, pharmacist, writer*
Westervelt, James Joseph *retired insurance company executive*
Westfall, Jeffrey N. *education educator*
Westheimer, Ruth Welling *retired management consultant*
Weston, Josh S. *retired data processing company executive*
Weston, Michael C. *retired lawyer*
Weston, Rebecca Lynn *forensic educator*
Weston, Saundra Olivia (Saundra Laidlaw) *quality assurance professional, minister*
Wetekam, Donald J. *career officer*
Wetherill, Eikins *lawyer, investment company executive*
Wetherill, George West *geophysicist, planetary scientist*
Wetzel, Heinz *foreign language educator*
Wetzel-Williams, Kimberly *lawyer*
Wexo, Alex *actor*
Weyl, Tom F. *advertising executive*
Weymouth, Elizabeth (Lally) Graham *editor, columnist*
Whack, Rita Coburn *television producer, writer*

Whalen, Charles William, Jr., author, business executive, educator
Whalen, Loretta Theresa religious educational administrator
Wharton, Thomas William medical products executive
Wheat, Brent Douglas music educator
Wheatley, George Milholland medical administrator
Wheaton, M. Gene investigator, consultant
Wheeler, Albin Gray retired military officer, retail executive, educator
Wheeler, Burton M. literature educator, higher education consultant, college dean
Wheeler, David Laurie university dean
Wheeler, George Charles, Jr., materials and processes engineer
Wheeler, John Oliver geologist
Wheeler, R(ichard) Kenneth lawyer, educator
Whelan, James Robert communications executive, international trade and investment consultant, author, educator, mining executive
Whelchel, Sandra Jane writer
Whipple, Judith Roy editor
Whisenhunt, Livia L. marketing executive
Whitburn, Merrill Duane English literature educator
Whitcomb, Richard Travis aeronautical consultant
White, Augustus Aaron, III, orthopedic surgeon
White, Bertram Milton chemicals executive
White, Charles Olds aeronautical engineer
White, Charles Sidney John retired humanities educator
White, Christine Allen elementary school educator
White, Daniel Ernest headmaster, educator, consultant
White, Eugene Vaden retired pharmacist
White, Gerald Andrew retired chemical company executive
White, Helene Nita federal judge
White, Jill Carolyn lawyer
White, John Joseph, III, lawyer
White, John Wesley, Jr., retired academic administrator
White, Kerr Lachlan retired hygiene and tropical medicine physician, medical educator, foundation administrator
White, Larry D. retired political science educator
White, Lerrill James clinical pastoral educator
White, Loray Betty TV talk show host, writer, television producer, vocalist, actress, television director
White, Martin Arthur utilities company executive
White, Raymond Burton former insurance executive
White, Rebecca E. advocate
White, Richard Thomas radiologist
White, Sandra Marie retired artist
White, Shelby Kathryn music educator
White, Stanley Archibald research electrical engineer
White, Thomas E. former federal agency administrator
White, William Nelson lawyer
White, Willis Sheridan, Jr., retired utilities company executive
Whitehead, Ian insurance company executive
Whitehead, Janice secondary school educator
Whitehead, Nehemiah, III, music educator
Whitehouse, Sheldon lawyer, former state attorney general
Whiteley, Benjamin Robert retired insurance company executive
Whitesell, John Edwin retired motion picture company executive
Whiting, Lucille Drake retired elementary school educator, consultant
Whitlock, Bennett Clarke, Jr., retired association executive
Whitman, Christine Todd former governor
Whitman, Gregory Theodore neurologist
Whitman, Meredith Ellis music educator
Whitmore, Bruce G. lawyer
Whitmore, Menandra M. librarian
Whitney, Edward Bonner retired investment banker
Whitney, Jane foreign service officer
Whitsell, John Crawford, II, general surgeon
Whittell, Polly (Mary Kaye Whittell) editor, journalist
Whittemore, John Douglas soccer coach, writer
Whitwam, David Ray appliance manufacturing company executive
Whitworth, J. Bryan, Jr., former oil company executive, lawyer
Whyte, Bruce Lincoln management executive, marketing professional
Wicke, Dallas Clyde retired aerospace engineer
Wicker, Thomas Carey, Jr., retired judge
Wicker, Thomas Grey retired journalist
Wicks, David O., Jr., communications executive
Wickstrom, Jon Alan telecommunications executive, consultant
Widmark, Richard actor
Wiebe, Leonard Irving radiopharmacist, educator
Wiebenson, Dora Louise architectural historian, editor, author
Wiehe, Fred writer
Wieland, William Dean healthcare consulting executive
Wiener, Jon history professor
Wiener, Russell Warren environmental scientist, researcher
Wies, Barbara editor, publisher
Wiesen, Donald Guy retired diversified manufacturing company executive
Wieser, Siegfried planetarium executive director
Wiessler, David Albert news correspondent
Wiest, Dianne actress
Wiginton, Jay Spencer sales executive
Wilburn, Mary Nelson retired lawyer, translator, poet
Wilcox, Brian James military analyst
Wilcox, Diane Marie educational psychologist, software designer
Wilcox, Robert Kalleen journalist
Wilde, Daniel Underwood computer engineering educator
Wilde, John artist, educator
Wilder, Eleanor Marie (Nora Roberts Wilder) writer
Wildhack, William August, Jr., lawyer
Wiley, Carl Ross timber company executive
Wiley, James Francis emergency medical technician, civilian military employee
Wiley, Richard Arthur lawyer
Wilhelm, John L. city health department administrator
Wilhelm, Morton retired surgery educator
Wilhelmsen, Harold John accountant, operations controller
Wilk, Ronald physician
Wilkening, Laurel Lynn academic administrator, planetary scientist
Wilkins, Barratt (George Wilkins) librarian
Wilkinson, Claude Henry writer, artist, English literature educator
Wilkinson, Doris medical sociology educator
Wilkinson, Grant Robert pharmacology educator
Wilkinson, Harry Edward management educator, consultant
Willauer, Whiting Russell retired manufacturing executive, systems engineer
Wille, Wayne Martin retired editor
Willenbecher, John artist
Willenz, June Adele writer, public affairs executive, playwright, screenwriter
Williams, Alfred Blythe retired management consultant
Williams, Anita Marie publishing executive, writer
Williams, B. John, Jr., former federal agency administrator, lawyer
Williams, Carolyn Elizabeth manufacturing executive
Williams, Charles Wesley technical executive, researcher
Williams, Deberrah Deithrisha elementary school educator, researcher
Williams, Diana news anchor, reporter, journalist
Williams, Dorothy Standridge soft drink company official, civic worker
Williams, Eleanor Claflin (Claffy Williams) artist
Williams, Erik George professional football player
Williams, Ervin Eugene religious organization administrator
Williams, George Christopher biologist, ecology and evolution educator
Williams, Howard Walter aerospace engineer, engineering executive
Williams, Jeffrey P. investment banker
Williams, Jimy professional athletics manager
Williams, John Charles, II, data processing executive
Williams, John Troy librarian, educator
Williams, John Zigler anesthesiologist
Williams, Lawrence (Judd) Marvin artist, education educator
Williams, Lewis T. (Rusty Williams) education educator
Williams, Louis Clair, Jr., public relations executive
Williams, Matt (Matthew Derrick Williams) former professional baseball player
Williams, Mildred Jane librarian
Williams, Niama Leslie JoAnn writer, educator
Williams, Phyllis Cutforth retired realtor
Williams, Richard Clarence retired librarian
Williams, Robert Leon psychiatrist, neurologist, educator
Williams, Robin actor, comedian
Williams, Ronald Oscar defense systems engineer
Williams, Spencer Mortimer federal judge
Williams, Stuart W. health facility administrator
Williams, Thomas W. electrical engineer
Williams, Treat (Richard Treat Williams) actor
Williams, William John, Jr., lawyer
Williams Maddox-Brown, Janice Helen nurse
Williamson, Edwin Dargan lawyer, former federal official
Williamson, Robert F. health products executive
Williamson, William Allen retired optometrist
Willig, Karl Victor computer firm executive
Willis, Selene Lowe electrical engineer, software consultant, project manager
Wills, Charles Francis former church executive, retired career officer
Wills, John Elliot, Jr., history educator, writer
Wills, Ritchie Jean hospital administrator
Wills, William Ridley, II, former insurance company executive, historian
Willson, Mary Frances ecology researcher, educator
Willson, Parker O. non-profit organization administrator
Wilmore, Douglas Wayne surgeon, educator
Wilpon, Fred professional baseball team executive, real estate developer
Wilson, Anne Judith writer, educator
Wilson, Bruce Duxbury lawyer
Wilson, C. Daniel, Jr., library director
Wilson, Carolyn Ross retired school system administrator
Wilson, Cheryl Yvonne elementary school educator, secondary school educator
Wilson, Colin Henry writer
Wilson, Delano Dee consultant
Wilson, Frances C. career military officer
Wilson, Glen Parten professional society administrator
Wilson, James Reid, Jr., publishing executive
Wilson, Jane artist
Wilson, Jerry Monty writer, educator
Wilson, Karen Lee researcher
Wilson, Kenneth Geddes physics research administrator
Wilson, Lanford playwright
Wilson, Lois M. minister
Wilson, Maron Loy nurse midwife
Wilson, Mary Elizabeth epidemiologist, physician, educator
Wilson, Melvin Edmond retired civil engineer
Wilson, Patricia Potter library science and reading educator, educational and library consultant
Wilson, Pete former governor
Wilson, Ralph Cookerly, Jr., professional football team executive
Wilson, Rhys Thaddeus lawyer
Wilson, Robert James Montgomery investment company executive
Wilson, Robert M. business executive
Wilson, Robin Scott retired academic administrator, writer
Wilson, S. Liane bank executive
Wilson, Samuel V. academic administrator
Wilson, Sloan writer, educator
Wilson, Walter Clinton retired gas industry executive
Wilson, Warren Samuel clergyman, bishop
Wiltrout, Ann Elizabeth foreign language educator
Wimmer, Kathryn retired elementary school educator
Wimpress, Gordon Duncan, Jr., corporate consultant, foundation executive
Winborne, Sheila Faye academic administrator
Winder, Robert Owen mathematician, computer engineer, geophysicist
Windom, Stephen Ralph former lieutenant governor, lawyer
Windom, William actor
Wingate, Bettye Faye librarian, educator
Wingate, William Peter theater executive
Wingham, Erma Doris secondary school educator
Winkelnkemper, Horst Elmar mathematician, educator
Winkler, Joseph Conrad former recreational products manufacturing executive
Winkler, Scott Alber literature educator
Winn, Herschel C. retired retail electronics company executive
Winslet, Kate actress
Winsley, William T. pharmacist, executive director
Winslow, David Allen chaplain, retired naval officer
Winslow, F. Dana (Francis Dana Winslow) judge, former record company owner
Winslow, John Franklin lawyer
Winslow, Julian Dallas retired lawyer, historian, writer
Winter, Arch Reese retired architect
Winter, Leigh Ellen artist, educator
Winter, Richard Samuel, Jr., computer training company owner, writer
Winterbottom, Goddard Williams retired editor
Winterstein, James Fredrick academic administrator
Winthrop, Sherman lawyer
Wintle, Rosemarie biomedical electronics engineer
Winwood, Stephen Lawrence musician, composer
Wirth, Mary L. Gibson writer
Wirth, Russell D. L., Jr., investment and merchant banker
Wirtz, William Willard lawyer
Wise, Patricia opera singer and educator
Wise, Sandra Casber lawyer
Wise, William Allen energy company executive
Wisehart, Mary Ruth retired religious organization administrator
Wiseman, Douglas Carl education educator, department chairman, dean
Wiseman, Jay Donald Donald photographer, inventor, mechanical designer and contractor, land developer, writer
Wishert, Martina nursing home administrator
Wishnick, Marcia Margolis pediatrician, geneticist, educator
Wisniewski, Thomas Joseph music educator
Wiswall, Dorothy Roller language educator
Witcher, Daniel Dougherty retired pharmaceutical company executive
Witt, Hugh Ernest technology consultant
Witt, James Lee business executive, former Cabinet member
Witte, Merlin Michael oil company executive
Witte, Owen Neil microbiologist, molecular biologist, educator
Wittebols, James Henry communications educator
Wittig, Raymond Shaffer lawyer, intellectual property technology manager
Wittmann, Dietmar H. surgery educator
Woerner, Louise hotel executive
Woestendiek, John, Jr., (William John Woestendiek) newspaper reporter
Wogen, Cathy Lynn academic director
Wohlgelernter, Beth organization executive
Wojahn, R. Lorraine retired state senator
Wolaner, Robin Peggy internet and magazine publisher
Wold, Margaret Barth religion educator, author
Wolf, Chadwick Linwood small business owner, firefighter
Wolf, Christine Strelow piano teacher
Wolf, Cynthia Tribelhorn librarian, library educator
Wolf, Dale Edward state official
Wolf, Edith Maletz retired educator
Wolf, Gary Wickert retired lawyer
Wolf, William Martin computer company executive, consultant
Wolfberg, Melvin Donald optometrist, educational administrator, consultant
Wolfe, Charles Morgan electrical engineering educator
Wolfe, Gregory Baker international relations educator
Wolfe, James Michael education educator, researcher
Wolfe, Joan non-profit organizations consultant
Wolfe, Linda writer
Wolfe, Townsend Durant, III, retired art museum director, curator
Wolff, Brian Richard metal products executive
Wolff, Cynthia Griffin humanities educator, author
Wolff, Manfred Ernst medicinal chemist, pharmaceutical company executive
Wolff, Peter Adalbert physicist, researcher
Wolfman, Ira Joel editor, writer
Wolford, Kathryn Frances religious organization executive
Wolfram, David Anthony computer scientist
Wolfson, Michael George lawyer
Wolin, Alfred M. former federal judge
Wollert, Gerald Dale retired food company executive, investor
Wolosonovich, Stephen violinist
Wolpert Richard, Chava artist
Wolsiffer, Patricia Rae retired insurance company executive
Wonders, William Clare geography educator
Wong, David Yue academic administrator, physics educator
Wong, Elaine Dang foundation executive
Wong, Liliane architect, architecture educator
Wong-Diaz, Francisco Raimundo lawyer, educator
Woo, Benson financial executive
Woo, Jonathan C. G. chemist, portfolio manager, management consultant
Woo, Savio Lau Ching molecular medical geneticist
Woo, Savio Lau-Yuen bioengineering educator
Wood, Allen John electrical engineer, consultant
Wood, Corinne Gieseke former lieutenant governor
Wood, Diane Pamela judge
Wood, Frank actor
Wood, John Arthur nurse
Wood, Marian Starr publishing company executive
Wood, Robert Charles lawyer, real estate developer
Wood, Robert Coldwell political scientist
Wood, Roberta Susan retired foreign service officer
Wood, Vivian Poates mezzo soprano, educator, writer
Wood, William Preston author, lawyer
Wood, Willis Bowne, Jr., retired utilities executive
Woodard, Alfre actress
Woodard, Deana Safford artist
Woodbridge, John Dunning history and church history educator
Woodcock, Richard Wesley educational psychologist
Wooden, John Robert former basketball coach
Woodland, N. Joseph retired optical engineer, retired mechanical engineer
Woodring, Margaret Daley architect, planner
Woodruff, Mary Brennan elementary school educator, educator
Woodruff, Truman O(wen) physicist, emeritus educator
Woodruff, Virginia broadcast journalist, writer
Woodrum, Patricia Ann librarian
Woods, Cheryl financial analyst
Woods, David Lyndon publishing and broadcast executive, former federal agency executive
Woods, Harriett Ruth retired political organization president
Woods, J. P. religious organization administrator
Woods, Phyllis Michalik librarian
Woods, Sandra Kay real estate executive
Woodson, Jacqueline writer
Woodsworth, Anne university administrator, librarian
Woodward, Thomas Morgan actor
Woodward, William Lee retired savings bank executive
Wooldridge, William Charles lawyer
Wooley, Geraldine Hamilton poet, writer
Woolsey, John Munro, Jr., retired lawyer
Woolworth, Susan Valk primary school educator
Woosnam, Ian Harold professional golfer
Wooten, Cecil Aaron retired religious organization administrator
Wooten, Frank Thomas retired research facility executive
Wooten, Joan Hedrich minister
Work, David R. pharmacist, executive director
Workman, Margaret Lee lawyer
Workman, Willard Allyn association executive
Worner, Theresa Marie internist, educator
Woronov, Mary Peter actress
Worrell, Richard Vernon orthopedic surgeon, college dean, dean
Worrell, Stewart Phillip lawyer, trust executive
Worth, Gary James communications executive
Worthen, John Edward retired academic administrator
Worthington, Deborah Eckhardt language educator
Wozniak, Stephen Gary computer scientist, philanthropist
Wren, Stephen Corey mathematician, inventor
Wright, Brian Theodore retired engineering executive
Wright, David Allen mechanical engineer, councilman
Wright, Dell residential care and treatment facility executive
Wright, Dixie Lee special needs persons consultant
Wright, Donald Franklin retired newspaper executive
Wright, Elizabeth Rebecca humanities educator
Wright, Ethel secondary school educator
Wright, Franz Paul poet, writer, translator
Wright, Gladys Stone music educator, composer, writer
Wright, Jacquelyn Dianne special education educator, performing arts educator
Wright, James David sociology educator, writer
Wright, Josephine Rosa Beatrice musicologist, educator
Wright, Judith Rae retired accountant
Wright, Linda Jean manufacturing executive
Wright, Randolph Earle retired petroleum company executive
Wright, Robert Payton lawyer
Wroblowa, Halina Stefania electrochemist
Wrong, Dennis Hume sociologist, educator
Wruble, Bernhardt Karp lawyer
Wruble, Brian Frederick private investor
Wruck, Erich-Oskar retired foreign language educator, administrator
Wu, Margaret Anne computer scientist, educator
Wu, Xinglu writer
Wuhl, Robert actor
Wunsch, Kathryn Sutherland retired lawyer
Wuthnow, Sara Margery retired nursing educator
Wyatt, Brett Michael secondary school educator
Wyatt, Robert Lee, IV, lawyer
Wyatt, Rose Marie clinical social worker
Wyche, Ruth Skyler rehabilitation contractor, researcher
Wylan, Barbara artist
Wyle, Noah actor
Wynar, Bohdan Stephen librarian, writer, editor
Wyngaarden, James Barnes physician
Wyrtki, Klaus oceanography educator
Wyshak, Lillian Worthing lawyer
Xiang, Hui biochemist, researcher
Xiao, Jiarun mechanical engineer
Xiao, Jizhong engineering educator, researcher
Xie, Song musician, music educator
Xu, Biqiang engineer, researcher
Yacavone, David William military officer, consultant, researcher
Yack, Patrick Ashley editor
Yackel, James William mathematician, academic administrator
Yacoub, Jean cardiologist
Yadrick, Robert Martin occupational analyst
Yahn, Mimi writer
Yalam, Arnold Robert allergist, immunologist, consultant
Yale (Yeleyenide-Yale), Melpomene Fotine anthropologist, archaeologist, art historian, conservator, researcher
Yamaguchi, Kristi Tsuya ice skater
Yamamoto, Joe psychiatrist, educator
Yampolsky, Phyllis artist
Yang, Dennis Tao education educator
Yang, Xiangzhong research scientist, administrator, educator
Yannella, Donald literature and language professor
Yarbro, Alan David lawyer
Yarbrough, Kathryn Davis public health nurse
Yarchoan, Robert clinical immunologist, researcher
Yard, Molly social activist
Yared, Gabriel composer
Yarick-Cross, Doris voice educator, soprano
Yarington, Charles Thomas, Jr., surgeon, educator, health facility administrator
Yarrington, George A. retired public relations executive, advertising executive, writer
Yarrow, Peter folksinger

Yates, David John C. *chemist, researcher*
Yates, Gwendolyn Draper *mathematician, educator*
Yates, Steven A. *curator, artist, scholar*
Yates, William Tennyson, II, *educational consultant, management consultant*
Yeadon, Tammy Pamela *information specialist*
Yeager, Anson Anders *writer, retired editor, retired columnist*
Yeager, Kurt Eric *research institute official*
Yeager, Mark Leonard *lawyer*
Yeager, Phillip Charles *transportation company exeuctive*
Yearian, Mason Russell *retired physicist*
Yearwood, Trisha *country music singer, songwriter*
Yee, Nancy W. *travel consultant*
Yeliseev, Alexei Arkadievich *biochemist, researcher*
Yen, Bing Cheng *retired civil engineer, retired engineering educator*
Yen, Wen Liang *retired aerospace engineer*
Yeosock, John John *army officer*
Yglesias, Rafael Jose *novelist*
Yielding, K. Lemone *physician*
Yin, Gerald Zheyao *technology and business executive*
Yin, Zhiping *engineer*
Ying, Jackie *chemical engineer, educator*
Yiotis, Gayle *archivist, researcher, anthropologist, writer*
Ynda, Mary Lou *artist, educator*
Yocam, Delbert Wayne *retired software products company executive*
Yodaiken, Ralph E. *pathologist, occupational medicine physician, educator*
Yoder, Randall D. *music educator*
Yoh, Harold Lionel, Jr., *retired engineering, construction and management company executive*
Yollick, Bernard Lawrence *otolaryngologist, surgeon*
Yolton, John William *philosopher, educator*
Yong, Raymond Nen-Yiu *civil engineering educator*
Yontz, Kenneth Fredric *medical and chemical company executive*
Yood, Harold Stanley *retired internist*
Yook, Chong Chul *engineering educator*
Yopconka, Natalie Ann Catherine *computer specialist, educator, business owner*
York, Alexandra *lawyer*
York, Theodore Robert *retired consulting company executive*
Yoskowitz, Irving Benjamin *lawyer, merchant banker*
Yost, William Albert *psychology educator, hearing researcher*
Youmans, Julian Ray *neurosurgeon, educator*
Younathan, Janet N. *chemist*
Young, Amy Y. *school librarian, writer*
Young, Andrew Jackson *civil rights leader, clergyman, former mayor, former ambassador, former congressman*

Young, Charles Edward *former academic administrator*
Young, Deborah (Deborah Ayling Yanowitz) *social worker, librarian*
Young, Edwin S. W. *federal agency official*
Young, Grace May-En *pediatrician, educator*
Young, Jay Maitland *healthcare communications consultant*
Young, John Alan *electronics company executive*
Young, John Hardin *lawyer, corporate executive*
Young, Judith Anne *animal conservationist*
Young, Leo *electrical engineer*
Young, Marvin Richard *dermatologist, educator*
Young, Patrick *writer, editor*
Young, Richard Alan *association executive*
Young, Ruth Brooks *retired elementary education educator*
Young, Sean (Mary Sean Young) *actress*
Young, Steve G. *former labor union administrator*
Young, Teresa Gail Hilger *retired adult education educator*
Young, Virgil Monroe *education educator*
Youngblood, Daisy *ceramist*
Youngstrom, Paul Clarence *anesthesiologist*
Younker, Kathleen Teuber *pianist, music educator*
Youst, David Bennett *career development educator*
Yu, Jessica *director, producer, writer, editor*
Yu, Jun *biologist*
Yue, Alfred Shui-choh *metallurgical engineer, educator*
Yuen, Henry C. *former consumer electronics manufacturing company executi*
Yuly, Rudy LeRoy *writer, graphics designer*
Yun, James Kyoon *electrical engineer*
Yunis, Jorge Jose *anatomy, pathology, and microbiology educator*
Yurchak, Katherine Sasso *writer*
Yurchuck, Roger Alexander *retired lawyer*
Yuriko, (Yuriko Kikuchi) *dancer, choreographer*
Zacarías, Fernando R. K. *physician*
Zacharias, Donald Wayne *academic administrator*
Zack, Daniel Gerard *retired library director*
Zaferson, William S. *philosophy educator, publisher*
Zaffaroni, Alejandro C. *biochemist, medical research company executive*
Zagaski, Chester Anthony, Jr., *author, researcher*
Zaghloul, Dina Amal *quality assurance professional, consultant*
Zagorin, Janet Susan *legal firm administrator, marketing professional*
Zahedi, Caveh *filmmaker, video artist, video specialist*
Zahler, Adam Troy *theater director*
Zahner, Dorothy Simkin *elementary school educator*
Zais, Mitchell M. *career military officer*
Zajac, John *semiconductor equipment company executive*
Zakim, David *biochemist*

Zaky-Al-Hashimi, Hajjah Sakina Nura *writer*
Zaleski, Jan Franciszek *biochemist*
Zaleski, Jean *artist*
Zaltman, Mark Allen *federal agency administrator*
Zanes, George William *management, marketing, human resources consultant*
Zanfagna, Philip Edward *government executive, urban planner*
Zanjacomo, Paulo Regis *engineering executive*
Zapapas, James Richard *pharmaceutical company executive*
Zapf, Hermann *book and type designer*
Zapp, John S. *retired medical association administrator*
Zappa, Gail *record producer*
Zappe, John Paul *city editor, educator, newspaper executive*
Zavala, Albert *research psychologist*
Zawacki, Bruce Edwin *surgeon, educator, ethicist*
Zdanis, Richard Albert *academic administrator*
Zeffren, Eugene *toiletries company executive*
Zehnder, Frederick John *retired automotive executive*
Zehr, Norman Robert *retired association administrator*
Zehring, Karen *information executive*
Zeien, Alfred M. *former consumer products company executive*
Zeigler, L(uther) Harmon *political science educator*
Zeilberger, Doron *researcher, mathematics educator*
Zeilig, Nancy Meeks *writer, editor*
Zeilinger, Elna Rae *elementary educator, gifted-talented education educator*
Zeine, Rana R. *pathologist, research scientist*
Zekman, Terri Margaret *graphic designer*
Zeleke, Assefa *electrical engineer*
Zeleznak, Shirley Anne *psychotherapist*
Zelinski, Joseph John *engineering educator, consultant*
Zelinsky, Paul O. *illustrator, painter, author*
Zeller, Joseph Paul *advertising executive*
Zentz, Patrick James *artist, rancher*
Zhang, Lin *research scientist, educator*
Zhang, Liping *research scientist*
Zhang, Shu *statistician*
Zhang, Zhongjian *research scientist*
Zhao, Guang-Quan *developmental reproductive biologist, researcher*
Zhao, Hong *biomedical engineer, educator*
Zhao, Zhen *music educator*
Zheutlin, Dale *sculptor, educator*
Zhiyou, Wen *research scientist*
Zhou, Cheng Ji *neuroscientist*
Zhou, Yuanxin *mechanical engineer, educator*
Zhu, Yong *research scientist*
Zick, John Walter *retired accounting company executive*
Ziegenhagen, David Mackenzie *consultant, retired healthcare company executive*

Ziegler, Earl Keller *minister*
Ziegler, Jack (Jack Denmore) *cartoonist*
Ziegler, James L. *marketing executive*
Ziegler, William Alexander *lawyer*
Ziemba, Karen *actress*
Zierler, Neal *retired mathematician*
Ziese, Dennis Russell *protective services official, retired military officer*
Zilbert, Allen Bruce *education educator, computer consultant*
Zilkha, Ezra Khedouri *banker*
Zillman, Donald Norman *law educator, university official*
Zimet, Lloyd *sport psychologist, health planner, educator*
Zimm, Bruno Hasbrouck *physical chemistry educator*
Zimmerman, David Alan *cardiologist*
Zimmerman, Harold Samuel *retired state legislator, newspaper editor and publisher, state administrator*
Zimmerman, Helene Loretta *retired business educator*
Zimmerman, Jean *lawyer*
Zimmerman, Lynn Diann *language educator, literary forensic consultant*
Zimmermann, Thomas Callander Price *retired historian, educator*
Zimny, Max *labor union administrator, lawyer*
Zinnen, Robert Oliver *general management executive*
Ziolo, Ronald F. *research scientist, educator, academic administrator, writer*
Zischke, Douglas Arthur *foreign service officer*
Zivelonghi, Kurt Daniel *painter, computer graphics artist, designer*
Zoelleck, Robert Bruce *federal official*
Zoeller, Donald J. *lawyer*
Zohn, Andrew Eliot *musician, music educator*
Zohn, Martin Steven *lawyer*
Zuck, Alfred Miller *public administration educator*
Zuckerman, Harriet *sociologist, educator*
Zufryden, Fred S. *academic administrator, marketing educator, researcher*
Zuiches, James Joseph *sociologist, educator*
Zuick, Ernest Ronald, Jr., *career officer, advertising executive*
Zumwalt, Ross Eugene *forensic pathologist, educator*
Zupsic, Matthew Michael *insurance company executive*
Zwerling, Gary Leslie *investment bank executive*
Zwerling, Lisa *painter, educator*
Zwislocki, Jozef John *neuroscience educator, researcher*

Professional Index

AGRICULTURE

UNITED STATES

ALABAMA

Montgomery
Frazer, Stuart Harrison, III, *cotton merchant*

Tuskegee Institute
Hill, Walter A. *agricultural sciences educator, researcher*

ARIZONA

Sun City
Coffman, Harold Emerson *retired agricultural products supplier, retail merchant*

CALIFORNIA

Fresno
Epperson, Robert Dale *farmer*

Healdsburg
Merinoff, Herman I. *vintager, wine company executive*

Livingston
Foster, Ron *agricultural products supplier, agricultural products executive*

Modesto
Freedman, Louis *vintager executive*
Gallo, Ernest *vintner*
Gallo, Joseph E. *vintner*

Napa
Chiarella, Peter Ralph *vintner*

Pacific Palisades
Jennings, Marcella Grady *rancher, investor*

San Diego
Caughlin, Stephenie Jane *organic farmer*

San Francisco
Hills, Austin Edward *vineyard executive*

San Jose
D'Arrigo, Stephen, Jr., *agricultural company executive*

COLORADO

Denver
Decker, Peter Randolph *rancher, former state official*

Fort Collins
Heird, James C. *agricultural studies educator*

Kersey
Guttersen, Michael *rancher, investor*

Montrose
Kontny, Vincent L. *rancher, engineering executive*

Springfield
Wessler, Melvin Dean *farmer, rancher*

DISTRICT OF COLUMBIA

Washington
Schimmelpfennig, David Everett *agricultural studies educator, researcher*

FLORIDA

Gainesville
Hochmuth, George J. *horticultural educator*
Schmitz, Andrew *agricultural studies educator*

Lakeland
Griffiths, James Thompson, Jr., *agricultural products supplier*

GEORGIA

Atlanta
Stimpert, Michael Alan *agricultural products company executive*

HAWAII

Honolulu
Ching, Chauncey Tai Kin *agricultural economics educator*

Waialua
Singlehurst, Dona Geisenheyner *horse farm owner*

IDAHO

Boise
Simplot, John R. *agribusiness executive*

ILLINOIS

Decatur
Camp, William H. *agricultural products supplier*
Harjehausen, Edward A. *agricultural products supplier*
Peterson, Brian F. *agricultural products supplier*
Rice, John D. *agricultural products supplier*

East Peoria
Frison, Rick *agricultural company executive*

Northfield
Bruns, Nicolaus, Jr., *retired agricultural chemicals company executive, lawyer*

Pleasant Plains
Thomas, Evelyn B. *agricultural products supplier*

Quincy
Finlay, Timothy *agricultural products supplier*
Foster, Michael *agricultural products supplier*

Urbana
Bentley, Orville George *retired agricultural educator, dean emeritus*
Hill, Lowell Dean *agricultural marketing educator*

INDIANA

Hanover
Heck, Richard T. *tree farmer*

Indianapolis
Hegel, Carolyn Marie *farm bureau executive*

Muncie
Simmons, Carl Kenneth *cooperative executive*

West Lafayette
Lechtenberg, Victor L. *agricultural studies educator*

IOWA

Akron
Hultgren, Dennis Eugene *farmer, management consultant*

Ames
Jacobson, Norman L. *retired agricultural educator, researcher*
Mullen, Russell Edward *agricultural studies educator*
Pearce, Robert Brent *agricultural studies educator*
Topel, David Glen *agricultural studies educator*

Des Moines
Mertz, Dolores Mary *farmer, state legislator*

KANSAS

Brookville
Bohata, Emil Anton *rancher*

Claflin
Burmeister, Paul Frederick *farmer*

Garden City
Reeve, Lee M. *farmer*

Haven
Schlickau, George Hans *cattle breeder, professional association executive*
Schlickau, Lois Marie *farmer*

Iola
Strickler, Ivan K. *dairy farmer*

Lewis
Cross, David Rusk *farmer, livestock raiser*

Wellington
Ferguson, William McDonald *rancher, writer, banker, retired lawyer, former state official*

MARYLAND

College Park
Fretz, Thomas A. *agricultural studies educator*

Princess Anne
Acquah, Sarah Nipah *agricultural educator*

MASSACHUSETTS

Brockton
Sullivan, Brendan Paul *state official, communications educator*

MICHIGAN

Allegan
Drozd, Phyllis Ann *agricultural products supplier*

Ann Arbor
Heydon, Peter Northrup *farmer, educator, philanthropist*

Howell
Cotton, Larry *ranching executive*

MINNESOTA

Canby
Larson, Gary Arthur *farmer, financial consultant*

Saint Paul
Sviggum, Steven Arthur *farmer, state representative*

MISSISSIPPI

Starkville
Gregg, Billy Ray *seed industry executive, consultant*

MISSOURI

Nixa
Kreider, Jim *farmer, former state legislator*

Sturgeon
Fashing, Edward Michael *ranch owner, physical science educator*

MONTANA

Helena
Rabenberg, John *farmer, political organization worker*

Pony
Anderson, Richard Ernest *agribusiness development consultant, rancher*

NEVADA

Yerington
Scatena, Lorraine Borba *retired rancher, women's rights advocate*

NEW JERSEY

Belmar
Paetzold, Mary E. *agricultural products supplier*

Jackson
Rickabaugh, Vicki *horse farm owner, mayor*

NEW MEXICO

Las Cruces
Holechek, Jerry *agricultural studies educator*

Rowe
Cowles, William Sheffield, III, *rancher*

NEW YORK

South Dayton
Jones, Richard Allen *horse breeder, educator*

NORTH CAROLINA

Raleigh
McClure, William F. *agricultural studies educator*
Peacock, Charles H. *agricultural studies educator*

NORTH DAKOTA

Amidon
Bergquist, Gene Alfred *farmer, rancher, county commissioner, retired county commissioner*

OHIO

Chardon
Wollpert, Sandra Cox *horse breeder*

Columbus
Ockerman, Herbert W. *agricultural studies educator*

OKLAHOMA

Stillwater
Luper, Charles C. *agricultural studies educator*

OREGON

Beaverton
Ray, Ruth Alice Yancey *retired rancher, real estate developer*

Medford
Smith, Robert F. (Bob Smith) *rancher, former congressman*

PENNSYLVANIA

Dillsburg
Smith, William Raymond *farmer, horse breeder*

University Park
Hood, Lamartine Frain *agriculture educator, former dean*

SOUTH CAROLINA

Clemson
Wehrenberg, William Busse *agricultural studies educator*

Greer
Gregg, Marie Byrd *retired farmer*

Pawleys Island
Kay, Thomas Oliver *agricultural consultant*

SOUTH DAKOTA

Brookings
Moore, Raymond A. *consultant, retired agriculture educator*

Saint Lawrence
Lockner, Vera Joanne *farmer, rancher, legislator*

TENNESSEE

Cordova
Echols, James *agricultural products supplier*

Hickory Valley
Weaver, Peggy (Marguerite McKinnie Weaver) *plantation owner*

Nashville
Thompson, Dean Allan *cattleman*

TEXAS

Cleburne
Gorman, Charlotte A. *family and consumer sciences agent*

College Station
Christiansen, James Edward *agricultural educator*
Hesby, John Howard *agricultural educator*

Farnsworth
Gramstorff, Jeanne B. *retired farmer*

Houston
Shuart, Carey Chenoweth *farmer, volunteer*

Industry
Huitt, Jimmie L. *rancher, oil, gas, real estate investor*

San Antonio
Petty, Scott, Jr., *rancher*

Valley View
Wallace, Donald John, III, *rancher*

VERMONT

Windham
Partridge, Carolyn *farmer, state representative*

VIRGINIA

Blacksburg
Swiger, L. A. *agricultural studies educator*

Montross
Fountain, Robert Roy, Jr., *farmer, industrial executive, naval officer*

WEST VIRGINIA

Charles Town
McDonald, Angus Wheeler *farmer*

WYOMING

Lander
Raynolds, David Robert *buffalo breeder, writer*

Wheatland
Bunker, John Birkbeck *cattle rancher, retired sugar company executive*

ADDRESS UNPUBLISHED

Barrett, Barbara McConnell *ranch owner, community leader, lawyer*
Brooks, Kenneth N. *forestry educator*
Cannell, Robert Quirk *former agricultural sciences educator*
Erwin, Elmer Louis *vintager, cement consultant*
Hiler, Edward Allan *agricultural and engineering educator*
Hitchcock, Vernon Thomas *farmer, lawyer*
Johnson, Cyrus Edwin *retired farmer*
Stanley, Marlyse Reed *horse breeder*
Webb, O. Glenn *retired farm supplies company executive*

ARCHITECTURE & DESIGN

UNITED STATES

ALABAMA

Auburn
Millman, Richard George *architect, educator*

Birmingham
Barrow, Richard Edward *architect*
Giattina, Joseph P., Jr., *architectural firm executive*
Gilchrist, William Aaron *architect*
Millen, Kevin S. *architectural firm executive*

Huntsville
Collazo, Francisco J. *architectural firm executive*

Madison
Vo, Hieu N. *architect*

ARIZONA

Glendale
Uhlmann, Elenore Arlene *interior designer, writer*

Oro Valley
McConnell, Robert Eastwood *architect, educator*

Paradise Valley
Blumer, Harry Maynard *architect*

Payson
Hershberger, Robert Glen *architect, educator*

Phoenix
DeBartolo, Jack, Jr., *architect*
Elmore, James Walter *architect, retired university dean*
Gwozdz, Kim Elizabeth *interior designer*
Hawkins, Jasper Stillwell, Jr., *architect*
Schiffner, Charles Robert *architect*
Winslow, Paul David *architect*

Scottsdale
Brown, Shirley Margaret Kern (Peggy Brown) *interior designer*
Rutes, Walter Alan *architect*
Wong, Joe Bing *retired architect*

Sonoita
Cook, William Howard *architect*

Tucson
Nelson, Edward Humphrey *architect*
Seehausen, Richard Ferdinand *architect*
Wallach, Leslie Rothaus *architect*

ARKANSAS

Fort Smith
Guest, Gordon D. *architectural firm executive*

Little Rock
Burruss, Terry Gene *architect*
Levy, Eugene Pfeifer *architect*
Truemper, John James, Jr., *retired architect*

Winslow
Burggraf, Frank Bernard, Jr., *landscape architect, retired educator*

CALIFORNIA

Bakersfield
McAlister, Michael H. *architect*

Belvedere
Gale, Daniel Bailey *architect*
Hugenberg, Patricia Ellen Petrie *product designer*

Berkeley
Brocchini, Ronald Gene *architect*
Burger, Edmund Ganes *architect*
Cardwell, Kenneth Harvey *architect, educator*
Olsen, Donald Emmanuel *architect, educator*
Stoller, Claude *architect*
Walker, Peter *landscape architect*

Beverly Hills
Buchberg, Akiva *product designer, inventor, consultant*

Carlsbad
Cuthbert, Emilie Ann (Emilie Winthrop) *interior designer*

Ceres
Abbott, Dan-San *parachute designer*

Chula Vista
Weiss-Cornwell, Amy *interior designer*

Cobb
Budzinski, James Edward *interior designer*

Corona Del Mar
Muller, David Webster *architectural designer*
Yeo, Ron *architect*

Coronado
Wagener, Hobart D. *retired architect*

Costa Mesa
Dougherty, Betsey Olenick *architect*
Hepp, David Worthington *draftsman*

Culver City
Moss, Eric Owen *architect*
Sussman, Deborah Evelyn *designer, company executive*

El Cerrito
Komatsu, Shigego Richard *architect*

Encino
Rance, Quentin E. *interior designer*

Fresno
Darden, Edwin Speight, Sr., *architect*
Patnaude, William Eugene *architect*
Pings, Anthony Claude *architect*

Hanford
Moffett, Frank Cardwell *architect, civil engineer, real estate developer*

Highland
MacQueen, Cher *interior designer, retired newscaster, sportscaster*

Huntington Beach
Lans, Carl Gustav *architect, economist*

Indian Wells
Munyon, William Harry, Jr., *architect*

Irvine
Kraemer, Kenneth Leo *architect, educator, urban planner*
Wilkeson, Kevin M. *architect*

Laguna Niguel
Axon, Donald Carlton *architect*

Laguna Woods
Badgley, John Roy *architect*

Long Beach
Perkowitz, Simon (Sy) *architect, architectural firm executive*
Pullman, Alan *architect*

Los Angeles
Bobrow, Michael Lawrence *architect*
Cuff, Dana *architecture educator*
DeCherney, Deanna Saver *interior designer*
Dworsky, Daniel Leonard *architect, educator*
Eisenshtat, Sidney Herbert *architect*
Fickett, Edward Hale *architect, planner, arbitrator*
Gehry, Frank Owen *architect*
Holdsworth, Ray W. *architectural firm executive*
Johnson, Stephen *architectural firm executive*
Kline, Lee B. *retired architect*
Lavin, Sylvia *architecture educator*
Maltzan, Michael Thomas *architect*
Man, Lawrence Kong *architect, art dealer*
McCullagh, Grant Gibson *retired architect*
Moe, Stanley Allen *architect, consultant*
Murcutt, Glen *architect*
Myers, Barton *architect*
Neutra, Dion *architect*
Noble, Douglas *architecture educator*
Pfeiffer, Norman *architectural firm executive*
Phelps, Barton Chase *architect, educator*
Stout, Randall *architect*
Tucker, Robert Paul *landscape architect, city planner*

Los Gatos
Chapson, Lois Jester *interior designer*

Manhattan Beach
Blanton, John Arthur *architect, writer*

Marshall
Evans, Robert James *architect*

Mill Valley
D'Amico, Michael *architect, urban planner*

Mojave
Rutan, Elbert L. (Burt Rutan) *aircraft designer, aircraft company executive*

Mountain View
Kobza, Dennis Jerome *architect*

Newport Beach
Bissell, George Arthur *architect*
Richardson, Walter John *architect*
Savopoulos, Marios A. *architect, director*
Stoutenborough, J. Todd *architect*

Novato
Thompson, Peter Layard Hailey, Sr., *landscape and golf course architect, architectural firm executive*

Oakland
Bonutti, Alexander Carl *architect, urban designer*
Matsumoto, George *architect*
Nicol, Robert Duncan *architect*

Ontario
Endsley, Donal E. *architectural firm executive*
Gilliam, James L. *architectural firm executive*
Kain, Robert J. *architectural firm executive*
Taylor, Chris R. *architect*

Orange
Shirvani, Hamid *architect, educator, author, administrator, philosopher*

Oxnard
O'Connell, Hugh Mellen, Jr., *retired architect*

Pasadena
Goei, Bernard Thwan-Poo (Bert Goei) *architectural and engineering firm executive*
Thomas, Joseph Fleshman *retired architect*

Pleasant Hill
Hassid, Sami *architect, educator*

Redondo Beach
Shellhorn, Ruth Patricia *landscape architect*

Riverside
Deal, Kevin Paul *furniture designer*

Sacramento
Hallenbeck, Harry C. *architect*
Lionakis, George *architect*
Ross, Terence William *architect*
Wasserman, Barry L(ee) *architect*

San Diego
Angyal, Charles *architect*
Delawie, Homer Torrence *retired architect*
Henderson, John Drews *architect*
Livingston, Stanley C. *architect*
Naslund, Eric *architectural firm executive*
Paderewski, Sir Clarence Joseph *architect*

San Francisco
Bull, Henrik Helkand *architect*
Costa, Walter Henry *architect*
Del Campo, Martin Bernardelli *architect*
Dodge, Peter Hampton *architect*
Ellis, John *urban designer*
Field, John Louis *architect*
Friedrichs, Edward Charles *architect*
Judd, Bruce Diven *architect*
Kriken, John Lund *architect*
Leddy, William *architect*
Minar, Paul G. *design consultant*
Moris, Lamberto Giuliano *architect*
Parker, Derek *architectural firm executive*
Raeber, John Arthur *architect, construction consultant*
Ream, James Terrill *architect, sculptor*
Solomon, Daniel *architectural firm executive*
Swanson, Roger *architectural firm executive*
Thistlethwaite, David Richard *architect*
Torney, Anne *architectural firm executive*
Valentine, William Edson *architect*
Werner, William Arno *architect*
Worthen, William James *architect*

San Jose
Lotten, Larry Lynn *architect*
Tanaka, Richard Koichi, Jr., *architect, planner*

San Luis Obispo
Deasy, Cornelius Michael *retired architect*
Fraser, Bruce Douglas, Jr., *architect, artist*

San Mateo
Sadilek, Vladimir *architect*

San Rafael
Clark, Charles Sutter *interior designer*

Santa Barbara
Burgee, John Henry *architect*
Kruger, Kenneth Charles *architect*
Pochini, Judy Hay *interior designer, writer, editor*

Santa Monica
Eizenberg, Julie *architect*
Koning, Hendrik *architect*

Santa Rosa
Morris, Jack G. *architecture educator, writer*

Seal Beach
Rossi, Mario Alexander *architect*

South Pasadena
Girvigian, Raymond *architect*

Sun City
Holl, Walter John *architect, interior designer*

Tarzana
Smith, Mark Lee *architect*

Venice
Beal, Jason Eliot *architect*

Walnut
Muszynski, Jane *interior designer, colorist, space planner*

COLORADO

Boulder
Hoffman, Charles Fenno, III, *architect*

Broomfield
Williams, John James, Jr., *architect*

Centennial
Hunt, Gerald G., Jr., *architect, real estate broker*

Colorado Springs
Greenlaw, Roger Lee *interior designer*

Crestone
Temple, Lee Brett *architect, songwriter, writer*

Denver
Abo, Ronald Kent *freelance/self-employed architect*
Anderson, John David *architect*
Bradburn, James Henry *architectural firm executive*
Dominick, Peter Hoyt, Jr., *architect*
Fentress, Curtis Worth *architectural firm executive*
Fogg, Janet *architectural firm executive*
Fuller, Robert Kenneth *architect, urban designer*

Havekost, Daniel John *architect*
Hynek, Frederick James *architect*
Kung, Malgorzata Laptas *architect*
Nelson, Nevin Mary *interior designer*
Obermeier, Tom *architectural firm executive*
Prosser, John Martin *architect, educator, urban design consultant*
Robins, Judy Roselyn *interior designer*
Steenhagen, Robert Lewis *landscape architect, consultant*
Wirkler, Norman Edward *retired architectural, engineering, construction management firm executive*

Fort Collins
Grandin, Temple *industrial designer*

Fort Garland
Boyer, Lester Leroy, Jr., *architecture educator, consultant*

Littleton
Shepherd, Donna Lou *interior designer*

Longmont
Woollen, Evans *retired architectural firm executive*

Vail
Vosbeck, Robert Randall *architect*

CONNECTICUT

Branford
Blake, Peter Jost *architect*
Wright, Nancy Howell *interior designer*

Centerbrook
Harper, Robert Leslie *architect, educator*

Cheshire
Rowland, Ralph Thomas *retired architect*

Fairfield
Ingis, Gail *interior designer, educator, photographer, artist, writer*

Greenwich
Hershaft, Elinor *space planner, interior designer*
Marks, Charles *architect*

Hamden
Roche, Eamonn Kevin *architect*

Hartford
Amatuli, Robert Alexander *architect*

Lyme
Hoyt, Charles King *architect, editor*

Monroe
Paniccia, Mario Domenic *architect*

New Canaan
Dean, Robert Bruce *architect*
Risom, Jens *furniture designer, manufacturing executive*

New Haven
Chilton, William David *architect*
Clarke, Fred W., III, *architect, architectural firm executive*
Deamer, Peggy *architecture educator*
Jacobson, John D. *architecture educator*
Newick, Craig David *architect*
Pelli, Cesar *architect*
Platner, Warren *architect*
Roth, Harold *architect*

New Preston Marble Dale
Myers, Robert Luther *architect, artist*

Niantic
Butler, Jonathan Putnam *architect*

Northford
Gregan, Edmund Robert *landscape architect*

Old Greenwich
Whitlock, Veronica P. *interior designer, educator*

Stamford
Papp, Laszlo George *architect*

Stonington
Stoddard, Alexandra *designer, writer, lecturer*

Trumbull
Watson, Donald Ralph *architect, artist, educator, author*

Westport
Ferris, Roger Patrick *architect*

DELAWARE

Newark
Stick, Thomas Howard Fitchett *corporate architect, construction litigation consultant*

DISTRICT OF COLUMBIA

Washington
Barr-Kumar, Raj *architect*
Birnbaum, Charles A. *landscape architect*
Bowie, Calvert Sheriff *architect*
Coffin, Beatriz de Winthuysen *landscape architect*
Cox, Warren Jacob *architect*
Fry, Louis Edwin, Jr., *architect*
Goetz, Lewis J. *architect*
Gordon, Harry Thomas *architectural firm executive*
Greene, Thomas Hardy *architect*
Hartman, George Eitel *architect*
Hellmuth, George William *architect*
Holladay, Wilhelmina Cole *interior design and museum executive*
Jacobsen, Hugh Newell *architect*
Lewis, Anne McCutcheon *architect*

Miller, Iris Ann *landscape architect, urban designer, educator*
Minkoff, Alice Sydney *interior designer stylist*
Murray, Christopher Charles, III, *architect*
Oehme, Wolfgang Walter *landscape architect*
Oehrlein, Mary Lou *architect*
Ramberg, Walter Dodd *architect*
Sarring, Kevin Lee *architect, archaeologist*
Schlesinger, B. Frank *architect, educator*
Siegel, Lloyd Harvey *architect, real estate developer, consultant*
White, George Malcolm *architect*
Yerkes, David Norton *architect*

FLORIDA

Bal Harbour
Spiegel, Siegmund *architect*

Boca Raton
Balter, Murray *interior designer*
Kephart, Larry Robert *architect*

Bonita Springs
Trudnak, Stephen Joseph *landscape architect*

Boynton Beach
Stubbins, Hugh A(sher), Jr., *architect*

Daytona Beach
Xepapas, Angargyros *architect*

Delray Beach
Rippeteau, Darrel Downing *retired architect*

Doral
Feito, Jose *architect*

Fort Lauderdale
Walker, Barabara J. *interior designer, writer*

Fort Myers
Mair, Bruce Logan *interior designer, company executive*

Gainesville
Dasta, Anthony J. *architecture educator*
Hasell, Mary Joyce (Jo) *architecture educator*
Kohen, Martha *architecture educator*

Gulf Breeze
French, Jere Stuart *landscape architect*

Hobe Sound
Graham, Bruce John *architect*

Hollywood
Harringer, Olaf Carl *architect, museum consultant*

Indian River Shores
Ahrens, William Henry *architect*

Jacksonville
Morgan, William Newton *architect, educator*

Jupiter
Mock, Robert Claude *architect*

Longwood
Gasperoni, Ellen Jean Lias *interior designer*

Miami
Arango, Jorge Sanin *architect*
Duany, Andres *architectural firm executive*
Farcus, Joseph Jay *architect, interior designer*
Fort-Brescia, Bernardo *architect*
Hampton, Mark Garrison *architect*
Plater-Zyberk, Elizabeth Maria *architectural educator*
Schapiro, Jaime *architect*
Spear, Laurinda Hope *architect*

Naples
Jones, Richard Wallace *interior designer*
Lewis, Gordon Gilmer *golf course architect*
Lickhalter, Merlin *architect*
McDonald, Jinx *interior designer*

Orlando
Duda, Richard Frank *architect, engineering executive*

Ormond Beach
Cowley, Gerald Dean *architect*
Truitt, Richard byron *landscape architect*

Palm Beach
Wirtz, Willem Kindler *garden and lighting designer, public relations consultant*

Palmetto
Turlo, George Jerzy *architect, city planner, artist*

Pensacola
Bullock, Ellis Way, Jr., *architect*
Woolf, Kenneth Howard *architect*

Pompano Beach
Gui, James Edmund *architect*

Saint Augustine
Wilkes, Delano Angus *architect*

Saint Petersburg
Gross, Geoffrey Fries *systems architect*
Wedding, Charles Randolph *architect*

Sarasota
Smith, Mark Hallard *architect*

Stuart
Ankrom, Charles Franklin *golf course architect, consultant*

Tallahassee
Bird, Mark Douglas *magnet designer, engineering researcher*

Tampa
Abell, Jan Meisterheim *architect*
Howey, John Richard *architect, writer*
Jennewein, James Joseph *architect*

Venice
Tafel, Edgar *architect*

Vero Beach
Gibson, James Elliot *architect*
Lagin, Neil *landscape designer, consultant*

West Palm Beach
Marshall-Beasley, Elizabeth *landscape architect*
Ross, Edward Joseph *architect*

Winter Haven
Burns, Arthur Lee *architect*

GEORGIA

Atlanta
Allen, Douglas C. *architecture educator*
Bainbridge, Frederick Freeman, III, *architect*
Bull, Frank James *retired architect*
Cantley, Kevin Rilous *architectural firm executive*
Cogburn, Richmond *architect*
Cooper, Jerome Maurice *architect*
Dalia, Thomas A. *architectural firm executive*
Diedrich, Richard Joseph *architect*
Eastman, Charles (Chuck) M. *architecture educator*
Fash, William Leonard *retired architecture educator, college dean*
Guest, Rita Carson *interior designer*
Lewcock, Ronald Bentley *architect, educator*
McAfee, Cheryl *architect*
Miller, Roger L. *architectural firm executive*
Moynihan, James J. *architectural firm executive*
Muse, Gar *architectural firm executive*
Neuenschwander, Roger *architectural firm executive*
Portman, John C., Jr., *architect, developer*
Pulgram, William Leopold *architect, space designer*
Rekau, Richard Robert *architect*
Sizemore, Michael Maynard *architectural firm executive*
Smith, Markham H. *architectural firm executive*
Surber, Eugene Lynn *architect*
Swicegood, Stephen *architect*
Unger, Roberta *architect*

Augusta
Woodhurst, Robert Stanford, Jr., *architect*

Columbus
Simpson, Minnie Peach *interior designer*

Decatur
Mc Intosh, James Eugene, Jr., *interior designer*

Lagrange
Wilkes, George Gardner, Jr., *landscape architect*

Macon
Dunwody, Eugene Cox *architect*

Marietta
Moulthrop, Edward Allen *architect, artist*

Moultrie
McCall, John Clark, Jr., *interior designer*

Rome
Janowski, Thaddeus Marian *architect*

Saint Simons Island
Webb, Lamar Thaxter *architect*

Savannah
Ramsay, Linda *architect*

Smyrna
Passantino, Richard J. *architect*

Watkinsville
Morrison, Darrel Gene *landscape architecture educator*

HAWAII

Honolulu
Botsai, Elmer Eugene *architect, architecture educator, retired dean*
Hale, Nathan Robert *architect*
Hamada, Duane Takumi *architect*
Lau, Charles Kwok-Chiu *architect, architectural firm executive*
Noe, Joyce M. *architecture educator*
Vidal, Alejandro Legaspi (Andy Vidal) *architect*
Yeh, Raymond Wei-Hwa *architect, educator*

Kaneohe
Fisette, Scott Michael *landscape and golf course architect*

Waipahu
Chang, Walter Tuck, Sr., *draftsman, real estate agent, religious studies educator*

IDAHO

Boise
Hunsucker, Wayne (Carl Wayne Hunsucker) *architectural firm executive, educator*

Sun Valley
Bryant, Woodrow Wesley *architect*
McLaughlin, James Daniel *architect*

ILLINOIS

Bloomington
Switzer, Jon Rex *architect*

Bolingbrook
Caddy, Edmund H.H., Jr., *architect*

Champaign
Andrejasich, Michael J. *architecture educator*
Baker, Jack Sherman *architect, educator*
Boubekri, Mohamed *architecture educator*
Hopkins, Lewis Dean *architecture educator*
Riley, Robert Bartlett *landscape architect*

Chicago
Amstadter, Laurence *retired architect*
Ast, Bruno *architecture educator*
Balasi, Mark Geoffrey *architect*
Barney, Carol Ross *architect*
Beeby, Thomas H. *architect*
Belluschi, Anthony C. *architect*
Blankenship, Edward G. *architect*
Clark, Raymond S. *architectural firm executive*
Cook, Richard Borreson *architect*
Enquist, Philip *architectural firm executive*
Epstein, Sidney *architect, civil engineer*
Friedman, Daniel S. *architecture educator*
Gardunio, Joseph *landscaping company executive*
Garofalo, Douglas *architectural firm executive, educator*
Gold, Allan Harold *architect, structural engineer, educator*
Grunsfeld, Ernest Alton, III, *architect*
Hackl, Donald John *architect*
Hayes, Richard Donald *architect*
Holabird, John Augur, Jr., *retired architect*
Jahn, Helmut *architect*
Kerbis, Gertrude Lempp *architect*
Kirkegaard, R. Lawrence *architectural acoustician*
Legge Kemp, Diane *architect, landscape architect*
Matthei, Edward Hodge *architect*
McCurry, Margaret Irene *architect, educator, furniture designer, interior designer*
Phillips, Frederick Falley *architect*
Robertson, Donna Virginia *architect, educator, dean*
Robinson, Sidney K. *architecture educator*
Roubik, Susanne Eileen *architect*
Rugo, Steven Alfred *architect*
Schroeder, Douglas Fredrick *architect*
Smith, Adrian Devaun *architect*
Tigerman, Stanley *architect, educator*
Valerio, Joseph Mastro *architectural firm executive, educator*
VanderBeke, Patricia K. *architect*
Vinci, John Nicholas *architect, educator*
Weber, Hanno *architect*
Weese, Benjamin Horace *architect*
Whitney, Patrick Foster *design educator*

Evanston
Friedman, Hans Adolf *architect*
Macsai, John *architect*
Salzman, Arthur George *architect*

Glenview
Bradtke, Philip Joseph *architect*

Highland Park
Dubin, Arthur Detmers *architect*
Tobin, Calvin Jay *architect*
Weinstein, Barry Alan *architect*

Hinsdale
Anderson, Harry Frederick, Jr., *architect*

Lake Zurich
Krolopp, Rudolph William *retired industrial designer, consultant*

Lincolnshire
Dobrin, Sheldon L. *architect*

Lisle
Mehaffey, Scott Alan *landscape architect*

Mount Carroll
Rogers, Ward Junior *retired industrial designer*

Mount Prospect
Thulin, Adelaide Ann *design company executive, interior designer*

Northfield
Schneider-Criezis, Susan Marie *architect*

Oak Park
Heitzman, Frank Edward *architect*

Park Ridge
Sersen, Howard Harry *retired interior designer, cabinetry consultant*

Rockford
Bradley, Charles MacArthur *retired architect*

Skokie
Siegal, Burton Lee *product designer, consultant, inventor*

Winnetka
Piper, Robert Johnston *retired architect, urban planner*
Schlossman, John Isaac *architect*
Weber, John Bertram *architect*

INDIANA

Carmel
Eden, Barbara Janiece *commercial and residential interior designer*
McLaughlin, Harry Roll *architect*

Fortville
VanArsdel, Thomas Paul *architect, engineering consultant*

Indianapolis
Florestano, Dana Joseph *architect*

Michigan City
Brockway, Lee J. *architect*
Manny, Carter Hugh, Jr., *architect, foundation administrator*

Mishawaka
Ponko, William Reuben *architect*
Troyer, LeRoy Seth *architect*

Muncie
Ernstberger, Eric *landplanning architectural company executive*

South Bend
Horsbrugh, Patrick *architect, educator, environologist*
Smith, Thomas Gordon *architect*

IOWA

Cedar Rapids
Stone, Herbert Marshall *architect*

Clear Lake
Broshar, Robert Clare *architect*

Des Moines
Lewis, Calvin Fred *architect, educator*

Iowa City
Neumann, Roy Covert *architect*

Solon
Healey, Edward Hopkins *retired architect*

KANSAS

Lawrence
Grabow, Stephen Harris *architecture educator*
Penny, Paul Baldwin *landscape artist*

Manhattan
Foerster, Bernd *architecture educator*

Overland Park
Conrad, William Merrill *architect*

Topeka
Karst, Gary Gene *retired architect*
Slemmons, Robert Sheldon *architect*

KENTUCKY

Lexington
Halley, Samuel Hampton, III, *architect, architectural firm executive*
Romanowitz, Byron Foster *architect, engineer*
Sherman, Steven S.J. *architectural firm executive*

Liberty
Wright, Rodney H. *architect*

Louisville
Godsey, H. Carleton, Jr., *architectural firm executive*

LOUISIANA

Arnaudville
Matas, Myra Dorothea *interior architect, designer, consultant*

Baton Rouge
Desmond, John Jacob *retired architect*
Lee, Betty Redding *architect*
Reich, Robert Sigmund *landscape architect*

Bogalusa
Gallaspy, Dixie *interior designer, innkeeper*

New Orleans
Blitch, Ronald Buchanan *architect*
Bookhardt, Fred Barringer, Jr., *architect*
Eskew, R. Allen *architect, director*
Filson, Ronald Coulter *architect, educator, college dean*
Frantz, Phares Albert *architect*
Hence, Jane Knight *designer*
Latorre, Robert George *naval architecture and engineering educator*
Mathes, Edward Conrad *architect*
Perez, August, III, *architectural firm executive*
Steinmetz, Robert Charles *architect*
Wisznia, Walter *architectural firm executive*

MAINE

Edgecomb
Carlson, Suzanne Olive *architect*

New Gloucester
Jaccaci, August Thayer, Jr., *social architect, educator*

Rockport
Hinrichs, Stephen *design educator, consultant*

Seal Harbor
Forbes, Peter *architect*

York
Lyman, William Welles, Jr., *retired architect*

MARYLAND

Annapolis
Jansson, John Phillip *architect, consultant*
Miller, Richards Thorn *naval architect, engineer*

Baltimore
Adams, Harold Lynn *architect*
Askew, Laurin Barker, Jr., *architect*
Brodie, M. J. (Jay Brodie) *architect, city planner, government executive*
Donkervoet, Richard Cornelius *architect*
Ford, John Gilmore *interior designer*
Snead, James Arrington *architect*
Toomey, Sister Stephana *liturgical space designer, nun*

Bethesda
Popescu, Daniel *interior designer*

Bowie
Stone, Edward Harris, II, *landscape architect*

Chevy Chase
Auerbach, Seymour *architect*
Oudens, Gerald Francis *architect, architectural firm executive*

Fort Washington
Miller, John Richard *interior designer*

Montgomery Village
Zabrek, Albert Samuel *architect*

Olney
Delmar, Eugene Anthony *architect*

Rockville
Morgan, William Bruce *naval architect*

Salisbury
Oldland, Kevin Bradley *architect*

Severna Park
Allison, John Langsdale *naval architect, marine engineer*

MASSACHUSETTS

Amherst
Cornish, Geoffrey St. John *golf course architect*

Bedford
Payne, Harry Morse, Jr., *architect*
Shepley, Hugh *architect*

Boston
Alexander, James Garth *architect*
Anis, Wagdy A.Y. *architect*
Anthony, Ethan *architect*
Collins, James H., Jr., *architectural firm executive*
Costa, Daniel Lawrence *architect*
Elkus, Howard Felix *architect*
Ericson, Elizabeth (Zibby) *architect*
Finegold, Maurice Nathan *architect*
Flansburgh, Earl Robert *architect*
Goody, Joan Edelman *architect*
Harkness, John Cheesman *architect*
Jackson, Ralph T. *architect*
Joseph, J. Jonathan *interior designer*
Kearns, Thomas D. *architect*
Klema, Donald David *architect*
Manfredi, David Peter *architect*
Mattox, Robert F. *architectural firm executive*
Rawn, William Leete, III, *architect*
Tappé, Albert Anthony *architect*
Twomey, Timothy *architect*
Wedge, Carole C. *architectural firm executive*

Boxboro
Berry, Robert John *architect*

Cambridge
Anderson, Stanford Owen *architect, architectural historian, educator*
Baird, George *architecture educator*
Barnes, Edward Larrabee *architect*
Bruck, Phoebe Ann Mason *landscape architect*
Bush, Michael *architectural firm executive*
Campbell, Robert *architect, writer*
Chiles, Carol S. *architectural firm executive*
Cohen, Preston Scott *architecture educator*
Dewart, Christopher *architectural educator, furniture maker*
Downes, Gregory *architectural organization executive*
Green, Richard John *architect*
Hamner, W. Easley *architect*
Hass, Michael Shepherdson *architect*
Hays, K. Michael *architecture educator*
Jones, Mary M. *landscape architect*
Kobus, Richard Lawrence *architect, designer, executive, photographer*
Krieger, Alex *architecture and design educator*
Kruger, Kenneth *architect*
Moneo, José Rafael *architecture educator*
Mori, Toshiko *architecture educator*
Owens, David M. *architect*
Pollock, Wilson F. *architectural firm executive*
Porter, William Lyman *architect, educator*
Rowe, Peter Grimmond *architecture educator, researcher*
Schodek, Daniel L. *architecture educator*
Tsoi, Edward Tze Ming *architect, interior designer, urban planner*

Edgartown
Rosenfeld, Walter David, Jr., *architect, writer*

Lexington
Frey, John Ward *landscape architect*

North Andover
Goldstein, Charles Henry *architect, consultant*

Plymouth
Merrill, Vincent Nichols *retired landscape architect*

Somerville
Safdie, Moshe *architect*

Springfield
Engebretson, Douglas Kenneth *architect, interior designer*

Waltham
Brooker, Richard I. *architect*
Notkin, Leonard Sheldon *architect*

Wayland
Huygens, Remmert William *architect*

Wellesley
Merguerian, Arshag *architect*

West Newbury
Taylor, Bruce Stevenson *architect, planner*

West Newton
Stahl, Marilyn Brown *interior designer*

Weston
Wood, Jeremy Scott *architect, urban designer*

Woods Hole
Newman, John Nicholas *naval architect educator*

MICHIGAN

Ann Arbor
Beckley, Robert Mark *architect, educator*
Benford, Harry Bell *naval architect*
Fry, Richard E. *architectural firm executive*
Kendall, Kay Lynn *interior designer, consultant*
Turner, James A. *architecture educator*
Wineman, Jean D. *architecture educator*

Bloomfield Hills
Allen, Maurice Bartelle, Jr., *architect*
Birkerts, Gunnar *architect*
Brown, Jack Wyman *architect*
Van Dine, Harold Forster, Jr., *architect, artist*

Chelsea
Paulsen, Serenus Glen *architect, educator*

Detroit
Francis, Edward D. *architect*
Roehling, Carl David *architect*

Eagle Harbor
Dawson, John Frederick *retired architect*

Farmington Hills
Reddig, Walter Eduard *architect, master cabinet maker*

Flint
Tomblinson, James Edmond *architect*

Grand Rapids
Dickerson, Allen Bruce *interior designer, consultant*
West, Terence Douglas *furniture company design executive*

Holland
Muyres, David Allen *industrial designer*

Kalamazoo
Carver, Norman Francis, Jr., *architect, photographer*

Saline
Frank, Richard Calhoun *architect*

South Haven
LaRocque, Linda Lou *interior designer, educator, playwright*

MINNESOTA

Duluth
Salmela, David Daniel *architect*
Whiteman, Richard Frank *architect*

Minneapolis
Clemence, Roger Davidson *landscape architect, educator*
Conway, William F. *architect, architecture educator*
Faricy, Richard Thomas *architect*
Fisher, Tom *architecture educator*
Fulop, Laszlo G. *architect*
Hollencamp, Greg *architectural firm executive*
Jacob, Bernard Michel *architect*
Martin, Roger Bond *landscape architect, department chairman*
Parker, Leonard S. *architect, educator*
Rand, Peter Anders *architect*
Solomonson, Katherine *architecture educator*
Swenson, Mark Gregory *architect*
Tollefson, Lee *architect*
Weeks, J. Stephen *architecture educator*

Minnetonka
Anderson, Tad Stephen *landscape designer, consultant, photographer*

Northfield
Sovik, Edward Anders *architect, consultant*

Saint Paul
Close, Elizabeth Scheu *retired architect*

Wayzata
Emison, Jane Bale Larson *interior designer*

MISSISSIPPI

Columbus
Kaye, Samuel Harvey *architect, educator*

Jackson
Burns, Robert, Jr., *architect, freelance writer, artist*
Canizaro, Robert Host *architect*
Dale, T.D. *architectural firm executive*

Mississippi State
Martin, Edward Curtis, Jr., *landscape architect, educator*

Starkville
Ford, Robert MacDonald, III, *architect, educator*

MISSOURI

Branson
Ownby, Jerry Steve *landscape architect, educator*

Clayton
Christner, Theodore Carroll *architect*

Columbia
Tofle, Ruth Brent *design educator, researcher*

Independence
Marsh, Gary W. *interior designer*

Kansas City
Baker, Robert Thomas *interior designer*
Seligson, Theodore H. *architect, art appraiser, interior designer*

Saint Louis
Bextermiller Metzger, Theresa Marie *architect, computer engineer*
Chivetta, Anthony Joseph *architect*
Lovelace, Eldridge Hirst *retired landscape architect, city planner*
MacKeith, Peter *architecture educator*
Michaelides, Constantine Evangelos *architect, educator*
Obata, Gyo *architect*
Thalden, Barry R. *architect*
Weese, Cynthia Rogers *architect, educator*

Springfield
Gardner, Steven *instructional designer*

Webster Groves
Becker, Rex Louis *architect*

MONTANA

Bozeman
DeHaas, John Neff, Jr., *retired architecture educator*

Great Falls
Davidson, David Scott *retired architect*

NEBRASKA

Lincoln
Handa, Rumiko *architect, educator*
Mutunayagam, N. Brito *architecture and planning educator*
Stange, James Henry *architect*
Steward, Weldon Cecil *architecture educator, architect, consultant*

Omaha
Polsky, Donald Perry *architect*
Ryan, Mark Anthony *architect, lawyer*

NEVADA

Las Vegas
Eich, Jerry L. *architectural firm executive*
Kastle, Kenneth Dimitrius *interior designer, educator, writer*
Marnell, Anthony Austin, II, *architect*

NEW HAMPSHIRE

Exeter
Richardson, Artemas P(artridge) *retired landscape architect*

Goffstown
Gillmore, Robert *landscape designer, author, editor, publisher*

Hanover
Brooks, H. Allen *architectural educator, author, lecturer*

Hollis
Nolin, John Charles *product specialist, engineering consultant*

New London
Sheerr, Deirdre McCrystal *architectural firm executive*

NEW JERSEY

Bloomsbury
Rohloff, Claire Marie *interior designer, educator*

Bound Brook
Shive, Richard Byron *architect*

Cape May Point
Jordan, Joe J. *architect*

Colonia
Wiesenfeld, Bess G. *interior designer*

East Orange
Fielo, Muriel Bryant *interior designer*

Englewood
Schmidt, Ronald Hans *architect*

Morristown
Nadaskay, Raymond *architect*

Princeton
Allen, Stanley T. *architect, dean, educator*
Boyer, M. Christine *architecture educator*
Diller, Elizabeth E. *architect, educator, artist*
Ford, Jeremiah, III, *architect*
Graves, Michael *architect, educator*
Hillier, J(ames) Robert *architect*
Holt, Philetus Havens, III, *architect*
Kehrt, Allan William *architect*
Lerner, Ralph *architect, university dean*
Mills, Michael James *architect*
Nichols, Karen *architect*

South Orange
DeVaris, Panayotis Eric *architect*

Upper Saddle River
Cappitella, Mauro John *architect*

NEW MEXICO

Albuquerque
Gutierrez, Gabriella *architecture educator*
Gutierrez, Joni Marie *landscape architect, political organization worker*
Pressman, Andy *architecture educator*
Sabatini, William Quinn *architect*
Schluntz, Roger *architecture educator*

Hobbs
Ritchie, Fran A. *interior designer, small business owner*

Placitas
Pirkl, James Joseph *industrial designer, educator, writer*

Santa Fe
Leon, Bruno *architect, architecture educator*

NEW YORK

Binghamton
Bearsch, Lee Palmer *architect, city planner*

Bridgehampton
Coy, Christopher James *architect*

Bronxville
Frost, A. Corwin *architect, consultant*

Brooklyn
Katavolos, William *architecture educator, furniture designer*
Nadel, Monroe Stanley *retired architect, landscape architect*
Palermo, Robert James *architect, consultant, inventor*
Rice, John Thomas *architecture educator*
Weston, I. Donald *architect*

Buffalo
Coles, Robert Traynham *architect*

Chester
Karen, Linda Tricarico *interior designer*

Cortlandt Manor
Frischmuth, Robert Alfred *landscape planner, filmmaker*

Cranberry Lake
Glavin, James Edward *landscape architect*

Cross River
Thorn, Susan Howe *interior designer*

Dobbs Ferry
Guggenheimer, Tobias Immanuel Simon *architect*

East Hampton
Delson, Sidney Leon *architect*

Elizaville
Koeppel, Harry Saul *interior designer, educator*

Grand Island
Mendell, Mark *architect*

Hastings On Hudson
Weinstein, Edward Michael *architect, consultant*

Hensonville
Newman, Oscar *architect, city planner, sculptor*

Ithaca
Olpadwala, Porus *architecture educator, dean*
Seraji-Bozorgzad, Nasrine *architecture educator*

Jamaica
Gati, William Eugene *architect, designer and planner*

Katonah
Baker, John Milnes *architect*

Kew Gardens
Aldea, Patricia *architect*

Locust Valley
Bentel, Carol Rusche *architect*
Bentel, Frederick Richard *architect, educator*
Bentel, Paul Louis *architect, educator*

Long Island City
Sadao, Shoji *architect*

Manhasset
Grossi, Olindo *architect, educator*
Schiller, Arthur A. *architect, educator*

Middletown
Fucci, Joseph Leonard *editor, consultant, school librarian*

New Lebanon
Baker, James Barnes *architect*

New Rochelle
Menzies, Henry Hardinge *architect*

New Windsor
Minuta, Joseph J. *architect*

New York
Aliotta, Joseph J. *architect, director*
Anderson, Ross S. *architectural firm executive*
Arad, Michael Sahar *architect*
Bader, Ian *architectural firm executive*
Baird, Penny Drue *interior designer*
Bakker, Ron *architect*
Beckmann, John *architect, designer, writer*
Beer, David Wells *architect*
Beyer, John H. *architectural firm executive*
Bland, Frederick Aves *architect*
Blumenfeld, Joan *architect*
Bond, J. Max, Jr., *architect, educational administrator*
Borrelli, John Francis *architect*
Breger, William N. *architect, educator*

Buatta, Mario *interior designer*
Buttrick, Harold *architect*
Carlson, Richard A. *interior designer*
Cavaglieri, Giorgio *architect*
Chan, Lo-Yi Cheung Yuen *architect*
Charles, Michael Harrison *architectural interior designer*
Childs, David *architectural firm executive*
Cioppa, Robert *architectural firm executive*
Clement, Gregory *architect*
Cobb, Henry Nichols *architect*
Cohn, Ian J. *architect*
Cracauer, Cynthia Phifer *architectural firm executive*
Cutler, Laurence Stephan *architect, urban designer, museum founder, advertising executive, educator*
Czajka, James Vincent *architect*
Daniels, J. Yolande *architectural firm executive, educator*
David, Theoharis Lambros *architect, educator*
Davis, Diane Arlene (Diane A. Davis) *architect, energy and environmental civil engineer, educator*
Davis, Lewis *architectural firm executive*
Davis, Steven M. *architectural firm executive*
Dennis, Diane Joy Milam *retired architect*
De Vido, Alfredo Eduardo *architect*
Djerejian, Robert Asbed *architect*
Edelman, Judith H. *architect*
Eisenman, Peter David *architect, educator*
Fleischer, Joseph Linden *architect*
Flynn, Michael D. *architectural firm executive*
Franzen, Ulrich J. *architect*
Freed, James Ingo *architect*
Galan, Leonidez Vindollo *architect*
Gastil, Raymond Wesley *urban designer*
Gath, Jean Marie *architectural firm executive*
Gatje, Robert Frederick *architect, writer*
Gaveras, Harry *architect*
Giddens-Jones, Emily Jane *architectural and interior designer, consultant*
Ginsberg, David Lawrence *architect*
Grabé, Christopher K. *architectural firm executive*
Guise, David Earl *architect, educator*
Gwathmey, Charles *architect*
Halsband, Frances *architect*
Hardy, Hugh *architect*
Hariri, Gisue *architect, educator*
Hayden, Richard Seth *architectural firm executive*
Hinz, Theodore Vincent *architect*
Holl, Steven Myron *architect, educator*
Holub, Martin *architect*
Hoog, Marjorie *architect*
Huxtable, Ada Louise *architecture critic*
Ivy, Robert Adams, Jr., *architect, editor-in-chief*
James, Warren A. *architect*
Joseph, Wendy Evans *architect*
Karlin, Susan *design company executive*
Kasakove, Susan *interior designer*
Kliment, Robert Michael *architect*
Kliment, Stephen Alexander *architect, editor, journalist*
Kohn, A. Eugene *architect*
Krebs, Carl F. *architectural firm executive*
Kuhl, William Bernard *landscape architect*
Lau, Harry Hung-Kwan *acoustical and interior designer, consultant*
Leavitt, David Livingstone *architect*
Lefferts, Gillet, Jr., *architect*
Leigh, Stephen *industrial designer*
Lerner, Jill *architect*
Lewis, Paul *architecture educator*
Libeskind, Daniel *architect*
Liebman, Theodore *architect*
Logan, Thaddeus Sumner, III, *architect*
Louie, William C. *architect*
Marpillero, Sandro *architectural firm executive*
Masey, Jack *exhibition designer*
Michielli, Frank V. *architectural firm executive*
Miller, George H. *architectural firm executive*
Mosellie, Anthony *architect*
Moss, Douglas *architectural firm executive*
Mui, Jimmy Kun *architect*
Olcott, Richard M. *architectural firm executive*
Paxson, William H. *architectural firm executive*
Pei, Ieoh Ming *architect*
Perkins, Lawrence Bradford, Jr., *architect*
Pomeroy, Lee Harris *architect*
Quennell, Nicholas *landscape architect, educator*
Robinson, James LeRoy *architect, educator, developer*
Rosenblatt, Arthur Isaac *architect, former museum director*
Sagan, M. J. *architectural firm executive*
Slomanson, Lloyd Howard *architect, musician, photographer*
Smotrich, David Isadore *architect*
Stern, Robert Arthur Morton *architect, educator, writer*
Strasser, Robert *architectural firm executive*
Stubbs, John Howell *architectural educator, preservationist*
Szeto, Yvonne *architectural firm executive*
Taylor, Marilyn Jordan *architectural firm executive*
Tozer, Elizabeth Farran *interior and floral designer*
Tschumi, Bernard *architect*
Varney, Carleton Bates, Jr., *interior designer, columnist, educator*
Vidler, Anthony *architecture educator, dean*
Voorsanger, Bartholomew *architect*
Wauford, J. Ben. *architect*
Wexler, Allan *architect, art educator*
Wigley, Mark Antony *architecture educator*
Willis, Beverly Ann *architect*

Northport
De Carolis, Philip Joseph *space designer, educator*

Nyack
Degenshein, Jan *architect, planner*

Old Westbury
Friedman, Jonathan Block *architect, educator, writer*

Penfield
Kraft, Donald Eugene *architecture and engineering company executive*

Pleasantville
Annese, Domenico *landscape architect*
Montgomery, Susan W *interior designer*

Rensselaerville
Dudley, George Austin *architect, planning consultant, educator*

Rye
Anderson, Allan *architectural firm executive*

Scarsdale
Bayar, Julia Beryl *interior designer*

Syracuse
Skoler, Louis *architect, educator*
Smardon, Richard Clay *landscape architecture and environmental studies educator*

Tarrytown
Kenney, John Michel *architect*

Troy
Balfour, Alan *architecture educator*
Haviland, David Sands *architectural educator, researcher, administrator*

Wappingers Falls
Johnson, Jeh Vincent *architect*

Weedsport
Cichello, Samuel Joseph *architect*

Westhampton Beach
Flood, Angela *interior designer, artist*

NORTH CAROLINA

Asheville
King, Joseph Bertram *architect*

Boone
Oelberg, Robert Nathan *landscape architect*

Chapel Hill
Dixon, Frederick Dail *architect*
Godschalk, David Robinson *architect, urban development planner, educator*
Stipe, Robert Edwin *design educator*

Charlotte
Ferebee, Stephen Scott, Jr., *architect*
Huberman, Jeffrey Allen *architect*
Little, William B. *architectural firm executive*
Montague, Edgar Burwell, III, (Monty Montague) *industrial designer*

Greensboro
Irvin, Helen Adcock *interior designer*
Murrelle, Ronald Kemp *architectural firm executive*

High Point
Schwartz, Robert Terry *industrial design executive*

Kitty Hawk
Elliott, Candice K. *interior designer*

Lexington
Younts, Patty Lou *interior design executive,inventor, researcher*

Pisgah Forest
Albyn, Richard Keith *retired architect*

Raleigh
Clarke, Lewis James *landscape architect*
Flournoy, William Louis, Jr., *landscape architect*
Godwin, James Beckham *retired landscape architect*
Malecha, Marvin John *architect, academic administrator*
Peele, Katherine N. *architect*

Research Triangle Park
Atkins, John L., III, *architect*
Freelon, Philip G. *architectural firm executive*

Robbinsville
Ginn, Ronn *architect, urban planner, general contractor*

Southern Shores
Vander Myde, Philip Louis *architectural design firm executive*

OHIO

Akron
Castronovo, Thomas Paul *architect, consultant*

Celina
Fanning, Ronald Heath *architect, engineer*

Cincinnati
Chatterjee, Jayanta *architecture and planning educator*
Glendening, Everett Austin *architect*
Goetzman, Bruce Edgar *architecture educator*
Luckner, Herman Richard, III, *interior designer*
Nielsen, George Lee *architect*
Roomann, Hugo *architect*
Senhauser, John Crater *architect*

Cleveland
Behnke, William Alfred *retired landscape architect*
Bowen, Richard Lee *architect*
Eberhard, William Thomas *architect*
Gellert, Edward Bradford, III, *architect*
Gibans, James David *architect*
Hancock, James Beaty *interior designer*
Kelly, John Terence *architect*
Little, Robert Andrews *architect, artist*
Madison, Robert Prince *architect*
Melsop, James William *architect*
Sande, Theodore Anton *architect, educator, foundation executive*
Zung, Thomas Tse-Kwai *architect*

Columbus
Bohm, Friedrich (Friedl) K.M. *architectural firm executive*
Kirk, Ballard Harry Thurston *architect*
Osgood, Robert T., Jr., *architect, strategic planner*
Oubrerie, José R. *architecture educator*
Tyne, Michael D. *architectural firm executive*
Voss, Jerrold Richard *architecture educator*
Weinhold, Virginia Beamer *interior designer*

Cuyahoga Falls
Haag, Everett Keith *architect*

Reynoldsburg
Serraglio, Mario *architect*

Toledo
Hills, Arthur W. *architectural firm executive*
Martin, Robert Edward *architect*

OKLAHOMA

Norman
Fillpot, Bob G. *architecture educator*
Henderson, Arnold Glenn *architect, educator*
Henkle, James L. *industrial designer*
Kudrna, James *architecture educator*
Sorey, Thomas Lester, Jr., *architect, educator*

Oklahoma City
Frankfurt, William W. *architectural firm executive*
Halpin, Anna Marie *architect, wrter*

Tulsa
Ball, Rex Martin *urban designer, architect*
Broach, David E. *architectural firm executive*

OREGON

Ashland
Mularz, Theodore Leonard *architect*

Chiloquin
Harreld, Karen L. *jewelry designer, photographer*

Eugene
Theodoropoulos, Christine O. *architecture educator*
Utsey, Glenda Fravel *architecture educator*

Lorane
Plésums, Guntis *architect, retired educator*

Medford
Skelton, Douglas H. *architect*
Straus, David A. *architectural firm executive*

Otter Rock
Eaton, Leonard Kimball *retired architecture educator*

Portland
Allen, Rex Whitaker *retired architect*
Frasca, Robert John *architect*
Gunsul, Brooks R. W. *architect*
Hacker, Thomas Owen *architect*
Kilbourn, Lee Ferris *architect, specfications writer*

Springfield
Lutes, Donald Henry *architect*

Tualatin
Broome, John William *retired architect*

Turner
Davenport, Linnea Maibrit *design educator*

Welches
Merrill, William Dean *retired architect, medical facility planning consultant*

PENNSYLVANIA

Ambler
Swansen, Donna Maloney *landscape designer, consultant*

Bala Cynwyd
Bentivegna, Peter Ignatius *architectural company executive*
Wheatley, William Arthur *architect, musician*

Bethlehem
Spillman, Robert Arnold *architect*

Butler
Kosar, John E. *architectural firm executive*

Camp Hill
Anderson, Dorothy Kentner *interior designer*

Chadds Ford
Milner, John D. *architectural firm executive, educator*
Werner DeNadai, Mary *architectural firm executive*

East Stroudsburg
Hoyt, Earl Edward, Jr., *industrial designer*

Greencastle
Scott, Leighton Reeves *interior designer, artist, writer*

Harrisburg
Knackstedt, Mary V. *interior designer*

Hershey
Rogowicz, Edward Joseph *industrial arts, technology educator*

Narberth
Grenald, Raymond *architectural lighting designer*

New Cumberland
Peters, Ralph Edgar *architectural firm executive, engineering executive*

Philadelphia
Barnett, Jonathan *architect, urban planner, educator*
Brown, Denise Scott *architect, urban planner*
Dagit, Charles Edward, Jr., *architect, educator*
DeLong, David G. *architect, urban planner, educator*
Eiswerth, Barry Neil *architect, educator*
Greenberger, Alan *architectural firm executive*
Hamme, David Codrington *architect*
Harris, Samuel Y. *architect, educator*
Hayes, John Freeman *architect*
Keefe, Mary *architectural firm executive*
Kelley, Daniel *architectural firm executive*
Kise, James Nelson *architect, urban planner*
Kolker, James Hamilton *architect*
Lawson, John Quinn *architect*
Magaziner, Henry Jonas *architect, writer*
Maxman, Susan Abel *architect*
Mertins, Detlef *architect, educator*
Mitchell, Ehrman Burkman, Jr., *architect*
Perkins, George Holmes *architectural educator, architect*
Rauch, John Keiser, Jr., *architect*
Rybczynski, Witold Marian *architect, educator, writer*
Rykwert, Joseph *architecture and art history educator*
Santos, Adele Naude *architect, educator*
Saylor, Peter M. *architect*
Shuman, Robert Z. *architect*
Venturi, Robert *architect*
Winkler, Gail Caskey *design historian, writer, educator*

Pittsburgh
Becherer, Richard John *architecture educator*
Carter, Donald K. *architectural firm executive*
Gindroz, Raymond L. *architect*
Hoglund, J. David *architectural firm executive*
Lam, Khee Poh *architecture educator, consultant*
Loftness, Vivian Ellen *architecture educator, department chairman*
Rico-Gutierrez, Luis F. *architecture educator*
Simonds, John Ormsbee *landscape architect*

Slatington
Heffelfinger, Karl William *retired draftsman*

State College
Haas, John C. *architect*

University Park
Wheeler, C. Herbert *architect, consultant, educator*

Willow Grove
Suer, Marvin David *architectural consultant*

Wyomissing
Kessler, Leona Hanover *interior designer*

RHODE ISLAND

Bristol
Hendrix, John Shannon *architecture educator*

Jamestown
Todd, Thomas Abbott *architect, urban designer, city planner*

Newport
Burgin, William Lyle *architect*
Wurman, Richard Saul *architect*

Providence
Barnum, William Milo *architect*
Kagan, Marilyn D. *retired architect*
St. Florian, Friedrich Gartler *architect, educator*

SOUTH CAROLINA

Beaufort
Frederick, Jane Y. *architect*

Charleston
Goff, R. Garey *architect*

Clemson
Bauerle, William L. *landscape architect, educator*
Halfacre, Robert Gordon *ombudsman, landscape architect, horticulturist, educator*

Columbia
Turk, John Cobb *architect, educator*

Greenville
Hultstrand, Charles John *architect*
LeBlanc, L(ouis) Christian *architect*
Neal, James Austin *architect*

Myrtle Beach
Pegram, J.J. *architectural firm executive*

TENNESSEE

Chattanooga
Derthick, Alan Wendell *architect, architectural firm executive*

Memphis
Adsit, Russell Allan *landscape architect*
Evans, James Mignon *architect*

Nashville
Miller, Richard L. *architectural executive*
Swensson, Earl Simcox *architect*

TEXAS

Arlington
Ferrier, Richard Brooks *architecture educator, architect*
Fouse, David Jesse *architect*
Gatzke, Donald Frank *architecture educator*
Wright, C(arroll) Lee, Jr., *architecture educator*

Austin
Alexander, Drury Blakeley *architectural educator*
Alter, Kevin S. *architecture educator*
Box, John Harold *architect, educator*
George, Walter Eugene, Jr., *architect*

Kahn, Terry D. *architecture educator*
Little, Emily Browning *architect*
Pateron, Robert G. *architecture educator*
Speck, Lawrence W. *architect, educator*

Bellaire
Lundy, Victor Alfred *architect, educator*

Carrollton
Hill, B. Don *office interiors company executive*

College Station
Clayton, Mark J. *architecture educator*
Downing, Frances E. *architecture educator*
Huang, Chang-Shan *landscape architect, educator*
Reed, Raymond Deryl *architect*
Regan, J. Thomas *architecture educator*
Shepley, Mardelle McCuskey *architect, educator*
Vandiver, Renee Lillian Aubry *interior designer, architectural preservator*
Woodcock, David Geoffrey *architect, educator*

Corpus Christi
Angell, Ellen *interior designer*

Dallas
Charriere, Suzanne *architectural firm executive*
Hawkins, H. Ralph *architectural firm executive*
Josal, Lance K. *architectural firm executive*
Kolb, Nathaniel Key, Jr., *architect*
Rees, Frank William, Jr., *architect*
Schwartz, Irving Donn *architect*
Shipley, Dan *architect*
Skaggs, Ronald Lloyd *architect*
Spencer, Mary Helen *interior designer*
Stacy, Dennis William *architect*
Wilson, Trisha *interior architectural designer*

Denton
Gough, Clarence Ray *retired designer, educator*

El Paso
Benning, Mary Etzold *interior designer*
Korth, Charlotte Williams *furniture and interior design firm executive*
Stanley, Duffy B. *architect, planner*

Flower Mound
Morrish, Thomas Jay *golf course architect*

Granbury
Garrison, Truitt B. *architect*

Houston
Bair, Royden Stanley *retired architect*
Bentsen, Kenneth Edward *architect*
Blackstone, W.C. *architectural firm executive*
Brents, Daniel *architectural firm executive*
Bryan, Mary Ann *interior designer*
Casbarian, John J. *architecture educator*
Colbert, Thomas *architecture educator*
Crane, John S. *architectural firm executive*
Cutler, John Earl *landscape architect*
Douglas, Frank Fair *architect, graphic designer*
Dumont, Edward Abdo *architect, interior designer*
Fannin, Tom *architectural firm executive*
Gloriod, Paul *architectural firm executive*
Hamilton, D. Kirk *architectural firm executive*
Hines, Gerald D. *architectural firm executive*
Ivanov, Lyuben Dimitrov *naval architecture researcher, educator*
Kirkland, Lannis *architecture educator*
Lerup, Lars G. *architecture educator, college dean*
Marchand, Wayne *architectural firm executive*
Mashburn, Joseph L. *architecture educator*
Mc Ginty, John Milton *architect*
Moorhead, Gerald Lee *architect*
Neuhaus, William Oscar, III, *architect*
Obiora, Chris Sunny *architect*
Turner, Leland *architectural firm executive*
Walton, Conrad Gordon, Sr., *retired architect*

San Antonio
Baron, Robert M. *architecture educator*
Blonkvist, Tim *architectural firm executive*
Davis, George Edward *industrial designer*
Frazer, Robert Lee *landscape architect*
Graves, Kenneth Martin *architect*
Gribou, Julius M. *architecture educator*
Haywood, Norcell Dan *architect*
Lowe, Douglas Howard *architect*

UTAH

Salt Lake City
Beall, Burtch W., Jr., *architect*
Brems, David Paul *architect*
Chong, Richard David *architect*
Christopher, James Walker *architect, educator*
Miller, William Charles *architect, educator*

VERMONT

Brattleboro
Gorman, Robert Saul *architect*

VIRGINIA

Alexandria
Cross, Eason, Jr., *architect*
Jackson, Nancy Morrison *architect*
Kitchens, David *architect*
Vosbeck, William Frederick, Jr., *architect*

Arlington
Adreon, Harry Barnes *architect*
Ankudinov, Vladimir Konstantinovich *naval architect*
DeBernard, Michael *architectural firm executive*
Draeger, Susanne Yarbrough *interior designer*
Freschi, Bruno Basilio *architect, educator*
Hassett, Valerie Jane *interior designer, architect, educator*
Sheridan, Frederick *architectural firm executive*
Stewart, Gordon Mead *architect*
Tarpgaard, Peter Thorvald *naval architect*

Blacksburg
Bliznakov, Milka Tcherneva *architect, educator*
Crawford, Peggy Smith *design educator*
Knox, Paul L. *architecture educator, dean*
Pittman, Hunter *architecture educator, department chairman*
Poole, Scott *architecture educator*
Rodriguez-Camilloni, Humberto Leonardo *architect, historian, educator*
Rott, Hans C. *architect, educator*
Weiner, Frank H. *architect, educator*

Boston
Engle, Reed Laurence *landscape architect*

Charlottesville
Anderson, Robert Barber *architect*
Bednar, Michael John *architecture educator*
Root, James Benjamin *landscape architect*
Sherman, William *architecture educator*
Swofford, Donald Anthony *architect*

Fairfax
Ward, George Truman *architect*

Falls Church
Barkley, Paul Haley, Jr., *architect*

Mc Lean
Mortensen, Robert Henry *landscape architect, golf course architect*

Mechanicsville
Peterson, William Canova *architect*

Orlean
Kulski, Julian Eugeniusz *architect, planner, educator*

Reston
Scheeler, James Arthur *architect*

Richmond
Jamgochian, Victoria *interior designer*
Joel, William Lee, II, *interior and lighting designer*
Morris, James Carl *architect*

Staunton
Firehock, Barbara A. *interior designer*

Virginia Beach
Bell, Janet S. *product designer, interior designer*
Stanton, Pamela Freeman *interior designer, writer*

Williamsburg
Herbert, Albert Edward, Jr., *interior and industrial designer*

Winchester
Hall, Ralph C. *retired architect, mechanical engineer*

Woodbridge
Peck, Dianne Kawecki *architect*

WASHINGTON

Bainbridge Island
Bowden, William Darsie *retired interior designer*

Gig Harbor
McMillan, John Howard *industrial designer, consultant*

Kennewick
Morris, Rusty Lee *architectural consulting firm executive*

Kirkland
Mitchell, Joseph Patrick *architect*
Steinmann, John Colburn *architect*

Mill Creek
Latta, Diana Lennox *retired interior designer*

Mount Vernon
Hall, David Ramsay *architect*
Klein, Henry *architect*

Olympia
Bagg, Carter Davis *architect, urban planner*

Redmond
Sowder, Robert Robertson *architect*

Seattle
Bain, William James, Jr., *architect*
Bosworth, Thomas Lawrence *architect, educator*
Buursma, William F. *architect*
Clark, Dawn A. *architect*
Deines, Katrina *architecture educator*
Dubrow, Gail Lee *architecture educator*
Epple, Steven *architectural firm executive*
Gish, John C. *architect*
Hinshaw, Mark Larson *architect, urban planner*
Johnson, Spencer A. *architect*
Johnston, Norman John *retired architecture educator*
Jonassen, James O. *architect*
Jones, Grant Richard *landscape architect, planner*
Karst, William B. *architectural firm executive*
Kolb, Keith Robert *architect, educator*
Kreager, William *architect*
Lacey, William Paul *architect*
Laegreid, Stanley T. *architect*
Lovett, Wendell Harper *architect, educator*
Ludtka, J. Mark *architect*
Meyer, C. Richard *architect*
Miles, Don Clifford *architect*
Mugerauer, Robert W., Jr., *architecture educator*
Olson, James William Park *architect*
Perthou, Alison Chandler *interior designer*
Piven, Peter Anthony *architect, management consultant*
Prakash, Vikramaditya (Vikram) *architecture educator*
Thomas, John Val Faia *architect*
Tindall, Robert J. *architectural firm executive*

Tacoma
Liddle, Alan Curtis *retired architect*

WEST VIRGINIA

Charleston
Gokcen, Uner *architectural firm executive*

Wheeling
Hooker, William *architectural firm executive*

WISCONSIN

Eau Claire
Larson, Brian Foix *architect*

Kenosha
Potente, Eugene, Jr., *interior designer*

La Crosse
Hogan, Kerry F. *design educator*

Madison
Buchholz, Ronald Lewis *architect*
Nisbet, Thomas K. *architect*
Tishler, William Henry *landscape architect, educator*

Milwaukee
Dumas, Tyrone Pierre *architect, consultant*
Frank, Nancy *architecture educator*
Greenstreet, Robert Charles *architect, educator*
Hanlon, Donald *architecture educator*
Hubbard, Nancy *architecture educator*

Soldiers Grove
Quebe, Jerry Lee *retired architect*

TERRITORIES OF THE UNITED STATES

PUERTO RICO

San Juan
Marvel, Thomas Stahl *architect*

VIRGIN ISLANDS

Saint John
Fradley, Frederick Macdonell *retired architect*

CANADA

BRITISH COLUMBIA

Vancouver
Erickson, Arthur Charles *architect*

NOVA SCOTIA

Halifax
Fowler, Charles Allison Eugene *retired architect, civil engineer*

ONTARIO

Ottawa
Rutt, James P. *design company executive*

Toronto
Budrevics, Alexander *landscape architect*
Fife, Edward H. *landscape architecture educator*
McKenna, Marianne *architect*
van Ginkel, Blanche Lemco *architect, educator*

QUEBEC

Montreal
Davidson, Colin Henry *architect, educator*

ENGLAND

Ely Cambridgeshire
March, Lionel John *architecture educator, researcher*

FRANCE

Roques
White, Norval Crawford *architect*

TURKEY

Istanbul
Ongan, Nilgün Erdal *decorator, architect, artist*

ADDRESS UNPUBLISHED

Accordino, Frank Joseph *architect*
Adler, Richard Melvin *architect, planner*
Alexander, James H. *industrial designer*
Alexander, Ruth Batchelder *interior decorator, environmental activist*
Anderson, Ruth Lucille *interior designer, educator, artist, librarian, archivist*
Armistead, Katherine Kelly (Mrs. Thomas B. Armistead III) *interior designer, travel consultant, civic worker*
Balke, Robert Roy *architect*
Berman, Siegrid Visconti *interior designer*
Berry, Sharon Elaine *interior designer*
Bower, Marilyn Kay *landscape artist*
Brent, Rebecca Kemp *product designer, writer*
Brotman, David Joel *retired architectural firm executive, consultant*
Bunch, Franklin Swope *retired architect*
Carpenter, Derr Alvin *landscape architect*
Case, Gerard Ramon *drafting technologist, paleontologist*
Chao, James Min-Tzu *architect*
Cleaveland, John Riddle *retired architect*
Crowther, Richard Layton *architect, consultant, researcher, author, lecturer*
DeFrancis, Suellen Maria *interior architect*
Degenhardt, Robert Allan *architectural firm executive, engineering executive*
Dermanis, Paul Raymond *architect*
Dibner, David Robert *architect, writer*
Dobbel, Rodger Francis *interior designer*
Doby, Margaret Gail *interior designer*
Ensign, William Lloyd *architect*
Fisher, Steven Jay *architect*
Flipse, John Edward *naval architect, mechanical engineer*
Friedman, Mildred *architectural and design educator, curator, consultant*
Gaillard, George Siday, III, *architect*
Gantz, Carroll Melvin *industrial design consultant, consumer product designer*
Geddes, Robert *architect, educator*
Genaro, Donald Michael *industrial designer*
Gensler, M. Arthur, Jr., *architect*
Gerou, Phillip Howard *architect*
Gillmer, Thomas Charles *retired naval architect*
Girgus, Signe Linscott *interior designer*
Glikin, Anton Arkadievich *architectural designer, artist*
Gordon, Ezra *architect, educator*
Green, Thomas George *retired architect*
Greenfield, Sanford Raymond *architect*
Grossman, Robert James *retired architect*
Grotta, Sandra Brown *interior designer*
Hakim, Besim Selim *architecture and urban design educator, researcher and consultant*
Hardison, Donald Leigh *retired architect*
Hastings, L(ois) Jane *architect, architecture educator*
Herzig, Julie Esther *designer*
Hooper, Roger Fellowes *retired architect*
Hutchins, Robert Ayer *architectural consultant*
Kahn, Charles Howard *architect, educator*
Kailian, Aram Harry *architect, consultant*
Kane, Diane Grinkevich *architectural historian, educator, planner*
Keech, Elowyn Ann *interior designer*
Kelalis, Barbara Anna Lisa *interior design company executive*
Keune, Russell Victor *retired architect*
Knoll, Florence Schust *architect, designer*
Korobkin, Barry Jay *architect*
Kultermann, Udo *architectural and art historian, educator, author*
Langeloh, Jean Kleppinger *interior designer*
Lederer, Paul Edward *landscape architect*
Lee, Sarah Tomerlin *design executive*
Leung, Roderick Chi-tak *architect*
Lin, Maya *architect, sculptor*
Liskamm, William Hugo *architect, urban planner, educator*
Loss, John C. *architect, retired educator*
Lyn, Jean *interior designer*
Lypka, Gerald L. *product designer, artist*
Macon, Irene Elizabeth *interior designer, consultant*
McCabe, Linda Rae *interior designer, artist, writer*
McFadden, Robbyn Kilbane *interior designer, public policy specialist, artist, advocate*
McGee, Humphrey Glenn *architect*
McGunigle, Dorothy Greene *interior designer, artist*
McIntosh, Molly *interior designer*
Mc Pheeters, Edwin Keith *architect, educator*
Meyers, Richard James *landscape architect*
Miller, Jack Conway *landscape artist, art gallery director, owner*
Millican, Kirk *architect*
Molnar, Donald Joseph *landscape architecture educator*
Moore, Richard Alan *landscape architect*
Mujica, Mauro E. *architect*
Mumma, Albert Girard, Jr., *architect*
Munson, Virginia Aldrich *interior designer, decorator*
Murray, David George *architect*
Myer, Donald Beekman *architect*
Naidorf, Louis Murray *architect*
Odermatt, Robert Allen *architect*
Oles, Paul Stevenson (Steve Oles) *architect, perspectivist, educator*
Omholt, Bruce Donald *product designer, mechanical engineer, consultant*
Orr, Frank Howard, III, *architect*
Park Spencer, Karen Lynn *architect, jewelry designer*
Pastor, Millie A. *interior designer, consultant*
Perkins, Nancy Jane *industrial designer*
Peters, Robert Woolsey *architect*
Pettitt, Jay S. *architect, consultant*
Pfanstiel Parr, Dorothea Ann *interior designer*
Pieretti, Michael *product designer*
Poss, Jeffery Scott *architect, educator*
Rabon, William James, Jr., *architect*
Ramirez, Martin Ruben *architect, engineer, educator, cognitive scientist, consultant*
Rasic, Janko *architect*
Reid, Joseph Browning *retired architect*
Rice, Richard Lee *retired architect*
Rogers, Kate Ellen *interior design educator*
Ross, Molly Owings *jewelry designer, sculptor, small business owner*
Ryan, John Michael *landscape architect*
Smolek, Rochelle Thérèse *interior designer*
Strombom, David Glen *designer*
Tachi, Douglas Paul *architect, interior designer*
Tharp, Benjamin Carroll, Jr., *retired architect*
Thiel, Philip *design educator*
Tomasi, Donald Charles *architect*
Tyng, Anne Griswold *architect*
Van Housen, Thomas Corwin, III, *retired architect*
Wiebenson, Dora Louise *architectural historian, editor, author*
Winter, Arch Reese *retired architect*

Wong, Liliane *architect, architecture educator*
Woodring, Margaret Daley *architect, planner*

ARTS: LITERARY *See also* COMMUNICATIONS MEDIA

UNITED STATES

ALABAMA

Auburn
Chris, Forhan *poet, educator*

Birmingham
Lide, Neoma Jewell Lawhon (Mrs. Martin James Lide Jr.) *poet*

Decatur
Sandlin, Anathalee Gray *writer, music company owner*

Florence
McDermott, David (John) *writer, marketing professional, artist*

Huntsville
Francis, Herbert Edward, Jr., *writer*

Tuscaloosa
Martone, Michael *writer*

ALASKA

Anchorage
Strohmeyer, John *writer, former editor*
Thomas, Lowell, Jr., *writer, lecturer, former lieutenant governor, former state senator*

Arctic Village
Tritt, Lincoln C. (Lincoln C. Gwich'in) *writer, educator, musician*

Delta Junction
Noble, Alice L. *writer, researcher*

Lake Clark Park
Kroll, Henry F. *writer, small business owner*

North Pole
McGee, Michael Vanhook *writer*

Wasilla
Brunke, Dawn Baumann *writer, editor*

ARIZONA

Kykotsmovi
Honan, Raena *writer*

Mesa
Kiefer, Don Russell *writer, researcher*
St. Cyr, Margaret Ann (Peggy St. Cyr) *writer*

Phoenix
Avila, Bridgett Bernice *writer*
Ellison, Cyril Lee *literary agent, retired publisher*
Prewitt, Alan Jay *playwright, performing company executive*

Prescott
Gose, Celeste Marlene *writer*

Scottsdale
Taylor, James C. *writer*

Sedona
Frankel, Jennie Louise *writer, composer, playwright*

Tempe
Cortright, Barbara Jean *writer*
Raby, William Louis *writer, consultant*

Tucson
Butcher, Russell Devereux *author, photographer*
Kingsolver, Barbara Ellen *writer*
Martin, Marci *writer, former advertising specialist*
Mason, Judith Ann *freelance writer*
Ratoff, Michael Barton (Nico Ratoff) *writer, poet, publishing executive*
Woods, James Melvin *writer*

Yarnell
Rogers, Barbara Jean *writer, costume designer*

ARKANSAS

Fayetteville
Shafer, Carol Larsen *retired book reviewer*
Williams, Miller *poet, fiction writer, translator*

Little Rock
Nunn, Patarica Dian *poet*

Morrilton
Lord, Penny *writer*
Lord, Robert *writer*

Springdale
Richards, Dusty *writer*

West Memphis
Coley, Jeannette Cabell *writer*

CALIFORNIA

Alameda
Grzanka, Leonard Gerald *writer, consultant*
Ngo, Tung Thanh *writer, photographer*

Alamo
Reed, John Theodore *writer, publisher*

Altadena
Burden, Jean Prussing *retired poet, writer, editor*

Arcadia
Coulombe, Charles Aquila *writer, educator*
Sloane, Beverly LeBov *writer, consultant*

Atascadero
Locke, Virginia Otis *writer*

Bay Point
Karasch, Jack (John) *writer, educator*

Belmont
MacLennan, Amy Marie *poet*

Berkeley
Brooke, Tal (Robert Taliaferro) *writer*
Callenbach, Ernest *writer, editor*
Dundes, Alan *writer, folklorist, educator*
Guest, Barbara *author, poet*
Katzen, Mollie *writer*
Kluger, Richard *author, editor*
Meltzer, David *author, musician, educator*
Mukherjee, Bharati (Mrs. Clark Blaise) *author, English educator*
Russell, Charlie L. *writer*
Scott, Peter Dale *writer, retired English language educator*
Temko, Allan Bernard *writer*
Thompson, Bernadette Maria *poet*

Beverly Hills
Ball, Alan *screenwriter*
Basichis, Gordon Allen *writer, scriptwriter, marketing consultant, media consultant*
Bass, Ronald *screenwriter*
Chase, David *scriptwriter, television producer, television director*
Crowe, Cameron *screenwriter, film director*
Darabont, Frank *screenwriter, director*
David, Larry *television scriptwriter, producer, actor*
Farrelly, Bobby (Robert Leo Rarrelly Jr.) *writer, producer, director*
Gelbart, Larry *writer, producer*
Goldman, William *writer, scriptwriter*
Hamilton, Laurell K. *writer*
Kaufman, Charlie *writer*
Maitland-Lewis, Stephen *writer*
Meyers, Nancy Jane *screenwriter, producer, director*
Rabe, David William *playwright*
Roth, Eric *screenwriter*
Schulian, John (Nielsen Schulian) *screenwriter, author*
Shepard, Sam (Samuel Shepard Rogers) *playwright, actor*
Sorkin, Aaron *scriptwriter*
Ward, David Schad *screenwriter, film director*
Williamson, Kevin *writer, producer, director*

Big Bear Lake
Brueske, Charlotte *poet, composer*

Bonita
Laverents, Sidney Nicklas *writer*

Burbank
Goldstein, Kenneth F. *entertainment executive, software publisher*

Calabasas
Carner, Charles Robert, Jr., *screenwriter, director*

Camarillo
Alexander, John Charles *editor, writer*

Cameron Park
Vorce-Tish, Helene R. *writer*

Canoga Park
Alexander, Sue *writer*

Capitola
Wolff, Jean Walton *writer*

Carlsbad
Farrell, Warren Thomas *author*

Cayucos
Shahan, Sherry Jean *writer, educator*

Cazadero
Tuggle, Mike *writer, secondary school educator*

Chatsworth
Dunwich, Gerina *writer, magazine editor, astrologer*

Chico
Cooper, Erwin *writer*
Livingston, Myran Jay *author, film writer, director and producer*

Chino Hills
Sanders, Nancy Ida *writer*

Chula Vista
Ryan, Candace Irene *writer, director, editor*

Citrus Heights
Daves, Sandra Lynn *poet, lyricist*

Claremont
Espinosa, Gaston E. *writer, educator*
Riley, Judith Merkle *writer, educator*
Tilden, Wesley Roderick *writer, retired computer programmer*
Wachtel, Albert *writer, educator*
Wolf, Kenneth Baxter *writer, educator*

Clovis
Shields, Allan Edwin *writer, photographer, retired educator*

Compton
Shiloh, Allen *writer*

Concord
Headding, Lillian Susan (Sally Headding) *writer, forensic clairvoyant*

Corona
Amato, Carol Joy *writer, anthropologist*

Coronado
Stockdale, James Bond *writer, research scholar, retired naval officer*

Cotati
Hill, Debora Elizabeth *writer, journalist, screenwriter*

Crescent City
Ruffer, Joyce Sellars *poet, artist*

Cromberg
Kolb, Ken Lloyd *writer*

Cupertino
Zobel, Louise Purwin *author, educator, lecturer, writing consultant*

Cypress
Edmonds, Ivy Gordon *writer*

Dana Point
Walker, Doris Isaak *writer, historian, educator*

Davis
Bunch, Richard Alan *writer, educator, poet, philosopher*
Lescroart, John Thomas *writer, composer, singer*
Major, Clarence Lee *poet, novelist, educator, artist*
Rooks, George Malcolm *writer, educator, company executive*

Del Mar
Morton, Frederic *author*
Smith, Robert Hamil *writer, fund raiser*

El Cajon
Cossairt, Joseph Arthur, Jr., *writer*

Elk Grove
McDonald, William Hector, Jr., *writer*

Escondido
Friedman, Alan Howard *writer, educator*

Fontana
Tong, Freda Madeline *writer*

Fresno
Garrison-Finderup, Ivadelle Dalton *writer, educator*
Lanter, Lanore *writer, educator*
Levine, Philip *poet, retired educator*

Garden Valley
Price, Lew Paxton *writer, engineer, scientist*

Glendale
Burr Stienon, Elaine *writer, minister, private school educator*

Grass Valley
Dodd, Lisa Lehr *writer, literature educator*

Healdsburg
Castellini, Mary Mercer *author*
Erdman, Paul Emil *author*
Myers, Robert Eugene *writer, educator*

Hollywood
Kurlander, Carl Litman *screenwriter*
Melchior, Ib Jorgen *author, television and motion picture writer, director*
Sacre, Antonio *playwright*

Huntington Beach
Flakes, Susan *playwright, screenwriter, director*

Idyllwild
Schneider, Paul *writer*

Irvine
Shusterman, Neal Douglas *writer, screenwriter*

Jacumba
Johnson, Crane *writer, lawyer*

Kensington
Littlejohn, David *writer*

La Jolla
Antin, David *poet, critic*
Havis, Allan Stuart *playwright, theatre educator*
Iddings, Kathleen *poet, editor, publisher, consultant*

La Mesa
Mitry, Darryl Joseph *writer, educator*

Laguna Beach
Ghiselin, Brewster *author, English language educator emeritus*
Taylor, Theodore Langhans *author*

Landers
Landers, Vernette Trosper *writer, educator, association executive*

Los Altos Hills
Robbins, Doren Gurstein *poet, educator, artist*

Los Angeles
Basil, Douglas Constantine *writer, educator*
Carothers, A.J. *scriptwriter*
Cohen, Leonard (Norman Cohen) *poet, novelist, musician, songwriter*
Corwin, Norman *writer, director, producer*
Dew, Joan King *freelance/self-employed writer*
Eisenberg, Gary Julius *writer, musician, printmaker*
Freedman, Deborah Colette *playwright, actress*
Good, Edith Elissa (Pearl Williams) *writer*
Hethmon, Robert H. *writer, educator*
Johnson, Carole A. *writer, artist*
Kaplan, Nadia *writer*
Messerli, Douglas *writer, publisher*
Noguchi, Thomas Tsunetomi *writer, pathologist*

Los Gatos
Dahlberg, Thomas Robert *writer, lawyer, educator, software company executive*

Mammoth Lakes
Fitzgerald, Timothy K. *writer, political organizer, non-profit administrator*

Marina Del Rey
Minanel, Shelley *writer, artist*

Modesto
Norton, Max C. *writer, educator*
Turner-Silvia, JoAnn *writer, vocalist, actress, music producer*

Moffett Field
Kwong, Jennifer *writer*

Monrovia
Salaman, Maureen Kennedy *writer, nutritionist*

Newport Beach
Wentworth, Diana von Welanetz *author*

North Hollywood
Campos, Luis *puzzle writer*
Kuter, Kay E. *writer, actor*

Oakland
Foley, Jack (John Wayne Harold Foley) *poet, writer, editor*
Halpern, Mark *writer*
Knox, Helene Margrethe *writer*
Massachi, Dalya Faith *writer, consultant*
Schacht, Henry Mevis *writer, consultant*
Silverberg, Robert *author*
Turner, Tom *writer, editor*

Oceano
Scott, Donald Michael *writer, educator*

Orinda
Strong, Susan Clancey *writer, communication consultant, editor*

Palm Desert
Friesz, Mary Lee *freelance/self-employed poet*

Palm Springs
Martin, Lisa Ann *literary agent, writer*
Racina, Thom (Thomas Frank Raucina) *television writer, author*

Palo Alto
Wright, Kirby Michael *writer, editor*

Pasadena
Brogden-Stirbl, Shona Marie *writer, researcher*
Bunting, Anne Evelyn (Eve Bunting) *author*

Petaluma
Hass, Robert L. *writer, literature educator*
Pronzini, Bill John (William Pronzini) *writer*
Sebold, Alice *writer*
Spiegelman, Art *author, cartoonist*

Placerville
Wilkinson, Rosemary Regina Challoner *poet, writer*

Playa Del Rey
McNeill, Daniel Richard *writer*

Pomona
Mezey, Robert *poet*

Rancho Mirage
Olderman, Murray *columnist, cartoonist*

Rancho Palos Verdes
Zar, Judith L. (Mickey McBride) *writer*

Rancho Santa Fe
Byrd, Betty Rantze *writer*
Simon, William Leonard *film and television writer and producer, writer*

Red Bluff
Peters, Michael Morgan *playwright, consultant, theater director, theater critic, educator*

Redondo Beach
Battles, Roxy Edith *novelist, consultant, educator*

Reedley
Carey, Ernestine Gilbreth (Mrs. Charles E. Carey) *writer, lecturer*

Rohnert Park
Haslam, Gerald William *writer, educator*

Rolling Hills Estates
Price, Lia Scott *writer*

Ross
Godwin, Sara *writer*

Sacramento
Gerringer, Elizabeth (The Marchioness de Roe Devon) *writer, lawyer*
Kennedy, B. L. *poet, archivist*

Saint Helena
Wiggins, Rita Cassidy *poet*

San Anselmo
Harper Haines, Jan Frances *writer, educator*

Torbet, Laura *writer, artist, photographer, graphic designer*

San Diego
Brennan-Sparks, Jennifer Anne *writer*
Chun Fat, George *writer*
Crumpler, Hugh Allan *author*
Cunningham, Chester Grant *writer*
Krull, Kathleen *writer*
Lederer, Richard Henry *writer, educator, columnist*
Mahdavi, Kamal B. *writer, researcher*
Prescott, Lawrence Malcolm *medical and health science writer*
Skwara, Erich Wolfgang *novelist, poet, educator, literary critic*
Sturman, George *poet*
Turov, Daniel *financial writer, investment executive*
Valdez, Jose Carbajal, Jr., *poet, lyricist*
Yarber, Robert Earl *writer, retired educator*

San Francisco
D'Arpino, Tony *poet*
Donnally, Patricia Broderick *writer*
Ferlinghetti, Lawrence *poet*
Ferris, Russell James, II, *writer*
Gold, Herbert *author*
Inman, Robert Anthony *writer*
Kirschner, Ruth Fay *writer, artist*
Kraus, Krandall Anthony *writer*
O'Connor, Sheila Anne *freelance writer*
Sachs, Marilyn Stickle *author, lecturer, editor*
Sterkina, Sofiya *writer*

San Jose
Bleznick, Susan Risa *writer, television producer, photographer*
Loventhal, Milton *writer, playwright, lyricist*

San Leandro
Wycoff, Charles Coleman *writer, retired anesthesiologist*

San Luis Obispo
Bunge, Russell Kenneth *writer, poet, editor*

San Rafael
Brett, Peter D. *writer*
Hart, John *writer*
Nelson, James Carmer, Jr., *writer, editor, advertising executive*
Turner, William Weyand *writer*

Santa Barbara
Bock, Russell Samuel *writer*
Cunningham, Julia Woolfolk *author*
Jackson, Beverley Joy Jacobson *columnist, lecturer*
Mitchell, Shawne Maureen *author*
Poynter, Dan *author, publisher, speaker*
Ramsay, William Charles *writer, composer*

Santa Clara
Simmons, Janet Bryant *writer, publisher*
Singh, Loren Chan *writer, educator*

Santa Clarita
Ayres, Glenn Alex *scriptwriter, film producer*

Santa Maria
Meehan, Lil Euphrasia Therese *poet*

Santa Monica
Crichton, Michael (John Crichton) *author, film director*
Grubisich, Tom *screenwriter, editor, writer*
Mora, Philippe *screenwriter, producer, director, painter*
Pezzullo, Ralph Michael *writer, playwright*
Quinn, Patricia K. *literary agent*
Roney, Alice Lorraine Mann *poet*
Sipos, Thomas M. *writer*
Spataro, Janie Dempsey Watts *writer*
Stone, Oliver *screenwriter, director*

Santa Rosa
Guglielmino, Jude Patch *writer, humanitarian aid worker*

Sausalito
Hyde, Catherine Ryan *writer, short story writer*

Seal Beach
Olechno-Huszcza, Czeslaw *retired translator and educator*

Sebastopol
Arnold, Marsha Diane *writer*
Marler, Joan *writer, educator*

Sherman Oaks
Ellison, Harlan Jay *author, screenwriter*
LeBlanc, Rena *writer*

Simi Valley
Hochheiser, Marilyn *author, actress*

Somis
Premack, Ann J. *writer*

Sonoma
Kizer, Carolyn Ashley *poet, educator*

Soquel
Murray, Barbara Olivia *writer, retired psychologist*

South Pasadena
White, W. Robin *writer*

Stanford
Berger, Joseph *author, educator, counselor*
Wolff, Tobias (Jonathan Ansell Wolff) *writer*

Studio City
Parish, James Robert *author, cinema historian*
Shavelson, Melville *writer, theatrical producer and director*

Sugarloaf
Black, Victoria Lynn *writer, artist*

Sunnyvale
McAlister, Cynthia Swensen *writer*

Sylmar
Hayes, Cynthia Ann (C.A. Hayes) *writer*

Ukiah
Van Dusen, Wilson M. *writer, psychologist*

Valencia
McQuown, Mark *scriptwriter*
Parks, Suzan Lori *playwright*
Webb, Margot *writer*

Van Nuys
Becker, Frawley *writer, dialogue director, location manager*

Venice
Eliot, Alexander *author, mythologist*
Padilla, Mario René *literature educator, writer, actor*

Vernon
Kim, Ho Gill *poet*

Vista
Owen, Daniel Hugh *writer*

Walnut Creek
Chu, Valentin Yuan-ling *author*

West Hollywood
Grasshoff, Alex *writer, producer, director*
Schnabel, Timothy Brian *writer, publishing executive*
Slade, Bernard *playwright*

Yorba Linda
Medland, Maurice Blue *writer*

Yucaipa
D'Amelio, Dan Anthony *writer, journalist, educator*

COLORADO

Aurora
Fisher, Patricia Anne *writer, publishing executive*

Boulder
Carlson, Rhonda *writer, law educator*
Hurd, Jerrie *writer*
Waldman, Anne Lesley *poet, performer, editor, publisher, educational administrator*

Colorado Springs
Dassanowsky, Robert von *educator, producer, writer, editor*
Murphy, James Rodney *playwright*
Rhodes, Daisy Chun *writer, researcher, oral historian*
Whalin, W. Terry *writer, editor*

Crestone
Wooten-Green, Ronald Clarence *writer*

Denver
Avi, (Avi Wortis) *author*
Buckstein, Caryl Sue *writer*
Ducker, Bruce *novelist, lawyer*
Howse, Cathy L. *writer, researcher, entrepreneur*
MacGregor, George Lescher, Jr., *freelance writer*
Nemiro, Beverly Mirium Anderson *author, educator*
Osborn, Susan Chaney *writer, educator*
Vosevich, Kathi Ann *writer, editor, scholar*

Durango
Korns, Leota Elsie *writer, mountain land developer, insurance broker*

Grand Junction
Nizalowski, John Anthony *writer, educator*

Greeley
Willis, Connie (Constance E. Willis) *author*

Highlands Ranch
Margolis, Bette Shula *writer, educator*

Ignacio
Craig, Roy Phillip *writer, educator, rancher*

Lafayette
Hollaran, Carolyn Rada *writer, small business owner*

Lyons
Spring, Kathleen *writer*

Montrose
Gates, Viola R. *writer*

Pueblo
Shomaker, Gordon Alexander, Jr., *poet, writer*

Vail
Knight, Constance Bracken *writer, realtor, corporate executive*

Westminster
Lingle, JoLynn Fleishman *writer, educator*

Wheat Ridge
Morriss, Frank *writer, educator*

CONNECTICUT

Canton
Jordan, Evora Ruth *writer, researcher, publishing executive*

Chester
Stark, Evelyn Brill *poet, musician*

Darien
Hailey, Arthur *author*

East Hampton
Tucceri, Clive Knowles *science writer and educator, consultant*

Easton
Maloney, John Joseph *writer*

Fairfield
Barone, Rose Marie Pace *writer, retired educator, entertainer*

Greenwich
Ewald, William Bragg, Jr., *author, consultant*
Hoberman, Mary Ann *author*
Walker, Robert Martin *writer, minister*
Wallach, Magdalena Falkenberg (Carla Wallach) *writer*

Guilford
Peters, William *author, producer, director*

Hamden
Davis, Lorraine Jensen *writer, editor*

Hanover
Cheney, Glenn Alan *writer, educator*

Hartford
Hedrick, Joan Doran *writer, university educator*

New Canaan
Fredericks, Jeanne Maria Judson *literary agent*

New Haven
Hayden, Dolores *author, architect, educator*
Scarf, Margaret (Maggie Scarf) *author*

New London
Espinosa, Resurreccion *playwright, theater director, writer*

Norwalk
Bortolot, Gary *writer, educator*

Old Lyme
St. George, Judith Alexander *author*

Roxbury
Gurney, Albert Ramsdell *playwright, novelist, educator*

Suffield
Sullivan, Edmund Bertram *writer*

Waterford
Commire, Anne *playwright, writer, editor*

West Hartford
Calip, Roger *writer, educator*
Schweitzer, N. Tina *fiction writer, photojournalist, television producer, director, international consultant public relations, media relations, government relations*

Weston
Diforio, Robert George *literary agent*
Kilty, Jerome Timothy *playwright, stage director, actor*
Wiseman, Carter Sterling *writer, educator*

Westport
Hotchner, Aaron Edward *author*

Wilton
Nugent, Gordon Walker *writer*

Woodbury
McHale-Hendricks, Cynthia *writer*

DELAWARE

Newark
Snair, Roger Clifford *writer, comedian*

Wilmington
Ziolkowska-Boehm, Aleksandra *writer*

DISTRICT OF COLUMBIA

Washington
Alperovitz, Gar *author, educator*
Alvarez de DeClaris, María Clemencia *writer, educator*
Angell, Lois Louise *writer, comedienne, poet*
Arndt, Richard Tallmadge *writer, consultant, cultural organization administrator*
Atlas, Liane Wiener *writer*
Barnet, Richard Jackson *author, educator*
Behrman, Greg *writer, health policy coordinator*
Birnbaum, Norman *author, humanities educator*
Brownstein, Elizabeth Smith *writer*
Burnham, David Bright *writer, educator*
Burns, David Mitchell *writer, retired diplomat, musician*
Carter, Yvonne Johnson *writer, editor, English educator*
Cavnar, Samuel Melmon *writer, publisher, activist*
Conroy, Richard Timothy *writer, retired foreign service officer*
Darr, Ann Russell *poet, educator*
Dessaso, Deborah Ann *freelance/self-employed writer, corporate communications specialist*
Dunbar, Leslie Wallace *writer, consultant*
Friedan, Betty *writer, feminist leader*
Furgurson, Ernest Baker, Jr., (Pat Furgurson) *writer*
Gioia, (Michael) Dana *poet, literary critic*
Goldberg, Kirsten Boyd *science journalist*
Hecht, Anthony Evan *poet*
Innis, Pauline *writer, publishing company executive*
Jasper, John A. *writer, lawyer*
King, Mary Elizabeth *writer, educator*
Kramer, Simon Paul *writer*
MacLeish, Roderick *novelist, screenwriter, television producer*
May, Stephen *writer, former government official*
Merrell, Jesse Howard *writer*
Miller, Hope Ridings *author*
Murphy, Joanne Becker *writer*
Nash, James Lee *poet, security official*
Robb, Lynda Johnson *writer*
Shaw, Russell Burnham *author, journalist*
Smith, Stuart Seaborne *writer, government official, union official*
Steinem, Gloria *writer, editor, lecturer, activist*
Taminiaux, Pierre Simon *writer, educator*
Tannen, Deborah Frances *writer*
Williams, Leaford Clemetson *writer, political scientist*
Williamson, Michael *photographer*
Wouk, Herman *writer*
Yarrow, Andrew Louis *writer, journalist, educator, international relations consultant*
Zietz, Karyl Lynn Kopelman *writer, opera critic, television correspondent, producer, documentary filmmaker*

FLORIDA

Babson Park
Morrison, Kenneth Douglas *author, columnist*

Belle Glade
Oeffner, Barbara Dunning *writer, educator, scriptwriter*

Belleair Beach
Fuentes, Martha Ayers *playwright*

Boca Raton
Keyes, Daniel *author*

Cape Canaveral
Hess, Terry Lee *writer, educator, logistician*

Daytona Beach
Chesnut, Nondis Lorine *screenwriter, consultant, reading and language arts educator, instructor, counselor*
Mc Collister, John Charles *writer, clergyman, educator, executive producer*

Delray Beach
Robinson, Richard Francis *geneaologist, personal historian, writer*

Destin
Schuster, Julia Horst *writer, publishing executive*

Edgewater
Collard, Eugene Robert *writer*

Eustis
Chorosinski, Eugene Conrad *writer, poet, author*

Fort Myers
Monear, Edwin Everett *writer*
Wall, Robert J. *author, researcher*

Gainesville
Holland, Norman Norwood *literary critic*
Leahy, Thomas Melvin, Jr., *writer*
Leavitt, David Adam *writer, English educator*
Smith, Jo Anne *writer, retired educator*

Hallandale Beach
Geller, Bunny Zelda *poet, author, publisher, sculptor, artist, photographer*

Highland Beach
Tolf, Robert Walter *writer*

Homosassa
Carmichael, Roberta Kay *writer*

Homosassa Springs
Burch, Annetta Jane *writer*

Islamorada
Papy, Frank Marin, III, *writer, editor*

Jacksonville
Fracis, Sohrab Homi *writer, education educator*
Murphy, Nickie Latrice *writer, insurance adjuster*

Key Largo
Benestante, Vincenzo *writer*

Kissimmee
McEnaney, Sherrie Jeanine *writer, marketing professional, advertising executive*

Longboat Key
Hazan, Marcella Maddalena *writer, educator, consultant*

Melbourne
Allington, Maynard *writer*
Fiore, Carmen Anthony *writer*
Lederer, William Julius *author*
Stone, Elaine Murray *author, composer, television producer*

Miami
Abril, Marcia (Ela I. Cardinas) *writer*
Alschuler, Al *freelance/self-employed writer, marketing professional*
Camner, Howard *author, poet*
Goin-Harding, Cecilia Margaret *poet*
Laje, Zilia L. *writer, publisher, translator*
Morgan, Marabel *writer*

Naples
Capelle-Frank, Jacqueline Aimee *writer*
Cook, Robin *author*
Thompson, Didi Castle (Mary Bennett) *writer, editor*

Navarre
Starratt, Patricia Elizabeth *writer, actress, composer, pianist*

New Smyrna Beach
Zink, Joan Wilson *writer, poet, composer*

Niceville
Hinze, Vicki Kay *writer, educator*

Ocala
Boston, Bruce David *writer, book designer*
DeSilva, Ann Marie *writer*

Orange Park
Goss, William Allan *author, speaker*

Sundick, Sherry Small *author, journalist, poet*

Princess Anne
du Nord, Jeanne *writer, publishing executive*

Rockville
Madle, Robert Albert *writer*

Saint Marys City
Clifton, Lucille Thelma *author*

Salisbury
Booker, Betty Mae *poet*

Severna Park
Davis, Clayton *writer, pilot, photographer*
Windsor, Patricia (Katonah Summertree, Perrin Winters, Anna Seeling) *author, educator, lecturer*

Silver Spring
Briese, Michael W. *writer*
Kellner, Mark Allen *writer*
Vanzant, Iyanla *writer*
Whitten, Leslie Hunter, Jr., *author, newspaper reporter, poet*

MASSACHUSETTS

Amherst
Glazier, Lyle *writer, educator*
Holland, Noy *writer, educator*
Sandweiss, Martha A. *author, American studies and history educator*

Andover
Murray, Sabina *writer*

Barre
Sullivan, James Edward *poet*

Belchertown
Lester, Julius B. *author*

Belmont
Rand, Peter *writer, editor, educator*
Ruocchio, Patricia Jeanne *writer*

Boston
Angelou, Maya (Marguerite Johnson) *writer, playwright, actress, activist*
Carroll, James *author*
Lahiri, Jhumpa *writer*
Lowry, Lois (Lois Hammersberg) *writer*
Martin, Jacqueline Briggs *author juvenile prose*
Payack, Peter *poet, writer, artist, educator*
Pinsky, Robert Neal *poet, educator*
Polizzotti, Mark *writer, translator, publishing executive*
Say, Allen *children's writer, illustrator*
Sklar, Holly L. *nonfiction writer*
Terrill, Ross Gladwin *writer, educator*
Van Allsburg, Chris *author, artist*
Warren, Rosanna *poet*
Wiesel, Elie *writer, educator*
Zelnick, Carl Robert Robert *writer, educator*

Byfield
Kozol, Jonathan *writer*

Cambridge
Bercaw, Roy *freelance/self-employed writer*
Blake, Patricia *writer*
DiCamillo, Kate *writer*
Graham, Jorie *writer, educator*
Kaplan, Justin *author*
Leonard, James Patrick *writer, editor, communications consultant, instructor*
Rhoda, Janice Tucker *writer, educator, musician*
Roazen, Paul *writer*
Yergin, Daniel Howard *writer, consultant*

Chestnut Hill
Valette, Jean Paul *writer*

Chicopee
Stevens, Joyce Ann *author, publisher, writer, speaker*

Cummington
Smith, William Jay *author*
Wilbur, Richard Purdy *writer, educator*

East Dennis
Ely, David (David E. Lilienthal Jr.) *writer*

Hatfield
Yolen, Jane *author*

Lexington
Kennedy, X. J. (Joseph Kennedy) *writer*
Topalian, Naomi Getsoyan *writer*

Lincoln
Donald, David Herbert *author, history educator*

Lowell
Pike, Jonathan Hamilton *writer*

Medfield
Phillips, Marion Grumman *writer, civic worker*

Medford
Dubus, Andre, III, *writer*
SSarno, Christopher Ed *writer*

Needham
Walworth, Arthur *author*

North Adams
Cruse, Howard *writer, illustrator*
Howe, Candace Jo-Lynn *writer*

North Chelmsford
Erkkila-Ricker, Barbara Howell *writer, photographer*

Northampton
Bartók-Baratta, Edward *poet, artist*

Osterville
El-Fayoumy, J. P. Quinn *writer, poet, teacher*

Provincetown
Cook, Molly Malone *literary agent*
Oliver, Mary *poet*

Revere
Recupero-Faiella, Anna Antonietta *poet*

Shelburne Falls
Bagg, Robert Ely *poet, educator, translator*

Somerset
Manchester, Steven Herbert *writer, educator*

Somerville
Auspitz, Josiah Lee *writer, consultant*

South Hadley
Shaw, Robert Burns *poet, educator*
Viereck, Peter *poet, historian, educator*

South Hamilton
Kroeger, Catherine C. *writer, educator, editor*

Southborough
Mylotte, John Arnold *writer, educator*

Truro
Woolley, Catherine (Jane Thayer) *writer*

Watertown
Pirolli, John Paul *poet, writer, building materials company executive*

Wellesley
Jacobs, Ruth Harriet *poet, playwright, sociologist, gerontologist*

Wellfleet
Piercy, Marge *poet, writer*

West Newbury
Dooley, Ann Elizabeth *freelance writers cooperative executive, editor*

West Newton
Porter, Jack Nusan *writer, sociologist, educator, political activist*

West Roxbury
Ellenbogen, George *poet, educator*
Seltzer, Richard Warren, Jr., *writer, editor, consultant*

Worcester
Vick, Susan *playwright, educator, director, actress*

MICHIGAN

Allendale
Osborn, William Palmer *writer, English language educator*

Ann Arbor
Gregerson, Linda Karen *poet, language educator, critic*

Battle Creek
Cline, Charles William *poet, pianist, rhetoric and literature educator*

Canton
Wiloch, Thomas *writer, editor*

Detroit
Madgett, Naomi Long *poet, editor, publisher, educator*

Dowagiac
Sweet, Margaret Ellen *writer*

East Lansing
Perrin, Robert *editorial consultant, writer*
Wakoski, Diane *poet, educator*

Grand Rapids
Henry, Karen Lee *writer, lecturer*

Holland
Nieuwsma, Milton John *writer, journalist*

Kalamazoo
Light, Christopher Upjohn *writer, computer musician, photographer*
Skipper, Jason Edward *writer, educator*

Mackinac Island
Mc Cabe, John Charles, III, *writer*

Mount Pleasant
Smallwood, Carol *writer*

Okemos
Klunzinger, Thomas Edward *writer, actor, director*

Republic
Wixtrom, Donald Joseph *translator*

Sodus
Handy, Virginia Mae *writer*

Southfield
Riley, Rochelle Rosalind *writer*

University Center
Puia, George M. *writer, educator*

West Bloomfield
Brin, David *writer, astronomer*

MINNESOTA

Duluth
Bakk-Hansen, Heidi K. *writer, researcher*

Edina
Christensen, Nadia Margaret *writer, translator, editor, educator*
Schwarzrock, Shirley Pratt *writer, educator*

Minneapolis
Baker, John Stevenson (Michael Dyregrov) *writer*
Bly, Robert *poet*
Hendra, Tony *writer, comedian, actor*
Kapelac, Samuel James *writer, sales executive*
Korotkin, Fred *writer, philatelist*
Mathy, Robin Michelle *writer*
St. Germaine-Lattig, Charles Edwin *political writer*

Northfield
Benkowski, Ann Marie *writer*

Ortonville
Schrom, Elizabeth Ann *retired writer*

Richfield
Thompson, Steve Allan *writer*

Saint Paul
Keillor, Garrison Edward *writer, radio host*

MISSISSIPPI

Hattiesburg
Barthelme, Frederick (Rick) *writer, literature educator*

Jackson
McElvaine, Robert Stuart *writer, educator*

Oxford
Neal, Mary Darlin' *writer, education educator*

Southaven
White, Marguerite *writer*

MISSOURI

Ballwin
Haller, Karen Sue *writer*

Bloomfield
Ferrell, Paul Cleveland *writer*

Carthage
Potter, Jacqueline Jean *writer*

Des Peres
Sadlo, Kenneth Louis *poet, writer*

Higbee
Holdren, James G. *writer*

Jefferson City
McDaniel, Sue Powell *writer, speaker*

Kansas City
Martin-Bowen, Lindsey *freelance writer*
Shindler, Dorman Truett, Jr., *writer, journalist, critic, photographer, cartoonist*
Vando, Gloria *poet, publishing executive*

Lees Summit
Plantz, Jerry Anthony *writer, consultant, consumer products company executive*

Mountain Grove
Allmon, Sandra J. *writer*

Saint Joseph
Constable, Jane *writer, small business owner*

Saint Louis
Broeg, Bob (Robert William Broeg) *writer*
Gass, William H. *writer, educator*
Lubbock, James Edward *retired writer, photographer, publicity consultant*
Lutz, John Thomas *author*
Miller, Judith Braffman *writer*
Schlafly, Phyllis Stewart *writer*
Sheffield, DeBorah Lagreta *poet, writer*
Smith, C. Grant *scriptwriter, film producer*

Sweet Springs
Long, Helen Halter *writer, educator*

Trenton
Ensminger, John Jay *writer, poet, minister, counselor*

Viburnum
West, Roberta Bertha *writer*

Wentzville
Poe, Judith A. Joyce *writer*

Willow Springs
Hinds, C. Robert (Bob) *retired writer*

MONTANA

Bonner
Smith, Annick *writer*

Missoula
Haines, John Meade *poet, translator, writer*
Yee, Albert Hoy *writer, retired psychologist, educator*

Red Lodge
McJunkin, Shirley Anne *writer*

NEBRASKA

Kearney
Fendt, Gene J. *poet, philosopher, educator*

Lincoln
Magorian, James *poet, writer*

Norfolk
Nielsen, Daniel C. *poet*

NEVADA

Cold Springs
Turner VanLydegraf, Claudia Beth *writer, researcher*

Incline Village
O'Connor, Thomas Patrick *screenwriter*

Las Vegas
Ashbaugh, Nancy Gould *writer, performing arts educator*
Latimer, Heather *writer*
Palmer, Lynne *writer, astrologer*
Patterson, William T. *writer*

Reno
Grady, Sean Michael *writer*
Scrimgeour, Gary James *writer, educator*

Zephyr Cove
Camille, Pamela *writer, educator*

NEW HAMPSHIRE

Brentwood
Bunker, Dusty *writer*

Cornish
Atkinson, James Blakely *writer, editor*

Durham
Ford, Daniel (Daniel Francis Ford) *writer*

Peterborough
Thomas, Elizabeth Marshall *writer*

Walpole
Fargnoli, Patricia B. *poet, educator*
Gooding, Judson *writer*

NEW JERSEY

Bergenfield
Clark, Fred *legal writer, editor*

Cape May Court House
Cohen, Daniel Edward *writer*
Cohen, Susan Lois *writer*

Cherry Hill
Gardner, Joel Robert *writer, historian*

Elizabeth
Lucco, James Perry *writer*

Englewood
Albee, Gloria *playwright*
Beltran, Elio F. *writer, painter*

Fair Haven
Derchin, Dary Bret Ingham *writer*

Franklin Lakes
Albright, Judith Anne *writer, educator*

Haddonfield
Halscheid, Therese Anne *poet*

Harrington Park
Manafette, Michael *writer*

Hazlet
Shea, James Bryan *writer*

Highland Park
Cheiten, Marvin Harold *playwright, manufacturing executive*

Hoboken
Paradise, Paul Richard *writer, editor*

Jersey City
Pratt, Minnie Bruce *writer, educator*

Lebanon
Barto, Susan Carol *writer*

Leonardo
Bianchi, Hollis Dolce *writer, artist*

Livingston
Simon, Sheryl Joy *writer, astrologer*

Long Branch
Stewart, Georgiana Liccione *writer*

Long Valley
Collins, Kathleen *writer*

Madison
Perriman, Wendy Karen *poet, educator*

Mahwah
King, Lis Sonder *writer*

Maplewood
Cousineau, Kelley Cunningham *writer, artist*
Lally, Michael David *writer, actor*

Medford
Henderson, Rita Elizabeth *literary agent, journalist*

Metuchen
Smyth, David *writer, editor*

Montclair
Delgado, Ramon Louis *theater educator, author, director, playwright, lyricist*

Mountainside
Nielsen, Gwyn English *writer, illustrator, publishing executive*

Lunardini, Christine Anne *writer, historian, school administrator*
Macer-Story, Eugenia Ann *writer*
MacLachlan, Patricia *author*
Maguire, Gregory *writer*
Manning, Martha Mary *writer, psychologist*
Mason, Bobbie Ann *novelist, short story writer*
Mathews, Norman *playwright, composer*
Maupin, Armistead Jones, Jr., *writer*
McCourt, Frank (Francis McCourt) *writer*
McCullough, David *writer, educator*
McDermott, Alice *writer*
Mcdonald, Gregory Christopher *author*
McGonigle, Thomas *writer, humanities educator*
McMurtry, Larry Jeff *author*
McNally, Terrence *playwright*
McQuown, Judith Hershkowitz *author, financial advisor*
McWhorter, Diane *writer*
Meadows, Denis John *writer, director*
Meltzer, Milton *author*
Menza, Claudia Marcella *literary agent*
Mercado, Nancy *writer, educator*
Mills, Stephanie Ellen *writer*
Minarik, Else Holmelund (Bigart Minarik) *author*
Mitchard, Jacquelyn *writer*
Monk Kidd, Sue *writer*
Mooney, Richard Emerson *writer*
Morrison, Patricia Kennealy *author*
Mosley, Walter *writer*
Munro, Alice *author*
Murphy, Patrice Ann (Pat Murphy) *writer*
Navarra, Tova *writer*
Nelson, Richard John *playwright, film director, screenwriter*
Nesbit, Lynn *literary agent*
Neugeboren, Jay *author*
Newberg, Esther *literary agent*
Nicol, Dominik *writer, photographer*
Nixon, Agnes Eckhardt *television writer, producer*
Noonan, Peggy *writer*
Oates, Joyce Carol *author*
O'Brien, Dan *writer*
O'Brien, Tim *writer*
O'Doherty, Brian *writer, filmmaker*
Offit, Sidney *writer, educator*
Okrent, Daniel *writer*
Olafsson, Olafur Johann *writer, media company executive*
Oltion, Jerry *author science fiction*
Oppenheimer, Paul *English comparative literature educator, poet, author*
Osborne, Mary Pope *writer*
Pall, Ellen Jane *writer*
Papell, Helen Gertrude *poet, retired librarian*
Park, Barbara *writer*
Park, Linda Sue *writer*
Parkhurst, Carolyn *writer*
Patchett, Ann *writer*
Paterson, Katherine Womeldorf *writer*
Patterson, James Brendan, Jr., *writer, former advertising agency executive*
Peck, Richard Wayne *novelist*
Pérez-Rivera, Francisco (Frank Rivera) *writer*
Pierce, Tamora *writer*
Pirsig, Robert Maynard *author*
Pogrebin, Letty Cottin *writer, lecturer*
Policoff, Stephen Phillip *writer, educator*
Pollack, Barbara Grace *writer*
Pomerantz, Charlotte *writer*
Pool, Mary Jane *writer, lecturer*
Poole, William Daniel *writer, editor*
Pottlitzer, Joanne *freelance/self-employed writer, theater producer, theater director*
Price, Reynolds *novelist, poet, playwright, essayist, educator*
Proulx, (Edna) Annie *writer*
Rathmann, Peggy *writer, illustrator*
Reed, Ishmael Scott (Emmett Coleman) *writer*
Reig, June Wilson *scriptwriter, television director, television producer*
Rhodes, Richard (Lee) *writer*
Rice, Anne *writer*
Rice, Luanne *writer*
Rich, Adrienne *writer*
Rigney, James Oliver, Jr., (Robert Jordan, Chang Lung, Reagan O'Neal, Jackson O'Reilly) *writer*
Roberts, Nora *writer*
Robinson, Kim Stanley *science fiction author*
Rollin, Betty *writer, television journalist, lecturer*
Ronde, John Herman *author, translator*
Rooney, Andrew Aitken *writer, columnist*
Root, William Pitt *poet, educator*
Rothenberg, Jerome *author, visual arts and literary educator*
Roy, Arundhati *writer*
Rumaker, Michael *writer, English educator*
Rylant, Cynthia *author*
Sachar, Louis *writer*
Salinger, J(erome) D(avid) *author*
Salter, Mary Jo *poet*
Sandum, Howard E. *literary agent*
Sargent, Herb *writer, television producer*
Sargent, Pamela *writer*
Saul, John Woodruff, III, *writer*
Schaffner, Cynthia Van Allen *writer, curator, lecturer*
Schine, Cathleen *writer*
Schisgal, Murray *playwright*
Schlesinger, Arthur, Jr., (Arthur Meier Schlesinger) *writer, educator, historian*
Seaman, Barbara (Ann Rosner) *author*
Secrest, Meryle *writer*
Sedaris, David Raymond *writer*
Segal, Lore *writer*
Sendak, Maurice Bernard *writer, illustrator*
Shaffer, Peter (Sir Peter Shaffer) *playwright*
Sheehan, Susan *writer*
Sheehy, Gail Henion *author*
Shulevitz, Uri *author, illustrator*
Simon, Neil *playwright, screenwriter, television writer*
Smiley, Jane Graves *author, educator*
Smith, Betty *writer, nonprofit foundation executive*
Smith, Warren Allen *writer*
Smith, Zadie *writer*
Soering, Jens *writer*
Solnit, Rebecca *writer, art critic*
Sontag, Susan *writer*
Sparks, Nicholas *writer*
Spillane, Mickey (Frank Morrison Spillane) *author*
Steel, Danielle Fernande *author*
Stein, Joseph *playwright*
Stone, Robert Anthony *author*
Talese, Gay *writer*
Tan, Amy Ruth *writer*
Taylor, Mildred D. *author*
Thomason, Dustin *writer*
Tillman, Lynne (Merrill) *writer*
Tomkins, Calvin *writer*
Toobin, Jeffrey Ross *writer, legal analyst*
Trillin, Calvin *writer, journalist*
Turner, Megan Whalen *author*
Uhry, Alfred Fox *playwright*
Urban, Amanda (Binky Urban) *literary agent*
Vidal, Gore *writer*
Vonnegut, Kurt, Jr., *writer*
Walker, Alice *writer*
Wallace, Daniel *writer*
Waller, Robert James *writer*
Ward, Geoffrey Champion *author, editor*
Wasserman, Albert *film producer, writer, director*
Wasserstein, Wendy *playwright*
Watt, Douglas (Benjamin Watt) *writer, critic*
Wender, Phyllis Bellows *literary agent*
West, Paul Noden *author, playwright*
Whitehead, Colson *writer*
Whitehouse, Anne Cherner *writer*
Whitney, Phyllis Ayame *author*
Whitty, Jeff *playwright, actor*
Wiener, Solomon *writer, consultant, former city official*
Wilds, Bonnie *author, community volunteer*
Wilson, August *playwright*
Wolfe, Thomas Kennerly, Jr., *writer, journalist*
Wolff, Virginia Euwer *writer*
Wren, Gayden *playwright, theater director*
Wright, Douglas *playwright*
Wright, Sarah Elizabeth *writer, poet*
Yaffe, James *writer*
Yglesias, Helen Bassine *author, educator*
Yorinks, Arthur *children's author, writer, director*
Zha, Jianying *writer, educator*

Newburgh
Begley, Vincent Joseph *writer, educator*
Severo, Richard *writer*

North Tonawanda
Powers, Bruce Raymond *writer, English language educator, consultant*

Nyack
Hendin, David Bruce *literary agent, writer, consultant, numismatist*

Olivebridge
Osborne, Seward Russell *writer*

Oneonta
Girshin, Mark Danilovich *writer, historian*
Wank, Martin *writer*

Painted Post
Kirk, Connie Ann *writer*

Palisades
Davis, Dorothy Salisbury *writer*

Pearl River
Pieterse, Natalie L. *writer, literature educator*

Pittsford
Schooler, Shirley Jean *writer*

Plainview
Sherwood, James Webster, III, *author, limousine company owner*

Pleasantville
Nelson, K. Bonita *literary agent*

Potsdam
DeGhett, Stephanie Coyne *writer, educator, poet*

Poughkeepsie
Willard, Nancy Margaret *writer, educator*

Purchase
Phillips, Carly *writer*

Red Hook
Altshuler, Miriam R. *literary agent*
Fitzpatrick, John *poet*

Rochester
Hoch, Edward Dentinger *writer*
Rothberg, Abraham *author, educator, editor*

Rockville Centre
Schwartz, Arthur *playwright, poet*

Rocky Point
Stever, Edward W. *writer, English language educator*

Rye
Hurwitz, Sol *writer, consultant*
Ketchum, William Clarence *author, educator*

Sag Harbor
Pashman, Susan Ellen *writer*

Sagaponack
Cedering, Siv *poet, writer*

Saratoga Springs
Millhauser, Steven *writer*
Sainer, Arthur *writer, theater educator*

Saugerties
de Mare, George *author*

Sayville
Leuzzi, Linda *writer*

Shady
Malkine-Falvey, Fern Sylvie *writer, journalist, painter*

Shelter Island
Mayer, Martin Prager *writer*

Sidney
Rivers Baker, Dawn *writer, publisher, consultant*

Southold
Small, Bertrice W. *writer*

Staten Island
Foster, Paul *playwright*
Popp, Lilian Mustaki *writer, educator*
Porter, Darwin Fred *writer*

Stony Brook
Roth, Susan Austin *author, photographer*

Syracuse
Albino, Joseph Xavier *writer, educator, photographer*
Jankiewicz, Henry John *writer, educator, musician*

Tarrytown
Loxley, Alice Anne *writer, educator*

Valley Stream
Rachlin, Harvey Brant *writer*

Vestal
Cohen, Marvin A. *writer*

Wainscott
Herzog, Arthur, III, *author*

Warwick
Linnéa, Sharon *writer, playwright*

West Nyack
Pringle, Laurence Patrick *writer*

Whitesboro
O'Hara, Cynthia O'Connor *writer, columnist, food consultant*

Woodstock
Godwin, Gail Kathleen *writer*

Yonkers
Baumel, Joan Patricia French *educator, writer, lecturer*

NORTH CAROLINA

Angier
Carwell, Gloria Jean *writer*

Boone
Stahl, Ray Emerson *freelance writer, historian, researcher*

Chapel Hill
Spencer, Elizabeth *author*

Charlotte
Finley, Glenna *writer*

Columbus
Blate, Michael *author, lecturer*
Sauvé, Carolyn Opal *writer, journalist, poet*

Cullowhee
Crowe, Thomas Rain *poet*
Stripling Byer, Kathryn *poet*

Flat Rock
Kay, Madeleine H. *writer, consultant, adult education educator*

Fletcher
Roe, Richard Steven *writer, illustrator*

Greensboro
Flynt, Candace Lambeth *writer*
Gilbert, Marie Rogers *poet*
Watson, Robert Winthrop *poet*

Greenville
Gilham, Hanna Kaltenbrunner *writer*

Kill Devil Hills
Lautermilch, Steven J. *poet, writer, photographer, educator*

Midland
Voncannon, Brian Everett *writer, scriptwriter, radio personality*

Morrisville
Clancy, Thomas L., Jr., *novelist*

Mount Olive
Rigsbee, David E. *poet, educator*

Pittsboro
Betts, Doris June Waugh *writer, English language educator*

Rutherfordton
Isbell, Robert *writer*

Southern Pines
Kaufman, Bernhard Barken *writer, educator*
Yarborough, William Pelham *writer, lecturer, retired army officer, consultant*

Wilkesboro
Barnhill, Anne Clinard *writer, educator*

Winston Salem
Ehle, John Marsden, Jr., *writer*
Hanes, Frank Borden *writer, former business executive, farmer*

OHIO

Athens
Dodd, Wayne D. *poet, editor*

Beachwood
Liebow, Joanne Elisabeth *poet and freelance publicist*

Centerville
Alexander, Lora Kay *writer, composer*

Cincinnati
Birmingham, Stephen *writer*
Braman, Heather Ruth *technical writer, editor, consultant, antiques dealer*
Teasley, John Ray Sanders, Jr., *writer*

Cleveland
Finn, Robert *writer, lecturer, broadcaster*
Gleisser, Marcus David *writer, lawyer, journalist*
Kovel, Ralph M. *writer, antiques expert*
Kovel, Terry Horvitz (Mrs. Ralph Kovel) *writer, antiques authority*

Cleveland Heights
Sandburg, Helga *author*

Columbus
Hilliard, Andrea Leigh *writer*

Dayton
Hayes, Stephen Kurtz *writer*
Jelus, Susan Crum *writer, editor*

Fairborn
Szucs, Andrew Eric *freelance/self-employed writer*

Gallipolis
Ferguson, A. H. *poet, medical/surgical nurse*

Glendale
Strom, Kristina Chase *writer, consultant*

Kent
Cielinski-Kessler, Audrey Ann *writer, publishing executive, small business owner*
Okantah, Mwatabu S. *writer, educator*

Middletown
McClain, Michael H. *writer*

Mount Vernon
Wells-Maxwell, Violet *writer, artist*

Napoleon
Meekison, MaryFran *writer*

North Royalton
Pamin, Diana Dolhancyk (Diana Dolhancyk) *poet*

Oberlin
Taylor, Robert Larry *author, freelance writer*

Parma
Peck, Andrea Sue *writer, educator*

Perrysburg
Celeste, Ardella Hazel *retired writer*
Weaver, Richard L., II, *writer, speaker, educator*

Stockport
Winebrenner, William Patrick *writer*

Westfield Center
Bock, Carolyn A. *writer, consultant, small business owner*

OKLAHOMA

Cleveland
Anderson, Patricia Sue *writer*

Lawton
Goetz, Gary D., Sr., *writer, retired chef, restaurateur*

Lone Wolf
Cole, Burna L. *writer, retired curator*

Mustang
Wood, Jean Carol *poet, lyricist*

Norman
MacFarland, Miriam Katherine (Mimi MacFarland) *writer*

Oklahoma City
Mather, Ruth Elsie *writer*

Shawnee
Stoddard, Allan Lee *writer, musician*

Tulsa
Mojtabai, Ann Grace *author, educator*
Price, Alice Lindsay *writer*
Shurley, Jay Talmadge *writer, retired psychiatrist, medical educator, administrator, behavioral scientist, polar explorer, genealogist*
Upton, Howard B., Jr., *writer, lawyer*

OREGON

Beatty
Nettelbeck, Fred Arthur *poet*

Bend
Connolly, Brian Anthony *writer*

Cannon Beach
Hellyer, Constance Anne (Connie Anne Conway) *writer, musician*

Chiloquin
Lane, Colette Marie *writer*

Corvallis
Birdseye, Thomas Earl *freelance/self-employed writer*

Culver
Siebert, Diane Dolores *author, poet*

Eugene
Wilhelm, Kate (Katy Gertrude) *author*

Klamath Falls
Koch, Margaret Rau *writer, artist, historian*
Korson, Victoria Lynn *writer*

Newberg
Hockett, Betty May *writer, educator*

Portland
Brewin, Michael K. *writer, publisher, musician*
Freeman, Sarah Elisabeth *poet, literature and language educator*
Larson, Wanda Z. *writer, poet*
Porter, Elsa Allgood *writer, lecturer*
Sachs, Harley Luther *writer, educator*
Tuska, Jon *author, publisher*

Tigard
Scarbrough, Allen Lee *writer, philosopher*

PENNSYLVANIA

Bloomsburg
Keyser, Leslie D. *writer*

Broomall
Saunders, Sally Love *poet, educator*

Brownsville
Nantus, Sheryl *writer*

California
Langham, Norma E. *playwright, educator, poet, composer, inventor*

Downingtown
Kovach, George Daniel *writer*

Drexel Hill
Alexander, Lloyd Chudley *author*

Erie
Mercer, Christina Marie *writer, artist*

Flourtown
Dressler, Mark Christopher *writer*

Glenside
Powlison, David A. *writer*

Greensburg
Shafer-Kenney, Jolie E. *writer, columnist*

Harrisburg
Cooper, Jane Todd (J. C. Todd) *poet, writer, educator*
Grobman, Gary M. *writer*

Kennett Square
Martin, George (George Whitney Martin) *writer*

King Of Prussia
Schumann, Paula M. L. *writer*

Lancaster
Shenk, Lois Elaine Landis *writer*

Maple Glen
Jacobson, Bonnie Brown *writer, energy executive, statistician, researcher*

Milford
Le Guin, Ursula Kroeber *writer*

New Kingstown
DiSipio, Rocco Thomas *writer*

Newfoundland
Grotta, Daniel *writer, editor*

Paoli
Yake, Sarah Louise *poet*

Pen Argyl
Martocci, Lewis Nicholas, III, *writer*

Philadelphia
Carasik, Michael *writer, researcher*
Connor, Bernadette Yvonne *retired writer*
Fussell, Paul *author, English literature educator*
Granato, Carol Anne *writer*
Kinsella, Thomas *poet*
Nickels, Thom *writer, journalist*
Owens, Rochelle *poet, playwright*
Paglia, Camille *writer, humanities educator*
Pipes, Daniel *writer*
Stewart, Susan *writer*
Wallace, Emily Mitchell *writer, editor, educator*

Pittsburgh
Daniels, James R. *poet, English language educator*
Faigen, Anne Gussin *writer, educator*
Hodges, Margaret Moore *author, educator*
Verlich, Jean Elaine *writer, public relations consultant*

Pottstown
Hylton, Thomas James *author*

Southampton
Bendiner, Robert *writer, editor*

Spring Mills
Gillan, Garth Jackson *writer, psychotherapist, deacon, emeritus educator*

Valley Forge
Miller, Betty Brown *freelance writer*

Wayne
Collin, Frances W. *literary agent*

Wynnewood
Meyers, Mary Ann *foundation administrator, writer, consultant*

RHODE ISLAND

Barrington
Deakin, James *writer, former newspaperman*

Johnston
Merolla, Carol Ann *writer, consultant*

Little Compton
Bamberger, Lauren R. *writer, photojournalist*

Newport
Scoll, Eulalie Elizabeth *writer, researcher*

Providence
Creeley, Robert White *author, English educator*
Eltringham, Dana Kristin *writer*
Goldstein, Joshua S. *writer, educator*
Lopez-Morillas, Frances M. *translator*
Schevill, James Erwin *poet, playwright*
Steinbach, Meredith Lynn *writer, educator*
Vogel, Paula Anne *playwright*

Tiverton
Frost, John Mason *writer, educator, retired protective services official*

SOUTH CAROLINA

Aiken
Naifeh, Steven Woodward *writer*
Smith, Gregory White *writer*

Anderson
Baughman, Janet Irene *writer*
Kline, George Louis *author, translator, retired philosophy and literature educator*

Charleston
Siddons, Anne Rivers (Sybil Anne Rivers Siddons) *writer*

Clover
Montgomery, Connie Roger *writer*

Columbia
Newton, Rhonwen Leonard *writer, microcomputer consultant, data processing executive, consultant*

Edgefield
Blossom, Laurel *poet, writer*

Hilton Head Island
Reed, Frances Boogher *writer, actress*

Kiawah Island
Harrigan, Anthony Hart *author*

Little River
Ehrlich, John Gunther *writer*

Myrtle Beach
Nirenstein, Jack *writer*

Rock Hill
Bristow, Robert O'Neil *writer, educator*

Seneca
Byars, Betsy (Cromer) *writer*

Summerville
Reisman, Rosemary Moody Canfield *writer, retired humanities educator*

Sumter
Justus, Adalu *writer, designer*

TENNESSEE

Blaine
Bull, James C. *poet*

Brentwood
Mitchell, Marilyn June *writer, lyricist*

Chattanooga
Callahan, North *author, educator*
Jackson, Richard P. *writer, educator*

Cleveland
Breuer, William Bentley *author*

Collegedale
Crosby, Berna *freelance/self-employed writer*

Henning
Parker, Joann Maudie *freelance/self-employed writer, retired reporter*

Knoxville
Lammers, Laura Bea *writer, communications executive*

Loudon
Randall, Marilyn Mae *writer*

Madison
Campbell, Chester Douglas *writer*

Memphis
Cohen, Susan Perlman *literary agent*
Foote, Shelby *author*
Quinn, Amelia Turner *writer*

Nashville
Bird, Caroline *author*
Bransford, Helen M. *writer, jewelry designer*
Flippo, Chet *writer, editor*
Hoekstra, Douglas Anthony *writer, educator, musician*
Pearson, Sela *poet, speaker*
Smith, Agnes Eyvonda *writer*
Winstead, Elisabeth Weaver *poet, writer, English language educator*

Sevierville
Koff, Shirley Irene *writer*

TEXAS

Addison
Cohn, Linkie Seltzer *professional speaker, author*

Arlington
Brown, Sandra *writer*

Austin
Barnes, Thomas Joseph *writer*
Beazley, Hamilton *writer, educator*
Gustafsson, Lars Erik Einar *writer, educator*
Parker, Drue A. *writer, educator*
Porter, Jenny Lind *writer*
Shefelman, Janice Jordan *writer*

Bertram
Albert, Susan Wittig *writer, English educator*

Boerne
Price, John Randolph *writer*

Burleson
Ballard, Barry Lynn *poet*

Cedar Hill
Stowers, Carlton Eugene *writer*

Chireno
Mayhar, Ardath Frances (Frank Cannon) *author*

Cibolo
Strojny, Joan Elizabeth *writer*

Corpus Christi
Foster, Bayard Everson *writer*

Crowley
Sizemore, Deborah Lightfoot *writer, editor*

Dallas
Bartlett, Richard Chalkley *writer, conservationist*
Dee, Ronda *poet, photographer, small business owner*
Gillett, Grover *author*
Murray, John William, Jr., *writer, legal investigator*
Phillips, Betty Lou (Elizabeth Louise Phillips) *writer, interior designer*
Rhodes, Samuel Earl *writer*
Sherrod, Danny Troy *writer, educator*
Sundgaard, Arnold Olaf *playwright*
Wolfe, Jane *writer*

Denton
Wood, Jane Roberts *writer*

El Paso
Cummings, Patricia Anne (Felicitas Cruz) *writer, journalist, poet*

Euless
Roark, Sheila B. *writer*

Fort Worth
de Toledo, Catherine Holt *medical writer*
Douglas, Carole Nelson *writer*
Munday, Stephen Dale *writer, artist*

Garland
Preston, Harry *writer, scriptwriter*

Houston
Fox, Connie Steitz *freelance writer, editor, graphic designer*
Hoagland, Tony *writer*
Parle, Bertha Ibarra *writer*
Plunkett, Jack William *writer, publisher*
Summers, Joseph Frank *author, publisher*
Wood, Susan *poet, literature educator*

Kyle
Atkinson, Valerie J. *writer, webmaster*

Lufkin
Billingsley, Shirley Ann *writer, poet*

Mansfield
Parnell, Charles L. *speechwriter*

Marfa
McBride, Elizabeth Anne Wilmore *writer*

Mcallen
Spyker, Leola Edith *writer, educator*

Odessa
Moseley, Clifford Wayne *writer, poet*

Pasadena
Thompson, Marian Nell *poetry, historical, non-fiction and fiction writer, educator, poet*

San Antonio
Ammann, Lillian Ann Nicholson *writer, editor, small business owner*
Fehrenbach, T(heodore) R(eed) *author, businessman*
Heidelberg, Paul *writer*
Holl, Kristi Diane *writer, educator*
Swiggett, Harold E. (Hal Swiggett) *writer, photographer*

Smithville
Clark, LaVerne Harrell *writer*

Springtown
Marrs, James F., Jr., (Jim Marrs) *author, journalist, educator*

Terrell
Whitaker, Kay *poet*

Texarkana
Presley, James Wright *writer, environmentalist*

UTAH

Park City
Solomon, Dorothy Jeanne Allred *writer, communications executive*

Provo
Hart, Edward LeRoy *poet, educator*

Salt Lake City
Osherow, Jacqueline Sue *poet, English language educator*
Straughn, Joanna Marzia *poet*

VERMONT

Bennington
Bernard, April *poet, literature educator*

Brattleboro
Lappe, Frances Moore *author, lecturer*

Burlington
Carlisle, Lilian Matarose Baker (Mrs. E. Grafton Carlisle Jr) *writer, lecturer*
Hearon, Shelby *writer, lecturer, educator*

Chester
Coleman, John Royston *writer*

Dorset
Pember, John Scott *poet*

Guilford
Olle, David Arthur *writer, researcher*

Marlboro
Stevenson, Laura Caroline *writer, educator*

Middlebury
MacDonald, Kenneth R., Jr., *author, artist*

Morrisville
Besser, Gretchen Rous *writer, educator*

Shaftsbury
Sugarman, Robert Edward *writer*

South Royalton
Powers, Thomas Moore *writer*

Stamford
Stevens, Lauren Rogers *writer, environmentalist*

Thetford
Paley, Grace *author, educator*

Wilmington
Reeve, Franklin D. *writer, literature educator*

VIRGINIA

Abingdon
Clifton, D. Renee *writer, educator*

Aldie
Weaver, Kitty Dunlap *author*

Alexandria
Byrne, John Edward (JEB Byrne) *writer, retired government official*
Justesen, Benjamin Ray, II, *writer*
Kaye, Ruth Lincoln *historical researcher*
Malott, John Raymond *writer, consultant*
Wallace, Barbara Brooks *writer*
Weinhagen, Eric John *writer, musician*

Arlington
Bowers, Ray Landis *writer*
Cinca, Silvia (Roberta King) *writer, producer*
England, Robert Stowe *writer*
Hittle, James Donald *writer, business consultant*
Jones, Edward Paul *writer, editor*
Timperlake, Edward Thomas *writer*

Ashburn
Boyne, Walter James *writer, former museum director*

Burke
Gelb, Sidney *writer*

Chantilly
Priem, Richard Gregory *writer, information systems executive*

Charlottesville
Casey, John Dudley *writer, English language educator*
Dove, Rita Frances *poet, English language educator*
Fiser, Karen B. *poet*
McCrimmon, Barbara Smith *writer, librarian*
Monaghan, Charles *writer, editor*

Clifton
Cavileer, Sharon E. *writer, public relations executive, consultant*

Fairfax
Bausch, Richard Carl *writer, educator*
Cosing, Arthur Paul, Jr., *writer, artist*
Parrish-St. John, Florence Tucker *writer, educator, retired government official*

Falls Church
Leighton, Frances Spatz *writer, journalist*
Orben, Robert *editor, writer*
Walker, Scot William P. *writer, real estate investor*
Whitehead, Kenneth Dean *author, translator, retired federal government official*

Fredericksburg
Marler, Helen *writer, actress*

Free Union
LeBoutillier, Megan *writer*

Leesburg
Johnson, Julia A. *writer*

Lexington
Stuart, Dabney *poet, author, English language educator*

Mc Lean
Waller, John Henry *author*

Middleburg
Grove, Noel Randall *writer*

Norfolk
Berent, Irwin Mark *writer, software executive*

Portsmouth
Mapp, Alf Johnson, Jr., *writer, historian, educator*
Nolen, Crystal Me'Kelle *poet, educator*

Reston
Smith, Ralph Lee *author, musician*

Richmond
Reynolds, Sheri *writer*

Stephenson
Johnson, Eva Maria *retired translator*

Sterling
Bernal-Labrada, Emilio *writer, poet, translator*

Vienna
Olshaker, Mark Bruce *author, film maker*

Virginia Beach
Seward, William W(ard), Jr., *writer, retired educator*

Warrenton
Estaver, Paul Edward *writer, poet*

Williamsburg
Myers, Roger Paul *writer, playwright, actor*
Smith, William Henry Preston *freelance/self-employed writer, editor, former telecommunications industry executive*

Woodbridge
Englert, Helen Wiggs *writer*

Woodville
Mc Carthy, Eugene Joseph *writer, former senator*

WASHINGTON

Arlington
Bullington, Gayle Rogers *writer, researcher*

Bellevue
Olson, Robert William *writer, retired counselor*

Bellingham
Hansen, Leonard Joseph *writer, journalist, editor, communications executive*

Freeland
Meador, Jo Guasasco *writer, retired information technology manager*

Issaquah
Cain, Coleen W. *writer, educator*

Kent
Raymond, Eugene Thomas *technical writer, consultant, retired aircraft engineer*

Kirkland
Szablya, Helen Mary *writer, language professional, lecturer*

La Conner
Robbins, Thomas Eugene *writer*

Leavenworth
Taub, Alex A.G. *writer, educator*

Lynnwood
Bear, Gregory Dale *writer, illustrator*

Medical Lake
Barber, Devin *writer*

Otis Orchards
Pfeiffer, Patricia Ruth *writer, consultant*

Port Angeles
Muller, Willard C(hester) *writer*

Poulsbo
Wayne, Kyra Petrovskaya *writer*

Seattle
Butler, Octavia Estelle *free-lance writer*
Evans, Jack R. (J. Glenn Evans) *writer, poet*
Kunkel, Georgie Bright *freelance writer, retired school counselor*
McHugh, Heather *poet*
Mini, Anne Alexandra Apostolides *writer, educator*
Singer, Sarah Beth *poet*
Thomas, Irv *journalist, publisher*
Wagoner, David Russell *writer, educator*

Shelton
Maddux, Carolyn L. *writer, educator*

WEST VIRGINIA

Little Birch
Harman, Brenda Kay *writer, researcher*

Teays
Lamb, Carl Vernon *writer, retired engineer*

WISCONSIN

Argyle
Daley, Ron (Ronald Eugene Daley) *playwright, poet, director, producer*

Brookfield
Schmitz, John J. *writer, educator*

Elkhorn
Dunn, Walter Scott, Jr., *writer, former museum director, consultant*

Green Bay
Elwell, Mark W. *writer*

Greenfield
Helland, Sherman M. *writer*

Janesville
Axtell, Roger E. *writer, retired marketing professional*

Menasha
Mills, Laurel *writer*

Milwaukee
Connelly, Mark *writer, educator*

Oshkosh
Alderson, Jo Bartels *writer, poet*

Racine
Wright, Betty Ren *children's book writer*

Saukville
Gulan, Bonnie Marion *writer, researcher*

Shawano
Mutter, John J., Jr., *writer, researcher*

WYOMING

Buffalo
Graham, Violet Joyce *writer*

Laramie
Boresi, Arthur Peter *writer, educator*

Mountain View
Silva, Alana G *writer, speech professional*
Connelly, Michael *writer*

CANADA

BRITISH COLUMBIA

Heriot Bay
Bringhurst, Robert *poet*

Vancouver
Bowering, George Harry *writer, English literature educator*

MANITOBA

Winnipeg
Oberman, Sheldon Arnold *writer, educator*

ONTARIO

Holland Landing
Dempster, Barry (Edward) *writer, poet*

Toronto
Colombo, John Robert *poet, editor, writer*
Moore, Christopher Hugh *writer*
Peacock, Molly *poet, educator*
Reaney, James Crerar *dramatist, poet, educator*

QUEBEC

Montreal
Becker, Herbert Lawrence *writer, accountant*
Bruemmer, Fred *writer, photographer*

AUSTRALIA

Norfolk Island
McCullough, Colleen *author*

Paddington
Keneally, Thomas Michael *author*

DENMARK

Charlottenlund
Garner, Fradley Hamilton *freelance writer, editor, narrator*

ENGLAND

Cambridge
Steiner, George (Francis Steiner) *author, educator*

London
Alvarez, A. (Al Alvarez) *writer*
Amis, Martin Louis *author*
Chevalier, Tracy Rose *writer*
Cleese, John Marwood *writer, comedian*
Cope, Wendy *poet*
Deighton, Len *author*
Desai, Anita *writer*
Drabble, Margaret *writer*
Fine, Anne *author*
Fowles, John *author*
Galloway, Janice *writer, editor*
Gibson, William Ford *author*
Gray, Simon James Holliday *writer, educator*
Hare, David *playwright*
Harwood, Ronald *screenwriter, playwright*
Hunter Blair, Pauline Clarke *author*
James, P(hyllis) D(orothy) (Baroness James of Holland Park of Southwold in County of Suffolk) *author*
Lessing, Doris (Doris May) *writer*
Naipaul, Vidiadhar Surajprasad *author*
Paton Walsh, Jill *writer*
Phillips, Caryl *writer*
Read, Piers Paul *author*
Rowling, J.K. (Joanne Kathleen Rowling) *writer*
Stoppard, Tom (Tomas Straussler) *playwright*

Stevenage
Follett, Kenneth Martin *author*

Whitchurch
Adams, Richard George *writer*

FRANCE

Paris
Gallant, Mavis *author*
Horovitz, Israel Arthur *playwright*
Reza, Yasmina *author, playwright*

Ramatuelle
Collins, Larry *author, journalist*

IRELAND

Donegal
Friel, Brian (Bernard Patrick Friel) *author*

Mullingar
Donleavy, James Patrick *writer, artist*

ITALY

Venice
Pasinetti, Pier Maria *author*

NETHERLANDS

Krimpen
Houtzager, Marianne Johanna (Marian de Boyen) *writer, artist, photographer*

NIGERIA

Abeokuta Ogun State
Soyinka, Wole *writer*

RUSSIA

Moscow
Solzhenitsyn, Aleksandr Isayevich *writer*

SWITZERLAND

Bern
Carlson, Dale Bick *writer*

TRINIDAD AND TOBAGO

Diego Martin
Walcott, Derek Alton *poet, playwright*

ADDRESS UNPUBLISHED

Adams, Deanna Ruth *writer, educator*
Aladjem, Henrietta H. *writer*
Alderman, Annabel (Elsie Higgs Griner Jr.) *writer*
Alexander, Amir Roi *writer*
Alinder, Mary Street *writer, lecturer*
Alipio, Gary Glynn *writer, consultant*
Allen, Ralph Gilmore *dramatist, producer, drama educator*
Allen, Roberta *fiction and nonfiction writer, conceptual artist, photographer*
Aloff, Mindy *writer*
Anderson, N. C. *writer, artist*
Anderson-Spivy, Alexandra *writer, editor*
Anselmo, Robert Louis *writer*
Anton, Barbara *writer*
Antonelli, Rosemary *writer*
Argers, Helen *novelist, playwright*
Arlen, Michael J. *writer*
Ashley, Renee *writer, creative writing educator, consultant*
Avery, Stephen Neal *playwright, writer*
Aziel, Barbie-dae *writer, artist, poet*
Bahr, Jane Marie *writer, retired English educator*
Bailey, Blake *writer*
Bailey, William Waddell *writer, communications executive*
Baker, Lucinda *writer*
Baldrige, Letitia *writer, management training consultant*
Balliett, Whitney *writer, critic*
Banks, Russell *writer, educator*
Barcus, Nancy B. *fine arts educator, writer*
Barney, Donna Nadyne *writer*
Barrett, Katherine *writer, multimedia producer*
Barzun, Jacques *author, literary consultant*
Bassett, Elizabeth Ewing (Libby Bassett) *writer, editor, consultant*
Baum, Roger S. *writer*
Beatts, Anne Patricia *writer, producer*
Bellow, Saul C. *writer, educator*
Benedict, Stewart H. *writer, playwright*
Berquist, Angela Su *writer, philosopher*
Berry, Richard Lewis *writer, magazine editor, lecturer, programmer*
Bertram, Jean DeSales *writer*
Billingsley, Franny *writer*
Black, David *writer, educator, producer*
Blake Ramos, Debra Barbara *writer*
Block, Lawrence *author*
Blos, Joan W. *author, critic, lecturer*
Bodsworth, Fred *author, naturalist*
Bova, Benjamin William *author, editor, educator*
Bracken, Michael Patrick *writer, editor*
Bracken, Peg *writer*
Brady, Sally Ryder *writer, literary agent*
Brookner, Anita *writer, educator*
Brown, Crystal Jeanine *writer*
Brown, Denise *poet*
Brown, Marcia Joan *author, artist, photographer*
Brown-Banks, Jennifer Elaine *writer, educator*
Brubach, Holly Beth *writer*
Bruce, Debra *poet, English language educator*
Bryant, John *author, publisher*
Bulla, Clyde Robert *writer*
Burgess, James Edward *writer*
Burke, Doug *author, director, producer, inventor*
Burke, Edgar P. *writer*
Busch, Frederick Matthew *writer, literature educator*
Cáceres, Franklin Thomas *writer*
Caldwell-Smith, Gaetana Lee *writer*
Caletti, Deb L. *writer*
Callan, Jamie *writer, educator*
Calore, Paul *retired writer*
Campanelli, Michele Wallace *writer*
Campbell, Addison James, Jr., *writer*
Carcaterra, Lorenzo Gabriel *writer*
Carlisle-Frank, Pamela L. *writer, researcher, consultant*
Carrigan, William Thomas, III, *writer*
Carroll, Mary Patricia *writer*
Carter, Danita M. *writer, securities trader*
Cavileer, Denise Marie *poet*
Chang, Lan Samantha *writer, educator*
Chapin, Miles Whitworth *writer, actor*
Cheatham, Belzora *writer*
Chesney, Susan Talmadge *writer, developer*
Choukas-Bradley, Melanie *writer, photographer*
Christensen, Madonna Dries *writer*
Claes, Gayla Christine *writer, editorial consultant*
Clark, Mary Higgins *writer, communications executive*
Clark, Matt *science writer*
Clarke, Sir Arthur Charles *author*
Clifford, Brian Elliott *writer, researcher*
Coburn, D(onald) L(ee) *playwright*
Cochrane, Shirley Graves *writer, educator*
Cohen, Cafi Fischer *writer, music educator*
Cole, Barry Michael *writer, writer*
Collins, William J. *poet, educator*
Colmes, Doris Harriett *writer*
Conklin, William Frank *writer*
Connell, Evan Shelby, Jr., *writer*
Coonts, Stephen Paul *novelist*
Cowan, Andrew Glenn *television writer, producer, performer*
Cowan, Mary Morton *writer*
Crisman Collier, Ruth Marie *writer*
Croswell, Katrina Antoinette *writer*
Cullen, Paula Bramsen *writer*
Curtis, Dolores Rogers *writer*
Cussler, Clive Eric *author*
Dailey, Janet *writer*
Damiano, Mary *scriptwriter, journalist*
Daren, Sylvia *poet*
Davidson, Chris Clark *writer*
Davidson, Mark *writer, educator*
Davis, Luther *writer, producer*
Davis, Maggie (Marie Hill) *writer*
Davis, Mamie (Denise Davis) *writer*
Davis, Michelle Denise *writer*
Davis, Ruth Marie *retired writer*
Deal, Gaye Follmer *writer*
DeBeers, Roger Norman *writer*
DeMille, Nelson Richard *writer*
Desio, Delores Jean *writer, artist, retired elementary school educator*
Dewey, Donald Charles *writer*
Diamant, Anita *writer*
Diprato, Jim *writer, video editor*
Disch, Thomas M(ichael) *author*
Dolan, Edward Francis *writer*
Dolby, Tom Eric *writer*
Donnelly, Patrick Stefan *writer, editor*
Drucker, Peter Ferdinand *writer, consultant, educator*
Dunlap, James *poet, writer*
Dunn, Robert Giddings *writer, educator*
Durnell, Laura *writer, educator*
Eberwein, Thomas K. *writer, reporter*
Egelston, Roberta Riethmiller *writer*
Eglee, Charles Hamilton *television and movie writer, producer*
Ephron, Nora *writer*
Erenberger, Timothy *writer*
Erwin, Judith Ann (Judith Ann Peacock) *writer, photographer, lawyer*
Esther, Queen *playwright, scriptwriter, songwriter, solo performer, actor, musician*
Esty, John Cushing, Jr., *writer, teacher, advisor to non-profit boards*
Evangelista, Anita Loretta *freelance writer, psychologist, nurse, publishing executive*
Evanovich, Janet *writer*
Ewing, Susan M. *writer*
Farrelly, Peter John *screenwriter*
Farronato, Cristina *writer, researcher*
Fearrington, Ann Peyton *writer, illustrator, newspaper reporter, portraitist*
Feldman, David Edward *playwright*
Filer, Tom Hanford *writer, educator*
Finder, Joseph Alan *writer*
Fisher, Nancy *writer, producer, director*
Foote, Horton *playwright, scriptwriter*
Foster, Ken *writer, educator*
Fraser, Kathleen Joy *poet, creative writing educator*
Freedman, Russell Bruce *author*
French, Marilyn *writer, critic*
Friday, Nancy *author*
Friedman, Donald M. *writer, lawyer*
Fritz, Ethel Mae Hendrickson *writer*
Fryer, Thomas Waitt, Jr., *writer and editor*
Frymer, Murry *writer, theater and film critic*
Fuentes, Carlos *writer, former ambassador*
Fuller, Charles H, Jr., *playwright*
Gallimore, Margaret Martin *poet*
Garfield-Woodbridge, Nancy *writer*
Garfinkle, Elaine Myra *writer*
Gebauer, Phyllis Victoria Feltskog *writer, educator*
Gellis, Willard Leon *poet, English educator*
George, Gerald William *author, administrator*
Gersoni-Edelman, Diane Claire *author, editor*
Giffin, Marjie G. *writer*
Gilbert, Elayne Rhoda *writer*
Gilchrist, Ellen Louise *writer*

ARTS: PERFORMING

UNITED STATES

ALABAMA

Auburn
Gilbreath, Jeffrey Lynn *music educator*

Auburn University
Powell, Rosephanye Dunn *composer, music educator*

Bay Minette
Grabill, Tim *band director, paramedic*

Birmingham
Chapman, Wes *dancer, performing company executive*
Eady, Charles Edward *music educator*
Gilmore, Catherine Rye *arts administrator*
Hall, Jessica L. *music educator*
Turner, Kevin Paul *music educator*
Westerfield, Richard *music director*

Cottonwood
Smith, Christopher M. *music educator*

Eutaw
Turner, Marvin Lesere *musician*

Huntsville
Mohan, Annette Imelda *producer, educator*
Mohan, Tungesh Nath *television and film producer, film educator*
Snodgrass, Jonathan Wayne *music educator, pastor*
Spencer, William David *music educator*

Mobile
Habib, Thomas Mark *musician, educator*

Montgomery
Copeland, Jacqueline Turner *music educator*
Lowe, Brian Wesley *music educator*

Muscle Shoals
Ownby, Terry Scott *music educator, director*

Normal
Hall, Doris Spooner *music educator*

Point Clear
Englund, Gage Bush *dancer, educator*

Vestavia Hills
Coleman, Travis Brent *music educator*

Wadley
Caldwell, Ann B. *music educator*

ALASKA

Anchorage
Gazaway, Barbara Ann *music educator, art educator*

Eagle River
Lange, Ron Q. *music educator*

Indian
Wright, Gordon Brooks *musician, conductor, educator*

ARIZONA

Chandler
Carpenter, Ron D. *music educator*
Faust, Donny D. *music educator*
Simon, Diane Rose *music educator, writer, poet*

Cortaro
Wyatt, Roland Gratts *music educator, voice educator, consultant*

Cottonwood
Masters, Arlene Elizabeth *singer*

Flagstaff
Levin, Mike Douglas *performing arts educator*
Weidenaar, Gary Alan *music educator*

Fountain Hills
Tyl, Noel Jan *baritone, astrologer, writer*

Lakeside
Stidham, Lucas Wesley *music educator*

Mesa
Moorhead, Nila Katherine *music educator*
Porter, Christy Lee *music educator*
Skoldberg, Phyllis Linnea *music educator, musician*

Phoenix
Anderson, Gary Gene *music educator*
Anderson, Ib *performing company executive*
Cook, Douglas Neilson *theater educator, producer, artistic director*
Hoerber, Michael David *music educator, conductor*
Jones, Isola Charlayne *mezzo soprano, voice educator*
Long, Michael Alan *musician, writer*
Nijinsky, Tamara *actress, puppeteer, author, librarian, educator*
Thomas, Jim Gus *music educator*
Wheaton, Marilyn *music educator, pianist, organist*

Scottsdale
Ash, Fayola Foltz *musician, music educator*
Baack, Paula D. *music educator*
Broe, Carolyn Waters *conductor, violist, music educator*
Newman, Ursula Irene *music educator*
Peterson, John Willard *composer, music publisher*
Wolfgang, Bonnie Arlene *musician, bassoonist*

Sierra Vista
Boughan, Zanetta Louise *music educator*

Surprise
Eastman, Donna Kelly *composer*

Tempe
Landschoot, Thomas V. *musician, educator*
Lombardi, Eugene Patsy *retired orchestra conductor, violinist, educator*
Wytko, Joseph Rudolph *music educator*

Tucson
Aurand, Charles Henry, Jr., *music educator, educator*
Birdman, Jerome Moseley *drama educator, consultant*
Boyle, Michael Frederick *retired television producer, actor*
Nelson, Mark A. *music educator*
Ostromencki, Nancy Lee *music educator*
Rees, Jay Carlyle *conductor, composer, music educator*
Seaman, Arlene Anna *retired musician, educator*

Vail
Cardieri, Alexander M. *music specialist, music educator*

ARKANSAS

Arkadelphia
Cai, Lei *music educator, pianist*

Conway
Showell, Jeffrey Adams *music educator, academic administrator, musician*

Fayetteville
Caldwell, Sarah *opera producer, conductor, stage director and administrator*
Commer, John Andrew *video director*

Fort Smith
Husarik, Stephen *music educator*

Jonesboro
Bartee, Neale *music educator, musician, conductor*

Little Rock
Brack, Robert Louis *retired music educator*
Itkin, David *music director, conductor*
Munoz, Olivier *artistic director*
Raney, Miriam Day *actress*
Vickery, William *arts administrator*

Magnolia
Campbell, Robert Gordon *music educator*

Pine Bluff
Sewald, Carl Martin *music educator*

CALIFORNIA

Agoura Hills
Homer, Raymond Rodney *film producer, director*
Klugman, Jack *actor*

Albany
Boris, Ruthanna *dancer, choreographer, dance therapist, educator*

Antioch
Adams, Liliana Osses *music performer, harpist*
Molina, Ron Joseph *music educator*

Apple Valley
Deller, Gerald Stephen *professional magician, former insurance company executive*
Lavallee, Charles Phillip *music educator, musician*

Arcadia
Zimmerman, Amy J. *television producer, television director*

Arroyo Grande
Mott, Robert Lewis *writer, sound effects artist*

Bakersfield
Provencio, Roberto Enrique *music educator, music minister*

Bell
Jackman, Hugh *actor*

Bellflower
de Thouars, Victor Ivan Charles *professional martial artist, educator*

Belmont
Musmann, Lois S. *conductor, music educator*

Berkeley
Dresher, Paul Joseph *composer, music educator, performer*
Imbrie, Andrew Welsh *composer, educator*
Matsumura, Vera Yoshi *pianist*
Reid, Frances Evelyn Kroll *cinematographer, director, film company executive*
Talbot, Stephen Henderson *television producer, documentary filmmaker, writer*
Thow, John H. *music educator, composer*

Beverly Hills
Adams, Joey Lauren *actress*
Alexander, Jason (Jay Scott Greenspan) *actor*
Allen, Debbie *actress, choreographer, dancer, television director*
Allen, Joan *actress*
Allen, Ted *television personality*
Allen, Tim (Timothy Allen Dick) *actor, comedian*
Ambrose, Lauren *actress*
Ames, Edmund Dantes *singer, actor, producer*
Amiel, Jon *film director, film producer*
Anders, Allison *film director, screenwriter*
Anderson, Gillian *actress*
Anderson, Pamela *actress*
Anderson, Wes *film director*
Aniston, Jennifer *actress*
Ann-Margret, (Ann-Margret Olsson) *actress, performer*
Armstrong, Gillian May *film director*
Arnold, Tom *actor, comedian, producer*
Astin, Sean Patrick *actor, film director, film producer, writer*
August, Bille *film director*
Avary, Roger Roberts (Frank Brauner) *film director, producer, writer*
Azaria, Hank *actor*
Bacon, Kevin *actor*
Badham, John MacDonald *motion picture director*
Bailey, John *cinematographer*
Baker, Kathy Whitton *actress*
Bancroft, Anne (Mrs. Mel Brooks) *actress, scriptwriter, television director*
Banderas, Antonio *actor*
Bassett, Angela *actress*
Bates, Kathy *actress*
Bay, Michael Benjamin *film director*
Beal, John Everett *composer, conductor*
Beatty, (Henry) Warren *actor, producer, director*
Becker, Harold *film director, producer*
Bedelia, Bonnie *actress*
Bello, Maria Elana *actress*
Belushi, James A. *actor*
Bening, Annette *actress*
Berg, Jeffrey Spencer *talent agency executive*
Bergman, Andrew *motion picture director*
Berkus, James *talent agent*
Berry, Halle M. *actress*
Bird, Antonia *film director*
Blanchett, Cate *actress*
Bogdanovich, Peter *film director, writer, producer, actor*
Bonham-Carter, Helena *actress*
Bosworth, Kate *actress*
Boyle, Lara Flynn *actress*
Braff, Zach *actor, director, scriptwriter*
Branch, Michelle *musician*
Bratt, Benjamin *actor*
Braun, Zev *motion picture and television producer*
Brenneman, Amy *actress*
Bridges, Jeff *actor*
Brillstein, Bernie J. *producer, talent manager*
Brockie, Pamela *motion picture executive*
Broderick, Matthew *actor*
Brokaw, Norman Robert *talent agency executive*
Burnett, Carol *actress, comedienne, singer*
Burnett, Charles *film director, screenwriter, producer*
Burnham, John Ludwig *agent*
Burns, Edward J., Jr., *actor, film director*
Burstyn, Ellen (Edna Rae Gillooly) *actress*
Buscemi, Steve *actor*
Busfield, Timothy *actor*
Bynes, Amanda *actress*
Byrne, Gabriel *actor*
Caan, James *actor, director*
Campbell, Neve *actress*
Capshaw, Kate (Kathy Sue Nail) *actress*
Carpenter, John Howard *director, screenwriter*
Carreras, José *tenor*
Carrey, Jim *actor*
Carroll, Diahann *actress, singer*
Carter, Chris *producer, director*
Carter, Dixie *actress*
Carter, Lynda *actress, entertainer*
Casey, Sue (Suzanne Marguerite Philips) *actress, real estate broker*
Castellaneta, Dan (Daniel Louis) *actor*
Castle-Hughes, Keisha *actress*
Caton-Jones, Michael *film director, film producer*
Cattrall, Kim *actress*
Caviezel, James Patrick *actor*
Channing, Carol *actress*
Chapelle, Dave *comedian*
Cheadle, Don *actor*
Cher, (Cherilyn Sarkisian) *singer, actress*
Christensen, Hayden *actor*
Chritton, George A. *theater producer*
Clooney, George *actor*
Close, Glenn *actress*
Coen, Ethan *film director, writer*
Coen, Joel *film director, writer*
Cole, Natalie Maria *singer*
Collette, Toni *actress*
Columbus, Chris *film director, screenwriter*
Connelly, Jennifer *actress*
Connery, Sir Sean (Thomas Connery) *actor*
Corbett, John *actor*
Corman, Eugene Harold *motion picture producer*
Cox Arquette, Courteney *actress*
Crawford, Cindy (Cynthia Ann Crawford) *model, actress*
Crowe, Russell *actor*
Cruz, Penelope *actress*
Culkin, Macaulay *actor*
Curtis, Jamie Lee *actress*
Cusack, Joan *actress*
Cusack, John *actor*
Dahl, John *film director*
Daly, Tyne *actress*
Damon, Matthew Paige *actor*
DeBont, Jan *cinematographer, director*
Delaney, Kim *actress*
Demme, Jonathan *director, producer, writer*
De Niro, Robert *actor, film producer, film director, restaurant owner*
Dennehy, Brian *actor*
Depp, Johnny *actor*
Dern, Bruce MacLeish *actor*
DeVito, Danny Michael *actor, director, producer*
Diaz, Cameron *actress*
Diesel, Vin (Mark Vincent) *actor*
Dillon, Matt *actor*
Donaldson, Roger *film director, film producer*
Dorff, Stephen *actor*
Dotrice, Roy Louis *actor*
Douglas, Michael Kirk *actor, film producer, director*
Drescher, Fran *actress*
Dreyfuss, Richard Stephan *actor*
Driver, Minnie *actress*
Duchovny, David *actor*
Dunaway, Faye (Dorothy Dunaway) *actress*
Duncan, Michael Clarke *actor*
Dussault, Nancy *actress, singer*
Duvall, Robert *actor*
Duvall, Shelley *actress*
Eastwood, Clint *actor, film director, former mayor*
Eden, Barbara Jean *actress*
Emmerich, Roland *director, producer, writer*
Everett, Rupert *actor*
Falco, Edie *actress*
Feldshuh, Tovah S. *actress*
Ferrell, Will *actor*
Filicia, Thom *television personality, interior designer*
Finstad, Suzanne Elaine *writer, producer, lawyer*
Flaum, Marshall Allen *television producer, writer, director*
Fleder, Gary *film director, producer*
Foch, Nina *actress, creative consultant, film director, educator*
Foley, David *television and film actor*
Foley, James *film director*
Fonda, Jane *actress*
Foster, Lawrence *concert and opera conductor*
Fox, Michael J. *actor*
Fox, Vivica *actress*
Foxx, Jamie *actor, comedian*
Fraser, Brendan *actor*
Garofalo, Janeane *actress, comedienne*
Garr, Teri (Ann) *actress*
Gellar, Sarah Michelle *actress*
Gilpin, Peri *actress*
Glover, John *actor*
Glover, Savion *actor, dancer*
Goodman, John *actor*
Graham, Heather *actress*
Graham, Lauren *actress*
Grant, Hugh *actor*
Graves, Peter *actor*
Green, Seth *actor*
Gregg, Rodman Walter *motion picture and television producer, publisher*
Grey, Brad *producer, agent*
Griffin, Merv Edward *former entertainer, television producer, entrepreneur*
Griffiths, Rachel *actress*
Gyllenhaal, Jake *actor*
Gyllenhaal, Maggie *actress*
Hackford, Taylor *film director, producer*
Hackman, Gene (Eugene Alden Hackman) *actor*
Hallstrom, Lasse *director*
Hamilton, Lisa Gay *actress*
Hanks, Tom *actor, producer, director*
Hannah, Daryl *actress*
Hanson, Curtis *film director, scriptwriter*
Harden, Marcia Gay *actress*
Harmon, Angie (Angie Sehorn) *actress*
Harrelson, Woody *actor*
Hartnett, Josh *actor*
Haskell, Peter Abraham *actor*
Hawn, Goldie *actress*
Heaton, Patricia *actress*
Helgeland, Brian Thomas *film director, writer, producer*
Herek, Stephen *film director, producer*
Hershey, Barbara (Barbara Herzstein) *actress*
Heston, Charlton (John Charlton Carter) *actor*
Hewitt, Jennifer Love *actress, singer*
Hill, Walter *film director, writer, producer*
Hines, Cheryl *actress*
Hoffman, Dustin Lee *actor*
Holmes, Katherine Noelle (Katie Holmes) *actress*
Hopkins, Sir Anthony (Philip) *actor*
Hopkins, Stephen *film director, producer*
Hopper, Dennis *actor, writer, photographer, film director*
Hounsou, Djimon Gaston *actor*
Howard, Ron *director, actor, producer*
Hughes, John W. *film producer, screenwriter, film director*
Hunt, Bonnie *actress*
Hunt, Helen *actress*
Hurd, Gale Anne *film producer*
Hurley, Elizabeth *actress, model, film producer*
Hurt, William *actor*
Huston, Anjelica *actress*
Hutton, Timothy *actor*
Huvane, Kevin *talent agent*
Imperioli, Michael *actor*
Jackson, Janet Damita Jo *vocalist, dancer*
Jackson, Mick *film director, producer*
Jackson, Peter *film director*
Jenkins, Patty *film director, scriptwriter*
Johansson, Scarlett *actress*
Jolie, Angelina *actress*
Jones, Cherry *actress*
Jonze, Spike *film director*
Jordan, Glenn *film director, television director, theater director*
Josephson, Nancy *talent agent*
Judd, Ashley *actress*
Keaton, Diane *actress*
Keaton, Michael *actor, comedian*
Keith, David Lemuel *actor*
Kelly, Moira *actress*
Kerns, Joanna de Varona *actress, writer, director*
Kidman, Nicole *actress*
Kilmer, Val *actor*
Kingsley, Ben *actor*
Kingston, Alex(andra) *actress*
Klum, Heidi *model, actress*
Knoxville, Johnny *actor*
Konchalovsky, Andrei *film director*
Krause, Peter *actor*
Kravitz, Lenny *singer, guitarist*
Kressley, Carson *television personality*
Kutcher, Ashton *actor*
Lahti, Christine *actress*
Lane, Nathan (Joseph Lane) *actor*
Lange, Jessica *actress*
Langella, Frank *actor*
Lansbury, Angela Brigid *actress*
LaPaglia, Anthony *actor*
La Vette, Maureen C. *actress, writer*
Law, Jude *actor*
Lawrence, Martin *actor, comedian*
Lear, Norman Milton *producer, writer, director*
Leary, Denis *actor, comedian*
Leder, Mimi *television director, film director, film producer*
Lee, Ang *filmmaker*
Leguizamö, John *actor*
Leigh, Jennifer Jason (Jennifer Leigh Morrow) *actress*
Levy, Eugene *actor, director, screenwriter*
Lewis, Juliette *actress*
Limato, Edward Frank *talent agent*
Linkletter, Arthur Gordon *radio and television broadcaster*
Linney, Laura *actress*
Liotta, Ray *actor*
Liu, Lucy *actress*
Lloyd, Christopher *actor*
Loggins, Kenny (Kenneth Clarke Loggins) *singer, songwriter*
Lopez, Jennifer *actress, singer, dancer*
Lourd, Bryan *talent agent*
Lovett, Richard *talent agency executive*
Lowe, Rob *actor*
Lucas, Josh (Josh Maurer) *actor*
Lyne, Adrian *film director*
Mac Dowell, Andie (Rose Anderson Mac Dowell) *actress*
MacLaine, Shirley *actress*
Macy, William H. *actor*
Madsen, Michael *actor*
Maher, Bill *talk show host, comedian, producer*
Malkovich, John *actor*
Manheim, Camryn *television and film actress*
Mann, Michael K. *producer, director, writer*
Mantello, Joseph *theater director*
Margulies, Julianna *actress*
Marsden, James (James Paul Marsden) *actor*
Marshall, Penny (C. Marshall) *director, actress*
Martin, Kellie (Noelle) *actress*
Martin, Steve *comedian, actor*
Martinson, Constance Frye *television personality, television producer*
Masterson, Mary Stuart *actress*
Mathis, Samantha *actress*
Matlin, Marlee *actress*
McAdams, Rachel *actress*
McCarthy, Jenny *actress*
McDormand, Frances *actress*
McGowan, Rose *actress*
Mc Kean, Michael *actor*
McShane, Ian *actor*
Messing, Debra *actress*
Meyer, Breckin *actor*
Midler, Bette *singer, entertainer, actress*
Milius, John Frederick *film writer, director*
Miller, Dennis *comedian*
Molina, Alfred *actor*
Moore, Demi (Demi Guynes) *actress*
Moore, Julianne (Julie Anne Smith) *actress*
Moore, Mary Tyler *actress*
Moore, Michael *film director, writer*
Moorhouse, Jocelyn Denise *film director*
Morissette, Alanis *musician*
Mortensen, Viggo *actor*
Morton, Samantha *actress*
Mullally, Megan *actress*
Mulroney, Dermot *actor*
Muniz, Frankie (Francisco James Muniz IV) *actor*
Murray, Bill *actor, writer*
Najimy, Kathy *actress*
Nava, Gregory *film director, screenwriter, producer*
Neeson, Liam *actor*
Neuwirth, Bebe (Beatrice Neuwirth) *dancer, actress*
Nicita, Rick *agent*
Nixon, Cynthia *actress*
Norton, Edward *actor*
Novak, Kim (Marilyn Novak) *actress*
O'Connor, David *talent agent*
O'Connor, Pat *film director*
O'Donnell, Chris *actor*
O'Donnell, Rosie *television personality, actress, comedienne*
Ormond, Julia *actress*
Pacino, Al (Alfredo James Pacino) *actor, film director, film producer*
Palance, Jack *actor*
Paltrow, Gwyneth *actress*
Pantoliano, Joe *actor*
Parker, Alan (William) (Sir Alan Parker) *film director, writer*
Parker, Mary-Louise *actress*
Parker, Sarah Jessica *actress*
Patinkin, Mandy *actor, singer*
Patric, Jason *actor*
Peet, Amanda *actress*
Penderecki, Krzysztof *composer, conductor*

Petersen, Wolfgang *film director*
Pfeiffer, Michelle *actress*
Phillippe, Ryan *actor*
Piscopo, Joseph Charles *actor*
Pitt, Brad *actor*
Plummer, Christopher (Orme) (Arthur Plummer) *actor*
Polanski, Roman *film director, writer, actor*
Pollack, Sydney *film director*
Pollak, Kevin *actor*
Portman, Natalie *actress*
Posey, Parker *actress*
Priestley, Jason *actor*
Ptak, John *talent agent*
Pullman, Bill *actor*
Quinn, Aidan *actor*
Raimi, Samuel M. *film director*
Redgrave, Vanessa *actress*
Reese, Della (Deloreese Patricia Early) *singer, actress*
Reeves, Keanu *actor*
Reiner, Carl *director, actor, writer*
Reiner, Rob *director, writer, actor*
Renfro, Brad *actor*
Rhames, Ving (Irving) *actor*
Ricci, Christina *actress*
Richardson, Patricia *actress*
Riley, Jack *actor, writer*
Ringwald, Molly *actress*
Rivers, Joan *entertainer*
Roberts, Julia Fiona *actress*
Rodriguez, Jai *television personality*
Romijn-Stamos, Rebecca *actress, model*
Ruffalo, Mark *actor*
Rush, Geoffrey *actor*
Russell, Keri *actress*
Russell, Kurt Von Vogel *actor*
Russo, Rene *actress*
Ryan, Meg *actress, film producer*
Sagal, Katey *actress*
Saget, Bob *director, actor, comedian, writer*
Sandrich, Jay H. *television director*
Schneider, Rob *actor*
Schroder, Rick *actor*
Schroeder, Barbet G. *director*
Scott, Ridley *film director*
Scott-Thomas, Kristin *actress*
Seagal, Steven *actor*
Sedgwick, Kyra *actress*
Sellecca, Connie *actress*
Seymour, Jane *actress*
Shadyac, Thomas *film director, producer*
Shalhoub, Tony *actor, television producer*
Shandling, Garry *comedian, scriptwriter, actor*
Sharif, Omar (Michael Shalhoub) *actor*
Sheen, Charlie (Carlos Irwin Estevez) *actor*
Short, Martin *actor, comedian*
Shue, Elisabeth *actress*
Shuler Donner, Lauren *film producer*
Shyamalan, Manoj Night *film director*
Silverman, Jonathan *actor*
Simpson, Mike *talent agent*
Sinise, Gary *actor, director*
Skerritt, Tom *actor*
Smith, Jaclyn *actress*
Smith, Kevin *film director, writer, actor*
Smith, Will *actor, rap artist*
Smith, Yeardley *actress*
Snipes, Wesley *actor, film producer*
Snyder, Liza *actress*
Sommers, Stephen *film director, scriptwriter, film producer*
Sonnenfeld, Barry *director, cinematographer*
Sorvino, Mira *actress*
Sorvino, Paul *actor*
Spacek, Sissy (Mary Elizabeth Spacek) *actress*
Spade, David *actor*
Spielberg, Steven *motion picture director, producer*
Spottiswoode, Roger *film director, film producer*
Stamos, John *actor*
Steenburgen, Mary *actress*
Stefano, Joseph William *film and television producer, writer*
Stern, Sandor *film writer, director*
Stewart, Jon (Jonathan Stewart Leibowitz) *comedian, actor*
Stiers, David Ogden *actor, conductor*
Stiles, Julia *actress*
Stowe, Madeleine *actress*
Streep, Meryl (Mary Louise Streep) *actress*
Sutherland, Donald *actor*
Sutherland, Kiefer *actor*
Suvari, Mena *actress*
Swank, Hilary Ann *actress*
Swayze, Patrick *actor, dancer*
Tamblyn, Amber Rose *actress*
Tambor, Jeffrey *actor, theatre director, educator*
Taylor, Christine *actress*
Taylor, Lili *actress*
Theron, Charlize *actress*
Thomas, Marlo (Margaret Julia Thomas) *actress*
Thompson, Caroline Warner *film director, screenwriter*
Thompson, Emma *actress*
Thompson, Larry Angelo *motion picture and TV producer, lawyer, personal manager, author, lecturer*
Thurman, Uma Karuna *actress*
Tierney, Maura *actress*
Tilly, Jennifer *actress*
Tomei, Marisa *actress*
Travolta, John *actor*
Trueba, Fernando *film director and producer, screenwriter*
Tucci, Stanley *actor*
Turlington, Christy *model*
Turner, Kathleen *actress*
Turturro, Nicholas *actor*
Tyler, Liv *actress*
Underwood, Blair *actor, director*
Valentine, Dean *film producer*
Van Ark, Joan *actress*
Van Dyke, Dick *actor, comedian*
Van Sant, Gus, Jr., *director, screenwriter*
Van Zandt, Steven *actor, musician, radio personality*
Vardalos, Nia *actress, screenwriter*
Vaughn, Vince *actor*
Verhoeven, Paul *film director*
Ward, Sela *actress*
Waters, John *film director, writer, actor*
Watts, Naomi *actress*
Wayans, Marlon *actor, film producer, writer*
Wayans, Shawn *actor, film producer, writer*
Weaver, Sigourney (Susan Alexandra Weaver) *actress*
Webb, Veronica *fashion model, journalist*
Weir, Peter Lindsay *film director*
Weisz, Rachel *actress*
Weitz, Bruce (Peter Weitz) *actor*
White, Betty *actress, comedienne*
Whitesell, Patrick *agent*
Wiatt, James Anthony *theatrical agency executive*
Willis, Walter Bruce (Bruce Willis) *actor, singer, writer*
Wilson, Luke *actor*
Wilson, Owen *actor*
Winger, Debra *actress*
Winkler, Irwin *motion picture producer*
Winningham, Mare *actress*
Winokur, Marissa Jaret *actress*
Winters, Shelley (Shirley Schrift) *actress*
Wirtschafter, David *agent*
Witherspoon, Reese (Laura Jean Witherspoon) *actress*
Witt, Alicia *actress*
Wood, Elijah *actor*
Woods, James Howard *actor*
Wright, Jeffrey *actor*
Wright Penn, Robin *actress*
Wu, Yusen (John Woo) *film director*
Yorn, Rick *talent agent*
Zanuck, Lili Fini *film director, producer*
Zellweger, Renee *actress*
Zeta-Jones, Catherine *actress*
Zwick, Edward M. *director, producer, scriptwriter*

Burbank
Bader, Diedrich *actor*
Baker, Rick *make-up artist*
Berman, Bruce *entertainment company executive, television producer*
Bloomberg, Stu *television producer*
Bright, Kevin S. *producer*
Bush, Billy *television personality*
Clapton, Eric *musician*
Cole, Paula *pop singer, songwriter*
Costner, Kevin *actor*
Crane, David *producer*
DeMent, Iris *vocalist, songwriter*
Donner, Richard *film director, producer*
Fishburne, Laurence, III, *actor*
Franco, James *actor*
Gibson, Mel *actor, film director, producer*
Henley, Don *singer, drummer, songwriter*
Horn, Alan *motion picture company executive*
Janney, Allison *actress*
Jovovich, Milla (Natasha Militza Jovovich) *model, actress*
Kauffman, Marta *producer, writer*
Kinney, Kathy *actress*
Lamas, Lorenzo *actor, director*
Lang, K. D. (Katherine Dawn Lang) *country music singer, composer*
Levinson, Barry L. *film director*
McGraw, Tim *country music singer*
Mc Vie, Christine Perfect *musician*
McVie, John *musician*
Meyer, Barry Michael *motion picture executive*
Milmore, Jennifer *actress*
Mitchell, Joni (Roberta Joan Anderson) *singer, songwriter*
Nagra, Parminder *actress*
Neill, Ve *make-up artist*
O'Dell, Nancy *television personality*
Petty, Tom (Thomas Earl Petty) *rock guitarist, band leader, composer*
Remini, Leah *actress*
Rimes, LeAnn *country music singer*
Rzeznik, Johnny *singer, musician*
Sajak, Pat *television game show host*
Schneider, Peter *theater producer*
Schumacher, Joel *director, writer*
Silver, Joel *film producer*
Stewart, Roderick David *singer*
Stiles, Ryan *actor*
Thompson, Lea *actress*
Wachowski, Andy *film director*
Wachowski, Larry *film director*
Wells, John Marcum *producer, writer*
Wonder, Stevie (Stevland Morris) *singer, musician, composer*

Calabasas
Bernhard, Sandra *actress, comedienne, singer*
Isham, Mark *composer, jazz musician*
Landau, Martin *actor*
Levy, Dena Christine *television producer, director*
Menteer, David Hilton *producer, production manager*
Phillips, Teddy Steve, Sr., *conductor, saxophone player, production company executive*

Carlsbad
Missett, Judi Sheppard *dancer, jazzercise company executive*

Carmel
Gordon, David Jamieson *tenor*

Carmel Valley
Meckel, Peter Timothy *arts administrator, educator*

Claremont
Doty, Horace Jay, Jr., *theater administrator, arts consultant*

Corona Del Mar
Karson, Burton Lewis *musician, educator*
Morisseau, Nan Kruger *television personality*

Coronado
Neblett, Carol *soprano*

Costa Mesa
Chambers-Belida, Candace R. *radio personality, writer, television producer*
McEnary, John Walter *music educator*
Mumford, Lawrence R. *composer, educator*

Culver City
Brooks, James L. *writer, director, producer*
Brooks, Mel *producer, director, writer, actor*
Chaffin, Cean *producer*
Coolio, (Artis Ivey Jr.) *popular musician*
Evans, Linda *actress*
Ewing, Michael Snyder *producer, film company executive*
Fisher, Lucy *film producer*
Guber, Peter *executive producer*
Hall, Barbara *television producer*
Kaufman, Richard Stuart *conductor, music director*
Mark, Laurence Maurice *film producer*
Sakai, Richard *motion picture and television executive, producer*
Tisch, Steven Elliot *television and movie producer*
Trebek, Alex *television game show host*
Wayans, Damon *actor*
Wick, Douglas *producer*
Ziskin, Laura *television producer, film producer*

Davis
Handel, Darrell Dale *composer, retired music educator*

Diamond Bar
Dogg, Snoop (Calvin Broadus) *vocalist, actor*

El Cerrito
Mendoza, Lydia *vocalist*

Encinitas
Litvin, Inessa Elizabeth *piano educator*
Rockwell, Elizabeth Goode *dance company director, consultant, educator*

Encino
Conway, Tim *comedian*
Franklin, Bonnie Gail *actress*
Ingels, Marty *theatrical agent, television and motion picture production executive*
Medak, Peter *film director*
Pryor, Richard *actor, writer*
Shire, David Lee *composer*
Taylor, Renee *actress, writer*
Westmore, Michael George *make-up artist, writer*
Zsigmond, Vilmos *cinematographer, director*

Escondido
Ehrhart, Joseph Edward *retired television broadcast engineer*

Frazier Park
Edwards, Sarah Anne *radio, cable TV personality, clinical social worker*

Fresno
Korkmazian, Gayane K *music educator*
Whitehead, Corey Ennis *music educator*

Fullerton
Wiley, David Cole *producer*

Glendale
Astvatsatrian, Gaiane *musician*
Furtado, Nelly Kim *vocalist*
Grillo, Leo *actor, photographer, animal rescuer*
Sherman, Eric *director, writer, educator*
Sprosty, Joseph Patrick *producer, writer, weapons specialist*

Glendora
Prukesatonkul, Kamol *music educator*

Hawthorne
Rasch, Karen *film editor*

Hollywood
Berryman, Guy *musician*
Buckland, Jon (Jonny) *musician*
Calva, Robert Baraquiel *music educator*
Champion, Will *musician*
Greenwood, Colin Charles *musician*
Greenwood, Jonathan Richard Guy (Jonny Greenwood) *musician*
Lewis, Huey (Hugh Anthony Cregg III) *singer, composer, bandleader*
Lynne, Shelby (Shelby Lynn Moorer) *country singer*
Martin, Chris *vocalist*
Miles, Joanna *actress, playwright, director*
Minnelli, Liza *singer, actress*
O'Brien, Edward John *musician, vocalist*
Salzman, David Elliot *entertainment industry executive*
Seacrest, Ryan *television and radio personality*
Selway, Phillip James *musician*
Warren, Diane *song writer*
Yorke, Thomas Edward *musician, vocalist*

Huntington Beach
Pieper, Michael Joseph *freelance/self-employed television producer*

Irvine
Davis, Clifton Duncan *actor, composer*
Luzko, Daniel *music educator*
Ruyter, Nancy Lee Chalfa *dance educator*

Kaweah
Foster, Joseph Kevin, IV, *entertainer, scribe*

Kentfield
Halprin, Anna Schuman (Mrs. Lawrence Halprin) *dancer*

King City
Ettinger, Steve Joel *music educator*

La Crescenta
Purcell, Lee *actress, film producer*

La Habra Heights
Agajanian, Gilda *pianist*

La Jolla
Harkins, Edwin L. *music educator, performer*
Lewis, George *music educator*
Pasler, Jann C. *music educator*
Reynolds, Roger Lee *composer, educator*

Laguna Beach
Englund, Robert *actor, director, producer*

Laguna Woods
McClure, Hal H. *film producer*

Lake Forest
Blackley, Daniel John *theater educator, theater director*

Lake View Terrace
Coolidge, Martha *film director*

Lancaster
Bell, Gary Lynn *owner production company, video and audio producer*

Littleriver
Van Dyck, Wendy *dancer*

Livermore
Darter, Thomas Eugene, Jr., *composer, musician, writer*

Long Beach
Engle, Robert Irwin *music educator, musician, composer, writer, translator*
Fischler, Sandy Lynn *event producer*
MacDonald, Patricia Geneve *theater director*

Los Altos
Collins, Gordon Dent *recording company executive*

Los Angeles
Abdul, Paula (Julie) *singer, dancer, choreographer*
Avedon, Loren Rains *actor*
Bain, Conrad Stafford *actor*
Ballard, Glen *composer*
Barker, Robert William (Bob Barker) *television personality*
Begley, Ed, Jr., *actor*
Bell, Lee Phillip *television personality, television producer*
Benatar, Pat (Pat Andrzejewski) *rock singer*
Bergman, Marilyn Keith *lyricist, writer*
Berman, Richard Keith *television producer, film producer*
Biel, Jessica *actress, model*
Biggs, Jason *actor*
Black, Lisa Hartman *actress, singer*
Bloom, Claire *actress*
Borda, Deborah *symphony orchestra executive*
Boyle, Danny *film director*
Brolin, James (James Brunderlin) *actor*
Brown, Carol *make-up artist*
Burrows, James *television and motion picture director, producer*
Burton, Tim *film director*
Butler, Brett *comedienne, actress*
Buzzi, Ruth *comedienne*
Caine, Michael *actor*
Calman, Craig David *writer, actor, director*
Cannon, Dyan *actress*
Carlin, George Denis *comedian, actor*
Cassavetes, Nick *film director, actor*
Catanzarite, David M. *theater educator, director*
Cates, Gilbert *film, theater, television producer and director*
Champlin, Charles Davenport *television host, book critic, writer*
Chapman, Carolyn *broadcasting director*
Charles, Ray *musician, composer, lyricist, arranger, conductor*
Chiklis, Michael *actor*
Cho, Margaret *comedienne, actress*
Combs, Holly Marie *actress*
Cooper, Chris *actor*
Corman, Roger William *motion picture producer, director*
Coston, Suzanne *television producer*
Crockett, Donald Harold *composer, university educator*
Crystal, Billy *comedian, actor*
D'Accone, Frank Anthony *music educator*
Davis, John A. *film producer*
Davis, Kristin *actress*
Dee, Ruby (Ruby Dee Davis) *actress, writer, director*
Diehl, Dolores *performing company executive*
Donahue, Ann M. *television producer*
Douglas, Kirk (Issur Danielovitch) *actor, motion picture producer*
Dr. Dre, (Andre Young) *rapper, record producer*
Dunst, Kirsten *actress*
Edwards, Blake *film director*
Elrod, Lu *emerita music educator, actress, author*
Everhart, Angie *model*
Ferrell, Conchata Galen *actress, performing arts educator*
Fincher, David *film director, film producer*
Fitz-Gerald, Kevin G. *music educator, musician*
Flanagan, Fionnula Manon *actress, writer, theater director*
Fleischmann, Ernest Martin *music administrator*
Flockhart, Calista *actress*
Foster, Jodie (Alicia Christian Foster) *actress, film director, film producer*
Franz, Dennis *actor*
Franz, Elizabeth *actress*
Gandolfini, James *actor*
Garrett, Betty *actress*
Garrett, Brad *actor, comedian*
Gibbons, Leeza *television talk show host, entertainment reporter*
Gooding, Cuba, Jr., *actor*
Gordon, Allen Barry *musician, composer*
Gordon, Mark, II, *film producer*
Gosling, Ryan (Ryan Thomas Gosling) *actor*
Grammer, Kelsey *actor*
Greenberg, Barry Michael *talent executive*
Guillaume, Robert *actor*
Haines, Randa *film director*
Hancock, Herbert Jeffrey (Herbie Hancock) *composer, pianist, publisher*
Harry, Deborah Ann *singer*
Hart, Mary *television talk show host*
Hart, Melissa Joan Catherine *actress*
Hartke, Stephen Paul *composer, educator*
Helms, Ed *comedian, actor*
Henderson, Florence *actress, singer*
Henkel, Kathy *composer*
Hoblit, Gregory *film director, television executive*
Hoffman, Philip Seymour *actor*
Horovitz, Adam (King Adrock) *recording artist*
Howard, Sandy *motion picture producer*
Hu, Kelly *actress*
Hudson, Richard Albert *music educator, musicologist, composer*
Jackson, Kate *actress*
Jackson, Randy *music producer, television personality, musician*
Jacobs, Stephen Jay *musician, composer, writer*
Jagger, Sir Mick (Michael Philip Jagger) *singer, musician*

Jennings, Willbur *musician, popular*
Johnson, Charles Floyd *television executive, producer*
Jones, Tom *singer*
Kaczmarek, Jane *actress*
Keith, David *symphony orchestra conductor*
Kellerman, Sally Claire *actress*
Kelley, David E. *producer, writer*
Kimmel, Jimmy (James Christian Kimmel) *television personality*
Klauss, Kenneth Karl *composer, educator*
Kurtz, Swoosie *actress*
Kyles, Cedric Antonio (Cedric the Entertainer) *comedian, actor*
Landers, Audrey *actress, singer*
Lansing, Sherry Lee (Heimann) *motion picture executive*
LeBeau, Mary Delle *dancer, educator, writer*
Ledger, Heath *actor*
Leeves, Jane *actress*
Levinsohn, Gary *producer*
Livingston, Larry J. *conductor, music educator*
London, Andrew Barry *film editor*
Lopez, George *actor, comedian*
Lovitz, Jon *actor, comedian*
Lunden, Joan *television personality*
MacLachlan, Kyle *actor*
Maguire, Tobey (Tobias Vincent Maguire) *actor*
Malden, Karl (Malden Sekulovich) *actor*
Malick, Terrence (David Whitney II) *film director*
Malone, Nancy *actress*
Mason, Andrew *film producer*
Matthews, Melony Kerry *opera singer, actress*
McCarthy, Nobu *actress, performing company executive, educator*
McQueen, Justice Ellis (L. Q. Jones) *actor, director*
Merlis, George *television producer*
Metheny, Patrick Bruce *musician*
Michelson, Sonia *music educator, author*
Milchan, Arnon *film producer*
Mueller, Carl Richard *theater arts educator, author*
Muldaur, Diana Charlton *actress*
Mulligan, Robert *film director, producer*
Nelligan, Kate (Patricia Colleen Nelligan) *actress*
Newhart, Bob *entertainer*
Newman, Randy *singer, songwriter, musician*
Nicholson, Jack *actor*
Nielsen, Leslie *actor*
Noble, James Wilkes *actor*
O'Brien, Pat *television personality*
O'Connell, Taaffe Cannon *actress, publishing executive*
O'Day, Anita Belle Colton *entertainer, musician, vocalist*
O'Hara, Maureen (Maureen FitzSimons) *actress*
Ohlmeyer, Donald Winfred, Jr., *film and television producer*
Oldham, Granville Murl, Jr., *conductor, educator*
Olmos, Edward James *actor*
Olsen, Ashley Fuller *actress*
Olsen, Mary-Kate *actress*
Orbach, Jerry *actor, singer*
Parkinson, Dian *actress*
Paxton, Bill *actor, writer, director*
Peña, Elizabeth *actress*
Penn, Sean *actor*
Perez, Rosie *actress*
Perry, Luke (Coy Luther Perry III) *actor*
Peterson, Lowell *cinematographer*
Pickett, Wilson *vocalist, composer*
Plummer, Amanda *actress*
Pollack, Daniel *concert pianist*
Ponty, Jean-Luc *violinist, composer, producer*
Presley, Priscilla *actress*
Quaid, Dennis *actor*
Quan, Denise Alane *music educator*
Rabinovitz, Jason *film and television consultant*
Rashad, Phylicia *actress, singer, dancer*
Richmond, Rocsan *television and video producer, director, publicist, actress, dancer, inventor, teacher*
Rickles, Donald Jay *comedian, actor*
Rohrer, Susan Earley *film producer, writer, director*
Rosenberger, Carol *concert pianist*
Ross, Marion *actress*
Roth, Tim *actor*
Rubin, Stanley Creamer *producer*
Ruskin, Joseph Richard *actor, director*
Samaha, Elie *producer, film company executive, business owner*
Scarl, Hilari Brooke *actress, writer, television producer*
Schmidt, Arthur *film editor*
Schmit, Timothy Bruce *musician*
Schwimmer, David *actor*
Scott, Tony *film director*
Selleck, Tom *actor*
Shatner, William *actor*
Shay, Anthony Victor *choreographer, dance historian*
Sheedy, Ally (Alexandra Elizabeth Sheedy) *actress*
Sheindlin, Judith *television personality, judge*
Silverstone, Alicia *actress*
Singleton, John *director, screenwriter*
Smits, Jimmy *actor*
Spelling, Aaron *film and television producer, writer, actor*
Spinotti, Dante *cinematographer*
Stevenson, Robert Murrell *music educator*
Streisand, Barbra Joan *singer, actress, director*
Stuart, Gloria *actress*
Swit, Loretta *actress*
Takei, George Hosato *actor*
Tarantino, Quentin *film director, screenwriter*
Taylor, Timothy Dean *music educator*
Termini, Olga Ascher *music educator*
Thompson, Sada Carolyn *actress*
Thornton, Billy Bob *actor, film producer*
Townley, John Joe *music educator, writer, musician*
Townsend, Robert *film director*
Trembly, Dennis Michael *musician*
Tyson, Cicely *actress*
Ullman, Tracey *actress, singer*
Van Der Beek, James *actor*
Wahlberg, Mark *actor*
Waits, Thomas Alan *composer, actor, singer*
Waterston, Samuel Atkinson *actor*
Watson, Emily *actress*
Watt, Robert Lee *music educator*
Webber, Peggy *actress, producer, director, writer*
Welch, Raquel *actress*
Whitaker, Forest *actor, director, producer*
White, Meg (Megan Martha White) *musician, vocalist*
Williams, Paul Hamilton *composer, singer*
Winters, Barbara Jo *musician*
Winters, Dean *actor*
Wise, Robert *film producer, director*
Zemeckis, Robert L. *film director*

Los Osos
Kreitzer, Jacalyn Bower *vocalist, voice educator*

Malibu
Almond, Paul *film director, producer, screenwriter, novelist*
Carson, Johnny *television personality*
Harris, Ed(ward Allen) *actor*
Keach, Stacy, Jr., *actor, director, producer, writer, musician, composer*
Murphy, Benjamin Edward *actor*
Wilson, Rita *actress*

Marina Del Rey
Fash, Michael William *cinematographer, director*

Mendocino
Woelfel, Robert William *broadcast executive, mayor*

Menlo Park
Baez, Joan Chandos *folk singer*

Mill Valley
Padula, Fred David *filmmaker*

Modesto
Martin, Anne Louise *music educator*

Monrovia
Brown, Gwendolyn (Williams) *music educator*

Monterey Park
Hogan, Kelley Maureen *theater educator, actress*

Moorpark
Kessner, Dolly Eugenio *music educator, concert pianist*

Moraga
Peterson, Gene David *music educator*

Mountain View
Sultanov, Namig, 2d Baronet, *musician, music educator*

Murrieta
Cloud, Mark F. *video producer, director, writer, musician*

Newhall
Baity, Cameron B. *film director, writer*

Newport Beach
Steinberg, Leigh W. *sports agent*

North Hollywood
Balmuth, Bernard Allen *retired film editor*
Busch, Estelle Winston *theater director*
Downey, Roma *actress*
Fanning, Dakota *actress*
Gallardo, Sandra Silvana *producer*
Holmes, Michael *performing company executive, performing arts educator*
Reynolds, Debbie (Mary Frances Reynolds) *actress*
Stone, Sharon *actress*
Taravella, Rosie *actress*
Thomas, Tony *producer*
Toplitt, Gloria H. *voice educator, singer, actress*
Toussieng, Yolanda *make-up artist*

Northridge
Cartwright, Nancy *actress, television producer*
Loudon, Craig Michael *video specialist*
Roscigno, John Anthony *music educator, conductor*

Norwalk
Betancourt, David Apodaca *music educator*
Schreiner, Gregory Lee *music educator*

Oakland
Brown, Karen *performing company executive*
DeFazio, Lynette Stevens *dancer, educator, choreographer, violinist, actress*
Elliott, Jack *folk musician*
Lake, Suzanne *singer, music educator*
Zschau, Marilyn *singer*

Oceanside
Swoger, James Wesley *magician*

Ojai
Cusumano, James Anthony *filmmaker, retired pharmaceutical company executive, former recording artist*
Paxton, Glenn Gilbert *composer*

Orange
Matthews, Joseph Virgil *pianist, music educator*

Oxnard
Engels, Gerhard *music educator, composer*

Pacific Palisades
Kirkgaard, Valerie Anne *media group executive, syndicated talk radio host, writer, producer, consultant*

Palm Springs
Gordon, Stewart Lynell *musician, educator*

Palo Alto
Lo, Yee On *composer*

Palos Verdes Peninsula
Bailey-Klein, Katheryn Elizabeth *music educator, musician*

Pasadena
Hicklin, Ronald Lee *music production company executive*
Horak, Jan-Christopher *film studies educator, curator*
Menefee, John William, III, *cinematographer, producer*
Robinson, Roger *actor, director*
Worby, Rachael Beth *conductor*
Worby, Rachel *conductor*

Penn Valley
Accardi, James Leonard *musician*

Pleasanton
Goddard, John Wesley *cable television company executive*

Pomona
Kopplin, David F. *music educator, composer*
Perez, Francisco, Jr., *music educator*

Port Hueneme
Schneider, Arthur Paul *retired videotape and film editor, author*

Quartz Hill
McKain, Mary Margaret *musician*

Redding
Waterbury, Elizabeth Floria *conductor*

Redondo Beach
Richards, Denise *actress*

Richmond
Lasseter, John P. *film director, computer animator*

Riverside
James, Etta *recording artist*

Sacramento
Condon, Frank *theater director, playwright*
Gore, Robert William *performing arts educator*
Howard, Dina Elaine *performing company executive, writer*
Mazzaferro, James Joseph *music educator*
Nice, Carter *conductor, music director*
Piper, Jami Kathleen *music educator, composer*

Salinas
Rosen, Jacqueline I. *flutist, music educator*

San Diego
Arova, Sonia *artistic director, ballet educator*
Bonn, Ronald Sheldon *TV news producer, journalism educator*
Burge, David Russell *concert pianist, composer, piano educator*
Campbell, Ian David *opera company director*
Flettner, Marianne *opera administrator*
Langer, Eva Marie *video specialist*
Lau, Maureen Treacy *television producer*
Mahon, Maxine *performing company executive*
Noehren, Robert *organist, organ builder*
O'Brien, Jack George *artistic director*
Overton, Marcus Lee *performing arts administrator, actor, writer*
Pagan, Keith Areatus *music educator, academic administrator*
Pfiffner, Patrick Meehan *musician, educator*
Ransom, Bryan Kenneth *music educator*
Reynolds, Rosina Widdowson *actress, theater director*
Ward-Steinman, David *composer, music educator, pianist*

San Francisco
Bennett, William *oboist*
Bratton, Christopher Alan *video and art educator*
Breeden, David *clarinetist*
Caniparoli, Val William *choreographer, dancer*
Cisneros, Evelyn *dancer*
Etheridge, Melissa Lou *singer, songwriter*
Festinger, Richard *music educator, composer*
Greenawald, Sheri *performing company executive*
Gregory, Sara Susan (Sudie) *musician, singer, lyricist, poet, recording industry executive, sound recording engineer, archivist*
Gropman, Saul I. *music educator*
Hastings, Edward Walton *theater director*
Jenkins, Margaret Ludmilla *choreographer, dancer*
King, Alonzo *artistic director, choreographer*
LeBlanc, Tina *dancer*
Lee, Iara *filmmaker*
Maffre, Muriel *ballet dancer*
Neve, Victoria J. *music educator*
Nichols, William J. *film studies educator*
Perloff, Carey *performing company executive, theater director, playwright*
Peterson, Wayne Turner *composer, pianist*
Rosenberg, Pamela *performing company executive, conductor*
Runnicles, Donald *conductor*
Scaggs, Boz (William Royce Scaggs) *musician*
Schechter, Joel *magazine editor, writer, educator*
Shorenstein Hays, Carole *theater producer*
Smuin, Michael *choreographer, director, dancer*
Tiano, Anthony Steven *television producer, book publishing executive*
Tomasson, Helgi *dancer, choreographer, dance company executive*

San Jose
Dalis, Irene *mezzo-soprano, opera company administrator, music educator*
Near, Timothy *theater director*
Shuster, Diana *former artistic director*
Slater, Stewart Eugene *theatre producer*
Weiner, Claire Zundell *theatrical director*

San Marcos
Houk, Benjamin Noah *performing company executive, choreographer*

San Rafael
Brubeck, David Warren *musician*
Lucas, George W., Jr., *film director, producer, screenwriter*
Noah, Nuer *filmmaker*
Santana, Carlos *guitarist*

Santa Ana
Freeman, James Michael *musician, vocalist*

Santa Barbara
Ben-Dor, Gisselle *conductor, musician*
Brodhead, James E(aston) *actor, writer*
Feigin, Joel *composer, education educator*
Hontos, Margaret Ellen *music educator*
Roads, Curtis *music educator, composer*
Sebastian, Suzie *producer*

Santa Cruz
Hester, Karlton Edward *composer, musician, educator*
Martinez, Alma R. *actress, theater director, educator*
Winston, George *solo pianist, guitarist, harmonica player*

Santa Monica
Angel, Steven *musician*
Bruckheimer, Jerry *producer*
Burrell, Orville Richard (Shaggy) *popular musician*
Cameron, James *film director, screenwriter, producer*
Chartoff, Robert Irwin *film producer*
Cooper, Jackie *actor, director, producer*
Diamond, Neil Leslie *singer, composer*
Eve, (Eve Jihan Jeffers) *rap artist, actress*
Fisher, Frances *actress*
Frot-Coutaz, Cecile *television producer*
Hersh, Kristin *vocalist, musician*
Kaminski, Janusz *cinematographer*
Leaf, Paul *film producer, writer*
Lohner, Henning *composer, filmmaker*
Louis-Dreyfus, Julia *actress*
Marin, Mindy *casting agent, entrepreneur, film producer, writer*
Minghella, Anthony *film director, screenwriter*
Redford, Robert (Charles Robert Redford) *actor, director*
Roberts, Tony (David Anthony Roberts) *actor*
Simpson, India.Arie *musician*
Smith, Anna Deavere *actress, educator, playwright*
Stewart, Patrick *actor*
Summer, Donna (La Donna Adrian Gaines) *singer, songwriter, actress*
Suschitzky, Peter *cinematographer*
Sussman, Peter Alan *entertainment company executive*
Tinturin, Peter *composer*
Watanabe, Ken *actor*
Watson, Doc (Arthel Lane Watson) *vocalist, guitarist, banjoist, recording artist*
Wexler, Haskell *film producer, cameraman*
Wilder, Gene *actor, film director, writer*
Winkler, Henry Franklin *actor*
York, Michael (Michael York-Johnson) *actor*

Santa Rosa
Daniel, Gary Wayne *motivation and behavior consultant*

Sebastopol
Snyder, Allegra Fuller *dance educator*

Sherman Oaks
Bergman, Alan *lyricist, writer*
Clark, Susan (Nora Goulding) *actress*
Elfman, Danny *composer*
Gibbs, Antony (Tony Gibbs) *film editor*
Goldenthal, Elliot *composer*
Horner, James *composer*
Karras, Alex *actor, former professional football player*
Norwood, Brandy Rayana (Brandy) *singer, actress*
Schlessinger, Laura *radio talk show host*
Shore, Howard Leslie *composer*
Williams, John Towner *composer, conductor*
Wood, Evan Rachel *actress*

Sonora
Carter, John Robert *music educator*

South Lake Tahoe
Williams, Mark Didrik *music educator, composer*

Stanford
Cohen, Albert *musician, educator*

Stevenson Ranch
Krainin, Julian Arthur *film director, producer, writer, cinematographer*

Stockton
Pope, Andy *musician, educator*

Studio City
Basinger, Kim *actress*
Boyle, Peter *actor*
Carsey, Marcia Lee Peterson *television producer*
Gautier, Dick *actor, writer*
Johnston, Kristen *television personality*
Kaye, Lori *actress, news reporter, producer*
Kenney, H(arry) Wesley, Jr., *producer, director*
King, Carole (Carole Klein) *songwriter, singer*
Kingi, Henry Masao *actor, stuntman*
Rubin, Saul *producer, writer, labor and civil rights organizer*
Sinbad, (David Adkins) *actor, comedian*
Steinberg, Roy Bennett *television producer, director, educator*
Werner, Tom *television producer, professional baseball team executive*

Sun Valley
Taesch, Richard Edmond *music educator*

Sylmar
Foster, Dudley Edwards, Jr., *musician, educator*
Powers, Mala *actress*

Tarzana
Jones, Dean Carroll *actor*
Richman, Peter Mark *actor, painter, writer, producer*

Thousand Oaks
Gary, Russell Lee *sound recording engineer, music company executive*
Loren, Sophia *actress*
Rooney, Mickey (Joe Yule Jr.) *actor*
Sloane, J.P. *television producer, writer, entertainer, theologian*
Washburn, Nan *conductor*

Toluca Lake
Morton, Hugh Wesley *producer, director*

Topanga
Bridgewater, Dee Dee *jazz singer, diplomat*

PROFESSIONAL INDEX 5515 ARTS: PERFORMING

Tustin
Kollias, Jim Harry *music educator*

Universal City
Crow, Sheryl *singer, songwriter, musician*
Merkerson, S. Epatha *actress*
Rapke, Jack *agent*
Reitman, Ivan *film director, producer*
Torres, Jacqueline *television director, actress*
Wolf, Dick (Richard A. Wolf) *television producer, film company executive*

Valencia
Finley, Greg Ronald *actor, scriptwriter*
Millar, Michael William *musician*
Windsor, William Earl *consulting engineer, sales representative*

Valley Center
Camp, Joseph Shelton, Jr., *film producer, director, writer*

Valley Village
Barkin, Elaine Radoff *composer*
Diller, Phyllis *actress, writer*

Van Nuys
Boone, Deborah Ann (Debby Boone) *singer*

Venice
Bill, Tony *producer, director*

Ventura
Gay, Marilyn Fanelli Martin *television producer, writer, talk show hostess, journalist*

Villa Park
Murphy, Patrick Christopher *music educator*

Walnut Creek
Stapp, Olivia Brewer *opera singer*

Watsonville
Dehner, David Anthony *music educator, voice educator*

West Covina
Lavruk, Alexander E. *music educator, sales consultant*

West Hollywood
Annakin, Kenneth Cooper *film director, writer*
Baker, Anita *singer*
Cage, Nicolas (Nicolas Coppola) *actor*
De Palma, Brian Russell *film director, writer*
Harper, Robert *actor*
Innes, Laura *actress*
Madonna, (Madonna Louise Veronica Ciccone) *singer, actress, producer*
Shaye, Robert Kenneth *cinema company executive*
Sherman, Robert B(ernard) *composer, lyricist, screenwriter*
Stein, Benjamin J. *television personality, writer, lawyer, economist*
Thomas, Rob *singer, songwriter*

Whittier
Korf, Jean Prinz *retired theater educator*
Spencer, Williametta *composer, retired music educator*

Woodland Hills
Berger, Phil *musician*
Chiodini, John Allen *musician, composer*
Levy, Norman *motion picture company executive*
O'Connor, Brian D. A. *music educator, French Horn musician*
Pendergrass, Teddy (Theodore D. Pendergrass) *musician*

Yucca Valley
Styles, Beverly (Juanita Robins Carpenter) *entertainer, composer, musician*

COLORADO

Aspen
Berkeley, (Ed)ward *performing arts association administrator, music educator*
Hardy, Gordon Alfred *music educator, music school president*
Roth, Don *music executive*

Aurora
Heisler, Traciann *music educator, musician*
Hughes, Christopher Adam *conductor, educator*

Boulder
Boydston, James Christopher *composer*
Duckworth, Guy *musician, pianist, educator*
Fink, Robert Russell *music theorist, former university dean*
Korevaar, David *musician, educator*
Mooney, William Piatt *actor*
Riis, Thomas Laurence *music educator*
Sable, Barbara Kinsey *retired music educator*
Sarson, John Christopher *television producer, director, writer*

Colorado Springs
Williamson, Paul Michael *music educator*

Denver
Albig, Irina S. *music educator*
Alsop, Marin *conductor*
Bearden, Thomas Howard *news program producer, correspondent*
Burshtan, John Willis *television producer*
Ceci, Jesse Arthur *violinist*
Fredmann, Martin *ballet artistic director, educator, choreographer*
Meininger, Steven Robert *music educator*
Morales, John Paul *television services producer*
Newman, Bob *radio personality, security consultant*
Robinson, Cleo Parker *artistic director*
Schwartz, Cherie Anne Karo *storyteller, writer*
White, John David *composer, theorist, cellist*

Fort Collins
Kenney, Wes, III, *conductor*
Kraus, David (Dirk) Bruce *musician, educator*

Highlands Ranch
Fiess, Stephen Charles Edward *musician, music educator*

Littleton
Alykova, Valentina *musician, music educator*
Johansson, Alicia Barbara *musician*
Keats, Donald Howard *composer, educator*
Reinker, Mary Stefanich *musician, music educator*
Zwilling, Mark C. *music director*

Loveland
Balsiger, David Wayne *television-video director, researcher, producer, writer*

Niwot
Buss, Kathleen E. *music educator*

Pritchett
Hall, Carol Ann *music educator*

Walsenburg
Mellott, George Kenneth *retired music educator*

Westminster
Callier, Maria Cecile *writer, actress*

CONNECTICUT

Branford
Smith, Richard Emerson (Dick Smith) *make-up artist*

Bridgeport
Williams, Yotisse R. *music educator*

Burlington
Ghiglia, Oscar Alberto *classical guitarist*

Canton
Richardson, Dana Roland *technology consultant*

Chaplin
Wood, Wendy Deborah *filmmaker*

Colchester
Winter, John Dawson, III, *blues guitarist, singer*

Danbury
Jennings, Alfred Higson, Jr., *music educator, actor, singer*
Nelson, Willie Hugh *musician, songwriter*

East Haddam
Borton, John Carter, Jr., (Terry Borton) *theatrical producer*

Ellington
Adams, Timothy Gene *music educator*

Greenwich
Tiegs, Cheryl *model, designer*

Hartford
Lyman, Peggy *artistic director, dancer, choreographer, educator*
Mc Lean, Jackie *jazz saxophonist, educator, composer, community activist*
Wood, Margaret *performing company executive*

Ledyard
Hammond, Russell Paul *music educator*

Middletown
Kordonskiy, Yuriy *performing arts educator, actor, director*

Milford
Basso, Jason Michael *film producer, actor*

Mystic
Bobruff, Carole Marks *radio producer, radio personality*

New Haven
Baker, Robert Stevens *organist, educator*
Morgan, Robert P. *music theorist, educator*
Nolan, Victoria *theater director*
Piehler, Wendell Howard *organist, choir director, fund raiser*
Tirro, Frank Pascale *music educator, author, composer*
Warshaw, Marvin D. *conductor, educator, musician*

New London
Harper, Patricia Louise *music educator*

New Preston Marble Dale
Grizzard, George *actor*

Old Saybrook
Listorti, Irene M. *music educator*

Ridgefield
Kantor, James Graham *music educator, composer*

Southbury
Bergen, Polly *actress*

Southport
Walker, Charles Dodsley *conductor, organist*

Stamford
Eagan, Sherman G. *producer, communications executive*
Karp, Steve *producing director*

Stonington
Gilliland-McEnerney, Tressa Mae *performing arts educator*

Storrs Mansfield
Crow, Laura Jean *design educator, costume designer*

Vernon Rockville
Williams, Julius Penson *composer, conductor*

Washington Depot
Pendleton, Moses Robert Andrew *dancer, choreographer*
Tracy, Michael Cameron *choreographer, performer, educator*
Wolken, Jonathan *performing company executive*

Waterford
White, George Cooke *theater director, foundation executive*

Weston
Fredrik, Burry *theatrical producer, director*

Westport
Feliciano, José *entertainer*
Newman, Paul *actor, professional race-car driver, food company executive*
Solum, John Henry *flutist, educator, author*

Wethersfield
Rioux, Scott Paul *music educator*

Windsor
Woodard, Peter Clark *music educator, musician*

Woodbridge
Just, Jennifer Ramsay *television and video producer, writer*

DELAWARE

Camden Wyoming
Pfeuffer, Robert John *musician*

Millville
Zinman, David Joel *conductor*

Wilmington
Amado, David *conductor*
Brown Leatherberry, Thomas Henry *gospel music company executive, clergy member*
Butterfield, Margaret Anne Davis *music educator, vocalist*
Cason, June Macnabb *musician, educator, arts administrator, fundraiser*
Syer, Fontaine *theater director*
Wesler, Ken *performing arts company executive*

DISTRICT OF COLUMBIA

Washington
Ames, Frank Anthony *percussionist, film producer*
Anderson, Mary Ann Grasso *theater association executive*
Battis, Emery John *actor*
Begala, Paul Edward *television personality, political scientist, consultant*
Byers, Paul Heed *television news producer, consultant*
Crawford-Mason, Clare Wootten *television producer, journalist*
Crosby, Thomas Anthony *radio producer, broadcaster*
Day, Doris (Doris von Kappelhoff) *singer, actress*
Day, Mary *artistic director, ballet company executive*
Domingo, Placido *tenor*
Donlon, Claudette *performing company executive*
Drizin, Julie Merle *public radio producer*
Findley, Mary Baker *violinist*
Fischer, Elizabeth (Betsy) *television producer*
Forrest, Sidney *clarinetist, music educator*
Gersh, Darren *television correspondent*
Goldberg, Jonah Jacob *television producer, writer*
Hamlisch, Marvin *composer, conductor, pianist, entertainer*
Harpham, Virginia Ruth *violinist*
Kahn, Michael *stage director*
Kaiser, Michael M. *performing company executive*
Kaltchev, Ivo *musician, educator*
Leissner, Janet *television news bureau chief*
Lewis, Stephen Joseph *television producer*
Makris, Andreas *composer*
Massey, Jeanne Kelly *music festival producer*
Moore, Elvi *performing company executive*
Mosettig, Michael David *television producer, writer*
Poxon, Stephanie Lyn *music specialist, accompanist*
Ratner, Ellen Faith *radio talk show host, writer*
Royle, David Brian Layton *television producer, journalist*
Russell, Mark *comedian*
Smith, Molly D. *theater director*
Snider, David Andrew *theater educator, theater director, actor*
Snyder, Andrea *performing arts association administrator*
Sproul, Robin *television news bureau chief*
Walsh, John *television show host*
Webre, Septime *ballet company artistic director, choreographer*
Weidenfeld, Sheila Rabb *television producer, author*
Woods, Stephanie *television producer, reporter*
Yurko, Michiko Kathleen *music educator, writer*

FLORIDA

Apopka
Reinecke, William T. *conductor, educator*

Bayonet Point
Errington, Norman *television producer, photographer*

Boca Raton
Castillo, William John *music educator*
Dower Gold, Catherine Anne *music history educator*
Fengler, John Peter *television producer, director, advertising executive*
Snyder, Mark Steven *theater educator*
Waxman, Donald *composer*
Yelin, Robert Bruce *musician, recording artist, composer, lyricist*

Bradenton
Bjorklund, Nancy Margarette Watts *music educator*
Lister, Thomas Mosie *composer, lyricist, publishing company executive, minister*

Cape Coral
Wendel, Joan Audrey *music educator*

Coral Gables
Miller, Bruce J. *performing arts educator, director*

Coral Springs
Hoffman, Avi *performing company executive*

Daytona Beach
Dumm, Robert Wayne *musician, educator, writer*

Deerfield Beach
Allaire, Gaston George *music educator, researcher*

Deland
Musco, Lynn Ann *music educator*
Robinson, Stephen A. *music educator, musician*

Delray Beach
Horowitz, Fedora Cohen *music educator, pianist*
Spyker, Harry A., III, *music educator*

Englewood
Brainard, Paul Henry *musicologist, retired music educator*

Fort Lauderdale
LeRoy, Miss Joy *model, apparel designer*
Randi, James (Randall James Hamilton Zwinge) *magician, writer, educator*
Spangler, David Sheridan *composer, director, creative arts educator, writer*

Fort Myers
Diers, Hank H. *drama educator, playwright, director*
Renfroe, W. Douglas *musician, conductor, music educator*

Fort Pierce
Norton, Robert Howard *entertainer, musical arranger, author*

Fort Walton Beach
Lindegren, Cecile Keyser *music educator*

Frostproof
Alia, Stephen Louis *music educator*

Gainesville
Estrin, Mitchell Stewart *musician*
McConn, William Everett *music educator*
Phoenix, Joaquin Raphael *actor*

Green Cove Springs
Davidson, Joy Elaine *mezzo-soprano*

Hallandale
Vaserstein, Ludmila *music educator*

Jacksonville
Homsley, Denise Louise *music educator*
Huber, Mary Susan *music educator*
Smith, Stephen Mark *music educator*
Stanley, Helen Camille *composer, musician*
Stewart, Sandra Kay *music educator*
Taylor, Gavin Hall *music educator*
Weikle, Paul Eugene, Jr., *music educator, musician*

Key West
Buffett, Jimmy (James William Buffett) *singer, songwriter, writer*
Mitchell, John Dietrich *theatre arts institute executive*

Lake Buena Vista
Sereno, Keala *musician*

Lake City
Montgomery, June C. *musician, composer*

Lake Helen
Finn, Stephen Martin *producer*

Lake Wales
Walton, Madalyn Carol *music educator*

Lecanto
Max, Buddy (Boris Max Pastuch) *musician*
Moyer-Staker, Denise Elane *music educator*

Melbourne
Kreines, Joseph Melvin *conductor*

Miami
Allen, Charles Norman *television, film and video producer*
Batson, Dawn Kirsten *music educator, cultural consultant*
Berman, Mona S. *actress, playwright, theater director, theater producer*
Catanzaro, Tony *dancer*
Ellis, Ryan Deane *conductor, musician*
Feinberg, Wendie *producer*
Hardy, Michael C. *performing arts administrator*
Harmon, Monica Renee *music educator*
Heuer, Robert Maynard, II, *opera company executive*
Kahn, Jack Merrill *television producer*
Kwiat, David Mark *educator, actor*
Madurga, Gonzalo F. *artistic director, actor, singer*
Petorak, Bryan Thomas *music educator, musician*
Reed, Alfred *composer, conductor*
Stephan, Egon, Sr., *cinematographer, film equipment company executive*

Miami Beach
Gardiner, Pamela Nan *performing arts company executive*
Gibb, Robin *vocalist, songwriter*
Lawson, Eve Kennedy *dancer*

Milton
Arnold, Margaret Morelock *music specialist, educator, performer*
Losee, Michael Patrick *music director*

Miramar
Walsh, Thomas Francis, Jr., *producer, writer, director*

Naples
Kirby, Charles William, Jr., *dancer, choreographer*
White, Roy Bernard *theater executive*

North Miami
Stills, Stephen *musician, vocalist, composer*

North Palm Beach
Hayman, Richard Warren Joseph *conductor*

Orlando
Haxton, David *filmmaker, photographer*
Yonetani, Ayako *music educator, entertainer*

Ormond Beach
Hodkinson, Sydney Phillip *composer, educator*

Palm Beach
Cole, Carol Alma Tomlinson *classical musician*

Palm Harbor
Katzen-Guthrie, Joy *performance artist, engineering services executive*
Krawczynski, Tony Edward *music educator*

Panama City
Fejer, T. William *pianist, composer, architect, furniture designer*

Pembroke Pines
Hudson, Brenda Louise *soprano, opera singer, vocal coach*

Pensacola
Jaffe, Alberto P. *musician, educator*
Lanier, Gregory Warren *theater educator*
Odell, M. Carol *music educator*
Rawlins, Joseph T. *music educator*
Rubardt, Peter Craig *conductor, educator*

Pinellas Park
Benedict, Gail Cleveland *music educator*

Pompano Beach
McPherson, Michael *entertainer, theater producer*

Ponte Vedra Beach
Yessin, Gerson *musician, educator*

Port Richey
Fry, Ronald Sylvan *music educator, director*

Saint Augustine
Gilmer, Jeriel Marcus *music educator*
Gilmore, H. James *film producer, educator*
Rahner, Jean A. *performing company executive, educator*

Saint Petersburg
Brightbill, Timothy R. *music educator*
Carroll, Charles Michael *music educator*

Sarasota
McCollum, John Morris *tenor*
Mizer, Joyce Taylor *music educator*
Ramsier, Paul *composer, psychotherapist*
Sarakatsannis, Leonidas Nicholas *musician, concert pianist, music educator, composer, conductor*
Schwartz, Francis *music educator, composer*

Spring Hill
Burnim, Kalman Aaron *theatre educator emeritus*

Summerland Key
Dallas, Joseph Anthony, Jr., *music educator*

Tallahassee
Harsanyi, Janice *soprano, educator*
Monahan, Patrick *singer*
Nalley, James H., II, *music educator, musician*
Ohlsson, Eric Paul *music educator*
Ondrasik, John *singer, songwriter*
Perry-Camp, Jane *music educator, pianist*
Stebleton, Michelle Marie *music educator, musician*
Streem, James Kenneth *musician, educator*

Tamarac
Bergman, Harold Everett *actor, retired lawyer, banker*

Tampa
Dickson, Tim *music educator*
Edberg, Judith Florence *music educator*
Fogarty, William Joseph, Jr., *performing arts organization executive*
Hankenson, E(dward) Craig, Jr., *performing arts executive*
Hankins, Phillip R. *music educator*
Harris, Dudley Michael *film producer, writer, director*
Scialdo, Mary Ann *music educator, musician*

Treasure Island
Dunn, Craig Andrew *entertainer, conductor, composer, writer, educator*

Trinity
Donataccio, Dean Michael *music educator, secondary school educator*

Venice
Gabriele, Charles *composer, educator*
Tausan, Carol A. *music educator*

West Palm Beach
Bezerra, Márcio *musician, educator*
Escalante, Juan *performing company executive*
Hale, Marie Stoner *artistic director*
Phillips, Kenneth Wayne *music educator*
Robinson, Raymond Edwin *conductor, music educator, writer*
Uzan, Bernard *artistic director*

Winter Springs
McKinney, Frank *music educator*

GEORGIA

Albany
Rodriguez, Sergio Raul *music educator, conductor*

Athens
Carey, Katherine M. *theater educator*
Criste, Mirla *theater educator, director, choreographer*
Longman, Stanley Vincent *retired performing arts educator*
Lupis, Giuseppe *musician*
Staub, August William *drama educator, theatrical producer, director*
Stipe, Michael *musician*

Atlanta
50 Cent, (Curtis Jackson) *rap artist*
Benjamin, Andre Lauren (André 3000) *vocalist*
Booth, Susan Virginia *theater director*
Chen, Joie *cable news anchor*
Clark, Faye Louise *retired drama and speech educator*
Duncan, Dale Scott *music educator*
Flannery, James William *performing arts educator, vocalist, theater director*
Gibson, Michael Allen *music educator*
Hanthorn, Dennis Wayne *performing arts association administrator*
Kingsbury, Michael Bryant *organist, retired elementary and secondary education educator*
McFall, John *artistic director*
McKnight, Terrance Thales *music educator*
Patterson, James Hardy *entertainer, conductor, musician, educator, arranger, composer*
Patton, Antwan Andre (Big Boi) *vocalist*
Raymond, Usher (Usher) *vocalist, actor*
Rex, Christopher Davis *classical musician*
Spano, Robert *conductor*
Tillotson, Mary *cable television host*
Vulgamore, Allison *performing arts administrator*
Wylly, Barbara Bentley *performing arts association administrator*

Augusta
Colton, Zanne Beaufort *performing company executive*

Austell
Fuller, Carol S. *theater educator, writer*

Blairsville
Dittman, Robert Allan *retired music educator*

Carrollton
Hibbard, Kevin Robert *music educator*

Conyers
King, Lori Ann *performing company executive*
Waters, Roger Allen *music educator*

Cordele
Helms, Bobby Gillespie *music educator, consultant*

Decatur
Cartman, Shirley Eleise *retired music educator*
Downs, Jon Franklin *drama educator, director, writer*
Hamilton, Frank Strawn *jazz musician, folksinger, composer and arranger, educator*

Douglas
Tucker, Maureen Ann *musician*

Duluth
Brasher, Earlene D. *music educator, church organist*
McClung, Samuel Brenton *music educator, consultant*

East Point
Bridgewater, Herbert Jeremiah, Jr., *radio host*

Ellaville
Frontz, Howard Clinton, III, *music educator*

Fayetteville
Hood, Barbara W. *musician, educator*

Flowery Branch
Congdon, Jon Harvey *music educator*

Gainesville
Jones, David Leland *music educator*

Hartwell
Rushing, Tonnie Austin Page *musician, educator*

Hazlehurst
Reed, John Cash *music educator, researcher*

Jonesboro
Demster, Dawna Kay *orchestra director*

Kennesaw
Adams, Dean (Lewis Adams) *theater director*
Kruger, Harry *retired conductor, retired music educator*
Moses, Oral *music educator*

Kingston
Dugger, Wanda Howard *music educator*

Macon
Bell, Andrew C. *music educator*
Waddy, Calista Anne *music educator, musician*

Madison
Neidlinger, Sheri Kim *music educator*

Marietta
Morisco, Jerid Simon *music educator, conductor*
Poor, Andrew Ford *music educator*
Taylor, Frederick Jerome *music educator, consultant*
Wells, Palmer Donald *performing arts executive*
Wimberly, Linda Roberts *music educator, artist*

Moultrie
McLendon, Richard Charles *music educator*

Mount Berry
Davis, John Edward *music educator, musician*

Mount Vernon
Eernisse, Glenn P. *music educator*

Peachtree City
Day, Annette J. *music educator*
Green, Franklin Pasco *music educator*

Quitman
Carter, Roger Alan *music educator, director*

Rincon
Carter, Charles Henry, III, *music educator*

Roberta
Clark, Donald *music educator*

Rome
Pethel, Stanley Robert *composer, music educator*
Potts, Glenda Rue *music educator*

Roswell
Lawler-Johnson, Dian L. *singer, instructor of voice, vocal technician*
Siepi, Cesare *opera singer*

Savannah
Greenberg, Philip B. *symphony orchestra conductor and music director*
Simmonds, Jimmie Neil *theater educator*

Smyrna
Rife, Elizabeth *musician, music educator*

Statesboro
Bryan, Carolyn J. *music educator, saxophonist*
Whitaker, Mical Rozier *theater director, educator*

Suwanee
Frey, Glenn *songwriter, vocalist, guitarist*
Harriman, John *music educator*

Sylvania
Harper, Michael Christopher *music educator*

Thomaston
Mauney, James Thomas, Jr., *music educator, musician*

Valdosta
Farwell, Doug George *music educator*
Phillips, Taurence Lamar *music educator*

HAWAII

Honolulu
Abe, Gregg Koyei *music educator*
Langhans, Edward Allen *drama and theater educator*
Li, Bichuan *music educator*
Moulin, Jane Ann Freeman *ethnomusicology educator, researcher*
Smith, Barbara Barnard *music educator*
Wessendorf, Markus *theater educator*

Kaneohe
Young-Pohlman, Colette Lisa *music educator*

Kapolei
Dudley, Doris S. *music educator, small business owner*

IDAHO

Boise
Holt, Isabel Rae *radio program producer*
Houle, Arthur Joseph *music educator*
Kent, E(verett) Allen *performing arts administrator, theatrical producer*
Parkinson, Del R. *music educator, pianist*
Pimble, Toni *artistic director, choreographer, educator*

Buhl
Blaszkiewicz, David Albin *theater educator, performing company executive*

Hagerman
Lipskoch, Christy Michelle *music educator*

Heyburn
Barson, Ross J. *music educator, assistant principal*

Pocatello
Ronk, Jay H. *music educator, department chairman*
Stanek, Alan Edward *retired music educator, performer, administrator*

Rexburg
North, Danny L. *music educator*
Wayne, Barbara Ann *music educator, classical guitar performer*

ILLINOIS

Algonquin
Carter, Jeanie *performing company executive*

Alton
Plummer, Laura A. *music educator*

Arlington Heights
Lim, Cheryl Cheon-Ae *music educator*

Aurora
McCarthy, Mary Elizabeth (Beth) Constance *conductor, educator, music educator*

Bement
Kepley, Douglas Neil *music educator*

Bloomington
Brown, Jared *theater director, educator, writer*
Hining, Michael Lynn *music educator, conductor*
Niles, Kevin Bryan *music educator*
Setchell, Charles Marshall *retired music educator*
Streeter, Thomas Wayne *music educator*
Vayo, David Joseph *composer, music educator*

Bolingbrook
Tot, Zvonimir *musician, composer, music educator*

Bourbonnais
Ball, Karen Michele *music educator, musician, composer*

Bunker Hill
Kramer, Barbara K. *musician, educator*

Carbondale
Townsend, Gregory Williams *music educator*

Carthage
Ward, Roger Allen *music educator, musician*

Champaign
Fredrickson, L(awrence) Thomas *composer*
Garvey, John Charles *violist, conductor, retired music educator*

Charleston
Szabó, István *music educator*

Chicago
Ahern, Joseph James, Jr., *television station executive*
Aitay, Victor *concert violinist, music educator*
Akos, Francis *violinist, conductor*
Arpino, Gerald Peter *performing company executive*
Basden, Cameron *ballet mistress, dancer*
Berryman, Diana (Kapnas) *radio personality*
Black, Robert Durward *television producer*
Brauer, Sasha Gerritson *church musician, music educator*
Conte, Lou *artistic director, choreographer*
Dabrowski, Edward John *television technical director*
Duell, Daniel Paul *artistic director, choreographer, lecturer*
Eaton, John C. *composer, educator*
Emmons Jr., Charles N. *music educator*
Falls, Robert Arthur *artistic director*
Freidheim, Ladonna *dance company director*
Gaines, Barbara *theater director*
Graddy, Julia Harder *music educator, researcher*
Gulbrandsen, Norman Ralph *retired music educator*
Hamarstrom, Patricia Ann *director, animation/multimedia specialist*
Higgins, Ruth Ellen *theatre producer*
Kalver, Gail Ellen *dance company executive, musician*
Katsman, Zinaida *musician, music educator*
Lavey, Martha *theater director*
Leifer, Lyon A. *musician, educator*
Leone, Gustavo *composer*
Lustrea, Anita *radio personality*
Mason, William *general director of opera company*
May, Aviva Rabinowitz *music educator, linguist, musician*
Moffatt, Joyce Anne *performing company executive*
Myers-Rami, Masequa *theatrical company executive, theater producer*
Naegele, Elizabeth Marie *musician, educator*
Padberg, Helen Swan *violinist*
Palermo, James W. *artistic director*
Ponné, Nanci Teresa *entertainment promoter, writer*
Rami, Pemon *theatrical company executive, theater producer*
Ran, Shulamit *composer*
Ratner, Carl Joseph *theater director*
Richter, Julia Maureen *music educator, musician*
Rode, Glenn G. *music educator, secondary school educator*
Sato, Junichi Steven *musician, music educator*
Savage, Terry *television personality, journalist, stockbroker*
Schmitt, Natalie Crohn *theater educator*
Scott, Stephen Brinsley *theater producer*
Sedelmaier, John Josef *filmmaker*
Sexton, Brenda *film agency director*
Stifler, Venetia Chakos *dancer, educator, choreographer*
Stratman, Deborah *filmmaker, film and video educator*
Tallchief, Maria *ballerina*
Taylor, Koko *singer*
Trogani, Monica *ballet dancer*
Tyson, Terri Lynn *television programming producer, consultant*
Vincent, Jim *performing company executive*
Wang, Albert James *violinist, educator*
Wasson, Jeffrey *music educator*
Winfrey, Oprah *television talk show host, actress, producer*
Woods, Nikki *radio personality*
Wooten, Robert E. *musician, educator*
Yost, Emery Joseph *music industry producer, educator*
Yu, Linda *newswoman, television anchorwoman*
Zajicek, Jeronym *retired music educator*

Chicago Heights
Reed, Scott C. *music educator, writer*

Country Club Hills
McClelland, Helen *music educator*

Crystal Lake
Dalzell, Scott D. *photo editor*

Decatur
Flores, Amy Claire Catron *music educator, musician*

Dekalb
Goldenberg, William Bruce *music educator, musician*
Meikle, Karen L. *music educator, musician*
Teague, Liam Richard *musician, researcher*

Dixon
Hertel, William John *music educator*

Downers Grove
Hornish, Ronald Frederick *music educator*

East Saint Louis
Dunham, Katherine *choreographer, anthropologist, dancer*

Edwardsville
Anderson, Mary Jane *music educator*
Schultz, Norbert J. *retired music educator*

Elgin
Dodohara, Jean Noton *music educator*
Jakle, Kenneth Richard *broadcasting executive*
McNeill, Holly Mary *theater educator, scriptwriter*

Elmhurst
Hays, Timothy Odell *musician, educator, writer*
Hirna-Levycka, Olena Romanivna *musician, music educator*

Eureka
West, Nancy Lee *music educator, performance artist, entertainer*

Evanston
Fherley, Helen-Kay *opera singer, classical record company executive, poet*
Fischer Monastero, Elizabeth *voice educator*
Hemke, Frederick L. *music educator, university administrator*
Kujala, Walfrid Eugene *musician, educator*
McDonough, Bridget Ann *music theatre company director*
Persons, Fern *actress*
Peters, Gordon Benes *retired musician*
Reimer, Bennett *music educator, writer*
Zimmerman, Mary Alice *performing arts educator*

Flossmoor
Barnas, Raymond Scott *music educator*
Day, Gregory Lynn *music educator*

Galesburg
Pahel, Tim Allen *music educator*
Polay, Bruce *music educator, conductor*

Geneva
Gallagher, Kent Grey *theater arts educator*
Klenke, Deborah Ann *band director, choral director, department chairman*

Glencoe
Boyell, Gloria *musician, music educator*

Gurnee
Myren, Allen W(illiam) *retired music educator*

Hickory Hills
Haustein, Janis M. *musician, music educator*

Homewood
Villari, Jack C. *performing arts executive, arts entrepreneur*

Jacksonville
Hayter, John Eldon *music educator*

Lake Zurich
Holdhusen, J. David *music educator*

Lawrenceville
LeGrand, Robin Lea *music educator*

Lemont
Marx, Kenneth R. *music educator*

Lisle
Kiener-Barnett, Lisa M. *music educator*

Lombard
Lindsay, Diane Miller *music educator*

Macomb
Romig, James *composer, educator*

Melrose Park
Hillert, Richard Walter *composer, educator, author*

Monmouth
Hiveley, Kelly Marie *music educator*

Niles
Kessell, Charles Arthur *music educator, musician*
Martinez, Euri Anthony *music educator, small business owner*

Northbrook
Slattery, James Joseph (Joe Slattery) *actor*

Oak Park
Leitch, Stuart *music educator, musician*

Park Ridge
Barnett, Patrick Shawn *music educator*

Princeton
Tillman, June Torrison *musician*

Quincy
Bohn, Donna May *music educator*

River Grove
Nestor, Larry *songwriter, musician*

Rockford
Lien, Hsien-Lian *music educator, conductor*
Robinson, Donald Peter *musician, retired electrical engineer*

Saint Charles
Stovall, April Leanne *music educator*

Saint Jacob
Carter, Dennis R. *music educator, band director, musician*

Springfield
Deal, Karen Lynne *conductor*

Streator
Cassady, Zoe Anne *theater educator, director*

Tinley Park
Data, Linda Laski *music educator*

Urbana
Brozak, George A. *music educator*
Davis, Ollie Watts *music educator*
Hedlund, Ronald *baritone*
Schleis, Thomas Henry *music educator, organist*
Temperley, Nicholas *music educator, writer*
Von Gunden, Heidi *music educator*
Weidner, Robert Wright *musician, music educator, musicologist*

Villa Park
Antonelli, Joseph K. *musician, educator*

Wheaton
Payne, Mary Louise *music educator, musician*

Wilmette
Blake, Douglas Munro *music educator*
Jampole, Michael *music educator, composer*
Merrier, Helen *actress*
Miller, Frederick Staten *retired music educator, academic administrator*
Montgomery Tobias, Karen Twerdahl *music educator*

Winnetka
Hausfeld, James Frank *executive director*

INDIANA

Anderson
Long, Brian Thomas *music educator*

Bloomington
Biss, Paul Martin *music educator*
Brown, Keith *musician, educator*
Mac Watters, Virginia Elizabeth *singer, music educator, actress*
McGibbon, Murray Lewis James *theater educator, theater director*
Phillips, Harvey G. *musician, soloist, music educator, arts consultant*
Spera, Dominic Gregorio *music educator, writer*
Svetlova, Marina *ballerina, choreographer, educator*
Ward-Steinman, Patrice Madura *music educator*
Williams, Camilla *soprano, voice educator*

Carmel
Thomas, John David *musician, composer, arranger, graphic designer, recording engineer, producer, photographer*

Columbus
Kuehl, Jeffry Steven (Jeff Keel) *performing arts association administrator, actor*

Evansville
Savia, Alfred *conductor*

Fort Wayne
Sack, James McDonald, Jr., *radio and television producer, marketing executive*
Stolba, K. Marie *music educator*

Goshen
Roberts, Mary Lois *music educator*

Hammond
Hansen, Jack Winsor *musician, educator*

Hanover
Batchvarova, Madlen Todorova *music educator, conductor*
Nickels, Ruth Elizabeth *band director*

Indianapolis
Aliev, Eldar *artistic director, choreographer, educator*
Bolin, Daniel Paul *music educator*
Booth, Nancy Davis *voice educator*
Coomer, Steven Robert *music educator, musician*
Everly, Jack *conductor*
Ilgen, Dorothy L. *arts foundation executive*
Johnson, David Allen *vocalist, minister, lyricist, investment advisor*
McIntyre, Lola Mazza *music educator*
Sowers, Jodi Louise *music educator*
Suzuki, Hidetaro *violinist*
Turner, Barbara A. *former dance company executive*
Venzago, Mario *conductor*
Zurick, John *consultant, former dance company director*

Knox
Weiss, Randall A. *television and radio producer, supermarket executive*

Kokomo
Highlen, Larry Wade *music educator, piano rebuilder, tuner*

Lafayette
Bodine, Gerald Bradley *composer, educator*

Muncie
Scheib, John W. *music educator, conductor*

Newburgh
Reese, Jerry Wayne *music educator, band director*

Remington
Legler, Christine Kay *music educator*

Richmond
Bordo, Guy Victor *conductor*

Royal Center
Blume, Craig Lee *music educator*

South Bend
Walters, Isaac Clayton *theater educator, director*

Tell City
Rutherford, Michael Francis *retired music educator*

Upland
Parker, Richard Allan *music educator*

Valparaiso
Bognar, Joseph Andrew *music educator, musician*

West Lafayette
Wright, Alfred George James *band symphony orchestra conductor, educator*

Zionsville
Garfunkel, Art *singer, actor*

IOWA

Ames
Adams, Andrew David *music educator*
Work, George Paul *cellist*

Anita
Everhart, Robert Phillip (Bobby Williams) *entertainer, songwriter, recording artist*

Cedar Falls
Fanelli, Michael Paul *music educator*

Cedar Rapids
Hall, Kathy L. *orchestra executive*
Nassif, Gary Tannus *singer and entertainer, art and special education educator, sculptor*
Tiemeyer, Christian *conductor*

Council Bluffs
Kurt, Johnny Thomas *music educator*

Davenport
Dcamp, Charles Barton *educator, musician*
Schleicher, Donald *music director*
Willett, Lance *orchestra executive*

Denison
Bekkerus, Perry Charles *music educator*

Des Moines
Blank, Myron Nathan *theater executive*
Erickson, Elaine Mae *composer, poet*
Giunta, Joseph *conductor, music director*
Mill, Jeth *performing company executive*

Dubuque
Hemmer, Paul Edward *musician, composer, broadcasting executive*
Hughes, Brian Lee *music educator*

Fort Dodge
Cassady, Daniel Bennet *music educator*

Fort Madison
Chapman, Allen D. *music educator*

Indianola
Duke, Michael Liston *music educator, musician*
Larsen, Robert LeRoy *artistic director*
Mace, Jerilee Marie *opera company executive*
Poulsen, James Viggo, III, *music educator, composer*

Iowa City
Hovland, Jody *theater director*
Kottick, Edward Leon *music educator, harpsichord maker*
Mather, Roger Frederick *music educator, writer*
Paredes, Robert Wesley *music educator*
Thompson, Basil F. *ballet master*

Le Mars
Cottrell, David Milton *sound recording engineer*

Mallard
Heldt, Kristin R. *conductor*

Mason City
Backlin, William Wayne *music educator, composer*

Pella
Bouler, Steven William *theater educator*

Pleasant Valley
Myatt, William Howard *theater educator, director, actor*

Storm Lake
Larson, Bethany Ann *theater educator, actress*

Sumner
Wright, James Timothy *music educator, composer*

Tipton
Farwell, Walter Maurice *vocalist, educator*

Waterloo
Eilers, Bruce Dean *music educator*
Lueders, Sara Jeanne *music educator, director*

Winterset
Feirer, Alan David *music educator, organizational development consultant*

KANSAS

Caldwell
Robinson, Alice Jean McDonnell *retired drama and speech educator*

Dodge City
Ross, Connie L. *music educator*

El Dorado
Mack, Valerie Lippoldt *music educator, performing arts educator, freelance/self-employed choreographer*

Emporia
Barham, Terry J. *music educator*
DeBauge, Janice B. *musician*

Hutchinson
Wendelburg, Norma Ruth *composer, pianist, educator*

Independence
Ellenstein, Peter *theater director, theater producer*

Lawrence
Castle, Joyce *mezzo soprano*
Duerksen, George Louis *music educator, music therapist*
Hilding, Jerel Lee *music and dance educator, former dancer*
Pozdro, John Walter *music educator, composer*
Tsubaki, Andrew Takahisa *theater director, educator*

Madison
Clark, Doris Ellen *music educator*

Manhattan
Mortenson, Kristin Oppenheim *violinist*

Offerle
Herrmann, Lorena Joyce *retired music educator*

Olathe
Prestley, Mark Douglas *video director*
Smith, Katheryn Jeanette *music educator*

Ottawa
Davidson, Medora Lea *dance educator*

Overland Park
Lamb, Gordon Howard *music educator*
McCready, Matt *music educator*
Pretzel, Mark William *musician*

Pittsburg
Berger, Reena *musician, music educator*

Rossville
Budden, Frederick Richard *music educator*

Shawnee Mission
Talley, Douglas Eric *music educator*

Topeka
Rivers, Julie Elaine *concert pianist, composer, recording industry executive*
Schultz, LeAnne *violinist, performer, music educator*

Viola
Sanderson, Kimberly Lea *dancer, educator, small business owner*

Wichita
Berman, Mitchell A. *orchestra executive*
Byers, Stephen Wesley *music educator*
Johnson, C. Nicholas *dance company executive*
Sewell, Andrew *music director*

Winfield
Yau, Oi Yan Eugenia *music educator*

KENTUCKY

Beaver Dam
Morris, Theresa Janette (TJ Morris) *vocalist, writer, composer, publishing executive*

Bowling Green
Berry, Mark Sean *music educator*
Tutino, Thomas James *theater educator, set designer*

Campbellsville
Gaddis, John Robert *music educator*
McArthur, Lisa R. *music educator, musician*
Roberts, M. Wesley *musician, educator*

Danville
Haigh, Anthony R. *performing arts educator, actor*

Frankfort
Fletcher, Winona Lee *theater educator*
Griffith, Patricia Barnes *music educator, pianist*

Highland Heights
Forman, Sandra H. *theater educator*
Hagner, Carolyn Zepf *music educator*
Pennington, Randy Keith *music educator*

Horse Cave
Brock, Robert F. *performing company executive, educator*

Lexington
Dewees, Kathy Paxton *music educator*
Grubbs, Misty D. *music educator*
Monsen, Ronald Peter *musician, music educator, artist*
Zack, George J. *conductor, music director*

Louisville
Atz, Sarah J. *music educator*
Fassett, Frances Nicholas (Kitty Fassett) *pianist, record producer*
Foster, Teresa E. *choral director, piano teacher*
Hernandez, John E. *musician, music educator*
Kee, Brenda Eltrine *music educator, concert pianist*
King, Tim *orchestra executive*
Lloyd, Kimcherie *performing company executive*
Miller, Marilee Hebert *arts administrator, producer, director, consultant*
Mowery, Ward Franklin *retired music educator*
Oliphant, Naomi Joyce *music educator, performer*
Sandler, Deborah *performing company executive*
Segal, Uriel *music director*
Shaver, Kathryn *retired performing company executive, design educator*
Sherman, Mildred Mozelle *music educator, vocalist, actress, opera director*

Morehead
Detweiler, Greg Jeffrey *music educator*

Murray
Steffa, John Amon *music educator, composer*

Nicholasville
Jones, Coletta Marie *music educator, composer*

Owensboro
Ruckdeschel, David Claude *music educator*

Williamsburg
Smoak, Jeff C., Jr., *music educator*

LOUISIANA

Alexandria
Burns, Ronald C. *music educator*

Baton Rouge
Buchmann, Molly O'Banion *choreographer, ballet educator*
Constantinides, Dinos Demetrios (Constantine Constantinides) *music educator, composer, conductor*
Hartzog, Elizabeth Windham *music educator*
Mathews, Sharon Walker *artistic director, secondary school educator*
McCoy, Wesley Lawrence *musician, conductor, educator*
Norem, Richard Frederick, Sr., *musician, music educator*
Smith, Richard James *retired music educator*
Sutherland, Wade Alan *music educator, director*
Willett, Anna Hart *composer, painter*
Yarbrough, Martha Cornelia *music educator*

Destrehan
Toups, Byron Joseph *musician, educator*

Hammond
Johansen, David Alan *musician, educator*

Lafayette
Taylor, Brian Stevon *music educator*

Lake Charles
Buckles, Michael Kim *music educator, musician*

Marrero
Brown, Courtney Allison *composer, writer, singer*

Metairie
deMoruelle, Charmaine *music educator*

Monroe
Thompson, Myrrah McCully Terzolas *music educator, director*

Natchitoches
Kuroda, Masahito *music educator*

New Orleans
Barreiro, Elias *music educator, researcher*
Barroso, Luis Q. *actor, educator, theater director*
Beck, Guy Leon *music educator*
Jazwinski, Barbara Marie *composer, educator*
Litwin, Sharon *orchestra executive*
St. Julien, Thais Mary *soprano, musician*
Seibel, Klauspeter *conductor*
Villia, Morris Sabastian *music producer, publishing executive, writer*
Walsh, James Paton *composer*

Patterson
Wilkinson III, Elwyn Nathaniel *music educator*

Ruston
Barker, Jon Albert *music educator*

Shreveport
DeRousse, Cathy Lynn *composer, music educator*
Simons, Dennis *performing company executive*
Stone, Thomas D. *music educator, composer*

Sulphur
Fuller, Betty Stamps *music educator*

Zachary
Rogillio, Kathy June *musician, piano rebuilder, educator*

MAINE

Augusta
Jenkins, Pamela Lynn *music educator*

Bethel
Farrar, Susan Clement *choreographer, performing company executive, writer*

Brunswick
Schwartz, Elliott Shelling *composer, author, music educator*

Cary Plt
Geishecker, Rueline Taylor *music educator*

Castine
Davis, Peter Frank *filmmaker, author*
Hall, David *sound archivist, writer*

Morrill
Hitt, Robert Willaim *actor*

Newcastle
Waterman, Charles Albert *actor, director, retired sales executive*

Orono
MacDonald, Elizabeth Helen *bassoonist, educator*

Portland
Bucci, Thomas Vincent *music educator, pianist, composer*
Miller, Buffy *dancer*
Russell, Robert Jackson *music educator, conductor*

Scarborough
Shulman, Richard *musician, composer, recording label owner*

Surry
Sopkin, George *cellist, music educator*

Waterville
Box, Laura Diane Chakravarty *theater educator*

West Baldwin
Simmonds, Rae Nichols *musician, composer, educator*

MARYLAND

Baltimore
Bryn-Julson, Phyllis *soprano, music educator*
Cornett, Stanley Orin *music educator*
Fleisher, Leon *concert pianist, conductor*
Harrison, Michael *opera company executive*
Huggins, Amy Branum *music educator*
Hughes, Catherine L. (Cathy Hughes) *radio personality, broadcast executive*
Huntoon, Ann Kristen *performing arts association administrator, music educator*
Jacobson, Katherine Louise *musician, music educator*
Jeffcoat, Cathleen Merle *musician, educator*
Moran, John Gregory *musician*
Temirkanov, Yuri *music director*

Bel Air
Kramer, Keith Allan *music educator, composer*

Bethesda
Burkhalter, Susan Shively *music educator, organist*

Bowie
Angebrandt, Betsy Jo *music educator, composer*
Gottlieb, Sylma R. *music educator, performing arts educator*

Brandywine
Briggs, John H., Sr., *music educator*

Chestertown
Clarke, Garry Evans *composer, educator, musician, administrator*

College Park
DeLio, Thomas *music educator, composer*

Columbia
Spicknall, Joan *music educator*
Weems, Helen Rachel *piano teacher, accompanist*

Ellicott City
Benjamin, Thomas Edward *music educator, composer, conductor*
Wann, Michael Stephen *music educator*

Frederick
McKewen Amato, Mary Patricia *musician*

Gambrills
White, Elizabeth G. *music educator*

Germantown
Hartley, James R. *musician, writer*

Glen Burnie
Ruth, Shiela Grant *music educator*

Highland
Varga, Deborah Trigg *music educator, entertainment company owner*

Huntingtown
Wilson-Dawes, Judy Ann *music educator*

Largo
Mahaffey, Redge Allan *movie producer, director, writer, actor, scientist*

Lexington Park
White, Donna C *music educator, director*

Potomac
Chang, Ya-Ting *pianist, music educator*

Rockville
Kurkul, Wenyi Wang *musician, educator, administrator*

Silver Spring
Korth, Thomas A. *musician, educator*
Neumann, Alfred John *music director*
Secular, Sidney *writer, weather forecaster, actor, model, fundraiser, consultant*

Westminster
Rogers, Jeffery Paul *music educator*

MASSACHUSETTS

Allston
Burton, Gary *musician*
Spencer, Lara *television personality, journalist*

Amherst
Donohue, Therese Brady *artistic director, choreographer, designer*
May, Ernest Dewey *university administrator, musician, executive*

Ashfield
Klein, Stacy A. *theater director*

Belmont
Gabrieli, Anna *voice educator*

Boston
Ahlbeck, Laura A. *musician, educator*
Anderson, Jewelle Lucille *musician, educator*
Bacon, A. Smoki *television host*
Barker, Edwin Bogue *musician*
Beatty, Carl *music educator*
Del Sesto, Janice Mancini *opera company executive*
Harvey, Mark Sumner *composer, minister, educator, musician*
Jochum, Veronica *pianist*
Kalogeras, Alexandros *composer, music educator*
Lesser, Laurence *musician, educator*
Lockhart, Keith Alan *conductor, musician, teacher*
McPhee, Jonathan *music director, conductor, composer, interim artistic coordinator*
Mitchell, Jon Ceander *music educator, conductor*
Moriarty, John *opera administrator, artistic director*
Nissinen, Mikko Pekka *dancer*
Palmer, Anthony John *music educator, composer, writer*
Rochinski, Stephen James *musician, educator*
Rotenberg, Sheldon *violinist*
Sonnenschein, David *music educator, composer*
Totenberg, Roman *violinist, music educator*
Vila, Robert Joseph *television host, designer, real estate developer*
Wheeler, W(illiam) Scott *composer, conductor, music educator*
Woodard, Jr., Fredrick James *music educator, musician*
Young, Laura *dance educator, choreographer*
Zander, Benjamin *conductor, educator*

Brewster
Johnson, Jill Ann *lyricist, actress*

Brimfield
Curtis, William Edgar *conductor, composer*

Brookline
Epstein, Alvin *actor, mime, theater director, make-up artist*
Kliman, Sylvia May Stern *film executive, editor, realtor*
Sho, Jennifer Yu-Fei *music educator, musician*

Cambridge
Chin, Wayman *musician, educator*
Cleary, David Michael *composer, critic, library assistant*
Clement McKinley, Sandi *performing arts association administrator, not-for-profit fundraiser*
Connick, Harry, Jr., *musician, actor, vocalist, composer, lyricist*
de Varon, Lorna Cooke *choral conductor*
Erdely, Stephen Lajos *music educator*
Glaser, Victoria Merrylees *retired music educator*
Harbison, John *composer*
Hoyt, Herbert Austin Aikins *television producer*
Martino, Donald James *composer, clarinetist, educator*
Orchard, Robert John *theater producer, educator*
Pinkham, Daniel *composer*
Russell, George Allen *composer, theoritician, author, conductor*
Sims, Ezra *composer*

Concord
Gomberg, Sydelle *dancer educator*

Dedham
Firth, Everett Joseph *timpanist*

Foxboro
Kennedy, Susan Marie *music educator*

Framingham
Bogard, Carole Christine *lyric soprano*
Struyk, Pieter M. *music educator*

Great Barrington
Curtin, Phyllis *music educator, dean, vocalist*

Greenfield
Nix, Michael Charles *musician, educator*

Hanover
Garrett, Matthew Langley *music educator*

Jamaica Plain
Florio, Christopher John *multimedia producer*

Lexington
O'Connell, Brian Morgan *music educator*

Lincoln
Giles, Allen *pianist, composer, music educator*

Ludlow
Szlosek, Elaine Marie (Saloio) *music educator*

Lynnfield
Hodgkins, Douglas Wendell *music educator*

Medford
Anderson, Thomas Jefferson, Jr., *composer, educator*
Bernstein, Jane Agar *music educator, writer*

Nantucket
Rorem, Ned *composer, author*

Needham
Di Domenica, Robert Anthony *musician, composer*

Newton
Li, Fan *pianist, music educator*

Newton Center
Schuller, Gunther Alexander *composer*

North Amherst
Plaček, Roman *cellist, music educator*

North Dartmouth
Noel, Barbara Hughes McMurtry *retired music educator*

North Easton
Keogh, Martin Jay *dancer, educator*

Northampton
Levy, Ralph Jacob, Jr., *retired theater educator*
Naegele, Philipp Otto *violinist, violist, music educator*
Snedeker, James Peter *music educator*
Wheelock, Donald F. *music educator, composer*

Norton
Crutcher, Ronald Andrew *academic administrator, music educator, musician*

Osterville
Faris, Stacey Elise *music educator*

Paxton
Hellman, Daniel Stuart *music educator*

Plymouth
Gregory, Dick *comedian, civil rights activist*

Roxbury
Martinborough, Samuel Neil *music educator, conductor, musician*

Salem
Melby, John B. *composer, educator*

Shrewsbury
McCluskey, James Francis *music educator, musician*

Somerville
Romanoff, Richard Arthur *music educator, musician*

Southbridge
Rutanen, Roy Stewart *producer, television personality*

Stockbridge
Silverstein, Joseph Harry *conductor, musician*

Swansea
Deston, Albert, III, *musician, educator*

Waltham
Boykan, Martin *composer, music educator*
Chasalow, Eric David *composer, educator*
Wyner, Yehudi *composer, pianist, conductor, educator*

Watertown
Langstaff, John Meredith *musician*

West Springfield
Eaton, Danny *theater producer, director*

Westborough
Rappaport, Jonathan C. *composer, educator, conductor*

Weston
Tenney, Sarah G. *music educator*

Williamstown
Shainman, Irwin *music educator, musician*

Worcester
Corbin, Frank Wayne *music educator*
Delorey, John Francis *music educator*
Falco, Richard Gerard *music educator*
Hagar, Richard Joseph *music educator, musician*
Kempskie, Jeffrey T. *music educator*
Lamothe, Donat Romeo *music educator*

Worthington
Schrade, Rolande Maxwell Young *composer, pianist, educator*

Wrentham
Cohen, Donna Lynn *music educator*

MICHIGAN

Allendale
Campbell, Arthur J. *music educator*
De La Barrera, Carlos Eduardo *music educator*
Reichert, Aviram *concert pianist, educator*
Vanden Wyngaard, Julianne Marguerite *music educator*

Ann Arbor
Aikman, James Whitton *composer, music educator*
Bengtsson, Erling Blöndal *classical cellist, educator*
Bolcom, William Elden *musician, composer, educator, pianist*
Korsyn, Kevin Ernest *music educator*
Matjias, Christian *music educator, musician*
Scavarda, Donald Robert *composer, artist*
Scharp-Radovic, Carol Ann *choreographer, classical ballet educator, artistic director*
Verrett, Shirley *soprano*

Berrien Springs
Caceres, Hernan Marcelo *composer, educator*

Bloomfield Hills
Haidostian, Alice Berberian *concert pianist, volunteer, not-for-profit fundraiser*
Swift, Jonathan *educator, television personality*

Dearborn
D'Alessio, Gina Maria *music educator*
David, Daniel *musician, social studies educator*

Detroit
Bryant, Marchelle Dionne *performing arts educator*
Calarco, N. Joseph *theater educator*
Di Chiera, David *general director of opera company*
Duensing, Dorothy Jean *music educator, vocalist*
Kang, Emil J. *orchestra executive*
Parsons, Anne *performing company executive*

East Lansing
Kirk, Edgar Lee *musician, educator*
Whiting Dobson, Lisa Lorraine *video production educator, producer, director*

Farmington Hills
Goslin, Gerald Hugh *concert pianist, educator*
Kalib, Sholom (Sylvan Kalib) *conductor, educator*

Frankfort
Storrer, William Allin *consultant*

Grand Blanc
Byerly, Carl Wesley *music educator, academic administrator*

Grand Rapids
Horn, Joyce Elaine *music educator*

Lockington, David *conductor*
Schmidt, Gordon Peirce *artistic director*
Taylor, Mark Lyman *music educator*
Williams, Glenn Carl *music educator, secondary school educator*

Hillsdale
Knecht, Melissa *music educator, musician*

Kalamazoo
Spradling, Robert Ledford *music educator, conductor*

Laingsburg
Zabriskie, Sherry LaFollette *filmmaker, author, actress*

Lansing
Kluge, Len H. *director, actor, theater educator*

Mason
Yoakam, Lynn Kelly *harpist, educator*

Midland
Diehl, Ann *radio personality*

Monroe
Nuechterlein, James Howard *music educator*

Mount Pleasant
Orlik, Christina Bear *music educator*

Northport
Scripps, Douglas Jerry *music educator, conductor*

Rochester
Alston, Lettie Beckon *music educator, musician*
Varani, Flavio *musician, music educator*

Rochester Hills
Eisenhower, Laurie *performing company executive*
Thoma, August John *music educator*

Roscommon
Carton, Gary L. *performing arts association administrator*

Saginaw
Leppert-Largent, Anna M. *church musician*

Scottville
Meyers, Daniel Michael *music educator, researcher*

Swartz Creek
Russell, Charles Harry *music educator, restaurant manager*

Traverse City
Faulmann, Roger Ray *retired music educator*

Troy
Okun, Maury *dance company executive*

MINNESOTA

Alexandria
DeGier, Gregory Alan *music educator*

Andover
Rudzitis, Roland Talis *music educator*

Bemidji
Wettstein, Shannon Leigh *music educator*

Big Lake
Fillafer, Richard *music educator*

Bloomington
Smith, Henry Charles, III, *symphony orchestra conductor*

Brainerd
Wannamaker, Mary Ruth *music educator*

Champlin
Lyons, Steven Gerard *music educator*

Chanhassen
Prince, (Prince Rogers Nelson) *musician, actor*

Coon Rapids
Wilson, Sylvia Alyce *musician, educator*

Duluth
Fields, Allen *artistic director*

Milaca
Wig, Robert Curtis *retired music educator, conductor*

Minneapolis
Fetler, Paul *retired composer*
Filloon, Karen *radio personality*
Houlton, Lise *performing company executive*
Jackson, Donna Cardamone *music educator*
Jeffries, Kim *radio personality*
Jones, Susie *radio personality*
Kaess, John Philip *music educator, choir director*
Maloney, Rita *radio personality*
Mamayek, Telly *radio personality*
Miller, John William, Jr., *bassoonist*
Oakes, Laura *radio personality*
Peterson, Patty *radio personality*
Reuler, Jack *theater director*
Rousseau, Eugene Ellsworth *musician, music educator, consultant*
Severinsen, Doc (Carl H. Severinsen) *conductor, musician*
Skrowaczewski, Stanislaw *conductor, composer*
Stanfield, Rebecca *radio personality*
Thurman, Virgil Leon *voice educator*
Vanska, Osmo *music director*
Walsh, David Allan *theater director*
Williams, Yolanda Yvette *music educator*
Wollan, Curtis Noel *theater producer, theater director*
Zahler, Noel Barry *composer, music educator*

Minnetonka
Jarvis, Linda Marie *music director, music educator*

Moorhead
Brekke, Kathrine Lydia *music educator*
Eyler, David Paul *music educator*
Rothlisberger, Rodney John *music educator*

Northfield
Gao, Hong *music educator*

Saint Cloud
Verrilli, Catherine Jean *music educator, soprano*

Saint Paul
Calkins, Mark R. *tenor, educator*
Coppock, Bruce *orchestra executive*
Dahlberg, Eric Ross *music educator*
Fairweather, Scott James *music educator*
Sawyer, Timothy Kenneth *music educator*
You, Yali *music educator*

Stillwater
Lindsay, Dennis R. *music educator, director*

Vadnais Heights
Martinez, Kathryn Marie *music educator*

Wabasso
Meyer, Sheldon Elliott *music educator*

Winona
Draayer, Suzanne Rhodes *music educator, writer*
Ramsdell, Bruce D. *music educator*

MISSISSIPPI

Brandon
Morgan, Helen Gayle *music educator*

Clinton
Sclater, James Stanley *music educator, composer, musician*

Greenwood
Wiley, Shelia Gilbert *music educator*

Hattiesburg
De Chiaro, John Paul *music educator*

Hernando
Freeman, Sherry Henderson *music educator*

Itta Bena
Goldman, Lawrence *music educator*

Jackson
Beck, Crafton *music director*
Bobo, Len Davis *musician, educator*
Keary, David *artistic director*

Perkinston
Douglas, Sam Lister *musician, writer*

University
Steel, David Warren *music history educator, organist, harpsichordist*

MISSOURI

Arrow Rock
Bollinger, Michael *artistic director*

Bolivar
Harrison, Carol L. *music educator*
Hooper, William Loyd *music educator, university administrator*
Thaller, Gregg P. *music educator*

Bowling Green
Bruce, Judith Esther *retired music educator, elementary education educator*

Branson
Bradley, Leon Charles *musician, educator, consultant*

Burlington Junction
Mathers, Bradley L. *music educator*

California
Lewis, Philip Henry *music educator*

Canton
McSpadden, David Larry *music educator*

Columbia
Baldwin, Timothy Kenneth *music educator*

Creve Coeur
Randle, Bernadette *musician, composer, graphics designer*

Dixon
Jackson, David Williams *music educator*

Doniphan
McCann, Lawrence Alton *music educator*

Florissant
Davis, Jan Malinda *music educator*

Joplin
Mahn, Timothy Wayne *music educator*

Kansas City
Altman, Peter A. *theater director*
Bentley, Jeffrey *performing company executive*
Blake, Darcie Kay *radio news director, anchor*
Bolender, Todd *choreographer*
Buford, Ronetta Marie *music educator*
Kuenn, Marjorie Asp *music educator*
Londré, Felicia Mae Hardison *theater educator*
Louis, William Joseph (Jonn Garvie Monks) *theater educator, actor, director, artist, poet*
Mancusi, Roberto Francesco Constantino *vocalist, educator*
Manson, Anne *music director*

Mobberley, James *music educator, composer*
Parcell, John Cleo *music educator*
Rich, Ruthanne *musician, educator*
Robertson, Kenneth Carl *music educator*
Valliere, Roland Edward *performing company executive*
Whitener, William Garnett *dancer, choreographer*

Liberty
Harriman, Richard Lee *performing arts association administrator, educator*
Seward, Nancy H. *retired band director, composer*

Maryville
Kramer, Ernest Joachim *music educator, composer*
Schultz, Patricia Bowers *vocal music educator, performer*
Sergel, Alfred E., III, (Al Sergel) *music educator*

Miller
Spencer, Jane Rene *music educator*

Point Lookout
Hardin, Garry Joe, II, *music educator*

Saint James
Stevens, Helen Jean *music educator*

Saint Louis
Boddie, Don O'Mar *recording company executive, producer, recording artist*
Briccetti, Joan Therese *theater manager, arts management consultant*
Carlin, Seth A. *music educator, musician*
Di Bisceglie, Laureen Gail *pianist, educator*
Haley, Johnetta Randolph *musician, educator, university official*
Hirsch, Arthur (Buzz Hirsch) *film producer, educator*
Montgomery, Alice Elizabeth *vocalist, speech pathologist*
Nelly, (Cornell Haynes Jr.) *rap artist*
Onovwerosuoke, Fred *music educator, musicologist*
Schindler, Laura Ann *piano teacher, accompanist*
Stewart, John Harger *music educator*
Woolf, Steven Michael *artistic director*

Saint Peters
Brandes, Gary Wayne *music educator*

Springfield
Alberti, Marie Joyce *musician, educator, entertainer*
Hawkins, Kevin Andrew *music educator*
Henry, Jack Allen, Jr., *music educator*
Moulder, T. Earline *musician*
Shirley, George William *retired music educator, farmer*
Spicer, Holt Vandercook *retired speech and theater educator*

Union
Rice, Douglas M. *music educator*

Warrensburg
Resch, Rita Marie *music educator*

Wentzville
Berry, Chuck (Charles Edward Anderson Berry) *musician, composer*

MONTANA

Billings
Barnea, Uri N. *music director, conductor, composer, violinist*

Bozeman
Vick, Jeffrey Harrison *music educator, musician*

Emigrant
Morsell, Frederick Albert *performing company executive, educator, consultant*

Great Falls
Johnson, Gordon James *artistic director, conductor*

Missoula
Knowles, William Leroy (Bill Knowles) *television news producer, journalism educator*

Richey
Baker, Kimberly Ann *music educator*

Whitefish
DeFranco, Boniface Ferdinand Leonard (Buddy DeFranco) *clarinetist, bandleader*

NEBRASKA

Chadron
Schaefer, George W. Sandy *musician, educator*

Crete
Monson, Larry Lee *music educator*

Grand Island
Maupin, Larry D. *retired music educator, musician*

Kearney
Buckner, Nathan Andrew *music educator, musician*
Schnoor, Neal Henry *music educator*

Lincoln
Blanke, Henry H., Jr., *retired theater educator*
Collier, Nathan Morris *musician, music educator*
Dixon, Wheeler Winston *film and video studies educator, writer*

Lyons
Rose, Dwight Dean *music educator*

North Platte
Mueller, Wayne Dennis *music educator*

Omaha
Cleary, Pamela Ann *symphony executive*
Eisenhardt, James William *performing arts educator, department chairman*

Johnson, James David *concert pianist, organist, educator*
Yampolsky, Victor *conductor*

Schuyler
Johnson, Dolores DeBower *consultant*

Scottsbluff
Rogers, Cindy L. *music educator*

NEVADA

Boulder City
Schultheis, Adam John *music educator, consultant*

Carson City
Bugli, David *conductor, arranger, composer*

Henderson
DeVol, Luana *vocalist, consultant*
Riske, William Kenneth *producer, cultural services consultant*

Las Vegas
Borovicka, Marsha Lorraine *music educator*
Castro, Joseph Armand *music director, pianist, composer, orchestrator*
Davies, Alma (Alma Rosita) *producer, playwright, lyricist, composer, designer, sculptor*
Gjurich, Michael John *music educator*
Goulet, Robert Gerard *singer, actor*
Healy, Mary (Mrs. Peter Lind Hayes) *singer, actress*
Kalb, Benjamin Stuart *television producer, director*
Knight, Gladys (Gladys Maria Knight) *singer*
Lewis, Jerry (Joseph Levitch) *comedian*
Lovern, Terrance Lee *production manager*
Sopko, Andrew S.J. *musician, educator*
Wiemer, Robert Ernest *film and television producer, writer, director*

North Las Vegas
Kennedy-Talley, Brenda S. *performing arts center executive, theatrical light designer*

Reno
Lee, H. Helen *music educator*

Sparks
McKenzie, Wesley Melvin, Jr., *music educator, composer*

NEW HAMPSHIRE

Alstead
Holloway, Robert Charles *orchestrator, arranger, composer*

Bath
Page, Patti (Clara Ann Fowler) *vocalist*

Durham
Kempster, William Geoffrey *conductor, music educator*

Hanover
Dong, Kui *music educator, composer*
Ehrlich, David Gordon *film director, educator*

New London
Twombly, Jean Sawyer *musician, educator*

Northwood
Lynne-O'Brien, Vincent *stage manager, director, actor*

Orford
Karol, John J., Jr., *producer, filmmaker*

Plymouth
Bourgelais, Paul *music educator*
Graff, Carleen *music educator*

Somersworth
Tully, Hugh Michael *music educator*

Walpole
Burns, Kenneth Lauren *filmmaker, historian*

NEW JERSEY

Allendale
Ruth, Rodney *musician, music consultant, contractor, educator*

Allenhurst
Tognoli, Era M. *performing company executive, artistic director*

Allentown
Sulyok, Paul David *music educator, composer*

Bayonne
McMahon, Eileen Marie *artist agent*

Cape May Court House
Weber, Lesley Elizabeth *music educator*

Cherry Hill
Clauser, Donald Roberdeau *musician*

Clayton
Bertenshaw, William Howard, III, *radio and television producer*

Cliffside Park
Perhacs, Marylouise Helen *musician, educator*

Colts Neck
Borisov, George P. *music educator*

Deal Park
Meisels, Judith A. *piano instructor, classical pianist*

Denville
Fisher, Sharon Mary *musician*
Veech, Lynda Anne *musician, educator*

East Brunswick
Hurst, Gregory Squire *director, producer, investment executive*
Kupchynsky, Jerry Markian *orchestra conductor, educator*
Savio, Frances Margaret Cammarotta *music educator*
Yttrehus, Rolv Berger *composer, educator*

East Hanover
Iovel, Alla *music educator, writer, pianist*

Edison
Fan, Shirley Tsui-Yu *music educator*

Englewood
Svezia, Vera Tisheff *concert pianist*
Zwilich, Ellen Taaffe *composer*

Englewood Cliffs
Van Gelder, Rudolph *sound recording engineer*

Ewing
Sirbaugh, Nora B. *performing arts educator, vocalist*

Fords
Brown, James *singer, broadcasting executive*

Fort Lee
Amara, Lucine *opera and concert singer*
Herera, Sue *television host*
Thomopoulos, Michael *music educator*

Glassboro
Robinette, Joseph Allen *theater educator, playwright*

Glenwood
Donald, William Robert, Jr., *performing arts educator, theater director, consultant*

Hamilton
Pucciatti, Sandra Milstein *opera company director*

Jackson
McCormick, Harold J. *music educator*

Jersey City
Hayes, Isaac *rhythm and blues singer, composer*
Queen Latifah, (Dana Owens) *recording artist, actress*
Stinchcomb, Albert Monroe *producer, designer/realtor*

Lawrenceville
Frantz, Charles Frederick *music educator*

Leonia
Deutsch, Nina *pianist, vocalist*
Dondysh, Victoria *pianist*
Victoria, Dondysh L. *piano educator*

Lincroft
Benham, Helen *music educator*

Livingston
Clark, Carolyn *performing company executive*

Long Valley
Landis, Daniel Scott *music educator*

Madison
Monte, Bonnie J. *performing arts company executive, director, educator*
Pietrowski, John A. *performing company executive, educator*

Matawan
Cohen, Robert L. *film producer*

Monmouth Junction
Lien, Ting-Ting *music educator*

Montclair
Cioffi, Patrizia *soprano, voice educator, arts consultant*
Walker, George Theophilus, Jr., *composer, pianist, music educator*

Newark
Macal, Zdenek *conductor*
Martin, Henry John *music educator, composer*
Monty, Gloria *former television producer, film executive*
Silipigni, Alfredo *opera conductor*

North Bergen
Schumacher, Barret *motion picture propman, writer*

Paramus
Gordon, Scott (Harry Scott Buehlmeier) *entertainer, actor*

Perth Amboy
Richardson-Melech, Joyce Suzanne *music educator, singer*

Pitman
Carpenter, Hoyle Dameron *music educator emeritus*

Plainfield
Ireland, Christopher P. *music educator*

Pomona
Poorman, Ronald James *music educator*

Port Elizabeth
Gross, Robert Floyd *music educator, composer*

Princeton
Graham, Nancy Love *music educator*
Kawarsky, Jay A. *music educator, conductor, composer*
Levy, Kenneth *music educator*
Lustig, Graham *artistic director*
Orphanides, Nora Charlotte *ballet educator*
Rosen, Marvin Abraham *music educator*

Raritan
Bower, David Norman *music educator, researcher*

Red Bank
Hughes, Barnard *actor*

Ridgefield
Tracey, Matthew Sean *music educator, musician*

Rivervale
Moderacki, Edmund Anthony *music educator, conductor*

Rockaway
Laine, Cleo (Clementina Dinah Dankworth) *singer*

Rumson
Topham, Sally Jane *ballet educator*

Rutherford
Baker, Don L. *band director*

Secaucus
Pinsker, Penny Collias (Pangeota Pinsker) *television producer*

Skillman
Hackel, Adam William *music educator*

Somerset
Sell, Noel Bruce *music educator*

South Orange
Nowik, John David *music educator, musician*

Springfield
Reeve, Christopher *actor*

Teaneck
Bullough, John Frank *organist, music educator*
Donato, Jeanne Gilam *musician*
Jackson, Millie *vocalist, songwriter, playwright, producer*

Trenton
Iszard, Calvin Oscar, Jr., *television production executive, public relations manager, former county freeholder*

Upper Montclair
Bergen, Christopher Brooke *opera company administrator, translator, editor*

Warren
Maull, George Marriner *music director, conductor*

Wayne
Kresky, Jeffrey *music educator, writer, composer*
Sullivan, Glenn D. *music educator*

West Orange
Atkins, Richard Bart *film, television producer*
Lieberman, Rob *performing company executive*

Westfield
Schlosberg, Theodore K. *music educator*

Westwood
French, Phyllis Olivia *artistic director, dance instructor*

Woodbridge
Qiu, Li-Hui *music educator, actress*

NEW MEXICO

Albuquerque
Evans, Bill (James William Evans) *dancer, choreographer, educator, arts administrator*
Lipka, Ronald C. *music educator, musician*
Mock, Joan Bodet *music educator*
Steinbach, Falko *musician, music educator*

Corrales
Radcliffe, Glena Eloise *lyricist, poet, composer*

Edgewood
Hamilton, Jerald *musician*

Fort Wingate
Neff, Patrick Lee (Pat Neff) *music educator*

Portales
Dal Porto, Mark Daniel *music educator*
Seifert, Dustin David *conductor, music educator*
Wozencraft-Ornellas, (Betty) Jean *singer, music educator*

Roswell
Hedin, Edna Jenks *musician, music educator*

Santa Fe
Ballard, Louis Wayne *composer*
Gaddes, Richard *performing arts administrator*
Gilbert, Alan *conductor*
McIntosh, Kathleen Ann *music educator*
Rubenstein, Bernard *orchestra conductor*
Zlatoff-Mirsky, Everett Igor *violinist*

Tesuque
MacGraw, Ali *actress*

NEW YORK

Albany
Burian, Jarka Marsano *performing arts educator*
Kristofferson, Kris *singer, songwriter, actor*
Mancinelli-Cahill, Maggie *theater director*
Zonder, Adam Steven *theater educator, production manager*

Annandale On Hudson
Miyagawa, Chiori *theater educator, playwright*

Armonk
Scotto, Renata *soprano*

Astoria
Carroll, David Joseph *stage manager*

Astoria
Sirignano, Monica Ann *performing company executive, playwright*

Aurora
Thoburn, Crawford Randall *music educator, composer*

Babylon
Kroll, Brian Walter Thomas *music educator*

Bayside
Zinn, William *musician, composer*

Bedford
Chase, Chevy (Cornelius Crane Chase) *comedian, actor, author*

Binghamton
Smales, Joel Robert *music educator*
Villecco, Anthony Charles *tenor, travel company executive, consultant*

Bloomington
Culver, Michael Patrick *music educator, composer*

Briarcliff Manor
Kennell, Richard Wayne *recording artist, business manager*

Brightwaters
Zayas, Elinor Abrams *music educator*

Brockport
Prioleau, Darwin E. *dance educator, choreographer*

Bronx
Casiano, Américo, Jr., *grants administrator, poet*
Goldstein, Eugene Bernard *comedian, educator*
Lewis, Darin John *music educator, composer*
Mittler, Diana (Diana Mittler-Battipaglia) *music educator, administrator, pianist*
Sherman, Judith Dorothy *producer, recording company owner, recording engineer*
Susso, Alhaji Papa *musician*

Bronxville
Biscardi, Chester *composer, educator*

Brooklyn
Baehr, Sonya Kay *theater educator, theater director*
Giuliano, Steven *filmmaker*
Ham, Karen *musician, music educator*
Harpham, Heather Elise *performing arts educator*
Hopkins, Karen Brooks *performing arts executive*
Lee, Spike (Shelton Jackson Lee) *filmmaker*
Mannheimer, Zachary R. *performing company executive*
Morris, Mark William *choreographer*
Niesen, James Louis *theater director*
Paton, Bob *theater director, writer*
Richmond, Eero *composer, music librarian*
Rumohr, Floyd *performing company executive, educator*
Salzman, Eric *composer, writer*
Skrobela, Katherine Creelman *music producer*
Smith, Bernadine M. *radio announcer, filmmaker, writer, producer, director*
Thomson, David *dancer, vocalist*
Vidal, Maureen Eris *theater educator, actress*

Buffalo
Boyar, Benjamin *music educator*
DiFranco, Ani *music executive, musician*
Knopf, Robert Michael *theater educator, theater director*
Manes, Stephen Gabriel *concert pianist, educator*
Reed, Janet *dance educator, choreographer*
Weekes, Rey *theater educator*

Camillus
Alvaro, Anthony Joseph *music educator*

Carmel
Calegari, Maria *ballerina*

Cicero
Pink, (Alecia Moore) *singer*

Commack
Ohman, Franklin Eric *ballet educator, choreographer*

Cooperstown
Cossa, Joanne *performing company executive*
Robertson, Stewart *conductor*

Corning
Peters, Linda S. *musician, music educator*

Crugers
Norman, Jessye *soprano*

Deer Park
Amend, Stephen J. *guitarist*
D'Amore, Victor *director, choreographer, dance educator*

Dix Hills
Mymit, Chuck W. *music educator, musician*

Dobbs Ferry
Briskin, Efrem *music educator*

Dunkirk
Levan, Kimberly Ann *music educator*

East Hampton
Dello Joio, Norman *composer*
Gladstone, Josh Adam *theater director, actor*

Fairport
Stewart, Barbara Dean *writer, musician, educational consultant*

Flushing
Electra, Carmen *actress*
Li, Qin *television anchor, reporter, director, producer*
Smaldone, Edward Michael *composer*

Forest Hills
Ashvil-Bibi, Sigalit *musician, artist*
Polakoff, Abe *baritone*
Rosenhaus, Steven L. *composer, conductor, music educator*

Garden City
Moravec, Paul *composer*

Germantown
Farberman, Harold *conductor, composer*
Rollins, Sonny (Theodore Rollins) *composer, musician*

Getzville
Clare, Roy Wallace *music educator, musician, bookseller*

Gilbertsville
Roos, Casper *actor*

Glen Cove
Carbuto, Nicholas *music educator*
Joel, Billy (William Martin Joel) *musician*

Greenfield Center
Conant, Robert Scott *harpsichordist, music educator*

Greenvale
Senft, Mason George *musician*

Hartsdale
McMann, Edith Brozak *dancer, artist*

Hastings On Hudson
D'Antoni, Philip *producer*
Del Colle, Paul Lawrence *communications administrator, journalist*
Sharpe, Robert Kent *writer, director, producer, photographer*
Wolfe, Stanley *composer, educator*

Hempstead
Chapman, Ronald Thomas *musician, educator*
Graffeo, Mary Thérèse *music educator, performer*

Hewlett
Wolff, Eleanor Blunk *actress*

Hicksville
Estrin, Morton *pianist, music educator*

Holbrook
Galijan-Simovic, Kamelija *music educator*

Homer
Bull, Beverly Jane *piano and voice educator*

Houghton
Hijleh, Mark *composer, educator*

Hunter
Khanzadian, Vahan *tenor*

Huntington
Masear, Claude *music educator, musician*

Hurley
O'Boyle, Maureen *television show host*

Ithaca
Aiosa, Vincent Nestor *music educator*
Arquit, Nora Harris *retired music educator, writer*
Borden, David *composer, educator*
Gearhart, Pamela Caum *conductor, educator*
Husa, Karel *composer, conductor, educator*
Tucker, Scott Arthur *music educator*

Jackson Heights
Morrow, Nana Kwasi Scott Douglas *choreographer, director, writer, filmmaker, educator*
Stevenson, Amanda (Sandy Stevens) *librettist, composer, document examiner*

Jamaica
Heckstall, Robyn Amina *performing arts educator, choreographer*
Lee, Joseph *musician, educator*
Retzel, Frank *music educator, composer*

Katonah
Brownlee, Delphine *actress, musician*

Kingston
Abrams, Bruce D. *music educator*

Levittown
Romano, Joseph Scott *music educator*

Lindenhurst
Farrell Logan, Vivian *actress*

Locust Valley
Peek, William DeWitt, Jr., *music educator*

Long Eddy
Hoiby, Lee *composer, concert pianist*

Manhasset
Brand, Oscar *folksinger, writer, educator*

Massapequa
Turk, Elizabeth Ann *music educator*

Massena
Schroll, Edwin John *retired secondary educator, stage director*

Melville
Sobol, Elise Schwarcz *music educator*

Merrick
Sardo, Sanford *music educator*

Millbrook
Flexner, Josephine Moncure *musician, educator*

Millerton
Hastings, Donald Francis *actor, writer*

Mount Vernon
Lando, Mary Alice music educator
Lemos, Arthur retired music educator

Narrowsburg
Krause, Gloria Rose music educator

New Rochelle
Cleary, James C. audio-visual producer

New York
Adams, John Coolidge composer, conductor
Adler, Richard composer, lyricist
Affleck, Ben actor
Aguilera, Christina vocalist
Ahrens, Lynn lyricist
Ailes, Roger Eugene television producer, consultant
Alexander, Jane actress, former federal agency administrator, producer, author, theater educator
Allen, Betty (Mrs. Ritten Edward Lee III) mezzo-soprano
Allen, Nancy musician, educator
Alt, Carol A. actress, model, entrepreneur, writer
Altman, Robert B. film director, writer, producer
Ameen, Robert musician, educator
Anagnost, Dino artistic director
Ananiashvili, Nina ballerina
Andrade, Andres vocalist, educator
Anthony, Marc (Marco Antonio Muniz) singer, composer, actor
Armitage, Karole dancer
Arnon, Baruch pianist, educator
Asakawa, Takako dancer, dance teacher, director, choreographer
Ashley, Elizabeth actress
Atkins, John concert pianist, voice teacher, model
Avgerakis, George Harris film director
Ax, Emanuel pianist
Bacall, Lauren (Betty Joan Perske) actress
Badu, Erykah singer, songwriter
Bana, Eric actor
Banks, Helen Augusta singer, actress
Banks, Tyra model, actress
Barber, Russell Brooks Butler television producer
Barbour, Catherine Jean actress, director, mime, set designer
Bardos, Karoly television and film educator, writer, director
Barino, Fantasia singer
Barrio, Soledad dancer
Barsalona, Frank Samuel theatrical agent
Bart, Roger actor
Bartoli, Cecilia soprano
Baryshnikov, Mikhail ballet dancer, actor
Bashkow, Jack Simon musician
Beauford, Carter musician
Beck, Jill dance educator, director
Beckerman, Michael Brim music educator, writer, television personality
Bednar, Rudy television producer, director
Bee, Samantha comedian, actress
Beeson, Jack Hamilton composer, educator, writer
Behar, Joy television personality
Belotserkovsky, Maxim dancer
Bennett, Dave W. talent agent, consultant
Bennett, Tony (Anthony Dominick Benedetto) entertainer
Benton, Nicholas theater producer
Bergman, Lowell television news producer
Berman, Rachel dancer
Bernardi, Mario conductor
Besterman, Douglas composer, orchestrator
Beyoncé, (Beyoncé Giselle Knowles) singer
Biedel, Alexis actress
Bikel, Theodore actor, singer
Birkenhead, Thomas Bruce theatrical producer and manager, educator
Black, Jack actor
Black, Shawn Morgado dancer
Blackman, Cindy musician, composer
Blakemore, Michael Howell theatre and film director
Blige, Mary Jane recording artist
Bohrman, David Ellis television news producer
Bolotowsky, Andrew Ilyitch flutist, composer
Bolton, Michael singer, songwriter
Borree, Yvonne dancer
Boston, Gretha actress, vocalist
Boxill, Edith Hillman music therapist, educator, writer
Bracco, Lorraine actress
Bradford, Robert Ernest motion picture producer, financier
Brant, Henry composer
Braxton, Toni popular musician
Brecker, Michael saxophonist
Brendel, Alfred concert pianist
Brewster, Robert Gene concert singer, educator
Brightman, Sarah singer, actress
Brinkley, Christie model, spokesperson, designer
Brohn, William David conductor, orchestrator
Brooks, Michael music archivist
Brothers, Joyce Diane television personality, psychologist
Brown, David motion picture producer, writer
Brown, Trisha dancer
Bumbry, Grace soprano
Bundchen, Giselle model
Burrell, Pamela actress
Bush, Lauren model
Butler, Kerry actress
Byer, Diana performing arts company executive
Cahill, Catherine M. orchestra executive
Caldwell, Zoe actress, film director
Campbell, Naomi model
Cano, Brian Joseph television producer, graphics designer
Cantrell, Lana actress, lawyer, singer
Capalbo, Carmen theater director and producer
Caples, Richard James dance company executive, lawyer
Capucilli, Terese performing company executive
Carell, Steve comedian, actor
Carlson, Marvin Albert theater educator
Carney, Michael orchestra leader
Carpenter, Mary Chapin singer, songwriter
Carter, Elliott Cook, Jr., composer
Carthay, R. Jon hand model, actor
Cash, Rosanne country singer, songwriter
Castel, Nico tenor, educator
Cazeaux, Isabelle Anne Marie retired musicology educator
Cesar, Kamala dancer, educator
Chang, Marian S. filmmaker, composer
Channing, Stockard (Susan Stockard) actress
Chappell, Wallace performing company executive
Chappelle, David (Dave Chappelle) actor, comedian
Charnin, Martin theatrical director, lyricist, producer
Chenoweth, Kristin actress
Chesler, Gail arts organization development executive
Chianese, Dominic actor
Christensen, Dieter ethnomusicologist
Church, Charlotte vocalist
Ciarrocchi, Maya dancer
Clarkson, Kelly Brianne singer
Clarkson, Patricia actress
Colbert, Stephen comedian, actor
Coleman, Cy pianist, composer, producer
Coleman, George Edward tenor, alto and soprano saxophonist
Colligan, John Aloysius music director, composer
Collins, Judy Marjorie singer, songwriter
Collins, Phil (Philip David Charles Collins) singer, songwriter, drummer, record producer
Colvin, Shawn recording artist, songwriter
Comissiona, Sergiu conductor
Conroy, Frances actress
Conway, Kevin actor, director
Cooper, Kenneth harpsichordist, pianist, music educator, conductor, musicologist
Cooperman, Alvin television and theatrical producer
Copeland, Stewart composer, musician
Coppola, Sofia Carmina film director, scriptwriter, actress
Corbin, Patrick dancer
Corddry, Rob comedian, actor
Corsaro, Frank Andrew theater, musical and opera director
Costello, Elvis (Declan Patrick McManus) musician, songwriter
Craven, Frank John actor, playwright, poet
Craven, Wes film director
Crawford, Bruce Edgar performing company executive
Creshevsky, Noah Ephraim composer, music educator
Cunningham, Merce dancer
Curran, Leigh actress, playwright
Currie, Russell composer, educator
Curtin, Jane Therese actress, writer
Curtis, Paul James mime director
Curtis, Tony (Bernard Schwartz) actor
D'Abruzzo, Stephanie actress
D'Addario, Edith performing company executive
Dakin, Christine Whitney dancer, educator
Daltrey, Roger musician
Danitz, Marilynn Patricia choreographer, videographer
D'Antuono, Eleanor ballet director, teacher, coach
David, Hal lyricist
Davidovsky, Mario composer
Davidson, Jack actor
Davis, Leonard violist
Deen, Paula H. television personality, restaurant owner, chef
DeFord, Ruth I. music educator
de Kenessey, Stefania Maria composer
De Luca, Eva vocalist, writer, composer, entrepreneur
de Matteo, Drea actress
Dendy, Mark choreographer
DiBiasio, Adolf R entertainment company executive
Dichter, Misha concert pianist
Dickson, James Edward actor
Diggins, Peter Sheehan arts administrator
Dion, Celine musician
DiScala, Jamie Lynn actress
Dissette, Alyce Marie television multimedia and theatrical producer, non-profit foundation executive
Di Vittorio, Salvatore music educator, composer, conductor
Dlugoszewski, Lucia artistic director
Domino, Fats (Antoine Domino) pianist, singer, songwriter
Doty, Shayne Taylor organist
Douglas, Ashanti S. (Ashanti) vocalist
Douglas, Kyan television personality
Downs, Hugh Malcolm radio and television broadcaster
Duchin, Peter Oelrichs musician
Duff, Hilary Ann actress, singer
Dukakis, Olympia actress
Dulaine, Pierre ballroom dancer
Dunham, Christine dancer
Dutoit, Charles conductor
Dylan, Bob (Robert Allen Zimmerman) singer, composer
Edmunds, Kenny (Babyface) popular musician
Elliott, Missy musician
Ellis, Scott theatrical director
Ellis, Terry vocalist
Eminem, (Marshall Mathers III) rap artist
Emme, model, apparel designer
Entremont, Philippe conductor, pianist
Epstein, Matthew performing company director
Eschenbach, Christoph conductor, pianist
Essman, Susie actress
Estes, Simon Lamont opera singer, bass-baritone
Evangelista, Linda model
Evans, Albert dancer
Evans, Faith singer
Falletta, Jo Ann conductor
Farley, Carole soprano
Fecteau, Christopher M. performing company executive, conductor
Feit, Barberi Paull composer, lyricist, psychotherapist, author, speaker
Feld, Eliot dancer, choreographer
Felious, Odetta vocalist
Feuer, Cy motion picture and theatrical producer, director
Fey, Tina actress
Filarski Hasselbeck, Elizabeth television host/personality
Fiorato, Hugo conductor
Flack, Roberta singer
Flaherty, Stephen composer, orchestrator
Fleming, Renée L. opera singer
Fogel, Henry orchestra administrator
Fontana, Thomas Michael producer, scriptwriter
Ford, Eileen Otte (Mrs. Gerard W. Ford) modeling agency executive
Foreman, Richard theater director, playwright
Formento, Daniel radio company executive, writer
Foster, Sutton actress
Fowler, Beth actress
Frankel, Gene theater director, writer, producer, educator
Franklin, Aretha singer
Freeman, Morgan actor
Freizer, Louis A. radio news producer
Frisell-Schröder, Sonja Bettie opera producer, stage director
Fuchs, Lillian classical musician, educator, composer
Gaines, Boyd actor
Galway, James flutist
Garcia, Andy actor
Garlin, Jeff actor
Gerard, Ian performing arts association administrator
Gibson, Jon Charles composer, musician, artist
Giraldi, Robert Nicholas film director
Glasberg, Lisa radio personality
Glass, Philip composer, musician
Goines, Leonard music educator, consultant
Goldsmith, Merwin actor, theater director
Goodacre, Jill model
Goode, Daniel S. composer, performing arts educator
Goodman, Roger Mark television director
Goto, Midori classical violinist
Graff, Randy actress
Graziano, John Michael music educator
Grenrock-Woods, Stacey comedian, actress
Griffel, L. Michael music educator, researcher
Groban, Josh vocalist
Grunschlag, Toni pianist, researcher
Guettel, Henry Arthur retired arts executive
Hadley, Jonathan Charles actor, director
Haimes, Todd artistic director
Hall, Michael C. actor
Halmi, Robert film producer, television producer
Hammett, Kirk Lee musician
Hample, Henry music educator, musician
Hardee, Lewis Jefferson, Jr., theater educator
Hargitay, Mariska actress
Harmon, Jane producer
Harris, Harriet actress
Harris, Julie (Julie Ann Harris) actress
Harrow, Nancy (Mrs. Jan Krukowski) jazz singer, songwriter, editor
Harter, Theo C. music educator, composer
Hartley, Hal film director
Harvey, Steven Patrick (Steve Harvey) comedian, actor
Hatfield, Juliana vocalist
Hawke, Ethan actor
Hebert, Bliss Edmund opera director
Herrera, Paloma dancer
Herron, Cindy actress, vocalist
Hewitt, Don S. television news producer
Heyward, Andrew John television producer
Hill, Lauryn vocalist, actress
Hilse, Walter Bruno music educator, organist
Holder, Geoffrey Lamont dancer, actor, choreographer, director
Holmes, Anna-Marie ballerina, ballet mistress
Holt, Thelma theatrical producer
Horn, Shirley vocalist, pianist
Horne, Marilyn Berneice mezzo-soprano
Houghton, James performing company executive
Hurlin, Dan actor, theater director
Hutchinson, Lynda Ronette vocalist, musician, comedian, actress
Hynde, Chrissie musician
Iler, Robert actor
Imus, Don (John Donald Imus Jr.) radio host
Intilli, Sharon Marie television director, small business owner
Isaacs, Robert conductor, tenor
Isbin, Sharon classical guitarist, guitar educator
Istomin, Marta Casals performing arts administrator, former educator
Ivory, James Francis film director
Jablonsky, Stephen music educator, composer, artist, writer
Jackson, Anne (Anne Jackson Wallach) actress
Jackson, Kristin choreographer, educator
Jacobs, Jim actor, playwright, composer, lyricist
Jacobson, Lawrence Seymour television executive producer
Jaffe, Susan ballerina
James, Belinda Sue choreographer
James, Cheryl vocalist
Jamison, Judith dancer
Jasperse, John performing company executive
Jefferson, Denise dance school director
Jett, Joan (Joan Larkin) musician
Jewel, (Jewel Kilcher) folk singer, songwriter
Jones, Bill T. dancer, choreographer
Jones, Maxine vocalist
Jung, Doris dramatic soprano
Kahane, Jeffrey conductor, pianist
Kaltin, Robert Z. theater director
Kalmanoff, Martin composer
Kamlot, Robert performing arts executive
Karchin, Louis Samuel composer, educator
Kassel, Virginia Weltmer television producer, writer
Keating, Isabel actress
Kellogg, Paul performing company executive
Kent, Julie ballet dancer, actress, model
Kent, Linda Gail dancer
Kern, Heath Thayer producer
Kernis, Aaron Jay composer
Keys, Alicia vocalist, musician, songwriter
Kinberg, Judy television producer, director
King, B. B. (Riley B. King) singer, guitarist
Kiser, Molly musician
Kitahata-Sporn, Amy movement educator
Kitt, Eartha Mae actress, singer
Kline, Kevin Delaney actor
Knight, Shirley actress
Knightley, Keira actress
Kono, Toshihiko cellist
Kowroski, Maria dancer
Kraut, Harry John music producer, consultant
Krizer, Jodi performing arts executive
Krosnick, Joel cellist
LaBelle, Patti (Patricia Louise Holt) singer, entertainer
Lake, Ricki talk show host, actress
Lampert, Zohra actress
Lane, Kenneth Robert producer, distributor
Lane, Louis musician, conductor
Lang, Pearl dancer, choreographer
Lansbury, Edgar George theatrical producer
Larmore, Jennifer mezzo-soprano
Last, Ruth Edith actress
Lauper, Cyndi musician
Leach, Robin producer, writer, television host
LeCompte, Elizabeth theater director
Lee, Amy singer
Lee, Dai-Keong composer
Legrand, Michel Jean composer
Leich Galland, Claire film and theatre indexer
Leppard, Raymond John conductor, harpsichordist
Leritz, Lawrence R. choreographer, singer, actor, dancer, producer
Lessard, Stefan musician
Letterman, David television personality, producer, comedian, writer
Levine, James conductor, pianist, artistic director
Lewis, Marcia actress
Libin, Paul theatre executive, producer
LiBretto, John Charles television director
Liebermann, Lowell composer, pianist, conductor
Lightfoot, Gordon Meredith singer, songwriter
Limbaugh, Rush Hudson radio and talk show host
Lipscomb, James Chapman film producer
Lipton, James television personality
Loeb, Lisa singer, songwriter
Loney, Glenn Meredith drama educator
Lopez, Robert composer, lyricist
Lopez-Cobos, Jesus conductor
Love, Laura singer, songwriter
Loveless, Patty (Patty Ramey) country music singer
Lubovitch, Lar dancer, choreographer
Lucas, James E(vans) operatic director
Lucci, Susan actress
Lunn, Kitty Elizabeth actress
Luvisi, Lee concert pianist
Ma, Yo-Yo cellist
Maazel, Lorin conductor, composer, violinist
Macpherson, Elle model
Macurdy, John Edward bass
Malakhov, Vladimir dancer
Malkin, Barry film editor, consultant
Malm, Mia actress
Mamlok, Ursula composer, educator
Manahan, Anna actress
Mandabach, Caryn television producer
Manilow, Barry (Barry Alan Pincus) singer, composer, arranger
Mann, Aimee singer, songwriter
Mansouri, Lotfollah (Lotfi Mansouri) retired performing company executive
Maraynes, Allan Lawrence filmmaker, television producer
Marsalis, Branford musician
Marshall, Kathleen choreographer, theater director, theater producer
Marshall, Robert film director, television director, theater director, choreographer
Martin, Elliot Edwards theatrical producer
Martini, Richard K. theatrical producer
Martins, Peter ballet master, choreographer, dancer
Marx, Jeff composer, lyricist
Mason, Marshall W. theater director, educator
Massey, Andrew John conductor, composer
Matthews, Dave singer, musician
Maxwell, Carla Lena dancer, choreographer, educator
May, Elaine actress, theatre and film director
Mayer, John vocalist
Mays, Jefferson actor
Mays, Linda performing arts association administrator
Maysles, Albert H. filmmaker
Mazzo, Kay ballet dancer, educator
Mazzola, John William former performing arts center executive, consultant
McDermott, Dylan actor
McDonald, Audra Ann actress
McGrady, Phyllis television producer
McKenzie, Kevin Patrick artistic director
McKerrow, Amanda ballet dancer
McLachlan, Sarah composer, musician
Mc Lean, Don singer, instrumentalist, composer
McPartland, Marian pianist, composer
Meadow, Lynne (Carolyn Meadow) theater producer
Mehta, Zarin performing company executive
Mellencamp, John (John Cougar) singer, songwriter
Meltzer, Harold performing company executive, composer
Menken, Alan composer
Menzel, Idina actress, singer
Merchant, Ismail Noormohamed film producer, film director
Merchant, Natalie Anne musician, singer
Meunier, Monique dancer
Meyer, Edgar musician, composer
Michaels, Lorne television writer, producer
Miller, Bebe choreographer
Miller, Beth McCarthy television director
Miller, Erika on-air business news reporter
Milnes, Sherrill E. baritone
Mintz, Shlomo conductor, violist
Mitchell, Arthur dancer, choreographer, educator
Mollica, Santo percussionist, songwriter, performer
Monk, Meredith Jane artistic director, composer, choreographer, filmmaker, director
Moore, Leroi musician
Moore, Mandy (Amanda Leigh Moore) singer, actress
Moore, Michael Watson musician, educator
Moore, Rachel Suzanne performing company executive, dancer
Morath, Max Edward entertainer, composer, writer
Morris, James Peppler bass
Morris, John composer, conductor, arranger
Morton, Joëlle musician, editor
Moskovitz, Jim radio, television and film producer, writer
Moyers, Judith Davidson television producer
Muller, Jennifer choreographer, dancer
Munzer, Cynthia Brown mezzo-soprano
Muradian, Vazgen violist, composer
Murphy, Carolyn model
Murphy, Donna actress
Murphy, Rosemary actress
Nagano, Kent George conductor
Naito, Akemi composer
Nash, Graham William singer, composer
Nederlander, James Morton theater executive
Nelson, Barry actor
Nelson, Edwin Stafford actor, educator
Nelson, Stanley film director, writer, film producer
Nugent, Nelle theater, film and television producer
Nussbaum, Jeffrey Joseph musician
O'Brien, Conan writer, performer, talk show host
Ohira, Kazuto theatre company executive, writer
O'Horgan, Thomas Foster composer, director
Olivieri Jr., Vincent Ronald sound designer
Olyphant, Timothy actor

O'Neal, Hank *entertainment producer, business owner*
Oremus, Stephen *composer*
Osborne, Joan (Elizabeth) *singer, songwriter*
Osbourne, Ozzy (John Osbourne) *vocalist*
Oz, Frank (Frank Richard Oznowicz) *puppeteer, film director*
Parker, Alice *composer*
Parker, Trey *actor, producer, director*
Parks, Gordon Roger Alexander *film director, author, photographer, composer*
Parsons, David *artistic director, choreographer*
Parsons, Estelle *actress, director, theater producer*
Paul, Les *entertainer, inventor*
Pavarotti, Luciano *lyric tenor*
Payton-Wright, Pamela *actress*
Penn, Arthur Hiller *film and theatre director*
Perahia, Murray *pianist*
Peress, Maurice *symphony conductor, musicologist*
Perlman, Itzhak *violinist*
Perlmutter, Alvin Howard *television and film producer*
Perry, Douglas *opera singer*
Peters, Bernadette (Bernadette Lazzara) *actress*
Peters, Roberta *soprano*
Pettibon, Raymond *video artist*
Phair, Liz *recording artist, pop vocalist*
Philbin, Regis *television personality*
Pinkins, Tonya *actress*
Plant, Robert Anthony *singer, composer*
Poor, Peter Varnum *producer, director*
Porter, Karl Hampton *orchestra musical director, conductor*
Porter, Stephen Winthrop *stage director*
Posin, Kathryn Olive *choreographer*
Powers, Scott *producer, actor*
Pratt, Suzanne *producer, reporter*
Presser, Michael *performing company executive*
Previn, Andre *composer, conductor*
Price, Leontyne (Mary Violet Leontyne Price) *retired concert and opera singer, soprano*
Prince, Harold *theatrical director, producer*
Pritchett, Gil, III, *actor*
Queler, Eve *conductor*
Quivers, Robin *radio personality*
Ramey, Samuel Edward *bass soloist*
Ramirez, Tina *artistic director*
Ramsay, Gustavus Remak *actor*
Randolph, David *conductor*
Raphael, Sally Jessy *talk-show host*
Rauch, Paul David *television producer*
Reed, Lou *musician*
Reich, Steve *composer*
Reinhart, Charles Lawrence *performing company executive*
Reinking, Ann H. *dancer, actress*
Renick, Kyle *artistic director*
Rennie, Milbrey Tower *television news producer*
Reuben, Gloria *actress*
Rhodes, Samuel *violist, educator*
Richard, Ellen *theater executive*
Richards, Keith *musician*
Richards, Lloyd George *theatrical director, university administrator*
Richards, Martin *theatrical producer*
Rigg, Dame Diana *actress*
Ringer, Jennifer *dancer*
Ripa, Kelly Maria *television personality*
Rivera, Chita (Conchita del Rivero) *actress, singer, dancer*
Rivera, Geraldo *television personality, journalist*
Rizer, Maggie *model*
Robbins, Timothy (Francis) *director, actor*
Roberts, Denise (Denise Roberts Hurlin) *dancer*
Robertson, Andrew *dancer*
Rodriguez, Freddy *actor*
Ronstadt, Linda Marie *singer*
Rosen, Nathaniel Kent *cellist*
Ross, Diana Ernestine Earle *singer, actress, entertainer, fashion designer*
Rossellini, Isabella *actress, model*
Rostropovich, Mstislav Leopoldovich *conductor, music director, musician*
Roth, Daryl *theater producer*
Rothman, Carol *theater director*
Rothschild, Amalie Randolph *filmmaker, producer, director, digital artist, photographer*
Rouse, Christopher Chapman, III, *composer, educator*
Rudel, Julius *conductor*
Rudin, Scott *film and theatre producer*
Rudolph, Maya *actress, comedienne*
Russell, David O. *film director, film producer, scriptwriter*
Saddler, Donald Edward *choreographer, dancer*
Sainte-Croix, Judith Lynn *composer, performing arts educator, consultant*
St. Patrick, Matthew *actor*
Salerno-Sonnenberg, Nadja *violinist*
Salomon, Frank Ernest *classical music administrator*
Salonen, Esa-Pekka *conductor*
Salonga, Lea *actress, singer*
Sandler, Adam *actor*
Sarandon, Susan Abigail *actress*
Schafer, Milton *composer, pianist, educator*
Schechner, Richard *theater director, author, educator*
Scheeder, Louis *theater producer, director, educator*
Schickele, Peter *composer*
Schifrin, Lalo *composer*
Schoonmaker Powell, Thelma *film editor*
Schorer, Suki *ballet teacher*
Scorsese, Martin *film director*
Scott, Campbell *actor*
Seary, Lawrence Anthony *cinematographer, news assignment editor, field operations administrator*
Seidelman, Susan *film director*
Seldes, Marian *actress*
Seligson, Gary Marc *musician*
Seltzer, Leo *documentary filmmaker, educator, lecturer*
Serebrier, José *musician, conductor, composer*
Severs, William Floyd *actor*
Seymour, Stephanie *model*
Shaffer, Paul *musician, bandleader*
Shane, Rita *opera singer, educator*
Sheik, Duncan *singer, songwriter*
Shelley, Carole *actress*
Sherman, Arthur *theater educator, writer, actor, composer, sculptor*
Shocked, Michelle *vocalist, songwriter*
Shuman, Earl Stanley *songwriter, music publisher*
Siegel, Marc Monroe *television and film producer, writer, director*
Silver, Joan Micklin *film director, screenwriter*
Silvers, Sally *choreographer, performing company executive*
Simmons, Gene *musician*
Simon, Abbey *pianist*
Simon, Carly *singer, composer, author*
Simpson, Jessica Ann *vocalist*
Sinclair, Daisy *casting executive*
Sirico, Genaro *actor*
Sitomer, Sheila Marie *television producer, director*
Smith, Anna Nicole (Vickie Lynn Hogan) *television personality, model*
Smith, Malcolm Sommerville *bass*
Snyder, Arlen Dean *actor*
Snyder, Donald Ivandale *music educator, musician*
Soley, David Benjamin *composer*
Solomon, Maynard Elliott *music historian, former recording company executive*
Solomons, Gus, Jr., (Gustave Martinez) *choreographer, dancer, writer*
Solov, Zachary *choreographer, ballet artist*
Somogyi, Jennie *dancer*
Soto, Jock *dancer*
Soyer, David *cellist, music educator*
Spacey, Kevin *actor*
Spears, Britney *singer*
Speller, Robert Ernest Blakefield, Jr., *choreographer*
Springsteen, Bruce *singer, songwriter, guitarist*
Stang, Arnold *actor, director, writer*
Stang, Rolf Kristian *vocalist, actor, educator, writer, advertising executive*
Stern, Howard Allan *radio personality, television show host*
Stevens, Risë *performing arts company administrator*
Stiefel, Ethan *dancer*
Sting, (Gordon Matthew Sumner) *musician, songwriter, actor*
Stoltzman, Richard Leslie *clarinetist*
Stoney, George Cashel *film educator*
Storch, Arthur *theater director*
Strasfogel, Ian *stage director, playwright*
Stratas, Teresa (Anastasia Strataki) *opera singer, soprano*
Stroman, Susan *choreographer, theater director*
Stuart, Ned *film producer*
Studdard, Ruben (Christopher Ruben Studdard) *singer*
Sullivan, Kathryn Ann *performing arts educator*
Sutherland, Dame Joan *retired soprano*
Swan, William *actor*
Tabatsky, David *theater educator, director*
Talmi, Yoav *conductor, composer*
Taylor, Paul B. *choreographer*
Taymor, Julie *theater, film and opera director and designer*
Tesori, Jeanine *composer*
Thomas, Richard *actor*
Thorne, Francis *composer*
Tilson Thomas, Michael *symphony conductor*
Timberlake, Justin *vocalist*
Tinsley, Boyd Calvin *musician*
Tischler, Judith Blanche *retired music publishing executive, educator*
Tkacz, Virlana Maria *theater director, writer, translator*
Torn, Rip (Elmore Rual Torn Jr.) *actor, director*
Torres, Dalys E. *music educator, consultant*
Tree, Michael *violinist, violist, educator*
Trujillo, Robert *musician*
Tucker, Allan Marc *mastering engineer*
Tuckwell, Barry Emmanuel *musician, music educator*
Turturro, Aida *actress*
Turturro, John *actor*
Tuttle, Ashley *dancer*
Uggams, Leslie *entertainer*
Ulrich, Lars *drummer*
Uppman, Theodor *concert and opera singer, voice educator*
Valletta, Amber *model*
Van Bellinghen III, Julian *composer, writer, actor, film company executive*
Vandross, Luther *singer*
Van Halen, Eddie *guitarist, rock musician*
Vedder, Eddie *singer*
Vendela, *model*
Vieira, Meredith *television personality*
Volpe, Joseph *opera company general manager*
Von Stade, Frederica *mezzo-soprano*
Wadsworth, Oliver *actor, playwright*
Wagner, Alan Cyril *television and film producer, consultant, performing arts educator*
Walden, Shelton Harrison *radio personality, educator*
Wallace, Michele *media company executive*
Wallach, Eli *actor*
Warrick, Ruth *actress*
Warwick, Dionne *singer*
Waters, Crystal *vocalist, songwriter*
Waters, Sylvia *dance company artistic director*
Watts, André *concert pianist*
Waxman, Anita *producer*
Weaver, John Borland *organist, composer*
Wedgeworth, Ann *actress*
Weese, Miranda *dancer*
Weiland, Scott Richard *singer*
Wein, George Theodore *music festivals producer, pianist, singer*
Weinstein, Ellen *performing company executive*
Weissler, Fran *theatrical producer*
West, James Reyenard *dance educator, health educator*
White, Lillias *actress*
Wilcox, T.J. *filmmaker*
Wile, Joan *composer, lyricist, singer*
Wilhjelm, Christian *conductor, artist*
Williams, Lucinda *country musician*
Williams, Montel *television talk show host*
Williams, Pharrell *music producer, arranger, vocalist*
Williams, Terrie Michelle *publicity agency executive*
Williams, Vanessa *recording artist, actress*
Wilson, Cassandra *singer*
Wittstein, Edwin Frank *stage and film production designer*
Wolfe, George C. *theater director, producer, playwright*
Wong, B.D. *actor*
Wood, Ronald *musician*
Woodward, Joanne Gignilliat *actress*
Wright, Steven *comedian*
Wuorinen, Charles Peter *composer*
Yamaguchi, Masaya *musician, educator*
Yellin, Victor Fell *composer, music educator*
Zirinsky, Susan *television producer*
Zucker, Stefan *tenor, writer, editor, radio broadcaster*
Zukerman, Pinchas *concert violinist, violist, conductor*

Newcomb
Chatzky, Herbert *music educator*

Niagara Falls
Towey, Augustine Denis *theater educator, theater director*

North Bangor
Hastings, Ralph B. *music educator*

Nyack
Bryant, George Bernard *music educator, musician*
Kenote, Marie Herseth *music educator, musician*

Orangeburg
Wagoner, Russell A. *music educator*

Owego
Kearney, Andrew William *music educator, musician*

Pawling
Jones, James Earl *actor*
Utter, Donald L. *music educator*

Pelham
Borzova, Alla Aleksandra *composer, conductor, pianist*

Penfield
Bagale, John R. *music educator*
Benson, Warren Frank *composer, educator*

Penn Yan
Stempien, Joseph Jeffrey *music educator*

Pleasant Valley
Becofsky, Arthur Luke *arts administrator, writer*

Port Washington
Starr, Ringo (Richard Starkey) *musician, actor*
Tarleton, Robert Stephen *producer and distributor fine arts videos*

Poughkeepsie
Wilson, Richard Edward *composer, pianist, music educator*

Purchase
Bannon, Nancy *performing arts educator*
Magaziner, Elliot Albert *musician, conductor, educator*
Mizelle, Dary John *composer, educator*

Putnam Valley
Amram, David Werner *composer, conductor, musician*

Rochester
Atkins, Carl J. *conductor, educator*
Diamond, David Leo *composer*
Schwantner, Joseph *composer, educator*

Rocky Point
Knapp, Craig Brian *music educator, musician*

Rosendale
Goldpaugh Brown, Bethany J. *theater educator, writer, costume designer*

Roslyn
Rosegarten, Rory *personal manager, television producer, theater producer*

Rye
Fumasoli, John *music educator*

Rye Brook
Levy, Howard Alan *music educator*

Saratoga Springs
Porter, David Hugh *pianist, classicist, academic administrator, liberal arts educator*
Winne, Elizabeth (Lise) *lyricist*

Schenectady
Hermance, Jr., Myron E. *conductor, educator*
Szokody, Aniko *pianist, educator*

Schroon Lake
Williams, Wayne M. *music educator*

Sea Cliff
Mourashkin, Boris V. *composer, sound therapist, poet, performer, producer*
Popova, Nina *dancer, choreographer, director*

South Salem
Knijff, Jan-Piet *musician, educator*

Sparkill
Dahl, Arlene *actress, writer, apparel designer, cosmetics executive*

Sparrow Bush
Murray, William Bruce *opera singer*

Spencer
Grunberg, Slawomir *film and television producer and director, director of photography*

Staten Island
Miller, Wayne *actor, designer, producer, impresario*
Robison, Paula Judith *flutist*
Thomas, Charles Columbus *dance educator, artist*

Stony Brook
Suchoff, Benjamin *music educator*

Sunnyside
Gil Orrios, Angel *theater director, lighting designer, translator*

Syracuse
Elms, Ben *actor, director*
Wolff, Catherine Elizabeth *opera company executive*

Troy
Snyder, Patricia Di Benedetto *theater director and administrator*

Wallkill
Strauser, Susan Parkyn *performing arts educator, singer*

Walton
Bartlett, Raymond L. *music educator*

Warwick
Gould, Keely Ann *music educator, conductor*

Watertown
Machuga, Thomas Richard *music educator*

Weedsport
English, Richard Paul *music educator*

West Chazy
Slosson, Constance Sweet *retired music educator*

West Hempstead
Dillmon, Robert Otho *music educator, editor*

West Hurley
Martucci, Vincent James *composer, pianist*

West Islip
Keller, Joyce *television and radio host, counselor, writer*

White Plains
Sedelmaier, J. J. *filmmaker*
Wedge, Chris *animation director, studio executive*

Williamsville
Whitcomb, James Stuart *videographer, photographer, production company executive*

Willow
Bley, Carla Borg *composer*

Yonkers
Baumel, Herbert *violinist, conductor*

NORTH CAROLINA

Andrews
Cozart, Kimberly Marie *music educator*

Asheville
Weed, Maurice James *composer, retired music educator*

Banner Elk
Tilden, Ralph Fulton *retired music educator, organist*

Blowing Rock
Kay, Kenneth *performing company executive*

Boone
Cole, Susan Stockbridge *theater educator*

Brevard
Effron, David Louis *conductor, music director*

Chapel Hill
Froeber, Sarah Marjorie *actress, playwright, educator*
Hammond, David Alan *stage director, educator*
Neff, Severine *music educator*
Powell, Carolyn Wilkerson *retired music educator*

Charlotte
Bonazzi, Elaine Claire *mezzo-soprano*
Bonnefoux, Jean-Pierre *artistic director, choreographer, dancer*
Iley, Martha Strawn *music educator*
Reese, Annette Evelyn *music educator*

Cherryville
Barger, Linda Kale *choral director*

Durham
Caesar, Shirley *gospel singer, evangelist*
Nakarai, Charles Frederick Toyozo *music educator, adjudicator*
Paolantonio, Edmund Joseph *musician, music educator*
Ward, Robert *composer, conductor, educator*

Fayetteville
Bridenstine, Evan M. *theater educator*
Curtis, Marvin Vernell *music educator*
Spena, Ronda Gale *music educator*

Franklinton
Elmore, Cenieth Catherine *music educator*

Greensboro
Middleton, Herman David, Sr., *theater educator*
Russell, Peggy Taylor *soprano, educator*
Ward, Angie *radio personality*

Havelock
Bolish, Cameron Adam *composer, music educator, musician*

Hickory
Kiser, Daniel *music educator, musician*

High Point
Huss, Donald Edwin, Jr., *musician*
Wilson, Donna Rae *music educator*

Mars Hill
Corley, Alton L. *music educator*
Newton, Paul George *musician, retired librarian*

Mooresville
Stewart, Patricia Canup *vocal music and performing arts educator*

Raleigh
Aiken, Clayton Holmes *singer*
Brown, Marilyn Shull *music educator*

Thompson Cornwall, Lonieta Aurora *music educator, consultant*

Salisbury
Higbee, Dale (Strohe) *musician, retired psychologist*

Swannanoa
Whittington, Lorin Dale *music educator*

Waynesville
Wise, Timothy Lee *music educator*

Wilmington
Cameron, Kay *conductor, music director, arranger*
Lavin, Linda *actress*

Wingate
Bostic, Polly Thomas *music educator*
Bostic, Ronald David *music educator*

Winston Salem
Chumbley, Robert Edward *performing arts association administrator*
Frazelle, Kenneth *composer, educator*
Lister-Sink, Barabara Ann *musician, education educator*
Mitchener, John Edward *music educator, musician*
Mueller, Margaret S. *musician, educator*
Peeples, Mary Louise *music educator, musician*
Trautwein, George William *conductor, educator*

Youngsville
Riggs, Susan Dunnagan *music educator, musician*

NORTH DAKOTA

Bismarck
Lundberg, Susan Ona *musical organization administrator*
Tornow, L. William *musician*
Wellin, Thomas *music director*

Dickinson
Vranna, Jeffrey *music educator*

Fargo
Olson, Robert Wallace *voice educator*

Grand Forks
Gallo, Sergio Roberto *music educator, researcher*
Popejoy, James Richard *music educator*

Hazen
Harvey, Chris S. *music educator*

OHIO

Ada
Altstaetter, Dean Edward *music educator, musician*
Neeley, Vernon Dean *music educator*

Akron
Slowiak, James *theater director, educator*
Wang, Ya-Hui *conductor*
Weaver, Thomas Jay *music educator*
Wilding, James *music educator, composer*

Alliance
DeStefano, L. Timothy *music educator, conductor*

Athens
Stomberg, Eric W *musician*

Berea
Ginn-Paster, Sophie Lillian *mezzo soprano, educator*

Boardman
Querin, Jeffrey David *theater educator*

Bowling Green
Kuehn, Mikel *composer, music educator*
Wolcott, Nancy Bookout *music director*

Bratenahl
DesRosiers, Anne Booke *performing arts administrator, consultant*

Canton
Honnold, Michael Edward *music educator*
Moorhouse, Linda Virginia *symphony orchestra administrator*

Cedarville
Winteregg, Steven Lee *composer, musician, educator*

Centerville
Wasson-Shaw, Carol R. *music teacher*

Cincinnati
Anderson, Simon V. *music educator*
Beggs, Patricia Kirk *performing company executive*
Bell, David Maxwell *music educator, consultant*
Costigan-Kerns, Louise E. *musician*
Haney, Michael Evan *theater director*
Hills, Alan *performing company executive*
Ingle, Gary L. *performing arts association administrator*
James, Jefferson Ann *performing company executive, choreographer*
Jarvi, Paavo *conductor*
Kalagayan, Jay B. *theater producer, director*
Klingshirn, David *performing arts association administrator*
Kunzel, Erich, Jr., *conductor, arranger, educator*
Milligan, Terence Gilbert *music educator*
Monder, Steven I. *orchestra executive*
Morgan, Victoria *performing company executive, choreographer*
Paavo, Jarvi *conductor*
Tocco, James *pianist*

Cleveland
Adams, H. Leslie *composer*
Erb, Donald *composer*
Lawrence, Estelene Yvonne *musician, transportation executive*

Morris, Thomas William *symphony orchestra administrator*
Nahat, Dennis F. *performing company executive, choreographer*
Spivey, Terrence *performing company executive, educator, actor, theater director, playwright*
Weir, Dame Gillian Constance *concert organist, harpsichordist*
Welser-Möst, Franz *conductor*

Columbus
Allen, Lois Arlene Height (Mrs. James Pierpont Allen) *musician*
Charles, Gerard *performing company executive, choreographer*
Drvota, Mojmir *cinema educator, author*
Harris, Donald *composer*
Hart, Daniel *orchestra executive*
Mollenhauer, Jude *musician, music educator*
Satoh, Yuko *music educator*
Siciliani, Alessandro Domenico *conductor*
Wagner, Robert Walter *photography, cinema and communications educator, media producer, consultant*
Wang, Tianshu *music educator, musician*
Zugger, Thomas W. *music educator, musician*

Creston
Ratica, Eric David *music educator*

Dayton
Hanna, Marsha L. *artistic director*
Walters, Jefferson Brooks *musician, retired real estate broker*
Wasson, Barbara Hickam *music educator*
Wasson, Steven *music educator, piano technician*

Defiance
Wiemken, Patricia E. *music educator, consultant*

Delaware
Jamison, Roger W. *pianist, piano educator*

Dublin
Ma, Hengwei *music educator*

Euclid
Matthews, Eric Joddy *film director*

Fairfield
Tumbleson, Stephan Norman *music educator*

Fairfiled
Flick, Debra Renee *music educator*

Findlay
Hanson, David Alan *music educator*

Grafton
Barber, Clarence E. *music educator*

Hamilton
Glass, Robert Edward *retired music educator*

Hilliard
Griffith, Gail *performing arts educator, actress*
Pyles, Selma Broadway *music educator*

Hiram
Bane, James Wallace *music educator*

Holland
Conlin, Thomas *conductor*

Kent
Kinney, Daryl Wayne *music educator*
Madden, Elisabeth Anne *theater director*

Kirtland
Petrone, John R. *music educator, composer*

Lexington
Maxwell, Mark *music educator*

Mansfield
Sturts, Donna Jean *music educator*

Medina
Liauba, Danute *music educator*

Mount Vernon
Tocheff, Robert Dale *music educator*

New Concord
Schumann, Laura Elaine *conductor*

North Olmsted
Janson, Patrick *singer, actor, conductor, educator*

Oberlin
Kennedy, Laurie Jean *music educator, musician*
Rutstein, Sedmara Zakarian *piano educator, concert pianist*
Sakakeeny II, George J. *music educator, musician*

Oregon
Knorr, John Christian *entertainment executive, bandleader, producer*

Orwell
Carlson, Timothy A. *music educator*

Parma
Laycock, Randolph Philip *music educator, conductor*

Peninsula
Shaw, Doris Beaumar *film and video producer, executive recruiter, management consultant*

Pepper Pike
Snell, James Blaine *music educator*

Pettisville
Beck, Duane J. *choir director*

Pickerington
Parulekar, Marc Samir *music educator*

Roseville
Carney, Karen Rose *music educator, pianist*

Spring Valley
Atkins, Laura Jane *music educator*

Springfield
Chen, Peng Hsin *composer, music educator*
Faber, Trudy *music educator*

Toledo
Bell, Robert *orchestra executive*
Finkbeiner, Carlton S. (Carty Finkbeiner) *radio personality, former mayor*
Girgis-Hanna, Mary Fahim *music educator*

Vandalia
Korte, Genevieve L *music educator*

West Chester
Pease, Stacey Lyn *music educator*

Westerville
Swinehart, Timothy E. *music educator*

Whitehall
Van Camp, Diana J. *music educator*

Whitehouse
Boyle, Daniel Robert *musician, delivery service executive*

Willoughby
Baker, Charles Stephen *music educator*
Elias, Judith Helen *music educator*
Primavera, Fred Joseph *music educator*

Yellow Springs
Rinehart, John McLain *composer, education educator*

Zanesville
Brown, Karen Rima *orchestra manager, Spanish language educator*

OKLAHOMA

Altus
Carson, S. Kirk *music educator*

Anadarko
Kidd, Lovetta Monza *music educator*

Bethany
Ballweg, David Brent *music educator, conductor*
Halpain, Sue R. *music educator, musician*

Choctaw
Howard, David L. *music educator, conductor*

Clinton
Askew, Penny Sue *choreographer, artistic director, ballet instructor*

Durant
Gregg, David Christopher *music educator*

Edmond
Remy-Schumacher, Tess *music educator, musician*

Enid
Record, Donald D. *music educator, literature educator*

Lawton
Ragan, Marilyn Kay *performing arts educator, costume designer*

Mounds
Fellows, Esther Elizabeth *musician, music educator*
Halsey, James Albert *international entertainment impresario, theatrical producer, talent manager*

Muskogee
Ehlers, Deborah Layne *theater director*
Wiles, James Steven *music educator*

Norman
Daniel, Sean *retired voice educator, baritone, artist*
Herstand, Theodore *theatre artist, educator*
Magrath, Jane *music educator*
Matlick, Eldon R. *music educator*
Meiller, James R. *music educator*
Ross, Allan Anderson *music educator, university official*

Oklahoma City
Holeman, Lora White *music educator*
Levine, Joel *music director, conductor*
Moore, Billy Don *video scriptwriter, producer*
Pitts, Bryan *performing company executive*
Thomas, Gary Wayne *actor*

Sapulpa
Weinstock Rad, Katheryn Louise *music educator*

Stillwater
te Velde, Rebecca Groom *organist, music educator, composer*

Tulsa
Angelini, Marcello *artistic director*
Cottingham, Barbara J. *music educator*
Guthrie, Joseph Randall *music educator*
Larkin, Moscelyne *retired artistic director, dancer*
Liggitt, Lonnie Robert *music educator, researcher*
Owens, Jana Jae *entertainer*
Reed, Robert A. *performing arts executive*
Saied, James Guy *conductor, consultant*
Slaucitajs, Andrew Paul *videographer, video producer*
Sowell, Laven *retired music educator*

Vinita
Lollman, Matthew Tobias *music educator*

Weatherford
Strickler, Steve P *theater educator*
Widen, Dennis Charles *music educator*

OREGON

Ashland
Appel, Libby Eve *theater director*

Bend
Gillem, Elise (Elise Michaels) *radio and television personality*
Seed, Brian Bruce *music educator*

Brookings
Shepherd, William Michael *music educator, musician*

Corvallis
Conatser, Brian Keith *music educator, musician*

Eugene
Bailey, Exine Margaret Anderson *soprano, educator*
Bergquist, Peter *music educator emeritus*
Majdic, Michael James *film producer, director*
Vacchi, Steve *music educator*

Fairview
Muller jr., Thomas G *music educator*

Forest Grove
Burch-Pesses, Thomas Michael *music educator*

Medford
Drysdale, John Edwin *retired music educator, performing arts association administrator, director*

Portland
Ainslie, Coln Dayle *retired music educator*
Bailey, Robert C. *opera company executive*
Berentsen, Kurtis George *music educator, choral conductor*
Blumberg, Naomi *symphony musician, educator*
Canfield, James *artistic director*
DePreist, James Anderson *conductor*
Harris, Charles David *music educator*
Hull, Samuel Logan, Jr., *theater educator*
Kleszynski, Kenneth *music educator, conductor*
Love, Edith Holmes *theater producer*
Mittelstaedt, Janet Rugen *music educator, composer*
Ryberg, William A. *orchestra executive*
Stowell, Christopher R. *artistic director, choreographer, retired dancer*
Tolon, Michael Oded *music educator, director*

Salem
Bauer, Richard LeRoy *music educator, musician*

Springfield
Ozab, David *composer, music educator*

PENNSYLVANIA

Allentown
Beltzner, Gail Ann *music educator*
Mealey, Grace Eleanor *music educator*

Annville
Condran, Cynthia Marie *gospel musician*

Beaver Falls
Copeland, Robert Marshall *music educator, department chairman*

Berwyn
Gingles, Marjorie Stanke *music educator*

Bethlehem
Allen, Beatrice *music educator, pianist*

Boswell
Croft, Daniel Thomas *music educator*

Bryn Mawr
Hoaglund, Susan Elizabeth *music educator*
Stucky, Steven (Edward) *composer, conductor*

California
O'Donnell, William W. *theater educator, lighting designer*

Chadds Ford
Swensson, Evelyn Dickenson *conductor, composer, librettist*

Cheyney
Ellis-Scruggs, Jan *theater arts educator*

Clearfield
Mandell, Raymond Andrew *music educator*

Danville
Bower, Jack R. *music educator*

Dingmans Ferry
Bartle, Barrie G. *music educator*

Drexel Hill
Martino, Michael Charles *entertainer, musician, actor*

East Stroudsburg
Miller, Robert W. *music educator, musician*

Easton
DeGrandis, Ronald Wayne *music educator*
Hay, Samuel Arthur *theater educator, playwright*

Elizabethtown
Chambers, David Lee *music educator*
Kitchen, Otis Dorsey *music educator*

Elizabethville
McCartney, Chad Edward *music educator*

Ephrata
Ohlinger, Kristie L *music educator*

Erie
George, Annmarie Irene *music educator*
Myers, Jeffrey Daniel *concert pianist, music educator*

Ford City
Skamai, Robert Walter *music educator*

Fredericksburg
Daubert, Harlan Aaron *music educator, director*

Grove City
Groves, Edgar Stephens *music educator, conductor*

Hatboro
Carroll, Lucy Ellen *choral director, music coordinator, educator*

Horsham
Schopp, David L. *music educator*

Indiana
Horner, Ronald George *music educator, musician*
Jeckavitch, David M. *music educator*
Perlongo, Daniel James *composer, educator*

King Of Prussia
Helmetag, Diana *music educator*

Kingston
Weisberger, Barbara *artistic director, educator, choreographer*

Lancaster
Buchanan, Lovell *entertainer*
Grochowski, Jelsia *music educator*
Heil, Paul Samuel *radio program producer*
Watson, Mark S. *music educator*

Lebanon
Copenhaver, John Edward *music educator*

Malvern
Bedford, Anne Marie *musician, educator, insurance agent*
Prichard, Joyce S. *music educator*

Mansfield
Dettwiler, Peggy Diane *music educator*

Milford Square
Sewell, Gloriana *piano teacher*

Monaca
Soltes, Joann Margaret *retired music educator, realtor*

Monroeville
Read, Robert Allen *music educator*

Mountaintop
Pendziwiatr, William J. *music educator*

Muncy
West, Thomas James *music educator*

New Bethlehem
Reefer, Russell Charles *music educator*

New Hope
Stahl, Stephen Lee *theater director, writer, producer*

New Oxford
Rohrbaugh, Nova R *retired music educator*

New Wilmington
Taylor, Gary B. *music educator*

Newtown
Nowak, Jerry (Gerald C. Nowak) *music educator, musician, writer*
Sheridan, John J. *musician, music educator*

Norristown
Reilley, Gail Goodwin *soprano, music educator, musician*

Oakdale
Humbert, Darren Mark *music educator*

Philadelphia
Blavat, Jerry (Gerald Joseph Blavat) *radio and television personality, actor*
Bookspan, Michael Lloyd *musician*
Colson, Rosemary *music educator*
Cornelius, Jeffrey Michael *music educator*
Crumb, George Henry *composer, educator*
Davis, Paige (Mindy Paige Davis) *television host/personality*
Dileo, Cheryl *music therapist*
Driver, Robert Baylor, Jr., *opera company administrator*
Garonzik, Sara Ellen *stage producer*
Graffman, Gary *pianist, music educator*
Harris, Rennie *choreographer*
Ingolfsson-Fassbind, Ursula G. *music educator*
Kaiser, Roy *artistic director*
Mason, Rodney *performing arts educator*
Mostovoy, Marc Sanders *conductor, music director*
Myers Brown, Joan *dance company executive*
Ross, Darrin *composer*
Sawallisch, Wolfgang *conductor*
Scaglione, Louis, III, *music educator, conductor*
Smith, Lloyd *musician*
Stallman, Robert *concert flutist, recording artist, editor, arranger*

Pittsburgh
Balada, Leonardo *composer, educator*
Bardyguine, Patricia Wilde *ballerina, ballet theatre executive*
Cardenes, Andres Jorge *violinist, music educator*
Desiree, Laura *dancer*
Feindel, Janet Madelle *performing arts educator*
Harth, Sidney *musician, educator*
Hollingsworth, Samuel Hawkins, Jr., *bassist*
Jansons, Mariss *orchestra conductor*
Keeling, Kenneth Augustus, Sr., *music educator*
Kraus, Stephen J. *music educator*
Li, Hanna Wu *music educator*
Li, Ying *dancer*
Neft, Suzi Terry *television producer, marketing, public relations executive, advertising executive*
Orr, Terrence S, *dancer, ballet master, artistic director*
Posvar, Mildred Miller *opera singer*

Taylor, Mark Chandlee *choreographer*
Wehr, David Allen *musician, educator*
Wilde, Patricia *retired artistic director*
Wilson, Wanda Lee Davis *casting director*

Plymouth Meeting
O'Neill, David A *music educator, musician*

Reading
Kremser, Harold L. *music educator*
Scollick, Bryan Robert *music educator, market research consultant*
Zug, Elizabeth E. *concert pianist, educator*

Reedsville
Garner, Douglas *music educator*

Robesonia
Hackett, Sean P. *music educator, conductor*

Scranton
Moyer, James Arthur *music educator, department chairman*

Selinsgrove
Powers, William Douglas *theater director, actor, educator*

State College
Pennock, Elizabeth H. *retired music educator*

Swarthmore
Devin, Lee (Philip Lee Devin) *dramaturg, author*
Freeman, James Douglas *music educator*
Redden, Taylor Tilghman *musician*

University Park
Baisley, Robert William *music educator*
Broyles, Michael E. *music history educator, writer*
Cook, Kim Diane *concert cellist*

Upper Darby
Kahler, Nancy J. *music educator, director*

Walnutport
Fister, Michael J. *music educator*

Warminster
VanBuren, Michael Paul *music educator*

West Chester
Burton, John Bryan *music educator*
Pennington, Robert Edgar *music educator*

West Grove
Allman, William Berthold *musician, engineer, consultant*

Wilkes Barre
Hill, Adam Aloysius *theater educator*

Williamsport
Boone, Daniel Lee *retired music educator*

Yardley
Castellanos, Diego Antonio *television personality*

Youngwood
Duvall, Hollie Jean *music educator*

RHODE ISLAND

Chepachet
Jubinska, Patricia Ann *ballet instructor, choreographer, artist, anthropologist, archaeologist*

Cumberland
Rossi, Joseph Anthony *film and television make-up artist, educator*

East Greenwich
Spivack, Gloria Jean *music educator*

Esmond
Seabra, James Joseph *music educator, professional musician*

Greenville
Hopkins, Catherine Lee *music educator*

Kingston
Ladewig, James L. *music history educator, reseacher*

Lincoln
Enos, David Michael *music educator, coach*
Marsden, Herci Ivana *classical ballet artistic director*

Newport
Malkovich, Mark Paul, III, *musician, artistic director, scientist, sports agent*

Pawtucket
Orson, Barbara Tuschner *actress*

Providence
Barnhill, James Orris *theater educator*
Dempsey, Raymond Leo, Jr., *radio and television producer, moderator, writer*

Warwick
Kiley, Peter Michael *music educator*

SOUTH CAROLINA

Cayce
Tucker, Kelly H. *music educator*

Charleston
Bonds, John Bledsoe *musician, educator*
Cantwell, Don *artistic director*
Edwards, Darrell *orchestra executive*
Rivas, Fernando *composer*

Clinton
Stokes, James Porter, II, *music educator*

Columbia
Bell, Isaac, Jr., *music educator*
Douglas, Samuel Osler *musician, educator*
Jesselson, Robert *musician, educator*
Olenchak, Frank Richard *music educator, musician*
Ruth, Deborah Ann *music educator*
Shearer, Ellen Marie *music educator*
Starrett, William *dancer, artistic director*

Conway
Stegall, Gary Miles *musician, music educator*

Duncan
Clarke, Jean Alderman *orchestra director*

Edisto Island
Van Metre, Margaret Cheryl *artistic director, dance educator*

Elgin
Cochran, Myrtie Winchester *music educator*

Goose Creek
Vogt, Kathleen Cunningham *musician, music educator*

Greenville
Tchivzhel, Edvard *music director*

Hilton Head Island
Brock, Karena Diane *dancer, educator*

Landrum
Bridwell, Barry Dean *music educator, director, musician*

Lexington
Russell, Candace Leigh *musician, educator*

Newberry
McGinnis, Barry Eugene *music educator, musician*
Wagner, John Waldorf *music educator, researcher*

Orangeburg
Dingle, Rosetta *music educator*
Montgomery, Amanda E. *music educator*
Price, Johnnie Ulmer *retired music educator*

Pendleton
Landreth, James Mack *elementary school music educator*

Pickens
White, Leeanne J. *music educator*

Simpsonville
Selvy, Barbara *dance instructor*

Spartanburg
Bolton, Calvin *music educator*
Feinstein, Marion Finke *artistic director, dance instructor*
Law, Kenneth Ray *music educator, dean*
Lucktenberg, Jerrie Cadek *music educator*

Summerville
Capps, Phillip Lewis *music educator*

Taylors
Riddle, Thad (Tad) W., III, *music educator, webmaster*

Travelers Rest
Hall, Gregory Blake *music educator*

Walterboro
Meshach, Joseph Robert *music educator*

SOUTH DAKOTA

Aberdeen
Manhart, Grant Lee *music educator*

Mitchell
Almjeld, Paul F. *conductor, music educator*

Sioux Falls
Haig, Susan *conductor*
McDowell, Robert James *music educator, composer*

Vermillion
Schou, Larry Brian *music educator*

TENNESSEE

Antioch
Ely, Joe *singer, songwriter*

Brentwood
Taylor, Nicole Renée (Niki Taylor) *model*
Tucker, Tanya Denise *singer*

Chattanooga
Bernhardt, Robert *music director, conductor*

Cleveland
Benson, Will E. *music educator*
Manley, Douglas Heath *music educator*

Clinton
Coker, Stephanie Ila *school choir director*

Columbia
Scheusner, Ronald L. *music educator*

Cordova
Griffin, Walton W. *performing company executive*
Pugh, Dorothy Gunther *artistic director*

Dayton
Luther, Sigrid *music educator*

Fairview
Hutchison, Barbara Bailey *singer, songwriter*

Franklin
Bull, Sandy (Alexander Benjamin Bull) *musician, composer*

Greeneville
Cook, Marshall Alan *theater producer, theater director, consultant*

Henderson
Hay, Thomas Franklin *music educator*

Jackson
McRoberts, Terry Allan *music educator*

Johnson City
Jenrette, Thomas Shepard, Jr., *music educator, choral director*
Rice-See, Lynn *music educator*
Sanderbeck, Rande Paul *music educator, musician*
Self, Jimmie Everette *music educator, musician*

Knoxville
Baldwin, Wesley Hale Barrick *music educator*
Chambers, Robert Ben *music educator, conductor*
Jacobs, Kenneth A. *composer, educator*
Speas, Bruce Orburn *theater educator*
Trevor, Kirk David Niell *orchestra conductor, cellist*

Lawrenceburg
Hayes, Sylvia Richmond *music educator*

Lebanon
Daniels, Charlie *musician, songwriter*

Martin
Wade, Reba *music teacher, pianist*

Memphis
Brewer, Jeffery Burt *music educator*
Chester, James A. *music educator*
Ching, James Michael *artistic director opera company, composer, conductor*
Dixon, Samuel B. *retired comedian, film director, film producer*
McRee, Celia *composer, singer, actress, writer, producer*
Piazza, Marguerite *opera singer, actress, entertainer*
Presley, Lisa Marie *musician*
Williams, David Russell *retired music educator*
Yow, Asuka Taga *music educator, researcher*

Morristown
Rowland, Kyla Faye *gospel songwriter*

Nashville
Anderson, Lynn (Rene Anderson) *singer*
Bentley, Dierks *country singer, songwriter*
Brooks, Kix *musician*
Chesney, Kenny *country singer, songwriter*
Clark, Terri *country singer*
Cleveland, Ashley *musician*
Demarcus, Jay (Stanley Demarcus) *country musician, songwriter*
Dunn, Ronnie *musician*
Estrin, Kari (Karen Ruth Estrin) *artist and tour manager, acoustic radio promoter*
Evans, Sara *country singer, songwriter*
Fabian, Jane *former ballet company executive*
Fleck, Bela *country musician*
Grant, Amy *singer, songwriter*
Griffith, Nanci *singer, songwriter*
Harris, Emmylou *singer*
Hill, Faith *musician*
Judd, Naomi *country music entertainer, singer, songwriter, writer*
Kaine, Paul *performing company executive*
Keith, Toby (Toby Keith Covel) *country singer, songwriter, producer*
Krauss, Alison *country musician*
Lawrence, Tracey *country singer, songwriter*
Lee, Douglas A. *music educator*
Levox, Gary (Gary Wayne Vernon Jr.) *country/rock singer*
Loyd, Stan *music specialist*
Lynn, Loretta Webb (Mrs. Oliver Lynn Jr.) *singer*
Maguire, Martha Elenor Erwin (Martie Maguire) *musician*
Maines, Natalie Louise *musician*
Mandrell, Barbara Ann *singer, entertainer, actress, producer, writer*
McBride, Martina *vocalist*
McDonald, Reginald Adrian *musician, educator*
Penterman, Carol A. *opera company executive*
Richey, Kimberly Kay *singer, actress, composer*
Robison, Emily Burns *musician*
Rooney, Joe Don *country musician*
Schermerhorn, Kenneth *music director*
Twain, Shania (Eilleen Regina Edwards) *country musician*
Urban, Keith *country singer, songwriter*
Valentine, Alan Darrell *symphony orchestra executive*
Vasterling, Paul *artistic director*
Watkins, Sara *musician*

Oak Ridge
van Tol, Jenifer *music educator, musician*

Pigeon Forge
Parton, Dolly Rebecca *singer, composer, actress*

Sevierville
Hicks, Deborah *music educator*

TEXAS

Abilene
Puckett, Lauren Joy *music educator*
Tolosa, Gustavo Alberto *music educator*

Alice
Taylor, Bryce B *music educator, consultant*

Amarillo
Busch, Mildred Moorman *music educator*
Laur, Noel Paul Douglas *music educator*
Rauscher, James Francis *music educator*

Arlington
Carey, Milburn Ernest *musician, educator*

PROFESSIONAL INDEX 5525 ARTS: PERFORMING

Forbes, Catherine Ann *music educator, musician*
Lau, Irene B. *music educator*
Thomas, Lois C. *musician, educator, religious organization administrator*

Aubrey
Pizzamiglio, Albert Theodore (Al Pierson) *conductor*

Austin
Antokoletz, Elliott Maxim *music educator*
Aubery, Stephen Royston Edmund *film producer*
Brockett, Oscar Gross *theater educator*
Douglas, Lucien Zabielski *performing arts educator, theater director*
Douglas, Susan Hickok *music educator*
Gimble, Johnny *country musician*
Hancock, Gerre Edward *musician, educator*
Henley, Paul Thomas *music educator, researcher*
Hinojosa, Tish (Leticia Hinojosa) *vocalist*
Holtzman, Joan King *musician, composer*
Kennan, Kent Wheeler *composer, educator*
Linklater, Richard *film director, actor, screenwriter*
Mills, Stephen *artistic director*
Mueller, Peggy Jean *dance educator, choreographer, rancher*
Robbins, Mary *concert pianist*
Ruiz, Cookie *performing company executive*
Scott, Laurie P. *music educator*
Slavin, Alexandra Nadal *artistic director, educator*

Beaumont
Brailsford, June Evelyn *musician, educator*

Beeville
Switzer, Linda Thrall *music educator*

Belton
Wood, Connie Garrison *music educator*

Borger
Strecker, Judy Ellen *music educator*

Brownwood
Banks, Patricia Anne *music educator, minister*

Canyon
Sheffield, Jovonna Michele *music educator*

Carthage
Brumley, Larry Gene *music educator*

College Station
Sikes, Paul Leon *music educator*

Commerce
Chang, Fenia I-fen *music educator, pianist*

Conroe
Harrison, Paula Jean *music educator*

Corpus Christi
Allison, Joan Kelly *music educator, pianist*
Fregoso, Marco Antonio *advertising producer, director*
Wojcik, John Casimir *music educator, director*

Dallas
Atkinson, Bill *artistic director*
Bronstein, Fred *orchestra executive*
Clinkscale, Martha *music educator, researcher*
Etgen, Ann *ballet educator, artistic director, choreographer*
Johnson, Mary Elizabeth *music educator, pianist*
Karayanis, Plato Steven *opera company executive*
Litton, Andrew *musical director*
Palmer, Christine (Clelia Rose Venditti) *operatic singer, pianist, vocal educator*
Pell, Jonathan Laurence *artistic administrator*
Stone, Karen *theater director*
Thomas, Paul Lindsley *composer, organist, music director*
Turocy, Catherine *performing company executive*

Deer Park
Wester, R. Glen *music educator, director*

Denton
Cooper, John Michael *music educator*
McTee, Cindy *classical musician, educator*
Nestler, Eric M. *music educator*

Edinburg
Grossman, Morley Keith *music educator*

El Paso
Harrison, Armin Otmar *music educator*

Farmers Branch
Walsh, Elizabeth Jameson *musician*

Fort Worth
Cliburn, Van (Harvey Lavan Cliburn Jr.) *concert pianist*
Dressler, Oscar H. *music educator*
Faherty, David Miles *musical instrument repairman*
Galaganov, Misha *music educator*
Harth-Bedoya, Miguel *conductor*
Hill, John David *television producer*
Lipkin, Seymour *pianist, conductor, educator*
Mallette, David *performing company executive*
Patteson, Charles Lynn *musician, retired music educator*
Raessler, Kenneth Ray *music educator*
Stevenson, Ben *artistic director*
Yacante, Maria Lucy *music educator, researcher*

Frisco
de Veritch, Nina *cellist, music educator*

Fulshear
Grantham, Nan L. *music educator, writer*

Georgetown
Teat, Herbert Leroy *retired music educator*

Houston
Auchter, Norma Holmes *musician, music educator*
Baranovich, Diana Lea *music educator*
Brosh, Rita *performing company executive*
Brown, Glenda Ann Walters *ballet director*
Clark, Ron D(ean) *cosmetologist*
Conner, Cecil C., Jr., *performing company executive*
Douglas, P.C. *producer, director, reporter, editor*
Englesmith, Tejas *actor, producer, curator*
Girouard, Peggy Jo Fulcher *ballet educator*
Gockley, David (Richard David Gockley) *opera director*
Graf, Hans *conductor*
Hazelip, Linda Ann *musician, small business owner, executive assistant*
Jackson, Donna Ann *musician, piano instructor*
Jones, Florence M. *music educator*
Krajewski, Michael *conductor*
Palmer, Willard Aldrich, III, *magician, writer, actor*
Rose, Beatrice Schroeder (Mrs. William H. Rose) *harpist, educator*
Singleton, Robert M. *theater educator, secondary school educator*
Sugars, Janeal M. *opera singer, vocal educator*
Talbert, Arthur Thomas *music educator*
Welch, Stanton *performing company executive*

Huntsville
Plugge, Scott Douglas *music educator, saxophonist*
Russell, George Haw *video production company executive*

Keene
Doroftei, Mugur Gideon *music educator, conductor, composer, musician*

Killeen
Bryan, Arthur Lee *music educator*

Kingwood
Hagen, Barbara C. *music educator*

Laredo
Crabtree, Joseph Craig *voice educator, vocalist*
Stone, Michael John *music educator, conductor*

Lewisville
Mebane, Barbara Margot *artistic director, choreographer*

Longview
Haymes, Jerry Lynn *entertainment industry executive*

Lorena
Maricle, Robyn LuAnn (Ford) *band director, choir director*

Lubbock
Aker, Suzanne Deverse *physical movement educator*
Arnold, Sue *music educator*
Chung, Ya-Li *music educator*
Lucas, Don John *music educator*
van Appledorn, Mary Jeanne *composer, music educator, pianist*

Marshall
Tapp, Paul Wayne *music educator*

Meadowlakes
Wilcox, Mary Reba *music educator*

Mesquite
Nye, Randall Wayne *music educator*

Midland
Celia, George *composer, writer*

Mineral Wells
Warfield, Gerald Alexander *composer, writer*

Nacogdoches
Dean, Michael *conductor, church music minister*
Jacobsen, Jeffrey Richard *music educator*

Olton
Carson, Harold Dean *music educator, composer*

Pampa
Cooley, Loralee Coleman *professional storyteller*
Willingham, Jeanne Maggart *dance educator, ballet company executive*

Pasadena
Gilley, Mickey Leroy *musician*

Plainview
Kelley, Timothy Shawn *music educator*

Plano
Cronauer, Gail Ann *theater educator, actress*

Rockwall
Wallace, Mary Elaine *opera director, author*

San Angelo
Curtin, David *music educator*

San Antonio
Balentine, James Scott *music educator, composer*
Hornsby, David McMillan *musician, music educator*
Jiménez, Leonardo *popular accordionist*
Massengale, Hope Vega *music educator*
Murphy, Cathy *music educator*
Oppenheim, Martha Kunkel *pianist, educator*
Peters, Richard Spencer *musician*
Robertson, Sterling Clifton *music educator, pianist*
Wilkins, Christopher Putnam *conductor*

San Marcos
Laumer, Jack C. *musician, educator*
Oxford, William Todd *music educator*
Schmidt, John Charles *music educator*

Sugar Land
Victor, Ann Michele *musician, educator*

The Woodlands
Crain, Richard Charles *school district music director, retired*

Tyler
Baker, Rebecca Louise *musician, music educator, consultant*
Cooper, Kelli D. *music educator*
Oxler, Cora Jean *voice educator*
Rogers, Cheryl Lynn *music and dance educator*
Rumbley, Philip Lee *music educator, musician, photographer*

Waco
Abbott-Kirk, Jane *music educator*
Colvin, Herbert, Jr., (Otis Herbert Colvin) *musician, educator*
Jones, (Anita) Joyce *musician, composer, music educator*
Ullman, Beth Robin *vocalist, voice educator*

Wharton
George, Lila Gene Plowe Kennedy *music educator*

Wichita Falls
Cook, Marcella Kay *retired theater educator*
Schaffer, Candler Gareld *conductor, hornist, educator*

UTAH

Cedar City
Modesitt, Carol Ann *music, voice educator, opera director*

Draper
Thacker, Catherine A. *music educator*

Ogden
Van Mason, Raymond *dancer, choreographer*

Orem
Riley, Dyanne *music professor*

Provo
Asplund, Christian Thomas *music educator, composer*
Brown, Shauna Kirsti *music educator, researcher, composer*
Powley, Edward Harrison, III, *musicology educator*

Salt Lake City
Chuaqui, Miguel Basim *composer, educator*
Conner, Heather J. *music educator*
Ewers, Anne *opera company director*
Lu, Ning *music educator*
Morey, Charles Leonard, III, *theatrical director*
Roens, Steven Thomas *music educator, dean*
St. John, Katherine Iva *artistic director, dance educator*

Sundance
Grant, Raymond Thomas *arts administrator*

Woods Cross
Blackley, Cheryl Ann *freelance/self-employed music educator, musician*
Hendriksen, Neil Evan *music educator*

VERMONT

Brattleboro
Brofsky, Howard *musician, music educator*

Burlington
Read, Thomas Lawrence *music educator, composer*
Tamarkin, Kate *conductor*
Toner, Donald Thomas *music educator*

Johnson
Whitehill, Angela Elizabeth *artistic director*

Lyndonville
Dodson, Daryl Theodore *ballet administrator, arts consultant*

Marlboro
Brelsford, Edmund Munger, III, *musician, educator*

Norwich
Stetson, Eugene William, III, *film producer*

Tunbridge
Stewart, Donald George *musician, composer, music industry executive*

Weston
Stettler, Stephen F. *performing company executive*

VIRGINIA

Alexandria
Eluhow, Ljiljana Skoric *musician, educator*
Hary, Douglas Alan *actor, educator*
Mishra, Sanjay *music educator*

Annandale
Hudson, William L. *conductor*

Arlington
Mc Donald, Gail Faber *musician, educator*
Orkis, Lambert *musician, music educator*
Southern, Hugh *retired performing arts manager*

Blacksburg
Leonard, Robert Haigh *theater educator, stage director*

Centreville
Kim-Yi, Sungsook *music educator, pianist*

Charlottesville
Bishop, Ruth Ann *coloratura soprano, voice educator*
Chapel, Robert Clyde *stage director, theater educator*

Chesapeake
Dixon, Timothy Kaine *music educator*
Lambert, H. Scott *music educator*
Scarangella, Jessica Ruthanne *music educator*

Chester
Gray, Frederick Thomas, Jr., ('Rick Gray) *actor, educator, playwright*

Fairfax
Mann, Laura Ann *soprano*
Miller, Patricia A. *music educator, opera and concert artist*
Wenner, Debby Linn *music educator, mezzo soprano*

Farmville
Kinzer, Charles Edward *music educator*

Gloucester Point
Sandridge, Donald Otis *music educator*

Hampton
Harris, Carl G. *music educator*
Rummel, Andrew Thomas *music educator, musician*

Harrisonburg
Arthur, Thomas Hahn *theater educator, director*
Kluesner, James Francis *musician, educator*
Reid, Susan L. *conductor*

Herndon
Walker, Lawrence Howard, Jr., *music educator, department chairman*

Leesburg
Mahood, Ken *music educator*

Lexington
Myers, Gerald C. *music educator*
Young, Bruce Kenneth *film director*

Lynchburg
Marra, Anthony Tullio *audio visual specialist*

Mc Lean
Skantze, Pat *model, consultant*

Newport News
Breese, Steven *theater director, actor, director, playwright*
Lenwell, John D. *music educator*

Norfolk
Kasparov, Andrey Rafailovich *composer, pianist, conductor, educator*
Mark, Peter *director, conductor*
Musgrave, Thea *composer, conductor*
Nixon, Patricia Saunders *music educator, performer*
Sanders, Stephanie Kenyatta *music educator*

Oak Hill
Ritter, Elza K. *music educator*

Oakton
Drummond, Carol Cramer *voice educator, singer, artist, writer*

Purcellville
Reaves, Richard Bruce *music educator*

Radford
James, Clarity (Carolyne Faye James) *mezzo-soprano*

Reston
Cravey, Clara *dancer, performing arts association administrator*
Hepworth-Woolston, Connie Jo *choreographer*
Wawrejko Cochran, Diane *performing arts association administrator*

Richmond
Barnes, Milton Millard *musician*
Campbell, Neal Franklin *music educator*
Carlton, Buzz (Clyde Gordon Carlton Jr.) *singer, songwriter, entertainer, recording artist*
Clatterbuck, John David *music educator*
Lohuis, Ardyth June *musician, educator*
Sennett, David *theater educator, actor*
Winslett, Stoner *artistic director*

Salem
Sandborg, Marianne M. *voice educator, musician*

Spotsylvania
Hoovler, Christopher Paul *music educator*

Staunton
Balsley, Philip Elwood *entertainer*

Sterling
Jefferson, Sandra Traylor *choreographer*
Lacey, Aaron Michael *actor, director, screenwriter, executive producer*

Vienna
Kinsolving, Sylvia Crockett *musician, educator*

Virginia Beach
Cehelska, Olga M. *music educator, flight instructor*
Panoff, Stephen Edward *music educator*
Prescott, David L. C., Jr., *music educator*
Price, Celes E. *retired music educator*
Smead, Kenneth William *music educator*

Williamsburg
Hornsby, Bruce Randall *composer, musician*

WASHINGTON

Bellevue
Rundell, Arden Grabke *musician*

Bellingham
Terey-Smith, Mary *music educator, conductor*
Whyte, Nancy Marie *performing arts educator*

Clarkston
Torgerson, Linda Belle *music educator*

College Place
Mariani, Evelyn Julia *music educator*

Coupeville
Lotzenhiser, George William *music educator, university administrator, composer*

Endicott
Ray, Billy John, Jr., *music educator*

Everett
Rimbach, Evangeline Lois *retired music educator*

Lacey
Louis, Glenn *music educator*

Longview
Correll, Donald Albert *theater educator*

North Bend
Brumbaugh, Harley Aaron *retired music educator, conductor, composer, poet*
Pope, Frances Elaine *music educator*

Olympia
Macduff, Ilone Margaret *music educator*

Othello
Bowerly, Daniel Kent *music educator, musician*

Port Angeles
Grier, George Edward *music educator, musician*

Portland
Webster, Gerald Best *musician, music educator*

Pullman
Yasinitsky, Gregory Walter *music educator*

Richland
Powell, David Charles *music educator, meteorologist*

Seattle
Anang, Amma Cecilia *dance company administrator*
Beale, Jane Guthrie *music publisher, music educator, pianist*
Card, Deborah Frances *orchestra administrator*
Collier, Tom Ward *musician, educator*
Dally, Lynn *choreographer, performing company executive, educator*
Denke, Conrad William *motion picture producer*
Elyn, Mark *retired opera singer, educator*
Forbes, David Craig *musician*
Jenkins, Speight *opera company executive, writer*
Jones, Samuel Leander *conductor*
Mahdaviani, Miriam *choreographer, educator*
Matesky, Nancy Lee *music educator*
Moore, Benjamin *theatrical producer*
Mull, Robert W. *filmmaker, curator*
Ott, Sharon *artistic director*
Ozaki, Nancy Junko *performance artist, performing arts educator*
Patrick, Julian Earnest *vocalist*
Russell, Francia *ballet director, educator*
Ryder, Hal *theater educator, director*
Staryk, Steven Sam *violinist, concertmaster, educator*
Stowell, Kent *ballet director*
Talachian, Reza *filmmaker*
Talvi, Ilkka Ilari *violinist*
Thomas, Karen P. *composer, conductor*
Van Lierop, John Henry, Jr., *music educator*

Silverdale
Raum, Mary Beth *ballet educator*

Snohomish
Philpott, Larry La Fayette *horn player*

Spokane
Baker, Sylvia Halldorson *music educator*
Fowler, Betty Janmae *dance company director, editor*
Gunning, Patricia Ann *music educator*
Halvorson, Marjory *opera educator*
Phillips, John Grant (Jack Phillips) *theatre director*

Tacoma
Gorbman, Claudia L. *performing arts educator, researcher*

Washougal
Harness, William Edward *tenor*

Woodinville
Sanders, Richard Kinard *actor*

WEST VIRGINIA

Athens
Westbrook, Gary Wayne *music educator, consultant*

Buckhannon
Wright, David Andrew *music educator*

Charles Town
Jones, Jay *television producer, television director, educator*

Charleston
Brightbill, Janet M. *music educator*
Cooper, Grant *composer, conductor, music educator*
Helfrich, Paul A. *orchestra executive*

Craigsville
James, Gregory Clark *music educator*

Huntington
Saunders, Martin Wesley *music educator*

Inwood
Rizzetta, Carolyn Teresa *musical instrument, sound recording entrepreneur*

Mannington
Reese, Katherine Rose *music educator*

Morgantown
Brosky, John Michael *music educator, director*
Kinsey, Donna Lee *music educator*
Lee, Keith D. *music educator*
Wilson, Mary Alice *violinist, music teacher*

Parkersburg
Gunter, Norma *artistic director*

Young III, Harmon Griffith *music educator*

Salem
Raad, Virginia *pianist, lecturer*

Shenandoah Junction
Showen Jr., Donald Eugene *music educator*

Wellsburg
Turner, Timothy Thomas *music educator, musician*

WISCONSIN

Cameron
Joosten, Michael John *music educator*

Delavan
Lepke, Charma Davies *musician, educator*

Dodgeville
Dentinger, Ronald Lee *comedian, speaker, freelance writer*

Dunbar
Habing, Brett William *music educator*

Eau Claire
Klopfenstein-Fletcher, Kristine Sue *music educator, librarian, bassoonist*
Patterson, Donald Lee *music educator*
Yasuda, Nobuyoshi *music educator*

Elkhart Lake
Schmidt, Lewis A. *retired music educator*

Fall River
Barker, David Matthew *music educator*

Green Bay
Balsley, Robert Lown *musician, writer*

Greenfield
McKillip, Patricia Claire *operatic soloist*

Hartford
Vandermeuse, David C. *music educator*

Horicon
Gasner, Donn Allan *music educator*

La Crosse
Grill, Joyce L. *musician, educator, composer*

Madison
Bartley, Linda L. *musician, music educator*
De Main, John *orchestra musical director*
Faulkner, Julia Ellen *opera singer*
Furumoto, David John *theater educator*
Mackie, Richard H. *orchestra executive*
Rosser, Annetta Hamilton *composer*

Marinette
Malmstadt, Mary Jane *music educator*

Menomonee Falls
Chicorel, Ralph *composer, lyricist, playwright*

Middleton
Semmes, Sally Peterson *choreographer, educator, performer*

Milwaukee
Blau, Richard Miles (Dick Blau) *performing arts educator, photographer, film director*
Cheatham, Wallace McClain *music educator*
Crocker, Ray Dean *musician, musical director*
Delfs, Andreas *conductor, musical director*
Downey, John Wilham *composer, pianist, conductor, educator*
Harris, Christine *dance company executive*
Heinrichs, William C. *music educator, composer*
Ovitsky, Steven Alan *musician, symphony orchestra executive*
Pink, Michael *performing company executive*
Samson, Richard Max *theater director, investment company executive*
Uecker, Bob *actor, radio announcer, former baseball player, television personality*

Neenah
Orm, Sally S. *music educator, consultant*

Onalaska
Reedy, David H. *music educator, musician*

Racine
Schoening, Ruth Irene *retired music educator, musician*

Reedsburg
Miotke, David Roy *music educator*

River Falls
Hedahl, Gorden Orlin *theatre educator, university dean*

Rudolph
Heywood, Gail Anne *music educator, musician*

Spooner
Cosmano, Vincent James *retired music educator*

Stevens Point
Holland, Patricia Christine *music educator, musician*
Teeple, Scott D. *conductor, music educator, director*

Washington Island
Schweikert, Norman Carl *retired musician*

Waukesha
Demerath, Julie Ellen *music educator*

Whitewater
Joseph, Stacey Ann McGraw *music educator, church choir director*
Tuinstra, John S. *music educator, consultant*

WYOMING

Casper
Empey, Thomas Henry *theater educator*
Unruh, Eric W. *music educator, academic administrator*

Dubois
Glasser, Pamela Jean *musician, music educator*

Sheridan
van Houten, Janet E. *music educator*
Cardarelli, Dr Diane *music educator, conductor*
Damjanovich, Chaslav M. (Casey Diamond) *filmmaker, television producer, writer*
Kaplan, James *composer*
Lowe, Vevlyn Parks *music educator*

TERRITORIES OF THE UNITED STATES

PUERTO RICO

Bayamon
Ortiz, William *composer, music educator*

San Juan
Guilermo, Figueroa *conductor*
San Miguel, Lolita *artistic director*

CANADA

ALBERTA

Calgary
Monk, Allan James *baritone*
Raeburn, Andrew Harvey *performing arts association executive, record producer*

BRITISH COLUMBIA

Vancouver
Jones, Norah *vocalist, musician*
Lavigne, Avril *singer*
Murray, Anne *singer*

Victoria
Turner, Robert Comrie *composer*

MANITOBA

Winnipeg
Birtwhistle, Tara *dancer*
Chang, Johnny W. *dancer*
Corrales, Jesús *dancer*
Lewis, André Leon *artistic director*
Reyes, Reyneris *dancer*
Vargas, Arionel P. *dancer*

ONTARIO

Kitchener
Coles, Graham *conductor, composer*
Eldred, Gerald Marcus *retired performing arts association executive*

London
Brian, Jackson *artistic director*
William, David *director, actor*

Mississauga
Peterson, Oscar Emmanuel *pianist*

Ottawa
Gillingham, Bryan Reginald *music educator*

Toronto
Antonijevic, Aleksandar *dancer*
Beckwith, John *musician, composer, educator*
Bertram, Victoria Elaine *dancer*
Boorne, Ryan *ballet dancer*
Bradshaw, Richard James *performing company executive*
Colgrass, Michael Charles *composer*
Egoyan, Atom *film director*
Eklof, Svea Christine *ballet dancer*
Freedman, Harry *composer*
Goh, Chan Hon *ballerina*
Hodgkinson, Greta *dancer*
Hon Goh, Chan *dancer*
Israelievitch, Jacques H. *violinist, conductor*
Kudelka, James *choreographer, artistic director*
Marrié, William *dancer*
Nan Yu, Xiao *dancer*
Oundjian, Peter *conductor*
Rasky, Harry *producer, director, writer*
Rodriguez, Sonia *dancer*
Schramek, Tomas *ballet dancer, educator*
Shearing, George Albert *pianist, composer*
Shirley, George Irving *tenor*
Sirman, Robert *performing company executive*
Staines, Mavis Avril *artistic director, ballet principal*
Van Der Wyst, Geon *dancer*
Yu, Xiao Nan *dancer*

QUEBEC

Montreal
Bissonnette, Anik *dancer*
Girard, Francois *film director*
Guérard, Geneviève *dancer*
Gulkin, Harry *arts administrator, film producer*
Lacombe, Jacques *conductor, music educator*
Lagacé, Bernard *performing company executive*
Pankov, Gradimir Krunislav *ballet artistic director*
Radacovský, Mário *dancer*

Calgary
Grand-Maitre, Jean *performing company executive*

Montreal
Labadie, Bernard *performing company executive*
Lock, Edouard *performing company executive*

MEXICO

Mexico City
Soberon Kuri, Alejandro *performing company executive*

AUSTRALIA

Darlinghurst
Davis, Judy *actress*

Perth
Dow, Simon *artistic director, coreographer*

Redfern
Campion, Jane *director, screenwriter*

AUSTRIA

Portland
Kalmar, Carlos *music director*

COSTA RICA

San José
Hoffman, Irwin *orchestra conductor*

DENMARK

Copenhagen
Martin, Vivian *soprano*

Holstebro
Schaufuss, Peter *dancer, producer, choreographer, ballet director*

ENGLAND

Askett
Irons, Jeremy John *actor*

Cambridge
Hogwood, Christopher Jarvis Haley *music educator*

Charlbury
Belkin, Boris David *violinist*

East Sussex
Katin, Peter Roy *pianist*

Isle of Wight
Stigwood, Robert Colin *theater, movie, television and record producer*

Leeds
Ichino, Yoko *ballet dancer*
Nixon, David *dancer*

London
Alexeev, Dmitri Konstantinovich *pianist*
Andsnes, Leif Ove *concert pianist*
Arman Gelenbe, Deniz *concert pianist*
Ashkenazy, Vladimir Davidovich *concert pianist, conductor*
Bertolucci, Bernardo *film director*
Bevan, Tim *film producer*
Bloom, Orlando *actor*
Bono, (Paul Hewson) *singer, songwriter*
Bourne, Matthew *performing company executive, artistic director*
Clay, Clifton Ford *motion picture producer, writer*
Codron, Michael Victor *theatrical producer*
Conti, Tom *actor, writer, director*
Day-Lewis, Daniel Michael Blake *actor*
Dohnányi, Christoph von *musician, conductor*
Duncan, Lindsay Vere *actress*
Fellner, Eric *film producer*
Flor, Claus Peter *conductor*
Fox, James *actor*
Gervais, Ricky *actor*
Harney, Kathryn Ann *opera singer*
John, Sir Elton Hercules (Reginald Kenneth Dwight) *musician*
Leigh, Mike *film director*
Levi, Yoel *orchestra conductor*
Mackerras, Sir Charles (Alan Maclaurin) *conductor*
Mackintosh, Cameron *musical theater producer*
Masur, Kurt *conductor*
McCowen, Alec *actor*
McGregor, Ewan Gordon *actor*
Mendes, Sam (Samuel Alexander Mendes) *film director, theater director*
Miller, Jonathan Wolfe *theater and film director, physician*
Minton, Yvonne Fay *mezzo-soprano*
Moody, Ron *actor, writer*
Moss, Kate *model*
Newell, Mike *film director*
Palin, Michael Edward *actor, screenwriter, writer*
Plowright, Joan Anne *actress*
Pryce, Jonathan *actor*
Radcliffe, Daniel *actor*
Ricci, Ruggiero *violinist, educator*
Rice, Sir Timothy Miles Bindon *lyricist*
Richardson, Ian William *actor*
Richardson, Miranda *actress*
Shankar, Ravi *musician, sitar player, composer*
Slatkin, Leonard Edward *conductor, music director, pianist*
Spillane, Mary Catherine *television producer*
Uchida, Mitsuko *pianist*
Winner, Michael Robert *film director, writer, producer*

Manchester
Wilson, Keith Dudley *media and music educator, consultant, dean*

North Wales
Hands, Terence David (Terry Hands) *theater and opera director*

Norwich
Aston, Peter George *music educator, composer, conductor*

Richmond
Te Kanawa, Kiri *opera and concert singer*

Saint Margaret's
Attenborough, Baron Richard Samuel *actor, producer, director, goodwill ambassador*

Warwickshire
Warbeck, Stephen *composer*

Wiltshire
Gabriel, Peter *vocalist, composer*

FRANCE

Collonges
Morgenstern, Sheldon Jon *symphony orchestra conductor*

Lyon
Robertson, David *conductor*

Paris
Annaud, Jean-Jacques *film director, screenwriter, producer*
Christensen, Helena *model*
de Havilland, Olivia Mary *actress*
Deneuve, Catherine (Catherine Dorleac) *actress*
Jolas, Betsy *composer, educator*
Kurtz, Eugene Allen *composer, educator, consultant*
Raimondi, Ruggero *opera singer*

GERMANY

Berlin
Saraste, Jukka-Pekka *conductor*

Dresden
Haitink, Bernard J. H. *conductor*
Schreier, Peter *tenor*

Hamburg
Neumeier, John *choreographer, ballet company director*

Hannover
Schnaus, Peter *musical history educator*

Luebeck
Pagels, Jürgen Heinrich *balletmaster, dance educator, dancer, choreographer, writer*

Munich
Araiza, Francisco (José Francisco Araiza Andrade) *opera singer*

Radevormwald
Sergi, Arturo *tenor, music educator, academic administrator*

Stuttgart
Anderson, Reid Bryce *performing company executive*

IRELAND

Dublin
Farrell, Colin James *actor*
Sheridan, Jim *director, screenwriter*

Galway
Hynes, Garry *theatre director*
Mullen, Marie *actress*

ITALY

Pesaro
Surian, Elvidio *music educator*

Rome
Piovani, Nicola *composer*

JAPAN

Tokyo
Ozawa, Seiji *conductor, music director*

LATVIA

Riga
Strautins, Vilnis *flute educator, past symphony orchestra executive*

MONACO

Monte Carlo
Marton, Eva *opera singer*

NEW ZEALAND

Wellington
Paquin, Anna *actress*

Wellington
Judd, James *conductor, music director*

REPUBLIC OF KOREA

Seoul
Han, Oksoo *pianist, music educator*

RUSSIA

Moscow
Kogan, Pavel *conductor*

SCOTLAND

Edinburgh
McMaster, Brian John *artistic director*

SPAIN

Barcelona
de Larrocha, Alicia *concert pianist*

Madrid
Almodovar, Pedro *filmmaker*
Frühbeck de Burgos, Rafael *conductor*

SWEDEN

Lund
Janacek, Bedrich *organist*

Stockholm
Soederstrom, Elisabeth Anna *opera singer*

SWITZERLAND

Geneva
Barenboim, Daniel *conductor, pianist*

ADDRESS UNPUBLISHED

Aberlin, Betty Kay *actress*
Abernathy, Corbin Brett *music educator, theater educator*
Adams, Hilary Shiels *theater director*
Adams, Mason *actor*
Adler, Samuel Hans *retired conductor, composer*
Aghdashloo, Shohreh *actress*
Alda, Alan *actor, writer, director*
Aleandri, Emelise Francesca *producer, director, television personality, actress*
Aliga, Olivia R. *music teacher, choral director*
Allard, Michael Alan *music educator, conductor*
Allen, Joseph T. *musician, educator*
Allen, Marilyn Myers Pool *theater director, video producer*
Allen, Woody (Allen Stewart Konigsberg) *director, actor, writer*
Alley, Kirstie *actress*
Allison, Glorietta Travis *vocal educator, soprano*
Alonso-Crespo, Eduardo *composer, conductor*
Alvare, Charles Daguerre *television producer*
Anderson, Jerry Lee *pianist, music educator*
Anderson, PT (Paul Thomas IV) *film director*
Andreu, Helene C. *dancer, educator*
Andrews, Dame Julie (Julia Elizabeth Wells) *actress, singer*
Andujar, Antonia *performing company executive*
Antioco, John F. *entertainment company executive*
Applegate, Christina *actress*
Apted, Michael David *film director*
Arenal, Julie (Mrs. Barry Primus) *choreographer*
Aron, Judy *music educator, composer*
Aronson, Luann Marie *actress*
Arthur, Beatrice *actress*
Arvold, David Allen *music educator*
Atherton, William *actor*
Auberjonois, René Murat *actor*
Avian, Bob *choreographer, producer*
Bach, Jan Morris *composer, educator*
Bacharach, Burt *composer, conductor*
Baerwald, Susan Grad *television broadcasting company executive producer*
Baksa, Robert Frank *composer*
Ball, Marcia *vocalist*
Ballard, Kelly Elizabeth *music educator*
Balser, Robert Edward *animation film producer, director*
Bank, Marji D. *actress*
Baranski, Christine *actress*
Barbera, Joseph *motion picture and television producer, cartoonist*
Barnett, Peggy G. *music educator*
Barranger, Milly Slater *theater educator, writer*
Barry, Miranda Robbins *internet and television producer, writer, educator*
Barrymore, Drew *actress*
Bassett, Leslie Raymond *composer, educator*
Bateman, Charles Gregory *music educator*
Baxter, Elizabeth Palm *music educator*
Becker, Wendy Jeanne *music and drama educator, songwriter, singer*
Behlmer, Rudy H., Jr., *director, writer, film educator, scriptwriter*
Belafonte, Harry (Harry George Belafonte Jr.) *singer, concert artist, actor*
Belin, Frances *music educator*
Beloff, Zoe *filmmaker, educator, photographer*
Bencini, Sara Haltiwanger *concert pianist*
Benner, Charles Henry *retired music educator*
Bennett, Sharon Kay *music educator*
Bennett, Thomas *orchestra executive*
Bennici, Antonino C. *music educator*
Beresford, Bruce *film director*
Berezin, Tanya *acting coach, educator, actress*
Bergen, Candice *actress, writer, photojournalist*
Bergeron, Earleen Fournet *actress*
Berlind, Roger Stuart *stage and film producer*
Berlinger, Warren *actor*
Berman, Sanford Solomon *motion picture sound designer, composer, arranger, artist*
Berman, Shari Springer *film director, scriptwriter*
Bethke, Louise Virginia *music educator, writer*
Birch, Patricia *choreographer, director*
Bissell, James Dougal, III, *motion picture production designer*
Biziou, Peter *cinematographer*
Bjerknes, Michael Leif *dancer*
Blanco, Laura *film producer*
Bloom, Frances Virginia *retired music educator*
Bloomquist, Kenneth Gene *music educator, university bands director*
Blossom, Beverly *choreographer, dance educator*
Boardman, Eunice *retired music educator*
Bobel, Mary *video development company financial executive*
Bock, Jerry (Jerrold Lewis) *composer*
Boe, David Stephen *musician, educator, dean*
Bohland, Eugene R., Jr., *music educator*
Bohn, James Matthew *video editor, educator*
Bohoskey, Bernice Fleming *actress, dancer, model*
Bond, Victoria Ellen *conductor, composer*
Bonfils, Darcy Reyne *television producer*
Bon Jovi, Jon (John Francis Bongiovi Jr.) *musician, actor*
Bonnard, Raymond *theater director*
Borgnine, Ernest *actor*
Bosco, Philip Michael *actor*
Boulez, Pierre *composer, conductor*
Brady, Donna Elizabeth *performing arts company executive*
Branagh, Kenneth *actor, director*
Brandon, Liane *filmmaker, educator*
Brewer, Wesley Douglas *music educator*
Bridges, John Robin *retired music educator*
Brock, Gordon R. *music educator*
Brody, Adrien *actor*
Bronson, James B. *music educator*
Brooks, (Troyal) Garth *country music singer*
Brooks-Turner, Myra *music educator*
Brosnan, Pierce *actor*
Brown, Charles Samuel *singer, composer, educator*
Browne, Jackson *singer, songwriter*
Buck, William Joseph *theatrical designer, educator*
Buckles, Boriana Kojouharova *musician, educator*
Bullock, Sandra *actress*
Burchard, Ellen Williams *actress, producer, artist, writer*
Burge, Constance M. *television producer*
Burger, David Mark *composer, educator, multimedia designer*
Burns, Karyl Lynn *actress, theater producer*
Burns, Kevin Michael *editor*
Burton, Al *producer, director, writer*
Bush, Ellen D. *music educator*
Buskirk, Kay N. *musician, music educator*
Butt, Sameer *filmmaker, writer*
Button, Richard Totten *television and stage producer, former figure skating champion*
Byrd, Jeffery *performance artist*
Capice, Philip Charles *television production executive*
Capone, Joseph Vincent *actor, theater educator, theater director*
Carey, Drew *actor*
Carmichael, Judy Lea *record industry executive, concert jazz pianist*
Carney, Kate *actor, director, educator, playwright, storyteller*
Carr, Paul Wallace *actor*
Carvey, Dana *actor, stand up comedian*
Casei, Nedda *mezzo-soprano*
Castellano, Mark Joseph *music educator*
Caswell, Dorothy Ann Cottrell *visual artist, arts administrator*
Chalcraft, Elena Marie *actress, singer*
Chambers, Audley C. *music historian, educator, researcher*
Chan, Jackie *actor, director, stuntman*
Chang, Gail Cathryn May (G. Gordan Chang) *music educator*
Chang, Helen Chung-Hung Hsiang *music educator*
Chapman, William *baritone*
Charette, Cecile M. *music educator*
Charles, Walter *actor*
Charlton, Catherine Marie *musician, composer*
Charry, Michael R(onald) *musician, conductor*
Cheadle, Louise *concert pianist, educator*
Child, Abigail *filmmaker, educator*
Childs, Lucinda *choreographer*
Christianson, Paul Alan *music educator*
Christopher, Russell Lewis *baritone*
Church, Joseph *music educator, conductor, composer*
Cionek, Edmund *composer, educator*
Clark, Nancy Lucinda Brown *retired music teacher*
Clark, Richard Eugene *music educator*
Clark, Teri Lynn *actress, trading department manager*
Clausen, Jeanne Lorraine *musician*
Claver, Robert Earl *television director, producer*
Cobb, Edward Ray *actor*
Coburn, Steven D. *composer, musicologist, educator, pianist*
Cody, Judith *composer, writer*
Cohen, Larry *film director, producer, screenwriter*
Cojbasic, Ivana R. *pianist, music educator*
Collins, Drew *music educator*
Collins, Kathleen Anne *artistic director*
Cone, Edward Toner *composer, emeritus music educator*
Consoli, Marc-Antonio *composer*
Constantine, Michael *actor*
Cooper, Hal *television director*
Cooper, Judith Kase *retired theater educator, playwright*
Copeland, Cori Studebaker *music educator*
Coppola, Francis Ford *film director, producer, writer*
Cordell, Bobbie B. *music educator*
Cosby, Bill *actor, entertainer*
Cosenza, Arthur George *opera director*
Cossa, Dominic Frank *baritone*
Costa-Gavras, (Constantin Gavras) *director, writer*
Cotrubas, Ileana *opera singer, retired lyric soprano*
Coukis, Peter George *musician, composer*
Cromer, Bruce Byron *actor, performing arts educator*
Cromwell, James *actor*
Crosby, Kathryn Grandstaff (Grant Crosby) *actress*
Crosby, Norman Lawrence *comedian*
Cross, Richard B. *bass, educator*
Crotty Guile, Julianne Marie *musician, educator, composer, writer*
Crouse, Lindsay *actress*
Crow, Todd William *pianist*
Cruise, Tom (Tom Cruise Mapother IV) *actor*
Cruz-Romo, Gilda *soprano*
Csurgai-Schmitt, Jacqueline *musician, educator*
Cuaron, Alfonso *film director*
Cummins, Wilma Jeanne *actress*
Cunningham, Michael Gerald *composer, music educator*
Currie, Fergus Gardner *performing arts educator*
Currier, Ruth *dancer, choreographer and educator*
Curry, Daniel Francis Myles *filmmaker*
Curson, Theodore *musician*
Dabbs, Henry Erven *television and film producer, educator*
Dafoe, Willem *actor*
Dailey, Irene *actress, educator*
Danaher, Mallory Millett (Mallory Jones) *actress, photographer, film producer, theater producer*
Danes, Claire *actress*
Dangerfield, Rodney (Jack Roy Dangerfield) *comedian, actor, author*
Daniels, Ronald George *theater director*
Daniels, Sydney Robert *theater director, educator*
Darling, Robert Edward *designer, stage director*
Darvarova, Elmira *musician, concertmaster*
Davis, Geena (Virginia Davis) *actress*
De Angelis, Rosemary Eleanor *actress*
de Blasis, James Michael *artistic director, producer, stage director*
Debus, Eleanor Viola *retired business management company executive*
De Felitta, Frank Paul *producer, writer, director*
DeGeneres, Ellen *actress, comedienne*
Demissie, Yemane I. *filmmaker*
Dench, Judith Olivia *actress*
Denny, Jera Cecilia Jane Elizabeth *musician, graphics designer*
Dern, Laura *actress*
Deutsch, Herbert Arnold *music educator*
Deutz, Natalie Rubinstein *actress, consultant*
Devlin, Michael Coles *bass-baritone*
DeVries, Linda Jane *music educator*
Diaz, Oscar, Jr., *voice educator, music institute director*
DiCaprio, Leonardo *actor*
Dick, James Cordell *concert pianist*
Diemer, Emma Lou *composer, educator*
DiGirolamo, Glen Francis *actor*
Ding, Ai-Yue *conductor, music educator*
Dixon, William Robert *musician, composer, educator*
Doherty, Shannon *actress*
Domenico, Anthony Wayne *conductor, music educator*
Donaldson, Myrtle Norma *music educator, musician*
Dorsky, Nathaniel *filmmaker*
Dossin, Alexandre Saggin *pianist, educator*
Douglass, Lori *music educator*
Downey, Robert, Jr., *actor*
Doyle, Gillian *actress*
Drake, Ervin Maurice *composer, author*
Dunlap, Richard Donovan *artistic director*
Durfee, Kevin Lee *music educator*
Dysart, Richard A. *actor*
Earnest, Matthew Eric *theater director*
Edwards, Anthony *actor*
Edwards, Ryan Hayes *baritone*
Eger, Joseph *conductor, music director*
Ehrling, Sixten *orchestra conductor*
Eisenberg, Daniel *filmmaker*
Elfman, Jenna *actress*
Elgart, Larry Joseph *orchestra leader*
Elias, Lori Anne *music educator, journalist, photojournalist*
Elias, Rosalind *mezzo-soprano*
Elisha, Larisa *musician, performer, educator*
Elizondo, Hector *actor*
Epcar, Richard Michael *actor, writer, director*
Erbe, Yvonne Mary *music educator, marketing specialist, guidance counselor*
Erdely-Sayo, Sandrine *musician, educator*
Eubank, Christopher Wade *music educator*
Eubanks, Kevin *jazz guitarist*
Evdokimova, Eva *prima ballerina assoluta, choreographer, director, producer, actress*
Everett, Tom *actor*
Fabian, D'Arline D. *music educator*
Fairleigh, James Parkinson *music educator*
Fan, Cong *music educator*
Farrell, Mike *actor*
Farrell, Suzanne *ballerina*
Fawcett, Farrah Leni *actress, model*
Feinstein, Martin *performing arts consultant, art director*
Feng, Chung-Chiang *music educator*
Ferguson, Ted *music educator, composer*
Fichandler, Zelda *director*
Field, Sally *actress*
Fiennes, Ralph Nathaniel *actor*
Filerman, Michael Herman *television producer*
Fischer, William Samuel *composer, lecturer*
Fisher, Carrie Frances *actress, writer*
Fleming, Rhonda *actress, singer*
Fletcher, Louise *actress*
Flory, Louise Michell *actress*
Foldi, Andrew Harry *retired singer, educator*
Foley, Mary Kathleen *theater arts educator*
Fonda, Bridget *actress*
Fonda, Peter *actor, director, producer*
Ford, Harrison *actor*
Ford, Nancy Louise *composer, scriptwriter*
Forsythe, Henderson *actor*
Foss, Lukas *composer, conductor, pianist*
Foster, Mary Christine *film producer*
Foster, Sonja Marguerite *musician, educator*
Franciosa, Anthony (Anthony Papaleo) *actor*
Franken, Al *humorist, actor, writer*
Frankish, Brian Edward *film producer, director*
Frazier, DuEwa M. *actor, educator, playwright*
Frick, Shadi A. *music educator, sound recording engineer*
Friedkin, William *film director*
Friedrich, Su G. *filmmaker, educator*
Friendly, Ed *television producer*
Froebel, Boo *performing company executive*
Fuerstner, Fiona Margaret Anne *ballet company executive, ballet educator*
Fukasawa, Natsuki *music educator*
Gabor, Zsa Zsa (Sari Gabor) *actress, cosmetics executive*
Galante, Jane Hohfeld *pianist, music historian*
Galt, John William *actor, writer*
Garner, James (James Scott Bumgarner) *actor*
Garner, Jennifer *actress*

Garniss, Joan Brewster *musician, educator*
Gehm, Denise Charlene *ballerina, arts administrator*
Gelman, Larry *actor, television director*
Gere, Richard *actor*
Gibaldi, Louis Milo *composer, marketing professional*
Gilbert, Melissa *actress*
Glynn, Carlin (Carlin Masterson) *actress*
Goen, Bob *television show host*
Goetzinger, Laurel Eldredge *music educator*
Goldberg, Whoopi (Caryn Elaine Johnson) *actress*
Goldblum, Jeff *actor*
Goldman, Barbara Deren *film and theatrical producer*
Goldstein, Tamara Beth *musician*
Gomez, Mirta *musician, educator*
González, Ibrahim *radio producer, educator, musician*
Gooden, Gregory Allen *music educator*
Goodman, Erika *dancer, actress*
Gordon, Marjorie *lyric coloratura soprano, opera producer, teacher*
Gordon, Myles Adam *television producer, writer*
Grant, Alexander Marshall *retired ballet director*
Grant, Lee (Lyova Haskell Rosenthal) *actress, television and film director*
Grant, Merrill Theodore *producer*
Graves, Denyce Antoinette *mezzo-soprano*
Graves, Lorraine Elizabeth *dancer, educator, coach*
Greco, Christopher Jon *musician, composer, educator*
Greer, Suzanne Michelle *music educator*
Gregory, Claire Distelhorst *television producer*
Gregory, Theodore Nathan *performing company executive, performing arts educator*
Greigg, Cathryn O. *music educator, musician*
Grelle, Bridget Anne *music educator*
Griffith, Melanie *actress*
Grittner, Michael Curtis *theater educator, theater director*
Grody, Donald *actor, judge, lawyer, arbitrator*
Grosbard, Ulu *director*
Groskopf, Aubrey Bud *motion picture television executive, lawyer*
Gruen, Margaret *actress*
Guerrero, Jeannie *music educator*
Gustafson, Craig Thomas *theatrical director, playwright, graphic artist*
Haeberle, Rosamond Pauline *retired music educator*
Hain, Patricia A. *music educator*
Halfvarson, Lucille Robertson *music educator*
Hall, Anthony Michael *actor*
Hall, James Stanley *jazz guitarist, composer*
Hall, Monty *television producer, actor*
Hanover, Donna (Donna Ann Kofnovec) *actress*
Harding, Philip Andreae *communications and marketing researcher*
Harper, Richard Henry *film producer, director*
Harris, Robert A. *retired music educator*
Harris, Terence Royer *theater educator*
Hart, Matthew Aaron *music educator*
Hathcock, John Edward *vocalist*
Hathorne, Gayle Gene *musician, family historian*
Hay, George Austin *actor, artist, musician, writer*
Hayek, Salma *actress*
Headley, Heather A. *actress*
Heard, Ronald Roy *motion picture producer*
Heche, Anne *actress*
Helgenberger, Marg *actress*
Heller, George Norman *music educator*
Helm, Lenora Zenzalai *musician, music educator*
Hendl, Walter *conductor, pianist, composer*
Henes, Donna *celebration artist, ritualist, writer*
Hennessey, Patrick Daniel *musician, educator, musicologist*
Herbig, Günther *conductor*
Hergo, Jane Antoinette *piano educator, composer*
Herson, Arlene Rita *television producer, journalist, television personality, commentator*
Hiller, Arthur *motion picture director*
Hilton, Paris *actress*
Hingle, Pat *actor*
Hirsch, Judd *actor*
Hirshtal, Edith *retired concert pianist, educator, chamber musician*
Hislop, Kare Elizabeth *music director, educator*
Hodges, Ann *actress, singer, dancer*
Hodges, Ann *retired television editor, newspaper columnist*
Hoggard, Lara Guldmar *conductor, educator*
Holland, Beth *actress*
Holliday, Polly Dean *actress*
Hollow, Steven Morry *entertainer, educator, theater director*
Holm, Celeste *actress*
Holm, Sir Ian *actor*
Holman, Bill *composer*
Holmes, Susan G. *music educator*
Hooper, Josh *screen actor, director, media producer, writer*
Hooper, Robert Alexander *television producer, international educator*
Hornyak, Roy Robert *music educator, minister*
Horsman, Lenore Lynde (Eleanora Lynde) *soprano, educator, actress*
Horton, Patricia Mathews *artist, violist and violinist*
Hosman, Sharon Lee *music educator*
Houghton, Diane Murley *actress, vocalist*
Houghton, Katharine *actress*
Housewright, Wiley Lee *music educator*
Houston, Whitney *vocalist, recording artist*
Howard, David *ballet school administrator*
Howells, Michelle C. *music educator*
Hubbard, Elizabeth *actress*
Huber, David G. *theater educator, actor*
Hudson, Alan C.H. *music educator, tropical fruit farmer*
Hudson, Kate *actress*
Huffman, Cady *actress*
Huggett, Monica *performing company executive*
Hughes, Michaela Kelly *actress*
Hunsberger, J. N. *music educator, musician*
Hunter, Holly *actress*
Hurt, John Vincent *actor*
Hutton, Lauren (Mary Laurence Hutton) *model, actress*
Hyman, Gary Scott *music educator*
Hymer, Tabitha Kim *music educator, writer, photographer*
Iman, (Iman Abdulmajid) *model*
Imboden, Elisabeth Sue *performing company executive*
Irving, George Steven *actor*
Issari, M(ohammad) Ali *film producer, writer, consultant*
Jackson, Felicity Anne *performing arts organization administrator*
Jackson, Michael Joseph *singer*
Jackson, Nagle *stage director, playwright*
Jackson, Samuel L. *actor*
Jackson, Victoria Lynn *actress, comedienne*
Jamini, Deborah *singer, music educator, writer, pianist*
Janis, Conrad *actor, jazz musician, art dealer, film producer, director*
Jarmusch, Jim *director, actor*
Jarrett, Keith *pianist, composer*
Jarvi, Neeme *conductor*
Jenkin, James Thomas *videotape editor*
Jenkins, Leroy *violinist, composer*
Jensen, Nancy Daggett *music educator*
Johnson, Timothy D. *music educator, composer, poet*
Jones, Shirley *actress, singer*
Jones, Tommy Lee *actor*
Joyner, Philip Andrew, Jr., *musician, educator*
Kåge, Jonas *ballet company artistic director*
Kane, Michael Joseph *director*
Kantor, Mary Louise *music educator*
Kaplan, Richard James *producer, director, writer, educator, consultant*
Karlins, M(artin) William *composer, educator*
Kasdan, Lawrence Edward *film director, screenwriter*
Kaspar, Frances Wolf *music educator*
Kavanaugh, Frank James *film producer, educator*
Kavner, Julie *actress*
Kaylan, Howard Lawrence *musical entertainer, screenwriter, composer*
Kellaigh, Kathleen *conservatory artistic director*
Kendall, Gavin Starr *actor*
Kennedy, Kathleen *film producer*
Kennedy, Linda Dale *music educator, pianist, organist*
Kenny, H. Sharie *music educator*
Kent, Gary Warner *film director, writer*
Kernochan, Sarah M. *film director, scriptwriter, composer*
Keyes, Alan L. *radio and talk show host, former federal government official*
Kietzman, Kris *music educator*
Kim, Jong-Hyun *music educator, conductor*
Kinnear, Greg *actor, producer*
Kirby, David Stephen *music educator*
Kirby, Frank Eugene *musicology educator, author, editor*
Kirby, George R., III, *music educator*
Kirkland, Geoffrey Alan *motion picture production designer*
Klampe, Craig Allen *composer*
Klein, Stephen Thomas *performing arts executive*
Kline, James Edgar *actor*
Kloves, Steven *film director, scriptwriter*
Koerber, Dolores Jean *music educator, musician*
Komlos, Peter *violinist*
Kopelson, Arnold *film producer*
Koszarski, Richard *film historian, writer*
Koutrouvelis, Alexis Andrea *music educator*
Kriegsman, Sali Ann *arts executive, artistic director, writer, consultant*
Kudrow, Lisa (Lisa Marie Diane Kudrow) *actress*
Kuo, Michelle Chen (Chou-hsia Chen) *musician, educator*
Kurahashi, Yuko *theater educator*
Kuriansky, Judy *television personality, radio personality, reporter, psychologist, writer, educator*
Kutrzeba, Joseph S. *theatrical and film producer, director*
Ladd, Rose Diane *actress*
Lane, Diane *actress*
LaSalle, Eriq *actor, film director*
Latimer, James Harold *percussionist, conductor, composer, consultant, educator*
LeBlanc, Matt *actor*
Lee, Christopher Frank Carandini *actor, author, singer*
Lefferts, George *producer, writer, director*
Lehman, Paul Robert *retired music educator*
Leiber, Jerry *songwriter*
Leno, Jay (James Douglas Muir Leno) *television personality, comedian, writer*
León, Tania Justina *composer, music director, pianist*
Leoni, Tea (Elizabeth Tea Pantaleoni) *actress*
Lepage, Robert *actor, director, playwright*
Lerner, Neil William *music educator*
Leventhal, Nathan *performing company executive, lawyer, municipal official*
Levine, Alan J. *entertainment company executive*
Levitas, Miriam C. Strickman *documentary filmmaker, producer, writer, designer, consultant intergenerational relationships*
Levy, Todd Robert *musician, music educator*
Lewis, Mary Jane *film producer, director, scriptwriter*
Lewis, Richard *actor, comedian*
Lichtenstein, Harvey *performing arts executive*
Light, April Gene *music educator*
Linden, Gordon Lowell *music educator*
Lipke, William Alan *music educator, musician*
Lithgow, John Arthur *actor, director*
Little, Loren Everton *musician, ophthalmologist*
Liu, Kexi *music educator*
Liu, Margaret C. *music educator*
Livingstone, Trudy Dorothy Zweig *dancer, educator*
Locklear, Heather *actress*
Locricchio, Matthew *actor, writer*
Lohan, Lindsay *actress*
Lord, Valerie Arlene *music educator, musician*
Loring, Gloria Jean *vocalist*
Love, Courtney *singer, actress*
LoVetri, Jeannette Louise *voice educator*
Lubin, Steven *concert pianist, musicologist*
Ludwig, Christa *mezzo-soprano*
Lukasiewicz, Paul Manus *music educator*
Lupu, Radu *pianist*
Madeira, Francis King Carey *conductor, educator*
Maffia, Roma *actress*
Magor, Louis Roland *conductor*
Mahoney, John *actor*
Manchevski, Milcho *film director, scriptwriter*
Mannes, Elena Sabin *film and television producer, director*
Manning, Michael Nicholas *actor, singer*
Marceau, Yvonne *ballroom dancer, educator*
Marchant, David Brian *music educator*
Marderosian, Armena Pearl *music educator*
Mark, Judi *actress, choreographer*
Mark, Michael Laurence *retired music educator*
Marks, Bruce *performing company executive, choreographer*
Marsalis, Wynton *musician*
Marsee, Susanne Irene *mezzo-soprano*
Marsh, Joan Knight *educational film, video and computer software company executive, publisher children's books*
Martin, Ace *music educator*
Martin, Andrea Louise *actress, comedienne, writer*
Martin, Helen Schatkowski *music educator, television producer*
Martinez, Gary Steven *actor*
Marx, Richard *vocalist, musician*
Mason, J. Murphy *theater director*
Mason, Marsha *actress, theater director, writer*
Masterson, Peter *actor, director*
Mastroianni, Thomas Owen *musician, music educator*
Matthau, Charles Marcus *film director*
McCann, Elizabeth Ireland *theater, television and motion picture producer, lawyer*
McClain, Richard Stan *cinematographer*
McCoy, Maureen B. *music educator*
McCready, Sam *theatre educator, actor, director, writer*
McDonald, Tanny *actress*
McDowell, Malcolm *actor*
McEntire, Brad *theater director, performing artist, educator*
McEntire, Reba N. *country singer*
McEwen, Joan Grace (Joanie Lawrence) *actress, recording industry executive*
McGegan, Nicholas *music director*
McKellen, Sir Ian *actor*
McKinney, Renovia M. *music educator*
McLean, Julianne Drew *concert pianist, educator*
McNown, Edythe S. *music educator*
Mc Tiernan, John *film director*
Meara, Anne *actress, playwright, writer*
Melillo, Joseph Vincent *producer, performing arts*
Melito, Thomas *music educator, musician*
Melnick, Jodi *dancer*
Mendelsohn, Carol S. *television producer*
Menotti, Gian Carlo *composer*
Merrill, Robert *baritone*
Meserve, Walter Joseph *drama studies writer, publisher*
Messier, Michael C. *television director, actor, writer*
Meyerink, Victoria Paige *film producer, actress*
Mezacapa, Edna S. *music educator, elementary school educator*
Mikulas, Dana Cameron *voice educator, music educator*
Milano, Alyssa *actress*
Minnix, Bruce Milton *television and theatre director*
Miranda-Levi, Jason *film producer, writer*
Mitchell, Brian Stokes *actor*
Moffatt, Katy (Katherine Louella Moffatt) *musician, vocalist, songwriter*
Montgomery, Jack Sherwood *performing company executive, director*
Moore, Terry Edward *actor, performing company executive*
Mordecai, Benjamin *theatrical producer, drama educator*
Morelan, Paula Kay *choreographer*
Morello, Joseph Albert *musician, educator*
Morgan, Linda Gail *producer*
Morgan, Michael B. *retired music educator*
Morrison, Shelley *actress*
Morrison, Van *musician, songwriter*
Moseley, Carlos DuPre *music executive, musician*
Moseley, Julia W. *music teacher, historic preservationist*
Moss, Carrie-Anne *actress*
Muren, Dennis E. *visual effects director*
Murphy, Eddie *comedian, actor*
Murphy, George *special effects expert*
Musante, Tony (Anthony Peter Musante Jr.) *actor*
Musgrave, Michael G. *musicologist, musician*
Myers, Margaret Jane (Dee Dee Myers) *television personality, editor*
Myers, Mike *actor, writer, producer*
Myerson, Alan *film and television director*
Nair, Mira *film producer, film director*
Nardini, Luisa *music educator*
Narita, Hiro *cinematographer*
Neame, Ronald *director, producer*
Neary, Patricia Elinor *ballet director*
Nederlander, James Laurence *theater owner, producer*
Neilson, Linda Emerson *theater educator, writer*
Nelson, Kelly Edward *actor, writer*
Nelson, Ron *composer, conductor, educator*
Neuerburg-Denzer, Ursula *theater director, educator, actress*
Neville, Phoebe *choreographer, dancer, educator*
Nevins, Sheila *television programmer and producer*
Newmar, Julie Chalane *actress, dancer, real estate businesswoman*
Nichols, Mike *stage and film director*
Nicks, Stevie (Stephanie Lynn Nicks) *singer, songwriter*
Niedung, Helen Bovbjerg *voice educator*
Nixon, Marni *singer*
Nolte, Nick *actor*
Norris, Chuck (Carlos Ray) *actor*
O'Brien, Kevin *musician, radio producer*
O'Brien, Orin Ynez *musician, educator*
Oettinger, Regina Marie *music educator*
O'Hara, Catherine *actress, comedienne*
O'Keefe, Gary Raymond *actor*
Olsson-Hume, Irena *music educator*
Oppenheim, David Jerome *musician, retired university dean*
Oppewall, Jeannine Claudia *motion picture production designer*
Orbit, William (William Wainwright) *record producer*
O'Reilly, Sally *musician, educator*
Ormai-Buza, Ildiko *soprano, composer, organist, music educator*
Osborne, Barrie M. *motion picture producer*
Oshita, John Takao *musician*
Osmond, Marie *singer*
Ostrow, Stuart *theatrical producer, educator, writer*
Page, Willis *conductor*
Palileo, Hazel Valencia *videographer*
Palmier, Darice *music educator*
Parks, Heather Jewel *music educator*
Pasquier, Joël *music educator*
Patterson, Seth Matthew *music educator*
Pensis, Henri Bram *music educator, conductor*
Percy, Lee Edward *motion picture film editor*
Perez, Gabriel Felan *music educator*
Perini, Jennifer Mary *television producer*
Perkins, Leeman Lloyd *music educator, musicologist*
Perle, George *composer*
Perry, Matthew *actor*
Persoff, Nehemiah *actor, artist*
Pesci, Joe *actor*
Phillips, Michelle Gilliam *actress, writer*
Phillips, Winifred Patricia *radio producer, composer*
Pierce, David Hyde *actor*
Pierce, Ponchitta Ann *TV host, producer, journalist, writer, consultant*
Pinkett-Smith, Jada *actress*
Pirkle, George Emory *television and film actor, director*
Plant, Linda R. *music educator*
Poitier, Sidney *actor, director*
Poledouris, Basil K. *composer*
Poll, Heinz *choreographer, artistic director*
Poll, Martin Harvey *film producer*
Polonchak, Richard *music educator*
Pop, Iggy (James Newell Osterberg) *composer, singer, musician*
Prausnitz, Frederik William *conductor*
Preston, Kelly *actress*
Price, Betty Jeanne *choirchime soloist, writer*
Price, Ruthe Geier *actress, writer, educator*
Price, Thomas Frederick *theatre educator*
Primosch, James Thomas *music educator, composer, musician*
Prosky, Robert Joseph *actor*
Puhekker, Kristin Rose *music educator*
Quaid, Randy *actor*
Qualls, Randall Wade *music educator*
Quam, Dori *music educator, paralegal*
Quinlan, Kathleen *actress*
Quirk, I-fan *filmmaker*
Ragland, Kathryn Marie *dancer, educator*
Raitt, Bonnie Lynn *blues singer, guitarist*
Rajski, Peggy *film director, film producer*
Rand, Calvin Gordon *arts and education consultant*
Ransom, Tasha Elana *news production assistant*
Ravin, Linda *actress*
Redman, Walter Dewey *musician, educator*
Reich, Ellen Judith *actress, writer*
Reilly, John C. *actor*
Remlinger, Rolf *music educator, composer*
Reynolds, Harrah (H.) Robert *conductor, artistic director*
Rhodes, Lawrence *artistic director*
Richards, Ann *actress, educator, poet*
Richardson, Natasha Jane *actress*
Richie, Lionel B., Jr., *singer, songwriter, producer*
Richie, Nicole *television personality*
Rideout, Patricia Irene *operatic, oratorio and concert singer*
Ridolfi, Patrick Murphy *music educator, tenor*
Rinella, Barbara *book dramatist*
Rino, Barbara Elizabeth *music educator, musician*
Ripley, Robert *actor, writer*
Robbins, Andrew Charles *sound recording engineer, music producer*
Roberts, Doris *actress*
Robinson, Dorothy Marie *theater producer, director, actress*
Robinson, Mark Allen *music educator*
Rocco, Jamie Alexander *choreographer, theater director, actor*
Rochberg, George *composer, educator*
Rock, Chris *actor, comedian*
Rodrigues, Azael Magalhaes, Jr., *musician*
Roeg, Nicolas Jack *film director*
Rolland, Clara *pianist, educator*
Romano, Ray *actor, comedian*
Rook, Judith Rawie *television producer, writer*
Rose, Michael Leonard *film, television and video producer*
Roseanne, (Roseanne Barr) *actress, comedienne, television producer, writer*
Rosen, Marcy B. *music educator*
Rosen, Myor *harpist, educator*
Rosenfeld, Steven Ira *artistic director, music publisher*
Rosten, Irwin *writer, producer, director*
Rothaar, Susanne Elisabeth *music educator, musician*
Rourke, Mickey (Philip Andre Rourke Jr.) *actor*
Rouse, Mikel *composer*
Rowe, Hahn *composer*
Rowlands, Gena *actress*
Rucinski, Robert Lawrence *musician, educator*
Rudner, Sara *dancer*
Ruggiero, Matthew John *bassoonist*
Russo, Vincent Barney *music educator*
Rutan, Charles R. *musician*
Ryan, Jeanne Vanyo *music educator*
Ryder, Winona (Winona Laura Horowitz) *actress*
Sabree, Yahya Agin *music educator*
Saint, Eva Marie *actress*
Saint-Girard, Christian *theatre director, choreographer, actor, educator, theater producer*
St. John, David A. *actor*
Saks, Eric Maurice *film producer, film director*
Saks, Gene *theater and film director, actor*
Saltzman, Barry *actor*
Saltzman, Philip *television writer, producer*
Salvatore, Richard John *cinematographer, company executive*
Samuelson, M. Kristin *music educator, vocalist*
Sandor, Gyorgy *pianist*
Sansbury, Olin Bennett, Jr., *retired university/orchestra administrator*
Sarry, Christine *ballerina*
Satterwhite, Marc *music educator, composer*
Scarth, Bruce Worden *music educator*
Scarwid, Diana Elizabeth *actress*
Schallert, William Joseph *actor*
Schexnayder, Brian Edward *opera singer, voice educator*
Schiffer, Claudia *model*
Schiller, Lawrence Julian *writer, motion picture producer, director*
Schlesser, Ethan Marc *music educator, musician*
Schmidt, Sheri Lynn *band director*
Schoof, Robert Norman *music educator*
Schubert, Barbara Schuele *retired performing company executive*
Schuur, Diane Joan *vocalist*
Schwartz, Stephen Lawrence *composer, lyricist*
Schwary, Ronald Louis *motion picture producer*
Schwarz, Gerard *conductor, musician*
Sciorra, Annabella *actress*

ARTS: VISUAL

UNITED STATES

Lafayette
Monheit, Molly Jane *artist*
Shurtleff, Akiko Aoyagi *artist, consultant*

Laguna Beach
Powers, Runa Skötte *artist*

Lagunitas
Holman, Arthur Stearns *artist*

Lancaster
Emch, Brian Kelly *photographer*

Larkspur
Napoles, Veronica *graphic designer, consultant*

Long Beach
Pizzo, Pia *artist, educator*
Viola, Bill *artist, writer*

Los Altos
Sherwood, Patricia Waring *artist, educator*
Spangler, Dorothy Benita *artist*

Los Angeles
Apple, Jacki (Jacqueline B. Apple) *artist, writer, educator*
Apt, Charles *artist*
Baca, Judith F. *art educator*
Benedict, Cheyann *apparel designer*
Caroompas, Carole Jean *artist, educator*
Curran, Darryl Joseph *photographer, educator*
De Larios, Dora *artist*
Dismukes, Valena Grace Broussard *photographer, former physical education educator*
Galanos, James *retired fashion designer*
Hamilton, Patricia Rose *art dealer*
Hess, Frederick Scott *artist*
Hockney, David *artist*
Johnston, Ynez *artist, educator*
Kupper, Ketti *artist*
Lark, Raymond *artist, art scholar*
Layton, Harry Christopher *artist, lecturer, consultant*
Lem, Richard Douglas *painter*
Lockhart, Sharon *artist*
Park, Lee (Lee Parklee) *artist*
Pastor, Jennifer *sculptor*
Sasaki, John Eric *art company executive, artist*
Schnitzler, Beverly Jeanne *designer, art educator, writer*
Serafin, Thomas Joseph *photographer, writer*
Stansfield, Claire *apparel designer*
Stone, George *artist, art educator*
Wells, Annie *photographer*
Williams, Clarence J, III, *photographer*

Los Gatos
Carson, Sol Kent *artist, educator*

Malibu
Bowman, Bruce *art educator*

Mammoth Lakes
Mager, Ingrid Irina *artist*

Mariposa
Bruce, John Anthony *artist*
Rogers, Earl Leslie *artist, educator*

Mckinleyville
Berry, Glenn *educator, artist*

Mill Valley
Jones, Pirkle *photographer, educator*

Modesto
Bucknam, Mary Olivia Caswell *artist, educator*

Monarch Beach
Mackaig, Janet Brownlee *artist, printmaker, educator*

Monterey
Lewis, Sharyn Lee *sculptor*

Moraga
O'Brien, Bea Jae *artist*

Morgan Hill
Freimark, Robert (Bob Freimark) *artist*

Newport Beach
Spitz, Barbara Salomon *artist*

North Hollywood
Miller, Philip Gray *artist*
Price, Joe (Joe Allen) *artist, former educator, actor*

Northridge
Bassler, Robert Covey *artist, educator*
Weatherup, Wendy Gaines *graphic designer, writer*

Oakdale
Saletta, Mary Elizabeth (Betty Saletta) *sculptor, rancher*

Oakhurst
Cantwell, Christopher William *artist*

Oakland
Alba, Benny *artist*
Beasley, Bruce Miller *sculptor*
Gonzalez, Arthur Padilla *artist, educator*
Rath, Alan T. *sculptor*

Oceanside
Sarkisian, Pamela Outlaw *artist*

Orange
Torres, Rudy Arnold *artist*

Orinda
Epperson, Stella Marie *artist*

Oxnard
Perrier, Barbara Sue *artist*
Sweet, Harvey *theatrical set designer, lighting designer*

Pacific Grove
Elinson, Henry David *artist, language educator*

Pacific Palisades
Casady, Dorothea Jane *artist, educator, sculptor*
Chesney, Lee Roy, Jr., *artist*

Palm Desert
Bass, Betty Zoe Passmore (Mrs. Eric Bass) *artist*
Kaufman, Charlotte King *artist*

Palo Alto
McCluskey, Lois Thornhill *photographer*
Rich, Lesley Mosher *artist*
Richardson, Tom (Edward Thompson Richardson) *artist*
Saegesser, Marguerite M. *artist*
Survilo, Francine Marion *painter, sculptor*

Palos Verdes Estates
Sharp, Jane Shriver *artist*

Panorama City
Janis, Elinor Raiden *artist, educator*

Pasadena
Gill, Gene *artist*
Iturbide, Graciela *photographer*
Pashgian, Margaret Helen *artist*
Sanchez, Pauline Stella *artist*

Pebble Beach
Mortensen, Gordon Louis *artist, printmaker*

Petaluma
McChesney, Robert Pearson *artist*
Reichek, Jesse *artist*
Skalagard, Hans Martin *artist*

Piedmont
Mayeri, Beverly *artist, ceramic sculptor, educator*

Richmond
Wessel, Henry *photographer*

Riverside
Smith, Dorothy Ottinger *jewelry designer, civic worker*

Ross
Pierce, Carole Jean *artist*

Sacramento
Hull, Frederick Albert *artist, writer*
Nye, Gene Warren *retired artist*
Skoor, John Brian *art educator, art consultant*
Thomas, Laura Marlene *artist, retired private antique dealer*

Salinas
Puckett, Richard Edward *artist, consultant, former recreation executive, former hotel executive*
Wu, Wayne Wen-Yau *artist*

San Carlos
Oliver, Nancy Lebkicher *artist, retired elementary education educator*
Sullivan, Shirley Ross (Shirley Ross Davis) *art collector*

San Diego
Barone, Angela Maria *artist, researcher*
Beaumont, Mona *artist*
Cook, Stephen Barton *art educator, artist*
Farmer, Janene Elizabeth *artist, educator*
Krupchak, Tamara *artist*
Riffenburgh, Gerrye H. *artist, educator*

San Francisco
Babcock, Jo *artist, educator*
Barber, Malcolm *auction house executive*
Beall, Dennis Ray *artist, educator*
Calvin, Carolina *apparel executive, designer*
Carmi, Sofia *artist, educator*
Chin, Sue Soone Marian (Suchin Chin) *conceptual artist, portraitist, photographer, community affairs activist*
DeSoto, Lewis Damien *art educator*
Dickinson, Eleanor Creekmore *artist, educator*
Goldstein, Sydney Rachel *photographer, writer, producer*
Hershman, Lynn Lester *artist*
Howard, David E. *artist*
Martin, Fred *artist, college administrator*
McClintock, Jessica *fashion designer*
Muranaka, Hideo *artist, educator*
Pfaff, Laura King *auction house executive*
Presniakov, Alexander *painter, sculptor, inventor, novelist, writer*
Raciti, Cherie *artist*
Rascón, Armando *artist*
Stermer, Dugald Robert *designer, illustrator, writer, consultant*
Thiebaud, Wayne *artist*
Van Hoesen, Beth Marie *artist, printmaker*

San Jose
Ellner, Michael William *art educator*
Estabrook, Reed *artist, educator*
Porter, John Paul *artist, educator*

San Juan Capistrano
Burns, Toni Anthony *artist*

San Mateo
Huxley, Mary Atsuko *artist*

San Pedro
Crutchfield, William Richard *artist, educator*

Santa Barbara
Corbani, Candace Bedford *antiques broker, political campaign consultant*
Hayward, Jean *artist, musician, interior designer, performance artist*

Santa Clara
Lane, Holly Diana *artist*

Santa Cruz
Aschbacher, James Carl *artist, consultant*

Moose, Brian David *illustrator, art director*
Podesta, Robert Edward *artist*
Summers, Carol *artist*

Santa Monica
Fukuhara, Henry *artist, educator*
Giannulli, Mossimo *designer, apparel business executive*
Haroon, Nasreen *artist*

Santa Rosa
Fields, Tina Rae *artist, ecopsychologist*
Monk, Diana Charla *artist, stable owner*

Santa Ynez
Rymer, Ilona Suto *artist, retired art educator*

Saratoga
Ogle, David William *art educator, sculptor, ceramist, printmaker*

Shadow Hills
Bangs, Cate (Cathryn Margaret Bangs) *film production designer, interior designer*

Sherman Oaks
Alcott-Jardine, Susan *artist, writer*
Atwood, Colleen *costume designer*
Beck, Brent Alan *graphics designer*
Hoover, Richard *set designer, art director, actor*
Platus, Libby *artist, sculptor, speaker*
Powell, Sandy *costume designer*
Weiss, Julie *costume designer*

Sierra Madre
Converse, Elizabeth *artist, writer*

Somis
Kehoe, Vincent Jeffré-Roux *photographer, author, cosmetic company executive*

Sonoma
Fellows, Alice Combs *artist*

Sonora
Sharboneau, Lorna Rosina *artist, educator, author, poet, illustrator*

South Pasadena
Askin, Walter Miller *artist, educator*

Stockton
Oak, Claire Morisset *artist, educator*
Sumida, Gregory Zio *artist, photographer, musician, astronomer*
Wright, Evelyn Louise *artist*

Studio City
Boyett, Joan Reynolds *arts administrator*
Easterson, Sam *artist*

Sunnyvale
Daltchev, Ana Ranguel *sculptor*

Sylmar
Scheib, Gerald Paul *fine art educator, jeweler, metalsmith*

Templeton
Foster-Wells, Karen Margaret *artist*

Thousand Oaks
Heyer, Carol Ann *illustrator*

Tustin
Coronel, Raul Angulo *sculptor*

Upper Lake
Twitchell, Kent *artist*

Van Nuys
Cook, Jenik Esterm (Jenik Esterm Cook Simonian) *artist, educator*
Graham, Roger John *photography and journalism educator*

Venice
Alf, Martha Joanne *artist*
Chipman, Jack *artist*
Eversley, Frederick John *sculptor, engineer*

Vista
Tadeo, Elvia *artist*

Walnut Creek
Reimann, Arline Lynn *artist*

Westlake Village
Weiss, Barbara G. *artist*

Wrightwood
Frame, John Fayette *sculptor*

Yucca Valley
Dockendorff, Robert Lawrence *computer graphics designer*

COLORADO

Arvada
Halley, Diane Esther *artist*

Aspen
Mitchell, Karen Frances *artist, jewelry designer*
Soldner, Paul Edmund *artist, ceramist, educator*

Boulder
Bolomey, Roger Henry *sculptor*
Glasergreen, Lawson Scott *designer*
Valdovino, Luis Hector *art educator*

Canon City
Fisher, Neal Foster *artist, writer*

Colorado Springs
Goehring, Kenneth *artist*
Owen, Thomas James *artist, educator*
Williams, Joyce Marilyn *artist, business owner*

Crestone
Jaynes, Jefferson S. *artist*

Denver
Daniels, Martha K. *artist*
Enright, Cynthia Lee *illustrator*
Graham, Pamela Smith *artist, distributing company executive*
Lockspeiser, Nancy Flanders *artist, designer*
McElhinney, James Lancel *artist, educator*
Ragland, Bob *artist, educator*
Shwayder, Elizabeth Yanish *sculptor*

Englewood
Brennan, Joann *photographer, educator*
Kristin, Karen *artist*
Lamb, Darlis Carol *sculptor*

Greeley
Jenkins, Virginia *visual arts educator, artist*

Hotchkiss
Blackstock, Virginia Harriett *artist*

La Veta
Zehring, Peggy Johnson *artist*

Lake George
Norman, John Barstow, Jr., *designer, educator*

Laporte
Riba, Shirley *artist*

Loveland
Bierbaum, Janith Marie *artist*
Weresh, Thelma Faye *sculptor, artist*

Norwood
Hollinbeck, Ethel Lindell *sculptor*

Paonia
Noonan, Robert Harry *art and music educator*

Snowmass Village
Casebeer, Douglas Kelley *artist, ceramist, consultant*

Westcliffe
Merfeld, Gerald Lydon *artist*

Woodland Park
Cockrille, Stephen *art director, business owner*

CONNECTICUT

Avon
Drapeau, Suzanne Eva *art educator*

Berlin
Pulito, Francis N. *artist*

Branford
LeVasseur, Lee Allan *artist*

Colebrook
Ash, Hiram Newton *graphic designer*

Cos Cob
Kane, Margaret Brassler *sculptor*
Neal, Irene Collins *artist, educator*

Danbury
Saghir, Adel Jamil *artist, painter, sculptor*

Darien
Ossi, James Matthew *artist*

Fairfield
Bullard, Roger Perrin *artist*

Falls Village
Cronin, Robert Lawrence *painter*

Gaylordsville
Dunn, Virginia *artist, community volunteer*

Georgetown
Roberts, Priscilla Warren *artist*

Greenwich
Cassidy, Denis Andrew *artist, architect*
Perless, Robert L. *sculptor*
Pope, Ingrid Bloomquist *sculptor, poet, painter*

Guilford
Pease, David Gordon *artist, educator*

Hartford
Carey, Ellen *artist*
Hammer, Alfred Emil *artist, educator*
Martin, Ionis B. *artist, educator*

Ivoryton
Osborne, Judith Barbour *artist*

Madison
Nebel, Sara Drought *artist, poet*

Meriden
Bertolli, Eugene Emil *sculptor, goldsmith, designer, consultant*

Milford
Curt, Denise Morris *artist, limner, photographer*

Mystic
Rooney, Maria Dewing *photographer*

Naugatuck
Mannweiler, Mary-Elizabeth *painter*

New Canaan
Christensen, Donna Radovich *needlecraft designer, consultant, educator*
Kovatch, Jak Gene *artist*
Richards, Walter DuBois *artist, illustrator*

New Haven
Bailey, William Harrison *artist, educator*

Feinstein, Rochelle *artist, educator*
Grausman, Philip *sculptor*
Johnson, Lester Fredrick *artist*
Lindroth, Linda (Linda Hammer) *artist, curator, writer*

Niantic
White, Katherine Ann *artist*

North Grosvenordale
Kornbluth, Frances Helen Schachter *artist*

Norwalk
Babcock, Catherine Evans *artist, educator*
Kahn, Wolf *artist*

Redding
Isley, Alexander Max *graphic designer, lecturer*

Sharon
Johns, Jasper *artist*

Sherman
Goodspeed, Barbara *artist*

Stamford
Babson, Jane Frances *artist, writer*
Roberts, Victoria Lynn P. *antique expert*
Rudman, Joan Eleanor *artist, educator*

Stonington
Elliott, Inger McCabe *designer, textile company executive, design consultant*

Storrs Mansfield
Jones, Clyde Adam *art educator, artist*

Torrington
McKenzie, Kathleen Julianna *artist*

Voluntown
Caddell, Foster *artist*

Wallingford
Lauttenbach, Carol *artist*

Washington
Grimes, Margaret Whitehurst *artist, educator*
Renouf, Edda *artist*

Weston
Bleifeld, Stanley *sculptor*

Westport
Chernow, Ann Levy *artist, art educator*
Fisher, Leonard Everett *artist, writer, educator*
Reilly, Nancy (Anne Caulfield Reilly) *painter*
Siff, Marlene Ida *artist, designer*

DELAWARE

Greenville
Cooch, Nancy duPont (Mrs. Edward W. Cooch Jr.) *sculptor*

Lewes
Costigan, Constance Frances *artist, educator*

New Castle
Almquist, Don *illustrator, artist*

Newark
Brown, Hilton *visual arts educator, artist, writer*
Rowe, Charles Alfred *artist, designer, educator*

Rockland
Harvey, Andre *sculptor*

Wilmington
Bounds-Seemans, Pamella J. *artist*
Lanyon, E. Jean *artist, poet*

DISTRICT OF COLUMBIA

Washington
Allard, William Albert *photographer*
Basch, Richard Vennard *photographer, producer, writer, director*
Baughman, J. Ross *photographer, writer, educator*
Biddle, Catharina Baart *artist*
Blair, James Pease *retired freelance photographer*
Boucher, Jack Edward *architectural photographer, writer*
Bowman, Dorothy Louise *artist*
Brown, Pamela Wedd *artist*
Cleary, Manon Catherine *artist, educator*
Coppola, John Francis *exhibits director*
DiPerna, Frank Paul *photographer, educator*
Douglas, Lydia Ann *photographer, educator*
Ferrell, James T. *sculptor*
Forrester, Patricia Tobacco *artist*
Gumpert, Gunther *artist*
Ihrie, John Richard, III. *art educator*
Jecklin, Loise Underwood *art corporation executive, consultant*
Kapikian, Catherine Andrews *artist*
Kobersteen, Kent *photographer, director, editor-in-chief*
Koller, Shirley Leavitt *sculptor*
Maletsky, Alfred F. *sculptor, engraver*
Mercanti, John M. *sculptor, engraver*
Nemeth, Norman E. *sculptor, engraver*
Olson, Randy *photographer*
Puryear, Martin *artist, educator*
Schaap, Aletta Johanna *artist*
Shinolt, Eileen Thelma *artist*
Steadham, Richard Lynn *magazine art director*
Stockdale, Sally Boyd *artist, real estate agent*
Summerford, Ben Long *retired artist, educator*
Tacha, Athena *sculptor, artist, educator*
Truitt, Anne Dean *artist*
Weaver, Donna L. *engraver*

FLORIDA

Atlantic Beach
Gartland, Alice Johnson *artist*

Bal Harbour
Bernay, Betti *artist*

Boca Raton
Ortlip, Paul Daniel *artist*
Wertheimer, Esther *sculptor*

Bonita Springs
McNamara-Ringewald, Mary Ann Thérèse *artist, educator*

Bradenton
French, Richard Paul *artist*
Melcher, Sandra J. *artist*
Voorhees, Stephanie Robin Faught *retired art educator*

Citra
Parisi, Marita *artist, art gallery director*

Clearwater
Slade, Roy *artist, college president, museum director*

Coconut Creek
Casey, Thomas Warren *graphic design company executive, architect*
Marshak, Arthur *artist, sculptor*

Dania
Satin, Claire Jeanine *sculptor, book artist*

Daytona Beach
Alvarez, Marianne *artist, photographer, educator*

Daytona Beach Shores
Dalia, Vesta Mayo *artist*

Debary
Pelosi, Haydee *sculptor*

Delray Beach
Mills, Agnes Eunice Karlin *artist, printmaker, sculptor*
Ross, Beatrice Brook *artist*
Schwarz, Rose Oberman *artist*

Dunedin
Allison, Brooke Hastings *artist, educator*

Edgewater
Schubert, Jeanne *artist*

Fort Lauderdale
Ambrose, Judith Ann *designer*
Duke, James T *art educator, consumer products company executive*
Moorhead, Rolande Annette Reverdy *artist, educator*
Simon, Robert Stephen *artist*

Fort Myers
Dean, Jean Beverly *artist*
Schwartz, Carl Edward *artist, printmaker*

Gainesville
Morgan, Anne Margaret Barclay *artist, author, psychologist*
Rowe, Bobby Louise *art educator*

Hialeah
Gil de Gibaja, Susana *artist, small business owner*

Hobe Sound
Houser, Jim (James Cowing Houser Jr., Jim Houser) *painter, art educator*

Hollywood
Sadowski, Carol Johnson *artist*

Indialantic
Pavlakos, Ellen Tsatiri *sculptor*

Indian Harbor Beach
Rains, Baxter Smith *sculptor, consultant*
Traylor, Angelika *stained glass artist*

Jacksonville
Eden, F. Brown *artist*
Schultz, Nancy Reilly *artist*

Jensen Beach
Gruppe, Charles Camille *artist*
Skrupky, Elaine Charlotte *art educator*
Traines, Rose Wunderbaum *sculptor, educator*

Key Largo
Kennedy, Mary Sussock *artist*

Key West
McIntosh, Jon Charles *illustrator, graphics designer, painter*
Taylor, Victoria *sculptor*

Kissimmee
McCann, Jean Friedrichs *artist, educator*

Lake Mary
Bachmann, Bill *photographer*

Lake Park
Heaton, Janet Nichols *artist, art gallery director*

Lakeland
Rogers, James Gordon, Jr., *art educator*
Stark, Bruce Gunsten *artist*

Melrose
Harley, Ruth *artist, educator*

Merritt Island
Ollie, Pearl Lynn *artist, singer, scriptwriter*

Miami
Bannard, Walter Darby *artist, art critic*
Chambers, Elenora Strasel *artist*
Dorn, Gordon Joseph *artist, art educator*
Kislak, Jean Hart *art director*
Maddern, David *artist*
Mendieta, Raquelín Maria de la Concepción *artist*

Moran, Kate *sculptor, photographer*
Pietrocarlo, Nick *artist, consultant*
Salinas, Baruj *artist, architect*
Urban, Alan Gene *painter, art executive*

Miami Beach
Gordon, Conni *artist, educator*

Mount Dora
Kirton, Jennifer Myers *artist*

Naples
Eldridge, David Carlton *art and antique appraiser*
York, Tina *painter*

Okeechobee
Mercer, Frances deCourcy *artist, educator*

Orlando
Warren, Dean Stuart *artist*

Osprey
Gross, Marilyn Agnes *artist, business owner, speech audiologist*

Palm Beach
Ness, Evaline (Mrs. Arnold A. Bayard) *illustrator, writer*

Palm Beach Gardens
Samuels, Fern Jacqueline *artist, educator*

Parkland
Janice, Barbara *illustrator*

Plantation
Ballantyne, Maree Anne Canine *artist*

Safety Harbor
Banks, Allan Richard *artist, art historian, researcher*

Saint Augustine
Connaway, Robert Wallace *artist, computer programmer*
Quirke, Lillian Mary *retired art educator*

Saint Petersburg
Rigg, Carol Margaret Elizabeth Ruth *calligrapher, graphics designer, art educator*
Stedman, R VanGorden *artist, art historian radio and television personality*

Sarasota
Altabe, Joan Augusta Berg *artist, writer, art and architecture critic*
Harmon, Foster (Loren Foster Harmon) *arts consultant*
Makau, John *artist*
Plunket, Dolores *art and archaeology educator*

Sebastian
Pieper, Patricia Rita *artist*

Stuart
Geng, Lisa Fernandez *artist*

Tampa
Cardoso, Anthony Antonio *artist, educator*

Tavernier
Fundora, Thomas *artist, journalist, composer*

Temple Terrace
Kashdin, Gladys Shafran *painter, educator*

Venice
Girman, Dee-Marie *iconographer, artist*

Vero Beach
Billeci, Andre George *art educator, sculptor*
Sprout, Francis *artist, educator*

West Palm Beach
Gronlund, Robert B. *art collector, fund raising consultant*
Longhofer, Gordan Allen *art educator, performance artist*
Lozito, Gilda Lelia *artist, painter*

Weston
Napp, Gudrun F. *artist*

Winter Springs
San Miguel, Manuel *painter, historian, composer, poet, art collector*

GEORGIA

Alpharetta
Bolton, Robin Jean *artist, painter*

Athens
Carnes, Jill Andrea *artist*
Clements, Robert Donald *sculptor*
DeZurko, Edward Robert *retired art educator*
Herbert, James Arthur *artist, filmmaker*
Kaufman, Glen Frank *art educator*
Olsen, Richard James *artist, educator*
Paul, William Dewitt, Jr., *artist, educator, photographer, videographer, museum director*

Atlanta
Brown, Sarah M. *artist, gallery owner, educator, publisher*
Gibson, Michael *artist*
Malone, James Hiram *graphic artist, painter, writer*
Parrish, Carl E. *artist, educator*
Rodríguez, Rocío *artist*

Augusta
Hand, Maryanne Kelly *artist, educator*

Columbus
Nix, Jeffrey Alan *photographer*

Darien
Davis, Ann Richardson *artist, sculptor, book dealer, writer*

Franklin Springs
Pettyjohn, Emma Kennedy *fine arts educator*

Hawkinsville
Whipple, Woodrow Thomas *artist, educator*

Jasper
Sutter, Jean *sculptor*

Lithia Springs
Jackson, Mitchell Alexander *artist, writer*

Macon
Weaver, Jacquelyn Kunkel Ivey *artist, educator*

Mount Berry
Mew, Thomas Joseph, III, (Tommy Mew) *artist, educator*

Roswell
Christopher, Lin *artist*

Savannah
Aja-Herrera, Marie *fashion designer, educator*
Aquadro, Jeana Lauren *graphic designer, educator*
Foley, Marilyn Lorna *artist*

Scottdale
Borochoff, Ida Sloan *artist*

Wildwood
Dombrowski, Bob *artist, publisher*

HAWAII

Honolulu
Betts, Barbara Stoke *artist, educator*
Chang, Rodney Eiu Joon *artist, dentist*
Guthrie, Edgar King *artist*
Pickens, Frances Jenkins *artist, educator*
Uhl, Philip Edward *artist, photographer, cinematographer*
Wolfe, Suzanne L. *artist, art educator*

Kapaa
duPont, Nicole *artist*

Kapaau
Jankowski, Theodore Andrew *artist*

Kihei
Galesi, Deborah Lee *fine artist*

Makawao
Keliiaa, Paul Bertrand *artist*

IDAHO

Harrison
Carlson, George Arthur *artist*

Lewiston
Esparsen, Ray Pat *art educator*

Meridian
Shaffer, Mary Louise *art educator*

Osburn
Bardelli, Frederick Ketchell *artist, art educator*

ILLINOIS

Bourbonnais
Wilkey, Elmira Smith *illustrator, artist, publisher, writer, educator*

Champaign
Jackson, Billy Morrow *artist, retired art educator*

Chicago
Alcantara, Anita Luisa *artist*
Altman, Edith G. *sculptor*
Anderson, Craig Allen *retired art educator, artist*
Aubin, Barbara Jean *artist*
Bowman, Leah *fashion designer, consultant, photographer, educator*
Campos-Pons, Maria Magdalena *artist*
Castillo, Mario Enrique *artist, educator*
Coffey, Susanna Jean *art educator*
Crane, Barbara Bachmann *photographer, educator*
Gray, Richard *art dealer, consultant, holding company executive*
Gunning, Tom *art educator*
Harris, Thomas Liston *art educator*
Himmelfarb, John David *artist*
Hindman, Leslie Susan *auctioneer*
Kearney, John Walter *sculptor, painter*
Kenney, Estelle Koval *artist, educator*
King, Andre Richardson *architectural graphic designer*
Look, Dona Jean *artist*
Malham, Joseph Mario *artist, writer*
McGrail, Jeane Kathryn *artist, educator, poet, curator*
Olin, Margaret *art educator*
Sigler, Hollis *artist, educator, author*
Smith, Harry Buchanan, Jr., *graphic designer, painter, photographer, writer*
Tessing, Louise Scire *graphic designer*
Thall, Robert *photographer, educator*
Wilson, Anne Gawthrop *artist, educator*
Workman, Robert Peter *artist, cartoonist*

Dekalb
Tió, Adrian Ricardo *artist, art educator*

Des Plaines
Banach, Art John *graphic artist*
Henrikson, Arthur Allen *political cartoonist, educator*

Dixon
Huber, Marianne Jeanne *art dealer, appraiser*

East Dundee
Simons, Gail S. *artist, educator, librarian*

Edwardsville
Hampton, Phillip Jewel *artist, art educator*
Malone, Robert Roy *artist, art educator*

Evanston
Conger, William Frame *artist, educator*
Hirshfield, Pearl *artist*

Frankfort
Sandlin, Dorothy *artist*

Highland Park
Slavick, Ann Lillian *retired art educator*

Hinsdale
Pantuso, Michael Vincent *graphic design company executive*

Hudson
Mills, Frederick VanFleet *art educator, educator, watercolorist*

Lake Forest
Weston, Dawn Thompson *artist, researcher*

Lombard
Ahlstrom, Ronald Gustin *artist*
Hudson, Samuel Campbell, Jr., *art educator, artist, sculptor, portraitist*
Sapulich, Joseph M. *art director*

Mchenry
Chisu, Ioan *artist*

Morton Grove
Goldsmith, Barbara Cecile *sculptor, curator*

Normal
Mau, Benjamin *artist*

Oak Lawn
Jachna, Joseph David *photographer, educator*

Park Ridge
Charewicz, David Michael *photographer*

Scales Mound
Lieberman, Archie *photographer, writer*

Table Grove
Thomson, Helen Louise *artist*

Techny
Vanderstappen, Harrie Albert *Far Eastern art educator*

Wheaton
Lowrie, Pamela Burt *educator, artist*

Willowbrook
Burrows, Donald Albert *artist, painter, photographer, dean*

Winnetka
Plowden, David *photographer*

INDIANA

Anderson
Olson, Carol Lea *lithographer, educator*

Beverly Shores
Collins, Moira Ann *graphics and communications company executive, calligrapher*

Bloomington
Connally, Sandra Jane Oppy *retired art educator, artist*
Markman, Ronald *artist, educator*
O'Hearn, Robert Raymond *stage designer*
Stines, Betty Irene *artist*

Evansville
Baker, Gloria Marie *visual artist, art educator*
Roth, Carolyn Louise *art educator*

Fort Wayne
Ushenko, Audrey Andreyevna *painter, art historian, educator*

Greensburg
Black, Marsha Jean *art educator, writer*

Indianapolis
Rutledge, Joanne *artist, consultant*

Kokomo
Ranney, Sandra Kay *artist, fine arts and humanities educator*

Lagro
Lynn, Richard Jo *freelance/self-employed illustrator, journalist, cartoonist*

Nashville
Kriner, Sally Gladys Pearl *artist*

Terre Haute
Lamis, Leroy *artist, retired educator*

Valparaiso
Olson, Lynn *sculptor, painter, writer*

West Lafayette
Ichiyama, Dennis Yoshihide *design educator, consultant, administrator*

Winamac
Ligocki, Gordon Michael *artist, educator*

IOWA

Ankeny
Stahr, Curtis Brent *photographer, art association administrator, educator*

Britt
Castillo, Leanne Marlow *artist, geriatrics nurse*

Cedar Falls
Echeverria, Frje *art educator, artist*

Coralville
Allen, (Edwin) Lee *artist*

Des Moines
Reece, Maynard Fred *artist, writer*

Iowa City
Hettmansperger, Sue *artist*
Myers, Virginia Anne *art educator*
Schmidt, Julius *sculptor*

KANSAS

Dodge City
Rosel, Carol Ann *artist*

Lawrence
Dooley, Patrick John *graphic designer, design educator*

Leawood
Kordash, Dorothy Mae *artist*

Ottawa
Howe, William Hugh *artist*

Topeka
Lee, Karen *art appraiser*
Navone, Edward William *artist, educator*
Peters, Barb Waterman *artist, educator*

KENTUCKY

Fort Wright
Sullivan, Connie Castleberry *artist*

Frankfort
Lanham, Sallie Clay *artist, educator*

Lexington
Sandoval, Arturo Alonzo *art educator*
Snowden, Ruth O'Dell Gillespie *artist*

Louisville
Brugioni, David Michael *graphic designer, illustrator, artist*

LOUISIANA

Cecilia
Girouard, Tina *artist, curator*

Choudrant
Ford, John Charles *artist*

Lake Charles
Roy, Donald *artist, poet*

Metairie
Banton, Kathleen Ariatti *artist, educator*
Crosby, Deborah Berry *artist*

New Orleans
Bailey, Barry Stone *sculptor, educator*
Best, Susan Marie *artist, educator*
Thornell, Jack Randolph *photographer*
Wegmann, Mary Katherine *art director*

Shreveport
Hughes, Mary Sorrows *artist*
Wray, Geraldine Smitherman (Jerry Wray) *artist*

Slidell
Neale, Zahidi Sahaj *artist, educator*

MAINE

Biddeford
Riley, Pamela Janerico *artist*

Cushing
Magee, Alan *artist*

Gorham
Bearce, Jeana Dale *artist, educator*

New Harbor
Lyford, Cabot *sculptor*

Ogunquit
Carpenter, George Robert *artist*
West, Norman Ellsworth *artist*

Portland
Bushell, Agnes *art educator, writer*

South Portland
Huntoon, Abby Elizabeth *artist, educator*

Trevett
Mathias, Cordula *art dealer*

West Southport
Barker, Walter William, Jr., *artist, writer*

Yarmouth
Clark, Gail Theroux *artist*

York
Haley, Priscilla Jane *printmaker*
Hallam, Beverly (Beverly Linney) *artist*

MARYLAND

Annapolis
Alderdice, Cynthia Lou *artist*
Fry, Virginia Milne *artist, poet*

Thoms, Josephine Bowers *artist*

Baltimore
Carper, Gertrude Esther *artist, marina owner*
Duncan, Lionel Sebastian *artist, educator*
Tapper, Leona (Leela) Siff *artist*

Balto
Ayala, Michelle *computer graphics designer, minister*

Bethesda
Dox, Ida *author, medical illustrator*
Elliott, George Armstrong, III, *artist, journalist*
Fleming, Patricia Stubbs *artist*
Koenig, Elizabeth Barbara *sculptor*
Perlmutter, Jack *artist, lithographer*
Sarnoff, Lili-Charlotte (Lolo Sarnoff) *artist*

Brentwood
Kaskey, Raymond John *sculptor*

Centreville
Amos, James Lysle *photographer*

Chestertown
Kellogg-Smith, Peter *sculptor, educator*

Chevy Chase
Duvall, Bernice Bettum *artist, exhibit coordinator, jewelry designer*
Kranking, Margaret Graham *artist*
Wright, Frank *artist, educator*

Denton
Doster, Rose Eleanor Wilhelm *artist*

Gaithersburg
Jevtic, Milomir *artist, sculptor*

Galena
Hunsperger, Elizabeth Jane *art and design consultant, educator*

Germantown
Bu, Rulei *artist, educator*

Glen Echo
Stevenson, A. Brockie *retired artist*

Lutherville
Kissel, William Thorn, Jr., *sculptor*

Potomac
Keil, Marilyn Martin *artist*

Silver Spring
Peiperl, Adam *kinetic sculptor, photographer*
Woolard, Connie Ward *artist, retired art gallery manager*

Whitehaven
Scott, David Winfield *artist, museum consultant*

Woodbine
Nuss, Barbara Gough *artist*

MASSACHUSETTS

Amherst
Anderson, Ronald Trent *artist, educator*
Dabrowski, Thaddeus E. *art educator, art consultant, painter*
Elman, Naomi Geist *artist, producer*
Kimball, Justin *photographer, educator*
Lasch, Pat *artist, educator*
Liebling, Jerome *photographer, educator*
Yarde, Richard Foster *art educator*

Ashland
Jost, David Nelson *art educator*

Auburn
Berg, G. Vivian *artist*

Barnstable
Lummus, Carol Travers *artist, printmaker*

Belmont
Hilt, Mary Louise *artist*

Beverly
Manning, William Frederick *retired wire service photographer*
Roy, Robert William *artist, educator*

Bolton
Keane, Karen M. *auction house executive*

Boston
Ablow, Joseph *artist, educator*
Ablow, Roz Karol (Roselyn Karol Ablow) *painter, curator*
Fink, Aaron *artist*
Gallagher, Ellen *artist*
Gibran, Kahlil *sculptor*
MacLean, Alex Stokes *aerial photographer*
Parker, Olivia *photographer*
Wiesner, David *illustrator, children's writer*

Brookfield
Couture, Ronald David *art administrator, design consultant*

Brookline
Barron, Ros *artist*
Kay, Reed *artist, educator*
Rubin-Katz, Barbara *sculptor, human services administrator*
Swirnoff, Lois *artist, color theorist*

Burlington
DeCrosta, Susan Elyse *graphic designer*

Cambridge
Ackerman, James Sloss *fine arts educator*
Alcalay, Albert S. *artist, design educator*
Bakanowsky, Louis Joseph *visual arts educator, architect, artist*
Chandler, Fay Martin *artist*

Feininger, Theodore Lux *artist*
Handford, Martin John *illustrator, author*
Mazur, Michael *artist*
Mc Kie, Todd Stoddard *artist*
Shubart, Dorothy Louise Tepfer *artist, educator*
Slosburg-Ackerman, Jill Rose *artist, educator*
Thompson, Samuel G. *artist*
Wodiczko, Krzysztof *artist, architect, educator*

Chilmark
Low, Joseph *artist*

Concord
Ihara, Michio *sculptor*

Dover
Rankine, V.V. *sculptor, painter*

East Bridgewater
Heywood, Anne *artist, educator, author*

East Orleans
Burkert, Robert Randall *artist*

Framingham
Aronson, Benjamin *artist*

Great Barrington
Yanoff, Arthur Samuel *artist, art therapist educator*

Harwich
Geberth, Frances White *painter*
Steward, Aleta Joanna *fine artist, digital artist*

Humarock
Murphy, Ann Marguerite *artist*

Lexington
Burwen, Barbara R. *painter*
Dietrich, Melinda *visual arts administrator*

Lynn
Farris, Robert Harold, Jr., *artist, educator*

Marblehead
Heins, Esther *botanical artist, painter*

Marshfield
Arapoff, John Richard *artist*

Marshfield Hills
Krause, Dorothy Simpson *fine artist*

Natick
Geller, Esther (Bailey Geller) *artist*

Needham
Carr, Iris Constantine *artist, writer*

Newtonville
Polonsky, Arthur *artist, educator*

Northampton
Knapp, Lucretia A *artist, educator, filmmaker*
Rayevsky, Robert *illustrator*
Rupp, Sheron Adeline *photographer, educator*

Norwell
Brett, Jan Churchill *illustrator, author*

Orleans
Baird, Julian Thompson, Jr., *art dealer*

Osterville
Kennedy, Michele Lyn *artist*

Plymouth
Freyermuth, Virginia Karen *art educator*

Provincetown
Hutchinson, Peter Arthur *artist*

Reading
Frey, Joanne Alice Tupper *art educator*
Nordstrand, Nathalie Elizabeth Johnson *artist*

Rockport
Calabro, Joanna Joan Sondra *artist*
Mosher, Donald Allen *artist*

Seekonk
Backes, Joan *artist, educator*

Sheffield
Schmehl Morley, Susan Linda *fine arts educator, artist*

Sherborn
Pickhardt, Carl Emile, Jr., *artist*

Somerville
Halevi, Marcus *photographer*
Yu, Shan *artist*

Southampton
Slater, Jess Everett *artist*

Springfield
Frey, Mary Elizabeth *artist*

Sudbury
Aronson, David *artist, retired art educator*

Townsend
Thorpe, Samuel Stanley, Jr., *artist*

Wakefield
Fioravanti, Jeff *artist*

Wayland
Dergalis, George *artist, educator*

Wellesley
Copplestone, David Wesley *artist, business owner*
McGibbon, Phyllis Isabel *art educator, artist*

West Brookfield
Higgins, Brian Alton *art gallery owner, pastel artist*

NEW MEXICO

Albuquerque
Antreasian, Garo Zareh *artist, lithographer, art educator*
Barry, Steve *sculptor, educator*
Coleman, Barbara McReynolds *artist*
Feinberg, Elen Amy *artist, educator*
Green, Mae Maera *artist*
Hahn, Betty *artist, photographer, educator*
Hovel, Esther Harrison *art educator*
Keating, David *photographer*
Lee-Smith, Hughie *artist, educator*
Miera, Lucille Catherine Miera *artist, retired art educator*
Multhaup, Merrel Keyes *artist*
Nelson, Mary Carroll *artist, writer*
Nevin, Jean Shaw *artist*
Qualley, Charles Albert *art educator*
Steider, Doris *artist*
Witkin, Joel-Peter *photographer, poet*

Alto
Zeitelhack, Gloria Jeanne *artist*

Belen
Chicago, Judy *artist*

Corrales
Eaton, Pauline *artist, educator*

Gallup
Cattaneo, Jacquelyn Annette Kammerer *artist, educator*

Hobbs
Garey, Patricia Martin *artist*

Jemez Springs
Brandon, John Boyd *artist*

Nogal
Moeller, Susan Elaine *artist*

Pinos Altos
Rogers, Linda Lee *artist*

Ranchos De Taos
Marx, Nicki Diane *sculptor, painter*

Roswell
Wiggins, Kim Douglas *artist, art appraiser, art dealer*

Sandia Park
Weitz, Jeanne Stewart *artist, educator*

Santa Fe
Allen, Page Randolph *artist*
Harroun, Dorothy Sumner *painter, educator*
Malone, Roxanne Enyeart *artist, educator*
Randolph, Somers *sculptor*
Sloan, Jeanette Pasin *artist*
Villela, Khristaan David *art educator*

Silver City
McCray, Dorothy Westaby *artist, printmaker, educator*

Taos
Becker, Elisabeth Maria *artist, educator*
Bell, Larry Stuart *artist*
Farnsworth, John Edward *artist, educator*
Harmon, Barbara Sayre *artist*
Martin, Agnes *artist*

Tesuque
Novak, Joe *artist*

NEW YORK

Afton
Schwartz, Aubrey Earl *artist, educator*

Albany
Lawton, Nancy *artist*
Meo, Diane Sue *artist, writer*

Alfred
Higby, Wayne (Donald Higby) *artist, educator*
Scheer, Joseph H. *artist, education educator*

Amenia
Hale, Nathan Cabot *sculptor, artist, poet*

Ancram
Blechman, R. O. *artist, filmmaker*

Ancramdale
Weinstein, Joyce *artist*

Armonk
Tantillo Elton, Nina *artist, graphics designer, educator*

Batavia
Grieger, Donald L. *artist*

Bayside
Adoquei, Sam *art educator, artist*

Bearsville
Ruellan, Andree *artist*

Briarcliff Manor
Lew, Leslie *artist*

Bronx
Adams, Alice *sculptor*
Behnken, William Joseph *art educator, artist*
Gillison, David Andrew *artist, educator*
Gonzalez, Rose A-Navarro *artist*
Juszczyk, James Joseph *artist*
Kassoy, Hortense (Honey Kassoy) *artist, sculptor, painter*
Kitt, Olga *artist*
Robinson, Nadine Caroline *artist*
Schwam, Marvin Albert *graphic design company executive*

Brookhaven
Grucci Butler, Donna *fireworks company executive*

Brooklyn
Adler, Lee *artist, educator, marketing executive*
Amendola, Sal John *artist, educator, writer*
Aquino, Humberto *painter, artist*
Argie, Jenny Lynn *artist*
Baker, Richard Joseph *artist*
Brody-Lederman, Stephanie *artist*
Clark, James O. *sculptor, art educator*
Collier, Sadikisha Saundra *artist, educator*
Dantzic, Cynthia Maris *artist, educator*
Diamond, Jessica *artist*
Dinnerstein, Harvey *artist*
Dinnerstein, Simon Abraham *artist, educator*
Fischer, R. M. *sculptor*
Fuller, Marney Cecelia *painter, graphics designer*
Gianlorenzi, Nona Elena *painter, art dealer, educator*
Giusti, Karin F. *artist, educator*
Haber, Ira Joel *artist, art educator*
Ivens, Rosalind *artist*
Jemisin, Noah *artist, educator*
Jones, Susan Emily *fashion educator, administrator, educator emeritus*
Kemp, James William *graphic artist*
Kjok, Sol *artist, art historian, linguist, translator*
Ortiz, Lori J. *painter, writer*
Otterness, Tom *artist*
Pearlstein, Seymour *artist*
Peker, Elya Abel *artist*
Pitynski, Andrzej Piotr *sculptor*
Rauschenbusch, Stephanie *artist, educator, poet*
Roach, Kevin Joseph *set designer*
Schaefer, Marilyn Louise *artist, writer, educator*
Shaw, Kendall (George Shaw) *artist, educator*
Silverstein, Louis *art director, designer, editor*
Sonenberg, Jack *artist*
Swirsky, Judith Perlman *arts administrator, consultant, writer*
Tomaselli, Fred *artist*
Turtz, Marilyn Joan *artist, painter, educator*
von Rydingsvard, Ursula Karoliszyn *sculptor*
Williams, Alun *artist, curator, art gallery director*
Woodham, Joseph Ed *artist, art educator*
Zakanitch, Robert Rahway *artist*
Zollar, Jawole Willa Jo *artist, choreographer*
Zweig, Janet *artist*

Buffalo
Houseknecht, Stephen *artist, educator*
McKibbin, William Alex *artist*
Naylon, Betsy Zimmermann *artist*
Rogovin, Milton *documentary photographer, retired optometrist*
Wise, Roland *retired art educator, artist*

Buskirk
Johanson, Patricia Maureen *artist, architect, park designer*

Cambridge
Tougias, Mark A. *artist*

Campbell Hall
Greenly, Colin *artist*

Canaan
Knebel, Constance *potter, ceramist*
Walker, William Bond *painter, retired librarian*

Catskill
Green, Francis Eugene *artist, educator*

Central Square
BuMann, Sharon Ann *sculptor*

Chatham
Squier, Rita Ann Holmberg *graphic designer*

Corning
Buechner, Thomas Scharman *artist, retired glass manufacturing company executive, museum director*

Cornwall On Hudson
Abrams-Collens, Vivien *artist*

Cortlandt Manor
Rosenberg, Marilyn Rosenthal *artist, visual poet*

Croton On Hudson
Johann, Anne Dorothy *visual artist, painter, printmaker, graphic artist*
Rubinfien, Leo H. *photographer, filmmaker*

Cutchogue
Dank, Leonard Dewey *medical illustrator, audio-visual consultant*
Strimban, Robert *graphic designer*

Dix Hills
Fouladvand, Hengameh *artist*

East Hampton
Delson, Elizabeth *artist*
Jaudon, Valerie *artist*
Scott, Rosa Mae *art educator, artist*

East Quogue
Setlow, Neva Delihas *artist, research biologist*

East Setauket
Badalamenti, Fred Leopoldo *artist, educator*

Eastchester
Gottschall, Edward Maurice *graphic arts company executive*

Fayetteville
Hadyk-Wepf, Sonia Margaret *artist, real estate manager*
Serafin, John Alfred *art educator*

Flushing
Flechner, Roberta Fay *graphic designer*
Yeo, Kim Eng *artist*

Fly Creek
Dusenbery, Walter Condit *sculptor*

Forest Hills
Fernandez, Amy *artist, illustrator, writer, educator*

Franklin Square
Indiviglia, Salvatore Joseph *artist, retired naval officer*

Fredonia
Conradi, Janet K. *art educator*

Gilbertsville
Greefkes, Roland Cornelis *artist*

Great Neck
Blanda, Sandi *artist*
Seidler, Doris *artist*

Hartsdale
Feigenbaum, Eric Seth *display designer, educator*

Hillsdale
Richards, Joseph Edward *artist*

Hudson
Artschwager, Richard Ernst *artist*

Hudson Falls
Leary, Daniel *artist*

Huntington
Tar, Laszlo *artist*
Twardowicz, Stanley Jan *artist, photographer*

Ithaca
Garrison, Elizabeth Jane *artist*
Gillis, Andrew J. *photographer*
Grady, James Michael, Jr., *art educator, theater director*
Grippi, Salvatore William *artist*
McCue, Arthur Harry *artist, educator*
Mikus, Eleanore Ann *artist*
Poleskie, Stephen Francis *artist, retired educator, writer*
Squier, Jack Leslie *sculptor, educator*

Jackson Heights
Dacey, Paul *artist*

Jamaica
Cade, Walter, III, *artist, actor, musician, vocalist*
Fogel, Jacqueline *artist*

Jamestown
White, Rae Alison *artist, writer*

Jeffersonville
Harms, Elizabeth Louise *artist*

Jordanville
Durham, Jeanette Randall *artist, educator*

Kenmore
Auerbach, Rita Argen *artist, educator*

Locust Valley
DeRegibus, William *artist*

Long Island City
Donneson, Seena Sand *artist*

Mahopac
Gonzalez-Tornero, Sergio *artist*

Mamaroneck
Katz, Babette *artist*

Marcellus
Baker, Bruce Roy *retired art educator, artist*

Marlboro
Cash, Sydney *sculptor, jewelry designer*

Merrick
Cariola, Robert Joseph *artist*

Miller Place
Sanger, Eileen *artist*

Mount Kisco
Michael, Creighton *artist, educator*

Napanoch
Kooistra, Andrew J. *painter, sculptor*

Naples
Gelder, Donald Clifford Barnard *artist*

New Hampton
Sinnard, Elaine Janice *painter, sculptor*

New Paltz
Azank, Roberto *artist*
Goodell, Kathy Susan *artist, educator*

New Rochelle
Buster, Larry Vincent *art director*
Slotnick, Mortimer H. *artist*

New York
Abboud, Joseph M. *fashion designer*
Abish, Cecile *artist*
Adams, Dennis Paul *artist*
Adams, Edward Thomas (Eddie Adams) *photographer*
Adri, (Adri Steckling Coen) *fashion designer*
Aitken, Doug *artist*
Allner, Walter Heinz *graphics designer, painter, art director*
Alpert, William Harold (Bill Alpert) *artist, painter*
Alvarado-Juárez, Francisco *visual artist*
Amelan, Bjorn G. *sculptor, set designer*
Anastasi, William Joseph *artist*
Andre, Carl *sculptor*
Anthony, William Graham *artist*
Antonakos, Stephen *sculptor*
Aptekar, Ken *painter*
Ashkin, Michael *artist*
Avedon, Richard *photographer*
Bachner, Barbara LaVerdiere *artist*
Bailey, Xenobia (Sherilyn Bailey) *artist, educator*
Banerjee, (Bimal Banerjee) *artist, educator*
Barnet, Will *artist, educator*
Bastidas, Hugo Xavier *painter*
Baumgardner, Matthew Clay *artist*
Beal, Jack *artist*
Benglis, Lynda *artist, sculptor*
Ben-Haim, Zigi *artist*
Berlind, Robert Elliot *artist, educator*
Berman, Ariane R. *artist*
Bernstein, Carl *jewelry designer, artist*
Berthot, Jake *artist, educator*
Bhavsar, Natvar Prahladji *artist*
Boardman, Seymour *artist*
Bochner, Mel *artist*
Bonino, Fernanda *art dealer*
Bordiga, Lord Benno *art dealer*
Botero, Fernando *artist*
Bourgeois, Louise *sculptor*
Boutis, Tom *artist, painter, print maker*
Bradley, Lisa M. *artist*
Bradshaw, Dove *artist*
Brett, Nancy Heléne *artist*
Bruder, Harold Jacob *artist, educator*
Brumer, Miriam *artist, educator*
Bull, Helen May *artist*
Bunts, Frank Emory *artist*
Byron, Eric Howard *sculptor, museum researcher and administrator*
Caivano, Ernesto *artist*
Cajori, Charles Florian *artist, educator*
Campbell, Ronald Neil *retired magazine designer*
Cardile, Paul Julius *fine arts dealer*
Castoro, Rosemarie *sculptor*
Celmins, Vija *artist*
Cesarani, Sal *fashion designer*
Chen, James Tsing-fang *artist, educator, cultural center administrator*
Chermayeff, Ivan *graphic designer*
Chwast, Seymour *graphic artist*
Chwatsky, Ann *photographer, educator*
Clutz, William (Hartman Clutz) *artist, educator*
Cohen, Cora *artist*
Cole, Willie *artist*
Colp, Norman Barry *photographic artist, curator*
Coraggio, Linus *sculptor, consultant*
Cowles, Charles *art dealer*
Cutler, Ronnie *artist*
Dana, F(rank) Mitchell *theatrical lighting designer*
Daphnis, Nassos *artist*
Davis, Lisa Corinne *artist*
de Champlain, Vera Chopak *artist, painter*
Deem, George *artist*
de la Renta, Oscar *fashion designer*
DeMonte, Claudia Ann *artist, educator*
Denes, Agnes C. *environmental artist*
Dennis, Donna Frances *sculptor, art educator*
Di Meo, Dominick *artist, sculptor, painter*
Dobbs, John Barnes *artist, educator*
Dolinsky, Rebecca *artist, educator*
Dolman, Edward James *auction house executive*
Donegan, Cheryl *artist*
Drucker, Mort *commercial artist*
Duff, John Ewing *sculptor*
Dunbar, Leila *antiques appraiser, auction house executive*
Dunkelman, Loretta *artist*
Eade, Michael Gregory *painter*
Edelson, Mary Beth *artist, educator*
Egielski, Richard *illustrator*
Eins, Stefan *painter, conceptual artist, sculptor, arts curator*
Eisenberg, Sonja Miriam *artist*
Enders, Elizabeth McGuire *artist*
Estes, Richard *artist*
Fazal, Sheikh *photographer*
Feigen, Richard L. *art dealer, collector, writer*
Feldschuh, Jonathan Adam *artist*
Ferri, David *lighting designer*
Feuerman, Carole A. *sculptor, artist*
Field, Patricia *apparel designer*
Findlay, Michael Alistair *art dealer, poet*
Fiore, Joseph Albert *artist*
Fischer, Carl *graphic designer, photographer, actor*
Foley, Maura *picture editor*
Fournier, Nicole D *graphics designer, photographer*
Frankenthaler, Helen *artist*
Fugate-Wilcox, Tery *artist*
Gage, Beau *artist*
Garrett, Wendell *antiques appraiser, auctioneer, editor*
Geismar, Thomas H. *graphic designer*
Geissbuhler, Stephan *graphics designer*
Georges, Paul Gordon *artist, educator*
Gerstein, Mordicai *illustrator*
Gertjejansen, Doyle *artist, educator*
Giannini, A. Christina *costume designer, set designer*
Gibson, Ralph H(olmes) *photographer*
Ginzel, Andrew H. *artist*
Goell, Abby Jane *painter, collage artist, art appraiser*
Goertz, Augustus Frederick, III, *artist*
Gold, Albert *artist*
Gold, Sharon Cecile *artist, educator*
Goldin, Leon *artist*
Goldsmith, Caroline L. *arts executive*
Gordon, Douglas *artist*
Granne, Regina *artist, educator*
Griefen, John Adams *artist, educator*
Grossman, Nancy *artist*
Gursky, Andreas *artist*
Gutman, Robert William *retired educator*
Guzman, Kathleen McFadden *antiques appraiser, auctioneer*
Haacke, Hans Christoph Carl *artist, educator*
Haessle, Jean-Marie Georges *artist*
Halaby, Samia Asaad *artist, educator, computer artist*
Hale, Stephen Michael *artist*
Hamoy, Carol *artist*
Harbutt, Sarah *photographer, director*
Hauser, Sarah B. *artist*
Henselmann, Caspar Gustav Fidelis *sculptor*
Herrera, Arturo *artist*
Herrera, Carolina *fashion designer*
Herring, Oliver *artist*
Highstein, Jene Abel *sculptor*
Hilfiger, Tommy *fashion designer*
Hohauser, Marilyn *artist*
Holder, Donald *lighting designer*
Holton, William *artist*
Hornbacher, Sara S. *visual artist, educator, video producer*
Houghtelling, Ayres *artist, architect, engineer*
Howard, Mildred *sculptor*
Hull, Cathy *artist, illustrator*

Ichikawa, Akiko *artist, editor*
Incandela, Gerald Jean-Marie *artist*
Ireland, Patrick *artist*
Jacquette, Yvonne Helene *artist*
Jenkins, Paul *artist*
Jetter, Frances S. *illustrator, educator, artist*
Johnson, Betsey Lee *fashion designer*
Johnston, Lynn Beverley *animator*
Jones, Kristin Andrea *artist*
Joo, Michael *artist, educator*
Kaish, Luise Clayborn *sculptor, former educator*
Kaish, Morton *artist, educator*
Kamali, Norma *fashion designer*
Kan, Diana Artemis Mann Shu *painter, art educator, writer*
Karan, Donna (Donna Faske) *fashion designer*
Kardon, Dennis *artist, educator*
Katz, Alex *artist*
Keno, Leigh R. *antiques dealer, appraiser*
Keno, Leslie B. *antiques dealer, appraiser*
Kersels, Martin *artist*
Khedoori, Toba *artist*
King, Marcia Gygli *artist*
Kinstler, Everett Raymond *artist*
Klein, Calvin Richard *fashion designer*
Klotz, Florence *costume designer*
Knepper, Ronald Alan *sculptor, educator*
Koppelman, Chaim *artist, educator*
Koppelman, Dorothy Myers *artist, consultant*
Korot, Beryl *artist*
Krauss, Judith Scheer *art dealer*
Krementz, Jill *photographer, author*
Kushner, Robert Ellis *artist*
Kushnir, Andrei *artist, consultant*
Kutosh, Sue *artist*
Kuwayama, Teru *photographer*
LaChapelle, David *photographer*
Lange, Liz Steinberg *apparel designer and executive*
Lash, Stephen Sycle *auction company executive*
Lasker, Jonathan Lewis *artist*
Lauren, Ralph *fashion designer*
Lee, Catherine *sculptor, painter*
LeGrady, George *photographer, educator*
Leibovitz, Annie *photographer*
Leonard, Zoe *artist*
Levine, David *artist*
Lewin, Betsy R. *illustrator*
LeWitt, Sol *artist*
Lipsky, Pat *artist*
Loengard, John Borg *photographer, editor*
Loring, John Robbins *artist, writer*
Lou, Liza *artist*
Lovell, Whitfield *artist*
Mackie, Robert Gordon *costume and fashion designer*
Madsen, Loren Wakefield *sculptor*
Mallet, Jacques Robert *art dealer*
Manglano-Ovalle, Inigo *sculptor*
Mann, Frank Bert *visual artist, painter*
Marcus, Gwen Ellen *sculptor*
Marden, Brice *artist*
Marello, Matt *artist*
Margolin, Jean Spielberg *artist*
Mayer, Rosemary *artist*
McCredie, James Robert *fine arts educator*
McDarrah, Fred William *photographer, editor, writer*
Mc Gowin, William Edward *artist*
McHugh, Caril Eisenstein Dreyfuss *art dealer, art gallery director, consultant*
McKenzie, Mary Beth *artist*
McKinley-Haas, Mary *artist*
Mendelson, Haim *artist, educator, art gallery director*
Mesa, Nilda *artist*
Miller, Harry Brill *scenic designer, actor, director, acting instructor, lyricist, interior designer*
Miller, Nicole Jacqueline *fashion designer*
Miller, Richard Kidwell *artist, actor, educator*
Miller, Richard McDermott *sculptor*
Milonas, Minos *artist, designer, poet*
Morgan, Jacqui *illustrator, painter, educator, writer*
Mori, Mariko *artist*
Murray, Elizabeth *artist*
Neiman, LeRoy *artist*
Newman, Arnold *photographer*
Ney, Alexander *artist, sculptor*
Niccolini, Dianora *photographer*
Notarbartolo, Albert *artist*
Ohlson, Douglas Dean *artist, educator*
Okuhara, Tetsu *artist, photographer*
Oldham, Todd *fashion designer*
Ono, Yoko *conceptual artist, singer, recording artist*
Opie, Catherine *photographer*
Oratofsky, Paul *photographer, application developer*
Orozco, Gabriel *artist*
Ortman, George Earl *artist*
Osorio, Pepon *artist*
Pace, Stephen Shell *artist, educator*
Parker, Nancy Winslow *artist, writer*
Pask, Scott *set designer*
Peckolick, Alan *painter, photographer, graphic designer*
Pelli, Leemour *artist*
Pionk, Richard Cletus *artist, educator*
Piper, J.E. *artist, photographer, historian*
Plavinskaya, Anna Dmitrievna *artist*
Polsky, Cynthia Hazen *artist, art collector, art dealer*
Poons, Larry *artist*
Porter, Liliana Alicia *artist, photographer, painter, printmaker, filmmaker*
Porter, Marc Bennett *auction house executive*
Posen, Zac *apparel designer*
Prieto, Monique N. *artist*
Pujol, Ernesto *artist*
Quackenbush, Robert Mead *artist, author, psychoanalyst*
Rauschenberg, Robert *artist*
Recanati, Dina *artist*
Reddy, Krishna Narayana *artist, educator*
Reiback, Earl Martin *artist*
Reininghaus, Ruth *retired artist*
Remington, Deborah Williams *artist*
Resika, Paul *artist*
Ringgold, Faith *artist*
Robbins, Carrie F(ishbein) *costume designer, educator*
Roberts, Nancy Cohen *art dealer, marketing professional*
Rodriguez, Geno (Eugene Rodriguez) *artist, arts administrator*
Rose, Aaron *artist*

Rosenberg, Alex Jacob *art dealer, curator, fine arts appraiser, educator*
Ross, Charles *artist*
Ross, Rhoda *artist*
Ruscha, Edward *artist*
Russell, Maryanne *photographer*
Ryman, Robert Tracy *artist*
St. Lifer, Jane M. *art appraiser*
Saru, George *artist*
Schnabel, Julian *artist*
Schneider, JoAnne *artist*
Schwartz, Daniel Bennett *artist*
Seborovski, Carole *artist*
Shambroom, Paul *artist, photographer*
Shapiro, Joel Elias *artist*
Sharp, Anne Catherine *artist, educator*
Sherman, Cindy *artist*
Shurdut, Jeffrey Hayden *artist*
Sigal-Ibsen, Rose *artist*
Sikander, Shahzia *artist*
Silver, John L. *artist, educator, poet*
Silverman, Burton Philip *artist*
Simonds, Charles Frederick *artist*
Singer, Barbara Helen *photographer*
Sis, Peter *illustrator, children's book author, artist, filmmaker*
Size, Dennis Michael *lighting and scenery designer*
Skupinski, Bogdan Kazimierz *artist*
Slavin, Arlene *artist*
Sleigh, Sylvia *artist, educator*
Slone, Sandi *artist*
Smith, Kiki *artist*
Smith, Mimi *artist*
Smith, Shirley *artist*
Sobell, Nina R. *artist*
Sonneman, Eve *artist*
Sopanen, Jeri Rainer *photography director*
Southworth, Linda Jean *artist, critic, educator, poet*
Spade, Kate (Katherine Noel Spade) *apparel designer*
Spence, Sique (Mary Stewart Spence) *art dealer*
Sperakis, Nicholas George *artist*
Starr, Steven Dawson *photographer*
Stewart, Jack *artist, educator, writer*
Stone, Caroline Fleming *artist*
Stone, Matt *animator*
Storrs, Immi Casagrande *sculptor*
Swain, Robert *artist*
Tagliarino, Salvatore *set designer, educator*
Thomasos, Denyse *artist*
Tobey, Peter C. *art dealer, conservator, consultant*
Tooker, George *artist*
Trueblood, Emily Herrick *artist, librarian*
Tsao, Vivian J. *artist, educator*
Tscherny, George *graphic designer*
Unruh, Richard Greenwood, III, *artist*
Upright, Diane Warner *art dealer*
Vass, Joan *apparel designer*
Von Betzen, Valerie *artist*
Wald, Sylvia *artist*
Walker, Kara *artist*
Walton, Anthony John (Tony Walton) *theater and film designer, book illustrator*
Wang, Vera *fashion designer*
Wechsler, Gil *lighting designer*
Weems, Carrie Mae *photographer*
Weiner, Lawrence Charles *artist*
Weinstein, Todd Jay *photographer*
Wenegrat, Saul S. *arts administrator, art educator, consultant*
Wesley, John Mercer *artist*
White, Roger L., Jr., *graphic designer, art director*
Wick, Tamara *photographer, artist, writer*
Williams, Sue *artist*
Willis, Thornton Wilson *painter*
Wilson, Robert Frank *graphics designer, property manager*
Winters, Terry *artist*
Wixom, Max Valentine *artist*
Wright, Faith-dorian *artist*
Wunderman, Jan Darcourt *artist*
Wurmfeld, Sanford *artist, educator*
Wyeth, James Browning *artist*
Zimmerman, Kathleen Marie *artist*

Newburgh
Ochs, Richard Wayne *artist, gallery owner*

Northport
Wingerter, John Parker *artist, photographer*

Nyack
Chien, Jennie *sculptor*

Oakdale
Iberti, Elissa Tatigikis *painter, costume designer, educator, independent curator*

Old Westbury
Tiscornia, Ana Maria *artist, educator, writer*

Oneonta
Wentworth, Murray Jackson *artist, educator*

Orchard Park
Mariani, David Frank *retired artist*

Ossining
Hill, Nils Arvid *artist, educator*
Sadan, Mark *photographer, film producer, artist*

Oswego
Baitsell, Wilma Williamson *artist, educator, lecturer*
Fox, Michael David *retired art educator*

Oyster Bay
Mooney, James David, Jr., *aerial photographer*
Prey, Barbara Ernst *artist*

Palisades
Knowlton, Grace Farrar *sculptor, photographer, painter*
Porta, Siena Gillann *sculptor, educator*

Peekskill
Brody, Jo-Ann *artist, educator*
Osyczka, Bohdan Danny *painter*

Penn Yan
Berlyn, Sheldon *art educator, artist*

Piermont
Berkon, Martin *artist*

Poughkeepsie
McCormack, Dan *photographer, educator*

Pound Ridge
Ferro, Walter *artist*
Schwebel, Renata Manasse *sculptor*

Red Hook
Pfeiffer, Werner Bernhard *artist, educator*

Rensselaer
Nack, Claire Durani *artist, author*

Riverhead
Mehling, Robert R. *artist*

Rochester
Giebel, Douglas Richard *art educator, artist*
Lotta, Tom (Anthony Tom Lotta) *artist*
Merritt, Howard Sutermeister *retired art educator*
Sheller, G. A. *artist, educator*
Singer, Alan Daniel *artist*
Sodervick, Bruce Werner *sculptor, art educator*

Roslyn Heights
Newmark, Marilyn *sculptor*

Rye
Lehman, Myra Harriet *sculptor, dental hygienist*
Troller, Fred *graphic designer, painter, visual consultant, educator*

Sag Harbor
Blanc, Peter (William Peters Blanc) *sculptor, painter*
de Cordova, Hector Armando *artist, consultant, art educator*

Saint Albans
Xu, Ying-Pei *artist*

Sanborn
Hill, Rosemary Louise *artist*

Saratoga Springs
Fenton, Michael I. *artist, educator*
Upton, Richard Thomas *artist*

Sayville
Wurtz, Margaret Johnston *artist, calligrapher*

Scarsdale
Carnase, Thomas Paul *graphic designer, typographic consultant*
Newman, Stacey Clarfield *artist, curator*

Schenectady
Banjamin, Martin E. *photographer, art educator*

Shelter Island Heights
Culbertson, Janet Lynn *artist*

Shushan
Witten, Anita *artist, editor*

Snyder
Breverman, Harvey *artist*

Somers
Bensen, Annette Wolf *graphic art company consultant*

Southampton
Kanovitz, Howard *artist, educator*

Sparkill
Myers, Adele Anna *artist, educator, nun*

Staten Island
Gennari, Flint *photographer*
Manister, Craig Alan *artist, educator*

Stony Brook
Dinkins, Stephanie A. *artist, educator*
Pindell, Howardena Doreen *artist*

Syracuse
King, Marcia Jones *potter, physicist, photographer*
Muters, Michael C. *printmaker*
Phillips, Larry Arthur *artist*
Thomas, Sidney *fine arts educator, researcher*

Tappan
Dell, Robert Christopher *geothermal sculptor, educator*

Troy
Canier, Caren R. *painter, educator*
Oatman, Michael James *artist, art educator*

Tuxedo Park
Domjan, Joseph *artist*

Utica
Fiori-Blanchfield, Joan *artist, art historian*

Wading River
Marlow, Audrey Swanson *artist, designer*

Wainscott
Russo, Alexander Peter *artist, educator*

Wantagh
Glaser, David *painter, sculptor*

Warwick
Franck, Frederick Sigfred *artist, author, dental surgeon*

Watertown
Ingalsbe, Marie Esther *artist*

Webster
Nicastro, Kathleen Wanda *artist, educator*

Westbury
Sherbell, Rhoda *artist, sculptor*

White Plains
Erla, Karen *artist, painter, collagist, printmaker*

Woodhaven
Zizi, *artist*

Woodmere
Winick, Bernyce Alpert *artist, photographer*

Woodstock
Banks, Rela *sculptor*
Currie, Bruce *artist*

Yonkers
Speirs, Greg *artist*

Yorktown Heights
Jones, Lauretta Marie *artist, designer, computer science researcher*
Witt, John J. *artist*

NORTH CAROLINA

Asheville
Chapman, Gary H. *artist, educator*

Brevard
Dillon, Doris (Doris Dillon Kenofer) *artist, art historian, educator*

Burnsville
Doyle, John Lawrence *artist*

Chapel Hill
Mangum, William Goodson *artist*

Davidson
Grosch, Laura Dudley *artist, educator*
Jackson, Herb *artist, educator*
Kamp, Barbara Ann *artist, poet, photographer, educator*

Greenville
Wallin, Leland Dean *artist, educator*

Landis
Lynch, Samuel Curlee, Jr., (Sir Sami Lynch) *painter*

Leland
Karch, Jacqueline *artist*

Newport
Burge, Larry Brady *artist*

Pittsboro
Kachergis, Joyce W. *designer*
Schwinn-Jordan, Barbara (Barbara Schwinn) *painter*

Raleigh
Green, Richard Bertram *sculptor*
Robinson, Charlotte Hill *artist*

Sanford
Higgins, George Edward *sculptor*

Whispering Pines
Catullo, Doris Jane *sculptor*

Whitsett
Fennell, Richard Arthur *artist*

Winston Salem
Faccinto, Victor Paul *artist, gallery administrator*

Zebulon
Ruffing, Anne Elizabeth *artist*

NORTH DAKOTA

Mandan
Hodge, Ann Linton *artist*

Taylor
Miller, Jean Patricia Salmon *art educator*

OHIO

Akron
Borowiec, Andrew *art educator, photographer*

Aurora
Lawton, Florian Kenneth *artist, educator*

Bowling Green
Ocvirk, Otto George *artist*

Chagrin Falls
Cox, Cynthia A. *art education specialist*
Held, Lila M. *art appraiser*

Chesterland
Wood, Kenneth Anderson *artist, designer, consultant*

Cincinnati
Bollen, Sharon Kesterson *artist, educator*
Brod, Stanford *graphic designer, educator*
Enstice, Wayne *artist, art educator, writer*
Rexroth, Nancy Louise *photographer*
Strohmaier, Thomas Edward *designer, educator, photographer*
Wygant, Foster Laurance *art educator, educator*

Cleveland
Cassill, Herbert Carroll *artist*
Fallon, Pat *artist, educator*
Taylor, Nellie Ruby *artist, poet*

Cleveland Heights
Weinbaum, Batya *artist, writer*

Columbus
Russell, Nas'Naga R. *illustrator*
Simson, Bevlyn *artist*
Sunami, John Soichi *designer*
Yancey-Jones, Floristine Darlene *artist, educator*
Zex, Damon *artist*

Dayton
Zahner, Mary Anne *art educator*

Greenville
Alexander, Paul Richard *illustrator*

Hilliard
Cupp, David Foster *photographer, journalist*

Hudson
Carducci, Judith Weeks Barker *artist, former social worker*

Lisbon
Berthoff, Frederic Warner *painter*

Loveland
Newton, Baldwin Charles *artist, educator*

Oberlin
Reinoehl, Richard Louis *artist, scholar, martial artist*

Olmsted Falls
Hohman, Lawrence Henry *graphics designer, publishing executive*

Oxford
Ewing, Susan R. *art educator, artist*

Perrysburg
Autry, Carolyn *artist, art history educator*

Richfield
Fry, W. Logan *artist*

Sandusky
Rothermel, Joan Ashley *artist*

Seven Hills
Stanczak, Julian *artist, educator*

Strongsville
Myers, Jack Fredrick *artist, educator, author*

Toledo
Brower, James Calvin *graphic artist, painter*
Cousino, Joe Ann *sculptor*
Danko-McGhee, Katherina Elaine *art educator, consultant*
McGlauchlin, Tom *artist*

Wadsworth
Neumann, Jeffrey Jay *photographer, minister*

Warren
Corson, Joseph Martin *multimedia designer*

West Carrollton
McLaughlin, Daniel R. *display designer, lighting designer*
Rabold, Barbara Ann *artist, writer, illustrator, systems analyst*

OKLAHOMA

Midwest City
Gonzalez, Richard Theodore *photographer*

Oklahoma City
Alaupovic, Alexandra Vrbanic *artist, educator*
Boston, Billie *costume designer, costume history educator*
Sorrin, Mary Louise *artist*
Whitener, Carolyn Raye *artist*

Ponca City
Wood-Warren, Maxine *artist, art educator*

Shawnee
Hicks, Steve L. *artist, art educator*

Tulsa
Frazier, Mary Ann *artist*
Hess, Stanley O. *retired art educator*

OREGON

Ashland
Kostka, Robert Anton *artist, educator*

Bandon
Lindquist, Louis William *artist, researcher, writer*

Cannon Beach
Greaver, Harry *artist*

Cheshire
Antikajian, Sarkis Serop *artist, retired pharmacist*

Depoe Bay
Blacketer, James Richard *artist*

Grants Pass
Roberts, Susan Sturgeon *art educator, writer*

Medford
Schubert, Ruth Carol Hickok *artist, educator*

Newberg
Campbell, Douglas G. *art educator*
Keith, Pauline Mary *artist, illustrator, writer*

Newport
Gilhooly, David James, III, *artist*

Pendleton
Williams-Steinwender, Karin Mae *artist*

Portland
Finch, Rob *photographer*
Hinckley, Gregory Keith *software industry executive*
Lorenz, Nancy *artist*
Mazzola, Michael *lighting designer*
Ramsby, Mark Delivan *lighting designer and consultant*
Thompson, Terrie Lee *graphic designer*

Salem
Pierre, Joseph Horace, Jr., *commercial artist*

PENNSYLVANIA

Allentown
Battle, Turner Charles, III, *art educator, educational association administrator*

Ardmore
Levy, Rochelle Feldman *artist*

Bally
Bertoia, Val *artist*

Bethlehem
Ackerman, Rudy Schlegel *artist, educator*

Bowmansville
Weinhold, Clifford Lee *photographer*

Bryn Mawr
Kline, John Charles *painter, educator*

Camp Hill
Rowe, Michael Duane *artist*

Cochranville
Sazegar, Morteza *artist*

Easton
Delong, Ronald *artist, educator*

Elkins Park
Erlebacher, Martha Mayer *artist, educator*
Romberg, Osvaldo *artist*

Erdenheim
Murphy, Mary Marguerite *artist*

Exton
Webber, Helen *artist, designer*

Fairless Hills
Marable, Simeon-David *artist*

Glen Mills
Turner, Janet Sullivan *painter, sculptor*

Glenshaw
Guentner, James Francis, Jr., *art educator, artist*

Glenside
Frudakis, Zenos Antonios *sculptor, artist*
Medel, Rebecca Rosalie *artist*

Glenwillard
Milne, Christopher McQuiston Wilmoth *photographer, journalist, educator*

Havertown
Craley, Carol Ruth *art educator, academic administrator*

Hawley
Persche, Henry-Peter *art consultant, artist*

Huntingdon Valley
Edelman, Janice *artist, educator*

Indiana
LaRoche, Lynda *artist, educator*

Jessup
Karluk, Lori Jean *craft designer, copy editor*

Kimberton
Williams, Lawrence Soper, Jr., *photographer*

Kinzers
Blake, Richard E. *sculptor, art educator*

Lancaster
Kermes, Constantine John *artist, industrial designer*
Stewart, Arlene Jean Golden *designer, stylist*

Lederach
Hallman, H(enry) Theodore, Jr., (Ted Hallman) *artist, textile designer*

Lumberville
Katsiff, Bruce *artist*

Media
Steinhardt Gutman, Bertha *artist, educator*
Turner, Letitia Rhodes *artist*

New Hope
Freyer, Victoria C. *fashion and interior design executive*

Oxford
Palser, Beth Anne *painter*

Philadelphia
Beck, Christine Safford *photographer, publisher, volunteer, school system administrator, academic administrator*
Camp, Donald Eugene *experimental photographer, educator*
Di Falco, Gerard A. *visual artist*
Franklin, Harold Leroy *graphic artist, filmmaker*
Le Clair, Charles George *artist, retired university dean*
McCormick, Rod *sculptor, art educator*
Paone, Peter *artist*
Saul, April *photographer*
Spandorfer, Merle Sue *artist, educator, author*
Willet, E. Crosby (Everett Crosby Willet) *artist*
Yaros, Constance Greenberg *painter, sculptor*
Zlowe, Florence Markowitz *artist*

Pittsburgh
Bickel, Minnette Duffy *artist*
Burgess, David Lowry *artist*
Kamienska-Carter, Eva Hanna *designer, artist*
Schwalb, Harry *artist*
Wilkins, David George *fine arts educator*

Pottstown
Mitchell, Eric Ehrman *photographer, stock broker*

Richboro
Burtt, Larice Annadel Roseman *artist*

Roscoe
O'Hara, Paul Anthony, Jr., *retired art educator, artist*

Selinsgrove
Connolly, Elma Troutman *artist, contractor, designer*

Shickshinny
Luksha, Rosemary Dorothy *art educator*

Slippery Rock
Bruya, John Robert *art educator*

Solebury
Anthonisen, George Rioch *sculptor, artist*

Spring Grove
Helberg, Shirley Adelaide Holden *artist, educator*

Swarthmore
Hungerford, Constance Cain *art educator*

Wellsboro
Driskell, Lucile G. *artist*

West Grove
Allman, Margo Hutz *sculptor, painter*

Yardley
Ahrens, Henry William *art educator, consultant, puppeteer*

York
Laucks, Therese Elaine *commercial art instructor*

RHODE ISLAND

Charlestown
Rohm, Robert Hermann *sculptor, educator*

Jamestown
Worden, Katharine Cole *sculptor*

Narragansett
Bentley-Scheck, Grace Mary *artist*
Sammis, Anne Mimi *sculptor, artist*

Newport
Nash, Karen Marsteller Myers *sculptor, designer, systems analyst*

North Kingstown
Kilguss, Elsie Schaich *artist, gallery owner*

Providence
Heyman, Lawrence Murray *printmaker, painter*
Howes, Lorraine de Wet *fashion designer, educator*
Leviten, Riva Shamray *artist*

Smithfield
Kosowski, Mary *artist, educator*

Wakefield
Leete, William White *artist*

SOUTH CAROLINA

Camden
Buckley, Claude Langford *artist*

Central
Smith-Cox, Elizabeth Shelton *art educator*

Charleston
Kitner, Harold *artist, educator*

Clover
Easter, Jr., Willie *artist, writer*

Columbia
Hansen, Harold John (Harry Hansen) *artist, educator*
Robbins, Emmalee Elizabeth *fine arts director, speech and theater coach, choreographer, writer*

Greenwood
Transue, David Lowell *illustrator, writer*

Hilton Head Island
Shepard, Steven Louis *graphic artist, painter*

Lexington
Holland, Gene Grigsby (Scottie Holland) *artist*

Mount Pleasant
Ayres, Paul Erdman *artist*

SOUTH DAKOTA

Huron
Clatworthy, Catherine Lynn *educational trainer, graphics designer*

Rapid City
Clark, Lynda Kay *artist*

Rosebud
MacKichan, Margaret Anna *artist, art educator*

Sioux Falls
Aldern, Robert Judson *architectural, liturgical and landscape artist*

TENNESSEE

Chattanooga
Martin, Chester Y. *sculptor, painter*

Mills, Olan, II, *photography company executive*
Swanger, Daniel Anthony-Ignatius *artist*

Cordova
Huang, Ken Shen *art educator*

Dandridge
Weatherly-McWaters, Barbara Cannon *artist*

Knoxville
Drinnon, Janis Bolton *artist, poet, volunteer*
Markert, Cynthia Allin *artist*
Sublett, Carl Cecil *artist, educator*

Lookout Mountain
Wyeth, Andrew *artist*

Memphis
Burton, Fred Clifford *visual artist, educator*
Carroll, Billy Price *artist*
De Mere-Dwyer, Leona *medical illustrator*
McPherson, Larry E(ugene) *photographer, educator*
Riss, Murray *photographer, educator*

Murfreesboro
Reed, Angelica Denise *sculptor, writer, illustrator*

Nashville
LeQuire, Alan Russell *sculpting educator*
Oates, Sherry Charlene *portraitist, artist, photographer*

Oak Ridge
Regan-Stanton, Christa Maria *artist*
Runtsch, Clarence Frederick *sculptor*

TEXAS

Austin
Fearing, William Kelly *art educator, artist*
Hatgil, Paul Peter *artist, sculptor, educator*
Long, Bert Louis, Jr., *artist*
McCoy, John Denny *artist*
Moreno, David *artist*
Reese, Claudia *artist*
Smith, Jeffrey Chipps *art educator*
Weismann, Donald Leroy *art educator, artist, filmmaker, writer*

Brownsville
Gómez, Carlos Guillermo *artist, educator, curator*

College Station
Martin, Carol Jacquelyn *artist, educator*

Corpus Christi
Worden, Elizabeth Ann *artist, author, comedy writer, singer, musician, playwright, screenwriter*

Dallas
Dealey, Lynn Townsend *artist*
Lawrence, Annette *artist*
Norman, Bobby Don *artist, writer, research scientist*
Penn, Linda *computer animator*
Rushton, Lynn Noelle *artist*
Schulz, Sandra E. *art educator*

Dripping Springs
Pellicone, William *artist, sculptor, architect, writer*

Elgin
Hallenbeck, Pomona Juanita *artist*

Euless
Leding, Anne Dixon *artist, educator*

Fort Worth
Allen, William Marion, III, *retired graphic designer, artist*
Kellerman, Shirley Rose *artist*
Rickett, Carolyn Kaye Master *artist, criminologist*

Houston
Camfield, William Arnett *art educator, educator*
Davenport, Bill *sculptor*
Hamilton, Jacqueline *art consultant*
Honeycutt, George Leonard *retired photographer*
Long, Meredith J. *art dealer*
Loro, Antonio *artist*
O'Neil, John *artist*
Orr, Carole *artist*
Reid, Katherine Louise *artist, educator, author*
Shelley, Clyde Burton *artist*
Twombly, Cy (Edwin Parker Twombly Jr.) *artist*

Huntsville
Lea, Stanley E. *artist, educator*

Kerrville
Chance, F. Earlayne *artist*
Frudakis, Evangelos William *sculptor*

Lakehills
Spears, Diane Shields *artist, retired art academy administrator*

Laredo
Gómez, Angela González *art educator*
Watson, Helen Richter *artist, educator*

Lometa
Thompson, Mary Koleta *sculptor, non-profit organization management consultant*

Lufkin
Mott, Earl *artist, poet, writer*

Mabank
Smith, Thelma Tina Harriette *gallery owner, artist*

Marfa
Edge, Daniel *art educator, artist, consultant*

Mission
McClendon, Maxine Nichols *artist*

Odessa
Phillips, Barry *artist, educator*

Plano
Cotter-Smith, Cathleen Marie *art educator, artist*
Litwin, Ruth Ann Forbes *artist*

Port Aransas
Van Baalen, Donna Gale *artist, retired pharmacist*

Post
Killian, Lawrence Harding, II, (Larry H. Killian) *sculptor*

San Antonio
Von Honts, Jacqueline Jay *artist, educator*

Spicewood
Carreli, Hammel Lee *jewelry designer*

UTAH

Castle Valley
Zavada, Barbara Johanna *artist*

Logan
Rasmuson, Brent J. *photographer, graphic artist, lithographer*

Salt Lake City
Dibaiyan, Fatemeh Mariam *artist*

Springville
Francis, Rell Gardner *artist, photographer, writer*

West Jordan
Wyness, Steven Charles *illustrator*

VERMONT

Bomoseen
Ressler, Robert *sculptor*

Cavendish
Shapiro, David *artist, art historian*

Charlotte
Robinson, Sally Winston *artist*

Danby
Peel, Harris *art gallery owner, retired diplomat*

Enosburg Falls
Svendsen, Alf *artist, art educator*

Hardwick
Holtz, Laurence *artisan, photographer*

Manchester Center
Armstrong, Jane Botsford *sculptor*

Newark
Van Vliet, Claire *artist*

Newbury
McGarrell, James *artist, educator*

North Pomfret
Shepherd, Gaal *artist*

Putney
Bass, Eric *artist, performing company executive*

Randolph
Zimet, Matthew *graphic arts and science educator*

Weston
Kasnowski, Chester Nelson *artist, educator*

Winooski
Essman, Robert Norvel *artist, graphic designer*

VIRGINIA

Alexandria
Kim, Sook Cha *artist*
Wasko-Flood, Sandra Jean *artist, educator*
Whitson, Elizabeth Temple *graphics designer*

Arlington
McCoart, Janice Greenberg *art educator*
Reed, Paul Allen *artist*

Blacksburg
Gablik, Suzi *art educator, writer*

Charlottesville
Priest, Hartwell Wyse *artist*
Weinberger, Adrienne *artist, appraiser*

Clifton
Hennesy, Gerald Craft *artist*

Colonial Heights
Grizzard-Barham, Barbara Lee *artist*

Draper
Whitehurst, Mary Tarr *artist, poet, writer*

Falls Church
Kotler, Wendy Illene *art educator, social studies educator, grants coordinator*

Fredericksburg
Schmutzhart, Berthold Josef *sculptor, educator, art and education consultant*

Great Falls
Ganley, Betty *artist*

Harrisonburg
Theodore, Crystal *artist, retired educator*

Independence
Craig, James Hicklin *fine arts consultant*

Leesburg
Robertson, Ruth *artist, art gallery owner*

Leon
Han, Nong *artist, sculptor, painter*

Lynchburg
Hudson, Walter Tiree *artist*
Massie, Anne Adams Robertson *artist*

Mc Lean
Francis, Karen *painter, television producer*
Safer, John *artist, lecturer, banker, real estate developer*
Youngs, William Ellis *photographer, motion picture engineer, projectionist*

Newport News
Abbott, Beverly Stubblefield *artist*
Camp, Hazel Lee Burt *artist*
Kyte, Shannan Dyan *multimedia designer*

Norfolk
Jones, Leon Herbert, Jr., (Herb Jones) *artist*

Reston
Ovissi, Nasser *artist*

Richmond
Freed, David Clark *artist*
Kevorkian, Richard *artist*
Savedge, Anne Creery *artist, photographer*
Vaughn, Ann Marie *art educator, artist*
Worden, Marny *artist, musician*

Roanoke
Osterhaus, Greg S. *artist, graphic designer*

Stanardsville
Gladstone, Arthur M. *artist, author, aerospace engineer*

Swoope
Avery, Robert Newell *sculptor*

Vienna
Yamaguchi, Yuriko Fujita *artist*

Virginia Beach
Drozda, Donna Jean *artist, educator, inventor*
Edmonds, William Bentley *artist, writer*
Ruben, Leonard *retired art educator*
Wasserman, Kathryn *photographer*

Wachapreague
Wilkins, Guy (Ira Wilkins) *painter, art teacher*

Williamsburg
Coleman, Henry Edwin *art educator*
Lorenz, Hans Ernest *photographer*
Robinson, Jay (Jay Thurston Robinson) *artist*
Roseberg, Carl Andersson *sculptor, educator*
Stanley, Shirley Davis *artist*

WASHINGTON

Anacortes
Mc Cracken, Philip Trafton *sculptor*

Battle Ground
Hansen, James Lee *sculptor*

Camano Island
Thayer, Thomas Manor, Jr., *artist*

Edmonds
Johnson, d'Elaine Ann Herard *artist, consultant*

Kent
Pierce, Danny Parcel *artist, educator*

Leavenworth
Caemmerer, Richard Rudolph *art educator*

Lilliwaup
McGrady, Corinne Young *design company executive*

Mercer Island
Langhout-Nix, Nelleke *artist*

Mukilteo
Black, Jackie John *artist*

North Bend
Kaplan, Donna Elaine *artist, educator*

Ocean Park
Lee, Martha *artist, writer*

Olympia
Haseltine, James Lewis *artist, consultant*
Randlett, Mary Willis *photographer*
Russman, Irene Karen *artist*

Richland
Ristow, Gail Ross *art educator, paralegal, children's rights advocate*
Sinerius-Rupp-Bloor, Sharon Kay *painter, photographer, sculptor*

Seattle
Berger, Paul Eric *artist, photographer*
Bibaud, Rene *artist, performer, consultant*
Blomdahl, Sonja *artist*
Chihuly, Dale Patrick *artist*
De Alessi, Ross Alan *lighting designer*
Farbanish, Thomas *sculptor*
Feldman, Roger Lawrence *artist, educator*
Gardiner, T(homas) Michael *artist*
Garvens, Ellen Jo *art educator, artist*
Tift, Mary Louise *artist*
Washington, James Winston, Jr., *artist, sculptor*

Silverdale
Balcomb, Mary Nelson *design studio owner*

Snohomish
Guzak, Karen Jean Wahlstrom *artist*

Tacoma
Harris, Robert Gaylen *art director, graphic designer, illustrator*

Vancouver
Hulburt, Lucille Hall *artist, educator*

WEST VIRGINIA

Charleston
Moore, Mark Tobin *art educator, artist, retired museum curator*

Parkersburg
Gilbert, Kenneth G. *art educator*

Wheeling
Phillis, Marilyn Hughey *artist*

WISCONSIN

Elkhorn
Herr, Richard Joseph *sculptor, educator*

Germantown
Hargan, Charles James *retired lithographer, village official*

Grafton
Duback, Sally Wood *artist, educator*

Hartland
Stamsta, Jean F. *artist*

Hollandale
Colescott, Warrington Wickham *artist, printmaker, educator*

Iola
Rosenberger, Carolyn Ann *art educator*

Janesville
Detert-Moriarty, Judith Anne *graphic designer, educator, volunteer*

Johnson Creek
Quest, Kristina Kay *art educator, small business owner*

Madison
Ardissone, Mary Jean *art director, writer*
Becker, David *artist, educator*
Cooper, Peggy (Mary Margaret) *artist, educator, poet, composer, choreographer*

Milwaukee
Thrall, Arthur Alvin *artist, educator*
Webb, Sheila Menzies *art educator*
Weisner, David *illustrator*

New Richmond
Schwan, LeRoy Bernard *artist, retired art educator*

Oconomowoc
Conrader, Constance Ruth *artist, writer, librarian*
Driscoll, Virgilyn Mae (Schaetzel) *retired art educator, artist, consultant*
Vespa, Ned Angelo *photographer*

Oshkosh
Hu, Li *art educator*

Osseo
Crowell, Rebecca A. *artist*

Wausau
Loftus, Stephen Edward *elementary art educator*

Whitewater
Gauger, Michele Roberta *photographer, studio administrator, corporate executive*

WYOMING

Casper
Ryan, Linda Lee *sculptor, art educator*

Centennial
Russin, Robert Isaiah *sculptor, educator*

Cheyenne
Moore, Mary French (Muffy Moore) *potter, advocate*

Cody
Jackson, Harry Andrew *artist*

Laramie
Reif, David (Frank David Reif) *artist, educator*

CANADA

ALBERTA

Calgary
Besant, Derek Michael *artist, educator*

BRITISH COLUMBIA

Duncan
Hughes, Edward John *artist*

Salt Spring Island
Raginsky, Nina *artist*

Vancouver
Bonifacho, Bratsa *artist*

Victoria
Harvey, Donald *artist, educator*

MANITOBA

Winnipeg
Eyre, Ivan *artist*

NEWFOUNDLAND

Torbay
Dabinett, Diana Frances *visual artist*

NOVA SCOTIA

Halifax
Kulyk, Karen Gay *visual artist*

Wolfville
Colville, David Alexander *artist*

ONTARIO

London
Livick, Stephen *fine art photographer*

Peterborough
Dumas, Michael Godfrey Joseph *artist*

Red Lake
Zaikow, Larry J. James *painter*

Scarborough
Cetín, Anton *artist*

Toronto
Astman, Barbara Ann *artist, educator*
Bolley, Andrea *artist*
Braswell, Paula Ann *artist*
Elder, Richard Bruce *artist, writer*
Jaworska, Tamara *painter, tapestry maker*
Kooluris Dobbs, Linda Kia *artist*
Kramer, Burton *graphic designer, educator*
Semak, Michael William *photographer, educator*
Tolmie, Kenneth Donald *artist, author*
Winter, Frederick Elliot *fine arts educator*

Waterloo
Urquhart, Tony *artist, educator*

QUEBEC

Beaconsfield
Harder, Rolf Peter *graphic designer, painter*

Montreal
Charney, Melvin *artist, architect, educator*
Hopkins, Tom *artist*
Krausz, Peter Thomas *artist, gallery director, educator*

Saint-Adele
Rousseau-Vermette, Mariette *artist*

SASKATCHEWAN

Saskatoon
Bornstein, Eli *artist, sculptor*

MEXICO

Mexico City
De La Riva, Myriam Ann *artist*
Friedeberg, Pedro *painter, sculptor, designer*

Patzcuaro
di Cori, Pat Miller *painter, sculptor*

AUSTRALIA

Camberwell
Base, Graeme Rowland *illustrator, author*

Malanda
Cooper, William Thomas *natural history artist*

AUSTRIA

Vienna
Higgins, William Woods *painter, art educator*

EGYPT

Cairo
Morsi, Abd el Wahab *artist*

ENGLAND

Chiswick
Adams, Norman *artist, educator*

London
Edwards, Sylvia Ann *artist*
Hiller, Susan *artist*
Vicari, Andrew *artist*

Richmond
Armfield, Diana Maxwell *artist, educator*

FRANCE

Arles
Clergue, Lucien Georges *photographer*

Paris
Lacroix, Christian Marie Marc *fashion designer*

Ungaro, Emanuel Matteotti *fashion designer*

Saint Ceols
Saisselin, Remy Gilbert *fine arts educator*

GERMANY

Berlin
Iannone, Dorothy *visual artist, writer*

Frankfurt
Ammann, Jean-Christophe *art director*

ISRAEL

Jerusalem
Menses, Jan *artist, draftsman, etcher, lithographer, muralist*

ITALY

Florence
Cecil, Charles Harkless *artist, educator*

Milan
Honegger, Federico *artist*

Pietrasanta
Swarz, Sahl *sculptor*

JAPAN

Kanagawa
Kato, Tomiko *artist*

Tokyo
Arzouman, David *artist, composer*

PAKISTAN

Lahore
Geoffrey, Iqbal (Mohammed Jawaid Iqbal Jafree) *artist, educator, lawyer*

POLAND

Warsaw
Abakanowicz, Magdalena *artist, sculptor*

SPAIN

Seville
Sanchez, Leonedes Monarrize Worthington (His Royal Highness Duke de Leonedes of Spain Sicily Greece) *fashion designer*

SWEDEN

Bralanda
Emilson, Henry Bertil *artist*

TUNISIA

Carthage
Sehili, Mahmoud *artist*

ADDRESS UNPUBLISHED

Abbe, Elfriede Martha *sculptor, graphic artist*
Abbott, Linda Joy *stained glass artisan, educator, photographer*
Abeles, Kim Victoria *artist*
Abeles, Sigmund M. *painter, printmaker, sculptor*
Aldredge, Theoni Vachliotis *costume designer*
Alexander, Marjorie Anne *artist, art consultant*
Ancona, George Efrain *photographer, author*
Andrade, Edna *artist, art educator*
Andrews, Jean *artist*
Aronson, Marc *artist*
Arrigo, Jan Elizabeth *photographer, writer*
Arrott, Patricia Graham *artist, art instructor*
Aschheim, Eve Michele *artist, educator*
Atkin, Edith *artist, poet*
Azarian, Mary *illustrator*
Babailov, Igor V. *artist, educator*
Ballaine, Jerrold Curtis *artist*
Barnes, Robert Vincent *retired elementary and secondary school art educator*
Barrow, Thomas Francis *artist, educator*
Barsky, Irene J. *art director*
Barth, Frances *artist*
Bartosik, Kimberly Michele *artist*
Bateman, Robert McLellan *artist*
Beckmann-Wells, Patricia G. *animator, writer*
Beerman, Miriam *artist, educator*
Bell, Patricia Ann *photographer, artist, writer*
Bellamy, Jennifer Wiggins *artist*
Benzle, Curtis Munhall *artist, art educator*
Bierman, Sandra *artist*
Bing, Xu *artist*
Birchard, Catherine Suzanne Sieh *artist*
Block, Amanda Roth *artist*
Bowen-Forbes, Jorge Courtney *artist, author, poet*
Boyer, Daniel Christopher *artist, writer*
Brach, Paul Henry *artist*
Bradford, Peter Corey *design consultant*
Bronkar, Eunice Dunalee *artist, educator*
Brown, Alice Elste *artist*
Brown, Carol Rose *artist*
Browne, Diana Gayle *artist, social worker*
Buck, John E. *sculptor, print maker, educator*
Buell, Dexter *artist, sculptor*
Bundi, Renee *art director, graphic designer*
Burns, Leslie Kaye *artist*
Busch, Nancy Elizabeth *artist, educator*
Butler Yank, Leslie Ann *artist, writer, editor*
Butterfield, Deborah Kay *sculptor*
Byrd, Marc Robert *designer, florist*
Cabot, Hugh, III, *painter, sculptor*
Calamar, Gloria *artist*
Campbell, Demarest Lindsay *artist, writer, interior designer*
Campbell, Patton *stage designer, educator*
Cape, Francis *artist*
Carrado, Joseph Michael *painter, sculptor*
Carter, Nanette Carolyn *artist*
Casanova, Aldo John *sculptor*
Caseiras, Jo Ann Striga *artist, educator*
Cassara, Frank *artist, art educator, printmaker*
Cerri, Robert Noel *photographer*
Chinni, Peter Anthony *artist, poet*
Christopher, Roy *set designer, production designer*
Claiborne, Liz (Elisabeth Claiborne Ortenberg) *fashion designer*
Cline, Ann *artist, designer*
Cobb, Ruth *artist*
Colker, Edward *artist, educator*
Conklin, Eric Linwood *artist*
Conley, Helen Donovan *artist, poet*
Conroy, Tamara Boks *artist, special education educator, former nurse*
Cooper, Elva June *artist*
Cooper, Rebecca *art dealer*
Corey, Claire *artist*
Coughlin, Jack *printmaker, sculptor, art educator*
Craw, Freeman (Jerry) *graphic artist*
Crawford, Sheila Jane *elementary education librarian, reading consultant*
Cumming, Robert Hugh *artist, photographer*
Cummings, David William *artist, educator*
Curington, Thomas Franklin, III, *photographer, writer*
Curnutte, Mary E. *artist, restorer of painting, educator*
Currie, Steven Ray *artist*
Dahlstrom, Patti *art educator, writer*
Daisy, Kyran Maxwell *artist, writer*
Dandarov, Robert *artist, educator*
Dangremond, David W. *fine arts educator*
Dave, Vinod C. *art educator*
Davidson, David Isaac *artist, educator*
Davidson, Jeannie *costume designer*
Davis Greivell, Judith Ann *artist*
DeAngelo, Judith *artist*
Debevoise, A. Clay *artist*
De Blasi, Tony (Anthony Armando De Blasi) *artist*
Dechar, Peter Henry *artist*
DeGeus, Wendell Ray *photographer*
DeJack, Jacqueline Elvadeana *artist, educator*
De Looper, Willem Johan *artist, museum curator*
Denison, Julian Rain *lighting designer, writer*
diCorcia, Philip-Lorca *artist, photographer*
Di Giacomo, Fran *artist*
Dill, Laddie John *artist*
Di Suvero, Mark *sculptor*
Dittmer, Linda Jean *photographer, computer artist, retired photojournalist*
Dixon, Michael Wayne *designer, writer, researcher*
Dogançay, Burhan C. *artist, photographer, sculptor*
Dominguez, Eddie *artist*
Dompke, Norbert Frank *retired photography studio executive*
Downes, Rackstraw *artist*
Doyle, Tom *sculptor*
Drasler, Gregory John *artist*
Duval-Carrié, Edouard *artist*
Ebata, Masako *artist*
Eddy, Don *artist*
Egas, Eric *artist*
Elcik, Elizabeth Mabie *fashion illustrator*
Engle, Steve Eugene *artist*
Erickson, James Gardner *retired artist, cartoonist*
Ewing, Edgar Louis *artist, educator*
Exton, Peter Walker *artist, writer*
Farrar, Elaine Willardson *artist*
Faxon, Alicia Craig *art educator, department chairman*
Ferreira, Armando Thomas *sculptor, educator*
Fillmore, John Dillon *artist*
Finn, Mary Ralphe *artist*
Fish, Janet Isobel *artist*
Fisher, Margaret *artist, researcher*
Fouché, Helen Strother *editorial design executive*
Fratkin, Leslie *photographer*
Frauenhoffer, Rose Marie *visual artist, cosmetologist*
Frederick, Elizabeth Eleanor Tatum *watercolor artist, retired educator*
Freilicher, Jane *artist*
Friday, Katherine Orwoll *artist*
Friedman, Marcia L. *photographer, writer*
Fumagalli, Barbara Merrill *artist, art educator, printmaker*
Furth, Karen J. *artist*
Galen, Elaine *painter*
Gallagher, Cynthia *artist, educator*
Gallup, David Craig *artist*
Gamble, Desirata *artist, poet*
Gerhardt, Carol Ashby *visual artist*
Glasson, Lloyd *sculptor, educator*
Glen, Niki *artist*
Gloman, David J. *artist*
Godbee, Gary Russell *artist*
Goldberger, Blanche Rubin *sculptor, jeweler*
Golden, Judith Greene *artist, educator*
Goulet, Lorrie *sculptor*
Graham, K(athleen) M. (K. M. Graham) *artist*
Grames-Lyra, Judith Ellen *artist*
Grande, Alexander, IV, *artist*
Greenberg, Albert *art director*
Guevarra, Manuel Robinson *artist, retired military officer*
Gurwitz-Hall, Barbara Ann *artist*
Haley, Sally Fulton *artist*
Hall, Susan Laurel *artist, educator, writer*
Hamilton, Ann Katherine *artist*
Hammond, Mary Sayer *art educator*
Hannaman, Alberta Anna *artist*
Hanson, Jo *artist, lecturer, writer*
Hardwicke, Catherine Helen *motion picture production designer*
Hasen, Burton Stanley *artist*
Hayes, David Vincent *sculptor*
Heginbotham, Jan Sturza *sculptor*
Heidenheimer, Kylie Lynn *artist*
Helander, Bruce Paul *artist*
Helpern, Joan (Joan Marshall) *designer, business executive*
Henry, John Raymond *sculptor*
Herman, David Henry *artist, violin restorer and dealer*
Herranen, Kathy *artist*
Herzberg, Thomas *artist, illustrator, art educator*
Hickman, Patricia *artist, craftswoman*
Higgins, Larkin Maureen *artist, poet, educator*
Hilton, Nicky (Nicholai Olivia Hilton) *apparel designer*
Hintzke, Teresa Anna *illustrator*
Hornbeck, Carrie L. *photographer*
Hsieh, Tsui-Hsia *artist, educator*
Huffington, Anita *sculptor*
Humann, Richard *artist*
Huo, Bonnie Kwan *artist*
Hyman, Trina Schart *illustrator*
Iacono, Bruce R. *painter*
Janus, Judith *artist*
Jay, Norma Joyce *artist*
Johnson, Elaine Lucille *artist, director*
Johnson, Ursula Anne *artist*
Jones, John Harding *photographer*
Josephson, Kenneth Bradley *artist, retired educator*
Kabakov, Ilya *artist*
Kahn, Susan *artist*
Kaplan, Phyllis *artist, composer*
Kazan, Alexandra Khan *photographer, web site designer*
Kearns, James Joseph *artist*
Kehew, George Mansir *artist*
Kehlmann, Robert *artist, critic*
Khvost-Vostrikova, Natalia S *art educator, consultant*
Kipniss, Robert *artist*
Kipniss MacDonald, Betty Ann *artist, educator*
Kirkland-Cuffee, Rana Antoinette *art educator*
Kirsch, Roslyn Ruth *art educator, painter, printmaker*
Kleiman, Alan Boyd *artist*
Klein, Lynn Ellen *artist*
Klement, Vera *artist*
Knox, Simmie Lee *artist*
Komar, Vitaly *artist*
Krulik, Barbara S. *director, writer, curator*
Kyle, Gene Magerl *merchandise presentation artist*
Landi, Diane Marie *graphics designer, consultant*
Lanson, Dennis *art educator*
La Rocca, Isabella *artist, educator*
Lassiter, Kenneth T. *photography educator, consultant*
Laufer, William Hervey *artist, printmaker*
Lawrence, Mary Josephine (Josie Lawrence) *artist, retired library official, retired library director*
LÊ, An-My *photographer, educator*
Lear, M. Kathleen *artist, music educator, small business owner*
Lebensohn, Jeremy *sculptor*
Lebron, Roberto *artist, educator*
Leeds, Nancy Brecker *sculptor, lyricist*
Lefranc, Margaret (Margaret Schoonover) *artist, illustrator, editor, writer*
Lehrer, Leonard *artist, educator*
Leiber, Judith Maria *designer, manufacturer*
Leipzig, Arthur *photographer, educator emeritus*
Leiva, Nicolas *artist*
Lembark, Connie Wertheimer *art consultant*
LeRoy, G. Palmer *art dealer*
Levi, Josef Alan *artist*
Levin, Morton D(avid) *artist, printmaker, educator*
Levine, Jack *artist*
Lewie, Reva Goodwin *artist, educator*
Lewis, Karen E. *artist, writer*
Lieberman, Louis (Karl Lieberman) *artist*
Liman, Ellen *painter, writer, arts advocate*
Linhares, Judith Yvonne *artist, educator*
Littleton, Harvey Kline *artist*
Liu, Katherine Chang *artist, art educator*
Logan, Earl Steven *artist*
Lopez Heredia, Hubert *artist*
Ludwig, Allan Ira *photographer, artist, author*
Lund, David Nathan *artist*
Lundgren, Cissi *artist, poet*
Lynd, Phyllis *artist, educator*
Magoni, Despo *artist*
Mahmud, Shireen Dianne *photographer*
Majore, Frank *artist*
Mallo, Luis *artist, art director, photographer*
Malloy, John Edward *media artist, writer*
Mangold, Sylvia Plimack *artist*
Mann, Sally *photographer*
Marlowe, Willie *artist, fine arts educator*
Marsh, Merrilyn Delano *sculptor, painter*
Marti, Virgil *artist*
Martin, Noel *graphic design consultant, educator*
Martyl, (Mrs. Alexander Langsdorf Jr.) *artist*
Masi, Robin *artist, writer, educator*
Mason, Lois E. (J. Day Mason) *painter, poet, actress, educator*
Massey, Stephen Charles *rare books and manuscripts appraiser, auctioneer*
Mathieu, Georges Victor Adolphe *artist*
Mauney, Thomas Lee *theater designer*
Mayer, Susan Martin *art educator*
McCargar, Eleanor Barker *artist*
McCully, Emily Arnold *illustrator, writer*
McCurdy, Michael Charles *illustrator, author*
McGee, Carrie L. *artist*
McKay, Renee *artist*
McKnight, Thomas Frederick *artist*
McLaughlin, Jean Wallace *art director, artist*
McMillen, Elizabeth Cashin *artist*
McPeters, Sharon Jenise *artist, writer*
McVicker, Jesse Jay *artist, educator*
Mead, Elizabeth *artist*
Medinger, C. Wynn *design and branding consultant*
Mehling, Emily *artist*
Melvin, Patricia E. *artist*
Meneeley, Edward Sterling *artist*
Menefee, Linnea-Norma *antique dealer*
Merritt, Eleanor Lynette *artist, educator*
Middaugh, Robert Burton *artist*
Mishler, John Joseph *sculptor, art educator*
Misrach, Richard Laurence *photographer*
Mohns, Judith *artist, art educator*
Montgomery, Linda Boudreaux *artist*
Morning, John *graphic designer*
Morse, Ann Lawrance *photographer*
Murray, Ernest Don *artist, educator*
Murray, Robert Gray *sculptor*
Nash, Mary Harriet *artist, educator*
Natkin, Robert *painter*
Nemiroff, Maxine Celia *art educator, gallery owner, consultant*
Newman, Alyse Maxine *artist, writer, lyricist*
Newman, Bruce Murray *antiques dealer*
Newman, Muriel Kallis Steinberg *art collector*
Nichols, Iris Jean *illustrator*
Nix, Patricia *artist*
Nodelman, Nancy Ziegler *sculptor, designer*
Noland, Kenneth Clifton *artist*
Nuss, Joanne Ruth *sculptor, artist*
O'Donnell, Kathleen C. *artist*
Okoshi-Mukai, Sumiye *artist*
Oldenburg, Claes Thure *artist*
Olitski, Jules *artist*
Olkinetzky, Sam *artist, retired museum director and educator*
O'Mara, Hugh *artist*
Ord, Linda Banks *artist*
Owen, Carol Thompson *artist, educator, writer*
Pack, Susan Joan *art consultant*
Palmer, George Thomas *artist*
Pate, Virginia Frances *artist, educator*
Paul, Arthur *artist, graphic designer, illustrator, art and design consultant*
Pearlstein, Philip *artist*
Peckham, Ellen *artist, poet*
Péladeau, Marius Beaudoin *art and history consultant, retired museum director*
Permuth, Jaime *artist, educator*
Peters, Evelyn Joan *artist*
Petterson, Margo *artist*
Pfaff, Judy *artist*
Phelan, Ellen *artist*
Phillips, Ronald Edward *artist, sales executive*
Piazza, Jo Ann Christine *sculptor*
Pidgeon, Leslea Sharon *artist, writer*
Pierce, Diane Jean *artist*
Pierce, Hilda (Hilda Herta Harmel) *painter*
Pipkin, Mary Margaret *artist*
Pozzatti, Rudy Otto *artist*
Priore, Christopher Anselmo *artist*
Provensen, Alice Rose Twitchell *artist, author*
Psillos, Susan Rose *artist, educator*
Pulitizer, Lilly (Lillian McKim Rousseau) *apparel designer, writer*
Purcell, George Richard *artist, postal employee*
Putnam, Marlene Evans *artist*
Putterman, Florence Grace *artist, printmaker*
Quayle, Jackie M. *artist*
Randall, Herbert Eugene *photographer, consultant*
Reid, Geraldine Wold (Geraldine Reid Skjervold) *artist*
Remington, Mary *artist, author*
Rendl-Marcus, Mildred *artist, economist*
Reynolds, Robert *artist, educator*
Richenburg, Robert Bartlett *artist, retired art educator*
Roberts, Russell L. *artist*
Roberts, Suzanne Catherine *artist*
Robinson, Linda Schultz *art educator, artist*
Robinson, Lynda Hickox *artist*
Rock, Mary Ann *artist, educator*
Rockburne, Dorothea Grace *artist*
Ronay, Matthew *sculptor*
Rose, Patricia *artist, educator*
Rosenbaum, Belle Sara *appraiser, interior designer, museum director, educator*
Rosenberg, Carole *art dealer, real estate broker, foundation executive*
Rosenberg, Herb *sculptor, educator*
Rossman, Ruth Scharff *artist, educator*
Rothschild, Jennifer Ann *artist, educator*
Rubello, David Jerome *artist*
Rubin, Sandra Mendelsohn *artist*
Rubinstein, Eva (Anna) *photographer*
Ruehlicke, Cornelia Iris *painter*
Ruffo, Michael *painter*
Rush, Julia Ann Halloran (Mrs. Richard Henry Rush) *artist, writer*
Rutschke, Annamarie *artist*
Sakai, Kiyoko *artist*
Saks, Judith-Ann *artist*
Salerno, Cherie Ann (C. S. Mau) *artist*
Santini, Debrah Ann *art educator, artist*
Santoso, Irene *art director, graphics designer*
Savedra, Jeannine Evangeline *artist, art educator*
Savulich, Andrew Michael *photographer*
Scharf, William *artist*
Schmalz, Carl Nelson, Jr., *artist, educator, printmaker*
Schreiber, Eileen Sher *artist*
Schultz, Eileen Hedy *graphic designer*
Schultz, William John *artist, educator*
Schwartz, Lillian Feldman *artist, filmmaker, art analyst, writer, nurse*
Scofidio, Ricardo *artist*
Scott, Deborah L. *costume designer*
Searles, Edna Lowe *artist, illustrator, composer*
Seddon, Priscilla Tingey *painter*
Seliger, Mark Alan *photographer*
Seligson, Judith *artist*
Serig, Daniel *art educator, researcher*
Shaughnessy, Marie Kaneko *artist*
Sheets, Nelda *artist*
Sheridan, Sonia Landy *artist, retired art educator*
Sherwood, Gloria N. *graphic and literary artist, genealogy researcher*
Shore, Stephen *photographer*
Shulman, Mildred *artist*
Siejka, George John *artist*
Siena, James *artist*
Sillmanm, Amy *painter, art educator*
Simons, Anneke Prins *artist, educator*
Sims, Pauline Andrée Villarico *artist*
Smith, Karen Ann *visual artist*
Smith, Leila Hentzen *artist*
Smith, Leonard Glenn *artist, educator, hypnotherapist*
Smith, Leonore Rae *artist*
Smith, Serafina Gangemi *artist, drug counselor*
Snelson, Kenneth Duane *sculptor*
Sniffen, Frances P. *artist*
Softic, Tanja *artist*
Solman, Joseph *artist*
Sorel, Edward *artist*
Sorensen, Jean *artist*
Souders, Jean Swedell *artist, educator*
Spence, Andrew *artist, painter*
Stanley, Robert Anthony *artist, educator*
Steel, Kuniko June *retired artist*
Stern, Marilyn *photographer, writer, picture editor*
Stevens, May *artist*
Stinsmuehlen-Amend, Susan *artist*
Stockar, Helena Marie Magdalena *artist*
Straus, Laura *photographer, art association administrator*
Strider, Marjorie Virginia *artist, educator*

Stroud, Betsy Dillard *artist*
Struble, Susan C. *artist, volunteer art therapist*
Studer, Carol A. *creative director, graphic designer, photographer, consultant*
Styler, Anda Jasamine *artist, educator*
Sukopp, Karl Martin *sculptor, painter, graphic artist*
Sullivan, Mary Ann *artist*
Swartz, Julianne *artist*
Swensen, Mary Jean Hamilton *graphic artist*
Switzer, Toccoa *artist*
Sze, Sarah *sculptor*
Szyszka, Roswita Evelyn *artist*
Taddei, Lois Annette Magowan *artist, decorator*
Taft, Nellie Leaman *artist*
Tagliente, Josephine Marlene *artist*
Talbot, Nina Isadora *artist, educator*
Taylor, Margaret Turner *apparel designer, economist, writer, architectural designer*
Thomson, Caroline Helen *artist*
Tiravanija, Rirkrit *sculptor*
Tomkow, Gwen Adelle *artist*
Torak, Elizabeth Lichtenstein *artist*
Tresslar, Nola V. *artist, retired marketing professional, retired foundation administrator*
Tsai, Wen-Ying *sculptor, painter, engineer*
Turner, Bracha *Naive Landscape painter*
Turner, Florence Frances *ceramist*
Tyrrell, Lilian *craftsperson, artist*
Ullberg, Kent Jean *sculptor*
Unithan, Dolly *visual artist*
Vanderbilt, Gloria Morgan *artist, actress, fashion designer*
Van Hooser, Patricia Lou Scott *art educator*
Vergara, Camilo José *photographer*
Vernazza, Trish Brown (Trish Eileen Brown) *visual artist, art therapist, sculptor*
Versch, Esther Marie *artist*
Vogel, Conrad David *artist*
Von Furstenberg, Diane Simone Michelle *fashion designer, writer, entrepreneur*
Walsh, Nan *artist, painter, sculptor, consultant*
Waltner, Beverly Ruland *artist*
Warach, Marie *artist*
Ward, Nari *sculptor*
Warren, Alice Louise *artist*
Wasserman, Helene Waltman *art dealer, artist*
Watts, Ginny (Virginia C. Watts) *artist*
Wayne, Lynn *photographer, writer*
Wegman, William George *artist*
Westbie, Barbara Jane *retired graphics designer*
White, Sandra Marie *retired artist*
Wilde, John *artist, educator*
Willenbecher, John *artist*
Williams, Eleanor Claflin (Claffy Williams) *artist*
Williams, Lawrence (Judd) Marvin *artist, education educator*
Wilson, Jane *artist*
Winter, Leigh Ellen *artist, educator*
Wiseman, Jay Donald Donald *photographer, inventor, mechanical designer and contractor, land developer, writer*
Wolpert Richard, Chava *artist*
Woodard, Deana Safford *artist*
Wylan, Barbara *artist*
Yampolsky, Phyllis *artist*
Yates, Steven A. *curator, artist, scholar*
Ynda, Mary Lou *artist, educator*
Youngblood, Daisy *ceramist*
Zaleski, Jean *artist*
Zapf, Hermann *book and type designer*
Zekman, Terri Margaret *graphic designer*
Zelinsky, Paul O. *illustrator, painter, author*
Zentz, Patrick James *artist, rancher*
Zheutlin, Dale *sculptor, educator*
Zivelonghi, Kurt Daniel *painter, computer graphics artist, designer*
Zwerling, Lisa *painter, educator*

ASSOCIATIONS AND ORGANIZATIONS *See also* specific fields

UNITED STATES

ALABAMA

Birmingham
Bonfield, Barbara Goldstein *non-profit organization administrator*
Carter, Frances Tunnell (Fran Carter) *fraternal organization administrator*
Connors, Marty *political party administrator, small business owner*
Diasio, Ilse Wolfartsberger *volunteer*
Gross, Iris Lee *not-for-profit association executive*
Newton, Don Allen *real estate broker, economic development consultant*
Rynearson, W. John *foundation administrator*

Huntsville
Motz, Kenneth Lee *former farm organization official*

Selma
Galloway, Robert Michael

Semmes
McCann, Clarence David, Jr., *museum curator and director, artist*

ALASKA

Anchorage
Jones, Jewel *social services administrator*
Jones, Mark Logan *educational association executive, educator*
O'Regan, Deborah *association executive, lawyer*
Ruedrich, Randy *political party official*
Thorsness, Julia Marie *hospice administrator*
Wilkniss, Peter E. *foundation administrator, researcher*
Williams, Deborah Lee *foundation administrator*

Sitka
Blood, Lawrence Preston *chamber of commerce executive*

ARIZONA

Chandler
Rossi, Mark Antony *political consultant, writer*

Marana
Green, Laura Lorraine *foundation administrator*

Paradise Valley
Moya, Sara Dreier *educational association administrator*

Parker
Carnicom, Gene E. *health services administrator*

Phoenix
Fannin, Paul Robert *political party official*
Genrich, Mark L. *retired foundation administrator*
Swartz, Jack *chamber of commerce executive*
Waas, Andrea Sue *nonprofit foundation administrator*

Prescott
Garvey, Daniel Edward *foundation administrator, educator, academic administrator*

Scottsdale
Dorland, Byrl Brown *retired volunteer*
Ferree, John Newton, Jr., *fundraising specialist, consultant*
Jacobson, Frank Joel *cultural organization administrator*
Marshall, Jonathan *charitable foundation administrator, journalist*
Milanovich, Norma JoAnne *training and development company executive*
Mohraz, Judy Jolley *foundation administrator*
Morrison, James William, Jr., *lobbyist, government relations consultant*
Nelson, Florence Ely *civic leader*

Tempe
Cochran, Mary Leffler *volunteer*

Tubac
Chilcote, Samuel Day, Jr., *trade association administrator*

Tucson
Grand, Marcia *civic worker*
Hechler, Pauline Urbano King *fundraiser*
Lovejoy, Jean Hastings *social services counselor*
Riggs, Lew *foundation executive*
Schevill, Edward *social services agency director*
Tirrell, John Albert *organization executive, consultant*

ARKANSAS

Fort Smith
Howard, Jeff David *volunteer, retired military officer*

Heber Springs
Niehaus, Sherry M. *social welfare administrator*

Little Rock
Adams, Rose Ann *nonprofit administrator*
Elders, (Minnie) Joycelyn *public health administrator, endocrinologist*
Kilgore, Nancy *educational association administrator*
Malone, David Roy *educational association administrator, director*

CALIFORNIA

Alameda
Kohgadai, Shukrullah *foundation administrator, editor*

Belvedere Tiburon
Collins, Dennis Arthur *retired foundation administrator*

Berkeley
McLaughlin, Sylvia Cranmer *volunteer, environmentalist*
Myers, Miles Alvin *educational association administrator, educator*
Odermatt, Diana B. *development consultant*
Pope, Alexander H. *former lawyer, county assessor and non-profit administrator*

Beverly Hills
Pavlik, John Michael *performing arts association executive*
Schaff, Manya *foundation administrator*
Siciliano, Rocco Carmine *institute executive*

Brea
Bosse, Mark Thomas *social services administrator*
Tamura, Cary Kaoru *consultant*

Burbank
Rawlinson, Joseph Eli *foundation executive, lawyer*
Steel, Shawn *political party official*

Canoga Park
Lederer, Marion Irvine *cultural administrator*

Carmel
Pippi, Mikel Eugene *cultural attache, television producer, arts administrator, television director*

Citrus Heights
Leisey, Donald Eugene *educational materials company executive, educator*

Concord
Misner, Charlotte Blanche Ruckman *retired community organization administrator*

Culver City
Netzel, Paul Arthur *fund raising management executive, consultant*

Daly City
Malifrando, Frank *foundation executive director, theater producer, consultant*

Elk Grove
McIntyre, Mary Maureen *social services consultant*

Encino
Baker, William Morris *cultural organization administrator*

Fairfax
Urquhart, Karin May *foundation administrator, environmentalist*

Folsom
Peck, Raymond Charles, Sr., *behavior research specialist, consultant*

Fullerton
Sadrudin, Moe *humanitarian organization executive*

Glendale
Lund, John Richard *entertainment company executive*

Irvine
Fouste, Donna H. *association executive*

Keene
Rodriguez, Arturo Salvador *labor union official*

Kentfield
Blum, Joan Kurley *fundraising executive*

Laguna Beach
Forry, Steven *not-for-profit fundraiser*

Loma Linda
Pendergraft, Janice Gayle *volunteer*

Long Beach
Lee, Isaiah Chong-Pie *social worker, educator*

Los Altos
Farber, Geraldine Ossman *civic worker*
Orr, Susan Packard *business owner*
Wilbur, Colburn Sloan *foundation consultant and trustee, former executive*

Los Angeles
Cislowski, Joseph A. *association executive*
Erichsen, Peter Christian *foundation administrator*
Glasschild, Boe *cultural organization administrator, educator*
Harris, Barbara Hull (Mrs. F. Chandler Harris) *social agency administrator*
Hirsch, Daniel Oren *nonprofit nuclear policy organization executive*
Hubbs, Donald Harvey *foundation executive*
Jaggers, Velma Mary Lee *foundation administrator, educator*
Kipke, Michele Diane *education and social services administrator, former hospital director*
Lindley, F(rancis) Haynes, Jr., *foundation executive, lawyer*
Mack, J. Curtis, II, *civic organization administrator*
Marshall, Mary Jones *civic worker*
Meier, Stephen Charles *foundation executive*
Munitz, Barry *arts and foundation administrator*
Orsatti, Alfred Kendall *organization executive*
Poole, Robert William, Jr., *foundation executive*
Prewitt, Jean *not-for-profit organization executive*
Scarlett, P. Lynn *foundation administrator, writer*
Shakely, John Bower (Jack Shakely) *foundation executive*
Smith, Jean Webb (Mrs. William French Smith) *civic worker*
Warder, Michael Young *non-profit executive*
Williams, Harold Marvin *foundation official, former government official, former university dean, former corporate executive*
Wilson, Gayle Ann *civic worker*
Wlaschin, Ken *cultural organization administrator, writer*
Wright, Connie Hotchkiss *educational association administrator, researcher*

Marina Del Rey
Stebbins, Gregory Kellogg *foundation executive*

Menlo Park
Altman, Drew E. *foundation executive*
Brown, Charles Dickson *not-for-profit fundraiser, consultant*
Collins, Nancy Whisnant *foundation administrator*
Madding, Bruce Wallace *foundation executive*
Nichols, William Ford, Jr., *foundation executive, business executive*
Pallotti, Marianne Marguerite *foundation administrator*
Smith, Marshall Savidge *foundation executive*

Mill Valley
Burke, Kathleen J. *foundation administrator*

Modesto
Barnes, William David *non-profit charities consultant, publisher*
Mattos, William Harold *trade association executive, newspaper publisher*
Whiteside, Carol Gordon *foundation executive*

Mount Shasta
Mann, Karen *consultant, educator*

Mountain View
Bills, Robert Howard *political party executive*
Serra, Patricia Janet *social services administrator*

Napa
Loar, Peggy Ann *foundation administrator, museum administrator*

Newbury Park
McCune, Sara Miller *foundation executive, publisher*

Newport Beach
Martin, Joseph Chekel *not-for-profit developer*
Poole, Thomas Richard *endowment capital campaign director, fund raising counsel*

Norwalk
Gould, D. Joy *social services administrator*

Oakland
Clemons, Robert Earl *non-profit organization administrator*
Hawkins, Robert B. *think-tank executive*
Lazar, John Edward *administrator non-profit organization*
Macmeeken, John Peebles *foundation executive, educator*
Smith, Mark D. *foundation administrator*

Oceanside
Roberts, James McGregor *retired professional association executive*

Orinda
Fisher, Robert Morton *foundation administrator, university administrator*

Pacific Palisades
Holberg, Eva Maria *volunteer*

Palo Alto
Lee, Virginia Fern *community volunteer*
Robinson, Agnes Claflin *educational administrator*
Skoll, Jeffrey *philanthropist, Internet company executive*

Palos Verdes Peninsula
Vanderlip, Elin Brekke *philanthropic executive*

Pasadena
Ellner, Carolyn Lipton *not-profit organization executive, dean, consultant*
Staehle, Robert L. *foundation executive*

Pleasanton
Whisnand, Rex James *association housing executive*

Porterville
Mullen, Rod *nonprofit organization executive*

Rancho Mirage
Wyatt, Lenore *civic worker*

Redding
Potter, James Vincent *association executive*

Redwood City
McFarland, Kevin John *foundation administrator*
Spangler, Nita Reifschneider *volunteer*

Riverside
Smith, Richard Charles *not-for-profit administrator, educator*

Sacramento
Alberson, Barbara *health services professional*
Patino, Douglas Xavier *foundation, government agency, and university administrator*
Ross, Jean M. *think-tank executive*

Salinas
Chester, Lynne *foundation administrator, artist*

San Andreas
Breed, Allen Forbes *correctional administrator*

San Diego
Grosser, T.J. *administrator, developer, fundraiser*
Krejci, Robert Harry *not-for-profit developer, consultant*
Lane, Gloria Julian *foundation administrator*
Repetti, Anamaria *healthcare foundation executive*
Sanders, Jerry *social services executive*
Sheldon, Lois Elizabeth *social services administrator*
Spira, Patricia Goodsitt *association executive*
Swanson, Mary Catherine *educational reform program founder*
Van Schoik, D. Rick *think-tank executive*
Wojcik, Martin Henry *not-for-profit executive*

San Francisco
Barzelatto, Jose S. *social welfare organization executive*
Bitterman, Mary Gayle Foley *foundation executive*
Canales, James Earl, Jr., *foundation administrator*
Chang, Patti *foundation administrator*
Clarey, Patricia *association executive*
Delaney, Martin *not-for-profit developer*
Eastham, Thomas *foundation administrator*
Giovinco, Joseph *nonprofit administrator, writer*
Grose, Andrew Peter *foundation executive*
Harvey, Glen H. *educational association administrator*
Hoganson, Susan Cook *non-profit organization executive*
Lord, Mia W. *advocate*
Madson, David John *fundraising executive*
Maracek, Leigh *association administrator*
Mattern, Douglas James *think-tank executive*
Metz, Mary Seawell *foundation administrator, retired academic administrator*
Newirth, Richard Scott *cultural organization administrator*
Pipes, Sally C. *think-tank executive*
Pope, Carl *professional society administrator*
Reading, Phyllis Ann *social welfare administrator*
Simon, Lateefah *foundation administrator, director*
Soler, Esta *foundation administrator*
Steele, Shari *think-tank executive*
Tobin, Gary Allan *cultural and community organization educator*

San Luis Obispo
Jamieson, James Bradshaw *foundation administrator*

San Pedro
Daniels, Kathleen Angela *educational administrator*

San Rafael
Burks, Rocky Alan *disability access coordinator, consultant*

Santa Ana
Prizio, Betty J. *volunteer, retired property manager*
Zepeda, Susan Ghozeil *foundation executive*

Santa Barbara
McCoy, Lois Clark *emergency services professional, retired county official, magazine editor*
Rehm, Susan J. *social services professional*

Santa Clarita
Boyer, Carl, III, *non-profit organization executive, former mayor, city official, secondary education educator*

Santa Monica
Abarbanel, Gail *social service administrator, educator*
Foley, Jane Deborah *foundation executive*
Hosie, Stanley William *foundation executive*
Klowden, Michael Louis *think-tank executive*
Milken, Michael R. *think-tank executive, philanthropist*
Rich, Michael David *research corporation executive, lawyer*
Thomson, James Alan *think-tank executive*

Santa Rosa
Ingerman, Michael Leigh *development director*

Sherman Oaks
Leighton, Carolyn *foundation administrator*

Sonoma
Stadtman, Verne August *former foundation executive, editor*

Stanford
Lyman, Richard Wall *foundation and university executive, historian*

Studio City
Frumkin, Simon *political activist and columnist*

Sun City
Peterson, Arthur Laverne *foundation administrator*

Susanville
McCoy, Douglas Michael *social services administrator, clergyman*

Sylmar
Froelich, Beverly Lorraine *foundation administrator*

Temecula
Angel, Michael Gonzalez *cultural organization administrator*

Torrance
Carey, Kathryn Ann *foundation administrator, editor, consultant*
Kallman, Burton Jay *foods association director*

Trinidad
Marshall, William Edward *historical association executive*

Union City
Reyes, Luzviminda Canuto *social welfare administrator*

Valencia
Anguiano, Lupe *advocate*

Ventura
Downs, Floella McIntyre *civic worker, ferry pilot, instructor and flight examiner*

West Hollywood
Hoffenblum, Allan Ernest *political consultant*

Whittier
Meardy, William Herman *retired educational association administrator*

Yorba Linda
Stavropoulos, Rose Mary Grant *community activist, volunteer*

COLORADO

Arvada
Meiklejohn, Mindy June (Lorraine Meiklejohn) *political organizer, realtor*

Boulder
Heath, Josephine Ward *foundation administrator*
Hess, John Warren *professional society administrator*
Johnston, Laurance Scott *foundation director*

Broomfield
Flanders, Eleanor Carlson *community volunteer*

Centennial
Bryan, A(lonzo) J(ay) *retired service club official*

Colorado Springs
Hawley, Nanci Elizabeth *association administrator*
Killian, George Ernest *educational association administrator*
Miller, Zoya Dickins (Mrs. Hilliard Eve Miller Jr.) *civic worker*

Denver
Gates, Chris *not-for-profit developer, political organization worker*
Gloss, Lawrence Robert *fundraising executive*
Halaby, Theodore S. *political organization worker, retired lawyer*
Hirschfeld, Arlene *civic worker, homemaker*
Hogan, Curtis Jule *union executive, industrial relations consultant*
Knaus, Tim *political organization administrator*
Low, Merry Cook *civic worker*
Nelson, Bernard William *foundation executive, educator, physician*
Raughton, Jimmie Leonard *education consultant, public administrator, urban planner*
Ward, Lester Lowe, Jr., *arts executive, lawyer*

Eldorado Springs
Lovins, L. Hunter *public policy institute executive*

Englewood
Keesling, Ruth Morris *foundation administrator*
Lessey, Samuel Kenric, Jr., *foundation administrator*

Estes Park
Cope, James Dudley *retired trade association executive*

Golden
Dickinson, Carol Rittgers *arts administrator, writer, executive director*

Greeley
Schrenk, Gary Dale *foundation executive*

Greenwood Village
Chesser, Al H. *union official*

Guffey
Ward, Larry Thomas *social program administrator*

Littleton
Graf, Joseph Charles *retired foundation executive*
Keogh, Heidi Helen Dake *advocate*

Louisville
Jonsen, Richard Wiliam *retired educational administrator*

Loveland
Rosa, Linda *advocate*

Mancos
Brown, Joy Alice *social services administrator*

CONNECTICUT

Canaan
Kettenhofen, Gretchen Maria *development executive*

Danbury
Meyers, Abbey S. *foundation administrator*

Darien
Penrose, Charles, Jr., *professional society administrator*

Fairfield
Evans, Margaret A. *volunteer*
Ford, Maureen Morrissey *civic worker*

Falls Village
Toomey, Jeanne Elizabeth *animal activist*

Greenwich
Bjornson, Edith Cameron *foundation administrator, communications consultant*
Kovner, Kathleen Jane *civic worker, portrait artist*
Stauffer, Valerie Vilas *civic volunteer*

Groton
Kennedy, Evelyn Siefert *foundation executive, textile specialist*

Hartford
Decko, Kenneth Owen *trade association administrator*
Gibbons, Mary Peyser *civic volunteer*

Madison
Houghton, Alan Nourse *association executive, educator, consultant*

New Britain
Baker, Patricia *health foundation administrator*

New Canaan
Bartlett, Dede Thompson *association executive*
Brakeley, George Archibald, Jr., *fundraising consultant*
Giusti, Kathy *foundation administrator*
McNamara, Francis Joseph, Jr., *retired foundation executive, lawyer*
Pifer, Alan (Jay Parrish) *former foundation executive*

New Haven
Anderson, Carl Albert *association executive, lawyer, dean*

Newington
Hadley, Nancy Lynne *community foundation executive, municipal official*
Sumner, David George *association executive*

North Branford
Logan, John Arthur, Jr., *retired foundation executive*

Old Lyme
Bond, Niles Woodbridge *cultural institute executive, former foreign service officer*

Riverside
Coulson, Robert *retired association executive, arbitrator, author*

Rocky Hill
Olsen, John William *political organization administrator*

Roxbury
Styron, Rose *human rights activist, poet, journalist*

South Windsor
Carman, Gary Olen *child welfare company executive*

Stamford
Chisholm, Andrea Lynne *business association administrator, foundation administrator*
Sharp, Daniel Asher *foundation executive*
Stillings, Irene Ella Grace Cordiner *foundation executive*
Wunsch, Bonnie Rubenstein *fraternal organization executive*

Vernon Rockville
Roden, Jon-Paul *retired educator, labor union organizer, educational consultant*

Waterbury
Harper, Barbara Clara *counselor, educational program administrator, counselor*

Westport
Stolz, Alan Jay *youth camp executive*

Wilton
Forger, Robert Durkin *retired professional association administrator*
Hughes, Joan Mottola *education association representative*

DELAWARE

Lewes
Spence, Sandra *retired professional society administrator*
Warden, Richard Dana *government labor union official*

Newark
Townsend, Brenda S. *educational association administrator*

Wilmington
Battaglia, Basil Richard *former political party official, company executive*
Emmert, Richard Eugene *retired industrial and professional association executive*
Peterson, Russell Wilbur *former association executive, former state governor*
Spence, Janet Blake Conley (Mrs. Alexander Pyott Spence) *civic worker*

DISTRICT OF COLUMBIA

Washington
Aall, Pamela R. *foundation administrator*
Able, Edward H. *association executive*
Alberts, Bruce Michael *President National Academy of Sciences, biochemist*
Alexander, Richard C. *association administrator*
Andrews, Laureen E. *foundation administrator*
Andrews, Lewis Davis, Jr., *trade association executive*
Arlook, Ira Arthur *non-profit association executive, communications firm administrator*
Armacost, Michael Hayden *research institution executive, ambassador*
Arnold, William Edwin *health advocate, consultant*
Auerbach, Stuart Charles *development loan fund administrator, journalist*
Avery, Byllye Yvonne *health association administrator*
Babby, Ellen Reisman *education administrator*
Bahr, Morton *labor union administrator*
Barry, John J. *labor union leader*
Bartlett, Charles Leffingwell *foundation executive, former newspaperman*
Bass, Gary D. *advocate, director*
Bednash, Geraldine Polly *educational association administrator*
Bell, Jerry Alan *science education association administrator*
Bender, David Ray *library association executive*
Berger, Brian Daniel *lobbyist, diversified financial services company executive*
Berry, Morrell John *cultural organization administrator*
Betancourt Lopez, Antonio L. *association executive*
Binkley, Marilyn Rothman *educational research administrator*
Blair, Louis Helion *foundation executive*
Boaz, David Douglas *foundation executive*
Bonosaro, Carol Alessandra *professional association executive, former government official*
Brady, Patricia G. *volunteer*
Brobeck, Stephen James *consumer advocate*
Brown, Ann W. *not-for-profit developer*
Buckles, Bradley A. *trade association administrator*
Bulger, Peggy Anne *cultural organization administrator*
Burrus, William Henry *labor union administrator*
Bushkin, Kathryn A. *foundation administrator*
Calhoun, John Alfred *social services administrator*
Calingaert, Michael *nonprofit organization executive*
Callahan, Debra Jean *professional society administrator*
Canja, Esther *foundation administrator*
Carr, John S. *trade association administrator*
Case, David Randall *trade association executive*
Cavaney, Red *trade association executive*
Chavez-Thompson, Linda *labor union administrator*
Cino, Maria *political organization administrator, former federal agency administrator*
Colbert, Robert Ivan *education association administrator*
Comstock, Amy L. *social services administrator*
Crane, Edward Harrison, III, *institute executive*
Crawford, Stephen *think tank executive*
Dallara, Charles H. *think-tank executive, financial analyst*
Damgard, John Michael *trade association executive*
Daschle, Linda Hall *transportation industry lobbyist*
Davis, Deidre *advocate*
Deal, Timothy *association executive, former diplomat*
DeKuyper, Mary Hundley *non-profit consultant*
DeMuth, Christopher Clay *think-tank executive*
DiConti, Michael Andrew *trade organization executive*
Dierlam, Bryan Douglas *trade association administrator*
Ditlow, Clarence M. *think-tank executive*
Dolibois, Robert Joseph *trade association administrator*
Donahue, Thomas Reilly *trade union official*
Dooley, Betty Parsons *educational association administrator*
Dority, Douglas H. *association executive*
Dorn, Jennifer Lynn *charitable organization administrator*
Dorsey, David Byard *non-profit executive*
DuBois, Paul Martin Joseph *non-profit organization executive*
DuVall, Jack *advocate*
Edelman, Marian Wright *not-for-profit organization administrator, lawyer*
Edwards, Steve *attorney, former political organization executive*
Eisenberg, Pablo Samuel *non-profit organization executive*
Ekman, Richard *association executive, educator*
Elliott, Thomas Michael *retired association executive, educator, consultant*
Elsey, George McKee *retired foundation administrator*
Emely, Mary Ann *association executive*
Evans, Joy *foundation administrator*
Evans, Marsha Johnson *non-profit association administrator, former career officer*
Fai, Ghulam Nabi *cultural organization administrator*
Feldman, Sandra *labor union executive*
Finkle, Jeffrey Alan *professional association executive*
Finley, Julie Hamm *political party official*
Fire, Edward *labor union administrator*
Fisher, William Pierre *association executive*
Flake, L. Gordon *think-tank executive*
Flavin, Christopher *think-tank executive*
Foard, Douglas W. *educational association administrator*
Foreman, Carol Lee Tucker *consumer advocate*
Forkan, Patricia Ann *foundation executive*
French, Hilary F. *foundation administrator*
Fried, Bruce Merlin *health care lawyer*
Friend, Patricia A. *trade association administrator*
Fries, Helen Sergeant Haynes *civic leader*
Fuller, Kathryn Scott *environmental association executive, lawyer*
Gage, John *labor union administrator*
Gans, Curtis B. *think tank administrator*
George, Warren S. *labor union administrator*
Gershman, Carl Samuel *foundation administrator*
Gillespie, Ed *political organization executive*
Goldman, Neil *association administrator*
Golodner, Jack *labor association official*
Gorham, William *organization executive*
Gough, Samuel Nathanael, Jr., *fund-raising executive*
Griffenhagen, George Bernard *trade association executive*
Griffin, Janice *political organization professional*
Hahn, Lorna *political organization executive, author*
Hall, Betty Jean *public interest group executive, lawyer*
Halstead, Edward Allen (Ted Halstead) *think-tank executive*
Hamilton, Lee Herbert *educational organization administrator, former congressman*
Hamre, John J. *think-tank executive*
Handman, Bobbie (Barbara Handman) *foundation executive*
Hanley, Frank *labor union official*
Hansen, Charles Martin, III, *lobbyist*
Hansen, Joseph T. *labor union administrator*
Harrison, Ronald O. *association administrator*
Heinz Kerry, Teresa F. *foundation administrator*
Hense, Donald Langford *educational association administrator*
Hentges, Harriet *not-for-profit developer*
Herson, Michael Harry *lobbyist, consultant*
Hill, Edwin D. *trade association administrator*
Hills, John Merrill *educational administrator, consultant, former public policy research center executive*
Hoehn, Richard Albert *association executive, clergyman*
Hoffa, James P. *labor union administrator*
Holmer, Alan Freeman *trade association executive, lawyer*
Howard, Barbara Viventi *research foundation executive*
Howard, Glen Scott *foundation executive, lawyer*
Hoyt, John Arthur *cultural organization administrator, minister*
Huband, Frank Louis *educational association executive*
Hudnut, William Herbert, III, *senior resident fellow, political scientist*
Hudson, Melinda B. *foundation administrator*
Hughes, Sharon Mary *trade association executive*
Hughes, Thomas Lowe *foundation executive*
Ingram, Richard Thomas *educational association executive*
Ireland, Patricia *not-for-profit developer*
Isaacs, Amy Fay *political organization executive*
Isaacson, Walter Seff *think-tank executive*
Ivey, William James *foundation executive, writer, producer*
Jacobson, Michael Faraday *consumer advocate, writer*
Janes, Jackson *research institute executive*
Jarboe, Kenan Patrick *think-tank executive, researcher*
Jensen, James E. *director congressional and government affairs*
Johnson, Gloria *labor union administrator*
Johnson, Karen *professional society administrator*
Kamber, Victor Samuel *political consultant*
Karpinski, Gene Brien *non-profit group administrator, think tank executive*
Kavanaugh, Everett Edward, Jr., *trade association executive*
Kearns, Kevin Lawrence *political association executive, lawyer*
Keegel, C. Thomas *labor union administrator*
Keeny, Spurgeon Milton, Jr., *association executive*
Kelley, Colleen M. *labor union administrator*
Keltz, Amy Lynn *foundation administrator*
Kim, Charles Changyoung *trade association executive, lawyer*
King, Jacqueline Elizabeth *policy analyst, researcher*
Knapp, Richard Maitland *association executive*
Knippers, Diane LeMasters *association executive*
Kolb, Charles Chester *humanities administrator*
Kovach, Bill *educational foundation administrator*
Kreig, Andrew Thomas *trade association executive*
Lachance, Janice Rachel *educational association administrator, former federal agency administrator, lawyer*
Lacour, Nat *labor union administrator*
Lampl, Peggy Ann *public policy administrator*
Langfeld, Patricia Ann *trade association executive, marketing and event planner*
La Sala, James *labor union administrator*
Lasher, Craig Richard *policy analyst*

Lenn, Marjorie Peace *education association administrator, consultant*
Leshner, Alan Irvin *science administrator*
Leskes, Andrea *educational association administrator, educator*
Levin, George Martin *association and organization administrator, aeronautical engineer*
Levine, Felice *educational association administrator*
Lichtman, Judith L. *lawyer, organization administrator*
Lief, Beth *educational association administrator*
Limon, Lavinia *social services administrator*
Low, Stephen *foundation executive, educator, former diplomat*
Loyless, Betsy Seymour *political organization worker*
Lucas, C. Payne *development organization executive*
Lynch, Robert L. *art association administrator*
Maddaloni, Martin J. *labor union administrator*
Magrath, C. Peter *educational association executive*
Makins, Christopher James *foreign policy institute administrator*
Marks, Susan Collin *foundation administrator*
Marshall, Brian Laurence *trade association executive*
Marshall, William, III, *think-tank executive*
Martin, Jerry Lee *organization executive, educator*
Masters, Edward E. *association executive, former foreign service officer*
Maynes, Charles William *foundation executive*
McAuliffe, Terry (Terence Richard McAuliffe) *political organization administrator*
McCarron, Douglas J. *labor union administrator*
McElroy, Edward J. *labor union administrator*
McEntee, Gerald W. *labor union official*
McGinnis, Patricia Gwaltney *nonprofit organization executive*
Mc Kay, Emily Gantz *civil rights professional*
McLaughlin, David *foundation administrator*
Meyerson, Adam *foundation administrator*
Michelman, Kate *advocate*
Moore, Jacquelyn Cornelia *labor union official, editor*
Moore, Minyon *political organization worker*
Mueller, Sharon Lee (Sherry Mueller) *educational organization executive*
Muir, Patricia Allen *professional association administrator*
Munson, Richard Jay *congressional policy analyst*
Murphy, Gerard Norris *trade association executive*
Murray, James Joseph, III, *association executive*
Musil, Robert Kirkland *professional society administrator*
Nader, Ralph *consumer advocate, lawyer, author*
Neverson, Norman Carl *political organization administrator*
Nicholson, Jim *political organization administrator*
Nicholson, Richard Selindh *educational association administrator*
Nickens, Paula *political organization administrator*
Obrecht, Margaret M. H. *cultural organization administrator*
O'Flaherty, James Daniel *council executive*
Ohlke, Amanda Anne *museum association administrator, museum educator*
O'Kane, Margaret E. *non-profit organization executive*
O'Neill, Catherine *cultural organization administrator*
O'Sullivan, Terence M. *labor union administrator*
Otremba, Geraldine Marie *congressional and international relations executive*
Ottley, William Henry *professional association director, consultant*
Pearson, Roger *organization executive*
Pelavin, Sol Herbert *research company executive*
Pensky, Carol *political organization administrator*
Petito, Margaret L. *foundation administrator*
Pierce, David R. *educational administrator*
Platts, Howard Gregory *scientific, educational organization executive*
Pleasure, Robert Jonathan *association director, lawyer*
Portney, Paul Rogers *research and educational organization executive*
Radin, Alex *former association executive, consultant*
Raizen, Senta Amon *educational administrator, researcher*
Rasmus, John Charles *trade association executive, lawyer*
Reger, Lawrence Lee *trade association administrator*
Reich, Alan Anderson *foundation administrator*
Reinsch, William Alan *association executive, educator*
Rich, Dorothy Kovitz *writer, educational administrator*
Richardson, Ann Bishop *foundation executive, lawyer*
Ridings, Dorothy Sattes *association executive*
Riedel, Bunnie *not-for-profit organization executive*
Riehle, B. Hudson *trade association executive*
Robinson, Leonard Harrison, Jr., *international government consultant, business executive*
Robinson, Sharon Porter *professional society administrator*
Rodman, Peter Warren *government official*
Roemer, Timothy J. *think-tank executive, former congressman*
Roessel, Faith *Indian arts and crafts administrator*
Rogers, Julie *foundation administrator*
Rosenstein, Peter D. *educational association administrator, consultant*
Rotenberg, Marc Steven *public interest advocate, lawyer*
Rother, John Charles *association executive, lawyer*
Ruskin, Robert Sterling *association executive*
Russell, William Joseph *educational association administrator*
Saffuri, Khaled Ahmad *cultural organization executive*
Salisbury, Dallas L. *research institute executive*
Sandler, Bernice Resnick *women's rights specialist*
Satloff, Robert B. *think-tank executive*
Saunders, Harold Henry *foundation administrator*
Scanlon, Terrence Maurice *public policy foundation administrator*
Schlickeisen, Rodger Oscar *non-profit environmental organization executive*
Schneider, Carol Geary *educational association administrator*
Schroeder, Patricia Scott *trade association administrator, retired congresswoman*
Scruggs-Leftwich, Yvonne *association executive*
Sewall, Sarah Lee *foundation administrator*
Sewell, John Williamson *research association executive*
Sheekey, Kathleen D. *advocate, director*
Shields, Carole *foundation administrator*
Shriver, Eunice Mary Kennedy (Mrs. Robert Sargent Shriver Jr.) *foundation administrator, volunteer, social worker*
Slade, John Danton *lobbyist*
Smith, Elise Fiber *international non-profit development agency administrator*
Smith, Jessie P. Dowling *retired social services administrator*
Smith, William S., Jr., *education association administrator*
Snyder, John Michael *lobbyist, public relations director*
Snyder, Wallace S. *advertising association executive, lawyer*
Sombrotto, Vincent R. *postal union executive*
Sparks, Kenneth R. *association executive*
Splete, Allen Peterjohn *association executive, educator*
Staats, Elmer Boyd *foundation executive, former government official*
Stern, Andrew L. *labor union administrator*
Stern, Paula *international trade advisor*
Strong, Henry *foundation executive*
Stump, E. Gordon *association administrator*
Sullivan, John David *business association executive*
Sullivan, Michael J. *labor union administrator*
Sweeney, John Joseph *labor union administrator*
Swenson, Sue *foundation administrator, former health and education administrator*
Talbott, Strobe *think-tank executive*
Tedeschi, George *labor union administrator*
Teich, Albert Harris *professional society administrator*
Theodore, Eustace D. *educational advancement consultant, management consultant*
Tipton, E. Linwood *trade association executive*
Tobias, Robert Max *labor leader, lawyer*
Tolu, Tolu *foundation administrator*
Tonkin, Leo Sampson *educational foundation administrator*
Torkelson, Jodie Rae *charitable organization executive*
Tosi, Gloria C. *labor union administrator*
Towle, Alexis Charles (Lex Towle) *education advocate*
Townsend, Ann Van Devanter *foundation administrator, art historian*
Tracy, Alan Thomas *trade association administrator*
Trumka, Richard Louis *labor leader, lawyer*
Tse, Man-Chun Marina *educational association administrator*
Unsell, Lloyd Neal *energy organization executive, former journalist*
Utley, Jon Basil *think-tank executive, journalist*
Vanderryn, Jack *philanthropic foundation administrator*
Van Metre, Lauren *foundation administrator*
Veatch, Elizabeth Wilson *educational administrator*
Wali, Sima *foundation administrator*
Walker, Barbara Dodson *cultural organization administrator, consultant, lecturer, researcher*
Warren, David Liles *educational association executive*
Watts, Glenn Ellis *union official*
Weaver, Reg *National Education Association president*
Weinstein, Allen *educator, historian, non-profit administrator*
Werronen, Betsy Warren *political organization administrator*
Wertheimer, Fredric Michael *public policy advocate*
Wesley, LaTonya Rashawn *legislative assistant*
West, Jake *labor union administrator*
Weyrich, Paul Michael *political organizations executive*
Whitehead, Alfred K. *labor union administrator*
Wilhelm, John W. *labor union administrator*
Wilkie, Edith B. *foundation administrator*
Williams, Eddie Nathan *research institution executive*
Williams, James A. *labor union administrator*
Williams, Jody *political organization administrator*
Williams, Lori Anne *foundation administrator, vocalist*
Williams, Maurice Jacoutot *development organization executive*
Wise, William Harvey, IV, *human service executive*
Wiseman, Laurence Donald *foundation executive*
Wolfe, Leslie R. *think-tank executive*
Woolley, John Edward *trade association executive*
Yost, Paul Alexander, Jr., *foundation executive, retired coast guard officer*
Young, William H. *labor union administrator*
Yzaguirre, Raul Humberto *civil rights leader*
Zielinski, Paul Bernard *grant program administrator, civil engineer*

FLORIDA

Boca Raton
Dembowski, Frederick Lester *educational administrator, educator, consultant*
Jessup, Jan Amis *arts volunteer, writer*

Boynton Beach
Rogers, John S. *retired union official*

Celebration
Wilson, George Peter *international organization executive*

Coconut Grove
Martinez-Carbonell, Karelia *not-for-profit fundraiser*

Coral Gables
Landon, Robert Kirkwood *philanthropist, retired insurance company executive*

Coral Springs
Burg, Ralph *art association executive*

Davenport
Vaughn, Rosalyn Mae *educational association administrator*

Delray Beach
Stewart, Patricia Carry *foundation administrator*

Destin
De Revere, David Wilsen *retired professional society administrator*

Estero
Brown, William Robert *association executive, consultant*

Fort Lauderdale
Bowen, Judith Reina *fundraising executive*
Donoho, Tim Mark *not-for-profit developer*
Washington, Alice Hester *human services professional*

Gulf Breeze
Rainwater, Freddie Barrett *volunteer worker*
Walker, Peggy Jean *retired social work agency administrator*
Williams, Betty *peace activist*

Holmes Beach
Dunne, Nancy Anne *retired social services administrator*

Jacksonville
Duvall, Janet Ann *volunteer*
Magill, Sherry *foundation administrator*

Jacksonville Beach
Morris, Max King *foundation executive, former naval officer*

Lady Lake
Akins, Zane Vernon *association executive*

Lake Worth
Goldstein, Jerome Charles *retired professional association executive, surgeon, otolaryngologist*

Lakeland
Spencer, Mary Miller *civic worker*

Lauderdale By The Sea
Wynne, Brian James *former association executive, consultant*

Longboat Key
Dorsey, Eugene Carroll *former foundation and communications executive*

Marco Island
Hollenbeck, Karen Fern *foundation consultant*

Melbourne
James-McKinney, Jodi Kaye *drug policy reformer, political organization worker*

Miami
Blanco, Josefa Joan-Juana (Jossie Blanco) *social services administrator*
Cullom, William Otis *trade association executive*
Culmer, Leome Frances *volunteer*
Dickason, John Hamilton *retired foundation executive*
Franklin, Phyllis *retired professional society administrator*
Lynch, Catherine Gores *social work administrator*
Shipp, Theta Wanza *social service organization administrator, educator, consultant, minister*

Naples
Rowe, Herbert Joseph *retired trade association executive*

Nocatee
Turnbull, David John (Chief Piercing Eyes-Penn) *cultural association executive*

North Palm Beach
Crawford, Roberta *association administrator*

Okeechobee
Bishop, Sid Glenwood *union official*

Orlando
Glynn, Gerard Francis *not-for-profit developer*
Murrah, Ann Ralls Freeman *historical association executive*

Ormond Beach
Lively, Carol A. *retired professional society administrator*

Osprey
Harrington, Nancy O'Connor *volunteer*

Palm Beach
Elson, Suzanne Goodman *community activist*
Hope, Margaret Lauten *civic worker*
Moloney, Thomas Walter *consulting firm executive*
Rinker, Ruby Stewart *foundation administrator*

Palm Beach Gardens
Falk, Bernard Henry *trade association executive*

Palm Coast
Cook, Gloria Houston *civic leader*

Pensacola
Furlong, George Morgan, Jr., *museum foundation consultant, retired naval officer*

Ponte Vedra Beach
Slayton, Gus *foundation administrator*
Watson, John Lawrence, III, *former trade association executive*

Punta Gorda
Clinton, Mariann Hancock *educational association administrator*

Saint Petersburg
Allshouse, Merle Frederick *educational organization administrator*

Sanibel
Ball, Armand Baer *former association executive, consultant*

Sarasota
Bausch, James John *foundation executive*
Boersma, Lawrence Allan (Larry Allan) *animal welfare administrator, photographer*
Culkin, Charles Walker, Jr., *retired trade association administrator*
Dobosz, Mark Joseph *fundraiser*
O'Connor, Sylvia Cannon *association legislative liaison, analyst, retired*
Spencer, Lonabelle (Kappie Spencer) *political agency administrator, lobbyist*

Tallahassee
Brady, Terrie *political organization executive*
Campbell, Frances Harvell *educational association administrator*
Dinnen, Maureen *educational association administrator, educator*
Hammer, Marion Price *association executive*
Humphrey, Louise Ireland *civic worker, equestrienne*
Turnbull, Marjorie Reitz *foundation executive, former state legislator*

Tampa
Lowe, Peter Stephen *non-profit company executive*

Titusville
VanBrode, Derrick Brent, IV, *trade association administrator*

West Palm Beach
Coppock, Mark Stephen *not-for-profit fundraiser*

Wilton Manors
Kaufmann, Vicki Marie *social services administrator*

Windermere
Russell, Robert Leonard *professional association executive*

Winter Park
Myers, Norman Lewis *fund development consultant*
Olsson, Nils William *former association executive*

GEORGIA

Americus
Fuller, Millard Dean *charitable organization executive, lawyer*
Williams, David Anthony *not-for-profit executive*

Atlanta
Birdsong, Alta Marie *volunteer*
DeConcini, Barbara *association executive, religious studies educator*
Kelly, William Watkins *educational association executive*
King, Coretta Scott (Mrs. Martin Luther King Jr.) *educational association administrator, lecturer, writer, concert singer*
King, Dexter Scott *foundation administrator*
Mays, Jill Duncan *social services administrator, counselor*
McTier, Charles Harvey *foundation administrator*
Philipp, Alicia *community foundation executive*
Ross, Loretta J. *human rights association executive*
Smyre, Calvin *political organization executive, state legislator*
Spillett, Roxanne *social services administrator*
Starr, Charles Christopher *foundation executive, priest*
Stuart, Joan Martha *fund raising executive*
Weatherly, Alvis Morrison, Jr., *retired association developer*

Duluth
Reed, Ralph Eugene, Jr., *political party official*

Lagrange
Gresham, James Thomas *foundation executive*

Norcross
LaFramboise, Patrick Joseph *trade association administrator*

Roswell
Thibaudeau, Mary Frances *cultural organization administrator*

Saint Simons Island
Bell, Ronald Mack *university foundation administrator, consultant*

Savannah
Beals, L(oren) Alan *association executive*

Stone Mountain
McNair, Nimrod, Jr., *foundation executive, consultant*

West Point
Barnwell, Madge Owen *volunteer*

HAWAII

Honolulu
Kane, Micah *political party official*
Morrison, Charles E. *think-tank executive*
Ogburn, Nancy Wrenn *civic volunteer*
Schoenke, Marilyn Leilani *foundation administrator*
White, Emmet, Jr., *retirement community administrator*

Naalehu
Carroll, Mary Colvert *corporate executive, honorary trade representative of Nepal*

Volcano
Nicholson, Marilyn Lee *arts administrator*

IDAHO

Boise
Boyce, Carolyn *political organization administrator*

Olson, A. Craig *foundation administrator, former retail executive, retail executive*
Sandy, John A. *political organization administrator, state legislator*

ILLINOIS

Arlington Heights
Nerlinger, John William *retired trade association administrator*

Belvidere
Luhman, William Simon *community development administrator*

Carlinville
Bellm, Joan *civic worker*

Chicago
Benedict, Kennette Mari *foundation executive, researcher*
Berkson, Sadie *volunteer*
Bindenagel, James Dale *foundation executive*
Bloch, Ralph Jay *professional association executive, marketing consultant*
Bourdon, Cathleen Jane *professional society administrator*
Brandt, Gene Stuart *fundraising consultant*
Chacko, Samuel *association official*
Connelly, John Dooley *social service organization executive*
Cook, Robin Nathaniel *organizational development consultant*
Crenshaw, Carol *charitable organization administrator*
Crown, Susan M. *social services administrator*
Dan, Bernard W. *trade association administrator*
Dolan, Thomas Christopher *professional society administrator*
Donohue, Craig S. *trade association administrator*
Edelman, Ruth Rozumoff *volunteer*
Franke, Richard James *arts advocate, former investment banker*
Froetscher, Janet *social services administrator*
Harvey, Katherine Abler *civic worker*
Helpingstine, Daniel Wallace *organization official, freelance writer*
Jones, Mary Laura *developer, fundraiser*
Kelly, Jerry Bob *social services administrator*
Knapp, Paul Raymond *think-tank executive*
Kudo, Irma Setsuko *not-for-profit executive director*
Lerner, Barbara *think-tank executive, researcher*
MacDougal, Gary Edward *corporate director, foundation trustee*
Mahaffey, John Christopher *professional society administrator*
McDonald, William Brice *educational association administrator*
Minow, Josephine Baskin *civic volunteer*
Munger, Benson Scott *former professional society administrator*
Murphy, Ellis *association management executive*
Olsen, Rex Norman *trade association executive*
Richman, Harold Alan *social welfare policy educator*
Rielly, John Edward *educational association administrator*
Rodgers, James Foster *association executive, economist*
Scherer, Karla *foundation executive, venture capitalist*
Schimberg, Barbara *organizational development consultant*
Sigmon, Joyce Elizabeth *professional society administrator*
Simmons, Adele Smith *foundation executive, former educator*
Smith, Kent Ernest *non-profit organization executive*
Swanson, Patricia Klick *foundation administrator*
Wright, Helen Kennedy *retired professional association administrator, publisher, editor, librarian*
Wyant, Carol Shumaker *not for profit management consultant*

Cicero
Moreno Delgadillo, Mario E. *educational association administrator, educator*

Crystal Lake
Chamberlain, Charles James *railroad labor union executive*

Evanston
Abnee, A. Victor *trade association executive*
Arrington, Michael Browne *foundation administrator*
Gordon, Julie Peyton *foundation administrator*
Korn, Jenny *social activist*
Thrash, Patricia Ann *educational association administrator*

Jacksonville
Mathews, Jack Sherman *foundation administrator, retired insurance company executive*

La Grange Park
Webster, Lois Shand *association executive*

Lake Bluff
Schreiber, George Richard *association executive, writer*

Lake Forest
Fetridge, Bonnie-Jean Clark (Mrs. William Harrison Fetridge) *civic volunteer*

Lansing
McKeown, Mary Elizabeth *educational administrator*

Lincolnshire
Michalik, John James *legal educational association executive*

Maywood
Barbato, Anthony *educational association administrator, medical educator*

Mooseheart
Ross, Donald Hugh *fraternal organization executive*

Naperville
L'Allier, James Joseph *educational multimedia company executive, instructional designer*

Northbrook
Siegal, Judy A. *social services administrator*

Oak Brook
John, Richard C. *enterprise development organization executive*

Ottawa
Thornton, Edmund B. *philanthropist*

Peoria
Smith, Barbara Roderick *health and social services administrator, nursing consultant*

Riverside
Dengler, Robert Anthony *professional association executive, educator*

Rosemont
Good, William Allen *professional society executive*

Schaumburg
Little, Bruce Washington *professional society administrator*
Tompson, Marian Leonard *professional society administrator*

Skokie
Gleason, John Patrick, Jr., *trade association executive*
Weidmann, K. Timothy *not-for-profit fundraiser, writer*

Springfield
Steiner, Janet *educational association administrator*

Sycamore
Stone, Van Courtright *not-for-profit developer*

Vandalia
Low, Louise O. *volunteer*

Waukegan
Drapalik, Betty R. *volunteer, artist, educator*

Wheaton
Votaw, John Frederick *educational foundation executive, educator*

Wilmette
Brink, Marion Francis *trade association administrator*
Hansen, Andrew Marius *retired library association executive*

INDIANA

Bloomington
Brinkman, Paul Del(bert) *foundation executive, university administrator*
Mobley, Tony Allen *foundation administrator, former dean, recreation educator*
Wells, Kimberly K. *not-for-profit organization executive*

Columbus
Brunner, Ellen Margaret *not-for-profit fundraiser*

Fishers
Gatto, Louis Constantine *educational association administrator*

Hagerstown
Bex, Brian William Louis *educational administrator*

Indianapolis
Alvarez, Thomas *foundation administrator, writer, consultant*
Barcus, Robert Gene *retired educational association administrator*
Blaydes, June Louise *volunteer*
Braun, Robert Clare *retired association and advertising executive*
Finley, Katherine Mandusic *professional society administrator*
Maxwell, Florence Hinshaw *civic worker*
McLaughlin, Sherry *association administrator*
Palmer, Robert P. *professional association executive*
Quarles, Beth *civil rights administrator*
Recker, Thomas Edward *fraternal organization executive*
Santos, Richard J. *association administrator*
Shaffer, Alfred Garfield (Terry Shaffer) *retired service organization executive*
Sparks, Donald Eugene *interscholastic activities association executive*
Sweezy, John William *political party official*
Vereen, Robert Charles *retired trade association executive*

Lawrenceburg
Edwards, Marie D. *social services administrator*

Martinsville
Smith, Peg L. *foundation administrator*

Muncie
Bakken, Douglas Adair *foundation executive*
Shoemaker, Helen E. Martin Achor *civic worker*

North Manchester
Myers, Anne M. *developer*

Terre Haute
Aldridge, Sandra *civic volunteer*

West Lafayette
Baumgardt, Billy Ray *professional society administrator, agriculturist*

IOWA

Cedar Rapids
Arnold-Olson, Helen B. *nonprofit consultant*
Huber, Rita Norma *civic worker*
Whipple, William Perry *foundation administrator*

Des Moines
McGuire-Riggs, Sheila *chairman Democratic party*
Nelson, Charlotte Bowers *public administrator*

Sioux City
Waller, Ephraim Everett *retired association executive*

West Branch
Forsythe, Patricia Hays *development professional*

KANSAS

Fort Riley
Spurrier-Bright, Patricia Ann *professional society administrator*

Kansas City
Jones, Charles W. *labor union executive*
Steineger, Margaret Leisy *non-profit organization officer*

Lawrence
Bowman, Laird Price *retired foundation administrator*

Shawnee Mission
Green, John Lafayette, Jr., *education executive*
Slater, William Adcock *retired social services organization executive*

Topeka
Frahm, Sheila *association executive, former government official, academic administrator*

Wichita
Rueb, Sheree A. *social services administrator*

Winfield
Gray, Ina Turner *fraternal organization administrator*

KENTUCKY

Corbin
Barton-Collings, Nelda Ann *political activist, newspaper, bank and nursing home executive*

Frankfort
Mone, Michael A. *social welfare administrator*
Patton, Nicki *former political organization executive*
Williams, Ellen C. *political party official*
Williamson, Deborah McKibben *social services administrator, educator*

Hardin
Morrow, Bruce William *educational administrator, business executive, consultant, author*

Lexington
Lewis, Robert Kay, Jr., *fundraising executive*
Sexton, Robert Fenimore *educational organization executive*

Louisville
Andrews, Adam Gregory *lobbyist, political scientist, educator*
Appleberry, James Bruce *higher education consultant*
Early, Jack Jones *foundation executive*
Hoffer, Debra Humes *educational association administrator*
Watts, Beverly L. *civil rights executive*

Utica
Mountjoy, Helen W. *educational association administrator*

LOUISIANA

Alexandria
Bradford, Louise Mathilde *social work administrator*

Baton Rouge
Brister, Pat *political party executive*
Davis, Carol *educational association administrator, educator*
Jeffers, Ben *political organization executive*

Lafayette
Ceballos, Jacqui Michot *feminist activist, organizer, administrator*

Mandeville
Landry, Joseph L., Jr., *retired affirmative action specialist*

New Orleans
Benjamin, Adelaide Wisdom *community volunteer and activist, retired lawyer*
Cody, Wilmer St. Clair *retired educational administrator, educational policy consultant*
Cohen, Rosalie *civic worker*
Ledbetter, Linda Carol *professional society administrator*

Ruston
Sabin, Paul Edgar *not-for-profit developer*

Shreveport
Goodman, Sylvia Klumok *volunteer*

MAINE

Augusta
Gervais, Paul Nelson *foundation administrator, psychotherapist, public relations executive, author*
Melanson, Dorothy *political organization administrator*
Raths, Barbara *political organization worker*

Bangor
Coffman, Michael S. *international organization official, ecologist*

Brunswick
Rosser, Richard Franklin *higher education consultant*

Cape Elizabeth
Gelzer, Lois Auge *foundation administrator*

Falmouth
Gulliver, Jean K. *educational association administrator*
Hathaway, Lynn McDonald *education advocate, administrator*

Georgetown
Chapin, Maryan Fox *civic worker*

Old Town
Scribner, Princess Rose-Marie *not-for-profit developer*

Portland
Boyle, John Edward Whiteford *cultural organization administrator*
Konkel, Harry Wagner *civic volunteer, retired career officer*

South Portland
Harris, Penny Smith *fundraising consultant*

Waterford
Stockwell, William F. *fundraiser, management consultant*

West Baldwin
Pierce, Elizabeth Gay *civic worker*

York
Smart, Mary-Leigh Call (Mrs. J. Scott Smart) *civic worker*

York Harbor
Rust, Libby Karen *fundraising and public relations counsel*

MARYLAND

Aberdeen Proving Ground
Tobin, Aileen Webb *educational administrator*

Annapolis
Josephson, Diana Hayward *not-for-profit company executive*
Kane, John *political organization administrator*
Rogers, Wayne L. *political organization administrator*

Baltimore
Brock, Roslyn McCallister *association executive*
Coleman, Carolyn Quilloin *association executive*
Davis, Linda L. *social welfare executive director*
Deffenbaugh, Ralston H., Jr., *immigration agency executive, lawyer*
Dickinson, Jane W. *social services administrator*
Ephross, Paul Hullman *social work educator*
Fuentealba, Victor William *professional society administrator*
Hahn Waranch, Helene *educational association administrator*
Levine, Audrey Pearlstein *foundation administrator*
Lungaro Cid, Lisa *educational association administrator*
Mfume, Kweisi *civil rights advocate, former congressman*
Pinkard, Anne Merrick *foundation administrator*
Rosen, Wendy Workman *arts management and publishing executive*
Thomas, Margaret Ann *not-for-profit developer*
Wahington, Anthony William *volunteer coordinator*
Wilmot, Louise C. *charitable organization executive, retired career officer*

Bel Air
Thursfield, Fred Falconer, II, *foundation administrator*

Bethesda
Augustine, Norman Ralph *organization executive, educator*
Beall, Robert Joseph *foundation executive*
Cleary, Timothy Finbar *professional society administrator*
Day, Robert Dwain, Jr., *foundation executive, lawyer*
Dulin, Maurine Stuart *volunteer*
Grady, Patricia A. *health institute director, researcher*
Grau, John Michael *trade association executive*
Jonas, Gary Fred *healthcare executive*
Kochanski, Lois Whidden *foundation administrator*
Oddis, Joseph Anthony *associations executive*
Salisbury, Tamara Paula *foundation executive*
Saunders, Charles Baskerville, Jr., *retired association executive*
Sprott, Richard Lawrence *foundation administrator, researcher*
Stearman, William Lloyd *military association executive, author*
Stone, Jeremy Judah *public interest activist*
Tape, Gerald Frederick *former association executive*

Bowie
Francois, Francis Bernard *retired professional society administrator, lawyer, transportation consultant*

Chevy Chase
Binder, Mildred Katherine *retired public welfare agency executive*
Hunt, Frederick Talley Drum, Jr., *association executive*
Wright, Helen Patton *professional society administrator*

College Park
Brazile, Donna *advocate*
Stover, Carl Frederick *foundation executive*

Columbia
Bailey, John Martin *retired transportation planner, educator*
Gray, Kirk Lamond *social investment firm executive, anthropologist*
Purcell, James Nelson, Jr., *international organization administrator*
Rogers, Thomas Francis *foundation administrator*

Crofton
Ross, E(dwin) Clarke *association executive, educator*

Damascus
Nelligan, William David, III, *professional association executive*

Fort Washington
Coffey, Matthew B. *trade association executive*

Gambrills
Messner, Howard Myron *professional association executive*

Greenbelt
Miller, Alwin Vermar *educational advisor, consultant*

Kensington
Hurt, Frank *labor union administrator*
Mintz, Suzanne *association executive*

Lanham Seabrook
Littlefield, Roy Everett, III, *association executive, law educator*

Lusby
Sprague, Edward Auchincloss *retired association executive, economist*

Mitchellville
Ball, Robert M(yers) *social security, welfare and health policy specialist, writer, lecturer*

North Bethesda
Sherman, Deane Murray *culture organization administrator*

Owings Mills
Tapp, Mamie Pearl *educational association administration*

Pasadena
Murphy, Alma Shirley *political organization worker*

Port Republic
Sugarman, Jule Meyer *children's services consultant, former public administrator*

Potomac
Johnson, Anne Hale *educational association administrator, director*
Keefe, Arthur Thomas, III, *non-profit fund raising executive*
Marincola, Elizabeth Mark *scientific society executive*
Rosenberg, Sarah Zacher *retired cultural organization administrator*

Rockville
Clancy, Carolyn M. *social services administrator, former science foundation director*
Futrovsky, Cheryl Jean *foundation administrator, performing company executive*
Grandy, Fred *foundation administrator, former congressman, former actor*
Kline, Raymond Adam *professional organization executive*
Marcuccio, Phyllis Rose *retired association executive, editor*
Power, A. Kathryn *social services administrator*
Scardelletti, Robert A. *labor union officer*
Spahr, Frederick Thomas *association executive*
Standing, Kimberly Anna *educational researcher*
Sumberg, Alfred Donald *professional association executive*

Salisbury
Leonard, Joseph Howard *association organization executive*

Severna Park
Hall, Marcia Joy *non-profit organization administrator*

Silver Spring
Camphor, James Winky, Jr., *educational administrator*
Fockler, Herbert Hill *foundation executive*
Fustero, Robert Raymond *retired political organization worker*
Gandy, Kim Allison *feminist organization executive, lawyer*
Hayman, Harry *association executive, electrical engineer*
Hermanson Ogilvie, Judith *foundation executive*
Junemann, Gregory J. *labor union administrator*
Smedley, Lawrence Thomas *retired organization executive*
Winston, Michael Russell *foundation executive, historian*
Zakheim, Barbara Jane *development professional*

Stevenson
Middendorf, Alice Carter *volunteer*

Suitland
Smith, Lois Ann (L.A. Smith) *foundation administrator, consultant*

Takoma Park
Richie, Robert Douglas *not-for-profit executive*

Upper Marlboro
Buffenbarger, Robert Thomas *labor union administrator*

MASSACHUSETTS

Belmont
Harris, William Wolpert *foundation administrator*

Boston
Cabot, Louis Wellington *foundation trustee*
Chung, Jennifer M. *not-for-profit executive*
Crate, Darrell *political organization administrator*
Deissler, Mary Alice *foundation executive*
Garcia, Frieda *community foundation executive*
Glass, Renée *educational health foundation executive*
Inman, Jean A. *political party official*
Jennings, Jon Paul *nonprofit foundation executive*
Knight, Norman *philanthropist, former broadcast executive*
Leff, Deborah *government executive*
McClung, William Alexander *foundation administrator, educator*
Shaheen, C. Jeanne *political organization administrator, former governor*
Shea, Dermot P. *consumer advocate, lawyer*
Sullivan, James Leo *organization executive*
Tate, Randall J. (Randy Tate) *former congressman*
Trumbull, David Lewis Kitchen *trade association executive*
Walsh, Peter L. *arts administrator, writer, consultant, researcher, art critic*

Cambridge
Berlowitz, Leslie *cultural organization administrator*
Bloomfield, Steven B. *think-tank executive*
DiGiustini, Antonetta Anna *educational association administrator, educator*
Sallee, Marguerite *association executive*
Tocio, Mary Ann *association executive*
Tucker, Louis Leonard *retired historical society administrator*

Framingham
Harrington, Joseph Francis *educational company executive, history educator*
Welte, A. Theodore *chamber of commerce executive*

Great Barrington
Gilmour, Robert Arthur *foundation executive, educator*

Greenfield
Hutcheson, Thomas Worthington *trade association administrator*

Groton
Anthony, Sylvia *social welfare organization executive*

Hull
Anderson, Timothy Christopher *educational association administrator*

Ipswich
Munro, Donald William, Jr., *non-profit organization executive*
Wilson, Doris H. *volunteer*

Lexington
Garing, Ione Davis *civic worker*

Lincoln
Searle, Andrew Barton *fund raising consultant*

Malden
Guild, Richard Samuel *trade association management company executive*

Medford
O'Connell, Brian *community organizer, public administrator, writer, educator*

Middleboro
Cacciatore, Sharen Wendy *educational administrator*

New Bedford
Bullard, John Kilburn *educational association administrator*

Orleans
Bast, James Louis *retired trade association executive*
Putnam, Allan Ray *association executive*

Quincy
Holway, David *labor union administrator*
Wilson, Blenda Jacqueline *foundation administrator*

Sharon
Reilley, Dennen *research agency administrator, educator*

Wayland
Humphrey, Diana Young *fund raiser*

Wellesley
Fuccillo, Ralph *foundation administrator, consultant*
Henderson, Mary Louise *civic worker*

Weston
Daly, Charles Ulick *foundation executive*

Winchester
Reno, John F. *foundation administrator*

MICHIGAN

Ann Arbor
Diana, Joseph A. *retired foundation executive*
Guardo, Carol J. *association executive*
Kennedy, David Boyd *foundation executive, lawyer*
Radock, Michael *foundation executive*
Ramírez-Betances, Beatriz Eugenia *student activist*
Ware, Richard Anderson *foundation executive*

Battle Creek
Davis, Laura Arlene *retired foundation administrator*
Mawby, Russell George *retired foundation executive*

Birmingham
VanDeusen, Bruce Dudley *educational association administrator*

Detroit
Gettelfinger, Ron *labor union administrator*
Neithercut, Mark Edward *foundation executive*
Parks, Rosa Louise *civil rights activist*

East Lansing
Mitstifer, Dorothy Irwin *honor society administrator*

Flint
Belcher, Max *social services administrator, college dean*
Maynard, Olivia P. *foundation administrator*
Munerlyn, Lorraine *administrative secretary, writer*
White, William Samuel *foundation executive*

Grand Rapids
Sieger, Diana R. *foundation administrator*

Kalamazoo
Petersen, Anne C.(Cheryl) *foundation administrator, educator*

Lansing
Lobenherz, William Ernest *container company/association executive, lawyer*
McKeague, Nancy Palmer *trade association executive*

Manistee
Behring, Daniel William *educational and business professional, consultant*

Oak Park
Piper, Annette Cleone *social services administrator, researcher*

Presque Isle
Kinney, Mark Baldwin *cultural organization administrator, educator*

Saint Clair Shores
Smith, Frank Earl *retired association executive*

Shelby Township
Schultz, Arthur Joseph, Jr., *retired trade association executive*

Southfield
Fleming, Mac Arthur *labor union administrator*

Troy
Marshall, John Elbert, III, *foundation executive*

Waterford
Laing, James Thomas *retired not-for-profit developer*

Whitehall
Weber, Alban *association executive, lawyer*

MINNESOTA

Chaska
Burke, Steven Francis *organization executive*

Minneapolis
Bell, Constance Conklin *child care association administrator*
Fawcett, Marie Ann Formanek (Mrs. Roscoe Kent Fawcett) *civic leader*
Herbison, Priscilla Joan *public policy and law educator, consultant*
Isaak, Larry A. *educational association administrator*
Johnson, John Warren *retired association executive*
King, Reatha Clark *community foundation executive*
Voss, Melinda *health care association administrator*

Minnetonka
Fogelberg, Paul Alan *continuing education company executive*

Owatonna
Groff, Stanley Allen *social services administrator, educator*

Rochester
Riggs, Jeanette Templeton *civic worker*
Shulman, Carole Karen *professional society administrator*

Saint Paul
Anderson, Gordon Louis *foundation administrator*
Archabal, Nina M(archetti) *historical society director*
Archer, Joan M. *trade association administrator*
Eibensteiner, Ron *political organization administrator, venture capitalist*
Kurtz, Harold Paul *foundation executive*
Pampusch, Anita Marie *foundation administrator*
Skillingstad, Constance Yvonne *social services administrator, educator*

Saint Peter
Nelsen, William Cameron *retired not-for-profit developer*

MISSISSIPPI

Crystal Springs
Bates, Lura Wheeler *retired trade association executive*

Fayette
La Salle, Arthur Edward *historic foundation executive*

Jackson
Cole, Ricky *political organization worker*
Herring, James H. *political organization administrator, lawyer*
Marks, Michael *association administrator*
Risley, Rod Alan *education association executive*
Sullivan, Bettye Yarborough *foundation administrator*

Long Beach
Kanagy, Steven Albert *foundation administrator*

Tougaloo
Whittington, Felicia Trenise *social services administrator, educator*

MISSOURI

Bridgeton
Kenison, Raymond Robert *fraternal organization administrator, director*

Chesterfield
Henderson, William J. *association executive*

Columbia
McDermott, Dennis Michael *trade association executive*

Defiance
LeMaster, Sherry Renee *fundraising administrator, foundation administrator, consultant*

Earth City
Anderhalter, Oliver Frank *educational organization executive*

Independence
Potts, Barbara Joyce *retired historical society executive*

Jefferson City
Ridenhour, Cory Todd *association executive, consultant, accountant*
Wagner, Ann *political organization executive*

Kansas City
Benner, Richard Edward, Jr., *community service volunteer, investor*
Bugher, Robert Dean *professional society administrator*
Paden, John Bruce *community resource executive*
Yarmo, Fanny F. *not-for-profit fundraiser*

Kirksville
French, Michael Francis *non-profit education agency administrator*

Lees Summit
Carter, William Gerald *non-profit corporation executive*

Moline Acres
Hinton, Velecia Ann *social welfare administrator*

Richmond Heights
Chandler, James Barton *international education consultant*

Rolla
Bagnall, Lindsay Lomax *not-for-profit developer*

Saint Louis
Anderson, Bruce John *foundation administrator*
Bascom, C. Perry *retired foundation administrator*
Brauer, Camilla Thompson (Kimmy Thompson Brauer) *civic leader*
Breckenridge, Joanne *political organization administrator*
Duhme, Carol McCarthy *civic worker*
Hall, Mary Taussig *professional volunteer*
Horn, Joan Kelly *political research and consulting firm executive*
Hunter, Earle Leslie, III, *retired professional association executive*
Kimmey, James Richard, Jr., *foundation administrator*
Nelson, Ronald Erwin *not-for-profit fundraiser*
Pope, Robert E(ugene) *fraternal organization administrator*
Robins, Marjorie McCarthy (Mrs. George Kenneth Robins) *civic worker*
Winter, Mildred M. *educational administrator*

Springfield
Morris, Ann Haseltine Jones *social welfare administrator*

MONTANA

Billings
Sample, Joseph Scanlon *foundation executive*

Helena
Ream, Bob *political organization administrator*

Manhattan
Sanddal, Nels Dodge *foundation executive, consultant*

Missoula
Kemmis, Daniel Orra *cultural organization administrator, author*

NEBRASKA

Harrison
Coffee, Virginia Claire *civic worker, former mayor*

Lincoln
Hardin, Martha Love Wood *civic leader*
Rosenow, John Edward *foundation executive*

Lyons
Hassebrook, Chuck *not-for-profit developer*

Ogallala
Bourque, Richard Michael *foundation administrator*

Omaha
Bell, C(lyde) R(oberts) (Bob Bell) *foundation administrator*
Burris, Janice Elaine *educational administrator*

Strawhecker, Paul Joseph *fundraising consultant*

NEVADA

Carson City
Ayres, Janice Ruth *social services administrator*

Henderson
Freyd, William Pattinson *fund raising executive, consultant*

Incline Village
Johnston, Bernard Fox *foundation executive, writer*

Las Vegas
Martin, Myron Gregory *foundation administrator*
Martinez, Adriana *political organization worker, photographer*
Nicholson, R. Stephen *organization administrator*
Reid, Rory *former political organization administrator*
Segerblom, Sharon B. *social services administrator*

NEW HAMPSHIRE

Concord
Crosier, John David *trade association administrator*

Manchester
Sullivan, Kathleen N. *political organization administrator, lawyer*

Peterborough
Eppes, William David *arts/humanities supporter*

Pike
Teschner, Douglass Paul *project administrator*

Randolph
Bradley, William Lee *retired foundation executive, educator*

NEW JERSEY

Atlantic City
Jamieson, John Edward, Jr., *social services administrator, minister*
McMaster, Art *beauty pageant organization executive*

Basking Ridge
Probert, Edward Whitford *foundation executive, volunteer*

Beach Haven
Houlihan, Gail Lanier *child advocate, educator*

Bloomfield
McCulloch, George McQuillan *retired foundation executive, fundraiser*

Bridgewater
Feldman, Margit *volunteer*

Cliffside Park
Pushkarev, Boris S. *research foundation director, writer*

East Brunswick
Goldberg, Bertram J. *social agency administrator*

East Orange
Caldwell, Toni Lucille *not-for-profit developer*

Glen Ridge
Pendley, Donald Lee *association executive*

Glen Rock
D'Angelo, Thomas J. *not-for-profit developer, financial consultant*
Sirower, Bonnie Fox *fundraising executive*

Lebanon
O'Neill, Elizabeth Sterling *trade association administrator*

Livingston
Friedman, Frances Wolf *political fund raiser*

Medford
Isaacson, Edith L. *civic leader*

Millburn
Tinning, Herbert Peter *association executive*

Montclair
Blooston, Roselee *cultural organization administrator, writer*
Campbell, Stewart Fred *foundation executive*

New Brunswick
Bunch, Charlotte *advocate*

New Vernon
Dugan, John Leslie, Jr., *foundation executive*

Pennington
Calvo, Roque John *professional society administrator*
Mitchell, Janet Aldrich *fund raising executive, reference materials publisher*

Plainfield
Limpert, John H., Jr., *fund raising executive*

Princeton
Balch, Stephen Howard *professional society administrator*
De Lung, Jane Solberger *independent sector executive*
Freeman, Bruce George *fundraising consultant*
Hearn, Ruby Puryear *foundation executive*
Johnson, Barbara Piasecka *philanthropist, art historian and collector, business investor*
Kassof, Allen H. *foundation administrator*
Kenyon, Regan Clair *educational research executive*
Orrill, Robert Thomas *foundation executive, former history educator*
Plaks, Livia Basch *foundation executive*
Silverman, Jane Aresty *not-for-profit organizational consultant*
Stern, Gail Frieda *historical association director*

Rumson
Brenner, Theodore Engelbert *retired trade association executive*
Swartz, Renee Becker *civic volunteer*

Shiloh
Garrison, John Raymond *organization executive*

South Orange
Stringile, Marie Elizabeth *educational administrator*

Trenton
Binder, Elaine Kotell *associations consultant*
Dahme, Maud *educational association administrator*

Union Beach
Gilmartin, Clara T. *volunteer*

West Caldwell
Giblin, Thomas Patrick *labor union administrator, political organization administrator*

West Orange
Rinsky, Judith Sue Lynn *foundation administrator, educator consultant*

NEW MEXICO

Albuquerque
Cole, Terri Lynn *organization administrator*
Dendahl, John *political organization administrator*
Koch, Jamie *political party official*
Roberts, Dennis William *association executive*
Sinnott, Linda Johnettee *educational association administrator*

Rio Rancho
Brown-Grayson, Ron *foundation administrator, writer*

Roswell
Anderson, Sally Midgette *social services administrator, linguist*

Santa Fe
Charles, Cheryl *non-profit and business executive*
Lukac, George Joseph *not-for-profit fundraiser*

NEW YORK

Albany
Bellizzi, John J. *law enforcement association administrator, educator, pharmacist*
Huxley, Carole Frances Corcoran *educational adminstrator*
Williman, Pauline *shorthand reporter, farm foundation administrator*

Amagansett
Frankl, Jeanne Silver *association executive, lawyer*

Amherst
Clark, Donald Malin *professional association executive*

Arkville
Downing, Darlene L. *non-for-profit organization executive*

Bayside
Madden, Joseph Daniel *trade association executive*

Binghamton
Crocker, Margaret Suydam Smith *art association executive director, art historian*

Bronx
Vassel, Lee Hylton *urbanist, social services administrator, writer*

Brooklyn
Horowitz, Sara *labor organizer*
Lovett, Edward Richardson *not-for-profit developer, writer*
Maslow, Jeffrey R. *not-for-profit fundraiser*
Morgan, Mary Louise Fitzsimmons *fund raising executive, lobbyist*

Buffalo
Clarkson, Elisabeth Ann Hudnut *volunteer*
Spengler, Paul Albert *grants and foundation administrator*

Centereach
Chassman, Karen Moss *educational administrator*
Greene, Marc Elliot *educational association administrator*

Commack
Price, Amelia Ruth *not-for-profit foundation president, artist, small business owner*

Corning
Cicerchi, Eleanor Ann Tomb *fundraising executive*

Dobbs Ferry
Cassella, William Nathan, Jr., *retired organization executive*
Miss, Robert Edward *fundraiser*

East Hampton
Hope, Judith H. *former political organization administrator*

East Quogue
Weiss, Elaine Landsberg *community development management official*

Elmhurst
Matsa, Loula Zacharoula *social services administrator, educator*

Flushing
Fichtel, Rudolph Robert *retired association executive*

Hampton Bays
Komoski, Paul Kenneth *community activist, educational research executive*

Harrison
Wadsworth, Frank Whittemore *foundation executive, literature educator*

Hawthorne
Cantor, Arnold *labor relations official*

Hudson
Miner, Jacqueline *political consultant*

Larchmont
Hinerfeld, Ruth G. *civic organization executive*

Long Island City
Hoffman, Merle Holly *political activist, social psychologist, author*

Manhasset
Foerst, John George, Jr., *retired fundraising executive*

Montauk
Butler, Thomas William *retired health and social services administrator*

New Rochelle
Black, Page Morton *civic worker, vocalist, musician*

New York
Aborn, Richard Mark *organization executive, lawyer*
Amitin, Mark Hall *cultural organization administrator, educator, writer, actor, director*
Anderson, Richard Theodore *trade association administrator, urban planner*
Annan, Kofi A. *Secretary General of the United Nations*
Appel, Marsha Ceil *association executive*
Aronson, Esther Leah *retired foundation administrator, psychotherapist*
Baird, Zoë *foundation president, lawyer*
Baker, William W. *nonprofit company executive*
Beardsley, Theodore S(terling), Jr., *professional society administrator*
Belden, David Leigh *professional association executive, engineering educator*
Belknap, Norton *foundation administrator*
Bellamy, Carol *international organization executive*
Bergman, Charles Cabe *foundation executive*
Berkley, Seth Franklin *epidemiologist, international health specialist*
Berresford, Susan Vail *philanthropic foundation executive*
Bertini, Catherine Ann *international organization official*
Bird, Mary Lynne Miller *professional society administrator*
Bischoff, Theresa A. *not-for-profit association administrator, former medical center executive*
Bishop, Frances Blackburn *civic worker*
Blake, Grace *cultural organization administrator*
Blum, Barbara B. *foundation administrator*
Booth, Barbara Ribman *civic worker*
Brainerd, Michael Charles *international exchange organization executive*
Braverman, Robert Jay *international consultant, public policy educator*
Brindle, Lewis Carver *administrator,fundraiser, consultant*
Brown, Mark Malloch *international organization official*
Brown, Terrence Charles *art association executive, researcher, lecturer*
Buckman, Thomas Richard *foundation executive, educator*
Cahan, Cora *not-for-profit developer*
Calhoun, Craig Jackson *social scientist, educator*
Carlson, Donna *art association administrator, director*
Carroll, David Paul *social welfare administrator*
Catley-Carlson, Margaret *not-for-profit executive*
Chapin, Schuyler Garrison *cultural affairs executive, university dean*
Chatfield-Taylor, Adele *historic preservationist*
Christensen, Kathleen Elizabeth *foundation administrator*
Christopher, Maurine Brooks *foundation administrator, writer, editor*
Coffin, Anne Gagnebin *art association administrator, editor*
Conarroe, Joel Osborne *foundation administrator, educator, editor*
Conway, Gordon Richard *foundation executive*
Cook, John Wesley *foundation administrator*
Dajani, Virginia *arts association administrator*
Dauer, Sheila A. *human rights program director*
Davis, Karen *fund executive*
Davis, Kathryn Wasserman *foundation executive, writer, lecturer*
Dennis, Everette Eugene, Jr., *foundation executive, educator, writer*
Desai, Nitin Dayalji *international organization official*
Dewhurst, David Litchfield *university administrator*
Drake, Owen Burtch Winters *association administrator*
Easum, Donald Boyd *consultant, educator, former institute executive, diplomat*
Eisenberg, Alan *professional society administrator*
Elliott, Eleanor Thomas *foundation executive, civic leader*
Ellis, Ross *non-profit organization executive*
Engelhardt, Sara Lawrence *organization executive*
Evans, Eli Nachamson *foundation administrator*
Feldt, Gloria A. *social service administrator*
Felicitas, C.S. *foundation director, library director*
Ferry, Martha Morton *nonprofit executive*
Feurey, Claudia Packer *not-for-profit executive*
Finberg, Barbara Denning *not-for-profit developer*
Flicker, John *foundation executive*
Fox, Daniel Michael *foundation executive, writer*
Foxman, Abraham Henry *advocacy organization administrator*
Freidheim, Lynn *not-for-profit fundraiser*
Fulweiler, Patricia Platt *civic worker*
Gallagher, Edward Peter *foundation executive*
Goldman, Fatima *social services administrator*
Goodwin, Michael *labor union administrator*
Grabois, Neil Robert *foundation administrator, former college president*
Grayer, Jonathan *education company executive*
Greene, Frank Edward Wade *writer, philanthropy adviser*
Gregorian, Vartan *foundation administrator*
Grimaldi, Nicholas Lawrence *fundraising executive*
Grumet, Louis *professional society administrator*
Guenther, Paul Bernard *volunteer*
Harris, David Alan *not-for-profit organization executive*
Hart, Kitty Carlisle *arts administrator*
Hesselbein, Frances Richards *foundation administrator, consultant, editor*
Hessinger, Greg *trade association administrator*
Heyzer, Noeleen *international organization official*
Hoffman, Linda R. *social services administrator*
Holtzman, Ellen A. *foundation executive*
Hundley, James W., III, *think-tank executive, consultant, researcher*
Ilchman, Alice Stone *foundation administrator, former college president, former government official*
Innis, Roy Emile Alfredo *organization executive*
Iselin, John Jay *foundation president*
Jackson McCabe, Jewell *not-for-profit developer*
Jacobsen, Theodore H. (Ted H. Jacobsen) *labor union administrator, secondary school educator*
Jordan, Richard Thomas *environmental organizations consultant*
Kaggen, Lois Sheila *non-profit organization executive*
Kahan, Marlene *professional association executive*
Kahn, Alfred Joseph *social worker and policy scholar, educator*
Kaskell, Peter Howard *association executive, lawyer*
Katzowitz Shenfield, Lauren *philanthropic consultant, foundation executive*
Kriegel, Jay L. *Olympic organizing committee executive, public relations executive*
Kuyper, Joan Carolyn *foundation administrator*
Labunski, Stephen Bronislaw *professional society administrator*
Lamberg, Carol *housing fund executive*
Lanier, Richard Sanders *foundation administrator*
Lawson-Johnston, Peter Orman *foundation executive*
Lee, Clement William Khan *trade association administrator*
Lee, David Hee-Don *trade association administrator, educator*
Lee, Thomas F. *art association administrator*
Luce, Henry, III, *foundation administrator*
Luckman, Sharon Gersten *arts administrator*
Luers, William Henry *foundation administrator, former art museum administrator*
Luks, Allan Barry *executive director*
Mahoney, Margaret Ellerbe *foundation executive*
Manuell, Lynn Marie *booking agent, singer, actress*
Marchi, Lorraine June *social services administrator*
Mathisen, Harold Clifford *foundation administrator*
Maynard, Virginia Madden *foundation administrator*
McCrary, Eugenia Lester (Mrs. Dennis Daughtry McCrary) *civic worker, writer*
McNamara, Mary E. *nonprofit executive, asset manager, minister*
McPherson, Mary Patterson *charitable foundation executive*
Melancon, Barry C. *professional society adminstrator*
Milbank, Jeremiah *foundation executive*
Miller, Harvey S. Shipley *foundation trustee, private investor*
Moran, Martin Joseph *fundraising company executive*
Neman, Eileen *not-for-profit organization executive*
Obaid, Thoraya Ahmed *international organization official*
Odenweller, Robert Paul *philatelist, association executive, retired airline pilot*
O'Neil Bidwell, Katharine Thomas *fine arts association executive, performing arts executive*
Osborn, Frederick Henry, III, *foundation executive*
Park, Leslie Desmond *health organization executive*
Peters, Elizabeth *media organization director*
Phillips, Russell Alexander, Jr., *retired foundation executive*
Polin, Jane L. *foundation official*
Preston, Frances Williams *performing rights organization executive*
Qiang, Xiao *advocate*
Raynor, Bruce S. *labor union administrator*
Redd, J. Diane *professional fundraiser and grants management executive*
Riordan, John Thomas *trade association executive*
Robinson, Nan Senior *not-for-profit organization consultant*
Robinson, Russell F. *foundation administrator*
Rose, Joanna Semel *cultural activist*
Rosenstein, Brad *cultural organization administrator, playwright*
Rosenthal, Jacob (Jack Rosenthal) *foundation executive*
Rosenthal, Joel Howard *think-tank executive*
Roth, Kenneth *human rights advocate*
Rover, Edward Frank *foundation administrator, lawyer*
Rowe, Elizabeth Webb *community volunteer*
Sard, Susannah Ellen *non-profit executive*
Sasman, Irene Deak Handberg *educational publishing executive*
Schlesinger, Stephen Cannon *think-tank executive*
Shelp, Ronald Kent *non-profit, business and trade association executive, author, lecturer, consultant*
Sherrod, Lonnie Ray *foundation administrator, researcher, psychologist*
Short, Thomas C. *theatre union executive*
Sidamon-Eristoff, Anne Phipps *community trust executive*
Sills, Beverly (Mrs. Peter B. Greenough) *performing arts organization executive, coloratura soprano*
Singh, Jyoti Shankar *international organization executive*
Slutsky, Lorie A(nn) *foundation executive*
Smith, Barry Hamilton *foundation administrator, physician*

PROFESSIONAL INDEX 5545 ASSOCIATIONS AND ORGANIZATIONS

Snyder, Jack L. *international relations educator*
Spero, Joan Edelman *foundation president*
Spindler, James Andrew *not-for-profit executive*
Stack, Edward William *business management and foundation executive*
Steedman, Doria Lynne Silberberg *organization executive*
Stein, Marcia *not-for-profit executive*
Stern-Larosa, Caryl M. *advocate, educational association administrator*
Steuer, Gary Paul *art association administrator*
Straus, Oscar S., II, *foundation executive*
Strubel, Deborah Weaver *think-tank associate*
Sullivan, Mary Brosnahan *advocate, social services administrator*
Sussman, Leonard Richard *foundation executive*
Symonette, Lys *foundation executive, musician, writer*
Tapia, Mario Eduardo *cultural organization administrator*
Tobin, Eugene Marc *foundation administrator, retired academic administrator*
Toldalagi, Marianne *foundation administrator*
Trump, Martha Lindley Blaine Beard *philanthropist*
Tudryn, Joyce Marie *professional society administrator*
Van de Bovenkamp, Sue Erpf *charitable organization executive*
Walker, Jennie Louise *not-for-profit fundraiser, consultant*
Wang, John *not-for-profit company executive*
Wanner, Eric *foundation executive*
Wattleton, Faye (Alyce Faye Wattleton) *research and education institute administrator, advocate*
Weisl, Edwin Louis, Jr., *foundation executive, lawyer*
Wellington, Sheila Wacks *foundation administrator, psychiatry educator*
Wheatley, Steven Charles *educational association administrator*
Wilson, Marie C. *foundation administrator*
Wylde, Kathryn S. *business organization executive*
Zelin, Madeleine *think-tank executive*

Oyster Bay
Russell, Mary Wendell Vander Poel *non-profit organization executive*

Poughkeepsie
Millett, Kate (Katherine Murray Millett) *political activist, sculptor, artist, writer*

Rochester
Klinke, Louise Hoyt *volunteer*
Lebman, Robert Richard *social services administrator*
Pacala, Leon *retired association executive*
Robbins, Nancy Slinker *volunteer*

Roslyn Heights
Malekoff, Andrew *social services administrator, writer*

Saranac
Smith, J. Kellum, Jr., *foundation executive, lawyer*

Saratoga Springs
Carey, Margot Beckmann *fundraiser*
Richardson, Elaina *foundation administrator, former magazine editor*

Scarsdale
Bruck Lieb Port, Lilly *retired consumer advisor, broadcaster, columnist*
Hemley, Eugene Adams *trade association executive*
Paulin, Amy Ruth *civic activist, consultant*

Spring Valley
Cacciola, Patrick Barry *art association administrator*

Staten Island
Lutkenhouse, Anne *non-profit executive*

Stony Brook
Brandwein, Ruth Ann *social welfare educator, administrator, author*

Syracuse
Furze, Edward William *fundraising consultant*

Tarrytown
Bergson, Henry Paul *professional society administrator*

Tonawanda
Glickman, Marlene *non-profit organization administrator*

Troy
Carovano, John Martin *not-for-profit administrator, conservationist*

Upton
Melucci, Richard Charles *research institute administrator*

White Plains
David, Miles *association and marketing executive*
Heimerdinger, John Frederick *association executive*
Howse, Jennifer Louise *foundation administrator*
Slaughter, John Brooks *professional society administrator*

Yonkers
Halloran, Jean *advocate*
Karpatkin, Rhoda Hendrick *retired consumer information organization executive, lawyer*
Neal, Leora Louise Haskett *social services administrator*

NORTH CAROLINA

Asheville
Fobes, John Edwin *international organization official*
Jones-Rafferty, Brenda Anne *personal growth and development company executive*

Cary
Martin, William Royall, Jr., *retired association executive*

Chapel Hill
Ferris, William Reynolds *humanities organization administrator, folklore educator*
Grayson, Mark *organization executive*
Kenan, Thomas Stephen, III, *philanthropist*
Krasno, Richard Michael *foundation executive, educator*
MacGillivray, Lois Ann *organization executive*

Charlotte
Bolick, Ryan *lobbyist, consultant*
Locke, Elizabeth Hughes *foundation executive*
McClure, Howard Jean, Jr., *advocate*
Pyle, Gerald Fredric *medical geographer, educator*

Clinton
Griffin, Betty Lou *not-for-profit developer, educator*

Durham
Bevan, William *retired foundation executive*
Semans, Mary Duke Biddle Trent *foundation administrator*

Greensboro
Kornegay, Horace Robinson *retired trade association executive, former congressman, lawyer*
Ohlott, Patricia J. *cultural organization administrator*

Raleigh
Allen, Barbara Kirkman *politcal organization administrator*
Cobey, William Wilfred, Jr., *political organization administrator*
Daubert, Erik Joseph *organization administrator*
McKinney, Carolyn *educational association administrator, educator*

Waynesville
Cole, James Yeager *foundation administrator*

Wilmington
Dickman, Catherine Crowe *retired human services administrator*
Nubel, Marianne Kunz *cultural administrator, writer, composer*
Seapker, Janet Kay *museum and architectural history consultant*

Wilson
McCain, Betty Landon Ray (Mrs. John Lewis McCain) *political party official, state official*

Wingate
Dodd, John Robert *non-profit organization administrator*

Winston Salem
Jones, F(rancis) Whitney *fund raising executive, consultant*

Woodland
Wilson, Lloyd Lee *organization administrator*

NORTH DAKOTA

Bismarck
Cramer, Kevin *foundation administrator*
Kleingartner, Larry *agricultural association executive*
Stoller, Rose *think-tank executive*
Thompson, Vern *political organization executive*

OHIO

Akron
Collier, Alice Elizabeth *retired community organization executive*
Donehey, Marilyn Moss *foundation administrator*
Frank, John V. *foundation administrator*
Gregoire, Larry V. *labor union administrator*
Martino, Frank Dominic *union executive*

Athens
Rudy, Joel S. *retired fraternal organization administrator*

Canton
Fernandez, Kathleen M. *cultural organization administrator*

Chagrin Falls
Vail, Iris Jennings *civic worker*

Cincinnati
Clay, Howard James, Jr., *foundation administrator*
Marx, Marjorie McCullough *service organization executive*
McAusland, Randolph M. N. *arts consultant*
Ruehlmann, Virginia Juergens *foundation creativity director, writer*
Sowder, Fred Allen *foundation administrator, alphabet specialist*
Tenbosch, Gerald John *fundraising executive*
Wilson, Arthur Henry *charitable institution executive*

Cleveland
Bergholz, David *foundation administrator*
Boyd, Byron A. *labor union administrator*
Calkins, Hugh *foundation executive*
Carter, John Dale *organizational development coordinator*
Distelhorst, Garis Fred *trade association executive*
Fallcreek, Stephanie Jean *non-profit organization executive*
Garrison, William Lloyd *cemetery executive*
Hartley, Duncan *fundraising executive*
Jenson, Jon Eberdt *association executive*
Pike, Kermit Jerome *cultural organization administrator*
Smith, Jerome *not-for-profit developer, film producer, writer*
Thompson, Paul C. *labor union administrator*

Cleveland Heights
Caswell Harris, Lucky Jean *community service administrator*

Columbia Station
Bender, Peggy Wallace *charitable gift planning consultant*

Columbus
Akers, Saundra Ruth *disability rights advocate*
Chu, Roderick Gong-Wah *educational administrator*
De Maria, Paolo *policy advisor*
Franano, Susan Margaret Ketteman *arts consultant and adminstrator, musician*
Luck, James I. *foundation executive*
Newman, Diana S. *development consultant*
Selby, Diane Ray Miller *fraternal organization administrator*
Sharp, Paul David *institute administrator*
White, Dennis L. *political organization administrator*

Cuyahoga Falls
Smith, Margaret A. (Maggie Carroll Smith) *community volunteer*

Dayton
Daley, Robert Emmett *retired foundation executive*
Mathews, David *foundation executive*
Schwartzhoff, James Paul *foundation executive*
Thomas, Marianna *volunteer community activist, writer, speaker*
Williams, Walker Richard, Jr., *social services administrator*

Dublin
Needham, George Michael *association executive*

Fairview Park
Fordyce, James Stuart *non-profit organization executive*

Hamilton
Gruenwald, James Howard *association executive, consultant*

Oberlin
Cartier, Brian Evans *association executive*
Young, Margaret Helen *educational association administrator, writer*

Olmsted Falls
Faller, Dorothy Anderson *international agency administrator*

Oxford
Becker, Stephen Bradbury *fraternal organization administrator*
Miller, Robert James *educational association administrator*

Richfield
Lewis, Sylvia Davidson *foundation executive*

Yellow Springs
Graham, Jewel Freeman *social worker, lawyer, educator*

OKLAHOMA

Edmond
Wylie, Quineta G. Beagle *state political party executive*

Enid
McCobb, Allan Paul *not-for-profit organization executive*

Oklahoma City
Brooks, Gene (Leslie Gene Brooks) *cultural association administrator*
Crowder, Carolyn *educational association administrator, educator*
Gumerson, Jean Gilderhus *health foundation executive*
Kerr, Lou C. *foundation administrator*
Parmley, Jay *political organization administrator*
Wynn, Brenda Reneau *trade association executive*

Sallisaw
Crowson, Watie Dee *foundation administrator*

OREGON

Bandon
Millard, Esther Lound *foundation administrator, educator*

Bend
Evers-Williams, Myrlie *cultural organization administrator*

Corvallis
Wilkins, Caroline Hanke *consumer agency administrator, political worker*

Eugene
Cone, June Elizabeth *civic worker*

Lake Oswego
Bruce, John Allen *foundation executive, educator*
Miller, Barbara Stallcup *development consultant*

Lincoln City
Decker, Mary Duryea *volunteer, educator, retired social worker*

Medford
Sours, James Kingsley *association executive, former college president*

Portland
Buckstein, Steve *think-tank executive*
Collins, Maribeth Wilson *foundation president*
Edmunson, James L. *political organization administrator*
Milton, Catherine Higgs *social service entrepreneur*
Patterson, Beverly Ann Gross *not-for-profit fundraiser, consultant, social services administrator*
Pine, William Charles *foundation executive*
Rooks, Charles S. *foundation administrator*

Thomas, Carol F. *educational association administrator*

Salem
Atkinson, Perry *political organization administrator*
Frank, Gerald Wendel *civic leader, journalist*
Kirk, Jill *educational association administrator*

Summerville
Hopkins, Gerald Frank *trade association administrator*

PENNSYLVANIA

Ben Avon
Gibson, Samuel Norris *educational organization executive, retired clergy*

Bridgeville
Fox, Debra L. *educational association administrator, business owner*

Bryn Mawr
Cooney, Patricia Ruth *civic worker*

Carlisle
Anderson, Howard Wayne, Jr., *training company executive*

Carnegie
Dybeck, Alfred Charles *labor arbitrator*

Chadds Ford
King, M. Jean *association executive*

Chambersburg
Lesher, Richard Lee *retired association executive*

Darby
Wardell, Lindy Constance *nonprofit organization administrator*

Dillsburg
Bowers, Glenn Lee *retired professional society administrator*

Drexel Hill
Schiazza, Guido Domenic (Guy Schiazza) *educational association administrator*

Easton
Danjczek, Michael Harvey *social service administrator*

Elizabethtown
Madeira, Robert Lehman *professional society administrator*

Elkins Park
Pak, Hyung Woong *community advocate*

Erie
Hauck, Barbara Jean *fund raising executive, writer, artist*

Gibsonia
Haas, Eileen Marie *homecare advocate*

Glenside
Block, Isaac Edward *professional society administrator*
Doman, Janet Joy *professional society administrator*

Harrisburg
Breslin, Michael Joseph, III, *social services administrator, educator*
Novak, Alan P. *political organization administrator*
Staub, Shalom David *cultural organization administrator*

Havertown
Wing, Kennard Thompson *educational organization official*

Huntingdon
Tuten, James H. *educational association administrator, educator*

Indiana
Steelman, Sara Gerling *art association administrator*

Kempton
Lenhart, Cynthia Rae *conservation organization executive*

Kingston
Friedman, Pauline Poplin *civic worker, consultant*

Lewisburg
Neuman, Nancy Adams Mosshammer *civic leader*
Schlegel, Richard LaMar *advocate, writer*

Macungie
Farr, Lona Mae *non-profit executive, business owner*
Nenstiel, Susan Kisthart *fundraising professional*

Mechanicsburg
Gibbons, Miles Joseph, Jr., *foundation administrator*

Merion Station
Freeze, James Donald *administrator, clergyman*

Monroeville
Skolnick, Marilyn *civic worker*

Newtown
Keenan, Terrance *foundation executive*

Penn Valley
Newhall, John Harrison *retired non profit company executive*

Philadelphia
Barnes, Vaughn Lamont, Jr., *social services administrator, social worker*
Bodine, James Forney *retired civic leader*

Byrnes, Maureen K. *foundation administrator*
Connor, Nancy L. *foundation executive*
Friedman, Murray *civil rights official, historian*
Makous, Bruce B. *fundraiser*
Mallery, David *education association executive, consultant*
Meyerson, Margy Ellin *urbanist, civic volunteer*
Ray, Evelyn Lucille *arts facilitator, small meetings planner*
Reed, Sally Gardner *cultural organization administrator*
Sicherman, Harvey *think-tank executive*
Tucker, Cynthia Delores Nottage (Mrs. William M. Tucker) *political party official, former state official*
Urahn, Susan K. *foundation administrator*
Vredenburgh, Judy *youth organization executive*
Watson, Bernard Charles *educator, foundation administrator*
Williams, Elizabeth A.W. *foundation administrator*

Pittsburgh
Becker, George *labor union administrator*
Gerard, Leo W. *labor union executive*
Lloyd, Robert Albert *retired foundation administrator*
Petersen, Jean Snyder *association executive*
Swallow, Frederick Richard *retired educational association administrator*
Ziegler, Arthur P., Jr., *foundation executive*

State College
Book, Edward R. *consultant, retired association executive*
DeVoss, James Thomas *community foundation administrator, retired*
Phillips, Janet Colleen *retired educational association executive, editor*

Uniontown
Eberly, Robert Edward *foundation administrator*

Villanova
Friend, Theodore Wood, III, *foundation executive, historian, writer*
Smith, Standish Harshaw *not-for-profit developer*

Warren
Johnson, Newkirk Lynn *not-for-profit developer*

Warrendale
Rumbaugh, Max Elden, Jr., *professional society administrator*
Scott, Alexander Robinson *engineering association executive*

Wayne
Etris, Samuel Franklin *trade association research consultant*

RHODE ISLAND

Warwick
Jennings, Julianne *cultural organization administrator*

West Warwick
Lancellotta, John Jerry-Louis *foundation administrator*

SOUTH CAROLINA

Aiken
Ely, Duncan Cairnes *non profit/human services executive, civic leader*

Charleston
Bailey, Dawn Marie *fund raising systems consultant*
Ferguson, Esther B. *philanthropist*
Hughes, Blake *retired architectural institute administrator, publisher*

Columbia
Bjontegard, Arthur Martin, Jr., *foundation executive*
Dawson, Katon *political organization administrator*
McGill, Jennifer Houser *non-profit association administrator*

Green Pond
Ittleson, H(enry) Anthony *foundation executive*

Greenville
Hendrix, Susan Clelia Derrick *civic worker*

Hilton Head Island
Ponder, Henry *educational association administrator*

Lancaster
Bundy, Charles Alan *foundation executive*

Spartanburg
Glassick, Charles Etzweiler *academic foundation administrator*
Richards, Marty Grover *foundation administrator, director*

Woodruff
Childers, Bob Eugene *educational association executive*

SOUTH DAKOTA

Pierre
Collins-Adler, Catherine Kay *social services professional*

Yankton
Piper, Kathleen *former political organization administrator*

TENNESSEE

Athens
Brown, Sandra Lee *arts management consultant, watercolorist*

Brentwood
Lodowski, Charles Alan *business association executive*

Cleveland
Lockhart, Madge Clements *educational organization executive*

Franklin
Jowdy, Jeffrey William *development executive*

Knoxville
Adaku, Chioma *non-profit organization administrator*
Froula, James DeWayne *national honor society executive, engineer*

Memphis
Jalenak, Peggy Eichenbaum *volunteer*
Kaplan, Claudette S. (Claudia Kaplan) *volunteer*
Patrick, Jane Austin *association executive*
Tibbs, Martha Jane Pullen *civic worker, retired social worker*

Nashville
Benson, Edwin Welburn, Jr., *trade association executive*
Farmer, William H. *political organization worker, lawyer*
Goetz, Dave *trade association administrator*
Harwell, Beth H. *political organization worker*
Henderson, Milton Arnold *professional society administrator*
Johnson, Hollis Eugene, III, *foundation executive*
Saltsman, John B. *former political party executive, commissioner*
Siegfried, John *association officer*
Turk, Thomas Liebig *cultural organization administrator*
Young, Boyd D. *labor union administrator*

TEXAS

Amarillo
Berry, Jacob Obadiah *not-for-profit developer, rancher*
Crain, Mary Tom *volunteer*
Utterback, Will Hay, Jr., *retired labor union administrator, genealogist*

Arlington
Eudaly, Olivia Coggin *not-for-profit executive, educator*

Austin
Banks, Virginia Anne (Ginger Banks) *association administrator*
Boles, Billye Gayle *program administrator*
Bonjean, Charles Michael *foundation executive, sociologist, educator*
Cleaves, Peter Shurtleff *foundation official*
Dougherty, Molly Ireland *organization executive*
Fisk, Doris Rosalie Scanlan *volunteer*
Fraser, Troy *development officer, state legislator*
Green, Shirley Moore *retired public affairs and communications executive*
Houston, Ron *professional society administrator*
Hughes, Judy Lynne *political organization executive*
Mathias, Reuben Victor (Vic Mathias) *chamber of commerce executive, real estate investor*
Mc Kinney, Michael Whitney *trade association executive*
Meredith, Thomas J. *civic leader, philanthropist, former computer company executive*
Pettigrew, Jo Arnold *educational association administrator*
Romero, Jesse Charles *political consultant*
Stoner, James Lloyd *retired foundation executive, clergyman*
Weddington, Susan *political party official*
White, Alice Virginia *college campaign program administrator*

Carrollton
Hart, Elizabeth Ann *foundation administrator*

Cedar Park
Love, Ben Howard *retired organization executive*

Colleyville
Tigue, Virginia Beth (Ginny Tigue) *volunteer*

Corpus Christi
French, Dorris Towers Bryan *volunteer*

Dallas
Bonner, Cathy *foundation administrator*
Braun, Susan J. *foundation administrator*
Cockerham, Sidney Joe *professional society administrator*
Evans, Dvorah A. *organization executive, professional organizer*
Evans, Linda Perryman *foundation adminstrator*
Goodman, John C. *think-tank executive*
Hamilton, Wendy J. *foundation administrator*
Hay, Betty Jo *civic worker*
Santos, Charles Daniel *cultural organization administrator*
Wassenich, Linda Pilcher *retired health policy analyst, fund raiser*
Wilber, Robert Edwin *trade association administrator*

El Paso
Goodman, Gertrude Amelia *civic worker*

Fort Worth
Davis, Alan Tucker *foundation administrator, philanthropist, minister*
Dilley, Carol *association administrator*
Prather, Robert Franklin *fund administrator*
Saenz, Nancy Elizabeth King (Mrs. Michael Saenz) *civic worker*

Galveston
Baker, Robert Ernest, Jr., *retired foundation executive*

Georgetown
Busfield, Roger Melvil, Jr., *retired trade association executive, educator*

Houston
Black, Marilyn Hammer *non-profit organization executive*
Grace, Priscilla Anne *labor union executive*
Grayson, Charles Jackson, Jr., *research association executive*
Handy, Robert Truman *association administrator, finance consultant*
Heckler, Walter Tim *association executive*
Menninger, Roy Wright *medical foundation executive, psychiatrist*
Tarlov, Alvin Richard *former philanthropic foundation administrator, physician, educator, researcher*

Irving
Olson, Herbert Theodore *trade association executive*
Wilkerson, H. Dean, Jr., *association and organization executive*

Lancaster
Stanley, Rosalind Marie Caldwell *social welfare administrator, consultant, writer*

Lubbock
Baiza, Mary Pesina *development management consultant*

Odessa
Boyd, Claude Collins *educational specialist, consultant*

Plano
Carver, Rita *fundraising consultant*

San Antonio
Crichton, Flora Cameron *volunteer*
Jacobson, Helen Gugenheim (Mrs. David Jacobson) *civic worker*
Kickbusch, Consuelo Castillo *educational association administrator, consultant, former military officer*
Krier, Joseph Roland *chamber of commerce executive, lawyer*
Moder, John Joseph *non-profit administrator*
Montecel, Maria Robledo (Cuca Robledo Montecel) *educational association administrator*
Williams, Tywanda Monceil *social services administrator*

Sugar Land
Hosley, Marguerite Cyril *civic worker*

Texarkana
Malcolm, Molly Beth *political party official, counselor*

UTAH

Brigham City
Bishop, Robert *former political organization administrator, secondary school educator*

Ogden
Davis, Lori *foundation executive*
Pappas, Leah Aglaia *civic worker, political consultant*

Orem
Hatch, Steven Graham *foundation administrator*

Salt Lake City
Clark, Deanna Dee *civic leader and volunteer*
Cofield, Philip Thomas *educational association administrator*
Dahmen-Ray, Patricia *professional society administrator*
Holbrook, Meghan Zanolli *fundraiser, public relations specialist, political organization chairman*
Julander, Paula Foil *health care and political consultant, state senator*
Lee, Blaine Nelson *executive consultant, educator, author*
Melich, Doris S. *public service worker*
Mendenhall, Robert W. *education technology executive*

Woods Cross
Ingles, Joseph Legrand *social services administrator, political science educator*

VERMONT

Bennington
Perin, Donald Wise, Jr., *former association executive*

Burlington
Neale, Gail Lovejoy *non-profit organization management consultant*

Ludlow
Nitka, Alice W. *social services administrator, state representative*

Middlebury
McGlashan, Amy Gibans *educational association administrator, consultant*

Montpelier
Barbieri, Christopher George *professional society administrator*
Metcalf, Cindy W. *political organization administrator*

Peacham
Barnes, Harry G., Jr., *human rights activist, conflict resolution specialist, retired ambassador*

Plymouth
Bittinger, Cynthia Douglas *foundation executive*

Shelburne
Ryerson, William Newton *non profit organization executive*

Williston
Podhajski, Blanche Rita *language foundation administrator*

VIRGINIA

Alexandria
Bachus, Walter Otis *retired army general, former association executive*
Baroody, Michael Elias *trade association executive*
Bezold, Clement *think tank executive*
Bolger, Robert Joseph *retired trade association executive*
Brown, Quincalee *professional society administrator*
Bryant, Anne Lincoln *educational association executive*
Carter, Gene Raymond *professional association executive*
Cooper, David Earl Kaleoikaika *foundation executive*
Cooper, Edythe E.D. *political organization administrator*
Crane, Stephen Charles *professional society administrator*
De Barbieri, Mary Ann *nonprofit management consultant*
Diachenko, Marge *political organization administrator*
Engler, Brian David *association executive*
Faenza, Michael M. *mental health association administrator*
Fisher, Colleen M. *trade association administrator*
Greenstein, Ruth Louise *research institute executive, lawyer*
Hodgkins, Allen Ray, III, *cultural organization administrator, director*
Kaufman, Beverly *political organization administrator*
Kolar, Mary Jane *trade and professional association executive*
Kratovil, Jane Lindley *think tank associate, developer/fundraiser*
LeBlanc, James Leo *business executive, consultant*
Lendsey, Jacquelyn L. *foundation administrator*
Lenz, Edward Arnold *trade association administrator, lawyer*
Magazine, Alan Harrison *association executive, consultant*
McCulloch, William Leonard *trade association administrator*
Miller, Marian *professional society administrator*
Murray, Robert John *think-tank executive*
Pugh, Jennifer Serafin *lobbyist*
Rabun, John Brewton, Jr., *criminal justice agency administrator*
Rector, John Michael *association executive, lawyer*
Riel, Pauline *association executive*
Schubert, Richard Francis *consultant*
Smith, Heidi *political organization administrator*
Thayer, Marilyn *political organization executive, civic worker*
Thomas, Ramonia *political organization executive, civic worker*
Turner, Mary Jane *educational administrator*
Welburn, Brenda Lilienthal *professional society administrator*

Annandale
Herbst, Robert LeRoy *organization executive*

Arlington
Anderson, Dean William *educational administrator*
Asbell, Fred Thomas *health industry association executive*
Bossman, David A. *trade association administrator*
Ericsson, Sally Claire *not-for-profit organization administrator*
Fujito, Wayne Takeshi *international business company executive*
Futrell, John William *environmental agency executive, lawyer*
Goetze, Richard B., Jr., *association administrator*
Hendrickson, Daniel C. *association administrator*
Hickman, Elizabeth Podesta *retired counselor, educator*
Hunter, Jody Jean *association executive, naturalist*
Hunter, J(ohn) Robert *insurance consumer advocate*
Jankowski, John Edward, Jr., *government administrator*
Langworthy, Everett Walter *association executive, natural gas exploration company executive*
McKee, Thomas J. *association administrator*
McKinnon, Russel Francis Daniel *professional society administrator*
McMasters, Paul Kenneth *foundation executive*
McShane, Michael John *lobbyist*
Newburger, Beth Weinstein *historical association administrator*
O'Day, Paul Thomas *trade association executive*
Paynter, Harry Alvin *retired trade association executive*
Politi, John J. *association administrator*
Price, Jack C. *association administrator*
Rubottom, George Milton *foundation administrator, chemist*
Shannon, Jacqueline *association executive*
Shannon, Thomas Alfred *retired educational association administrator emeritus*
Smeal, Eleanor Cutri *civil rights executive*
Stonner, David Moore *foundation administrator*
Tarr-Whelan, Linda *policy center executive*
Tugwell, Franklin *think-tank executive*
Uncapher, Mark Elson *lawyer, trade association administrator*
Watson, Alexander Fletcher *organization executive, former ambassador*

Basye
Stanley, Robert Warren *association executive*

Boston
Fisher, John Morris *association official, business executive, educator*

Burke
Woodruff, C(harles) Roy *consultant, retired professional association executive*

Chantilly
Sroka, John Walter *trade association executive*

Charlottesville
Brownell, Blaine Allison *educational association administrator, former university administrator, history educator*
Friedman, Susan Lynn Bell *economic development professional*
Hendrickson, Jerome Orland *trade association administrator, lawyer*
Jordan, Daniel Porter, Jr., *foundation administrator, history educator*
Thompson, Kenneth W(inifred) *educational association administrator, writer, editor, social sciences educator*
Wilson, Mitchell B. *fraternal organization administrator*

Colonial Heights
Thomson, Gary R. *political organization administrator, accountant*

Fairfax
Chafuen, Alejandro Antonio *think-tank executive*
Cullison, Alexander C. (Doc Cullison) *mediator, arbitrator*
Gray, William H., III, *association executive, former congressman*
Hollans, Irby Noah, Jr., *retired association executive*
Jones, George Fleming *international consultant*
Lomax, Michael Lucius *non-profit association administrator*
Molino, Michael Anthony *trade association executive*
Roberts, Cecil Edward, Jr., *labor union administrator*
Robinson, Kayne B. *lobbyist, former political organization officer*

Falls Church
Jones, Linda R. Wolf *company executive*
Rodgers, Kirk Procter *international environmental consultant*
Thomsen, Samuel Borron *non-profit executive, consultant*

Flint Hill
Dietel, William Moore *former foundation executive*
Williamson, Richard Hall *association executive*

Franktown
Kellam, Caramine *volunteer*

Fredericksburg
Ivey, David Lamar *trade association executive*

Garrisonville
Emely, Charles Harry *trade association executive, consultant*

Great Falls
DiBona, Charles Joseph *retired trade association executive*
Klimczuk, Stephen John *business executive, foundation director*

Herndon
Woerth, Duane E. *labor union administrator*

Keswick
Nosanow, Barbara Shissler *art association administrator*

Louisa
Small, William Edwin, Jr., *association and recreation executive*

Lynchburg
Johnson, Robert Bruce *historic preservationist*

Manassas
Cypess, Raymond Harold *bioscience organization executive*

Mc Lean
Bragg, Lynn Munroe *trade association administrator, former federal commissioner*
Canes, Michael Edwin *research economist*
Lovaas, John L. *foreign aid executive, community activist*
McInerney, James Eugene, Jr., *trade association executive*
Stackpole, Kerry Clifford *association executive*
Trout, Margie Marie Mueller *civic worker*

Merrifield
Earley, Mark Lawrence *not-for-profit administrator, former state attorney general*

Middleburg
Sodolski, John *retired association administrator*

Newport News
Mazur, Rhoda Himmel *community volunteer*

Oakton
Rees, Clifford Harcourt, Jr., (Ted Rees) *retired association executive, retired air force officer*

Reston
Brennan, Norma Jean *professional society publications director*
Chattman, Raymond Christopher *foundation executive*
Gates, James David *retired association executive, consultant*
Hope, Samuel Howard *accreditation organization executive*
Mahlmann, John James *music education association administrator*
Minton, Joseph Paul *retired safety organization executive*
Mogge, Harriet Morgan *educational association executive*

Richmond
Bankos, Jean *educational association administrator, educator*
Brackenridge, N. Lynn *not-for-profit developer*
Dell, Willie Jones *social services executive, educator*
Framme, Lawrence Henry, III, *political organization administrator, lawyer*

Wheelan, Belle S. *educational association administrator*
Wood, Jeanne Clarke *charitable organization executive*

Roanoke
Logan Lawson, Anna *social services administrator*

Spotsylvania
Clower, William Dewey *retired trade association executive*
Hardy, Dorcas Ruth *business and government relations executive*

Springfield
Bartlow, Gene Steven *association executive, retired air force officer*
Larson, Reed Eugene *foundation administrator*
Spencer, William Courtney *foundation executive, international business executive*

Stafford
Sedlak, James William *organization administrator*

Sterling
Chavez, Linda *civil rights organization executive*
Munger, Paul David *company executive, educational administrator*

Upperville
Smart, Edith Merrill *civic worker*

Vienna
Gerson, Elliot Francis *foundation administrator*
Marx, Gary Dean *international education consultant, association executive, futurist*
Spiro, Robert Harry, Jr., *foundation and business executive, educator*
Sturm, John F. *trade association administrator*
Thompson, Louis Milton, Jr., *association executive, horse breeder*

Virginia Beach
Reece-Porter, Sharon Ann *international human rights educator*

Warrenton
Fox, Raymond Graham *educational technologist*

Williamsburg
Campbell, Colin Goetze *foundation president*

Woodbridge
Bastas, Thomas G. *labor union administrator*
Garon, Richard Joseph, Jr., *political organization worker*

WASHINGTON

Bainbridge Island
Oechsli, Christopher George *foundation administrator*

Bellevue
Arnold, Ronald Henri *nonprofit organization executive, consultant*

Bellingham
St. James, Margaret Jean *not-for-profit developer*

Edmonds
Monroe, James Walter *retired organization executive*

Kenmore
Patten, Richard E. *not-for-profit developer, director*

Olympia
Stohl, Esther A. *senior citizen advocate*

Port Townsend
Woolf, William Blauvelt *retired association executive*

Puyallup
Muchmore, Don Moncrief *retired museum, foundation, educational, financial fund raising and public opinion consulting firm administrator, banker*

Seattle
Arthur, William Lynn *environmental/political program director*
Berendt, Paul *political organization worker*
Davidson, Robert William *not-for-profit executive*
Donnelly, Peter F. *art association administrator*
Farrell, Anne Van Ness *foundation executive*
Foster, Barry Alan *cultural organization researcher, educator*
Gates, Melinda French *foundation administrator*
Gates, William Henry, Sr., *foundation administrator*
Martínez, Yolanda R. *social services administrator*
Mathews, Sylvia Mary *foundation administrator*
Stonesifer, Patricia Q. *foundation administrator*
Vance, Christopher *political organization worker*

Spokane
Coker, Charlotte Noel *political activist*
Herzer, Marian Day *not-for-profit developer, educator*

Tacoma
Rieke, William Oliver *foundation director, medical educator, former university president*

Vancouver
Smith, Sam Corry *retired foundation executive, consultant*

WEST VIRGINIA

Charleston
Chapman, John Andrew *retired chamber of commerce executive*

Fairmont
Ford, Alma Regina *union official, educator*

South Charleston
Warner, Kris *political organization administrator*

Wheeling
Hogan, Susan Cox *association executive*

WISCONSIN

Altoona
James, Henry Thomas *former foundation executive, educator*

Appleton
Hlukens, Kay L. *social services association executive*

Balsam Lake
Mattson, Carol Linnette *social services administrator*

Hayward
Yakes, Penny Anne *advocate, writer*

Kenosha
Adler, Seymour Jack *social services administrator*

Madison
Brennan, Robert Walter *association executive*
Honold, Linda Kaye *political organization executive, human resources development executive*
Spring, Terri *political organization executive*

Milwaukee
Fradkin, Hillel Gideon *foundation official, educator*
Joyce, Michael Stewart *foundation executive, political science educator*
Rader, I. Andrew *foundation administrator*
Schneider, Thomas Paul *non-profit agency administrator*
Zeidler, Frank P. *former association administrator, mayor, arbitrator, mediator, fact-finder*

Onalaska
Pertzsch, Evelyn Maria *civic worker*

Pewaukee
Carlson, Kathleen *not-for-profit fundraiser, writer, journalist*

Shawano
Lyon, Thomas L. *agricultural organization administrator*

Whitewater
Connor, James Richard *retired foundation administrator*
Kolda, Thomas Joseph *non-profit organization executive*

WYOMING

Casper
Constantino, Becky *political organization administrator*
Gierau, Mike *political organization worker, small business owner*
Stoval, Linda *political party official*

Cheyenne
Noe, Guy *retired social services administrator*

Laramie
Darnall, Roberta Morrow *association executive*

TERRITORIES OF THE UNITED STATES

GUAM

Agana
San Agustin, Joe Taitano *political organization worker, educator*

PUERTO RICO

San Juan
Castro-Blanco, James *professional society administrator*
Prats Palerm, Robert L. *political party chairman*

VIRGIN ISLANDS

St Thomas
Creque, Linda Ann *non-profit educational and research executive, former education commissioner*

CANADA

MANITOBA

Winnipeg
Runnalls, David *think-tank executive*

NEW BRUNSWICK

Fredericton
Lewell, Peter A. *international technology executive, researcher*

Saint John
Mowatt, E. Ann *women's voluntary leader, lawyer*

ONTARIO

Ottawa
Maxwell, Judith *think-tank executive, economist*
O'Neil, Maureen *think-tank executive*
Plumptre, Tim *think tank executive*
Rodger, Ginette *professional association executive, nurse*
Wilson, Ian Edwin *cultural organization administrator, archivist*

Toronto
Goodenow, Robert W. *labor union administrator*
Goold, Douglas *think-tank executive*
Mintz, Jack Maurice *think-tank executive, economics professor*

QUEBEC

Outremont
Letourneau, Jean-Paul *business association executive and consultant*

Rosemere
Hopper, Carol *meeting and incentive trip administrator*

MEXICO

Mexico City
Bruton, John Macaulay *trade association executive, consultant*

ARGENTINA

Buenos Aires
Levy, Joseph Bruno *foundation administrator, educator*

AUSTRIA

Vienna
al-Omair, Saleh *trade association administrator*

BELGIUM

Brussels
Berna, Marie-Rose *international organization executive*

CZECH REPUBLIC

Prague
Zharikov, Alexander Nikolaevich *trade union federation executive*

ENGLAND

London
Chadwick, Derek James *foundation administrator*
Hazell, Robert John Davidge *policy institute director, government educator*
Nelson, Elizabeth Hawkins *public association administrator*

FRANCE

Paris
Janicot, Daniel Claude Emmanuel *foundation administrator*

GERMANY

Hamburg
Lüst, Reimar *foundation president*

Mayen
Gartz, Rolf Fritz *foundation administrator*

HUNGARY

Budapest
Varkonyi, Anna *cultural organization administrator, management consultant, educator*

ISRAEL

Ashqelon
Hansen, Peter *international organization executive*

Herzlia
Gruder, Yaron E. *foundation administrator*

NORTHERN IRELAND

Belfast
Corrigan-Maguire, Mairead *peace worker*

NORWAY

Trondheim
Lunde, Øivind *cultural organization administrator, archaeologist*

PHILIPPINES

Paranaque
Mabasa, Teresa Albar *social welfare association administrator*

POLAND

Warsaw
Rotfeld, Adam Daniel *research institute administrator, government official, government agency administrator*

REPUBLIC OF KOREA

Seoul
Park, Won Kuk *foundation administrator*

SWEDEN

Stockholm
Altéus, Åke *foundation administrator*
Sohlman, Michael *foundation administrator*

SWITZERLAND

Bern
Leavey, Thomas Edward *international organization administrator*

Geneva
Chow, Jack C. *international organization administrator*
Evans, Timothy Grant *international organization administrator*
Rossier, William *trade association administrator*
Schweitzer, Theodore Gottlieb, III, *United Nations administrator*
Sommaruga, Cornelio *humanitarian services organization administrator, diplomat*

ADDRESS UNPUBLISHED

Adams, Jim Michael *foundation administrator*
Allerton, John Stephen *association executive*
Alves, Kyrin Jean *cultural organization administrator, educator*
Ambach, Gordon Mac Kay *educational association executive*
Anderson, Ned, Sr., *Apache tribal chairman*
Apfel, Meri F *not-for-profit developer*
Aron, Peter Arthur *charitable foundation executive, private investor*
Astor, Brooke *foundation administrator, philanthropist, writer*
Atchison, Richard Calvin *trade association director*
Bahret, Mary Ellen *lobbyist*
Balter, Frances Sunstein *civic worker*
Bard, Marjorie *social welfare administrator*
Barr, Marlene Joy *volunteer*
Barrow, Robert Earl *retired agricultural organization administrator*
Bashore, Irene Saras *art association administrator*
Beatty, Frances *civic worker*
Becerra, Rosina Madeline *social welfare educator*
Beck, Irene Clare *educational consultant, writer*
Berenbeim, Jane Rosen *not-for-profit executive*
Berger, Arthur Seymour *organization executive, city official*
Biddle, Albert G. W. *trade association executive*
Bieber, Owen F. *labor union official*
Blair, Fred Edward *social services administrator*
Blair, Kathie Lynn *social services worker*
Blondin, C. J. *trade association administrator*
Blum, Barbara Meddock *retired association executive*
Blumstein, Susan Bender *fundraiser*
Boal, Dean *retired arts center administrator, educator*
Bond, Julian *civil rights leader*
Bordner, Marjorie Rich *educator, civic worker*
Boysen, Thomas Cyril *educational association administrator*
Bray, Charles William, III, *foundation executive*
Brim, Orville Gilbert, Jr., *former foundation administrator, writer*
Brinker, Nancy Goodman *social service administrator*
Brooke, Francis John, III, *foundation administrator*
Brown, Bruce Maitland *philanthropy consultant*
Browning, Jane Louise *social services administrator*
Brundtland, Gro Harlem *former international organization executive*
Brune, Eva *fundraiser*
Buhl, Cynthia Maureen *foreign policy educator and advocate*
Bundy, Cheryl LaSota *non-profit executive, consultant*
Burki, Fred Albert *labor union official*
Campbell, Edwin Denton *consultant*
Carey, Ronald *former labor union leader*
Carr, Larry Dean *not-for-profit executive*
Carter, Henry Moore, Jr., *retired foundation executive*
Carter, Hodding, III, (William Hodding Carter) *foundation executive, former journalist, public official and educator*
Carter, Mandy *professional organization administrator*
Cesnik, James Michael *union official, newspaperman, printer, consultant*
Chan, Wing-Chi *cultural organization administrator, musicologist*
Chang, Debbie I-Ju *health services director*
Chase, Robert F. *educational association executive*
Chassman, Leonard Fredric *retired labor union administrator*
Chernish, Lelia Margaret *fundraiser*
Chowdhury, Anwarul Karim *international organization official*
Clark, Alicia Garcia *political party official*
Clark, Stan *association executive*

Collyer, Robert B. *trade association administrator*
Connell, Hugh P. *foundation executive*
Connor, Joseph E. *former international organization official*
Cooper, Charles Donald *association executive, editor, retired career officer*
Cooper, Josephine Smith *trade association and public affairs executive*
Cornwell, Jimmy Lee *fundraising executive, retired air force officer*
Couper, Richard Watrous *retired foundation administrator*
Dasch, Pat (Anne) *professional society administrator*
Dechant, Virgil C. *retired fraternal organization administrator*
Dees, Bowen Causey *institute executive, retired*
DeVos, Elisabeth (Betsy) *political association executive*
DeVries, Robert Allen *foundation administrator*
Donnell, Harold Eugene, Jr., *retired professional society administrator*
Dorman, Richard Frederick, Jr., *association executive, consultant*
Dozier, Therese Knecht *educational association administrator, educator*
Drennen, William Miller, Jr., *cultural organization administrator, freelance producer, writer*
Easton, Michelle *foundation executive*
Eberhard, Franz Valentin *association executive*
Eliot, Theodore Lyman, Jr., *international consultant*
Ellis, Anne Elizabeth *fundraiser*
Elliston, Kristine *not-for-profit fundraiser*
Engstrom, Marlene M. *volunteer*
Evans, Lucy Lee Custis (Lucy Lee Grimes) *family planning activist, writer*
Fahlbeck, Douglas Alan *corporate development executive*
Fields, Jerri Lynn *foundation administrator*
Fink, Matthew Pollack *trade association executive, lawyer*
Fluth, John Adam *educational administrator*
Flynn, Paul Bartholomew *foundation executive*
Foshay, Maxine Valentine Shottland *civic worker, public relations executive*
Foster, Charles Henry Wheelwright *former foundation officer, consultant, author*
Fréchette, Louise *international organization official*
Freeman, Glenn *political organization worker, retired non-commissioned military officer*
French, Stephanie Taylor *corporate philanthropist*
Friedman, Miles *trade association executive, financial services company executive, university lecturer*
Fuller, Norine Leas *lobbyist, educational administrator*
Gabria, Joanne Bakaitis *health and education volunteer*
Gammon, Samuel Rhea, III, *association executive, former ambassador*
Garner, Carlene Ann *fundraising consultant*
Gasper, Jo Ann *consulting firm executive*
Gereau, Mary Condon *political corporate executive*
Gilchrest, Thornton Charles *retired association executive*
Gleisner, Henry Heinz *retired advocate, writer*
Goerz, Mary Elizabeth Larsen *civic worker*
Goldman, Rachel Bok *civic volunteer*
Grell, Lewis Adam *retired association executive*
Griggs, Bobbie June *civic worker*
Hamilton, Shirley Siekmann *arts administrator*
Hammer, Susan W. *educational foundation executive, former mayor*
Hanford, George Hyde *retired educational administrator*
Hardy, Clarence Earl, Jr., *government, nonprofit and corporate sector executive*
Harnage, Bobby L. *former labor union administrator*
Harrison, John Raymond *foundation executive, retired newspaper executive*
Harvey, Glenn Francis *association manager*
Hays, E. Earl *youth organization administrator*
Helm, DeWitt Frederick, Jr., *consultant, professional association administrator*
Hester, James McNaughton *retired foundation administrator, artist*
Himes, Diane Adele *buyer, fundraiser, actress, lobbyist*
Hines, JoAnn R. *professional association executive and consultant*
Holloway, James Lemuel, III, *foundation executive, retired naval officer*
Holmes, Joan *retired social welfare administrator*
Horn, Howard M. *labor union administrator, consultant*
Huerta, Dolores Fernandez *labor union administrator*
Hyatt-Smith, Ann Rose *non-profit organization executive, consultant*
Ikeda, Tsuguo (Ike Ikeda) *social services center administrator, consultant*
Jacobson, Richard M. *not-for-profit fundraiser, researcher*
Jaffeson, Richard Charles *association executive administrator*
Johnson, Marlene M. *nonprofit executive*
Jones, Elaine R. *civil rights advocate*
Kahmann, Sarah Stuber *retired foundation administrator*
Kahrmann, Robert George *educational administrator*
Kajosevic, Indira *cultural organization administrator*
Kaskowitz, Edwin *social services executive*
Keil, M. David *retired international association executive*
Kelly, Cheryl Ann *healthcare administrator*
Kelly, Nancy Folden *art association administrator*
King, Jane Cudlip Coblentz *volunteer educator*
King, Marielle Elisabeth *educational research association administrator, writer, mathematics educator*
Kinslow, Margie Ann *volunteer*
Klarich, David John *political organization executive, lawyer*
Klopfleisch, Stephanie Squance *social services agency administrator*
Knauer, Virginia Harrington (Mrs. Wilhelm F. Knauer) *consumer consultant, former government official*
Kunstadter, Geraldine Sapolsky *foundation executive*
Kurtz, Dolores May *retired civic worker*

Kussrow, Nancy Esther *educational association administrator*
LaHaye, Beverly *cultural organization administrator*
Langer, Edward L. *trade association administrator*
LaPidus, Jules Benjamin *educational association administrator*
Ledwig, Donald Eugene *association executive, former broadcasting executive, former naval officer*
Leggett, Roberta Jean (Bobbi Leggett) *retired social services administrator*
LePome, Penelope Marie *rehabilitation counselor, educator*
Liddell, Jane Hawley Hawkes *civic worker*
Little, Judith *cultural organization administrator*
Livingston, Margaret Gresham *civic leader*
Losey, Michael Robert *retired professional society administrator*
Luckey, Doris Waring *civic volunteer*
MacCarthy, Talbot Leland *civic volunteer*
Mack, Charles Daniel, III, *labor union executive*
Mahoney, Ann Dickinson *fundraiser*
Maroney, Thomas P. *lawyer, political party executive*
Maxwell, Dorothea Bost Andrews *volunteer*
Maxwell, Patricia Joy *fund raising executive*
Mazur, Jay J. *trade union official*
Mazza, Terilyn McGovern *finance executive*
McCloskey, J(ohn) Michael *retired association administrator*
McDaniel, Mike *former political association executive*
McDonald, Douglas Robert *non profit agency executive*
McFate, Kenneth Leverne *trade association administrator*
McFate, Patricia Ann *foundation executive, science educator*
McLauchlan, Sylvia June *charity organization executive*
McWethy, Patricia Joan *educational association administrator*
Mende, Robert Graham *retired engineering association executive*
Menzel, Marybelle Proctor *volunteer*
Metcalf, Karen *retired foundation executive*
Meyer, Rachel Abijah *foundation director, artist, theorist, poet*
Mishel, Lawrence *economics research director*
Mitchell, Carolyn Cochran *foundation administrator's executive assistant*
Moore, Robert William *professional organization executive*
Muller, H(enry) Nicholas, III, *retired foundation administrator*
Munson, Lynne Ann *cultural critic*
Murphy-Pilon, Monica *cultural organization administrator*
Neel, Judy Murphy *association executive*
Neumann, Deborah Brochi *not-for-profit fundraiser*
Niemiec, Edward Walter *retired professional association executive*
O'Connor, Doris Julia *non-profit fundraiser, consultant*
O'Donnell, Kathleen Mary *social services administrator*
Olyphant, David *cultural, educational association executive*
O'Neill, Mary Jane *not-for-profit administrator, consultant*
Orosz, Joel J. *philanthropist, educator*
Ovadiah, Janice *non-profit organization consultant, cultural institute executive*
Owens, Luvie Moore *association consultant*
Palmer, Jocelyn Beth *volunteer*
Palmer, Robert Erwin *association executive*
Parkel, James G. *former health association administrator*
Peck, Robert David *educational foundation administrator*
Poe, Bob *political organization worker, communications company executive*
Porter, John Wilson *education executive*
Prescott, Barbara Lodwich *educational administrator*
Prins, Carol *not-for-profit developer, consultant*
Pritchard, Kathleen Jo *not-for-profit association administrator*
Pruzan, Irene *arts administrator, music educator, flutist, marketing and public relations specialist*
Pullen, Penny Lynne *non-profit organization administrator, former state legislator*
Quehl, Gary Howard *consultant*
Ramo, Virginia M. Smith *civic worker*
Ramsden, Willa Oldham *retired organization executive, columnist, historian, consultant*
Ramsey, Lynn Allison *trade association, public relations professional*
Rattazzi, Serena *retired art association administrator*
Reed, Leon Samuel *writer, photographer*
Reggie, Doris Boustany *volunteer*
Rheinfrank, Sally Lyman *volunteer*
Rice, Susan F. *fundraising consultant*
Rickerd, Donald Sheridan *foundation executive*
Rimel, Rebecca Webster *foundation administrator*
Riskin, Victoria *former trade association administrator*
Roberson, James O. *foundation executive*
Robinson, David Zav *non-profit agency consultant*
Roethel, David Albert Hill *consultant*
Rogers, Margaret Ellen Jonsson *civic worker*
Rosenberg, Alison P. *public policy official*
Ross, Charlotte Pack *social services administrator*
Ryall, Marty *former political organization administrator*
Ryan, John William *association executive*
Sabinson, Harvey Barnett *theatrical organization administrator*
Sampson, Robert Neil *natural resources consultant*
Sanford, Sarah J. *healthcare executive*
Schiaffino, S(ilvio) Stephen *retired medical society executive, consultant*
Schulberg, Jay William *foundation official*
Schulz, William Frederick *human rights association executive*
Schumacher, Philip Gerard *fundraising executive*
Schuster, Elaine *civil rights professional*
Schwartz, John J. *association executive, consultant*
Schweiker, Richard Schultz *trade association executive, former senator, former cabinet secretary*

Scott, Jacqueline Delmar Parker *educational association administrator, business administrator, consultant, fundraiser, educator*
Scott, Sandra J. *not-for-profit executive*
Seggerman, Anne Crellin *foundation executive*
Seldman, Neil Norman *cultural organization administrator*
Shevlin, Michael W. *retired cultural organization administrator*
Sims, Elizabeth LaNeal *association executive*
Singer, Markus Morton *retired trade association executive*
Smith, Margaret Taylor *volunteer*
Smith, Wendy L. *foundation executive*
Stanley, George Joel *social services administrator, advocate*
Stearns, Stewart Warren *charitable association executive*
Stevens, Sheila Maureen *retired teachers union administrator*
Sulc, Jean Luena (Jean L. Mestres) *lobbyist, consultant*
Swig, Roselyne Chroman *community consultant*
Takanishi, Ruby N. *foundation administrator, researcher*
Teoli-Phelps, Brook Elaine *advocate, dance educator*
Tipping, William Malcolm *social services administrator*
Tise, Larry Edward *association executive, historian*
Toms, Justine Willis *educational organization executive*
Townsend, Susan Elaine *religious organization officer*
Trinchero, Agnes Theresa *social services consultant, administrator, educator*
Ulrich, Werner Richard *union education administrator*
Vander Horst, Kathleen Purcell *nonprofit association administrator*
Vickers, George Ross *non-profit organization executive, sociology educator*
Wachtell, Esther *non-profit management executive, consultant*
Walker, Nathan C. *foundation administrator, minister, educator*
Walter, J. Jackson *consultant*
Ward, JoAnn Boettner *convention and tourist bureau administrator*
Warren, John William *professional society administrator*
Wasserheit, Judith N. *social services administrator*
Watson, Kathy *political organization administrator*
Webb, Wellington Edward *political organization administrator, former mayor*
Whalen, Loretta Theresa *religious educational administrator*
White, Rebecca E. *advocate*
Whitlock, Bennett Clarke, Jr., *retired association executive*
Willson, Parker O. *non-profit organization administrator*
Wilson, Glen Parten *professional society administrator*
Wohlgelernter, Beth *organization executive*
Wolfe, Joan *non-profit organizations consultant*
Wong, Elaine Dang *foundation executive*
Woods, Harriett Ruth *retired political organization president*
Wooten, Frank Thomas *retired research facility executive*
Workman, Willard Allyn *association executive*
Yard, Molly *social activist*
Young, Andrew Jackson *civil rights leader, clergyman, former mayor, former ambassador, former congressman*
Young, Steve G. *former labor union administrator*
Zehr, Norman Robert *retired association administrator*
Zimny, Max *labor union administrator, lawyer*
Zuck, Alfred Miller *public administration educator*

ATHLETICS

UNITED STATES

ALABAMA

Birmingham
Del Greco, Albert Louis, Jr., *former football player*
Flowers, Vonetta *Olympic athlete*

ARIZONA

Phoenix
Agler, Brian *professional basketball coach*
Bell, Jay Stuart *professional baseball player*
Bidwill, William V. *professional football executive*
Brenly, Bob *professional sports team executive, broadcaster*
Colangelo, Jerry John *professional sports team executive*
D'Antoni, Mike *professional athletics coach*
Garagiola, Joe, Jr., *baseball team executive*
Gillom, Jennifer *professional basketball player*
Green, Dennis *professional football coach*
Helling, Ricky Allen *professional baseball player*
Johnson, Kevin Maurice *professional basketball player*
Johnson, Randy (Randall David Johnson) *professional baseball player*
Marion, Shawn *professional basketball player*
Sexson, Richmond Lockwood *professional baseball player*
Sharp, Linda *professional basketball coach*
Smith, Emmitt J., III, *professional football player*
Stoudemire, Amare Carsares *professional basketball player*
Swann, Eric Jerrod *professional football player*
Taurasi, Diana *college basketball player*

Scottsdale
Amonte, Anthony Lewis *professional hockey player*
Barnett, Michael *professional sports team executive*
Boucher, Brain *professional hockey player*
Doan, Shane *professional hockey player*

PROFESSIONAL INDEX 5549 ATHLETICS

Francis, Robert *professional hockey coach*
Fuhr, Grant *professional hockey player*
Gretzky, Wayne Douglas *retired professional hockey player, businessman*
Hull, Brett A. *professional hockey player*
Lemieux, Claude *professional hockey player*
Numminen, Teppo *professional hockey player*

Tucson
Bonvicini, Joan M. *women's college basketball coach*
Kearney, Joseph Laurence *retired athletic conference administrator*

ARKANSAS

State University
Comeau, Matthew J. *athletic training program director, educator*

CALIFORNIA

Alameda
Collins, Kerry *professional football player*
Davis, Allen *professional football team executive*
Gannon, Rich *professional football player*
Harbaugh, James Joseph *former professional football player*
Herrera, John *professional football team executive*
Rice, Jerry Lee *professional football player*
Sapp, Warren Carlos *professional football player*
Turner, Norv *professional football coach*

Aliso Viejo
Cohen, Sasha (Alexandra Pauline Cohen) *ice skater*

Anaheim
Anderson, Garret *professional baseball player*
Glaus, Troy *professional baseball player*
Guerrero, Vladimir *professional baseball player*
Salmon, Timothy James *professional baseball player*
Sykora, Petr *professional hockey player*

Beverly Hills
Johnson, Magic (Earvin Johnson) *professional sports team executive, development company executive, former professional basketball coach and player*
Lott, Ronnie (Ronald Mandel Lott) *retired professional football player, television broadcaster*

Carmel
Epstein-Shepherd, Bee *coach, hypnotist, speaker*

Carson
Cienfuegos, Mauricio *professional soccer player*
Del Prado, Sergio *professional soccer team executive*
Schmid, Sigi *professional soccer coach*

Coronado
Axelson, Joseph Allen *professional athletics executive, publisher*

Cypress
Dorn, Marian Margaret *sports management administrator, educator*

El Segundo
Bryant, Kobe *professional basketball player*
Byears, Latasha *professional basketball player*
Divac, Vlade *professional basketball player*
Leslie, Lisa DeShaun *professional basketball player*
Malone, Karl *professional basketball player*
Milton-Jones, DeLisha *professional basketball player*
Odom, Lamar Joseph *professional basketball player*
Richmond, Mitchell James *professional basketball player*
Toler, Penny *former professional basketball player, sports team executive*
Tomjanovich, Rudolph *professional basketball coach*
Weatherspoon, Teresa Gaye *professional basketball player*

Felton
Wughalter, Emily Hope *physical education educator*

Fountain Valley
Treadway-Dillmon, Linda Lee *athletic trainer, actress, stuntwoman*

Fullerton
Curry, Denise *women's college basketball coach*

Inglewood
Buss, Jeanie *professional sports team executive*
Dixon, Tamecka *professional basketball player*

Jamul
Smith, Akili *professional football player*

La Jolla
Bavasi, Peter Joseph *sports management executive*

Los Angeles
Allison, Jason *professional hockey player*
Brand, Elton *professional basketball player*
Brown, James Kevin *professional baseball player*
Carroll, Pete *college football coach*
Daly, Robert Anthony *professional baseball team executive, former film executive*
Dantzscher, Jamie *gymnast*
DeFrantz, Anita *sports association executive, lawyer*
Dunleavy, Mike, Sr., *professional basketball coach*
Gagne, Eric *professional baseball player*
Green, Shawn *professional baseball player*
Hershiser, Orel Leonard, IV, *professional baseball player*
Hundley, Todd Randolph *professional baseball player*
Johnson, Davey (David Allen Johnson) *professional baseball team manager*
Karros, Eric Peter *professional baseball player*
Lasorda, Thomas Charles (Tommy Lasorda) *professional baseball team manager*
Lavin, Stephen Michael *university basketball coach*
Leiweke, Timothy *sports executive, marketing professional*
Leyritz, James Joseph *professional baseball player*
Maloney, Kristen *gymnast*
Murray, Andy *professional hockey coach*
Olivier, Kathy Ricks *college basketball coach*
Palffy, Zigmund (Ziggy Palffy) *professional hockey player*
Park, Chan Ho *professional baseball player*
Potvin, Felix *professional hockey player*
Roski, Edward P., Jr., *professional sports team executive*
Scates, Allen Edward *professional volleyball coach*
Sterling, Donald T. *professional basketball team executive*
Tracy, Jim *professional sports team executive*

Marina Del Rey
Banks, Ernest (Ernie Banks) *retired professional baseball player*

Menlo Park
Montana, Joseph C., Jr., *former professional football player*

Monrovia
Stevens, Gary *retired jockey*

Oakland
Appier, Kevin (Robert Kevin Appier) *professional baseball player*
Cohan, Christopher *professional sports team executive*
Cowens, David William (Dave Cowens) *professional basketball coach, insurance executive, retired professional basketball player*
Montgomery, Mike *professional baseball coach*
Richardson, Jason Anthoney *professional basketball player*
Zito, Barry *professional baseball player*

Palm Springs
Jumonville, Felix Joseph, Jr., *physical education educator, realtor*

Palo Alto
McHugh, Maura *professional basketball coach*

Sacramento
Adelman, Rick *professional basketball coach*
Griffith, Yolanda Evette *professional basketball player*
Hardmon, Lady *professional athlete*
Maitoza, Colleen *professional sports team executive*
Penicheiro, Ticha Nunes *professional basketball player*
Reynolds, Jerry Owen *sports team executive*
Totton, Gayle *professional sports team executive*
Webber, Chris, III, (Mayce Edward Christopher Webber) *professional basketball player*

San Diego
Alch, Mark Lee *organization executive, educator*
Bochy, Bruce *professional sports team manager, coach*
Boone, Bret Robert *professional baseball player*
Flutie, Douglas Richard (Doug Flutie) *professional football player*
Gwynn, Anthony Keith (Tony Gwynn) *former professional baseball player*
Hoffman, Trevor William *professional baseball player*
Klesko, Ryan *professional baseball player*
Lucchino, Lawrence *sports team executive, lawyer*
Magadan, David Joseph *professional baseball player*
Moores, John *professional sports team executive*
Nevin, Phillip *professional baseball player*
Phillips, Wade *professional football team coach*
Schottenheimer, Martin Edward *professional football coach*
Spanos, Dean A. *professional sports team executive*
Wells, David Lee *professional baseball player*

San Francisco
Alou, Felipe Rojas *professional baseball manager*
Bonds, Barry Lamar *professional baseball player*
Cepeda, Orlando *retired professional baseball player*
Magowan, Peter Alden *professional sports team executive, retail executive*
McCovey, Willie Lee *former professional baseball player*
Nen, Robert Allen (Robb Nen) *professional baseball player*

San Jose
Cerritos, Ronald *professional soccer player*
Damphousse, Vincent *professional hockey player*
Selanne, Teemu *professional hockey player*
Wilson, Ronald Lawrence *professional hockey coach*

Santa Clara
Chastain, Brandi Denise *professional soccer player*
DeBartolo-York, Denise *sports team executive*
Erickson, Dennis *professional football coach*
Hearst, Garrison (Gerald Garrison Hearst) *professional football player*
McNown, Cade *professional football player*

Sausalito
Casals, Rosemary *retired professional tennis player*

Stanford
Van Derveer, Tara *university athletic coach*

Stockton
Murphy, Jeremiah T. *professional sports team executive/constuction services*

COLORADO

Colorado Springs
Arsenault, Samantha *Olympic athlete*
Barton, Gregory Mark *Olympic athlete, kayak racer*
Beard, Amanda *swimmer, Olympic athlete*
Bedford, Barbara J. *Olympic athlete*
Benko, Lindsay *Olympic athlete*
Bennett, Brooke *Olympic athlete*
Bobek, Nicole *professional figure skater*
Buckner-Davis, Annett *professional volleyball player*
Cash, Swin (Swintayla Marie Cash) *professional basketball player*
Clay, Bryan Ezra *Olympic track and field athlete*
Corwin, Amber *figure skater*
Coughlin, Natalie *Olympic athlete*
Crocker, Ian *Olympic athlete*
Cutone, Kathaleen Kelly *figure skater, former skating judge, athletic representative*
D'Entremont, Amy *professional figure skater*
Dolan, Tom *Olympic athlete*
Ervin, Anthony *Olympic athlete*
Evans, Janet *former Olympic swimmer*
Gatlin, Justin *track and field athlete, Olympic track and field athlete*
Granato, Catherine (Cammi Granato) *Olympic athlete*
Halber, Diane *professional figure skater*
Hall, Gary, Jr., *Olympic athlete*
Hamilton, Tyler *professional cyclist, Olympic athlete*
Hamm, Morgan *Olympic athlete*
Hamm, Paul *Olympic athlete*
Hayes, Joanna *Olympic track and field athlete*
Hughes, Sarah *figure skater*
Hyman, Misty Dawn *Olympic athlete*
Krayzelburg, Lenny *Olympic athlete*
Kupets, Courtney *Olympic athlete*
Kwan, Karen *professional figure skater*
Kwan, Michelle *professional figure skater*
Lang, Naomi *ice skater*
Malchow, Thomas A *Olympic athlete*
May, Misty *Olympic athlete*
McCool, Courtney *Olympic athlete*
McDonough, Ann Patrice *ice skater*
Munz, Diana *Olympic athlete*
Nikodinov, Angela *professional figure skater, Olympic athlete*
Pappas, Tom *Olympic track and field athlete*
Patterson, Carly *Olympic athlete*
Peirsol, Aaron *Olympic athlete*
Phelps, Michael *Olympic athlete*
Quann, Megan *Olympic athlete*
Riley, Ruth Ellen *professional basketball player*
Rouse, Jeff *Olympic athlete, swimmer*
Schultz, Richard Dale *national athletic organization executive*
Scott, Tiffany *ice skater*
Shealy, Courtney *Olympic athlete*
Torres, Dara *Olympic athlete*
Tueting, Sarah *professional hockey player*
Walsh, Kerri Lee *Olympic athlete*
Wariner, Jeremy *Olympic track and field athlete*
Woolridge, Orlando *former professional basketball coach, Olympic coach*

Craig
Chason, Renee Lynn *coach, legal coordinator*

Denver
Alomar, Sandy, Jr., (Santos Velazquez Alomar) *professional baseball player*
Anthony, Carmelo F. *professional basketball player*
Balboa, Marcelo *professional soccer player*
Beuerlein, Steve Taylor *professional football player*
Bourque, Ray *professional hockey player*
Evans, Mike *professional basketball coach*
Forsberg, Peter *professional hockey player*
Hankinson, Tim *soccer coach*
Hardaway, Timothy Duane *professional basketball player*
Helton, Todd *professional baseball player*
Hurdle, Clint *professional athletics manager*
Kariya, Paul *professional hockey player*
Martin, Kenyon *professional basketball player*
Quenneville, Joel *professional hockey coach*
Sakic, Joe (Joseph Steve Sakic) *professional hockey player*
Walker, Larry Kenneth Robert *professional baseball player*

Englewood
Bailey, Champ *professional football player*
Bowlen, Pat(rick)(Dennis) *professional sports team executive, holding company executive, lawyer*
Davis, Terrell *former professional football player*
Griese, Brian *professional football player*
Lynch, John Terrence *professional football player*
McGlockton, Chester *professional football player*
Plummer, Jason Steven (Jake Plummer) *professional football player*
Shanahan, Mike *professional football coach*
Smith, Neil *professional football player*
Smith, Rod *professional football player*

U S A F Academy
DeBerry, Fisher *college football coach*

CONNECTICUT

Bristol
Reynolds, Harold Craig *professional baseball player*

Cos Cob
Leamy, Nancy M. *professional athletics coach*

Farmington
DiCicco, Tony *soccer coach*

Stamford
Goldsmith, Donna *sports association executive*
Johnson, Dwayne Douglas (The Rock) *professional wrestler, actor*
McMahon, Linda E. *sports association executive*
Stevenson, Alexandra *professional tennis player*
Valentine, Robert John (Bobby Valentine) *former professional baseball manager*

Storrs Mansfield
Auriemma, Geno *women's college basketball coach*
Calhoun, Jim *college basketball coach*

Uncasville
Lobo, Rebecca *professional basketball player*

West Haven
Hatch, Annia *gymnast*

DELAWARE

Milton
Scott, Phyllis Wright *coach, music educator*

Newark
Wilson, Deborrah *physical education educator*

DISTRICT OF COLUMBIA

Washington
Bullett, Vicky *professional basketball player*
Button, Katy *professional athletics manager*
Chin, Allen E., Sr., *athletic administrator, educator*
Ewing, Patrick Aloysius *professional basketball coach*
Hamilton, Richard Clay *professional basketball player*
Hanlon, Glen *professional athletics coach*
Hargrove, Linda *professional basketball coach*
Holdsclaw, Chamique Shaunta *professional basketball player*
Jordan, Eddie *professional basketball coach*
Kolzig, Olaf *professional hockey player*
McCray, Nikki Kesangame *professional basketball player*
McPhee, George *professional sports team executive*
Oakley, Charles *professional basketball player*
O'Malley, Susan *professional basketball team executive*
Patrick, Richard M. *professional hockey team executive*
Pollin, Abe *professional basketball team executive, builder*
Shriver, Sargent *sports association executive*
Shriver, Timothy P. *sports association executive*
Stanley, Marianne *professional athletics coach*
Upshaw, Gene *sports association executive*

FLORIDA

Bradenton
Kournikova, Anna *professional tennis player*

Coral Springs
Singh, Vijay *professional golfer*

Davie
Boston, David *professional football player*
Madison, Sam A., Jr., *professional football player*
Mare, Olindo Franco *professional football player*
Martin, Tony Derrick *professional football player*
McDuffie, Otis James (O.J. McDuffie) *professional football player*
Seau, Junior (Tiana Seau Jr.) *professional football player*
Thomas, Thurman Lee *professional football player*
Thomas, Zach Michael *professional football player*
Wannstedt, David Raymond *professional football coach*

Daytona Beach
Andrews, Donna L. *professional golfer*
Barrett, Tina *professional golfer*
Bodine, Brett *race car driver*
Bodine, Geoff *race car driver*
Davies, Laura *professional golfer*
DeLuca, Annette *professional golfer*
Figg-Currier, Cindy *professional golfer*
France, William Clifton, Jr., *professional sports team executive*
Gordon, Jeff *race car driver*
Helton, Mike *professional sports team executive*
Inkster, Juli *professional golfer*
Jones, Rose *professional golfer*
Kane, Lorie *professional golfer*
King, Betsy *professional golfer*
Klein, Emilee *professional golfer*
Kuehne, Kelli *professional golfer*
Mallon, Meg *professional golfer*
Moodie, Janice *professional golfer*
Neumann, Liselotte *professional golfer*
Pak, Se Ri *professional golfer*
Pepper, Dottie *professional golfer*
Robbins, Kelly *professional golfer*
Rudd, Ricky *race car driver*
Schrader, Ken *race car driver*
Sheehan, Patty *professional golfer*
Sorenstam, Annika *professional golfer*
Steinhauer, Sherri *professional golfer*
Tschetter, Kris *professional golfer*
Votaw, Ty M. *golf association commissioner*
Wallace, Rusty *race car driver*
Webb, Karrie *professional golfer*
Whitworth, Kathrynne Ann *professional golfer*
Wie, Michelle Sung *amateur golfer*
Yarborough, William Caleb *retired race car driver*

Deerfield Beach
King, Don *boxing promoter*

Fort Lauderdale
Lassiter, Roy *professional soccer player*
Melo, Welton *professional soccer player*
Searcy, Leon, Jr., *professional football player*
Torchetti, John *professional athletics coach*

Gainesville
Donovan, Billy *university basketball coach*

Hollywood
King, Alma Jean *retired physical education educator, healthcare educator*

Jacksonville
Brady, Kyle James *professional football player*
Del Rio, Jack *professional football coach, former professional football player*
Leftwich, Byron Antron *professional football player*
Smith, Jimmy, Jr., *professional football player*
Taylor, Fred *professional football player*

Lady Lake
Hartzler, Genevieve Lucille *physical education educator*

Melbourne
Rose, Peter Edward *former professional baseball player and manager*

Miami
Benitez, Armando German *professional baseball player*

Brondello, Sandy *professional basketball player*
Fiedler, Jay *professional football player*
Loria, Jeffrey H. *sports team executive*
Martin, Jacques *professional hockey coach*
McKeon, John Aloysius (Jack McKeon) *professional baseball manager*
Meadors, Marynell *former professional basketball coach, sports team executive*
O'Neal, Shaquille Rashaun *professional basketball player*
Strickland, Rodney *professional basketball player*
Wade, Dwyane *professional basketball player*
Willis, Dontrelle *professional baseball player*

Miami Beach
Shula, Don Francis *former professional football coach, team executive*

Naples
Frazer, John Howard *tennis association executive*

North Palm Beach
Nicklaus, Jack William *professional golfer*

Opa Locka
Beckett, Joshua Patrick *professional baseball player*
Castillo, Luis Antonio Donato *professional baseball player*
Kotsay, Mark Steven *professional baseball player*
Lee, Derrek Leon *professional baseball player*
Perez, Tony *former baseball player*

Orlando
Davis, Johnny Reginald *professional basketball coach*
De Vos, Daniel G. *sports team executive, marketing professional*
Francis, Steve *professional basketball player*
Hill, Grant *professional basketball player*
Janzen, Lee *professional golfer*
Peck, Carolyn *professional basketball coach*
Vander Weide, Cheri DeVos *sports team executive, marketing professional*
Weisbrod, John *professional sports team executive*

Ormond Beach
Wendelstedt, Harry Hunter, Jr., *umpire*

Palm Bch Gdns
Wadkins, Lanny Lanston *professional golfer*

Palm Beach
Floyd, Raymond Loran *professional golfer*

Palm Beach Gardens
Awtrey, Jim L. *sports association executive*
Couples, Frederick Steven *professional golfer*
Daly, John Patrick *professional golfer*
Duval, David Robert *professional golfer*
Hamilton, Todd *professional golfer*
Henninger, Brian Hatfield *professional golfer*
Leonard, Justin (Justin Charles Garret Leonard) *professional golfer*
Love, Davis Milton, III, *professional golfer*
Maggert, Jeffrey Allan *professional golfer*
Mickelson, Phil *professional golfer*
Miller, John Laurence *professional golfer*
O'Meara, Mark *professional golfer*
Stankowski, Paul Francis *professional golfer*
Strange, Curtis Northrop *professional golfer*
Verplank, Scott Rachal *professional golfer*
Westwood, Lee *professional golfer*
Woods, Tiger (Eldrick Woods) *professional golfer*

Palm City
Mc Hale, John Joseph *baseball club executive*

Ponte Vedra Beach
Agassi, Andre Kirk *professional tennis player*
Faxon, Brad *professional golfer*
Finchem, Tim *sports association executive*
Pavin, Corey Allen *professional golfer*
Sluman, Jeff (Jeffrey George Sluman) *professional golfer*
Stricker, Steve *professional golfer*
Triplett, Kirk Allen *professional golfer*

Saint Petersburg
Alvarez, Wilson Eduardo *professional baseball player*
Castilla, Vinivio Soria *professional baseball player*
Craybas, Jill *professional tennis player*
Gooden, Dwight Eugene *professional baseball player*
Granville, Laura *professional tennis player*
Harkleroad, Ashley *professional tennis player*
Martinez, Tino *professional baseball player*
McGriff, Fred (Frederick Stanley McGriff) *professional baseball player*
Piniella, Louis Victor *professional baseball team manager*
Reeves, Samantha *professional tennis player*
Sharapova, Maria *professional tennis player*
Shaughnessy, Meghann *professional tennis player*
Vaughn, Gregory Lamont *professional baseball player*
Wilson, Paul *professional baseball player*
Zimmer, Donald William *professional baseball coach, former professional baseball manager*

Sunrise
Keenan, Michael E. *professional hockey team executive*
Larionov, Igor *professional hockey player*
Luongo, Roberto *professional hockey player*
Ozolinsh, Sandis *professional hockey player*
Torrey, William Arthur *professional hockey team executive*
Worrell, Peter *professional hockey player*

Tallahassee
Bowden, Bobby *college football coach*
Hamilton, J. Leonard *collegiate basketball coach, former professional basketball coach*

Tampa
Alstott, Michael Joseph (Mike Alstott) *professional football player*
Andreychuk, David *professional hockey player*
Brooks, Derrick Dewan *professional football player*
Brown, Timothy Donell *professional football player*
Christy, Jeff *professional football player*
Galloway, Joe *professional football player*
Glazer, Malcolm *professional sports team executive*
Gruden, Jon *professional football coach*
Johnson, Brad *professional football player*
Khabibulin, Nikolai *professional hockey player*
Kubina, Pavel *professional hockey player*
Lecavalier, Vincent *professional hockey player*
McCardell, Keenan *professional football player*
McDaniel, Randall Cornell *retired professional football player*
Modin, Fredrik *professional hockey player*
Richards, Brad *professional hockey player*
St. Louis, Martin *professional hockey player*
Tortorella, John *professional athletics coach*

GEORGIA

Athens
Dishman, Rodney King *physical education educator*

Atlanta
Aaron, Hank (Henry L. Aaron) *professional baseball team executive*
Arani, Ardy A. *professional sports marketing executive, lawyer*
Babcock, Peter Heartz *professional sports executive*
Bellamy, Walter *retired basketball player*
Cox, Bobby (Robert Joe Cox) *professional baseball manager*
Ferraro, Ray *professional hockey player*
Gailey, Thomas Chandler (Chan), Jr., *college football coach*
Hartley, Bob *professional hockey coach*
Heatley, Dany *professional hockey player*
Hewitt, Paul Harrington *basketball coach*
Jones, Andruw Rudolf *professional baseball player*
Jones, Chipper (Larry Wayne Jones Jr.) *professional baseball player*
Kovalchuk, Ilya *professional hockey player*
Kozlov, Vyacheslav *professional hockey player*
Kruger, Lon *coach*
Rhodes, Damian *professional hockey player*
Schuerholz, John Boland, Jr., *professional baseball executive*
Smoltz, John Andrew *professional baseball player*
Thompson, Wallace Reeves, III, *physical education educator*

Flowery Branch
Blank, Arthur M. *professional sports team executive, retired home and lumber retail chain executive*
Vick, Michael *professional football player*

Suwanee
Anderson, Jamal Sharif *professional football player*

HAWAII

Honolulu
Murata, Nathan M. *physical education educator, researcher*

Kamuela
Biondi, Matt *Olympic athlete*

ILLINOIS

Belleville
Connors, Jimmy (James Scott Connors) *former professional tennis player*

Chicago
Agoos, Jeff *professional soccer player*
Aguilera, Richard Warren (Rick Aguilera) *professional baseball player*
Akers, Michelle Anne *professional soccer player*
Alomar, Roberto Velazquez *professional baseball player*
Alou, Moises *professional baseball player*
Arena, Bruce *professional soccer coach*
Artest, Ron *professional basketball player*
Baker, Dusty (Johnnie B. Baker Jr.) *professional baseball team manager*
Baumgardt, Justi Michelle *professional soccer player*
Baylor, Don Edward *former professional baseball manager*
Bradley, Bob *professional soccer coach*
Buehrle, Mark *professional baseball player*
Cromwell, Amanda Caryl *former soccer player, coach*
Daze, Eric *professional hockey player*
Ducar, Tracy *former soccer player*
Fawcett, Joy Lynn *professional soccer player*
Fotopoulos, Danielle *former soccer player*
Foudy, Julia Maurine *professional soccer player, Olympic athlete*
Gabarra, Carin Leslie *professional soccer player, professional soccer coach*
Garciaparra, Nomar (Anthony Nomar Garciaparra) *professional baseball player*
Girardi, Joseph Elliott *professional baseball player*
Gregg, Lauren *women's soccer coach*
Guillen, Oswaldo Jose Barrios (Ozzie Guillen) *professional baseball team manager*
Hamm, Mia (Mariel Margaret Hamm) *professional soccer player*
Heinrichs, April *coach*
Housley, Phil F. *professional hockey player*
Hucles, Angela Khalia *professional soccer player*
Jones, Cobi *professional soccer player*
Keller, Deborah Kim *former soccer player*
Konerko, Paul *professional baseball player*
Lenti Ponsetto, Jean *athletic director*
Lilly, Kristine Marie *professional soccer player*
Little, William Grady (Grady Little) *professional baseball coach*
MacMillan, Shannon Ann *professional soccer player*
Maddux, Gregory (Gregory Alan Maddux) *professional baseball player*
Mercer, Ron *professional basketball player*
Milbrett, Tiffeny Carleen *professional soccer player*
Myernick, Glenn *professional soccer coach*
O'Reilly, Heather Ann *Olympic athlete*
Overbeck, Carla Werden *soccer player, coach*
Parlow, Cynthia Maria *professional soccer player*
Pearce, Christie Patricia *professional soccer player*
Pizer, Howard Charles *sports and entertainment executive*
Reddick, Catherine Anne (Cat Reddick) *Olympic athlete*
Reinsdorf, Jerry Michael *professional sports teams executive, real estate executive, lawyer, accountant*
Reyna, Claudio *professional soccer player*
Roberts, Tiffany Marie *former soccer player*
Rose, Jalen *professional basketball player*
Savard, Denis Joseph *former professional hockey player, coach*
Schwartz, Alan Gifford *sport company executive*
Schwoy, Laurie Annette *professional soccer player*
Scurry, Briana Collette *professional soccer player*
Skiles, Scott Allen *professional basketball coach*
Slaton, Danielle Victoria *professional soccer player*
Sobrero, Kate (Kathryn Michele Sobrero) *professional soccer player*
Sosa, Samuel (Sammy Sosa) *professional baseball player*
Staples, Thori Yvette *former soccer player*
Streiffer, Jenny *former soccer player*
Thomas, Frank Edward *professional baseball player*
Venturini, Tisha Lea *professional soccer player*
Wagner, Alyson Kay (Aly Wagner) *professional soccer player*
Wambach, Abby (Mary Abigail Wambach) *Olympic athlete*
Whalen, Sarah Eve *professional soccer player*
Wood, Kerry *professional baseball player*
Zelepukin, Valeri *professional hockey player*

Elk Grove Village
Meyer, Raymond Joseph *former college basketball coach*

Glenview
King, Billie Jean Moffitt *former professional tennis player*

Lake Forest
Hampton, Daniel Oliver *professional football player*
McCaskey, Michael B. *professional football team executive*

Libertyville
Trzyna, Chris *physical education educator*

Lincolnshire
Schauble, John Eugene *physical education educator*

Mahomet
Thompson, Margaret M. *physical education educator*

Westmont
Tricase, Elizabeth *gymnast*

INDIANA

Granger
Thomas, Debi (Debra J. Thomas) *ice skater*

Indianapolis
Abdul-Jabbar, Karim *retired professional football player*
Batten, Kimberly Jane *Olympic athlete*
Bird, Larry Joe *professional athletics manager, former professional basketball coach*
Buford-Bailey, Tonja Yevette *Olympic athlete*
Carlisle, Rick *professional basketball coach*
Catchings, Tamika Devonne *professional basketball player*
Colander-Richardson, LaTasha *Olympic athlete*
Dawes, Dominique *Olympic athlete*
Dempsey, Cedric W. *former sports association administrator*
Dimas, Trent *Olympic athlete, gymnast*
Donovan, Anne *professional basketball coach, coach*
Drummond, Jon *Olympic athlete*
Dungy, Tony *professional football coach*
Favor-Hamilton, Suzanne Marie *track and field athlete, Olympian*
Fortner, Nell *professional athletics coach*
Ganassi, Chip *professional race car executive, owner*
Greene, Maurice *Olympic athlete, track and field athlete*
Harrison, Alvin *Olympic athlete*
Harrison, Calvin *Olympic athlete*
Harrison, Marvin *professional football player*
Hennagan, Monique *Olympic athlete*
Irsay, James Steven *professional football team owner*
James, Edgerrin *professional football player*
Johnson, Michael *former international athlete*
Jones, Marion *track and field athlete*
Lewis, Brian *Olympic athlete*
Manning, Peyton *professional football player*
Marsh, Michael Lawrence *track and field athlete*
Miles-Clark, Jearl *olympic athlete, track and field*
Miller, Reginald Wayne *professional basketball player*
Pettigrew, Antonio *Olympic athlete*
Phelps, Jaycie *gymnast, Olympic athlete*
Taylor, Angelo *Olympic athlete*
Torrence, Gwen *Olympic athlete*
Tracy, Paul Anthony *race car driver*
Vasser, Jimmy *professional race car driver*
Wilkinson, Laura *Olympic athlete*
Williams, Bernard *Olympic athlete*

Marion
DeMichael, Mark Joseph *physical education educator, baseball coach*

West Lafayette
Sims-Curry, Kristy *women's college basketball coach*

IOWA

Ames
Fennelly, William *basketball coach*

Davenport
Foster, James Franklin *professional sports management executive*

Iowa City
Alford, Steve *college basketball coach*
Bowlsby, Bob *athletic director*
Lee, Angie *basketball coach*

KANSAS

Lawrence
Washington, Marian *women's college basketball coach*

Manhattan
Patterson, Deb *women's college basketball coach*

Mission
Trevino, Lee Buck *professional golfer*
Watson, Thomas Sturges *professional golfer*

Overland Park
Voska, Kathryn Caples *consultant, facilitator*

Saint Marys
Byers, Walter *athletic association executive*

KENTUCKY

Central City
McMurray, Jamie *race car driver*

Louisville
Crum, Denny (Denzel Edwin Crum) *retired collegiate basketball coach*
Pitino, Richard *collegiate basketball coach, former professional basketball coach*

Richmond
Inman, Larry Joe *basketball coach*

LOUISIANA

Grambling
Robinson, Eddie Gay *college football coach*

Metairie
Brooks, Aaron Lafette *professional football player*
Haslett, Jim *professional football coach*
McAllister, Deuce *professional football player*
Reed, Jake *professional football player*

New Orleans
Scelfo, Chris *university football coach*
Scott, Byron Alton *professional basketball coach, former professional basketball player*

Shreveport
Shemwell, Mary Anne *adapted physical education specialist*
Sutton, Hal Evan *professional golfer*

MAINE

Bangor
Kelley, Barbara Bannin *physical education educator*

Portland
Chow, Amy *gymnast, Olympic athlete*
Powers, Ross *Olympic athlete*

MARYLAND

Baltimore
Anderson, Brady Kevin *professional baseball player*
Angelos, Peter G. *professional sports team executive, lawyer*
Belle, Albert Jojuan *professional baseball player*
Fassel, Jim (James E. Fassel) *professional football coach*
Lewis, Jamal *professional football player*
Lewis, Ray *professional football player*
Mazzilli, Lee *professional baseball coach*
Modell, Arthur B. *professional football team executive*
Murray, Eddie Clarence *baseball batting coach*
Ogden, Jonathan *professional football player*
Palmeiro, Rafael Corrales *professional baseball player*
Sanders, Deion Luwynn *professional football player*
Smith, Janet Marie *sports and entertainment executive*
Tejada, Miguel *professional baseball player*

Bethesda
Palmer, James Alvin *baseball commentator*

Bowie
Silva, Lawrence Kehinde *physical education educator*

Hunt Valley
Mussina, Michael Cole *professional baseball player*

Owings Mills
Billick, Brian *professional football coach*
Coates, Ben Terrence *professional football player*
Newsome, Ozzie *manager professional athletics*

Towson
Shriver, Pamela H. *retired professional tennis player, sports analyst*

MASSACHUSETTS

Arlington
Samuelson, Joan Benoit *professional runner*

Boston
Auerbach, Arnold Jacob (Red Auerbach) *professional basketball team executive*
Baker, Vincent Lamont *professional basketball player*
Dafoe, Byron Jaromir *professional hockey player*

Williams, Serena *professional tennis player*
Williams, Ted Vaughnell *physical education educator*
Williams, Venus *professional tennis player*

Yorktown Heights
Bogdanoff, Stewart Ronald *physical education educator, coach*

NORTH CAROLINA

Chapel Hill
Smith, Dean Edwards *university basketball coach*

Charlotte
Bates, Michael *professional football player, former Olympic athlete, track and field*
Davis, Stephen *professional football player*
Delhomme, Jake Christopher *professional football player*
Fox, John *professional football coach*
Hendrick, Ricky *race car driver*
Johnson, Jimmie *race car driver*
Lacey, Trudi *professional athletics coach*
Mapp, Rhonda *professional basketball player*
Means, Natrone Jermaine *professional football player*
Metcalf, Eric Quinn *professional football player*
Muhammad, Muhsin, II, *professional football player*
Nadeau, Jerry *race car driver*
Okafor, Emeka *professional basketball player*
Reid, Tracy *professional basketball player*
Robinson, Shawna *race car driver*
Sprague, Jack *race car driver*
Staley, Dawn Michelle *professional basketball player*
Stinson, Andrea Maria *professional basketball player*
Walls, Wesley (Charles Wesley Walls) *professional football player*
Weinke, Chris *professional football player*

Concord
Biffle, Greg *race car driver*
Busch, Kurt *race car driver*

Conover
Jarrett, Dale *race car driver*

Durham
Goestenkors, Gail *basketball coach*
Krzyzewski, Mike *university athletic coach*

Fairview
Bradley, Edward William *sports foundation executive*

Harrisburg
Labonte, Terry *race car driver*

High Point
Burton, Ward *professional race car driver*
Stricklin, Hut *race car driver*
Wimmer, Scott *race car driver*

Huntersville
McLaughlin, Mike *race car driver*
Stewart, Tony *professional race car driver*

Mooresville
Atwood, Casey *race car driver*
Blaney, Dave *race car driver*
Compton, Stacy *race car driver*
Cope, Derrike *race car driver*
Earnhardt, Dale, Jr., *race car driver*
Earnhardt, Kerry *race car driver*
Earnhardt, Teresa *race team owner*
Elder, Christian *race car driver*
Foyt, Larry *race car driver*
Keller, Jason *race car driver*
LaJoie, Randy *race car driver*
Little, Charles Glen, Jr., *professional race car driver*
Marlin, Sterling *race car driver*
Martin, Mark *race car driver*
Münter, Leilani Maaja *race car driver*
Nemechek, Joe *race car driver*
Newman, Ryan *race car driver*
Park, Steve *race car driver*
Riggs, Scott *race car driver*
Wallace, Mike *race car driver*
Waltrip, Michael *professional race car driver*

Raleigh
Brind'Amour, Rod Jean *professional hockey player*
Irbe, Arturs *professional hockey player*
Laviolette, Peter *professional hockey coach*
O'Neill, Jeff *professional hockey player*
Rutherford, Jim *professional sports team executive*

Randleman
Andretti, John *professional race car driver*

Statesville
Mayfield, Jeremy *race car driver*

Trinity
Labonte, Bobby *race car driver*

Welcome
Gordon, Robby *race car driver*
Green, Jeff *race car driver*
Harvick, Kevin *race car driver*
Purvis, Jeff *race car driver*
Sauter, Johnny *race car driver*
Skinner, Mike *professional race car driver*

OHIO

Berea
Campo, Dave *professional football coach*
Clark, Dwight Edward *sports team executive, former professional football player*
Davis, Butch *professional football coach*
Garcia, Jeff *professional football player*
Policy, Carmen A. *professional sports team executive*

Canton
Elliott, Peter R. *retired athletic organization executive*
Long, Howie *former pro football player*
Mack, Tom *retired professional football player*
Shaw, Billy *retired professional football player*

Cincinnati
Brown, Mike *professional sports team executive*
Griffey, Ken, Jr., (George Kenneth Griffey Jr.) *professional baseball player*
Huggins, Bob *college basketball coach*
Kitna, Jon *professional football player*
Larkin, Barry Louis *professional baseball player*
Miley, David *professional baseball coach*
Neagle, Dennis Edward (Denny Neagle) *professional baseball player*
Pirtle, Laurie Lee *women's college basketball coach*
Santiago, Benito Rivera *professional baseball player*
Warrick, Peter *professional football player*

Cleveland
Bell, David Gus (Buddy) (Buddy Bell) *professional baseball manager*
Boland, James C. *sports association executive*
Edwards, Michelle Denise *professional basketball player*
Fijalkowski, Isabelle *professional basketball player*
Finley, Chuck (Charles Edward Finley) *professional baseball player*
Fryman, David Travis *professional baseball player*
Gardocki, Christopher *professional football player*
Hargrove, Mike (Dudley Michael Hargrove, Mike Hargrove) *former professional baseball team manager*
Hart, John *professional sports team executive*
Hill, Tyrone *professional basketball player*
James, LeBron *professional basketball player*
Johnston, Alastair J. *sports association executive*
Lopez, Nancy *former professional golfer*
Manuel, Charlie Fuqua, Jr., *professional baseball manager*
Nemcova, Eva *professional basketball player*
Seles, Monica *professional tennis player*
Silas, Paul *professional basketball coach*
Thome, Jim *professional baseball player*
Vizquel, Omar Enrique *professional baseball player*

Columbus
Cooper, John *university football coach*
McBride, Brian *professional soccer player*
Pastore, Donna Lee *physical education educator*
Sanderson, Geoff *professional hockey player*

Fairfield
Robertson, Oscar Palmer (Big O Robertson) *chemical company executive, former professional basketball player*
Sheehan, Samantha *gymnast*

Hilliard
Herta, Bryan *race car driver*

Oxford
Pont, John *football coach, educator*

Shaker Heights
Eakin, Thomas Capper *sports promotion executive*

Somerset
Green, Tammie *professional golfer*

Tiffin
Spellerberg, Elinor M. *riding instructor*

Westlake
FitzRandolph, Casey *Olympic athlete*
Ohno, Apolo Anton *Olympic athlete*
Parra, Derek *Olympic athlete*

Worthington
Whitney, Ray *professional hockey player*

Youngstown
DeBartolo, Edward John, Jr., *professional football team owner, real estate developer*

OKLAHOMA

Edmond
Miller, Shannon *Olympic athlete*

Enid
Abdul-Jabbar, Kareem (Lewis Ferdinand Alcindor) *professional basketball coach*

Oklahoma City
Berg, Laura *Olympic athlete*
Binning, Bette Finese (Mrs. Gene Hedgcock Binning) *athletic association official*
Bustos, Crystl *softball player*
Douty, Sheila *softball player*
Fernandez, Lisa *softball player*
Finch, Jennie *softball player*
Flowers, Tairia Mims *softball player, Olympic athlete*
Freed, Amanda Louise *Olympic athlete*
Harrigan, Lori *Olympic athlete*
Jung, Lovieanne *Olympic athlete*
Kretschman, Kelly *Olympic athlete*
Lappin, Lauren *Olympic athlete*
Mendoza, Jessica *Olympic athlete*
Nuveman, Stacey *Olympic athlete*
Osterman, Catherine *Olympic athlete*
O'Brien-Amico, Leah *Olympic athlete*
Richardson, Dot (Dorothy Gay) *softball player, physician*
Topping, Jennifer *Olympic athlete*
Watley, Natasha *Olympic athlete*

Tulsa
Smith, Betty Gene *physical education educator*

OREGON

Eugene
Sisley, Becky Lynn *physical education educator*

Portland
Daniels, Antonio *professional basketball player*
Dunleavy, Michael Joseph *professional basketball coach*
Patterson, Steve *professional basketball team executive*
Pippen, Scottie *professional basketball player*
Van Exel, Nickey Maxwell *professional basketball player*
Witherspoon, Sophia *professional basketball player*

West Linn
Harris, Debra Coral *physical education educator*

PENNSYLVANIA

Clifton Heights
Pagano, Richard Donald *physical education educator, researcher*

Easton
Holmes, Larry, Jr., *retired professional boxer*

Flourtown
Reneberg, Richard (Richey Reneberg) *professional tennis player*

Philadelphia
Abreu, Bobby *professional baseball player*
Bowa, Lawrence Robert (Larry Bowa) *professional baseball manager*
Boyer, Lisa *basketball coach*
Burke, Sean *professional hockey player*
Clarke, Robert Earle (Bobby Clarke) *hockey executive*
Croce, Pat *author, fitness trainer, former sports team executive*
Hitchcock, Ken *professional hockey coach*
Holmgren, Paul *professional hockey coach*
Iverson, Allen *professional basketball player*
Kearse, Jevon *professional football player*
Kukoc, Toni *professional basketball player*
LeClair, John Clark *professional hockey player*
Lurie, Jeffrey *professional sports team executive*
McNabb, Donovan *professional football player*
O'Brien, Jim *professional basketball coach*
Owens, Terrell *professional football player*
Primeau, Keith *professional hockey player*
Reid, Andy *professional football coach*
Roenick, Jeremy *professional hockey player*
Rollins, James Calvin *professional baseball player*
Snider, Edward Malcolm *professional hockey club executive*
Vanbiesbrouck, John *professional hockey player*
Wade, Ed *professional sports team executive*
Zhamnov, Alexei *professional hockey player*

Pittsburgh
Bettis, Jerome Abram *professional football player*
Cowher, Bill *professional football coach*
Giles, Brian Stephen *professional baseball player*
Kendall, Jason Daniel *professional baseball player*
LeBeau, Dick *professional football coach, retired professional football player*
Lemieux, Mario *professional sports team executive, professional hockey player*
Littlefield, David *professional sports team executive*
Mathis, Terance *professional football player*
McClatchy, Kevin S. *professional sports team executive*
Olcyzk, Ed *professional athletics coach*
Patrick, Craig *professional hockey team executive*
Recchi, Mark *professional hockey player*
Rooney, Daniel M. *professional football team executive*
Straka, Martin *professional hockey player*
Ward, Hines, Jr., *professional football player*

Reading
Unser, Alfred, Jr., *race car driver*

Rydal
Fernberger, Marilyn Friedman *events organizer, consultant, civic leader*

University Park
Paterno, Joseph Vincent *college football coach*

Youngstown
Palmer, Arnold Daniel *retired professional golfer*

RHODE ISLAND

Cranston
Perna, Marie Immaculate *retired physical education educator*

Newport
Brown, Jane G. *sports association executive*

SOUTH CAROLINA

Columbia
Holtz, Louis Leo *college football coach*

TENNESSEE

Greeneville
Ford, Sally J. *physical education educator*

Knoxville
Fulmer, Phillip *university football coach*

Memphis
Brown, Hubert Jude *professional athletics coach*
West, Jerry Alan *professional basketball team executive*
Williams, Jason *professional basketball player*

Nashville
Fisher, Jeff *professional football coach*
Johnson, Greg *professional hockey player*
Legwand, David *professional hockey player*
Leipold, Craig L. *professional sports team executive*
Mason, Derrick *professional football player*
McNair, Steve LaTreal *professional football player*
Snoddy, Chris Raymond *athletic trainer*
Trotz, Barry *professional hockey coach*

TEXAS

Arlington
Alicea, Luis Rene *professional baseball player*
Alvarez, Juan M. *professional baseball player*
Guerin, Bill *professional hockey player*
Showalter, Buck (William Nathaniel Showalter III) *major league baseball team manager*
Soriano, Alfonso Guilleard *professional baseball player*

Austin
Armstrong, Lance *professional cyclist*
Barnes, Richard Dale *college basketball coach*
Conradt, Jody *basketball coach*
Crenshaw, Ben *professional golfer*

Carrollton
Lieberman-Cline, Nancy *sports commentator, former professional basketball coach, former player*

Clutch City
Rice, Glen Anthony *professional basketball player*

College Station
Slocum, Richard Copeland (R.C. Slocum) *university athletic coach*

Dallas
Cuban, Mark *professional sports team executive, Internet company executive*
Dir, Dave *professional soccer coach*
Hamilton, David Lee *sports association administrator, retired environmental company executive*
Hudel, Chestella Alvis *athletics educator*
Laettner, Christian Donald *professional basketball player*
Nelson, Donald Arvid (Nellie Nelson) *professional basketball coach*
Stackhouse, Jerry *professional basketball player*
Turgeon, Pierre *professional hockey player*
Zubov, Sergei *professional hockey player*

Frisco
Modano, Mike (Michael Modano) *professional hockey player*

Galveston
Foster, William Edwin (Bill Foster) *nonprofessional basketball coach*

Houston
Alexander, Leslie Lee *professional sports team owner*
Bagwell, Jeff (Jeffrey Robert Bagwell) *professional baseball player*
Beltran, Carlos *professional baseball player*
Biggio, Craig *professional baseball player*
Capers, Dominic *professional football coach*
Chancellor, Van *professional basketball coach*
Clemens, Roger (William Roger Clemens) *professional baseball player*
Cooper, Cynthia *professional basketball player*
Garner, Phil
Howard, Juwan *professional basketball player*
Kent, Jeffrey Franklin *professional baseball player*
Kim, Pyung-Soo *martial arts educator*
Lamont, Gene *professional baseball coach, former professional baseball team manager*
McGrady, Tracy *professional basketball player*
Ming, Yao *professional basketball player*
Mutombo, DiKembe (Dikembe Mutombo Mpolondo Mukamba Jean Jacque Wamutombo) *professional basketball player*
Oswalt, Roy E. *professional baseball player*
Palmer, Chris *professional football coach*
Pettitte, Andrew Eugene (Andy Pettitte) *professional baseball player*
Swoopes, Sheryl Denise *professional basketball player*
Thompson, Tina Marie *professional basketball player*
Van Gundy, Jeff *professional basketball coach*
Wagner, Billy *professional baseball player*

Irving
Aikman, Troy *professional football player*
Coakley, Dexter *professional football player*
Coslet, Bruce N. *professional football coach*
George, Eddie (Edward Nathan George) *professional football player*
Hardy, Kevin Lamont *professional football player*
Hatcher, Darien *professional hockey player*
Irvin, Michael Jerome *professional football player*
Ismail, Raghib (Rocket Ismail) *professional football player*
Johnson, Keyshawn *professional football player*
Jones, Jerry (Jerral Wayne Jones) *professional football team executive*
Lites, James R. *professional hockey team executive*
Parcells, Bill (Duane Charles Parcells) *professional football coach*
Testaverde, Vincent Frank (Vinny Testaverde) *professional football player*

Leander
Erickson, Ralph D. *retired physical education educator, small business owner, consultant*

Lubbock
Knight, Bob *college basketball coach*
Sharp, Marsha *basketball coach*
Wilson, Margaret Eileen *retired physical education educator*

Round Rock
Ryan, Nolan *former professional baseball player*

San Antonio
Azzi, Jennifer L. *professional basketball player*
Duncan, Tim *professional basketball player*
Harvey, Candi *professional basketball coach*
Holt, Peter M. *sports team executive*
Johnson, Shannon *professional basketball player*
Popovich, Gregg *professional basketball coach*

Robinson, David Maurice *professional basketball player*
Smith, Steven Delano *professional basketball player*

Waco
Tomey, Dick *university football coach*

UTAH

Murray
Witworth, Clark L. *sports team executive*

Park City
Clark, Kelly *Olympic athlete*
Dunn, Shannon *Olympic athlete*
Shea, Jim *Olympic athlete*
Stone, Nikki *motivational speaker, retired Olympic athlete*
Witty, Christine (Chris Witty) *speed skater*
Young, Steven *former professional football player*

Salt Lake City
Boozer, Carlos Austin, Jr., *professional basketball player*
Dydek, Margo *professional basketball player*
Hlede, Korie *professional basketball player*
Miller, Larry H. *professional sports team executive, automobile dealer*
Sloan, Jerry (Gerald Eugene Sloan) *professional basketball coach*
Williams, Natalie *professional basketball player, restaurant executive*

VERMONT

South Royalton
McLaughlin, Rosemary *horse trainer, state representative*

VIRGINIA

Abingdon
Hamilton, Bobby *professional race car driver*

Ashburn
Arrington, Lavarr *professional football player*
Brunell, Mark Allen *professional football player*
Coles, Laveranues *professional football player*
Gibbs, Joe Jackson *professional football coach*
Murrell, Adrian Bryan *professional football player*
Portis, Clinton *professional football player*
Smith, Bruce *professional football player*
Snyder, Daniel *professional sports team executive, communications executive*
Williams, Gregg E. *professional football coach*

Blacksburg
Henrickson, Bonnie *college basketball coach*

Dublin
Clark, Shelia Roxanne *sports association executive, legislative analyst*

Falls Church
Theismann, Joseph Robert *former professional football player, announcer*

Herndon
Rongen, Thomas *professional soccer coach*

Lynchburg
Cushman, Valerie Jean *athletic director*

Mc Lean
Blair, Bonnie *former professional speedskater, former Olympic athlete*
Chang, Michael *professional tennis player*

Richmond
Mast, Rick *race car driver*

Stuart
Sadler, Elliott *race car driver*

Wise
Wasem, Bruce William *football coach, educator*

WASHINGTON

Everett
Constantine, Kevin *professional hockey coach*

Kirkland
Alexander, Shaun *professional football player*
Dilfer, Trent *professional football player*
Holmgren, Mike *professional football coach*
Randle, John *professional football player*
Watters, Richard James *professional football player*

Pullman
Bennett, Dick *college basketball coach*

Seattle
Armstrong, Charles G. *professional baseball executive, lawyer*
Bird, Sue (Suzanne Brigit Bird) *professional basketball player*
Buhner, Jay Campbell *former professional baseball player*
Ellis, John W. *professional baseball team executive, utilities executive*
Henderson, Rickey Henley *professional baseball player*
Jackson, Lauren *professional basketball player*
Suzuki, Ichiro *professional baseball player*
Walker, Walter Frederick *professional basketball team executive*
Westphal, Paul *professional basketball coach*

Spokane
Ueberroth, Peter Victor *former baseball commissioner*

WISCONSIN

Green Bay
Favre, Brett Lorenzo *professional football player*
Green, Ahman *professional football player*
Harlan, Robert Ernest *professional football team executive*
Nickerson, Hardy Otto *professional football player*
Sherman, Michael Francis *professional football coach*

Greendale
Kuhn, Roseann *sports association administrator*

Milwaukee
Cassell, Samuel James *professional basketball player*
Hernandez, Jose *professional baseball player*
Lopes, Davey *former professional baseball manager*
Porter, Terry *professional basketball coach*
Selig-Prieb, Wendy *sports team executive*
Steinmiller, John F. *professional basketball team executive*
Van Horn, Keith *professional basketball player*

WYOMING

Newcastle
Engle, Kathleen Faye *elementary education educator*
Gardner, Rulon E. *Olympic athlete*

CANADA

ALBERTA

Calgary
Hotchkiss, Harley N. *professional hockey team owner*
Sutter, Darryl John *professional hockey coach*
Turek, Roman *professional hockey player*

Edmonton
Lowe, Kevin Hugh *professional sports team executive, former hockey player and coach*
MacTavish, Craig *professional hockey coach, former hockey player*

BRITISH COLUMBIA

Richmond
Zeigler, Earle Frederick *physical education-kinesiology educator*

Surrey
Igali, Baraladei Daniel *Olympic athlete*

Vancouver
Abdul-Rahim, Shareef *professional basketball player*
Crawford, Marc *professional hockey coach*
McCaw, John E., Jr., *professional sports team executive*

ONTARIO

Dorchester
Fanning, William James *professional baseball team executive, radio and television broadcaster*

Gloucester
Pelletier, David *Olympic athlete, ice skater*
Salé, Jamie *Olympic athlete, ice skater*

Kanata
Hasek, Dominik *professional hockey player*
Murray, Bryan Clarence *professional sports team executive*

Ottawa
Bédard, Éric *Olympic athlete*
Bryden, Roderick M. *professional sports team executive*
Gagnon, Marc *Olympic athlete*
Guilmette, Jonathan *Olympic athlete*
Lemay-Doan, Catriona *Olympic speed skater*
Tremblay, Francois-Louis *Olympic athlete*
Turcotte, Mathieu *Olympic athlete*

Toronto
Bailey, Donovan *Olympic athlete*
Barber, Aaron *professional golfer*
Belfour, Ed *professional hockey player*
Berezin, Sergei *professional hockey player*
Bohn, Jason *professional golfer*
Bugg, Jace *professional golfer*
Carter, Vince *professional basketball player*
Davenport, Paul *professional golfer*
Dryden, Ken *sports team executive*
Espinosa, Carlos *professional golfer*
Francis, Ron *professional hockey player*
Fregosi, James Louis *professional baseball team manager*
Gaston, Cito *former professional baseball manager*
Halladay, Roy *professional baseball player*
Khristich, Dimitri *professional hockey player*
Leetch, Brian Joseph *professional hockey player*
Mogilny, Alexander *professional hockey player*
Mondesi, Raul *professional baseball player*
Nolan, Owen *professional hockey player*
Quinn, Pat (John Brian Patrick Quinn) *professional sports team manager*
Ricciardi, J.P. *professional sports team executive*
Slawter, Mark *professional golfer*
Stavro, Steve A. *professional hockey team executive*
Sundin, Mats Johan *professional hockey player*
Whitfield, Simon *Olympic athlete*
Willis, Kevin Alvin *professional basketball player*

PRINCE EDWARD ISLAND

Charlottetown
Vigneault, Alain *professional hockey coach*

QUEBEC

Montreal
Corson, Shayne *professional hockey player*
Gainey, Robert Michael *professional hockey coach, former player*
Julien, Claude *professional athletics coach*
Kovalev, Alexei *professional hockey player*
Minaya, Omar *professional sports team executive*
Tavares, Tony *professional hockey and baseball leagues executive*
Theodore, Jose *professional hockey player*

MEXICO

La Noria
Campos, Jorge *professional soccer player*

Mexico City
Chavez, Julio Cesar *professional boxer*

ENGLAND

London
Goosen, Retief *professional golfer*

Surrey
Els, Ernie (Theodore Ernest Els) *professional golfer*
Olazabal, Jose Maria *professional golfer*

SPAIN

Santander
Ballesteros, Severiano *professional golfer*

SWITZERLAND

Zurich
Groebli, Werner Fritz *professional ice skater, realtor*

ADDRESS UNPUBLISHED

Ali, Muhammad (Cassius Marcellus Clay) *retired professional boxer*
Andretti, Mario *retired race car driver*
Barkley, Charles Wade *sports broadcaster, retired professional basketball player*
Bennett, Cornelius *retired professional football player*
Bjornsrud, Marlene *professional athletics manager*
Blackwell, Jerry Alexander *professional golfer*
Boitano, Brian *Olympic athlete*
Boles, John *professional baseball coach, manager*
Bolton-Holifield, Alice Ruth *professional basketball player*
Boone, Robert Raymond *former professional baseball coach*
Bordick, Michael Todd *professional baseball player*
Bowe, Riddick Lamont *professional boxer*
Burton, Jeff *race car driver*
Camacho, Hector *boxer*
Caminiti, Kenneth Gene *professional baseball player*
Carroll, John *professional basketball coach*
Carter, Cris *retired professional football player, sportscaster*
Cartwright, James William (Bill Cartwright) *former professional basketball coach*
Chaney, Don *professional basketball coach*
Checketts, David Wayne *sports executive*
Collins, Paul Douglas (Doug Collins) *former professional basketball coach*
Cook, Ben Trelowe *sports performance specialist*
Crocker, Evelyne Marie *retired physical education educator*
Dallenbach, Wally, Jr., *professional race car driver*
Daniel, Beth *professional golfer*
Darsch, Nancy *former professional basketball coach*
Davidson, Bonnie Jean *gymnastics educator, sports management consultant*
Desjardins, Eric *professional hockey player*
Diaz-Arce, Raul *professional soccer player*
Dickerson, Eric Demetric *former professional football player*
Ditka, Michael Keller *former professional football coach*
Douglas, James (Buster) *boxer*
Dudley, Rick (Richard C. Dudley) *professional sports team executive*
Eckersley, Dennis Lee *former professional baseball player*
Elliott, Bill *race car driver*
Elway, John Albert *retired professional football player*
Evangelista, Nick Forrest *fencing master, writer, illustrator, publisher*
Evert, Chris (Christine Marie Evert) *retired professional tennis player*
Fleury, Theoren *professional hockey player*
Floyd, Tim *former professional basketball coach*
Foreman, George *former boxer, minister, boxing broadcaster*
Gambill, Jan-Michael Charles *professional tennis player*
Gilbert, Greg *former professional hockey coach*
Gilmour, Doug *professional hockey player*
Graham, John Hamilton, II, *professional athletics manager*
Guthrie, Janet *professional race car driver*
Hatchell, Sylvia *basketball coach*
Hicks, Ritchie B. *physical education educator*
Hornacek, Jeffrey John *professional basketball player*
Howe, Gordon *former professional hockey player, sports association executive*
Irwin, Kenny *professional race car driver*
Jackson, Philip Douglas *professional basketball coach*
Jansen, Daniel Ervin *former professional speedskater, marketing professional, former Olympic athlete*
Johnson, Frank(lin) Lenard *former professional basketball coach*
Johnson, Jimmy *sports broadcaster, former professional football coach*
Jones, Roy, Jr., *professional boxer*
Jordan, Michael Jeffrey *retired professional basketball player, former professional sports team executive, retired baseball player*
Karl, George *professional basketball coach*
Kavalek, Lubomir *chess expert*
Kitchen, Paul Howard *hockey historian*
Kite, Thomas O., Jr., *professional golfer*
Kluka, Darlene Ann *human performance educator, researcher*
Kumar, Sanjay *professional sports team executive, former computer company executive*
Kundla, John Albert *retired coach*
Lacroix, Pierre *professional sports team professional*
Langer, Bernhard *professional golfer*
Layden, Scott *former basketball executive*
Leonard, Sugar Ray (Ray Charles Leonard) *retired professional boxer*
Levens, Dorsey (Herbert Levens) *professional football player*
Lewis, Carl (Frederick Carlton Lewis) *Olympic track and field athlete*
Lindner, Carl Henry, Jr., *professional sports team executive, insurance company executive*
Lipinski, Tara Kristen *retired professional figure skater*
Littler, Gene Alec *professional golfer*
Ludzik, Steve *former professional hockey coach*
Lukian, Robert Hermann *professional tennis player, educator*
Manahan, Joan Elsie *health and physical education educator*
Manuel, Jerry *former professional sports team manager*
Martinez, Edgar *retired professional baseball player*
Mason, Linda *physical education educator, softball and basketball coach*
Matthews, Bruce Rankin *former professional football player*
Maurice, Paul *former professional hockey coach*
McCarthy, Jean Jerome *retired physical education educator*
McGhee, Carla Renee *professional basketball player*
McGinnis, Dave *former professional football coach*
McGwire, Mark David *retired professional baseball player*
Miller, Cheryl DeAnn *former professional basketball coach, broadcaster*
Montgomery, David Paul *professional baseball team executive*
Mora, James Ernest *former professional football coach*
Morgan, Lynn *sports association executive*
Moses, Edwin *former track and field athlete*
Mourning, Alonzo *retired professional basketball player*
Murray, Terry (Terence Rodney Murray) *former professional hockey team coach*
Musselman, Eric *professional basketball coach*
Navratilova, Martina *professional tennis player*
Norman, Gregory John *professional golfer*
Nott, Tara Lee *Olympic athlete*
Olajuwon, Hakeem Abdul *former professional basketball player*
O'Neill, Kevin *professional athletics coach*
Parins, Robert James *professional football team executive, judge*
Price, Nick *professional golfer*
Reeves, Daniel Edward *former professional football coach*
Rhode, Kim *Olympic athlete*
Rhodes, Raymond Earl *professional sports team executive*
Riley, Patrick James *former professional basketball coach*
Ripken, Calvin Edwin, Jr., (Cal Ripken) *retired professional baseball player*
Robinson, Crystal *professional basketball player*
Robinson, Larry Clark *professional hockey coach*
Roddick, Andy *professional tennis player*
Rodenberg, Joy D. *sports association executive*
Rothschild, Larry *former professional baseball executive*
Roy, Patrick *professional hockey player*
Rutherford, John Sherman, III, (Johnny Rutherford) *professional race car driver*
Safrit, Margaret *physical education educator*
Sanders, Barry *retired football player*
Seifert, George *retired professional football coach*
Sharman, William *professional basketball team executive*
Sharpe, Sterling *former professional football player, sports commentator*
Slay, Brandon *Olympic athlete*
Smits, Rik *retired professional basketball player*
Spitz, Mark *Olympic athlete*
Spurrier, Steve (Steven Orr Spurrier) *former professional football coach*
Stadler, Craig Robert *professional golfer*
Stewart, Kordell *professional football player*
Stockton, John Houston *retired professional basketball player*
Street, Picabo *Olympic athlete*
Stringer, C. Vivian *college basketball coach*
Summitt, Patricia Head *basketball coach*
Therrien, Michel *former professional hockey coach*
Thomas, Steve *professional hockey player*
Thompson, Jennifer B. *Olympic swimmer*
Timms, Michele *retired professional basketball player*
Tobin, Vincent Michael *professional football coach, former sports team executive*
Tyson, Mike G. *boxer*
Van Dyken, Amy *Olympic athlete*
Wagner, Richard *athletics consultant, former baseball team executive*
Waltrip, Darrell Lee *race car driver*
Whittemore, John Douglas *soccer coach, writer*
Williams, Erik George *professional football player*
Williams, Jimy *professional athletics manager*
Williams, Matt (Matthew Derrick Williams) *former professional baseball player*
Wilpon, Fred *professional baseball team executive, real estate developer*
Wilson, Ralph Cookerly, Jr., *professional football team executive*
Wooden, John Robert *former basketball coach*
Woosnam, Ian Harold *professional golfer*

Yamaguchi, Kristi Tsuya *ice skater*

BUSINESS *See* **FINANCE: INDUSTRY**

COMMUNICATIONS *See* **COMMUNICATIONS MEDIA; INDUSTRY: SERVICE**

COMMUNICATIONS MEDIA *See also* **ARTS: LITERARY**

UNITED STATES

ALABAMA

Andalusia
Biggs, Jeffery Ladon *editor*

Anniston
Ayers, Harry Brandt *editor, publisher, columnist*

Athens
Sandefur III, James *publishing executive*

Auburn
Audet, Barbara Anne *photojournalist, educator*

Birmingham
Adams, Kaye Mabry *periodical editor*
Allen, Christopher C. *publishing executive*
Bozzelli, Richard *publishing executive*
Crichton, Douglas Bentley *editor, writer*
Francavilla, Donna T. *journalist*
Griffin, Eleanor *publishing executive, editor*
Hanson, Victor Henry, II, *newspaper publisher*
Hickson, Marcus Lafayette, III, *communication educator, consultant*
Kennedy, Joe David, Jr., (Joey Kennedy) *editor*
Nunnelley, Carol Fishburne *editor newspaper*
Powell, Larry *communications educator*
Scarritt, Thomas Varnon *newspaper editor*
Seitz, Karl Raymond *editor*
Sheppard, Scott *magazine publisher*
Smyth, Rich *publishing executive*
Stephens, James T. *publishing executive*

Gadsden
Smothers, Jimmy *editor, sportswriter*

Jacksonville
Merrill, Martha *library media educator*

Madison
Cazavan, Larry O. *television executive*

Mobile
Clark, Veronica Ann Wilds (Ronni Patriquin Clark) *journalist*

Pelham
Harvey, James Mathews, Jr., *communications specialist*

Trussville
Jacobson, James Edmund *retired newspaper editor*

Tuscaloosa
Reinhart, Kellee Connely *journalist*
Ross, Daniel J.J. *publishing executive*

ALASKA

Anchorage
Cowell, Fuller A. *newspaper publisher*
Dougherty, Patrick *editor*
Hill, Erik Bryan *newspaper photographer*
Pagano, Rosanne V. *journalism professor, media consultant*
Pearson, Larry Lester *journalism educator*
Tobin, William Joseph *newspaper editor*

ARIZONA

Bisbee
Eppele, David Louis *columnist, author*

Carefree
Mangouni, Norman *publishing executive*

Gilbert
Kenney, Thomas Frederick *broadcast executive*

Glendale
Joseph, Gregory Nelson *media critic, writer, actor*

Green Valley
Macafee, Susan Diane *reporter*

Phoenix
Bushee, Ward *newspaper editor*
Clark-Johnson, Sue *publishing executive*
Clark Johnson, Susan *publishing executive*
Early, Robert Joseph *magazine editor*
Edens, Gary Denton *broadcast executive*
Elliott, Steve *newspaper editor*
Granato, Heather Breuninger *editor*
Leach, John F. *editor, journalism educator*
Lovely, Randy *editor*
Moyer, Alan Dean *retired newspaper editor*
Pyle, Thomas Alton *instructional television and motion picture executive*
Reyes, Anna Maria *broadcast executive*

Schatt, Paul *newspaper editor*
Steckler, Phyllis Betty *publishing company executive*
Turi, Louis *publishing executive*

Prescott
Anderson, Parker Lynn *columnist, playwright*

Scottsdale
Faer, A.M. *magazine publishing consultant, poet*
Murian, Richard Miller *book company executive*
Weil, Louis Arthur, III, *retired newspaper publishing executive*

Sedona
Chicorel, Marietta Eva *publishing company executive, consultant*
Sasmor, James Cecil *publishing representative, educator*

Tempe
Rankin, William Parkman *communications educator, academic administrator*
Richards, Gale Lee *communications educator*

Tucson
Davis, Cathy *publishing executive*
Hale, William Bryan, Jr., *newspaper editor*
Hayt, Therese D. *newspaper executive*
Hutchinson, Charles Smith, Jr., *book publisher*
Martin, June Johnson Caldwell *journalist*

ARKANSAS

Arkadelphia
Addington, Ronald Paul *mass media educator*
Grogan, Michael Wayne *columnist, editor-in-chief, poet*

Cedarville
Whitaker, Ruth Reed *state legislator, retired newspaper editor*

Fayetteville
Smith, Stephen Austin *communications educator*

Hot Springs Village
Smith, W. Preston *publishing executive, educator, real estate broker*

Little Rock
Bell, James Winfred *retired publishing executive*
Greenberg, Paul *editor*
Hussman, Walter E., Jr., *publishing executive*
Portis, Charles McColl *reporter, writer*
Shaw, Robert *newspaper editor*
Smith, Griffin *editor*

Rogers
Angleman, Sharon Ann *journalist*

Springdale
Parks, Michelle *journalist*

CALIFORNIA

Agoura Hills
Chagall, David *journalist, writer*
Teresi, Joseph *publishing executive*

Alameda
Billings, Thomas Neal *computer and publishing executive, management consultant, entrepreneur, journalist, writer*

Albany
Madgalene, David *editor, writer*

Alhambra
Duke, Donald Norman *publishing executive*

Alpine
Greenberg, Byron Stanley *newspaper and business executive, consultant*

Anaheim
Kelley, Lee *publishing executive*
Laderman, Kathleen Ann *magazine publisher*
Rizzo, James *editor*

Arcadia
Belnap, David F. *journalist*

Atascadero
Rios, Evelyn Deerwester *columnist, musician, artist, writer*

Bakersfield
Beene, Richard Stuart *newspaper editor*
Jenner, Mike *newspaper editor*

Belvedere Tiburon
Kramer, Lawrence Stephen *journalist*
Rosenthal, Robert Jon *newspaper editor, journalist*

Berkeley
Bagdikian, Ben Haig *journalist, emeritus university educator*
Browne, G.M. Walter Shawn *journalist, publisher, organizer*
Drechsel, Edwin Jared *retired magazine editor*
Helson, Henry Berge *publisher, retired mathematics educator*
Hertelendy, Paul *critic, writer, poet*
Lehmkuhl, Lynn *publishing executive*
Lesser, Wendy *editor, writer, consultant*
Lewis, Andrea Elen *editor*
Matthews, Mildred Shapley *scientific editor, freelance writer*
Shahani, Sapna *broadcast executive*

Beverly Hills
Berney, Bob *film company executive*
Bradshaw, Terry *sports announcer, former professional football player*
Corwin, Stanley Joel *book publisher*
Fernandez, Giselle *newscaster, journalist*
Friedman, Robert Lee *film company executive*
Gerber, William Norman *motion picture executive*

Grazer, Brian *film company executive*
Heller, Paul Michael *film company executive, producer*
Hill, David *broadcast executive*
Israel, David *journalist, screenwriter, producer*
Lond, Harley Weldon *editor, publisher*
Rothman, Thomas Edgar *production executive*
Schneider, Charles Ivan *newspaper executive*
Serletic, Matthew *recording industry executive*
Wallace De Cornwall, Clinton H. *media consultant*
Wolper, David Lloyd *motion picture and television executive*
Zanuck, Richard Darryl *motion picture company executive*

Burbank
Ancier, Garth Richard *television broadcast executive*
Barber, Gary *motion picture company executive*
Daniels, Susanne *broadcast executive*
DiBonaventura, Lorenzo *film company executive*
Eisner, Michael Dammann *entertainment company executive*
Evanitsky, Stephan E. *film company executive*
Hashe, Janis Helene *editor*
Iger, Robert A. *broadcast executive*
Jacobson, Nina *film company executive*
Janollari, David *television broadcasting executive, cable producer, television producer*
Jonas, Tony *television executive*
Kaye, Jhani *radio station manager, owner production company*
Kellner, Jamie *broadcast executive*
Lang, Laurie *entertainment company executive*
Lee, Paul *broadcast executive*
Letterie, Kathleen *broadcast executive*
Mack, Kelly *newscaster*
Madison, Paula *broadcast executive*
Marinelli, Janice *broadcast executive*
McPherson, Stephen *broadcast executive*
Michel, Donald Charles *editor*
Pedowitz, Mark *broadcast executive*
Robertson, Richard Trafton *entertainment company executive*
Ross, Rich *broadcast executive*
Roth, Peter *broadcast executive*
Ruiz, Michele *newscaster*
Schumacher, Thomas *film company executive*
Shapiro, Angela *broadcast executive*
Staggs, Thomas *entertainment company executive*
Sweeney, Anne M. *cable television company executive*
Sweeny, Anne *broadcast executive*
Taubin, Dawn *film company executive*
Thyret, Russ *recording industry executive*
Valdez, Denise *newscaster*
Wallau, Alex *broadcast executive*
Williams, Colleen *newscaster*
Younger, Laurie *broadcast executive*
Zucker, Jeffrey *broadcast executive*

Burlingame
Mendelson, Lee M. *film company executive, writer, producer, director*

Carlsbad
Allison, Stephen Galender *broadcast executive*
Howard, Robert Staples *newspaper publisher*
Owen, Charles Theodore *journalist, publishing executive*

Carmel
Koeppel, Gary Merle *publishing executive, art gallery owner, writer*
Mollman, John Peter *book publisher, consultant electronic publishing*

Chatsworth
Faerber, Charles N. *editor*

Chula Vista
Blankfort, Lowell Arnold *newspaper publisher*

Clearlake
Schoenherr, Bob *communications educator, consultant*

Costa Mesa
Sykes, Jolene *former publishing executive*

Culver City
Harris, Mel *broadcast executive*
Lynton, Michael *film company executive*
Michaels, Helene *broadcast executive*
Neufeld, Mace *film company executive*
Pascal, Amy *film company executive*
Wigan, Gareth *film company executive*

Daly City
Batlin, Robert Alfred *retired newspaper editor*

Davis
Brown, Hershel M. *retired newspaper publisher*

Del Mar
Faludi, Susan C. *journalist, scholarly writer*

Dobbins
Giles, Marjorie Briggs *publishing executive, writer*

Downey
Wayman, Joseph McKelden *editor, researcher*

El Segundo
Carey, Chase *broadcast executive*
Conrad, Paul Francis *editorial cartoonist*

Emeryville
Bax, Simon Tristan *film company executive*
Mather, Ann *film company executive*

Encino
Glickman, Daniel Robert *motion picture executive, former congressman*
Holman, Harland Eugene *retired motion picture company executive*
Rawitch, Robert Joe *journalist, educator*

Fair Oaks
Carrier, Lynne Thomson *journalist*
Stewart, William Thomas *communications educator*

Fresno
Lumbye, Betsy *editor*
Moyer, J. Keith *newspaper editor*
Waters, Charles R., Jr., *executive editor*
Wilson, James Ross *communications educator, broadcasting executive*

Glendale
Bishop, Debbie *publisher, business owner*
Dandor, Denise *newscaster*
DeLuca, Michael *film company executive*
Katzenberg, Jeffrey *motion picture studio executive*
Leyva, Ellen *newscaster*
MacDonald, Laurie *film company executive*
Parkes, Walter *film company executive*
Tuzee, Michelle *newscaster*

Glendora
Thornburg, Lee Ellis *film executive, director*

Hanford
Harris, Mildred Staeger *retired broadcast executive*

Hollywood
Malcom, Shawna L. *journalist*
McAdams, Frank Joseph, III, *communications educator*
Perth, Rod *network entertainment executive*

Huntington Beach
De Massa, Jessie G. *media specialist*

Imperial
Lokey, Frank Marion, Jr., *broadcast executive, consultant*

Inglewood
Sludikoff, Stanley Robert *publisher, writer*

Irvine
Bartkus, Richard Anthony *magazine publisher*
Kaplan, Arline Ray *editor, writer*
Lesonsky, Rieva *editor*
Power, Francis William *newspaper publisher*
Stein, M(eyer) L(ewis) *journalist, magazine editor, writer*

La Canada
Paniccia, Patricia Lynn *journalist, writer, lawyer, educator*

La Crescenta
Loehwing, Lord Rudi Charles, Jr., *publicist, radio broadcasting executive, journalist*

La Habra
Oliver, Joyce Anne *journalist, editorial and film consultant, columnist*

La Jolla
Copley, David C. *newspaper publishing company executive*
Freedman, Jonathan Borwick *journalist, writer, lecturer, educator*
Hallin, Daniel Clark *communications educator*
Harris, T. George *editor*
Jones, Charlie *television sports announcer*

La Quinta
Gassman, Andrea C. *journalist, artist*

Lake Elsinore
Corral, Jeanie Beleyn *journalist, school board administrator*

Long Beach
Adler, Jeffrey D. *political consultant, public affairs consultant, crisis management expert*
Bond, Frances Curtis *retired editor*
Ruszkiewicz, Carolyn Mae *newspaper editor*
Stevens, Mark *publishing executive*

Los Angeles
Askin, Richard Henry, Jr., *entertainment company executive*
Baquet, Dean Paul *newspaper editor*
Barberie, Jillian *newscaster, meteorologist*
Bart, Peter Benton *newspaper editor, film producer, novelist*
Berman, Gail *broadcast executive*
Bernstein, William *film company executive*
Berry, Nancy *recording industry executive*
Berry, Stephen Joseph *reporter*
Bouju, Jean-Marc *photojournalist*
Boyle, Barbara Dorman *motion picture company executive*
Camron, Roxanne *retired magazine editor, consultant*
Carroll, John Sawyer *newspaper editor*
Chernin, Peter *motion picture company executive*
Churgin, Amy *publishing executive*
Clarke, Peter *communications and health educator*
Cohn, Gary Dennis *journalist*
Cole, Carolyn *photojournalist*
Cross, Sue *newspaper editor*
Darling, Juanita Marie *correspondent*
Delugach, Albert Lawrence *journalist*
Devine, Christine *newscaster*
Diaz, Laura *newscaster*
Dolan, Mary Anne *journalist, columnist*
Dwyre, William Patrick *journalist, public speaker*
Fein, Irving Ashley *television and motion picture executive*
Field, Ted (Frederick Field) *film and record industry executive*
Findley, John Allen, Jr., *publishing executive*
Firstenberg, Jean Picker *film institute executive*
Fisher, Barbara *broadcast executive*
Flanigan, James J(oseph) *journalist*
Friedman, Robert G. *film company executive*
Gardner, Joseph Lawrence *editor, writer*
Garza, Oscar *newspaper editor*
Gauff, Lisa *broadcast journalist*
Gianopulos, Jim *film company executive*
Goldwyn, John *film company executive*
Griego, Linda *media executive*
Gross, Larry Paul *communications educator*
Groves, Martha *newspaper writer*
Hamlin, Doug *publishing executive*
Harbert, Ted (Edward W. Harbert III) *broadcast executive*
Hart, John Lewis (Johnny Hart) *cartoonist*

PROFESSIONAL INDEX 5555 COMMUNICATIONS MEDIA

Hefner, Hugh Marston *editor-in-chief*
Herzog, Doug *broadcast executive*
Horowitz, David Charles *consumer commentator, newspaper columnist*
Iovine, Jimmy *recording industry executive*
Ivins, Molly *columnist, writer*
Jacobson, Sidney *editor*
Johnson, John Malcolm, Jr., *reporter*
Jones, Quincy *producer, composer, arranger, conductor, trumpeter*
Kallet, Judith S. *publishing executive*
Kaplan, Andy *broadcast executive*
Knapp, Cleon Talboys *publishing executive*
Knittle, William Joseph, Jr., *media executive, psychologist, religious leader, management and marketing consultant, educator*
Kraft, Scott Corey *correspondent*
Kranwinkle, Conrad Douglas *broadcast executive*
Langguth, Arthur John *writer, journalism educator*
Larson, Gary *cartoonist*
Lazano, Monica *publishing executive*
Lazarus, Mell *cartoonist*
Levine, Jesse E. *publishing executive*
Lewis, Tommi *magazine editor*
Lozano-Centanino, Monica Cecilia *publishing executive*
Maltin, Leonard *television commentator, writer*
Mann, Wesley F. *editor, writer, reporter*
Margulies, Lee *newspaper editor*
Martin, Ann *newscaster*
Martinez, Jean *newscaster*
McCluggage, Kerry *film and television executive*
Mestres, Ricardo A., III, *motion picture company executive*
Miles, Jack (John Russiano) *journalist, educator*
Morgan, Dirck *broadcast journalist*
Nagy, Bob *editor*
Nazario, Sonia *reporter*
Neil, Daniel *journalist*
Nelson, Bryce Eames *journalist, educator*
O'Neil, William J. *newspaper executive*
O'Neil, William Scott *publishing executive*
O'Reilly, Richard Brooks *journalist*
Parisi, Paula Elizabeth *writer, photographer, editor*
Parks, Michael Christopher *journalist*
Paul, Charles S. *motion picture and television company executive*
Perenchio, Andrew Jerrold *film and television executive*
Perlmutter, Donna *music critic, dance critic*
Philips, Chuck *journalist*
Phillips, Geneva Ficker *academic editor*
Plate, Thomas Gordon *columnist, educator*
Press, Beth *publishing executive*
Puerner, John P. *newspaper publishing executive*
Raksin, Alex *reporter*
Reich, Kenneth Irvin *journalist*
Rense, Paige *editor, publishing company executive*
Rich, Alan *music critic, editor, author*
Richmond, Ray S(am) *journalist*
Rico, Suzanne *newscaster*
Rosenzweig, Richard Stuart *publishing company executive*
Rosett, Daniel J. *film company executive*
Rush, Herman E. *television executive*
Rust, Patricia Joan *television/film production company executive, writer, producer*
Salmon, Beth Ann *magazine editor in chief*
Saltzman, Joseph *journalist, producer, educator*
Sarnoff, Thomas Warren *television executive*
Saylor, Mark Julian *newspaper editor*
Scott, Kelly *newspaper editor*
Shaw, David Lyle *journalist, columnist*
Shuster, Alvin *journalist, newspaper editor*
Siegel, Barry *reporter*
Sigband, Norman Bruce *management communication educator*
Sinay, Hershel David *publishing executive*
Sing, Bill *editor*
Sipchen, Bob *reporter*
Sloan, L. Lawrence *publishing executive*
Somerson, Paul *editor-in-chief*
Spirtos, Maria *magazine publisher*
Steptoe, Sonja *journalist*
Stern, Leonard Bernard *television and motion picture production company executive*
Tellem, Nancy Reiss *broadcast executive*
Thompson, Anne Kathleen *entertainment journalist*
Tobias, Anita *publishing executive*
Ut, Huynh Cong *photojournalist*
Van Buren, Abigail (Jeanne Phillips) *columnist, lecturer*
Vargas, Diana Lisa *television station executive*
Walden, Dana *broadcast executive*
Ward, Leslie Allyson *journalist, editor*
Wardlow, Bill *record industry consultant, entertainer*
Warfel, Susan Leigh *editor*
Wilson, Charles Zachary, Jr., *newspaper publisher*
Zacchino, Narda *newspaper editor*

Los Gatos
Hastings, Reed *film company executive, educational association administrator*
Meyers, Ann Elizabeth *sports broadcaster*

Malibu
McCall, Elizabeth Kaye *columnist, consultant, writer*

Marina Del Rey
Lindheim, Richard David *television company executive, university official*

Menlo Park
Lynch, Kevin J. *publishing executive, media planner*

Merced
Boese, Sandra Jean *publishing executive*

Mill Valley
Cohn, Bruce *film and television company executive*
Leslie, Jacques Robert, Jr., *journalist*
McNamara, Stephen *newspaper executive*

Modesto
Smith, Chester *broadcast executive*
Vasche, Mark *newspaper editor*

Monterey
Gotshall, Cordia Ann *publishing company executive, distributing executive*
Miller, Richard Connelly *publishing executive, writer*

Monterey Park
Stapleton, Jean *journalism educator*

Mount Shasta
Stienstra, Stephani Ann *editor, writer*

National City
Beauchamp, Miles Philip *newspaper editor, columnist, education consultant*

Newport Beach
Bryant, Thomas Lee *magazine editor*
Doan, Paul John *magazine editor*
McMahon, Brian *publishing executive*

Newport Coast
Evanoff, George C. *retired publishing executive*

North Palm Springs
Mowry, Frank Henry *journalist, photojournalist*

Northridge
Dart, John Seward *journalist, writer*

Oakland
Brevetti, Francine Clelia *journalist*
Dailey, Garrett Clark *publisher, lawyer*
Foster (Anderson), Margaret Howard *editor, archivist*
George, Donald Warner *online columnist and editor, freelance writer*
Haiman, Franklyn Saul *author, communications educator*
McKinney, Judson Thad *broadcast executive*
Schrag, Peter *editor, writer*
Wood, Larry (Mary Laird) *journalist, writer, public relations executive, educator, environmental consultant*

Oceanside
Beck, Marilyn Mohr *columnist*
Delienne, Jacquelyn E. *e-commerce consultant, publisher*

Ontario
Rappaport, Michael Paul *columnist*

Pacific Grove
Davis, Robert Edward *retired communication educator*

Pacific Palisades
Hadges, Thomas Richard *media consultant*
Price, Frank *motion picture and television company executive*

Pacifica
Kelly, Kevin *editor*

Palm Desert
Ayling, Henry Faithful *writer, editor, consultant*

Palm Springs
Gerard, James Wilson *publishing consultant*

Palo Alto
Diamond, Diana Louise *editor, graphic artist*
Hamilton, David Mike *publishing executive*

Pasadena
Spector, Phil *record company executive*

Paso Robles
Baron, Adelaide Josephine *newswriter, artist*
Brown, Benjamin Andrew *retired journalist*

Placentia
Zweifel, Donald Edwin *retired newspaper editor, lobbyist, consultant*

Playa Del Rey
Cairns, Diane Patricia *motion picture executive*

Pomona
Wirsig, Woodrow *magazine editor, trade association administrator*

Rancho Mirage
Sheldon, Deena Lynn *television camera operator*

Rancho Palos Verdes
Hillinger, Charles *journalist, writer*

Redlands
Heiss, David James *editor*

Redwood City
Hearst, William Randolph, III, *newspaper publisher*

Riverside
McLaughlin, Leighton Bates, II, *journalism educator, former newspaperman*
Rodrigue, George P. *newspaper editor*
Sokolsky, Robert Lawrence *journalist, entertainment writer*

Sacramento
Baltake, Joe *film critic*
Belyn, David Neves *journalist, editor*
Block, Alvin Gilbert *publishing executive*
Glackin, William Charles *arts critic, editor*
Heaphy, Janis Besler *newspaper executive*
Hendricks, Chris *publishing executive*
Jones, Mark Alan *broadcast technician*
Knudson, Thomas Jeffery *journalist*
Lundstrom, Marjie *newspaper editor and columnist*
McClatchy, James B. *newspaper publisher, editor*
Proud, Robert Donald (Robert Payton) *broadcast executive*
Rodriguez, Rick *newspaper executive editor*
Shriver, Maria Owings *news correspondent*
Stall, William Read *writer*
Terhaar, Joyce *editor*
Walsh, Denny Jay *reporter*

San Bernardino
McAfee, I. Paul, III, *editor*

San Diego
Bell, Gene *newspaper publishing executive*
Benedyk, Mika Ono *editor, writer*
Charat, Jennifer Nicole *editor*
Da Rosa, Alison *travel editor*
Fike, Edward Lake *newspaper editor*
Kaufman, Julian Mortimer *broadcasting company executive, consultant*
Klein, Herbert George *newspaper editor*
Krulak, Victor Harold *newspaper executive*
Kyle, Robert Campbell, II, *publishing executive*
Morgan, Neil *writer, newspaper editor, lecturer, columnist*
O'Laughlin, Joanie *broadcast executive*
Pincus, Robert Lawrence *art critic, cultural historian*
Rowe, Peter A. *newspaper columnist*
Scripps, Robert P. *publishing executive*
Steen, Paul Joseph *retired broadcasting executive*
Walton, Bill (William Theodore Walton III) *sportscaster, former professional basketball player*
Welsh, Anne Marie *theater critic, writer, educator*
Willis, Norman Hunt *author, writer, director, producer*
Winders, Glenda *publishing executive*
Winner, Karin E. *editor*

San Francisco
Bentley, Lisa *publisher*
Blakey, Scott Chaloner *journalist, writer*
Boyle, Antonia Barnes *electronic learning consultant, writer*
Bronstein, Phil *executive editor*
Cameron, Heather Anne *publishing executive*
Chapin, Dwight Allan *columnist, writer*
Chase, Marilyn *journalist*
Dickey, Glenn Ernest, Jr., *sports columnist*
Dowling, Meaghan Hundley *editor*
Duscha, Julius Carl *journalist*
Ellery, Tracey *internet company executive*
Falk, Steven B. *newspaper publishing executive*
Fernald, Thomas A. *publishing executive*
Fox, Steve *editor-in-chief*
Garchik, Leah Lieberman *journalist*
German, William *newspaper editor*
Gore, Andrew *editor-in-chief periodical*
Graysmith, Robert *political cartoonist, author*
Hale, Cecil *communications educator, business educator*
Hamilton, Joan Nice *editor-in-chief*
Hochschild, Adam *writer, commentator, journalist*
Hubbell, Linda *publishing executive*
Klein, Marc S. *newspaper editor and publisher*
Lara, Adair *columnist, writer*
Louderback, Jim *editor-in-chief*
Mason, Greg *publishing executive*
McKean, Kevin S. *editor-in-chief, writer*
Minton, Torri *journalist*
Pazour, Don *publishing executive*
Perkins, Anthony B. *editor-in-chief, writer, educator*
Perlman, David *science editor, journalist*
Pimentel, Benjamin Impelido *journalist*
Randazzo, Gary Wayne *newspaper executive*
Rennie, I. Drummond *periodical editor, medical educator*
Riggenbach, Jeff *journalist*
Rosen, Evan Mark *executive communication advisor, journalist*
Rubenstein, Steven Paul *newspaper columnist*
Rusher, William Allen *writer, commentator*
Saunders, Debra J. *columnist*
Schwarz, Glenn Vernon *newspaper editor*
Sias, John B. *former multi-media company executive, newspaper publisher, publishing executive*
Singh, Jai *online news executive*
Taylor, Wendy *magazine editor*
Thornley, Evan *internet company executive*
Warrick, Sheridan *magazine editor*
Winn, Steven Jay *critic*

San Gabriel
Fry, Donald Owen *broadcasting company executive*

San Jose
Carey, Peter Kevin *reporter*
Ceppos, Jerome Merle (Jerry Ceppos) *newspaper editor*
Doctor, Kenneth Jay *publishing executive*
Elder, Robert Laurie *newspaper editor*
Goldberg, Susan *editor*
Harris, Jay Terrence *communications educator*
McDonald, Susan *publishing executive*
Mendoza, Martha *reporter*
Migielicz, Geralyn *photojournalist*
Nardi, Glen *publishing executive*
Rossi, Steven B. *newspaper publishing company executive*
Woldt, Harold Frederick, Jr., *newspaper publishing executive*
Yarnold, David *editor*

San Mateo
McLucas, Kate *magazine editor*
Nizard, Michael *editor-in-chief*
Reed, Sandy *former magazine editor*

San Pedro
Bowling, Lance Christopher *record producer, publishing executive*

San Rafael
Morgan, Michael Brewster *publishing company executive*
Sansweet, Stephen Jay *journalist, author, marketing executive*

Santa Ana
Anderson, N. Christian, III, *newspaper publisher*
Balzer, Robert Lawrence *journalist*
Brusic, Ken *editor*
Gudea, Darlene *publishing company executive*
Katz, Tonnie *newspaper editor*
Lehrer, John *editor*
Treshie, R. David *former newspaper publishing executive*
Weiermiller, Kathy *publishing executive*

Santa Barbara
Ackerman, Marshall *publishing company executive*
Brantingham, Barney *journalist, writer*
Brilliant, Ashleigh Ellwood *writer, cartoonist, publisher, educator*
Brown, J'Amy Maroney *journalist, media relations consultant, investor*
Campbell, William Steen *publishing executive, writer, speaker*
Dubroff, Henry Allen *newspaper editor, publisher*
Gibney, Frank Bray *publisher, editor, writer, foundation executive*
Roberts, Jerry *newspaper editor*
Segal, Helene Rose *periodical editor*
Tapper, Joan Judith *magazine editor*

Santa Clarita
Sturges, Sherry Lynn *recording industry executive*

Santa Monica
Adelson, Merv Lee *entertainment and communication industry executive*
Alpert, Herb *composer, recording artist, producer, painter*
Baer, Walter S. *research executive*
Block, Bill *film company executive*
Feltheimer, Jon *entertainment company executive*
Halperin, Stuart *entertainment company executive*
Lewis, Leslie Joy *music company executive, artist*
Littlefield, Warren *television executive*
Malin, Amir *former film company executive*
Mancuso, Frank G. *entertainment and communications company executive*
McGurk, Christopher J. *film company executive*
Osbourne, Sharon Arden *music manager, actress, television personality*
Palmatier, Malcolm Arthur *editor, consultant*
Rifkin, Arnold *film company executive*
Snedaker, Catherine Raupagh (Kit Snedaker) *editor*
Whalley, Tom *recording industry executive*
Yemenidjian, Alex *film company executive*

Santa Rosa
Callum, Myles *magazine editor, writer*
Person, Evert Bertil *newspaper and radio executive*
Swofford, Robert Lee *newspaper editor, journalist*

Sausalito
Brand, Stewart *editor, writer*
Hansen, Charles Morton *editor, retired military officer*

Seaside
May, James Harvey *communications educator*

Sherman Oaks
Yasnyi, Allan David *communications company executive*

Sonoma
Beckmann, Jon Michael *publishing company executive*

South Pasadena
Mantell, Suzanne Ruth *editor*

Stanford
Andreopoulos, Spyros George *writer*
Baker, Patricia Ann *publishing executive*
Kennedy, Donald *editor, environmental scientist, educator*
Pope, Norris *publishing executive*
Roberts, Donald Frank, Jr., *communications educator*
Suppes, Christine Johnson *publishing executive*

Stockton
McGrath, Murray Franklin *publishing executive*

Summerland
Cannon, Louis Simeon *journalist, writer*
Hall, Lee Boaz *publishing company consultant, author*

Sunnyvale
Coleman, Gregory G. *former magazine publisher*
Hurtado, Ernest R. *media specialist, educator*

Sylmar
Roth, Joe *motion picture company executive*

Tehachapi
Mitchell, Betty Jo *writer, publisher*

Thousand Oaks
Ferber, Samuel *publishing executive*
Rife, Douglas M. *publishing executive*

Torrance
Adelsman, Jean (Harriette Adelsman) *newspaper editor*
Sperling, Irene R. *publishing executive*
Wafer, Thomas J., Jr., *newspaper publisher*

Tracy
Coursey, David *columnist, management consultant*

Ukiah
Toms, Michael Anthony *broadcast journalist, editor, writer, producer*

Universal City
Fleishman, Susan Nahley *film company executive*
Geffen, David *recording company executive, producer*
Gill, Libby *television executive*
Hahn, Helene B. *motion picture company executive*
Hammer, Bonnie *broadcast executive*
Menendez, Belinda *broadcast executive*
Meyer, Ron *film company executive*
Nelson, Ronald L. *film company executive*
Parent, Mary *film company executive*
Randall, Karen *film company executive*
Rocco, Nikki *film company executive*
Schulz, Diana *film company executive*
Snider, Stacey *film company executive*
Stuber, Scott *film company executive*

Valley Springs
Anema-Garten, Durlynn C. *communications educator, counselor, writer*

Van Nuys
Harnsberger, Lindsey Carleton *music company executive, composer*

Ventura
Gallagher, Timothy J. *newspaper editor*
Greig, William Taber, II, *publishing company executive*
Howry, Joe R. *newspaper editor*

Vista
Linhart, Letty Lemon *editor*

Walnut Creek
Anderberg, Roy A. *journalist*
Pfeiffer, Phyllis Kramer *publishing executive*
Satz, Louis K. *publishing executive*
Trousdale, Stephen Richard *newspaper editor*

West Hollywood
De Line, Donald *film company executive*

West Los Angeles
Hirschhorn, Charles *media company executive*

West Point
tenZeldam, Justine Cubbage *publishing executive, editor-in-chief*

Whittier
Loughrin, Jay Richardson *mass communications educator, consultant*

Wilton
Harrison, George Harry, III, (Hank Harrison) *publishing executive, author*

Woodland Hills
Anastasi, Michael Anton *journalist*
Deters, Thomas C. *publishing executive, educator*
Harris, Barbara S. *publishing executive*
Lund, Robert W. *newspaper editor*
Murphy, Irene Helen *publishing executive*
Rafter, Tracy *publishing executive*
Schueler, John R. *newspaper executive*

Yreka
Smith, Vin *sports editor, business owner, novelist*

COLORADO

Aspen
Hayes, Mary Eshbaugh *editor, writer*

Aurora
Whelchel, Anita E. *publishing executive*

Berthoud
Davis, Donald Alan *news correspondent, writer, lecturer*

Boulder
Clos, Lynne Mobley *magazine publisher, paleontologist*
El Mallakh, Dorothea Hendry *editor, publishing executive*
Rienner, Lynne Carol *publishing executive*
Rinehart, Amy Hutchinson *publishing executive, consultant*

Centennial
Ulevich, Neal Hirsh *photojournalist*

Cherry Hills Village
Stapleton, Katharine Hall (Katie Stapleton) *food broadcaster, writer*

Colorado Springs
Brander, Bruce George *international journalist, author*
Fleming, Terri *newspaper editor*
Mehlis, David Lee *publishing executive*
Wright, Laura Keith *editor, writer*
Zapel, Arthur Lewis *book publishing executive*

Craig
Gray, Ann Maynard *broadcasting company executive*

Denver
Barbour, Alton Bradford *human communication studies educator*
Bates, James Robert *newspaper editor*
Britton, Dennis A. *former newspaper editor, newspaper executive*
Brom, Libor *journalist, educator*
Chavez, Jeanette *editor*
Clark, Gary R. *newspaper editor*
Cubbison, Christopher Allen *newspaper editor*
Dance, Francis Esburn Xavier *communications educator*
Drake, Sylvie (Jurras Drake) *theater critic*
Elliman, Donald M., Jr., *magazine company executive*
Engdahl, Todd Philip *editor*
Esposito, Joseph John *publishing company executive*
Giffin, Glenn Orlando, II, *music critic, writer, newspaper editor*
Goeken, Deborah *editor*
Grilly, Gerald E. *publishing executive*
McDonald, Kirk *publishing executive*
Moore, Gregory L. *editor*
Price, Kathleen McCormick *book editor, writer*
Rothman, Paul Alan *publishing executive*
Saltz, Howard Joel *newspaper editor*
Scudder, Richard B. *newspaper executive*
Singleton, William Dean *publishing executive*
Temple, John R. *publishing executive*
Wolman, Jonathan Paley *journalist*
Zimmer, Larry William, Jr., *sports announcer*

Durango
Ballantine, Morley Cowles (Mrs. Arthur Atwood Ballantine) *editor*
Reid-Bills, Mae *magazine editor, historian*
Van Mols, Brian *publishing executive*

Englewood
Peters, Janice C. *cable company executive*

Evergreen
Dobbs, Gregory Allan *journalist*

Fort Collins
Christiansen, Norman Juhl *retired newspaper publisher*
Hallahan, Kirk Edward *journalism educator*
MacLauchlin, Robert Kerwin *communications artist, educator*
May, Stephen James *communications educator, writer*
Sons, Raymond William *journalist*

Georgetown
Stern, Mort(imer) P(hillip) *journalism and communications educator, academic administrator, consultant*

Golden
Baron, Robert Charles *publishing executive*

Granby
Johnson, William Potter *publishing executive, director*

Greenwood Village
Cooper, Ronald *broadcast executive*

Highlands Ranch
Harris, Douglas Clay *retired newspaper executive*

Littleton
Bennett, Janice Lynn *publisher, educator*
Ergen, Charles *communications professional*
Udevitz, Norman *publishing executive*

Longmont
Pattyn, Sue *publishing executive*

Loveland
Goldberg, Laurie Lane *editor*

Morrison
Myers, Harry J., Jr., *retired publisher*

Pueblo
Gregory, Leonard *publishing executive*

Sedalia
McKee, John Morrison *broadcast executive*

CONNECTICUT

Bethel
Shepard, Jean Heck *retired publishing consultant*

Bridgeport
Simoneau, Cynthia Lambert *newspaper editor, journalism educator*

Bridgewater
Crooke, Robert Andrew *media consultant, writer, educator*

Bristol
Bodenheimer, George *broadcast executive*
Driessen, Christine F. *broadcast executive*
Eisen, Rich *reporter*
Melrose, Barry James *sportscaster, former professional hockey team coach*
Patrick, Dan *sportscaster*
Roberts, Robin *sportscaster*

Brookfield
Reynolds, Jean Edwards *publishing executive*

Cos Cob
Barnard, Charles Nelson *editorial consultant, author*
Hauptman, Michael *broadcasting company executive*

Danbury
Annesi, Adele Mary *editor, writer*

Darien
Brooke, Avery Rogers *publisher, writer*

Deep River
Cobb, Hubbard Hanford *magazine editor, writer*

Easton
Enos, Randall *cartoonist, illustrator*
Lorenz, Lee Sharp *cartoonist*

Fairfield
Hodgkinson, William James *publishing executive*
Kaff, Albert Ernest *reporter, writer*
Spence, Barbara E. *publishing company executive*
Wright, Robert C. *broadcast executive*

Greens Farms
Deford, Frank *sportswriter, television and radio commentator, author*

Greenwich
Collins, Richard Lawrence *magazine editor, publisher, author*
Engstrom, Erik *private equity investor*
Keogh, James *journalist*
Moffly, John Wesley, IV, *magazine publishing executive*
Reisch, Marc *publishing executive*
Rukeyser, Louis Richard *economic commentator*
Sweeney, Michael Andrew *newspaper editor*
Welling, Kathryn Marie *editor*

Hartford
Davis, Jack Wayne, Jr., *publishing executive*
Englehart, Robert Wayne, Jr., *cartoonist*
Golden, Louis Joseph *former business news editor, newspaper executive*
Harden, Jon Bixby *publishing executive*
Noel, Don Obert, Jr., *retired editor, columnist*
Pach, Peter Barnard *columnist, editor*
Roessner, Barbara *journalist*
Teutsch, Clifford L. *publishing executive*
Toolan, Brian Paul *newspaper editor*

Ivoryton
Bendig, William Charles *editor, artist, publisher*

Lakeville
Estabrook, Robert Harley *journalist*

Madison
Egbert, Emerson Charles *retired publisher*
Purcell, Bradford Moore *publishing company executive*

Mansfield Center
Petrus, Robert Thomas *internet business owner, real estate investor*

Middletown
Balay, Robert Elmore *editor, reference librarian*

Milford
Henderson, Albert Kossack *publishing company executive, dairy executive, consultant*

Moodus
Cumming, Robert Emil *editor, writer*

New Britain
Martin, Vivian Bonita *journalist, educator*

New Haven
Leeney, Robert Joseph *newspaper editor*
McClatchy, J. D. *editor, writer, educator*
Ryden, John Graham *publishing executive*

Norwalk
DeCesare, Donald E. *broadcast executive*
White, Rick *publishing executive*

Old Greenwich
Dixon, John Morris *magazine editor*

Rocky Hill
Powers, Helen *columnist, writer*

Sharon
Gordon, Nicholas *broadcast executive*

Sherman
Cowley, Robert William *editor, writer, lecturer, consultant*
Valeriani, Richard Gerard *news broadcaster*

Southbury
Barry, Edward William *retired publisher*
Vega, Marylois Purdy *journalist*

Stamford
Beck, Angel C. *columnist, screenwriter, educator, film director*
Britt, Glenn Alan *media company executive*
Burke, Alexander James, Jr., *publishing company executive, scripture scholar*
Evans, Thomas R. *magazine publisher*
Fein, Ronnie *writer, journalist*
Frese, Alan D.R. *publishing executive*
Harrington, Richard J. *information business executive*
Kisseberth, Paul Barto *retired publishing executive*
Lane, Hana Umlauf *editor*
Pardue, Bill *publishing executive*
Rowe, William John *retired newspaper publishing executive*
Wilensky, Julius M. *publishing company executive*

Stonington
Elliott, Osborn *journalist, educator, urban activist, former dean*

Storrs Mansfield
Croteau, Maureen Elizabeth *journalism educator*
Maier, Romulus *journalist*

Stratford
Cox, Richard Joseph *former broadcasting executive*

Vernon Rockville
Orr, Jim (James D. Orr) *editor, writer*

Waterbury
Pape, William James, II, *newspaper publisher*

West Hartford
Whitman, Mara Arden *publishing executive*

Westport
Carvalko, Debora G. *editor, writer*
Kramer, Sidney B. *publisher, lawyer, literary agent*
McCormack, Donald Paul *newspaper consultant*
Murphy, Thomas John *publishing executive*
Stern, Robert D. *publishing executive*

Wethersfield
Jenks, Dennis *publishing executive*
Osborne, Louise *publishing executive*

Wilton
Bair, Tom *publishing executive*
Binder, Steven F. *publishing executive*
Fox, Mitchell B. *magazine publisher*
Harty, Thomas H. *publishing executive*
Seitz, Nicholas Joseph *magazine editor, journalist*
Tarde, Gerard (Jerry) *magazine executive*

Woodbridge
Menchaca, Frank *editorial director*

DELAWARE

Dover
Lewis, Larry *communications educator, video producer*
Smyth, Joel Douglas *newspaper executive*

Millsboro
Kettinger, David John *broadcast executive*

New Castle
Cansler, Leslie Ervin *retired newspaper editor*
Henley, Deborah S. *newspaper editor*
von Hoelle, John Jacob Lewis *publisher, commercial developer*

Newark
Jackson, M.(arvin) Dennis *journalism educator, writer*

Wilmington
Lewis, Mary Therese *publisher*

DISTRICT OF COLUMBIA

Washington
Adams, Lorraine *reporter*
Adams, Robert Edward *journalist*
Aguirre-Baca, Francisco *publisher, consultant*
Allen, William L. *editor*
Andrews, John Frank *editor, author, educator*
Angier, Natalie Marie *science journalist*
Apple, Raymond Walter, Jr., *journalist*
Applebaum, Anne *journalist, writer*
Arana, Marie *editor, writer*
Archibald, George *reporter*
Arena, Kelli *news correspondent*
Arnold, Gary Howard *film critic*
Arnovitz, Benton Mayer *editor*
Asker, James Robert *magazine editor*
Atcheson, Richard *editor*
Atkinson, Lawrence Rush, IV, (Rick Atkinson) *journalist*
Atlas, Terry *journalist*
Attkisson, Sharyl T. *newscaster, correspondent, writer*
Bailey, Charles Waldo, II, *journalist, author*
Balz, Daniel John *newspaper editor, journalist*
Bandow, Douglas Leighton *editor, columnist, policy consultant*
Barber, Ben Bernard Andrew *journalist*
Beach, Walter Eggert *retired publishing organization executive*
Beale, Betty (Mrs. George K. Graeber) *columnist, writer*
Benson, Miles Richard *journalist*
Bern, Paula Ruth *columnist*
Berry, Chris *broadcast executive*
Biannic, Georges *news service executive*
Blitzer, Wolf *anchor, news correspondent*
Bohannon, Camille *news anchor*
Boo, Katherine *newswriter*
Borger, Gloria *journalist, editor*
Bourke, Dale Hanson *publishing company owner*
Boyce, Clayton Winfred *magazine publisher, editor*
Boyle, Patrick Kevin *journalist*
Bradlee, Benjamin Crowninshield *executive editor*
Branegan, James Augustus, III, *journalist*
Brazaitis, Thomas Joseph *journalist*
Broder, David Salzer *reporter, writer*
Brown, John Patrick *newspaper executive, financial consultant*
Bruzelius, Nils Johan Axel *journalist*
Butler, Patrick Harold *publishing executive*
Butterworth, Ritajean Hartung *broadcast executive*
Buzbee, Sally Streff *news correspondent*
Carlson, Tucker *political analyst, writer, television host*
Clift, Eleanor *magazine correspondent*
Clurman, Michael *newspaper publishing executive*
Clymer, Adam *newspaper correspondent*
Cohen, Richard Edward *journalist*
Cohen, Sarah *reporter*
Coll, Stephen Wilson *editor*
Cook, Charles Edward, Jr., *editor, political analyst*
Cook, David *editor*
Copeland, Peter *editor*
Cosgrove, John Patrick *editor*
Cowan, Edward *journalist, editor*
Cowen, Eugene Sherman *broadcast executive*
Cox, Kathleen *broadcast executive, lawyer*
Crenshaw, Albert Burford *journalist*
Crewdson, John Mark *journalist, writer*
Crock, Stanley Miles *journalist*
Curry, George Edward *former journalist*
Curtiss, Richard Holden *magazine editor, writer*
Cutler, Bernard Joseph *editor-in-chief, writer*
Cutler, Carol Ann *food writer, consultant*
Davidson, Susan Bettina *editor, writer*
Davis, Garry (S. Gareth Davis) *publishing executive, writer*
de Borchgrave, Arnaud *editor, writer, lecturer*
Deeb, Mary-Jane *editor, educator*
Denlinger, John Kenneth *journalist*
Dewar, Helen *reporter*
Dillin, John Woodward, Jr., *retired newspaper editor, correspondent*
Doan, Michael Frederick *editor*
Donaldson, Samuel Andrew *journalist*
Donlan, Thomas Garrett *journalist*
Donohoe, Cathryn Murray *journalist*
Dorn, James Andrew *editor*
Dowd, Maureen *columnist*
Downie, Leonard, Jr., *editor, writer*
Drew, Elizabeth *television commentator, journalist, author*
Duffy, Brian *editor*
Dujack, Stephen Raymond *editor*
Eaton, Sabrina Catherine Elizabeth *journalist*
Edsall, Thomas Byrne *reporter*
Edwards, Bob (Robert Alan Edwards) *radio news anchor*
Elfin, Mel *magazine editor*
Elsasser, Glen Robert *journalist*
Elsberg, John William *editor-in-chief*
Elving, Ronald Dwight *journalist, educator*
Epstein, Kalman Noel *newspaper publishing company executive*
Faherty, Robert Louis *publishing executive*
Fahey, John M., Jr., *book publishing executive*
Faucheux, Ronald Anthony *publisher, editor*
Feld, Karen Irma *columnist, journalist, broadcaster, public speaker*
Fields, Suzanne Bregman *syndicated columnist*
Folkerts, Jean *journalism educator*
Franzen, Byron T. (John Franzen) *media specialist*
Friedman, Thomas Loren *foreign correspondent*
Fritts, Edward O. *broadcast executive*
Frommer, Frederic Jason *journalist, writer*
Galloway, Joseph Lee, Jr., *writer, journalist*
Garling, Scipio *editor*
Garrels, Anne *news correspondent*
Geyer, Georgie Anne *syndicated columnist, educator, author, biographer, TV commentator*
Gibson, Florence Anderson *talking book company executive, narrator*
Glaser, Vera Romans *journalist*
Glass, Andrew James *newspaper editor*
Glassman, James Kenneth *editor, writer, publishing executive*

Gorman, Patricia Jane *editor*
Graham, Donald Edward *publishing company executive*
Grebow, Edward *media specialist, finance company executive*
Greenhouse, Linda Joyce *journalist*
Greenwood, William Warren *journalist*
Gregory, Bettina Louise *journalist*
Grosvenor, Gilbert Melville *journalist, educator, business executive*
Gutman, Roy William *reporter*
Guzy, Carol *photojournalist*
Gwaltney, Corbin *editor, publishing executive*
Halsey, Ashley, III, *newspaper editor*
Hartman, Carl (Howard Carl Hartman) *reporter*
Hassan, Aftab Syed *education specialist, author, editor*
Headden, Susan M. *editor*
Hecht, Marjorie Mazel *editor*
Henry, John Cooper *journalist*
Herman, Andrea Maxine *newspaper editor*
Herman, George Edward *radio and television correspondent*
Hiatt, Fred *editorial editor*
Hiebert, Ray Eldon *educator, author, consultant*
Higham, Scott *reporter*
Hinden, Stanley Jay *newspaper editor*
Hoagland, Jimmie Lee *newspaper editor*
Hopper, V. Linda *communications educator, writer*
Horwitz, Sari *reporter*
Howell, Deborah *editor*
Hoyt, Clark Freeland *journalist, newspaper editor*
Hume, Brit (Alexander Britton Hume) *journalist*
Hunt, Albert R. *newspaper executive*
Hunter, Stephen *film critic, writer*
Irvine, Reed John *media critic, corporation executive*
Jacobson, Louis Alan *journalist*
James, Bruce Richard *information specialist*
Johnson, Richard Kent *publishing executive*
Johnson, Robert Louis *cable television company executive, professional sports team owner*
Johnson, Sandra K. *journalist*
Jones, Boisfeuillet, Jr., *publishing executive*
Joo, Douglas D.M. *newspaper and video production executive*
Jordan, Mary *editor-in-chief, reporter*
Joyce, Anne Raine *editor, director of publications*
Judd, Jacqueline Dee (Jackie Judd) *journalist, reporter*
Julien, Janelle E.D. *editor, writer*
Kaiser, Robert Greeley *newspaper editor*
Kilborn, Peter Thurston *journalist*
Kilian, Michael David *journalist, columnist, writer*
Kimmitt, Robert Michael *broadcast executive*
King, Colbert Isaiah *editor*
King, Larry (Larry Zeiger) *broadcaster, radio personality*
King, Llewellyn Willings *publisher, lecturer, journalist, commentator*
King, Nina Davis *journalist*
Kiplinger, Knight Austin *journalist, publisher*
Kirk, Donald *journalist*
Klose, Kevin *broadcast executive*
Knight, Athelia Wilhelmenia *journalist*
Koppel, Ted *broadcast journalist*
Kristol, William *editor, political analyst*
Laessig, Walter Bruce *publishing executive*
Lamb, Brian P. *broadcast executive*
Lambro, Donald Joseph *columnist*
Lardner, George, Jr., *journalist, writer*
Larson, George Charles *magazine editor, writer*
Lawson, Jennifer *broadcast executive*
LeBrecht, Thelma Jane Mossman *reporter*
Lee, Debra L. *broadcast executive*
Leeds, Charles Alan *publishing executive*
Lehrman, Margaret McBride *television news executive, producer*
Leubsdorf, Carl Philipp *publishing executive*
Levey, Robert Frank *newspaper columnist, fundraiser*
Lewis, Charles Joseph *journalist*
Lewis, Robert David Gilmore *retired editor*
Lindberg, Tod Marshall *editor, writer*
Loker, Elizabeth St. John *newspaper executive*
Lorsung, Thomas Nicholas *news service editor*
Lubar, Jeffrey Stuart *journalist, trade association executive*
Lynker, John Paul *newscaster*
Mankiewicz, Frank F. *journalist, writer*
Margolis, Doris May Rosenberg *editor, writer*
Marimow, William Kalmon *editor*
Matthiesen, Lance *publishing executive*
May, Clifford Daniel *director of communications, newspaper editor, journalist*
McBee, Susanna Barnes *retired journalist*
McCormally, Kevin Jay *editor*
McCune, Greg E. *communications media executive*
McFeatters, Ann Carey *journalist*
McLaughlin, John J. *broadcast executive, television producer, journalist, political commentator*
Means, Marianne *political columnist*
Melendy, David Russell *broadcast journalist*
Merry, Robert William *publishing executive*
Miller, Alan *newswriter*
Milner Anderson, Katherine *broadcast executive*
Mitchell, Andrea *journalist*
Moore, Miles David *journalist*
Moser, Donald Bruce *magazine editor*
Moss, Madison Scott *editor*
Mowlana, Hamid *international relations and communication educator*
Murphy, Caryle Marie *foreign correspondent*
Murray, Alan Stewart *publishing executive*
Nesmith, Jeff *journalist*
Novak, Robert David Sanders *newspaper columnist, television commentator*
O'Brien, Soledad *newscaster, news anchor*
O'Brien, Timothy Andrew *writer, journalist, lawyer, educator*
Oka, Takashi *journalist, consultant, educator*
Older, Susan *editor*
Ong, Laureen E. *broadcast executive*
Ottaway, David Blackburne *journalist*
Overby, Peter M. *journalist*
Padden, Preston *broadcast executive*
Page, Clarence E. *newspaper columnist*
Page, Tim *music critic, writer, producer*
Palmer, Stacy Ella *periodical editor*
Pancake, John *newspaper editor*
Panero, Hugh Edward *broadcast executive*
Paxson, Richard *newspaper editor*
Peck, Louis Moses *editor*
Perkins, Lucian *photographer*
Peters, Charles Given, Jr., *editor*
Pincus, Walter Haskell *editor*
Porter, Barbara *anchorwoman, writer, educator*
Potter, Deborah Ann *news correspondent, educator*
Pratt, Carin *television executive*
Prina, L(ouis) Edgar *journalist*
Putzel, Michael *journalist, editor*
Rankin, Robert Arthur *journalist*
Richman, Phyllis Chasanow *newspaper critic*
Ridgeway, James Fowler *journalist*
Rosen, Carol *editor*
Rosen, Gerald Robert *editor*
Russert, Timothy John *broadcast journalist, executive*
Safire, William *journalist, writer*
Samsot, Robert Louis *newspaper editor, consultant*
Scheibel, Kenneth Maynard *journalist*
Schieffer, Bob *broadcast journalist*
Schiff, Margaret Scott *newspaper publishing executive*
Scholz, Jane *newspaper publisher*
Schram, Martin Jay *journalist*
Schulman, Heidi *broadcast executive*
Seidman, L(ewis) William *television commentator, publisher*
Semas, Philip Wayne *editor*
Shadid, Anthony *journalist*
Shales, Thomas William *television and film critic, writer, journalist*
Shanks, Hershel *editor, writer*
Shanks, Judith Weil *editor*
Shannon, Donald Hawkins *retired editor*
Shapinsky, David Frazier *journalist, historian*
Shapiro, Walter Elliot *political columnist*
Shaw, Gaylord *newspaper executive*
Shearer, Alan *newspaper editor*
Sheehan, Neil *reporter, scholarly writer*
Shenon, Philip *journalist*
Sidey, Hugh Swanson *correspondent*
Siegel, Robert Charles *broadcast journalist*
Silver, Brian Quayle *broadcast journalist, musician, educator*
Simons, Carol Lenore *magazine editor*
Slafka, Kristi Lynne *journalist*
Slater, Jim *sportswriter, journalist*
Smith, Dean *communications advisor, arbitrator*
Smith, Mignon C. *publishing executive*
Smith, Stephen Grant *communications executive*
Snow, Robert Anthony *journalist*
Sperling, Godfrey, Jr., *journalist*
Stamberg, Susan Levitt *radio broadcaster*
Stepp, Laura Sessions *journalist*
Stern, Carl Leonard *former news correspondent, federal official*
Sullivan, Kevin *bureau chief, reporter*
Sweet, Lynn D. *journalist*
Terzian, Philip Henry *journalist*
Tiede, Tom Robert *journalist*
Toedtman, James Smith *newspaper editor, journalist*
Tolchin, Martin *retired newspaper reporter, author*
Toledano, Ralph de *columnist, author, poet*
Toles, Thomas Gregory *editorial cartoonist*
Totenberg, Nina *journalist*
Trafford, Abigail *columnist, editor, writer*
Turner, Douglas Laird *writer, editor, columnist*
Turner, Ted (Robert Edward Turner) *former television executive, philanthropist*
Warren, Albert *publishing executive*
Warren, Clay *communications educator*
Watson, William Hughes *news service publisher, network executive*
Weinberger, Caspar Willard *publishing executive, former secretary of defense*
Wiener, Leonard *journalist*
Will, George Frederick *editor, political columnist, news commentator*
Winfrey, Carey Wells *journalist, magazine editor*
Winter, Thomas Swanson *editor, newspaper executive*
Witcover, Jules Joseph *newspaper columnist, author*
Woodruff, Judy Carline *broadcast journalist*
Woodward, Robert Upshur *newspaper reporter, writer*
Yardley, Jonathan *journalist*
Zahn, Paula *newscaster*
Zwadiuk, Oleh *radio executive*

FLORIDA

Amelia Island
Britt, David Van Buren *retired educational communications executive*

Aventura
Babson, Irving K. *publishing company executive*
Perkel, Robert Simon *photojournalist, educator*

Belleair
Szep, Paul Michael *editorial cartoonist*

Boca Grande
Heffernan, John William *retired journalist*

Boca Raton
Levine, Irving R. *commentator, dean, writer, educator*
McQueen, Scott Robert *broadcasting company executive*
Myers, Michelle *publishing executive*

Boynton Beach
Jacobs, Wendy *editor, writer, translator*
Klein, Bernard *publishing company executive*
Oppler, Ralph Leo *retired publishing executive, advertising executive*

Braden River
Wilkerson, Janet Stafford *publishing executive, educator*

Bradenton
Crouthamel, Thomas Grover, Sr., *editor, consultant*
McFarland, Richard Macklin *retired journalist*
White, Dale Andrew *journalist*

Brandon
Landry, Richard *publishing executive*

Christmas
Fowler, Ronald James *journalist*

Clearwater
VanMeer, Mary Ann *publisher, writer, researcher, webmaster*

Clermont
Jolley, Franklin David, Jr., *journalist, writer*

Coral Gables
Roberto, Samuel Smith *television news executive*

Coral Springs
Medina-Salinas, Elizabeth *publishing executive, writer*

Daytona Beach
Davidson, Herbert M., Jr., (Tippen Davidson) *newspaper owner*
Wanjohi, Elsie Wairimu *communications educator*

Delray Beach
Salsberg, Arthur Philip *publishing company executive*
Siegel, Ira T. *publishing executive*

Dover
Pearson, Walter Donald *editor, columnist*

Fort Lauderdale
Bolanos, Michael Templeton *new media executive*
Eisner, Will *publishing company executive*
Greenberger, Sheldon Lee *newspaper advertising executive*
Gremillion, Robert *publishing executive*
Hartz, Deborah Sophia *editor, writer*
Markus, Robert Michael *retired journalist*
Maucker, Earl Robert *newspaper editor, newspaper executive*
Reisinger, Sandra Sue *columnist*
Schulte, Frederick James *newpaper editor*
Skellings, Edmund *communications educator, poet*
Williamson, William Paul, Jr., *journalist*

Fort Myers
Barbour, William Rinehart, Jr., *retired book publisher*

Gainesville
Barber, Charles Edward *newspaper executive, journalist*
Hollien, Harry Francis *speech and communications scientist, educator*
Kaid, Lynda Lee *communications educator*
Kaplan, John *photojournalist, educator, consultant*
Maple, Marilyn Jean *educational media coordinator*
Ross, Melanie Fridl *journalist, writer*

Hallandale
Schatken, Nancy Leah *medical editor*
Yigit, Nuyan *journalist*

Heathrow
Argirion, Michael *editor*

Hialeah
Hernandez, Roland *broadcast executive*

Highland Beach
Settler, Eugene Brian *recording industry executive*
Zagoria, Sam D(avid) *reporter, government official, educator*

Hillsboro Beach
Gibbons, Celia Victoria Townsend (Mrs. John Sheldon) *editor, publisher*

Hollywood
Blakley, John Clyde *telecommunications consultant*

Holmes Beach
McCartney, James Harold *newspaper columnist, journalist, educator*

Jacksonville
Barrow, Sally Settle *media specialist, librarian*
Bedell, Elizabeth Snyder (Betty Bedell) *editor-in-chief, marketing professional*
Brown, Lloyd Harcourt, Jr., *newspaper editor*
Cannon, Carl *publishing executive*
Davis, Fred *journalist, educator*
Hartmann, Frederick William *newspaper editor*
Koeppel, Mary Sue *communications educator, writer*
Kress, Mary Elizabeth *retired newspaper editor*
Lehmbeck, John Pierce *journalist*
Vincent, Norman Fuller *broadcast executive*
Walters, John Sherwood *retired newspaperman*

Key Biscayne
Pope, John Edwin, III, *newspaper sports editor, columnist*
Smith, Harrison Harvey *journalism consultant*

Kissimmee
Cody, Aldus Morrill *journalist, retired editor, typographer*

Lake Worth
Asher, Kathleen May *communications educator*
Pecker, David J. *magazine publishing company executive*

Longboat Key
Gilbert, Hamlin Miller, Jr., *publishing executive*

Longwood
O'Keefe, Maurice Timothy *editor, writer, photographer, educator*

Merritt Island
Klass, Philip Julian *technical journalist, electrical engineer*

Miami
Alperin, Stanley I. *publisher, writer, editor, consultant*
Balmaseda, Liz *columnist*
Barry, Dave *columnist, author*
Birsh, Arthur Thomas *publishing executive*
Black, Creed Carter *newspaper executive*
Chapman, Alvah Herman, Jr., *newspaper executive*
Dahlburg, John-Thor Theodore *newspaper correspondent*
de Leon, Lidia Maria *magazine editor*
Diaz, Alan *photojournalist*
Dickey, Arden *newspaper publishing executive*
Doane, Harold Everett *recording executive*
Fichtner, Margaria *journalist*
Fiedler, Tom *editor-in-chief*
Garvin, Glenn *journalist, writer*
Hampton, John Lewis *retired newspaper editor*
Ibarguen, Alberto *newspaper executive*
Lawrence, David, Jr., *journalist*
Lew, Salvador *radio station executive*
Lewis, John Milton *cable television company executive*
McSwan, Angus *news agency executive*
Miller, Gene Edward *newspaper reporter and editor*
Muir, Helen *journalist*
O'Bryon, Linda Elizabeth *television station executive*
Pitts, Leonard Garvey, Jr., *columnist, writer*
Russell, James Webster, Jr., *newspaper editor, columnist*
Savage, James Francis *editor*
Terilli, Samuel A., Jr., *newspaper publishing executive*
Walsh, Kevin *newspaper editor*
Wax, William Edward *photojournalist*

Miami Beach
Roseman, Martin Richard *publisher, consultant, lecturer*

Naples
Blevins, Charles Russell *publishing executive*
Burdick, Robert W. *newspaper editor*
Clapp, Roger Howland *retired publishing executive*
Clarke, John Patrick *retired newspaper publisher*
Cobb, Brian Eric *broadcast executive*
Dill, John Francis *retired publishing company executive*
Penniman, Nicholas Griffith, IV, *retired newspaper publisher*
Wyant, Corbin A. *newspaper publisher*

North Palm Beach
Edwards, William James *broadcast executive*
Lavine, Alan *columnist, writer*

North Port
Coe, Laurie Lynne Barker *photojournalist, artist*
Hill, Wallace Harry *sports television consultant*

Ocala
Stock, Stephen Michael *broadcast journalist*

Orlando
Boyar, Jay Mitchell *film critic*
Bredin, Brenda Ann *communications educator*
Dunn, William Bruna, III, *journalist*
Healy, Jane Elizabeth *newspaper editor*
Maupin, Elizabeth Thatcher *theater critic*
Potter, Ronald Neal, Jr., *newspaper distribution specialist*
Waltz, Kathleen M. *publishing executive*
Waltz, Kathy *publishing executive*

Palm Beach
Monath, Norman *publishing company executive*
Pryor, Hubert *editor, writer*
Willis, Clayton *broadcaster, author, former government official, educator, arts consultant*

Palm Beach Gardens
Rigby, Paul Crispin *artist, cartoonist*

Palm Coast
Franco, Annemarie Woletz *editor*

Palm Harbor
Barker, Larry Lee *communications educator*

Parrish
Wood, Rev. Dr. Benton *retired editor, priest*

Pensacola
Bowden, Jesse Earle *newspaper editor, author, cartoonist, journalism educator*
Ivey, Denise H. *publishing executive*

Pensacola Beach
Jenkins, Louis (Woody) *television executive, state legislator*

Pompano Beach
Roen, Sheldon R. *publisher, psychologist*

Port Saint Lucie
Sommers, Robert Thomas *editor, publisher, author*

Punta Gorda
Miles, Frank Charles *retired newspaper executive*

Saint Augustine
Nolan, Joseph Thomas *journalism educator, communications consultant*

Saint Petersburg
Barnes, Andrew Earl *newspaper executive*
Belich, John Patrick, Sr., *journalist*
Corty, Andrew P. *publishing executive*
Favre, Gregory *publishing executive*
Haiman, Robert James *newspaper editor, journalism educator, media consultant, media critic, expert witness*
Hooker, Robert Wright *journalist*
Johnson, Edna Ruth *editor*
Leavell, William A. *publisher, editor*
Martin, Susan Taylor *newspaper editor*
Naughton, James Martin *journalist*
Patterson, Eugene Corbett *retired editor, publisher*
Petty, Marty *publishing executive*
Pittman, Robert Turner *retired newspaper editor*
Tash, Paul Clifford *editor, publishing executive*

Sanford
Scott, Mellouise Jacqueline *retired media specialist*

Sanibel
Ray, Charles Albert *photojournalist*

Sarasota
Allen, George Howard *publishing management consultant*
Hughes, Allen *music critic*
Marino, Eugene Louis *publishing company executive*
North, Marjorie Mary *columnist*

Proffitt, Waldo, Jr., *newspaper editor*
Stevens, Elisabeth Goss (Mrs. Robert Schleussner Jr.) *writer, journalist, graphic artist*
Tennant, Diane P. *editor*
Wetstone, Janet Meyerson *designer, journalist*

Satellite Beach
Covault, Craig *editor*

Sebring
DeWitt, Carol A. *publishing executive, writer*

Tallahassee
Ash, Jim C. *news service executive*
Dadisman, Joseph Carrol *newspaper executive*
Grier, Barbara G. (Gene Damon) *editor, lecturer, writer*
Morgan, Lucy Ware *journalist*
Pettijohn, Fred Phillips *retired newspaper executive, consultant*
Sanchez, Robert Francis *journalist*

Tampa
Barrow, Lionel Ceon, Jr., *communications and marketing consultant*
Culpepper, Mary Kay *publishing executive*
Denton, Frank M. *newspaper editor*
Fernandez, Yolanda *newscaster*
Friedlander, Edward Jay *journalist, educator*
Guyardo, Gayle *newscaster*
Maher, Irene *newscaster*
Prest, Nerissa *newscaster*
Reed, Donna Marie *editor, newspaper*
Roberts, Edwin Albert, Jr., *newspaper editor, journalist*
Schaible, Stacie *newscaster*
Sharp, Robert R. *publishing executive*
Sierens, Gayle *newscaster*
Thelen, Gil *newspaper publisher*
Tully, Darrow *newspaper publisher*
Weaver, Janet S. *newspaper editor*
Weaver, Steven M. *publishing executive*
Witwer, Bruce *former newspaper editor*

Tarpon Springs
Leisner, Anthony Baker *publishing company executive*

Venice
Corrigan, William Thomas *retired broadcast news executive*

Vero Beach
Parkyn, John William *editor, writer, columnist*

West Palm Beach
Bergmann, Arthur M. *writer, former county official, former newspaperman*
Passy, Charles *arts critic*
Pedersen, Paul Mark *sportswriter, educator, columnist*
Rukeyser, M. S., Jr., *television consultant, writer*
Sears, Edward Milner, Jr., *newspaper editor*

Winter Haven
Benton, Obie Folsom *publishing executive, writer*

GEORGIA

Athens
Agee, Warren Kendall *journalism educator*
Feldman, Edmund Burke *art critic*
Greenman, John Frederick *newspaper executive*

Atlanta
Allen, Natalie *cable news anchor*
Anstrom, Decker *broadcast executive*
Berry, Dennis *newspaper publishing executive*
Bisher, James Furman *journalist, writer*
Bruner, Michael Lane *communications educator*
Campbell, Colin McLeod *journalist*
Chambers, Anne Cox *newspaper executive, former diplomat*
Charles, Cory Anne *television guest booking director*
Clark, Gary *newspaper editor*
Clayton, Xernona *media executive*
Connelly, Terrence John, Sr., *television and cable station executive*
Davis, Amanda *newscaster*
Davis, Sterling Evan *television executive*
Dobson, Bridget McColl Hursley *television executive, writer*
Dupri, Jermaine *music company executive, music producer*
Ellis, Elmo Israel *broadcast executive, consultant, columnist*
Evans, Gail Hirschorn *television news executive*
Fortin, Judy *cable news anchor*
Furnad, V. Robert (Bob Furnad) *television news executive*
Grogan, Paula Cataldi *newspaper editor*
Grubic, Adrianne *journalist*
Hiett, Joe *publishing executive, writer, editor*
Holsendolph, Ernest *newspaper editor*
Johnson, W. Thomas, Jr., *media executive*
Jones, J. Kenley *journalist*
Kaufman, Monica *newscaster*
Kennedy, James C. *publishing and media executive*
Kintzel, Roger S. *publishing executive*
Kloer, Philip Baldwin *popular culture critic*
Landess, Mike (Malcolm Lee Landess III) *television news anchorman*
Martin, Ron *newspaper editor-in-chief*
Merdek, Andrew Austin *publishing/media executive, lawyer*
Neil, Robert F. *broadcast executive*
O'Leary, Robert C. *publishing and media executive*
Polk, James Ray *journalist*
Puckett, Susan *newspaper editor*
Robelot, Jane *anchor*
Roth, Teresa Ann *broadcast executive*
Sack, Kevin *news correspondent*
Schwartz, Sandy *publishing executive*
Scott, Marian Alexis *journalist*
Simao, Paul *news agency executive*
Sloan, Mary Jean *retired media specialist*
Smith, Jay *publishing executive*
Stewart, Michael McFadden *professional speaker*
Teepen, Thomas Henry *newspaper editor, journalist*
Toner, Michael F. *journalist*
Tucker, Cynthia Anne *journalist*
Vadlamani, Suchita *newscaster*
Wallace, Julia Diane *newspaper editor*
Walter, John *newspaper editor*
Ward, Janet Lynn *magazine editor, sports wire reporter*
Waters, Lou *anchorman, correspondent*
Whitt, Richard Ernest *reporter*
Whitworth, Wendy Walker *cable network executive*
Wilson, Debora J. *broadcast executive*
Wussler, Robert Joseph *broadcasting executive, media consultant*

Augusta
Morris, William Shivers, III, *newspaper executive*

Barnesville
Wilcox, Rhonda V. *media studies educator*

Clarkesville
Dowden, Thomas Clark *telecommunication executive*

Columbus
Siddall, Pam *publishing executive*

Decatur
Knight, Walker Leigh *editor, publisher, clergyman*
Shaw, Jeanne Osborne *editor, poet*

Fayetteville
Turnipseed, Barnwell Rhett, III, *journalist, public relations consultant*

Fort Valley
Archer, Lloyd Daniel *communications educator*

Jekyll Island
Bentley, James Luther *former journalist*
McKinley, Douglas Webster (Webb McKinley) *consultant*

Loganville
Daly, Joe Ann Godown *publishing company executive*

Mableton
Rowe, Bonnie Gordon *music company executive*

Macon
McQueen, Michael Anthony *journalism educator*
Savage, Randall Ernest *journalist*

Marietta
Dunwoody, Kenneth Reed *magazine and book editor*
Hays, Robert William *communications consultant, educator, writer*
Opre, Thomas Edward *retired editor, retired film company executive*

Oxford
Sitton, Claude Fox *newspaper editor*

Richmond Hill
Budde, Neil Frederick *publishing company executive, editor, publisher*

Roswell
Peterson, Donald Robert *magazine editor, vintage automobile consultant*

Savannah
Edeawo, Gale Sky *publishing company executive, writer*
Gusby, Kim *newscaster*
Parker, Sheila *newscaster*
Thorne, Kristan *newscaster*
Tyus-Shaw, Tina *newscaster*
Wilder, Ginger *newscaster*

Watkinsville
Williams, Vivian (Vinnie) Marie *publishing executive, editor, writer*

HAWAII

Honolulu
Black, Cobey *journalist*
Flanagan, John Michael *editor, publisher*
Gatti, Jim *editor*
Jellinek, Roger *editor*
Keyes, Saundra Elise *newspaper editor*
Platte, Mark *editor*
Rexner, Romulus *publishing executive*
Sakamoto, Gordon *newspaper editor*
Shapiro, David *newspaper editor*
Simonds, John Edward *retired newspaper editor*
Sparks, Robert William *retired publishing executive*
Tehranian, Majid *political economy and communications educator*

Kahului
Yamamoto, Irwin Toraki *editor, publishing executive*

Kailua
Bone, Robert William *writer*

Kaneohe
McGlaughlin, Thomas Howard *publisher, retired naval officer, marine surveyor*

IDAHO

Boise
Boren, Robert Reed *communications educator*

Idaho Falls
Harris, Darryl Wayne *publishing executive*

McCall
Romano, Michael *publishing executive, consultant*

Moscow
Anderson, Clifton Einar *writer, communications consultant*

Sandpoint
Bowne, Martha Hoke *publishing consultant*

ILLINOIS

Arlington Heights
Baumann, Daniel E. *publishing executive*
Lampinen, John A. *newspaper editor*
Ray, Douglas Kent *newspaper executive*

Barrington
Bash, Philip Edwin *publishing executive*

Bartlett
Markle, Sandra *publishing company executive*

Belleville
Berkley, Gary Lee *newspaper publisher*
Couch, Jeffry *editor*
Richmond, Richard Thomas *journalist*
Tebbe, Jay *publishing executive*

Berwyn
Forst, Edmund Charles, Jr., *communications educator, administrator, consultant*

Bloomington
Merwin, Davis Underwood *newspaper executive*

Buffalo Grove
Kuennen, Thomas Gerard *journalist*

Carol Stream
Franzen, Janice Marguerite Gosnell *magazine editor*
Taylor, Kenneth Nathaniel *publishing executive, writer*

Champaign
Gajda, Amy *columnist, educator, writer*
Hansen, Kathryn Gertrude *editor, former state official*
Kroner, Fred L. *journalist*
McCulloh, Judith Marie *editor*
Meyer, August Christopher, Jr., *broadcasting company executive, lawyer*
Pierce, Walter J. *publishing executive*
Schiller, Daniel Toby *communications educator*
Turquette, Frances Bond *editor*
Watts, Robert Allan *publisher, lawyer*
Yates, Ronald Eugene *newspaper editor, journalist, educator, author*

Chicago
Adams, Rosemary Kathleen *publishing executive*
Agema, Gerald Walton *publishing executive*
Ahern, Mary Ann *reporter*
Allen, Richard Blose *legal editor, lawyer*
Anderson, Jon Stephen *newswriter*
Anderson, Karl Stephen *editor*
Baca, Stacey *newscaster*
Barr, Emily L. *television station executive*
Barron, John *publishing executive*
Bratcher, Juanita *journalist*
Breen, Neil Thomas *publishing executive*
Brock, Kathy *newscaster*
Brooks, Marion *newscaster*
Brotman, Barbara Louise *columnist, writer*
Brumback, Charles Tiedtke *retired newspaper executive*
Burns, Diann *newscaster*
Burton, Cheryl *newscaster*
Callaway, Karen A(lice) *journalist*
Camper, John Jacob *speech writer*
Cappo, Joseph C. *journalist, writer*
Childers, Mary Ann *newscaster*
Claiborne, William *journalist*
Connors, Dorsey *television and radio commentator, newspaper columnist*
Cooke, Michael *editor-in-chief*
Cooper, Ilene Linda *magazine editor, author*
Cross, Robert Clark *journalist*
Cruickshank, John Douglas *publishing executive*
Curwen, Randall William *journalist, editor*
Darby, Edwin Wheeler *retired newspaper financial columnist*
Dee, Ivan Richard *book publisher*
DeLong, Ray *editor*
Dold, Robert Bruce *journalist*
Eastabrook, Dianne *news correspondent*
Ebert, Roger Joseph *film critic*
Essex, Joseph Michael *visual communication planner*
Evans, Mariwyn *periodical editor*
Feder, Robert *television and radio columnist*
Ferguson, Renee *news correspondent, reporter*
Fetridge, Clark Worthington *publishing executive*
Flanagan, Sylvia *editor*
Flock, Jeffrey Charles *news bureau chief*
Francuch, Paul Charles *broadcast journalist*
Fuller, Jack William *writer, publishing executive*
Gomez, Sylvia *newscaster*
Grant, Dennis *newspaper publishing executive*
Grumman, Cornelia *newswriter*
Guillen, Alita (Alita Haytayan) *newscaster*
Hallinan, Joseph Thomas *journalist, reporter*
Hano, Randy *publishing executive*
Harvey, Paul *news commentator, author, columnist*
Hast, Adele *editor, historian*
Hefner, Christie Ann *multi-media entertainment executive*
Hill, Darlene *newscaster*
Hlavacek, Roy George *publishing executive, magazine editor, association executive*
Hsu, Judy *newscaster*
Huntley, Robert Stephen *newspaper editor*
Idol, Anna Catherine *magazine editor*
Iglauer, Bruce *record company executive*
Jones, Christopher N. *journalist, educator*
Jones, Linda *communications educator*
Jordan, Karen *newscaster*
Judge, Bernard Martin *editor, publisher*
Kelly, Curtis Hartt *retired publishing executive*
Kelly, Maura Anne *reporter*
Kim, Daniel J. *publishing executive, editor*
King, Jennifer Elizabeth *editor*
Kisor, Henry Du Bois *newspaper editor, critic, columnist, writer*
Klatt, Wayne Roy *editor, writer*
Klaviter, Helen Lothrop *magazine editor*
Koppes, Steven Nelson *science writer, editor*
Kotulak, Ronald *newspaper science writer*
Kramer, Weezie Crawford *former broadcast executive*
Krueger, Bonnie Lee *editor, writer*
Kwan, Nesita *newscaster*
Leckey, Andrew A. *financial columnist*
Lenehan, Michael Daniel *editor, writer*
Lipinski, Ann Marie *newspaper editor*
Loesch, Katharine Taylor (Mrs. John George Loesch) *communication and theatre educator*
Longworth, Richard Cole *journalist*
Lythcott, Marcia A. *newspaper editor*
Madigan, John William *publishing executive*
Martinez, Natalie *newscaster*
McNally, Andrew, IV, *publishing executive, director*
Melnick, Jane Fisher *journalist, educator, photographer, literature educator*
Migala, Lucyna J. *journalist, arts administrator, radio station executive*
Nault, William Henry *publishing executive*
Needleman, Barbara *newspaper executive*
Neubauer, Charles Frederick *investigative reporter*
Oakes, Fred D. *editor*
O'Dell, James E. *newspaper publishing executive*
O'Shea, James *managing editor*
Peerman, Dean Gordon *magazine editor*
Pender, Nancy *newscaster*
Pendley, Kevin *communication media executive*
Peres, Judith May *journalist*
Perez, Sylvia *newscaster, reporter*
Pilchen, Ira A. *editor*
Pitt, Judson Hamilton *publisher, author*
Plotnick, Harvey Barry *publishing executive*
Plotnik, Arthur *author, columnist*
Pope, Kerig Rodgers *magazine executive*
Price, Henry Escoe *broadcast executive*
Primm, Earl Russell, III, *publishing executive*
Reardon, Patrick Thomas *reporter*
Reindl, James *newspaper editor*
Rice, Linda Johnson *publishing executive*
Rice, William Edward *journalist*
Rico, Maria L. *publishing executive*
Robinson, Robin *newscaster*
Roeser, Thomas Francis *columnist, commentator*
Rosati, Allison *newscaster*
Roth, Robert A. *newspaper executive*
Rynkiewicz, Stephen Michael *journalist*
Scanlan, Thomas Cleary *publishing executive, editor*
Schmeltzer, John C. *financial writer*
Smith, Sam *columnist, author*
Sneed, Michael (Michele Sneed) *columnist*
Towers, Kenneth Dale *journalism educator*
True, Alison Cochran *newspaper editor*
Tyner, Howard A. *publishing executive, newspaper editor, journalist*
Veres, Bob *editor*
von Rhein, John Richard *music critic, editor*
Vukas, Ronald *publishing executive*
Wade, Nigel *former editor in chief*
Wasiolek, Edward *literary critic, language and literature educator*
Weinberg, Lila Shaffer *writer, editor*
Weintraub, Joseph Barton *publishing executive*
Wier, Patricia Ann *publishing executive, consultant*
Wille, Lois Jean *retired newspaper editor*
Wilson, Gahan *cartoonist, author*
Winker, Margaret A. *editor*
Winnecke, Joycelyn *editor*
Wolfe, Sheila A. *journalist*
Working, Russell Craig *reporter, writer*
Wright, Sharon *reporter*
Youngman, Owen Ralph *newspaper executive*
Zekman, Pamela Lois (Mrs. Fredric Soll) *reporter*
Zwecker, William Rene, Jr., (Bill Zwecker) *newspaper columnist, television reporter*

Crystal Lake
Keller, William Francis *publishing consultant*

Des Plaines
Henrikson, Lois Elizabeth *photojournalist*

Elmhurst
Pruter, Margaret Franson *editor*

Evanston
Borcover, Alfred Seymour *journalist*
Buck, Tom *journalist*
Deming, Thomas Edward *publishing executive*
Downing, Joan Forman *editor, writer*
Felknor, Bruce Lester *editorial consultant, writer*
Galvin, Kathleen Malone *communications educator*
Jacobs, Norman Joseph *publishing company executive*
Jones, Robert Russell *magazine editor*
Kuenster, John Joseph *editor*
McCarron, John Francis *editor*
Otwell, Ralph Maurice *retired newspaper editor*
Peck, Abraham *editor, writer, educator, media consultant*
Wefler, Wilson Daniel *management consultant*
Wilhelm, Frank Leo *publisher, writer*
Ziomek, Jonathan S. *journalist, educator*

Glen Ellyn
Beers, V(ictor) Gilbert *publishing executive*

Glenview
Mabley, Jack *newspaper columnist, communications consultant*
Martin, James Frederick *media consultant*

Greenville
Flowers, Creole Duane *publishing executive*

Highland Park
Johnson, Curtis Lee *publisher, editor, writer*
Pattis, Mark R. *publishing company executive*
Pattis, S. William *publishing executive*
Rutenberg-Rosenberg, Sharon Leslie *retired journalist*

Huntley
Balk, Alfred William *journalist*

Kenilworth
Cook, Stanton R. *media company executive*
Ewing, Raymond Peyton *educator, author, management consultant*
Hayes, M. M.M. *publishing executive*

La Salle
Vickrey, Robert Fischer *publishing executive, broadcast executive*

Lake Forest
Schulze, Franz, Jr., *critic, educator*

Lake In The Hills
Kay, Dennis Matthew *retired publishing company official*

Libertyville
True, Raymond Stephen *writer, editor, analyst, consultant*

Litchfield
Jackson, David Alonzo *retired newspaper editor*

Mount Vernon
Withers, W. Russell, Jr., *broadcast executive*

Naperville
Spiotta, Raymond Herman *editor*

Northbrook
Pesmen, Sandra (Mrs. Harold William Pesmen) *editor*
Snader, Jack Ross *publishing company executive*

Northfield
Hotze, Charles Wayne *publisher, printer*
Quaal, Ward Louis *broadcast executive*

Oak Brook
Biedron, Theodore John *newspaper advertising executive*

Oak Park
Bedrossian, Ursula Kay Kennedy *editor*

Oregon
Haynes, Gary Allen *photographer, journalist, newspaper editor*

Pekin
Dancey, Charles Lohman *newspaper executive*

Peoria
Harkrader, Alan Dale, Jr., *retired photojournalist*
McConnell, John Thomas *newspaper executive, publisher*
Murphy, Sharon Margaret *communications educator*

Peru
Carus, Andre Wolfgang *educational publishing firm executive*
Carus, Milton Blouke *publisher children's periodicals*

Plainfield
Cook, Bruce Lawrence *editor*
Diercks, Eileen Kay *educational media coordinator, elementary school educator*

Prospect Heights
Robinson, Martin (Marty Robinson) *television and radio broadcaster, media consultant*

River Forest
Harvey, Lynne Cooper *broadcasting executive, civic worker*

Rockford
Fleming, Thomas J. *editor, publishing executive*
Jacobi, Fredrick Thomas *newspaper publisher*

Skokie
Feinberg, Henry J. *publishing executive*
Manos, John *editor-in-chief*
Wasik, John Francis *editor, writer, publisher*
Weber, Randy *publishing executive*

Tinley Park
Flanagan, John F. *publishing executive*

University Park
McMaster, Michele *communications educator*

Urbana
Christians, Clifford Glenn *communications educator*
Dash, Leon DeCosta, Jr., *journalist*

Westmont
Hansen, Donald Marty *journalist, retired accountant*

Wheaton
Hollingsworth, Pierce *publishing executive*
Taylor, Mark Douglas *publishing executive*

Winnetka
Burke, John Edward *communications editor*

INDIANA

Bloomington
Cookman, Claude *journalist, educator*
Gough, Pauline Bjerke *magazine editor*
Hogan, Jeremy Robert *photojournalist*
Jacobi, Peter Paul *journalism educator, author*
Lee, Don Yoon *publisher, academic researcher and writer*
Schurz, Scott Clark *journalist, publisher*
Walling, Donovan Robert *educational book editor*
Weaver, David Hugh *journalism educator, communications researcher*

Cambridge City
Slonaker, Mary Joanna King *columnist*

Evansville
Pate, Jack D. *publishing executive*

Fort Wayne
Inskeep, Richard Glenn *publishing executive*
Klugman, Stephan Craig *newspaper editor*
Oxley, Ann *television executive*
Pellegrene, Thomas James, Jr., *editor, researcher*

Franklin
Nuwer, Henry Joseph (Hank Nuwer) *journalist, educator*

Greencastle
Hall, David *newspaper editor*

Hammond
Kamalipour, Yahya R. *communications educator*

Indianapolis
Adamak, M. Jeanelle *broadcast executive*
Caperton, Albert Franklin *retired newspaper editor*
Chase, Alyssa Ann *editor*
Clanin, Douglas Edward *editor, researcher*
Coffey, Charles Moore *communication research professional, writer*
Cohen, Gabriel Murrel *editor, publisher*
Comiskey, Nancy *newspaper editor*
Cortopassi, Ray *newscaster*
Fine, Pamela B. *newspaper editor*
Fleming, Marcella *journalist*
Ganote, Angela *newscaster*
Garmel, Marion Bess Simon *retired arts journalist*
Henry, Barbara A. *publishing executive*
Lee, Kristi *broadcast executive, reporter*
Lyst, John Henry *former newspaper editor*
McKeand, Patrick Joseph *newspaper publisher, educator*
Pursley, Julie *newscaster*
Raughter, John B. *editor*
Robinson, Keith *newspaper editor*
Russell, Frank Eli *retired newspaper publishing executive*
Ryerson, Dennis *editor*
Tedesco, Kristi *newscaster*
Truhan, Grace *newscaster*
Weaver, Martha *newscaster*
Weisfeld, Eric *newscaster*
Wheeler, Daniel Scott *management executive, editor*
Wright, David Burton *retired newspaper publishing company executive*

Knightstown
Richardson, Shirley Maxine *editor*

Kokomo
Hockney, Dean Wesley *editor, writer*

Martinsville
Kendall, Robert Stanton *newspaper editor, journalist, automotive executive*

Muncie
Bell, Stephen Scott (Steve Bell) *journalist, educator*

Munster
Colander, Patricia Marie *newspaper editor*
Neff, Bonita Dostal *communication development facilitator*
Potempa, Philip Matthew *journalist, columnist, communications educator*

North Manchester
Strode, Scott K. *communications educator*

South Bend
Smith, E. Berry *television and radio consultant*

Terre Haute
Chesebro, James William *communications educator*
Kondras, Holly Witten *publishing executive*

West Lafayette
Greene, John Oscar *communications educator*

IOWA

Ames
Alumbaugh, JoAnn McCalla *magazine editor*

Cedar Rapids
Keller, Eliot Aaron *broadcast executive*

Davenport
Brocka, Bruce *editor, educator, application developer*
Gottlieb, Richard Douglas *media executive*

Des Moines
Byal, Nancy Louise *food editor*
DeWulf Nickell, Karol *editor*
Gartner, Michael Gay *editor, television executive, baseball executive*
Graham, Diane E. *newspaper editor*
Kerr, William T. *publishing and broadcasting executive*
Kruidenier, David *retired newspaper executive*
Lacy, Stephen M. *broadcast and publishing executive*
Leach, Dave Francis *editor, musician*
Myers, Mary Kathleen *publishing executive*
Rhein, Dave *newspaper editor*
Sheehan, Carol Sama *magazine editor*
Stier, Mary P. *publishing executive*
Van Zante, Shirley M(ae) *magazine editor*
Witke, David Rodney *retired newspaper editor, consultant*

Mason City
Collison, Jim *publishing executive*

Mount Ayr
Smith, Howard Alan *editor, publishing executive*

Moville
Baker, Kent Alfred *broadcasting, publishing company executive*

Spirit Lake
Hedberg, Paul Clifford *broadcast executive*

West Des Moines
Burnett, Robert A. *retired publisher*

Zearing
Britten, William Harry *editor, publisher*

KANSAS

Arkansas City
Rowen, Sharon Marie *journalist, photographer*

Atchison
Lowry, Patrick Emmet *journalist*

Hutchinson
Baumer, Beverly Belle *journalist*
Buzbee, Richard Edgar *retired newspaper editor*

Iola
Lynn, Emerson Elwood, Jr., *retired newspaper editor/publisher*

Lawrence
Dickinson, William Boyd, Jr., *editorial consultant*
Hale, Richard Lee *magazine editor*
Pickett, Calder Marcus *retired journalism educator*
Simons, Dolph Collins, Jr., *newspaper executive and editor*

Manhattan
Seaton, Edward Lee *editor, publishing executive*

Marion
Meyer, Bill *publishing executive, editor*

North Newton
Snider, Marie Anna *syndicated columnist*

Olathe
Dodd, James B. *internet executive*

Overland Park
Kuppuswamy, Cathy *news analyst*

Salina
Entriken, Robert Kersey, Jr., *editor, writer*

Shawnee Mission
Martin, Donna Lee *retired publishing company executive*

Wichita
Dill, Sheri *publishing executive*
Hatteberg, Larry Merle *photojournalist*

KENTUCKY

Carlisle
Wolf, John Howell *retired publisher*

Crescent Springs
Ott, James Daniel *journalist, educator*

Fort Knox
Barnes, Larry Glen *journalist, editor, educator*

Fort Mitchell
Silvers, Gerald Thomas *retired publishing executive*

Georgetown
Allison, James Claybrooke, II, *broadcasting executive*
Chi, Keon Soo *editor, educator, researcher*

Glasgow
Knicely, Carroll Franklin *publishing executive*

Goshen
Strode, William Hall, III, *photojournalist, publisher*

Lexington
Cross, Alvin Miller (Al Cross) *journalist*
Donohew, Robert Lewis, Sr., *communications educator*
Keeling, Larry Dale *journalist*
Kelly, Timothy Michael *newspaper publisher*
Kissling, Fred Ralph, Jr., *publishing executive, insurance agency executive*

London
Giles, William Elmer *retired newspaper editor*

Louisville
Hawpe, David Vaughn *newspaper editor, journalist*
Ivory, Bennie *editor*
Lewis, Ronald Chapman *record company executive*
Manassah, Edward E. *publishing executive*
Staats, Howard E. *newspaper editor*
Towles, Donald Blackburn *retired publishing executive*

Paducah
Stice, Dwayne Lee *broadcasting company executive*

Pewee Valley
Gill, George Norman *newspaper publishing company executive*

Prospect
Shipley, Alden Peverly *broadcaster, broadcasting executive*

LOUISIANA

Alexandria
Smith, Joe Dorsey, Jr., *retired newspaper executive*

Baker
Roberson, Patt Foster *mass communications educator*

Baton Rouge
Gilmore, Clarence Percy *writer, magazine editor*
Wu, H. Denis *communications educator*

Gonzales
Young, David Nelson *media and communications consultant*

Gretna
Calhoun, Milburn *publishing executive, rare book dealer, physician*

La Place
Fiffie Proctor, JoAnn *media and technology specialist*

Lake Charles
Beam, James Carroll (Jim Beam) *retired newspaper editor*
Stacey, Truman *journalist, consultant*

New Orleans
Amoss, Walter James (Jim), III, *editor*
Ball, Millie (Mildred Porteous Ball) *editor, journalist*
Boswell, Stephanie *newscaster*
Corey, Orlin Russell *publisher, editor*
Crumley, David Oliver *publishing executive, writer, corporate executive*
Fairbairn, Kriss *newscaster*
Ferguson, Charles Austin *retired newspaper editor*
Kemp, John Randolph *journalist, writer*
Moreno, Helena *newscaster*
Orr, Margaret *newscaster*
Phelps, Ashton, Jr., *newspaper publisher*
Pope, John M. *journalist*
Roberts, Shauna S. *editor, writer*
Roesler, Robert Harry *media consultant*
Sanders, Melanie *newscaster*

Shreveport
Beaird, Charles T. *former publishing executive*
Lazarus, Allan Matthew *retired newspaper editor*
Robinson, Garry Lewin *television news executive*

Slidell
Lovell, Emily Kalled *retired journalist*

MAINE

Bangor
Warren, Richard Jordan *newspaper publisher*
Warren, Richard Kearney *newspaper publisher*

Belfast
Griffith, Patricia King *journalist*

Camden
Fisher, Craig Becker *film and television executive*

Castine
Bernstein, Lester *editorial consultant*

Chebeague Island
Traina, Albert Salvatore *publishing executive*

Damariscotta
Blake, Bud (Julian Watson) *cartoonist*

Georgetown
Ludgin, Donald Hugh *editor*

Kennebunkport
Ray, Virginia H. S. *columnist, writer*

Lincoln
Kneeland, Douglas Eugene *retired newspaper editor*

Rockland
Platt, David Day *journalist, editor*

Sebago Lake
Murray, Wallace Shordon *publisher, educator*

Sedgwick
Schroth, Thomas Nolan *editor*

Sunset
Knowlton, Leslie Brooks *journalist*

MARYLAND

Annapolis
Casey, Edward Dennis *newspaper editor*
Chambers, Ronald D. *book publishing executive*
Holston, A. Frank *retired broadcaster, communications educator*
Nelson, Charles Arthur *publishing executive, writer*

Baltimore
Broening, Walter Stephens, Jr., *journalist, history educator*
Donovan, Dianne Francys *journalist*
Dorsey, John Russell *journalist*
Franklin, Timothy A. *editor*
Giuliano, Michael Philip *arts journalist, educator*
Hirsh, Allan T., III, *book publisher*
Hirsh, Allan Thurman, Jr., *publishing executive*
Kesselring, Linda J. *medical editor, writer*
Leary, Michael Warren *journalist*
Mears, Frances R. *communications media executive*
Palmer, Denise *publishing executive*
Pollak, Lisa *columnist*
Rousuck, J. Wynn *theater critic*
Scott, Frederick Isadore, Jr., *editor, business executive*
Steinbach, Alice *journalist*
Sterne, Joseph Robert Livingston *newspaper editor, educator*
Sugg, Diana K. *reporter*
Tepper, Michael Howard *publishing company executive*
Thomas, Jacqueline Marie *journalist, editor*
Waller, Michael E. *publishing executive*

Bethesda
Brant, Donna Marie *journalist*
Chronister, Gregory Michael *newspaper editor*
Cornish, Edward Seymour *magazine editor*
English, Michela *entertainment company executive*
Frank, Richard Sanford *retired magazine editor*
Hartmann, Robert Trowbridge *newspaperman, presidential counselor*
Hendricks, John S. *broadcast executive*
Herman, Edith Carol *journalist*
Kaplan, Marjorie *broadcast executive*
Kesaris, Paul *publishing executive*
Larrabee, Donald Richard *publishing company executive*
McHale, Judith A. (Judith Ottalloran) *broadcast executive, lawyer*
Nelson, John Howard (Jack Howard Nelson) *journalist*
Olson, Lynn *editor*
Pickerell, James Howard *photojournalist*
Pratt, Dana Joseph *publishing consultant*
Schaeffer, Charles Perry *newswriter, editor*
Wagner, Cynthia Gail *editor, writer*

Cheverly
Miller, Mark Karl *journalist*

Chevy Chase
Adler, James Barron *publishing executive*
Bruno, Harold Robinson, Jr., *retired journalist, writer*
Epstein, Sidney *retired editor*
Jones, Philip Howard *broadcast journalist*
Kingsley, Nathan *journalist, consultant, educator*
Kriegsman, Alan M. *retired critic*
Shipler, David Karr *journalist, correspondent, author*
Shogan, Robert *news correspondent*
Toth, Robert Charles *retired polling consultant, journalist, writer*

College Park
Beasley, Maurine Hoffman *journalism educator, historian*
Gomery, Douglas *communications educator, writer*
Grunig, James Elmer *communications educator, researcher, public relations consultant*
Johnson, Haynes Bonner *author, journalist, television commentator*
Martin, L(eslie) John *retired journalism educator and dean*
Winik, Jay B. *writer, political scientist, consultant*

Columbia
Drummond, LaCreda Renee *journalist*

Easton
Potter, Blair Burns *editor*

Frederick
Delaplaine, George Birely, Jr., *newspaper editor, cable television executive*
Weincek, Craig James *communications educator, writer*

Gaithersburg
Wicklein, John Frederick *journalist, educator*

Garrett Park
Franklin, Benjamin A. *editor, reporter*

Hollywood
Powledge, Fred Arlius *freelance writer*

Landover
Maduka, Chikezie *journalist*

Lanham
Godwin, Mary Jo *editor, librarian consultant*
Heiserman, Alice E. *publishing executive, editor*
Lyons, James Edward *publishing executive*
Rodgers, Johnathan *broadcast executive*

Lanham Seabrook
Hill, Ben *broadcast executive*
Ojinnaka, Becky *publishing executive*

Lutherville Timonium
Cedrone, Louis Robert, Jr., *critic*

North Potomac
Lide, David Reynolds *handbook and database editor*

Odenton
Aho, Brien *photojournalist*

Owings Mills
Holdridge, Barbara *book publisher*

Potomac
Christian, John Kenton *organization executive, publisher, writer, marketing consultant*
Fox, Arthur Joseph, Jr., *editor*
Karnow, Stanley *journalist, writer*
Rehns, Marsha Lee *magazine editor, writer*

Rockville
Hoar, William Patrick *editor, author*
Kohlmeier, Louis Martin, Jr., *newspaper reporter*
Miller, Claire Ellen *children's writer, editor, educator*

Salisbury
Kleiman, Gary Howard *broadcast, advertising and cellular communications consultant*

Severna Park
Moore, John Leo, Jr., *journalist, writer, editor*

Silver Spring
Bennett, Carol(ine) Elise *retired reporter, actress*
Carson, Steven Lee *newspaper publisher*
Eiserer, Leonard Albert Carl *publishing executive*
Kurata, Phillip Cedomir *journalist*
Speights, Michael David *newsletter editor*
Vernon, Weston, III, (Wes Vernon) *broadcaster, writer, actor*

Street
Spangler, Ronald Leroy *retired television executive, aircraft executive, automobile collector*

Sunderland
Franklin, Jon Daniel *writer, journalist, educator*

Takoma Park
Conroy, Sarah Booth *columnist, writer, educator*

University Park
Beckenstein, Myron *journalist*

MASSACHUSETTS

Acton
Kittross, John Michael *retired communications educator*

Allston
Becton, Henry Prentiss, Jr., *broadcasting company executive*

Arlington
Thomas, Patricia Joanne *journalist, writer*

Bedford
Goodman, William Beehler *editor, literary agent*

Beverly
Daya, Jackie *publishing company executive*

Boston
Ackroyd, Peter Warwick *publishing company executive*
Adams, Phoebe-Lou *journalist*
Baldassano, Corinne Leslie *radio executive*
Baughman, James Carroll *information and communication educator*
Bennett, Clay *cartoonist*
Bourne, Katherine Day *journalist, educator*
Caldwell, Gail *book critic*
Cohen, Rachelle Sharon *journalist*
Collins, Monica Ann *journalist*
Convey, Kevin R. *editor*
Costello, Andrew F. *newspaper editor*
Darehshori, Nader Farhang *publishing sales executive*
Davison, Peter Hubert *editor, poet*
Donovan, Helen W. *newspaper editor*
Eder, Richard Gray *newspaper critic*
Feder, Donald Albert *syndicated columnist*
Flaherty, Lois Talbot *editor, psychiatrist, educator*
Flanders, Jefferson *publishing executive*
Foreman, Judy *journalist*
Gendron, George *magazine editor*
Gevirtz, Leslie *communications media executive*
Gibson, Barry Joseph *magazine editor*
Gilman, Richard H. *newspaper publishing executive*
Grimes, Heilan Yvette *publishing executive*
Grossfeld, Stan *newspaper photography executive, author*
Harris, Roy Jay, Jr., *editor, business journalist*
Hoffman, Stanley Marc *editor, composer*
Hostetter, Amos Barr, Jr., *cable television executive*
Kauffman, Godfrey *former newspaper publishing executive*
Kimball, George Edward, III, *sports columnist*
Klarfeld, Jonathan Michael *journalism educator*
Krakoff, Robert Leonard *publishing executive*
Kuttner, Robert Louis *editor, columnist, writer*
Larkin, Alfred Sinnott, Jr., *newspaper editor*
Larkin, Michael John *newspaper editor, journalist*
Lawrence, Merloyd Ludington *editor*
Lee, Donald Young (Don Lee) *publishing executive, editor, writer*
Leland, Timothy *retired newspaper executive*
Lisman, Eric *publishing executive, lawyer*
Lyman, Henry *retired publisher, marine fisheries consultant*
Manning, Robert Joseph *editor*
Mason, Charles Ellis, III, *magazine editor*
McGinn, Daniel F. *journalist*
Menzies, Ian Stuart *newspaper editor*
Morris, Gerald Douglas *newspaper editor*
Moyes, Norman Barr *journalism educator, writer, photographer*
Norment, Eric Stuart *newspaper editor*
Purcell, Patrick Joseph *newspaper publisher*
Raeder, William Munro *publishing executive*
Schulz, John Joseph *communications educator*
Schwartz, Lloyd *music critic, poet*
Stevens, Marilyn Ruth *editor*
Strothman, Wendy Jo *book publisher*
Taylor, Stephen Emlyn *publishing executive*
Taylor, William Osgood *newspaper executive*
Whitworth, William A. *magazine editor*

Cambridge
Aronson, Michael Andrew *editor*
Berners-Lee, Tim *web inventor*
Effron, Seth Alan *editor, journalist*
Emsley, Sarah Louise Baxter *critic, educator*
Giles, Robert Hartmann *journalist, educator*
Goodman, Ellen Holtz *journalist*
Jones, Alex S. *journalist, writer, broadcaster*
Lenger, John Richard *journalism educator*
Nordell, Hans Roderick *journalist, retired editor*
Urbanowski, Frank *publishing company executive*
Wilcox, Maud *editor*

Chicopee
Elleman, Barbara *editor*

Cohasset
Replogle, David Robert *publishing company executive*

Concord
Wang, Arthur Woods *retired publisher*

Dorchester
Baron, Martin *editor*
Brelis, Matthew Dean Burns *journalist*

Dover
Salhany, Lucille S. *broadcast executive*

Easton
Chichetto, James William *editor, educator*

Forestdale
Bissell, Phil (Charles P. Bissell) *cartoonist*

Framingham
Johnson, Maryfran *editor*
Kenealy, Patrick *publishing company executive*
Levy, Joseph Louis *publishing company executive*
Ostrow, Robert *publishing executive*
Twombly, Stephen Doane *magazine publisher*

Franklin
Maril, David C. *editor*

Gardner
Koller, John Dryden *media educator, scriptwriter*

Hudson
Osoff, Jeffrey Arlin *media executive*

Hyannis
Makkay, Albert *broadcast executive*
Makkay, Maureen Ann *broadcast executive*

Jamaica Plain
Howland, Llewellyn, III, *publishing executive, writer*

Leeds
Deane, James Garner *magazine editor, conservationist*

Lincoln
Nenneman, Richard Arthur *retired publishing executive*

Marblehead
Quigley, Stephen Howard *executive editor*

Mashpee
Porter, John Stephen *retired television executive*

Needham
Greenway, Hugh Davids Scott *journalist*
Kardon, Brian *music company executive*
Meisner, Mary Jo *editor*

Newton
Brown, Michael Robert *communications educator, poet*
Hume, Ellen Hunsberger *media analyst, journalist*
Knez, Brian J. *publishing executive*

North Adams
Thurston, Donald Allen *broadcast executive*

North Attleboro
Reed, Douglas H. *editor, publishing executive*

Northampton
Garvey, Richard Conrad *journalist*

Pittsfield
Rich, Philip Dewey *publishing executive*

Plymouth
Flood, H(ulda) Gay *editor, consultant*

Quincy
Lippincott, Joseph P. *photojournalist, educator*

Roslindale
Driscoll, Kathleen J. *writer*

Salisbury
Berggren, Dick *editor*

Sharon
Blaszkowsky, David M. *publishing executive*

South Deerfield
Bete, Channing Lindquist, Jr., *publishing company executive*

Springfield
Gordon, Ronni Anne *journalist*
Haggerty, Thomas Francis *newspaper editor*
McDermott, Larry Arnold *newspaper publisher, newspaper editor*
Morse, John M. *book publishing executive*
Starr, David *newspaper editor, publisher*

Sudbury
Hillery, Mary Jane Larato *columnist, television personality, television producer, writer, military officer*

Waltham
Davis, Robert J. *internet company executive*

Wayland
Huff, William Braid *retired publishing company executive*

Wellesley
Myers, Arthur B. *journalist*

Wellfleet
Limpitlaw, John Donald *retired publishing executive, clergyman*

West Falmouth
King, Richard Hood *newspaper executive*

Westfield
Gardner, Thomas Neville *communications educator*

Weston
Sanzone, Donna S. *publishing executive*

Westport
Gormley, Robert John *publishing executive*

Westwood
Borgman, George Allan *journalist*

Williamstown
Bleezarde, Thomas Warren *retired magazine editor*

Winchester
Ockerbloom, Richard C. *newspaper executive*

Woburn
Lundquist, Eric *editor-in-chief*

Worcester
Bennett, Bruce S. *publishing executive*

MICHIGAN

Ann Arbor
Beaver, Frank Eugene *communication educator, film critic and historian*
Bedard, Patrick Joseph *editor, writer, consultant*
Csere, Csaba *magazine editor*
Eisendrath, Charles Rice *journalism educator, farmer, consultant*
Fitzsimmons, Joseph John *publishing executive*
Hessler, David William *information and multimedia systems educator*
Lewis, Robert Enzer *lexicographer, educator*
Markman, Jon *business journalist*
Martin, Bruce James *newspaper editor*

Beverly Hills
Dalka-Prysby, Sandra Sue *news correspondent*

Birmingham
Berman, Laura *journalist, writer*
Moss, Charles Joseph, III, (Chuck Moss) *writer, broadcaster*

Bloomfield Hills
James, William Ramsay *broadcast executive*

Bloomfield Township
Brown, Lynette Ralya *journalist, publicist*

Dearborn
Hogan, Brian Joseph *editor*

Detroit
Albom, Mitch David *sports columnist*
Alpert, Daniel *television executive*
Ashenfelter, David Louis *reporter*
Bennett, Grace *publishing executive*
Bullard, George *newspaper editor*
Burzynski, Susan Marie *newspaper editor*
Colby, Joy Hakanson *critic*
Diebolt, Judith *newspaper editor*
Fladung, Thom *managing editor*
Hill, Charles *newspaper editor*
Hutton, Carole Leigh *newspaper editor*
James, Sheryl Teresa *journalist*
Kohn, Martin F. *theater critic, journalist*
Laughlin, Nancy *newspaper editor*
Parry, Dale D. *newspaper editor*
Smyntek, John Eugene, Jr., *editor*
Stark, Susan R. *film critic*
Taylor, Jeff *reporter, editor*
Teagan, John Gerard *newspaper executive*
Vega, Frank J. *newspaper publishing executive*
White, Joseph B. *reporter*

East Lansing
Freedman, Eric *journalist, educator, writer*
Greenberg, Bradley Sander *communications educator*
Ralph, David Clinton *communications educator*

Farmington Hills
Bryfonski, Dedria Anne *publishing company executive*
Olendorf, Donna *editor*

Flint
Samuel, Roger D. *newspaper publishing executive*

Grand Rapids
Baker, Richard Lee *book publishing company executive*
Bolinder, Scott W. *publishing company executive*
Fortner, Robert Steven *media educator, researcher*
Kaczmarczyk, Jeffrey Allen *journalist, classical music critic*
Kregel, James R. *publishing executive*
Mayo, David Wayne *sportswriter*
Ryskamp, Bruce E. *publishing executive*

Grosse Pointe
Hill, Draper *editorial cartoonist*
Ruffner, Frederick G., Jr., *book publisher*
Whittaker, Jeanne Evans *former newspaper columnist*

Grosse Pointe Farms
Christian, Edward Kieren *broadcasting station executive*

Grosse Pointe Park
Elsila, David August *editor*

Grosse Pointe Woods
McWhirter, Glenna Suzanne (Nickie McWhirter) *retired newspaper columnist*

Kalamazoo
Jamison, Frank Raymond *independent video producer, retired communications educator*

Lansing
Brown, Nancy Field *editor*

Manistee
Trussell, Charles Tait *columnist*

Marquette
Manning, Robert Hendrick *media consultant*

Mears
Binder, L. James *retired magazine editor, journalist*

Mount Pleasant
Petrick, Michael Joseph *journalism educator*

Petoskey
Winter, Kenneth Michael *editor, publishing executive, educator*

Pontiac
Moss, Edward R. *publishing executive*

Royal Oak
Bohy, Ric *magazine editor, consultant, broadcast commentator*

Saginaw
Chaffee, Paul Charles *newspaper editor*

Saint Clair Shores
Shine, Neal James *journalism educator, former newspaper editor, publisher*

Southfield
Catallo, Heather *newscaster*
Dickerson, Brian *columnist*
Gayle, Monica *broadcast journalist*
Makupson, Amyre Porter *television station executive*
Margolis, Sherry *newscaster*
Stinger, Fanchon *newscaster*
Thomas, Judy Janet *reporter, health services professional*

Sturgis
Hair, Robert Eugene *editor, writer, historian*

PROFESSIONAL INDEX 5561 COMMUNICATIONS MEDIA

Troy
Moore, Oliver Semon, III, *publishing executive, consultant*

Waterford
Hallemann, James Raymond *media specialist, educator*

West Bloomfield
Starr, Monica *company executive*

Ypsilanti
Evans, Gary Lee *communications educator and consultant*
Okafor, Victor O. *journalist, educator*

MINNESOTA

Belle Plaine
Townsend, C. Edward *publishing executive*

Bloomington
Larson, Michael Len *newspaper editor, hospital administrator, publishing executive*

Circle Pines
Barott, Pat Robert *broadcast technician*

Duluth
Gruver, Nancy *publishing executive*
Latto, Lewis M. *broadcasting company executive*

Eagan
Collier, Ken O. *editor*

Eden Prairie
Thompson, Sally Ann *editor*

Edina
Bisping, Bruce Henry *photojournalist*
Steinberg, Michael *music critic, educator*

Minneapolis
Buoen, Roger *newspaper editor*
Cope, Lewis *journalist*
Cowles, John, Jr., *publisher, women's sports promoter*
Crosby, Jacqueline Garton *newspaper editor, journalist*
Flanagan, Barbara *journalist*
Gyllenhaal, Anders *publishing executive, editor*
Haverkamp, Judson *editor*
Johnson, Gary L. *publishing executive*
Jones, Will(iam) (William Arnold Jones) *writer, former newspaper columnist*
Kramer, Joel Roy *journalist, newspaper executive*
Laing, Karel Ann *magazine publishing executive*
Lerner, Harry Jonas *publishing company executive*
Marshall, Sherrie *newspaper editor*
McDaniel, Jan *television station executive*
McGuire, Tim *editor*
Meador, Ron *newspaper editor, writer*
Miller, Alan M. *editor, educator, writer*
Moyer, Keith J. *publishing executive*
Murphy, Joseph Edward, Jr., *broadcast executive*
Pyle, Dave *newspaper editor*
Randall, Roger David *publishing executive*
Roloff, Marvin L. *publishing executive*
Salyer, Stephen Lee *media executive*
Scallen, Thomas Kaine *broadcast executive*
Watson, Catherine Elaine *journalist*
Werner, Bill *communication media executive*
Werner, Lawrence H. *editor*
White, Robert James *newspaper columnist*
Wright, Frank Gardner *retired newspaper editor*
Zelickson, Sue *newspaper and cookbook editor, television reporter and host, food consultant*

Minnetonka
Weisman, Eric *music company executive*

New Hope
Johnson, David Paul *publishing executive, writer*

Rochester
Shampo, Marc Anthony *retired medical editor, writer*

Saint Cloud
Porter, Laurinda Wright *communications educator, consultant*

Saint Joseph
Rowland, Howard Ray *mass communications educator*

Saint Louis Park
Harstad, Carl Leslie *consultant, writer*
Kalman, Marc *radio station executive*

Saint Paul
Amidon, Paul Charles *publishing executive*
Blanchard, J. A., III, *publishing executive*
Bree, Marlin Duane *publisher, author*
Fruehling, Rosemary Therese *publishing executive, author*
Griffin, Michael Scott *communications educator, writer*
Hubbard, Stanley Stub *broadcast executive*
Kling, William Hugh *broadcast executive*
Maitland, Margaret Todd *editor*
Oliver, Marlys Mae *retired editor, writer*
Sadowski, Richard J. *former publishing executive*
Straight, Cathy *editor*
Wehrwein, Austin Carl *newspaper reporter, editor, writer*
Weschcke, Carl Llewellyn *publishing executive*

Two Harbors
McMillion, John Macon *retired newspaper publisher*

West Saint Paul
Cento, William Francis *retired newspaper editor*

MISSISSIPPI

Biloxi
Weeks, Roland, Jr., *newspaper publisher*

Clinton
Fortenberry, Jack Clifton (Cliff Fortenberry) *mass communications educator*

Greenwood
Jones, Carolyn Ellis *publishing executive*

Hattiesburg
Hickman, Ronald Lee *media broker, broadcast executive*

Jackson
Anderson, Roslyn *newscaster*
Frazel-Lasseter, Cheryl *newscaster*
Lindsay, Arnold Arness *reporter*
Petty, David *newspaper editor*
Segal, Jane *newscaster*
Srinivasan, Seetha *publishing company executive*
Thompson, Marsha *newscaster*
Wade, Maggie *newscaster*

Kosciusko
Shoemaker, William C. *journalist*

MISSOURI

Chesterfield
Higgins, Edward Aloysius *retired newspaper editor*

Clayton
Costas, Bob (Robert Quinlan Costas) *sportscaster*

Clinton
Wentz, Wendell Franklin *columnist, writer*

Columbia
Helvey, William Charles, Jr., *communications specialist*
Loory, Stuart Hugh *journalist*
Sanders, Keith Page *journalism educator*
White, Robert M., II, *newspaper executive, editor, publisher*

Jefferson City
Brown, Vicki Knasel *newswriter*

Joplin
Massa, Richard Wayne *retired communications educator*

Kansas City
Anderson, James Keith *retired magazine editor*
Batiuk, Thomas Martin *cartoonist*
Brisbane, Arthur Seward *newspaper publisher*
Busby, Marjean (Marjorie Jean Busby) *retired journalist*
Cahill, Patricia Deal *radio station executive*
Davis, James Robert *cartoonist*
Diuguid, Lewis Walter *newspaper executive, columnist*
Guisewite, Cathy Lee *cartoonist*
Gusewelle, Charles Wesley *journalist, writer, documentary maker*
Lindenbaum, Sharon *publishing executive*
McDermott, Alan *newspaper editor*
Mc Meel, John Paul *newspaper syndicate and publishing executive*
McSweeney, William Lincoln, Jr., *retired publishing executive*
Oliphant, Patrick *cartoonist*
Palmer, Cruise *newspaper editor*
Roush, Sue *newspaper editor*
Stevens, Paul *newspaper editor*
Tammeus, William David *journalist, columnist*
Thornton, Thomas Noel *publishing executive*
Zieman, Mark *newspaper editor*

Saint Louis
Bennett, Patricia Ann *radio executive*
Domjan, Laszlo Karoly *newspaper editor*
Egger, Terrance C.Z. *publishing executive*
Ehrlich, Ava *television executive*
Elkins, Ken Joe *retired broadcast executive*
Engelhardt, Thomas Alexander *editorial cartoonist*
Gauen, Patrick Emil *newspaper correspondent*
Goldberg, Norman Albert *music publisher, writer*
Green, Joyce *book publishing company executive*
Hays, Howard H. (Tim Hays) *editor, publisher*
Kanne, Marvin George *newspaper publishing executive*
Killenberg, George Andrew *newspaper consultant, former newspaper editor*
Korando, Donna Kay *journalist*
Martínez-Solís, Luis Fernando *journalist, writer, historian*
Perkins, Norris Lynwood, III, (Terry Perkins) *columnist and writer*
Pollack, Joe *retired newspaper critic and columnist, writer*
Randolph, Jennings, Jr., (Jay Randolph) *sportscaster*
Rice, Patricia Jane *journalist*
Soeteber, Ellen *journalist, editor*
Waters, Richard *retired publishing company executive*

Springfield
Champion, Norma Jean *communications educator, state legislator*
Glazier, Robert Carl *publishing executive*
Harris, Ralph William *religious journalist*

Warrensburg
Carr, Richard Raymond *editor, public relations executive*
Jones, Robert Claude *editor*

Weston
McPherson, James Alden *publishing executive*

MONTANA

Billings
Schile, Wayne *newspaper publishing executive*
Svee, Gary Duane *newspaper editor, writer, journalist*

Missoula
Weber, Jonathan *editor, journalist, educator*

Whitefish
James, Marion Ray *magazine founder, editor*

NEBRASKA

Chadron
Buschkopf, Debora J. *court reporter*

Friend
De Bevoise, Lee Raymond *editor, writer*

Hastings
Bush, Marjorie Evelynn Tower-Tooker *educator, media specialist, librarian*

Lincoln
Dyer, William Earl, Jr., *retired newspaper editor*
Raz, Hilda *editor-in-chief, educator, English educator*
Royster, Paul Barnett *publishing executive*

Norfolk
Huse, Eugene Franklin *newspaper publisher*

Omaha
Batchelder, Anne Stuart *retired publishing executive, political organization worker*
Danielson, Mary Ann *communications educator, department chairman*
Gottschalk, John E. *newspaper publishing executive*
King, Larry *editor*
Nicol, Brian *publishing executive*
Sands, Deanna *editor*
Simon, Paul H. *newspaper editor*

York
Givens, Randal Jack *communications educator*

NEVADA

Boulder City
Kidd, Hillery Gene *educational publisher*

Henderson
Kelley, Michael John *newspaper editor*
Wills, Robert Hamilton *retired newspaper executive*

Incline Village
Diederich, J(ohn) William *internet publisher*

Las Vegas
Frederick, Sherman *publishing executive*
Jaffe, Herb *retired newspaper editor, columnist*
Miller, Valerie Carol *journalist*
Norman, Jean Reid *journalist*
Paine (Williams), Alan (Al) K. *recording industry executive*
Scherf, Dietmar *publishing executive, artist, minister*
Steckler, Larry *publisher, editor, writer*
Wooten, Glen Donovan *media consultant*
Zobell, Charles W. *newspaper managing editor*

Reno
Cunning, Tonia *newspaper managing editor*
Feinhandler, Edward Sanford *writer, photographer, art dealer, sports mentor, consultant, educator*
Hengstler, Gary Ardell *publisher, editor, lawyer*
Miller, Newton Edd, Jr., *communications educator*
Weniger-Phelps, Nancy Ann *media specialist, photographer*

Sparks
Boyer, Patricia W. *publishing executive, editor*

NEW HAMPSHIRE

Bristol
Peirce, Neal R. *journalist*

Concord
Brown, Tom Christian *newspaper publisher*
Laughlin, Larry *communications media executive*

Dublin
Carlton, Michael *magazine editor*
Hale, Judson Drake, Sr., *publishing executive, editor, writer*

Lebanon
Linnell, Robert Hartley *editor-in-chief*

Lyme
Dwight, Donald Rathbun *newspaper publisher, corporate communications executive*

Manchester
Perkins, Charles, III, *newspaper editor*

Merrimack
Kotelly, George Vincent *editor, writer, electrical engineer*

Portsmouth
Hopkins, Jeannette Ethel *book publisher, editor*

NEW JERSEY

Allendale
DiBlasi, Dianne Clark *editor*

Asbury Park
Sandberg-Morgan, Barbara *retired communication and women's studies educator*

Belmar
Landeck, Carl *cable company executive*

Blackwood
Cloyd, Thomas Earl *broadcast designer, consultant*

Caldwell
Mann, Robert Christopher *communications educator, television host, producer*

Cape May
Fox, Matthew Ignatius *publishing company executive*

Cedar Grove
O'Keefe, Paul *editor*

Chatham
Meagher, James Proctor *editor*

Cherry Hill
Rudman, Solomon Kal *magazine publisher*

Cranbury
Yoseloff, Julien David *publishing company executive*

Deal
Becker, Richard Stanley *music publisher*

Delran
Parker, Michael J. *editor, writer, researcher*

Dover
Kassell, Paula Sally *editor, publisher*

Dumont
Sadock, Karen *editor, writer*

East Windsor
Adams, Stephen M. *publishing company executive*

Edison
Calder, John Mackenzie *publisher, theatre director, writer*
Currence, Anna *publishing executive*
Hunter, Michael *publishing executive*

Englewood
Hoexter, Corinne Rosenfelder Katz *author, editor*

Englewood Cliffs
Dobrzynski, Judith Helen *journalist, commentator*
Faber, David *broadcast business news network correspondent*
Fisher, Andrew, IV, *newswriter, television producer*
Haltiwanger, Robert Sidney, Jr., *book publishing executive*
Kernen, Joe *broadcast business news network correspondent*
Saible, Stephanie Irene *magazine editor*
Vane, Dena *magazine editor-in-chief*

Englishtown
Dorfman, Dan *news correspondent*

Fair Haven
Wyndrum, Ralph William, Jr., *communications executive consultant*

Fair Lawn
Mazel, Joseph Lucas *publishing executive, consultant*

Fanwood
Berger, Ivan Bennett *magazine editor, writer*
Whitaker, Joel *publisher, editor, elected public official*

Flemington
Thomas, Anne Moreau *former newspaper owner*
Zulker, Charles Bates *broadcasting company executive*

Fords
Blond, Stuart Richard *newsletter editor*

Fort Lee
Bohner, Kate *correspondent*
Bolster, William Lawrence *broadcast executive*
Epperson, Sharon *television correspondent*
Insana, Ronald Gerard *newscaster*
MacCallum, Martha *correspondent*
Nadeine, Vladimir *journalist, editor*
Orman, Suze *news correspondent, writer*
Stuart, Carole *publishing executive*
Stuart, Lyle *publishing company executive*

Gillette
Nathanson, Linda Sue *publisher, author, technical writer*

Hackensack
Ahearn, James *newspaper columnist*
Barry, Jan *journalist, poet*
Borg, Malcolm Austin *publishing executive*
Margulies, James Howard *editorial cartoonist*
Waixel, Vivian *journalist*

Hackettstown
Scalza, Margaret T. *publishing executive*

Haworth
Biesel, David Barrie *publishing executive*
Biesel, Diane Jane *editor, publishing executive*

Hightstown
Wham, George Sims *retired publishing executive*

Hillsborough
Yuster-Freeman, Leigh Carol *broadcast executive*

Hoboken
Spring, Michael *editor, writer*
Tardiff, Jill Alexandria *publishing executive*
Ubell, Robert Neil *editor, publisher, educator, consultant*

Jackson
Wagner, Edward Kurt *publishing company executive*

Jersey City
Hitchcock, John C. *communications media executive*
Ingrassia, Paul Joseph *publishing executive*
Levine, Richard James *publishing executive*
Lipschutz, Neal *editor*
Scharfstein, Sol *publishing executive*
Stine, Rick D. *editor*

Lakewood
Forbes, Gordon Maxwell *sports journalist, commentator*

Leonia
Greenwald, Martin *publishing company executive*

Linden
Ball, William Lee (Atley Fall) *sportswriter*

Little Falls
Glasser, Stephen Andrew *publishing executive, lawyer*

Long Branch
Attardi, Michael Daniel *publisher, animation developer, retired professional football player*
Lagowski, Barbara Jean *writer, book editor*

Madison
Goodman, Michael B(arry) *communications educator*

Maplewood
Laramee, Elaine R. *magazine editor*
Peabody, William W., Jr., *publishing executive*

Martinsville
Squire, Laurie Rubin *media consultant*

Middletown
Bishop, Gordon Bruce *journalist*
Purcell, James Joseph *publishing executive, public relations executive*

Monmouth Junction
Prestbo, John Andrew *newspaper editor, journalist, author*

Monroe Township
Reichek, Morton Arthur *retired magazine editor, writer*

Montclair
Gollob, Herman Cohen *retired publishing company, editor*
Jacoby, Tamar *journalist*

Montvale
Politi, Beth Kukkonen *publishing services company executive*

Montville
Coleman, Earl Maxwell *publishing company executive*
Teubner, Ferdinand Cary, Jr., *retired publishing company executive*

Morris Plains
O'Neill, Robert Edward *business journal editor*

Mountainside
Holton, Carlotta *editor-in-chief, writer*
Horner, Shirley Jaye *columnist, writing and publishing consultant*

Neptune
Breen, Stephen P. *editorial cartoonist*
Siegel, Harris G. *managing editor*

Neptune City
Axelrod, Glen Scott *publishing company executive, pet product company executive*

New Brunswick
Horowitz, Irving Louis *publisher, educator*
Katz, James E. *communications educator*
Wilson, Donald Malcolm *publishing executive*

New Milford
Nesoff, Robert (Bob Nesoff) *newspaper publisher*

New Providence
Cooper, Carol Diane *publishing company executive*
Hollister, Dean *publishing company executive*

Newark
Aregood, Richard Lloyd *editor*
Arwady, George E. *publishing executive*
Dauth, Frances Kutcher *journalist, newspaper editor*
Dennery, Linda *newspaper publishing executive*
Everett, Richard G. *newspaper editor*
Fleury, Ronald J. *editor*
Holt, Donald Dale *magazine editor*
Newhouse, Mark William *publishing executive*
Steinbaum, Robert S. *publisher, lawyer*
Willse, James Patrick *newspaper editor*

Oldwick
Snyder, Arthur *publishing executive*

Parsippany
Smay, Connie R. *educational media specialist, educator*

Passaic
Cash-Clark, Regina L. *writer, editor*

Paterson
Deffaa, Chip *jazz critic*

Piscataway
Fogiel, Max *publishing executive*

Plainfield
Allen, Stuart (Stuart Allen Sup) *film and television company executive*
Johnson, Lonnie L., Jr., *information specialist*

Plainsboro
Tenner, Edward *publishing executive, writer*

Pleasantville
Applewhite, Kim *music company executive, educator*

Princeton
Crawford, Franklin David *publishing company executive*
Lincoln, Anna *publishing executive, language educator*
Lippincott, Walter Heulings, Jr., *publishing executive*
Nied, Thomas H. *media company executive*
O'Donnell, Laurence Gerard *editorial consultant, former managing editor The Wall Street Journal*
Sandman, Peter M. *risk communication consultant, speaker*
Weiss, Renée Karol *editor, musician*

Ramsey
Underwood, Steven Clark *publishing executive*

Ridgefield Park
D'Avella, Bernard Johnson, Jr., *publishing company executive, lawyer*

Ridgewood
Mitgang, Lee David *journalist, writer, educator, foundation administrator*

Saddle River
Noyes, Robert Edwin *publisher, writer*

Secaucus
Bailey, Steven Frederick *publishing executive*
Blackman, Brenda *newscaster*
Cho, Alina *anchor*
Williams, Brian *news anchor, correspondent*

Short Hills
Soderlind, Sterling Eugene *newspaper industry consultant*
Winter, Ruth Grosman (Mrs. Arthur Winter) *journalist*

Skillman
Eiger, Richard William *retired publisher*

Somerville
Dunbar, Holly Jean *communications and public relations executive*

Southampton
Callaway, Ben Anderson *journalist*

Sparta
Spence, Robert Leroy *publishing executive*

Stockholm
dePaolo, Ronald Francis *editor, writer*

Teaneck
Goldman, Eric A. *film company executive*
Solá, Victoria M. *announcer, writer*

Trenton
Christopherson, Elizabeth Good *broadcast executive*
Jelenic, Robert M. *newspaper publishing executive*
Mittelstadt, Mark *news service executive*

Upper Saddle River
Jovanovich, Peter William *publishing executive*

Vineland
DeVivo, Sal J. *newspaper executive*

Weehawken
Hobson, Burton Harold *publishing company executive*

West New York
Knopf, Claire *editor, writer*

West Orange
Petrokubi, Marilyn *film company executive, researcher, film producer, writer*

Westfield
Jannotti, Gene Patrick *business consultant, telecommunications professional*

Woodcliff Lake
Jacobs, Charles Nathan *editor, writer*

NEW MEXICO

Albuquerque
Blake, Renée *broadcast executive*
Danziger, Jerry *broadcast executive*
Hadas, Elizabeth Chamberlayne *editor*
Lang, Thompson Hughes *publishing company executive*
Moses, Karen *editor*
Moskos, Harry *writer, former newspaper editor*
Rhetts, Paul Fisher *publishing executive*
Walz, Kent *publishing executive*

Los Alamos
Mendius, Patricia Dodd Winter *editor, educator, writer*

Raton
Carroll, William *publishing company executive*

Santa Fe
Bowman, Jon Robert *magazine editor, film critic*
Burke, Lawrence J. *editor-in-chief*
Dirks, Lee Edward *newspaper executive*
Groseclose, Everett Harrison *retired editor*
Lichtenberg, Margaret Klee *publishing company executive*
Stieber, Tamar *journalist*

Silver City
Fryxell, David Allen *publishing executive*
Hall, Jean Quintero *communications and history educator*

NEW YORK

Albany
Kermani, Peter Rustam *recording industry executive*
Morga Bellizzi, Celeste *editor*
Mueller, I. Lynn *strategic planning and communications consultant*
Rosenfeld, Harry Morris *editor*
Tyksinski, Eugene Kory *broadcast executive*

Amherst
Goldhaber, Gerald Martin *communication educator, author, consultant*

Armonk
Sharpe, Myron Emanuel *publisher, editor, writer*

Astoria
Salzberg, Russ *sportscaster*

Bainbridge
Goerlich, Shirley Alice Boyce *publishing executive, educator, media consultant*

Beacon
Mc Keown, William Taylor *magazine editor, author*

Bedford
Bowman, James Kinsey *publishing company executive, rare book specialist*

Bellport
Townsend, Terry *publishing executive*

Bethpage
Albergo, Margaret *broadcast executive*
Dolan, Charles Francis *media and entertainment company executive*
Mahony, Sheila Anne *broadcast executive*
McEnroe, Kate *broadcast executive*
Ratner, Hank J. *broadcast executive*
Schwartz, Jonathan *broadcast executive*

Binghamton
Marella, Philip Daniel *broadcasting company executive*

Brewster
Simon, Andrew L. *educational publishing executive*

Bridgehampton
Phillips, Warren Henry *publishing executive*

Bronx
Ahmose, Nefertari A. *journalism educator*
Ellentuck, Elmer *journal editor*
Lomke, Evander *publishing executive*
Stein, Bernard L. *journalist*
Strate, Lance Adam *communications educator*
Zalaznick, Sheldon *editor, journalist*

Bronxville
Civiello, Mary *correspondent*
Lombardo, Philip Joseph *broadcasting company executive*
Rosenthal, Lucy Gabrielle *writer, educator, editor*

Brooklyn
Bianco, Anthony Joseph, III, *newswriter*
Burlacu, Constantin *journalist, educator*
Chambers, William Edmond *telephone techician, writer*
Davis, Lawrence James *editor, writer*
Ensminger, John J. *publishing executive, lawyer*
Newbauer, John Arthur *editor*
Ortner, Everett Howard *magazine editor, writer*
Quick, Walter Curtis *music company executive*
Sanford, David Boyer *writer, editor*
Walsh, George William *publishing company executive, editor, author*
Wiener, Hesh (Harold Frederic Wiener) *publisher, editor, consultant*

Buffalo
Epstein, Jonathan Daniel *journalist*
Leist, Susan Mondschein *communications educator, consultant*
Robinson, David Clinton *reporter*
Sullivan, Margaret M. *editor*
Trotter, Herman Eager, Jr., (Herman Trotter) *retired music critic*
Urban, Henry Zeller *newspaperman*
Vogel, Michael N. *journalist, writer, historian*

Campbell Hall
Austin, Danforth Whitley *newspaper executive*
Ottaway, James Haller, Jr., *newspaper publisher*

Centerport
Tunick, Laraine Donisi *publishing executive*

Chappaqua
Caranicas, Peter *editor*
Melvin, Russell Johnston (Jay Melvin) *magazine publishing consultant*
Ujifusa, Grant Masashi *editor*

Cherry Valley
Sapinsky, Joseph Charles *magazine executive, photographer*

Clifton Park
Elken, Alar E. *publishing executive*

Clinton
Behrens, John (Jack) *editor, writer, columnist, educator*

Croton On Hudson
Straka, Laszlo Richard *publishing consultant*
Turner, David Reuben *publisher, author*

Dobbs Ferry
Anbinder, Paul *publishing company executive*
Simon, Lothar *publishing company executive*

East Hampton
Metz, Robert Roy *publisher, editor*

East Syracuse
Duffy, Nancy Keogh *television broadcast professional*

Elba
Kauffman, William Joseph *writer, editor*

Elmsford
Miranda, Robert Nicholas *publishing company executive*

Flushing
Chook, Paul Howard *publishing executive*

Forest Hills
Prager, Alice Heinecke *music company executive*
Reis, Don *publishing executive*

Fresh Meadows
Cohen, Robert L. *editor*

Garden City
Egan, Frank T. *writer, editor*
Rhein, John Hancock Willing, III, *publishing executive*

Geneseo
Strong, Michael Corrin *publishing executive, writer*

Glen Head
Fairman, Joel Martin *broadcasting consultant*

GrandView-on-Hudson
Meriwether, Heath J. *newspaper consultant, retired newspaper publisher*

Great Neck
Fiel, Maxine Lucille *journalist, behavior analyst, educator*
Kahn, David *editor, author*
Panes, Jack Samuel *publishing company executive*
Rosenthal, Irving *journalism educator*
Roth, Harvey Paul *publishing executive*

Greenwich
Fung, Paul, Jr., *cartoonist, illustrator*

Hamilton
Edmonston, William Edward, Jr., *publisher, educator*

Hastings On Hudson
Considine, Russel A. *publisher, real estate consultant*
Landau, Peter Edward *editor*
Reich, Herb *editor*

Hempstead
Masheck, Joseph Daniel *art critic, educator*

Hewlett
Cirker, Blanche *retired publishing executive*

Hicksville
Horowitz, Barry Allan *music company executive*

Holmes
Conyers, Claude Brunson *publishing consultant, editor, dance historian*

Howard Beach
Krein, Catherine Cecilia *broadcast and journalism educator*

Huntington
Connor, Joseph Robert *editor*

Hyde Park
Pragman, Kurt Daniel *media specialist*

Irvington
Yablon, Leonard Harold *publishing company executive*

Ithaca
Benson, Frances Goldsmith *publishing executive*
Bourne, Russell *publisher, author*
Hardy, Jane Elizabeth *communications educator*
Kendler, Bernhard *editor*
Mackin, Jeanne Ann *journalist, educator*
Schwartz, Donald Franklin *communication scientist*

Jackson Heights
Cayón, José C. *editor-in-chief, artist, sculptor*

Jericho
Dore, Kathleen A. *broadcast executive*

Katonah
Fry, John *magazine editor*

Kew Gardens
Breslin, Jimmy *columnist, author*

Kings Park
Greene, Robert William *journalism educator, media consultant*

Lake George
Gordon, H. William *media specialist*

Latham
Condon, Joseph Dennis *broadcasting executive*

Levittown
Massie, Clifford Michael *music company executive*

Locust Valley
Zulch, Joan Carolyn *retired medical publishing company executive*

Long Beach
Robbins, Jeffrey Howard *media consultant, research writer, educator*

Long Island City
Moran, Kevin J. *book publisher*

Mahopac Falls
Travis, Alice Dimery *journalist*

Malverne
Pollio, Ralph Thomas *managing editor, writer, magazine publishing consultant*

Manhasset
Evans, Robert (Bob) *publishing executive*
Friedenberg, Mike *publishing executive*
Vizard, Michael *periodical editor*
Wallace, Richard *editor, writer*

Koppelman, Charles A. *record company executive*
Korman, Lewis J. *entertainment/media company executive, entrepreneur*
Korvin, Catherine Madeleine *editor*
Koster, Elaine Landis *publishing executive*
Koteff, Ellen *periodical editor*
Koten, John *editor-in-chief*
Kozodoy, Neal *magazine editor*
Kramer, Marc Z. *publishing executive*
Kramer, Michelle *reporter*
Kravitz, Lee *publishing executive*
Kristof, Nicholas Donabet *journalist*
Kroeger, Brooke W. *journalist, writer*
Kroft, Steve *news correspondent, editor*
Krulwich, Robert *broadcast news correspondent*
Kunes, Ellen *magazine executive*
Kupper, William P., Jr., *publishing executive*
Lack, Andrew R. *music company executive*
Lagani, Daniel *publishing executive*
Lamm, Donald Stephen *publishing company executive*
Lamont, Lansing *journalist, public affairs executive, author*
Landau, Sidney Ivan *lexicographer*
Landro, Laura *editor*
Lane, Nancy *editor, human rights activist*
Lapham, Lewis Henry *editor, author, television host*
Larsen, Jonathan Zerbe *journalist*
Lauer, Matt *broadcast journalist*
Laventhol, David Abram *newspaper editor*
Lawhon, Charla *editor*
Laybourne, Geraldine B. *broadcast executive*
Leaf, Clinton *publishing executive*
Leahey, Lynn *editor-in-chief*
Leahy, Michael Joseph *newspaper editor*
LeDoux, Harold Anthony *cartoonist, painter*
Lee, Bruce *editor, writer*
Lee, Frances Helen *editor*
Lee, Sally A. *editor-in-chief*
Lees, Alfred William *writer, former magazine editor*
Lehmann-Haupt, Christopher Charles Herbert *book reviewer*
Leive, Cindi *editor-in-chief*
Lelyveld, Joseph Salem *writer, retired newspaper editor, correspondent*
Lemann, Nicholas B. *journalist, writer*
Lenzner, Robert L. *journalist*
Levin, Alan M. *television journalist*
Levine, Ellen R. *editor-in-chief*
Levinson, Warren Mitchell *broadcast journalist*
Levitz, Paul Elliot *publishing executive*
Levy, Alan Joseph *editor, journalist, writer*
Levy, Clifford J. *reporter*
Lewis, Russell T. *publishing executive*
Liftin, Joan R. *photojournalist, educator*
Lingeman, Richard Roberts *editor, writer*
Linz, Werner Mark *international publishing executive*
Lipscomb, Thomas Heber, III, *media executive*
Lisovicz, Susan *anchor, correspondent*
Loeb, Marshall Robert *journalist*
Logan, Don *publishing executive*
Long, Lisa Valk *communications company executive*
Longley, Marjorie Watters *newspaper executive*
Longobardi, David *editor-in-chief*
Loomis, Carol J. *journalist*
Lord, Robert Wilder *retired editor, retired writer*
Love, Robert *editor*
Low, Richard H. *broadcasting executive, producer*
Lundberg, George David, II, *medical editor in chief, pathologist*
Lurie, Ranan Raymond *political cartoonist, political analyst, artist, lecturer*
Lynne, Michael *film company executive*
Lyons, Nick *publishing executive*
Mabrey, Vicki *news correspondent, anchor*
MacBain, Louise T. Blouin *publishing executive*
MacGowan, Sandra Firelli *publishing executive, publishing educator*
Macri, Theodore William *book publisher*
Madden, John *television sports commentator, former professional football coach*
Maidment, Paul *publishing executive*
Mandel, Michael *editor*
Mann, Maria *photojournalist, director*
Mapes, Glynn Dempsey *newspaper editor*
Mardin, Arif *music industry executive, musician*
Marsh, Michele *former newscaster*
Marshall, Tom *publishing executive*
Martin, Denise Belisle *magazine editor*
Martin, Judith Sylvia *journalist*
Martin, Kelli Alyse *editor*
Martin, Paul Ross *editor*
Marzorati, Gerald *editor*
Mathews, Jack Wayne *journalist, film critic*
Mazzola, Anthony Thomas *editor, art consultant, designer, writer*
McAniff, Nora P. *publishing executive*
McCarrick, Edward R. *magazine publisher*
McCarthy, Pamela Maffei *magazine editor*
McCarthy, Patrick *magazine publishing executive*
McCarty, V.K. *publisher, chaplain, librarian*
McConnico, John *photojournalist*
McCormack, Thomas Joseph *playwright, retired publishing company executive*
McCrie, Robert Delbert *editor, publisher, educator*
McDonell, Robert Terry *magazine editor, novelist*
McDonell, Terry *publishing executive, writer, editor*
McFadden, Robert Dennis *reporter*
McFeely, William Drake *publishing company executive*
McGill, Jay *magazine publisher*
McGrath, Eleanor Burns *editor, writer*
McGrath, Judith *broadcast executive*
McGraw, Harold Whittlesey, Jr., *publishing executive*
Mc Kay, Jim *television sports commentator*
McPherson, David *music company executive*
Means Coleman, Robin Renee *communications educator*
Medenica, Gordon *publication executive*
Mehta, A. Sonny *publishing company executive*
Meigs, James B. *editor-in-chief*
Melloan, George Richard *editor, columnist, writer*
Menaker, Daniel *publishing executive*
Mencher, Melvin *journalist, retired educator*
Mendini, Douglas A. *publishing company executive, writer*
Mercado-Valdes, Frank *broadcast executive*
Meyer, Karl Ernest *journalist*
Meyers, John Allen *magazine publisher*
Michaels, Alan Richard *sports commentator*
Mikita, Joseph Karl *broadcast executive*
Miller, Michael Jeffrey *editor, columnist*
Millstein, Lincoln *digital media company executive*
Minick, Michael *publishing executive*
Mohler, Mary Gail *magazine editor*
Moldow, Susan *publishing executive*
Montorio, John Angelo *magazine editor*
Moonves, Leslie *broadcast executive*
Moore, Ann S. *magazine executive*
Morehouse, Ward, III, *theater critic, writer, playwright*
Morgan, Mary E. *publishing executive*
Morgenson, Gretchen C. *reporter*
Morris, David *publishing executive*
Morris, Douglas Peter *recording company executive*
Morris, Valerie *news correspondent*
Morrison, Stacy Lynne *magazine editor*
Moskin, John Robert *historian, editor, writer*
Moss, Adam Wender *editor*
Mossberg, Walter *columnist*
Moyers, Bill D. *journalist*
Moylan, Steve *publishing executive*
Muller, Henry James *journalist, magazine editor*
Murdoch, Lachlan Keith *publishing executive*
Murphy, Helen *recording industry executive*
Murray, Brian *publishing executive*
Myers, Roberta *editor-in-chief*
Nagourney, Herbert *publishing company executive*
Nathan, Paul S. *editor, writer*
Navasky, Victor Saul *magazine editor, publisher*
Nederlander, Robert E. *entertainment and television executive, lawyer*
Needham, Ed *editor*
Newcomb, Jonathan *publishing executive*
Newhouse, Nancy Riley *newspaper editor*
Newman, Nancy *publishing executive*
Nibley, Andrew Mathews *editorial executive*
Nielsen, Nancy *publishing executive*
Nocera, Joseph *editor, writer*
Norman, Christina *broadcast executive*
Norris, Floyd Hamilton *financial journalist*
Norville, Deborah Anne *news correspondent*
Novitz, Charles Richard *television executive*
Novogrod, Nancy Gerstein *editor*
Nyren, Neil Sebastian *publisher, editor*
O'Brien, Geoffrey Paul *editor, writer*
O'Kelley, Winnie *editor*
Oldham, Joe *editor*
Olson, Peter *publishing executive*
O'Reilly, William, Jr., (Bill O'Reilly) *commentator*
Osgood, Charles *news broadcaster, journalist*
Osnos, Peter Lionel Winston *publishing executive*
Ostling, Richard Neil *journalist*
Pace, Eric Dwight *journalist, writer*
Packard, George Randolph *journalist, educator*
Pak, SuChin *newscaster*
Palmer, Marcella *reporter*
Palsho, Dorothea Coccoli *information services executive*
Paneth, Donald Joseph *editor, writer*
Parisotto, Gloria *publishing executive, poet*
Parmelee, Scott *publishing executive*
Passano, William M., III, *publishing executive*
Patterson, Perry William *publishing company executive*
Paul, Kenneth *newspaper editor*
Pearlstine, Norman *editor*
Peck, Thomas *newspaper publishing executive*
Penn, Stanley William *journalist*
Perlis, Michael Steven *magazine publisher*
Pesin, Ella Michele *journalist, public relations professional*
Petersen, Barry Rex *news correspondent*
Petranek, Stephen Lynn *editor*
Petzal, David Elias *editor, writer*
Pfeiffer, Jane Cahill *former broadcasting company executive, consultant*
Philips, Jeremy *media company executive*
Phillips, Reneé *editor-in-chief, writer, educator*
Phillips, Stone *television journalist*
Pines, Burton Yale *media executive*
Pinkerton, W. Stewart, Jr., *editor*
Pinkwater, Julie *publishing executive*
Plagemann, Susan *publishing executive*
Podd, Ann *newspaper editor*
Poleway, Christoper J. *publishing executive*
Pope, Liston, Jr., *writer, journalist*
Porterfield, Christopher *magazine editor, writer*
Post, David Alan *media executive*
Poster, Meryl *film company executive*
Potter, Ned *science journalist, writer*
Pressman, Gabe Stanley *television reporter*
Price, Robert *media and communications executive, investment banker, lawyer*
Prozes, Andrew *publishing executive*
Pulos, Virginia Kate *communications consultant*
Quindlen, Anna *journalist*
Quinn, Jane Bryant *journalist, writer*
Quinson, Bruno Andre *publishing executive*
Quittner, Josh *editor-in-chief*
Rabinowitz, Dorothy *television critic*
Rather, Dan *broadcast journalist*
Rauch, Rudolph Stewart, III, *periodical editor, arts education executive*
Raven, Abbe *broadcast executive*
Rawson, Eleanor S. *publishing company executive*
Raymond, Jack *journalist, public relations executive, foundation executive*
Reed, Susan K *editor-in-chief*
Regan, Judith Terrance *publishing executive*
Regazzi, John James, III, *publishing executive*
Reice, Sylvie *columnist, editor, author*
Reichl, Ruth Molly *editor*
Reid, Antonio (L.A. Reid) *music company executive*
Reilly, William Francis *media company executive*
Remnick, David J. *journalist, editor*
Rescigno, Richard Joseph *editor*
Resnick, Rosalind *multimedia executive*
Reuther, David Louis *retired children's book publisher, writer*
Reynolds, Fredric G. *broadcasting company executive*
Rhoads, Geraldine Emeline *editor, consultant*
Rich, Frank Hart *newscaster*
Richardson, Paul *publishing executive*
Ridell, Carol Anne *reporter*
Riggio, Leonard *book publishing executive*
Rigney, Jane *copy editor, writer*
Roach, Margaret *editor-in-chief*
Roberts, John *news anchor*
Robinson, Janet L. *publishing executive*
Robinson, Maurice Richard, Jr., *publishing executive*
Robinson, Richard *publishing company executive*
Rodriguez, Darlene *newscaster*
Rogin, Gilbert Leslie *editor, author*
Roker, Al *broadcast journalist*
Roland, John *newscaster*
Roosevelt, Phil *periodical editor*
Rosado, Rossana *publishing executive, editor-in-chief*
Rose, Charles *television journalist*
Rosenthal, Jane *film company executive*
Rosenthal, Shirley Lord *cosmetics magazine executive, novelist*
Rosset, Barnet Lee, Jr., *publishing executive*
Rothberg, Gerald *editor, publisher, editor-in-chief*
Rubenstein, Atoosa Behnegar *editor-in-chief*
Rubin, Harry Meyer *entertainment and software industry executive*
Rubin, Harvey *publishing executive*
Rubin, Stephen Edward *publishing executive, editor, journalist*
Russo, Melissa *reporter*
Sabat, Robert Hartman *magazine editor*
Safer, Morley *journalist*
Safian, Robert *managing editor*
Salembier, Valerie Birnbaum *publishing executive*
Samelson, Judy *editor*
Sanchez, Hazel *reporter*
Sanders, Richard Louis *executive editor*
Sandler, Irving Harry *art critic, art historian*
Sareyan, Andy *publishing executive*
Sawyer, Diane (L. Diane Sawyer) *newscaster, journalist*
Scannell, Herb *broadcast executive*
Scarborough, Charles Bishop, III, *broadcast journalist, writer*
Schlosser, Herbert S. *broadcasting company executive*
Schmemann, Serge *journalist*
Schmertz, Mildred Floyd *editor, writer*
Schmidt, Stanley Albert *editor, writer*
Schnittman, Evan Randolph *publishing executive*
Schrader, Michael Eugene *columnist, editor*
Schuch, Beverly *anchor*
Schulz, Susan *magazine editor*
Schuman, Patricia Glass *publishing company executive, educator*
Scotto, Rosanna *newscaster*
Scribner, Charles, III, *publisher, art historian, writer*
Seelig, Jill *publishing executive*
Segal, Jonathan Bruce *editor*
Seligman, Daniel *editor*
Seligman, Nicole K. *broadcast executive, lawyer*
Semple, Robert Baylor, Jr., *newspaper editor, journalist*
Sengupta, Somini *reporter*
Sereyan, Andy *publishing executive*
Servodidio, Pat Anthony *broadcast executive*
Seymour, Lesley Jane *magazine editor-in-chief*
Shaffler, Rhonda *news correspondent*
Shaine, Frederick Mordecai *newspaper executive, consultant*
Shandler, Geoff *publishing executive*
Shanks, David *publishing executive*
Shapiro, Gary Evan *newspaper journalist*
Shapiro, Neal *broadcast executive, television producer*
Sharbel, Jean M. *editor*
Sharpe, Shannon *commentator, retired professional football player*
Sheinman, Mort *editor, consultant, writer, photographer*
Shepard, Stephen Benjamin *journalist, magazine editor*
Shepherd, Kathleen Shearer Maynard *television executive*
Sheridan LaBarge, Joan Ruth *publishing executive*
Sherman, Robert *broadcaster*
Shier, Shelley M. *production company executive*
Shnayerson, Robert Beahan *editor, consultant*
Shortz, Will *puzzle editor*
Shreve, Elizabeth Steward *publishing executive*
Shull, Mikki *media consultant*
Siegal, Allan Marshall *newspaper editor*
Siegel, Joel Steven *television news correspondent*
Siegel, Marvin *newspaper editor*
Siegel, Max Laurence *recording industry executive*
Siegel, Randy *publishing executive*
Sifton, Elisabeth *book publisher*
Silverman, Al *editor*
Silvers, Robert B. *editor*
Simmons, Sue *newscaster*
Simon, Bob *news correspondent, anchor*
Simon, Peter J. *editor*
Simons, James *publishing executive*
Singer, Niki *media consultant*
Singleton, Donald Edward *journalist*
Sischy, Ingrid Barbara *editor, art critic*
Sivy, Michael *journalist*
Skinner, Peter Graeme *publishing executive, lawyer*
Sleed, Joel *columnist*
Sloan, Allan Herbert *journalist*
Smith, Corlies Morgan *publishing executive*
Smith, Dennis (Edward Smith) *author, publisher*
Smith, Harry *newscaster*
Smith, Joseph Phelan *film company executive*
Smith, Liz (Mary Elizabeth Smith) *newspaper columnist, broadcast journalist*
Smith, Patrick John *editor, writer*
Smith, Richard Mills *editor-in-chief*
Soriano, Nancy Mernit *editor-in-chief*
Spanfeller, James John, Jr., *publishing executive*
Speller, Robert Ernest Blakefield *publishing executive*
Spence, James Robert, Jr., *television sports executive, educator*
Squires, John *publishing executive*
Stahl, Lesley R. *news correspondent*
Stanger, Ila *writer, editor*
Steck, Jodi *photojournalist*
Steiger, Paul Ernest *newspaper editor, journalist*
Stephanopoulos, George Robert *political reporter*
Stern, Mitchell *broadcast executive*
Stern, Roslyne Paige *magazine publisher*
Steves, Gale C. *marketing professional, writer, editor-in-chief, publishing executive*
Stokes, Lori *newscaster*
Stone, Amy *reporter*
Storm, Hannah *newscaster*
Stringer, Howard *media executive*
Studin, Jan *publishing executive*
Sturtevant, Peter Mann, Jr., *television news executive*
Sugihara, Kenzi *publishing executive*
Sulzberger, Arthur Ochs *newspaper executive*
Sulzberger, Arthur Ochs, Jr., *newspaper publisher*
Susskind, Emily H. *broadcast executive*
Sussman, Gerald *publishing company executive*
Swartz, Steven R. *publishing executive*
Sweed, Phyllis *publishing executive*
Syler, Rene *newscaster*
Tafoya, Michele *sports reporter*
Talese, Nan Ahearn *publishing company executive*
Tamony, Katie *editor-in-chief*
Tanenhaus, Sam *editor*
Tanner, Lois *magazine editor*
Tarnofsky-Ostroff, Dawn *broadcast executive*
Tarr, Robert Joseph, Jr., *publishing executive, retail executive*
Taylor, Felicia *newscaster*
Taylor, Sherril Wightman *broadcasting company executive*
Taylor, Terry R. *editor, educator*
Teren, Marc *publishing executive*
Tetzeli, Rick *editor*
Thierry, Lauren *anchor*
Thomas, Brooks *publishing company executive*
Thomas, Helen A. (Mrs. Douglas B. Cornell) *columnist, former White House correspondent*
Thompson, Martin Christian *news service executive*
Thorn, Rod *professional basketball executive*
Tober, Barbara D. (Mrs. Donald Gibbs Tober) *editor*
Toepfer, Susan Jill *editor*
Toff, Nancy Ellen *book editor*
Tomlinson, James Francis *retired news agency executive*
Tong, Kaity *anchor*
Torchin, Mimi *periodical editor*
Toussaint, Allen Richard *recording studio executive, composer, pianist*
Townsend, Alair Ane *publisher, municipal official*
Townsend, Charles H. *publishing executive*
Trauthwein, Christina *editor-in-chief*
Tucker, Diane Straus *publishing executive*
Turner, Alice Kennedy *editor*
Tyler, Dana *anchor*
Uchitelle, Louis *journalist*
Umansky, Diane *publishing executive*
Ungaro, Susan Kelliher *magazine editor*
Urdang, Alexandra *book publishing executive*
Vanden Heuvel, Katrina *magazine editor*
Vaughan, Linda *publishing executive*
Velshi, Ali *news correspondent*
Vick, James Albert *publishing executive, consultant*
Vickers, Marcia *journalist*
Vlamis, Susan (Suzanne) Anne *editor, photographer*
Wackermann, William *publishing executive*
Wald, Richard Charles *broadcasting executive*
Walker, Mort *cartoonist*
Wallace, Carol *editor at large*
Wallace, Ken *magazine publisher*
Wallace, Mike *television interviewer and reporter*
Wallace, Thomas C(hristopher) *editor, literary agent*
Walters, Barbara Ann *television journalist*
Waricha, Joan *publishing executive*
Warner, Peter David *publishing executive*
Wasow, Omar *reporter*
Watson, Marlan *reporter*
Weber, Robert Maxwell *cartoonist*
Weeks, Brigitte *publishing executive*
Weinstein, Harvey *film company executive, film producer*
Weinstein, Robert *film company executive*
Weiss, Barry *recording industry executive*
Wells, Linda Ann *editor-in-chief*
Wen, George Walter Sun *editor*
Wenner, Jann Simon *editor, publisher*
West, Betsy *broadcast executive*
Wetschler, Ed *editor*
Whitaker, Mark Theis *magazine editor*
White, Kate *editor-in-chief*
White, Russell *publishing executive*
Whitney, Craig Richard *journalist*
Wiggers, Charlotte Suzanne Ward *magazine editor*
Wilford, John Noble, Jr., *science news correspondent*
Wilkins, Amy P. *publishing executive*
Williams, Lena *sportswriter*
Williams, Michael G. *publishing executive*
Willis, Gerri *news correspondent*
Willis, John Alvin *editor*
Wils, Madelyn *film company executive*
Wilson, Edwin *theater critic, editor*
Winkler, Matthew Adam *editor-in-chief, reporter, editor*
Winship, Frederick Moery *journalist*
Winston, Mary A. *publishing executive*
Wintour, Anna *editor*
Witherell, Mary *editor*
Wogan, Robert *broadcasting company executive*
Wolper, Allan *journalist, educator*
Woodruff, Jay Noel *editor, writer*
Woodruff, Mark Reed *magazine editor*
Wössner, Mark Matthias *retired publishing company executive*
WuDunn, Sheryl *journalist, correspondent*
Young, Genevieve Leman *publishing executive, editor*
Young, Steve *correspondent, anchor*
Zackheim, Adrian Walter *editor*
Zagat, Nina *publishing executive*
Zagat, Tim *publishing executive*
Zarghami, Cyma *broadcast executive*
Zerman, Melvyn Bernard *publishing company executive, author*
Zevon, Susan Jane *editor*
Zimmerman, William Edwin *newspaper editor, publisher, writer*
Zinczenko, David *publishing executive*
Zuckerman, Mortimer Benjamin *publisher, editor, real estate developer*

North Salem
Burlingame, Edward Livermore *book publisher*

Nyack
Oursler, Fulton, Jr., *editor, writer*

Old Westbury
Matarazzo, Patricia Ann *media specialist*

Oneonta
Jensen, Paul M. *communications educator*

Oswego
Loveridge-Sanbonmatsu, Joan Meredith *communication studies and women's studies educator, poet*

Pittsford
Utterback, Betty Harris *editor*

Pleasantville
Geltzeiler, Michael S. *publishing executive*

Leo, Jacqueline M. *editor-in-chief*
McEwen, Laura *publishing executive*
Pia, Pamela Carmel *editor, director*
Reddicliffe, Steven *periodical editor-in-chief*
Rockwood, Marcia *magazine editor*
Schrier, Eric *publishing executive*
Willcox, Christopher Patrick *magazine editor*

Port Washington
Candido, Arthur Aldo *publishing and distribution company executive*
Jay, Frank Peter *retired writer, lexicographer, educator*

Poughkeepsie
Kim, David Sang Chul *publishing executive, evangelist, retired academic administrator*

Remsenburg
Billman, Irwin Edward *publishing company executive*

Richmondville
Bartholomew, Debra Lee *publishing executive*

Riverdale
Chimsky-Lustig, Mark Evan *publishing consultant*

Riverhead
Banfelder, Robert Joseph *novelist, lecturer*
Roland, David Leonard *retired broadcast production educator*

Rochester
Kaidy, Mitchell *journalist, writer, legislative staff member*
Magnuson, Karen M. *editor*
Moore, Matthew Scott *publisher, deaf advocate, author*
Pitoniak, Scott Michael *sportswriter*
Simmons, Russell *recording industry executive*
Sutter, Jane E. *editor*

Rome
Waters, George Bausch *newspaper publisher*

Rosedale
Affleck, Gilbert Leslie *editor, journalist*

Rye
Nelson, Vita Joy *editor, publisher*
Schmitz, Robert Allen *publishing executive, investor*

Sag Harbor
Brody, Jacqueline *editor*
Epstein, Jason *publishing company executive*

Scarborough
Byrne, Robert Eugene *chess columnist*

Scarsdale
Erbsen, Claude Ernest *retired journalist*
Goodman, Jordan Elliot *journalist*
Heese, William John *music publishing company executive*
O'Neill, Michael James *editor, author*
Pope, Leavitt Joseph *broadcast company executive*
Rothschild, Eric *editor, consultant*
Shaw, Grace Goodfriend (Mrs. Herbert Franklin Shaw) *publisher, editor*
Topping, Audrey Ronning *photojournalist*
Topping, Seymour *author, educator*

Schenectady
Pearson, Timothy Alfred *newspaper circulation executive*

Selkirk
Christoph, Peter Richard *historical editor, archivist*

Setauket
Dunaief, Leah S. *newspaper editor, publisher, writer*
Robinson, Richard M. *technical communication specialist*

Sleepy Hollow
Flynn-Connors, Elizabeth Kathryn *editor*

Somers
Cohn, Howard *retired magazine editor*

South Setauket
Poli, Kenneth Joseph *editor, writer, photographer*

Southampton
Graham, Howard Barrett *publishing company executive*

Staten Island
Choo, Kristin E. *journalist*
Kahn, Jim *former magazine publisher*
Newhouse, Donald E. *newspaper publishing executive*
Newhouse, Samuel I., Jr., *publishing executive*
Prince, Danforth *publishing executive, journalist*
Silverstein, Arthur *publishing executive*

Stony Brook
Booth, George *cartoonist*
Harvey, Christine Lynn *publishing executive*

Stony Point
Carter, Richard *publisher, writer*

Syracuse
Bunn, Timothy David *newspaper editor*

Tarrytown
Bunton, Phil *editor-in-chief*
Kaplan, Richard *magazine editor*
LeGrice, Stephen *magazine editor*
Neill, Richard Robert *retired publishing company executive*
Stein, Sol *publisher, writer, editor in chief*

Troy
Friedman, Sue Tyler *technical publications executive*

Unionville
Kemnitz, Myrna Kay *publishing executive*

Valley Cottage
Lazecko, David John *broadcast executive*

Valley Stream
Lehner, Remy D. *publishing executive*

Waccabuc
Krefting, Robert J(ohn) *publishing company executive*

Wainscott
Henderson, William Charles *editor*

Warwick
Simon, Dolores Daly *copy editor*
Tinney, Diane Linda *publishing executive*

Watertown
Brett, James Clarence *retired journalism educator*

White Plains
Davies, Matt *cartoonist*
Royle, Cynthia *editor*

Williamsville
Levite, Laurence A. *publishing executive*

Yonkers
Denver, Eileen Ann *retired magazine editor*
Fyle, Clifford Nelson *publishing executive, educator*
Kagan, Julia Lee *magazine editor*
Lieberman, Trudy *healthcare journalist*
Slade, Margot *editor*

Yorktown Heights
Wade, James O'Shea *editor, writer*

NORTH CAROLINA

Asheville
De Bruhl, A. Marshall *writer, editor, publishing consultant*

Brevard
Phillips, Euan Hywel *publishing executive*

Burlington
Buckley, J. Stephen *newspaper publisher*

Chapel Hill
Bailey, Herbert Smith, Jr., *retired publisher*
Hauser, Charles Newland McCorkle *newspaper consultant*
Lauder, Valarie Anne *editor, educator*
Ravenel, Shannon *book publishing professional*

Charlotte
Abels, Debbie *publishing executive*
Barrows, Frank Clemence *editor*
Dunlap, Edward *broadcast executive, transportation executive*
Ethridge, Mark Foster, III, *writer, publisher, media consultant*
Haines, Kenneth H. *sports television broadcasting and marketing executive*
Horner, Robert (Bob) *broadcast executive*
Neill, Rolfe *retired newspaper executive*
Ridder, Peter B. *publishing executive*
Stobbe, Michael *reporter*
Thames, Rick *publishing executive, editor*
Williams, Edwin Neel *newspaper editor*

Davidson
Turner, Kathleen J. *communications educator, consultant*

Durham
Cayne, Bernard Stanley *editor*
Fiske, Edward B. *editor, journalist, educational consultant*
Harrell, Carlton (Benjamin Carlton Harrell) *writer, retired editor*
Hawkins, William E. N. *newspaper editor*
Rollins, Edward Tyler, Jr., *newspaper executive*
Rossiter, Alexander, Jr., *news service executive, editor*

Greensboro
Blackwell, William Ernest *broadcast executive*
Gill, Evalyn Pierpoint *editor, writer, publisher*
Hester, Martin Luther *publishing executive*
Jellicorse, John Lee *communications and theatre educator*

Greenville
Eribo, Festus *mass communication educator, journalist*

Harrisburg
Economaki, Chris Constantine (Christopher Economaki) *publisher, editor*
Handy, William Russell *newspaper executive*

Hendersonville
McCormick, Robert Matthew, III, *newspaper executive*

Jefferson
Franklin, Robert McFarland *book publisher*

Laurel Springs
Gilbert-Strawbridge, Anne Wieland *journalist*

Lawndale
Williams, Robert Leonard *publishing executive, photographer*

Lincolnton
Kempster, Norman Roy *journalist*

New Bern
Hawley, Nancy Ann *editor, writer*

Pembroke
Jordan, Chester I. *communication educator, theater educator*

Raleigh
Anderson, Jala *newscaster*
Byrd, Emily *newscaster*
Crawford, Jennifer Chapman *editor*
Crisp, Fred *retired publishing executive*
Daniels, Frank Arthur, Jr., *newspaper publisher*
Daniels, Frank Arthur, III, *internet publishing executive*
Deja, Heidi *newscaster*
Delaney, Sharon *newscaster*
Entman, Robert Mathew *communications educator, consultant*
Genardo, Kim *newscaster*
Harrison-Jervay, Evelyn Yvonne *publishing executive*
Jones, Janice *newscaster*
Kauffman, Terry *broadcast and creative arts communication educator, artist*
Marsh, Melissa *newscaster*
McKinney, Donald Lee *magazine editor*
Parker, Joseph Mayon *retired publishing executive*
Quarles, Orage, III, *publishing executive*
Reeves, Ralph Bernard, III, *publisher, editor*
Shaw, Sandra *newscaster*
Sill, Melanie *editor*
Thorton, Angelica *newscaster*
Whitworth, Camille *newscaster*
Wilson, Sue *newspaper editor*

Research Triangle Park
Greenwell, Arnold *editor, photographer*
Reid, Rosalind *magazine editor*

Saluda
McCutcheon, John Tinney, Jr., *retired journalist*

Winston Salem
Graybeal, Barbara *editor, writer*
King, Wayne Edgar *journalist, educator*
Pera, McCall *newscaster*
Somerville, Atwell Wilson, Jr., *medical editor, director*

Wrightsville Beach
Mc Ilwain, William Franklin *newspaper editor, writer*

NORTH DAKOTA

Fargo
Littlefield, Robert Stephen *communications educator, training consultant*
Marcil, William Christ, Sr., *publisher, broadcast executive*

Grand Forks
Glassheim, Eliot Alan *editor, state legislator*

OHIO

Akron
Burbach, Mike *editor*
Simmons, Debra Adams *editor*

Athens
Metters, Thomas Waddell *sports writer*
Scott, Charles Lewis *retired photojournalist*
Stempel, Guido Hermann, III, *journalism educator*

Beachwood
Cozzarin, James Robert *editor, writer*
Wells Bradley, Charlena Renee *editor, writer*

Bowling Green
Clark, Robert King *communications educator emeritus, lecturer, consultant, actor, model*

Cincinnati
Beckwith, Barbara Jean *journalist*
Buchanan, Margaret *publishing executive*
Burleigh, William Robert *newspaper executive*
Burroughs, Thomas, Jr., *media consultant*
Callinan, Tom *editor*
Flanagan, Martha Lang *publishing executive*
Knue, Paul Frederick *newspaper editor*
McMullin, Ruth Roney *publishing executive, trustee, management fellow*
Mechem, Charles Stanley, Jr., *former broadcasting executive, former golf association executive*
Petty, Priscilla Hayes *writer, columnist, producer*
Porte, Michael Sheldon *communication educator, consultant*
Sedgwick, Sally Belle *publishing company executive*
Steinberg, Janet Eckstein *journalist*
Whipple, Harry M. *newspaper publishing executive*

Cleveland
Bingham, Richard Donnelly *journal editor, director, educator*
Clifton, Douglas C. *newspaper editor*
Conrad, Robert David *broadcast executive, educator*
Fabris, James A. *journalist*
Giannetti, Louis Daniel *film critic, educator*
Greer, Thomas H. *newspaper executive*
Jensen, Kathryn Patricia (Kit) *public radio and television station executive*
Kanzeg, David George *radio station executive*
Kovacs, Rosemary *newspaper editor*
Lebovitz, Harold Paul (Hal Lebovitz) *journalist*
Lee, Jae-won *journalism educator, political campaign consultant*
Long, Robert M. *newspaper publishing executive*
Lowry, Joan Marie Dondrea *broadcaster*
Machaskee, Alex *newspaper publishing company executive*
Michaels, Alex P. *film company executive*
Molyneaux, David Glenn *newspaper travel editor*
O'Hara, Thomas Patrick *managing editor*
Pascarella, Perry James *author, editor, speaker*
Raven, Hyacinthe L. *publishing executive, editor*
Strang, James Dennis *editor*
Torgerson, Katherine P. *diversified business media company executive*

Columbus
Barry, James P(otvin) *writer, editor*
Charles, Bertram *radio broadcasting executive*
Cox, Mitchel Neal *editor*
Fornshell, Dave Lee *educational broadcasting executive*
Fox, Kate Templeton *editor, writer*
Gribble, Charles Edward *editor, Slavic languages educator*
Grossberg, Michael Lee *theater critic, writer*
Johnston, Jeffery W. *publishing executive*
Kapenda, Simon Shidule *broadcast executive*
Kefauver, Weldon Addison *publishing executive*
Kiefer, Gary *newspaper editor*
Lowe, Clayton Kent *radio film critic, educator*
Massie, Robert Joseph *publishing company executive*
Meckler, Michael Louis *historian, journalist*
Miller, Alan D. *editor*
Murphy, Andrew J. *managing news editor*
Sherrill, Thomas Boykin, III, *retired newspaper publishing executive*
Strode, George K. *sports editor*

Dayton
Franklin, Douglas E. *publishing executive*
Hamlin, Tom *sportscaster*
Matheny, Ruth Ann *editor*
Tillson, John Bradford (Brad), Jr., *newspaper publisher*

Kent
Tiene, Drew *communications educator, consultant*

Lakewood
Condon, George Edward *journalist*

Lorain
Pérez-Rodríguez, Juan Esteban, II, (Esteban de Lares) *journalist, writer, historian, researcher*

Mason
Smith, C. LeMoyne *publishing company executive*

North Canton
Pollock, Rachel Rebecca *publishing executive, educator*

Oxford
Sanders, Gerald Hollie *communications educator, educator*

Pataskala
Caw, Thomas William *retired publisher and editor*

Pepper Pike
Vail, Thomas Van Husen *retired newspaper publisher and editor*

Perrysburg
Schwier, Priscilla Lamb Guyton *television broadcasting company executive*

Seaman
Cartaino, Carol Ann *editor*

Sidney
Laurence, Michael Marshall *magazine publisher, writer*
Stevens, Robert Jay *magazine editor*

Toledo
Block, John Robinson *newspaper publisher*
Block, William K., Jr., *media executive*
Mahr, Joe *journalist*
Royhab, Ronald *journalist, editor*
Sallah, Michael D. *journalist*
Weiss, Mitch *journalist*
Willey, John Douglas *retired newspaper executive*

Westerville
Grover, Kevin Patrick *publishing executive, consultant*

Willoughby
Corrigan, Faith *journalist, educator, historian*

Wooster
August, Robert Olin *retired journalist*

Yellow Springs
Cawood, Albert McLaurin (Hap Cawood) *retired newspaper editor*

OKLAHOMA

Ada
Reese, Patricia Ann *retired editor, columnist*

Bethany
Murrow, Wayne Lee *retired communications educator, dean*

Chouteau
Sasser, Charles Wayne *journalist, educator, writer*

Cyril
Rains, Scott Wyatt *editor, musician*

El Reno
Hughey, Billy *publishing executive*

Norman
Dary, David Archie *journalism educator, author*
Drayton, John N. *publishing executive*

Oklahoma City
Gourley, James Leland *editor, publishing executive*
Gourley, Vicki Clark *publishing executive*
Hale, Sue A. *editor*
Hutson, Lindel G. *newspaper editor*
Kelley, Ed *editor*
Mitrovgenis, James William, Jr., *journalist*
Thompson, David *publishing executive*
Triplett, E. Eugene *editor*

Ponca City
Collins, Walter Lloyd George *editor*

Tulsa
Beck, Robert James *editor, writer, economist, consultant*
Bender, John Henry, Jr., (Jack Bender) *editor, cartoonist*
Ellerbach, Susan *editor*
Fleming, Ken *publishing executive*
Haring, Robert Westing *newspaper editor*

Jones, Jenk, Jr., editor, educator
Lorton, Robert E., Jr., publishing executive
Worley, Joe editor

Warr Acres
Engle, Richard Victor publishing executive

Wewoka
Trimble, Vance Henry retired newspaper editor

OREGON

Albany
Wood, Kenneth Arthur retired editor, writer

Ashland
Risser, James Vaulx, Jr., journalist, educator

Bend
Loewenthal, Nessa Parker intercultural communications consultant

Canby
Jarvey, Paulette Sue publishing executive

Corvallis
Coffin, Chris managing editor
Hall, Don Alan editor, writer
Zwahlen, Fred Casper, Jr., journalism educator

Eugene
Baker, Alton Fletcher, III, newspaper editor, publishing executive
Baker, Bridget Downey publishing executive
Green, Paul John critic
Tykeson, Donald Erwin broadcast executive
Wilson, Jackman Lee editor

Milton Freewater
Gipson, Stephen Richard journalist, construction executive

Portland
Bhatia, Peter K. newspaper editor, journalist
Bottomly, Therese editor
Bunza, Linda Hathaway editor, writer, composer, institution director
Crabbs, Roger Alan publisher, consultant, small business owner, educator, military officer
Dolan, William J. media executive
Holtz, Andrew health care journalist
Hooker, Elaine Norton news executive
Johnston, Richard C. newspaper editor
Johnston, Virginia Evelyn retired editor
Kyles-Omari, Cynthia Lee editor, career consultant
Mapes, Jeffrey Robert journalist
Nokes, John Richard retired newspaper editor, writer
Rowe, Sandra Mims editor
Stickel, Frederick A. publishing executive
Stickel, Patrick Francis publishing executive, newspaper
Woodward, Stephen Richard newspaper reporter

Salem
Bentley, Sara newspaper publishing executive
Mainwaring, William Lewis publishing company executive, author

Wallowa
Wizard, Brian publisher, author

Woodburn
Luse, Dorecia S. radio station executive, writer, producer

PENNSYLVANIA

Allentown
Hunt, L. Susan publishing executive

Altoona
Nemanic, Mary Lou communications educator, film producer, photographer

Bala Cynwyd
Perkins, Russell Alexander publisher, consultant

Beaver
Ferrick-Roman, Karen L. journalist

Bellwood
Broadwater, Robert Paul publishing executive, writer

Bensalem
Kang, Benjamin Toyeong writer, clergyman

Bloomsburg
Bertelsen, Dale Alan communications educator

Broomall
Cohen, Philip D. book publishing executive

Butler
Hawk, Kathleen Patricia broadcast consultant
Wise, Vernon L., Jr., publishing executive

Carlisle
Fish, Chester Boardman, Jr., retired editor
Talley, Carol Lee newspaper editor

Clearfield
Krebs, Margaret Eloise publishing executive

Easton
Stitt, Dorothy Jewett journalist

Emmaus
Bricklin, Mark Harris magazine editor, publisher
Favorule, Denise publishing executive
Rodale, Ardath Harter publishing executive
Teufel, Robert J. publishing executive

Felton
Shoemaker, Eleanor Boggs television production company executive

Flourtown
Lee, Adrian Iselin, Jr., journalist

Gettysburg
Gritsch, Ruth Christine Lisa editor

Gwynedd Valley
Strasburg, William Edward retired newspaper publisher

Harleysville
Smagalski, Carolyn M publishing executive, webmaster, director

Harrisburg
Antoun, Annette Agnes newspaper editor, publisher
Barron, Cate editor
DeKok, David writer, reporter
Gover, Raymond Lewis retired newspaper executive

Havertown
Hendrickson, Paul Joseph journalist, author, writing educator

Honesdale
Algieri, Sal Edward sportswriter
Brown, Kent Louis, Jr., magazine editor
Clark, Christine May editor, author

Horsham
Fisher, Darryl information services company executive

Kennett Square
Landstrom, Elsie Hayes retired editor

King Of Prussia
Broido, Arnold Peace music publishing company executive

Lancaster
Shaw, Charles Raymond journalist
Shenk, Willis Weidman newspaper executive

Levittown
Halberstein, Joseph Leonard retired associate editor

Marshalls Creek
Johnson, Loren Charisse publishing executive, writer

Millville
Shoup, Michael C. newspaper reporter, editor

Montoursville
Woolever, Naomi Louise retired editor-in-chief

New Kensington
Demmler, Albert William, Jr., retired editor, metallurgical engineer

Philadelphia
Alchin, John Reginald cable company executive
Bennett, Amanda editor
Biddle, Daniel R. editor, reporter
Binzen, Peter Husted columnist
Bonner-Coles, Rochelle Denise journalist, educator
Bradley, Kevin J. publishing company executive
Brodsky, Julian A. broadcast executive, telecommunications industry executive
Caggiula, Samuel Matthew publishing executive, consultant
Carey, Arthur Bernard, Jr., editor, writer, columnist
Cooper, Richard Lee newspaper editor, journalist
Gontarek, Leonard Andrew editor, writer
Gordon, Anne Kathleen editor
Hale, Zan editor, publisher
Hall, Robert J. newspaper executive
Halpern, Eric Franklin university publishing director
Hatch, Denny (Alden Denison) newsletter editor and publisher, copywriter
Hebble, Nancy L. editor
Hillgren, Sonja Dorothy journalist
Jackson, Harold journalist
Klein, Julia Meredith freelance journalist
Leiter, Robert Allen journalist, magazine editor
Lent, John Anthony journalist, educator
Libkind, Jean Sue Johnson (Jean Sue Johnson-Libkind) publishing executive
Lundy, Walker newspaper editor
Lyon, William Carl sports columnist
McQuade, Andrew John journalist
Morgan, David communications media executive
Nalle, Peter Devereux publishing company executive
Natoli, Joeseph T. (Joe) newspaper publishing executive
Parry, Lance Aaron newspaper executive
Pedersen, Darlene Delcourt publishing executive, psychotherapist
Porter, Jill journalist
Rorer, John Whiteley publisher, consultant
Shapiro, Howard newspaper editor
Stalberg, Zachary newspaper editor
Vitez, Michael reporter
Ward, Butch newspaper editor
Wilkinson, Signe cartoonist
Winfrey, Marion Lee retired television critic

Pittsburgh
Apone, Carl Anthony journalist
Froehlich, Fritz Edgar communications educator, telecommunications scientist
Graham, Laurie editor, writer
Harrell, Edward Harding newspaper executive
Leo, Peter Andrew newspaper columnist, writing educator
Lopes, Jerry broadcast executive
Rial, Martha photographer
Roof, Robert L. broadcast executive, sales executive
Ross, Madelyn Ann newspaper editor
Shribman, David Marks editor

Saint Davids
Denenberg, Herbert Sidney journalist, lawyer, educator, retired state official

Scranton
Lynett, George Vincent newspaper publisher
Lynett, William Ruddy publishing, broadcasting company executive

Sewickley
Swann, Lynn Curtis sportscaster, former professional football player

Warrington
Ward, Hiley Henry journalist, educator

Washington Crossing
Roche, Gail Connor editor

Wayne
Fabbri, Anne R. art critic, curator
Youman, Roger Jacob editor, writer

West Chester
Gallagher, Terrence Vincent editor
Mahoney, William Francis editor, writer

West Conshohocken
Lenfest, Harold Fitz Gerald former cable television executive, lawyer

Worcester
Curtis, Alton Kenneth film company executive, clergyman

Wynnewood
Bernfeld, Gerald E. editor, writer, retired nursing educator

Yardley
Huret, Marilynn Joyce editor

RHODE ISLAND

Charlestown
Ungaro, Joseph Michael newspaper publishing executive, consultant

Newport
Uhlig, Frank, Jr., editor, writer

Portsmouth
Needham, Richard Lee magazine editor
Parker, Nancy Knowles (Mrs. Cortlandt Parker) retired publishing executive

Providence
Dujardin, Richard Charles journalist
Farmer, Susan Lawson broadcasting executive, former secretary of state
Monaghan, John J. managing editor
Rosenberg, Alan Gene newspaper editor
Sutton, Howard G. publishing executive

Wakefield
Wyman, James Vernon newspaper executive

Warwick
Halperson, Michael Allen publishing executive

Woonsocket
Eno, Paul Frederick editor, writer

SOUTH CAROLINA

Anderson
Urakami, Akio manufacturing company executive

Barnwell
Nichols, M(arian) Theresa radio station executive

Bennettsville
Kinney, William Light, Jr., newspaper editor, publisher

Blackstock
King, Robert Thomas editor, freelance writer

Cayce
McElveen, William Lindsay broadcasting executive, lecturer

Charleston
Schreadley, Richard Lee writer, retired newspaper editor
Tarleton, Larry Wilson editor
Williams, Barbara Stambaugh editor
Wyrick, Charles Lloyd, Jr., publisher, writer, editor

Clemson
Denham, Bryan Errol communications educator

Columbia
Breedin, Berryman Brent journalist, public relations, historian, consultant
Fry, Catherine Howard publishing executive
Holmes, Cecile Searson religion editor
Lett, Mark editor
Mott, Frederick B., Jr., publishing executive

Easley
Failing, George Edgar editor, clergyman, educator

Greenville
Eskew, Rhea Taliaferro newspaper publisher
Hipp, William Hayne broadcast executive
Lloyd, Wanda Smalls newspaper editor

Hilton Head Island
Baumgardner, Barbara Borke publishing consultant
Shaheen, Jack George communications educator

Mount Pleasant
Abbott-Lyon, Frances Dowdle journalist, civic worker

Orangeburg
Sims, Edward Howell editor, publisher

Simpsonville
Kanzler, George journalist, critic

SOUTH DAKOTA

Pierre
Callahan, Patrick communication media executive

Sioux Falls
Garson, Arnold Hugh publishing executive
Haraldson, Tena newspaper editor
Masters, Lee broadcast executive

Spearfish
Wishard, Della Mae former newspaper editor

TENNESSEE

Brentwood
Flanagan, Van Kent journalist

Chattanooga
Holmberg, Albert William, Jr., retired publishing company executive
Lutgen, Robert Raymond newspaper editor
Sachsman, David Bernard communications educator

College Grove
Battle, William Robert (Bob Battle) retired newspaper executive

Crossville
Moser, Michael R. newspaper editor

Franklin
Duduit, Michael editor, university administrator

Hermitage
Higgs, Mary Phil Egerton editor

Kenton
Jenkins-Brady, Terri Lynn publishing executive, journalist

Knoxville
Aguilar, Julia Shell publishing executive
Cagle, Frank editor
Edge, Lara editor
Hartmann, Bruce publishing executive
Howard, Herbert Hoover broadcasting and communications educator
Pulliam, Walter Tillman newspaper publisher
Rukeyser, William Simon journalist
Siler, Susan Reeder communications educator
Teeter, Dwight Leland, Jr., journalism educator

Lewisburg
Poole, Rhonda Ann editor, reporter

Maryville
Bradford, Tutt Sloan retired publisher

Maynardville
Upton, Chris L. publishing executive

Memphis
Kushma, David William journalist
Stokes, Henry Arthur journalist
Vetscher, Timothy John reporter, television anchorman
Wilcox, John P. publishing executive

Nashville
Boyd, Theophilus Bartholomew, III, publishing company executive
Du Bois, Tim recording industry executive
Giallombardo, Leslie publishing executive
Green, Lisa Cannon online editor
Ingram, Martha Rivers publishing executive
Lowe, Harold Gladstone, Jr., photojournalist, small business owner, farmer
Mayhew, Aubrey music industry executive
Policinski, Eugene Francis foundation executive, newspaper editor, radio and television host, producer
Roberts, Sandra editor
Rogers, Barbara Jean (B.J. Rogers) writer, editor
Shaw, Carole editor, publisher
Shaw-Cohen, Lori Eve magazine editor
Sherborne, Robert editor
Stone, Lawrence Mynatt publishing executive
Sullivan, Dennis James, Jr., hospitality and music executive
Sutherland, Frank publishing executive, editor

TEXAS

Abilene
Boyll, David Lloyd broadcasting company executive
Marler, Charles Herbert journalism educator, historian, consultant

Arlington
Otto, Ludwig publisher, educator, consultant, evangelist
White, Alisa communications educator, consultant

Austin
Anderson, Nadeane Walker journalist
Carmical, Phil editor
Conine, Ernest newspaper commentator, writer
Danielson, Wayne Allen journalism and computer science educator
Dorsch, Jeffrey Peter journalist
Hankins, Michael James-Edwin broadcast executive
Henson, Glenda Maria newspaper writer
King, Kelley Jones editor
Laosa, Mike publishing executive
Mayes, Wendell Wise, Jr., former broadcasting company executive
Oppel, Richard Alfred newspaper executive
Spielman, Barbara Helen New retired editor
Stout, Patricia A. communications educator
Williamson, Thomas Arnold publishing executive

Bacliff
Kahn, Kathleen Pica photojournalist, journalist, mediator, arbitrator

Beaumont
Baker, Mary Alice communication educator, consultant
Roth, Lane communications educator

WASHINGTON

Auburn
Overholt, Miles Harvard *cable television consultant*

Bellingham
Meals, Pamela F. *publishing executive*

Blaine
Miller, Ronald *writer, critic*

Bothell
Scannell, John R. *publishing consultant*

Edmonds
Owen, John *retired newspaper editor*

Lynnwood
Krause, Thomas Evans *record promotion and radio consultant*

Olympia
Harmon, Lynn Astrid *broadcaster, writer*

Port Angeles
Brewer, John Charles *journalist*

Port Ludlow
Trzaska, Joyce Anne *publishing executive*

Port Townsend
Buhler, Jill Lorie *editor, writer*
MacLean, Barbara Hutmacher *author, retired journalist*

Redmond
Pawlosky, Mark A. *broadcast executive*

Seattle
Blethen, Frank A. *newspaper publisher*
Boardman, David *newspaper editor*
Bruner, Nancy J. *publishing executive*
Buckner, Philip Franklin *newspaper publisher*
Bunting, Kenneth Freeman *newspaper editor*
Cochran, Wendell Albert *science editor*
Duncan, Dale A. *publishing executive*
Ellegood, Donald Russell *publishing executive*
Fancher, Michael Reilly *newspaper editor, newspaper publishing executive*
Godden, Jean W. *columnist*
Gouldthorpe, Kenneth Alfred Percival *publisher, state official*
Grimley, Janet Elizabeth *newspaper editor*
Gwinn, Mary Ann *newspaper reporter*
Hills, Regina J. *journalist*
Horsey, David *editorial cartoonist*
Johnson, Wayne Eaton *writer, editor, former drama critic*
Kelly, Carolyn Sue *newspaper executive*
MacLeod, Alex *newspaper editor*
Medved, Michael *film critic, author, talk show host*
Nalder, Eric Christopher *investigative reporter*
Nash, Cynthia Jeanne *journalist*
Oglesby, Roger *publishing executive*
Parks, Michael James *publisher, editor*
Payne, Ancil Horace *retired broadcasting executive*
Perry, Michael Wiley *editor, writer*
Shenkman, Richard Bennett *journalist, historian*
Sizemore, Herman Mason, Jr., *newspaper executive*
Soden, John P. *publishing executive*
Stanton, Michael John *newspaper editor*
Steele, Cynthia *literary critic, translator, educator*
Strahilevitz, Meir *inventor, researcher, psychiatry educator*

Spokane
Cowles, William Stacey *newspaper publisher*
Kafentzis, John Charles *journalist, educator*
Kunkel, Richard Lester *public radio executive*
Steele, Karen Dorn *journalist*

Tacoma
Brenner, Elizabeth (Betsy Brenner) *publishing executive*
Mladenich, Ronald E. *publishing executive*
Mowery, Gerald Eugene *publishing executive, writer*
Zeeck, David *newspaper editor*

Tukwila
Lamb, Ronald Alfred *editor*

Vancouver
Campbell, Scott *newspaper publishing company executive*

Woodinville
Alvarez, Bryan *newsletter editor, writer*

WEST VIRGINIA

Bunker Hill
Marple, Thomas Franklin *columnist, reporter*

Charleston
Beary, Kimberly *newscaster, writer*
Bolt, John A. *newspaper editor*
Chilton, Elizabeth Easley Early *newspaper executive*
Grimes, Richard Stuart *newswriter*
Haught, James Albert, Jr., *journalist, newspaper editor, author*

Greenville
Warner, Kenneth Wilson, Jr., *editor, association and publications executive*

Huntington
Ritchie, Garry Harlan *television broadcast executive*

Shepherdstown
Snyder, Joseph John *editor, historian, author, lecturer, consultant*
Wilson, Miriam Janet Williams *publishing executive*

Weston
Billeter, Robert James *newspaper publisher*

WISCONSIN

Appleton
Oppmann, Andrew James *newspaper editor*

Brookfield
Fibich, Howard Raymond *retired newspaper editor*

Eau Claire
Clark, Judy *newscaster*
Rupnor, Jennifer *journalist*
Tuckner, Michelle *newscaster*

Fort Atkinson
Knox, Brian Victor *newspaper publisher, editor*
Knox, William David *publishing company executive*
Meyer, Eugene Carlton *retired editor*

Green Bay
Daley, Arthur James *retired magazine publisher*

Greendale
Kaiser, Ann Christine *magazine editor*
Pohl, Kathleen Sharon *editor*
Reiman, Roy J. *publishing executive*

Iola
Krause, Chester Lee *publishing executive*

Janesville
Fitzgerald, James Francis *cable television executive*

Kenosha
Leeds-Hurwitz, Wendy *communications educator*

La Crosse
Thomas-Williams, Pamela Rae *publishing executive, writer*

Madison
Brann, Edward R(ommel) *editor*
Burgess, James Edward *newspaper publisher, executive*
Burns, Elizabeth Murphy *media executive*
Drechsel, Robert Edward *journalism educator*
Foley Mullaney, Ellen Madaline *journalist*
Gruber, John Edward *editor, railroad historian, photographer*
Haslanger, Philip Charles *journalist*
Hastings, Joyce R. *editor*
Hopson, James Warren *publishing executive*
Hoyt, James Lawrence *journalism educator, athletic administrator*
McNelly, John Taylor *retired journalist, educator*
Miller, Frederick William *publisher, lawyer*
Wolman, J. Martin *retired newspaper publisher*
Zweifel, David Alan *newspaper editor*

Menomonie
Cutnaw, Mary-Frances *retired communications educator, writer, editor, publisher*

Middleton
Rowland, Pleasant *publisher, toy company executive*

Milwaukee
Auer, James Matthew *art critic, journalist*
Behrendt, David Frogner *retired journalist*
Dawson, Kim *reporter*
Elliot, Tammy *newscaster*
Farris, Trueman Earl, Jr., *retired newspaper editor*
Foster, Richard *journalist*
Garbaciak-Bobber, Joyce Katherine *news anchor*
Garcia, Astrid J. *newspaper executive*
Hinkley, Gerry *newspaper editor*
Hughes, T. Lee *newspaper editor*
Jallings, Jessica *reporter, newscaster*
Kaiser, Martin *newspaper editor*
Kleefisch, Rebecca *reporter*
Kritzer, Paul Eric *media executive, communications lawyer*
Leonard, Richard Hart *journalist, educator*
Mykleby, Kathy *newscaster, reporter*
Rollins, Timothy Christopher *editor, policy analyst*
Spore, Keith Kent *newspaper executive*
Stafford, Lori *reporter*
Sullivan, Edward *periodical editor*

Oregon
Uphoff, Charles Maynard *news correspondent, writer*

Pewaukee
Lee, Jack (Jim Sanders Beasley) *broadcast executive*

Racine
Miller, Yolanda *publisher, writer*

Schofield
Gettelman, Robin Claire *media specialist*

Waukesha
Korach, Alice F. *editor, artist*
Larson, Russell George *magazine publisher*
LeBlanc, Julie A. *editor*
Popp, David A. *editor, educator*

West Bend
Fraedrich, Royal Louis *magazine editor, publisher*

WYOMING

Jackson
Decker, Carol Arne *magazine publishing executive*

Kelly
Harrice, Cy (Nicholas Psiharis) *commercial radio and television announcer*

Riverton
Peck, Robert A. *newspaper publisher, state legislator*

Las Vegas
Luquette, Elise Roshau *recording industry executive*

Texas City
Bernard, Lora Marie *journalist*

TERRITORIES OF THE UNITED STATES

GUAM

Mangilao
Cohen, Arlene Guretzky *editor, librarian*

PUERTO RICO

San Juan
Casiano, Kimberly *publishing executive*
Sepúlveda, Sandra *communications educator*

VIRGIN ISLANDS

St John
Walker, Ronald R. *writer, editor, educator*

CANADA

ALBERTA

Calgary
Shaw, Jim, Jr., *broadcast executive*

Edmonton
Hughes, Linda J. *newspaper publisher*

BRITISH COLUMBIA

Vancouver
Yaffe, Barbara Marlene *journalist*

ONTARIO

Don Mills
French, William Harold *retired newspaper editor*

London
Cornies, Larry Alan *journalist, educator*

Mississauga
Gelfond, Richard L. *film company executive*

North York
Gasparrini-Etheridge, Claudia *publishing company executive, scientist, writer*

Ottawa
Beatty, Perrin *business association executive*
Davey, Clark William *newspaper publisher*

Saint Catharines
Miller, John Peter (Jack Miller) *journalist*

Toronto
Berton, Pierre *journalist, author*
Black, Lord Conrad Moffat *former publishing corporate executive*
Dean, Geoffrey *book publisher*
Downing, John Henry *columnist, journalist*
Galloway, David Alexander *publishing company executive*
Geiger, John Grigsby *editor, writer, reporter*
Hanna, William Brooks *literary agent*
Landsberg, Michele *journalist*
Lewis, Robert *journalist, media executive*
Roberts, William D. *broadcast executive*
Slaight, Gary *broadcast executive*
Thall, Burnett Murray *retired newspaper executive*
Thomson, Kenneth R. (Lord Thomson of Fleet) *publishing executive*

Willowdale
Kerner, Fred *book publisher, writer*

QUEBEC

Montreal
Webster, Norman Eric *journalist, charitable foundation administrator*
Moss, David *music company executive*

AUSTRALIA

Double Bay Sydney
Guerin, Didier *magazine executive*

BELGIUM

Brussels
Kempe, Frederick Schumann *newspaper editor, columnist, author*

ENGLAND

Cambridge
Kermode, Frank (John Kermode) *literary critic, educator*

London
Davis, Crispin *publishing company executive*
Oliver, Diane Frances *publisher, writer*
Scardino, Marjorie Morris *publishing company executive*

FRANCE

Croupieres Lethor
Salinger, Pierre Emil George *journalist*

Neuilly
Goldmark, Peter Carl, Jr., *publishing executive*

HONG KONG

Hong Kong
Laurie, James Andrew *journalist, broadcaster*

ICELAND

Reykjavik
Hallmundsson, Hallberg *editor*

INDIA

New Delhi
Watson, Paul *photojournalist, correspondent*

ISRAEL

Jerusalem
Singer, Suzanne Fried *editor*

Savyon
Bushinsky, Jay (Joseph Mason) *journalist, radio/TV correspondent, columnist*

JAPAN

Tokyo
Akutsu, Yoshihiro *communications educator*
Chang, Steve *internet security company executive*
Krisher, Bernard *foreign correspondent*
Nagata, Akira *publishing executive*

NETHERLANDS

Aerdenhout
Vinken, Pierre Jacques *publishing executive*

SOUTH AFRICA

Johannesburg
Berk, Philip Woolf *journalist*

SWITZERLAND

Zollikerberg
Bocker, Hans Jurgen *editor, analyst, consultant, management educator*

ADDRESS UNPUBLISHED

Abrams, Roz *newscaster*
Achorn, Robert Comey *retired newspaper publisher*
Adams, Wilburn Clifton *communications educator*
Addison, Kalim J. *music company executive, consultant*
Albrizio, Eileen Marie *commentator, poet*
Aldrich, Patricia Anne Richardson *retired magazine editor*
Aldridge, Amy N. *communications educator*
Alexander, Jasper D. *publishing executive*
Altschul, David Edwin *record company executive, lawyer*
Anders, George Charles *writer, journalist*
Anderson, Glen Robert *editor, publisher*
Anderson, Ivan Verner, Jr., *newspaper publisher*
Anderson, Janice M. *freelance/self-employed photojournalist*
Andrisani, John Anthony *editor, author, golf consultant*
Ankrom, Barbara Burke *journalist*
Arden, Sherry W. *publishing company executive*
Armstrong, Douglas Dean *journalist*
Arnold, Henri *cartoonist*
Aronson, Norman Leonard *publishing executive, consultant*
Ashby, Norma Rae Beatty *journalist, beauty consultant*
Ashkenaz, Judith *editor*
Ashton, Betsy Finley *broadcast journalist, author, lecturer*
Audet, Paul Andre *retired newspaper executive*
Avnet, Jonathan Michael *motion picture company executive, film director*
Backowski-Dawson, Therese Marie *editor*
Baggett, Donnis Gene *journalist, editor*
Baker, Wendy Beth *editor, writer*
Bane, Bernard Maurice *publishing company executive*
Barnes, Harper Henderson *movie critic, editor, writer*
Behrmann, Joan Gail *newspaper editor*
Beierle, Andrew W.M. *journalist, writer*
Bennack, Frank Anthony, Jr., *publishing company executive*
Bennett, Lerone, Jr., *retired magazine editor, author*
Bennett, Ronald Thomas *photojournalist, government official*
Berger, William Ernest *newspaper publisher*
Berkowitz, Steve *publishing company executive*
Berlin, Meredith Rise *editor*
Berman, William H. *publishing company executive*
Bernheimer, Martin *music critic*
Bernt, Joseph Philip *communications educator*
Betts, Katherine *editor-in-chief, publisher*
Bieber-Roberts, Peggy Eilene *communications educator, editor, journalist, researcher*
Bingham, Jinsie Scott *broadcast company executive*
Blackburn, Robin Ann *editor, writer*
Block, William *newspaper publisher*
Blount, Delores Overman *publishing executive*
Blyth, Myrna Greenstein *publishing executive, editor, author*

Ruvituso, Donna M. *editor, publishing executive*
Sackett, Susan Deanna *film and television production associate, writer*
Sakihama, Dean Sho *communications educator*
Salvatore, Diane J. *editor-in-chief*
Sanders, Marlene *anchor, journalism educator, news correspondent*
Sapsowitz, Sidney H. *entertainment and media company executive*
Sarris, Andrew George *film critic*
Schmaler, Tracy Alice *newspaper journalist, writer*
Schorr, Daniel Louis *broadcast journalist, author, lecturer*
Schrand, Richard Henry *broadcaster, writer*
Schulz, Ralph Richard *publishing consultant*
Schurenberg, Eric *magazine editor*
Sciolino, Elaine *reporter*
Scogin, Troy Pope *publishing company executive, accounts executive*
Scruggs, Charles G. *editor*
Seigenthaler, John Lawrence *retired newspaper executive*
Serwatka, Walter Dennis *publishing executive*
Seymore, James W., Jr., *magazine editor*
Seymour, Sloan *publishing executive*
Shacter, James Detmers *editor, writer*
Shao Collins, Jeannine *magazine publisher*
Shapiro, Richard Charles *publishing executive, sales executive, marketing professional*
Sharp, Timothy Allen *editor*
Shaw, Eleanor Jane *newspaper editor*
Shelton, Stephani *broadcast journalist, consultant*
Shere, Dennis *lawyer, retired publishing executive*
Shoemaker, Marjorie Patterson *textbook editor, consultant*
Shrader, Alan Ross *editor, writer*
Shuler, Sally Ann Smith *retired media consultant*
Shulgasser-Parker, Barbara *writer*
Sifton, David Whittier *retired magazine editor*
Silvey, Anita Lynne *editor*
Simms, Maria Kay *writer, non-profit organization executive*
Simon, Peter E. *publishing executive*
Simons, Lewis Martin *journalist*
Simonson, Lee Stuart *broadcast company executive*
Simpson, Hugh L. *news correspondent, newswriter*
Sinclair, Carole *publisher, editor, author*
Singer, Kurt Deutsch *news commentator, writer, publisher*
Skinner, Thomas *broadcasting and film executive*
Smardz, Zofia Jadwiga *editor, writer*
Smith, A. Robert *editor, author*
Smith, George Drury *publisher, editor, collagist, writer*
Smith, Hedrick Laurence *journalist, television producer, correspondent, author, lecturer*
Smith, Martin Bernhard *journalist*
Sparlin, Jennifer Robin *communications educator, writer*
Speerstra, Karen M. *former publishing executive*
Spencer, Frederick Gilman *former newspaper editor*
Stamaty, Mark Alan *cartoonist, writer, artist*
Stamper, Malcolm Theodore *publishing company executive*
Stanley, Scott, Jr., *editor*
Stanton, John Jeffrey *editor, writer, print and broadcast journalist, government programs director, analyst, professional society administrator*
Staton, Johanna Bilbo *editor, writer*
Stauderman, Albert Philip, Jr., *media consultant*
Stauffer, Stanley Howard *retired newspaper and broadcasting executive*
Stennett, William Clinton (Clint Stennett) *television station executive, state legislator*
Stephens, Edward Carl *communications educator, writer*
Stephenson, Toni Edwards *publishing executive, investment management executive, communications executive*
Stiff, Robert Martin *newspaper editor*
Stolley, Richard Brockway *journalist*
Strothman, James Edward *editor*
Strutton, Larry D. *former newspaper executive*
Stuart, Nancy Rubin (Nancy Zimman Stetson) *journalist, author, writer, producer*
Stutz, Pearl Hewlett *retired photojournalist*
Sullivan, Daniel Joseph *theater critic*
Summerall, Pat (George Allan Summerall) *sportscaster*
Sund, Jeffrey Owen *retired publishing company executive*
Suskind, Ronald Steven *journalist*
Sustendal, Diane *media executive*
Sutton-Straus, Joan M. *journalist*
Switzer, Maurice Harold *journalist*
Taishoff, Lawrence Bruce *publishing company executive*
Taliaferro, Theresa Lynn *reporter, educator, artist*
Talkington, William Ale *retired publishing company executive*
Tate, Sonsyrea *journalist, writer*
Taylor, George Frederick *newspaper publisher, editor*
Teison (Bass-Teitelbaum), Herbert J. *editor, publisher*
Telnaes, Ann *cartoonist*
Terry, Clifford Lewis *journalist*
Thomas, Jo *journalist, educator*
Thomas, Patricia Goodnow *journalist*
Thompson, Andrea *TV host, former newscaster, actress*
Threlkeld, Richard Davis *broadcast journalist*
Tiedge-Lafranier, Jeanne Marie *editor*
Toay, Thelma M. *columnist, poet*
Tobias, Andrew Previn *columnist, lecturer*
Todd, Jay Marlyn *retired editor*
Triece, Anne Gallagher *magazine publisher*
Trudeau, Garretson Beekman (Garry Trudeau) *cartoonist*
Trueman, William Peter Main *broadcaster, newspaper columnist*
Turek, Sonia Fay *journalist*
Turnley, David Carl *photojournalist*
Twigg-Smith, Thurston *newspaper publisher*
Tyrity, Kathy Milica *reporter, editor*
Ucciardo, Frank Joseph *television journalist, reporter*
Urbano, Juan Antonio *broadcast executive, television producer, television director*
Urdang, Laurence *lexicographer, publisher*
Uviller, Daphne Rachel *journalist*
Valenti, Jack Joseph *former motion picture executive*
Vandenberg, Peter Ray *publishing executive*
Van Susteren, Greta Conway *news anchor, lawyer*
Varro, Barbara Joan *retired editor*
Vaughan, Samuel Snell *editor, author, publisher*
Vedder, Robert Allen *publishing executive*
Verdery, David Norwood *broadcast programming executive*
Vincent, Charles Eagar, Jr., *sports columnist*
Wagman, Robert John *journalist, writer*
Wagner, Julia A(nne) *retired editor*
Walden, Philip Michael *recording company executive, publishing company executive*
Waldmeir, Peter Nielsen *journalist*
Walker, Fred Elmer *broadcast executive*
Walls, Carmage Lee, Jr., *newspaper publisher/executive, consultant*
Waters, Betty Lou *newspaper reporter, writer*
Watson, George Henry, Jr., *broadcaster, journalist*
Wearn, Wilson Cannon *retired media executive*
Weaver, Franklin Thomas *retired newspaper executive*
Weaver, Howard C. *newspaper executive*
Weaver, Leah Ann *journalist, speech writer*
Weber, Arthur *magazine executive*
Weckesser, Ernest Prosper, Jr., *publisher, educator*
Weissman, Jack (George Anderson) *retired editor*
Welsome, Eileen *journalist*
Werman, Thomas Ehrlich *record producer*
Weymouth, Elizabeth (Lally) Graham *editor, columnist*
Whipple, Judith Roy *editor*
Whitesell, John Edwin *retired motion picture company executive*
Whittell, Polly (Mary Kaye Whittell) *editor, journalist*
Wicker, Thomas Grey *retired journalist*
Wies, Barbara *editor, publisher*
Wiessler, David Albert *news correspondent*
Wilcox, Robert Kalleen *journalist*
Wille, Wayne Martin *retired editor*
Williams, Anita Marie *publishing executive, writer*
Williams, Diana *news anchor, reporter, journalist*
Wilson, James Reid, Jr., *publishing executive*
Winterbottom, Goddard Williams *retired editor*
Wittebols, James Henry *communications educator*
Woestendiek, John, Jr., (William John Woestendiek) *newspaper reporter*
Wolaner, Robin Peggy *internet and magazine publisher*
Wolfman, Ira Joel *editor, writer*
Wood, Marian Starr *publishing company executive*
Woodruff, Virginia *broadcast journalist, writer*
Woods, David Lyndon *publishing and broadcast executive, former federal agency executive*
Wright, Donald Franklin *retired newspaper executive*
Yack, Patrick Ashley *editor*
Young, Patrick *writer, editor*
Young, Richard Alan *association executive*
Zappe, John Paul *city editor, educator, newspaper executive*
Zeilig, Nancy Meeks *writer, editor*
Ziegler, Jack (Jack Denmore) *cartoonist*

EDUCATION *See also* specific fields for postsecondary education

UNITED STATES

ALABAMA

Albertville
Sheets, Dorothy Jane *school librarian, retired elementary school educator*

Alexander City
Graham, Betty Carol *community college administrator*

Auburn
Boosinger, Timothy R. *dean*
Galbraith, Ruth Legg *retired university dean, home economist*
Katz, Jeffrey Steven *education educator*
Miller, Wilbur Randolph *university educator and administrator*
Osei, Joseph *education educator, minister*
Philpott, Harry Melvin *former university president*
Voitle, Robert Allen *college dean, physiologist*

Auburn University
Ansell, Joseph Paul *director, art educator*
Dodge, Timothy de K. *college librarian*

Bay Minette
Palmer, Mary S. *education educator, writer*

Birmingham
Berte, Neal Richard *academic administrator*
Carter, John Thomas *retired educational administrator, writer*
Corts, Thomas Edward *university president*
Coyne, Edward James, Sr., *international business educator*
Deal, William Brown *physician, educator, author, medical school dean*
Garrison, Carol Z. *academic administrator*
Hahn, Beatrice A. *education educator*
Mayne, Richard *educator*
Mc Callum, Charles Alexander *academic administrator*
Reynolds, W(ynetka) Ann *academic administrator, educator*
Sloan, Albert *college president*

Decatur
Smith, Trina *academic administrator*

Dothan
Fleming, Jennie M *retired education educator*
Fletcher, Sarah Lee *retired elementary school educator*
Flowers, V. Anne *academic administrator emerita*

Evergreen
Dailey, Marilyn *elementary school educator*

Florence
Thompson, Ermis Armenter *retired education educator*
Williams, Joyce Hall *secondary school educator*

Huntsville
Franz, Frank Andrew *university president, physics educator*
Hawley, Harold Patrick *educational consultant*
Krueger, Kathleen Susan *special education administrator*
Lundquist, Charles Arthur *university official*
Moore, Ann Roy *school system administrator*
Morgan, Beverly Hammersley *middle school educator, artist*

Jacksonville
Dunaway, William Preston *retired educator*

Jasper
Rowland, David Jack *retired academic administrator*

Livingston
Green, Asa Norman *university president*

Madison
Brannan, Eulie Ross *educational consultant*

Maylene
Copes, Marvin Lee *college president*

Mobile
Byrd, Gwendolyn Pauline *school system superintendent*
Kreisberg, Robert A. *dean, medical educator*
Phan, Anh-Vu *adult education educator, researcher*
Rewak, William John *former academic administrator, clergyman*

Montevallo
Simone, Sam Paul *education educator, researcher*

Montgomery
Cox, Cathy A. *elementary school educator*
Kline, John Alvin *academic administrator*
May, Cecil Richard, Jr., *academic administrator*
Richardson, Edward R. *school system administrator*
Ritvo, Roger Alan *vice chancellor, health management-policy educator*

Normal
Gibson, John Thomas *academic administrator, consultant*

Phenix City
Jinright, Noah Franklin *vocational school educator, security firm executive*

Prattville
Burrows, Henry Peter, III, *secondary school educator*

Seale
Harris-Stokes, Joyce A. *secondary school educator*

Troy
Davidson, Barry Sheldon *academic administrator, education educator*
Rinehart, James Forrest *international relations professor*

Tuscaloosa
Bonner, Judy L. *academic administrator*
Randall, Kenneth C. *dean, law educator*
Thomas, Joab Langston *retired university president, biology educator*

Tuscumbia
Hutchens, Eugene Garlington *college administrator*

Tuskegee
Green, Elbert P. *retired university official*
Payton, Benjamin Franklin *college president*

ALASKA

Anchorage
Anthony, Susan *secondary school educator*
Bowie, Phyllis *secondary school educator*
Byrd, Milton Bruce *college president, former business executive*
Chapman, James Paul *university official*
Davis, Bettye Jean *academic administrator, state official*
DeTerra, Sandra Lee Shivers *secondary school educator*
Maimon, Elaine Plaskow *academic administrator*
Matsui, Dorothy Nobuko *elementary school educator*
Mitchell, Michael Kiehl *elementary school educator, secondary school educator, security officer, minister*
Narang, Deborah Lynn *education educator*
North, Douglas McKay *academic administrator*
Wedel-Cowgill, Millie Redmond *secondary school educator, performing arts educator, communications educator, education educator*

Fairbanks
Alexander, Vera *dean, marine science educator*
Doran, Timothy Patrick *educational administrator*
Gold, Carol *education educator*
Hamilton, Mark R. *academic administrator*
Lind, Marshall L. *academic administrator*
Reichardt, Paul Bernard *provost, chemistry educator*

Juneau
Pugh, John Robert *chancellor, former state health administrator*

Kotzebue
O'Brien, Annmarie *education educator*

Tuntutuliak
Daniel, Barbara Ann *retired elementary school educator*

ARIZONA

Apache Junction
Maher, John *adult education educator, writer*

Arizona City
Donovan, Willard Patrick *retired elementary education educator*

Camp Verde
Wagner, Gary Wayne *educational administrator*

Casa Grande
Landers, Patricia Glover *reading specialist*

Chandler
Anderson, Melanie Sue *special education educator*
Barnard, Annette Williamson *elementary school principal*
Canham, Jeanne M. *secondary school educator*
Casteel, Camille *school system administrator*
Rowe, Ernest Ras *education educator, academic administrator*

Flagstaff
Baron, Patricia Burrell *university director*
Haeger, John Denis *academic administrator*

Fort Huachuca
Adams, Frank *education specialist*

Fountain Hills
Wright, C. T. Enus *former academic administrator*

Glendale
Altersitz, Janet Kinahan *principal*
Avila, Lidia D. *principal*
Cole, James W. *academic administrator*
Edwards, Vicki Ann *elementary school principal*
Staczek, John Joseph *academic administrator, consultant*
Stauffer, Thomas Michael *former university president*
Thrasher, Jacqueline F. *elementary school educator*

Green Valley
Smith, Raymond Lloyd *former university president, consultant*

Lake Havasu City
Brydon, Ruth Vickery *history educator*

Mesa
Cassalata, Richard William *secondary school educator*
Christiansen, Larry K. *college president*
Dillenberg, Jack *dean*
Duvall, Debra *school system administrator*
Garwood, John Delvert *former college administrator*
Ramirez, Janice L. *assistant school superintendent*

Miami
Ladendorff, Linda Hardin-Reed *early childhood education educator*

Phoenix
Coor, Lattie Finch *university president*
Culnon, Sharon Darlene *reading specialist, special education educator*
Erwin, Barbara F. *school system administrator*
Fitzgerald, Joan *principal*
Fleenor, Geneva Lucille *retired elementary school educator*
Karabatsos, Elizabeth Ann *career counseling services executive*
Klor de Alva, Jorge *education company executive*
McConnell, Albert Lynn *dean*
McKay, Kay *academic administrator*
Noone, Palmer *academic administrator*
Palacios, Christina *academic administrator*
Stewart, Nancy Sue Spurlock *education educator*
Thorne, Ann LaRayne *secondary school educator*
Udall, Vesta Hammond *special education educator*
Van Fleet, David Dominic *educator*
Yamamoto, Alice M. *educator*

Picacho
Cortright, Lewis Stephen *elementary school educator*

Pinetop
Colgate, Catharine Pamella *secondary school educator*

Prescott
Waterer, Bonnie Clausing *retired secondary school educator*

Rio Verde
Vanselow, Neal Arthur *academic administrator, internist*

Scottsdale
Hill, Louis Allen, Jr., *former university dean, consultant*
Pacheco, Manuel Trinidad *retired academic administrator*
Stone, Alan Jay *retired academic administrator*

Sedona
Mastor, Helen *career planning administrator, educator*

Sierra Vista
Plummer, Val J. *education educator, chaplain*

Sun Lakes
Johnson, Marian Ilene *education educator*
Smith, Eleanor Jane *retired university chancellor, consultant*
Thompson, Loring Moore *retired college administrator, writer*

Surprise
Bradford, Mariah *elementary school educator, consultant*
Horner, Jennie Linn *retired educational administrator, nurse*
Orenstein, Fran M. *director, writer*

Tempe
Codell, Julie Francia *academic administrator, educator*

PROFESSIONAL INDEX 5571 EDUCATION

Crow, Michael *academic administrator*
Durand, Barbara *dean*
Haggerson, Nelson Lionel, Jr., *education educator*
Krahenbuhl, Gary Stuart *university administrator*
Rivers, Patrick A. *education educator, researcher*
Wallen, Carl Joseph, Jr., *education educator*
Walters, Kathy *elementary school educator*
White, Patricia Denise *dean*
Wills, J. Robert *academic administrator, drama educator, writer*

Tucson
Chandola, Anoop C. *educator, writer*
Dyer-Raffler, Joy Ann *special education diagnostician, educator*
Garner, Girolama Thomasina *retired educational administrator, educator*
Gottfredson, Michael Ryan *criminal justice educator*
Humphrey, John Julius *university program director, historian, writer*
Johnson, John Gray *retired university chancellor*
Kaltenbach, C(arl) Colin *dean, educator*
Larson, L. Jean *educational administrator*
Likins, Peter William *university administrator*
Massaro, Toni Marie *dean, law educator*
Peirce, Karen Patricia *education educator*
Sakall, Daniel *education educator*
Stoffle, Carla Joy *university library dean*
Thomson, Donald Arthur *education educator*
Tombaugh, Dorothy Elve *retired secondary school educator, author, lecturer*

Window Rock
Deschinny, Isabel *elementary school educator*

ARKANSAS

Arkadelphia
Dunn, Charles DeWitt *academic administrator*
Elrod, Ben Moody *academic administrator*
Grant, Daniel Ross *retired academic administrator*

Blytheville
Fulling, Sharon S. *college nursing program director*

Camden
Bradshaw, Otabel *retired primary school educator*
Owen, Larry Gene *academic administrator, educator, electronic and computer integrated manufacturing consultant*

Conway
Cloyd, J. Timothy *academic administrator*
Thompson, Winfred Lee *university president, lawyer*

De Valls Bluff
Arnold, Elliott O. (Bill Arnold) *secondary school educator*

Fayetteville
Jones, Louis, Jr., (Bucky Jones) *academic administrator*
Schoppmeyer, Martin William *education educator*
Smith, Robert Victor *university administrator*
Van Patten, James Jeffers *education educator*
Williams, Doyle Z. *university dean, educator*

Forrest City
Coleman, Catherine Towne *counseling administrator*

Fort Smith
Gooden, Benny L. *school system administrator*

Harrison
Street, Susan Lee *elementary school educator*

Hindsville
Bayley, Carolyn Sue *primary school educator, writer, artist*

Jonesboro
Smith, Eugene Wilson *retired university president and educator*

Little Rock
Anderson, Joel E., Jr., *university administrator*
Caldwell, Bettye McDonald *education educator, director*
Chesser, Thelma Jo Sykes *early childhood educator, administrator*
Fribourgh, James Henry *retired university administrator*
Hathaway, Charles E. *academic administrator*
Hester, D. Micah *education educator*
Kibbe-Reed, Trudie *academic administrator*
Moore, Helen Lucille *adult education educator, consultant*
Robison, Judy A. *grants officer, research administrator*
Truex, Dorothy Adine *retired university administrator*
Wilson, I. Dodd *dean*

Magnolia
Gamble, Steven G. *academic administrator*

Nashville
Hall, Jaree Elayne *elementary school educator, musician*

Pine Bluff
Davis, Lawrence A., Jr., *academic administrator*

Rogers
Spainhower, James Ivan *retired college president*
Wright, I. Melissa *secondary school educator*

Russellville
Morris, Lois Lawson *retired education educator*

Searcy
Burks, David Basil *academic administrator, educator*

Springdale
Cordell, Beulah Faye *special education educator*

State University
McClain, Veda *education educator, department chairman*
Wyatt, Leslie, III, *academic administrator*

White Hall
Scott, Vicki Sue *school system administrator*

CALIFORNIA

Agoura Hills
Kuzmanovic, Jane Violet *academic administrator*

Alameda
Carter, Roberta Eccleston *therapist, counselor*
Hwang, Michael Tian-Chung *university president*

Alhambra
Austin, Elizabeth Ruth *retired elementary school educator*
Schuster, Darleen Victoria *director*
Suzuki, Bob H. *retired academic administrator*

Aliso Viejo
Carroll, Adeline F. *special education educator*

Alta Loma
Haskvitz, Alan Paul *elementary education educator, consultant*

Anaheim
Barry, Sandra *school system administrator*
Goodspeed, Kathryn Ann *pre-school educator*
Guajardo, Elisa *counselor, educator*
Jantolak, Laura Jean *elementary school educator*
Unan, George Vincent *adult education educator*

Aptos
Bohn, Ralph Carl *educational consultant, retired educator*
Hirsch, Bette G(ross) *college administrator, foreign language educator*

Arcadia
Baltz, Patricia Ann (Pann Baltz) *elementary school educator*

Arcata
McCrone, Alistair William *retired academic administrator*

Atherton
Lane, Joan Fletcher *educational administrator*

Azusa
Aguilar, Gladys Maria *counselor, educator*
Gray, Paul Wesley *university dean*
Lee, Chang Soo *education educator*
Liegler, Rosemary Menke *dean*

Bakersfield
Arciniega, Tomas Abel *university president*
Fuller, Jean *school system administrator*
Hancock, Tapp *elementary school educator*
Kennedy, Joseph Paul, Jr., *retired elementary school educator*
Saucier, Bonnie L. *dean, pediatrics nurse*

Banning
Finley, Margaret Mavis *retired elementary school educator*
Gladden, Garnett Lee *educator, health consultant, psychologist*

Bell
Turner, Laraine Elizabeth *elementary school educator*

Ben Lomond
Sikora, James Robert *educational business consultant, financial analyst*

Berkeley
Bastrenta, Brigitte Elisabeth *school administrator*
Birgeneau, Robert Joseph *academic administrator, physicist, researcher*
Bowker, Albert Hosmer *retired university chancellor*
Cieslak, William *academic administrator*
diSessa, Andrea A. *education educator*
Freedman, Sarah Warshauer *education educator*
Heathcock, Clayton Howell *chemistry educator, researcher*
Johnson, Mary Katherine (Katie Johnson) *elementary school educator*
Kay, Herma Hill *education educator*
King, C. Judson *academic administrator*
LaBelle, Thomas Jeffrey *academic administrator*
Leonard, Thomas *dean, educator, librarian*
Maslach, George James *former university official*
McCoy, Charles Sherwood *university president, former theology educator*
Miles, Raymond Edward *former university dean, organizational behavior and industrial relations educator*
Rice, Robert Arnot *school administrator*
Shortell, Stephen Michael *dean, health services researcher*
Tyson, Laura D'Andrea *dean, economist, educator*

Beverly Hills
Grant, Michael Ernest *educational administrator, institutional management educator*

Big Bear City
Pipes, Doris Perry *secondary school educator, consultant*

Boulevard
Charles, Blanche *retired elementary education educator*

Brentwood
Groseclose, Wanda Westman *retired elementary school educator*
Paul, Yvonne C. *retired elementary school educator*

Bryn Mawr
Gilbert, Jeremiah Abraham *education educator, writer*

Burbank
Doud, Jacqueline Powers *academic administrator*
Neumann, Nancy Ruth *studio educator*
Nielsen, Kenneth Ray *academic administrator*

Camarillo
Rush, Richard R. *academic administrator*

Capitola
Jackson, Kingsbury Temple *educational contract consultant*

Carmel
Faul, June Patricia *education specialist*

Carmichael
Cunningham, Brenda R. *secondary school educator, editor*

Carson
Fisher, Farah Lee *education educator*
Mori, Allen Anthony *academic administrator, consultant*
Stuart, Nancy Giovinazzo *secondary school educator*

Cathedral City
Satcher, Clement Michael *elementary school educator*

Chatsworth
Miller, Robert Steven *secondary school educator*
Wilson, Darlene Anderson *elementary school educator*

Chico
Esteban, Manuel Antonio *academic administrator, language educator*
Zingg, Paul Joseph *academic administrator*

Chino
Forsyth, Barbara Jean *elementary reading specialist, writer, poet*
Kennedy, Mark Alan *secondary school educator*

Claremont
Alexander, John David, Jr., *college administrator*
Bekavac, Nancy Yavor *academic administrator, lawyer*
Douglass, Enid Hart *educational program director*
Gann, Pamela Brooks *academic administrator*
Kates, Gary *academic administrator*
Liggett, Thomas Jackson *retired seminary president*
Maguire, John David *academic administrator, educator, writer*
Platt, Joseph Beaven *former college president*
Riggs, Henry Earle *academic administrator, engineering educator*
Stanley, Peter William *former academic administrator*
Strauss, Jon Calvert *academic administrator*
Wettack, F. Sheldon *academic administrator*

Clayton
Bower, Fay Louise *academic administrator, nursing educator*

Corte Madera
Dalpino, Ida Jane *retired secondary school educator*

Costa Mesa
Dempster, Murray Wayne *academic administrator, religion educator, minister*
Hara, Tadao *educational administrator*
Tillman, Barbara Ann *education educator, consultant*

Culver City
Chammou, Eliezer *education educator, school librarian*
Maxwell-Brogdon, Florence Morency *school administrator, educational consultant*

Cupertino
Lyon, Mary Lou *retired secondary school educator*

Cypress
Henrickson, Leslie Ann *educational consultant, education educator*

Danville
Cross, Christopher T. *education consultant*

Davis
Biggart, Nicole Woolsey *dean*
Carter, Colin Andre *education educator*
Hinshaw, Virginia *academic administrator*
Mann, Susan Louise *education educator*
Osburn, Bennie I. *dean*
Perschbacher, Rex Robert *dean, law educator*
Pritchard, William Roy *former university system administrator*
Sandoval, Jonathan Hough *education educator*
Springer, Sally Pearl *university administrator*
Vanderhoef, Larry Neil *academic administrator*

Del Mar
Walshok, Mary Lindenstein *academic administrator, sociology educator*

Downey
Brooks, Lillian Drilling Ashton (Lillian Hazel Church) *adult education educator*
Robles, Darline P. *school system administrator*

El Cajon
Anthony, Roy Sanford, Jr., *secondary school educator*
Ostermeyer, Maryann *secondary school educator, writer*
Thomas, Esther Merlene *elementary and adult education educator*

El Cerrito
Herzberg, Dorothy Crews *secondary school educator*

El Dorado Hills
Bartlett, Robert Watkins *educator, consultant, metallurgist*

Elk Grove
Moe, Janet Anne *elementary school educator, church organist*
Sparks, Jack Norman *college dean*

Escondido
Duguid, Iain Moir *education educator*
Hannam-Oosterbaan, Maria Gertrude *secondary school educator*
Moore, Marc Anthony *university administrator, writer, retired military officer*
Sanders, Adrian Lionel *educational consultant*

Fair Oaks
Lemke, Herman Ernest Frederick, Jr., *retired elementary education educator, consultant*

Folsom
Sarraf, Shirley A. *secondary school educator*

Forestville
Kielsmeier, Catherine Jane *school system administrator*

Fountain Valley
Otto, Marie (Bertha Otto) *educational administrator, educational consulting company executive*
Purdy, Leslie *community college president*

Fremont
Le, Thuy Trong *educator, researcher*

Fresno
Dandoy, Maxima Antonio *education educator emeritus*
Girvin, Shirley Eppinette *retired elementary education educator, journalist*
Klassen, Peter James *academic administrator, history educator*
Stewart, Deborah Claire *dean*
Welty, John Donald *academic administrator*

Fullerton
Donoghue, Mildred Ransdorf *education educator*
Fischer, Robert Blanchard *university administrator, researcher*
Gordon, Milton Andrew *academic administrator*
Smith, Ephraim Philip *academic administrator, former university dean, educator*

Garden Grove
Schwalm, Laura *school system administrator*

Gardena
Harvey, Cyril Leslie *education educator*
Hume-Dawson, Rodney Babatune *education educator*

Glendale
Edwards, Kathryn Inez *educational consultant*
Whalen, Lucille *retired academic administrator*
Witt, Nancy Ann *secondary school educator*

Glendora
Schiele, Paul Ellsworth, Jr., *education business owner, writer*

Goleta
Gilbert, Richard Keith *education educator, researcher*

Hanford
Hazen, William A. *secondary school educator*
Levin, Eric Mathew *secondary school educator*
Park, Penny Sheran *elementary school educator, writer*

Hawthorne
Brann, Donald Lewis, Jr., *school superintendent*

Hayward
Getz, Melissa B. *secondary school educator*
Laycock, Mary Chappell *gifted and talented education educator, consultant*
McCune, Ellis E. *retired university system chief administrator, higher education consultant*
Raack, Richard Charles *retired education educator, writer, researcher*
Rees, Norma S. *academic administrator*

Hollister
Turpin, Calvin Coolidge *retired university administrator, educator*

Huntington Beach
Agadjanyan, Michael Grant *education educator*
Davidson-Shepard, Gay *secondary school educator*
Shishkoff, Muriel Mendelsohn *education writer*
Yglesias, Kenneth Dale *college president*

Indian Wells
Trotter, F(rederick) Thomas *retired academic administrator*

Indio
Houghton, Robert Charles *secondary school educator*

Inglewood
Cato, Gloria Maxine *retired secondary education educator, school program administrator*

Irvine
Cicerone, Ralph John *academic administrator, geophysicist*
Fleischer, Everly Borah *academic administrator*
McCubbin, Sharon A *elementary school educator*
Peltason, Jack Walter *foundation executive, educator*

La Canada Flintridge
Lamson, Robert Woodrow *retired school system administrator*

La Habra
Ahn, Peter Pyung-choo *dean*

La Jolla
Atkinson, Richard Chatham *retired academic administrator, educator*

Carty, Heidi Marlene *educator, researcher*
Cavenee, Webster K. *director*
Chandler, Marsha *academic administrator, educator*
Foxe, Marye Anne *university chancellor, chemistry educator*
Henig, Suzanne *retired educator, writer, editor*
Holmes, Edward Warren *dean, physician, medical educator*
Lee, Jerry Carlton *university administrator*
Lowe, Lisa *education educator, department chairman*
Masys, Daniel Richard *medical school director*
Miller, David R. *academic administrator*
North, Kathryn E. Keesey (Mrs. Eugene C. North) *retired secondary school educator*
Savoia, Maria Christina *vice dean*
Stefan, Vladislav Alexander *academic administrator, educator, research scientist, writer*

La Mesa
Browne, Juanita Maria *academic administrator, social sciences educator*

La Mirada
Krotinger, Sheila M. *secondary school educator*
Lock, William Rowland *director, educator, conductor*
Pennoyer, F. Douglas *dean*

La Quinta
Farber, Patricia Ann *secondary school educator*
Tebbs, Carol Ann *secondary school educator, academic administrator*

La Verne
Fleck, Raymond Anthony, Jr., *retired university administrator*
Morgan, Stephen Charles *academic administrator*

Laguna Beach
Fry, Edward Bernard *education educator, retired*
Martinez, Vera *academic administrator*

Laguna Niguel
Teitelbaum, Marilyn Leah *retired special education educator*

Lancaster
Walsh, Patricia Maack *special education educator*

Lodi
Bishop-Graham, Barbara *secondary school educator, journalist*
Reinold, Christy Diane *school counselor, consultant*

Loma Linda
Goodacre, Charles J. *academic administrator*
King, Helen Emori *dean*
Klooster, Judson *academic administrator, dentistry educator*

Long Beach
Collins, Aristide J., Jr., *academic administrator*
Cook, Karla Joan *elementary school educator*
Cotner, Douglas Monroe *provost, mathematics and environmental science educator*
Culton, Paul Melvin *retired counselor, educator, interpreter*
Fleming, Jane Williams *retired educator, writer*
Lathrop, Irvin Tunis *retired academic dean, educator*
Lauda, Donald Paul *dean*
Maxson, Robert C. *university president*
McDonough, Patrick Dennis *academic administrator*
Reed, Charles Bass *chief academic administrator*
Reichard, Gary Warren *university administrator, history educator*
Rutherford, Vicky Lynn *special education educator*
Singhal, Meena *education educator*
Strafaci, Samuel Anthony *academic administrator, consultant*
Writer, Sharon Lisle *secondary school educator*

Los Altos
Fong, Bernadine Chuck *academic administrator*

Los Angeles
Agnew, John A. *education educator*
Armstrong, Lloyd, Jr., *university official, physics educator*
Astin, Alexander William *education educator*
Bernstein, Leslie *academic administrator, biostatistician*
Bice, Scott Haas *dean, lawyer, educator*
Campo, Todd Russell *principal, law enforcement educator*
Carnesale, Albert *academic administrator*
Chapman Collins, Janice *elementary school educator, supervisor, educational consultant*
Darmstaetter, Jay Eugene *secondary school educator*
Dewey, Donald Odell *dean, academic administrator*
Fitz-Carter, Aleane *elementary school educator, composer*
Gothold, Stuart Eugene *school system administrator, educator*
Gupta, Yash *dean*
Gurval, Robert Alan *education educator*
Haley, Roslyn Trezevant *educational program director*
Hamilton, Katrina Hasan *educational consultant, writer*
Harris, F. Chandler *retired director*
Harvey, James Gerald *educational consultant, researcher*
Hayes, Robert Mayo *university dean, library and information science educator*
Heath, Berthann Jones *education administrator*
Henderson, Brian Edmond *dean, physician, educator*
Hoi, Samuel Chuen-Tsung *art school president*
Hubbard, John Randolph *retired academic administrator*
Kaback, Elaine *career counselor, family therapist, consultant*
Kleingartner, Archie *founding dean, educator*
Lieber, David Leo *university president*
Lynch, Beverly Pfeifer *education and information studies educator*
Martin, Shane Patrick *education educator, consultant*
McCabe, Edward R. B. *academic administrator, educator, physician*
McLinn, Anna Ruth *educator*
Mitchell, Theodore Reed *academic administrator*
Morin, JoyAnn Hauge *education educator*
Morisky, Donald E. *director, medical educator*
Park, No-Hee *academic administrator*
Pierskalla, William Peter *university dean, management-engineering educator*
Romer, Roy R. *Superintendent Los Angeles Unified School District, former governor*
Rosser, James Milton *academic administrator*
Sample, Steven Browning *university executive*
Saunders, Myra Kathleen *dean, law librarian, educator*
Shearer, Derek Norcross *international studies educator, diplomat, administrator*
Slavkin, Harold Charles *dean, biologist*
Small, Gary W. *academic administrator, psychiatrist, educator*
Sohaili, Monira *special education educator, writer*
Spangler, Mary *college president*
Steinberg, Warren Linnington *school principal*
Strippoli, William Peter *academic administrator*
Varat, Jonathan D. *dean, law educator*
Wagner, William Gerard *university dean, physicist, consultant, information scientist, investment manager*
Wang, Jia *educator*
Waterman, Christopher *dean*
Wazzan, A(hmed) R(assem) Frank *engineering educator, dean*
Westerfield, Randolph W. *university dean, business educator*
Wexler, Robert *university administrator*
Wilkerson, LuAnn *dean, medical educator*
Willison, Bruce Gray *dean*
Zexter, Eleanor M. *secondary school educator*

Los Gatos
Dunham, Anne *educational institute director*
Rudolph, Allen *secondary school educator, consultant*

Malibu
Benton, Andrew Keith *university administrator, lawyer*
Phillips, Ronald Frank *university administrator*
Raine, Melinda L. *library manager*
Starr, Kenneth Winston *dean, lawyer*

Menifee
Balow, Irving Henry *retired education educator*

Menlo Park
Chapin, June Roediger *education educator*
Zercher, Craig Allen *special education educator, researcher*

Merced
Tomlinson-Keasey, Carol Ann *university administrator*

Mill Valley
Maubert, Jacques Claude *retired school superintendent*

Mission Viejo
Hodge, Kathleen O'Connell *academic administrator*

Mojave
Shelby, Tim Otto *secondary school educator*

Monterey
Kadushin, Karen Donna *dean*
Oder, Broeck Newton *school emergency management consultant*

Monterey Park
Moreno, Ernest H. *college president*

Morro Bay
Scholer, Margaret D. *adult education educator*

Mountain View
Craig, Joan Carmen *secondary school educator, performing arts educator*

Northridge
Curzon, Susan Carol *university administrator*
Falk, Heinrich Richard *theater and humanities educator*
Koester, Jolene *academic administrator*
McHenry, Leemon Benton *education educator, writer*
Mitchell, James Andrew *education educator*

Norwalk
Matsuura, Kenneth Ray *counselor, articulation officer*

Novato
Jaeger, Patsy Elaine *retired secondary education educator, artist*
Patterson, W. Morgan *college president*
White, Linda Lee Locy *secondary educator*

Oakland
Anderson, Brother Timothy Mel *academic administrator*
Dibble, David Van Vlack *visually impaired educator, lawyer*
Dynes, Robert C. *academic administrator*
Gomes, Wayne Reginald *academic administrator*
Griffin, Betty Jo *elementary school educator*
Holmgren, Janet L. *college president*
Howatt, Sister Helen Clare *former human services director, former college library director*
Isaac Nash, Eva Mae *secondary school educator*
Krause, Marcella Elizabeth Mason (Mrs. Eugene Fitch Krause) *retired secondary school educator*
Stewart, John Lincoln *university administrator*

Oceanside
LaRosa, John Paul *education educator*
Pena, Maria Geges *academic services administrator*

Ojai
Shagam, Marvin Hückel-Berri *private school educator*

Ontario
Küeng, Christian Roulland *elementary school educator, principal*
McGehee, Sharon *school system administrator*
Peters, Jacqueline Mary *secondary school educator*

Orange
Cooper, Steven Harold *education educator*
Doti, James L. *academic administrator*
Hamilton, Harry Lemuel, Jr., *atmospheric science professor*
Stuewe, Isabel *elementary school educator*
Tuggle, Francis Douglas *dean, consultant*

Oxnard
Auston, David Henry *former academic administrator, electrical engineer, educator*

Pacific Grove
Longman, Anne Strickland *special education educator, consultant*

Pacific Palisades
Georges, Robert Augustus *retired educator, researcher, writer*

Palm Desert
Baxter, Betty Carpenter *educational administrator*
Bratrud, Linda Kay *secondary school educator*
Heydman, Abby Maria *academic executive*
Hoffmann, Joan Carol *retired academic dean*
Sexson, Stephen Bruce *education writer, educator*

Palm Springs
Hartman, Rosemary Jane *retired special education educator*
Owings, Thalia Kelley *elementary school educator*

Palo Alto
Bohrnstedt, George William *educational researcher*
Gong, Mamie Poggio *elementary school educator*
Loveless, Edward Eugene *education educator, musician*

Palos Verdes Estates
Lazzaro, Anthony Derek *university administrator*

Paramount
Williams, Vivian Lewie *retired counseling administrator*

Pasadena
Almore-Randle, Allie Louise *special education educator*
Baltimore, David *academic administrator, microbiologist, educator*
Brooks, Edward Howard *retired academic administrator*
Everhart, Thomas Eugene *retired university president, engineering educator*
Gilman, Richard Carleton *retired college president*
Hoffmann, Michael R. *dean*
Lingenfelter, Sherwood Galen *university provost, anthropology educator*
Meye, Robert Paul *retired seminary educator, administrator, writer*
Pings, Cornelius John *educational consultant, director*
Siemon-Burgeson, Marilyn M. (Marilyn Burgeson) *education administrator*
Stolper, Edward Manin *secondary school educator*
Wise, Mark B. *education educator*

Pebble Beach
Hoffman, Sharon Lynn *adult education educator*

Penn Valley
Longan, Suzanne M. *retired elementary school educator*

Petaluma
Mulkern-Kolosey, Sandy Kathleen *college counselor, educator, realtor*
O'Hare, Sandra Fernandez *education educator*

Pinole
Grogan, Stanley Joseph *educational and security consultant*

Pleasant Hill
Edelstein, Mark Gerson *college president*

Pleasanton
Roshong, Dee Ann Daniels *dean, educator*

Pomona
Charney, George *academic administrator*
Demery, Dorothy Jean *secondary school educator*
Dishman, Rose Marie Rice *academic administrator, researcher*
Lenz, Craig *academic administrator*
Rhodes, Rhonda Lynn *business educator*
Tunison, Elizabeth Lamb *education educator*

Porterville
Hayes, Shirley Ann *special education educator*

Quartz Hill
Nettelhorst, Robin Paul *academic administrator, writer*

Ramona
Van Zant, Susan Lucille *principal*

Red Bluff
Kennedy, James William, Jr., (Sarge Kennedy) *special education administrator, consultant*

Redding
Spawn, Kevin Lewis *education educator*

Redlands
Appleton, James Robert *university president, educator*
Burgess, Charlotte Gaylord *dean*

Rialto
Jackson, Betty Eileen *music and elementary school educator*

Richmond
Cushnie, Michele *academic administrator*

Riverside
Boldt, William Gregory *academic administrator, consultant*
Deese, E(thel) Helen *English educator*
Geraty, Lawrence Thomas *academic administrator, archaeologist, educator*
Hendrick, Irving Guilford *education educator*
Prosser, Michael Joseph *college librarian*
Rainey, Susan J. *school system administrator*
Yacoub, Ignatius I. *university dean*

Rocklin
Hyde, Geraldine Veola *retired secondary school educator*
Womack, Joseph Darryl *academic administrator*

Rohnert Park
Arminana, Ruben *academic administrator, educator*
Babula, William *university dean*

Ross
Matan, Lillian Kathleen *secondary school educator, consultant, interior designer*

Sacramento
Amezcua, Esther Hernandez *elementary school educator*
Drummond, Marshall "Mark" Edward *academic administrator*
Gerth, Donald Rogers *university president, educator*
Gray, John Douglas *education educator, researcher*
Lam, Siuwa Monica *education educator, consultant*
O'Leary, Marion Hugh *university dean, chemist*
Sanborn, Kathy *career planning administrator, consultant*
Shoemaker, Cameron David James *dean, educator*
Silva, Joseph, Jr., *dean, medical educator*
Smith, Marie B. *college president*
Zaidi, Emily Louise *retired elementary school educator*

San Anselmo
Crawley, Cheryl K. *school system administrator*

San Bernardino
Caballero, Sharon *academic administrator*
Hwang, Young S. *education educator*

San Diego
Conant, Kim Untiedt *elementary school educator*
Early, Teri Wilson (Denise Wilson) *elementary school educator, consultant*
Golding, Brage *university president*
Kahan, David Michael *education educator*
Kitchen, James R. *academic administrator*
Lyons, Mary E. *academic administrator*
Mayer, George Roy *education educator*
McBrayer, Sandra L. *educational director, homeless outreach educator*
Naschak, Bruce Stephen *education educator, consultant*
Pastoor, Robertus Antonius *academic administrator*
Pohan, Cathy Ann *education educator, consultant*
Schwartz, Alfred *university dean*
Travaglini, Joseph *educational consultant*
Ulen, Gene Eldridge *elementary school educator*
Walker, Donald Ezzell *retired academic administrator*
Weber, Stephen Lewis *university president*
Williams, Carolyn *secondary school educator*

San Francisco
Ackerman, Arlene *school system administrator*
Bertolami, Charles Nicholas *dean, dental educator, oral surgeon*
Bishop, John Michael *academic administrator, biomedical researcher, educator*
Boyden, Jaclyne Witte *university vice dean*
Corrigan, Robert Anthony *academic administrator*
Fleishhacker, David *school administrator*
Goldstine, Stephen Joseph *college administrator*
Harris, Daniel Y. *private school educator, poet, artist*
Kane, Mary Kay *dean*
Kessler, David Aaron *dean, medical educator*
Kozloff, Lloyd M. *university dean, educator, scientist*
Lane, Mary B. *education educator, writer*
Laret, Mark R. *school system administrator, health facility executive*
Lo, Bernard *education educator*
Naegele, Carl Joseph *university academic administrator, educator*
Privett, Stephen A. *academic administrator*
Rumjahn, Diana *academic administrator*
Stephens, Elisa *college president*
Wara, Diane *dean*
Zingale, Donald Paul *academic administrator, educator*

San Gabriel
Tomich-Bolognesi, Vera *secondary school educator*

San Jose
Bain, Linda L. *academic administrator*
Cryer, Rodger Earl *educational administrator*
Holyer, Erna Maria *adult education educator, writer, artist*
Jordan, Bernice Bell *retired elementary school educator*
Lobig, Janie Howell *special education educator*
Madigan, Jennifer Caroline *education educator*
Ogawa, Joichi Raphael *director, consultant*
Okerlund, Arlene Naylor *university official*
Yu, Paul *academic administrator*

San Juan Capistrano
Larwood, Susan Elizabeth *elementary school educator*

San Luis Obispo
Bailey, Philip Sigmon, Jr., *university official and dean, chemistry educator*
Baker, Warren J(oseph) *university president*
Ericson, Jon Meyer *academic administrator, rhetoric theory educator*
Girard, Sally F. *education educator*
Haile, Allen Cleveland *educator and administrator*

San Marcos
Coleman, Dorothy Jones *retired educator*
Haynes, Karen Sue *academic administrator, educator*
Lilly, Martin Stephen *university dean*

San Marino
Footman, Gordon Elliott *educational administrator*

San Pedro
Gaines, Jerry Lee *retired secondary education educator*

San Rafael
Adcock, Muriel W. *special education educator*
Fink, Joseph Richard *academic administrator*
Henry, Joseph Louis *dean*
Thomas, Mary Ann McCrary *counselor, school system administrator*

San Ramon
Peebles, Lucretia Neal Drane *policy and administration educator*

Santa Ana
Beal, Dennis *academic administrator*
Ellis, Gregory Scott *elementary school educator*
Kato, Terri Emi *elementary school and gifted and talented educator*
Moore, David Gene *academic administrator*
Wilson, Beth A. *college official*

Santa Barbara
Allaway, William Harris *retired academic administrator*
Anderson, Carol Ann *retired secondary school educator, lawyer, political organization worker*
Barry, Robert Michael *education educator*
Boyan, Norman J. *retired education educator*
Cirone, William Joseph *educational administrator*
Lucas, Gene *academic administrator*
O'Dowd, Donald Davy *retired university president*
Sinsheimer, Robert Louis *retired academic administrator, educator*
Yang, Henry T. *academic administrator, educator*
Zwick, Rebecca *education educator*

Santa Clara
Facione, Peter Arthur *dean, philosophy and education educator*
Ling, Nam *educator*
Locatelli, Paul Leo *academic administrator*

Santa Clarita
Lavine, Steven David *academic administrator*

Santa Cruz
Chemers, Martin M. *academic administrator, psychologist, educator*
Delaney, Margaret L. *academic administrator*
Greenwood, M. R. C. *college dean, biologist, nutrition educator*
Mirk, Judy Ann *retired elementary school educator*

Santa Rosa
Christiansen, Peggy *principal*
Webb, Charles Richard *retired university president*

Santee
Morris, Henry Madison, Jr., *education educator*

Saratoga
Baratta-Lorton, Robert *mathematics educator*
Houston, Elizabeth Reece Manasco *correctional education consultant*

Saugus
Grishman, Lee Howard *college program administrator*

Seaside
Paget, Ruth Pennington *academic administrator, educator, writer*

Sherman Oaks
O'Neill, Sallie Boyd *educational consultant, business owner, sculptor*

Signal Hill
Vandament, William Eugene *retired academic administrator*

Silverado
Mamer, James Michael *secondary school educator*

Solana Beach
Beck-von-Peccoz, Michele *retired secondary school educator, writer*

South Pasadena
Fuller, Kathy J. *special education educator, consultant, researcher*
Yett, Sally Pugh *elementary school educator, gifted and talented educator*

Stanford
Ball, Arnetha *education educator*
Barron, Brigid *education educator*
Boaler, Jo *education educator*
Bridges, Edwin Maxwell *education educator*
Byerwalter, Mariann *academic administrator*
Casper, Gerhard *law educator, former academic administrator*
Cohen, Elizabeth G. *education and sociology educator, researcher*
Darling-Hammond, Linda *education educator*
Etchemendy, John *academic administrator*
Evers, Williamson Moore *education policy analyst, political scientist*
Gross, Richard Edmund *education educator*
Hennessy, John L. *academic administrator*
Henriksen, Thomas Hollinger *university official*
Joss, Robert L. *dean*
Kamil, Michael *education educator*
Kays, William Morrow *university administrator, mechanical engineer*
Kirst, Michael Weile *education educator, researcher*
Loeb, Susanna *education educator*
Lotan, Rachel *education educator*
Naimark, Norman M. *academic administrator*
Palm, Charles Gilman *university official*
Perry, William James *education educator, former federal official*
Raisian, John *academic administrator, economist*
Spence, A(ndrew) Michael *dean, finance educator*
Stipek, Deborah *education educator, dean*
Stone, William Edward *academic administrator, consultant*
Strober, Myra Hoffenberg *education educator, consultant*
Sullivan, Kathleen Marie *former dean, law educator*
Turner, Frederick Clair, Jr., *education educator*
Walker, George Edward *academic administrator, physicist*
Wotipka, Christine Min *education educator*

Stockton
DeRicco, Lawrence Albert *college president emeritus*
Gilbertson, Philip *academic administrator*
Haines, Joybelle *retired elementary school educator*
Kareem, A'isha *educational consultant, counselor*
Sorby, Donald Lloyd *university dean*

Sun Valley
Mayhue, Richard Lee *provost, dean, pastor, writer*

Tehachapi
Sprinkle, Martha Clare *elementary school educator*

Temple City
Anderson, Paulette Elizabeth *retired elementary school educator*

Thousand Oaks
Gillette, Dennis C. *academic administrator, mayor*

Torrance
Kuc, Joseph A. *research scientist*
McNamara, Brenda Norma *secondary school educator*

Trinidad
Conant, Ralph Wendell *educator, consultant, author*

Turlock
Hughes, Marvalene *academic administrator*

Twentynine Palms
Clemente, Patrocinio Ablola *secondary school educator*

Upland
Berger, Stanley Christ *secondary school educator*

Vallejo
Murillo, Carol Ann *secondary school educator*
Zeliger, Bernard *dean*

Van Nuys
Altshiller, Arthur Leonard *secondary school educator*

Ventura
Jaeger, Kenneth Michael *secondary school educator*
Renger, Marilyn Hanson *elementary school educator*

Victorville
Scott, Deborah Elizabeth *school system administrator, poet*

Visalia
Singh, Daljit *dean, business and public administration educator*

Walnut Creek
Dea, Norman *secondary school educator*
Lilly, Luella Jean *academic administrator*

Waterford
Reed, Thomas W. *secondary school educator*

Weimar
Kerschner, Lee R(onald) *academic administrator, political science educator*

West Covina
Fuller, George Stuart *secondary school educator*

Whittier
Drake, E. Maylon *academic administrator*
Gosfield, Margaret *secondary school educator, school system administrator, consultant, editor*

Woodland Hills
Zeitlin, Herbert Zakary *retired academic administrator, real estate consultant*

Yountville
Bedell, Jay Dee *educator, writer*

Yucaipa
Gomez, Louis Salazar *college president*

COLORADO

Arvada
Bert, Carol Lois *retired educational assistant*
Reed, Joan-Marie *special education educator*

Aurora
Beckman, L. David *university chancellor*
Du, Yiping P. *education educator*
Lassen, Betty Jane *gifted and talented educator*
Sorenson, Katherine Ann *elementary school educator*
Walker, Joyce Marie *secondary school educator*

Boulder
Anderson, Ronald Delaine *education educator*
Borko, Hilda *education educator*
Bruff, Harold Hastings *dean*
Buechner, John C. *academic administrator*
Burke, Thomas Sebastian, Jr., *educator, writer*
Byyny, Richard Lee *academic administrator, physician*
Dilley, Barbara Jean *college administrator, choreographer, educator*
DiStefano, Philip *academic administrator*
Enarson, Harold L. *retired academic administrator*
Hoffman, Elizabeth *academic administrator*
Sirotkin, Phillip Leonard *education administrator*

Calhan
Fuller, Janice Marie *secondary school educator*
Henderson, Freda LaVerne *elementary school educator*

Colorado Springs
Adams, Bernard Schroder *retired college president*
Celeste, Richard F. *academic administrator, former ambassador, former governor*
Guy, Mildred Dorothy *retired secondary school educator*
Hinkle, Betty Ruth *educational administrator*
Kettner Polley, Richard Brian *director*
Matzke, Rex Kay *education educator*
Olivas, Phil *secondary school educator*
Shockley-Zalabak, Pamela Sue *academic administrator*
Vandenberg, Sara E. *secondary school educator*

Commerce City
Baker, Maria Luise *retired secondary school educator*

Denver
Bosworth, Bruce Leighton *school administrator, educator, consultant*
Brown, Hank *foundation administrator, former university administrator, former senator*
Burrows, Bertha Jean *retired academic administrator*
Caldwell, Richard A. *director*
Coombe, Bob *academic administrator*
Driggs, Margaret *educator*
Ernewein, Philippe *educational consultant, educator*
Fielden, C. Franklin, III, *early childhood education consultant*
Fulkerson, William Measey, Jr., *college president*
Gibson, Elisabeth Jane *retired principal*
Halgren, Lee A. *academic administrator*
Jarles, Ruth Sewell *education educator*
Kaplan, Sheila *academic administrator*
Landesman, Howard M. *academic administrator*
Messer, Donald Edward *theological school president, theology educator*
Pearson, Michelle Line *private school educator, not-for-profit fundraiser*
Pointer, Marsha G. *principal*
Ritchie, Daniel Lee *academic administrator*
Rubin, Cathy Ann *retired educator*
Vogel, Robert Lee *retired college administrator, clergyman*
Wright, Carole Dean *reading specialist*

Durango
Jones, Joel Mackey *academic administrator*

Englewood
Graves, Nada Proctor *retired elementary school educator*
Shields, Marlene Sue *elementary school educator*

Estes Park
Guest, Linda Sand *education educator*

Fort Collins
Baldwin, Lionel Vernon *retired university president*
Harper, Judson Morse *retired university administrator, consultant, educator*
Karbula, John Charles *principal*
Maher, Thomas George *academic administrator, producer, media educator*
Nicholls, Peter J. *academic administrator*
Perryman, Lance *dean*
Savage, Eldon Paul *retired environmental health educator*
Yates, Albert Carl *academic administrator, chemistry educator*

Fort Morgan
Raines, Louis Edward *school administrator*

Fruita
Bowles, Kelley Kay *secondary school educator, writer*

Golden
Bickart, Theodore Albert *university president emeritus*
Klug, John Joseph *secondary school educator, director*
Shea, Dion Warren Joseph *university official, fund raiser*
Truly, Richard H. *academic administrator, former federal agency administrator, former astronaut*

Greeley
Bond, Richard Randolph *foundation administrator, legislator*
Duff, William Leroy, Jr., *university dean emeritus, business educator*

Greenwood Village
Lynn, Patricia Anne *student services representative*

Henderson
Sauceda, Augustina Jo *pre-school educator*

Lakewood
Hummel, Carol Lucille *education educator, writer*
Joy, Carla Marie *history educator*
McBride, Guy Thornton, Jr., *college president emeritus*

Littleton
Greenberg, Elinor Miller *university official, consultant*
Kennedy, Jack *secondary education journalism educator*
Lesh-Laurie, Georgia Elizabeth *university administrator, biology educator, researcher*
Rothenberg, Harvey David *educational administrator*
Tucker, James Raymond *primary education educator*

Loveland
Lee, Evelyn Marie *elementary school educator, secondary school educator*

Morrison
DeMiro, Diane Mollie *parochial school educator*

Nederland
Gibson, Lena S. *secondary school educator*
Lutz, Frank Wenzel *education administration educator*
Morrison, K. Jaydene *education counseling firm executive*

Pueblo
Sisson, Ray L. *retired dean, author*

Snowmass Village
DiBiaggio, John A. *university president*

Westminster
Eaves, Stephen Douglas *high school and vocational administrator, educator, consultant*
Hartman, Susan P(atrice) *adult education administrator*

CONNECTICUT

Bloomfield
Foster, Benjamin, Jr., *educational administrator*

Branford
Milgram, Richard Myron *music school administrator*

Bridgeport
Hendricks, Edward David *education director, consultant, speaker, trainer*
Lanci, Janet Mead *academic administrator, educator*

Bristol
Copeland, Karin A. *training director*

Coventry
Ferguson, Ronald Max *chemistry educator, researcher*

Danbury
Hawkes, Carol Ann *academic administrator*
Jensen-Ruopp, Helga Spitko *school program administrator, consultant*
Roach, James Richard *university president*

Fairfield
Cernera, Anthony Joseph *academic administrator*
Howell, Karen Jane *private school educator*
Kelley, Aloysius Paul *university administrator, priest*
Miles, Leland Weber *university president*
Paolini, Claire Jacqueline *dean, educator*

Falls Village
Purcell, Dale *college president, consultant*
Purcell, Mary Louise Gerlinger *retired adult education educator*

Farmington
Cutler, Leslie Stuart *academic administrator, educator*
Deckers, Peter John *dean*

Glastonbury
Hatch, D. Patricia P. *principal*

Greenwich
Behr, Meredith Allison *private school educator*
Pursley, Carol Roberts *admissions director*

Groton
English, James Fairfield, Jr., *former college president*

Guilford
Speth, James Gustave *dean, environmental studies educator, lawyer*

Hamden
Brown, Jay Marshall *retired secondary school educator*

Hartford
Brown, W. Miller *dean (faculty)*
Cibes, William Joseph, Jr., *chancellor, educator*
Frost, James Arthur *former university president*
Hassett, Patricia *university administrator*
Newton, Nell Jessup *dean, law educator*
Reynolds, Scott Walton *academic administrator*
Rosa, Peter Manuel *academic administrator, researcher, education educator*
Skerker, Arthur J. *secondary school educator*
Stuart, Ann *academic administrator, writer, educator*

Middletown
Bennet, Douglas Joseph, Jr., *university president*
Brown, Judith *academic administrator*
Craig, Barbara Kinkson *academic administrator*

Monroe
Kranyik, Elizabeth Ann *secondary school educator*

Mystic
Chace, William Murdough *former university administrator*

New Britain
Lunn, Charles Paul *secondary school educator*

New Fairfield
Lambrech, Régine M. *college program administrator, language educator*

New Haven
Alpern, Robert J. *dean, medical educator*
Garten, Jeffrey E. *college dean, educator, marketing professional*
Gaudiani, Claire Lynn *retired academic administrator*
Hennah, Vivian Lisa *school system administrator*
Krasner, David *education educator*
Kronman, Anthony Townsend *law educator, dean*
Lamar, Howard Roberts *educational administrator, historian*

Levin, Richard Charles *academic administrator, economist*
Lorimer, Linda Koch *university educator*
McNamara, Julia Mary *academic administrator, foreign language educator*
Norton, Cheryl J. *academic administrator*
Pepper, John Ennis, Jr., *academic administrator*
Seilacher, Adolf *special education educator*
Soderstrom, Edward Jonathan *academic administrator, consultant*
Waxman, Merle *dean*
Whitman, James Quick *education educator*
Yandle, Stephen Thomas *dean*

New London
Fainstein, Norman *college president*
Olsen, Robert C., Jr., *academic administrator, military officer*

North Haven
Fuggi, Gretchen Miller *education educator*
Hudson, Richard L. *retired adult education educator, minister*

North Stonington
Keane, John Patrick *retired secondary education educator*

Norwalk
Nelson, Paula Morrison Bronson *gifted and talented educator, consultant*

Ridgefield
Brewster, Carroll Worcester *former academic administrator*
Leonard, Sister Anne C. *superintendent, education director*
Lindsay, Dianna Marie *educational administrator*

Storrs
Lee, Hanho *educator, researcher*
Siegle, Del *education educator*

Storrs Mansfield
Austin, Philip Edward *university president*
Kerr, Kirklyn M. *university administrator, veterinary pathologist, researcher*
MacDonald, John Thomas *educational administrator*
Maryanski, Fred *academic administrator*
Price, Glenda Delores *university dean*

Trumbull
Lang, James Richard *education consultant*
Madigan, Rita Duffy *career education coordinator*
Nevins, Lyn (Carolyn A. Nevins) *educational supervisor, trainer, consultant*
Norcel, Jacqueline Joyce Casale *educational administrator*
Potter, Andrew Harold *secondary school educator*

Waterbury
Brown, Lillian Hill *retired academic administrator*

West Hartford
Anderson, Michael *education educator*
Echols, Ivor Tatum *retired educator, assistant dean*
Gaumond, Lynn E. *elementary school educator*
Harrison, Walter Lee *university president*
Malone, Thomas Francis *academic administrator, meteorologist*
Tonkin, Humphrey Richard *academic administrator, educator*

West Haven
DeNardis, Lawrence J. *academic administrator*
Farquharson, Patrice Ellen *primary school educator*
Singh, Parbudyal *dean, educator*

Willimantic
Carter, David George, Sr., *university administrator*
Wilson, Margaret Sullivan *retired executive dean, consultant*

Wilton
Grunewald, Donald *former college president, educator*

Windsor Locks
Coelho, Sandra Signorelli *secondary school educator, consultant*

Winsted
Baccus, R. Eileen Turner *academic administrator*

DELAWARE

Bear
Hersi, Dorothy Talbert *education educator*
McLain, William Tome *principal, educator*
Stewart, Shirley Anne *educational administrator*

Dover
Braverman, Ray Howard *secondary school educator*
Delauder, William B. *academic administrator*
Ferrari, Mercedes V *secondary school educator*
Gorum, Jacquelyne W. *dean, social work educator*
Sessoms, Allen Lee *academic administrator, former diplomat, physicist*
Smith, Charles Nathaniel *academic administrator*
Sorenson, Liane Beth McDowell *women's affairs director, state legislator*
Wagner, Nancy Hughes *secondary school educator, state legislator*

Laurel
Kile, Kenda Jones *educational consultant*

Millsboro
Gallite-McGinnis, Anne Rita *elementary school educator*

New Castle
Brownson, Kenneth C. *university dean*
Doberstein, Audrey K. *college president*

Newark
Carter, Mae Riedy *retired academic official, consultant*
Clayton, John Middleton, Jr., *development officer*
Gehrlein, William Vincent *business education educator*
Hockersmith, Charles Edwin *information technology educator*
Huang, Chin-pao *education educator*
Rich, Daniel *provost*
Roselle, David Paul *university president, mathematics educator*
Schiavelli, Melvyn David *academic administrator, science educator, researcher*

Wilmington
Chagnon, Lucille Tessier *workforce development and literacy specialist*
Higgins, Roxanne Snelling *educational consultant*
Olson, Leroy Calvin *retired educational administration educator*

DISTRICT OF COLUMBIA

Washington
Alatis, James Efstathios *university dean emeritus*
Aleinikoff, Thomas Alexander *dean, law educator*
Allan, Ronald Gage *university research coordinator*
Arnez, Nancy Levi *educational leadership educator*
Barrett, Richard David *university director, consultant, bank executive*
Beckham, Edgar Frederick *educational consultant*
Bernstein, Melvin *provost*
Biggs, Jeffrey Robert *educator*
Boggs, George Robert *academic administrator*
Brown, Priscilla Ann *elementary school educator*
Bulger, Roger James *academic health center executive*
Bullock, Alice Gresham *university dean*
Burgin, Walter Hotchkiss, Jr., *educational administrator*
Burris, James Frederick *federal healthcare administrator, educator*
Caputo, Anne Spencer *knowledge and learning programs director*
Chamberlain, Mary *retired academic administrator, translator*
Chambers, Franklin Delano *academic administrator*
Christian, Mary Jo Dinan *educational administrator, educator*
Churchill, John Hugh *college academic administrator*
Cleland, Joseph Maxwell (Max Cleland) *education educator, retired state official*
Collins, Michael John *education educator*
Convey, John J. *academic administrator*
Crosby, David S *statistics educator, consultant*
DeGioia, John J. *university president*
Dixon, Michel L. *educational administrator*
Donley, Rosemary *university official*
Duffey, Joseph Daniel *academic administrator*
Elliott, Emerson John *education consultant, policy analyst*
Feder, Judith *dean*
Felbinger, Claire Louise *research administrator*
Fisher, Miles Mark, IV, *education and religion educator, minister*
Flaherty, Sister Mary Jean *dean*
Fosler, R. Scott *academic administrator*
French, Roderick Stuart *university chancellor*
Gaff, Jerry Gene *academic administrator*
Geiselman, LucyAnn *college president*
Hagan, Philip Edward, Jr., *academic administrator*
Halperin, Samuel *education and training policy analyst*
Hayes, Kevin Gregory *university administrator*
Herbert, James Charles *academic administrator*
Jarvis, Charlene Drew *university administrator, former scientist*
Jenkins, Timothy L. *university president, communications executive*
Johnson, Judith A. *educational administrator*
Jones, Judith Miller *director*
Jordan, Irving King *university president*
Kang, Young Woo *special education educator, dean*
Karelis, Charles Howard (Buddy Karelis) *former academic administrator, humanities educator*
Katsapis, Christine Campbell Anne *university research administrator*
Keeley, Robert Vossler *retired academic administrator, retired ambassador*
Kerwin, Cornelius Martin *provost, dean, public affairs educator*
Kirkien-Rzeszotarski, Alicja Maria *academic administrator, researcher, educator*
Ladner, Benjamin *university president*
Lebel, Gregory Galen *educator, consultant*
Lefton, Lester Alan *dean, psychology educator*
Longstreth, Richard Washington *education educator, consultant*
Lovett, Clara Maria *university administrator, historian*
Luttwak, Edward Nicolae *academic administrator, educator, policy and business consultant*
Malveaux, Floyd Joseph *dean*
Manley, Audrey Forbes *retired academic administrator, pediatrician, military officer*
Mayo, John W. *dean, educator, researcher*
Mohrman, Kathryn J *academic administrator*
Nelson, Jacqueline Dunham *elementary school educator*
Nwagbaraocha, Joel Onukwugha *academic administrator, educator*
Obiedat, Mohammad Ahmad *education educator, researcher*
O'Connell, David M. *academic administrator*
O'Donovan, Leo Jeremiah *former academic administrator, priest, theologian*
Pagel, Scott B. *dean, law librarian, law educator*
Peck, Malcolm Cameron *educational exchange specialist*
Petty, Rachel *academic administrator*
Ramos, Flavia Sales *education educator, consultant*
Ranck, Edna Runnels *academic administrator, researcher*
Reddel, Carl Walter *educational administrator*
Riccards, Michael Patrick *academic administrator*
Rouse, Leo E. *dean, dental educator*
Sanders, Charles F. *dean*
Santoro, Miléna *education educator*
Schmoke, Kurt L. *dean, former mayor*
Sedmak, Daniel D. *academic administrator*
Smith, Abbie Oliver *college administrator, educator*
Smuckler, Ralph Herbert *dean, political scientist, educator*
Solomon, Henry *university dean*
Steigman, Andrew L. *academic dean*
Stewart, Debra Wehrle *academic administrator*
Stopford, Michael John *university administrator*
Studds, Susan Martin *education educator*
Sweeting, Sharon Howe *school librarian, editor*
Swygert, Haywood Patrick *academic administrator*
Thompson, Bernida Lamerle *principal, consultant, educator*
Timpane, Philip Michael *education educator, policy analyst*
Titus-Dillon, Pauline Yvonne *associate dean academic affairs, medical educator*
Trachtenberg, Stephen Joel *university president*
Tucker, Marc Stephen *education policy analyst, author*
Van Ummersen, Claire A(nn) *academic administrator, biologist, educator*
Ward, David *academic administrator, educator*
Weiss, Charles, Jr., *educator*
Westmoreland, Timothy M. *education educator*
Williams, Jackie L. *public administrator*
Zhao, Quansheng *university administrator, educator*

FLORIDA

Babson Park
Warner, Steven S. *dean*

Boca Raton
Arden, Eugene *retired university provost*
Boykin, Anne J. *dean*
Capps, David Edward, Jr., *assistant dean*
Connor, Frances Partridge *retired education educator*
Connor, Leo Edward *special education administrator*
Decker, Larry E. *education educator*
Leary, William James *educational administrator*
Lowe, Benno Powers, II, *History professor*
Miller, Eugene *university official, business executive*
Ross, Donald Edward *university administrator*
Tennies, Robert Hunter *headmaster*
Warshaw, Carole Klein *education educator, consultant*

Bokeelia
Adams, Alfred Hugh *retired college president*

Bonita Springs
Becker, Richard Charles *retired college president*
Johnson, Franklyn Arthur *academic administrator*
McManigal, Shirley Ann *university educator, dean emerita*

Bradenton
Driscoll, Constance Fitzgerald *education educator, writer, consultant*
Pillot, Gene Merrill *retired school system administrator*

Cape Coral
Graham, Minnie Dorothy *elementary school educator*

Clearwater
Jacobs, Marilyn Arlene Potoker *gifted education educator, consultant, author*

Cocoa
Gamble, Thomas Ellsworth *academic administrator*

Coconut Creek
Brenner, Egon *university official, education consultant*
Rogge, James Alan *education educator*

Coconut Grove
Soto, Patricia McFarlane *elementary school educator*

Coral Gables
Horner, Diane L. *dean*
Murfin, Ross C *university dean, English educator*
Shalala, Donna E. *university administrator, former federal official, political scientist, educator*

Coral Springs
Becker, Allienne R. *education educator, writer*

Dania
Fernander, Karen Geneine *secondary school educator*

Davie
Jackson, Lisa Keisha *educational consultant*
Silva, Yvonne N. *registrar*

Daytona Beach
Brady, Tim *dean*
Ebbs, George Heberling, Jr., *university executive*
Fuqua, Muriel *education educator*
Hartsell, Horace Ed *college president*
Libbey, James K. *education educator*
Sharples, D. Kent *college administrator*

Deerfield Beach
Hoppenstedt, Elbert M. *retired school system administrator*

Deland
Brakeman, Louis Freeman *retired university official*
Dascher, Paul Edward *university dean, accounting educator*
Gill, Donald George *retired education educator*
Langston, Paul T. *music educator, university dean, composer*
Lee, Howard Douglas *academic administrator*
Morland, Richard Boyd *retired educator*
Wittich, John Jacob *retired academic administrator, business executive*

Destin
Asher, Betty Turner *academic administrator*

Dunnellon
Fonseca, Julio *retired secondary school educator*

Estero
Brush, George W. *college president*

Fort Lauderdale
Edmund, Norman Wilson *educational researcher*
Fischler, Abraham Saul *retired academic administrator, educator*
Ginn, Vera Walker *director*
Hanbury, George Lafayette, II, *academic administrator*
Klein, Stacy Lynn *educational consultant*
McCan, James Lawton *education educator*
Miller, Stephen Warren *dean*
Sanderson, Rita Marye *history educator*
Spungin, Charlotte Isabelle *retired secondary education educator, writer*
Tolchin, Karen Rebecca *adult education educator*
Trubey, Lillian Priscilla *secondary education educator, retired*
Uchin, Robert Allen *dean, endodontist*

Fort Myers
Canham, Pruella Cromartie Niver *retired educator*
Pouliot, Assunta Gallucci *retired business school owner and director, consultant*

Fort Pierce
Massey, Edwin R. *college president*

Fort Walton Beach
Sanders, Jimmy Devon *public administration and health services educator*

Gainesville
Brodeur, Michael Stephen *dean*
Bryan, Robert Armistead *university administrator, educator*
Challoner, David Reynolds *academic administrator, endocrinologist*
Cheek, Jimmy Geary *university administrator, agricultural education and communications educator*
Colburn, David R. *academic administrator*
DiPietro, Joseph A. *dean, educator*
Dolan, Teresa A. *dean, educator, researcher*
Gets, Lispbeth Ella *educational administrator*
Hay-Roe, Mirian Medina *education educator, researcher*
Lane, Jodi *education educator*
Lowenstein, Ralph Lynn *university dean emeritus*
Machen, James Bernard *academic administrator*
Mills, Jon *dean, law educator*
Pham, Andrea Hoa *educator, writer*
Phillips, Winfred Marshall *university administrator, biomedical research executive, mechanical engineer, educator*
Rosenberger, Margaret Adaline *retired elementary school educator, writer*
Viessman, Warren, Jr., *civil engineering educator emeritus, researcher*
York, E. Travis *academic administrator, former university chancellor, consultant*

Goulds
Taylor, Millicent Ruth *elementary school educator*

Graceville
Kinchen, Thomas Alexander *college president*

Gulfport
Athanson, Mary Catheryne *school system administrator*

Hialeah
Agrawal, Piyush C. *school system administrator*
Palacios, Olga *director*

Homestead
Davis, Scott Michael *director, music educator*
Horton, Thelma White *educational administrator, author*

Jacksonville
Cornelius, Jacquelyn H. *high school principal, educator*
Corse, John Doggett *university official, lawyer*
Delaney, John Adrian *academic administrator*
Dumbleton, Duane Dean *college president, educator*
Fine, Cory R. *education educator, consultant*
Jamrich, John Xavier *retired university administrator*
Jenkins, Jimmy Raymond *university president*
Kinne, Frances Bartlett *academic administrator*
Leonard, Thomas Michael *university program director, educator*
Main, Edna Dewey (June Main) *education educator*
Olin, Marilyn *secondary school educator*
Osborn, Marvin Griffing, Jr., *educational consultant*
Sandercox, Robert Allen *college official, clergyman*
Simms, Jacqueline Kamp *secondary school educator*
Vadnal, John Louis *dean, mathematician, educator*
Wallace, Steven R. *college president*

Kennedy Space Center
Feldman, Stephen *academic administrator*

Kissimmee
Haynes, Ulric St. Clair, Jr., *retired dean*
Rattie, Margaret Elizabeth (Beth Rattie) *elementary school educator*
Toothe, Karen Lee *elementary and secondary school educator*

Lake Worth
Gallon, Dennis P. *college president*
Taylor, Clifford Otis *retired principal*

Lakeland
Herron, Robert Wilburn, Jr., *academic administrator, educator*
Mooney, Burton Lee *retired secondary school educator, editor*
Tate, Robert Hale *academic administrator*
Wade, Ben Frank *college administrator*

Lakeland,
Washington, Gloria Dunn *secondary school educator*

Lecanto
Mathia, Mary Loyola *parochial school educator, nun*

Longwood
Johnson, Nancy Plattner *secondary school educator*

Manalapan
Phipard, Nancy Midwood *retired special education educator, poet*

Marco Island
Ballou, Mildred Oralee *elementary school educator, pre-school educator*
Henry, Sally *assistant principal*

Marianna
Standland, Jamie *director, music educator*

Melbourne
Bailey, J. Ronald *dean, engineering educator*
Catanese, Anthony James *academic administrator*
Hollingsworth, Abner Thomas *university dean*
Stark, Norman *secondary school educator*
Weaver, Lynn Edward *academic administrator, consultant, editor*

Merritt Island
McClanahan, Leland *university director*
Thompson, Hugh Lee *academic administrator*
Walter, George Anthony *elementary school educator*

Miami
Bachmeyer, Steven Allan *secondary school educator*
Banas, Suzanne *middle school educator*
Brooten, Dorothy *nursing educator, former dean*
Butterworth, Robert A. *dean, former state attorney general*
Clarkson, John G. *academic administrator, ophthalmologist*
Foote, Edward Thaddeus, II, *university president, lawyer*
Halberg, F. David *principal*
Johnson, Channey *elementary school educator*
Jones, Janice Cox *elementary school educator, writer*
Kaplan, Betsy Hess *school board member*
Lee, J. Patrick *academic administrator*
Love, Mildred Allison *retired secondary school educator, historian, writer, volunteer*
Maidique, Modesto Alex *academic administrator*
McCabe, Robert Howard *college president*
Rodriguez-Walling, Matilde Barcelo *special education educator*
Stiehm, Judith Hicks *university official, political science educator*
Vielot, Alain J. *elementary school educator*
Wright, Pamela Jean *academic administrator*

Miami Beach
Gitlow, Abraham Leo *retired dean*

Milton
Seaton, Carolle Carter *educator, writer*

Montverde
Carlo-Melendez, Arnaldo *mathematics educator*

Mount Dora
Scharfenberg, Margaret Ellan *retired elementary school educator*

Naples
Finger, Iris Dale Abrams *elementary school educator*

New Port Richey
Hardway, Wendell Gary *retired academic administrator*

Newberry
Thornton, J. Ronald *technology consultant*

Nokomis
Lockledge, Jack E. *retired principal*

North Lauderdale
Altman, Miriam Elizabeth *director, music educator*

North Miami
Pierre-louis, Rosaire *elementary school educator, educator*

North Miami Beach
Sorosky, Jeri Ruth *academic administrator*

Ocala
Delozier, Doris M. *retired secondary school educator*
Gatison, Karen Ann *private school educator*
Ovrebo, Judith *retired physical education educator*
Renda, Rosa A. *special education educator*

Opa Locka
Smith, Albert E. *college president*
Wilson, Isabel Gomez *elementary school educator, consultant*

Orange Park
Miller, Martin Eugene *school system consultant, negotiator, lobbyist*

Orlando
Avery, Kay Beth *secondary school educator*
Clinton, Stephen Michael *academic administrator*
Colbourn, Trevor *retired university president, historian*
Gianini, Paul C., Jr., *academic administrator*
Guzman, Marie Elvira *school guidance counselor*
Hitt, John Charles *academic administrator*

Oviedo
MacKenzie, Charles Sherrard *academic administrator*

Palatka
Embree, Mary Evelyn *retired secondary school educator*

Palm Bay
Colman, Charles Kingsbury *academic administrator, criminologist*

Palm Beach Gardens
Brosemer, Jim P *education educator*
Orr, Joseph Alexander *educational administrator*

Pembroke Pines
Embergher, Mary Louise *elementary school educator*

Pensacola
Kimball, Bob *education educator, writer*

Plantation
Young, William Benjamin *retired special education educator*

Pompano Beach
Bookbinder, Robert Max *superintendent of schools*
Hellwege, Nancy Carol *special education educator*
Johnson, Dorothy Curfman *elementary school educator*

Ponte Vedra Beach
Hartzell, Karl Drew *retired university dean, historian*
Patterson, Oscar, III, *university program administrator*
Tyler, Diane Lazzelle *elementary school educator*

Port Charlotte
Hill, Richard Earl *academic administrator*

Port Saint Lucie
Guglielmino, Lucy Margaret Madsen *education educator, researcher, consultant*

Punta Gorda
Eliason, Nancy Carol *education consultant*
Kampa, William *retired elementary school educator, writer*
Klarik, Bela William James Clark *retired school system administrator*
Spaulding, Mar *retired special education educator, therapist*

Rockledge
Sutton, Betty Sheriff *elementary school educator*

Saint Augustine
Proctor, William Lee *college chancellor*
Sappington, Sharon Anne *retired school librarian*

Saint Petersburg
Armacost, Peter Hayden *academic administrator*
Dunlap, Karen F. Brown *academic administrator*
Griffin, Dennis Joseph *middle school principal*
Kerlin, Max L. *academic administrator*
Kuttler, Carl Martin, Jr., *academic administrator*
Meyer, Robert Allen *human resource management educator*
Nussbaum, Leo Lester *retired college president, consultant*
Sebastien, Anya Celita *academic administrator, consultant*
Southworth, William Dixon *retired education educator*
Wetzel, Laura Reiser *educator*

Sanford
Tossi, Alice Louise *special education educator*

Sarasota
Atwell, Robert Herron *higher education executive*
Christ-Janer, Arland Frederick *college president*
Cleland, Sherrill *college president*
Martia, Dominic Francis *academic administrator*
Stevens, Leonard Berry *educational consultant*
Thompson, Annie Figueroa *retired academic director, educator*

Sebastian
Mauke, Otto Russell *retired college president*

Spring Hill
Hopkins, Thomas Charles *behavior specialist*
Rojas, Victor Hugo Macedo *retired vocational education educator*
Wood, Shelton Eugene *education educator, consultant, minister*

Stuart
Maktouf, Samir *education company executive*

Summerfield
Shaw, Danny Wayne *educational consultant, musician*

Sun City Center
Gummere, Walter Cooper *educator, consultant*

Sunrise
Stalker, Jacqueline D'Aoust *academic administrator, educator*

Tallahassee
Bailey, Theresa L. *director, consultant*
Burkman, Ernest, Jr., *education educator*
Burnette, Ada M. Puryear *retired educational administrator*
D'Alemberte, Talbot (Sandy D'Alemberte) *academic administrator, lawyer*
Friedman, Max Paul *education educator*
Grant, Sydney R. *education educator, consultant*
Leon, Karen Renée *elementary school educator*
Lick, Dale Wesley *educational leadership educator*
Losh, Susan Carol *education educator, researcher*
Mills, Belen Collantes *early childhood education educator*
Morgan, Robert Marion *educational research educator*
Riley, Kenneth Jerome *athletic director*
Sliger, Bernard Francis *academic administrator, economist, educator*
Wetherell, Thomas Kent *college president*

Tampa
Barrow, Frederica Harrison *education educator, social worker*
Daugherty, Robert Melvin, Jr., *dean, medical educator*
Givens, Paul Ronald *former university chancellor*
Harlow, Carol Jean *prospect researcher*
Hegarty, Thomas Joseph *academic administrator, history educator*
Luddington, Betty Walles *library media specialist*
McCook, Kathleen de la Peña *university educator*
Meisels, Gerhard George *academic administrator, chemist, educator*
Sanchez, Mary Anne *retired secondary school educator*
Ziegler, Robert Oliver *retired music and special education educator*

Tarpon Springs
Byrne, Richard Hill *counselor, educator*

The Villages
Phillips, Patricia Jeanne *retired school system administrator*

Tierra Verde
Schmitz, Dolores Jean *primary education educator*

Titusville
Arnold, Betty Bunnell *secondary school educator*

Valrico
Straub, Susan Monica *special education educator*

Venice
Finlay, Susan Sparling *education educator*

Weeki Wachee
Jernstrom, Joan *retired secondary school educator*

West Palm Beach
Corts, Paul Richard *college president*
Mims, Lloyd Lee *dean, conductor, vocalist*

Wewahitchka
Stryker, Terence Wayne *secondary school educator*

Winter Garden
Gillet, Pamela Kipping *special education educator*

Winter Haven
Peck, Maryly VanLeer *retired academic administrator, chemical engineer*

Winter Park
Bornstein, Rita *academic administrator*
Sinclair, Gail D. *education educator*

Zephyrhills
Barron, Ilona Eleanor *reading educator, consultant*

GEORGIA

Albany
Coats-Hardy, Janice Ellen *counseling administrator, educator*
Ellis, Mark E. *school librarian*
Keith, Carolyn Austin *secondary school counselor*
Shields, Portia Holmes *academic administrator*
Stanley-Chavis, Sandra Ornecia *special education educator, consultant*

Americus
Capitan, William Harry *university president emeritus*
Nichols, Harold James *university dean*
Stanford, Henry King *college president*

Athens
Adams, Michael Fred *university president, political communications specialist*
Andrews, Grover Jene *adult education educator, administrator*
Benson, P. George *dean, finance educator*
Coley, Linda Marie *retired secondary school educator*
Crowley, John Francis, III, *university dean*
Feldman, Daniel Charles *adult education educator*
Golembiewski, Robert Thomas *educator, management consultant*
Herrman, Margaret Susan *university official, sociologist*
Mace, Arnett Clay, Jr., *university administrator*
Marable, Robert Blane *secondary school educator, agricultural studies educator*
Prasse, Keith W. *dean*
Reid, Leonard N. *academic administrator*
Shipley, David Elliott *dean, lawyer*
Smagorinsky, Peter *education educator*
Wraga, William Gerard *educator*

Atlanta
Aaberg, Thomas Marshall, Sr., *academic administrator*
Affonso, Dyanne D. *dean*
Alexander, Cecil Abraham *college official, architect, consultant*
Bailey, Joy Hafner *counselor educator*
Beik, William H. *education educator, writer*
Blum, Terry C. *dean*
Bright, David Forbes *academic administrator, classicist, educator*
Chameau, Jean-Lou *academic administrator*
Clough, Gerald Wayne *academic administrator*
Cole, Thomas Winston, Jr., *chancellor, college president, chemist*
Curry, Toni Griffin *counseling center executive, consultant*
Denmark, Darron B. *compliance specialist*
Galloway, Thomas D. *dean*
Geil, Mark D. *education educator*
Hall, Beverly L. *school system administrator*
Harris, Eon Nigel *dean, rheumatologist, internist*
Henry, Ronald James Whyte *academic administrator, physicist, educator*
Hogan, John Donald *retired college dean, finance educator*
Hunter, Howard Owen *academic administrator, law educator*
Ignatonis, Sandra Carole Autry *special education educator*
Jolley, Samuel Delanor, Jr., *academic administrator*
Keiller, James Bruce *college dean, clergyman*
Lawley, Thomas Joseph *dean, medical educator*
Lee, Hamilton H. *education educator*
Lewis, Earl *academic administrator*
Lovewell, Marjorie Klingensmith *secondary school educator*
Lucas-Tauchar, M. Frances *university administrator*
Maddox-Adams, Sherry *secondary school educator*
Meredith, Thomas C. *academic administrator*
Meyer, Ellen L. *academic administrator*
Meyer, Richard W. *school librarian*
Myrick, Cecilia Jane *education educator, consultant*
Nentwich, Michael Andreas Erhart *educator, consultant*
Orenstein, Walter Albert *director*
Patton, Carl Vernon *academic administrator, educator*
Richey, Russell E. *university dean*
Robertson, Thomas Sinclair *dean, marketing educator*
Rogers, Brenda Gayle *educational administrator, educator, consultant*
Towslee, Janet L. *special education educator*
Wagner, James Warren *academic administrator, engineering educator*
Xu, Shucheng *chemistry educator, research scientist*
Yancey, Carolyn Dunbar *educational policy maker*
Zhao, Yichuan *education educator*

Augusta
Lewis, Shirley Ann Redd *college president*
Potter, Brad J. *dean, researcher, educator*
Puryear, Joan Copeland *academic administrator*
Stern, David Mark *dean, educator*
Tedesco, Francis Joseph *retired academic administrator, medical educator*

Avondale Estates
Fowler, Andrea *teachers academy administrator*

Bishop
Bower, Douglas William *pastoral counselor, psychotherapist, clergyman*

Brunswick
Hanson, Carol Hall *elementary school educator*
Pittman, Catherine Sylvia *secondary school educator*
Spencer, Shirley Ann *secondary school educator, speech educator, literature educator*

Carrollton
Brewer, A. Bruce *university administrator*
Morgan, Harry New *education educator*
Sethna, Beheruz Nariman *university president, marketing, management educator*

Cartersville
Wang, Pinghua *education educator*

Chatsworth
Beasley, Troy Daniel *secondary education educator*

College Park
Ferguson, Wendell *private school educator*

Columbus
Brown, Frank Douglas *academic administrator*
Montgomery, Anna Frances *elementary school educator*
Riggsby, Dutchie Sellers *education educator*
Ripple, Rochelle Poyourow *educational administrator, educator*

Conyers
Bouchillon, John Ray *education coordinator*

Cumming
Benson, Betty Jones *retired school system administrator*

Dahlonega
Hansford, Nathaniel *academic administrator, lawyer*

Decatur
Baker, Stephen Monroe *school system administrator*
Bullock, Mary Brown *college president*

Demorest
Rogers, Elizabeth (Betty) Carlisle *education educator, consultant*

Duluth
Pickett, Christa Langford *elementary school counselor*

East Point
Johnson, Hardwick Smith, Jr., *school psychologist*

Fairburn
Hughes, Cheryl Peck *elementary school educator, director*

Folkston
Knowles, Julie Nall *secondary school educator*

Forest Park
Lambert, Ethel Gibson Clark *secondary school educator*

Gainesville
Burd, John Stephen *retired academic administrator, music educator*
Mills, Hugh Milton, Jr., *retired college president*

Gainesville Georgia
Teem, Clayton L(aVerne), II, *education educator, psychologist*

Jonesboro
Blevins, Andrea Elizabeth *secondary school educator*

Kennesaw
Siegel, Betty Lentz *university president*

Lagrange
Ault, Ethyl Lorita *special education educator, consultant*

Lake Park
Blanton, Vallye J. *elementary school educator*

Lawrenceville
Crain, Mary Ann *elementary school educator*

Lithonia
Smith, Shaunte Renee *secondary school educator, poet*

Macon
Godsey, R(aleigh) Kirby *university president*
Jobe, Ann Connor *dean, educator*
Steeples, Douglas Wayne *retired university dean, consultant, researcher*

Marietta
Houston, Dorothy Middleton *elementary school educator*
Laframboise, Joan Carol *middle school educator*
Murray, Barry Wayne *economics educator*
Oliver, Ann Breeding *secondary school educator*
Rivers, Alma Faye *secondary school educator*
Rossbacher, Lisa Ann *university president, geology educator, writer*
Segerhammar, Sharon K. *special education administrator*

Metter
Farmer, DeWayne Mark *director, photographer*

Milledgeville
Deal, Therry Nash *college dean*
Harshbarger, D. Bruce, Sr., *director, educator*
Leland, Dorothy *academic administrator*
Reed, Harold Wayne *university program coordinator*

Monroe
Sewell, Joan Marshall *retired elementary school educator*

Morrow
Smith-Jones, Mary Emily *elementary school physical education educator*

Mount Vernon
Jossey, Laurie A. *education educator*
Smith, David Robert *higher education administrator, minister, writer*

Peachtree City
Barnes, Marylou Riddleberger *retired academic administrator, educator*
Wilde, Mary *secondary school educator*

Rome
Sheeley, Steven M. *academic administrator, minister, education educator*

Saint Marys
Hall, Lois Bremer *retired educator, volunteer*

Saint Simons Island
Mathis, Luster Doyle *college administrator, political scientist*

Savannah
Brown, Carlton E. *college president*
Dirlam, David Kirk *education educator*
Leighton, Richard Frederick *retired dean*
Polite, Evelyn C. *retired middle school educator, counselor, evangelist*
Taggart, Helen M. *adult education educator, nurse*
Thompson, Larry James *retired gifted and social studies education educator*
Wallace, Paula S. *academic administrator*

Smyrna
Bean, Susan Montgomery *secondary school educator*

Snellville
Magill, Dodie Burns *early childhood education educator*

Statesboro
Ngai, Sze-Man *education educator*

Stone Mountain
Dees, Julian Worth *retired academic/research administrator*
Gary, C. Ceci *primary school educator*

Swainsboro
Edenfield, Cynthia Smith *pre-school educator*

Toccoa Falls
Alford, Paul Legare *college and religious foundation administrator*
Gardner, Donna Rae (Diehl) *education educator*

Valdosta
Aronson-Friedman, Amy Ilene *education educator*
Bailey, Hugh Coleman *university president*

Winterville
Anderson, David Prewitt *retired university dean*

Zebulon
Bizzell Yarbrough, Cindy Lee *school counselor*

HAWAII

Aiea
Suyenaga, Elsie Sakae *secondary school educator*

Hilo
Tseng, Rose *academic administrator*

Honolulu
Agrusa, Jerome *tourism studies educator, consultant*
Cadman, Edwin Clarence *dean, health facility administrator, medical educator*
Chee, Gloria Y.M. *secondary school educator*
Chock, Raelene *school system administrator*
Gee, Chuck Yim *dean*
Gonsalves, Margaret Leboy *elementary school educator*
Hamamoto, Patricia *school system administrator, educator*
Keith, Kent Marsteller *academic administrator, writer, lawyer, recreational facility executive*
King, Arthur R., Jr., *education educator, researcher*
Leton, Donald A. *counseling administrator*
Masters, Elaine *educator, writer*
Mortimer, Kenneth P. *retired academic administrator*
Neubauer, Deane *academic administrator*

Perkins, Frank Overton *university official, marine scientist*
Pickens, Alexander Legrand *retired education educator*
Sloane, James R.W. *academic administrator, writer*
Thurston, Kathleen *academic administrator*
Walsh, Janice Maureen *counselor, educator*
Wee, Christine Dijos *elementary school educator*
Wesselkamper, Sue *academic administrator*
Wright, Chatt Grandison *academic administrator*

Kailua Kona
Clewett, Kenneth Vaughn *college official*
Diama, Benjamin *retired educator, artist, composer, writer*
Spitze, Glenys Smith *retired educator*

Kamuela
Najita, Kiyoshi Young *education educator*

Kaneohe
Ko, Seung Kyun *international relations educator, consultant*
Timbers, Judith Ann *academic administrator, writer*

Kapaa
Outcalt, David Lewis *academic administrator, mathematician, educator, consultant, musician*

Laie
Miller, Ronald Mellado *education educator*
Shumway, Eric *academic administrator*

Paia
Loomis, James Cook *educator, navigator*

IDAHO

Boise
Andrus, Cecil Dale *academic administrator*
Ellis-Vant, Karen McGee *elementary and special education educator, consultant*
Griffin, Sylvia Gail *reading specialist*
Howard, Marilyn *school system administrator*
Kaupins, Gundars Egons *education educator*
Maloof, Giles Wilson *academic administrator, educator, author*
Ruch, Charles P. *academic administrator*

Caldwell
Hendren, Robert Lee, Jr., *academic administrator*
Hoover, Robert Allan *university president*

Lewiston
Duley, Charlotte Dudley *vocational counselor*
Thomas, Dene *academic administrator, educator*

Moscow
Hendee, John Clare *university research educator*

Nampa
Hagood, Richard A. *academic administrator, educator*

Ola
Farr, Reeta Rae *special education administrator*

Pocatello
Bowen, Richard Lee *academic administrator, political science educator*
Eichman, Charles Melvin *school counselor, career assessment educator*
Lawson, Jonathan Nevin *academic administrator*
Smith, Elaine E. *school system administrator*

Sun Valley
Cassell, William Comyn *retired college president*

Twin Falls
McGregor, Wendolyn Suzanne *elementary school educator, mathematician*

Wendell
Anderson, Marilyn Nelle *elementary education educator, librarian, counselor*

ILLINOIS

Argonne
Vivio, Frank Michael *education educator, researcher*

Arlington Heights
Placek-Zimmerman, Ellyn Clare *school system administrator, educator, consultant*

Belleville
Hanna, Phyllis Ann *elementary school educator*

Bloomington
Kindle, Otis T. *secondary school educator*
Wilson, Richard F. *academic administrator*

Carbondale
Barrette, Linda Jones *dean*
Covington, Patricia Ann *university administrator*
Dixon, Billy Gene *academic administrator, educator*
Hammond, Charles E *education educator*
Mead, John Stanley *university administrator*
Quisenberry, Nancy Lou *university administrator, educator*
Snyder, Carolyn Ann *education educator, librarian*

Carlinville
Pride, Miriam R. *college president*

Champaign
Cohen, Dov Joseph *education educator, researcher*
Dulany, Elizabeth Gjelsness *university press administrator*
Ghosh, Avijit *dean*
Gomez, Terrine *school director*
Harris, Zelema M. *academic administrator*
Herman, Richard H. *academic administrator*
Ikenberry, Stanley Oliver *education educator, former university president*
Pillay, Anand *education educator, researcher*
Spodek, Bernard *early childhood educator*

Charleston
Hencken, Louis V. *academic administrator*
Moler, Donald Lewis *educational psychology educator*
NeSmith, Richard A. *education educator, consultant*
Rives, Stanley Gene *university president emeritus*
Surles, Carol D. *academic administrator*
Thornburgh, Daniel Eston *retired university administrator, journalism educator*

Chicago
Adelman, Pamela Bernice Kozoll *education educator*
Ayman, Iraj *educational consultant*
Beane, Marjorie Noterman *academic administrator*
Bell, Dean Phillip *dean*
Birnbaum, Barry William *special education educator*
Borges, Dain *education educator*
Bouton, Marshall Melvin *academic administrator*
Buniak, Raymond *educational professional*
Collens, Lewis Morton *university president, legal educator*
Cook, Sandy *dean*
Cooper, Jo Marie *elementary school principal*
Coy, Patricia Ann *special education director, consultant*
Craine, Thomas Knowlton *non-profit administrator*
Crockett, George Ephriam *secondary school educator*
Cross, Dolores Evelyn *former university administrator, educator*
Culp, Kristine Ann *dean, theology educator*
Daniel, Elnora D. *academic administrator*
Di Prima, Stephanie Marie *educational administrator*
Driskell, Claude Evans *college director, educator, dentist*
Einoder, Camille Elizabeth *retired secondary school educator*
Felton, Cynthia *educational administrator*
Fish, Stanley Eugene *university dean, English educator*
Garanzini, Michael J. *academic administrator*
Getz, Godfrey Shalom *dean, pathologist, educator*
Gold, Carol R. *dean, nursing educator*
Graham, Bruce S. *dean, educator*
Graner, Evan *academic administrator*
Gross, Theodore Lawrence *university administrator, author*
Hamada, Robert S(eiji) *dean, educator, economist, entrepreneur*
Harris, Shirley *elementary, secondary and adult education educator*
Hart, Katherine Miller *college dean*
Hawkins, Loretta Ann *retired secondary school educator, playwright*
Hayes, Alice Bourke *academic administrator, biologist, researcher*
Henikoff, Leo M., Jr., *academic administrator, educator, medical educator*
Holliday, Patricia A. *elementary school educator*
Holtschneider, Dennis H. *university official, priest*
Johnson, Barbara Elaine Spears *retired education educator*
Johnson, Mary Ann *vocational school owner*
Keiderling, Timothy Allen *chemistry educator, researcher*
Kim, Mi Ja *dean, academic administrator*
Kubistal, Patricia Bernice *educational consultant*
Lund-Molfese, Nicholas C. *academic administrator*
Madara, James Lee *dean, pathologist, educator, epitheliologist*
Malcolm, Christine Anne *university hospital administrator*
Martin-Liamazares, Carlos *academic administrator*
Mason, Gregory Wesley, Jr., *secondary school educator, educator*
Matasar, Ann B. *former dean, business and political science educator*
McCray, Curtis Lee *academic administrator*
McPherson, Michael Steven *former academic administrator, economist*
Meisels, Marlene *literacy and special education educator, editor*
Mell, Patricia *dean*
Miceli, William Cyril, Sr., *director*
Mindes, Gayle Dean *education educator*
Minogue, John P. *academic administrator, educator, priest*
Mirza, Leona Lousin *elementary school educator, director*
Morris-Rogers, Cheryl-Ann *daycare provider, director, educator*
Moss, Gerald S. *dean, medical educator*
O'Brien, Gregory Michael St. Lawrence *academic administrator*
Orden, Alex *management science educator emeritus*
O'Reilly, Charles Terrance *university dean*
Osby, Iris *education educator*
Pappas, David Wayne *guidance counselor, consultant*
Petitan, Debra Ann Burke *elementary school educator, counselor, design engineer, writer*
Piderit, John J. *university educator*
Randel, Don Michael *academic administrator, musicologist*
Rawal, Viresh *education educator*
Roberts, Jo Ann Wooden *school system administrator*
Roizen, Michael F. *dean, medical educator, internist*
Schieser, Hans Alois *education educator*
Schubert, William Henry *curriculum studies educator*
Scribner, Margaret Ellen *educational consultant, consultant*
Scrimshaw, Susan Crosby *dean*
Shahidehpour, Mohammad *dean, academic administrator, engineering educator*
Shaver, Joan Louise Fowler *dean*
Simoni, Christopher *dean, law educator*
Sinha, Raj P. *education educator, researcher*
Snyder, Edward Adams *dean, economics professor*
Steinberg, Salme Elizabeth Harju *academic administrator, historian*
Stovall-Brooks, Patricia *elementary school educator, writer*
Stowell, Joseph, III, *academic administrator*
Sulkin, Howard Allen *college president*
Swanson, Don Richard *university dean*
Traudt, Mary B. *elementary school educator*
Tukes, Jamu Wayne *educational consultant*
Van Zandt, David E. *dean*
Wasan, Darsh Tilakchand *university official, chemical engineer educator*

Wham, David Buffington *secondary school educator*
Yamakawa, Allan Hitoshi *academic administrator*
Youm, Yoosik *education educator*
Young, Lauren Sue Jones *education educator*

Clarendon Hills
Choice, Priscilla Kathryn Means (Penny Choice) *retired international educational consultant*

Collinsville
Daugherty, Phyllis Lyn *secondary school educator*

Country Club Hills
Scherer, George Robert *retired secondary school educator*

Crystal Lake
Davidson, Shirley Jean *elementary and secondary educator*

Decatur
Munoz, Joseph Mark *education educator, consultant*
Rinchiuso, Diana Lynn *academic administrator*
Weinstein, Susan Ann *secondary school educator*

Deerfield
Meyer, Mara Ellice *special education consultant, principal*

Dekalb
Monat, William Robert *university official*
Morrison, Harriet Barbara *retired education educator*
Stahl, Norman A. *educator*

Des Plaines
Coburn, James LeRoy *educational administrator*
Lee, Margaret Burke *college president, English educator*

Dixon
Behrendt, Richard Louis *academic administrator*

Downers Grove
Nichols, Karen *academic administrator*
Punt, Leonard Cornelis *educational services company executive*

East Saint Louis
Wright, Katie Harper *educational administrator, journalist*

Elgin
Turnquist, Jerry L. *teacher, journalist*

Elk Grove Village
Edmiston, Cheryl Lee *educator, clergywoman*

Elmhurst
Begando, Joseph Sheridan *retired university chancellor, educator*

Eureka
Hearne, George Archer *academic administrator*

Evanston
Beljan, John Richard *university administrator, medical educator*
Bienen, Henry Samuel *academic administrator, political science educator*
Boye, Roger Carl *academic administrator, journalism educator, writer*
Christian, Richard Carlton *university dean, former advertising agency executive*
Connie, Leslie Lynn *secondary school educator*
Dumas, Lawrence B. *academic administrator*
Jacobs, Donald P. *dean emeritus, banking and finance educator*
Jain, Dipak Chand *dean, marketing educator, consultant*
Jennings, Hamlin Manson *materials consultant*
Lewis, Dan Albert *education educator*
Musa, Samuel Albert *university executive*
Weber, Arnold Robert *academic administrator*

Galesburg
Haywood, Bruce *retired academic administrator*
Taylor, Roger Lee *academic administrator, lawyer*

Glen Carbon
Lazerson, Earl Edwin *academic administrator emeritus*

Glen Ellyn
Bollendorf, Robert Fredrick *retired education educator, psychologist*
Gage, Nancy Elizabeth *college administrator, accountant, educator*
Patten, Ronald James *university dean*

Glenview
Corley, Jenny Lynd Wertheim *elementary school educator*

Godfrey
Zilm, Karl Miller *education educator*

Granite City
Eftimoff, Anita Kendall *educational consultant*
Humphrey, Owen Everett *retired education administrator*

Hartford
Shelton, Michael Patrick *principal*

Hazel Crest
Freed, Melvyn Norris *retired higher education administrator and educator, writer*

Hinsdale
Taylor, Ronald Lee *academic administrator*
Taylor, T(homas) Roger *educational consultant, educator*

Hoffman Estates
Larson, John M. *educational consultant*

Homewood
Schillings, Denny Lynn *retired history educator, educational and grants consultant*

Ingleside
Krentz, Eugene Leo *university president, educator, minister*

Jacksonville
Anderson, Michael R. *elementary school educator, writer*
Johns, Beverley Anne Holden *special education administrator*
Moe-Fishback, Barbara Ann *counseling administrator*
Welch, Rhea Jo *special education educator*

Joliet
Bartow, Barbara Jené *university program administrator*

Lake Forest
Feinberg, Jeffrey Enoch *educator, author*
Ferrari, Michael Richard, Jr., *university administrator*
Herron, Orley R. *college president*
Hotchkiss, Eugene, III, *retired academic administrator*

Lincolnshire
Martin, John Driscoll *school administrator*

Lincolnwood
Greenblatt, Deana Charlene *elementary school educator*

Lisle
Huffman, Louise Tolle *middle school educator*

Macomb
Adams, John Quincy *educator, consultant*
Kyllonen Rose, Julie Frances *college program administrator*
Witthuhn, Burton Orrin *retired university official*

Madison
Purdes, Alice Marie *retired adult education educator*

Maple Park
Callaghan, Barney *secondary school educator*

Markham
Peacock, Marilyn Claire *primary education educator*

Maywood
Higgs, Rosa Lee *special education educator, writer*

Monmouth
Bruce, Mary Hanford *academic administrator, educator, writer*

Morton
Corey, Judith Ann *retired elementary school educator*

Naperville
Briseno, Kathleen *education educator*
Florence, Ernest Estell, Jr., *special education educator*
Heuer, Michael Alexander *dean, endodonist educator*
Rosenthal, Edward Leonard *secondary school educator*
Wilde, Harold Richard *college president*

New Baden
Franke, Louise Anna *early childhood educator, farmland manager*

Normal
Bowman, C. Alvin *academic administrator*
Hickrod, George Alan Karnes Wallis *educational administration educator*
Miller, Wilma Hildruth *education educator*
Parette, Howard P. *school system administrator, special education educator*
Presley, John Woodrow *academic administrator*
Temple, Mark Allen *adult education educator, consultant*

Northbrook
Ben-Arie, Ronit Peleg *elementary school educator*

Oak Lawn
Jandes, Kenneth Michael *superintendent of schools*

Oak Park
Adelman, William John *university labor and industrial relations educator*
Venerable, Shirley Marie *gifted education educator*

Oakbrook Terrace
Levine, Norman M. *academic administrator*

Olympia Fields
Means-Willis, Emily W. *secondary school educator, writer*
Strong, Dorothy Swearengen *school system administrator*

Ottawa
Benning, Joseph Raymond *principal*

Palos Hills
Crawley, Vernon Obadiah *academic administrator*

Peoria
Kelly, Grace Dentino *secondary school educator*
Wiltse, Mark Edward *academic administrator, director*

Peoria Heights
Bergia, Roger Merle *school system administrator*

Richton Park
Burt, Gwen Behrens *elementary school administrator*

River Forest
Bush, Gail *library educator, librarian*
Carroll, Donna M. *academic administrator*
Coe, Donald Kirk *retired university official*

Eisel, Jean Ellen *university educational administrator*

River Grove
Rodriguez, Ileana P. *academic administrator, director*
Stein, Thomas Henry *social science educator*

Rock Island
Bahls, Steven Carl *academic administrator, educator*
Horstmann, James Douglas *retired academic administrator*
Tredway, Thomas *college president*

Rockford
Howard, John Addison *former college president, institute executive*
Pribbenow, Paul C. *higher education administrator, consultant*
Steele, Carl Lavern *academic administrator*

Schaumburg
Westlund, Maribeth *secondary school educator*

Skokie
Sloan, Judi C. *former physical education educator*

Springfield
Dorsey, John Kevin *dean*
Poorman, Robert Lewis *education consultant, former college president*

Sterling
Donahue, Shirley Ohnstad *elementary school educator*

Sycamore
Johnson, Yvonne Amalia *elementary education educator, science consultant*

Tinley Park
Baker, Betty Louise *retired secondary school educator*
Kostka, Elmer Bohumil *secondary school educator*

Tuscola
Henderson, E. Suzanne *elementary school educator*

University Park
Keys, Paul Ross *university provost/academic affairs official*
Peterson, Kenneth Allen, Sr., *retired superintendent*

Urbana
Glick, Karen Lynne *college administrator*
Henderson, Stanley Elwood *academic administrator, consultant*
Johnson, Duane D. *education educator, researcher*
Leggett, Anthony J. *education educator*
Stukel, James Joseph *academic administrator, mechanical engineer, educator*
Whiteley, H. E. *dean*

Vernon Hills
Cho, Yong Hyo *public administrator, educator*

Wayne City
Blank, Stanley Bruce *secondary school educator*

West Peoria
McBride, Sharon Louise *counselor, technical communication educator*

Wheaton
Litfin, A. Duane *academic administrator*

Wilmette
McNeill, Thomas B. *director, retired lawyer*
Smutny, Joan Franklin *academic director, educator*

Winnetka
Bundy, Blakely Fetridge *early childhood educator, advocate*
Huggins, Charlotte Susan Harrison *secondary school educator, author, travel specialist*

Woodstock
Levandowski, Barbara Sue *educational administrator*

Worden
Dole, Thomas Brader *retired secondary school educator, musician*

INDIANA

Anderson
Neidert, David Lynn *administrator*

Angola
Reynolds, R. John *academic administrator, educator*

Batesville
Volk, Cecilia Ann *elementary school educator*

Bloomington
Arnove, Robert Frederick *education educator*
Barnes, A. James *academic dean*
Bornholdt, Laura Anna *university administrator*
Chafel, Judith Ann *education educator*
Collins, Dorothy Craig *retired educational administrator*
Herbert, Adam William, Jr., *academic administrator, educator*
Johnson, Kevin LaMont *educator*
Louis, Kenneth R.R. Gross *academic administrator*
Mehlinger, Howard Dean *education educator*
Palmer, Judith Grace *university administrator*
Ryan, John William *academic administrator*
Webb, Charles Haizlip, Jr., *retired university dean*

Carmel
Rand, Leon *academic administrator*

Chesterton
Nelson, Paul James *educator*

Crawfordsville
Ford, Andrew Thomas *academic administrator*

Crown Point
Harder, Heather Anne *education educator*

Demotte
Mitchell, Timmy J. *principal*

East Chicago
Fortenberry, Delores B. *dean*

Elwood
Barnett, Marilyn Doan *secondary education business educator*

Evansville
Dean, K. Matthew *elementary school educator*
Jennings, Stephen Grant *academic administrator*

Fort Wayne
Andorfer, Donald Joseph *university president*
Balthaser, Linda Irene *retired academic administrator*
Cutshall-Hayes, Diane Marion *elementary school educator*
Robinson, Wendy Y. *school system administrator*
Wartell, Michael Alan *academic administrator*

Gary
Hall, James Rayford, III, *political science educator*
Smith, Vernon G. *education educator, state representative*

Goshen
Meyer, Albert James *educational researcher*
Stoltzfus, Victor Ezra *retired university president*

Granger
Morgan, Ardys Nord *school improvement consultant*

Greencastle
Bottoms, Robert Garvin *academic administrator*

Hammond
Fehring, Mary Ann *secondary school educator*
Weber, Elsa Koenig *pre-school educator*
Woodson, Adrianne Marie *secondary school educator and coordinator*

Highland
DeVaney, Cynthia Ann *retired elementary school educator, real estate instructor*

Hobart
Hanley, Roberta Lynn *alternative education coordinator, educator*

Indianapolis
Bepko, Gerald Lewis *university administrator, law educator, lecturer, consultant, lawyer*
Brand, Myles *academic administrator*
Brash, Susan Kay *principal*
Brater, Donald Craig *dean, educator*
Brenner, Mark Lee *academic administrator, physiologist, educator*
Broome, Marion *dean*
Clark, Charles M., Jr., *medical school administrator*
D'Amico, Carol *educational administrator*
Dykstra, Clifford Elliot *chemistry educator, researcher*
Fletcher, Brady Jones *vocational education career specialist*
Goldblatt, Lawrence I. *dean, educator, researcher*
Gooldy, Patricia Alice *retired elementary education educator*
Kennedy, Russell Edward *academic administrator*
Metzner, Barbara Stone *university counselor*
Reed, Suellen Kinder *school system administrator*
Solomon, Marilyn Kay *educator, consultant*
Speth, Gerald Lennus *education and business consultant*
Watkins, Sherry Lynne *elementary school educator*
Wolfe, Elaine Claire Daughetee *junior high school educator*
Woody, John Frederick *retired secondary education educator*

Kokomo
Person, Ruth Janssen *academic administrator*

Kouts
Miller, Sarabeth *secondary school educator*

La Porte
Johnson, Bruce Ross *elementary school educator*

Lafayette
Chen, Qingyan *educator*
Troutner, Joanne Johnson *director, consultant, secondary school educator*

Marion
Barnes, James Byron *university president*

Markle
Strait, Nick Edward *elementary school educator*

Mishawaka
Harmon, David Edward *education educator, artist*

Monroeville
Sorgen, Elizabeth Ann *retired educator*

Muncie
Gora, JoAnn M. *academic administrator*
Kitchens, Frederick Lynton, III, *education educator, researcher*
Lawhead, Victor Bernard *education educator*
Stewart, Rita Joan *academic administrator*

New Albany
Riehl, Jane Ellen *education educator*

New Harmony
Rice, David Lee *university president emeritus*

North Manchester
Mason, Stephen Olin *academic administrator*
Switzer, Jo Young *academic administrator, dean*

Notre Dame
Bederman, Gail *education educator, historian*
Burke, Leo *dean, director*
Crosson, Frederick James *retired dean, humanities educator*
Haenggi, Martin *education educator, researcher*
Hatch, Nathan Orr *university administrator*
Hyder, Anthony K. *academic administrator, science educator*
Kselman, Thomas *education educator*
Malloy, Edward Aloysius *academic administrator*
O'Hara, Patricia A. *dean, law educator*
O'Meara, Onorato Timothy *academic administrator, mathematician*
Scheidt, W. Robert *chemistry educator, researcher*
Woo, Carolyn Yauyan *dean*

Pendleton
Phenis-Bourke, Nancy Sue *educational administrator*

Plainfield
Lucas, Georgetta Marie Snell *retired educator, artist*

Richmond
Bennett, Douglas Carleton *academic administrator*

Schererville
Platis, Chris Steven *educator*

South Bend
Cerny, William *retired education educator, musician*
House, Harold Von *education educator, consultant*
Karns, Elizabeth (Libby) A. *retired daycare administrator*
Redmond, Mark Leroy *secondary school educator*
Schreiber, Roy Edward *education educator, writer*
Storin, Matthew Victor *academic administrator, educator, retired editor*

Terre Haute
Hulbert, Samuel Foster *college president*
Hunt, Effie Neva *former college dean, former English language educator*
Landini, Richard George *university president emeritus, English educator*
Leach, Ronald George *education educator, librarian*
Miller, Maurice Dean *special education educator*
Olsen, Christopher John *education educator*
Van Til, William *education educator, writer*

Upland
Kesler, Jay Lewis *retired academic administrator*

Valparaiso
Harre, Alan Frederick *academic administrator*
Mundinger, Donald Charles *retired college president*
Scales, Freda S. *dean, nursing educator*
Schnabel, Robert Victor *retired academic administrator*

Wabash
Whitehead, Wendy Lee *special education educator*

West Lafayette
Asher, J. William *education educator, psychology professor*
Beering, Steven Claus *academic administrator, medical educator*
Carney, Thomas Quentin *academic administrator, educator, pilot*
Cosier, Richard A. *dean, business educator, consultant*
Frick, Gene Armin *university administrator*
Gappa, Judith M. *university administrator*
Gennett, Timothy *academic administrator*
Jischke, Martin C. *academic administrator*
Moskowitz, Herbert *management educator*
Moyars-Johnson, Mary Annis *university official*
Plante, Robert Donald *dean*
Rebar, Alan H. *dean*
Ringel, Robert Lewis *university administrator*
Shertzer, Bruce Eldon *education educator*

Winona Lake
Henry, Ronald O. *academic administrator*

IOWA

Ames
Allen, Benjamin J. *academic administrator*
Crabtree, Beverly June *retired dean*
Ebbers, Larry Harold *education educator*
Geoffroy, Gregory L. *academic administrator, educator*
Manatt, Richard *retired education educator*
Mattila, Mary Jo Kalsem *elementary and art educator*
Schuh, John Howard *higher education educator, academic administrator*

Bettendorf
Hanzelka, Richard Louis *education educator*

Burlington
Lundy, Sherman Perry *secondary school educator*

Cedar Falls
Lettow, Lucille Jane *school librarian, education educator*
Price, Nancy *education educator, writer*

Cedar Rapids
Condon, Sherri Kay *secondary school educator*
Rosberg, Merilee Ann *education educator*

Davenport
Hudson, Celeste Nutting *education educator, reading clinic administrator, consultant*
Rogalski, Edward J. *university administrator*

Des Moines
Gaines, Ruth Ann *secondary school educator*
Maxwell, David E. *academic executive, educator*
Paterik, Frances Sue *secondary school educator, actress*
Teitelbaum, Howard S. *academic administrator*
Webb, Mary Christine *reading recovery educator, in-class reading specialist*

Dubuque
Collins, Barbara Louise *retired elementary school educator*
Dunn, M. Catherine *college administrator, educator*
Keller, Robert Scott *education educator*
Kerrigan, John E. *academic administrator*
Toale, Thomas Edward *school system administrator, priest*

Epworth
Wozniak, John S. *dean*

Fort Dodge
Pratt, Diane Adele *talented and gifted education educator*

Grinnell
Knight, Rita Cecilia *school librarian*
Osgood, Russell King *academic administrator*

Iowa City
Boyd, Willard Lee *academic administrator, educator, lawyer, museum director*
Brennan, Robert Lawrence *educational director, psychometrician*
Buckwalter, Kathleen C. *academic administrator, educator*
Dreher, Melanie Creagan *dean, nursing educator*
Duffy, William Edward, Jr., *retired education educator*
Feldt, Leonard Samuel *university educator and administrator*
Fethke, Gary C. *dean*
Gray, George Trumon *test development professional*
Hines, N. William *dean, law educator, administrator*
Hogan, Michael *academic administrator*
Johnsen, David C. *dean, dentistry educator*
King, Jeri Ripley *academic administrator*
McGovern, Jennifer Anne *education educator*
Robillard, Jean Eugene *dean, educator*
Roe, Gerald Bruce *director, writer*
Skorton, David Jan *academic administrator*
Spriestersbach, Duane Caryl *academic administrator, speech pathology/audiology services professional, educator*

Keokuk
Hardy, Julia Irene *elementary school educator*

Newton
Ponder, Marian Ruth *retired mathematics educator*

Oskaloosa
Burrow, Paul Irving *secondary school educator*
Clovis, Samuel Harvey *academic administrator*

Pacific Junction
Krogstad, Jack Lynn *associate dean, accounting educator*

Sheldon
Gifford, Carla J. *education educator*

Sioux City
Deeds, William Charles *university dean, executive*
Hamilton, Ruth Milton Green *retired college administrator, consultant*
Rants, Carolyn Jean *college official*
Wick, Sister Margaret *former college administrator*

Waterloo
Hasek, Jane Ellen *academic administrator*
Kober, Arletta Refshauge (Mrs. Kay L. Kober) *supervisor*

Waverly
Rose, Mary Mabel *elementary school educator*

West Des Moines
Holderness, Susan Rutherford *at-risk educator*

KANSAS

Atchison
Seago, Diana Marie *college administrator*

Baldwin City
Lambert, Daniel Michael *academic administrator*

Carbondale
McCollum, Susan *elementary school educator*

Clearwater
Taverner, Pamela Johnson *secondary school educator*

Concordia
Kalthoff, Theodore Joseph *academic administrator*

Emporia
Mehring, Teresa Ann *dean, education educator*
Schallenkamp, Kay *academic administrator*

Great Bend
Rittenhouse, Nancy Carol *elementary school educator*

Hays
Hammond, Edward H. *university president*
Harbin, Calvin Edward *retired educator*
Vesely, Suzanne Araas *school librarian, educator*

Kansas City
Atkinson, Barbara F. *dean, medical educator, academic administrator*
Hagen, Donald Floyd *university administrator, former military officer*
Miller, Karen L. *dean, nursing educator*
Warne, Alan M. *adult education educator, consultant*
Wendel, Shirley Anne *college dean*

Lawrence
Berry, James Lee *retired educator*
Capps, Jason Scott *education educator, researcher*
Frederickson, Horace George *former college president, public administration educator*
Hemenway, Robert E. *academic administrator, language educator*
Hilt, Betty Marie *special education educator*
Locke, Carl Edwin, Jr., *academic administrator, engineer, educator*
Peterson, Nancy *special education educator*
Rury, John Leslie *education educator*
Sheridan, Rick D. *educator*
Turnbull, Ann Patterson *special educator, consultant, research director*
Wiechert, Allen LeRoy *educational planning consultant, architect*

Lindsborg
Humphrey, Karen Ann *college director*

Manhattan
Amtoft, Torben *adult education educator, researcher*
Coffman, James Richard *academic administrator, veterinarian, educator*
Muir, William Lloyd, III, *academic administrator*
Nellis, M. Duane *dean*
Richardson, Ralph C. *dean*
Shanklin, Carol Williams *academic administrator, researcher*
Wefald, Jon *university president*

Mcpherson
Stevens, Leota Mae *retired elementary education educator*

Meade
Brannan, Cleo Estella *retired elementary education educator*

Mission
Sheets, Cynthia Ann *elementary school educator, gifted and talented educator*

North Newton
Ediger, Marlow *education educator*

Olathe
Goodwin, Becky K. *educational technology resource educator*
Stevens, Diana Lynn *elementary school educator*

Overland Park
Whelan, Richard J. *retired academic administrator*

Pittsburg
Runyan, Charles Kent *education educator*

Pomona
Gentry, Alberta Elizabeth *elementary school educator*

Pratt
Hart, Don Lee *academic administrator, writer*

Shawnee Mission
Barton, Betty Louise *school system administrator*
Crooks, Lisa Zahn *elementary school educator*

Sublette
Swinney, Carol Joyce *secondary school educator*

Topeka
Jennings, Nancy Ann *retired elementary education educator*
Smith, Loran Bradford *education educator*
Varner, Robert Bernard *counselor, educator*

Wichita
Beggs, Donald Lee *academic administrator*
Mitchell, Linda Marlene *education educator*
Platt, George Milo *university administrator*
Sherwood, Joan Karolyn Sargent *retired career counselor*

KENTUCKY

Berea
Krug, John Carleton (Tony Krug) *college administrator, library consultant*

Bowling Green
Atwell, Nedra Wheeler *education educator, consultant*
Burch, Barbara G. *academic administrator*

Cecilia
Thompson, Kathy Self *secondary school educator*

Danville
Breeze, William Hancock *college administrator*
Kennan, Elizabeth Topham *academic administrator, retired historian*
Roush, John A. *academic administrator*

East Point
Whitaker, Herbert Loyd *retired special education educator*

Frankfort
Shabazz, David Lorenzo *vocational school educator*

Harlan
Greene, James S., III, *school administrator*

Harrodsburg
Semones, Charles W. *retired elementary school educator, writer*

Lexington
Assael, Leon A. *dean, educator*
Cole, Henry Philip *educational psychology educator*
Gill, Karen V. *secondary school educator, consultant*
Robinson, Thomas Christopher *academic administrator, educator*
Salisbury, Holly Buckner *university arts director*
Sharkey, Michael Joseph *education educator, researcher*
Thelin, John Robert *academic administrator, education educator, historian*
Turner, Sharon P. *dean, dental educator, dentist*
Vestal, Allan W. *dean, law educator*
Wethington, Charles T., Jr., *academic administrator*
Williams, Carolyn Antonides *university dean*
Wilson, Emery Allen *university dean, obstetrician-gynecologist, educator*
Zinser, Elisabeth Ann *academic administrator*

Louisville
Bratton, Ida Frank *retired secondary school educator*
Cecil, Bonnie Susan *elementary school educator*
DeVitis, Joseph L. *education educator*
Kaplan, Joel A. *academic administrator*
Kmetz, Donald R. *retired academic administrator*
Mohler, Richard Albert, Jr., *academic administrator, theologian*
Oates, Thomas R. *university executive*
Popp, Shaun Raymond *secondary school educator, music educator*
Rockey, Eugene A., Jr., *vocational school educator, scriptwriter*
Smith, J. Lea *education educator, researcher*
Swain, Donald Christie *retired university president, history educator*
Taylor, Robert Lewis *management educator*
Thomas, Riedel *education educator*
Wagoner, Ruth R *education coach*
Williams, John N. *dean, dental educator*

Middlesboro
Marcum, Joseph Susong *education educator*

Murray
Pearson, Kelly Jeanne *education educator*

Newport
Clinkenbeard, James Howard *principal*

Owensboro
Roberts, Brian Wayne *middle school educator, minister*

Pikeville
Johnson, Amy M. *elementary school educator*
Smith, Harold Hasken *university administrator*
Strosnider, John *dean*

Prestonsburg
Wells, Zella Faye *school system administrator*

Richmond
Blanchard, Paul *academic administrator, educator*

Saint Catharine
Collins, Martha Layne *college president, former governor*

Shelbyville
Hedrick, William David *secondary school educator, musician, educator*

Versailles
Taylor, Elizabeth *elementary school educator*

Whitley City
Stephens, Robert Ernest *retired educator*

Williamsburg
Trickett, Paula J. *assistant principal*

LOUISIANA

Baker
Steward, Alfred *education educator, researcher*

Baton Rouge
Bellinger, Michael Craig *education educator, musician*
Bensman, Stephen J. *school librarian, researcher*
Caffey, H(orace) Rouse *academic administrator, agricultural company executive*
Giger, Andreas *education educator*
Groves, Michael G. *dean*
Harrelson, Clyde Lee *retired secondary school educator*
Jones, Mary Elizabeth *school counselor*
Maxcy, Spencer John *education educator*
Mc Cameron, Fritz Allen *retired university administrator*
Ngandu, Pius Nkashama *education educator*
Perkins, Huel Davis *academic administrator*
Prestage, James Jordan *university chancellor*
Rami, Janet Simmons *university dean, nursing educator*
Smith, Michael *college president*

Benton
Hudson, Marguerite W. *secondary school educator*

Bossier City
French, Holly Lynn *education educator*

Chalmette
Williamson, Ramona Diane *special education educator*

Convent
Deroche, Kathleen Samrow *elementary educator, mathematics consultant, assistant principal*

Covington
Bourgeois, Priscilla Elzey *educational administrator*

Denham Springs
Perkins, Arthur Lee, Sr., *retired principal, real estate broker, insurance agent*

Franklin
Fairchild, Phyllis Elaine *school counselor*

Grambling
Favors, Steve Alexander *academic administrator*
Judson, Horace Augustus *academic administrator, chemistry educator*
Porter, Wilma Jean *educational consultant*
Stentiford, Barry Maxfield *education educator, military officer*
Warner, Neari Francois *university president*

Gretna
Weekley, Judy Liddington *special education educator*

Hammond
Kulkin, Heidi Sharon *education educator*
Nauman, Ann Keith *education educator, department chairman*
Parker, Clea Edward *retired university president*

Lacombe
Hendricks, Donald Duane *retired school librarian*

Lafayette
Authement, Ray P. *college president*
Colbert-Cormier, Patricia A. *secondary school educator*
Petry, Ruth Vidrine *principal*
Redding, Evelyn A. *dean*
Rieck, William Albert *education educator, academic administrator*

Lake Arthur
Dronet, Judy Lynn *elementary school educator, librarian*

Lake Charles
Fields-Gold, Anita *retired dean*
Hebert, Robert D. *academic administrator*

Metairie
Chambers, Thomas Edward *college president, psychologist*
Johnson, Beth Michael *school administrator*
St. John, Bridgette Alayne *secondary school educator*

Monroe
Foreman, Teresa *educational consultant, educator*

Natchitoches
Wolfe, George Cropper *retired private school educator, artist, writer*

New Orleans
Bennett-Johnson, Earnestine Rose *education educator, consultant*
Cowen, Scott S. *academic administrator*
Folse, Henry Joseph, Jr. *education educator*
Francis, Norman C. *academic administrator*
Gery, John Roy Octavius *secondary school educator, poet*
Gordon, Joseph Elwell *university official, educator*
Hassenboehler, Donalyn *principal*
Hebert, Thomas Joseph *university educator*
Hovland, Eric Jeffrey *dean, endodontics educator*
Kelly, Eamon Michael *university president emeritus*
Le Blanc, Alice Isabelle *academic administrator*
Longstreet, Wilma S. *curriculum and instruction educator*
McCall, John Patrick *college president, educator*
McFarland, James W. *dean, finance educator*
Mosier, John *education educator, writer*
Novakov, George John, Jr., *gifted and talented educator, consultant, administrative assistant*
Puri, Pratap *educator, researcher*
Ryan, Timothy P. *academic administrator*
Sherman, Edward Francis *dean, law educator*
Stanton, Vivian Brennan (Mrs. Ernest Stanton) *retired guidance counselor*
Taylor, Ian Logan *dean*
Thompson, Martyn Philip *political and literary studies educator, translator*
Watson, James Raymond *education educator*

Newllano
Boren, Lynda Sue *gifted education educator*

Ruston
Freasier, Aileen W. *special education educator*
Maxfield, John Edward *retired university dean*
Reneau, Daniel D. *academic administrator*
Taylor, Foster Jay *retired university president*

Shreveport
Bogue, Ernest Grady *academic administrator, educator*
Joshua, Percy *English educator*
Watts, Jessica Milan *director*

Slidell
Faust, Marilyn B. *middle school principal*

Sorrento
Welch, Joe Ben *academic administrator*

Springhill
Thomas, Faye Evelyn J. *elementary and secondary school educator*

Thibodaux
Hulbert, Stephen Thompson *academic administrator*

MAINE

Ashland
Morrow, David Andrew *secondary school educator*

Auburn
Umpierre, Luz María *women studies educator, foreign language educator*

Augusta
Lyons, Charles M. *academic administrator*

Bangor
MacTaggart, Terrence Joseph *professor, former university chancellor*
McKinnon, Carolyn Ann *child care center director*
Westphal, Joseph W. *academic administrator*

Bar Harbor
Krevans, Julius Richard *academic administrator, internist*
Swazey, Judith Pound *academic administrator, sociomedical science educator*

Biddeford
Featherman, Sandra *academic administrator, political science educator*
Shannon, Stephen Curtis *dean, occupational health physician*

Bremen
Wilson, Linda Smith *academic administrator*

Brownfield
Kloskowski, Vincent John, Jr., *educational consultant, writer, educator*

Brunswick
Greason, Arthur LeRoy, Jr., *retired university administrator*
McEwen, Craig A. *dean*
Tautz, Birgit *education educator, researcher*

Corea
Harward, Donald West *retired academic administrator*

Cumberland Foreside
Dill, William Rankin *college president*

Farmington
Kalikow, Theodora June *university president*

Glenburn
Rauch, Charles Frederick, Jr., *retired university official and business educator*

Gorham
Canniff, Julie G. *education educator, researcher*

Lewiston
Hansen, Elaine Tuttle *academic administrator*
Reich, Jill *dean*

Lubec
Hudson, Miles *retired special education educator*

Mount Desert
Singleton, Francis Seth *international educator*

North Yarmouth
Fecteau, Rosemary Louise *educational administrator, educator, consultant*

Old Town
Alex, Joanne DeFilipp *elementary school educator*

Orono
Allen, Anne Elliott *academic administrator*
Estler, Suzanne E. *education educator*
Hoff, Peter Sloat *academic administrator*
Rice, Edward Perry *secondary school educator*
Wiersma, G. Bruce *dean, forest resources educator*

Portland
Chandler, Patricia Ann *retired special education educator*
Gilmore, Roger *college consultant*
Khoury, Colleen A. *dean*
Pattenaude, Richard Louis *university administrator*
Rhinehardt, Peter Kevin *elementary school educator, writer, artist*

Presque Isle
Hensel, Nancy H. *academic administrator*

Skowhegan
Ross, James Owen *education educator, researcher*

Veazie
Kennedy, Robert Alan *educational administrator*

Waterville
Adams, William D. *academic administrator*
Armstrong, Darlene L. *elementary school educator*
Cook, Susan Farwell *associate director planned giving*

Yarmouth
Bischoff, David Canby *retired university dean*
Hart, Loring Edward *academic administrator*

MARYLAND

Adamstown
Church, Martha Eleanor *retired academic administrator, scholar*

Adelphi
Heeger, Gerald Arthur *university president*

Annapolis
Bowen, Linnell R. *director*
Burnett, Calvin Wilks *academic administrator*
Farmer, Martha Louise *retired college administrator*
Jacobs, Linda Joan *secondary school educator*
Parham, Carol Sheffey *school system administrator*
Stern, Margaret Bassett *retired special education educator, author*

Arnold
Smith, Martha A. *academic administrator*

Baltimore
Adams, Clara I. *academic administrator*
Allan, Janet D. *dean*
Ball, Marion Jokl *academic administrator*
Behm, Mark Edward *university administrator, consultant*
Boughman, Joann Ashley *dean*
Brewster, Gerry Leiper *educator, lawyer*
Brody, William Ralph *academic administrator, radiologist, educator*
Browne, Lovetie W. *special education educator, small business owner*
Buser, Carolyn Elizabeth *correctional education administrator*
Ellis, Brother Patrick (H. J. Ellis) *academic administrator*
Freedman, Janet Whittle *retired academic administrator, writer*
Gifford, Donald George *legal educator*
Gleichmann, Frances Evangeline *retired elementary educator*
Grasmick, Nancy S. *school system administrator*
Helfman, Carolyn Rae *middle school educator*
Heller, Barbara R. *former dean, nursing educator*
Hrabowski, Freeman Alphonsa, III, *university president*
Hsu, Cornelia Wang Mei-Chih *education educator*
Isable, Alisha *elementary school educator*
Jackson, Stanley Edward *retired special education educator*
Jones, Dan L. *academic administrator*
Keller, George Charles *higher education consultant, writer*
Klitzke, Theodore Elmer *former college dean, arts consultant*
Knapp, Steven *provost*
Lazarus, Fred, IV, *college president*
McPartland, James Michael *university official*
Reid, Lauretta Glasper *retired principal*
Richardson, Earl Stanford *university president*
Roby, Mary Lorraine *special education educator*
Ross, Richard Starr *retired medical school dean, cardiologist, educator*
Rothenberg, Karen H. *dean, law educator*
Sawyer, David Jonathan *educator*
Seurkamp, Mary Pat *college president*
Simmons, Howard L. *education educator*
Sugiyama, Toku Mary *retired school administrator*
Tiefenwerth, William Philip *university program director*

Bel Air
Larsen, Kevin Wayne *education educator*
Phillips, Bernice Cecile Golden *retired vocational education educator*

Beltsville
Lewis, Bette Louise *school principal*

Bethesda
Buccino, Alphonse *university dean emeritus, consultant*
Corn, Milton *academic dean, physician*
Gleazer, Edmund John, Jr., *retired education educator*
Hemming, Val G. *retired dean, educator*
Jameson, Sanford Chandler *education educator*
Laughlin, Larry W. *academic administrator, military officer*
Sanoff, Alvin Paul *education consultant, writer*

Chestertown
Tipson, Lynn Baird (Baird Tipson) *academic administrator, religion educator*

Chevy Chase
Curris, Constantine William *university president*
Mathis, Laurelle Sheedy *academic administrator, volunteer*
Ostar, Allan William *academic administrator, higher education consultant*
Towsner, Cynthia Merle *vocational school educator*

Clarksville
Peirce, James Walter *secondary school educator, historian*

College Park
Amershek, Kathleen *education educator*
Destler, William W. *academic administrator*
Dieter, George Elwood, Jr., *university official*
Finkelstein, Barbara *education educator*
Frank, Howard *dean, educator, systems company executive*
Hey, Nancy Henson *educational administrator*
Langenberg, Donald Newton *retired academic administrator, physicist*
Malen, Betty *education policy and leadership educator*
Modarres, Mohammad *education educator*
Mote, Clayton Daniel, Jr., *university president, mechanical engineer, educator*
Prentice, Ann Ethelynd *university dean*
Qu, Gang *education educator, researcher*
Ramsey, S. Robert *education educator*
Schwab, Susan Carroll *dean*
Sedlacek, William *education educator*
Souza, Gilvan Castro *operations and management educator*
Stumpff, Robert Thomas *academic administrator*
Szymanski, Edna Mora *dean*
Toll, John Sampson *university president, physics educator*

Columbia
Bruley, Duane Frederick *academic administrator, consultant, engineer*
Folkenberg, Lois Waxter *principal, educator, psychologist*
Hartman, Lee Ann Walraff *secondary school educator, consultant*
Jones-Wilson, Faustine Clarisse *retired education educator*
Strain, Lucille Brewton *education educator, researcher*
Whiting, Albert Nathaniel *former university chancellor*

Cumberland
Jancuk, Kathleen Frances *educational administrator*

Ellicott City
Powell, Lillian Marie *retired music educator*

Essex
Bunn, Wm. Jeffrey *secondary school educator, director*

Frederick
Aaslestad, Halvor Gunerius *retired dean*
Hamilton, Rhoda Lillian Rosén *guidance counselor, language educator, consultant*
Klein, Elaine Charlotte *school system administrator*

Frostburg
Childs, William Parker *education educator*
Gira, Catherine Russell *university president*
Root, Edward Lakin *education educator, academic administrator*

Greenbelt
Kalnay, Eugenia *university administrator, meteorologist*
Linn, Terry Ann Noffsinger *secondary school educator*

Hagerstown
Warner, Charles David, III, *academic administrator*

Hunt Valley
Collier, Stephen N *educational consultant*

Indian Head
Price, Teresa Annette *elementary school educator*

Joppa
Bates, Charles Benjamin *elementary school administrator*

Kennedyville
Schiff, Gary Stuart *academic administrator, educator, consultant*

Kensington
Holloway, William Jimmerson *retired educator*

Laurel
Dorsey, John Wesley, Jr., *university administrator, economist*

Lusby
Ladd, Culver Sprogle *secondary school educator*

Mardela Springs
Harcum, Louise Mary Davis *retired elementary education educator*

Marion Station
Handy, Mary Thomas *retired elementary school educator*

Ocean Pines
Crawford, Norman Crane, Jr., *academic administrator, consultant*

Owings
Oring, Stuart August *visual information specialist, writer, photographer, researcher*

Phoenix
Hairston, Walter Albert *school system administrator*

Potomac
Bremenstuhl, David P. *elementary school educator*
Karch, Karen Brooke *principal*
Kuykendall, Crystal Arlene *educational consultant, lawyer*
Schuessler, Isabelle Sweeny *school administrator*

Princess Anne
Nnadi, Eucharia E. *academic administrator*

Rockville
Rankin, Rachel Ann *retired media specialist*
Sparks, David Stanley *university administrator*

Saint Michaels
Feisel, Lyle Dean *retired dean, electrical engineer, educator*

Severna Park
Chatelaine, Kenneth Leo *education educator, psychoanalyst*

Silver Spring
Burgos-Sasscer, Ruth *chancellor emeritus*
Coles, Anna Louise Bailey *retired dean, nurse*
Holcomb, Minnie Irby *elementary school educator, educator*
Jackson, Mary Jane McHale Flickinger *principal*
Latson, Richard Charles *retired audio-visual specialist*
McGinn, Cherie M. *secondary school educator*
Schick, Irvin Henry *academic administrator, educator*
Whalen, John Philip *retired educational administrator, clergyman, lawyer*
Williams, Barbara Ivory *educational researcher*

Stevenson
Hyman, Mary Bloom *science education programs coordinator*
Manning, Kevin James *academic administrator*

Swanton
Cummins, Delmer Duane *academic administrator, historian*

Temple Hills
Curry, Emma Beatrice *elementary school educator*

Towson
Caret, Robert Laurent *academic administrator*
Hoch, David Allen *athletic director*
Lund, Mark Fifield *secondary school educator*

Waldorf
Hastings, Lee L. *secondary school educator*

Westminster
Dundes, Lauren *education educator*
Pappalardo, Faye *academic administrator*
Rosenthal, Michael Ross *academic administrator, consultant*

MASSACHUSETTS

Amherst
Call, Gregory S. *academic administrator*
Feldman, Allan *education educator*
Immerman, Neil *academic administrator, computer science educator*
Lombardi, John V. *university administrator, historian*
Marx, Anthony W. *academic administrator*
Prince, Gregory Smith, Jr., *academic administrator*
Seymour, Charlena *academic administrator*

Arlington
Fulmer, Vincent Anthony *retired college president*

Ashburnham
Von Deck, Joseph Francis *secondary school educator, researcher*

Auburndale
Doran, Kathleen Brewer *dean, consultant*

Bedford
Wasson, Lila Elizabeth *educational consultant*

Beverly
Eastman, W. Dean *secondary school educator*

Billerica
Furlong, Patrick David *educator, researcher*

Boston
Berk, Lee Eliot *academic administrator*
Berkman, Lisa F. *public health educator*
Bloom, Barry R. *dean*
Boodram, Mohan David *academic administrator*
Caldwell, Ann Wickins *academic administrator*
Chobanian, Aram *medical school dean, cardiologist*
Chou, Laisheng *education educator*
Clark, Kim Bryce *dean, business educator*
Cotter, William Reckling *foundation president*
Cox, Malcolm *academic administrator, medical educator*
Davies, Don *education educator*
DePaola, Dominick Philip *academic administrator*
Dluhy, Deborah Haigh *college dean*
Doyle, Mathias Francis *academic administrator, political scientist, educator*
Eisner, Sister Janet Margaret *college president*
Fitzmaurice, Garrett Martin *education educator, researcher*
Freeland, Richard Middleton *academic affairs administrator, historian*
Grant, Barbara Hurwitz *educator*
Harris, Andrew Michael *director*
Hedlund, Ronald David *academic administrator, researcher, educator*
Henderson, Jeffrey J. *dean, educator*
Juusela, Kari Henrik *dean*
Keusch, Gerald Tilden *academic administrator*
Khazanov, Marina Boris *academic administrator, educator*
Kirkpatrick, Edward Thomson *academic administrator, mechanical engineer*
Lataif, Louis Edward *dean*
Le Quesne, Philip William *chemistry educator, researcher*
Liebergott, Jacqueline W. *academic administrator*
Love, Carol *dean*
Martin, Joseph Boyd *dean, neurologist, educator*
Matarazzo, James M. *dean, educator*
Meier, Deborah *principal*
Morris, Robert *education educator*
Norris, Lonnie Harold *dean*
Novotny, Vladimir *educator, consultant*
Paine, Lynn *academic administrator*
Pei, Lowry Cheng-Wu *education educator, writer*
Penney, Sherry Hood *university president, educator*
Prothrow-Stith, Deborah *academic administrator, public health educator*
Reede, Joan Yvonne *academic administrator, medical educator, pediatrician*
Ronayne, Michael Richard, Jr., *academic dean*
Sargent, David Jasper *academic administrator*
Shore, Eleanor Gossard *medical school dean*
Silber, John Robert *retired academic administrator, law educator, philosophy educator*
Silverman, Robert Alan *college official, historian*
Simmons, Sylvia Jeanne Quarles (Mrs. Herbert G. Simmons Jr.) *university administrator, educator, executive*
Standard, John Robert *academic administrator*
Stefanos, Asgedet *educational consultant*
Upton Puccinelli, Nancy Marie *education educator, researcher*
Van Domelen, John Francis *academic administrator*
Vernon, Heidi *international business educator*
Wagle, Udaya *educator*
Westling, Jon *university administrator*
Wood, Peter Wyatt *education educator, writer*
Xu, Xiping *adult education educator, director*
Zungolo, Eileen H. *dean*

Bridgewater
Jeffries, Frances Moore *academic administrator*
Tinsley, Adrian *college president*

Brookline
Ruthchild, Rochelle Goldberg *education educator*

Cambridge
Clay, Phillip L. *academic administrator*
Emanuel, Kerry Andrew *academic administrator, meteorologist, oceanographer, educator*
Eurich, Nell P. *education educator*
Fischer, Kurt Walter *education educator*
Fox, John Bayley, Jr., *university dean*
Graham, Patricia Albjerg *education educator*
Gray, Paul Edward *academic official*
Greyser, Linda Lorraine *education educator*
Harris, Joseph C. *education educator*
Hockfield, Susan *academic administrator, medical educator*
Johnson, Howard Wesley *former university president, business executive*
Khoury, Philip S. *academic administrator*
Lagace, Paul Alfred *college educator*
McKenna, Margaret Anne *university president*
Mitchell, William J. *academic administrator, architecture educator*
Mullainathan, Sendhil *education educator, researcher*
Nye, Joseph Samuel, Jr., *dean, political science educator*
Power, Samantha *academic administrator, writer*
Rowe, Mary P. *organizational ombudsman, management educator*
Schmalensee, Richard Lee *dean, economist, former government official, educator*
Shinagel, Michael *dean, English literature educator*
Summers, Lawrence H. *academic administrator, former government official*
Thiemann, Ronald Frank *dean, religion educator*
Thompson, William Irwin *educational consultant, writer*
Vafa, Cumrun *education educator*
White, Alan Frederick *academic administrator*
Whitlock, Charles Preston *former university dean*

Centerville
Kiernan, Owen Burns *educational consultant*

Chestnut Hill
Altbach, Philip *director, educator*
Bando, Patricia Alice *director*

Gaiser, Ted Joseph *academic administrator, minister*
Keating, Patrick J. *academic administrator*
Leahy, William P. *academic administrator, historian, educator*
Monan, James Donald *university chancellor*
Nemerowicz, Gloria *academic administrator*

Cummington
Bannister, Geoffrey *academic administrator, geographer*

Danvers
Clark, Sharon Jackson *private school administrator*

Dighton
Buote, Rosemarie Boschen *retired special education educator*

Fairhaven
Rose, Anita Carroll *retired educator*

Fitchburg
Kemp, Deborah K. *primary school educator*
Mara, Vincent Joseph *college president*
Schilling, Thomas Harold *education educator*

Framingham
Heineman, Helen L. *provost*
Kennedy, Samantha Ann *special education educator*
Valakis, M. Lois *retired elementary school educator*

Granville
Fields, Margaret Mary *elementary school educator, paralegal*

Hingham
Mackiewicz, Theresa Ann *special education educator*

Holden
O'Neil, William Francis *academic administrator*

Holland
McGrory, Mary Kathleen *retired academic administrator, humanities educator*

Housatonic
Charpentier, Gail Wigutow *private school executive director*

Hubbardston
Marceau, Judith Marie *retired elementary school educator, small business owner*

Hyde Park
Harris, Emily Louise *special education educator*

Indian Orchard
Daley, Veta Adassa *educational administrator*

Lakeville
Barry, Marilyn White *retired special education educator, dean*

Leominster
Cucchiara, Sandra Chiavaras *special education educator*

Lexington
McFarland, Philip James *educator, writer*

Lincoln
Baum, Laura *secondary school educator*

Longmeadow
Katz, Barbara Stein *special education educator*
Leary, Carol Ann *academic administrator*

Lynn
Astuccio, Sheila Margaret *educational administrator*
Ryder, Edward Francis *secondary school educator*

Marion
Latham, Christopher Robert *alumni and development director*

Marlborough
Wheeler, Diana D. *educational consultant*

Marstons Mills
Martin, David Standish *education educator*

Mattapoisett
Andersen, Laird Bryce *retired university administrator*

Maynard
Holway, Ellen Twombly Hay *primary education educator*

Medford
Bacow, Lawrence Seldon *academic administrator, environmental educator*
Bosworth, Stephen Warren *dean, former ambassador*
Gittleman, Sol *university official, humanities educator*
Jamshed, Bharucha *academic administrator*

Methuen
Stanley, (Malchan) Craig *school superintendent, psychologist*

Milton
Warren, John Coolidge *private school administrator, history educator*
Wengler, Marguerite Marie *educational therapist*

Needham
Zambone, Alana Maria *special education educator, consultant*

Newton
Matteson, Carol J. *academic administrator*

Newton Center
Garvey, John Hugh *dean, law educator*

North Adams
Rodrigues, Raymond Joseph *academic administrator*

North Andover
Volpe, Ellen Marie *secondary school educator*

North Dartmouth
Khanna, Gaurav *education educator, researcher*

North Easton
Varella, Hazel L. *education educator, historian*

Northampton
Christ, Carol Tecla *academic administrator*
Lightburn, Anita Louise *dean, social work educator*
Mahoney, Maureen A. *academic administrator*

Norton
Marshall, Dale Rogers *academic administrator, political scientist, educator*
Woods, Susanne *academic administrator, educator*

Norwood
Reilley, Margaret Randall *secondary school educator*

Oak Bluffs
Harris, Margaret T. *school system administrator*

Peabody
Bakrow, William John *college president emeritus*

Plymouth
Paul, Carol Ann *retired academic administrator, biology educator*

Plympton
Smith, Robert Rutherford *university dean, communication educator*

Provincetown
Wolfman, Brunetta Reid *education educator*

Quincy
Adams, Ronald G. *middle school educator*
Chisholm, Maureen *academic administrator*
Henck, Anita Fitzgerald *academic administrator, educator*

Reading
Terilli, Joseph Anthony *secondary school educator*

Salem
Harrington, Nancy D. *college president*

Saugus
Austill, Allen *dean emeritus*

Scituate
Spangler, Stanley Eugene *international relations educator*

Shelburne Falls
Merrill, Deane Whitney, Jr., *secondary school educator, consultant*

Shrewsbury
Onorato, Nicholas Louis *retired program director, economist*

South Dartmouth
Ward, Richard Joseph *university dean, educator, author*

South Deerfield
Fritz, Nancy H. *educational researcher, administrator*

South Hadley
Bowie, Lee *academic administrator, philosopher, educator*
Creighton, Joanne Vanish *academic administrator*
Kaltenbach, Jane Couffer *biology educator*

Springfield
Caprio, Anthony S. *academic administrator*
Cook, Kathryn Anne *secondary school educator*
Mantoni, Philip Joseph *principal*
Mariani, Marita C. *secondary school educator*
Miller, Leroy Paul, Jr., *secondary English educator*

Stonehill College
Conboy, Katie (Sheila C. Conboy) *academic administrator*

Sudbury
Thompson, Mary Lou *elementary school educator*

Swansea
Curry, Thomas John *academic administrator*

Waltham
Adamian, Gregory Harry *academic administrator*
Jaffe, Adam Benjamin *education educator*
Krauss, Marty Wyngaarden *academic administrator*
Mc Menimen, Kathleen Brennan *secondary school educator, consultant*
Reinharz, Jehuda *academic administrator, history educator*
Shonkoff, Jack P. *dean, educator*
Tchaicha, Jane Davagian *education educator, consultant*

Wayland
Anderson, Monica Luffman *school librarian, educator, real estate broker*

Wellesley
Auerbach, Jerold S. *university educator*
Cuba, Lee *dean*
Heartt, Charlotte Beebe *university official*
Ragone, David Vincent *former university president*
Walsh, Diana Chapman *academic administrator, sociologist, educator*

Wenham
Baker, Ruth Holmes *retired secondary education educator*
Beauregard, John *college librarian, consultant*

West Roxbury
Roach, Maureen S. *primary school educator*

Westborough
Antalek, Eileen Elizabeth *educational consultant*

Westfield
Niles, DeBorah Olive *veteran benefits coordinator*

Wilbraham
Woloshchuk, Candace Dixon *secondary school educator, artist, consultant*

Williamstown
Chandler, John Wesley *educational consultant*
Schapiro, Morton Owen *university administrator*

Woods Hole
Farrington, John William *academic administrator, dean, research scientist*

Worcester
Angel, David *academic administrator*
Bassett, John E. *academic administrator, English educator*
Brooks, John Edward *college president emeritus*
Carney, John F., III, *academic administrator*
Johnson, Nancy Ann *education educator*
Lazare, Aaron *dean, psychiatrist*
Loew, Franklin Martin *college president, biologist, consultant*
Mardilovich, Ivan P *education educator, researcher*
McFarland, Michael C. *academic administrator*
Palmer, John Anthony, III, *secondary school educator, music educator*
Schmalz, Mathew Nelson *academic administrator*
Vellaccio, Frank *academic administrator*

MICHIGAN

Adrian
Caine, Stanley Paul *college administrator*
Lamprecht, Elizabeth Ann *educator*

Algonac
Paquet, Gary Lee *elementary school educator*

Allendale
Kindschi, P. Douglas *dean, educator*

Alma
Swanson, Robert Draper *college president*
Tracy, Saundra J. *academic administrator*

Ann Arbor
Alfred, Richard Lincoln *education educator, educational association administrator, consultant, researcher*
Ball, Deborah Loewenberg *education educator*
Beutler, Suzanne A. *retired secondary school educator, artist*
Chin, Chen Ooi *dean*
Copeland, Carolyn Abigail *retired dean*
Dolan, Robert J. *dean*
Duderstadt, James Johnson *academic administrator, engineering educator*
Dumas, Rhetaugh Etheldra Graves *university official*
Ellis, Charles Norman *professor, researcher*
Fishback, Robert Lawrence *retired secondary education educator*
Fleming, Suzanne Marie *academic administrator, freelance/self-employed writer*
Hinshaw, Ada Sue *dean, nursing educator*
Kelch, Robert Paul *former dean, pediatric endocrinologist*
La Fountain-Stokes, Lawrence M. *education educator*
Omenn, Gilbert Stanley *academic administrator, internist*
Paul, Ara Garo *university dean*
Perkins, George *educator, writer*
Polverini, Peter J. *dean, dental educator*
Ross, Theresa Mae *secondary school educator*
Rowley, Larry Lee *education educator*
Sullivan, Thomas Patrick *academic administrator*
Tharney, Leonard John *education educator, consultant*
Tice, Carol Hoff *intergenerational specialist, consultant*
Warner, Robert Mark *university dean, archivist, historian,*
White, B. Joseph *former dean, business educator*
Xie, Yu *adult education educator*

Armada
Kummerow, Arnold A. *superintendent of schools*

Auburn Hills
De Martin, Colleen Dianne *college official, interior designer, consultant*

Bay City
Zuraw, Kathleen Ann *special education and physical education educator*

Benzonia
Acker, Nathaniel Hull *retired educational administrator*

Berrien Springs
Cotro, Hugo Antonio *education educator, researcher*
Lesher, William Richard *retired academic administrator*
Lundgren, Dennis D. *elementary school educator*

Birch Run
Thompson-Christie, Heather Marie *adult education educator*

Bloomfield Hills
Thompson, Richard Thomas *academic administrator*

Brighton
Jensen, Baiba *principal*

Dearborn
Dziuba, Henry Frank *retired university official*
Fair, Jean Everhard *retired education educator*
Meyer, Lisa Marie *elementary school educator*
Shamoon, Montaha Jirges *educator, researcher*

Dearborn Heights
Carter, Julia Marie *secondary school educator*
Johns, Diana *secondary school educator*

Detroit
Barrett, Nancy Smith *university administrator*
Booth, Betty Jean *retired daycare administrator, poet*
Burnley, Kenneth Stephen *school system administrator*
Connellan, William Wesley *higher education educator*
Corbitt, Eumiller Mattie *elementary and secondary education educator, special education educator*
Edelstein, Tilden Gerald *university official, history educator*
Fay, Sister Maureen A. *university president*
Green, Charles Adam *retired education educator, psychologist*
Jones, James Allen *secondary school educator*
Jordan, Napoleon Bonaparte *educational consultant*
Mika, Joseph John *program director, educator, consultant*
Mitchell, Connie *director*
Pietrofesa, John Joseph *education educator*
Reid, Irvin D. *academic official*
Steiman, H. Robert *dean, dental educator*

Dowagiac
Mulder, Patricia Marie *education educator*

East Lansing
Brophy, Jere Edward *education educator, researcher*
Byerrum, Richard Uglow *college dean*
Gift, David Ayres *academic administrator*
Harrison, Jeremy Thomas *dean, law educator*
Honhart, Frederick Lewis, III, *academic director*
Jackson-Elmoore, Cynthia *director, educator*
King, Lonnie J. *dean*
Petropoulos, Evangelos *former health institute director, educator, researcher*
Raper, Kellie Curry *education educator, researcher*
Rothert, Marilyn L. *dean, nursing educator*
Schwille, John Robert *education educator, researcher*
Simon, Lou Anna Kimsey *academic administrator*
Snoddy, James Ernest *education educator*
Strampel, William Derkey *dean, medical educator*
Velicer, Janet Schafbuch *retired elementary school educator*

Escanaba
Karweick, June Klees *education educator*

Farmington
Fleming, Jill Louise *education educator*

Farmington Hills
Barry, Essie Marilyn *elementary school educator, writer*
Faxon, Jack *headmaster*

Flint
Lorenz, John Douglas *college official*

Franklin
Reinhart, Anne Christine *special education educator, consultant*

Garden City
Polin, Colleen Marie *special education educator*

Grand Rapids
Diekema, Anthony J. *college president, educational consultant*
Lubbers, Arend Donselaar *retired academic administrator*
Yarington, David Jon *retired educator*

Grosse Pointe Woods
Robie, Joan *elementary school principal*

Gwinn
Lasich, Vivian Esther Layne *secondary school educator*

Hancock
Puotinen, Arthur Edwin *college president, clergyman*

Harbor Springs
Cappel, Constance *educational consultant, writer*

Haslett
Hotaling, Robert Bachman *community planner, educator*
Warrington, Willard Glade *former university official*

Hillsdale
Grassl, Wolfgang *adult education educator*

Holland
Nyenhuis, Jacob Eugene *college official*
Schieringa, Paul Kenneth *special education educator, entertainer*
Van Wylen, Gordon John *former college president*

Houghton
Mroz, Glenn D. *academic administrator*
Wray, Kent *academic administrator*
Wright, Debra Denise *education educator*

Inkster
Hall, Andrea Jenella *special education educator*

Jackson
Reid, Mona Gay *education educator*

Kalamazoo
Bailey, Judith Irene *university official, consultant*
Chateauneuf, John Edward *chemistry educator, researcher*
Cody, Frank Joseph *secondary school educator*
Haenicke, Diether Hans *academic administrator emeritus, educator*
Jones, James Fleming, Jr., *academic administrator, Roman language and literature educator*
Palchick, Bernard S. *academic administrator, art educator*
Showalter, Shirley H. *academic administrator*
Stufflebeam, Daniel LeRoy *education educator*

PROFESSIONAL INDEX 5581 EDUCATION

Kentwood
Yovich, Daniel John *education educator*

Lanse
Berggren-Moilanen, Bonnie Lee *education educator*

Lansing
Kissling, Paul Joseph *academic administrator, religious studies educator, minister*
Nguyen, Hoa Thai *academic administrator*
Straus, Kathleen Nagler *education administrator, consultant*

Livonia
Kujawa, Sister Rose Marie *academic administrator*
Van de Vyver, Sister Mary Francilene *academic administrator*

Ludington
Puffer, Richard Judson *retired college chancellor*

Macomb
Farmakis, George Leonard *education educator*

Maple City
Morris, Donald Arthur Adams *college president*

Marquette
Roy, Michael Joseph *higher education administrator*
Saville, Kathleen Jo *instructional technologist*
Stulz, Karin M. *educator*

Midland
Barker, Nancy Lepard *university official*
Grzesiak, Katherine Ann *primary educator*

Monroe
Siciliano, Elizabeth Marie *secondary school educator*

Mount Pleasant
Kopp, Stephen James *academic administrator*

North Branch
Sorensen, Shawn Richard *secondary school educator*

Ontonagon
Clark, Raymond John *academic administrator*

Pentwater
Noffke, Frank Edward *educational planner, writer, educator*

Petoskey
Baird, Gregory Ross *residence life/student activities director, theater educator*

Pleasant Ridge
Sneed, Marie Eleanor Wilkey *retired secondary school educator*

Pontiac
Decker, Peter William *academic administrator*
Love, Sharon Irene *elementary school educator*

Rochester
Appleton, Sheldon Lee *education educator*
Burke, Richard John *education educator*
Gallagher, Edward Arthur *retired academic administrator, real estate developer*
Packard, Sandra Podolin *education educator, consultant*
Russi, Gary D. *academic administrator*
Zeppelin, Mary Frances *special education educator, elementary school educator, consultant*

Rochester Hills
Mills, Helene Audrey *education educator*

Saginaw
Scharffe, William Granville *academic administrator, educator*

Saint Clair Shores
Skoney, Sophie Essa *educational administrator*

Saugatuck
Blair, John Raymond *educational psychology educator*

Sault Sainte Marie
Youngblood, Betty J. *academic administrator*

South Lyon
Palmer, Kimberly Anne *director*

Southfield
Chambers, Charles MacKay *academic administrator, lawyer, consultant*
Lee, James Edward, Jr., *educational consultant*

Sparta
McDonald, Lois Alice *elementary school educator*

Spring Lake
Bussard, Janice Wingeier *retired educator, inventor*

Stanton
Winchell, George William *curriculum and technology educator*

Traverse City
Zimmerman, Paul Albert *retired college president, minister*

Trenton
Wukovits, John Francis *secondary school educator, writer*

University Center
Boyse, Peter Dent *academic administrator*
Gilbertson, Eric Raymond *academic administrator, lawyer*

Warren
Lorenzo, Albert L. *academic administrator*

Waterford
Anderson, Francile Mary *secondary school educator*

Wayne
Carpenter, Arthur Lloyd *education educator*

Wellston
Spain, Frederick William *retired secondary school educator, writer*

West Bloomfield
Simpson, Robert Lee *university official, biology educator*

Williamston
Johnson, Tom Milroy *academic dean, medical educator, physician*

Ypsilanti
Boone, Morell Douglas *information and communications technology educator*
Gwaltney, Thomas Marion *education educator, writer*
Robbins, Jerry Hal *educational administration educator*

MINNESOTA

Ada
Sillerud, Arlen Roger *retired educator*

Andover
Peterson, Jill Susan *elementary school educator*

Bemidji
Rogers, Patricia Louise *education educator, consultant*

Blaine
Yecke, Cheri Pierson *education policy fellow, columnist, author*

Bloomington
Kuntz, Lila Elaine *secondary business education educator*

Collegeville
Reinhart, Dietrich Thomas *academic administrator, social studies educator*

Duluth
Martin, Kathryn A. *academic administrator*
Ziegler, Richard J. *dean, educator*
Zinn, Gesa *education educator*

Falcon Heights
Kreuter, Gretchen V. *academic administrator*

Fridley
Larson, Marilyn J. *retired elementary music educator*

Grand Rapids
King, Sheryl Jayne *secondary education educator, counselor*

Hopkins
Ramberg, Patricia Lynn *college president*

Long Lake
Lowthian, Petrena *academic administrator*

Mankato
Moldstad, Joslyn M. *pre-school educator, writer*
Nickerson, James Findley *retired educator*
Preska, Margaret Louise Robinson *education historian, administrator*

Maple Grove
Kirpes, Anne Irene *elementary school educator*

Marine On Saint Croix
Gavin, Robert Michael, Jr., *education consultant*

Marshall
Danahar, David C. *academic administrator, historian, educator*

Minneapolis
Atwood, John Brian *dean*
Avella, Joseph Ralph *university educator*
Benveniste, Lawrence *dean*
Bowie, Norman Ernest *university official, educator*
Bruininks, Robert H. *academic administrator, psychologist, educator*
Cerra, Frank Bernard *dean*
Cline, Richard Ryan *education educator*
DiGangi, Frank Edward *academic administrator*
Eckberg, E. Daniel *secondary school educator*
Edwardson, Sandra *dean, nursing educator*
Fruen, Lois *secondary school educator*
Gardebring, Sandra S. *academic administrator*
Hollis, Martha *director, researcher*
Johnson, Carol R. *school system administrator*
Johnson, David Chester *university chancellor, sociology educator*
Lindell, Edward Albert *former college president, religious organization administrator*
Matson, Wesley Jennings *educational administrator*
Maziar, Christine M. *academic administrator*
Mengler, Thomas M. *dean*
O'Keefe, Thomas Michael *academic administrator*
Osander, John *secondary school educator*
Redmon, Rose Marie *secondary school educator*
Rogers, Karen Beckstead *gifted studies educator, researcher, consultant*
Rothausen-Vange, Teresa Jean *director, educator*
Schuh, G(eorge) Edward *university dean, agricultural economist*
Sullivan, Alfred Dewitt *academic administrator*
Svendsbye, Lloyd August *college president, clergyman, educator*
Veldey, Bonnie *special education educator*
Wilhelm, Gretchen *retired secondary school educator, volunteer*

Minnetonka
Moon, James Russell *technology education educator*

Wigfield, Rita L. *elementary school educator*

Moorhead
Dille, Roland Paul *college president*
Treumann, William Borgen *university dean*

Mounds View
Calvin, Stafford Richard *academic administrator*
Huber, Tonya *education educator*

Northfield
Boardman, Shelby J. *academic administrator*
Edwards, Mark U., Jr., *academic administrator, history educator, author*
Oden, Robert A., Jr., *academic administrator*
Priore, Jr, Charles Frank *school librarian*

Preston
Hokenson, David Leonard *secondary school educator*

Proctor
Scheibe, Margaret Helen *elementary school educator, librarian*

Richfield
Devlin, Barbara Jo *school district administrator*
Reilly, Jill Marlene *school system administrator*

Rochester
Talley, Nicholas Joseph *educator, physician, scientist*
Windebank, Anthony J. *dean*

Rushford
Stras, Penny Lynn *director*

Saginaw
Stauber, Marilyn Jean *retired secondary school educator, retired elementary school educator*

Saint Cloud
Frank, Jan L. H. *education educator, consultant*
Wertz, John Alan *retired secondary school educator*

Saint Paul
Brushaber, George Karl *academic administrator, minister*
Dykstra, Robert *retired education educator*
Gleason, Bruce Philip *education educator, writer*
Graham, Charles John *university educator, former university president*
Harvey, Patricia A. *school system administrator*
Hornbach, Daniel J. *academic administrator, biologist, educator*
Huber, Sister Alberta *college president*
Klausner, Jeffrey *dean*
Kurzer, Mindy Susan *educator*
Lee, Andrea Jane *academic administrator, nun*
McCormick, James Harold *academic administrator*
Osnes, Larry G. *academic administrator*
Rosenberg, Brian C *academic administrator*
Scapanski, Gene Albert *academic administrator, educator*
Stroud, Rhoda M. *elementary school educator*

Saint Peter
Mosbo, John Alvin *dean*

Sartell
Van Nostrand, Catharine Marie Herr *consultant, speaker, educator, writer*

Waseca
Frederick, Edward Charles *university official*

Winona
Beyer, Mary Edel *primary education educator*
Boseker, Barbara Jean *education educator*
DeThomasis, Brother Louis *academic administrator*
Krueger, Darrell William *academic administrator*
Nasstrom, Roy Richard *retired education educator*

MISSISSIPPI

Ackerman
Coleman, Frances McLean *secondary school educator*

Alcorn State
Bristow, Clinton, Jr., *academic administrator*

Batesville
Neal, Joseph Lee *vocational school educator*

Biloxi
Manners, Pamela Jeanne *secondary school educator*

Brandon
Okojie, Felix A. *research administrator*

Clarksdale
Presley, Vivian Mathews *junior college administrator*

Cleveland
Potter, David L. *academic administrator*

Clinton
Ottis, Sherri Danielle Greene *secondary school educator, historian*
Whitlock, Betty *retired secondary school educator*

Glen
Wigginton, Lisa Benderman *elementary school educator*

Gulfport
White, Barbara Lee *education educator*

Hattiesburg
Bedenbaugh, Angela Lea Owen *chemistry educator, researcher*
Lucas, Aubrey Keith *retired university president*
Noonkester, James Ralph *retired college president*

Hazlehurst
Blakeney, Margaret Elizabeth Fleming *counselor, educator*

Holly Springs
Beckley, David Lenard *academic administrator*

Itta Bena
Ahanonu, Chukwuma Smart *education educator*

Jackson
Anglin, Linda McCluney *retired elementary school educator*
Broome, Kathryn *secondary school educator*
Collins, Deloris Williams *secondary school educator*
Creel, Sue Cloer *secondary school educator*
Harmon, George Marion *academic administrator*
Harrison, Esther M. *elementary school educator, state representative*
Hupp, James R. *dean, dental educator*
McLeod, Stephen Glenn *education educator, language educator*
Rogers, Oscar Allan, Jr., *college president*

Long Beach
Williams, James Orrin *university administrator, educator*

Mendenhall
Cockrell, Jean D. *elementary school educator*

Mississippi State
Mabry, Donald Joseph *university administrator, history educator*
Rabideau, Peter Wayne *university administrator, chemistry educator*
Rent, Clyda Stokes *academic administrator*

Natchez
Marion, Ann *school psychologist, educator*

Oxford
Moorhead, Sylvester Andrew *retired education educator*

Perkinston
Mellinger, Barry Lee *community college president, vocational educator*

Starkville
Martin, Theodore Krinn *former university administrator*

Thaxton
Dillard, Faye Graham *education educator*

Tylertown
Barrett, Dawn Dillon *counseling administrator, journalist, editor*

University
Khayat, Robert Conrad *academic administrator*
Martin, Jeanette St. Clair *adult education educator*

Vicksburg
Keulegan, Emma Pauline *special education educator*

Yazoo City
Hawthorne, Minnie *elementary school educator*

MISSOURI

Ballwin
Guinther, Christine Louise *special education educator*

Bethel
Coonrod, Delberta Hollaway (Debbie Coonrod) *retired elementary education educator, consultant, freelance writer*

Blue Eye
Anderson, Ruth G. *retired education educator, educational consultant*

Bonne Terre
Mitchell, Bart Allen *secondary school educator*

Butler
Cochran, Beth *gifted and talented educator*

Cape Girardeau
Eom, Sean Bock *education educator, researcher*

Chesterfield
Crock, Winifred Woodard *director, music educator, conductor, musician*
McLain, Donald J. *retired academic administrator, educational consultant*
Reid, Lorene Frances *middle school educator*

Clayton
Mach, Ruth *principal*

Columbia
Ballard, Bruce W. *philosophy educator, religious studies educator*
Brouder, Gerald T. *academic administrator*
Crist, William Miles *dean, pediatrician, educator*
Deaton, Brady J. *academic administrator*
George, Melvin Douglas *retired university president*
Gysbers, Norman Charles *education educator*
Libby, Wendy B. *academic administrator*
Miller, Paul Ausborn *adult education educator*
Payne, Thomas L. *university official*
Wallace, Richard Lee *chancellor*

Farmington
Massie, Maureen Teresa *elementary school educator*

Fayette
Inman, Marianne Elizabeth *college administrator*

Forsyth
Klinefelter, Sarah Stephens *retired division dean, radio station manager*

Fort Leonard Wood
Campbell, Sonya Beth *elementary school educator*

Fulton
Jones, David Keith *education educator*
Lamkin, Fletcher M., Jr., *academic administrator*

Hillsboro
Adkins, Gregory D. *higher education administrator*

Independence
Henley, Patricia Joan *principal*
Starks, Carol Elizabeth *retired principal*

Jamesport
Franklin, Linda Ann *education educator*

Jefferson City
Henson, David B. *university administrator*
Novotney, Donald Francis *superintendent of schools*

Kansas City
Byers-Pevitts, Beverley *college administrator, educator*
Caulfield, Joan *director, educator*
Churchman, Michael Steele Bright *educational consultant, educator*
Drees, Betty *dean, educator*
Guilliland, Martha W. *academic administrator*
Hamilton, Richard Alfred *university administrator, marketing educator*
Hoffer, Sharon Marie *secondary school educator*
McCollum, Clifford Glenn *college dean emeritus*
Schuchman, Philip Melchor *education educator*
Schulkin, Carl Roger *secondary school educator*
Sizemore, William Christian *retired academic administrator, county official*
Slaughter, Rochelle Denise *elementary school educator*
Wilkins, Arthur Norman *retired academic administrator*
Willsie, Sandra K. *dean, internist, educator*

Kimberling City
Stovall, Richard L. *retired academic administrator*

Lees Summit
Linder, Beverly L. *elementary school educator*

Liberty
Tanner, Jimmie Eugene *retired dean*

Maryville
Clayton, John Andrew *director, coroner*
Hubbard, Dean Leon *academic administrator*
Strating, Sharon L. *elementary school educator, professional staff developer, educational consultant*

Mexico
Teague, Deborah Gant *elementary school educator*

Neosho
Allman, Margaret Ann Lowrance *counseling administrator*

Rich Hill
Laughlin, Jo Ann *elementary school educator*

Rolla
Shah, Y. T. *academic administrator*
Thomas, Gary L. *academic administrator*
Warner, Don Lee *dean emeritus*

Saint Charles
Delicath, Timothy A. *academic administrator*
Segelhorst, Cindy Marie *pre-school educator*

Saint Joseph
Mclear, Patrick Edward *education educator*
Murphy, Janet Gorman *college president*

Saint Louis
Baker, Shirley Kistler *university administrator*
Biondi, Lawrence *university administrator, priest*
Brown, Travis Lamonte, Sr., *principal*
Byrnes, Christopher Ian *academic dean, researcher*
Danforth, William Henry *retired academic administrator, physician*
Dodge, Paul Cecil *academic administrator*
George, Thomas Frederick *academic administrator*
Gilligan, Sandra Kaye *private school director*
Hrubetz, Joan *dean, nursing educator*
Jordan, Julia Crawford *secondary school educator*
Kalyanaraman, Ramki *education educator, researcher*
Kennelly, Sister Karen Margaret *retired academic administrator, church administrator, nun*
Lackey, Kayle Diann *elementary school educator*
Leonard, Judith Price *educational advisor*
Lovin, Keith Harold *academic administrator, philosophy educator*
Luebbert, Karen Merritt *academic administrator*
Mahan, David James *retired university official*
Monteleone, Patricia *dean*
Nedwek, Brian *academic administrator*
Nickolai, Beatrice Rose *education educator*
O'Neill, Sheila *principal*
Ramming, Michael Alexander *retired school system administrator*
Scheffing, Dianne Elizabeth *special education educator*
Seligman, Joel *dean*
Ware, Judith Boyd *education educator*
Weir, Thomas Albert *education educator*
Weiss, Robert Francis *former academic administrator, religious organization administrator, consultant*
Welch, Michael John *chemistry educator, researcher*
Williams, Nellie James Batt *secondary school educator, educator*
Williamson, Marilyn *retired secondary school educator*
Wiltenburg, Robert Edward *university dean*

Sedalia
Hazen, Elizabeth Frances *retired special education educator*

Springfield
Fritts, Josephine Ann *education educator*
Keiser, John Howard *academic administrator*
Matthews, Charles Leroy, Jr., *director*
Moore, John Edwin, Jr., *academic administrator*
Toste, Anthony Paim *chemistry educator, researcher*

Union
Martin, Joyce E. *education educator*

Verona
Youngberg, Charlotte Anne *education specialist, clergywoman*

Vienna
Byrd, Mickey Joe *secondary school educator, singer*

Webb City
James, Kathryn A. *secondary school educator*

Webster Groves
Schenkenberg, Mary Martin *principal*

Windyville
Condron, Daniel Ralph *academic administrator, metaphysics educator*

MONTANA

Billings
Park, Janie C. *provost*

Bozeman
Acord, Lea *dean*
Gamble, Geoffrey *academic administrator*

Butte
Haugen, Margaret Ellen *daycare administrator*
L'heureux, Richard Allen *academic administrator, consultant*

Crow Agency
Pease-Pretty On Top, Janine B. *community college administrator*

Dayton
Catalfomo, Philip *retired university dean*

Great Falls
Messick, Edward Burton *elementary school educator, secondary school educator*

Helena
Crofts, Richard A. *academic administrator*

Lewistown
Edwards, Linda L. *former elementary education educator*

Lolo
Stewart, JoAnne *retired director*

Missoula
Brown, Perry Joe *university dean*
Dennison, George Marshel *academic administrator*

NEBRASKA

Bellevue
Kayne, Jon Barry *industrial psychologist*
Muller, John Bartlett *university president*
Wydeven, Joseph Jude *university dean, educator*

Blair
Christopherson, Myrvin Frederick *college president*

Grand Island
Weseman, Vicki Lynne *elementary school educator*
Zichek, Shannon Elaine *retired secondary school educator*

Gretna
Druliner, Marcia Marie *education educator*

Hastings
Kort, Betty *secondary school educator*

Kearney
Johnston, Gladys Styles *university official*

Lincoln
Bradley, Richard Edwin *retired academic administrator*
Grew, Priscilla Croswell *university official, geology educator*
Hardin, Clifford Morris *retired academic administrator*
Janzow, Walter Theophilus *retired college administrator*
Koubek, Ekaterina N. *education educator*
Kraus, Joseph C. *education educator*
Milligan, Cynthia Hardin *university dean, lawyer*
Nelson, Darrell Wayne *university administrator, scientist*
Reinhardt, John W. *dean, dental educator*
Robak, Kim M. *academic administrator, lawyer*
Smith, L. Dennis *former academic administrator*
Tonack, DeLoris *elementary school educator*

Norfolk
Mortensen-Say, Marlys *school system administrator*

Omaha
Barkmeier, Wayne W. *academic administrator*
Belck, Nancy Garrison *dean, educator*
Bruckner, Martha *academic administrator*
Gollan, John Lachlan *dean, educator*
Haselwood, Eldon LaVerne *retired education educator*
Kuhlman, Thomas Ashford *American studies educator, writer*
Lindsey, Ada Marie *dean, nursing educator*
Newton, John Milton *academic administrator, psychologist, educator*
O'Brien, Richard L(ee) *medical educator, academic administrator, physician, cell biologist*
Ross, Larry *education educator, researcher*
Ryan, Sheila A. *nursing educator, former dean*
Sample, Lisa L. *education educator*
Schlegel, John P. *academic administrator*

Papillion
James, Geneva Behrens *secondary school educator*

NEVADA

Carson City
Brant, James William *educational consultant, mathematician, educator*
Wadman, William Wood, III, *educational director, technical research executive, consulting company executive*

Elko
Lovell, Walter Benjamin *secondary education educator, radio broadcaster*

Gardnerville
Smith, Roderick Joel *behavioral consultant, researcher, educator*

Henderson
Chairsell, Christine *academic administrator*
Moore, Richard *former academic administrator, educator*
Thomas, James Patrick *special education educator*

Incline Village
Timinsky, Dale *academic administrator*

Las Vegas
Ananias, José *retired school system administrator*
Brown, Lori Lipman *secondary school educator*
Carroll, Rossye O'Neal *college administrator*
Chance, Patti Lynn *school leadership educator*
Edler, Lisa Ann *middle school educator*
Ferrillo, Patrick J., Jr., *dean, endodontist*
Gaffga, Timothy Frederick *elementary school educator*
Gaspar, Anna Louise *retired elementary school educator, consultant*
Harter, Carol Clancey *university president, English language educator*
Holmes, BarbaraAnn Krajkoski *secondary school educator*
Mancl, Dustin Bernard *elementary school educator, language educator*
Pierce, Thresia Korte (Tish Pierce) *primary school educator*
Shuman, R. Baird *academic program director, writer, English language educator, educational consultant*
Singer, Kathryn J. *assistant principal*

Minden
Tyndall, Gaye Lynn *secondary school educator*

North Las Vegas
Kelly, Christopher Pat *dean, educator*

Panaca
Soderborg, Martin Todd *elementary school educator*

Reno
Cathey-Gibson, Sharon Sue Rinn *school principal, college administrator*
Crowley, Joseph Neil *university president, political science educator*
Dale, Debra Eileen *elementary school educator*
Dietrich, Dean Forbes *academic administrator*
Gillies, John Angus *education educator*
Huckle, Norman Matthew *school librarian*
Humphrey, Neil Darwin *retired academic administrator*
Lilley, John Mark *academic administrator*
McFarlane, Stephen C. *dean, researcher*
Perry, Jean Louise *dean*

Sparks
Tran, Can Ngoc *educator, researcher*

NEW HAMPSHIRE

Alton Bay
Scott, Susan Shattuck *retired secondary school educator*

Boscawen
Clarke, Claire Diggs *academic counselor*

Concord
Twomey, Elizabeth Ann Molloy *education educator*

Dover
Pelletier, Marsha Lynn *secondary school educator, poet*

Durham
Berona, David A. *computer systems librarian, educator*
DeMitchell, Todd Allan *education educator*
Farrell, William Joseph *university chancellor*
Greenberg, Arthur *dean, chemistry professor*
Hart, Ann Weaver *academic administrator*
Mallory, Bruce *academic administrator*

Exeter
Cole, Donald Barnard *education educator*

Farmington
Meyers, James B. *secondary school educator*

Hanover
Danos, Paul *dean, accounting educator*
Freedman, James Oliver *former university president, lawyer*
Hennessey, John William, Jr., *academic administrator, educator*
Platt, James David *academic administrator, educator*
Spielberg, Stephen Paul *dean, educator*
Wright, James Edward *academic administrator, historian, educator*

Lempster
Jillette, Arthur George, Jr., *school system administrator, educator*

Manchester
Desrosiers, Aprylle Lynn *director, consultant*
Merideth, Susan Carol *business administration educator*

Nashua
Johnson, Arthur V., II, *secondary school educator*
Mitsakos, Charles Leonidas *education educator, consultant*

New London
Vulgamore, Melvin L. *retired college president*

Plaistow
Goddu, Kevin Albert *secondary school educator*
Wilder, Dwight Safford *academic administrator*

Rindge
Dangelantonio, Sarah Teresa *academic administrator, educator*

West Lebanon
Halperin, George Bennett *education educator, retired naval officer*

Wilton
Ritchie-Dunham, James Loomis *academic administrator, researcher*

Windham
Nease, Stephen Wesley *college president*

NEW JERSEY

Asbury Park
Avella, John Thomas *educational administrator*

Basking Ridge
Besch, Lorraine W. *special education educator*

Bayonne
Lo Re, Vincent, Jr., *retired academic administrator, municipal official*
Zuckerman, Nancy Carol *learning disabilities specialist, consultant*

Bellmawr
Wilke, Constance Regina *elementary school educator*

Berkeley Heights
Shaffer, Gail Dorothy *secondary school educator*

Bernardsville
Cooperman, Saul *educational administrator*
Robinson, Maureen Loretta *retired elementary school educator*
Salinger, Anthony Wilshire *educator, organization consultant*

Beverly
Taylor, Lyn Ann *principal*

Brigantine
Kickish, Margaret Elizabeth *elementary school educator*

Browns Mills
Di Nunzio, Dominick *educational administrator*

Buena
Monastra, Richard J. *secondary school educator*

Burlington
Matlack, Maria Theresa *elementary school educator*

Caldwell
Ott, Walter Richard *academic administrator*
Werner, Patrice (Patricia Ann Werner) *academic administrator*

Camden
Daniels, Albertina Diana *secondary school educator*
Gordon, Walter Kelly *retired provost, English language educator*
Lawrence, Francis Leo *former university president, language educator*

Cherry Hill
Kapel, David Edward *retired academic administrator, education educator*

Chester
Di Battista, Anthony Paul *secondary school educator*

Clark
Hasselman, San D *secondary school educator*

Colts Neck
Ridoux, Denise C. *director, educator*

East Brunswick
Meningall, Evelyn L. *educational media specialist*

East Hanover
Tamburro, Peter James, Jr., *secondary school educator*

East Orange
Jones-Gregory, Patricia *secondary art educator*

Edison
Maeroff, Gene I. *academic administrator, journalist*

Egg Harbor City
Farris, Vera King *former college president*

Englewood Cliffs
Kim, Jae Taik *educator*

Ewing
Gitenstein, Donna M. *academic administrator*
Hamm, Claire Rose *development information services administrator*

Fair Lawn
Aitchison, Suann *elementary school educator*

Fort Lee
Sugarman, Alan William *educational consultant, national speaker*
Young, Vera Lee Hall *educational administrator, association executive*

Freehold
Soto-Fernandez, Liliana *education educator*

Frenchtown
Fogelson, Brian David *educational administrator*

Garfield
Rosenberg, Raymond David *special education educator, consultant*

Glassboro
Davis, Ronald P. *secondary school administrator*
Detofsky, Louis Bennett *secondary school educator*
Gephardt, Donald Louis *university official*
James, Herman Delano *former college administrator*

Green Brook
Balsamello, Melissa (Marley) *elementary school educator*

Hackensack
Parisi, Cheryl Lynn *elementary school educator*

Hackettstown
Boody, Kathleen Marie *dean*
Grigsby, Bryon Lee *dean*

Haddon Heights
Gwiazda, Stanley John *retired university dean*

Hoboken
Moeller, Joseph John, Jr., *university official*
Raveché, Harold Joseph *university administrator, physical chemist*

Jackson
Carney, Rita J. *educational administrator*
Vacchiano, Julie Catherine *special education educator*

Jersey City
Farrior, Evan Bell *special education educator, writer*
Miller, Adele Engelbrecht *educational administrator*

Lakewood
Williams, Barbara Anne *retired academic administrator*

Lawrenceville
Stehle, Edward Raymond *secondary education educator, school system administrator*
Warner, Jean Rockwell *education educator*

Linden
Bedrick, Bernice *retired science educator, consultant*

Little Falls
Blanton, Lawton Walter *retired dean*

Madison
Kean, Thomas H. *academic administrator, former governor*
Mertz, Francis James *university president*

Mahwah
Davis, Henry Vance *education educator*
Geiling, Louise Elizabeth *elementary school educator, secondary school educator*

Marlboro
Kayafas, Stephanie Ann *special education educator, consultant, supervisor, actress*

Martinsville
Raby, John Cornelius *secondary school educator*

Matawan
Liggett, Twila Marie Christensen *academic administrator, public television executive*
Rivera-Dominguez, Alberto *chemistry educator, mechanical engineer*

Mays Landing
May, John T. *college president*

Mendham
Posunko, Barbara *retired elementary education educator*
Sagurton, Wilma *retired secondary school educator, musician, historian*

Monroe Township
Wolfe, Deborah Cannon Partridge *government education consultant, educator, minister*

Montclair
Coffin, Charlsa Lee *director, writer, artist*
Cole, Susan A. *university president, English language educator*
Lynde, Richard A. *academic administrator*

Moorestown
Weeks, Maurice Richard, Jr., *educational consultant, academic administrator*

Morristown
Venezia, William Thomas *school system administrator, counseling consultant*

Mount Holly
Denniston, Marjorie McGeorge *retired elementary school educator*

Neptune
Alston, Goldie Venessa *early childhood educator*

New Brunswick
Durnin, Richard Gerry *education educator*
Garner, Charles William *educational administration educator, consultant*
Kansfield, Norman J. *seminary president*
McCormick, Richard Levis *academic administrator*
Morrow, Lesley Mandel *literacy and elementary education educator*
Nelson, Jack Lee *education educator*
Paz, Harold Louis *dean, educator, internist*
Strickland, Dorothy *education educator*
Tanner, Daniel *curriculum theory educator*

New Milford
Rosato, Melissa Anne *educator*

New Monmouth
Santos, Sharon Lee *parochial school educator*

Newark
Altenkirch, Robert A. *academic administrator*
Bergen, Stanley Silvers, Jr., *retired university president, physician*
Bloom, Joel S. *academic administrator*
Bolden, Marion A. *superintendent*
Docarmo, Jerry Soares *academic administrator*
Feldman, Cecile Arlene *dean, dental educator*
Fenster, Saul K. *university president emeritus*
Flagg, E(loise) Alma Williams *educational administrator*
Griffith, Hurdis M. *dean*
Hollander, Toby Edward *education educator*
Joffe, Russell T. *dean*
Liman, Joan Pamela *university dean*
Rollino, John *academic administrator, writer, physicist, educator*
Ryan, Lisa Kathleen *education educator, consultant*
Schachter, Hindy Lauer *public management educator*
Shaw, Earl D. *academic administrator, physics educator*

Newton
Gallo, Nancy R. *educational consultant*
MacMurren, Margaret Patricia *secondary education educator, consultant*

Northfield
Watkins, Joan Frances *retired elementary school educator*

Oakland
Butterfield, Charles Edward, Jr., *educational consultant*

Parsippany
Kapfer, Miriam Bierbaum *technical documentation and training specialist*

Paterson
Fields, Marvin Leon *secondary school educator*
Murez, John *music education director, educator*

Phillipsburg
Johnson, Laurie Lynn *history educator*

Piscataway
Colaizzi, John Louis *dean*
Dill, Ellis Harold *university dean*
Goetz, George Edward *adult education educator*
Klein, Michael Tully *university dean, chemical engineer, consultant*
Trontell, Marie Celestine *dean*
You, Aleta *education educator*

Plainfield
Reeder, Hubert *elementary school educator*
Thomas, William Joseph *secondary school educator, administrator*

Pleasantville
London, Charlotte Isabella *secondary education educator, reading specialist*

Pomona
Colijn, Geert Jan *academic administrator, political scientist*
Sutman, Francis Xavier *university dean*

Princeton
Cooper, Michael R. *dean*
Gillespie, Thomas William *theological seminary administrator, religion educator*
Howarth, William (Louis Howarth) *education educator, writer*
Malkiel, Nancy Weiss *dean, historian, educator*
Sandoval, Amada *education program director*
Shapiro, Harold Tafler *former academic administrator, economist*
Tilghman, Shirley Marie *academic administrator, biology professor*

Rockaway
Allen, Dorothea *secondary school educator*

Roselle
Di Marco, Barbaranne Yanus *principal*
Meister, Karen Olivia *secondary school educator*

Roselle Park
Scarpelli, Vito *adult education educator, administrator*

Short Hills
Robbins-Wilf, Marcia *educational consultant*

Sicklerville
Miller, Audrey Thornton *retired educational administrator*

Skillman
Rhett, Haskell Emery Smith *educator*

Somerville
Thompson, William *director*
Weisblatt, Barbara Ann *secondary school educator*

South Amboy
Moskal, Anthony John *former dean, professor, management and education consultant*

South Hackensack
Wille, Rosanne Louise *higher education administrator*

South Orange
Deyrup, Marta Mestrovic *academic librarian, writer*
Hanbury, Kevin M. *dean, priest*
Sheeran, Robert *academic administrator*

Stratford
Gallagher, R. Michael *academic administrator*

Summit
Rossey, Paul William *school superintendent, university president*
Starks, Florence Elizabeth *retired special education educator*

Teaneck
Baldwin, Dorothy Leila *secondary school educator*
Dewey, Ralph Jay *school system administrator*
Lewis, Karen Ann *director*
Pischl, Adolph John *school administrator*
Smith, Susan Elizabeth *guidance director*
Walker, Lucy Doris *secondary school educator, writer*

Toms River
Finale, Frank Louis *retired elementary school educator, writer*

Trenton
Jones, Sarah Lucille *supervisor, consultant, principal*
Kaminski, Isabelle *pre-school educator, music educator*
Pruitt, George Albert *college president*
Scheiring, Michael James *college official*
Smallwood, Robert Albian, Jr., *secondary education educator*

Union
Applbaum, Ronald Lee *academic administrator*
Black, Jappie King *education educator, artist*
Lederman, Susan Sturc *public administration educator*

Union City
Bull, Inez Stewart *pianist, editor, author, music educator, curator, coloratura soprano*
Sheehy, Janice Ann *education technology coordinator*

Vernon
Megna, Steve Allan *secondary school educator*

Waldwick
Lynch, Carol *director special services, psychologist*

Wall
Petrovich, Dorothy *elementary school educator*

Warren
Hennings, Dorothy Grant (Mrs. George Hennings) *education educator*

Washington
De Sanctis, Vincent *college president*

Wayne
Cheo, Li-hsiang S. *education educator*
Edelstein, Melvin *education educator*
Garcia, Ofelia *dean*
Speert, Arnold *academic administrator, chemistry educator*

West Long Branch
Gaffney, Paul Golden, II, *academic administrator, military officer*
Lutz, Francis Charles *university dean, civil engineering educator*

West New York
Avello, Alfredo J. *retired secondary school educator*

West Orange
Pollara, Joanne *learning disabilities educator consultant*

West Paterson
DeLouise, Tia Caputi *university executive*

Westampton
Patel, Anjana *education educator, consultant*

Willingboro
Denslow, Deborah Pierson *primary education educator*

Woodbury
Duffield-Myers, Arlene Anna *elementary school educator*

NEW MEXICO

Alamogordo
McFadin, Helen Lozetta *retired elementary education educator*

Albuquerque
Abraham, Karen A. *university administrator*
Anaya, Rudolfo *educator, writer*
Arthur, Michelle Marie *education educator*
Caldera, Louis Edward *academic administrator, former federal official*
Caplan, Edwin Harvey *university dean, accounting educator*
Cliff, Norman *psychology educator, consultant, writer*
Everitt, Elizabeth M. *school system administrator*
Garcia, F. Chris *academic administrator, political science educator, public opinion researcher*
Graff, Pat Stuever *secondary school educator*
Hansen, Harold B., Jr., *elementary school educator*
Lattman, Laurence Harold *retired academic administrator*
Sena, Kathleen F. *academic administrator*
Stuart, Cynthia Morgan *university administrator*
Travelstead, Chester Coleman *former educational administrator*
Zink, Lee Berkey *retired academic administrator, economist, educator*

Gallup
Zongolowicz, Helen Michaeline *education and psychology educator*

Hobbs
Dill, Gary A. *academic administrator*
DiUlus, Frederick Alfonso-Edward *business educator*

Payton-Robinson, Constance Marian *educational consultant, writer*

Las Cruces
Conroy, William B. *retired university administrator*
Egginton, Everett *educational administrator*
Gale, Thomas Martin *university dean*
Heger, Herbert Krueger *education educator*

Montezuma
Geier, Philip Otto, III, *academic administrator*

Portales
Cobb, Jeanne Beck *education educator, researcher, consultant*
Howard, Carolyn F. *elementary school educator*

Rio Rancho
Weber, Alois Hughes *principal*

Roswell
Franzoni, Delaina Day *special education educator, department chairman*

Ruidoso
Pittman, Kathleen M. *education educator, consultant*

Santa Fe
Cerny, Charlene Ann *director*
Hanson, Linda N. *academic administrator, educator*
Harcourt, Robert Neff *educational administrator, journalist, genealogist*
Sandoval, Isabelle Medina *education educator*

Shiprock
Atcitty, Fannie L. *elementary school educator, education educator*
Austin-Garrison, Martha A. *educator, researcher*

Silver City
Snedeker, John Haggner *university president*

Taos
Garcia, Christine *academic administrator, educator, researcher*

NEW YORK

Albany
Brademas, John *retired university president, former congressman*
Langer, Judith Ann *literacy educator*
Lessner, Lawrence *education educator*
Mills, Richard Paul *school system administrator*
Mumpower, Jeryl L. *academic administrator*
Quackenbush, Roger E. *retired secondary school educator*
Robbins, Cornelius (Cornelius Van Vorse) *educational administration educator*
Rosenthal, Irene L. *education educator, consultant*
Salins, Peter D. *academic administrator*
Schell, Lawrence M. *education educator, biologist*
Stenson, Brian T. *academic administrator*

Alfred
Coll, Edward Girard, Jr., *university president*

Amherst
Anisman, Martin Jay *academic administrator*

Amityville
Palumbo, Anthony *education educator*
Wright, Nannie Bell *retired secondary school educator*

Annandale On Hudson
Botstein, Leon *academic administrator, conductor, historian*

Aurora
Ryerson, Lisa M. *academic administrator*

Batavia
Steiner, Stuart *college president*

Bedford
Kluge, Steve *secondary school educator*

Bellmore
Feldman, Harriet Ruth *dean*
Rosenstein, Elyse S. *secondary school educator*

Bellport
Schultheis, Edwin Milford *dean, business educator*

Bethpage
Martin, Darryl James *audio-visual specialist*

Binghamton
Clark, Clifford Dale *university president*
Coffey, Margaret Tobin *education educator, county official*
DeFleur, Lois B. *university president, sociology educator*
Meador, John Milward, Jr., *university dean*
Swain, Mary Ann Price *university official*

Briarwood
Benedict, Joseph Harold, Jr., *academic administrator, management consultant*
Takacs, Michael Joseph *secondary school educator*

Bridgeport
Sheldon, Thomas Donald *academic administrator*

Brockport
Gemmett, Robert J. *university dean, English language educator*
Stier, William Frederick, Jr., *academic administrator, educator*

Bronx
Currie, Joseph Aloysius *campus ministry director, theology studies educator*
Fernandez, Ricardo R. *university administrator*
Hauser, Bernice Worman *director*
Lerner, Laurence M. *college administrator*
McShane, Joseph Michael *academic administrator, priest*

Mercurio, Mia Lynn *education educator*
Mobasher, Maher Attia *academic administrator*
Purpura, Dominick P. *dean, neuroscientist*
Rothstein, Anne Louise *education educator, college official*
Scanlan, Thomas Joseph *college president, educator*
Todd, Thomas Alexander *secondary school educator*
Wertheim, Mary Danielle *elementary education coordinator*

Bronxville
Myers, Michele Tolela *academic administrator*

Brooklyn
Arcuri, Leonard Philip *elementary school educator*
Birenbaum, William M. *former university president*
Bugliarello, George *academic administrator, educator*
Burrows, Edwin G. *education educator*
Chung, Ping Tsai *education educator*
Clayton, Julia B. *academic administrator, musician*
D'Elia, Nicholas *secondary school educator*
Douglass, Melvin Isadore *middle school administrator, educator, clergyman*
Feigelson, Eugene B. *dean*
Greene, Gladstone Fitzpatrick *educator, consultant*
Hill, Elizabeth Anne *academic administrator, lawyer*
Ierardi, Eric Joseph *school system administrator*
Kimmich, Christoph Martin *academic administrator, educator*
Mc Clenney, Byron Nelson *community college administrator*
O'Connor, Sister George Aquin (Margaret M. O'Connor) *academic administrator, sociology educator*
Peruggi, Regina S. *academic administrator*
Rosario-Olmedo, Carmen Gloria *principal*
Schutte, Thomas Frederick *academic administrator*
Thoering, Robert Charles *elementary school educator*
Wilson, Arthur Theodore *education consultant*
Wolfe, Ethyle Renee (Mrs. Coleman Hamilton Benedict) *college administrator*

Buffalo
Armfield, Felix L. *education educator, consultant*
Bernardino, Michael E. *academic administrator, physician, educator*
Buchanan, Richard N. *dean, dental educator*
Cañedo, Marion *school system administrator*
Cathey, Patrice Antoinette *secondary school educator, director*
Cryan, Richard James, Jr., *academic administrator*
Fuda, Siri Narayan K.K. (Elaine T. Barber) *director*
Greiner, William Robert *university administrator, educator, lawyer*
Gress, Edward J(ules) *educator, consultant*
Holm, Bruce Allen *academic administrator, researcher*
Howard, Muriel A. *academic administrator*
McClary, Glen David *education educator*
Metzger, Erika Alma *education educator*
Mitchell, Mike L. *academic administrator*
Neuner, Jerome Lawrence *academic administrator, educator*
Schmidli, Keith William *vocational education administrator, educator, researcher*
Simpson, John Barclay *academic administrator*
Triggle, David John *dean, pharmacist, consultant*
Tucker, Melvin Jay *education educator, researcher*
Wilbur, Barbara Marie *elementary school educator*
Zhang, Jie *education educator, researcher*

Burke
Crippen, Juanita Witherell *elementary school educator*

Camillus
Davis, Lynn Harry *secondary school educator*

Canandaigua
Love, Robert Lyman *educational consulting company executive*

Canton
Shuman, James C. *education educator*
Sullivan, Daniel F. *academic administrator, sociologist, educator*

Castleton On Hudson
Kienzle, John Fred *history educator*
Lanford, Oscar Erasmus, Jr., *retired university vice chancellor*

Catskill
Wolfe, Geraldine *academic administrator*

Cedarhurst
Van Raalte, Polly Ann *reading and writing specialist, photojournalist*

Centerport
Rogers, Ailene Kane *retired secondary school educator*

Chazy
Ratner, Gayle *special education educator*

Churchville
Balch, Glenn McClain, Jr., *academic administrator, minister, writer*

Clarence
Johnston, Joan Lawler *director, consultant*

Clinton
Paris, David C. *academic administrator, political scientist, educator*

Cold Spring
Battersby, Katherine Sue *elementary school educator*

Commack
Cohen, Judith W. *retired academic administrator*

Corinth
Winslow, Norma Mae *elementary school educator*

Corning
Bonomo, Timothy Paul *education educator, consultant*

Cortland
Valentine, Gordon Carlton *retired secondary school educator*

Delhi
Duncan, Mary Ellen *academic administrator*

Delmar
Houghton, Raymond Carl, Jr., *education educator*
Yeara, James Carroll *secondary school educator, writer*

Dix Hills
Braun, Ludwig *educational technology consultant*

Douglaston
Palatnick, Frank Sidney *educational consultant*

Downsville
Hornick, Susan Florence Stegmuller *secondary education educator, fine arts educator, curriculum specialist, artist*

East Aurora
Weidemann, Julia Clark *retired principal, educator*
Woodard, Carol Jane *educational consultant*

East Hampton
Osterweil, Adam Matthew *elementary school educator, writer*
Schetlin, Eleanor M. *retired university official*

East Islip
Donohue, Claire P. *retired school librarian*

East Northport
Ambrosio, Joseph Michael *secondary school educator, composer*

East Setauket
Maffia, Christina *elementary school educator, consultant*

Elmira
Meier, Thomas Keith *college president, English educator*

Fairport
Holtzclaw, Diane Smith *elementary school educator*

Falconer
Benke, Paul Arthur *academic administrator*

Fallsburg
Sperber, Marilyn Janice *special education educator*

Far Rockaway
Sussman, Laureen Glicklin *junior high school educator*

Flushing
Erickson, Raymond *music historian, musician*
Roberts, Kathleen Joy Doty *secondary school educator*
Totakura, Satyanarayana Raju *secondary school educator*
Yoshida, Roland Kiyoshi *academic dean, special education educator*

Frankfort
Conigilaro, Phyllis Ann *retired elementary education educator*

Fredonia
Vassoler-Froeligh, Ivani *education educator, journalist*

Freeport
Martorana, Barbara Joan *secondary school educator*
Walker, Lula Noriega *secondary administrator*

Fresh Meadows
Castellano, Joseph P. *assistant principal*

Garden City
Fanelli, Sean A. *college president*
Gorin, Robert Murray, Jr., *history educator*
Kline, Eileen Mary *secondary school educator*
Scott, Robert Allyn *academic administrator*
Shuart, James Martin *retired academic administrator*
Webb, Igor Michael *academic administrator*

Geneva
Stranahan, Patricia *dean*

Ghent
Rich, Donna L. *school system administrator*

Glen Cove
Compton, Roger H. *dean, engineering educator*

Great Neck
Fried, Belle Warshavsky *education educator*
Gross, Beatrice Schaap *writer*
Hecht, Marie Bergenfeld *retired educator, author*
Peterson, Jon A. *education educator*

Greenport
Monsell, Thomas Oliver *secondary English educator, writer*

Greenvale
Megay-Nespoli, Karen Patricia *elementary school educator*
Shenker, Joseph *academic administrator*
Steinberg, David Joel *academic administrator, historian, educator*
Westermann-Cicio, Mary Louise *academic administrator, library studies educator*

Guilderland
Escobar, Deborah Ann *gifted and talented education educator*

Hamilton
Chopp, Rebecca S. *university president*

Jones, Howard Langworthy *retired educational administrator, consultant*

Harrison
Northcutt, Marie Rose *elementary, secondary, & special education educator*

Hartsdale
Aker, Susan K. *elementary school educator*

Hempstead
Berliner, Herman Albert *university provost and officer, economics educator*
Salten, David George *academic administrator*

Holland
Loockerman, William Delmer *retired educational administrator*

Horseheads
Andrake, Nancy Carolyn *secondary school educator*

Houghton
Chamberlain, Daniel Robert *college president*
Luckey, Robert Reuel Raphael *retired academic administrator*

Huntington
D'Addario, Alice Marie *school administrator*
Moglia, Greg *education educator*

Hurley
Opdahl, Viola Elizabeth *secondary school educator*

Ithaca
Ben Daniel, David Jacob *entrepreneurship educator, consultant*
Carpenter, Barry Keith *chemistry educator, researcher*
Firebaugh, Francille Maloch *university official*
Green, Edward Thomas, Jr., *education educator*
Halpern, Bruce Peter *academic administrator, researcher, educator*
Lehman, Jeffrey Sean *academic administrator, educator*
Lovelace, Richard Van Evera *education educator, research scientist*
Martin, Carolyn A. (Biddy Martin) *provost*
Nesheim, Malden C. *academic administrator, nutrition educator*
Pinch, Trevor J. *education educator*
Rhodes, Frank Harold Trevor *academic administrator, geologist*
Sass, Stephen Louis *education educator*
Schwab, Stewart Jon *dean*
Scott, Norman Roy *academic administrator, agricultural engineering educator*
Smith, Donald F. *dean*
Streett, William Bernard *retired university dean, engineering educator*
Swieringa, Robert Jay *dean, accountant, educator*
Ullrich, Robert Albert *academic administrator*
Williams, Peggy Ryan *academic administrator*

Jamaica
Cline, Janice Claire *education educator*
Davis-Jerome, Eileen George *educational consultant, principal*
Delener, Nejdet *college dean, marketing and international business educator*
Faust, Naomi Flowe *education educator*
Harrington, Donald James *university president*
Malewitz, Joan *elementary school educator, multi-media specialist*
Ramos, Alice M *education educator*
Sciame, Joseph *university administrator*
Skirde, Edward George *academic administrator, consultant*

Kendall
Rak, Linda Marie *elementary education educator, consultant*

Krumville
Nagi, Catherine Raseh *retired educational administrator, financial planner*
Schuckman, Nancy Lee *retired principal*

Lake Placid
Reiss, Paul Jacob *academic administrator*

Lake Ronkonkoma
Spahr, Clinton S., Jr., *retired elementary education educator*

Lawrence
Press, Marlyn Rothman *special education and literacy educator*

Le Roy
Sovocool, Mary Anne Elizabeth Cranston *secondary school educator*

Lewiston
Kelly, Sean Q *education educator*

Lido Beach
Shear, Richard Gary *education administrator*

Lockport
Spero, Joseph J. *secondary school educator*

Locust Valley
Mathews, Walter Michael *educational consultant*

Long Beach
Thompson, Dorothy Barnard *elementary school educator*

Long Island City
Lieberman, Janet Elaine *academic administrator*

Loudonville
Toal, James Francis *academic administrator*

Mahopac
McCluskey, Frank Bryce *director*

Mamaroneck
Feigin, Nancy J. *guidance counselor*

Merrick
Garfinkel, Lawrence Saul *academic administrator, educator, television producer*

Middle Island
Sanfilippo, Stephen Nicholas *retired secondary school educator*

Middletown
McCord, Jean Ellen *secondary art educator, coach*
Moore, Virginia Lee Smith *elementary school educator*

Montrose
Matthias, George Frank *retired educator*

New Kingston
St. George, Joyce *conflict and crisis management educator, writer*

New Paltz
Emanuel-Smith, Robin Lesley *special education educator*
Flanagan Kelly, Anne Marie *academic administrator*
Lavallee, David Kenneth *chemistry educator, researcher*

New Rochelle
Cohen, Saul Bernard *retired academic administrator, geographer*
Donahue, Richard James *secondary school educator*
Gallagher, John Francis *education educator*
Sweeny, Stephen Jude *academic administrator*

New York
Alfano, Michael Charles *dental school dean*
Anspacher, Stephen John *university official*
Arndt, Cynthia *educational administrator*
Benhabib, Jess *adult education educator*
Benson, Thomas Luther *academic administrator*
Bollinger, Lee Carroll *academic administrator, law educator*
Boylan, Elizabeth Shippee *academic administrator, biologist, educator*
Brinkley, Alan David *provost, historian*
Brown, Joyce F. *academic administrator*
Buckley, Robert John *academic research administrator*
Budig, Gene Arthur *former chancellor, professional sports executive*
Burns, Red *academic administrator*
Burton, John Campbell *university dean, educator, consultant*
Campbell, Mary Schmidt *dean*
Caputo, David Armand *university president, political scientist educator*
Clarke, Lewis Ryland *history educator*
Claster, Jill Nadell *university administrator, history educator*
Cochran, Raymond Martin *university auditor*
Cohen, Steven Alan *program director*
Consagra, Sophie Chandler *academic administrator*
Cooley, Thomas F. *dean, economist, educator*
Daly, George Garman *college dean, educator*
Davidson, Anthony R. *education educator, consultant*
Durkin, Dorothy Angela *university official*
Essandoh, Hilda Brathwaite *kindergarten educator*
Fabian, Larry Louis *university administrator*
Feldberg, Meyer *university dean*
Finegold, Amy Beth *elementary school educator, consultant*
Gatto, John Taylor *educational consultant, writer, speaker*
Gemorah, Solomon *education educator, historian*
Gerety, Tom *academic administrator, lawyer, educator, philosopher*
Gillespie, John Thomas *university administrator*
Goldstein, Matthew *academic administrator*
Gorelick, Steven Michael *academic administrator, writer, sociologist*
Gottschalk, Alfred *retired college chancellor, museum executive*
Grant, Sonia Vivienne *secondary school educator*
Haboush, Jahyun Kim *education educator*
Haffner, Alden Norman *academic administrator*
Harris, Marilyn *retired academic administrator*
Hickey, Catherine Josephine *school system administrator*
Hoffner, Marilyn *university administrator*
Hood, Donald Charles *university administrator, psychology educator*
Horowitz, Frances Degen *academic administrator, psychology educator*
Howard, David *educational administrator*
Ilchman, Warren Frederick *university administrator, foundation director, educator*
Jelinek, Vera *university director*
Jeynes, Mary Kay *college dean*
Joel, Richard Marc *academic administrator, law educator, dean*
Kase, Nathan Ginden *dean*
Kerrey, Bob (J. Robert Kerrey) *academic administrator, former senator*
Klein, Joel Irwin *school system administrator*
Konner, Joan Weiner *academic administrator, educator, television producer, writer*
Kopp, Wendy *teaching program administrator*
Kozlowski, Cheryl M. *principal*
Lamm, Norman *academic administrator, rabbi*
Lamster, Ira Barry *academic administrator*
Lange, Phil C. *retired education educator*
Lao, Joseph R. *education educator, researcher*
Leebron, David Wayne *dean, law educator*
Leiman, Joan Maisel *university administrator, hospital administrator*
Levine, Arthur Elliott *academic administrator, educator*
Levine, Naomi Bronheim *academic administrator*
Lloyd, Jean *retired early childhood educator*
Logue, Alexandra Woods *higher education administrator, psychologist*
Lowengrub, Morton *academic administrator*
Lynch, Gerald Weldon *academic administrator, psychologist*
Macchiarola, Frank Joseph *academic administrator, educator*
Marcuse, Adrian Gregory *academic administrator*
Marks, Lillian Shapiro *secretarial studies educator, author*
Mayer, Robert Anthony *retired college president*
McLaughlin, David *academic administrator*
Mills, Barry *academic administrator, lawyer*

Minotti, Mark Anthony *assistant principal*
Mitterand, Henri C. *education educator, writer*
Monson, Robert Joseph *education educator*
Morgan, Arlene Notoro *university administrator*
Morreale, Joseph Constantino *higher education administrator, public administration educator, economic and financial consultant*
Nelson, Iris Dorothy *retired guidance and rehabilitation counselor*
Newman, Phyllis *adult education educator, psychologist*
Nissim, Shai *special education educator, consultant*
Nurse, Sir Paul M. *academic administrator*
Oliva, Lawrence Jay *former academic administrator, history educator*
Oremland, Melvyn J. *education educator, director*
Parkin, Gerard Francis Ralph *chemistry educator, researcher*
Pawliczko, George Ihor *academic administrator*
Perelman, Michael A *education educator, psychologist*
Polisi, Joseph W(illiam) *academic administrator*
Prager, Leslie Beth *career counselor*
Pulanco, Tonya Beth *special education educator*
Rabb, Harriet Schaffer *academic administrator, educator, lawyer, government official*
Reutter, Eberhard Edmund, Jr., *education and law educator*
Rhodes, David J. *academic administrator*
Robinson, Joyce McPeake *administrator*
Rowland, Esther E(delman) *retired dean*
Rubino, Victor Joseph *academic administrator, lawyer*
Rudenstine, Neil Leon *former academic administrator, educator*
Rupp, George Erik *not-for-profit administrator*
Scaffidi, Judith Ann *academic administrator*
Schaller-Demers, Debra Susan *education coordinator, health facility administrator*
Seitz, Frederick *former university administrator*
Selby, Cecily Cannan *dean, educator, scientist*
Sexton, John Edward *academic administrator, law educator*
Shapiro, Judith R. *academic administrator, anthropology educator*
Shields, James Joseph *academic administrator, educator, writer*
Silverman, Martin Morris Bernard *secondary school educator*
Socol, Sheldon Eleazer *university official*
Soros, Susan Weber *educational administrator*
Takamura, Jeanette Chiyoko *dean*
Taylor, Diana Lancaster *school system administrator*
Travis, Jeremy *academic administrator*
Walton, R. Keith *academic administrator, lawyer*
Walzer, Judith Borodovko *academic administrator, educator*
Waren, Stanley Arnold *university administrator, theatre and arts center administrator, director*
Weinstein, Sidney *retired university program director*
Wylie, James Malcolm *adult education educator*
Yetman, Leith Eleanor *academic administrator*
Yu, Pauline Ruth *former dean, educational association administrator*

Newburgh
Conner, Susan *elementary school educator*
Joyce, Mary Ann *principal*
Sakac, Sister Ann *academic administrator*

Newfield
Rawlings, Hunter Ripley, III, *academic administrator, classicist*

Niagara University
O'Leary, Daniel Francis *academic administrator, priest*

Niskayuna
Bish, L. Ann *retired secondary school educator*

North Tonawanda
Beach, Sandra Marie Yudichak *secondary school educator*

Northport
McGarry, Frances Lorraine *education educator*

Ogdensburg
Smith, Carol Ann *academic administrator*

Old Westbury
Christofides, Fotine *parochial school educator*
Schure, Matthew *academic administrator*
van Wie, Paul David *secondary school educator, historian*

Oneonta
Donovan, Alan Barton *college president*
Nishida, Mieko *educator*

Orangeburg
Filoramo, Dorothy Christine *academic administrator*
Hsu, Donald Kung-Hsing *education educator, management consultant*

Oswego
Moody, Florence Elizabeth *education educator, retired college dean*

Oyster Bay
Hoxie, Ralph Gordon *educational administrator, author*

Patchogue
Orlowski, Karel Ann *elementary school educator*

Peconic
Aldcroft, George Edward *guidance counselor*

Pittsford
Bernstein, Paul *retired academic dean*
Sproull, Robert Lamb *retired university president, physicist*
Thompson, Brian John *university administrator, optics educator*

Plattsburgh
Worthington, Janet Evans *retired academic dean, English language educator*

Pleasantville
Cleary, Edward Louis *university administrator*
Kahn, Beverly L. *academic administrator*
Tao, Lixin *computer scientist, computer science educator*

Pomona
Frelow, Robert Dean *retired school system administrator, writer*

Port Jefferson Station
Shockley, Alonzo Hilton, Jr., *school system administrator*

Port Washington
Gordon-Tennant, Jennifer Jay *secondary school educator*
Mittelstaedt, Arthur Howard, Jr., *educational educator*

Potsdam
Collins, Anthony G. *academic administrator*
Rudiger, Lance Wade *secondary school educator*
Sarnoff, Joseph C. *academic administrator*
Scott, Jean A. *university president*

Poughkeepsie
Bjork, Christopher Brian *education educator*
Brakas, Nora Jachym *education educator*
Conklin, Donald David *academic administrator*
Fergusson, Frances Daly *college president, educator*
Hadaller, David Lawrence *dean*
Jackson, Judy Faye *academic administrator*
Opdycke, Leonard Emerson *retired elementary, secondary and college-level educator, publisher*

Purchase
Lacy, Bill *academic administrator, architect*
Vardin, Patricia Anne *education educator*
Wepner, Shelley Beth *education educator, software developer*

Rexford
Schmitt, Roland Walter *retired academic administrator*

Riverhead
Buck, Leslie Elizabeth *mathematics educator, poet*

Rochester
Cohen, Jules *physician, educator, former academic dean*
Demers, Elizabeth Anne *education educator*
Everett, Claudia Kellam *retired special education educator*
Flynn, R. Thomas *academic administrator*
Goldfarb, Barry Joseph *education educator*
Guzick, David S. *dean, educator*
Jackson, Thomas Humphrey *academic administrator, lawyer*
Joynt, Robert James *academic administrator, physician*
Kirschenbaum, Howard *education educator*
Mahar, Jason *education educator*
McKenzie, Stanley Don *academic administrator, English educator*
Munson, Harold Lewis *education educator*
Palmer, Harvey John *dean*
Shirley, Bonnie J. *secondary school educator*
Simone, Albert Joseph *academic administrator*
Zupan, Mark A. *dean, business professor*

Roosevelt
Adams, Mary A. *retired assistant principal*

Roslyn
Stracher, Dorothy Altman *education educator, consultant*

Roslyn Heights
Jordan, Patricia James *secondary school educator*

Rotterdam Junction
Cox, Paulyn Mae *retired elementary school educator*

Rush
Smith, Katherine Teresa *history educator*

Saint Albans
Bess, Olean *educator, counselor*

Saint James
Kelly, Michael Joseph *academic administrator, consultant*

Saint Johnsville
Dillenbeck, Marianne Frances *elementary school educator*

Sands Point
Cullinan, Bernice E(llinger) *education educator*

Saratoga Springs
Glotzbach, Philip A. *academic administrator*
McKnight, Joyce Sheldon *adult educator, community organizer, mediator*

Scarsdale
Naughton, Ann Elsie *primary school educator*

Schenectady
Hull, Roger Harold *academic administrator*

Sea Cliff
Hassani, Mojdeh *special education educator*
Martin, David S. *retired secondary school educator, administrator*

Seaford
Moore, Sister Mary Francis *parochial school educator*

Selden
Connors, William Francis, Jr., *academic administrator*

Setauket
McClean, Lenora James *nursing educator, dean*

Shirley
Harper, Catherine B. *primary school educator*

South Salem
Tafrate, Polly Hare *retired elementary school educator*

Southampton
Rodas, Daniel *academic administrator, management educator*

Staten Island
Brady, Christine Ellen *education coordinator*
Springer, Marlene *university administrator, educator*
Wilson, Alice McAteer *secondary school educator*

Stony Brook
Cochran, James Kirk *dean, oceanographer, geochemist, educator*
Kenny, Shirley Strum *academic administrator*
McGrath, Robert L. *academic administrator*
Rifkin, Barry R. *dean, dental educator, researcher*
Shamash, Yacov *dean, electrical engineering educator*

Syracuse
Burstyn, Joan Netta *education educator*
Cantor, Nancy *academic administrator*
Charters, Alexander Nathaniel *retired adult education educator*
Chickadonz, Grace Harlow *dean*
Eastwood, Gregory Lindsay *academic administrator*
Federman Stein, Ruth *educational consultant*
Freund, Deborah A. *academic administrator*
Krathwohl, David Reading *retired education educator*
Miles, Kenneth Ontario *academic program director*
Murphy, Cornelius B., Jr., (Neil Murphy) *academic administrator*
Rubin, David M. *dean, educator*
Shaw, Kenneth Alan *university president*
Soyars, M. Douglas *academic administrator, music educator*
Ware, Bennie *university administrator*
Weiss, Volker *university administrator, educator*
Witkin, Jerome *education educator, painter*

Tarrytown
Marcus, Sheldon *adult education educator*

Troy
De, Suvranu *education educator*
Jackson, Shirley Ann *academic administrator, physicist*
Judd, Gary *university administrator*
Kahl, William Frederick *retired college president*
Nagy, George *education educator*
Neff, Jeanne Henry *academic administrator*
Peterson, G. P. "Bud" *academic administrator*
Wait, Samuel Charles, Jr., *academic administrator, educator*

Utica
Boyle, William Leo, Jr., *educational consultant, retired college president*

Valhalla
Hankin, Joseph Nathan *college president*
O'Connell, Ralph Anthony *dean, psychiatrist, educator*

Valley Stream
Rodgers, John Joseph, III, *educational administration consultant, educator*

Vestal
Day, Stephen Fred *school system administrator, writer*

Wallkill
Leopold, Richard William *middle school educator*

Wantagh
Marcatante, John Joseph *educational administrator*

Watertown
Faunce, Russ *educator, musician*

West Hempstead
Conway-Gervais, Kathleen Marie *reading specialist, educational consultant*

West Nyack
Coffey, Kimberly E. *secondary school educator*

Westbury
Ross-Lee, Barbara *dean, educator*

White Plains
Ottinger, Richard Lawrence *dean emeritus*

Whitestone
Lodico, Cheryl Madeline *secondary school educator*

Woodmere
Seyfert, Wayne George *secondary education educator, anatomy educator*

Yonkers
Liggio, Jean Vincenza *adult education educator, artist*
Trentanelli, John Anthony *educational administrator*
Weston, Francine Evans *secondary school educator*

Yorktown Heights
Delmoro, Ronald Anthony *elementary school principal*

NORTH CAROLINA

Asheville
Brown, David G. *academic administrator*
Carver, Peter James *education educator, director*
McGrotty, Carole Weaver *elementary school educator, parochial school educator*
Reed, Patsy Bostick *former academic administrator*
Sgro, Beverly Huston *day school administrator, educator, state official*

Banner Elk
Robinson, Earl James *academic administrator, information systems and statistics educator, consultant*

Belmont
Abernathy, Dixie Friend *elementary school educator, principal*

Boiling Springs
White, Martin Christopher *academic administrator*

Boone
Duke, Charles Richard *academic dean*
Hay, Fred J. *education educator, librarian, editor*
Land, Ming Huey *college dean*
Lugo, Emil J. *retired secondary school educator*
McFadden, Margaret H. *education educator, writer*
Morris, Robert Darrell *reading education educator*
Pollard, William Barlow, III, *university educator*
Woollcombe, Graham Douglas *dean*

Buies Creek
Johnson, George Lloyd *education educator, consultant, writer*
Martin, James Ingram *education educator*
Wiggins, Norman Adrian *university administrator, legal educator*

Chapel Hill
Broad, Margaret Corbett (Molly Broad) *academic administrator*
Campbell, Bobby Jack *university official*
Carroll, Roy *retired academic administrator*
Cole, Richard Ray *university dean*
Cronenwett, Linda Houk *dean*
Cunningham, James William *literacy education educator, researcher*
Edwards, Richard LeRoy *dean, social sciences educator, management consultant*
Fordham, Christopher Columbus, III, *dean, academic administrator, medical educator*
Freund, Cynthia M. *dean*
Ganley, Oswald Harold *retired director*
Hobson, Fred Colby, Jr., *English educator, author*
Jones, W. S. (Steve Jones) *dean*
Magill, Samuel Hays *academic administrator, higher education consultant*
McCoy, William O. *former academic administrator, retired telecommunications executive*
Mc Kean, John Rosseel Overton *university dean*
Moeser, James Charles *university chancellor, musician*
Nichol, Gene Ray, Jr., *dean, department chairman*
Roper, William Lee *dean, physician*
Satterfield, John Roberts, Jr., *retired college president and music educator*
Stewart, Sarah *elementary school educator*
Sullivan, Robert S. *college dean*
Ware, William Brettel *education educator*

Charlotte
Bradley, Dana Burr *educational researcher, consultant*
Clark, Ann Blakeney *educational administrator*
Colvard, Dean Wallace *emeritus university chancellor*
Fretwell, Elbert K., Jr., *retired university chancellor, consultant*
Kirkpatrick, James Alexander *education educator, writer*
Mercer, Evelyn Lois *retired guidance counselor*
Stephens, Kitty Frances *academic administrator*
Tyson, Cynthia Haldenby *academic administrator*
Woodward, James Hoyt *academic administrator, engineer*
Yancy, Dorothy Cowser *college president*

Chocowinity
Castle, William Eugene *retired academic administrator*

Clayton
Scott, Stephen Carlos *academic administrator*

Cullowhee
Bardo, John William *university administrator*
Coulter, Myron Lee *retired academic administrator*
Reed, Alfred Douglas *retired academic administrator*

Davidson
Spencer, Samuel Reid, Jr., *education consultant, former college president*
Vagt, Robert F. *academic administrator*

Denver
Eppley, Frances Fielden *retired secondary education educator, writer*

Dobson
Smith, Richard Jackson *elementary school educator*

Durham
Adams, Rex *dean*
Brodhead, Richard H. *academic administrator*
Champagne, Mary T. *dean*
Denlinger, Ann T. *school system administrator*
Huestis, Charles Benjamin *former academic administrator*
Jeffreys, Arcelia Taylor *education educator*
Kuniholm, Bruce Robellet *university administrator*
Lange, Peter *academic administrator*
Schmalbeck, Richard Louis *university dean, lawyer*
Wescott, Joseph Warren, II, *academic administrator, education educator*
Williams, Robert Sanders (Sandy Williams) *dean, academic administrator, educator, researcher*

Elizabeth City
Beloat, Hollis A *education educator*
Burnim, Mickey L. *academic administrator*
White, Leon Samuel *college administrator*

Elon
Tolley, Jerry Russell *university administrator*

Fayetteville
Cook Wike, Lauren Markland *academic administrator*
Hagans, Valerie Mae Gee *special education educator*

Jordan, Karla Salge *early childhood education educator*
Watt, Willis Martin *academic administrator, communications, adult education, leadership educator*

Greensboro
Bynum, Magnolia Virginia Wright *retired secondary school educator*
Chabotar, Kent John *academic administrator*
Cole, Johnnetta Betsch *academic administrator, educator*
Derosa, Donald V. *academic administrator*
Godard, Jerry Holton Caris *psychology educator, college dean*
Miller, Robert Louis *university dean, chemistry educator*
Moran, William Edward *academic administrator*
Oliver, Donna H. *secondary school educator*
Pearcey, Lynne G. *university dean, nursing educator*
Renick, James Carmichael *academic administrator, educator*
Sullivan, Patricia A. *academic administrator*
Williams, Craven Edward *academic administrator*
Zopf, Evelyn LaNoel Montgomery *guidance counselor*

Greenville
Ballard, Steven C. *academic administrator*
Bearden, James Hudson *university official*
Eakin, Richard Ronald *academic educator, mathematics educator*
Guidry, Allen Owen *secondary school educator*
Howell, John McDade *retired university chancellor, political science educator*
Kragel, Peter J. *academic administrator*
Leggett, Donald Yates *academic administrator*
Muse, William Van *academic administrator*

Hendersonville
Payne, Gerald Oliver *retired elementary education educator*

High Point
Howard, Lou Dean Graham *elementary school educator*

Holly Springs
Booth, Penelope Partridge *secondary school educator, writer, principal*

Jamestown
Cameron, Donald W. *academic administrator*

Kinston
Petteway, Samuel Bruce *college president*
Richardson, Vanessa *education educator*

Lake Junaluska
Stanton, Donald Sheldon *academic administrator*

Laurinburg
Deegan, John, Jr., *academic administrator, educator, researcher*

Matthews
Kocsis, Joan Bosco *elementary education educator, administrative assistant, assistant principal*

Monroe
Rorie, Nancy Catherine *retired elementary and secondary school educator*

Montreat
Stackhouse, Eunice Wonderly *education educator, musician*
Struble, Dan *academic administrator*

Mount Olive
Raper, William Burkette *retired college president*

Pembroke
Meadors, Allen Coats *health administrator, educator*

Raleigh
Baker, Stanley Beckwith *education educator*
Barnhardt, Robert Alexander *college dean*
Boylan, Winnie Carleen *secondary school educator, writer*
Bruck, Robert Ian *education educator*
Burris, Craven Allen *retired college administrator, educator*
Dolce, Carl John *education administration educator*
Dornan, John Neill *public policy center professional*
Drew, Nancy McLaurin Shannon *counselor, consultant*
Fletcher, Oscar Jasper, Jr., *dean*
Hartford, Maureen A. *academic administrator*
Howell, Bruce Inman *academic administrator*
Jarrett, Polly Hawkins *secondary education educator, retired*
Kimbrough, Lorelei *elementary school educator*
Mac Cormac, Earl Ronald *retired education educator*
Maidon, Carolyn Howser *director*
Memory, Jasper Durham *academic administrator, physics educator*
Oblinger, James L. *academic administrator*
Page, Anne Ruth *gifted education educator, education specialist*
Parramore, Barbara Mitchell *education educator*
Robinson, Prezell Russell *academic administrator*
Steed, Michelle Elnora *special education educator, counselor*
Suber, Dianne Boardley *educational administrator*
Whitaker, Bruce Ezell *college president*
Winstead, Nash Nicks *university administrator, phytopathologist*

Salisbury
Freeman, Algeania Warren *academic administrator*
Hall, Telka Mowery Elium *retired educational administrator*

Sanford
York, Carolyn Pleasants Stearns *English educator*

Shelby
Edgar, Ruth R. *retired elementary school educator*

Smithfield
Wiggs, Shirley JoAnn *retired secondary school educator*

Southport
Spain, Sheryl Scarbrough *school counselor, educator*

Taylorsville
Leonhardt, Debbie Ann *counselor, writer, minister*

Wake Forest
Buchanan, Edward A. *education educator*

Wilmington
Rorison, Margaret Lippitt *reading consultant*

Winston Salem
Applegate, William Brown *dean, medical educator, researcher, physician*
Crowder, Lena Belle *retired special education educator*
Gordon, William Charles *college administrator*
Hauser, Charlie Brady *elementary school educator*
Hearn, Thomas K., Jr., *university president*
Hobgood, E(arl) Wade *college chancellor*
Linster, Michelle Lynn *education educator, consultant*
Patel, Ajay *dean*
Roth, Marjory Joan Jarboe *special education educator*
Schexnider, Alvin J. *academic administrator*
Walsh, Robert K. *dean*
Zubov, Lynn *special education educator, researcher*

Yanceyville
Wiggins, Sarah *assistant principal, secondary school educator*

NORTH DAKOTA

Bismarck
Joersz, Fran Woodmansee *secondary school educator*
Potts, Robert Leslie *academic administrator*
Sanstead, Wayne Godfrey *school system administrator*

Dickinson
Medlar, Deborah Starkey *history and political science educator*

Ellendale
Schlieve, Hy C. J. *school administrator*

Fargo
Lardy, Sister Susan Marie *academic administrator*
Sanford, Glenda Levonne *educational administrator*
Wegenast, Judy H. *elementary school educator, consultant*

Grand Forks
Alfonso, Peter J. *educator*
Ashe, Kathy Rae *special education educator*
Aune, Adonica Schultz *education educator, consultant*
Kupchella, Charles Edward *academic administrator, author, educator*
Page, Sally Jacquelyn *university official, management educator*
Porter, Kimberly K. *education educator, consultant*
Vitton, John Joseph *education educator*
Wilson, H. David *dean*

Minot
Jermiason, John Lynn *elementary school educator, farmer, rancher*
Shaar, H. Erik *academic administrator*

OHIO

Ada
Baker, Kendall L. *academic administrator*

Akron
Barker, Harold Kenneth *former university dean*
Bowman-Dalton, Burdene Kathryn *education testing coordinator, computer consultant*
Buzzelli, Charlotte Grace *special education educator*
Capers, Cynthia Flynn *dean, nursing educator*
Dietz, Margaret Jane *retired public information director*
Duan, Zhong-Hui *education educator, researcher*
Hodakievic, James Joseph *retired secondary education educator*
Jana, Sadhan C *education educator, researcher*
Linberger, Peter *school librarian*
Ruebel, Marion A. *university president*

Andover
Mathay, John Preston *elementary school educator*

Ashland
Drushal, Mary Ellen *education educator, former academic administrator*
Shelly, Ann Converse *education educator, administrator*
Suggs, Robert Chinello *academic administrator, educator*

Athens
Bugeja, Michael Joseph *educator, writer*
Glidden, Robert Burr *academic administrator, musician, educator*
Krendl, Kathy *dean*
Mantione, Meryl E. *director, education educator*
McDavis, Roderick J. *academic administrator*
Neiman, Gary S. *university administrator*
Tymas-Jones, Raymond *dean*

Austintown
Kope, Joseph B. *retired humanities educator, consultant*

Berea
Canfield, Nanette Gay *director*

Bexley
Beller, Stephen Mark *retired university administrator*

Bowling Green
Dobb, Linda Sue *university official, librarian*
Ribeau, Sidney A. *academic administrator*
Zwierlein, Ronald Edward *athletics director*

Broadview Heights
Jergens, Maribeth Joie *school counselor*

Chagrin Falls
Brown, Jeanette Grasselli *retired university official*
Robertson, Linda F. *educational adminstrator*

Cincinnati
Briggs, Henry Payson, Jr., *headmaster*
Dionysiou, Dionysios Demetriou *adult education educator, researcher*
Greengus, Samuel *academic administrator, religion educator*
Hall, Michael Davis *principal*
Harrison, Donald Carey *university official, cardiology educator*
Hoffman, Donna Coy *learning disabilities educator*
Kelz, Rochelle Shelle K. *academic administrator*
Lindell, Andrea Regina *dean, nurse*
Martin, William Joseph, II, *dean, educator*
McFarlan, Rebecca Collins *secondary school educator, consultant*
Morrow, Ardythe Luxion *adult education educator, researcher*
Nester, William Raymond, Jr., *retired academic administrator and educator*
Palmer, Paul Richard *school librarian, archivist, curator*
Sheffield, Elizabeth Baker *special education educator, lecturer, consultant*
Silberstein, Edward Bernard *nuclear medicine educator, oncologist, researcher*
Smith, Gregory Allgire *college administrator*
Steger, Joseph A. *university president*
Thompson, Adrienne *secondary school educator*
Tomain, Joseph Patrick *dean, law educator*
Turner, Joan Dale *elementary school educator*
Winkler, Henry Ralph *retired academic administrator, historian*
Zimpher, Nancy Lusk *academic administrator*

Cleveland
Berger, Nathan Allen *academic administrator*
Boboc, Marius *education educator*
Byrd-Bennett, Barbara *school system administrator*
Cavanagh, Peter Robert *academic administrator, science educator, researcher*
Cerone, David *academic administrator*
Goldberg, Jerold S. *dean*
Grabowski, John Joseph *education educator, researcher*
Hansman, Catherine Ann *adult education educator, researcher*
Hundert, Edward M. *academic administrator*
Johnson, Victoria Houston *elementary school educator, poet*
McArdle, Richard Joseph *retired academic administrator*
McCullough, Joseph *college president emeritus*
Parker, Robert Frederic *university dean emeritus*
Queen, Joyce Ellen *elementary school educator*
Quigney, Theresa Ann *special education educator*
Rutledge, Virgie Marilyn *elementary school educator*
Thornton, Jerry Sue *community college president*
Weidenthal, Maurice David (Bud Weidenthal) *educational administrator, journalist*
Wertheim, Sally Harris *academic administrator, dean, education educator, consultant*
Wykle, May L. *dean, educator, researcher*

Columbia Station
Goll, Paulette Susan *education educator*

Columbus
Alutto, Joseph Anthony *dean, management educator*
Armes, Walter Scott *vocational school administrator*
Bagby, Ross Frederick *educational consultant*
Barsky, Constance Kay *education educator*
Cole, Clarence Russell *college dean*
Culbertson, Jack Arthur *education educator*
Eckert, Douglas *academic administrator, educator*
Foucht, Joan Lucille *retired elementary school educator, retired counseling administrator*
Kerns, Allen Franklin *education educator*
Koenigsknecht, Roy A. *education administrator*
Kronmiller, Jan E. *academic administrator*
Lee, Robert J. *education educator, consultant*
Lehto, Gail S. *education educator, musician*
Leitzel, Joan Ruth *university president emerita*
Lisko (Dozer), Bonnie Lee *education educator*
Otte, Paul John *academic administrator, consultant, trainer*
Rezin, Andrew Anthony *academic administrator, educator*
Riedinger, Edward Anthony (Ted Riedinger) *international educator, Brazilianist*
Ritchey, Kenneth William *administrator*
Rogers, Nancy Hardin *dean, law educator*
Sanfilippo, Alfred Paul *dean, medical educator, pathologist*
Snyder, Barbara Rook *academic administrator*
Stephens, Thomas M(aron) *education educator*
Stewart, Mac A. *educator*
Stull, Gary Evan *secondary school educator, writer*
Warmbrod, Catharine Phelps *educational researcher, consultant*
Washington, Christopher L. *education educator*
Willke, Thomas Aloys *university official, statistics educator*
Zelman, Susan Tave *school system administrator*

Dayton
Allen, Rose Letitia *special education educator*
Carson, Dora A. *secondary school educator*
Curran, Daniel J. *academic administrator, sociologist, educator*
Dermody, Diana Dorothy *elementary school educator*
Fitz, Brother Raymond L. *university president*
Goldenberg, Kim *academic administrator, internist*
Heft, James Lewis *academic administrator, theology studies educator*

Lasley, Thomas J., II, *education educator*
Martin, Patricia *dean, nursing educator*
Part, Howard Mitchell *dean*
Pestello, Fred P. *academic administrator*
Ponitz, David H. *former academic administrator*
Taylor, Elisabeth Coler *retired secondary school educator*
Uphoff, James Kent *education educator*

Delaware
Pettigrew, Carolyn Landers *theological school official, minister*

Delta
Miller, Beverly White *former college president, educational consultant, consultant*

Dublin
Bordelon, Carolyn Thew *elementary school educator*

Fairview Park
Flynn, Patricia M. *director, special education educator, gifted and talented educator*

Findlay
Freed, DeBow *academic administrator*

Fremont
Johnson, Laurence F. *college executive*

Gambier
Nugent, S. Georgia *academic administrator*
Ponder, Anne *dean*
Spaid, Gregory P. *academic administrator, art educator*

Hamilton
Zahner-Krach, Anne Colette *preschool educator*

Hiram
Oliver, G(eorge) Benjamin *educational administrator, philosophy educator*

Holgate
Oberhaus, James Edward *secondary school educator*

Howard
Griffith, Jason Scott *education educator*

Hudson
Goheen, Janet Moore *counseling administrator, sales executive*
Hallenbeck, Linda S. *elementary school educator*

Ironton
Curry, Estella Roberta *education educator, consultant*

Kent
Buttlar, Rudolph Otto *retired college dean*
Cartwright, Carol Ann *university president*
Gaston, Paul Lee *academic administrator, language educator*
Gosnell, Davina J. *dean, nursing educator*
Lilly, Erica Barditch *academic librarian*
Odell-Scott, David Winfield *education educator*
Schwartz, Michael *university president, sociology educator*

Lancaster
Young, Paul Garlin *principal*

Lewis Center
Heinlen, Daniel Lee *alumni organization administrator*

Lima
Meek, Violet Imhof *retired dean*

Loveland
Stanger, Nora Lynn *educational consultant*

Maineville
Cook, Janice Eleanor Nolan *retired elementary school educator*

Mansfield
Ash, Thomas Phillip *superintendent of schools*
Gregory, Deirdre Dianne *secondary educator*
Olinger, Angela Marie *adult education educator*
Riedl, John Orth *university dean*
Sturgill, Judith Lynn *education educator, lawyer*

Marietta
Montgomery, Jerry Lynn *retired education educator*

Medina
Feola, David Craig *secondary school administrator*
Neiman, Marcus Lawrence *educational consultant*

Mentor
Schock, Trisha Kay *primary school educator*

Middleburg Heights
Molnar, Bela *school administrator*

Moreland Hills
Hardie, James Carl *college administrator, consultant*

Mount Vernon
Shriver, William Russell *secondary school educator*
Wallace, Geri Lynn *special education educator, landscape architect*

New Matamoras
Brown, Blanche Y. *secondary education educator, genealogy researcher*

New Philadelphia
Doughten, Mary Katherine (Molly Doughten) *retired secondary school educator*
Goforth, Mary Elaine Davey *secondary school educator*

Niles
Linden, Carol Marie *special education educator*

North Olmsted
Werner, Wade W. *secondary school educator*

PROFESSIONAL INDEX 5587 EDUCATION

Oak Harbor
Randels, David George *retired secondary school educator*

Oberlin
Dye, Nancy Schrom *academic administrator, historian, educator*
Koppes, Clayton R. *academic administrator*
MacKay, Alfred F. *dean, philosophy educator*

Orrville
Hennell, Robert William, III, *secondary school educator*
Warner, Patricia Ann *secondary school educator*

Oxford
Garland, James C. *academic administrator*
Shriver, Phillip Raymond *academic administrator*
Thompson, Bertha Boya *retired education educator, antique dealer and appraiser*

Painesville
Davis, Barbara Snell *education educator*

Parma
Cratty, David Michael *education educator*
Scheffel, Donna Jean *elementary school educator*
Tener, Carol Joan *retired secondary school educator*

Patriot
Riggle, Patricia Carol *special education educator*

Paulding
Moore, Pamela Rae *elementary school educator*

Pepper Pike
Stano, Sister Diana *academic administrator*

Pickerington
Collins, Arlene *secondary school educator*

Plymouth
Hartman, Ruth Campbell *director, educator*

Portsmouth
Johnson, Janice E. *education educator, writer*
Turner, Elvin L. *retired educational administrator*

Ravenna
Felton, Robert O'Neil, II, *secondary education educator*

Richmond
Radinsky, Troy D. *assistant principal*

Shaker Heights
Trefts, Joan Landenberger *retired educator, administrator*

Sidney
Seitz, James Eugene *retired college president, freelance writer*

Springfield
Dominick, Charles Alva *college official*
Kinnison, William Andrew *retired university president*

Stow
Jahn, Cynthia Patton *secondary school educator*

Strongsville
Berkey, Donald Frederick *counseling administrator*

Struthers
Noble, Robert William, Jr., *retired elementary school educator, minister*

Sylvania
Helmer, Robert C. *academic administrator*
Sampson, Earldine Robison *education educator*

Toledo
Billups, Norman Fredrick *college dean, pharmacist, educator*
Condon, Elizabeth M. *education educator*
Gutteridge, Thomas G. *academic administrator, consultant and labor arbitrator*
Pham, David Lan *secondary school educator, writer*
Rabideau, Margaret Catherine *retired media center director*
Romanoff, Marjorie Reinwald *retired education educator*
Weinblatt, Charles Samuel *university administrator, employment consultant*

University Heights
Glynn, Edward *college administrator*
Seaton, Shirley Smith *academic administrator, consultant*
Starcher-Dell'Aquila, Judy Lynn *special education educator*

Valley View
Miller, Susan Ann *retired school system administrator*

Wellston
Loxley, Kathryn *retired elementary school educator*

Westerville
Chivington, Amy Doan *education educator*
DeVore, C. Brent *college president, educator*
Husarik, Ernest Alfred *educational administrator*
Kerr, Thomas Jefferson, IV, *academic official*

Westfield Center
Spinelli, Anne Catherine *elementary school educator*

Westlake
Loehr, Marla *spiritual care coordinator*

Willoughby
Grossman, Mary Margaret *elementary school educator*

Yellow Springs
Straumanis, Joan *academic administrator*

Youngstown
Atwater, Tony *provost,dean, educator*
Loch, John Robert *university administrator*
McCollum, Everett *retired school system administrator, music educator*
Zorn, Robert Lynn *education educator*

OKLAHOMA

Ada
Frye, Linda Beth (Linda Beth Hisle) *elementary, secondary education educator*
Harris, Kim A. *elementary school educator*

Altus
Brown, Roger Dale *academic administrator*

Bartlesville
Chambers, Imogene Klutts *school system administrator, financial consultant*
Risner, Anita Jane *vocational school educator*

Bethany
Crabtree, John Michael *college administrator, consultant*

Billings
Matthiesen, Robert L. *education educator, farmer, rancher*

Broken Arrow
Steeley, Jill Edwards *education educator*

Choctaw
Uselton, Bill W. *secondary school educator*

Coalgate
Willis, Tricia Lee *special education educator*

Disney
Hamilton, Carl Hulet *retired academic administrator*

Durant
Spencer, Mark Benner *education educator*

Edmond
Harryman, Rhonda L. *education educator*
Sibley, William Arthur *academic administrator, physics educator, consultant*
Zabel, Vivian Ellouise *secondary school educator*

Langston
Holloway, Ernest Leon *university president*

Lawton
Cates, Dennis Lynn *education educator*
McKeown, Rebecca J. *principal*
Smiley, Frederick Melvin *education educator, consultant*

Muskogee
Edwards, Terri Lyn Wilmoth *education educator*
Peddy, Lisa Lynn *secondary school educator*

Norman
Boren, David Lyle *academic administrator*
Croft, Janet Brennan *academic librarian*
Dalton, Deborah Whitmore *dean*
Haring, Kathryn Ann *special education educator, research scientist*
Mergler, Nancy L. *academic administrator*
Nelson, Donna Jean *chemistry educator, researcher*
Pappas, James Pete *university administrator*
Sharp, Paul Frederick *former university president, education consultant*
Zapffe, Nina Byrom *retired elementary education educator*

Oklahoma City
Alexander, Patrick Byron *university administrator*
Blackburn, Debbie *elementary school educator, state representative*
Boomer, Dennis Keith *college official, clergyman*
Easley, Mary *retired elementary school educator, state representative*
Faltyn, Timothy Wayne *education educator, writer*
Garrett, Sandy Langley *school system administrator*
Hall, Nancy K. *college dean*
Kraker, Deborah Schovanec *special education educator*
Risser, Paul Gillan *academic administrator, botanist*
Voth, Douglas W. *dean, educator*
Wiles, Edwin McKinley *education educator, librarian*
Williamson, Marvel *dean, nursing administrator, sexologist, educator, writer*
Woods, Pendleton *college director, author*
Young, Stephen K. *academic administrator*

Ponca City
Gallagher, Gary W(ayne) *educational services executive*
Rice, Sue Ann *dean, industrial and organizational psychologist*
Surber, Joe Robert *assistant superintendent*

Prague
Stefansen, Peggy Ann *special education educator*

Pryor
Burdick, Larry G. *school system administrator*

Shawnee
Hill, Bryce Dale *school administrator*
Wilks, Jacquelin Holsomback *campus ministries director*

Stillwater
Chung, Jong-Moon *education educator*
Curl, Samuel Everett *university dean, agricultural scientist*
Eastman, Kenneth Karl *academic administrator*
Gunzenhauser, Michael Gerard *educator, researcher*
Vestal, Theodore Merrill *education educator*

Tahlequah
Alexander, Grant *education educator, consultant*
Howard, James Kenton *academic administrator, journalist*

Williams, Larry Bill *academic administrator*

Tulsa
Buthod, Mary Clare *school administrator*
Donaldson, Robert Herschel *university administrator, educator*
Lawless, Robert William *academic administrator*
Roger, Jerry Lee *academic administrator*
Trennepohl, Gary Lee *university administrator, finance educator*
Wood, Emily Churchill *special education educator, social studies educator, consultant*

Weatherford
Aspedon, Mary D. *education educator*

Woodward
Fisher, Deena Kaye *social studies education administrator*

OREGON

Albany
Smart, Ann Catherine *dean*

Ashland
Kreisman, Arthur *higher education consultant, humanities educator emeritus*

Beaverton
de Sá e Silva, Elizabeth Anne *secondary school educator*

Clackamas
Woods, Dennis Oliver *headmaster, market and political research analyst*

Corvallis
Arnold, Roy Gary *academic administrator*
Byrne, John Vincent *higher education consultant*
Davis, John Rowland *university administrator*
Healey, Deborah Lynn *education administrator*
McKee-Ryan, Frances M. *education educator*
Parker, Donald Fred *college dean, human resources management educator*
Verts, Lita Jeanne *university administrator*
Young, Roy Alton *university administrator, educator*

Eugene
Frohnmayer, David Braden *academic administrator*
Gall, Meredith Damien (Meredith Mark Damien Gall) *education educator, writer*
Moseley, John Travis *university administrator, research physicist*
Newton, Julianne H *education educator, photographer*
Pickett, Stephen Wesley *academic administrator, consultant*
Piele, Philip Kern *education infosystems educator*
Tobin, Tary Jeanne *educational consultant, researcher*
Upham, Steadman *academic administrator, anthropologist, educator*
Warpinski, Terri L. *academic administrator, artist*
Womack, James Errol *college president*

Gresham
Light, Betty Jensen Pritchett *former college dean*
Vela, Joel E. *college president*

Jacksonville
Langworthy, William Clayton *college official*

Joseph
Gilbert, David Erwin *retired academic administrator, physicist*

La Grande
Woodward, Ralph Frederick, Jr., *elementary school educator, consultant, education educator*

Lake Oswego
Lenderman, Joanie *elementary school educator*

Mcminnville
Bull, Vivian Ann *college president*
Walker, Charles Urmston *retired university president*

Medford
Dixon, Andrew Derart *retired academic administrator*
Tracy, Harold Dewayne *retired secondary school educator*

Monmouth
Dunn, Doris Marjory *retired educator, volunteer*

Newberg
Johnson, Thomas Floyd *former academic administrator, educator*

Oceanside
Wadlow, Joan Krueger *retired academic administrator, construction executive*

Portland
Bartlett, Thomas Alva *retired educational administrator*
Bennett, Charles Leon *vocational and graphic arts educator*
Bloom, Joseph D. *medical educator, psychiatrist*
Blumel, Joseph Carlton *university president*
Braun, Stephen Baker *academic administrator*
Brown, James Chandler *retired education educator*
Cantelon, John Edward *retired university chancellor*
Clinton, Jack W. *dean*
Cox, Joseph William *former academic administrator, education educator*
Diver, Colin S. *academic administrator, educator*
Franklin, Dolores Roberts *elementary school educator*
Frolick, Patricia Mary *retired elementary school educator*
Jarvis, Richard S. *academic administrator*
Koblik, Steven S. *academic administrator*
Leupp, Edythe Peterson *retired education educator*
McClave, Donald Silsbee *academic administrator*
Mooney, Michael Joseph *college president*
Phillips, Vicki L. *school system administrator*
Potempa, Kathleen *dean*
Rushen, Elizabeth Rae Marshall *director*
Tyson, David T. *academic administrator*
Unger, Karen Virginia *director*
Whitlow, Lillian *retired elementary school educator, poet*
Wilson, Thomas Dale *philanthropic fundraising consultant*

Salem
Bauer, James Richard *academic administrator*
Castillo, Susan *school system administrator*
Hoff, Reno R. *academic administrator*
Page, Cheryl Miller *elementary school educator*
Pelton, M. Lee *academic administrator*

Yachats
Robeck, Mildred Coen *education educator, writer*

PENNSYLVANIA

Abington
Magison, Deborah Helen *elementary school educator*
Montemurro, Elizabeth A *education educator*

Allentown
Blaney, Dorothy Gulbenkian *academic administrator*
Haddon, Eva W. *principal*

Allison Park
Guffey, Barbara Braden *elementary school educator*

Annville
McGill, William James, Jr., *university official, writer*

Bala Cynwyd
Oswald, James Marlin *education educator*
Sutnick, Alton Ivan *dean, educator, researcher, physician*

Beaver
Strock, Robert S. *retired education educator*

Bellefonte
Dupuis, Victor Lionel *retired curriculum and instruction educator*

Bethel Park
Douds, Virginia Lee *elementary school educator*

Bethlehem
Bergethon, Kaare Roald *retired college president*
Farrington, Gregory C. *university administrator*
Traupman-Carr, Carol Ann *dean, musicologist*

Bloomsburg
Kozloff, Jessica S. *university president*
Liu, Hsien-Tung *dean*
Perner, Darlene E. *special education educator, consultant, editor*

Blue Bell
Brendlinger, LeRoy R. *academic administrator*

Broomall
DiRosa, Steven Joseph *primary and secondary school educator*

Brownsville
Martin, Richard H. *principal*

Bryn Mawr
Baird, John Absalom, Jr., *retired academic administrator*
Frank, Edward David, II, *history educator*
Kuncl, Ralph *provost*
Opendak, Irene *academic administrator*
Salisbury, Helen Holland *education educator*
Vickers, Nancy J. *academic administrator*

Canonsburg
Mascetta, Joseph Anthony *principal*

Carlisle
Durden, William G. *academic administrator*

Center Valley
Bartolacci, Paulette Marie *middle school educator, aerobics instructor*
Turner, Brian Allen *sport management director, educator*

Chester
Bruce, Robert James *retired academic administrator*
Buck, Lawrence Paul *academic administrator, educator*
Carnwath, Thomas Howlan *academic administrator*
Harris, James Thomas, III, *college administrator, educator*

Claridge
Perich, Terry Miller *secondary school educator*

Clarion
Reinhard, Diane L. *university president*

Coatesville
Rodkey, Frances Theresa *elementary school educator*
Smith, Patricia Anne *special education educator*

Collegeville
Richter, Richard Paul *academic administrator*
Strassburger, John Robert *academic administrator*

Cooperstown
Hogg, James Henry, Jr., *retired education educator*

Cranberry Township
MacDonald, Barbara Katic *secondary school educator*

Cresson
D'Emilio, Deanne A. *education educator, lawyer*

Dallas
Comitz, John Joseph *retired secondary school educator*

Dingmans Ferry
Haas, Karen Marie *secondary school educator*

Downingtown
Hemingway, David C. *elementary school principal*
Romanosky, LuAnn *elementary school educator*

Doylestown
Rodenbaugh, Marcia Louise *retired elementary school educator*

Drums
Frask, Robin Ann Kostanesky *secondary school educator*

Dunmore
Krogh-Jespersen, Mary-Beth *academic administrator*
McDonald, Nancy E. *retired secondary school educator*

East Stroudsburg
Braithwaite, Barbara J. *secondary school educator*
Dillman, Robert John *academic administrator*

Easton
Hughes, Michael P. *principal*
Rothkopf, Arthur J. *college president*

Edinboro
Cox, Clifford Laird *retired academic administrator*

Edwardsville
Lukas, Edward Michael *retired secondary school educator*

Elizabethtown
Sample, Frederick Palmer *former college president*

Elkins Park
Burnley, June Williams *secondary school educator*

Erie
Belfiore, Phillip Joseph *education educator, researcher*
Dever, Merrill Thomas *academic administrator, retired police chief*
Ferretti, Silvia *dean*
Henry, Martin Daniel *university president*
Taylor, Margaret Uhrich *educational administrator*

Exeter
Stocker, Joyce Arlene *retired secondary school educator*

Franklin
Sauer, Mary Julia *special education educator*

Gettysburg
Will, Katherine Haley *academic administrator*

Glenside
Landman, Bette Emeline *academic administrator*

Greenville
Parmiter, Karen Lynn *education educator*

Gwynedd Valley
Owens, Kathleen C. *academic administrator*

Harrisburg
Baehre, Edna Victoria *college president*
Brown, John Walter *vocational education supervisor*
Hample, Judy G. *academic administrator*
Pringle, Rebecca *elementary school educator*

Harrison City
McWilliams, Samuel Robert *secondary school educator*

Hatfield
Jesberg, Robert Ottis, Jr., *educational consultant, science educator*

Haverford
Brownlow, Donald Grey *private school educator*
Dawson, John David *academic administrator, religious studies educator*
Stuard, Susan Mosher *education educator*
Tritton, Thomas Richard *academic administrator, biologist, educator*

Hazleton
Ambrose, Sherry L *principal, elementary school educator*

Hershey
Butterfield, Andrea Christine *elementary school educator, adult education educator, psychology educator*
Hortman, David Jones *secondary school educator*
Jones, Marshall Bush *education educator, researcher*
Kirch, Darrell Gene *academic administrator, dean*
Lingle, Virginia Ann *school librarian*

Honesdale
Barbe, Walter Burke *education educator*

Houston
Briggs, Rich *secondary school educator*

Huntingdon
Kepple, Thomas Ray, Jr., *college administrator*

Immaculata
Fadden, Sister R. Patricia *academic administrator, nun*

Indiana
Bowers, Fredalene Barletta *education educator, consultant*
Pettit, Lawrence Kay *university president*
Princes, Carolyn Diane Wilbon *educational director*
Thibadeau, Eugene Francis *education educator, consultant*

Johnstown
Alcamo, Frank Paul *retired educational administrator*
Lindberg, Stephen *secondary school educator*

Kennett Square
Brigman, Dorothea Jane Pengelly *secondary and elementary education educator*

King Of Prussia
Martini, Perry James *educational consultant*

Kingston
Marko, Andrew Paul *school system administrator*

Knox
Rupert, Elizabeth Anastasia *retired dean*

Kutztown
Laub, Mary Lou *elementary school educator*
Watrous, Robert Thomas *academic director*

La Plume
Boehm, Edward Gordon, Jr., *college administrator, educator*

Lafayette Hill
Delacato, Janice Elaine *learning consultant, educator*
King, Diane Averbach *education educator*

Lancaster
Drum, Alice *academic administrator, educator*
Ebersole, Mark Chester *emeritus college president*
Fry, John Anderson *academic administrator*
Kneedler, Richard (Alvin Kneedler) *former academic administrator*
Linton, Joy Smith *primary school educator*

Langhorne
Babb, Wylie Sherrill *college president*

Lewisburg
Huffines, Marion Lois *academic administrator, linguist, educator, language educator*

Lincoln University
Nelson, Ivory Vance *academic administrator*

Lock Haven
Almes, June *retired education educator, librarian*
Moyer, Anna Blackburn *retired secondary and elementary school educator*
Willis, Craig Dean *academic administrator*

Macungie
Rubin, Arthur Herman *retired university official, consultant*

Malvern
Clariana, Roy Boris *education educator*

Maple Glen
Weaver-Stroh, Joanne Mateer *education educator, consultant*

Martinsburg
Neff, Robert Wilbur *academic administrator, educator, minister*

Meadville
Dixon, Armendia Pierce *school program administrator*

Mechanicsburg
Hoffman, Diane Mae *special education educator*

Media
Hornet, Andrea *education educator, consultant*

Mercersburg
Tompkins, Christopher Robin *director, educator*

Milford
Reynolds, Edwin Wilfred, Jr., *retired secondary education educator*

Montgomeryville
Detwiler, Christine Wendler *special education educator*

Mount Pleasant
Dangelo, Eugene Michael *elementary school educator*

Nanticoke
Domzalski, Ronald Laurence *audio-visual specialist, educator*
Donohue, Patricia Carol *academic administrator*

Nescopeck
Shultz, Jack Ellsworth *education educator*

New Castle
Roux, Mildred Anna *retired secondary school educator*

New Hope
Knight, Douglas Maitland *educational administrator, optical executive, writer*

New Kensington
Kalavar, Jyotsna Mirle *education educator*

New Wilmington
McCormick, Kimberly A *elementary school educator*
McKee, Delber L. *retired education educator*

Newtown
Booraem, Hendrik, V, *education educator, historian*
Duncan, Stephen Robert *elementary school educator*

Oil City
Sabousky, Richard Anthony *adult education educator*

Perkasie
Ferry, Joan Evans *school counselor*

White, Michael R. *secondary school educator, consultant*

Philadelphia
Aversa, Dolores Sejda *educational administrator*
Bass, Aaron *school system administrator*
Bates, James Earl *academic administrator*
Blumberg, Baruch Samuel *academic research scientist*
Brucker, Paul C. *academic administrator, physician*
Capers, Gregg *secondary school educator, musician*
Christman, Jolley Bruce *educational research executive, educator*
Cohen, David Walter *academic administrator, educator, periodontist*
Cooperman, Barry S. *educational administrator, educator, scientist*
Donnelly, Gloria Ferraro *university dean*
Drake, Jayne Kribbs *university administrator, English educator*
Drucker, Richard M. *educational consultant*
Dunn, Mary Maples *former university dean*
Fernandez, Happy Craven (Gladys Fernandez) *academic administrator*
Giegengack, Robert *university administrator*
Gur, Raquel E. *academic administrator*
Gutmann, Amy *academic administrator, political science and philosophy educator*
Guyer, Hedy-Ann Klein *special education educator*
Hack, Gary Arthur *dean*
Hackney, Francis Sheldon *university president*
Harker, Patrick Timothy *dean, management educator*
Houshmand, Ali A. *academic administrator*
Jamieson, Kathleen Hall *dean, communications educator*
Jamieson, Patrick E. *researcher, writer*
Kelly, Alan M. *dean*
Klaiber, Karen Elaine *education educator*
Krewer, Julie-Ann *scholar*
Liacouras, Peter James *academic administrator, educator, lawyer, arbitrator*
Meyerson, Martin *university educator, urban and regional planner*
Nasca, Thomas Joseph *dean*
Onley, Sister Francesca *academic administrator*
Padulo, Louis *university administrator*
Papadakis, Constantine N. *university executive*
Powers, Michael Roland *educator, insurance consultant*
Presseisen, Barbara Zemboch *retired educational director, researcher*
Reid, Mary Wallace *retired secondary school educator*
Riley, B. Gresham *college president*
Romer, Daniel *university official, psychologist, educator*
Ross, Warren E. *dean*
Rubenstein, Arthur Harold *academic administrator, educator, dean, internist*
Rudczynski, Andrew B. *academic administrator, medical researcher*
Schaubroeck, John Michael *education educator, academic administrator*
Sibolski, Elizabeth Hawley *higher education administrator*
Slaughter-Defoe, Diana Tresa *education educator*
Tansy, Martin F. *dean*
Veit, Kenneth *dean, educator*
Wachman, Marvin *retired academic administrator*
Walker, Valaida Smith *university administrator*
Zheng, Robert Zhiwei *educational technology educator*
Zimmer, Janie Louise *mathematics educator, administrator*

Philipsburg
Genesi, Susan Petrovich *school system administrator*

Pittsburgh
Barazzone, Esther Lynn *academic administrator, educator*
Boyce, Doreen Elizabeth *lecturer, civic development foundation executive*
Braun, Thomas W. *academic administrator*
Brockmann, Stephen Matthew *education educator*
Cohon, Jared L. *academic administrator*
Cooper, Rory Alan *engineering educator, researcher*
Dunn, Douglas Murray *university dean*
Dunn, Kenneth B. *dean*
Eckert, Jean Patricia *elementary school educator*
Geibel, Sister Grace Ann *college president*
Giannoukakis, Nick *educator*
Hunker, Jeffrey *dean*
Kelly, Mary *education educator, secondary school educator*
Krackhardt, David Michael *education educator*
Marsh, Gary Martin *environmental biostatistician, epidemiologist, educator*
McHoes, Ann McIver *academic administrator, computer systems consultant*
Michalopoulos, George Konstantine *academic administrator*
Miller, Ronald Lynn *director*
Praytor, Kent Dwayne *career planning administrator*
Rago, Ann D'Amico *academic administrator, public relations executive*
Richard, Jean-Francois *education educator, consultant*
Smartschan, Glenn Fred *educational consultant*
Sobehart, Helen C *academic administrator, educator*
Van Dusen, Albert Clarence *university official*
Weidman, John Carl, II, *education and sociology educator, consultant*

Quarryville
Armerding, Hudson Taylor *retired college president, consultant*

Radnor
Iadarola, Antoinette *college president*

Reading
Bowles, Patricia Mary *secondary school educator*
Devlin, Karin L *education educator*
Yoder, James Dale *adult education educator*

Russellton
Curtis, Paula Annette *elementary and secondary education educator*

Saint Davids
Miles, Sara Joan *dean*

Saltsburg
Pidgeon, John Anderson *headmaster*

Schuylkill Haven
Sarno, Patricia Ann *biology educator*

Scranton
Nee, Sister Mary Coleman *college president emeritus*
Panuska, Joseph Allan *retired academic administrator*
Passon, Richard Henry *English language educator, former administrator*
Reap, Sister Mary Margaret *college administrator*

Selinsgrove
Lemons, L. Jay *academic administrator*

Shippensburg
Ceddia, Anthony Francis *university administrator*

Slippery Rock
Smith, Grant Warren, II, *university administrator, physical sciences educator*
Smith, Robert Mason *academic administrator*

State College
Hoffa, Harlan Edward *retired university dean, art educator*
Link, Phoebe Forrest *secondary school educator, writer, social worker, poet*
Max, Elizabeth *educator*
Mills, Rilla Dean *university administrator, consultant*
Remick, Forrest Jerome, Jr., *former university official*

Swarthmore
Bloom, Alfred Howard *academic administrator, educator*

Titusville
Campasino, Ellen Marie *elementary school educator*

Unionville
Martin, Helen Elizabeth *educational consultant*

University Park
Askov, Eunice May *adult education educator*
Fuhrman, Susan H *education educator*
Hammond, J. D. *dean emeritus, corporate director*
Herr, Edwin Leon *educator, academic administrator*
Larson, Russell Edward *university provost emeritus, consultant agriculture research and development*
Olian, Judy D. *dean*
Shannon, Barbara *dean, nutrition educator*
Spanier, Graham Basil *university president*
Wormley, David *dean*
Yoder, Edgar Paul *education educator*

Upper Darby
Hudiak, David Michael *academic administrator, lawyer*
Leiby, Bruce Richard *secondary education educator, writer*

Upper Saint Clair
Dunkis, Patricia B. *school system administrator*

Verona
Bruno, Louis Vincent *principal*

Villanova
Amin, Moeness Gamal *education educator, director*
Dobbin, Edmund J. *university administrator*
Fitzpatrick, M. Louise *dean, nursing educator*
Savitz, Fred *education educator*

Warminster
Ciao, Frederick J. *school system administrator, educator*

Washington
Mitchell, Brian Christopher *academic administrator*

West Chester
Adler, Madeleine Wing *academic administrator*
Bove, Patrice Magee *elementary school educator*
Hammonds, Jay A. *retired secondary education educator, administrator*

West Lawn
Partridge, David Edward *secondary school educator*

Westtown
Jackson, Katherine Church *elementary school educator, reading educator*

Williamsport
Douthat, James Evans *college administrator*
Garner, Ron A. *vocational school educator*

Willow Grove
Burtt, Anne Dampman *special education educator*

Yardley
Breitenfeld, Frederick, Jr., *retired educational consultant, former public broadcasting executive*
Elliott, Frank Nelson *retired college president*

York
Aarestad, James Harrison *retired educational administrator, army officer*
Caffrey, Lynn Regina *education educator*
Owens, Marilyn Mae *elementary school educator, secondary school educator*
Zortman, Mark Albert *secondary school educator, director*

Youngwood
Henry, Candy A. *education educator, writer*

RHODE ISLAND

Kingston
Carothers, Robert Lee *academic administrator*

PROFESSIONAL INDEX 5589 EDUCATION

Middletown
Jackson, John Edward *educator, logistician, retired naval officer*

Newport
Wood, Berenice Howland *retired secondary school educator*

Providence
Deal, Joseph Maurice *academic administrator, art educator, photographer*
Duncan, David Frank *community health specialist, educator*
Gaebe, Morris J. *academic administrator*
Greer, David S. *dean, educator, physician*
Johnson, Melody *school system administrator*
Mandle, Earl Roger *design school president, former museum executive*
Marsh, Donald Jay *medical school dean, medical educator*
Nazarian, John *academic administrator, mathematics educator*
Robert, Stephen *academic administrator*
Simmons, Ruth J. *academic administrator*
Smith, Philip A. *academic administrator*
Sweeney, Judith Kiernan *secondary school educator*
Waite-Franzen, Ellen Jane *academic administrator*
Yena, John A. *academic administrator*

Saunderstown
Donovan, Gerald Alton *retired academic administrator, former university dean*

Warwick
Gambardella, Mary Jo *secondary school educator, music educator*
Izzi, John *mathematics educator, writer*

Woonsocket
Stubbs, Donald Clark *retired secondary school educator*

SOUTH CAROLINA

Aiken
Hickey, Delina Rose *retired education educator*
Moore, Edna Googe *primary school educator*
Ritchie, Charles Michael *education educator, consultant*
Santos, Karey Michale *elementary school educator*

Anderson
Martin, Terrell Owen *retired university administrator*

Beaufort
Raines, Karen Cornell *secondary school educator*

Bennettsville
Best, Carolyn Anne Hill *elementary school educator*

Blythewood
Daniels, James Douglas *retired academic administrator*

Central
Holcombe, Joseph Steven *academic administrator, educator*

Charleston
Appleget, Terri Lynn *elementary school educator*
Gunn, Morey Walker, Jr., *secondary education educator, choir director, organist*
Henson, Kenneth Tyrone *education educator*
Hunter, Jairy C., Jr., *academic administrator*
Morris, Valerie Bonita *performing arts administrator*
O'Bryant-Seabrook, Marlene Loretta Linton *retired educator*
Simms, Lois Averetta *retired secondary school educator*
Sutusky, John Charles *higher education educator*
Worthington, Ward Curtis, Jr., *university dean, anatomy educator*

Clemson
Bailey, Beatrice Naff *researcher and educator in English*
Barker, James F. *academic administrator*
Felder, Frankie Ottowiess *academic administrator*
Helms, Doris R. *academic administrator*
Kelly, John William, Jr., *university administrator*
Kimmel, Robert Michael *education educator, consultant*
Skaar, Eric Christen *education educator, consultant*
Sluss, Dorothy Louise *education educator, researcher*
Vogel, Henry Elliott *retired university dean and physics educator*

Clinton
Griffith, John Vincent *academic official*

Columbia
Aelion, C. Marjorie *adult education educator*
Faulkner, Larry R. *dean, educator, researcher, writer*
Friedman, Myles Ivan *education educator*
Mash, Samuel David *dean*
McCulloch, Anne Merline Jacobs *college dean*
Odom, Jerome D. *academic administrator*
Palms, John Michael *academic administrator, physicist*
Petty, Donna Matthews *middle school educator*
Rekers, George Alan *education educator, clinical psychologist*
Sinclair, Linda Drumwright *educational consultant*
Sorensen, Andrew Aaron *university president*
Swinton, David Holmes *academic administrator*
Tunstall, Dorothy Fiebrich *early childhood educator*

Conway
Squatriglia, Robert William *university dean, educator*

Denmark
Boyd-Scotland, Joann *college president*

Due West
Gettys, James Wylie, Jr., *education educator*

Koonts, Jones Calvin *retired education educator*

Florence
Carter, Luther Fredrick *university president*
Fitzkee, Thomas L. *education educator*

Gaffney
Griffin, Walter Roland *college president, historian, educator*
Suttle, Helen Jayson *retired education educator*

Greenville
Hill, Grace Lucile Garrison *education educator, consultant*
Jones, Bob, III, *academic administrator*
Lawson, Darren Patrick *academic administrator, educator*
Shi, David E. *academic administrator, historian*

Greenwood
Jackson, Larry Artope *retired college president*
Williams, Sylvester Emanual, III, *secondary school educator, consultant*

Iva
Gentry, Margaret Burton *retired elementary school teacher*

Kiawah Island
Warren, Russell Glen *academic administrator*

Ladson
Cannon, Major Tom *special education educator*

Lexington
Floyd, Ann R. *elementary school educator*

Little River
Sarvis, Elaine Magann *retired assistant principal*

Marion
Kirkpatrick, Donald Robert *secondary school educator*

Mount Pleasant
Gilbert, James Eastham *academic administrator*

North Charleston
Reilly, David Henry *university dean*

Orangeburg
Hill, Howard Darnell *educator, university administrator*

Pawleys Island
Proefrock, Carl Kenneth *academic medical administrator*

Piedmont
Winter-Neighbors, Gwen Carole *special education educator, art educator, consultant*

Prosperity
Hause, Edith Collins *college administrator*

Richburg
Cox, Kevin Monterey *school administrator*

Rock Hill
Di Giorgio, Anthony J. *college president*
Russell, Cynthia M. *college president*

Ruffin
Lambright, Marilyn *elementary school educator*

Spartanburg
Dunlap, Benjamin Bernard *academic administrator*
McDaniel, Thomas Robb *academic administrator, educator*
McGehee, Larry Thomas *university administrator*
Stephens, Bobby Gene *college administrator, consultant*

SOUTH DAKOTA

Aberdeen
Fouberg, Glenna M. *career planning administrator*
Tebben, Sharon Lee *education educator*

Brookings
Miller, Peggy Gordon Elliott *university president*

Madison
Knowlton, Douglas D. *academic administrator*

Rapid City
Hughes, William Lewis *former university official, electrical engineer*
Schleusener, Richard August *college president*

Selby
Akre, Donald J. *school system administrator*

Sioux Falls
Ashworth, Julie *elementary school educator*
Balcer, Charles Louis *college president emeritus, educator*
Talley, Robert Cochran *medical school dean and administrator, cardiologist*
Wagoner, Ralph Howard *academic administrator*

Yankton
Foster, James Caldwell *academic dean, historian*

TENNESSEE

Bristol
Gaines, John Strother *retired educator, writer, municipal official*

Camden
Sayles, Kristi Renee *elementary school educator, writer, application developer*

Chapel Hill
Christman, Luther Parmalee *retired dean, consultant*

Chattanooga
Obear, Frederick Woods *academic administrator*
Stacy, Bill Wayne *academic administrator*

Clarksville
Chartrand, Danny Lewis *secondary school educator, coach*
Newby, Earl Fernando *educator*
Stoddard, Peter Hawkins *education educator, consultant*

Cleveland
Suttles, David Clyde *educator*

Columbia
Cantrell, Sharron Caulk *principal*

Cookeville
Elkins, Donald Marcum *dean, agronomy educator*
Peters, Ralph Martin *academic administrator*
Volpe, Angelo Anthony *former university president, chemistry educator*

Dickson
Thomas, Janey Sue *elementary school principal*

Gainesboro
Ramsey, Catherine Louise *secondary school educator, horse trainer*

Goodlettsville
Vatandoost, Nossi Malek *art school administrator*

Harriman
Hoppe, Sherry Lee *academic administrator*

Henderson
England, Richard C., Jr., *special education educator*

Henning
Sadler, Dennis *supervisor*

Hermitage
Quaintance, Alice Lynn *elementary school media specialist*

Jackson
Agee, Bob R. *academic administrator, educator, minister*
Johnsey, Geryl Lynn *elementary school educator, musician*
McClure, Wesley C. *academic administrator*
Myatt, Dottie Woodard *education educator*

Johnson City
Alfonso, Robert John *university administrator*
Bishop, Wilsie Sue *dean, nursing educator*
Edwards, Joellen Beckett *dean, community health nurse educator*
Franks, Ronald Dwyer *dean, psychiatrist, educator*
Pumariega, JoAnne Buttacavoli *mathematics educator*

Knoxville
Armistead, Willis William *academic administrator, veterinarian*
Boling, Edward Joseph *retired academic administrator*
Crabtree, Loren William *chancellor, academic administrator, history educator*
Creasia, Joan Catherine *dean, nursing educator*
Galligan, Thomas C., Jr., *dean, law educator*
Gilley, James Wade *university president*
Hatton, Barbara R. *academic administrator*
Kim, Hyunjoong *education educator*
Levy, Robert A. *academic administrator*
Mankel, Francis Xavier *former principal, priest*
Moran, James D., III, *university administrator*
nes, Sherman J. *academic administrator, management educator, investment executive*
Petersen, John D. *academic administrator*
Romeo, Joanne Josefa Marino *mathematics educator*
Snyder, William T. *university chancellor*
South, Stephen A. *academic administrator*
Yeomans, Gordon Allan *retired education educator*

Lebanon
King, Kevin William *secondary school educator*

Martin
McCracken, Kenneth Donald *retired education educator*

Maryville
Simpson, Terry L. *education educator, department chairman*

Memphis
Call, M. Douglas *former university administrator*
Daughdrill, James Harold, Jr., *academic administrator*
Donahue, Joan Elizabeth *elementary school educator*
Dunathan, Harmon Craig *college dean*
Gourley, Dick R. *college dean*
Hardy, Joy Miller *academic administrator, consultant*
Herrod, Henry Grady, III, *dean, allergist, immunologist*
Hunt, James Calvin *academic administrator, physician*
Jones, Jerry C. *special education educator, counselor*
Moffitt, Carolyn Mullins *university official*
Nesin, Jeffrey David *academic administrator*
Pezeshki, S. Reza *education educator*
Raines, Shirley Carol *academic administrator*
Ranta, Richard Robert *university dean*
Sigler, Lois Oliver *retired secondary school educator*
Swofford, Joel David *education educator*
Taylor, Marilyn Horton *secondary school educator*
Troutt, William Earl *academic administrator*

Morristown
Hopper, Peggy F. *education educator*

Murfreesboro
Doyle, Delores Marie *retired principal*
Gilbert, Linda Arms *education educator, educational administrator*

Walker, James E. *academic administrator, educator*

Nashville
Butler, William Blaine *dean, dental educator*
Cerjan, Martin *dean, law educator*
Chapman, John Edmon *academic administrator, pharmacologist, educator*
Clinton, Barbara Marie *university health services director, social worker*
Collins, Joe Lena *retired secondary school educator*
Coney, PonJola *dean, researcher, educator*
Conway-Welch, Colleen *dean, nurse midwife*
Gabbe, Steven Glenn G. *dean, educator, obstetrician, gynecologist*
Gee, Elwood Gordon *academic administrator*
Guha, Sujata *education educator*
Hazelip, Herbert Harold *academic administrator*
Heard, Alexander *retired educator and chancellor*
Hefner, James A. *academic administrator*
Longhurst, Robert Russell *retired secondary school educator*
Loper, Linda Sue *special collections librarian*
Manning, Charles W. *university chancellor*
Marcic, Dorothy Anne *education educator*
Maupin, John E., Jr., *college president*
McKerley, Annette Elizabeth *school system administrator*
McMurry, Idanelle Sam *educational consultant*
Moon, Fletcher Free *college librarian, multi-media artist, minister*
Porter, Andrew Calvin *academic administrator, psychologist, educator*
Ramer, Hal Reed *academic administrator*
Reschly, Daniel J. *education educator, psychologist*
Rivera, Maximiano Marquez *academic administrator, writer*
Schoenfeld, Michael *academic administrator, education educator*
Singh, Surendra P. *agricultural economics professor, consultant*
Swan, Patricia Brintnall *research administrator*
Syverud, Kent Douglas *dean*
Treible, Kirk *retired academic administrator, foundation administrator*
Womack, Steven James *education educator, writer*
Wyatt, Joe Billy *academic administrator*
Zepos, Nicholas S. *academic administrator*

Newport
Ball, Travis, Jr., *educational consultant, editor*

Oak Ridge
Cragle, Donna Lynne *university administrator, researcher*

Pleasant Hill
Hull, Charles William *retired special education educator*

Sewanee
Alvarez, Laurence Richards *education educator*
Croom, Frederick Hailey *academic administrator, mathematician, educator*
Cunningham, Joel Luther *university president, vice-chancellor*
Patterson, William Brown *dean, history professor*

Telford
Mashburn, Donald Eugene *education educator*

White House
Warpool, Christopher Paul *elementary school educator, freelance/self-employed musician*

Whiteville
Allen, Yvonne *principal*

TEXAS

Abilene
Christopher, Mary M. *education educator, consultant*
McCaleb, Gary Day *university official*
Turner, Stafford *education educator, baritone*
Wheeler, Floyd Larry *education educator*

Allen
Williams, Bryan *dean, medical educator*

Alpine
Morgan, Raymond Victor, Jr., *university administrator, mathematics educator*
Snyder, John Edward, Jr., *education educator*

Alvin
Roberson, Deborah Kay *secondary school educator*

Arlington
Dillard, John James *school librarian*
Pickard, Myrna Rae *dean*
Pomerantz, Martin *chemistry educator, researcher*
Poster, Elizabeth C. *dean*
Sobol, Harold *retired dean, manufacturing executive, consultant*
Spaniolo, James D. *academic administrator*
Witt, Robert E. *academic administrator*

Austin
Auvenshine, Anna Lee Banks *school system administrator*
Ayres, Robert Moss, Jr., *retired university president*
Brewer, Thomas Bowman *retired university president*
Cannon, William Bernard *retired university educator*
Cardozier, Virgus Ray *higher education educator*
Cunningham, William Hughes *former academic administrator, marketing educator*
DuBose, Gaylan Ray *elementary school educator, musician, writer*
Ehrlich, Stacy Wheeler *school fundraiser, administrator*
Faulkner, Larry Ray *university official, chemistry educator*
Fonté, Richard W. *university administrator*
Franklin, G(eorge) Charles *retired academic administrator*
Gau, George W. *dean*
Harris, Ben M. *education educator*
Jordan, Bryce *retired university president*
Keto, John Wayne *education educator, researcher*

Lafferty, Joyce G. Zvonar *retired elementary school educator*
Lehmann-Carssow, Nancy Beth *secondary school educator, coach*
Livingston, William Samuel *university administrator, political scientist*
Martin, Earin Miller *grant administrator, program director, educator, trainer*
Matwiczak, Kenneth Matthew *university educator, consultant*
May, Robert George *dean, accounting educator*
Powers, William Charles, Jr., *dean, law educator*
Rogers, Lorene Lane *university president emeritus*
Roueche, John Edward, II, *education educator, leadership program director*
Royal, Darrell K. *university official, former football coach*
Sands, Dolores S. *dean*
Shiff, Richard Allen *director, art historian*
Shilling, Roy Bryant, Jr., *academic administrator*
Sorber, Charles Arthur *academic administrator*
Warner, David Cook *public affairs educator*
Wurzbach, Linda *educational consultant*
Yansky, Brian Lee *education educator, writer*

Bastrop
Carpenter, Delbert Stanley *educational administration educator*

Beaumont
Brentlinger, William Brock *college dean*
Doblin, Stephen Alan *academic administrator, mathematician, educator*
Gagne, Mary *academic administrator*
Hargove, William Richard *education educator, lawyer*

Bedias
Williamson, Norma Beth *adult education educator*

Belton
Guess, David Lynn *education educator*

Blanco
Dudley, Brooke Fitzhugh *educational consultant*

Boerne
Goode, Bobby Claude *retired secondary education educator, writer*

Bonham
Gerner, Leonard Arthur *elementary school educator, minister*
Youree, Cheryl Ann *secondary school educator*

Brownsville
Boze, Betsy Vogel *dean, marketing professional, educator*
Chamberlain, Steven Paul *special education educator*
Garcia, Juliet Villarreal *university administrator*
Santa-Coloma, Bernardo *secondary school educator, counselor*
Wagner, Mary Satterwhite *education educator*

Bryan
Hanks, Clay David *academic administrator*

Canyon
Long, Russell Charles *academic administrator*

College Station
Adams, H. Richard *dean*
Adkisson, Perry Lee *university system chancellor*
Bowen, Ray Morris *academic administrator, engineering educator*
Calhoun, John C., Jr., *academic administrator*
Cantrell, Carol Whitaker *educational administrator*
Cocanougher, Arthur Benton *academic administrator*
Dickey, Nancy Wilson *chancellor, physician*
Edwards, Janine C. *educational administrator*
Erlandson, David Alan *education administration educator*
Lynn, Laurence Edwin, Jr., *university administrator, educator*
Monroe, Haskell Moorman, Jr., *retired university educator*
Prior, David B. *academic administrator*
Sadoski, Mark Christian *education educator*
Strawser, Jerry *dean*
Vandiver, Frank Everson *institute administrator, former university president, author, educator*

Colleyville
Hodgell, Murlin Ray *university dean*

Commerce
Scott, Joyce Alaine *university official*

Conroe
Gray, Janet Ethel *elementary school educator*
Marsh, Sue Ann *special education educator*

Coppell
Griffin, Jim *secondary school educator*

Corpus Christi
Abdelsamad, Moustafa Hassan *dean*
Cassidy, Jack *academic administrator, educator*
Harper, Sandra Stecher *university administrator*

Dallas
Attanasio, John Baptist *dean, law educator*
Blankenbaker, Zarina *adult education educator, consultant*
Campaigne, Linda Mary *special education educator*
Cirilo, Amelia Medina *educational consultant, supervisor*
Cole, James S. *dean, dental educator*
Cook, Gary Raymond *university president, clergyman*
Dumerer, Lorraine JoAnne Lori *social studies educator, clinician, consultant*
Early, James *education educator*
Friedheim, Jan V. *education administrator*
Friedheim, Stephen Bailey *educational consultant*
Giggleman, Gene Felton *academic administrator, veterinarian*
Haayen, Richard Jan *university official, insurance company executive*
Hansen, William *educational consultant*
Harrison, Frank *former university president*
Hernandez, Christine *educational consultant*
Hester, Linda Hunt *retired dean, counseling administrator, sociology educator, physical education educator*
Hill-Foster, Ialine *retired secondary school educator*
Karns, Phyllis J. Spear *dean*
Kesterson, Ray Brent *college dean, retired air force officer*
McCartor, Sheila Smith *secondary school educator*
Mittelstet, Stephen *academic administrator*
Mulcahy, Joan Catherine *elementary school educator*
Reynolds, Annette *secondary school educator*
Scott, John Roland *business law educator*
Shambaugh, Irvin Calvin, Jr., *aptitude test firm executive*
Shelton, Virginia Kaye *director*
Sosa, Kena *primary school educator, writer*
Turner, Robert Gerald *university president*
Wrucke-Nelson, Ann C. *elementary school educator*

Denton
Carlson, William Dwight *college president emeritus*
Hurley, Alfred Francis *historian, academic administrator emeritus, retired air force officer*
Katsinas, Stephen Gregory *academic administrator, education educator*
McDonald-West, Sandi MacLean *headmaster, consultant*
Pinson, Joseph *education educator, entertainer*
Smith, Howard Wellington *education educator, dean emeritus*
Tanner, Harold Miles *education educator, researcher*
Williams, Cheryl A. *secondary school educator*

Edinburg
Nevarez, Miguel A. *academic administrator*
Zeng, Liang *education educator*

Egypt
Wynn, John Thomas *retired academic administrator, farming executive, economic consultant, oil and gas producer*

El Paso
Armitage, Shelley Sue *American studies educator*
Burnham, Albert David *education educator, researcher, historian, consultant*
Erskine, William Crawford *retired academic administrator, accountant, health facility administrator*
Hernandez, Roberto Reyes *secondary school educator*
Natalicio, Diana Siedhoff *academic administrator*
Patty, William Robert *secondary school educator, principal*
Renteria, Victor Manuel *secondary school educator*
Small, Ray *university administrator*
von Tungeln, George Robert *retired university administrator, economics consultant*

Elgin
Shelby, Nina Claire *special education educator*

Emory
Cates, Sue Sadler *educational diagnostician*

Fort Sam Houston
Robinson, Naomi Jean *educational training systems educator*

Fort Worth
Boschini, Victor John, Jr., *academic administrator*
Collins Block, Cathy *education educator, writer, educational consultant*
Donovan, Nowell *academic administrator*
Saenz, Michael *college president*
Slater, Carmen Rochelle *elementary school educator*
Tucker, William Edward *academic administrator, minister*
Wilson-Webb, Nancy Lou *education administration consultant, director*

Fredericksburg
Chase, John David *retired dean, retired internist*

Freeport
Baskin, William Gresham *counselor, music educator, vocalist*

Friendswood
Kennedy, Priscilla Ann *elementary school educator*

Galveston
Banet, Charles Henry *academic administrator, clergyman*
Carrier, Warren Pendleton *retired university chancellor, writer*
Clayton, William Howard *retired university president*
Goodwin, Sharon Ann *academic administrator*
Hawkins, Ida Faye *elementary school educator*
Stobo, John David *dean, educator, physician*

Georgetown
Abegg, Martin Gerald *retired academic administrator*
Schrum, Jake Bennett *university administrator*

Grand Prairie
Puckett, Mary Alice *primary school educator, consultant*

Grapevine
Hirsh, Cristy J. *principal*

Hale Center
Courtney, Carolyn Ann *school librarian*

Henderson
Knapp, Virginia Estella *retired secondary school educator*

Houston
Alfini, James Joseph *dean, educator, lawyer*
Anderson, Claire W. *gifted and talented educator*
Ballard, Linda Christine *financial aid director*
Bott, Simon Gregory *chemistry educator, researcher*
Brinkley, William R. *dean*
Brooks, Philip Russell *chemistry educator, researcher*
Bui, Khoi Tien *college counselor*
Butler, William Thomas *academic administrator, physician, educator*
Caram, Dorothy Farrington *educational consultant*
Carroll, Michael M. *academic dean, mechanical engineering educator*
Davis, Bruce Gordon *retired principal*
Djerejian, Edward Peter *institute director, former diplomat*
Douglas, James M. *university president*
Fisher, Janet Warner *secondary school educator*
Flaitz, Catherine M. *dean, dental educator*
Gonzalez, Antonio *academic administrator, mortgage company executive*
Hammond, DeAnna *elementary school educator*
Hodo, Edward Douglas *university president*
Hoffman, Philip Guthrie *former university president*
Hubert, Frank William Rene *retired university system chancellor*
Jackson, Wanda Britton *educator*
Kapadia, Asha Seth *education educator, consultant*
Lewis, Cleotrice O. Ney Tillis *retired elementary education educator*
Ligon-Borden, Betty Lee *academic director*
Mansell, Joyce Marilyn *retired special education educator*
Miller, Harry Freeman *university administrator*
Netsiri, Chaiyapoj *academic administrator, researcher*
O'Rourke, Marylyn Kay *counseling administrator, consultant*
Paul, Alida Ruth *arts and crafts educator*
Pickering, James Henry, III, *academic administrator, educator*
Pinson, Artie Frances *retired elementary school educator*
Poats, Lillian Brown *education educator*
Rapoport, Nancy B. *dean, law educator*
Rawlinson, Gayla *director, consultant*
Rice, Lynda Lu *elementary school educator, writer*
Roos, Sybil Friedenthal *retired elementary school educator*
Shaffer, Anita Mohrland *counselor, educator*
Sheehan, Linda Suzanne *education administrator*
Smith, Arthur Kittredge, Jr., *academic administrator, political science educator*
Smith, Roland Blair, Jr., *university administrator*
Stripling, Kaye *school system administrator*
Traber, Peter George *academic administrator, educator*
Urbina, Febe Gloria *elementary school principal*
Wagner, Paul Anthony, Jr., *education educator*
Webb, Marty Fox *principal*
Weber, Wilford Alexander *education educator*
Whitaker, Gilbert Riley, Jr., *academic administrator, business economist*
Whiting, Martha Countee *retired secondary education educator*
Wiley, Shirley Winona Walters *adult education educator, artist*
Williames, Lee John *university official, history educator*

Huntsville
Payne, David Emer *university administrator*
Payne, Richard Harold *university research administrator*
Ward, Richard Hurley *dean, writer*
Warner, Laverne *education educator*

Irving
Chase, Pearline *adult education educator*
Lazarus, Francis Martin *academic administrator*
Martin, Thomas Lyle, Jr., *academic administrator*
McVay, Barbara Chaves *mathematics educator*

Johnson City
Pollock, Margaret Landau Peggy *elementary school educator*

Katy
Hughes, Sandra Michelle *education administrator, educator*

Kemp
Chalk, J. Lee *secondary school educator, writer*

Killeen
Anderson, James Raymond *academic administrator*

Kingsville
Arnold, Mitylene B. *special education educator, consultant*
Hines, Gladys H. *academic administrator*
Ibanez, Manuel Luis *university official, biological sciences educator*
Kinkel, Doreen Heather *education educator*
Wiley, Millicent Yoder *realtor, pianist, accompanist, retired secondary school choir director*

La Porte
Svambera, Beatrice Alice *secondary school educator*

Lake Jackson
Tasa, Ken *college dean*

Laredo
Black, Clifford Merwyn *academic administrator, sociologist, educator*
Heimes, Charmaine Marie *elementary school educator, poet, writer*
Keck, Ray Marvin, III, *academic administrator*
Reuthinger, Georgeanne *special education educator*

Longview
Gentry, Vernessa Diana *principal, consultant*
Roller, Robert H. *dean, finance educator*

Lubbock
Burns, John Mitchell *academic administrator*
Daniels, Bruce C *education educator*
Gelca, Razvan *education educator*
Glasscock, Herlinda Martinez *dean*
Haragan, Donald Robert *university administrator, geosciences educator*
Irons, Brian K. *education educator, pharmacist*
Schmidly, David J. *university president, biology educator*
Schneider, Andreas *education educator, researcher*
Yoder-Wise, Patricia Snyder *education educator*

Mabank
Beets, Hughla Fae *retired secondary school educator*

Marfa
Chambers, Johnnie Lois (Tucker Chambers) *elementary school educator, rancher*

Marshall
Shaw, Dianne Elizabeth *school administrator*

Mart
Mathews, B. J. *secondary school educator*

Maxwell
Peters, Carol Ann *secondary school educator*

Mcallen
Friedman, Bruce David *academic administrator, educator, social worker*

Mercedes
Alaniz, Theodora Villarreal *elementary school educator*

Mesquite
Gant, Linda Gayle *elementary school educator*
Holt, Mildred Frances *special education educator*
Patrick, Pamela Ann *research consultant*
Reid, Helen Veronica *dean*
Vaughan, Joseph Lee, Jr., *education educator, consultant*
Wenrich, John William *college president*

Mount Pleasant
Caskey, Judith Ann *educational director*

New Braunfels
Barragán, Celia Silguero *elementary school educator*
Oestreich, Charles Henry *retired university president*

Odessa
Grubbs, Donald Ray *educational director, educator, welder*

Orange
Odom, Sarah Bernice *elementary school educator*

Paige
Trevino, Jerry Rosalez *retired secondary school principal*

Pasadena
Blue, Monte Lynn *college president*
Fogo, Peter C. *educator, novelist, poet*

Perryton
Doerrie, Bobette *secondary school educator*

Plano
Rhodes, Doris Chaney *freelance/self-employed secondary school educator*

Prairie View
Hines, Charles A. *academic administrator*

Rancho Viejo
Garza, Roberto Jesus *retired education educator*

Richardson
Bray, Carolyn Scott *education educator*
Dunn, David E. *university dean*
Heath, Mary Ann *elementary school educator*
Kelly, Rita Mae *academic administrator, researcher*
Wildenthal, Bryan Hobson *university administrator*

Roma
Martinez, Adolfo Roberto *secondary school educator*

Rosenberg
White, Gretchen Nance *education educator, writer*

Round Rock
Ledbetter, Sharon Faye Welch *retired educational consultant*

Royse City
Borden, William Vickers *education educator, writer*

San Angelo
Davison, Elizabeth Jane Linton *education educator*
Smith, Karen B. *educational consultant*

San Antonio
Barrera, Elvira Puig *counselor, therapist, educator*
Bennett, Sister Elsa Mary *retired secondary education educator*
Brazil, John Russell *academic administrator*
Faules, Barbara Ruth *retired elementary education educator*
Foerster, Paul A. *secondary school educator, writer*
Goelz, Paul Cornelius *university dean*
Hall, Denise *special education educator*
Henderson, Dwight Franklin *dean, educator*
Horowitz, Rosalind *education educator, researcher*
Jerralds, Oswald Clarence *elementary school educator*
Kalkwarf, Kenneth Lee *dean, dental educator*
King, Kandi Jaye *secondary school educator, consultant*
Kosty, Carlita *secondary school educator*
Leal, J. Terri *academic facility administrator*
Madrid, Olga Hilda Gonzalez *retired elementary education educator, association executive*
Maxwell, Diana Kathleen *early childhood education educator*
McBee, Lucy Armijo *retired elementary education educator, administrator, singer, actress, writer*
McDonald, Mary Helen *special education educator*
Messina, Paul Francis *education consultant*
Orange, Carolyn *education educator*
Recker, Patricia Bullion *secondary school educator*
Robertson, Samuel Luther, Jr., *special education educator, therapist, researcher*
Sobre, Judith Berg *education educator*
Wartman, Steven *dean, educator*
White, Charles B. *academic administrator*
Wilson, Stephen Edward *academic administrator*

Young, James Julius *academic administrator, retired military officer*

San Diego
Pena, Modesta Celedonia *retired principal*

San Juan
Guzmán, Belinda F. *elementary school educator*

San Marcos
Carman, Mary Ann *retired special education educator*
Fite, Kathleen Elizabeth *education educator*
Moore, Betty Jean *retired education educator*

Sherman
Bueno, Lourdes *education educator*
Jarma, Donna Marie *secondary school educator*
Page, Oscar C. *academic administrator*

Snyder
Hall, Sandra J. *education educator*

Spade
Davis, Thomas Pinkney *secondary school educator*

Stephenville
Swanson, Jacqueline V. *academic administrator, educator, women's health nurse practitioner*

Sugar Land
Ramos, Rose Mary *elementary school educator*

Sulphur Springs
Gibson, Jannette Poe *educational consultant*

Texarkana
Austin, Sandra Jenelle *school librarian, language educator*
Davis-Sutton, Rosiland *secondary school educator*

Trophy Club
Hardy, Vicki *elementary school principal*

Tyler
Davidson, Jack Leroy *academic administrator*
Dunlap, Martha McKinzie *middle school educator*
McGarry, Sandra Alethea *elementary school educator*
Peters, Robert K. *dean, newscaster, newswriter, journalist*
Waller, Wilma Ruth *retired secondary school educator and librarian*

Victoria
Williams, Debra Ann *assistant principal*

Waco
Belew, John Seymour *academic administrator, chemist*
Brooks, Roger Leon *retired academic administrator*
Emanuel, Gloria Page *retired secondary school educator*
Hollingsworth, Martha Lynette *secondary school educator*
Lindsey, Jonathan Asmel *university official, librarian, educator*
Reynolds, Herbert Hal *university administrator*

Weatherford
Colton, James Patrick *community college administrator*

West Columbia
Walker, Phyllis LeVonne *elementary school educator*

Wichita Falls
Leavell, Landrum Pinson, II, *seminary administrator, clergyman, educator*
Rodriguez, Louis Joseph *academic administrator, economist, educator*
Stange, Terrence V. *education educator*

UTAH

Kaysville
Dickson, Marjorie Wagers Thatcher *secondary school educator*

Logan
Dobson, Dorothy Lynn Watts *elementary school educator*
Emert, George Henry *former academic administrator, biochemist*
McKell, Cyrus M. *retired college dean, plant physiologist*
Shaver, James Porter *education educator, university dean*

Ogden
Eisler, David Lee *provost*
Thompson, Paul Harold *university president*

Provo
Boyter, Scott M. *academic administrator*
Bradshaw, Jerald Sherwin *chemistry educator, researcher*
Bullough, Robert Vernon, Jr., *educational studies professor*
Densley, Colleen T. *principal*
Fleming, Joseph Clifton, Jr., *dean, law educator*
Hansen, H. Reese *dean, educator*
Hill, Ned Cromar *dean, finance educator, consultant*
Peterson, Erlend Dean *dean*
Samuelson, Cecil O. *academic administrator*

Salem
Hahn, Joan Christensen *retired secondary education educator, travel agent*

Salt Lake City
Bassis, Michael Steven *academic administrator*
Bennion, John Warren *urban education educator*
Betz, A. Lorris *dean, educator, pediatrician, consultant*
Cannell, Cyndy Michelle *elementary school principal*
Christensen, Bruce LeRoy *former academic administrator, commercial broadcasting executive*
Drew, Clifford James *university administrator, special education and educational psychology educator*
Keefe, Maureen Ruth *dean*
Markham, Reed B. *education educator, consultant*
McCleary, Lloyd E(verald) *education educator*
Stock, Peggy A(nn) *college president, educator*
Young, Michael Kent *dean, lawyer, educator*

West Jordan
Shepherd, Paul H. *school system administrator*

VERMONT

Bennington
Coleman, Elizabeth *college president*

Burlington
Allard, Judith Louise *secondary school educator*
Della Santa, Laura *principal*
Ferrari, Dennis M. *secondary school educator*
Willis, Russell Edward *academic administrator*

Colchester
Edmundson, Lorna Duphiney *academic administrator*
vanderHeyden, Marc A. *academic administrator*

Essex Junction
Bisson, Roger *middle school educator*

Lower Waterford
Burnham, Robert Alan *academic administrator, educator*

Lyndonville
Moore, Carol A. *academic administrator*

Middlebury
Liebowitz, Ronald D. *academic administrator*
O'Brien, George Dennis *retired academic administrator*

Moretown
Hartshorn, Brenda Bean *elementary school educator*

Northfield
Schneider, Richard William *academic administrator*

Plainfield
Jervis, Jane Lise *college official, science historian*

Poultney
Pentkowski, Raymond J. *principal*

South Royalton
Doria, Anthony Notarnicola *college dean, educator*

Strafford
Williams, William Magavern *headmaster*

Williston
Foss, Jean Mitchell *school system administrator*

VIRGINIA

Alexandria
Bartlett, Elizabeth Susan *audio-visual specialist*
Dubin, Martin Steven *principal*
Gil, Libia Socorro *school system administrator*
Jenkins, John Smith *retired academic dean, lawyer*
Kierscht, Marcia Selland *academic administrator, psychologist*
Pastin, Mark Joseph *association executive*
Schiff, Charlene *adult education educator*
Stevens, Alice Marie *educational consultant*
Wright, Mary James *senior education consultant*

Amherst
Campbell, Catherine Lynn *elementary school educator*
Copp, Cindy Pierce *education educator*

Annandale
Bohen, Dolores Boylston *retired school system administrator*
Del Conte, L. Catherine *special education educator*
Di'Metrius, Simpson Kevin *elementary school educator*
Morales, Iris C. *secondary school educator*
Wilhelmi, Mary Charlotte *education educator, college official*

Arlington
Grady, Mark F. *dean, law educator*
Haggett, Rosemary Romanowski *academic administrator*
Hill, Donald Wain *education accreditation commission executive*
McTique, Maurice P. *director*
Price, Donald Ray *university official, agricultural engineer*
Ramaley, Judith Aitken *former university president, endocrinologist*
Rogers, Sharon J. *education consultant*
Rosenblatt, Louise Michel *emerita educator*
Stout, Mary Webb *education program specialist*
Trombley, Edward Francis, III, *registrar*

Ashland
Bruce, Jennifer Elaine *education educator*
Rice, Adrian Clifford *adult education educator*

Blacksburg
Barksdale, Mary Alice *education educator*
Bosniak, Murray Eli *vocational school educator*
Brown, Gregory Neil *university administrator, forest physiology educator*
Campbell, Joan Virginia Loweke *secondary school educator, language educator*
Edwards, Patricia Klobus *former dean, architecture/urban studies educator*
Eyre, Peter *dean*
McNamee, Mark *academic administrator*
Meszaros, Peggy S. *academic administrator*
Pearson, Ronald Earl *educator, researcher*
Porter, Duncan MacNair *editor, educator*
Smoot, Raymond D., Jr., *academic administrator*
Steger, Charles William *university administrator*
Torgersen, Paul Ernest *academic administrator, educator*

Bridgewater
Barkley, Terrell Wayne *school librarian, archivist, curator*
Geisert, Wayne Frederick *educational consultant, retired administrator*

Burke
Emery, Vicki Morris *school library media administrator*

Charlottesville
Ayers, Edward *dean*
Casteen, John Thomas, III, *university president*
Garson, Arthur, Jr., *dean, medical educator*
Harris, Robert Shields *dean*
Matson, Robert Edward *public management educator, leadership consultant*
Miller, Margaret Alison *education educator*
O'Neil, Robert Marchant *university administrator, law educator*
Scott, Robert Edwin *dean, law educator*
Smith, Clyde Ray *dean*

Chesapeake
Lewter, Helen Clark *retired elementary school educator*
Niemeyer, Antonio Bilisoly, Jr., *school system administrator*
Pearce, Patsy Beasley *elementary education educator*
Webb, Julia Jones *elementary school educator, minister*

Chester
Law, Thomas Melvin *college president*

Christiansburg
Patty, Anna Christine *retired elementary school educator, tax specialist*

Clifton
Latt, Pamela Yvonne *school system administrator*

Clifton Forge
Allen, M(ilford) Ray *secondary school educator*

Danville
Aaron, Larry Gene *secondary education educator, writer, minister*
Pfau, Richard Anthony *university president*

Dulles
Hegarty, George John *university rector, English educator*

Fairfax
Carty, Rita Mary *dean, nurse*
Kettlewell, Gail Biery *academic administrator*
Merten, Alan Gilbert *academic administrator*
Silcox, Gordon Bruce *executive coach*

Falls Church
Johnson, William David *retired university administrator*
Lambert, Vickie Ann *dean emerita, international nursing consultant*
Todd, Shirley Ann *school system administrator*

Farmville
Cormier, Patricia Picard *academic executive*

Fort Lee
Simmonds, Robert Maurer *education educator*

Fredericksburg
Emory, Samuel Thomas *retired educator*
Jenks-Davies, Kathryn Ryburn *retired daycare provider and owner, civic worker*
Potter, Sylvia *education educator*

Gainesville
Tuck, Russell R., Jr., *former college president*

Great Falls
Andrews, Betty Bauserman *retired secondary school educator, property manager*
Cass, Ronald Andrew *dean*

Grundy
Davis, W. Jeremy *dean, law educator, lawyer*

Hamilton
Shoremount, Paul Erik *secondary school educator*

Hampton
Bhuiyan, Mohammad Ali *university administrator, educator, consultant*
Fox, Margaret Louise *retired secondary education educator*
Harvey, William Robert *university president*
Moser, Eugene Paul, Jr., *retired secondary school educator*

Harrisonburg
Carrier, Ronald Edwin *academic administrator, director*
Wang, Greg G. *education educator, consultant*

Herndon
Jones, Reba (Becki) Pestun *elementary school educator, music educator*

Hillsville
Becker, Elizabeth Anne *secondary school educator*

Hollins College
O'Brien, Jane Margaret *academic administrator*

Leesburg
Alwani, Ahmed J. *dean, consultant*

Lexington
Ball, Gordon Victor *education educator, writer, editor, filmmaker, photographer*
Burish, Thomas Gerard *academic administrator*
McCloud, Anece Faison *academic administrator*
Partlett, David F. *dean, law educator*
Squire, James C. *adult education educator, engineer, consultant*
Velasquez, Eduardo A *education educator*
Williams, H. Thomas (Tom) *academic administrator, physicist, educator*
Young, Kenneth Evans *educational consultant*

Locust Grove
Ingalls, Jane *university program director*

Lynchburg
Bowman, Kathleen Gill *academic administrator*
Herndon, Merle Puckette *principal*
Husted, Stewart Winthrop *dean, marketing educator, consultant*
Schewel, Rosel Hoffberger *education educator*

Manassas
Archer, Chalmers, Jr., *retired education educator*

Marion
Groseclose, Joanne Stowers *special education educator*

Mc Dowell
Harkleroad, Jo-Ann Decker *special education educator*

Mc Lean
Kropp, Edward H. *education educator, consultant*

Mechanicsville
Watkins, Carol A. *special education educator*

Melfa
Harmon, Patricia Marie *special education educator*

Midland
Andes, Donna M. *adult education educator, community health nurse*

Newport News
Eastman, John Robert *education educator*
Hightower, John Brantley *arts administrator*
Powell, Jouett Lynn *college dean, philosophy and religious studies educator*
Tracy, Tracy Faircloth *special education educator*

Norfolk
Byrne, William Andrew *education educator, historian*
Combs, Charles Donald *academic administrator*
Epplein, Lawrence Elliott *hospitality management educator*
Farmer, Evan R. *academic administrator, dermatologist, researcher*
Jones, Franklin Ross *education educator*
Koch, James Verch *academic administrator, economist*
McDemmond, Marie Valentine *academic administrator, consultant*
Opfer, Steven Earl *education educator, researcher*
Runte, Roseann *academic administrator*
Sebren, Lucille Griggs *retired private school educator, public school educator*
Steele, James Eugene *retired school system administrator*
Taylor Claud, Andrea *educational consultant*

Orange
Daniel, Daniele Mallison *elementary school educator*

Partlow
Papapetrou, Paula Bartello *special education educator, writer*

Petersburg
Wyatt, Bryant Nelson *education educator, writer*

Radford
Templeton, Dennie, III, *educational administrator, consultant*

Reston
Keefe, James Washburn *educational writer, researcher, consultant*

Richlands
Stacy, Curtis Alan *secondary school educator*

Richmond
Archer, Kellie Jo *education educator*
Blank, Florence Weiss *literacy educator, editor*
Budd, Richard Wade *university official, communications scientist, priest*
Drain, Cecil B. *university dean, nurse anesthetist educator, retired army officer*
Ellis, Anthony John *education educator*
Hamel, Dana Bertrand *academic administrator*
Harris, Grace E. *academic administrator*
Heilman, E. Bruce *academic administrator*
Hunt, Ronald J. *dean, dental educator*
James, Allix Bledsoe *retired university president*
Jewell-Sherman, Deborah *school system administrator*
Jones, Jeanne Pitts *pre-school administrator*
Langston, Nancy Sue Friedrich *dean*
McGee, Henry Alexander, Jr., *university official*
Minor, Marian Thomas *elementary and secondary school educational consultant*
Morrill, Richard Leslie *university administrator*
Newsome, Heber H. *academic administrator*
Spindler, Judith Tarleton *elementary school educator*
Trani, Eugene Paul *university president, educator*

Roanoke
Cole, Evelyn Marie *day care administrator*

Rocky Mount
Flora, Jenny Shreves *special education educator*

Salem
Fisher, Charles Harold *chemistry educator, researcher*

Springfield
Leavitt, Mary Janice Deimel *special education educator, civic worker*

Stafford
Lambert, Linda Margaret *reading specialist*

Suffolk
Logan-Sutton, Floretta R. *elementary school educator*

Surry
Sprouse, Earlene Pentecost *special education educator*

Sweet Briar
Muhlenfeld, Elisabeth S. *college president, educator, author*

Tazewell
Claytor, Katherine W. Moss *secondary school educator*

Urbanna
Salley, John Jones *retired academic administrator, oral pathologist*

Virginia Beach
Jones, Robert Clair *middle school educator*
Kunzinger, Robert Stephen *education educator, writer*
Morgan, Raymond Franklin *education educator*
Selig, William George *university official*

Waynesboro
Dillon, William Henry *retired secondary school educator*

Williamsburg
Aldrow-Liput, Priscilla Reese *retired elementary education educator*
Calver, Richard Allen *retired college dean*
Chandler, Kimberley Lynn *educational administrator*
Feiss, P. Geoffrey *university dean*
Hight, Orian Langley *retired education educator*
Reveley, Walter Taylor, III, *dean*

Wise
Smiddy, Joseph Charles *retired academic administrator*

Woodberry Forest
Campbell, Dennis Marion *academic administrator, educator, theologian*

WASHINGTON

Anacortes
Felger, Ralph William *education educator, retired military officer*

Bellevue
Clark, Richard Walter *education consultant*
Van Vactor, Myra Florendo *school librarian, director*
Westergaard, George Henry *secondary school educator*

Bellingham
Morse, Karen Williams *academic administrator*

Centralia
Kirk, Henry Port *academic administrator*

Cheney
Jordan, Stephen M. *university president*
Stearns, Susan A *education educator*
Toneva, Elena T. *education educator, researcher*

College Place
Anderson, Clarence Glen *dean*

Darrington
Powell, Gregory David *secondary school educator, coach, musician*

Davenport
Lonn, Suzanne Dallas *secondary school educator*

Ellensburg
McIntyre, Jerilyn Sue *university administrator*
Nethery, Vincent Michael *adult education educator*

Everett
Hundley, Ronnie *academic administrator*

Federal Way
Simpson, Shawn Marie *secondary school educator*

Friday Harbor
Hoyt, James *education educator*

Gig Harbor
Minnerly, Robert Ward *retired headmaster*

Kelso
Janke, John Eric *secondary educator*

Kenmore
Jennerich, Edward John *university official and dean*

Kirkland
Argue, Don Harvey *college president, minister*
Rich, Clayton *retired academic administrator, educator*
Tyllia, Frank Michael *university official, educator*

Lakewood
Oakes, DuWayne Earl *retired principal*

Leavenworth
Smith, G(odfrey) T(aylor) *retired academic administrator*

Lynnwood
Floten, Barbara Jean *educational dean*
Oharah, Jack *academic administrator*

Mercer Island
Davis, Tinka Guerguieva *secondary school educator*

Mount Vernon
Witmer, Michael Douglas *education educator*

Olympia
Bergeson, Teresa *school system administrator*

Pullman
Bates, Robert C. *academic administrator*
Lewis, Norman G. *academic administrator, researcher, consultant*
Rawlins, V. Lane *university president*
Walter, Scott *school librarian*

Renton
Gaolach, Brad Wayne *academic administrator, director*
Wong, Jee K *education educator, music consultant*

Richland
Miller, James Vince *university president*

Seattle
Banks, James Albert *educational research director, educator*
Carlson, Dale Arvid *university dean*
Cox, Frederick Moreland *retired university dean, social worker*
Debro, Julius *education educator, sociologist*
Denny, Brewster Castberg *retired university dean*
Emmert, Mark Allen *academic administrator, educator*
Gardiner, John Jacob *leadership educator, writer, speaker, philosopher*
Gerberding, William Passavant *retired university president*
Ginorio, Angela Beatriz *university research administrator, educator*
Goodlad, John Inkster *education educator, writer*
Hampton, Shelley Lynn *hearing impaired educator*
Hegyvary, Sue Thomas *nursing school dean, editor, nursing educator*
Kelley, Lucille Marie Kindely *dean, psychosocial nurse*
Knight, W.H., Jr., (Joe Knight) *dean, law educator*
Mitchell, Gloria Jean *principal, educator*
Murdock, Tullisse Antoinette (Toni Murdock) *academic administrator*
Plotnick, Robert David *educator, economic consultant*
Proctor, Richard Macfarlane *art educator, artist, writer, gallery owner*
Ramsey, Paul Glenn *dean, internist*
Ray, Charles Kendall *retired university dean*
Silver, Michael *education educator*
Somerman, Martha J. *dean, dental educator*
Stringer, William Jeremy *university official*
Sundborg, Stephen V. *academic administrator*
Terrell, W(illiam) Glenn *university president emeritus*
Thorud, David B. *academic administrator*
Tschernisch, Sergei P. *academic administrator*
Voegtlin-Anderson, Mary Margaret *secondary school educator, music educator*
Woods, Nancy Fugate *dean, women's health nurse, educator*

Shelton
Milander, Henry Martin *educational consultant*

Spanaway
Roberts-Dempsey, Patricia E. *secondary school educator*

Spokane
Coughlin, Bernard John *university chancellor*
Hansen, Laurel D. *elementary school educator*
Hirsch, Anne *dean*
Hosking, Neville John *educational administrator*
Matters, Clyde Burns *former college president*
McManus, Patrick Francis *educator, writer*
Nyman, Carl John, Jr., *university dean and official*
Robinson, William P. *academic administrator, consultant, speaker*
Spitzer, Robert J. *academic administrator*

Sumner
Wickizer, Cindy Louise *retired elementary school educator*

Tacoma
King, Gundar Julian *retired university dean*

Toppenish
Ross, Kathleen Anne *academic administrator*

Walla Walla
Cronin, Thomas Edward *academic administrator*

Yakima
Ullas, Yvonne Lee *primary school educator*
Walker, Lorene *retired elementary school educator*

WEST VIRGINIA

Athens
Beasley, Jerry Lynn *academic administrator*
Marsh, Joseph Franklin, Jr., *emeritus college president, educational consultant*

Belmont
Drane, A. D. *adult education educator*

Bluefield
Blevins, Thomas E. *college administrator, educator*
Loundmon-Clay, Juanita L. *academic administrator, educator, dean*

Charleston
Arrington, Carolyn Ruth *education consultant*
Davis, Billie Johnston *school counselor*
Welch, Edwin Hugh *academic administrator*

Clarksburg
Leuliette, Connie Jane *secondary educator*

Dunbar
Russell, James Alvin, Jr., *college administrator*

Fairmont
Dudley-Eshbach, Janet *university president*

Glenville
Schmetzer, Frances Myers *secondary school educator*

Huntington
Anderson, Lorraine Pearson *dean*
Cole, Patricia Aluise *elementary school educator*
Gould, Alan Brant *academic administrator*
Hayes, Robert Bruce *former college president, educator*
Kent, Calvin Albert *university administrator*
McKown, Charles Henry *dean*
Welch, Lynne Brodie *nursing school dean*

Lewisburg
Adelman, Michael *dean*

Morgantown
Allamong, Betty D. *retired academic administrator*
Bajura, Richard Albert *university administrator, engineering educator*
Biddington, William Robert *academic administrator, dental educator*
Bucklew, Neil S. *former academic administrator, educator*
D'Alessandri, Robert M. *dean*
Hardesty, David Carter, Jr., *university president*
Jackson, Ruth Moore *academic administrator*
Koelbl, James J. *dean*
Mei, Betty Muichi *director*

Mount Gay
Pierce, Calisa A. *director*

Parkersburg
Meadows, Lois Annette *elementary school educator*

Saint Albans
Whiteley, John Frederick *education educator, consultant*

Vienna
Hamm, David B. *dean*
Terry, Ralph Bruce *education educator*

Wheeling
Campbell, Clyde Del *academic administrator*

WISCONSIN

Appleton
Meidl, Kevin *secondary school educator*

Beloit
Burris, John Edward *academic administrator, biologist, educator*
Melvin, Charles Alfred, III, *superintendent of schools*
Wheeler, Karla *education educator*

Burlington
Roeschen, Marlene Y. *retired elementary school educator*

Crivitz
Gerhart, Lorraine Pfeiffer *reading specialist, educator*

De Forest
O'Neil, J(ames) Peter *computer software designer, educator*

De Pere
Manion, Thomas A. *chancellor*

Delafield
Kurth, Ronald James *university president, retired naval officer*

Eau Claire
Brill, Donald Maxim *educator, writer, researcher*
Brummer, James J. *adult education educator, writer*
Kozbial, Richard James *retired elementary education educator*
Mash, Donald J. *college president*
Richards, Jerry Lee *academic administrator, religious educator*

Elkhorn
Reinke, Doris Marie *retired elementary school educator*

Fish Creek
Zvara, Christine C. *middle school education educator*

Fort Atkinson
Schumacher, Mabel G. *director, consultant*

Freedom
Moscinski, David Joseph *educational administrator, school psychologist*

Glendale
Schenker, Eric *university dean, economist*

Green Bay
Hardy, Deborah Lewis *dean, educator, dental hygienist*
Perkins, Mark L. *university chancellor*
Shepard, W. Bruce *academic administrator*
Weidner, Edward William *university chancellor, political scientist*

Green Lake
Mitchell, Tawnia Juanita *elementary school educator, music educator*

Holmen
Meyer, Karl William *retired university president*

Howards Grove
Houston, Angela Marie *director*

Hudson
Dahle, Johannes Upton *retired academic administrator*

Kenosha
Campbell, F(enton) Gregory *college administrator, historian*
Helman, Iris Barca *elementary school educator, consultant*
Iaquinta, Leonard Phillip *former university official, not-for-profit fundraiser*

La Crosse
Hitch, Elizabeth *academic administrator*
Lentz, Kirby Warren *academic administrator*
Medland, William James *university president*

Laona
Sturzl, Alice A. *school library administrator*

Madison
Burmaster, Elizabeth *school system administrator*
Busby, Edward Oliver *retired dean*
Davis, Kenneth Boone, Jr., *dean, law educator*
Hamers, Robert J. *chemistry educator, researcher*
Jackson, Jerlando F.L. *education educator*
Knetter, Michael Mark *dean, economics professor*
Policano, Andrew J. *dean, finance educator*
Reilly, Kevin P. *academic administrator*
Skochelak, Susan E. *college dean*
Spear, Peter D. *academic administrator*
Suri, Jeremi A. *education educator*
Wiley, John D. *academic administrator*

Menomonee Falls
Hinnrichs-Dahms, Holly Beth *middle school educator*

Menomonie
Furst-Bowe, Julie *academic administrator*

Mequon
Dohmen, Mary Holgate *retired primary school educator*
Ellis, William Grenville *academic administrator, management consultant*

Middleton
Conaway, Jane Ellen *elementary school educator*

Milwaukee
Aman, Mohammed Mohammed *dean, library and information science educator*
Barth, Karl Luther *retired seminary president*
Beck, Kim Christopher *director*
Conner, David Lee *secondary educator*
Dunn, Michael J. *dean*
Hansen, John Herbert *university administrator, accountant*
Hatton, Janie R. Hill *principal*
Hill, James Warren *university dean*
Jenkins, Clarence William, Jr., *academic administrator*
Lobb, William K. *dean, dental educator*
O'Brien, Kathleen Ann *academic administrator*
Rheams, Annie Elizabeth *education educator*
Rhoten, Juliana Theresa *retired principal*
Sankovitz, James Leo *retired development director, lobbyist*
Schneider, Mary Lea *college administrator*
Schroeder, John H. *university chancellor*
Setright, Mildred Alberta *educator*
Viets, Hermann *college president, consultant*
Weiner, Wendy L. *elementary school educator, writer*
Wild, Robert Anthony *university president*

Nekoosa
Ramirez, Mary Catherine *retired secondary school educator*

Oconto
Watson-Boone, Rebecca A. *library and information studies researcher, educator*

Oshkosh
Earns, Lane Robert *academic administrator, historian, educator*
Olejniczak, Bernard Charles *education educator*

Palmyra
Hammiller, Ruth Ellen *school official and psychologist*

Platteville
Markee, David James *university official, education educator*

Racine
Bradley, Paul N. *special education educator*
Hayward, Tamerin M. *secondary school educator*

River Falls
Thibodeau, Gary A. *academic administrator*

Sheboygan
Fulop, Timothy *academic administrator*

Shorewood
Lietz, Jeremy Jon *educational administrator, writer*

Somerset
Gabrick, Robert William *educational consultant, writer*

Spencer
Herder, Paul O. *secondary school educator*

Stevens Point
Grahn, Lance R. *education educator, historian*
Shade, Linda Bunnell *university chancellor*
Walker, Hugh Dyson *educator, deacon*

Sun Prairie
Schmidt, Glenn Norbert *special education educator*

Superior
Morden, Annette Sonja Knudson *education educator*
Vance, Mary Lee *academic administrator*

Washburn
Krutsch, Phyllis *academic administrator*

Waukesha
Falcone, Frank S. *academic administrator*
Gustafson, Mardel Emma *secondary school educator, writer*
Trebon, Thomas *academic administrator*

West Bend
Rodney, Joel Morris *dean, campus executive officer*

Whitewater
Busse, Eileen Elaine *special education educator*
Greenhill, H. Gaylon *retired academic administrator*
Kolb, Sharon Marie *educator, cognitive disabilities director*

Wisconsin Rapids
Olson-Hellerud, Linda Kathryn *elementary school educator*

WYOMING

Casper
Ibach, Kim L. *secondary school educator*
Moler, Mary *secondary school educator*
Richardson, Bruce Alan *academic administrator*

Cheyenne
Hart, Kerry *college administrator, music educator*
Simons, Lynn Osborn *educational consultant*
Weigner, Brent James *secondary school educator*

Glendo
Burton, Eva Ella Mary *primary school educator*

Green River
Albers, Dolores M. *secondary school educator*

Jackson
Massy, William Francis *education educator, consultant*
Ninnemann, Thomas George *secondary school educator*

Laramie
Dubois, Philip Leon *university administrator, political science educator*
McBride, Judith *elementary school educator*
Sepnafski, Bill G. *secondary school educator, consultant*

TERRITORIES OF THE UNITED STATES

GUAM

Talofofo
Taylor, James John *academic administrator*

NORTHERN MARIANA ISLANDS

Saipan
Inos, Rita Hocog *school system administrator*
Kaufer, Connie Tenorio *retired reading specialist*

PUERTO RICO

Aguadilla
Jaramillo, Juana Segarra *chancellor*

Bayamon
Rosa, Helen *dean*

Cayey
Acevedo-Loubriel, Suzette *adult education educator*

Ramey
Aponte, Abraham *secondary school educator*

San German
Mojica, Agnes *academic administrator*

San Juan
Carreras, Francisco José *retired university president, foundation executive*
Joglar, Francisco *academic administrator*
Lopez, Angel R. Pagan *dean, dentist*
Matheu, Federico Manuel *university chancellor*
Pedreira, Mark Alan *education educator*

VIRGIN ISLANDS

St Thomas
Kean, Orville *retired academic administrator*
Morse, Theodore Freeman *dean, writer*
Ragster, LaVerne E. *academic administrator*

MILITARY ADDRESSES OF THE UNITED STATES

EUROPE

APO
Knudsen, Gene Arthur *school system administrator*

CANADA

ALBERTA

Calgary
Neale, E(rnest) R(ichard) Ward *retired university official, consultant*
Smith, Rowland James *educational administrator*

Edmonton
Adams, Peter Frederick *university president, civil engineer*
Kratochvil, Byron George *chemistry educator, researcher*
Tyrrell, D. Lorne J. *university dean*

BRITISH COLUMBIA

Cobble Hill
Cox, Albert Reginald *academic administrator, physician, retired*

Kelowna
Muggeridge, Derek Brian *dean, engineering consultant*

Vancouver
Finnegan, Cyril Vincent *retired university dean, zoology educator*
Haycock, Kenneth Roy *educator, consultant, administrator*
McNeill, John Hugh *pharmaceutical sciences educator*
Snider, Robert F. *chemistry educator, researcher*
Webber, William Alexander *university administrator, physician*

MANITOBA

Winnipeg
Poettcker, Henry *retired academic administrator*

NEWFOUNDLAND

Saint John's
May, Arthur W. *retired academic administrator, educator*

NOVA SCOTIA

Halifax
Jaeger, Leslie Gordon *university administrator*
Murray, Thomas John (Jock Murray) *medical humanities educator, medical researcher, neurologist*
Ozmon, Kenneth Lawrence *retired university president, educator*

Timberlea
Verma, Surjit Kumar *retired school system administrator*

Wolfville
Ogilvie, Kelvin Kenneth *university president, chemistry educator*

ONTARIO

Belleville
Buckley, Edward Joseph *retired academic dean*

Gloucester
Malouin, Jean-Louis *university educator*

London
Davenport, Paul *academic administrator, economics educator*

Ottawa
Jordan, Joseph Louis *education educator, government official*
Kroeger, Arthur *former university chancellor, former government official*
Labarge, Margaret Wade *medieval history educator*
Philogene, Bernard J. R. *academic administrator, science educator*
Prevost, Roxane Lise *music theory educator*

Peterborough
Theall, Donald Francis *retired university president*

Toronto
Evans, John Robert *academic administrator, cardiologist*
Hayhurst, James Frederick Palmer *career and business consultant, inspirational speaker, author*
Knowlton, Thomas A. *university dean, retired food products executive*
Kushner, Eva *academic administrator, educator, author*
Macdonald, Hugh Ian *university president emeritus, economist, educator*
Marks, Ray *education educator, researcher*
Ostry, Sylvia *academic administrator, economist*
Sessle, Barry John *adult education educator, researcher*

Waterloo
Berczi, Andrew Stephen *academic administrator, educator*
Wright, Douglas Tyndall *business executive, university executive emeritus*

Willowdale
Wolfe, Rose *former academic administrator*

QUEBEC

Brossard
Allen, Harold Don *mathematics educator, science writer, monetary historian*

Montreal
Freedman, Samuel Orkin *university official*
Granger, Luc Andre *university dean, psychologist*
Lowy, Frederick Hans *academic administrator, psychiatrist*

Saint-Laurent
Jundi, Bilal *principal*

SASKATCHEWAN

Regina
Barber, Lloyd Ingram *retired university president*

Saskatoon
Knott, Douglas Ronald *college dean, agricultural sciences educator, researcher*

MEXICO

Distrito Federal
de la Fuente Ramirez, Juan Ramon *academic administrator*

San Pedro Garza García
Defiore, Perry Dennis *director, small business owner*

AUSTRALIA

Canberra
Harris, Stuart Francis *international relations educator, researcher*

East Perth
Young, Deidra Jane *educational researcher*

Melbourne
Searby, Richard Henry *academic administrator, lawyer*

Parkville Victoria
Chambers, Robert Hunter, III, *college president, American studies educator, consultant*

EGYPT

Cairo
Miller, Harry George *education educator*

ENGLAND

Durham
Galloway, David Malcolm *retired education educator*

London
Peckham, Michael John *academic administrator*

Oxford
May, Robert McCredie *biology educator*

Richmond-upon-Thames
Smith, Norman Raymond *academic administrator*

FRANCE

Paris
Teicher, Henry Earl *retired education educator*

GERMANY

Bochum
Meyers, Albert Thomas Marie *academic counsellor*

Braunschweig
Fricke, Reiner *education educator*

Dortmund
Vogt, Hartmut *education educator*

GUINEA

Hagatna
Flores, Juan P. *school system administrator*

ITALY

Rome
Wales, Patrice *school system administrator*

JAPAN

Tokyo
Nakajima, Hiroshi *education educator*

Tsukuba-shi
Shimizu, Kazuhiko *education educator*

NORWAY

Trondheim
Søvik, Nils *education educator*

POLAND

Gdańsk
Mokrzecki, Lech Marian *history of education educator*

Poznan
Skrzypczak, Jozef Aleksander *education educator*

REPUBLIC OF KOREA

Seoul
Lee, Sungho H. *education educator, consultant, dean, academic administrator*

SCOTLAND

Dundee
Black, Sir James (Sir James Whyte Black) *academic administrator, pharmacologist*

SOUTH AFRICA

Parklands
Koekemoer, Carl Lodewicus *college official, business consultant*

Port Elizabeth
Botha, Maria Magdalena *education educator, researcher*

SWEDEN

Stockholm
Lindström, Lars Ernst Simon *education educator*

THAILAND

Bangkok
Kruck, Donna Jean *special education educator, consultant*

ADDRESS UNPUBLISHED

Adams, Leocadia *secondary school educator, writer*
Adams-Passey, Suellen S. *retired elementary school educator*
Agreen, Linda Kerr *secondary school educator*
Agresto, John Thomas *former college president, education consultant*
Albino, Judith Elaine Newsom *university president*
Allen, Charles Eugene *university administrator, agriculturist, educator*
Allen, Charlotte *secondary school educator*
Alraban, Munther Francis *education educator, consultant*
Amos, Linda K. *academic administrator*
Anderson, Gregory Thomas *secondary school educator, researcher, historian*
Anderson, Susan Elaine Mosshamer *educational consultant, organization consultant, musician, mezzo soprano*
Andretti, Daniel *secondary school educator*
Applegate, Edward C. *education educator, researcher, writer*
Apps, Jerold Willard *adult education educator, writer*
Aretz, Barbara Jane *reading specialist, educator*
Armacost, Mary-Linda Sorber Merriam *former academic administrator, consultant*
Armstrong-Law, Margaret *school administrator*
Arnett, Edward McCollin *chemistry educator, researcher*
Arnold, P. A. *special education educator*
Ascher, William *program and policy educator*
Avant, Gayle *political science educator*
Azuma, Shoji *education educator*
Babbitt, Samuel Fisher *retired university official*
Backlar, Patricia *education educator*
Baldwin, Marie Hunsucker *retired secondary school educator*
Ball, Howard Guy *education specialist educator*
Barceló, Nancy Virginia (Rusty Barceló) *academic administrator*
Barone, John Anthony *academic administrator emeritus*
Barrett, Evelyn Carol *retired secondary education educator*
Basham, Garlyn Argabright *retired academic administrator*
Baxter, Cecil William, Jr., *retired college president*
Baxter, Judith Lee *academic administrator, mathematics professor*
Bayard, Susan Shapiro *adult education educator, small business owner*
Beals, Mark Graden *dean*
Beatty, Marilyn Barton *special education educator*
Beck, Barbara Nell *elementary school educator*
Beckwith, Sidney Johnson *director special programs*
Behre, Patricia Elizabeth *education educator*
Belanger, Cherry Churchill *elementary school educator*
Belcher, Charles William *education educator*
Berdahl, Robert Max *academic administrator, historian, educator*
Berger-Knorr, Lawrence *education educator, information technology manager*
Bergman, Hermas John (Jack Bergman) *retired college administrator*
Bernstein, Andrea S. *school system administrator, psychologist*
Bernstein, I. Melvin *university official and dean, materials scientist*
Bertram, Joan M. *school system administrator*
Beston, Rose Marie *retired academic administrator*
Betts, Elaine Wiswall *retired headmistress*
Beyersdorf, Marguerite Mulloy *retired secondary school educator*
Bishop, Charles Edwin *university president emeritus, economist*
Bishop, Sue Marquis (Ina Sue Marquis Bishop) *retired dean*
Black, Recca Marcele *elementary school educator*
Blackledge, David William *retired academic administrator*
Blakley, Earnestine *elementary school educator*
Blecke, Arthur Edward *retired principal*
Bloch, Julia Chang *adult education educator*
Blood, Peggy A. *academic administrator*
Bloodworth, Gladys Leon *elementary school educator*

Boesch, Diane Harriet *retired elementary education educator*
Bohannan, Lillian Muriel *elementary school educator*
Boise, Audrey Lorraine *retired special education educator*
Bolton, Marie *elementary school educator, minister*
Bondi, Joseph Charles, Jr., *education educator, consultant*
Boothe, Leon Estel *academic administrator emeritus, consultant*
Borchert, Carol Ann *school librarian*
Borkowski, Francis Thomas *university chancellor*
Borntrager, John Sherwood *principal*
Borst, Philip West *academic administrator*
Bosse, Margaret Fisher Ishler *education educator*
Bost, Raymond Morris *retired college president*
Bowens, Gloria Furr *educational administrator*
Bowling, John C. *academic administrator*
Bragdon, Paul Errol *educator*
Brain, George Bernard *university dean*
Brannon, Jean *education educator*
Brewer, Carey *retired academic administrator*
Brooks, Avery *education educator, actor*
Brown, Alvenice Hortense *elementary school educator, writer*
Brown, David Richard *school system administrator, minister*
Brownlee, Paula Pimlott *higher education consultant, former academic administrator*
Bruttomesso, Kathleen Ann *dean, nursing educator, researcher*
Bryan, Lawrence Dow *college president*
Bryant, Janice Ann *special education department administrator*
Buckler, Marilyn Lebow *school psychologist, educational consultant*
Bullock, Cheryl Davis *academic administrator, educator*
Burke, Joseph C. *former university official*
Burnett, Howard Jerome *academic administrator emeritus*
Burns, James Milton *retired educator*
Burrell, E. William *retired university admnistrator, educator*
Burton, Lavon D. *education educator*
Bush, Janice *principal*
Bush, Sandi Tokoa *elementary school educator*
Byerly, Steven Lee *educational consultant*
Cahill, Charles L. *retired university administrator, chemistry educator*
Caldwell, William Edward *educational administration educator, arbitrator*
Cambiano, Renee Leigh *education educator*
Cameron, J. Elliot *retired parochial educational system administrator*
Cameron, Lucille Wilson *retired dean*
Caputo, Joseph Anthony *retired university president*
Cardinal, Bradley John *educational researcher*
Carey, John Jesse *academic administrator, religion educator*
Carlin, Betty *education educator*
Carr, Bessie *retired elementary school educator*
Carter, Herbert Edmund *former university official*
Cartwright, Talula Elizabeth *education educator, consultant*
Case, Elizabeth Joy *special education administrator*
Castellanos-Brandon, Alba G. *secondary school educator*
Castiglia, Patricia Anne Thorson *dean, nursing educator*
Castor, Betty *academic administrator*
Cauthen, Rebecca Ann *secondary school educator*
Chandler, Alice *higher education consultant, university president*
Chappell, Annette M. *higher education consultant, minister*
Charlton, Shirley Marie *educational consultant*
Chase, James Richard *retired college president*
Chatelain, Dalia de la Paz *elementary education educator, counselor*
Christensen, Caroline "Connie" *vocational educator*
Christian, Juan Lee *elementary school educator, translator*
Cimino, Ann Mary *education educator*
Clark, Barbara June *elementary school educator*
Clark, James Milford *retired college president*
Clarke, Lambuth McGeehee *retired academic administrator*
Clawson, Roxann Eloise *college administrator, computer company executive*
Clements, Cathy J. *education educator*
Cline, Pauline M. *educational administrator*
Close, Thomas James *school administrator*
Cochrane, Walter E. *academic administrator, music educator, conductor*
Coffee, Joseph Denis, Jr., *retired college chancellor*
Cohen, Gloria Ernestine *elementary education educator*
Cole, Nancy Stooksberry *educational research executive*
Colella, Antonia Klara *reading specialist, educator*
Coleman, Gary William *retired elementary school educator*
Coleman, Mary Sue *academic administrator*
Collier, Herman Edward, Jr., *retired college president*
Compton, Norma Haynes *retired university dean, artist*
Concialdi, Michael F. *secondary school educator, speech educator*
Connell, George Edward *former university president, scientist*
Cook, Edward Joseph *college president*
Cook, Sister M(ary) Mercedes *secondary school educator, principal*
Cook, Michelle Westerman *special education educator*
Cooper, James Michael *education educator*
Copeland, Henry Jefferson, Jr., *former college president*
Copeland, Phillips Jerome *former academic administrator, former air force officer*
Courtney, Mark Edward *education educator, researcher*
Craiglow, James Hawkins *academic administrator*
Cramer, Robert Vern *retired college administrator, consultant*
Crissman, John D. *dean, pathologist*
Cronholm, Lois S. *academic administrator*
Crosby, Marena Lienhard *retired college administrator*
Cross, Kathryn Patricia *education educator*
Crouse, Carol K. Mavromatis *elementary school educator*
Cucciniello, Dawn Grace *elementary and secondary school educator*
Curry, Everett William, Jr., *college official, minister*
Cusimano, Adeline Miletti *educational consultant*
Damianakos, Phaedra Vasiliki *secondary school educator*
Daugherty, Paul D.A. *higher education executive director*
Davenport, Lawrence Franklin *academic administrator*
Dávila, Rafael Angel, III, *college counselor, educator*
Dávila, Susan *guidance counselor*
Davion, Ethel Johnson *school system administrator, curriculum specialist*
Davis, Anna Jane Ripley *elementary school educator*
Davis, Hiram Joe *public school administrator*
Davis, Joseph Lloyd *educational administrator, consultant*
Davis, Karen Ann (Karen Ann Falconer) *special education educator*
Davis, Patricia May *primary school educator, writer*
Davison, Helen Irene *secondary education educator, counselor*
de Abreu, Sue *elementary school educator*
Debs, Barbara Knowles *former college president, consultant*
De Jong, Arthur Jay *education consultant, former university president*
Delahanty, Rebecca Ann *school system administrator*
DePriest, Jon *academic administrator, department chairman*
Derrickson, Denise Ann *secondary school educator*
de Russy, Candace Uter *education reformer*
Detwiler, Christina LeFevre *elementary school educator*
DeVera, Gertrude Quenano *education educator*
Devoe, Dorothy S. *elementary school educator*
DeWolfe, Susan *elementary school educator*
Diamond, Richard *retired secondary education educator*
Diamond, Robert Mach *higher education administrator*
Dickerson, Quincy René *secondary school educator*
Dickeson, Robert Celmer *retired university president, foundation executive, political science educator*
DiSalle, Michael Danny *secondary school educator*
Dobelle, Evan Samuel *former academic administrator*
Dobler, Donald William *retired dean*
Dockery, J. Lee *retired medical school administrator*
Donaldson, Wilma Crankshaw *elementary school educator*
Donoff, R. Bruce *dean, oral surgeon, dental educator*
Dorsey, Rhoda Mary *retired academic administrator*
Doviak, Ingrid Ellinger *elementary school educator*
Drake, George Albert *college president, historian*
Dresbach, Mary Louise *state educational administrator*
Dubé, Ronald Norman *elementary school educator*
Duff, John Bernard *academic administrator, former city official*
Duffey, Rosalie Ruth *elementary school educator*
Duffy, John Joseph *retired academic administrator, history educator*
Duncan, Robert Bannerman *dean, strategy and organizations educator*
Dunn, Helen Elizabeth *retired secondary school educator*
Dunworth, John *retired college president*
Duplessis, Audrey Joseph *school system administrator*
Dutson, Thayne R. *university dean*
DuVall, Patricia Arlene *secondary school educator*
Dwinell, Ann Jones *retired special education educator*
Dycus, Elizabeth Rasmussen *academic administrator*
Eads, Albert E., Jr., *school system administrator*
Eason-Watkins, Barbara June *principal*
Edelman, Norman Herman *dean, medical educator, academic administrator*
Edens, Betty Joyce *reading recovery educator*
Edwards, Ardis Lavonne Quam *retired elementary education educator*
Edwards, Barbara *academic administrator*
Edwards, Lynn A. *retired school system administrator*
Edwards, Robert Hazard *retired college president*
Edwards-Mitchum, Lillian (Red the Poet) *secondary school educator, writer*
Egipciaco, Rosa Elena *secondary school educator*
Eliot, Charles William John *former university president*
Elliott, Tommy *secondary school educator*
Enssle, Marilyn E. *primary school educator*
Erfani, Shervin *academic administrator, engineering educator*
Espiricueta, Sylvia *counseling administrator*
Essegaier, Skander *education educator, researcher*
Estes, Laurie Lynn *educational program developer and administrator*
Evans, Bonita Dianne *adult education educator*
Evans, Geraldine Ann *academic administrator*
Evans, James Handel *university administrator, architect, educator*
Evans, Margaret Utz *secondary school educator*
Evosevich, Carey Lynn *elementary school educator, music educator*
Falk, Marshall Allen *retired university dean, physician*
Farquhar, Robin Hugh *former university president*
Feldstein, Joshua *educational administrator*
Felicetti, Daniel A. *academic administrator*
Felix, Arthur Martin *chemistry educator, researcher*
Fernández-Velazquez, Juan Ramon *university chancellor*
Field, Michael Jay *education educator*
Fietzer, William Harold *school librarian, writer*
Fife, Jonathan Donald *education educator*
Filchock, Ethel *education educator*
Filomeno, Linda Jean Harvey *elementary school educator*
Fink, Alma *retired elementary education educator*
Fishburn, Janet Forsythe *university dean*
Fleury, Paul Aimé *university dean, physicist*
Foldesi, Robert Stephen *education administrator, management educator*
Ford, Loretta C. *retired dean, educator, consultant, nurse*
Forney, Ronald Dean *elementary school educator, consultant, educational therapist*
Foronda, Elena Isabel *secondary school educator*
Forsyth, Ben Ralph *academic administrator, medical educator*
Foutris, Christine S. *secondary school educator*
Frankel, Albert J. *registrar*
Franklin, Billy Joe *international higher education specialist*
Franklin, Mary Ann Wheeler *educator, higher education and management consultant*
Freeman, Meredith Norwin *former college president, education educator*
Frick, Ivan Eugene *college president emeritus, education consultant*
Fricklas, Richard Leon *roofing educator, educational institute administrator*
Frost, Everett Lloyd *anthropologist, academic administrator*
Fuller, Maxine Compton *retired secondary school educator*
Fullerton, Gail Jackson *retired academic administrator*
Gabel, Katherine *retired academic administrator*
Gamsky, Neal Richard *academic administrator, psychology educator*
Garcia, Julia Theresa *secondary school educator*
Garcia-Mely, Rafael *retired education educator*
Gardner, David Chambers *adult education educator, psychologist, business executive, author*
Garner, Doris Traganza *education educator, director*
Genovese, Vincent James *educational consultant*
Gibson, Lisette L. *elementary school educator, music educator*
Gillis, Malcolm (Stephen Gillis) *former academic administrator*
Giusti, Joseph Paul *retired academic administrator, consultant*
Glasser, Charles Edward *university president emeritus*
Glaze, Lynn Ferguson *development consultant*
Glennen, Robert Eugene, Jr., *retired university president*
Gleue, Lorine Anna *elementary school educator*
Glismann, Clementine *elementary school educator, researcher*
Goerke, Glenn Allen *university administrator*
Goertz, Roger Lamar *retired education counselor*
Goetz, Jack Ralph *dean*
Goff, Jane E. *secondary school educator*
Goode, Janet Weiss *elementary school educator*
Goodman, Lillian Rachel *retired dean, nursing educator*
Goodman, Rebecca Gruver *education educator, writer*
Goodrich, Kenneth Paul *retired college dean*
Goodsell, Charles True *retired educator*
Gordis, David Moses *academic administrator, rabbi*
Gore, Carolyn Williams Gardner *special education educator, reading specialist*
Gorman, Joseph Batterton *elementary school educator*
Gorsuch, Edward Lee *former chancellor*
Graff, Arthur Steven *educational consultant*
Graves, Wallace Billingsley *retired university executive*
Gray, Richard Moss *retired college president*
Grebstein, Sheldon Norman *university administrator*
Green, Patricia Pataky *school system administrator, consultant*
Greenberg, Raymond Seth *academic administrator, educator, health facility administrator*
Greenway, Joan M. *dean*
Grey, Robert Dean *academic administrator, biology educator*
Groves, Bernice Ann *retired elementary and secondary school coordinator, educator*
Gruberg, Cy *educational administrator*
Guerrero, Olive Ciridon *retired educator, civic worker*
Gunning, Carolyn Sue *dean, provost, nursing educator*
Guskin, Alan E. *university president*
Gustafson, Richard Alrick *university president emeritus*
Haaland, Gordon Arthur *former academic administrator*
Haas, Carolyn Buhai *elementary education educator, publisher, writer, consultant*
Haden, Clovis Roland *retired academic administrator, engineering educator*
Hadley, William Melvin *retired dean*
Hagan, Joseph Henry *higher education consultant*
Hageman, Richard Philip, Jr., *educational administrator*
Hall, Kathryn Marie *elementary school educator*
Hall, Zach Winter *academic administrator*
Hamlet, Richard Graham *education educator, researcher*
Hammer, Joyce Mae *gifted and talented education educator*
Hampton, Nanette Davina *private school educator, writer*
Han, Xianlin *education educator, consultant*
Haneke, Dianne Myers *retired education educator*
Hardage, Page Taylor *elementary school educator*
Harding, Robert William *academic administrator*
Harper, Janet Sutherlin Lane *retired educational administrator, writer*
Harrington, Jean Patrice *college president*
Harris, Ann *elementary school teacher*
Harris, Dolores M. *retired academic administrator, adult education educator*
Harris, Merle Wiener *college administrator, educator*
Harrison, Earl Grant, Jr., *educational administrator*
Harrison, Neil David *education educator*
Hart, James Warren *retired academic administrator, retired professional football player*
Hartley, Philip. L. *academic administrator, psychology educator*
Haskin, Larry Allen *academic administrator, geochemist, educator*
Hasselmo, Nils *academic administrator, linguistics educator*
Hatfield, Jane Stauff *secondary school educator*
Haugland, Susan Warrell *education educator, consultant*
Haupt, Patricia A. *principal*
Hawkins, Brian L. *academic administrator, educator*
Haynes, Cheryl Lynn *secondary school educator*
Hazel, Mary Belle *university administrator*
Heaggans, Raphael Chesare *education educator*
Heap, Sylvia Stuber *adult education educator*
Heck, James Baker *retired education educator*
Heidenfelder, Kathryn M. *educational administrator*
Heinrichs, Mary Ann *former dean*
Helm, Peyton Randolph *academic administrator, educator*
Helman, Alfred Blair *retired college president, education consultant*
Henderson, Catherine Lynn *retired secondary education educator, writer*
Henley, Robert Lee *school system administrator*
Henry, Robert E. *dean, educator*
Hensley, Patricia Drake *principal*
Hereford, Pamela Ann *elementary school educator*
Herensztat, Greta *retired elementary school educator*
Herf, Jeffrey *education educator, writer*
Herge, Donna Carol *secondary school educator*
Herge, Henry Curtis, Sr., *education educator, dean emeritus*
Hernandez, Gema G. *education educator, consultant*
Hersh, Richard H. *academic administrator*
Hertel, Suzanne Marie *training and development specialist*
Hext, Kathleen Florence *college administrator*
Hill, Emita Brady *academic administrator, consultant*
Hill, Jerry Dean *secondary school educator*
Hill, Virgil Lusk, Jr., *academic administrator, naval officer*
Hilsabeck, Larry L. *education educator*
Hing, Barbara Lim *elementary school educator, assistant principal, data processing executive*
Hiraldo, Carlos *education educator, poet*
Hitchcock, Walter Anson *educational consultant, retired educational administrator*
Hixson, Marcia Jeanne *retired educational administrator*
Hoffman, Judy Greenblatt *preschool director*
Hoffman, Neil James *academic administrator*
Hoffsis, Glen F. *dean*
Hogue, James Larry *retired academic administrator, business executive*
Holcomb, Mildred Geneva Comrie *elementary school educator*
Holgate, George Jackson *university president*
Hooper, Henry Olcott *retired academic administrator, physicist*
Hopkins, Kevin W. *education educator*
Hopp, Phillip Edward *gifted and talented educator*
Hopping, Richard Lee *college president emeritus*
Horner, Matina Souretis *retired academic administrator, corporate financial executive*
Horst, Jason Matthew *director*
House, Ernest Robert *education educator, educational evaluator*
Houseman, Ann Elizabeth Lord *educational administrator, state official*
Howard, Diane Elizabeth *education educator, consultant*
Hubbard, Robert Glenn *academic administrator, former federal agency administrator*
Huffman, Durward Roy *college system official, electrical engineer*
Huffman, Janice Kay *middle school educator, curriculum coordinator*
Hughes, Paul *elementary school educator*
Huie, Carol P. *information systems educator*
Hull, Louise Knox *retired elementary educator, administrator*
Hull, McAllister Hobart, Jr., *retired university administrator*
Huntsman, Lee L. *former academic administrator, director*
Hurlbut, Geraldine *retired elementary education educator*
Hurley, Mary Jo *elementary school educator, gas industry executive*
Huttenback, Robert Arthur *academic administrator, educator*
Inniss, Morgan Z. *director*
Insalaco-De Nigris, Anna Maria Theresa *middle school educator*
Iverson, Thomas Edwin *retired academic administrator, mathematician, educator*
Ivey, Lisa Ann *elementary school educator*
Jack, Patricia Ann *assistant principal*
Jackson, Grace Louise *education educator, writer*
Jackson, Miles Merrill *retired university dean*
Jacobowitz, Chana M. *director*
Jakubauskas, Edward Benedict *college president*
Janeway, Richard *retired academic administrator*
Jean, Claudette R. *retired elementary school educator*
Jenkins, Brenda Gwenetta *early childhood and special education specialist*
Jenkins, Sebetha *college president*
Johnson, Linda Sue *academic administrator, state agency administrator, retired state legislator*
Johnson, Melvin *academic administrator, economist*
Johnson, Sylvia Sue *university administrator, educator*
Jones, Lawrence Neale *university dean, minister*
Jordan, James Lowell *educator, writer*
Kanada, Gary N. Kahaho'omalu *adult education educator*
Kappner, Augusta Souza *academic administrator*
Keebler, Lois Marie *elementary school educator*
Keiper, Marilyn Morrison *elementary school educator*
Kelley, Patricia Colleen *education educator, researcher*
Kelly, Sister Dorothy Ann *Ursuline Provincial college chancellor*
Kempner, Maximilian Walter *law school dean, lawyer*
Kennedy, Christopher *director*
Keohane, Nannerl Overholser *university president emerita, political scientist*
Kern, Charles William *retired university official, chemistry educator*
Keskinocak, Pinar *adult education educator*
Ketron, Carrie Sue *secondary school educator*
Keyes, Joan Ross Rafter *education educator, writer*
Khan, Maryam *educator*
King, John Ethelbert, Jr., *retired academic administrator*
King, Maxwell Clark *former academic administrator*
Kinney, Michele A. *education educator, lawyer*
Kinney, Thomas J. John *adult education educator*
Kirk, Rea Helene (Rea Helene Glazer) *special education educator*
Klein, Irma Molligan *career planning administrator, consultant*
Klein, Mary Ann *special education educator*

Warder, Richard Currey, Jr., *dean, mechanical aerospace engineering educator*
Watkins, Esther Sherrod *secondary school educator, school librarian*
Watts, John Ransford *university administrator*
Watts, Mary Ann *retired elementary education educator*
Webb, Robert David *school system administrator*
Weintraub, Sam *reading educator*
Weir, Morton Webster *retired academic administrator, educator*
Wendt, Marilynn Suzann *elementary school educator, principal*
Werner, Robert Joseph *dean, music educator*
Wernet, Patricia A. *director*
Westfall, Jeffrey N. *education educator*
Weston, Rebecca Lynn *forensic educator*
Wheeler, David Laurie *university dean*
White, Christine Allen *elementary school educator*
White, Daniel Ernest *headmaster, educator, consultant*
White, John Wesley, Jr., *retired academic administrator*
Whitehead, Janice *secondary school educator*
Whiting, Lucille Drake *retired elementary school educator, consultant*
Wilkening, Laurel Lynn *academic administrator, planetary scientist*
Williams, Deberrah Deithrisha *elementary school educator, researcher*
Williams, Lewis T. (Rusty Williams) *education educator*
Wilson, Carolyn Ross *retired school system administrator*
Wilson, Cheryl Yvonne *elementary school educator, secondary school educator*
Wilson, Robin Scott *retired academic administrator, writer*
Wilson, Samuel V. *academic administrator*
Wimmer, Kathryn *retired elementary school educator*
Winborne, Sheila Faye *academic administrator*
Wingham, Erma Doris *secondary school educator*
Winterstein, James Fredrick *academic administrator*
Wiseman, Douglas Carl *education educator, department chairman, dean*
Wogen, Cathy Lynn *academic director*
Wolf, Edith Maletz *retired educator*
Wolfe, James Michael *education educator, researcher*
Wong, David Yue *academic administrator, physics educator*
Woodruff, Mary Brennan *elementary school educator, educator*
Woodsworth, Anne *university administrator, librarian*
Woolworth, Susan Valk *primary school educator*
Worthen, John Edward *retired academic administrator*
Wright, Dixie Lee *special needs persons consultant*
Wright, Ethel *secondary school educator*
Wright, Jacquelyn Dianne *special education educator, performing arts educator*
Wyatt, Brett Michael *secondary school educator*
Yang, Dennis Tao *education educator*
Yates, William Tennyson, II, *educational consultant, management consultant*
Young, Amy Y. *school librarian, writer*
Young, Charles Edward *former academic administrator*
Young, Ruth Brooks *retired elementary education educator*
Young, Teresa Gail Hilger *retired adult education educator*
Young, Virgil Monroe *education educator*
Zacharias, Donald Wayne *academic administrator*
Zahner, Dorothy Simkin *elementary school educator*
Zdanis, Richard Albert *academic administrator*
Zeilinger, Elna Rae *elementary educator, gifted-talented education educator*
Zilbert, Allen Bruce *education educator, computer consultant*
Zufryden, Fred S. *academic administrator, marketing educator, researcher*

ENGINEERING

UNITED STATES

ALABAMA

Andalusia
Grantham, Charles Edward *broadcast engineer*

Auburn
Clement, T. Prabhakar *computer engineer, educator*
Cochran, John Euell, Jr., *aerospace engineer, educator, lawyer*
Crocker, Malcolm John *mechanical engineer, noise control engineer, educator*
Haneman, Vincent Siering, Jr., *consulting engineer, educator, university dean*
Hanley, Thomas Richard *engineering educator*
Irwin, John David *electrical engineering educator*
Jaeger, Richard Charles *electrical engineer, educator, science center director*
Sforzini, Richard Henry *aerospace engineer, educator*

Birmingham
Edmonds, William Fleming *retired engineering and construction company executive*
Flakes, Larry Joseph *civil engineer*
Goldman, Jay *industrial engineer, educator, former dean*
Goodrich, Thomas Michael *engineering and construction executive, lawyer*
Parma, Edward Scott *engineer, surgeon*
Potter, John Leith *mechanical and aerospace engineer, educator, consultant*
Sain, Charles (Hack Sain) *civil engineer, surveyor*
Uddin, Nasim *civil engineer, educator*

Daphne
Jeffreys, Elystan Geoffrey *geological engineer, petroleum consultant and appraiser, gemologist*

Decatur
Smith, Troy Alvin *aerospace research engineer*

Florence
Badger, Phillip Charles *agricultural engineer*

Fort Rucker
Fraser, Stuart *engineer*

Huntsville
Archuleta, Nancy E. *engineering executive*
Bendickson, Marcus J. *engineering company executive*
Daussman, Grover Frederick *electrical engineer, consultant*
Hunter, Herbert Erwin *aerospace engineer*
Mazumder, Sandip *engineer, researcher*
Moore, Fletcher Brooks *retired engineering company executive*
Morgan, John Derald *electrical engineer*
Pastrick, Harold Lee *aeronautical engineer*
Pittman, William Claude *electrical engineer*
Reece, Wanda G. *space station training engineer, writer*
Sackheim, Robert Lewis *aerospace engineer, educator*
Schroer, Bernard Jon *industrial engineering educator*
Stephenson, Arthur G. *aerospace engineer*
Vaughan, Otha H., Jr., *retired aerospace engineer*
Watson, Raymond Coke, Jr., *engineering executive, academic administrator*
Wu, Susan Ying Chu Lin (Ying-chu Lin) *engineering company executive, engineer*

Loachapoka
Schafer, Robert Louis *agricultural engineer, researcher*

Madison
Dannenberg, Konrad K. *aeronautical engineer*
Emerson, William Kary *engineering company executive*

Mobile
Hamid, Michael *electrical engineering educator, consultant*
Hsiao, Kuang-Ting *mechanical engineer, educator, researcher*
Perry, Nelson Allen *retired radiation safety engineer, radiological consultant*

Montgomery
Pan, Chai-Fu *engineering educator*

Somerville
Johnson, Loyd *agricultural engineer, researcher*

Spanish Fort
van Aken, John Henry *retired marine surveyor, engineer, consultant*

Thomasville
Davis, Gene *retired civil engineer*

Tuscaloosa
Barfield, Robert F. *retired mechanical engineer, educator, dean*
Bryan, Colgan Hobson *aerospace engineering educator*
Fonseca, Daniel J. *engineering educator*
Greene, Timothy James *industrial engineering educator*
Griffin, Marvin Anthony *industrial engineer, educator*
Morley, Lloyd Albert *electrical engineering educator*
Moynihan, Gary Peter *industrial engineering educator*
Polites, Michael Edward *aerospace engineer, educator*
Ray, Paul S. *engineering educator, researcher*

ALASKA

Anchorage
Baker, Grant Cody *civil engineering educator*
Mandell, Gordon Keith *aerospace engineer*
Pressley, James Ray *electrical engineer*
Thomas, Howard Paul *civil engineer, consultant*

Fairbanks
Tilsworth, Timothy *retired environmental/civil engineering educator*

ARIZONA

Apache Junction
Campbell, John Carl *retired engineering educator*

Chandler
Fordemwalt, James Newton *microelectronics engineering educator, consultant*
Meieran, Eugene Stuart *material scientist*

Flagstaff
Collins, Galen Robert *technology educator*

Gilbert
Stephenson, Frank Alex *engineer, consultant*

Goodyear
Taylor, Richard L., Jr., *engineer, consultant*

Hereford
Hirth, John Price *metallurgical engineering educator*

Lake Havasu City
Hurt, Nathan Hampton, Jr., *mechanical engineer*

Mesa
Baxter, Gene Kenneth *mechanical engineer, engineering company executive*
Burgess, Robert Kingsley *aeronautical engineer*
Rummel, Robert Wiland *aeronautical engineer, writer*

Paradise Valley
Ratkowski, Donald J. *mechanical engineer, consultant*
Russell, Paul Edgar *electrical engineering educator*

Phoenix
Bachus, Benson Floyd *mechanical engineer, consultant*
Blevins, Willard Ahart *electrical engineer*
Freyermuth, Clifford L. *structural engineering consultant*
Miller, Michael Jon *survey engineer*
Quddus, Mohammed Tanvir *electrical engineer, researcher*
Ragland, Samuel Connelly *industrial engineer, management consultant*
Sochacki, Andrzej *mechanical engineer, researcher, tourism educator*

Prescott
Bieniawski, Zdzislaw Tadeusz Richard *engineering educator emeritus, writer, consultant*
Chesson, Eugene *civil engineering educator, consultant*
Kahne, Stephen James *systems engineer, educator, academic administrator, engineering executive*

Scottsdale
Cai, Weizhong (Will) *electronics engineer, researcher, physicist*
Fisher, John Richard *engineering consultant, former naval officer*
Gilson, Arnold Leslie *retired engineering executive, consultant*
Gookin, Thomas Allen Jaudon *civil engineer*
Jeffe, Sidney David *automotive engineer*

Sun City
Davies, Percy (Pete) Charles *mechanical engineer*
Tijmann, Willem Bert *civil engineer, consultant*
Vander Molen, Jack Jacobus *engineering executive, industrial facility planner, consultant*

Sun City West
Brown, Ruth Geisler *engineering supervisor*

Tempe
Balanis, Constantine Apostle *electrical engineering educator*
Berman, Neil Sheldon *chemical engineering educator*
Black, John Arthur, Jr., *electrical engineer, computer scientist, publisher*
Carpenter, Ray Warren *materials scientist and engineer, educator*
Chawla, Nikhilesh *engineering educator*
Chiriac, Victor Adrian *aerospace engineer, researcher*
Ferry, David Keane *electrical engineering educator*
Harris, Warren Lynn *computer engineer*
Karady, George Gyorgy *electrical engineering educator, consultant*
Mays, Larry W. *civil engineering educator, hydrologist*
Morrison, John Haddow, Jr., *engineering company executive*
Robertson, Samuel Harry, III, *transportation safety research engineer, educator*
Schroder, Dieter Karl *electrical engineering educator*
Shah, Jami J. *mechanical engineering educator, researcher*
Shaw, Milton Clayton *mechanical engineering educator*
Tseng, Ampere An-Pei *mechanical engineer, educator, administrator*

Tucson
Arnell, Walter James William *engineering educator, consultant*
Bjorhovde, Reidar *structural engineer, educator*
Brunton, Daniel William *mechanical engineer*
Contractor, Dinshaw N. *civil engineer, educator*
Cook, Paul Christopher *engineering psychologist*
Eigel, James Anthony *environmental engineer*
Gaither, William Samuel *civil engineering executive, consultant*
Ganapol, Barry Douglas *nuclear engineering educator, consultant*
Harrington, Roger Fuller *electrical engineering educator, consultant*
Jones, Roger Clyde *retired electrical engineering educator*
Kececioglu, Dimitri Basil *reliability engineering educator, consultant*
Kerwin, William James *electrical engineering educator, consultant*
Mense, Allan Tate *research and development engineering executive*
Ogilvie, T(homas) Francis *engineer, educator*
Prince, John Luther, III, *engineering educator*
Slack, Donald Carl *agricultural engineer, educator*
Smerdon, Ernest Thomas *engineering educator*
Wyant, James Clair *engineering company executive, educator*

ARKANSAS

Black Rock
Plunkett, Joseph Charles *electrical engineer, consultant*

Fayetteville
Andrews, John Frank *civil and environmental engineering educator*
Gaddy, James Leoma *chemical engineer, educator*
LeFevre, Elbert Walter, Jr., *civil engineering educator*
Rossetti, Manuel David *engineering educator, consultant*

Hot Springs National Park
Ray, Arliss Dean *retired environmental consultant*

Little Rock
Bhattacharyya, Abhijit *engineering educator*

CALIFORNIA

Aliso Viejo
Boeckmann, Alan L. *engineering and construction management company executive*

Alpine
Doliber, Darrel Lee *retired engineering consultant, innkeeper*
Roberts, Dwight Loren *engineering consultant, writer*

Altadena
Coles, Donald Earl *retired aeronautics educator*

Anaheim
Elchert, Kenneth Clarence *aerospace engineer*
Gaglani, Jitendra A. *aerospace engineer*
Uyehara, Otto Arthur *mechanical engineering educator emeritus, consultant*
Watson, Oliver Lee, III, *aerospace engineering manager*

Antioch
Granik, Vladimir *mechanics researcher, educator*

Arroyo Grande
Hoffmann, Jon Arnold *retired aeronautical engineer, educator*

Atherton
Lowry, Larry Lorn *engineering company executive*
Morel-Seytoux, Hubert Jean *civil engineer, educator*

Benicia
Farnham, Timothy *training and education administrator*

Berkeley
Bajcsy, Ruzena *computer engineer*
Birdsall, Charles Kennedy *electrical engineer*
Bogy, David B(eauregard) *mechanical engineering educator*
Cairns, Elton James *chemical engineering educator*
Dornfeld, David Alan *engineering educator*
Filippou, Filip C. *engineering educator*
Frisch, Joseph *mechanical engineer, educator, consultant*
Fuerstenau, Douglas Winston *mineral engineering educator*
Garrison, William Louis *civil engineering educator*
Greif, Ralph *mechanical engineer, educator*
Hodges, David Albert *electrical engineering educator*
Hsu, Chieh Su *applied mechanics engineering educator, researcher*
Kastenberg, William Edward *engineering educator, science educator*
Kuh, Ernest Shiu-Jen *electrical engineering educator*
Leitmann, George *mechanical engineer, educator*
Lewis, Edwin Reynolds *biomedical engineering educator*
May, Adolf Darlington *civil engineering educator*
McMains, Sara A. *engineering educator*
Monismith, Carl Leroy *civil engineering educator*
Muller, Richard Stephen *electrical engineer, educator*
Newman, John Scott *chemical engineer, educator*
Newton, A. Richard *engineering educator*
Ott, David Michael *engineering company executive*
Pagni, Patrick John *mechanical and fire safety engineering science educator*
Pawsey, Stuart Frederick *structural engineer, retired*
Penzien, Joseph *structural engineering educator*
Pigford, Thomas Harrington *nuclear engineering educator*
Pister, Karl Stark *engineering educator*
Polak, Elijah *engineering educator, computer scientist*
Rakas, Jasenka Milan *aviation engineer*
Schultz, E. Eugene, Jr., *computer engineer*
Whinnery, John Roy *electrical engineer, educator*
White, Richard Manning *electrical engineering educator*
Wiegel, Robert Louis *consulting engineering executive*
Xi, Xuemei *electrical engineer, researcher*
Yeung, Ronald Wai-Chun *engineering educator, researcher*

Berry Creek
Miller, Joseph Arthur *manufacturing engineer, consultant*

Beverly Hills
Dragan, Alexandra *mechanical engineer, consultant, environmental engineer, researcher, engineering educator*

Brea
Brown, Ronald Malcolm *engineering corporation executive*

Brentwood
Rawson, Eric Gordon *optical engineer*

Buellton
Porter, Bruce Jackman *military engineer, computer software engineer, application developer, investment broker, civil engineer*

Buena Park
Wiersema, Harold LeRoy *aerospace engineer*

Burbank
Granlund, Thomas Arthur *engineering executive, consultant*

Calabasas
Moule, William Nelson *electrical engineer, consultant*

Campbell
Levy, Salomon *mechanical engineer*
Ross, Hugh Courtney *electrical engineer*

Carlsbad
Nahavandi, Amir Nezameddin *retired engineering firm executive*

Carmel
Alsberg, Dietrich Anselm *electrical engineer, consultant*

Youngdahl, Paul Frederick *mechanical engineer*

Cayucos
Theurer, Byron W. *aerospace engineer, business owner*

Chatsworth
Levine, Arnold Milton *retired electrical engineer, documentary filmmaker*

Chico
Allen, Charles William *mechanical engineering educator*

Claremont
Dym, Clive Lionel *engineering educator*
Molinder, John Irving *engineering educator, consultant*
Monson, James Edward *electrical engineer, educator*
Presecan, Nicholas Lee *environmental and civil engineer, consultant*
Tanenbaum, Basil Samuel *engineering educator*

Clovis
Brahma, Chandra Sekhar *civil engineering educator*

Compton
Wang, Charles Ping *engineering executive*

Concord
Crandall, Ira Carlton *consulting electrical engineer*
Lee, Low Kee *electronics engineer, consultant*
Middleton, Michael John *civil engineer*

Cool
Trybul, Theodore Nicholas *engineering educator*

Corona
Tillman, Joseph Nathaniel *engineering executive*

Coronado
Crilly, Eugene Richard *engineering consultant*

Corte Madera
Scott, John Walter *chemical engineer, research management executive*

Coto De Caza
Sheehy, Jerome Joseph *electrical engineer*

Crockett
Leporiere, Ralph Dennis *retired quality engineer*

Cupertino
Chung, Jin Soo *ocean mining and ocean engineer*
Edson, William Alden *retired electrical engineer, researcher*
Fan, Chien *aerospace engineer, researcher*
Lam, Cheung-Wei *electrical engineer*

Dana Point
Olvera, Carlos Nelson *mechanical engineer, executive*

Davis
Akesson, Norman Berndt *agricultural engineer, emeritus educator*
Bellie, Sivakumar *engineer, researcher*
Brandt, Harry *mechanical engineering educator*
Chancellor, William Joseph *agricultural engineering educator*
Chang, Daniel Pan Yih *environmental engineering educator*
Cheney, James Addison *civil engineering educator*
Hess, Ronald Andrew *aerospace engineer, educator*
Kavvas, M. Levent *civil engineering educator*
Krener, Arthur J. *systems engineering educator*
Marino, Miguel Angel *engineering educator*
Pan, Ning *engineering educator*
Sperling, Daniel *engineering educator, transportation studies director*
Tchobanoglous, George *civil engineering educator*
Wang, Shih-Ho *electrical engineer, educator*

Del Mar
Wilkinson, Eugene Parks *nuclear engineer, director*

Desert Hot Springs
Halasz, Stephen Joseph *retired electro-optical systems engineer*

Diamond Bar
Mirisola, Lisa Heinemann *air quality engineer*

Dinuba
Leps, Thomas MacMaster *civil engineer, consultant*

Downey
Baumann, Theodore Robert *aerospace engineer, consultant, military officer*

Edwards AFB
Baer-Riedhart, Jenny *aeronautical engineer*

El Cerrito
Wilson, Edward Lawrence *civil engineer, educator, structural engineering consultant*

El Segundo
Abbassian-Kashi, Mandana *industrial engineer, systems engineer*
Agrawal, Suphal P. *engineering company executive*
Bauer, Jerome Leo, Jr., *chemical engineer*
Jacobs, Michael Moises *aerospace engineer, consultant*
McDonald, Rosa Nell *engineering executive*
Puckett, Allen Emerson *aeronautical engineer*
Rosen, Harold A. *retired aeronautical engineer*
Sterling, Warren Martin *engineering director*
Webb, Darryl Willard *systems engineer*

Emeryville
Zwoyer, Eugene Milton *retired consulting engineering executive*

Encinitas
Frank, Michael Victor *risk assessment engineer*

Encino
Friedman, George Jerry *aerospace engineer, engineering executive*
Knuth, Eldon Luverne *engineering educator*

Escondido
Ellenberger, William Joseph *retired engineering consultant*
Ghandhi, Sorab Khushro *electrical engineering educator*
Grew, Raymond Edward *mechanical engineer*
Kennedy, Robert Philip *civil engineer*
Pantos, William Pantazes *mechanical engineer, consultant*

Fair Oaks
Agerbek, Sven *mechanical engineer*

Fallbrook
Harsha, Philip Thomas *retired aerospace engineer*

Folsom
Ettlich, William F. *electrical engineer*
Majorkumar, Govindaraju *human factors engineer*
Ryu, Woong Hwan *electrical engineer*

Foster City
Ham, Lee Edward *civil engineer*

Fountain Valley
Hosokawa, Koichi *engineering company executive*

Fremont
Chen, Wai-Kai *electrical engineering and computer science educator, consultant*
Duan, Xiaodong *engineer*
Engelbart, Doug *engineering executive*
Fotouhi, Bahram *electrical engineer*
Majumder, Sabir Ahmed *process engineer*
Mian, Guo *electrical engineer*
Ramirez-Mireles, Fernando *electrical engineer*
Wu, James Chen-Yuan *aerospace engineering educator*

Fresno
Ransom, Gaylord Rick *structural engineer*

Fullerton
Bradburn, David Denison *engineer, retired air force officer*
Rao, Prasada *engineering educator*
Tehrani, Fleur Taher *electrical engineer, educator, researcher*

Gardena
Stuart, Jay William *retired engineer*

Glendale
Knoop, Vern Thomas *civil engineer, consultant*

Glendora
Haile, Benjamin Carroll, Jr., *retired chemical engineer, retired mechanical engineer*

Goleta
Lea, Wayne Adair *electrical engineer, linguist*
Sullivan, Kevin Joseph *mechanical engineer*

Granite Bay
Hunnicutt, Richard Pearce *metallurgical engineer*

Hacienda Heights
Love, Daniel Joseph *consulting engineer*

Hawthorne
McRuer, Duane Torrance *aerospace engineering executive*

Hermosa Beach
Teshirogi, Jerry Takahide *aerospace engineer*

Hollywood
Mkhitarian, Marine *chemical engineer*

Huntington Beach
Grooms, Henry Randall *civil engineer*
Leveton, Ian Sinclair *civil engineer*
Nash, Richard Eugene *aerospace engineer*
Nguyen, Han Van *mechanical engineer*
Stillman, Alfred William, Jr., *electrical engineer*

Indian Wells
Jorgensen, Gordon David *retired engineering company executive*

Irvine
Ang, Alfredo Hua-Sing *civil engineering educator*
Chang, Ying Chih *engineering educator, researcher*
Chelapati, Chunduri Venkata *civil engineering educator*
Lin, Amy Yuh-Mei *industrial engineer, real estate investor*
Orme, Melissa Emily *mechanical engineering educator*
Samueli, Henry *electrical engineering educator, entrepreneur*
Sirignano, William Alfonso *aerospace and mechanical engineer, educator*
Stubberud, Allen Roger *electrical engineering educator*
Ting, Albert Chia *bioengineering researcher*
Xu, Tao *electrical engineer, biomedical researcher*
Zabsky, John Mitchell *engineering executive*

Irwindale
Lu, Guiyang *electrical engineer*

Kensington
Oppenheim, Antoni Kazimierz *mechanical engineer*

La Canada Flintridge
Macmillan, Robert Smith *electronics engineer*

La Crescenta
Otoshi, Tom Yasuo *electrical engineer, consultant*

La Jolla
Chang, William Shen Chie *electrical engineering educator*
Chien, Shu *physiology and bioengineering educator*
Coler, Myron A(braham) *chemical engineer, educator*
Counts, Stanley Thomas *retired naval officer, retired electronics company executive*
Elgamal, Ahmed *geotechnical and structural engineering educator*
Fung, Yuan-Cheng Bertram *bioengineering educator, writer*
Hall, Harold Robert *retired computer engineer*
Karin, Sidney *computer science and engineering educator*
Levy, Ralph *engineering executive, consultant*
Lubarda, Vlado *mechanical engineer, researcher, educator*
Milstein, Laurence Bennett *electrical engineering educator, researcher*
Penner, Stanford Solomon *engineering educator*
Rudee, Mervyn Lea *engineering educator, researcher*
Saldivar, Enrique *bioengineer, researcher*
Schmid-Schoenbein, Geert Wilfried Wilfried *biomedical engineer, educator*
Williams, Forman Arthur *engineering science educator, combustion theorist*
Wolf, Jack Keil *electrical engineer, educator*

Lafayette
Krueger, Robert Edward *manufacturing executive, mechanical engineer*
Peirano, Lawrence Edward *civil engineer*

Laguna Hills
Hammond, R. Philip *chemical engineer*

Laguna Niguel
Eber, Lorenz *aeronautical engineer, civil engineer*

Laguna Woods
Waaland, Irving Theodore *retired aerospace design executive*

Lancaster
Hodges, Vernon Wray *mechanical engineer*

Livermore
Johnson, Roy Ragnar *electrical engineer, researcher*
King, Ray John *electrical engineer, educator, business executive*
Yoh, Jack Jai-ick *mechanical engineer*

Lomita
Balcom, Orville *engineer*

Lompoc
Means, James Andrew *engineer*

Long Beach
Davis, Mark Hezekiah, Jr., *electrical engineer*
Dillon, Michael Earl *engineering executive, mechanical engineer, educator*
Kumar, Rajendra *electrical engineering educator*
Moroso, Michael Joseph *aerospace engineer*

Los Alamitos
Eckelman, Richard Joel *engineering specialist*

Los Altos
Carlson, Warren Ore *civil engineer, consultant*
Gough, William Cabot *engineer*
Moll, John Lewis *retired electronics engineer*
Peterson, Victor Lowell *aerospace engineer, consultant*
Sharpe, Roland Leonard *structural engineer, consultant*
Zebroski, Edwin Leopold *risk management consultant*

Los Altos Hills
Fondahl, John Walker *civil engineering educator*

Los Angeles
Ballhaus, William Francis, Jr., *aerospace industry executive, research scientist*
Buffington, Gary Lee Roy *safety engineer, construction executive*
Cheng, Tsen-Chung *electrical engineering educator*
Chobotov, Vladimir Alexander *aerospace engineer, educator*
Crombie, Douglass Darnill *aerospace communications system engineer*
Danziger, Bruce Edward *structural engineer*
Dhir, Vijay K. *mechanical engineering educator*
Dorman, Albert A. *consulting engineer executive, architect*
Friedlander, Sheldon Kay *chemical engineering educator*
Hovanessian, Shahen Alexander *electrical engineer, educator, consultant*
Incaudo, Joseph August *engineering company executive*
Itoh, Tatsuo *engineering educator*
Jacobson, Marcus J. *retired mechanical engineer*
Jacoby, Neil Herman, Jr., *astronautical engineer, scientific consultant*
James, William Langford *aerospace engineer*
Johnston, Roy G. *consulting structural engineer*
Ju, Jiann-Wen *mechanics educator, researcher*
Kelly, Robert Edward *engineer, educator*
Kim, Jeongbin John *mechanical engineering educator*
King-Ning, Tu *materials science and engineering educator*
Kuang, Jun *aeronautical engineer, researcher, fluid mechanics engineer*
Kuehl, Hans Henry *electrical engineering educator*
Lavine, Adrienne Gail *mechanical engineering educator*
Leal, George D. *engineering company executive*
Lin, Tung Hua *civil engineering educator*
Marmarelis, Vasilis Zissis *engineering educator, writer, consultant*
Martin, J(ohn) Edward *architectural engineer*
Maxworthy, Tony *mechanical and aerospace engineering educator*
Mendel, Jerry Marc *electrical engineering educator*
Muntz, Eric Phillip *aerospace and mechanical engineering and radiology educator, consultant*
Newman, Richard G. *engineering company executive*
Nobe, Ken *chemical engineering educator*
Okrent, David *engineering educator*
O'Neill, Russell Richard *engineering educator*
Parker, Alice Cline *computer engineering educator, consultant*
Perrine, Richard Leroy *environmental engineer, educator*
Ramo, Simon *retired engineering executive*
Rauch, Lawrence Lee *aerospace and electrical engineer, educator*
Robson, Glenn R. *engineering and design company executive*
Rubinstein, Moshe Fajwel *engineering educator*
Russell, Joseph Allen *instrumentation and controls engineer, consultant*
Safadi, Mohammad Oussama *engineering educator*
Safonov, Michael George *electrical engineering educator, consultant*
Scholtz, Robert Arno *electrical engineering educator*
Settles, F. Stan, Jr., *engineering educator, manufacturing executive*
Sklansky, Jack *electrical and computer engineering educator, researcher*
Udwadia, Firdaus Erach *engineering educator, consultant*
Vesely, Ivan *biomedical engineer*
Wagner, Christian Nikolaus Johann *materials engineering educator*
Weber, Charles L. *electrical engineering educator*
Welch, Lloyd Richard *electrical engineering educator, communications consultant*
Willner, Alan Eli *electrical engineer, educator*
Yablonovitch, Eli *electrical engineering educator*
Yan, Lianshan *optical engineer, scientist*
Yang, Fan *electrical engineering research scientist*
Yen, Teh Fu *civil and environmental engineering educator*

Los Banos
York, Courtney Carter *retired engineering executive, genealogist*

Los Gatos
Kazan, Benjamin *research engineer*
Naymark, Sherman *consulting nuclear engineer*
Rosenheim, Donald Edwin *electrical engineer*

Malibu
Ancker, Clinton James, Jr., *emeritus systems and industrial engineering educator*
Bedrosian, Edward *electrical engineer*
Kirby, Deborah Janice *electrical engineer, researcher*

Marina del Rey
Abebe, Henok *engineer, researcher*

Martinez
Sepulveda, Eduardo Solideo *chemical engineer*

Menifee
Morshed, Moqbul Monty *civil and environmental engineer*

Menlo Park
Honey, Richard Churchill *retired electrical engineer*
McCarthy, Roger Lee *mechanical engineer*
Ross, Bernard *engineering consultant, educator*

Mission Hills
Cramer, Frank Brown *engineering executive, combustion engineer, systems consultant*

Moffett Field
Bilimoria, Karl D. *aerospace engineer*
Denery, Dallas G. *aeronautical engineer, researcher*
Kerr, Andrew W. *aerodynamics researcher*
Park, Chul *aerospace engineer*
Shaw, Tianna *biomedical engineer*
Statler, Irving Carl *aerospace engineer*
Yamauchi, Gloria *aerospace engineer*
Zuniga, Fanny *aerospace engineer*

Monarch Beach
Dougherty, Elmer Lloyd, Jr., *retired chemical engineering educator, consultant*

Monrovia
Edwards, Kenneth Neil *chemical engineering executive*
Pray, Ralph Emerson *metallurgical engineer*

Monterey
Butler, Jon Terry *computer engineering educator, researcher*
Marto, Paul James *retired mechanical engineering educator, consultant, researcher*
Newberry, Conrad Floyde *aerospace engineering educator*
Sarpkaya, Turgut *mechanical engineering educator*

Moorpark
Bahn, Gilbert Schuyler *retired mechanical engineer, researcher, novelist*

Mountain View
Chandramouli, Ramamurti *electrical engineer*
Johnson, Conor Deane *mechanical engineer*
Malachowsky, Chris Alan *electrical engineer*
Perrella, Anthony Joseph *electronics engineer*

Murrieta
Geffe, Philip Reinhold *electrical engineer, consultant*
Plachno, Ronald John *electrical engineer*

Newark
Shah, Haresh Chandulal *civil engineering educator*

Newport Beach
Kraus, John Walter *former aerospace engineering company executive*
Parks, Fredrick Scott *systems engineer*

North Hollywood
de la Houssaye, Brette Angelo-Pepe *electronics engineer, researcher*

Northridge
Bradshaw, Richard Rotherwood *engineering executive*
Kiddoo, Robert James *engineering service company executive*
Torgow, Eugene N. *electrical engineer*

Oakland
Kint, Arne Tonis *industrial engineer, mechanical engineer*
Musihin, Konstantin K. *electrical engineer*
Youngs, Robert Riggs *engineer*

Occidental
Rumsey, Victor Henry *electrical engineering educator emeritus*

Oceanside
McLean, Arthur Frederick *mechanical engineer*
Yurist, Svetlan Joseph *mechanical engineer*

Orange
Fisk, Edward Ray *retired civil engineer, author, educator*
Monsees, James Eugene *engineering executive, consultant*

Oroville
Cella, Paul *civil engineer, consultant*

Oxnard
Zhou, Sophia Huai *biomedical engineering scientist*

Pacific Palisades
Herman, Elvin E. *retired consulting electronic engineer*

Palm Desert
Osborne, Bartley Porter, Jr., *aeronautical engineer*

Palmdale
Farr, Donald Eugene *engineering scientist*

Palo Alto
Brown, David Randolph *electrical engineer*
Casati, Fabio *engineer*
Hodge, Philip Gibson, Jr., *mechanical and aerospace engineering educator*
Kim, Wan Hee *electrical engineering educator, business executive*
Lender, Adam *electrical engineer*
Luh, Howard H. *aerospace engineer*
McHugh, Stuart Lawrence *materials engineer*
Quate, Calvin Forrest *engineering educator*
Taylor, John Joseph *nuclear engineer, researcher*
Vassar, Richard Holt *aerospace engineer*
Watson, David Colquitt *electrical engineer, educator*

Palos Verdes Estates
Abbott, A. Dwight *retired astronautical engineer*
Perry, Robert Michael *engineering company executive*
Raue, Jorg Emil *electrical engineer*
Yarbrough, Allyson Debra *electrical engineer*

Palos Verdes Peninsula
Denke, Paul Herman *retired aircraft engineer*
Lowi, Alvin, Jr., *mechanical engineer, consultant*
Mirels, Harold *aerospace engineer*
Seide, Paul *civil engineering educator*

Pasadena
Bower, Curtis A. *engineering executive*
Breckinridge, James Bernard *optical engineer*
Bridges, William Bruce *electrical engineer, researcher, engineering educator*
Chiang, Wen-Li *hydrodynamicist*
Ching, Jianye *civil engineer, researcher*
Dallas, Saterios (Sam Dallas) *aerospace engineer, researcher, consultant*
DeMartino, Frank A. *engineering company executive*
Elachi, Charles *aerospace engineer*
Gould, Roy Walter *engineering educator*
Hall, William E. *engineering and construction company executive*
Harris, Jennifer A. *aerospace engineer*
Hilbert, Robert S(aul) *optical engineer*
Hornung, Hans Georg *aeronautical engineering educator, science facility administrator*
Housner, George William *retired civil engineering educator, consultant*
Hwang, Li-San *technology executive*
Jacobs, Joseph John *engineering company executive*
Jennings, Paul Christian *civil engineering educator, academic administrator*
Knowles, James Kenyon *applied mechanics educator*
Kornfield, Julia Ann *chemical engineering educator*
Liebe, Carl Christian *aerospace engineer, researcher*
List, Ericson John *environmental engineering science educator, engineering consultant*
Martin, Craig Lee *engineering company executive*
Newell, Michael Alfred *electrical engineer*
Poon, Peter Tin-Yau *engineer, physicist*
Roshko, Anatol *aeronautical engineer*
Sabersky, Rolf Heinrich *mechanical engineer*
Schlinger, Warren Gleason *retired chemical engineer*
Scott, Ronald Fraser *civil engineering educator, engineering consultant*
Seinfeld, John Hersh *chemical engineering educator*
Shimada, Katsunori *retired electrical engineer*
Smith, Michael Robert *electro-optical engineer, physicist*
Tan-Wang, Grace *aeronautical engineer*
Tolaney, Murli *environmental engineering executive*
Weisbin, Charles Richard *nuclear engineer*
Wood, Lincoln Jackson *aerospace engineer*
Yariv, Amnon *electrical engineering educator, scientist*
Yeh, Paul Pao *electrical and electronics engineer, educator*

Penn Valley
Throner, Guy Charles, Jr., *engineering executive, scientist, engineer, inventor, consultant*

Penryn
Bryson, Vern Elrick *nuclear engineer*

Pleasanton
Novak, Randi Ruth *engineer, computer scientist*
Van Dreser, Merton Lawrence *ceramics engineer*

Pomona
Kucij, Timothy Michael *engineer, minister, musician*
Teague, Lavette Cox, Jr., *systems educator, consultant*

Rancho Cordova
Carleone, Joseph *business executive*

Rancho Cucamonga
Alvarez, Tirso Reyes, Jr., *engineer*

Rancho Mirage
Kramer, Gordon *mechanical engineer*

Rancho Palos Verdes
Frassinelli, Guido Joseph *retired aerospace engineer*

Redondo Beach
Brodsky, Robert Fox *aerospace engineer, educator, author*
Grzesik, Jan Alexander *electronics engineer, mathematician*
Kich, Rolf *communications scientist, consultant*

Richmond
Moehle, Jack P. *civil engineer, engineering executive*

Riverside
Beni, Gerardo *electrical and computer engineering educator, robotics scientist*
Hackwood, Susan *electrical and computer engineering educator*
Mulchandani, Ashok Kimatrai *chemical engineer, educator*

Rocklin
Tovar, Nicholas Mario *mechanical engineer*

Rodeo
Emmanuel, Jorge Agustin *chemical engineer, environmental consultant*

Rolling Hills Estates
Diaz-Zubieta, Agustin *nuclear engineer, engineering executive*
Wong, Sun Yet *engineering consultant*

Running Springs
Liddle, Sidney George *retired mechanical engineer, researcher*

Sacramento
Bailey, Michael Glenn *engineer*
Crimmins, Philip Patrick *retired metallurgical engineer, lawyer*
Forsyth, Raymond Arthur *civil engineer, consultant*
Kerri, Kenneth Donald *civil engineering educator*
Lathi, Bhagawandas Pannalal *retired electrical engineering educator*
Roberts, James E. *civil engineer*
Simeroth, Dean Conrad *chemical engineer*

San Bernardino
Kirkland, Bertha Theresa *project engineer*

San Carlos
Robinson, Neil *materials engineer, consultant*
Symons, Robert Spencer *electronic engineer*

San Diego
Anderson, Karl Richard *aerospace engineer, consultant*
Anderson, Paul Maurice *electrical engineering educator, researcher, consultant*
Auld, Robert Henry, Jr., *biomedical engineer, educator, consultant, author*
Basso, Robert J. *manufacturing engineer, inventor*
Beyster, John Robert *engineering company executive*
Conly, John Franklin *engineering educator, researcher*
Dean, Richard Anthony *mechanical engineer, engineering executive*
Evans, Ersel Arthur *consulting engineer executive*
Foreman, John Patrick *electrical engineer*
Friedman, Arthur Daniel *electrical engineering and computer science educator, investment management company executive*
Gaal, Peter *electrical engineer, researcher*
Gupta, Madhu Sudan *electrical engineering educator*
Inoue, Michael Shigeru *industrial engineer, electrical engineer*
Ito, Carl Susumu *computer engineer*
Larson, Arvid Gunnar *electrical engineer*
Lieber, Richard Louis *biomedical engineering scientist, educator*
McLeod, John Hugh, Jr., *mechanical and electrical engineer*
Paget, John Arthur *mechanical engineer*
St. Clair, Hal Kay *electrical engineer*
Schmidt, Thomas Charles *biomedical engineer, researcher*
Schultz, Kenneth Robert *nuclear engineer, researcher*
Sell, Robert Emerson *electrical engineer*
Slate, John Butler *biomedical engineer*
Suycott, Mark Leland *aerospace engineer, retired military officer*
Tricoles, Gus Peter *electromagnetic engineer, physicist, consultant*
Ward, Charles Raymond *systems engineer*
Youngs, Jack Marvin *cost engineer*

San Francisco
Abramson, Norman *engineering educator*
Ainsworth, Kent P. *engineering company executive*
Bechtel, Riley Peart *engineering company executive*
Bechtel, Stephen Davison, Jr., *engineering company executive*
Bell, Chester Gordon *computer engineering company executive*
Cheng, Wan-Lee *mechanical engineer, industrial technology educator*
Dolby, Ray Milton *engineering company executive, electrical engineer*
Eliaz, Rom Ezer *chemical engineer, educator*
Gerwick, Ben Clifford, Jr., *construction engineer, educator*
Keller, Edward Lowell *electrical engineer, educator*
Koffel, Martin M. *engineering company executive*
Laspa, Jude *engineering company executive*
Lolli, Andrew Ralph *industrial engineer, former army officer*
Luft, Rene Wilfred *civil engineer*
Vreeland, Robert Wilder *retired electronics engineer*
Wong, Stephen T.C. *radiology, neurology, computer scientist, and bioengineer educator*
Yuan, Shao Wen *aerospace engineer, educator*

San Jose
Dennison, Ronald Walton *engineer*
Der Torossian, Papken *engineering executive*
Eastburn, Martin Howard *engineer*
Gill, Hardayal Singh *electrical engineer*
Hoang, Loc Bao *electrical engineer*
Hoff, Marcian Edward, Jr., *electronics engineer*
Jain, Raj *engineering educator*
Jonaris, George G. *electrical engineer, computer engineer*
Kirk, Donald Evan *electrical engineering educator, dean*
Kring, Charles Udell *retired civil engineer*
Rosenblum, Frank Michael *civil engineer, consultant, surveyor*
Shaw, Charles Alden *engineering executive*
Takeuchi, Tetsuya *materials engineer*
Tatipamula, Mallikarjun *telecommunications and networking engineer*
Tran, Jack Nhuan Ngoc *gas and oil reservoir engineer*
Tretz, Christophe Robert *electrical engineer*
Wickramasinghe, Hemantha Kumar *electrical engineer, physicist*
Zhang, G. Z. (Guangzhi Zhang) *electro-optics engineer*
Zheng, Min *engineer*

San Lorenzo
Thompson, Lyle Eugene *electrical engineer*

San Luis Obispo
Anderson, Warren Ronald *electrical engineering educator*

San Luis Rey
Melbourne, Robert Ernest *civil engineer*

San Marcos
Purdy, Alan Harris *biomedical engineer*

San Mateo
Hur, Stephen Ponyi *civil engineer, management consultant, educator*

San Pedro
Ellis, George Edwin, Jr., *chemical engineer*
McCarty, Frederick Briggs *electrical engineer, consultant*

San Rafael
Douglas, James *construction engineering educator*

San Ramon
Morrison, Cheryl Lynn *petroleum engineer, project manager*

Sand City
Coile, Russell Cleven *electrical engineer, consultant*

Santa Ana
Amoroso, Frank *retired communication system engineer, consultant*
Bauer, Bruce F. *former aerospace engineer*
Kelly, James Patrick, Jr., *retired engineering and construction executive*
Toeppe, William Joseph, Jr., *retired aerospace engineer*

Santa Barbara
Bruch, John Clarence, Jr., *engineer, educator*
Chmelka, Bradley Floyd *chemical engineering educator*
Coldren, Larry Allen *engineering educator, consultant*
Crispin, James Hewes *engineering and construction company executive*
Gilbert, Paul Thomas *chemical development engineer*
Hu, Evelyn Lynn *electrical and computer engineering educator*
Iselin, Donald Grote *civil engineering and management consultant*
Kokotovic, Petar V. *electrical and computer engineer, educator*
Kramer, Edward John *materials science and engineering educator*
Kroemer, Herbert *electrical engineering educator*
Lawrance, Charles Holway *retired civil and sanitary engineer*
Lick, Wilbert James *mechanical engineering educator*
Mitra, Sanjit Kumar *electrical and computer engineering educator*
Nakamura, Shuji *engineering educator*
Parhami, Behrooz *engineering educator, consultant*
Sensiper, Samuel *electrical engineer*
Theofanous, Theo G. *engineering educator, consultant*
Thomas, Bertram David *retired chemical engineer*
Wade, Glen *electrical engineer, educator*
Wooldridge, Dean Everett *engineering executive, scientist*

Santa Clara
Aitken, Robert Campbell *engineer*
Chan, Shu-Park *electrical engineering educator*
Kamal, Abu Hena M. *electrical engineer, researcher*
Kelley, Robert Suma *network engineer*
Parden, Robert James *engineering educator, management consultant*
Roy, Abhra *process engineer, researcher*
Vakanas, George P. *process engineer, research scientist, consultant, entrepreneur*
Vu, Quat Thuong *electrical engineer*
Weinberg, William Henry *chemical engineer, chemical physicist, educator*

Santa Clarita
Garcia, Andrew B. *chemical engineer*

Santa Cruz
Bollinger, Kenneth John *aerospace engineer, computer and space scientist*
Kang, Sung-Mo (Steve Kang) *electrical engineering educator*
Wiberg, Donald Martin *electrical engineering educator, consultant*

Santa Monica
Brauner, Marygail K. *engineer, systems analyst*
Gritton, Eugene Charles *nuclear engineer, director*
Kayton, Myron *engineering company executive*
McGuire, Michael John *environmental engineer*
Roney, Robert Kenneth *retired aerospace company executive*
Sherman, Zachary *civil engineer, aerospace engineer, consultant*

Saratoga
Syvertson, Clarence Alfred *engineering and research management consultant*

Seal Beach
Robinson, Michael R. *aeronautical engineer*
Wiley, Dianne *aeronautical engineer*

Sebastopol
Norman, Arnold McCallum, Jr., *engineer*

Sonoma
Muchmore, Robert Boyer *engineering consultant executive*
Sasaki, Y(asunaga) Tito *engineering executive*

South Pasadena
Glad, Dain Sturgis *aerospace engineer, consultant*
Kopp, Eugene Howard *electrical engineer*

South San Francisco
Niehaus, Ed *engineering executive*
Tananbaum, James *medical engineering company executive*

Stanford
Aziz, Khalid *petroleum engineering educator*
Boudart, Michel *chemical engineer, chemist, educator, consultant*
Bracewell, Ronald Newbold *electrical engineering educator*
Bryson, Arthur Earl, Jr., *retired aerospace engineering educator*
Cannon, Robert Hamilton, Jr., *aerospace engineering educator*
Cornell, Carl Allin *civil engineering educator*
Cox, Donald Clyde *electrical engineering educator*
Eshleman, Von Russel *electrical engineering educator*
Eustis, Robert Henry *mechanical engineer*
Franklin, Gene Farthing *engineering educator, consultant*
Glynn, Peter Winston Gunnar *engineering educator*
Goodman, Joseph Wilfred *electrical engineering educator*
Harris, Stephen Ernest *electrical engineering and applied physics educator*
Herrmann, George *mechanical engineering educator*
Hesselink, Lambertus *electrical engineering and physics educator*
Hillier, Frederick Stanton *industrial engineer, educator*
Howard, Ronald A. *systems engineer, educator*
Kailath, Thomas *electrical engineer, educator*
Kino, Gordon Stanley *electrical engineering educator*
Kruger, Paul *nuclear civil engineering educator*
Landau, Ralph *chemical engineer*
Linvill, John Grimes *engineering educator*
Macovski, Albert *electrical engineer, educator*
Mathews, Max V. *acoustical engineer, educator*
McCarty, Perry Lee *civil and environmental engineering educator*
Mitchell, Reginald Eugene *mechanical engineering educator*
Orr, Franklin Mattes, Jr., *petroleum engineering educator*
Ott, Wayne Robert *environmental engineer*
Parkinson, Bradford Wells *astronautical engineer, educator*
Paulson, Boyd Colton, Jr., *civil engineering educator*
Saraswat, Krishna *electrical engineering educator*
Siegman, Anthony Edward *electrical engineer, educator*
Springer, George Stephen *mechanical engineering educator*
Steele, Charles Richard *biomedical and mechanical engineering educator*
Street, Robert Lynnwood *civil, mechanical and environmental engineer*
Van Dyke, Milton Denman *aeronautical engineering educator*
Vincenti, Walter Guido *aeronautical engineer, emeritus educator*
White, Robert Lee *electrical engineer, educator*
Zahedi, Sina *electrical engineer, researcher*

Stockton
Cassens, Nicholas, Jr., *ceramics engineer*

Sunnyvale
Choi, Hoon *electrical engineer*
Lang, John Joseph *systems engineer, program manager*
Lopatin, Sergey Dmitrievich *microelectronic scientist, electrochemist*
Saha, Samar Kanti *electronics engineer, educator*
Shirvani, Alireza *electrical engineer*
Siddiqee, Muhammad Waheeduddin *electrical engineer*

Sylmar
Bridges, Robert McSteen *mechanical engineer*
Madni, Asad Mohamed *engineering executive*

Tarzana
Hansen, Robert Clinton *electrical engineering consultant*
Lindley, Charles Alexander *aerospace engineer, consultant*
Portney, Joseph Nathaniel *retired aerospace executive, navigation consultant*

Temecula
Bathaee, Soussan *engineering technician*
Minogue, Robert Brophy *retired nuclear engineer*

Thousand Oaks
Vizcaino, Henry P. *mining engineer, consultant*

PROFESSIONAL INDEX 5599 ENGINEERING

Wiktorowicz, Andrew Charles *engineer*

Torrance
Gran, Robert *engineering company executive*
Lee, Francis Cho-Kuen *aerospace engineering analyst*
Mende, Howard Shigeharu *mechanical engineer*
Sorstokke, Susan Eileen *systems engineer*

Trabuco Canyon
Larson, Harry Thomas *electronics engineer, executive, consultant*

Tustin
Prasad, Birendra (Brian) *mechanical engineer*

Vallejo
Brooks, William George *retired aeronautical engineer*

Ventura
Gaynor, Joseph *chemical engineer, technical-management consultant*

Victorville
Sedeño, Eugene Raymond *electronics engineer, consultant*

Walnut
Cheng, Shide *engineer, researcher*

Walnut Creek
Cassidy, John Joseph *hydraulic and hydrologic engineer*
Hanson, Robert Duane *civil engineering educator*

Watsonville
Brown, Alan Charlton *retired aeronautical engineer*

Westlake Village
Caligiuri, Joseph Frank *retired engineering executive*

Westminster
Armstrong, Gene Lee *systems engineering consultant, retired aerospace company executive*

Wilmington
Hatch, Ronald Ray *engineer*

Wilton
Felts, Margaret Clemen *environmental engineer, consultant*

Woodland Hills
Hokana, Gregory Howard *engineering executive*
Piersol, Allan Gerald *mechanical engineer*

Wrightwood
Caudron, John Armand *accident reconstructionist, forensic examiner*

Yorba Linda
Lynch, Frank Thomas *aeronautical engineer, consultant*
Porcello, Leonard Joseph *engineering research and development executive*

COLORADO

Arvada
Ferguson, Lloyd Elbert *retired manufacturing engineer*
Smith, Paul Tillman *engineering executive, writer*

Aurora
Fisk, Charles Carroll *retired civil engineer, consultant*
Heller, Austin Norman *chemical and environmental engineer*
Osterberg, Jorj O. *retired civil engineer*
Robertson, James Mueller *civil engineer, educator*
Schwartz, Lawrence *aeronautical engineer*

Bayfield
Haug, Edward Joseph, Jr., *engineering educator, director*

Boulder
Avery, Susan Kathryn *electrical engineering educator, research administrator*
Barnes, Frank Stephenson *electrical engineer, educator*
Breddan, Joe *systems engineering consultant*
Cathey, Wade Thomas *retired electrical engineering educator*
Corotis, Ross Barry *civil engineering educator, academic administrator*
Greschik, Gyula *structural engineer*
Hanna, William Johnson *electrical engineering educator*
Hauser, Ray Louis *research engineer, entrepreneur*
Hill, David Allan *electrical engineer*
Joy, Edward Bennett *electrical engineer, educator*
Mahajan, Roop L. *engineering educator*
Mulhern, Martin Robert *engineer*
Peacock, Neil T. *engineer*
Peters, Max Stone *chemical engineer, educator*
Ramirez, W. Fred *chemical engineering educator*
Reitsema, Harold James *aerospace engineer*
Rodriguez, Juan Alfonso *technology corporation executive*
Sani, Robert LeRoy *chemical engineering educator*
Smith, Ernest Ketcham *electrical engineer*
Sodal, Ingvar Edmund *electrical engineer, scientist*
Timmerhaus, Klaus Dieter *chemical engineering educator*
Uberoi, Mahinder Singh *aerospace engineer, researcher*

Broomfield
Crawford, Caren Lee *computer engineer*

Centennial
Brown, Steven Harry *engineering executive*
Goughnour, Roy Robert *civil engineer, consultant*

Colorado Springs
Adnet, Jacques Jim Pierre *astronautical and electrical engineer, consultant*
Heilman, John Edward *engineering consultant*
Littlejohn, John Joseph *petroleum engineer*
McMillan, Larry Donald *engineering executive*
Morris, Steven Lynn *engineering consultant, retired career officer*
Prochaska, Frank Joseph *industrial engineer, educator*
Vallado, David Anthony *aerospace engineer*
Watts, Oliver Edward *engineering consultancy company executive*
White, Gayle Clay *aerospace company executive*
Ziemer, Rodger Edmund *electrical engineering educator, consultant*

Columbine Valley
Gagin, Lawrence Vincent *ceramics engineer, consultant*

Denver
Abu-Hejleh, Naser M. *civil engineer, researcher*
Bialasiewicz, Jan Tadeusz *electrical engineering educator*
Chamberlain, Adrian Ramond *transportation engineer*
Colvis, John Paris *aerospace engineer, mathematician*
Cook, Frank Richardson *aeronautical engineer, social scientist*
Emery, Henry Alfred *petroleum engineer*
Fay, Richard James *mechanical engineer, executive, educator*
Haliw, Jerome Michael *civil engineer*
Long, Francis Mark *retired electrical engineer*
McCandless, Bruce, II, *aerospace engineer, retired astronaut*
Perez, Jean-Yves *engineering company executive*
Poirot, James Wesley *engineering company executive*
Porter, J. Reid *engineering executive*
Smith, William French, II, *safety engineer, special projects administrator*
Stephens, Larry Dean *engineer, consultant*
Walker, Radford *computer system architect*

Durango
Langoni, Richard Allen *civil engineer*

Englewood
Barbezat, Eugene LaVar *computer systems engineer, retired air force officer*
Bingham, Paris Edward, Jr., *electrical engineer, computer consultant*
Grant, Paul *chemical engineer, manufacturer's representative, real estate broker*
Peterson, Ralph Randall *engineering executive*
Sideman, Jill *engineering executive*

Estes Park
Ojalvo, Morris *civil engineer, educator*
Webb, Richard C. *engineering company executive*

Evergreen
Rodolff, Dale Ward *engineer, sales executive, consultant*

Fort Collins
Abt, Steven R. *civil engineering educator, dean*
Cermak, Jack Edward *engineer, educator*
Emslie, William Arthur *electrical engineer*
Evans, Norman Allen *retired civil engineering educator*
Garvey, Daniel Cyril *mechanical engineer*
Grigg, Neil S. *civil engineering educator*
Matthies, Frederick John *civil and environmental engineer*
Richardson, Everett Vern *hydraulic engineer, educator, administrator, consultant*
Roesner, Larry August *civil engineer*
Sandborn, Virgil Alvin *civil engineer, educator*
Thierstein, Gerald E. (Gerry Thierstein) *retired agricultural engineer*

Golden
Gosink, Joan P. *engineering educator*
Myers, Daryl Ronald *engineer*
Sloan, Earle Dendy, Jr., *chemical engineering educator*
Spurck, Richard Francis *materials engineer*

Grand Junction
Rybak, James Patrick *engineering educator*
Tavossi, Hasson M. *physics and engineering educator, consultant*

Greenwood Village
Arvizu, Dan Eliab *mechanical engineer*

Highlands Ranch
Brierley, Corale L. *geological engineer*
Hastey, Joe *engineering executive*

Lafayette
Middlebrooks, Eddie Joe *environmental engineer*

Lakewood
Barrett, Michael Henry *civil engineer*

Littleton
Annandale, George William *engineer*
Kielmeyer, William Henry *ceramics engineer, researcher*
Kullas, Albert John *management and systems engineering consultant*

Loveland
Fleischer, Gerald Albert *industrial engineer, educator*
Stewart, James Michael *engineer*

Palmer Lake
Dixon, Robert Clyde *systems engineer, consultant*

Pueblo
Giffin, Walter Charles *retired industrial engineer, educator, consultant*

Telluride
Kuehler, Jack Dwyer *engineering consultant*

Thornton
Kane, Sean Patrick *computer engineer, consultant*

Wheat Ridge
Parrish, Peter Trasel *retired civil engineer*
Scherich, Erwin Thomas *civil engineer, consultant*

CONNECTICUT

Bethel
DeLugo, Ernest Mario, Jr., *electrical engineer*

Bloomfield
Cornell, Robert Witherspoon *engineering consultant*
De Maria, Anthony John *electrical engineer*
Kissa, Karl Martin *electrical engineer*

Bolton
Banas, Conrad Martin *mechanical engineer, chief scientist*

Branford
Sipprell, George Sidney *engineering professional*
Wegener, Peter Paul *engineering educator, author*

Danbury
Layton, Howard Manton *electrical engineer*

Darien
Forman, J(oseph) Charles *chemical engineer, consultant, writer*

East Hartford
Pfeifer, Howard Melford *mechanical engineer*
Vacher, Clive Graham *aerospace executive*

Farmington
DiFrancesco, John *design engineering services company executive*

Groton
Helm, John Leslie *retired mechanical engineer, company executive*
Sheets, Herman Ernest *marine engineer*
Stoddard, Patrick Clare *retired military systems consultant, computer engineer*

Hartford
Bronzino, Joseph Daniel *electrical engineer*
Gieras, Jacek Franciszek *electrical engineering educator, scientist*

Jewett City
Pucel, Robert Albin *electronics research engineer*

Litchfield
Ellison, William Theodore *marine engineer*

Madison
Atkinson, Neil Norman *mechanical engineer*

Mystic
Lincoln, Walter Butler, Jr., *marine engineer, educator*
Thompson, Robert Allan *aerospace engineer*

New Britain
Czajkowski, Eva Anna *aerospace engineer, educator*

New Haven
Baltayan, Ara M. *engineering executive*
Narendra, Kumpati Subrahmanya *electrical engineer, educator*
Staib, Lawrence Hamilton *biomedical engineer*

North Haven
Sawyer, Charles S. *environmental engineer, engineering educator*

Norwalk
Bays, John Theophanis *consulting engineer*
Levy, Jeffrey M. *engineering company executive*
Swift, Richard J. *engineering company executive*

Old Lyme
Doersam, Charles Henry, Jr., *engineer, educator, entrepreneur*

Orange
Lobay, Ivan *mechanical engineering educator*

Redding
Binger, Wilson Valentine *civil engineer*
Halverstadt, Robert Dale *mechanical engineer, metals manufacturing company*

Ridgefield
McConnell, John Edward *electrical engineering company executive*

Rocky Hill
Chuang, Frank Shiunn-Jea *engineering executive, consultant*
McCullough, Jefferson Walker *industrial engineering consultant*

South Windsor
Hobbs, David Ellis *mechanical engineer*

Stamford
Sahota, Gurcharn Singh *mechanical engineer*

Storrs Mansfield
Bzymek, Zbigniew Marian *engineering educator*
Pitkin, Edward Thaddeus *aerospace engineer, consultant*
Shaw, Montgomery Throop *chemical engineering educator*
Stephens, Jack Edward *civil engineer, consultant*

Vernon
Collins, Shawn Thomas *mechanical engineer*

Waterbury
Dreisbach, Mary Elizabeth *manufacturing engineer*
Wu, Zheng Y. *hydroinformatics engineer, hydrologist, consultant*

Waterford
Hinkle, Muriel Ruth Nelson *naval warfare analysis company executive*

West Mystic
Hoagland, Porter, Jr., *electrical and mechanical engineer, consultant*

Wilton
Juran, Joseph Moses *engineer, consultant*

DELAWARE

Newark
Allen, Herbert Ellis *environmental chemistry educator*
Barteau, Mark Alan *chemical engineering and chemistry educator*
Christy, Charles Wesley, III, *industrial engineering educator*
Kaler, Eric William *chemical engineer, educator*
Kim, Hee June *engineer*
Kobayashi, Nobuhisa *civil and coastal engineer, educator*
Ritter, William Frederick *civil and agricultural engineering educator*
Sandler, Stanley Irving *chemical engineering educator*

Rehoboth Beach
Bischoff, Kenneth Bruce *chemical engineer, educator*

Smyrna
Hutchison, James Arthur, Jr., *architectural and engineering company executive*

Wilmington
Murphy, Arthur Thomas *systems engineer*
Naylor, Craig G. *engineering company executive*
Sutton, Ernest Shaw *chemical engineer*

DISTRICT OF COLUMBIA

Washington
Anthony, Donald Barrett *engineering executive*
Arkilic, Galip Mehmet *mechanical engineer, educator*
Bainum, Peter Montgomery *aerospace engineer, consultant*
Blanchard, Bruce *civil engineer, federal official*
Bresee, James Collins *chemical engineer*
Bruckman, Richard R. *aerospace engineer*
Burton, William Joseph *engineering executive*
Chalmers, Franklin Stevens, Jr., *engineering consultant*
Chen, Ho-Hong H. H. *industrial engineering executive, educator*
Cleave, Mary L. *environmental engineer, former astronaut*
Cohen, Gregory Michael *civil engineer, transportation executive*
Cromer, Donald L. *aerospace engineer*
Deason, Jonathan Pierce *environmental engineer, federal agency administrator*
Eisner, Howard *engineering educator, engineering executive*
Englar, Kenneth G. *aerospace engineer*
Giallorenzi, Thomas Gaetano *optical engineer*
Hershey, Robert Lewis *mechanical engineer, management consultant*
Jones, Howard St. Claire, Jr., *electronics engineering executive*
Kao, Timothy Wu *civil engineering educator*
Khozeimeh, Issa *electrical engineer, educator*
Koester, Frederick H. *aviation systems engineer*
Larsson, Erik G. *engineering educator*
Monroe, Robert Rawson *engineering construction executive*
O'Neil, Robert S. *engineering executive*
Page, Robert Wesley *engineering and construction company executive, federal official*
Paulhus, Norman Gerard, Jr., *aerospace engineer*
Pawley, Carl John *laser engineer, physicist*
Pickholtz, Raymond Lee *electrical engineering educator, consultant*
Plusquellec, Herve Louis *irrigation and agricultural engineering consultant*
Quinn, Pat Maloy *engineering company executive*
Replogle, Michael A. *civil engineer, urban planner, environmentalist*
Rust, William David, Jr., *retired structural engineer*
Shapiro, Paul Sauveur *chemical engineer, researcher*
Sieck, Robert *aerospace engineer*
Skinner, Robert Earle, Jr., *civil engineer, engineering executive*
Skolnik, Merrill I. *electrical engineer*
Townsend, Marjorie Rhodes *aerospace engineer, engineering executive*
Wang, John Cheng Hwai *communications engineer, researcher*
Warnick, Walter Lee *mechanical engineer*
Weiner, Edward *civil engineer, federal agency administrator*
White, Robert Roy *retired chemical engineer*
Whitworth, Horace Algernon *mechanical engineer*
Williamson, Carl Augustus *engineering executive*

FLORIDA

Amelia Island
Jesser, Benn Wainwright *retired chemical engineering and construction company executive*

Aventura
Alisetti, Edwin Luis *engineer, financial executive*

Boca Raton
Kotheimer, William Conrad *consulting engineer*
Lin, Yukweng M. *engineer, educator*
Reynolds, George Anthony, Jr., *engineering executive*

Bonita Springs
Katzen, Raphael *consulting chemical engineer*

Brandon
Cartlidge, Edward Sutterley *mechanical engineer*

Brooksville
Lauer, Harry Curtis *retired civil engineer*

Cape Coral
Longo, Paul Albert *retired industrial engineer, consultant*

Cocoa
Block, David L. *solar engineering executive*

Coral Gables
Aljifri, Hassan *engineering educator, consultant*
Crespo, Fernando Calderon *retired civil engineer*
Mantell, Murray I. *engineering educator*
Modestino, James William *electrical engineering educator*
Saffir, Herbert Seymour *structural engineer, consultant*
Sumanth, David Jonnakoty *industrial engineer, educator*
Young, Tzay Y. *electrical and computer engineering educator*

Davie
Upadhiaya, Umesh Chandra *engineer, consultant*

Daytona Beach
Sloane, James Robert *chemical engineer*
Tiblier, Fernand Joseph, Jr., *municipal engineering administrator*

Deland
Gross, Mitchell Neal *ceramics engineer*
Rattman, William John *electronics and electro-optic engineer*

Delray Beach
Smith, Charles Oliver *engineer*
Zepnick, Seymour *civil engineer, consultant*

Destin
Harmuth, Henning F. *electrical engineer, educator*

Dunedin
Goodale, Arthur Worthington *civil engineer, researcher*

Fernandina Beach
Lilly, Wesley Cooper *marine engineer, surveyor*

Fort Lauderdale
Schear, Betty Z. *engineering executive, consultant*

Fort Myers
Mergler, Harry Winston *retired engineering educator*
Moeschl, Stanley Francis *electrical engineer, management consultant*
Scott, Kenneth Elsner *mechanical engineering educator*

Gainesville
Anderson, Timothy J. *chemical engineering educator*
Capehart, Barney Lee *industrial and systems engineer*
Cristescu, Nicolaie Dan *engineering educator*
Delfino, Joseph John *environmental engineering sciences educator*
Fossum, Jerry George *electrical engineering educator*
Huang, Jinhua *mechanical engineer, researcher*
Isaacs, Gerald William *retired agricultural engineering educator, consultant*
Kurzweg, Ulrich Hermann *engineering science educator*
Law, Mark Edward *electrical engineer, educator*
Lindholm, Fredrik Arthur *electrical engineering educator*
Peebles, Peyton Zimmermann, Jr., *electrical engineer, educator*
Polasek, Edward John *retired electrical engineer, consultant*
Ruth, Byron Edward *civil engineering educator*
Sah, Chih-Tang *electrical and computer engineering educator*
Schmertmann, John Henry *civil engineer, educator, consultant*
Sherif, S. A. *engineering educator*
Shyy, Wei *aerospace and mechanical engineering researcher, educator*
Tia, Mang *civil engineering educator*
Verink, Ellis Daniel, Jr., *metallurgical engineering educator, consultant*
Wethington, John Abner, Jr., *retired nuclear engineering educator*
Xie, Huikai *electrical engineer, educator*

Hialeah
Rhee, Sorah *biomedical engineer*

Jacksonville
Arbogast, Gordon Wade *systems engineer, educator, consultant, retired military officer*
Costin, Rea-Silvia *civil engineer*
Mueller, Edward Albert *retired transportation engineer executive*
Reagan, James Raymond *safety and ergonomics consultant*
Russell, David Emerson *mechanical engineer, consultant, writer*

Jupiter
Migliaro, Marco William *electrical engineer*
Wolff, Edward Alvin *electronics engineer*

Keystone Heights
Ohanian, Mihran Jacob *nuclear engineering educator, research dean*

Kissimmee
Gagne, Antoine F. *retired mechanical engineer, writer*

Lady Lake
Dore, Stephen Edward, Jr., *retired civil engineer*
Granger, Robert Alan *mechanical and aerospace engineering educator*

Lake Placid
Rew, William Edmund *civil engineer*

Lake Worth
Cohen, Edward *civil engineer*

Lantana
Schmaus, Siegfried H. A. *engineering executive, consultant*

Lauderhill
Swisher, Charles Francis *electrical engineer, consultant*

Longboat Key
Workman, George Henry *structural engineering consultant*

Melbourne
Maloratsky, Leo G. *electrical engineer*

Merritt Island
Morgan, Ronald Brian *retired aerospace engineer, advocate, writer*

Miami
Barthel, William Frederick, Jr., *electrical engineer*
Chang-Mota, Roberto *electrical engineer*
de la Guardia, Mario Francisco *electrical engineer*
Jones, William Kinzy *materials engineering educator*
Ural, Oktay *civil engineering educator*
Veziroglu, Turhan Nejat *mechanical engineering educator, energy researcher*
Wolfenson, Azi U. *electrical, mechanical and industrial engineer, consultant*

Naples
Lynn, Larry (Verne Lauriston Lynn) *engineering executive*
Sowman, Harold Gene *ceramic engineer, researcher*
Suziedelis, Vytautas A. *engineering corporation executive*
Thampi, Mohan Varghese *environmental health and civil engineer*
Williams, George Earnest *engineer, retired business executive*

Nokomis
Beck, George William *retired industrial engineer*

North Fort Myers
Callanan, Kathleen Joan *internet consultant and marketer, retired electrical engineer*

North Miami Beach
Roif, Henry Irving *aeronautical engineer, electronic engineer, air transportation executive*

North Palm Beach
Sooy, William Ray *information technology executive*

North Port
Lazich, Daniel *aerospace engineer*

Orlando
Bauer, Maria Casanova *computer engineer*
Figner, William James *instructional systems designer*
Ha, Yonggang *optical engineer*
Landaeta, Rafael Ernesto *industrial engineer, researcher*
Lucariello, Georgann *engineer*
Marsh, Malcolm Roy, Jr., *electronics engineer*
Rosenbach, Leopold *engineer, consultant*
Whitehouse, Gary *industrial engineer, educator*
Wu, Thomas Xinzhang *engineering educator*

Osprey
Boldt, Heinz *aerospace engineer*
Jones, George Steven *civil engineer*

Palm Beach
Callahan, Edward William *chemical engineer, retired manufacturing executive*

Palm Beach Gardens
Gillette, Frank C., Jr., *retired mechanical engineer*

Palm Harbor
Warfield, John Nelson *retired engineering educator, consultant*

Panama City
Campbell, Regan Helen *engineer*
D'Arcy, Gerald Paul *engineering executive, consultant*

Patrick AFB
Beauregard, Adam *aerospace engineer*

Pensacola
Clare, George *safety engineer, systems safety consultant*
Mazzeo, Daniel Patrick *aerospace engineer, aviation consultant*
Olsen, Richard Galen *biomedical engineer, consultant*

Plantation
Chou, Chung-Kwang *bio-engineer*

Port Charlotte
Kok, Hans Gebhard *consulting engineer*

Port Orange
Millar, Gordon Halstead *mechanical engineer, agricultural machinery manufacturing executive*

Saint Augustine
Lund, Frederick Henry *aerospace and electrical engineer*

Saint Cloud
Everett, Woodrow Wilson *electrical engineer, educator*

Saint Petersburg
Collins, Carl Russell, Jr., *industrial engineer*

Sarasota
Deutsch, Sid *bioengineer, educator*
Long, Robert Radcliffe *fluid mechanics educator*
Metzger, Sidney *retired communications engineer*
Michejda, Oskar *civil engineer, structural engineer, consultant*
Mitchell, John Noyes, Jr., *retired electrical engineer*
Pender, Michael Roger *engineering consultant*
Ross, Gerald Fred *engineering executive, researcher*

Satellite Beach
Clark, John F. *aerospace research and engineering educator*
Van Arsdall, Robert Armes *engineer, retired air force officer*

Sun City Center
Edwards, Paul Beverly *retired science and engineering educator*
Jeffries, Robert Joseph *retired engineer, educator, business executive*

Sunny Isles Beach
Brunetto, Frank *electrical engineer*

Tallahassee
AbdelRazig, Yassir A. *engineering educator*
Coloney, Wayne Herndon *civil engineer*
De Forest, Sherwood Searle *agricultural engineer, agribusiness services executive*
Hall, Houghton Alexander *electrical engineer, city official*
Islam, A.K.M. Anwarul *civil engineer, consultant*

Tampa
Carnahan, Robert Paul *civil engineer, educator, researcher, consultant*
Ghiu, Silvana Melania Stefania *environmental engineer*
Hunter, Larry Lee *retired electrical engineer*
Stephens, Robert David *environmental engineering executive*
Wade, Thomas Edward *electrical engineering educator, university research administrator*

Tavares
Kaiser, Robert Lee *retired engineering executive*

Titusville
Stewart, David Witherington *aerospace engineer*

Valrico
Melconian, Jerry Ohanes *engineering executive*

Venice
Przemieniecki, Janusz Stanislaw *engineering executive, former government senior executive and college dean*
Slate, Floyd Owen *retired engineering educator*

West Palm Beach
Aaron, M. Robert *electrical engineer*
Davis, Paul B. *retired mechanical engineer, civil engineer,*

Weston
Gonzalez, Juan Guillermo *electrical engineer*

Winter Haven
Johnson, Gordon Selby *consulting electrical engineer*

Winter Park
Granberry, Edwin Phillips, Jr., *safety engineer, consultant*
Kerr, James Wilson *engineer*

GEORGIA

Albany
Marbury, Ritchey McGuire, III, *engineering executive, surveyor*

Athens
Marlar, John Thomas *environmental engineer*
McCutcheon, Steven Clifton *environmental and ecological engineer, hydrologist*
Nelson, Stuart Owen *agricultural engineer, researcher, educator*

Atlanta
Abdel-Khalik, Said Ibrahim *nuclear and mechanical engineering educator*
Bacon, Louis Albert *retired consulting civil engineer*
Barksdale, Richard Dillon *civil engineer, educator*
Bellanca, Joseph Paul *engineering construction executive*
Bevins, Karl Alten *retired engineer, musician, educator*
Caseman, Austin Bert *civil engineering educator*
Ellingwood, Bruce Russell *structural engineering researcher, educator*
Forney, Larry J. *chemical engineer, educator*
Giddens, Don Peyton *engineering educator, researcher*
Hess, Dennis William *chemical engineering educator*
Hodges, Dewey Harper *aerospace engineer, educator*
Jin, Zhenrong *electrical engineer, researcher*
Johnson, Richard Clayton *engineer, physicist*
Koros, William John *chemical engineering educator*
Loewy, Robert Gustav *aeronautical engineering executive, engineering educator*
Loven, Andrew Witherspoon *environmental engineering company executive*
Ludovice, Peter John *chemical engineer*
McIntire, Larry Vern *biomedical engineering educator*
Meindl, James Donald *electrical engineering educator, administrator*
Nemhauser, George L. *industrial, systems engineer, operations research educator*
Nerem, Robert Michael *engineering educator, consultant*
O'Kon, James Alexander *engineering company executive*
Pence, Ira Wilson, Jr., *material handling research executive, engineer*
Porter, Alan Leslie *industrial and systems engineering educator*
Price, Edward Warren *aerospace engineer, educator*
Rouhani, Shahrokh *civil engineering/environmental consultant, educator*
Salant, Richard Frank *mechanical engineer, educator*
Schafer, Ronald William *electrical engineering educator*
Scovil, Roger Morris *international business consultant*
Simitses, George John *retired engineering educator, consultant*
Sommerfeld, Jude Thomas *chemical engineer, educator*
Stacey, Weston Monroe, Jr., *nuclear engineer, physicist, educator*
Stancell, Arnold Francis *chemical engineering educator, retired oil industry executive*
Su, Kendall Ling-Chiao *engineering educator*
Tentzeris, Emmanouil Manos *engineering educator, researcher*
Thuesen, Gerald Jorgen *industrial engineer, educator*
Tincher, Wayne Coleman *engineering educator*
Vachon, Reginald Irenee *mechanical engineer*
Winer, Ward Otis *mechanical engineer, educator*
Yoganathan, Ajit Prithiviraj *biomedical engineer, educator*
Zeng, Wei *environmental engineer*
Zinn, Ben T. *engineer, educator, consultant*

Big Canoe
Bendelius, Arthur George *engineering firm executive*

Columbus
Cummins, James Donald *retired electrical engineer*
Gibbons, Dona Alden Coe *electrical engineer*
Sweeney, Robert David *communications engineer*

Decatur
Holtzman, Mary *engineering company executive*
Tan, Li-Zhe *engineering educator, researcher*

Doraville
Wempner, Gerald Arthur *engineering educator*

Dublin
McCord, James Richard, III, *chemical engineer, mathematician*

Duluth
Colwell, Gene Thomas *engineering educator*
Luger, Donald R. *engineering company executive*

Gainesville
Jones, William Benjamin, Jr., *electrical engineering educator*

Macon
Aldridge, Melvin Dayne *engineering educator*
Leonard, Michael Steven *industrial engineering educator*

Marietta
Fitzgerald, John Edmund *civil engineering educator*
Miles, Thomas Caswell *aerospace engineer*
Ranu, Harcharan Singh *biomedical scientist, administrator, orthopaedic biomechanics educator*

Murrayville
Morris, Donald G. *engineering company executive*

Norcross
Ballard, Robert Clifford *automation engineer, failure analysis consultant*
Harrison, Gordon Ray *engineering executive, consultant, research scientist*
Moore, Christopher Barry *industrial engineer*
Puente, Jose Garza *safety engineer*
Sutherland, Mitchell Alsobrook, Jr., *mechanical engineer, consultant*

Peachtree City
Liang, Yue *engineer*
Snyder, Franklin Farison *hydrologic engineering consultant*

Rome
Lewis, Wayne Walton *industrial engineer*

Savannah
Hsu, Ming-Yu *engineering educator*

Smyrna
Michelson, Robert C. *engineering educator, researcher*

Townsend
Hicks, Harold Eugene *chemical engineer*

Warner Robins
DePriest, C(harles) David *engineering executive, retired military officer*

HAWAII

Honolulu
Adachi, Athan Ken *civil engineer*
Chen, Wai-Fah *civil engineering educator*
Choi, Song K. *mechanical engineer, educator*
Cox, Richard Horton *civil engineering executive*
Hamada, Harold Seichi *civil engineer, educator*
Kohloss, Frederick Henry *retired consulting engineer*
Koide, Frank Takayuki *electrical engineering educator*
Ma, Kougen *engineering educator, researcher*
Morioka, Brennon T. *engineering executive, political organization worker*
Ogburn, Hugh Bell *chemical engineer, consultant*
Sato, Richard Michio *consulting engineering company executive*
Saxena, Narendra K. *marine research educator*
Wang, Jaw-Kai *bioengineering educator*
Wataru, Weston Yasuo *civil engineer*
White, Gary Richard *electrical engineer*
Yee, Alfred Alphonse *structural engineer, consultant*

Kaneohe
Hanson, Richard Edwin *civil engineer*

Kapaau
McFee, Richard *electrical engineer, physicist*

Kilauea
McDowell, Edward R. H. *chemical engineer*

Wahiawa
Camery, John William *computer engineer*

IDAHO

Boise
Cory, Wallace Newell *retired civil engineer*
Zarges, Thomas H. *engineering executive*

Idaho Falls
Jacobsen, Richard T. *mechanical engineering educator*
Miller, Gregory Kent *structural engineer*
Riemke, Richard Allan *mechanical engineer*

Inkom
Ambrose, Tommy W. *chemical engineer, executive*

Moscow
DeShazer, James Arthur *biological engineer, educator, administrator*
Jackson, Melbourne Leslie *chemical engineering educator and administrator, consultant*
Johnson, Brian Keith *electrical engineering educator*

Pocatello
Valentine, Ralph Schuyler *chemical engineer, research director*

Pollock
Rubbert, Paul Edward *engineering executive*

Rigby
Peterson, Erle Vidaillet *retired metallurgical engineer*

ILLINOIS

Argonne
Chang, Yoon Il *nuclear engineer*
Jody, Bassam Jamil *energy engineer, researcher*
Kumar, Romesh *chemical engineer*
Miller, Shelby Alexander *chemical engineer, educator*

Aurora
Koopman, Richard Nelson *engineer, consultant*

Belleville
Thien-Stasko, Vicki Lynn *civil engineer*

Carbondale
Alghazo, Jaafar M. *computer engineer, educator*
Mohanty, Manoj K. *mineral engineer, educator*

Champaign
Davisson, Melvin Thomas *consulting engineer*
Kim, Sung O. *electrical engineer, researcher*
Korst, Helmut Hans *mechanical engineer, educator*
Sohn, Chang Wook *energy systems researcher, educator*

Chicago
Babcock, Lyndon Ross, Jr., *environmental engineer, educator*
Banerjee, Prashant *industrial engineer, educator, computer scientist*
Ben-Arie, Jezekiel *electrical engineer, computer scientist, educator*
Cheng, Paul Hung-Chiao *civil engineer*
Chung, Paul Myungha *mechanical engineer, educator*
Davis, DeForest P. *architectural engineer*
Dix, Rollin C(umming) *mechanical engineering educator, consultant*
Epstein, Raymond *engineering and architectural executive*
Erricolo, Danilo *engineering educator*
Fabisch, Gale Warren *environmental engineer*
Feng, Yinshan *mechanical engineer, researcher*
Fortuna, William Frank *architectural engineer, architect*
Gerstner, Robert William *structural engineering educator, consultant*
Gupta, Krishna Chandra *mechanical engineering educator*
Guralnick, Sidney Aaron *civil engineering educator*
Hartnett, James Patrick *engineering educator*
Jaramillo, Carlos Alberto *civil engineer*
Kennedy, Lawrence Allan *mechanical engineering educator*
Lin, James Chih-I *biomedical and electrical engineer, educator*
Linden, Henry Robert *chemical engineer, researcher*
Miller, Irving Franklin *chemical engineer, educator, biomedical engineer, educator, academic administrator*
Miller, Verne William *computer engineer, consultant*
Minkowycz, W.J. *mechanical engineering educator*
Minneste, Viktor, Jr., *retired engineering executive*
Mohammadian, Abolfazl *civil engineer, educator*
Murad, Sohail *engineer educator*
Murata, Tadao *engineering and computer science educator*
Nassos, George P. *chemical engineer, educator*
Nickel, Melvin Edwin *metallurgical engineer*
Omosheyin, Rotimi *electronics specialist, real estate company executive*
Rikoski, Richard Anthony *engineering executive, electrical engineer*
Rozenblat, Anatoly Isaacovich *manufacturing engineer, inventor*
Wong, Thomas Tang Yum *engineering educator*
Wyslotsky, Ihor *engineering company executive*

Chicago Heights
Kavis, George *engineer, photographer*

Clarendon Hills
Moritz, Donald Brooks *mechanical engineer, consultant*

Crete
Cosme, Luke George *retired structural engineer*

Darien
Hanson, Martin Philip *mechanical engineer, farmer*

Decatur
Graf, Karl Rockwell *nuclear engineer*
Koucky, John Richard *metallurgical engineer, manufacturing executive*

Deerfield
Saida, Toyoyasu *chemical and biochemical engineer*

Des Plaines
Alley, David Wayne *corrosion engineer*
Gahan, Brian C. *petroleum engineer, researcher*
Lyu, Seung Won *metallurgical engineer, environmental scientist*
Winfield, Michael D. *engineering company executive*

Downers Grove
Bogett, William R. *accident reconstructionist, investigator and safety engineer*

Dunlap
Reinsma, Harold Lawrence *design consultant, engineer*

Elmhurst
Burton, Darrell Irvin *engineering executive*
Parker, James John *engineering and marketing manager*

Evanston
Achenbach, Jan Drewes *engineering educator, director*
Bazant, Zdenek Pavel *engineering educator*
Belytschko, Ted *engineering educator*
Bobco, William David, Jr., *consulting engineering company executive*
Carr, Stephen Howard *materials engineer, educator*
Daskin, Mark Stephen *engineering educator*
Fessler, Raymond R. *metallurgical engineering consultant*
Fine, Morris Eugene *materials engineer, educator*
Fourer, Robert Harold *industrial engineering educator, consultant*
Frey, Donald Nelson *industrial engineer, educator, retired manufacturing executive*
Goldstick, Thomas Karl *biomedical engineering educator*
Keer, Leon Morris *engineering educator*
Krizek, Raymond John *civil engineering educator, consultant*
Murphy, Gordon John *electrical engineer, educator*
Ottino, Julio Mario *engineering educator*
Packman, Aaron Ian *environmental engineer, educator*
Rubenstein, Albert Harold *industrial engineering and management sciences educator*
Shah, Surendra Poonamchand *engineering educator*
Smith, Spencer Bailey *engineering and business educator*
Sobel, Alan *electrical engineer, physicist*
Taflove, Allen *electrical engineer, educator, researcher, consultant*
Van Ness, James Edward *electrical engineering educator*
Wachs, Alan L *quality assurance engineer*

Gilman
Ireland, Herbert Orin *retired engineering educator*

Glencoe
Dean, H. Clark *retired civil engineer, professional genealogist*

Glendale Heights
Rawal, Darshan Lal *civil engineer, structural engineer, consultant*

Glenview
Panarese, William C. *civil engineer*
Russell, Henry George *structural engineer*
Speer, David Blakeney *industrial executive*
Van Zelst, Theodore William *civil engineer, engineering company executive*

Gurnee
Sommerlad, Robert Edward *environmental research engineer*

Highland
Orthwein, William Coe *mechanical engineer*

Hillside
Hayes Jr., Richard J. *engineering company executive*

Hinsdale
Copley, Stephen Michael *materials science and technology engineer, consultant, manufacturing executive*

Joliet
Vandevender, Robert Lee, II, *nuclear engineering consultant*

La Grange
Mehlenbacher, Dohn Harlow *civil engineer, consultant*

Lake Forest
Lambert, John Boyd *chemical engineer, consultant*

Libertyville
Gallopoulos, Nicholas Efstratios *chemical engineer*

Machesney Park
Hornby, Robert Ray *mechanical engineer*

Mahomet
Sundy, George Joseph, Jr., *retired engineering executive*

Moline
Harrington, Roy Edwards *agricultural engineer, author*
Norris, William Robert *engineer, researcher*

Naperville
Crawford, Raymond Maxwell, Jr., *nuclear engineer*
McCaul, Joseph Patrick *chemical engineer*
Vora, Manu Kishandas *chemical engineer, quality consultant*

Normal
Devinatz, Victor Gary *industrial relations educator*

Northbrook
Adler, Robert *electronics engineer*
Boettcher, Robert Walter *civil engineer*
Pertz, Douglas A. *engineering executive*

Oak Brook
Degerstrom, James Marvin *retired engineering executive*

Oak Forest
Kogut, Kenneth Joseph *consulting engineer*

Oak Park
Clark, John Peter, III, *engineering consultant*

Oakbrook Terrace
Savage, Murray *engineering executive*

Palatine
Kieft, Gerald Nelson *mechanical engineer*

Park Forest
Williams, Jack Raymond *civil engineer*

Peoria
Kroll, Dennis Edwards *industrial engineering educator*

Plainfield
Chakrabarti, Subrata Kumar *marine research engineer*

Quincy
Centanni, Ross J. *engineering executive*

Rockford
Eliason, Jon Tate *electrical engineer*
Shepler, John Edward *engineering executive*

Rolling Meadows
Eckel, James J. *flight test engineer*
Theis, Steven Thomas *safety engineer*

Roselle
Marshall, James Andrew *civil engineer, real estate developer*

Rushville
Zingher, Harry Lee *chemical engineer*

Saint Joseph
Valencia, Rogelio Pasco *electronics engineer*

Schaumburg
De Lerno, Manuel Joseph *electrical engineer*
Hambley, Douglas Frederick *geological and environmental engineer*
Kornowski, Robert Richard *engineer, science educator*
Talukdar, Anup Kumar *computer engineer, researcher*

Scott Air Force Base
Fox, Leonard Dean *civil engineer, air force officer*

Skokie
Corley, William Gene *engineering research executive*
Siegal, Rita Goran *engineering company executive*

Springfield
Ballenger, Hurley René *electrical engineer*

Tinley Park
West, David Wayne *mechanical engineer*

Urbana
Addy, Alva Leroy *mechanical engineer*
Axford, Roy Arthur *nuclear engineering educator*
Bergeron, Clifton George *ceramics engineer, educator*
Blahut, Richard Edward *electrical and computer engineering educator*
Braatz, Richard Dean *chemical engineer*
Chao, Bei Tse *mechanical engineering educator*
Chato, John Clark *mechanical and bioengineering educator*
Coleman, James J. *electrical engineer, educator*
Conry, Thomas Francis *mechanical engineering educator, consultant*
Cusano, Cristino *mechanical engineer, educator*
Daniel, David Edwin *civil engineer, educator*
Dick, William Allen *engineering educator*
Eden, James Gary *electrical engineer, educator, physicist, researcher*
Gaddy, Oscar Lee *electrical engineering educator*
Hall, William Joel *civil engineer, educator*
Hannon, Bruce Michael *engineering educator*
Hess, Karl *electrical and computer engineering educator*
Holonyak, Nick, Jr., *electrical engineering educator*
Huang, Thomas Shi-Tao *electrical engineering educator, researcher*
Krier, Herman *mechanical and industrial engineering educator*
Kumar, Panganamala Ramana *electrical and computer engineering educator*
Mayes, Paul Eugene *engineering educator, consultant*
Miley, George Hunter *nuclear and electrical engineering educator*
Miller, Robert Earl *engineering educator*
Rao, Nannapaneni Narayana *electrical engineer*
Ravaioli, Umberto *electrical engineer, educator*
Sauer, Peter William *electrical engineer, educator*
Snoeyink, Vernon L. *civil engineer, educator*
Walker, William Hamilton *civil engineer, educator*

Washington
Hallinan, John Cornelius *mechanical engineering consultant*

Westchester
Tutins, Antons *electrical and audio engineer*

Wheaton
Astrup, Jens Leo *retired civil engineer*

Wilmette
Muhlenbruch, Carl W. *civil engineer*
Wadden, Richard Albert *environmental engineer, educator, science administrator, consultant*

Wood Dale
Bullen, Daniel Bernard *mechanical engineering educator*

INDIANA

Albany
White, William Richard *manufacturing engineer, consultant*

Angola
Lin, Ping-Wha *engineering educator, consultant*
Meeks, Kenneth W. *civil engineer, educator*

Carmel
Kalwara, Joseph John *engineer*

Columbus
Matthews, Drexel Gene *quality control executive*

Corydon
Speth, Camille *engineer*

Evansville
Blandford, Dick *electrical engineering and communications educator*
Stamps, Douglas *mechanical engineer, educator*

Fort Wayne
Hannigan, John Dennis *logistics engineer*
Lyons, Jerry Lee *mechanical engineer*
Streeter, Robert Davenport *electrical engineer, consultant*
Weatherford, George Edward *civil engineer*

Gary
Johnson, Jerome *engineer*

Hammond
Kopischke, Chris David *mechanical engineer*
Pierson, Edward Samuel *engineering educator, consultant*

Indianapolis
Griffith, Roy Lloyd *design engineer*
Ramos, Jose A. *engineering educator*
Svirsky, Mario Alfredo *biomedical engineer*

Lafayette
Caldwell, Barrett Scott *industrial engineering educator*
Etzel, James Edward *environmental engineering educator*
Finch, Robert Jonathan *communications engineer, consultant*
Geddes, Leslie Alexander *engineering educator, forensic engineer, physiologist*
Gustafson, Winthrop Adolph *aeronautical and astronautical engineering educator*
Huynh, Victor C. *process engineer*
Liley, Peter Edward *retired mechanical engineering educator*
Lindenlaub, John Charles *electrical engineer, educator*
Osborn, John Robert *retired mechanical engineer*
Ott, Karl Otto *nuclear engineer, consultant*
Smith, Kenneth Dale *civil engineer, consultant*

Leavenworth
Kreisle, William Eckman *civil engineer, surveyor, research cartographer, writer*

Mount Vernon
Moll, Joseph Eugene *chemical engineer, chemical company executive*

Muncie
Seymour, Richard Deming *technology educator*

Noblesville
Evans, Richard James *mechanical engineer*
Monical, Robert Duane *engineering company executive*

Notre Dame
Gray, William Gucrin *civil engineering educator*
Incropera, Frank Paul *mechanical engineering educator*
Jerger, Edward William *engineering educator, dean*
Merz, James Logan *electrical engineering and materials educator, researcher*
Michel, Anthony Nikolaus *electrical engineering educator, researcher*
Mueller, Thomas James *engineering educator, researcher*
Ovaert, Timothy Christopher *mechanical engineering educator*
Schmitz, Roger Anthony *chemical engineer, educator, academic administrator*
Stadtherr, Mark A. *chemical engineer, educator*

Purdue University
Ramkrishna, Doraiswami *chemical engineering educator, researcher*

Syracuse
Blakesley, Wayne Lavere, Jr., *retired production engineer*

Terre Haute
Malooley, David Joseph *electronics and computer technology educator*
Wheelock, Larry Arthur *retired engineer, consultant*

West Lafayette
Albright, Lyle Frederick *chemical engineering educator*
Altschaeffl, Adolph George *civil engineering educator, retired*
Andres, Ronald Paul *chemical engineer, educator*
Barany, James Walter *industrial engineering educator*

Chao, Kwang-Chu *chemical engineer, educator*
Cohen, Raymond *mechanical engineer, educator*
Delleur, Jacques William *civil engineering educator*
Greenkorn, Robert Albert *chemical engineering educator*
Jackson, Mark James *engineering educator*
Ladisch, Michael R. *engineering educator*
Landgrebe, David Allen *electrical engineer*
Lin, Pen-Min *electrical engineer, educator*
Marshall, Francis Joseph *aerospace engineer*
Mc Laughlin, John Francis *civil engineer, educator*
Ong, Chee-Mun *engineering educator*
Peeta, Srinivas *civil engineering educator, consultant*
Salvendy, Gavriel *industrial engineer, educator*
Schwartz, Richard John *electrical engineering educator, researcher*
Solberg, James Joseph *industrial engineering educator*
Sweet, Arnold Lawrence *industrial engineering educator*
Taber, Margaret Ruth *engineering educator*
Thomas, Marlin Uluess *industrial engineer, educator, academic administrator*
Tomovic, Mileta Milos *mechanical engineer, educator*
Varma, Arvind *chemical engineering educator, researcher*
Viskanta, Raymond *mechanical engineering educator*
Wankat, Phillip Charles *chemical engineering educator*
Williams, Theodore Joseph *engineering educator*
Yao, Bin *mechanical engineering educator*

Westfield
Tanov, Romil Raykov *mechanical engineer, researcher*

IOWA

Ames
Anderson, Robert Morris, Jr., *electrical engineer*
Baumann, Edward Robert *environmental engineering educator*
Black, James Robert *industrial engineer*
Brown, Robert Grover *engineering educator*
Colvin, Thomas Stuart *agricultural engineer, farmer*
Johnson, Howard Paul *agricultural engineering educator*
Jones, Edwin Channing, Jr., *electrical and computer engineering educator*
Kanwar, Rameshwar Singh *agricultural engineer, researcher, educator*
Larsen, William Lawrence *engineering educator*
Melvin, Stewart Wayne *engineering educator*
Okiishi, Theodore Hisao *mechanical engineering educator*
Reilly, Peter John *chemical engineer, educator*
Sanders, Wallace Wolfred, Jr., *civil engineer*
Wilder, David Randolph *materials engineer, consultant*

Bettendorf
Heyderman, Arthur Jerome *engineer, civilian military employee*

Cedar Falls
Rao, Posinasetti Nageswara *manufacturing engineering educator*

Cherokee
Clark, Larry Dalton *civil engineer*

Davenport
Chowdhury, Ali Asraf *electrical engineer, researcher*
Pedersen, Karen Sue *electrical engineer*

Iowa City
Marshall, Jeffrey Scott *mechanical engineer, educator*
Park, Joon Bu *biomedical engineer, researcher, educator*
Patel, Virendra Chaturbhai *mechanical engineer, educator*
Sun, Lizhi *engineering educator, researcher*

Madrid
Handy, Richard Lincoln *civil engineer, educator*

Muscatine
Stanley, Richard Holt *consulting engineer*
Thomopulos, Gregs G. *consulting engineering company executive*

Orange City
Hancock, Albert Sidney, Jr., *engineering executive*

KANSAS

Garden City
Buchele, Wesley Fisher *retired agricultural engineering educator*

Lawrence
Benjamin, Bezaleel Solomon *architectural engineer, educator*
Darwin, David *civil engineering educator, researcher, consultant*
Green, Don Wesley *chemical and petroleum engineering educator*
Grzymala-Busse, Jerzy Witold *engineering educator*
McCabe, John Lee *engineer, educator*
McCabe, Steven Lee *structural engineer*
Moore, Richard Kerr *electrical engineering educator*
Muirhead, Vincent Uriel *retired aerospace engineer*
Roskam, Jan *aerospace engineer*
Rowland, James Richard *electrical engineering educator*

Leawood
Karmeier, Delbert Fred *engineer, consultant, realtor*

Manhattan
Cai, Liang-Wu *engineering educator*
Chung, Do Sup *agricultural engineering educator*
Hagen, Lawrence Jacob *agricultural engineer*
Johnson, William Howard *agricultural engineer, educator*
Lee, E(ugene) Stanley *engineering educator*
Pei, Zj *engineer, educator, researcher*
Russell, Eugene Robert, Sr., *engineering educator, administrator*
Simons, Gale Gene *nuclear and electrical engineer, educator*

Overland Park
Daniel, Karen *engineering and design company executive*
Tubbs, David Eugene *mechanical engineer, marketing professional*
Vaughan, Brad *engineering and design company executive*
Voeller, John George *engineer*

Salina
Selm, Robert Prickett *engineer, consultant*
Sigai, A. Gary *engineer*

Shawnee Mission
Bartlett, Roger Danforth *engineering executive*
Gaboury, David *engineering company executive*

Topeka
Nason, Barry Mark *systems engineer, mathematician, educator*
Sutherland, John Bennett *chemical engineer*

Wichita
Koch, Charles de Ganahl *engineering company executive*
McKee, George Moffitt, Jr., *civil engineer, consultant*
Siginer, Dennis A. *mechanical engineering educator, university dean*
Wilhelm, William Jean *civil engineering educator*

KENTUCKY

Ashland
Scharp, Robert Charles *mining engineer, energy company executive*

Bellevue
Lemlich, Robert *chemical engineer, educator*

Lexington
Baker, Merl *engineering educator*
Brock, Louis Milton, Jr., *engineering educator, researcher*
Caroland, William Bourne *structural engineer*
Chen, Zhi *electrical engineering educator*
Drake, Vaughn Paris, Jr., *electrical engineer, retired telephone company executive*
Male, Alan Thomas *engineering educator, association executive*
Teegavarapu, Ramesh Satya *engineering educator, researcher*
Todd, Lee Trover, Jr., *electrical engineer*

Louisville
Cornelius, Wayne Anderson *electrical and computer engineering consultant*
Garcia, Rafael Jorge *retired chemical engineer*
Longuet, Gregory Arthur *automation engineer, consultant*
Siewert, Robin Noelle *planning engineer*
Tran, Long Trieu *industrial engineer*
Wang, Chung-Hsiao *industrial engineer*

Prospect
Kehlbeck, Joseph H. *software developer and consultant*

Radcliff
Jarvis, John Michael *logistical engineer, writer*

Winchester
Studebaker, John Milton *utilities engineer, consultant, educator*

LOUISIANA

Baker
Cross, James Edward *electrical engineering educator*

Baton Rouge
Arman, Ara *civil engineering educator*
Avent, Raymond Richard, Jr., *civil engineering educator*
Bengtson, Richard Lee *agricultural engineer, educator*
Bernhard, James M., Jr., *engineering executive*
Chen, Peter Pin-Shan *electrical engineering, computer science and internet/web educator, data processing executive*
Corripio, Armando Benito *chemical engineering educator*
de Queiroz, Marcio S. *engineering educator*
Gammon, Malcolm Ernest, Sr., *surveying and engineering executive*
Khonsari, Michael M. *mechanical engineering educator*
Lima, Marybeth *engineering educator*
Moody, Gene Byron *engineering executive, small business owner, minister*
Pike, Ralph Webster *chemical engineer, educator, university administrator*
Reible, Danny David *environmental chemical engineer, educator*
Sinclair, Glenn Bruce *mechanical engineering educator, researcher*
Tipton, Kenneth Warren *agricultural administrator, researcher*
Tumay, Mehmet Taner *geotechnical consultant, educator, research administrator*
Vaidyanathan, Ramachandran *computer engineer, educator*
Voyiadjis, George Zino *civil engineer, educator*

Dubach
Straughan, William Thomas *engineering educator*

Elm Grove
Livingston, John H. *retired engineer, retired military officer*

Hammond
Parish, Richard Lee *engineer, consultant*

Harvey
Simon, Keith R. *safety engineer, petroleum engineer, professional disc jockey*

Jennings
Moniruzzaman, Mohammed *chemical engineer*

Kenner
Hallila, Bruce Allan *welding engineer*
Siebel, Mathias Paul *mechanical engineer, consultant*

Lafayette
Darwish, Tarek *computer engineer*
Domingue, Emery *retired consulting engineering company executive*
Fang, Cheng-Shen *chemical engineering educator*
Marshak, Alan Howard *electrical engineer, educator*
Rickey, Horace B., Jr., *retired engineer*
Salters, Richard Stewart *engineering company executive*

Lake Charles
Levingston, Ernest Lee *engineering company executive*

New Orleans
Boh, Robert Henry *civil engineer, construction company executive*
Lannes, William Joseph, III, *electrical engineer*
Lintinger, Gregory John *electrical engineer, educator*
McCorquodale, J. Alexander *civil and environmental engineer, educator*
Michaelides, Efstathios Emmanuel *mechanical engineer*
Nelson, Waldemar Stanley *civil engineer, consultant*
Quirk, Peter Richard *engineering company executive*
Wafer, Douglas Drew *environmental engineer*
Wang, Ting *mechanical engineering educator*

Ruston
Hale, Paul Nolen, Jr., *engineering administrator, educator*
Selmic, Rastko R. *engineering educator*
Sterling, Raymond Leslie *civil engineering educator, researcher, consultant*
Thompson, Ronald H. *chemical engineer, educator*

Slidell
Tewell, Joseph Robert, Jr., *electrical engineer*

MAINE

Bangor
Hsu, Yu Kao *aerospace scientist, mathematician, educator*

Falmouth
Rohsenow, Warren Max *retired mechanical engineer, educator*

Orono
Matthews, Larryl Kent *mechanical engineering educator*

Scarborough
Raisbeck, Gordon *systems engineer, consultant*

Waterville
Laurence, Robert Lionel *chemical engineering educator*

MARYLAND

Aberdeen Proving Ground
Berry, Patrick Lowell *chemical engineer*
Cozby, Richard Scott *electronics engineer, military officer*
Gupta, Aaron Das *mechanical engineer*
Waugh, John Douglas *engineer, researcher*

Adelphi
Bayne, Stephen B. *electronics engineer, researcher*
Mait, Joseph N. *electrical engineer, educator*
Torrieri, Don Joseph *electronics engineer, mathematician, researcher*

Annapolis
DiAiso, Robert Joseph *civil engineer*
Johnson, Bruce *engineering educator*
Rogers, David Freeman *aerospace engineering educator*

Baltimore
Bero, Joseph Martin *manufacturing engineer*
Culurciello, Eugenio *research engineer, educator*
Emerick, Norman Cooper *consulting engineer*
Girovich, Mark Jacob *mechanical engineer*
Jelinek, Frederick *electrical engineer, educator*
Jenniches, F. Suzanne *engineering executive*
Kattel, Bheem Prakash *engineering educator, consultant*
Katz, Joseph Louis *chemical engineer, educator*
Knoedler, Elmer L. *retired chemical engineer*
Lemer, Andrew Charles *engineer, economist*
Nathanson, Harvey Charles *electrical engineer*
O'Melia, Charles Richard *environmental engineer, educator*
Sharpe, William Norman, Jr., *mechanical engineer, educator*
Washington, Strother Lee, Jr., *mechanical engineer, design engineer*

Bethesda
Burdeshaw, William Brooksbank *engineering executive*
Fuller, Joseph, Jr., *aeronautical engineer*
Kemelhor, Robert E(lias) *mechanical engineer*
Kutemeyer, Peter Martin *industrial engineering executive*
Saville, Thorndike, Jr., *coastal engineer*

Chevy Chase
Cheng, David Keun *engineering educator*

Cooley, William Crockett *mechanical engineer, retired educator*
Hirschhorn, Joel Stephen *engineer*
Lebow, Irwin Leon *communications engineering consultant*
Rockwell, Theodore *nuclear engineer*
Short, Steve Eugene *engineer*

Cockeysville Hunt Valley
Barr, Irwin Robert *retired aeronautical engineer*

College Park
Aggour, Mohamed Sherif *civil engineer, educator*
Anderson, John David, Jr., *aerospace engineer*
Ayyub, Bilal M. *civil engineering educator, researcher, executive*
Barbe, David Franklin *electrical engineer, educator*
Datta, Madhumita *electrical engineer, researcher*
Granatstein, Victor Lawrence *electrical engineer, educator*
Gupta, Ashwani Kumar *mechanical engineering educator*
Lathan, Corinna Elisabeth *aerospace engineer*
Levine, William Silver *electrical engineer, educator*
Lin, Hung C. *electrical engineer educator*
Marcus, Steven Irl *electrical engineering educator*
Newcomb, Robert Wayne *electrical engineer educator*
Qi, Jianwei *mechanical engineer, researcher*
Rao, Jaganmohan Boppana Lakshimi *electrical engineer*
Taylor, Leonard Stuart *engineering educator, consultant*
Vankatesan, Thirumalai *engineering educator*

Columbia
Doi, Yutaka *electrical engineer*
Moulton, Paul Douglas (Pete Moulton) *information technology consultant*
Straja, Sorin Radu *chemical engineer, mathematician, computer programmer*
Van Buiten, Robert D. *aerospace engineer*

Crofton
Laurenson, Robert Mark *mechanical engineer*

Elkton
Chen, Oliver Tsung-Yu *chemical engineer, researcher*

Finksburg
Konigsberg, Robert Lee *electrical engineer*

Fort Washington
Caveny, Leonard Hugh *mechanical engineer, aerospace scientist, consultant*

Frederick
Bryan, John Leland *retired engineering educator*
Kelsey, Ronald Grant *retired environmental engineer*
Wolf, Donald Joseph *industrial engineer, consultant*

Gaithersburg
Cookson, Alan Howard *electrical engineer, researcher*
Ferrell, Charles Madison *retired nuclear engineer, health physicist*
Gu, Xiaohong *polymer engineer, chemist*
Jahanmir, Said *materials scientist, mechanical engineer*
Levine, Robert Sidney *chemical engineer, consultant*
Marin, Cynthia Myers (Cheryl Marin) *systems engineer*
Presser, Cary *research engineer*
Ulbrecht, Jaromir Josef *chemical engineer*
Wiederhorn, Sheldon M. *materials engineer*
Wright, Richard Newport, III, *retired engineering executive, engineering educator*

Glenwood
Billig, Frederick Stucky *mechanical engineer*

Greenbelt
Amato, Deborah Douglass *aerospace engineer*
Bryant, Paul T. *electronics engineering manager*
Healey, John Joseph *engineering executive, civil engineer*
Levitt, Gerald Steven *engineering executive*
Vranish, John Michael *electrical engineer, researcher*

Hunt Valley
Kinstlinger, Jack *engineering executive, consultant*
Plaks, Albert I. *electrical engineer, educator*

Hyattsville
Kirk, James Allen *mechanical engineering educator*

Indian Head
Latimer, Paul Jerry *non-destructive testing engineer*

Jessup
Hsiao, Chao-Tsung *engineer*

Lanham Seabrook
Cooper, Robert Alfred *electrical engineer*

Laurel
Dallman, Paul Jerald *engineer, writer*
Darrell, Charles G. *engineer*
Eaton, Alvin Ralph *aeronautical and systems engineer, research and development administrator*
Westhaver, Lawrence Albert *electronics engineer, consultant*

Linthicum
Metzel, Alan Barry *manufacturing engineer*

Linthicum Heights
Skillman, William Alfred *consulting engineering executive*

Patuxent River
Adams, Richard Eugene *aerospace engineer, project manager*

Potomac
Lawrence, Robert Edward *electrical engineer*
Peters, Frank Albert *retired chemical engineer*

Williams, Peter MacLellan *nuclear engineer*

Queenstown
Corn, Morton *environmental engineer, educator*

Reisterstown
Broadbent, J. Streett *engineering executive*

Rockville
Burdick, William MacDonald *biomedical engineer*
McDonald, Capers Walter *biomedical engineer, manufacturing executive, educator*
Menendez, Adolfo *engineering company executive*
Reddy, Thikkavarapu Ramachandra *electrical engineer*
Seagle, Edgar Franklin *environmental engineer, consultant*
Sorensen, John Noble *retired mechanical and nuclear engineer*

Silver Spring
Hermach, Francis Lewis *consulting engineer*
Koltnow, Peter Gregory *engineering consultant*
Mok, Carson Kwok-Chi *structural engineer*
Okigbo, Franklin C. *engineering company executive*
Scipio, L(ouis) Albert, II, *retired aerospace science engineering educator, architect, military historian*
Shalowitz, Erwin Emmanuel *civil engineer*
Yanushevsky, Rafael Tovie *electromechanical engineer, scientist, consultant, educator*

Suitland
Brooks, Richard C. *electrical engineer, federal government executive*
Cheng, Jian-Yu *mechanical engineer, researcher, application developer*

Towson
Huang, Joseph Chen-Huan *civil engineer*

Upper Marlboro
Freeman, Ernest Robert *engineering executive*

West Bethesda
Sevik, Maurice *acoustical engineer, researcher*

MASSACHUSETTS

Acton
Hicks, Walter Joseph *electrical engineer*

Amherst
Bobba, Kumar Manoj *engineer, researcher*
Franks, Lewis E. *electrical and computer engineering educator, researcher*
Koren, Israel *electrical and computer engineering educator*
Nash, William Arthur *civil engineer, educator*
Schaubert, Daniel Harold *electrical engineering educator*
Swift, Calvin Thomas *electrical and computer engineering educator*
Terpenny, Janis P. *engineering educator, researcher*
Vogl, Otto *polymer science and engineering educator*
Winter, Horst Henning *chemical engineer, educator*

Andover
Jakes, William Chester *electrical engineer*
Marsh, Robert Buford *chemical engineer, consultant*

Attleboro
Brodeur, Russell P. *design engineer*

Attleboro Falls
Kulwicki, Bernard Michael *ceramics engineer, researcher*

Bedford
An, Hong *engineer*
Fante, Ronald Louis *engineering scientist*
Jelalian, Albert V. *electrical engineer*
Johansen, Jack T. *engineering company executive*
Labudovic, Marko *research scientist, consultant*
Winter, David Louis *systems engineer, human factors scientist, retired*

Belmont
Haralampu, George Stelios *electric power engineer, former engineering executive electric utility company*
Merrill, Edward Wilson *chemical engineering educator*

Billerica
Akhavan, Farhad *electrical engineer*
Kinsman, Robert Preston *biomedical plastics engineer*

Boston
Baillieul, John Brouard *aerospace engineering and applied mathematics educator*
Buchanan, Walter Woolwine *electrical engineer, educator, academic administrator*
Chen, Chih-Fan *electrical engineer*
Choo, Arthur C.S. *structural engineer, consultant*
De Luca, Carlo John *biomedical engineer, educator*
Frank-Kamenetskii, Maxim D. *biomedical engineer*
Jain, Rakesh K. *chemical engineer, tumor biology educator*
Langer, Robert Martin *retired chemical engineering company executive, consultant*
Miaoulis, Ioannis Nikolaos *mechanical engineer, educator*
Moore, Richard Lawrence *structural engineer, consultant*
Pierce, Allan Dale *engineering educator, researcher, editor*
Teich, Malvin Carl *electrical engineering educator*
Wiegner, Allen Walter *biomedical engineering educator, researcher*
Zaldastani, Othar *structural engineer*

Boxford
Yates, John Robert, Jr., *engineer, educator*

Brookline
Eden, Murray *electrical engineer, emeritus educator*
Felsen, Leopold B. *engineering educator*

Burlington
Nananukul, Soracha *electrical engineer*

Cambridge
Abelson, Harold *electrical engineer, educator*
Abernathy, Frederick Henry *mechanical engineering educator*
Argon, Ali Suphi *mechanical engineering educator*
Baggeroer, Arthur Bernard *electrical engineering educator*
Bathe, Klaus-Jurgen *mechanical engineering educator, science association director*
Battin, Richard Horace *astronautical engineer*
Beér, János Miklós *engineering educator*
Ben-Akiva, Moshe Emanuel *civil engineering educator*
Benedict, Manson *chemical engineer, educator*
Beranek, Leo Leroy *acoustical consultant*
Bras, Rafael Luis *engineering educator*
Brenner, Howard *chemical engineering educator*
Brown, Robert Arthur *chemical engineering educator*
Carmichael, Alexander Douglas *engineering educator*
Chen, Sow-Hsin *nuclear engineering educator, researcher*
Cohen, Morris *engineering educator*
Cohen, Robert Edward *chemical engineering educator, consultant*
Colton, Clark Kenneth *chemical engineering educator*
Covert, Eugene Edzards *aerospace engineer, physics educator*
Crandall, Stephen Harry *engineering educator*
de Neufville, Richard Lawrence *engineering educator*
Dewey, Clarence Forbes, Jr., *engineering educator*
Drake, Elisabeth Mertz *chemical engineer, consultant*
Duffy, Robert Aloysius *aeronautical engineer*
Dugundji, John *aeronautical engineer*
Eagleson, Peter Sturges *civil engineer, environmental engineer, educator*
Fantone, Stephen Dennis *electrical engineer*
Fay, James Alan *mechanical engineering educator*
Flemings, Merton Corson *engineering educator, materials scientist*
Fujimoto, James G. *electrical engineering educator*
Furman, Thomas D., Jr., *engineering company executive*
Gallager, Robert Gray *electrical engineering educator*
Gatos, Harry Constantine *engineering educator*
Greitzer, Edward Marc *aeronautical engineering educator, consultant*
Gyftopoulos, Elias Panayiotis *mechanical and nuclear engineering educator*
Hansen, Kent Forrest *nuclear engineering educator*
Hansman, Robert John, Jr., *aeronautics and astronautics educator*
Harris, Wesley L. *aeronautical engineer, educator*
Heywood, John Benjamin *mechanical engineering educator*
How, Hoton *electrical engineer*
Ippen, Erich Peter *electrical engineer, educator, physicist*
Kazimi, Mujid Suliman *nuclear engineer, educator*
Ladd, Charles Cushing, III, *civil engineer, educator*
Langer, Robert Samuel *chemical, biomedical engineering educator*
Latanision, Ronald Michael *materials science and engineering consultant*
Leveson, Nancy G. *aeronautical engineer*
Lim, Jae Soo *engineering educator, information systems*
Magee, Christopher L. *systems engineer*
Mann, Robert Wellesley *biomedical engineer, educator*
Marini, Robert Charles *environmental engineering executive*
Markey, Winston Roscoe *aeronautical engineering educator*
Marks, David Hunter *civil engineering educator*
Milgram, Jerome H. *marine and ocean engineer, educator*
Nightingale, Deborah Seifert *systems engineer, consultant*
Penfield, Paul Livingstone, Jr., *electrical engineering educator*
Pian, Theodore Hsueh-Huang *engineering educator, consultant*
Probstein, Ronald Filmore *mechanical engineering educator*
Reid, Robert Clark *chemical engineering educator*
Rogers, Peter Phillips *environmental engineering educator, city planner*
Roos, Daniel *engineering educator*
Ruina, Jack Philip *electrical engineer, educator*
Russell, Kenneth Calvin *metallurgical engineer, educator*
Samson, Leona D. *biological engineering educator, research center director, researcher*
Satterfield, Charles Nelson *chemical engineer, educator*
Smith, Kenneth Alan *chemical engineer, educator*
Staelin, David Hudson *electrical engineering educator, consultant*
Stevens, Kenneth Noble *electrical engineer, educator*
Suh, Nam Pyo *mechanical engineering educator*
Todreas, Neil Emmanuel *nuclear engineering educator*
Triantafyllou, Michael Stefanos *ocean engineering educator*
Trilling, Leon *aeronautical engineering educator*
Tuller, Harry Louis *materials science and engineering educator*
Ungar, Eric Edward *mechanical engineer*
Vander Velde, Wallace Earl *aeronautical and astronautical educator*
White, David Calvin *electrical engineer, energy educator, consultant*
Whitman, Robert Van Duyne *civil engineer, educator*
Williams, James Henry, Jr., *mechanical engineer, educator, consultant*
Wuensch, Bernhardt John *ceramic engineering educator*
Yannas, Ioannis Vassilios *polymer scientist, educator*

Canton
Costa, Pat Vincent *automation sciences executive*

Carlisle
Drew, Philip Garfield *retired engineering company executive, consultant*

Concord
Davidson, Frank Paul *retired macroengineer, retired lawyer*
Villers, Philippe *mechanical engineer*
Woll, Harry J. *electrical engineer*

Danvers
Shenai, Deodatta Vinayak *chemical engineer*

Dartmouth
Notaros, Branislav M. *electrical engineer, educator*

Fall River
Alam, Akm A. *ceramics engineer*

Foxboro
Cai, Hongzhi *electrical engineer, researcher*
Pierce, Francis Casimir *civil engineer*

Framingham
Bose, Amar Gopal *electrical engineering educator*
Crossley, Frank Alphonso *retired metallurgical engineer*
Kendall, Julius *consulting engineer*
Lindsay, Leslie *packaging engineer*

Gloucester
Baxter, Larry K. *electrical engineer, consultant*

Hanscom AFB
Schmitt, Stephen Richard *electronics engineer*

Holbrook
Crandlemere, Robert Wayne *engineering executive*

Hopkinton
DiDomenico, Angela Terese *industrial engineer, researcher*

Jamaica Plain
Shapiro, Ascher Herman *mechanical engineer, educator, consultant*

Lawrence
Devaney, Robert James, Jr., *environmental engineer*

Lenox
Coffin, Louis Fussell, Jr., *mechanical engineer*

Lexington
Aldrich, Nancy Cook *engineer, administrator*
Aronin, Lewis Richard *metallurgical engineer*
Bailey, Fred Coolidge *retired engineering consulting company executive*
Beusch, John Ulrich *engineer, researcher*
Brookner, Eli *electrical engineer*
Bussgang, Julian Jakub *electronics engineer*
Dinneen, Gerald Paul *electrical engineer, former government official*
Freed, Charles *engineering consultant, researcher*
Gelb, Arthur *electrical and systems engineering executive*
Glaser, Peter Edward *mechanical engineer, consultant, educator*
Haldeman, Charles Waldo, III, *aeronautical engineer*
Keicher, William Eugene *electrical engineer*
Marchilena, Frank S. *engineering company executive*
Martinez, David R. *electrical engineer, science educator*
Morrow, Walter Edwin, Jr., *electrical engineer, university laboratory administrator*

Lincoln
Kerrebrock, Jack Leo *aeronautics and astronautics engineering educator*
Kusik, Charles Lembit *chemical engineer*

Longmeadow
Lemnios, Andrew Zachery *aerospace engineer, educator, researcher*

Lynn
Chow, Humphrey Wai *mechanical engineer*
D'Entremont, Edward Joseph *infosystems engineer, educator*

Manchester
Arntsen, Arnt Peter *engineer, consultant*

Marlborough
Bennett, C. Leonard *electrical engineer*
Hunt, Philip Charles *engineer, consultant*

Medford
Abriola, Linda M. *civil engineer, environmental engineer*
Greif, Robert *mechanical engineering educator*
Howell, Alvin Harold *engineering executive, educator*
Nelson, Frederick Carl *mechanical engineering educator*
Uhlir, Arthur, Jr., *electrical engineer, university administrator*

Medway
Hoag, David Garratt *aerospace engineer*

Milford
Carson, Charles Henry *microwave engineer*

Nantucket
Kales, Paul Albert *engineering educator, cartoonist*

Natick
Myers, Timothy James *chemical engineer, consultant*

Newton
Fragala, Guy Andrew *safety engineer, educator*
Sheridan, Thomas Brown *mechanical engineering and applied psychology educator, researcher, consultant*

Newton Center
Mark, Melvin *consulting mechanical engineer, educator*

Northborough
Jeas, William C. *aerospace engineering executive, consultant*
Licht, Robert H. *ceramics engineer*

Norwood
Fuller, Samuel Henry, III, *computer engineer*
Sheingold, Daniel H. *electrical engineer*

Paxton
Clarke, Edward Nielsen *engineering science educator*

Peabody
Peters, Leo Francis *environmental engineer*

Pittsfield
Feigenbaum, Armand Vallin *systems engineer, systems equipment executive*
Shammas, Nazih Kheirallah *environmental engineer, consultant, engineering educator*

Quincy
Colgan, Sumner *manufacturing engineer, chemical engineer*

Sharon
Wisotsky, Serge Sidorovich *engineering executive*

Shutesbury
Abbott, Douglas Eugene *engineering educator*

Somerset
Bower, John *retired fluid mechanics engineer, commissioner*

South Deerfield
Waluk, Stanley Peter *corporate engineering official*

Stoughton
Graber, Samuel David *environmental and water resources engineer, consultant*
Ural, Erdem A. *engineering executive, educator*

Sudbury
Fowler, Charles Albert *electronics engineer*

Swampscott
Kaufman, William Morris *engineer consultant*

Waban
Christian, John Thomas *civil engineer*

Waltham
Guerra, John Michael *optical engineer*
Gumpertz, Werner Herbert *structural engineering company executive*
Liu, Huamin Patrick *industrial engineer, researcher*

Wellesley
Weil, Thomas Alexander *electronics engineer, retired*

Westborough
Gionfriddo, Maurice Paul *aeronautical engineer, research and development company executive*

Weston
Katz, William Emanuel *retired chemical engineer*

Wilmington
Eldada, Louay A. *fiber optic engineer*

Winchester
Hansen, Robert Joseph *civil engineer*
Koppel, Lowell B. *chemical engineer*

Worcester
Katz, Robert Nathan *ceramic engineer, educator*
Parrish, Edward Alton, Jr., *electrical and computer engineering educator, academic administrator*
Rong, Yiming *manufacturing engineering educator*

Wrentham
Bittenbender, Brad James *safety and health engineer*

MICHIGAN

Adrian
Coleman, John Wesley *fluid mechanics engineer, heat transfer engineer*

Ann Arbor
Adamson, Thomas Charles, Jr., *aerospace engineering educator, consultant*
Becher, William Don *retired electrical engineer, engineering educator, writer*
Bilello, John Charles *engineering educator, director*
Bitondo, Domenic *engineering executive*
Carnahan, Brice *chemical engineer, educator*
Chaffin, Don Brian *industrial engineering educator, research director*
Director, Stephen William *electrical and computer engineering educator, academic administrator*
England, Anthony Wayne *engineering educator, dean, educator, science educator*
Faeth, Gerard Michael *aerospace and mechanical engineering educator, researcher*
Friedmann, Peretz Peter *aerospace engineer, educator*
Gerlitz, Frank Edward *engineer*
Gibala, Ronald *metallurgical engineering educator*
Gilbert, Elmer Grant *aerospace engineering educator, control theorist*
Gillespie, R. Brent *engineering educator*
Hayes, John Patrick *electrical engineering and computer science educator, consultant*
Johnson, Neil Monroe *test engineer*
Koc, Muammer *engineering educator, researcher*
Kozma, Adam *electrical engineer*
Leith, Emmett Norman *electrical engineer, educator*
Lyons, Harvey Isaac *mechanical engineering educator*
Martin, William Russell *nuclear engineering educator*

Mazumder, Jyotirmoy *mechanical and materials engineering educator*
Meitzler, Allen Henry *electrical engineering educator, automotive scientist*
Meyer, John Frederick *engineering educator*
Motoyama, Keiichi *mechanical engineer, consultant*
Petrick, Ernest Nicholas *mechanical engineer, researcher*
Pollock, Stephen Michael *operations research engineer, educator, consultant*
Pradhan, Sandeep *engineering educator*
Root, William Lucas *electrical engineering educator*
Savari, Serap Ayse *engineering educator, researcher*
Senior, Thomas Bryan A. *electrical engineering educator, researcher, consultant*
Tsimhoni, Omer *engineering educator*
Wilson, Richard Christian *engineering firm executive*
Yagle, Andrew Emil *engineering educator*
Young, Edwin Harold *chemical and metallurgical engineering educator*

Auburn Hills
Bahman, Mujibur *engineer*

Battle Creek
Risukhin, Vladimir Nikolayevich *aeronautical engineer, educator*

Big Rapids
Thapa, Khagendra *survey engineering educator*

Bingham Farms
Gratch, Serge *mechanical engineering educator*

Bloomfield
Gabriel, Martin George *engineering consultant*

Bloomfield Hills
Cuffe, Stafford Sigesmund *engineering company executive, consultant in E-business, E-commerce, technology, manufacturing & management*
Putchakayala, Hari Babu *engineering company executive*
Stivender, Donald Lewis *mechanical engineering consultant*

Dearborn
Cairns, James Robert *mechanical engineering educator*
Gandhi, Haren S. *chemical engineer*
Gu, Jianmin *mechanical engineer, researcher*
Haskara, Ibrahim *electronics engineer, researcher*
Irick, Brett D *manufacturing engineer*
Jie, Min *mechanical engineering educator, researcher*
Little, Robert Eugene *engineering educator*
Wagner, Harvey Arthur *nuclear engineer, consultant*
Yang, Guangbin *engineer*

Detroit
Batcha, George *retired mechanical and nuclear engineer*
Harden, Daniel Alexander, Jr., *chemical engineer*
Holness, Gordon Victor Rix *engineering executive, mechanical engineer*
Kline, Kenneth Alan *mechanical engineering educator*
Kummler, Ralph H. *chemical engineer, educator, dean*
Rathod, Mulchand *mechanical engineering educator*
Taraza, Dinu *engineering educator, researcher*
Trim, Donald Roy *consulting engineer*

East Lansing
Andersland, Orlando Baldwin *civil engineering educator*
Beck, James V. *mechanical engineering educator*
Chen, Kun-Mu *electrical engineering educator*
Cutts, Charles Eugene *civil engineering educator*
Foss, John Frank *mechanical engineering educator*
Goodman, Erik David *engineering educator*
Lloyd, John Raymond *mechanical engineering educator*
Pierre, Percy Anthony *engineering educator*
Saul, William Edward *civil engineering educator*
Segerlind, Larry J. *agricultural engineering educator*
von Bernuth, Robert Dean *agricultural engineering educator, consultant*
Von Tersch, Lawrence Wayne *engineering educator, dean*

Eastport
Tomlinson, James Lawrence *mechanical engineer*

Farmington
Chou, Clifford Chi Fong *research engineering executive*
Neyer, Jerome Charles *consulting civil engineer*

Farmington Hills
Hurd, Mary K. *civil engineer, writer*

Flint
Echempati, Raghu *mechanical engineering educator, consultant*
Novak, Jo-Ann Stout *chemical engineer*

Grand Blanc
Riley, Ronald Jim *industrial engineer, consultant*

Grand Rapids
Garver, Frederick Merrill *industrial engineering executive*

Greenbush
Paulson, James Marvin *engineering educator*

Grosse Pointe
Beltz, Charles Robert *retired engineering executive*

Harrison Township
Rivard, Jerome G. *engineering executive*

Holland
Stynes, Stanley Kenneth *retired chemical engineer, educator*

Houghton
Crittenden, John Charles *engineering educator*
Heckel, Richard Wayne *metallurgical engineering educator*
Huang, Eugene Yuching *civil engineer, educator*
Pelc, Karol Ignacy *engineering and technology management educator, researcher*
White, Calvin Lamont *engineer*

Kalamazoo
Ahmad, Shah Mahmood *chemical engineer, consultant*
Fang, Yichuan *aeronautical engineer, researcher*
Joyce, Margaret *chemical engineer, educator*
Litynski, Daniel Mitchell *engineering educator, retired military officer*

Lansing
Severin, Blaine Frank *environmental engineer*
Shirtum, Earl Edward *retired civil engineer*

Leland
Soutas-Little, Robert William *mechanical engineer, educator*

Livonia
Uicker, Joseph Bernard *retired engineering company executive*

Madison Heights
Xia, Jiding *chemical engineering educator*

Midland
Leng, Douglas Ellis *chemical engineer, scientist*
Meister, Bernard John *chemical engineer*

Niles
Marshall, Gerald Francis *optical engineer, consultant, physicist*

North Branch
Stevenson, James Laraway *communications engineer, consultant*

Okemos
Giacoletto, Lawrence Joseph *electronics engineering educator, researcher, consultant*

Pontiac
Hampton, Philip Michael *consulting engineering company executive*

Redford
Hu, Weilong *engineer*

Rochester
Loh, Robert N. K. *engineering educator*
Yang, Lianxiang *optical engineer, educator*

Shelby Township
Nagy, Louis Leonard *engineering executive, researcher*

Southfield
Hanisko, John-Cyril Patrick *electronics engineer, physicist*
McKeen, Alexander C. *retired engineering executive, foundation administrator*

Sterling Heights
Burke, Thomas Joseph *civil engineer*

Troy
Hsi, Morris Yu *mechanical engineer, educator*
Lan, Xuekui *engineer*

Walled Lake
Williams, Sam B. *engineering executive*

Warren
Lett, Philip W. *engineering executive*
Nefske, Donald Joseph *engineer*

Washington
Chatterley, James Philip *retired automotive development engineer*

Waterford
Morgan, Paul William *engineer, researcher*

MINNESOTA

Bloomington
Tsu, I-Fei *materials engineer*

Burnsville
Lai, Juey Hong *chemical engineer*

Chanhassen
Shanahan, Eugene Miles *flow measurement instrumentation company executive*

Coleraine
Ersayin, Salih *engineering educator, researcher*
Iwasaki, Iwao *engineering educator*

Eden Prairie
Higgins, Robert Arthur *electrical engineer, educator, consultant*

Grand Marais
Napadensky, Hyla Sarane *engineering consultant*

Lakeville
Setterholm, Jeffrey Miles *systems engineer*

Madison
Husby, Donald Evans *engineering company executive*

Minneapolis
Abi-Ghanem, Georges Victor *engineer, scientist*
Anderson, John Edward *mechanical engineering educator*
Bae, Seongtae *electrical engineer*
Bakken, Earl Elmer *electrical engineer, bioengineering company executive*
Cussler, Edward Lansing, Jr., *chemical engineer, educator*
Davis, Howard Ted *engineering educator*
Ernst, James Allan *safety engineer*
Fletcher, Edward Abraham *engineering educator*
French, Catherine E. Wolfgram *engineering educator, researcher*
Galambos, Theodore Victor *civil engineer, educator*
Gulliver, John Stephen *civil engineering educator, consultant*
Guo, Meiwen *structural engineer*
He, Bin *biomedical engineer, educator*
Hillstrom, Thomas Peter *engineering executive*
Johnson, Walter Kline *civil engineer*
Joseph, Daniel Donald *aeronautical engineer, educator*
Keller, Kenneth Harrison *engineering educator*
Kulacki, Francis Alfred *engineer, educator*
Kvalseth, Tarald Oddvar *mechanical engineer, educator*
Lambert, Robert Frank *electrical engineer, consultant*
Lee, E. Bruce *electrical engineering educator*
Ogata, Katsuhiko *engineering educator*
Oriani, Richard Anthony *metallurgical engineer, educator*
Persson, Erland Karl *electrical engineer, engineering executive*
Pfender, Emil *mechanical engineering educator*
Sapiro, Guillermo *engineering educator, consultant*
Tennyson, Joseph Alan *engineering executive*
Viegas, Herman Hermogio *mechanical engineer*

Minnetonka
Johnson, Lennart Ingemar *materials engineering consultant*

Oakdale
Tran, Nang Tri *engineering executive, electrical engineer*

Plymouth
Peterson, Donn Neal *forensic engineer*

Rochester
Huffine, Coy Lee *retired chemical engineer*
O'Hare, Daniel John *electrical engineer*

Shoreview
Liu, Benjamin Young-hwai *engineering educator*

South Saint Paul
Fairhurst, Charles *engineering educator*

Winona
Nastek, Thomas Edward *engineer, researcher, writer*

Woodbury
Beck, Warren Randall *retired glass technologist*
Exe, David Allen *electrical engineer*

MISSISSIPPI

Bay Saint Louis
Corbin, James H. *engineering executive, meteorologist, oceanographer*
Rahman, Shamim A. *engineering executive*

Biloxi
Brinsmade, Akbar Fairchild *chemical engineering consultant*

Lorman
Hylander, Walter Raymond, Jr., *retired civil engineer*

Madison
Priest, Melville Stanton *retired consulting hydraulic engineer*

Mississippi State
Cliett, Charles Buren *aeronautical engineer, educator, academic administrator*
Taylor, Clayborne Dudley *engineering educator*
Thompson, Joe Floyd *aerospace engineer, researcher*
Truax, Dennis Dale *civil engineer, educator, consultant*

Oxford
Costner, Charles Lynn *retired civil engineer*
Horton, Thomas Edward, Jr., *mechanical engineering educator*

Pascagoula
Chapel, Theron Theodore *retired quality assurance engineer*

Starkville
Jacob, Paul Bernard, Jr., *electrical engineering educator*

University
Cheng, Alexander Hung-Darh *engineering educator, consultant*
Fox, Garey A. *civil engineer, educator*
Smith, Allie Maitland *engineering educator*
Wang, Sam Shu-Yi *mechanical engineer, educator*

Vaiden
Murphy, Ben Carroll *engineering company executive*

Vicksburg
McRae, John Leonidas *civil engineer, consultant*

MISSOURI

Ballwin
Cornell, William Daniel *mechanical engineer*

Chesterfield
Metzler, Paul Raymond *electrical engineer, consultant*

Cleveland
Dunham, Michael D. *design engineer*

Columbia
Day, Cecil LeRoy *agricultural engineering educator*
Frisby, James Curtis *agricultural engineering educator*
Keyvan, Shahla *nuclear engineer, educator*
O'Connor, John Thomas *civil engineering educator*
Pringle, Oran Allan *mechanical and aerospace engineering educator*
Schuder, John Claude *biomedical engineer, educator*
Shende, Rajesh V. *chemical engineer, materials scientist, researcher*
Tzou, Robert Da *engineering educator*
Waidelich, Donald Long *electrical engineer, consultant*
Wu, Bin *industrial engineering, professor*
Yasuda, Hirotsugu Koge *engineering educator, director*

Ferguson
Bruns, Billy Lee *electrical engineer, consultant*

Florissant
Stevens, Robert Edward *engineering company executive*
Tomazi, George Donald *retired electrical engineer*

Fortuna
Ramer, James LeRoy *civil engineer*

Four Seasons
Bivins, Susan Steinbach *systems engineer*

Kansas City
Acheson, Allen Morrow *retired engineering executive*
Davis, F(rancis) Keith *civil engineer*
Green, Frank Earl *civil engineer*
Hall, Wayne F. *engineering company executive*
Leigh, Cheri J. *engineering consulting executive*
Rodman, Leonard C. *civil and communication engineering executive*
Wade, Robert Glenn *engineering executive*

Kirkwood
Holsen, James Noble, Jr., *retired chemical engineer*

Maryland Heights
Ramanuja, Teralandur Krishnaswamy *retired structural engineer*

Rolla
Chen, Genda *engineering educator*
Crosbie, Alfred Linden *mechanical engineering educator*
Day, Delbert Edwin *ceramic engineering educator*
Jagannathan, Sarangapani *engineering educator, researcher*
Lehnhoff, Terry Franklin *mechanical engineering*
Saperstein, Lee Waldo *mining engineering educator*
Sauer, Harry John, Jr., *mechanical engineer, educator, academic administrator*
Tsoulfanidis, Nicholas *engineering educator, dean*
Yu, Wei-Wen *retired engineering educator*

Saint Charles
Martin, Edward Brian *electrical engineer*

Saint Louis
Antonacci, Anthony Eugene *engineer*
Briggs, William Benajah *aeronautical engineer*
Condoor, Sridhar S. *mechanical engineer, educator*
Cox, Jerome Rockhold, Jr., *electrical engineer*
Dreifke, Gerald Edmond *electrical engineering educator*
Dudukovic, Milorad P. *chemical engineering educator, consultant*
Goldstein, Julius Lester *biomedical engineer, consultant*
Gould, Phillip Louis *civil engineering educator, consultant*
Izuchukwu, John Ifeanyichukwu *industrial engineer, mechanical engineer*
McKelvey, James Morgan *chemical engineering educator*
Olsen, Tava Maryanne Lennon *industrial and operations engineering educator*
Orton, George Frederick *aerospace engineer*
Peters, David Allen *mechanical engineering educator, consultant*
Richardson, Thomas Hampton *design consulting engineer*
Ross, Monte *electrical engineer, researcher*
Shrauner, Barbara Wayne Abraham *electrical engineer, educator*
Sutera, Salvatore Philip *mechanical engineer, educator*
Szabo, Barna Aladar *engineering educator*
Winter, David Ferdinand *electrical engineering educator, consultant*
Zurheide, Charles Henry *consulting electrical engineer*

Springfield
Brady, Steven L. *civil engineer, consultant*
Maples, Jimmie Kay *mechanical engineer*

University City
McVey, Francis Daniel *mechanical engineer, software developer, educator*

Webb City
Nichols, Robert Leighton *civil engineer*

MONTANA

Bozeman
Chen, Shi-Jie (Gary) *industrial engineer, educator*
Cokelet, Giles Roy *biomedical engineering educator*
Kaiser, Todd Jeffrey *electrical engineer, educator*
Nehrir, M. Hashem *electrical engineer, educator*
Sanks, Robert Leland *environmental engineer, emeritus educator*
Stanislao, Joseph *consulting engineer, educator*

Butte
Nikolic-Tirkas, Bojana *aerospace engineer, researcher*

Darby
Rusconi, Louis Joseph *marine engineer*

Great Falls
Walker, Leland Jasper *civil engineer*

Harlem
Brekke, Alan Lee *industrial engineer*

Helena
Johnson, David Sellie *civil engineer*

NEBRASKA

Alliance
Riemenschneider, Albert Louis *retired engineering educator*

Clay Center
Hahn, George LeRoy *agricultural engineer*

Lincoln
Burnham, Stephen John *civil engineer*
Edison, Allen Ray *electrical engineer, educator*
Edwards, Donald Mervin *systems engineer, educator, dean*
Elias, Samy E. G. *engineering executive*
Gitelson, Anatoly Avraam *engineering educator*
Goddard, Steve *computer engineer, educator*
Hanna, Milford A. *agricultural engineering educator*
Mohebbi, Esmail *industrial engineer*
Splinter, William Eldon *agricultural engineering educator*
Woollam, John Arthur *electrical engineering educator*

Omaha
Durham, Charles William *civil engineer, director*
Howard, Walter Burke *chemical engineer*
Kostecki, Martin Paul *industrial engineer*
Liu, Mingsheng *engineering educator*
Tunnicliff, David George *civil engineer, consultant*
Zerbs, Stephen Taylor *communications engineer*

NEVADA

Boulder City
Wyman, Richard Vaughn *engineering educator, exploration company executive*

Carson City
Klippert, Richard Hobdell, Jr., *engineering executive*

Dayton
Clements, Linda L. *materials engineer, educator, journalist*

Henderson
Wennerstrom, Arthur John *aeronautical engineer*

Incline Village
Merdinger, Charles John *civil engineer, naval officer, academic administrator*
Thompson, David Alfred *industrial engineer*

Las Vegas
Culp, Gordon Louis *consulting engineer*
Dastin, Samuel J. *aerospace engineer, consultant*
Haas, Robert John *aerospace engineer*
Herzlich, Harold J. *chemical engineer*
Kam, James Ting *engineer, consultant, scientist*
Massier, Paul Ferdinand *mechanical engineer*
Mc Elroy, John Harley *electrical and industrial engineering educator*
Messenger, George Clement *engineering executive, consultant*
Mulvihill, Peter James *fire protection engineer*
Neumann, Edward Schreiber *transportation engineering educator*
Philips, John Chase *retired process engineer*
Ramos, Albert A. *electrical engineer*

Minden
Bently, Donald Emery *electrical engineer*
Yu, John Junyao *mechanical engineer, researcher*

Reno
Byrd, Ronald Dallas *civil engineer*
Danko, George *engineering educator*
Fuerstenau, M(aurice) C(lark) *metallurgical engineer*
Haupt, Randy Larry *electrical engineering educator*
Kleppe, John Arthur *electrical engineering educator, business executive*
Krenkel, Peter Ashton *engineer, educator*
Raja, Krishnan Selva *materials engineer*

Sparks
Lagasse, Bruce Kenneth *retired structural engineer*

NEW HAMPSHIRE

Farmington
Panek, William Dominick *systems engineer executive*

Hanover
Garmire, Elsa Meints *electrical engineering educator, consultant*
Graves, Robert John *industrial engineering educator*
Hutchinson, Charles Edgar *engineering educator*
Kennedy, Francis Edward *engineering educator*
Long, Carl Ferdinand *retired engineering educator*
Queneau, Paul Etienne *metallurgical engineer, educator*

Hillsboro
Pearson, William Rowland *retired nuclear engineer*

Jaffrey
Foster, Walter Herbert, III, *mechanical and manufacturing engineer, executive*

Lee
Blidberg, D. Richard *marine engineer*

Manchester
Hower, Philip Leland *semiconductor device engineer*
Kamen, Dean *biomedical engineer*

Nashua
Seifer, Arnold David *systems engineer*
Woodruff, Thomas Ellis *electronics consulting executive*

New London
Crane, Robert Kendall *engineering educator, researcher, consultant*

Peterborough
Farnham, Sherman Brett *retired electrical engineer*

Portsmouth
Baumann, Hans D. *engineering executive*
Sinaisky, Nicholas Alekseevich *mechanical engineer, researcher, consultant*

Wolfeboro
Hutchins, Carleen Maley *acoustical engineer, consultant*

NEW JERSEY

Atco
Beard, Richard Burnham *engineering educator emeritus, researcher*

Basking Ridge
Drewry, Don Neal *fire protection engineer*

Bedminster
David, Edward Emil, Jr., *electrical engineer, business executive*

Berkeley Heights
Rabiner, Lawrence Richard *electrical engineer, educator*
Rabinovich, Eliezer M *retired ceramics engineer*

Bloomfield
Hutcheon, Forbes Clifford Robert *engineer, company executive*

Boonton
Lin, Ping *mechanical engineer*

Burlington
Kennedy, Christopher Robin *ceramic engineer, director*

Camden
Madan, Deepak S. *engineering executive*

Cherry Hill
Batterman, Steven Charles *engineering mechanics and bioengineering educator, forensic engineering and biomechanics consultant*
Camardo, Michael F. *engineering company executive*
Fuentevilla, Manuel Edward *chemical engineer*

Clinton
Milchovich, Raymond J. *engineering executive*

Columbus
Litman, Bernard *electrical engineer, consultant*

East Orange
Masucci, Nicholas J. *engineering company executive*

Edison
Selvakumar, Ariamalar *environmental engineer*

Englewood
Deresiewicz, Herbert *mechanical engineering educator*

Ewing
Brunda, Daniel Donald *retired aerospace engineer, consultant, inventor, writer*

Fairfield
Govic, Rudolf *structural engineer*
Purcell, Fenton Peter *engineering consultant*

Fort Lee
Screpetis, Dennis *retired nuclear engineer, consultant*
Treskov, Yakov Maks *engineer*

Fort Monmouth
Perlman, Barry Stuart *electrical engineering executive, researcher*
Su, Wei *electrical engineer*

Freehold
Christ, Duane Marland *retired computer systems engineer*
Schwartz, Perry Lester *information systems engineer, consultant*
Stirrat, William Albert *electronics engineer*

Green Village
Castenschiold, René *engineering executive, consultant, writer*

Hackensack
Mavrovic, Ivo *chemical engineer*
Yagoda, Harry Nathan *system engineering executive*
Zimmerman, Marlin U., Jr., *chemical engineer*

Haddonfield
Chu, Horn Dean *chemical engineer*
Harris, Stuart Innes *construction equipment engineer, marketing professional*
Siskin, Edward Joseph *engineering and construction company executive*

Helmetta
Gabay, Eleonora V. *mechanical engineer, educator*

Hewitt
Selwyn, Donald *engineering administrator, researcher, inventor, educator*

Highland Park
Spencer, Herbert Harry *structural engineering researcher, computer analyst*

Hightstown
Johnson, Ernest Frederick *chemical engineer, educator*
Johnson, Walter Curtis *electrical engineering educator*

Hoboken
Boesch, Francis Theodore *electrical engineer, educator*
Fernandez, Fernando Lawrence *aeronautical engineer, research and development company executive*
Griskey, Richard George *chemical engineering educator*
Pochiraju, Kishore *mechanical engineer, educator*
Savitsky, Daniel *engineer, educator*
Sisto, Fernando *mechanical engineering educator*

Holmdel
Lang, Howard Lawrence *electrical engineer*
Papadias, Constantinos Basil *electrical engineer*
Ross, Ian Munro *electrical engineer*

Hopatcong
Ferderber-Hersonski, Boris Constantin *process engineer*

Hopewell
VanMarcke, Erik Hector *civil engineer, educator*

Jersey City
Klyatis, Lev Matusovich *test and reliability scientist*
Vasmatzidis, Ioannis *systems engineer*

Kearny
Shin, John Joongsung *mechanical nuclear engineer, consultant*

Kinnelon
Haller, Charles Edward *engineering consultant*

Lincroft
Heirman, Donald Nestor *training engineering company executive, consultant*

Little Falls
Viil, Heino *retired engineer*

Livingston
Daman, Ernest Ludwig *mechanical engineer*
DeGhetto, Kenneth Anselm *engineering executive, construction executive*

Lodi
Melignano, Carmine (Emanuel Melignano) *video engineer*

Madison
Chang, Darwin Ray *civil engineer*

Manasquan
Abate, John E. *electrical and electronic engineer, communications consultant*

Matawan
Fennessy, James Gerard *retired engineer*

Middletown
Granstrom, Marvin Leroy *civil and sanitary engineering educator*
Kodali, Nageswararao *human factors engineer, researcher*

Montclair
Eager, George Sidney, Jr., *electrical engineer, engineering executive*

Moorestown
Atilgan, Timur Faik *structural engineer*

Morris Plains
Bennett, John Charles *former engineering and construction executive*
Kagan, Val Alexander *engineer, researcher, educator*

Morristown
Kittelberger, Larry E. *engineering executive*
Lieberman, Lester Zane *engineering company executive*
Pavlovich, John Stephen *civil engineer*
Rainal, Attilio Joseph *retired electronics engineer, researcher*

Mount Laurel
Vidas, Vincent George *engineering executive*

Murray Hill
Fleming, James William *ceramics engineer*

New Brunswick
Jaluria, Yogesh *mechanical engineering educator*
Weng, George Jueng-Cious *engineering educator*

New Providence
Cho, Alfred Yi *electrical engineer*
West, James E. *acoustical engineer*

Newark
Bar-Ness, Yeheskel *electrical engineer, educator*
Barrett, Kirk Robert *environmental engineer, educator*
Brazil, Aine M. *engineering company executive*
Carpinelli, John Dominick *computer engineering educator*
Dhawan, Atam Prakash *engineering educator, dean*
Friedland, Bernard *engineer, educator*
Hanesian, Deran *chemical engineer, chemistry and environmental science educator, consultant*
Hrycak, Peter *mechanical engineer, educator*
Rosato, Anthony Dominick *mechanical engineer, educator*
Shi, Yun Qing *electrical engineer*
Spillers, William Russell *civil engineering educator*
Van Buskirk, William Charles *engineering educator*

Newfoundland
Van Winkle, Edgar Walling *retired electrical engineer, computer consultant*

North Caldwell
Stevens, William Dollard *consulting mechanical engineer*

Ocean
Reich, Bernard *retired telecommunications engineer*

Ocean City
Weir, William Thomas *retired engineer, educator*

Oradell
Roe, W. Barton *engineering executive*

Pennington
Kelly, Quentin Thorn *water company executive, inventor, writer*

Pennsauken
Alday, Paul Stackhouse, Jr., *retired mechanical engineer*

Piscataway
Balaguru, Perumalsamy *civil engineering educator*
Elsayed, Elsayed Abdelrazik *industrial engineer, educator*
Flanagan, James Loton *electrical engineer, researcher, engineering educator*
Freeman, Herbert *computer engineering educator*
Frenkiel, Richard Henry *retired systems engineer, consultant*
Hsiao, Michael S. *electrical engineer, educator*
Mammone, Richard James *engineering educator*
Poses, Frederic M. *engineering company executive*
Shanefield, Daniel Jay *ceramics engineering educator*
Sincoskie, W. David *computer engineer*
Welkowitz, Walter *biomedical engineer, educator*
Yuen, Wing Ho *electrical engineer, researcher*
Zhang, Li *engineer, researcher*

Princeton
Bartolini, Robert Alfred *electrical engineer, researcher*
Billington, David Perkins *civil engineering educator*
Blair, David William *mechanical engineer*
Debenedetti, Pablo Gaston *chemical engineering educator*
File, Joseph *research physics engineer*
Galloway, Patricia Denese *civil engineer*
Gillham, John Kinsey *chemical engineering educator*
Glassman, Irvin *mechanical and aeronautical engineering educator, consultant*
Hough, Robert Alan *civil engineer*
Jackson, Roy *chemical engineering educator*
Lechner, Bernard Joseph *consulting electrical engineer*
Linke, Richard A. *systems engineer, researcher*
Liu, Bede *electrical engineering educator*
Lo, Arthur Wu-nien *electrical engineering educator*
Miles, Richard Bryant *mechanical and aerospace engineering educator*
Poor, Harold Vincent *electrical engineering educator*
Russel, William Bailey *engineering educator*
Salkind, Alvin J. *electrochemical engineer, biomedical engineer, educator, dean*
Saville, Dudley Albert *chemical engineering educator*
Stengel, Robert Frank *engineering and applied science educator*
Tsui, Daniel C. *electrical engineer, physicist*
Vahaviolos, Sotirios John *electrical engineer, researcher, engineering executive*
Verdu, Sergio *engineering educator*
Wei, James *chemical engineering educator, academic dean*
Whipple, William, Jr., *government policy consultant, writer*
Zatz, Irving J. *structural engineer*

Princeton Junction
Bair, William Alois *engineer*
Denlinger, Edgar Jacob *electronics engineering research executive*
Haddad, James Henry *chemical engineer, consultant*
Lull, William Paul *engineering consultant*

Rancocas
Rowan, Henry M. *electrical engineer*

Red Bank
Lucky, Robert Wendell *electrical engineer*
Schneider, Sol *electronic engineer, consultant, researcher*

Rumson
Rowe, Harrison Edward *electrical engineer*

Scotch Plains
Marlowe, Chris Sean *safety engineer*

Secaucus
Lynch, Joseph Michael *engineer, consultant*

Short Hills
Wharton, Lennard *engineering company executive*

Skillman
Brill, Yvonne Claeys *engineer, consultant*

South Plainfield
Kennedy, John William *engineering company executive*

Sparta
Truran, William Richard *electrical engineer*

Summit
Fukui, Hatsuaki *electrical engineer, art historian*

Swedesboro
Lovell, Theodore *electrical engineer, consultant*

Teaneck
Ehrlich, Ira Robert *mechanical engineering consultant*
Pfeffer, Robert *chemical engineer, academic administrator, educator*

Tinton Falls
Schink, Frank Edward *electrical engineer*

Tague, Charles Francis *retired engineering, construction and real estate development company executive*

Titusville
Cooper, Paul *retired mechanical engineer, research director*

Toms River
Fanuele, Michael Anthony *retired electronics engineer, research engineer*

Trenton
Rahman, Mohammed Siddiqur *environmental engineer, researcher*

Union
Newman, Stephen Alexander *chemical engineer, thermodynamicist*

Upper Saddle River
Wallace, William, III, *engineering executive*

Watchung
Michaelis, Paul Charles *engineering physicist executive*
Tornqvist, Erik Gustav Markus *chemical engineer, research scientist, consultant*

Wayne
Meeldijk, Victor Anthony *engineering professional*
Schmidt, Barnet Michael *communications and electronic engineer*

West New York
Gruenberg, Elliot Lewis *electronics engineer and company executive*

West Orange
Dohr, Donald R. *metallurgical engineer, researcher*

Westfield
Bhagat, Phiroz Maneck *mechanical engineer*

NEW MEXICO

Albuquerque
Anderson, Lawrence Keith *electrical engineer, consultant*
Davis, Jon L. *logistics consultant*
Dorato, Peter *electrical and computer engineering educator*
Haddad, Edward Raouf *civil engineer, consultant*
Hall, Jerome William *research engineering educator*
Herrera, Gilbert Victor *engineering executive*
Hulsbos, Cornie Leonard *civil engineering educator*
Lederer, John Martin *retired aeronautical engineer*
Lee, David Oi *engineer*
Moulds, William J. *retired aeronautical engineer*
Peck, Ralph Brazelton *civil engineering educator, consultant*
Studer, James Edward *geological engineer*

Belen
Toliver, Lee *mechanical engineer*

Carlsbad
Piper, Lloyd Llewellyn, II, *engineer, government and service industry executive*

Cerrillos
Lutz, Raymond Price *retired industrial engineer, educator*

Cloudcroft
Hadfield, Michael James *electrical engineer*

Embudo
Rogers, Benjamin Talbot *former consulting engineer, solar energy consultant*

Farmington
Lewis, Homer Dick *retired nuclear engineer*

Holloman Afb
Minto, David W. *aeronautical engineer*

Las Cruces
Ford, Clarence Quentin *mechanical engineer, educator*
Strickland, Jennifer Laura *engineer*

Los Alamos
Dudziak, Donald John *nuclear engineer, educator*
Jackson, James F. *nuclear engineer, educator*
McDonald, Thomas Edwin, Jr., *retired electrical engineer*
Nunz, Gregory Joseph *aerospace engineer, program manager, educator, entrepreneur*
Stoddard, Stephen Davidson *ceramic engineer, former state senator*
Van Tuyle, Gregory Jay *nuclear engineer*

Placitas
Hidy, George Martel *chemical engineer, executive*

Rio Rancho
Delahanty, Carlos Anthony *industrial engineer*
Sei, Ibrahim *process engineer*

Santa Fe
Amtmann, Hans Henry *retired aeronautical engineer, architect*
Goorley, John Timothy *nuclear engineer*

White Sands Missile Range
Arthur, Paul Keith *electronic engineer*

NEW YORK

Albany
Fanuele, Frank John *engineering executive*
Happ, Harvey Heinz *electrical engineer, educator*

Alfred
Spriggs, Richard Moore *ceramic engineer, research center administrator*

Amherst
Hu, Yun Hang *chemical engineer*
Kutsin, Leonid *engineering educator, researcher*

Armonk
Donofrio, Nicholas M. *computer engineer*

Auburn
Mochel, Myron George *mechanical engineer, educator*

Bethpage
Conti, James Joseph *retired chemical engineer, educator*

Big Flats
Orsillo, James Edward *computer systems engineer, company executive*

Bloomfield
Hansen, Widmer Case *retired weapons systems engineer, analyst*

Brewster
Nadel, Norman Allen *civil engineer*

Bronx
Reynolds, Joseph Patrick *chemical engineering educator, consultant*

Bronxville
Brunale, Vito John *aerospace engineer*

Brooklyn
Beaufait, Frederick W(illiam) *civil engineering educator*
Birenbaum, Leo *retired engineering educator*
Crânganu, Constantin *engineer*
Das, Nirod K. *engineering educator*
Goodman, Alvin S. *engineering educator, consultant*
Helly, Walter Sigmund *engineering educator*
Iskander, Magued *engineering educator, consultant*
Kempner, Joseph *aerospace engineering educator*
Leonard, James Kevin *mechanical engineer*
McLean, William Ronald *retired electrical engineer, consultant*
Nakanishi, Yuko Julie *engineering educator, consultant*
Parlamis, Michael Frank *civil engineer, construction company executive*
Shaw, Leonard Glazer *retired electrical engineering educator, consultant*

Buffalo
Anderson, Wayne Arthur *electrical engineering educator*
Chang, Ching Ming (Carl Chang) *engineering executive, mechanical engineer, educator*
Karwan, Mark Henry *engineering educator, dean*
Landi, Dale Michael *industrial engineer, academic administrator*
Meredith, Dale Dean *civil engineering educator*
Metzger, Ernest Hugh *aerospace engineer, research scientist*
Reinhorn, Andrei M. *civil structural engineering educator, consultant*
Reismann, Herbert *engineer, educator*
Ruckenstein, Eli *chemical engineering educator*
Shaw, David Tai-Ko *electrical and computer engineering educator, university administrator*
Swihart, Mark Thomas *chemical engineer, educator*
Tsai, Christina W. *civil engineer, educator*
Weber, Thomas William *chemical engineering educator*
Weller, Sol William *chemical engineering educator*

Cato
Sheckler, Ross David *engineering executive*

Chappaqua
O'Neill, Robert Charles *inventor, consultant*
Pomerene, James Herbert *retired computer engineer*

Cheektowaga
Wozniak, Richard Anthony *computer engineer*

Clarence
Greatbatch, Wilson *biomedical engineer*

Clinton
Pagani, Albert Louis *aerospace system engineer*

Cold Spring
Pugh, Emerson William *electrical engineer*

Coram
Uh, David Keun *civil engineer*

Corning
Beall, George Halsey *ceramics engineer*

Delmar
Campas, Anna Penelope *civil engineer, architect*
Shen, Thomas To *environmental engineer*

East Amherst
Soong, Tsu-Teh *engineering science educator*

East Norwich
Rosen, Meyer Robert *chemical engineer*

East Syracuse
Mohan, Sankar Krishnan *mechanical engineer*

Farmingdale
Bandyopadhyay, Amitabha *engineering educator*

Fayetteville
Dosanjh, Darshan S(ingh) *aeronautical engineer, educator*

Flushing
Goldenshteyn, Vladimir Lev *civil engineer*
Kopp, Ilya Zinovij *energy and environmental researcher*
Stahl, Frank Ludwig *civil engineer*

Franklin Square
Cantilli, Edmund Joseph *safety engineering educator, translator, writer, consultant*

Glen Cove
Makris, Constantine John *computer engineer*

Glenville
Anderson, Roy Everett *retired electrical engineer*

Great Neck
Abraham, Carl Joel *corporate executive, safety specialist, inventor, consultant*

Greenlawn
Bachman, Henry Lee *electrical engineer, engineering company executive*

Harrison
Schulz, Helmut Wilhelm *chemical engineer, environmental executive*

Hauppauge
Buckley, Robert Matthew *electrical engineer*

Hawthorne
Lavenberg, Stephen S. *electrical engineer, researcher*

Hempstead
Goldstein, Stanley Philip *engineering educator*

Hewlett
Haralick, Robert Martin *electrical engineering educator*

Hopewell Junction
Park, Byeongju *engineer*
Sikka, Kamal K. *engineering executive*

Huntington
Chmelev, Vsevolod *engineer, consultant*
Christiansen, Donald David *electrical engineer, editor, publishing consultant*
LaTourrette, James Thomas *retired electrophysics, electrical engineering and computer science educator*

Huntington Station
Agosta, Vito *mechanical and aerospace engineering educator*

Ithaca
Berger, Toby *electrical engineer, educator*
Carlin, Herbert J. *electrical engineering educator, researcher*
De Boer, Pieter Cornelis Tobias *mechanical and aerospace engineering educator*
Dick, Richard Irwin *environmental engineer, educator*
Eastman, Lester Fuess *electrical engineer, educator*
Harriott, Peter *chemical engineering educator*
Leibovich, Sidney *engineering educator*
Linke, Simpson *electrical engineering educator*
Loucks, Daniel Peter *environmental systems engineer*
Maxwell, William Laughlin *retired industrial engineering educator*
McGuire, William *civil engineer, educator*
Meyburg, Arnim Hans *transportation engineer, educator, consultant*
O'Rourke, Thomas Denis *civil engineer, educator*
Phelan, Richard Magruder *mechanical engineer*
Rodríguez, Ferdinand *chemical engineer, educator*
Smith, Julian Cleveland, Jr., *chemical engineering educator*
Stedinger, Jery Russell *civil and environmental engineer, researcher*

Jackson Heights
Parascos, Edward Themistocles *engineering consultant*

Jericho
Shinners, Stanley Marvin *electrical engineer*

Katonah
Bashkow, Theodore Robert *electrical engineering consultant, former educator*

Kew Gardens
Chipkin, Frederick *textile designer, consultant*

Lansing
Dalman, Gisli Conrad *electrical engineering educator*

Liverpool
Hamlett, James Gordon *electronics engineer, management consultant, educator*

Long Island City
Barbanel, Sidney William *engineering consulting firm executive*

Manlius
Jefferies, Michael John *retired electrical engineer*

Melville
Bongiorno, Joseph John, Jr., *electrical engineering educator*
Bultan, Aykut *communications systems engineer*
Horton, Theodore G. *industrial engineer*
Schmid, Charles Ernest *acoustical engineer, administrator*
Sullivan, Kenneth Wayne *engineer*
Taub, Jesse J. *electrical engineering researcher*

Middle Island
Crowder, Lillie Mae Brown *retired architectural engineer*

Mineola
Newman, Malcolm *mechanical and civil engineering consultant*

Mohegan Lake
Paik, John Kee *structural engineer*

Mount Kisco
Green, Paul Eliot, Jr., *optical communications consultant*

New Hyde Park
Huebscher, Herbert *electrical engineer, educator*
Hyman, Abraham *electrical engineer*

New Rochelle
Schwarz, Ralph Jacques *retired engineering educator*

New York
Acrivos, Andreas *chemical engineering educator*
Ahmad, Jameel *civil engineer, researcher, educator*
Asadorian, Diana C. *electrical engineer, educator*
Baum, Richard Theodore *engineering executive*
Boley, Bruno Adrian *engineering educator*
Bove, John Louis *chemistry and environmental engineering educator, researcher*
Brazinsky, Irv(ing) *chemical engineering educator*
Briskman, Robert David *engineering executive*
Chen, Tak-Ming *civil engineer, consultant*
Chowdhury, Shoaib *engineer*
Cowin, Stephen Corteen *biomedical engineering educator, consultant*
Daniel, Charles Timothy *transportation engineer, consultant*
DiMaggio, Frank Louis *civil engineering educator*
Fawcett, Christopher Babcock *civil engineer, construction and water resources company executive*
Fennell, Thomas Edward, Jr., *engineering educator*
Fogel, Irving Martin *consulting engineer*
Freiman, Charles Visvald *engineering foundation administrator*
Greenfield, Seymour Stephen *mechanical engineer*
Grunes, Robert Lewis *consulting engineer company executive*
Haratunian, Michael *engineering company executive*
Harris, Colin Cyril *mineral engineer, educator*
Hennessy, John Francis, III, *engineering executive, mechanical engineer*
Kim, Se Jung *civil engineer*
Knobler, Alfred Everett *ceramic engineer, manufacturing company executive, publisher*
Lammie, James Louis *engineering executive, retired military officer*
Laufer, Mark Vladimir *retired engineering educator*
Levy, Matthys Paul *structural engineer*
Manassah, Jamal Tewfek *electrical engineer, educator, management consultant*
Morfopoulos, V. *metallurgical engineer, materials engineer*
Mow, Van C. *engineering educator, researcher*
Nasr, George Elias *electrical engineer, consultant, computer engineer, educator*
Nusim, Stanley Herbert *chemical engineer, consultant*
O'Neill, Thomas J. (Tom O' Neill) *engineering company executive*
Paaswell, Robert Emil *civil engineer, educator*
Rubenstein, Leonard *engineering company executive*
Rumschitzki, David Sheldon *chemical engineering educator*
Sadegh, Ali M. *mechanical engineering educator, researcher, consultant*
Schoenfeld, Robert Louis *biomedical engineer*
Schrader, Richard Allen *engineering company executive*
Schwartz, Mischa *electrical engineering educator*
See, Saw-Teen *structural engineer*
Servedio, Dominick Michael *engineering executive*
Shinnar, Reuel *chemical engineering educator, industrial consultant*
Sivakumaran, Kumaraswamy *civil engineer, consultant, lawyer*
Smith, Gordon H. *civil engineer, consultant, forensic engineer consultant*
Soejima, Daisuke *international trade engineer, economist*
Subak-Sharpe, Gerald Emil *electrical engineer, educator*
Tamaro, George John *consulting engineer*
Tamboli, Akbar Rasul *consulting engineer*
Tsividis, Yannis P. *electrical engineering educator*
Villela, Daniel Antunes Maciel *electrical engineer, researcher*
Vogelman, Joseph Herbert *scientific engineering company executive*
Watkins, Charles Booker, Jr., *mechanical engineering educator*
Weinbaum, Sheldon *biomedical engineer*
Weinstein, Herbert *chemical engineer, educator*
Yao, David Da-Wei *engineering educator*
Yapijakis, Constantine *environmental engineer, educator, consultant*
Yegulalp, Tuncel M. *mining engineer, educator*
Zuck, Alfred Christian *consulting mechanical engineer*

Niskayuna
Huening, Walter Carl, Jr., *retired consulting application engineer*
Saak, Yungyee Jennifer Su *materials engineer*

North Syracuse
Roberts, Robert *engineering organization executive, think-tank executive*

Northport
Weber, Ray Everett *engineering executive, consultant*

Norwood
Church, Richard Dwight *electrical engineer, scientist*

Old Bethpage
Buzzelli, Dennis Kevin *mechanical engineer*

Oxford
Ryan, Kenneth Eugene *engineer*

Palisades
Lenton, Roberto Leonardo *research facility and environmental administrator*

Phoenix
Ackerman, Roger G. *ceramics engineer*

Pittsford
Strella, Eve G. *industrial engineer, consultant*

Plainview
Snyder, Joel Bennett *engineering executive, educator*

Plattsburgh
Treacy, William Joseph *electrical and environmental engineer*

Pleasantville
Pike, John Nazarian *optical engineering consultant*
Urban, Joseph Jaroslav *engineer, consultant*

Port Jefferson
Gilmore, Arthur Warham *retired aeronautical engineer*

Port Washington
Gaddis, M. Francis *mechanical and marine engineer, environmental scientist*

Potsdam
Chin, Der-Tau *chemical engineer, educator*
Galo, Gary A. *audio engineer*
Rengaswamy, Raghunathan *chemical engineering researcher, educator*
Shen, Hung Tao *hydraulic engineering educator*

Poughkeepsie
Chu, Richard Chao-Fan *mechanical engineer*
Katopis, George A. *electrical engineer*
Logue, Joseph Carl *electronics engineer, consultant*
Simons, Robert Edward *mechanical engineer, consultant*
Turgeon, Paul R. *computer program manager*

Rochester
Carstensen, Edwin Lorenz *biomedical engineer, biophysicist*
Drummond, Malcolm McAllister *electronics engineer*
Hetnarski, Richard Bozyslaw *mechanical engineering educator*
Joos, Felipe Miguel *mechanical engineer, researcher*
Loewen, Erwin G. *precision engineer, educator, consultant*
Nasr, Nabil Zaki *national center executive*
Niznik, Carol Ann *electrical engineer, educator, consultant*
Oldshue, James Y. *chemical engineering consultant*
Parker, Kevin James *electrical engineer, educator*
Shah, Ramesh Keshavlal *researcher, engineering educator*
Smoral, Vincent J. *electrical engineer*
Stratton, John Alfred *electrical engineer, educator*

Rye
Lehman, Lawrence Herbert *consulting engineering executive*

Rye Brook
Landegger, George F. *engineering executive*

Scarsdale
Borg, Robert Frederic *civil engineer*
Florman, Samuel Charles *civil engineer*

Schenectady
Fischer, Michael David *civil engineer*
Greskovich, Charles D. *retired materials engineer*
Mikata, Yozo *mechanical engineer, application developer*
Ringlee, Robert James *consulting engineering executive*
Sutherland, Peter Edward *electrical engineer*

Setauket
Levine, Sumner Norton *industrial engineer, educator, editor, author, financial consultant*

Smithtown
Rockensies, John William *mechanical engineer*

Somers
Anderson, John Erling *chemical engineer*

Stony Brook
Bennett, Tyrone LaMont *engineer, director*
Gambino, Richard Joseph *materials science engineering*
Judex, Stefan *biomedical engineer, educator*
Zemanian, Armen Humpartsoum *electrical engineer, mathematician*

Syracuse
Drucker, Alan Steven *mechanical engineer*
Konski, James Louis *civil engineer*
Levy, Alan Joseph *mechanical engineer, educator*
Pennock, Donald William *retired mechanical engineer*
Sargent, Robert George *engineering educator*
Tully, William P. *civil engineer, academic administrator*

Tarrytown
Farrell, Gregory Alan *biomedical engineer*

Tonawanda
Drozdziel, Marion John *aeronautical engineer*

Troy
Ajayan, Pulickel M. *materials engineering educator*
Arcak, Murat *engineering educator, consultant*
Belfort, Georges *chemical engineering educator, consultant*
Bergles, Arthur Edward *mechanical engineering educator*
Block, Robert Charles *nuclear engineering educator, engineering physics educator*
Boyina, Ramana Prasad Venkata *civil engineering educator, researcher*
Duquette, David Joseph *materials science and engineering educator*
Dvorak, George J. *mechanics and materials engineering educator*
Feeser, Larry James *civil engineering educator, researcher*
Gerhardt, Lester A. *engineering educator, dean*
Gill, William Nelson *chemical engineering educator*
Glicksman, Martin Eden *materials engineering educator*
Hsu, Cheng *decision sciences and engineering systems educator*
Lahey, Richard Thomas, Jr., *nuclear engineer, fluid mechanics engineer*
Linton, Jonathan D *management researcher, educator*
Littman, Howard *chemical engineer, educator*
McDonald, John Francis Patrick *electrical engineering educator*
Messac, Achille *mechanical engineer, aerospace engineer*
Nelson, John Keith *electrical engineer, educator*
Sanderson, Arthur Clark *engineering educator*
Saridis, George Nicholas *electrical, computers and system engineering educator, robotics and automation researcher*
Shephard, Mark Scott *civil and mechanical engineering educator*
Shuey, Richard Lyman *engineering educator, consultant*
Woods, John William *electrical, computer and systems engineering educator, consultant*
Xu, Xie George *engineering educator*
Zimmie, Thomas Frank *civil engineer, educator*

Upton
Foerster, Conrad Louis *project engineer*
Fthenakis, Vasilis *chemical engineer, consultant, educator*
Steinberg, Meyer *chemical engineer*
Susskind, Herbert *biomedical engineer, educator*

Valatie
Smith, Albert Aloysius, Jr., *electrical engineer, consultant*

Webster
McWilliams, C. Paul, Jr., *engineering executive*

Wellsville
Fuller, Bruce E. *mechanical engineer*
Tezak, Edward George *mechanics educator*

West Kill
Dwon, Larry *retired electrical engineer, educator, consultant*

White Plains
Dee, William *engineering executive*
Foster, John Horace *consulting environmental engineer*
Freed, Arthur *civil engineer*
Frieling, Jerry *engineering executive*
Haines, Daniel Webster *engineering consultant, educator*
Mitchell, Robert Dale *consulting engineer*
Westerhoff, Garret Peter *environmental engineer, executive*

Whitesboro
Kwiat, Kevin Anthony *computer engineer*

Woodside
Unsal-Tunay, Nuran *geological engineer, researcher*

Yorktown Heights
Dennard, Robert Heath *engineering executive, scientist*
Terman, Lewis Madison *electrical engineer, researcher*

NORTH CAROLINA

Asheville
Jaslow, Howard *engineer*

Cary
Briggs, Joseph Jay *communications engineer*
Conrad, Hans *materials engineering educator*
Odum, Jeffery Neal *mechanical engineer*
Pchelnikov, Yuriy Nikitich *microwave engineer*
Vick, Columbus Edwin, Jr., *retired civil engineering design firm executive*
Wright, Robert G. *engineering executive*

Chapel Hill
Kusy, Robert Peter *biomedical engineering and orthodontics educator*
Leith, David *engineering educator*
McKinney, Ross Erwin *civil engineering educator*
Okun, Daniel Alexander *environmental engineering educator*
Singer, Philip Charles *environmental engineer, educator*
Stidham, Shaler, Jr., *operations research educator*

Charlotte
Elanayar, Sunil K. *research and development engineer*
Fitzpatrick, James Ward, Jr., *engineering technology educator*
Griffith, Dewey Maurice *mechanical engineer, investor*
Rodite, Robert R.R. *engineering scientist*
Valasquez, Joseph Louis *industrial engineer*

Columbus
Brooks, Jerry Claude *safety engineer, educator*

Durham
Bejan, Adrian *mechanical engineering educator*
Casey, H(orace) Craig, Jr., *electrical engineering educator*
Goodwin, Frank Erik *materials engineer*
Harman, Charles Morgan *mechanical engineer*
Hochmuth, Robert Milo *mechanical and biomedical engineer, educator*
Pamula, Vamsee K. *electrical engineer, researcher*
Petroski, Henry *engineer educator, writer*
Plonsey, Robert *electrical and biomedical engineer*
Vatavuk, William Michael *chemical engineer, writer*

Granite Falls
Humphreys, Kenneth King *engineer, educator, association executive*

Greensboro
Cazel, Hugh Allen *industrial engineer, educator*

Hendersonville
Thomas, Stephen *retired industrial engineer*

Murphy
Kerr, Walter Belnap *retired electrical engineer, English language researcher, consultant*

New Bern
Baughman, Fred Hubbard *aeronautical engineer, retired military officer*
Moeller, Dade William *environmental engineer, educator*
Painter, Jack Timberlake *civil engineer*
Whitehurst, Brooks Morris *chemical engineer*

Raleigh
Barrett, Rolin Farrar, Jr., *mechanical engineer, consultant*
Beatty, Kenneth Orion, Jr., *chemical engineer, educator*
Bitzer, Donald Lester *electrical engineering educator, retired research laboratory administrator*
Davis, Joseph Randall *engineer, ergonomist*
Gardner, Robin Pierce *engineering educator*
Grantham, Donald James *chemical engineer, educator, author*
Hauser, John Reid *electrical engineering educator*
Havner, Kerry Shuford *civil engineering and solid mechanics educator*
Heidari, Amir Homayoun *computational mechanic*
Holton, William Coffeen *electrical engineering executive*
Kolbas, Robert Michael *electrical engineering educator*
Larsen, Ralph Irving *environmental research engineer*
Lin, Changqing *chemical engineer, researcher*
Meier, Wilbur Leroy, Jr., *industrial engineer, educator, former university chancellor*
Noori, Mohammad Noori *mechanical engineering educator*
Sneed, Ronald Ernest *engineering educator emeritus*
Turinsky, Paul Josef *nuclear engineer, educator*
Velev, Orlin D. *chemical engineer, educator*
Wahls, Harvey Edward *civil engineer, educator*
Wehring, Bernard William *nuclear engineering educator*
Whitaker, Thomas Burton *agricultural engineer, educator*
Williams, Hugh Alexander, Jr., *retired mechanical engineer, consultant*
Zorowski, Carl Frank *engineering educator, university administrator*

Research Triangle Park
Johnson-Payton, Lori Renee *systems engineer*

Sunset Beach
Mattson, Clarence Russell *safety engineer*

Swannanoa
Stuck, Roger Dean *electrical engineering educator*

Washington
Hackney, James Acra, III, *industrial engineer, consultant, retired manufacturing company executive*

Whispering Pines
Kuhn, Matthew *retired engineering company executive*

Winston Salem
Bayram, Ersin *electrical engineer, researcher*
Bourne, Henry Clark, Jr., *electrical engineering educator, former academic official*

NORTH DAKOTA

Fargo
Helweg, Otto Jennings *civil engineer, educator*
Li, Kam Wu *mechanical engineer, educator*
Reitan, Daniel Kinseth *electrical and computer engineering educator*
Rogers, David Anthony *electrical engineer, educator, researcher*

OHIO

Akron
Brown, David Rupert *engineering executive*
Isayev, Avraam Isayevich *polymer engineer, educator*
Pipes, Robert Byron *mechanical engineer, educator*
Symens, Ronald Edwin *electrical engineer, consultant*

Athens
Irwin, Richard Dennis *electrical engineering educator*
Robe, Thurlow Richard *engineering educator, dean*

Aurora
Kirchner, James William *retired electrical engineer*

Barberton
Kitto, John Buck, Jr., *mechanical engineer*

Brecksville
Forsyth, T. Henry *plastic researcher*

Canton
Pedoto, Gerald Joseph *supplier quality specialist*

Cincinnati
Adams, Donald Scott *engineer, pharmacist*
Agrawal, Dharma Prakash *engineering educator*
Bahr, Donald Walter *retired chemical engineer*
Barrett, William Martin *environmental engineer, chemical engineer, researcher*
Bruno, David Joseph, Jr., *chemical engineer, researcher*
Greenberg, David Bernard *chemical engineering educator*
Hodge, Bobby Lynn *mechanical engineer, manufacturing executive*
Jones, Mark Allen *structural engineer*
Kowel, Stephen Thomas *electrical engineer, educator*
Krantz, William Bernard *chemical engineering educator*
Madson, Philip Ward *engineering executive, consultant*
Morgan, William Richard *mechanical engineer*
Ratliff, Thomas Asbury, Jr., *retired engineer*
Toftner, Richard Orville *engineering executive*
Wachenfeld, Timothy H. *aeronautical engineering executive*
Weisman, Joel *retired engineering educator*
Wilson, William Alexander *manufacturing engineer, consultant*
Wisler, David Charles *aerospace engineer*

Cleveland
Angus, John Cotton *chemical engineering educator*
Bahniuk, Eugene *mechanical engineering educator*
Bansal, Narottam Prasad *ceramic research engineer*
Burghart, James Henry *electrical engineer, educator*
DellaCorte, Christopher *engineer*
Hardy, Richard Allen *mechanical engineer, engineering executive*
Heuer, Arthur Harold *ceramics engineer, educator*
Ko, Wen-Hsiung *electrical engineering educator*
Madden, James D. *forensic engineer*
Okojie, Robert Sylvester *electronics engineer, researcher, aerospace scientist*
Qutubuddin, Syed Abu Shams *chemical engineer, educator*
Reshotko, Eli *aerospace engineer, educator*
Rich, Lawrence Vincent *manufacturing and engineering company executive*
Rudy, Yoram *biomedical engineer, biophysicist, educator*
Saada, Adel Selim *civil engineer, educator*
Saidel, Gerald Maxwell *biomedical engineering educator*
Savinell, Robert Francis *engineering educator*
Wilson, Jack *aeronautical engineer*

Columbus
Adeli, Hojjat *engineer, educator, computer scientist*
Alexander, Carl Albert *ceramics engineer, educator*
Altan, Taylan *engineering educator, director*
Applegate, Ralph Asa *engineering educator*
Bailey, Cecil Dewitt *aerospace engineer, educator*
Bechtel, Stephen E. *mechanical engineer, educator*
Bhushan, Bharat *mechanical engineer*
Brodkey, Robert Stanley *chemical engineering educator*
Collins, Jack Adam *mechanical engineer*
Cooper, Stuart Leonard *chemical engineering educator, researcher, consultant*
Cruz, Jose Bejar, Jr., *engineering educator*
Duckworth, Winston Howard *retired ceramic engineer*
Ensminger, Dale *mechanical engineer, electrical engineer*
Fan, Liang-Shih *chemical engineering educator*
Fenton, Robert Earl *electrical engineering educator*
Gozon, Jozsef Stephan *engineering educator*
Grant, Michael Peter *electrical engineer*
Harris, Ronald David *chemical engineer*
Houser, Donald Russell *mechanical engineering educator, consultant*
Jacox, John William *retired mechanical engineer and consulting company executive*
Ksienski, Aharon Arthur *electrical engineer*
Miller, Don Wilson *nuclear engineering educator*
Moulton, Edward Quentin *civil engineer, educator*
Ozkan, Umit Sivrioglu *chemical engineering educator*
Peters, Leon, Jr., *engineering educator*
Rapp, Robert Anthony *metallurgical engineering educator, consultant*
Rich, Joseph William *engineering educator, consultant*
Rubin, Alan J. *engineering educator*
St. Pierre, George Roland, Jr., *materials science and engineering administrator, educator*
Singh, Rajendra *mechanical engineering educator*
Smith, Philip John *industrial and systems engineering educator*
Uotila, Urho Antti Kalevi *engineering educator*
Utkin, Vadim I. *electrical engineer, educator*
Volakis, John Leonidas *engineering educator*
Ware, Brendan John *retired electrical engineer and utility executive*
Zakin, Jacques Louis *chemical engineering educator*
Zhu, Xiankui *mechanical engineer, researcher*

Concord
Baid, Kushalkumar M. *chemical engineer*

Continental
Dranchak, Lawrence John *retired mechanical engineer*

Dayton
Crabtree, Mark S. *engineer, director*
Houpis, Constantine Harry *retired electrical engineering educator*
Phillips, Chandler Allen *biomedical/human factors engineer*
Schmitt, George Frederick, Jr., *materials engineer*
Soon, Boon Yi *engineer*

Delaware
Arnold, Jay *retired engineering executive, educator*

Dublin
Major, Coleman Joseph *chemical engineer*

Fairborn
Conklin, Robert Eugene *electronics engineer*

Fairfield
Walsh, Thomas James *environmental engineer, consultant*

Gates Mills
Enyedy, Gustav, Jr., *chemical engineer*
Pace, Stanley Carter *retired aeronautical engineer*

Kent
Anderson, William John, II, *engineering and business management consultant*

Lakeside Marblehead
Haering, Edwin Raymond *chemical engineering educator, consultant*

Logan
Carmean, Jerry Richard *broadcast engineer*

Mansfield
Burnell, Elvin Wallace *industrial engineer, security specialist*

Miller, Kenneth William, II, *research and development engineering executive*
Sheridan, Mark William *mechanical engineer, strategic planner*

Marion
Nutbrown, Edwin Emanuel *safety engineer, writer*

Marysville
Baik-Kromalic, Sue S. *metallurgical engineer*

Medina
Rog, Joseph W. *engineering company executive*

Middletown
Newby, John Robert *metallurgical engineer*

Milford
Weyand, William J. *engineering executive*

North Olmsted
Bluford, Guion Stewart, Jr., *engineering company executive*
Lundin, Bruce Theodore *engineering and management consultant*

Oxford
Ward, Roscoe Fredrick *engineering educator*

Poland
Murphy, Thomas Michael *civil engineer*

Shaker Heights
Siegel, Robert *heat transfer engineer*

Shauck
Garvick, Kenneth Ryan *broadcast engineer, announcer, educator*

Springboro
Saxer, Richard Karl *metallurgical engineer, retired air force officer*

Springfield
Moore, Florian Howard *retired electronics engineer*

Toledo
Diehl, Dean R. *engineering company executive*
Wolff, Edwin Ray *retired construction engineer, consultant*

West Chester
Mital, Anil *engineering educator*

Wilberforce
Elali, Taan *engineering and computer science educator*

Worthington
Compton, Ralph Theodore, Jr., *electrical engineering educator*
Wu, Tien Hsing *civil engineering educator, consulting engineer*

Yellow Springs
Trolander, Hardy Wilcox *engineering executive, consultant*

Youngstown
Cernica, John N. *engineering educator, civil engineer, consultant*
Fok, Thomas Dso Yun *civil engineer*
Lacivita, Michael John *safety engineer*

OKLAHOMA

Bartlesville
Johnson, Marvin Merrill *chemical engineer, chemist*
Mihm, John Clifford *chemical engineer*

Broken Arrow
Paden, Larry J. *consulting electronics engineer, lawyer*

Norman
Bert, Charles Wesley *mechanical and aerospace engineer, educator*
Campbell, John Morgan *retired chemical engineer*
Egle, Davis Max *mechanical engineering educator*
Mallinson, Richard Gregory *chemical engineering educator*
O'Rear, Edgar Allen, III, *chemical engineering educator*
Papavassiliou, Dimitrios Vassilios *chemical engineer, educator*
Striz, Alfred Gerhard *aerospace engineer, educator*
Zelby, Leon Wolf *electrical engineering educator, consulting engineer*

Oklahoma City
Coll, Mario M *engineering company executive*
Mikkelson, Dean Harold *geological engineer, writer*
Miller, Herbert Dell *petroleum engineer*
Reynolds, Edwin Clinton, Jr., *engineering manager*
Wickens, Donald Lee *engineer executive, consultant, rancher*

Perry
Gard, Michael Floyd *research engineer*

Ponca City
Gong, Xiaoyi *engineer*

Stillwater
Case, Kenneth Eugene *industrial engineering educator*
Gasem, Khaled A.M. *chemical engineer, educator*
Hoberock, Lawrence Linden *mechanical engineer, educator*
Hughes, Michael *civil engineer*
Huhnke, Raymond Leroy *engineering educator*
Maddox, Robert Nott *chemical engineer, educator*
Mize, Joe Henry *industrial engineer, educator*
Noyes, Ronald Tacie *agricultural engineering educator*
Thompson, David Russell *engineering educator, academic dean*

Tulsa
Chung, I-Ping *mechanical engineer*
Cobbs, James Harold *engineer, consultant*
Earlougher, Robert Charles, Sr., *petroleum engineer*
Fleifil, Mahmoud Mohamed *acoustical engineer, researcher*
Williams, John Horter *civil engineer, oil, gas, telecommunications and allied products distribution company executive*

OREGON

Beaverton
Cassidy, Richard Arthur *environmental engineer, governmental water resources specialist*
Chartier, Vernon Lee *electrical engineer*
Edlich, Richard French *biomedical engineering educator*

Corvallis
Engelbrecht, Rudolf *electrical engineering educator*
Forbes, Leonard *engineering educator*
Temes, Gabor Charles *electrical engineering educator*

Florence
Ericksen, Jerald Laverne *retired engineering scientist, educator*

Hillsboro
Venkatesan, Raguraman *computer engineer*

John Day
Tuttle, Kenneth Lewis *engineering educator, consultant*

Klamath Falls
Woodall, David Monroe *research engineer, dean*

Lake Oswego
Gehrig, Edward Harry *electrical engineer, consultant*

Medford
Horton, Lawrence Stanley *electrical engineer, apartment developer*

Myrtle Point
Walsh, Don *marine consultant, executive*

Portland
Albright, Robert James *electrical engineering educator*
Becker, Bruce Douglas *mechanical engineer*
Dinh, Hoat Khang *mechanical engineer, educator*
Forsberg, Charles Alton *computer, information systems engineer*
Kennedy, R(obert) Evan *engineering executive, consultant, retired structural engineer*
Khalil, Mohammad Aslam Khan *environmental science and engineering educator, physics educator*
Kocaoglu, Dundar F. *engineering management educator, industrial and civil engineer*
Lall, B. Kent *civil engineer, educator*
Li, Fu *electrical engineering educator, editor*
Yamayee, Zia Ahmad *engineering educator, dean*

Salem
Butts, Edward Perry *civil engineer, environmental consultant*
Dixon, Robert Gene *retired manufacturing engineering educator, retired mechanical engineering company executive*

Sunriver
Clough, Ray William, Jr., *civil engineering educator*

Woodburn
Oliver, Madison E. *retired engineering executive, mechanical engineer*

PENNSYLVANIA

Allentown
Agrawal, Rakesh *industrial researcher*
Alici, Semra *engineer, researcher*
Foster, Edward Paul (Ted Foster) *process industries executive*
Gaensler, Tomas Fritz *engineering executive*
Gewartowski, James Walter *retired electrical engineer*
Hansel, James Gordon *engineer, educator*
Lesak, David Michael *safety engineer, educator, consultant*
Moore, Robert Byron *chemical engineer, consultant*

Allison Park
Lagnese, Joseph F. *environmental engineer*

Apollo
Musselman, Larry L. *chemical engineer*

Bala Cynwyd
Staley, Kenneth Bernard *civil engineer*

Beaver
Vogeley, Clyde Eicher, Jr., *engineering educator, artist, consultant*

Berwyn
Lund, George Edward *retired electrical engineer*

Bethel Park
Korchynsky, Michael *metallurgical engineer*
O'Donnell, Thomas P. *mechanical engineer*

Bethlehem
Anderson, David Martin *environmental health scientist and engineer*
Chen, John C. *chemical engineering educator*
Durkee, Jackson Leland *civil engineer*
Fisher, John William *civil engineering educator*
Karakash, John J. *engineering educator*
Mirro, John *engineering company executive*
Neti, Sudhakar *mechanical engineering educator*
Ostapenko, Alexis *civil engineer, educator*
Pense, Alan Wiggins *metallurgical engineer, academic administrator*
Roberts, Richard *mechanical engineering educator*
Shi, Wei *engineering educator, researcher*
Tuzla, Kemal *mechanical engineer, scientist*

Boalsburg
Gettig, Martin Winthrop *retired mechanical engineer*

Broomall
Emplit, Raymond Henry *electrical engineer*

Camp Hill
Drnevich, Ronald *engineering executive*

Carnegie
Moretti, Edward Charles *environmental engineer, consultant*

Chadds Ford
Isakoff, Sheldon Erwin *chemical engineer*

Cheltenham
Weinstock, Walter Wolfe *systems engineer*

Cheswick
Nair, Bala Radhakrishnan *engineer*

Clearfield
Singh, Shiwendra Prasad *civil engineer*

Conshohocken
Senturk, Ufuk *ceramics engineer, researcher*

Coopersburg
Bolle, Donald Martin *retired engineering educator*
Peserik, James E. *electrical, controls and computer engineer, consultant, forensics and safety engineer, fire cause and origin investigator*
Siess, Alfred Albert, Jr., *engineering executive, management consultant*

Coraopolis
Kay, George Paul *environmental engineer*
Shaw, Richard Leslie *engineering company executive*

Erie
Crankshaw, John Hamilton *mechanical engineer*
Dockstader, Emmett Stanley *engineer, construction executive*

Glen Mills
Churchill, Stuart Winston *chemical engineering educator*

Harrisburg
Dietz, John Raphael *consulting engineer executive*

Havertown
Kostkiewicz, Krzysztof *electrical engineer, journalist*

Hummelstown
Creswell, Charles Alexander *process engineering and management consultant*

Huntingdon Valley
West, A(rnold) Sumner *chemical engineer*

Indiana
Soule, Robert D. *safety and health educator, administrator*

Irwin
Kuhn, Howard Arthur *engineering executive, educator*

Jamison
Touhill, C. Joseph *environmental engineer*

Johnstown
Depra, Alan Jay *mechanical engineer*

Kennett Square
Dwyer, Francis Gerard *chemical engineer, researcher*

King Of Prussia
Hegedus, L. Louis *chemical engineer, research and development company executive*
Lee, Robert *engineer*

Lancaster
Ebersole, J. Glenn, Jr., *engineering, marketing, management and public relations executive*

Lewisburg
Aldrich, Robert Adams *agricultural engineer, consultant*
Orbison, James Graham *civil engineer, educator*

Meadville
Gilles, Bruce Carlson *civil engineer*

Media
Garrison, Walter R. *engineering executive, director*

Merion Station
Coppa, Anthony Patrick *engineer, consultant*

Monroeville
Di Gioia, Anthony Michael, Jr., *civil engineer, business executive*
Hribar, John Anthony *civil engineer, consultant*
Jacobi, William Mallett *nuclear engineer, consultant*
Mandel, Herbert Maurice *civil engineer*

Moon Township
Rabosky, Joseph George *engineering consulting company executive*

New Cumberland
Scheiner, James Ira *engineering company executive*

New Kensington
Jarrett, Noel *chemical engineer, researcher*

Newtown
Schroeder, Alfred Christian *electronics research engineer*
Woods, Howard James, Jr., *civil engineer*

Newtown Square
Perrone, Nicholas *mechanical engineer, business executive*

Philadelphia
Cohen, Ira Myron *aeronautical and mechanical engineering educator*
El-Sherif, Mahmoud A. *electrical engineering educator*
Falkie, Thomas Victor *mining engineer, mining executive*
Fegley, Kenneth Allen *systems engineering educator*
Flicker, Eric Lee *civil engineer, consultant*
Giorgio, Robert *engineering executive*
Jaron, Dov *biomedical engineer, educator*
Kritikos, Haralambos Nicholas *electrical engineering educator*
Kuruvilla, Kollanparampil *electrical engineer*
Lawley, Alan *materials engineering educator*
Lewin, Peter Andrew *electrical engineer, educator*
Litt, Mitchell *chemical engineer, educator, bioengineer*
Mulford, Richard Albert *mechanical engineer, professional society administrator*
Munson, Janis Elizabeth Tremblay *engineering company executive*
Popovics, Sandor *civil engineer, educator, researcher*
Quinn, John Albert *chemical engineering educator*
Schwan, Herman Paul *electrical engineering and physical science educator, research scientist*
Seider, Warren D. *engineering educator*
Sun, Hun H. *electrical engineering and biomedical engineering educator*
Terzian, Karnig Yervant *retired civil engineer*
Tomiyasu, Kiyo *consulting engineer*
Van der Spiegel, Jan *engineering educator*
Walker, Allen Lyon *engineer*
Winston, Flaura K. *engineering researcher*
Zavaliangos, Antonios *mechanical engineer, educator*

Pittsburgh
Anderson, John Leonard *chemical engineering educator*
Bloom, William Millard *furnace design engineer*
Borovetz, Harvey Selwyn *biomedical engineer, educator*
Casasent, David Paul *electrical engineering educator, data processing executive*
Cendes, Zoltan Joseph *electrical engineer, educator*
Charap, Stanley Harvey *electrical engineering educator*
Chiu, Chao-Lin *civil engineer*
Desai, Niranjan A. *chemical engineer*
Diamond, Fred I. *electronic engineer*
Di Martino, Elena Stefania *engineering educator, researcher*
Dzombak, David Adam *environmental engineering educator*
Hendrickson, Chris Thompson *civil and environmental engineering educator, researcher*
Hoburg, James Frederick *electrical engineering educator*
Hoover, George Charles *engineer, broadcast technician*
Humphrey, Watts Sherman *technical executive, author*
Jordan, Angel Goni *electrical and computer engineering educator*
Kadow, Clemens Martin Joachim *engineer, researcher*
Karacan, Cevat Ozgen *petroleum engineer, researcher*
Li, Ching-Chung *electrical engineering and computer science educator*
McAvoy, Bruce Ronald *engineer, consultant*
Mickle, Marlin Homer *electrical engineer, educator*
Milnes, Arthur George *electrical engineer, educator*
Morrison, L. Warren *computer engineer*
Moura, José Manuel Fonseca *electrical engineer, educator*
Neuman, Charles P. *electrical and computer engineering educator*
Nielsen, Paul Douglas *engineering executive, retired military officer*
O'Donnell, William James *engineering executive*
Peterson, Robert Scott *electrical engineer*
Pettit, Frederick Sidney *metallurgical engineering educator, researcher*
Reznik, Alan A. *petroleum engineering educator*
Ruh, Edwin *ceramic engineer, consultant, researcher*
Russell, Alan James *chemical engineering and biotechnology educator*
Schultz, Jerome Samson *biochemical engineer, educator*
Shea, John Joseph *electrical engineer*
Simaan, Marwan *electrical engineering educator*
Stahl, Laddie L. *electrical engineer, manufacturing company executive*
Trumble, Dennis Robert *biomedical engineer*
Westerberg, Arthur William *retired chemical engineering educator*
Yang, Wen-Ching *chemical engineer*

Reading
Lacki, Allan Vincent *industrial engineer*
Moriarty, John Klinge *electronics engineer, consultant*

Sewickley
Fells, Charles Dayton *civil engineer, educator*
Hartwig, Thomas Leo *civil engineer, environmental engineer, sports association administrator*

Sinking Spring
Heffner, William Rudolph *engineer, consultant*

Souderton
Silvestri, George J., Jr., *retired thermodynamics engineer*

State College
Barnoff, Robert Mark *civil engineering educator*
Foderaro, Anthony Harolde *nuclear engineering educator*
Grimes, Dale Mills *physics and electrical engineering educator*
Mutmansky, Jan M. *retired engineering educator*
Olson, Donald Richard *mechanical engineering educator*
Shaikh, Nazrul Islam *industrial engineer, researcher*

Sibul, Leon Henry *electrical engineer*
Sinha, Sunil K. *engineer, educator*

Swarthmore
Krendel, Ezra Simon *systems and human factors engineering consultant*

University Park
Aplan, Frank Fulton *metallurgical engineering educator*
Austin, Leonard George *mineral engineer*
Bose, Nirmal Kumar *electrical engineering, mathematics educator*
Brown, John Lawrence, Jr., *electrical engineering educator*
Cross, Leslie Eric *electrical engineering educator*
Davids, Norman *engineering science and mechanics educator, researcher*
Duda, John Larry *chemical engineering educator*
Elliott, Herschel *agricultural engineer, educator*
Ertekin, Turgay *petroleum engineer educator, researcher, consultant*
Feng, Tse-yun *computer engineer, educator*
Grimes, Craig Alan *electrical engineering educator*
Guo, Ruyan *engineering educator, researcher*
Ham, Inyong *industrial engineering educator*
Hogg, Richard *process engineer*
Holl, John William *engineering educator*
Irwin, Mary Jane *engineering educator*
Kabel, Robert Lynn *chemical engineering educator*
Knott, Kenneth *engineering educator, consultant, expert witness*
Lauchle, Gerald Clyde *acoustics educator*
Manbeck, Harvey B. *agricultural and biological engineer, educator*
McCormick, Barnes Warnock *aerospace engineering educator*
McDonnell, Archie Joseph *environmental engineer*
Mentzer, John Raymond *electrical engineer, educator*
Ramani, Raja Venkat *mining engineering educator*
Ruud, Clayton Olaf *engineering educator*
Thompson, William, Jr., *engineering educator*
Tikalsky, Paul J. *civil engineering educator, structural engineer*
Tittmann, Bernhard Rainer *engineering science and mechanics educator*
Todd Copley, Judith A. *materials and metallurgical engineering educator*
Vannice, M. Albert *chemical engineering educator, researcher*
Vennam, Venkata Surya Prakash *engineering educator, researcher*
Vrentas, James Spiro *chemical engineering educator*
Witzig, Warren Frank *nuclear engineer, educator*
Wysk, Richard A. *engineering educator, researcher*

Villanova
McLaughlin, Philip VanDoren, Jr., *mechanical engineering educator, researcher, consultant*
Tomlinson, J. Richard *engineering services company executive*

Waynesboro
Martin, Harold G. *engineering consultant*

West Grove
Fuller, Jack Glendon, Jr., *retired plastics engineer*

West Mifflin
Ardash, Garin *mechanical engineer*

West Point
Buckland, Barry Christopher *chemical engineer*

Willow Grove
Chatterjee, Hem Chandra *electrical engineer*

York
Blair, William David *retired electrical engineer*
Horn, Russell Eugene *engineering executive, consultant*

RHODE ISLAND

Bristol
Danzberger, Alexander Harris *chemical engineer, consultant*

Fiskeville
Mc Feeley, John Jay *chemical engineer*

Kingston
Lee, Kang-Won Wayne *engineer, educator*

Narragansett
Potty, Gopu Ramachandran *marine engineer, researcher*

Newport
Ehrlich, Stanley Leonard *acoustical engineer, consultant*

Portsmouth
Becken, Bradford Albert *engineering executive*

Providence
Dobbins, Richard Andrew *engineering educator, researcher*
Freund, Lambert Ben *engineering educator, researcher, consultant*
Glicksman, Maurice *engineering educator, former dean and provost*
Hazeltine, Barrett *electrical engineer, educator*
Khrushchev, Sergei Nikitich *engineering educator*
Kimia, Benjamin B. *engineering educator*
Needleman, Alan *mechanical engineering educator*
Richman, Marc Herbert *forensic engineer, educator*
Symonds, Paul Southworth *mechanical engineering educator, researcher*
Weiner, Jerome Harris *mechanical engineering educator*

Wakefield
Boothroyd, Geoffrey *industrial and manufacturing engineering educator*

SOUTH CAROLINA

Aiken
Hootman, Harry Edward *retired nuclear engineer, consultant*
Zirps, George Thomas *marine engineer, consultant*

Beaufort
Pinkerton, Robert Bruce *mechanical engineer*

Camden
Sindler, Allan Jay *chemical engineer, sculptor, educator*

Charleston
Bolin, Edmund Mike *electrical engineer, franchise engineering consultant*
Chapman, Howard Reed *city and county transportation engineer, consultant*

Clemson
Golan, Lawrence Peter *mechanical engineering educator, energy researcher*
Grady, C.P. Leslie, Jr., *engineering educator*
Paul, Frank Waters *mechanical engineer, educator, consultant*
Pursley, Michael Bader *electrical engineering educator, communications systems research and consulting*
Wagner, John Russell *mechanical engineering educator, researcher*
Williamson, Robert Elmore *engineering educator*
Xu, Xiao-Bang *engineering educator*
Zumbrunnen, David Arnold *mechanical engineering and materials science educator, consultant*

Columbia
Baskin, C. R. *civil engineer*
Graulty, Robert Thomas *engineer, consultant*
Harries, Kent Alexander *engineering educator, structural engineer, consultant*
White, Ralph Edward *chemical engineer, educator*

Easley
Luo, Nianzhu *mechanical engineer*

Edisto Island
Cannon, David C. *mechanical engineer, consultant*

Greeleyville
Collins, Almon Winslow *retired engineer*

Greenville
Fernandez, Miguel Angel *process safety and design engineer, energy consultant*
Wang, Ming De *engineer*

Hartsville
Menius, Espie Flynn, Jr., *electrical engineer*

Hilton Head Island
Bruun, Per Moller *civil engineer, consultant*
Huckins, Harold Aaron *chemical engineer*
Windman, Arnold Lewis *retired mechanical engineer*

North Charleston
Fei, James Robert *engineering executive, consultant*

Orangeburg
Graule, Raymond (Siegfried) *metallurgical engineer*
Hong, Jae-Dong *industrial engineering educator*
Sriskanda, Nesan Sithamparapillai *engineering educator, researcher*

Salem
Darnell, William Headen *chemical engineer, medical/surgical nurse, nursing educator*

Spartanburg
Cogan, Jerry Albert, Jr., *chemical engineer, engineering executive*

SOUTH DAKOTA

Madison
Mukhopadhyay, Indranath *communications engineer, researcher*

Rapid City
Lefevre, Donald Keith *electrical engineer*
Pillay, Gautam *chemical engineer, chemist, academic administrator*
Ramakrishnan, Venkataswamy *civil engineer, educator*
Scofield, Gordon Lloyd *mechanical engineer, educator*

TENNESSEE

Arnold AFB
Davis, John William *government science and engineering executive*

Brownsville
Stevenson, William Edward *chemical engineer*

Chattanooga
Duckworth, Jerrell James *electrical engineer*
Foster, Edwin Powell, Jr., *structural engineer, educator*
Hensley, Marble John, Sr., *civil engineer, consultant*

Cookeville
Black, Gary William *industrial engineer*
Chowdhuri, Pritindra *electrical engineer, educator*
Sissom, Leighton Esten *engineering educator, dean, consultant*
Velu, Yogeshwar Karunakaran *industrial engineer, researcher*

Crossville
Bell, Charles Eugene, Jr., *retired industrial engineer*
Hovmand, Svend *chemical engineer, engineering executive*

Dandridge
Menzel, William Clarence, Jr., *nuclear quality engineer*

Greenbrier
Newell, Paul Haynes, Jr., *engineering educator, former college president*

Kingsport
Siirola, Jeffrey John *chemical engineer*

Knoxville
Badiru, Adedeji Bodunde *industrial engineer*
Bose, Bimal Kumar *electrical engineering educator*
Bressler, Marcus Nathan *consulting engineer*
Brown, Donald Vaughn *technical educator, engineering consultant*
Cliff, Steven Burris *engineering executive*
Garrison, Arlene Allen *engineering executive, engineering educator*
Kress, Tyler A. *biomedical engineer*
LeVert, Francis Edward *nuclear engineer, researcher*
Mc Dow, John Jett *biosystems engineering educator*
Mise, Jesse Sherden *structural engineer, consultant*
Oakes, Thomas Wyatt *environmental engineer, computer engineer*
Prados, John William *engineering educator*
Roth, J(ohn) Reece *electrical engineer, educator, researcher, inventor*
Schuler, Theodore Anthony
Uhrig, Robert Eugene *nuclear engineer, educator*

Loudon
Lownsdale, Gary Richard *mechanical engineer*

Maryville
Oakes, Lester Cornelius *retired electrical engineer, consultant*

Memphis
Bhattacharya, Syamal Kanti *biomedical scientist, educator*
Born, Robert Heywood *consulting civil engineer*
Demir, Semahat Siddika *engineering educator*
Hochstein, John Isaac *mechanical engineer, educator*
Williams, Edward F(oster), III, *environmental engineer*

Midway
Kutbay, Cihat *process engineer*

Nashville
Basu, Prodyot Kumar *civil engineer, educator*
Cadzow, James Archie *engineering educator, researcher*
Galloway, Kenneth Franklin *engineering educator*
Hahn, George Thomas *materials engineering educator, researcher*
Harris, Thomas Raymond *biomedical engineer, educator*
LeVan, Martin Douglas *chemical engineering educator*
Schnelle, Karl Benjamin, Jr., *chemical engineering educator, consultant, researcher*
Speece, Richard Eugene *civil engineer, educator*

Oak Ridge
David, Stanislaus Antony *metallurgical engineer*
Wang, Hong *engineer, researcher*

Signal Mountain
Makansi, Munzer *chemical engineer, researcher*

Tullahoma
Hill, Susan Sloan *safety engineer*

TEXAS

Allen
Lim, Jae Doeg *systems engineer, researcher*

Alpine
Kittlitz, Rudolf Gottlieb, Jr., *chemical engineer, researcher*

Amarillo
Elkins, Lloyd Edwin, Sr., *petroleum engineer, energy consultant*
Von Eschen, Robert Leroy *electrical engineer, consultant*

Arlington
Anderson, Dale Arden *aerospace engineer, educator*
Clark, Dayle Meritt *civil engineer*
Everard, Noel J. *structural engineer, educator*
Lewis, Frank Leroy *electrical engineer, educator, researcher*
Liu, Hanli *biomedical engineer, educator*
Rollins, Albert Williamson *civil engineer, consultant*
Stevens, Gladstone Taylor, Jr., *industrial engineer*

Austin
Abraham, Jacob A. *computer engineering educator, consultant*
Al-Omari, Ra'ed M. *computer engineer, consultant, computer scientist, researcher*
Armstrong, Neal Earl *civil engineering educator*
Baker, Lee Edward *biomedical engineering educator*
Banerjee, Sanjay Kumar *electrical engineer, director*
Blackstock, David T. *acoustical engineer, educator*
Brannon-Peppas, Lisa *chemical engineer, researcher*
Breen, John Edward *civil engineer, educator*
Brock, James Rush *chemical engineering educator*
Bronaugh, Edwin Lee *electromagnetic compatibility engineer, consultant*
Brown, Stephen Neal *computer engineer*
Burns, Ned Hamilton *civil engineering educator*
Carlton, Donald Morrill *research, development and engineering executive*
Castaldi, Frank James *environmental engineer, consultant*
Cywar, Adam Walter *management engineer*
Dodabalapur, Ananth *electrical engineer*
Dougal, Arwin Adelbert *electrical engineer, educator*
Ell, Travis Eugene *electronics engineer*
Epright, Charles John *retired aerospace engineer*
Erengil, Mehmet Erdal *aeronautical engineer, researcher*
Evans, Walter Reed *retired engineering executive, consultant*

Fair, James Rutherford, Jr., *chemical engineering educator, consultant*
Freeman, Benny Dean *engineering educator*
Furlong, Richard W. *structural engineer, educator*
Gloyna, Earnest Frederick *environmental engineer, educator*
Gomes, Norman Vincent *retired industrial engineer*
Harris, Richard Lee *engineering executive, retired army officer*
Himmelblau, David Mautner *chemical engineer*
Hixson, Elmer L. *retired engineering educator*
Howell, John Reid *mechanical engineering educator*
Hughes, Thomas J.R. *mechanical engineering educator, consultant*
Hull, David George *aerospace engineering educator, researcher*
Jensen, Paul Allen *mechanical engineer*
Koen, Billy Vaughn *mechanical engineering educator*
Koepsel, Wellington Wesley *electrical engineering educator*
Lamb, Jamie Parker, Jr., *retired mechanical engineer, educator*
Li, Hong-Jyh *process engineer, researcher*
Luedecke, William Henry *mechanical engineer*
Mc Ketta, John J., Jr., *chemical engineering educator*
Naimi-Tajdar, Reza *petroleum engineer*
Nichols, Steven Parks *mechanical engineer, lawyer, educator, academic administrator*
O'Connor, James T. *civil engineering educator*
Oden, John Tinsley *engineering educator, mathematician, consultant*
O'Geary, Dennis Traylor *retired contracting/engineering company executive*
Peppas, Nikolaos Athanassiou *chemical and biomedical engineering educator, consultant*
Reese, Lymon Clifton *civil engineering educator*
Richards-Kortum, Rebecca Rae *biomedical engineering educator*
Rylander, Henry Grady, Jr., *mechanical engineering educator*
Sandberg, Irwin Walter *electrical and computer engineering educator*
Schechter, Robert Samuel *chemical engineer, educator*
Sciance, Carroll Thomas *chemical engineer, educator*
Steinfink, Hugo *chemical engineering educator*
Stokoe, Kenneth H., II, *civil engineer, educator*
Streetman, Ben Garland *electrical engineering educator*
Swartzlander, Earl Eugene, Jr., *engineering educator, former electronics company executive*
Tesar, Delbert *machine systems and robotics educator, researcher, manufacturing consultant*
Thurston, George Butte *mechanical and biomedical engineering educator*
Truchard, James J. *engineering executive*
Tucker, Richard Lee *civil engineer, educator*
Walton, Charles Michael *civil engineering educator*
Welch, Ashley James *engineering educator*
Wells, Jon Barrett *engineer*
Wittliff, Danny Joe *environmental engineer*
Woodson, Herbert Horace *retired electrical engineering educator*

Bacliff
Bacani, Nicanor-Guglielmo Vila *civil and structural engineer, consultant*

Baird
Rodenberger, Charles Alvard *aerospace engineer, consultant*

Beaumont
Hopper, Jack Rudd *chemical engineering educator*
Koehn, Enno *engineering educator, researcher*
Morales, Emmitt *mechanical consultant*

Bellaire
Wisch, David John *structural engineer*

Boerne
Mitchelhill, James Moffat *retired civil engineer*

Bryan
Samson, Charles Harold, Jr., (Car Samson) *retired engineering educator, consultant*

College Station
Buth, Carl Eugene *civil engineer*
Button, Joe Wade *civil engineer, researcher, consultant*
Cohen, Aaron *aerospace engineer*
Ehsani, Mehrdad (Mark Ehsani) *electrical engineering educator, consultant*
El-Halwagi, Mahmoud M. *chemical engineer, educator*
Fletcher, Leroy Stevenson *mechanical engineer, educator*
Hall, Kenneth Richard *chemical engineering educator, consultant*
Hann, Roy William, Jr., *civil engineer, educator*
Isdale, Charles Edwin *chemical engineer*
Jayasuriya, Suhada *mechanical engineering educator*
Kunze, Otto Robert *retired agricultural engineering educator*
Kuo, Way *industrial engineer, researcher*
Lee, William John *petroleum engineering educator, consultant*
Lowery, Lee Leon, Jr., *civil engineer*
Lu, Mi *computer engineer, educator*
Lytton, Robert Leonard *civil engineer, educator*
Mannan, M. Sam *chemical engineer, educator, consultant*
Mathewson, Christopher Colville *engineering geologist, educator*
Mercer, Melvin Ray *electrical engineer, educator*
Page, Robert Henry *engineering educator, researcher*
Painter, John Hoyt *electrical engineer*
Parnell, Calvin Boyd, Jr., *agricultural engineering educator*
Patton, Alton DeWitt *electrical engineering consultant*
Reddy, J. N. *mechanical engineering educator*
Richardson, Herbert Heath *mechanical engineer, educator, institute director*
Riskowski, Gerald Lee *engineering educator*
Seyed-Yagoobi, Jamal *mechanical engineering educator*

Sue, Hung-Jue *engineer, educator*
Weese, John Augustus *mechanical engineer, educator*

Dallas

Anim-Appiah, Kofi Dankwa *electrical engineer, researcher*
Brown, Phillip James *systems engineer*
Bruene, Warren Benz *electronic engineer*
Cruikshank, Thomas Henry *energy services and engineering executive*
Eberhart, Robert Clyde *biomedical engineering educator, researcher*
Fix, Douglas Martin *electrical engineer*
Fontana, Robert Edward *electrical engineering educator, retired air force officer*
Gass, Wanda *engineering executive*
Hansen, John Paul *retired metallurgical engineer*
Huang, Yen Ti *civil engineer*
Kilby, Jack St. Clair *electrical engineer*
Lersch, DeLynden Rife *computer engineering executive*
McLane, William Delano *mechanical engineer*
Rainwater, R. Steven *systems engineer*
Schulze, Richard Hans *engineering executive, environmental engineer*
Szygenda, Stephen A. *electrical and computer engineering educator, researcher*
Williams, Charles Edward *engineer*
Zhou, Desheng *petroleum engineer*
Zimmerman, S(amuel) Morton (Mort Zimmerman) *engineering executive*

Denton

Golding, Terry David *engineering educator, researcher*

El Paso

Fahy, Michael P. *civil and environmental engineer*
Grieves, Robert Belanger *engineering educator*
Heide, John Wesley *engineering executive*
Nava, Patricia Ann *electrical engineering educator, researcher*
Peterscheck, Walter Hermann *chemical engineer*

Fort Worth

Buckner, John Kendrick *aerospace engineer*
Cunningham, Atlee Marion, Jr., *aeronautical engineer*
Deaver, Pete Eugene *civil and aeronautical engineer*
Nichols, James Richard *civil engineer, consultant*
Palmer, Jeffery Dean *systems engineering manager, consultant*
Pray, Donald George *retired aerospace engineer*
Thornton, Anthony L *aerospace engineer*

Galveston

Otis, John James *civil engineer*

Garland

Christensen, Allan Robert *electrical engineer, enrolled agent*

Georgetown

Moore, Pat Howard *engineering and construction company executive*

Grapevine

Blair, Sylvia H. *computer systems project engineer, small business owner*
Shue, Shyh-Pyng Jack *aerospace engineer, researcher, electrical engineer, consultant*

Hollywood Park

Smith, Richard Thomas *retired electrical engineer*

Houston

Antalffy, Leslie Peter *mechanical engineer*
Bovay, Harry Elmo, Jr., *retired engineering company executive*
Bozeman, Ross Elliot *engineering executive*
Cheatham, John Bane, Jr., *retired mechanical engineering educator*
Chiquelin, David Bryan *mechanical engineer*
Devoy, Stephen Douglas *marine engineer*
Duerr, David *civil engineer*
Dunbar, Bonnie J. *engineer, astronaut*
Ehlig-Economides, Christine A. *petroleum engineer*
Focht, John Arnold, Jr., *geotechnical engineer*
Fossati, Humberto Mario *electrical engineer, researcher*
Frankhouser, Homer Sheldon, Jr., *engineering and construction company executive*
Geer, Ronald Lamar *mechanical engineering consultant, retired oil company executive*
Gunsel, Selda *chemical engineer, researcher*
Henley, Ernest Justus *chemical engineering educator, consultant*
Hirasaki, George Jiro *chemical engineer, educator*
Hsu, Thomas Tseng-Chuang *civil engineer, educator*
Huang, Hsien-Lu *electrical engineer*
Huang, Shawn Shaoping *engineer*
Itaketo, Umana Thompson *systems and control engineer*
Johnson, Sandra G. *engineering company executive*
Karger, Walter *mechanical engineer*
Kavandi, Janet Lynn *aerospace power engineer, chemist*
Kobayashi, Riki *chemical engineer, educator*
Learned, Vincent Roy *electrical engineer, educator*
Lienhard, John Henry, IV, *mechanical engineer, educator*
Litvinov, Dmitri *engineering educator*
Luss, Dan *chemical engineering educator*
Matthews, Charles Sedwick *petroleum engineering consultant, research advisor*
McLeod, Harry O'Neal, Jr., *retired petroleum engineer, consultant*
Miele, Angelo *engineering educator, researcher, consultant, author*
Morris, Owen Glenn *engineering corporation executive*
Nance, Weldon Bailey *petroleum engineer*
Nelson-Thorpe, Carlon Justine *engineering and operations executive*
Nordgren, Ronald Paul *engineering educator, researcher*
Pearson, James Boyd, Jr., *electrical engineering educator*
Peng, Liang-Chuan *mechanical engineer*
Powell, Alan *scientist-engineer*
Prats, Michael *petroleum engineer, educator*

Rhodes, Allen Franklin *engineering executive*
Scott, Carl Douglas *aerospace engineer*
Shen, Liang Chi *electrical engineer, educator, researcher*
Spanos, Pol Dimitrios *engineering educator*
Talapatra, Dipak Chandra *aerospace engineer*
Tezduyar, Tayfun Ersin *engineering educator*
Tsai, Tom Chunghu *chemical engineer*
Vaughn, Donald C. *engineering executive*
Vazquez, Luis *electronics engineer*
Wilton, Donald Robert *engineering educator*
Wren, Robert James *aerospace engineering manager*
Yelich, Louis James *engineering executive*
Yiu, Fang *structural engineer, researcher*
Yu, Aiting Tobey *engineering executive*
Zhao, Zhongshan *structural engineer, researcher*

Humble

Brown, Samuel Joseph, Jr., *engineer, scientist*

Irving

McCormack, Grace Lynette *civil engineering technician*
Papakostas, Achilleas *telecommunications engineer, researcher*
Potter, Robert Joseph *technical and business executive*
Walley, James Marvin, Jr., *engineering executive, management consultant, real estate company executive*

Katy

Chavez, Victor Manuel *process engineer*

Kemah

Sneider, Robert M. *petroleum exploration engineer*

Kingsville

Du, Qian *electrical engineer, educator*
Li, Shuhui *engineer, educator*

Kyle

Akins, Vaughn Edward *retired engineering company executive*

League City

Kanuth, James Gordan *chemical engineer*

Lindale

Wilson, Leland Earl *petroleum engineering consultant*

Livingston

Hayes, Gordon Glenn *civil engineer*

Lubbock

Archer, James Elson *engineering educator*
Dudek, Richard Albert *engineering educator*
Kiesling, Ernst Willie *civil engineering educator*
Kristiansen, Magne *electrical engineer, educator*

Mc Kinney

Gill, David Brian *electrical engineer, educator*

Midland

Helms, Micky *engineering executive*

Mission

Capener, Regner Alvin *electronics engineer, minister, writer, inventor*

Pasadena

Martinez, Fernando V. *civil engineer*

Plano

Hiegel, James Edward *mechanical engineer*
Warburton, Ralph Joseph *architect, engineer, planner, educator*

Port Aransas

Lehmann, William Leonardo *electrical engineer, educator*

Prairie View

Akujuobi, Cajetan Maduabuchukwu *systems engineer, electrical engineering educator, researcher*

Richardson

Rogers, Mal David, Jr., *chemical engineer*

Rockport

Minor, Joseph Edward *civil engineer, educator*
Stachiw, Jaroslaw (Jerry) Drahomyr *mechanical engineer, consultant*

Rockwall

Griffith, James William *systems engineer, consultant*

Rosenberg

Tourtellotte, Mills Charlton *mechanical and electrical engineer*

Round Rock

O'Connor, Clint Haynie *electrical engineer*

San Antonio

Abramson, Hyman Norman *engineering and science research executive*
Atchley, Curtis Leon *mechanical engineer*
Hubbard, Walter Bryan *chemical engineer, consultant*
Prengle, Herman William, Jr., *chemical engineer, educator*
Redfield, Carol Ann Luckhardt *engineering educator*
Singh, Yesh Pal *mechanical engineering educator, consultant*
Weinbrenner, George Ryan *aeronautical engineer*

Seabrook

Young, Kenneth Alden *aerospace engineer, consultant*

Spring

Szymczak, Edward Joseph *mechanical engineer*
Woodward, Clifford Edward *chemical engineer*

Stafford

Le, Duy-Loan *electrical engineer*

Temple

Carroll, Irwin Dixon *engineer*
Patureau, Arthur Mitchell *chemical engineer, consultant*

Tyler

Mountain, Jeffrey Richardson *engineering educator*

Waco

Bradley, Walter Lee *mechanical engineer, educator, researcher, consultant*
Farison, James Blair *electrical biomedical engineer, educator*

Webster

Kobayashi, Herbert Shin *electrical engineer*

UTAH

Bluffdale

Bliss, Rick Wayne *engineer*

Brigham City

Krejci, Robert Henry *aerospace engineer*
Tolle, Melinda Edith *engineer, scientist*

Dugway

Benson, Morgan *energy engineer, military officer*

Holladay

Silver, Barnard Joseph Stewart *mechanical and chemical engineer, consultant, inventor*

Logan

Bowles, David Stanley *engineering educator, engineering consultant*
Hargreaves, George Henry *civil and agricultural engineer, researcher*
Keller, Jack *agricultural engineering educator, consultant*
Subprasom, Kitti *civil engineer*

Murray

Volberg, Herman William *electronics engineer, consultant*

Ogden

Davidson, Thomas Ferguson *chemical engineer*

Orem

Harris, Michael James *software engineer*
Nordgren, William Bennett *engineering executive*

Provo

Howell, Larry L. *mechanical engineer, educator*
Merritt, LaVere Barrus *engineering educator, civil engineer*
Smoot, Leon Douglas *chemical engineering educator, former dean*
Youd, T. Leslie *retired civil engineer*

Salt Lake City

Anderson, Charles Ross *civil engineer*
Barney, Kline Porter, Jr., *engineering company executive, consultant*
Bousfield, Kenneth Harold *civil engineer*
Chung, You Chung *electrical engineer, educator*
De Vries, Kenneth Lawrence *mechanical engineer, educator*
Gandhi, Om Parkash *electrical engineer*
Ghosh, Sambhunath (Sam Ghosh) *civil engineering educator, environmental engineer*
Kopecek, Jindrich *biomedical scientist, biomaterials and pharmaceutics educator*
McMullin, Paul Wayne *structural engineer*
Pershing, David Walter *chemical engineering educator, researcher*
Sandquist, Gary Marlin *engineering educator, researcher, consultant, writer*
Seader, Junior DeVere (Bob Seader) *chemical engineering educator*
Sohn, Hong Yong *chemical engineer, educator, metallurgical engineer, educator*
Stringfellow, Gerald B. *engineering educator*

VERMONT

Burlington

Outwater, John Ogden *mechanical engineering educator*
Pinder, George Francis *engineering educator, scientist*

Essex Junction

Eshun, Ebenezer E *electrical engineer*
Ishaq, Mousa Hanna *materials engineer*

Jericho

Bolin, Henry Robert *retired engineer*

Rutland

Thompson, Marie Angela *computer engineer, consultant*

Shelburne

Anderson, Richard Louis *electrical engineer*

White River Junction

Japikse, David *mechanical engineer, manufacturing executive*

VIRGINIA

Afton

Anderson, Donald Norton, Jr., *retired electrical engineer*

Alexandria

Cook, Charles William *aerospace engineer, consultant, educator*
Eckhart, Myron, Jr., (Max Eckhart) *retired marine engineer*
Garrett, James F. *engineering company executive*
Glynn, Ernest B. *civil engineer, environmental engineer*
Gould, Phillip *engineer*
Jokl, Alois Louis *electrical engineer*

Kemble, James Richard *retired engineering services executive*
Krambeck, Frederick J. *chemical engineer*
Lasser, Howard Gilbert *chemical engineer, consultant*
Mandil, I. Harry *nuclear engineer*
Murray, Russell, II, *aeronautical engineer, security consultant*
Poehlein, Gary Wayne *retired chemical engineering educator*
Weisberg, Leonard R. *retired engineering executive, researcher*
Wilcox, David Eric *electrical engineer, educational consultant*

Annandale

Geiger, Richard Bernard *engineer, retired federal agency administrator*
Ochs, Walter J. *civil engineer, consultant*

Arlington

Allen, David *systems engineer*
Atkins, Walter J. *electrical engineer*
Beck, Buddy *systems engineer*
Bordogna, Joseph *engineer, educator*
Brighton, John A. *mechanical engineer, academic administrator*
Brown, Gardner Russell *engineering executive*
Hall, Carl William *agricultural and mechanical engineer*
Hazelrigg, George Arthur, Jr., *systems engineer, educator*
Heineken, Frederick George *biochemical engineer*
Kappaz, Michael H. *engineering and energy executive*
Katona, Peter Geza *biomedical engineer, educator*
Kinsey, John Allen *systems engineer, director*
Kumar, Srikanta Ponnathpur *electrical engineer, researcher*
Lala, Jaynarayan Hotchand *computer engineer*
Rahman, Muhammad Abdur *mechanical engineer*
Reagan, Lawrence Paul, Jr., *systems engineer*
Salmon, William Cooper *mechanical engineer, engineering academy executive*
Sewell, William George, III, *electronics engineer, writer*
Shortal, Terence Michael *systems company executive*
Stevens, Donald King *retired aeronautical engineer, consultant*
Stuart, Charles Edward *electrical engineer, oceanographer*

Ashburn

Nickle, Dennis Edwin *electronics engineering consultant, deacon*

Bedford

Ramsey, Forrest Gladstone, Jr., *retired engineering company executive*

Blacksburg

Aref, Hassan *fluid mechanics educator*
Batra, Romesh Chander *engineering mechanics educator, researcher*
Brown, Gary Sandy *electrical engineering educator*
de Wolf, David Alter *electrical engineer, educator*
Disney, Ralph L(ynde) *retired industrial engineering educator*
Fabrycky, Wolter Joseph *engineering educator, author, industrial and systems engineer*
Glasser, Wolfgang Gerhard *chemical engineering, wood science researcher, educator*
Gray, Festus Gail *electrical engineer, educator, researcher*
Inman, Daniel John *mechanical engineer, educator*
Jones, James Beverly *retired mechanical engineering educator, consultant*
Lee, Fred C. *electrical engineering educator*
Mitchell, James Kenneth *civil engineer, educator*
Randall, Clifford Wendell *civil engineer, educator*
Schetz, Joseph Alfred *aerospace engineer, educator*
Squires, Arthur Morton *chemical engineer, educator*
Vikesland, Peter John *environmental engineering educator, researcher*
Walker, Richard David *civil engineer, educator*

Blue Ridge

Elmore, Walter A. *electrical engineer, consultant*

Burke

Lynch, Charles Theodore, Sr., *materials science engineering researcher, consultant, educator*

Chantilly

Tian, Yonglai *electrical engineer*

Charlottesville

Bly, Charles Albert *nuclear engineer, research scientist*
Brewer, Philip Warren *retired civil engineer*
Gaden, Elmer Lewis, Jr., *chemical engineering educator, retired*
Haimes, Yacov Yosseph *systems and civil engineering educator, consultant*
Hoel, Lester A. *civil engineering educator*
Hudson, John Lester *chemical engineering educator*
Inigo, Rafael Madrigal *retired electrical engineering educator*
Krzysztofowicz, Roman *systems engineering and statistical science educator, consultant*
Laurencin, Cato Thomas *biomedical engineer, orthopaedic surgeon*
Lee, Jen-shih *biomedical engineering educator*
McGinnis, Charles Irving *civil engineer*
Norris, Pamela Marie *mechanical engineer, educator*
Reynolds, Albert Barnett *nuclear engineer, educator*
Theodoridis, George Constantin *biomedical engineering educator, researcher*
Townsend, Miles Averill *aerospace and mechanical engineering educator*
White, K(ing) Preston, Jr., *systems engineering educator, researcher, consultant*

Chesapeake

Hampton, John Philip *systems engineer, retired naval officer*

Dulles

Lovell, Robert R(oland) *engineering executive*

Fairfax
Boone, James Virgil *retired engineering executive, researcher*
Bowman, Bruce Alan *civil engineer*
Chen, Chun-Hung *engineering educator*
Cook, Gerald *electrical engineering educator*
Dewberry, Sidney O. *engineering executive*
Fowler, John P. *engineering executive*
Gertler, Janos John *electrical engineer, educator*
Gollobin, Leonard Paul *chemical engineer*
Larsen, Phillip Nelson *electrical engineer*
Levis, Alexander Henry *systems engineer, educator, consultant*
Pedersen, George J. *engineering company executive, computer support company executive*

Fairfax Station
Coaker, James Whitfield *mechanical engineer*
Duff, William Grierson *electrical engineer, educator*

Fairfield
Harrawood, Paul *civil engineering educator*

Falls Church
Jones, Russel Cameron *civil engineer, educator*
Jordan, Mark Henry *retired consulting civil engineer*
Lorenzo, Michael *engineer, government official, real estate broker*
Poza, Hugo Bernardo *aerospace company executive*
Thomas, Lydia Waters *research and development executive*
Villarreal, Carlos Castañeda *engineering executive*

Fort Belvoir
Barnholdt, Terry Joseph *chemical, industrial, and general engineer*

Fredericksburg
Anderson, Roberta June *computer engineer*
Hasenfus, Harold Joseph *retired mechanical engineer, naval technical director*
Medding, Walter Sherman *retired environmental engineer*

Great Falls
Skeen, David Ray *systems engineer, consultant, engineering executive, educator*

Halifax
Dunavant, Samuel Jackson, Jr., *civil engineer, contractor*

Hampton
Amer, Tahani R. *aerospace engineer*
Bangert, Linda S. *aeronautical engineer*
Bartels, Robert Edwin *aerospace engineer*
Dwoyer, Douglas Leon *engineering executive*
Fay, Catharine C. *aerospace engineer*
Joshi, Suresh Meghashyam *research engineer*
Kludze, Ave K.P., Jr., *aerospace engineer*
Mehrotra, Sudhir C. *engineering company executive*
Meyers, James Frank *electronics engineer*
Singleterry, Robert Clay, Jr., *aerospace technologist, physicist*
Sobieski, Jaroslaw *aerospace engineer*
Spearman, Morris Leroy *aeronautics and aerospace researcher*
Weiser, Erik Saul *materials research engineer, project manager*

Hayes
Martinez Fallon, Alma Urania *mechanical engineer*

Lynchburg
Barkley, Henry Brock, Jr., *research and development engineering executive*
Groshner, Maria Star *nuclear engineer*

Mc Lean
Carnicero, Jorge Emilio *aeronautical engineer, transportation executive*
Dobson, Donald Alfred *retired electrical engineer*
Halik, Eugene Egon *engineering consultant*
Klopfenstein, Rex Carter *electrical engineer*
McCambridge, John James *civil engineer*
Metters, Samuel *engineering executive*
Park, Sunwoo *engineer*
Rosenbaum, David Mark *engineering executive, consultant, educator*
Schauer, Franz Peter *civil and nuclear engineer, educator*

Middleburg
Langley, Rolland Ament, Jr., *retired engineering technology company executive*

Newport News
Donaldson, Coleman duPont *aeronautical engineer, consultant, aerospace engineer*
Hubbard, Harvey Hart *aeroacoustician, noise control engineer, consultant*
Noblitt, Nancy Anne *aerospace engineer*

Norfolk
Donohue, David Patrick *engineering executive, retired navy rear admiral*
Samuels, John M., Jr., *industrial engineer*
Wei, Benjamin Min *engineering educator*
Wiltse, James Clark *civil engineer*

Oakton
Curry, Thomas Fortson *electronics engineer, defense industry executive*

Penhook
Coar, Richard John *mechanical engineer, aerospace consultant*

Radford
Phelps, George Graham *computer systems engineer, consultant*

Reston
Choi, Michael Kamwah *aerospace engineer, mechanical engineer, researcher*
Kahn, Robert E. *electrical engineer*

Richmond
Aiken, Peter Haynes *systems engineer, educator*
Compton, Olin Randall *consulting electrical engineer, researcher*
Lingerfelt, Alan Thomas *civil engineer, real estate executive*
Mattauch, Robert Joseph *electrical engineering educator*
McCune, John Brian *broadcast engineer*
Morkoç, Hadis *electrical engineer, educator*
Reed, Christopher Robert *civil engineer*
Rowe, James William, Sr., *engineer*
Sprinkle, William Melvin *audio-acoustical engineer, engineering administrator*
Wynne, Kenneth J. *chemical engineer, educator*

Roanoke
Goad, Danny Harlan *mechanical engineer*
Landis, John William *engineering and construction executive, government advisor*
Stadler, Donald Arthur *management engineer*

Salem
Shaffner, Patrick Noel *retired architectural engineering executive*

Springfield
Casazza, John Andrew *electrical engineer, energy executive*
Galvin, Cyril Jerome, Jr., *coastal engineer*
Meikle, Philip G. *engineer, retired government agency executive*
Sonnemann, Harry *electrical engineer, consultant*

Staunton
Smith, Rodney Wike *engineering executive*

Sterling
Coulter, David Creswell *research engineer*

Vienna
Keiser, Bernhard Edward *engineering company executive, consulting telecommunications engineer*
Mujumdar, Vilas Sitaram *structural engineer, researcher*
Salah, Sagid *retired nuclear engineer*
Woodward, Kenneth Emerson *retired mechanical engineer*

Virginia Beach
Bradshaw, Denis James *engineer, graphics designer*
Denyes, James Richard *industrial engineer*
Spivak, Maurice Sidney *chief project management, consultant*

Waynesboro
Lane, Lawrence Jubin *retired electrical engineer, consultant*

Williamsburg
Aaron, Bertram Donald *engineering executive, management consultant*
Dunn, Ronald Holland *civil engineer, management executive, consultant*

Woodbridge
Kreipke, Merrill Vincent *civil engineer, consultant*

Zacata
Gardiner, William Ralph *electronics engineer, consultant*

WASHINGTON

Auburn
Whitmore, Donald Clark *retired engineer*

Bellevue
Hibbard, Richard Paul *industrial ventilation consultant, educator*
Neuzil, Dennis R. *civil engineer*
Parks, Donald Lee *mechanical engineer, human factors engineer*
Shushkewich, Kenneth Wayne *structural engineer*
Wang, Xing *power systems engineer*

Bellingham
Albrecht, Albert Pearson *electronics/systems engineer, consultant*
Jansen, Robert Bruce *consulting civil engineer*

Clinton
Jacobs, Harold Robert *mechanical engineer, educator*

Dupont
Pettit, Ghery St. John *electronics engineer*

Edmonds
Peckol, James Kenneth *consulting engineer*
Schmit, Lucien André, Jr., *structural engineer*
Terrel, Ronald Lee *civil engineer, business executive, educator*

Federal Way
Gates, Thomas Edward *civil engineer, researcher, waste management administrator, lawyer*
Holman, Kermit Layton *chemical engineer*
Studebaker, Irving Glen *mining engineering consultant*

Issaquah
Reid, John Mitchell (Jack Reid) *biomedical engineer, researcher, consultant*

Kenmore
Guy, Arthur William *electrical engineering educator, researcher*

Kingston
Longwell, John Ploeger *chemical engineering educator*

Kirkland
Szablya, John Francis *electrical engineer, consultant*

Lummi Island
Ewing, Benjamin Baugh *environmental engineer, educator, consultant*

Mercer Island
Bridgforth, Robert Moore, Jr., *aerospace engineer*

Mill Creek
Sengupta, Mritunjoy *mining engineer, educator*

Mukilteo
Bohn, Dennis Allen *electrical engineer, executive*

Olympia
Das, Tapas Kumar *chemical and environmental engineer*
Sesonske, Alexander *nuclear and chemical engineer*

Pullman
Funk, William Henry *retired environmental engineering educator*
Stock, David Earl *mechanical engineering educator*

Redmond
Egner, John David *electrical engineer*
Forsen, Harold Kay *retired engineering executive*
Willard, H(arrison) Robert *electrical engineer*

Renton
Majors, James Edward *electrical engineer*

Richland
Trent, Donald Stephen *thermo fluids engineer*

Sammamish
Yocam, Eric Wayne *engineer*

Seattle
Babb, Albert Leslie *biomedical engineer, educator*
Bowen, Jewell Ray *chemical engineering educator*
Burges, Stephen John *civil engineer, hydrologist*
Christiansen, Walter Henry *aeronautics educator*
Clark, Robert Newhall *electrical and aeronautical engineering educator*
Davis, Earl James *chemical engineering educator*
Davis, Jennie Sue *aerospace engineer*
Finlayson, Bruce Alan *chemical engineering educator*
Gilbert, Paul H. *engineering executive, consultant*
Hands, Eric William *civil engineer, general engineer, researcher*
Hertzberg, Abraham *aeronautical engineering educator, university research scientist*
Hoffman, Allan Sachs *chemical engineer, educator*
Ishimaru, Akira *electrical engineering educator*
Kalonji, Gretchen *engineering educator*
Kapur, Kailash Chander *industrial engineering educator*
Kobayashi, Albert Satoshi *mechanical engineering educator*
Mc Feron, Dean Earl *mechanical engineer, educator*
Murphy-Daniels, Karen Ilene *environmental, safety and health professional*
Oman, Henry *retired electrical engineer, engineering executive*
Parker, Donald Edward *aeronautics and aerospace educator*
Raisbeck, James David *engineering company executive*
Ratner, Buddy Dennis *bioengineer, educator*
Rojas, Eddy M. *engineering educator*
Shankar, Venky N. *transportation engineer, educator*
Sleicher, Charles Albert *chemical engineer*
Spindel, Robert Charles *electrical engineering educator*
Sutter, Joseph F. *aeronautical engineer, consultant, retired air transportation executive*
Wenk, Edward, Jr., *civil engineer, policy analyst, educator, writer*
Woodruff, Gene Lowry *nuclear engineer, university dean*
Yeh, Ying Chin *electrical engineer*

South Bend
Heinz, Roney Allen *civil engineering consultant*

Tacoma
Sloan, Daniel Kay *electrical engineer*

Vancouver
Taylor, Carson William *electrical engineer*

WEST VIRGINIA

Charleston
Bolen, Charles Paul *systems engineer*
Lewis, Charles Raymond, II, *traffic engineer, consultant*

Montgomery
Sathyamoorthy, Muthukrishnan *engineering researcher, educator*
Zatar, Wael Abdelhalim *civil engineer, educator*

Morgantown
Eck, Ronald Warren *civil engineer, educator*
Guthrie, Hugh Delmar *chemical engineer*
Halabe, Udaya Bhatta *civil engineering educator, researcher*
Kemp, Emory Leland *civil engineering educator*
Mazaheri, Ali Reza *engineer, researcher*
Mucino-Quintero, Victor Hugo *mechanical engineering educator, consultant*

Parkersburg
Sperati, Carleton Angelo *retired industrial scientist*

Ravenswood
Hamrick, Leslie Wilford, Jr., *metallurgy supervisor*

South Charleston
Nielsen, Kenneth Andrew *chemical engineer*

WISCONSIN

Brookfield
Curfman, Floyd Edwin *retired engineering educator*
Thomas, John *mechanical engineer*

Genoa
Parkyn, John Duwane *nuclear engineer*

Glendale
Kadel, Lee A. *computer engineer*

Green Bay
Panchalavarapu, Poornachandra Rao *industrial engineer, consultant*

Hudson
Johnson, James Robert *ceramic engineer, educator*

La Crosse
Davy, Michael Francis *civil engineer, consultant*

Madison
Beachley, Norman Henry *mechanical engineer, educator*
Berthouex, Paul Mac *civil and environmental engineer, educator*
Bird, Robert Byron *chemical engineering educator, author*
Boyle, William Charles *civil engineering educator*
Carbon, Max William *nuclear engineering educator*
Dietmeyer, Donald Leo *retired electrical engineer, educator*
Duffie, John Atwater *chemical engineer, educator*
Emmert, Gilbert Arthur *engineer, educator*
Grogan, Paul J. *retired engineering educator*
Gustafson, David Harold *industrial engineering and preventive medicine educator*
Hill, Charles Graham, Jr., *chemical engineering educator*
Kulcinski, Gerald LaVerne *nuclear engineer, educator, dean*
Langer, Stanley Harold *chemical engineer, educator*
Lasseter, Robert Haygood *electrical engineering educator, consultant*
Lightfoot, Edwin Niblock, Jr., *retired chemical engineering educator*
Long, Willis Franklin *electrical engineering educator, researcher*
Lovell, Edward George *mechanical engineering educator*
Novotny, Donald Wayne *electrical engineering educator*
Skiles, James Jean *electrical engineer, computer engineer, educator*
Smith, Michael James *industrial engineering educator*
Stewart, Warren Earl *chemical engineer, educator*
Thesen, Arne *industrial engineering educator*
Vanderheiden, Gregg C. *engineering educator, research scientist*
Webster, John Goodwin *biomedical engineer, researcher, biomedical engineer, educator*

Milwaukee
Chandler, Edward William *communication systems engineer, electrical engineer, electrical engineering educator*
Demerdash, Nabeel Aly Omar *electrical engineer*
Fournelle, Raymond Albert *engineering educator*
Gaggioli, Richard Arnold *mechanical engineering educator*
Graef, Luther William *civil engineer*
Heinen, James Albin *electrical engineering educator*
Landis, Fred *mechanical engineering educator*
Widera, Georg Ernst Otto *mechanical engineering educator, consultant*

Oconomowoc
Dupies, Donald Albert *retired civil engineer*

Richland Center
Heinen, John Timothy *environmental engineer*

Wisconsin Rapids
Drew, Richard Allen *retired electrical and instrument engineer*

WYOMING

Laramie
Bellamy, John Cary *civil engineer, meteorologist*
Mingle, John Orville *engineer, educator, lawyer, consultant*
Rechard, Paul Albert *retired civil engineering company executive, consultant*

Wilson
Lawroski, Harry *nuclear engineer*
Muftu, Sinan *mechanical engineer, educator*

TERRITORIES OF THE UNITED STATES

PUERTO RICO

Gurabo
Kuruganty, Sastry Pratap *electrical engineering educator*

MILITARY ADDRESSES OF THE UNITED STATES

PACIFIC

Apo
Tsau, William Wen-Shiung *civil engineer, consultant, structural engineer*
Turner, David Lowery *system safety engineer*

CANADA

ALBERTA

Calgary
Glockner, Peter G. *civil and mechanical engineering educator*
Heidemann, Robert Albert *chemical engineering educator, researcher*
Lam, Galen Ka-Ron *electrical engineer*

Malik, Om Parkash *electrical engineering educator, researcher*
McDaniel, Roderick Rogers *petroleum engineer, consultant*

Edmonton
Lock, Gerald Seymour Hunter *retired mechanical engineering educator*
Morgenstern, Norbert Rubin *civil engineering educator*
Offenberger, Allan Anthony *electrical engineering educator*
Otto, Fred Douglas *chemical engineering educator*
Zuo, Ming Jian *industrial engineering educator*

BRITISH COLUMBIA

Coquitlam
Fei, Lin *engineering educator, engineering executive*

Vancouver
Salcudean, Martha Eva *mechanical engineer, educator*
Young, Lawrence *electrical engineering educator*

Victoria
Antoniou, Andreas *electrical engineering educator*
Lind, Niels Christian *civil engineering educator*

Westbank
Wedepohl, Leonhard Martin *electrical engineering educator*

MANITOBA

Winnipeg
Cohen, Harley *engineering educator*
Kuffel, Edmund *electrical engineering educator*
Mufti, Aftab A. *civil engineering educator*

NEW BRUNSWICK

Fredericton
Bray, Dale Irving *civil engineering educator*

NEWFOUNDLAND

Saint John's
Clark, Jack Ivor *civil engineer, researcher*
Meisen, Axel *chemical engineering educator, university dean*

NOVA SCOTIA

Kentville
Baker, George Chisholm *engineering executive, consultant*

ONTARIO

Burlington
Begum, Shaila Luxmy *environmental engineer*
Harris, Philip John *engineering educator*

Hamilton
Bandler, John William *electrical engineering educator, consultant*
Campbell, Colin Kydd *electrical and computer engineering educator, researcher*
Crowe, Cameron Macmillan *chemical engineering educator*

Kingston
Batchelor, Barrington de Vere *civil engineer, educator*

London
Davenport, Alan Garnett *civil engineer, educator*
Inculet, Ion I. *electrical engineering educator, research director, consultant*

Mississauga
Chen, Xi-Qing *mechanical engineer*
Gupta, Rajesh *engineer, consultant*
John, Leonard Keith *aerospace and mechanical engineer*
Rygiel, Edward K. *chemical engineer*

North York
Buzacott, John Alan *engineering educator*

Ottawa
Bozozuk, Michael *civil engineer*
Georganas, Nicolas D. *electrical engineering educator*
Moore, William John Myles *retired electrical engineer, researcher*
Pachner, Jaroslav (Frantisek) *nuclear engineer, consultant*

Saint Catharines
Picken, Harry Belfrage *aerospace engineer*

Scarborough
Huang, Wei *engineer, researcher*

Toronto
Davison, Edward Joseph *electrical engineering educator*
Endrenyi, Janos *research engineer, educator*
Ganczarczyk, Jerzy Jozef *civil engineering educator, wastewater treatment consultant*
Goring, David Arthur Ingham *chemical engineering educator, scientist*
Janischewskyj, Wasyl *electrical engineering educator*
Kunov, Hans *biomedical and electrical engineering educator*
Meagher, George Vincent *mechanical engineer*
Salama, C. Andre Tewfik *electrical engineering educator*

Slemon, Gordon Richard *electrical engineering educator*
Smith, Peter William Ebblewhite *electrical engineering educator, scientist, physicist*
Venetsanopoulos, Anastasios Nicolaos *electrical engineer, educator*
Wonham, Walter Murray *electrical engineer, educator*
Zeng, Hong *audio system architect, researcher*

Waterloo
Penlidis, Alexander *chemical engineering educator*
Sedra, Adel Shafeek *electrical engineering educator, academic administrator*
Vlach, Jiri *electrical engineering educator, researcher*

Windsor
Hackam, Reuben *electrical engineering educator*
Kennedy, John Baptist *civil engineer*

QUEBEC

Montreal
Dealy, John Michael *chemical engineer, educator*
Haccoun, David *electrical engineering educator*
Ladanyi, Branko *civil engineer, educator*
Lamarre, Bernard *engineering executive*
Paidoussis, Michael Pandeli *mechanical engineering educator*
Ramachandran, Venkatanarayana Deekshit *electrical engineering educator*
Saint-Pierre, Guy *engineering executive*
Van Dyke, Donald Lee *systems engineer, consultant*

Mount Royal
Couture, Armand *civil engineer*

Saint-Lambert
Terreault, Charles *engineer, management educator, researcher*

Sainte-Anne-de-Bellevue
Broughton, Robert Stephen *irrigation and drainage engineering educator, consultant*

Sainte-Foy
LeDuy, Anh *engineering educator*

Sillery
La Rochelle, Pierre-Louis *civil engineering educator*

Varennes
Bartnikas, Raymond *electrical engineer, educator*

Westmount
Kalaycioglu, Serdar *space robotics engineer, manager*

SASKATCHEWAN

Regina
Mollard, John Douglas *engineering and geology executive*

Saskatoon
Billinton, Roy *engineering educator*
Smith, C. D. *civil engineering educator*

Mississauga
Runnalls, Oliver John Clyve (John Runnalls) *nuclear engineering educator*

Montreal
Selvadurai, Antony Patrick Sinnappa *civil engineering educator, applied mathematician, consultant*

MEXICO

Mexico City
Porraz, Mauricio Jimenez Labora *civil engineer, researcher*

AUSTRALIA

Cammeray
Besley, Morrish Alexander (Tim Besley) *civil engineer*

BELGIUM

Roeselare
Libbrecht, Gaspar Joseph *civil engineer, educator*

CHINA

Shanghai
Yun, Liang *marine engineer, educator*

DENMARK

Vedbaek
Svensson, Sven Eilif *civil engineer, consultant*

ENGLAND

Cambridge
Hawthorne, Sir William (Sir William Rede Hawthorne) *aerospace and mechanical engineer, educator*

Coulsdon
Vijayaratnam, Kanapathipillai *civil and environmental engineer, consultant, director, educator*

Liverpool
Sawko, Felicjan *civil engineering educator*

London
Gelenbe, Sami Erol *engineering educator*

Southampton
Brebbia, Carlos Alberto *educator, engineering consultant*

Westminster
Broers, Lord Alec Nigel *engineering educator*

FRANCE

Grenoble
Dussopt, Laurent *electrical engineer*

GERMANY

Aachen
Pischinger, Franz Felix *engineer, researcher*

Dortmund
Freund, Eckhard *electrical engineering educator*

Munich
Hein, Fritz Eugen *engineer, consultant, architect*

GREECE

Athens
Arnis, Efstathios Constantinos *mechanical engineer, space naval designer*

HONG KONG

Greenvale Village
Chan, Kit Yu Evan *civil engineer*

Hong Kong
Kao, Charles Kuen *electrical engineer, educator*

IRELAND

Dublin
Dooge, James Clement Ignatius *civil engineer, hydrologist, former senator*

ISRAEL

Beer Sheva
Brosilow, Coleman Bernard *chemical engineering educator*

Tel Aviv
Eliaz, Noam *materials engineer, researcher*

JAPAN

Nagoya
Sendo, Takeshi *mechanical engineering educator, researcher, author*

Shizuoka
Anma, So *engineer consultant*

Tokyo
Hori, Yukio *engineering educator, scientific association administrator*
Kaneko, Hisashi *engineering executive*
Kato, Shuichi *information engineering educator*
Saito, Shuzo *electrical engineering educator*
Sakuta, Masaaki *engineering educator, consultant*

PAKISTAN

Lahore
Rai, Maqbool Ahmad *civil engineer, consultant*

PORTUGAL

Algés
Horta, José Carlos de Oliveira Sousa *civil engineering consultant*

REPUBLIC OF KOREA

Pusan
Ha, Chang Sik *polymer science educator*

Seoul
Zi, Goangseup *engineering educator*

Taejon
Kang, Kyungin *electronics engineer, researcher*
Park, Seok-Kyun *civil engineer, educator*

SAUDI ARABIA

Dhahran
Allen, John Timothy *mechanical engineer*

Riyadh
Alsubaie, Abdulaziz Mohamed *civil engineer*

SINGAPORE

Singapore
Yeo, Yee-Chia *engineering educator, consultant*
Zhou, Wei *engineer, educator*

SLOVAKIA

Bratislava
Fristacky, Norbert *computer engineering educator, researcher*

SWEDEN

Askim
Bakhuizen, Willem Anthonie Hendrik Johannes *civil engineer*

SWITZERLAND

Zurich
Morari, Manfred *chemical engineer, educator*

TAIWAN

Tainan
Huang, Ting-Chia *chemical engineering educator, researcher*
Lin, Jiin-Huey Chern *engineering educator*

Taipei
Sheu, Jiuh-Biing *transportation engineer, educator*

TURKEY

Bilkent
Akman, Varol *computer engineer, educator*

WALES

Porthmadog
Owen, Walter Shepherd *materials science and engineering educator*

ZIMBABWE

Harare
Salahuddin, Ahmad *civil engineer, educator*

ADDRESS UNPUBLISHED

Abdulla, Mostafa Naguib *communications engineer*
Abetti, Pier Antonio *consulting electrical engineer, technology management and entrepreneurship educator*
Ackerman, Daniel L. *audio engineer, writer*
Adar, Eytan *computer engineer, researcher*
Aguinsky, Richard Daniel *electrical engineer, engineering executive*
Ahsan, Omar Faruk *computer engineer, manager, consultant*
Alexander, Melvin Taylor *quality assurance engineer, statistician*
Allison, John McComb *retired aeronautical engineer*
Amancio, Ruth Carson *safety engineer*
Amann, Charles Albert *mechanical engineer, researcher*
Amlani, Islamshah *engineering scientist*
Anderson, John Gaston *electrical engineer, consultant*
Anderson, Thomas Patrick *mechanical engineer, educator*
Andrea, Mario Iacobucci *engineer, scientist, gemologist, appraiser*
Archer, Hugh Morris *consulting engineer, retired manufacturing executive*
Arcot, Prakash Kumar B *engineer, consultant*
Argo, Robert Wayne *electrical engineer*
Armaingaud, Franck *engineer*
Azar, Fred S. *biomedical engineer, researcher*
Baddour, Raymond Frederick *chemical engineer, educator, entrepreneur*
Baker, Jack Thomas *design engineer, environmental scientist, consultant*
Bakht, Baidar *civil engineer, researcher, educator*
Balagurunathan, Yoganand *electrical engineer, researcher*
Baltazzi, Evan Serge *engineering research consulting company executive*
Banerjee, Kaustav *electrical and computer engineering educator*
Bar-Cohen, Avram *mechanical engineering educator*
Baron, Barton Leonard *engineer*
Baron, Seymour *engineering and research executive*
Bartlett, Desmond William *engineering company executive*
Battaglia, Francine *mechanical engineering educator, researcher*
Bauer, Richard Carlton *nuclear engineer*
Baum, Eleanor *electrical engineering educator, academic administrator*
Beach, Harry Lee, Jr., *mechanical engineer, aerospace engineer*
Beard, Leo Roy *retired civil engineer*
Beckjord, Eric Stephen *nuclear engineer, energy researcher*
Berger, Frederick Jerome *electrical engineer, educator*
Bers, Abraham *electrical engineering and physics educator*
Bershad, Neil Jeremy *electrical engineering educator*
Bertin, John Joseph *aeronautical engineer, educator, researcher*

Beumer, Richard Eugene *retired engineering executive*
Bhatia, Rajan *engineer, physicist, researcher*
Bierley, Paul Edmund *aeronautical engineer, musician, author, publisher*
Birmingham, Thomas Harlan *civil engineer, writer*
Bishop, Paul Leslie *civil and environmental engineering educator, environmental engineering consultant*
Bissell, Allen Morris *engineer, consultant*
Blakemore, Dwayne, II, *electrical engineer*
Bloch, Erich *retired electrical engineer, former science foundation administrator*
Bodensieck, Ernest Justus *mechanical engineer*
Bolie, Victor Wayne *engineering consultant*
Bornhorst, Kenneth Frank *electromagnetics and systems engineer*
Bose, Anjan *electrical engineering educator, academic administrator*
Bowman, Charles Hay *retired engineering educator, petroleum company executive*
Boyd, John T. *engineering executive*
Boyle, Bryan Douglas *computer and network systems architect*
Bradshaw, Peter *engineering educator*
Braun, Edward Louis *engineer, writer*
Brennan, Lawrence Edward *retired electronics engineer*
Brickell, Charles Hennessey, Jr., *marine engineer, retired military officer*
Bridger, Baldwin, Jr., *electrical engineer*
Briggs, James Henry, II, *engineering administrator*
Brown, Teion O'Dell *engineering executive*
Brozowski, Laura Adrienne *mechanical engineer*
Brubaker, James Edward *mechanical engineer*
Brungraber, Robert J. *civil engineer, educator*
Brustman, Richard D. *civil engineer, consultant*
Bueno, Pablo Cesar *aeronautical engineer, educator*
Bunch, Jennings Bryan, Jr., *retired electrical engineer*
Burchard, John Kenneth *retired chemical engineer*
Burhans, Frank Malcolm *mechanical engineer*
Byrd, Lloyd Garland *retired civil engineer*
Calder, Robert Mac *aerospace engineer*
Canter, Howard Raphael *nuclear engineer*
Carlson, Robert Codner *industrial engineering educator*
Carroll, Philip Joseph, Jr., *engineering company executive*
Cerny, Louis Thomas *civil engineer, railway engineering consultant*
Cha, Soyoung Stephen *mechanical engineer, educator*
Chae, Heeyeop *chemical engineer, researcher*
Champa, John Joseph *telecommunications engineer, consultant, writer*
Chandra, Abhijit *engineering educator*
Charwat, Andrew Franciszek *engineering educator*
Chen, Shoei-Sheng *retired mechanical engineer*
Chouery, Farid Alexandre *electrical engineer, structural engineer, consultant*
Chow, Winston *engineering research executive*
Chu, Jack J. (Jack J. Zhu) *electrical engineer*
Claridge, Elmond Lowell *retired engineering educator, consultant*
Clewett, Raymond Winfred *mechanical design engineer*
Concordia, Charles *consulting engineer*
Conway, Richard Ashley *environmental engineer*
Corallo, N. Ralph *retired health care products design engineer*
Councill, William Thomas, III, *computer engineer, consultant*
Crespo, Luis Guillermo *aerospace engineer, educator*
Crossley, Francis Rendel Erskine *former engineering educator*
Curtis, James Richard *flight engineer*
Dajani, Jarir Subhi *retired civil engineer, consultant*
Dally, James William *mechanical engineering educator, consultant*
Daly, Donald F. *retired engineering company executive*
Dargan, Pamela Ann *electrical engineer*
Davis, Keigh Leigh *aerospace engineer*
Day, Donald Lee *retired engineering educator, researcher*
De Ford, Douglas Atmetlla *biochemical, biomechanical and industrial engineer*
Derby, Robert Allen *acoustical engineer*
Dewhurst, Peter *industrial engineer, educator*
Diao, Yixin *electrical engineer, researcher*
Dickerson, John Robert *retired automotive engineer*
Dix, Gary Errol *engineering executive*
Dix, Samuel Morman *industrial engineer, physical economist, appraiser*
Dizer, John T., Jr., *engineering educator*
Dodd, Steven Louis *systems engineer*
Donohue, George L. *mechanical engineer, educator*
Donohue, Marc David *chemical engineering educator*
Dorighi, Nancy S. *computer engineer*
Dorning, John Joseph *nuclear engineering, engineering physics and applied mathematics educator*
Dougherty, Floyd Wallace *design engineer*
Douglas, Karin Nadja *engineer*
Dransite, Brian Robert *product engineer manager*
Dull, William Martin *retired engineering executive*
Durrani, Sajjad Haidar *retired space communications engineer*
Dyer, Ira *ocean engineering educator, consultant*
Eaglet, Robert Danton *electrical engineer, aerospace consultant, retired military officer*
Eberstein, Arthur *former biomedical engineering educator, researcher*
Edgar, Thomas Flynn *chemical engineering educator*
Edwards, Victor Henry *chemical engineer*
Eissmann, Robert Fred *retired manufacturing engineer*
Ellis, Michael David *aerospace engineer*
Engelmann, Rudolph Herman *electronics consultant, writer*
Ernst, Edward Willis *retired electrical engineering educator*
Ettinger, Harry Joseph *industrial hygiene engineer, consultant*
Evans, Maria D. *mechanical engineer*
Everett, Robert Rivers *electrical engineer*
Fischer, Maxim *electronics engineer*
Fish, Andrew Joseph, Jr., *electrical engineering educator, researcher*
Fishman, Bernard *mechanical engineer*
Flick, Carl *electrical engineer, consultant*
Foley, Gary J. *research chemical engineer, computer scientist, federal agency administrator*
Fontana, Mario H. *nuclear engineer*
Ford, Mark Lee *aerospace engineer, researcher*
Forman, Edgar Ross *mechanical engineer*
Fox, Joan Phyllis *environmental engineer*
Frantiska, Joseph John, Jr., *systems engineer, educator*
Fraser, Brent DeWayne *industrial engineer, researcher*
Fraser, Donald C. *engineering executive, educator*
Fridley, Robert Bruce *agricultural engineer, educator*
Galli, Stefano *electrical engineer, researcher, consultant*
Gamble, Scott L. *civil engineer*
Garriott, Owen Kay *astronaut, scientist*
Geiger, David E *engineer*
Gens, Ralph Samuel *electrical engineering consultant*
Gere, James Monroe *civil engineering educator*
Germany, Daniel Monroe *aerospace engineer*
Ghausi, Mohammed Shuaib *electrical engineering educator, university dean*
Gidley, John Lynn *engineering executive*
Gildart, Charles Rolland, Jr., *mechanical engineer*
Gill, Rebecca LaLosh *aerospace engineer*
Goldberger, Arthur Earl, Jr., *industrial engineer, executive*
Gouse, S. William, Jr., *engineering executive, scientist*
Graessley, William Walter *retired chemical engineering educator*
Grandi, Attilio *engineering consultant*
Gray, Gavin Campbell, II, *computer information engineer*
Gray, Harry Joshua *retired engineering educator*
Green, Leon, Jr., *mechanical engineer*
Groce, William Henry, III, *environmental engineer, consultant*
Gray, Henry Jones *engineering company executive, petroleum engineer*
Gubbins, Keith Edmund *chemical engineering educator*
Guymon, Gary LeRoy *civil engineering educator, consultant*
Haberman, Charles Morris *mechanical engineer, educator*
Hallett, William Jared *retired nuclear engineer*
Halpin, Daniel William *civil engineering educator, consultant*
Hammam, M. Shawky *electrical engineer, educator*
Hanneman, Rodney Elton *metallurgical engineer*
Hansen, Rex Cossey *mechanical engineer*
Hanson, John M. *civil engineering and construction educator*
Hanson, Wendy Karen *retired chemical engineer*
Hardy, Chester Alfred *engineer*
Haywood, John William, Jr., *manufacturing engineering consultant*
Hecker, Michael Hanns Louis *retired electrical engineer, speech scientist*
Heilmeier, George Harry *electrical engineer, researcher*
Helstrom, Carl Wilhelm *electrical engineering educator*
Henderson, Charles Brooke *research company executive*
Heney, Joseph Edward *environmental engineer*
Herbel, LeRoy Alec, Jr., *telecommunications engineer*
Herman, William Arthur *engineering and physics laboratory director*
Herrlinger, Stephen Paul *flight test engineer, air force officer, educator*
Higby, Edward Julian *safety engineer*
Hillman, Leon *electrical engineer*
Hinderliter, Richard Glenn *electrical engineer*
Ho, Teh Chung *chemical engineer, researcher*
Hockeimer, Henry Eric *business executive*
Holeman, Russell Kent *civil engineer*
Hornby-Anderson, Sara Ann *metallurgical engineer, marketing professional*
Howard, Dean Denton *electrical engineer, researcher, consultant*
Hsu, John S. *electrical engineer, researcher*
Huang, Shouhua *electronics engineer*
Hughes, Kevin Dewayne *electronics engineer, educator*
Hung, James Chen *engineer, educator, consultant*
Hunsucker, Robert Dudley *physicist, electrical engineer, educator, researcher*
Hutchinson, John Woodside *mechanical engineer, educator*
Israelachvili, Jacob Nissim *chemical engineer*
Jackson, Michael P. *engineering company executive, former federal agency administrator*
James, Charles Franklin, Jr., *engineering educator*
Jarvik, Robert K. *biomedical research scientist*
Jasper, Norman Hans *engineer*
Jensen, Marvin Eli *retired agricultural engineer, science administrator*
Johnson, Noel Lars *biomedical engineer*
Johnson, Stewart Willard *civil engineer*
Jones, Everett Bruce *retired civil engineer, hydrologist*
Jordan, Howard Emerson *retired engineering executive, consultant*
Juricic, Davor *mechanical engineering educator*
Kahn, Irwin William *industrial engineer*
Kamgaing, Telesphor *electrical engineer, researcher*
Kaufman, Irving *retired engineering educator*
Kemper, John Dustin *mechanical engineering educator*
Kenderian, Shant *engineer, consultant*
Kennedy, Leo Raymond *engineering executive*
Kercher, David Max *mechanical engineer*
Kesselring, Debbie Anne *systems engineer*
Khan, Aurangzeb *engineering educator*
Kice, John Edward *engineer, educator, consultant*
Kinsman, Frank Ellwood *engineering executive*
Kirkland, Virgil Wayne *electrical engineer*
Kleinsorge, William Peter *metallurgical engineer*
Klink, Robert Michael *consulting engineer, management consultant, financial consultant, property developer*
Klohn, Earle Jardine *retired engineering company executive, consultant*
Knott, Wiley Eugene *electronic engineer*
Kolbe, Ronald Lynn *research engineer*
Kopp, Richard Edgar *electrical engineer*
Kozak, Alexander L. *engineer*
Kreith, Frank *research engineer, consultant*
Kretschmer, Frank Frederick, Jr., *electrical engineer, researcher, consultant*
Krishnamoorti, Ramanan *chemical engineer, educator*
Kriz, George James *former agricultural research administrator*
Krol, Stanley Joseph, Jr., *electrical engineer*
Kuesel, Thomas Robert *civil engineer*
Kurfess, Thomas Roland *mechanical engineering educator*
Lafferty, Brad Donadl *communications engineer*
Lancaster, John Howard *civil engineer, consultant*
Langston, James Leland *electronics engineer*
Laskai, Laszlo *electrical engineer, consultant*
Lecat, Robert J. *retired aeronautical engineer*
Levinson, Herbert Sherman *civil and transportation engineer*
Levinson, Stephen Eliot *engineering educator, electrical engineer*
Lewitt, Miles Martin *computer engineering company executive*
Li, Tingye *electrical engineer*
Li, Yao En *chemical engineer*
Liang, Junxiang *retired aeronautics and astronautics engineer, educator*
Liew, Fah Pow *mechanical engineer*
Liu, Weiping *materials engineer, research scientist*
Liu, Xuan *computer engineer, researcher*
Lodge, Arthur Scott *mechanical engineering educator*
Longobardo, Anna Kazanjian *engineering executive*
Loper, Carl Richard, Jr., *metallurgical engineer, educator*
Lou, Gang *engineer, researcher*
Lou, Janet *electrical engineer, researcher*
Lovell, Walter Carl *engineer, inventor*
Lowe, John, III, *consulting civil engineer*
Lui, Eric Mun *civil engineering educator, practitioner*
Lund, Rita Pollard *aerospace engineer, consultant*
Luo, Wenbin *computer engineer, educator*
Luthy, Richard Godfrey *environmental engineering educator*
Lyon, Martha Sue *research engineer, retired military officer*
MacGregor, James Grierson *retired civil engineering educator, structural engineering consultant*
Madhavan, Guruprasad *biomedical engineer*
Madix, Robert James *chemical engineer, educator*
Magnabosco, Louis Mario *chemical engineer, researcher, consultant*
Mahle, Christoph Erhard *electrical engineer*
Mai, Chao Chen *engineer*
Mak, Ben Bohdan *engineer*
Marshall, John Paul *broadcast engineer*
Mason, John Latimer *engineering executive*
Mataric', Maja *engineering educator*
Mates, Robert Edward *mechanical engineering educator*
McClellan, Robert Edward *civil engineer*
McDonald, Mark Douglas *electrical engineer*
McFadden, Peter William *retired mechanical engineering educator*
McLaughlin, William Irving *space technical manager, writer*
McNair, John William, Jr., *civil engineer*
Meadors, Howard Clarence, Jr., *electrical engineer*
Meiksin, Zvi H. *electrical engineering educator*
Merriam, Robert W. *engineering executive, educator*
Meunier, Robert Raymond *research electrical engineer, optical engineer*
Meyer, John Edward *nuclear engineering educator*
Michel, Bernard *civil engineering educator, consultant*
Miele, Joel Arthur, Sr., *civil engineer*
Miller, Martin E. *engineer, consultant*
Milligan, Victor *consulting engineer*
Miskus, Michael Anthony *electrical engineer*
Mitzner, Kenneth Martin *electrical engineering consultant*
Moazed, Khosrow L. *retired engineering educator*
Mohler, Ronald Rutt *electrical engineering educator*
Moll, David Carter *civil engineer*
Moore, Fay Linda *systems engineer*
Morgan, James John *environmental engineering educator*
Mortimer, David William *electronics engineer*
Mortimer, Richard Walter *mechanical engineer, educator*
Moscicka, Dorota *engineer*
Munger, Elmer Lewis *civil engineer, educator*
Munger, Paul R. *civil engineering educator*
Munoz, Mario Alejandro *civil engineer, retired consultant*
Munzner, Robert Frederick *biomedical engineer*
Myers, Phillip Samuel *mechanical engineering educator*
Myerson, Allan Stuart *chemical engineering educator, university dean*
Nahman, Norris Stanley *electrical engineer*
Nakayama, Wataru *engineering educator, consultant*
Narasimhan, Ravi *electrical engineer*
Nawy, Edward George *civil engineer, educator*
Nellums, Robert O. *retired chemical engineer*
Nelson, Robert Arthur *civil engineer*
Nelson, Thomas Adams *electrical engineer, transportation consultant*
Newkirk, John Burt *retired metallurgical engineer, administrator*
Nguyen, Charles Cuong *engineering educator, researcher, dean*
Nguyen, Quoc *mechanical engineer*
Nicholas, Henry Thompson, III, *former communications engineering executive*
Nicholls, Robert Lee *civil engineer, educator*
Nielsen, Jakob *computer interface engineer*
Oberai, Assad A. *engineer, researcher*
Odar, Fuat *nuclear engineer*
Ortolano, Ralph J. *engineering consultant*
Padin, Jeffry *aerospace engineer*
Partington, James Wood *engineering executive*
Patel, Anil S. *biomedical engineer, researcher, medical products executive*
Perrenod, Douglas Arthur *engineer, astronaut*
Peters, Douglas Cameron *mining engineer, geologist*
Pham, Duc *engineering executive*
Phan, Long Thanh *structural engineer, researcher*
Pniakowski, Andrew Frank *structural engineer*
Polliack, Adrian A. *biomedical engineer, researcher*
Ponton, Michael Kamano *engineer, educator*
Porter, Philip Thomas *retired electrical engineer*
Pott, James Thomas *civil engineer, consultant*
Potvin, Alfred Raoul *engineering executive*
Poucher, John Scott *systems engineer, physicist*
Pruden, Ann Lorette *chemical engineer, researcher, management consultant*
Pun, Suzie *biomedical engineer, educator*
Puri, Ishwar Kanwar *engineering educator, researcher*
Rainer, Rex Kelly *civil engineer, educator*
Rand, Robert Stephen *electrical engineer, physicist, statistician*
Raven, Francis Harvey *mechanical engineer, educator*
Reaves, Ray Donald *civil engineer*
Reid, Robert Lelon *engineering educator, dean*
Ren, Ying *engineer*
Reynik, Robert John *materials scientist, research and education administrator*
Guzman, Jose Javier *aeronautical engineer*
Richards, Earl Frederick *electrical engineer, educator*
Richards-Barnard, Sandra L. *control systems engineer, computer graphics consultant*
Riden, Michael David *nuclear engineer*
Robillard, Jean Jules *engineering educator, researcher*
Rodgers, Billy Russell *chemical engineer, research scientist*
Rohr, Davis Charles *aerospace consultant, business executive, retired air force officer*
Rollins, Andrew Martin *biomedical engineer, educator*
Rooke, Allen Driscoll, Jr., *civil engineer, consultant*
Ross, Donald Edward *engineering company executive*
Rousey, Jennifer Ann *engineer*
Rudd, D(ale) F(rederick) *chemical engineering educator*
Russo, Roy Lawrence *retired electronic design automation engineer*
Saeks, Richard Ephraim *engineering executive*
Saha, Arun Kumar *engineering educator, researcher*
Salamon, Miklos Dezso Gyorgy *mining engineer, educator*
Salvatorelli, Joseph J. *engineer, consultant*
Samorek, Alexander Henry *electrical engineer, mathematics and technology educator*
Schell, Allan Carter *retired electrical engineer*
Scherrer, George M. *electrical engineer*
Schlegelmilch, Reuben Orville *electrical engineer, consultant*
Schmidt, Robert *retired mechanics and civil engineering educator*
Schnelle, Phillip David *electrical engineer, consultant*
Schoen, Allen Harry *retired aerospace engineering executive*
Schultz, Albert Barry *engineering educator*
Schurmeier, Harris McIntosh *aeronautical engineer*
Scott, Charles David *chemical engineer, consultant*
Seaden, George *civil engineer*
Seamans, Robert Channing, Jr., *astronautical engineering educator*
Seccombe, Stephen Dana *computer engineer*
Sechrist, Chalmers Franklin, Jr., *electrical engineering educator*
Sells, Kevin Dwayne *marine engineer*
Sethi, Sandeep *environmental engineer*
Seymour, Frederick Prescott, Jr., *industrial engineer, consultant*
Shaffer, Bernard William *mechanical and aerospace engineering educator*
Shank, Maurice Edwin *aerospace engineering executive, consultant*
Shartle, Stanley Musgrave *engineering executive, consultant, surveyor*
Sheaffer, Richard Allen *electrical engineer*
Shur, Michael *electrical engineer, educator, consultant*
Sievenpiper, Daniel Frederic *engineer*
Siljak, Dragoslav D. *engineering educator, researcher*
Silsby, Graham Forbes *mechanical engineer, consultant*
Simpson, Murray *electrical engineer, consultant*
Singhal, Rajan *engineering executive, consultant*
Sise, Karen H. *acoustical engineer*
Sitnyakovsky, Roman Emmanuil *scientist, writer, inventor, translator*
Skelland, Anthony Harold Peter *chemical engineering educator*
Skov, Arlie Mason *petroleum engineer, consultant*
Skromme, Lawrence H. *consulting agricultural engineer*
Smally, Donald Jay *consulting engineering executive*
Smith, Virgil Baker *retired electrical engineer*
Smith, Wayne Calvin *chemical engineer, consultant*
Somasundaran, Ponisseril *surface and colloid engineer, applied science educator*
Sowers, William Armand *civil engineer*
Spanovich, Milan *retired civil engineer*
Sreenivasan, Katepalli Raju *mechanical engineering educator*
Srivatsan, Tirumalai Srinivas *engineering educator*
Stallings, Viola Patricia Elizabeth *systems engineer, educational systems specialist, retired information technology manager*
Starks, Kelly George *systems engineer, consultant*
Stever, Horton Guyford *aerospace scientist and engineer, educator, consultant*
Stiffler, Jack Justin *electrical engineer*
Stovall, Julia Connor *industrial engineer*
Stumpe, Warren Robert *county official, retired scientific, engineering and technical services company executive*
Su, Hung-Jue *mechanical engineer, educator*
Suarez, Michael Anthony *civil engineer, consultant*
Swalm, Thomas Sterling *aerospace executive, retired military officer*
Taylor, Anthony Baldwin *civil engineer*
Terry, Reese, Jr., *engineering executive*
Thackston, Edward Lee *engineer, educator*
Thomas, Matthew Shawn *civil engineer*
Tokerud, Robert Eugene *retired electrical engineer*
Tonapi, Sandeep Shrikant *engineer*
Tontiruttananon, Channarong *electrical engineer, researcher*
Trauger, Donald Byron *nuclear engineering laboratory administrator*
Trujillo-Cuthrell, Loretta Marie *chemical engineer*
Tsygan, Leonid Iosifovich *civil engineer, writer*
Turchi, Peter John *aerospace and electrical engineer, physicist, educator*
Upatnieks, Juris *retired optical engineer*
Urbanik, Thomas, II, *civil engineering educator, researcher*
Utlaut, William Frederick *electrical engineer*

Vér, István László *acoustical engineer, consultant*
Verbov, Lev Falkovich *metallurgical engineer, writer, translator*
Viest, Ivan M(iroslav) *consulting structural engineer*
Voldman, Steven Howard *electrical engineer*
Walton, Harold Vincent *former agricultural engineering educator, academic administrator*
Wang, Gaofeng *engineer, educator*
Wang, Leon Ru-Liang *civil engineer, educator*
Wang, Qigui *materials engineer, researcher*
Wang, Qin *computer engineer, researcher*
Wang, Xi Cheng (David Wang) *mechanical engineer*
Wang, Zhishun *biomedical engineer, consultant*
Washington, Anthony Nathaniel *mechanical engineer*
Washington, Charles Henderson *laser systems designer, consultant*
Washington, Donna Janel *engineer*
Waxman, Ronald *computer engineer*
Wei, John Hua-Fang *engineering executive*
Weil, Randolph Allen *engineering executive*
Weinberger, Arnold *retired electrical engineer*
Weingarten, Joseph Leonard *aerospace engineer*
Weiss, Alvin Harvey *chemical engineering educator, catalysis researcher and consultant*
Weldon, William Forrest *electrical and mechanical engineer, educator*
Wentz, William Henry, Jr., *aerospace engineer, educator*
Wheeler, George Charles, Jr., *materials and processes engineer*
Whitcomb, Richard Travis *aeronautical consultant*
White, Charles Olds *aeronautical engineer*
White, Stanley Archibald *research electrical engineer*
Wicke, Dallas Clyde *retired aerospace engineer*
Wilde, Daniel Underwood *computer engineering educator*
Williams, Charles Wesley *technical executive, researcher*
Williams, Howard Walter *aerospace engineer, engineering executive*
Williams, Ronald Oscar *defense systems engineer*
Williams, Thomas W. *electrical engineer*
Willis, Selene Lowe *electrical engineer, software consultant, project manager*
Wilson, Melvin Edmond *retired civil engineer*
Wintle, Rosemarie *biomedical electronics engineer*
Wolfe, Charles Morgan *electrical engineering educator*
Woo, Savio Lau-Yuen *bioengineering educator*
Wood, Allen John *electrical engineer, consultant*
Woodland, N. Joseph *retired optical engineer, retired mechanical engineer*
Wright, Brian Theodore *retired engineering executive*
Wright, David Allen *mechanical engineer, councilman*
Xiao, Jiarun *mechanical engineer*
Xiao, Jizhong *engineering educator, researcher*
Xu, Biqiang *engineer, researcher*
Yeager, Kurt Eric *research institute official*
Yen, Bing Cheng *retired civil engineer, retired engineering educator*
Yen, Wen Liang *retired aerospace engineer*
Yin, Gerald Zheyao *technology and business executive*
Yin, Zhiping *engineer*
Ying, Jackie *chemical engineer, educator*
Yong, Raymond Nen-Yiu *civil engineering educator*
Yook, Chong Chul *engineering educator*
Young, Leo *electrical engineer*
Yue, Alfred Shui-choh *metallurgical engineer, educator*
Yun, James Kyoon *electrical engineer*
Zanjacomo, Paulo Regis *engineering executive*
Zeleke, Assefa *electrical engineer*
Zelinski, Joseph John *engineering educator, consultant*
Zhao, Hong *biomedical engineer, educator*
Zhou, Yuanxin *mechanical engineer, educator*

FINANCE: BANKING SERVICES
See also **FINANCE: INVESTMENT SERVICES**

UNITED STATES

ALABAMA

Birmingham
Banton, Julian Watts *banker*
Bottorff, Dennis C. *banker*
Coley, Thomas H. *banker*
Horsley, Richard David *banker*
Jones, Carl E., Jr., *bank executive*
Jones, D. Paul, Jr., *banker, lawyer*
Malone, Wallace D., Jr., *bank executive*
Morgan, Hugh Jackson, Jr., *bank executive*
Nash, Warren Leslie *banker*
Northen, Charles Swift, III, *retired bank executive*
Page, Ruffner *bank executive*
Powell, William Arnold, Jr., *retired bank executive*
Weatherly, Robert Stone, Jr., *banker*

Dothan
Peterson, Roger *community bank executive, retired international investment banker, retired manufacturing executive, retired Air Force officer*

Montgomery
Hoffman, Richard William *retired banker*
Lowder, Robert E. *bank executive*
Taylor, Watson Robbins, Jr., *investment banker*

ALASKA

Anchorage
Cuddy, Daniel Hon *bank executive*
Rasmuson, Edward Bernard *banker*
Reed, Frank Metcalf *bank executive, director*

Fairbanks
Heckman, Jyotsna (Jo) L. *bank executive*

ARIZONA

Paradise Valley
Unruh, James Arlen *bank executive*

Phoenix
Ralston, Barbara Jo *bank executive*
Welborn, R. Michael *bank executive*

Scottsdale
Carpenter, Peter Rockefeller *retired bank executive*
Garfield, Ernest *bank consultant*

Surprise
Koessel, Donald Ray *retired bank executive*

Tubac
Miller, Frederick Robeson *banker, director*

Tucson
Bernmúdez, Carmen *trust company executive*
Bradley, Gilbert Francis *retired bank executive*
Markman, Sherman *investment banker, venture capitalist, financial consultant*
O'Brien, Kevin James *investment banking executive*

ARKANSAS

Conway
Daugherty, Billy Joe *retired banker*

Little Rock
Bowen, William Harvey *banker, lawyer*
Gulley, Wilbur Paul, Jr., *retired savings and loan association executive*

CALIFORNIA

Bakersfield
Sawyer, Nelson Baldwin, Jr., *credit union executive*

Beverly Hills
Goldsmith, Bram *banker*
Walker, William Tidd, Jr., *investment banker*

Burbank
Miller, Clifford Albert *merchant banker, business consultant*

Carmel
Barton, Hugh Perry *bank executive*
Dobey, James Kenneth *banker*

Concord
Miller, John Nelson *banker, educator*

Costa Mesa
Giannini, Valerio Louis *investment banker*

Encinitas
Ford, William Francis *retired bank holding company executive*

Escondido
Newman, Barry Ingalls *retired banker, lawyer*

Fallbrook
David, Ward S. *bank officer, retired federal agency executive*

Fresno
Smith, Richard Howard *banker*

Glendale
Cross, Richard John *bank executive*

La Mesa
Schmidt, James Craig *retired bank executive, savings and loan association executive*

Lafayette
Dethero, J. Hambright *banker*

Lake Arrowhead
Fitzgerald, John Charles, Jr., *investment banker*

Long Beach
Hancock, John Walker, III, *banker*
Keller, J(ames) Wesley *credit union executive*

Los Angeles
Badie, Ronald Peter *banker*
Barren de Serres, Bruce Willard (H.R.H. The Duke Bruce Willard Barren de Serres) *merchant banker*
Brown, Kathleen *bank executive, lawyer*
Buchman, Mark Edward *banker*
Koffler, Stephen Alexander *investment banker*
McDonough, Richard Aloysius, IV, *investment banker*
Riordan, George Nickerson *investment banker*
Schwartzberg, Gil N. *apparel executive, lawyer*
Takakura, Tamio *bank official*
Wu, Li-Pei *banker*

Malibu
DeMieri, Joseph L. *retired bank executive*

Manhattan Beach
Magner, Rachel Harris *retired banker*

Manteca
Meckler, Mary McStroul *mortgage company executive, writer*

Menlo Park
Chamberlain, Paul Edward *investment banker*
Grimes, Michael D. *investment banker*
Hazen, Paul Mandeville *banker*
Schmidt, Chauncey Everett *banker, director*

Newport Beach
Casey, Thomas Clark *retired trust company executive, investment advisor*
Frederick, Dolliver H. *merchant banker*
Woollatt, Paul G. *financial company executive*

Oakland
Kettell, Russell Willard *banker*
Nelson, Shirley W. *bank executive*
Sandler, Herbert M. *savings and loan association executive*
Sandler, Marion Osher *savings and loan association executive*

Orinda
Trowbridge, Thomas, Jr., *mortgage banking company executive*

Pasadena
Patton, Richard Weston *retired mortgage company executive*

Rolling Hills Estates
Chuang, Harold Hwa-Ming *banker, consultant, finance educator*

San Diego
Blakemore, Claude Coulehan *banker*
Kendrick, Ronald H. *banker*
Reinhard, Christopher John *merchant banking, venture capital and biotechnology executive*
Wiesler, James Ballard *retired banker*

San Francisco
Armacost, Samuel Henry *bank executive*
Atkins, Howard Ian *bank executive*
August-deWilde, Katherine *banker*
Baumhefner, Clarence Herman *retired bank executive*
Bee, Robert Norman *banker*
Callahan, Patricia R. *bank executive*
Dellas, Robert Dennis *investment banker*
Demarest, David Franklin, Jr., *banker, retired government official*
Edwards, C. Webb *bank executive*
Ehrlich, Susan Patricia *bank executive*
Gillette, Frankie Jacobs *retired savings and loan executive, social worker, government administrator*
Hewitt, Conrad W. *bank executive*
Ho, Doreen Woo *bank executive*
Hoyt, David A. *bank executive*
Kari, Ross *bank executive*
Kovacevich, Richard M. *bank executive*
Lee, Pamela Anne *bank executive, accountant, business analyst*
Luikart, John Ford *investment banker*
Matthews, Gilbert Elliott *investment banker*
McGettigan, Charles Carroll, Jr., *investment banker*
Mehta, Shailesh J. *banker*
Munio, David J. *bank executive*
Murray, Michael J. *bank executive*
Oman, Mark C. *bank executive*
Ostler, Clyde W. *banker*
Petrini, David J. *bank executive*
Rosenberg, Richard Morris *banker*
Saavedra, Charles James *banker*
Stumpf, John G. *bank executive*
Tolstedt, Carrie L. *bank executive*
Trafton, Stephen J. *bank executive*
Warner, Harold Clay, Jr., *banker, investment management executive, brokerage house executive*
Webb, Carl B. *banker*
Yellen, Janet Louise *bank executive*

San Jose
Hall, Robert Emmett, Jr., *investment banker, realtor*
Myer, Warren Hitesh *mortgage broker, internet advertising executive*

San Rafael
Djordjevich, Miroslav-Michael *bank executive*

Santa Barbara
Anderson, Donald Meredith *bank executive*
Tilton, David Lloyd *savings and loan association executive*

Santa Clara
Kamm, Barbara B. *bank executive*

Santa Monica
Heimbuch, Babette E. *bank executive*

Santa Rosa
Elam, John Richard *mortgage company executive*

Tarzana
Weil, Leonard *banker*

Upland
Horton, Michael L. *mortgage company executive, publishing executive*

Walnut Creek
McGrath, Don John *banker*
Rhody, Ronald Edward *banker, communications executive*

COLORADO

Colorado Springs
Olin, Kent Oliver *banker*

Denver
Berg, Gordon Hercher *banker*
Grant, William West, III, *banker*
Imhoff, Walter Francis *investment banker*
Nicholson, Will Faust, Jr., *bank holding company executive*
Oullian, B. LaRae *bank executive*
Rockwell, Bruce McKee *retired banker and foundation executive*

Englewood
Rosser, Edwin Michael *mortgage company executive*

Estes Park
Piper, Mark Harry *retired banker*

Fowler
Fox, Jonathan Randall *banker, real estate broker, insurance agent*

Georgetown
Hildebrandt-Willard, Claudia Joan *banker*

Greenwood Village
Davidson, John Robert (Jay) *bank executive*
Sims, Douglas D. *bank executive*

Highlands Ranch
Hoover, Gary Lynn *banker*

Lakewood
Corboy, James McNally *investment banker*
Fugate, Ivan Dee *banker, lawyer*
Weskamp, Kelley S. *loan account manager, real estate company executive*

Palisade
Barnewall, Marilyn MacGruder *banker, writer*

CONNECTICUT

Cobalt
Stevens, Robert Edwin *bank executive, former insurance company executive*

Cos Cob
Kane, Jay Brassler *banker*

Darien
Mapel, William Marlen Raines *retired banking executive*

Essex
Miller, Elliott Cairns *retired bank executive, lawyer*

Fairfield
Brett, Arthur Cushman, Jr., *banker*

Greenwich
Caruso, Victor Guy *investment banker*
Clark, Thomas Carlyle *banker*
de Visscher, Francois Marie *investment banker*
Lebec, Alain *investment banker*
Long, Thomas Michael *investment banker*
Nevin, Crocker *investment banker*
Scaturro, Peter K. *investment banker*
Shanks, Eugene Baylis, Jr., *banker*
Smith, Phillips Guy *banker*
Stockman, David Alan *investment banker*
Swarz, Jeffrey Robert *investment banker, biotechnologist, neuroscientist*

Hamden
Williams, Edward Gilman *retired bank executive*

Hartford
Fiszel, Geoffrey Lynn *investment banker, investment advisor*
Klinger, Douglas Evan *money management executive*

Litchfield
Booth, John Thomas *investment banker*

New Canaan
MacEwan, Nigel Savage *merchant banker*
Stewart, James Montgomery *retired bank executive*

New Haven
Miller, Walter Richard, Jr., *banker*
Patterson, Peyton R. *bank executive*

Norwalk
Baylis, Robert Montague *investment banker*

Ridgefield
Mesznik, Joel R. *investment banker*

Rowayton
Piper, Thomas Laurence, III, *banker*

Southport
Sheppard, William Stevens *investment banker*

Stamford
Lewis, Perry Joshua *investment banker*

Weston
Harmon, James Allen *bank executive*
Zimmerman, Bernard *investment banker*

Westport
Donaldson, James Neill *banker*
Kelly, Paul Knox *investment banker*
Santoro, Charles William *investment banker*
Weyher, Harry Frederick, III, *merchant banker*

Windsor
Ferraro, John Francis *investment banker*

DELAWARE

Montchanin
Freytag, Richard Arthur *banker*

New Castle
Hill, J. Nathan *trust company executive*

Wilmington
Cochran, John R. *bank executive*
Hammonds, Bruce L. *bank executive*
Hartwick, Paul S., Jr., *bank executive, writer*
St. Clair, Jesse Walton, Jr., *retired savings and loan executive*
Wright, Vernon Hugh Carroll *bank executive*

DISTRICT OF COLUMBIA

Washington
Aguirre-Sacasa, Francisco Xavier *international banker, diplomat*
Aninat, Eduardo *international banking official*

Assad, George John *investment banker*
Baxter, Nevins Dennis *bank consultant*
Carson, Thomas Bode *bank executive, consultant*
Couper, William *bank executive*
D'Aniello, Daniel *merchant banker*
Dervis, Kemal *bank executive*
Douglas, Leslie *investment banker*
Ferguson, Roger W., Jr., *bank executive, federal agency administrator*
Graham, William Pierson *investment banker, entrepreneur*
Greenspan, Alan *bank executive, economist*
Guenther, Jack Donald *banker*
Helfer, Ricki Tigert *banking consultant*
Heumann, Judith *bank executive*
Hoyes, Louis W. *mortgage company executive*
Kesterman, Frank Raymond *investment banker*
Levin, Robert J. *mortgage company executive*
Linn, Johannes *bank executive*
Marzol, Adolfo *mortgage company executive*
Mathias, Edward Joseph *merchant banker*
McDonough, William J. *banker*
McNamara, Robert Strange *former banking executive, former Secretary of Defense*
Miller, G(eorge) William *merchant banker, business executive*
Mudd, Daniel H. *mortgage company executive*
Niculescu, Peter S. *mortgage company executive*
Ogilvie, Donald Gordon *bankers association executive*
Olson, Mark Walter *investment banker, federal agency administrator*
Palmer, R(obie) Mark (Robie Marcus Hooker Palmer) *banker*
Picciotto, Robert *bank executive*
Pollock, Alexander John *retired banker*
Razavi, Hossein *bank executive*
Relch, John *banker, federal agency administrator*
Ring, James Edward Patrick *mortgage banking consulting executive*
Rotberg, Eugene Harvey *investment banker, lawyer*
St. John, Julie *mortgage company executive*
Shelly, Thaddeus Rubez, III, *trust company executive*
Sugisaki, Shigemitsu *international bank official*

FLORIDA

Boca Raton
Cannon, Herbert Seth *investment banker*
Goldberger, Melvin Tobias *executive investment banker*
Hoppenstein, Abraham Solomon *investment and merchant banker, consultant*

Boynton Beach
Davant, James Waring *investment banker*

Coral Gables
Herald, Sara Barli *bank executive*
Weiner, Morton David *banker, insurance agent*

Dunedin
Rosa, Raymond Ulric *retired banker*

Englewood
Simis, Theodore Luckey *investment banker, information technology executive*

Fort Lauderdale
Leach, Ralph F. *banker*
Stewart, John Murray *retired bank executive*
Thayer, Charles J. *investment banker*

Groveland
Miles, Doris Cooper *bank executive*

Jacksonville
Lane, Edward Wood, Jr., *retired banker*
Rice, Charles Edward *bank executive*

Key Biscayne
Wilson, Robert Gordon *investment banker*

Lantana
Barrett, Robert James, III, *investment banker*

Marco Island
Cooper, Thomas Astley *bank executive*

Miami
Brownell, Edwin Rowland *banker, land surveyor, civil engineer*
Jackson, Wilfried *banker*

Naples
Craighead, Rodkey *banker, director*
Kley, John Arthur *banker*
Kvetko, Colleen M. *bank executive*
Martinuzzi, Leo Sergio, Jr., *banker*

Nokomis
Hawley, Phillip Eugene *investment banker*

North Palm Beach
Lynch, William Walker *banker*

Orlando
Hoepner, Theodore John *banker*
Shirek, John Richard *retired savings and loan executive*

Ormond Beach
Franchini, Roxanne *bank executive*

Palm Beach
Harper, Mary Sadler *financial advisor*
Levine, Laurence Brandt *investment banker*

Pompano Beach
Calatchi, Ralph Franklin *investment banker, writer*
Kester, Stewart Randolph *banker*

Ponte Vedra Beach
de Selding, Edward Bertrand *retired bank executive*
O'Brien, Raymond Vincent, Jr., *banker*

Punta Gorda
Haswell, Carleton Radley *banker*

Saint Petersburg
Godbold, Francis Stanley *investment banker, securities firm executive*

Sarasota
Geithner, Paul Herman, Jr., *retired banker*
Phillips, Howard William *investment banker*

Tarpon Springs
Johnson, Randall Clyde *mortgage banker*

Temple Terrace
Rink, Wesley Winfred *retired bank executive*

Tequesta
Turrell, Richard Horton, Sr., *banker*

Vero Beach
Glassmeyer, Edward *investment banker*

Wellington
Guillama-Alvarez, Noel Jesus *merchant banker, healthcare executive*

West Palm Beach
Addison, Ferguson Lofton Lightbourne *retired bank executive*

GEORGIA

Atlanta
Barron, Patrick Kenneth *bank executive*
Biggins, J. Veronica *bank executive*
Chapman, Hugh McMaster *banker*
Chau, Pin Pin *bank executive*
Dowling, Roderick Anthony *investment banker*
Forrestal, Robert Patrick *banker, lawyer*
Hollis, Timothy Martin *bank executive*
Humann, L. Phillip *bank executive*
Long, Robert Richard *banker*
Snelling, George Arthur *banker*
Spiegel, John William *banker*
Watts, Anthony Lee *bank executive*
Williams, James Bryan *banker*
Young, James E. *banker*

Columbus
Anthony, Richard E. *bank executive*
James, Elizabeth R. *bank executive*
Prescott, Thomas W. *bank executive*
Yancey, James D. *bank executive*

Flowery Branch
Monroe, Melrose *retired bank executive*

Kennesaw
Whittingham, Harry Edward, Jr., *retired banker*

Macon
McCook, Thomas H. *savings and loan association executive*

Marietta
Bond, Barbara J. *bank executive*
Burnett, Christopher H. *bank executive*
Hines, P. Harris *bank executive*
Milligan, Edward C. *bank executive*

Savannah
Clemmons, John B. *bank executive, director, retired mathematics educator*
Howard, Constance Adair *banker*

Sea Island
LaWare, John Patrick *retired bank executive, federal agency administrator*

HAWAII

Honolulu
Davis, Stephen Edward Folwell *banker*
Dods, Walter Arthur, Jr., *bank executive*
Hoag, John Arthur *retired bank executive*
Johnson, Lawrence M. *retired bank executive*
Keir, Gerald Janes *banker*
Midkiff, Robert Richards *financial and trust company executive, consultant*
Tanoue, Donna A. *bank executive, former federal agency administrator*
Wolff, Herbert Eric *banker, former army officer*

IDAHO

Ketchum
McElhinny, Wilson Dunbar *banker*

ILLINOIS

Bloomington
Dietz, William Ronald *management executive*

Blue Island
Yager, Vincent Cook *bank executive*

Burr Ridge
McCormack, Robert Cornelius *investment banker*

Chicago
Adams, Austin A. *bank executive*
Bakwin, Edward Morris *banker*
Bartter, Brit Jeffrey *investment banker*
Blair, Edward McCormick *investment banker*
Bobins, Norman R. *banker*
Bobrinskoy, Charles Kellogg *investment banker*
Fox, David Wayne *banker*
Gibbons, John *mortgage company executive*
Glickman, Robert Jeffrey *bank executive*
Hart, Pamela Heim *banker*
Heagy, Thomas Charles *banker*
Istock, Verne George *retired bank executive*
Kearney, Michael John *banker*
Kincaid, Richard D. *bank executive*
Leszinske, William O. *bank executive*
McKay, Neil *banker*
McNally, Alan G. *bank executive*

Montgomery, Charles Howard *retired bank executive*
Roberts, Theodore Harris *banker*
Scharf, Charles W. *bank executive*
Schroeder, Charles Edgar *investment management executive*
Schulte, David Michael *investment banker*
Scully, John Edward, Jr., *banker*
Seaman, Irving, Jr., *banker*
Stevens, Mark *banker*
Stirling, James Paulman *investment banker*
Susman, Louis *investment banker*
Swift, Edward Foster, III, *investment banker*
Techar, Frank J. *bank executive*
Theobald, Thomas Charles *banker*
Thomas, J. Mikesell *bank executive*
Thomas, Richard Lee *banker*
Weston, Roger Lance *banker*

Fox River Grove
Abboud, Alfred Robert *banker, consultant, investor*

Golf
Fellingham, Warren Luther, Jr., *retired banker*

Grayslake
Jacobson, Earl James *lawyer, investment banker*

Highwood
Brown, Lawrence Haas *retired banker*

Hinsdale
Kinney, Kenneth Parrish *retired banker*

Kenilworth
Corrigan, John Edward, Jr., *retired banker, lawyer*

Lake Bluff
Anderson, Roger E. *bank executive*

Lake Forest
Rahe, Maribeth Sembach *bank executive*
Ross, Robert Evan *bank executive*

Northbrook
Gratalo, John, Jr., *banker, small business owner*
Keehn, Silas *retired bank executive*

Oak Brook
Khoshabe, Steven Y. *mortgage company executive*

Oak Park
Kinzie, Raymond Wyant *banker, lawyer*

Palatine
Fitzgerald, Gerald Francis *retired banker*
Hershenhorn, Robert Gene *bank executive*

Peoria
Bussone, Frank Joseph *bank executive, television broadcaster, director*

Springfield
Ferguson, Mark Harmon *banker, lawyer*

Tinley Park
Keenan, Robert Arthur *bank executive, consultant*

Winnetka
Fenton, Clifton Lucien *investment banker*
Klapperich, Frank Lawrence, Jr., *investment banker*

INDIANA

Columbus
Abts, Henry William *retired banker*

Evansville
Giancola, James J. *bank executive*

Fort Wayne
Shaffer, Paul E. *retired banker*

Greenwood
Broscoe, Peter A. *mortgage company executive, consultant*

Indianapolis
Heger, Martin L. *bank executive*

Muncie
Anderson, Stefan Stolen *banker*

IOWA

Cedar Rapids
Wax, Nadine Virginia *retired bank executive*

Dubuque
Dunn, Frank M. (Francis Michael Dunn) *banker*

Maquoketa
Tubbs, Edward Lane *banker*

Mason City
Rodamaker, Marti Tomson *bank executive*

KANSAS

Coldwater
Adams, Elizabeth Herrington *banker*

Manhattan
Stolzer, Leo William *bank executive*

Olathe
Fraser, David Charles *investment banker*

Overland Park
Whitaker, Freda N. *trust company executive*

Pratt
Loomis, Howard Krey *banker, director*

Shawnee Mission
McEachen, Richard Edward *banker, lawyer*

Stockton
Kollman, Chris L. *bank executive*

Topeka
Bunten, William Daniel *retired banker*
Dicus, John Carmack *savings bank executive*

KENTUCKY

Inez
Duncan, Robert Michael *banker, lawyer, Republican national committeeman*

Louisville
Grissom, J. David *private investor, bank executive*
Guillaume, Raymond Kendrick *banker*
Marsh, Donald Louis *investment banker*
Thompson, Kathy C. *bank executive*

Shepherdsville
Pike, Burlyn *retired bank director, lawyer*

Wilmore
Savage, William Earl *savings and loan executive, religious educator*

LOUISIANA

Baton Rouge
Travis, John D. *bank commission official*

Covington
Blossman, Alfred Rhody, Jr., *banker*

Lafayette
Stuart, Walter Dynum, III, *banker*

Shreveport
Nelson, George Dalman, Jr., *banker*

MAINE

Andover
Ellis, George Hathaway *retired bank executive, utilities executive*

Bangor
Bullock, William Clapp, Jr., *banker*

Cape Elizabeth
Cotter, Joseph Francis *retired hotel and bank executive*

Farmington
Downs, Gary M. *bank executive*

Portland
Saufley, William Edward *banker, lawyer*

MARYLAND

Annapolis
McGuirk, Ronald Charles *retired bank executive, economic advisor*

Baltimore
Baldwin, Henry Furlong *banker*
Barnhill, Gregory Hurd *investment banker*
Bramble, Frank P. *bank executive*
Dunn, Edward K., Jr., *banker*
Jacobs, Richard James *banker, educator*
Liberto, Joseph Salvatore *retired bank executive*
Morrel, William Griffin, Jr., *banker*
Murray, Joseph William *banker*
Schaefer, Robert Wayne *banker*
Wieler, Scott Alan *investment banker*

Bethesda
Rosenbaum, Greg Alan *merchant banker, consultant*
Saul, B. Francis, II, *bank executive, director*

Columbia
DeRosa, Thomas J. *investment banker, investment company executive*

Darnestown
Lightner, Gene Cleek *investment banker*

Elkton
Harrington, Benjamin Franklin, III, *retired business consultant*

Frederick
Cannon, Faye E. *bank executive*

North East
Goldbach, Jennifer D. *bank executive*

Owings Mills
Sanner, George Bradley *bank executive*

Potomac
Schonholtz, Joan Sondra Hirsch *banker, civic worker*

Rockville
Meyer, F. Weller *bank executive*

Saint Michaels
Shipley, L. Parks, Jr., *banker*

Sparks Glencoe
Swackhamer, Gene L. *bank executive*

MASSACHUSETTS

Boston
Alden, Vernon Roger *corporate director, trustee*
Aquilino, Leo R. *banker*
Breitman, Leo R. *banker*
Brown, William L. *banker*
Carter, Marshall Nichols *retired banker*
Comeau, Susan *bank executive*

Fallon, John Golden *banker*
Finnegan, Neal Francis *banker*
Gifford, Charles Kilvert *banker*
Higgins, Robert Joseph *bank executive*
Hill, Richard Devereux *retired banker*
Mullin, Patricia Jones *banker*
Murray, Terrence *bank executive*
Phillips, Daniel Anthony *trust company executive*
Sarles, H. Jay *bank executive*
Sax, Kenneth J. *bank executive*
Vermilye, Peter Hoagland *banker*

Cambridge
Edgerly, William Skelton *banker*

Dover
Aldrich, Frank Nathan *banker*

Duxbury
Safe, Kenneth Shaw, Jr., *fiduciary firm executive*

Gloucester
Fioravanti, Nancy Eleanor *retired banker*

Lenox
Newton, Frank George *bank executive*

Longmeadow
Lo Bello, Joseph David *bank executive*

Medford
Sloane, Marshall M. *banker*

Newton
Teig, Marlowe Gilman *investment banker*

Pittsfield
Fawcett, Gayle P. *bank executive*

Reading
Burbank, Nelson Stone *investment banker*

Salem
McLaughlin, Michael Angelo *mortgage consultant, author*

Wellesley
Small, Parker Adams, III, *investment banker*

Westport
Nichols, C. Walter, III, *retired trust company executive*

Westwood
Riley, Henry Charles *banker*

Winchester
Brennan, Francis Patrick *banker*

Worcester
Hunt, John David *retired bank executive*
Spencer, Harry Irving, Jr., *retired bank executive*

MICHIGAN

Ann Arbor
Nelson, Jason Craig *company executive*

Bay City
Van Dyke, Clifford Craig *retired bank executive*

Bloomfield Hills
McQueen, Patrick M. *bank executive*
Miller, Eugene Albert *retired bank executive*
Stepp, James Michael *business executive*

Dearborn
Musson, Warren R. *investment banker*

Detroit
Babb, Ralph W., Jr., *banker*
Beran, John R. *banker*
Greenwood, Harriet Lois *environmental banker, researcher*
Jeffs, Thomas Hamilton, II, *retired bank executive*
Lewis, John D. *banking official*

Frankfort
Foster, Robert Carmichael *banker*

Grand Rapids
Canepa, John Charles *banking consultant*

Grosse Pointe Farms
Surdam, Robert McClellan *retired banker*

Saginaw
Evans, Harold Edward *banker*

Southfield
Shields, Robert Emmet *merchant banker, lawyer*

Waterford
Houston, E. James, Jr., *banker, consultant*

MINNESOTA

Chanhassen
Severson, Roger Allan *bank executive*

Eden Prairie
Hanson, Dale S. *retired bank executive*

Edina
Campbell, James Robert *retired bank executive*

Golden Valley
Lester, Susan E. *bank executive*

Minneapolis
Carlson, Jennie Peaslack *bank executive*
Cecere, Andrew *bank executive*
Cooper, William Allen *bank executive*
Griffith, Sima Lynn *investment banker, consultant*
Grundhofer, Jerry A. *bank executive*
Grundhofer, John F. *bank executive*
Mitau, Lee R. *bank executive*
Moffett, David McKenzie *bank executive*
Morrison, John M. *bank executive*
Rahn, Alvin Albert *former banker*
Walters, Glen Robert *banker*

Northfield
Talen, William Claire *bank executive, financial consultant*

Rosemount
Morrison, James R. *retired banker*

Saint Paul
Rothmeier, Steven George *merchant banker, investment manager*

Wayzata
Rich, Willis Frank, Jr., *banker*

MISSISSIPPI

Gulfport
Thatcher, George Robert *banker, author, journalist, columnist*

Tupelo
Patterson, Aubrey Burns, Jr., *banker*
Ramage, Martis Donald, Jr., *banker*

MISSOURI

Chesterfield
Hinrichs, Charles A. *commercial banker*

Clayton
Kemper, David Woods, II, *banker*

Kansas City
Green, Jerry Howard *investment banker*
Hoenig, Thomas M. *bank executive*
Kemper, Jonathan McBride *banker*
Reiter, Robert Edward *banker*

Saint Joseph
Jeppesen, Floyd S. *banker*

Saint Louis
Barksdale, Clarence Caulfield *banker*
Blake, Allen *bank executive*
Bryant, Ruth Alyne *banker*
Costigan, Edward John *investment banker*
Dierberg, James F. *bank executive*
Edwards, Benjamin Franklin, III, *investment banker*
Joyner, Dee Ann *bank official*
Maurer, Frederic George, III, *banker*
Poole, William *bank executive*
Rasche, Robert Harold *banker, retired economics educator*
Stann, John Anthony *investment banker*
Stoecker, David Thomas *banker*

Springfield
Budzinsky, Armin Alexander *investment banker*

Walker
Martin, Phillip Dwight *bank consulting company executive, mayor*

NEBRASKA

Lincoln
Lundstrom, Gilbert Gene *banker, lawyer*
Young, Dale Lee *banker*

Omaha
Fitzgerald, William Allingham *savings and loan association executive, director*
Harvey, Jack K. *holding company executive*
Lauritzen, Bruce Ronnow *banker*

Waterloo
O'Brien, Nancy Lynn *bank executive*

NEVADA

Logandale
Smiley, Robert William, Jr., *investment banker*

Reno
Binns, James Edward *retired banker*

Smith
Weaver, William Merritt, Jr., *investment banker*

Zephyr Cove
Peters, Raymond Robert *bank executive*

NEW HAMPSHIRE

Sanbornville
Berg, Warren Stanley *retired bank executive*

Silver Lake
Tregenza, Norman Hughson *investment banker*

NEW JERSEY

Bay Head
O'Brien, Robert Brownell, Jr., *investment banker, consultant, yacht broker, opera company executive*

Chatham
Leonett, Anthony Arthur *banker*

Cherry Hill
Hill, Vernon W., II, *bank executive*

Cinnaminson
Johnson, Victor Lawrence *banker, director*

Cliffside Park
Goldstein, Howard Bernard *investment banker*

Denville
O'Keefe, Robert James *retired bank executive*

Edison
Dore, James Francis *financial services executive*

Englewood Cliffs
Kim, Soo-Ryong *investment banker*
Murray, Brian Victor *investment banker*

Hamilton
Blohm, Robert *investment banker, economist, statistician*

Jersey City
Goldberg, Arthur Abba *merchant banker, financial advisor*

Little Falls
Casey, Karen Anne *banker*

Madison
Armstrong, Richard William *bank executive, management consultant*

Manasquan
Sbarbaro, Robert Arthur *banker*

Morristown
Kearns, William Michael, Jr., *investment banker*
Moore, Milo Anderson *banker*

Newton
Case, Tammy *bank executive*

Princeton
Feeney, John Robert *banker*
Ganoe, Charles Stratford *banker, consultant*
Semrod, T. Joseph *banker*

Short Hills
Lohse, Austin Webb *banker*

Shrewsbury
Jones, Charles Hill, Jr., *banker*

Spring Lake
D'Luhy, John James *investment banker*

Summit
Lewis, Donald Emerson *banker*
Mueller, Paul Henry *retired bank executive*
Singleterry, Gary Lee *investment banker*

Tenafly
Levy, Norman Jay *investment banker, financial consultant*

Trenton
Bakke, Holly C. *bank commission official*

Vineland
Bracken, Thomas *bank executive*

NEW MEXICO

Deming
Rogers, Alice Louise *retired bank executive, writer, researcher*

Santa Fe
Clyde, Larry Forbes *banker*
Dreisbach, John Gustave *investment banker*
Morrissey, Michael Joseph *investment banker*

NEW YORK

Bedford
Philip, Peter Van Ness *former trust company executive*

Bolton Landing
Crosby, John Griffith *investment banker*

Brooklyn
Cohen, Alan *investment banker*
Singer, Eric T. *investment banker*

Buffalo
Pett, John Lyman *banker*
Wilmers, Robert George *banker*

Cherry Valley
Humes, Graham *investment banker*

De Witt
Belden, Sanford Adams *banker*

Elmont
Cusack, Thomas Joseph *retired banker*

Farmingville
Olson, Gary Robert *banker*

Garden City
Lovely, Thomas Dixon *banker*

Great Neck
Katz, Edward Morris *banker*

Hartsdale
Katz, John *investment banker*

Ithaca
Smith, Robert Samuel *banker, former agricultural finance educator*

Katonah
Grunebaum, Ernest Michael *investment banker*

Larchmont
Kaufmann, Henry Mark *mortgage banker*

Long Island City
Markus, Maura *bank executive*

Mattituck
Kanas, John Adam *banker*

Melville
Newman, Samuel *retired trust company executive*

Miller Place
Leedom, E. Paul *banker*

New Paltz
Smith, Kathleen Tener *bank executive*

New York
Adams, John Brett *investment banker, company executive*
Agostinelli, Robert Francesco *investment banker*
Alemany, Ellen *investment banker*
Allen, Claxton Edmonds, III, *investment banker*
Bagatelle, Warren Denis *investment banker*
Bains, Leslie Elizabeth *banker*
Baird, Douglas James *investment banker*
Ballard, Charles Alan *investment banker*
Barrett, William Joel *investment banker*
Barry, Nancy Marie *bank executive*
Beim, David Odell *investment banker, educator*
Bellanger, Serge René *bank executive*
Bermudez, Jorge Alberto *bank executive*
Biglari, Hamid *investment banker*
Blankfein, Lloyd C. *investment banker*
Bloom, Jack Sandler *investment banker*
Boothby, Willard Sands, III, *retired bank executive*
Brenner, Howard Martin *banker*
Brody, Kenneth David *investment banker*
Burke, James Joseph, Jr., *investment banker*
Calello, Paul *banker*
Carey, Francis James *investment banker*
Carey, William Polk *investment banker*
Casey, Thomas Jefferson *business executive, investment banker, venture capitalist, social entrprеneur, environmental activist*
Castellanos, Julio J. *banker, consultant*
Castle, John Krob *merchant banker*
Cayne, James E. *investment banker*
Childs, John Farnsworth *consultant, retired investment banker*
Clayton, Jonathan Alan *banker*
Clifford, Stewart Burnett *banker, director*
Cohen, Jonathan Little *investment banker*
Collins, Adriana Delia *banker*
Comfort, William Twyman, Jr., *banker*
Considine, Jill *banker*
Corrigan, E(dward) Gerald *investment banker*
Coulter, David A. *investment banker*
Creamer, German Gonzalo *bank executive, educator*
Crockett, Andrew Duncan *bank executive*
Cromwell, Oliver Dean *investment banker*
Curtin, John Paul, Jr., *investment banker*
Daniel, Richard H. *trust company executive*
David-Weill, Michel Alexandre *investment banker*
Davin, James Manson *investment banker*
Davis, George Linn *banker*
Davis, Thomas W. *investment bank executive*
Davison, Daniel P. *retired banking executive*
Deans, Patricia Herrmann *investment banker*
Debs, Richard A. *investment banker*
DeGroff, Ralph Lynn, Jr., *investment banker*
DelliBovi, Alfred A. *bank executive*
DeNunzio, Ralph Dwight *investment banker*
Djeddah, Richard Nissim *investment banker*
Dooley, Douglas John *bank executive*
Douglass, Robert Royal *banker, lawyer*
Drew, Ina R. *bank executive*
Dublon, Dina *bank executive*
DuGan, Gordon F. *investment banker*
Dwek, Cyril S. *bank executive*
Enders, Anthony Talcott *banker*
Eshleman, Diane Varrin *bank executive*
Farley, Terrence Michael *banker*
Fisher, Richard B. *investment banker*
Flaherty, Pamela Potter *bank executive*
Flinn, Michael de Vlaming *investment banker, former state legislator*
Flynn, Elizabeth E. *bank executive*
Fried, Albert, Jr., *investment banker*
Friedberg, Barry Sewell *investment banker*
Friedman, W. Robert, Jr., *investment banker*
Fruitman, Frederick Howard *investment banker*
Furman, Roy Lance *investment banker*
Gamble, Theodore Robert, Jr., *investment banker*
Gant, Donald Ross *investment banker*
Garner, Albert Headden *investment banker*
Geithner, Timothy F. *bank executive*
Gellert, Michael Erwin *investment banker*
Godridge, Leslie V. *bank executive*
Gonzalez, Eugene Robert *investment banker*
Gorter, James Polk *investment banker*
Gossett, Robert Francis, Jr., *merchant banker*
Greenhill, Robert Foster *investment banker*
Greenstein, Abraham Jacob *mortgage company executive, accountant*
Griffith, Alan Richard *banker*
Haddon, James Francis *banker*
Halpern, Merril Mark *investment banker*
Harlan, Leonard Morton *merchant banker*
Harrison, Gilbert Warner *investment banker*
Hedstrom, Mitchell Warren *banker*
Heimann, John Gaines *investment banker*
Herregat, Guy-Georges Jacques *banker*
Hill, J(ames) Tomilson *investment banker*
Hilliard, Landon *banker*
Horowitz, Gedale Bob *investment banker*
Hricik, Lorraine E. *bank executive*
Hughes, Norah Ann O'Brien *bank securities executive*
Hurley, Dean C. *bank executive, lawyer*
Jack, Bradley H. *investment banker*
Janiak, Anthony Richard, Jr., *investment banker*
Johnson, Scott Stuart *merchant banker*
Johnson, Thomas Stephen *banker*
Jones, Thomas E. *bank executive*
Joseph, Frederick Harold *investment banker*
Kaplan, Robert S. *investment banker*
Kardon, Robert *mortgage company executive*
Kaufmann, Mark Steiner *banker, director*
Keilin, Eugene Jacob *investment banker, lawyer*
Kilburn, H(enry) T(homas), Jr., *investment banker*
Kirdar, Nemir Amin *banker*
Klamm de Betas, Ullrich *investment banker*
Klein, Michael *investment banker*
Klenikov, Vlad *investment banker*
Krimendahl, Herbert Frederick, II, *investment banker*
Lagomasino, Maria Elena *bank executive*
Lattin, Albert Floyd *banker*

Reading
Roesch, Clarence Henry *banker*
Sidhu, Jay S. *bank executive*

Saint Davids
Sheftel, Roger Terry *merchant banker*

Sewickley
Ostern, Wilhem Curt *retired holding company executive*

Sinking Spring
Bausher, Verne C(harles) *retired bank executive*

Souderton
Hoeflich, Charles Hitschler *banker*

Telford
Hagey, Walter Rex *retired bank executive*

West Chester
Taylor, Bernard J., II, *banker, director*

West Conshohocken
Boenning, Henry Dorr, Jr., *investment banker*

Wyomissing
Mohn, Richard E. *bank executive*
Moll, Lloyd Henry *banker*

RHODE ISLAND

East Greenwich
Hunter, Garrett Bell *investment banker*
Stark, Dennis Edwin *bank executive, director*

Little Compton
Middendorf, J. William, II, *investment banker*

Newport
Sands, Harold Winthrop *banker, financial adviser*

Providence
Burns, Robert E. *bank executive*
Fish, Lawrence Kingsbaker *banker*
Higginbotham, Richard A. *investment banker*
Lohrum, Frederick *bank executive*

SOUTH CAROLINA

Columbia
Boggs, Jack Aaron *banker, publisher, municipal government official, mayor*

Greenville
Whittle, Mack Ira, Jr., *bank executive*

Greenwood
Boxx, Rita McCord *banker*

Hilton Head Island
Ostergard, Paul Michael *not-for-profit executive*

SOUTH DAKOTA

Sioux Falls
Engen, Lee Emerson *retired savings and loan executive*

TENNESSEE

Clinton
Birdwell, James Edwin, Jr., *retired banker*

Gray
Surface, James Louis, Sr., *trust officer, lawyer*

Harrogate
Robertson, Edwin Oscar *banker*

Knoxville
Barker, Keith Rene *investment banker*
Blake, Gerald Rutherford *retired banker*
Lawson, Fred Raulston *banker*

Memphis
Garrott, Thomas M. *bank executive*
Glass, J. Kenneth *bank executive*
Horn, Ralph *bank executive*

Murfreesboro
Ford, William F. *banker*

Nashville
Andrews, Holdt *investment banker*
Burch, John Christopher, Jr., *investment banker*
Clay, John W., Jr., *bank executive*
Daane, James Dewey *banker*
Harrison, Clifford Joy, Jr., *banker*
Heard, Edwin Anthony *banker*
Shell, Owen G., Jr., *retired bank executive*

TEXAS

Abilene
Bentley, Clarence Edward *savings and loan executive*

Amarillo
Burgess, C(harles) Coney *bank executive*

Austin
Carner, William John *banker*
Deal, Ernest Linwood, Jr., *banker*
Lemens, William Vernon, Jr., *banker, finance company executive, lawyer*
Stone, Leon *banker*
West, Glenn Edward *investment banking executive*

Dallas
Bishop, Gene Herbert *financial corporate executive*
Cochran, George Calloway, III, *retired bank executive, lawyer*

Gumbiner, Anthony Joseph *investment banker, lawyer*
McTeer, Robert D., Jr., *banker*
Philipson, Herman Louis, Jr., *investment banker*
Reid, Langhorne, III, *merchant banker*
Smerge, Raymond G. *mortgage company executive*

Houston
Elkins, James Anderson, Jr., *banker, director*
Elkins, James Anderson, III, *investment professional*
Ghiglieri, Catherine A. *auto loan company executive*
Knapp, David Hebard *investment banker*
Neuhaus, Philip Ross *investment banker*
Thomas, M. Ann *bank executive*
Tilghman, Richard Granville *bank executive*

Pasadena
Moon, John Henry, Sr., *banker*

Plano
Day, Kevin Thomas *retired bank executive*

San Antonio
Condos, J. Alexander *mortgage company executive*
Crichton, John Hayes *investment banker*
Duncan, A. Baker *investment banker*
Frost, Thomas Clayborne *banker, director*

Tyler
Bell, Henry Marsh, Jr., *bank executive*
Blasingame, Donald Ray (Don Blasingame) *banker*

UTAH

Ogden
Browning, Roderick Hanson *banker*

Park City
Montgomery, James Fischer *savings and loan association executive*

Saint George
Strobell, Dan F. *bank executive, writer*

Salt Lake City
Eccles, Spencer Fox *banker, director*
Simmons, Roy William *banker, director*

VERMONT

Charlotte
Sim, Craig Stephen *retired investment banker*

Chester
Carey, Erron J. *merchant banker, state representative*

Lyndon Center
Dame, William Page, III, *bank executive, educational administrator*

Manchester
Carey, James Henry *banker*

VIRGINIA

Alexandria
Birely, William Cramer *investment banker*

Arlington
Leland, Marc Ernest *trust advisor, lawyer*
Ochoa-Brillembourg, Hilda Margarita *investment banker*
Rogers, James Frederick *banker, management consultant*
Watkins, Birge Swift *investment banker*

Charlottesville
Bull, George Albert *retired banker*

Lynchburg
Quillian, William Fletcher, Jr., *retired banker, former college president*

Mc Lean
Baumann, Martin F. *savings and loan association executive*
Kimberly, William Essick *investment banker*
Paul, Peterson T. *savings and loan association executive*
Schools, Charles Hughlette *banker, lawyer*

Purcellville
Kok, Frans Johan *investment banker*

Reston
Fitzpatrick, Thomas J. *mortgage company executive*

Richmond
Black, Robert Perry *retired banker, executive*
Broaddus, John Alfred, Jr., *retired bank executive, economist*
Henley, Vernard William *banker*
Miller, Lewis Nelson, Jr., *banker*
Moore, Andrew Taylor, Jr., *banker*
Talley, Charles Richmond *commercial banking executive*
Wells, James M., III, *bank executive*

Salem
Ramsey, Lloyd Brinkley *retired savings and loan executive, retired army officer*

Urbanna
Garey, Francis Benjamin *retired merchant banker*

Virginia Beach
Duke, Elizabeth (Betsy) A. *bank executive*

WASHINGTON

Coupeville
Piercy, Gordon Clayton *bank executive*

Everett
Nelson, Carol Kobuke *bank executive*

Lakewood
Owen, Thomas Walker *banker, broker*

Port Angeles
McCormick, Karen Louise *savings and loan association executive*

Seattle
Andrew, Lucius Archibald David, III, *bank executive*
Arnold, Robert Morris *banker*
Bley, John L. *financial executive*
Campbell, Robert Hedgcock *investment banker, lawyer*
Faulstich, James R. *retired bank executive*
Fetters, Norman Craig, II, *banker*
Green, Joshua, III, *retired banker*
Greenwood, W. R., III, *investment banker*
Helms, Luke *bank executive*
Killinger, Kerry Kent *bank executive*
Oppenheimer, Deanna Watson *bank executive*
Rice, Norman B. *bank executive, former mayor*
Vanasek, James George *commercial banker*

Sequim
Laube, Roger Gustav *retired trust officer, financial consultant*

Spokane
Horton, Susan Pittman *bank executive*
McWilliams, Edwin Joseph *banker*

Tacoma
Anderson, Lynn L. *trust company executive*

WEST VIRGINIA

Charleston
Martin, Jerry Harold *bank examiner*

WISCONSIN

Brookfield
Bauer, Chris Michael *banker*

Delafield
Walters, Ronald Ogden *mortgage banker*

Madison
Kitchen, Michael B. *bank executive*

Milwaukee
Becker, John Alphonsis *retired bank executive*
Chenevich, William L. *bank executive*
Murphy, Judith Chisholm *trust company executive*
Wigdale, James B. *bank executive*

Pewaukee
Long, Robert Eugene *banker*

Sauk City
Lins, Debra *bank executive*

Walworth
Carlson, Victoria Thilda *merchant banker*

Zenda
Sills, William Henry, III, *investment banker*

WYOMING

Cheyenne
Knight, Robert Edward *bank executive, educator*

TERRITORIES OF THE UNITED STATES

PUERTO RICO

Hato Rey
Carrion, Richard *bank executive*

San Juan
Arsuaga, Juan Arenado *banker*

CANADA

BRITISH COLUMBIA

Vancouver
Gardiner, William Douglas Haig *bank executive, director*
Lyons, Terrence Allan *merchant banking, investment company executive*

ONTARIO

Hamilton
Robinson, Daniel Baruch *retired banker*

Mississauga
Palmer, Patrick Asa *former banker, lecturer*

Ottawa
Freedman, Charles *retired bank executive*

Sault Sainte Marie
Stinson, Deane Brian *financial executive, consultant*

Toronto
Augustine, Jerome Samuel *merchant banker*
Cleghorn, John Edward *business executive*
Comper, Tony *banker*
Fullerton, R. Donald *banker*
Godsoe, Peter Cowperthwaite *banker*

Gordon, Harold P. *bank executive*
Greenwood, Lawrence George *banker*
Lawson, Jane Elizabeth *bank executive*
MacDougall, Hartland Molson *trust company executive, retired bank executive*
Mulholland, William David, Jr., *retired bank executive*
Storey, Susan *investment banker*
Taylor, Allan Richard *retired banker*
Thomson, Richard Murray *retired bank executive*
Waugh, Richard Earl *banker*
Webb, Anthony Allan *banker, director*
Wilson, Michael Holcombe *investment banker, former Canadian government official*

QUEBEC

Laval
Pichette, Claude *former banking executive, university rector, research executive*

Montreal
Torrey, David Leonard *investment banker*

Mount Royal
Elie, Jean André *investment banker*

Sutton
Bolduc, J. Emilien *bank executive*

SASKATCHEWAN

Saskatoon
Martell, Keith *bank executive*

MEXICO

Col Lomas de Chapultepec
Guajardo Touché, Ricardo *bank executive*

Mexico City
Ortiz, Guillermo *banker*

BERMUDA

Hamilton
Johnston, Malcolm (Calum) *bank executive*

ENGLAND

London
Binney, Robert Harry *bank executive*
Collins, Paul John *banker*
Gulliver, Stuart *bank executive*
Jourdren, Marc Henri *investment banking company executive*
Keevil, Philip Clement *investment banker*
Pennant-Rea, Rupert Lascelles *banker, economist*
Studzinski, John Joseph Paul *investment banking executive*

FRANCE

Paris
Bujon de L'Estang, Francois *bank executive*

GERMANY

Munich
Viermetz, Kurt F. *banker*

GREECE

Athens
Papadakis, Panagiotis Agamemnon *financier, international business executive*

INDIA

Fort Mumbai
Woodard, Nina Elizabeth *banker*

LUXEMBOURG

Luxembourg
Warner, Scott Dennis *investment banker*

NETHERLANDS

Amsterdam
Rizzi, Joseph Vito *banker*

SCOTLAND

Tighnabruaich
Reisinger, Ronald Busch (Baron of Inneryne, Baron of Culbin, Laird of Ascog Castle, Laird of Eilean Na Beithe, *bank executive*

SINGAPORE

Singapore
Olds, John Theodore *banker*

TAIWAN

Taipei
Hsieh, Rudy Ru-Pin *banker*
Yeh, Kuo Hsing *bank executive*

ADDRESS UNPUBLISHED

Ackerman, Jack Rossin *investment banker*
Alvord, Joel Barnes *retired bank executive*
Andreas, David Lowell *retired banker*
Applegarth, Paul Vollmer *investment and finance executive*
Armstrong, Michael David *investment banker*
Ashton, Thomas Walsh *investment banker*
Ashworth, Lawrence Nelson *retired bank executive*
Baker, Henry S., Jr., *retired bank executive*
Bansak, Stephen A., Jr., *investment banker, financial consultant*
Baramova, Irina Antonova *investment banker*
Barrow, Charles Herbert *investment banker*
Bedrij, Orest *investment banker, scientist*
Bibby, Douglas Martin *mortgage association executive*
Biklen, Stephen Clinton *retired student loan company executive*
Birky, John Edward *banker, financial advisor*
Bitner, John William *banker*
Boykin, Robert Heath *retired banker*
Boyle, Richard James *banker*
Boyles, James Kenneth *retired banker*
Britt, John Roy *banker*
Browning, Colin Arrott *retired banker*
Buckels, Marvin Wayne *savings and loan executive*
Burden, Ordway Partridge *investment banker*
Busch, Noel Henry *banker*
Busse, Leonard Wayne *banker, financial consultant*
Campbell, William Yates *investment banker*
Carlisle, Patricia Kinley *mortgage company executive, paralegal, real estate broker*
Cawley, Charles M. *retired bank executive*
Chalsty, John Steele *investment banker*
Christenson, Gregg Andrew *bank executive*
Clark, Raymond Oakes *banker*
Clifton, Russell B. *banking and mortgage lending consultant, retired mortgage company executive*
Cockrum, William Monroe, III, *investment banker, consultant, educator*
Coleman, Lewis Waldo *bank executive*
Colwell, Bryan York *private investor, philanthropist*
Conner, Lindsay Andrew *investment banker*
Cook, Charles Wilkerson, Jr., *retired banker, former county official*
Cooney, John Thomas *retired banker*
Costanzo, Hilda Alba *retired banker*
Costello, Daniel Walter *retired bank executive*
Cotsakos, Christos Michael *former internet financial services company executive*
Cottrell, Mary-Patricia Tross *bank executive*
Crozier, William Marshall, Jr., *bank holding company executive*
Crumrine, Cecil Vernon, Jr., *bank officer*
Curry, John Michael *investment banker*
DeMartini, Richard Michael *retired bank executive*
Derrico, Georgia Santangelo *banker*
Dimon, James (Jamie Dimon) *bank executive*
Ding, Chen *investment banker*
Dittenhafer, Brian Douglas *banker, economist*
Dodson, Samuel Robinette, III, *investment banker*
Doyle, L. F. Boker *retired trust company executive*
Eaton, Curtis Howarth *banker, lawyer*
Elliott, Steven G. *bank executive*
Fahringer, Catherine Hewson *retired savings and loan association executive*
Fennebresque, Kim Samuel *investment banker*
Finocchiaro, Alfonso G. *bank executive*
Fitzmaurice, Laurence Dorset *retired bank executive*
Fix, John Neilson *banker*
Foster, Stephen Kent *banker, director*
Freeman, Richard Francis *banker*
Frischkorn, David Ephraim Keasbey, Jr., *investment banker*
Gaffney, Thomas *banker*
Gainor, Thomas Edward *bank executive*
Gallagher, Robert P. *bank executive*
Giblin, Patrick David *retired banker*
Glenn, David Wright *former mortgage company executive*
Goodsell, Douglas Charles *bank executive*
Graham, Cynthia Armstrong *banker*
Grant, James Colin *banker*
Greene, Richard Thaddeus *bank executive*
Greer, K. Gordon *banker*
Gregg, David, III, *investment banker*
Grosland, Emery Layton *retired banker*
Harrison, William Burwell, Jr., *bank executive*
Hayes, Mary Phyllis *retired savings and loan association executive*
Henkel, Arthur John *investment banker*
Hess, Dennis John *investment banker*
Hetland, James Lyman, Jr., *banker, lawyer, educator*
Hickey, Joseph Michael *investment banker*
Hogan, Robert Henry *trust company executive, investment strategist*
Hooper, John Allen *retired banker*
Howard, Donald Searcy *banker*
Hower, Frank Beard, Jr., *retired banker*
Hughes, Keith William *banking and finance company executive*
Huntington, Lawrence Smith *investment banker*
Ingersoll, Paul Mills *banker*
Ingraham, John Wright *banker, director*
Jennings, Joseph Ashby *banker*
Jensen, Edmund Paul *retired bank holding company executive*
Jepson, Robert Scott, Jr., *international investment banking specialist*
Jones, Richard Melvin *bank executive, former retail executive*
Kane Hittner, Marcia Susan *bank executive*
Kaplan, Grisel Arias *bank executive*
Kapnick, Stewart *investment banker*
Keith, Robert William *banker*
Klett, Gordon A. *retired savings and loan association executive*
Kooken, John Frederick *retired bank holding company executive*
Korpal, Eugene Stanley *banker, military officer*
Kotler, Steven *investment banker*
Kulesha, Kevin John *investment banker*
Lafley, Alan Frederick *retired banker*
Lantis, Donna Lea *retired banker, art educator, artist*

Larr, Peter *retired banker, consultant*
Lawer, Betsy *banker*
Masa, George John *retired bank executive*
McColl, Hugh Leon, Jr., *former bank executive*
McGough, Brian Edward *investment banker, lawyer*
McHugh, Robert Daniel *bank executive, writer*
Meeker, Guy Bentley *banker*
Menaker, Ronald Herbert *retired bank executive*
Meyer, Donald Robert *state agency administrator, banker, lawyer*
Milligan, Arthur Achille *retired banker*
Mograbi, Robert *bank executive*
Moore, Andrew Given Tobias, II, *investment banker, law educator*
Moriarty, Donald William, Jr., *bank executive*
Moyse, Hermann, III, *banker*
Muñoz, Carlos Ramón *retired bank executive*
Najarian, Jack George *investment banker*
Nash, Charles D. *investment banker*
O'Brien, Thomas Henry *former bank holding company executive*
O'Neill, Michael E. *former bank executive*
Ortiz Mena, Antonio *banker*
Osborn, William George *savings and loan executive*
Otto, Ingolf Helgi Elfried *banking institute fellow*
Owen, Suzanne *retired savings and loan association executive*
Parks, Grace Susan *bank official*
Parseghian, Gregory J. *former mortgage company executive*
Peretsman, Nancy B. *investment banker*
Peters, Ralph Frew *investment banker*
Place, Janey *banking consultant, former bank executive*
Poehner, Raymond Glenn *retired bank executive*
Pontius, Stanley N. *bank holding company executive*
Pool, Philip Bemis, Jr., *investment banker*
Porter, Walter Thomas, Jr., *retired bank executive*
Rank, Larry Gene *retired bank executive*
Renyi, Thomas A. *bank executive*
Reuber, Grant Louis *banking insurance company executive*
Rice, Joseph Albert *retired bank executive*
Rishel, Richard Clinton *retired bank executive*
Roby, Joe Lindell *investment banker*
Rogers, Nathaniel Sims *retired banker*
Romero-Rainey, Rebeca *bank executive*
Ross, Wilbur Louis, Jr., *investment banker*
Schaut, Joseph William *retired bank executive*
Searle, Philip Ford *banker*
Seeds, Sharon Lynn *bank processor*
Shelton, James Douglas *banker*
Silberstein, Alan Mark *financial services executive*
Simon, Leonard Samuel *banker*
Skillern, Frank L., Jr., *bank executive*
Solar, Richard Leon *banker*
Solomon, Jack D. *investment banker*
Stansell, Ronald Bruce *retired investment banker*
Stephens, Elton Bryson *bank executive, service and manufacturing company executive*
Stephenson, Herman Howard *retired banker*
Stewart, Carleton M. *bank executive, director*
Stotter, Harry Shelton *banker, lawyer, savings and loan association executive*
Sweet, Philip W. K., Jr., *former banker*
Swope, Donald Downey *retired banker*
Tabussi, Stephen John *banker*
Tatlock, Anne M. *trust company executive*
Taylor, David George *retired banker*
Thaler, Richard Winston, Jr., *investment banker*
Thurm, Kevin L. *bank executive*
Thurmond, John Peter, II, *bank executive, rancher, archaeologist*
Tily, Stephen Bromley, III, *bank executive*
Tyrrell, Gerald Gettys *banker*
Tyson, H. Michael *retired bank executive*
Vennat, Michel *former bank executive, lawyer*
Vitale, David J. *former banker*
Wall, Mark Emanuel *banker, engineer, consultant*
Walton, Alice L. *bank executive*
Weatherstone, Sir Dennis *bank executive*
Weisman, Lorenzo David *investment banker*
West, Rexford Leon *retired bank executive*
Whitney, Edward Bonner *retired investment banker*
Williams, Jeffrey P. *investment banker*
Wilson, S. Liane *bank executive*
Wirth, Russell D. L., Jr., *investment and merchant banker*
Woodward, William Lee *retired savings bank executive*
Zilkha, Ezra Khedouri *banker*
Zwerling, Gary Leslie *investment bank executive*

FINANCE: FINANCIAL SERVICES

UNITED STATES

ALABAMA

Alpine
Abbott, Benjamin Edward, Jr., *corporate executive*

Birmingham
Culp, Charles Allen *financial executive*
Gibson, Sloan D., IV, *corporate financial executive*
Hendley, Dan Lunsford *retired finance executive*
Jordan, D. Bryan *corporate financial executive*
Lockamy, Archie, III, *operations management educator*
Nowlan, Charles F. *controller*
Ritter, C. Dowd *diversified financial services company executive*
Sellers, Fred Wilson *accountant*

Decatur
Mason, Loretta Ann *accountant assistant*
Michelini, Sylvia Hamilton *auditor*
Talley, Richard Woodrow *accountant*

Dothan
Bailey, Chip *investment advisor, former state senator*
Cross, Steven Jasper *finance educator*

Huntsville
Graves, Benjamin Barnes *business administration educator*
Morgan, Ethel Branman *accountant, retired electronics engineer*
Stewart, Verlindsey Laquetta *accounting educator*

Mobile
McConnell, Roger *investment representative, political party official*

Montevallo
Jarrett, Cynthia S. *accountant*

Montgomery
Frazer, Nimrod Thompson *financial services company executive*
McLeod, Purser L., Jr., *financial executive*

Tuscaloosa
Gup, Benton Eugene *banking educator*
Mayer, Morris Lehman *marketing educator*

ALASKA

Anchorage
Ashcraft, Charles Olin *business educator*
Riendl, Robin Wendy *financial consultant*
Rose, David Allan *portfolio manager*
Rylander, Robert Allan *financial service executive*

Fairbanks
Lan, Ping *business educator*
Wichmann, Henry, Jr., *accounting educator, researcher*

ARIZONA

Carefree
Smoot, David Paul *finance company executive*

Chino Valley
Norton, Douglas Ray *former auditor general*

Goodyear
Eppen, Gary Dean *business educator*

Mesa
Allen, David Harlow *business educator, logistician, consultant*
Linxwiler, Louis Major, Jr., *retired finance company executive*

Paradise Valley
Chrisman, William Herring *property tax consultant*

Phoenix
Campbell, Jon R. *financial services executive*
Castleberry, W. Thomas *financial company executive*
Clark, John *corporate financial executive*
Cole, John *controller*
Daniel, James Richard *accountant, corporate financial executive*
Hovis, John *corporate financial executive*
Jovicic, Dusko *financial analyst*
Lemon, Leslie Gene *retired diversified services company executive, lawyer*
Mullen, Daniel Robert *finance executive*
Proffitt, Dennis Lewis *finance educator*
Richardson, Judy McEwen *education administrator, consultant, cartoonist*
Shaw, Richard Glenn *financial analyst*
Smith, Gordon *finance company executive*
Upson, Donald V. *retired corporate financial executive*

Scottsdale
Breyne, Matthew M. *finance company executive*
Hansen, Donald W. *insurance and financial services executive*
Hathaway, Peter S *corporate financial executive*
Ryan, Thomas W. *treasurer manufacturing company*
Washburn, Jerry Martin *accountant, corporate executive*
Williamson, R. Max *diversified financial services company executive*

Sun City West
Person, Robert John *financial management consultant*
Schrag, Adele Frisbie *business education educator*

Tempe
Kaufman, Herbert Mark *finance educator*
Pany, Kurt Joseph *accounting educator, consultant*
Reckers, Philip Merle *accounting and business educator*
Roy, Asim *business educator*

Tucson
Brasswel, Kerry *tax accountant*
Cain, Vernon *retired information services executive*
Carleton, Willard Tracy *retired finance educator*
Crawford, Richard Eben, Jr., *former investment advisor*
Fajardo, Sarah Elizabeth Johnson *financial consultant*
Hellon, Michael Thomas *tax consultant, political party official*
Nixon, Robert Obey, Sr., *business educator*
Ruscher, Charles B. *finance educator, consultant*
Taveggia, Thomas Charles *business educator*

ARKANSAS

Arkadelphia
Webster, Robert Lee *accounting educator, researcher*

Conway
Horton, Joseph Julian, Jr., *economics and finance educator*
McNew, Bennie Banks *retired finance educator*
Moore, Herff Leo, Jr., *management educator*

Fayetteville
Ellstrand, Alan Edwin *finance educator*
Hay, Robert Dean *retired management educator*
Rosenberg, Leon Joseph *marketing educator*

Fort Smith
Hembree, Hugh Lawson, III, *diversified holding company executive*

Higden
George, James Edward *accountant*

Hot Springs Village
Lihs, Marilyn Louise *retired accountant*

Little Rock
Fahoum, Yousef Arfan *financial analyst, educator*
Goodner, Norman Wesley *governmental relations specialist*
Scivally, Bart Murnane *accountant, auditor*

CALIFORNIA

Anaheim
Lano, Charles Jack *retired financial executive*

Apple Valley
Watkin, Virginia Ruth *financial professional*

Atherton
Barker, Robert Jeffery *financial executive*

Bakersfield
Bacon, Leonard Anthony *accounting educator*

Bell Canyon
Labbett, John Edgar *senior financial executive*

Berkeley
Bucklin, Louis Pierre *business educator, consultant*
Staubus, George Joseph *accounting educator*

Beverly Hills
Korn, Lester Bernard *diversified financial services company executive*
Lyle, Freeman A. *finance company executive*
McGagh, William Gilbert *financial consultant*
McMorrow, William J. *finance company executive*
Widaman, Greg *financial executive, accountant*

Brea
Barbas, Jeffrey Lawrence *finance company executive*
Oh, Tai Keun *business educator*

Brentwood
Defield, Charleen K. *accountant*
Fridley, Saundra Lynn *private investigator*

Buena Park
Kristy, James E. *financial management consultant*

Burbank
Gold, Stanley Phillip *diversified investments executive*
Murphy, Peter E. *corporate financial officer*
Sherbert, Sharon Debra *financial services executive*

Calabasas
Anderson, Joe D. *diversified financial services company executive*
Boone, Thomas H. *diversified financial services company executive*
Garcia, Carlos M. *financial services company executive*
Goldfield, Emily Dawson *finance company executive, artist*
Kurland, Stanford L. *financial lending company executive*
McLaughlin, Thomas Keith *diversified financial services company executive*
Mozilo, Angelo R. *diversified financial services company executive*
Sambol, David *diversified financial services company executive*
Samuels, Sandor E. *diversified financial services company executive*
Sieracki, Eric P. *diversified financial services company executive*

Canoga Park
Brandenburg, Stanley C. *financial company executive*

Carmichael
Areen, Gordon E. *finance company executive*

Chico
Moore Jr, Cletus B. *financial consultant, hotel executive*

Claremont
Christian, Suzanne Hall *financial planner*
Forti, William Bell *finance educator*

Corona Del Mar
Helphand, Ben J. *actuary, consultant*
Indiek, Victor Henry *finance corporation executive*

Coronado
Baumer, Edward Ferdinand *financial services executive*

Costa Mesa
Metzger, Vernon Arthur *management educator, consultant*

Culver City
Marcus, Richard Andrew *accountant, mayor*

Daly City
Dee, Jon Facundo *financial services executive*

Dana Point
Kesselhaut, Arthur Melvyn *financial consultant*

Davis
Tsai, Chih-Ling *management educator*

Encino
Dor, Yoram *accountant*
Ribac, Catalino Tagatac *retired accountant*

Fallbrook
Freeman, Harry Lynwood *retired accountant*

Fountain Valley
Penderghast, Thomas Frederick *business educator*

Fremont
Jensen, Paul Edward Tyson *business educator, consultant*
Lyons, Irving (Bud), III, *corporate financial executive*

Fresno
Tellier, Richard Davis *management educator*

Fullerton
Foote, Paul Sheldon *business educator, administrator, forecasting consultant*
Peralta, Joseph Soriano *financial planner*

Granada Hills
Lehtihalme, Larry K. (Lauri Lehtihalme) *financial planner*

Grass Valley
Connell, Will *financial consultant*

Hayward
McKenzie, Brian Bruce *finance educator*

Hemet
Rowe, Mary Sue *accounting executive*

Huntington Beach
Hamilton, Allen Philip *financial advisor*

Inglewood
Patmore, Kimberly S. *financial services executive*

Irvine
Farrar, Donald Keith *retired financial executive*
Feldstein, Paul Joseph *management educator*
Parnes, Andrew H. *financial executive*
Premchand, Arigapudi *retired financial consultant*

La Canada
Tookey, Robert Clarence *actuary, consultant*

La Crescenta
Fisk, Irwin Wesley *financial investigator*

La Habra
Schoppa, Elroy *accountant, financial planner*

La Jolla
Dorsey, Dolores Florence *retired corporate treasurer, business executive*
Jeub, Michael Leonard *financial consultant*
Purdy, Kevin Moore *estate planner*

Laguna Niguel
Bauer, Barbara A. *financial consultant*

Lake Forest
Smith, William Hugh, Sr., *retired audit manager, consultant*

Larkspur
Aster, Richard (Rick) F., Jr., *diversified financial services company executive*

Lincoln
Dorn, Mary Ann *retired auditor*

Los Altos
Yu, Oliver Shukiang *corporate executive, educator, technology strategist*

Los Angeles
Allen, Sharon *accounting firm executive*
Allen, Suzanne *financial planning executive, insurance agent, writer*
Allison, Laird Burl *business educator*
Anderson, John Edward *diversified holding company executive, lawyer*
Bennis, Warren Gameliel *business administration educator*
Borsting, Jack Raymond *business administration educator*
Broad, Eli *financial services executive*
Caskie, William Wirt *accountant, securities broker*
Chan, David Ronald *tax specialist, lawyer*
Crane, Steven *financial company executive*
Ellsworth, Frank L. *business executive*
Garrison, P. Gregory *diversified financial services company executive*
Karmarkar, Uday Sadashiv *management educator*
Leach, Anthony Raymond *financial executive*
Lin, Thomas Wen-shyoung *accounting educator, researcher, consultant*
Mock, Theodore Jaye *accounting educator*
Moffatt, Robert Henry *accountant, publisher, writer, consultant*
More, Philip Harvey Birnbaum *business administration educator*
Morrison, Donald Graham *business educator, consultant*
Morrow, Winston Vaughan *financial executive*
Mosich, Anelis Nick *accountant, writer, educator, consultant*
O'Toole, James Joseph *business educator*
Ownbey, Vance Scott *corporate financial executive*
Porper, Mary *comptroller*
Roth, Gary Neal *accountant*
Roussey, Robert Stanley *accountant, educator*
Stancill, James McNeill *finance educator, consultant*
Stewart, David Wayne *marketing educator, psychologist, consultant*
Tellis, Gerard J. *business educator*
Udvar-Hazy, Steven F. *leasing company financial executive*
Walendowski, George Jerry *accounting and business educator*
Weston, John Frederick *business educator, consultant*
Williams, Julie Ford *mutual fund officer*

Malibu
Baskin, Otis Wayne *business educator*
Hill, Lawrence Sidney *finance educator*

Manhattan Beach
Pettersen, Thomas Morgan *accountant, finance executive*

Marina Del Rey
Allmon, Michael Bryan *financial consultant*

Martinez
Withrow, Sherrie Anne (Jimie Jean Pearl) *financial specialist*

Marysville
Larson, Billy Dell *finance company executive*

Menlo Park
McDonald, Warren George *retired accountant, former savings and loan executive*
Messmer, Harold Maximilian, Jr., (Max Messmer) *financial services executive*
Scholes, Myron S. *financier, former law and finance educator*
Scifres, Donald Ray *finance company executive*

Mill Valley
Mumford, Christopher Greene *corporate financial executive*
Ware, David Joseph *financial consultant*

Napa
Gillespie, Marcia Lou *tax specialist, accountant, musician*

Newark
Call, John G. *corporate financial executive*

Newport Beach
Bruggeman, Terrance John *financial corporate executive*
Gross, William H. (Bill Gross) *financial analyst, investment company executive*
Randolph, Steven *financial advisor*
Tracy, James Jared, Jr., *accountant, financial executive, law firm administrator*

North Hollywood
Boulanger, Donald Richard *financial services executive*
Chang, Wung *business advisor, researcher, lecturer*

Northridge
Roberts, Teri Alane *accountant, educator, civic activist*

Oakland
Lee, Jong Hyuk *accountant*
Randisi, Elaine Marie *accountant, educator, writer*
Tyndall, David Gordon *business educator*

Oceanside
Garfin, Louis *retired actuary*
McIntyre, Louise S. *income tax consultant*

Pacific Palisades
Hagenbuch, Rodney Dale *financial consultant*

Palo Alto
Herrick, Tracy Grant *fiduciary*
Ivy, Benjamin Franklin, III, *financial and real estate investment advisor*
Kohler, Fred Christopher *tax specialist*

Palos Verdes Peninsula
Manning, Christopher Ashley *finance educator, consultant*

Pasadena
Axelson, Charles Frederic *retired accounting educator*
Gillis, Christine Diest-Lorgion *financial planner, stockbroker*
O'Connor, William Charles *automobile agency finance executive*

Pittsburg
Williams, Elizabeth A. *financial planner, business consultant*

Pleasanton
Edwards, Robert L. *corporate financial executive*

Pollock Pines
Johnson, Stanford Leland *marketing, international business educator*

Pomona
Driebe, Michael D. *corporate financial executive*
Lin, Lianlian *management educator, researcher*
Patten, Thomas Henry, Jr., *management, human resources educator*

Poway
Mueller, Gerhard G(ottlob) *retired financial accounting standard setter, retired educator*
Uke, Alan Kurt *company executive*

Rancho Mirage
Brimble, Alan *business executive*
Steele, Charles Glen *retired accountant*

Rancho Santa Margarita
Parth, Frank R. *consulting company executive, educator*

Redlands
Pick, James Block *business educator, demographer*

Reseda
Chavez, Albert Blas *finance company executive*

Riverside
Giroir, Leo Jean Jr. *accountant*
Mc Cormac, Weston Arthur *retired educator, retired career officer*

Rocklin
Dwyer, Darrell James *finance company executive*

Sacramento
Gardner, Jerry Lee *financial consultant*

Salinas
Mehta, Siddarth N. *credit services company executive*
Sprude, Margaret *credit services company executive*
Stevens, Wilbur Hunt *accountant*

San Bernardino
Estes, James Paul *financial services company executive*
Seitz, Victoria Ann *marketing educator*

San Clemente
Petruzzi, Christopher Robert *business educator, consultant*

San Diego
Gengor, Virginia Anderson *financial planning executive, educator*
Markowitz, Harry Max *finance and economics educator*
Pierson, Albert Chadwick *business management educator*
Riedy, Mark Joseph *finance educator*
Russell, Cristel Antonia *finance educator*
Stambaugh, Larry G. *finance executive*
Standifird, Stephen Scott *finance educator*
Tennent, Valentine Leslie *accountant*

San Francisco
Barlow, William Pusey, Jr., *accountant*
Burkey, Marcia B. *corporate financial executive*
Chatterjee, Sharmila *marketing educator*
Dawson, Peter A. *corporate financial executive*
Dodds, Christopher V. *finance company executive*
Du Bain, Myron *financial services executive*
Duncan, Deborah L. *finance company executive*
Friedman, Tully Michael *corporate financial executive*
Fuller, James William *financial director*
Grubb, Edgar Harold *financial services industrial executive*
Gruber, George Michael *accountant, financial systems consultant*
Herringer, Frank Casper *diversified financial services company executive*
Lee, Yikuan *finance educator*
MacNaughton, Angus Athole *finance company executive*
McKeever, Michael Pierce, Sr., *economics and business educator*
McWhinney, Deborah *finance company executive*
Moe, Michael *diversified financial services company executive*
Paterson, Richard Denis *financial executive*
Penney, Geoff *finance company executive*
Richey, Ellen *credit card company executive*
Saunders, Joseph W. *financial services company executive*
Savage, Thomas Joseph *executive development company executive, priest*
Silverman, Victoria Lillian *consultant, fundraiser, cultural organization administrator*
Tornese, Judith M. *financial institution executive*
Vuoto, Anthony *corporate financial executive*
Weihrich, Heinz *management educator*
Yang, Nini *finance educator, researcher*

San Jose
Effren, Gary Ross *financial executive*
Jiang, William Yuying *business educator, consultant, researcher*
Kelly, Robert D *finance company executive*
Landis, Kevin *diversified financial services company executive*
Morrison, William Fosdick *business educator, retired electrical company executive*
Osland, Joyce Marie *finance educator, consultant*
Smith, David Eugene *business administration educator*
Yee, Keith Philip *accountant, finance company executive*

San Luis Obispo
Blakeslee, Diane Pusey *financial planner*
Sena, James Anthony *finance educator, department chairman*

San Marino
Gouw, Julia Suryapranata *accountant*
Grantham, Richard Robert *financial consultant*

San Mateo
Baio, James R. *diversified financial services company executive*
Hopkins, Cecilia Ann *business educator*
Johnson, Charles Bartlett *mutual fund executive*
Johnson, Gregory E. *diversified financial services company executive*
Johnson, Rupert Harris, Jr., *finance company executive*

San Rafael
Purcell, Stuart McLeod, III, *financial planner*

San Ramon
Crowe, Stephen J. *comptroller*
King Hauser, Ann Marie B. *retired controller, artist*
Vaughn, John Rolland *auditor*

Santa Ana
Ricketts, James F. *treasurer*

Santa Barbara
Abbinante, Christopher *finance company executive*
Maudsley, Ronald R. *finance company executive*

Santa Clara
Bronson, Joseph R. *manufacturing company executive*
Paisley, Christopher B. *business educator*
Splinter, Michael R. *corporate financial executive*

Santa Monica
Markoff, Steven C. *finance company executive*
Ozaki, Joseph *finance company executive*

Santa Rosa
Biderman, Charles Israel *diversified financial services company executive*

Brigham, John Allen, Jr., *financial executive, environmentalist, polition*
Leong, Stephanie Mei *financial planner*

Sherman Oaks
Kerr, Gib *financial planner*

Sonora
Wheeler, Elton Samuel *financial executive*

South Lake Tahoe
Dean, John Randall *financial consultant, general building contractor*

Stanford
Beaver, William Henry *accounting educator*
Holloway, Charles Arthur *public and private management educator*
McDonald, John Gregory *financial investment educator*
Montgomery, David Bruce *marketing educator*
Pfeffer, Jeffrey *business educator*
Porterfield, James Temple Starke *business administration educator*
Saloner, Garth *management educator*
Segal, Ilya R. *finance educator*

Stockton
Post, Gerald V. *business educator*
Taylor, Francis Michael *auditor, municipal official*
Weick, Cynthia Wagner *business educator*

Tarzana
Goldberg, Harvey *financial executive*
Kagan, Stephen Bruce (Sandy Kagan) *chief financial officer*

Thousand Oaks
Keller, James Robert *business development director*

Torrance
Antkiewicz, Charmian Elizabeth *controller*

Truckee
Sanwick, James Arthur *corporate financial executive*

Ukiah
Patel, Bharat *financial executive*

Upland
Cullen, Robert John *financial planner, investment advisor*

Valencia
Werkheiser, Steven Lawrence *financial executive*

Visalia
Neeley, James Kame *credit agency executive*
O'Leary, Deanna Kay *analyst, consultant*

Vista
Ferguson, Margaret Ann *tax consultant*

Walnut
Budzak, Stephen Howard *tax specialist, consultant*

Walnut Creek
McCauley, Bruce Gordon *financial consultant*
Palmer, William Joseph *accountant*

West Sacramento
Anderson, William Wallace *financial executive*

Westlake Village
Detterman, Robert Linwood *financial planner*

Willits
Akins, George Charles *accountant*

Woodland Hills
Babayans, Emil *financial planner*
Harmon, David *finance company executive*
Tuthill, Walter Warren *financial executive, international business consultant*
Wiesner, Carol A. *financial services company executive*

COLORADO

Aurora
Bauman, Earl William *accountant*

Boulder
Bangs, F(rank) Kendrick *former business educator*
Baugh, L. Darrell *financial executive*
Baughn, William Hubert *former business educator and academic administrator*
Melicher, Ronald William *finance educator*
Stanton, William John, Jr., *marketing educator, author*
Thomas, Daniel Foley *retired financial services company executive*

Broomfield
Seabrook, Raymond J. *corporate financial executive*

Castle Rock
Barnard, Rollin Dwight *retired financial executive*

Centennial
Milliken, Douglas Gordon *financial consultant, municipal official*

Clifton
Konola, Claudette June *finance company executive, financial consultant*

Colorado Springs
Bressan, Robert Ralph *accountant*
Shambo, James Alan *accountant*
Spicer, Ronald L. *financial services educator*

Columbine Valley
Wittbrodt, Edwin Stanley *consultant, former bank executive, former air force officer*

Denver
Cook, Albert Thomas Thornton, Jr., *financial advisor*

Dancik, Jo Marie *accountant, accounting company executive*
Eppler, Jerome Cannon *private financial advisor*
Felser, Louis A. *retired corporate financial executive, writer*
Hall, Richard Murray, Jr., *finance executive, consultant*
Knights, Ronald Michael *business educator*
Leraaen, Allen Keith *financial executive*
Levinson, Shauna T. *financial services executive*
Lincoln, Alexander, III, *financial analyst, lawyer, private investor*
Sandler, Thomas R. *accountant*
Seiple, John W., Jr., *corporate financial executive*
Zanecchia, Thomas Edward *financial executive*

Dillon
Townsend, James Douglas *accountant*

Englewood
Bondi, Bert Roger *accountant, financial planner*
Iapalucci, Samuel H. *financial executive*

Erie
Alpers, John Hardesty, Jr., *financial planning executive, retired military officer*

Fort Collins
Ewing, Jack Robert *accountant*
Kinnison, Robert Wheelock *retired accountant*

Lakewood
Barber, Larry Eugene *financial planner*
Keller, Shirley Inez *accountant*
Nichols, Vicki Anne *financial consultant, librarian*

Littleton
Hadley, Marlin LeRoy *direct sales financial consultant*

Trinidad
Veltri, Sandra Kay *finance educator*

Twin Lakes
Homan, Ralph William *finance company executive*

Wheat Ridge
Gerlick, Helen J. *tax practitioner, accountant*
Leino, Deanna Rose *business educator*

CONNECTICUT

Avon
Mazur, Edward John, Jr., *financial planner*

Bridgeport
Huo, Yangchung Paul *business educator*

Cos Cob
Halvorsen, Ole Andreas *financier*

Danbury
Gezurian, Dorothy Ellen *accounting executive*
Moskowitz, Stanley Alan *financial executive*
Proctor, Richard Jerome, Jr., *business educator, accountant, expert witness*

Darien
Lim, Ralph Wei Hsiong *finance educator*
Nava, Eloy Luis *financial planner, financial consultant*
Schell, James Munson *financial executive*

East Hartford
Barredo, Rita M. *auditor*

Fairfield
Harris, Wiley Lee *financial services executive*

Greenwich
Cook, Jay Michael *accounting company executive*
Fleisher, Jerrilyn *financial planner*
Hewitt, Dennis Edwin *financial executive*
Horton, Jared Churchill *retired corporation executive*
Kolb, Jerry Wilbert *accountant*
Macaulay, William Edward *financial executive*
Mandel, Stephen, Jr., *financier*
Smith, Rodger Field *financial executive*
Tarantino, Dominic A. A. *retired professional services firm executive*
von Braun, Peter Carl Moore Stewart *business executive*
Wyman, Ralph Mark *finance company executive*

Hamden
He, Xiaohong *finance educator*
Nehrt, Chadwick C. *business educator*
Tomasko, Edward A. *financial planner*

Hartford
Bennett, Alan M. *corporate financial executive*
Campbell, Timothy Reid *financial services company executive*
Glover, Ann B. *finance company executive*
Johnson, David M. *finance company executive*
Olejiniczak, Ronald M *corporate financial executive*
Olson, Peter Wesley *international business educator*
Price, Robert J *corporate financial executive*
Quirk, Alfred P, Jr., *corporate financial executive*
Rounce, Rob *controller*
Souza, Diane D *corporate financial executive*
Veale, John Edmond (Jack Veale) *business executive*

Litchfield
Kenagy, Robert Coffman *planning consulting company executive*

Madison
James, John Whitaker, Sr., *financial services executive*

Meriden
Frederick, Paul G. *financial services systems company executive*

Middletown
Malkin, Moses Montefiore *employee benefits administration company executive*

Mystic
Nolf, David M. *financial consultant*

New Haven
Abdelsayed, Wafeek Hakim *accounting educator*
Buck, Donald Tirrell *retired finance educator*
Buckley, Richard Bennett *asset management company executive*
Fried, Charles A. *retired accountant, financial executive*

North Stonington
Mills, Joshua Redmond *financial executive*

Norwalk
Chesser, Leicle E. *corporate financial executive*
Garten, Wayne Philip *financial executive*
Schmalzried, Marvin Eugene *financial consultant*

Old Lyme
Fairfield-Sonn, James Willed *management educator and consultant*

Rowayton
Tropin, Kenneth G. *fund management executive*

South Windsor
Tedoldi, Robert Louis, Jr., *financial planner, consultant*

Stamford
Frishkorn, David Loy *finance company executive*
Godfrey, Robert R. *financial services executive*
Gonnelli, Patrick M. *finance company executive*
Lessin, Andrew Richard *accounting executive*
Loh, Arthur Tsung Yuan *finance company executive*
Mactas, Mark V. *diversified financial services company executive*
Mahony, Edward B. *corporate financial executive*
Morgan, William J. *accounting company executive*
Pansini, Michael Samuel *tax and financial consultant*
Parke, James A. *corporate financial executive*
Rand, A. Barry *financial services executive*
Tully, Daniel Patrick *financial services executive*
Wilson, Mark *corporate financial executive*
Zimmerman, Lawrence A. *corporate financial executive*

Stonington
Rees, Charles H. G. *retired finance company executive, investor, consultant*

Thompson
Fisher, William Thomas *business administration educator*

West Haven
Ellis, Lynn Webster *retired finance educator, retired media consultant*
Haley, Usha C.V. *international business educator*
Suster, Zeljan *business educator, dean*

West Simsbury
Ross, Coleman DeVane *accountant, insurance company executive*

Westport
Baliban, Jeffrey Lee *accountant, economist*
Ready, Robert James *financial company executive*

Wilton
Hersh, Ira Paul *tax specialist, financial consultant*
Kangas, Edward A. *former diversified financial services company executive*

DELAWARE

Newark
Davis, Darwin Jacob *operations management educator*
Sawyer, John Edward *management educator*

Wilmington
Copeland, Tatiana Brandt *accountant*
Griffin, Jo Ann Thomas *retired financial planner, tax specialist*
Lerner, Randolph D. *finance company executive*
Mand, Martin G. *financial executive*
Moore, Brian Clive *actuary*
Rogoski, Patricia Diana *financial executive*

DISTRICT OF COLUMBIA

Washington
Aguirre-Sacasa, Rafael Eugenio *international consultant*
Amyx, Terry Don *corporate financial executive*
Anjaria, Shailendra J. *international finance official*
Armstrong, Alexandra *financial advisor*
Arnold, G. Dewey, Jr., *accountant*
Arundel, John Howard *financial consultant*
Buzzell, Robert Dow *management educator*
Dacey, Robert Frank *accountant, executive*
DiGanci, Todd T. *stock exchange executive*
Droms, William George *finance educator, investment advisor*
Finneran, John Patrick, Jr., *finance company executive, educator*
Glauber, Robert R. *stock exchange executive*
Goldstein, Jeffrey A. *corporate financial executive*
Gould, W. Scott *financial administrator*
Howard, J. Timothy *finance company executive*
Jackson, Brian D. *diversified financial services company executive*
Johnson, James A. *financial organization executive*
Kanter, Arnold Lee *international businesss consultant, policy analyst*
Knight, Linda K. *financial company executive*
Larsen, Richard Gary *accounting firm executive*
Levy, Michael B. *business educator*
Logan, Ann D. *financial company executive*
Ludwig, Eugene Allan *financial consultant, former US Comptroller of the Currency, lawyer*
MacLaury, Bruce King *financial institution executive*
Malek, Frederic Vincent *finance company executive*
Maul, Kevin Jay *financial consultant*
Merrifield, Dudley Bruce *business educator, former government official*
Morse, John B., Jr., *corporate financial executive*
Mosso, Lyle David *financial executive*
Musick, Anthony *financial executive*
Noll, Richard Allan *strategy consultant*
Overend, Mark G. *diversified financial services company executive*
Parde, Duane Arthur *association executive*
Riffee, Stephen *corporate financial executive*
Springer, Linda *portfolio manager, controller*
Taylor, David Kerr *international business educator, consultant*
Teng, Bing-Sheng *finance educator, researcher*
Tuttle, Marv *finance association executive*
Walker, David A(lan) *finance educator*
Wesberry, James Pickett, Jr., *financial management consultant, auditor, international organization executive*
Woicke, Peter *corporate financial executive*
Zeidman, Fred S. *corporate financial executive*
Zenker, Wendy *financial executive*
Zhang, Shengman *corporate financial executive*
Zoeller, Jack Carl *financial executive*

FLORIDA

Auburndale
Mercer, Earnest Brant *retired finance educator*

Aventura
Fishel, Peter Livingston *accounting business executive*
Goodman, Neal Robert *international management consultant and educator*
Kliger, Milton Richard *financial services executive*

Belleview
Bellis, Arthur Albert *financial executive, government official*

Boca Grande
de Saint Phalle, Thibaut *investment banker, educator, lawyer, financial consultant*

Boca Raton
Jessup, Joe Lee *business educator, management consultant*
Karmelin, Michael Allen *financial executive*
Kleinberg, Brian *financial services executive*
Miles, Jesse Mc Lane *retired accounting company executive*
Ortiz, Jaime *business educator*
Owen, Daniel Bruce *financial consultant*
Peterson, Mark F. *business educator*
Pradere, Sonia *accounting administrator*
Sigel, Marshall Elliot *financial consultant*

Boynton Beach
Bartholomew, Arthur Peck, Jr., *accountant*

Clearwater
Campolettano, Thomas Alfred *international contract manager*
Crites, Richard Ray *financial planner, investment advisor, financial services company executive*
Hibbard, Frank V. *diversified financial services company executive*
Loos, Randolph Meade *financial planner*

Cocoa Beach
Kennedy, Thomas Patrick *financial executive*
Wirtschafter, Irene Nerove *tax specialist, consultant*

Crestview
Scott, George Gallmann *accountant*

Deerfield Beach
Moran, Patricia Genevieve *corporate financial executive*
Siegel, Steven L. *finance company executive, consultant*

Dunnellon
Martell, Thomas Stewart *accountant*

Fort Lauderdale
Cobb, David Keith *accountant*
Dörken, Uwe R. *finance company executive*
Feldman, Les J. *finance educator*
Lampert, Wayne Morris *corporate financier*
Pohlman, Randolph A. *business administration educator, dean*
Shoemaker, William Edward *financial executive*
Stephan, John *finance educator*

Fort Myers
Kleman, Charles J. *finance company executive*
Oligario, Max *retired accountant*

Hobe Sound
Caspersen, Finn Michael Westby *diversified financial services company executive*

Hollywood
Harkin, Daniel John *controller*
Mendelson, Laurans Adam *accountant*

Jacksonville
Adams, Scott Leslie *accountant*
Duncan, Shirley A. *portfolio manager*
Edwards, Marvin Raymond *investment counselor, economic consultant*
Munoz, Oscar *corporate financial executive*
Patel, Vinod Motibhai *accountant*
Tomlinson, William Holmes *management educator, retired army officer*
Vane, Terence G., Jr., *finance company executive, lawyer*

Lake Wales
Luing, Gary Alan *financial management educator*

Largo
Shillinglaw, Gordon *accounting educator, consultant*

Lighthouse Point
Shein, Jay Lesing *financial planner*

Longboat Key
Van Dyke-Cooper, Anny Marion *retired financial company executive*

Lutz
Hacker, Michelle Wendy *auditor, researcher, finance educator*

Manalapan
Gatewood, Robert Payne *retired financial planning executive*

Melbourne
Roub, Bryan R(oger) *financial executive*

Miami
Capraro, Franz *accountant*
Coton, Carlos David *finance manager*
Ehrlich, Morton *international finance executive*
Esteves, Vernon Xavier *financial consultant, investment advisor*
Flinn, David Lynfield *financial consultant*
Forgione, Dana Anthony *healthcare accounting educator*
Guerra, Charles Albert *financial consultant, real estate investor*
Ibler, Gerold *finance company executive, consultant*
Kregg, Judith Lynne *accountant*
Miyazaki, Anthony D. *marketing educator, consultant*
Mouly, Eileen Louise *financial planner*
Nunez-Lawton, Miguel G. *international finance specialist*
Pomeranz, Felix *accounting educator*

Miami Shores
Diener, Betty Jane *business educator*

Naples
Handy, Charles Brooks *accountant, educator*
Madigan, Joseph Edward *financial executive, consultant, director*
Ordway, John Danton *retired pension administrator, lawyer, accountant*
Thomas, Gary Lynn *financial executive*

New Port Richey
Assini, Vincent Paul *financial executive*
Deasy, Theresa *accountant, financial and administrative executive*

New Smyrna Beach
Plane, Donald Ray *management science educator*

Nokomis
Meyerhoff, Jack Fulton *financial executive*

North Miami
Tate, Stanley G. *diversified business executive, expert witness*

North Palm Beach
Frevert, James Wilmot *financial planner, investment advisor*
Higgins, Jay F. *financial executive*

Orlando
Armacost, Robert Leo *management educator, former coast guard officer*
Bearman, David *corporate financial executive*
Deli, Steven Frank *business investment and development executive*
Gray, Anthony Rollin *retired finance company executive*

Oviedo
Drummer, Donald Raymond *financial services executive*

Palm Beach
Banks, Russell *financial planner, consultant*
Fitilis, Theodore Nicholas *portfolio manager, retired financial analyst*

Palm Beach Gardens
Howard, Melvin *financial executive*
Werner, Joanne Loucille *financial executive*

Palmetto
Patton, Ray Baker *financial consultant, real estate broker*

Pompano Beach
Vasquez, William Leroy *business educator, consultant*

Ponte Vedra Beach
Roland, Melissa Montgomery *accountant*

Saint Augustine
DeLaughter, Thomas Glenn *business administration educator, consultant*

Saint Petersburg
Bryant, Timothy Clark *investment brokerage executive*
Davenport, Jeffrey Paton *financial planner, investment advisor*
Geiger, Scott William *finance educator*
Godwin, Benjamin Braxton *finance company executive*
Keistler, Betty Lou *accountant, tax consultant*
Putnam, J. Stephen *financial executive*
Shuck, Robert F. *financial executive*
Wasserman, Susan Valesky *accountant, artist, yoga instructor*

Sarasota
Arreola, John Bradley *financial planner*
Bailey, Robert Elliott *financial executive*
Berman, Lewis Paul *financial executive*
Drake, Diana Ashley *retired financial planner*
Goodman, Tracy Annette *financial consultant*
Miles, Arthur J. *financial planner, consultant*
Morris, Gordon James *financial company executive, consultant*

Stuart
Bygate, Wayne Ian *controller*

Tallahassee
Keister, Beverly Jane *accountant*

Tampa
Alexander, William Olin *finance company executive*
Bear, Marca Marie *business educator, management consultant*
Bradish, Warren Allen *retired internal auditor, operations analyst, management consultant*
DeVane, Mindy Klein *financial planner*
Hanford, Agnes Rutledge *retired financial adviser*
Hernandez, Gilberto Juan *accountant, auditor, management consultant*
Hlavay, Jay Alan *financial analyst*
Lebouitz, Martin Frederick *financial services industry executive, consultant*
Nord, Walter Robert *business administration educator, researcher, consultant*
Peiser, Robert Alan *financial executive*
Sendrow, Jerrold B. *financial services executive*
Taylor, Thomas S. *diversified financial services company executive*

Vero Beach
Conway, Earl Cranston *business educator, retired manufacturing company executive*
Danforth, Arthur Edwards *finance executive*
Fetter, Robert Barclay *retired administrative sciences educator*
Koontz, Alfred Joseph, Jr., *financial and operating management executive, consultant*
Riefler, Donald Brown *financial consultant*
Satuloff, Barth *accounting executive, dispute resolution professional, investment strategist, publisher*
Simon, Donald John *employee benefits administrator, insurance and investment broker*

Wesley Chapel
Mendelsohn, Louis Benjamin *financial analyst*

West Palm Beach
Doto, Paul Jerome *retired accountant*
Eppley, Roland Raymond, Jr., *retired financial services executive*
Herrick, John Dennis *financial consultant, former law firm executive, retired food products executive*
Livingstone, John Leslie *accountant, management consultant, business economist, educator*

Weston
Holtzman, Gary Yale *retired administrative and financial executive*

Winter Park
Alon, Ilan *international business educator*
Matulich, Serge *accounting educator, author*
Pearson, R. Scott *investment advisor, editor*
Therrien, Francois Xavier, Jr., *business and tax consultant*

GEORGIA

Alpharetta
Bickell, Cliff O. *financial company executive*

Athens
Carroll, Archie Benjamin, III, *finance educator*
Miller, Herbert Elmer *accountant*

Atlanta
Ackerman, Arlene Alice *accountant, business consultant, artist, writer*
Appeadu, Charles Edward *finance educator, researcher*
Argenbright, Frank A., Jr., *diversified financial services company executive*
Averitt, Richard Garland, III, *financial services company executive*
Brown, Terry Steven *accountant*
Chambers, Robert William *business broker*
Cook, Don Lloyd *marketing educator, lawyer, consultant*
Cook, John M. *finance company executive*
Craig, Anna Maynard *financial educator, consultant*
Davis, D. Scott *corporate financial executive*
Gross, Stephen Randolph *accountant*
Gundersen, Mary Lisa Kranitzky *finance company executive*
Hanna, Frank Joseph, Jr., *credit company executive*
Hays, William Grady, Jr., *corporate financial and bank consultant*
Hogan, William Jephtha, Jr., *financial consultant*
Hudson, Dean *tax accountant*
Johnson, Phillip Murray *treasurer, lumber company executive, paper company executive, chemicals executive, consumer products company executive*
Kringelis, Kurt *portfolio manager*
Lane, Brian David *accountant*
Lobb, William Atkinson *financial services executive*
Lustig, Michael A. *finance company executive*
Mamrack, William H. *tax specialist*
Moore, Daniel D. *finance company executive*
Oliver, Robert C. *financial company executive*
Parsons, Leonard Jon *marketing educator, consultant*
Reid, Joseph William *consultant*
Ricketson, Michael E. *financial company executive*
Robertson, Sandra Dee (Graen) *tax director*
Seto, William Roderick *public accounting company executive*
Sheth, Jagdish Nanchand *finance educator*
Terrel, James E. *controller*
Tome, Carol *corporate financial executive*
Whittington, Frederick Brown, Jr., *business administration educator*

Carrollton
Cochran, J. Guyton, Jr., *corporate financial executive*

Columbus
Blanchard, James Hubert *finance company executive*

Dahlonega
Faulkner, James A. *financial executive*

Dalton
Turner, Jackson Parks *financial company executive*
Winter, Larry Eugene *accountant*

Decatur
Myers, Clark Everett *retired business administration educator*

Fayetteville
Brown, L(arry) Eddie *tax practitioner, business accountant, real estate broker, financial planner*

Hinesville
Wise, Carl Stamps *accounting educator*

Kennesaw
Robinson, Kenneth Charles *management educator*

Lawrenceville
Neaton, Marcia Lynne *accountant, financial analyst*

Macon
Hall, David L. *finance company executive*
Hatcher, Robert F. *financial executive*
Molloy, George A. *finance company executive*

Marietta
Edwards, Charle Mundy, III, *financial consultant*
Kiger, Ronald Lee *contract negotiator*
Simmons, Stephen Gregory *accountant*

Milledgeville
Engerrand, Doris Dieskow *business educator*

Monroe
Altherr, Jack Richard, Jr., *accountant*

Norcross
Kight, Peter J. *financial services company executive*
Massey, Lewis *finance company executive*
Plummer, Michael Kenneth *financial consultant*
Shulman, Allen L. *financial services company executive*
Sinisgalli, Peter F. *financial company executive*

Oakwood
Martin, Johnny Benjamin *accountant*

Savannah
Goodwyn, George Waverly, Jr., *corporate financial executive, educator*

Statesboro
Murkison, Eugene Cox *finance educator*

Woodstock
Austin, John David *retired financial executive*

HAWAII

Honolulu
Fukushima, Barbara Naomi *financial advisor*
Haig, David M. *property and investment manager*
Hirai, Craig Kazuo *accountant*
Hook, Ralph Clifford, Jr., *business educator*
Kawamura, Georgina K. *finance company executive*
Liu, Roger Kim Sing *accountant*
Ng, Wing Chiu *accountant, educator, application developer, lawyer, educator, advocate*
Palia, Aspy Phiroze *marketing educator, researcher, consultant*
Pilar, L. Prudencio R. *financial services executive*
Solidum, James *finance and insurance executive*
Villinger, Niti *management educator*

IDAHO

Boise
Ingram, Cecil D. *accountant, state legislator*
Juetten, George H. *company executive*

Idaho Falls
Riddoch, Hilda Johnson *accountant*

ILLINOIS

Ashmore
Bagwell, Kim Diane *accountant*

Bellwood
Miller, Denyce Karlina *tax specialist*

Bloomington
Friedman, Joan M. *accounting educator*

Buffalo Grove
Leonetti, Michael Edward *financial planner*
McConville, Rita Jean *finance executive*
Yacktman, Donald Arthur *financial executive, investment counselor*

Cahokia
Healy, Steven Michael *accountant, city official*

Champaign
Brighton, Gerald David *accounting educator*
Ganguly, Ananda Roop *business management educator*

Chicago
Berardino, Joseph Francis *accounting company executive*
Brooksher, K. Dane *accounting, management company executive*
Carlson, Richard Gregory *accountant*
Chapman, Alger Baldwin *finance company executive, lawyer*
Chookaszian, Dennis Haig *retired financial executive*
Christianson, Stanley David *finance company executive*
Chromizky, William Rudolph *accountant*
Falkowski, Patricia Ann *investment counsel*
Fensin, Daniel *diversified financial service company executive*
Fischer, Paul *corporate financial executive*
Fitzgerald, Robert Maurice *financial executive*
Fleming, Richard H. *finance executive*
Forbes, John Edward *financial consultant*
Forehand, Joseph W. *finance company executive*
Garrigan, Richard Thomas *finance educator, consultant, editor*
Gluth, Robert C. *management company executive*
Goldfein, Iris *financial company executive*
Goodman, Robert Stanley *management educator*
Hansen, Claire V. *financial executive*
Haydock, Walter James *banker*
Herting, Claireen LaVern *financial planner*
Hooton, James G. *finance company executive*
Ibbotson, Roger G. *financial educator*
Jaffe, Howard Allen *financial company executive*
Koltin, Allan David *accountant*
Kudish, David J. *financial executive*
Kullberg, Duane Reuben *accounting firm executive*
London, Justin Joshua *portfolio manager, consultant*
Lorch, Robert K. *corporate financial executive*
Mallory, Robert Mark *controller, finance executive*
Mayer, Raymond Richard *business administration educator*
McDonnell, David Croft *diversified financial services company executive*
McGrath, Michael G. *finance company executive*
Mendenhall, Candice *former finance company executive*
Miller, Heidi G. *diversified financial company executive*
Pavelich, Daniel L. *retired account, tax management consulting executive*
Perlmutter, Norman *finance company executive*
Pump, Bernard John *finance company executive, consultant*
Rappaport, Anna M. *actuary*
Rasin, Rudolph Stephen *corporate financial executive*
Reed, M. Scott *accounting company executive*
Reynolds, James, Jr., *finance company executive*
Rosenbaum, Michael A. *investor relations consultant*
Schornack, John James *accountant*
Schueppert, George Louis *financial executive*
Schumann, William Henry, III, *financial executive*
Siegel, Laurence B. *investment research company executive, consultant*
Sjogren, Bengt B *corporate financial executive*
Smith, Adrian J.R. *management company executive*
Smith, Marcia Jean *accountant, tax specialist, financial consultant*
Stirling, D. Leslie *corporate financial executive*
Szypulski, Wayne R. *controller, food products executive*
Varma, Arup *finance educator, consultant*
Verschoor, Curtis Carl *business educator, consultant*
Vitale, Gerald Lee *financial services executive*
Williams, Marsha C. *corporate financial executive*
Wittenberg, Jon Albert *accountant*
Young, Scott Thomas *business management educator*
Zech, Ronald H. *financial services executive*
Zingales, Luigi G. *finance educator*
Zorko, Mark A. *financial executive*

Crestwood
Cowie, Norman Edwin *credit manager*

Decatur
Loebl, Maragaret Margo *corporate financial executive*
Mulhollem, Paul B. *finance company executive*

Deerfield
Boyd, Joseph Don *financial services executive*
Heiman, Marvin Stewart *finance company executive*
Holter, Gary S. *finance executive*
Lifschultz, Phillip *financial and tax consultant, accountant, lawyer*
Park, Jeffrey Bryan *controller*

Dixon
Metka, Phillip Edward *comptroller*

Evanston
Corey, Gordon Richard *financial advisor, former utilities executive*
Kalai, Ehud *finance educator, economist, researcher*
Oranove, David *business educator, consultant, economist*
Powers, Marian *accounting educator*
Prince, Thomas Richard *accountant, educator*
Scott, Walter Dill *management educator*
Seaman, Jerome Francis *actuary*
Stern, Louis William *marketing educator, consultant*

Geneva
Young, Jack Allison *financial executive*

Glencoe
Silver, Ralph David *financial consultant and arbitrator*

Glendale Heights
Cook, Doris Marie *retired accountant, educator*

Glenview
Levin, Donald Robert *business and finance executive, motion picture producer, professional sports team owner*

Highland Park
Afterman, Allan B. *accountant, educator, researcher, consultant*

Hinsdale
Ciccarone, Richard Anthony *financial executive*
Self, Madison Allen *finance company executive*
Urbik, Jerome Anthony *financial consultant*

Hoffman Estates
Baier, Lucinda *corporate financial executive*

Jacksonville
Kirchhoff, Michael Kent *economic development executive*

Kenilworth
Bott, Harold Sheldon *accountant, management consultant*

Lincolnshire
Hays, Thomas Chandler *holding company executive*

Lisle
Ruyle-Hullinger, Elizabeth Smith (Beth Ruyle) *consultant, municipal financial advisor*

Macomb
Bauerly, Ronald John *marketing educator*

Mchenry
Koehl, Camille Joan *accountant*

Mundelein
Abington, William K *corporate financial executive*

Naperville
Calamos, Nick P. *diversified financial services company executive*
Tan, Li-Su Lin *accountant, insurance executive, investment consultant*

Northbrook
Feibel, Frederick Arthur *financial consultant*
Hale, Danny Lyman *financial executive*
Lane, William Noble, III, *financial executive*
Mandel, Karyl Lynn *accountant*
Newman, Lawrence William *financial executive*
Pilch, Samuel H. *controller, corporate financial executive*

Northfield
Shillestad, John Gardner *financial services company executive*

Oak Brook
Bossmann, Laurie *controller, hardware company executive*
Koufis, John Theodore *accountant*

Oakbrook Terrace
Catalano, Gerald *accountant*

Oswego
Eberhardt, Robert Michael *diversified financial services company executive, sales executive*

Palatine
Butler, John Musgrave *financial consultant*
Spinner, Lee Louis *accountant*

Park Ridge
Russell, William Steven *finance executive*

Peoria
George, Carl R. *accounting company executie*
Vaughan, David John *corporate financial executive*

Prospect Heights
Aldinger, William F., III, *diversified financial services company executive*
Harvey, Kenneth M *corporate financial executive*
McDonald, Steven L. *controller*
Schoenholz, David A. *diversified financial services company executive*

Quincy
Mallory, Troy L. *accountant*

Riverdale
Hoekwater, James Warren *treasurer*

Riverside
Perkins, William H., Jr., *retired finance company executive*

Rockford
Albert, Janyce Louise *human resources specialist, retired business educator, banker, consultant*
Wallem, Paul Sigurd *financial planner*

Rosemont
Macioch, James Edward *investment consultant, financial planner*

Schaumburg
Devonshire, David W. *financial executive*
Hanna, Nessim *marketing educator*

Spring Grove
York, Karen Kay *accountant, farmer*

Springfield
Kuhn, Kathleen Jo *accountant*
O'Shea, Helene Claire *bookkeeper*
Travis, Lawrence Allan *accountant*

Westmont
Moor, Roy Edward *finance educator*

Wheaton
Holman, James Lewis *financial and management consultant*

Wilmette
Wishner, Maynard Ira *retired finance company executive, lawyer*

INDIANA

Bloomington
Belth, Joseph Morton *retired business educator*
Dalton, Dan R. *finance educator, former dean*
DeHayes, Daniel Wesley *management executive, educator*
Gordon, Paul John *management educator*
Hustad, Thomas Pegg *marketing educator*
MacKay, David B. *finance educator*
Smith, Daniel C. *finance educator*
Wentworth, Jack Roberts *business educator, consultant*

Carmel
Mahoney, Margaret Ellis *accountant*
Wendt, Gary Carl *finance company executive*

Columbus
Binkley, John Frey, Jr., *financial consultant, writer*
Miller, William Irwin *finance company executive*

Evansville
Gaither, John Francis *accountant, consultant*
McGuire, Brian Lyle *educator, consultant*

Fort Wayne
Owen, Dave A. *finance executive*

Goshen
Whitcraft, James Richard, Jr., *accountant*

Medford
Goldberg, Pamela Winer *business professor, director*

Monson
Krach, Mitchell Peter *retired financial services executive*

Nantucket
Louderback, Peter Darragh *accountant, consultant*

Newton
Temkin, Robert Harvey *accountant*

North Chatham
Wilson, E. B. *business executive, consultant, writer*

Norton
Nicolas, John Scott (Jack Nicolas) *benefits company executive*

Osterville
Silk, Alvin John *business educator, management consultant*

Plymouth
Madonna, Jon C. *accounting firm executive*

Quincy
Britt, Margaret Mary *finance educator*
Somers, Susan Eileen *business educator*

Randolph
Cammarata, Richard John *financial advisor*

Spencer
Goldman, Ethan Harris *finance executive*

Springfield
O'Connell, Robert John *diversified financial services company executive*

Sudbury
Meltzer, Donald Richard *treasurer*

Swampscott
Wolff, Richard Carl *financial planner, insurance agency and pension planning company executive*

Swansea
Hjerpe, Edward Alfred, III, *finance and banking executive*

Tewksbury
Black, Richard Bruce *business executive, consultant*

Waban
Tofias, Allan *accountant*

Waltham
Farb, Thomas Forest *financial executive*
Gittell, Jody Hoffer *finance educator, writer*
Kasputys, Joseph Edward *finance company executive, economist*
McClary, Loretta Mary *accountant*
O'Connell, Jeanne *financial planner, insurance broker*
Thamhain, Hans Jurgen *management educator*

Wellesley
Maxwell, J. B. *financial consultant, marketing professional, consultant*

Weston
Valente, Louis Patrick (Dan Valente) *business and financial executive*

Woburn
Offermann, Peter *financial executive*

Worcester
Banks, McRae Cave, II, *management educator, consultant*
Coonan, Cathleen A. *controller, accountant*
Eppinger, Frederick H., Jr., *finance company executive*
Greenberg, Nathan *accountant*
Zeng, Amy Z. *finance educator, engineering educator*

MICHIGAN

Ann Arbor
Elger, William Robert, Jr., *accountant*
Foster, Alan Herbert *financial consultant, educator*
Kim, E. Han *finance and business administration educator*
Wilhelm, Edward W. *corporate financial executive*

Auburn Hills
Knight, Jeffrey Alan *finance executive*
Kulesza, Chester Stephen (Bud Kulesza) *finance executive*

Birmingham
Helppie, Charles Everett, III, *financial consultant*
McCuen, John Joachim *finance company executive, columnist, educator*

Bloomfield Hills
Poth, Stefan Michael *retired sales financing company executive*

Canadian Lake
Cawthorne, Kenneth Clifford *retired financial planner*

Dearborn
Bannister, Michael E. *corporate financial executive*

Detroit
Acton, Elizabeth S *corporate financial executive*
Adams, Robin J. *corporate financial executive*
Adams, William Johnston *financial and tax consultant*
Clarke, James T. *financial company executive*
Kahalas, Harvey *business educator*

East Lansing
Arens, Alvin Armond *accountant, educator*

Farmington Hills
Smith, Isabel Francis *financial planner*

Flint
Stone, Pamela Ann *accountant*

Grand Rapids
Hermann, William M. *finance company executive*
Mavima, Paul *finance educator*
Staples, David M. *corporate financial executive*

Grosse Pointe Farms
Fromm, Joseph L. *financial consultant*

Kalamazoo
Tang, Roger Yin Wu *accounting educator*

Livonia
McHard, James Lorin *corporate financial executive*
Valerio, Michael Anthony *diversified financial services company executive*

Maple City
Duff, James George *retired autotobile industry and financial services executive*

Marquette
Camerius, James Walter *marketing educator, corporate researcher*

Midland
Morgan, Frank T. *business educator, consultant*

Monroe
Mlocek, Sister Frances Angeline *financial executive*

Mount Clemens
Vosburg, Kathy D *tax specialist, consultant*

Muskegon
DeLong, Donald R. *accountant*

Oak Park
Agboruche, William *accountant, educator, toxicologist, philosopher*

Oxford
Smith, Jay Lawrence *planning company executive*

Plymouth
Stafeil, Jeff *corporate financial executive*

Portage
Zhang, Charles C. *financial planner*

Portland
Rich, Joseph John *accountant*

Southfield
Boyce, Daniel Hobbs *finance company executive*
Miller, Robert Stevens, Jr., *finance professional*
Rawden, David *financial services company executive*
Selis, Stuart L. *financial consultant, underwriter*

Three Rivers
Truesdell, Timothy L. *private investor*

West Bloomfield
Meyers, Gerald Carl *finance educator, writer, expert witness, consultant*
Rauwerdink, William Jay *accountant*

MINNESOTA

Duluth
Feroz, Ehsan Habib *accounting educator, researcher, writer*
Nelson, Dennis Lee *finance educator*

Edina
Taylor, Scott Maxfield *business educator*

Elk River
Goss, Cynthia Lee *tax accountant*

Golden Valley
Harrison, David D. *corporate financial executive*

Minneapolis
Benson, Donald Erick *holding company executive*
Berry, David J. *former financial services company executive*
Berryman, Robert Glen *accounting educator, consultant*
Buckley, John William *financial company executive*
Cracchiolo, James M. *diversified financial services company executive*
Davis, Richard K. *corporate financial executive*
Doyle, Michael J. *corporate financial executive*
Duff, Andrew S. *corporate financial executive*
Elm, Dawn Rae *management educator*
Goldberg, Luella Gross *corporation executive*
Hasten, Joseph E. *corporate financial executive*
Hoffmann, Thomas Russell *business management educator*
Kinney, Earl Robert *mutual funds company executive*
Kuplic, David Michael *portfolio manager*
Martin, Frederick Kane *portfolio manager, investor*
Mohanty, Sunil K. *finance educator, researcher*
Moller, Andrew K. *finance company executive*
Montgomery, Henry Irving *financial planner*
Petersen, Douglas Arndt *financial consultant*
Pillsbury, George Sturgis *investment adviser*
Prange, Michael J. *finance company executive*
Robbins, Larry A. *finance company executive*
Schwartz, Howard Wyn *business/marketing educator, consultant*
Stein, Paul Clinton *financial planner*

Minnetonka
Wesselink, David Duwayne *finance company executive*

Nevis
Stibbe, Austin Jule *accountant*

Nisswa
Marmas, James Gust *retired business educator, retired college dean*

Plymouth
Hauser, Elloyd *finance company executive*

Saint Cloud
Reha, Rose Krivisky *retired finance educator*
Supanvanij, Janikan *finance educator*

Saint Paul
Baukol, Ronald Oliver *retired finance company executive*
Bessette, Andy F. *diversified financial services company executive*
Crittenden, Bruce A. *finance company executive*
Dutcher, Judi *state auditor*
McDonough, Paul H. *corporate financial executive*
Rudelius, William *marketing educator*
Wheelock, Pam *financial executive*

Sleepy Eye
Ruddy, James Vincent, Jr., *tax advocate*

Winona
Haas, James Wayne *accountant*
McCallum, Shelly Yvonne *marketing and international business educator, consultant*

Worthington
Meyer, Helen Bernadine *financial services company executive*

MISSISSIPPI

Clinton
Dubel, John S. *corporate financial executive*

Hattiesburg
Doty, Duane Harold *business educator*
Duhon, David Lester *business educator, management consultant*

Meridian
Thomas, Kenneth Eugene *auditor*

Ocean Springs
Furlow, William Lawrence *manufacturing and financial consultant*

Starkville
George, Ernest Thornton, III, *financial consultant*
Thomas, Garnett Jett *accountant*

Tupelo
Nash, Henry Warren *marketing educator*

University
Flesher, Dale Lee *accounting educator, dean*
Frink, Dwight David *management educator*

MISSOURI

Ballwin
Bond, Dennis Earl *auditor*

Cape Girardeau
Haugland, Jerry Lee *accounting educator*
Potter, Richard Kevin *accountant, controller, consultant*

Chesterfield
Armstrong, Theodore Morelock *financial executive*
Henry, Roy Monroe *financial planner*
Hunter, Buddy D. *holding company executive*

Clayton
Bartmann, William R. *financial services company executive*

Columbia
Cunningham, Billie M. *accounting educator*
Lansford, Raymond William *finance educator, retired*
Nikolai, Loren Alfred *accounting educator, writer*
Stockglausner, William George *accountant*

Fenton
Powers, James G. *corporate financial executive*

Grain Valley
Love, Gary Duane *financial consultant, music educator*

Hazelwood
Kostecki, Mary Ann *financial tax consultant, small business consultant*

Jefferson City
Liese, Christopher A. *benefits and financial consulting company owner, state legislator*
McCaskill, Claire *auditor*

Kansas City
Bloch, Henry Wollman *tax preparation company executive*
Boysen, Melicent Pearl *finance company executive*
Brandmaier, Jeff *diversified financial services company executive*
Ernst, Mark A. *diversified financial services company executive*
Ingraham, James H. *diversified financial services company executive*
Johnson, Sondra Lea *accountant*
Jones, Charles Calhoun *estate and business planning consultant*
Pruitt, Stephen Wallace *finance educator*
Rowland, Landon Hill *diversified holding company executive*
Salizzoni, Frank L. *finance company executive*
Shaw, Richard David *marketing and management educator*
Stevens, James Hervey, Jr., *retired financial advisor*
Streek, Dan *corporate financial executive*
Yabuki, Jeffrey W. *diversified financial services company executive*

Lees Summit
Foudree, Charles M. *financial consultant*

North Kansas City
Staloff, Arnold Fred *financial executive*

Saint Louis
Badalamenti, Anthony *financial planner*
Bagby, Robert L. *finance company executive*
Bloemer, Rosemary Celeste *bookkeeper*
Brockhaus, Robert Herold, Sr., *business educator, consultant*
Brown, Melvin F. *finance company executive*
Carlson, Arthur Eugene *accounting educator*
Crider, Robert Agustine *international financier, protective services official*
Green, Darlene *controller, municipal official*
James, William W. *financial consultant*
Liggett, Hiram Shaw, Jr., *retired diversified industry financial executive*
Lock, Albert Larry, Jr., *financial services company executive*
Novik, Steve *finance company executive*
Paz, George *accountant*
Rainwater, Gary L. *corporate financial executive*
Rich, Harry Earl *corporate financial executive*
Ricks, David Artel *business educator, editor*
Schmidt, Robert Charles, Jr., *finance executive*
Schumm, Steven A *corporate financial executive*
Shepperd, Thomas Eugene *accountant*
Snyder, William W. *corporate financial executive*
Tei, Takuri *accountant*
Tyree, Donald Andrew *financial educator*
Weldon, Virginia V. *retired corporate executive, pediatrician*
Wildhaber, Michael Rene *accountant*
Winter, Richard Lawrence *financial and health care company executive*

Saint Peters
Pring, Robert Bradford *financial consultant*

Springfield
Scroggins, Wesley Allen *finance educator, researcher*

MONTANA

Billings
Elser, Danny R. *financial planner*
Stapleton, Corey *financial planner*

Bozeman
Davis, Nicholas Homans Clark *finance company executive*

Helena
Craig, Mary Lauri *accountant*

Missoula
Uhlenbruck, Nikolaus Theodor *finance educator*

Rollins
Greer, Willis Roswell, Jr., *accounting educator*

Troy
Sherman, Signe Lidfeldt *portfolio manager, former research chemist*

NEBRASKA

Fremont
Dunklau, Rupert Louis *personal investments consultant*

Lincoln
Byrd, Lorelee *state treasurer*
Digman, Lester Aloysius *management educator*
Lee, Sang M. *management educator*
Lienemann, Delmar Arthur, Sr., *accountant, real estate developer*

Norfolk
Wehrer, Charles Siecke *business and education educator*

Omaha
Fairfield, Bill L. *finance company executive*
Miller, Larry Thomas *accountant*
Munger, Charles T. *diversified company executive*
Pitts, Robert Eugene, Jr., *marketing educator, consultant*

Scottsbluff
DiBacco, T. Jay *financial services planner, retired military officer*

NEVADA

Las Vegas
Arend, Richard J *finance educator, consultant*
Duva-Mikhail, Donna Marie *financial executive*
Goldin, Martin Bruce *financial executive, consultant*
Hobbs, Guy Stephen *financial executive*
Kobberoe, Birthe *corporate financial executive, accountant*
Pollak, Norman Lee *accountant*
Rodgers, Steven Edward *tax practitioner, educator*
Rogers, David Hughes *finance executive*
Tan, Keah-Choon *finance educator*

North Las Vegas
Jones, Terri Ann *hotel management educator*

Reno
Holder, Anna Maria *holding company executive*
Neidert, Kalo Edward *accountant, educator*

NEW HAMPSHIRE

Amherst
Atwater, Verne Stafford *finance educator*

Gilmanton
Osler, Howard Lloyd *retired controller*

Bowie, Angie *accounting company official*
Brown, Clifford Bryant *financial consultant*
Brown, Richard Martin *financial consultant*
Browning, Candace *corporate financial executive*
Brustein, Lawrence *financial executive*
Buttner, Jean Bernhard *diversified financial services company executive*
Calio, Nicholas E. *diversified financial services company executive*
Canes, Brian Dennis *retirement benefits systems specialist*
Caputo, Lisa M. *finance company executive*
Carmichael, Douglas Roy *accountant, educator*
Carpenter, Michael A. *financial services executive*
Chenault, Kenneth Irvine *financial services company executive*
Clark, Howard Longstreth, Jr., *finance company executive, director*
Cockrell, Sanford Alonza, III, *accountant*
Cogliano, Dan *tax accountant*
Connolly, Judith *financial consultant*
Conway, E. Virgil *financial consultant, banker, lawyer*
Corbet, Kathleen A. *financial information company executive*
Coughlin, Christopher J. *financial executive*
Craig, Charles Samuel *marketing educator*
Cramer, Jim *online financial information executive*
Crawford, Stephen S. *financial services executive*
Cristea, Ruxandra Maria *corporate financial executive*
Crittenden, Gary Lewis *diversified financial services company executive*
Cronson, Caroline Mary *financial executive*
Cumming, Ian M. *holding company executive*
Cummings, John W. *diversified financial services company executive*
Daidone, Lewis Eugene *financial services company executive*
Dean, G. Hilton *financial company executive*
Dehn, James Keith *financial advisor*
De Lisi, Nancy *corporate financial executive*
DiPiazza, Samuel, Jr., *finance company executive*
Dougan, Brady W. *diversified financial services company executive*
Druskin, Robert A. *diversified financial services company executive*
Duch, Stephen *corporate financial executive*
Edwards, James D. *accounting company executive*
Efrat, Isaac *financial analyst, mathematician*
Eisner, Richard Alan *accountant*
Ellegard, Roy Whitney *appraiser*
Ellis-Simon, Amy *diversified financial services company executive*
Elmer, Russell S. *diversified financial services company executive*
Emmerman, Michael N. *financial analyst*
Englander, Israel A. *financier*
Engle, Robert F. *finance educator*
Etienne, Michele *financial consultant*
Fakahany, Ahmass L. *finance company executive*
Farley, Peggy Ann *finance company executive*
Feldstein, Eric A. *finance company executive*
Felix, Ted Mark *accountant*
Fink, Laurence D. *diversified financial services company executive*
Finkel, Robert *finance company executive*
Finn, Brian D. *financial services executive*
Fishman, Jay Steven *financial services executive*
Fleming, Gregory J. *finance company executive*
Fowler, John M. *financial services executive*
Fowler, William A. *accounting firm executive*
Freiberg, Steven J. *diversified financial services company executive*
Fridson, Martin Steven *finance executive*
Friedman, Steven M. *investment company executive*
Frye, Clayton Wesley, Jr., *finance executive*
Galletti, Scott M. *finance company executive*
Gardner, H. McIntrye *diversified financial services company executive*
Garrett, Robert *financial advisory executive*
Gaughan, Eugene Francis *retired accountant, lawyer*
Geller, Jeffrey Lawrence *financier*
Gilligan, Edward P. *diversified financial services company executive*
Gladstone, William Louis *accountant*
Glaeser, Betsy *financial services company executive*
Goldberg, Edward L. *financial services executive*
Golden, William Theodore *trustee, corporate director*
Goldstein, Steve *corporate financial executive*
Golub, Gerald Leonard *accounting company executive*
Goodman, Bennett J. *diversified financial services company executive, investment banker*
Goodman, Roy Matz *corporate president, chief executive officer, former state senator*
Gorman, James P. *finance company executive*
Gottlieb, Paul Mitchel *corporate financial executive*
Gowens, Walter, II, *financial and business services executive*
Graf, John A. *finance company executive*
Graf, Peter Gustav *accountant, lawyer*
Greifeld, Robert A. *corporate financial executive*
Groves, Ray John *accountant*
Guillaume, Juanita Connor *financial analyst, minister*
Guthrie, Roy A. *financial company executive*
Hajim, Edmund A. *financial services executive*
Harris, Ethan S. *diversified financial services company executive*
Harrison, Warren *finance company executive*
Hayes, John D. *diversified financial services company executive*
Heasley, Philip *financial services company executive*
Heintz, Joseph E. *financial services company executive*
Hines, Walter James *stock exchange executive*
Hintz, Charles B. *finance company executive*
Hirschberg, D. Jeffrey *former financial company executive*
Hopkins, Deborah C. *diversified financial services company executive*
Hornstein, Mark *financial executive*
House, David C. *diversified financial services company executive*
Isaacs, Jeremy M. *finance company executive*
Jacobs, Mark Neil *financial services corporation executive, lawyer*
Jamison, Sheila Ann English *stockbroker, retirement planning specialist*
Johnson, Clarke Courtney *financial consultant, educator*
Johnson, J. Chester *financial executive, poet*
Jones, Thomas Wade *financial services executive*
Kapito, Robert S. *diversified financial services company executive*
Karpen, Marian Joan *financial executive*
Karr, Robert A. *financier*
Kaufman, Henry *financial services executive*
Kaye, Walter *financial executive*
Kearns, Richard P. *diversified financial services company executive*
Keefe, Diane Marie *portfolio manager*
Keegan, Peter W. *diversified financial services company executive*
Kellner, George *securities executive*
Kelly, Alfred F., Jr., *diversified financial services company executive*
Kenneally, Michael E. *diversified financial services company executive*
Kennedy, Kevin W. *finance company executive*
Kent, Jr., Thomas Jefferson, Jr., *corporate financial executive*
Kessler, Michael George *forensic accountant*
Kessler, Stuart *accountant, financial planner*
Kim, Dow *finance company executive*
Kimsey, William L. *diversified financial services company executive*
Kirsch, Arthur William *financial consultant*
Kirsch, Donald *financial consultant, writer*
Kirschenbaum, Lisa L. *portfolio manager, financial advisor*
Knapp, Ellen M. *financial company executive*
Knerr, Anthony David *strategic consultant*
Koeppel, Noel Immanuel *financial planner, securities and real estate broker*
Kolesar, Peter John *business and engineering educator, entrepreneur*
Kopelman, Richard Eric *management educator*
Kruse, Douglas Charles *financial industry consultant, educator*
Ladjevardi, Hamid *fund manager*
Laliberte, Antonio M. *financial company executive*
Lamb, Robert Boyden *finance and management educator*
Langbert, Mitchell Berke *business educator*
Lappin, Joan E. *financial executive*
Laue, Bruce Antonio *financial consultant, writer*
Lessing, Brian Reid *actuary*
Lessing, Stephen M. *finance company executive*
Lewis, W. Walker *strategic and financial advisory company executive*
Libby, John Kelway *financial services company executive*
Lilien, Robert Jarrett *diversified financial services company executive*
Lindegren, Lennart S. *diversified financial services company executive*
Linen, Jonathan S. *diversified financial services company executive*
Lipton, William James *accountant, lawyer*
Ljungqvist, Alexander *finance educator*
Loeb, Peter Kenneth *money manager*
Lowell, Stanley Edgar *accountant*
MacDonald, Alan S. *diversified financial services company executive*
MacDonald, Ronald Francis *diversified financial services company executive*
Madden, Michael Daniel *finance company executive*
Maggiotto, Rocco J. *financial company executive*
Maheras, Thomas G. *finance company executive*
Malernee, James Kent, Jr., *finance and securities consultant*
Mandelbaum, Harold Neil *accountant*
Mankin, Robert Stephen *financial executive*
Margolis, Jeffrey Robert *financial services executive*
Marlas, James Constantine *holding company executive*
Mason, Eli *accountant*
Masterson, Ellen Hornberger *accountant*
Maurer, Jeffrey Stuart *finance executive*
Mayforth, Lee J. *finance company executive, consultant*
McCall, H. Carl *finacial services executive, former state comptroller*
McCutchen, William Walter, Jr., *management educator*
McDade, Herbert H., III, *finance company executive*
McDaniel, Raymond W., Jr., *financial information company executive*
McDonald, Thomas Paul *controller*
McGovern, Donald A. *diversified financial services company executive*
McGraw, Harold Whittlesey, III, (Terry McGraw) *information company executive*
Meehan, Sandra Gotham *corporate financial executive, consultant*
Merin, Mitchell M *corporate financial executive*
Meyer, Fred Josef *financial executive*
Miller, John R. *accountant*
Mockler, Robert Joseph *management educator*
Monrad, Elizabeth A. *corporate financial executive*
Morano, Kevin R. *mining company executive*
Moshkin, Nickolay V. *financial consultant, litigation consultant*
Mosse, Peter John Charles *financial services executive*
Moyles, Philip Vincent, Jr., *financial services company executive*
Nachum, Lilach *international business educator*
Nally, Dennis Mathew *accountant, finance company executive*
Nickell, Frank (Nick) T. *diversified financial services company executive*
Nicoll, Edward J. *internet financial company executive*
Nides, Thomas Richard *diversified financial services company executive*
Norman, Stephen Peckham *financial services company executive*
O'Kelly, Eugene D. *accounting company executive*
Oler, Wesley M., IV, *portfolio manager*
Openshaw, Jennifer *finance company executive*
Osmont, Ghyslain Louis *accountant*
Paddock, Anthony Conaway *financial consultant*
Papps, Bruce William *financial analyst, investment company executive*
Perry, Richard C. *financier*
Phillips, J. Douglas *financial company executive*
Powlen, David Michael *finance company executive, director*
Presby, J. Thomas *financial advisor, director, arbitrator*
Prestia, Michael Anthony *accounting executive*
Purcell, Philip James *financial services company executive*
Purdum, Dennis R. *financial company executive*
Quigley, James H. *finance company executive*
Rafaloff, Gary B. *financial company executive*
Raskin, Joshua R. *financial analyst, researcher*
Rebell, Arthur L. *corporate financial executive*
Reinganum, Marc Richard *finance educator*
Reiss, Dale Anne *accounting executive, investment company executive*
Ritch, Kathleen *diversified company executive*
Roberts, John J. *accounting firm executive*
Robinson, Barry E. *financial company executive*
Robinson, James D., III, *finance company executive, investor*
Roethenmund, Otto Emil *financial and banking executive*
Rosen, Scott Alan *corporate financial executive, financial analyst*
Rosenberg, Alan David *accountant*
Rosenberg, Michael Joseph *financial executive*
Rosenthal, Charles Michael *financial executive*
Rowe, David Lee *financial advisor*
Ruda, Howard *lawyer, finance company executive*
Rutherfurd, John *financial information company executive*
Salom, Roberto *financial executive*
Salow, Glen *diversified financial services company executive*
Salzman, Robert Jay *accountant*
Scarcella, Vincent A. *finance company executive*
Schaefer, John H. *finance company executive, securities company executive*
Schick, Thomas *diversified financial services company executive*
Schlein, Michael Edward *diversified financial services company executive*
Schlosstein, Ralph L. *diversified financial services company executive*
Schoenhut, Frederick W. *stock exchange executive*
Schubert, Scott E. *corporate financial executive*
Schwartz, Bart *diversified financial services company executive*
Schwartz, Robert *finance educator*
Scott, Robert *financial services company executive*
Segal, Martin Eli *retired actuarial and consulting company executive*
Seltzer, Jeffrey Lloyd *diversified financial services company executive*
Shafir, Robert S. *finance company executive*
Shallcross, Deanne J. *finance company executive*
Shapoff, Stephen H. *financial executive*
Sharp, J(ames) Franklin *finance educator, portfolio manager*
Shaw, Alan Roger *financial executive, educator*
Shenkman, Mark Ronald *investment and finance executive*
Siegel, Arthur Herbert *finance company executive*
Siguler, George William *financial services executive*
Simmons, John Derek *retired financial consultant*
Simmons, Robert J. *treasurer*
Simons, Eric Ward *financial executive*
Skwiersky, Paul *accountant*
Slazberg, Barry *accounting firm executive*
Slotkin, Todd *holding company executive*
Sonders, Elizabeth Ann *diversified financial services company executive*
Soros, George *fund management executive*
Starbuck, William Haynes *business management educator*
Steel, Robert K. *finance company executive*
Sutton, Mark B. *diversified financial services company executive*
Tavel, Mark Kivey *money management company executive, economist*
Thomson, Todd Stuart *corporate finance executive*
Tillman, Vickie A. *diversified financial services company executive*
Tisch, James Solomon *diversified holding company executive*
Tisch, Preston Robert *finance and sports executive*
Toben, Doreen A. *corporate financial executive*
Toohey, Edward Joseph *financial services company executive, retired*
Tortora, Leslie C. *finance company executive*
Toy, Stephen J. *corporate financial executive*
Trapp, Peter Jarl Rudolf *portfolio manager, farmer*
Treitel, David Henry *financial consultant*
Trinkaus, John William *management educator*
Turley, James S. *corporate financial executive*
Vanderbeek, Jeffrey *diversified financial services company executive*
Volk, Norman Hans *financial executive*
Volk, Stephen Richard *diversified financial services company executive, investment banker, lawyer*
Warren, David P. *stock exchange executive*
Wax, David Louis *corporate financial executive*
Wayne, Andrew Mark *diversified financial services company executive*
Weiner, Ronald Gary *accounting firm executive*
Weingrow, Howard L. *financial executive, investor*
Whiting, Anthony *executive search consultant*
Whitman, Martin J. *portfolio manager*
Wiesenthal, Robert S. *corporate financial executive*
Williams, Simon *diversified financial services company executive*
Wilson, Pamela K. *corporate financial executive*
Wong, Y. S. *diversified financial services company executive*
Wyss, David Alen *financial service executive*
Yastine, Barbara A. *diversified financial services company executive*
Zand, Dale Ezra *business management educator*

Niagara Falls
Askins, Arthur James *accountant, finance management and auditing executive*

Northport
Krahel, Thomas Stephen *account executive*

Old Westbury
Barbera, Anthony Thomas *accountant, educator*

Orchard Park
Oliver, Dominick Michael *business educator*

Pearl River
Bryant, Karen Worstell *financial advisor, investment company executive*

Pittsford
Herge, Henry Curtis, Jr., *consulting firm executive*

Plainview
Feller, Benjamin E. *actuary*

Plattsburgh
Dossin, Ernest Joseph, III, *credit consulting company executive*

Pomona
Landau, Lauri Beth *accountant, tax consultant*

Port Washington
Phelan, Arthur Joseph *financial executive*

Potsdam
Bommer, Michael Roger William *finance educator*

Pound Ridge
Darcy, Keith Thomas *finance company executive, educator*
Sacco, John Michael *accountant*
Webb, Richard Gilbert *financial executive, antique selling service executive*

Purchase
Noonan, Frank Russell *business executive*
Xiao, Shuyi *finance company executive*

Queens Village
Cook, Michael Anthony *financial services executive*

Queensbury
Bitner, William Lawrence, III, *retired banker, educator*

Rego Park
Thomas, James Edward *accountant*

Rochester
Cameros, Alan Lee *financial services executive*
Ford, Marcia Marie *financial consultant*
Garg, Devendra *financial executive*
Golisano, B. Thomas *finance company director, human resources director*
Marriott, Marcia Ann *business and economics educator, health facility administrator*
Schwert, G(eorge) William, III, *finance educator*
Watts, Ross Leslie *accounting educator, consultant*

Rye
Gabelli, Mario J. *diversified financial services company executive*
Mahoney, Thomas Henry, IV, *finance executive*

Saratoga Springs
Auriemmo, Frank Joseph, Jr., *financial holding company executive*
Dickinson, Richard Henry *accountant*

Scarsdale
Gollin, Stuart Allen *accountant*
Paige, Susanne Lynn *financial consultant*

Sleepy Hollow
Ferguson, Douglas Edward *finance company executive*

Southampton
Needham, James Joseph *retired financial services executive, consultant*

Spencertown
Hawkins, Robert Garvin *management educator*

Staten Island
Clark, Sylvia Dolores *business educator*
Gelbein, Jay Joel *accountant*

Sunnyside
Privo, Alexander *finance educator, department chairman*

Syracuse
Marcoccia, Louis Gary *accountant, university administrator*
Vitharana, Padmal M. *management educator*

Tarrytown
Ferrari, Robert Joseph *business educator, former banker*
Hyman, Leonard Stephen *financial consultant, economist, writer*

Troy
Murtagh, James Patrick *finance educator, consultant*

Valhalla
Christesen, John Denis *business educator*

Vestal
Piaker, Philip Martin *accountant, educator*

Wappingers Falls
Hogan, Edward Robert *financial services executive*
Kells, Albert John *financial consultant*

Water Mill
Kreimer, Michael Walter *financial planner, investment company executive*

Waterloo
Schreck, Richard Thomas *accountant*

Webster
McCormack, Stanley Eugene *financial consultant*
Nicholson, Douglas Robert *accountant*
Southard, Paul Raymond *financial executive*

Westbury
Lorber, Howard Mark *investments executive*

White Plains
Beldock, Donald Travis *corporate financial executive*
Doyle, John McCormick *actuary, pension plan consultant*
Isaak, Robert Allen *international management and political economy educator, writer*
Kroner, Arnold Friedrich *financial consultant, economist*
Prabhu, Vasant *corporate financial executive*
Zuckerman, Marc Abraham *accountant, educator*

Greencastle
Horst, Carolyn Diane *accountant*

Greensburg
Foreman, John Daniel *financial executive*

Haverford
Merrill, Arthur Alexander *financial analyst*

Havertown
Brinker, Thomas Michael *finance executive*

Horsham
Johnson, G. Carol *financial services executive*

Jamison
O'Hanlon, Michael A. *finance company executive*

Kennett Square
Bell, Philip Wilkes *accounting and economics educator*

King Of Prussia
Anderson, Jerry Allen *financial analyst*
Filton, Steve G. *corporate financial executive*

Kutztown
Ogden, James Russell *marketing educator, consultant, lecturer, writer*

Lafayette Hill
King, Leon *financial services executive*

Lancaster
Freeman, Clarence Calvin *financial executive*

Macungie
Moore, Joyce Kristina *financial planner, director*

Malvern
Hendrix, Stephen C. *financial executive*

Media
Hemphill, James S. *investment management executive, financial advisor*

Nazareth
Rayner, Robert Martin *financial executive*

Newtown
Fiore, James Louis, Jr., *accountant, educator*
Golub, Harvey *financial services company executive*
Grubbs, Donald Shaw, Jr., *retired actuary*

Newtown Square
Graf, Arnold Harold *employee benefits executive, financial planner*

Parkesburg
Zevtchin, J. Mark *financial executive, consultant*

Philadelphia
Alexander, Elmore Rosebur, III, *business educator, dean*
Alexander, William Herbert *business educator, former construction executive*
Anderson, Rolph Ely *finance educator*
Andrisani, Paul J. *business educator, management consultant*
Babbel, David Frederick *finance and insurance educator*
Blume, Marshall Edward *finance educator*
Booth, Anna Belle *accountant*
DiTrolio, Joseph *controller*
Fisher, Marshall Lee *operations management educator*
Friedman, Sidney A. *financial services executive*
Gerrity, Thomas P. *management educator*
Glazier, Jason S. *finance company executive*
Hindelang, Thomas Joseph *finance educator, dean*
Kandel, Donald Harry *financial analyst*
Keim, Donald Bruce *finance educator*
Kim, Seung-Lae *management science educator, researcher*
Kimberly, John Robert *management educator, consultant*
Knott, Anne Marie *finance educator*
Ksansnak, James Edward *service management company executive*
Leimkuhler, Gerard Joseph *crisis management and finance company executive*
Lodish, Leonard Melvin *marketing educator, entrepreneur*
Logue-Kinder, Joan *consultant*
Malhotra, Davinder Kumar *finance educator, consultant, researcher*
Mazzarella, James Kevin *business administration educator*
Micko, Alexander S. *financial executive*
Montemara, William J. *accountant*
Moore, Faye L. Mitchell *executive*
Rose, Robert Lawrence *financial services company executive*
Rosenbloom, Bert *marketing educator, consultant, writer*
Rosenthal, Edward Charles *management science educator*
Rowan, Richard Lamar *business management educator*
Sanyour, Michael Louis, Jr., *diversified financial services company executive*
Saul, Ralph Southey *financial service executive*
Selles, Robert Hendrikus *retired actuary*
Shils, Edward B. *finance educator, lawyer, arbitrator, mediator*
Siegel, Jeremy James *finance educator, consultant*
Webber, Ross Arkell *management educator*
Ziegler, Donald Robert *accountant*
Zucker, William *retired business educator*

Pittsburgh
Bernt, Benno Anthony *business executive, entrepreneur and investor*
Bly, James Charles, Jr., *financial services executive*
Bryson, Michael A *corporate financial executive*
Czuszak, Janis Marie *former credit company official, researcher*
Demchak, William S. *corporate financial executive*
Franklin, Kenneth Ronald *franchise company executive, consultant*
Giliberti, Michael Richard *financial planner*
Guna, Edward Francis *financial executive*

Haggerty, Gretchen R. *accounting and finance executive*
Haley, Roy W. *finance company executive*
Ijiri, Yuji *accounting and economics educator*
Kahn, Herman L. (Bud Kahn) *financial advisor*
King, William Richard *business educator, consultant*
Kriebel, Charles Hosey *management sciences educator*
Rohr, James Edward *diversified financial services company executive*
Saykiewicz-Sajkiewicz, Jan Napoleon *marketing educator*
Thorne, John Reinecke *business educator, venture capitalist*
Wagner, Lawrence M. *diversified financial services company executive*

Richboro
Higginbotham, Kenneth James *financial services executive*

Saint Davids
Bertsch, Frederick Charles, III, *business executive*

Scranton
Eckersley, Richard Laurence *accountant*

Sewickley
Jehle, Michael Edward *financial executive*

Slippery Rock
Mukherjee, Pracheta *management educator, researcher, consultant*

Tarentum
McGuire, Timothy William *economics and management educator, dean*

University Park
De Jong, Gordon Frederick *finance educator, consultant*
Enis, Charles Richard *accountant, educator*
Junker, Edward P., III, *retired diversified financial services company executive*
Kilduff, Martin James *finance educator*
McKeown, James Charles *accounting educator, consultant*
Muscarella, Christopher James *finance educator*

Valley Forge
Phelizon, Jean Francois *business executive*

Volant
Moore, Janet Marie *accountant, state official*

West Chester
Blasiotti, Robert Vincent *accountant, consultant*

Wynnewood
Robinson, Robert L. *former financial service company executive, lawyer*

Wyomissing
Gebbia, Robert James *tax executive*

Yardley
Gilmour, D(avid) James *financial analyst, systems analyst*

York
Day, Ronald Richard *retired financial executive*
Kornblatt, David *corporate financial executive*

RHODE ISLAND

Kingston
Mazze, Edward Mark *marketing educator, consultant*

Lincoln
Carter, Wilfred Wilson *financial executive, controller*

Pawtucket
Davison, Charles Hamilton *financial executive*
Ready, Christopher James *accountant*

Providence
Harris, Richard John *diversified holding company executive*
McNeil, Paul Joseph, Jr., *employment security interviewer*

Warwick
Morgan, Patricia *financial consultant, former Republican party chairman*

SOUTH CAROLINA

Columbia
Edwards, James Benjamin *accountant, educator*
Hollis, Charles Eugene, Jr., *finance company executive*
Monahan, Thomas Paul *accountant*
Outin, Mary Louise *business, multi-cultural history and geneology educator*
Pritchett, Samuel Travis *finance and insurance educator, researcher, consultant*
Wheeler, Hoyt Noland *finance educator*

Conway
Nale, Robert D. *finance educator*

Darlington
Bischoff, Frederick Christopher, III, *retired accountant*

Georgetown
Bowen, William Augustus *financial consultant*
McGrath, James Charles, III, *financial services company executive, lawyer, consultant*

Graniteville
Learnard, James Michael *middle school educator, former finance company executive, special education educator*

Greenville
Aston, James A. *financial services company executive*
Porter, Charles Michael (Mike Porter) *diversified financial services company executive*
Rogers, Jon Martin *financial consultant, finance company executive*

Rock Hill
Cornick, Michael F(rederick) *accounting educator*

Spartanburg
Pate, John Gillis, Jr., *financial consultant, accounting educator*

Summerville
Sexton, Donald Lee *retired business administration educator*

Sumter
Van Bulck, Hendrikus Eugenius *accountant*

West Columbia
Byars, Merlene Hutto *accountant, visual artist, writer*
Moore, Shirley Throckmorton (Mrs. Elmer Lee Moore) *accountant*

Williamston
Alewine, James William *financial executive*

SOUTH DAKOTA

Aberdeen
Hollingsworth, John Arthur *business educator*

TENNESSEE

Alamo
Finch, Evelyn Vorise *financial planner*

Brentwood
McClary, Jim Marston *accounting executive, consultant*

Brighton
Iles, Roger Dean *business educator*

Chattanooga
Dawson, Gail Alesia *management educator*
Russe, Conrad Thomas Campbell *accountant*

Crossville
Lansford, Edwin Gaines *accountant*

Franklin
Sloan, W(ilson) Keith *actuary*

Jackson
Holt, Michael Kenneth *management and finance educator, consultant, city councilman*
Roth, Georgia Middlebrooks *accounting educator*

Johnson City
Morgan, Robert George *accounting educator, researcher*

Martin
Lemons, Mary A. *finance educator*

Mc Kenzie
Blasick, James David *finance educator*

Memphis
Brandon, Elvis Denby, Jr., *financial planner*
Brandon, Elvis Denby, III, *financial planner*
Brandon, Raymond Wilson *financial planner, securities principal*
Forell, David Charles *financial executive*
Haslam, Edward T. *finance company executive*
Horn, D. Ralph *corporate financial executive*
Isaacson, Bond R. *finance company executive*
Kiphart, Richard P. *finance company executive*
Labry, Edward A., III, *finance company executive*
Palmer, Dan M. *finance company executive*
Umholtz, Clyde Allan *financial analyst*

Munford
Harrington, Herbert H. *accountant*

Murfreesboro
Lee, John Thomas *finance educator, financial planner*

Nashville
Bracken, Richard M. *corporate financial executive*
Brophy, Jeremiah Joseph *former financial company official, former army officer*
Christie, William Gary *finance educator, dean*
Freudenthal, Ernest Guenter *technology and business educator*
Gore, Steven Lowell *business development manager*
Hazen, Samuel N *corporate financial executive*
Richmond, Samuel Bernard *management educator*
Rutherford, William B. *corporate financial executive*
Shallcross, Richard *corporate financial executive*
Ullestad, Merwin Allan *tax services executive*
Van, George Paul *international money management consultant*
Weingartner, H(ans) Martin *finance educator*

Pikeville
Wright, Donald Gene *accountant*

Soddy Daisy
Randall, Kay Temple *accountant, retired real estate agent*

TEXAS

Addison
Rinehart, Neil *financial consultant*

Aledo
Reilly, Michael Atlee *financial company executive, venture capital investor*

Argyle
Pettit, John Douglas, Jr., *management educator*

Arlington
Swanson, Peggy Eubanks *finance educator*

Austin
Alpert, Mark Ira *marketing educator*
Anderson, Urton Liggett *accounting educator*
Cundiff, Edward William *marketing educator*
Doenges, Rudolph Conrad *finance educator*
Granof, Michael H. *accounting educator*
Graydon, Frank Drake *retired accounting educator, university administrator*
Haunschild, Pamela Rausch *finance educator*
Kimberlin, Sam Owen, Jr., *financial institutions consultant*
Larson, Kermit Dean *accounting educator*
Mitte, Roy F. *finance company executive*
Nixon, Drew *accountant, state legislator*
Parrino, Robert *finance educator*
Peterson, Robert Allen *marketing educator*
Shifrin, Kenneth Steven *financial service executive*
Strayhorn, Carole Keeton *comptroller*
Wolf, Harold Arthur *finance educator*

Brenham
Rothermel, James Douglas *retired finance educator*

Brownwood
Bell, Mary E. Beniteau *accountant*

Burton
Knauss, Robert Lynn *international business educator, corporate executive*

Cedar Hill
Ebozue, Benson Obian *financial analyst*
Shower, Robert Wesley *financial executive*

College Station
Wichern, Dean William *business educator*

Commerce
Avard, Stephen Lewis *finance educator*
Carraher, Shawn Michael *management educator*

Cypress
Hlozek, Carole Diane Quast *finance company executive*

Dallas
Bayne, James Elwood *investor and financial consultant*
Briesch, Richard Allen *finance educator*
Coldwell, Philip Edward *financial consultant*
Grant, Joseph Moorman *finance executive*
Guthrie, M. Philip *corporate financial executive*
Gyemant, Robert Ernest *diversified financial services company executive, merchant*
Hay, Jess Thomas *retired finance company executive*
Howland, Grafton Dulany *financial counselor*
Jimenez, Mercy *corporate financial executive*
Jobe, Larry Alton *financial company executive*
Kelley, Terry *financial executive*
Lam, Chun Hung *finance educator, consultant*
McElvain, David Plowman *retired manufacturing company financial executive*
McElyea, Jacquelyn Suzanne *accountant, real estate consultant*
Morgan, Gregory Paul *financial planner*
Peiser, John George *accountant, consultant*
Rossel, Cary *corporate financial executive*
Shimer, Daniel Lewis *treasurer*
Shultz, Brian Michael *diversified financial services company executive*
Skinner, James E. *corporate financial executive*
Smiles, Ronald *management educator*
Solender, Robert Lawrence *real estate executive, retired newspaper executive*
Tannebaum, Samuel Hugo *accountant*
Ulrich, Richard William *finance executive*
Walker, Gordon Beverley Moore, Jr., *business educator*

Denton
Wallace, William Hall *economic and financial consultant*

Diboll
Jastrow, Kenneth M. *financial executive*

Eagle Pass
May, Mitchell Johnson *controller*

Edinburg
Kaynak, Hale *finance educator, researcher*

El Paso
Beard, Jane Alida *retired accountant*
Kelley, Sylvia Johnson *financial services firm executive*

Fort Worth
Bass, Robert Muse *financier*
Bonzelaar, Gregory Scott *accountant*
Clark, Emory Eugene *financial planning executive*
Dominiak, Geraldine Florence *accounting educator, retired*
Hendricks, Scott *corporate budget specialist*
Karnes, Keith Dale *portfolio manager*
Rainwater, Richard *financial consultant, investor*

Frisco
Bloskas, John D. *retired finance company executive*

Garland
Lord, Jacqueline Ward *accountant, photographer, artist*
McGill, Maurice Leon *financial executive*

Georgetown
Sellers, Fred Evans *accounting educator*

Hondo
Bryant, Jannie *corporate financial executive*

Houston
Arnold, Daniel Calmes *lawyer, former finance company executive*
Ayadi, Olusegun Felix *finance educator*

Barnett, Donald Blake *corporate financial executive*
Bowen, Raymond M., Jr., *corporate financial executive*
Clark, Geoffrey *accountant*
D'Agostino, James Samuel, Jr., *financial executive*
Duganier, Barbara J. *corporate financial executive*
Getz, Lowell Vernon *financial advisor*
Griffith, Martha *controller*
Harris, Venita Van Caspel *retired financial planner*
Horvitz, Paul Michael *finance educator*
Janssens, Joe Lee *controller, consultant*
Jones, Eli, III, *marketing/sales educator*
Larkin, William Vincent, Jr., *corporate financial executive*
McEachern, Stephen Matthew *accountant*
Nolen, Norman W. *financial executive*
Olstead, Christopher Eric *financial consultant, entertainment executive*
Plank, Raymond *investment corporation executive*
Rawson, Jim Charles *business executive*
Salam, Debera Jean *accounting company executive*
Scott, D. Dwight *corporate financial executive*
Sims, Rebecca Gibbs *accountant, certified fraud examiner, journalist, editor*
Van Dusen, Glenn T. *business executive*
Watkins, Lisa M. *financial analyst*
Williams, James Lee *financial industries executive*
Wilson, Gerald Everette *financial executive*
Zeff, Stephen Addam *accounting educator*

Irving
Forson, Norman Ray *controller*
Sensabaugh, Mary Elizabeth *financial consultant*

Keene
Stembridge, Allen Frederick *management educator*

Laredo
Nixon, Dennis E. *financial company executive*

Lubbock
Sears, Robert Stephen *finance educator, university dean*

Mcallen
Roney, Glen E. *finance company executive*

Midland
Tom, James Robert *accountant*

Navasota
Smith, Jo Ann Costa *retired comptroller*

New Braunfels
Griffin-Thompson, Melanie *accounting firm executive*

Pasadena
Scott, William Floyd *accountant*

Plano
Bode, Richard Albert *retired financial executive*
Swan, Robert H. *corporate financial executive*

Richardson
Burke, Thomas William *executive benefits consulting company official*
Liu, Shelby *financial advisor, chemist*
Merville, Lawrence Joseph *finance educator*

Rosharon
Jenkins, Judith Alexander *bank consultant*

Round Rock
Puri, Rajendra Kumar *business and tax specialist, consultant*

San Antonio
Edelman, Asher Barry *financier*
Evans, Richard W. *finance company executive*
Fonseca, Joseph Mojica, Jr., *financial analyst, educator*
Herres, Robert Tralles *financial services executive*
Jensen White, Teresa *financial planner*
Jones, James Richard *business administration educator*
Lien, Da-Hsiang Donald *finance educator*
Marvin, Catherine A. *financial consultant*
Melson, Marvin E. *finance company executive*
Stevens, Dennis Max *audit director*

San Marcos
Palmer, Roger Raymond *accounting educator*
Taylor, Ruth Arleen Lesher *marketing educator*

Stephenville
Collier, Boyd Dean *finance educator, management consultant*

Sugar Land
Keefe, Carolyn Joan *tax accountant*

Sweetwater
Woodrow, Natile Latreece *accountant, educator*

Waco
Rose, John Thomas *finance educator, department chairman*

Wimberley
Skaggs, Wayne Gerard *financial services company executive, retired*

UTAH

Bountiful
Brooke, Edna Mae *retired business educator*

Provo
DeTienne, Kristen Bell *finance educator*
Hunt, H(arold) Keith *business management educator, marketing consultant*

Salt Lake City
Johnson, Auston Gilbert, III, *auditor*
Nelson, Roger Hugh *management educator, corporate consultant, business executive*
Nicolatus, Stephen Jon *financial consultant*
Snell, Ned Colwell *financial planner*

VERMONT

Quechee
Vitty, Roderic Bemis *retired financial planner, publishing executive*

Rutland
Haley, John Charles *financial executive*

Woodstock
Churchill, James Garton *retired international finance consultant*

VIRGINIA

Abingdon
Graham, Howard Lee, Sr., *financial services company executive*

Alexandria
Berkowitz, Martin A. *diversified financial services company executive*
Collins, William L., III, *financial executive*
Henderson, Paul Bargas, Jr., *economic development consultant*
Inman, Stephen Eugene *finance officer*
Smith, Robert Luther *management educator*

Annandale
Connair, Stephen Michael *financial analyst*
Jones, David Charles *international financial and management consultant*

Arlington
Caplan, Mitchell H. *diversified financial services company executive*
Davis, Maynard Kirk *accountant*
Gelbard, Arlen W. *diversified financial services company executive*
Lewis, Hunter *investment advisor, publisher*
Page, Harry Robert *business administration educator*
Petersen, John Laurens *future research and strategic planner*

Blacksburg
Moore, Laurence John *business educator*
Patterson, Douglas MacLennan *finance educator*
Uysal, Muzaffer Shamil *management educator*

Broad Run
Kube, Harold Deming *retired financial executive*

Chantilly
Carlson, Robert Charles *financial advisor, writer*
Young, M. Dendy *finance company executive*

Charlottesville
Davis, Edward Wilson *business administration educator*
Ellett, John Spears, II, *retired taxation educator, accountant, lawyer*
Laseter, Timothy Marks *finance educator*
Minehart, Jean Besse *tax accountant*
Scott, Charlotte H. *business educator*
Shenkir, William Gary *business educator*
Sihler, William Wooding *finance educator*
Thompson, David William *business educator*

Chesterfield
Garnett, Douglas Acree *financial analyst, researcher*

Crozet
Rosenblum, John William *finance educator*

Fairfax
Bowden, Howard Kent *accountant*
Burnett, Michael Bruce *benefits compensation analyst*
Fulton, Diann Marie *financial consultant*
Lee, Hun *finance educator, consultant*
Meamber, Laurie Ann *marketing educator*

Falls Church
Bruck, Bill *business executive*
Morris, Nigel W. *financial executive*
Purvis, Ronald Scott *financial counselor, real estate professional*
Rosenberg, Theodore Roy *financial executive*

Keswick
Pochick, Francis Edward *financial consultant*

Mc Lean
Blazer, Randolph C. *diversified financial services company executive*
Drew, K. *financial advisor, management consultant*
Edgar, Janelle Diane Ward *financial services executive*
Fairbank, Richard D. *diversified financial services company executive*
Falcone, Robert S. *diversified financial services company executive*
Kautt, Glenn Gregory *financial planner, consultant*
Pho, Long Ambrose Ba *business educator, consultant*
Saville, Paul C. *financial executive*
Syron, Richard Francis *finance company executive, economist*

Newport News
Le Mons, Kathleen Ann *securities company executive, branch manager, investment officer, portfolio manager*

Norfolk
Bullington, James Richard *business educator, former ambassador*
McKee, Timothy Carlton *taxation educator*
Shumadine, Anne Ballard *financial advisor, lawyer*

Palmyra
Sahr, Morris Gallup *financial planner*

Quantico
Evans, Gaye Lois *comptroller*

Reston
Fox, Edward A. *finance company executive*
Lister, Harry Joseph *finance company executive*
Lord, Albert L. *diversified financial services company executive*
Polemitou, Olga Andrea *accountant*

Richmond
Ashworth, D. Neil *business educator*
Austin, John D. *corporate financial executive*
Capps, Thos E. *diversified financial services company executive*
Harris, Ruth Hortense Coles *retired accounting educator*
King, Robert Leroy *business administration educator*
Mann, Stephen Ashby *financial consultant*
Narula, Subhash Chander *management science and statistics educator*
Neal, Stu M. *finance educator, writer*
Palmer, Robert J. *corporate financial executive*
Scott, Sidney Buford *financial services company executive*
Wagner, Jody M. *treasurer*

Sterling
Hough, Lawrence A. *former financial organization executive*

Upperville
Smart, Stephen Bruce, Jr., *business and government executive*

Vienna
Townsend, Irene Fogleman *accountant, tax specialist*
Urbanas, Alban William *estate planner*

Virginia Beach
Martin, William Raymond *retired financial manager*

Waterford
Harper, James Weldon, III, *finance consultant*

Williamsburg
Gottfried, Mark Ellis *accountant, consultant*
Holstein, William Kurt *business administration educator*
Kottas, John Frederick *business administration educator*
McLennan, Barbara Nancy *international tax specialist*
Messmer, Donald Joseph *business management educator, marketing consultant*
Montgomery, Joseph William *finance company executive*
O'Connell, William Edward, Jr., *finance educator*

Woodbridge
Denison, Cynthia Lee *accountant, tax specialist*
Dillaber, Philip Arthur *budget and resource analyst, consultant*

WASHINGTON

Bellevue
Graham, John Robert, Jr., *financial executive*

Bellingham
Globerman, Steven *finance educator*
Ross, Steven Charles *business administration educator, consultant*

Federal Way
Taggart, Richard J. *corporate financial executive*

Gig Harbor
Cuzzetto, Charles Edward *accountant, financial analyst, educator*

Kirkland
Etcheson, Warren Wade *business administration educator*

Medical Lake
Grub, Phillip Donald *business educator*

Mount Vernon
Gaston, Margaret Anne *retired business educator*

Mukilteo
Brown, Bruce Baden *accountant*

Olympia
Myers, Sharon Diane *auditor*

Seattle
Awasthi, Vidya Nidhi *accounting educator*
Baker, Roland Jerald *finance educator*
Bunting, Robert Louis *accounting firm executive, management consultant*
Casey, Thomas W. *finance company executive*
Chapman, Craig J. *finance company executive*
Collett, Robert Lee *financial company executive*
Covey, Joy D. *finance and administration executive*
David, Daryl D. *finance company executive*
Dively, Dwight Douglas *finance director*
Fry, John Craig, Jr., *portfolio manager*
Gaskill, Herbert Leo *accountant, engineer*
Gorans, Gerald Elmer *retired accountant*
Gross, Jeremy V. (Jerry Gross) *finance company executive*
Klein, Jonathan D. *finance company executive*
MacLachlan, Douglas Lee *marketing educator*
Pitts, Barbara Towle *accountant, painter*
Roley, V. Vance *finance educator, academic administrator*
Saxberg, Borje Osvald *management educator*
Szkutak, Tom *corporate financial executive*
Tall, Craig E. *finance company executive*

Shelton
McNabb, David E. *business educator, writer*

Shoreline
Hanson, Kermit Osmond *business administration educator, university dean emeritus*

Spokane
Burton, Robert Lyle *accounting firm executive*
Cameron, Alex Brian *accounting educator*
Hoyt, Bradley James *financial advisor*

Vancouver
Regan, Elizabeth Anne *bail bond agent*
Tripp, Thomas Murray *finance educator*

WEST VIRGINIA

Elkins
Payne, Gloria Marquette *business educator*

Huntington
Wenzel, Loren Alvin *accounting educator*

Kenova
Adkins, Garry Prentice *retired accountant*

Lewisburg
Campbell, Thomas Wood *accountant*

Morgantown
Beu, Danielle *management educator*
Dawley, David Daniel *finance educator*

Wheeling
Gracey, Robert William *financial advisor, minister*

WISCONSIN

Appleton
Stellmacher, Jon Michael *corporate financial executive*

Eau Claire
Weil, D(onald) Wallace *business administration educator*

Kenosha
Infusino, Achille Francis *financial and administrative support executive*
Manion, Michael T. *finance educator*

Madison
Aldag, Ramon John *management and organization educator*
Durcan, Deborah Ann *finance company executive*
Eisler, Millard Marcus *financial executive*
Hickman, James Charles *finance educator, dean*
Nevin, John Robert *business educator, consultant*
Prieve, E. Arthur *arts administration educator*

Mequon
Berry, William Martin *financial consultant*

Middleton
Foss, Karl Robert *auditor*

Milwaukee
Kendall, Leon Thomas *finance and real estate educator, retired insurance company executive*
Klappa, Gale E. *corporate financial executive*
Redlin, Bruce Michael *financial consultant*
Schnoll, Howard Manuel *financial consultant, investment company executive*
Simoneau, Daniel Robert *accountant, watercolorist, educator, application developer*
Stewart, Alex *finance educator*
Zore, Edward John *financial services executive*

Oconomowoc
Kneiser, Richard John *accountant*

Superior
Robek, Mary Frances *business education educator*

Waupun
Wendt, Thomas *finance executive*

West Bend
VanBrunt-Kramer, Karen *business administration educator*

Whitewater
Parboteeah, Kaviraj Praveen *finance educator*

WYOMING

Cody
Riley, Victor J., Jr., *financial services company executive*

Laramie
Spiegelberg, Emma Jo *business education educator, academic administrator*

Sheridan
Ryan, Michael Louis *controller*

Wheatland
Whitney, Ralph Royal, Jr., *financial executive*
Carney, Michael T. *financial services executive*

TERRITORIES OF THE UNITED STATES

PUERTO RICO

Hato Rey
Vilches-O'Bourke, Octavio Augusto *accounting company executive*

San Juan
Rosso de Irizarry, Carmen (Tutty Rosso de Irizarry) *finance executive*

MILITARY ADDRESSES OF THE UNITED STATES

PACIFIC

Fpo
Tarpeh-Doe, Linda Diane *controller*

CANADA

BRITISH COLUMBIA

Burnaby
Tung, Rosalie Lam *business educator, consultant*

Salt Spring Island
Kandler, Joseph Rudolph *financial executive*

Vancouver
Mattessich, Richard Victor (Alvarus) *business administration researcher*

MANITOBA

Winnipeg
McCallum, John Stuart *finance educator, columnist*

NEW BRUNSWICK

Saint Andrews
Anderson, John Murray *operations executive, former university president*

ONTARIO

Ancaster
Smith, Newman Donald *retired financial executive*

Arva
Weldon, David Black *company director*

London
Osbaldeston, Gordon Francis *business educator, former government official*

Toronto
Cockwell, Jack Lynn *business executive*
Cook-Bennett, Gail *pension fund administrator*
Cunningham, Gordon Ross *financial executive*
Hirst, Peter Christopher *consulting actuary*
Mann, George Stanley *real estate and financial services corporation executive*
Mercier, Eileen Ann *corporate financial executive*
Morneau, William *pension and benefits company executive*
Oliphant, Randall *financial executive*
Pollock, Samuel *diversified financial services company executive*
Poprawa, Andrew *financial services executive, accountant*
Price, Timothy R. *accountant*
Schwartz, Gerald Wilfred *financial executive*
Silk, Frederick C.Z. *financial consultant*
Sloan, David Edward *retired finance company executive*
Steinberg, Gregg Martin *financial and management consultant, investment banker*
Stymiest, Barbara *stock exchange executive*
Weston, W. Galen, Sr., *diversified holdings executive*

Willowdale
Sze, Michael Ming-Chih *actuary, consultant*

QUEBEC

Montreal
Crowston, Wallace Bruce Stewart *management educator*
Daly, Gerald *accountant*
Desmarais, Paul *holding company executive*
Gratton, Robert *diversified financial services company executive*
Joly, Clément *accountant*
Laurin, Pierre *finance company executive*
Nadeau, Bertin Felix *diversified financial services company executive*
Picard, Laurent A(ugustin) *retired management educator, administrator, consultant*
Speirs, Derek James *diversified corporation financial executive*
Thompson, John Douglas *financier*

Verdun
Lessard, Michel M. *finance company executive*

SASKATCHEWAN

Saskatoon
Deng, Shengliang *marketing educator*
Irvine, Vernon Bruce *accounting educator, administrator*

AUSTRALIA

Melbourne
Batrouney, Clive M. *corporate financial executive*

THE BAHAMAS

Nassau
Crone, John Thomas, IV, *portfolio manager, financial analyst*

BRAZIL

Sao Paulo
Kim, Kwang Wook *corporate financial executive*

CYPRUS

Nicosia
Aloneftis, Andreas *financial and investment executive*

ENGLAND

Coventry
Thomas, Howard *business educator*

London
Akin, Steven Paul *financial company executive*
Ellis, Claud M. Buddy *diversified financial services company executive*
Eustace, Dudley Graham *diversified financial services company executive*
Furse, Clara *stock exchange executive*
Sarkis, Ziad Joseph *private equity executive*
Vanniasingham, Samuel Kanagasabapathy *accountant*
Waldegrave, Lord (Lord Waldegrave of North Hill) *financial services company executive*

Stokenchurch
Barratt, Eric George *accountant*

FRANCE

Paris
Vandame, Jean-Marie Richard *diversified financial services company executive*

HONG KONG

Hong Kong
Pacter, Paul Allan *accounting standards researcher*

Wanchai
Iwasawa, Isoo (Francis Iwasawa) *accountant, management consultant*

ISRAEL

Jerusalem
Shrensky, Don Steven *accountant, consultant*

JAPAN

Kumatori
Ohashi, Shoichi *business administration educator*

Tokyo
Kobayashi, Noritake *business educator*
Makihara, Minoru *diversified corporation executive*
Nishimura, Masao *diversified financial services company executive*
Yamamoto, Yoshiro *former diversified financial services company executive*

Yokohama
Tokutani, Masao *risk management educator*

SCOTLAND

Dundee
Lee, Thomas Alexander *accountant, educator*

SINGAPORE

Singapore
Frank, Ronald Edward *marketing educator*

SWEDEN

Bjuv
Persson, Ronny Anders *accountant, historian*

TAIWAN

Taipei
Tsung, Christine Chai-yi *financial executive*

ADDRESS UNPUBLISHED

Abbott, Edward Leroy *finance executive*
Alexander, Barbara Toll *financial consultant*
Allbritton, Joe Lewis *diversified holding company executive*
Almeida, Richard Joseph *finance company administrator*
Alper, Merlin Lionel *finance company executive*
Amdahl, Byrdelle John *business consulting executive*
Anaya, Richard Alfred, Jr., *accountant, investment banker*
Arenberg, Julius Theodore, Jr., *retired accounting company executive*
Ashby, Franklin Charles, Jr., *business executive, author*
Astill, Robert Michael *office manager*
Atcheson, Sue Hart *business educator*
Balakrishnan, P.V. (Sundar) *finance educator*
Barbee, George E.L. *financial services and business executive*
Barney, Austin Dunham, II, *estate planner*
Bartlett, Shirley Anne *accountant*
Barton, Ann Elizabeth *retired corporate financial executive*
Becker, Edward A. *accounting educator, consultant*
Beller, Luanne Evelyn *accountant*
Belluomini, Frank Stephen *accountant*
Benenson, Claire Berger *investment and financial planning educator*
Bennett, Peter Dunne *retired marketing educator*
Bertucelli, Robert Edward *accountant, educator*
Betts, James William, Jr., *financial analyst, consultant*
Black, David deLaine *retired investment consultant*
Blausey, Jeanne Martha *accountant, financial systems analyst, fraud examiner*
Bobbitt, Juanita Crawford *international organization executive*
Bobrow, Richard S. *former diversified financial services executive*
Bolt, Dawn Maria *financial coach, stock trader*
Borum, Rodney Lee *financial business executive*
Bowne, Shirlee Pearson *finance and housing consultant*
Boxer, Alan Lee *accountant*
Boyd, Danny Douglass *financial counselor*
Boyd, Edward Lee *retired financial executive*
Boyd, Francis Virgil *retired accounting educator*
Boyer, Heidi Hild *public policy consultant*
Brainard, Melissa *accountant*
Branson, Harley Kenneth *finance executive*
Breitling, Julius *financial executive*
Brennan, Ciaran Brendan *accountant, oil industry executive*
Brittain, Willard Woodson, Jr., (Woody Brittain) *diversified financial services company executive*
Broome, Oscar Whitfield, Jr., *accounting educator, administrator*
Brown, Henry Bedinger Rust *financial management company executive*
Brown, James Nelson, Jr., *retired accountant*
Brown, Michael Robert *finance specialist*
Canedy, Nancy Gay *comptroller, accountant, educator*
Carter, Richard Duane *business educator*
Casey, Micheal William *portfolio manager*
Chadwell, James Russell, Jr., *retired controller*
Charlton, Jesse Melvin, Jr., *management educator, lawyer*
Cheesman, John Michael *corporate financial executive*
Chelberg, Bruce Stanley *holding company executive*
Clapp, Beverly Booker *accountant*
Claspill, James Louis *finance company executive*
Clayton, Richard Reese *retired holding company executive*
Coates, Shirley Jean *finance educator, secondary school educator*
Cohen, William Alan *marketing educator, author, consultant*
Coleman, Henry James, Jr., *management educator, consultant*
Collette, Frances Madelyn *retired tax specialist, lawyer, consultant, advocate*
Conner, William J. *diversified financial services company executive*
Conrad, David Paul *business broker, retired restaurant chain executive*
Conti, Indalicio Palomar *accountancy educator*
Contillo, Lawrence Joseph *financial and computer company executive*
Cooper, John Arnold *financial analyst*
Coulter, Jack Benson, Jr., *financial planner*
Cramp, Lori Angell *finance executive*
Crook, Robert Wayne *retired mutual funds executive*
Culp, Mildred Louise *corporate executive*
Dean, Thompson *diversified financial services company executive, investment banker*
Denn, Cyril Joseph *retired financial advisor*
Denning, Karen Craft *finance educator*
Derchin, Michael Wayne *portfolio manager and financial analyst*
Diaz, Linda Heidi *portfolio manager*
DiCandilo, Michael D *corporate financial executive, accountant*
Dickman, James Earl *financial services executive*
Dickson, Eva Mae *credit manager*
Doherty, Thomas Joseph *financial services industry consultant*
Dolan, Peter J. *corporate financial consultant*
Donlon, James D, III, *controller, corporate financial executive*
Doty, Philip Edward *accountant*
Downing, M. Scott *budget systems analyst*
Dozier, Glenn Joseph *diversified financial services company executive*
Eggan, Hugh Melford *retired accountant*
Ellen, Martin M. *financial services executive*
Ernsthal, Henry L. *management educator*
Estrin, Herbert Alvin *financial consultant, entertainment company executive*
Everett, Donna Raney *finance educator*
Fansler, Brian Caldwell *budget analyst*
Farrar, John Edson, II, *business executive, consultant, investment adviser*
Faucette, Gloria Marie *accountant, educator*
Fisher, David Andrew *merchant banker, lawyer, venture capitalist*
FitzSimons, Sharon Russell *international financial and treasury executive*
Fletcher, Denise Koen *strategic and financial consultant*
Fortune, Annetta *management educator, accountant*
Fowler, Robert Joseph *financial company executive, consultant*
Fox, Kelly Diane *financial advisor*
Frank, Charles Raphael, Jr., *financial advisor*
Frank, Edgar Gerald *retired financial executive*
Franklin, William Emery *international business educator*
Frazee, James T. *financial associate*
Freimark, Jeffrey Philip *corporate financial executive*
Frey, Francis M. *finance educator*
Gaines, Brenda *retired financial services company executive*
Galda, Dwight William *financial company executive*
Gallagher, Tom *finance company executive*
Gardner, William Lansing, III, *business educator*
Geissinger, Frederick Wallace *finance company executive*
Genét, Barbara Ann *accountant, travel counselor*
Giles, James Francis *financial executive*
Gilmore, Merle *diversified financial services company executive*
Goehring, Maude Cope *retired business educator*
Goeltz, Richard Karl *finance company executive*
Goldberger, George Stefan *finance company executive*
Goodson, Raymond Eugene *business educator, retired automotive executive*
Grey, Francis Joseph *accountant, accounting company executive, educator*
Griffin, Carleton Hadlock *accountant, educator*
Gruber, Fredric Francis *financial planning and investment research executive*
Haddock, Harold, Jr., *retired accounting firm executive*
Hand, Herbert Hensley *finance educator, writer, entrepreneur*
Handy, Edward Otis, Jr., *retired financial services executive*
Hanson, J. Donald *retired diversified financial services company executive*
Hanson, Tamara Shields *accountant*
Harper, W(alter) Joseph *financial consultant*
Hayek, Carolyn Jean *financial consultant, retired judge*
Heller, H(einz) Robert *financial executive*
Henry, William Ray *business administration educator*
Hickson, Ernest Charles *financial executive*
Hild, Matthias *finance educator*
Hintz, Charles Bradley *diversified financial executive*
Hirschhorn, Sidney *accountant, educator*
Hites, Becky E. *financial executive*
Holland, Joseph John *financial manager*
Holloran, Thomas Edward *business educator*
Holsclaw, Jason Scott *financial analyst*
Holton, Grace Holland *accountant*
Horwitz, William J. *treasurer*
Hoy, Harold Joseph *marketing educator, author, management consultant, retail executive, military officer*
Hubbe, Henry Ernest *financial forecaster, funds manager*
Hudak, Thomas F(rancis) *finance company executive*
Ivezaj, Viktor N. *auditor, consultant*
Jacobsen, Karsten E. *accountant*
Jamison, John Callison *business educator, investment banker*
Johnson, Freda S. *public finance consultant*
Johnson, Margaret Kathleen *business educator*
Ju, Xiongwei *portfolio manager*
Kaplan, Leonard Eugene *accountant*
Kass, David Norman *accountant, lawyer*
Kelley, Albert Joseph *global management strategy consultant*
Khuong, Loc Huu *corporate financial executive*
Kilmann, Ralph Herman *business educator*
King, Algin Braddy *retired marketing educator*
Kingsbery, Walton Waits, Jr., *retired accounting firm executive*
Kipper, Richard E. *retired financial services executive, association executive*
Kirk, Donald James *accountant, consultant*
Kohn, David Samuel *accountant, educator, banker*
Kulak, Daryl Wayne *holistic health business educator*
Kushmar, Neal *accountant*
La Blanc, Robert Edmund *consulting company executive*
Lamont, Alice *accountant, consultant*
Larson, Dorothy Ann *business educator*
Latta, Jean Carolyn *financial analyst, chemist*
Lavengood, Lawrence Gene *management educator, historian*
Leaptrott, John *accountant*
Lee, Jonathan Owen *financial services company executive, lawyer*
Leibler, Kenneth Robert *financial service executive*
Lerner, Herbert J. *tax consultant*
Lesher, John Lee, Jr., *consulting services company executive*
Lester, Alicia Louise *financial analyst*
Leventhal, Ellen Iris *portfolio manager*
Levy, Louis Edward *retired accounting firm executive*
Lewis, James Lee, Jr., *actuary*
Loken, Barbara *marketing educator, social psychologist*
Lopgue, Ronald *finance company executive*
Lucas, Karen Williams *controller*
Macaskill, Bridget *finance company executive*
Macdonald, Sheila de Marillac *company executive*
Mack, John J. *diversified financial services company executive*
Magnano, Salvatore Paul *retired financial executive, treasurer*
Malhotra, Pulin *financial infrastructure consultant*
Marks, Leonard, Jr., *retired corporate financial executive*
Marot, Lola *retired accountant*
Martin, Preston *financial services consultant*
Maruyama, Magoroh *business educator, researcher, consultant*
Mason, George Henry *business educator*
Massura, Edward Anthony *accountant*
Mattingly, James Edward *finance educator, writer*
Maxwell, Raymond Roger *retired accountant*
May, Phyllis Jean *financial executive*
Mayoras, Donald Eugene *corporate executive, writer, consultant, educator*
McBride, Jack J. *retired diversified financial services company executive*
McCafferty, Michael *corporate financial executive*
McCall, Louis Charles John *financial advisor, executive, accountant*
McClinton, Donald George *retired diversified holding company executive*
McGovern, John Francis *former financial executive*
McLennan, Robert Gordon *asset management company executive*
Measelle, Richard Leland *accountant*
Mednick, Robert *accountant*
Millard, Donald Rex *financial executive*
Miller, Donald Muxlow *accountant*
Miller, Ross M. *financial services company executive*
Mitchem, Cheryl E. *accounting educator*
Mobley, William Hodges *management educator, researcher, author, executive*
Moore, Robert Henry *financial services executive*
Morman, Dean Smith *accountant, consultant*
Morris, Stanley E. *international financial consultant*
Morton, Scott Vincent *finance company executive*
Mudry, Michael *pension and benefit consultant*
Munhall, Ruth Beatrice *business and financial consultant*
Needles, Belverd Earl, Jr., *accountant, educator*
Neff, John Brown *financial portfolio manager*
Nehrt, Lee Charles *management educator*
Nelson, Mary Ellen Dickson *retired actuary*
Newman, Jay Hartley *finance company executive*
Norton, Karen Ann *accountant*
Norwood, B.J. Scott *business and management educator, Russian affairs educator*
O'Brien, Erin *auditor*
Oldman, Alfred Maurice *accountant, management consultant*
Ologbenla, Adesoji Olaposi *financial advisor*

Osborn, Kenneth Louis *financial executive*
Pacor, Victor J. *diversified financial services company executive*
Pagel, Inga Ann *accountant*
Palmeri, Michael Thomas *financial analyst, equity trader*
Parrish-Porter, Vallerie *controller*
Paulose, Anil Chiramel *financial market data/trading systems software infrastructure consultant*
Payton, Thomas William *corporate finance consultant executive*
Pefley, Norman Gordon *corporate financial executive*
Pfeister, Raymond Lynn *diversified financial services company executive*
Phillips, Charles Alan *accounting firm executive*
Pierre, Natasha Unada *accountant*
Plimpton, Peggy Lucas *trustee*
Ponce, Arnoldo A. *financial analyst, poet*
Powers, Michael J. *retired financial company executive*
Preudhomme, Marcia Denrique *finance company executive, writer*
Propp, Steven H. *benefits compensation analyst*
Prudhomme, James Larry *financial consultant, writer*
Puryear, Alvin Nelson *management educator*
Pyle, Robert Milner, Jr., *financial consultant*
Quant, Harold Edward *retired financial services company executive, rancher*
Rader, Patrick Neil *accountant*
Ragland, William C. *accountant*
Rail, Kathy Lynn Parish *accountant*
Raines, Franklin Delano *finance company executive*
Rastegar-Djavahery, Nader E. *private equities investor*
Reidy, Thomas Michael *financial executive*
Rich, David Barry *financial executive, accountant, entertainer, publishing executive*
Richardson, Margaret Milner *former accounting firm executive, lawyer*
Robertson, A. Haeworth *actuary, benefit consultant, foundation executive*
Robertson, Jack Clark *accounting educator*
Rockwell, Elizabeth Dennis *retirement specialist, financial planner*
Rowe, William Davis *financial services company executive*
Rush, Richard Henry *financial executive, writer, lecturer*
Ryan, Leo Vincent *business educator*
Ryan, Patrick G. *diversified financial services company executive, director*
Sagafi-Nejad, Tagi *business educator*
Sayles, Leonard Robert *management educator, consultant*
Scanlon, Peter Redmond *accountant*
Scheel, Nels Earl *finance company executive, accountant*
Schellenberger, Robert Earl *retired management educator and department chairman*
Schnese, Carsten B. *corporate financial executive*
Schoen, William Jack *financier*
Schwyn, Charles Edward *retired accountant*
Sexton, Carol Burke *consultant*
Shankar, Gautham *associate, financial services & sales trader*
Shepherd, Steven Stewart *auditor, consultant*
Sheridan, Patrick Michael *finance company executive, retired*
Shoop, Glenn Powell *investment consultant*
Shore, Harvey Harris *business educator*
Showery, Charles George, Jr., *financial services company executive, consultant*
Shultis, Robert Lynn *finance educator, cost systems consultant, retired professional association executive*
Simon, Ronald I. *financial executive*
Skaggs, Tina Marie *accountant*
Skinner, Alastair *retired accountant*
Smith, Harold Charles *private pension fund executive*
Smith, Ronald Emory *financial executive*
Snare, Carl Lawrence, Jr., *retired accountant, financial planner*
Snelling, Robert Orren, Sr., *franchising and employment executive*
Snyder, Alan Carhart *financial services executive*
Sonnier, Patricia Bennett *business management educator*
Sproull, Lee S. *finance educator*
Srinivasan, Venkataraman *marketing and management educator*
Stanfill, Dennis Carothers *business executive*
Stephens, Brooke *financial commentator, writer*
Stofferson, Terry Lee *financial officer*
Sundaramurthy, Chamundeswari *finance educator, educator*
Taylor, Linda Rathbun *investment manager*
Taylor, Wilson H. *retired diversified financial company executive*
Thomson, Alexander Bennett, Jr., *financial planner, tax and management consultant*
Tongue, Paul Graham *financial executive*
Trail, Margaret Ann *retired employee benefits company executive, beef cattle producer, sterling silver merchant*
Trent, Robert Harold *retired business educator*
Treynor, Jack Lawrence *financial advisor, educator*
Tripoli, Masumi Hiroyasu *financial consultant*
Turner, Henry Brown *finance executive*
Tyler, Richard James *personal and professional development educator*
Tyler, W(illiam) Ed *finance company executive*
Vadaparty, Kumar Venkata *finance company executive, director*
Vago, Anthony Scott *investment representative*
Van Nostrand, C. Alexandra *finance educator, consultant*
Vu, Joseph Duong *financial educator*
Wain, Christopher Henry Fairfax Moresby *retired actuary, insurance and investment consultant*
Wall, M. Danny *financial services company executive*
Waller, Jim D. *former holding company executive*
Walsh, John E., Jr., *business educator, consultant*
Webster, John Daniel *corporate financial executive*
Weil, John David *financial executive*
Wilhelmsen, Harold John *accountant, operations controller*
Wilkinson, Harry Edward *management educator, consultant*
Wilson, Robert M. *business executive*
Woo, Benson *financial executive*
Woods, Cheryl *financial analyst*
Wright, Judith Rae *retired accountant*
Zick, John Walter *retired accounting company executive*
Zimmerman, Helene Loretta *retired business educator*

FINANCE: INSURANCE

UNITED STATES

ALABAMA

Anniston
Currie, Larry Lamar *insurance agent*

Birmingham
Coleman, Gary L. *insurance company executive*
Johns, John D. *insurance company executive, lawyer*
Ritchie, Allen W. *insurance company executive*
Rushton, William James, III, *insurance company executive, director*
Tucker, Russell B. *insurance company executive*

Foley
Russell, Ralph Timothy *insurance company executive, mayor*

Tuscaloosa
Bickley, John S. *insurance association executive, educator, writer*

ARIZONA

Phoenix
Foley, William Patrick, II, *title insurance company executive*
Fugiel, Frank Paul *insurance company executive*

Scottsdale
Burr, Edward Benjamin *life insurance company executive, financial executive*
Tyner, Neal Edward *retired insurance company executive*
Vairo, Robert John *insurance company executive*

Sun City
Reynolds, John Francis *insurance company executive*

Tucson
Haney, Robert Locke *retired insurance company executive*
Ziehler, Tony Joseph *insurance agent*

ARKANSAS

Cherokee Village
Payne, Howard James *retired insurance company executive*

El Dorado
Hardy, Charlotte B. *insurance agent*

Pine Bluff
Bradford, Jay Turner *insurance executive, state legislator*

Sherwood
Keaton, Frances Marlene *insurance sales representative*

CALIFORNIA

Alhambra
Fried, Elaine June *insurance company executive*

Auburn
Jeske, Howard Leigh *retired life insurance company executive, lawyer*

Calabasas
Christensen, Donn Wayne *insurance executive*

Cupertino
Knapp, George Griff Prather *retired insurance executive*

Encino
Parrott, Dennis Beecher *retired insurance executive*
Seiden, Paul *insurance agent, consultant*

Garden Grove
Williams, J(ohn) Tilman *insurance executive, real estate broker, city official*

Glendale
Erickson, Richard Beau *insurance and financial company executive*

Gold River
Gray, Myles McClure *insurance company executive*

La Quinta
Adolph, Diane Joyce *retired underwriter*

Los Angeles
Houston, Ivan James *insurance company executive*
Inman, James Russell *claims consultant*
Johnson, E. Eric *insurance executive*
McNamara, Aida Shahid *insurance executive*

Newark
Gupta, Anju *risk management consultant*

Newman
Carlsen, Janet Haws *retired insurance company executive*

Newport Beach
Fries, Arthur Lawrence *life health insurance broker, disability claim consultant*
Gerken, Walter Bland *insurance company executive*
Marcoux, Carl Henry *former insurance executive, writer, historian*
Schafer, Glenn S *insurance company executive*
Sutton, Thomas C. *insurance company executive*
Tran, Khanh T. *insurance company executive*

Novato
Carendi, Jan R. *insurance company executive*

Oakland
Halvorson, George Charles *health care insurance company executive*

Orange
Godeke, Raymond Dwight Cook *insurance company executive, accountant*

Paso Robles
Webster, David Arthur *retired life insurance company executive*

Rancho Mirage
Fromm, Erwin Frederick *retired insurance company executive*

San Diego
Baxter, Robert Hampton *insurance executive*
Hayes, Robert Emmet *retired insurance company executive*
Purcifull, Robert Otis *insurance company executive*
Rotter, Paul Talbott *retired insurance executive*
Vasudevan, Sriram *risk management professional*

San Francisco
Enfield, Donald Michael *insurance company executive*
Lamberson, John Roger *insurance company executive*

San Rafael
Keegan, Jane Ann *insurance executive, consultant*

Santa Ana
Klemens, Thomas A. *insurance company executive*

Santa Barbara
Evans, Thomas Edgar, Jr., *title insurance agency executive*

Sherman Oaks
Holden, William Willard *insurance executive*
Milgrim, Darrow A. *insurance company executive*

Sunnyvale
Merrill, Wendy Jane *insurance company executive*

Thousand Oaks
O'Rourke, John A. *insurance company executive*
Ponder, Ron J. *insurance company executive*
Weinberg, D. Mark *health insurance company executive*

Toluca Lake
Hardy, Wayne Russell *insurance and investment broker*

Vista
Fuhlrodt, Norman Theodore *retired insurance company executive*

Woodland Hills
Erwin, Steven P. *insurance company executive*
Greaves, Roger F. *health maintenance organization executive*
Helwig, David S. *insurance company executive*

Woodside
Freitas, Antoinette Juni *insurance company executive*

COLORADO

Aurora
Nelson, Marvin Ray *retired life insurance company executive*

Colorado Springs
Duvall, Lawrence Delbert *insurance company executive*

Denver
Axley, Hartman *underwriter*
Volpe, Richard Gerard *insurance accounts executive, consultant*

Fort Collins
Schendel, Winfried George *insurance company executive*

Golden
Lott, Brenda Louise *insurance company executive*

Superior
Forshee, Gladys Marie *writer, insurance agent*

CONNECTICUT

Essex
Miller, Walter Neal *insurance company consultant*

Glastonbury
Budd, Edward Hey *retired insurance company executive*

Greenwich
Berkley, William Robert *insurance holding company executive*
Clements, Robert *insurance executive*
Fuller, Theodore *retired insurance executive*

Hartford
Ahn, Dong H *insurance company executive*
Ayer, Ramani *insurance company executive*
Benanav, Gary G. *insurance company counsel*
Bermel, John J *insurance company executive, corporate financial executive*
Bertolini, Mark T *insurance company executive*
Bolton, Roger *insurance company executive*
Brown, C Timothy *insurance company executive*
Casazza, William James *insurance company executive, lawyer*
Cheng, Wei-Tih *insurance company executive*
deRaismes, Ann M. *insurance company executive, human resources specialist*
Elliott, Eric S *insurance company executive*
Entrekin, David W *insurance company executive*
Fisher, Russell D *insurance company executive*
Geyer, James A *insurance company executive*
Haylon, Michael E. *insurance company executive*
Hebert, Paul B *insurance company executive*
Hudson, Calvin *insurance company executive*
Kokulis, George *insurance company executive*
Lautzenheiser, Barbara Jean *insurance company executive*
Mullane, Denis Francis *insurance executive*
Popik, William C *insurance company executive*
Redmond, Arthur J *insurance company executive*
Reese, Stuart Harry *insurance company executive*
Roth, William H *insurance company executive*
Rowe, John Wallis *health insurance executive, medical executive*
Sargent, Joseph Denny *insurance executive*
Scully, John Carroll *life insurance marketing research company executive*
Searfoss, David W. *insurance company executive*
Smith, Lowndes A. (Lon) *insurance company executive*
Wilde, Wilson *insurance company executive*
Williams, Ronald A. *insurance company executive*
Wise, Richard Evans *corporate executive*
Wright, Elease *insurance company executive*
Zwiener, David K. *insurance company executive*

Meriden
Licata, Ronald Charles *insurance company executive*

New Canaan
Cohen, Richard Norman *insurance executive*

Norwalk
Hickey, Kevin Francis *healthcare executive*

Southington
Rudolph, Kathleen Ann *insurance company executive*

Stamford
Block, Ruth *retired insurance company executive*
Brandon, Joseph P. *reinsurance company executive*
Chickering, Howard Allen *insurance company executive, lawyer*
Ferguson, Ronald Eugene *reinsurance company executive*
Fraizer, Michael D. *insurance company executive*
Hudson, Harold Jordon, Jr., *retired insurance executive*

Trumbull
Berg, Charles G. *insurance company executive*

Vernon Rockville
Wolff, Gregory Steven *insurance company executive*

West Hartford
DeLibero, Mary Smellie *insurance company professional, pianist, soprano*
Wilder, Michael Stephen *former insurance company executive*

Weston
Thompson, N(orman) David *insurance company executive*

DELAWARE

Hockessin
Dombeck, Harold Arthur *insurance company executive*

Wilmington
Nottingham, Robinson Kendall *insurance company executive*

DISTRICT OF COLUMBIA

Washington
Canapary, Herbert Carton *insurance company executive*
Haley, John *risk management consultant*
Martin, Julie A. *retired insurance company executive*
Nicely, Olza M. (Tony) *insurance company executive*
Schiller, Harvey W. *risk management company executive*
Simpson, Louis A. *insurance company executive*

FLORIDA

Boca Raton
Kaye, Barry *insurance company executive*
Richardson, R(oss) Fred(erick) *insurance executive*

Boynton Beach
Bryant, Donald Loyd *insurance company executive*
Caras, Joseph Sheldon *life insurance company executive*

Coral Gables
Rodriguez, Nestor Joaquin *insurance broker*

Daytona Beach
Adams, John Carter, Jr., *insurance executive*

Destin
Linn, James Eldon, II, *insurance company executive*

Fort Lauderdale
Hull, Richard Franklin *insurance brokerage executive*

Zumbano, Anthony Ralph *risk, claims management executive*

Fort Myers
Blomquist, Robert Oscar *retired insurance company executive*
Dockins, George Joel *retired insurance and securities company executive*
Mc Queen, Robert Charles *retired insurance executive*

Gainesville
Boothroyd, Herbert J. *insurance company executive*

Gulf Breeze
DeBardeleben, John Thomas, Jr., *retired insurance company executive*

Holiday
Peterson, George F. *retired insurance company executive, writer*

Hollywood
Martinez, Carlos *insurance adjuster, company manager*

Indian Harbor Beach
Phelan, John Densmore *insurance executive, consultant*

Jacksonville
Lyon, Wilford Charles, Jr., *insurance executive*
Morehead, Charles Richard *insurance company executive*
Rader, David *insurance company executive*

Juno Beach
Holmes, Melvin Almont *insurance company executive*

Key Largo
Daenzer, Bernard John *insurance company executive, legal consultant*
Lynn, James Thomas *insurance company executive, government executive, lawyer, investment banker*

Lakeland
Jay, James Albert *retired insurance company executive*

Largo
Eisele, William David *insurance agency executive*

Longwood
Cooper, Brian Reginald *insurance company executive*

Miami
Gabor, Frank *insurance company executive*
Heggen, Arthur William *insurance company executive*
Shusterman, Nathan *underwriter, financial consultant*
Van Wyck, George Richard *insurance company executive*

Naples
Clark, William James *retired insurance company executive*

New Port Richey
Hanahan, James Lake *retired insurance executive*

Ocean Ridge
Bates, Edward Brill *retired insurance company executive*

Oldsmar
Caronis, George John *insurance executive*

Orlando
Kellison, Stephen George *actuarial consultant*

Ormond Beach
Burt, Wallace Joseph, Jr., *insurance company executive*

Oviedo
Brethauer, William Russell, Jr., *claim investigator*

Palm Beach Gardens
Deppe, Henry A. *insurance company executive*

Ponte Vedra Beach
MacKowski, John Joseph *retired insurance company executive*

Punta Gorda
McDaniel, Norwood Allan *insurance broker*

Redington Beach
Alpert, Barry Mark *insurance company and banking executive*

Sarasota
Best, Jerry Lavon *insurance consultant*
Bushey, Alan Scott *retired insurance holding company executive*

Spring Hill
Vanderburg, Paul Stacey *insurance executive, consultant*

Tallahassee
Gabor, Jeffrey Alan *insurance and financial services executive*

Tampa
Poe, William Frederick *insurance agency executive, former mayor*
Sullivan, Joseph Peter *risk and insurance management consultant*

Vero Beach
Burton, Arthur Henry, Jr., *insurance company executive*
Feagles, Robert West *retired insurance company executive*

Winter Park
Kraft, Kenneth Houston, Jr., *insurance agency executive*

GEORGIA

Alpharetta
Curling, Douglas *insurance company executive*
Fowler, Vivian Delores *insurance company executive*
Smith, Derek V. *risk management consultant*

Atlanta
Black, Kenneth, Jr., *retired insurance executive and educator, author*
Cornelius, Charles H. *insurance company executive*
Davis, Grover L. *risk management consultant*
Gregory, Mel Hyatt, Jr., *retired insurance company executive*
Hubbell, Fred Shelton *insurance company executive*
Meyers, Archie L., Jr., *risk management consultant*
Peacock, George Rowatt *retired life insurance company executive*
Watts, John, Jr., *insurance company executive*

Columbus
Amos, Daniel Paul *insurance company executive*
Amos, Paul Shelby *insurance company executive*
Cloninger, Kriss, III, *insurance company executive*
Loudermilk, Joey M. *insurance company executive, lawyer*
Spencer, Kathelen V. *insurance company executive*

Duluth
Burns, Carroll Dean *insurance company executive*

Gainesville
Clary, Ronald Gordon *insurance agency executive*

Lagrange
Hudson, Charles Daugherty *insurance executive*

Norcross
Atkinson, A. Kelley *insurance company executive*

Savannah
Dodge, William Douglas *insurance company consultant*

Smyrna
Buck, Lee Albert *retired insurance company executive, evangelist*

HAWAII

Honolulu
Kanehiro, Kenneth Kenji *insurance educator, risk analyst, consultant*
Metcalf, Wayne C., III, *insurance commissioner*
Noguchi, Hideo *insurance company executive*

IDAHO

Idaho Falls
Parkinson, Howard Evans *insurance company executive*

ILLINOIS

Bloomington
Axley, Dixie L. *insurance company executive*
Brunner, Kim M. *insurance company executive*
Curry, Alan Chester *insurance company executive*
Johnson, Earle Bertrand *insurance executive*
Joslin, Roger Scott *insurance company executive*
Rodman, Raymond G. *insurance company executive*
Rust, Edward Barry, Jr., *insurance company executive, lawyer*
Tipsord, Michael L. *insurance company executive*
Trosino, Vincent Joseph, Sr., *insurance company executive*

Calumet City
Parks, Corrine Frances *insurance company executive*

Chicago
Adams, John S. *insurance company executive*
Bartholomay, William C. *insurance brokerage company executive, professional baseball team executive*
Beemster, Joseph Robert *risk management consultant*
Bolger, David P. *insurance company executive*
Chang, Yi-Cheng *insurance agent*
DeMoss, Jon W. *insurance company executive, lawyer*
Draut, Eric J. *insurance company executive*
Engel, Philip L. *retired insurance company executive*
Hughes, Martin P. *insurance company executive*
Janecek, Lenore Elaine *insurance specialist, consultant*
Jerome, Jerrold V. *retired insurance company executive*
Lerner, Alexander Robert *insurance company executive*
Lorenz, Hugo Albert *retired insurance executive, consultant*
McCaskey, Raymond F. *insurance company executive*
Preble, Robert Curtis, Jr., *insurance executive*
Southwell, Donald G. *insurance company executive*
Tyree, James C. *insurance company executive*
Vie, Richard Carl *insurance company executive*
Zucaro, Aldo Charles *insurance company executive*

Darien
Bland, Robert S. *insurance company executive*

Des Plaines
Pannke-Smith, Peggy *long term care insurance and annuity agency executive*

Evanston
Peponis, Harold Arthur *insurance agent, broker*

Galena
Crandall, John Lynn *insurance consultant, retired insurance company executive*

Gilberts
Barilich, Thomas Anthony *loss control specialist*

Hinsdale
Denton, Ray Douglas *insurance company executive*

Itasca
Gallagher, J. Patrick, Jr., *insurance company executive*
Gallagher, Robert E. *risk management marketing company executive*
Gallgher, J. Patrick, Jr., *risk management marketing company executive*

Lake Forest
Brown, Cameron *insurance company consultant*
Eckert, Ralph John *insurance company executive*
Peterson, Donald Matthew *insurance company executive*

Long Grove
Mathis, David B. *insurance company executive*

Naperville
Desch, Theodore Edward *retired health insurance company executive, lawyer*

Northbrook
Cruikshank, John W., III, *insurance agent*
Liddy, Edward M. *insurance company executive*
McCabe, Michael J. *insurance executive*
Pike, Robert William *insurance company executive, lawyer*
Wilson, Rita P. *insurance company executive*
Wilson, Thomas Joseph *insurance company executive*
Young, R. James *insurance company executive*

Park Ridge
Ewald, Robert Frederick *insurance company executive, consultant*

Peoria
Michael, Jonathan Edward *insurance company executive*

Rock Island
Cheney, Thomas Ward *retired insurance company executive*
Lardner, Henry Petersen (Peter Lardner) *insurance company executive*

Schaumburg
Muhich, Brian William *insurance broker*

Skokie
Hedien, Wayne Evans *retired insurance company executive*
Hoopis, Harry Peter *insurance executive, entrepreneur*

Springfield
Dodge, Edward John *retired insurance company executive*
Simpson, William Arthur *insurance company executive*

Wheaton
Hamilton, Robert Appleby, Jr., *insurance company executive*

INDIANA

Batesville
Rockwood, Frederick Whitney *insurance company executive*

Carmel
Chokel, Charles B. *insurance company executive*
Dick, Rollin Merle *insurance company executive*
Hagerty, Thomas M. *insurance executive*
Hilbert, Stephen C. *former insurance company executive*
Husman, Catherine Bigot *retired insurance company executive, actuary*
Kilian, Thomas J. *insurance company executive*
Shea, William J. *insurance company executive*

Fort Wayne
Dunsire, P(eter) Kenneth *insurance company executive*
Robertson, Richard Stuart *insurance holding company executive*
Sasko, Nancy Ann *insurance agent*
Steiner, Paul Andrew *retired insurance executive*
Vachon, Marilyn Ann *retired insurance company executive*

Indianapolis
Cramer, Betty F. *life insurance company executive*
Funk, James William, Jr., *insurance agency administrator, business owner*
Gaunce, Michael Paul *insurance company executive*
Glasscock, Larry Claborn *insurance company executive*
Lytle, L(arry) Ben *insurance company executive, lawyer*
McCarthy, Harold Charles *retired insurance company executive*
McKinney, E. Kirk, Jr., *retired insurance company executive*
Norman, LaLander Stadig *retired insurance company executive*

Pendleton
Kischuk, Richard Karl *insurance company executive*

Valparaiso
Collie, John, Jr., *insurance agent*

IOWA

Des Moines
Brooks, Roger Kay *insurance company executive*
Ellis, Mary Louise Helgeson *retired insurance company executive, business consultant*
Gersie, Michael H. *insurance company executive*
Griswell, J. Barry *insurance company executive*
Kelley, Bruce Gunn *insurance company executive, lawyer*
Schneider, William George *former life insurance company executive*
Williams, Carl Chanson *insurance company executive*
Williamson, Rose Ann *insurance agent*

Oskaloosa
Mangold, Archie Wayne, II, *insurance agent*

KANSAS

De Soto
Strubbe, Thomas R. *insurance industry executive*

Eudora
Miller, David Groff *insurance agent*

Lenexa
Grant, W. Thomas, II, *insurance company executive*

Manhattan
Ball, Louis Alvin *insurance company executive*

Shawnee Mission
Miller, Stanford *retired reinsurance executive, lawyer*

Wichita
Van Milligen, James M. *health care administrator*

KENTUCKY

Crestview Hills
Cory, Edward William, Jr., *underwriting executive*

Louisville
Haddaway, James David *retired insurance company official*
McCormick, Steven Thomas *insurance company executive*
Rosky, Theodore Samuel *insurance company executive*

LOUISIANA

Harvey
Pete, Eric E. *claims representative, writer*

New Orleans
Grau, Jean Elizabeth *retired insurance agent*
Marks, Charles Dennery *insurance consultant*
Purvis, George Frank, Jr., *life insurance company executive*
Trapolin, Frank Winter *retired insurance executive*

Shreveport
Harbuck, Edwin Charles *insurance agent*

MAINE

Portland
Candage, Howard Everett *insurance management consultant, agent, broker*
Reid, Rosemary Anne *insurance agent*

MARYLAND

Baltimore
Goodman, William Richard *insurance adjusting company executive*
Hecht, Alan Dannenberg *insurance executive*
Tocco, Elaine Kay *insurance policy specialist*

Chester
Dabich, Eli, Jr., *insurance company executive*

Columbia
Messina, Daniel S. *insurance company executive*

Derwood
Blank, Leta Sondra *health and long term care insurance specialist*

Emmitsburg
Howes, Theodore Clark *claims examiner*

Gaithersburg
Boddiger, George Cyrus *insurance corporate executive, consultant*

Hanover
Roenigk, Martin Allen *insurance company executive*

Hunt Valley
Carney, Stephen Patrick *insurance company executive*

Mitchellville
Ball, Robert M. *social security and health insurance specialist*

Owings Mills
Disharoon, Leslie Benjamin *retired insurance executive*

Oxford
Radcliffe, George Grove *retired life insurance company executive*

Parkton
Cummins, Paul Zach, II, *insurance company executive*

Reisterstown
Tirone, Barbara Jean *health insurance administrator*

Severna Park
Ebersberger, Arthur Darryl *insurance company executive, consultant*

Silver Spring
Jaskot, John Joseph *retired insurance company executive*

MASSACHUSETTS

Boston
Aborn, Foster Litchfield *insurance company executive*
Brown, Stephen Lee *retired insurance company executive*
Bunker, Beryl H. *retired insurance company executive, volunteer*
Chilvers, Derek *insurance company executive*
Condrin, J. Paul *insurance company executive*
Conner, Terry L *insurance company executive*
D'Alessandro, David Francis *insurance company executive*
D'Allesandro, David F. *insurance company executive*
Farnam, Walter Edward *insurance company executive*
Ford, Maureen R. *insurance company executive*
Kamer, Joel Victor *insurance company executive, actuary*
Kelley, Kevin H. *insurance company executive*
Kelly, Edmund Francis *insurance company executive*
Maloney, Thomas E. *insurance executive*
Mansfield, Christopher Charles *insurance company legal executive*
McAneny, Deborah H. *insurance company executive*
Moloney, Thomas E. *insurance company executive*
Morton, Edward James *insurance company executive*
Shafto, Robert Austin *retired insurance company executive*
Shemin, Barry L. *insurance company executive*
Taylor, Edward Michael *insurance, enterprise risk management consultant*
Van Faasen, William C. *health insurance company executive*

Brewster
Adam, John, Jr., *insurance company executive emeritus*

Duxbury
Wangler, William Clarence *retired insurance company executive*

Framingham
Oleskiewicz, Francis Stanley *lawyer, retired insurance executive*

Needham
Rodman, Sumner *insurance company executive*

North Attleboro
Koussa, Harold Alan *insurance account executive*

North Chatham
O'Brien, Robert Emmet *insurance company executive*

North Dighton
Silvia, David Alan *insurance broker*

Pittsfield
Cornelio, Albert Carmen *insurance executive*

South Orleans
Hale, Margaret Smith *insurance company executive, educator*

Springfield
Burkett, Lawrence V. *insurance company executive, lawyer*
Gunton, Howard E. *insurance company executive*
Johnson, Robert Allison *life insurance company executive*
Modie, Christine M. *insurance company executive*

Wellesley
Baker, Charles D. *health insurance company executive*

West Hyannisport
Gingold, George Norman *insurance company executive, lawyer*

Weston
Fish, David Earl *insurance company executive*

Worcester
Angelini, Michael P. *insurance company executive*
Parry, Edward Jones, III, *insurance company executive*

MICHIGAN

Caledonia
Antonini, Richard Lee *insurance executive*

Chelsea
Kitchens, Frederick Lynton, Jr., *retired insurance company executive*

Detroit
Schwartz, Michael Robinson *insurance company executive*
Webb, Bobbie James *insurance broker*
Whitmer, Richard E. *insurance company executive*

Kalamazoo
Curry, John Patrick *insurance company executive, management consultant*

Lansing
Arends, Herman Joseph *insurance company executive*
Fisher, John W. *insurance company executive*

Naubinway
Smith, Richard Ernest *retired insurance company executive*

Southgate
Torok, Margaret Louise *insurance company executive*

MINNESOTA

Bemidji
Bridston, Paul Joseph *strategic consultant*

Bloomington
Matlon, David Michael *insurance agent, treasurer*

Coon Rapids
Bordner, Patricia Anne *insurance agent, writer*

Minneapolis
Barnhill, Howard Eugene *insurance company executive*
Keets, John David, Jr., *insurance company executive*
Nicholson, Bruce J. *insurance company executive*
Sourdiff, Gerald *retired insurance company executive*
Turner, John Gosney *insurance company executive, director*

Minnetonka
Dapper, L. Robert *healthcare insurance company executive*
McGuire, William W. *insurance company executive*
Rivet, Jeannine M. *health plan administrator*
Robbins, Orem Olford *insurance company executive*

Saint Paul
Bradley, Thomas A. *insurance company executive*
Connly, Michael R. *insurance company executive*
Johnson, James Erling *insurance executive*
Kane, Stanley Phillip *insurance company executive*
Senkler, Robert L. *insurance company executive*
Treacy, John C. *insurance company executive*
Urness, Kent D. *insurance company executive*
Yessman, Timothy *insurance company executive*
Zuraitis, Marita *insurance company executive*

MISSISSIPPI

Clinton
Montgomery, Keith Norris, Sr., *insurance executive, state legislator*

Madison
Dean, Jack Pearce *retired insurance company executive*

MISSOURI

Earth City
Buselmeier, Bernard Joseph *insurance company executive*

Kansas City
Lakin, Scott Bradley *insurance agent*
Mc Gee, Joseph John, Jr., *former insurance company executive*

Saint Louis
Liddy, Richard A. *insurance company executive*
Mullens, William Reese *retired insurance company executive*
Ott, David T. *insurance company executive*
Van Trease, Sandra Ann *insurance company executive*
Werner, Burton Kready *insurance company executive*
Winer, Warren James *insurance executive*

NEBRASKA

Holdrege
Hendrickson, Bruce Carl *life insurance company executive*

Lincoln
Angle, John Charles *retired life insurance company executive*
Arth, Lawrence Joseph *insurance executive*

Omaha
Conley, Eugene Allen *retired insurance company executive*
Hamburg, Marc D. *insurance company executive*
Jetter, Arthur Carl, Jr., *insurance company executive*
Lechowicz, Lisa Marie *retired insurance company executive*
Neary, Daniel *insurance company executive*
Sigerson, Charles Willard, Jr., *insurance agency executive*
Sturgeon, John Ashley *insurance company executive*
Weekly, John William *insurance company executive*

NEW HAMPSHIRE

Hanover
Kemp, Karl Thomas *insurance company executive*

Kingston
Saunders, Janet McGee *small business owner, healthcare administrator*

Rochester
Dworkin, Gary Steven *insurance company executive*

NEW JERSEY

Augusta
Martin, Richard L. *retired insurance executive*

Englewood
Volk, Austin N. *insurance company executive*

Fort Lee
Adler, Earl *insurance executive*

Glen Rock
Mc Elrath, Richard Elsworth *retired insurance company executive*

Jersey City
Coyne, Frank J. *insurance industry executive*

Little Silver
Redden, Harral Arthur, Jr., *broker*

Lumberton
Friedberg, Thomas Harold *insurance company executive*

Madison
Calligan, William Dennis *retired life insurance company executive*
Leak, Margaret Elizabeth *insurance company executive*
Parker, Henry Griffith, III, *insurance executive*

Morristown
Galeotti, Steven *insurance executive*
Newhouse, Robert J., Jr., *insurance executive*

New Brunswick
Mills, George Marshall *insurance consultant*

New Vernon
McCormack, John Joseph, Jr., *insurance executive*

Newark
Banta, Vivian L. *insurance company executive*
Carbone, Richard *insurance executive*
Caulfield, E. Michael *insurance company executive*
Koster, Barbara *insurance company executive*
Marino, William J. *insurance executive*
Myers, Priscilla A. *insurance company executive*
Ryan, Arthur Frederick *insurance company executive*
Winters, Robert Cushing *insurance company executive*

Parsippany
Broatch, Robert E. *company executive*

Plainfield
Cox, Robert C. *insurance company executive*
Krump, Paul J. *insurance company executive*

Rumson
Creamer, William Henry, III, *retired insurance company executive*

Short Hills
MacKinnon, Malcolm D(avid) *retired insurance company executive*

Somerset
Brophy, Joseph Thomas *information company executive*

Spring Lake
Bonhag, Thomas Edward *insurance company executive, financial planner, financial consultant*

Summit
Gerathy, E. Carroll *former insurance executive, real estate developer*

Warren
Chubb, Percy, III, *insurance company executive*
Finnegan, John D. *insurance company executive*
Kelso, David Blair *insurance company executive*
Motamed, Thomas Firouz *insurance company executive*

Whitehouse Station
Fiscus, Philip Wayne *underwriter*

Wyckoff
Munson, William Leslie *insurance company executive*

NEW MEXICO

Albuquerque
Liss, Norman Richard *insurance executive*
Matros, Richard K. *insurance company executive*
Pendergest, Kevin W. *insurance company executive*
Roseman, Steven A. *insurance company executive*

Tucumcari
Woodard, Dorothy Marie *insurance broker*

NEW YORK

Albany
Cole, John Adam *insurance executive*

Amityville
Imbert, Richard Conrad *insurance company executive, real estate developer*

Armonk
Dunton, Gary C. *insurance company executive*

Bemus Point
Ross, Roderic Henry *insurance company executive*

Binghamton
Best, Robert Mulvane *insurance company executive*

Bronx
Elkins, Alfred David *insurance company executive*

Brooklyn
Faison, Seth Shepard *retired insurance broker*

Cohocton
Sarfaty, Wayne Allen *insurance agent, financial planner*

Dolgeville
Riedman, James Robert *insurance company executive*

Dryden
Baxter, Robert Banning *insurance company executive*

Glens Falls
Trombley, Joseph Edward *insurance company executive, underwriter*

Lindenhurst
Hungerford, Gary A. *insurance company executive, columnist, writer, editor*

Malverne
Knight, John Francis *retired insurance company executive*

Merrick
Cherry, Harold *insurance company executive*

Mineola
Gibson, William Shepard *insurance company executive*
Miller, Loring Erik *insurance agent, broker*

New York
Agnew, William Harold *insurance company executive*
Akhoury, Ravi *insurance company executive*
Baker, George R. *insurance industry executive*
Benmosche, Robert H. *insurance company executive*
Berdick, Leonard Stanley *insurance broker*
Biggs, John Herron *retired insurance company executive*
Borelli, Francis J(oseph) (Frank Borelli) *insurance brokerage and consulting firm financial executive*
Buchmueller, Ross J. *insurance company executive*
Burns, John Joseph, Jr., *financial and insurance holding company executive*
Callahan, Dennis S. *insurance company executive*
Campbell, Judith E. *retired insurance company executive*
Cavanaugh, Daniel J. *insurance company executive*
Crystal, James William *insurance company executive*
Davis, Charles A. *insurance company executive*
Devlin, Robert Manning *insurance company executive*
Dolan, Raymond Bernard *insurance company executive*
Earls, Kevin Gerard *insurance company executive*
Foti, Samuel J. *insurance company executive*
Freiberg, Lowell Carl *insurance company executive*
Frenkel, Jacob Aharon *insurance company executive*
Gammill, Lee Morgan, Jr., *retired insurance company executive*
Gamper, Albert R., Jr., *insurance executive*
Gibbs, Richard L. *insurance company executive*
Greenberg, Maurice Raymond (Hank Greenberg) *insurance company executive*
Harris, David Henry *retired life insurance company executive*
Herrikson, C. Robert *insurance company executive*
Hildebrand, Phillip J. *insurance company executive*
Hohn, Harry George *retired insurance company executive, lawyer*
Hutchings, Peter Lounsbery *retird insurance company executive, director*
Jacobson, Sibyl C. *insurance company executive*
Jones, Frank Joseph *insurance company executive*
Kanak, Donald Perry, Jr., *insurance company executive, lawyer, diversified financial services company executive*
Kaplan, Keith Eugene *insurance company executive, lawyer*
Knapp, Amy K. *insurance company executive*
Manning, Dennis J. *insurance company executive*
Manton, Edwin Alfred Grenville *insurance company executive*
Martens, Erwin W. *risk management consultant*
Martin, Rodney O., Jr., *insurance company executive*
Martino, Cheryl Derby *insurance company secretary*
Matthews, Edward E. *insurance company executive*
McCarthy, Gloria M *insurance company executive*
Melone, Joseph James *retired insurance company executive*
Milton, Christian Michel *insurance executive*
Moor, Kristian P. *insurance company executive*
Murray, Richard Maximilian *insurance executive*
Nagler, Stewart Gordon *insurance company executive*
Neuger, Win J. *insurance company executive*
Olsen, David Alexander *insurance executive*
Piccione, Tal P. *insurance company executive*
Rein, Catherine Amelia *insurance company executive, lawyer*
Remshard, John W. *insurance company executive*
Ross, Donald Keith *retired insurance company executive*
Sandler, Robert Michael *insurance company executive, actuary*
Savage, Frank *insurance executive*
Schwartz, Robert George *retired insurance company executive*
Scott, Bertram *insurance company executive*
Sievert, Frederick *insurance company executive*
Smith, Howard I. *insurance company executive*
Somers, John Arthur *insurance company executive*
Sproule, Michael E. *insurance company executive*
Sternberg, Seymour *insurance company executive*
Stocker, Michael Aubrey *health insurance company executive*
Sullivan, Martin J. *insurance company executive*
Toppeta, William John *insurance company executive, lawyer*
Underhill, Jacob Berry, III, *retired insurance company executive*
Vidal, David Jonathan *insurance company executive, journalist*
Washington, Clarence Edward, Jr., *insurance company executive*
Weber, Alan J. *insurance company executive*
Weber, Lisa M. *insurance company executive*
Wendlandt, Gary E. *insurance company executive*
Wintrob, Jay S. *insurance company executive*
Wisner, Frank George *insurance company executive, former ambassador*
Wolf, James Anthony *insurance company executive*
Yalen, Gary N. *retired insurance company executive*

Northport
Miller, Philip John *insurance consultant*

Oakdale
Mackenzie, Maureen L *insurance company executive*

Oceanside
Rubin, Hanan *retired insurance company executive*

Point Lookout
Stack, Maurice Daniel *retired insurance company executive*

Pound Ridge
Bennett, Edward Henry *reinsurance executive*

Rock Hill
Lombardi, Kent Bailey *insurance company administrator*

Saratoga Springs
Ford, Dexter *retired insurance company executive*

Scarsdale
Decaminada, Joseph Pio *retired insurance company executive*

Schenectady
Murray, Edward Rock *insurance broker*

Southampton
Dublis, Raymond Anthony *insurance executive*

Staten Island
Gavrity, John Decker *insurance company executive*

Syosset
Barry, Richard Francis *retired life insurance company executive*
Kniffin, Paula Sichel *insurance sales executive*

Utica
Austin, Michael Charles *insurance company executive*

White Plains
Greer, Robert E. *retired insurance executive*

Yonkers
Wolfson, Irwin M. *insurance company executive*

NORTH CAROLINA

Burlington
Blevins, James Ray *lawyer, insurance company claims executive*

Camden
Hammond, Roy Joseph *reinsurance company executive*

Chapel Hill
Fine, J(ames) Allen *insurance company executive*
Stewart, Richard Edwin *insurance consulting company executive*

Charlotte
Howard, Grazell *risk management executive*

Durham
Clark, Arthur Watts *insurance company executive*

Greensboro
Glass, Dennis Robert *financial company executive*
Hall, William Edward, Jr., *insurance agency executive*
Soles, William Roger *insurance company executive, director*
Stonecipher, David A. *insurance company executive*

Pinehurst
O'Loughlin, John Kirby *retired insurance executive*

Winston Salem
Beardsley, Charles Mitchell *retired insurance company executive*
Jesseph, Steven Austin *risk management consultant*

NORTH DAKOTA

Grand Forks
Wogaman, George Elsworth *insurance company executive, financial consultant*

OHIO

Canton
Bower, Ronald Edward *insurance agency owner*
Repp, Ronald Stewart *insurance company executive*
Schauer, Thomas Alfred *insurance company executive*

Cincinnati
Horrell, Karen Holley *insurance company executive, lawyer*
Klein, Jerry Emanuel *insurance and financial planning executive*
Klinedinst, Thomas John, Jr., *insurance agency executive*
Krohn, Claus Dankertsen *insurance company executive*
Runk, Fred J. *insurance company executive*

Cleveland
Lewis, Peter Benjamin *insurance company executive*
Renwick, Glenn M. *insurance company executive*

Columbus
Barnes, Galen R. *insurance company executive*
Duryee, Harold Taylor *insurance consultant*
Gasper, Joseph J. *insurance company executive*
Jurgensen, W.G. *insurance company executive*
Oakley, Robert Alan *insurance executive*
Wilhelmy, Odin, Jr. *insurance agent*

Hamilton
Marcum, Joseph LaRue *insurance company executive*

Mayfield
Forrester, W. Thomas, II, *insurance company executive*
Jarrett, Charles Elwood *insurance company executive, lawyer*

Powell
Emanuelson, James Robert *retired insurance company executive*

Rocky River
Riedthaler, William Allen *risk management professional*

Shreve
Denman, Nicholas Werner *insurance executive*

OKLAHOMA

Oklahoma City
Hamilton, Thomas Allen *independent insurance agent, securities representative*
Ille, Bernard Glenn *insurance company executive, director*
Jenkins, Sherry L. *state insurance program administrator*

Tulsa
Abbott, William Thomas *private investigator*
Watson, Eric N. *corporate executive*

OREGON

Portland
Blachly, Beverly Jean *retired vocational and insurance consultant*
Clemens, Charles Joseph *retired insurance agent*
Galbraith, John Robert *insurance company exeuctive*
Hill, James Edward *insurance company executive*
Lang, Philip David *former state legislator, insurance company executive*
Timpe, Ronald Ernest *insurance company executive*

Wilsonville
DeHart, David Floyd *retired insurance company executive*

PENNSYLVANIA

Bala Cynwyd
Shepard, Geoffrey Carroll *insurance executive*

Berwyn
McIntyre, James Owen *insurance executive*

Bethlehem
Schumacher, Susan Louise *underwriter*

Bushkill
Garretto, Leonard Anthony, Jr., *insurance company executive*

Camp Hill
Mead, James Matthew *insurance company executive*

Elkins Park
Hart, William C. *underwriter, educator, writer*

Erie
Garcia, Philip A. *insurance company executive*
Ludrof, Jeffrey A. *insurance company executive*

Harrisburg
Patterson, Robert Eugene *insurance company executive*

King Of Prussia
Anderson, Eric E. *healthcare services executive*
Volpe, Ralph Pasquale *retired insurance company executive*

Newtown Square
Staats, Dean Roy *retired reinsurance executive*

Philadelphia
Anania, Andrea *insurance company executive*
Bell, Michael W. *insurance company executive*
Boscia, Jon Andrew *insurance company executive*
Hanway, H. Edward *insurance company executive*
Hochberg, Edward S. *insurance executive*
Jones, Thomas Chester, III, *insurance company executive*
Kendall, Terry *insurance company executive*
Kim, John Y. *insurance company executive*
Murabito, John *insurance company executive*
Pastore, William M. *insurance company executive*
Romasco, Robert G. *insurance company executive*
Soltz, Judith E. *insurance company executive, lawyer*
Stewart, James Gathings *insurance company executive*
Vaughan, Richard C. *insurance company executive*
Welch, Patrick *health insurance company executive*
Wolf, Gregory H. *insurance company executive*

Pittsburgh
Melani, Kenneth R. *insurance company executive*

Radnor
Pappas, Thomas Nicholas *insurance brokerage executive, consultant*

Spring House
van Steenwyk, John Joseph *health care plan consultant, educator*

Wayne
Yoskin, Jon William, II, *insurance company executive*

West Chester
Dzury, Stephen Daniel *insurance company executive*

Wynnewood
Waber, Harry Edward *insurance agency executive*

RHODE ISLAND

Johnston
Bosman, Ruud H. *insurance company executive*
Hurley, Brian J. *insurance company executive*
Subramaniam, Shivan Sivaswamy *insurance company executive*

SOUTH CAROLINA

Columbia
Averyt, Gayle Owen *retired insurance company executive*

SOUTH DAKOTA

Aberdeen
Stoia, Viorel G. *life underwriter*

Mitchell
Widman, Paul Joseph *insurance agent*

TENNESSEE

Chattanooga
Copeland, Floyd Dean *insurance company executive, lawyer*
Greving, Robert C. *insurance company executive*
Watjen, Thomas Ros *insurance company executive*

Nashville
Carson, Paul Eugene *insurance examiner*
Howell, John Floyd *insurance company executive*
Leatherwood, Thomas *insurance agent, state legislator*
Womack, David Andrew (Andy Womack) *insurance agent, state legislator*

Rockwood
Bane, Charles E *insurance broker, writer*

Seymour
Steele, Ernest Clyde *retired insurance company executive*

TEXAS

Austin
Golden, Edwin Harold *insurance company executive*
Madla, Frank, Jr., *insurance and real estate broker, state legislator*
Moody, Robert Lee *insurance company executive*
Moody, Ross R. *life insurance company executive*
Mullen, Ron *insurance company executive*
Payne, Tyson Elliott, Jr., *retired insurance executive*
Truan, Carlos F. *insurance agent, state legislator*
Watson, Brenda Bennett *insurance company executive*

Bryan
Valdez-Flores, Ciriaco *risk assessment consultant*

Dallas
Arizaga, Nicolas Antonio *insurance company executive*
Cline, Bobby James *insurance company executive*
Hogan, Thomas Victor *insurance company executive*
Hudson, C. B., Jr., *insurance company executive*
Rinne, Austin Dean *retired insurance company executive*
Weakley, Clare George, Jr., *insurance executive, theologian, entrepreneur*

Fort Worth
Blackburn, Wyatt Douglas *insurance executive*
Cooper, Alcie Lee, Jr., *entrepreneur, former insurance executive*
Mitchell, Robert Joseph *insurance executive*
St. John, Evert Eugene *insurance company executive*

Frisco
Forêt, Randy Blaise *insurance executive, consultant*

Houston
Alexander, Harold Campbell *insurance consultant*
Bickel, Stephen Douglas *former insurance company executive*
Couch, Jesse Wadsworth *retired insurance company executive*
Davis, Rex Lloyd *insurance company executive*
Dean, Robert Franklin *insurance company executive*
Harris, Richard Foster, Jr., *insurance company executive*
Hook, Harold Swanson *former management consulting executive*
King, Willis T., Jr., *insurance company executive*
Lindsey, John Horace *insurance agency executive*
Poulos, Michael James *insurance company executive*
Rasmussen, Nicholas Roberts *insurance company executive*

Irving
Clemens, Alvin Honey *insurance company executive*
Eudaly, Nathan H. *insurance company executive*
Halbert, Jon S. *insurance company executive*
Phillips, T. Danny *insurance company executive*

Lake Jackson
Elbert, James Peak *independent insurance agent, minister*

Lubbock
Blake, Robert Wade *retired insurance company executive*

North Richland Hills
Mutz, Gregory Thomas *insurance company executive*

Plano
Jensen, Ronald L. *insurance company executive*

San Antonio
Colyer, Kirk Klein *insurance executive, real estate investment executive*
Davis, Robert G. *insurance executive*
Reid, Demetra Adams *insurance company executive*
Rich, Bradford Whitman *insurance executive*
Robles, Josue, Jr., *insurance company executive*
Wellberg, Edward Louis, Jr., *insurance company executive*

Temple
Gillett, Victor William, Jr., *title insurance company executive*

Tyler
Guin, Don Lester *insurance company executive*

Waco
Rapoport, Bernard *life insurance company executive*

UTAH

Ogden
Buckner, Elmer La Mar *insurance executive*

VERMONT

East Calais
Harding, John Hibbard *retired insurance company executive*

Moscow
Kende, Stephen James *insurance sales executive*

VIRGINIA

Arlington
Clarke, Frederic B., III, *risk analysis consultant*

Charlottesville
Long, Charles Farrell *insurance company executive*

Fairfax
Tringale, Anthony Rosario *insurance executive*

Glen Allen
Jones, Carolyn *insurance company executive*
Rogal, Andrew L. *insurance company executive*

Lynchburg
McRorie, William Edward *lawyer, retired life insurance company executive*

Mc Lean
Connelly, Mary Creedon *insurance company executive*

Newport News
Miller, W. Marshall, II, *insurance broker*

Penhook
Hahn, John William *retired insurance company executive*

Williamsburg
Herrmann, Benjamin Edward *former insurance executive*
Sisk, Albert Fletcher, Jr., *retired insurance agent*

WASHINGTON

Bellevue
Clay, Orson C. *insurance company executive, director*

Olympia
Senn, Deborah *insurance commissioner*

Seattle
Armstrong, Mary M. *insurance company executive*
Duckworth, Tara Ann *insurance company executive*
Eigsti, Roger Harry *retired insurance company executive*
Koster, John Frederick *insurance executive*
McGavick, Michael S. *insurance and financial services company executive*
Patulot, Jun J. R. *insurance company executive*
Pierson, Rodney *insurance company executive*

Walla Walla
Perry, Louis Barnes *retired insurance company executive*

Woodland
Hansen, Walter Eugene *insurance executive*

WEST VIRGINIA

Clarksburg
Mollish, Jack James *retired insurance executive*

Morgantown
Oliverio, Michael Angelo, II, *insurance agent, state legislator*

WISCONSIN

Appleton
Anderson, Ronald Gordon *insurance company executive*
Gilbert, John Oren *insurance company executive*
Rudolph, Carl J. *insurance company executive*

Eau Claire
Rusch, Gerald Allen *financial representative*

FINANCE: INVESTMENT SERVICES

Rosemead
Goddard, Jo Ann *investment advisor*

Roseville
Grant, Barbara *venture capitalist*

San Diego
Dunn, David Joseph *financial executive*
Ellsworth, Robert Fred *investment executive, former government official*
Molina Villacorta, Rafael Antonio *technology management investment company executive*

San Francisco
Bauch, Thomas Jay *financial/investment advisor, lawyer, retired apparel executive*
Buckner, John Knowles *investor*
Dachs, Alan Mark *investment company executive*
Da Silva, Delio P. *investment advisor*
DeFeo, Phillip D. *brokerage house executive*
Draper, William Henry, III, *venture capitalist*
Dunn, Patricia C. *investment company executive*
Dunn, Richard Joseph *retired investment counselor*
Gale, Michael Johnathan *entrepreneur*
Gardner, James Harkins *venture capitalist*
Gund, George, III, *financier, professional sports team executive*
Hagenbuch, John Jacob *investor*
Halliday, John Meech *investment company executive*
Hellman, F(rederick) Warren *investment advisor*
Hsieh, Michael Thomas *venture capitalist*
Mahoney, Michael James *investment and software executive*
Marduel, Alix *venture capitalist*
Morgan, Christina *venture capital firm executive*
Nedelman, Adam *entrepreneur*
Redo, David Lucien *investment company executive*
Rock, Arthur *venture capitalist*
Rosenberg, Claude Newman, Jr., *investment adviser*
Schwab, Charles R. *brokerage house executive*
Shansby, John Gary *investor*
Steinberg, David M. *securities analyst*
Steyer, Thomas Fahr *investment company executive*
Turner, Ross James *investment corporation executive*
Vilar, Alberto W. *investment company executive*
Weisel, Thomas W. *investment company executive*
Winblad, Ann *investment company executive*
Wolf, Christopher Robin *investment executive*

San Mateo
Most, Nathan *mutual fund executive*
Strohm, David *venture capitalist*

Santa Barbara
Bartlett, James Lowell, III, *investment company executive*
Egan, Susan Chan *securities analyst*
Emmeluth, Bruce Palmer *investment company executive, venture capitalist*
Sipprelle, Dudley Gene *investor*

Santa Clara
Raghavan, Harsha *investment company executive*

Santa Monica
DeBard, Roger *investment executive*
Unterman, Thomas *venture capitalist, lawyer*

Sausalito
Apatoff, Michael John *entrepreneur*

Sherman Oaks
Koonce, John Peter *investment company executive, educator*

Tarzana
Lauter, James Donald *retired stockbroker*
Neece, Olivia Helene Ernst *investment company executive, consultant*

Templeton
Guenther, Robert Stanley, II, *investment and property executive*

Truckee
Turner, George Pearce *consulting company executive*

West Covina
Tuck, Edward Fenton *venture capitalist*

Westlake Village
Valentine, Gene C. *securities dealer*

Woodland Hills
Feiman, Thomas E. *investment manager*

Woodside
Fisher, Kenneth Lawrence *investment management firm executive*
Markkula, A.C., Jr., *entrepreneur, computer company executive*

COLORADO

Aurora
Ton, Paul *investor, educator*

Boulder
Kahn, Herta Hess (Mrs. Howard Kahn) *retired securities trader*
Mehalchin, John Joseph *entrepreneur, finance executive*

Cherry Hills Village
Sutton, Robert Edward *investment company executive*

Crested Butte
Fletcher, Donn Wallace *retired investor*

Denver
Gampel, Elaine Susan *investment company executive, consultant*
Scheid, Steven L. *investment company executive*
Stephenson, Arthur Emmet, Jr., *corporate and investment company executive*
Wagner, Judith Buck *investment firm executive*

Englewood
Guggenheim-Boucard, Alan Andre Albert Paul Edouard *business executive, international consultant*
Keegan, James Joseph *financial executive*
Van Loucks, Mark Louis *venture capitalist, business advisor*

Estes Park
Marr, James Joseph *venture capitalist*

Evergreen
Jackson, William Richard *entrepreneur*

Grand Junction
Skogen, Haven Sherman *investment company executive*

Placerville
Treat, John Elting *entrepreneur*

Snowmass Village
Bancroft, Paul, III, *investment company executive*

CONNECTICUT

Bristol
Morgan, Joe Leonard *investment company executive, retired professional baseball player, commentator*

Collinsville
Whitney, Carol Marie *securities sales professional*

Danbury
Balmaseda, Ricardo Antonio *stockbroker*

Darien
Koontz, Carl Lennis, II, *investment counselor*
Moltz, James Edward *investment brokerage company executive*

Farmington
Estes, George L., III, *investment company executive*
Halligan, Howard Ansel *investment management company executive*

Glastonbury
Orr, Richard Clayton *financial modeler, futures trader*

Greenwich
Birle, James Robb *investor*
Lampert, Edward *investment company executive*
Marram, Ellen R. *investment company executive*
Miller, Donald Keith *venture capitalist, asset management executive*
Schneider, John Arnold *investor*
Winkler, Charles Howard *investment company executive*

Hartford
Giamalis, John N *investment company executive*
Kurtz, Grant W. *investment company executive*
Lilienthal, Martin M. *investment company executive*
Marra, Thomas M *investment company executive*
O'Keefe, James William, Jr., *investment manager and banker*
Znamierowski, David M *investment company executive*

Litchfield
Sherva, Dennis G. *retired investment company executive*

New Canaan
Babcock, Warner King *entrepreneur, venture capitalist, investment advisor*
Bisbee, Gerald Elftman, Jr., *investment company executive*
Gilbert, Steven Jeffrey *venture capitalist, screenwriter*
Grace, Julianne Alice *retired investor relations firm executive*
Mountcastle, Kenneth Franklin, Jr., *retired stockbroker*
Pike, William Edward *business executive*

Norwalk
Alderman, Rhenus Hoffard, III, *investment company executive*
Hathaway, Carl Emil *investment management company executive*
Maisano, Phillip Nicholas *investment company executive*

Old Greenwich
Lee, Ann Yuk *investment company executive*

South Kent
Keehner, Michael Arthur Miller *investment bank executive*

Southport
Wilbur, E. Packer *investment company executive*

Stamford
Christophe, Cleveland Aleridge *investment company executive*
Cohen, Steven A. *investment company executive*
Hawley, Frank Jordan, Jr., *venture capital executive*

West Hartford
Bigler, Harold Edwin, Jr., *retired investment company executive*

Westport
Frey, Dale Franklin *financial investment company executive, manufacturing company executive*
O'Keefe, John David *investment specialist*
Rudd, Nicholas *investor, consultant*
Walton, Alan George *venture capitalist*

Wilton
Danvers, David Bell *equity broker*

DELAWARE

Greenville
DeWees, Donald Charles *securities company executive*

Millsboro
Lasher, Hiram Nelson *international biological consultant, entrepreneur*

Wilmington
Kalil, James, Sr., *investment executive*

DISTRICT OF COLUMBIA

Washington
Abramson, Patty *investment company executive*
Akerson, Daniel F. *investment company executive*
Ansary, Cyrus A. *investment company executive, lawyer*
Caldwell, John L. *international company executive*
Coreth, Joseph Herman *investment advisor*
Darman, Richard *investor, former government official, former educator*
Farr, Michael Keogh *investment company executive*
Fenn, Scott Alan *investor*
Fisher, Robert Dale *stockbroker, retired naval officer*
Flügelman, Máximo Enrique *financier, composer*
Galvin, Michael Paul *venture capital executive*
Gibson, Paul Raymond *international trade and investment development executive*
Hartwell, Stephen *investment company executive*
Hillman, Devlin *entrepreneur, researcher*
Kelly, Charles J., Jr., *investment company executive*
Kent, Jill Elspeth *entrepreneur, art dealer, lawyer*
Lurton, Horace VanDeventer *brokerage house executive*
Macomber, John D. *investment company executive*
McCaul, Elizabeth *investment advisor, former state agency administrator*
McIlwain, John Knox *housing policy fellow*
Nordlinger, Gerson *investor*
Selin, Ivan *entrepreneur*
Shrier, Adam Louis *investment firm executive, consultant*
Spears, David D. *trading commission executive*
Tanous, Peter Joseph *investment advisor*
Tomlinson, Alexander Cooper *investment banker, consultant*
Van de Water, Mark E. *investment company executive*
Wortley, George Cornelius *government affairs consultant, investor*

FLORIDA

Alva
Darlow, George Anthony Gratton *investor*

Anna Maria
Hall, Edwin Huddleston, Jr., *retired investment company executive*

Boca Grande
Maguire, John Patrick *investment company executive*

Boca Raton
Batmasian, Marta Tersakian *investment company owner*
Bell, Marc H. *investment company executive*
Chestnov, Richard Franklin *private investor*
Ohlman, Douglas Ronald *commodities and securities trader, investment consultant, lawyer*

Bradenton
Nelson, Ralph Erwin *investment company executive, coin dealer*

Clearwater
Benavente, Javier Edgar *venture technology executive*
Grala, Jane M. *securities firm executive*

Coral Gables
Nunez-Portuondo, Ricardo *investment company executive*
Steinberg, Alan Wolfe *investment company executive*

Delray Beach
DeMueller, Lucia *investment consultant*
Schaffer, Marvin W. *investor*

Fort Lauderdale
Huizenga, H. Wayne *entrepreneur, professional sports team executive*

Highland Beach
Lane, James McConkey *retired investment executive*

Hobe Sound
Parker, H. Lawrence *investor, rancher, retired investment banker*

Islamorada
Hawkins, Frank Nelson, Jr., *investor relations consultant, writer*

Jacksonville
Monsky, John Bertrand *investment banking executive*
Schultz, Frederick Henry *investor, former government official*

Jacksonville Beach
Tempelman, Jerry Henry *investment funds trader, financial analyst*

Jupiter
Kulok, William Allan *entrepreneur, venture capitalist*
Malm, Rita H. *securities executive*

Longwood
Goddard, Edward Dean *stockbroker, accountant*

Marco Island
Blackwell, John Wesley *securities industry executive, consultant*
Pettersen, Kjell Will *stockbroker, consultant*

Miami
Batcheller, Joe Ann *entrepreneur*
Bishopric, Karl *investment banker, real estate executive, advertising executive*
Dorion, Robert Charles *entrepreneur, investor*
Ferré, Maurice A. *entrepreneur*
Kuczynski, Pedro-Pablo *investor*

Naples
Elliott, Edward *investment executive, financial planner*
Fogg, Joseph Graham, III, *investment banking executive*
Frantzen, Henry Arthur *retired investment company executive*
Gulda, Edward James *business acquisitions executive*
Oliver, Robert Bruce *retired investment company executive*

New Smyrna Beach
Grummer, Eugene Merrill *commodity futures market development executive*

North Palm Beach
Jaffe, Melvin *securities company executive*

Palm Beach
Bagby, Joseph Rigsby *financial investor*
Gundlach, Heinz Ludwig *investment banker, lawyer*
Halmos, Peter *entrepreneur*
Johnson, Theodore Mebane *investment executive*
McCarter, Thomas Nesbitt, III, *investment counseling company executive*

Palm Beach Gardens
Hannon, John Robert *investment company executive*
Kleinberg, Lawrence H. *investor, consultant*
Mergler, H. Kent *investment counselor*

Pensacola
Lovoy, Joseph T. *investment advisor*

Pompano Beach
Rifenburgh, Richard Philip *investment company executive*

Ponte Vedra Beach
Keeler, Ross Vincent *securities company executive*

Punta Gorda
Presley, Brian *investment company executive*

Saint Petersburg
Emerson, William Allen *retired investment company executive*
Franke, Thomas *investment company executive*
James, Thomas A. *investment company executive*
Julien, Jeffrey P. *investment company executive*
Nichols, Katie *investment company executive*
Scott, Lee Hansen *retired holding company executive*

Sarasota
Balliett, John William *entrepreneur, real estate executive*

Tallahassee
Handy, F. Philip *investment company executive, educational association administrator*

Tampa
Meek, Mark Alan *investment executive*
Michaels, John Patrick, Jr., *investment banker, media broker*
Sigety, Charles Birge *investment company executive*

Tierra Verde
Gaffney, Thomas Francis *private investor*

Venice
Hackett, Edward Vincent *investment research company executive*

Vero Beach
Clawson, John Addison *financier, investor*

GEORGIA

Atlanta
Banks, Marvin R., Jr., *investment company executive*
Blackwell, Michael Sidney *broker, financial services executive*
Bromley, Marcus E. *investment company executive*
Clark, C. Jordan *investment company executive*
Dees, Lafon Carabo *brokerage house executive*
Green, Holcombe Tucker, Jr., *investment company executive*
Keough, Donald Raymond *investment company executive, director*
McMahon, Donald Aylward *investor, corporate director*
Merkel-Moran, Christa Ilse *investor, linguist, educator*
Mitchell, Stephen Milton *investment company executive*
Moore, Darla D. *investment company executive*
Ottley, John K., Jr., *entrepreneur*
Prater, Robert Stanley, Jr., *broker*
Roberts, Thomasene Blount *entrepreneur*
Sands, Jerome D. *investment company executive*
Wheeler, Chris D. *investment company executive*
Whitman, Homer William, Jr., *retired investment counseling company executive*
Williams, Ralph Watson, Jr., *retired securities company executive*

Austell
Orr, Zellie *entrepreneur, educator, writer, researcher*

Columbus
Diaz-Verson, Salvador, Jr., *investment advisor*

Cumming
Drew, Paul S. *entrepreneur*

Duluth
Street, David Hargett *investment company executive*

Dale, John Sorensen *investment company executive, portfolio manager*
Falker, John Richard *investment advisor*
Fauth, John J. *venture capitalist*
Gallagher, Gerald Raphael *venture capitalist*
Horsager, Kent *brokerage house executive*
Lindau, Philip *commodities trader*
Piper, Addison Lewis *securities executive*
Schreck, Robert *commodities trader*
Sit, Eugene C. *investment executive*

Saint Paul
Heyman, William Herbert *financial services executive*

Savage
Bean, Glen Atherton *entrepreneur*

Stillwater
Horsch, Lawrence Leonard *venture capitalist, corporate revitalization executive*

Waubun
Christensen, Marvin Nelson *venture capitalist*

MISSOURI

Joplin
Huffman, Patricia Nell *entrepreneur*

Kansas City
Latshaw, John *entrepreneur, director*
Morgison, F. Edward *investment broker*
Petersen, Robert R. *brokerage house executive*
Stowers, James Evans, Jr., *investment company executive*

Lees Summit
Korschot, Benjamin Calvin *retired investment executive*

Saint Louis
Aldridge, Charles Ray *brokerage house executive, trade director*
Anagnostopoulos, Constantine Emmanuel *venture capitalist, former company executive*
Bachmann, John William *securities firm executive*
Bernstein, Donald Chester *brokerage company executive, lawyer*
Bickel, Floyd Gilbert, III, *investment counselor*
Foster, Scarlett Lee *investor relations executive*
Holway, George J. *holding company executive*
Mendel, Mark J. *venture capitalist*
O'Neill, Eugene Milton *retired investor*

Springfield
O'Block, Robert *entrepreneur, publishing executive*

MONTANA

Missoula
Liston, Albert Morris *investor, administrator, educator*

Polson
Marchi, Jon *former investment brokerage executive, cattle rancher, exporter, venture capitalist*

NEBRASKA

Lincoln
Knox, Arthur Lloyd *investor*
Laphen, James A. *investment company executive*

Omaha
Buffett, Warren Edward *entrepreneur, investment company executive*
Wild, Stephen Kent *securities broker, dealer*

NEVADA

Carson City
Reid, Belmont Mervyn *brokerage house executive*

Incline Village
Johnson, James Arnold *business consultant, venture capitalist*

Las Vegas
Di Palma, Joseph Alphonse *investment company executive, lawyer*
Jabara, Michael Dean *technology and business development entrepreneur*
Roberts, Lia *investor, political organization worker*

Sparks
Holder, Harold Douglas, Sr., *investor, hotel executive*

NEW HAMPSHIRE

Derry
Sapareto, Frank Vincent, II, *investment advisor, state legislator*

Dover
Parks, Joe Benjamin *entrepreneur, former state legislator*

Melvin Village
Allison, Dwight Leonard, Jr., *investor*

NEW JERSEY

Avenel
Berg, Louis Leslie *investment executive*

Berkeley Heights
Webster, John Kimball *investment executive*

Bridgewater
Lowman, Tyrone David *entrepreneur*

Fort Lee
Kramer, Orin Stuart *investment services company executive*
Lippman, William Jennings *investment company executive*

Hackensack
Heilborn, George Heinz *investor*

Haddonfield
Carter, Joan Pauline *investment company executive*

Jamesburg
Olmsted, David John *capital management company executive*

Jersey City
Balsamo, Stephen *brokerage house executive*
Breuer, Ronald Karl, Sr., *investment banking executive*
Gopikrishnan, Parameswaran *investment company executive*
Kontos, Arthur *investment company executive*
Smith, James Frederick *securities executive*
Tang, C. Mark *investment banker, venture capitalist, writer*

Lincoln Park
Sichuk, George *entrepreneur, theoretical biologist*

Madison
Kirby, Jefferson W. *investment company executive*

Mendham
Kirby, Allan Price, Jr., *investment company executive*
Pierson, Robert David *investor*

Morristown
Hedley, David Van Houten *retired investment banker*

New Brunswick
Knapp, J. Barclay *entrepreneur*

Newark
O'Flynn, Thomas M. *investment company executive*
Scott, James Hunter, Jr., *investment executive*

North Brunswick
Mahajan, Sanjiv Rai *entrepreneur*

Parsippany
Moch, Kenneth Ian *entrepreneur*
Winograd, Bernard *real estate and financial adviser*

Pennington
Gundeck, Caroline Nyklewicz *investment company executive*

Plainsboro
Schreyer, William Allen *retired investment firm executive*

Princeton
Chamberlin, John Stephen *investor, former cosmetics company executive*
Fernholz, Erhard Robert *investment executive*
Gund, Gordon *venture capitalist, professional sports team executive*
Johnston, Robert Fowler *venture capitalist*
Schafer, Carl Walter *investment executive*
Treu, Jesse Isaiah *venture capitalist*

Red Bank
Dreman, David Nasaniel *investment counselor, security analyst*
Hertz, Daniel Leroy, Jr., *entrepreneur*

Ridgewood
Ege, Hans Alsnes *securities company executive*
O'Leary, Paul Gerard *investment executive*
Tuthill, Jay Dean, II, *investment executive*

Rumson
Strong, George Hotham *private investor, consultant*

Scotch Plains
Plumeri, Joseph James, II, *financial executive*

Seaside Heights
Cone, Michael McKay *venture capitalist*

Short Hills
Howe, James Everett *investment company executive*

Summit
Keith, Garnett Lee, Jr., *investment executive*
Malin, Robert Abernethy *investment management executive*

Upper Saddle River
Oolie, Sam *manufacturing and investment company executive*

Westfield
Simon, Martin Stanley *commodity marketing company executive, economist*

NEW MEXICO

Santa Fe
Colvin, Greta Wilmoth *entrepreneur*
Davis, Shelby Moore Cullom *investment executive, consultant*
Schuyler, Robert Len *investment company executive*
Thompson, Waite *investment company executive, researcher*

NEW YORK

Babylon
Brackett, Ronald E. *investment company executive, lawyer*

Bay Shore
Williams, Tonda *entrepreneur, consultant*

Bedford Corners
Singer, Craig *entrepreneur, inventor, investor, consultant*

Binghamton
Taylor, Kenneth Douglas *stockbroker, finance and computer consultant, educator*

Blue Point
Owen, Thomas Llewellyn *investment executive*

Brooklyn
Ross, Randolph Ernest *investor*
Wilson, Robert Warne *philanthropist, investor*

Buffalo
Irwin, Robert James Armstrong *investment company executive*
Littlewood, Douglas Burden *business brokerage executive*

Cooperstown
Gavey, James Edward *investment company executive*

Glen Cove
Pettersen, Kevin Will *investment company executive*

Great Neck
Appel, Gerald *investment advisor*
Hampton, Benjamin Bertram *brokerage house executive*

Greenwich
Smethurst, E(dward) William, Jr., *investment manager*

Ithaca
Hojnowski, Jules Austin *entrepreneur*

Manhasset
Calvin, Donald Lee *business executive, stock exchange consultant*
Gardner, Robert *financial services executive*

Massapequa
De Micoli, Salvatore *metals commodity executive*

Merrick
Poppel, Seth Raphael *entrepreneur*

Mount Kisco
Eastburn, John S., Jr., *venture capitalist*
Frieder, Samuel P. *venture capitalist*
Kohlberg, James A. *venture capitalist*
Kohlberg, Jerome, Jr., (Jerry Kohlberg) *venture capitalist, lawyer*
Lacovara, Christopher *venture capitalist*
Romeyn, Prescott C. *venture capitalist*
Wildstein, Evan *venture capitalist*

New Hyde Park
Richards, Bernard *investment company executive*

New York
Acampora, Ralph Joseph *brokerage firm executive*
Adler, Cyrus A *entrepreneur, writer, educator*
Allison, Herbert Monroe, Jr., *investment firm executive*
Andersen, K(ent) Tucker *investment executive*
Aronson, Edgar David *venture capitalist*
Barry, Thomas Corcoran *investment counselor*
Bartlett, Peter B. *investment company executive*
Beinecke, Frederick William *investment company executive*
Bell, Martin Allen *investment company executive*
Bellas, Albert Constantine *investment banker, advisor*
Bendelac, Roger E. *investment executive, financial consultant*
Bergreen, Bernard D. *investment company executive*
Berkowitz, Brad Alan *stock analyst*
Berkowitz, Susan J. *investment banking executive*
Berris, Brian A. *investment company executive*
Bewkes, Eugene Garrett, Jr., *investment company executive, consultant*
Biggs, Barton Michael *investment company executive*
Birkelund, John Peter *investment banking executive*
Blalock, Sherrill *investment advisor*
Bodenchak, Frank Leslie *investment company executive*
Brandford, Napoleon *securities firm executive*
Britz, Robert G. *stock exchange executive*
Britz Lotti, Diane Edward *investment company executive*
Brody, Alan Jeffrey *investment company executive*
Brotman, Steven *venture capitalist*
Brown, Ronald *retired stockbroker*
Brown, Walter H. *investment company executive*
Bruce, Duncan Archibald *investor, writer*
Brunie, Charles Henry *investment manager*
Buckles, Robert Howard *retired investment company executive*
Butte, Amy S. *securities trader*
Cader, Andrew *brokerage house executive, investment company executive*
Cecil, Donald *retired investment company executive*
Cerrone, Gabriele M. *investment company executive*
Chapin, Samuel R. *investment company executive*
Chapman, Peter Herbert *investment company executive*
Clay, John Peter *investment company executive*
Clemente, Lilia Calderon *capital company executive*
Cohen, Abby Joseph *investment strategist*
Cohen, Alan M. *investment company executive*
Cohen, Claire Gorham *investors service company executive*
Cohen, Joseph M. *investment company executive*
Cole, Carolyn Jo *brokerage company executive*
Collins, Timothy Clark *holding company executive*
Condron, Christopher (Kip Condron) *investment company executive*
Conway, Richard Francis *investment company executive*
Cooperman, Leon G. *investment company executive*
Cortez, Ricardo Lee *investment management executive*
Crane, Charles Grant *securities analyst*
Crawford, R. George *investment manager, educator, filmmaker*
Cruz, Zoe *investment company executive*
Dallen, Russell Morris, Jr., *investment company executive, lawyer, publishing company executive*
Daly, John Neal *investment company executive*
Dantzker, David Roy *venture capitalist*
Darlington, Henry, Jr., *investment broker*
Darst, David Martin *investment company executive, educator, writer*
Davis, Jordan S. *venture capitalist*
Dimond, Thomas *investment advisory company executive*
Dorsett, Burt *investment company executive*
Dumler, Richard J. *venture capitalist*
Edlow, Kenneth Lewis *securities brokerage official*
Ehinger, Albert Louis, Jr., *securities trader*
Ehinger, John Anthony *securities trader*
Eig, Norman *investment company executive*
Elkman, Steven Munro *stockbroker*
Elvey, Malcolm *venture capitalist*
Ercklentz, Alexander Tonio *investment executive*
Evnin, Anthony Basil *venture capital investor*
Fahey, James Edward *brokerage house executive*
Fahour, Ahmed *investment company executive*
Feeley, Michael John *investment counselor*
Filimonov, Mikhail Anatolyevitch *investment company executive*
Fisher, Peter R. *investment company executive*
Forst, Edward C. *investment company executive*
Forstmann, Theodore J. *investment firm executive*
Fort, Randall Martin *investment banking executive*
France, Joseph David *securities analyst*
Franklin, Edward Ward *international investment consultant, lawyer, actor*
Freidheim, Stephen C. *investment company executive*
Friedenberg, Daniel Meyer *financial investor, writer*
Friedman, Alvin Edward *investment executive*
Friedman, Robert Laurence *investment professional*
Fuld, Richard Severin, Jr., *investment banking executive*
Gavin, Paula Lance *investment company executive*
Gero, Anthony George *securities and commodities trader*
Goelet, Robert G. *investment executive*
Gold, Jeffrey Mark *investment banker, financial adviser*
Goldfarb, David *investment banking executive*
Goldring, Gary Floyd *securities industry executive*
Goldsmith, John H. *investment company executive*
Goodman, Edwin A. *venture capitalist*
Gottesman, David Sanford *investment executive*
Grano, Joseph J., Jr., *securities industry executive*
Gray, James L. *investment company executive*
Greenberg, Alan Courtney (Ace Greenberg) *securities trader*
Gregory, Joseph M. *investment company executive*
Grusky, Robert R. *investor*
Gubert, Walter Alexander *investment company executive*
Gupta, Gautam *commodities trader*
Haas, Eleanor A. (Mrs. Peter Ralph Haas) *business advisor*
Haggerty, Rosanne *entrepreneur*
Hamdan, Lawrence Anise *investment banker, lawyer*
Hanauer, Linda *venture capitalist*
Hansmann, Ralph Emil *investment executive*
Harris, Carla Ann *investment company executive*
Harris, Charles E. *venture capital investment executive*
Harris, D. George *entrepreneur*
Hart, Gurnee Fellows *investment counselor*
Hashimoto, Kyosuke *investment company executive*
Haskell, John Henry Farrell, Jr., *investment banking company executive*
Havens, John P *investment company executive*
Head, Glenn Oakes *investment company executive*
Healey, Thomas J. *former government official, brokerage house executive*
Healy, James P. *securities trader*
Helsby, Keith R. *stock exchange executive*
Hennessy, John M. *brokerage house executive*
Hensel, Katherine Ruth *portfolio manager, investment strategist, securities analyst*
Herbst, Edward Ian *brokerage firm executive*
Herrmann, Lacy Bunnell *investment company executive, entrepreneur, venture capitalist*
Hertog, Roger *investment company executive*
Herzog, John E. *commodities trader*
Hieber, William George, Jr., *stockbroker*
Hillman, Rita *investor*
Hilton, Andrew Carson *investor, management consultant, former manufacturing company executive*
Hochschild, Roger C *investment company executive*
Hodges, Deborah *investment company executive*
Holland, Michael Francis *investment company executive*
House, Karen Elliott *company executive, former editor, reporter*
Howard, Nathan Southard *investment banker, lawyer*
Hurst, Robert Jay *securities company executive*
Ilacqua, Rosario Salvatore *securities analyst*
Jacobs, Harry Allan, Jr., *investment firm executive*
James, Hamilton Evans (Tony James) *investment banking firm executive*
James, Marc Stephen *brokerage house executive*
James, Robert Gregory *investment company executive*
Jamison, Douglas W. *venture capitalist*
Janney, Stuart Symington, III, *investment company executive*
Jepson, Hans Godfrey *investment company executive, director*
Jones, Abbott C. *investment banking executive*
Kane, William Jeffrey *investment firm executive*
Kavovit, Barbara *entrepreneur*
Kehoe, John P. *investor relations and corporate development consultant*
Kelly, William Michael *investment executive*
Kennan, Christopher James *investment executive, not-for-profit fundraiser*
Ketchum, Richard G. *stock exchange executive, lawyer*
Kinney, Catherine R. *stock exchange executive*
Klein, Jeffrey Peter *investor*
Kolm, Petter N. *investment advisor, mathematician*
Kovacs, James *brokerage house executive*
Kovner, Bruce *investment company executive*
Kravis, Henry R. *venture capitalist*
Krawcheck, Sallie L. *investment company executive*
Kraynak, Michael, Jr., *investment company executive*
Kreitman, James E. *securities trader*
Kressel, Henry *venture capitalist*
Kuttner, Neil *investment company executive*

Lakatos, Susan Carol *investment banker, artist*
Lamport, Anthony Matthew *investments and venture capitalist*
Lane, Jeffrey Bruce *financial services company executive*
Lang, Everett Francis, Jr., *brokerage house executive*
Langone, Kenneth *investment company executive*
Lasser, Joseph Robert *investment company executive*
Lauder, Ronald Stephen *investor*
Lawrence, Bryan Hunt *investment banking executive*
Lebenthal, Alexandra *investment firm executive*
Leibowitz, Martin L. *investment company executive*
Levy, Matthew Degen *investment banking technology and operations company executive, consumer products business development and planning executive, management consultant*
Lin, Yiling Ellen *investment advisor*
Liu, Xinyu *securities trader, financial analyst*
Loeb, John Langeloth, Jr., *investment counselor*
Logan, J. Murray *investment manager*
Lubin, Daniel C. *venture capitalist*
Luke, Douglas Sigler *business executive*
Lynch, Gary G. *investment company executive, lawyer*
MacAllaster, Archie *investment company executive*
Macdonald, R. Fulton Smith *venture capitalist, advertising executive, consultant, finance educator*
Mager, Ezra Pascal *investment management company executive*
Main, Patricia Englander *investor*
Mariotti, Steve J. *entrepreneur, finance educator*
Mayer, William Emilio *investor*
McCann, Robert J. *investment company executive*
McConnell, Michael W. *investment company executive*
McDonald, James S. *investment company executive*
McGlynn, William Charles *brokerage house executive*
McKay, Geoff *private equity investor*
Meeker, Mary *stock brokerage executive*
Meguid, Terry F *investment company executive*
Mendez, Albert Orlando *industrialist, financier*
Metz, Emmanuel Michael *investment company executive, lawyer*
Meyers, Michael E. *venture capitalist*
Miller, Corbin Russell *investment company executive*
Mintz, Walter *investment company executive*
Moore, William H., III, *investment company executive*
Morris, William Charles *investor*
Morse, Robert Parker *investment company executive*
Murphy, Donald B. *investment company executive*
Murphy, John B. *investment advisor*
Murphy, John Joseph, Jr., *investment company executive*
Murray, Eileen K. *investment company executive*
Nabi, Stanley Andrew *investment executive*
Nadelberg, Eric Paul *brokerage house executive*
Nazem, Fereydoun F. *venture capitalist*
Neustein, Robin *investment company executive*
Newhouse, Stephan F. *securities company executive*
Newsome, James E. *commodity futures exchange executive*
Nielsen, John A. *investment company executive*
Niemiec, David Wallace *investment management executive*
Obernauer, Marne, Jr., *business executive*
Obolensky, Ivan *investment banker, foundation consultant, writer, publisher*
Offit, Morris Wolf *investment advisory executive*
O'Grady, Beverly Troxler *investment executive, counselor*
Olinger, Chauncey Greene, Jr., *investment company executive, editorial consultant*
O'Neal, E. Stanley (Stan O'Neal) *investment company executive*
Orben, Jack Richard *investment company executive, director*
Pados, Frank John, Jr., *investment company executive*
Pandit, Vikram S *investment company executive*
Pappas, Milton J. *venture capitalist*
Paul, Andrew Mitchell *private equity investor*
Paulson, Henry Merritt, Jr., (Hank Paulson) *venture capitalist, investment company executive*
Perlmutter, Louis *investment banker, lawyer*
Peterson, Peter G. *investment company executive*
Pfinsgraff, Martin *investment company executive*
Pietri, Todd T. *venture capitalist*
Pittman, Robert Warren *investor*
Pollack, Stephen J. *stockbroker*
Pouschine, John Laurence *private equity investment executive*
Purjes, Dan *investment company executive*
Queally, Paul B. *venture capitalist*
Quick, Peter *former brokerage firm executive*
Quick, Thomas Clarkson *brokerage house executive*
Quigley, James R. *investment company executive*
Quirk, John James *investment company executive*
Rahl, Leslie *risk advisor, entrepreneur*
Rand, Lawrence Anthony *investor, financial relations executive*
Reed, John Shepard *stock exchange executive*
Ritterseiser, Robert *investment company executive*
Rizzuto, Richard Peter *entrepreneur*
Rogers, James Beeland, Jr., *investment company executive*
Rogers, Theodore Courtney *investment company executive*
Rosenbloom, Daniel *investment banker, lawyer*
Rothfeld, Michael B. *theatrical productions executive, investor*
Rothstein, Gerald Alan *retired investment company executive*
Schafer, Oscar S. *investment company executive*
Schick, Harry Leon *investment company executive*
Schiff, Frank *investment company executive*
Schiff, Marlene Sandler *entrepreneur*
Schoen, Rem *retired investment executive*
Shalom, Liliane Winn *investment company executive, consultant*
Shapiro, Robert Frank *investment banking company executive*
Sharp, Rob *investment company executive*
Shavin, Helene B. *venture capital company executive*
Sheffery, Michael B. *investment company executive*
Shern, Stephanie Marie *investment company executive, accountant*

Siebert, Muriel (Mickie) *brokerage house executive, former state banking official*
Smith, Malcolm Bernard *investment company executive*
Sodano, Salvatore F. *stock exchange executive*
Sorte, John Follett *investment firm executive*
Speciale, Richard *investment company executive*
Spira, Robert Alan *securities company executive*
Stead, Jerre L. *investment company executive*
Steffens, John Laundon *brokerage house executive*
Stein, David Fred *investment executive*
Steinberg, Saul Phillip *holding company executive*
Sterling, Robert Lee, Jr., *investment company executive*
Stern, Walter Phillips *investment executive*
Stevens, Jerome Hebert *entrepreneur*
Stewart, E(dward) Nicholson *investment management executive*
Stoddard, George Earl *investment company financial executive*
Taylor, Richard William *investment banker, securities broker*
Thain, John A. *stock exchange executive*
Tishman, Danel R *entrepreneur*
Tizzio, Thomas Ralph *brokerage executive*
Toffolon, John, Jr., *investment company executive*
Tozer, W. James, Jr., *investment company executive*
Train, John *investment counselor, writer, government official*
Tucker, Lawrence C. *investment company executive*
Turner, Patrick Noel Waddington *fund manager*
Tutwiler, Margaret DeBardeleben *stock exchange executive, former federal agency administrator*
Ule, Guy Maxwell, Jr., *stockbroker*
Updike, Helen Hill *investment manager, financial advisor*
Valbuena, Vivian *brokerage house executive*
Virtue, Ted *investment company executive*
Vogelstein, John L. *venture capitalist*
Wages, Robert Coleman *equity investor*
Walker, Jeffrey Clemens *venture capitalist*
Wareham, Raymond Noble *investment professional*
Weintz, Jacob Frederick, Jr., *retired investment banker*
Williams, Christopher *investment company executive*
Williams, Dave Harrell *investment executive*
Wilson, Stephen R. *financial infromation executive*
Wit, Harold Maurice *investment banker, lawyer, investor*
Witmer, Richard H. *investment company executive*
Wood, Jerry *investment company executive*
Woods, Ward Wilson, Jr., *investment company executive*
Xia, Lulin *private equity investor*
Yetman, Gary *investment company executive*
Zachem, Tyler *investment company executive*
Zeuschner, Erwin Arnold *investment advisory company executive*
Zwickler, Allen *investment advisor, educator*

Oyster Bay
Zarb, Frank Gustave *investment executive*

Pittsford
Green, Martin Lincoln *investor, retired financial analyst*

Purchase
Black, Leon David *private investment firm executive*

Rochester
Fielding, Ronald Herbert *investment company executive*
Rulison, Joseph Richard *investment advisor*

Rye
Casson Madden, Chris *entrepreneur, interior designer*

Sag Harbor
Brody, Eugene David *investment company executive*

Shirley
Kruk, Barbara Guarino *entrepreneur, public relations executive*

Southampton
Culp, Michael Bronston *investor, writer, publisher*

Wantagh
Zinder, Newton Donald *stock market analyst, consultant*

White Plains
Gottlieb, Lester M. *entrepreneur*
McCulloch, James Callahan *corporate executive*

Woodstock
Ober, Stuart Alan *investment consultant, book publisher*

Yonkers
Smith, Aldo Ralston, Jr., *brokerage house executive*

NORTH CAROLINA

Boone
Mackorell, James Theodore, Jr., *entrepreneur, small business owner*

Charlotte
Cummings, Stephen Emery *investment banking executive*
Dalton, Parks H. *investment company executive*
Grimaldi, James Thomas *investment fund executive*
May, Benjamin Tallman *securities specialist, administrator*
Morgan, James H. *investment company executive*
Ragan, Robert Allison *private investment executive, financial consultant*
Ruff, Edward Carr *retired investment company executive*

Denton
Tuttle, Bynum R., Jr., *brokerage house executive*

Greensboro
Johnson, Marshall Hardy *investment company executive*

Hendersonville
Garcia, Ron B. *securities trader, professional golfer*

High Point
Phillips, Earl Norfleet, Jr., *diplomat, financial services executive*

Raleigh
McKinney, Charles Cecil *investment company executive*

Winston Salem
Smunt, Marsha Lynn Haeflinger *financial executive*
Strickland, Robert Louis *former retail company executive*

NORTH DAKOTA

Fargo
Tallman, Robert Hall *investment company executive*

Grand Forks
Gjovig, Bruce Quentin *entrepreneur coach, consultant, entrepreneur*

OHIO

Alpha
James, Francis Edward, Jr., *investment counselor*

Bryan
Oberlin, Earl Clifford, III, *securities brokerage company executive*

Cincinnati
Anning, Robert Doan Hopkins *brokerage company executive*
Bell, Sandra Elizabeth *commercial and investment banker*
James, George Barker, II, *investment executive*
Lucke, Robert Vito *merger and acquisition executive*
Price, Thomas Emile *investment company executive*
Sekhar, Jainagesh Akkaraja *entrepreneur, educator*

Cleveland
Acheampong, Robert Kwabena *investment consultant*
Brentlinger, Paul Smith *venture capital executive*
Charnas, Michael (Mannie Charnas) *investment company executive*
Gelfand, Ivan *investment advisor*
O'Donnell, Thomas Michael *former brokerage firm executive*
Summers, William B., Jr., *brokerage house executive*

Columbus
Barthelmas, Ned Kelton *investment and commercial real estate developer*

Dayton
Klein, Sophia H. *entrepreneur*

Galion
Cobey, Ralph *industrialist*

Hudson
Ashcroft, Richard Carter *investment company executive*
Kempe, Robert Aron *venture management executive*

Kent
Juvan, Dennis Paul *securities trader*

OKLAHOMA

Bethany
McGowan, Bernard W. *venture capitalist, writer*

Oklahoma City
Sulc, Dwight George *investment advisor*

Tulsa
Healey, David Lee *investment company executive*
Neas, John Theodore *investment company executive*
Sanditen, Edgar Richard *investment company executive*

OREGON

Bend
Fain, Jay Lindsey *brokerage house executive, consultant*

Chiloquin
Reed, David George *entrepreneur*

Medford
Hennion, Carolyn Laird (Lyn Hennion) *investment executive*

Portland
Corbett, Alice Catherine *investor*
Rutherford, William Drake *investment executive*

PENNSYLVANIA

Ambler
Cannon, John *investment consultant*

Bethlehem
Stella, John Anthony *investment company executive*

Blue Bell
Giordano, Nicholas Anthony *stock exchange executive*

Camp Hill
Custer, John Charles *investment broker*

Collegeville
Barnes, Jo Anne *investment advisor*

Easton
Lear, Floyd Raymond, III, *entrepreneur*

Feasterville Trevose
Schwartz, Theodore A. *investment company executive*

Gladwyne
Geisel, Cameron Meade, Jr., *investment professional*

Lancaster
Carlisle, James Patton *entrepreneur*

Ligonier
Mellon, Seward Prosser *investment executive*

Linwood
Cogan, Marshall S. *entrepreneur*

Moscow
Shotko, Kurt Joseph *entrepreneur, music entertainer*

Murrysville
Maurer, Richard Michael *investment company executive*

New Hope
Sergey, John Michael, Jr., *investment company executive*

Newtown Square
Lewis, James Earl *investor*

Paoli
Denny, William Murdoch, Jr., *investment management executive*

Philadelphia
Chen, Philip Minkang *investment banker, corporate executive, lawyer, engineer*
Cunningham, Jessie Jerome *entrepreneur*
Frucher, Meyer S. (Sandy Frucher) *brokerage house executive*
Gowa, Andrew *investor, lawyer*
Neff, P(aul) Sherrill *venture capitalist*
Palmer, Russell Eugene *investment executive*
Savitz, Samuel J. *actuarial consulting firm executive*
Wilde, Norman Taylor, Jr., *investment banking company executive*
Wolitarsky, James William *securities industry executive*
Woosnam, Richard Edward *venture capitalist, lawyer*

Pittsburgh
Casturo, Don James *venture capitalist*
Donahue, J. Christopher *investment company executive*
Donahue, John Francis *investment company executive*
Hillman, Henry L. *investment company executive*
Hyman, Lewis Neil *investment company executive, investment advisor*
Knapp, George Robert *investment executive, business advisor, lawyer*
Schliebs, Charles Allan *venture capitalist, lawyer*
Walton, James Mellon *investment company executive*
Walton, Joseph Carroll *investor*

Quarryville
Bird, L. Raymond *investor*

Radnor
Buck, James Mahlon, Jr., *venture capital executive*

Scranton
Janoski, Henry Valentine *investment advisor, former banker*

Valley Forge
Bogle, John Clifton *investment company executive*
Brennan, John Joseph *mutual fund company executive*

Villanova
Lewis, Wayne H. *investment company executive*

West Chester
Branman, M. Jeffrey *investment fund company executive*

West Conshohocken
Taylor, Martha Elizabeth (Betsy Taylor) *investment company executive*

West Grove
Seder, Jeffrey A. *entrepreneur*

Wilkes Barre
Yarmey, Richard Andrew *investment manager*

York
Thornton, George Whiteley *investment company executive*
White, Timothy Paul *brokerage house executive*

RHODE ISLAND

Newport
Higgins, Harriet Pratt *investment advisor*
Stone, Edward Luke *private equity investor, realtor*

Providence
Hall, Almon C., III, *investment company executive*
Joukowsky, Artemis A. W. *private investor*
Richardson, Julie G. *investment company executive*

Wakefield
Mason, Scott MacGregor *entrepreneur, inventor, consultant*

SOUTH CAROLINA

Charleston
Brown, Ann Catherine *investment company executive*

Columbia
Brockelsby, Jeffrey Lind *investment executive*
Edens, Joe *investment company executive*
McLean, Jodie W. *investment company executive*

Fort Mill
Prud'homme, Albert Fredric *securities company executive, financial planner*

Greenville
Oxner, Glenn Ruckman *financial executive*

Hilton Head Island
Scott, Kerrigan Davis *private investor, philanthropist*

Johns Island
Cameron, Thomas William Lane *investment company executive*

Orangeburg
Dalton, Cheryl Renee *entrepreneur*

Pawleys Island
Hudson-Young, Jane Smither *investor*

Sullivans Island
Romaine, Henry Simmons *investment consultant*

TENNESSEE

Johnson City
Wilkes, Clem Cabell, Jr., *stockbroker*

Memphis
Deupree, William W. *investment company executive*
Reaves, Charles Durham *investment company executive, lawyer*

Nashville
Bradford, James C., Jr., *brokerage house executive*
Byrd, Andrew Wayne *investment company executive*
Hanselman, Richard Wilson *entrepreneur*
Kuhn, Paul Hubert, Jr., *investment counsel*
Nelson, Edward Gage *merchant banking investment company executive*
Roberts, Kenneth Lewis *investor, lawyer, foundation administrator*
Wagner, Michael Grafton *investor, management consultant*

TEXAS

Abilene
Owen, Dian Grave *investment corporation executive*

Addison
Smith, Cece *venture capitalist*

Amarillo
Horton, Thomas Mark *futures and options trader, commodity consultant*

Austin
Baumgartner, Robert *consultant*
Salimena, Kathleen Elizabeth *investor, writer*

Cibolo
Smith, Harry Leroy *securities firm executive*

Corsicana
Dyer, James Mason, Jr., *investment company executive*

Dallas
Bond, Myron Humphrey *investment executive*
Brown, Benjamin A. *investment advisor*
Buchholz, Donald Alden *stock brokerage company executive*
Byrne, Susan M. *investment company executive*
Crockett, Dodee Frost *brokerage firm executive*
Durham, Michael Jonathan *investment professional*
Edmondson, James Howard *investor, former insurance executive*
Fisher, Richard Welton *investor, ambassador*
Glatstein, David *investment company executive*
Hicks, Thomas O. *buyout firm executive, professional baseball team executive*
Lynch, William Wright, Jr., *investment company executive, engineer*
Owen, Daniel Thomas *entrepreneur, venture capitalist*
Quinn, William Francis *investment company executive, accountant*
Whitson, James Norfleet, Jr., *retired diversified company executive*

El Paso
Prendergast, Thomas A. *investments and management consultant*
Wootten, John Robert *investor*

Fort Worth
Bonderman, David *investment company executive*
Dunn, Bill *entrepreneur*
Mitchell, Patrick John *financial executive*

Garland
McGrath, James Thomas *real estate investment company executive*

Groveton
Pyle, Benjamin Malrey *investor*

Horseshoe Bay
Anderson, Kenneth Ward *investor, consultant*

Houston
Barrere, Clem Adolph *business brokerage company executive*
Bollich, Elridge Nicholas *brokerage house executive*
Crispin, Andre Arthur *international trading company executive*
Cunningham, Ronnie Walter *venture capitalist*
Currie, John Thornton (Jack Currie) *retired investment banker*
Duncan, Charles William, Jr., *investor, former government official*
Glassell, Alfred Curry, Jr., *investor*

O'Connor, Ralph Sturges *investment company executive*
Olajuwon, Akinola *investment company executive*
Parsons, Edmund Morris *investment company executive*
Richards, Leonard Martin *investment executive, consultant*
Vaughan, Eugene H. *investment company executive*
Wells, Damon *investment company executive*
Williams, Edward Earl, Jr., *entrepreneur, educator*
Williams, Robert Lyle *investor, retail executive*

Irving
Wooldridge, Raymond *former investment company executive*

Lakeway
Boswell, Gary Taggart *investor, former electronics company executive*

Midland
Roberts, David Glen *prospector, investor*

Orange
Jackson, Cynthia Ann *entrepreneur*

San Antonio
McClane, Robert Sanford *former bank holding company executive, entrepreneur*

UTAH

Salt Lake City
Ballard, Melvin Russell, Jr., *investment executive, church official*
Brady, Rodney Howard *holding company executive, broadcast company executive, former college president, former government official*
Meldrum, Peter Durkee *venture capitalist, biotechnology company executive*
Wallace, Matthew Walker *retired entrepreneur*

VERMONT

Middlebury
Pardee, Scott Edward *securities dealer*

Quechee
DeRouchey, Beverly Jean *investment company executive*

VIRGINIA

Alexandria
Furash, Edward Elliott *investment company executive, banker, lecturer, writer, theater producer*
Rainwater, Joan Lucille Morse *investment company executive*
Tucker, Howard McKeldin *investment banker, consultant*

Arlington
Choksi, Mary *investment company executive*

Charlottesville
Gunter, Bradley Hunt *capital management executive*

Edinburg
Zirkle, William Denman *investment company executive*

Falls Church
Han, Syung D. *international trade consultant, financier*
Isaac, William Michael *investment firm executive, former government official*

Herndon
Burns, Patrick Owen *venture capital company executive*

Mc Lean
Smith, Thomas Eugene *investment company executive, financial consultant*

Middleburg
Parkinson, James Thomas, III, *investment consultant*

Reston
Mitchell, Ellen Clabaugh *investment executive*

Richmond
Gorr, Louis Frederick *investment consultant*
Hong, James Ming *former industrialist, venture capitalist*
Phillips, Thomas Edworth, Jr., *financial advisor, investment mangement consultant*
Scott, George Cole, III, *investment advisor*
Washburn, John Rosser *entrepreneur*

Stanardsville
Anns, Philip Harold *international trading executive, former pharmaceutical company executive*

Suffolk
Holloway, Christopher Matthew *brokerage house executive*

Williamsburg
Gordon, Baron Jack *stockbroker*
Roberson, Robert S. *investment company executive*

WASHINGTON

Bellevue
Kocher, Cynthia *investment specialist*
Wells-Henderson, Ronald John *investment counselor*

Kirkland
Ryles, Gerald Fay *private investor, business executive*

Olympia
Shin, Paull Hobom *investment company executive, state legislator*

Port Townsend
Jones, John Wesley *entrepreneur*

Redmond
Pacholski, Richard Francis *retired securities company executive, financial advisor, consultant*

Seattle
Bayley, Christopher T. *public affairs consultant*
Heath, Richard Raymond *retired investment company executive*
Nelson, Allen F. *proxy solicitation company executive*
Ruckelshaus, William Doyle *investment company executive*
Schultz, Howard *entrepreneur, professional basketball team owner*

Sequim
Kretschmer, Keith Hughes *investor*

WISCONSIN

Madison
Chu, Hsien Ming *investment company executive*

Mequon
Bloom, James Edward *commodity trading and financial executive*

Milwaukee
Kasten, G. Frederick, Jr., *investment company executive*
O'Neill, James Martin *venture capitalist*
Samson, Allen Lawrence *investor, bank executive*

WYOMING

Casper
True, Jean Durland *entrepreneur, oil industry executive, gas industry executive*

Cheyenne
Myers, Rolland Graham *investment counselor*

Jackson
Hirschfield, Alan James *entrepreneur*

Wilson
Chrystie, Thomas Ludlow *investor*
Sage, Andrew Gregg Curtin, II, *corporate investor, manager*

TERRITORIES OF THE UNITED STATES

PUERTO RICO

Hato Rey
Ferrer, Miguel Antonio *brokerage firm and investment bank executive*

San Juan
Uribe, Javier Miguel *investment executive*

CANADA

ALBERTA

Calgary
Cumming, Thomas Alexander *stock exchange executive*

BRITISH COLUMBIA

Vancouver
Saunders, Peter Paul *investor*

MANITOBA

Winnipeg
Watchorn, William Ernest *venture capitalist*

NOVA SCOTIA

Bedford
Hennigar, David John *investment broker*

ONTARIO

Chatham
McKeough, William Darcy *investment company executive, director*

Ottawa
Morand, Peter *investment company executive*

Toronto
Bloomberg, Lawrence S. *securities executive, art collector*
Dey, Peter J. *investment company executive*
Fox, Wayne C. *brokerage house executive, corporate financial executive*
Hore, John Michael *commodity futures educator*
Leech, James William *investment company executive*
Lindsay, Roger Alexander (Baron of Craighall) *investment executive*
Magford, Mary *investment company executive*
Tilley, Shermaine Ann *investment company executive*

QUEBEC

Montreal
Cedraschi, Tullio *investment management company executive*
Gillespie, Thomas Stuart *investment company executive*
Lemire, Andre *investment company executive*
Nadeau, Jacques O. *brokerage house executive*

SASKATCHEWAN

Regina
Vanderhooft, Rob *investment company executive*

MEXICO

Mexico City
Trevino, Guillermo Prieto *brokerage house executive*

AUSTRALIA

Sydney
Lucas, Peter Charles *investment company executive*

AUSTRIA

Kitzbuehel
Newman, Claire Poe *private investor*

Vienna
Liebscher, Klaus *stock exchange executive, banker*

BELGIUM

Brussels
Baxon, Paul Henri Maria *company executive*

BERMUDA

Tuckers Town
Heizer, Edgar Francis, Jr., *venture capitalist*

BRAZIL

Sao Paolo
Leighton, Robert Bruce *investment company executive*

ENGLAND

London
Flint, Douglas J. *business executive*
Scheinman, Stanley Bruce *international financial executive, lawyer*

Oxford
Doyle, William Stowell *venture capitalist*

FRANCE

Neoules
Masurel, Jean-Louis Antoine Nicolas *investment company executive*

GERMANY

Frankfurt am Main
von Rosen, Rüdiger *stock exchange executive*

HONG KONG

Hong Kong
Li, Ka-Shing *international entrepreneur*

ITALY

Milan
DeBenedetti, Carlo *entrepreneur*

JAPAN

Tokyo
Kondo, Masanobu *investment company executive*
Yonezu, Takehiko *retired investment company executive*

MONGOLIA

Ulaanbaatar
Mandel, Leslie Ann *investment advisor, business owner, author*

NEW ZEALAND

Wellington
von Kohorn, Baron Ralph Steven *retired investment banker, author*

NIGERIA

Lagos
Omole, Gabriel Gbolabo *international venture capitalist*

REPUBLIC OF KOREA

Seoul
Hyun, Myung-Kwan *investment company executive*

SAUDI ARABIA

Riyadh
Al-Saud, Alwaleed Bin Talal Bin Abdulaziz *investment company executive*

SLOVENIA

Ljubljana
Rotar, Tomaz *stock exchange executive*
Veselinovič, Draško *stock exchange executive*

SWITZERLAND

Geneva
Farman-Farmaian, Ghaffar *investment company executive*

Lausanne
Bloemsma, Marco Paul *investor*

ADDRESS UNPUBLISHED

Ackerman, Don Eugene *venture capital executive*
Ackerman, Melvin *investment company executive*
Albers, Charles Edgar *retired investment manager*
Aljian, James Donovan *investment company executive*
Allen, Donald Vail *investment executive, writer, concert pianist*
Arbuckle, John Finley, Jr., *retired investment advisor*
Auerbach, Jonathan Louis *securities trader*
Aurin, Robert James *entrepreneur*
Bacharach, Melvin Lewis *retired venture capitalist*
Bacon, Caroline Sharfman *investor relations consultant*
Bagwill, John Williams *retired pension fund company executive*
Bailey, Rita Maria *investment advisor, psychologist*
Bantry, Bryan *entrepreneur, producer, director*
Becker, Paul Albert *investment executive*
Berkley, Stephen Mark *entrepreneur, investor*
Berlin, Howard Richard *investment advisory company executive*
Beyman, Jonathan Eric *investment company executive*
Blum, Barbara Davis *investor*
Bowles, Barbara Landers *investment company executive*
Bratt, Nicholas *investment management and research company executive*
Brown, Herbert Graham *entrepreneur*
Burks, Jack D. *investment executive*
Callard, David Jacobus *investment company executive*
Carr, Harold Noflet *investment company executive*
Cassidy, Donald L. *investment analyst*
Cathey, Catharine Mellon *investment company executive*
Chang, Kevin C. *securities trader*
Chatham, Rosemary Gail Moog *entrepreneur, musician, volunteer, composer*
Chryssis, George Christopher *entrepreneur*
Clemmensen, Larry P. *former investment company executive*
Czarnecki, Gerald Milton *investment banker, venture capitalist*
Daie, Jaleh *investment company executive*
D'Arcy, John P. *investment company executive*
Davies, Michael S. *security analyst*
Dean, Edwin Becton *entrepreneur*
De Lutis, Donald Conse *investment adviser, consultant*
Dietz, Arthur Townsend *investment counseling company executive*
Doherty, Charles Vincent *investment counsel executive*
Drake, Rodman Leland *investment company executive, consultant*
Duarte, Prospero Villacin *retired entrepreneur*
Duff, Philip *investment company executive*
Dunn, John Raymond, Jr., *stockbroker*
Edgreen, Robert J. *equity company executive*
Engelbreit, Mary *art licensing entrepreneur*
Fitts, Catherine Austin *investment advisor*
Fiumefreddo, Charles A. *investment management company executive*
Frankenberger, Bertram, Jr., *investor, consultant*
Freed, Eva Praeger *investment advisor*
Freeman, Ralph Carter *investment banker, management consultant*
Froehlke, Robert Frederick *financial services executive*
Glasberg, Laurence Brian *private investor, business executive*
Godwin, Pamela June *financial services executive*
Goldberg, David Alan *investment banker, lawyer*
Goldman, Alan Ira *investment banking executive*
Good, Walter Raymond *investment executive*
Gouletas, Evangeline *investment executive*
Grasso, Richard A. *former stock exchange executive*
Greber, Robert Martin *retired financial investments executive*
Greene, Frank Sullivan, Jr., *investment management executive*
Grijns, Laine *investment company executive*
Haber, Warren H. *investment company executive*
Hansen, Hal T. *retired investment company executive*
Hanson, John C. *investment company executive*
Hapner, Mary Lou *securities trader and dealer, writer*
Harte, Christopher McCutcheon *investment manager*
Heaton, Larry Cadwalder *securities company executive*
Heine, Leonard M., Jr., *investment executive*
Hentic, Yves Frank Mao *investment banker, industrial engineer*
Hochheimer, Frank Leo *brokerage and financial industry executive*
Holte, Debra Leah *investment executive, financial analyst*
Hom, Doris Soo *consultant, investment manager*
Howard, James Webb *investment banker, lawyer, engineer*
Hudson, Donald J. *retired stock exchange executive*
Ihlanfeldt, William *investment company executive, consultant*
Jaenike, William F. *retired securities industry executive*
Jerrytone, Samuel Joseph *financial broker*
Johnson, Michael Warren *international relations specialist*
Jones, Paul Tudor, II, *investment executive*
Kalita, Dwight Kenton *securities trader*
Kawano, James Conrad *investment analyst*
Kellogg, Peter R. *securities dealer*
Kimmel, Mark *author, venture capital company executive*
Knox, Lance Lethbridge *venture capital executive*
Korins, Leopold *stock exchange executive*
Kuhens, Brian Scott *investment company executive, publishing executive*
Lack, Randall *brokerage house executive*
Lambert, Rebecca Fotouhi *investment company executive*
Landis, Robert Kumler, III, *investment banker, lawyer*
Landsman, Richard *investment company executive, finance educator*
Lasser, Lawrence J. *former investment company executive*
Lavington, Michael Richard *venture capital company executive*
Lee, Thomas H. *buyout firm executive*
Levins, John Raymond *investment advisor, management consultant, educator*
Levinson, Kathy *former investment company executive, philanthropist*
Levitt, Arthur, Jr., *investment company executive*
Lewis, Brock *investment company executive*
Lieberman, Gail Forman *investment company executive*
Logan, Dan *investor, writer*
Lohrer, Richard Baker *investment consultant*
Lynch, Thomas Peter *securities executive*
Mace, Stephen Alan *investment advisor*
Madison, T. Jerome *business executive*
Mayer, Anthony John *investment company executive*
McCausland, Thomas James, Jr., *brokerage house executive*
McNeill, Robert Patrick *investment counselor*
Mikitka, Gerald Peter *investment banker, financial consultant*
Millsaps, Fred Ray *investor*
Molitor, Michael A. *entrepreneur, consultant*
Moran, Charles A. *securities executive*
Morgenroth, Earl Eugene *entrepreneur*
Nadel, Elliott *investment firm executive*
Newberg, William Charles *stock broker, real estate broker, automotive engineer*
Nichols, Carl Michael *venture capital executive*
Niehoff, Karl Richard Besuden *financial executive*
Nordley, Gerald David *investor, writer*
O'Sullivan, Lawrence Joseph *retired investment counselor*
Othman, Talat Mohamad *financial consultant, investment banker*
Page, Jonathan Roy *investment analyst*
Pardue, Dwight Edward *venture capitalist*
Patrick, Thomas H. *investment company executive*
Pauken, Thomas Weir *venture capital executive, mediator*
Paup, Martin Arnold *real estate and securities investor*
Petrillo, Leonard Philip *retired corporate securities executive, lawyer*
Pilkington, Mary Ellen *stockbroker, trader*
Pinkney, D. Timothy *investment company executive*
Pottruck, David Steven *brokerage house executive*
Pulling, Thomas Leffingwell *investment advisor*
Quirk, Raymond R *investment company executive*
Renouf, Anne *technology commercialization financier*
Robinson, Bob Leo *retired international investment service executive*
Roland, Catherine Dixon *entrepreneur*
Rondeau, Doris Jean *entrepreneur, consultant*
Rosenthal, Daniel *investment company executive*
Rosenwald, E. John, Jr., *former brokerage house executive, former investment banker*
Ross, Darius Alexander *arbitrager and commodities trader, philanthropist, investment banker*
Rydén, Bengt Gunnar *retired stock exchange executive*
Samberg, Arthur (Art) J. *investment company executive*
Santilli, Anthony J., Jr., *investment company executive*
Scher, Laura Susan *financial company executive*
Schwartz, Carol Ann *investment company executive*
Sells, Boake Anthony *private investor*
Sener, Joseph Ward, Jr., *securities company executive*
Shah, Arvind *trade consultant, industrial designer*
Sherrill, H. Virgil *securities company executive*
Shinn, George Latimer *investment banker, consultant, educator*
Shivers, Mitchell Everett *retired investment advisor*
Shuler, Jon Emmett *securities industry professional*
Simmons, Hardwick *stock exchange executive*
Snyder, Nathan *entrepreneur*
Sowa, Frank Xavier *entrepreneur, futurist, educator, speaker*
Steen, Carlton Duane *private investor, retired food products executive*
Stephens, Donald R(ichards) *investor*
Stewart, Thomas Clifford *trading and investment company executive*
Stiles, Thomas Beveridge, II, *retired investment banking executive*
Stuart, Gerard William, Jr., *investment company executive, city official*
Swanson, Lauren A. *consultant, entrepreneur, educator, researcher*
Thomas, James Edward, Jr., *brokerage house executive*
Trongale, Nicholas Albert *entrepreneur, researcher*
Uchida, Prentiss Susumu *entrepreneur, management executive*
Urato, Barbra Casale *entrepreneur*
Urciuoli, J. Arthur *investment executive*
Uys, Jurgen Peter Brinker *securities analyst*
Vallee, Jacques Fabrice *venture capitalist*
Wadsworth, Jacqueline Dorèt *private investor*
Welch, Martin E., III, *investor, retail executive*
Wilson, Robert James Montgomery *investment company executive*
Wruble, Brian Frederick *private investor*

GOVERNMENT: AGENCY ADMINISTRATION

UNITED STATES

ALABAMA

Birmingham
Wheeler, Cathy Jo *federal agency administrator*

Decatur
Little, Thomas Walker *retired protective services official*

Huntsville
Schumann, J. Paul *federal agency administrator*

Mobile
Cunningham, Julian Antonia *retired protective services official*

Montgomery
Baker, Jimmy H. *former state finance administrator*
Cauthen, Florence M. *protective services official*
Mandry, Christine M. *public adminstator*
Parker, Susan D. *state official, auditor*

ALASKA

Anchorage
Burke, Marianne King *state agency administrator, financial executive, consultant*
Demarco, Patricia M. *state agency administrator*
Lacy, Gregory Lawrence *protective services official*
Sandvik, Helvi *state agency administrator*
Sedwick, Deborah *state agency administrator*
Thompson, G. Nanette *state agency administrator*

Juneau
Perdue, Karen *state agency administrator*
Usera, Vincent L. *state agency administrator*

ARIZONA

Goodyear
Carlson, Norman A. *government official*

Phoenix
Brunacini, Alan Vincent *protective services official*
Chavez, Nelba R. *state agency administrator, former federal agency administrator*
Dickey, Ginny Grace *state agency administrator*
Foutz, Claudia *state agency administrator*
Houseworth, Richard Court *state agency administrator*
Karnas, Fred G., Jr., *policy advisor*
Martin, Douglas Kenton *state agency administrator*
North, Warren James *government official*

Tucson
Emerson, Kirk *government agency administrator*

ARKANSAS

Little Rock
Green, Johnnie D. *government finance officer, finance educator*
Greene, Tristan Dorian *state agency administrator*

CALIFORNIA

Alpine
Oliverio, Ponzio *protective services official, educator*

Bakersfield
Bernard, Alexander *protective services official*

Beverly Hills
Snowden, David L. *protective services official*

Castaic
Burkhart, Stephanie Gloria *protective services official, writer*

City Of Industry
Cavanaugh, Janis Lynn *protective services official, educator*

Corona
Hall, Harlan *federal agency administrator*

Culver City
Mastro, Danny Frank *protective services official*

Cupertino
Compton, Dale Leonard *retired space agency executive, consultant*

Edwards
Larson, Jo Ann *government agency administrator*
McCarthy, Marianne *government agency administrator*
Petersen, Kevin *federal agency administrator*

El Centro
Steensgaard, Anthony Harvey *federal agency administrator*

Fresno
Haddix, Charles Brian *state agency administrator*
Rank, Everett George *government official*

La Jolla
Butterfield, Alexander Porter *government agency administrator, air transportation executive*
Petersen, Richard Herman *federal agency administrator, aeronautical engineer*

Los Angeles
Bratton, William J. *police chief, former police commissioner*
Fisher, Barry Alan Joel *protective services official*
Garthwaite, Thomas Leonard *city health department administrator*
Lake, Randall Alan *forensic specialist, educator*
Robinson, James W. *fire captain*

Moffett Field
Bingham, Nancy F. *government agency administrator*
Dolci, Wendy Whiting *government agency administrator*
Grymes, Rose *government agency administrator*

Pasadena
Means, Tina *police officer, consultant*
Parker, Robert Allan Ridley *federal agency administrator, astronaut*
Schander, Mary Lea *retired protective services official, educator, consultant*

Redwood City
O'Keefe, Donald Martin *detective-lieutenant*

Sacramento
Brown, Craig L. *state agency administrator*
Gage, B. Timothy *state finance department administrator*
Muehleisen, Gene *retired protective services administrator, state official*
Myrrdin, Terry A. *state agency administrator*
Roberts, Paul Dale *state agency administrator, writer*

Salinas
Liebersbach, Norbert John *protective services official*

San Bernardino
Curry, Paul Russell *law enforcement official, lobbyist*

San Diego
Bejarano, David *protective services official*
Lansdowne, William M. *police chief*
Lum, Rodger G. *city health department administrator*
Osby, Robert Edward *protective services official*
Yokley, Richard Clarence *protective services official*

San Francisco
Coye, Molly Joel *state agency administrator*
Fong, Heather J. *protective services official*
Fujii, Sharon M. *federal agency administrator*
Katz, Mitchell H. *city health department administrator*
Lynch, Loretta *state agency administrator*
Muñoz, Calise I. *federal agency administrator*
Tarnoff, Peter *former federal agency administrator, business consultant*

San Jacinto
Willis, Ralph Walker *retired firefighter*

San Jose
Fenstersheib, Martin *city health department administrator*
Monica, Martin J. *law enforcement officer, educator*

Santa Barbara
Aylesworth, Owen Roy *firefighter*

Santa Monica
Timmer, Barbara *state agency administrator*

Stockton
Chavez, Edward *protective services official*

COLORADO

Aurora
Moser, Jeffery Richard *state agency administrator, public affairs and public management executive, artist, writer, former state official*

Colorado Springs
Young, Larry, Sr., *protective services official, educator, investigator*

Denver
Adkins, Jeanne M. *state agency administrator*
Cooke, Paul Lewis *state fire marshal*
Fulkerson, Richard *state agency administrator*
Logan, James Scott, Sr., *federal agency administrator*
Mathews, Laurie A. *state agency administrator*
Maurstad, David Ingolf *federal agency administrator, insurance company executive*
Nuñez, Joe C. *federal agency administrator*
Page, Polly E. *state agency administrator*
Ponzi, James Doughlas *police officer, computer specialist*
Wade, Karen *federal agency administrator*
Woerner, Robert Eugene *federal agency administrator, editor*

Englewood
McGraw, Jack Wilson *federal agency administrator*

Golden
Olson, Marian Katherine *management executive, consultant, publisher*
Stewart, Frank Maurice, Jr., *federal agency administrator*

Monument
Miele, Alfonse Ralph *former government official*

Vail
McGee, Michael Jay *protective services official, educator*

CONNECTICUT

Bloomfield
Shimelman, Susan Fromm *state policy administrator*

Cheshire
McKee, Margaret Jean *federal agency administrator*

East Granby
Kozlowski, Michael *state agency administrator*

Hartford
Burke, John P. *state agency administrator*
Morgan, William Francis, Jr., *police chief*

Southbury
Foxworth, Johnnie Hunter *retired state agency administrator*

Suffield
Hanzalek, Astrid Teicher *public information officer, consultant*

Wethersfield
Bussiere, Bruce Emile *protective services official*

DELAWARE

Dover
Britt, Maisha Dorrah *protective services official*
Glen, Robert Alexander *state agency administrator*
Williams, Donna Lee H. *state agency administrator*

Newark
Le Min, Thomas Francis *protective services official, educator*

Washington
Comey, James B., Jr., *federal agency administrator*

Wilmington
Vattilana, Joseph William *retired chief state safety inspector*

DISTRICT OF COLUMBIA

Washington
Abernathy, Kathleen Q. *government agency administrator*
Aguirre, Eduardo, Jr., *federal agency administrator*
Albernathy, Kathleen Q. *federal agency administrator*
Albright, Penrose Carballo *federal agency administrator*
Aldonas, Grant D. *federal agency administrator*
Allen, Charles E. *federal agency administrator*
Allen, Claude Alexander *federal agency administrator*
Allgeier, Peter F. *federal agency administrator*
Altenhofen, Jane Ellen *federal agency administrator, auditor*
Alvillar-Speake, Theresa *federal agency administrator*
Andersen, Margo K. *federal agency administrator*
Anderson, David Wayne *federal agency administrator*
Anfinson, Thomas Elmer *government financial administrator*
Antonelli, Angela Maria *federal agency administrator*
Apple, Daina Dravnieks *government agency official*
Armendariz, Tony *federal agency administrator*
Armitage, Richard Lee *federal agency administrator*
Ayres, Judith Elizabeth *federal agency administrator*
Azar, Alex Michael, II, *federal agency administrator*
Bacon, Kenneth H. *federal agency administrator, editor, journalist*
Badger, Doug *federal agency administrator*
Baginski, Maureen A. *federal agency administrator*
Bailey, Sue *federal agency administrator, osteopath*
Bailey, Vicky A. *federal agency administrator*
Bair, Sheila Colleen *federal agency administrator*
Banfield, Marian D. *federal agency administrator*
Barreto, Hector V. *federal agency administrator*
Barthwell, Andrea G. *federal agency administrator*
Bartuska, Ann *government official, biologist*
Bateman, Paul William *government official, business executive*
Baxter, Sandra L *government agency administrator*
Beato, Cristina V. *government agency administrator*
Beck, Richard Thomas *government agency administrator*
Becker, Brenda L. *federal agency administrator*
Beckner, Everet Hess *federal agency administrator*
Benitez, Juan Carlos *federal agency administrator*
Bernanke, Ben S. *federal agency administrator*
Bernardi, Romolo Albert (Roy A. Bernardi) *federal agency administrator*
Berry, Mary Frances *federal agency administrator, history and law educator*
Bhatia, Karan K. *federal agency administrator*
Bies, Susan Schmidt *federal agency administrator*
Bigelow, Donald Nevius *educational administrator, historian, consultant*
Bingham, Jeff *federal agency administrator*
Black, J. Cofer *government agency administrator*
Blair, Dan Gregory *federal agency administrator, lawyer*
Blakey, Marion C. *federal agency administrator*
Bloomfield, Lincoln Palmer *federal agency administrator*
Bodman, Samuel Wright, III, *federal agency administrator, former specialty chemicals and materials company executive*
Bolton, Claude M., Jr., *federal agency administrator, retired military officer*
Bolton, John Robert *federal agency administrator, lawyer, government official*
Bond, Phillip J. *federal agency administrator*
Bonner, Robert Cleve *federal agency administrator, lawyer*
Bost, Eric M. *federal agency administrator*
Bosworth, Dale N. *federal agency administrator*
Boucher, Richard A. *federal agency administrator*
Brenner, Robert David *federal agency administrator*
Briggs, Ethel DeLoria *federal agency administrator*
Brookins, Carole L. *federal agency administrator*
Brooks, Linton Forrestall *federal agency administrator*
Brouillette, Dan R. *former federal agency administrator*
Brown, Dale Susan *government administrator, educational program director, writer*
Brown, Harold *former secretary of defense, corporate director*
Brown, Michael DeWayne *federal agency administrator, lawyer*
Brown, Reginald Jude *federal agency administrator*
Brownell, Nora Mead *federal agency administrator*
Browner, Carol M. *former federal agency administrator*
Bryant, Daniel J. *federal agency administrator*
Bryson, Nancy S. *federal agency administrator*
Buford, James A. *city health department administrator*
Burnham, Christopher Bancroft *federal agency administrator*
Burns, William Joseph *federal agency administrator*
Cabaniss, Dale *government agency administrator*
Campanelli, Richard M. *federal agency administrator*
Campoverde, Rebecca O. *federal agency administrator*
Canterbury, Charles *protective services official, labor union administrator*
Caproni, Valerie E. *government agency administrator*
Carbonell, Josefina G. *federal agency administrator*
Card, Robert Gordon *federal agency administrator*
Carmody, Carol J. *government agency professional*
Carnes, Bruce M. *federal agency administrator*
Carpenter, David G. *federal agency administrator*
Caruso, Guy *federal agency administrator*
Casteel, Steven W. *federal agency administrator*
Chao, Elaine L. *secretary of labor*
Cherry, Schroeder *federal agency administrator*
Christenson, Michael D. *federal agency administrator*
Christie, Thomas Philip *federal agency administrator, research manager*
Chu, David S.C. *federal agency administrator, economist*
Chu, Margaret S. Y. *federal agency administrator*
Chun, Shinae *federal agency administrator*
Church, Cynthia R. *federal agency administrator*
Chute, Mary L. *federal agency administrator, library director*
Clapp, Joseph Mark *federal agency administrator*
Clark, Cynthia Zang Facer *federal agency administrator*
Clark, Kathryn *government agency administrator*
Clarke, Kathleen Burton *federal agency administrator*
Claussen, Eileen Barbara *federal agency administrator*
Clement, Paul D. *federal agency administrator, lawyer*
Cobb, Robert W. *federal agency administrator*
Cole, Bruce Milan *federal agency administrator, art historian*
Combs, Ann L. *federal agency administrator*
Combs, Linda Morrison *federal agency administrator*
Conlin, Linda Mysliwy *federal agency administrator*
Connaughton, James L. *federal agency administrator*
Conway, John Thomas *government official, lawyer, engineer*
Cook, Beverly *federal agency administrator*
Cooper, Daniel L. *federal agency administrator*
Cooper, Kathleen Bell *federal agency administrator*
Copps, Michael Joseph *federal agency administrator*
Corrigan, Dara *federal agency administrator*
Cowen, William B. *government agency administrator*
Crane, Barry D. *federal agency administrator*
Creel, Harold Jennings, Jr., *federal commission administrator, lawyer*
Cronin, Patrick M. *federal agency administrator*
Crouch, Jack Dyer, II, *federal agency administrator*
Curry, Thomas J. *former state agency administrator*
Daniels, Deborah Jean *federal agency administrator*
Daniels, Stephen M. *government official*
Davies, J. Clarence (Terry Davies) *government agency administrator*
Davis, Michele *federal agency administrator*
Davis, Ruth A. *federal agency administrator*
Day, Elizabeth Agall *press secretary*
Dearborn, Rick A. *federal agency administrator*
Decker, Michael H. *government agency administrator*
Deering, Mary Jo *federal agency administrator*
de Kanter, Adriana Alison *federal agency administrator*
Dempsey, Joan *federal agency administrator*
DeRocco, Emily Stover *federal agency administrator*
Devaney, Earl E. *federal agency administrator*
Dewey, Arthur Eugene *federal agency administrator*
Diaz, Nils Juan *federal agency administrator*
Dobriansky, Paula Jon *federal agency administrator*
Dominguez, Cari M. *government agency administrator*
Dominguez, Michael L. *federal agency administrator*
Dominiquez, Cari M. *federal agency administrator*
Donaldson, William Henry *federal agency administrator, corporate financial executive, insurance company executive*
Donnelly, Shaun Edward *government agency administrator*
Donohue, Kenneth M. *federal agency administrator*
Donohue, Thomas Joseph *federal agency administrator, transportation association executive*
Dorfman, Cynthia Hearn *government agency administrator*
Dorn, Jennifer L. *federal agency administrator*
Duggan, Joseph Patrick *federal agency administrator*
Duncan, John M. *federal agency administrator*
Eastham, Alan Walter, Jr., *foreign service officer, lawyer*
Eaton, William A. *federal agency administrator*
Eggenberger, Andrew Jon *federal agency administrator*
Engleman, Ellen G. *federal agency administrator*
Ennis, Michael E. *government agency administrator*
Ervin, Clark Kent *federal agency administrator*
Everson, Mark W. *federal agency administrator*
Feith, Douglas Jay *federal agency administrator*
Fennel, Melody H. *federal agency administrator*
Figueroa, Orlando *federal agency executive*
Findlay, Donald Cameron *federal agency administrator, lawyer*
Fine, Glenn *federal agency administrator*
Fisher, Richard *federal agency administrator*
Fleischer, Rebecca *federal agency administrator*
Flores, J. Robert *federal agency administrator*
Fong, Phyllis Kamoi *federal agency administrator, lawyer*
Ford, Carl W., Jr., *federal agency administrator*
Ford, Cecilia S. *federal agency administrator*
Fore, Henrietta Holsman *federal agency administrator*
Forman, Lori Ann *federal agency administrator*
Fourquet, Jose A. *federal agency administrator*
Fox, James Edward, Jr., *federal agency administrator*
Francis, Shari *federal agency administrator*
Franco, Adolfo Alberto *federal agency administrator, lawyer*
Freeman, Chas. W., Jr., *government official, ambassador, writer*
Freeman, Sharee M. *federal agency administrator*
French, Richard Vaughn *federal agency administrator*
Frieden, Lex *government agency administrator*
Gall, Mary Sheila *federal agency administrator*
Gallagher, Patricia E. *government agency administrator*
Gallegos, Lou *federal agency administrator*
Gannon, John C. *federal agency administrator*
Garcia, Michael J. *federal agency administrator*
Garcia, Michael P. *federal agency administrator*
Garman, David Kline *federal agency administrator*
Garnette, Cheryl Petty *government agency administrator*
Gearan, Mark D. *former federal agency administrator*
Gebhardt, Bruce J. *federal agency administrator*
Gensler, Gary *federal agency administrator*
Gianni, Gaston Louis, Jr., *federal agency administrator*
Gibbs, Nelson F. *federal agency administrator*
Gilbert, Pamela *strategic services company executive*
Gilleran, James E. *federal agency administrator*
Gillis, John W. *federal agency administrator*
Gilman, J. Paul *federal agency administrator*
Goldin, Daniel S. *former federal agency administrator*
Goldsmith, Jack Landman, III, *federal agency administrator*
Goldway, Ruth Y. *federal agency administrator*
Gore, Patricia W. *federal agency administrator*
Gottlieb, James Rubel *federal agency administrator, lawyer*
Graham, John David *federal agency administrator*
Grandmaison, J. Joseph *federal agency administrator*
Green, Grant S., Jr., *federal agency administrator*
Greenfield, Michael A. *federal agency administrator*
Griffin, Richard J. *federal agency administrator*
Griles, James Steven *federal agency administrator*
Guard, Patricia J. *federal agency administrator*
Hale, Janet *federal agency administrator*
Hall, Michael Lee *federal government agency grants administrator*
Hall, Thomas Forrest *federal agency administrator, naval officer*
Halpern, Cheryl F. *federal agency administrator*
Hammerschmidt, John Arthur *federal agency administrator*
Hanford, John V., III, *federal agency administrator*
Harrington, Kathleen M. *federal agency administrator*
Harrison, Patricia de Stacy *federal agency administrator*
Hart, Clyde J., Jr., *federal agency administrator*
Hart, Sarah V. *federal agency administrator*
Harty, Maura *federal agency administrator, former ambassador*
Harvey, Edith M. *federal agency administrator*
Hauser, Richard Alan *Federal Agency Administrator, Lawyer*
Havens, Arnold I. *federal agency administrator*
Hawks, William T. *federal agency administrator*
Hayes, Paula Freda *governmental official*
Heddell, Gordon S. *federal agency administrator*
Helgerson, John Leonard *federal agency administrator*
Henshaw, John Lester *federal agency administrator*
Herraiz, Domingo S. *federal agency administrator*
Hevel, Gary Francis *public information officer, consultant*
Higgins, Robin L. *federal agency administrator*
Hill, Jefferson Borden *regulatory oversight officer, lawyer*
Hill, Kent Richmond *federal agency administrator*
Hobbs, Ira *federal agency administrator*
Holcomb, Lee *federal agency administrator*
Holmstead, Jeffrey Ralph *federal agency administrator*
Horinko, Marianne Lamant *former federal agency administrator*
Horn, Sharon K. *government agency administrator*
Horn, Wade Frederick *federal agency administrator*
Horner, Constance Joan *federal agency administrator*
Hove, Andrew Christian *federal agency administrator*
Howard, John *federal agency administrator*
Hundt, Reed Eric *information industry advisor, lawyer*
Hunt, Earl Stephen *federal agency administrator*
Hunt, Lynne *federal agency administrator*
Huntsman, Jon Meade, Jr., *federal agency administrator*
Hutchinson, Asa *federal agency administrator*
Hutchison, Claude B., Jr., *federal agency administrator*
Iklé, Fred Charles *former federal agency administrator, policy advisor, defense expert*
Iverson, Kristine Ann *federal agency administrator*
Jackson, Alphonso R. *secretary of housing and urban development*
Jackson, Beverly Roberson *state agency administrator, consultant*
Jackson, Jacquelyn C. *federal agency administrator*
Jacobs, David Ernest *federal agency administrator*
James, Kay Coles *federal agency administrator*
Jarrett, Jeffrey D. *federal agency administrator*
Jen, Joseph Jwu-Shan *federal agency administrator*
Jennings, Jerry D. *federal agency administrator*
Jenson, William G. *federal agency administrator*
Jochum, James J. *federal agency administrator*
John, Darwin A. *federal agency administrator*
Johnson, Allen Frederick *federal agency administrator*
Johnson, Stephen L. *federal agency administrator*
Jones, A. Elizabeth *federal agency administrator*
Jones, Linda W. *federal agency administrator*
Juarbe, Frederico, Jr., *federal agency administrator*
Juster, Kenneth Ian *federal agency administrator*
Kansteimer, Walter H., II, *federal agency administrator*
Karp, Naomi Katherine *United States government administrator*
Karpan, Kathleen Marie *former state official, lawyer, journalist*
Kassinger, Theodore William *federal agency administrator*
Keane, Kevin W. *federal agency administrator*
Keegan, Lisa Graham *state agency administrator*
Keegan, Richard *federal agency administrator*
Keisler, Peter Douglas *federal agency administrator, lawyer*
Kelly, James Andrew *federal agency administrator, former policy reseach executive*
Kelly, Paul V. *federal agency administrator*
Kelly, Stanley N. *federal agency administrator*
Keys, John W., III, *federal agency administrator*
Kicklighter, Claude Milton *federal agency administrator, retired army officer*
Kicza, Mary E. *federal agency administrator*
Kilgore, Edwin Carroll *retired government official, consultant*
Kincannon, Louis *federal agency administrator*
Kinney, Anne *federal agency administrator*
Kinney, Stephanie S. *state agency administrator*
Klein, Dale Edward *federal agency administrator*
Klepner, Jerry D. *federal agency administrator*
Korb, Donald Lee *federal agency administrator, lawyer*
Korsmo, John Thomas *federal agency administrator*
Kroszner, Randall Scott *federal agency administrator, economist*
Krueger, Anne O. *international agency executive, economist*
Larson, Alan Philip *federal agency administrator*
Lash, William Henry, III, *federal agency administrator, law educator, lawyer*
LaSpada, Carmella *government agency administrator*
Laurie, Rich M. *federal agency administrator*
Law, Steven J. *federal agency administrator*
Lawson, Kenneth *federal agency administrator*
Leahy, Daniel F. *federal agency administrator*
Leary, Thomas Barrett *federal agency administrator*
Leavitt, Michael Okerlund *federal agency administrator*
Ledbetter, Kenneth W. *federal agency administrator*
Legg, Hilda Gay *federal agency administrator*
Lengyel, David *federal agency administrator*
Lenkowsky, Leslie *federal agency administrator*
Lentini, Joseph Charles *government agency management analyst*
Levinson, Daniel Ronald *federal agency administrator, lawyer*
Libutti, Frank *federal agency administrator*
Lichtenbaum, Peter *federal agency administrator*
Liebman, Wilma B. *government agency administrator*
Lim, Jeanette J. *federal agency administrator*
Lipnic, Victoria A. *federal agency administrator*
Liu, Michael Minoru Fawn *federal agency administrator*
Lloyd, James D. *federal agency administrator*
Lockhart, James Bicknell, III, *federal agency administrator*
Lord, Jerome Edmund *education administrator, writer*
Lowery, W. Wilson, Jr., *federal agency administrator*
Loy, James Milton *federal agency administrator, retired coast guard officer*
Lozada, Jacob *federal agency administrator*
Luther, Michael R. *federal agency administrator*
Mackay, Leo Sidney, Jr., *federal agency administrator*
Maco, Paul Stephen *securities and exchange administrator*
Magaw, John W. *former federal agency administrator*
Magnee, Tom *federal agency administrator*
Magwood, William D. *federal agency administrator*
Mahone, Glenn *federal agency administrator*
Mainella, Frances P. *federal agency administrator*
Maizel, Roy *federal agency administrator*
Mansfield, Gordon Hall *federal agency administrator*
Manson, Harold Craig *federal agency administrator*
Marburger, Darla A. *federal agency administrator*
Marburger, John Harmen, III, *federal agency administrator*
Marshall, John *federal agency administrator*
Marshall, Susanne T. *government agency administrator*
Martin, Jack *federal agency administrator*
Martin, Kevin J. *federal agency administrator*
Martin, Robert Sidney *federal agency administrator*
Mason, Eileen B. *federal agency administrator*
Maxwell, David Ogden *former government official and financial executive*
Mc Afee, William *government official*
McCallum, Robert D., Jr., *federal agency administrator*
McClain, Tim S. *federal agency administrator*
McClellan, Mark B. *federal agency administrator*
McCutchen, Tammy Dee *federal agency administrator*

PROFESSIONAL INDEX 5643 GOVERNMENT: AGENCY ADMINISTRATION

McDonald, Frances D. *government official, editor, lawyer*
McFarland, Patrick E. *federal agency administrator*
McFarland, Robert N. *federal agency administrator*
McLaughlin, John E. *federal agency administrator*
McNamara, Robert M., Jr., *federal agency administrator, lawyer*
McPherson, Edward Russell *federal agency administrator*
McSlarrow, Kyle E. *federal agency administrator*
Mead, Kenneth Minor *federal agency administrator*
Meadows, Vickers B. *federal agency administrator*
Mehan, George Tracey, III, *federal agency administrator*
Mehlman, Bruce P. *federal agency administrator*
Mencer, C. Suzanne *federal agency administrator*
Mendelowitz, Allan Irwin *federal agency administrator*
Merritt, Carolyn *government agency administrator*
Meyers, Linda Dee *federal agency administrator*
Miller, John Ripin *federal agency administrator, former congressman*
Mok, Samuel T. *federal agency administrator*
Monro, Elizabeth (Betty Monro) *federal agency administrator*
Monroe, Jane D. *federal agency administrator*
Montelongo, Michael *business executive, army officer*
Moore, Marilyn *federal agency administrator*
Moore, Powell Allen *federal government official*
Morello, Steven J. *federal agency administrator, lawyer*
Morse, Jerome Samuel *government administrator, trade specialist*
Moseley, James R. *federal agency administrator, farmer*
Mosley, Everett L. *federal agency administrator*
Mosley, Raymond A. *federal agency administrator*
Mueller, Robert Swan, III, *federal agency administrator, lawyer*
Mulville, Daniel R. *federal agency administrator*
Murano, Elsa A. *federal agency administrator*
Murphy, Frances M. *government agency administrator*
Myers, Julie L. *federal agency administrator*
Nason, Nicole *federal agency administrator*
Natsios, Andrew *federal agency administrator*
Navas, William Antonio, Jr., *federal agency administrator, retired military officer*
Neal, Darwina Lee *government official*
Nelson, Kimberly Terese *federal agency administrator*
Nesmith, Steven B. *congressional and intergovernment relations secretary*
Nethery, John Jay *government official*
Neuman, Susan B. *federal agency administrator*
Newman, Constance Berry *federal agency administrator*
Newman, Sherryl A. Hobbs *secretary of the district*
Nicholson, John W. *federal agency administrator*
Noriega, Roger Francisco *federal agency administrator*
Norris, Andrea *government agency administrator*
O'Connor, Eileen J. *federal agency administrator*
O'Grady, Michael J. *federal agency administrator*
Ohl, Joan E. *federal agency administrator*
O'Hollaren, Sean B. *federal agency administrator*
O'Keefe, Sean Charles *federal agency administrator*
Okun, Deanna T. *government agency administrator*
O'Leary, John *international trade consultant, former ambassador*
Oliver, LeAnn Michelle *government official*
Olsen, Josephine K. *federal agency administrator*
Olsen, Kathie Lynn *federal agency administrator*
Palast, Geri Deborah *federal agency administrator, Lawyer*
Parker, Michael (Mike Parker) *federal agency administrator*
Pastorek, Paul G. *federal agency administrator*
Patrick, Susan D. *government agency administrator*
Patron, June Eileen *former government official*
Patterson, Sally Jane *government affairs consultant*
Peoples, Carolyn Y. *federal agency administrator*
Perper, Michael Joseph *federal agency administrator*
Peters, Mary E. *federal agency administrator*
Peterson, E. Anne *federal agency administrator*
Peterson, Katherine H. *federal agency administrator, former ambassador*
Pincus, Ann Terry *federal agency administrator, editor, writer*
Pizzella, Patrick *federal agency administrator*
Polito, Robert J. *federal agency administrator*
Pope, Anne B. *agency head, business executive, lawyer*
Posner, Paul Leonard *government official*
Potok, Nancy Ann Fagenson *federal agency administrator*
Powell, Donald E. *federal agency administrator*
Powell, Michael Kevin *federal agency administrator*
Principi, Anthony Joseph *secretary of veterans affairs*
Prosper, Pierre-Richard *federal agency administrator*
Prouty, Charles S. *federal agency administrator*
Quello, James Henry *government official*
Rademaker, Stephen Geoffrey *federal agency administrator, lawyer*
Railton, William Scott *federal agency administrator*
Raley, Bennett W. *federal agency administrator*
Ramsey, Charles H. *police chief*
Rato Figaredo, Rodrigo *international official*
Reed, Anne F. Thomson *government official*
Reese, George W. *federal agency administrator*
Ressel, Teresa Mullett *federal agency administrator*
Rey, Mark E. *federal agency administrator*
Reyna, Benigno G. *federal agency administrator*
Reynolds, Gerald *federal agency administrator*
Riegler, Guenter *federal agency administrator*
Rivlin, Alice Mitchell *federal agency administrator, economist*
Roberson, Jessie Hill *federal agency administrator*
Rocca, Christina B. *federal agency administrator*
Rogan, James E. *federal agency administrator, former congressman*
Roseboro, Brian Carlton *federal agency administrator*
Rosen, Jeffrey Adam *federal agency administrator, lawyer*
Rosendhal, Jeffrey David *federal science agency administrator, astronomer*
Rosenfeld, Arthur F. *federal agency administrator*
Rosenfeld, Ronald A. *federal agency administrator*
Rosenker, Mark Victor *federal agency administrator*
Rosenstock, Linda *federal agency administrator, medical educator*
Roswell, Robert H. *federal agency administrator*
Roth, Stanley Owen *federal agency administrator*
Rottman, Ellis *public information officer*
Runge, Jeffrey William *federal agency administrator*
Rush, Jeffrey, Jr., *federal agency administrator*
Russell, Judy C. *government agency administrator*
Russell, Richard M. *federal agency administrator*
Rutledge, Peter J. *federal agency administrator*
Rutter, Alan *federal agency administrator*
Sabelhaus, Melanie R. *government agency administrator*
Saleeba, David A. *federal agency administrator*
Sambur, Marvin *federal agency administrator*
Sampson, David Allan *federal agency administrator*
Sansonetti, Thomas L. *federal agency administrator*
Scarlett, Patricia Lynn *federal agency administrator*
Schagh, Catherine *federal agency administrator*
Schaitberger, Harold *protective services official, labor union administrator*
Schapiro, Mary *federal agency administrator, lawyer*
Schaumber, Peter C. *government agency administrator*
Schieck, Frederick W. *federal agency administrator*
Schneider, Mark Lewis *government official*
Schoenberg, Mark George *government agency administrator*
Schoettle, Enid C.B. *government agency administrator*
Schubert, William G. *federal agency administrator*
Sclafani, Susan K. *federal agency administrator*
Scolese, Christopher *federal agency administrator*
Sebejais, Melanie *federal agency administrator*
Sessions, William Steele *former government official, lawyer*
Shearer, Paul Scott *government relations professional*
Sibolski, John Alfred, Jr., *educational association executive*
Silverman, Leslie E. *federal agency administrator*
Simmons, Emmy B *federal agency administrator*
Simmons, Enid Brown *retired state agency administrator*
Simon, James M. *federal agency administrator*
Slater, Eve *federal agency administrator*
Smith, Carl Michael *federal agency administrator, lawyer*
Smith, Dennis G. *federal agency administrator*
Solberg, Mary Ann *federal agency administrator*
Sontag, Ed W. *federal agency administrator*
Sorrels, Carrie L. *federal agency administrator*
Spear, Chris *federal agency administrator*
Springer, Michael Louis *federal agency administrator*
Stadd, Courtney *federal agency administrator*
Steele, Ana Mercedes *former government official*
Stenbit, John Paul *federal agency administrator*
Stevenson, Katherine Holler *federal agency administrator*
Stillman, Robert Donald *government official*
Stone, David M. *federal agency administrator, retired career military officer*
Stoner, John Richard *federal government executive*
Stroup, Sally *federal agency administrator*
Sturgell, Robert A. *government agency administrator*
Styles, Angela B. *federal agency administrator*
Sullivan, Thomas M. *federal agency administrator*
Taft, William Howard, IV, *federal agency administrator*
Tamargo, Mauricio J. *federal agency administrator*
Taylor, John Brian *federal agency administrator*
Teets, Peter B. *federal agency administrator*
Tether, Anthony J. *government agency administrator*
Thompson, Lawrence Hyde *federal agency official*
Tinsley, Nikki Lee *federal agency administrator*
Tomb, Diane Lenegan *federal agency administrator*
Towey, Carroll Francis *senior education specialist*
Townsend, Frances Fragos *federal agency administrator*
Truscott, Carl J. *federal agency administrator*
Tuck, John Chatfield *former federal agency administrator, public policy advisor*
Turner, John Freeland *federal agency administrator*
Van Tine, Kirk Kelso *federal agency administrator*
Vasques, Victoria L. *federal agency administrator*
Vasquez, Gaddi *federal agency administrator*
Venneri, Samuel L. *federal agency administrator*
Verstandig, Toni Grant *federal agency administrator*
Victory, Nancy *federal agency administrator*
Walker, David Michael *US government officer*
Walker, Mary L. *federal agency administrator, lawyer*
Walsh, Dennis P. *government agency administrator*
Walsh, John F. *government agency administrator*
Warshawsky, Mark Joel *federal agency administrator, economist*
Washburn, Kathryn Hazel *government agency executive*
Waters, Mary Brice Kirtley *federal agency administrator*
Watson, Harlan L(eroy) *federal official, physicist, economist*
Watson, Peter S. *federal agency administrator*
Watson, Rebecca Wunder *federal agency administrator, lawyer*
Wayne, Earl Anthony *federal agency administrator*
Weems, Kerry N. *federal agency administrator*
Weicher, John Charles *federal agency administrator*
Weiler, Edward J. *federal agency administrator*
Weinberger, Mark *federal agency administrator*
Weiner, Robert Stephen *federal agency administrator*
Wenzel, Bob *federal agency administrator*
Whitaker, Scott *federal agency administrator*
Williams, David C. *federal agency administrator*
Williams, Steven A., Jr., *federal agency administrator*
Wilson, Joanne *federal agency administrator*
Winkenwerder, William, Jr., *federal agency administrator*
Winn, Morris X. *federal agency administrator*
Winter, Michael Alex *federal agency administrator*
Winter, Roger Paul *federal agency administrator*
Withrow, Mary Ellen *federal agency administrator*
Wolanin, Thomas Richard *educator, researcher*
Wolfensohn, James David *government agency administrator*
Wolff, Otto *federal agency administrator*
Wood, Patrick Henry, III, *federal agency administrator*
Wright, Sylvia *government agency administrator*
Yaklin, Lori Stillwagon *government agency administrator*
Young, Jennifer B. *federal agency administrator*
Zaragoza, Lawrence Jay *government manager*
Ziglar, James W. *federal agency administrator, investment banker, lawyer, educator*

FLORIDA

Boca Raton
Boggess, Jerry Reid *protective services official*
Lazar, Charna L. *retired protective services official, private investigator, consultant*

Bonita Springs
Dunning, Herbert Neal *government industry official, physical chemist*

Boynton Beach
Hill, Patricia Jo *workforce development specialist*

Delray Beach
Schenkel, Suzanne Chance *retired natural resource specialist*

Fort Lauderdale
Jean, Alain *protective services official*

Fort Pierce
Belcher, Dorothy S. *state correctional department administrator*

Gulf Stream
Nalen, Craig Anthony *government official*

Indian Rocks Beach
DeLucia, Gene Anthony *government administrator, computer company executive*

Jacksonville
Glover, Nathaniel, Jr., *sheriff*
Goldhagen, Jeffrey Lee *city health department administrator*

Kennedy Space Center
Malone, Lisa A. *federal agency administrator*

Lakeland
Mahr, Aaron Lee *retired government executive*

Largo
Hasen-Sinz, Susan Katherine *state agency administrator, actress*

Miami
Grist, John *retired government official, engineering executive*

Niceville
Crawford, Jackie R. *retired federal agency administrator*
Culver, Dan Louis *federal agency administrator*

Pinellas Park
Cramer, Kenneth Lee *protective services official, consultant*

Plantation
Gay, John Marion *federal agency administrator, organization-personnel analyst*

Saint Petersburg
Burnette, Charles Galyon *protective services official*

Stuart
Laska, Paul Robert *protective services official, writer, educator*

Tallahassee
Ashler, Philip Frederic *international trade and development advisor*
Buford, Barbara Fest *retired state agency employee*
Milligan, Robert Frank *state agency administrator*
Struhs, David B. *state agency administrator*
Thomas, James Bert, Jr., *government official*

Tampa
Liedke, Guy Arthur *public administrator*

GEORGIA

Atlanta
Broadnax, Walter D. *public policy educator*
Cochi, Stephen L. *federal agency administrator*
Cox, Kathy *education commissioner*
Crockett, Delores *federal agency administrator*
Dallas, Robert F. *state agency administrator*
Dortch, Carole A. *federal agency administrator*
Finley, Michael Valton *foundation executive*
Ford-Roegner, Patricia A. *health services professional*
Gerberding, Julie Louise *federal agency administrator*
Hakes, Jay Edward *federal agency administrator*
Harvard, Beverly Joyce Bailey *protective service official*
Jaffe, Harold W. *federal agency administrator*
Miskis, Constantinos I. *federal agency administrator*
Palmer, James I. *government agency administrator*
Pennington, Richard J. *police chief*
Rucker, Kenneth Lamar *law enforcement officer, educator, military officer*
Smith, Suzanne M. *federal agency administrator*
Sorrell, David G. *state agency administrator*
Thomas, Lee Muller *former government offical*
Toomey, Kathleen Elizabeth *state agency administrator*

Augusta
Cheng, Wu C. *retired patent examiner*

Conyers
Bugg, Owen Bruce *state agency administrator*

Jonesboro
Colburn, Donald Eugene *protective services official*

Kennesaw
Paterson, Paul Charles *retired private investigator, security consultant*

Lawrenceville
Lynn, Thomas Edward *retired government agency administrator*

Peachtree City
Ebneter, Stewart Dwight *utility industry management consultant*

HAWAII

Honolulu
Devaney, Donald Everett *law enforcement official*
Kudo, Emiko Iwashita *former state official*
Miyahira, Neal *state budget and finance administrator*
Miyasaki, Nola *state agency administrator*
Saiki, Patricia (Mrs. Stanley Mitsuo Saiki) *former federal agency administrator, former congresswoman*
Tsukayama, Derrick Kawika *police sergeant, consultant*

IDAHO

Boise
Ahrens, Pamela *state government administrator*
Gee, Gavin M. *state agency administrator*
Jones, Donna Marilyn *state agency administrator, former legislator*
Smith, Marsha H. *state agency administrator, lawyer*

Idaho Falls
Rydalch, Ann *federal agency administrator*

ILLINOIS

Chicago
Cline, Philip J. *protective services official*
Dickman, Martin J. *federal agency administrator*
Henderson, William J. *former postmaster general*
Jones, Stephanie J. *federal agency administrator*
Kuczwara, Thomas Paul *postal inspector, lawyer*
Nava, Roxanne *state agency administrator*
Schmidt, Paul Jeffrey *federal government official*
Sen, Ashish Kumar *government administrator, urban planner, educator, statistician*
Skinner, Thomas V. *government agency administrator*
Thomas, Cherryl T. *former federal agency administrator*
Van Pelt, Robert Irving *retired firefighter*

Decatur
Erlanson, Deborah McFarlin *state program administrator*

Effingham
Bower, Glen Landis *lawyer*

Fairview Heights
Tenpas, Ronald J. *federal agency administrator, lawyer*

Lake Forest
Muldoon, James Peter, Jr., *government agency administrator*

Northlake
Haack, Richard Wilson *retired police officer*

Palatine
Hellyer, Timothy Michael *protective services officer*

Peoria
Jibben, Laura Ann *state agency administrator*

Riverdale
Kruszynski, Timothy Edward *retired corrections officer, poet*

Springfield
Doyle, Rebecca Carlisle *state agency administrator*
Mogerman, Susan *state agency administrator*
Phelps, David Dwain *state agency administrator, former congressman*
Schroeder, Joyce Katherine *state agency administrator, research analyst*

Taylorville
Garner, John Lee *protective services official, educator*

INDIANA

Anderson
Harris, Ronald *state agency administrator*

East Chicago
Ramos, John C., Jr., *protective services official, educator*

Gary
Isla, Exu Reidemer Quero *corrections professional, lawyer, author*

Indianapolis
Baker, Jerry L. *protective services official*
Boehm, Peggy *state agency administrator*
Caine, Virginia A. *city health department administrator*
Gerdes, Ralph Donald *fire safety consultant*
Jarvis, Debra Jean *fire chief, consultant*
Landis, Larry Seabrook *state agency administrator*
Phillips, Charles W. *state agency administrator*
Smith, Keith *protective services official*

Martinsville
Fritsche, Volitta *county detective*

Schererville
Opacich, Milan *protective services official, musician*

IOWA

Des Moines
Bair, Gerald D. *state government official*
Brickman, Kenneth Alan *state lottery executive*
Henry, Phylliss Jeanette *marshal*
Martens, Harvey Arthur *retired government worker, academic administrator*

Treynor
Guttau, Michael K. *state agency administrator, banker*

Waterloo
Newcomer, James Henry *retired federal agency administrator*

KANSAS

Kansas City
Gulliford, James B. *government agency administrator*
Nastri, Wayne *government agency administrator*

Overland Park
McCann, Vonya B. *federal agency administrator, telecommunications industry executive*

Topeka
Parks, Blanche Cecile *public administrator*

Wichita
Etter, Gregg Wayne, Sr., *police officer, educator*

KENTUCKY

Bowling Green
Wells, Jerry Wayne *protective services official*

Frankfort
Robinson, Ella D. *state agency administrator*

Lexington
Calvert, C(lyde) Emmett *former state agency administrator*

Louisville
Adams, Robert Waugh *state agency administrator, economics educator*
Lilly, Charles G. *protective services official, consultant*

LOUISIANA

Baton Rouge
Parks, James William, II, *public facilities executive, lawyer*

New Orleans
Collins, Harry David *forensic engineer, mechanical engineer, nuclear engineer, claims consultant*

MAINE

Saco
Mason, Nancy Tolman *retired state agency director*

MARYLAND

Annapolis
Galvin, Michael Francis *state agency administrator, arborist*
Hunkele, Lester Martin, III, *retired federal agency administrator*
Snyder, Kathleen Theresa *state agency administrator*

Baltimore
Barnhart, Jo Anne B. *federal agency administrator*
Clark, Kevin P. *police commissioner*
Crawford, Fred Lee *public affairs officer*
Dorsey, Donna Morgan *state agency administrator*
Fox, Claude Earl *former federal health official*
Gooden, Eric *government agency administrator, real estate agent*
Hart, Robert Gordon *federal agency administrator*
Huse, James G. *federal agency administrator*
McNally, David D. *federal agency administrator*
Uhl, Scott Mark *state agency administrator*

Beltsville
Tso, Tien Chioh *federal agency official, plant physiologist*

Bethesda
Alexander, Duane Frederick *federal agency administrator, pediatrician, research administrator*
Alving, Barbara *federal agency administrator, hematologist, oncologist*
Battey, James F., Jr., *federal agency administrator, neurologist*
Berg, Jeremy Mark *federal agency administrator, biochemist, researcher*
Chen, Philip S., Jr., *government official*
Clapper, James R., Jr., *government agency administrator*
Collins, Francis S. *federal agency administrator, medical research scientist*
Fauci, Anthony Stephen *federal agency administrator, allergist, immunologist*
Fefferman, Hilbert *government official, lawyer*
Gorden, Phillip *federal agency administrator*
Hodes, Richard J. *federal agency administrator, immunologist, researcher*
Hrynkow, Sharon Hemond *federal agency administrator, neuroscientist, researcher*
Insel, Thomas R. *federal agency administrator, psychiatrist*
Joyce, Bernita Anne *former federal government agency administrator*
Katz, Stephen Ira *federal agency administrator, dermatologist, immunologist*
Kington, Raynard S. *federal agency administrator*
Landis, Story C. *federal agency administrator, neurobiologist*
Larrabee, Barbara Princelau *retired intelligence officer*
Li, Ting-Kai *federal agency administrator, biologist*
Millstein, Richard Allen *federal agency administrator*
O'Callaghan, Jerry Alexander *government official*
Penn, Audrey S. *federal agency administrator*
Pettigrew, Roderic I. *federal agency administrator, radiologist, researcher*
Pinn, Vivian W. *federal agency administrator, pathologist*
Rabson, Alan Saul *federal agency administrator, physician, educator*
Richardson, John *retired international relations executive*
Ruffin, John *federal agency administrator, researcher*
Sieving, Paul A. *federal agency administrator, ophthalmologist, educator*
Singer, Dinah S. *federal agency administrator, immunologist, researcher*
Skirboll, Lana R. *federal health policy director*
Spiegel, Allen *federal agency administrator, internist*
Stanfield, Brent B. *federal agency administrator*
Stith, Kenneth *federal agency administrator*
Strausberg, Robert L. *federal agency administrator*
Tabak, Lawrence *federal agency administrator, dentist*
von Eschenbach, Andrew C. *director National Cancer Institute, oncologist*
Whaley, Storm Hammond *retired government official, consultant*
Whitescarver, Jack Edward *federal agency administrator*
Zerhouni, Elias Adam *Director National Institutes of Health*

Bowie
Alvarez, Aida *former federal agency administrator*

Boyds
Kammer, Raymond Gerard, Jr., *government official*

Chevy Chase
Gaines, Michael Johnston *parole commissioner*
Pitofsky, Robert *federal agency administrator, law educator*

Emmitsburg
Paulison, R. David *federal agency administrator*

Fort George G Meade
Black, William B., Jr., *government agency administrator*

Frederick
Swanson, Norma Frances *federal agency administrator*

Gaithersburg
Hertz, Harry Steven *government official*

Kensington
Suraci, Charles Xavier, Jr., *retired federal agency administrator, aerospace education consultant*

Laurel
Chrismer, Ronald Michael *federal agency administrator*

Potomac
Foord, Robert LaVerne *intelligence executive, consultant*

Rockville
Aamodt, Roger Louis *federal agency administrator*
Carmona, Richard Henry *Surgeon General of the US*
Couig, Mary Patricia *federal agency administrator*
Croyle, Robert T. *federal agency administrator, psychologist, educator*
Curie, Charles G. *federal agency administrator*
Davis, Beverly Watts *federal agency administrator*
Epstein, Jay Stuart *federal regulator*
Grim, Charles W. *federal agency administrator*
Lumpkin, Murray M. *federal agency administrator*
Manderscheid, Ronald William *federal program administrator*

Silver Spring
Kline, Jerry Robert *government official, ecologist*
Maas, Joe (Melvin Joseph Maas) *retired federal agency administrator*
Mahoney, James R. *federal agency administrator*
Telesetsky, Walter *government official*
Williams, Paul *retired federal agency administrator*

MASSACHUSETTS

Boston
Auerbach, John M. *city health department administrator*
Crimlisk, Jane Therese *probation officer*
Laskey, Frederick A. *state agency administrator*
O'Toole, Kathleen M. *police commissioner*
Torkildsen, Peter G. *state agency administrator*
Varney, Robert W. *government agency administrator*

Cambridge
Cuomo, Andrew *former federal agency administrator*
Deutch, John M. *former federal agency administrator, chemistry educator*
Donahue, John David *public official, educator*
White, John P *federal agency administrator*

Fall River
Liebenow, Larry Albert *federal agency administrator, textile company executive*

Fitchburg
Lee, Robert Dorwin *retired public affairs educator, administrator*

New Bedford
Cordeiro, Elizabeth Dalein *law enforcement training educator*

Saugus
Maillet, Martin Joseph, Sr., *retired police captain*

Westborough
Horwitz, Eleanor Catherine *information and education official*

MICHIGAN

Ann Arbor
Funk, Sherman Maxwell *former government official, writer, consultant*

Dearborn
Van Kirk, Donald John *forensic specialist, engineering executive, consultant, writer*

Detroit
Bully-Cummings, Ella M. *protective services official*
Dale, Shirley Marie *protective services official*
Maseru, Noble A.W. *city health department administrator*
Moss, Leslie Otha *protective services official*

Houghton
Fink, William Orman *federal agency administrator, management consultant*

Lansing
Wilbur, Kathleen *state agency administrator*

Midland
Adams, Thomas Walton *corrections official*

New Haven
Shaw, Charles Rusanda *retired government investigator*

Southfield
Gleichman, John Alan *safety and loss control executive*

Wyandotte
Kaurin, Douglas Edward *protective services official*

Ypsilanti
Lottie, Adrian Jerome *public policy educator, consultant*

MINNESOTA

Minneapolis
Aanerud, Melvin Bernard *federal agency administrator*

Saint Paul
Beers, Anne *protective services official*
O'Brien, Odessa Louise *protective services official*

MISSISSIPPI

Clarksdale
Johnson, P. H. *federal agency administrator*
Schmidt, John Frederick, III, *government agency administrator, consultant*

Jackson
Hoban-Moore, Patricia A. *federal agency administrator*

Southaven
Johnson, Joyce Thedford *state agency administrator*

MISSOURI

Clayton
Davenport, Dennis Lynn *protective services official*

Jefferson City
Mahfood, Stephen Michael *governmental agency executive*

Kansas City
English, R(obert) Bradford *marshal*
Parker, Dennis Gene *former sheriff, martial arts instructor*
Schuster, Fred *federal agency administrator*

Saint Louis
King, Joseph, Jr., *government administrator, educator, consultant*
Warner, Susan *federal agency administrator*

Springfield
Luttrull, Shirley JoAnn *protective services official*

Troy
Burkemper, Sarah B. *state agency administrator*

MONTANA

Helena
Keenan, Nancy A. *state agency administrator*

NEBRASKA

Lincoln
Baird, Samuel P. *state finance director*
Fleharty, Mary Sue *state government staff member*
Gray, Joni Nadine *state agency administrator*

Omaha
Hansen, James Allen *state agency administrator*
Patrick, Erline M. *federal agency administrator*

Oneill
Hedren, Paul Leslie *national park administrator, historian*

NEVADA

Carson City
Chanos, Adriana Escobar *state agency administrator*
Peterson, Mary L. *state agency official*

Henderson
Perkins, Richard D(ale) *police official, state legislator*

Las Vegas
Lally, Norma Ross *retired federal agency administrator*
Wieting, Gary Lee *federal agency executive*

North Las Vegas
Marchand, Russell David, II, *retired protective services official*

Reno
Griffin, Jeff *federal agency administrator, mayor*
Svahn, John Alfred *government official*

NEW HAMPSHIRE

Concord
Day, Russell Clover *state agency administrator*
Hildreth, Peter C. *state agency administrator*
Lohmann, Keith Henry *police department official, consultant*
Mevers, Frank Clement *state archivist, historian*
Millerick, Jayne Marcucci *Republican party chairman*

NEW JERSEY

Adelphia
Carter, Harry Robert *fire protection consultant*

Bordentown
Lowery, William Odell *personnel services executive*

Cape May Court House
Pierson, Jeffrey Lynn *protective services officer*

East Orange
Ilogienboh, Caroline O. *protective services official, publishing executive*

Hamilton
Lacy, John Russell *retired state government administrator, public affairs counselor*

Jersey City
Connolly, Theodore Daniel *protective services official, councilman*

Lawrenceville
Hunt, Wayne Robert, Sr., *state government official*

Lodi
D'Onofrio, Dominick Anthony *police officer, acting police chief*

Maplewood
Rabadeau, Mary Frances *protective services official*

Mays Landing
Connor, Wilda *government health agency administrator*

Mountainside
Weigele, Richard Sayre *police officer*

Newark
Traier, John *state agency administrator*

Toms River
Luzky, Leonard *law enforcement official, national guard officer, educator*

Trenton
Caspersen, Sidney J. *state agency administrator*
Suter, Karen L. *former state banking department administrator*
Tucci, Mark A. *state agency administrator*

NEW MEXICO

Albuquerque
Eichenberg, Peter Thompson *retired state agency administrator*
Gutierrez, Sidney M. *federal agency administrator*
Jaramillo, Mari-Luci *retired federal agency administrator*
Montoya, Patricia T. *federal agency administrator*
Williams, Marion Lester *government official*

Santa Fe
Chambers, Letitia Pearl Caroline *state agency administrator*
Field, Harold *state finance administrator*
Harris, David W. *state agency administrator*
Lovejoy, Lynda M. *state agency administrator*
Otten, Robin Dozier *state agency administrator*
Verant, William J. *state agency administrator*

NEW YORK

Albany
Bradley, Edward James *state official, computer programmer and analyst*
Cross, Robert Francis *commissioner*
Gilliam, Marsha Sampson *state agency administrator*
Novello, Antonia Coello *state health commissioner, former surgeon general, pediatric nephrologist, educator, retired federal agency administrator*

Bronx
Sedacca, Angelo Anthony *police investigator, educator, notary public*

Brooklyn
Von Essen, Thomas *protective services official*

Flushing
Ghazarbekian, Sahak *retired civil servant, consultant*

Garden City
Laureano, Mari *government agency administrator, writer*

Great Neck
Blumberg, Barbara Salmanson (Mrs. Arnold G. Blumberg) *retired state housing official, housing consultant*

Harrison
Nardone, Dennis M. *protective services official, radio personality*

New York
Beausoleil, Doris Mae *federal agency housing specialist*
Blix, Hans Martin *retired international atomic energy official*
Esposito, Joseph J. *chief of police*
Haass, Richard Nathan *federal agency administrator, educator*
Hirsch, Charles S. *city health department administrator*
Holzer, Harold *public affairs officer, historian, writer*
Kelly, Raymond W. *police commissioner*
Kenny, Jane Marie *government agency administrator*
Konopko, Deborah *federal agency administrator*
Oshunrinade, Adeyemi Olusegun *public information officer, writer*
Sorensen, Gillian Martin *United Nations official*
Talbot, Phillips *Asian affairs specialist*
Turso, Vito Anthony *government and public affairs executive*

Rochester
Boehly, Thomas *forensic specialist*
Mars, John Eugene *protective services official, artist*

Springfield Gardens
Moore, Deborah Chantay *protective services official, psychotherapist*

Staten Island
Gonzalez, Richard *maritime safety officer*

Valhalla
Czarnecki, Anthony J. *correction administrator, educator*

Valley Stream
Viegas, Louis Paul *real estate salesperson, retired postmaster*

NORTH CAROLINA

Canton
Roberts, Bill Glen *retired fire chief, investor, consultant*

Charlotte
Wright, Wayne Kenneth *federal agency statistician*

Corolla
Schrote, John Ellis *retired government executive*

Davidson
Brown, Douglas Ivan *law enforcement officer, educator, consultant*

Durham
Peele, Anne Marie *government relations administrator*

Fayetteville
Bickram, Ronald *protective services official*

Franklinton
Moran, John Bernard *retired government official*

Greensboro
Reed, William Edward *government official, educator*
Wallace, Becky Whitley *protective services official*

Raleigh
Maness, Edwin Clinton, III, *highway patrol officer, video coordinator*
Neenan, Peter Anthony *state agency administrator*
Sanford, Jo Anne *state agency administrator*

Research Triangle Park
Olden, Kenneth *federal agency administrator, medical researcher*

NORTH DAKOTA

Williston
Casler, Michael M. *protective services official*

OHIO

Cleveland
Crandall, Karen *government agency administrator*
Grabow, Raymond John *mayor, lawyer*
Jettke, Harry Jerome *retired government official*

Columbus
Gerhardstein, Samuel Edward *public utility administrator*
Gillmor, Karen Lako *state agency administrator*
Jackson, James G. *police chief*
Long, Teresa C. *city health department administrator*
McInturff, Floyd M. *retired state agency administrator*
O'Donnell, F. Scott *state agency administrator*

Dayton
Cannon, Cris A. *protective services official*

Delaware
Ciochetty, John Bryan *protective services official*

Galloway
Barner, Bruce Monroe *former state agency administrator, not-for-profit company chairman*

Montpelier
Deckrosh, Hazen Douglas *retired state agency educator and administrator*

Newark
Billy, Gerry Dee *protective services official*

Pomeroy
Brockert, Joseph Paul *government executive, writer, editor, designer*

Reynoldsburg
Dailey, Fred L. *state agency administrator*

Rocky River
Nisenson, James Howard *retired government agency administrator*

Toledo
McClair, Annette *protective services official*
Smith, Robert Nelson *former government official, anesthesiologist*

Zanesville
O'Sullivan, Christine *retired executive director social service agency, consultant*

OKLAHOMA

Oklahoma City
Bush, William Arden *federal agency administrator*
Collins, William Edward *aeromedical administrator, researcher*
Daxon, Tom *state agency administrator*

Tulsa
Deihl, Michael Allen *federal agency administrator*

OREGON

Eugene
Jiler, Linda Cerise *retired fire and aviation program support specialist, fire emergency dispatcher, consultant, researcher, writer*

Portland
Thompson, Jill Lynette Long *federal agency administrator, former congresswoman*

Salem
Lanter, Floyd G. *state agency administrator*

PENNSYLVANIA

Beach Lake
Farr, Jesse F. *federal agency administrator*

Camp Hill
Nowak, Jacquelyn Louise *state agency administrator, artist, realtor, consultant*

Carlisle Barracks
Metz, Steven Kent *federal agency administrator, writer*

Gettysburg
Roach, James Clark *government official*

Hanover Township
Ginyard, Caleb Nathaniel, III, *government agency administrator*

Harrisburg
Cortés, Pedro *secretary to commonwealth*
Margolis, David Leslie *government agency administrator*
Wentzel, Paul H., Jr., *state agency administrator*

Lancaster
Hudak, Joseph David *forensic engineer, educator, police investigator*

Norristown
Raquet, Maureen Graham *protective services official, educator*

Philadelphia
Brown, Betty Marie *government agency administrator*
Domzalski, John F. *city health department administrator*
Hackney, Sheldon *former federal agency administrator, history educator*
Hairston, Harold B. *protective services official*
Johnson, Sylvester *police commissioner*
Welsh, Donald S. *government agency administrator*
Zimmerman, Robert S., Jr., *federal agency administrator*

Unionville
De Marino, Donald Nicholson *former federal agency administrator*

Wallingford
Cook, Harvey Carlisle *law enforcement official*

RHODE ISLAND

Providence
Hittner, Barry G. *state agency administrator*

Saunderstown
Knauss, John Atkinson *former federal agency administrator, oceanographer, educator, former university dean*

SOUTH CAROLINA

Chapin
Freitag, Carol Wilma *state official, political scientist*

Clemson
Nielsen, Barbara Stock *state educational administrator*

Columbia
Duffie, Virgil Whatley, Jr., *retired state agency administrator*
Inkley, Scott Russell, Jr., *state agency administrator*

Lexington
Resch, Mary Louise *town agency administrator*

Swansea
Inabinet, George Walker, Jr., *retired state agency administrator*

SOUTH DAKOTA

Pierre
Duncan, Dick *state agency administrator*
Olson, Judith Mary Reedy *retired public information officer, former state senator*

TENNESSEE

Knoxville
Andrews, Rosalind *probation officer*
Baxter, William *federal agency administrator*
Harris, Skila *government agency administrator*

Memphis
Knight, H. Stuart *law enforcement official, consultant*
Madlock, Yvonne *city health department administrator*
Walters, Jane *state agency administrator*

Nashville
Bailey, Stephanie B.C. *city health department administrator*
Kyle, Sara *state agency administrator*
Neel, C. Warren *state finance department commissioner*

TEXAS

Amarillo
Bull, Walter Stephen *police officer*

Austin
Ashworth, Kenneth Hayden *public affairs specialist*
James, Randall S. *state banking department commissioner*
Knee, Stanley La Moyne *police chief*
Watson, Elizabeth Marion *protective services official*

Belton
Smith, Marcia K. *government agency administrator*

Bryan
Owens, Harold B. *former state agency consultant*

Carrollton
Varner, Bruce H., Jr., *fire department official, educator*

Dallas
Bolton, Terrell *protective services official*
Cain, Sally H. *federal agency administrator*
Garreans, Leonard Lansford *protective services official, criminal justice professional*
Hill, Jesse Hoyt *training specialist, economics & business educator*
Kunkle, David M. *police chief*
Lancaster, Karine R. *city health department administrator*
Thompson, Zachary *city health department administrator*

Duncanville
Fewel, John Gerrard *government agency administrator, director*

Fort Worth
De Leon, Sergio Leon *protective services official*
Jackson, Stephen Eric *public speaker, life strategist*

Houston
Asher, Jerry L. *retired government agency administrator*
Bradford, C.O. *protective services officer*
Corral, Edward Anthony *fire marshal*
Dillon, Jimi *protective services official*
Hurtt, Harold L. *police chief*

Pasadena
Mondich, Edward H. *protective services official*

Pharr
Medina, Jesse James *protective services official, educator*

San Antonio
Alvey, Dennis H. *government agency administrator*
Dean, Jack *protective services official*
Hatcher, Donald W. *government agency administrator*
Ortiz, Albert *police chief*

UTAH

Salt Lake City
Sparks, Mildred Thomas *state agency administrator, educator*

Tooele
Jansen, Lambertus *state agency administrator, retired judge, criminal justice educator*

VERMONT

Montpelier
Peterson, Julie *public information officer*

Springfield
Putnam, Paul Adin *retired government agency official*

VIRGINIA

Alexandria
Cabral, Sam A. *protective services official, labor union administrator*
Connell, John Gibbs, Jr., *former government official*
Courtney, William Harrison *government agency administrator*
Danaher, James William *retired federal government executive*
Guevara, Rogelio E. *federal agency administrator*
Hughes, Grace-Flores *federal agency administrator*
Johnson, JoAnn Mardelle *federal agency administrator*
Kalder, Frank M. *federal agency administrator*
Knowlton, William Allen *political and military consultant, educator*
Leestma, Robert *federal agency administrator, educator*
Leonhart, Michele Marie *government agency administrator*
Matz, Deborah *federal agency administrator*
Parker, C. Danielle *government agency administrator*
Senese, Donald Joseph *former government official, research administrator*
Simpkins, William B. *federal agency administrator*
Tandy, Karen P. *government agency administrator*
Williams, Justin W. *government official*

Annandale
Greinke, Everett Donald *government agency administrator, educator*

Arlington
Alford, Paula N. *federal agency administrator*
Askey, Thelma J. *federal agency administrator*
Bement, Arden Lee, Jr., *federal agency administrator*
Cohen, Jay *government agency administrator*
Covington, James Edwin *government agency administrator, psychologist*
Kearney, Stephen Michael *corporate executive*
Lauriski, Dave D. *federal agency administrator*
Lieberman, Robert J. *federal audit agency administrator*
McDonald, Bernard Robert *retired federal agency administrator*
Milkman, Beverly L. *federal agency administrator*
Moore, Guy Will *retired public information officer, historian, writer*
Rascon, Alfred *federal agency administrator*
Walker, Robert S. *government agency administrator*

Burgess
Towle, Leland Hill *retired government official*

Charlottesville
Roseberry, Edwin Southall *retired state agency administrator*

Chesterfield
Peterson, Glen Raymond *protective services official*

Crozet
Reswick, James Bigelow *former government official, rehabilitation engineer, educator, biomedical engineer*

Fairfax Station
Kaminski, Paul Garrett *federal agency administrator, investment banker*

Falls Church
Cole, Patricia A. *federal agency administrator*
Dunne, Mary Maguire *federal agency administrator, lawyer*
Padden, Anthony Aloysius, Jr., *federal government official*

Fort Belvoir
Molholm, Kurt Nelson *federal agency administrator*

Fredericksburg
Kusserow, Richard Phillip *government official, corporate financial executive*

Glen Allen
Chittum, Loretta Petty *federal agency administrator*

Hampton
Bridges, Roy Dubard, Jr., *federal agency administrator*

Leesburg
Ink, Dwight A. *government agency administrator*

Mc Lean
DeCell, Hal C. *federal agency administrator*
Hale, Robert Fargo *government consultant*
Hill, Jimmie Dale *retired government official*
Lion, Linda N. *retired federal agency administrator*
Mahan, Clarence *retired government official, writer*
Spaulding, Wallace Holmes *retired federal agency professional*
Verhalen, Robert Donald *consultant*
Yancik, Joseph John *government official*

Mineral
Donald, James Robert *federal agency official, economist, outdoors writer*

Oakton
Entzminger, John Nelson, Jr., *federal agency administrator, electronic engineer, researcher*
Mosemann, Lloyd Kenneth, II, *business executive*

Quantico
Mangan, Terence Joseph *federal agency professional, retired protective services official*

Richmond
Crouch, Robert P., Jr., *state agency administrator, former prosecutor*
Face, E. Joseph, Jr., *state agency administrator*
Pollard, Overton Price *retired state agency executive, lawyer*

Roanoke
Burcham, Darlene *state agency administrator*

Springfield
Basham, W. Ralph *federal agency administrator*
Turner, Stansfield *former government official, lecturer, writer, teacher*

Williamsburg
Dunn, Keith A. *government agency administrator, consultant*
Flanders, Raymond Alan *dentist, governmental health agency administrator*
Gentry, James William *retired state official*

WASHINGTON

Bellevue
O'Keefe, Kathleen Mary *state government official*

Bothell
Anders, Harley Dillon, Sr., *retired federal agency administrator*

Freeland
Calio, Anthony John *scientist, business executive*

Issaquah
Wright, Theodore Otis *forensic engineer*

Lynden
Vigil, Eugene Leon *retired federal agency administrator, cell biologist*

Olympia
Howell, Helen *state agency administrator*
Showalter, Marilyn Grace *state agency administrator*

Seattle
Krochalis, Richard F. *federal agency administrator*
Melendez, Rosa Maria *protective services official*
Plough, Alonzo L. *city health department administrator*

Sequim
Meacham, Charles Harding *government official*

WEST VIRGINIA

Charleston
Douglass, Gus Ruben *state agency administrator*

WISCONSIN

Madison
Deer, Ada E. *former federal agency official, social worker, educator*
Kundert, John F. *state finance administrator*
Leckie, Carol Mavis *retired state government administrator*
Mach, Michael J. *state agency administrator*
Parrino, Cheryl Lynn *federal agency administrator*

Milwaukee
Hegerty, Nannette H. *police chief*

Oshkosh
Poberezny, Tom *federal agency administrator*

Sturtevant
Marschke, Sean M. *police commander, emergency management director*

WYOMING

Cheyenne
De Herrera, Juan Abran (Age) *federal judicial security official*
Fecht, Robert David *protective services official, educator*
Friess, Lynn *state agency administrator*
Green, Laurie *state agency administrator*
Law, Carlene *state agency administrator*
Moser, Diane *state agency administrator*

Powell
Bruscino, Leah *state agency administrator*

TERRITORIES OF THE UNITED STATES

VIRGIN ISLANDS

Kingshill
Llanos, Luis Socorro *retired public administrator, mediator, arbitrator, public affairs consultant*

MILITARY ADDRESSES OF THE UNITED STATES

EUROPE

APO
Ohman, Diana J. *government agency administrator, former state official*

CANADA

NOVA SCOTIA

Lawrencetown
Pottie, Roswell Francis *Canadian federal science and technology consultant*

ONTARIO

Ottawa
MacFarlane, John Alexander *former federal housing agency administrator*
Murray, Larry *government agency administrator*
Penner, Keith *former Canadian government official*
Withers, Ramsey Muir *retired federal agency administrator*

Toronto
Fraser, William Neil *government official, retired*
Tsubouchi, David H. *Canadian provincial official*

Quebec City
Morin, Louis *government agency administrator*

COTE D'IVOIRE

Abidjan
Perry, Cynthia Shepard *federal agency administrator*

EGYPT

Garden City
Norris, James Arnold *federal agency administrator, consultant*

SAUDI ARABIA

Riyadh
Faraidy, Abdulaziz Abdullah *national public security officer*

SCOTLAND

Melrose
Russell, Thomas *retired British government official*

ADDRESS UNPUBLISHED

Adler, Alexander *former federal government health service executive*
Aldridge, Edward Cleveland, Jr., *former federal agency administrator*
Allbaugh, Joe M. *federal agency administrator*
Anderson, Larry J. *federal agency administrator, researcher*
Anderson, Wayne Carl *public affairs officer, former corporate executive*
Arveson, Raymond Gerhard *retired state official*
Baquet, Charles R., III, *former federal agency administrator, international studies educator*
Barca, James Joseph *fire department administrative services executive*
Bayer, Robert Edward *retired defense department official, consultant*
Beers, Charlotte Lenore *former federal agency administrator*
Beers, R. Rand *former narcotics and law enforcement administrator*
Benton, Marjorie Craig *federal agency administrator*
Billings, Judith A. *state education official*
Bishop, C. Diane *state agency administrator, educator*
Blackwill, Robert D. *government agency administrator*
Bolling, Amy L. *federal agency administrator*
Brown, John B., III, *former federal agency administrator*
Brubaker, Crawford Francis, Jr., *federal agency official, aerospace consultant*
Burgess, Marjorie Laura *retired protective services official*
Campbell, Arthur Andrews *retired government official*
Cantu, Jose Francisco *retired postal worker*
Cassidy, Esther Christmas *retired government official*
Clark, Thomas Ryan *retired federal agency executive, business and technical consultant*
Clarke, Richard Alan *former national security specialist*
Claytor, Richard Anderson *retired federal agency executive, consultant*
Conway, James Valentine Patrick *forensic document examiner, former postal service executive*
Crowell, Craven H., Jr., *retired federal agency administrator*
Daniels, Mitchell Elias, Jr., *federal agency administrator*
Dingle, Carol A. *state agency administrator, writer*
Fella, Marie Ann *intelligence analyst, drug enforcement administration*
Fisher, Linda J. *federal agency administrator*
FitzAlan-Howard, Bennett-Thomas Henry Robert *public administration and policy analyst, political theorist, theologian*
Flint, Lou Jean *retired state agency administrator*
Forbes-Richardson, Helen Hilda *state agency administrator*
Frank, Marshall *protective services official, writer*
Frazier, Henry Bowen, III, *retired judge, government official, lawyer*
Frazier, Thomas C. *protective services official*
Friday, Elbert Walter, Jr., *federal agency administrator, meteorologist*
Gauss, John A. *former federal agency administrator, retired naval officer*
Golding, Carolyn May *former government senior executive, consultant*
Grandguist, Betty L. *former director elder affairs*
Grossman, Marc *federal agency administrator*
Helms, J. Lynn *former government agency administrator*
Hervey, Homer Vaughan *retired federal agency administrator*
Heyman, Ira Michael *federal agency administrator, museum executive, law educator*
Hodsoll, Francis Samuel Monaise *government official*
Jameson, Patricia Marian *government agency administrator*
Johnstone, Stowell *former state agency administrator*
Keilty, Bryan T. *government agency administrator*
Kelley, Edward Watson, Jr., *former federal agency administrator*
Kelso, John Hodgson *former government official*
Kemble, Penn *government official*
Kezer, Pauline Ryder *state government executive, management consultant*
Knapp, Edward Alan *retired government agency administrator, scientist*
KÖhler, Horst *former international official*
Korologos, Ann McLaughlin *public policy, communications executive*
Kott, Alan *state agency administrator*
Kutscher, Ronald Earl *retired federal government executive*
Kwame, Guy Allen *protective services official*
LaBarre, Carl Anthony *retired government official*
Lau, Fred H. *protective services official*
Lawler, Thomas Comerford *intelligence agency official*
Lewis, Samuel Winfield *retired government official, former ambassador*
Lissakers, Karin Margareta *former federal agency administrator*
Lovelace, Rose Marie Sniegon *federal space agency administrator*
Low, Paul Charles *protective services specialist*
Loy, Frank Ernest *retired government official*
Marin, Rosario *former federal agency administrator*
Mazzoni, Kerry *former state agency administrator*
McCaleb, Neal A. *former federal agency administrator*
McClain, Lena Alexandria *protective services official*
Mc Coy, Tidal Windham *former government official*
McDowell, Elaine *retired federal government executive, educator*
Mc Fee, Thomas Stuart *retired government agency administrator*
McGarry, Marcia *retired community service coordinator*
Millman, Amy J. *government official*
Minners, Howard Alyn *federal agency administrator, preventive medicine physician, researcher*
Moose, Charles A. *former protective services official*
Morales, Diane K. *former federal agency administrator*
Morgan, Linda Joan *former federal agency administrator*
Muris, Timothy Joseph *former federal agency administrator*
Murr, James Coleman *retired federal government official*
Nedelkoff, Richard R. *former federal agency administrator*
Nyquist, Maurice Otto *federal agency administrator, scientist*
Oliver, Jerry Alton *former police chief*
Panetta, Michael Jon *retired state agency administrator, educator, writer, researcher*
Pearson, Jennie Sue *retired government administrator*
Philippus, Al A. *protective services official*
Pitt, Harvey Lloyd *federal agency administrator*
Polisar, Joseph Michael *protective services official*
Port, Arthur Tyler *retired government administrator, lawyer*
Reilly, Edward Francis, Jr., *federal agency administrator, former state senator*
Rhodes, Karren *public information officer*
Rockett, John Alexander *fire safety consultant*
Rossotti, Charles Ossola *former federal agency administrator*
Saddler, George Floyd *government economic adviser*
Schoenberger, James Edwin *retired federal agency administrator*
Schrenko, Linda C. *former state agency administrator*
Scott, Jeffrey Lyle *protective services official*
Shanahan, Michael George *police officer*
Shasteen, Donald Eugene *government official*
Shelton, Henry H. *former chairman of joint chiefs*
Shirzad, Faryar *federal agency administrator*
Shute, Richard Emil *government official, engineer*
Skaff, Joseph John *retired state agency administrator, army officer*
Sloat, Jane Roberts DeGraff *government official, civic worker, consultant*
Smith, Nancy Angelynn *federal agency administrator*
Smith, Sarah Jane (Sally Smith) *state agency administrator*
Smith, Wendy Haimes *federal agency administrator*
Sorter, Bruce Wilbur *federal program administrator, educator, consultant*
Stagliano, Vito Alexander *federal agency administrator, utilities executive, writer*
Steffy, Marion Nancy *state agency administrator*
Stefko, Joseph V. *government agency administrator*
Tenet, George John *former CIA Director*
Thompson, Larry Dean *former federal agency administrator, lawyer*
Truesdale, John Cushman *government executive*
van Schilfgaarde, Jan *retired agricultural engineer, government agricultural research service administrator*
Waggener, Theryn Lee *retired law enforcement professional*
Walker, Gordon Davies *former government official, writer, lecturer, consultant*
West, Mary Beth *federal agency administrator*
White, Thomas E. *former federal agency administrator*
Wilhelm, John L. *city health department administrator*
Williams, B. John, Jr., *former federal agency administrator, lawyer*
Young, Edwin S. W. *federal agency official*
Zaltman, Mark Allen *federal agency administrator*
Ziese, Dennis Russell *protective services official, retired military officer*

GOVERNMENT: EXECUTIVE ADMINISTRATION

UNITED STATES

ALABAMA

Birmingham
Boomershine, Donald Eugene *bureau executive, development official*
Siegelman, Don Eugene *former governor*

Huntsville
Williams, Phillip Wayne *former state official and army officer, securities and diversified company executive, consultant*

Mobile
Bostwick, Robert Otis *municipal staff member*
Delaney, Thomas Caldwell, Jr., *city official*
Higginbotham, Prieur Jay *city official*
Lee, Christopher Luke *municipal official*

Montgomery
Baxley, Lucy *lieutenant governor*
Bennett, James Ronald *state official*
Bright, Bobby *mayor*
Ivey, Kay Ellen *state official*
King, Troy *state attorney general*
Riley, Robert *governor*
Williamson, Donald Ellis *state official*
Worley, Nancy L. *secretary of state*
Young, Caron L *county official*

Semmes
Phelps, James Franklin *retired county official*

Warrior
Johnson, Barbara L. *retired municipal official*

ALASKA

Anchorage
Brown, Dean Naomi *state official, geologist*
Knowles, Tony *former governor*
Leman, Loren Dwight *lieutenant governor, civil engineer*

Juneau
Murkowski, Frank Hughes *governor*
Renkes, Gregg *state attorney general*

Kodiak
Selby, Jerome M. *mayor*

ARIZONA

Anthem
MacMillan, Hoke *former state attorney general*

Chandler
Dunn, Boyd *mayor, lawyer*

Glendale
Scruggs, Elaine M. *mayor*

Mesa
Brown, Wayne J. *former mayor*
Hawker, Keno *mayor, trucking company executive*
Wong, Willie *former mayor, automotive executive*

Phoenix
Brewer, Janice Kay *state official*
Goddard, Terry *state attorney general*
Gordon, Phil *mayor*
McClennen, Miriam J. *former state official*
Napolitano, Janet Ann *governor*
Takata, Lisa D. *city manager, artist*

San Carlos
Talgo, Harrison *chief administrator tribal government*

Scottsdale
Dobronski, Mark William *judge, justice of the peace*
Manross, Mary *mayor*
Quayle, Dan (James Danforth Quayle) *former vice president United States, entrepreneur*
Quayle, Marilyn Tucker *wife of former vice president of United States, lawyer*

South Tucson
Eckstrom, Daniel William *retired county official*

Sun City
Smith, Stanford Sidney *former state treasurer*

Sun Lakes
Sharpless, Joseph Benjamin *retired county official*

Tempe
Giuliano, Neil Gerard *mayor, academic administrator*

Tucson
Miller, Elizabeth Rodriguez *city official*
Scott, Shirley *city council*
Walkup, Robert E. *mayor*

Wickenburg
Henry, John Charles *county official*

ARKANSAS

Bella Vista
Medin, Myron James, Jr., *city manager*

Heber Springs
Rawlings, Paul C. *retired government official*

Little Rock
Beebe, Mike *state attorney general*
Cheek, James Richard *ambassador*
Daniels, Charlie *state official*
Fisher, Jimmie Lou *state official*
Huckabee, Michael Dale *governor*
Priest, Sharon Devlin *association executive, former state secretary of state*
Rockefeller, Winthrop P. *lieutenant governor*
Weiss, Richard A. *state official*

CALIFORNIA

Albany
Thomsen, Peggy Jean *mayor, educator*

Anaheim
Jung, Charlene *city treasurer*
Pringle, Curt *mayor*

Aptos
Trounstine, Philip John *communications consultant, institute administrator*

Bakersfield
Hall, Harvey L. *mayor, medical transportation company executive*

Bellflower
Bermudez, Rudy *state official*

Benicia
von Studnitz, Gilbert Alfred *state official*

Berkeley
Hamilton, Randy Haskell *city manager*
Taylor, John Lockhart *former city official*

Beverly Hills
Covitz, Carl D. *state official, real estate and investment executive*

Brea
Daucher, Lynn M. *state official*

Carson
Oropeza, Jenny *state official*

Cathedral City
Garcia, Bonnie *state official*

Chula Vista
Madigan, Laurie Anne *municipal official*

City Of Industry
Pacheco, Robert *state official*

Claremont
Pedersen, Richard Foote *diplomat and academic administrator*

Coronado
Hostler, Charles Warren *former ambassador, international affairs consultant*

Costa Mesa
Maddox, Ken *state official*

Davis
Sanderson, Janet A. *ambassador*

El Cajon
Thigpen, Mary Cecelia *city official, consultant*

Elk Grove
Garth-Lewis, Kimberley *state official, public policy educator*

Felicity
Istel, Jacques Andre *mayor*

Folsom
Peck, Ellie Enriquez *retired state administrator*

Fremont
Morrison, Gus (Angus Hugh Morrison) *mayor, engineer*

Fresno
Autry, Alan *mayor, actor, former professional football player, film company executive*

Garden Grove
Broadwater, Bruce A. *mayor*

Gardena
Hardison, Dee *former mayor*

Grass Valley
Cassella, Dennis Gene *retired county official*

Hayward
Cooper, Roberta *mayor*

Hollister
Gray, Robert Donald *retired mayor*

Huntington Beach
Boardman, Connie *former mayor, biologist, educator*
Harman, Thomas *state official*

Inglewood
Horton, Jerome E. *state official*

Irvine
Agran, Larry *mayor, lawyer*
Campbell, John B. T., III, *state official*

Kensington
Huddle, Franklin Pierce, Jr., *diplomat*

La Mesa
La Suer, Jay *state official*

Laguna Niguel
Bates, Patricia C. *state official*

Laguna Woods
Hussey, William Bertrand *retired foreign service officer*

Littlerock
Haas, Sir Russell (Duke of Elbasan) *ambassador*

Livermore
Brown, Cathie *city official*

Long Beach
Lowenthal, Alan *state official*
O'Neill, Beverly Lewis *mayor, former college president*
Sato, Eunice Noda *former mayor, consultant*

Los Angeles
Antonovich, Michael Dennis *county official*
Davis, Michael Rico *county official*
Galanter, Ruth *city official*
Hahn, James Kenneth *mayor, lawyer*
Helm, Robert Wilbur *federal official*
Morris, Sharon Hutson *city manager*
Reagan, Nancy Davis (Anne Francis Robbins) *former First Lady of the United States, volunteer*
Smith, Ann Delorise *municipal official*
Toman, Mary Ann *federal official*
Torres-Gil, Fernando M. *federal official, academic administrator*

Marina
Mettee-McCutchon, Ila *municipal official, retired career army officer*

Mckinleyville
Schoettger, Theodore Leo *city official*

Menlo Park
Lane, Laurence William, Jr., *retired ambassador, publisher*

Modesto
Sabatino, Carmen *mayor*

Monrovia
Mountjoy, Dennis Lee *state official*

Montclair
Negrete McLeod, Gloria *state official*

Montebello
Calderon, Ronald *state official*

Monterey Park
Smith, Betty Denny *county official, administrator, fashion executive*

Moreno Valley
White, Charles R. *former mayor*

Murrieta
McClellan, Barry Dean *city manager*

Napa
Battisti, Paul Oreste *retired county supervisor*

Oakland
Brown, Jerry (Edmund Gerald Brown Jr.) *mayor, former governor*

Oceanside
Lyon, Richard *mayor emeritus, retired naval officer*

Ontario
Dastrup-Hamill, Faye Myers *city official*
Ovitt, Gary C. *mayor*

Orange
Lungren, Daniel Edward *former state attorney general*
Spitzer, Todd *state official*

Oroville
Curry, William Sims *county official*
Davis, Frederick Charles *county official*

Oxnard
Lopez, Manuel M. *mayor*
Takasugi, Nao *state official, business developer*

Pasadena
Bean, Maurice Darrow *retired diplomat*
Bogaard, William Joseph *mayor, lawyer, educator*

Pomona
Cortez, Edward S. *mayor*

Rancho Cucamonga
Dutton, Robert D. *state official*

Rancho Mirage
Ford, Betty Ann (Elizabeth Ann Ford) *former First Lady of the United States, health facility executive*
Ford, Gerald Rudolph, Jr., *38th President of the United States*

Redlands
Hanson, Gerald Warner *retired county official*

Richmond
Corbin, Rosemary MacGowan *former mayor*

Riverside
Benoit, John J. *state official*
Stewart, Richard A. *former mayor*

Sacramento
Betts, Bert A. *former state treasurer, accountant*
Burton, John *state official*
Bustamante, Cruz M. *lieutenant governor*
Connell, Kathleen *state official*
Corbett, Ellen M. *mayor*
Covin, David L. *political science educator*
Dunnett, Dennis George *retired state official*
Fargo, Heather *mayor*
Hunter, Patricia Rae (Tricia Hunter) *state official*
Lockyer, Bill *state attorney general*
Schwarzenegger, Arnold Alois *governor*
Shelley, Kevin *state official*
Shirey, John Frederick *local government administrator*

Salinas
Wong, Walter Foo *county official*

San Bernardino
Giralt-Cabrales, Carlos Ignacio *consul of Mexico*
Valles, Judith *mayor, former academic administrator*

San Diego
Bliesner, James Douglas *municipal/county official, consultant*
Golding, Susan G. *former mayor*
Jacob, Dianne *county official*
Kehoe, Christine T. *state official*
Murphy, Dick *mayor, former superior court judge*
Plescia, George A. *state official*
Rahmani, Reza Mossaver *writer, retired Iranian Air Force officer, banker, tour operator*

San Francisco
Achtenberg, Roberta *former federal official*
Frank, Anthony Melchior *federal official, former financial executive*
Islambouly, Hagar Abdel-Hamid *consul general*
Low, Donald *diplomat, financial investor*
Newsom, Gavin *mayor*
Ward, Doris M. *county official*

San Jose
Edwards, Frances Lavinia *city official*
Gonzales, Ron *mayor, former county supervisor*

San Luis Obispo
Shlaudeman, Harry Walter *retired diplomat*

Santa Ana
Correa, Lou *state official*
Daly, Tom *county official*
Pulido, Miguel Angel *mayor*

Santa Monica
Aaron, David L. *diplomat, author*
Rice, Donald Blessing *business executive, former secretary of air force*

Santa Paula
Kay, Hazel T. *local commissioner*

Seaside
Panetta, Leon Edward *federal official, former congressman*

Solana Beach
Beard, Ann Southard *diplomat, oil company executive*
Gildred, Theodore E. *former diplomat, real estate developer*

South Gate
Firebaugh, Marco Antonio *state official*

Stanford
Shultz, George Pratt *former government executive, economics educator*

Stockton
Lewis, Mark Earldon *city manager*
Meissner, Katherine Gong *city official*
Podesto, Gary A. *mayor*

Torrance
Walker, Dan *mayor, business consultant*

Ventura
Smith, Bill *city manager*

Vista
Wyland, Mark *state official*

Yuba City
Kemmerly, Jack Dale *retired state official, aviation consultant*

Yucaipa
Bogh, Russell *state official*

COLORADO

Aurora
Sheffield, Nancy *city agency administrator*
Tauer, Paul E. *mayor, educator*

Colorado Springs
Chestnutt, Ellen Joanne *state official*
Makepeace, Mary Lou *former mayor*
Milton, Richard Henry *retired diplomat, children's advocate*
Rivera, Lionel *mayor*

Denver
Barnhart, Arthur L. *state official*
Brown, Keith Lapham *retired ambassador*
Cuba, Stanley L. *government official*
Davidson, Donetta *secretary of state*
Hickenlooper, John W. *mayor*
Minger, Terrell John *public administration and natural resource institute executive*
Moulton, Jennifer T. *city official, architect*
Norton, Jane E. *lieutenant governor*
Owens, Bill *governor*
Rogers, Joe *former lieutenant governor*
Rowe, Tina L. *government official*
Salazar, Kenneth L. *state attorney general*

Lakewood
Burkholder, Steve *mayor*

Pueblo
Occhiato, Michael Anthony *city official*

CONNECTICUT

Brookfield
Foncello, Martin John, Jr., *municipal official*

Canton Center
Humphrey, Samuel Stockwell *town official, physicist*

Chester
Hilsman, Roger *government educator*

Darien
McIntire, William Tredick, II, *municipal official, investment banker*

Easton
Meyer, Alice Virginia *state official*

Hartford
Blumenthal, Richard *state attorney general*
Bysiewicz, Susan *secretary of state*
Killian, Robert Kenneth *former lieutenant governor*
Nappier, Denise L. *state official*
Perez, Eddie A. *mayor*
Rell, M. Jodi *governor*
Sullivan, Kevin B. *lieutenant governor, former state legislator*
Vacchelli, Robert Francis *lawyer*

Litchfield
Privitera, Joseph F. *retired foreign service officer, writer-researcher*

New Haven
Zedillo Ponce de León, Ernesto *former president of Mexico*

New Milford
Peitler, Arthur Joseph *mayor, lawyer*

North Haven
Westerfield, Carolyn Elizabeth Hess *city planner*

Northford
James, William Hall *former state official, educator*

Norwalk
Willcox, Roger *city planner, consultant*

Stamford
Dennies, Sandra Lee *city official*
Malloy, Dannel Patrick *mayor*

DELAWARE

Dover
Carney, John C., Jr., *lieutenant governor*
Minner, Ruth Ann *governor*
Windsor, Harriet Smith *state official*
Woodruff, Valerie *secretary of education*

Newark
Freel, Edward J. *former state official*
Woo, S. B. (Shien-Biau Woo) *former lieutenant governor, physics educator*

Wilmington
Brady, M. Jane *state attorney general*
Ianni, Francis Alphonse *state official, former army officer*

DISTRICT OF COLUMBIA

Washington
Abraham, Spencer *secretary of energy*
Abrams, Elliott *governmental official*
Abshire, David Manker *diplomat, research executive*
Andersen, Robert Allen *retired government official*
Anthony, Sheila Foster *government official*
Argrett, Loretta Collins *assistant attorney general, educator*
Argyros, George L. *ambassador, former development company executive, former professional sports team owner*
Ashcroft, John David *attorney general*
Atherton, Charles Henry *federal commission administrator*
Atkins, Paul S. *commissioner*
Austin, Roy L. *ambassador*
Ayres, Mary Ellen *government official*
Baasan, Ragchaa *diplomat*
Babbitt, Bruce Edward *former federal official, lawyer*
Baker, Howard Henry, Jr., *ambassador, former senator, lawyer*
Baldyga, Leonard J. *retired diplomat, international consultant*
Bandar, Prince bin Sultan bin Abd al-Aziz Al Saud *Saudi Arabian ambassador to United States*
Bandler, Donald Keith *diplomat*
Barbosa, Rubens Antonio *Brazilian ambassador*
Bassin, Jules *foreign service officer*
Battle, Vincent M. *ambassador*
Bellows, Michael Donald *foreign service officer*
Berg, Stephen Warren *government official*
Bernstein, Stuart A. *ambassador*
Bivins, Miles Teel *ambassador, former state legislator*
Blackman, Sir Courtney Newlands *diplomat*
Block, John Rusling *former secretary of agriculture*
Blust, Steven R. *commissioner*
Boehm, Peter Michael *ambassador*
Bolten, Joshua Brewster *federal official*
Bond, Clayton Alan *foreign affairs fellow*
Boyce, Ralph L. *ambassador*
Brazeal, Aurelia Erskine *ambassador*
Breathitt, Linda K. *federal commissioner*
Brewster, Robert Charles *diplomat, consultant*
Bridgewater, Pamela E. *ambassador*
Burns III, Matthew J. *diplomat*

Burson, Charles W. *former federal official, former state attorney general, lawyer*
Bush, George Walker *43d President of the United States*
Bush, Laura Welch *First Lady of United States*
Bushnell, Prudence *diplomat, former management consultant, trainer*
Campbell, John *ambassador*
Campos, Roel C. *commissioner*
Card, Andrew Hill, Jr., *federal official*
Carlucci, Frank Charles, III, *former secretary of defense*
Cheney, Richard B. (Dick Cheney) *Vice President of the United States*
Chesser, Judy Lee *municipal official*
Chrétien, Raymond A.J. *retired diplomat*
Churchill, Malcolm Hughes *retired diplomat, investment analyst*
Coats, Daniel Ray *ambassador, former senator*
Cohen, William Sebastian *consultant, former federal official, former senator*
Collins, James Franklin *retired ambassador*
Collins, Keith *federal executive*
Cook, Michael Blanchard *government executive*
Cowal, Sally Grooms *diplomat, association administrator*
Coy, Curtis L. *federal official*
Craner, Lorne Whitney *federal official*
Crocker, Chester Arthur *diplomat, scholar, federal agency administrator*
Cropp, Linda W. *city official*
Cutler, Steven *federal official*
Cutler, Walter Leon *diplomat, foundation executive*
Damelin, Harold *federal official*
Danzig, Richard Jeffrey *former government official, lawyer*
Dawson, Horace Greeley, Jr., *former diplomat, government official*
Dell, Christopher William *ambassador*
Deming, Rust M. *ambassador*
Donilon, Thomas E. *federal official*
Duemling, Robert Werner *diplomat, museum director*
Duffy, Michael F. *commissioner*
Echaveste, Maria *government official, lawyer*
Eddy, John Joseph *diplomat*
Edelman, Eric Steven *ambassador*
Einaudi, Luigi Roberto *diplomat, educator*
Eizenstat, Stuart Elliot *ambassador*
Eliasson, Jan K. *Swedish diplomat*
El-Nakib, Hesham Moussa *diplomat*
Emmanuel, Rahm *former federal official, investment banker, congressman*
Ensenat, Donald Burnham *ambassador, lawyer*
Evans, Donald L. *secretary of commerce*
Federspiel, Ulrik *diplomat*
Ferrier, Maria Hernandez *federal official, educator*
Fishel, Andrew S. *director, federal*
FitzGerald, William Henry G. *diplomat, corporation executive*
Fleisher, Eric Wilfrid *retired foreign service officer*
Francke, Rend Rahim *ambassador*
Franco, Omar *governmental relations administrator*
Frankel, Emil H. *transporation policy secretary*
Franklin, Barbara Hackman *former government official, health products executive*
Frawley Bagley, Elizabeth *government advisor, ambassador*
Frazer, Jendayi *ambassador*
Freeman, Russell Fuller *ambassador*
Fried, Daniel *retired ambassador*
Frierson, Robert DeV. *federal official*
Fritsche, Claudia *diplomat, ambassador*
Gantt, Harvey B. *former mayor*
Garthoff, Raymond Leonard *diplomat, diplomatic historian*
Gates, Robert M. *government official*
Gatons, Anna-Marie Kilmade *government official*
Gaviria Trujillo, Cesar *international organization administrator, former president of Colombia, economist*
Gelbard, Robert Sidney *ambassador*
Gergen, David Richmond *federal official, magazine editor*
Gerry, Dale Francis *defense adviser, legislative consultant*
Gessaman, Donald Eugene *government executive, federal official, consultant*
Giffin, Gordon D. *former ambassador, lawyer*
Gilliom, Judith Carr *government official*
Ginsberg, Marc Charles *former diplomat, investment company executive*
Glassman, Cynthia A. *commissioner*
Gregorian, Raffi *diplomat*
Grove, Brandon Hambright, Jr., *diplomat*
Hall, Kathryn Walt *ambassador*
Hammond, Anthony *commissioner*
Harrop, William Caldwell *retired ambassador, foreign service officer*
Hawke, John Daniel, Jr., *United States Comptroller of the Currency*
Hayes, Allene Valerie Farmer *government executive*
Hecklinger, Richard E. *ambassador*
Herbst, John Edward *ambassador*
Hernreich, Nancy *federal official*
Hill, Christopher R. *ambassador*
Hillman, Jennifer Anne *commissioner, federal official, trade negotiator*
Hooks, Aubrey *ambassador*
Horowitz, Herbert Eugene *retired diplomat*
Hull, Edmund J. *ambassador*
Hunter, Michael James *state government official, lawyer, educator*
Iglesias, Enrique V. *bank executive, former government minister*
Indyk, Martin S. *diplomat*
Irvin, Necole S *government relations director*
Itoh, William H. *former ambassador*
Ivry, David *diplomat*
Jacobs, Susan S. *ambassador*
Jarque, Carlos M. *former federal official*
Johnson, Darryl Norman *ambassador*
Johnson, David Timothy *diplomat*
Johnson, Jennifer J. *federal official*
Jones, Brian W. *federal official*
Jones, James Robert *ambassador, retired congressman, lawyer*
Jordan, Mary Lucille *commissioner*
Kaiser, Philip Mayer *retired diplomat*
Kampelman, Max M. *former ambassador, lawyer*
Kantor, Michael (Mickey Kantor) *federal official*
Karaer, Arma Jane *ambassador*
Kauzlarich, Richard Dale *retired ambassador, political scientist, consultant*

Keating, Francis Anthony, II, *former governor, lawyer*
Keating, Robert B. *ambassador*
Keevey, Richard Francis *government official, educator*
Kilberg, Bobbie Greene *govenment official*
Killgore, Andrew Ivy *former ambassador*
Kolb, Charles Edward Mealey *federal government official, lawyer*
Koplan, Steven *federal government commissioner*
Koskinen, John Andrew *government executive*
Kotil, Rostislav *defense attache*
Kraemer, Sylvia Katharine *government official, historian*
Kyerematen, Alan *ambassador*
Lake, Anthony *former federal official*
La Rocque, Gene Robert *retired naval officer, government official, author*
Lastowka, James Anthony *former federal agency executive, lawyer*
Leidinger, William John *federal official*
Levy, Leah Garrigan *federal official*
Lewis, Ann Frank *former government official*
Lieberman, Evelyn S. *diplomat*
Lilly, William Eldridge *government official*
Livingood, Wilson S. *law enforcement official*
Loftis, Robert G. *ambassador*
Lovell, Malcolm Read, Jr., *public policy institute executive, educator, former government official, former trade association executive*
Lowe, Mary Frances *government official*
Lowenstein, James Gordon *former diplomat, international consultant*
Lowrey, Barbara R. *federal official*
Lucas, James Walter *federal government official*
Lukken, Walt *commissioner*
MacKay, Kenneth Hood, Jr., (Buddy MacKay) *federal official*
Magee, Charles Thomas *international consultant, retired diplomat*
Maisto, John F. *ambassador*
Malinowski, Michael E. *ambassador*
Malott, Frank Stephen *foreign service officer*
Mangano, Michael F. *federal official*
Marcotte, Michael Steven *municipal administrator*
Marcoullis, Erato Kozakou *ambassador*
Martinez, Carmen M. *ambassador*
Mathews, Jessica Tuchman *executive, foreign policy expert*
McCargar, James Goodrich *diplomat, writer*
McDonald, Jackson *ambassador*
McElveen-Hunter, Bonnie *ambassador*
McHale, Paul F., Jr., *federal official, former congressman*
McLarty, Thomas F., III, (Mack McLarty) *former governement advisor, business executive*
McMichael, Guy H., III, *federal official*
McQueary, Charles E. *federal official*
Meece, Roger A. *ambassador*
Meyer, Armin Henry *retired diplomat, author, educator*
Meyer, Laurence Harvey *former federal official*
Michaud, Michael Alan George *diplomat, writer*
Milam, William Bryant *former ambassador, senior policy scholar, economist*
Miller, Judith A. *federal official*
Miller, Marcia E. *federal government official*
Miller, William Green *ambassador*
Mineta, Norman Yoshio *secretary of transportation*
Moorefield, Kenneth P. *ambassador*
Morrissey, Patricia A. *commissioner*
Moschella, William Emil *state attorney general*
Mulford, David Campbell *ambassador, former finance company executive*
Myers, Richard B. *Chairman of the Joint Chiefs of Staff*
Nesbitt, Wanda L. *ambassador*
Ness, Susan *federal official*
Newhouse, Alan Russell *federal government executive*
Nitze, William Albert *government official, lawyer, not-for-profit developer, energy executive*
Norland, Donald Richard *retired foreign service officer*
Norton, Gale Ann *Secretary of the Interior*
Oakley, Phyllis Elliott *retired diplomat*
O'Day, Kathleen M. *federal official*
Olson, Lyndon Lowell, Jr., *ambassador*
Ordway, John *ambassador*
Orr, Bobette Kay *diplomat*
Owen, Henry *former ambassador, consultant*
Paige, Roderick R. *secretary of education*
Parris, Mark Robert *former ambassador, policy advisor*
Pascual, Carlos *ambassador*
Passage, David *diplomat*
Pearce, Drue *government official, former state legislator*
Pearson, W. Robert *former ambassador*
Pendleton, Miles Stevens, Jr., *diplomat*
Perle, Richard Norman *former government official*
Peters, F. Whitten *lawyer, former federal official*
Phillips, James D. *retired diplomat*
Phillips, Jeanne L. *ambassador*
Pibulsonggram, Nitya *diplomat*
Piccininno, Anthony Ray *government administrative executive*
Pierce, Margaret Hunter *government official*
Placke, James A(nthony) *foreign service officer, international affairs consultant*
Plaisted, Joan M. *diplomat*
Powell, Colin Luther *secretary of state, retired military officer, author, public speaker*
Quainton, Anthony Cecil Eden *diplomat*
Quinn, Maureen E. *ambassador*
Randt, Clark Thorp, Jr., *ambassador, lawyer*
Raphel, Robin *ambassador*
Reed, John Hathaway *former ambassador*
Reef, Grace *government official*
Rees, Nina Shokraii *federal official, writer*
Remez, Shereen G. *government executive*
Reyes Heroles, Jesus *former Mexican government official*
Ricciardone, Francis J. *ambassador*
Rice, Condoleezza *national security advisor*
Rich, Laurie M. *federal official, educator*
Ridge, Thomas Joseph (Tom Ridge) *secretary of homeland security*
Roby, Cheryl J. *deputy assistant secretary*
Rogers, Thomasina Venese *federal commissioner*
Rogowsky, Robert Arthur *trade commission operations director, educator*
Romani, Paul Nicholas *government official*
Rossin, Lawrence G. *ambassador*
Rove, Karl Christian *government advisor, consultant*

Rumsfeld, Donald Henry *secretary of defense*
Ryan, Mary A. *diplomat*
Sackster, Frederick Henry *former foreign service officer*
Sakoda, Robin (Sak Sakoda) *government official*
Saleh, Ali-Abdullah *state official*
Saliba, George Maltese *government official*
Sarros, P. Peter *diplomat, consultant*
Sayre, Robert Marion *ambassador*
Scarbrough, Frank Edward *government official*
Schieffer, John Thomas *ambassador, former professional baseball team executive*
Searing, Marjory Ellen *government official, economist*
Seck, Mamadou Mansour *ambassador, military officer*
Sellin, Theodore *foreign service officer, consultant*
Sembler, Melvin F. *ambassador, real estate developer*
Shane, Jeffrey Neil *government official, lawyer*
Sharpless, Mattie R. *ambassador*
Shaw, Theresa (Terri) S. *federal official*
Shelly, Christine Deborah *foreign service officer*
Shinn, David Hamilton *educator, author, former diplomat*
Shumate, John Page *diplomat*
Silverstein, Martin J. *ambassador*
Simmons, Anne L. *federal official*
Slater, Rodney E. *former federal official, lawyer*
Smith, Elaine Diana *foreign service officer*
Smith, Pamela Hyde *ambassador*
Smith, Patricia Grace *government official*
Snow, John William *secretary of treasury*
Somerville, Walter Raleigh, Jr., *government official*
Sommerfelt, Soren Christian *foreign affairs, international trade consultant, former Norwegian diplomat, lawyer*
Sonnenfeldt, Helmut *former government official, educator, consultant, author*
Spagnoletti, Robert J. *state attorney general*
Spellings, Margaret LaMontagne *assistant to US President on domestic policy*
Stadtler, Walter Edward *diplomat*
Stapleton, Craig Roberts *ambassador*
Stock, Ann *federal official*
Sutter, Eleanor Bly *retired diplomat*
Tarrants, William Eugene *federal official*
Taylor, William B., Jr., *ambassador*
Teare, Richard Wallace *retired foreign service officer*
Tefft, John *ambassador*
Terpeluk, Peter, Jr., *ambassador*
Thawley, Michael *diplomat*
Thomas, Gerald E. *ambassador*
Thomas, Harry K., Jr., *ambassador*
Thomas, Ralph Charles, III, *federal official*
Thomas, Scott E. *federal government executive, lawyer*
Thompson, Sally Engstrom *state official*
Thompson, Tommy George *secretary of health and human services*
Tobias, Randall Lee *ambassador, retired pharmaceutical executive*
Toner, Michael E. *commissioner*
Truman, Edwin Malcolm *federal official*
Ushakov, Yuri Viktorovich *diplomat*
Veneman, Ann M. *secretary of agriculture*
Verville, Elizabeth Giavani *federal official*
Vos, Joris Michael *ambassador*
Wahba, Marcelle M. *ambassador*
Walker, Edward S., Jr., *diplomat*
Walston, Roderick Eugene *federal official*
Walters, John P. *federal official*
Watson, Arthur Dennis *federal official*
Wayne, Stephen J. *government educator, writer*
Weintraub, Ellen L. *commissioner*
West, Togo Dennis, Jr., *lawyer, former cabinet member, former aerospace executive*
Wexler, Anne *government relations and public affairs consultant*
Wheatley, Katherine Holbrook *federal official*
Whiting, Meredith Armstrong *public affairs executive*
Wilkinson, Sharon P. *department of state official, former administrator*
Willeford, Pamela P. *ambassador*
Williams, Anthony A. *mayor*
Wills, E. Ashley *ambassador*
Wilson, Joseph Charles, IV, *former ambassador*
Wolf, John S. *ambassador, federal agency administrator*
Wolfowitz, Paul Dundes *federal official, former ambassador to Indonesia*
Won, Delmond Jack Hing *commissioner*
Wulf, Norman *federal official*
Yanai, Shunji *former diplomat*
Yates, Mary Carlin *ambassador*

FLORIDA

Bal Harbour
Horton, Jeanette *municipal government official*

Boca Raton
Brogan, Frank T. *former lieutenant governor*

Bonita Springs
Mehuron, William Otto *retired government official, consultant*

Boynton Beach
Polinsky, Janet Naboicheck *retired state official, former state legislator*

Brooksville
Anderson, Richard Edmund *city manager, management consultant*

Daytona Beach
Betancourt, Ralph Ernest *mayor*

Delray Beach
Warshaw, Stanley Irving *federal official, consultant*

Fort Lauderdale
Burleigh, A. Peter *ambassador*
Gunzburger, Suzanne Nathan *municipal official, social worker*
Parrish, Lori Nance *commissioner*

Gainesville
Heflin, Martin Ganier *foreign service officer, international political economist*

Jones, Elizabeth Nordwall *county government official*

Hollywood
Giulianti, Mara Selena *mayor, civic worker*

Jensen Beach
Peterson, David Frederick *government agency executive*

Kennedy Space Center
Banks, Lisa Jean *government official*

Miami
Bouri, Michael *civil servant*
Carey-Shuler, Barbara *county commissioner*
Cefaratti, Anthony Joseph *retired diplomat*
Diaz, Manuel A. *mayor*
Margolis, Gwen *county commissioner*
Penelas, Alex *mayor*
Pinder, Renee Monique *diplomat*
Reno, Janet *former attorney general*
Rocha, V. Manuel *former diplomat, international trade consultant*
Sorenson, Katy *county commissioner*

Naples
Edwards, Jennifer Jones *county official*

Ormond Beach
Burton, Alan Harvey *city official*

Palm City
Henry, David Howe, II, *retired diplomat*

Palmetto
Angulo, Charles Bonin *foreign service officer, lawyer*

Punta Gorda
Smith-Mooney, Marilyn Patricia *city government official, management consultant and facilitator*

Saint Augustine
Bourne, John David *retired city finance executive*

Sarasota
Hartman, Karen Marie *municipal official*
Morrow, William Earl *retired government official*

Tallahassee
Bush, John Ellis (Jeb Bush) *governor*
Crist, Charles (Charlie Crist) *state attorney general*
Hetrick, Charles Brady *retired county official*
Hood, Glenda E. *state official*
Jaber, Lila A. *state official*
Jennings, Toni *lieutenant governor*
Mortham, Sandra Barringer *former state official*
Ramsey, Sally Ann Seitz *retired state official*
Smith, James Cloudis *secretary of state, former state attorney general*

Tampa
Bucella, Donna Ann *federal official*
Freedman, Sandra Warshaw *former mayor*
Iorio, Pam *county official*
Platt, Jan Kaminis *county commissioner*
Studer, William Allen *county official*

Vero Beach
Cochrane, William Henry *former city official*

GEORGIA

Atlanta
Baker, Thurbert E. *state attorney general*
Bell, Griffin B. *lawyer, former attorney general*
Bowers, Michael Joseph *former state attorney general*
Carter, Jimmy (James Earl Carter Jr.) *39th President of the United States*
Cox, Cathy *state official*
Franklin, Shirley Clarke *mayor*
Howard, Pierre *former state official*
Jeter, Howard F. *former ambassador*
Perdue, George (Sonny Perdue) *governor, state legislator*
Scott, Donald Lavern *city manager, former army officer*
Streeb, Gordon Lee *diplomat, economist*
Sullivan, Louis Wade *former secretary health and human services, physician*
Taylor, Mark *lieutenant governor*

Cartersville
Harris, Joe Frank *former governor*

Conyers
Kelly, John Hubert *diplomat, business executive*

Saint Simons
Douglas, William Ernest *retired government official*

Statesboro
Wood, George Ambos *city manager*

HAWAII

Honolulu
Aiona, James R., Jr., *lieutenant governor*
Bennett, Mark J. *state attorney general*
Bronster, Margery S *state attorney general*
Goto Sabas, Jennifer *state official*
Harris, Jeremy *mayor*
Lingle, Linda *governor*
Okimoto, Glenn Michiaki *state official*
Wakatsuki, Lynn Y. *commissioner*

Lihue
Kusaka, Maryanne Winona *mayor*

Mililani
Olsen, Harris Leland *diplomat, writer, real estate company executive, educator*

Wailea
Thompson, Travis Ogden *retired county official*

IDAHO

Boise
Kempthorne, Dirk Arthur *governor*
Lance, Alan George *former state attorney general*
Risch, James E. *lieutenant governor, former state legislator, lawyer*
Wasden, Lawrence *state attorney general*
Wilson, Jack Fredrick *retired federal government official*
Ysursa, Ben T. *state official*

Idaho Falls
King, Ronald Amos *federal official, communications professional, retired*

Post Falls
Riggs, Jack Timothy *emergency physician, former state lieutenant governor*

ILLINOIS

Carbondale
Cole, Brad *mayor*

Champaign
Semonin, Richard Gerard *retired state official*

Chicago
Daley, Richard Michael *mayor*
Enenbach, Mark Henry *community action agency executive, educator*
Harris, Gregory Scott *municipal official*
Johnson, Donald Harry, Jr., *government official, educator*
Madigan, Lisa *state attorney general*
Moskow, Michael H. *federal official*
Natarus, Burton F. *lawyer, municipal legislator*
Olk, Frederick James *county official, paralegal*
Quinn, Patrick *lieutenant governor*
Robbins, Audrey *county official*
Sweis Mussa, Rafiq *consular general, activist*
Topinka, Judy Baar *state official, political organization worker*
Walker, Thomas Ray *city aviation commissioner*

Downers Grove
Jacklin, William Thomas *retired county official, educator*

Glenview
Olson, Roy Arthur *retired government official*

Kankakee
Ryan, George H. *former governor, pharmacist*

Quincy
Points, Roy Wilson *municipal official*

Springfield
Blagojevich, Rod R. *governor, former congressman*
Darr, William A. *commissioner*
Gamble, Douglas Irvin *state official, educator*
Hasara, Karen A. *mayor*
Lindley, Maralee Irwin *county official, consultant, speaker*
Morford, Lynn Ellen *state official*
White, Jesse *state official*

Urbana
Edgar, Jim *former governor*
Prussing, Laurel Lunt *public interest lobbyist, economist, auditor*

Wheeling
Kenny, James Casey *ambassador, construction company executive*

INDIANA

Columbus
Carter, Pamela Lynn *former state attorney general*

Fort Wayne
Helmke, Paul (Walter Paul Helmke Jr.) *mayor, lawyer*
Lee, Timothy Earl *international agency executive, paralegal*

Hammond
Curiel, Carolyn *ambassador*

Huntington
Brown, Robert Clark, Jr., *county official*

Indianapolis
Carter, Steve *state attorney general*
Davis, Katherine Lyon *lieutenant governor*
Kernan, Joseph E., III *governor*
Klika, Cristine M. *state official*
Nass, Connie Kay *state auditor*
Peterson, Bart *mayor*
Rokita, Todd *secretary of state*

IOWA

Cedar Rapids
Novetzke, Sally Johnson *former ambassador*
Reppert, Nancy Lue *retired municipal official, legal consultant*

Des Moines
Anderson, Eric Anthony *city manager*
Bergman, Bruce E. *municipal official*
Boal, Carmine *state official*
Buhr, Florence D. *county official*
Corning, Joy Cole *retired state official*
Culver, Chester J. *state official, educator*
Deluhery, Patrick John *state official*
Gaskill, Mary *state official*
Gronstal, Tom *commissioner, bank executive*
Heddens, Lisa *state official*
Huser, Geri D. *state official*
Jacobs, Libby Swanson *state official*
Miller, Thomas J. *state attorney general*
Pederson, Sally *lieutenant governor*
Tymeson, Jodi *state official*

Upmeyer, Linda *state official*
Vaughan, Therese Michele *insurance commissioner*
Vilsack, Thomas *governor*

Hiawatha
Pate, Paul Danny *mayor*

Oelwein
McFarlane, Beth Lucetta Troester *former mayor*

KANSAS

Arkansas City
Bruton, Rebecca Ann *mayor, commissioner*

Coffeyville
Garner, Jim D. *state official, lawyer*

Garden Plain
Stovall, Carla Jo *former state attorney general*

Hutchinson
Kerr, Dave *state official, marketing professional*

Topeka
Glasscock, Joyce H. *state official*
Jenkins, Lynn M. *state official, former state legislator*
Kline, Phillip D. *state attorney general*
Moore, John Eddy *lieutenant governor*
Nelson, Franklin W. *commissioner, retired banker*
Sebelius, Kathleen Gilligan *governor*
Thornburgh, Ron E. *secretary of state*

Wichita
Knight, Robert G. *mayor, investment banker*

KENTUCKY

Bowling Green
Cooper, Davis A. *city official*

Frankfort
Fletcher, Ernie (Ernest L. Fletcher) *governor, former congressman*
Greyson, Trey (C.M. Grayson) *state official*
Hamilton, John Kennedy *former state treasurer*
Nowland-Curry, Betsy *state official*
Palmore, Carol M. *state official*
Pence, Stephen Beville *lieutenant governor*
Sonego, Ian G. *assistant attorney general*
Stumbo, Gregory D. *state attorney general*

Lexington
Miller, Pamela Gundersen *mayor*
Whitmer, Leslie Gay *federal official*

Shelbyville
Miller, Mary Helen *retired public administrator*

Versailles
Farish, William S. *former United States ambassador to United Kingdom, horse breeder*

LOUISIANA

Baton Rouge
Blanco, Kathleen Babineaux *governor*
Bohlinger, Lewis Hall *state government official*
Foti, Charles C., Jr., *state attorney general*
Landrieu, Mitchell Joseph *lieutenant governor*
McKeithen, Walter Fox *secretary of state*

New Orleans
Gates, Audrey Castine *city government administrator*
Nagin, C. Ray *mayor*
Ortique, Revius Oliver, Jr., *city official, retired state supreme court justice*
Stansbury, Harry Case *state commissioner*

Slidell
Dearing, Reinhard Josef *city official*

MAINE

Augusta
Baldacci, John Elias *governor, former congressman*
Gendron, Susan Ann *commissioner, educator*
Gray, Howard R., Jr., *former commissioner*
Gwadosky, Dan A. *secretary of state*
Ketterer, Andrew *state commissioner, former state attorney general*
McCormick, Dale *state treasurer*
Rowe, G. Steven *state attorney general*
Waldron, Janet E. *state commissioner*

Belfast
Worth, Mary Page *mayor*

Brunswick
King, Angus S., Jr., *former governor*

MARYLAND

Annapolis
Andrews, Archie Moulton *government official*
Aumann, R. Karl *state official, lawyer*
Clagett, Virginia Parker *county official*
Coulter, James Bennett *state official*
Ehrlich, Robert L., Jr., *governor, former congressman*
Kopp, Nancy Kornblith *state official*
Steele, Michael *lieutenant governor*

Baltimore
Curran, J. Joseph, Jr., *state attorney general*
Daniels, Susan M. *commissioner*
Jones, Raymond Moylan *strategy and public policy educator*
O'Malley, Martin Joseph *mayor, former councilman, lawyer*
Willis, John T. *former secretary of state*

Bel Air
O'Bryon, James Fredrick *defense executive*

Bethesda
Bowsher, Charles Arthur *retired government official, business executive*
Gallagher, Hubert Randall *government consultant*
Green, Jerome George *federal government official*
Hempstone, Smith, Jr., *diplomat, journalist*
Kawazoe, Robin Inada *federal official*
Kirby, Harmon E. *retired ambassador*
Laingen, Lowell Bruce *diplomat*
MacKay, Charles Robert *federal official, consultant*
Morgan, John Davis *consultant*
Neill, Denis Michael *international consultant*
North, William Haven *foreign service officer*
Peck, Edward Lionel *retired foreign service officer, corporate executive*
Rowell, Edward Morgan *retired foreign service officer, lecturer*
Spector, Melbourne Louis *retired foreign service officer*
Stoddard, Philip Hendrick *foreign affairs analyst, consultant, writer*
Vest, George Southall *retired diplomat*

Cabin John
Ingraham, Edward Clarke, Jr., *retired foreign service officer*

Chevy Chase
Albright, Raymond Jacob *government official*
Bush, Frederick Morris *federal official*
Lukens, Alan Wood *retired ambassador and foreign service officer*
Prince, Julius S. (Bud Prince) *retired foreign service reserve officer*

Cockeysville
Barnes, Peter *federal official*

College Park
Benedick, Richard Elliot *diplomat*

Columbia
Cargo, William Ira *retired ambassador*
Scates, Alice Yeomans *former government official, consultant*

Crownsville
Hanna, James Curtis *state official*

Ellicott City
Galinsky, Deborah Jean *county official*

Fort Washington
Smoot, Burgess Howard *federal official*

Frederick
Baker, Joanne Evelyn *retired government official*

Gaithersburg
French, Judson Cull *government official*
Watson, Royce Andrew *retired federal official*

Greenbelt
Harris, Marion Hopkins *former government official*

Kensington
Rosenthal, Alan Sayre *government official*

Leonardtown
Smalley, Robert Manning *government official*

Lexington Park
Morgan, Dennis Alan *retired federal official, education educator*

Mitchellville
Sober, Sidney *retired diplomat, educator*

North Bethesda
Szabo, Daniel *government official*

Owings Mills
Nes, David Gulick *retired diplomat*

Oxford
Shepard, William Seth *government official, diplomat, writer*

Potomac
Kernan, Barbara Desind *senior government executive*

Rockville
Chiogioji, Melvin Hiroaki *retired federal official, entrepreneur*
Corley, Rose Ann McAfee *government official*
Woodcock, Janet *federal official*

Severna Park
Meima, Ralph Chester, Jr., *retired diplomat, real estate company executive*

Silver Spring
Ewing, Blair Gordon *federal official*
Goott, Daniel *government official, consultant*
Kelly, John Joseph, Jr., *government executive*
Ware, Thaddeus Van *government official*

Takoma Park
Lott, Alfred Davis *assistant city manager*

Upper Marlboro
Hewlett, Elizabeth M. *county official*

MASSACHUSETTS

Amesbury
Parker, William H., III, *federal official*

Boston
Fishman, Len *state commissioner*
Galvin, William Francis *state official*
Healey, Kerry Murphy *lieutenant governor*
Menino, Thomas M. *mayor*
O'Brien, Shannon Patricia *state treasurer*
Reilly, Thomas F. *state attorney general*
Romney, W. Mitt *governor*

Shattuck, John *diplomat, civil rights lawyer, educator, academic administrator*

Bridgewater
Heffernan, Peter John *state official*

Brookline
Qualls, Roxanne *mayor*

Cambridge
Hunt, Swanee G. *public policy educator, former ambassador*
Kelman, Steven Jay *management educator*
Martin, Lynn Morley *former secretary of labor*
Porter, Roger Blaine *government official, educator*

Canton
Fuchs, Lawrence Howard *government official, educator*

Concord
Rathore, Naeem Gul *retired United Nations official*

Dorchester
Garrison, Althea *government official*

Lowell
Donoghue, Eileen M. *former mayor*
Mercier, Rita *mayor*
Natsios, Nicholas Andrew *retired foreign service officer*

Lynn
McManus, Patrick J. *mayor, lawyer, accountant*

Roslindale
Sullivan, Dorothy Rona *state official*

Sherborn
Kennedy, Chester Ralph, Jr., *former state official, art director*

Springfield
Mazza Moriarty, Rosemarie *municipal official*

Worcester
Murray, Timothy P. *mayor*

Yarmouth Port
Nichols, Robert Lyman *retired foreign service officer, lecturer*

MICHIGAN

Ann Arbor
Sheldon, Ingrid Kristina *former mayor, bookkeeper*

Battle Creek
Baldwin, Susan Olin *commissioner, management consultant*

Cadillac
Walker, Dale Maxwell *city official*

Dearborn
Lin, Paul kuang-Hsien *assemblyman, educator*

Detroit
Bell Wilson, Carlotta A. *state official, consultant*
Kilpatrick, Kwame M. *mayor*

Dowagiac
Ott, C(larence) H(enry) *ambassador, accountant*

Fennville
Kamman, Curtis Warren *retired ambassador*

Grand Rapids
Logie, John Hoult *former mayor, lawyer*
Posthumus, Richard Earl *former lieutenant governor, farmer*

Lansing
Cannon, Patrick D. *federal offical, broadcaster*
Cherry, John D., Jr., *lieutenant governor*
Christian, Sandra Svec *retired state official*
Cox, Mike *state attorney general*
Fitzgerald, Frank Moore *commissioner*
Granholm, Jennifer Mulhern *governor*
Hills, Rusty *state official*
Johnson, Rick *state official*
Land, Terri Lynn *state official*

Mount Clemens
Kolakowski, Diana Jean *county commissioner*

Pinckney
Davis, Robert Leach *retired government official, consultant*

MINNESOTA

Chisholm
Peterson, Marjorie *former mayor*

Dellwood
Ventura, Jesse (James Janos) *former governor*

Golden Valley
Leppik, Margaret White *municipal official*

Minneapolis
Carlson, Arne Helge *former governor*
Fraser, Arvonne Skelton *former United Nations ambassador*
Mondale, Joan Adams *wife of former Vice President of United States*
Rybak, R.T. *mayor*

Northfield
Flaten, Robert Arnold *former ambassador*
Levin, Burton *diplomat*

Saint Paul
Bernstein, James C. *commissioner*
Hatch, Mike *state attorney general*
Kiffmeyer, Mary *state official*
Molnau, Carol *lieutenant governor*

Ortega, Rafael Enrique *county official, educator*
Pawlenty, Timothy J. *governor*

MISSISSIPPI

Gulfport
Mc Call, Jerry Chalmers *retired government official*

Jackson
Allison, John S. *commissioner*
Barbour, Haley Reeves *governor*
Clark, Eric C. *state official*
Hood, Jim *state attorney general*
Moore, Mike *former state attorney general*
Tuck, Amy *lieutenant governor*
Winter, William Forrest *former governor, lawyer*

Long Beach
Easton, Jill Johanna *state official*

MISSOURI

Jefferson City
Blunt, Matt *secretary of state*
Farmer, Nancy *state official*
Holden, Robert (Bob Holden) *governor*
Lumpe, Sheila *state commissioner, former state legislator*
Maxwell, Joe Edwin *lieutenant governor*
Nixon, Jeremiah W. (Jay Nixon) *state attorney general*

Kansas City
Barnes, Kay *mayor*
Danner, Kathleen Frances Steele *federal official*
Davis, Richard Francis *city government official*
Price, Charles H., II, *former ambassador*
Rocha, Catherine Tomasa *municipal official*
Stroup, Kala Mays *educational alliance administrator, former state higher education commissioner*

Saint Louis
Brauer, Stephen Franklin *diplomat, manufacturing company executive*
Carpenter, Sharon Quigley *municipal official*
Harmon, Clarence *former mayor, law educator*
Slay, Francis G. *mayor*

MONTANA

Billings
Larsen, Richard Lee *former mayor and city manager, business, municipal and labor relations consultant, arbitrator*

Clancy
Ekanger, Laurie *retired state official, contractor*

Helena
Brown, Robert J. (Bob Brown) *state official*
Cooney, Mike *former secretary of state*
Martz, Judy Helen *governor*
Mazurek, Joseph P. *lawyer, former state legislator*
McCulloch, Linda *state official*
McGrath, Mike *attorney general, lawyer*
Ohs, Karl *lieutenant governor*

NEBRASKA

Benkelman
Whiteley, Rose Marie *city clerk, treasurer*

Lincoln
Beermann, Allen J. *former state official*
Boyle, Anne C. *state commissioner*
Bruning, Jon Cumberland *state attorney general*
Gale, John A. *secretary of state*
Heineman, David *lieutenant governor*
Johanns, Michael O. *governor*
Moul, Maxine Burnett *state official*
Novoa, Yanira *diplomat*
Seng, Coleen Joy *mayor*

Omaha
Daub, Hal *former mayor, former congressman*
Fahey, Mike *mayor*
Moore, Scott *former state official*
Pirsch, Carol McBride *county official, former state senator, community relations manager*

South Sioux City
Conley, Randy Joe *city official, private investigator*

Wayne
Burge, Steven Donald *city administrator*

NEVADA

Carson City
Guinn, Kenny C. *governor*
Heller, Dean *state official*
Hunt, Lorraine T. *lieutenant governor*
Krolicki, Brian Keith *state official*
Walshaw, L. Scott *commissioner*
wSandoval, Brian *state attorney general*

Henderson
Gibson, James B. *mayor*
McKinney, Sally Vitkus *state official*

Las Vegas
Goodman, Oscar Baylin *mayor, lawyer*
Hammargren, Lonnie L. *former lieutenant governor*
Vandever, Judith Ann *county official*

Reno
Augustine, Kathy Marie *state controller, state legislator, secondary education educator*

NEW HAMPSHIRE

Concord
Ayotte, Kelly A. *state attorney general*
Benson, Craig Robert *governor*
Gardner, William Michael *state official*
Hill, Donald S. *commissioner, state*
Taylor, Stephen H. *state commissioner*
Thomas, Georgie A. *state official*

Grantham
Feldman, Roger Bruce *government official*

Hanover
Haselton, Mary Michelson *retired foreign service officer, artist*

Hooksett
Denaco, Parker Alden *state official, lawyer, arbitrator*

Manchester
Holden, Carol H. *county official*

New Durham
Herman, William George *municipal government executive*

NEW JERSEY

Atlantic City
Mora, Kathleen Rita *state judicial administrator*

Camden
Uhler, Walter Charles *government official, writer*

Cape May Point
Fraser, Malcolm Cavanagh *mayor*

Clifton
Anzaldi, James Anthony *mayor*

East Rutherford
DiEleuterio, James A. *state official*

Elizabeth
Bollwage, J. Christian *mayor*

Irvington
Paden, Harry *municipal official*

Jersey City
Schundler, Bret Davis *former mayor*

Kearny
John, Ricky *state official*

Maplewood
Bigelow, Page Elizabeth *public policy professional*

Mays Landing
Mooney, Lori *county official*

Morristown
MacKinnis, Ann Phelps *municipal government and land use management executive*

Newark
Davis, Yvonne D. *county official*
Martin, James Hanley *deputy state attorney general*
Scales, John Thomas *state official*

Princeton
Matlock, Jack Foust, Jr., *diplomat*

Rockaway
Catlin, Robert Thomas *city planning consultant*

Sea Isle City
Tull, Theresa Anne *retired diplomat*

Trenton
Caldwell, Dale Gilbert *state official*
Castro, Ida L. *state official, former federal official*
Farmer, John J. *state commissioner, former state attorney general*
Harvey, Peter C. *state attorney general*
McGreevey, James Edward *governor*
Palmer, Douglas Harold *mayor*
Thomas, Regena L. *secretary of state*

Vincentown
Trainor, Lillian (Midge Trainor) *elections official, campaign consultant*

NEW MEXICO

Albuquerque
Giller, Edward Bonfoy *retired government official, retired air force officer*
Kotchian, Sarah Bruff *municipal official*

Gallup
Lundstrom, Patricia *state government administrator*

Los Alamos
Gonzales, Stephanie *state official*

Mesilla
Lewis, Delano Eugene *ambassador, retired broadcast executive*

Santa Fe
Bradley, Walter D. *lieutenant governor, real estate broker*
Denish, Diane D. *lieutenant governor*
Kinderwater, Diane *state official*
Madrid, Patricia A. *state attorney general*
Montoya, Michael A. *state official, accountant*
Richardson, William Blaine *governor*
Vigil-Giron, Rebecca *state official*

NEW YORK

Albany
Berman, Carol *commissioner*
Casey, Glen P. *state official*
Castro, Bernadette *state official*
Clarey, Donald Alexander *government affairs consultant*
Croce, Alan J. *government agency executive*
Daniels, Randy A. *secretary of state*
Donohue, Mary *lieutenant governor*
Jennings, Gerald D. (Jerry Jennings) *mayor*
Pataki, George E. *governor*
Spitzer, Eliot Laurence *state attorney general*
Treadwell, Alexander F. *former state official, political party chairman & leader*

Brewster
Bates, Barbara J. Neuner *retired municipal official*

Bronx
Mendez, Ruben Policarpio *diplomat, educator, economist*

Buffalo
Giambra, Joel Anthony *county executive*
Masiello, Anthony M. (Tony Masiello) *mayor*

Canandaigua
Barden, George V. *county official, watershed specialist*

Chappaqua
Laun, Louis Frederick *government official*

Floral Park
Corbett, William John *government and public relations consultant, lawyer*

Flushing
Rusu, Sir Andrew Peter (Sir Andrew Rusu Baron Rochefort) *ambassador, lawyer*

Manlius
Cotter, William Donald *former state commissioner, former newspaper editor*

Medford
Saunders, Audrey Jayne *federal official*

Nedrow
Lyons, Oren *Native American chieftain, conservationist*

New York
Abulhasan, Mohammad Abdulla *ambassador*
Amenta, Joyce Ann *United Nations executive*
Anderegg, Julius Fidelis *diplomat, consul general*
Arias, Inocencio F. *diplomat*
Arystanbekova, Akmaral Khaidarovna *diplomat*
Atsada, Chaiyanam *diplomat*
Ayafor, Martin Chungong *ambassador*
Berruga-Filloy, Enrique *ambassador*
Blinken, Donald *ambassador, investment banker, brokerage house executive*
Bloomberg, Michael Rubens *mayor*
Boisson, Jacques Louis *diplomat, ambassador*
Bystryn, Marcia Hammill *city program administrator*
Chaves, Jose Maria *diplomat, foundation administrator, lawyer, educator*
Clinton, William Jefferson (Bill Clinton) *42d President of the United States*
Curley, Walter Joseph Patrick *diplomat, investment banker*
Danforth, John Claggett *ambassador, former senator*
Dangue Rewaka, Denis *diplomat*
Dayson, Diane Harris *superintendent, park ranger*
Doctoroff, Daniel L. *municipal official*
Dos Santos, Carlos *ambassador*
Doyle, Michael W. *federal official*
Durrant, M. Patricia *diplomat*
Eisenstadt, G. Michael *diplomat, writer, educator, researcher*
Ferguson, Sarah *The Duchess of York*
Finauri, Graciela Maria *foreign service professional*
Fowler, Robert Ramsay *former Canadian government official*
Gambari, Ibrahim Agboola *diplomat, international organization official*
Gardner, Richard Newton *diplomat, lawyer, educator*
Gelb, Bruce Stuart *city commissioner, consultant*
Giuliani, Rudolph W. *former mayor, consultant, lawyer*
Grunwald, Henry Anatole *ambassador, editor, writer*
Guillot, Cyril Etienne *international organization administrator*
Harris, Patricia E. *deputy mayor*
Holbrooke, Richard Charles Albert *ambassador, investment banker, writer*
Katz, Abraham *retired foreign service officer*
Kennedy, Patrick F. *federal official*
Kiwanuka, Semakula Mathias Mulumba *United Nations ambassador*
Koch, Edward I. *former mayor, lawyer*
Lehman, Orin *retired state official*
Levin, Herbert *retired diplomat, retired foundation executive*
Løj, Ellen Margrethe *ambassador*
Malone, David Michael *diplomat, educator*
McKenna, George Norton *government educator*
Morial, Marc Haydel *former mayor, association executive*
Murphy, Richard William *retired foreign service officer, Middle East specialist, consultant*
Neewoor, Anund Priyay *ambassador*
Ney, Edward N. *ambassador, advertising and public relations company executive*
Okun, Herbert Stuart *diplomat, educator*
Patterson, Anne Brevard Woods *ambassador*
Platt, Nicholas *Asia specialist, retired ambassador*
Raab, Jennifer J. *city commissioner*
Rabiu, Badru I.O. *federal official*
Ranald, Ralph Arthur *former government official, educator*
Rapoport, Miles S. *former state offical*
Robles-Roman, Carol A. *municipal official*
Rock, Allan Michael *ambassador, former Canadian government official*
Rzewnicki, Janet C. *state official*
Sadik, Nafis *United Nations administrator*
Siv, Sichan *Aun ambassador*
Streator, Edward *retired diplomat, management consultant*
Swing, William Lacy *ambassador*
Townsend, Kathleen Kennedy *former lieutenant governor*
Urroz-Rapold, Patricia Julia S. *retired diplomat, writer*
Vural, Volkan *Turkish representative to UN*
Wastberg, Olle M. *diplomat*
Wibisono, Makarim *diplomat*
Williamson, Richard Salisbury *ambassador*
Wyzner, Eugeniusz *diplomat*

Newburgh
Zarutskie, Andrew John *town official*

Newtonville
Conroy-LaCivita, Diane Catherine *city administrator*

Plainview
Bell, James Thomas *housing authority official*

Port Jefferson
Strong, Robert Thomas *former mayor, middle school educator*

Rochester
Huddleston, Vicki Jean *diplomat*

Rome
Sanders, Robin Renee *diplomat*

Romulus
Ostrander, Robert Edwin *retired United Nations interregional advisor, petroleum company executive*

Slingerlands
Herman, Robert S. *former state official, economist, author, educator*

Syracuse
Baker, Sandra Lynn *county official, minister*
Barclay, H(ugh) Douglas *ambassador, lawyer*
Driscoll, Matthew J. *mayor, real estate developer, small business owner*
Levitsky, Melvyn *former ambassador, professor*
Ortiz, Fernando, Jr., *commissioner*

Watertown
Coe, Benjamin Plaisted *retired state official*

NORTH CAROLINA

Chapel Hill
Schoonover, Brenda B. *ambassador*

Charlotte
Bowles, Erskine *former White House staff member, consultant*
Brynn, Edward Paul *former ambassador*
McCrory, Patrick *mayor*

Durham
Joseph, James Alfred *retired ambassador, political scientist, educator*

High Point
Pate, William Patrick *city manager*

Merritt
de Vos, Peter Jon *ambassador*

Mill Spring
Saunders, Barry Wayne *state official*

Pittsboro
Cotter, Michael William *retired ambassador, business consultant*

Raleigh
Berry, Cherie Killian *commissioner*
Boyles, Harlan Edward *former state official*
Cooper, Roy Asberry, III, *state attorney general, lawyer*
Easley, Michael F. *governor*
Faulkner, Janice H. *state official*
Freeman, Franklin Edward, Jr., *state governmental assistant*
Joyner, Lorinzo Little *commissioner*
Marshall, Elaine Folk *state official*
Perdue, Beverly E. *lieutenant governor, geriatric consultant*

Southern Pines
Toon, Malcolm *former ambassador*

Wilson
Wyatt, Edward Avery, V, *city manager*

NORTH DAKOTA

Bismarck
Clark, Tony *state commissioner*
Dalrymple, Jack *lieutenant governor*
Gilmore, Kathi *state treasurer*
Hoeven, John *governor*
Jaeger, Alvin A. (Al Jaeger) *secretary of state*
Stenehjem, Wayne Kevin *state attorney general, lawyer*
Wefald, Susan *state commissioner*

Edinburg
Myrdal, Rosemarie Caryle *state official, former state legislator*

OHIO

Akron
Plusquellic, Donald L. *mayor*

Alliance
Woods, Rose Mary *former presidential assistant, consultant*

Cincinnati
Kelley, Cleophus O. *city official*

Cleveland
Campbell, Jane Louise *mayor*
Chema, Thomas V. *consultant, government official, lawyer, academic administrator*
White, Michael Reed *former mayor*

Columbus
Blackwell, J(ohn) Kenneth *state official*
Bradley, Jennette *lieutenant governor*
Carter, Melinda *municipal official*
Coleman, Michael B. *mayor*
Hogan, Michael F. *state official*
Householder, Larry *state official, small business owner*
Lashutka, Gregory S. *mayor, lawyer*
Montgomery, Betty Dee *state auditor, former state attorney general, former state legislator*
Petro, James Michael *state attorney general*
Speck, Samuel Wallace, Jr., *state official*
Taft, Bob *governor*
Walcher, Kathleen *state official*

Dayton
Lashley, William Bartholomew *county official*
McLin, Rhine Lana *mayor, former state legislator*

Fremont
Recktenwald, Fred William *city financial official*

Hamilton
Kramer, Benjamin Robert *sheriff's deputy, accident reconstructionist*

Lakewood
Cain, Madeline Ann *mayor*

Mansfield
Converse, Sandra *city finance director, financial planner*

Sidney
Thompson, James W., Jr., *state official*

Walton Hills
Thellmann, Edward L. *mayor*

Wright Patterson Afb
Caudill, Tom Holden *governmental policy and analysis executive*

Youngstown
Gransee, Marsha L. *federal agency executive*

OKLAHOMA

Ada
Anoatubby, Bill *governor of Chickawaw Nation*

Bethany
Hendrick, Howard H. *state official*

Blanchard
Harris, Barbara Ellen *mayor*

Collinsville
Rogers, Jimmy Don *county official, writer*

Norman
Corr, Edwin Gharst *ambassador*
Perkins, Edward J. *diplomat*

Oklahoma City
Boyd, Betty *government official*
Butkin, Robert *state treasurer*
Cornett, Mick *mayor*
Edmondson, William Andrew *state attorney general*
Fallin, Mary Copeland *lieutenant governor*
Henry, C. Brad *governor*
Humphreys, Kirk *mayor*
McKenzie, Clif Allen *Indian tribe official, accountant*
Savage, Susan M. *state official, former mayor*
Thompson, Mick *state commissioner*

Park Hill
Mankiller, Wilma Pearl *tribal leader, retired*

Tulsa
LaFortune, Bill *mayor*
Madison, Eddie Lawrence, Jr., *public relations consultant, editor, writer*

OREGON

Eugene
Bascom, Ruth F. *retired mayor*
Torrey, James D. *mayor, communications executive, consultant*

Lake Oswego
Campbell, Colin Herald *former mayor*

Portland
Katz, Vera *mayor, former college administrator, state legislator*
Kitzhaber, John Albert *former governor, emergency physician, former state senator*
Kleim, E. Denise *city official*

Salem
Bradbury, William Chapman, III, *state official*
Kulongoski, Theodore Ralph *governor, former judge*
Myers, Hardy *state attorney general, lawyer*
Taylor, Janet R. *mayor*

PENNSYLVANIA

Bellefonte
Lamb, Robert Edward *retired diplomat, professional society administrator*

Canonsburg
Colaizzo, Anthony Louis *mayor, former state legislator, small business owner*

Donora
Todd, Norma Ross *retired government official*

Erie
Filippi, Richard *mayor, lawyer, real estate company executive*

Glen Mills
Dunion, Celeste Mogab *consultant, business manager, township official*

Harrisburg
Baker Knoll, Catherine *lieutenant governor*
Bittenbender, Robert A. *state official*
Hafer, Barbara *state official*
Houstoun, Feather O'Connor *state official*
Jubelirer, Robert C. *lieutenant governor*
Koken, M. Diane *state commissioner*
Pappert, Gerald J. (Jerry) *state attorney general*
Pizzingrilli, Kim *state official*
Rendell, Edward Gene *governor, former mayor, lawyer*
Wolfe, Gary Donald *library commissioner, retired state education official*

Lititz
Koch, Bruce R. *diplomat*

Newtown
Brennan, Thomas John *city and state official, consultant, educator*

Norristown
Biondi, Anthony *municipal official*

Philadelphia
Harris, Raymond Jesse *retired government official*
Kaplan, Barbara Jane *retired city planner*
Krycia, Shelly *state official*
Miller, Donna Reed *city official*
Murray, Kathleen *municipal official*
O'Connor, Charles Edward, Jr., *state government official, lawyer*

Pittsburgh
Mitchell, George Charles *diplomat, international consultant, mediator, educator, writer*
Murphy, Thomas J., Jr., *mayor*
O'Neill, Paul Henry *former government official*
Simpson, Daniel H. *ambassador*

West Chester
Dinniman, Andrew Eric *county commissioner, history educator, academic program director, international studies educator*

York
Wiles, William Wharton *retired federal government official*

RHODE ISLAND

Kingston
Sundlun, Bruce *former governor*

Providence
Brown, Matthew A. *state official*
Carcieri, Donald L. *governor*
Fogarty, Charles Joseph *lieutenant governor*
Franklin, Lawrence C. *state official*
Lynch, Patrick C. *state attorney general*
Pine, Jeffrey Barry *lawyer, former state attorney general*

SOUTH CAROLINA

Columbia
Bauer, R. Andre *lieutenant governor*
Clyburn, Mignon L. *commissioner*
Hammond, Mark *state official*
McMaster, Henry Dargan *state attorney general*
Page, Randall *state official*
Sanford, Marshall (Mark Sanford) *governor, former congressman*
Tenenbaum, Inez Moore *superintendent of education*
Zelenka, Donald John *lawyer*

Lexington
Morris, Earle Elias, Jr., *retired state official, business executive*

SOUTH DAKOTA

Pierre
Daugaard, Dennis M. *lieutenant governor*
Everson, Curt *commissioner, state*
Long, Larry *state attorney general*
Nelson, Chris A. *secretary of state*
Rounds, Michael *governor*
Schoenfelder, Laska *commissioner, farmer*

Rapid City
Eccarius, Scott *state official, eye surgeon*

TENNESSEE

Alcoa
Dunlap, Bill *municipal administrator*

Memphis
Herenton, Willie W. *mayor*
Pendleton, Mary Catherine *foreign service officer*

Nashville
Bredesen, Philip Norman *governor*
Darnell, Riley Carlisle *Secretary of State, lawyer*
Gore, Tipper (Mary Elizabeth Gore) *wife of the former vice president of the United States*
Houston, Bill *state commissioner*
Seivers, Lana C. *commissioner of education*
Summers, Paul *state attorney general*
Swing, Marilyn S. *metropolitan clerk*
Thomas, Hazel Beatrice *state official*
Wadley, Fredia Stovall *state commissioner*
Wilder, John Shelton *lieutenant governor*

Oak Ridge
Holloway, Jacqueline *county commissioner*

Springfield
Nutting, Paul John *city manager*

Townsend
Sundquist, Don *former governor, former congressman, sales corporation executive*

TEXAS

Austin
Abbott, Greg Wayne *state attorney general, former state supreme court justice*
Ables-Flatt, Jean Ann *commissioner*
Caldwell, Shirley W. *commissioner*
Clay, Lareatha H. *commissioner*
Combs, Susan *commissioner of agriculture*
Connor, Geoffrey Scott *state official, lawyer*
Cooke, Carlton Lee, Jr., *mayor*
Dewhurst, David *lieutenant governor*
Gates, Charles Woodley, Sr., *city official*
Johnson, Lady Bird (Mrs. Claudia Alta Taylor) *former First Lady of the United States*
Klein, Rebecca *commissioner*
McKnight, Mamie *commissioner*
Perry, Rick *governor*
Ratliff, William *former stae senator; lieutenant governor, civil engineer*
Richards, Ann Willis *former governor*
Wynn, Will *mayor*

Beaumont
Lord, Evelyn Marlin *mayor*

Brenham
Pipes, Paul Ray *county commissioner*

Buffalo
Standley, John Robert *city official*

Dallas
Baker, James Edward *city planner*
Jackson, Jimmy Lee *commissioner*
Lake, Joseph Edward *ambassador*
Miller, Laura *mayor, journalist*
Rubottom, Roy Richard, Jr., *retired diplomat and educator, consultant*

El Paso
Wardy, Joe *mayor*

Fort Worth
Moncrief, Michael Joseph *mayor, former state legislator*
Wilder, Thomas A. *county official*

Gainesville
Broyles, Stephen Douglas *public administrator*

Harlingen
Matz, James Richard *municipal official*

Houston
Baker, James Addison, III, *ambassador, lawyer, former government official*
Bush, George Herbert Walker *41st President of the United States*
Dedeaux, Jules A. *city official*
desVignes-Kendrick, Mary *municipal official*
Kendrick, Robert Warren *county official*
Lanier, Bob *mayor*
Sipahioglu, Hatice Elcin *diplomat, interpreter/translator*
White, William H. *mayor*

Lubbock
Sitton, Windy *mayor*
Stuart, Frank Adell *county official*

New Braunfels
Krueger, Robert Charles *former ambassador, former senator, congressman*

Plano
Evans, Pat *mayor*

San Antonio
Catto, Henry Edward *former government official, former ambassador*
Daley, William M. *former federal government official*
Garza, Ed *mayor*
Henderson, Connie Chorlton *city planner, artist and writer*
Peak, Howard W. *former mayor*

UTAH

Salt Lake City
Alter, Edward T. *state treasurer*
Anderson, Ross Carl *mayor, lawyer*
Deamer, Michael Lynn *mayor, lawyer, accountant*
Foxley, Cecelia Harrison *commissioner*
Leary, G. Edward *state financial commisioner*
McKeachnie, Gayle F. *lieutenant governor*
Quinn, Eugene Frederick *foreign service officer, clergyman*
Schow, Terry D. *state official*
Shurtleff, Mark L. *state attorney general*
Sorenson, Roger A. *international relations consultant*
Stephens, Martin R. *state official*
Varela, Vicki *state official*
Walker, Olene S. *governor*
White, Constance Burnham *state official*

VERMONT

Burlington
Clavelle, Peter *mayor*
Dean, Howard *political activist, former governor*
Kunin, Madeleine May *former ambassador to Switzerland, former governor*

Montpelier
Costle, Elizabeth Rowe *commissioner*
Douglas, James Holley *governor*
Dubie, Brian E. *lieutenant governor*
Markowitz, Deborah Lynn *state government official*
Pelham, Tom *commissioner*
Racine, Douglas A *former lieutenant governor*
Sorrell, William H. *state attorney general*

Peacham
Engle, James Bruce *ambassador*

South Londonderry
Spiers, Ronald Ian *diplomat*

VIRGINIA

Alexandria
Brotzman, Donald Glenn *government official, lawyer*
Connell, Mary Ellen *diplomat*
Costagliola, Francesco *retired government official*
Fitton, Harvey Nelson, Jr., *former government official*
Freeman-Wilson, Karen *former attorney general, prosecutor, educational association administrator*
Havens, Harry Stewart *former federal assistant comptroller general, government consultant*
Helman, Gerald Bernard *government official*
McCaffrey, Barry Richard *federal official, retired army officer*
McGuire, Roger Alan *retired foreign service officer*
McNicol, David Leon *retired federal official, consultant*
Pringle, Robert Maxwell *diplomat*
Saloom, Joseph A., III, *diplomat*
Tucker, Alvin Leroy *retired government official*

Annandale
Christianson, Geryld B. *government relations consultant*
Rogers, Stephen Hitchcock *former ambassador*

Arlington
Aggrey, Orison Rudolph *former ambassador, university administrator*
Allison, Graham Tillett, Jr., *federal government official*
Bolster, Archie Milburn *retired foreign service officer*
Bune, Karen Louise *criminal justice official*
Clutter, Mary Elizabeth *federal official*
Douglass, John W. *commissioner*
Edmondson, William Brockway *retired foreign service officer*
Galloway, William Jefferson *former foreign service officer*
Hamed, Martha Ellen *government administrator*
Heivilin, Donna Mae *retired government executive*
Hurley, John Arthur *former national security advisor*
Katzen, Jay Kenneth *retired diplomat, state legislator, government agency administrator*
Krys, Sheldon Jack *retired foreign service officer, career minister*
Mc Donald, John Warlick *diplomat, global strategist*
Ochmanek, David Alan *defense analyst*
Pickering, Thomas Reeve *diplomat*
Schneider, William, Jr., *commissioner*
Umminger, Bruce Lynn *government official, scientist, educator*
Winter, Harvey John *retired government official*
Wood, Heidi *commissioner*

Burke
Pfister, Cloyd Harry *consultant, former career officer*

Charlottesville
Newsom, David Dunlop *foreign service officer, educator*

Chesapeake
Myrick, Bismarck *diplomat*
Ward, William E. *mayor*

Dulles
Minikes, Stephan Michael *ambassador, lawyer, banker*
Montgomery, William D. *ambassador*
Yates, John Melvin *retired ambassador*

Dumfries
Wolle, William Down *foreign service officer*

Fairfax
Beckler, David Zander *government official, science administrator*
Haskett, Dianne Louise *former mayor, lawyer, consultant*
McCormick, Robert Junior *former government official, air transportation executive*
Pyatt, Everett Arno *government official*
Ruedy, Ralph H. *diplomat, consultant*

Falls Church
Beeman, Josiah Horton *diplomat*
Beyer, Donald Sternoff, II, *former state offical*
Morrison, H. Robert *municipal official*
Rostker, Bernard *federal official*
Ward, George Frank, Jr., *ambassador*

Haymarket
Doolittle, Warren T. *retired federal official*

King George
Newhall, David, III, *former government official*

Lynchburg
Stephens, Bart Nelson *former foreign service officer*

Manassas
Storing, Paul Edward *retired foreign service officer*

Mathews
Busby, Morris D. *former ambassador*

Mc Lean
Cahill, Harry Amory *diplomat, educator*

Cannon, Mark Wilcox *government official, business executive*
Chaplin, Stephen Michael *retired diplomat*
Healy, Theresa Ann *former ambassador*
Malley, Raymond Charles *retired foreign service officer, industrial executive*
Russell, Theodore Emery *diplomat*
Smith, Russell Jack *former intelligence official*
Trout, Maurice Elmore *diplomat*

Midlothian
Perkins, Raymond Lamont *retired government official*

Morattico
Dawson, Carol Gene *former commissioner, writer, consultant*

Norfolk
Andrews, Mason Cooke *mayor, obstetrician, gynecologist, educator*
Griffith, Charles Dee, Jr., *state official*

Oakton
Farwell, Albert Edmond *retired government official, consultant*
Pratsch, Lloyd Wilmer *government official*

Richmond
DeMary, Jo Lynne *state official, elementary school educator*
Hager, John Henry *state official, former lieutenant governor*
Jones-Atkins, DeBorah Kaye *state official*
Kaine, Timothy M. *lieutenant governor*
Kilgore, Jerry *state attorney general*
Linkonis, Suzanne Newbold *probation officer, counselor*
McCollum, Rudolph C., Jr., *mayor*
Petera, Anne Pappas *state official*
Warner, Mark R. *governor*
Wilder, Eunice *city official*
Wilder, L(awrence) Douglas *former governor*

Springfield
Hunt, Robert Gayle *former government official*
Stottlemyer, David Lee *government official*

Stafford
Williams, Carlisle M., Jr., *municipal official*

Stanardsville
Keel, Alton Gold, Jr., *ambassador*

Susan
Ambach, Dwight Russell *retired foreign service officer*

The Plains
Gibbons, John Howard (Jack Gibbons) *government official, physicist*

Vienna
Almaguer, Frank *ambassador*
DeWitt, Charles Barbour *federal government official*
Rossello, Pedro *former governor*

Virginia Beach
Oberndorf, Meyera E. *mayor*
Smith, Ruth Hodges *city clerk*

WASHINGTON

Bellevue
Mosher, Charles D. *mayor, real estate manager*

Chattaroy
Ezelle, Robert Eugene *diplomat*

Edmonds
Thyden, James Eskel *diplomat, educator, lecturer*

Everett
Vaughn, Kathy *municipal official*

Olympia
Chopp, Frank *state official*
Gregoire, Christine O. *state attorney general*
Locke, Gary *governor*
Long, Marsha Tadano *state official*
Markham, J. David *educator, writer, historical consultant*
O'Brien, Robert S. *state official*
Owen, Bradley Scott *lieutenant governor*
Reed, Sam *secretary of state*

Seattle
Kennedy, Mary Virginia *diplomat*
Nickels, Greg *mayor*
Nuxoll, Carla *federal official*
Schell, Paul E.S. *former mayor*
Skidmore, Donald Earl, Jr., *government official*

Sequim
Huntley, James Robert *government official, international affairs scholar and consultant*
McMahon, Terrence John *retired foreign service officer*

Spokane
Greenwood, Collette P. *municipal official, finance officer*

Sumas
Hemry, Larry Harold *former federal agency official, writer, inventor*

Tacoma
Ebersole, Brian *former mayor*
Sutherland, Douglass B. *former mayor, tent and awning company executive*

Vancouver
Ogden, Daniel Miller, Jr., *government official, educator*

WEST VIRGINIA

Charleston
Bias, Sharon G. *state commissioner*
Hechler, Ken *former state official, former congressman, political science educator, writer*
Manchin, Joe, III, *secretary of state*
Mc Graw, Darrell Vivian, Jr., *state attorney general*
Melton, G. Kemp *former mayor*
Stark, Larry A. *commissioner*
Wise, Robert Ellsworth, Jr., (Bob Ellsworth) *governor, former congressman*

WISCONSIN

Ashland
Smith, Jane Schneberger *retired city administrator*

Deerfield
Shakespeare, Frank *ambassador*

Janesville
Blazkowski, Phillip *community development and planning official*

Juneau
Carpenter, David Erwin *county official, land use planner*

Madison
Bauman, Susan Joan Mayer *mayor, lawyer*
Doyle, James E(dward) *governor*
Earl, Anthony Scully *former governor of Wisconsin, lawyer*
La Follette, Douglas J. *secretary of state*
Lautenschlager, Peggy A. *state attorney general*
Lawton, Barbara *lieutenant governor*
Shilling, Jennifer *state official*
Sinicki, Christine *state official*
Thompson, Barbara Storck *state official*
Voight, Jack C. *state official*

Milwaukee
Barrett, Thomas M. *mayor, former congressman*

Pewaukee
Farrow, Margaret Ann *former state official*

WYOMING

Cheyenne
Catchpole, Judy *state official*
Crank, Pat *state attorney general*
Freudenthal, David D. *governor*
Lummis, Cynthia Marie *state official, lawyer*
Meyer, Joseph B. *Secretary of State, former academic administrator*
Rodekohr, Diane E. *state official*
Thomson, Thyra Godfrey *former state official*
Vogel, Jeffrey C. *commissioner*
Woodhouse, Gay Vanderpoel *former state attorney general, lawyer*

Laramie
Dickman, Francois Moussiegt *former foreign service officer, educator*
Brown, Carroll *diplomat, association executive, consultant*

TERRITORIES OF THE UNITED STATES

AMERICAN SAMOA

Pago Pago
Mailo, Toetagata Albert *territory attorney general*
Sunia, Aitofele Toese F. *lieutenant governor*
Sunia, Muagututia Fiti *American Samoa attorney general*
Tulafono, Togiola T.A. *governor*

GUAM

Adelup
Moylan, Kaleo *lieutenant governor*

Hagatna
Camacho, Felix Perez *governor*
Moylan, Douglas *state attorney general*

NORTHERN MARIANA ISLANDS

Saipan
Benavente, Diego T. *lieutenant governor*
Brown, Pamela S. *attorney general*

PUERTO RICO

San Juan
Andujar, Norma Burgos *former state official*
Calderón, Sila M. *governor*
Encarnación, Jose M. Izquierdo *Secretary of State Puerto Rico*
Garcia, Marc Anthony *diplomat*
Padilla, Alfredo *commissioner*
Rodriguez, Annabelle *state attorney general*
Santini, Jorge *mayor*
Velez Silva, Xenia *Puerto Rican government official*

VIRGIN ISLANDS

Charlotte Amalie
Stapleton, Marylyn Alecia *diplomat*
Stridiron, Iver Allison *attorney general*

Christiansted
James, Gerard Luz Amwur, II, *former lieutenant governor*
Richards, Vargrave A. *lieutenant governor*

Saint Thomas
Turnbull, Charles W. *governor*

St Thomas
Michael, Noreen *commissioner, educator*

MILITARY ADDRESSES OF THE UNITED STATES

ATLANTIC

Apo
Brownfield, William R. *ambassador*
Danilovich, John J. *ambassador*
Jett, Dennis Coleman *foreign service officer*
Watt, Linda E. *ambassador*

EUROPE

APO
Carson, Johnnie *ambassador*
Cejas, Paul L. *diplomat, executive*
Fowler, Wyche, Jr., *ambassador*
Gnehm, Edward W., Jr., *ambassador*
Korologos, Tom Chris *ambassador*
McGowan, Gerald S. *diplomat*
Morella, Constance Albanese *ambassador, former congresswoman*
Oberwetter, James C. *ambassador*
Romero, Edward L. *diplomat, environmental engineering executive*
Webster, Christopher White *foreign service officer*

Apo
Untermeyer, Charles Graves (Chase Untermeyer) *ambassador, diplomat*

FPO
Benedict, Lawrence Neal *foreign service officer*
Gadsden, James Irvin *ambassador*

Fpo
Klosson, Michael *foreign service officer*

PACIFIC

Apo
Ray, Charles Aaron *foreign service officer*

CANADA

BRITISH COLUMBIA

Vancouver
Chan, Raymond *Canadian government minister*

MANITOBA

Winnipeg
Curtis, Charles Edward *Canadian government official*
Filmon, Gary Albert *Canadian provincial premier, civil engineer*
Liba, Peter Michael *Canadian provincial government official*

NOVA SCOTIA

Waverley
Grady, Wayne J. *government official*

ONTARIO

Belleville
Vanclief, Lyle *former Canadian government official*

Brantford
Stewart, Jane *former Canadian government minister*

Downsview
Eggleton, Arthur C. *former Canadian government official, member of Parliament*

Nobleton
Embleton, Tony Frederick Wallace *retired Canadian government official*

Ottawa
Almakky, Ghazy Abdulwahed Makky *diplomat, geography educator*
Anderson, David Leslie *member of parliament*
Angus, W. David *Queen's Counsel*
Armstrong, Henry Conner *former Canadian government official, consultant*
Augustine, Jean Magdalene *Canadian government official, member of parliament*
Austin, Jacob (Jack Austin) *Canadian government official*
Axworthy, Lloyd *Canadian government official*
Bailey, Roy H. *member of parliament*
Baker, George S. *federal official*
Bélisle, Paul Charles *Canadian government official*
Boudria, Don *Canadian government official*
Buchanan, John MacLennan *Canadian provincial official*
Caplan, Elinor *former Canadian government official*
Cauchon, Martin *former Canadian government official*
Cellucci, Paul (Argeo Paul Cellucci) *ambassador, former governor*
Clarkson, Adrienne *Governor General of Canada*
Coderre, Denis *Canadian government official*
Copps, Sheila *former Canadian government official*
Day, Stockwell Burt *government official*
Efford, R. John *Canadian government official*
Fairbairn, Joyce *Canadian government official*
Fitzpatrick, Brian *member of parliament*
Gold, Lorne W. *Canadian government official*
Goodale, Ralph E. *Canadian government official*
Graham, B. Alasdair *government official*
Graham, William C. *Canadian government official*
Gray, Herbert Eser (The Right Honourable Herbert Gray) *former federal official*
Grey, Deborah Cleland *Canadian government official*
Guarnieri, Albina *Canadian government official, Canadian legislator*
Harb, Mac *Canadian government official*
Keyes, Stan Kazmierczak *Canadian government official*
Kingsley, Jean-Pierre *government official*
Laliberte, Rick *member of parliament*
MacAulay, Lawrence A. *Canadian government official, member of Parliament*
MacDonald, Flora Isabel *Canadian government official*
Manley, John Paul *former Canadian government official*
Marleau, Diane *Canadian government official*
Martin, Paul *Prime Minister of Canada*
McGuire, Joseph *Canadian government official*
McLellan, A. Anne *Canadian government official*
McLure, John Douglas *federal official*
Mifflin, Fred John *Canadian government official*
Mills, Bob *member of Canadian parliament*
Minna, Maria *member of Canadian Parliament*
Mitchell, Andrew (Andy Mitchell) *Canadian government official*
Nystrom, Lorne *member of parliament*
Pagtakhan, Rey D. *Canadian government official*
Pankiw, Jim *member of parliament*
Paradis, Denis *Canadian government official, member of parliament*
Peterson, James Scott (Jim Peterson) *Canadian government official*
Pettigrew, Pierre S. *Canadian government official*
Poulin, Marie *Canadian government official*
Proctor, Dick *member of parliament*
Regan, Geoff *Canadian government official*
Robillard, Lucienne *Canadian government official*
Roland, Anne *registrar Supreme Court of Canada*
Scherrer, Helene Chalifour *Canada government official*
Scott, Andy *Canadian government official*
Sgro, Judy *Canadian government official*
Silverman, Ozzie *consulting strategist*
Stanford, Joseph Stephen *diplomat, lawyer, educator*
Stewart, Christine Susan *Canadian government official*
Valeri, Tony *Canadian government official*
Volpe, Joseph *Canadian government official*
Yalden, Maxwell Freeman *Canadian diplomat*
Yeomans, Donald Ralph *Canadian government official, consultant*

Toronto
Bartleman, James K. *lieutenant governor*
Gotlieb, Allan E. *former ambassador*
Holyday, Douglas Charles *city councillor*
Lastman, Melvin D. *mayor*
MacLaren, Roy *retired federal official*
Turner, John Napier *former prime minister of Canada, legislator*

PRINCE EDWARD ISLAND

Charlottetown
McCallum, John *Canadian government official*

QUEBEC

Chelsea
Warren, Jack Hamilton *former diplomat and trade policy adviser*

Hull
Anderson, David *Canadian government official*
Blondin-Andrew, Ethel D. *Canadian government official*
Bradshaw, Claudette *Canadian government official*
Gagliano, Alfonso *Canadian government official*

Montreal
Mulroney, Brian (Martin Brian Mulroney) *former prime minister of Canada*

Pointe-Claire
Lapointe, Lucie *Canadian government official*

SASKATCHEWAN

Regina
Clayton, Raymond Edward *government official*
Haverstock, Lynda M. *lieutenant governor*

Saskatoon
Blakeney, Allan Emrys *Canadian government official, lawyer, educator*

Ottawa
Owen, Stephen *Canadian government official*

MEXICO

Col Centro
Gil Diaz, Francisco *minister of finance for Mexico*

Colonia Cuauhtemoc
Garza, Antonio O. *ambassador*

Mexico City
Abascal Carranza, Carlos Maria *secretary of labor and social planning for Mexico*
Barrio Terrazas, Francisco *government official of Mexico*
Cerisola y Weber, Pedro *secretary of communications and transportation for Mexico*
Creel Miranda, Santiago *Mexican government official*
Derbez Bautista, Luis Ernesto *secretary of foreign affairs of Mexico*
Fox, Vicente (Vicente Fox Quesada) *President of Mexico*

Gurria Trevino, José Angel *former Mexican government official*
Herrera Tello, Maria Teresa *secretary of agrarian reform for Mexico*
Lichtinger, Victor *government official*
Macedo de la Concha, Rafael *attorney general of Mexico*
Navarro, Leticia *Mexican government official*
Peyrot Gonzalez, Marco A. *secretary of the navy of Mexico*
Tamez Guerra, Reyes S. *secretary of public education for Mexico*
Usabiaga Arroyo, Javier *secretary of agriculture, livestock and rural development for Mexico*
Vazquez Mota, Josefina *secretary of social development for Mexico*
Vega Garcia, Gerardo Clemente R. *Mexico Secretary of Defense*

Piso
Tellez Kuenzler, Luis *government official*
Arroyo Marroquin, Romárico *former federal official*
Carabias Lillo, Julia *government official*
Carrasco Altamirano, Diódoro *former federal official*
Farell Cubillas, Arsenio *former Mexican government official*
Limón Rojas, Miguel *former Mexican government official*
Lorenzo Franco, José Ramón *former Mexican government official*
Martens Rebolledo, Ernesto *secretary of energy for Mexico*
Robledo Rincón, Eduardo *former federal official*

AFGHANISTAN

Kabul
Khalilzad, Zalmay *ambassador*

ARGENTINA

Buenos Aires
Green Macias, Rosario *ambassador*

AUSTRALIA

Camberwell
Peterson, Douglas Pete (Pete Peterson) *ambassador, retired congressman*

Double Bay
Peacock, Penne Korth *ambassador*

AUSTRIA

Vienna
Brill, Kenneth C. *ambassador*

BELARUS

Minsk
Sychov, Alyaksandr *diplomat*

BELGIUM

Brussels
Burns, R. Nicholas *ambassador*
Kerber, Frank John *diplomat*
Schnabel, Rockwell Anthony *ambassador*

BRAZIL

Brasília
Amorim, Celso Luiz Nunes *government official*

CHAD

N'Djamena
Goldthwait, Christopher E. *ambassador*

CHILE

Santiago
Wilkey, Malcolm Richard *retired ambassador, former federal judge*

COSTA RICA

San José
Arias Sanchez, Oscar *former president of Costa Rica*

CZECH REPUBLIC

Prague
Kavan, Jan *member Czech Parliament, former president UN General Assembly*

EGYPT

Cairo
Elaraby, Nabil A. *Egyptian diplomat, judge*
Welch, C. David *ambassador*

ENGLAND

London
Elizabeth, Her Majesty, II, (Elizabeth Alexandra Mary) *Queen of United Kingdom of Great Britain, Northern Ireland and of her other Realms and Territories; Head of Commonwealth, Defender of Faith*
Meyer, Sir Christopher J.R. *former diplomat*
Navarrete, Jorge Eduardo *ambassador*
Paulus, Michael John *government official, bank executive, economist*

Oxford
Robinson, Mary *former United Nations official*

FRANCE

APO
Carner, George *foreign service executive, economic strategist*

Paris
Dean, John Gunther *diplomat*
Flack, Ronald David *diplomat, public service educator, banker*
Leach, Howard H. *ambassador, former health care products company executive*
Myerson, Jacob Myer *retired diplomat*

GERMANY

Berlin
Chrobog, Juergen *ambassador*

INDIA

New Delhi
Anderson, Michael Hugh *diplomat*

IRAQ

Baghdad
Negroponte, John Dimitri *ambassador*

ISRAEL

Tel Aviv
Kurtzer, Daniel C. *ambassador*

ITALY

Bologna
Lino, Marisa Rose *retired diplomat*

Rome
Hall, Tony P. *ambassador, retired congressman*
Sisulu, Sheila Violet Makate *diplomat*
Skodon, Emil Mark *diplomat*

JAPAN

Tokyo
Foley, Thomas Stephen *diplomat, former speaker House of Representatives*

LUXEMBOURG

Senningerberg
Fulci, Francesco Paolo *former diplomat*

NETHERLANDS

The Hague
Tomka, Peter *Slovakian diplomat, lawyer, judge, arbitrator*

NORWAY

Oslo
Ong, John Doyle *ambassador, retired manufacturing executive*

OMAN

Medinat Qaboos
Craig, John Bruce *ambassador*

PAKISTAN

Islamabad
Powell, Nancy J. *ambassador*

PERU

Lima
Struble, James Curtis *ambassador*

PHILIPPINES

Makati
Mabilangan, Felipe Hugo, Jr., *Philippine diplomat*

RUSSIA

Moscow
Vershbow, Alexander R. *ambassador*

SLOVENIA

Ljubljana
Rupel, Dimitrij *diplomat*

SOUTH AFRICA

Johannesburg
Dunn, David B. *ambassador*

SPAIN

Canary Islands
Wells, Melissa Foelsch *foreign service officer*

SWEDEN

Stockholm
Wachtmeister, Count Wilhelm H. F. *diplomat*

SWITZERLAND

Bern
Gonzalez, Guillermo Enrique *diplomat*

Geneva
Brown, Kent Newville *ambassador*
Deily, Linnet Frazier *ambassador*
Marchi, Sergio Sisto *Canadian government official*
Moley, Kevin Edward *ambassador*
Ogata, Sadako *United Nations official*

Versoix
Frenk, Julio Jose *secretary of health for Mexico, health systems researcher, consultant*
Boutros-Ghali, Boutros *former United Nations secretary general*

SYRIA

Damascus
Scobey, Margaret *ambassador*

TAIWAN

Taipei
Chang, Parris Hsu-cheng *law-maker, political science educator, writer*

TURKEY

Ankara
Ilkin, Baki *former diplomat, Turkish government official*

VIETNAM

Hanoi
Burghardt, Raymond Francis, Jr., *ambassador*

ADDRESS UNPUBLISHED

Abramowitz, Morton I. *former ambassador*
Adams, Edwin Melville *former foreign service officer, actor, author, lecturer*
Adams, Weston *former diplomat, lawyer*
Addo, Charles Kwame *municipal official*
Aguilar Zinser, Adolfo Miguel *former ambassador*
Albano, Michael J. *former mayor*
Albright, Madeleine Korbel *former secretary of state*
Allukian, Myron, Jr., *government administrator, public health educator, dental educator*
Almond, Lincoln *retired governor, retired lawyer*
Amato Chiaramonte Bordonaro, Baron Carlo Camillo *ambassador, consultant*
Anzai, Earl I. *former state attorney general*
Archulata, Margie Baca *city clerk*
Arcos, Cresencio S. *ambassador*
Armstrong, Anne Legendre (Mrs. Tobin Armstrong) *retired ambassador*
Arrington, Richard, Jr., *former mayor*
Atwater, Phyllis Y. *municipal administrator*
Baca, Jim *former mayor*
Barkley, Richard Clark *ambassador*
Barnett, Mark William *former state attorney general*
Barr, Kenneth L. *former mayor*
Bayless, Betsey *state official*
Beasley, David Muldrow *former governor, consultant*
Benson, Joanne E. *former lieutenant governor*
Bentsen, Lloyd *former government official, former senator*
Berlincourt, Marjorie Alkins *government official, retired*
Betti, John Anso *federal official, former automobile manufacturing company executive*
Bishop, Oliver Richard *retired state official*
Black, Shirley Temple (Mrs. Charles A. Black) *former ambassador, former actress*
Blanco Mendoza, Herminio *Mexican government official*
Blankenship, J. Richard *former ambassador*
Blood, Archer Kent *retired foreign service officer*
Bolen, David Benjamin *ambassador*
Bomer, Elton *former state official*

Botelho, Bruce Manuel *mayor, former state attorney general*
Boyatt, Thomas David *former ambassador*
Bremer, Lewis Paul, III *former diplomat*
Bremer Martino, Juan Jose *former ambassador*
Broadrick-Allen, Sandra Carol *retired city manager, consultant, civic worker*
Brown, June Gibbs *retired government official*
Brown, Kay (Mary Kathryn Brown) *retired state official, consultant*
Brown, Lee Patrick *former mayor, city official, law enforcement educator*
Brown, Willie Lewis, Jr., *former mayor, former state legislator, lawyer*
Bryant, Winston *former state attorney general*
Bumpas, Diane DeWare *commissioner*
Burchman, Leonard *government official, journalist*
Bush, Barbara Pierce *former First Lady of the United States, volunteer*
Carter, Rosalynn Smith *former First Lady of the United States*
Cayetano, Benjamin Jerome *former governor, former state senator and representative*
Cenarrusa, Pete T. *retired state official*
Chan, Wilma *county official*
Chen, Stephen S. F. *retired diplomat*
Cherry, Robert Steven, III, *municipal administrator*
Christie, Walter Scott *retired state official*
Chung, Caroline *foreign service officer*
Clark, William, Jr., *political advisor*
Clarke, Henry Lee *foreign service officer, former ambassador*
Cohen, Roberta Jane *government executive*
Condayan, John *foreign service officer*
Condon, Charles Molony *former state attorney general*
Cook, Rebecca McDowell *former state official*
Coop, Frederick Robert *retired city manager*
Coppie, Comer Swift *retired state official*
Corkery, James Caldwell *retired Canadian government executive, mechanical engineer*
Cornell, Robert Arthur *retired international government official, consultant*
Cornish, Richard Joseph *international affairs consultant, retired diplomat*
Cosman, Francene Jen *former government official*
Cougill, Roscoe McDaniel *mayor, retired air force officer*
Cunningham, James Blair *former ambassador*
Dalsimer, Anthony Stearns *retired foreign service officer, educator*
Dalton, John Howard *former secretary of the navy, financial consultant*
Daly, Paul Sylvester *mayor, retired academic administrator, management consultant*
Davis, Gray (Joseph Graham Davis) *former governor*
Del Papa, Frankie Sue *former state attorney general*
DeThomas, Joseph Michael *former ambassador*
Dillon, Robert Sherwood *retired government official*
Duelfer, Charles A. *weapons inspector*
Dyrstad, Joanell M. *former lieutenant governor, consultant*
Edwards, Lydia *Justice state official*
Egan, Wesley William *former ambassador*
Eisenhower, John Sheldon Doud *former ambassador, author*
Elson, Edward Elliott *diplomat*
Emmons, Robert Duncan *diplomat*
Engler, John M. *former governor*
Enkhsaikhan, Jargalsaikhany *former ambassador*
Eu, March Fong *ambassador*
Evatt, Parker *former state commissioner, former state legislator*
Ewing, Raymond Charles *retired ambassador*
Fiddick, Paul William *government official, broadcasting executive*
Foglietta, Thomas Michael *former diplomat, former congressman*
Ford, Christopher Ashley *state official, lawyer*
Ford, Ford Barney *retired government official*
Foster, Murphy James, Jr., (Mike Foster) *former governor*
Fowler, Robert Asa *diplomat, manufacturing executive*
Franke, Wayne Thomas *retired government affairs director, consultant*
Fraser, Donald MacKay *former mayor, former congressman, educator*
Galloway, Judy A. *deputy commissioner*
Gardom, Garde Basil *former lieutenant governor of British Columbia*
Gawf, John Lee *foreign service officer*
Geisel, Harold Walter *diplomat*
Glendening, Parris Nelson *former governor, political science educator*
Gore, Albert, Jr., *former Vice President of the United States*
Graves, William Preston *governor*
Growe, Joan Anderson *former state official*
Gumppert, Karella Ann *federal government official*
Haley, George W. *ambassador*
Hanmer, Stephen Read, Jr., *retired government executive*
Harder, Robert Clarence *state official*
Hauer, Jerome M. *city official*
Havel, Vaclav *former president of Czech Republic, playwright*
Hazeltine, Joyce *former state official*
Heimbold, Charles Andreas, Jr., *former ambassador*
Hennemeyer, Robert Thomas *diplomat*
Henry, Sherrye P. *former political advisor*
Henry, Stephen Lewis *orthopedic surgeon, educator, former lieutenant governor*
Herman, Alexis M. *former secretary of labor*
Hester, Nancy Elizabeth *county government official*
Hett, Joan Margaret *ecological consultant*
Heydt, William *former mayor*
Hirono, Mazie Keiko *former lieutenant governor*
Holiday, Edith Elizabeth *former presidential adviser, cabinet secretary*
Holmes, Genta Hawkins *former diplomat*
Holmes, Henry Allen *government official*
Howard, Robert Elliott *former federal official, consultant, educator*
Hubbard, Thomas C. *former ambassador*
Hughes, Karen Parfitt *former federal official*
Hull, Jane Dee *former governor, former state legislator*
Hume, Cameron R. *former ambassador*
Hunter, Sue Persons *former state official*
Inman, Edward Salisbury, III, *former secretary of state, secondary school educator*

James, Fob, Jr., (Forrest Hood James) *former governor*
Johnson, Gary Earl *former governor*
Jones, Bill *former state official, rancher*
Jones, Jan Laverty *mayor*
Joseph, Geri Mack (Geraldine Joseph) *former ambassador, educator, journalist*
Kattouf, Theodore E. *ambassador*
Kelley, Wayne Plumbley, Jr., *retired federal official*
Kendig, William Lamar *retired government official, accountant*
Kissinger, Henry Alfred *former secretary of state, international consulting company executive*
Kulstad, Guy Charles *public works official*
Landers, Sharon L.
Laney, James Thomas *former ambassador, educator*
Leader, Joyce E. *ambassador*
Ledogar, Stephen J. *retired diplomat*
Lee, James Matthew *Canadian politician*
Likins, Rose Marie *foreign service officer*
Loiello, John Peter *diplomat*
MacIsaac, John Anthony *retired municipal official*
Maestrone, Frank Eusebio *diplomat*
Manz, Johannes Jakob *Swiss diplomat*
Mariano, Raymond V. *former mayor*
Martin, James Kay *government official*
Martinez, Melquiades R. (Mel Martinez) *former secretary of housing and urban development*
Mattingly, Mack Francis *former ambassador, former senator, entrepreneur*
Mazankowski, Donald Frank *Canadian government official*
McBee, Robert Levi *retired federal government official, writer, consultant*
McCaughey Ross, Elizabeth P. (Betsy McCaughey) *former lieutenant governor*
McClinton, James Leroy *city administrator*
McCoy, Mary Ann *state official*
McLean, Hon. Walter Franklin *executive, pastor, legislator*
Mercado-Ramos, Ferdinand *former secretary of state*
Miles, Jim *former state offical*
Millane, Lynn *retired town official*
Miller, Thomas J. *former ambassador*
Milne, James F. *former secretary of state*
Mohler, Brian Jeffery *diplomat*
Mondale, Walter Frederick *former Vice President of United States, diplomat, lawyer*
Morris, Robert Gemmill *retired foreign service officer*
Morris, Ronald Anthony *county official*
Munro, Ralph Davies *former state official*
Murphy, Gerald *retired government official, consultant*
Musgrove, David Ronald (Ronnie Musgrove) *former governor*
Neal, Robert Lee, Jr., *government official*
Nelson, Norman Daniel *government official*
Nemfakos, Charles Panagiotis *defense industry executive, strategic consultant*
Neumann, Ronald Eldredge *former ambassador*
Normand, Gilbert *government official*
Norquist, John Olaf *former mayor*
Obermann, Richard Michael *governmental technology and policy analyst*
Ortiz, Francis Vincent, Jr., *retired ambassador*
Paliwal, Dinesh Kumar *diplomat, educational administrator*
Patterson, James *former mayor*
Patton, Paul E. *former governor*
Pearl, Laurence Dickson *retired federal government executive*
Peeler, Bob *lieutenant governor*
Peña, Federico Fabian *retired federal official*
Peters, Michael P. *former mayor*
Petrequin, Harry Joseph, Jr., *foreign service officer*
Peyton, John *mayor*
Pies, Ronald E. *retired city official*
Powers, John T., Jr., *former mayor*
Preis, Mary Louise *commissioner, former state legislator*
Price, Robert Otis *former mayor*
Pridmore, Roy Davis *government official*
Purcell, Bill *mayor*
Ramirez, Carlos Moises *former mayor*
Raynolds, Harold, Jr., *retired state education commissioner*
Reich, Robert Bernard *former federal official, political economics educator*
Reinhardt, John Edward *former international affairs specialist*
Render, Arlene *former ambassador*
Rice, Richard Campbell *retired state official, retired army officer*
Rickert, Jonathan Bradley *retired foreign service officer*
Ridgway, James Mastin *retired government official*
Ridgway, Rozanne LeJeanne *retired diplomat*
Ries, Charles P. *ambassador*
Rimsza, Skip *former mayor*
Rivers, Beverly D. *former district secretary*
Robinson, Laurie Overby *former assistant attorney general*
Rohatyn, Felix George *ambassador*
Rosenthal, Helen Nagelberg *county official, advocate*
Rosenthal, James D. *retired federal official, former U.S. ambassador*
Rubin, Robert E. *former secretary of treasury*
Rudin, Anne *retired mayor, nursing educator*
Ruggiero, Renato *former Italian government official*
Ryan, James E. *former state attorney general*
Sa, Julie (Shia Ri Xiang) *former councilwoman, former mayor, real estate developer*
Salleo, Ferdinando *former Italian diplomat*
Sampas, Dorothy Myers *retired government official*
Sauerbrey, Ellen Elaine Richmond *diplomat*
Scanlan, John Douglas *foreign service officer, former ambassador*
Schoettler, Gail Sinton *former ambassador*
Schunk, Mae Gasparac *former state official*
Schwartz, Carol Levitt *government official*
Seale, Robert L. *former state treasurer*
Segesváry, Victor Gyözö *retired diplomat*
Shea, Christina *former mayor*
Sheehan, Michael Andrew *diplomat*
Sherrer, Gary *former state lieutenant governor, bank executive*
Smith, Jean Kennedy *former ambassador*
Smith, Robert Powell *former ambassador, former foundation executive*
Snider, L. Britt *government executive*
Solomon, Connie Scott *chief of staff*
Sotirhos, Michael *ambassador*
Spielvogel, Carl *former ambassador, international business and marketing executive*
Stevens, Kenneth Allen *retired defense department worker*
Street, John F. *mayor*
Sudanowicz, Elaine Marie *government executive*
Swett, Richard Nelson (Dick Swett) *diplomat, former congressman*
Swift, Jane Maria *former governor*
Swoap, David Bruce *government affairs consultant*
Talbott, John *mayor*
Tambs, Lewis Arthur *diplomat, historian, educator*
Teater, Dorothy Seath *retired county official*
Tibshraeny, Jay *former mayor*
Tienken, Arthur T. *retired foreign service officer*
Tomasky, Susan *corporate officer*
Turner, Lisa Hill *county official*
Ulmer, Frances Ann *former lieutenant governor*
Underwood, Cecil H. *former governor, company executive*
Walker, George Herbert, III, *ambassador, former investment banking company executive*
Wallach, Patricia *councilwoman, retired mayor*
Watkins, James David *federal official, military officer*
Wendt, E. Allan *international affairs consultant*
Whitman, Christine Todd *former governor*
Whitney, Jane *foreign service officer*
Wilson, Pete *former governor*
Windom, Stephen Ralph *former lieutenant governor, lawyer*
Witt, James Lee *business executive, former Cabinet member*
Wolf, Dale Edward *state official*
Wood, Corinne Gieseke *former lieutenant governor*
Wood, Roberta Susan *retired foreign service officer*
Zischke, Douglas Arthur *foreign service officer*
Zoelleck, Robert Bruce *federal official*

GOVERNMENT: LEGISLATIVE ADMINISTRATION

UNITED STATES

ALABAMA

Birmingham
Allen, Maryon Pittman *former senator, journalist, lecturer, interior and clothing designer*
Hilliard, Earl Frederick *congressman, lawyer*

Jasper
Bevill, Tom *retired congressman, lawyer*

Mobile
Edwards, Jack *former congressman, lawyer*

Montgomery
Barron, Lowell Ray *state legislator*
Dixon, Larry Dean *state legislator*
Escott-Russell, Sundra *state legislator*
Figures, Vivian Davis *state legislator*
Hammett, Seth *state legislator*
Kennedy, Yvonne *state legislator*
Smith, Harri Anne *state legislator*

Tuscumbia
Heflin, Howell Thomas *former senator, lawyer, former state supreme court chief justice*

ALASKA

Anchorage
Sturgulewski, Arliss *state legislator, director*

Eagle River
Cotten, Samuel Richard *fisheries consultant, fisherman, former state legislator*

Homer
Phillips, Gail *state legislator*

Juneau
Cissna, Sharon *state representative*
Dahlstrom, Nancy *state representative*
Green, Lyda N. *state legislator*
Guess, Gretchen *state senator*
Heinze, Cheryll Boren *state representative*
Kapsner, Mary *state representative*
Kohring, Victor H. *state legislator*
Kott, Pete *state representative*
Lincoln, Georgianna *state legislator*
Mackie, Jerry *state legislator, business owner*
Masek, Beverly *state representative*
McGuire, Lesil L. *state representative*
Miller, Mike *state legislator, small business owner*
Phillips, Randy *state legislator, marketing professional*
Stevens, Gary Lee *state senator*
Therriault, Gene *state senator*
Ward, Jerry *state legislator, real estate executive*
Wilson, Peggy *state representative, registered nurse*

North Pole
James, Jeannette Adeline *state legislator, accountant*

ARIZONA

Chandler
Caccamo, Robert *councilman, retired principal*

Paradise Valley
Salmon, Matt *former congressman, communications company executive*

Phoenix
Aguirre, Linda *state senator*
Arzberger, Marsha *state senator*
Brown, Jack A. *state legislator, rancher, real estate broker*
Burns, Brenda *state senator*
Cheuvront, Kenneth David *state senator, construction executive, small business owner*
Cirillo, Edward J. *state legislator, retired financial manager*
Daniels, Lori S. *state legislator, insurance agent*
Day, Ann *state legislator*
Gerard, Susan *state senator*
Grace, Sue *state legislator*
Gray, Charles Dale (Chuck Gray) *state legislator, entrepreneur*
Hartley, Mary *state legislator*
Hellon, Toni *state senator*
Huppenthal, John *state senator, planning analyst*
Petersen, David A. *state legislator, financial advisor*
Weiers, Jim *state representative*
Wold, Kimberly G. *legislative staff member*

Tucson
Bartlett, David Carson *state legislator*

Waddell
Turner, Warren Austin *state legislator*

ARKANSAS

Dumas
Schexnayder, Charlotte Tillar *state legislator*

Fayetteville
Madison, Sue Wood *state legislator*

Foreman
Horn, Barbara B. *state legislator*

Greenwood
Walters, Bill *former state senator, lawyer*

Little Rock
Hill, Jim B. *state legislator*
Pollan, Carolyn Joan *state legislator, job research administrator*
Pryor, David Hampton *former senator*

Morrilton
Johnson, Bob W. *state senator*

Paris
Cleveland, Herschel *state representative*

Pine Bluff
Gullett, Brenda B. *state legislator*

Russellville
Trusty, Sharon *state legislator*

CALIFORNIA

Alamo
Baker, William P. (Bill Baker) *former congressman*

Bakersfield
Ashburn, Roy *state senator*
Florez, Dean R. *state senator*

Brentwood
Houston, Guy Spencer *state legislator*

Chico
Keene, Rick *state legislator*

Chula Vista
Moreno-Ducheny, Denise *state senator*

Compton
Dymally, Mervyn Malcolm *retired congressman*

El Cajon
Hollingsworth, Dennis *state senator*

Eureka
Berg, Patty *state legislator*

Fremont
Dutra, John A. *state legislator*

Garden Grove
Dornan, Robert Kenneth *former congressman*

Glendale
Moorhead, Carlos J. *former congressman*

Long Beach
Karentte, Betty *state legislator*
Karnette, Betty *state senator*

Los Angeles
Cedillo, Gilbert A. *state senator*
Chick, Laura *councilwoman*
Walters, Rita *councilwoman*

Martinez
Canciamilla, Joseph *state legislator*

Merced
Denham, Jeffrey *state senator*

Monterey
Browder, John Glen *former congressman, educator*

Ontario
Soto, Nell *state senator*

Redding
La Malfa, Doug *state representative*

Rosemead
McKinney, Michael Wayne *government and public affairs representative*

Sacramento
Aghazarian, Greg G. *state representative*
Alpert, Deirdre Whittleton (Dede Alpert) *state legislator*
Cogdill, David *state representative*
Cohn, Rebecca *state representative*
Cox, Dave *state legislator*
Diaz, Manny *state representative*
Frommer, Dario F. *state representative*
Goldberg, Jackie *councilwoman*
Hancock, Loni *state legislator, former mayor*
Holmes, Robert Eugene *legislative staff member, journalist*
Horton, Shirley A. *state legislator, former mayor*
Hughes, Teresa P. *state legislator*
Koretz, Paul *state representative*
Kuehl, Sheila James *state legislator*
Levine, Lloyd E. *state representative*
Lieber, Sally J. *state representative*
Liu, Carol *state representative*
Maze, Bill *state representative*
McCarthy, Kevin *state representative*
Montanez, Cindy *state representative*
Morrow, Bill *state legislator*
Nunez, Fabian *state representative*
Parra, Nicole M. *state representative*
Pavley, Fran J. *state representative*
Perata, Don *state legislator*
Reyes, Sarah *state representative*
Richman, Keith Stuart *state representative*
Runner, Sharon *state representative*
Simitian, Joe *state representative*
Steinberg, Darrell S. *state legislator*
Strickland, Anthony *state representative*
Torres, Art *former state legislator*
Wesson, Herb J. *state representative*
Wilson, E. Dotson *legislative staff member*
Wright, Cathie *state legislator*

San Diego
McCarty, Judy *councilman*
Stallings, Valerie Aileen *retired councilwoman, consultant*

San Francisco
Leno, Mark *state legislator*

San Mateo
Mullin, Gene *state legislator*

Santa Barbara
Jackson, Hannah Beth *state legislator*

Santa Rosa
King, Gwendolyn Bair *former government staff member, public speaker*

Stockton
Matthews, Barbara *state legislator*
Singleton, Marvin Ayers *state legislator, otolaryngologist*

Torrance
Kuykendall, Steven Thomas *former congressman*
McIntyre, Patricia Bowne *councilman*

Vacaville
Wolk, Lois *state legislator*

Van Nuys
Hertzberg, Robert M. *former state legislator*
Westall, Andrew Jon *legislative staff member, urban planner*

West Covina
Torres, Esteban Edward *former congressman, business executive*

COLORADO

Colorado Springs
McElhany, Andy *state senator*
Sinclair, William Donald *state legislator, former church official*

Denver
Anderson, Norma V. *state legislator*
Berry, Gayle *state representative*
Borodkin, Alice *state representative*
Boyd, Betty Ann *state representative*
Butcher, Dorothy *state representative*
Chlouber, Ken *state legislator*
Clapp, Lauri *state representative*
Coleman, Fran Natividad *state representative*
Dean, Doug *state representative*
Dennis, Ginette E. (Gigi) *state legislator*
Epps, Mary Ellen *state legislator*
Faatz, Jeanne Ryan *councilperson*
Fitz-Gerald, Joan *state senator*
Gordon, Ken *state senator*
Hefley, Lynn A. *state representative*
Hernandez, Robert Michael *state legislator, software engineer*
Hodge, Mary *state representative*
Hoppe, Phyllis Diane *state representative*
Jahn, Cheri E. *state representative*
Keller, Maryanne *state senator*
Lacy, Elsie *state legislator*
Marshall, Rosemary *state representative*
May, Ron *state senator*
McFadyen, Liane *state representative*
Meiklejohn, Alvin J., Jr., *state legislator, lawyer, accountant*
Nichol, Alice J. *state legislator*
Owen, David Turner *state legislator, owner, operator*
Ragsdale, Ann F. *state representative*
Reeves, Peggy *state legislator*
Rhodes, Pamela *state representative*
Rupert, Dorothy *state legislator*
Sandoval, Paula E. *state senator*
Spence, Nancy Joan *state representative*
Spradley, Lola *state representative*
Stafford, Debbie *state representative*
Takis, Stephanie *state senator*
Tanner, Gloria Travis *state legislator*
Tate, Penfield *state senator*
Tupa, Ron *state senator*
Veiga, Jennifer *state representative*
Williams, Suzanne *state representative*
Williams, Tambor *state representative*
Windels, Sue *state senator*

Golden
Hopper, Sally Hunter *former state legislator*

Grand Junction
Bishop, Tilman Malcolm *retired state legislator, college administrator*

Lakewood
Hanna, Deanna *state senator*

Steamboat Springs
Taylor, Jack *state senator*

CONNECTICUT

Branford
Gejdenson, Sam *former congressman*

Bridgeport
Garcia, Edna I. *state legislator, secondary education educator*

Glastonbury
Googins, Sonya Forbes *state legislator, retired banker*

Greenwich
Hess, Marilyn Ann *state legislator*

Groton
DeMarinis, Nancy Ann *state legislator*

Hartford
Carter, Annette Wheeler *state legislator*
Cocco, Jacqueline M. *state legislator*
Cook, Catherine Welles *state legislator*
Currey, Melody Alena *state legislator*
Daily, Eileen M. *state legislator*
Dandrow, Ann P. *state legislator*
Dillon, Patricia Anne *state legislator*
Eberle, Mary U. *state legislator*
Fahrbach, Ruth C. *state legislator*
Flaherty, Brian John *state legislator, editor*
Garvey, Jeanne Wolter *state legislator, realtor*
Gerratana, Theresa B. *state legislator*
Handley, Mary Ann *state legislator*
Harp, Toni N. *state legislator*
Kirkley-Bey, Marie Lopez *state legislator*
Lyons, Moira K. *state legislator*
McDonald, Anne B. *state legislator*
McGrattan, Mary K. *state legislator*
Mushinsky, Mary M. *state legislator*
Orefice, Gary James *state legislator*
Peters, Melodie M. *state legislator*
Prague, Edith G. *state legislator*
Sawyer, Pamela Z. *state legislator*
Scalettar, Ellen *state legislator*
Stillman, Andrea L. *state legislator*
Stratton, Jessie Gray *state legislator*
Truglia, Christel *state legislator*

Middlebury
Scarpetti, Angelina (Lee Scarpetti) *state legislator*

New Haven
DePino, Chris Anthoney *state legislator*
Dyson, William R. *state legislator, educator*

Plainville
Boukus, Elizabeth *state legislator*

Riverside
Powers, Claudia McKenna *state legislator*

Stafford Springs
Guglielmo, Anthony *state legislator, insurance agency executive*

Storrs Mansfield
Merrill, Denise *state legislator*

Tolland
Wyman, Nancy S. *state legislator*

Wallingford
Fritz, Mary G. *state legislator*

Westport
Freedman, Judith Greenberg *state legislator, importer*

DELAWARE

Dover
Adams, Thurman G., Jr., *state legislator*
Amick, Steven Hammond *state legislator, lawyer*
Cloutier, Catherine A. *state legislator*
Connor, Dorinda A. *state legislator*
Cook, Nancy W. *state legislator*
Fallon, Tina K. *state legislator*
Schroeder, John R. *state legislator, banker*
Spence, Terry R. *state legislator*
Still, John C., III, *insurance agent, state legislator*

Newark
Neal, James Preston *state senator, project engineer*

Washington
Diaz-Balart, Mario *congressman*
Hutchinson, Tim *former senator*

Wilmington
Blevins, Patricia M. *state legislator*

DISTRICT OF COLUMBIA

Washington
Abercrombie, Neil *congressman*
Acevedo-Vila, Anibal *congressional representative, state legislator, lawyer*
Ackerman, Gary Leonard *congressman*
Aderholt, Robert B. *congressman, attorney*
Akaka, Daniel Kahikina *senator*
Akin, W. Todd *congressman, former state legislator*
Alexander, Lamar (Andrew Lamar Alexander) *senator, former secretary of education, former governor, lawyer*
Alexander, Rodney M. *congressman*
Allard, Wayne (A. Wayne Allard) *senator, veterinarian*
Allen, George Felix *senator, former governor*
Allen, Thomas H. *congressman, lawyer*
Andrews, Robert E. *congressman*
Archer, William Reynolds, Jr., (Bill Archer) *lobbyist, former congressman*
Baca, Joe *congressman*
Bachus, Spencer T., III, *congressman, lawyer*
Baird, Brian N. *congressman*
Baker, Richard Hugh *congressman*
Baldwin, Tammy *congresswoman*
Ballenger, Thomas Cass (Thomas Ballenger) *congressman*
Barrett, James Gresham *congressman*
Bartlett, Roscoe G. *congressman*
Bass, Charles F. *congressman*
Baucus, Max S. *senator*
Bayh, Evan *senator, former governor*
Beauprez, Bob *congressman*
Becerra, Xavier *congressman, lawyer*
Bell, Robert Christopher (Chris Bell) *congressman*
Bennett, Robert F. *senator*
Bentsen, Kenneth E., Jr., *congressman*
Bereuter, Douglas Kent *congressman*
Berkley, Shelley *congresswoman*
Berman, Howard Lawrence *congressman*
Berry, Marion *congressman*
Biden, Joseph Robinette, Jr., *senator*
Biggert, Judith Borg *congresswoman, lawyer*
Bilirakis, Michael *congressman, lawyer, business executive*
Bingaman, Jeff *senator*
Bishop, Rob *congressman*
Bishop, Sanford Dixon, Jr., *congressman*
Bishop, Timothy H. *congressman*
Blackburn, Marsha *congresswoman*
Bliley, Thomas Jerome, Jr., *former congressman*
Blumenauer, Earl *congressman*
Blunt, Roy D. *congressman*
Boehlert, Sherwood Louis *congressman*
Boehner, John A. *congressman*
Bond, Christopher Samuel (Kit Bond) *senator, lawyer*
Bonilla, Henry *congressman, broadcast executive*
Bonner, Josiah Robins, Jr., (Jo Bonner) *congressman*
Bono, Mary Whitaker *congresswoman*
Boozman, John *congressman*
Bordallo, Madeleine Mary (Mrs. Ricardo Jerome Bordallo) *congresswoman*
Borski, Robert Anthony *former congressman*
Boswell, Leonard L. *congressman*
Boucher, Frederick C. *congressman, lawyer*
Boxer, Barbara *senator*
Boyd, F. Allen, Jr., *congressman, farmer*
Boykin, Richard Renarda *legislative staff member, lawyer*
Bradley, Jeb E. *US Congressman*
Brady, Kevin *congressman*
Brady, Robert A. *congressman*
Breaux, John B. *senator, former congressman*
Brown, Corrine *congresswoman*
Brown, Henry E., Jr., *congressman*
Brown, Sherrod *congressman, former state official*
Brownback, Sam *senator, lawyer*
Bumpers, Dale L. *former senator, former governor, lawyer*
Bunning, Jim *senator, former professional baseball player*
Burgess, Michael *congressman*
Burns, Conrad Ray *senator*
Burns, Max *congressman*
Burr, Richard M. *congressman*
Burton, Dan L. *congressman*
Butterfield, George Kenneth, Jr., *congressman, former state supreme court justice*
Buyer, Steven Earle *congressman, lawyer*
Byrd, Robert Carlyle *senator*
Calvert, Ken *congressman*
Camp, Dave *congressman*
Campbell, Ben Nighthorse *senator*
Cantor, Eric I. *congressman*
Cantwell, Maria E. *senator*
Capito, Shelley Moore *congresswoman*
Capps, Lois Ragnhild Grimsrud *congresswoman, former school nurse*
Capuano, Michael Everett *congressman*
Cardin, Benjamin Louis *congressman*
Cardoza, Dennis *congressman*
Carper, Thomas Richard *senator, former governor*
Carr, Bob *former congressman, lawyer*
Carson, Brad Rogers *congressman*
Carson, Julia M. *congresswoman*
Case, Ed *congressman*
Castle, Michael N. *congressman*
Chabot, Steven J. *congressman*
Chafee, Lincoln *senator*
Chambliss, Saxby *senator*
Chandler, Albert Benjamin, III, *congressman, former state attorney general*
Chapman, James L. (Jim Chapman) *former congressman, lawyer*
Chocola, Chris *congressman*
Christian-Christensen, Donna Marie *congresswoman*
Clark, Dick *former senator, ambassador, foreign affairs specialist*
Clay, William Lacy, Jr., *congressman*
Clinton, Hillary Rodham *senator, lawyer, former First Lady of United States*
Clyburn, James E. *congressman*
Cole, Tom *congressman*
Coleman, Norm *senator, former mayor*
Collins, Michael A. (Mac Collins) *congressman*
Collins, Susan M. *senator*
Conrad, Kent *senator*
Conyers, John, Jr., *congressman*
Cooper, James Hayes Shofner (Jim Cooper) *congressman*
Cornyn, John *senator*
Corzine, Jon Stevens *senator, former investment banker*
Costello, Jerry F., Jr., *congressman, former county official*
Cox, Christopher (Charles Cox) *congressman*
Craig, Larry Edwin *senator*
Cramer, Robert E., Jr., (Bud Cramer) *congressman*
Crane, Philip Miller *congressman*
Crapo, Michael Dean *senator, former congressman, lawyer*
Crenshaw, Ander *congressman*
Crowley, Joseph *congressman*
Cubin, Barbara Lynn *congresswoman*
Culberson, John *congressman*
Cummings, Elijah E. *congressman*
Cunningham, Randy *congressman*
Daschle, Thomas Andrew *senator*
Davis, Artur *congressman*
Davis, Jim *congressman, lawyer*
Davis, Jo Ann S. *congresswoman*
Davis, Lincoln *congressman*
Davis, Susan A. *congresswoman*
Davis, Thomas M., III, *congressman*
Dayton, Mark *senator*
Deal, Nathan J. *congressman, lawyer*
DeFazio, Peter A. *congressman*
Delahunt, William D. *congressman*
DeLauro, Rosa L. *congresswoman*
DeLay, Thomas D. (Tom DeLay) *congressman*
Dellums, Ronald V. *former congressman, health facility administrator*
Deutsch, Peter R. *congressman, lawyer*
DeWine, R. Michael *senator, lawyer*
Diaz-Balart, Lincoln *congressman, lawyer*
Dicks, Norman De Valois *congressman*
Dingell, John David *congressman*
Dodd, Christopher J. *senator*
Doggett, Lloyd *congressman, former state supreme court justice*
Dole, Elizabeth Hanford *senator, former charitable organization administrator, former federal official*
Domenici, Pete V. (Vichi Domenici) *senator*
Dooley, Calvin Millard *congressman*
Doolittle, John Taylor *congressman*
Dorgan, Byron Leslie *senator*
Doyle, Michael F. *congressman*
Dreier, David Timothy *congressman*
Duncan, John J., Jr., *congressman*
Dunn, Jennifer Blackburn *congresswoman*
Durbin, Richard Joseph *senator*
Edwards, Chet *congressman*
Edwards, John Reid *senator, lawyer*
Ehlers, Vernon James *congressman*
Emanuel, Rahm *congressman*
Emerson, Jo Ann *congresswoman*
Engel, Eliot L. *congressman*
English, Philip Sheridan *congressman*
Ensign, John E. *senator, former congressman*
Enzi, Michael Bradley *senator, accountant*
Eshoo, Anna Georges *congresswoman*
Etheridge, Bob *congressman*
Evans, Lane *congressman*
Everett, Terry *congressman*
Faleomavaega, Eni Fa'auaa Hunkin *congressman*
Farr, Sam *congressman*
Fattah, Chaka *congressman, former state legislator*
Feeney, Tom *congressman*
Feingold, Russell Dana *senator, lawyer*
Feinstein, Dianne *senator*
Ferguson, Michael *congressman*
Fidler, Shelley N. *legislative director*
Filner, Bob *congressman*
Fitzgerald, Peter Gosselin *senator, lawyer*
Flake, Jeff *congressman*
Foley, Mark Adam *congressman*
Forbes, J. Randy *congressman*
Ford, Harold Eugene, Jr., *congressman*
Fossella, Vito John *congressman*
Foust, Robert Schmertz *senior policy advisor*
Frank, Barney *congressman*
Franks, Trent *congressman*
Frelinghuysen, Rodney P. *congressman*
Frist, William H. *senator, thoracic surgeon*
Frost, (Jonas) Martin, III, *congressman*
Gallegly, Elton William *congressman*
Garrett, E. Scott *congressman*
Gephardt, Richard Andrew *congressman*
Gibbons, James Arthur *congressman*
Gibbons, Sam Melville *former congressman, business executive*
Gilchrest, Wayne Thomas *congressman, secondary school educator*
Gillmor, Paul E. *congressman, lawyer*
Gilman, Benjamin Arthur *former congressman, lawyer*
Gingrey, Phil *congressman*
Gingrich, Newt (Newton Leroy Gingrich) *former congressman*
Gonzalez, Charles A. *congressman*
Goode, Virgil H., Jr., *congressman*
Goodlatte, Robert William (Bob Goodlatte) *congressman, lawyer*
Gordon, Barton Jennings (Bart Gordon) *congressman, lawyer*
Goss, Porter Johnston *congressman*
Graham, Daniel Robert (Bob Graham) *senator, former governor*
Graham, Lindsey O. *senator*
Grassley, Charles Ernest *senator*
Graves, Samuel B. *congressman, former state legislator*
Green, Gene *congressman*
Green, Mark Andrew *congressman, lawyer*
Greenwood, James Charles *congressman*
Gregg, Judd *senator, former governor*
Grijalva, Raul *congressman*
Grucci, Felix J., Jr., *former congressman*
Gutierrez, Luis V. *congressman, elementary education educator*
Gutknecht, Gilbert William, Jr., *congressman, former state legislator*
Hagel, Charles *senator*
Hall, Ralph Moody *congressman*
Hansen, James Vear *former congressman*
Harkin, Thomas Richard *senator*
Harman, Jane *congresswoman*
Harris, Katherine *congresswoman*
Hart, Melissa Anne *congresswoman*
Hastert, Dennis (J. Dennis Hastert) *congressman*
Hastings, Alcee Lamar *congressman, former federal judge*
Hastings, Richard Doc *congressman*
Hattan, Susan K. *legislative staff member*
Hayes, Robert (Robin Hayes) *congressman*
Hayworth, J(ohn) D(avid), Jr., *congressman, former sportscaster*
Hefley, Joel M. *congressman*
Hensarling, Jeb *congressman*
Herger, Wally W. *congressman*
Herseth, Stephanie *congresswoman*
Hill, Baron P. *congressman*
Hinchey, Maurice D. *congressman*
Hinojosa, Ruben *congressman*
Hobson, David Lee *congressman, lawyer*
Hoeffel, Joseph M. *congressman, lawyer*
Hoekstra, Peter *congressman, manufacturing executive*
Hoglander, Harry R. *legislative staff member*
Holden, Tim *congressman, protective official*
Hollings, Ernest Frederick *senator*
Holt, Rush Dew *congressman, physics educator, researcher, consultant*
Honda, Michael M. *congressman*
Hooley, Darlene *congresswoman*
Hostettler, John N. *congressman*
Houghton, Amory, Jr., (Amo Houghton) *congressman*
Hoyer, Steny Hamilton *congressman*
Hulshof, Kenny *congressman*
Hyde, Henry John *congressman*
Inhofe, James M. *senator*
Inouye, Daniel Ken *senator*
Inslee, Jay R. *congressman*
Isakson, Johnny *congressman*
Issa, Darrell E. *congressman*
Istook, Ernest James, Jr., (Jim Istook) *congressman, lawyer*
Jackson, Jesse L., Jr., *congressman*
Jackson Lee, Sheila *congresswoman*
Jefferson, William J. (Jeff Jefferson) *congressman*
Jeffords, James Merrill *senator*
Jenkins, William L. (Bill Jenkins) *congressman*
John, Christopher *congressman*
Johnson, Eddie Bernice *congresswoman*
Johnson, Karen *legislation and congressional affairs secretary*
Johnson, Nancy Lee *congresswoman*
Johnson, Samuel (Sam Johnson) *congressman*
Johnson, Timothy Peter *senator*
Johnson, Timothy Vincent *congressman*
Johnston, John Bennett, Jr., *former senator, consultant*
Jones, Stephanie Tubbs *congresswoman, lawyer*
Jones, Walter Beaman *congressman*
Kanjorski, Paul Edmund *congressman, lawyer*
Kaptur, Marcia Carolyn *congresswoman*
Kassiday, Joel David *legislative staff member*
Kasten, Robert W., Jr., *former senator*
Keller, Ric *congressman, lawyer*
Kelly, Sue W. *congresswoman*
Kennan, Stephanie Ann *policy advisor*
Kennedy, Edward Moore (Ted Kennedy) *senator*
Kennedy, Mark R. *congressman*
Kennedy, Patrick J. *congressman*
Kennelly, Barbara B. *former congresswoman, federal agency administrator*
Kerry, John Forbes *senator*
Kildee, Dale Edward *congressman*
Kilpatrick, Carolyn Cheeks *congresswoman*
Kind, Ronald James *congressman*
King, Peter Thomas *congressman, lawyer*
King, Steve *congressman*
Kingston, Jack *congressman*
Kirk, Mark Steven *congressman*
Kleczka, Gerald D. *congressman*
Kline, John *congressman*
Knollenberg, Joseph (Joe Knollenberg) *congressman*
Kohl, Herbert *senator, professional sports team executive*
Kolbe, James Thomas *congressman*
Kucinich, Dennis J. *congressman*
Kyl, Jon L. *senator*
LaHood, Ray H. *congressman*
Lampson, Nick *congressman*
Landrieu, Mary L. *senator*
Langevin, James R. *congressman, former state official*
Lantos, Thomas Peter *congressman*
Larsen, Richard R. *congressman*
Larson, John Barry *congressman, insurance executive*
Latham, Tom *congressman*
LaTourette, Steven C. *congressman*
Laughlin, Gregory H. (Greg Laughlin) *former congressman*
Lautenberg, Frank R. *senator*
Leach, James Albert Smith *congressman*
Leahy, Patrick Joseph *senator*
Lee, Barbara *congresswoman*
Lent, Norman Frederick, Jr., *former congressman*
Levin, Carl *senator*
Levin, Sander M. *congressman*
Lewis, Charles Jeremy (Jerry Lewis) *congressman*
Lewis, John R. *congressman*
Lewis, Ron *congressman*
Lieberman, Joseph I. *senator*
Lincoln, Blanche Lambert *senator*
Linder, John E. *congressman, dentist*
Lipinski, William Oliver *congressman*
LoBiondo, Frank A. *congressman*
Lofgren, Zoe *congresswoman*
Lott, Trent *senator*
Lowey, Nita M. *congresswoman*
Lucas, Frank D. *congressman*
Lucas, Ken *congressman*
Lugar, Richard Green *senator*
Lynch, Stephen F. *congressman*
Mack, Connie, III, (Cornelius Mack) *former senator*
Majette, Denise *congresswoman*
Maloney, Carolyn Bosher *congresswoman*
Manley, James P. *congressional press secretary*
Manzullo, Donald A *congressman, lawyer*
Markey, Edward John *congressman*
Marshall, James Creel *congressman*
Martin, David O'Brien *congressman*
Matheson, Jim *congressman*
Matsui, Robert Takeo *congressman*
McCain, John Sidney, III, *senator*
McCarthy, Carolyn *congresswoman*
McCarthy, Karen P. *congresswoman, former state legislator*
McCollum, Betty *congresswoman*
McConnell, Mitchell, Jr., (Mitch McConnell Jr., Addison Mitchell McConnell Jr.) *senator, lawyer*
McCotter, Thaddeus G. *congressman*
McCrery, James (Jim McCrery) *congressman*
McDermott, James A. *congressman, psychiatrist*
McDonald, Patricia Ann *legislative administrator*
McGovern, James P. *congressman*
McGuire, Carole Baker *legislative staff member*
McHugh, John Michael *congressman, former state senator*
McInnis, Scott Steve *congressman, lawyer*
McIntyre, Douglas Carmichael, II, (Mike McIntyre) *congressman*
McKeon, Howard P. (Buck McKeon) *congressman, former mayor*
McNulty, Michael Robert *congressman*
Meehan, Martin Thomas *congressman, lawyer*
Meek, Kendrick B. *congressman*
Meeks, Gregory Weldon *congressman*
Menendez, Robert *congressman, lawyer*
Mica, John L. *congressman*
Millender-McDonald, Juanita *congresswoman, school system administration*
Miller, Candice S. *congresswoman*
Miller, Dan *retired congressman*
Miller, Emilie F. *former state senator, consultant*
Miller, Gary G. *congressman*
Miller, George *congressman*

Miller, Jeff *congressman*
Miller, Ralph Bradley *congressman*
Miller, Zell Bryan *senator, former governor*
Mitchell, George John *former senator, lawyer*
Molinari, Susan *congresswoman*
Mollohan, Alan B. *congressman*
Montoya-Aguilar, Carlos *congressman*
Moore, Dennis *congressman*
Moran, James Patrick, Jr., *congressman, stockbroker*
Moran, Jerry *congressman*
Murkowski, Lisa *senator*
Murphy, Timothy F. *congressman*
Murray, Patty *senator*
Murtha, John Patrick *congressman*
Musgrave, Marilyn N. *congresswoman*
Nadler, Jerrold Lewis *congressman, lawyer*
Napolitano, Grace F. *congresswoman*
Nardi Riddle, Clarine *legislative staff member*
Neal, Richard Edmund *congressman, former mayor*
Nelson, Benjamin *senator, former governor, lawyer*
Nelson, Bill *senator, former state treasurer*
Nelson, Gaylord Anton *former senator, association executive*
Nethercutt, George Rector, Jr., *congressman, lawyer*
Neugebauer, Randy *congressman*
Ney, Robert W. *congressman*
Nickles, Don (Donald Nickles) *senator*
Northup, Anne Meagher *congresswoman*
Norton, Eleanor Holmes *congresswoman, lawyer, educator*
Norwood, Charles W., Jr., *congressman*
Nunes, Devin *congressman*
Nunn, Samuel (Sam Nunn) *former senator, lawyer*
Nussle, James Allen *congressman*
Oberstar, James L. *congressman*
Obey, David Ross *congressman*
Olver, John Walter *congressman*
Ortiz, Solomon P. *congressman*
Osborne, Tom *congressman, former college football coach*
Ose, Douglas *congressman*
Otter, Clement Leroy (Butch Otter) *congressman*
Owens, Major Robert Odell *congressman*
Oxley, Michael Garver *congressman*
Pallone, Frank, Jr., *congressman*
Pascrell, William J., Jr., *congressman*
Pastor, Edward *congressman*
Paxon, L. William *former congressman*
Payne, Donald M. *congressman*
Pearce, Steve *congressman*
Pelosi, Nancy *congresswoman*
Pence, Michael Richard *congressman*
Peterson, Collin C. *congressman*
Peterson, John E. *congressman*
Petri, Thomas Evert *congressman*
Pickering, Charles W., Jr., *congressman*
Pitts, Joseph R. *congressman*
Platts, Todd Russell *congressman, state legislator*
Pombo, Richard *congressman, rancher, farmer*
Pomeroy, Earl R. *congressman, former state insurance commissioner*
Poppleton, Janet Waters *legislative staff member*
Porter, John Edward *former congressman*
Porter, Jon Christopher *congressman*
Portman, Rob *congressman*
Price, David Eugene *congressman, educator*
Pryce, Deborah D. *congresswoman*
Pryor, Mark Lunsford *senator*
Putnam, Adam Hughes *congressman, farmer, rancher*
Quinn, Jack *congressman, English language educator, coach*
Radanovich, George P. *congressman*
Rahall, Nick Joe, II, (Nick Rahall) *congressman*
Ramstad, James *congressman, lawyer*
Rangel, Charles Bernard *congressman*
Reed, John Francis (Jack Reed) *senator*
Regula, Ralph *congressman, lawyer*
Rehberg, Dennis R. *congressman*
Reid, Harry *senator*
Renzi, Rick *congressman*
Reynolds, Thomas M. *congressman*
Roberts, Charles Patrick (Pat Roberts) *senator*
Rockefeller, John Davison, IV, (Jay Rockefeller) *senator, former governor*
Rodriguez, Ciro Davis *congressman*
Rogers, Harold Dallas (Hal Rogers) *congressman*
Rogers, Mike *congressman*
Rohrabacher, Dana *congressman*
Ros-Lehtinen, Ileana *congresswoman*
Ross, Mike *congressman*
Rothman, Steven R. *congressman*
Roybal-Allard, Lucille *congresswoman*
Royce, Edward R. (Ed Royce) *congressman*
Rudman, Warren Bruce *former senator, lawyer, think tank executive*
Ruppersberger, Charles Albert, III, *congressman*
Rush, Bobby L. *congressman*
Ryan, Paul *congressman*
Ryan, Timothy *congressman*
Ryun, James Ronald *congressman*
Sabo, Martin Olav *congressman*
Sanchez, Linda T. *congresswoman*
Sanchez, Loretta *congresswoman*
Sanders, Bernard (Bernie Sanders) *congressman*
Sandlin, Max Allen, Jr., *congressman*
Santorum, Rick *senator*
Sarbanes, Paul Spyros *senator*
Saxton, H. James *congressman*
Schaffer, Robert (Bob Schaffer) *former congressman*
Schakowsky, Janice *congresswoman*
Schiff, Adam Bennett *congressman, lawyer*
Schrock, Edward L. (Ed Schrock) *congressman, former state senator*
Schumer, Charles Ellis *senator*
Scott, David Albert *congressman*
Scott, Robert Cortez *congressman, lawyer*
Sensenbrenner, F(rank) James, Jr., *congressman*
Serrano, Jose E. *congressman*
Sessions, Jefferson Beauregard, III, *senator*
Shadegg, John B. *congressman*
Shaffron, J. Janet *legislative administrator*
Shaw, E. Clay, Jr., (Clay Shaw) *congressman*
Shays, Christopher *congressman*
Shelby, Richard Craig *senator, former congressman*
Sherman, Bradley James *congressman*
Sherwood, Donald Lewis *congressman*
Shimkus, John Mondy *congressman*
Shuster, William (Bill Shuster) *congressman*
Simmons, Robert Ruhl *congressman*
Simpson, Michael K. *congressman*
Skelton, Isaac Newton, IV, (Ike Skelton) *congressman*
Slaughter, Louise McIntosh *congresswoman*
Smith, Christopher Henry *congressman*
Smith, D. Adam *congressman*
Smith, Gordon Harold *senator*
Smith, Lamar Seeligson *congressman*
Smith, Linda Gene *legislative staff member*
Smith, Nick *congressman, farmer*
Snowbarger, Vince *former congressman*
Snowe, Olympia J. *senator*
Snyder, Vic *congressman, physician*
Solis, Hilda Lucia *congresswoman, educational administrator*
Souder, Mark Edward *congressman*
Specter, Arlen *senator*
Spratt, John McKee, Jr., *congressman, lawyer*
Stabenow, Deborah Ann *senator, former congresswoman*
Stark, Fortney Hillman (Pete Stark) *congressman*
Stearns, Clifford Bundy *congressman, business executive*
Stenholm, Charles W. *congressman*
Stevens, Theodore Fulton *senator*
Strickland, Ted *congressman, clergyman, psychology educator, psychologist*
Stupak, Bart T. *congressman, lawyer*
Sullivan, John A. *congressman*
Sununu, John E. *senator*
Sweeney, John E. *congressman*
Talent, James M. *senator, former congressman, lawyer*
Tancredo, Thomas G. *congressman*
Tanner, John S. *congressman, lawyer*
Tauzin, W. J. Billy, II, (Wilbert J. Tauzin) *congressman*
Taylor, Charles H. *congressman*
Taylor, Gene *congressman*
Tenorio, Pedro A. *resident representative*
Terry, Lee R. *congressman, lawyer*
Thomas, Craig *senator*
Thomas, William Marshall (Bill Thomas) *congressman*
Thompson, Bennie G. *congressman*
Thompson, C. Michael *congressman*
Thornberry, Mac *congressman*
Tiahrt, W. Todd *congressman, former state senator*
Tiberi, Patrick J. *congressman, former state legislator*
Tierney, John F. *congressman, lawyer*
Toomey, Patrick J. *congressman*
Towns, Edolphus *congressman*
Turner, James *congressman*
Turner, Michael *congressman*
Udall, Mark *congressman*
Udall, Thomas (Tom Udall) *congressman*
Underwood, Robert Anacletus *former congressman, university official*
Upton, Frederick Stephen *congressman*
Van Hollen, Christopher, Jr., *congressman*
Vazirani-Fales, Heea *legislative staff member, lawyer*
Velazquez, Nydia M. *congresswoman*
Visclosky, Peter John *congressman, lawyer*
Vitter, David *congressman*
Voinovich, George V. *senator, former governor*
Walden, Greg *congressman*
Walker, Robert Smith *former congressman*
Walsh, James Thomas *congressman*
Wamp, Zach *congressman*
Warner, John William *senator*
Waters, Maxine *congresswoman*
Watson, Diane Edith *congresswoman*
Watt, Melvin L. *congressman, lawyer*
Waxman, Henry Arnold *congressman*
Weiss, Gail Ellen *legislative staff director*
Weldon, David Joseph, Jr., *congressman, physician*
Weldon, W(ayne) Curtis (Curt Weldon) *congressman*
Weller, Gerald C. *congressman*
Wexler, Robert *congressman*
Whitfield, Edward (Wayne Whitfield) *congressman*
Wicker, Roger F. *congressman, lawyer*
Wilson, Addison Graves (Joe Wilson) *congressman, former senator, lawyer*
Wilson, Charles *former congressman*
Wilson, Heather Ann *congresswoman*
Wofford, Harris *former senator, national service executive*
Wolf, Frank R. *congressman, lawyer*
Woolsey, Lynn *congresswoman*
Wu, David *congressman*
Wyden, Ron *senator*
Wynn, Albert Russell *congressman*
Yonts-Shepard, Susan *forest service administrator*
Young, C. W. (Bill Young) *congressman*
Young, Donald E. *congressman*

FLORIDA

Bradenton
Woodson-Howard, Marlene Erdley *former state legislator*

Coral Springs
Ritter, Stacy Joy *state legislator, lawyer*

Destin
Clary, Charles William, III, *state legislator, architect, consultant*

Fernandina Beach
Smeeton, Thomas Rooney *governmental affairs consultant*

Fort Lauderdale
Dawson, Muriel Amanda (Mandy Dawson) *state legislator*

Gainesville
Chestnut, Cynthia Moore *state legislator*

Jacksonville
Soud, Ginger *city councilwoman*

Miami
Bullard, Larcenia J. *state legislator*
Cosgrove, John Francis *lawyer, state legislator*

Ormond Beach
Lynn, Evelyn Joan *state senator, consultant*

Pensacola
Hutto, Earl *retired congressman*

Pinellas Park
Brennan, Mary M. *state legislator*

Tallahassee
Argenziano, Nancy *state legislator*
Betancourt, Annie *state legislator*
Blanton, Faye Wester *legislative official*
Bloom, Elaine *state legislator*
Boyd, Janegale *state legislator*
Burt, Locke *state legislator, insurance company executive*
Byrd, Johnnie, Jr., *state legislator*
Carlton, Lisa *state legislator*
Cowin, Anna P. *state legislator, educator*
Dockery, Paula *state legislator*
Edwards, Lori *state legislator*
Frankel, Lois J. *state legislator*
Heyman, Sally Anne *state legislator, crime/loss prevention specialist*
Jacobs, Suzanne *state legislator*
King, James E. "Jim", Jr., *state legislator, personnel executive, consultant*
Kosmas, Suzanne *state legislator, real estate company executive*
Kurth, Patsy Ann *state legislator*
Lawson, Alfred J., Jr., *state legislator, insurance agent*
Merchant, Sharon J. *state legislator*
Minton, O.R. (Rick Minton) *state legislator, real estate broker*
Morroni, John *state legislator, banker*
Murman, Sandra L. *state legislator, community activist*
Prewitt, Debra A. *state legislator*
Roberts-Burke, Beryl D. *state legislator, lawyer*
Spratt, Joseph R. (Joe Spratt) *state legislator, real estate developer*
Starks, Robert J. (Bob Starks) *state legislator, airline pilot, realtor*
Trovillion, Allen *state legislator, contractor*
Wasserman-Schultz, Debbie *state legislator*

Tampa
Davis, Helen Gordon *former state senator*

Wellington
Smith, Robert Clinton *former senator*

GEORGIA

Americus
Hooks, George Bardin *state legislator, insurance and real estate company executive*

Atlanta
Blitch, Peg *state legislator*
Buckner, Gail *state legislator*
Bunn, Barbara Jean *state legislator*
Butler, Gloria Singleton *state legislator*
Cable, Susan W. *state legislator*
Coleman, Terry Lewis *state legislator*
Davis, Grace W. *state legislator*
Felton, Dorothy *state legislator*
Gagne, Jeffrey P. *policy analyst*
Hegstrom, June *state legislator*
Jackson, Carol *state legislator*
James, Donzella *state legislator*
Jamieson, Mary Jeanette *state legislator*
Kemp, Rene D. *state legislator*
Manning, Judith Hubert *state legislator, real estate executive*
McBee, Mary Louise *state legislator, former academic administrator*
McClinton, JoAnn *state legislator*
Mobley, Barbara Jean *state legislator*
Mueller, Anne *legislator*
Oliver, Mary Margaret *state legislator*
Orrock, Nan *state legislator*
Purcell, Ann Rushing *state legislator, office manager*
Sinkfield, Georganna T. *state legislator*
Smith, Faye *state legislator*
Stanley, Lanett Lorraine *state legislator*
Stanley, Pamela Aurelia *state legislator*
Starr, Terrell *state senator*
Stokes, Connie *state legislator*
Tate, Horencena *state legislator, software company executive*
Taylor, Maretta Mitchell *state legislator*
Teague, Sharon Beasley *state legislator*
Thomas, Nadine *state senator, nurse*
Trense, Sharon *state legislator*

Columbus
Harbison, Ed *state legislator, broadcast journalist, motivational speaker*

Lawrenceville
Wall, Clarence Vinson *state legislator*

Marietta
Sauder, Randy James *state legislator, lawyer*

Savannah
Johnson, Eric B. *state legislator*
Thomas, Regina D. *state legislator*

Smyrna
Atkins, William Austin, Sr., (Bill Atkins) *former state legislator*

Snellville
Cleland, Max *former senator*

HAWAII

Honolulu
Aduja, Melodie Williams *state senator*
Arakaki, Dennis A. *state representative*
Baker, Rosalyn Hester *state senator*
Buen, Jan Yagi *state legislator*
Bukoski, Kika G. *state representative*
Bunda, Robert *state legislator*
Cachola, Romy Munoz *state legislator*
Caldwell, Kirk *state representative*
Espero, William (Willie C.) *state senator*
Fasi, Frank Francis *state legislator*
Fox, Galen W. *state representative*
Gabbard, Mike G. *councilman, small business owner*
Hale, Helene H. *state representative*
Ito, Ken *state representative*
Kawakami, Bertha C. *state representative*
Lee, Marilyn B. *state representative*
Leong, Bertha F.K. *state representative*
Magaoay, Michael Y. *state representative*
Matsunaga, Matthew Masao *state legislator, lawyer, accountant*
Moses, Mark S. *state representative*
Ontai, Guy Po'olanui *state representative*
Say, Calvin *state legislator*
Takumi, Roy Mitsuo *state legislator*

Kailua
Young, Jacqueline Eurn Hai *former state legislator, consultant*

Kapolei
Sakamoto, Norman Lloyd *state legislator, civil engineer*

IDAHO

Boise
Barrett, Lenore Hardy *state legislator, mining and investment consultant*
Black, Pete *retired state legislator, educator*
Boe, Donna H. *state representative*
Crow, Dolores J. *state representative*
Danielson, Judith A. *state legislator*
Douglas, Bonnie *state representative*
Dunklin, Betsy D. *state legislator*
Ellsworth, Julie *state representative*
Field, Debbie *state representative*
Field, Frances *state representative*
Geddes, Robert L. *state legislator*
Goedde, John W. *state senator*
Jaquet, Wendy S. *state representative*
Kellogg, Hilde *state representative*
Keough, Shawn *state legislator*
Lodge, Patti Anne *state senator*
McKague, Shirley *state representative*
McLaughlin, Marguerite P. *state legislator, logging company executive*
Newcomb, Bruce *state legislator, farmer, rancher*
Parry, Atwell J., Jr., *state legislator, retail executive*
Ringo, Shirley G. *state representative*
Shepherd, Mary Lou *state representative*
Wainwright Henbest, Margaret A. *state representative*
Wood, JoAn E. *state representative*

Glenns Ferry
King-Barrutia, Robbie L. *state senator*

Jerome
Bell, Maxine Toolson *state legislator, librarian*

Kooskia
Brandt, R. Skipper *state senator*

Moscow
St. Germain, Fernand Joseph *retired congressman*

Osburn
Calabretta, Marti Ann *senator*

Terreton
Burtenshaw, Don M. *state senator*

ILLINOIS

Carbondale
Poshard, Glenn W. *former congressman*

Chicago
Berman, Arthur Leonard *retired state senator*
Bugielski, Robert Joseph *state legislator*
Cohen, Ira *legislative staff member*
Colom, Vilma *alderman*
Davis, Danny K. *congressman*
Doherty, Brian Gerard *alderman*
Jones, Emil, Jr., *state legislator*
Stern, Grace Mary *former state legislator*

Crestwood
Rita, Robert *state representative*

Jacksonville
Findley, Paul *former congressman, author, educator*

Lake Forest
Frederick, Virginia Fiester *state legislator*

Lincolnwood
Carroll, Howard William *lawyer, retired state senator*

Northbrook
Parker, Kathleen Kappel *state legislator*

Palos Hills
Zickus, Anne *state legislator*

Pontiac
Ewing, Thomas William *former congressman, lawyer*

Quincy
Donahue, Laura Kent *former state senator*

Springfield
Beaubien, Mark H., Jr., *state representative*
Bowles, Evelyn Margaret *state legislator*
Bradley, Richard T. *state representative*
Brady, Daniel P. *state representative*
Collins, Annazette R. *state representative*
Collins, Jacqueline Y *state senator*
Crotty, M. Maggie *state senator*
Cultra, Shane *state representative*
Currie, Barbara Flynn *state legislator*
Daniels, Lee Albert *state legislator*
Dunn, Joe *state representative*
Eddy, Roger L. *state representative*
Erwin, Judy *state legislator*
Forby, Gary F. *state representative*
Fritchey, John A. *state representative*
Garrett, Susan *state senator*
Haine, William R. *state senator*

Hamos, Julie E. *state representative*
Hannig, Gary L. *state representative*
Howard, Constance A. *state representative*
Jakobsson, Naomi D. *state representative*
Jefferson, Charles E. *state representative*
Jones, Shirley M. *state legislator*
Karpiel, Doris Catherine *state legislator*
Kelly, Robin L. *state representative*
Klingler, Gwendolyn Walbolt *state representative*
Kosel, Renée *state representative*
Kurtz, Rosemary *state representative*
Lightford, Kimberly A. *state legislator*
Lyons, Joseph M. *state representative*
Martinez, Iris *state senator*
Mathias, Sidney H. *state representative*
McCarthy, Kevin A. *state representative*
McKeon, Larry J. *state representative*
Meeks, James T. *state senator*
Miller, David E. *state representative*
Moore, Andrea S. *state legislator*
Nekritz, Elaine *state representative*
Obama, Barack H. *state legislator*
Pankau, Carole *state legislator*
Parke, Terry Richard *state legislator*
Pihos, Sandra M *state representative*
Reitz, Dan *state representative*
Righter, Dale A. *state senator*
Sacia, Jim *state representative*
Schaffer, Jack *former state senator*
Slone, Ricca C *state representative*
Smith, Margaret *state legislator*
Washington, Eddie *state representative*
Yarbrough, Karen A. *state representative*

Sycamore
Burzynski, James Bradley *state legislator*
Vance Siebrasse, Kathy Ann *legislative staff member*

INDIANA

Columbus
Garton, Robert Dean *state legislator*

Fort Wayne
Moses, Winfield Carroll, Jr., *state legislator, construction company executive*
Schmidt, Donald J. *councilman, educator*

Indianapolis
Antich-Carr, Rose Ann *state legislator*
Austin, Terri Jo *state representative*
Becker, Vaneta G. *state representative*
Bowser, Anita Olga *state legislator, education educator*
Broden, John E. *state legislator*
Budak, Mary Kay *state legislator*
Dembrowski, Nancy J. *state senator*
Dickinson, Mae *state legislator*
Gard, Beverly J. *state legislator*
Hershman, Brandt *state legislator*
Kenley, Luke *state legislator*
Kittle, Jim, Jr., *state representative, political party administrator*
Klinker, Sheila Ann J. *state legislator, middle school educator*
Landske, Dorothy Suzanne (Sue Landske) *state legislator*
Lawson, Connie *state legislator*
Lawson, Linda *state senator*
Leuck, Claire M. *state legislator*
Lubbers, Teresa S. *state legislator, public relations executive*
Marendt, Candace L. *state legislator*
Mays, Carolene *state representative*
Merritt, James W., Jr., *state legislator, real estate developer*
Noe, Cindy J. *state representative*
Nugent, Johnny Wesley *state legislator, tractor company executive*
Richardson, Kathy Kreag *state legislator*
Rogers, Earline S. *state legislator*
Scholer, Sue Wyant *state legislator*
Simpson, Vi *state senator*
Sipes, Connie W. *state legislator, educator*
Skillman, Becky Sue *state legislator*
Summers, Vanessa *state legislator*
Welch, Peggy *state representative*
Wheeler, Harold H. *state legislator, utility contractor*
Willing, Katherine *former state legislator*
Wolf, Katie Louise *state legislator*
Young, Richard D. *state legislator*

Muncie
McIntosh, David M. *former congressman*

Shoals
Boyd, Earl E., Jr., *councilman*

South Bend
Bauer, Burnett Patrick *state legislator*

IOWA

Ames
Rosenberg, Ralph *former state senator, lawyer, consultant, educator, foundation administrator*

Chariton
McKinley, Paul *state legislator*

Davenport
Tinsman, Margaret Neir *state legislator*

Des Moines
Berry, Deborah *state representative*
Boettger, Nancy J. *state legislator*
Bukta, Polly *state representative*
Dandekar, Swati *state representative*
DeBoef, Betty *state representative*
Drake, Richard Francis *state legislator*
Freeman, Mary Louise *state legislator*
Garman, Teresa Agnes *state legislator*
Granzow, Polly *state representative, language educator*
Greimann, Jane *state representative, elementary school educator*
Grundberg, Betty *state legislator, property manager*
Holveck, Jack *state legislator*
Hosch, Julie *state senator*
Jochum, Pam *state representative*
Kramer, Mary Elizabeth *state legislator, health services executive*
Larson, Chuck, Jr., *state representative, political organization administrator*
Lensing, Vicki *state representative, funeral home business owner*
Miller, Helen *state representative, lawyer*
Oldson, Jo *state representative, lawyer*
Petersen, Janet *state representative*
Ragan, Amanda *state senator*
Rants, Christopher C. *state representative*
Rehberg, Kitty *state legislator*
Smith, Neal Edward *congressman*
Soukup, Betty A. *state legislator*
Szymoniak, Elaine Eisfelder *retired state senator*
Winckler, Cindy *state representative*

Keota
Greiner, Sandra *state legislator*

Sioux City
Andersen, Leonard Christian *former state legislator, real estate investor*
Doyle, Donald Vincent *retired state senator, lawyer*

West Des Moines
Churchill, Steven Wayne *former state legislator, marketing professional*

KANSAS

Clay Center
Braden, James Dale *former state legislator*

Clifton
Taddiken, Mark *state legislator*

Concordia
Freeborn, Joann Lee *state legislator, farmer, former educator*

Haddam
Hardenburger, Janice *state legislator*

Herington
Weber, Shari *state legislator*

Hutchinson
O'Neal, Michael Ralph *state legislator, lawyer*

Junction City
Craft, Barbara J. *state representative*

Kansas City
Steineger, Chris *state legislator*

Lawrence
Ballard, Barbara W. *state legislator*
Winter, Winton Allen, Jr., *lawyer, state senator*

Manhattan
Glasscock, Kenton *state legislator*

Neodesha
Chronister, Rochelle Beach *former state legislator*

Olathe
O'Connor, Kay F. *state legislator*

Overland Park
Vratil, John Logan *state legislator, lawyer*

Prairie Village
Langworthy, Audrey Hansen *state legislator*

Salina
Horst, Deena Louise *state legislator*

Shawnee Mission
Sader, Carol Hope *former state legislator*

Topeka
Barbieri-Lightner, Patricia *state representative*
Bleeker, Laurie *state legislator*
Bunten, William Wallace *state senator*
Burroughs, Tom L. *state representative*
Campbell, Larry L. *state representative*
Carlin, Sydney *state representative*
Carter, Eric *state representative*
Dahl, Donald L. *state representative*
Dan, Johnson *state representative*
Dillmore, Nile *state representative*
Dreher, Stanley E., Jr., *state representative*
Faber, John M. *state representative*
Findley, Troy Ray *former state legislator, bank officer*
Flaharty, Geraldine *state representative*
Gatewood, Doug *state representative*
Gilmore, Phyllis *state legislator*
Goodwin, Greta Hall *state legislator*
Gordon, Lana G. *state representative*
Grant, Robert *state representative*
Hill, Don *state representative*
Jackson, David D. *state legislator*
Kirk, Nancy A. *state legislator, nursing home administrator*
Krehbiel, Carl *state representative*
Kuether, Annie *state representative*
Lee, Janis K. *state legislator*
Light, Bill *state representative*
Long-Mast, Peggy *state representative*
Mays, M. Douglas *state legislator, financial consultant*
McClure, Laura *state legislator*
McCreary, Bill *state representative*
Merrick, Raymond F. *state representative*
Newton, Dean *state representative*
Oleen, Lana *state legislator*
Owens, Thomas C. *state representative*
Patterson, Doug *state representative*
Pauls, Janice Long *state legislator*
Petty, Marge D. *state senator*
Praeger, Sandy *state legislator*
Reardon, William J. *state representative*
Rehorn, Rick *state representative*
Reitz, Roger *state representative*
Ruff, L. Candy *state legislator*
Salisbury, Alicia Laing *state senator*
Schmidt, Derek *state legislator*
Schodorf, Jean *state legislator*
Schwartz, Sharon J. *state representative*
Showalter, Judy *state representative*
Storm, Suzanne *state representative*
Tafanelli, Lee *state representative*
Thull, Tom *state representative*
Toelkes, Dixie E. *state legislator*
Ward, Jim *state representative*
Welshimer, Gwen R. *state legislator, real estate broker, appraiser*
Williams, Daniel A. *state representative*
Wilson, R. J. *state representative*
Winn, Valdenia C. *state representative*

Wichita
Jennison, Robin L. *former state legislator, lobbyist*
Landwehr, Brenda *state legislator, corporate financial executive*
Pottorff, Jo Ann *state legislator*
Wagle, Susan *state legislator, small business owner*

KENTUCKY

Caneyville
Embry, C B, Jr., *state representative*

Crestview Hills
Harper, Kenneth Franklin *retired state legislator, real estate broker*

Frankfort
Adams, John W. *state representative*
Arnold, Adrian King *state representative*
Barrows, Joseph Howard *state representative*
Bather, Paul *state representative*
Belcher, Carolyn R. *state representative*
Burch, Thomas Joseph *state representative*
Casebier, Lindy *state legislator*
Cherry, Mike E. *state legislator*
Clark, Lawrence D. *state representative*
Comer, James R., Jr., *state representative*
Cornett, Howard *state representative*
Crimm, Ronald E. *state representative*
Damron, Robert R. *state representative*
DeWeese, Bob M. *state representative*
Draud, Jon E. *state representative*
Feeley, Timothy E. *state representative*
Ford, Danny R. *state representative*
Graham, Derrick W. *state representative, educator*
Gray, J. R. *state representative*
Haydon, Joseph A. (Jodie) *state representative*
Jenkins, Joni Lynn *state legislator*
Johns, Susan D. *state senator*
Johnson, Jerry D. *legislative staff member*
Liler, Charles L. *state representative*
Marcotte, Paul Henry *state representative*
McKee, Thomas M. *state representative*
Miller, Charles W. *state representative*
Nunn, Stephen R. *state representative*
Palumbo, Ruth Ann *state legislator*
Pullin, Tanya *state representative*
Richards, Jody *state legislator, journalism educator, small business owner*
Stein, Kathy W. *state representative*
Stine, Katie Kratz *state legislator*
Tapp, Gary L. *state senator*
Wayne, Jim *state representative*
Williams, David Lewis *state senator*

Lebanon
Higdon, Jimmy *state representative*

Lexington
Kerr, Alice Forgy *state legislator*

LOUISIANA

Alexandria
DeWitt, Charles Woodrow *state legislator*

Baton Rouge
Hainkel, John J., Jr., *state senator*

Deridder
Iles, Kay C. *state representative*

Grambling
Wilkerson, Pinkie Carolyn *state legislator, lawyer*

Harahan
Bowler, Shirley *state legislator*

Lake Charles
Mount, Willie Landry *state legislator*

Monroe
Cooksey, John Charles *former congressman, ophthalmic surgeon*

New Orleans
Bajoie, Diana E. *state legislator*
Boggs, Corinne Claiborne (Lindy Boggs) *retired congresswoman*
Irons, Paulette Riley *state legislator, lawyer*
Pratt, Renee Gill *state legislator*

Parks
Durand, Sydnie Mae M. *state legislator*

Slidell
Schedler, John Thomas, Jr., *state legislator, bank executive*

MAINE

Auburn
Douglass, Neria Gay *state legislator, lawyer*

Augusta
Amero, Jane Adams *state senator*
Barstow, Christopher R. *state representative*
Bennett, Richard A. *state senator*
Bromley, Lynn *state legislator*
Cathcart, Mary R. *state legislator*
Daggett, Beverly Clark *state legislator*
Dunlap, Matthew Gordon *legislator*
Edmonds, Beth A. *state legislator*
Hatch, Pamela H. *state legislator*
Kontos, Carol A. *state senator, educator*
Ledwin, Mary Ellen *state legislator*
Libby, James Delmas *state senator, educator, marketing consultant*
Martin, John Lewis *state legislator*
Mitchell, Betty Lou *state legislator, retired operations director*
Paradis, Judy *state legislator*
Pendleton, Peggy A. *state legislator, nurse education consultant*
Rotundo, Margaret R. *state legislator*
Savage, Christine R. *state legislator*
Saxl, Jane Wilhelm *state legislator*
Small, Mary E. *state legislator*
Townsend, Elizabeth *state legislator*

Bangor
Donnelly, James Owen *state legislator, bank executive*

Bar Harbor
Goldthwait, Jill Murdoch *state legislator*

Brunswick
Pfeiffer, Sophia Douglass *state legislator, lawyer*

Cape Elizabeth
Simonds, Stephen Paige *former state legislator*

East Millinocket
Michaud, Michael Herman *congressman*

Eliot
Lawrence, Mark W. *former state legislator, lawyer*

Gardiner
Treat, Sharon Anglin *state legislator*

North Haven
Pingree, Rochelle M. *state legislator*

Westbrook
O'Gara, William B. *state legislator, real estate agent*

MARYLAND

Annapolis
Benson, Joanne C. *state legislator*
Busch, Michael *state legislator*
Cadden, Joan *state legislator*
Conroy, Mary A. *state legislator*
Conway, Joan Carter *state legislator*
Forehand, Jennie Meador *state senator*
Harrison, Hattie N. *state senator*
Healey, Anne *state legislator*
Hixson, Sheila Ellis *state legislator*
Hoffman, Barbara A. *state legislator*
Hollinger, Paula Colodny *state legislator*
Howard, Carolyn J. B. *state legislator*
Jacobs, Nancy *state legislator*
Kelley, Delores Goodwin *state legislator*
Kirk, Ruth M. *state legislator*
Klima, Martha Scanlan *state legislator*
Krysiak, Carolyn *state legislator*
Madden, Martin Gerard *former state legislator*
McIntosh, Maggie *state legislator*
Miller, Thomas V. Mike, Jr., *state legislator*
Ruben, Ida Gass *state senator*
Snodgrass, Louise Virginia *state legislator, dental assistant*
Teitelbaum, Leonard H. *state legislator*

Baltimore
Hughes, Brenda Bethea *state legislator*

Bethesda
Gude, Gilbert *former state and federal legislator, nurseryman, writer*
Metzenbaum, Howard Morton *former senator, consumer organization official*
Morrison, Bruce Andrew *government executive, public affairs consultant*
Reed, Miriam Bell *legislative staff member*

Cambridge
Eckardt, Adelaide Campbell *state legislator, psychiatric nurse*

Frederick
Byron, Beverly Butcher *retired congresswoman*

Rockville
Leventhal, George L. *councilman, consultant*
Petzold, Carol Stoker *state legislator*

Temple Hills
Lawlah, Gloria Gary *state legislator, educator*

MASSACHUSETTS

Boston
Atkins, Cory *state legislator, writer*
Balser, Ruth B. *state legislator, psychologist*
Blumer, Deborah *state legislator*
Callahan, Jennifer *state legislator, education educator*
Canavan, Christine Estelle *state legislator*
Candaras, Gale D. *state legislator, lawyer*
Chesky, Evelyn G. *state legislator*
Creedon, Geraldine *state legislator*
Creem, Cynthia Stone *state legislator, lawyer*
Donovan, Carol Ann *state legislator*
Fargo, Susan C. *state legislator*
Fennell, Robert F. *state legislator, small business owner*
Finegold, Barry R. *state legislator, banker, lawyer*
Finneran, Thomas M. *state legislator, lawyer*
Flavin, Nancy Ann *state legislator*
Fox, Gloria L. *state representative, state legislator*
Garry, Colleen M. *state legislator*
Gobi, Anne *state legislator, lawyer*
Gomes, Shirley *state legislator*
Haddad, Patricia A. *state legislator*
Hahn, Celia Ferner *state representative, broadcaster*
Harkins, Lida E. *state legislator, educator*
Hyland, Barbara Claire *state legislator*
Jacques, Cheryl Ann *state legislator*
Jehlen, Patricia D. *state legislator*
Kaprielian, Rachel *state legislator*

L'italien, Barbara A. *state legislator, social worker*
Malia, Elizabeth A. *state representative, state legislator*
Melconian, Linda Jean *state legislator, lawyer*
Menard, Joan M. *state legislator*
Murray, Therese *state legislator*
Owens-Hicks, Shirley *state legislator*
Paulsen, Anne M. *state legislator*
Peisch, Alice Hanlon *state legislator*
Poirier, Elizabeth A. *state representative, state legislator*
Pope, Susan W. *state legislator*
Provost, Ruth W. *state legislator*
Reinstein, Kathi-Anne *state representative, state legislator*
Resor, Pamela P. *state legislator*
Rivera, Cheryl A. *state representative, lawyer*
Rogeness, Mary Speer *state legislator*
St. Fleur, Marie P. *state representative, state legislator*
Simmons, Mary Jane *state legislator*
Spiliotis, Joyce A. *state legislator*
Spilka, Karen *state legislator, lawyer*
Sprague, Jo Ann *state legislator*
Stanley, Harriett Lari *state legislator*
Story, Ellen *state legislator*
Teahan, Kathleen M. *state legislator, educator*
Travaglini, Robert E. *state legislator*
Tucker, Susan Carol *state legislator*
Walrath, Patricia A. *state legislator*
Walsh, Marian C. *state legislator*
Weygand, Bob A. *former congressman*
Wilkerson, Dianne *state legislator*
Williams Gifford, Susan *state legislator*
Wolf, Alice K. *state legislator, former mayor*

Gardner
Hawke, Robert Douglas *retired state legislator*

Hingham
Hedlund, Robert L. *state legislator, automobile executive*

Newton
Khan, Kay *state legislator*

MICHIGAN

Allendale
Jellema, Jon *state legislator, educator*

Detroit
Bonior, David Edward *congressman*
Mahaffey, Maryann *councilwoman*
Stallworth, Alma Grace *former state legislator*

Dowling
Perricone, Charles *former state legislator*

Lansing
Barcia, James A. *state senator, former congressman*
Brater, Elizabeth *state legislator*
Byrum, Dianne *state legislator, small business owner*
DeHart, Eileen *state legislator*
Emmons, Joanne *state legislator*
Hammerstrom, Beverly Swoish *state legislator*
Rogers, Mike *congressman*
Schwarz, John J.H. *state legislator, surgeon*
Scott, Martha G. *state legislator*
Van Regenmorter, William *state legislator*

Mount Clemens
Rocca, Sue *state legislator*

Rochester
Crissman, Penny M. *state legislator*

MINNESOTA

Apple Valley
Knutson, David Lee *state legislator, lawyer*

Brainerd
Samuelson, Donald B. *former state legislator*

Brandon
Bettermann, Hilda *state legislator*

Erskine
Moe, Roger Deane *former state legislator, secondary education educator*

Fairmont
Fowler, Chuck *former state legislator*

Forest Lake
Broecker, Sherry *state legislator*

Lakeland
Larsen, Peg *state legislator*

Maple Grove
Limmer, Warren E. *state legislator, real estate broker*

Minneapolis
Greenfield, Lee *state legislator*
Mickelson, Stacey *state legislator*
Oliver, Edward Carl *retired state legislator, retired insurance company executive, small business owner*
Reichgott Junge, Ember D. *former state senator, lawyer, writer, broadcast analyst, radio personality*
Spear, Allan Henry *former state senator, historian, educator*

Ottertail
Anderson, Bob *state legislator, business executive*

Rush City
Jennings, Loren G. *state legislator, business owner*

Saint Paul
Anderson, Ellen Ruth *state legislator*
Bachmann, Michele *state legislator*
Berglin, Linda *state legislator*
Boudreau, Lynda L. *state legislator*

Chaudhary, Satveer *state senator*
Clark, Karen *state legislator*
Fischbach, Michelle L. *state legislator*
Flynn, Carol *state legislator*
Greiling, Mindy *state legislator*
Hanson, Paula E. *state legislator*
Harder, Elaine Rene *state legislator*
Higgins, Linda I. *state legislator*
Johnson, Alice M. *state legislator*
Kahn, Phyllis *state legislator*
Kiscaden, Sheila M. *state legislator*
Krentz, Jane *state legislator, elementary school educator*
Lesewski, Arlene *state legislator, insurance agent*
Lessard, Robert Bernard *state legislator, recreational facility executive*
McGuire, Mary Jo *state legislator*
Minge, David *former congressman, lawyer, law educator*
Murphy, Mary C. *state legislator*
Olson, Gen *state legislator*
Pappas, Sandra Lee *state senator*
Pariseau, Patricia *state legislator*
Ranum, Jane Barnhardt *state senator, lawyer*
Rest, Ann H. *state legislator*
Ring, Twyla L. *state legislator, newspaper editor*
Robertson, Martha Rappaport *state legislator, consultant*
Robling, Claire A. *state legislator*
Runbeck, Linda C. *state legislator*
Rydell, Catherine M. *former state legislator*
Scheid, Linda J. *state legislator*
Seagren, Alice *state legislator*
Wejcman, Linda *state legislator*

Shakopee
Kelso, Becky *former state legislator*

Side Lake
Janezich, Jerry R. *state legislator, small business owner*

South Saint Paul
Metzen, James P. *state legislator, bank executive*

Woodbury
Luther, William P. *former congressman*

MISSISSIPPI

Brookhaven
Hyde-Smith, Cindy *state legislator*

Canton
Blackmon, Barbara Martin *state senator, lawyer*

Gulfport
Gex, Lucien Marion, III, (Beau Gex) *legislative staff member*

Jackson
Carlton, Neely C. *state legislator, lawyer*
Clarke, Alyce Griffin *state legislator*
Coleman, Linda *state legislator*
Coleman, Mary H. *state legislator*
Dickson, Reecy L. *state legislator*
Ford, Timothy Alan *state representative*
Fredericks, Frances M. *state legislator, nurse*
Harden, Alice V. *state legislator*
Hudson, Joe E. *state legislator, pharmacist*
Jennings, Wanda T. *state legislator*
Little, Travis Lane *state senator, motel management executive*
Martinson, Rita R. *state legislator*
Mettetal, H. Nolan *state legislator, pharmacist*
Peranich, Diane C. *state legislator*
Read, John O. *state legislator, pharmacist*
Robertson, Valeria Brower *state legislator, land developer*
Scott, Eloise Hale *state legislator*
Scott, Omeria McDonald *state legislator*
Smith, (Floyd) Clayton *state legislator, business owner*
Stevens, Mary Ann *state legislator*
Thomas, Sara R. *state legislator*

Pass Christian
Dawkins, Deborah Jeanne *state legislator*

Philadelphia
Williamson, Gloria *state legislator*

MISSOURI

Florissant
Stokan, Lana J. Ladd *state legislator*

Jefferson City
Backer, Gracia Yancey *state legislator*
Bland, Mary Groves *state legislator*
Bray, Joan *state legislator*
Carter, Paula J. *state legislator*
Days, Rita Denise *state legislator*
Hagan-Harrell, Mary M. *state legislator*
Hanaway, Catherine *state representative, lawyer*
Kasten, Mary Alice C. *state legislator*
Kauffman, Sandra Daley *state legislator*
Kelly, Glenda Marie *state legislator*
Kinder, Peter D. *state legislator*
Long, Elizabeth L. *state legislator, small business owner*
Mays, Carol Jean *state legislator*
McClelland, Emma L. *state legislator*
Murray, Connie Wible *state official, former state legislator*
Ostmann, Cindy *state legislator*
Ridgeway, Luann *state legislator*
Robirds, Estel *state legislator*
Sallee, Mary Lou *state legislator*
Scheve, May E. *state legislator, political organization worker*
Sims, Betty *state legislator*
Westfall, Morris *state legislator*
Williams, Deleta *state legislator*
Williams, Marilyn *state legislator*

Kansas City
Lyon, Bob *state legislator*

Licking
Katz, Aya *jurist, linguist, writer*

Rolla
Steelman, Sarah *state legislator*

Saint Louis
Yeckel, Anita T. *state legislator*

MONTANA

Anaconda
McCarthy, Bea *state legislator*

Augusta
Cobb, John Richardson *state senator*

Bigfork
Keenan, Bob *state legislator*

Billings
Johnson, Royal Calvin *state senator*

Butte
Harrington, Dan W. *state senator*
Shea, Debbie Bowman *state legislator*

Columbia Falls
O'Neil, Jerry *state senator*

Cut Bank
Roush, Glenn A. *state senator*

Dillon
Tash, Bill *state senator*

Glasgow
Kitzenberg, Sam L. *senator*

Great Falls
Franklin, Eve *state legislator*
Ryan, Don *state legislator*

Helena
Bartlett, Sue *retired state legislator*
Beck, Tom *state legislator, rancher*
Cocchiarella, Vicki Marshall *state legislator*
Eck, Dorothy Fritz *state legislator*
Hanson, Marian W. *state legislator*
Hill, Rick Allan *former congressman*
Mahlum, Dale Duane *state legislator, small business owner*
Mercer, John A. *former state legislator*
Miller, Ken *state legislator*
Stonington, Emily S. *state legislator*
Toole, Kenneth R., Jr., *state senator*

Laurel
McGee, Dan(iel) W. *state legislator*

Lodge Grass
Pease, Gerald *state legislator*

Medicine Lake
Nelson, Linda J. *state legislator*

Miles City
Zook, Tom *state senator*

Missoula
Williams, Pat *former congressman*

Trout Creek
Elliott, Jim *state senator*

Winifred
Butcher, Edward Bernie *state senator*

NEBRASKA

Hastings
Bohlke, Ardyce *state legislator*

Lincoln
Bromm, Curt *state legislator*
Brown, Pam *state legislator*
Crosby, LaVon Kehoe Stuart *state legislator, civic leader*
Erdman, Philip *state legislator, farmer*
Exon, J(ohn) James *former senator*
Kramer, David J. *state representative, lawyer*
Kristensen, Douglas Allan *former state legislator*
Krogh, Rodney S. *legislative staff member*
Landis, David Morrison *state legislator*
Maxwell, Chip *state legislator*
Preister, Donald George *state legislator, greeting card manufacturer*
Price, Marian L. *state legislator*
Redfield, Pamela A. *state legislator*
Robak, Jennie *state legislator*
Schimek, DiAnna Ruth Rebman *state legislator*
Smith, Adrian M. *state legislator, real estate agent*
Stuhr, Elaine Ruth *state legislator*
Suttle, Deborah S. *state legislator*
Thompson, Nancy P. *state legislator*
Witek, Kate *state senator, trucking company executive*
Withem, Ronald E. *state senator, trade association executive*

NEVADA

Carson City
Amodei, Mark E. *state legislator, lawyer*
O'Connell, Mary Ann *state legislator, small business owner*
Titus, Alice Costandina (Dina Titus) *state legislator*

Hawthorne
Chenoweth-Hage, Helen P. *former congresswoman*

Henderson
Tiffany, Sandra L. *state legislator*

Las Vegas
Care, Terry *state legislator, lawyer*
Carlton, Maggie *state legislator*

Coffin, James Robert *state legislator, small business owner*
Wiener, Valerie *state senator, writer, positioning strategist, communications executive*

Reno
Mathews, Bernice Martin *state legislator, small business owner*
Raggio, William John *state legislator*

NEW HAMPSHIRE

Barrington
DeChane, Marlene M. *state legislator*

Bartlett
Chandler, Gene G. *state legislator*

Bow
Sytek, Donna P. *former state legislator*

Center Harbor
Patten, Betsey Leland *state legislator*

Concord
Arnold, Thomas Ivan, Jr., *state legislator*
Clark, Martha Fuller *state legislator, architectural historian, preservation consultant*
Clemons, Jane Andrea *state legislator*
Colantuono, Thomas Paul *state legislator*
Cote, David Edward *state legislator*
Cote, Patricia L. *state legislator*
Crosby, Toni M. *state legislator*
Drabinowicz, A. Theresa *state legislator*
Dunlap, Patricia C. *state legislator*
Eaton, Thomas R. *state legislator*
Ferland, Brenda L. *state representative*
Flanagan, Natalie Smith *state representative*
Flora, Kathleen M. *state representative*
Foster, Linda Timberlake *state representative*
Francoeur, Sheila T. *state representative*
Fraser, Marilyn Anne *state legislator*
Ginsburg, Ruth *state representative*
Griffin, Mary E. *state representative*
Hager, Elizabeth Sears *state legislator, social services organization administrator*
Hall, Betty B. *state legislator, manufacturing executive*
Hutchinson, Rebecca *state representative*
Kaen, Naida *state representative*
Kane, Cecelia Drapeau *state legislator, registered nurse*
Keans, Sandra B. *state legislator*
Larsen, Sylvia B. *state legislator*
Lozeau, Donnalee M. *state legislator*
Lynch, Margaret A. *state legislator*
Lynott, Margaret *state legislator*
Martin, Mary Ellen *state legislator, human development specialist*
McCarley, Caroline *state legislator*
McRae, Karen K. *state legislator*
Merritt, Deborah Foote *state legislator, vocational coordinator*
Messier, Irene M. *state legislator*
Moore, Carol *state legislator*
Nichols, Avis B. *state legislator*
Nordgren, Sharon L. *state legislator*
Norelli, Terie Thompson *state legislator*
Nowe, Ronald John *state legislator, small business owner*
O'Hearn, Jane E. *state legislator*
O'Keefe, Patricia M. *state legislator*
Packard, Bonnie Bennett *former state legislator*
Pilliod, James P. *state legislator, physician*
Pratt, Irene Agnes *state legislator*
Reardon, Tara G. *state legislator*
Richardson, Barbara Hull *state legislator, social worker*
Roberge, M. Sheila *state legislator*
Seldin, Gloria *state legislator*
Smith, Marjorie K. *state legislator*
Snyder, Clair A. *state legislator*
Stickney, Nancy Carver *state legislator*
Wall, Janet G. *state legislator*
Wallin, Jean R. *state legislator*
Wallner, Mary Jane *state legislator, director child care organization*
Weatherspoon, Jackie K. *state legislator*
Wiggins, Celestine K. *state legislator*
Williams, Carol Ann *state legislator*

Derry
Katsakiores, George Nicholas *state legislator, retired restauranteur*

Dover
Pelletier, Arthur Joseph *state legislator, data processing executive, educator*

Durham
Estabrook, Iris W. *state representative*
Wheeler, Katherine Wells *retired state legislator*

Gorham
Guay, Lawrence J. *state legislator, business owner*

Hanover
Copenhaver, Marion Lamson *former state legislator*
Crory, Elizabeth L. *former state legislator*

Henniker
French, Barbara C. *state representative*

Hollis
Durham, Susan B. *state legislator*

Keene
Robertson, Timothy N. *state legislator, retired real estate agent*

Lancaster
Horton, Lynn C. *state legislator*
Pratt, Leighton Calvin *state legislator*

Lebanon
Guest, Robert Henry *former state legislator, management educator*

Littleton
Eaton, Stephanie *state legislator*

Winkler, Cheryl J. *state legislator*
Woodard, Claudette J. *state representative, retired educational association administrator*

Tiffin
Galipeau, Peter Armand *city councilman*

OKLAHOMA

Muskogee
Coburn, Tom A. *former congressman*

Oklahoma City
Adair, Larry E. *state representative*
Coleman, Carolyn *state legislator*
Cox, Kevin *state representative*
Ford, Charles Reed *state legislator*
Greenwood, Joan *state representative*
Hamilton, Rebecca *state representative*
Hefner, Jerry W. *state legislator, concrete block plant executive*
Hobson, Calvin J., III, *state legislator, real estate firm executive*
Horner, Maxine Edwyna Cissel *state legislator*
Johnson, Mike *state legislator, automobile agency executive*
Lawler, Daisy *state senator, elementary school educator, farmer, rancher*
Martin, Caroline June *state senator*
Mass, Michael Don *state legislator*
Monson, Angela Zoe *state legislator*
Riley, Nancy C. *state legislator*
Staggs, Barbara *state representative*
Taylor, Stratton *state legislator, lawyer*
Tibbs, Sue *state representative*
Weedn, Trish *state legislator*
Wilcoxson, Kathleen Louise *state legislator, educator*

Tahlequah
Rozell, Herbert *state legislator, construction executive*

Tulsa
Williams, Penny *state legislator*

OREGON

Beaverton
Deckert, Ryan P. *state senator*

Coos Bay
Messerle, Kenneth C. *state senator*

Grants Pass
Adams, Brady *bank executive, former state legislator*

Hillsboro
Furse, Elizabeth *former congresswoman, small business owner*

Mcminnville
Nelson, Donna Gayle *state representative*

Portland
Gordly, Avel Louise *state legislator, community activist*
Hatfield, Mark Odom *former senator*
Wilde, Thomas Andrew *state legislator, home remodeler, writer*

Redmond
Clarno, Beverly Ann *state legislator, farmer*

Salem
Anderson, Laurie Monnes *state representative*
Atkinson, Jason A. *state senator*
Berger, Vicki *state representative*
Beyer, Elizabeth Terry *state representative*
Beyer, Roger *state senator*
Brown, Kate *state legislator*
Burdick, Ginny Marie *state legislator*
Close, Betsy L. *state representative*
Courtney, Peter C. *state legislator*
Dingfelder, Jackie *state representative*
Dukes, Joan *state legislator*
Fisher, William G.E. *state legislator, rental investor, assisted living facility owner*
Flores, Linda *state representative*
Gallegos, Mary *state representative*
Harper, Steven V. *state senator*
Hopson, Elaine M. *state representative*
Kafoury, Deborah *state representative*
Minnis, Karen *state representative*
Morgan, Susan H. *state representative*
Nolan, Mary *state representative*
Qutub, Eileen *state legislator, real estate appraiser*
Rosenbaum, Diane M. *state representative*
Shannon, Marylin Linfoot *state legislator, educator*
Simmons, Mark *state representative*
Smith, Patti *state representative*
Smith, Tootie *state representative*
Tomei, Carolyn *state representative*
Verger, Joanne *state representative*
Walker, Vicki L. *state senator*
Wirth, Kelley K. *state representative*
Yih, Mae Dunn *state legislator*

Sunriver
Whisnant, C. Gene *state representative, retired military officer*

PENNSYLVANIA

Abington
Bard, Ellen Marie *state legislator, former small business owner*

Chalfont
Wilson, Jean L. *retired state legislator*

Easton
Reibman, Jeanette Fichman *retired state senator*

Erie
Earll, Jane *state legislator, lawyer*

Harrisburg
Bebko-Jones, Linda *state legislator*
Bishop, Louise Williams *state legislator*
Boscola, Lisa M. *state legislator*
Cohen, Lita Indzel *state legislator*
Crahalla, Jacqueline R. *state representative*
Forcier, Teresa Elaine *state legislator*
Gerlach, James William *congressman*
Gingrich, Mauree A. *state representative*
Greenleaf, Stewart John *state legislator*
Herman, Lynn Briggs *state legislator*
Kukovich, Allen Gale *state legislator, lawyer*
Laughlin, Susan *state legislator*
Lederer, Marie A. *state legislator*
Mackereth, Beverly D. *state representative*
Mann, Jennifer L. *state representative*
Miller, Sheila *state legislator*
Perzel, John Michael *state legislator*
Pickett, Tina L. *state representative*
Schwartz, Allyson Y. *state legislator*
Tartaglione, Christine M. *state legislator*
Taylor, Elinor Zimmerman *state legislator*
True, Katie *state legislator*
Vance, Patricia H. *state legislator*
Watson, Katharine M. *state representative*
Weber, Melissa Murphy *state representative*
White, Mary Jo *state legislator, lawyer*
Williams, Constance *state senator*

Lewisberry
Smith, Bruce I. *state legislator*

Monroeville
Klink, Ron *former congressman, reporter, newscaster*

Philadelphia
Josephs, Babette *legislator*
Kitchen, Shirley *state legislator, social worker*
Roebuck, James Randolph, Jr., *state legislator*

Reading
Kiehne, Frank Charles, Jr., *foreign affairs adviser*

Wayne
Rubley, Carole A. *state legislator*

RHODE ISLAND

Adamsville
Quick, Joan B. *state legislator*

Bristol
Parella, Mary A. *state legislator*

Charlestown
Walsh, Donna M. *state legislator*

Cranston
Hetherington, Nancy *state legislator*
Lanzi, Beatrice A. *state legislator*

North Kingstown
Benson, Melvoid J. *state legislator*

Providence
Ajello, Edith H. *state legislator*
Algiere, Dennis Lee *state legislator*
Anderson, Mabel M. *state legislator*
Callahan, Christine H. *state legislator*
Cambio, Bambilyn Breece *state legislator*
Coderre, Elaine Ann *state representative*
Gallo, Hanna M. *state legislator*
Gibbs, June Nesbitt *state legislator*
Goodwin, Maryellen *state legislator*
Henseler, Suzanne Marie *state legislator, social studies educator, majority whip*
Iannitelli, Susan B. *state legislator*
Lima, Charlene *state legislator*
Lopes, Maria J. *state legislator*
Murphy, William J. *state legislator*
Paiva-Weed, M. Teresa *state legislator*
Roberts, Elizabeth H. *state legislator*
Sasso, Eleanor Catherine *state senator*
Sosnowski, V. Susan *state legislator*
Williams, Anastasia P. *state legislator*

Rumford
Irons, William V. *state legislator*

Saunderstown
Carter, Kenneth *state legislator, restauranteur*

Warwick
Revens, John Cosgrove, Jr., *state legislator, lawyer*

SOUTH CAROLINA

Bluffton
Cork, Holly A. *former state legislator*

Columbia
Alexander, Thomas C. *state legislator, office supply company executive*
Allison, Merita Ann *state legislator*
Arias-Haskins, Gloria *state representative*
Ceips, Catherine C. *state representative*
Cobb-Hunter, Gilda *state representative, social worker*
Courson, John Edward *state legislator, insurance company executive*
Drummond, John W. *state legislator, oil company executive*
Elliott, Dick *state legislator, real estate developer*
Fair, Michael L. *state legislator, insurance company executive*
Ford, Robert *state legislator, black community developer*
Freeman, Mary Beth *state representative*
Gilham, JoAnne *state representative*
Glover, Maggie Wallace *state legislator*
Grooms, Lawrence K. *state legislator, petroleum marketer*
Harvin, Charles Alexander, III, *state legislator, lawyer*
Hinson, Shirley Rogers *state representative*
Jackson, Darrell *state legislator, company executive, clergyman*

Leatherman, Hugh Kenneth, Sr., *state legislator, business executive*
Lee, Brenda *state representative*
Martin, Becky Rogers *state representative, realtor*
Martin, Larry A(nthony) *state legislator, textile company executive*
McConnell, Glenn F. *state legislator, lawyer, art gallery executive*
McGill, J. Yancey *state legislator, real estate broker, homebuilder*
Mescher, William Clarence *state legislator, management consultant*
Miller, Vida O. *state representative, art gallery owner*
Moody-Lawrence, Bessie *state representative, education educator*
Moore, Thomas L. *state legislator*
O'Dell, William H. *state legislator, manufacturing executive*
Parks, J. Anne *state representative, funeral director*
Richardson, Becky D. *state representative*
Ryberg, W. Greg *state legislator, food store executive*
Short, Linda Huffstetler *state legislator*
Wilkins, David Horton *state legislator*
Young, Annette D. *state representative*

Greenville
Inglis, Robert D. (Bob Inglis) *former congressman, lawyer*
Manly, Sarah Letitia *retired state legislator, ophthalmic photographer, angiographer*
Mann, James Robert *former congressman*

Hardeeville
Flexon, Courtney Sprague *alderman*

Inman
Reese, Glenn G. *state legislator, food products executive*

Mc Cormick
Clayton, Verna Lewis *retired state legislator*

SOUTH DAKOTA

Black Hawk
Maicki, G. Carol *former state senator, consultant*

Brandon
Hunt, Roger *former state legislator*

Brookings
Brown, Arnold M. *state legislator*
McClure-Bibby, Mary Anne *former state legislator*

Gettysburg
Schreiber, Lola F. *former state legislator*

Miller
Morford, JoAnn (JoAnn Morford-Burg) *state senator, investment company executive*

Mud Butte
Ingalls, Marie Cecelie *former state legislator, retail executive*

Pierre
Adam, Patricia Ann *legislative aide*
Diedtrich, Elmer *state legislator*
Everist, Barbara *state legislator*
Fiegen, Kristie K. *state legislator*
Ham, Arlene H. *state legislator*
Pederson, Gordon Roy *state legislator, retired military officer*

Sioux Falls
Dunn, Rebecca Jo *state legislator*
Koetzle, Gil *state legislator, fire fighter, professional association administrator*

Watertown
Drake, Robert Alan *state legislator, animal nutritionist, mayor*

Wentworth
Kringen, Dale Eldon *state legislator, transportation executive*

TENNESSEE

Chattanooga
Turner, Brenda Kaye *state legislator*

Hermitage
Thompson, Fred Dalton *former senator*

Memphis
Ford, Harold Eugene *consultant, former congressman*

Nashville
Burchett, Tim *state legislator, small business owner*
Burks, Charlotte *state legislator*
Clabough, William C. *state legislator, small business owner*
DeBerry, Lois Marie *state legislator*
Dixon, Roscoe *state legislator, consultant, insurance company executive*
Eckles, Mary Ann *state legislator*
Graves, Jo Ann *state legislator*
Halteman Harwell, Beth *state legislator*
Harper, Thelma *state legislator*
Haun, Tommy George *state legislator, insurance agent*
Kurita, Rosalind *state legislator*
Naifeh, James O. (Jimmy Naifeh) *state legislator, speaker of the house*
Person, Curtis S., Jr., *state legislator, lawyer*
Ramsey, Ronald L. *state legislator, realtor*

TEXAS

Austin
Danburg, Debra *state legislator*
Denny, Mary Craver *state legislator, business owner*
Jackson, Mike *state legislator, contracting company executive*

Lucio, Eduardo Andres, Jr., *state legislator*
Nelson, Jane Gray *state legislator, small business owner, educator*
Shapiro, Florence *state legislator, advertising, public relations executive*

Beaumont
Brooks, Jack Bascom *former congressman*

Dallas
Bryant, John Wiley *former congressman*

Fort Worth
Geren, Pete (Preston Geren) *former congressman*
Harris, Christopher J. *state legislator, lawyer*
Mowery, Anna Renshaw *state legislator*

Garland
Driver, Joe L. *state legislator, insurance agent*

Hale Center
Laney, James Earl (Pete Laney) *state representative, speaker of the house, farmer*

Houston
Ellis, Rodney Glenn *state legislator, investment banking firm director*

Laredo
Zaffirini, Judith *state legislator, small business owner*

Midland
Craddick, Thomas Russell *speaker of state house of representatives*

Round Rock
Carter, John Rice *congressman*

San Antonio
Montford, John Thomas *state legislator, academic administrator, lawyer*

Temple
Jones, Grant *retired state legislator, lawyer, insurance agent*

Tyler
Berman, Leo *state legislator, retired military officer*

UTAH

Bountiful
Burningham, Kim Richard *former state legislator*

Clearfield
Minson, Dixie L. *legislative staff member*

Corinne
Ferry, Miles Yeoman *state legislator*

Logan
Hillyard, Lyle William *state legislator, lawyer*

Midvale
Greene, Enid *retired congresswoman*
Mansell, L. Alma *state legislator*

Provo
Cannon, Christopher Black *congressman*
Valentine, John Lester *state legislator, lawyer*

Salt Lake City
Black, Wilford Rex, Jr., *former state senator*
Bowen, Melanie *legislative staff administrator*
Carnahan, Orville Darrell *retired state legislator, retired college president*
Evans, Beverly Ann *state legislator, school system administrator*
Garn, Edwin Jacob (Jake Garn) *former senator*
Hale, Karen *state legislator*
Moore, Annette B. *legislative staff member*
Peterson, Millie M. *state senator*
Shepherd, Karen *retired congresswoman*
Walker, Carlene Martin *state senator*

Tooele
Allen, Ronald Carl *state senator, computer consulting executive, visual artist*

VERMONT

Bellows Falls
Obuchowski, Michael J. *state legislator*

Bennington
Morrissey, Mary *state representative*

Burlington
Donovan, Johannah L. *state representative, educator*
Lafayette, Karen Moran *state legislator*
Miller, Hinda *state senator, management consultant*
Sullivan, Mary Margaret *state legislator*
Tracy, John Patrick *state legislator*

Chelsea
Kennedy, Sylvia C. *state representative*

Colchester
Dakin, Maureen P. *state representative*
Sweeney, Joyce C. *state representative*

Enosburg Falls
Gervais, Avis L. *state representative, consumer products company executive*

Essex Junction
Kirker, Linda *state representative, health facility administrator*

Fairfield
Kittell, Sara Branon *state legislator*

Georgia
Branagan, Carolyn W. *state representative*

Hinesburg
Snelling, Diane *state senator, artist*

Hyde Park
Bartlett, Susan J. *state legislator*
Bourdeau, Stephanie *state representative*

Jericho
Symington, Gaye R. *state representative*

Middlebury
Ginevan, Anne V. *state representative*
Nuovo, Betty A. *state representative*

Milton
Rivero, Marilyn Elaine Keith *state legislator*

Montpelier
Backus, Jan *state legislator*
Crowley, John P. *state legislator, lawyer, accountant*
Cummings, Ann E. *state legislator*
Emmons, Alice M. *state legislator*
Fox, Sally G. *state legislator, lawyer*
Mazza, Richard T. *state legislator, small business owner*
Munt, Janet S. *state legislator*
Paquin, Edward H., Jr., *former state legislator, non-profit organization executive*
Peaslee, Janice L. *state legislator, agricultural products executive*
Ready, Elizabeth M. *state legislator*
Riehle, Helen S. *state senator*
Rivers, Cheryl P. *state legislator*
Seibert, Ann *state legislator, physical therapist*
Sheltra, Nancy J. *state legislator, legal assistant, auditor*
Towne, Ruth H. *state legislator*

Moretown
Grad, Maxine J. *state representative, law educator*

Pittsford
Flory, Margaret K. *state representative, lawyer*

Putney
White, Jeanette K. *state senator, health facility administrator*

Rutland
Doyle, Patricia R. *state representative*
Duffy, Virginia *state representative, artist*
Ferraro, Betty Ann *former state senator*
Mazzariello, Mary C. *state representative*

Saint Albans
Keenan, Kathleen *state legislator*

South Burlington
Head, Helen *state representative, management consultant*
Pugh, Anne D. *state legislator*

South Hero
Johnson, Mitzi *state representative*

Swanton
LaVoie, Kathy L. *state representative*

Tinmouth
Fallar, Gail M. *state representative, town clerk*

Underhill
Hummel, Margaret P. *state representative*

Vergennes
Houston, Constance T. *state legislator*

Vernon
O'Donnell, Pat A. *state representative*

Warren
Connell, Kinny *state representative*

Waterbury
Vincent, Val D. *state legislator*

West Rutland
Crowley, Judy B. *state representative*

Westford
Heath, Martha *state legislator*

Weybridge
Ayer, Claire D. *state representative, women's health nurse*

White River Junction
Welch, Peter F. *state legislator*

Williston
Ankeney, Jean B. *state legislator*
Lyons, Virginia *state legislator*
Peterson, Mary N. *state representative, lawyer*

Windsor
Sweaney, Donna *state representative*

Woodstock
Crocker, Patricia Conway *former state legislator*

VIRGINIA

Alexandria
Collins, Cardiss *retired congresswoman*
Goodling, William F. *former congressman*
Montgomery, Gillespie V. (Sonny Montgomery) *former congressman*

Arlington
Robb, Charles Spittal *former senator, former governor, lawyer, educator*

Fairfax
Woods, Jane Haycock *state legislator*

Falls Church
Byrne, Leslie Larkin *state legislator*

Fredericksburg
Goolrick, John Cole *congressional staff member, writer, consultant*

Leesburg
Mims, William Cleveland *state legislator, lawyer*

Mc Lean
Burke, Sheila P. *federal administrator*
Callahan, Vincent Francis, Jr., *state legislator, publisher*
Kim, Jay *former congressman*
Paul, Andrew Robert *defense and legislative consultant*

Newport News
Keator, Margaret Whitley *legislative aide*
Trible, Paul Seward, Jr., *former United States senator*

Norfolk
Sears, Winsome Earle *congressman*

Portsmouth
Randall, Marlene Dietrich *councilwoman, retired school system administrator*

Reston
Plum, Kenneth Ray *state legislator*

Richmond
Chichester, John H. *state legislator*
Crittenden, Flora Davis *state legislator*
Darner, Leslie Karen *state legislator*
Devolites, Jeanne Marie Aragona *state legislator*
Drake, Thelma Day *state legislator*
Howell, William James *state legislator*
McQuigg, Michele Berger *state legislator*
Puckett, Phillip P. *state legislator, insurance agency executive*
Puller, Linda Todd *state legislator*
Putney, Lacey Edward *state legislator*
Rapp, Melanie L. *state legislator, primary school educator*
Rhodes, Anne Gregory (Panny Rhodes) *state legislator*
Rimler, Anita A. *secretary of state*
Suit, Terrie L. *state representative*
Whipple, Mary Margaret *state legislator*

Vienna
Higginbotham, Wendy Jacobson *political adviser, writer*

WASHINGTON

Langley
Metcalf, Jack *former congressman, retired state senator*

Olympia
Ballard, Clyde *state legislator*
Brown, Lisa J. *state legislator, educator*
Carlson, Don M. *state senator*
Constatine, Dow *state senator*
Costa, Jeralita *state legislator*
Eide, Tracey J. *state legislator*
Fairley, Darlene *state legislator*
Franklin, Rosa G. *state legislator, retired nurse*
Fraser, Karen *state legislator*
Gardner, Georgia Anne *state legislator*
Hale, Patricia S. *state legislator*
Haugen, Mary Margaret *state legislator*
Hewitt, Mike *state senator*
Kastama, Jim *state senator*
Kessler, Lynn Elizabeth *state legislator*
Long, Jeanine Hundley *retired state legislator*
McAuliffe, Rosemary *state legislator*
Parlette, Linda Evans *state senator*
Patterson, Julia *state legislator*
Prentice, Margarita *state legislator, nurse*
Rasmussen, Marilyn *state legislator*
Regala, Debbie *state senator*
Roach, Pam *state legislator*
Rossi, Dino J. *state legislator, real estate broker*
Sheldon, Betti L. *state legislator*
Snyder, Sid *state legislator, retail executive*
Spanel, Harriet *state legislator*
Stevens, Val *state legislator*
Thibaudeau, Patricia *state legislator*
Winsley, Shirley J. *state legislator, insurance agent*

Seattle
Law, Marcia Elizabeth *aide*
Oakley, Carolyn Le *state legislator, city manager, director*

Tacoma
Bunney, Shawn I. *councilman*

Vancouver
Benton, Donald Mark *state legislator, political organization chairman*
Smith, Linda A. *retired congresswoman*

WEST VIRGINIA

Charleston
Anderson, Leonard W. *state legislator, small business owner*
Ball, Homer K. *state senator*
Boley, Donna Jean *state legislator*
Helmick, Walt *state legislator*
Kiss, Robert *state legislator*
McCabe, Brooks Fleming, Jr., *state legislator*
Minard, Joseph M. *state legislator*
Minear, Sarah M. *state legislator*
Plymale, Robert H. *state legislator, lumber company executive*
Redd, Marie E. *state legislator, criminal justice educator*
Sharpe, William R. *state legislator, electrical contractor*
Snyder, Herb *state legislator*
Tomblin, Earl Ray *state legislator*
Walker, Martha Yeager *state senator, businesswoman*

Parkersburg
Brum, Brenda *state legislator, librarian*

Shinnston
Spears, Jae *state legislator*

Wheeling
White, Lawrence Gilbert *state legislator, insurance company executive*

WISCONSIN

Black Earth
Klug, Scott Leo *former congressman*

De Pere
Lasee, Alan J. *state legislator*

Eau Claire
Kreibich, Robin G. *state legislator*

Fort Atkinson
Lorman, Barbara K. *former state senator*

Green Bay
Kelso, Carol *state legislator*

Madison
Barish, Lawrence Stephen *nonpartisan legislative staff administrator*
Berceau, Terese L. *state representative*
Darling, Alberta Statkus *state legislator, marketing executive, former art museum executive*
Gronemus, Barbara *state legislator*
Gunderson, Scott Lee *state legislator*
Hanson, Doris J. *state legislator*
Huelsman, Joanne B. *state legislator*
Hundertmark, Jean L. *state representative*
Jeskewitz, Suzanne E. *state representative*
Kerkman, Samantha *state representative*
Krawczyk, Judy *state representative*
Krug, Shirley *state legislator*
Krusick, Margaret Ann *state legislator*
Lassa, Julie M. *state representative*
McCormick, Terri *state legislator*
Nischke, Ann M. *state legislator*
Owens, Carol *state legislator*
Panzer, Mary E. *state legislator*
Plache, Kimberly Marie *state legislator*
Pope-Roberts, Sondy *state legislator*
Rhoades, Kitty *state legislator*
Risser, Fred A. *state legislator*
Robson, Judith Biros *state legislator*
Roessler, Carol Ann *state legislator*
Rosenzweig, Peggy A. *state legislator*
Seratti, Lorraine M. *state legislator*
Stepp, Cathy *state senator*
Towns, Debi *state legislator*
Turner, Robert Lloyd *state legislator*
Vruwink, Amy Sue *state legislator*
Vukmir, Leah *state legislator*
Weber, Becky *state legislator*
Williams, Annette Polly *state legislator*
Williams, Mary *state legislator*
Young, Rebecca Mary Conrad *retired state legislator*

Menomonie
Clausing, Alice *state legislator*

Milwaukee
Potter, Rosemary *state legislator*

Nashotah
Neumann, Mark W. *former congressman, real estate developer*

Peshtigo
Gard, John *state legislator*

Racine
Ladwig, Bonnie L. *state legislator*

Rice Lake
Hubler, Mary *state legislator*

River Falls
Harsdorf, Sheila Eloise *state legislator, farmer*

WYOMING

Buffalo
Madden, Cheryl Beth *state legislator*

Casper
Donley, Russell Lee, III, *former state legislator*
Hawks, Bill *state legislator, oil company executive*
Tempest, Rick *state representative*

Cheyenne
Berger, Rosie M. *state representative*
Devin, Irene K. *state legislator, nurse*
Erb, Richard A. *state legislator, real estate executive*
Gentile, Liz *state representative*
Harvey, Elaine *state representative*
Johnson, Lorna *state representative*
Kunz, April Brimmer *state legislator, lawyer*
Mockler, Esther Jayne *state senator*
Parady, Fred *state representative*
Robinson, Ann *state representative*
Sessions, Kathryn L. *state legislator, educator*
Warren, Jane *state representative*

Cody
Coe, Henry H. R. *state legislator*
Simpson, Alan Kooi *former US senator, lawyer*

Douglas
Twiford, Jim *former state legislator*

Glenrock
Anderson, James *senator*

Laramie
Hansen, Matilda *former state legislator*
Maxfield, Peter C. *state legislator, law educator, lawyer*

Rock Springs
Job, Rae Lynn *state legislator*

Worland
Geis, Gerald E. *state legislator, trucking company executive*
Edwards, Sarah R. *state representative*

TERRITORIES OF THE UNITED STATES

NORTHERN MARIANA ISLANDS

Saipan
Babauta, Juan Nekai *governor*

PUERTO RICO

San Juan
Romero-Barceló, Carlos Antonio *former congressman, former governor of Puerto Rico, former mayor of San Juan*

VIRGIN ISLANDS

St Thomas
Berry, Lorraine L. *state senator*

CANADA

BRITISH COLUMBIA

Vancouver
McWhinney, Edward Watson *Canadian government legislator*

ONTARIO

Brampton
Malhi, Gurbax Singh *legislator*

Don Mills
Collenette, David Michael *legislator, former Canadian government official*

Essex
Whelan, Susan *member of parliament*

Ottawa
Bélanger, Mauril *member Canadian Parliament*
Bevilacqua, Maurizio *member of Canadian parliament*
Carroll, M(argaret) Aileen *member of Canadian parliament*
Catterall, Marlene *Canadian legislator*
Dhaliwal, Herb (Harbance Singh) *legislator, former Canadian government official*
Hart, Jim *member of Canadian parliament*
Kilgour, David *Canadian member of parliament*
Maheu, Shirley *Canadian legislator*
Murray, Lowell *Canadian senator*
Nault, Robert Daniel *legislator*
Ritz, Gerry *member of parliament*
Saada, Jacques *legislator*
Skelton, Carol *member of parliament*
Telegdi, Andrew *member of parliament*
Vellacott, Maurice *member of parliament*
Yelich, Lynne *member of parliament*

Toronto
Eyton, John Trevor *senator, business executive*

QUEBEC

St Laurent
Dion, Stéphane *legislator*

SASKATCHEWAN

Regina
Spencer, Larry *member of parliament*

ADDRESS UNPUBLISHED

Abromson, Irving Joel *state legislator, financial services professional*
Albers, Sheryl Kay *state legislator*
Alfano, Elaine *state representative*
Armey, Richard Keith (Dick Armey) *former congressman*
Baker, Nancy Kassebaum (Nancy Kassebaum) *former senator, foundation official*
Barrett, William E. *former congressman*
Barton, Joe Linus *congressman*
Beals, Nancy Farwell *former state legislator*
Bennett, John O. *former state legislator*
Benoit, Nancy Louise *former state legislator, secondary school educator*
Benson, Loyd *retired state legislator*
Bilbray, Brian P. *former congressman*
Bilbray, James Hubert *former congressman, lawyer, consultant*
Binienda, John J. *state legislator*
Blanchard, MaryAnn N. *state legislator*
Bodem, Beverly A. *state legislator*
Bonsack, Rose Mary Hatem *state legislator, physician*
Boyd, Barbara *state legislator*
Bradley, Bill *former senator*
Braun, Richard Freeman *legislative staff member*
Brightbill, David John *state legislator, lawyer*
Broderick, B. Michael, Jr., *state legislator, banker*
Brown, Mary Ellen *former state legislator, accountant*
Browne, Ray *congressman, insurance broker*
Brown-Waite, Virginia (Ginny Brown-Waite) *congresswoman*
Bryant, Edward *former congressman, lawyer*

Burton, R. Johnnie Medinger *state official, data processing executive, finance company executive*
Callahan, Sonny (H.L. Callahan) *former congressman*
Campbell, Tom *former congressman, dean*
Carnahan, Jean *former senator*
Carpenter, Dorothy Fulton *retired state legislator*
Carstairs, Sharon *legislator*
Charlton, Betty Jo *retired state legislator*
Chrysler, Richard R. *former congressman*
Churchill, Robert Wilson *state legislator, lawyer*
Clayton, Eva M. *retired congresswoman, former commissioner*
Clement, Bob *former congressman*
Clinger, William Floyd, Jr., *retired congressman*
Coble, Howard *congressman, lawyer*
Cochran, Thad *senator*
Combest, Larry Ed *retired congressman*
Condit, Gary Adrian *former congressman*
Connelly, Elizabeth Ann *retired state legislator*
Coyne, William Joseph *former congressman*
Crippen, Bruce D. *former state legislator, real estate manager*
Curtis, Candace A. *former state legislator*
Daggett, Roxann *state legislator*
Danner, Patsy Ann (Mrs. C. M. Meyer) *former congresswoman*
De Gette, Diana Louise *congresswoman, lawyer*
DeMint, James Warren *congressman, marketing professional*
Dickey, Jay W., Jr., *former congressman, lawyer*
Duncan, Cleo *state legislator*
Duniphan, J. P. *state legislator, small business owner*
Fantin, Arline Marie *state legislator*
Federing, Eric K. *congressional communications director, motion picture preservationist, educator, public policy advisor*
Fields, Cleo *state legislator*
Finestone, Sheila *former legislator*
Forbes, Michael Patrick *former congressman*
Fox, Jon D. *former congressman*
Fraguela, Rafael J. *assemblyman*
Ganske, J. Greg *former congressman, plastic surgeon*
Gekas, George William *former congressman*
Grams, Rodney D. *former senator, former congressman*
Granger, Kay *congresswoman*
Groscost, Jeff *former state legislator, small business owner*
Hammerschmidt, John Paul *retired congressman, lumber company executive*
Hatch, Orrin Grant *senator*
Hawkins, Mary Ellen Higgins (Mary Ellen Higgins) *former state legislator, public relations consultant*
Haytaian, Garabed (Chuck Haytaian) *state legislator*
Hearn, Joyce Camp *retired state legislator, educator, consultant*
Helms, Jesse *retired senator*
Henry, Margaret Rose *state legislator*
Hickey, Winifred E(spy) *former state legislator, social worker*
Hilleary, Van *former congressman, lawyer*
Holliday, Robert Kelvin *retired state senator, former newspaper executive, educator*
Hollingworth, Beverly A. *former state legislator*
Horn, Stephen *congressman, political science educator*
Howard, Janet C. *former state legislator*
Howell, Janet D. *state legislator*
Hudkins, Carol L. *state legislator*
Hugley, Carolyn Fleming *state legislator*
Hunter, Duncan Lee *congressman*
Hutchison, Kay Bailey *senator*
Hutmacher, James K. *state legislator, water drilling contractor*
Ipsen, Grant Ruel *state legislator, insurance and investments professional*
Janakiraman, Savitha *legislative staff member*
Johnson, Jay Withington *former congressman*
Kasich, John R. *former congressman*
Kerns, Brian D. *former congressman*
Kiel, Shelley *state senator*
Klusman, Judith Anderson *state legislator*
Konnyu, Ernest Leslie *former congressman*
La Falce, John Joseph *former congressman, lawyer*
Lazio, Rick A. *former congressman, lawyer, association administrator*
Lebowitz, Catharine Koch *state legislator*
Maloney, James Henry *community development executive, former congressman*
Mandel, Adrienne Abramson *state legislator*
Markey, Margaret M. *state legislator*
Maroney, Jane P. *former state legislator, consultant*
Martinez, Matthew Gilbert *former congressman*
Mascara, Frank R. *former congressman*
Matsunaka, Stanley T. *former state legislator*
Matusow, Naomi C. *state legislator*
May, Edgar *former state legislator, nonprofit administrator*
Mc Collum, Ira William, Jr., (Bill Mc Collum) *former congressman*
McCoy, Matthew William *state legislator, human resource manager*
McDade, Joseph Michael *former congressman*
McGovern, George Stanley *former senator*
McKay, John M. *former state senator*
Meek, Carrie P. *former congresswoman*
Meshel, Harry *former state senator, political party official*
Meyers, Jan *retired congresswoman*
Mikulski, Barbara Ann *senator*
Miller, Alice *state representative*
Miller, Patricia Louise *state legislator, nurse*
Mizuguchi, Norman *former state senator*
Moseley-Braun, Carol *former senator, former ambassador*
Myers, Connie *assemblywoman*
Myers, John Thomas *retired congressman*
Nielsen, Linda Miller *city councilwoman*
Ortiz, Felix W. *state legislator*
Packard, Ronald C. *former congressman*
Pappas, Michael *former congressman*
Pascoe, Patricia Hill *former state legislator*
Passailaigue, Ernest L., Jr., *state legislator, accountant*
Patrick, Michele Mary *government official*
Patterson, Elizabeth Johnston *retired congresswoman*
Paul, Ron *congressman*
Pease, Edward A *former congressman*
Pell, Claiborne *former senator*
Pettis-Roberson, Shirley McCumber *retired congresswoman*
Pevear, Roberta Charlotte *retired state legislator*
Philip, James (Pate Philip) *retired state legislator*
Powers, Ray Lloyd *former state senator, dairy farmer, rancher*
Pressler, Larry *former senator, lawyer*
Quinby, Harold Eugene *retired councilman*
Reyes, Silvestre *congressman*
Richardson, Elaine *state legislator*
Rivers, Lynn N. *former congresswoman*
Roman, Twyla I. *state legislator*
Roukema, Margaret Scafati *congresswoman*
Rudy, Ruth Corman *former state legislator*
Salerno, Amy *state legislator*
Satterthwaite, Helen Foster *retired state legislator*
Saucier, Gene Duane *retired state legislator*
Sawyer, Thomas C. *former congressman*
Scarborough, Joe *former congressman*
Schaefer, Dan L. *former congressman*
Searle, Rodney Newell *state legislator, farmer, insurance agent*
Sessions, Pete *congressman*
Shea, Gwyn *former secretary of state*
Sherrill, Thomas Beck *former state legislator, financial planner*
Shows, Ronnie *former congressman*
Shuster, Bud *business executive, former congressman*
Simpers, Mary Palmer *state legislator*
Skinner, Patricia Morag *state legislator*
Smith, Alma Wheeler *state legislator*
Smith, Patricia *state representative*
Smith, Wayne Alan *state legislator, financial executive*
Snelling, Barbara W. *retired state legislator*
Soles, Ada Leigh *former state legislator, government advisor*
Sorensen, Sheila *state legislator*
Stickney, Jessica *former state legislator*
Sykora, Barbara Zwach *state legislator*
Tauscher, Ellen O. *congresswoman*
Tavares, Charleta B. *former state legislator*
Taylor, Kathleen N. *state legislator*
Tebedo, MaryAnne *state legislator*
Teichman, Ruth *state senator*
Thune, John *former congressman*
Thurman, Karen L. *former congresswoman, lobbyist*
Tochtrop, Lois *state legislator, nurse consultant*
Treppler, Irene Esther *retired state senator*
Van Engen, Thomas Lee *state legislator*
Vellenga, Kathleen Osborne *retired state legislator*
Vucanovich, Barbara Farrell *retired congressman*
Walkup, Mary Roe *state legislator*
Watkins, Wesley Wade *retired congressman*
Watts, J. C., Jr., *former congressman, retired professional football player*
Wojahn, R. Lorraine *retired state senator*
Zanfagna, Philip Edward *government executive, urban planner*
Zimmerman, Harold Samuel *retired state legislator, newspaper editor and publisher, state administrator*

HEALTHCARE: DENTISTRY

UNITED STATES

ALABAMA

Birmingham
Fullmer, Harold Milton *dentist, educator*
King, Charles Mark *dentist, educator*
Thomas, Huw Francis *dental educator, dean*

ARIZONA

Tucson
Hawke, Robert Francis *dentist*
Kassman, Andrew Lance *orthodontist*
Mondragon, Marc Rene *dentist, pharmacist, consultant*
Oro, Robert John *dentist, consultant, writer*
Pearson, Gary Dean *dentist*

CALIFORNIA

Anaheim
Kishiyama, Craig Akira *orthodontist*

Arcadia
Gamboa, George Charles *retired oral surgeon, educator*

Claremont
Valdez, Arnold *dentist, lawyer*

Irvine
Kim, Han Pyong *dentist, researcher*

Loma Linda
Boyne, Philip J. *dental association administrator, oral surgeon*
Feller, Ralph Paul *dentist, educator*

Los Angeles
Dorfman, William M. *dentist*
Drury, Gerald Irwin *periodontist, educator*
Dummett, Clifton Orrin *dentist, educator*
Etessami, Hirbod (Hiri Etessami) *endodontist, educator*
Evans, Caswell Alves, Jr., *dentist*

Manteca
Tonn, Elverne Meryl *pediatric dentist, dental benefits consultant, forensic odontologist*

Monterey Park
Sekiguchi, Eugene *dentist, dental association executive*

Northridge
Logan, Lee Robert *orthodontist*

Pasadena
Mc Carthy, Frank Martin *oral surgeon, surgical sciences educator*

Richmond
Anderson, Vera Strong *retired dentist*

San Francisco
Bensinger, David August *dentist, university dean*
Dugoni, Arthur A. *orthodontics educator, dean*
Gekelman, Diana *dentist, dental educator, researcher*
Greenspan, John S. *dental and medical educator, scientist, administrator*
Khosla, Ved Mitter *oral and maxillofacial surgeon, educator*
Olsen, Steven Kent *dentist*

San Jose
Lee, Stanley Tak *dentist*
Yoshizumi, Donald Tetsuro *dentist*

San Rafael
Greene, John Clifford *dentist, retired dean*
Gryson, Joseph Anthony *orthodontist*

Scotia
Hise, Mark Allen *dentist*

Tulare
Birtcil, Robert Franklin, Jr., *dental educator*

COLORADO

Denver
Doida, Stanley Y. *dentist*

Golden
Christensen, Robert Wayne *oral maxillofacial surgeon, minister*

CONNECTICUT

Avon
Weiss, Robert Michael *dentist*

Brookfield
Cohen, Mark Steven *dentist*

Farmington
Robinson, Peter J. *dean, periodontal educator, pathologist*

Sharon
Nweeia, Martin Thomas *dentist, musician, composer, anthropologist*

Southbury
Hopf, Frank Rudolph *retired dentist*

Vernon Rockville
Putnam, Richard *dentist, educator*

DISTRICT OF COLUMBIA

Washington
Calhoun, Noah Robert *oral maxillofacial surgeon, educator*
Melendez, Rodrigo Cuauhtemoc *dentist, read admiral US Navy*
Richeson, James G., Jr., *dentist*

FLORIDA

Bay Harbor Islands
Rosenbluth, Morton *periodontist, educator*

Boca Raton
Armstrong, Edward Bradford, Jr., *oral and maxillofacial surgeon, educator*
Lerner, Theodore Raphael *dentist*

Boynton Beach
Kronman, Joseph Henry *orthodontist, educator*

Bradenton
Engelman, Melvin Alkon *retired dentist, dental products executive*

Fort Lauderdale
Oliet, Seymour *endodontics educator, dean, dentist*
Siegel, Michael Alan *dental educator*

Fort Myers
Laboda, Gerald *oral and maxillofacial surgeon*

Gainesville
Catalanotto, Frank A. *dentist, association executive*

Jupiter
Nessmith, H(erbert) Alva *dentist*

Madison
Shaw, Roderick Kirkpatrick, III, *dentist*

Melbourne
Elder, Stewart Taylor *dentist, retired naval officer*

Miami
Higley, Bruce Wadsworth *orthodontist*
Iver, Robert Drew *dentist*
Parnes, Edmund Ira *oral and maxillofacial surgeon, educator*

Naples
Rehak, James Richard *orthodontist*
Rosen, Michel *retired prosthodontist*

Pinellas Park
Frantzis, Theodosios George *periodontist*

Tampa
Pasetti, Louis Oscar *retired dentist*
Perret, Gerard Anthony, Jr., *orthodontist*

West Melbourne
Vance, Jimie A. *dentist*

Winter Park
McKean, Thomas Wayne *dentist, retired military officer*

GEORGIA

Atlanta
Freedman, Louis Martin *dentist*

Augusta
Drisko, Connie Lee Hastings *dental educator, dean*
Rippert, Eric Theodore *oral and maxillofacial surgeon*
Rogers, Michael Bruce *orthodontist*

Macon
Walton, DeWitt Talmage, Jr., *dentist*

Tucker
Osborne, Thomas Eugene *oral and maxillofacial surgeon*

HAWAII

Honolulu
George, Peter T. *orthodontist, consultant*
Nishimura, Pete Hideo *oral surgeon*
Scheerer, Ernest William *dentist*

Pearl City
Sue, Alan Kwai Keong *dentist*

ILLINOIS

Alton
Boyle, Ann M. *dental educator, dean*

Bloomington
Milligan, Michael Lee *dentist*

Chicago
Bramson, James B. *dentist, dental association administrator*
Chandler, John D. *dentist*
Glenner, Richard Allen *dentist, dental historian*
Graber, Thomas M. *orthodontist, researcher*
Hardaway, Ernest, II, *oral and maxillofacial surgeon, public health service officer*
Hirsch, Martin *dentist*
Howley, Thomas A. *dentist*
Mao, Jeremy J *orthodontist, educator*
Santangelo, Mario Vincent *dentist*
Yale, Seymour Hershel *dental radiologist, educator, university dean, gerontologist*

Geneva
Kallstrom, Charles Clark *dentist*
Lazzara, Dennis Joseph *orthodontist*

Kenilworth
Edson, Wayne E. *retired dentist, consultant*

Lake Forest
Jones, Gordon Kempton *dentist*

Naperville
Grimley, Jeffrey Michael *dentist*

Park Ridge
Kenney, John Patrick *dentist*

INDIANA

Evansville
Fritz, Edward Lane *dentist*
Raibley, Parvin Rudolph *dentist*

Gary
Stephens, Paul Alfred *dentist*

Indianapolis
Christen, Arden Gale *dental educator, researcher, consultant*
Hartsfield, James Kennedy, Jr., *orthodontist, geneticist*
Roberts, Wilbur Eugene *dental educator, research scientist, wine importer*

Lafayette
Buckles, Judith Ann *dental educator, program administrator*

Terre Haute
Roshel, John Albert, Jr., *orthodontist*

IOWA

Ankeny
Weigel, Ollie J. *dentist, former mayor*

Iowa City
Bishara, Samir Edward *orthodontist*
Bjorndal, Arne Magne *endodontist*
Olin, William Harold *orthodontist, educator*

KANSAS

Topeka
Fyler, Carl John *dentist*
Stroud, Herschel Leon *retired dentist*

KENTUCKY

Danville
Morris, Alvin Leonard *retired dentist, educational administrator*

Lackland A F B
Dunn, William Jackson *dental educator, researcher*

Livingston
Davidson, John Robert *dentist*

Missouri City
Chang, Jeffrey Chai *dentist, educator, researcher*

Mount Pleasant
McCauley, Dan Paul *dentist*

Plainview
Crawford, Felix Conkling *dentist*

Plano
Findley, John Sidney *dentist*
Taylor, Paul Peak *pediatric dentist, educator*

Salado
Willingham, Douglas Barton *dentist*

San Antonio
Langland, Olaf Elmer *retired dental educator*
Mealey, Brian L. *periodontist, military officer*
Palmer, Hubert Bernard *dentist, retired military officer*
Schmitz, John Phillip *maxillofacial surgeon, researcher*

VERMONT

Essex Junction
Lampert, S. Henry *retired dentist*

Shelburne
Sawabini, Wadi Issa *retired dentist, educator*

VIRGINIA

Pearisburg
Morse, F. D., Jr., *dentist*

Richmond
Laskin, Daniel M. *oral and maxillofacial surgeon, educator*

Virginia Beach
Lowe, Cameron Anderson *dentist, endodontist, educator*

WASHINGTON

Bellevue
Carlson, Curtis Eugene *orthodontist, periodontist*

Everett
Oliver, William Donald *orthodontist*

Seattle
Herring, Susan Weller *dental educator, oral anatomist*
Hollender, Lars Gösta *dental educator*
Johnson, Marcia J. *dental hygienist*

Spokane
Kolsrud, Henry Gerald *dentist*
Steadman, Robert Kempton *oral and maxillofacial surgeon*

WISCONSIN

Beloit
Green, Harold Daniel *dentist*

Racine
Sikora, Suzanne Marie *dentist*

Shawano
Swetlik, William Philip *orthodontist*

WYOMING

Casper
Keim, Michael Ray *dentist*

CANADA

QUEBEC

Fossambault Sur Le Lac
Maranda, Guy *retired oral maxillofacial surgeon, Canadian health facility executive, educator*

ENGLAND

London
MacClean, Walter Lee *dentist*

GERMANY

Witten
Gaengler, Peter Wolfgang *dentist, researcher*

TAIWAN

Lung-tan
Shen, E-Chin *dentist, periodontist*

ADDRESS UNPUBLISHED

Bates, Richard Mather *dentist*

Beagrie, George Simpson *dentist, educator, dean emeritus*
Bentley, Kenneth Chessar *oral surgeon, educator*
Brooke, Ralph Ian *dental educator*
Carroll, La Shun La Rue *dental surgeon*
Collins, Frank, Jr., *dentist, educator*
Elzay, Richard Paul *retired dental school administrator*
Farrell, Edward Wagner *retired dentist, educator*
Garnick, Jerry Jack *periodontist, educator*
Geistfeld, Ronald Elwood *dental educator*
Hammer, Wade Burke *retired oral and maxillofacial surgeon, educator*
Herman, David Jay *orthodontist*
Hill, Maurice B., Jr., *dentist*
Hoffman, Jerry Irwin *retired dental educator*
Lippert, Christopher Nelson *dentist, consultant*
Listgarten, Max Albert *periodontics educator*
Löe, Harald *retired dentist, educator, researcher*
McNeely, Carol J. *dentist*
Meffert, Roland Matthew *periodontist, educator*
Molinaro, Joseph Daniel *dentist*
Nabers, Claude Lowrey *retired periodontist, writer*
Nery, Edmundo Barbin *periodontist, researcher*
Newbrun, Ernest *oral biology and periodontology educator*
Paris, David Andrew *dentist*
Park, Jon Keith *dentist, educator*
Rodin, Howard Alan *periodontist*
Sinkford, Jeanne Craig *dental association administrator, retired dentist, retired dean, educator*
Slaughter, Freeman Cluff *retired dentist*

HEALTHCARE: HEALTH SERVICES

UNITED STATES

ALABAMA

Auburn
Barker, Kenneth Neil *pharmacy administration educator*
Gropper, Sareen Annora Stepnick *dietitian, educator*

Birmingham
Booth, Rachel Zonelle *nursing educator*
Crittenden, Martha A. *disability specialist*
Devane, Denis James *healthcare company executive*
Gibbs, Sydney Royston *health facility administrator*
Grinney, Jay *health facility company executive*
Hoidal, David *health facility administrator*
Holmes, Suzanne McRae *nursing supervisor*
Hullett, Sandral *hospital administrator, health facility administrator*
Mann, Joel Franklin *medical technologist*
May, Robert P. *health facility company executive*
Nichols, Sandra B. *public health service officer*
Perry, Helen *medical/surgical nurse, secondary school educator*
Pickett, Stephen Alan *hospital executive*
Roth, William Stanley *hospital foundation executive*
Snow, Michael D. *health facility administrator*
Stephens, Deborah Lynn *health company executive*
Tieszen, Ralph Leland, Sr., *hospital administrator, educator*
Weinsier, Roland Louis *nutrition educator and director*

Chelsea
Culpepper, Michael Irving *researcher, educator*

Daphne
Curreri, Peter William *health policy consultant*

Decatur
Mardis, Elizabeth Williams *occupational health nurse*

Florence
Foote, Dorothy Gargis *nursing educator*

Hamilton
Vinson, Leila Terry Walker *retired gerontological social worker*

Hanceville
Hazard, Lynn Marchetti *occupational therapist*

Hoover
Bishop, Joan H. *health facility administrator*

Huntsville
Ingram, Shirley Jean *social worker*
McCaleb, John E. *public health environmentalist, biologist*
Steinbuchel, Carla Faye *pediatrics nurse, nursing educator*

Irondale
Karr, Beverly Ann *counselor*

Mobile
Clark, Jack *retired hospital company executive, accountant*

Opelika
Smith-Sanders, Carol Ann *music therapist, psychologist*

Oxford
Johnson, Mary Murphy *social worker, writer*

Ozark
DuBose, Elizabeth (Bettye DuBose) *community health nurse*

Pelham
Lee, James A. *health facility finance executive*

Scottsboro
Flarity, Edith Lynne *medical/surgical nurse*

Sulligent
Burleson, Emily Jane *nursing administrator*

Talladega
Swain, Mary Madgalene *pediatrics nurse*

Tuscaloosa
Orcutt, Ben Avis *retired social work educator*

Tuskegee Institute
Cooley, Fannie Richardson *counselor, educator*

ALASKA

Anchorage
Teague, Bruce Williams *chiropractor*

Fairbanks
Blake, Robert Philip *human services administrator, music therapist*

Kotzebue
Dakai, Steven Henry *alcohol/drug abuse services professional*

Soldotna
Moore, Hubert J. *addictions counselor, consultant*

Valdez
Devens, John Searle *natural resources administrator*

ARIZONA

Chandler
Graham, Anita Louise *correctional and legal nurse consultant, community health nurse*

Cornville
White, Judith Louise *social worker, counselor*

Glendale
Amador, Fred L. *counselor*
McDonald, Barbara Ann *retired psychotherapist*
Thomas, Bruce Larry *counselor*

Hereford
Schenk, Quentin Frederick *retired social work educator, mayor, psychologist*

Mesa
Boyd, Leona Potter *retired social worker*
Evans, Don A. *healthcare company executive*
Gantz, Nancy Rollins *hospital administrator, nursing administrator, consultant*
Trejos, Franklin Anthony *physician assistant*
Zaharia, Eric Stafford *health facility administrator*

Parker
Grazier, Diana Lynn *community health nurse, medical/surgical nurse, writer*

Payson
Lasys, Joan *medical nurse, writer, educator, publisher*

Phoenix
Allen, Janice Faye Clement *nursing administrator*
Hutchinson, Edna M. *home care nurse*
Metzler, Jerry Don *retired nursing administrator*
Mitchell, Wayne Lee *health care administrator*
Norris, John Steven *healthcare company executive*
Orr, Steven R. *health facility administrator*
Powell, Suzanne K. K. *nurse, consultant*
Seiler, Steven Lawrence *health facility administrator*
Welliver, Charles Harold *hospital administrator*

Rio Verde
Ramsey, David Selmer *retired health facility administrator*

Scottsdale
Brown, Frederick Lee *health care executive*
Timmons, Evelyn Deering *pharmacist*
Weaver, Linda Marie *pharmacist, education educator*

Sedona
Catterton, Marianne Rose *occupational therapist*

Sonoita
Scott, William Coryell *medical executive*

Sun City West
Czarny, Frank Silvey *social problems specialist, human and organizational systems consultant*
Holloway, Diane Elaine *psychological consultant, psychotherapist, writer*

Surprise
Wargo, Andrea Ann *retired public health official, commissioned officer*

Tempe
Playford, Nancy Jean *medical staff administrator*

Tucson
Arcus, Sam George *social worker, educator, writer*
Bootman, J. Lyle *pharmacy educator, dean*
Deutsch, Maurice Mayer *healthcare educator, consultant, medical librarian*
Glueck, Mary Audrey *retired psychiatric and mental health nurse*
Horan, Mary Ann Theresa *retired medical/surgical nurse*
Joseph, David Martin *medical administrator*
Ledin, Patricia Ann *nurse, nurse legal consultant*
Shropshire, Donald Gray *hospital executive*
Thompson, Kathleen Shambaugh *marriage and family counselor*
Valentine, Anna Mae *retired nurse*
Weber, Charles Walter *nutrition educator*

Yuma
Houggard, Santa Carol Hall *family nurse practitioner*
Kiley, Thomas *rehabilitation counselor*

ARKANSAS

Eureka Springs
McCullough, V. Beth *pharmacist, educator*

Fayetteville
Banks, David Russell *former health care executive*
Farley, Roy Carl *counselor educator*
Mullen, Maureen Ann *social worker*

Fort Smith
Decker, Josephine I. *health clinic official*
Floyd, William R. *health facility administrator*
Tabakin, Scott M. *healthcare executive*

Hot Springs Village
Cawood, Jenny Lind *social worker, poet*

Jonesboro
Douglas, John T. *pharmacist, state agency administrator*

Little Rock
Harmon, Kay Madelon *occupational therapist*
Jacobi, Sandra E. *medical/surgical nurse, researcher*
Thomas, Lestene *nurse*

North Little Rock
Wilson, LaVerne *nursing administrator*

Sherwood
Eddy, Nancy C. *counselor*

Springdale
Phillips, Linda Lou *pharmacist*

CALIFORNIA

Agoura Hills
Merchant, Roland Samuel, Sr., *health facility administrator, educator*

Alameda
Vaughn, Donna Becker *retired social worker*

Albany
Daniels, Lydia M. *health care administrator*

Aliso Viejo
Dunn, Dana-Lori *counselor*

Altadena
Montanez, Mary Ann Chavez *counselor, consultant, writer*

Anaheim
Gregg, James R. *optometrist, educator*

Arcata
Janssen-Pellatz, Eunice Charlene *healthcare facility administrator*

Arroyo Grande
Bekey, Shirley White *psychotherapist*

Bakersfield
Wong, Wayne D. *nutritionist*

Berkeley
Carpenter, Kenneth John *nutrition educator*
Cohn, Theodore Elliot *optometry educator, vision scientist, biomedical engineer*
Enoch, Jay Martin *optometrist, vision scientist*
Gilbert, Neil Robin *social work educator, writer, consultant*
Harris, Michael Gene *optometrist, educator, lawyer*
Hill, Lorie Elizabeth *psychotherapist*
Holder, Harold D. *public health administrator, communications specialist, educator*
Lashof, Joyce Cohen *public health educator*
Margen, Sheldon *public health educator*
Tutashinda, Kweli (Brian P. Altheimer) *chiropractic physician, educator*
Westheimer, Gerald *optometrist, educator*

Beverly Hills
Mindell, Earl Lawrence *nutritionist, writer*
Seymour, Racheal *human services administrator*

Burbank
Hartshorn, Terry O. *health facility administrator*

Canoga Park
Meier, Sue A. *marriage and family therapist, director*

Carlsbad
Benjamin, Theresa Mary *retired psychotherapist*
Royston, Ivor *scientific director*

Cathedral City
Berry, Ester Lorée *vocational nurse*

Chico
Akimoto, Martin Wayne *mental health services professional*

City Of Industry
Requeno, Nestor Danilo *human services administrator*

Claremont
Hartford, Margaret Elizabeth (Betty Hartford) *social work educator, gerontologist, writer*
Martin, Jay Herbert *psychoanalyst, English and political science educator*

Crockett
Silverman, Mervyn F. *health science association administrator, consultant*

Davis
Schneeman, Barbara Olds *nutritionist, educator*
Stern, Judith Schneider *nutritionist, researcher, educator*
Turnlund, Judith Rae *nutritionist*

PROFESSIONAL INDEX 5665 HEALTHCARE: HEALTH SERVICES

Diamond Bar
Johnson, Leonidas Alexander *optometrist, minister*

Downey
Diaz, Consuelo *health facility administrator*

Duarte
Riggs, Arthur D. *health facility administrator, research scientist*

El Cajon
Swanson-Perrelet, Donna Kay *speech pathology/audiology services professional*

El Segundo
Thiry, Kent J. *health facility administrator*

Emeryville
Goldstein, Jack *health science executive, microbiologist*

Encino
House-Hendrick, Karen Sue *nursing consultant*
Vogel, Susan Carol *nursing administrator*

Escondido
Garcia, Luis F. *social worker, photographer*
Gentile, Robert Dale *optometrist, consultant*
Kelley, George Lorenze *psychologist, consultant*

Foster City
Denny, James M. *health care services company executive*

Fremont
Richter, Hans Jürgen *technologist, researcher*
Sahatjian, Manik *retired nurse, retired psychologist*

Fresno
Antrim, Minnie Faye *residential care facility administrator*
Cole, Jessie Mae *nursing assistant, writer*
Corless, Dorothy Alice *nursing educator*
Ezaki-Yamaguchi, Joyce Yayoi *dietician*
Schroeder, Rita Molthen *retired chiropractor*
Scott, David Allen *mental health services professional, writer*

Fullerton
Montgomery, Thom Mathew *health program administrator, counselor*

Glendale
Asaturyan, Robert *mental health services professional, counselor*
Ebert, Gerard (Gerry Ebert) *hypnotherapist, freelance/self-employed writer*

Glendora
Lasko, Allen Howard *pharmacist*

Greenbrae
Neuharth, Daniel J., II, *psychotherapist*

Hanford
Cardens, Jeanice Wynclare Maylen *geriatrics nurse*

Hawthorne
Fila, John Charles *psychoanalyst*

Highland
Tacal, Jose Vega, Jr., *retired public health official, veterinarian*

Inglewood
Epstein, Marsha Ann *public health administrator, physician*

Irvine
Cotman, Carl W. *health science association administrator*
Ruttenberg, Susann I. *health sciences administrator*

Kingsburg
Quaday-Gray, Ailene Diann *retired speech pathology/audiology services professional*

La Jolla
Fritz, Chris *health facility administrator*
Grobstein, Ruth H. *health facility administrator*
Harrison, Larry J. *health facility administrator*
Koob, George *health science association administrator*

Laguna Beach
Frenzel, Frances Johnson *registered nurse, educator, lecturer, poet, real estate broker*

Laguna Niguel
Carr, Bernard Francis *hospital administrator*
Smith, Leslie Roper *hospital administrator, health facility administrator*

Laguna Woods
Leonard, Elizabeth Adney *social worker*

Lake Elsinore
Young, Patricia Janean *speech pathology/audiology services professional*

Lake Forest
Boccia, Judy Elaine Stacy *home health agency executive, consultant*

Lake View Terrace
McCraven, Eva Stewart Mapes *health service administrator*

Lakewood
Woodson-Glenn, Yolanda *social worker*

Lawndale
Matsushima, Teresa Takaki *school nurse practitioner*

Lincoln
Helzer, James Dennis *retired health facility administrator*

Loma Linda
Bleidt, Barry Anthony *pharmacy educator*
Bullock, Weldon Kimball *health facility administrator, pathologist, pathology educator*

Lompoc
Wagner, Geraldine Marie *nursing educator, consultant*

Long Beach
Brown, Lester B. *social worker, educator*
Ferreri, Michael Victor *optometrist*
Molina, Joseph Mario *medical administrator*
Mullins, Ruth Gladys *nurse*
Welch, Ronnie Scott *health facility administrator*

Los Angeles
Andersen, Ronald Max *health services educator, researcher*
Ash, Lawrence Robert *public health educator, administrator*
Baron, Melvin Farrell *pharmacy educator*
Barsugli, Jesse Benjamin *lab administrator*
Boswell, James Douglas *medical research executive*
Brodwin, Martin George *counselor, educator*
Caldwell, Alethea Otti *health care systems executive*
Chen, Peter Wei-Teh *mental health services administrator*
Chuksorji, Jean Caulfield *nursing educator*
Cohn, Daniel Howard *laboratory director*
Compton, William Henry, Jr., *mental health services professional*
Cowan, Marie Jeanette *nurse, pathology and cardiology educator*
Greene, Albert Lawrence *healthcare executive*
Harrison, Gail G. *public health educator*
Haughton, James Gray *medical facility administrator, municipal health department administrator, consultant, physician*
Horowitz, Ben *health facility administrator*
Jin, Yan *university educator, researcher, consultant*
Katchur, Marlene Martha *nursing administrator*
Katzin, Carolyn Fernanda *nutritionist, consultant*
Lloyd-Jones, Dadiva Bocobo *nursing assistant, writer*
Looney, Claudia Arlene *healthcare administrator*
Noce, Walter William, Jr., *hospital administrator*
Priselac, Thomas M. *health facility executive, educator*
Roberts, Robert Winston *social work educator, dean*
Rosenthal, J. Thomas *hospital administrator, medical educator*
Swartz, Allan Joel *pharmacist, educator, hospital administrator*
Territo, Mary C. *health facility administrator, oncologist, educator*
Thompson, Judith Kastrup *nursing researcher*
Tulloch-Reid, Elma Deen *nurse, consultant*
Utz, Sarah Winifred *nursing educator*
van Dam, Heiman *psychoanalyst*
Ver Steeg, Donna Lorraine Frank *nurse, sociologist, educator*
Walla, Catherine Anne *nursing administrator, educator*
White-Whitfield, Lisa Denise *social worker, grant writer*
Williams, Bradley Robert *pharmacy and gerontology educator, consultant*

Malibu
Palacio, June Rose Payne *nutritional science educator*

Manteca
Hirning, Fredric Carl *pharmacist*

Marina
Cornell, Annie Aiko *nurse, administrator, retired military officer*

Marysville
Gray, Katherine *marriage, family and child therapist, writer, educator*
Myers, Elmer *psychiatric social worker*

Menlo Park
Reamy, Michaelin *marriage and family therapist, educator, consultant*

Mission Viejo
Glasky, Alvin Jerald *retired medical research scientist*

Modesto
Ponko, Anne Marie *adult nurse practitioner*
Smith, Heather Lynn *psychotherapist, recreational therapist*

Moffett Field
Hughes, Gregory L. *human services manager*

Monterey Park
Ly, Allan Q. *medical technician*

Moorpark
Young, Victoria E. *occupational health nurse, lawyer*

Moraga
Allen, Richard Garrett *healthcare and education consultant*

Moreno Valley
Hadfield, Tomi Senger *hospital administrator*

Mount Shasta
Mariner, William Martin *chiropractor*

Newport Beach
Stephens, Michael Dean *hospital administrator*

Novato
Kratka-Schneider, Dorothy Maryjohanna *psychotherapist*

Oakland
Bouska Lee, Carla Ann *nursing and health care educator*
Chodorow, Nancy Julia *psychoanalyst, psychotherapist, educator*
Cole, Joan Hays *social worker, clinical psychologist*
DeMoro, Rose Ann *nursing administrator*
Hafey, Joseph Michael *health association executive*
Miller, Barry *research administrator, psychologist*
O'Hara, Delia Iglauer *family nurse practitioner*
Slack, Vickie *human services administrator*

Oceanside
Downer, William John, Jr., *retired health facility administrator*

Ontario
Hull, Jane Laurel Leek *retired nurse, administrator*

Orange
Todsen, Dana Rognar *health care executive*

Oxnard
Dimitriadis, Andre C. *health care executive*

Pacific Palisades
Bilson, Wesley *healthcare company executive*

Palm Springs
Boyajian, Timothy Edward *public health officer, educator, consultant*
Loya, Ranaldo *senior physician assistant*

Palo Alto
Skeff, Kelley Michael *health facility administrator*

Pasadena
Brotman, Richard Dennis *counselor*
Chan, Peter Wing Kwong *pharmacist*
Holmes, Louis Ira *physician assistant, educator, photojournalist*

Placerville
Wall, Sonja Eloise *nursing administrator*

Pleasanton
Shen, Mason Ming-Sun *medical center administrator*

Redlands
Coleman, Arlene Florence *retired pediatrics nurse*

Richmond
Terrill, Karen Stapleton *retired medical planning consultant*

Riverside
Chang, Sylvia Tan *health facility administrator, educator*
Meadows, Joyce Katherine *nurse*
Smith, Jeffry Alan *health administrator, physician, consultant*

Rohnert Park
Johnson, Herman Leonall *retired research nutritionist, researcher*

Roseville
Ammon, Donald R. *hospital administrator*
Madden, Wanda Lois *nurse*
Wright, Carole Yvonne *chiropractor*

Running Springs
Fangerow, Kay Elizabeth *nurse*

Sacramento
Armacost, Mary Jane *healthcare company executive*
Chason, Robert *health facility administrator*
Dager, William Erling *pharmacist specialist, educator*
Drachnik, Catherine Meldyn *recreational therapist, artist, counselor*
Farrell, Francine Annette *psychotherapist, educator, author*
Friedman, Kenni *healthcare company official, councilwoman*
Johnson, Van R. *health facility administrator*
Merwin, Edwin Preston *healthcare educator, consultant*
Woo, Sharon Y. *healthcare organization executive*

San Anselmo
Ellenberger, Diane Marie *nurse, consultant*

San Bernardino
Neighbors, Ira Arthell *social work educator*

San Diego
Bakko, Orville Edwin *retired health care executive, consultant*
Batey, Sharyn Rebecca *clinical research scientist*
Doan, Tai Danh *social worker, director*
Edwards-Tate, Laurie Ellen *human services administrator, educator*
Francisco, Edith Gaba *medical/surgical nurse*
Haverly, Pamela Sue *nursing administrator*
Johnson, Kenneth Owen *retired speech pathology/audiology services professional*
Klamerus, Karen Jean *pharmacist, researcher*
Larson, Vernon Dale *audiologist, researcher*
Maier-Lorentz, Madeline Marie *nurse educator*
Nenner, Victoria Corich *nurse, educator*
Norling, Richard Arthur *health care executive*
Rezin, Joyce June *pediatric nurse practitioner*
Rodgers, Maryann Ahalt *nursing educator, dean*
Rosen, Peter *health facility administrator, emergency physician, educator*
Schmidt, Terry L. *health care executive*
Smith, Raymond Edward *retired health care administrator*
Whittington, Anne Elizabeth *diabetes educator*

San Francisco
Chater, Shirley Sears *health educator*
Dracup, Kathleen Anne *nursing educator*
Eng, Catherine *health care facility administrator, physician, medical educator*
Green, Robert Leonard *hospital management company executive*
Harrington, Charlene Ann *sociology and health policy educator*
Holzemer, William L. *nursing educator*
Kirincic, Paul E. *human services administrator*
Mahley, Robert W. *health facility administrator*
Nix, Katherine Jean *medical case manager*
Rosales, Suzanne Marie *hospital coordinator*
Salbec, Patricia R. *emergency medical technician*
Sheiner, Lewis B. *pharmacist, educator*
Smith, Cecilia May *hospital official*
Styles, Margretta Madden *nursing educator*
Wilhelm-Hass, Elaine *operating room nurse*
Wu-Chu, Stella Chwenyea *nutritionist, consultant*
Young, Lowell Sung-yi *medical administrator, educator*

San Jose
Carruth, Patti Jo *nursing director*
Hathcock, Bonita Catherine (Bonnie Hathcock) *managed health care company executive*
Lu, Nancy Chao *nutrition and food science educator*
Luna, Michael Donovan *speech language pathologist*

San Marcos
Ball, Betty Jewel *retired social worker, consultant*

San Pedro
McMullen, Sharon Joy Abel *life coach, marriage and family therapist*

San Rafael
Amada, Gerald *retired psychotherapist*
Friesecke, Raymond Francis *health company executive*

Santa Ana
Chenhalls, Anne Marie *nurse, educator*
Folick, Jeffrey M. *healthcare systems company executive*
Lyons, Linda *health science association administrator*
Reed, David Andrew *managed health care company executive*
Schmitz, Stephen E. *mental health specialist, writer*
Schub, Craig S. *health science association administrator*

Santa Barbara
Brown, Stephen F. *health facility administrator*
Dennis, David L. *healthcare executive*
Farber, Stephen D. *health facility administrator*
Fetter, Trevor *healthcare industry executive*
Focht, Michael Harrison *health care industry executive*
Mackey, Thomas B. *health facility administrator*
Salotti, Kathryn E. *marriage and family therapist*
Schochet, Barry P. *health care executive*

Santa Fe Springs
Hanzel, Mimi S. *psychotherapist*

Santa Maria
Phillips, Dorothy Lowe *nursing educator*
Walton, Maurine Isabel *social worker*

Santa Monica
Brook, Robert Henry *health services researcher, physician, educator, internist, educator*
Magnabosco-Bower, Jennifer Lynn *mental health professional*

Santee
Schenk, Susan Kirkpatrick *nursing educator, consultant, small business owner*

Sausalito
Groah, Linda Kay *nursing administrator, educator*

Sepulveda
Burton, Paul Floyd *social worker*

Shaver Lake
Hatmaker, Grace Marie *nurse, writer*

Sherman Oaks
Krueger, Kenneth John *nutritionist, educator*

Simi Valley
Trager, D. David *retired pharmacist, general consultant*

Sonoma
Markey, William Alan *healthcare administrator, consultant*

Stanford
Marsh, Martha *hospital administrator*
Mc Namara, Joseph Donald *researcher, retired police chief, novelist*

Stockton
Norton, Linda Lee *pharmacist, educator*
Shek, Allen *pharmacist, educator*

Studio City
Herrman, Marcia Kutz *child development specialist*
Stoughton, W. Vickery *healthcare executive*

Sun City
Olim, August Souza *counselor*

Sunnyvale
Gordon, Marc Stewart *pharmacist, research scientist*

Tarzana
Rinsch, Maryann Elizabeth *occupational therapist*

Temecula
Keenan, Retha Ellen Vornholt *retired nursing educator*

Thousand Oaks
Gaus, Clifton R. *healthcare executive*
Herman, Joan Elizabeth *healthcare company executive*
Johnson, Shirley Amagna *health system executive*
Schaeffer, Leonard David *healthcare executive*
Souza, Lawrence M. *health facility administrator*

Trabuco Canyon
Jessup, R. Judd *health care executive*

Upland
Likens, John David *rehabilitation services professional*

Vallejo
Crosley-Mayers, Diane *social worker*
Toms, Kathleen Moore *nurse*

Vandenberg Afb
Huggins, Elaine Jacqueline *nurse, retired army officer*

Visalia
Phillipe, Chester Tolleson *alcohol/drug abuse services professional, educator, substance abuse facility administrator*

Walnut Creek
Burns, Francis Raymond *medical facility administrator, researcher*
Foster, Bonnie Gayle *operating room nurse, real estate agent*
Nolan, Janiece Simmons *health care company executive*
Schneider, Gisela Helga *medical technician*

Whittier
Rosenstein, Mary Elisabeth Mallory *retired social worker*

Woodland Hills
Funari, Robert Glenn *health care services executive*
John Robert, Bruce *healthcare company executive*
Pettit, John W. *administrator*
Rich, Marvin P. *health association executive*
Tellez, Cora *healthcare company executive*
Yates, Gary L. *marriage and family therapist*

COLORADO

Aurora
Brown, Anne Sherwin *speech pathologist, educator*

Boulder
Arnold, Janet Nina *health care consultant*
Braddock, David Lawrence *health science educator*
Copeland, Poppy Carlson *psychotherapist*
Holdsworth, Janet Nott *women's health nurse*
Middleton-Downing, Laura *psychiatric social worker, artist, small business owner*

Broomfield
Scott, John Atwood, Jr., *hypnoanalyst, psychologist, marriage and family therapist*

Buena Vista
Herb, Edmund Michael *optometrist, educator*

Canon City
Honaker, Charles Ray *health facility administrator*
McCaslin, Kathleen Denise *child abuse educator*

Colorado Springs
DiPadova, Regina Maria *counselor*
Driscoll, David Lee *chiropractor*
Haas, Julian L. *researcher, educator*
Lokken, Steven Lee *chiropractor, nutritionist, internist*
Olson, Kenneth Paul *vocational consultant*
Oman, Virginia Mills *psychotherapist*
Orner, Linda Price *family therapist, counselor*

Denver
Brimhall, Dennis C. *hospital executive*
Carroll, Kim Marie *nurse*
Edelman, Joel *health facility administrator*
Joyce, Mary Holt *retired social worker*
Judson, Franklyn Nevin *physician, educator*
Parker, Catherine Susanne *psychotherapist*
Plummer, Ora Beatrice *nursing educator, trainer*
Rael, Henry Sylvester, Sr., *retired health administrator, financial and management consultant*
Schultz, Janet K. *nursing consultant, business executive*
Taussig, Lynn Max *healthcare administrator, pulmonologist, pediatrician, educator*
Thompson, Cathy Joanne *nursing educator, consultant, acute care nurse practitioner*
Wilkinson, Joan Kristine *nurse, pediatric clinical specialist*
Witt, Catherine Lewis *neonatal nurse practitioner, writer*

Englewood
Bradshaw, Beverly Jean *psychotherapist, consultant, educator*

Fort Carson
Stanbro, Heather Aspen *emergency medical technician*

Fort Collins
Hultgren, Glenn M. *chiropractor*
Tyler, Gail Madeleine *nurse*

Grand Junction
Pantenburg, Michel *hospital administrator, health educator, holistic health coordinator*

Idledale
Brown, Gerri Ann *physical therapist*

Lakewood
Buckelew, Larry C. *lab administrator*
Johnson, Ramey Kayes *community health nurse*
Mellstig, Sören *lab administrator*

Longmont
Jones, Beverly Ann Miller *nursing administrator, retired patient services administrator*

Louisville
Shively, Merrick Lee *pharmaceutical scientist, consultant*

Meeker
Omer, Robert Wendell *hospital administrator*

Peyton
Dunn, Doris *retired critical care nurse, artist, rancher*

Pueblo
Avery, Julia May *speech pathologist, organizational volunteer*
Hawkins, Robert Lee *health facility administrator*
Levy, Patricia Anne *psychotherapist, educator*

Yuma
Hertneky, Randy Lee *optometrist*

CONNECTICUT

Avon
Dahl, Andrew Wilbur *health services executive*

Branford
Carroll, Deirdre Holden *psychiatric nurse practitioner, clinical researcher, educator*

Bridgeport
Macdonald, Karen Crane *occupational therapist, geriatric counselor*
Trefry, Robert J. *healthcare administrator*

Bristol
Morales, Mary E. *social worker*

Danbury
Finkelstein, Annette Anuhid *nurse*

Derby
Jekel, James Franklin *physician, public health educator*

East Hartford
Young, Albert Frederick Antonio *grants coordinator*

Fairfield
Mead, Philomena *mental health nurse*

Farmington
Houchin, John Frederick, Sr., *human services administrator*

Greenwich
Krauser, Robert Stanley *health care executive*
LLangley, Patricia Coffroth *retired psychiatric social worker*

Hamden
Cole-Schiraldi, Marilyn Bush *occupational therapy educator*

Hartford
Furniss, Wendy Hagstrom *public health services administrator*
Wheeler, Robert Channing, Jr., *health maintenance organization executive*

Higganum
Twachtman-Cullen, Diane *communication disorders and autism specialist*

Meriden
Molder, Sybil Ailene *retired occupational health nurse*
Shemchuk, Mary Elizabeth *occupational therapist*

Milford
Muth, Eric Peter *ophthalmic optician*

New Britain
Foster, Patrick *technologist, educator, writer, educational consultant*
Fothergill, William Corey *counselor, therapist*

New Haven
Armbruster, Paula *child mental health educator, university director*
Benfer, David William *hospital administrator*
De Rose, Sandra Michele *psychotherapist, educator, supervisor, administrator*
Diers, Donna Kaye *nursing educator*
Gilliss, Catherine Lynch *nursing educator*
Krauss, Judith Belliveau *nursing educator*
McCorkle, Ruth *oncological nurse, educator*
Reyes, Marcia Stygles *medical technologist*
Stiber, Julie Anne *social worker*
Zaccagnino, Joseph Anthony *hospital administrator*
Zilber, Irene *counselor*

New London
Larson, Richard Everett *lab technician*

Newington
Zeldes, Benjamin *optometrist*

North Branford
Womer, Charles Berry *retired hospital executive, management consultant*

North Haven
Hogan, James Carroll, Jr., *public health administrator, research biologist*

Putnam
Desaulniers, Rene Gerard Lesieur *retired optometrist*

Redding
Benyei, Candace Reed *psychotherapist*

Simsbury
Long, Ann Marie *health facility administrator*

Stamford
Bostin, Marvin Jay *hospital and health services consultant*
Scott, Gregory Alan *pharmacist, writer*

Storrs
Cirakoglu, Menderes *researcher*

Storrs Mansfield
Chinn, Peggy Lois *nursing educator, editor*
Jensen, Robert Gordon *nutritionist, consultant*
Xu, Yu *nursing educator*

Suffield
Bianchi, Maria *critical care specialist, adult and acute care nurse practitioner, nursing administrator*

Trumbull
Kole, Marc M. *healthcare provider executive*

Schneider, Charles M. *healthcare provider company executive*
Thompson, Kurt B. *healthcare provider executive*

Wallingford
Spero, Barry Melvin *health facility administrator*

West Hartford
Gitterman, Alex *social work educator*
Hugg, Geraldine Bertha Novotny *retired gerontology specialist, journalist*

West Haven
Druss, Benjamin George *health services researcher, psychiatrist*

Wilton
Kriss, Patricia Anne *health services executive*

DELAWARE

Dover
McCabe, Margaret Clark *family nurse practitioner*

Hockessin
Croyle, Barbara Ann *health care management executive*

Lewes
Fried, Jeffrey Michael *health care administrator*

Newark
Talbert, Dorothy Georgie Burkett *social worker*

Wilmington
Martin, Patricia Carmella *counselor, entrepreneur*
Schmerling, Erwin Robert *counselor, retired physicist*

DISTRICT OF COLUMBIA

Washington
Acord, Bobby *health science association administrator*
Adams-Campbell, Lucille L. *health facility administrator*
Alleyne, George A.O. *public health administrator, educator*
Alward, Ruth Rosendall *nursing consultant*
Angotti, Catherine Marie *occupational health director*
Arling, Donna Dickson *social worker*
Auerbach, Judith Diane *public health service officer*
Baigis, Judith Ann *nursing educator, academic administrator*
Bailar, John Christian, III, *retired public health educator, physician, statistician*
Beale, Susan Yates *social worker*
Behney, Clyde Joseph *health policy researcher*
Chalk, Rosemary Anne *health science association administrator*
Corrigan, Janet M. *health science association administrator*
Daalder, Ivo H. *foreign policy researcher*
Delbanco, Suzanne F. *human services administrator*
Eckenhoff, Edward Alvin *healthcare administrator, educator*
Fineberg, Harvey Vernon *president Institute of Medicine, preventive medicine physician, educator*
Fitzgerald, Helen Teresa *grief therapist, writer*
Flax, Jane *psychotherapist, educator*
Garfunkel, Sanford M. *medical administrator*
Gary, Lawrence Edward *social work educator*
Gaston, Marilyn Hughes *health facility administrator*
Gaynor, Suzanne Marie *health care executive, researcher*
Ginsburg, Paul *health facility administrator*
Golden, Olivia A. *human service agency administrator*
Goldstein, Murray *health organization official*
Gray, Bradford Hitch *health policy researcher*
Grob, George Frederick *health, social services association administrator*
Hackbarth, Glenn M. *human services administrator*
Hager, Mary Hastings *nutritionist, educator, consultant*
Hannett, Frederick James *healthcare consulting company executive*
Hartmann, Robert Sankey *hospital administrator, communications and fundraising executive*
Heller, (Douglas) Brian *human services administrator*
Holland, Joy *health care facility executive*
Hudson, Timothy Leon *nursing educator*
Ignagni, Karen *healthcare association executive*
Johnson, Cheryl L. *nursing administrator*
Jones, Stanley Boyd *health policy analyst, priest*
Lee, Shew Kuhn *retired optometrist*
Lewis, Benjamin Pershing, Jr., *pharmacist, public health service officer*
Llubién, Joseph Herman *psychotherapist, counselor*
Lombardo, Fredric Alan *pharmacist, educator*
Lynch, John Joseph *health facility administrator*
Mahaffey, Kathryn Rose *risk assessor*
Martin, Kathleen *medical center administrator*
Martinez, Rose Marie *health science association administrator*
Masi, Dale A. *research company executive, social work educator*
McCarter, Katherine Sauter *association executive*
McCarthy, John F. *healthcare administrator*
Michnich, Marie E. *health policy analyst, consultant, educator*
Miller, Linda B. *administrator*
Nightingale, Stuart Lester *physician, public health officer*
Njie, Veronica P.S. *clinical nurse, educator*
Oak, Jeffrey Charles *ethicist*
Obrams, Gunta Iris *medical officer*
O'Neill, Joseph F. *health science association administrator*
Pappas, Gregory *health agency administrator*
Pollack, Ronald F(rank) *healthcare organization executive, lawyer*
Pope, Andrew *health science association administrator*
Porter, John Weston *counselor, consultant, hospital administrator*

Rheintgen, Laura Dale *research center official*
Richman, Joseph Herbert *retired public health services official*
Samet, Kenneth Alan *hospital administrator*
Sanchez-Way, Ruth Dolores *health services administrator*
Satcher, David *former public health service officer*
Schorr, Lisbeth Bamberger *child and family policy analyst, author, educator*
Seelman, Katherine Dolores *institute administrator*
Southby, Richard McKellar Fairfax *health services educator, consultant*
Spencer, Harrison Clark, Jr., *public health administrator, educator*
Stoiber, Susanne A. *health science organization administrator*
Theiss, Patricia Kelley *public health researcher, educator*
Thomas, Tracey Williams *researcher*
Valentine, Nancy Marie *nursing administrator, educator*
Walder, Debby Jean *program director, quality manager, nursing service administrator, nurse, educator*
Wells, Samuel Fogle, Jr., *research center administrator*
Woteki, Catherine Ellen *nutritionist*
Zechman, Edwin Kerper, Jr., *medical facility administrator*

FLORIDA

Altamonte Springs
LeBlanc, Janet M. *addictions and relationship counselor*
Linberger, Lara Jane *marriage and family therapist, music educator*

Avon Park
Cranfill, Virginia May *retired nursing administrator*

Boca Raton
Baumgarten, Diana Virginia *gerontological nurse*
Garland, Joan Bruder *social worker, psychologist*
Goodstone, Erica Mae *sex therapist, psychotherapist*
Rothberg-Blackman, June Simmonds *retired nursing educator, psychotherapist, psychoanalyst*

Boynton Beach
Machtiger, Harriet Gordon *retired psychoanalyst*

Clearwater
Barry, Joyce Alice *dietician, consultant*
Graves, Robert Lee *health facility administrator*
Whedon, George Donald *medical administrator, researcher*

Coral Gables
Keeley, Brian E. *hospital administrator*
Weiner, Ruth Eileen Blower Kassewitz *retired public relations executive*

Crystal River
Stone, Fred Lyndon *retired human resources administrator*

Daytona Beach
Cardwell, Harold Douglas, Sr., *retired rehabilitation specialist*
Richards, Virginia (Ginnie) *social worker*

Deerfield Beach
Solomon, Barry Jason *healthcare administrator*

Delray Beach
Weiner, Anne Lee *social worker*

Deltona
Bondinell, Stephanie *counselor, academic administrator*

Ellenton
Edson, Herbert Robbins *retired foundation and hospital executive*

Englewood
Clark, Carolyn Chambers *nurse, educator, publishing executive*

Fernandina Beach
Kurtz, Myers Richard *hospital administrator*

Fort Lauderdale
Alpert, Martin Jeffrey *chiropractic physician*
Chapman, Erie, III, *hospital administrator*
Geronemus, Diann Fox *social work consultant*
Kornblau, Barbara L. *physical therapist*
Marine, Michael R. *healthcare company executive*
Rentoumis, Ann Mastroianni *psychotherapist*
Stern, Edith Lois *counselor, hypno-therapist*
Sundel, Sandra Stone *social worker*

Fort Myers
Johnson, Sally A. *nurse, educator*
Nugent, Timothy Scott *alcohol/drug abuse services professional*
Thurman, Cynthia Denise *human services administrator*
Woodbridge, Norma Jean *registered nurse, writer*

Fort Walton Beach
Bolt, Lynda Elaine *alcohol/drug abuse services professional*

Gainesville
Brushwood, David Benson *pharmacy educator, lawyer*
Bzoch, Kenneth Rudolph *speech and language educator, department chairman*
Chmielewski, Terese Lynn *physical therapist, educator*
Doering, Paul Louis *pharmacist, educator*
Gaintner, Richard J. *health facility administrator*
Kersey, Talana S. *mental health counselor*
Long, Kathleen Ann *nursing educator, dean, consultant*
Malasanos, Lois Julanne Fosse *nursing educator*
Puckett, Ruby Parker *nutritionist, hospital food service administrator, consultant, author*
Randall, Malcom *health care administrator*

Ray, Timothy Britt *social worker, lawyer, administrator*
Small, Natalie Settimelli *pediatric mental health counselor*
Thompson, Neal Philip *food science and nutrition educator*
Watson, Robert Joe *health facility administrator, retired career officer*

Hialeah
Perez, Leyanee C. *nutritionist, consultant*

Hillsboro Beach
Marshall, Jo Taylor *social worker*

Hollywood
Tucker, Nina Angella *hospital administrator*

Homosassa
Acton, Norman *international organization executive*

Inverness
Dowdell, Michael Francis *critical care nurse, forensic and anesthesia nurse practitioner*

Jacksonville
Fulton-Quindoza, Debra Ann *emergency nurse practitioner*
Langford, Cecilia Motes *nursing educator*
Mason, William Cordell, III, *hospital administrator*
Pavlick, Pamela Kay *nurse, consultant*
Sanders, Marion Yvonne *retired geriatrics nurse*
Stiehl, Ruth Rasco *nursing educator*
Williams, Leola Wilkerson *social worker, writer*
Wilson, C. Nick *health educator, consultant, researcher, lecturer*

Jensen Beach
Gamble, Raymond Wesley *marriage and family therapist, clergyman*

Lake City
Norman, Alline L. *health facility administrator*

Lakeland
Hixon, Andrea Kaye *healthcare quality specialist*

Largo
Bush, Debra W. *occupational health nurse*
Hamlin, Robert Henry *public health educator, management consultant*
Simmons, Deborah Jo *pharmacy executive*

Lauderhill
Bathurst, Debra Lynnette *physical therapist assistant*

Lecanto
Gessner, Donald Robert *healthcare consultant*

Melbourne
Fox, Thomas George *health science educator*
Hughes, A. N. *psychotherapist*

Miami
Cekauskas, Cynthia Danute *social worker*
Chisholm, Martha Maria *dietitian*
Clark, Ira C. *hospital association administrator, educator*
Dann, Oliver Townsend *psychoanalyst, psychiatrist, educator*
Embden, Dawn Terris *cardiovascular nurse, writer*
Getz, Morton Ernest *medical facility director, gastroenterologist*
Himburg, Susan Phillips *dietician, educator*
Huysman, James David *healthcare executive, consultant*
Jones-Wills, Eunice Stephanie *mental health nurse, researcher*
Kaiser, Gerard A. *hospital administrator*
Kooima, Linda Kay *neonatal and pediatrics nurse*
Nadeau, Joseph Eugene *health care management consultant, information systems consultant*
Newton, Terry Fernando *health information specialist, writer*
Osinski, Martin Henry *healthcare consultant*
Rozek, Thomas M. *health facility administrator*
Schor, Olga Seemann *mental health counselor, real estate broker*
Strinko, Thomas Edward *medical services administrator*
Yaffa, Jack Ber *healthcare administrator, educator, surgeon*

Mount Dora
Crone, Eugene N. *addictions specialist, retired educator*
Moretto, Jane Ann *nurse, public health officer, consultant*
Shyers, Larry Edward *mental health counselor, educator*

Naples
Barkley, Marlene A. Nyhuis *nursing educator*
Farnham, Robert E. *health facility administrator*
Holland, Earl P. *health services executive*
Ray, Stephen M. *health services executive*
Seavey, Christopher Gordon *psychotherapist, addiction counselor*
Sekowski, Cynthia Jean *corporate executive, contact lens specialist*
Vumbacco, Joseph V. *health services executive*

New Port Richey
Charters, Karen Ann Elliott *critical care nurse, health facility administrator*

North Bay Village
Levine, Jane Sheila *nurse, health insurance consultant*

Ocala
Roberts, Mary Belle *clinical social worker*

Orange Park
Rice, Ronald James *hospital administrator*

Orlando
Byrnes, John Francis, Jr., *physician assistant*
Camoes, Norma Arcamo *school nurse*
Eastmond-Robinson, June Patricia *public health nurse*
Fottler, Myron David *health services educator*
Jacinto, George Anthony *social worker, counselor, educator, consultant*
Vanryckeghem, Martine *speech pathology/audiology services professional, educator*

Ormond Beach
Moore, Frederick Appel *administrator*

Palm Beach Gardens
Holloway, Edward Olin *human services manager*

Palmetto
Carter, Elizabeth Wackerman *retired mental health nurse*

Panama City
Reedy-Dewey, Madeline Anne *retired occupational therapist*

Panama City Beach
Nelson, Edith Ellen *dietitian*

Pensacola
Appleyard, Diane Paige *human service administrator*
Loesch, Mabel Lorraine *social worker*
Maygarden, Jerry Louis *health care foundation executive*
Raisler, Mary E. *nurse*
Shimmin, Margaret Ann *women's health nurse*
Taggart, Linda Diane *women's health nurse*

Plant City
Henry, J. Myrle *pharmacist*

Plantation
Gonshak, Isabelle Lee *nurse, civic worker*

Pompano Beach
Goldberg, Lois D. *health facility administrator, disability analyst*

Ponte Vedra Beach
Church, Barbara Ryan *organizational psychologist*

Port Charlotte
Kidd, A. Paul *hospital administrator, government official*

Port Saint Lucie
Beatrice, Ruth Hadfield *hypnotherapist, retired educator, financial administrator*
Verfaillie, Roland Bruce *mental health professional*

Riviera Beach
Sonnier, Joseph A. *lab administrator, physician*

Rockledge
Means, Michael David *hospital administrator*

Saint Petersburg
Freeman, Corinne *financial services, former mayor*
Keller, Natasha Matrina Leonidow *nursing administrator*
McNeill, Felita Gale *nurse, military officer*

Sarasota
Carr, Patricia Ann *community health nurse*
Green, Karen Danielle *psychotherapist*
Harris, Judith Ann White *health occupations vocational educator, nurse*
Middleton, Norman Graham *social worker, psychotherapist*
Schoenhals, Katherine Viola *social worker*
Scott, Charles Francis *health facility administrator*
Tucci, Steven Michael *health facility administrator, physician, recording industry executive*

South Miami
Bauman, Sandra Spiegel *nurse practitioner, mental health counselor*

Stuart
Cocoves, Anita Petzold *psychotherapist*

Sun City Center
Ballard, Mildred Louise *retired adult nurse practitioner*
Ward, Jacqueline Ann Beas *nurse, healthcare administrator*

Tallahassee
Ivory, Peter B. C. B. *retired medical administrator*
Molinari, Joseph Francis *oculist*
Robbins, Brenda Jean *music therapist*
Soliman, Karam Farah Attia *pharmacy educator*
Taylor, John D. *pharmacist, health services executive*

Tamarac
Krause, John L. *optometrist*

Tampa
Arfsten, Betty-Jane *nurse*
Berarducci, Adrienne *nursing educator, researcher*
Boutros, Linda Nelene Wiley *medical/surgical nurse*
Mahan, Charles Samuel *public health educator*
Plawecki, Judith Ann *nursing educator*
Price, Douglas Armstrong *chiropractor*

Tarpon Springs
Georgiou, Ruth Schwab *retired social worker*

Trenton
Ivey, James Frederick, Jr., *physician, health facility administrator*

Venice
Barritt, Evelyn Ruth Berryman *nurse, educator, dean*

Vero Beach
Christopher, Robert Paul *retired physical medicine and rehabilitation physician, educator*
Kornicks, Margot Susan *nursing administrator*

West Palm Beach
Bernhardt, Marcia Brenda *mental health counselor*
Bohn, Barbara Ann *retired laboratory director*

Winter Haven
Porter, Howard Leonard, III, *health and education policy consultant*

Winter Park
Jernigan, Donald *hospital administrator*
Werner, Thomas Lee *hospital administrator*

Winter Springs
San Miguel, Sandra Bonilla *social worker*

GEORGIA

Alpharetta
Mock, Melinda Smith *orthopedic nurse specialist, consultant*
White, Carl Edward, Jr., *pharmaceutical administrator*

Atlanta
Baird, Marianne Saunorus *critical care clinical nurse specialist, administrator*
Bales, Virginia Shankle *health administrator*
Barker, William Daniel *hospital administrator*
Beaton, Rebecca Andrea *psychotherapist*
Chandler, Robert Charles *healthcare consultant*
Churchwell, Andre *health science association administrator*
Dahl, Alan C. *health facility administrator*
Dykstra, Gary James *administrator*
Foege, William Herbert *public health administrator, educator*
Fox, John T. *health facility administrator*
Fricks, Larry *mental health services professional*
Ganzarain, Ramon Cajiao *psychoanalyst*
Gay, Robert Derril *behavioral health consultant*
Henry, John Dunklin, Sr., *hospital executive*
Holloway, Barbara R. *health science association administrator*
Honaman, J. Craig *health facility administrator*
Hopkins, Donald Roswell *public health physician*
Johnson, Carl Frederick *marriage and family therapist*
Marks, James S. *public health service administrator*
Martin, David Edward *health sciences educator*
Polhamus, Barbara *nutritionist, educator*
Renford, Edward J. *hospital administrator*
Salmon, Marla E. *nursing educator, dean*
Seffrin, John Reese *health science association administrator, educator*
Tkaczuk, Nancy Anne *cardiovascular services administrator*
Walton, Carole Lorraine *clinical social worker*
Weed, Roger Oren *rehabilitation services professional, educator*
Winkle, C. Christian *health facility administrator*
Woody, Mary Florence *nursing educator, university administrator*

Augusta
Feldman, Elaine Bossak *medical nutritionist, educator*
Gillespie, Edward Malcolm *hospital administrator*
Whittemore, Ronald Paul *hospital administrator, retired army officer, nursing educator*

Brunswick
Herndon, Alice Patterson Latham *public health nurse*

Covington
Litkea, Carole Lynn *paramedic*

Dahlonega
Miller, Carol Ann *physical therapist, educator*

Decatur
Gregory, Sharon E. *neonatal clinical nurse specialist, nurse practitioner*
Hinman, Alan Richard *public health administrator, epidemiologist*
Rosenberg, Mark L. *health agency administrator*

Duluth
Weldon, Thomas David *medical products manufacturer*

Evans
Fournier, Joseph Andre Alphonse *nurse, social worker, psychotherapist*

Fayetteville
Cokuslu, Lynda Elizabeth McCord *medical assistant*

Grayson
Nease, Judith Allgood *marriage and family therapist*

Hiawassee
Bayless, Carolyn Cotton *nurse*

Jonesboro
Finley, Sarah Maude Merritt *social worker*

Kennesaw
Hetrick, Joan Willette *critical care nurse, administrator*

Lagrange
Davidson, Joeline Dillard *laboratory services administrator*

Lawrenceville
Meehan, Patrick John *public health officer*

Macon
Brown, Nancy Childs *marriage and family therapist*
Camp, Shirley A. *nursing consultant, lawyer*
Drysdale, Joyce A *substance abuse counselor*
Fickling, William Arthur, Jr., *health care manager*

Marietta
McEntire, Betty *health facility administrator*
Neff, Marilyn Lee *nursing consultant*
Petit, Parker Holmes *health care corporation executive*

Norcross
Barrow, Pamela H. *health services administrator*
Nabors, David *health facility executive*

Port Wentworth
Ivie, Shirley Bridges *nurse anesthetist*

Redan
Bennett-Williams, Sharon K. *mental health services professional, writer*

Rome
Kines, Joan Elaine *human services administrator, consultant*
Massing, Virginia Reeves *surgical nurse and administrator*

Savannah
Baker, Brinda Elizabeth Garrison *infectious disease nurse*
DiClaudio, Janet Alberta *health information administrator*

Statesboro
Bartels, Jean Ellen *nursing educator*
Beasley, John Julius *child and family development educator*

Stone Mountain
Roth, Edie Cowan *rehabilitation services professional*

Warner Robins
Beck, Rhonda Joann *paramedic, educator, writer*

HAWAII

Hanalei
Snyder, Francine *psychotherapist, registered nurse, writer*

Hilo
Clark, Janet *retired health services executive*
Skorikov, Vladimir B. *researcher, educator*

Honolulu
Fischer, Joel *social work educator*
Kadohiro, Jane K. *educator, nurse, diabetes consultant*
Kennedy, Faye *retired social worker, author*
Lum, Jean Loui Jin *nursing educator*
Simon, Gary B. *health care manager, investor*
Wilson, William James *healthcare executive*
Yokouchi, Kathy *nursing administrator*

Kailua
Lundquist, Dana Richard *healthcare executive*
Westerdahl, John Brian *nutritionist, health educator*

IDAHO

Hope
Meyers, Marlene O. *retired health facility administrator*

Idaho Falls
Lee, Glenn Richard *medical administrator, educator*

Meridian
Thorsted, V. Darleene *neonatal and community health nurse*

Naples
Soss, Daniel Lee *social work educator*

ILLINOIS

Alton
Kessler, William Eugene *health care executive*

Arlington Heights
Baptist, Allwyn J. *healthcare consultant*
Lemke, Sherry Ellen *therapist*
Telleen, Judy *counselor*

Barrington
Stoutenburg, Jane Sue Williamson *nurse practitioner, fund raiser, actress*

Belleville
Shim, Sang Koo *mental health services professional*

Berwyn
Hudik, Martin Francis *hospital administrator, educator, consultant, writer*

Bolingbrook
Day, Mary Ann *medical/surgical nurse*
Price, Theodora Hadzisteliou *individual, child and family therapist*

Buffalo Grove
Rai, Rajat *health facility administrator*

Burr Ridge
Daly-Gawenda, Debra *health facility administrator, nursing educator*

Carbondale
Kawewe, Saliwe Moyo *social work educator, researcher*
Sarvela, Paul D. *health facility administrator, educator*

Cary
Blevins, Steven W. *chiropractor*

Centralia
Whitten, Mary Lou *nursing educator*

Champaign
Schiro-Geist, Chrisann *rehabilitation counselor*

Chatham
Chew, Keith Elvin *healthcare services administrator*

Chicago
Andreoli, Kathleen Gainor *nurse, educator, dean*
Bauman, Jerry L. *pharmacy researcher, educator*
Berman, Laura *sex therapist*
Bosma, Jennifer *nursing association administrator*
Bracken, Kathleen Ann *nurse*
Bristo, Marca *human services administrator*
Brown, Charles Eric *health facility administrator, biochemist*
Cain, Harry P. *health science association administrator*
Chen, David *rehabilitation services professional*
Cox-Hayley, Deon Melayne *geriatrics services professional*
Crawford, Jean Andre *clinical therapist*
Easley, Cheryl Eileen *nursing educator, department chairman*
Finley, Yvonne Smith *social worker*
Gaynes, Bruce Ira *optometrist, pharmacist, educator*
Goldsmith, Ethel Frank *medical social worker*
Goodman, Larry J. *health facility administrator*
Hill, Barbara Benton *healthcare executive*
Kopytko, Edwin Edward *nursing administrator*
Lerner, Wayne M. *health care executive*
Levin, Arnold Murray *social worker, psychotherapist*
Lim, Len Gui Remolona (Mark Lim) *critical care and emergency nurse*
Logemann, Jerilyn Ann *speech pathologist, educator*
Massura, Eileen Kathleen *family therapist*
McDermott, Mary Ann *nursing educator*
Mecklenburg, Gary Alan *hospital executive*
Mullner, Ross Michael *healthcare educator*
Nielsen, Nancy H. *health organization executive*
Peters, Elizabeth Anne *nutrition educator*
Reed, Vastina Kathryn (Tina Reed) *child and adolescent psychotherapist, family development specialist*
Riordan, Michael C. *hospital administrator*
Rojek, Kenneth John *health facility administrator, hospital*
Rosenheim, Margaret Keeney *social welfare policy educator*
Sandler, Richard H. *lab administrator, gastroenterologist*
Schwartz, John Norman *human services administrator*
Scott, Nancy L. *health facility administrator, consultant*
Simon, Bernece Kern *retired social work educator*
Spergel, Irving Abraham *social worker, researcher*
Szerlag, Chester Theodore *health facility administrator*
Walton, Carmelita Noreen *retired nursing administrator*
Williams, Alexander Hazard, III, *health care executive, consultant*

Crystal Lake
Schaefer, Mary Ann *health facility administrator, consultant*

Deerfield
Moon, John C. *healthcare company executive*

Dekalb
Frank-Stromborg, Marilyn Laura *nursing educator*

Des Plaines
D'Anca, John Arthur *psychotherapist, educator*

Downers Grove
Thomas, Daniel J. *health services executive*
Wristen, Edward L. *health facility administrator*

East Saint Louis
Martin, Betty J. *speech, language pathologist*

Effingham
Heth, Diana Sue *psychotherapist*

Elgin
Beyer, Karen Haynes *social worker*
Ollayos, Clare M. *chiropractor*

Elmhurst
Dallas, Daniel George *social worker*
Fry, Evelyn Leona *clinical social worker*
Moffitt, Ray *social worker, consultant*

Evanston
Neaman, Mark Robert *hospital administrator*

Fairfield
Thomason, Nola Faye *critical care-emergency supervisor*

Freeport
Weaver, Michael Glenn *pharmacist*

Galena
Alexander, Barbara Leah Shapiro *clinical social worker*

Galesburg
Kowalski, Richard Sheldon *hospital administrator*

Glenview
Coulson, Elizabeth Anne *physical therapy educator, state representative*

Hampshire
Hirn, Doris Dreyer *health service administrator*

Harrisburg
Rushing, Philip Dale *retired social worker*

Highland Park
Eldridge, Amy Helene *clinical social worker, academic dean*

Hillside
Morrison, Jelena *technologist, educator*

Hines
Cummings, Joan E. *health facility administrator, educator*

Homewood
Ramirez, Ralph Henry *nurse, corporate executive*

La Grange
Mahoney, Donna Marie *psychotherapist*

Lake Forest
Damico, Joseph F. *medical company executive*

Litchfield
Deaton, Beverly Jean *nursing administrator, educator*

Lombard
Holgers-Awana, Rita Marie *electrodiagnosis specialist*

Macomb
Hopper, Stephen Rodger *hospital administrator*

Matteson
van der Hoek, Sherry A. *counselor*

Mchenry
Duel, Ward Calvin *retired health care consultant*

Morton Grove
Labunski, Alma Joel *nursing educator*

Mount Prospect
Rueggeberg, Erna M. *nursing consultant, nursing administrator, researcher*

Naperville
Dhar, Promila *researcher*

Northbrook
Betz, Ronald Philip *pharmacist*
Hicks, Judith Eileen *nursing administrator*
Kahn, Sandra S. *psychotherapist*
Lever, Alvin *health science association administrator*
Noeth, Carolyn Frances *speech and language pathologist*

Northfield
Lubawski, James Lawrence *healthcare consultant*

Oak Brook
Baker, Robert J(ohn) *hospital administrator*
Bower, Barbara Jean *nurse, consultant*
Risk, Richard Robert *health care executive*
Skogsbergh, James H. *health facility administrator*

Oak Park
Varchmin, Thomas Edward *environmental health administrator*

Oregon
Cates, Jeffrey R. *chiropractor*
Hayes, Randy Alan *family therapist*

Palos Hills
Healy, Judith Ann *social worker*

Park Forest
Steinmetz, Jon David *mental health executive, psychologist*

Park Ridge
Boe, Gerard Patrick *health science association administrator, educator*
Campbell, Bruce Crichton *hospital administrator*
Catizone, Carmen A. *health science association administrator, secretary*

Peoria
McCollum, Jean Hubble *medical assistant*
Walker, Philip Chamberlain, II, *health care executive*

Plainfield
Schinderle, Robert Frank *retired hospital administrator*

Prophetstown
Williamsen, Dannye Sue *personal development educator, health facility administrator*

Rockton
Pennell, Danny Joe *social worker*

Round Lake
Abdullah, Bashar Y. *pharmacist, researcher*

Saint Anne
Holtzman, Michael *alcohol abuse professional*

Saint Francisville
Harezi, Ilonka Jo *medical technology research executive*

Schaumburg
Uhrik, Steven Brian *clinical social worker, psychotherapist, employee assistance professional, behavioral science consultant*

Silvis
Bobb, Harold Daniel *chiropractor, consultant*

Skokie
Guillermo, Linda Sue *clinical social worker*
Langguth, Margaret Witty *health facility administrator*
McCarthy, Michael Shawn *health care company executive, lawyer*

Springfield
Hundley, Elaine E. *retired nursing education administrator*
Voycheck, Gerald Louis *nursing home administrator, social worker*

Tinley Park
Basit, Abdul *mental health services professional*
Daniels, Kurt R. *speech and language pathologist*

Urbana
Baker, David Hiram *nutritionist, nutrition educator*
Erdman, John W. *nutritionist, educator*
Tripp, April *special education services professional*
Visek, Willard James *nutritionist, animal scientist, physician, educator*

Vernon Hills
Curns, Eileen Bohan *counselor, author, speaker*

Walnut
Meisenheimer, Sharon Lee *nurse*

Waukegan
Martis, Leo *healthcare researcher*

Westchester
Clarke, Richard Lewis *health science association administrator*
Shaffer, Susan E. *nutrition specialist*

Western Springs
Tiefenthal, Marguerite Aurand *school social worker*
Walsh, Robert Joseph *psychotherapist*

Wheaton
Kaenel, Rosemary Therese *community health nurse, educator*
Pape, Patricia Ann *social worker, consultant*

Wilmette
Ellis, Helene Rita *social worker*

Winfield
Young, Quentin Hayse *family counselor*

INDIANA

Beech Grove
Byrkett, Gary Lee *hospital engineer*

Berne
Habegger, Cynthia A. *medical/surgical nurse*

Bloomington
Austin, Joan Kessner *mental health nurse*
Bartleson, Amy Aileen *psychotherapist*

Bluffton
Brockmann, William Frank *medical facility administrator*

East Chicago
Psaltis, Helen *medical and surgical nurse*

Fort Wayne
Rhoad, Richard E. *healthcare executive*
Ridderheim, Mary Margaret *psychotherapist*

Gary
Bennett, Richard Carl *social worker*
Woodson, Porsha Marie *speech pathology/audiology services professional*

Hammond
Chandler, Melanie Lynn *surgical technologist, paralegal*
Smokvina, Gloria Jacqueline *nursing educator*

Indianapolis
Buhner, Byron Bevis *health science facility administrator*
Corley, William Edward *hospital administrator*
Davis, Edgar Glenn *science and health policy executive*
Dickenson-Hazard, Nancy Ann *pediatric nurse practitioner, consultant*
Handel, David Jonathan *healthcare administrator*
Harden, Anita Joyce *nurse*
Hitchens, William Randolph (Randy Hitchens) *health care executive*
Humphreys, Katie *health agency administrator*
Khurana, Poonam *neonatologist*
Loveday, William John *hospital administrator*
Moelhman, Amy Jo *social worker*
Pesut, Daniel J. *nursing educator*
Riegsecker, Marvin Dean *pharmacist, state senator*
SerVaas, Cory *health sciences association administrator*
Shi, Lizheng *health economist*
Smith, Donald Eugene *healthcare facility management administrator owner*
Stern, Phyllis Noerager *nursing educator*
Storm, Janet S. *psychiatric social worker*
Torres, Judith *lab administrator*
Walther, Joseph Edward *health facility administrator, retired physician*
Waymire, Bonnie Gladine *nursing administrator*
Yip-Schneider, Michele Terrell *researcher*

Jeffersonville
Walburn, John Clifford *mental health services professional*

Kokomo
Coppock, Janet Elaine *mental health nurse*

La Porte
Morris, Leigh Edward *mayor, retired hospital executive officer*

Lafayette
Geddes, LaNelle Evelyn *nurse, physiologist*
McBride, Angela Barron *nursing educator*

Michigan City
Brown, Arnold *physical therapy consultant*
Moldenhauer, Nancy A. *social worker, educator*

Mishawaka
Erdel, Sally Elizabeth *nurse*

Muncie
Hoffman, Mary Catherine *retired nurse, anesthetist*
Irvine, Phyllis Eleanor *nursing educator, administrator*

New Albany
Rhodes, Betty Fleming *rehabilitation services professional, nurse*

Newburgh
Haley, David Alan *healthcare executive*

Plymouth
Stiver, James Frederick *pharmacist, health physicist, administrator, scientist*

Richmond
Rains, Joanne Warner *nursing educator*

Rockport
Davis, Karen Sue *hospital nursing supervisor*

Seymour
Lake, Nancy Jean *nursing educator, medical/surgical nurse*

South Bend
Bella, Dantina Carmen Quartaroli *human services consultant*

Terre Haute
Anderson, Louise A. *public health service officer*
Tomey, Ann Louise Marriner *nursing educator*

West Lafayette
Belcastro, Patrick Frank *pharmaceutical scientist*
Christian, John Edward *health science educator*
Kirksey, Avanelle *nutrition educator*
Peck, Garnet Edward *pharmacist, educator*

IOWA

Ames
Kaplan, Murray Lee *nutritionist, educator*

Camanche
Stearns, Roxann Lynn *social worker*

Cedar Rapids
Brooks, Debra L. *healthcare executive, neuromuscular therapist*
Stephens, Ralph Renne *massage therapy educator*
Ziese, Nancylee Hanson *social worker*

Davenport
Goudy, Josephine Gray *social worker*

Des Moines
Abbott, Aloris Jean *retired medical/surgical nurse, retired nursing administrator*
Dukes, Vanessa Johnson *dietician*
Inman, Lorinda K. *nursing administrator*
Jessen, Lloyd K. *pharmacist, lawyer*
Wallace, Samuel Taylor *health system administrator*

Dubuque
Barker, Barbara Yvonne *nursing home administrator*

Glenwood
Campbell, William Edward *mental hospital administrator*

Iowa City
Banker, Gilbert Stephen *industrial and physical pharmacy educator, administrator*
Berg, Mary Jaylene *pharmacy educator, researcher*
Colloton, John William *university health care executive*
Craft-Rosenberg, Martha Jane *nursing educator, researcher*
Cyphert, Stacey Todd *health facilities administrator*
Katen-Bahensky, Donna *health facility administrator*
Muir, Ruth Brooks *counselor, substance abuse service coordinator*
Nesbitt, John Arthur *recreational therapist, writer, educator, researcher*
Wurster, Dale Eric *pharmacy educator*
Wurster, Dale Erwin *pharmacist, educator, retired dean*

Lamoni
Kirkpatrick, Sharon Minton *nursing educator, college administrator*

West Des Moines
Goldsmith, Janet Jane *pediatric nurse practitioner*
Zimmerman, Jo Ann *health services and educational consultant, former lieutenant governor*

KANSAS

Colby
Morrison, James Frank *optometrist, state legislator*

Courtland
Johnson, Dorothy Phyllis *retired counselor, art therapist*

Emporia
Frogge, Beverly Ann *nurse, consultant*

Fort Leavenworth
Oliver, Thornal Goodloe *health care executive*

Hays
Bustos, Rudolph R. *health facility administrator*
Hassett, Mary Ruth *nursing educator*

Humboldt
Finney, Paul David *acupuncturist, Chinese herbologist, entrepreneur*

Hutchinson
Davis, Mary Elizabeth *speech pathologist, educator, counselor*

Kansas City
Godwin, Harold Norman *pharmacist, educator*
Jerome, Norge Winifred *nutritionist, anthropologist*
Sanders-Hall, Patricia E. *health facility administrator*
Starling, Carol King *nursing educator*

Lawrence
Canda, Edward R. *social work educator*
Mc Coin, John Mack *social worker*
Siemsen, Susan Anne *physician assistant*

Leavenworth
Heim, Dixie Sharp *family practice nurse practitioner*

Manhattan
Shanklin, Carol W. *dietician*
Spears, Marian Caddy *dietetics and institutional management educator*

Oskaloosa
Flower, Joann *nurse, former state legislator*

Ottawa
DeShazer, Ruth Shomler *health facility administrator, consultant*

Pratt
Westerhaus, Catherine K. *social worker*

Shawnee Mission
Breen, Katherine Anne *speech and language pathologist*
Picciano, R J. *renal technician*

Topeka
Bauman-Bork, Marceil *health services administrator*
Sheffel, Irving Eugene *psychiatric institution executive*
Varner, Charleen LaVerne McClanahan *nutritionist, educator, administrator, dietitian*

Wichita
Da'Luz Vieira-Jones, Lorraine Christine C. *acupuncturist, researcher*
Dorr, Stephanie Tilden *psychotherapist*
Guthrie, Diana Fern *nursing educator*
Hicks, M. Elizabeth (Liz Hicks) *pharmacist*
Hull, Spring Sasha *researcher*
Korf, Clifford Dean *physician assistant*
Park, Chan Hyung *cell biologist, physician*
Rogers, Rita Doris Luck *family nurse practitioner*

Winfield
Hall, Lydia Jane *geriatrics nurse*

KENTUCKY

Calvert City
Butler, Sheila Morris *occupational health nurse*

Covington
Gemunder, Joel Frank *healthcare company executive*

Edgewood
Gross, Joseph Wallace *hospital administrator*

Fort Thomas
Besier, James Louis *pharmacist, educator*

Frankfort
Fleming, Juanita Wilson *nursing educator, academic administrator*

Henderson
Logan, John A., III, *hospital administrator*

Highland Heights
Moss, Nancy Evans *nurse midwife, women's health nurse*

Kings Mountain
Gill, Allen (Dale Gill) *health facility administrator*

Lexington
Davis, George A. *pharmacologist, medical researcher*
DeLuca, Patrick Phillip *pharmaceutical scientist, educator, administrator*
Farrar, Donna Beatrice *hospital official*
Karpf, Michael *medical administrator*
Leukefeld, Carl George *researcher, educator*
Rowe, Melinda Grace *public health service officer*

Louisville
Anderson, Linda Jean *critical care nurse, psychiatric nurse practitioner*
Bloem, James H. *managed health care executive*
Carlisle, Douglas R. *managed health care executive*
DeKay, Barbara Ann *social worker*
Diaz, Paul J. *service industry executive*
Eighmey, Douglas Joseph, Jr., *hospital administrator*
Force, Jill L. *health facility executive*
Gillenwater, James H. *health facility administrator*
Goodman, Bruce *managed health care company executive*
Hanson, Dennis Michael *medical imaging executive*
Hipwell, Art *managed health care company executive*
Kuntz, Edward Lawrence *healthcare executive*
Lechleiter, Richard A. *service industry executive*
Lofton, Kevin Eugene *medical facility administrator*
Lunsford, W. Bruce *health facility administrator, health and medical products executive*
Margulis, Heidi *managed health care company executive*
Mather, Elizabeth Vivian *healthcare executive*
Matuschka, Paul R. *pharmacist*
McCallister, Michael B. *managed health care executive*
Moya, Steve *managed health care company executive*
Murray, James E. *managed health care company executive*
Shield, Gene *managed health care company executive*
Weisenbeck, Sharon M. *healthcare regulatory administrator*

Mount Olivet
Dorton, Truda Lou *medical/surgical nurse, geriatrics nurse*

Murray
Brown, Jonathon Andrew *healthcare executive*

Richmond
Hall, Kathy *nursing official*

Russellville
Harper, Shirley Fay *nutritionist, educator, consultant, lecturer*

LOUISIANA

Baton Rouge
Davidge, Robert Cunninghame, Jr., *hospital administrator*
Finan, John Joseph *hospital administrator*
Mohan, Brij *social work educator*
Palmer, Curtis Dwayne *cardiopulmonary practitioner, microbiologist, researcher, builder*
Wallyn, Joan M. *social worker, writer*

Belle Chasse
Arimura, Akira *biomedical research laboratory administrator, educator*

Delhi
House, Ann *home health nurse, administrator*

La Place
Lodwick, Judith Lynne *nursing educator*

Leesville
Gutman, Lucy Toni *school social worker, educator, counselor*

Mandeville
Pittman, Jacquelyn *retired mental health nurse, nursing educator*
Treuting, Edna Gannon *retired nursing administrator, retired nursing educator*

Metairie
Evans, Carol Rockwell *nursing administrator*
Friedman, Lynn Joseph *counselor*
Morvant, Barbara L. *nursing administrator*

Monroe
Corder, Jan Busby *nursing educator, university dean*

Natchitoches
Egan, Shirley Anne *retired nursing educator*

New Orleans
Brown, Mary Willoughby *health facilities administrator*
Buddington, Steve Apalong *social worker, educator*
Culbertson, Richard Allen *healthcare educator, health system director*
Henault, Richard A. *healthcare hospital administrator*
Humphrey, Elizabeth Ann *women's health nurse*
Layman, Kim Florinda Marie *pharmacist, writer*
Marier, Robert L. *dean, hospital administrator*
Oliver, Ronald *retired medical technologist*
Remley, Theodore Phant, Jr., *counseling educator, lawyer*
Rigby, Perry Gardner *medical center administrator, educator, former university dean, physician*
Setlow, Valerie Petit *health science association director*

Pineville
Jones, Syble Thornhill *retired dietitian*

Ruston
Bourgeois, Patricia McLin *women's health and pediatrics nurse, educator*

Shreveport
Carter, Louvenia McGee *nursing educator*
Heacock, Donald Dee *social worker*
Hummel, Kay Jean *physical therapist*
St. Aubyn, Ronald Anthony *pediatrics nurse*

MAINE

Bangor
Beaupain, Elaine Shapiro *psychiatric social worker*
Swanson, Lisa Tucker *human services manager, consultant*

Belgrade Lakes
Kany, Judy C(asperson) *health policy analyst, former state senator*

Brooklin
Schmidt, Lynda Wheelwright *psychotherapist*

Brunswick
Fiori, Michael J. *pharmacist*

Caribou
Swanson, Shirley June *emergency room nurse, travel nurse, adult education educator*

East Boothbay
Eldred, Kenneth McKechnie *acoustical consultant*

Fort Fairfield
Shapiro, Joan Isabelle *lab administrator, medical/surgical nurse*

Freeport
Cushman, Margaret Jane *herbalist, nurse*

Jackman
Thomas, Paulette Suzanne *holistic health practitioner, physician assistant*

Old Town
Nelligan, Annette Frances *clinical coordinator*

Orono
Marston-Scott, Mary Vesta *nurse, educator*

Portland
McDowell, Donald L. *hospital administrator*

Scarborough
Connolly, Elaine Alexander Paterson *nurse*

South Portland
Baker, Arlene Ann *speech pathology/audiology services professional, consultant*

Starks
Medeiros, M. Joyce *community health educator*

MARYLAND

Adamstown
Munson, John Christian *acoustician*

Annapolis
Goldwater, Marilyn R(ubin) *medical/surgical nurse, state legislator*
Kushner, Jack *retired physician executive*
Levin, Gilbert Victor *health services administrator*

Arnold
Teklu, Dawit *researcher*

Baltimore
Abeloff, Martin David *medical administrator, educator, researcher*
Amos, Helen *hospital administrator*
Applebaum, Gary E. *medical director, executive*
Baker, Nadine Lois *cardiovascular technician*
Beilenson, Peter Lowell *public health official*
Block, James A. *hospital administrator, pediatrician*
Boston, Wallace Ellsworth, Jr., *healthcare executive, financial consultant*
Brieger, Gert Henry *medical historian, educator*
Brown, Patricia Mary Clare *health facility administrator*
Campbell, Jacquelyn C. *community health nurse*
Cohen, Eric *optometrist*
Donaldson, Sue Karen *nursing educator, researcher*
Gary, Tiffany L. *healthcare educator*
Henderson, Donald Ainslie *public health educator*
Hwang, Wenke *health services researcher*
Kaplan, Abner J. *social worker, public relations executive*
Knapp, David Allan *pharmaceutical educator, researcher*
Kumin, Libby Barbara *speech language pathologist, educator*
Larch, Sara Margaret *chief operating officer*
Maultsby, Marilyn D. *health science association administrator*
Metzger, Delores Virginia *social services professional*
Palley, Howard A. *social work educator*
Peterson, Ronald R. *health service administrator*
Pointer, Michelle Phillips *counselor, educator, consultant*
Ringel, Shoshana *psychotherapist, educator*
Sachs, Murray B. *audiologist, educator*
Steinwachs, Donald Michael *public health educator*

Bethesda
Cohen, Lois Ruth Kushner *research institute administrator*
Dyer, Doris Anne *nursing consultant*
Gabelnick, Henry Lewis *medical research director*
Gonzalez, Frank J. *health science association administrator*
Govern, Frank Stanley *health facility administrator, consultant, healthcare educator, writer*
Graeff, Alan S. *health association executive*
Greenwood, Naomi *social worker*
Hoyer, Mary Louise *social worker, educator*
Koslow, Stephen Hugh *science administrator, pharmacologist*
Malone, Winfred Francis *health scientist*
Martin, Malcolm A. *health facility administrator*
McCray, Alexa T. *health science association administrator, director*
McDonough, Thomas P. *health facility administrator*
Metzger, Henry *federal research institution administrator*
Monjan, Andrew Arthur *health science association administrator, educator*
Nakamura, Richard *mental health research professional*
Nee, Linda Elizabeth *social science analyst*
Polsby, Gail K. *psychotherapist*
Robinson, Sharon Beth *health science association administrator*
Shekar, Sam *health facility administrator*
Sher, Alan *health science association administrator, immunologist*
Stover, Ellen L. *health scientist, psychologist*
Talbot, Bernard *government medical research facility official, physician*
Taylor, Lindsay David, Jr., *health care executive*
Tracy, Thomas Miles *international health organization official*
Willoughby, Anne *health facility administrator, researcher, educator*
Wise, Allen F. *health care administrator*
Wolman, Sandra R. *health science association administrator, pathologist, geneticist*

Bowie
Speller-Brown, Barbara Jean *pediatric nurse practitioner*

Catonsville
Woolley, Alma Schelle *nursing educator*

Chillum
Malbon, Louise *nursing educator, hypnotherapist*

Clarksville
Hung, Mei-Jong Chow *social worker*

College Park
Morris, Joseph Anthony *retired health science association administrator*
Vanderveen, John E. *nutritionist, federal agency administrator*

Colora
Borland, Raymond M. *researcher*

Columbia
Harbin, Henry T. *health facility administrator*
Latkin, Carl *healthcare educator*
Pacifico, Joseph Carl *counselor*
Starks, Doris N. *nursing educator, administrator*
Wilson, Imogene R. *counselor*

Crofton
Boland, Gerald Lee *health facility administrator*

Frederick
Devineni, Mohan *pharmacist*
Kung, Hsiang-fu *health facility administrator*
Wickizer, Stephen Wesley *pharmacist*

Gaithersburg
Dowd, Carolyn Lay *social worker*
Peele, Roger *hospital administrator*
Quraishi, Mohammed Sayeed *retired health scientist, administrator*
Reynolds, Frank Miller *retired government administrator*

Glen Burnie
Barteet, Barbara Boyter *retired social worker*
Rubin, Amy Rochelle *speech-language pathologist*

Greenbelt
Tate, Antoinette Cooper *marriage and family therapist*

Hagerstown
Harrison, Lois Smith *hospital executive, educator*

Hanover
Feng, Lan *health analyst*
Rochdi, Myriam *pharmacist, researcher*

Hyattsville
Sondik, Edward J. *health science administrator*

La Plata
Core, Mary Carolyn W. Parsons *health facility administrator*

Lanham Seabrook
Pleasant-Jackson, Tonya *therapist, consultant*

Laurel
Landis, Donna Marie *nursing administrator, women's health nurse*

Leominster
Markham, John Thomas *social worker, educator*

Marriottsville
Strange, Donald Ernest *health care company executive*

Mitchellville
Chilman, Catherine Earles Street *social welfare educator, author*
Kendall, Katherine Anne *social worker*

Newburg
Mason, Christine Chapman *psychotherapist*

Ocean City
O'Hanlon, Richard Thomas *counseling educator*

Olney
Michael, Jerrold Mark *public health specialist, former university dean, educator*
Westerman, Rosemary Matzzie *nurse, administrator*

Potomac
Heller, Peggy Osna *psychotherapist, poetry therapist*
Leva, Neil Irwin *psychotherapist, hypnotherapist*
Wolman, Eric *health care consultant*

Rockville
Balbier, Thomas E., Jr., *health facility administrator*
Barbera, Thomas P. *health care company executive*
Barnette, Doris *public health services professional*
Clark, H. Westley *health facility administrator*
Duke, Elizabeth M. *health facility administrator*
Foss, Robert E. *health care company executive*
Goodman, Jesse *health facility administrator*
Greenberg, Jerrold Selig *health education educator*
Groban, Mark D. *health care company executive*
Howard, Lee Milton *international health consultant*
Kiger, F. Louise *nursing administrator*
Kopf, Randi *family and oncology nurse practitioner, lawyer*
Long, Cedric William *health research executive*
McCormick, Kathleen Ann Krym *geriatrics nurse, computer information specialist, federal agency administrator*
Moore, Melinda *public health physician*
O'Donnell, James Francis *retired health science administrator*
Parham-Hopson, Deborah *health administrator*
Rasmussen, Caren Nancy *hospital executive*
Scully, Martha Seebach *speech and language pathologist*
van Dyck, Peter Cuyler *health services administrator, pediatrics educator*

Severna Park
Daly, Charles Arthur *health services administrator*
Simonds, Valerie Deverse *healthcare educator*
Sundeen, Sandra Joan *mental health nurse*

Silver Spring
Kelley, Patrick W. *health science association administrator, preventive medicine physician*
Mashin, Jacqueline Ann Cook *medical sciences administrator, nursing administrator*
Nevans, Laurel S. *rehabilitation counselor*

Takoma Park
Stephenson, Patricia Ann *public health researcher, educator*

Towson
Evangeliou, Christos C. *researcher, educator*
Linz, James G. *health facility administrator*
Serpick, Arthur Allen *health facility administrator, physician*

MASSACHUSETTS

Acton
Buck-Moore, Joanne Rose *nursing administrator, educator*

Amherst
Breslin, Eileen Theresa *women's health nurse*

Attleboro
Bischoff, Marilyn Brett *clinical social worker, personal life coach*

Auburndale
Kibrick, Anne *retired nursing educator and university dean*

Bedford
Abbott, John Cope *forensic research administrator*
Herlihy, Maura Ann *psychology technician*
Taylor, Cora Hodge *social worker*

Belmont
Junger, Miguel Chapero *acoustics researcher*

Beverly
DeVore, Dale Paul *scientific research organization executive*

Boston
Attar, Eyal *physician assistant*
Bebo, Joseph Anthony *counselor, educator*
Berwick, Donald M. *administrator*
Blakeney, Barbara A. *public health service officer*
Blendon, Robert Jay *health policy educator*
Blumenthal, David *health policy expert*
Bonanno, Theresa M. *nursing administrator*
Cohen, Alan Barry *researcher, educator*
Drought, James Henry *healthcare business owner, exercise physiologist*
Dwyer, Johanna Todd *nutrition research scientist, clinical nutritionist, educator*
Fein, Rashi *health sciences educator*
Fowler, Floyd Jackson, Jr., *researcher*
Frank, Richard G. *health educator*
Gewirtz, Henry *health facility administrator, medical educator*
Gonyeau, Michael J. *pharmacy professor, internal medicine clinical pharmacist*
Kasper, Dennis Lee *health facility administrator, educator*
Levy, Paul Finanque *health facility administrator*
Liang, Matthew Heng *medical director*
Lowenstein, Arlene Jane *nursing educator, health facility administrator*
Mandell, James *health facility executive, urologist, educator*
Nicholson, Britain W. *health facility administrator, physician, educator*
Noble, Mildred M. *retired social worker*
Portney, Leslie Gross *physical therapist*
Powers, Francis J. *physical therapist*
Reinherz, Helen Zarsky *researcher, social services educator*
Riendeau, Theresa Frances *rehabilitation nurse*
Sapirie, Stephen Alan *public health administrator*
Slavin, Peter L. *hospital administrator*
Smith, F. Curtis *health facility executive*
Stevens, Joyce West *social worker, educator, researcher*
Ullian, Elaine S. *health facility administrator*
Weinstein, Milton Charles *health policy educator, decision scientist*
Woods, Cathi L. *human services administrator*

Boylston
Larson, Roland Elmer *healthcare executive*

Bridgewater
Cavanaugh, Deborah Jean *mental health services professional*

Brockton
Lawrence, Janice Elaine *psychiatric and mental health nurse*

Cambridge
Botkin, James W. *leadership and life coach*
Burns, Virginia *social worker*
Clifton, Anne Rutenber *psychotherapist, educator*
Narayanamurti, Venkatesh *research administrator*
Quane, James *human services administrator*

Canton
Bihldorff, John Pearson *hospital director*
Sawtelle, Carl S. *psychiatric social worker*

Charlestown
Tansey, Robert Paul, Sr., *pharmaceutical chemist*

Chestnut Hill
Burgess, Ann Wolbert *nursing educator*
Hawkins, Joellen Margaret Beck *nursing educator*
Munro, Barbara Hazard *nursing educator, dean, researcher*

Chicopee
Dame, Catherine Elaine *acupuncturist*

Concord
Domar, Carola Rosenthal *social worker*

Fairhaven
Merolla, Michele Edward *chiropractor, broadcaster*

Framingham
Austin, Sandra Ikenberry *nursing educator, consultant*
Bilsky, Edward Gerald *clinical social worker*
Vermette, Raymond Edward *clinical laboratories administrator*

Georgetown
Ramseur, T. Michael *social worker*

Greenfield
Curtiss, Carol Perry *healthcare consultant*

Haverhill
Walker, Robert Ross *social worker*

Hyannis
Nicholson, Ellen Ellis *clinical social worker*

Lexington
Bombardieri, Merle Ann *psychotherapist*
Densmore, Ann *speech pathology/audiology services professional, audiologist, writer*
Otten, Jeffrey *former hospital administrator*

Lowell
Sweed, Art *social worker, adult education educator*

Ludlow
Budnick, Thomas Peter *social worker*

Lynn
Donovan, Elaine F. *social worker*

Malden
Kemp, Loretta Christine *human services administrator*

Marion
McPartland, Patricia Ann *health educator and administrator*

Monterey
Frye-Moquin, Marsha Marie *social worker*

Nantucket
Bartlett, Cheryl Ann *public health service administrator*

Natick
Lebowitz, Charlotte Meyersohn *social worker*

Needham
Ryan, Una Scully *health sciences professional, medical educator*

New Bedford
LaPorte, Adrienne Aroxie *nursing administrator*

Newton
Pill, Cynthia Joan *social worker*

North Easton
Paul, Donald W. *audiologist*

Rockland
LaFerney, Michael C. *mental health nurse, mental health counselor*

Salem
Everitt, Amy Lynn *healthcare educator*
Mendoza, Laurie Parker *social worker*

Shrewsbury
Falter, Robert Gary *long-term care administrator, educator*

Southbridge
Mangion, Richard Michael *health care executive*

Sterling
Garafalo, Lynne Mary *audiologist, speech and language pathologist*

Swampscott
Smith, Carl Dean, Jr., *rehabilitation services professional, young adult advocate*

Taunton
Anderson, Peter D. *pharmacist, forensic scientist*

Tiverton
Brock, Dawn Marie *counselor*

Waltham
Mitchell, Janet Brew *health services researcher*
Roosevelt, James, Jr., *health plan executive, lawyer*
Wallack, Stanley S. *healthcare administrator*

Watertown
Pellegrom, Daniel Earl *international health and development executive*

Wellesley
Montague, Joel Gedney *public health officer*

West Roxbury
Cohen, Carolyn Alta *healthcare educator*

Weymouth
Parks, Kristin M. *pediatrics health nurse, educator and practitioner*

Woods Hole
Speck, William T. *former physician, health facility administrator*

Worcester
Joshi, Harihar S. *medical laboratory executive*
Ravnikar, Veronika A. *reproductive endocrinologist, educator*
Snyder, L. Michael *hospital administrator*

Yarmouth Port
Phelps, Judson Hewett *health facility administrator, marketing professional*
Terrill, Robert Carl *hospital administrator*

MICHIGAN

Allen Park
Kirby, Dorothy Manville *social worker*

Ann Arbor
Bashshur, Rashid L. *health facility administrator, educator*
Clark, Noreen Morrison *behavioral science educator, researcher*
El-Kattan, Ayman Fawzi *pharmacist, researcher*
Griffith, John Randall *health services administrator, educator*
Ketefian, Shaké *nursing educator*
McLaughlin, Catherine G. *healthcare educator*
Meezan, William Alan *social work educator, consultant*
Mosberg, Henry I. *pharmacist, educator, medicinal chemist*
Reame, Nancy *nursing educator*
Romani, John Henry *health administration educator*
Rupp, Ralph Russell *audiologist, educator, author*
Samons, Sandra Lea *psychotherapist*
Warner, Kenneth E. *public health educator, consultant*

Charlotte
Herrick, Kathleen Magara *social worker*

Clarkston
Pieknik, Rebecca Anne *technologist, educator*

Dearborn
Barnhart, Mary C. *health facility administrator*
Beauford, Sandra *registered nurse, data processing executive*

Detroit
Abramson, Hanley Norman *pharmacy educator*
Alvarez, Ann Rosegrant *social worker, educator, dean*
Davis, Catherine Diane *health science association administrator*
Duggan, Michael E. *health facility administrator*
Jacox, Ada Kathryn *nurse, educator*
Johnson, Kalimah *social worker, consultant*
Krouse, Helene June *nursing educator*
Moses, Gregory H., Jr., *health services administrator*
Redman, Barbara Klug *nursing educator*
Talley, Susan Ann *physical therapist, educator*
Velick, Stephen H. *medical facility administrator*
Warden, Gail Lee *health care executive*

Dexter
Hanamey, Rosemary T. *nursing educator*

East Lansing
Schemmel, Rachel Anne *food science and human nutrition educator, researcher*

Farmington
Burns, Sister Elizabeth Mary *hospital administrator*

Farmington Hills
Bauser, Nancy *social worker*
Rinker, Marianne Marie *rehabilitation nurse*

Flint
Williams, Veronica Myres *psychotherapist, social worker*

Franklin
Sax, Mary Randolph *speech and language pathologist*

Grand Haven
Disbrow, Sidney Arden, Jr., *chiropractor*

Grand Ledge
Evert, Sandra Florence (Sandra Wheeler) *medical/surgical nurse*

Grand Rapids
Brent, Helen Teressa *school nurse*
Chase, Sandra Lee *clinical pharmacist, consultant*

Grosse Pointe
Marshall, Douglas William *medical administrator, educator*

Grosse Pointe Park
Knapp, Mildred Florence *retired social worker*

Hastings
Adrounie, V. Harry *public health administrator, scientist, educator, environmentalist*

Holland
Franken, Darrell *counselor, writer, publisher*

Ionia
Ulmer, Evonne Gail *health science facility executive*

Kalamazoo
Bennett, Arlie Joyce *clinical social worker emeritus*
Fredericks, Sharon Kay *nurse's aide*
Lander, Joyce Ann *nursing educator, medical/surgical nurse*
Lawson, Gary D. *audiology educator*
Ortiz-Button, Olga *social worker*

Leland
Hamelin, Paul Robert *pharmacist, pharmaceutical executive, consultant*

Lincoln Park
Russell, Harriet Shaw *social worker*

Livonia
Gepford, Barbara Beebe *retired nutrition educator*

Marquette
Sherony, Cheryl Anne *dietician*

Novi
Pelham, Judith *health system administrator*

Pinckney
McNamara, Ann Dowd *medical technologist*

Redford
Aubertin, Madeline Katherine *retired nursing educator, medical/surgical nurse, mental health services professional*

Rochester Hills
Romero, Josefino Tabernilla *nurse anesthetist*

Royal Oak
Matzick, Kenneth John *hospital administrator*

Southfield
Martin, Marcella Edric *retired community health nurse*
Sedler, Rozanne Friedlander *social worker, educator*
Tripp, James E. *psychotherapist, educator*

Traverse City
VanderKolk, Mary DeDecker *nursing educator*

Troy
Arking, Lucille Musser *nurse, epidemiologist*
Potts, Anthony Vincent *optometrist, orthokeratologist*
White, James, Jr., *psychiatric, mental health nurse, consultant*

West Bloomfield
Barr, Martin *health care and higher education administrator*
Myers, Kenneth Ellis *hospital administrator*

Westland
Coates, Dianne Kay *social worker*

Ypsilanti
Brown-Chappell, Betty L. *social worker, educator*

MINNESOTA

Bemidji
Christenson, Eileen Esther *geriatrics nurse*
Martinson, Ida Marie *nursing educator, physiologist, medical/surgical nurse*

Bloomington
Nichols, Donna Mardell *nurse anesthetist*

Circle Pines
Davis, Richard Carlton *rehabilitation services administrator*

Duluth
Salmela, Lynn Marie *clinical nurse specialist*

Eagan
Wendler, M. Cecilia *nursing educator*

Eden Prairie
Harmon, Robert Gerald *health company executive, educator*

Elysian
Thayer, Edna Louise *medical facility and nursing administrator*

Golden Valley
Dahl, Gerald LuVern *psychotherapist, educator*

Mankato
Bell, Sue Ellen *research analyst, administrator, nursing educator*

Minneapolis
DeNavaez, Denny *health facility administrator*
Farr, Leonard Alfred *hospital administrator*
Feldman, Nancy Jane *health organization executive*
Gerdner, Linda Ann *nursing researcher, educator*
Grant, David James William *pharmacy educator*
Kralewski, John Edward *health service research educator*
Murphy, Edrie Lee *laboratory administrator*
Sprenger, Gordon M. *hospital administrator*
Steen-Hinderlie, Diane Evelyn *social worker, musician*
Suryanarayanan, Raj Gopalan *pharmacist, researcher, consultant, educator*
Toscano, James Vincent *medical institute administration*

Minnetonka
Colby, Ronald B. *health facility administrator*
Coyle, Michael J. *medical administrator*
Hornfeldt, Carl S. *pharmacist, toxicologist*
Pearson, Kevin *health facility administrator*
Penshorn, John S. *health facility administrator*
Quam, Lois *healthcare company executive*
Sheehy, Robert J. *health facility administrator*

New Brighton
Appel, William Frank *pharmacist*
Heston, Renate *nursing administrator*

Palisade
Kilde, Sandra Jean *nurse, anesthetist, educator, consultant*

Robbinsdale
Anderson, Scott Robbins *hospital administrator*

Rochester
Frusti, Doreen Kaye *nursing administrator*
Gervais, Sister Generose *hospital consultant*
Goodman, Julie *nurse midwife*
McConnell, Joseph Paul *lab administrator, researcher, biochemist, consultant*
Prendergast, Franklyn G. *health facility administrator, medical educator*
Williams, Arthur Ross *health service and public administrator*

Saint Louis Park
Croll, Jillian Kathleen *dietician, researcher*

Saint Paul
Abrams, Laura Sue *social worker, educator*
Barry, Anne M. *public health officer*
Braun, Richard J. *lab administrator*
Gilgun, Jane Frances *social work educator*
Hollister, Clifton David *social work educator*
Owens, B. Mitchell *lab administrator*
Schoonover, James A. *lab administrator*
Shepherd, Terry L. *health facility administrator*
Simmons, Lawrence William *healthcare company executive*
Wiersma, Kevin *lab administrator*

MISSISSIPPI

Amory
Walden, Mary L *nurse, educator*

Brandon
Baltz, Richard Jay *health care company executive*

Centreville
Nelson, Janie Rish *hospital executive*

Hattiesburg
Saucier Lundy, Karen *nursing educator*

Jackson
Malloy, James Matthew *health management executive, healthcare consultant*
Roberts, Kristie *researcher*
Tchounwou, Paul Bernard *environmental health specialist, toxicologist, educator*
Thornton, Larry Lee *psychotherapist, author, educator, minister*

Mississippi State
Or, Ka Lun *research assistant*

Ocean Springs
Lee, Kathleen Mary *administration and nursing executive*

Tupelo
Zurawski, Jeanette *rehabilitation services professional*

MISSOURI

Arcadia
Davis, Jo *nurse, writer, professional speaker, small business owner, photographer*

Cape Girardeau
MohdZain, A. Zaidy *counselor, educator*

Chesterfield
Ashworth, Ronald Broughton *health facility executive, accountant*

Columbia
Dellande, William Drew *optometrist*
Galambos, Colleen Marie *social worker, educator, director*
Hensley, Elizabeth Catherine *nutritionist, educator*
Stewart, Bobby Gene *laboratory director*

Crystal City
Sita, Michael John *pharmacist, educator*

Independence
Sturges, Sidney James *pharmacist, educator, investment and development company executive*

Jefferson City
Winegar, Anthony C. *health care worker*

Kansas City
Begleiter, Michael L. *genetic counselor*
DeParle, Nancy-Ann Min *former federal agency administrator, lawyer*
Devanny, E.H. (Trace) III *healthcare informatics executive*
Eddy, Charles Alan *chiropractor*
Lannigan, James William *voluntary service officer*
McKelvey, John Clifford *mental health services professional*
Piepho, Robert Walter *pharmacy educator, researcher*

Kirbyville
Burch, Lori Ann *obstetrics nurse*

Kirksville
Schwend, Michael T. *hospital administrator*

Liberty
Kersten, Joanne Wilkerson *nursing educator*
Samuel, Robert Thompson *optometrist*

Louisiana
Warner, Eleanore Joyce *nurse, educator*

Macon
Maddox, Wilma *health facility administrator*

Maryland Heights
Cacchione, Patrick Joseph *health association executive*

O Fallon
Gross, Stanley Merhl *chiropractor*
Jamison, Darlene *geriatrics nurse, artist*

Saint Louis
Baum, M(ary) Carolyn *occupational therapist*
Borders, John Gillespie *psychotherapist, former corporate executive*
Chignoli, C(elso) William *health care center administrator*
Ezenwa, Josephine Nwabuoku *social worker*
Farrell, John Timothy *former hospital administrator*
Fitch, Rachel Farr *health policy analyst*
Foy, Betsy D. *health facility administrator, educator*
French, Douglas Dewitt *medical facility administrator*
Friedberg, Michael A. *healthcare executive*
Grawitch, Matthew J. *educator, consultant*
Hancock, Camilla Ann *pharmacist*
Molloff, Florence Jeanine *speech and language therapist*
Ozawa, Martha Naoko *social work educator*
Place, Michael D. *health association administrator*
Pryor, David Bram *health science association administrator*
Ryan, Sister Mary Jean *health facility executive*
Schoenhard, William Charles, Jr., *health care executive*
Smith, Gladys Ann *counselor, military medic*
Stencer, Mark Joseph *healthcare administrator, consultant*
Stretch, John Joseph *social work educator, management and evaluation consultant*

Sedalia
Gingerich, Naomi R. *emergency room nurse*

Springfield
Catapang, Gerald Porciungula *physical therapist*

West Plains
Bakken, Jennifer Susan *community health nurse, writer*

MONTANA

Helena
Wickham, Dianne *nursing administrator*

Poplar
Gabrielson, Shirley Gail *nurse*

Victor
Davenport, Anne Marilyn *dietician*

NEBRASKA

Lincoln
Drullinger, Leona Pearl Blair *obstetrics nurse*
Steffan, Judy Mae *medical/surgical nurse*

Omaha
Baldwin, Jeffrey Nathan *pharmacy educator*
Corbin, David E. *health education and public health educator*
Graves, Maureen Ann *self esteem and spirituality consultant*
Hachten, Richard Arthur, II, *health system executive*
Leininger, Madeleine Monica *nursing educator, consultant, anthropologist, theorist, editor, writer*

NEVADA

Carson City
Hull, Dennis Jacques *counselor*

Henderson
Van Noy, Terry Willard *health care executive*

Las Vegas
Close, Jack Dean, Sr., *physical therapist*
Duncombe, Patricia Warburton *retired social worker*
Francis, Timothy Duane *chiropractor*
Gilchrist, Ann Roundey *hospice nurse*
MacDonald, Erin E. *healthcare company executive*
Marlon, Anthony M. *healthcare company executive, cardiologist*
Michel, Mary Ann Kedzuf *nursing educator*

Reno
Bramwell, Marvel Lynnette *mental health nurse, social worker*
Graham, Denis David *marriage and family therapist, educational consultant*
Middlebrooks, Deloris Jeanette *nurse, educator*
Pinson, Larry Lee *pharmacist*

NEW HAMPSHIRE

Amherst
Buff, Margaret Anne *psychiatric nurse practitioner*

Bedford
Demers, Nancy Kae *nursing educator*

Campton
Scrimshaw, Nevin Stewart *physician, nutrition and health educator*

Concord
Boisseau, Paul G. *pharmacist, executive secretary*
MacKay, James Robert *psychiatric social worker, mayor, educator, state legislator*
White, Jeffrey George *healthcare consultant*

Hanover
Burgess, Robert Sargent *retired human services consultant*
Sporn, Michael Benjamin *cancer researcher*

Lebanon
Thompson, Pamela A. *nurse administrator*
Varnum, James William *hospital administrator*

Manchester
Bolduc, Diane Eileen Mary Buchholz *psychotherapist*

Nashua
Descoteaux, Carol J. *health facility administrator*

Plymouth
Gorin, Stephen H. *social worker, educator*

Sandown
Densen, Paul Maximillian *former health administrator, educator*

Sunapee
Springer, John Kelley *hospital administrator*

NEW JERSEY

Atlantic Highlands
Royce, Paul Chadwick *medical administrator*

Basking Ridge
McNamee, James M. *lab administrator*

Bedminster
Delehanty, Martha *human services administrator*

Belle Mead
Sarle, Charles Richard *health facility executive*

Belvidere
Walsh, John Alfred *retired social worker*

Branchville
Johanson, Gregory John *psychotherapy trainer, minister*

Bridgewater
Weingast, Marvin *laboratory executive*

Brigantine
Holl, James Andrew *prehospital care administrator*

Budd Lake
Davis-Kalugin, Dorinne Sue *audiologist*

Burlington
Rowlette, Henry Allen, Jr., *social worker, counseling psychologist*

Chatham
Murphy, Joseph James *chiropractic physician*

Cherry Hill
Berman, Steven Eric *audiologist*
Betchen, Stephen Jay *marital, family and sex therapist*
Grado-Wolynies, Evelyn (Evelyn Wolynies) *clinical nurse specialist, educator*
Israelsky, Roberta Schwartz *speech pathologist, audiologist*

Deptford
Johns, Michael Douglas *health care corporate executive, writer, former federal government offical*

East Hanover
Purkayastha, Das D. *biostatistician*

East Orange
Brown, Rosa Elizabeth *social worker, writer*
Hudson-Zonn, Eliza *nurse, psychologist*

Edison
Blumengold, Jeffrey Gene *health facility administrator*
Islam, Naushad S. *pharmacist, government agency administrator*
Lunt, Alan Nicholas *psychiatric rehabilitation counselor*

Elmwood Park
Grodman, Marc D. *lab administrator, physician, medical educator*

Erial
Browna, Jo McIntyre *nurse*

Florham Park
Oths, Richard Philip *health systems administrator*

Franklin Lakes
Ludwig, Edward J. *medical technology company executive*

Green Brook
Spoeri, Randall Keith *healthcare company executive*

Hackensack
Dent, Thompson S. *health care organization executive*
Ferguson, John Patrick *health facility administrator*
Imus, Deirdre *health facility administrator*

Hamilton Square
Ridolfi, Dorothy Porter Boulden *nurse, real estate broker*

Highland Park
Grady, Joyce (Marian Joyce Grady) *psychotherapist, consultant*

Hillsborough
Weinman, Steven Alan *emergency nurse, researcher, writer, educator, consultant*

Hoboken
Sniffen, Michael Joseph *hospital administrator*

Kenilworth
Yang, Tsong-Toh (T.T.) *pharmacist, researcher*

Kinnelon
Preston, Andrew Joseph *pharmacist, drug company executive*

Livingston
Adelsberg, Harvey *hospital administrator*

Long Branch
Vandebunte, Eileen J. *health facility administrator*

Madison
Ellenbogen, Leon *nutritionist, pharmaceutical company executive*

Manalapan
Garger, Morris William *pharmacist, historian, educator*

Manasquan
Kelman, Marybeth *health care consultant, health policy analyst*

Marlton
Stack, Robert Timothy *health facility administrator*

Montville
Leeson, Lewis Joseph *pharmacist, researcher*

Moorestown
McDaniel, Joanava B. *medical/surgical nurse*

Morganville
Lechtanski, Cheryl Lee *chiropractor*

Morris Plains
Inez, Donna Lee *hospital administrator*

Murray Hill
Case, Christopher *technologist*

New Brunswick
Barone, Dean *physician assistant, small business owner*
Brilliant, Eleanor Luria *social work educator*
Greenberg, Michael Richard *urban studies and community health educator*
Momah, Ethel Chukwuekwe *women's health nurse*

Newark
Mercado, Lillian Amensina *counselor*

Savage, Joseph George *hospital administrator*

Newfield
Dreher, Jr., Frank H. *retired optician*

North Haledon
McGill, Kenneth, Jr., *mental health services professional*

Nutley
Andreula-Ortiz, Jo-Ellen *pharmaceutical company administrator, cosmetologist*
Podosheva, Olga *lab administrator, researcher*

Parsippany
Gannon, Peter M. *healthcare executive*

Paterson
Daniels, Cheryl Lynn *pediatrics nurse, case manager*
McEvoy, Lorraine Katherine *oncology nurse*

Pequannock
Blanchard, Kevin Joseph *social worker*

Piscataway
Kipen, Howard Matthew *environmental and occupational health educator*

Plainfield
Holdorf, Harry Hulbert *health services administrator*
Mattson, Joy Louise *oncological nurse*

Plainsboro
Dezii, Christopher Michael *medical researcher, organ transplant nurse*

Pleasantville
Etim, Terris *geriatrics nurse*

Princeton
Bergman, Richard Isaac *health information company executive*
Gu, Henry Hongsheng *pharmacist, researcher*
Kelly, Paul J. *lab administrator, physician, researcher*
Logue, Judith Felton *psychoanalyst, educator, professional coach*
Pechura, Constance Mary *foundation official*
Spicer, Michael E. *lab administrator*

Red Bank
Brown, Valerie Anne *psychiatric social worker, educator*
Gutentag, Patricia Richmand *social worker, family counselor, occupational therapist*

Ridgewood
Arnt, Georgia Lee *psychiatric social worker*
Clements, Lynne Fleming *marriage and family therapist, application developer*

Roseland
Malafronte, Donald *health executive*

Saddle Brook
Clifton, Nelida *social worker*

South Orange
Hansell, Phyllis Shanley *nursing educator, administrator, researcher, consultant*
Hecht, Marion B. *mental health counselor, mental health therapist*
Wright, Barbara Wincklhofer *nursing educator*

Teaneck
Alperin, Richard Martin *social worker, psychoanalyst*

Teterboro
Freeman, Kenneth W. *laboratory executive*
Hagemann, Robert A. *health facility administrator*
Mohapatra, Surya N. *laboratory executive*
Prevoznik, Michael E. *health facility administrator*

Trenton
Miller, Velvet G. *healthcare administrator*
Terrill, Thomas Edward *health facility administrator*

Union
Nesoff, Irwin *social work educator, management consultant*

Warren
Kozberg, Donna Walters *rehabilitation administration executive*

West Caldwell
Schiff, Robert *healthcare consulting company executive*

West New York
Kelly, Lucie Stirm Young *nursing educator*
Schmidt, Nancy Anne *psychotherapist*

West Orange
Bornstein, Lester Milton *retired health facility administrator*
De Lisa, Joel Alan *rehabilitation physician, rehabilitation research executive*

Willingboro
Green, Riva Lee *social worker, minister*

NEW MEXICO

Albuquerque
Burrows, Kathy S. *health facility administrator*
Gordon, Larry Jean *environmental health educator*
Gupchup, Gireesh Vijay *pharmacist, educator*
Hancock, Don Ray *researcher*
Lowrance, Muriel Edwards *program specialist*
Sanderlin, Terry Keith *counselor*
Solomon, Arthur Charles *pharmacist*
White, Jennifer Phelps *counselor*

Clovis
Rehorn, Lois M(arie) (Lois Marie Smith) *nursing administrator*

Farmington
Thompson, Joseph T., Jr., *health facility administrator*

Las Cruces
Adaime, Hamed Nazin *counselor*
Welsh, Mary McAnaw *family mediator, educator*

Mountainair
Woodruff, Joan Leslie *occupational therapist, counselor*

Santa Fe
Feist-Fite, Bernadette *international health education consultant*
Hyde, Pamela Suzon *housing and human services administrator*
Melnick, Alice Jean (AJ Melnick) *counselor*
Pulitzer, Roslyn Kitty *social worker, psychotherapist*
Ruybalid, Louis Arthur *social worker, community development consultant*

Truth Or Consequences
Rush, Domenica Marie *health facilities administrator*

NEW YORK

Albany
DeNuzzo, Rinaldo Vincent *pharmacy educator*
Elwell, Rowland John *pharmacist, researcher*
Kelley, Sister Helen *health facility executive*
Reaulo, Arthur Robert *mental health specialist, advocate*
Travers, W. Lawrence *healthcare executive*

Ardsley
Mohl, Allan S. *social worker*

Astoria
Aquino, Robert Joseph *health care executive, consultant*
Matheson, Linda *retired social worker*

Bedford
Margolin, Carl M. *psychotherapist*

Binghamton
Collins, Mary Shaffer *community nursing educator*

Bronx
Clary, Roy *hospital administration executive*
Cubeñas, José Antonio *social worker, consultant*
Horan, Gary S. *healthcare executive*
Iezza, Anita Kay *physician assistant*
Yadeka, Theophilus Adeniyi *hospital administrator*

Brooklyn
Abraham, Teena *pharmacist, educator*
Baker, Kristina Marie *adult nurse practitioner*
Brenner, Beryl H. *arts therapist*
Browne, Ruth *health science association administrator*
Cammarata, Jerry Frank *hospital administrator, speech pathology/audiology services professional*
Donovan, Rita R. *nurse anesthetist, trauma and critical care nurse, educator*
Eisenberg, Karen Sue Byer *nurse*
Eliasi, Jennifer Rebecca *dietician, consultant*
Graham, RosaLind Carlies *nursing educator*
Gross, Stephen Mark *pharmacist, academic dean*
Gustin, Mark Douglas *health facility administrator*
Harris, Fred *prosthetist*
Heisler, Norma Boodman *psychotherapist*
Logan, Janet Artisam *mental health nurse*
Morales, Jose *psychotherapist, writer*
Murillo-Rohde, Ildaura Maria *marriage and family therapist, consultant, educator, dean*
Peters, Mercedes *psychoanalyst*
Phillips, Gretchen *social worker*
Pine, Bessie Miriam *social worker, editor, columnist*
Samuel, Carren C. *hospital administrator*
Stellman, Jeanne Mager *public health educator*
Twining, Lynne Dianne *clinical psychologist and psychoanalyst, professional society administrator, educator, writer*
Wrotten, Marylean *medical coordinator, counselor*

Buffalo
Blane, Howard Thomas *research institute administrator*
Catalano, James Anthony *social worker, consultant*
Hoffman, Faith Louise *social worker*
Jusko, William Joseph *pharmaceutical scientist, educator*
McGuire, William Dennis *health facility administrator*
Perry, J. Warren *health sciences educator, administrator*
Schentag, Jerome John *pharmacy educator*

Canandaigua
Chappelle, Lou Jo *physical therapist assistant*

Cedarhurst
Lipsky, Linda Ethel *health facility administrator*

Chappaqua
Boal, Lyndall Elizabeth *social worker*

Clayton
Blassingame, Ronald Jay *social worker*

Clinton Corners
McDermott, Patricia Ann *nursing administrator*

Eastchester
Giuliano, Robert Paul *pharmacist*

Elmira
Wright, Linda Ellen *nursing educator*

Farmingdale
Vainder, Melanie *speech pathology/audiology services professional, educator*

Garden City
Lederer, Susan Hendler *speech/language pathologist, educator*
Nicklin, George Leslie, Jr., *psychoanalyst, educator, physician, author*
Scollard, Patrick John *hospital executive*

Glen Oaks
Miller, Rachel L. *social worker, consultant*

Glens Falls
Vitvitsky, Jack *physician assistant*

Grand Central
Freedman, Mollie Cecille *researcher*

Great Neck
Feldman, Gary Marc *nutritionist, consultant*
Gallagher, John S. T. (Jack Gallagher) *health facility executive*
Mayer, Susan Lee *nurse, educator*

Greenfield Center
Templin, John Leon, Jr., *healthcare consulting executive*

Hastings On Hudson
Stillman, Jeanne Betsock *public health administrator, consultant*

Hempstead
Ades, Janet *social worker*

Huntington
Sparacino, Philip William *psychotherapist, consultant*

Huntington Station
Williams, Una Joyce *psychiatric social worker*

Hurley
Petruski, Jennifer Andrea *speech and language pathologist*

Hyde Park
Rider, Kathleen Mary *dietician*

Ithaca
Cawley, John Horan *health policy educator*
Habicht, Jean Pierre *public health educator*
Mueller, Betty Jeanne *social work educator*

Jackson Heights
Chang, Lydia Liang-Hwa *social worker, educator*
Lippman, Susan E. *social worker, psychotherapist, educator*
Macia, Nanette *social worker, secondary school educator*

Jamaica
Morrill, Joyce Marie *social worker, educator*

Jamestown
DJang, Arthur H.K. *physician, scientist*

Johnstown
Gibson, Jahnn Hansen Swanker *mental health nurse*

Lincolndale
Morton, Mary Madeline *family nurse practitioner*

Medford
Brower, Robert Charles *rehabilitation counselor, small business owner*

Melville
Collura, John J. *health care services company executive*
Forsyth, Stephen A. *lab administrator, venture capitalist*
Gothard, Paul *lab administrator*

Middletown
Ojeda, Joseph A. *psychotherapist*
Radeboldt-Daly, Karen Elaine *medical nurse*

Mineola
Christiansen, Colleen M. *physician assistant*

Mount Vernon
Coombes, David Harrison *health facility administrator*

New Paltz
Pine, Patricia Palmer *aging services administrator*

New York
Aaronson, Stuart A. *health facility administrator, medical educator*
Agard, Emma Estornel *psychotherapist*
Bailey, Darlyne *social worker, educator*
Barnum, Barbara Stevens *writer, retired nursing educator*
Barrett, Elizabeth Ann Manhart *nursing educator, psychotherapist, consultant*
Batavia, Mitchell *physical therapist, educator*
Bendor, Susan Julia *social worker, educator*
Berman, Michael Allen *hospital administrator, pediatric cardiologist*
Billig, Robert Emanuel *psychiatric social worker*
Blau, John *retired social worker*
Blum, Diane S. *human services manager*
Boufford, Jo Ivey *health and human services administrator*
Breslow, Jan Leslie *scientist, educator, physician*
Bressman, Susan Berliner *health facility administrator*
Brownell, Patricia Jane *social worker, educator*
Buehler, Thomas *psychotherapist, expressive therapist, artist*
Campbell, David James *hospital administrator*
Cardinale, Kathleen Carmel *retired medical center administrator*
Carver, John H. *medical science organization administrator*
Chu, Benjamin K. *hospital administrator*
Connolly, John Joseph *healthcare company executive*
Corcoran, Joseph P. *health facility administrator*
Corwin, Steven *hospital administrator*
Costa, Max *health facility administrator, pharmacology educator, environmental medicine educator*
Cox, Carole Beth *social worker, educator*
Daines, Richard *health services executive*
Daniel, Samuel J. *hospital administrator, medical educator*
Dinerman, Miriam *social work educator*
Dorn, Sue Bricker *consultant, retired hospital administrator*
Drayer, Burton Paul *hospital administrator, neuroadiologist*
Ethan, Carol Baehr *psychotherapist*
Feldman, Ronald Arthur *social work educator, researcher*
Fenchel, Gerd Herman *psychoanalyst*
Fink, Matthew E. *health facility executive, educator*
Flannelly, Laura T. *mental health nurse, nursing educator, researcher*
Flores, Clemente, Jr., *counselor, educator*
Flynn, Laurie M. *social worker*
Giordano, Bill A. *psychotherapist*
Goff, Robert Edward *health care executive*
Gold, William Elliott *health care management consultant, educator*
Gorevic, Jason N. *health science association administrator*
Gottdiener, William Henry *psychotherapist, psychologist*
Green, Barbara Strawn *psychotherapist*
Haseley, Dennis *psychoanalyst, writer*
Hoskins, Carol Noll *nursing educator, researcher*
Isaacs, Richard B. *investigative and protective services professional*
Kahn, Charlotte *psychotherapist, marriage and family therapist*
Kalayjian, Anie *psychotherapist, nurse, educator, consultant*
Kamerman, Sheila Brody *educator, social worker*
Kapoor, Neera *optometrist, vision scientist*
Kassel, Catherine M. *community, maternal, and women's health nurse, consultant*
Kent, Deborah Warren *hypnotherapist, consultant, lecturer*
Labovitz, Deborah Rose Rubin *occupational therapist, educator*
Lawrence, Lauren *author, dreams expert, psychoanalytical theorist, psychoanalyst*
Leone, Rose Marie *psychotherapist*
Levitt, Harry *speech and hearing scientist*
Lopez, Pedro Felipe *social worker, educator, playwright, writer*
Madsen, Libbe Hurvitz *clinical social worker*
Matseoane, Carol *social worker*
Mattson, Marlin Roy Albin *health facility administrator, psychiatry educator*
Mayeux, Richard *hospital administrator, neurologist*
McGonagle, Duncan Francis *mental health nurse, substance abuse counselor*
Mulvihill, William J. *former health science association administrator*
Mundinger, Mary O'Neil *nursing educator*
Murphy, Stacia *health service association executive*
Naegle, Madeline Anne *mental health nurse, educator*
Neubauer, Peter Bela *psychoanalyst*
O'Connor Vos, Lynn *healthcare group executive*
O'Neill McGivern, Diane *nursing educator, educator*
Pakter, Jean *maternal and child health consultant*
Patterson Dehn, Cathleen *pediatrics administrator*
Paulson, Loretta Nancy *psychoanalyst*
Pennisi, Liz *women's health nurse*
Perez, Carlos F. *health facility administrator*
Piombino, Nicholas *psychotherapist*
Pyle, Rolanda *social worker*
Rackow, Eric C. *health facility administrator*
Radwin, Jerome *public health service officer*
Resnick, Rhoda Brodowsky *psychotherapist*
Reynolds, John R. *hospital executive*
Rhodes, Dorothy Lee *public health service officer*
Riggin, Donald L. *health science association administrator*
Roglieri, John Louis *health facility administrator*
Rosenthal, Donna Myra *social worker*
Saffar, Jean-Marc *healthcare consultant*
Scherman, Susan Louise *nurse*
Scott, Mimi Koblenz *psychotherapist, actress, publicist, journalist, playwright*
Shohen, Saundra Anne *health care communications and public relations executive*
Sigety, Cornelius Edward *family office manager*
Silber, Steven A. *lab administrator, physician*
Simmons, Richard Milton Teagle *physical fitness specialist, television personality*
Solomon, Libertina *pharmacist, educator*
Stark, Robin Caryl *psychotherapist, consultant*
Stein, Zena A. *health facility administrator, psychiatry educator*
Stich, June Jeacoma *psychotherapist*
Storm, Jackie *nutritionist, health education specialist*
Trent, Charles H., Jr., *social work educator*
Van Etten, Peter Walbridge *foundation executive*
Varmus, Harold Eliot *former health science association administrator, research scientist, health facility executive, educator*
Victor, Jack *former health association executive, consultant*
Vladeck, Bruce Charney *health services administrator, policy educator*
Watson, Anthony L. *health facility executive*
Weiss, Phillip W. *social worker, writer*

Newburgh
Weintraub, Arthur E. *health service association executive*

Norwich
Garzione, John Edward *physical therapist*

Ossining
Robinson, Karen Vajda *dietician*

Ozone Park
Catalfo, Betty Marie *health service executive, nutritionist*

Painted Post
Ogden, Anita Bushey *nursing educator*

Pittsford
Taub, Aaron Myron *retired healthcare administrator, consultant*

Pomona
Downey, Bruce L. *medical company executive, lawyer*

Poughkeepsie
Heller, Mary Bernita *psychotherapist*
Henley, Richard James *health facility administrator*

Queens
Geffner, Donna Sue *speech pathology/audiology services professional, audiologist, educator*

Queens Village
Maroney-Davoren, Danette Edna *pharmacist, writer, publishing executive*

Rochester
Agrawal, Govind Prasad *optics educator*
Aydelotte, Myrtle Kitchell *retired nursing administrator*
Braley, Oleta Pearl *home health care provider*
Chiverton, Patricia Ann *nursing educator, dean*
De Mattia, Marlene J. *psychotherapist*
Hoffman, Nancy Yanes *medical author, patient educator, writer, pharmaceutical editor, health care consultant, lecturer*
Hurlbut, Robert Harold *health care services executive*
Huston, Samuel Richard *health facility executive*
King, Kathleen Bernadette *nursing educator*
McClurg, Robert James *emergency nurse practitioner, educator*
Moore, Duncan Thomas *optics educator*
Parrinello, Kathleen Ann Mulholland *nursing administrator, educator*

Rockville Centre
Erland, Shirley May *nurse*

Roslyn Heights
Rubrum, Erica Courtney *family therapist, school counselor*

Rye
Davis, Samuel *hospital administrator, educator, consultant*
Newburger, Howard Martin *psychoanalyst*
Wilmot, Irvin Gorsage *former hospital administrator, educator, consultant*

Saranac Lake
Caguiat, Carlos Jose *health facility administrator, priest*

Saratoga Springs
O'Baire, Marika *nurse, writer*

Scarsdale
Liston, Mary Frances *retired nursing educator*
Rogalski, Lois Ann *speech and language pathologist*

Schenectady
Oliker, David William *healthcare management administrator*
Weiner, Clare Frances *social worker, psychotherapist*

Seaford
Tuzil, Teresa Jordan *clinical social worker, psychotherapist*

Seneca Falls
Norman, Mary Marshall *alcohol/drug abuse services professional*

Sleepy Hollow
Resnick, Adrienne Jo *psychotherapist*

Slingerlands
Jacobs, Karen Louise *medical technologist*

Staatsburg
Reagan, Paul Terrence *retired social worker*

Staten Island
De Luca, Anthony James *psychoanalyst, theologian*
Nadler, Nona Jean *social worker*
Spada, Dominick *pharmacist*

Suffern
Raven, Luisa Antonia *nurse, psychotherapist*

Syracuse
Fitzgerald, Harold Kenneth *social work educator, consultant*
Fluck, Robert R., Jr., *respiratory therapist, educator*
Guharoy, Roy Sudip *pharmacist*
Pirozzi, Mildred Jean *nursing administrator*
Rabuzzi, Daniel D. *medical administrator*

Tarrytown
Gutheil, Irene A. *social work educator, researcher*
Safian, Keith Franklin *hospital administrator*
Singh, Brahma Nand *pharmaceutical scientist*
Yancopoulos, George *health facility administrator*

Troy
Fusfeld, Herbert Irving *research management and public policy executive*

Truxton
Schultz, Helen Welkley *marriage and family therapist, minister*

White Plains
Dvorak, Roger Gran *health facility executive*
Fowlkes, Nancy Lanetta Pinkard *social worker*
Leung, Betty Brigid *nursing administrator*

Woodmere
Cohen, Lawrence Alan *health facility administrator*

Woodside
VanArsdale, Diana Cort *social worker*

Wyandanch
Hodges-Robinson, Chettina M. *nursing administrator*

Yaphank
Digilio, Jr., John Thomas *health care executive, consultant*

Yonkers
Lawson, Beverly Elaine *nursing administrator*
Roberson, Doris Jean Herold *retired social worker*

NORTH CAROLINA

Advance
Walser, Sandra Teresa Johnson *rehabilitation nurse, preceptor*

Asheville
McKeown, Peter Philip *medical center administrator, medical educator, cardiothoracic surgeon*

Buies Creek
Blalock, Mary Wright *counselor*

Burlington
Knesel, Ernest Arthur, Jr., *diagnostic company executive*
Mark, Edna Brown *health facility administrator, writer*
Powell, James Bobbitt *biomedical laboratories executive, pathologist*

Chapel Hill
Martikainen, A(une) Helen *retired health education specialist*
Munson, Eric Bruce *hospital administrator*
Murray, Michael Dennis *pharmacist*
Soltys, Florence Gray *social worker*
Usher, Charles Lindsey *social work educator, public policy analyst*
Zeisel, Steven H. *nutritionist, scientist, educator*

Charlotte
Fussell, Tracey Mattox *medical/surgical nurse*
Kuehnert, Deborah Anne *medical center administrator*
Latimer, Ben William *healthcare executive*
Martin, James Grubbs *medical executive, former governor*

Davidson
Plyler, John Laney, Jr., *retired healthcare management professional*

Durham
Brantley, Jeffrey Garland *health science facility administrator*
Colvin, O. Michael *medical director, medical educator*
Córdoba Montoya, Daniel Amado *psychologist, researcher, educator*
Fulkerson, William *health facility executive, pulmonologist*
Gosselin, Tracy Karen *nursing administrator*
Holzworth, Donald A. *lab administrator*
LeGrand, Chris *lab administrator*
Pericak-Vance, Margaret A. *health facility administrator*
Ware, Ruth Winchester *social worker*
Wilson, Ruby Leila *nursing educator*

Elizabeth City
Deaton, Fae Adams *clinical social worker, counselor*

Fayetteville
Jansen, Michael John *healthcare executive*

Greensboro
Barry, Dennis Robert *hospital administrator*
McDaniel, James Mark, Jr., *health care executive*
Rice, Arther Mae *dietician*
Scearse, Patricia Dotson *nurse educator, college dean*
Schwenn, Lee William *retired medical center executive*
Shotwell, Sheila Murray *medical/surgical nurse*
Smith, Rebecca McCulloch *human relations educator*

Hendersonville
Deskin, William C. *healthcare educator*
Heil, Mary Ruth *former counselor*

Morrisville
Cannon, Alice Grace *counselor*

Murphy
Dickey, Jeannetta Burkett *social worker*

New Bern
Forrester, Ann *nurse*

Newland
Lustig, Susan Gardner *occupational therapist*

Oxford
Harvey, Gloria-Stroud *physician assistant*

Raleigh
Bailey, Mary Beatrice *retired nursing information systems director*
Berry, Joni Ingram *hospice pharmacist, educator*
Geller, Janice Grace *nurse*
Johnson, Janet Gray Andrews *clinical social worker*
O'Brien, Helen Margaret *healthcare educator, environmentalist*
Quiambao, Dalisay Lelay *dietician, consultant, surveyor*

Research Triangle Park
Parra, William *administrator*
Uhrig, Jennifer Dee *researcher*

Rockingham
Evans, Patricia McCormick *clinical therapist*

Shelby
Blanton, Madge Brantley *family practice nurse practitioner*

Southport
Richmond, Jonathan Y. *public health administration officer*

Sylva
Babel, Deborah Jean *social worker, paralegal*

Tarboro
Andrews, Claude Leonard *psychotherapist*

Wilmington
Israel, Margie Olanoff *psychotherapist*

Wilson
Setliffe, Charles David *hospital administrator*

Winston Salem
Kannry, Sybil *retired psychotherapist, consultant*
Preslar, Len Broughton, Jr., *hospital administrator*
Wiles, Paul Martin *hospital administration executive*
Yeatts, Dorothy Elizabeth Freeman *nurse, educator, retired county official*

NORTH DAKOTA

Fargo
Ghatta, Srinivas *pharmacist, researcher*
Nickel, Janet Marlene Milton *geriatrics nurse*
Rice, Jon Richard *managed care administrator, physician*

Grand Forks
Nielsen, Forrest Harold *research nutritionist*
Ransom, Michael T. *counselor*

Maddock
Aadland, Kathleen A. *counselor, army intelligence officer*

Williston
Benson, Robert John *physical therapist, department chairman, massage therapist*

OHIO

Akron
Bentley, Bonnie J. *retired medical and oncological nurse*
O'Brien, Gayle Ann *nurse*
West, Michael Alan *retired hospital administrator*

Bowling Green
Scherer, Ronald Callaway *voice scientist, educator*

Bratenahl
Jones, Trevor Owen *biomedical industry executive, management consultant*

Bucyrus
Cooper, April Helen *family nurse practitioner*

Canton
Bartlette, Donald Lloyd *social worker, counselor, educator*

Cincinnati
Angeline, Michael E. *social worker, bereavement facilitator*
Bacher, Susan Lorraine *nursing educator*
Cook, Jack McPherson *hospital administrator*
Curtin, Leah Louise *publisher, editor, author, nurse, educator*
Daraiseh, Nancy M. *researcher, educator*
Derstadt, Ronald Theodore *health care administrator*
Goldstein, Sidney *pharmaceutical scientist*
Henney, Jane Ellen *health facility administrator, educator, oncologist*
Hensgen, Herbert Thomas *medical technologist*
Koebel, Sister Celestia *health care system executive*
Lang, Jackie Ann *nursing consultant*
Lichtin, Leon (Judah Leon Lichtin) *pharmacist*
Lippincott, Jonathan Ramsay *healthcare executive*
Monroe, Erin *psychiatric nurse practitioner*
Morgan, John Bruce *hospital care consultant*
Schubert, William Kuenneth *hospital medical center executive*
Sierra-Amor, Rosa Isabel *health facility administrator*
Stinson, Mary Florence *retired nursing educator*
Trofe, Jennifer *pharmacist, educator*
Weinrich, Alan Jeffrey *occupational hygienist*

Cleveland
Baker, Melvin *hospital pharmacy administrator*
Blum, Arthur *social worker, educator*
Bridges, John Francis Patrick *healthcare educator, researcher*
Cosgrove, Delos M. *health facility administrator, surgeon*
Cotleur, Mark A. *hospital administrator*
Crispin, Patricia Lynnette *social worker*
Curran, Phyllis Marie *counselor*
Dadley, Arlene Jeanne *sleep technologist*
Douglas, Janice Green *physician, educator*
Fitzpatrick, Joyce J. *nursing educator, former dean*
Hokenstad, Merl Clifford, Jr., *social work educator*
Johnson, Mattiedna *medical/surgical nurse*
Kohn, Mary Louise Beatrice *nurse*
Mazgalev, Todor Nikolov *health science association administrator, research scientist*
Rothstein, Fred C. *health facility administrator*
Schlotfeldt, Rozella May *nursing educator*
Schrott, Norman *retired clinical social worker*
Schultz, Jeffrey Eric *optometrist*
Shakno, Robert Julian *hospital and social services administrator*
Simmons, Clinton Craig *human resources executive*
Stark, George Robert *health science association administrator*
Taylor, Harris C. *consultant endocrinologist, diabetologist*
Vega, Manuel Thomas *medical/surgical nurse*
Walcott, Robert *health facility administrator, priest*
Womack, John W. *pharmacist*

Columbus
Anderson, Carole Ann *nursing educator, academic administrator*
Bachman, Sister Janice *healthcare executive, religious order administrator*

Banasik, Robert Casmer *nursing home administrator, educator*
Blom, Dave *healthcare industry executive*
McConnell, Donald Patrick *research institute executive*
Murden, Robert A. *medical administrator, physician*
Schuller, David Edward *cancer center administrator, otolaryngologist*
Sims, Richard Lee *hospital administrator*
Tripodi, Tony *social work educator, author, editor*

Dayton
Hitch, Melanie Audrey *orthopaedic nurse*
Kiser, Sharon Ann *health facility professional*
McKelvey, Alan Curtis *pharmacist*
Murphy, Martin Joseph, Jr., *cancer research center executive*
Nixon, Charles William *acoustician*
Stefanics, Charlotte Louise *retired mental health nurse*
Versic, Linda Joan *nurse educator, research company executive*

Dublin
Dolch, Gary D. *health facility administrator*
Ford, Brendan A. *health facility administrator*
Kane, John C. *retired health care products company executive*
Labrum, Ronald K. *health facility administrator*
Parrish, Mark *health facility administrator*
Thomas, Stephen S. *health facility administrator*
Troup, Gordon A. *health facility administrator*
White, Kathy Brittain *medical association executive*

Findlay
Stephani, Nancy Jean *social worker, journalist*

Gallipolis
Niehm, Bernard Frank *retired health facility administrator*

Granville
Pollard, Jeffrey Wallace *college counseling, health services director*

Hamilton
Fein, Linda Ann *nurse anesthetist, consultant*

Hudson
Wooldredge, William Dunbar *health facility administrator*

Independence
Van Kirk, Robert John *nursing case manager, educator*

Ironton
Oakes, Maria Spachner *nurse*

Kent
Biordi, Diana L. *healthcare educator, dean*

Lancaster
Varney, Richard Alan *health facility administrator*

Lima
Miller, Roy Raymond *optician, oculist*

Little Hocking
Corbin, David P. *counselor*

Mason
Clements, Michael Craig *health services consulting executive, retired renal dialysis technician*
Jackobs, Miriam Ann *dietitian*

Mayfield Heights
Billick, Steven M. *emergency medical technician*
Rhein, Arthur *emergency medical technician*

Middletown
Gordon, Sandy Gale Combs *medical/surgical nurse, community health nurse*

Oxford
Weinrich, Barbara Diane *speech pathology/audiology services professional, educator*

Pemberville
Sterling, William Carlisle *physician assistant*

Perrysburg
Billnitzer, Bonnie Jeanne *nurse, gerontologist*

Plain City
Karrer, Carol Converse *nursing educator, consultant*

Ravenna
Turcotte, Margaret Jane *retired nurse*

Richmond
Mills, Holly Lynn *registered nurse*

Sidney
Leffler, Carole Elizabeth *mental health nurse, women's health nurse*

Spencer
Snyder, Teresa Ann *medical/surgical nurse*

Strongsville
Lamberton, Jacquelyn E. *psychotherapist*

Tallmadge
Kaul, Mohan Lal *social worker, educator*

Toledo
Brass, Alan W. *healthcare executive*
Hyman, Melvin *speech-language pathologist, consultant*
Kneen, James Russell *health care administrator*
Lessick, Mira Lee *nursing educator*
Ormond, Paul A. *healthcare company executive*
Talmage, Lance Allen *obstetrician/gynecologist, career military officer*
Weikel, Malcolm Keith *healthcare company executive*

Worthington
Bernhagen, Lillian Flickinger *retired school health consultant*
Lentz, Edward Allen *consultant, retired health administrator*

Youngstown
Iannucci, Marleen *physical therapist, educator*

Zanesville
Ray, Susanne Gettings *counselor*

OKLAHOMA

Ada
Davenport, Ann Adele Mayfield *retired home care agency administrator*

Broken Arrow
Cruzan, Clarah Catherine *dietitian*

Edmond
Lewis, Gladys Sherman *nursing educator*

El Reno
Buendia, Imelda Bernardo *health facility administrator, physician*

Healdton
Eck, Kenneth Frank *pharmacist*

Lawton
Dishman, Bob N. *pharmacist*

Mangum
Bronson, William Cavolt, Jr., *counselor*

Newkirk
Newport, L. Joan *clinical social worker, retired psychotherapist*

Oklahoma City
Forni, Patricia Rose *nursing educator*
Harper, Robbie Jane *critical care nurse, administrator*
Henley, Everett Scott *health care marketing firm executive*
McClellan, Mary Ann *pediatric nurse practitioner*
McEwen, Irene Ruble *physical therapy educator*
McIntyre, Judy *social worker, state representative*
Mustion, Alan Lee *pharmacist*
Nakagawara, Van B. *optometrist, researcher*
Paris, Wayne *social worker, researcher*
Schroyer, Michael Kevin *critical care nurse and hospital administrator*
Schwemin, Joseph *retired pharmacist*
Spencer, Melvin Joe *health facility administrator, lawyer*

Tulsa
Carpenter, Nancy J. *health science association administrator*
Cherry, Andrew Lawrence, Jr., *social work educator, researcher*
Gray, Karen Kay *counselor*
Lewis, Corinne Hemeter *psychotherapist, educator*
McCall, Charles Barnard *health facility administrator, educator*

OREGON

Albany
Chowning, Orr-Lyda Brown *dietician*

Ashland
Masters, Robert Edward Lee *psychotherapist, neural researcher, human potential educator, philosopher*

Bend
Irwin, Kerri Lynne *pharmacist, writer, small business owner*

Central Point
Brown, Christopher Patrick *health care administrator, educator*

Corvallis
Oldfield, James Edmund *nutrition educator*

Cove
Kerper, Meike *family violence, sex abuse and addiction educator, consultant*

Eugene
Acker, Martin Herbert *psychotherapist, educator*
Camp, Delpha Jeanne *counselor*

Florence
Van Horn, O. Frank *retired counselor, consultant*

Hebo
Kesey, Jimmy Marvin *counselor, writer*

Klamath Falls
Klepper, Carol Herdman *mental health therapist*

Lake Oswego
Tyler, Darlene Jasmer *retired dietitian*

Lyons
Acuff, L. (Lewis) Steven *nutritionist, educator*

Milwaukie
Orloff, Barbara-Lee Marguerite Hewitt *social worker*

Pendleton
Smiley, Richard Wayne *researcher*

Phoenix
Dodd, Darlene Mae *retired nurse, retired military officer*

Portland
Fritz, Barbara Jean *occupational health nurse*
Goldfarb, Timothy Moore *hospital administrator*

Greenlick, Merwyn Ronald *health services researcher*
King, John G. *health service administrator*
Mendelson, Lottie M. *retired pediatric nurse practitioner, writer*
Pfeifer, Larry Alan *public health service coordinator*
Pladel, John Gerald *psychiatric nurse practitioner, psychologist, psychotherapist*
Plonski, Halina Maria *retired pharmacist*
Richens, Muriel Whittaker *marriage and family therapist, educator*
Shireman, Joan Foster *social work educator*
Sims, Kathleen Marie Eichner *nursing educator*

Redmond
Dey, Charlotte Jane *retired community health nurse*

Salem
Edge, James Edward *health care administrator*
Zumwalt, Roger Carl *hospital administrator*

The Dalles
Cooper, Rickey Eugene *medical transcriptionist, educator*

PENNSYLVANIA

Abington
Roediger, Paul Margerum *hospital administrator*

Acme
Babcock, Marguerite Lockwood *addictions treatment therapist, educator, writer*

Allentown
Flores, Robin Ann *social worker, social services administrator*
Halberstadt, Robert Bilheimer *optometrist*

Aston
Mirenda, Rosalie M. *nursing educator, administrator*

Bala Cynwyd
Cawthorn, Robert Elston *health care executive*

Berwick
Smith, Clara Jean *retired nursing home administrator*

Bethlehem
Herrenkohl, Roy Cecil *psychology educator*

Blue Bell
Baine, Richard Joseph *vocational rehabilitation counselor*

Bryn Mawr
Maehl, Jane Cecilia *social worker, administrator*

Camp Hill
Crider, Rudyard Lee *psychotherapist*
Parry-Solá, Cheryl Lee *critical care nurse*
Roach, Ralph Lee *human services and rehabilitation consultant*

Carbondale
Niles, John Southworth, III, *counselor, farmer*

Chambersburg
Mehrmann, CraigAnn *nurse practitioner*

Coatesville
Zarychta, William Alex *physician assistant*

Coopersburg
Kohler, Deborah Diamond *dietitian, food service executive*

Doylestown
Meyer, Diane Christine *social worker*

East Stroudsburg
Boyd, Katherine Ann *clinical therapist*

Easton
Pysher, Zane Kermit *counselor*

Elkins Park
Verma, Satya Bhushan *optometrist, educator*

Erie
Nihill, Karen Bailey *nursing home executive, nurse clinician*
Sensor, Mary Delores *hospital official, consultant*

Export
Carter, Linda Whitehead *oncology nurse, educator, consultant, researcher*

Gladwyne
Cathcart, Harold Robert *hospital administrator*

Grantham
Kreamer, Carolyn Lee *nursing educator, community health nurse*

Hamburg
Schappell, Abigail Susan *speech, language, hearing and massage therapist*

Hanover
Conway, Samuel Anthony *retired chiropractor*

Harrisburg
Brewer, Steven Gregory *human services administrator*
Stwalley, Brian David *pharmacist*

Harveys Lake
Wolensky, Joan *occupational therapist, interfaith minister*

Herman
Dittmer, Sylvester Stephen Wess *retired nursing administrator*

Hershey
Christensen, Dawn Michelle *family practice nurse practitioner, consultant*
Moskowitz, Jay *health sciences administrator*

Hopwood
Syphers, James Edgar *retired social worker*

Hulmeville
Jackson, Mary L. *health services executive*

Huntingdon Valley
Cohen, Michael R. *health facility administrator, pharmacist*
Isard, Phillip Isaac *medical nutritionist, consultant*

Jenkintown
DiSandro, Linda Anita *counselor*

Johnstown
Babik, Dennis Allen *social worker, consultant*

Kennett Square
Hager, George V. *health services executive*
Souney, Paul Frederick *pharmacist*

King Of Prussia
Miller, Alan B. *hospital management executive*

Lancaster
Brunner, Lillian Sholtis *nurse, writer*

Lititz
Hartz, Brian David *physical therapist, educator, small business owner*

Malvern
Hilzinger, Kurt John *healthcare company executive*

Martinsburg
Keith, Tammy Leah *geriatrics nurse*

Millersville
Heintzelman, Carol Ann *social work educator*

Newtown Square
Cordes, Eugene Harold *pharmacy and chemistry educator*

Norristown
Hess, Wanda Jean *health facility administrator*

Oil City
Loring, Richard William *psychotherapist*

Philadelphia
Aiken, Linda Harman *nurse, sociologist, educator*
Alaigh, Poonam *health facility administrator*
Altschuler, Steven M. *health facility executive, pediatrician, gastroenterologist*
Anyanwu, Chukwukre *alcohol/drug abuse services professional*
Austan, Frank Acosta *clinician, educator*
Broytman, Vladislav I. *hygenist*
Carpenter, Nathaniel Dennard *resident health services director*
Charney, Natalie J. *behavioral health services administrator, researcher, educator and clinician*
Clarkin, John Francis *health care management executive*
Fagin, Claire Mintzer *nursing educator, nursing administrator*
Freeman, Sharon Elizabeth *psychiatric nurse practitioner*
Holman, Larry Dean *health care administrator*
Jemmott, Loretta Sweet *nursing educator*
Joe, Sean *social work educator*
Kagan, Sarah Hope *geriatrics services professional, educator*
Kumanyika, Shiriki K. *nutrition epidemiology researcher, educator*
Lang, Norma M. *nursing educator*
Lowery, Barbara J. *psychiatric nurse, educator*
Meleis, Afaf Ibrahim *nurse sociologist, educator, clinician, researcher*
Micozzi, Marc Stephen *health executive, physician, educator*
Muller, Ralph W. *hospital administrator*
Newman, Francine M. *healthcare company executive*
Peck, Susan Nell *pediatric nurse*
Piccolo, Joseph Anthony *hospital administrator*
Potter, Alice Catherine *clinical laboratory scientist*
Scheib, Garry L. *hospital administrator*
Solomon, Phyllis Linda *social work educator, researcher*
Steinberg, Janet DeBerry *optometrist, educator, researcher*
Tegenu, Mesfin *health services administrator, consultant*
Trojanowski, John Q. *health facility administrator*
Williams, Francine Anita *community outreach worker*
Williams, Sankey Vaughan *health services researcher, internist*

Pittsburgh
Constantino-Bana, Rose Eva *nursing educator, researcher, lawyer*
Dato, Virginia Marie *public health physician*
Ferrara-Love, Roseann *nurse*
George, John Anthony *health corporation executive*
Goertzen, Irma *hospital executive*
Goldstein, Bernard David *physician, educator*
Granati, Diane Alane *ophthalmic nurse*
Maguire, Lambert *social worker, educator*
Maiolini, Gloria J. *nurse case manager, poet, writer*
Miller, Laura Jean *medical center director*
Mokotoff, Michael *pharmaceutical sciences educator*
Moore, Pearl B. *nursing educator*
Pennell, Daniel Mark *researcher*
Romoff, Jeffrey Alan *health care executive*
Rudy, Ellen Beam *nursing educator*
Smith, Ryan Arthur Harold *mental health services professional, writer*
Trauth, Jeanette M. *healthcare educator*
Zanardelli, John Joseph *healthcare services executive*

Pottsville
Blossey, Maureen B. *mental health administrator*

Reading
Bell, Frances Louise *medical technologist*
Sauer, Elissa Swisher *nursing educator*

Scranton
Lukasik, John Peter, Jr., *therapist, counselor, school psychologist*
Turock, Jane Parsick *nutritionist*

Slippery Rock
Fulton, Jane *health science institution administrator*

State College
Henshaw, Beverly Ann Harsh *women's health nurse, consultant*

University Park
Guthrie, Helen A. *nutrition educator, registered dietitian*
Holt, Frieda M. *nursing educator, former academic director*
Jung, Myung-Chul *researcher*
Lorence, Daniel *healthcare educator*
Mayers, Stanley Penrose, Jr., *public health educator*
Murray-Kolb, Laura Elaine *nutritionist, researcher*

Villanova
Beletz, Elaine Ethel *nurse, educator*
Haynor, Patricia Manzi *nursing educator, consultant*

Washington Bord
Snyder, John Jacob *researcher*

Wayne
Rolleri, Denise Marie *radiation therapist, business owner*

West Chester
Cinelli, Bethann *school health educator*

Wilkes Barre
Legg, Timothy James *nursing educator*
Stokes, Kimberly Ann *counselor*

Willow Street
Wesbury, Stuart Arnold, Jr., *health administration and policy executive, educator*

Wyncote
Schaffner, Roberta Irene *retired medical, surgical nurse*

Wyomissing
Rosello, Jacqueline DeLapp *occupational therapist*

York
Bartels, Bruce Michael *health care executive*
Keiser, Paul Harold *retired hospital administrator*
Minissale, Anthony A. *hospital administrator*
Rosen, Raymond *health facility executive*

RHODE ISLAND

Cranston
Mathewson, Doris May *retired medical/surgical nurse*

East Greenwich
Jordan, Ronald P. *pharmacist, pharmaceutical executive, consultant*

Newport
Cicilline, J. Clement *mental health services professional, state legislator*
Mullaney, Joann Barnes *nursing educator*
Woods, Donald E. *healthcare executive*

Providence
Boekelheide, Kim *pathologist*
Kane, Steven Michael *psychotherapist, educator*
Metrey, George David *social work educator, academic administrator*
Monteiro, Lois Ann *medical science educator*
Murphy, Christine *medical facility administrator*
Nolan, Patricia Ann *public health officer*
Parris, Thomas Godfrey, Jr., *medical facility administrator*
Recupero, Patricia Ryan *hospital administrator, psychiatrist, lawyer, health facility executive*

Warwick
Horn, Donna M. *pharmacist, medical association administrator*

SOUTH CAROLINA

Cayce
Paynter, Vesta Lucas *pharmacist*

Charleston
Austin, Charles John *health services educator*
Hollis, Bruce Warren *experimental nutritionist, industrial consultant*
KilPatrick, Anne Osborne *health administration and policy educator*
Smith, W. Stuart *strategic planning director*
Stanley, Karen M. *mental health nurse, consultant*

Clemson
Logan, Barbara N. *nursing educator*

Columbia
Amidon, Roger Lyman *retired health administration educator*
Bowman, Ned David *medical administrator*
Bristow, Thomas Cole, Jr., *social work educator*
Bryant, Douglas E. *public health service official*
Ettel, Zita Moak *nursing administrator, food services executive*
Rabb, Gael Caution *mental health consultant*
Ruff, Cheryl Anderson *health facility administrator*
Seigler, Ruth Queen *college nursing administrator, educator, consultant, nurse*
Wieland, Gilbert Darryl *health facility administrator, researcher*

Greenville
Burkhardt, J. Bland, Jr., *hospital administrator*
Cargill, Paula Marie *social worker, gerontologist*

Hilton Head Island
Wesselmann, Glenn Allen *retired hospital executive*

Irmo
Stewart, Alexander Constantine *medical technologist*

Jonesville
Summer-Strait, Beth *mental health services professional*

Marion
Inabinet, Lawrence Elliott *retired pharmacist*
Manning, Leslie Carlton *counselor*

Myrtle Beach
Fowler, Marilyn S. Atlas *social worker*
Killian, Greg *mental health services professional*

Rock Hill
Benson, Keith J. *healthcare management educator*
Bessinger, Raymond Carlton *nutritionist, educator*

Simpsonville
Davis, Shirley Harriet *social worker, editor*

Spartanburg
Jones, William Osborne, II, *physician assistant*

Summerville
Deavers, James Frederick *optometrist*
Young, Margaret Aletha McMullen (Mrs. Herbert Wilson Young) *social worker*

SOUTH DAKOTA

Pierre
Weyer, Dianne Sue *health facility administrator*

Rapid City
Corwin, Bert Clark *optometrist*

Sioux Falls
McMillin, Joan Austin *social worker*
Nygaard, Lance Corey *nurse, data processing consultant*
Richards, LaClaire Lissetta Jones (Mrs. George A. Richards) *social worker*
VanDemark, Michelle Volin *critical care, neuroscience nurse*

TENNESSEE

Antioch
Huff, Jimmy Laurence *nurse*

Bartlett
Huffman, D. C., Jr., *pharmacy association executive*

Brentwood
Chapdelaine, Perry Anthony, Jr., *public health and preventive medicine physician, educator*
Rash, Martin S. *health facility administrator*
White, Michael James *healthcare facilities administrator*

Cleveland
Preston, Forrest L. *health care executive*
Watson, S. Michele *school nurse*
Ziegler, Steve *health care services/centers executive*

Clinton
Seib, Billie McGhee Rushing *nursing administrator, consultant*

Columbia
Cline, Shawn Fredrick *social worker*

Cookeville
Reynolds, Barbara C. *mental health educator, academic dean, retired*

Crossville
Sower, Milene A. *nursing educator*

Franklin
Miller, Dennis Edward *health medical executive*

Germantown
Nolly, Robert J. *pharmacist, health facility administrator, educator*

Goodlettsville
Harper, Jewel Benton *pharmacist*

Hendersonville
Davis, Robert Norman *hospital administrator*

Jackson
Barlow, Richard Clay *nurse, consultant*
Woodall, Gilbert Earl, Jr., *medical administrator*

Jellico
Hausman, Keith Lynn *hospital administrator, physical therapist*

Knoxville
Erickson, Mary (Molly) Louise *speech pathology/audiology services professional, educator*
Guy, Allen C. *health facility administrator*
Matteson, Karla J. *health science association administrator*
McGuire, Sandra Lynn *nursing educator*
Moore, Louise Hill *surgical technologist*
Trout, Monroe Eugene *hospital systems executive*

Lewisburg
Gonzalez, Raquel Maria *pharmacist*

Linden
Mitchell, Elizabeth Marelle *family nurse practitioner, nursing educator, medical, surgical nurse*

Lynchburg
Koss, Jacqueline Jarrell *women's health nurse practitioner, educator*

Memphis
Bargagliotti, Lillian Antoinette *nursing dean*
Boucher, Bradley Albert *pharmacist, educator*
Carter, Michael Allen *nursing educator*
Diggs, Walter Whitley *health science facility administrator*
Gourley, Greta Ann Kimbrough *pharmaceutical sciences educator*
Ihle, James N. *health facility administrator*
Mahato, Ram Ishwar *pharmacist, educator*
Mulholland, Kenneth Leo, Jr., *health care facility administrator*
Reynolds, Stephen Curtis *hospital administrator*
Shorb, Gary Seymour *hospital administrator*
Winters, Darcy LaFountain *medical management company executive*

Millington
Fletchall, Sandra Kay *occupational therapist*

Morristown
Harmon, David Eugene *optometrist, geneticist*

Nashville
Anderson, David C. *healthcare company executive*
Bolian, George Clement *health care executive, physician*
Brown, Tommie Florence *social work educator*
Buerhaus, Peter I. *nursing administrator*
Carlson, Robert Marshall *hospital professional services official*
Dalton, James Edgar, Jr., *health facility administrator*
Donahey, Kenneth C. *hospital management company executive*
Doyal, Linda E. *clinical pharmacist*
Jacobsen, Harry R. *hospital administrator, physician*
Johnson, David *medical administrator*
Johnson, R. Milton *healthcare executive*
Kaiser, Allen Bernard *health facility administrator*
Mauksch, Ingeborg Grosser *nursing educator*
McNally, James Rand (Randy McNally) *pharmacist, state legislator*
Sergent, John S. *hospital administrator, medical educator*
Silver, Heidi Jaye *nutritionist, educator, researcher*
Sloan, Reba Faye *dietitian, consultant*
Stringfield, Charles David *hospital administrator*
Urmy, Norman B. *hospital administrator*
Warner, Tokesha L *health facility administrator*

Oak Ridge
Jones, Virginia McClurkin *retired social worker*
Slusher, Kimberly Goode *researcher*

Saulsbury
Jacobs, Henry Madison, Jr., *researcher, writer*

Trenton
McCullough, Kathryn T. Baker *social worker*

TEXAS

Abilene
Waters, Michael Cooper *medical center and development corporation executive*

Amarillo
Arnold, Winnie Jo *retired mental health nurse, nursing administrator*
Simpson, Chad W. *pharmacist, educator*

Arlington
Adams, Phyllis Curl *nursing educator*
Rainey, Claude Gladwin *retired health care executive*

Austin
Attal, Gene (Fred Eugene Attal) *hospital executive*
Austin, David Mayo *social work educator*
Davis, Donald Robert *nutritionist, researcher, consultant*
Doluisio, James Thomas *pharmacy educator*
Durbin, Richard Louis, Sr., *healthcare administration consultant*
Easley, Christa Birgit *nurse, researcher*
Golden, Kimberly Kay *critical care nurse*
Hall, Beverly Adele *nursing educator*
Hayes, Patricia Ann *health facility administrator*
Heffley, James Dickey *nutrition counselor*
Herrington-Borre, Frances June *sign language school director*
Kirk, Lynda Pounds *biofeedback therapist, neurotherapist, counselor*
Larkam, Beverley McCosham *clinical social worker, family therapist*
Martin, Frederick Noel *audiology educator*
McClintic, James A. *lab administrator*
McGinity, James W. *pharmacy educator*
Rider, Katherine Loveta Thompson *clinical social worker*
Smith, Bert Kruger *retired mental health services professional*
Taylor, Mildred Lois *nursing home administrator*

Bryan
Buckley, John Joseph, Jr., *health care executive*
Guitry, Loraine Dunn *community health nurse*
Parrott, Thena Elizabeth *nurse educator*

Bulverde
Blasingim, Charlotte Oren DeShazor *counselor, consultant*

Carrollton
Withrow, Lucille Monnot *nursing home administrator*

Chandler
Wilson, Michael Paul *pharmacist*

Chillicothe
Brock, Helen Rachel McCoy *retired mental health and community health nurse*

Colleyville
Donnelly, Barbara Schettler *retired medical technologist*

Conroe
Sowers, Amelia Barnet *speech and language pathologist*

Copperas Cove
Haas, Lu Ann *counselor*

Corpus Christi
Stowers, Russell Brent *physical therapy educator*

Dallas
Anderson, Ron Joe *health facility administrator, internist, educator*
Baker, James Guy *health facility administrator*
Banchereau, Jacques *health facility administrator*
Bradley, John Andrew *hospital management company executive*
Carson, Jo Ann Simon *dietitian*
Dykes, Virginia Chandler *occupational therapist, educator*
France, Newell Edwin *former hospital administrator, consultant*
Goldmann, James Allen *healthcare consultant*
Haynes, Linda C. *nursing educator*
Hitt, David Hamilton, Sr., *retired hospital executive*
Johnson, Murray H. *optometrist, researcher, consultant, lecturer*
Marentette, Elijah Chandler *health services executive*
McLean, Lynne Marie *social worker*
Miller, Jo Carolyn Dendy *family and marriage counselor, educator*
O'Bannion, Mindy Martha Martin *nurse*
Parsons, Terry Thomas *psychotherapist, educator*
Powell, Boone, Jr., *hospital executive*
Purkey, Thomas Eugene *social worker*
Richardson, Dennise Marie *physician assistant*
Schecter, Arnold Joel *public health educator*
Smith, William Randolph (Randy Smith) *health care management executive*
Solomon, Risa Greenberg *clinical social worker, child and family therapist, former entertainment industry executive*
Taulbee, Thomas Lester *psychotherapist, educator*
Wheeler, M. Cass *health science association administrator*

Denton
Lawhon, Tommie Collins Montgomery *child development and family living educator*
McCuistion, Robert Wiley *hospital administrator, management consultant, lawyer*
Ryan, Melbagene T. *retired food and nutrition service director*

Dyess Afb
Chester, Linnes Lee, Jr., *healthcare association administrator*

Edinburg
Wilson, Bruce Keith *men's health nurse*

El Paso
Allen, Anna J. *chiropractor*
Dombrowski, Frank Paul, Jr., *pharmacist*
Edmonds, Velma McInnis *nursing educator*
Hedrick, Wyatt Smith *pharmacist*
Juarez, Antonio *psychotherapist, consultant, counselor, educator*
Mitchell, Paula Rae *nursing educator, college dean*

Fort Sam Houston
Nelson, James Harold *health sciences administrator*

Fort Worth
Brockman, Leslie Richard *social worker*
Brodale, Louise Lado *medical, post surgery and geriatrics nurse*
Taylor, Elizabeth R. *counselor, educator*
Tubb, Larry *health facility administrator*

Galveston
Hargraves, Martha Ann *health services administrator, researcher*
Lemon, Stanley M. *hospital administrator*
Protas, Elizabeth J. *physical therapist, academic administrator*
Rassin, David Keith *nutrition educator, researcher*

Georgetown
Smitheram, Margaret Etheridge *health facility administrator, director*

Haltom City
Irwin, Richard D. *lab administrator, venture capitalist*

Hondo
Swort, Arlowayne *retired nursing educator and administrator*

Houston
Adkins, Susan *health services administrator*
Aitken, Iam *health facility administrator*
Altman, William Carl *health facility administrator, merger and acquisitions specialist, investment manager, consultant*
Arcilla, Demetrio Ballares, Jr., *health facility administrator, rehabilitation services professional, writer, genealogist*
Battin, R. Ray (Rosabell Harriet Ray) *audiologist, neuropsychologist*
Becker, Frederick Fenimore *cancer center administrator, pathologist*
Berry, Martha Frances *counselor*
Bleiberg, Efrain *medical clinic executive*
Burdine, John A. *hospital administrator, nuclear medicine educator*
Caskey, Caroline *lab administrator*
Chima, Felix O. *social work educator*
Cunningham, Terence Thomas, III, *hospital administrator*
Davis-Lewis, Bettye *nursing educator*
Fine, David Jeffrey *hospital executive, educator, consultant, lecturer*
Florian-Lacy, Dorothy *therapist, educator*
Frison, Paul Maurice *health care executive*
Golinkin, Webster Fowler *healthcare executive, media consultant*
Grimes, Richard Michael *public health educator*
Gunn, Joan Marie *health facility administrator*
Hanrahan, Lawrence Martin *healthcare consultant*
Hempfling, Linda Lee *nurse*
Holmes, Harry Dadisman *health facility administrator*
Hrna, Daniel Joseph *pharmacist, lawyer*
Jhin, Michael Kontien *health care executive*
Johnson, Sandra Ann *counselor, educator*
Latting, Jean Kantambu *social worker, educator*
Leichtman, Maria Luisa *mental health services professional*
Mallia-Hughes, Marianne *medical writer*
Montgomery, Denise Karen *nurse*
Moore, Lois Jean *health science facility administrator*
Munsell, Debra S. *physician assistant, educator*
Nicklas, Theresa Ann *nutritionist, educator, researcher*
Nora, Hope *healthcare consultant*
Page, David Randall *hospital administrator*
Peabody, Arlene L. Howland Bayar *retired, nurse*
Potluri, Venkateswara Rao *medical facility administrator*
Poulton, Beverly Ann *medical/surgical nurse*
Reed, Kathlyn Louise *occupational therapist, educator*
Rives, Terry Edward *public health service officer, researcher, epidemiologist*
Robbins, Susan Paula *social work educator*
Schiflett, Mary Fletcher Cavender *retired health facility executive, researcher, educator*
Stokes, Jim D. *psychotherapist*
Turner, Kelley Bailey *non profit consultant, volunteer program administrator*
Wagner, Donald Bert *healthcare consultant*
Wallace, Mark Allen *hospital executive*
Wilford, Dan Sewell *hospital administrator*
Wissel-Littmann, Jeffrey G. *health facility executive*

Irving
Hicks, Allen Morley *hospital administrator*
Jorden, Yon Yoon *health services company executive*
Smith, C. Thomas, Jr., *hospital administrator*
Turner, Carlton Edgar *pharmacist, presidential advisor*

Karnes City
Davis, Troy Arnol *reflexologist, hypnotherapist*

Keene
Adams, Lavonne Marilyn Beck *critical care nurse, nursing educator*

Kingsville
Robins, James Dow *counselor*

La Porte
Fotsch, George Bernard, III, *chemical addiction counselor*

Lago Vista
Garcia y Carrillo, Martha Xochitl *pharmacist*

Lubbock
Allison, Jane Shawver *medical school administrator, management consultant*
Broselow, Linda Latt *medical office technician, aviculturist*
Dersch, Charette Alyse *marriage and family therapist*

Mcallen
Arredondo, Jenna Dolores *speech pathology/audiology services professional*
Tupper, Ron *public health, policy, and management educator*

Mexia
Chambers, Linda Dianne Thompson *social worker*

Midland
Fredrickson, Mark Allan *health facility administrator, physician*
Ienatsch, Gayleen Elizabeth *nursing educator*

Normangee
Rector, M. Eugene *community pharmacist*

Panhandle
Sherrod, Lloyd Bruce *nutritionist*

Pasadena
Kenagy, Cheri Lynn *nurse*

Plainview
Misa, Elena May *physical therapist*

Plano
Parsons, Michael J. *health facility administrator*
Shelton, James D. (Denny Shelton) *hospital management company executive*

Port Arthur
Vinecour, Oneida Agnes *nurse*

Post
Warren, Jennifer Elizabeth *family nurse practitioner*

Red Oak
Jones, Genia Kay *emergency supervising nurse, consultant*

Richardson
Avadhut, HitendranandaAcarya *spiritual counselor, yoga teacher*
Krauss, Henry Frederick, Jr., *optometrist*

Rockwall
Crooks, Patricia Kay *counselor*

San Antonio
Champion, Michael Edward *physician assistant, clinical perfusionist*
Crabtree, Ben C. *neuromuscular therapy clinic director*
Dacbert-Friese, Sharyn Varhely *social worker, evangelist*
Davis, Sarah Jane *health care professional*
DeNice, Marcella L. *counselor*
Gonzalez, Hector Hugo *nurse, educator, consultant*
Hawken, Patty Lynn *retired nursing educator, dean of faculty*
Junek, Heather Diane *medical/surgical nurse*
Pysher, Alan Guy *nurse anesthetist*
Rojo, Ruth M. *nutritionist, alternative medicine consultant*
Swansburg, Russell Chester *nursing educator, consultant, health facility administrator*
Van de Putte, Leticia *pharmacist, state senator*
Walsh, Nicolas Eugene *rehabilitation medicine physician, educator*
Wilson, Janie Menchaca *nursing educator, researcher*
Wood, Thomas Willard *health care industry executive*

San Marcos
Watkins, Ted Ross *social work educator*
Wetter-Kubeck, Daisy Fisher *dietitian, consultant*

Snyder
Barnes, Maggie Lue Shifflett (Mrs. Lawrence Barnes) *nurse*

Temple
Erickson, Richard A. *health facility administrator, medical educator*
Hoffer, J. Lee *health facility administrator, medical educator*
Koehler, Bruce D. *health facility administrator, medical educator*
McDavid, Andrew J. *health facility administrator, medical educator*

Tyler
Mastern, Dean Scott *personal growth and development consultant*

Universal City
Lamoureux, Gloria Kathleen *nurse, consultant, retired military officer*

Van Horn
Dodson, Hersha Rhee *psychiatric and mental health nurse*

Waco
Christy, Kimbera Mills *acute care nurse practitioner, educator*
Scott, Richard Elton *health facility administrator*

Weatherford
Scott, Geneva Lee Smith *nursing educator*

Wheeler
Love, Wanda Jo *hospital administrator*

Whiteface
Marshall, Robert Wayne *human services administrator*

Wortham
Lee, Gordon Kenneth *physician assistant*

Yoakum
Leahy, Lawrence Marshall *health care administrator, marketing consultant*

UTAH

Kaysville
Ashmead, Allez Morrill *retired speech, hearing, and language pathologist, orofacial myologist, consultant*

Murray
Webster, Linda Jane *clinical social worker, consultant*

Ogden
Jones, Galen Ray *physician assistant*
Seager, Dauna Gayle Olson-Stokes *speech therapist*

Saint George
Chilow, Barbara Gail *social worker*

Salt Lake City
Hull, Grafton Hazard, Jr., *social work educator*
Jorgensen, Lou Ann Birkbeck *social worker*
Kjeldsberg, Karl R. *lab administrator, physician, educator*
Mason, James Ostermann *public health administrator*
Melton, Arthur Richard *healthcare executive*
Weiss, Ronald L. *lab administrator*
Wolf, Harold Herbert *pharmacy educator*

VERMONT

Brattleboro
Bussino, Melinda Holden *human services administrator*
Smiley, Carol Anne *home health administrator, sculptor*

Burlington
Erno, Margaret Jean *social worker, consultant*
Mead, Philip Bartlett *healthcare administrator, obstetrician, educator*

East Thetford
Cummings Rockwell, Patricia Guilbault *psychiatric nurse*

Morrisville
Roberts, Carolyn C. *former hospital administrator*

Winooski
Higgins, Margaret Ann *home health nurse, operating room nurse*

VIRGINIA

Abingdon
Beil, Clark Raymond *hospital executive*

Alexandria
Fisher, Donald Wayne *medical association executive*
Gormley, Dennis Michael *research scholar*
Graham, John H., IV, *health science association administrator*
Henry, Catherine Ann *health science association administrator*
Mallon, Francis J. *health science association administrator*

Mathias, Melvin Merle *nutrition scientist*
Penrose, Cynthia C. *retired health care consultant*

Annandale
Abdellah, Faye Glenn *retired public health service executive*

Arlington
Adreon, Beatrice Marie Rice *pharmacist*
Contis, George *medical services company executive*
Donnelly, Mary Beth *research analyst*
Lurie, Nicole *former health science association administrator*
May, Sterling Randolph *health association executive*

Blacksburg
Callison, Myrna C. *occupational therapist*

Bristow
Onufrock, Richard Shade *pharmacist, researcher*

Burke
Werfel, Sandra Diane *clinical social worker*

Centreville
Malouff, Frank Joseph *health care association executive*

Charlottesville
Bouchard, Ronald A. *health care administrator*
Hanft, Ruth S. Samuels *healthcare consultant, educator, economist*
Hinnant, Clarence Henry, III, *health care executive*
Howell, Robert Edward *hospital administrator*
Pate, Robert Hewitt, Jr., *counselor educator*
Wiggins, Barbara Sue *pharmacy clinical specialist, educator*

Chesapeake
Skrip, Linda Jean *nurse*

Culpeper
Goddard, Frances Byrd *clinical social worker*

Danville
Johnson, Gerald Lee *health facility administrator*

Fairfax
Drenkard, Karen Neil *nursing administrator*
Fitzgerald, Darlene *technologist, writer*
Harper, Doreen C. *nursing educator*
Knee, Ruth Irelan (Mrs. Junior K. Knee) *social worker, health care consultant*

Fairfax Station
Barringer, Joan Marie *counselor, educator, artist, writer*

Falls Church
Adams, Nancy R. *nurse, retired military officer*
Fink, Charles Augustin *behavioral systems scientist*
Grabenstein, John Douglas *pharmacist, army officer*
Seifert, Patricia Clark *cardiac surgery nurse, educator, consultant*

Farmville
Terry, Wayne Gilbert *healthcare executive, hospital administrator, mediator*

Fredericksburg
Unison-Pace, Wendy Jane *nursing educator*

Glen Allen
Smith, Craig R. *medical equipment company executive*

Hampton
Davis, Bertha Lane *psychiatric nursing educator*

Keswick
Johansen, Eivind Herbert *special education services executive, former army officer*

Locust Grove
Walsh, Geraldine Frances *nursing administrator*

Mc Lean
Filerman, Gary Lewis *health educator*
Walsh, Marie Leclerc *nurse*

Newport News
Brink, Gerald R. *hospital executive*
Warren, Daniel Churchman *health facility administrator*

Norfolk
Anderson, Darleen Shircliffe *hospital system administrator*
Bernd, David LeMoine *multi-hospital system executive*
Davis, Russell Haden *consultant*
Hartman, Deanna Mears *retired family counselor, addiction counselor*
Nichols, Brenda Sue *nursing educator*

Portsmouth
Barnes, Judith P. *nursing administrator*

Radford
Scartelli, Joseph Paul *music therapy educator, dean*

Richmond
Barker, Thomas Carl *retired health care administration educator, executive*
Beaman, Mary Anina *psychiatric nurse, educator*
Bovender, Jack Oliver, Jr., *hospital management company executive*
Durrett, Nancy Kashner *health science association administrator*
Freund, Emma Frances *technologist*
Gandy, Gerald Larmon *rehabilitation counseling educator, psychologist, writer*
Hardy, Richard Earl *rehabilitation counseling educator*
Luke, Roice D. *health science association administrator*
McCarthy, Charles R. *bioethicist, consultant*
Northrop, Mary Ruth *retired mental health nurse*
Schall, Carol Marie *special education services professional*
Winter, Joan Elizabeth *psychotherapist*

Roanoke
Dagenhart, Betty Jane Mahaffey *nursing educator, administrator*
Fralino, W. Heywood *health facility administrator*
Klein, Deborah Rae *health facility administrator*
Robertson, Thomas L. *health facility administrator*

Springfield
Dake, Marcia Allene *retired nursing educator, university dean*
Williams, Cecilia Lee Pursel *optometrist*

Staunton
Sweetman, Beverly Yarroll *physical therapist*

Suffolk
Glasson, Linda *hospital security and safety official, healthcare*

Vienna
Kader, Nancy Stowe *nurse, consultant, bioethicist*
Welters, Anthony *health services executive*

Virginia Beach
Denzler, James Wyatt *pharmacist*
Eleuterius, Nancy Lea *health administrator*
McWaters, Jeffrey L. *healthcare executive*

Waynesboro
Glaser, Elisabeth *psychotherapist, historian*

Williamsburg
Farrar, John Thruston *health facility administrator*

Winchester
Halseth, Michael James *medical center administrator*

Woodbridge
Monaco, Anthony John *retired health facility administrator, writer*

WASHINGTON

Camano Island
Hartley, Celia Love *nursing consultant, writer, retired nursing educator, nursing administrator*

Centralia
Gimbel, Hervey Willis *public health physician, medical administrator*

Clarkston
Smith, Phyllis Mae *healthcare consultant, educator*

Federal Way
Ketchersid, Wayne Lester, Jr., *medical technologist*
Mail, Patricia Davison *public health specialist*

Issaquah
Duncan, Elizabeth Charlotte *retired marriage and family therapist, educational therapist, educator*

Kennewick
Fann, Margaret Ann *counselor*

Kirkland
Gerstman, Hubert Louis *retired speech and language pathologist, audiologist, otolaryngology educator, humorist*

Long Beach
McClintock, William Thomas *health care administrator*

Mukilteo
Atal, Bishnu Saroop *retired speech research executive*

Oak Harbor
Miller, Robert Scott *mental health administrator, social worker*

Port Angeles
Barker, Barbara *registered nurse, medical researcher*
Muller, Carolyn Bue *physical therapist, volunteer*

Poulsbo
Carle, Harry Lloyd *social worker*

Pullman
Baugh, Bradford Hamilton *occupational and environmental health advisor*
Chermak, Gail D. *audiologist, educator*

Redmond
Sasenick, Joseph Anthony *animal health and food safety company executive*

Seattle
Barnard, Kathryn Elaine *nursing educator, researcher*
Berni, Rosemarian Rauch *rehabilitation and oncology nurse*
Blomstrand, Doreen Kathryn *retired physician assistant*
Dear, Ronald Bruce *social work educator*
de Chesnay, Mary *nursing educator*
de Tornyay, Rheba *nursing educator, retired dean*
Dorpat, Theodore Lorenz *psychoanalyst*
Ellis, Janice Rider *nursing educator, consultant*
Hellström, Ingegerd *business executive, medical researcher*
Katz, Treuman P. *health facility administrator*
Kolbeson, Marilyn Hopf *holistic practitioner, educator, artist, poet, advertising executive, poet*
Monsen, Elaine Ranker *nutritionist, educator, editor*
Perkin, Gordon Wesley *international health executive*
Perrin, Edward Burton *health services researcher, biostatistician, public health educator*
Peterson, Jane White *nursing educator, anthropologist*
Sandahl, Bonnie Beardsley *human services administrator, educator*
Sellick, Kathleen A. *hospital administrator*

Seaview
McNeil, Helen Jo Connolly *nursing educator, public health administrator*

Shoreline
Gilchrist, Garrett Alexander *psychotherapist*

Spokane
Hendershot, Carol Miller *physical therapist*
Murphy, Mary Ann *human services administrator*
Robinson, Herbert Henry, III, *educator, psychotherapist*

Tacoma
Neff Balch, Betty Marie *retired nursing educator*

Tahuya
Quesinberry, Bonita Mae *counselor, writer, editor*

Vancouver
Woodward, Jonathan Morgan *mental health specialist*

Yakima
Simonson, Susan Kay *hospital clinical care coordinator*

WEST VIRGINIA

Charleston
Border, Larry Willis *pharmacist*
Richardson, Sally Keadle *health care administrator*

Given
Hamon, Janice M. *social worker, educator*

Huntington
Henderson, Dan W. *psychiatric therapist, educator*

Institute
Richards, John Dale *social worker, educator, counselor*

Kearneysville
Smith, Gene Marcus *mental health services professional*

Morgantown
Beresford, Annette Diana *researcher*

Moundsville
McCraken, Vickie Darlene *nursing assistant*

Parkersburg
Bush, Roberta B. *retired psychotherapist, accountant*

Ranson
Rudacille, Sharon Victoria *medical technologist*

Wheeling
Good, Laurance Frederic *hospital administrator*
Hofreuter, Donald H. *health facility administrator*
Urval, Krishna Raj *health facility administrator, educator*

WISCONSIN

Beaver Dam
Bleifuss, Karen K *technologist, educator*

Burlington
Oestmann, Mary Jane *retired senior radiation specialist*

Columbus
Brinkman, Michael Owen *health care consultant, educator*

Eau Claire
Biegel, Eileen Mae *retired hospital executive*

Green Bay
McIntosh, Elaine Virginia *nutrition educator*

Madison
Berven, Norman Lee *counselor, psychologist, educator*
Brennan, Patricia Flatley *nursing educator, systems engineer, educator*
Derzon, Gordon M. *hospital administrator*
Fryback, Dennis G. *health services research educator*
Gavin, Mary Jane *medical and surgical nurse*
Johnson, Jean Elaine *nursing educator*
Littlefield, Vivian Moore *nursing educator, administrator*
Maersch, Nancy Kay *health facility administrator*
Marlett, Judith Ann *nutritional sciences educator, researcher*
Satter, Larry Dean *nutritionist*
Schoeller, Dale Alan *nutrition research educator*

Marshfield
Wesbrook, Frederic P. *health facility administrator, physician*

Menomonee Falls
Janzen, Norine Madelyn Quinlan *medical technologist*
Siegel, Hildegarde Julia *retired nursing educator*

Milwaukee
Babcock, Janice Beatrice *healthcare coordinator*
Brideau, Leo Paul *healthcare executive*
Fluharty, George Mark *speech pathology/audiology services professional*
Frank, Dennis *psychotherapist, educator*
Harvieux, Anne Marie *psychotherapist*
Howe, G. Edwin *healthcare executive*
Lange, Marilyn *social worker*
Loehr, Stephanie Schmahl *social worker*
Mancuso, Joseph Edward *medical psychotherapist*
Platt, Jeb Buchanan *health facility administrator*
Waller, Mary Bellis *psychotherapist, education educator, consultant*
White-Winters, Jill Mary *nursing educator*

Minocqua
Jaye, David Robert, Jr., *retired health facility administrator*

New Berlin
Winkler, Dolores Eugenia *retired health facility administrator*

Rhinelander
Van Brunt-Bartholomew, Marcia Adele *retired social worker*

River Falls
Hayden, Paul Allan *speech pathology educator, consultant, researcher*

Shawano
Wilson, Douglas *genetics company executive*

Superior
Rodne, Kjell John *healthcare administrator*

Waukesha
Wallskog, Joyce Marie *nursing educator, psychologist*

Wausau
Moore, Alfred P. *health facility administrator, benefits compensation analyst*

West Allis
Fiorelli, Karen Lynn *registered nurse*

Whitehall
Nordhagen, Hallie Huerth *nursing home administrator*

WYOMING

Bondurant
Ellwood, Paul Murdock, Jr., *health policy analyst, consultant*

Cheyenne
Dale, Marcia Lyn *nursing educator*
Laycock, Anita Simon *psychotherapist*
Nisbet, Toma A. *nursing administrator*

Ethete
Tepper, Marcy Elizabeth *drug education director*

Jackson Hole
Farkas, Carol Garner *nurse, administrator*

TERRITORIES OF THE UNITED STATES

GUAM

Barrigada
Cruz, Teofila Perez *nursing administrator*

Mangilao
Duenas, Laurent Flores *health and nursing consultant*

PUERTO RICO

Arecibo
Bravo LaLuz, Yamilete N. *pharmacist*

Carolina
López-Hernández, Ledyana *substance abuse counselor*

Fajardo
Millan, Alvin *speech pathology/audiology services professional, educator*

VIRGIN ISLANDS

Charlotte Amalie
Garfield, Winifred L. *nursing administrator*

St Thomas
Clark, Jessie Dona *social worker*

CANADA

ALBERTA

Edmonton
Fields, Anthony Lindsay Austin *health facility administrator, oncologist, educator*
Kovalyov, Mikhail *researcher, educator*

BRITISH COLUMBIA

Vancouver
Desapriya, Ediriweera B.R. *public health expert, researcher*
Riedel, Bernard Edward *retired pharmaceutical sciences educator*

MANITOBA

Winnipeg
Schultz, Harry *health science organization administrator*

NEW BRUNSWICK

Sussex
Secord, Lloyd Douglas *healthcare administrator*

PROFESSIONAL INDEX 5677 HEALTHCARE: HEALTH SERVICES

ONTARIO

Brantford
Inns, Harry Douglas Ellis *retired optometrist*

Etobicoke
Scholefield, Peter Gordon *health agency executive*

Owen Sound
Jones, Phyllis Edith *nursing educator*

Toronto
Turnbull, John Cameron *retired pharmacist, consultant*

QUEBEC

Montreal
Messing, Karen *occupational health researcher*

MEXICO

Reynosa
Asomoza, Miguel A. *researcher, educator*

CHANNEL ISLANDS

Guernsey
Schere, Jean *researcher*

ENGLAND

London
de Savorgnani, Adriane Aldrich *health care administrator, nurse*

Tunbridge Wells
Singer, Norbert *health services professional, educational consultant*
Kingsley, James Gordon *college administrator*

JAPAN

Abiko Chiba
Sakaguchi, Takehiro *healthcare educator, researcher*

Tokyo
Murray, Julia Kaoru (Mrs. Joseph E. Murray) *occupational therapist*

REPUBLIC OF KOREA

Seoul
Chung, Ick-Joong *social worker, educator*

Taegu
Kim, Doohie *retired public health educator*

RUSSIA

Moscow
Collins, Mary *health science association administrator, retired legislator*

SWITZERLAND

Geneva
Maglacas, A. Mangay *nursing researcher, educator*

Versoix
Mahler, Halfdan Theodor *physician, health organization executive*

TAIWAN

Kaohsiung
Chien, Yie W. *pharmaceutical science educator, university dean, academic administrator*

Taipei
Chen, Chien-hsing *Chinese traditional health practices educator*

ZAMBIA

Nangoma
Hansen, Florence Marie Congiolosi (Mrs. James S. Hansen) *social worker*

ADDRESS UNPUBLISHED

Aalberts, Nola Jean *social worker, administrator*
Abbott, Regina A. *neurodiagnostic technologist, consultant, business owner*
Abernathy, Ronald Fitz *pharmacist*
Ackerson, Barry James *social worker*
Adekson, Mary Olufunmilayo *therapist, counselor, educator*
Aehlert, Barbara June *health services executive*
Alberts, Renée Miller *substance abuse and mental health professional*
Allen, Bonnie Lynn *optometrist*
Alton, N. Kirby *health facility administrator*
Alvarez-Galloso, Roberto C. *mental health professional*
Anderson, Ernest Frederick *social worker, educator*
Angermeier, Patricia *occupational therapist*
Antoun, Mikhail *medicinal chemistry and pharmacognosy educator*
Austin, James H(oward), Jr., *healthcare executive*
Austin, John H. *health care administrator*
Babao, Donna Marie *retired community health and psychiatric nurse, educator*
Babitzke, Theresa Angeline *health facility administrator*
Baier, Edward John *former public health official, industrial hygiene engineer, consultant*
Baldwin, William Russell *optometrist, foundation administrator*
Ball, John Robert *healthcare executive*
Banks, Anthony D'Wayne *ergonomist*
Barnett, Major Alex *counselor, educator*
Barry, Camille T. *health and human services director*
Bass, Lynda D. *retired medical/surgical nurse, nursing educator*
Bast, Kenneth George *healthcare executive*
Baymiller, Lynda Doern *social worker*
Bear, Geraldine M. *nursing assistant, poet*
Becich, Raymond Brice *healthcare consultant, mediator, trainer, educator*
Becker, Nancy May *nursing educator*
Bell, Rebecca *psychotherapist, journalist*
Bell, Susan Jane *nurse*
Belles, Donald Arnold *pastoral therapist, mental health counselor*
Belmont, Larry Miller *retired public health executive*
Bennett, Harriet Cook *social worker, educator*
Berger, Miriam Roskin *creative arts therapy director, educator, therapist*
Berger-Kraemer, Nancy *speech and language pathologist, artist*
Berkley, Gail Winnick *psychotherapist*
Berman, Richard Angel *health and educational administrator*
Bertram, Susan *rehabilitation counselor*
Biegel, David Eli *social worker, educator*
Bieron, Louise T. *physician placement executive*
Blackson, Benjamin F(ranklin) *clinical social worker*
Blonz, Edward Robert *nutritionist, biochemist*
Blumberg, Mark Stuart *health services researcher*
Bockius, Ruth Bear *nursing educator*
Boone, Donna Clausen *physical therapist, biostatistician, researcher*
Borg, Ruth I. *home nursing care provider*
Boswell, Dan Alan *health maintenance organization executive, health care consultant*
Bottone, JoAnn *health services executive*
Braun, Mary Lucile Dekle (Lucy Braun) *therapist, consultant, counselor, educator*
Brewer, Barbara Bagdasarian *nursing administrator*
Brodie, Alice Velma *health and ethics advocate*
Brokaw, Meredith A. *women's health care company director*
Bronzi, Philip A. *retired social worker, educator*
Brosz, Margaret Headley *pediatrics nurse*
Brown, April Schlea *pharmacist*
Brown, Barbara June *hospital and nursing administrator*
Brown, Billye Jean *retired nursing educator*
Brown, Geraldine *nurse, freelance writer*
Brown, Stephen Hayze, Jr., *human services caseworker*
Brunett, Emery Walter *pharmacist, educator*
Bryant, Bertha Estelle *retired medical/surgical nurse*
Budnicki, Michael J. *nurse*
Bullough, Vern LeRoy *sexologist, nursing educator, researcher, historian*
Bundy, Mary Lothrop *retired clinical social worker*
Burke, Grace Dora Reynolds *medical/surgical nurse*
Büsch, Annemarie *retired mental health nurse*
Byrd, Lorenda Sue *nursing administrator*
Campbell, Claire Patricia *nurse practitioner, educator*
Campbell, Edward Wallace *nutritionist*
Caples, Lakeisha Lalaine *researcher*
Carman, Susan Hufert *nurse coordinator*
Carney, Robert Alfred *retired health care administrator*
Carson, Mary Silvano *career counselor, educator*
Carter, James Harvey, Jr., *physician assistant*
Casey, Nancy J. *women's healthcare company executive*
Casso, James C. *social worker, mental health services professional*
Castleman, Breaux Ballard *health management company executive*
Cauthorne-Burnette, Tamera Dianne *family nurse practitioner, healthcare consultant*
Centafont, Lucy Ann Alexander *occupational therapy consultant*
Chait, Fay Klein *health administrator*
Chambers-Steinberg, Wanda *researcher*
Chapman, Thomas William *hospital executive*
Chin, Jennifer Young *public health educator*
Cholewka, Patricia Anne *health services administrator*
Chow, Rita Kathleen *nursing consultant*
Christiansen, David K. *healthcare administrator*
Clendinen, Cynthia A.A. *healthcare professional, compliance specialist*
Cohen, Norman Girard *retired social worker, writer*
Coleman, Jean Black *nurse, physician assistant*
Condry, Robert Stewart *retired hospital administrator*
Conley, Sarah Ann *health facility administrator*
Cooper, Eugene Bruce *speech, language pathologist, educator*
Cortright, Louise Vera *retired medical technologist, small business owner*
Cosby, Stephanie Bennett *health services professional*
Cotruvo, Joseph Alfred *environmental and public health consultant*
Couch, Daniel Michael *healthcare executive*
Couchman, Robert George James *foundation executive director*
Cox, John Curtis *healthcare and educational administrator*
Crawford, Debra P. *women's healthcare company executive*
Crawford, Randi *women's healthcare company executive*
Crocker, Barbara Jean *clinical nurse specialist*
Cromwell, Florence Stevens *occupational therapist*
Curt, Gregory A. *clinical director*
da Fonseca, Augusto J. *social worker*
Darkovich, Sharon Marie *nurse administrator*
Daus, Victoria Lynn *nurse midwife*
Davis, Bertha *emergency nurse practitioner, emergency medical technician*
Davis, Carolyne Kahle *health care consultant*
Davis, Charles S. *biostatistician*
Davis, Crystal Michelle *state health administrator*
Davis, June Fiksdal *medical facility owner, floral designer*
Davis, Margaret Thacker *retired critical care, medical and surgical nurse*
Dawson, Karen Oltmanns *nursing educator*
Day, Steven Matthew *researcher, consultant*
De Antoni, Edward Paul *lab administrator*
Deely, Maureen Cecelia *community health nurse*
DeLapp, Tina Davis *retired nursing educator*
DeMille, Dale Esther *medical/surgical nurse, educator*
Desjardins, Judith Anne *psychotherapist*
Dickens, Alycia Thompson *nurse practitioner*
Dickens, Joyce Rebecca *addictions therapist, educator*
Diedrick, Geraldine Rose *retired nurse*
Dincecco, Jennie Elizabeth Williams Swanson *healthcare administrator, mentor, healthcare educator, volunteer*
Doberenz, Alexander R. *nutrition educator, chemist*
Dogoloff, Lee Israel *clinical social worker, psychotherapist, consultant*
Donahue, Mary Beth *human services administrator*
Doniger, Jay *health information executive*
Donnelly, PaJa Lee *nursing educator and nurse practitioner*
Dorman, Arthur *optometrist, state legislator*
Downing, Cynthia Hurst *therapist, addiction and abuse specialist*
Dressel, Irene Emma Ringwald *alcoholism and family therapist*
Drews, Jürgen *pharmaceutical researcher*
Dryden, David W. *pharmacist, executive secretary*
Dubé, Susan E. *women's healthcare company executive*
Duffy, Mary Kathleen *neonatal nurse*
Dunlap, Tanya Louise *nurse, writer*
Dyer, Wayne Walter *psychologist, writer, radio and television personality*
Eason, Karen E. *public health service officer, researcher*
Ebinger, Linda Ann *nurse*
Edelsberg, Sally Comins *physical therapy educator and administrator*
Edelstein, Rosemarie (Rosemarie Hublou) *medical/surgical nurse, educator, gerontological nurse, medical and legal consultant*
Eichel, Edward William *psychotherapist, painter*
Elkins, Robert N. *association executive*
Elliott-Zahorik, Bonnie *nurse, administrator*
Emerson, Ann Parker *retired dietitian, educator*
Engle, Jane *research nurse, artist, chaplain*
Erenstein, Alan *emergency nurse practitioner*
Essex, Lauren S. *women's health care company executive*
Farrington, Bertha Louise *retired nursing administrator*
Farthing, Aliana M. *critical care nurse, writer*
Feathers, Gail M. Wratny *social worker*
Feigal, David W., Jr., *health science association administrator*
Felhofer, Marylouise Katherine *nursing administrator*
Ferguson, Paula Irene *nursing administrator*
Finder-Stone, Patricia Ann *nurse, health educator, volunteer*
Findling, Rhonda Barbara *psychotherapist*
Fischer, Carl Robert *retired health care facility administrator*
Fogelman, Ann Florence *nutrition consultant, educator, researcher*
Forest, Eva Brown *nursing administrator, songwriter*
Franciosa, Joseph Anthony *health care consultant*
Francke, Gloria Niemeyer *pharmacist, editor, publisher*
Frank-Fitzner, Fontaine Lynne *geriatrics nurse, insurance company executive*
Franklin-Griffin, Cathy Lou Hinson *nursing educator*
Frederick-Mairs, T(hyra) Julie *administrative health services official*
Freese, Barbara Tapp *nursing educator*
Froiland, Kathryn Grace *nursing educator*
Fuller, Richard Kenneth *retired alcohol/drug abuse services professional*
Gable, Karen Lynn *social worker*
Gardner, Clyde Edward *healthcare executive, consultant, educator*
Gardner, Judith Sturgen *nursing administrator, educator*
Garza, Cutberto *nutrition educator*
Gerald, Michael Charles *pharmacy educator, dean*
Gerry, Debra Prue *psychotherapist, recording artist, writer*
Giannella, Susanne *women's health, medical, and surgical nurse*
Gibson, Scott Russell *nursing administrator*
Giles, Melva Theresa *nursing educator*
Gilmore, David Schneiter *administrator*
Gladden, Vivianne Cervantes *healthcare consultant, writer*
Glenn, Lois A *paramedic*
Glynn, Peter Alexander Richard *healthcare consultant*
Godager, Jane Ann *retired social worker*
Gonzales, Richard Robert *counselor*
Goodman, Robert Lee *nursing administrator*
Goodwin, Phillip Hugh *hospital administrator*
Gordon, Ruby Daniels *retired nursing educator, counselor*
Gottlieb, Gary L. *hospital administrator*
Govan, Gladys Vernita Mosley *retired critical care and medical/surgical nurse*
Graham, Warren Kenyon *counselor*
Grant, Richard Earl *retired medical and legal consultant*
Gray, Barbara Bronson *nurse, foundation administrator, writer, public relations executive*
Greene, Monica Lynn Banks *recreational therapist, director*
Greenfield, Linda Sue *nursing educator*
Greenhaw, Judith Yvonne *health facility administrator, medical/surgical nurse*
Greggs, Elanora *social worker*
Gregory, Jackie Sue *critical care nurse, family nurse practitioner*
Grenier, Laura Margiotta *medical/surgical nurse*
Grolli, Frank Thomas *retired pharmacist*
Grunder, Fred Irwin *industrial hygienist, consultant*
Guedes, Alessandra Casanova *public health service officer*
Hammond, Robie Lee *health science association administrator*
Han, Timothy Wayne *drug abuse professional, public health educator*
Hansen-Carter, Marilyn Ray *retired mental health nurse*
Hansen-Kyle, Linda L *managed health care nurse, nursing educator*
Hanson, Elayne June *medical information administrator*
Hardy, James Chester *speech pathologist, educator*
Harman, Donald Lee *nurse, educator, consultant*
Harms, Nancy Ann *nursing educator*
Harrell, Carolyn Hardison *nursing home administrator*
Hart-Duling, Jean Macaulay *clinical social worker*
Hartman, Lenore Anne *physical therapist*
Harvey, Michelle Mauthe *researcher, consultant*
Harvey, Paul Thomas *healthcare executive*
Hasselmeyer, Eileen Grace *medical research administrator*
Hayes, Daphne L. *researcher*
Hays, Patrick Gregory *health care executive*
Headlee, Raymond *retired psychoanalyst, educator*
Healy, Patricia Colleen *social worker*
Healy, Sonya Ainslie *retired health facility administrator*
Helrich, Amy Louise *medical/surgical nurse*
Henneman, Stephen Charles *psychotherapist*
Henry, Sue *social worker, educator*
Herren, Chris *mental health services professional, psychologist, researcher*
Hertz, Kenneth Theodore *health care executive*
Hickman, Lucille *physical therapist*
Hill, Martha N. *community health nurse*
Hofmann, Paul Bernard *healthcare consultant*
Hollis, Mary Fern Caudill *nurse educator, music educator, writer*
Holtzman, David H. *technologist, security and privacy expert*
Honea, Joyce Clayton *critical care nurse*
Hooker, Renée Michelle *perinatal and perianesthesia nurse*
Houtz, Duane Talbott *hospital administrator*
Howe, John Prentice, III, *health facility administrator, physician*
Howe, Virginia Hoffman *nurse administrator*
Hui, Sai-Hung *emergency medical professional*
Hutzler, Lisa Ann *mental health nurse, adult clinical psychologist*
Inscho, Jean Anderson *retired social worker, landscape artist*
Iriart, Celia Beatriz *healthcare educator, consultant, researcher*
Isong, Enó *public health service officer*
Jackson-Tkac, Stephanie Ann *nurse*
Jarvis, Irene *retired medical/surgical nurse*
Jew, Henry *pharmacist*
John, Gerald Warren *pharmacist, educator*
Johnson, Barbara Ann *health services educator*
Johnson, Wendy S. *women's healthcare company executive*
Jones, Donna Lee Noble *emergency nurse*
Jones, Jolene Rebecca *medical transcriptionist, educator*
Joseph, Eleanor Ann *health science association administrator, consultant*
Juenemann, Sister Jean *hospital executive*
Kaiser, Nina Irene *health care consultant*
Kampf, Marilyn Jeanne *medical analyst*
Kapalcik, Michele Lida *therapist, guidance counselor*
Karp, Rosanne *oncology and women's health nurse*
Kerr, Frederick Hohmann *retired health care company executive*
King, Imogene M. *retired nursing educator*
King, Sheldon Selig *health facility administrator, educator*
Kirkpatrick, Charles Harvey *physician, immunology researcher*
Kiszka, Sonia Ann *nurse practitioner, educator*
Kline-Koenig, Barbara A. *nursing case manager*
Knies, Robert Carl, Jr., *critical care nurse*
Kohn, Jean Gatewood *retired health facility administrator, pediatrician*
Kolasa, Kathryn Marianne *food and nutrition educator, consultant*
Kopec-Garnett, Linda *nurse, researcher*
Kortepeter, Karl Nuri *dietician*
Krehtinkoff-Yarlovsky, Nina *nursing administrator, medical-legal consulting firm owner*
Kruger, Nancy R. *university program director, nurse*
Kuhler, Deborah Gail *grief therapist, former state legislator*
Lacedra, Christine A. *medical/surgical nurse, educator*
Langenkamp, Sandra Carroll *retired human services administrator*
Lanphear, Bruce Perrin *health facility administrator, educator*
Larson, Vicki Lord *communication disorders educator*
Latiolais, Minnie Fitzgerald *retired nurse, health facility administrator*
Lawrence, David M. *health facility administrator*
Leddy, Susan *nursing educator*
Lee, Sarena Janeen *buyer, disaster preparedness professional*
Lehmann, Danica Maria *psychotherapist*
Leigh, Vincenta M. *health administrator*
Lenart, Paul Alan *respiratory therapist*
L'Eplattenier, Nora Sweeny Hickey *nursing educator*
Levin, Peter J. *hospital administrator, public health educator*
Ligenza, Andrea Angela *nurse*
Loarie, Thomas Merritt *healthcare executive*
Logan, David Bruce *health care administrator, nurse*
Loop, Floyd D. *retired healthcare executive*
Lopez Lysne, Robin *counselor, writer, artist*
Louise, Lynette *counselor, writer*
Lowinsky, Naomi Ruth *psychoanalyst, poet*
Lubic, Ruth Watson *health facility administrator, nurse midwife*
Luce, Donald Sanders *social worker*
Luddy, Paula Scott *nursing educator*
Lund, Doris Hibbs *retired dietitian*
Lung, Christine *health science association administrator*
Lynch-Polansky, Patricia *health services executive*
Lyngbye, Jørgen *hospital administrator, researcher*
Lyons, Anthony Patrick *acoustician, acoustical engineer, researcher*

MacKenzie, Donald Murray *healthcare administrator*
MacMullen, Jean Alexandria Stewart *nurse, administrator*
Magnuson, Robert Martin *retired health facility administrator*
Majors, Nelda Faye *physical therapist*
Malek, Marlene Anne *healthcare advocate, foundation administrator*
Malin, Harold Martin, Jr., *sexologist, educator*
Manning, Joan Elizabeth *health association administrator*
Maplesden, Carol Harper *marital and family therapist, music educator*
Marchan, Marissa L. *social worker*
Marcinek, Margaret Ann *nursing educator*
Marcoux, Julia A. *midwife*
Markle, Cheri Virginia Cummins *nurse*
Marquez, Jennifer Trachsel *health facility administrator*
Marquis, Harriet Hill *social worker*
Marselis-Moore, Jadeh *emergency room nurse, alcohol/drug abuse nurse*
Marshall, Donald Thomas *retired medical technician, theology studies educator*
Marshall, Phyllis Ellinwood *health facility administrator, consultant*
Martin, Julie *women's healthcare company executive*
Martin, Karen Siebenthal *community health nurse*
Martin, William Collier *hospital administrator*
Maslanka, Sandra Karen *social worker, educator, educational consultant*
Mata, Josefina *health education coordinator*
Materia, Kathleen Patricia Ayling *nurse*
Matherlee, Thomas Ray *health care consultant*
May, Joan Verner *nursing consultant*
McCarthy, Rhoda Ann *nursing administrator, medical/surgical nurse*
McCraven, Carl Clarke *health service administrator*
McCuistion, Peg Orem *retired hospice administrator*
McGeer, James Peter *research executive, consultant*
McGrath, Eileen Marie *pediatric nurse*
McNulty, Kathleen Anne *clinical social worker, psychotherapist, business consultant,*
Medina, Sandra *social worker, educator*
Meehan, John Joseph, Jr., *hospital administrator*
Meyer, Harry Martin, Jr., *retired health science facility administrator*
Mikan, Kathleen Joyce Kehrer *medical/surgical nurse, educator*
Mikel, Thomas Kelly, Jr., *laboratory administrator*
Milewski, Barbara Anne *pediatrics nurse, neonatal/perinatal nurse practitioner, critical care nurse*
Millar, John Donald *occupational and environmental health consultant, essayist, musician*
Miller, Lenore Wolf Daniels *speech-language pathologist*
Miller, Steven *medical administrator*
Miller-Young, Corriene Calhoun *nursing educator*
Milnor, Hazel *nurse*
Milunas, J. Robert *health care organization executive*
Minniti, Martha Jean *home healthcare company executive*
Miracle, Doris Jean *retired medical/surgical nurse*
Misner, Lorraine *laboratory technologist*
Mitchell, Carol Ann *nursing educator*
Mitchell, Geneva Brooke *hypnotherapist*
Moffatt, Hugh McCulloch, Jr., *hospital administrator, physical therapist*
Molnar, Violet *mental health nurse*
Monck, Maureen F. *psychoanalyst*
Moreland, Diane Christina *researcher*
Morgan, Evelyn Buck *retired nursing educator*
Morrison, Richard Drury *health policy consultant, medical educator*
Mortimer, Mary R. *counselor*
Mosqueira, Charlotte Marianne *dietitian*
Mullette, Julienne Patricia *health facility administrator*
Munic, Rachelle Ethel *health services administrator*
Munier, William Boss *medical service executive*
Muñoz Dones De Carrascal, Eloisa *hospital administrator, pediatrician, consultant, educator*
Murphy, Margaret A. *nursing educator, adult nurse practitioner*
Nakagawa, Allen Donald *radiologic technologist*
Narayanan, Mohanram *health facility administrator, medical educator*
Nardozzi, Peter Michael *pharmacist, clinical educator, lecturer, entrepreneur*
Nashif, Taysir N. *researcher*
Neumann, Forrest Karl *retired health facility administrator*
Newcomb, Robert Douglas *optometrist, clinician, educator*
Nichols, Elizabeth Grace *nursing educator, dean*
Nidetz, Myron Philip *health care delivery systems consultant*
Nightengale, Rochelle M. *rehabilitation services professional*
Norbeck, Jane S. *retired nursing educator*
Norkin, Cynthia Clair *retired physical therapist*
Nuttelman, Doris Graves *nursing administrator*
O'Connor Taylor, Sheryl Ann *medical services administrator*
Oerter, Cynthia Lynn *medical technologist*
Okolski, Cynthia Antonia *psychotherapist, social worker*
O'Neill, Donald Edmund *health science executive*
O'Neill, James F. *retired health facility administrator*
O'Quinn, Nancy Diane *nurse, educator, consultant*
Otis, Jack *social work educator*
Parham, Ellen Speiden *nutrition educator*
Pariag, Haimwattie Ramkistodas *information management administrator*
Parker, Susan Brooks *healthcare executive*
Parkman, Cynthia Ann *medical and surgical nurse, nursing educator*
Paskawicz, Jeanne Frances *pain specialist*
Penachio, Anthony Joseph, Jr., *psychotherapist, hypnotherapist, behavioral therapist*
Pepelea, Kimberli Rae *case manager*
Peters, Carol Ann Dudycha *counselor*
Peters, Douglas Alan *medical-legal consultant, health law attorney*
Pierce, Shaheeda Laura *midwife, consultant*
Pipchick, Margaret Hopkins *advance practice nurse, marriage and family therapist*
Pitts, Deborah Krueger *healthcare consultant*
Plummer, Leone Poindexter *marriage and family therapist, nursing educator, nurse practitioner*
Poe, Laura *nursing educator, administrator*
Poulton, Roberta Doris *nurse, consultant*
Price, Donna B. *special education services professional*
Przybylski, Sandra Marie *speech pathologist*
Quattrone-Carroll, Diane Rose *clinical social worker*
Quilala, Joanna Caneda *physician assistant, researcher*
Ragsdale, Richard Elliot *healthcare management executive*
Ramsey, Janet Louise *public health service officer*
Rand, Joella Mae *retired nursing educator, counselor*
Randolph, Donald Phillip *nurse anesthetist*
Reece, Sheila Marlene *health facility administrator, writer*
Reid, Virginia Anne *school nurse*
Reilly, Robert Joseph *counselor*
Rella, Francis John *paramedic, writer*
Rickert, Janet E. *medical/surgical nurse*
Rimer, Barbara K. *health facility administrator, educator*
Rindone, Joseph Patrick *clinical pharmacist, educator*
Ritter, Elise Dawn *therapist, clinical social worker, writer, artist, artist*
Ritter, Madeliene *practical nurse, surgical technologist*
Robinson, Gail Patricia *retired mental health counselor*
Robinson, William Andrew *health service executive, physician*
Rodriguez, Donna Jeanne Anglin *dietician, writer*
Rollins, Diann E. *nurse, occupational health nurse*
Rosenfeld, Martin Jerome *healthcare executive, educator*
Rubin, Phyllis Getz *health association executive*
Ruskaup, Calvin *therapist, history professor*
Sabatini, Nelson John *health care executive*
Salerno, Sister Maria *nursing educator, adult and gerontological nurse*
Samuels, Marc *health care consultant*
Sandorsen, Cassiopeia *public health service officer*
Santina, Dalia *nutritionist, writer, skin care specialist*
Santos, Lisa Wells *critical care nurse*
Sastrowardoyo, Teresita Manejar *nurse*
Savoy, Suzanne Marie *advanced practice nurse*
Sawyer-Morse, Mary Kaye *nutritionist, educator*
Scala, James *health care industry consultant, writer*
Schnabel, Gary A. *health facility administrator, director*
Schoenberg, April Mindy *nursing administrator*
Schuch, Cynthia Silleck *nurse*
Scott, Justine Ford *counselor, educator*
Shabot, Myron Michael *surgeon, critical care educator, informaticist*
Shane, Donea Lynne *retired nursing educator*
Shanks, Kathryn Mary *health care administrator*
Shannon, Margaret T. *nursing administrator, educator*
Shannon, Mary Lou *adult health nursing educator*
Shapiro, David Benjamin *researcher*
Shepherd, Douglas *hospital administrator*
Shores, Pearl Marie *health care company executive*
Simpson, Jack Benjamin *medical technologist, business executive*
Simpson, John Noel (Virginia Simpson) *healthcare administrator*
Slaughter, Djuanique Naté *healthcare analyst, project manager, consultant*
Smith, Angele Leora *school nurse practitioner, poet, artist*
Smith, Barbara Anne *health facility administrator, consultant*
Smith, Connie *hospital administrator*
Smith, Ethel Farrington *retired social worker, genealogist, writer*
Smith, Gloria Richardson *nursing educator*
Smith, Ronald Lynn *health system executive*
Sneider, Joyce Pappachristou *dietitian, educator*
Somes, Joan Marie *emergency nurse*
Sommerfeld, Marianna *retired social worker, writer*
Speer, Nancy Girouard *health care administrator*
Splane, Richard Beverley *social work educator*
Stancil, Irene Mack *family counselor*
Stash, Susan Michele *critical care nurse*
Steele, Dale F. *women's healthcare company executive*
Steelman, Deborah Macon *pharmaceutical consultant*
Stevens, Linda Doreen *intensive care nurse*
Stickles, Bonnie Jean *retired nurse*
Stillings, Dennis Otto *research association administrator, consultant*
Stoddard, M. Anita *psychiatric nurse*
Stratton, Mariann *retired naval nursing administrator*
Strauss, Dorothy Brandfon *marriage and family therapist*
Stutzman, Sandra Louise *advanced nurse practitioner*
Suber, Robin Hall *former medical and surgical nurse*
Suelto, Consuelo Quilao *retired nursing educator*
Tack, Theresa Rose *women's health nurse*
Talty, Kathryn Melene *women's health nurse, artist*
Tan, Marianne Mee-Ryung *pharmacist, medical liaison, consultant*
Tanner, Peggy *retired nurse*
Taylor, Edna Jane *retired employment program counselor*
Tewfik, Diane Burak *occupational therapist, educator*
Thiel, David Brian *physician assistant*
Thomas, Robert Rene *physician assistant, athletic trainer*
Thomas, Stephen Crawford *social worker*
Thome, Javier *medical/surgical nurse*
Thompson, Theodis *retired healthcare executive, health management consultant*
Thrasher, Rose Marie *critical care nurse, community health nurse*
Tinner, Franziska Paula *social worker, artist, apparel designer, educator, entrepreneur*
Tolliver, Glenda Reeder *social worker*
Towlen, Tracey *physical therapist*
Townsend, Frances (Fran Townsend) *healthcare educator, writer*
Tracy, Susanne Mary *nursing educator*
Tran, Henry Bang Q. *social work case manager*
Tucceri, Ellen Lee *medical/surgical nurse*
Uris, Patricia Firme *health science association administrator*
Varga, Jeanne-Marie *women's healthcare company executive*
Veyna, Adrienne Marie *exercise specialist*
Vince, April Renee *social worker*
Violet, Woodrow Wilson, Jr., *retired chiropractor*
Vogel, H. Victoria *psychotherapist, trauma, post-traumatic stress disorder and addiction recovery counselor and educator, author*
Vohs, James Arthur *health care program executive*
Walker, Henry Gilbert *health care executive, consultant*
Walston, Lola Inge *dietitian*
Weaver, Agnes Jin Ai *medical/surgical nurse*
Webb, Pharron R. *counselor, secondary school educator*
Weil, Thomas P. *health services consultant*
Westcarr, Linton Anthony *nurse, pharmacist, writer*
Wheatley, George Milholland *medical administrator*
White, Eugene Vaden *retired pharmacist*
Wiebe, Leonard Irving *radiopharmacist, educator*
Wieland, William Dean *healthcare consulting executive*
Wiley, James Francis *emergency medical technician, civilian military employee*
Williams, Stuart W. *health facility administrator*
Williams Maddox-Brown, Janice Helen *nurse*
Williamson, William Allen *retired optometrist*
Wills, Ritchie Jean *hospital administrator*
Wilson, Karen Lee *researcher*
Wilson, Maron Loy *nurse midwife*
Winsley, William T. *pharmacist, executive director*
Wishert, Martina *nursing home administrator*
Wolfberg, Melvin Donald *optometrist, educational administrator, consultant*
Wood, John Arthur *nurse*
Work, David R. *pharmacist, executive director*
Wright, Dell *residential care and treatment facility executive*
Wuthnow, Sara Margery *retired nursing educator*
Wyatt, Rose Marie *clinical social worker*
Wyche, Ruth Skyler *rehabilitation contractor, researcher*
Yarbrough, Kathryn Davis *public health nurse*
Young, Deborah (Deborah Ayling Yanowitz) *social worker, librarian*
Zeleznak, Shirley Anne *psychotherapist*
Ziegenhagen, David Mackenzie *consultant, retired healthcare company executive*

HEALTHCARE: MEDICINE

UNITED STATES

ALABAMA

Alexander City
Tyler, Eric Owen *pediatrician*

Auburn
Parsons, Daniel Lankester *pharmaceutics educator*

Birmingham
Avent, Charles Kirk *medical educator*
Bedwell, David M. *medical educator*
Bell, David Samuel Henry *medical educator*
Bueschen, Anton Joslyn *physician, educator*
Callahan, Alston *physician, author*
Caulfield, James Benjamin *pathologist, educator*
Clayton, Orville Woolford *surgeon*
Cooper, Max Dale *pediatrician, researcher*
Curtis, John J. *medical educator*
Davis, Richard Oliver *obstetrician-gynecologist, educator*
Diethelm, Arnold Gillespie *surgeon*
Dowdey, Benjamin Charles *physician*
Dubovsky, Eva Vitkova *nuclear medicine physician, educator*
Epstein, Andrew Ernest *cardiologist, educator*
Fine, Philip Russel *medical educator*
Finley, Wayne House *medical educator*
Fix, R. Jobe *plastic surgeon, reconstructive hand surgeon*
Greene, Ernest Rinaldo, Jr., *anesthesiologist, chemical engineer*
Hirschowitz, Basil Isaac *physician*
Johnston, Carden *emergency physician, pediatrician*
Kirby, Russell Stephen *epidemiologist, statistician, geographer*
Koopman, William James *medical educator, internist, immunologist*
Lochridge, Stanley Keith *cardiovascular and thoracic surgeon*
Meezan, Elias *pharmacologist, educator*
Nepomuceno, Cecil Santos *physician*
Oakes, Walter Jerry *pediatric neurosurgeon*
Omura, George Adolf *medical oncologist*
Oparil, Suzanne *cardiologist, researcher, educator*
Pacifico, Albert Dominick *cardiovascular surgeon*
Pittman, Constance Shen *endocrinologist, educator*
Pittman, James Allen, Jr., *endocrinologist, educator*
Pohost, Gerald Michael *cardiologist, medical educator*
Rousso, Daniel Elliott *facial plastic surgeon, educator*
Russell, Richard Olney, Jr., *cardiologist, educator*
Shaw, George M. *hematologist, educator*
Skalka, Harold Walter *ophthalmologist, educator*
Stevenson, Edward Ward *retired physician, surgeon, otolaryngologist*
Vickers, Selwyn M. *surgeon*
Warnock, David Gene *nephrologist*
Wells, Alan Hilary *biomedical researcher*

Fairfield
Hamrick, Leon Columbus *surgeon, medical director*

Fairhope
Mozley, Paul David *retired obstetrics and gynecology educator*
Ottensmeyer, David Joseph *retired neurosurgeon, retired healthcare executive*

Huntsville
Huber, Donald Simon *physician*
Nuessle, William Raymond *surgeon*
Robinson, Helen Margaret *emergency physician, internist*
Tietke, Wilhelm *gastroenterologist, educator*

Mobile
Atkinson, William James, Jr., *retired cardiologist*
Brogdon, Byron Gilliam *physician, radiology educator*
Cohen, Michael Victor *cardiologist*
DeBakey, Ernest George *physician, surgeon*
Eichold, Samuel *medical educator, medical museum curator*
Littleton, Jesse Talbot, III, *radiology educator*
LoCicero, Joseph *thoracic surgeon, researcher*
Pitcock, James Kent *head and neck surgical oncologist*
Rodning, Charles Bernard *surgeon*
Smith, Jesse Graham, Jr., *dermatologist, educator*

Montgomery
Adams, Robert Barry *pathologist*
Barnes, Harrey McGwinn, III, *internist, oncologist*
Frazer, David Hugh, Jr., *allergist*
Givhan, Edgar Gilmore *physician, writer*
Hunker, Fred Dominic *internist, medical educator*
Lee, Harry Antonius *allergist, immunologist*
Myers, Ira Lee *physician*

Orange Beach
Conrad, Marcel Edward *hematologist, educator*

Spanish Fort
Benjamin, Regina Marcia *physician, administrator*

Tuscaloosa
Koger, Michael Pigott *physician, writer*
Lumpkin, Thomas Riley *physician, educator*
Pieroni, Robert Edward *internist, educator, military officer*
Sinclair, Robert Ewald *retired physician*

ALASKA

Anchorage
Christensen, Ronald E. *physician*
Conway, George A. *medical epidemiologist, physician*
Park, Gloria *family physician, consultant*
Rogers, Donald Robert *retired pathologist*

Fairbanks
Hess, Richard Christian, Jr., *obstetrician/gynecologist, educator*

Valdez
Todd, Kathleen Gail *physician*

ARIZONA

Carefree
Hook, William Franklin *retired radiologist*

Casa Grande
Houle, Joseph Adrien *orthopedic surgeon*
Kapsos, Philip John *anesthesiologist*
Khan, Habib Urrehman *neurologist*

Flagstaff
Braunstein, Ethan Malcolm *skeletal radiologist, paleopathologist, educator*
Weston, Laurie Beth *psychiatrist*

Glendale
Michael, Cecil Francis, Jr., *pediatrician*

Green Valley
Moser, Robert Harlan *internist, educator, writer*

Mesa
Fiorino, John Wayne *podiatrist*
Hagen, Nicholas Steward *medical educator, consultant*
McGill, John J. *radiologist*
Thompson, Ronald MacKinnon *former family physician, artist, writer*

Paradise Valley
Buffmire, Donald K. *retired internist*
Burkholder, Peter Miller *physician, educator*
Lorenzen, Robert Frederick *ophthalmologist*
Morris, Stephen Owens *psychiatrist*
Targovnik, Selma E. Kaplan *physician*

Phoenix
Ammon, John Richard *anesthesiologist*
Bodensteiner, John Burton *neurologist*
Charlton, John Kipp *pediatrician*
Desser, Kenneth Barry *cardiologist, educator*
DuVal, Merlin Kearfott *health consultant*
Felicetta, James Vincent *endocrinologist, educator*
Fishburne, John Ingram, Jr., *obstetrician/gynecologist, educator*
Goldberg, Morris *internist*
Hammerschlag, Carl A *psychiatrist*
Hotz, Jeffrey Alan *anesthesiologist, educator*
Laufer, Nathan *cardiologist*
Lawrence, William Henry, Jr., *neurologist*
Levin, Warren Mayer *family practice physician*
Lovett, William Lee *surgeon*
McLoone, James Brian *psychiatrist, educator*
Reed, Wallace Allison *anesthesiologist*
Rudd, Gerald Patrick *ophthalmologist*
Sage, Webster LeGene, Jr., *ophthalmologist*
Singer, Jeffrey Alan *surgeon*
Stern, Stanley *psychiatrist*
Swafford, Leslie Eugene *physician assistant, consultant*
Teague, Robert Cole *physician*
Theodore, Nicholas *neurosurgeon, researcher*
Underwood, Paul Lester *cardiologist*
Wright, Richard Oscar, III, *pathologist, educator, clinical ethicist*
Zerella, Joseph T. *retired pediatric surgeon*

Scottsdale
Cawley, Leo Patrick *pathologist, immunologist*
Chaurasia, Vishal *physician, writer, computer programmer*
Clement, Richard William *plastic and reconstructive surgeon*

Dahl, Mark Victor *dermatologist, educator*
Evans, Tommy Nicholas *obstetrician/gynecologist, educator*
French, Lyle Albert *surgeon*
Friedman, Shelly Arnold *cosmetic surgeon*
Garcia-Buñuel, Luis *neurologist*
Kinney, Carolyn *physician*
Leighton, William D. *plastic and reconstructive surgeon*
Lewis, John Christopher *allergist*
Lillo, Joseph Leonard *osteopath, family practice physician*
Meland, N. Bradly *plastic surgeon*
Nadler, Henry Louis *pediatrician, geneticist, medical educator*
Orford, Robert Raymond *consulting physician*
Reznick, Richard Howard *pediatrician*
Sanderson, David R. *physician*
Steier, Jeffrey David *neurologist*
Watkins, Eugene Leonard *surgeon, educator*
Weisman, Avery *psychiatrist*

Sedona
Briney, Allan King *retired radiologist*
Hawkins, David Ramon *psychiatrist, writer, researcher, religious studies educator*
Metzner, Richard Joel *psychiatrist, psychopharmacologist, educator*
Reno, Joseph Harry *retired orthopedic surgeon*
Shors, Clayton Marion *cardiologist*

Sun City
Buchman, Elwood *internist, pharmaceutical company medical director*
Nicchi, Vincent, Jr., *cardiologist*

Tempe
Anand, Suresh Chandra *physician*
Boren, Kenneth Ray *endocrinologist, nephrologist*
Rowley, Beverley Davies *medical sociologist*
Schneller, Eugene Stewart *health administration and policy educator*

Tubac
Pardue, A. Michael *retired plastic and reconstructive surgeon*

Tucson
Alberts, David Samuel *physician, pharmacologist, educator*
Alpert, Joseph Stephen *physician, educator*
Ben-Asher, M. David *physician*
Capp, Michael Paul *physician, educator*
Carter, L. Philip *neurosurgeon, consultant*
Corrigan, James John, Jr., *pediatrician, educator, dean*
Dalen, James Eugene *cardiologist, educator*
DeLuca, Dominick *medical educator, researcher*
Elliott, Sean P. *pediatrician, infectious disease specialist*
Ewy, Gordon Allen *cardiologist, clinician, researcher, educator*
Gatenby, Robert A. *radiologist*
Graham, Anna Regina *pathologist, educator*
Harris, David Thomas *immunology educator*
Hattery, Robert Ralph *radiologist, educator*
Hess, Richard Neal *plastic surgeon*
Houser, Harold Byron *epidemiologist*
Huestis, Douglas William *physician, pathologist*
King, Joseph Willet *child psychiatrist*
Kischer, Clayton Ward *human embryologist, educator*
Levenson, Alan Ira *psychiatrist, physician, educator*
Levine, Norman *physician*
Marcus, Frank Isadore *cardiologist, educator*
Martin, Loren Winston *allergist*
Meislin, Harvey Warren *emergency healthcare physician, professional society administrator*
Pollack, Irwin William *psychiatrist, educator*
Rogers, Lee Frank *radiologist*
Ross, Robert *medical association administrator*
Sampliner, Richard Evan *physician*
Schumacher, Michael John *allergist*
Stearns, Elliott Edmund, Jr., *retired surgeon*
Theodorou, Andreas A. *pediatrician, educator*
Weil, Andrew Thomas *physician, educator*
Witte, Marlys Hearst *internist, educator*
Woolfenden, James Manning *nuclear medicine physician, educator*
Woosley, Raymond *pharmacologist, educator*

Vail
Reichlin, Seymour *physician, educator*

ARKANSAS

Arkadelphia
Fullerton, John C., III, *surgeon*

El Dorado
Tommey, Charles Eldon *retired surgeon*

Fayetteville
Fink, William James *retired surgeon*

Fort Smith
Coleman, Michael Dortch *nephrologist*
Drolshagen, Leo Francis, III, *radiologist, physician*
Howell, James Tennyson *allergist, immunologist, pediatrician*
Snider, James Rhodes *radiologist*

Helena
Kontos, George John, Jr., *surgeon*

Hot Springs National Park
Brunner, John Harry *surgeon*

Jonesboro
Jones, Kenneth Bruce *surgeon*

Little Rock
Anand, Kanwaljeet Singh *pediatrician, researcher*
Apuya, Jesus Serra *anesthesiologist*
Barnes, Robert Webster *medical educator*
Bates, Joseph Henry *internist, educator*
Bissada, Nabil Kaddis *urologist, educator, researcher, author*
Bruce, Thomas Allen *physician, educator*
Campbell, Gilbert Sadler *surgery educator, surgeon*
Ferrer, Thomas John *surgeon*

Hart, Ronald Wilson *radiobiologist, educator, toxicologist, researcher, corporate advisor*
Hough, Aubrey Johnston, Jr., *pathologist, physician, educator*
Jansen, G. Thomas *dermatologist*
Kemp, Stephen Frank *pediatric endocrinologist, educator, composer*
Lang, Nicholas Paul *surgeon*
Lucy, Dennis Durwood, Jr., *neurologist, educator*
Mehta, Jawahar Lal *cardiologist*
Mrak, Robert Emil *neuropathologist, educator, electron microscopist*
Reece, E. Albert *dean, obstetrician, gynecologist, perinatologist*
Sherman, Jerome Kalman *retired anatomy educator*
Sotomora-von Ahn, Ricardo Federico *pediatrician, educator*
Ward, Harry Pfeffer *hematologist, retired academic administrator*
Wenger, Galen Rosenberger *pharmacology educator*
Westbrook, Kent Coleman *surgeon, educator*

North Little Rock
Clothier, Jeffrey Lane *neuropsychiatrist, educator*
Lawson, William Bradford *psychiatrist*

Rogers
Summerlin, William Talley *allergist, immunologist, dermatologist*

Scranton
Uzman, Betty Ben Geren *retired pathologist*

Van Buren
Stone, David Mark *plastic surgeon*

CALIFORNIA

Agoura Hills
deCiutiis, Alfred Charles Maria *oncologist, television producer*
Havlicek, Michael W *medical association administrator*

Alameda
Whorton, M. Donald *occupational and environmental health physician, epidemiologist*

Alhambra
Xie, Bin *epidemiologist, research scientist*

Arcadia
Fisher, Alan J. *otolaryngologist, plastic surgeon*
Soleimani, Massoud *internist, rheumatologist*

Arroyo Grande
Grisez, James Louis *physician, plastic surgeon*

Artesia
Dhamija, Kailash Raj *physician, consultant*

Atherton
Weston, Jane Sara *plastic surgeon, educator*

Auburn
Henrikson, Donald Merle *forensic pathologist*

Bakersfield
Prunes, Fernando *plastic surgeon, educator*
Sio, Jimmy Ong *embryologist*

Bellflower
Lee, Paul Yue-Yan *surgeon*

Belvedere
Wallerstein, Robert Solomon *psychiatrist*

Belvedere Tiburon
Behrman, Richard Elliot *pediatrician, neonatologist, university dean*

Berkeley
Abbott, Myles Bruce *pediatrician*
Abel, Carlos Alberto *immunologist*
Allison, James Patrick *immunology educator, medical association administrator*
Budinger, Thomas Francis *radiologist, educator*
Buffler, Patricia Ann *epidemiologist, educator, dean emerita*
Diamond, Marian Cleeves *anatomy educator*
Duhl, Leonard *psychiatrist, educator*
Grimes, Michael David *podiatrist*
Grossman, Elmer Roy *pediatrician*
Poor, Clarence Alexander *retired physician*
Seitz, Walter Stanley *cardiovascular research consultant*
Syme, Sherman Leonard *epidemiologist, educator*
Tempelis, Constantine Harry *immunologist, educator*
Troxel, David B. *pathologist*
Winkelstein, Warren, Jr., *physician, educator*

Beverly Hills
Allen, Howard Norman *cardiologist, educator*
Arieff, Allen Ives *physician*
Bao, Katherine Sung *pediatric cardiologist*
Caster, Andrew Ian *ophthalmologist*
Catz, Boris *endocrinologist, educator*
Dennis, Karen Marie *plastic surgeon*
Fein, William *ophthalmologist*
Fisher, (Donald) Garth *plastic surgeon*
Goodman, Mark Paul *physician*
Griffin, Anthony *plastic surgeon*
Haworth, Randal Digby *plastic surgeon*
Hofbauer, John D. *ophthalmologist*
Karpman, Harold Lew *cardiologist, educator, writer*
Klein, Arnold William *dermatologist*
Marshak, Harry *plastic surgeon*
Menkes, John Hans *pediatric neurologist*
Moelleken, Brent Roderick Wilfred *surgeon*
Perlman, Jon Arthur *plastic surgeon*
Rosenthal, Richard Jay *psychiatrist*
Ryan, Frank Harry *plastic surgeon*
Seiff, Stephen S. *ophthalmologist*
Semel, George Herbert *plastic surgeon*

Bolinas
Remen, Rachel Naomi *pediatrician, integrative medicine physician*

Borrego Springs
Strong, John Oliver *plastic surgeon, educator*

Brawley
Jaquith, George Oakes *ophthalmologist*

Burbank
Renner, Andrew Ihor *surgeon*

Calabasas
Bursten, Stuart Lowell *physician, biochemist*

Canyon Lake
Sparks, Dale Boyd *allergist, health facility administrator*

Carlsbad
Bennett, C. Frank *molecular pharmacologist*
Chopra, Deepak *preventive medicine physician, writer*

Carmel
Felch, William Campbell *internist, editor*
Flanagan, Michael Brendan *obstetrician and gynecologist*

Carmel Valley
Chapman, Robert Galbraith *retired hematologist, administrator*

Carmichael
Wolfe, Bruce McLaren *surgery educator*

Chatsworth
Stephenson, Irene Hamlen *biorhythm analyst, consultant, editor, educator*

Chico
Ritter, Dale William *obstetrician, gynecologist*
Ward, Chester Lawrence *physician, consultant*

Chula Vista
Cohen, Elaine Helena *pediatrician, cardiologist, educator*
Gongora, Eduardo *plastic surgeon*

Claremont
Johnson, Jerome Linné *cardiologist, educator*

Clovis
Terrell, Howard Bruce *psychiatrist*

Concord
Rohra, Srikrishin Assardas *cardiologist*

Corona
Haynes, Moses Alfred *physician*
Shaffer, Audrey Jeanne *health information administrator, educator*

Corona Del Mar
Tobis, Jerome Sanford *physician*

Coronado
Mock, David Clinton, Jr., *internist*

Corte Madera
Epstein, William Louis *dermatologist, educator*
Serber, William *radiation oncologist, educator*

Cypress
Waite, Verner Stuart *retired surgeon*

Daly City
Baladi, Naoum Abboud *surgeon*

Davis
Cardiff, Robert Darrell *pathology educator*
Enders, Allen Coffin *anatomy educator*
Gardner, Murray Briggs *pathologist, educator*
Halsted, Charles Hopkinson *internist*
Hollinger, Mannfred Alan *pharmacologist, educator, toxicologist*
Jensen, Hanne Margrete *pathology educator*
Lipscomb, Paul Rogers *retired orthopedic surgeon, educator*
Luciw, Paul A. *medical educator*
Overstreet, James Wilkins *obstetrics and gynecology educator, administrator*
Palmer, Philip Edward Stephen *radiologist*
Richman, David Paul *neurologist, educator, researcher*
Schenker, Marc Benet *preventive medicine educator*

Deer Park
Hodgkin, John E. *pulmonologist*

Del Mar
Lesko, Ronald Michael *osteopathic physician*
Scherger, Joseph Edward *family physician, educator*

Delano
Salmassi, Sadegh *family practice physician*

Dixon
Hanowell, Ernest Goddin *physician*

Downey
Gong, Henry, Jr., *internist, researcher, educator*
Hackney, Jack Dean *physician*
Mishal, Devadatt M. *obstetrician/gynecologist*
Perry, Jacquelin *orthopedic surgeon*
Shapiro, Richard Stanley *physician*

Duarte
Sleeter, John William Higgs *retired physician, health service administrator*
Weiss, Lawrence Martin *pathologist, researcher*

El Dorado Hills
Sparks, Robert Dean *medical administrator, gastroenterologist*
Yao, John Sen *physician*

El Macero
Andrews, Neil Corbly *surgeon*
Stowell, Robert Eugene *pathologist, retired educator*

Emeryville
Hurst, Deborah *pediatric hematologist*

Penhoet, Edward *medical association administrator, biochemicals company executive, former dean*

Encino
Lesavoy, Malcolm A. *plastic surgeon, educator*

Escondido
Everton, Marta Ve *retired ophthalmologist*
McCarberg, Bill Harold *physician*

Fairfield
Martin, Clyde Verne *psychiatrist*
Munn, William Charles, II, *psychiatrist*

Folsom
Anderson, Jeffrey Lee *physician, anesthesiologist, consultant*
Ewing, Russell Charles, II, *physician*

Fontana
Johna, Samir *surgeon*
Resch, Charlotte Susanna *plastic surgeon*

Fountain Valley
Kieu, Quynh Dinh *pediatrician, not-for-profit developer*

Fremont
Amylon, Michael David *physician, educator*
Maynard, Catherine *medical researcher*

Fresno
Glassheim, Jeffrey Wayne *allergist, immunologist, pediatrician*
Kardashian, Jane Flora *dermatologist*
Leigh, Hoyle *psychiatrist, educator, writer*
Patton, Jack Thomas *family practice physician*
Shigyo, Tetsuo Ted *emergency physician*
Welch, Jack Hamill *retired internist*

Fullerton
Nitta, Douglas *family practice physician*
Steward, Marsh, Jr., *obstetrician, gynecologist*
Sugarman, Michael *physician, rheumatologist*

Glendale
Garcia, Serafin Montealto *physician*
Spring, Carl Chaffee, Jr., *medical writer*

Grass Valley
Ely, Parry Haines *dermatologist, educator*

Greenbrae
Cushing, Matthew *internist*
Levy, S. William *dermatologist, educator*
Parnell, Francis William, Jr., *otolaryngologist*

Gualala
Ring, Alice Ruth Bishop *retired preventive medicine physician*

Half Moon Bay
Robertson, Abel L., Jr., *pathologist*

Hanford
Gamboa, Lucito G. *physician, pathologist*

Hayward
Bachicha, Joseph Alfred *physician, educator*

Hemet
Galletta, Joseph Leo *physician*
Mata, David Joseph *physician*

Hillsborough
Kraft, Robert Arnold *retired medical educator, physician*
Packard, Peter *medical educator, retired internist*

Huntington Beach
Pacino, Frank George *physician, educator*
Welsh, William Daniel *geriatric medicine family practice physician*

Indian Wells
Hrabal, Antonin *physician, medical educator*

Irvine
de la Maza, Luis M. *pathology educator*
Friedenberg, Richard Myron *radiology educator, physician*
George, Kattunilathu Oommen *physician, educator*
Gupta, Sudhir *immunologist, educator*
Huang, Taosheng *biomedical researcher, educator, medical geneticist*
Korc, Murray *endocrinologist*
Lee, Eva *medical educator*
Quilligan, Edward James *obstetrician, gynecologist, educator*
Smith, Harold Raymond *neurologist, sleep medicine specialist, educator*
Tetef, Merry Lynn *internist, oncologist*
van-den-Noort, Stanley *neurologist, educator*
Weinstein, Gerald D. *dermatology educator*
Werlin, Lawrence B. *obstetrician, gynecologist, reproductive endocrinologist*

Jamul
Harwood, Ivan Richmond *retired pediatric pulmonologist*

Kentfield
Bruyn, Henry Bicker *physician*
Ramirez, Archimedes *neurosurgeon, educator*
Schmid, Rudi (Rudolf Schmid) *internist, educator, academic administrator*

La Canada Flintridge
Byrne, George Melvin *physician*

La Crescenta
Riccardi, Vincent Michael *pediatrician, researcher, educator, entrepreneur*

La Jolla
Bailey, David Nelson *pathology educator, dean, academic administrator*
Barlow, Carrolee *physician, scientist, educator*
Barnett, Faith Hemenway *neurosurgeon, researcher*
Barrett-Connor, Elizabeth Louise *epidemiologist, educator*

Beutler, Ernest *physician, research scientist*
Blanchard, Daniel G. *cardiologist*
Blantz, Roland C. *nephrologist, educator*
Block, Melvin August *surgeon, educator*
Bloom, Floyd Elliott *internist, research scientist*
Brown, Stuart I. *ophthalmologist, educator*
Buchta, Richard Michael *pediatrician*
Carmichael, David Burton *physician*
Chisari, Francis V. *pathologist*
Covell, Ruth Marie *medical educator, medical school administrator*
Dalessio, Donald John *internist, neurologist, educator*
Dixon, Frank James *medical scientist, educator*
Edgington, Thomas S. *pathologist, educator, molecular biologist, vascular biologist*
Edwards, Charles Cornell *surgeon, research administrator*
Friedmann, Theodore *physician*
Garland, Cedric Frank *epidemiologist, educator*
Gerber, Michael Lewis *cardiac surgeon*
Gill, Gordon N. *medical educator*
Gittes, Ruben Foster *urological surgeon*
Glass, Christopher Kevin *physician*
Hamburger, Robert N. *pediatrician, educator, consultant*
Han, Jiahuai *medical researcher*
Hench, Philip Kahler *physician*
Hendler, Sheldon Saul *internist, educator, biochemist, writer*
Hofmann, Alan Frederick *biomedical researcher, educator*
Horner, Anthony Adam *pediatrician, educator*
Jaffer, Adrian Michael *physician*
Joris-Quinton, Liesbet *internal medicine physician*
Judd, Lewis Lund *psychiatrist, educator*
Katzman, Robert *neurologist, medical educator*
Kripke, Daniel Frederick *psychiatrist, educator*
Lewis, Carson McLaughl *retired plastic surgeon*
Malhotra, Vivek *medical educator*
Masouredis, Serafeim Panagiotis *pathologist, educator*
Mayer, John M. *medical researcher, educator*
Mendoza, Stanley Atran *pediatric nephrologist, educator*
Moossa, A. R. *surgery educator*
Nakamura, Robert Motoharu *pathologist*
Oldstone, Michael Beauregard Alan *immunologist, educator*
Pashler, Harold E. *psychologist, educator*
Rapaport, Samuel I. *educator, physician*
Rearden, Carole Ann *clinical pathologist, educator*
Rosenfeld, Michael G. *medical educator*
Rubin, Lewis J. *physician, researcher*
Ruoslahti, Erkki *medical research administrator*
Schneider, Gerald L. *plastic surgeon*
Shabaik, Ahmed *pathologist, educator*
Singer, Robert *plastic surgeon*
Smith, Richard Alan *neurologist, medical association administrator*
Spiegelberg, Hans Leonhard *medical educator*
Steinberg, Daniel *preventive medicine physician, educator*
Takabe, Kazuaki *gastroenterology surgeon, research scientist*
Tan, Eng Meng *immunologist, biomedical researcher*
Tarin, David *oncologist, researcher*
Taylor, Palmer W. *pharmacology educator*
Terry, Robert Davis *neuropathologist, educator*
Tuszynski, Mark H. *neurologist*
Vogt, Peter K. *oncologist*
Walker, Richard Hugh *orthopaedic surgeon*
Yaksh, Tony L. *pharmacologist, educator, health facility administrator*
Yen, Samuel S(how)-C(hih) *obstetrics and gynecology educator, reproductive endocrinologist*

La Mesa
Behrend, Albert James *surgeon*
Boghairi, Anoushiravan *cardiologist*

La Mirada
Salinger, Charles *dermatologist*

La Quinta
Calvin, James Willard *thoracic and vascular surgeon*
Pitkin, Roy Macbeth *retired obstetrician, educator*

La Verne
McDonough-Treichler, Judith Dianne *medical educator, consultant*

Lafayette
Cobb, George Edward *surgeon*

Laguna Beach
Richard, Robert Max *cardiologist*

Laguna Hills
Ierardi, Stephen John *physician*
Widyolar, Sheila Gayle *dermatologist*

Laguna Woods
Berk, Jack Edward *gastroenterologist, educator*

Lincoln
Chong, Vernon *retired surgeon, retired military officer*

Livermore
Seward, James Pickett *internist, educator*

Loma Linda
Bailey, Leonard Lee *surgeon*
Behrens, Berel Lyn *physician, academic and healthcare administrator*
Briggs, Burton A. *medical educator*
Bull, Brian Stanley *pathology educator, medical consultant, business executive*
Bunnell, William Paul *orthopaedic surgery educator*
Chan, Philip J. *medical educator*
Coggin, Charlotte Joan *cardiologist, educator*
Condon, Stanley Charles *gastroenterologist*
Dayes, Lloyd Albert *neurosurgeon, minister*
Edwards, Lincoln Paul *pharmacologist, educator*
Hardesty, Robert Alan *plastic surgeon*
Hinshaw, David B., Jr., *radiologist*
Kirk, Gerald Arthur *nuclear radiologist*
Llaurado, Josep G. *nuclear medicine physician, scientist*
Mace, John Weldon *pediatrician*
Reeve, Ivan Leon *physician*
Rendell-Baker, Leslie *anesthesiologist, educator*
Roberts, Walter Herbert Beatty *anatomist, educator*
Slater, James Munro *radiation oncologist*
Smith, Aida Marissa *medical reference librarian*
Stilson, Walter Leslie *radiologist, educator*
Strother, Allen *biochemical pharmacologist, researcher*
Wareham, Ellsworth Edwin *cardiothoracic surgeon, educator*
Young, Lionel Wesley *radiologist*

Long Beach
Fagan, Frederic *neurosurgeon*
Friis, Robert Harold *epidemiologist, health science educator*
Kwaan, Jack Hau Ming *retired physician*
Macer, George Armen, Jr., *orthopedic hand surgeon*
Marks, Melvin I. *physician, educator, hospital administrator, consultant*
Mills, Don Harper *pathology and psychiatry educator, lawyer*
Nageotte, Michael Patrick *obstetrician*
Pineda, Anselmo *neurosurgery educator*
Stemmer, Edward Alan *surgeon, educator*
Wells, James H. *plastic surgeon*
Worcester, Howard Lester *internist*

Los Altos
Abrams, Arthur Jay *physician*
Martin, Leonardo S.J. *retired urologist, surgeon*
Orman, Nanette Hector *psychiatrist*

Los Angeles
Agarwal, Sanjay Kumar *physician*
Alkalay, Arie L. *pediatrician, neonatologist*
Alkon, Ellen Skillen *physician*
Ansell, Benjamin Jesse *physician*
Apt, Leonard *physician*
Apuzzo, Michael Lawrence John *neurological surgeon*
Aronowitz, Joel Alan *plastic and reconstructive surgeon*
Ashley, Sharon Anita *pediatric anesthesiologist*
Barker, Wiley Franklin *surgeon, educator*
Barrett, Cynthia Townsend *neonatologist*
Beart, Robert W., Jr., *colon and rectal surgeon, educator*
Becker, Donald Paul *surgeon, neurosurgeon*
Berek, Jonathan Samuel *surgeon, cancer researcher, gynecologist, writer*
Berman, Jennifer R. *urologist*
Bernstein, Sol *cardiologist, educator*
Bessman, Samuel Paul *pediatrician, biochemist*
Bhidayasiri, Roongroj *neurologist, researcher*
Biles, John Alexander *pharmacology educator, chemistry educator*
Blahd, William Henry *physician, nuclear medicine physician*
Bodey, Bela *immunologist, pathologist, oncologist*
Bondareff, William *psychiatry educator*
Borenstein, Daniel Bernard *psychiatrist, educator*
Brackmann, Derald E. *otolaryngologist*
Braunstein, Glenn David *physician, educator*
Breslow, Lester *preventive medicine physician, educator*
Brynes, Russell Kermit *pathologist, educator*
Buchwald, Nathaniel Avrom *neurophysiologist*
Caprioli, Joseph *ophthalmologist*
Chandor, Stebbins Bryant *pathologist*
Chen, William *surgeon*
Cherry, James Donald *pediatrician*
Chopra, Inder Jit *physician, endocrinologist*
Chui, Helena Chang *physician*
Cicciarelli, James Carl *immunology educator*
Clemente, Carmine Domenic *anatomist, educator*
Coates, Thomas J. *medical association administrator*
Cook, Ian Ainsworth *psychiatrist, researcher, educator*
Cooper, Edwin Lowell *anatomy educator*
Cote, Richard James *pathologist, researcher*
Danoff, Dudley Seth *surgeon, urologist*
Davidson, Ezra C., Jr., *obstetrician, gynecologist, educator, academic administrator*
De Cherney, Alan Hersh *obstetrics and gynecology educator*
Derebery, Mary Jennifer *otolaryngologist*
Detels, Roger *epidemiologist, retired dean*
Dignam, William Joseph *obstetrician, gynecologist, educator*
Edgerton, Bradford Wheatly *plastic surgeon*
Engel, William King *neurologist, educator*
Enstrom, James Eugene *epidemiologist*
Eshagian, Joseph *ophthalmologist*
Ettenger, Robert Bruce *physician, nephrologist*
Fahey, John Leslie *immunologist*
Feig, Stephen Arthur *pediatrics educator, hematologist, oncologist*
Ferrante, F. Michael *anesthesiologist, internist*
Fielding, Jonathan Evan *pediatrician*
Figlin, Robert Alan *hematologist, oncologist*
Fish, Barbara *psychiatrist, educator*
Fishbein, Michael Claude *physician, pathologist*
Fodor, Peter Bela *plastic surgeon*
Fogelman, Alan Marcus *internist*
Fonkalsrud, Eric Walter *pediatric surgeon, educator*
Fowler, Vincent R. *dermatologist*
Francis, Charles K. *medical educator*
Frasier, S. Douglas *medical educator*
Gabriel, Ronald Samuel *child neurologist*
Gale, Robert Peter *physician, scientist, researcher*
Gambino, Jerome James *nuclear medicine educator*
Geller, Stephen Arthur *pathologist, educator*
Giannotta, Steven Louis *neurosurgery educator*
Gonick, Harvey Craig *nephrologist, educator*
Goodwin, Scott Craig *interventional radiologist*
Gorney, Roderic *psychiatry educator*
Grody, Wayne William *physician*
Guze, Phyllis Arlene *internist, educator, academic administrator*
Han, Ken-ryu *urologist*
Haywood, L. Julian *physician, educator*
Henriksen, Eva H. *former anesthesiology educator*
Hirai, Denitsu *surgeon*
Hirsch, Anthony Terry *physician*
Hoang, Duc Van *theoretical pathologist, educator*
Holland, Gary Norman *ophthalmologist, educator*
Hollander, Daniel *gastroenterologist, medical educator*
Horwitz, David A. *rheumatologist, educator*
House, John William *otolaryngologist*
Huang, Sheng He *medical educator*
Huerta, Sergio *physician, researcher*
Ignarro, Louis J. *pharmacology educator*
Itabashi, Hideo Henry *neuropathologist*
Jacobson, Edwin James *medical educator*
Jalali, Behnaz *psychiatrist, educator*
Jarvik, Lissy F. *psychiatrist*
Jenders, Robert Allen *medical educator, researcher*
Johnson, Cage Saul *hematologist, educator*
Jones, Neil Ford *surgeon, educator*
Jones, Peter Anthony *medical research administrator*
Kamil, Elaine Scheiner *pediatric nephrologist, educator*
Kaplowitz, Neil *physician, educator*
Katz, Ronald Lewis *physician, educator*
Kaunitz, Jonathan Davidson *physician*
Kelly, Arthur Paul *physician*
Kleeman, Charles Richard *medical educator, nephrologist, researcher*
Kloner, Robert A. *cardiologist, researcher, educator*
Korsch, Barbara M. *pediatrician*
Kramer, Barry Alan *psychiatrist, educator*
Lamb, H. Richard *psychiatry educator*
Lawrence, Sanford Hull *physician, immunochemist, author*
Lazareff, Jorge Antonio *neurosurgeon, researcher*
Lechago, Juan *pathologist, educator*
Levey, Gerald Saul *dean, internist, educator*
Lewin, Klaus Jonathan *pathologist, educator*
Lewis, Charles Edwin *epidemiologist, educator*
Lim, David Jong-Jai *otolaryngology educator, researcher*
Linde, Leonard M. *pediatric cardiologist*
Macavinta-Tenazas, Gemorsita *family physician*
Malcolm, Dawn Grace *family physician*
Maloney, Robert Keller *ophthalmologist, medical educator*
Mandal, Ashis K. *cardiothoracic surgeon*
Maronde, Robert Francis *internist, clinical pharmacologist, educator*
Martinez, Miguel Acevedo *urologist, consultant, lecturer*
McCann, John David *physician, educator*
Mellinkoff, Sherman Mussoff *medical educator*
Mihan, Richard *retired dermatologist*
Miller, Timothy Alden *plastic and reconstructive surgeon*
Mishell, Daniel R., Jr., *obstetrician, gynecologist, educator*
Mondino, Bartly J. *ophthalmologist*
Monforte-Muñoz, Hector L. *pathologist*
Moser, Franklin George *neuroradiologist, researcher*
Moshfegh, Moussa *surgeon*
Moussavi, Ramyar *podiatrist*
Moxley, John Howard, III, *internist*
Moy, Ronald Leonard *dermatologist, surgeon*
Murphree, A. Linn *pediatric ophthalmologist*
Naqvi, Tasneem Zehra *cardiologist, researcher, consultant*
Nathwani, Bharat N. *pathologist, consultant*
Nelson, Marvin Dale, Jr., *radiologist, educator*
Newman, Anita Nadine *surgeon*
Nissenson, Allen Richard *physician, educator*
Noble, Ernest Pascal *pharmacologist, biochemist, educator*
Parker, Robert George *radiation oncology educator, academic administrator*
Parmelee, Arthur Hawley, Jr., *pediatric medical educator*
Patzakis, Michael J. *orthopaedic surgeon, educator*
Pike, Malcolm Cecil *preventive medicine educator*
Preston-Martin, Susan *epidemiologist, educator*
Pulec, Jack Lee *otolaryngologist*
Rachelefsky, Gary Stuart *medical educator*
Rao, Jian Yu *physician, cancer biologist, educator*
Rassman, William R. *plastic surgeon*
Reynolds, Charles Patrick *pediatric oncologist, researcher*
Richters, Arnis *medical educator, researcher*
Rimoin, David Lawrence *medical geneticist*
Ritvo, Edward Ross *psychiatrist*
Rodriguez, Ensor *physician, scientist, writer*
Rosenbaum, Arthur L. *ophthalmologist*
Roven, Alfred Nathan *surgeon*
Roy-Burman, Pradip *molecular biology and virology educator*
Ryan, Stephen Joseph, Jr., *ophthalmologist, educator*
Sarma, Radha J. *cardiologist, educator*
Sarnat, Bernard George *plastic surgeon, educator, researcher*
Sattin, Albert *psychiatry and neuropharmacology educator*
Sawyer, Charles Henry *anatomist, educator*
Scheibel, Arnold Bernard *psychiatrist, educator, research director*
Schelbert, Heinrich Ruediger *nuclear medicine physician*
Schiff, Martin *physician, surgeon*
Schneider, Edward Lewis *medicine educator, research administrator*
Schwartz, William Benjamin *internist, educator*
Sherman, Randolph *plastic and reconstructive surgeon, educator*
Shtengold, Yefim Shelichovich *medical educator, researcher*
Siegel, Michael Elliot *nuclear medicine physician, educator*
Siegel, Sheldon C. *pediatrician, allergist, immunologist*
Siegel, Stuart Elliott *physician, pediatrics educator, cancer researcher*
Small, Kent Wilson *ophthalmologist, educator*
Solomon, David Harris *geriatrician, educator*
Soo Hoo, Guy W. *internist, educator*
Spencer, Carole A. *medical association administrator, medical educator*
Stein, Tomiko *infectious disease specialist*
Stevanovic, Milan V. *surgeon*
Stiehm, E. Richard *pediatrician, educator*
Straatsma, Bradley Ralph *ophthalmologist, educator*
Streeter, Oscar Edward, Jr., *radiation oncologist*
Sullivan, Stuart Francis *anesthesiologist, educator*
Sutterby, Larry Quentin *internist*
Tabachnick, Norman Donald *psychiatrist, educator*
Tache, Yvette France *neurogastroenterologist*
Takahashi, Masato *pediatric cardiologist, educator*
Tolo, Vernon Thorpe *orthopedist, educator*
Toluie, Kamran *cardiologist, physiologist*
Tompkins, Ronald K. *surgeon*
Van Der Meulen, Joseph Pierre *neurologist*
Verma, Dinesh *ophthalmologist, researcher*
Vredevoe, Donna Lou *research immunologist, microbiologist, educator*
Wallach, Howard Frederic *psychiatrist*
Walts, Ann E. *pathologist*
Wasterlain, Claude Guy *neurologist*
Weiner, Leslie Philip *neurology educator, researcher*
Weiss, Martin Harvey *neurosurgeon, educator*
Whybrow, Peter Charles *psychiatrist, educator, director, author*
Wilkinson, Alan Herbert *nephrologist, educator*
Wilson, Miriam Geisendorfer *retired physician, educator*
Wincor, Michael Z. *psychopharmacology educator, clinician, researcher*
Withers, Hubert Rodney *radiotherapist, radiobiologist, educator*
Woodley, David Timothy *dermatology educator*
Yaffe, Sumner Jason *pediatrician, educator, science administrator*
Ziering, Craig L. *osteopath*

Malibu
Jenden, Donald James *pharmacologist, educator*
Morgenstern, Leon *surgeon*

Martinez
Barnard, William Marion *psychiatrist*
McKnight, Lenore Ravin *child psychiatrist, educator*

Menlo Park
Goodreau, Robert Charles *surgeon*
Harris, Edward Day, Jr., *physician*
Healy, Cynthia *pharmacologist, life scientist, researcher*
Holmquest, Donald Lee *physician, astronaut, lawyer*
Kovachy, Edward Miklos, Jr., *psychiatrist, consultant*
Wachtel, John Steven *obstetrician, gynecologist*

Mill Valley
Bolen, Jean Shinoda *psychiatrist, writer*
Harris, Jeffrey Saul *physician, executive, consultant*
Kolb, Felix Oscar *physician*

Milpitas
Chiu, Peter Yee-Chew *physician*

Mission Viejo
Hafner-Eaton, Chris *health services researcher, medical educator, policy analyst*

Modesto
Chan, Alexander *internist*
Cimino, Lewis R., Jr., *surgeon*
Khanna, Kanwal *rheumatologist*
Lewis, Marshall Edward *psychiatrist, administrator, educator*
Suntra, Charles Ratapol *surgeon, educator*

Moffett Field
Dismukes, Robert Key *medical scientist*

Monrovia
Comings, David Edward *physician, medical genetics scientist*
Deliman, Robert Michael *surgeon*

Montecito
Shehata, Said Ahmed *surgeon, researcher*

Monterey
Bhaskar, Surindar Nath *pathologist, periodontist*
Black, Robert Lincoln *pediatrician, educator*
Lehr, Jeffrey Marvin *immunologist, allergist*
Sunde, Douglas *plastic surgeon*

Morgan Hill
Tan, Lucas G. *anesthesiologist*

Morro Bay
Chandler, Bruce Frederick *internist*

Mountain View
Abel, Elizabeth A. *dermatologist*
Lowen, Robert Marshall *plastic surgeon*
Urman, Jeffrey David *physician, educator*
Warren, Richard Wayne *obstetrician, gynecologist*

Napa
Anderson, Richard Elliott *internist, educator*
Morgese, Vincent John *neurosurgeon*
Silver, Diane S. *dermatologist*
Zimmermann, John Paul *plastic surgeon*

National City
Morgan, Jacob Richard *cardiologist*

Newbury Park
Bleiberg, Leon William *surgical podiatrist*

Newhall
Stein, Karl N. *plastic and reconstructive surgeon*

Newport Beach
Amyes, Edwin Westby *neurosurgeon*
Chiu, John Tang *physician*
Connolly, John Earle *surgeon, educator*
Shamoun, John Milam *plastic surgeon*
Shohet, Jack A. *otolaryngologist*
Solmer, Richard *surgeon*
Viehe, Richard B. *podiatrist*

Newport Coast
Afifi, Alaa Youssef *cardiothoracic surgeon*

Norwalk
Armstrong, David Ligon *psychiatrist*
Bao, Joseph Yue-Se *orthopedist, microsurgeon, educator*

Oak Park
Caldwell, Stratton Franklin *kinesiology educator*

Oakland
Benton-Hardy, Lisa Renee *psychiatrist, educator*
Collen, Morris Frank *medical educator, administrator, physician, researcher*
Gruber, Ronald P. *plastic surgeon, researcher*
Hilsinger, Raymond L., Jr., *otolaryngologist*
Killebrew, Ellen Jane (Mrs. Edward S. Graves) *cardiologist, educator*
Klatsky, Arthur Louis *cardiologist, epidemiologist*

Le Noir, Michael A. *allergist*
Ng, Lawrence Ming-Loy *pediatrician*
Patton, Dennis David *radiologist, educator*
Rice, Frances Mae *physician*
Sharpton, Thomas *physician*
Sun, Peter P. *neurosurgeon*
Teufel, William Lockwood *emergency physician*
Weinmann, Robert Lewis *neurologist*

Oceanside
Curtin, Thomas Lee *ophthalmologist*

Orange
Anzel, Sanford Harold *orthopedic surgeon*
Armentrout, Steven Alexander *oncologist*
Ballard, Jeffrey Lawrence *surgeon, educator*
Barr, Ronald Jeffrey *dermatologist, pathologist*
Chang, Jae Chan *hematologist, oncologist, educator*
Cinat, Marianne Eva *surgeon*
Crumley, Roger Lee *surgeon, educator, otolaryngologist*
DiSaia, Philip John *obstetrician, gynecologist, radiology educator*
Fischel, Richard Jeffrey *thoracic surgeon*
Fisher, Mark Jay *neurologist, neuroscientist, educator*
Hubbell, Floyd Allan *internist, educator*
Kim, Moon Hyun *endocrinologist, educator*
Klassen, Henry John *ophthalmologist*
Milliken, Jeffrey *cardiothoracic surgeon*
Morgan, Beverly Carver *pediatrician, educator*
Mosier, Harry David, Jr., *physician, educator*
Rowen, Marshall *radiologist*
Smith, Ronald Edward *ophthalmologist*
Vatcher, James Gordon *retired physician*
Vaziri, Nosratola Dabir *internist, educator, nephrologist*
Wilson, Archie Fredric *medical educator*
Wong, Brian Jet-Fel *surgeon*
Yu, Jen *medical educator*

Oroville
Chandy, Mammen G. *surgeon*

Pacific Palisades
Beck, John Christian *physician, educator*
Claes, Daniel John *physician*
Love, Susan Margaret *surgeon, educator, writer*
Tourtellotte, Wallace William *neurologist, educator*

Palm Springs
Gaede, James Ernest *physician, medical educator*
Weil, Max Harry *internist, cardiologist, educator, medical researcher*
Wilson, Myron Robert, Jr., *retired psychiatrist*

Palo Alto
Adamson, Geoffrey David *reproductive endocrinologist, surgeon*
Babb, Richard Rankin *gastroenterologist, educator*
Bagshaw, Malcolm A. *radiation oncologist, educator*
Blessing-Moore, Joann Catherine *allergist*
Britton, M(elvin) C(reed), Jr., *rheumatologist*
Byrd, Thomas Russell *medical educator*
Chen, Stephen Shi-hua *pathologist, biochemist*
Cooke, John P. *cardiologist, medical educator, medical researcher*
Dafoe, Donald Cameron *surgeon, educator*
Daniels, John R. *oncologist, educator*
Dement, William Charles *medical researcher, medical educator*
Desai, Kavin Hirendra *pediatrician*
Forno, Lysia S. *neuropathologist*
Fortmann, Stephen Paul *medical educator, researcher, epidemiologist*
Fries, James Franklin *internal medicine educator*
Harkonen, Wesley Scott *physician, pharmaceutical company executive*
Hays, Marguerite Thompson *nuclear medicine physician, educator*
Hentz, Vincent R. *surgeon*
Holman, Halsted Reid *medical educator, physician*
Hubert, Helen Betty *epidemiologist*
Illes, Judy *medical researcher, neuroethicist*
Keeffe, Emmet Britton *medical educator*
Lane, Alfred Thomas *medical educator*
Linna, Timo Juhani *immunologist, researcher, educator*
Litt, Iris Figarsky *pediatrics educator*
Maffly, Roy Herrick *internist, educator, retired dean*
Matthews, Zakee *psychiatrist, educator*
Michie, Sara H. *pathologist, educator*
Ning, Shoucheng *cancer biologist, head and neck surgeon*
Pizzo, Philip A. *pediatrics educator, university administrator*
Salvatierra, Oscar, Jr., *transplant surgeon, urologist, educator*
Schrier, Stanley Leonard *hematologist, educator*
Schurman, David Jay *orthopedic surgeon, educator*
Shuer, Lawrence Mendel *neurosurgery educator*
Silverman, Norman Henry *cardiologist, educator*
Strober, Samuel *immunologist, educator*
Sunshine, Philip *pediatrician*
Swain, Judith Lea *cardiovascular physician, educator*
Tune, Bruce Malcolm *pediatrics educator, renal toxicologist*
Urquhart, John *medical researcher, educator*
Weng, Wen-Kai *oncologist, medical researcher*
Winkleby, Marilyn A. *medical researcher*
Zarins, Christopher Kristaps *surgery educator, vascular surgeon*

Palos Verdes Peninsula
Narasimhan, Padma Mandyam *physician*
Thomas, Claudewell Sidney *psychiatry educator*

Panorama City
Bass, Harold Neal *pediatrician, medical geneticist*
Jacob, Peter James *obstetrician-gynecologist*
Jasso, Nancy *dermatologist*
Sue, Michael Alvin *allergist*

Paradise
Haws, Hale Louis *medical consultant*

Paramount
Cohn, Lawrence Steven *physician, educator*

Pasadena
Carregal, Enrique J. *anesthesiologist, educator*

Dyck, Peter *neurosurgeon, educator*
Glovsky, Myron Michael *medical educator*
Harvey, Joseph Paul, Jr., *orthopedist, educator*
Lake, Kevin Bruce *medical association administrator*
Magnes, Harry Alan *physician*
Mathies, Allen Wray, Jr., *former pediatrician, hospital administrator*
Newman, Marjorie Yospin *psychiatrist*
Opel, William *medical research administrator*
Pitts, Ferris Newcomb *physician, psychiatry educator*
Shaw, Anthony *pediatric surgeon, retired educator*
Short, Elizabeth M. *internist, educator, retired federal agency administrator*
Wong, Raymond Shiu-Loong *radiologist*
Yeager, Caroline Hale *radiologist, consultant*

Piedmont
Hughes, James Paul *physician*
Montgomery, Theodore Ashton *physician*
Reich, Stanley Benjamin *radiologist, medical educator*

Pinole
Harvey, Elinor B. *child psychiatrist*
Naughton, James Lee *internist*

Placerville
Bonser, Quentin *retired surgeon*

Pleasant Hill
Hollister, Arthur Clair, Jr., *epidemiologist, consultant, retired public health service officer*

Pleasanton
Hisaka, Eric Tom *plastic surgeon*

Pomona
Vo, Huu Dinh *pediatrician, educator*

Portola Valley
Fogarty, Thomas James *surgery educator*

Rancho Mirage
Cone, Lawrence Arthur *medical educator*
Jacobson, John D. D. *anesthesiologist*

Rancho Palos Verdes
Kwan, Benjamin Ching Kee *ophthalmologist*

Rancho Santa Fe
Affeldt, John Ellsworth *retired physician*
Carr, David Turner *physician*
Levy, Michael Lee *neurosurgeon*
Rockoff, S. David *radiologist, physician, educator*

Redding
Renard, Ronald Lee *allergist*

Redlands
Adey, William Ross *physician*
Bangasser, Ronald Paul *physician*
Dexter, James Riley *internist, pulmonologist, critical care specialist*
Skoog, William Arthur *former oncologist, educator*

Redwood City
Ellis, Eldon Eugene *surgeon*

Rescue
Frey, Charles Frederick *surgeon, educator*

Richmond
Arnon, Stephen Soulé *epidemiologist, research scientist*

Riverside
Bricker, Neal S. *physician, educator*
Chang, Janice May *lawyer, naturopathic doctor, psychologist*
Jung, Timothy Tae Kun *otolaryngologist*
Linaweaver, Walter Ellsworth, Jr., *physician*
Shoji, Hiromu *orthopedic surgeon, educator*
Siambanes, David *orthopedic surgeon*
Stone, Herman Hull *internist*

Rolling Hills Estates
Bellis, Carroll Joseph *surgeon, educator*

Roseville
Jammal, Joseph Jamil *cardiologist*

Sacramento
Bogren, Hugo Gunnar *radiology educator*
Chapman, Michael William *orthopedist, educator*
Cunningham, Mary Elizabeth (Mary Cunningham-Lusby) *physician*
Dobie, Robert Alan *otologist*
Ellis, William Gene *neuropathologist*
Evans, David Alun *otolaryngologist*
Jackson, Richard Joseph *epidemiologist, educator, pediatrician, preventive medicine physician*
Leong, Albin B. *pediatric pulmonologist, allergist, educator*
Lilla, James A. *plastic surgeon*
Lim, Alan Young *plastic surgeon*
Lippold, Roland Will *retired surgeon*
Lynch, Peter John *retired dermatologist*
Malkin, Harold Marshall *medical researcher*
Nagy, Stephen Mears, Jr., *physician, allergist*
Richards, John Ray *emergency physician, educator*
Rounds, Barbara Lynn *psychiatrist*
Shapero, Harris Joel *pediatrician*
Sharma, Arjun Dutta *cardiologist*
Spann, Lawrence Henry (Chip Spann) *physician associate*
Stevenson, Thomas Ray *plastic surgeon*
Styne, Dennis Michael *physician, educator*
Tung, Prabhas *plastic surgeon*
Wisner, David Hamilton *surgeon, educator*
Wolfman, Earl Frank, Jr., *surgeon, educator*
Wolkov, Harvey Brian *oncologist, researcher*
Zil, J. S. *psychiatrist, physiologist*

Saint Helena
Herber, Steven Carlton *physician*

Salinas
Phillips, John P(aul) *retired neurosurgeon*

San Bernardino
De Haas, David Dana *emergency physician*
Gorenberg, Alan Eugene *physician*

San Bruno
Bradley, Charles William *podiatrist, educator*

San Clemente
Kim, Edward William *ophthalmic surgeon*

San Diego
Alksne, John F. *medical educator, former dean*
Bot, Adrian Ion *immunologist*
Chambers, Henry George *orthopedic surgeon*
DeMaria, Anthony Nicholas *cardiologist, educator*
Drummond, John C. *anesthesiologist, educator*
Ebbeling, William Leonard *physician*
Friedman, Paul Jay *radiologist, educator*
Garfin, Steven R. *orthopedic surgeon*
Goltz, Robert William *physician, educator*
Intriere, Anthony Donald *retired internist, gastroenterologist*
Jacoby, Irving *physician*
Jamieson, Stuart William *surgeon, educator*
Kaback, Michael *medical educator*
Kaplan, George Willard *urologist*
Kaweski, Susan *plastic surgeon, naval officer*
Kruggel, John Louis *plastic surgeon*
Leopold, George Robert *radiologist*
Levy, Jerome *dermatologist, retired military officer*
Magnuson, Harold Joseph *physician*
Meerson, Felix Zalmanovich *cardiologist*
Neuman, Tom S. *emergency medical physician, educator*
Olefsky, Jerrold M. *medical educator, researcher*
O'Malley, Edward *psychiatrist, consultant*
Pan, Henry Yue-Ming *clinical pharmacologist*
Parthemore, Jacqueline Gail *internist, educator, hospital administrator*
Peebles, Carol Lynn *immunology researcher*
Pitt, William Alexander *cardiologist*
Radke, Jan Rodger *pulmonologist, physician executive*
Ray, Albert *family physician, educator*
Reid, Robert Tilden *medical association administrator, internist*
Resnik, Robert *medical educator*
Ross, John, Jr., *cardiologist, educator*
Schmidt, Joseph David *urologist*
Seagren, Stephen Linner *oncologist*
Teguh, Collin *physician, educator*
Thoman, David Scott *surgeon*
Ware, Carl *immunologist*
Wasserman, Stephen Ira *allergist, immunologist, educator*
Widder, Kenneth Jon *pathologist, educator*
Zeiger, Robert S. *allergist*

San Francisco
Abbas, Abul K. *pathologist, educator*
Amend, William John Conrad, Jr., *physician, educator*
Ascher, Nancy Louise *surgeon*
Bachman, David Christian *orthopedic surgeon*
Bainton, Dorothy Ford *pathology educator, researcher*
Barondes, Samuel Herbert *psychiatrist, educator*
Behrens, M. Kathleen *medical researcher*
Benet, Leslie Zachary *pharmacokineticist, educator*
Berger, Mitchel Stuart *neurosurgeon*
Bernstein, Harold Seth *pediatric cardiologist, molecular geneticist*
Boles, Roger *otolaryngologist*
Bourne, Henry R. *medicine, cellular and molecular pharmacology educator*
Bradford, David S. *surgeon*
Brotman, Martin *gastroenterologist*
Brown, Donald Malcolm *plastic surgeon*
Brown, Eric Joel *biomedical researcher, researcher*
Callaham, Michael L. *emergency physician, educator*
Campbell, André Renay *surgical educator, internist*
Capozzi, Angelo *surgeon*
Chesney, Margaret A. *medical educator, medical researcher*
Clever, Linda Hawes *physician*
Cobbs, Price Mashaw *social psychiatrist*
Crawford, Michael Howard *cardiologist, educator, researcher*
David, George *psychiatrist, economic theory lecturer*
Dawson, Chandler Robert *ophthalmologist, educator*
Deicken, Raymond Friedrich *neuropsychiatrist, clinical neuroscientist*
Dillon, William Patrick *neuroradiologist, radiologist*
Engleman, Ephraim Philip *rheumatologist*
Epstein, Charles Joseph *physician, medical geneticist, pediatrics and biochemistry educator*
Epstein, John Howard *dermatologist*
Erskine, John Morse *surgeon*
Fessel, Walford Jeffrey *rheumatologist*
Fielder, David R. *medical research administrator*
Fields, Howard Lincoln *neurology and physiology educator*
Filly, Roy A. *radiologist*
Finberg, Laurence *pediatrician, educator, dean*
Fishman, Robert Allen *neurologist, educator, department chair*
Frick, Oscar Lionel *physician, educator*
Ganem, Donald E. *immunologist*
Gellin, Gerald Alan *dermatologist*
Gibbs, Patricia Hellman *physician*
Goldberg, Robert Lewis *preventive and occupational medicine physician, internet executive*
Gooding, Charles Arthur *radiologist, physician, educator*
Gooding, Gretchen Ann Wagner *physician, educator*
Gotway, Michael B. *radiologist, health facility administrator*
Gradinger, Gilbert Paul *plastic surgeon*
Greene, Warner Craig *medical educator, medical association administrator*
Greenspan, Francis S. *physician*
Grossman, William *medical researcher, educator*
Grumbach, Melvin Malcolm *pediatrician, educator*
Hauser, Stephen L. *medical educator*
Havel, Richard Joseph *physician, educator*
Henderson, Isaac Craig *oncologist, researcher*
Herbert, Chesley C. *psychiatrist, educator*
Hering, William Marshall *medical organization executive*

Higashida, Randall Takeo *radiologist, neurosurgeon, medical educator*
Hinman, Frank, Jr., *urologist, educator*
Hoffman, Julien Ivor Ellis *pediatric cardiologist, educator*
Hoffman, William Yanes *plastic surgeon*
Hsu, John Chao-Chun *retired pediatrician*
Ikeda, Clyde Junichi *plastic and reconstructive surgeon*
Jablons, David M. *surgeon, educator*
Jonsen, Albert R(upert) *retired medical ethics educator*
Kan, Yuet Wai *hematologist, educator*
Kaplan, Selna L. *medical educator*
Katz, Hilliard Joel *physician*
Katzung, Bertram George *pharmacologist*
Kenyon, Cynthia J. *medical researcher*
Kerman, Barry Martin *ophthalmologist, educator*
Kiefer, Renata Gertrud *physician, epidemiologist, economist, international health management consultant*
King, Talmadge E. *physician*
Koda-Kimble, Mary Anne *medical educator, pharmacologist, dean*
Koo, John Ying Ming *psychiatrist, dermatologist*
Kramer, Steven G. *ophthalmologist, educator*
Lam, Fung *obstetrician, gynecologist, medical educator*
Lee, Philip Randolph Randolph *medical educator*
Levy, Jay A. *medical educator*
Liu, Xiao *ophthalmologist, neurobiologist*
Low, Randall *internist, cardiologist*
Lucia, Marilyn Reed *physician*
Mason, Dean Towle *cardiologist*
Mathes, Stephen John *plastic and reconstructive surgeon, educator*
McAninch, Jack Weldon *urological surgeon, educator*
McNamara, Margaret M. *pediatrician*
Messina, Louis Michael *vascular surgeon, educator*
Miller, Walter Luther *pediatrician, educator*
Mustacchi, Piero *preventive medicine physician, educator*
Newacheck, Paul W. *medical educator, researcher*
Newfield, Philippa *anesthesiologist*
O'Connor, G(eorge) Richard *ophthalmologist*
Odom, Richard B. *dermatologist, educator*
O'Shea, Erin K. *biomedical researcher*
Owsley, John Quincy, III, *plastic surgeon, educator*
Perez-Stable, Eliseo *medical educator*
Perkins, Herbert Asa *hematologist, educator*
Peterlin, Boris Matija *physician*
Petrakis, Nicholas Louis *epidemiologist, oncologist, medical researcher, educator*
Phillips, Theodore Locke *radiation oncologist, educator*
Rabow, Michael Warren *physician, educator*
Raskin, Neil Hugh *neurology educator*
Resneck, Jack Selwyn, Jr., *dermatologist, medical educator*
Ristow, Brunno *plastic surgeon*
Roe, Benson Bertheau *surgeon, educator*
Rosinski, Edwin Francis *medical educator*
Rudolph, Abraham Morris *pediatrician, educator*
Schmidt, Robert Milton *physician, scientist, educator, administrator*
Schrock, Theodore R. *surgeon*
Schroeder, Steven Alfred *medical educator*
Seebach, Lydia Marie *physician*
Shaw, Richard Eugene *cardiovascular researcher*
Shinefield, Henry Robert *pediatrician*
Smith, David Elvin *physician*
Smith, Lloyd Hollingsworth *physician*
Snyderman, Nancy *surgeon, medical journalist*
Speidel, John Joseph *public health physician, educator*
Spivey, Bruce E. *ophthalmologist, integrated healthcare delivery systems management executive*
Stamper, Robert Lewis *ophthalmologist, educator*
Terr, Abba Israel *allergist, immunologist*
Terr, Lenore Cagen *psychiatrist, writer*
Van Dyke, Craig *psychiatrist, director*
Volberding, Paul Arthur *academic physician*
Volpe, Peter Anthony *surgeon*
Wallerstein, Ralph Oliver *physician*
Washington, A. Eugene *medical educator*
Watts, Malcolm S(tuart) M(cNeal) *retired internist, medical educator*
Way, E(dward) Leong *pharmacologist, toxicologist, educator*
Wayburn, Edgar *internist, environmentalist*
Wescott, William Burnham *oral maxillofacial pathologist, educator*
Wintroub, Bruce Urich *dermatologist, educator, researcher*
Woeber, Kenneth Alois *physician*
Wolff, Sheldon *radiobiologist, educator*
Zippin, Calvin *epidemiologist, educator*

San Gabriel
Chen, John Calvin *child and adolescent psychiatrist*
Ko, Cheng Chia Charles *obstetrician-gynecologist*
Wong, John Wing-Chung *psychiatrist*

San Jose
Avakoff, Joseph Carnegie *medical consultant, law consultant*
Boldrey, Edwin Eastland *retinal surgeon, educator*
Buechel, Donald Robert *anesthesiologist, educator*
Doty, Jeffrey Edward *surgeon*
Kramer, Richard Jay *gastroenterologist, educator*
Shatney, Clayton Henry *surgeon*
Stein, Arthur Oscar *retired pediatrician, small business owner*
Stevens, David Alec *medical educator*
Yavorkovsky, Leonid Lazar *oncologist, researcher, hematologist*

San Juan Capistrano
Braunstein, Herbert *pathologist, educator*
Fisher, Delbert Arthur *pediatric endocrinologist, educator, health facility administrator*
Zalta, Edward *otorhinolaryngologist, physician*

San Luis Obispo
Pinkel, Donald Paul *pediatrician*
Weaver, Karl E. *psychiatrist*

San Marino
Terry, Roger *retired pathologist, consultant*

San Mateo
Bell, Leo S. *retired physician*

Van Kirk, John Ellsworth *retired cardiologist*
Wong, Otto *epidemiologist*

San Pablo
Woodruff, Kay Herrin *pathologist, educator*

San Pedro
Kline, Frank Menefee *psychiatrist*

San Ramon
Litman, Robert Barry *physician, writer, television and radio commentator*

Santa Ana
Myers, Marilyn Gladys *pediatric hematologist and oncologist*
Vaccaro, Jerome Vincent *psychiatrist, educator, healthcare executive*

Santa Barbara
Bischel, Margaret DeMeritt *physician, managed care consultant*
Ellis, Eugene Joseph *cardiologist*
Fisher, Steven Kay *neurobiology educator*
Freidell, Hugh Vernon *internist, nephrologist*
Klakeg, Clayton Harold *cardiologist*
Kohn, Roger Alan *surgeon*
Liebhaber, Myron I. *allergist*
Lifshitz, Fima *pediatrician, endocrinologist*
Marcus, Joseph *child psychiatrist*
Mathews, Barbara Edith *gynecologist*
Mosely, Jack Meredith *thoracic surgeon*
Prager, Elliot David *surgeon, educator*
Reid, Robert Alfred *physician*
Rockwell, Don Arthur *retired psychiatrist*
Shackman, Daniel Robert *psychiatrist*
Steckel, Richard J. *radiologist, educator, academic administrator*

Santa Clara
Chin, Albert Kae *research physician*

Santa Clarita
Zuk, Carmen Veiga *psychiatrist*

Santa Cruz
Magid, Gail Avrum *neurosurgeon, neurosurgery educator*
Pletsch, Marie Eleanor *plastic surgeon*
Shorenstein, Rosalind Greenberg *internist*

Santa Monica
Alpern, Harvey L. *cardiologist*
Carr, Ruth Margaret *plastic surgeon*
Derose, Kathryn Pitkin *medical researcher, minister*
Gupta, Rishab Kumar *medical association administrator, educator, researcher*
Hoefflin, Steven M. *plastic surgeon*
Katz, Roger *pediatrician, educator, allergist, immunologist*
Kawamoto, Henry K. *plastic surgeon*
Lincoln, Thomas L. *pathologist, educator*
McGuire, Michael Francis *plastic surgeon*
Monosson, Ira Howard *physician*
Pieton, Richard *anesthesiologist*
Rand, Robert Wheeler *neurosurgeon, educator*
Resnick, Jeffrey I. *plastic surgeon*
Rivin, Arthur Udell *medical educator*
Safa, Afshin Akhavan *oncologist, researcher*
Schultz, Victor M. *physician*
Shamban, Ava T. *dermatologist*
Shim, Elisabeth K. *dermatologist, writer*
Singer, Frederick Raphael *medical researcher*
Stern, Walter Eugene *neurosurgeon, educator*
Thompson, Dennis Peters *plastic surgeon*
Warick, Lawrence Herbert *psychiatrist*
Wells, Kenneth B. *medical educator*
Zarem, Harvey Alan *plastic surgeon*

Santa Paula
Edwards, Samuel Roger *internist*

Santa Rosa
Leuty, Gerald Johnston *osteopathic physician and surgeon*
Lewis, Alvin Edward *pathology educator*
Smith, Thomas Kent *retired radiologist, viticulturist*
Trucker, Albert *plastic surgeon*

Sausalito
Ornish, Dean *medical educator, administrator*

Sepulveda
Yano, Elizabeth Martin *epidemiologist, researcher*

Sherman Oaks
Hershman, Jerome Marshall *endocrinologist*
Zemplenyi, Tibor Karol *cardiologist, educator*

Sierra Madre
Nation, Earl F. *retired urologist, educator*

Sonoma
Gelpi, Armand Philippe *internist*

South Laguna
Mowlavi, Arian S. *plastic surgeon*

South Pasadena
Whang, Sukoo Jack *pathologist, microbiologist*

South San Francisco
Caro, Ivor *dermatologist*
Dixit, Vishva M. *pathology educator*
Humphrey, Patrick Paul *pharmacologist*

Spring Valley
Long, David Michael, Jr., *biomedical researcher, cardiothoracic surgeon*

Stanford
Abrams, Herbert LeRoy *radiologist, educator*
Bauer, Eugene Andrew *dermatologist, educator*
Blaschke, Terrence Francis *medicine and molecular pharmacology educator*
Blau, Helen Margaret *pharmacology educator*
Brown, J. Martin *oncologist, educator*
Carstensen, Laura Lee *gerontology educator*
Chase, Robert Arthur *surgeon, educator*
Cohen, Harvey Joel *pediatric hematology and oncology educator*
Donaldson, Sarah Susan *radiologist*
Egbert, Peter Roy *ophthalmologist, educator*
Farquhar, John William *physician, educator*
Fee, Willard Edward, Jr., *otolaryngologist*
Fire, Andrew Z. *pathologist, educator, geneticist*
Friedman, Gary David *epidemiologist*
Garber, Alan Michael *internist, educator, economist*
Glazer, Gary Mark *radiology educator*
Goodman, Stuart B. *medical educator*
Greco, Ralph Steven *surgeon, researcher, medical educator*
Greenberg, Harry B. *gastroenterologist, educator*
Harsh, Griffith R., IV, *neurosurgeon, educator*
Henderson, Victor Warren *behavioral and geriatric neurologist, researcher, educator*
Hinckley, Mary de Raismes *reproductive endocrinologist, infertility specialist*
Hlatky, Mark Andrew *cardiologist, medical researcher*
Jacobs, Charlotte De Croes *medical educator, oncologist*
Jardetzky, Oleg *medical educator, researcher*
Kraemer, Helena Antoinette Chmura *psychiatry educator*
Levy, Ronald *medical educator, researcher*
Malenka, Robert C. *psychiatrist, educator*
Mansour, Tag Eldin *pharmacologist, educator*
Mark, James B. D. *surgeon, educator*
Marmor, Michael Franklin *ophthalmologist, educator*
McDevitt, Hugh O'Neill *immunologist, educator*
McDougall, Iain Ross *nuclear medicine educator*
Merigan, Thomas Charles, Jr., *internist, medical researcher, educator*
Oberhelman, Harry Alvin, Jr., *surgeon, educator*
Polan, Mary Lake *obstetrics and gynecology educator*
Powers, Rebecca Ann *psychiatrist, health facility administrator*
Raffin, Thomas A. *physician*
Reitz, Bruce Arnold *cardiac surgeon, educator*
Robbins, Robert Clayton *surgeon*
Rosenberg, Saul Allen *oncologist, educator*
Rubenstein, Edward *physician, educator*
Safer, Debra Lynn *psychiatrist*
Schatzberg, Alan Frederic *psychiatrist, researcher*
Schendel, Stephen Alfred *plastic surgery educator, craniofacial surgeon*
Shumway, Norman Edward *surgeon, educator*
So, Yuen T. *neurologist, educator*
Spiegel, David *psychiatrist*
Stamey, Thomas Alexander *urologist, educator*
Steinman, Lawrence *neurologist, educator*
Sugawara, Taku *neurosurgeon, researcher*
Wapnir, Irene Leonor *medical educator*
Weissman, Irving L. *medical researcher*
Whyte, Richard Ian *surgeon*

Stockton
Lilienstein, Robert Wolfgang *anesthesiologist*
Nakanishi, Alan *ophthalmologist*

Suisun City
Atiba, Joshua Olajide O. *internist, pharmacologist, oncologist, educator, philanthropist*

Sunnyvale
Castellino, Ronald Augustus Dietrich *radiologist, educator*
Saxena, Amol *podiatrist, consultant*

Sylmar
Corry, Dalila Boudjellal *internist, educator*
Liu, Paul Ishen *pathologist, educator*
Tully, Susan Balsley *pediatrician, medical educator*
Ziment, Irwin *medical educator*

Tarzana
Handelsman, Yehuda *endocrinologist, internal medicine physician*

Tehachapi
Melsheimer, Harold *obstetrician, gynecologist*

Templeton
Abernathy, Shields B. *allergist, immunologist, internist, medical missionary*

Thousand Oaks
Farshidi, Ardeshir B. *cardiologist, educator*
Shi, Zhi-Qing *endocrinologist*
Stolina, Marina *immunologist, research scientist*
Walker, Lorenzo Giles *surgeon, educator*

Torrance
Ananth, Jambur *psychiatrist, educator*
Birnbaumer, Diane Margaret *emergency physician, educator*
Brasel, Jo Anne *pediatrician, educator*
Brass, Eric Paul *internal medicine and pharmacology educator, director*
Emmanouilides, George Christos *physician, educator*
Hammer, Terence Michael *physician*
Howell, Irvin Wendell, Jr., *physician, consultant*
Keller, Margaret Anne Eikrem *pediatrician, educator*
Kram, Harry Bernard *surgeon*
Mehringer, Charles Mark *medical educator*
Mehrotra, Rajnish *nephrologist, researcher, medical educator*
Miller, Milton Howard *psychiatrist*
Myhre, Byron Arnold *pathologist, educator*
Shitabata, Paul Kent *pathologist*
Stabile, Bruce Edward *surgeon*
Stringer, William Warner *physician*
Sun, Nora Chi-Jun *pathologist*
Tanaka, Kouichi Robert *hematologist, educator*

Ukiah
McClintock, Richard Polson *dermatologist*

Vallejo
Gunn, Alexander N., II, *surgeon*

Van Nuys
Fox, James Michael *orthopedic surgeon*

Ventura
Abul-Haj, Suleiman Kahil *pathologist*
Greene, Warren W. *anesthesiologist*
Lovell, Frederick Warren *pathologist, medical legal consultant*
Villaveces, James Walter *allergist, immunologist*

Visalia
Hsu, Shu-Dean *hematologist, oncologist*
Riegel, Byron William *ophthalmologist*

Walnut Creek
Cannon, Grace Bert *retired immunologist*
Carson, Jay Wilmer *pathologist, educator*
Sheen, Portia Yunn-ling *retired physician*

Weimar
Ing, Clarence Sinn Fook *preventive medicine physician, ophthalmic surgeon*

West Hills
Hyde, M. Deborah *neurosurgeon*

Westlake Village
Levine, Donald Arthur *anesthesiologist*

Westminster
Nguyen, Lan Thi Hoang *physician, educator*

Whittier
Arenowitz, Albert Harold *psychiatrist*
Prickett, David Clinton *physician*

Woodland Hills
Herdeg, Howard Brian *physician*
Vokshoor, Amir *neurosurgeon*

Woodside
Blum, Richard Hosmer Adams *medical educator, writer*
Liebowitz, Daniel S. F. *retired medical educator*

Yreka
Nelson, Steven Leslie *surgeon*

COLORADO

Aspen
Oden, Robert Rudolph *surgeon*
Williams, Rhys A. *surgeon*

Aurora
Battaglia, Frederick Camillo *physician*
Green, Larry Alton *physician, educator*
Mellette, Julian Ramsey, Jr., *dermatologist, dermatologic surgeon*
Nora, Audrey Hart *physician*

Basalt
Weill, Hans *medical educator*

Boulder
Kinder, Eugene J(oseph) *psychiatrist, psychoanalyst*

Canon City
Mohr, Gary Alan *physician*

Castle Rock
Thornbury, John Rousseau *radiologist, physician*

Colorado City
Stelle, Robert E. *physician, retired educator*

Colorado Springs
Anderson, Paul Nathaniel *oncologist, educator*
Bohanon, Kathleen Sue *neonatologist, educator*
Gifford, Marilyn Joyce *emergency physician, consultant*
Sceats, D(onald) James, Jr., *neurological surgeon*
Simerville, James Jasper *pediatrician*
Storms, William Wallace *physician*
Todd, Harold Wade *retired association executive, retired air force officer*
Wong, Bert Yuan Shu *internist, cardiologist*

Denver
Accurso, Frank Joseph *physician, educator*
Adler, Charles Spencer *psychiatrist*
Aikawa, Jerry Kazuo *physician, educator*
Arend, William Phelps *medical researcher*
Beresford, Thomas Patrick *psychiatry educator, alcoholism researcher*
Brantigan, Charles Otto *surgeon*
Bunn, Paul A., Jr., *oncologist, educator*
Churchill, Mair Elisa Annabelle *medical educator*
Clayton, Mack Louis *surgeon, educator*
Cohn, Aaron I. *anesthesiologist, educator*
Covar, Ronina A. *medical educator*
Crowley, Thomas James *psychiatry educator*
Deitrich, Richard Adam *pharmacology educator*
Eickhoff, Theodore Carl *epidemiologist*
Fennessey, Paul Vincent *pediatrics and pharmacology educator, research administrator*
Filley, Christopher Mark *neurologist, researcher*
Fletcher, Courtney Vance *pharmacologist, educator*
Gabow, Patricia Anne *internist, health facility executive*
Gibbs, Ronald Steven *obstetrician/gynecologist*
Golitz, Loren Eugene *dermatologist, clinical administrator, educator, pathologist*
Greyson, Clifford Russell *internist*
Haase, Gerald Martin *pediatric surgeon*
Harris, Robert Adron *pharmacologist*
Hoehn, Margaret Maier *neurologist*
Hoehn, Robert J. *plastic surgeon, educator*
Hoffman, Murray Stanley *internist, cardiologist, educator*
Huang, Linda Chen *plastic surgeon*
Jafek, Bruce William *otolaryngologist, educator*
Johnson, Candice Elaine Brown *pediatrics educator*
Johnston, Richard Boles, Jr., *pediatrician, educator, biomedical researcher*
Jones, M. Douglas, Jr., *pediatrician, educator*
Kindt, Glenn W. *neurosurgeon, educator*
Krikos, George Alexander *pathologist, educator*
Krugman, Richard David *pediatrician, academic administrator, educator*
La Rosa, Francisco Guillermo *pathologist, researcher, educator*
Larsen, Gary Loy *physician, researcher*
Lee, Lela A. *dermatology educator, researcher*
Lillehei, Kevin Owen *neurosurgeon, educator*
Lindenfeld, JoAnn *physician, educator*
Lubeck, Marvin Jay *ophthalmologist*
Markovchick, Vincent J. *surgeon*
Martin, Richard Jay *medical educator*
McAtee, Patricia Anne Rooney *medical educator*
Mendez, William Humbert *family medicine physician*
Moore, Ernest Eugene, Jr., *surgeon, educator*
Moore, George Eugene *surgeon*
Mueller, Kathryn Lucile *occupational and environmental medicine educator*
Novins, Douglas K. *psychiatrist, educator*
Nutting, Paul Albert *medical educator, medical science administrator*
Petty, Thomas Lee *physician, educator*
Pomerantz, Marvin *thoracic surgeon*
Rabinovitch, Nathan *pediatrician, educator*
Rainer, William Gerald *cardiac surgeon*
Repine, John Edward *internist, educator*
Robertson, Lawrence Marshall, Jr., *neurosurgeon*
Ruge, Daniel August *retired neurosurgeon, educator*
Schiff, Donald Wilfred *pediatrician, educator*
Schrier, Robert William *physician, educator*
Shore, James H(enry) *psychiatrist*
Silverman, Arnold *pediatrician, educator*
Strand, Melford Lien *anesthesiologist*
Studevant, Laura *medical association administrator*
Sujansky, Eva Borska *pediatrician, geneticist, educator*
Szefler, Stanley James *pediatrics and pharmacology educator*
Takeda, Yasuhiko *pathologist*
Taylor, Edward Stewart *physician, educator*
Tyler, Kenneth Laurence *neurologist, researcher*
Waldstein, Gail P. *pediatric pathologist, writer*
Weatherley-White, Roy Christopher Anthony *surgeon, consultant*
Weston, William Lee *dermatologist*
Wiggs, Eugene Overbey *ophthalmologist, educator*

Dillon
Becker, Quinn Henderson *orthopedic surgeon, military officer*

Durango
Wigton, Chester Mahlon *family physician*

Englewood
Bartee, Roy McKinley, II, *anesthesiologist*
Knize, David Maurice *plastic surgeon*
Makowski, Edgar Leonard *obstetrician and gynecologist*
Woodward, John Simpson, Jr., *orthopedic surgeon*

Fort Collins
Anderson, John Albert *physician*
Gillette, Edward LeRoy *radiation oncology educator*
Kosoy, Michael Y. *biomedical researcher*
Reif, John Steven *epidemiologist, veterinarian*
Roehrig, John T. *immunologist, educator*

Golden
Karlin, Joel Marvin *allergist*

Grand Junction
Janson, Richard Anthony *plastic surgeon*

Greeley
Cook, Donald E. *pediatrician, educator*
Ebomoyi, William Ehigie *epidemiologist*
Jaouen, Richard Matthie *plastic surgeon*

Greenwood Village
Grainger, John R. *medical association administrator*
Lazarus, Jeremy A. *psychiatrist*
Magoun, Harold Ives, Jr., *osteopath*

Highlands Ranch
Bublitz, Deborah Keirstead *pediatrician*

La Jara
Portnoy, Darin Arthur *medical association administrator*

Lakewood
Goldman, L. Barton *physician*

Littleton
Brega, Kerry Elizabeth *physician, researcher*
Forstot, Stephan Lance *ophthalmologist*

Lone Tree
Washington, Reginald Louis *pediatric cardiologist*

Loveland
King, Joan Caluda *medical educator, neuroscientist*

Montrose
Boice, Judith Lynette *physician, writer, educator*
Yocum, Brian Lee *paramedic, educator*

Morrison
Pettee, Daniel Starr *retired neurologist*

Pueblo
Lewallen, William Marvin, Jr., *ophthalmologist*

Wheat Ridge
Brown, Steven Brien *radiologist*
Fleischaker, Gordon Henry, Jr., *pediatrician*
Hashimoto, Christine L. *physician*
Wells, Karen Kay *medical librarian*

Wolcott
Flacke, Joan Wareham *physician, anesthesiology educator*

CONNECTICUT

Avon
Hinz, Carl Frederick, Jr., *immunologist, educator*

Branford
Charlot, Joseph Leonce, Jr., *preventive medicine physician*
Cronin, Michael Thomas Ignatius *pathologist, educator*
Tchernev, Velizar Tzvetanov *physician and biomedical scientist*
Vietzke, Wesley Maunder *internist, educator*

Bridgeport
Lobdell, David Hill *pathologist*
Nijensohn, Daniel Edgardo *neurosurgeon*

Twist-Rudolph, Donna Joy *neurophysiology and neuropsychology researcher*

Cos Cob
Duncalf, Deryck *retired anesthesiologist*

Danbury
Johns, William David *nuclear medicine physician, internist*

Essex
Burris, Harriet Louise *emergency physician*
Goff, Christopher Wallick *pediatrician*

Fairfield
Burd, Robert Meyer *hematologist, oncologist, educator*
Levinson, Stephen Ronald *retired otolaryngologist*
Pinto, Edward Ralph *internist, cardiologist*

Farmington
Arnold, Andrew *medical researcher, physician*
Burki, Nausherwan *pulmonologist*
Cone, Robert Edward *immunologist, educator*
Cooperstein, Sherwin Jerome *medical educator*
Donaldson, James Oswell, III, *neurologist, educator*
Koulos, John *medical association administrator, medical educator*
Liebowitz, Neil Robert *psychiatrist*
McCawley, Austin *psychiatrist, educator*
Metersky, Mark L. *physician*
Owens, Guy *retired neurosurgeon*
Rothfield, Naomi Fox *physician*
Schenkman, John Boris *pharmacologist, educator*

Greenwich
Blumberg, Joel Myron *cardiologist*
Gordon, Neil Alan *facial plastic surgeon*
Haddad, Gabriel G. *pediatrician, educator*
Kalan, Gary Edward *anesthesiologist*
Kopenhaver, Patricia Ellsworth *podiatrist*

Groton
Harrigan, Edmund Patrick *physician, researcher*

Guilford
Springgate, Clark Franklin *physician, researcher*

Hamden
Beardsley, G(eorge) Peter *pediatric oncologist, biochemical pharmacologist*
Nuland, Sherwin *surgeon, writer*

Hartford
Bower, Carol E. *medical researcher, editor, writer*
Cole, Solon Robert *pathologist, educator*
Dworkin, Paul Howard *pediatrician*
Gibbons, John Martin, Jr., *physician, educator*
Gillam, Linda Dawn *cardiologist, researcher*
Gould, Bruce Elliott *physician, medical educator, academic administrator*
Jahiel, Rene Ino *physician*
Jung, Betty Chin *epidemiologist, research analyst, educator, medical/surgical nurse*
Kirton, Orlando Cecilio *surgeon, educator*
Klimek, Joseph John *physician, educator*
Lyons, Robert William *medical educator, infectious disease consultant*
Pachter, Lee M. *pediatrician*
Powers, Robert David *physician*
Robinson, Kenneth John *emergency medicine physician*

Killingworth
Buchanan, J(ohn) Robert *physician, educator*
Christy, Nicholas Pierson *physician*

Lyme
Bloom, Barry Malcolm *pharmaceutical consultant*

Madison
Snell, Richard Saxon *anatomist*

Meriden
Horton, Paul Chester *psychiatrist*
Perricone, Nicholas V. *dermatologist*

Middlebury
Arnold, William Parsons, Jr., *retired internist*

Middletown
Narad, Joan Stern *psychiatrist*
Torop, Paul *psychiatrist*

Mystic
Burrow, Gerard Noel *internist, educator*

New Canaan
Ackerman, Sigurd Howard *psychiatrist*
Coughlin, Francis Raymond, Jr., *surgeon, educator, lawyer*

New Haven
Aghajanian, George Kevork *medical educator*
Arons, Marvin Shield *plastic and hand surgeon*
Barash, Paul George *anesthesiologist, educator*
Bartoshuk, Linda J. *otolaryngologist, educator*
Behrman, Harold Richard *endocrinologist, physiologist, educator*
Boyer, James Lorenzen *physician, educator*
Braverman, Irwin Merton *dermatologist, educator*
Bunney, Benjamin Stephenson *psychiatrist, educator*
Cohen, Lawrence Sorel *internist, educator*
Collins, William F., Jr., *neurosurgery educator*
Comer, James Pierpont *psychiatrist, educator*
Cooper, Dennis Lawrence *oncologist, educator*
Cooper, Jack Ross *pharmacology educator, researcher*
Cullen, Mark Richard *medical educator*
Davey, Lycurgus Michael *neurosurgeon*
Dolan, Thomas Francis, Jr., *pediatrician, educator*
Dunkle, Lisa Marie *pharmaceutical research executive*
Ehrenkranz, Richard Allan *pediatrician*
Fei, Yijian *ophthalmologist, biomedical researcher*
Ferholt, J. Deborah Lott *pediatrician*
Fikrig, Erol *rheumatologist, medical educator*
Forster, Susan H. *ophthalmologist, educator*
Freedman, Gerald Stanley *radiologist, healthcare administrator, educator*
Genel, Myron *pediatrician, educator*
Glaser, Gilbert Herbert *neuroscientist, physician, educator*
Goodrich, Isaac *neurosurgeon, educator*
Gross, Ian *academic pediatrician, neonatologist*
Hines, Roberta Leigh *medical educator*
Horwich, Arthur L. *medical educator*
Hostetter, Margaret K. *pediatrician, medical educator*
Jacoby, Robert Ottinger *comparative medicine educator*
Jatlow, Peter I. *pathologist, medical educator, researcher*
Kashgarian, Michael *pathologist, educator*
Katz, Jay *psychiatry and law educator*
Kushlan, Samuel Daniel *physician, educator, hospital administrator*
Lannin, Donald Rowe *oncologist, surgeon*
Lee, Sin Hang *pathologist, educator*
Leffell, David Joel *dermatologist, surgeon, health facility administrator, educator, writer*
Lentz, Thomas Lawrence *biomedical educator, dean, researcher*
Levine, Robert John *physician, educator*
Lewis, Melvin *psychiatrist, pediatrician, psychoanalyst*
Lytton, Bernard *urology educator*
McGlashan, Thomas Hamel *psychiatry educator*
Miller, I. George *physician, educator, researcher*
Mukherjee, Sandip Kumar *cardiologist*
Musto, David Franklin *medical researcher, educator, historian, consultant*
Naftolin, Frederick *physician, reproductive biologist educator*
Nestler, Eric J. *psychiatry educator*
Niederman, James Corson *physician, educator*
Norbeck, Timothy Burns *medical association executive*
Nwangwu, John Tochukwu *epidemiologist, public health educator*
Petersen, Kitt Mia Falck *medical scientist*
Powsner, Seth *psychiatry educator, medical computing researcher*
Prusoff, William Herman *biochemical pharmacologist, educator*
Ritchie, J. Murdoch *pharmacologist, educator*
Sartorelli, Alan Clayton *pharmacologist, educator*
Sasaki, Clarence Takashi *surgeon, educator*
Schlessinger, Joseph *pharmacology educator*
Schowalter, John Erwin *child and adolescent psychiatry educator*
Seashore, Margretta Reed *physician, educator*
Shaywitz, Bennett Arthur *medical educator*
Shaywitz, Sally E. *pediatrics educator*
Shulman, Gerald I. *endocrinologist, educator, research scientist*
Silverstone, David Edward *ophthalmologist*
Smith, Brian Richard *hematologist, oncologist, pathologist*
Spencer, Dennis Dee *medical educator, director*
Spinner, Gary Frederick *physician assistant, healthcare administrator*
Stern, Robert *psychiatrist*
Volkmar, Fred Robert *psychiatrist, educator*
Waxman, Stephen George *neurologist, neuroscientist*
Weiss, Robert M. *urologist, educator*
Werdiger, Norman *neurologist*
Wessel, Morris Arthur *retired pediatrician*
Wright, Hastings Kemper *surgeon, educator*
Yanagisawa, Eiji *otolaryngologist, educator*
Zaret, Barry Lewis *cardiologist, medical educator*

New London
Schoenberger, Steven Harris *physician, research consultant*
Urbanetti, John Sutherland *internist, consultant*

Niantic
Douglas, Robert Gordon, Jr., *physician*

Norfolk
Mermann, Alan Cameron *retired pediatrics educator, chaplain*

Norwalk
Conosceñti, Craig Stephen *physician*
Floch, Martin Herbert *physician*
Vris, Thomas W. *surgeon*

Norwich
Chakrabarti, Jai *internist, cardiologist*

Putnam
Day, John Anthony, Jr., *pulmonologist*

Ridgefield
Egan, Kenneth J. *dermatologist*

Sacramento
Turner, Kathryn Claire *medical educator, writer*

Southington
Byeff, Peter David *hematologist, oncologist*

Stamford
Cook, Colin Burford *psychiatrist*
Goodhue, Peter Ames *obstetrician and gynecologist, educator*
Klein, Neil Charles *physician*
Klenk, Rosemary Ellen *pediatrician*
Masino, Frank A. *radiologist*
Walsh, Thomas Joseph *neuro-ophthalmologist*

Storrs
Piao, Daqing *biomedical researcher*

Storrs Mansfield
Skauen, Donald Matthew *retired pharmaceutical educator*

Stratford
Feinberg, Dennis Lowell *dermatologist*

Vernon Rockville
Brooks, Neil H. *physician*
Marmer, Ellen Lucille *pediatric cardiologist, mayor*

Waterbury
DeFrancesco, Mark Stephen *physician*
Dudrick, Stanley John *surgeon, scientist, educator*
Eisen, Steven Leslie *neurologist*
Fischbein, Charles Alan *pediatrician*
Garsten, Joel Jay *gastroenterologist*
Shetty, Jayakara *surgeon*

Waterford
Pierson, Anne Bingham *physician*

Watertown
Sherwood, James Alan *physician, scientist, educator*

West Hartford
Stavola, John Joseph *retired obstetrician-gynecologist*

West Haven
Ezekowitz, Michael David *physician*

Westport
Burns, John Joseph *pharmacology educator*
Clausman, Gilbert Joseph *retired medical librarian*
Sacks, Herbert Simeon *psychiatrist, educator, consultant*

Woodbridge
Bondy, Philip Kramer *physician, educator*

DELAWARE

Dover
Boardman, Iva J. *nursing association administrator*
Wilson, Samuel Mayhew *surgeon*

Milton
Provost, Thomas Taylor *dermatology educator, researcher*

Newark
Dadmarz, Kewmars Ebrahim *physician, educator*
Lemole, Gerald Michael *surgeon*

Rockland
Levinson, John Milton *obstetrician, gynecologist*

Seaford
Campbell, Eugene Paul *retired public health administrator*

Wilmington
Benes, Solomon *biomedical scientist, physician*
Cornelison, Floyd Shovington, Jr., *retired psychiatrist, former educator*
Dalziel, Sean Mark *pharmaceuticals researcher*
Frelick, Robert Westcott *physician, consultant*
Goldberg, Morton Edward *pharmacologist*
Gonzalez, Ricardo *surgeon, educator*
Gupta, Rakesh Kumar *internist*
Harley, Robison Dooling *ophthalmologist, educator*
Ikeda, Satoshi *thoracic and cardiovascular surgeon*
Inselman, Laura Sue *pediatrician, educator*
Mathieu, Henri-Pierre *physician*
Pahnke, Greg Randolph *surgeon*
Pell, Sidney *epidemiologist*
Sager, Philip Travis *research physician, cardiologist, cardiac electrophysiologist*
Smith, S(tewart) Gregory *ophthalmologist, inventor, product developer, consultant, author*
Stein, Robert Benjamin *biomedical researcher, physician*
Wallace, Jesse Wyatt *pharmaceutical scientist*
Wong, Pancras C. *biomedical researcher, educator*

DISTRICT OF COLUMBIA

Washington
Allen, Beverly E. *medical librarian*
Anthony, Virginia Quinn Bausch *medical association executive*
Arling, Bryan Jeremy *internist*
Ascensão, João Luis Afonso *physician, researcher*
Avery, Gordon Bennett *medical educator, neonatologist*
Belman, A. Barry *pediatric urologist*
Benjamin, Georges Curtis *emergency physician, consultant*
Benoit, Marilyn B. *psychiatrist, medical association administrator*
Bernstein, Lionel M. *gastroenterologist, educator*
Blumenthal, Susan Jane *psychiatrist, educator, public health official*
Borenstein, David Gilbert *physician, author*
Bourne, Peter Geoffrey *physician, educator, author*
Bryant, Thomas Edward *physician, lawyer*
Burris, Boyd Lee *psychiatrist, psychoanalyst, physician, educator*
Callaway, Clifford Wayne *physician*
Callender, Clive Orville *surgeon*
Catoe, Bette Lorrina *pediatrician, educator*
Cheng, Tsung O. *cardiologist, educator*
Chester, Alexander Campbell, III, *physician*
Chiapella, Anne Page *epidemiologist*
Chiappinelli, Vincent Alexander *pharmacology and physiology educator*
Cohen, Jordan Jay *medical association executive*
Collea, Joseph Vincent *perinatologist, educator*
Collins, Robert Ellwood *surgeon*
Cooper, Byron Stanley *physician, educator*
Curfman, David Ralph *neurosurgeon, educator, civic leader, musician*
Davidson, Richard J. *medical association administrator*
Davis, David Oliver *radiologist, educator*
Dennis, Gary C. *neurosurgeon, educator*
Deutsch, Stanley *retired anesthesiologist, educator*
Dey, Radheshyam Chandra *cytologist*
Dublin, Thomas David *retired physician*
Dym, Martin *medical educator*
Earll, Jerry Miller *internist, educator, endocrinologist*
Ein, Daniel *allergist*
Engler, Renata Johanna Martha *allergist, immunologist, internist, educator*
Epps, Roselyn Elizabeth Payne *pediatrician, educator*
Fairbanks, David Nathaniel Fox *otolaryngologist, surgeon, educator*
Fallon, Harold Joseph *physician, pharmacology and biochemistry educator*
Fenton, Wayne S. *psychiatrist*
Ficarra, Bernard Joseph *former surgeon, legal medicine and bioethics consultant*
Finkelstein, James David *physician, educator*
Foley, Mary E. *medical association administrator, nursing administrator*
Freis, Edward David *physician, medical researcher*
Galbis, Ricardo *psychiatrist*
Gardner, William Albert, Jr., *pathologist, medical foundation executive*
Gehrig, Leo Joseph *retired surgeon*
Gelmann, Edward Paul *oncologist, educator*
Goodwin, Frederick King *psychiatrist*
Gordon, James Samuel *psychiatrist*
Granados, Francisco D. *retired physician*
Gray, Sheila Hafter *psychiatrist, psychoanalyst*
Grealy, Mary R. *medical association administrator*
Hamburg, Margaret Ann (Peggy Hamburg) *public health administrator*
Hartman, Gary E. *pediatric surgeon*
Harvey, John Collins *physician, educator*
Helms, W. David *health research and policy organization administrator*
Herdman, Roger C. *physician, policy analyst*
Holden, Raymond Thomas *physician, educator*
Hussain, Syed Taseer *biomedical educator, researcher*
Ishak, Kamal George *pathologist, consultant, educator, researcher*
Jaffin, Jonathan Hunter *surgeon*
Jenkins, Renee R. *medical educator, pediatrician*
Kahn, Charles N., III, (Chip Kahn) *medical association administrator*
Kanda, Louis T. *cardiologist, health facility administrator*
Karcher, Donald Steven *medical educator*
Kark, John A. *medical educator, consultant*
Khachemoune, Amor *physician*
Kizer, Kenneth Wayne *emergency physician, educator, researcher, consultant, administrator*
Korn, David *pathologist, educator*
Kupersmith, Joel *physician, medical school dean*
Landau, Emanuel *epidemiologist*
Leach, Berton Joe *medical educator*
Leffall, LaSalle D(oheny), Jr., *surgeon, educator*
Lessin, Lawrence Stephen *hematologist, oncologist, educator*
Li, Theodore C.M. *medical educator*
Lindsay, Joseph, Jr., *cardiologist, educator*
Lippman, Marc Estes *pharmacology educator*
Little, John William *plastic surgeon, educator*
Luessenhop, Alfred John *neurosurgeon, educator*
Lynn, D. Joanne *physician, ethicist, health services researcher*
Mandel, H(arold) George *pharmacologist, educator*
Mann, Marion *pathologist, educator*
Mann, Oscar *retired physician, internist, educator*
Marcus, Devra Joy Cohen *internist*
Massaro, Donald John *medical educator, medical researcher*
Mattsson, Ake *psychiatrist, physician*
Maxey, Randall W. *medical researcher, health science association administrator*
McGill, Willis Alexander *anesthesiologist*
McLeod, David G. *urologist, educator*
Miller, Harry Charles, Jr., *physician, urologist, educator*
Monteiro, Maristela Goldnadel *physician, researcher*
Murray, Robert Fulton, Jr., *physician*
Musgrave, Franklyn Garfield *obstetrician, gynecologist*
Nelson, Alan Ray *internist, medical association administrator*
Neviaser, Robert Jon *orthopaedic surgeon, educator*
Novitch, Mark *physician, retired pharmaceutical executive, educator*
Nowak, Judith Ann *psychiatrist*
Oertel, Yolanda Castillo *pathologist, educator, diagnostician*
Packer, Roger Joseph *neurologist, neuro-oncologist*
Pasternack, Stefan Alan *psychiatrist, psychoanalyst*
Paulson, Jerome Avrom *pediatrician*
Pawlson, Leonard Gregory *physician*
Payne, Fred J. *physician, educator*
Pearse, Warren Harland *obstetrician and gynecologist, association executive*
Pellegrino, Edmund Daniel *internist, educator, retired academic administrator*
Perez, Lucille C. Norville *medical association administrator, pediatrician*
Perkins, Joseph S. *medical association administrator*
Phillips, Michael M. *gastroenterologist*
Piemme, Thomas Eugene *medical educator*
Pincus, Jonathan Henry *neurologist, educator*
Pincus, Stephanie Hoyer *dermatologist*
Potter, John Francis *surgical oncologist, educator*
Puchalski, Christina M. *physician, medical educator*
Quivers, Eric Stanley *physician*
Ramphele, Mamphela A. *medical educator*
Ramsey, Robert Leslie *oncologist*
Rayner, Victoria Leigh *medical educator, estheticist, consultant*
Reaman, Gregory Harold *pediatric hematologist, oncologist*
Redman, Robert Shelton *pathologist, dentist*
Rennert, Wolfgang Peter *pediatrician, educator*
Rhoades, Margaret *health care association executive*
Richert, John Rolin *neuroimmunologist, educator*
Ruckman, Roger Norris *pediatric cardiologist*
Ruehle, Charles Joseph *pathologist, military officer*
Sabshin, Melvin *psychiatrist, educator, medical association administrator*
Schechter, Geraldine Poppa *hematologist*
Schubert, Richard D. *medical educator, physician*
Schulke, David *medical association administrator*
Shanahan, Sheila Ann *pediatrician, educator*
Shrier, Diane Kesler *psychiatrist, educator*
Simmons, Henry E. *health care association executive*
Simon, Gary Leonard *internist, educator*
Sivasubramanian, Kolinjavadi Nagarajan *neonatologist, educator*
Sly, Ridge Michael *pediatrician, educator, allergist, immunologist*
Smith, Lee Elton *surgery educator, retired military officer*
Spagnolo, Samuel Vincent *internist, pulmonary specialist, educator*
Spear, Scott Lawrence *plastic surgeon*
Steinberg, William Mark *physician*
Stratton, Kathleen R. *medical association administrator*
Tomich, Paul *medical association administrator, obstetrician, gynecologist*
Valachovic, Richard W. *medical association administrator*

Walsh, Raymond John *medical educator*
Walton, Tracy Matthew, Jr., *radiologist*
Weinberg, Myrl *medical association administrator*
Weingold, Allan Byrne *obstetrician, gynecologist, educator*
Werkman, Sidney Lee *psychiatry educator*
Wiesel, Sam W. *medical educator, academic administrator*
Wilensky, Robert J. *plastic surgeon, historian*
Williams, John Franklin *anesthesiologist educator and administrator*
Winnie, Glenna Barbara *pediatric pulmonologist*
Witorsch, Philip *internist, educator*
Wolfe, Sidney Manuel *physician*
Young, Donald Alan *physician*
Zook, Bernard Charles *pathology educator, administrator, researcher*

FLORIDA

Amelia Island
Schiebler, Gerold Ludwig *pediatrician, educator*

Apopka
Rath, Maurice Monroe *retired physician*

Atlantic Beach
Walker, Richard Harold *pathologist, educator*

Atlantis
Louie, Steven J. *allergist, immunologist*

Bal Harbour
Katz, Shmuel *surgeon*

Bay Pines
Law, David Hillis *physician*
Stewart, Jonathan Taylor *psychiatrist, educator*

Belleair
Dexter, Helen Louise *dermatologist, consultant*
Goldenfarb, Paul Bennett *internist, oncologist*

Boca Raton
Friedland, Michael Lawrence *medical educator*
Friend, Harold Charles *neurologist*
Gagliardi, Raymond Alfred *physician*
Goldman, Stuart Miles *podiatrist*
Kramer, Cecile E. *retired medical librarian*
Weiner, Howard Marc *physician*
Zuckerman, Sidney *retired allergist, immunologist*

Bonita Springs
Dougherty, James *orthopedic surgeon, educator, author*

Boynton Beach
Glickman, Franklin Sheldon *dermatologist, educator*
Lemanski, Larry Fredrick *medical educator, university administrator*
Pataky, Paul Eric *ophthalmologist*
Srinath, Latha *physician*

Brandon
Mack, Arthur Neal *emergency medicine and family practice physician*

Cape Coral
Martin, Benjamin Gaufman *ophthalmologist*

Clearwater
Blumencranz, Peter William *surgeon*
Brown, Richard Christopher *retired epidemiologist*
Heid, Michael Patrick *surgeon*
Lansky, Zena *surgeon*
Thomas, Patrick Robert Maxwell *oncology educator, academic administrator*

Coral Gables
Brandt, Frederic Sheldon *dermatologist*
Perez, Josephine *psychiatrist, educator*
Quillian, Warren Wilson, II, *pediatrician, educator*
Suarez, George Michael *urologist*
Zand, Lloyd Craig *radiologist*

Coral Springs
Wechsler, Arnold *osteopathic obstetrician, gynecologist*

Daytona Beach
Brown, Benjamin Thomas *urologist, educator*
Di Nicolo, Roberto *allergist*

Deland
Goldberg, Paul Bernard *gastroenterologist, clinical researcher*

Delray Beach
Baine, Stuart Allan *cardiologist*
Ehrlich, S(aul) Paul, Jr., *physician, consultant, former government official*
Ellsweig, Phyllis Leah *retired psychotherapist*
Rosenfeld, Steven Ira *ophthalmologist*
Sherwood, Louis Maier *physician, scientist, pharmaceutical company executive*

Englewood
Sanders, W(illiam) Eugene, Jr., *internist, educator*

Fernandina Beach
Barlow, Anne Louise *pediatrician, medical research administrator*

Fisher Island
Rogers, Mark Charles *anesthesiologist, pediatrician, entrepreneur, educator*

Fort Lauderdale
Chernow, Bart *critical care physician*
Cox, Linda Susan *allergist, immunologist*
Crikelair, George Francis *retired plastic surgeon, educator, researcher*
Lodwick, Gwilym Savage *radiologist, educator*
Robb, James Arthur *pathologist*
Rubinson, Howard Alan *physician*
Silvagni, Anthony Joseph *dean, osteopath*
Thomas, John Melvin *retired surgeon*
Whitmore, Douglas Michael *physician*

Fort Myers
Simmons, Vaughan Pippen *medical consultant*
Steier, Michael Edward *cardiac surgeon*
Vera, Enrique *psychiatrist*

Fort Pierce
Partenheimer, Robert Chapin *emergency physician*
Starner, Don Edward *radiographer, educator*

Gainesville
Behnke, Marylou *pediatrician, educator*
Berns, Kenneth Ira *physician*
Burns, Theodore Weber *gastroenterologist*
Cance, William George *surgery educator*
Cassisi, Nicholas John *otolaryngologist, dean*
Copeland, Edward Meadors, III, *surgery educator*
Donnelly, William Henry *pathology educator*
Freund, Gerhard *medical educator*
Gold, Mark Stephen *psychopharmacologist, physician*
Greer, Melvin *medical educator*
LeVeen, Robert Frederick *radiologist*
Limacher, Marian Cecile *cardiologist*
Mahla, Michael E. *anesthesiologist, educator*
Mazzaferri, Ernest Louis *endocrinologist, educator*
Meakin, Faith Anne *medical library dictor*
Modell, Jerome Herbert *anesthesiologist, educator*
Neims, Allen Howard *pediatrician, educator, dean, researcher*
Pfaff, William Wallace *medical educator*
Reynolds, Richard Clyde *internist, educator*
Rhoton, Albert Loren, Jr., *neurological surgery educator*
Rubin, Melvin Lynne *ophthalmologist, educator*
Small, Parker Adams, Jr., *pediatrician, educator*
Suzuki, Howard Kazuro *retired anatomist, educator*
Talbert, James Lewis *pediatric surgeon, educator*
Taylor, William Jape *physician*
Tisher, C. Craig *nephrologist, educator, dean*
Toskes, Phillip Paul *gastroenterologist, educator, clinical researcher*

Greenacres
Goldfarb, Arthur A. *allergist, immunologist, educator*

Gulf Breeze
Pettyjohn, Frank Schmermund *cardiology and emergency medicine educator*

Hialeah
Economides, Christopher George *pathologist*

Hollywood
Constantinescu, Alex R. *pediatrician, nephrologist*
Duffner, Lee R. *ophthalmologist*

Inverness
Esquibel, Edward V. *psychiatrist, clinical medical program developer*

Jacksonville
Bartley, George B. *ophthalmologist, surgeon*
Boylan, Kevin Bernard *neurologist*
DeOrio, James Keith *orthopedic surgeon*
Dorsher, Peter T. *physician*
Earle, J.D. *physician*
Feinglass, Neil Gordon *anesthesiologist*
Gonwa, Thomas Arthur *nephrologist, educator, transplant physician*
Hecht, Frederick *pediatrician, educator, medical geneticist, researcher, consultant, writer*
Hered, Robert W. *ophthalmologist*
Johnson, Douglas William *radiation oncologist, educator*
Kimmich, Haydee Javier *orthopedist, consultant*
Mizrahi, Edward Alan *allergist*
Narayan, Vaduvur Srinivasan *preventive medicine physician*
Oldenburg, Warner Andrew *vascular surgeon*
Raynor, Eileen Margolies *otolaryngologist, educator*
Rodney, Roxanne Audrey *cardiologist, consultant*
Siegel, Steven Douglas *oncologist*
Stephenson, Samuel Edward, Jr., *retired physician*
Thorsteinsson, Gudni *physiatrist*
Threlkel, Robert Hays *pediatrician*
Van Cleve, Robert Baldwin *cardiologist*

Juno Beach
Zuckerman, Stuart *psychiatrist, forensic examiner, educator*

Jupiter
Ernst, Calvin Bradley *vascular surgeon, surgery educator*
Zelnick, Ronald Stuart *surgeon*

Key Biscayne
Aleniewski, Monica Irene *retired anesthesiologist*
Palmer, Roger Farley *pharmacology educator*

Kissimmee
Rajyaguru, Vrajlal Laljibhai *anesthesiologist*
Saha, Asis Kumar *cardiologist*

Lake Placid
Brightwell, Dennis Richard *psychiatrist*

Lake Worth
Stone, Ross Gluck *orthopedic surgeon*

Lakeland
Cassell, Robert Holland *internist, oncologist*
Tripi, Vincent James *physician*

Largo
Grove, Jeffrey Scott *family practice physician*
Wheat, Myron William, Jr., *cardiothoracic surgeon*

Leesburg
Moore, Wistar *cardiovascular surgeon*

Longboat Key
Frankel, Jack *pediatrician, allergist*
Kabara, Jon Joseph *biochemical pharmacology educator*

Lutz
Cualing, Hernani Del Mundo *physician, researcher*

Marco Island
Krause, Charles Joseph *otolaryngologist*

Margate
Ory, Steven Jay *physician, educator*

Melbourne
Greenblatt, Hellen Chaya *immunologist, microbiologist*
Minor, Mark William *allergist*
Pocoski, David John *cardiologist*

Miami
Anderson, Douglas Richard *ophthalmologist, educator, researcher*
Bancalari, Eduardo *pediatrician, educator*
Beck, Morris *allergist*
Block, Norman Louis *physician, medical educator*
Bolooki, Hooshang *cardiac surgeon*
Casariego, Jorge Isaac *psychiatrist, psychoanalyst, educator*
Cassel, John Michael *plastic surgeon*
Cassileth, Peter Anthony *internist*
Chakko, Simon C. *cardiologist, educator*
Cherniack, Evan Paul *geriatrician*
Ciancio, Gaetano *transplant surgeon, urologist*
Civantos, Francisco *pathologist, educator*
Conde, Cesar Augusto *cardiologist, educator*
Davis, Richard Edmund *facial plastic surgeon*
Eftekhari, Nasser *physiatrist*
Eisdorfer, Carl *psychiatrist, health care executive*
Engle, Mary Allen English *retired physician*
Enriquez, Cristino Catud *radiologist, internist, cardiologist*
Freshwater, Michael Felix *plastic surgeon, educator*
Furst, Alex Julian *thoracic and cardiovascular surgeon*
Gelband, Henry *pediatric cardiologist*
Ginsberg, Myron David *neurologist*
Goldberg, Lee Dresden *endocrinologist, medical educator*
Goodwin, W. Jarrard *otolaryngologist, educator*
Heros, Roberto Cosme *neurosurgeon*
Herz, Marvin Ira *psychiatrist, researcher*
Hicks, Dorothy Jane *obstetrician and gynecologist, educator*
Howell, Ralph Rodney *pediatrician, educator, geneticist*
Koller, William Carl *neurology educator*
Lam, Byron L. *ophthalmologist*
Lasseter, Kenneth Carlyle *pharmacologist*
Lemberg, Louis *cardiologist, educator*
Martínez, Luís Osvaldo *radiologist, educator*
Mc Kenzie, John Maxwell *physician*
Medina, Luis Santiago *radiologist, researcher*
Mendez, Luis Eduardo *medical educator, researcher*
Mintz, Daniel Harvey *endocrinologist, educator, academic administrator*
Mizel, Mark Stuart *orthopedic surgeon*
Morrison, Glenn *neurosurgeon*
Murray, Timothy Garrett *ophthalmologist*
O'Sullivan, Mary J. *physician, maternal fetal medicine educator*
Page, Larry Keith *neurosurgeon, educator*
Parrish, Richard Kenneth, II, *medical educator*
Pham, Si Mai *cardiothoracic surgeon, medical educator*
Porter, Wayne Randolph *dermatologist*
Puliafito, Carmen Anthony *ophthalmologist, healthcare executive*
Quencer, Robert Moore *neuroradiologist, researcher*
Raines, Jeff *biomedical scientist, medical research director*
Ricordi, Camillo *surgeon, transplant and diabetes researcher*
Roth, Michael Stewart *obstetrician-gynecologist*
Sanchez de Leon, Roberto J. *physician, educator, writer*
Schachner, Lawrence Alan *pediatric dermatologist*
Schiff, Eugene Roger *internist, gastroenterologist, educator*
Smith, Stanley Bertram *clinical pathologist, allergist, immunologist, anatomic pathologist*
Struhl, Theodore Roosevelt *surgeon*
Stuzin, James M. *plastic surgeon*
Sussmane, Jeffrey Brett *pediatrician*
Tejada, Francisco *physician, educator*
Temple, Jack Donald, Jr., *physician, medical educator*
Tzakis, Andreas Gerasimos *surgeon, educator, research scientist*
Viamonte, Manuel *surgeon*
Vilasuso, Francisco X. *anesthesiologist*
Wanner, Adam *medical association administrator, pulmonologist*
Wheeler, Steve Dereal *neurologist*
Wolff, Grace Susan *pediatrician, pediatric cardiologist*
Wolfson, Aaron Howard *radiation oncologist, educator*
Zwerling, Leonard Joseph *physician, educator*

Miami Beach
Agatston, Arthur Stephen *cardiologist*
Carmichael, Lynn Paul *family practice physician*
Krieger, Bruce Phillip *medical educator*
Lamas, Gervasio Antonio *cardiologist, educator*
Nash, Seymour Cy *surgeon, urologist*
Nixon, Daniel David. *internist*
Sackner, Marvin Arthur *physician*

Miami Shores
Sperry, Len Thomas *psychiatrist and preventive medicine educator*

Naples
Brooks, Joae Graham *psychiatrist*
Doyle, Joseph Thomas *preventive medicine physician*
Gehring, David Austin *physician, cardiologist, administrator*
Grove, William Johnson *physician, surgery educator*
Randall, Neil Warren *gastroenterologist*
Temple, Donald *retired allergist and dermatologist*
Wallace, Edward L. *biomedical researcher, consultant*
Wiegenstein, John Gerald *retired physician*

New Port Richey
Hauber, Frederick August *ophthalmologist*
Hu, Chen-Sien *surgeon*

North Palm Beach
Fierer, Joshua Allan *pathology educator*
Stein, Mark Rodger *allergist*

Ocala
Altenburger, Karl Marion *allergist*
Hunter, Oregon K., Jr., *physiatrist*

Oldsmar
Dyer, Allan M. *medical association administrator*

Orange Park
Fetchero, John Anthony, Jr., *otorhinolaryngologist*

Orlando
Carson, Thomas P. *pediatric cardiologist*
Hornick, Richard Bernard *physician*
Layish, Daniel T. *internist*
Marsh, Ella Jean *pediatrician*
Norris, Franklin Gray *thoracic and cardiovascular surgeon*
Okun, Neil Jeffrey *vitreoretinal surgeon*
Pollack, Robert William *psychiatrist*
Taitt, Earl Paul *psychiatrist, army officer*
Williamson, Paul Richard *medical educator, surgeon*

Ormond Beach
Cromartie, Robert Samuel, III, *thoracic surgeon*

Osprey
Gross, James Dehnert *pathologist*

Palm Beach
Lee, Robert Earl *retired physician*
Seggev, Meir *radiologist, educator*
Simon, Harold *radiologist*

Palm Beach Gardens
Seaman, William Bernard *physician, radiology educator*
Shapiro, Steven David *dermatologist*
Skinner, Margaret Sheppard *pathologist*
Small, Melvin D. *physician, educator*

Palm Harbor
O'Neal, Michael L. *physician*

Palm Springs
Abou-Sayed, Hatem *plastic surgeon*

Palmetto
Dielman, Ray Walter *radiologic scientist, natural hygienist, medical herbalist*

Panama City
Walters, George John *oral and maxillofacial surgeon*

Pensacola
Bradshaw, Bascom Kyle *surgeon, science educator*
Canady, Alexa Irene *pediatric neurosurgeon*
Dillard, Robert Perkins *pediatrician, educator*
Gill, Becky Lorette *retired psychiatrist*
Redmond, Michael R. *ophthalmologist*
Ricketson, George Manning, III, *retired surgeon*
Vuksta, Michael Joseph *surgeon*

Plantation
Gewirtzman, Garry Bruce *dermatologist*
Morris, James Bruce *internist*
Nickelson, Kim René *internist*
Wick, Mitchell A. *physician*

Pompano Beach
Bowsher, Dennis James *internist, cardiologist, pharmacologist*
Searle, Bernard G. *pharmacologist, dental educator*

Ponte Vedra Beach
ReMine, William Hervey, Jr., *retired surgeon*
Toker, Karen Harkavy *physician*

Port Charlotte
Al-Khatib, Tareq *surgeon*
Hollinshead, Ariel Cahill *research oncologist, educator*
McMullen, G. Arthur *physician, cardiologist*

Punta Gorda
Faerber, Abigail Hobbs *physician*

Saint Augustine
Walker, Robert Dixon, III, *retired surgeon, urologist, educator*

Saint Petersburg
Bercu, Barry Bernard *pediatric endocrinologist*
Betzer, Susan Elizabeth Beers *physician, geriatrician*
Bolhofner, Brett Robinson *orthopedist*
Collins, Paul Steven *vascular surgeon*
Donovan, Denis Miller *psychiatrist, author, lecturer*
Hamilton, John McFarland *plastic surgeon, real estate developer*
Lacson, Atilano G. *pathologist*
Larach, Fernando C. *rheumatologist, researcher*
Linhart, Joseph Wayland *retired cardiologist, educational administrator*
Pardoll, Peter Michael *gastroenterologist*
Pflum, William John *physician*
Quiroga, Alicia Espinosa *physiatrist*
Root, Allen William *pediatrician, educator*
Rosenblum, Martin Jerome *ophthalmologist*
Schmidt, Paul Joseph *physician, educator*
Simpson, Lisa Ann *physician, educator*

Sanford
Oostwouder, Peter Henry *family physician*

Sanibel
Davie, Joseph Myrten *physician, pathology and immunology educator, science administrator*

Sarasota
Bowers, Charles Richard *surgeon*
Cavanagh, Denis *gynecologist, obstetrician, educator, gynecological oncologist*
Cummings, Martin Marc *retired medical educator, physician, scientific administrator*
El Shahawy, Mahfouz *internist, cardiologist, educator*
Giordano, David Alfred *retired internist, gastroenterologist*
Iverson, Robert Louis, Jr., *internist, physician*
Jelks, Mary Larson *retired pediatrician*

Levy, Gerhard *pharmacologist*
Magenheim, Mark Joseph *physician, epidemiologist, educator*
Marks, Charles *surgeon, educator*
O'Malley, Thomas Anthony *gastroenterologist, internist*
Sturtevant, Ruthann Patterson *anatomy educator*
Welch, John Dana *retired urologist*
Zavon, Mitchell Ralph *occupational medicine physician*

Sebring
Ibrahim, George W. *physician, health facility administrator*

Stuart
Delagi, Edward Francis *physician, retired educator*
Maldonado, Carlos Manuel *surgeon*
Patterson, Robert Arthur *physician, health care consultant, retired health care company executive, retired air force officer*

Sun City Center
Crow, Harold Eugene *physician, family medicine educator*

Tallahassee
Conti, Lisa Ann *epidemiologist, veterinarian*
Deal, Charles Raymond *anesthesiologist*
Hernandez, Jose Yolando Balagtas *physician, surgeon*
Maguire, Charlotte Edwards *retired pediatrician*
Shamsham, Fadi Michel *cardiologist*

Tampa
Afield, Walter Edward *psychiatrist, service executive*
Barclay-Collett, Laurie Lynn *neurologist, consultant*
Barness, Lewis Abraham *physician*
Behnke, Roy Herbert *physician, educator*
Belsole, Robert John *surgeon*
Branch, William Terrell *urologist, educator*
Bunker-Soler, Antonio Luis *physician*
Ebel, Theron Arthur *physician*
Eichberg, Rodolfo David *orthopedic surgeon, educator*
Evangelista, Allan *podiatrist, medical researcher*
Fabri, Peter J. *surgeon, educator*
Figueroa, Tomas *internist*
Flynn, Michael Patrick *radiologist*
Frias, Jaime Luis *pediatrician, educator*
Gambone, Victor, Jr., *internist, geriatrician*
Gilbert Barness, Enid *medical educator*
Gilbert-Barness, Enid F. *pathologist, pathology and pediatrics educator*
Greenfield, George B. *radiologist*
Holfelder, Lawrence Andrew *pediatrician, allergist*
Hubbell, David Smith *surgeon, educator*
Jacobs, Timothy Andrew *epidemiologist, international health consultant, medical missionary*
Jacobson, Howard Newman *obstetrics and gynecology educator, researcher*
Ledford, Dennis Keith *physician*
Lockey, Richard Funk *allergist, immunologist, educator*
Malafa, Mokenge Peter *surgeon*
Malone, John I. *pediatrics educator, biomedical researcher*
Mantilla, Gonzalo, Jr., *pediatrician*
Martin, Robert Leslie *physician*
McCollough, Newton Clark, III, *orthopaedic surgeon*
Muroff, Lawrence Ross *nuclear medicine physician, educator*
Nagera, Humberto *psychiatrist, psychoanalyst, educator, author*
Nord, H. Juergen *gastroenterologist*
Older, Jay Justin *ophthalmic plastic surgeon*
Olson, Robert Eugene *physician, biochemist, educator*
Pollara, Bernard *pediatrician, educator*
Pomerance, Herbert Hart *pediatrician*
Powers, Pauline Smith *psychiatrist, educator, researcher*
Pupello, Dennis Frank *cardiac surgeon, educator*
Rhodin, Johannes Arne Gösta *medical educator*
Rifkin, Stephen *nephrologist*
Rowlands, David Thomas *pathology educator*
Shenefelt, Philip David *dermatologist*
Shephard, Bruce Dennis *obstetrician, educator, medical writer*
Siegel, Richard Lawrence *immunologist, allergist*
Silbiger, Martin L. *radiologist, educator, dean*
Sinnott, John Thomas *internist, educator*
Smith, David John, Jr., *plastic surgeon*
Spellacy, William Nelson *obstetrician, educator, gynecologist, educator*
Sullebarger, John Thompson *internist, cardiologist, educator*
Walling, Arthur Knight *orthopedist*
Watkins, Joan Marie *osteopath, occupational medicine physician*

Tarpon Springs
Mueller, Willys Francis, Jr., *retired pathologist*

Treasure Island
Hemadeh, Ossama Sharif *surgeon*

University Park
Wurlitzer, Fred Pabst *surgeon*

Venice
Hrachovina, Frederick Vincent *osteopathic physician and surgeon*

Vero Beach
Schwarz, Berthold Eric *psychiatrist*

Weeki Wachee
Finney, Roy Pelham, Jr., *urologist, surgeon, inventor*

West Melbourne
Grenevicki, Lance Francis *surgeon*

West Palm Beach
Brown, Paul A. *physician, business executive*
Brumback, Clarence Landen *physician*
Coloso, Victor Francisco *pediatrician*
Craft, Jerome Walter *plastic surgeon, health facility administrator*
Kapnick, S. Jason *oncologist*
Lichtstein, Daniel M. *medical educator*
Newmark, Emanuel *ophthalmologist*
Pottash, A. Carter *psychiatrist, hospital executive*
Stambaugh, Reginald Jack *ophthalmologist*
Whitfield, Graham Frank *orthopedic surgeon*
Wisnicki, Jeffrey Leonard *plastic surgeon*

Weston
Galvez-Jimenez, Nestor *neurologist*
Malave, Andres *pharmacologist, educator*
McAuliffe, John Anthony *hand surgeon*
Messa, Charles Angelo, III, *plastic surgeon*
Nogueras, Juan Jose *surgeon*
Weiss, Eric Glenn *physician*
Zlatkin, Michael Brian *physician*

Wimauma
Palmer, Louis Thomas *pathologist*

Winter Haven
Honer, Richard Joseph *surgeon*
Warner, Nelson Alfred *dermatologist*

Winter Park
Acierno, Louis Joseph *medical educator*
Baker, James L., Jr., *plastic surgeon*
Pineless, Hal Steven *neurologist*
Wilson, Cecil Bruce *internist*

GEORGIA

Albany
Erhardt, Walter L., Jr., *medical association administrator*

Alpharetta
Harris, James Herman *pathologist, neuropathologist, consultant, educator*

Ashburn
Swygert, Leslie Ann *epidemiologist, consultant*

Athens
Bowen, John Metcalf *pharmacologist, toxicologist, educator*
Masters, Orlan Vincent Wade *gynecologist*

Atlanta
Achiron, Leonard R. *ophthalmologist, educator*
Alexander, Robert Wayne *medical educator*
Ambrose, Samuel Sheridan, Jr., *retired urologist educator*
Amin, Mahul B. *physician, researcher, educator, consultant*
Barnett, Crawford Fannin, Jr., *internist, educator, cardiologist, travel medicine specialist*
Beasley, Ernest William, Jr., *endocrinologist*
Benian, Guy M. *medical educator*
Berkelhamer, Jay Ellis *pediatrician*
Bostwick, John, III, *plastic surgeon, department chairman, medical educator*
Branch, William Thomas, Jr., *medical educator*
Brandenburg, David Saul *gastroenterologist, educator*
Bremner, James Douglas *psychiatrist, researcher, education educator*
Brody, Harold Joseph *dermatologist*
Broome, Claire Veronica *epidemiologist, researcher*
Casarella, William Joseph *physician*
Cooper, Gerald Rice *clinical pathologist*
Cordero, Jose Fernando *pediatrician, federal agency administrator, USPHS officer*
Curran, James W. *epidemiologist, educator, academic administrator*
Davis, Lawrence William *radiation oncologist*
DeLong, Mahlon R. *neurologist, educator*
Dietz, William Harry *pediatrician*
Dobes, William Lamar, Jr., *dermatologist, educator*
Dowda, William F. *internist*
Dunston-Thomas, Frances Johnson *pediatrician, public health official*
Dutt, Kamla *medical educator*
Edelhauser, Henry F. *ophthalmologic researcher, educator, physiologist*
Elsas, Louis Jacob, II, *medical educator*
Eriksen, Michael *medical educator*
Falk, Henry *pediatrician, epidemiologist, researcher*
Fermanis, Ernest George *urologic surgeon*
Fosha, Kent C., Sr., *healthcare management company executive*
Franch, Harold August *nephrologist, researcher*
Frank, Erica *preventive medicine physician*
Fuller, Lonnie *medical educator*
Galambos, John Thomas *medical educator, internist*
Ganaway, George Kenneth *psychiatrist, psychoanalyst*
Gayles, Joseph Nathan, Jr., *administrator, fund raising consultant*
Godwin, John Thomas *pathologist, nuclear medicine specialist*
Goldman, John Abner *rheumatologist, immunologist, educator*
Gordon, Frank Jeffrey *medical educator*
Gude, Albert Valdemar *retired anesthesiologist*
Hardman, John B. *psychiatrist, director*
Hatcher, Charles Ross, Jr., *surgeon, health facility administrator*
Heimburger, Elizabeth Morgan *psychiatrist*
Heller, John Gaylord *orthopaedic surgery educator*
Holloway, Kelvin J. *allergist, immunologist, pediatrician*
Horsburgh, Charles Robert *allergist*
Houry, Debra *emergency physician, educator*
Hug, Carl Casimir, Jr., *anesthesiology and pharmacology educator*
Hughes, James Mitchell *epidemiologist*
Israili, Zafar Hasan *scientist, clinical pharmacologist, educator*
Johns, Michael Marieb Edward *otolaryngologist, academic administrator*
Jones, Herbert Cornelius, III, *otolaryngologist*
Jurkiewicz, Maurice John *surgeon, educator*
Karp, Herbert Rubin *neurologist, educator*
Kellermann, Arthur L. *medical educator*
Khuri, Fadlo Raja *oncologist, educator*
Kimani, Grace Alexandra *internist*
Klein, Luella Voogd *obstetrics-gynecology educator*
Klippel, John H. *physician, association executive*
Kokko, Juha Pekka *physician, educator*
Koplan, Jeffrey Powell *physician*
Ku, David Nelson *medical educator*
Kushner, Howard I. *public health and history of medicine educator*
Lee, John Everett *physician*
Letton, Alva Hamblin *surgeon, educator*
Levey, Allan I. *neurologist, educator, pharmacologist*
Lindsay, Michael Kenneth *obstetrics and gynecology educator*
Litt, Brian *neurologist, educator, biomedical engineer*
Louard, Rita Jean *endocrinologist, educator*
Lubin, Michael Frederick *physician, educator, researcher*
Lui, Victor King Shing *pediatrician*
Lybarger, Jeffrey Allen *epidemiology research administrator*
Majmudar, Bhagirath *medical educator*
Mandel, Jack Sheldon *epidemiologist, educator*
Mansour, Kamal A. *cardiothoracic surgeon*
Mantella, Tino J. *former medical association administrator*
Matsuura, John Henry *surgeon*
Mattox, Douglas E. *otolaryngologist*
Medford, Russell Marshall *physician*
Minneman, Kenneth Paul *pharmacology educator*
Murphy, Ana Alvarez *obstetrician, gynecologist*
Nahai, Foad *plastic surgery educator*
Nemeroff, Charles Barnet *neurobiology and psychiatry educator*
Nichols, Joseph J., Sr., *surgeon*
Oakley, Godfrey Porter, Jr., *medical educator, former health facility administrator*
O'Brien, Mark Stephen *pediatric neurosurgeon*
Olansky, Sidney *retired dermatologist*
Oyesiku, Nelson Mobolanle *neurosurgeon, neuroscientist*
Peacock, Lamar Batts *retired physician*
Reed, James Whitfield *physician, educator*
Rich, Robert Regier *immunology educator, physician*
Salomone, Jeffrey Paul *surgeon, educator*
Sexson, William Robert *pediatrician, educator*
Sherman, Roger Talbot *surgeon, educator*
Simsic, Janet M. *cardiologist*
Smith, Robert Boulware, III, *vascular surgeon, educator*
Sola, Augusto *pediatrician, educator*
Spangler, Dennis Lee *physician*
Steinhaus, John Edward *anesthesiologist, educator*
Stillwagon, Gary Bouldin *radiation oncologist*
Tait, C(olumbus) Downing, Jr., *physician, medical educator*
Taylor, Andrew T., Jr., *radiologist, educator*
Thacker, Stephen Brady *medical association administrator, epidemiologist*
Tissue, Mike *medical educator, respiratory therapist*
Udoff, Eric Joel *diagnostic radiologist*
Wang, Richard Y. *emergency physician, osteopath*
Wertheim, Steven Blake *orthopedist*
Willis, Isaac *dermatologist, educator*
Wulkan, Mark Lewis *pediatrician, surgeon*
Yancey, Asa Greenwood, Sr., *physician*
Yeargin-Allsopp, Marshalyn *medical epidemiologist, pediatrician*
Z, Chris *internist, medical educator*

Augusta
Chandler, Arthur Bleakley *pathologist, educator*
Cundey, Paul Edward, Jr., *cardiologist*
Dolen, William Kennedy *allergist, immunologist, pediatrician, educator*
Ellison, Lois Taylor *physician, medical educator and administrator*
Fincher, Ruth Marie Edla *medical educator, dean*
Gadacz, Thomas Roman *surgery educator*
Gambrell, Richard Donald, Jr., *endocrinologist, educator*
Given, Kenna Sidney *surgeon, educator*
Hooks, Vendie Hudson, III, *surgeon*
Horuzsko, Anatolij *medical research scientist*
House, Fredrick Crisler *allergist*
Imig, John David *medical educator*
Luxenberg, Malcolm Neuwahl *ophthalmologist, educator, retired*
Mahesh, Virendra Bhushan *endocrinologist*
Manganiello, Louis Otto Joseph *retired neurosurgeon*
McDaniel, George M. *pediatrician*
McDonough, Paul Gerard *obstetrician-gynecologist, educator*
Miller, Jerry Allan, Jr., *pediatrician*
Nesbit, Robert Raymond, Jr., *surgeon*
Ownby, Dennis Randall *pediatrician, educator, allergist, researcher*
Prisant, L(ouis) Michael *cardiologist*
Ryan, James Walter *physician, medical researcher*
Smith, Randolph Relihan *plastic surgeon*
Talledo, Oscar Eduardo *medical educator*
Wray, Betty Beasley *allergist, immunologist, pediatrician*
Xenakis, Stephen Nicholas *psychiatrist, army officer*

Austell
Halwig, J. Michael *allergist*

Brunswick
Mohr, Janet Ann *psychiatrist*
Perniciaro, Charles Vincent *dermatologist, educator, entrepreneur*

Buford
Byrd, Larry Donald *behavioral pharmacologist*

Colquitt
San Jose, Angel Molina *surgeon*

Columbus
Chan, Philip *retired dermatologist, retired military officer*

Dahlonega
Brown, Hugh Keith *medical researcher, educator*

Dalton
McKay, William Paul *oncologist, health facility administrator*

Decatur
Bain, James Arthur *pharmacologist, educator*
Brown, William Virgil *internal medicine educator*
Dreyer, Susan *orthopedist, educator*
Gann, Joyce Ann *obstetrician-gynecologist*
Harris, Maurice Daniel *internist*
Henderson, Ralph Hale *physician*
Rausher, David Benjamin *internist, gastroenterologist*

Doraville
Dean, Andrew Griswold *epidemiologist, consultant, medical educator*

Dublin
Nellis, Noel *thoracic surgeon, educator*

Duluth
Evans, Paul *osteopath*

Evans
Fischer, Paul M. *physician, educator*

Fort Valley
Swartwout, Joseph Rodolph *obstetrics and gynecology educator, administrator*

Gainesville
Givogre, John Lee *anesthesiologist*
Turner, John Sidney, Jr., *retired otolaryngologist, educator*
Vaughn, Betty Jean *obstetrician/gynecologist*

Kennesaw
Barnett, Benjamin Lewis, Jr., *retired physician, educator*

Lagrange
Copeland, Robert Bodine *internist, cardiologist*

Lawrenceville
Fetner, Robert Henry *radiation biologist*

Macon
Bagley, Cathy Lorraine *obstetrician, gynecologist*
Robinson, Joe Sam *neurosurgeon, educator*
White, John Joseph *surgery and pediatrics educator*
Young, Henry E. *tissue engineering medical educator*

Marietta
Chastain, Mark Alan *dermatologist, otolaryngologist, educator*
Hagood, Murl Felton *surgeon*
Meyer, Roger Albert *surgeon*
Thomas, Pamella Delores *medical director, physician, educator*
Wheatley, Joseph Kevin *physician, urologist*
Wheelock, Argil J. *urologist, medical company executive*

Martinez
Colborn, Gene Louis *anatomy educator, researcher*
Nesbitt, Robert Edward Lee, Jr., *physician, educator, scientific researcher, writer, poet*

Quitman
Baum, Joseph Herman *retired biomedical educator*

Reidsville
Saad, Fathy Zaki *medical association administrator, physician*

Roswell
Barnett, Florence Carsley *neurosurgeon*
McCloud, Melody Theresa *obstetrician-gynecologist, surgeon*

Savannah
Ferro, Alejandro F. *obstetrician, gynecologist*
Hemphill, John Michael *neurologist*
Hoskins, William John *obstetrician, gynecologist, educator*
Krahl, Enzo *retired surgeon*
Skelton, William Douglas *physician*
Taylor, Roslyn Donny *family physician*
Wirth, Fremont Philip, Jr., *neurosurgeon, educator*
Zoller, Michael *otolaryngologist, head and neck surgeon, educator*

Smyrna
Kell, Michael Jon *physician, researcher*

Stockbridge
Friedman, Robert Barry *neurosurgeon*

Stone Mountain
Gotlieb, Jaquelin Smith *pediatrician*

Tifton
Dorminey, Henry Clayton, Jr., *allergist*

HAWAII

Honolulu
Ahmed, Iqbal *psychiatrist, consultant*
Bauman, Kay A. *physician*
Brady, Stephen R.P.K. *physician*
Chee, Percival Hon Yin *ophthalmologist*
Chock, Clifford Yet-Chong *family practice physician*
Crowell, David Harrison *retired biomedical researcher, consultant*
Curb, Jess David *medical educator, researcher*
Edwards, John Wesley, Jr., *urologist*
Fitz-Patrick, David *endocrinologist, educator*
Fong, Bernard W.D. *physician, educator*
Goldstein, Sir Norman *dermatologist*
Goodhue, William Walter, Jr., *forensic pathologist, military officer, educator*
Hammar, Sherrel Leyton *medical educator*
Hay-Roe, Victor *plastic surgeon*
Herbich, Gregory J. *dermatologist, plastic surgeon*
Ho, Reginald Chi Shing *medical educator*
Ishii, Clyde Hideo *plastic surgeon*
Kane, Thomas Jay, III, *orthopaedic surgeon, educator*
Lau, H. Lorrin *obstetrician/gynecologist, inventor*
Lee, Yeu-Tsu Margaret *surgeon, educator*
Moreno-Cabral, Carlos Eduardo *cardiac surgeon*
Murray, Kevin Dennis *surgeon*
Parsa, Fereydoun Don *plastic surgeon*
Reilly, Kevin C., Sr., *radiologist*
Schatz, Irwin Jacob *cardiologist, educator*
Sia, Calvin Chia Jung *pediatrician*
Siegel, Richard Jay *plastic surgeon, consultant*
Sugiki, Shigemi *ophthalmologist, educator*

Takanishi, Jr., Danny M. *medical educator, department chairman*
Tseng, George Shihchi *anesthesiologist*
Vogel, Carl-Wilhelm Ernst *biomedical scientist, clinical pathologist*
Wallach, Stephen Joseph *cardiologist*

Kamuela
Mc Dermott, John Francis *psychiatrist, physician*
Morgan, Andrew Lane *urologist, educator*

Koloa
Donohugh, Donald Lee *physician*

Lihue
Culliney, John James *radiologist, educator*

Mililani
Gardner, Sheryl Paige *gynecologist*
Okita, George Torao *pharmacologist educator*

Wahiawa
Hazenfield, Hugh Norman *surgeon*

Waikoloa
Copman, Louis *radiologist*

IDAHO

Boise
Hoffman, William Kenneth *retired obstetrician, gynecologist*
Redshaw, James Douglas *neurologist*

Coeur D Alene
Gumprecht, Jane Caroline Doering *retired physician*

ILLINOIS

Arlington Heights
Ehrenpreis, Eli Daniel *physician, educator, biomedical researcher*
Jensen, Lynn Edward *retired medical association executive, economist*
Moser, Richard Peter *neurosurgeon*
Pochyly, Donald Frederick *physician, hospital administrator*

Belleville
Franks, David Bryan *internist, emergency physician*

Berwyn
Misurec, Rudolf *physician, surgeon*

Bloomington
Trefzger, Richard Charles *surgeon*

Carol Stream
Schmerold, Wilfried Lothar *dermatologist*

Centralia
Sharp, Elaine Cecile *obstetrician, gynecologist*

Champaign
Freedman, Philip *physician, educator*
Gold, Paul Ernest *psychology and behavioral neuroscience educator*
Risken, Jared Cleveland *physician*
Rosenblatt, Karin Ann *cancer epidemiologist*

Chester
Felthous, Alan Robert *psychiatrist*

Chicago
Abcarian, Herand *surgeon, educator*
Abelson, Herbert Traub *pediatrician, educator*
Adelman, Susan Hershberg *surgeon*
Adomavicius, Jonas *gastroenterologist, writer*
Albrecht, Ronald Frank *anesthesiologist*
Andersen, Burton Robert *immunologist, educator*
Astrachan, Boris Morton *psychiatry educator, consultant*
Bakay, Roy Arpad Earle *neurosurgeon, educator*
Bakris, George *nephrologist, educator*
Baldwin, DeWitt Clair, Jr., *physician, educator*
Balk, Robert A. *medical educator*
Barker, Walter Lee *thoracic surgeon*
Baron, Joseph Mandel *hematologist*
Barton, John Joseph *obstetrician, gynecologist, educator, health facility administrator, researcher*
Bassiouny, Hisham Sallah *surgeon, educator*
Beck, Robert N. *nuclear medicine educator*
Becker, Michael Allen *internist, rheumatologist, educator*
Beigl, William *physician, hypnotist, acupuncturist, consultant*
Bell, Carl Compton *psychiatrist, researcher*
Bendok, Bernard R. *neurosurgeon, researcher*
Benson, Al Bowen, III, *oncologist, educator*
Benzon, Honorio Tabal *anesthesiologist*
Beyer, Eric C. *pediatrician, researcher*
Black, Henry Richard *physician*
Bluefarb, Samuel Mitchell *retired physician*
Boddie, Arthur Walker, Jr., *surgeon, cancer researcher*
Boggs, Joseph Dodridge *pediatric pathologist, educator*
Bogolub, David Louis *physician*
Bonow, Robert Ogden *medical educator*
Bowman, James Edward *physician, educator*
Brandman, James Franklin *internist, oncologist*
Bransfield, James Joseph *surgeon*
Brendler, Charles Burgess *urologist, educator*
Bunn, William Bernice, III, *occupational health and environmental medicine executive, epidemiologist, lawyer*
Burck, Joseph Russell *medical educator, consultant, minister*
Burt, Richard K. *physician, educator*
Calenoff, Leonid *radiologist*
Calvin, James Eldon, Jr., *cardiologist, educator, researcher*
Caro, William Allan *physician, educator*
Cavallino, Robert P. *radiologist*
Celesia, Gastone Guglielmo *neurologist, neurophysiologist, researcher*
Champagne, Ronald Oscar *medical association administrator*
Chan, Lawrence Siu-Yung *dermatologist, educator*
Charles, Allan G. *physician, educator*
Charrow, Joel *pediatrician, educator, geneticist, director*
Chatterton, Robert Treat, Jr., *reproductive endocrinology educator*
Christoffel, Katherine Kaufer *pediatrician, epidemiologist, educator*
Coble, Yank David, Jr., *internist, endocrinologist*
Coe, Fredric L. *physician, educator, researcher*
Cohen, Melvin R. *physician, educator*
Colley, Karen J. *medical educator, medical researcher*
Conway, James Joseph *radiologist, educator*
Corlin, Richard F. *gastroenterologist*
Costa, Erminio *pharmacologist, cell biologist, educator*
Curry, Raymond Howard *physician*
Curtis, Arthur William *otolaryngologist*
Davison, Richard *internist, educator*
Derlacki, Eugene L(ubin) *retired otolaryngologist*
Deziel, Daniel J. *surgeon*
Diamond, Seymour *physician*
Dooley, Sharon L. *obstetrician, gynecologist*
Dunaif, Andrea Elizabeth *endocrinologist*
Dunea, George *nephrologist, educator*
Elias, Sherman *obstetrician, gynecologist, educator, clinical geneticist*
Epstein, Leon G. *neurologist*
Evans, Thelma Jean Mathis *internist*
Farhadi, Ashkan *physician, researcher*
Faxon, David Parker *cardiologist*
Feingold, Daniel Leon *anesthesiologist, consultant*
Feldman, Ted *cardiologist*
Fennessy, John James *radiologist, educator*
Ferguson, Donald John *surgeon, educator*
Ferguson, Mark Kendric *physician, educator, researcher*
Flaherty, Emalee Gottbrath *pediatrician*
Flaherty, Timothy Thomas *radiologist*
Fontanarosa, Phil Bernard *emergency physician*
Fragen, Robert Joseph *physician, anesthesiologist*
Franco, Carlo Diaz *surgeon, anatomist, anesthesiologist*
Frederiksen, Marilynn C. *physician*
Freitag, Frederick Gerald *osteopathic physician*
Galante, Jorge Osvaldo *orthopedic surgeon, educator*
Gapstur, Susan Mary *cancer epidemiologist, educator, researcher*
Gecht, Martin Louis *physician, bank executive*
Geha, Alexander Salim *cardiothoracic surgeon, educator*
Gerbie, Albert Bernard *obstetrician, gynecologist, educator*
Gewertz, Bruce Labe *surgeon, educator*
Gewurz, Anita Tartell *medical association administrator*
Ginsberg, Norman Arthur *physician, educator*
Giovacchini, Peter Louis *psychoanalyst*
Glassenberg, Myron *neurologist*
Golomb, Harvey Morris *hematologist, oncologist, educator*
Gorbien, Martin John *medical educator, geriatrician*
Gordon, Leo I. *hematologist, oncologist, educator*
Gould, Samuel Halpert *pediatrics educator*
Grammer, Leslie Carroll *allergist*
Grayhack, John Thomas *urologist, educator*
Green, David *hematologist*
Greenberger, Paul Allen *allergist, immunologist, educator, medical researcher*
Gregory, Stephanie Ann *hematologist, educator*
Hackett, Karen L. *medical association administrator*
Hambrick, Ernestine *retired colon and rectal surgeon*
Hand, Roger *physician, educator*
Harris, Jules Eli *medical educator, physician, clinical scientist, administrator*
Hasnain, Memoona *medical educator, medical researcher*
Hast, Malcolm Howard *biomedical scientist, medical educator*
Head, Louis Rollin *surgeon*
Hellman, Samuel *radiologist, educator*
Herbst, Arthur Lee *obstetrician, gynecologist*
Hibbard, Judith Usher *obstetrician*
Hill, Carlotta H. *physician*
Honig, George Raymond *pediatrician*
Horgan, Santiago *surgeon*
Hsueh, Wei *pathologist, educator*
Huckman, Michael Saul *neuroradiologist, educator*
Hughes, John Russell *neurologist, educator*
Hussey, Michael Jude *obstetrician, educator*
Ivankovich, Anthony D. *anesthesiologist, educator*
Jeevanandam, Valluvan *surgeon, educator*
Jensen, Harold Leroy *medical liability insurance administrator, physician*
Jilhewar, Ashok *gastroenterologist*
Johnson, Timothy Patrick *health and social researcher*
Jonasson, Olga *surgeon, educator*
Jones, Richard Jeffery *internist, educator*
Jordan, V. Craig *endocrine pharmacologist, educator*
Kahrilas, Peter James *medical educator, researcher*
Katz, Adrian Izhack *physician, educator*
Katz, Robert Stephen *rheumatologist, educator*
Kerth, Jack D. *otolaryngologist*
Kiani, Reza *endocrinology and internal medicine educator*
Kinslow, Monica M. *forensic scientist*
Kirschner, Barbara Starrels *pediatric gastroenterologist*
Kirsner, Joseph Barnett *physician, educator*
Kittle, Charles Frederick *surgeon*
Kloss, Linda L. *medical association administrator*
Knote, John A. *diagnostic radiologist*
Kowal-Vern, Areta *pathology and pediatrics educator*
Landsberg, Lewis *dean, endocrinologist, medical researcher*
Langman, Craig Bradford *nephrologist*
Lauth, William Brian *emergency physician, internist, educator*
Lee, Raphael Carl *plastic surgeon, biomedical engineer*
Leff, Alan Richard *medical educator, researcher*
Leventhal, Bennett Lee *psychiatry and pediatrics educator, administrator*
Lopez, Carolyn Catherine *physician*
Luchins, Daniel Jonathan *psychiatrist*
Lurain, John Robert, III, *gynecologic oncologist*
Mahood, William H. *gastroenterologist*
Malkinson, Frederick David *dermatologist, educator*
Martin, Gary Joseph *medical educator*
Maves, Michael Donald *medical association executive*
McDermott, Raymond, Jr., *physician*
McDonald, Larry William *neuropathologist educator*
McKinney, William T. *psychiatrist, educator*
McLawhon, Ronald William *pathology educator, biochemist*
Meadow, William Lee *medical educator*
Mehlman, David Joel *cardiologist, educator*
Mendelson, Ellen B. *radiologist, educator*
Merk, Bradley Robert *orthopedic surgeon*
Metz, Charles Edgar *radiology educator*
Meyer, Paul Reims, Jr., *orthopedic surgeon*
Miller, Albert J. *cardiologist, internist*
Miller, Richard J. *pharmacologist, educator*
Millichap, Joseph Gordon *neurologist, educator*
Mirkin, Bernard Leo *clinical pharmacologist, pediatrician*
Moawad, Atef *obstetrician, gynecologist, educator*
Moen, Ronald S. *medical association administrator*
Moore, Vernon John, Jr., *pediatrician, consultant, lawyer*
Morris, Naomi Carolyn Minner *clinical pediatrician, medical researcher, educator, health facility administrator*
Musacchio, Robert A. *medical association administrator*
Naclerio, Robert Michael *otolaryngologist, educator*
Nadler, Robert B. *medical educator*
Nahrwold, David Lange *surgeon, educator*
Nakajima, Yasuko *medical educator*
Narahashi, Toshio *pharmacology educator*
Nelson, Richard Lawrence *surgeon, educator*
Nguyen, Tuan Manh *internist, perinatologist, obstetrician, gynecologist*
Nyhus, Lloyd Milton *surgeon, educator*
Olson, Jack Conrad, Jr., *geriatrician*
Olson, Sandra Forbes *neurologist*
Onsager, David Ralph *cardiothoracic surgeon, educator*
Owens, Charles A. *cardiovascular and interventional radiologist*
Page, Ernest *medical educator*
Palmisano, Donald J. *surgeon, medical educator*
Pappas, George Demetrios *anatomy and cell biology educator, scientist*
Pasche, Boris Claude Roger *physician*
Plested, William G., III, *surgeon*
Poznanski, Andrew Karol *pediatric radiologist*
Prinz, Richard Allen *surgeon*
Pulido, Jose S. *physician*
Ramsey-Goldman, Rosalind *physician*
Reardon, Thomas R. *physician, medical association administrator*
Reddy, Janardan K. *medical educator*
Replogle, Robert Lee *cardiovascular and thoracic surgeon*
Rhone, Douglas Pierce *pathologist, educator*
Rice, Charles Lane *surgical educator*
Ridenour, Joey *medical association administrator, operations research specialist*
Robertson, William Wright, Jr., *orthopedist, educator*
Robinson, June Kerswell *dermatologist, educator*
Roizen, Nancy J. *physician, educator*
Rosen, Steven Terry *oncologist, hematologist*
Rosenthal, Ira Maurice *pediatrician, educator*
Rothschild, Steven K. *physician, medical educator, researcher*
Rowley, Janet Davison *physician*
Russell, Thomas R. *medical association administrator*
Sachs, Greg Alan *preventive medicine physician*
Salem, Riad *radiologist, consultant*
Sandlow, Leslie Jordan *gastroenterologist, educator*
Sarwark, John Francis *orthopaedic surgeon, educator*
Scarse, Olivia Marie *cardiologist, consultant*
Schade, Stanley Greinert, Jr., *hematologist, educator*
Schafer, Michael Frederick *orthopedic surgeon*
Schilsky, Richard Lewis *oncologist, researcher*
Schneidman, Barbara Sue *psychiatrist*
Schuler, James Joseph *vascular surgeon*
Schulman, Sidney *neurologist, educator*
Sciarra, John J. *obstetrician, gynecologist, educator*
Scommegna, Antonio *obstetrician, gynecologist, educator*
Scott, Bruce A. *otolaryngologist*
Seeler, Ruth Andrea *pediatrician, educator*
Serota, Scott *medical association administrator*
Shannon, Iris Reed *health consultant*
Shapiro, Richard Alan *surgeon*
Sheagren, John Newcomb *physician, educator*
Shields, Thomas William *surgeon, educator*
Short, Marion Priscilla *neurogenetics educator*
Siegler, Mark *internist, educator*
Silverstein, Jonathan Charles *surgeon, researcher*
Slavin, Konstantin Vladimirovich *neurosurgeon*
Smith, Earl Charles *nephrologist, educator*
Socol, Michael Lee *obstetrician, gynecologist, educator*
Soper, Nathaniel Jolas *surgeon*
Sorensen, Leif Boge *physician, retired educator*
Southgate, Marie Therese *physician, editor*
Sparberg, Marshall Stuart *gastroenterologist, educator*
Spargo, Benjamin H. *educator, renal pathologist*
Strassner, Howard Taft, Jr., *obstetrician, educator*
Straus, Francis Howe *pathologist, educator*
Swerdlow, Martin Abraham *pathologist, educator*
Tallman, Martin Stuart *hematologist, oncologist*
Tardy, Medney Eugene, Jr., *retired otolaryngologist, facial plastic surgeon*
Tatar, Arnold Marshall *internal medicine physician, educator*
Telfer, Margaret Clare *internist, hematologist, oncologist*
Thomas, Leona Marlene *health information educator*
Tomar, Russell Herman *pathologist, educator, researcher*
Toriumi, Dean Michael *facial, plastic and reconstructive surgery, educator*
Valle, Rafael F. *obstetrician-gynecologist*
Valvassori, Galdino E. *physician*
Valyi-Nagy, Tibor G. *neuropathologist, virologist*
Vazquez, Richard Michael *surgeon*
Walton, Robert Lee, Jr., *plastic surgeon*
Waxler, Beverly Jean *anesthesiologist, physician*
Webster, James Randolph, Jr., *physician*
Weichselbaum, Ralph R. *oncologist chairman*
Weigel, Thomas J. *pediatrician, cardiologist*
Weis, Mervyn J. *physician, gastroenterologist*
Weisenberg, Elliot *pathologist, educator*
Weiss, Robert Alan *surgeon*
Weldon-Linne, C. Michael *pathologist, microbiologist*
Whitington, Peter Frank *pediatrics educator, pediatric hepatologist*
Wied, George Ludwig *physician*
Williams, Philip Copelain *obstetrician, gynecologist*
Williamson, Wayne C. *preventive medicine physician*
Willoughby, William Franklin, II, *physician, researcher*
Winjum, Stephen J. *medical association administrator*
Winter, Jane *medical educator*
Wissler, Robert William *physician, cardiovascular pathologist, educator*
Witt, Thomas Roy *surgeon*
Yao, Tito Go *pediatrician*
Yogev, Ram *pediatrician, educator*
Yordan, Edgardo Luis *gynecologist*
Young, Nancy Melinda *otolaryngologist*
Zini, James E. *physician*
Zsigmond, Elemer Kalman *anesthesiologist*

Crystal Lake
Dy, Deana Lim *allergist*

Danville
Prabhudesai, Mukund M. *pathology educator, laboratory director, researcher, administrator*

Darien
Gardner, Howard Garry *pediatrician, educator*
Kulkarni, Bidy *reproductive endocrinologist, biomedical researcher, consultant*

Deerfield
Sanner, John Harper *retired pharmacologist*
Scheiber, Stephen Carl *psychiatrist*

Des Plaines
Quintanilla, Antonio Paulet *retired physician, educator*
Roukis, Thomas Sean *surgeon, podiatrist*

Dixon
Polascik, Mary Ann *ophthalmologist*

Downers Grove
Ozog, Diane L. *allergist*

Effingham
Kabbes, Douglas John *physician*

Elk Grove Village
Sanders, Joe Maxwell, Jr., *pediatrician, association administrator*

Elmhurst
Banich, Francis Edward *surgeon*
Blain, Charlotte Marie *internist, educator*
Fornatto, Elio Joseph *retired otolaryngologist, educator*

Elmwood Park
Oryshkevich, Roman Sviatoslav *retired physician, physiatrist, dentist, educator*

Evanston
Adelson, Bernard Henry *physician*
Bashook, Philip G. *medical association executive, educator*
Bloomer, William David *radiation oncologist, educator*
Crawford, James Weldon *psychiatrist, educator, administrator*
Enroth-Cugell, Christina Alma Elisabeth *neurophysiologist, educator*
Gaiha, Vishnu Das *cardiologist*
Golbus, Joseph *rheumatologist*
Hughes, Edward F. X. *preventive medicine physician, educator*
Kentor, Paul Martin *allergist*
Khandekar, Janardan Dinkar *oncologist, educator*
Langsley, Donald Gene *psychiatrist, medical board executive*
Langsley, Pauline Royal *psychiatrist*
Lloyd-Still, John Dashwood *pediatrician, educator*
Locker, Gershon Yehuda *oncologist, educator*
Mc Nerney, Walter James *health policy educator, consultant*
Mustoe, Thomas Anthony *physician, plastic surgeon*
Plaut, Eric Alfred *retired psychiatrist, educator*
Schwartz, Neena Betty *endocrinologist, educator*
Sprang, Milton LeRoy *obstetrician, gynecologist, educator*
Stumpf, David Allen *pediatric neurologist*
Traisman, Howard Sevin *pediatrician*
Vick, Nicholas A. *neurologist*
Zeman, Gregory Oswald *physician*

Evergreen Park
Hong, Kuhn *nuclear medicine physician*
Zumerchik, John *urologist*

Galesburg
Gupta, Madan Lal *cardiologist*
Mathew, James *cardiologist*
Tourlentes, Thomas Theodore *psychiatrist*

Glen Ellyn
Agruss, Neil Stuart *cardiologist*
Dieter, Raymond Andrew, Jr., *physician, thoracic and vascular surgeon*

Glencoe
Milloy, Frank Joseph, Jr., *surgeon*

Glenview
Casas, Laurie Ann *plastic surgeon*
Graff, Jeffrey G. *emergency physician*
Rubin, Susan M. *neurologist*

Godfrey
King, Ordie Herbert, Jr., *oral pathologist*

Greenville
Junod, Daniel August *podiatrist*

Harvey
Heilicser, Bernard Jay *emergency physician*

Highland Park
Epstein, Randy J. *physician, ophthalmologist*
Kaplan, Mark E. *allergist*
Rubin, David Neal *radiologist*
Saltzberg, Eugene Ernest *emergency physician, educator*

Hillsboro
Mulch, Robert F., Jr., *physician*

Hines
Best, William Robert *physician, educator, university official*
Fisher, Morris Alan *neurologist, medical educator*
Folk, Frank Anton *surgeon, educator*
Zvetina, James Raymond *pulmonologist*

Hinsdale
Allen, James Edward *preventive medicine physician*
Brueschke, Erich Edward *physician, researcher, educator*
Finley, Robert Coe, III, *interventional cardiologist, consultant, educator*
Gruft, James Harris *physiatrist, educator*
Gunn, Larry Charles *physician*
McConaughy, Joseph C. *surgeon*

Hoffman Estates
Sodt, Peter Christian *pediatrician, cardiologist*

Indianhead Park
Johnson, Anita (Mary Anita Johnson) *physician, medical service administrator*

Joliet
Layman, Dale Pierre *medical educator, researcher, writer*
Ring, Alvin Manuel *pathologist, educator*

Lake Barrington
Morris, Ralph William *chronopharmacologist*

Lake Bluff
Kyncl, John Jaroslav *pharmacologist*

Lake Forest
Jones, Philip Newton *internist, educator*
Kelly, Daniel John *physician*
Levy, Nelson Louis *physician, scientist, corporate executive*
Parker, Rebecca Bollinger *emergency physician*
Pawl, Ronald Phillip *neurosurgery educator*
Salter, Edwin Carroll *retired physician*
Sherman, Jeffrey Wayne *physician, clinical researcher*
Somberg, John Charin *cardiologist, medicine and pharmacology educator*
Weinberg, Milton, Jr., *cardiovascular and thoracic surgeon*
Wilbur, Richard Sloan *physician, executive*

Lincolnshire
Taub, Amy F. *dermatologist*

Lisle
Colbert, Marvin Jay *retired internist, educator*

Lombard
Bachop, William Earl, Jr., *retired anatomist, zoologist*
Henkin, Robert Elliott *nuclear medicine physician*
Kasprow, Barbara Anne *biomedical scientist, writer*

Long Grove
Ausman, Robert K. *surgeon, research executive*

Macomb
Dexter, Donald Harvey *surgeon, educator*

Marion
Munas, Falies A. *psychiatric physician*
Schaede, Richard Edwin *retired family practice physician*

Marshall
Mitchell, George Trice *physician*

Mattoon
Maris, Charles Robert *surgeon, otolaryngologist*

Maywood
Albain, Kathy S. *oncologist*
Barron, William M. *physician, educator*
Berman, James H. *pediatrician, gastroenterologist, educator*
Dado, Diane Valentina *plastic and reconstructive surgeon, pediatric plastic surgeon*
Eidem, Benjamin Walter *cardiologist*
Freeark, Robert James *surgeon, educator, health facility administrator*
Gamelli, Richard Louis *surgeon, educator*
Gaynor, Ellen Rose *hematologist*
Gianopoulos, John George *obstetrician*
Godwin, John E. *hematologist*
Hanin, Israel *pharmacologist, educator*
Light, Terry Richard *orthopedic hand surgeon*
Mittendorf, Robert *physician, epidemiologist*
Moran, John Francis *cardiologist*
Nand, Sucha *medical educator*
Newman, Barry Marc *pediatric surgeon*
O'Keefe, James Paul *epidemiologist*
Pickleman, Jack R. *surgeon*
Slogoff, Stephen *dean, anesthesiologist, educator*
Stiff, Patrick Joseph *internist, hematologist, oncologist, educator*
Tobin, Martin John *pulmonary and critical care physician*
Wilber, David James *cardiologist*
Zelby, Andrew S. *neurosurgeon*

Melrose Park
Klein, Lloyd William *cardiologist, researcher*

Moline
Arnell, Richard Anthony *radiologist*
Varela, Fernando *anesthesiologist*

Mundelein
McLeskey, Charles Hamilton *anesthesiologist, educator, pharmaceutical executive*

Naperville
Bleck, Phyllis Claire *surgeon, musician*
Bufalino, Vincent John *medical association administrator, cardiologist*
Schwab, Paul Josiah *psychiatrist, educator*

Niles
Kaden, Bruce Richard *hematologist, oncologist*

Normal
Cooley, William Emory, Jr., *radiologist*
Joyce, Larry Wayne *physician*

North Chicago
Barsano, Charles Paul *medical educator, dean*
Bush, Eugene Nyle *pharmacologist, research scientist*
Chedid, Antonio *pathologist, educator, researcher*
Gall, Eric Papineau *physician, educator*
Hawkins, Richard Albert *medical educator, administrator*
Kim, Yoon Berm *immunologist, educator*
Nair, Velayudhan *pharmacologist, medical educator, academic administrator*
Rogers, Eugene Jack *medical educator*
Rudy, David Robert *physician, educator*
Sierles, Frederick Stephen *psychiatrist, educator*

Northbrook
Cucco, Ulisse P. *retired obstetrician, gynecologist*
Hindo, Walid Afram *radiology educator, researcher*
Hirsch, Lawrence Leonard *physician, retired educator*
Hughes, William Franklin, Jr., *ophthalmologist, emeritus educator*

Oak Brook
Bryan, R. Nick *medical association administrator*
Christian, Joseph Ralph *physician*
Loughead, Jeffrey Lee *physician*

Oak Forest
Lee, David Chang *physician*

Oak Lawn
Byrnes, Michael Francis *podiatrist*

Oak Park
Matsuda, Takayoshi *surgeon, educator, biomedical researcher*

Oakbrook Terrace
Becker, Robert Jerome *allergist, health care consultant*

Palatine
Carranza, Cesar Augusto *surgeon*

Park Ridge
Bitran, Jacob David *internist*
Greenspahn, Bruce Robert *cardiologist*
Johnson, Glenn W. *medical association administrator*
Pielet, Bruce William *obstetrician*
White, John Vincent *surgeon, consultant*

Peoria
Lanzino, Giuseppe *physician*
Lorenz, Rodney Alan *physician, educator*
Meriden, Terry *physician*
Pollak, Raymond *general and transplant surgeon*

Pinckneyville
Cawvey, Clarence Eugene *retired physician*

Quincy
Barnes, Walter C., Jr., *physician*

River Grove
Hillert, Gloria Bonnin *anatomist, educator*

Riverside
Chmell, Samuel Jay *orthopedic surgeon*

Riverwoods
Douglas, Bruce Lee *oral and maxillofacial surgeon, public health educator, gerontology and workplace health consultant*

Rockford
Baptist, Errol Christopher *pediatrician, educator*
Heerens, Robert Edward *physician*
Schauer, Jeffrey Edward *surgeon*

Skokie
Levy, Mark Hirsch *internist, medical educator, researcher*

Springfield
Frank, Stuart *cardiologist*
Graham, Donald R. *epidemiologist*
Holland, John Madison *retired family practice physician*
Mikell, Frank Leonard *cardiologist*
Myers, Phillip Ward *otolaryngologist*
Rabinovich, Sergio *physician, educator*
Sumner, David Spurgeon *surgery educator*
Swartz, Conrad Melton *psychiatrist*
Woodson, Gayle Ellen *otolaryngologist*
Yaffe, Stuart Allen *physician*
Zaricznyj, Basilius *orthopedic surgeon*
Zook, Elvin Glenn *plastic surgeon, educator*

Sugar Grove
Debartolo, Hansel Marion, Jr., *otolaryngologist, plastic surgeon*

Sycamore
Fanning, Gary Lee *anesthesiologist*

Urbana
Kaufman, Jerome Benzion *neurosurgeon*
Kotynek, Jan George *surgeon*
Krock, Curtis Josselyn *pulmonologist*
Nelson, Ralph Alfred *physician*
Oliphant, Uretz John *physician, surgeon*
O'Morchoe, Charles Christopher Creagh *anatomical sciences educator, science administrator*

Washington
Stine, Robert Howard *retired pediatrician, allergist*

Waukegan
Keller, Richard Loran *physician*

West Chicago
Paulissen, James Peter *retired pediatrician, county official*

Westchester
Calder, Robert Austin *preventive medicine physician, administrator*

Wheaton
Bogdonoff, Maurice Lambert *physician*
McCartney, Charles Price *retired obstetrician-gynecologist*
Oesterle, Carolyn Scherer *pediatric ophthalmologist*

Wilmette
Erickson, James Clifford, III, *anesthesiologist, educator*
Hier, Daniel Barnet *neurologist*

Winnetka
Carrow, Leon Albert *physician*
Rossi, Ennio C. *physician, educator*
Rubnitz, Myron Ethan *pathologist, educator*

Yorkville
McEachern, Joan *medical association administrator*

Zion
Birdsall, Timothy Carroll *naturopathic physician*

INDIANA

Alexandria
Irwin, Gerald Port *physician*

Anderson
King, Charles Ross *physician*

Bedford
Hunter, Harlen Charles *orthopedic surgeon*

Beech Grove
Hughes, Charles E., III, *plastic surgeon*

Bloomington
Bishop, Michael D. *emergency physician*
Kunkler, Arnold William *retired surgeon, educator*
Moore, Ward Wilfred *medical educator*
Rink, Lawrence Donald *cardiologist*

Bluffton
Pitts, Neal Chase *rheumatologist*

Carmel
Cohen, Marlene Lois *pharmacologist*

Corydon
Kelty, Paul David *obstetrician, educator*

Decatur
Fitzgerald, Robert Hannon, Jr., *orthopedic surgeon*

Dune Acres
Martino, Robert Salvatore *orthopedic surgeon*

Evansville
Penkava, Robert Ray *radiologist, educator*

Fishers
Baach, Michael L. *internist*

Fort Wayne
Heger, James Joseph *internist, cardiologist*
Lee, Shuishih Sage *pathologist*
Richardson, Joseph Hill *physician, medical educator*

Gary
Iatridis, Panayotis George *medical educator*

Hammond
Ashbach, David Laurence *internist, nephrologist*

Highland
Steen, Lowell Harrison *retired physician*

Indianapolis
Allen, Stephen D(ean) *pathologist, microbiologist*
Atkins, Clayton H. *family physician, epidemiologist, educator*
Beltz, Homer Ferguson *radiologist, healthcare executive*
Bergstein, Jerry Michael *nephrologist*
Biller, Jose *neurologist*
Bloch, Richard *physician*
Bonaventura, Leo Mark *gynecologist, educator*
Brandt, Ira Kive *pediatrician, medical geneticist*
Brickley, Richard Agar *retired surgeon*
Broadie, Thomas Allen *surgeon, educator*
Brown, Edwin Wilson, Jr., *preventive medicine physician, educator*
Broxmeyer, Hal Edward *medical educator*
Burr, David Bentley *anatomy educator*
Cheng, Liang *pathologist*
Chuang, Tsu-Yi *dermatologist, epidemiologist, educator*
Cleary, Robert Emmet *gynecologist, infertility specialist*
Coleman, John Joseph, III, *surgery educator*
Corkins, Mark R. *physician, pediatric gastroenterologist*
Daly, Walter Joseph *medical educator*
Dere, Willard Honglen *internist, educator*
Dyken, Mark Lewis, Jr., *neurologist, educator*
Eble, John Nelson *pathologist, oncology researcher*
Eigen, Howard *pediatrician, educator*
Einhorn, Lawrence Henry *medical educator*
Eisenberg, Paul Richard *cardiologist, consultant, educator*
Feng, Gen-sheng *medical educator, researcher*
Ghetti, Bernardino Francesco *neuropathologist, neurobiology researcher*
Green, Morris *pediatrician, educator*
Greist, Mary Coffey *dermatologist*
Grosfeld, Jay Lazar *surgeon, educator*
Hansell, Richard Stanley *obstetrician, educator, gynecologist, educator*
Helveston, Eugene McGillis *pediatric ophthalmologist, educator*
Holden, Robert Watson *radiologist, educator, university dean*
Inui, Thomas Spencer *physician, educator*
Irwin, Glenn Ward, Jr., *medical educator, physician, university official*
Jackson, Valerie Pascuzzi *radiologist, educator*
Johnston, Cyrus Conrad, Jr., *medical educator*
Kaye, Gordon Israel *pathologist, anatomist, educator*
Knoebel, Suzanne Buckner *cardiologist, educator*
Lemberger, Louis *pharmacologist, physician*
Luerssen, Thomas George *pediatric neurosurgeon, educator*
Lumeng, Lawrence *physician, educator*
MacDougall, John Duncan *surgeon*
Madura, James Anthony *surgical educator*
Mahomed, Yousuf *physician, cardiothoracic surgeon*
Manders, Karl Lee *neurosurgeon*
Miyamoto, Richard Takashi *otolaryngologist*
Molitoris, Bruce Albert *nephrologist, educator*
Mosbaugh, Phillip George *urologist, educator*
Norins, Arthur Leonard *physician, educator*
Nurnberger, John I., Jr., *psychiatrist, educator*
Richter, Judith Anne *pharmacology educator*
Rogers, Robert Ernest *medical educator*
Ross, Edward *cardiologist*
Roth, Lawrence Max *pathologist, educator*
Ryder, Kenneth William *pathologist, educator*
Schamberger, Marcus S. *pediatric cardiologist*
Schmetzer, Alan David *psychiatrist*
Sherman, Stuart *internist, gastroenterologist*
Smith, James Warren *pathologist, educator, microbiologist, parasitologist*
Stehman, Frederick Bates *gynecologic oncologist, educator*
Surawicz, Borys *physician, educator*
Sutton, Gregory Paul *obstetrician, gynecologist*
Ware, J(oe) Anthony *cardiologist*
Watanabe, August Masaru *physician, medical educator*
Weber, George *oncology and pharmacology researcher, educator*
Weinberger, Myron Hilmar *medical educator*
Wilson, Fred M., II, *ophthalmologist, educator*
Winters, Peter Lee *dermatologist*
Woolling, Kenneth Rau *vascular internist*
Yee, Robert Donald *ophthalmologist*
Zipes, Douglas Peter *cardiologist, researcher*

Lafayette
Gordon, Irene Marlow *radiology educator*
Langston, Edward Lee *physician, pharmacist*
Maickel, Roger Philip *pharmacologist, educator*

Logansport
Brewer, Robert Allen *physician*

Marion
Fisher, Pierre James, Jr., *physician*
Lau, Patrick Hing-Leung *radiologist, educator*

Merrillville
Doumanian, Heratch Ohannes *radiologist*
Nguyen, Thach Ngoc *cardiologist*

Michigan City
Mothkur, Sridhar Rao *radiologist*

Muncie
Goswami, Ajanta *psychiatrist*
Roch, Lewis Marshall, II, *ophthalmic surgeon, medical entrepreneur*
Zemtsov, Alexander *dermatology and biochemistry educator, inventor*

Munster
Singh, Manmohan *orthopedic surgeon, educator*

Nappanee
Borger, Michael Hinton Ivers *osteopathic physician, educator*

New Albany
Chowhan, Naveed Mahfooz *oncologist*

Scottsburg
Kho, Eusebio *surgeon*

South Bend
Anderson, Kenneth Paul *nephrologist, administrator*
Beker, Bernardo Enrique *anesthesiologist*
Creps, Philp Lloyd *child psychiatrist*
Reed, Robert Frederick *physician*
White, Robert Dennis *pediatrician, director*

Sullivan
Chavez, Mary Ann *osteopathic family physician*

Terre Haute
Sawyer, Thomas Harrison *health, physical education and recreation director*
Siebenmorgen, Paul *retired family physician, lay church worker*

Valparaiso
Kobak, Alfred Julian, Jr., *obstetrician, gynecologist*
Poracky, Bernard Francis *radiologist*

Walton
Chu, Johnson Chin Sheng *retired physician*

West Lafayette
Bergstrom, Donald E. *medical educator*
Borch, Richard Frederic *pharmacology and chemistry educator*
Borowitz, Joseph Leo *pharmacologist, educator*
Frey, Harley Harrison, Jr., *retired anesthesiologist*
Poulos, James Thomas *endocrinologist, educator*
Robinson, Farrel Richard *pathologist, toxicologist*
Rutledge, Charles Ozwin *pharmacologist, educator*
Shaw, Stanley Miner *nuclear pharmacy scientist*

IOWA

Ames
Fleming, Jon Lee *gastroenterologist*

Burlington
Paragas, Rolando G. *physician*

Cedar Rapids
Houmes, Blaine V. *emergency physician, county medical examiner*
Krivit, Jeffrey Scot *surgeon*
Maikon, Marc Steven *podiatrist*
Norris, Albert Stanley *psychiatrist, educator*

Clinton
Vidal, Ronald Anthony *otolaryngology*
Woodman, Grey Musgrave *psychiatrist*

Clive
Neis, Arthur Veral *healthcare and development company executive*

Davenport
Edgerton, Winfield Dow *retired gynecologist*
Shammas, Nicolas Wahib *internist, cardiologist*

Des Moines
Elmets, Harry Barnard *retired osteopath, dermatologist*
Olds, John Ward *internist*
Rodgers, Louis Dean *retired surgeon*
Song, Joseph *pathologist, educator*
Wattleworth, Roberta Ann *physician, medical educator*

Iowa City
Abboud, Francois Mitry *physician, educator*
Afifi, Adel Kassim *physician*
Andreasen, Nancy Coover *psychiatrist, educator, neuroscientist*
Apicella, Michael Allen *physician, educator*
Bar, Robert S. *endocrinologist, educator*
Bedell, George Noble *physician, educator*
Buckwalter, Joseph Addison *orthopedic surgeon, educator*
Burns, C(harles) Patrick *hematologist, oncologist*
Butler, John Edward *biomedical sciences educator, consultant*
Clifton, James Albert *physician, educator*
Cooper, Reginald Rudyard *orthopedic surgeon, educator*
Damasio, Antonio R. *physician, neurologist*
Eckstein, John William *internist, educator, retired dean*
Erkonen, William E. *radiologist, medical educator*
Fellows, Robert Ellis *medical educator, medical scientist*
Folk, James Calvin *ophthalmologist, researcher*
Galask, Rudolph Peter *obstetrician and gynecologist*
Gantz, Bruce Jay *otolaryngologist, educator*
Gergis, Samir Danial *anesthesiologist, educator*
Grose, Charles Frederick *pediatrician, infectious disease specialist*
Hammond, Harold Logan *oral and maxillofacial pathologist, educator*
Hartz, Arthur J. *medical researcher*
Heistad, Donald Dean *cardiologist*
Helms, Charles Milton *medical educator, consultant*
Hussey, David Holbert *physician*
Kerber, Richard E. *cardiologist*
Kisker, Carl Thomas *pediatrician, educator*
Lamping, Kathryn G. *medical educator, medical researcher*
Lariviere, Gene Robert *surgeon*
Lauer, Ronald Martin *pediatric cardiologist, researcher*
LeBlond, Richard Foard *internist, educator*
Long, John Paul *pharmacologist, educator*
Lynch, Richard Gregory *medical educator*
Markham, Sanford Max *obstetrician-gynecologist, educator*
Mason, Edward Eaton *surgeon*
Medh, Jheem D. *medical educator, biochemist, researcher*
Merchant, James A. *medical educator*
Morriss, Frank Howard, Jr., *pediatrics educator*
Muller, Barbara Ann *allergist*
Niebyl, Jennifer Robinson *obstetrician, gynecologist, educator*
Noyes, Russell, Jr., *psychiatrist*
Peloso, Paul Michael *medical educator*
Richerson, Hal Bates *physician, internist, allergist, immunologist, educator*
Robinson, Robert George *psychiatry educator*
Smoker, Wendy Rue Kartinos *neuroradiologist, consultant, educator*
Snyder, Peter M. *medical educator, medical researcher*
Strauss, John Steinert *dermatologist, educator*
Sutphin, John E. *ophthalmologist, educator*
Tephly, Thomas Robert *pharmacologist, educator, toxicologist*
Thompson, Herbert Stanley *neuro-ophthalmologist*
Tsalikian, Eva *physician, educator*
Van Gilder, John Corley *neurosurgeon, educator*
Wallace, Robert B. *medical educator*
Weinberger, Miles M. *pediatrician, educator*
Weiner, George Jay *internist*
Weingeist, Thomas Alan *ophthalmology educator*
Weinstock, Joel Vincent *immunologist*
Weintraub, Neal L. *medical educator, cardiologist*
Welsh, Michael James *medical educator, biophysicist, educator*
Williams, Richard Dwayne *physician, educator, urologist*
Ziegler, Ekhard Erich *pediatrics educator*

Johnston
Thoman, Mark Edward *pediatrician*

Marshalltown
Cassidy, Eugene Patrick *pathologist*
Packer, Karen Gilliland *cancer patient educator, researcher*
Thomas, David Llewellyn *physician*

Sioux City
Ayi, Bertha Serwa *epidemiologist, internist*

West Des Moines
Alberts, Marion Edward *physician*

KANSAS

Coffeyville
Hawley, Raymond Glen *pathologist*

Concordia
Fowler, Wayne Lewis, Sr., *internist*

Hutchinson
Crater, Timothy Andrews *internist*

Kansas City
Anderson, Harrison Clarke *pathologist, educator, biomedical researcher*
Arakawa, Kasumi *physician, educator*
Ator, Gregory A. *otolaryngologist, consultant*
Damjanov, Ivan *pathologist, educator*
Dunn, Marvin Irvin *physician*
Grantham, Jared James *nephrologist, educator*
Hite, Pamela Rene *emergency medicine physician*
Hudson, Robert Paul *medical educator*
Johnson, Joy Ann *diagnostic radiologist*
Krantz, Kermit Edward *physician, educator*
Lawrence, Walter Thomas *plastic surgeon*
Lee, Kyo Rak *radiology educator*
Mathewson, Hugh Spalding *anesthesiologist, educator*
McCallum, Richard Warwick *medical researcher, clinician, educator*
Meyers, David George *internist, cardiologist, educator*
Mohn, Melvin Paul *anatomist, educator*
Neuberger, John Stephen *preventive medicine and epidemiology educator*
Pehlivanov, Nonko Dimitrov *gastroenterologist, researcher*
Rawitch, Allen Barry *medical educator, academic administrator*
Schloerb, Paul Richard *surgeon, educator*
Sciolaro, Charles Michael *cardiac surgeon*
Suzuki, Tsuneo *molecular immunologist*
Voogt, James Leonard *medical educator*
Waxman, David *internist, consultant, academic administrator*
Ziegler, Dewey Kiper *neurologist, educator*

Lawrence
Buck, Henry William, Jr., *obstetrician-gynecologist*

Manhattan
Durkee, William Robert *retired internist*
Oehme, Frederick Wolfgang *medical researcher, educator*

Overland Park
Dockhorn, Robert John *physician, educator*
Landry, Mark Edward *podiatrist, researcher*

Pittsburg
Sullivan, William John *osteopath*

Prairie Village
Fairchild, Robert Charles *pediatrician*

Shawnee Mission
Bell, Deloris Wiley *physician*
Fleming, Michael O. *physician*
Hartzler, Geoffrey Oliver *retired cardiologist*
Price, James Gordon *physician, educator*
Thomas, Christopher Yancey, III, *surgeon, educator*

Topeka
Johnson, Patsy *nursing association administrator*
Menninger, William Walter *psychiatrist*
Roy, William Robert *physician, lawyer, former congressman*

Westwood
Hart, Paul Vincent, Jr., *emergency and acute care physician, inventor*

Wichita
Brada, Donald Robert *psychiatrist*
Burket, George Edward, Jr., *retired family physician*
Cummings, Richard J. *retired otologist*
Frazier, Linda M. *medical educator*
French, James Edward *surgeon*
Guthrie, Richard Alan *physician*
McKenzie, Harry James *cardiothoracic surgeon, surgical researcher*
Oxley, Dwight K(ahala) *pathologist*

KENTUCKY

Ashland
Roth, Oliver Ralph *radiologist*

Berea
Lamb, Irene Hendricks *medical researcher*

Bowling Green
Jhamb, Indar Mohan *physician*

Danville
Nickens, Harry Carl *medical association administrator*

Edgewood
Martin, Kevin Douglas *surgeon*

Elizabethtown
Rahman, Rafiq Ur *oncologist, educator*

Frankfort
Holsinger, James Wilson, Jr., *physician*

Hindman
Bailey, Benny Ray *health care administrator, state senator*

Lexington
Anderson, James Wingo *physician*
Avant, Robert Frank *physician, educator*
Clawson, David Kay *orthopedic surgeon*
Davey, Diane Davis *pathologist, educator*
Gilliam, M(elvin) Randolph *retired urologist, educator*
Glenn, James Francis *urologist, educator*
Hagen, Michael Dale *family physician educator*
Hill, John Sylvester *allergist*
Hood, Gregory A. *internal medicine physician*
Kang, Bann C. *immunologist*
Kaplan, Martin P. *allergist, immunologist, pediatrician*
Kibler, William Benjamin *orthopedist, surgeon*
Markesbery, William R. *neurology and pathology educator, physician*
Mayer, Lloyd Dewald *allergist, immunologist, physician, medical educator*
Means, Robert Taylor, Jr., *hematologist, educator*
Mentzer, Robert Melvin, Jr., *surgeon*
Nikolova - Karakashian, Mariana *biomedical researcher*
Noonan, Jacqueline Anne *pediatrics educator*
Rowland, Randall G. *urologist*
Tollison, Joseph W. *family practice physician*
Van Meter, Woodford Spears *ophthalmologist, surgeon*
Weitzel, William David *psychiatrist*
Whayne, Thomas French, Jr., *cardiologist, educator*
Woodring, John Howell *radiologist*
Young, Paul Ray *medical board executive, physician*

Louisville
Amin, Mohammad *urology educator*
Andrews, Billy Franklin *pediatrician, educator*
Aronoff, George Rodger *medicine and pharmacology educator*
Bertolone, Salvatore J. *pediatric medicine educator*
Callen, Jeffrey Phillip *dermatologist, educator*
Chien, Sufan *surgeon, educator*
Cook, Larry Norman *pediatrician, neonatologist, educator*
Crum, John Evan *physician, executive*
Danzl, Daniel Frank *emergency physician*
DeMunbrun-Harmon, Donne O'Donnell *retired family physician*
Doyle, Michael Joseph *neurosurgeon*
Elin, Ronald John *pathologist, educator*
Farman, Allan George *radiologist, oral pathologist, educator*
Galandiuk, Susan *colon and rectal surgeon, educator*
Gall, Stanley Adolph *physician, immunology researcher*
Garretson, Henry David *neurosurgeon*
Garver, David L. *psychiatrist*
Gray, Laman A., Jr., *thoracic surgeon, educator*
Haddy, Richard Ian *family physician, educator*
Haynes, Douglas Martin *obstetrician, gynecologist, educator*
Holt, Homer Anthony, Jr., *urologist, educator*
Kaplan, Henry Jerrold *ophthalmologist, educator*
Kutz, Joseph Edward *hand surgeon, educator*
Lei, Zhenmin *endocrinologist, reproductive biologist, researcher*
Lord, Jonathan T. (Jack Lord) *medical association administrator*
Olson, William Henry *neurology educator, administrator*
Parker, Joseph Corbin, Jr., *pathologist, educator*
Pence, Hobert Lee *physician*
Polk, Hiram Carey, Jr., *surgeon, educator*
Raff, Martin Jay *internist, infectious diseases educator, lawyer*
Richardson, James David *surgeon*
Schwab, John Joseph *psychiatrist, educator*
Scott, Ralph Mason *physician, radiation oncology educator*
Syed, Ibrahim Bijli *medical educator and physicist, author, philosopher, theologist, public speaker, writer*
Tanguay, Peter Eugene *child and adolescent psychiatry educator*
Tasman, Allan *psychiatry educator*
Thongbookerd, Visith *nephrologist, researcher*
Waddell, William Joseph *pharmacologist, toxicologist*
Weisskopf, Bernard *pediatrician, child behavior, development and genetics specialist, educator*
Whitelaw, Christine Cappelle *pediatrician, aesthetic medicine educator*
Wright, Jesse Hartzell *psychiatrist, educator*

Mayfield
Viles, Henry *pathologist*

Radcliff
Flores, George H. *obstetrician-gynecologist*

Russellville
Arshad, Abrar Mehmood *physician*

LOUISIANA

Alexandria
Hanley, Henry Gorman *cardiologist*
Sampson, Jerome Mark *pulmonologist*

Arcadia
Cummings, Kenneth Ila *coroner, medical examiner*

Baton Rouge
Bray, George August *internist, researcher, educator*
Cherry, William Ashley *surgeon, state health officer, educator*
DiBenedetto, Robert Lawrence *retired obstetrician, gynecologist, insurance company executive*
Gettys, Thomas Wigington *medical researcher*
Kastin, Abba Jeremiah *endocrinologist, researcher*
Kidd, James Marion, III, *allergist, immunologist, educator*
Kisner, Wendell Howard, Jr., *plastic surgeon*
Le Vine, Jerome Edward *retired ophthalmologist*
Lovejoy, Jennifer Carole *medical educator*
Puyau, Francis Albert *retired physician, radiology educator*

Covington
Darr, Kevin F. *orthopedic surgeon*

Franklinton
Payne, Eric Alan *physician*

Harvey
Lamid, Sofjan *physician, educator*

Houma
Ferguson, Thomas Glen *internist*
Walker, Craig M. *cardiologist, medical association administrator*

Lake Charles
Clement, Richard Joseph *obstetrician-gynecologist*
Drez, David Jacob, Jr., *orthopedic surgeon, educator*
Gunderson, Clark Alan *orthopedic surgeon*

Mandeville
Young, Lucy Cleaver *physician*

Marrero
Kushner, Frederick Gary *cardiologist, medical educator*

Metairie
Dugan, Fortune Anthony *cardiologist, consultant*
Edisen, Clayton Byron *physician*
Johnston, William J., Jr., *neurosurgeon*
Lake, Wesley Wayne, Jr., *internist, allergist, educator*
Ochsner, Seymour Fiske *radiologist, editor*
Spruiell, Vann *psychoanalyst, educator, editor, researcher*

Minden
Kemmerly, James Robert *obstetrician, gynecologist*

New Orleans
Agrawal, Krishna Chandra *pharmacology educator*
Arshad, M. Kaleem *psychiatrist*
Beck, David Edward *surgeon*
Beckerman, Robert Cy *pediatrician, educator*
Bertrand, William Ellis *public health educator, academic administrator*
Brazda, Frederick Wicks *pathologist, educator*
Caldwell, Delmar Ray *ophthalmologist, educator*
Campeau, Richard John, Jr., *internal medicine and radiology educator*
Carey, Michael Emmett *neurosurgeon, educator*
Cargille, Charles M. *emergency physician, educator*
Cefalu, Charles A. *medical educator*
Chan, Albert W. *cardiologist*
Cohn, Isidore, Jr., *surgeon, educator*
Connolly, Edward S. *neurological surgeon*
Daniels, Robert Sanford *psychiatrist, administrator*
Domingue, Gerald James *medical scientist, microbiology, immunology and urology educator, researcher, clinical bacteriologist, artist*
Duncan, Margaret Caroline *physician*
Easson, William McAlpine *psychiatrist, educator*
Ensenat, Louis Albert *surgeon*
Epstein, Arthur William *physician, educator*
Espinoza, Luis Rolan *rheumatologist, researcher*
Ewin, Dabney Minor *surgeon*
Farris, Charles, Jr., *obstetrician, gynecologist*
Fisch, Bruce Jeffrey *physician, educator*
Fisher, James William *pharmacologist, medical educator*
Flórman, Sander Scott *transplant surgeon*
Fonseca, Vivian Andrew *physician*
Foundas, Anne Leigh *psychiatrist*
Frohlich, Edward David *medical educator*
Fuselier, Harold Anthony, Jr., *urologist, director, educator*
Gitlin, Melvin Charles *anesthesiologist, educator*
Griffin, Jeffrey Farrow *surgeon*
Hartz, Renee Semo *cardiothoracic surgeon*
Hicks, Terrell Cohlman *surgeon, educator, health facility administrator, academic administrator*
Hollier, Larry Harold *vascular surgeon, hospital administrator*
Howard, Richard Ralston, II, *medical health advisor, financial consultant*
Hyman, Albert Lewis *cardiologist, educator*
Hyslop, Newton Everett, Jr., *infectious disease specialist*
Incaprera, Frank Philip *internist*
Jaffe, Bernard Michael *surgeon, department chairman*
Kewalramani, Laxman Sunderdas *surgeon, consultant*
Kline, David Gellinger *neurosurgery educator*
Kolinsky, Michael Allen *emergency physician*
Krementz, Edward Thomas *surgeon*
LaRosa, John Charles *internist, educator, researcher*
Lewy, John Edwin *pediatric nephrologist*
Locke, William *retired endocrinologist*
Lopez, Manuel *immunology and allergy educator*
Martin, David Hubert *internist, epidemiologist, educator*
Martin, Louis Frank *surgery and healthcare outcomes analyst*
McKinnon, William Mitchell Patrick *surgeon*
Meekers, Dominique Armand *health and demographics researcher*
Millikan, Larry Edward *dermatologist*
Nelson, James Smith *pathologist, educator*
Nichols, Ronald Lee *surgeon, educator*
Ochsner, John Lockwood *thoracic-cardiovascular surgeon*
O'Quinn, April Gale *obstetrician, gynecologist, educator*
Pankey, George Atkinson *internist, educator, researcher*
Plavsic, Branko Milenko *radiology educator*
Puschett, Jules B. *medical educator, nephrologist, researcher*
Re, Richard Noel *endocrinologist*
Reisin, Efrain *nephrologist, researcher, educator*
Reyes, Raul Gregorio *surgeon*
Reza, Ali Hajmohammad *cardiologist*
Riddick, Frank Adams, Jr., *physician, health care administrator*
Rock, John Aubrey *gynecologist and obstetrician, educator*
Schally, Andrew Victor *endocrine oncologist, researcher*
Simakajornboon, Narong *physician*
Stewart, Gregory Wallace *physician*
Strong, Jack Perry *pathologist, educator*
Sullivan, Jerry Warner *educator, physician*
Szepeshazi, Karoly Istvan *pathologist*
Timmcke, Alan Edward *colon and rectal surgeon*
Tracy, Richard E. *medical educator*
Udall, John Nicholas, Jr., *pediatric gastroenterologist*
Usdin, Gene Leonard *psychiatrist*
Waring, William Winburn *pediatric pulmonologist, educator*
Webb, Watts Rankin *surgeon*
Willis, Gladden Williams *pathologist, scientific photographer, tree farmer*
Winstead, Daniel Keith *psychiatrist*

Opelousas
Lafleur, Kenneth Charles *ophthalmologist*
Pinac, André Louis, III, *obstetrician, gynecologist*

Scott
Bergeron, Wilton Lee *physician*

Shreveport
Albores-Saavedra, Jorge *pathologist, educator*
Blondin, Joan *nephrologist educator*
Brannon, Guy Emilio *physician*
Conrad, Steven Allen *critical care and emergency physician, biomedical engineer, educator*
Dhanireddy, Ramasubbareddy *neonatologist, researcher*
Fort, Arthur Tomlinson, III, *physician, educator*
Fowler, Marjorie Ellen Rees *pathologist*
Freeman, Arthur Merrimon, III, *psychiatry educator, dean*
Gallagher, Patrick Timothy *emergency physician*
Griffith, Robert Charles *allergist, educator, planter*
Jones, Kenneth B., Jr., *surgeon*
Levine, Steven Neil *endocrinologist*
London, Steve Norman *obstetrician-gynecologist, educator*
Misra, Raghunath Prasad *physician, educator*
Shelby, James Stanford *cardiovascular surgeon*
Thurmon, Theodore Francis *medical educator*
Wolf, Robert Edward *physician, educator*

Slidell
McBurney, Elizabeth Innes *dermatologist, physician, educator*
Muller, Robert Joseph *gynecologist*

Springfield
Annable, Charles Roy *pathologist*

MAINE

Augusta
Caron, Jean C. *nursing association administrator*
Cheng, Hsueh Ching *physician*
Hussey, John Francis *physician, geriatrician*

Bangor
Austin, Linda S. *psychiatrist*
Rosen, Clifford James *internist*

Bar Harbor
Nass, Meryl J. *physician, writer, research scientist*

Biddeford
Ford, Charles Willard *health science educator*

Deer Isle
Smith, Gardner Watkins *physician*

East Boothbay
Turndorf, Herman *anesthesiologist, educator*

Freeport
Lewis, Jessica Helen (Mrs. Jack D. Myers) *physician, educator*

Houlton
Levien, David Harold *surgeon*

Kennebunk
Sholl, John Gurney, III, *physician*

Kingfield
Collins, H(erschel) Douglas *retired physician*

Lewiston
Christie, Donald Melvin, Jr., *physician*

Lubec
Hayes, Ernest M. *podiatrist*

Northeast Harbor
Hafkenschiel, Joseph Henry, Jr., *cardiologist, educator*

Oakland
Rutherford, Robert Barry *vascular surgeon*

Orono
Weiss, Robert Jerome *psychiatrist, educator*

Portland
Clark, Gordon Hostetter, Jr., *physician*
Hotelling, David Rawson *endocrinologist, medical educator*
Rockefeller, Richard Gilder *medical association administrator*
Tooker, John Phillip *internist, educator*

Sanford
Collins, Thomas Michael *surgeon*

Scarborough
Devlin, John Tobey *physician, educator*

South Paris
Hamilton, Kenneth Hawley *surgeon, consultant*

South Portland
Lovett, E. J., III, *cytometrist, immunologist*
Wheeler, Hewitt Brownell *surgeon, educator*

Yarmouth
Mansmann, Paris Taylor *medical educator*
Northrup, Christiane *gynecologist-obstetrician*

MARYLAND

Andrews Air Force Base
Hall, Molly J. *psychiatrist, educator*

Annapolis
Essandoh, Louis Kofi *cardiologist*
Halpern, Joseph Alan *physician*
Holtgrewe, Henry Logan *urologist*
Hoyer, Leon William *physician, educator*
Welch, Robert Bond *ophthalmologist, educator*

Arnold
Harris, Roger Clark *psychiatrist, consultant*

Baltimore
Agre, Peter Courtland *medical educator*
Albuquerque, Edson Xavier *pharmacology educator*
Anderson, Jean R. *women's health physician*
Anthony, James Christopher *mental hygiene educator*
August, Joseph Thomas *pharmacology educator*
Bachur, Nicholas Robert, Sr., *research physician*
Baker, R. Robinson *surgeon*
Baker, Timothy Danforth *physician, educator*
Baramki, Theodore Atallah *gynecologist, reproductive endocrinologist*
Barnes, Kathleen Carole *medical educator*
Bartlett, John Gill *infectious disease physician*
Baumgartner, William Anthony *cardiac surgeon*
Bayless, Theodore M(orris) *gastroenterologist, educator, researcher*
Bigelow, George E. *psychology and pharmacology scientist*
Blakemore, Karin Jane *obstetrician, geneticist*
Blattner, William Albert *physician, epidemiology researcher*
Bochner, Bruce Scott *immunologist, educator*
Breitner, John C. S. *psychiatrist, educator, academic administrator*
Brem, Henry *neurosurgeon, educator, researcher*
Brody, Eugene Bloor *psychiatrist, educator*
Brookmeyer, Ronald *medical educator*
Brushart, Thomas Marshall *hand surgeon, neuroscience researcher*
Cameron, Duke Edward *cardiac surgeon, educator*
Carrier, France *medical educator*
Carson, Benjamin Solomon *neurosurgeon*
Chen, Yu *acupuncturist, Chinese herbologist*
Childs, Barton *retired physician, educator*
Clements, Mary Lou *epidemiologist, educator*
Colomer, Veronica *medical educator, researcher*
Cotter, Robert *pharmacology and science educator*
Crowel, Raymond L. *medical educator*
Cummings, Charles William *physician, educator*
Curl, Leigh Ann *orthopedist, surgeon*
Dang, Chi Van *hematology and oncology educator*
Dannenberg, Arthur Milton, Jr., *experimental pathologist, immunologist, educator*
DeAngelis, Catherine D. *pediatrics educator*
DeLateur, Barbara Jane *medical educator*
Dilsizian, Vasken *cardiologist, nuclear medicine physician*
Drachman, Daniel Bruce *neurologist, educator*
Eaton, William W. *mental hygiene educator*
Eisenberg, Howard Michael *neurosurgeon*
Faden, Ruth R. *medical educator, ethicist, researcher*
Felsenthal, Gerald *physiatrist, educator*
Ferencz, Charlotte *pediatrician, epidemiology and preventive medicine educator*
Ferentz, Kevin Scott *physician*
Fleisher, Lee Alan *anesthesiologist, medical educator*
Fox, Harold Edward *obstetrician, gynecologist, educator, researcher*
Freeman, John Mark *pediatric neurologist*
Freischlag, Julie Ann *surgeon*
Fried, Linda P. *medical educator*
Gallant, Joel Emanuel *physician*
Gambert, Steven Ross *geriatrician, internist*
Gimenez, Luis Fernando *physician, educator*
Godenne, Ghislaine Dudley *physician, psychoanalyst, educator*
Goldberg, Morton Falk *ophthalmologist, educator*
Goldman, Lynn Rose *medical educator*
Gordis, Leon *physician*
Greenough, William Bates, III, *medical educator*
Griffin, Diane Edmund *research physician, virologist, educator*
Griffith, Lawrence Stacey Cameron *cardiologist, educator*
Grossman, Stuart Alan *oncologist, medical educator*
Guilarte, Tomas R. *medical educator*
Gustafson, Thomas *medical association administrator*
Haq, Rizwan *oncologist, researcher*
Harris, James Carol Overton, Jr., *psychiatrist, pediatrician*
Hellmann, David Bruce *medical educator*
Higginbotham, Eve Juliet *ophthalmologist, educator*
Hildreth, James E.K. *pharmacology and molecular science educator, dean*
Hoffman, Elmer *surgeon*
Hofkin, Gerald Alan *gastroenterologist*
Holder, Lawrence Edward *radiologist, educator*
Hungerford, David Samuel *orthopedic surgeon, educator*
Johns, Richard James *physician, educator*
Johns, Roger *anesthesiologist, educator*
Johnson, Richard Tidball *neurology, microbiology and neuroscience educator, research virologist*
Karp, Judith Esther *oncologist, science administrator*
Kastor, John Alfred *cardiologist, educator*
Kellam, Sheppard G. *medical educator*
Kessler, Irving Isar *epidemiologist, consultant*
Kinzler, Kenneth *medical educator, director*
Kowarski, Allen Avinoam *endocrinologist, educator*
Krumholz, Allan *medical educator*
Kuppusamy, Periannan *medical educator, medical researcher*
Kwon, Chul Soo *psychiatrist*
Lawrence, Robert Swan *physician, educator*
Lawson, Edward Earle *neonatologist*
Lazarus, Gerald Sylvan *dermatologist, educator, dean*
Lesser, Ronald Peter *neurologist*
Lewison, Edward Frederick *surgeon*
Liang, Kung-Yee *medical educator*
Lichtenstein, Lawrence Mark *immunologist, allergist, educator*
Lion, John René *psychiatrist, educator*
Litrenta, Frances Marie *psychiatrist*
Longo, Dan Louis *internist, researcher, oncologist*
Mansfield, Carl Major *radiation oncology educator*
Manson, Paul Nellis *plastic surgeon*
Marshall, Fray Francis *urology educator*
Matheson, Nina W. *medical researcher*
Matjasko, M. Jane *anesthesiologist, educator*
Maumenee, Irene H. *ophthalmology educator*
McDonnell, Peter *ophthalmologist, health facility administrator, medical educator, researcher*
McHugh, Paul R. *psychiatrist, neurologist, educator*
McKhann, Guy Mead *pediatrician, educator*
McMillan, Julia A. *pediatrician*
Migeon, Barbara Ruben *pediatrician, geneticist*
Miller, Edward Doring *anesthesiologist*
Miller, Michael *physician, educator*
Miller, Stuart D. *surgeon*
Molmenti, Ernesto P. *surgeon*
Morford, Thomas *administrator*
Moser, Hugo Wolfgang *physician*
Mosley, Wiley Henry *medical educator*
Mower, Morton Maimon *cardiologist*
Mysko, William Kiefer *emergency physician, educator*
Myslinski, Norbert Raymond *medical educator*
Nichols, David Gregory *anesthesiologist, pediatrician, educator*
Noar, Mark David *internist, gastroenterologist, therapeutic endoscopist, consultant, inventor*
Noga, Stephen Joseph *oncologist, researcher*
Norman, Philip Sidney *physician*
Pass, Carolyn Joan *dermatologist*
Patz, Arnall *ophthalmologist*
Perman, Jay Allan *pediatrician, educator*
Piantadosi, Steven *medical researcher, statistical consultant*
Powe, Neil Richard *physician, educator, epidemiologist, health services researcher*
Price, Donald L. *pathology educator*
Pronovost, Peter J. *anesthesiology educator, health facility administrator*
Rayson, Glendon Ennes *internist, preventive medicine specialist, writer*
Rose, Noel Richard *immunologist, microbiologist, educator*
Rosenstein, Beryl Joel *physician*
Samet, Jonathan Michael *epidemiologist, educator*
Saudek, Christopher D. *medical educator*
Schoenrich, Edyth Hull *internal and preventive medicine physician*
Schuster, Marvin Meier *retired physician, educator*
Schwartz, Brian S. *medical educator, academic administrator*
Silbergeld, Ellen Kovner *environmental epidemiologist, researcher, toxicologist*
Siliciano, Robert F. *immunologist, medical educator*
Silverberg, Steven George *pathologist, educator*
Slavney, Phillip Richard *psychiatrist*
Smith, Stephen Ross *endocrinologist*
Snyder, Solomon Halbert *psychiatrist, pharmacologist*
Sommer, Alfred *ophthalmologist, medical educator, researcher*
Spannhake, Ernst William *medical educator, academic administrator*
Staats, Peter S. *pain medicine physician, surgeon*
Starfield, Barbara Helen *pediatrician, educator*
Stephens, Joseph *psychiatrist, researcher*
Swinson, Angela Anthony *physician*
Talalay, Paul *pharmacologist, educator*
Tamargo, Rafael J. *neurological surgeon, educator*
Taylor, Carl Ernest *preventive medicine physician, epidemiologist, educator*
Thomas, Claudia Lynn *orthopedic surgeon*
Trush, Michael A. *medical educator*
Vogel, James Edmond *plastic surgeon*
Vogelstein, Bert *oncology educator*
Wagner, Henry Nicholas, Jr., *physician*
Wahl, Richard Leo *radiologist, educator, nuclear medicine researcher*
Walsh, Patrick Craig *urologist*
Weisfeldt, Myron Lee *cardiologist, educator*
Weiss, James Lloyd *cardiology educator*
Welker, James Anthony *physician*
Wharam, Moody DeWitt, Jr., *physician, medical educator*
Williams, G(eorge) Melville *surgeon, medical educator*
Wilson, Donald Edward *internist, educator, dean*
Woodward, Theodore Englar *retired medical educator, internist*
Wu, Albert W. *medical educator*
Young, Barbara *psychiatrist, psychoanalyst, psychiatry educator, photographer*
Zizic, Thomas Michael *physician, educator*

Bethesda
Alter, Harvey J. *hematologist, educator*
Apud, Jose Antonio *psychiatrist, psychopharmacologist, educator*
Arons, Bernard S. *psychiatrist, educator, health services administrator*
Atkinson, Arthur John, Jr., *pharmacologist, educator*
Axelrod, Julius *pharmacologist, researcher*
Barrett, J. Carl *cancer researcher, molecular biologist*
Belyakov, Igor M. *immunologist, researcher*
Billingsley, Frank S. *gynecologist, obstetrician, educator*
Brodine, Charles Edward *physician*
Brown, Dudley Earl, Jr., *psychiatrist, educator, health executive, former federal agency administrator, former naval officer*
Brunell, Philip Alfred *physician, educator*
Cath, Stanley Howard *psychiatrist, psychoanalyst*
Chanock, Robert Merritt *pediatrician*
Charney, Dennis S. *psychiatrist*
Chase, Thomas Newell *neurologist, researcher, educator*
Christian, Michaele Chamblee *internist, oncologist*
Cohen, Robert Abraham *retired physician*
Cohen, Sheldon Gilbert *physician, historian, immunologist*
Crout, J(ohn) Richard *physician, pharmaceutical researcher*
Danforth, David Newton, Jr., *physician, scientist*
Dietrich, Robert Anthony *pathologist, medical administrator, consultant*
Fischbeck, Kenneth H. *medical researcher*
Fleisher, Thomas Arthur *physician*
Fox, Lawrence Michael *infectious diseases specialist*
Fraumeni, Joseph Francis, Jr., *epidemiologist, research scientist, educator, military officer*
Gallin, John I. *clinical investigator*
Gastwirth, Glenn Barry *medical association administrator*
Gershengorn, Marvin Carl *internist, researcher, educator*
Gottesman, Michael Marc *biomedical researcher*
Greenwald, Peter *physician, government medical research director*
Hallett, Mark *neurologist, educator, medical researcher, director*
Harlan, Linda Carol *epidemiologist*
Harris, Curtis C. *physician*
Haseltine, Florence Pat *obstetrician, gynecologist, research administrator*
Helke, Cinda Jane *pharmacology and neuroscience educator, researcher, academic administrator*
Herman, Mary Margaret *neuropathologist*
Heymsfield, Steven *medical association administrator*
Hutton, John Evans, Jr., *surgery educator, retired military officer*
Ito, Yoichiro *pathologist*
Javitt, Jonathan C. *physician, ophthalmologist, health information technologist*
Johnson, Joyce Marie *psychiatrist, epidemiologist, public health officer*
Joy, Robert John Thomas *medical history educator*
Keiser, Harry Robert *retired physician*
Kirschstein, Ruth Lillian *physician*
Klee, Claude Blenc *medical researcher*
Kramer, Barnett Sheldon *oncologist*
Krause, Richard Michael *medical scientist, government official, educator, senior researcher*
Kupfer, Carl *ophthalmologist, educator, science administrator*
Leon-Sarmiento, Fidias E. *neurologist, researcher*
Leppert, Phyllis Carolyn *obstetrician, gynecologist*
Liotta, Lance Allen *pathologist*
Lipman, David J. *medical association administrator, researcher*
Longfellow, David *administrator*
Lowry, Douglas R. *internist, dermatologist*
Lowy, Douglas Ronald *oncologist*
MacLean, Paul Donald *government institute medical research official*
Manolio, Teri A *physician*
Marini, Ann Marie *medical researcher, educator*
Masur, Henry *internist*
Mattison, Donald Roger *gynecologist, toxicologist, educator, medical association administrator, public health service officer*
McCurdy, Harry Ward *otolaryngologist*
Metcalfe, Dean Darrel *medical research physician*
Mullan, Fitzhugh *public health physician*
Muraro, Paolo A. *immunologist, neurologist*
Murphy, Dennis L. *psychiatrist*
Nabel, Elizabeth G. *medical researcher, cardiologist*
Neumann, Ronald Daniel *nuclear medicine physician, educator*
North, A. Frederick *physician*
Nyirjesy, Istvan *obstetrician, gynecologist*
Ognibene, Frederick Peter *internist*
Oldfield, Edward Hudson *neurosurgeon, researcher*
Ommaya, Ayub Khan *neurosurgeon, educator*
Paul, William Erwin *immunologist, researcher*
Perlin, Seymour *psychiatrist, educator*
Peterson, Charles Marquis *medical educator*
Pollard, Harvey B. *medical educator, neuroscientist*
Puck, Jennifer M. *physician, scientist*
Quinnan, Gerald Vincent, Jr., *medical educator*
Quon, Michael James *medical researcher, internist*
Rall, Joseph Edward *physician*
Ramm, Louise *administrator*
Rapoport, Judith *psychiatrist*
Rennert, Owen Murray *pediatrician, geneticist, educator*
Reynolds, Herbert Young *physician, internist*
Rhim, Johng Sik *physician, educator, medical researcher*
Robbins, John Bennett *medical researcher*
Roberts, Doris Emma *epidemiologist, consultant, public health nurse*
Rosenberg, Steven Aaron *surgeon, medical researcher*
Saffiotti, Umberto *pathologist*
SanGiovanni, John Paul *ophthalmic epidemiologist, eye and vision researcher*
Schneerson, Rachel *immunologist*
Shapeero, Lorraine G. *physician, researcher, educator*
Smoller, Bruce Melvyn *psychiatrist*
Sobel, Mark Esar *pathologist, researcher*
Sowell, R. Douglas *medical association administrator, podiatrist*
Spong, Catherine Yvonne *obstetrician, gynecologist, researcher*
Sternberg, Esther May *neuroendocrinologist, immunologist, rheumatologist*
Stetler-Stevenson, William George *pathologist*
Straus, Stephen Ezra *biomedical researcher*
Stutz, Donald Lee *physician, educator, naval officer*
Tavel, Jorge Alberto *internist, researcher*
Ursano, Robert Joseph *psychiatrist*
Volkow, Nora Dolores *medical research center director*
Waldmann, Thomas Alexander *medical researcher, physician*
Walsh, Thomas John *infectious disease physician, oncologist, researcher, educator*
Walters, Judith Richmond *neuropharmacologist*
Weinberger, Daniel R. *psychiatrist, neurologist*
Work, Henry Harcus *psychiatrist, educator*
Worth, Melvin H. *surgeon, educator*

Bowie
Dawodu, Segun Toyin *pain medicine and sports medicine physician, physiatrist*
Perkins, Dana Stela *pharmacologist, research scientist*

Chevy Chase
Alpert, Seymour *anesthesiologist, educator*
Feldman, Bruce Allen *otolaryngologist*
Gaasterland, Douglas E. *physician, ophthalmologist*
Hani, Antoine George *psychiatrist, psychoanalyst*
Harlan, William Robert, Jr., *internist, educator, researcher*
Hersh, Stephen Peter *psychiatrist, psycho-oncologist, educator*
Morgan, Elizabeth *plastic surgeon*
Pilkerton, Arthur Raymond, Jr., *surgeon, educator*
Pogue, John Marshall *physician*
Romansky, Monroe James *physician, educator*
Rose, John Charles *internist, educator*
Sanz, Luis E. *gynecologist, educator*
Silver, George Albert *preventive medicine physician, educator*
Tacket, Hall Sanford *retired internist*
Williams, Charles Laval, Jr., *physician, international organization official*

Clarksville
Zhu, Kangmin *epidemiologist*

Clinton
Davis, Mark Cameron *radiologist*

College Park
Katz, Ronald Alan *dermatologist*
Resnik, Harvey Lewis Paul *psychiatrist*
Sacks, Charles Bernard *physician, educator*

Columbia
Harrison, Elza Stanley *medical association executive*

Hyman, Lawrence Robert *psychiatrist*
Stolley, Paul David *medical educator, researcher*

Darnestown
Cohen, Sanford Irwin *physician, educator*
Gottlieb, Julius Judah *podiatrist*

Easton
Snow, James Byron, Jr., *otolaryngologist, research administrator, educator*

Fort Detrick
Maher, Cornelius Creedon, III, *neurologist, toxicologist, army officer*

Frederick
Anderson, Arthur Osmund *pathologist, immunologist, army officer*
Hanna, Michael George, Jr., *immunologist, pharmaceutical executive*
Malone, Robert Wallace *surgeon*

Gaithersburg
Bowen, Rafael Lee *dental materials researcher*
Dermody, William Christian *biomedical consultant*
Fratantoni, Joseph Charles *medical researcher, hematologist, biotechnology executive*
Gottlieb, H. David *podiatrist*
Lenfant, Claude Jean-Marie *physician*
Schwartzberg, Allan Zelig *psychiatrist, educator*

Glen Burnie
Wityk, Joseph John *radiologist*

Greenbelt
Obamogie, Mercy A. *physician*

Hagerstown
Strauss, Albert John, Jr., *pediatrician*

Hollywood
Shah, Nayan *internist*

Hyattsville
Clifford, Maurice Cecil *physician, former college president, foundation executive*
Rose, Deborah *epidemiologist*

Kensington
Mirkin, Gabe Baron *allergist, pediatrician, medical educator, writer, radio personality*
Szára, Stephen István *pharmacologist, consultant*

La Plata
Fisher, Gail Feimster *epidemiologist, researcher, government agency administrator*

Lutherville
Elma, Bayani Borja *physician*
Meyer, Jon Keith *psychiatrist, psychoanalyst, educator*
Morison, Warwick Lindsay *dermatologist, educator, consultant*

Lutherville Timonium
Park, Lee Crandall *psychiatrist*
Pierpont, Ross Z. *retired surgeon*
Sternberger, Ludwig Amadeus *neurologist, educator*

North Potomac
Geller, Ronald Gene *biomedical researcher, consultant*

Olney
Baker, Carl Gwin *research administrator*

Owings Mills
Heck, Albert Frank *retired neurologist*

Potomac
Bush, Mark Robert *physician*
Jones, Warren H. *physician, educator*
Waugaman, Richard Merle *psychiatrist, psychoanalyst, educator*

Randallstown
McDowell, Elizabeth Mary *retired pathology educator*

Riverdale
Kumar, Shailendra *urologist, educator*

Rockville
Barr, Solomon Efrem *allergist, educator*
Birns, Mark Theodore *physician*
Boice, John Dunning, Jr., *epidemiologist, science administrator*
Chretien, Paul Bernard *oncologist, medical researcher*
Culliton, Barbara J. *medical association administrator*
DuPont, Robert Louis *psychiatrist, physician*
Gonzalez-Licea, Augustin *pathologist, public health service officer*
Graham, Robert *medical association executive*
Gulya, Aina Julianna *neurotologist, surgeon, educator*
Hisada, Michie *physician, epidemiologist*
Leventhal, Carl M. *neurologist, consultant, retired government agency administrator*
Lincoln, Michael E. *administrator*
Littman, Burt A. *obstetrician-gynecologist*
Mofenson, Lynne Meryl *pediatrician*
Moritsugu, Kenneth Paul *physician, government official*
Robinowitz, Max *pathologist, consultant*
Rodriguez, William Julio *physician*
Temple, Robert *physician, federal agency administrator*
Veech, Richard Lewis *medical researcher, physician*

Silver Spring
Adams, Diane Loretta *physician*
Beard, Lillian B. McLean *pediatrician, consultant*
Cruze, Kenneth *retired surgeon*
Gaydos, Joel Carl *physician*
Gilbert, Charles Richard Alsop *obstetrician, gynecologist, surgeon, educator*
Heppner, Donald Gray, Jr., *immunology research physician, army officer*
Kriegel, Robin *medical association administrator*
Williams, James Thomas *physician, educator*

Stevenson
Hendler, Nelson Howard *physician, medical clinic director*

Sykesville
O'Connor, William Thomas *retired surgeon*

Takoma Park
Silverman, Charlotte *epidemiologist, educator*

Timonium
Forrester, Alfred Whitfield *psychiatrist, educator*

Towson
Ferrer, Roberto O. *surgeon*
Meny, Robert George *former medical research administrator, physician*
Spodak, Michael Kenneth *forensic psychiatrist*
Thompson, John Tilynn *ophthalmologist, medical educator*
Wilkinson, Charles P. *ophthalmologist*

Waldorf
Wiggins, Stephen Edward *physician, medical association administrator*

Westminster
Wheatley, Charles Henry, III, *education and technology company executive, lawyer*

Wheaton
White, Martha Vetter *allergy and immunology physician, researcher*

Woodbine
Mc Indoe, Darrell Winfred *retired nuclear medicine physician*

MASSACHUSETTS

Amesbury
Heyman, Joseph Martin *obstetrician, gynecologist*

Amherst
Fleischman, Paul Robert *psychiatrist, writer*

Arlington
Berkoben, John Perri *physician*
Birk, Lee (Carl Lee Birk) *psychiatrist, educator*

Bedford
Steinberg, James Jonah *physician, medical administrator, educator*

Belmont
Cohen, Bruce Michael *psychiatrist, educator, scientist, health facility administrator*
Coyle, Joseph Thomas *psychiatrist*
de Marneffe, Francis *psychiatrist, hospital administrator*
Ke, Yong *medical educator, researcher*
Onesti, Silvio Joseph *psychiatrist*
Pope, Harrison Graham, Jr., *psychiatrist, educator*
Sifneos, Peter Emanuel *psychiatrist, educator*
Zhang, Kehong *neuropharmacologist, educator*

Beverly
Chitre, Sharadchandra Raghunandan *physician*

Boston
Abrahm, Janet Lee *hematologist, oncologist, palliative care specialist, educator*
Abu-moustafa, Adel H. *medical educator, dean*
Adamis, Mary K. *medical educator*
Adelstein, S(tanley) James *pathologist, educator*
Akins, Cary Willard *surgeon, educator*
Albert, Martin Lawrence *behavioral neurologist*
Alpert, Joel Jacobs *medical educator, pediatrician*
Alt, Frederick W. *geneticist, pediatrician*
Ampola, Mary G. *pediatrician, geneticist*
Anderson, Kenneth Carl *physician, educator*
Angell, Marcia *pathologist, editor-in-chief*
Arky, Ronald Alfred *medical educator*
Auchincloss, Hugh, Jr., *transplant surgeon*
Austen, K(arl) Frank *internist, educator*
Austen, W(illiam) Gerald *surgeon, educator*
Avery, Mary Ellen *pediatrician, educator*
Axelrod, Lloyd *endocrinologist, diabetologist, educator*
Banks, Henry H. *orthopedic surgeon, educator, dean*
Barnett, Guy Octo *physician, educator*
Barouch, Dan Hung *physician, scientist*
Bates, David Westfall *internist, educator, medical researcher*
Baughman, Kenneth Lee *cardiologist, educator*
Beardslee, William Rigby *psychiatrist*
Becker, James Murdoch *surgeon, educator*
Benacerraf, Baruj *pathologist, educator*
Benz, Edward John, Jr., *internist, hematologist, educator, health facility executive*
Bern, Murray Morris *hematologist, oncologist*
Bernhard, William Francis *thoracic and cardiovascular surgeon*
Berson, Eliot Lawrence *ophthalmologist, medical educator*
Bieber, Frederick Robert *medical geneticist*
Bigby, JudyAnn *medical educator*
Bistrian, Bruce Ryan *internist, educator*
Black, Paul Henry *medical educator, researcher*
Black, Peter *surgeon, educator*
Bliss, Charles Michael *gastroenterologist*
Bloch, Kurt Julius *physician*
Bougas, James Andrew *physician, educator, surgeon*
Bousvaros, Athos *pediatric gastroenterologist*
Brain, Joseph David *biomedical scientist*
Braunwald, Eugene *physician, educator*
Brazelton, Thomas Berry *pediatrician, educator*
Breitbart, Roger Eric *pediatrician*
Brenner, Barry Morton *physician*
Brenner, Michael Barry *rheumatologist, educator*
Briggs, Susan Miller *surgeon*
Brugge, Joan S. *medical educator*
Buckley, Mortimer Joseph *physician*
Buxbaum, Robert C(ourtney) *internist*
Calkins, David Ross *physician, medical educator*
Callow, Allan Dana *surgeon*
Canellos, George Peter *physician educator*
Caplan, Louis Robert *neurologist, educator*
Carey, Martin Conrad *gastroenterologist, molecular biophysicist, educator, medical geneticist*
Carr, Daniel Barry *anesthesiologist, endocrinologist, medical researcher*
Chakravarti, Arnab *physician, researcher*
Chapman, Paul H. *pediatric neurosurgeon*
Ciraulo, Domenic Anthony *psychiatrist, educator*
Clouse, Melvin E. *radiologist*
Coffman, Jay Denton *physician, educator*
Cohen, Alan Seymour *internist*
Cohn, Lawrence H. *cardiothoracic surgeon*
Collier, R(obert) John *biomedical researcher, dean*
Connolly, James Leo *physician, pathologist*
Cosimi, A. Benedict *surgeon*
Costa, Mark E. *medical director, educator*
Cotran, Ramzi S. *pathologist, educator*
Crocker, Allen Carrol *pediatrician*
Crowley, William Francis, Jr., *medical researcher and educator*
Cursiefen, Claus *ophthalmologist, researcher*
Daly, Benedict Dudley Thomas, Jr., *cardiothoracic surgeon*
David, John R. *internist, educator*
Delbanco, Thomas Lewis *medical educator, researcher*
DeSanctis, Roman William *cardiologist, educator*
Dluhy, Robert George *physician*
Dolin, Raphael *medical educator*
Donahoe, Patricia Kilroy *surgeon*
Drazen, Jeffrey Mark *medical educator*
Duncan, Lyn M. *pathology educator*
Dvorak, Harold Fisher *pathologist, educator, scientist*
Dzau, Victor Joseph *cardiologist, educator, researcher*
Edelin, Kenneth Carlton *physician*
Egdahl, Richard Harrison *surgeon, medical educator, health science administrator*
Eisenberg, Leon *psychiatrist, educator*
Ellis, F. Henry, Jr., *surgeon, educator*
Epler, Gary Robert *physician, author, educator*
Epstein, Arnold M. *medical educator*
Epstein, Franklin Harold *physician, educator*
Essex, Max *epidemiology educator*
Farris, R. Wesley, II, *neurologist*
Federman, Daniel David *medical educator, academic administrator, endocrinologist*
Ferencik, Maros *medical researcher*
Fletcher, Robert Hillman *medical educator*
Flier, Jeffrey S. *endocrinologist*
Folkman, Moses Judah *surgeon, educator*
Franco, Ramon Arturo *medical educator*
Frazier, Howard Stanley *physician*
Frederick, Albert R., Jr., *ophthalmologist, surgeon*
Freedberg, A. Stone *physician*
Frei, Emil, III, *physician, medical researcher, medical educator*
Gargiulo, Antonio Rosario *reproductive endocrinologist, researcher, clinician*
Gelfand, Jeffrey Alan *physician, educator*
Gilchrest, Barbara Ann *dermatologist*
Glimcher, Melvin Jacob *orthopedic surgeon*
Goldberg, Irving Hyman *molecular pharmacology and biochemistry educator*
Goldberg, Marcia B. *medical educator*
Goldman, Peter *nutrition and clinical pharmacology educator*
Gottlieb, Leonard Solomon *pathology educator*
Greenberger, Norton Jerald *physician*
Greenblatt, David J. *pharmacologist*
Greene, Michael F. *obstetrician*
Greenes, Robert A. *medical educator*
Greiner, Jack Volker *ophthalmologist, physician, surgeon, scientist*
Grillo, Hermes Conrad *surgeon*
Groopman, Jerome *medical educator*
Grundfast, Kenneth Martin *otolaryngologist*
Habener, Joel Francis *medical educator, researcher*
Hall, John Emmett *orthopedic surgeon, educator*
Harlow, Edward E., Jr., *oncologist*
Harris, Jay Robert *radiation oncologist, educator*
Healy, Gerald Burke *otolaryngologist*
Hedley-Whyte, Elizabeth Tessa *neuropathologist*
Hedley-Whyte, John *anesthesiologist, educator*
Herndon, James Henry *orthopedic surgeon, educator*
Hiatt, Howard H. *physician*
Hickey, Paul Robert *anesthesiologist, educator*
Howley, Peter Maxwell *pathology educator*
Hutchinson, Bernard Thomas *ophthalmologist*
Hutter, Adolph Matthew, Jr., *cardiologist, educator*
Huvos, Andrew *internist, cardiologist, educator*
Iezzoni, Lisa I. *medical educator, healthcare educator, researcher*
Januzzi, James *cardiologist*
Jellinek, Michael Steven *psychiatrist, pediatrician*
Johnson, Michael Lewis *psychiatrist*
Jolesz, Ferenc A. *medical association administrator*
Jonas, Richard Andrew *medical educator*
Joyce-Brady, Martin Francis *medical educator, physician, researcher*
Kandarian, Susan Christine *medical educator*
Kaplan, Marshall Myles *medical educator, researcher, gastroenterologist*
Karnovsky, Morris John *pathologist, biologist*
Kasser, James R. *medical educator*
Kassirer, Jerome Paul *medical educator, editor-in-chief*
Kazemi, Homayoun *internist, educator*
Kelsey, Karl Timothy *medical educator*
Kiang, Nelson Yuan-sheng *medical educator*
Kieff, Elliott Dan *medical educator*
Kitz, Richard John *anesthesiologist, educator*
Kocher, Mininder Singh *pediatric orthopaedic surgeon, epidemiologist*
Korsmeyer, Stanley Joel *pathologist, educator*
Krane, Stephen Martin *rheumatologist, educator*
Kressel, Herbert Yehude *medical educator*
Laussen, Peter Charles *pediatric cardiac anesthesiologist, intensive care physician*
Lazar, Harold Lee *cardiothoracic surgeon*
Lee, Thomas Henry *internist, cardiologist, healthcare executive*
Levine, Deborah *radiologist*
Li, Frederick P. *medical educator*
Linfante, Italo *physician, medical educator*
Little, John Bertram *radiologist, radiobiology educator, researcher*
Livingston, David Morse *internist, biomedical researcher*
Lo Gerfo, Frank William *surgeon*
Loscalzo, Joseph *cardiologist, biochemist*
Mankin, Henry Jay *orthopedist, educator, health facility administrator*
Mannick, John Anthony *surgeon*
Manson, JoAnn Elisabeth *endocrinologist*
Maratos-Flier, Eleftheria *medical educator, physician*
Marshansky, Vladimir Nikolaevich *medical educator, biochemist, cell biologist*
Martuza, Robert L. *neurosurgeon*
Mathisen, Douglas J. *thoracic surgeon*
McConnell, Michael V. *medical educator, researcher*
McCormick, Marie Clare *pediatrician, educator*
McDougal, William Scott *urology educator*
McNeil, Barbara Joyce *radiologist, educator*
Meenan, Robert Francis *rheumatologist, researcher, academician*
Merk, Frederick Bannister *biomedical educator, medical researcher*
Messerle, Judith Rose *medical librarian, public relations director*
Meyer, Jack Edward *radiologist, educator*
Michel, Thomas Mark *internal medicine educator, scientist, physician*
Mihm, Martin Charles, Jr., *pathologist, educator*
Milunsky, Aubrey *geneticist, pediatrician, medical educator*
Moellering, Robert Charles, Jr., *internist, educator*
Mongan, James John *healthcare system administrator*
Morgan, James Philip *pharmacologist, cardiologist, educator*
Murphy, George Francis *dermatopathologist, educator*
Nadelson, Carol Cooperman *psychiatrist, educator*
Naimi, Shapur *cardiologist, educator*
Nathan, David Gordon *pediatrician, educator*
Nour, Nawal M. *obstetrician, gynecologist, health facility administrator*
O'Brien, J(ohn) Patrick *psychiatrist, educator*
Oddsson, Lars Ingimar Eugen *biomedical researcher*
Olubodun, Joel Oladapo *medical researcher, physician*
Pallotta, Johanna Antonia (Johanna Stephen) *physician, educator, researcher*
Papageorgiou, Panagiotis *medical educator*
Parrish, John Albert *dermatologist, research administrator*
Pauker, Stephen Gary *internist, cardiologist*
Paul, Oglesby *cardiologist, educator*
Petersen, Robert Allen *pediatric ophthalmologist*
Phipatanakul, Wanda *pediatrician, allergist, immunologist*
Prout, Curtis *internist, educator*
Quickel, Kenneth Elwood, Jr., *physician, medical center executive*
Rabkin, Mitchell Thornton *physician, educator, hospital administrator*
Rajewsky, Klaus *immunologist, educator*
Ravid, Katya *medical educator*
Reid, Lynne McArthur *pathologist*
Relman, Arnold Seymour *physician, educator, editor*
Reppert, Steven Marion *pediatrician, scientist, educator*
Richie, Jerome Paul *surgeon, educator*
Ridker, Paul M. *cardiologist, medical educator*
Rockoff, Mark Alan *pediatric anesthesiologist*
Rohrer, Richard Jeffrey *surgeon, educator*
Rosen, Fred Saul *pediatrics educator*
Rosenberg, Irwin Harold *physician, educator*
Rosenblatt, Michael *internist, researcher, academic administrator, educator*
Roth, Sanford Irwin *pathologist, educator*
Rubash, Harry E. *orthopedist, surgeon*
Russell, Paul Snowden *surgeon, educator*
Ryan, Thomas John *academic cardiologist, physician*
Ryser, Hugues Jean-Paul *pharmacologist, educator, cell biologist*
Sachs, David Howard *surgery and immunology educator, medical researcher*
Sadeghi-Nejad, Abdollah *pediatrician, educator*
Sahani, Dushyant V. *radiologist, educator*
Salant, David John *medical educator, nephrologist*
Sallan, Stephen E. *pediatrician*
Saper, Clifford Baird *neurobiology and neurology educator*
Scadden, David Thomas *hematologist, oncologist, research scientist*
Schaller, Jane Green *pediatrician*
Schlossman, Stuart Franklin *physician, educator, researcher*
Scott, James Arthur *radiologist, educator*
Seddon, Johanna Margaret *ophthalmologist, epidemiologist*
Seidman, Christine E. *medical educator*
Seidman, Jonathan G. *genetics educator*
Selkoe, Dennis Jesse *neurologist, researcher, educator*
Sellke, Frank William *cardiothoracic surgeon, researcher*
Shader, Richard Irwin *psychiatrist, pharmacologist, educator*
Sheikh, Javed *physician, educator*
Shi, Jialan *pathologist, educator*
Shields, Lawrence Thornton *orthopaedic surgeon, educator*
Shubrooks, Samuel Joseph, Jr., *cardiologist*
Shucart, William Arthur *neurosurgeon*
Siegel, Benjamin *pediatrician*
Silen, William *physician, surgery educator*
Sledge, Clement Blount *orthopedic surgeon, educator*
Snydman, David Richard *infectious diseases specialist, educator*
Sodroski, Joseph G. *medical educator*
Solomon, Caren Grossbard *internist*
Speizer, Frank E. *physician, researcher*
Spellman, Mitchell Wright *surgeon, academic administrator, educator*
Stair, Thomas Osborne *physician, educator*
Stossel, Thomas Peter *medical educator, medical researcher, director*
Suit, Herman Day *physician, medical educator*
Surman, Owen Stanley *psychiatrist*
Swartz, Morton Norman *medical educator*
Tang, Yi *radiologist, researcher*
Tashjian, Armen H., Jr., *medical educator*
Taubman, Martin Arnold *immunologist, educator*
Taylor, William C. *physician, medical educator*
Teich, Jonathan Marc *emergency medicine physician, internist, medical informatics specialist*
Theoharides, Theoharis Constantin *pharmacologist, physician, educator*
Thibault, George Edwin *medical educator, non-profit healthcare organization administrator*

Tilney, Nicholas Lechmere *surgery educator*
Tischler, Arthur Steven *pathologist, researcher*
Tompkins, Ronald Gary *surgeon, educator, biomedical investigator*
Trier, Jerry Steven *gastroenterologist, educator*
Urion, David Kimball *pediatric neurologist, researcher, educator*
Vacanti, Joseph Philip *pediatric surgeon, transplant surgeon*
Vachon, Louis *psychiatrist, educator*
Volpe, Joseph John *pediatric neurologist, educator*
Warshaw, Andrew Louis *surgeon, researcher*
Warth, James Arthur *physician, researcher*
Weinberg, Arnold N. *physician, educator*
Weinstein, Robert *hematologist, researcher*
Weiss, Earle Burton *physician*
Whittemore, Anthony Dunster *vascular surgeon, chief medical officer*
Willett, Walter Churchill *epidemiologist, educator*
Wyszynski, Diego Federico *epidemiologist, educator*
Young, Anne B. *neurologist, educator*
Young, Lucy H.Y. *physician, retina surgeon*
Yuan, Junying *medical educator, researcher*
Zaleznik, Abraham *psychoanalyst, management specialist, educator*
Zambrano, Eduardo Vicente *pathologist, researcher*
Zapol, Warren Myron *anesthesiologist*
Zarins, Bertram *orthopaedic surgeon*
Zervas, Nicholas Themistocles *neurosurgeon*
Zinner, Michael Jeffrey *surgeon, educator*
Zuckerman, Barry *medical educator*

Boylston
Hanshaw, James Barry *physician, educator*

Brockton
Carlson, Desiree Anice *pathologist*

Brookline
Alarcon, Rogelio Alfonso *physician, researcher*
Gurian, Bennett Sheppe *psychiatrist*
Jakab, Irene *psychiatrist*
Jordan, Ruth Ann *physician*
Koretsky, Sidney *internist, educator, paper historian*
Lown, Bernard *cardiologist, educator*
Schwartz, Bernard *physician*
Tyler, H. Richard *physician, educator*

Burlington
Barrett, David M. *urologist*
Choi, In-Sup *radiologist*
Freidberg, Stephen Roy *neurosurgeon*
Hurd, Joseph Kindall, Jr., *obstetrician, gynecologist*
Jones, Harvey Royden, Jr., *neurologist*
McLellan, Robert *gynecologist, oncologist, educator*
Moschella, Samuel L. *dermatology educator*
Oberfield, Richard Alan *oncologist*
Schoetz, David John, Jr., *colon and rectal surgeon, educator*

Cambridge
Amon, Angelika *medical researcher*
Anderson, William Henry *psychobiologist, educator*
Brusch, John Lynch *physician, educator, hospital administrator*
Buchwald, Jed Zachary *environmental health researcher, science history educator*
Chen, Lincoln Chin-ho *former medical educator*
Coles, Robert *child psychiatrist, educator, writer*
Eisen, Herman Nathaniel *immunology researcher, medical educator*
Eisenberg, Carola *psychiatry educator*
Ewing, Scott Edwin *physician, psychiatrist, educator, researcher*
Graybiel, Ann M. *medical educator*
Havens, Leston Laycock *psychiatrist, educator*
Hirsch, Martin Stanley *internist, educator, infectious disease physician, reseacher*
Liau, Gene *medical educator*
Lipsitt, Don Richard *psychiatrist, educator*
London, Irving Myer *physician, educator*
Mathews, Joan Helene *pediatrician*
Monath, Thomas Patrick *physician*
Nathanson, Larry *medical educator, physician*
Shore, Miles Frederick *psychiatrist, educator*
Wacker, Warren Ernest Clyde *physician, educator*
Wurtman, Richard Jay *physician, educator, inventor*
Young, Laurence R. *biomedical researcher, biomedical engineer, aeronautical engineer, aerospace engineer*

Charlestown
Ackerman, Jerome Leonard *radiology educator*
Brown, Robert Horatio *physician, neuromuscular research scientist*
Faustman, Denise L. *immunologist*
Gross, Jerome *physician, biologist, educator*
Hyman, Bradley T. *neurologist, educator*
Isselbacher, Kurt Julius *internist, educator*
Lamont-Havers, Ronald William *physician, research administrator*
Leaf, Alexander *preventive medicine physician, epidemiologist*
Potts, John Thomas, Jr., *physician, educator*
Zamecnik, Paul Charles *oncologist, medical research scientist*

Chestnut Hill
Bresnahan, James Francis *retired medical educator*
Cohen, David Joel *medical educator*
Dahlben, Salin Abraham *neuropsychiatrist*
Flax, Martin Howard *pathologist, retired educator*
Grossman, Jerome Harvey *medical educator, medical association administrator*
Kosasky, Harold Jack *fertility researcher*
Schildkraut, Joseph Jacob *psychiatrist, educator*
Stanbury, John Bruton *retired pharmacologist, educator*
Thier, Samuel Osiah *physician, educator*

Concord
Andrews, Joseph Lyon, Jr., *medical practitioner, educator, writer*
Boger, William Pierce, III, *ophthalmologist*
Meistas, Mary Therese *endocrinologist, diabetes researcher*

Dartmouth
Frothingham, Thomas Eliot *pediatrician*

Dover
Buyse, Marylou *pediatrician, geneticist, medical association administrator*
Kim, Ducksoo *radiologist, inventor and educator*

East Boston
Patinkin, Terry Allan *physician*

Falmouth
Funkhouser, John Jeremiah *urologist*
Heisler, Kenneth Avery *surgeon*
Sato, Kazuyoshi *pathologist*

Framingham
Capobianco, Anthony G. *physician*
Lavin, Philip Todd *medical educator, lab administrator*

Franklin
Rafal, Keith W.L. *physician*

Gardner
Du Buske, Lawrence Michael *immunologist, allergist, rheumotologist*

Gloucester
White, Harold Jack *pathologist*

Hingham
Calnan, Arthur Francis *ophthalmologist*

Hyannis
Chiotellis, Philip Nicos *cardiologist*

Jamaica Plain
Pierce, Chester Middlebrook *retired psychiatrist, educator*
Tsuang, Ming Tso *psychiatrist, educator*

Lenox
Pirani, Conrad Levi *pathologist, educator*

Lexington
Lacson, Eduardo K., Jr., *nephrologist*
Li, Tongchuan *pharmacologist, researcher*
Paul, Norman Leo *psychiatrist, educator*

Lincoln
Brandt, John Henry *physician*

Lowell
Wegman, David Howe *health science educator, consultant*

Marlborough
Miotto, Mary Elizabeth G. *pediatrician*

Medfield
Woolston-Catlin, Marian *psychiatrist*

Medford
Logan, Bernard J. *obstetrician*

Melrose
Desforges, Jane Fay *retired internist, hematologist, educator*
Hamburger, Ronald Daniel *dermatologist*

Monument Beach
Sullivan, Philip G. *retired obstetrician-gynecologist*

Natick
Gottlieb, Michael Norman *internist, educator, health facility administrator*

Needham
Weller, Thomas Huckle *physician, former educator*

Needham Heights
Hubbell, John Platt *pediatrician, educator*

Newbury
Ablow, Keith Russell *psychiatrist, journalist, author*

Newton
Bassuk, Ellen Linda *psychiatrist*
Blacher, Richard Stanley *psychiatrist*
Gryska, Paul Von Ryll *surgeon*
Monaco, Anthony Peter *surgery educator, medical institute administrator*
Sasahara, Arthur Asao *cardiologist, educator, researcher*

North Andover
Scully, Stephen J. *plastic surgeon*
Wessler, Stanford *physician, educator*

Northborough
Fulmer, Hugh Scott *physician, educator*

Norwood
Berliner, Allen Irwin *dermatologist*

Oak Bluffs
Schott, John William *psychiatrist*

Oxford
Schur, Walter Robert *physician*

Palmer
Ferriss, John Alden, III, *medical educator*

Peabody
Lipman, Richard Paul *pediatrician*

Petersham
Chivian, Eric Seth *psychiatrist, environmental scientist, educator*

Pittsfield
Fanelli, Robert D. *surgeon*
Malkani, Prakash *medical educator, neuroradiologist*

Plymouth
Pieters, Richard Sawyer, Jr., *radiation oncologist, educator*

Quincy
Luo, Hong Yuan *biomedical scientist, educator*

Reading
Hambartsoumian, Edouard *obstetrician, researcher, embryologist*

Rockland
Blethen, Sandra Lee *pediatric endocrinologist*

Roxbury
Berman, Marlene Oscar *neuropsychologist, educator*
Peters, Alan *anatomy educator*

Salem
Reich, Michael Ira *obstetrician/gynecologist*

Shrewsbury
Charney, Evan *pediatrician, educator*

South Wellfleet
Blau, Monte *retired radiology educator*

South Weymouth
Young, Michael Chung-En *allergist, immunologist, pediatrician*

Springfield
Burkman, Ronald Thomas, Jr., *physician administrator, medical educator*
Farkas, Paul Stephen *gastroenterologist*
Frankel, Kenneth Mark *thoracic surgeon*
Friedmann, Paul *surgeon, educator*
Kirkwood, John Robert *neuroradiologist*
Kottamasu, Mohan Rao (K.V.R. Mohan Rao) *physician, health facility administrator*
Liptzin, Benjamin *psychiatrist*
Lynn, Morton Daniel *orthopedist*
McGee, William Tobin *intensive care physician*
Petrone, William Francis *pediatrician, microbiologist, corporate executive*

Stockbridge
Shapiro, Edward Robert *psychiatrist, administrator educator psychoanalyst*

Stoneham
Adamson, Joyce Roberts *physician*
Igou, Raymond Alvin, Jr., *orthopedic surgeon*

Taunton
Bornstein, Myer Sidney *gynecologist*

Vineyard Haven
Jacobs, Gretchen Huntley *psychiatrist*

Waban
Rogoff, Jerome Howard *psychiatrist, psychoanalyst, forensic expert*

Waltham
Hayes, Ailish Maire *pediatrician*
Lackner, James Robert *aerospace medicine educator*
Leach, Robert Ellis *orthopedic surgeon, educator, department chair*
Mangano, Salvatore Nicholas *surgeon*
Reilly, Philip Raymond *medical research administrator*

Wellesley
Landaw, Stephen Arthur *physician, educator*
Murray, Joseph Edward *retired plastic surgeon*
Pierce, Donald Shelton *retired orthopedic surgeon, educator*
Sexton, John Joseph *oral and maxillofacial surgeon, educator*
Twitchell, Thomas Evans *neurologist, educator*

Wellfleet
Mashberg, Arthur *medical educator*

West Falmouth
Bass, Norman Herbert *neurologist, educator, research scientist, hospital adminstrator, healthcare executive, academic administrator*
Holz, George G., IV, *medical educator, research scientist*

West Springfield
Desai, Veena Balvantrai *obstetrician, gynecologist, educator*
Martorell, Claudia *infectious diseases physician*

Westwood
Bloomingdale, Lewis Morgan *retired psychiatrist*
Plimpton, Calvin Hastings *physician, university president*

Williamstown
Stuebner, Erwin August, Jr., *internist*
Wilkins, Earle Wayne, Jr., *surgery educator emeritus*

Winchester
Ericson, William B. *orthopedic hand surgeon*

Woods Hole
Laster, Leonard *internist, gastroenterologist, academic administrator, educator, writer*
Prendergast, Robert Anthony *pathologist educator*

Worcester
Appelbaum, Paul Stuart *psychiatrist, medical educator, department chairman*
Bernhard, Jeffrey David *dermatologist, educator*
Daly, Jennifer *physician*
Davis, Roger J. *medical educator*
Drachman, David Alexander *neurologist*
Fanale, James E. *geriatrician, educator*
Gandhi, Pritesh *medical educator*
Geller, Jeffrey L. *psychiatrist, educator*
Goss, Thomas Pixton *orthopaedic surgeon*
Hunter, Richard Edward *retired physician*
Lanza, Robert Paul *medical scientist*
Levine, Peter Hughes *physician, health facility administrator*
Mello, Craig C. *molecular medicine educator, researcher*
Morse, Leonard J. *epidemiologist, public health service officer*
Rothschild, Anthony Joseph *psychiatrist*
Santamarina, Rodrigo *surgeon, researcher*
Selin, Lisa K. *physician*
Smith, Thomas William *neuropathologist*
Smyrnios, Nicholas A. *physician, educator*
Stoff, Jeffrey S. *physician, educator*
Tonkonogy, Joseph Moses *physician, neuropsychiatrist, researcher*
Townes, Philip Leonard *pediatrician, educator*
Zurier, Robert Burton *medical educator, clinical investigator*

Yarmouth Port
Gordon, Benjamin Dichter *pediatrician, educator, health facility administrator*

MICHIGAN

Alma
Sanders, Jack Ford *physician*

Ann Arbor
Abrams, Gerald David *physician, educator*
Ansbacher, Rudi *physician*
Arneson, Wallace Aggergaard, Jr., *surgeon*
Arvan, Peter *endocrinologist, educator*
Bacon, George Edgar *pediatrician*
Baker, Laurence Howard *oncology educator*
Barsan, William George *emergency physician*
Bartlett, Robert Hawes *surgeon*
Bergstrom, Terry Joseph *medical educator, physician*
Bloom, Jane Maginnis *emergency physician*
Bodmer, Rolf A. *medical educator*
Bole, Giles G. *physician, researcher, medical educator*
Borer, Katarina T. *exercise endocrinologist*
Bowdler, Anthony John *physician, educator*
Burdi, Alphonse Rocco *anatomist*
Burke, Robert Harry *surgeon, educator*
Cameron, Oliver Gene *psychiatrist, educator, psychobiology researcher*
Carlson, Bruce Martin *anatomist*
Casey, Kenneth Lyman *neurologist*
Cerny, Joseph Charles *urologist, educator*
Cho, Kyung Jae *physician, radiologist, educator*
Coran, Arnold Gerald *pediatrician, surgeon*
Craig, Clifford Lindley *orthopaedic pediatric surgery educator*
Davis, Wayne Kay *medical educator*
Donabedian, Avedis *physician, educator*
Doyle, Constance Talcott Johnston *physician, educator, medical association administrator*
Eagle, Kim Allen *cardiologist*
Fajans, Stefan Stanislaus *retired internist*
Fekety, Robert *physician, educator*
Feldman, Eva Lucille *neurology educator*
Ferrara, James Lawrence Michael *medical educator, physician, scientist*
Frueh, Bartley Richard *surgeon*
Gebarski, Stephen S. *neuroradiologist, educator*
Gikas, Paul William *medical educator*
Gilman, Sid *neurologist*
Goldstein, Irwin Joseph *medical research executive*
Goldstein, Steven Alan *medical and engineering educator*
Greden, John Francis *psychiatrist, educator*
Greenfield, Lazar John *surgeon, educator*
Halter, Jeffrey Brian *internal medicine educator, geriatrician*
Hawthorne, Victor Morrison *epidemiologist, educator*
Hensinger, Robert Neil *orthopedist*
Hiss, Roland Graham *internist, educator*
Hoff, Julian Theodore *neurosurgeon, educator*
Hollenberg, Paul Frederick *pharmacology educator*
Horowitz, Samuel Boris *biomedical researcher, educational consultant*
Humes, H(arvey) David *nephrologist, educator*
Johnson, Timothy R. B. *obstetrician, gynecologist, educator*
Julius, Stevo *internist, physiologist, educator*
Kaplan, George A. *medical educator*
Kenyon, George Lommel *pharmaceutical educator, dean*
Kuhl, David Edmund *physician, nuclear medicine educator*
Kunkel, Steven *pathologist, educator*
La Du, Bert Nichols, Jr., *pharmacology educator, physician*
Lawrence, Merle *medical educator*
Lichter, Allen S. *oncology educator, university dean*
Lichter, Paul Richard *ophthalmology educator*
Lockwood, Dean H. *physician, pharmaceutical executive*
Lopatin, Dennis Edward *immunologist, educator*
Lusk, Sally L. *medical educator*
Margolis, Philip Marcus *psychiatrist, educator*
Markel, Howard *medical educator*
Mehta, Rajendra H *cardiologist, researcher*
Midgley, A(lvin) Rees, Jr., *reproductive endocrinology educator, researcher*
Miller, Josef M. *otolaryngologist, educator*
Modell, Stephen Mark *medical researcher, educator*
Monto, Arnold Simon *epidemiology educator*
Morgenstern, Lewis B. *medical educator*
Musch, David C. *epidemiologist*
Nabel, Gary J. *internal medicine and biological chemistry educator*
Nelson, Virginia Simson *pediatrician, educator, physiatrist*
Oliver, William John *pediatrician, educator*
Orringer, Mark Burton *surgeon, educator*
Owyang, Chung *gastroenterologist, researcher*
Pitt, Bertram *cardiologist, educator, consultant*
Powsner, Edward Raphael *physician*
Quint, Douglas Joseph *neuroradiology educator*
Raoof, Ameed Mohammed Saeed *anatomist*
Reddy, Venkat Narsimha *ophthalmologist, researcher*
Rosenthal, Amnon *pediatric cardiologist*
Russell, James William *neurologist, neuroscientist, electrophysiologist*
Schottenfeld, David *epidemiologist, educator*
Schteingart, David Eduardo *internist*
Seibold, James Richard *physician, educator*
Shapiro, Brahm *nuclear medicine physician, endocrinologist*
Sloan, Herbert Elias *physician, surgeon*
Smith, Donald Cameron *preventive medicine physician, educator*
Strang, Ruth Hancock *pediatric educator, pediatric cardiologist, priest*
Stross, Jeoffrey Knight *internist, educator*
Tandon, Rajiv *psychiatrist, educator*
Thompson, Norman Winslow *surgeon, educator*

Todd, Robert Franklin, III, *oncologist, educator*
Tran, Tuan Diep *pediatrician, educator*
Voorhees, John James *dermatologist, department chairman*
Ward, Peter Allan *pathologist, educator*
Weg, John Gerard *physician*
Weiss, Stephen J. *medical educator, researcher, oncologist*
Wicha, Max S. *oncologist, educator*
Wiggins, Roger C. *internist, educator, researcher*
Yamada, Tadataka *internist*
Yu, Mei-yu *medical researcher*

Au Gres
Dhawan, Vikas *plastic surgeon*

Bingham Farms
Giles, Conrad Leslie *ophthalmic surgeon*
Katz, Sidney Franklin *obstetrician, gynecologist*

Birmingham
Cohen, Adam J. *plastic surgeon*
Edwards, Michael Gerard *physician*

Bloomfield Hills
Ball, Patricia Ann *physician*
Mathog, Robert Henry *otolaryngologist, educator*
Prasad, Niru *physician, television personality*
Stunz, John Henry, Jr., *retired physician*

Chelsea
Yarows, Steven Allen *internist*

Clarkston
Wydra, Frank Thomas *healthcare executive*

Dearborn
Coburn, Ronald Murray *ophthalmic surgeon, researcher*
Myers, Woodrow Augustus, Jr., *physician, health care management director*

Detroit
Benninger, Michael Stephen *otolaryngologist*
Bock, Brooks Frederick *emergency physician*
Brooks, Beth Ann *psychiatrist*
Cohen, Sanford Ned *pediatrics educator, academic administrator*
Davis, Ronald Mark *preventive medicine physician*
Dhar, Josephine Patricia *medical educator*
Diaz, Fernando Gustavo *neurosurgeon*
Dombrowski, Mitchell Paul *physician, inventor, researcher*
Ehrinpreis, Murray Norman *gastroenterologist, educator*
Fromm, David *surgeon*
Gardin, Julius Markus *cardiologist, educator*
Hashimoto, Ken *dermatologist, educator*
Hood, Antoinette Foote *dermatologist*
Hurley, Harry James, Jr., *dermatologist, educator*
Jampel, Robert Steven *ophthalmologist, educator*
Jenkins-Anderson, Barbara Jeanne *pathologist, educator*
Kantrowitz, Adrian *surgeon, educator*
Kaplan, Joseph *pediatrician*
Kelley, Mark Albert *physician, educator, health care executive*
Krull, Edward Alexander *dermatologist*
Lawson, Noel Seymore *pathologist, consultant*
Lim, Henry Wan-Peng *dermatologist*
Lisak, Robert Philip *neurologist, researcher, educator*
Lupulescu, Aurel Peter *medical educator, researcher, physician*
Lusher, Jeanne Marie *pediatric hematologist, educator*
Maiese, Kenneth *neurologist, neuroscientist*
Marsh, Harold Michael *anesthesiologist*
Miller, Orlando Jack *obstetrician, gynecologist, educator, geneticist*
Newton, Kenneth Kurt *physician, educator, administrator*
O'Connell, John Bernard, Jr., *medical educator, chairman department of medicine*
Perez Arjona, Eimir Ariel *neurosurgeon, researcher*
Perry, Burton Lars *retired pediatrician*
Peters, William P. *oncologist, educator, science administrator, dean*
Porter, Arthur T. *oncologist, educator, medical administrator*
Shah, Aashit K. *neurologist*
Shields, Anthony Frank *oncologist, hematologist*
Silverman, Norman Alan *cardiac surgeon*
Simon, Michael Richard *allergist, immunologist, internist*
Slovis, Thomas Laurence *radiologist*
Smith, Wilbur Lazar *radiologist, educator*
Sokol, Robert James *obstetrician, gynecologist, educator*
Tolia, Vasundhara K. *pediatric gastroenterologist, educator*
Tse, Harley Y. *immunologist, educator*
Voudoukis, Ignatios John *internist, cardiologist*
White, Blaine C *medical educator, researcher, emergency physician*
Whitehouse, Fred Waite *endocrinologist, researcher*
Wiener, Joseph *pathologist*

East Lansing
Beckmeyer, Henry Ernest *anesthesiologist, pain management specialist, medical educator*
Brody, Howard *medical educator*
Brody, Theodore Meyer *pharmacologist, educator*
Davis, Glenn Craig *psychiatrist*
Gottschalk, Alexander *radiologist, diagnostic radiology educator*
Kumar, Ashir *pediatrician, medical educator*
Magen, Myron Shimin *osteopathic physician, educator, university dean*
Moore, Kenneth Edwin *pharmacology educator*
Pathak, Dorothy Rybaczyk *epidemiologist, biostatistician*
Rechtien, James Joseph *osteopath, educator*
Reinhart, Mary Ann *medical board executive*
Rosenman, Kenneth D. *medical educator*
Sato, Paul Hisashi *pharmacologist*
Waite, Donald Eugene *medical educator, consultant*
Walker, Bruce Edward *anatomy educator*
Wang, Donna Hui *investigative medicine director*
Watson, Ralph Edward *physician, educator*
Werner, Arnold *psychiatrist*

Farmington
Gordon, Craig Jeffrey *oncologist, educator*

Farmington Hills
Dobritt, Dennis William *physician, researcher, pain management specialist*
McQuiggan, Mark C. *urologist*
Sargent, Eric Winslow *otolaryngologist, surgeon*
Simpson, David Allen *osteopath*

Fife Lake
Knecht, Richard Arden *family practitioner*

Flint
Farrehi, Cyrus *cardiologist, educator*
Johnson, Gary Keith *pediatrician*

Fort Gratiot
Zimmer, Lawrence Joseph *psychiatrist, internist*

Frankenmuth
Shetlar, James Francis *physician*

Grand Rapids
Bartek, Gordon Luke *radiologist*
Swanson, Alfred Bertil *orthopaedic and hand surgeon, inventor, educator*
Verdier, David D'Ooge *ophthalmologist, educator*
Wilt, Jeffrey Lynn *pulmonary and critical care physician, educator*

Grosse Pointe
Dzul, Paul J. *physician, medical journal editor*
Sphire, Raymond Daniel *anesthesiologist, educator*

Grosse Pointe Woods
Sul, Yi Chul *neurologist*

Holland
Zuidema, George Dale *surgeon, educator*

Howell
Yanga, Ismael Duran *surgeon*

Kalamazoo
Gladstone, William Sheldon, Jr., *radiologist*
Greydanus, Donald Everett *pediatrician, consultant*
Lavery, J. Patrick *perinatologist*
Saber, Alan A. *surgeon*
Toledo-Pereyra, Luis Horacio *transplant surgeon, researcher, historian educator*

Kalkaska
Batsakis, John George *pathology educator*

Lake Angelus
Kresge, Bruce Anderson *retired physician*

Lansing
Kepros, John Paul *trauma surgeon*
Sauer, Harold John *physician, educator*
Vincent, Frederick Michael, Sr., *neurologist, educator*

Livonia
Rhoades Dumler, Kelly J. *medical educator*
Sobel, Howard Bernard *osteopath, educator*

Mancelona
Whelan, Joseph L. *neurologist*

Marine City
Brown, Ronald Delano *endocrinologist*

Milford
Oliveri, Eugene Alfred *gastroenterologist*

Niles
Gibbs, Denis Laurel *radiologist*
Kim, Chong-Man Joseph *radiologist*

Northport
Schultz, Richard Carlton *plastic surgeon*

Northville
Carhuapoma, Juan Ricardo *critical care neurologist, researcher*

Okemos
Monson, Carol Lynn *osteopath, psychotherapist*
Ristow, George Edward *neurologist, educator*

Petoskey
Beierwaltes, William Henry *physician, educator*
Meengs, William Lloyd *cardiologist*

Pleasant Ridge
Krabbenhoft, Kenneth Lester *radiologist, educator*

Pontiac
James, Reese Joseph *physician*

Portage
Chodos, Dale David Jerome *physician, consumer advocate*

Rochester Hills
Badalament, Robert Anthony *urologist, oncologist*

Royal Oak
Al-Sarraf, Muhyi *internist, oncologist*
Dworkin, Howard Jerry *nuclear medicine physician, educator*
Farhy, Rodolfo David *internist, cardiologist*
LaBan, Myron Miles *physician, administrator*
Malik, Ghaus Muhammad *neurosurgeon*
McCarroll, Kathleen Ann *radiologist, educator*
O'Neill, William Walter *physician, educator*
Proctor, Conrad Arnold *physician*

Saginaw
Ferlinz, Jack *cardiologist, medical educator*
Manning, John Warren, III, *retired surgeon, medical educator*

Saint Clair Shores
Field, Stephen Ira *dermatologist, educator*

Saint Joseph
Wood, Dirk Gregory *surgeon, physician, forensic consultant*

Southfield
Newman, Steven E. *neurologist*

O'Hara, John Paul, III, *orthopedic surgeon*
Perez-Cruet, Mick Jorge *neurological surgeon, educator*
Soo, Teck Mun *neurosurgeon*
Zubroff, Leonard Saul *surgeon*

Sterling Heights
Abbasi, Tariq Afzal *psychiatrist, educator*

Sturgis
Reiff, James Stanley *osteopathic physician, addictions and psychiatric physician, surgeon*

Taylor
Fleshman, James W. *medical association administrator*
Lavery, Ian C. *colon and rectal surgeon, medical association administrator*

Traverse City
Supanich, Barbara Ann *family practice physician*
Tobin, Patrick John *dermatologist*

Trenton
Go, Benedict Anthony *internist*

Troy
Barton, Stanley L. *ophthalmologist, consultant*
Golusin, Millard R. *obstetrician and gynecologist*
Meerschaert, Joseph Richard *physician*
Misra, Dwijen Cristobal *surgeon*

West Bloomfield
Jones, Lewis Arnold, Jr., *physician, radiologist, consultant*
Joseph, Ramon Rafael *physician, educator*
Sarwer-Foner, Gerald Jacob *psychiatrist, educator*
Sawyer, Howard Jerome *physician*

Woodhaven
Kim, Hyo Sook *anesthesiologist*

Ypsilanti
Sealy, Vernol St. Clair *scientist*

MINNESOTA

Austin
Rioux, Pierre August *psychiatrist*

Bloomington
Carpel, Emmett Franklin *ophthalmologist, consultant*

Burnsville
Lakin, James Dennis *allergist, immunologist, director*

Clarissa
Titrud, Oliver George *retired medical educator*

Detroit Lakes
Eginton, Charles Theodore *surgeon, educator*

Duluth
Aufderheide, Arthur Carl *pathologist*
McKee, David Charles *physician, neurologist*

Edina
Frys, Russell N. *obstetrician-gynecologist*
Justman, Richard Allen *pediatrician*
Sandy, Lewis Gordon *physician, healthcare executive*
Schroeder, Albert John *retired pediatrician*
Tagatz, George Elmo *retired obstetrician, gynecologist, educator*
Van Beek, Allen Lester *plastic surgeon*
Wilder, Walter Llewellyn *allergist, immunologist, pediatrician*

Lauderdale
Resch, Joseph Anthony *neurologist*

Madelia
Lucek, Donald Walter *surgeon*

Mankato
Huot, Rachel Irene *biomedical educator, research scientist, physician*

Melrose
Hammarsten, James Francis *internist, educator*

Minneapolis
Bache, Robert James *physician, medical educator*
Blackburn, Henry Webster, Jr., *retired epidemiologist*
Boudreau, Robert James *nuclear medicine physician, researcher*
Brown, David Mitchell *pediatrician, educator, dean*
Buchwald, Henry *surgeon, educator, researcher*
Burchell, Howard Bertram *retired physician, educator*
Burton, Charles Victor *neurosurgeon, inventor*
Charnas, Lawrence *neurologist*
Chavers, Blanche Marie *pediatrician, educator, researcher*
Cohn, Jay N. *cardiologist, educator*
Craig, James Lynn *physician*
Domino, Constance Mae *genetics researcher*
Dykstra, Dennis Dale *physiatrist*
Fisch, Robert Otto *medical educator*
Freese, Andrew *neurosurgeon, educator, scientist*
Gajl-Peczalska, Kazimiera J. *retired surgical pathologist, pathology educator*
Gerberich, Susan Goodwin *epidemiologist, educator, medical researcher*
Gorlin, Robert James *medical educator*
Gullickson, Glenn, Jr., *physician, educator*
Haines, Stephen John *neurological surgeon*
Hanson, Arthur Stuart *physician, consultant*
Hays, Thomas S. *medical educator, medical researcher*
Hom, David Brian *surgeon*
Humar, Abhinav *transplant surgeon, clinical researcher*
Joseph, Marilyn Susan *gynecologist*
Kane, Robert Lewis *public health educator*
Keane, William Francis *nephrology educator, research foundation executive*
Kump, Warren Lee *retired diagnostic radiologist*

Lederle, Frank Allen *medical educator*
Leon, Arthur Sol *research cardiologist, exercise physiologist*
Leppik, Ilo E. *neurologist, educator*
Levitt, Seymour Herbert *physician, radiology educator*
Litman, Theodor James *medical educator*
Loh, Horace H. *pharmacology educator*
Luepker, Russell Vincent *epidemiology educator*
Malmquist, Carl Phillip *psychiatrist*
Mandel, Sheldon Lloyd *dermatologist, educator*
Mazze, Roger Steven *medical educator, researcher*
McQuarrie, Donald Gray *surgeon, educator*
Moller, James Herman *pediatrician, educator*
Najarian, John Sarkis *surgeon, educator*
Palahniuk, Richard John *anesthesiology educator, researcher*
Peterson, Douglas Arthur *physician*
Peterson, Phillip Keith *physician, clinical investigator*
Phibbs, Clifford Matthew *surgeon, educator*
Powell, Deborah Elizabeth *pathologist, dean*
Quie, Paul Gerhardt *pediatrician, educator*
Rockswold, Gaylan Lee *neurosurgeon*
Rothenberger, David Albert *surgeon*
Schuman, Leonard M. *medical educator, academic administrator*
Slocum, Rosemarie *physician services consultant, recruiter*
Staba, Emil John *pharmacognosy and medicinal chemistry educator*
Thompson, Roby Calvin, Jr., *orthopedic surgeon, educator*
Thompson, Theodore Robert *pediatric educator*
Ulstrom, Robert A. *retired pediatrician*
Wang, Yang *cardiologist, educator, medical researcher*
Weir, Edward Kenneth *cardiologist, educator*
Willey, Andrea *surgeon, researcher*
Wirtschafter, Jonathan Dine *neuro-ophthalmology educator, scientist*

Minnetonka
Bahl, Tracy L. *healthcare executive*
Berlinger, Norman Thomas *physician, author*
Erlandson, Patrick J. *medical association administrator*

Morris
Lewis, Eric Joseph *dermatologist*

Olivia
Cosgriff, James Arthur *physician*

Pequot Lakes
Weaver, Arthur Lawrence *rheumatologist, consultant*

Rochester
Archibald, Reginald Mac Gregor *pediatrician, endocrinologist, chemist, educator*
Bartholomew, Lloyd Gibson *physician*
Beahrs, Oliver Howard *surgeon, educator*
Beckman, Thomas J. *physician*
Berry, Daniel John *orthopedist, surgeon*
Bowie, E(dward) J(ohn) Walter *hematologist, researcher*
Brimijoin, William Stephen *pharmacologist, educator, neuroscientist, researcher*
Brown, Arnold Lanehart, Jr., *pathologist, educator, university dean*
Charboneau, Joseph William *radiologist, medical educator*
Cofield, Robert Hahn *orthopedic surgeon, educator*
Cortese, Denis A. *medical educator, healthcare executive*
Czaja, Albert Joseph *physician, educator*
Danielson, Gordon Kenneth, Jr., *cardiovascular surgeon, educator*
DeRemee, Richard Arthur *physician, educator, researcher*
Dickson, Edgar Rolland *gastroenterologist*
Douglas, William W. *physician, consultant*
Douglass, Bruce E. *physician*
Du Shane, James William *physician, educator*
Engel, Andrew George *neurologist*
Fervenza, Fernando C. *nephrologist, educator*
Foote, Robert Leonard *oncologist, educator, researcher*
Fye, W. Bruce, III, *cardiologist*
Geda, Yonas Endale *neuropsychiatrist, researcher*
Gharib, Hossein *medical educator*
Gomez, Manuel Rodriguez *physician*
Gorman, Colum Alphonsus *retired endocrinologist*
Gracey, Douglas Robert *physician, physiologist, educator*
Haddy, Francis John *physician, educator*
Hodgson, Jane Elizabeth *obstetrician, gynecologist, consultant*
Hunder, Gene Gerald *physician, educator*
Jaffe, Allan S. *cardiologist, educator, medical researcher*
Jankowski, Christopher James *anesthesiologist, educator*
Kelemen, Linda Elizabeth *epidemiologist, dietician*
Knopman, David S. *neurologist*
Kyle, Robert Arthur *medical educator, oncologist*
Lanier, William Lovel, Jr., *anesthesiologist, educator*
LaRusso, Nicholas F. *gastroenterologist, educator, scientist*
Lofgren, Karl Adolph *surgeon, educator*
Loftus, Edward Vincent, Jr., *gastroenterologist, writer*
Lucas, Alexander Ralph *child psychiatrist, educator, writer*
Mackenzie, Ronald Alexander *anesthesiologist*
Malek, Reza Said *urological surgeon*
Malkasian, George Durand, Jr., *physician, educator*
Morlock, Carl Grismore *physician, medical educator*
Mrazek, David Allen *pediatric psychiatrist*
Mulder, Donald William *physician, educator*
Neel, Harry Bryan, III, *surgeon, scientist, educator*
Nelson, Audrey May *physician*
O'Driscoll, Shawn William *surgeon, researcher*
Pairolero, Peter Charles *surgeon, educator*
Perry, Harold Otto *dermatologist*
Phillips, Sidney Frederick *gastroenterologist, educator*
Piepgras, David G. *neurosurgeon, educator*
Pisansky, Thomas Michael *physician*
Pittelkow, Mark Robert *physician, dermatology educator, researcher*

Platt, Jeffrey Louis *surgeon, immunologist, educator, pediatric nephrologist*
Podratz, Karl C. *gynecologic surgeon, oncologist, educator*
Prakash, Udaya B.S. *internist, educator*
Reitemeier, Richard Joseph *physician*
Rogers, Roy Steele, III, *dermatologist, educator, dean*
Rosenow, Edward Carl, III, *medical educator*
Scanlon, Paul David *pulmonologist, educator*
Scott, John Paul *medical educator*
Siekert, Robert George *neurologist*
Sim, Franklin H. *orthopedic surgery educator*
Smith, Hugh Cadham *cardiovascular diseases physician*
Somers, Virend Kristen *physician, researcher*
Stegall, Mark D. *surgeon, medical educator*
Stickler, Gunnar Brynolf *pediatrician*
Tarvestad, Anthony M. *psychiatrist*
Varkey, Prathibha *preventive medicine physician, medical educator*
Ward, Louis Emmerson *retired physician*
Weinshilboum, Richard M. *pharmacologist, educator, biomedical researcher*
Wells, Lloyd Allan *psychiatrist, educator*
Whisnant, Jack Page *neurologist*
Wood, Michael Bruce *orthopedic surgeon, researcher, educator*
Woods, John Elmer *plastic surgeon*

Saint Cloud
Olson, Barbara Ford *physician*

Saint Paul
Cavert, Henry Mead *physician, retired educator*
Crabb, Kenneth Wayne *obstetrician, gynecologist*
Dennis, Clarence *surgeon, educator*
Edwards, Jesse Efrem *pathologist, educator*
Holter, Arlen Rolf *cardiothoracic surgeon*
Larkin, John Edward, Jr., *orthopedic surgeon*
Michael, Alfred Frederick, Jr., *pediatric nephrology educator*
Swaiman, Kenneth Fred *pediatric neurologist, educator*
Westermeyer, Joseph John *psychiatrist*
Wilson, Leonard Gilchrist *medical history educator*

Stillwater
Asch, Susan McClellan *pediatrician*

Virginia
Knabe, George William, Jr., *pathologist, educator*

Waseca
Barr, Leslie Glen *family practice physician*

Wayzata
Muschenheim, Frederick *retired pathologist*

MISSISSIPPI

Gautier
Egerton, Charles Pickford *anatomy and physiology educator*

Gulfport
Conrad, Harold Theodore *psychiatrist*
Fooladi, Mike M. *physician, educator*

Jackson
Bloom, Sherman *retired pathologist, educator*
Boronow, Richard Carlton *gynecologist, educator*
Corbett, James John *neurologist, neuroophthalmologist*
Cruse, Julius Major, Jr., *pathologist, educator*
Das, Suman Kumar *plastic surgeon, researcher*
de Shazo, Richard Denson *medical educator, academic administrator*
Freeland, Alan Edward *orthopedic surgery educator, physician*
Hall, John E. *medical educator*
Harisdangkul, Valee *physician*
Herndon, Robert McCulloch *neurologist, researcher*
Houston, Gerry Ann *oncologist*
Howard, William Percy *physician*
Kermode, John Cotterill *pharmacology educator, researcher*
Lewis, Robert Edwin, Jr., *pathology immunology educator, researcher*
Marshall, Gailen Daugherty, Jr., *physician, scientist, educator*
Moll, George William *pediatrician, educator*
Munera, Pedro Antonio *child and adolescent psychiatrist*
Poole, Galen Vincent *surgeon, educator, researcher*
Raila, Frank Arthur *radiologist*
Rawson, John Elton *neonatologist, educator*
Rhodes, Linda L. *medical transcriptionist, medical assistant*
Ross, Ian Beaudoin *neurosurgeon, educator*
Sawyer, Donald E. *urologist*
Shirley, Aaron *pediatrician*
Sneed, Raphael Corcoran *physiatrist, pediatrician*
Suess, James Francis *retired psychiatry educator*
Thigpen, James Tate *physician, oncology educator*
Vance, Ralph Brooks, Sr., *oncologist, educator*

Laurel
Lacey, Peeler Grayson *diagnostic radiologist*
Lindstrom, Eric Everett *ophthalmologist*

Mantachie
Marcy, William L. *physician, consultant*

Ocean Springs
Austin, Claude Lidell *retired surgeon*

Tupelo
Hill, J. Edward *physician, educator*

Vicksburg
Hopson, William Briggs, Jr., *surgeon*
Masterson, Chester W. *otolaryngologist, state representative*

MISSOURI

Belton
Blim, Richard Don *retired pediatrician, health facility administrator*

Blue Springs
McElroy, Michelle Marie *physician*
Sugarbaker, Stephen Philip *surgeon, educator*

Caruthersville
Puangsuvan, Somporn *surgeon, consultant*

Chesterfield
Qazi, Mujtaba A. *ophthalmologist*

Clayton
Post, Stephen Lightner *psychiatrist, psychoanalyst, educator*

Columbia
Aggarwal, Kul *internist, cardiologist, educator*
Allen, William Cecil *physician, educator*
Anderson, Ralph Robert *endocrinologist, educator*
Barrett, James Thomas *immunologist, educator*
Bothwell, Marcella Roper *pediatric otolaryngologist*
Colwill, Jack Marshall *physician, educator*
Dhand, Rajiv *physician*
Eggers, George William Nordholtz, Jr., *anesthesiologist, educator*
Hardin, Christopher Demarest *medical educator*
James, Elizabeth Joan Plogsted *pediatrician, educator*
König, Peter *pediatrician, educator*
Krause II, William John *medical educator, researcher*
Mehr, David Ralph *geriatrician, researcher*
Nolph, Georgia Bower *physician*
Perkoff, Gerald Thomas *physician, educator*
Perry, Michael Clinton *physician, medical educator, academic administrator*
Puckett, Charles Linwood *plastic surgeon, educator*
Silver, Donald *surgeon, educator*
Swan, Shanna Helen *epidemiologist, researcher*
Tarnove, Lorraine *medical association executive*
White, Harry Houston *neurologist*
Winship, Daniel Holcomb *medical educator, dean*
Witten, David Melvin *radiology educator*

Crystal City
Lourwood, David Lee, Jr., *pharmacotherapist, educator*

Florissant
Owen, Robert Frederick *internist, rheumatologist*
Tanphaichitr, Kongsak *rheumatologist, allergist, immunologist, internist*

Grandview
Hunzicker, Warren John *retired cardiologist, medical educator, consultant, health facility administrator*

Gravois Mills
Dunn, Floyd Emryl *psychiatrist, neurologist, consultant*

Independence
Dorshow-Gordon, Ellen *epidemiologist*

Joplin
Daus, Arthur Steven *neurological surgeon*
Habermann, James Herbert *retired pathologist*

Kansas City
Ardinger, Robert Hall, Jr., *physician, educator*
Butler, Merlin Gene *physician, medical geneticist, educator*
Dimond, Edmunds Grey *medical educator*
Fiorella, Russell Michael *pathologist*
Godfrey, William Ashley *ophthalmologist*
Hagan, John Charles, III, *ophthalmologist*
Heymach, George John, III, *physician, educator, health facility administrator, consultant*
Huston, Kent Allen *rheumatologist*
Jonas, Harry S. *medical education consultant*
Kagan, Stuart Michael *pediatrician*
Lofland, Gary Kenneth *cardiac surgeon*
Long, Edwin Tutt *surgeon*
Lotuaco, Luisa Go *pathologist*
Ma, O. John *emergency physician, editor*
Manimtim, Winston Mendoza *pediatrician, neonatologist*
McCoy, Frederick John *retired plastic surgeon*
McGregor, Douglas Hugh *pathologist, educator*
McKinsey, David Stephen *infectious diseases specialist*
McPhee, Mark Steven *medical educator, physician, gastroenterologist*
Mebust, Winston Keith *surgeon, educator*
Molteni, Agostino *pathology educator*
Poston, Walker Seward, II, *medical educator, researcher*
Sauer, Gordon Chenoweth *retired dermatologist, educator*
Stelmach, Walter Jack *physician, medical education administrator*
Treffer, Kevin Duane *physician, educator*
Truog, William Edward, III, *pediatrician, educator, researcher*
Van Way, Charles Ward, III, *surgery educator, research scientist*
Waeckerle, Joseph *emergency physician, educator*

Kearney
Waltz, James Richard *physician*

Kirksville
Osborn, Gerald Guy *dean, psychiatrist, educator*

Mexico
Tillman, Charles Herbert, Jr., *cardiologist*

Nevada
Goldberger, Stephen Henry *otolaryngologist*

North Kansas City
Hellman, Richard *endocrinologist*

Oak Grove
Davis, Jo *naturopath, hypnotherapist*

Saint Charles
Wang, William Weiqi *physician*

Saint Louis
Acharya, Jayant Narahari *neurologist, educator*
Albert, Stewart Gary *medical educator, internist, endocrinologist*
Alpers, David Hershel *internist, educator*
Bacharier, Leonard B. *allergist, researcher*
Bacon, Bruce Raymond *physician*
Ballinger, Walter Francis *surgeon, educator*
Berg, Leonard *retired neurologist, educator, researcher*
Berland, David I. *psychiatrist, educator*
Bjerregaard, Preben *cardiologist, educator*
Blumenthal, Herman Theodore *retired physician, educator*
Brink, David Scott *pathologist, educator*
Brodeur, Armand Edward *pediatric radiologist*
Case-Schmidt, Mary E. *pathologist, educator*
Chaplin, David Dunbar *medical research specialist, medical educator*
Chaplin, Hugh, Jr., *physician, educator*
Chole, Richard Arthur *otolaryngologist, department chairman*
Cloninger, Claude Robert *psychiatric researcher, educator, genetic epidemiologist*
Constantino, John Nicholas *medical educator, researcher*
Cross, Dewitte Talmadge, III, *neuroradiologist*
Cryer, Philip Eugene *medical educator, scientist, endocrinologist*
Dacey, Ralph Gerard, Jr., *internist, neurosurgeon*
Del Priore, Lucian V. *ophthalmologist, educator*
Dewald, Paul Adolph *psychiatrist, educator*
Donati, Robert Mario *physician, educational administrator*
Dougherty, Charles Hamilton *pediatrician*
Dykewicz, Mark Steven *physician*
Evens, Ronald Gene *radiologist, educator, health facility administrator*
Feman, Stephen S. *ophthalmologist*
Ferkol, Thomas William *medical educator, pediatrician*
Fitch, Coy Dean *internist, educator*
Fletcher, James Warren *physician*
Flye, M. Wayne *surgeon, immunologist, educator, writer*
Fonseca, Peter *surgeon*
Friedman, William Hersh *otolaryngologist, educator*
Gay, William Arthur, Jr., *thoracic surgeon*
Gelberman, Richard H. *orthopedist, surgeon*
Goebel, Joel Alan *otolaryngologist*
Goldberg, Anne Carol *physician, educator*
Goodenberger, Daniel Marvin *medical educator*
Griffing, George Thomas *medical educator, endocrinologist*
Grossberg, George Thomas *psychiatrist, educator*
Grubb, Robert L., Jr., *neurosurgeon*
Hammerman, Marc Randall *nephrologist, educator*
Hanley, Thomas Patrick *obstetrician-gynecologist*
Heiken, Jay Paul *physician*
Holmes, Nancy Elizabeth *pediatrician*
Holtzman, David Michael *neurologist*
Hsu, Chung Yi *neurologist*
Hsueh, Eddy C. *surgeon, oncologist*
Hyers, Thomas Morgan *physician, biomedical researcher*
Johnson, Eugene M. *neurologist, educator, molecular biologist, pharmacologist*
Johnson, Robert Graham *surgeon, educator, researcher*
Johnston, Marilyn Frances-Meyers *physician, medical educator*
Kaminski, Donald Leon *surgeon, educator, gastrointestinal physiologist*
Kass, Michael Allen *ophthalmologist, educator*
Kelly, Daniel P. *cardiologist, molecular biologist*
Kincaid, Marilyn Coburn *medical educator*
Kinsella, Ralph Aloysius, Jr., *physician*
Kipnis, David Morris *physician, educator*
Klahr, Saulo *nephrologist, educator*
Knutsen, Alan Paul *pediatrician, immunologist, allergist*
Kolker, Allan Erwin *ophthalmologist*
Kornfeld, Stuart A. *hematology educator*
Kouchoukos, Nicholas Thomas *surgeon*
Lacy, Paul Eston *pathologist*
Landau, William Milton *neurologist, department chairman*
Lewis, Robert David *ophthalmologist, educator*
Li, Ping *pharmacologist, educator, researcher*
Liapis, Helen *pathologist, researcher, medical educator*
Loeb, Virgil, Jr., *oncologist, hematologist*
Ludbrook, Philip Albert *cardiologist, clinical researcher, educator*
Majerus, Philip Warren *physician*
Mangelsdorf, Thomas Kelly *psychiatrist, consultant*
Manske, Paul Robert *orthopedic hand surgeon, educator*
Mantovani, John F. *pediatric neurologist*
Martin, Kevin John *nephrologist, educator*
McFadden, James Frederick, Jr., *surgeon*
McMahon, Robert M. *physician, lawyer*
Middelkamp, John Neal *pediatrician, educator*
Mooradian, Arshag Dertad *internist, educator*
Morley, John Edward *physician*
Myerson, Robert J. *radiation oncologist, educator*
Needleman, Philip *cardiologist, pharmacologist*
Neely, John Gail *otolaryngologist*
Olney, John William *psychiatry educator*
Owens, William Don *anesthesiology educator*
Payne, Meredith Jorstad *physician*
Peck, William Arno *internist, educator, dean, academic administrator*
Powers, William John *neurologist*
Prensky, Arthur Lawrence *pediatric neurologist, educator*
Purkerson, Mabel Louise *physician, physiologist, educator*
Rao, Dabeeru C. *epidemiologist, educator*
Ratner, Lee *medical educator*
Reh, Thomas Edward *radiologist, educator*
Riew, K. Daniel *cervical spine surgeon*
Riner, Ronald Nathan *cardiologist, business consultant*
Robins, Lee Nelken *medical educator*
Rosenblum, Barry Norton *physician*
Royal, Henry Duval *nuclear medicine physician*
Ryall, Jo-Ellyn M. *psychiatrist*
Schonfeld, Gustav *medical educator, researcher, administrator*
Schreiber, James Ralph *obstetrician, researcher*
Schwartz, Alan Leigh *pediatrician, educator*
Shapiro, Larry J. *pediatrician, scientist, educator*
Siegel, Barry Alan *nuclear radiologist*
Singh, Inderjit *nephrologist, internist, medical educator*
Slatopolsky, Eduardo *nephrologist, educator*
Slavin, Raymond Granam *allergist, immunologist*
Smith, Morton Edward *ophthalmology educator, dean*
Spector, Gershon Jerry *otolaryngologist, educator, researcher*
States, David Johnson *biomedical scientist, physician*
Stenson, William Frederick *gastroenterologist*
Stoneman, William, III, *physician, educator*
Sweet, Stuart C. *pediatrician*
Teitelbaum, Steven Lazarus *pathology educator*
Ternberg, Jessie Lamoin *pediatric surgeon*
Thach, William Thomas, Jr., *neurobiology and neurology educator*
Tiefenbrunn, Alan James *medical educator*
Trevathan, Edwin *neurologist, educator*
Unanue, Emil Raphael *immunopathologist*
Waterston, Robert Hugh *medical educator, researcher, medical geneticist, department chairman*
Weber, Mark F. *medical executive*
Wedner, H. James *physician, researcher*
Wickline, Samuel Alan *cardiologist, educator*
Willman, Vallee Louis *physician, surgery educator*
Willmore, Luther James, Jr., *neurologist, academic administrator, educator*
Wilson, Margaret Mary Georgiana *geriatrician, researcher, physician*
Young, Leroy *plastic surgeon*
Young, Paul Andrew *anatomist*

Springfield
Geter, Rodney Keith *plastic surgeon*
Hackett, Earl Randolph *neurologist*
Stratmann, Henry George *cardiologist*

Town And Country
Levin, Marvin Edgar *physician*

MONTANA

Billings
Glenn, Guy Charles *pathologist*

Bozeman
Quinn, Mark T. *medical educator*

Helena
Reynolds, James Francis, Jr., *physician*
Strickler, Jeffrey Harold *pediatrician*

Kalispell
Winkel, R. Dennis *family practice physician*

Missoula
Beckwith, John Bruce *pediatric pathologist*
Fawcett, Don Wayne *retired anatomist*
Swick, Herbert Morris *medical educator, humanist, neurologist*

Whitefish
Miller, Ronald Alfred *family physician*

NEBRASKA

Atkinson
Sutherland, John Campbell *pathologist, educator*

Fremont
Keasling, Gerald Frank *obstetrician-gynecologist, educator*

Hastings
Dungan, John Russell, Jr., (12th Viscount Dungan of Clane, Hereditary Prince of Fermoy and Arra) *anesthesiologist, health facility administrator*
Pankratz, Todd Alan *obstetrician, gynecologist*

Lincoln
Bernthal, John E. *medical association administrator*
Hill, Ronald Clair *anesthesiologist*
Koszewski, Bohdan Julius *retired internist, medical educator*
Wilson, Charles Stephen *cardiologist, educator*

Omaha
Armitage, James O. *medical educator*
Balaji, K.C. *urologist, researcher*
Benson, John Alexander, Jr., *internist, educator*
Brumback, Roger Alan *neuropathologist, researcher*
Casale, Thomas Bruce *medical educator*
Casey, Murray Joseph *physician, educator*
Chan, Wing-Chung *pathologist, educator*
Ferlic, Randolph *medical educator*
Fusaro, Ramon Michael *dermatologist, researcher*
Harned, Roger Kent *radiology educator*
Hartman, Herbert Arthur, Jr., *oncologist*
Hinder, Ronald Albert *surgeon, researcher*
Hodgson, Paul Edmund *surgeon, department chairman*
Howard, Thomas Clement *surgeon*
Huurman, Walter William *pediatric orthopaedic surgeon, educator*
Imray, Thomas John *radiologist, educator*
Jacobs, Danny O. *surgeon, medical educator*
Kessinger, Margaret Anne *medical educator*
Kobayashi, Roger Hideo *allergy and immunology educator*
Korbitz, Bernard Carl *retired oncologist, hematologist, educator, consultant*
Lynch, Henry Thomson *medical educator*
Lynch, Thomas Gerald *surgeon, educator*
Mardis, Hal Kennedy *urological surgeon, educator, researcher*
Maurer, Harold Maurice *pediatrician*
Mohiuddin, Syed Maqdoom *cardiologist, educator*
Mukherjee, Sandeep *gastroenterologist, educator*
Nairn, Roderick *immunologist, educator, biochemist*
Pearson, Paul Hammond *physician*
Quigley, Herbert Joseph, Jr., *pathologist, educator*
Shilling, Kay Marlene *psychiatrist*
Skoog, Donald Paul *retired pathologist, educator*
Smith, Philip W. *epidemiologist*
Sooriyaarachchi, Gamini Sarathchandra *oncologist, hematologist, educator, researcher*
Tinker, John Heath *anesthesiologist, educator*
Waggener, Ronald Edgar *radiologist*
Ward, Vernon Graves *internist*
Zardetto-Smith, Andrea *medical educator*

Papillion
Dvorak, Allen Dale *radiologist*

Scottsbluff
Kabalin, John Nicholas *urologist*

NEVADA

Glenbrook
Goldsmith, Harry Sawyer *surgeon, educator*

Henderson
Roth, Jeffrey Joseph *plastic surgeon*

Las Vegas
Bandt, Paul Douglas *physician, neurologist*
Buzard, Kurt Andre *ophthalmologist*
Canada, William H. *plastic surgeon*
Carter, Paul Richard *physician*
Cooper, Matthew Marc *cardiothoracic surgeon*
Gremse, David Albert *pediatrician, educator*
Hanson, Gerald Eugene *oral and maxillofacial surgeon*
Kurlinski, John Parker *physician*
Merkin, Albert Charles *pediatrician, allergist*
Moritz, Timothy Bovie *psychiatrist*
Noback, Richardson Kilbourne *medical educator*
Shires, George Thomas *surgeon, educator*
Speck, Eugene Lewis *internist*
Trigiano, Lucien Lewis *physician*
Wax, Arnold *physician*
Weiss, Robert Michael *dermatologist*
Zuspan, Frederick Paul *obstetrician, gynecologist, educator*

Reno
Barnet, Robert Joseph *cardiologist, ethicist*
Forbes, Kenneth Albert Faucher *urological surgeon*
MacKintosh, Frederick Roy *oncologist*
Small, Elisabeth Chan *psychiatrist, educator*
Zager, Bernard Solomon *physician, consultant*

NEW HAMPSHIRE

Bow
Emery, Paul Emile *psychiatrist*

Concord
Bagan, Merwyn *neurological surgeon*
Unger, Gere Nathan *emergency physician, lawyer*

Durham
Miller, Joseph Morton *internist*

Etna
Ferm, Vergil Harkness *anatomist, embryologist*
Rous, Stephen Norman *urologist, educator*

Exeter
Beeson, Paul Bruce *physician*

Grantham
Figley, Melvin Morgan *radiologist, physician, educator*

Hampstead
Moore, Raymond Edward *retired physician*

Hanover
Baldwin, John Charles *surgeon, researcher*
Chapman, Robert James *psychiatrist, educator*
Dietrich, Allen J. *medical educator*
Dmitrovsky, Ethan *oncologist, medical educator, researcher*
Fiering, Steven *medical educator*
Koop, Charles Everett *surgeon, educator, former surgeon general*
Likosky, Donald *epidemiologist, consultant*
Petitto, Laura-Ann *cognitive neuroscience educator*
Rawnsley, Howard Melody *pathologist, educator*
Rolett, Ellis Lawrence *medical educator, cardiologist*
Rueckert, Frederic *retired plastic, reconstructive and hand surgeon*
Wennberg, John E. *epidemiologist*
Zubkoff, Michael *medical educator*

Laconia
Brody, Spencer John *pediatrician*

Lebanon
Bernat, James Lawrence *neurologist, educator*
Clendenning, William Edmund *dermatologist*
Cohen, Jeffrey Allen *neurologist, educator*
Cronenwett, Jack LeMoyne *vascular surgeon educator*
Fanger, Michael W. *medical educator*
Fillinger, Mark F. *vascular surgeon, researcher*
Fromm, Hans *gastroenterologist, educator, researcher, hepatologist*
Glass, Donald David *anesthesiologist*
Gosselin, Benoit Jean *otolaryngologist, facial plastic surgeon, head and neck and reconstructive surgeon*
Greenberg, E. Robert *medical research administrator*
Kelley, Maurice Leslie, Jr., *gastroenterologist, educator*
McCollum, Robert Wayne *physician, educator*
Moeschler, John Boyer *physician, educator*
Schoolwerth, Anton C. *nephrologist, educator*
Silberfarb, Peter Michael *psychiatrist, educator*
von Reyn, C. Fordham *infectious disease physician*
Waugh, Theodore Rogers *orthopedic surgeon*

Lee
Young, James Morningstar *internist, military officer*

Lincoln
Seletz, Jules Mortimer *surgeon*

Lyme
Cornwell, Gibbons Gray, III, *retired internist, educator*
McIntyre, Oswald Ross *physician*

Manchester
Angoff, Gerald Harvey *cardiologist*
DesRochers, Gerard Camille *surgeon*

Nashua
Knights, Edwin Munroe *pathologist*
Siroty, William Charles *physician*

Portsmouth
Michelsen, W(olfgang) Jost *neurosurgeon, educator, retired*

Tamworth
Colten, Harvey Radin *pediatrician, educator*

West Lebanon
Day, Emerson *physician*

Windham
Levin, Murray Newman *retired surgeon*

NEW JERSEY

Bayonne
Pelosi, Marco Antonio *obstetrician and gynecologist*

Belle Mead
Goodnick, Paul Joel *psychiatrist*

Bernardsville
Dixon, Rosina Berry *physician, pharmaceutical development consultant*

Brick
Abel, Mark *dermatologist*

Bridgewater
Bernson, Marcella S. *psychiatrist*
Faruqi, Abdul Rab *physician, consultant*
Hirsch, Paul J. *orthopedist, surgeon, medical executive, educator, editor*
Maynard, Kenneth Irwin *medical educator, researcher*
Taylor, Duncan Paul *research neuropharmacologist*

Browns Mills
Cha, Se Do *internist*
Moore, Roger Addison *pediatrician, anesthesiologist*

Camden
Ances, I. G(eorge) *obstetrician, gynecologist, educator*
Bodofsky, Elliot Bruce *physician, researcher*
Parrillo, Joseph Edison, Jr., *allergist, immunologist, cardiologist*
Pello, Mark Joel *surgeon, educator*
Stahl, Gary Edward *neonatologist*

Cape May Court House
Altman, Brian David *pediatric ophthalmologist*

Cherry Hill
Barton, Diane *physician*
Brachfeld, Jonas *cardiologist, educator*
Kahn, Marc Leslie *orthopedic surgeon*
Margolis, Gerald Joseph *psychiatrist, psychoanalyst*
Olearchyk, Andrew *cardiothoracic surgeon, educator*
Proper, Michael Charles *cardiologist, educator*
Swibinski, Edward Thomas *internist, endocrinologist, educator*
Werbitt, Warren *gastroenterologist, educator*

Cliffside Park
Chryssanthou, Chryssanthos *pathologist, educator*
Zucker, Howard Alan *pediatric cardiologist, intensivist, anesthesiologist, government agency administrator*

Clifton
Pineda, Albert Anthony *obstetrician, gynecologist, educator*
Silber, Judy G. *dermatologist*

Demarest
Dornfest, Burton Saul *anatomy educator*

Denville
Husar, Walter Gene *neurologist, neuroscientist, educator*

East Orange
Brundage, Gertrude Barnes *pediatrician*
Fellus, Jonathan L. *neurologist*

Edison
Angelakos, Evangelos Theodorou *physician, physiologist, pharmacologist, educator*
Gizzi, Martin Sherman *neurologist, neurophysiologist*
Moussouttas, Michael M. *medical educator*
Salvati, Eugene Philip *retired surgeon*
Strax, Thomas E. *physiatrist*

Elizabeth
Berger, Harold Richard *physician*
Cinberg, James Zubow *otolaryngologist, educator*
Rosenstein, Neil *surgeon, genealogical researcher*
Sananman, Michael Lawrence *neurologist*
Wilchins, Sidney A. *gynecologist*

Englewood
Butler, David George *obstetrician, gynecologist*
Dardik, Herbert *vascular surgeon, general surgeon*
Frieden, Faith Joy *obstetrician*
Goldweit, Richard Scott *cardiologist*
Harish, Ziv *allergist, immunologist*
Herman, Steven Douglas *cardiothoracic surgeon, educator*
Hurst, Wendy R(obin) *obstetrician*
Rubin, Kenneth Phillip *gastroenterologist*
Tobias, Geoffrey *otolaryngologist, plastic surgeon*
Willner, Joseph H. *neurologist*
Wuhl, Charles Michael *psychiatrist*

Englewood Cliffs
Yu, Fei *internist*

Fair Lawn
Namerow, David Mark *pediatrician*

Flanders
Huang, Jacob Chen-ya *physician, educator, city health official*

Flemington
Rushton, Alan R. *physician, medical historian*

Florham Park
Weisberg, Lynne Willing *psychiatrist, consultant*

Forked River
Novak, Dennis E. *physician*

Fort Lee
Chessler, Richard Kenneth *gastroenterologist, endoscopist*
Goldfarb, Joel Peter *internist, gastroenterologist*
Li, Tien-Shun *obstetrician, gynecologist, educator*

Franklin Lakes
Ginsberg, Barry Howard *physician, researcher*

Franklin Park
Jones, Frank A., Jr., *psychiatrist, educator*

Glen Ridge
Rubin, Roberta Gail *pathologist*
Zbar, Lloyd Irwin Stanley *otolaryngologist, educator*

Green Brook
Bokhari, Sabahat *cardiologist*
Hertzberg, Henry *retired radiologist*

Guttenberg
Wright, Jane Cooke *oncologist, educator, consultant*

Hackensack
Davies, Richard John *surgical oncologist*
De Groote, Robert David *general and vascular surgeon*
Gross, Peter Alan *epidemiologist, researcher*
Haines, Kathleen Ann *pediatrician, educator*
Harris, Michael Bertram *pediatrician, educator*
Masullo, Alfredo Salvatore *dermatologist*
Pascal, Mark S. *oncologist*
Pecora, Andrew Louis *hematologist*
Perl, Harold *pediatrician*

Haddonfield
Capelli, John Placido *nephrologist, educator*
Gatti, Eugene Anthony *immunologist, pediatrician*

Hamilton
Sipski, Mary Leonide *physician, healthcare administrator*
Sporn, Aaron Adolph *physician, educator*

Highland Park
Glasgold, Alvin Irwin *physician*

Hillsborough
Nahass, Ronald G(eorge) *internist, educator*

Hillsdale
Copeland, Lois Jacqueline *physician*

Holmdel
Catanese, Vincent Joseph *internist*

Irvington
Akinsanmi, Lawrence Akintunde *medical researcher*
Treadwell, Kenneth, Jr., *obstetrician/gynecologist*

Lawrenceville
Pouleur, Hubert Gustave *cardiologist, consultant*
Rosenthal, Albert Lester *dermatologist, educator*

Livingston
Duberstein, Joel Lawrence *internist, pulmonologist, educator*
Fisher, Hyman Wendell *physician*
Krieger, Abbott Joel *neurosurgeon*
Rickert, Robert Richard *pathologist, educator*
Samojlik, Eugeniusz *medical educator, clinical researcher*
Templeton, Hilda B. *psychiatrist, educator*

Long Branch
Fisher, Margaret Catharine *pediatrician, epidemiologist, educator*
Luria, Martin Jay *endocrinologist*
Poch, Herbert Edward *retired pediatrician, educator*
Shagan, Bernard Pellman *endocrinologist, educator*
Zinterhofer, Louis *pathologist*
Zukaukas, Charles Lawrence *surgeon*

Lumberton
Campagnolo, Mary Frances *physician*
Lee, David Charles *neurologist, educator*

Mahwah
Bello, Mary *physician*

Maple Shade
Abidi, S. Manzoor *neurologist*

Maplewood
Shuttleworth, Anne Margaret *psychiatrist*

Margate City
Videll, Jared Steven *cardiologist*

Marlton
Born, Christopher T. *orthopedist, surgeon*
Kahn, Sigmund Benham *retired internist and dean*

Medford
Lawson-Ndu, Ovunda A. *emergency physician, surgeon*

Metuchen
Slobodien, Howard David *surgeon, educator*

Millburn
Heistein, Robert Kenneth *obstetrician and gynecologist*

Monmouth Junction
Brolin, Robert Edward *physician, surgeon*

Monroe Township
Drury, James Anthony Bartholomew *forensic psychiatrist, psychoanalyst*
Spierer, Robert *family practice physician*

Montclair
Kaiser, Richard Alan *surgeon*
Rosen, Allen David *plastic surgeon*

Montville
Keefe, Deborah Lynn *cardiologist, educator*

Moorestown
Cervantes, Luis Augusto *neurosurgeon*

Morris Plains
Elias, Salwa Emil Ghabrial *allergist, immunologist, pediatrician*
Fielding, Stuart *psychopharmacologist*
Goldenberg, David Milton *experimental pathologist, oncologist*

Morristown
Adler, Kenneth R. *oncologist*
De Rosa, William Thomas *internist, hematologist, oncologist*
Finkel, Marion Judith *internist, pharmaceutical administrator*
Papish, Steven William *internist*
Parr, Grant Van Siclen *surgeon*
Raska, Karel *internist, cardiologist*
Scott, Richard Thomas, Jr., *reproductive endocrinologist*
Starkman, Harold S. *physician, researcher*

Mount Laurel
Hayken, Gerald Dreux *orthopedic surgeon*
Sapega, Alexander A. *sports medicine physician, orthopedic surgeon*
Topiel, Martin Stanley *epidemiologist*

Mullica Hill
Bahal, Vishal *cardiologist*

Neptune
Ahmed, Nasim *surgeon*
Mann, William Joseph, Jr., *gynecologic oncologist*
Rice, Stephen Gary *medical educator, pediatrician, sports medicine physician*

New Brunswick
Aisenberg, Javier E. *endocrinologist, pediatrician*
Amorosa, Louis F. *endocrinologist*
August, David Allen *surgeon*
Bachmann, Gloria Ann *obstetrician, gynecologist, educator*
Bancila, Edita *pathologist, educator*
Bertino, Joseph Rocco *physician, educator*
Borah, Gregory Louis *plastic and reconstructive surgeon*
Boyarsky, Andrew Harold *surgeon*
Carson, Jeffrey L. *internist*
Castello, Frank V. *pediatrician*
Chandler, James John *surgeon, educator*
Choi, Young K. *anesthesiologist*
Corbett, Siobhan Aiden *surgeon*
Das, Kiron M. *gastroenterologist*
Day-Salvatore, Debra Lynn *medical geneticist*
DiPaola, Robert *internist*
Drachtman, Richard A. *pediatrician, educator*
Ettinger, Lawrence Jay *pediatric hematologist and oncologist, educator*
Golbe, Lawrence Ingram *neurologist*
Goldberg, Michael Ira *obstetrician, gynecologist*
Gorski, David Henry *surgeon, biomedical researcher*
Gottlieb, Alice B. *dermatologist*
Greenwald, Alfred Emanuel *retired cosmetic surgeon*
Grimes, Julia Patrice *physician, researcher*
Hait, William Neil *oncologist*
Harwood, David A. *orthopedist, surgeon*
Hegyi, Thomas *pediatrician*
Hiatt, I. Mark *pediatrician*
Holmes, Nathaniel J. *surgeon*
John, Joseph F., Jr., *internist*
Kairys, Steven W. *pediatrician, hospital administrator*
Karp, George Isaac *hematologist, oncologist*
Kaufman, Kenneth Roland *psychiatrist, educator*
Kemmann, Eckhard *obstetrician, gynecologist*
Kesarwala, Hermant H. *pediatrician, educator*
Khachadurian, Avedis *physician*
Knuppel, Robert Alan *obstetrics-gynecology educator, healthcare consultant*
Koniaris, Soula G. *pediatrician, educator*
Kostis, John Basil *cardiologist*
Kountz, David S. *physician, educator*
Krasna, Irwin H. *pediatric surgeon, educator*
Kugler, Steven L. *pediatrician, educator*
Kurer, Cheryl C. *pediatric cardiologist*
Kushins, Lawrence G. *anesthesiologist, educator*
Lacy, Clifton R. *internist, commissioner*
Laraya-Cuasay, Lourdes Redublo *pediatric pulmonologist, educator*
Leddy, Joseph Patrick *orthopedist*
Lepore, Frederick Everett *neurologist, educator*
Leventhal, Elaine A. *internist*
Lowry, Stephen Frederick *surgeon, educator*
Mann, Richard Alan *physician, educator*
Manoukian, Aram V. *gastroenterologist*
Mehta, Rajeev *neonatologist, researcher*
Moreyra, Abel E. *physician, medical educator*
Nissenblatt, Michael Jeffrey *medical oncologist*
Nosher, John Louis *radiologist*
Notterman, Daniel A. *pediatrician, educator, scientist*
Palmeri, Sebastian T. *cardiologist, educator*
Pinals, Robert Stanton *physician*
Pitchumoni, Capecomorin Sankar *gastroenterologist, educator*
Price, Mitchell R. *pediatric surgeon*
Raska, Karel Frantisek Julian, Jr., *pathologist, virologist, educator*
Rodgers, Denise V. *medical educator*
Rosenthal, Susan R. *pediatrician, educator*
Sachdeo, Rajesh C. *neurologist, educator*
Sage, Jacob I. *neurologist, educator*
Saidi, Parvin *hematologist, medical educator*
Salas, Max *pediatrician, educator*
Schneider, Stephen Harley *medical educator*
Scholz, Peter M. *surgeon*
Scully, John Thomas *obstetrician, gynecologist, educator*

Sisler, Glen E. *surgeon, educator*
Snyder, Barbara K. *pediatrician, educator*
Sommer, Warren K. *anesthesiologist, educator*
Sonnenberg, Frank A. *internist*
Spotnitz, Alan Jeffrey *cardiothoracic surgeon*
Strair, Roger K. *oncologist*
Swee, David Ethan *physician*
Treiman, David Murray *neurology educator*
Trelstad, Robert Laurence *pathology educator, cell biologist*
Vintzileos, Anthony Mark *obstetrician-gynecologist*
Weinstein, Melvin Phillip *physician educator*
Weiss, Lynne S. *pediatrician, educator*
Weiss, Robert Edward *urologist, educator*
Willett, Laura R. *internist*

Newark
Apuzzio, Joseph J. *obstetrician-gynecologist*
Baker, Herman *medical educator, writer*
Baker, Stephen R. *physician*
Benevena, Joseph *orthopedist*
Bethel, Colin Anthony Ivan *pediatric surgeon, educator*
Carmel, Peter W. *neurosurgeon*
Cherniack, Neil Stanley *pulmonologist, educator*
Cohen, Alice *hematologist*
Cohen, Stanley *pathologist, educator*
Cook, Stuart Donald *neurologist, educator*
Correia, Joaquim Jose *physician*
Donahoo, James Saunders *cardiothoracic surgeon*
Einzig, Stanley *pediatric cardiologist, researcher*
Ellner, Jerrold Jay *epidemiologist*
Evans, Hugh E. *pediatrician, educator*
Fu, Shoucheng Joseph *biomedicine educator*
Haggerty, Mary Ann *medical educator*
Haycock, Christine Elizabeth *retired medical educator, health educator*
Hobson, Robert Wayne, II, *surgeon*
Iffy, Leslie *medical educator*
Kirmani, Jawad F. *neurologist, surgeon, researcher*
Lama, Paul J. *surgeon, educator*
Leevy, Carroll Moton *medical educator, hepatology researcher*
Little, Alan Brian *obstetrician, gynecologist, educator*
Materna, Thomas Walter *ophthalmologist*
O'Connor, Brian Kevin *pediatric cardiac electrophysiologist, researcher*
Pletcher, Beth *medical geneticist*
Reichman, Lee Brodersohn *physician*
Rothbart, Stephen Tobias *cardiologist*
Schleifer, Steven J *psychiatrist, educator*
Smith, Leon G. *physician, educator*
Weiss, Gerson *reproductive endocrinologist, educator*
Zarbin, Marco Attilio *ophthalmologist, surgeon, educator*

Newton
Colizza, Wayne Anthony *orthopaedic surgeon*
Scales, James Leonard *orthopedic surgeon, health facility administrator*

North Brunswick
Cirillo, Vincent J. *medical historian, consultant*

Northfield
Margolis, Thomas Ira *vitreoretinal ophthalmologist*

Nutley
Gordon, Robert Dana *transplant surgeon*
Mostillo, Ralph *medical association administrator*

Ocean
Sher, Ellen *allergist*

Old Bridge
Yakubovich, Lidia *physician*

Orange
Agarwal, Shashi Kant *cardiologist*

Paramus
Fakharzadeh, Frederick F. *surgeon*
Faust, Michael Gregory *gynecologist, obstetrician*
Liva, Edward Louis *eye surgeon*

Park Ridge
Ablin, Richard Joel *immunologist, educator*

Parlin
Flick, Ferdinand Herman *surgeon, preventive medicine physician*
Fuks, Boris Borisovich *immunologist, researcher*

Passaic
Haddad, Jamil Raouf *retired physician*

Paterson
Malkin, Stanley Lee *neurologist*
Salcedo, Jose Rodolfo *nephrologist*
Stewart, Peter J. *general surgery, trauma and critical care physician*

Peapack
Eddey, Gary Erwin *physician, administrator, educator*

Phillipsburg
Drago, Joseph Rosario *urologist, educator*

Piscataway
Conney, Allan Howard *pharmacologist, researcher*
Escobar, Javier Ignacio *psychiatrist*
Gessner, Myron S. *psychiatrist, educator*
Lambert, George H. *pediatrician, educator*
Leibowitz, Michael Jonathan *medical educator*
Menza, Matthew A. *psychiatrist*
Rhoads, George Grant *medical epidemiologist*
Riley, David Joseph *medical educator*
Sahota, Amrik *medical researcher, educator, lab administrator*
Schwartz, Arthur Harold *psychiatry educator*
Schwartz, Stuart R. *psychiatrist*
Seiden, David *anatomist, academic administrator*
Upton, Arthur Canfield *experimental pathologist, educator*

Plainsboro
Lansing, Martha Hempel *internist*

Princeton
Carver, David Harold *physician, educator*
Forester, Gary P. *gastroenterologist*
Haynes, William Forby, Jr., *retired internist, cardiologist, educator*
Lavizzo-Mourey, Risa Juanita *medical foundation administrator, academic administrator*
McGinnis, James Michael *physician*
Scasta, David Lynn *forensic psychiatrist*
Sierocki, John Stanley *oncologist*
Sugerman, Abraham Arthur *psychiatrist, educator*
von der Schmidt, Edward, III, *neurosurgeon, veterinarian*
Wei, Fong *nephrologist*

Princeton Junction
Amenta, Peter Sebastian *pathologist*

Red Bank
Braddom, Randall Lee *physiatrist, educator*
Calabro, Joseph John, III, *physician*
Macdonald, Donald Arthur, Jr., *physician, surgeon*

Ridgewood
Baddoura, Rashid Joseph *emergency medicine physician*
Holt, Natalie Frances *physician*
Sumers, Anne Ricks *ophthalmologist, museum director*
Tohme, Jack Fouad *endocrinologist*

Roseland
Clemente, Celestino *physician, surgeon*
Panagides, John *pharmacologist*

Saddle River
Goodman, Jerome David *psychiatrist*
Weissmann, Heidi Seitelblum *radiologist, educator*

Scotch Plains
Kalischer, Alan Lester *cardiologist*

Shiloh
Dickson, Robert W., III, *internist*

Short Hills
Chaiken, Bernard Henry *internist, gastroenterologist*
Hurlbut, Terry Allison *pathologist*

Somers Point
Hunter, Kevin Edward *neurologist*

Somerset
De Salva, Salvatore Joseph *retired pharmacologist, toxicologist*
Ilogu, Noel Obiajulu *physician*
Sofia, R. D. *pharmacologist*

Somerville
Fox, James Allen *allergist, pediatrician, immunologist*
Herman, David J. *epidemiologist*

South Hackensack
Jacobs, George Braun *neurosurgeon*

South Plainfield
Barone, Joseph G. *surgeon, urologist, pediatrician*
Choi, Soon Chae *orthopaedic surgeon*

Spring Lake
Harrigan, John Thomas, Jr., *physician, obstetrician-gynecologist*

Springfield
Kerner, Michael Bernard *gastroenterologist*
Kwartler, Jed Aryeh *otolaryngologist*
Wosnitzer, Morey *urologist*

Stratford
Stein, T. Peter *medical educator*
Vitale, Patty A. *pediatrician, consultant, medical educator*

Summit
Carniol, Paul J. *plastic and reconstructive surgeon, otolaryngologist*
Halpern, Steven Lon *physician*
Hodosh, Richard M. *neurosurgeon*

Teaneck
Halper, June *medical center director*
Ladenheim, Jules Calvin *neurosurgeon*
Scotti, Dennis Joseph *educator, researcher, consultant*

Tenafly
Golomb, Frederick Martin *surgeon, educator*
Grieco, Michael Henry *allergy and infectious diseases physician*
Gritsman, Andrey *pathologist, poet*

Teterboro
Schwartz, Joyce Gensberg *pathologist*

Titusville
Bridge, T(homas) Peter *psychiatrist, researcher*

Toms River
Garcia, Jesus I. *medical association administrator, surgeon*
Marchese, Michael James, Jr., *radiation oncologist*

Trenton
Gomez, William *orthopedist*
Gupta, Rajendra Prasad *physician*
Samuel, Steven A. *cardiologist*
Taboada, Javier Gustavo *neurologist*
Thatsneyakul, Yaovares *physician, consultant*
Tolan, Robert Warren *pediatric infectious disease specialist*
Zanna, Martin Thomas *physician*

Turnersville
DePace, Nicholas Louis *physician*

Union
Jacobs-Carey, Sheila L. *immunologist*

Upper Montclair
Bluestein, Sanfurd G. *radiologist*

Vineland
Clinton, Lawrence Paul *psychiatrist*

Voorhees
Glasofer, Eric David *allergist, immunologist, pediatrician, educator*

Wall
Monaco, Robert Anthony *radiologist*
O'Neill, James Paul *psychiatrist*

Wayne
Bronstein, Jagoda Ewa *pediatrician*
Gollance, Robert Barnett *ophthalmologist*
Khoury, Hani *surgeon, educator*

West Orange
Brodkin, Roger Harrison *dermatologist, educator*
Casella, Anthony John *cardiologist*
Dispaltro, Franklin L. *plastic surgeon*
Gans, Bruce Merrill *physiatrist, educator, health facility administrator*
Ghali, Anwar Youssef *psychiatrist, educator*
Hill, George James *physician, educator*
Katz, Jeffrey Ivan *urologist*
Langsner, Alan Michael *pediatric cardiologist*
Linsenmeyer, Todd Alan *medical educator, physician*
Martin, Boston Faust *neurosurgeon*
Roseff, Scott *reproductive endocrinologist*
Wu, Nan Faion *pediatrician*

Westfield
Blum, Richard H. *obstetrician-gynecologist, educator*

Whitehouse Station
Mahmoud, Adel A. *infectious disease and tropical medicine physician, educator, pharmaceutical executive*

Woodbury
Stambaugh, John Edgar *oncologist, hematologist, pharmacologist, educator*

Wyckoff
Bauer, Theodore James *physician*
Marcus, Linda Susan *dermatologist*

NEW MEXICO

Alamogordo
Ashdown, Franklin Donald *physician, composer*
Lindley, Norman Dale *physician*

Albuquerque
Baack, Bret Rolyn *plastic surgeon*
Ballard, David Eugene *anesthesiologist*
Berman, Stanley Zissman *allergist, immunologist, internist, educator*
Borden, Thomas Allen *urologist, educator*
Bradshaw, Elaine A. *pediatrician*
Chang, Barbara Karen *medical educator*
Chilton, Lance Alix *pediatrician*
Cobb, John Candler *medical educator*
Eldredge, Jonathan DeForest *medical librarian, educator*
Fry, Donald Edmund *surgeon*
Harbert, Kenneth Ray *physician assistant*
Heffron, Warren A. *physician, educator*
Hudson, Patrick A. *plastic surgeon*
Keep, Marcus Floyd *neurosurgeon*
King, Lowell Restell *pediatric urologist*
Knospe, William Herbert *medical educator*
Mason, William vanHorn *dermatologist*
Mora, Federico *neurosurgeon*
Omer, George Elbert, Jr., *orthopaedic surgeon, educator*
Roth, Paul Barry *dean, educator, emergency medicine physician*
Saland, Linda Carol *anatomy educator, neuroscience researcher*
Smith, Edgar Benton *dermatologist*
Stevenson, James Richard *radiologist, lawyer*
Strasburger, Victor C. *pediatrician*
Summers, William Koopmans *neuropsychiatrist, researcher*
Twigg, Nancy L. *nursing association administrator*
Uhlenhuth, Eberhard Henry *psychiatrist, educator*
Waitzkin, Howard Bruce *internist, sociologist, educator*
Wimer, Mark G. *healthcare management company executive*
Winslow, Walter William *psychiatrist, educator*
Wong, Phillip Allen *osteopathic physician*
Worrell, Audrey Martiny *geriatric psychiatrist*

Farmington
Neidhart, James Allen *oncologist, educator*

Las Cruces
Jacobs, Kent Frederick *dermatologist*

Los Alamos
Smith, Fredrica Emrich *rheumatologist, internist*

Portales
Goodwin, Martin Brune *radiologist*

Rio Rancho
Goss, Jerome Eldon *cardiologist*

Rodeo
Scholes, Robert Thornton *physician, research administrator*

Roswell
Choudhary, Adil Mushtaq *gastroenterologist*
Tabrez, Shams S.M. *gastroenterologist*

Santa Fe
Alfidi, Ralph Joseph *retired radiologist*
Gilmour, Edward Ellis *retired psychiatrist*
Hoffmann, Louis Gerhard *immunologist, educator*
Kotin, Paul *pathologist*
Schiller, William Richard *surgeon*
Schwartz, George R. *physician, researcher*
Williams, Ralph Chester, Jr., *physician, educator*

Valdez
Jacobs, Roland William *psychiatrist*

NEW YORK

Akron
Hoover, Eddie Lee *cardiothoracic surgeon, educator*

Albany
Arseneau, James Charles *physician*
Bradley, Wesley Holmes *physician*
Clark, David Albert *pediatrician, consultant*
Conway de Macario, Everly *immunologist, molecular biologist*
Dal Col, Richard Herbert *cardiothoracic surgeon*
Davis, Paul Joseph *endocrinologist*
DeBuono, Barbara Ann *physician, state official*
Glazer, Joseph A. *medical association administrator*
Hoffmeister, Jana Marie *cardiologist*
Howard, Lyn Jennifer *medical educator*
Lepow, Martha Lipson *pediatric educator*
Macario, Alberto Juan Lorenzo *physician*
MacDowell, Richard T. *surgeon, educator*
Meyer, Dale Robert *ophthalmologist*
Snitkoff, Gail Goodman *immunologist, educator*
Swartz, Donald Percy *physician*
Tepper, Clifford *allergist, immunologist, educator*
Veille, Jean-Claude *maternal-fetal medicine physician, educator*
Verdile, Vincent Paul *dean, emergency physician*
Zimmerman, Earl Abram *physician, scientist, educator, neuroendocrinology researcher*

Amagansett
Fleetwood, M. Freile *psychiatrist, educator*

Amherst
Roehmholdt, John Michael *urologist, educator*

Amityville
Upadhyay, Yogendra Nath *physician, educator*

Ardsley
Utermohlen, Herbert Georg *dermatologist*

Armonk
Levere, Richard David *internist, educator*
Mellors, Robert Charles *physician, scientist, educator*

Bay Shore
Bloom, William Herman *neurosurgeon, author*
Kirsch, Scott Douglas *family practice physician*

Bayside
Roth, Joshua S. *obstetrician/gynecologist, educator*

Bayville
Arenberg, Irving Kaufman Karchmer *otolaryngologist*

Bedford
Tischler, Gary Lowell *psychiatrist, educator*

Bellmore
Bregman, Davis *physician, pain management specialist*

Binghamton
Bethje, Robert *retired general surgeon*
Peterson, Alfred Edward *family physician*

Briarcliff Manor
Pousada, Lidia *physician*

Bronx
Bella, Jonathan Noriega *cardiologist*
Bhalodkar, Narendra Chandrakant *cardiologist*
Bigal, Marcelo E *physician, researcher*
Billett, Henny Heisler *hematologist*
Blaufox, Morton Donald *hypertension specialist, educator, nuclear medicine physician*
Brandt, Lawrence Jay *internist, gastroenterologist, educator*
Burde, Ronald Marshall *neuro-ophthalmologist*
Burgio, Michael *medical researcher*
Buschke, Herman *neurologist*
Cohen, Herbert Jesse *physician, educator*
Cohen, Michael I. *pediatrician*
Correa, Nereida *women's health physician*
Coupey, Susan McGuire *pediatrician, educator*
Das, Ashoke Kumar *internist, consultant*
Drepaul, Loris Omesh *internist, infectious diseases physician*
Dutcher, Janice Jean Phillips *oncologist*
Eliasoph, Joan *radiologist, educator*
Foreman, Spencer *pulmonary specialist, hospital executive*
Freeman, Leonard Murray *radiologist, nuclear medicine physician, educator*
Fulop, Milford *physician*
Gerst, Paul Howard *physician*
Gillman, Arthur Emanuel *psychiatrist*
Goldberg, Gary L. *oncologist, medical educator*
Goldman, Israel David *hematologist, director, oncologist, educator*
Gurland, Judith E. *ophthalmologist, education educator*
Hamerman, David Jay *gerontologist, educator*
Heagarty, Margaret Caroline *retired pediatrician*
Hilaris, Basil S. *radiologist, educator*
Hirano, Asao *neuropathologist*
Hodgson, W(alter) John (Barry Hodgson) *surgeon*
Horwitz, Susan Band *molecular pharmacologist*
Jaffé, Ernst Richard *medical educator and administrator*
Kahn, Thomas *medical educator*
Kanofsky, Jacob Daniel *psychiatrist, educator*
Karkanias, George B. *neurologist, educator*
Koss, Leopold G. *physician, pathologist, educator*
Kuhn, Leslie Alvin *cardiologist*
Lieber, Charles Saul *physician, educator*
Macklin, Ruth *bioethics educator*
Margolin, Leon *physician*
Mendez, Hermann Armando *pediatrician, educator*
Nagler, Arnold Leon *pathologist, research scientist, educator*
Nitowsky, Harold Martin *physician, educator*
Ofodile, Ferdinand *plastic surgeon*
Okpalanma, Chika *psychiatrist*
Radel, Eva *pediatrician, hematologist*
Rapin, Isabelle *physician*
Reynolds, Benedict Michael *surgeon*
Reznik, Sandra Eve *physician, consultant*

Robinson, Bernard Pahl *retired thoracic surgeon, educator*
Romney, Seymour Leonard *physician, educator*
Ruben, Robert Joel *pediatric otorhinolaryngolist, educator*
Sable, Robert Allen *gastroenterologist*
Safyer, Steven Michael *medical administrator, educator*
Satir, Birgit H. *medical educator, medical researcher*
Scharff, Matthew Daniel *immunologist, cell biologist, educator*
Schaumburg, Herbert Howard *neurology educator*
Senturia, Yvonne Dreyfus *pediatrician, epidemiologist*
Shafritz, David Andrew *physician, research scientist*
Shapiro, Nella Irene *surgeon*
Shinnar, Shlomo *child neurologist, educator*
Spitzer, Adrian *pediatrician, educator*
Stein, Ruth Elizabeth Klein *physician*
Strauch, Berish *plastic surgeon, hand and cosmetic surgeon*
Sy, Stanley Peter Sison *internist*
Walsh, Christine Ann *cardiologist*
Wertenbaker, Christian T. *neuro-ophthalmologist, writer*
Wiernik, Peter Harris *oncologist, educator*

Bronxville
Bertles, John Francis *physician, educator*
Bottino, Clement Gino *surgeon*
DeMartino, Anthony Gabriel *cardiologist, internist*
Levitt, Miriam *pediatrician*

Brooklyn
Abott, Michael Larry *physician*
Ackerman, Jacob Lewis *ophthalmologist*
Afshinnia, Farsad *endocrinologist, researcher*
Avram, Morrell M. *nephrologist, educator, consultant*
Bandler, Martin *physician*
Barth, Robert Henry *nephrologist, educator*
Bhattacharya, Bhaswati *preventive medicine physician*
Biro, Laszlo *dermatologist*
Brown, Lawrence Stewart, Jr., *physician*
Chao, Tsai Chung *physician, residency program director*
Charchaflieh, Jean *physician, educator*
Cheung, Chi Pui *internist*
Cohen, Carl I. *psychiatry educator, researcher*
Collins, Ronald Leslie Leopold *physician, neurosurgeon*
Cottrell, James E. *anesthesiologist, medical educator*
Cracco, Roger Quinlan *medical educator, neurologist*
Crum, Albert Byrd *psychiatrist, consultant*
Cunningham, Joseph Newton, Jr., *cardiothoracic and vascular surgeon*
Dimant, Jacob *internist*
El Kodsi, Baroukh *gastroenterologist, educator*
Erber, William Franklin *gastroenterologist*
Fernandes, David Richard *physician*
Finger, Stephen *otolaryngologist*
Friedman, Eli A. *nephrologist, educator*
Furchgott, Robert Francis *pharmacologist, educator*
Gotta, Alexander Walter *anesthesiologist, educator*
Hamarman, Stephanie *psychiatrist, educator*
Haque, Dewan Nazimul *physician, anesthesiologist*
Imperato, Pascal James *physician, healthcare administrator, writer, historian*
Jacobowitz, Israel Jacob *cardiothoracic surgeon*
Jaffe, Eric Allen *physician, educator, researcher*
Kay, Arthur David *neurologist*
Kirshenbaum, Richard Irving *retired public health physician*
Lash, James *radiologist*
Levy, Norman B. *psychiatrist, educator*
Lichter, Stephen Marc *oncologist*
Lindo, J. Trevor *psychiatrist, consultant*
Lowery, Robert Chesley *thoracic surgeon, educator*
Mahler, Howard Samuel *psychiatrist*
Mark, Richard Kushakow *internist*
Mayer, Ira Edward *gastroenterologist*
Mezey, Andrew Peter *pediatrician, educator*
Mirra, Suzanne Samuels *neuropathologist, researcher*
Moosazadeh, Kioomars *orthopedist, educator, physiatrist, researcher*
Nurhussein, Mohammed Alamin *internist, geriatrician, educator*
Nussbaum, Arnold *pediatrician*
Pertschuk, Louis Philip *pathologist, consultant*
Ponnambalam, Ananthasekar *pediatrician, gastroenterologist*
Price, Ely *dermatologist*
Quinones, Jose Ramon, Jr., *obstetrician-gynecologist, educator*
Rachko, Maurice *cardiologist*
Ravitz, Leonard J., Jr., *physician, scientist, consultant*
Reich, Nathaniel Edwin *internist, educator, poet, artist*
Rezkalla, Laurence *internist*
Salwen, Martin J. *pathologist, educator*
Savits, Barry Sorrel *surgeon*
Schwarz, Richard Howard *obstetrician, gynecologist, educator*
Shalita, Alan Remi *dermatologist*
Shelov, Steven Patrick *pediatrician, educator*
Shulman, Abraham *otolaryngology educator, hospital administrator*
Sun, Wei Yue *internist*
Tunuguntla, Hari Siva Gurunadha Rao *urologist*
Viswanathan, Ramaswamy *physician, educator*
Weinstock, Judith *obstetrician/gynecologist*
Wolintz, Arthur Harry *neurologist, ophthalmologist*
Yogeswaran, Pararajasingam *physician*

Buffalo
Albert, Michael Salvatore *pathologist, medical laboratory executive*
Ambrus, Clara Maria *physician*
Ambrus, Julian L. *physician, medical educator*
Ballow, Mark *physician, educator*
Brody, Harold *neuroanatomist, gerontologist*
Butsch, John Lord *surgeon, educator*
Chu, Tsann Ming *immunochemist, educator*
Creaven, Patrick Joseph *physician, clinical pharmacologist*
Enhorning, Goran *obstetrician, gynecologist, educator*
Fallavollita, James A. *cardiologist, educator, cardiologist, researcher*
Genco, Robert Joseph *immunologist, periodontist, educator, scientist*
Hahn, Theresa *epidemiologist, researcher*
Halbreich, Uriel Morav *psychiatrist, educator*
Hohn, David *physician*
Hudson, Raymond Anthony *physician*
Kipping, Hans F. *dermatologist, educator*
Krzyzanski, Wojciech *pharmacokineticist, consultant, mathematician*
Kurlan, Marvin Zeft *retired surgeon*
Lele, Amol Shashikant *obstetrician and gynecologist*
Levy, Harold James *physician, psychiatrist*
Milgrom, Felix *immunologist, educator*
Mindell, Eugene Robert *surgeon, educator*
Naughton, John Patrick *cardiologist, medical educator*
Nolan, James Paul *internist, educator, medical researcher*
Piver, M. Steven *gynecologic oncologist*
Seller, Robert Herman *cardiologist, physician*
Shedd, Donald Pomroy *surgeon*
Sherris, David Allan *surgeon, medical researcher, educator*
Simpson, George True *surgeon, educator*
Stoll, Howard Lester, Jr., *dermatologist*
Trevisan, Maurizio *epidemiologist*
Vladutiu, Adrian O. *physician, educator*
Wright, John Robert *pathologist, educator*

Canaan
Rothenberg, Albert *psychiatrist, educator*

Canandaigua
Wormer, Thomas Andrew *surgeon*

Carthage
Ebbels, Bruce Jeffery *retired physician, health facility administrator*

Cedarhurst
Cohen, Harris L. *diagnostic radiologist, consultant*

Centerport
Fischel, Edward Elliot *physician, educator*

Cheektowaga
Woldman, Sherman *pediatrician*

Chester
Amelar, Richard Daniel *urologist, andrologist*

Chestnut Ridge
Day, Stacey Biswas *physician, medical educator*

Clifton Park
Blais, Bernard Raymond *ophthalmologist, occupational health physician, educator*

Cooperstown
Bordley, James, IV, *surgeon*
Franck, Walter Alfred *rheumatologist, medical administrator, educator*

Cortland
Gauss, Karl Frederik *internist, educator, geriatrician*

Cutchogue
Cottrell, Thomas Sylvester *pathology educator, university dean*

Dix Hills
Lin, Ching-Shen *pathologist*
Mastrogiannis, Dimitrios S. *obstetrician/gynecologist, perinatologist*

Dobbs Ferry
Kravath, Richard Elliot *retired pediatrician, educator*
Lavinder, Gale June *medical educator, physical therapist, clinician*

East Aurora
Carfagna, Vincent O. *physician*

East Hampton
Paton, David *ophthalmologist, educator*

East Meadow
Bleidner, Clifford W. *pharmacologist, chemist*

East Setauket
Malbon, Craig Curtis *pharmacology educator, university official*

East Syracuse
Nivarthi, Raju Naga *anesthesiology educator*

Elmhurst
Masci, Joseph Richard *medical educator, physician*

Elmira
Abderhalden, Robert Thomas *internist*
Graham, David Richard *orthopedic surgeon*
Nast, Edward Paul *cardiac surgeon*

Endicott
Szabo, Andras *internist*

Far Rockaway
Madhusoodanan, Subramoniam *psychiatrist, educator*

Farmingdale
Lieberman, Michael Jay *ophthalmologist*

Fayetteville
Chevli, Renate Naren *obstetrician, gynecologist*
Pirodsky, Donald Max *psychiatrist, educator*
Stewart, William A. *medical educator, neurosurgeon*

Fishers Island
Baue, Arthur Edward *surgeon, educator, retired health facility administrator*

Fishkill
Brocks, Eric *ophthalmologist, surgeon*

Floral Park
Mazlen, Roger Geoffrey *physician, clinical pharmacologist, nutritionist*

Flushing
Baik-Han, Won H. *pediatrician, educator, consultant*
Galdamez, Ricardo *internist*
Hon, John Wingsun *physician*
Lin, Pi-Tang *physician*
Morales, Michael Angelo *physician*
Nussbaum, Michel Ernest *physician*
Person, Philip *biomedical consultant, biochemist, dentist*

Forest Hills
Eden, Alvin Noam *pediatrician, writer*
Narasimhan, Parthasarathy *physician*
Sekler-Katz, Rudolfine *internist, psychiatrist*
Tvildiani, Dimitry *cardiologist*

Freeport
Burstein, Stephen David *neurosurgeon*

Fresh Meadows
Godfrey, Philip M. *plastic surgeon*
Kaplan, Barry Hubert *physician*

Garden City
Deane, Leland Marc *plastic surgeon*
DiGregorio, Vincent R. *plastic surgeon*
Good, Larry Irwin *gastroenterologist, educator*

Garrison
Callahan, Daniel John *biomedical researcher*

Geneva
Dickson, James Edwin, II, *obstetrician, gynecologist*

Glen Cove
Sheehy, John Paul *pediatrician*

Glen Oaks
Siris, Samuel Gidding *psychiatrist*

Goshen
Roncal, Rogelio *psychiatrist*

Great Neck
Breidbart, Rory Steven *endocrinologist*
Dines, David Michael *surgeon, educator*
Gold, Alan H. *plastic surgeon*
Goldman, Ira Steven *gastroenterologist*
Gross, Lillian *psychiatrist, educator*
Kechijian, Paul *dermatologist, educator*
Lieber, Constance E. *medical association administrator*
Packer, Samuel *ophthalmologist*
Rosenberg, Richard F. *physician, radiologist*
Rothbaum, David *obstetrician-gynecologist*
Samuel, Paul *retired cardiologist, educator*
Schlesinger, Irwin D. *neurologist*
Shons, Alan Rance *plastic surgeon, surgical oncologist, educator*
Simon, Arthur *pharmacologist, research laboratory executive*
Tosheff, Julij Gospodinoff *psychiatrist*

Great River
Hayman, Martin Arthur *psychiatrist, educator*

Greenport
Loomis, Earl Alfred, Jr., *psychiatrist*

Hamburg
Calkins, Evan *physician, educator*

Hartsdale
Chait, Maxwell Mani *physician*
Katz, David *gastroenterologist, educator*

Hastings On Hudson
Rosch, Paul John *internist, educator*

Hawthorne
Nandedkar, Sanjeev Dattatraya *medical researcher, educator*
Panitz, Lawrence *physician*

Hewlett
Cohen, David Leon *physician*
Steinfeld, Philip Sheldon *pediatrician*

Hollis Hills
Malis, Leonard Irving *neurosurgeon*

Hudson
Mustapha, Tamton *gastroenterologist*

Huntington
Alsop, Reese Fell *medical educator*
Engstrand, Beatrice C. *neurologist, educator*
Salcedo-Dovi, Hector Eduardo *anatomist, educator, surgeon*
Trager, Gary Alan *endocrinologist, diabetologist*
Vale, Margo Rose *physician*

Ilion
Gay, Douglas MacKenzie *pharmacologist*

Irvington
Bendixen, Henrik Holt *physician, educator, dean*

Ithaca
Dietert, Rodney Reynolds *immunology and toxicology educator*
Whitaker, Susanne Kanis *veterinary medical librarian*

Jamaica
Bakshi, Sanjiv *internist*
Duffoo, Frantz Michel *nephrologist, medical director*
Garner, Steven C. *radiologist, emergency physician*
Grünwald, Hans Wolfgang *internist, hematologist, oncologist*

Jamiaca
Kemeny, M. Margaret *oncologist, hospital administrator, surgeon*

Jericho
Schell, Norman Barnett *preventive medicine physician, consultant*

Johnson City
Goddard, Bryan Lance *physician, director*
McGovern, Thomas Boardman *physician, pediatrician*

Kenmore
Elibol, Tarik *gastroenterologist, educator*

Kingston
Johnson, Marie-Louise Tully *dermatologist, educator*

Lake Katrine
Dolamore, Michael John *physician*

Lancaster
Batt, Ronald Elmer *gynecologist, scientist, historian*

Larchmont
Rockland, Lawrence Howard *psychiatrist, educator*

Latham
Silverman, Warren *physician*

Liverpool
Cady, Duane Maynard *surgeon*

Lockport
Carr, Edward Albert, Jr., *medical educator, physician*

Lowville
Becker, Robert Otto *orthopedic surgery educator*
Herrman, John Clinton *surgeon*

Mamaroneck
Coleman, Marshall Donald *psychiatrist, psychoanalyst*
Halpern, Abraham Leon *psychiatrist*
Hoffert, Paul Washington *surgeon*

Manhasset
Boal, Bernard Harvey *cardiologist, educator, author*
Bosworth, Jay L. *radiation oncologist*
Bradley, Thomas Paul *internist*
Chaudhry, Saima *physician, educator*
D'Olimpio, James Thomas *oncologist*
Fountain, Karen Schueler *physician*
Milhorat, Thomas Herrick *neurosurgeon*
Nelson, Roy Leslie *cardiac surgeon, researcher, educator*
Pogo, Gustave Javier *cardiothoracic surgeon*
Scherr, Lawrence *internist, educator*
Wecksell, Alan *radiologist*

Manlius
Prior, John Thompson *pathology educator*

Massapequa
Zwanger, Jerome *physician*

Melville
Copperman, Stuart Morton *pediatrician, educator*

Merrick
Gutnik, Zhanna *physician, gastroenterology consultant*

Middletown
Broslovsky, Lewis *physician*

Mineola
Aloia, John F. *endocrinologist, academic administrator*
Gomolin, Irving Harold *medical educator*
Twist, Paul Francis, Jr., *neonatologist*

Monticello
Lauterstein, Joseph *cardiologist*

Mount Kisco
Geissinger-Robertson, Ruth Fabry *retired obstetrician, gynecologist*
Hayworth, Scott David *physician*
Schneider, Robert Jay *oncologist*
Stein, Mitchell Brian *physician*

Mount Sinai
Feinberg, Sheldon Norman *pediatrician, educator*

Mount Vernon
Kaufman, Alan *internist, allergist*
Zucker, Arnold Harris *psychiatrist*

Naples
Beal, Myron Clarence *osteopath*

Nesconset
Catena, Salvatore Vincent *family physician*

New City
Esser, Aristide Henri *psychiatrist*
Savitz, Martin Harold *neurosurgeon*

New Hyde Park
Bonagura, Vincent R. *pediatrician, educator, researcher*
Eberhard, Barbara Anne *pediatric rheumatologist, researcher*
Gelber, Philip Michael *cardiologist*
Goldberg, Itzhak D. *radiation oncologist*
Lanzkowsky, Philip *physician*
Lipton, Jeffrey M. *physician*
Mealie, Carl A. *physician, educator*
Palestro, Christopher J. *physician*
Prisco, Douglas Louis *physician*
Sagy, Mayer *critical care physician*
Seltzer, Vicki Lynn *obstetrician, gynecologist*
Shenker, Ira Ronald *physician*
Steinberg, Harry *pulmonologist*

New Rochelle
Eaton, Richard Gillette *retired surgeon, educator*
Gable, Carol Brignoli *health economics researcher*
Gitler, Bernard *cardiologist and critical care specialist*

Purcell, Karen Barlar *physician, nutritionist, vocalist, writer*
Quest, Donald O. *neurological surgeon*
Quimby, Fred William *pathology educator, veterinarian*
Quraishi, Nisar Ali *internist*
Rabbani, Farhang *urologic oncologist*
Rabinowitz, Jack Grant *radiologist, educator*
Rainess, Alan Edward *psychiatrist, neurologist, educator*
Ramsay, David Leslie *physician, dermatologist, medical educator*
Raskin, Keith B. *surgeon*
Rausen, Aaron Reuben *pediatric hematologist, oncologist*
Raynor, Richard Benjamin *neurosurgeon, educator*
Reader, George G. *retired internal-public health medicine educator*
Redo, S(averio) Frank *surgeon*
Reidenberg, Marcus Milton *physician, educator*
Reiffel, James *cardiologist, educator*
Reiner, Mark Allen *surgeon, educator*
Reisberg, Barry *geropsychiatrist, neuropsychopharmacologist*
Reisner, Milton *psychiatrist, psychoanalyst*
Reiss, Robert Francis *physician*
Reuter, Victor E. *pathologist, educator*
Rifkind, Arleen B. *pharmacologist, researcher, educator*
Ristich, Miodrag *psychiatrist*
Ritch, Robert Harry *ophthalmologist, educator*
Robertson, Hugh Dunbar *biomedical researcher, consultant*
Rodeo, Scott A. *surgeon, sports medicine specialist*
Rodriguez-Sains, Rene S. *physician, surgeon, educator*
Roen, Philip Ruben *urologist, surgeon, medical educator*
Romano, John Francis *dermatologist*
Romas, Nicholas Achilles *urologist, educator*
Romita, Mauro Charles *plastic surgeon*
Rosenberg, Harold Nmi *preventive medicine physician, consultant*
Rosenberg, Victor I. *plastic surgeon, educator*
Rosenfield, Allan *physician*
Rothe, Desider J. *gynecologist-obstetrician*
Rotman, Marvin *radiation oncologist, radiologist, educator*
Rovit, Richard Lee *neurological surgeon*
Rowland, Lewis Phillip *neurology educator, editor, clinical investigator*
Rubin, Albert Louis *internist, nephrologist, educator*
Rubin, Theodore Isaac *psychiatrist, writer*
Rubinstein, Ruth P. *medical educator, researcher*
Ruder, Usha C. *pathologist*
Rusch, Valerie Williams *thoracic surgeon*
Ruskin, Richard A. *obstetrician-gynecologist*
Sachar, David Bernard *gastroenterologist, educator*
Sacks, Oliver Wolf *neurologist, writer*
Sadick, Neil Scott *dermatologist*
Sadock, Benjamin James *psychiatrist, educator*
Safian, Leroy Scheller *radiologist*
Sager, Clifford J. *psychiatrist, educator*
Salans, Lester Barry *physician, scientist, educator*
Salgo, Peter Lloyd *internist, writer, anesthesiologist, journalist, commentator*
Sampson, Hugh Albert, Jr., *medical educator*
Sandhu, Harvinder Singh *spinal surgeon, educator*
Saphir, Richard Louis *pediatrician*
Saxena, Brij B. *endocrinologist, biochemist, educator*
Schaefer, Steven David *head and neck surgeon, physiologist*
Schaffner, Bertram Henry *psychiatrist*
Scheidt, Stephen Slaton *internist, cardiologist*
Scher, Howard S. *oncologist*
Schlegel, Peter Niles *urologist and educator*
Schley, William Shain *otorhinolaryngologist*
Schneck, Jerome M. *psychiatrist, medical historian, educator*
Schuster, Carlotta Lief *psychiatrist*
Schwartz, Irving Leon *physician, scientist, educator*
Schwarz, M. Roy *physician, administrator*
Sclafani, Anthony Paul *plastic surgeon, educator, biomedical researcher*
Scott, Susan Craig *plastic surgeon*
Sculco, Thomas Peter *surgeon*
Sedlin, Elias David *physician, orthopedic researcher, educator*
Seely, Robert Daniel *physician, medical educator*
Serle, Janet Barbra *ophthalmologist, educator*
Sessions, Roy Brumby *otolaryngologist, educator*
Shapiro, Theodore *psychiatrist, educator*
Shepherd, Gillian Mary *physician*
Sherman, John Eric *plastic surgeon*
Sherman, Spencer E. *ophthalmologist*
Shortliffe, Edward Hance *internist, medical educator, computer scientist*
Shungu, Dikoma Cyrille *radiology educator*
Silver, Richard Tobias *physician, educator*
Siris, Ethel Silverman *endocrinologist*
Sisti, Michael Brian *neurosurgeon*
Sitarz, Anneliese Lotte *pediatrics educator, physician*
Skolnik, Richard Alan *plastic surgeon*
Smith, Craig Richey *thoracic surgeon*
Smith, Daniel *oncologist, gynecologist*
Smits, Helen Lida *physician, medical administrator, educator*
Soave, Rosemary *internist*
Sobel, Howard D. *dermatologist*
Solomon, Gail Ellen *physician*
Spencer, Frank Cole *medical educator*
Speyer, James L. *oncologist*
Spiegel, Herbert *psychiatrist, educator*
Stark, Richard Boies *surgeon, artist*
Starren, Justin Bruce *medical educator*
Steadman, E. Thomas *gynecologist*
Steigbigel, Neal H. *medical educator*
Stein, Marvin *psychiatrist, historian*
Stein, Richard Alan *cardiologist, educator*
Steinman, Ralph M. *medical educator*
Stelzer, Paul *cardiac surgeon, educator*
Stern, Claudio Daniel *medical educator, embryological researcher*
Stimmel, Barry *cardiologist, internist, educator, university dean*
Stoopler, Mark Benjamin *physician*
Stübgen, Joerg-Patrick *neurologist*
Subramanian, Valavanur A. *surgeon, director, thoracic surgeon*
Sultan, Mark R. *plastic surgeon*
Sun, Tung-Tien *medical science educator*
Susser, Ezra Saul *psychiatry educator*
Susser, Mervyn Wilfred *epidemiologist, educator*
Suzuki, Wendy A. *neural science educator*
Sverdlik, Samuel Simon *physiatrist, physician*
Tabbal, Nicolas G. *plastic surgeon*
Taha, Assad M. *surgeon*
Temple, Donald Edward *medical association administrator*
Thomas, Stephen Jay *anesthesiologist*
Thomson, Gerald Edmund *physician, educator*
Thornton, Yvonne Shirley *physician, author, musician*
Tolchin, Joan Gubin *psychiatrist, educator*
Tortolani, Anthony John *surgeon, educator*
Tourlitsas, John Constantine *radiologist*
Tsai, James C. *ophthalmologist, researcher*
Turino, Gerard Michael *physician, medical scientist, educator*
Tzimas, Nicholas Achilles *orthopedic surgeon, educator*
Vaughan, Edwin Darracott, Jr., *urologist, surgeon*
Vilcek, Jan Tomas *immunologist, medical educator*
Waksman, Byron Halsted *neuroimmunologist, experimental pathologist, educator, medical association administrator*
Wallace, Joyce Irene Malakoff *internist*
Wallach, Robert Charles *obstetrician, gynecologist, educator*
Wang, Frederick Mark *pediatric ophthalmologist, medical educator*
Wang, Lu-Hai *medical educator, scientist, researcher*
Weiland, Andrew J. *orthopaedic surgeon*
Weinberg, Jeffrey Mitchell *dermatologist, researcher*
Weinshenker, Naomi Joyce *clinical psychiatrist, educator, researcher*
Weinstein, George William *retired ophthalmology educator*
Weinstein, I. Bernard *oncologist, director, geneticist, educator*
Weinstock, David Marc *bone marrow transplantation and infectious diseases physician, researcher*
Weiss, Paul Richard *plastic surgeon*
Weissman, Myrna M. *epidemiologist, researcher, medical educator*
Weissmann, Gerald *internist, medical educator, researcher, writer, editor*
Welch, Martha Grace *physician, researcher*
Werman, David Sanford *psychiatrist, psychoanalyst, educator*
West, Alexander Brian *pathologist*
Wexler, Patricia Susan *dermatologist, surgeon*
Wharton, Ralph Nathaniel *psychiatrist, educator*
Whitehead, Edgar Douglas *urology educator*
Winawer, Sidney J. *physician, clinical investigator, educator*
Winick, Myron *educator, physician*
Winn, H. Richard *surgeon*
Winters, Robert Wayne *medical educator, pediatrician, healthcare executive*
Wittes, Robert E. *physician, science foundation director*
Wolf, Carl F.W. *physician, biomedical engineer*
Wolfe, Scott W. *orthopedic hand surgeon*
Wolff, William I. *surgeon, educator*
Wood-Smith, Donald *plastic surgeon*
Worman, Howard Jay *internist, educator*
Yahalom, Joachim *radiologist, educator, oncologist, researcher*
Yeh, Hsu-Chong *radiology educator*
Yeh, Ming-Neng *obstetrician, gynecologist*
Young, Bruce K. *obstetrician, gynecologist, educator*
Young, Estelle Irene *dermatologist, educator*
Yu, Yi-Hao *endocrinologist, educator, physician, research scientist*
Yurt, Roger William *surgeon, educator*
Zatlin, Gabriel Stanley *physician*
Zimmerman, Sol Shea *pediatrician*
Zinn, Keith Marshall *ophthalmologist, educator*
Zitrin, Arthur *physician*
Zucker-Franklin, Dorothea *internist, educator*

Newburgh
Grossman, Stanley Lawrence *surgeon*

Niagara Falls
DeFelice, Eugene Anthony *physician, medical educator, author, consultant, magician*
Yun, Young Jae *neurosurgeon*

North Babylon
Zitt, Myron J. *allergist, immunologist*

North Tonawanda
Megahed, Mohamed Salah *neurologist, educator*

Ogdensburg
Madhok, Ashish Brij *pediatrician, cardiologist*

Old Westbury
Chaudhry, Humayun Javaid *physician, medical educator, writer, flight surgeon*

Olean
Lewis, Fred Harvey *allergist, immunologist*

Orangeburg
Citrome, Leslie Lucien *psychiatrist, educator*
Greenberg, William Michael *psychiatrist*
Levine, Jerome *psychiatrist, educator*
Nixon, Ralph Angus *psychiatrist, educator, research neuroscientist*

Orchard Park
Lee, Richard Vaille *physician, educator*

Ossining
Wolfe, Mary Joan *physician*

Pelham
Yurenev, Aleksey Pavlovich (Alexei Pavlovich Yurenev) *cardiologist, researcher*

Penn Yan
Strouse, Wayne Steven *physician*

Pittsford
Faloon, William Wassell *physician, educator*

Plainview
Kelemen, John *neurologist, educator*

Plattsburgh
Bedworth, David Albert *health educator*
Berggren, Jean R. *psychiatrist*
Medearis, Kenneth Robert *medical products manufacturing company executive*
Virostek, Robert Joseph *physician*

Pomona
Landa, George *cardiologist, internist*
Zugibe, Frederick Thomas *retired pathologist*

Port Jefferson
Dranitzke, Richard J. *surgeon*

Port Jefferson Station
Kaplan, Martin Paul *pediatrician, educator*

Port Washington
Brownstein, Martin Herbert *dermatopathologist*

Poughkeepsie
Berlin, Doris Ada *psychiatrist*
Bodack, Mark Peter *physician, medical educator*
Carino, Aurora Lao *psychiatrist, hospital administrator*
Hansraj, Kenneth Karamchand *surgeon, research scientist*

Purchase
Frost, Elizabeth Ann McArthur *physician*

Queensbury
De Pan, Harry McCarthy *retired surgeon*

Rego Park
Winter, Darius Gerjon *internist*

Rochester
Akiyama, Toshio *cardiologist, educator, researcher*
Anderson, Porter Warren, Jr., *retired pediatrics educator*
Baum, John *physician*
Berg, Robert Lewis *physician, educator*
Bidlack, Jean Marie *pharmacologist, educator, medical researcher*
Bonfiglio, Thomas Albert *pathologist, educator*
Brody, Bernard B. *internist, educator*
Brooks, Walter S. *dermatologist*
Burton, Richard Irving *orthopedist, educator*
Chey, William Yoon *physician*
Ciccone, J. Richard *psychiatrist, educator*
Cohen, Nicholas *immunologist, educator*
Danforth-Morningstar, Elizabeth *obstetrician, gynecologist*
DeWeese, James Arville *surgeon, educator*
Dye, Timothy De Ver *epidemiologist, anthropologist, educator*
Farmer, Richard Gilbert *physician, foundation administrator, medical advisor, healthcare consultant*
Frazer, John Paul *surgeon*
Friedman, Susan Marie *geriatrician, educator, medical researcher*
Galaria, Noreen Ahmad *physician, medical researcher, consultant*
Golden, Reynold Stephen *geriatrician, educator*
Goldstein, Marvin Norman *physician*
Griggs, Robert Charles *physician*
Hakim, Fares Samih *physician*
Klein, Jonathan David *physician, researcher*
Lichtman, Marshall Albert *internist, educator, medical researcher*
Lyman, Gary Herbert *epidemiologist, cancer researcher, educator*
McAnarney, Elizabeth R. *pediatrician, educator*
McDonald, Joseph Valentine *neurosurgeon*
McMeekin, Thomas Owen *dermatologist*
McQuillen, Michael Paul *neurologist, educator, clinical ethicist*
Messing, Edward M. *urologic surgeon*
Morgan, William Lionel, Jr., *physician, educator*
Moss, Arthur Jay *physician*
Nazarian, Lawrence Fred *pediatrician*
Panner, Bernard J. *pathologist, educator*
Pearson, Thomas Arthur *epidemiologist, educator*
Powers, James Matthew *neuropathologist*
Rowley, Peter Templeton *pediatrician, educator*
Schrock, Robert D., Jr., *orthopaedic surgeon, educator*
Schwartz, Seymour Ira *surgeon, educator*
Smith, Julia Ladd *medical oncologist, hospice physician*
Sparks, Charles Edward *pathologist, educator*
Sparks, Janet Lindsay Dehoff *pathology educator*
Utell, Mark Jeffrey *medical educator*
Wax, Paul Matthew *emergency medicine physician, educator, medical toxicologist*
Wheeless, Leon Lum *pathology educator*
Wiley, Jason LaRue, Jr., *neurosurgeon*
Williams, Thomas Franklin *physician, educator*

Rockville Centre
Meredith, Gary S. *physician*
Teyan, Frederick Gene *pediatrician*

Roslyn
Gulotta, Stephen J. *cardiologist*
Hartman, Nancy Lee *physician*
Lidonnici, Leslie *surgeon*

Roslyn Heights
Rogatz, Peter *retired physician*

Rye
Barker, Harold Grant *surgeon, educator*
Curtin, Brian Joseph *ophthalmologist*
Waltz, Joseph McKendree *neurosurgeon, educator*

Rye Brook
Kuntzman, Ronald *pharmacology research executive*
Lo Russo, Diane *radiologist*

Sands Point
Lear, Erwin *anesthesiologist, educator*

Saranac Lake
Hixson, Edward George *general surgeon*

Scarsdale
Dulit, Everett Paul *psychiatrist, educator*
Edis, Gloria Toby *pediatrician*
Fishbach, Mitchell Harvey *cardiologist*
Jacobs, Theodore Joseph *psychiatrist, educator*
Moser, Marvin *physician, educator, writer*
Perez, Louis Anthony *radiologist*

Schenectady
Schenck, John Frederic *physician*
Zhu, Yudong *medical imaging researcher*

Scotia
de la Rocha, Carlos A. *retired physician*

Sleepy Hollow
Chia, David Thien-Shing *internist, gastroenterologist*

Somers
Bauman, William Allen *pediatrician, educator, health systems consultant*
Reznick, Steven Michael *orthopedic surgeon, educator*
Rubin, Samuel Harold *internist, consultant*

Staten Island
Banner, Burton *pediatrician*
Bruckstein, Alex Harry *internist, gastroenterologist, geriatrician*
Ferzli, George Salem *surgeon*
Grodman, Richard Stephen *internist, cardiologist*
Jarrett, Mark Paul *rheumatologist, medical administrator*
Maiman, Mitchell *oncologist, gynecologist*
Pillari, Vincent Thomas *obstetrician-gynecologist, educator*
Popler, Kenneth *behavioral health services administrator, psychologist*
Silverberg, Michael Barry *anesthesiologist*
Stathopoulos, Peter *internist*
Winter, Steven *internist, cardiologist*

Stony Brook
Chandran, Latha *pediatrician, educator*
Corman, Marvin Leonard *surgeon, educator*
Fritts, Harry Washington, Jr., *physician, educator*
Jonas, Steven *public health physician, health policy analyst, writer*
Kuchner, Eugene Frederick *neurosurgeon, educator, neuroscientist*
Lane, Dorothy Spiegel *preventive medicine physician*
Leske, M. Cristina *medical educator, medical researcher*
Liang, Jerome Zhengrong *radiology educator*
Meyers, Morton Allen *physician, radiology educator*
Mirza, Humair *cardiologist, educator*
Priebe, Cedric Joseph, Jr., *pediatric surgeon*
Ricotta, John Joseph *vascular surgeon, educator*
Sokoloff, Leon *pathology educator*
Steigbigel, Roy Theodore *epidemiologist, educator, research scientist*

Suffern
Codispoti, Andre John *allergist, immunologist*
Oppenheim, Jeffrey Sable *neurosurgeon, educator*

Syracuse
Ashutosh, Kumar *pulmonologist, educator*
Baker, Bruce Edward *orthopedic surgeon, consultant*
Becker, Lorne Arthur *family physician*
Bornhurst, Robert Allan *radiologist*
Cohen, William Nathan *radiologist*
Daly, Robert W. *psychiatrist, medical educator*
Farah, Fuad Salim *dermatologist, educator*
Gold, Joseph *medical researcher*
Grant, William Davis *medical educator, dean*
Henry, John Bernard *pathologist, educator, academic administrator*
Horst, Pamela Sue *medical educator, family physician*
Kane, Peter Bayard *physician*
Kaplan, Eugene Alken *psychiatry educator, department chairman*
Meguid, Michael M. *medical educator, researcher*
Numann, Patricia Joy *surgeon, educator*
Phillips, Paul Everard *physician, medical educator*
Rogers, Sherry Anne *physician*
Sagerman, Robert Howard *radiation oncologist*
Scheinman, Steven Jay *medical educator*
Sheehan, Michael Gerard *allergist*
Smith, Robert L. *medical research administrator*
Streeten, Barbara Wiard *ophthalmologist, medical educator*
Szasz, Thomas Stephen *psychiatrist, educator, writer*
Threatte, Gregory Allen *pathology educator, academic director*
Vardan, Suman *medical educator*
Welch, Thomas Robert *pediatrician, educator*
Williams, William Joseph *physician, educator*
Wolff, L. Thomas *physician, educator*

Tarrytown
Field, Barry Elliot *internist, gastroenterologist*
Sullivan, Janet Nelson *dermatologist, department chairman, health facility administrator*

Tuxedo Park
Regan, Ellen Frances (Mrs. Walston Shepard Brown) *ophthalmologist, educator*

Upton
Carsten, Arland Leon *radiobiologist, researcher, educator, consultant*
Hamilton, Leonard Derwent *physician, molecular biologist*

Utica
Millet, John Bradford *retired surgeon*
Min, Balshik *pathologist*

Valhalla
Aronow, Wilbert Solomon *physician, educator*
Balazy, Michael *pharmacologist, educator*
Cimino, Joseph Anthony *preventive medicine physician, educator*
Del Guercio, Louis Richard Maurice *surgeon, educator*
Duan, Jiandong *neurologist, researcher*
Frishman, William Howard *cardiology educator, cardiovascular pharmacologist, gerontologist*

Goodman, Alvin Irwin *internist, nephrologist, educator*
Kline, Susan Anderson *medical school official and dean, internist*
Madden, Robert Edward *surgeon, educator*
Marks, Stephen J. *neurologist, educator*
McGoldrick, Kathryn Elizabeth *anesthesiologist, educator, writer*
Peterson, Stephen Joseph *internist*
Reed, George Elliott *surgeon, educator, dean*
Safai, Bijan *physician, investigator*
Slim, Michel S. *surgeon, educator, health facility administrator*
Stringel, Gustavo *pediatric surgeon*
Weinberg, Hubert *plastic surgeon*
Weisburger, John Hans *medical researcher*
Williams, Gary Murray *medical researcher, pathology educator*

Wappingers Falls
Aguero-Rosenfeld, Maria E. *pathologist, medical microbiologist*

Water Mill
Hagstrom, Jack Walter Carl Kling *retired pathology educator*

West Haverstraw
Cavaliere, Rossella *neurologist*

West Islip
Doganay, Kazim Levent *physician*
Elkowitz, Sheryl Sue *radiologist*

White Plains
Barland, Peter *rheumatologist, medical educator*
Bernard, Robert William *plastic surgeon*
Biers, Martin Henry *physician*
Blass, John Paul *psychiatrist, neurologist, geriatrician, educator*
Howson, Christopher Paul *medical association administrator, epidemiologist*
Katz, Michael *pediatrician, educator*
Liebert, Peter Selig *pediatric surgeon, consultant*
Marano, Anthony Joseph *cardiologist*
McDowell, Fletcher Hughes *physician, educator*
Morello, Daniel Conway *plastic surgeon*
Pfeffer, Cynthia Roberta *psychiatrist, educator*
Soley, Robert Lawrence *plastic surgeon*
Volpe, Bruce Thomas *neurologist*

Whitestone
Rosmarin, Leonard Alan *dermatologist*

Williamsville
Canfield, Cheryl Lucas *epidemiologist*
Ogra, Pearay L. *pediatrician, educator*
Reisman, Robert E. *physician, educator*
Rekate, Albert C. *physician*

Woodbury
Bleicher, Sheldon Joseph *endocrinologist, medical educator*

Yonkers
Chumaceiro, Rolando Jose Mendez *family practice physician*
Daman, Harlan Richard *allergist, educator*
Rosch, Elliott Carl *internist*
Spagnuolo, Mario *physician*

Yorktown Heights
Berk, George Ellis *cardiologist*
Gerard, Mayer J. *physician*

NORTH CAROLINA

Aberdeen
Jacobson, Peter Lars *neurologist, educator*

Advance
Guth, Caryl Joy *retired anesthesiologist*

Asheboro
Helsabeck, Eric H. *emergency physician*

Asheville
Astler, Vernon Benson *surgeon*
White, Terry Edward *physician*

Beech Mountain
Alea, Jorge Antonio *physician*

Blowing Rock
Littlejohn, Mark Hays *retired radiologist, artist*

Boone
Domer, Floyd Ray *pharmacologist, educator*

Brevard
Finnerty, Frances Martin *medical administrator*

Bullock
Stead, Eugene Anson, Jr., *physician*

Burlington
Malinda, Paul F. *emergency physician*
Wilson, William Preston *psychiatrist, educator*

Cary
Kimbrell, Odell Culp, Jr., *internist*

Chapel Hill
Aamoth, Gordon M. *medical association administrator*
Bailey, Donald B., Jr., *medical and special education educator*
Baker, Christopher Cameron *surgeon*
Bondurant, Stuart *physician, educational association administrator*
Briggaman, Robert Alan *dermatologist, medical educator*
Carson, Culley Clyde, III, *urologist, educator*
Clemmons, David Robert *internist, educator*
Coles, William Henry *ophthalmologist, educator*
Collier, Albert M. *pediatric educator, child development center director*
Crews, Fulton Timm *pharmacology educator*
Cromartie, William James *medical educator, researcher*
De Friese, Gordon H. *health services researcher*
De Rosa, Guy Paul *orthopedic surgery educator*
Droegemueller, William *gynecologist, obstetrician, medical educator*
Drossman, Douglas Arnold *medical investigator, educator, gastroenterologist*
Falk, Ronald J. *medical educator*
Fletcher, Suzanne Wright *epidemiologist, medical educator, editor*
Fowler, Wesley Caswell, Jr., *obstetrician, gynecologist*
Goldsmith, Lowell Alan *medical educator*
Goyer, Robert Andrew *pathology educator*
Graham, John Borden *pathologist, writer, educator*
Harden, T. Kendall *pharmacologist, educator*
Hawkins, David Rollo, Sr., *psychiatrist, educator*
Henson, O'Dell Williams, Jr., *retired anatomy educator*
Houpt, Jeffrey Lyle *psychiatrist, educator, former dean*
Howard, James Francis, Jr., *medical educator, neurologist*
Hulka, Barbara Sorenson *epidemiologist, educator*
Hulka, Jaroslav Fabian *obstetrician, gynecologist*
James, Alton Everette, Jr., *radiologist*
Juliano, Rudolph L. *medical educator*
Keagy, Blair Allen *surgery educator*
Lichtman, Steven N. *pediatrician, educator*
Lieberman, Jeffrey Alan *psychiatrist, educator*
Lohr, Jacob Andrew *physician, pediatrician, educator*
Marzluff, William Frank *medical educator*
McMillan, Campbell White *pediatric hematologist*
Miller, C. Arden *physician, educator*
Mitchell, Beverly Shriver *hematologist, oncologist, educator*
Pagano, Joseph Stephen *physician, researcher, educator*
Palmer, Jeffress Gary *hematologist, educator*
Peacock, Erle Ewart, Jr., *surgeon, lawyer, educator*
Pillsbury, Harold Crockett, III, *otolaryngologist*
Prange, Arthur Jergen, Jr., *psychiatrist, neurobiologist, educator*
Roberts, Harold Ross *medical educator, hematologist*
Sanders, Charles Addison *retired physician*
Senior, Brent Anthony *otolaryngologist, educator*
Sheldon, George Frank *medical educator*
Simmons, Michael Anthony *pediatrician*
Sorenson, James Roger *public health educator*
Spencer, Roger Felix *psychiatrist, psychoanalyst, medical educator*
Stockman, James Anthony, III, *pediatrician*
Sugioka, Kenneth *anesthesiologist, educator*
Thomas, Colin Gordon, Jr., *surgeon, medical educator*
Tilson, Hugh Hanna *epidemiologist*
Tolley, Aubrey Granville *psychiatrist, health facility administrator*
Trejo, JoAnn *medical researcher*
Tyroler, Herman Alfred *epidemiologist*
Wheeler, Clayton Eugene, Jr., *dermatologist, educator*
Wilcox, Benson Reid *cardiothoracic surgeon, educator*
Wilfert, Catherine M. *medical association administrator, medical educator*
Winfield, John Buckner *rheumatologist, educator*

Charlotte
Bosse, Michael Joseph *orthopedic trauma surgeon*
Colavita, Paul Gerard *cardiologist, medical educator*
Hutcheson, J. Sterling *allergist, immunologist, physician*
Lapp, Charles Warren *internal medicine physician, pediatrician*
Nicholson, Henry Hale, Jr., *surgeon*
Saikevych, Irene A. *pathologist*
Schafermeyer, Robert William *emergency physician, educator*
Thompson, John Albert, Jr., *dermatologist*
Visser, Valya Elizabeth *physician*

Clemmons
Maloney, Sean Robert *physician, biomedical engineer*

Cornelius
Wortman, William Jerome, Jr., *obstetrician-gynecologist*

Durham
Alexander, Michael Jozef *neurosurgeon, radiologist*
Anderson, William Banks, Jr., *ophthalmology educator*
Anlyan, William George *surgeon, educator, academic administrator*
Armstrong, Brenda Estelle *pediatric cardiologist, educator*
Bennett, Peter Brian *researcher, hyperbaric medicine*
Blazer, Dan German, II, *psychiatrist, epidemiologist*
Blazing, Michael August *internist*
Bollinger, Ralph Randal *surgeon, researcher*
Bradford, William Dalton *pathologist, educator*
Brodie, Harlow Keith Hammond *psychiatrist, educator, former university president*
Buckley, Charles Edward, III, *physician, educator*
Buckley, Rebecca Hatcher *allergist, immunologist, pediatrician, educator*
Burks, A. Wesley *pediatrics educator*
Carter, James Harvey *psychiatrist, educator*
Cohen, Harvey Jay *hematologist, oncologist, educator*
Coleman, Ralph Edward *nuclear medicine physician, educator*
Coppridge, Alton James *urological surgeon*
Dawson, Jeffrey Robert *immunology educator*
Dawson, Robert Edward, Sr., *ophthalmologist*
Edwards, Christopher Levon *medical association administrator*
Falletta, John Matthew *pediatrician, educator*
Foreman, John William *pediatrician, educator*
Frank, Michael M. *physician*
Freemark, Michael Scott *pediatric endocrinologist, educator*
George, Timothy Merrill *neurosurgeon*
Greenfield, Joseph Cholmondeley, Jr., *physician, educator*
Hamilton, Michael A. *medical educator*
Hammond, Charles Bessellieu *obstetrician, gynecologist, educator*
Harmel, Merel Hilber *anesthesiologist, educator*
Harris, Jerome Sylvan *pediatrician, pediatrics and biochemistry educator*
Heinz, E(dward) Ralph *neuroradiologist, educator*
James, Sherman Athonia *social epidemiologist, educator*
Katz, Samuel Lawrence *pediatrician, researcher*
Kirshner, Norman *pharmacologist, researcher, educator*
Klitzman, Bruce *physiologist, plastic surgery educator, researcher*
Koepke, John Arthur *hematologist, clinical pathologist*
Krishnan, Ranga Rama *psychiatrist*
Kurtzberg, Joanne *pediatrics educator*
Lack, Leon *pharmacology and biochemistry educator*
Lee, Paul P. *ophthalmologist, educator, consultant, lawyer*
Lefkowitz, Robert Joseph *physician, educator*
Levin, Lawrence Scott *plastic surgeon*
London, William Lord *pediatrician*
Marchuk, Douglas Alan *medical educator*
Mark, Daniel Benjamin *cardiologist*
Markert, Mary Louise *pediatrics educator*
Massey, Ben F., Jr., *medical association administrator*
Means, Anthony Ross *pharmacology educator*
Michener, James Lloyd *medical educator*
Miller, David Edmond *physician*
Murphy, Barbara Anne *emergency physician, surgery educator*
Murphy, Thomas Miles *pediatrician, educator*
Osterhout, Suydam *internist, educator*
Page, Bernadette Ryan *emergency physician*
Pinnell, Sheldon Richard *dermatologist, researcher, retired educator*
Pizzo, Salvatore Vincent *pathologist*
Prosnitz, Leonard R. *radiologist*
Ravin, Carl Eric *radiologist, educator, department chairman*
Robboy, Stanley J. *pathologist, educator*
Sabiston, David Coston, Jr., *surgeon, educator*
Schmechel, Donald E. *medical educator*
Serafin, Donald *plastic surgeon, educator*
Shelburne, John Daniel *pathologist*
Silvertooth, Erin J. *preventive medicine physician*
Soper, John Tunnicliff *obstetrician-gynecologist, educator*
Spach, Madison Stockton *cardiologist, educator*
Tedder, Thomas Fletcher *immunology educator, researcher*
Thompson, William Moreau *radiologist, educator*
Vaslef, Steven Nicholas *surgeon*
Warner, David Samuel *anesthesiologist, educator*
Weiner, Richard David *psychiatrist, researcher*
Wells, Samuel Alonzo, Jr., *surgeon, educator*
Wilkins, Robert Henry *neurosurgeon, educator, editor*
Willard, Huntington F. *medical association administrator, medical geneticist*
Williams, Redford Brown *medical educator*
Yancy, William Samuel *pediatrician*

Fairview
Gaffney, Thomas Edward *physician*

Fayetteville
Lowe, James Edward, Jr., *plastic and reconstructive surgeon*

Four Oaks
Jordan, Lyndon Kirkman *family practice physician*

Gastonia
Prince, George Edward *retired pediatrician*

Greensboro
Ganji, Jagadeesh (Jay Ganji) *cardiologist*
Hensel, William Arthur *family physician*
Houston, Frank Matt *dermatologist*
Stevens, Elliott Walker, Jr., *allergist, cardiologist, pulmonologist*

Greenville
Johnson, Cynda Ann *physician, educator*
Lee, Kenneth Stuart *neurosurgeon, educator*
Perkin, Ronald Murray *pediatrician, educator*
Pories, Walter Julius *surgeon, educator*
Saeed, Sy Atezaz *psychiatrist, physician*
Tingelstad, Jon Bunde *retired pediatrician, educator*
Winn, Francis John, Jr., *medical educator*

Hendersonville
Reinhart, John Belvin *retired child and adolescent psychiatrist, educator*
Roberts, James Allen *urologist*

Hickory
Lefler, Wade Hampton, Jr., *ophthalmologist*

High Point
Bardelas, Jose Antonio *allergist*
Cullom, Joseph William *surgeon*
Draelos, Zoe Diana *dermatologist, consultant*
Kandt, Raymond S. *neurologist*
Williams, Lawrence D. *surgeon*

Hillsborough
Johnston, William Webb *pathologist, educator*
Wallace, Andrew Grover *physician, educator, medical school dean*

Hope Mills
Henley, Douglas E. *medical association administrator*

Lincolnton
Gamble, John Reeves, Jr., *surgeon*

Lumberton
Jackson, Anita Louise *otolaryngologist, editor-in-chief*

Matthews
Freeman, Tyler Ira *physician*

Mebane
Langley, Ricky Lee *occupational medicine physician*

Monroe
Taylor, Jimmy Lynn *retired family practice physician, administrator*

Morehead City
Drury, Bradford David *surgeon*

New Bern
McKee, Francis John *medical association consultant, lawyer*
Sinning, Mark Alan *thoracic and vascular surgeon*

Otto
Able, Luke William *pediatric surgeon, consultant*

Pinehurst
Bussey, George Davis *psychiatrist*

Pisgah Forest
Kempe, Ludwig George *neurological surgeon*

Raeford
Abreu, Sue Hudson *physician, army officer, organizational and healthcare consultant*

Raleigh
Barish, Charles Franklin *internist, gastroenterologist, researcher*
Garrett, Leland Earl *nephrologist, educator*
Hughes, Francis P. *medical organization executive*
Levine, Ronald H. *physician, educator*
Parsons, William Jonathan *cardiologist*
Riviere, Jim Edmond *pharmacologist, educator, toxicologist*
Speer, Kevin Paul *surgeon*

Research Triangle Park
Qualls, Charles Wayne, Jr., *research pathologist*
Roses, Allen David *neurologist, educator*

Roanoke Rapids
Adiga, Giridhar U. *geriatrician, pharmacologist, researcher, internist*

Rocky Mount
Hendrix, Robert A. *otolaryngologist*

Roxboro
Olds, William Bellamy *physician*

Salisbury
Crowe, John Albert, Jr., *surgeon*

Salter Path
Wiley, Albert Lee, Jr., *physician, engineer, educator*

Southern Pines
Haserick, John Roger *retired dermatologist*

Spencer
Kiser, Glenn Augustus *retired pediatrician, investor*

Thomasville
Sprinkle, Robert Lee, Jr., *podiatrist*

Waynesville
McKinney, Alexander Stuart *retired neurologist*

Whispering Pines
Enlow, Donald Hugh *anatomist, educator, university dean*

Wilmington
De Maria, Alfred Anthony *neurologist*
Solomon, Robert Douglas *pathology educator*
Wilkins, Lucien Sanders *gastroenterologist*

Wilson
Kushner, Michael James *neurologist, consultant, educator*
Ladwig, Harold Allen *neurologist*

Winston Salem
Alexander, Eben, Jr., *neurological surgeon*
Bleecker, Eugene R. *internist, educator*
Butterworth, John Fauntleroy, IV, *anesthesiologist*
Clarkson, Thomas Boston *comparative medicine educator*
Dean, Richard Henry *surgeon, educator*
Donofrio, Peter Daniel *neurology educator*
Georgitis, John *allergist, educator*
Graham, Gloria Flippin *dermatologist*
Harle, Thomas Stanley *radiologist*
Henrichs, W(alter) Dean *dermatologist*
Hopkins, Judith Owen *oncologist*
Howell, Charles Maitland *dermatologist*
James, Francis Marshall, III, *anesthesiologist*
Jorizzo, Joseph L. *dermatology educator*
Kelly, David Lee, Jr., *neurosurgeon, educator*
Kohut, Robert Irwin *otolaryngologist, educator*
Little, William Campbell *cardiologist, physiologist*
Matlaga, Brian Richard *physician*
Maynard, Charles Douglas *radiologist*
Meis, Paul Jean *obstetrics and gynecology educator*
Moody, Dixon McGuire *radiologist*
Mueller-Heubach, Eberhard *medical educator*
Olympio, Michael Allen *anesthesiologist, researcher*
O'Steen, Wendall Keith *neurobiology and anatomy educator*
Peters, Stephen Paul *medical educator*
Pitovski, Dimitri Zivko *otolaryngologist, educator*
Pittaway, Donald Edward *endocrinology educator, gynecologist*
Podgorny, George *emergency physician*
Simon, Jimmy Louis *pediatrician, educator*
Stein, Barry Edward *medical educator*
Toole, James Francis *medical educator*
Torti, Frank Michael *physician, healthcare administrator*
Uhl, Henry Stephen Magraw *internist, educator*

NORTH DAKOTA

Bismarck
Schwartz, Judy Ellen *cardiothoracic surgeon*

Fargo
Mitchell, James Edward *physician, educator*

Grand Forks
Carlson, Edward C. *anatomy educator*
Lerma, Edgar Villaneuva *nephrologist*
Siegel, Mark Bernard *surgeon*

Sobus, Kerstin MaryLouise *physician, physical therapist*

Williston
Adducci, Joseph Edward *obstetrician, gynecologist*
Naranja, Rogelio Darusin, Sr., *psychiatrist*

OHIO

Akron
Aldana, Philipp Roque *neurosurgeon*
Allen, Marc Kevin *emergency physician, educator*
Bird, Forrest M. *retired medical inventor*
Emmett, John Colin *retired inventor, consultant*
Evans, Douglas McCullough *surgeon, educator*
Houston, Alma Faye *psychiatrist*
Levy, Richard Philip *physician, educator*
Milsted, Amy *biomedical educator*
Mubashir, Bashar A. *internist, oncologist, hematologist*
Seiwald, Robert J. *retired inventor*
Timmons, Gerald Dean *pediatric neurologist*

Aurora
Su, Sunyu *MRI scientist*

Beachwood
Moskowitz, Roland Wallace *internist*

Bellefontaine
Graber, Harry Lee *internist*

Bexley
Yashon, David *neurosurgeon, educator*

Brecksville
Ventenilla, Aurora Curamen *psychiatrist*

Brunswick
Kuchynski, Marie *physician*

Bryan
Carrico, Virgil Norman *physician*

Canfield
Price, William Anthony *psychiatrist*

Canton
Howland, Willard J. *radiologist, educator*
Kellermeyer, Robert William *physician, educator*
Nadas, John Adalbert *psychiatrist, educator*
Rubin, Patricia *internist*
Starchman, Dale Edward *medical educator*

Chagrin Falls
Bloser, Dieter *radiologist*
Lingl, Friedrich Albert *psychiatrist*

Chardon
Dobyns, Brown McIlvaine *surgeon, educator*
Kellis, Michael John *osteopathic physician*

Chillicothe
El-Zawahry, M.A. Moneim *retired epidemiologist, tropical medicine specialist*

Cincinnati
Adolph, Robert J. *physician, medical educator*
Alexander, James Wesley *surgeon, educator*
Balistreri, William Francis *pediatric gastroenterologist*
Baughman, Robert Phillip *physician*
Bell, Thomas Edwin *urologist, educator*
Bellet, Paul Sanders *pediatrician, educator*
Boat, Thomas Frederick *pediatrician, researcher, pulmonologist, educator*
Bommireddy, Ramireddy *immunologist, researcher*
Bower, Robert Hewitt *surgeon, educator, researcher*
Chin, Nee Oo Wong *reproductive endocrinologist*
Collins, Margaret Helen *pathologist*
Creaghead, Nancy A. *medical association administrator*
Cudkowicz, Leon *medical educator*
Datta, Sukdeb *anesthesiologist, pain management specialist*
De Courten-Myers, Gabrielle Marguerite *neuropathologist*
DeWitt, Thomas *pediatrician, educator*
Dunsker, Stewart B. *physician, neurosurgeon*
Eckman, Mark H. *physician, educator*
Finkelman, Fred D. *medical educator*
Gelfand, Michael Joseph *radiology educator*
Gerson, Myron Craig *cardiologist, researcher*
Greenwalt, Tibor Jack *physician, educator*
Griffith, John Francis *pediatrician, administrator, educator*
Heaton, Charles Lloyd *dermatologist, educator*
Heimlich, Henry J. *physician, surgeon, educator*
Hess, Evelyn Victorine *medical educator*
Heubi, James Edward *pediatrician, educator*
Ivey, Tom Dexter *cardiac surgeon*
Kereiakes, Dean James *cardiologist*
Khan, Sohaib Ahmed *cancer researcher, molecular cell biology educator*
Kulwin, Dwight Robert *surgeon, educator*
Kuntz, Charles, IV, *neurological surgeon*
Levinson, Joseph E. *physician, emeritus educator*
Loggie, Jennifer Mary Hildreth *medical educator, physician*
Lucas, Stanley Jerome *retired radiologist, physician*
Lucky, Anne Weissman *dermatologist*
Luse, Kimberly Ann *radiologic technologist, educator*
Maltz, Robert *surgeon*
Nasrallah, Henry Ata *psychiatry researcher, educator*
Neale, Henry Whitehead *plastic surgery educator*
Putnam, Frank William, Jr., *medical researcher*
Rapoport, Robert Morton *medical educator*
Rashkin, Mitchell Carl *internist, pulmonary medicine specialist*
Rudich, Steven Mark *surgeon*
Ryan, Richard J. *emergency medicine physician*
Sacher, Ronald Alan *hematologist*
Schreiner, Albert William *physician, educator*
Sherman, Kenneth Eliot *medicine educator, researcher*
Shott, Sally Richard *otolaryngologist*
Spinnato, Joseph Anthony, II, *obstetrician*
Thomas, Michael A. *endocrinologist, gynecologist*
Vilter, Richard William *internist, educator*
Welsh, George Franklin *plastic surgeon, educator, healthcare consultant*
West, Clark Darwin *pediatric nephrologist, educator*
Whitsett, Jeffrey Allen *pediatric educator*
Williams, Daniel Bryan *obstetrician/gynecologist, educator*
Wiot, Jerome Francis *radiologist*
Wood, Robert Emerson *pediatrics educator*
Wright, Creighton Bolter *cardiovascular surgeon, educator*
Zuccarello, Mario *neurosurgeon, researcher*

Cleveland
Abughali, Nazha *pediatrician, consultant*
Agani, Faton Hilmi *anatomist, educator*
Anderson, James M. *pathologist*
Awais, George Musa *obstetrician, gynecologist*
Badal, Daniel Walter *psychiatrist, educator*
Baker, Saul Phillip *geriatrician, cardiologist, internist*
Barnett, Gene Henry *neurosurgeon*
Bause, George Stephen Loneraven *anesthesiologist*
Berger, Melvin *allergist, immunologist*
Bodner, Donald Roger *urologist, medical educator*
Bowerfind, Edgar Sihler, Jr., *retired physician, medical administrator*
Boyd, Arthur Bernette, Jr., *surgeon, clergyman, beverage company executive*
Brody, Robert *dermatologist, educator*
Bronson, David Leigh *physician, educator*
Bruner, William Evans, II, *ophthalmologist, educator, researcher*
Budd, John Henry *physician*
Castele, Theodore John *radiologist*
Chae, Han *medical researcher*
Chao, Jason *family physician, educator*
Cola, Philip Andrew *research administrator*
Collis, John Stanley *neurosurgeon*
Cooper, Gregory Scott *epidemiologist, gastroenterologist, educator*
Cowan, Dale Harvey *internist, lawyer*
Daroff, Robert Barry *neurologist, educator*
Davis, Pamela Bowes *pediatric pulmonologist*
Doershuk, Carl Frederick *pediatrician, pediatrics educator*
Dweik, Raed A. *physician, researcher, educator*
Eiben, Robert Michael *pediatric neurologist, educator*
Ellis, Lloyd H., Jr., *emergency physician, art historian*
Esselstyn, Caldwell Blakeman, Jr., *physician*
Falcone, Tommaso *reproductive endocrinologist*
Fanaroff, Avroy A. *pediatrician, educator*
Fazio, Victor Warren *physician, colon and rectal surgeon*
Fei, Baowei *biomedical researcher*
Gambetti, Perluigi *pathologist*
Harding, Clifford Vincent, III, *medical educator*
Hermann, Robert Ewald *retired surgeon*
Holzbach, Raymond Thomas *gastroenterologist, educator, writer*
Horwitz, Ralph Irving *internist, medical educator, epidemiologist*
Jackson, Edgar B., Jr., *medical educator*
Kashyap, Vikram S. *vascular surgeon, military officer*
Kass, Lawrence *hematologist, oncologist, educator, hematopathologist*
Lamm, Michael Emanuel *pathologist, immunologist, educator*
Lefferts, William Geoffrey *internist, educator*
Luce, Edward Andrew *plastic surgeon*
Macklis, Roger Milton *physician, educator, researcher*
Malangoni, Mark Alan *surgeon, educator*
McCrae, Keith R. *medical educator, researcher*
McHenry, Martin Christopher *physician, educator*
McQuarrie, Irvine Gray *neurosurgeon, educator*
Medalie, Jack Harvey *physician*
Meziane, Moulay Ahmed *physician*
Minai, Omar Ahmad *physician*
Montague, Drogo K. *urologist*
Moravec, Christine D. Schomis *medical educator*
Neuhauser, Duncan vonBriesen *medical educator*
Novick, Andrew Carl *urologist*
Olness, Karen Norma *pediatrics and international health educator*
Ornt, Daniel B. *physician*
Papay, Francis Anthony *plastic surgeon, researcher*
Pina, Ileana *medical educator*
Pretlow, Thomas Garrett *physician, pathology educator, researcher*
Raaf, John Hart *surgeon, health facility administrator, educator*
Raghavan, Derek *oncologist, medical researcher and educator*
Rakita, Louis *cardiologist, educator*
Ransohoff, Richard Milton *neurologist, researcher*
Ratcheson, Robert Allan *neurological surgeon*
Ratnoff, Oscar Davis *physician, educator*
Rehm, Susan *physician*
Rose, Peter Graham *gynecologic oncologist*
Ruff, Robert Louis *neurologist, physiology researcher*
Scarpa, Antonio *medical educator, researcher, physiologist*
Schwartz, Michael Alan *physician*
Shuck, Jerry Mark *surgeon, educator*
Stange, Kurt C. *medical educator*
Stanton-Hicks, Michael D'Arcy *anesthesiologist, pain medicine specialist*
Stavitsky, Abram Benjamin *immunologist, educator*
Steinmetz, Michael Patrick *physician, neurosurgeon*
Stern, Robert C. *pediatrician, medical educator*
Strome, Marshall *otolaryngologist, educator*
Tetzlaff, John Edwin *physician*
Trapp, Bruce D. *neurologist*
Utian, Wulf Hessel *gynecologist, endocrinologist*
Walters, Mark Douglas *obstetrician, gynecologist*
Webster, Leslie Tillotson, Jr., *pharmacologist, educator*
Wish, Jay Barry *nephrologist, specialist*
Wolfman, Alan *medical educator, researcher*
Wolinsky, Emanuel *physician, educator*
Young, Jess Ray *retired internist*

Cleveland Heights
Byramjee, Aspi Minoo *surgeon*

Columbus
Balcerzak, Stanley Paul *hematologist, oncologist, director, retired medical educator*
Barth, Rolf Frederick *pathologist, educator*
Berntson, Gary Glen *psychiatry, psychology and pediatrics educator*
Beversdorf, David Quentin *neurologist, researcher*
Billings, Charles Edgar *physician*
Bloomfield, Clara Derber *oncologist, medical institute administrator*
Boudoulas, Harisios *physician, educator, researcher*
Boué, Daniel Robert *pediatric pathologist, neuropathologist, educator*
Bullock, Joseph Daniel *pediatrician, educator*
Christoforidis, A. John *radiologist, educator*
Cordle, Christopher T. *immunologist, race boat driver*
Cramblett, Henry Gaylord *pediatrician, virologist, educator*
Dull, Pamela *physician, educator*
Eaton, Antoinette Joan *pediatrician*
Ellison, Edwin Christopher *surgeon, educator*
Fass, Robert J. *epidemiologist, academic administrator*
Ferguson, Ronald Morris *surgeon, educator*
Furste, Wesley Leonard, II, *surgeon, educator*
Gahbauer, Reinhard A. *physician*
Gravlee, Glenn P(age) *anesthesiologist, educator*
Hansen, Thomas Nanastad *pediatrician, health facility administrator*
Haque, Malika Hakim *pediatrician*
Hilliard, Kirk Loveland *osteopathic physician, educator*
Huheey, Marilyn Jane *ophthalmologist, educator*
Kakos, Gerard Stephen *thoracic and cardiovascular surgeon*
Kukielka, Gilbert Leon *physician*
Ladinsky, Morissa Jean *medical educator, pediatrician*
Lander, Ruth A. *medical group and association administrator*
Laufman, Leslie Rodgers *hematologist, oncologist*
Leier, Carl Victor *internist, cardiologist*
Lewis, Richard Phelps *cardiologist, educator*
Long, Sarah Elizabeth Brackney *physician*
Magro, Cynthia Maria *pathologist*
McClung, Hugo Juhling *pediatrician, educator*
Morrison, Ashton Byrom *pathologist, medical school official*
Morrow, Grant, III, *medical research director, pediatrician*
Moser, Debra Kay *medical educator*
Mueller, Charles Frederick *radiologist, educator*
Munson, Robert Sydney *biomedical researcher*
Nappi, James Francis *hand surgeon, educator*
Newton, Herbert Bruce *neuro-oncologist*
Newton, William Allen, Jr., *pediatric pathologist*
Peterson, Larry James *medical educator, oral surgeon*
Rund, Douglas Andrew *emergency physician*
St. Pierre, Ronald Leslie *medical and public health educator, university administrator*
Sayers, Martin Peter *pediatric neurosurgeon*
Senhauser, Donald A(lbert) *pathologist, educator*
Sommer, Annemarie *pediatrician*
Speicher, Carl Eugene *pathologist*
Tzagournis, Manuel *endocrinologist, educator, retired dean, academic administrator*
Vogel, Thomas Timothy *surgeon, educator, lay worker*
Wexler, Randy *medical educator*
Whitacre, Caroline Clement *immunologist, researcher*
Wolfe, Claire V. *physiatrist*
Yu, Chack Yung *pediatrics educator, molecular biologist*
Zhao, Fang Li *medical researcher*

Dayton
Abromowitz, Herman I. *family physician, occupational medicine physician*
Dunn, Margaret M. *general surgeon, educator, university official*
Gillig, Paulette Marie *psychiatry educator, researcher*
Heller, Abraham *psychiatrist, educator*
Hitch, David Charles *pediatric surgeon*
Lee, Sung Ho *psychiatrist*
Lyman, John Leslie *emergency physician*
Maugans, Todd Allen *pediatric neurosurgeon*
Mohler, Stanley Ross *physician, educator*
Monk, Susan Marie *pediatrician, educator*
Nanagas, Maria Teresita Cruz *pediatrician, educator*
Pflum, Barbara Ann *pediatrician, allergist*
Ruegsegger, Donald Ray, Jr., *radiological physicist, educator*
Weinberg, Sylvan Lee *cardiologist, educator, author, editor*
Williams, Craig Foster *osteopathic emergency physician*
Wilson, William Campbell McFarland *gastroenterologist*
Wyderski, Richard Joseph *internist*

Edgerton
Wu, Lawrence Mg Hla Myin *physician*

Fairborn
Krane, Dan E *DNA expert, education educator*

Fairfield
Wilson, James Miller, IV, *cardiovascular surgeon, educator*

Fairview Park
Kothari, Purnima *obstetrician/gynecologist*

Galena
Berggren, Ronald Bernard *surgeon, retired educator*

Gallipolis
Senthil Nathan, Selvaraj *internist, geriatrician*

Grove City
Kilman, James William *surgeon, educator*

Hudson
Morris, Jeffrey Selman *orthopedic surgeon*

Kent
Ference-Valenta, Mary Jean *osteopath, health facility administrator*

Lancaster
Woodward, James Kenneth *retired pharmacologist*

Lima
Becker, Dwight Lowell *physician*

Madison
Stafford, Arthur Charles *medical association administrator*

Mansfield
Adair, Charles Valloyd *retired physician*
Houston, William Robert Montgomery *ophthalmic surgeon*

Mason
Beary, John Francis, III, *rheumatologist, researcher, pharmaceutical executive*

Massillon
Dishong, Morris William *forensic investigator, nurse*

Nelsonville
Davis, Mary W. Allen *medical secretary*

Newark
Pacht, Eric Reed *pulmonary and critical care physician*

North Canton
Di Simone, Robert Nicholas *radiologist, educator*

Norwalk
Gutowicz, Matthew Francis, Jr., *radiologist*

Portsmouth
Akhtar, Muhammad I. *neurologist, researcher*

Richfield
Pelagalli, James A. *surgeon*

Rootstown
Blacklow, Robert Stanley *internist, educator*
Brodell, Robert Thomas *internal medicine educator*
Campbell, Colin *obstetrician, gynecologist, school dean*
Nora, Lois Margaret *neurologist, educator, academic administrator, dean*

Saint Marys
Dallura, Sal Anthony *physician*

Shaker Heights
Smith, Jonathan David *medical educator*
White, Eugene A. *retired physician, neuroradiologist*

Springfield
Kurian, Pius *nephrologist, educator*

Steubenville
Reddy, Vardhan Jonnala *surgeon*

Sylvania
Burkhart, Craig Garrett *dermatologist*

Toledo
Alexander, Kenneth Saul *pharmaceuticals educator*
Barrett, Michael John *anesthesiologist*
Cardwell, Michael Steven
Comerota, Anthony James *vascular surgeon, biomedical researcher*
Goodenday, Lucy Sherman *physician, educator*
Howard, John Malone *surgeon, educator*
Jacobs, Lloyd A. *vascular surgeon*
Knotts, Frank Barry *physician, surgeon*
Lawrence, Edmund Pond, Jr., *neurosurgeon*
Martin, John Thomas *physician, author, educator*
Medhkour, Azedine *neurosurgeon, educator*
Mulrow, Patrick Joseph *medical educator*
Rejent, Marian Magdalen *retired pediatrician*
Shelley, Walter Brown *physician, educator*
Zrull, Joel Peter *psychiatry educator*

Troy
Savage, Joseph Scott *physician*

Uniontown
Krabill, Robert Elmer *osteopathic physician*

Westerville
Dawdy, W. David *pediatrician*

Willoughby
Carter, John Robert *physician*
Combs, Steven Paul *orthopedic surgeon*

Worthington
Winter, Chester Caldwell *physician, surgery educator, historian, writer*

Wright Patterson Afb
Reston, Rocky Russell *anesthesiologist, engineer, educator*

Yellow Springs
Von Gierke, Henning Edgar *biomedical science educator, former government official, researcher*

Youngstown
Ragland, Thomas Eugene *osteopath, protective services official*
Walton, Ralph Gerald *psychiatrist, educator*

Zanesville
Kopf, George Michael *retired ophthalmologist*
Ray, John Walker *otolaryngologist, educator, broadcast commentator*

OKLAHOMA

Ada
Mynatt, Cecil Ferrell *psychiatrist*

Altus
Stine, Earle John, Jr., *radiologist*

Claremore
Whinery, Michael Albert *physician*

Edmond
Haywood, B(etty) J(ean) *anesthesiologist*

Guymon
Lim, Jeffrey James *internist*

Kingfisher
Buswell, Arthur Wilcox *physician, surgeon*

Lawton
Webb, Orville Lynn *retired physician, pharmacologist, educator*

Muskogee
Kent, Bartis Milton *retired physician*

Norman
Cochran, Gloria Grimes *retired pediatrician*
Dille, John Robert *retired physician*

Oklahoma City
Andrews, M. Dewayne *dean, internist, educator*
Bahr, Carman Bloedow *internist*
Bogardus, Carl Robert, Jr., *radiologist, educator*
Bozalis, John Russell *physician*
Brandt, Edward Newman, Jr., *physician, educator*
Claflin, James Robert *pediatrician, allergist*
Comp, Philip Cinnamon *medical researcher*
Couch, James Russell, Jr., *neurology educator*
Everett, Mark Allen *dermatologist, educator*
Felton, Warren Locker, II, *surgeon*
Filley, Warren Vernon *allergist*
George, James Noel *hematologist, oncologist, educator*
Gilchrist, John Mark *otolaryngologist*
Halverstadt, Donald Bruce *urologist, educator*
Hampton, James Wilburn *hematologist, medical oncologist*
Jacocks, Mac Alexander *surgeon*
Johnson, Thomas Harold *radiologist*
Lo, Patrick Punchuk *physician*
Moffett, Sulinda *nursing association administrator*
Nour, Bakr M. *surgeon, health facility administrator*
Oehlert, William Herbert, Jr., *cardiologist, administrator, educator*
Pardo, Gabriel *neuro-ophthalmologist, neurologist, researcher*
Parke, David Wilkin, II, *ophthalmologist, educator, healthcare executive*
Pelofsky, Stan *neurosurgeon, educator*
Perez-Cruet, Jorge *physician, psychopharmacologist, psychophysiologist, psychiatrist, educator, addictionologist, geropsychiatrist*
Pfefferbaum, Betty Jane *psychiatrist, educator*
Prodan, Calin Ioan *physician*
Rahhal, Donald K. *obstetrician, gynecologist*
Robison, Clarence, Jr., *surgeon*
Rossavik, Ivar Kristian *obstetrician, gynecologist*
Skuta, Gregory Louis *ophthalmologist, educator*
Thadani, Udho *physician, cardiologist*
Wisdom, Peggy Jean *neurologist*
Wolraich, Mark Lee *pediatrician, educator*
Worsham, Bertrand Ray *psychiatrist*
Zuhdi, Nazih *former surgeon, administrator*

Owasso
Reed, Walter George, Jr., *osteopathic physician*

Shawnee
Wilson, Robert Godfrey *radiologist*

Stillwater
Cooper, Donald Lee *physician*

Tulsa
Brunk, Samuel Frederick *oncologist*
Calvert, Jon Channing *physician, department chairman*
de Leon, Antonio Carmelo, Jr., *retired internist, cardiologist*
Friedman, Mark Joel *cardiologist, educator*
Gregg, Lawrence J. *physician*
Kalbfleisch, John McDowell *cardiologist, educator*
Liebendorfer, Richard Arthur *internist*
McCullough, Robert Dale, II, *osteopath*
Nettles, John Barnwell *obstetrics and gynecology educator*
Nevinny-Stickel, Hans Boris *oncologist*
Plunket, Daniel Clark *pediatrician, department chairman*
Say, Burhan *physician*
Sherburn, Eric W. *neurosurgeon*
Wortmann, Dorothy Woodward *physician*

Vinita
Neer, Charles Sumner, II, *orthopedic surgeon, educator*

Weatherford
Wolgamott, Gary Dean *medical educator*

OREGON

Beaverton
Austin, Glenn *retired pediatrician, medical researcher*

Bend
Brundage, Bruce Howard *cardiologist*
Thow, George Bruce *surgeon*

Corvallis
Steele, Robert Edwin *orthopedic surgeon*

Eugene
Biglan, Anthony *medical educator*
Collis, Dennis K. *orthopedic surgeon*
Flanagan, Latham, Jr., *surgeon*
Jewell, Mark Laurence *plastic surgeon*
Loescher, Richard Alvin *gastroenterologist*
Roe, Thomas Leroy Willis *pediatrician*

Hillsboro
Abtin, Keyvan *neurosurgeon*

Klamath Falls
Novak, James F. *physician*

Lake Oswego
Hutchens, Tyra Thornton *physician, educator*
Thong, Tran *biomedical company executive*

Medford
Shekhar, Stephen S. *obstetrician, gynecologist*

Milwaukie
Sklovsky, Robert Joel *naturopathic physician, pharmacist, educator*

North Plains
Wood, James Anderson *cardiac surgeon*

Ontario
Tyler, Donald Earl *urologist*

Oregon City
Burke, William Romney *urologist*

Portland
Baker, Diane R.H. *dermatologist*
Bardana, Emil John, Jr., *allergist, immunologist, internist*
Barkhuizen, Andre *academic rheumatologist*
Barry, John Maynard *urologist*
Bennett, William Michael *internist, nephrologist, educator*
Berthelsdorf, Siegfried *psychiatrist*
Blank, Eugene *pediatrician, radiologist, educator*
Bouchard, Joan C. *nursing association administrator*
Burris, Terry Eugene *ophthalmologist, corneal specialist*
Connor, William Elliott *physician, educator*
Crawshaw, Ralph *psychiatrist*
Druker, Brian Jay *medical educator, researcher*
Fraunfelder, Frederick Theodore *ophthalmologist, educator*
Greer, Monte Arnold *endocrinologist, educator*
Guderian, Ronald Howard *pathologist*
Hedges, Jerris *medical educator, health services researcher*
Jacob, Stanley Wallace *surgeon, educator*
Julien, Robert Michael *anesthesiologist, writer*
Kendall, John Walker, Jr., *medical educator, researcher, university dean*
Kohl, Steve *pediatrician, infectious disease physician*
Kohler, Peter Ogden *internist, educator, academic administrator*
Layman, Charles Donald *plastic surgeon*
MacArthur, Carol Jeanne *pediatric otolaryngology educator*
Matejuk, Agata *immunologist*
Moorhead, John Couper *emergency physician*
Patterson, James Randolph *physician*
Prendergast, William John *ophthalmologist*
Press, Edward *consulting physician*
Riddle, Matthew C(asey) *physician, educator*
Robertson, Joseph E., Jr., *ophthalmologist, educator*
Rosenberg, Kenneth David *epidemiologist*
Schmidt, Waldemar Adrian *pathologist, educator*
Schumacher, Maria *biomedical researcher, educator*
Schwartz, Martin Lerner *physician*
Scott, John D. *pharmacologist*
Sells, Clifford Wayne *pediatrician*
Smith, Dennis B. *neurologist, educator*
Stevens, Wendell Claire *retired anesthesiology educator*
Sutherland, Donald Wood *cardiologist*
Swan, Kenneth Carl *surgeon*
Taylor, Robert Brown *medical educator, physician, writer*
Tolle, Susan W. *internist, educator, educational administrator*
Vernon, Jack Allen *otolaryngology educator, laboratory administrator*
Weleber, Richard Gordon *ophthalmologist, geneticist, medical educator, researcher*
Zerbe, Kathryn Jane *psychiatrist*
Zerzan, Charles Joseph, Jr., *retired gastroenterologist*

Roseburg
Oliphant, Charles Romig *retired physician*

Silverton
Centerwall, Willard Raymond *pediatrician, educator*

Wilsonville
Johnson, Martin Clifton *physician*

PENNSYLVANIA

Abington
Eskin, David J. *cardiologist*

Aliquippa
Twerski, Abraham Joshua *psychiatrist*

Allentown
Barrett, Stephen *psychiatrist, educator, consultant*
Gaylor, Donald Hughes *surgeon, educator*
Hess, Leonard Wayne *obstetrician gynecologist, perinatologist*
Khubchandani, Indru Tekchand *colon and rectal surgeon*
Lester, Mark Charles *neurosurgeon*
Maffeo, Alphonse A. *anesthesiologist*
Rienzo, Robert James *radiologist*
Weinstock, Michael S. *emergency physician, department chairman*

Allison Park
Hollerman, Charles Edward *retired pediatrician*

Altoona
Fochler, Francis John *surgeon*

Ardmore
Goodrich, Edward Olin *surgeon, educator*

Bakerstown
Beachley, Michael Charles *radiologist*

Bala Cynwyd
Chiusano, Michael Augustus *urologic surgeon, mechanical engineer*
Kirschner, Ronald Allen *osteopathic plastic surgeon, otolaryngologist, educator*
Masket, Samuel *medical association administrator*
Ringpfeil, Fraziska *dermatologist*

Bangor
Wolf, Stewart George, Jr., *physician, medical educator*

Berwick
Fiero, Patrick *physician*

Bethlehem
Benz, Edward John, Sr., *clinical pathologist*
Chang, Chris C.N. *pediatric surgeon*
Cole, Jack Eli *physician*
Rosenfeld, Joel Charles *surgeon*

Braddock
Lebovitz, Charles Neal *surgeon*

Bryn Mawr
Brunt, Manly Yates, Jr., *psychiatrist*
Huth, Edward Janavel *internist, educator, editor*
Levitt, Robert E. *gastroenterologist*
Noone, R. Barrett *plastic surgeon*
Price, Trevor Robert Pryce *psychiatrist, educator*

Camp Hill
Brouse, John S. *medical association administrator*
Swamidoss, Stephenson *pathologist, health facility administrator*
Tokuhata, George K. *retired medical educator, epidemiologist, consultant*
Yates, James Arthur *plastic surgeon*

Cecil
Keddie, Roland Thomas *physician, hospital administrator, lawyer*

Chalfont
Pederson, Linda Lue *epidemiologist, researcher*

Chester Springs
Scheer, R. Scott *physician*

Coatesville
Ainslie, George William *psychiatrist, behavioral economist*
Bell, Robert Lloyd *retired neurosurgeon*
Lee, Daniel *retired physician, public health service officer*
Makous, Norman *internist, cardiologist, educator*

Collegeville
Neylan, John Francis, III, *nephrologist, educator, scientist*
Stiles, Gary Lester *cardiologist, molecular pharmacologist, educator*

Conshohocken
Jacoby, Richard Allen *pathologist, dermatologist*
Johnson, Waine Cecil *dermatologist*

Danville
Bakri, Younes Noaman *surgeon, oncologist, gynecologist*
Cochran, William John *physician, pediatrician, gastroenterologist, nutritionist, consultant*
Franklin, David Perdue *vascular surgeon, educator*
Pierce, James Clarence *surgeon, educator*
Steele, Glenn Daniel, Jr., *oncologist, healthcare system executive*

Darby
Eiser, Arnold Robert *bioethicist, nephrologist, internist*

Devon
Porter, Roger John *medical research executive, educator, neurologist, pharmacologist*

Dillsburg
Jackson, George Lyman *retired nuclear medicine physician*

Downingtown
Newman, Richard August *psychiatrist, educator*

Doylestown
McGarvey, Joseph F. X., Sr., *cardiologist*

Dunmore
Sebastianelli, Mario Joseph *internist, nephrologist, health services administrator*

East Berlin
Greer, Robert Bruce, III, *retired orthopedic surgeon, educator*

Easton
Grunberg, Robert Leon Willy *nephrologist, educator*

Elizabethtown
Geder, Laszlo *retired neurologist, educator*

Elkins Park
Yun, Daniel Duwhan *physician, foundation administrator*

Erie
Mason, Gregg Claude *orthopedic surgeon, researcher*
Michaelides, Doros Nikita *internist, medical educator*

Etters
Garloff, Samuel John *psychiatrist*

Fort Washington
Pappas, Charles Engelos *plastic surgeon*

Forty Fort
Kopen, Dan Francis *surgeon, consultant*

Gaines
Beller, Martin Leonard *retired orthopaedic surgeon*

Gibsonia
Cauna, Nikolajs *physician, medical educator, scientist*
Krause, Helen Fox *otolaryngologist*

Gladwyne
Harkins, Herbert Perrin *otolaryngologist, educator*
Kaye, Donald *physician, educator*
Morrison, Gail *internist, nephrologist, educator*

Glenside
Reiss, George Russell, Jr., *physician*

Greensburg
Catalano, Louis William, Jr., *neurologist*
Kathuria, Nirmal Bhatia *psychiatrist*

Harrisburg
Cadieux, Roger Joseph *physician, mental health care executive*
Chernicoff, David Paul *osteopathic physician, educator*
Logue, James Nicholas *epidemiologist*

Haverford
Aronson, Carl Edward *pharmacology and toxicology educator*
Goppelt, John Walter *physician, psychiatrist*
Rosefsky, Jonathan Benensohn *pediatrician*

Havertown
Korényi-Both, András Levente *pathologist, educator*

Hershey
Adams, David R. *dermatologist*
Ballard, James Otis, III, *medical educator, physician*
Davis, Dwight *cardiologist, educator*
Domen, Ronald Eugene *physician*
Fyster, Mary Elaine *hematologist, educator*
Kees-Folts, Deborah *pediatrician, educator*
Leaman, David Martin *cardiologist, educator*
Madewell, John Edward *radiologist*
Marks, James Garfield, Jr., *dermatologist*
Marshall, Wayne Keith *anesthesiology educator*
Naeye, Richard L. *pathologist, educator*
Naides, Stanley J. *physician, educator, researcher*
Ouyang, Ann *physician, researcher, educator*
Pierce, William Schuler *cardiac surgeon*
Severs, Walter Bruce *pharmacology educator, researcher*
Tan, Tjiauw-Ling *psychiatrist, educator*
Uhde, Thomas Whitley *psychiatry educator, psychiatrist*
Vesell, Elliot Saul *pharmacologist, educator*
Waldhausen, John Anton *retired surgeon, educator, editor*
Wassner, Steven Joel *pediatric nephrologist, educator*
Zelis, Robert Felix *cardiologist, educator*

Hollidaysburg
Cottle, Harold Ranson *pathologist, laboratory owner*

Huntingdon Valley
Lefton, Harvey Bennett *gastroenterologist, educator, author*

Irwin
Brown, Donald Clyde *surgeon*

Jenkintown
Greenspan-Margolis, June E. *psychiatrist*
Sadoff, Robert Leslie *psychiatrist, educator*

Kingston
Denaro, Anthony Thomas *psychiatrist*

Lancaster
Brod, Roy David *ophthalmologist, educator*
Burlingame, Mark Wayne *cardiothoracic surgeon*
Falk, Robert Barclay, Jr., *anesthesiologist, educator*
Kendall, Leigh Wakefield *surgeon*
Lu, Milton Ming-Deh *plastic surgeon, consultant*
Rung, George W. *physician*

Lemoyne
Klein, Michael Elihu *physician*
Vickery, Jon Livingstone *neurologist*

Lower Gwynedd
Pendleton, Robert Grubb *pharmacologist*

Malvern
Rucker, Donald W. *emergency physician, educator, consultant*

Mc Murray
Diamond, Daniel Lloyd *surgeon*

Merion Station
Lewis, Paul Le Roy *pathology educator*

Mohnton
Hildreth, Eugene A. *physician, educator*

Mount Pleasant
Domit, John *surgeon*

Narberth
Chait, Arnold *retired radiologist*
Comer, Nathan Lawrence *psychiatrist, educator*
Goldstein, Martin Barne *osteopathic physician, psychiatrist*
Strom, Brian Leslie *internist, educator*

New Hope
Raabe, Gerhard Karl *epidemiologist*

New Tripoli
Hess, Darla Bakersmith *cardiologist, educator*

Newtown
Somers, Anne Ramsay *retired medical educator*

Newtown Square
de Rivas, Carmela Foderaro *retired psychiatrist, retired health facility administrator*
Lawrence, Theodore *physician*

Norristown
Garabedian, Joseph Andre *physician*

Olyphant
Batzel, Edward Lee *surgeon*

Philadelphia
Abrams, Charles S. *oncologist, hematologist, educator*
Amsterdam, Jay D. *psychiatrist, department chairman*
Arce, A. Anthony *psychiatrist, educator*
Asbury, Arthur Knight *neurologist, educator*
Aston-Jones, Gary S. *psychiatry educator*
Austrian, Robert *internist, medical educator, department chairman*
Ballard, Roberta A. *pediatrics educator*
Baltuch, Gordon Hirsh *neurosurgeon*
Barchi, Robert Lawrence *clinical neurologist, neuroscientist, educator*
Barker, Clyde Frederick *surgeon, educator*
Baserga, Renato Luigi *pathology educator*
Baum, Stanley *radiologist, educator*
Baxt, William Gordon *medical educator*
Bearn, Alexander Gordon *physician, researcher, retired pharmaceutical executive*
Beck, Aaron Temkin *psychiatrist, educator*
Beck, John Robert *pathologist, information scientist*
Bergelson, Jeffrey Michael *pediatrician, educator*
Berrettini, Wade H. *psychiatry educator*
Bibbo, Marluce *physician, educator*
Bigelow, Douglas C. *otolaryngologist*
Bilaniuk, Larissa Tetiana *neuroradiologist, educator*
Bjärngard, Bengt Erik *medical educator*
Black, Perry *neurological surgeon, educator*
Bleshman, Michael Henry *radiologist*
Bluemle, Lewis William, Jr., *medical educator*
Boden, Guenther *endocrinologist*
Bove, Alfred Anthony *medical educator*
Bowman, Marjorie Ann *family practice physician, educator*
Brady, Luther W., Jr., *physician, radiation oncology educator*
Brodeur, Garret M. *oncologist*
Broennle, A. Michael *anesthesiologist*
Brooks, John Samuel Joseph *pathologist, researcher*
Cassel, Christine Karen *physician*
Cawley, Michael J. *medical educator, pharmacist*
Clark, Christopher Michael *neurologist, educator, clinic director*
Clearfield, Harris Reynold *physician*
Colman, Robert Wolf *physician, medical educator, researcher*
Conn, Rex Boland, Jr., *physician, educator*
Cooper, Edward Sawyer *cardiologist, internist, educator*
Dalinka, Murray Kenneth *radiologist, educator*
Daly, John M. *surgeon, educator*
D'Angio, Giulio John *radiologist, educator*
Danzon, Patricia M. *medical educator*
Dasgupta, Indranil *physician, educator*
Dichter, Marc Allen *physician*
Dinoso, Vicente Pescador, Jr., *physician, educator*
DiPalma, Joseph Rupert *pharmacology educator*
Djerassi, Isaac *physician, medical researcher*
Dormans, John Paul *surgeon, educator*
Douglas, Steven Daniel *immunologist, educator, director*
Dunn, Linda Kay *physician*
Ehrlich, George Edward *rheumatologist, international pharmaceutical consultant*
Eisen, Howard Joel *internist, researcher*
Eisenberg, Burton L. *surgeon*
El-Deiry, Wafik S. *medical educator*
Eskin, Bernard Abraham *obstetrics and gynecology educator, medical researcher*
Esterhai, John Louis, Jr., *surgeon, medical educator*
Feldman, Arthur M. *cardiologist*
Feldman, Michael Saul *cardiologist, educator*
Ferrari, Victor Alfred *cardiologist*
Fisher, Robert *gastroenterologist, health facility administrator*
Fishman, Alfred Paul *physician*
FitzGerald, Garret Adare *medical educator*
Foti, Margaret *medical association administrator, editor, consultant*
Fraker, Douglas L. *oncologist, endocrinologist, surgeon, educator*
Frank, Barbara Balis *gastroenterologist, educator*
Friedman, Harvey Michael *infectious diseases educator*
Gaiser, Robert Raymond *obstetric anesthesiologist, educator*
Gardner, Timothy Joseph *surgeon, educator*
Gartland, John Joseph *physician, writer*
Gary, Nancy Elizabeth *nephrologist, academic administrator*
Glick, Jane Mills *biomedical researcher, educator*
Glick, John H. *oncologist, medical educator*
Goldberg, Martin *physician, educator*
Goldhamer, David J. *medical educator, researcher*
Gonnella, Joseph Salvator *medical educator, university dean and official, consultant, researcher*
Gonzalez-Scarano, Francisco Antonio *neurologist, virologist*
Gordon, Susan Joan *physician, educator*
Greenstein, Jeffrey Ian *neurologist*
Gueson, Emerita Torres *obstetrician, gynecologist*
Gulati, Gene L. *hematologist, educator, consultant*
Hallock, James Anthony *pediatrician, health facility administrator*
Hanks, Gerald E. *oncologist*
Hansen-Flaschen, John Hyman *medical educator, researcher*
Hargrove, Walter Clark, III, *cardiothoracic surgeon*
Hernandez, Enrique *gynecologist, educator*
Hillman, Alan L. *internist, educator, researcher*
Holzbaur, Erika L. *medical educator*
Hosalkar, Harish Sadanand *pediatrician, orthopedist, surgeon, consultant*
Hussain, M. Mahmood *medical educator*
Ildstad, Suzanne T. *transplant surgeon, immunologist, educator*
Ischiropoulos, Harry *medical researcher, educator*
Jackson, Laird Gray *internist, educator*
Jacobs, Eugene Gardner, Jr., *psychiatrist, psychotherapist, educator*
Jensh, Ronald Paul *anatomist, educator*
Jimenez, Sergio A. *internist, science educator, rheumatologist*
Johnson, Joseph Eggleston, III, *physician, educator*
Joseph, Rosaline Resnick *hematologist and oncologist*
June, Carl H. *pathologist, educator*
Kahn, Sandra J. *anesthesiologist*
Kaiser, Larry Robert *thoracic surgeon*
Katz, Julian *gastroenterologist, educator*
Kauffman, Leon A. *internist, educator*
Kaufman, Russel Eugene *hematologist, oncologist*
Kazanjian, Haig Hagop, Jr., *pediatrician, researcher, educator*
Kefalides, Nicholas Alexander *physician, educator*
Kelley, William Nimmons *physician, educator, science administrator, dean*
Kennedy, David William *otolaryngologist, educator, medical educator*
Kim, Kwan Eun *nephrologist, educator*
Kligerman, Morton M. *radiologist*
Knudson, Alfred George, Jr., *medical geneticist*
Kresh, J. Yasha *cardiovascular researcher, educator*
Kurtz, Alfred Bernard *radiologist*
Lee, Virginia M. Y. *medical educator, health science association administrator*
Le Roux, Peter David *neurosurgeon*
Leventhal, Lawrence Jay *rheumatologist, educator*
Levin, David C. *radiologist, educator, medical educator*
Levin, Ronald Mitchell *geriatrician*
Levinson, Arnold Irving *allergist, immunologist*
Levit, Edithe Judith *physician*
Levitt, Jerry David *medical educator*
Lewis, Frank Russell, Jr., *surgeon*
Li, Weiye *ophthalmologist, educator, biochemist*
Lippa, Carol Frances *neurologist*
Lipshutz, Laurel Sprung *psychiatrist*
Long, Sarah Sundborg *pediatrician, educator*
Longnecker, David Eugene *anesthesiologist, educator*
Lubiniecki, Gregory Michael *physician*
Ma, Xin-Liang *biomedical researcher, educator*
Madow, Leo *psychiatrist, educator*
Malkowicz, Stanley Bruce *urologist*
Mancall, Elliott Lee *neurologist, educator*
Marcotte, Paul John *neurosurgeon, educator*
Margo, Katherine Lane *family physician, educator*
Marino, Ignazio Roberto *transplant surgeon, educator, researcher*
Mastroianni, Luigi, Jr., *physician, educator*
Maurer, Alan Harvey *nuclear medicine physician*
Mayock, Robert Lee *internist*
McDonald, Walter J. *internist*
Ming, Si-Chun *pathologist, educator*
Monos, Dimitrios *medical educator, researcher*
Morrow, Monica *medical educator*
Most-Levin, Carol Lynn *physician, geriatrician*
Mulholland, S. Grant *urologist*
Myers, Allen Richard *rheumatologist*
Nash, David Bret *physician*
Nimoityn, Philip *cardiologist*
Norris, Charles Morgan *laryngologist, educator*
Nowell, Peter Carey *pathologist, educator*
O'Brien, Charles P. *psychiatrist, educator*
O'Malley, Bert William, Jr., *head and neck surgeon, educator, researcher*
Owens, Gary Mitchell *physician, educator, health facility administrator*
Pack, Allan I. *medical educator*
Permut, Stephen Robert *physician, lawyer*
Platsoucas, Chris Dimitrios *immunologist*
Potsic, William Paul *physician, educator*
Pugliese, Maria Alessandra *psychiatrist*
Pyeritz, Reed Edwin *medical geneticist, educator, research director*
Rabinowitz, Howard K. *physician, educator*
Randall, Peter *plastic surgeon*
Reddy, Eragam Premkumar *medical educator*
Rickels, Karl *psychiatrist, educator*
Ritchie, Wallace Parks, Jr., *retired surgeon, educator*
Ritter, Deborah Elizabeth *anesthesiologist, educator*
Rogers, Fred Baker *medical educator*
Rorke-Adams, Lucy Balian *pathologist, educator*
Rosen, Arye *microwave, optoelectronics and medicine researcher*
Ross, Leonard Lester *anatomist, educator*
Rovera, Giovanni Aurelio *medical educator, scientist*
Rubin, Stephen Curtis *gynecologic oncologist, educator*
Russo, Irma Haydee Alvarez de *pathologist*
Sabili, Erlinda Asa *internist, psychiatrist, pastoral care minister*
Saulino, Michael Francis *physiatrist*
Savage, Michael Paul *medicine educator, interventional cardiologist*
Scheff, Alice Mellors *nuclear medicine physician*
Schless, Guy Lacy *endocrinologist*
Schotland, Donald Lewis *retired medical educator, neurologist*
Schumacher, H(arry) Ralph *internist, rheumatologist, medical educator, researcher*
Schwartz, Gordon Francis *surgeon, educator*
Schwartz, Marshall Zane *pediatric surgeon*
Segal, Bernard Louis *physician, educator*
Sevy, Roger Warren *retired pharmacology educator*
Sharan, Ashwini D. *neurosurgeon, researcher*
Sheaffer, Steven L. *medical association administrator, medical educator*
Shields, Jerry Allen *ophthalmologist, educator*
Shore, Eric Eugene *internist, consultant, lawyer*
Silberberg, Donald H. *neurologist*
Silberman, Edward Kenneth *physician, educator*
Simpkins, Henry *medical educator*
Slipman, Curtis W. *rehabilitation medicine physician*
Smith, David Stuart *anesthesiology educator, physician*
Sox, Harold Carleton, Jr., *physician, educator, editor*
Spaeth, George Link *physician, ophthalmology educator, writer, educator*
Steinberg, Marvin Edward *orthopaedic surgeon, educator*
Strauss, Jerome Frank, III, *reproductive endocrinologist, educator*
Stuart, Marie Jean *physician, hematologist, researcher*
Stunkard, Albert James *psychiatrist, educator*
Sudak, Howard Stanley *physician, psychiatry educator*
Suzuki, Jon Byron *medical educator, periodontist, microbiologist*
Talerman, Aleksander *pathologist, educator*
Tannen, Richard Laurence *medical educator, nephrologist*
Tasman, William Samuel *ophthalmologist, educator*
Torg, Joseph Steven *orthopaedic surgeon, educator*
Tourtellotte, Charles Dee *internist, rheumatologist, educator*
Truant, Allan L. *medical educator, laboratory scientist, health science association administrator*
Vaccaro, Alexander R. *orthopedist, surgeon*
Van Arsdalen, Keith Norman *urologist*
Vergare, Michael J. *psychiatrist, department chairman*
Volgin, Denys V. *medical researcher*
Waldman, Scott Arthur *medical educator, medical association administrator*
Wang, Yen *nuclear medicine physician, radiologist*
Webber, John Bentley *orthopedic surgeon*
Wein, Alan Jerome *urologist, educator, researcher*
Weller, Elizabeth Boghossian *child and adolescent psychiatrist*
Whitaker, Linton Andin *plastic surgeon*
Willi, Steven Matthew *physician, educator, researcher*
Wivel, Nelson Auburn *physician, medical researcher, educator*
Yanoff, Myron *ophthalmologist*
Young, Donald Stirling *clinical pathology educator*
Young, Terri L. *ophthalmologist*
Yunginger, John W. *allergist*
Zorowitz, Richard David *physiatrics educator*
Zweiman, Burton *physician, scientist, educator*

Pittsburgh
Allen, Thomas E. *obstetrician, gynecologist*
Brito, Maximo Oscar *epidemiologist*
Busquets, Miguel Antonio *ophthalmologist*
Caritis, Steve Nick *obstetrician, gynecologist, educator*
Chang, Yuan *neuropathologist, researcher, educator*
Chengappa, Roy K. N. *psychiatrist, educator*
Cockerham, Kimberly Peele *ophthalmologist, educator*
Contractor, Farhad M. *diagnostic radiologist, educator*
Cooper, William Marion *physician*
Craig, Fiona Elizabeth *pathologist*
Culig, Michael H. *cardiologist, surgeon*
deGroat, William Chesney *pharmacology educator*
DeKosky, Steven Trent *neurologist*
Detre, Thomas *psychiatrist, educator*
Dixit, Balwant Narayan *pharmacology and toxicology educator*
Doria, Cataldo *transplant surgeon*
Einhorn, Jerzy *internist, endocrinologist, consultant*
Fireman, Philip *pediatrician, allergist, immunologist*
Fisher, Bernard *surgeon, educator*
Fisher, Edwin R. *pathologist*
Fontes, Paulo A. *surgeon, educator*
Frank, Ellen *medical educator, psychiatrist, psychologist, researcher*
Frezza, Ermenegildo Eldo *physician, surgeon*
Friday, Gilbert Anthony, Jr., *pediatrician*
Heckler, Frederick Roger *plastic surgeon*
Herberman, Ronald Bruce *medical research administrator, immunologist*
Jannetta, Peter Joseph *neurosurgeon, educator*
Joyner, Claude Reuben, Jr., *physician, medical educator*
Kalnicki, Shalom *radiologist, educator*
Kane-Gill, Sandra Lucille *medical educator*
Karol, Meryl Helene *medical educator, researcher, health facility administrator, science educator*
Kent, Georgia L. *obstetrician-gynecologist, healthcare executive, educator*
Klunk, William Edward *psychiatrist, educator*
Kochanek, Patrick Michael *pediatrician, educator*
Kondziolka, Douglas *neurosurgeon*
Kupfer, David J. *psychiatry educator*
Lasorda, David Michael *cardiologist*
Levine, Arthur Samuel *pediatric hematologist and oncologist, researcher, dean, educator*
Levine, Macy Irving *physician*
Lowery, Willa Dean *obstetrician, gynecologist*
Lyjak Chorazy, Anna Julia *pediatrician, medical administrator, educator*
MacLeod, Gordon Kenneth *physician, educator*
Magovern, James Anthony *thoracic surgeon*
McCafferty, Leo Raymond *plastic surgeon*
Meltzer, Carolyn Cidis *neuroradiology educator*
Merenstein, Joel Harvey *physician, researcher*
Mitre, Blima Kirmayer *pathologist, educator*
Moore, Patrick S. *epidemiologist, researcher, educator*
Mulsant, Benoit Henri *psychiatry educator, medical researcher*
Myers, Eugene Nicholas *otolaryngologist, educator*
Needleman, Herbert Leroy *psychiatrist, pediatrician*
Paterson, David Leslie *epidemiologist*
Perel, James Maurice *pharmacology and psychiatry educator, researcher*
Phillips, William Watson *gastroenterologist*
Pollock, Bruce Godfrey *psychiatrist, educator*
Roth, Loren H. *psychiatrist*
Rubin, Robert Terry *psychiatrist, researcher, educator*
Sanfilippo, Joseph Salvatore *physician, reproductive endocrinologist, educator*
Serene, Harry E. *surgeon*
Sherman, Frederick Scott *pediatric cardiologist*
Siker, Ephraim S. *anesthesiologist*
Simmons, Richard L. *surgeon*
Stanger, Robert Henry *psychiatrist, educator*
Starzl, Thomas Earl *physician, educator*
Swerdlow, Steven Howard *hematopathologist*
Toledo, Frederico Granchi Steidel *physician, scientist*
Vogel, Victor Gerald *medical educator, researcher*
Wald, Arnold *gastroenterologist*
Wald, Niel *public health educator*
Welch, William Charles *neurosurgeon*
Wenger, Sharon Louise *pediatrics educator, researcher, cytogeneticist*
Winter, Peter Michael *anesthesiologist, educator*
Zehel, Wendell Evans *surgeon*
Zitelli, Basil J. *pediatrician, educator*

Plymouth Meeting
Nobel, Joel J. *biomedical researcher*

Port Carbon
Boran, Robert Paul, Jr., *orthopedic surgeon*

Radnor
Templeton, John Marks, Jr., *retired pediatric surgeon, foundation executive*

Reading
Brigham, Robert Allan *surgeon, educator*
Lusch, Charles Jack *oncologist*

Sayre
Gu, Jeng Yul *radiologist*
Moody, Robert Adams *neurosurgeon*

Scranton
Rhiew, Francis Changnam *radiologist, physician*

Sellersville
Hollander, Irwin Joel *pathologist, educator*
Rilling, David Carl *surgeon*

Sewickley
Munoz, Alfredo Nectario *emergency medicine physician, pediatrician*

Somerset
Nair, Velupillai Krishnan *cardiologist*

Springfield
Arsht, Edwin David *physician*
Sing, Robert Fong *physician*

State College
Wilson, Keith B. *rehabilitation educator*

Swarthmore
Carey, William Bacon *pediatrician, educator*

Thorndale
Hodess, Arthur Bart *cardiologist*

Upper Darby
Toney, Angela M. *medical administrator and educator*

Upper Saint Clair
Raymond, Bruce Allen *medical association administrator*

Vandergrift
Bullard, Ray Elva, Jr., *retired psychiatrist, hospital administrator*

Warren
Bergstein, Jack Marshall *surgeon*

Wayne
Burget, Dean Edwin, Jr., *plastic surgeon*
Lief, Harold Isaiah *psychiatrist*

Waynesboro
Cryer, Theodore Hudson *ophthalmologist, educator*
Kirk, Daniel Lee *retired physician, consultant*

West Point
Chang, Raymond S. L. *pharmacologist*
Dorsey, Bruce David *medical researcher, research scientist*

Wilkes Barre
Casale, Alfred Stanley *thoracic and cardiovascular surgeon*
Schiowitz, Mark F. *surgeon*

Williamsport
Gouldin, Judith Ann *nuclear medicine physician*

Wyndmoor
Brown, Gary Christian *ophthalmologist, director*

Wynnewood
Alter, Milton *retired neurologist*
Brady, John Paul *psychiatrist*
Clarke, John Rodney *surgeon*
Frankl, William Stewart *cardiologist, educator*
Kenton, Edgar Jackson, III, *neurologist*

Wyomissing
Smith, Raymond Leigh *plastic surgeon*

Yardley
Fraser, David William *epidemiologist*
Newsom, John Harlan *family physician*

RHODE ISLAND

Barrington
Carpenter, Charles Colcock Jones *internist, educator*

Block Island
Gasner, Walter Gilbert *retired dermatologist*

East Providence
Guggenheim, Frederick Gibson *psychiatry educator*
Parziale, John R. *physiatrist*

Kingston
Mahammad, Riyaz Basha *biomedical researcher*

Pawtucket
Chopra, Pradeep *physician, educator*
Crowley, James Patrick *hematologist, medical educator, immunologist*
Friedman, Joseph Harold *neurologist*
Glicksman, Arvin S(igmund) *radiation oncologist*
Kiessling, Louise Sadler *pediatrician, medical educator*

Providence
Amaral, Joseph Ferreira *surgeon*
Aronson, Stanley Maynard *physician, educator*
Besdine, Richard William *medical educator, researcher*
Biron, Christine Anne *medical science educator, researcher*
Block, Stanley Hoyt *pediatrician, allergist*
Braman, Sidney Stuart *internist, educator*
Bristow, Lonnie Robert *physician*
Cady, Blake *surgical oncologist*
Davis, Robert Paul *physician, educator*
DiGiovanni, Christopher William *orthopedic surgeon*
Donahue, John Edward *physician*
Easton, J(ohn) Donald *neurologist, educator*
Erikson, G(eorge) E(mil) (Erik Erikson) *anatomist, archivist, historian, educator, information specialist*
Gilchrist, James Manning *neurologist, researcher, educator*

Gnepp, Douglas Robbin *pathologist*
Hamolsky, Milton William *physician*
Jackson, Benjamin Taylor *retired surgeon, educator, medical facility administrator*
Jenny, Carole *physician, researcher*
Kane, Agnes Brezak *pathologist, educator*
Knopf, Paul Mark *immunoparasitologist, neuro-immunologist*
Lewis, David Carleton *medical educator, university center director*
Magendantz, Henry Guenther *physician*
Mc Donald, Charles J. *dermatologist, educator*
Merlino, Anthony Frank *orthopedist*
Oh, William *physician*
Pueschel, Siegfried M. *pediatrician, educator*
Roesler, Thomas Allen *psychiatrist, researcher*
Shetty, Taranath *neurologist, educator*
Tracy, Thomas Francis, Jr., *pediatric surgeon, resarcher, educator*
Vezeridis, Michael Panagiotis *surgeon, educator*
Weitberg, Alan Barry *physician, researcher*

South Kingstown
Pembrook, Richard Charles *internist, cardiologist*

Wakefield
Fera, Steven Raymond *internist, cardiologist, educator*

Warwick
Lowe, David Alan *epidemiologist*

Westerly
Bachmann, William Thompson *dermatologist*

SOUTH CAROLINA

Anderson
Chipman, Dennis Clarence, Jr., *psychiatrist, consultant*
Woodall, Hunter Earl *physician, educator*

Charleston
Bell, Norman Howard *physician, endocrinologist, educator*
Brown, Carroll Smith *anesthesiologist*
Carek, Donald J(ohn) *child psychiatry educator*
Carter, James Folger *obstetrician-gynecologist, educator, consultant*
Chiaramida, Salvatore *cardiologist, educator, health facility administrator*
Daniell, Herman Burch *pharmacologist*
Dobson, Richard Lawrence *dermatologist, educator*
Finn, Albert Frank, Jr., *physician*
Hainer, Barry L. *physician*
Hoffman, Brenda Joyce *gastroenterology educator*
Hogan, Edward Leo *neurologist*
Jaffa, Ayad A. *medical educator, medical researcher*
Jaffe, Murray Sherwood *retired surgeon*
Kaplan, Allen P. *immunologist, educator, allergist, researcher*
Key, Janice Dixon *physician, medical educator*
Maize, John Christopher *dermatologist, educator*
Margolius, Harry Stephen *pharmacologist, physician*
Maricq, Hildegard Rand *physician, researcher*
Mayfield, Ronald Keith *endocrinologist, educator*
McCurdy, Layton *medical educator*
Mohr, Lawrence Charles *physician*
Oldham, John Michael *physician, psychiatrist, educator*
Osguthorpe, John David *otolaryngologist, educator*
Othersen, Henry Biemann, Jr., *surgeon, physician, educator*
Reves, Joseph Gerald *dean, anesthesiology educator*
Rustin, Rudolph Byrd, III, *surgeon, educator*
Saul, J. Philip *pediatrician, educator*
Schuman, Stanley Harold *epidemiologist, educator*
Simson, Jo Anne *retired anatomy and cell biology educator, biologist, educator*
Spinale, Francis G. *medical educator, research cardiologist*
Stuart, Robert Kenneth *internist, oncologist, hematologist, educator*
Underwood, Paul Benjamin *gynecologist, oncologist, educator*
Vela, Marcelo Fernando *gastroenterologist*
Waller, John Louis *anesthesiology educator*
Wilson, Frederick Allen *medical educator, medical center administrator, gastroenterologist*

Columbia
Almond, Carl Herman *surgeon, physician, educator*
Brooker, Jeff Zeigler *cardiologist*
Bryan, Charles Stone *internal medicine educator*
Cruikshank, Stephen Herrick *physician, consultant*
Cuffe, Steven Paul *psychiatrist*
da Silva, Ercio Mario *physician*
Donald, Alexander Grant *psychiatrist, educator*
Flanagan, Clyde Harvey, Jr., *psychiatrist, psychoanalyst, educator*
Horger, Edgar Olin, III, *obstetrics and gynecology educator*
Humphries, John O'Neal *physician, educator, university dean*
Hwang, Te-Long *neurologist, educator*
Sheppe, Joseph Andrew *surgeon*
Shmunes, Edward *dermatologist*
Still, Charles Neal *neurologist, consultant*
Sutherland-Abel, Anne Elizabeth *pediatrician*
Thornhill, Joshua Taylor, IV, *psychiatrist, academic administrator*
Wright, Harry Hercules *psychiatrist*

Conway
Delia, Claude William *retired physician, pathologist*

Florence
Agnew, Samuel Gerard *orthopaedic traumatologist*
Imbeau, Stephen Alan *allergist*

Fripp Island
Metcalf, David Roy *retired pediatrician*

Georgetown
Sprinkle, Ralph Stephen *podiatrist*

Greenville
Bonner, Jack Wilbur, III, *psychiatrist, educator, administrator*
Dreskin, Erving Arthur *pathologist, educator*
Hogg, Judith E. *neurologist, educator*
Kilgore, Donald Gibson, Jr., *pathologist*

Greer
Vaught, Richard Loren *urologist*

Hanahan
Langdale, Emory Lawrence *retired physician*

Hilton Head Island
Birk, Robert Eugene *retired physician, educator*
Duvall, Charles Patton *retired internist, retired oncologist*
Engelman, Karl *physician*
Field, James Bernard *internist, educator*
Hewes, Robert Charles *radiologist*
Humphrey, Edward William *surgeon, educator*
Jarvis, William Robert *epidemiologist, educator*
Roehrig, C(harles) Burns *internist, health policy consultant*
Slachta, Gregory Andrew *urologist*

Isle Of Palms
Elliott, Larry Paul *cardiac radiologist, educator*
Wohltmann, Hulda Justine *pediatric endocrinologist, diabetologist*

Myrtle Beach
Schwartz, Steve Wendelin *physician*

North Charleston
Mintzer, Jacobo E. *physician, researcher*

Orangeburg
Smoak, Randolph Duncan, Jr., *surgeon*

Pawleys Island
Brownlee, Robert Calvin *pediatrician, educator*

Seneca
Uden, David Elliott *cardiologist, educator*

Spartanburg
Parmley, Richard Turner *pediatric hematologist, oncologist*
Sovenyhazy, Gabor Ferenc *surgeon*

Sullivans Island
Brewerton, Timothy David *psychiatrist*

Surfside Beach
Favaro, Mary Kaye Asperheim *pediatrician, writer*

West Columbia
Carter, Saralee Lessman *immunologist, microbiologist*

SOUTH DAKOTA

Aberdeen
Gruca, Pawel Piotr *neuroradiologist*

Sioux Falls
Carpenter, Paul Lynn *cardiologist*
Fenton, Lawrence Jules *pediatric educator*
Jaqua, Richard Allen *pathologist*
Morse, Peter Hodges *ophthalmologist, educator*
Richards, George Alvarez *psychiatrist, educator*
Rossing, David Robert *internist*
Trujillo, Angelina *endocrinologist*
Zawada, Edward Thaddeus, Jr., *physician, educator*

TENNESSEE

Brentwood
Gray, Roland William *pediatrician*

Chattanooga
Alvarez, Richard G. *orthopedist*
Apyan, Paul M. *orthopedist*
Campbell, William O'Neal *retired physician*
Chandra, Channappa *orthopedist*
Enriquez, Manuel Hipolito *physician*
Kaplan, Hyman M. *internist, educator*
Norris, Brent Lane *orthopedist*
Shuck, Edwin Haywood, III, *surgeon*

Fayetteville
Ralston, J. Fred, Jr., *internist*

Franklin
Moessner, Harold Frederic *allergist*
Smolenski, Lisabeth Ann *family practice physician*

Germantown
Lieberman, Phillip Louis *allergist, educator*
Vastagh, George Frederick *physician*

Gray
Combs, Stephen Paul *pediatrician, health facility administrator*

Hendersonville
Burt, Alvin Miller, III, *anatomist, cell biologist, educator, writer*

Jackson
Kamso-Pratt, Jimmy Michael *physician, administrator*
Misulis, Karl Edward *physician*
Swaim, Mark Wendell *hepatologist, molecular biologist, gastroenterologist, educator, photographer*

Jefferson City
Muncy, Estle Pershing *physician*

Johnson City
Adebonojo, Festus O. *medical educator*
Coogan, Philip Shields *pathologist*
Cupp, Horace Ballard *surgeon, educator*
De Witt, Jan A. *emergency medicine physician*
Dunkelberger, Brian Herbert *physician*
Hamdy, Ronald Charles *geriatrician*
Kalin, George Bruno *pathologist, educator*
Kao, Race Li-Chan *medical educator*
Olsen, Martin E. *obstetrician, educator*
Shurbaji, M. Salah *pathologist*

Kingsport
Doty, Robert Douglas, Sr., *retired surgeon*
Grigsby, William P. *surgeon*
Hall, John Richard *surgery educator, researcher*
Mehta, Ashok Vallavdas *pediatric cardiologist*

Knoxville
Acker, Joseph Edington *retired cardiology educator*
DePersio, Richard John *otolaryngologist, plastic surgeon*
Filston, Howard Church *pediatric surgeon, educator*
Graber, Glenn C. *medical educator, educational consultant*
Howard, George Turner, Jr., *retired surgeon*
Kliefoth, A(rthur) Bernhard, III, *neurosurgeon*
Lett, James Chancey *retired surgeon*

Maryville
Howard, Cecil Byron *pediatrician*

Memphis
Amonette, Rex. A. *physician*
Anghelescu, Doralina Lucia *anesthesiologist*
Chesney, Russell Wallace *pediatrician*
Cox, Clair Edward, II, *urologist, medical educator*
Currey, Thomas Arthur *ophthalmologist*
Dagogo-Jack, Samuel E. *medical educator, physician scientist, endocrinologist*
Dickerson, Roland Nelson *pharmacy educator, clinical consultant*
Edmonson, Allen S. *orthopedist*
Eichner, Samantha Foster *medical educator, consultant, writer*
Frey, William Rayburn *healthcare educator, consultant*
Gerald, Barry *retired radiology educator, neuroradiologist*
Godsey, William Cole *physician*
Heimberg, Murray *pharmacologist, biochemist, physician, educator*
Hughes, Walter Thompson *physician, pediatrics educator*
Klesges, Robert C. *medical educator, clinical psychology researcher*
Korones, Sheldon Bernarr *pediatrician, educator*
Lazar, Rande Harris *otolaryngologist*
Martin, Daniel C. *surgeon, gynecologist, educator*
Mauer, Alvin Marx *physician, medical educator*
Morreim, E. Haavi *medical ethics educator*
Mowry, Robert Wilbur *pathologist, educator*
Nienhuis, Arthur Wesley *physician, researcher*
Robertson, James Thomas *neurosurgeon*
Sherr, Charles J. *medical educator*
Shochat, Stephen Jay *pediatric surgeon*
Simone, Joseph Vincent *physician, educator*
Solomon, Solomon Sidney *endocrinologist, pharmacologist, scientist*
Soskel, Norman Terry *physician*
Tonkin, Ina Lynn Dyer *cardiovascular radiologist, educator*
Waller, Robert Rex *ophthalmologist, educator, foundation executive*
Wilcox, Harry Hammond *retired medical educator*
Wingate, Robert Lee, Jr., *internist*

Nashville
Allen, George Sewell *neurosurgery educator*
Allison, Fred, Jr., *internist, retired medical educator*
Baldwin, Harold Scott *pediatrician*
Bates, George William *obstetrician, gynecologist, educator, medical products executive*
Bender, Harvey W., Jr., *cardiac and thoracic surgeon*
Bernard, Louis Joseph *surgeon, educator*
Brigham, Kenneth Larry *medical educator*
Brill, Aaron Bertrand *nuclear medicine educator*
Brown, Wendy Weinstock *nephrologist, educator*
Burk, Raymond Franklin, Jr., *physician, educator, researcher*
Burnett, Lonnie Sheldon *obstetrics and gynecology educator*
Byrd, Benjamin Franklin, Jr., *surgeon, educator*
Byrne, Daniel William *biostatistician, educator*
Carroll, Frank Edward *radiologist, medical researcher*
DeHart, Roy Lynch *physician, educator*
Donnelly, Edwin F. *radiologist*
Elam, Lloyd Charles *psychiatrist, educator*
Epps, Anna Cherrie *immunologist, educator, dean*
Etherington, Carol A. *medical association administrator*
Fazio, Sergio *medical educator, researcher*
Fenichel, Gerald Mervin *neurologist, educator*
Fields, James Perry *dermatologist, dermatopathologist, allergist, pharmacologist, pharmacist*
Fleischer, Arthur C. *medical educator, radiologist*
Foster, Henry Wendell *medical educator*
Franks, John Julian *anesthesiology educator, medical investigator*
George, Alfred L., Jr., *medical educator, researcher*
Graham, Thomas Pegram, Jr., *pediatric cardiologist*
Griffin, Patti Elaine *medical educator, consultant*
Jennings, Henry Smith, III, *cardiologist*
Kirshner, Howard S. *neurologist, medical educator*
Lawton, Alexander Robert *immunologist, educator*
Leftwich, Russell Bryant *allergist, immunologist, consultant*
Lynch, John Brown *plastic surgeon, educator*
Marney, Samuel Rowe, Jr., *immunologist, educator*
Martin, Peter Robert *psychiatrist, pharmacologist*
Mawn, Louise Ann *ophthalmologist, educator*
May, James M. *medical educator, medical researcher*
Morrow, Jason Drew *medical and pharmacology educator*
Moses, Harold L. *oncologist*
Neilson, Eric Grant *physician, educator, health facility administrator*
Oates, John Alexander, III, *medical educator*
O'Day, Denis Michael *ophthalmologist, educator*
Orth, David Nelson *physician, educator, sculptor*
Ossoff, Robert Henry *otolaryngological surgeon*
Petrie, William Marshall *psychiatrist*
Pinson, Charles Wright *transplant surgeon, healthcare administrator, educator*
Ray, Wayne Allen *epidemiologist, educator*
Riley, Harris DeWitt, Jr., *pediatrician, medical educator*
Robertson, David *physician, scientist, educator*
Roden, Dan Mark *clinical pharmacologist, cardiologist, medical educator*
Ross, Joseph Comer *physician, educator, academic administrator*
Saposnik, Ira Stephen *physician, historian*
Schwartz, Herbert S. *surgical oncology educator*
Shack, R. Bruce *plastic surgeon*
Smith, Bradley E. *anesthesiologist*
Spengler, Dan Michael *orthopedic surgery educator, researcher, surgeon*
Stahlman, Mildred Thornton *pediatrics and pathology educator, researcher*
Strupp, John Allen *oncologist*
Sullivan, James Nelson *physician*
Thornton, Spencer P. *ophthalmologist, educator*
van Eys, Jan *retired pediatrician, educator, administrator*
Wasserman, David H. *medical educator, researcher*

Oak Ridge
Spray, Paul Ellsworth *retired surgeon*

Signal Mountain
Swann, Nat Henderson, Jr., *physician*

Smyrna
Moore, Wesley Boyd *occupational physician*

Williamsport
Dysinger, Paul William *preventive medicine physician, educator*

TEXAS

Abilene
Dickerson, Russell Sturges *neurologist*
Morgan, Clyde Nathaniel *dermatologist*

Amarillo
Biggs, William Curtis *endocrinologist*
Laur, William Edward *retired dermatologist*
Marupudi, Sambasiva Rao *surgeon, educator*
Parker, Gerald M. *osteopath, researcher*
Pillai, Narayana Gopalakrishnan *internist, oncologist*
Pratt, Donald George *physician*
Saadeh, Constantine Khalil *internist, health facility administrator, educator*

Aransas Pass
Stehn, Lorraine Strelnick *physician*

Arlington
Adams, Quentin Mark *neurologist*
Kier, Carlos M. *rheumatologist*
Tingley, Floyd Warren *retired internist*

Austin
Bernstein, Robert *retired physician, state official, former army officer*
Elequin, Cleto, Jr., *retired physician*
Ersek, Robert Allen *plastic surgeon, inventor*
Fleeger, David Clark *colon and rectal surgeon*
Ivy, John L. *medical educator, researcher*
Mazzetti, Robert F. *real estate manager, retired orthopedic surgeon*
Painter, Theophilus Shickel, Jr., *internist, allergist*
Schleuse, William *retired psychiatrist, psychoanalyst*
Sutton, Beverly Jewell *psychiatrist*

Baytown
Williams, Drew Davis *surgeon*

Beaumont
Lozano, Jose *nephrologist*
McCord, Michael David *anesthesiologist*
Sooudi, Matthew M. *retired surgeon*

Bedford
Farhat, Georges Antoun *anesthesiologist*

Bellaire
Haywood, Theodore Joseph *physician, educator*
Pokorny, Alex Daniel *psychiatrist*

Bellville
Neely, Robert Allen *retired ophthalmologist*

Boerne
Wittmer, James Frederick *preventive medicine physician, educator*

Brownsville
Imperial, Henry L. *internist*
Walss, Rodolfo J. *obstetrician-gynecologist, artist*

Bryan
Anderson, Frank Gist, Jr., *ophthalmologist, educator*
Dirks, Kenneth Ray *pathologist, medical educator, army officer*

Camp Wood
Triplett, William Carryl *physician, researcher*

Carrollton
Kelly, Ralph Whitley *emergency physician, health facility administrator*

College Station
Kier, Ann Burnette *pathologist*
Tiffany-Castiglioni, Evelyn *biomedical science educator, researcher*

Corpus Christi
Cook, Kenneth Ray *radiologist*
Cox, William Andrew *cardiovascular thoracic surgeon*
Kylstra, Johannes Arnold *physician*
Lim, Alexander Rufasta *neurologist, clinical investigator, clinical neurophysiologist, educator, writer*
Sisley, Nina Mae *physician, public health service officer*
Van Burkleo, Bill Ben *osteopath, emergency physician*

Dallas
Allen, Terry Devereux *retired urologist*
Bashour, Fouad Anis *cardiology educator*
Beck, Jay M. *gynecologist*
Berbary, Maurice Shehadeh *physician, military officer, hospital administrator, educator*

Bergstresser, Paul Richard *dermatologist, educator*
Berry, Phil Hunter *orthopedic surgeon*
Bick, Rodger Lee *hematologist, researcher, oncologist, educator*
Blomquist, Preston Howard *ophthalmologist*
Bonte, Frederick James *radiologist, educator, physician*
Boswell, George Marion, Jr., *orthopedist, health care facility administrator*
Burns, Alton Jay *plastic surgeon*
Burnside, John Wayne *medical educator, university official*
Byrd, Henry Stephenson *plastic surgeon, educator*
Caetano, Raul *psychiatrist, educator*
Carman, George Henry *retired physician*
Cavanagh, Harrison Dwight Dwight *ophthalmic surgeon, medical educator*
Cloud, Robert Royce *surgeon*
Cox, Rody P(owell) *medical educator, internist*
Dees, Tom Moore, II, *internist*
Eichenwald, Heinz Felix *physician*
Einspruch, Burton Cyril *psychiatrist*
Feiner, Joel S. *psychiatrist*
Flatt, Adrian Ede *surgeon*
Fordtran, John Satterfield *physician*
Foster, Daniel Willett *medical educator*
Frenkel, Eugene Phillip *physician*
Friedberg, Errol Clive *pathology educator, researcher*
Gant, Norman Ferrell, Jr., *obstetrician, gynecologist, educator*
Gantt, James Raiford *thoracic surgeon*
Gilman, Alfred Goodman *pharmacologist, educator*
Goldstein, Joseph Leonard *physician, medical educator, molecular genetics scientist*
Grammer, John Colquitte *cardiologist*
Griffeth, Landis King *nuclear medicine physician*
Griffith, Rachel *neonatologist*
Gross, Gary Neil *allergist, physician*
Guy, L(eona) Ruth *medical educator*
Hayes, James Edwin *emergency physician, educator*
Helm, Phala Aniece *physiatrist*
Hilgemann, Donald William *medical educator*
Hinnant, Jerry Herbert *surgeon*
Holman, James *allergist*
Hurd, Eric Ray *rheumatologist, internist, educator*
Idris, Ahamed H. *emergency medicine physician*
Jessen, Michael Erik *surgeon, educator*
Jialal, Ishwarlal *medical educator*
Johnson, Jane Elaine *medical educator*
Johnson, Robert Lee, Jr., *physician, educator, researcher*
Kaiser, Fran Elizabeth *endocrinologist, gerontologist*
Karandikar, Nitin J. *physician, scientist, educator*
Khan, Amanullah *physician*
Kindberg, Shirley Jane *pediatrician*
Lewis, Jerry M. *psychiatrist, educator*
Lichliter, Warren Eugene *surgeon, educator*
Lister, George *pediatrician*
Maddrey, Willis Crocker *medical educator, internist, academic administrator, consultant, researcher*
Margolin, Solomon Begelfor *pharmacologist, consultant*
Martin, Jack *physician*
Mc Clelland, Robert Nelson *surgeon, educator*
Mitchell, Teddy Lee *physician*
Montgomery, Philip O'Bryan, Jr., *pathologist*
Mullins, Charles Brown *physician, academic administrator*
New, William Neil *physician, retired naval officer*
Odom, Floyd Clark *surgeon*
Pakes, Steven P. *medical school administrator*
Perry, Malcolm Oliver *vascular surgeon*
Phillips, Margaret A. *pharmacology educator*
Race, George Justice *pathology educator*
Rainey, William E., II, *medical educator*
Ramsay, Michael Anthony *anesthesiologist*
Romero, Jorge Antonio *neurologist, educator*
Rosenberg, Roger Newman *neurologist, educator, department chair*
Ross, Elliott M. *pharmacologist, researcher, educator*
Rush, Augustus John *psychiatrist, educator*
Sacco, David J. *neurosurgeon*
Salyer, Kenneth E. *surgeon*
Samson, Duke Staples *neurosurgeon*
Schneider, Nancy Reynolds *pathologist, educator*
Seldin, Donald Wayne *physician, educator*
Shapiro, Kenneth N. *neurosurgeon*
Simmang, Clifford Liles *surgeon*
Simon, Theodore Ronald *physician, medical educator*
Sklar, Frederick H. *neurosurgeon*
Smith, Barry Samuel *physiatrist*
Sprague, Charles Cameron *medical foundation president*
Stone, Marvin Jules *physician, educator*
Swift, Dale Matthew *neurosurgeon*
Taliaferro, Ellen *medical educator*
Thomas, James A. *pediatrician*
Thompson, James Nicholas *medical association administrator*
Thompson, Jesse Eldon *vascular surgeon*
Tong, Alex Waiming *immunologist*
Trivedi, Madhukar H. *psychiatrist*
Turner, Ralph James *obstetrician, gynecologist*
Uhr, Jonathan William *immunologist, educator, researcher*
Unger, Roger Harold *physician, scientist*
Van Ness, Paul C. *neurologist, educator*
Waddell, Douglas Howard *family physician*
Wang, Xiaodong *biomedical researcher, educator*
Wasserman, Richard Lawrence *pediatrician, educator*
Weprin, Bradley *neurosurgeon*
Wildenthal, C(laud) Kern *physician, educator*
Wilson, Jean Donald *endocrinologist, educator*
Zhou, Xin (Joseph Zhou) *medical educator*

Danville
Robertson, Rose Marie *cardiologist, educator*

El Paso
Crossen, John Jacob *radiologist, educator*
Harlass, Frederick E. *obstetrician, gynecologist, perinatologist*
Magana, Jorge Carlos *pediatrician*
Mrochek, Michael John *physician*
Mulla, Zuber *epidemiologist*
Simpson, Michael Homer *dermatologist*
Taber, David O. *urological surgeon*
Tyroch, Roxanne Marie *internist, educator*
Williams, Darryl Marlowe *medical educator*
Zaloznik, Arlene Joyce *oncologist, retired military officer*

Fort Sam Houston
Bauman, Wendall Carter, Jr., *ophthalmologist, career officer*
Hewitson, William Craig *physician, career officer*
Kragh, John Frederick, Jr., *orthopedist, educator*

Fort Worth
Bailey, Susan Rudd *physician*
Blanck, Ronald Ray *health science university administrator, internist, military officer*
Bradley, William Texas *neurologist*
Cottner, Donald *pathologist*
Cox, James Sidney *physician*
de Sousa, Byron N.S. *educator, physician, health and medical consultant*
Floyd, Judy Louise Casburn *anesthesiologist, political scientist*
Gillette, Paul Crawford *pediatric cardiologist*
Hahn, Marc B. *osteopath, academic administrator*
Lamensdorf, Hugh *urologist, educator*
Schussler, Irwin *psychiatrist, educator*
Suba, Steven Antonio *obstetrician, gynecologist*
Willard, Ralph Lawrence *surgery educator, physician, former college president*
Yanni, John Michael *pharmacologist*

Frisco
Gajraj, Noor *anesthesiologist, educator*
Hahn, Keith Worden *physiatrist*

Galveston
Bailey, Byron James *otolaryngologist, educator, medical association administrator*
Bello-Reuss, Elsa Noemi *physician, educator*
Bernier, George Matthew, Jr., *oncologist, educator, dean*
Brasier, Allan R. *medical educator*
Bryan, George Thomas *pediatrician, academic administrator*
Burns, Chester Ray *medical history educator*
Calverley, John Robert *physician, educator*
Dawson, Earl Bliss *obstetrics and gynecology educator*
Ernst, Randy *radiologist*
Gold, Daniel Howard *ophthalmologist, educator*
Goodwin, Jean McClung *psychiatrist*
Grant, J(ohn) Andrew, Jr., *medical educator, allergist*
Heggers, John Paul *surgery, immunology and microbiology educator*
Hudnall, Stanley David *pathology and laboratory medicine educator*
James, Thomas Naum *cardiologist, educator*
Mitch, William Evans *nephrologist*
Neugebauer, Volker Egdar *biomedical scientist, neuroscientist, physician*
Nusynowitz, Martin Lawrence *nuclear medicine physician*
Phillips, Linda Goluch *plastic surgeon, educator, researcher*
Sandstead, Harold Hilton *medical educator*
Schreiber, Melvyn Hirsh *radiologist*
Smith, David English *pathologist, educator*
Thompson, James Charles *surgeon*
Townsend, Courtney M. *surgeon*
Vedernikov, Yuri P. *pharmacologist, educator*
White, Robert Brown *medical educator*

Garland
Haynsworth, Robert Francis, Jr., *anesthesiologist*
Hockett, Sheri Lynn *radiologist*

Georgetown
Manning, Robert Thomas *physician, educator*
Sawyer, William Dale *physician, educator, university dean, foundation administrator*

Harlingen
Klein, Garner Franklin *cardiologist, internist*

Houston
Abbruzzese, James Lewis *medical oncologist*
Abramson, Stuart L. *pediatrics, microbiology and immunology educator*
Aguilar-Bryan, Lydia *medical educator, medical researcher*
Alexanian, Raymond *hematologist*
Alford, Bobby Ray *otolaryngologist, educator, academic administrator*
Allen, Steven Jeffrey *anesthesiologist, educator*
Amato, Paula *medical educator*
Appel, Stanley Hersh *neurologist, educator*
Arcilla, Juanita R. *physical rehabilitation physician*
Arens, James F. *anesthesiologist, educator*
Ayus, Juan Carlos *nephrologist*
Bailey, Harold Randolph *surgeon*
Barcenas, Camilo Gustavo *physician*
Barrett, Bernard Morris, Jr., *plastic and reconstructive surgeon*
Baskin, David Stuart *neurosurgeon, educator*
Bast, Robert Clinton, Jr., *medical researcher, medical educator*
Baumgartner, James Edumnd *pediatric neurosurgeon*
Beasley, Robert Palmer *epidemiologist, dean, educator*
Beaudet, Arthur L. *medical genetics researcher*
Bethea, Louise Huffman *allergist*
Bezold, Louis Irving, III, *pediatrician, pediatric cardiologist*
Bier, Dennis M. *medical educator*
Bodey, Gerald Paul *medical educator, physician*
Brenner, Malcolm K. *pediatric and medical educator*
Bricker, John Timothy *pediatric cardiologist*
Brody, Baruch Alter *medical educator, academic center administrator*
Brown, Jacqueline Elaine *obstetrician-gynecologist*
Buja, L. Maximilian *pathologist, academic administrator, educator*
Bungo, Michael William *physician, educator, science administrator*
Burdette, Walter James *surgeon, educator*
Burzynski, Stanislaw Rajmund *internist*
Buster, John Edmond *gynecologist, medical researcher*
Callender, David L. *medical educator, health facility administrator, surgeon*
Carabello, Blase Anthony *cardiology educator*
Catlin, Francis Irving *physician*
Chiou-Tan, Faye *physician, educator*
Clifton, Guy L. *neurosurgeon, educator*
Cooley, Denton Arthur *surgeon, educator*
Couch, Robert Barnard *physician, medical researcher, educator, microbiologist, immunologist*
DeBakey, Michael Ellis *cardiovascular surgeon, educator, scientist*
Deicios-Soler, Luis *medical educator, oncologist*
Deter, Russell Lee, II, *obstetrical ultrasonographer*
DiBardino, Daniel Jude *surgeon, researcher*
Dodd, Gerald Dewey, Jr., *radiologist, educator*
Doubleday, Charles William *dermatologist, educator*
Drutz, Jan Edwin *pediatrics educator*
DuPont, Herbert Lancashire *medical educator, researcher*
Elledge, Stephen Joseph *medical educator*
Engelhardt, Hugo Tristram, Jr., *physician, educator*
Ertan, Atilla *medical educator, physician, researcher, health facility administrator*
Esmaeli, BitA *ophthalmologist*
Esteva, Francisco Javier *physician, researcher*
Evans, Harry Launius *pathology educator*
Feig, Barry W. *surgeon, surgical oncologist*
Feigon, Judith Tova *ophthalmologist, surgeon, educator*
Ferrendelli, James Anthony *neurologist, educator*
Fischer, Craig Leland *physician*
Fisher, Anna Lee *physician, astronaut*
Fishman, Marvin Allen *pediatric neurologist, educator*
Fornage, Bruno Denis *radiologist, educator*
Freireich, Emil J. *hematologist, educator*
Gabbard, Glen Owens *psychiatrist, psychoanalyst*
Gardezi, Syed A. *medical researcher*
Gigli, Irma *dermatologist, educator, academic administrator*
Glassman, Armand Barry *physician, pathologist, scientist, educator, administrator*
Goldman, Stanford Milton *medical educator*
Gorry, G. Anthony *medical educator*
Graham, David Yates *gastroenterologist*
Grossman, Herbert Barton *urologist, researcher*
Grossman, Robert George *neurologist, educator*
Gunn, Albert Edward, Jr., *internist, educator, health facility administrator, lawyer*
Guynn, Robert William *psychiatrist, educator*
Ha, Chul S. *radiation oncologist*
Hall, Robert Joseph *physician, medical educator*
Hamilton, Carlos Robert, Jr., *clinical endocrinologist, educator, university official*
Hanania, Nicola Alexander *physician*
Haney, Peter Michael *pediatrics educator*
Harper, J. Wade *medical educator*
Harrell, James Earl, Sr., *radiologist, educator*
Haynie, Thomas Powell, III, *physician*
Heimberger, Amy Beth *neurosurgeon, researcher*
Herndon, John Wyatt *otolaryngologist*
Heslop, Helen E. *physician, educator, health facility administrator*
Ho, Ching *surgeon*
Hong, Waun Ki *medical oncologist, clinical investigator*
Jandhyala, Bhagavan S. *pharmacology educator*
Jankovic, Joseph *neurologist, educator, scientist*
Jemison, Mae Carol *physician, engineer, entrepreneur, philanthropist, educator, former astronaut*
Jhingran, Anuja *oncologist, educator*
Jones, Edith Irby *physician*
Jordon, Robert Earl *physician*
Juneja, Harinder Singh *hematologist*
Kaplan, Alan Leslie *gynecology educator, oncologist*
Kavanagh, John Joseph *medical educator*
Kelly, Dorothy Helen *pediatrician, educator*
Key, James Everett *ophthalmologist*
Kim, Han-Seob *pathologist*
Kirkland, Rebecca Trent *pediatric endocrinologist*
Kitowski, Vincent Joseph *medical consultant, former physical medicine and rehabilitation physician*
Kline, Mark Wendel *pediatric medicine educator*
Kraft, Irvin Alan *psychiatrist*
Krance, Robert A. *physician, educator, health facility administrator*
Kripke, Margaret Louise *immunologist, health facility executive*
Kutka, Nicholas *nuclear medicine physician*
Lanza, Frank Leo *gastroenterologist, researcher*
Leak, Jessie Aronow *anesthesiologist*
Lepow, Ronald S. *podiatrist*
Levin, Bernard *physician*
Levin, Victor A. *neurologist, oncologist, educator*
Low, Morton David *neuroscientist, educator, policy consultant*
Luna, Mario Armando *pathologist, consultant*
Max, Ernest *surgeon*
Mayor, Heather Donald *medical educator, molecular biologist*
McKechnie, John Charles *gastroenterologist, educator*
McPherson, Alice Ruth *ophthalmologist, educator*
Mendelsohn, John *oncologist, hematologist, educator, health facility executive*
Mentz, Henry A., III, *plastic surgeon*
Merrill, Joseph Melton *medical educator*
Meyer, John Stirling *neurologist, educator*
Milam, John Daniel *pathologist, educator*
Miles, Brian John *urologist*
Miller, Gary Evan *psychiatrist, mental health services professional*
Miller, Geoffrey *child neurologist*
Miller, Robert Harold *otolaryngologist, educator*
Miner, Michael E. *neurosurgery educator*
Mintz-Hittner, Helen Ann *physician, researcher*
Moody, Frank G. *surgeon*
Murad, Ferid *physician*
Murphy, William Alexander, Jr., *diagnostic radiologist, educator*
Nichols, Buford Lee, Jr., *pediatrician, physiologist*
Phung, Nguyen Dinh *medical educator*
Poplack, David G. *pediatric oncologist*
Portman, Ronald Jay *pediatric nephrologist, researcher*
Powers, William Edward *emergency physician, educator*
Rakel, Robert Edwin *internist, educator*
Rao, P. Syamasundar *pediatric cardiologist*
Rapini, Ronald Peter *dermatology educator*
Rassidakis, George Z. *pathologist, researcher*
Redmon, Agile Hugh, Jr., *allergist*
Ribble, John Charles *medical educator*
Robb, Geoffrey Lawrence *plastic surgeon*
Ross, Michael Wallis *public health educator*
Ross, Patti Jayne *obstetrics and gynecology educator*
Rudolph, Andrew Henry *dermatologist, educator*
Ruiz, Pedro *psychiatrist*
Sanderson, Mary Louise *medical association administrator*
Sargent, John *psychiatrist*
Satitpunwaycha, Pon *surgeon*
Sawaya, Raymond *neurosurgeon*
Sazama, Kathleen *pathologist, lawyer*
Schachtel, Barbara Harriet Levin *epidemiologist, educator*
Scharold, Mary Louise *psychoanalyst, educator*
Schoolar, Joseph Clayton *psychiatrist, pharmacologist, educator*
Sdringola-Maranga, Stefano *medical educator, researcher*
Sears, David Alan *medical educator*
Shan, Kesavan *cardiologist, researcher*
Shearer, William Thomas *pediatrician, educator*
Shook, Joan E. *medical educator*
Shulman, Robert Jay *pediatrician, educator, nutritionist*
Simpson, Joe Leigh *obstetrics and gynecology educator*
Singletary, Sonja Eva *surgeon, educator*
Smythe, Cheves McCord *internist, geriatrician, educator, dean*
Spira, Melvin *plastic surgeon*
Stehlin, John Sebastian, Jr., *surgeon*
Stewart, Michael Glenn *otolaryngologist, educator*
Talmage, Edward Arthur *anesthesiologist*
Tanous, Helene Mary *radiologist, educator*
Thomas, Orville C. *retired physician, consultant*
Torre-Amione, Guillermo *cardiologist, researcher*
Vallbona, Carlos *physician*
Vanderploeg, James M. *preventive medicine physician*
Varma, Datla G.K. *radiologist, researcher*
Vassilopoulou-Sellin, Rena *clinician investigator*
Walker, William Easton *surgeon, educator, lawyer*
Wall, Matthew J., Jr., *surgeon, research scientist*
Wallace, Sidney *radiologist*
Wheless, James Warren *neurologist*
White, Ronald Joseph *life and biomedical researcher, physiologist, educator*
Willerson, James Thornton *internist, educator*
Williams, Temple Weatherly, Jr., *retired internist*
Wray, Nelda Park *medical association administrator*
Wu, Kenneth Kun-Yu *physician, scientist*
Yung, Wai Kwan Alfred *neurology and neuro-oncology educator*
Zoghbi, Huda Y. *pediatric neurology and genetics educator*

Humble
Trowbridge, John Parks *physician*

Huntsville
Conwell, Halford Roger *physician*

Irving
Meyerson, Lawrence Bernard *physician*
Rorrie, Colin C., Jr., *emergency physician*

Jacksonville
Wonnacott, James Brian *physician*

Kerrville
Zuber, Randolph Clark *urologist*

La Grange
Collins, George J., Jr., *surgeon*

Lago Vista
Hilton, James Gorton *pharmacologist*

Laredo
Ali, Ashraf *psychiatrist*
Mandell, Marshall *pediatrician, allergist, consultant*

Longview
Frase, Larry Lynn *medical oncologist*

Lubbock
Barnette, Chris W. *medical association administrator*
Beck, George Preston *anesthesiologist, educator*
Buesseler, John Aure *ophthalmologist, management consultant*
Illner-Canizaro, Hana *physician, oral surgeon, researcher*
Kaye, Alan David *anesthesiologist, researcher*
Kurtzman, Neil A. *medical educator*
May, Donald Robert Lee *ophthalmologist, retina and vitreous surgeon, educator, farmer*
Mittemeyer, Bernhard Theodore *urology and surgery educator*
Prien, Samuel David *medical educator, researcher*
Schiffer, Randolph Brenton *physician*
Sharif, M. Alan *interventional cardiologist*
Varma, Surendra K. *pediatrician, educator*
Warren, Donald John *retired surgeon, educator*
Way, Barbara Haight *dermatologist*
Wilson, M. Roy *medical educator*
Woolam, Gerald Lynn *surgeon*

Magnolia
Girard, Louis Joseph *ophthalmologist, educator*

Marshall
Sudhivoraseth, Niphon *pediatrician, allergist, immunologist*

Mcallen
Casso, Ramiro Raul *retired family physician, college official*
Ramirez, Mario Efrain *physician*
Robalino, Benjamin David *cardiologist*

Midland
Van de Water, Susan D. *physiatrist*

Mineral Wells
Braun, Gustav Milan *facial plastic surgeon, otolaryngologist*

Nacogdoches
Bommanna, Vasudeva M. *allergist, immunologist*

Pampa
Powell, Dan Clayton *physician*

Pasadena
Shapiro, Edward Muray *dermatologist*

Pearland
Hammond, Raymond William *pharmacotherapy specialist*

Raymondville
Montgomery-Davis, Joseph *osteopathic physician*

Rockport
Johnson, Marilyn *retired obstetrician, gynecologist*

Rockwall
Kotas, Robert Vincent *research physician, educator*

Salado
Wilmer, Harry Aron *psychiatrist, educator*

San Angelo
Charlesworth, Ernest Neal *allergist, immunologist, dermatologist, educator*
Fischer, Duncan Kinnear *neurosurgeon*

San Antonio
Armstrong, John Hulse *surgeon*
Aust, Joe Bradley *surgeon, educator*
Bailey, Steven R. *cardiologist, researcher*
Baker, Floyd Wilmer *surgeon, retired army officer*
Beckmann, Charles Henry *cardiologist, educator*
Campbell, Robert Murray, Jr., *surgeon, researcher*
Croft, Harry Allen *psychiatrist*
Davis, Steven Andrew *dermatologist*
Dumitru, Daniel *physiatrist*
Espino, David V. *geriatrician, family practice physician*
Feldman, Marc D. *cardiologist, physiologist, biomedical engineer*
Guerra, Fernando A. *pediatrician, health facility administrator*
Hausheer, Frederick Herman *medical oncologist, researcher, pharmaceutical company officer*
Honore, Gerard Marcel *reproductive endocrinologist*
Horton, Granville Eugene *occupational medicine physician, retired air force officer*
Huff, Robert Whitley *obstetrician, gynecologist, educator*
Kamada-Cole, Mika M. *allergist, immunologist, medical educator*
Kaye, Celia Ilene *pediatrics educator*
Kolaparthi, VenkataSubbaRao *oncologist*
Kreisberg, Jeffrey I. *medical educator, researcher*
Ledford, Frank Finley, Jr., *surgeon, army officer*
Le Maistre, Charles Aubrey *retired internist, epidemiologist, educator*
Leon, Robert Leonard *psychiatrist, educator*
Marlin, Arthur Edward *pediatric neurosurgeon, educator*
Martin, James Charles *physician*
McFee, Arthur Storer *physician*
McGill, Henry Coleman, Jr., *pathologist, educator, researcher*
Mitchell, George Washington, Jr., *physician, educator*
Neel, Spurgeon Hart, Jr., *physician, retired army officer*
Ognibene, Andre John *physician, army officer, educator*
O'Rourke, Robert A. *cardiologist, educator*
Park, Myung Kun *medical educator*
Persellin, Robert Harold *physician*
Pestana, Carlos *surgeon, retired dean, educator*
Phillips, William Thomas *nuclear medicine physician, researcher*
Pruitt, Basil Arthur, Jr., *surgeon, retired military officer*
Ramos, Raul *surgeon*
Reuter, Stewart Ralston *retired radiologist, lawyer, educator*
Rhodes, Linda Jane *psychiatrist*
Roberts, James Lewis *medical sciences educator*
Schenker, Steven *internist, educator*
Schneider, Frank David *family physician*
Smith, John Marvin, III, *surgeon, educator*
Smith, Reginald Brian Furness *retired anesthesiologist, educator*
Solomon, Diane Hurst *neurologist*
Thomas, John Arlen *pharmacology educator, health science administrator*
Thompson, Robert Knox *surgeon*
Ujioka, Takeshi *endocrinologist*
Verghese, Abraham Cheeran *internist, educator, writer*
Von Hoff, Daniel Douglas *physician, oncologist*
Wang, Samuel James *physician*
Wolff, Hugh Lipman *urologist, educator*
Zilveti, Carlos Benjamin *preventive medicine physician, pediatrician*

Seabrook
Patten, Bernard Michael *neurologist, writer, educator*

Stafford
Polinger, Iris Sandra *dermatologist*

Temple
Allen, Steven R. *obstetrician, gynecologist, educator*
Buswell, Arthur Lee *psychiatrist*
Dyck, Walter Peter *gastroenterologist, educator, university official*
Gantt, David Scott *cardiologist, academic administrator*
Holleman, Vernon Daughty *physician, internist*
Knudsen, Kermit Bruce *physician*
Kuo, Lih *medical educator*
Lynch, Dennis James *plastic surgeon*
Stoebner, John Martin *physician*
Sulak, Patricia Jane *gynecologist, educator*

Texarkana
Harrison, James Wilburn *gynecologist*

Texas City
Korndorffer, William Earl *forensic pathologist*

The Woodlands
Desjardins, Raoul *medical association administrator, financial consultant*

Tyler
Hyman, William Jay *internist, oncologist*

Neuenschwander, Pierre Fernand *medical educator*
Wrenn, Christopher Jay *physician*

Waco
Dow, David Sontag *retired ophthalmologist*
Richie, Rodney Charles *critical care and pulmonary medicine physician*

Weatherford
Reitman, Sanford *radiologist*

Webster
Farnam, Jafar *allergist, immunologist, pediatrician*

West
Eisma, Jose A. *physician*

Willis
Rappaport, Martin Paul *internist, nephrologist, educator*

Wimberley
Koeppe, Patsy Poduska *internist, medical educator*
Cacayorin, Edwin D. *diagnostic and interventional neuroradiologist*

UTAH

Bountiful
Ross, Gerald Harvey *family practice and environmental medicine physician*

Logan
Roberts, Donald Wilson *pathologist, consultant*

Mapleton
Hillyard, Ira William *pharmacologist, educator*

Ogden
Maughan, Willard Zinn *dermatologist*

Orem
Roberts, Stanley Dwayne *physician, medical educator*

Park City
Carmichael, Paul Louis *ophthalmic surgeon*

Provo
Bott, Jay Cordell *oncologist, hematologist*
Latta, George Haworth, III, *neonatologist*
Ogden, Bruce E. *pediatrician, neonatologist*

Salt Lake City
Adashi, Eli Y. *obstetrician, gynecologist*
Bauer, A(ugust) Robert, Jr., *surgeon*
Black, Richard Eugene *pediatric surgeon*
Burke, John Patrick *internist, educator*
Carey, John Clayton *pediatrician, educator, medical geneticist*
Carroll, Karen Colleen *physician, infectious disease educator, medical microbiologist*
Clegg, Daniel Orme *rheumatologist, educator*
Cook, Joseph V. *physician*
Davis, Roy Kim *otolaryngologist, health facility administrator*
Dolcourt, John (Jack) Lawrence *pediatrician*
Fujinami, Robert Shin *neurology educator*
Graham, John Wallace *pathologist*
Grosser, Bernard Irving *psychiatry educator*
Jaskowski, Troy D. *immunologist, researcher*
Johnson, Spencer *physician, writer*
Knight, Joseph Adams *pathologist*
Krishna, Kishore Bellamkonda *biomedical researcher, educator*
Layfield, Lester James *pathologist, educator*
Legant, Patricia *internist, oncologist*
Leiferman, Kristin Marie *physician, educator, science association director*
Lloyd, Ray Dix *health physicist*
Middleton, Anthony Wayne, Jr., *urologist, educator*
Moser, Royce, Jr., *preventive medicine physician, educator*
Nelson, John C. *obstetrician/gynecologist*
Nelson, Russell Marion *surgeon, educator*
Parkin, James Lamar *otolaryngologist, educator*
Renzetti, Attilio David, Jr., *retired physician*
Stanford, Joseph Barney *medical educator, physician*
Thomas, David Snow *plastic surgeon*
Ward, John Robert *internist, educator*
Wilcox, Adam Benjamin *medical researcher, educator*

VERMONT

Brattleboro
Agallianos, Dennis Dionysios *psychiatrist*

Burlington
Brown, Kenneth Andrew *cardiologist, educator*
Cooper, Sheldon Mark *medical educator, immunologist, researcher, rheumatologist*
Davis, John Herschel *retired surgeon, educator*
Galbraith, Richard Anthony *physician, hospital administrator*
Krag, Martin Hans *physician, orthopaedist, educator, researcher*
Lucey, Jerold Francis *pediatrician*
Riddick, Daniel Howison *obstetrics and gynecology educator, priest*
Sobel, Burton Elias *physician, educator*
Tampas, John P. *radiologist*

Dorset
Bamford, Joseph Charles, Jr., *gynecologist, obstetrician, educator, medical missionary, author*

Jacksonville
Dell, Ralph Bishop *retired pediatrician, researcher*
Hein, Karen Kramer *pediatrician, epidemiologist*

Norwich
Katz, Arnold Martin *medical educator*

Randolph
Sax, Daniel Saul *neurologist, educator*

Shelburne
Foster, Roger Sherman, Jr., *surgeon, educator, health facility administrator*

South Burlington
Shinozaki, Tamotsu *retired physician, anesthesiologist*

Swanton
Wooding, William Minor *statistics consultant*

Underhill
Danforth, Elliot, Jr., *medical educator*

White River Junction
Myers, Warren Powers Laird *physician, educator*

Woodstock
Killian, Edward James *retired pediatrician*

VIRGINIA

Alexandria
Adams, Thomas L. *medical association administrator*
Balch, Charles M. *surgeon, educator*
Bumgarner, Robert Linville *pathologist, retired military officer*
Chapman, Anthony Bradley *psychiatrist*
Hallman, Linda D. *medical association administrator*
Hark, William Henry *medical executive, retired military officer*
Herrera, Clarita *medical association administrator*
Hurtado, Rodrigo Claudio *allergist*
Jones-Lukács, Elizabeth Lucille *physician*
Nicholas, Lynn B. *medical association administrator*
Wilhide, Stephen D. *medical association administrator*

Annandale
Lefrak, Edward Arthur *cardiovascular and thoracic surgeon*
Shamburek, Roland Howard *physician*
Simonian, Simon John *surgeon, scientist, educator, administrator*

Arlington
Adams, Hunter (Patch Adams) *internist, health facility administrator*
Dvorak, Josef Cermin *endocrinologist*
Ferraz, Francisco Marconi *neurological surgeon*
Harper, Michael John Kennedy *obstetrics and gynecology educator*
Lundeen, William Bruce *radiologist*
Nguyen-Dinh, Thanh *internist, geriatrician, acupuncturist*
Nirschl, Robert Phillip *orthopedic surgeon*
Shine, Kenneth Irwin *cardiologist, educator*

Blacksburg
Baudoin, Antonius B. A. M. *plant pathologist, educator*

Charlottesville
Barrett, Eugene Joseph *physician, educator, researcher*
Beller, George Allan *medical educator*
Brautigan, David L. *biomedical researcher*
Bruns, David Eugene *medical educator, researcher*
Cantrell, Robert Wendell *otolaryngologist, head and neck surgeon, educator*
Carey, Robert Munson *medical educator, physician*
Clayton, Anita Louise *psychiatrist, physician*
Crosby, Ivan Keith *cardiac surgeon, educator*
Doctor, Allan *physician, researcher*
Durbin, Charles G., Jr., *anesthesiologist, intensivist, educator*
Epstein, Robert Marvin *anesthesiologist, educator*
Flickinger, Charles John *anatomist, educator*
Gillenwater, Jay Young *urologist, educator*
Greer, Kenneth E. *dermatologist*
Guerrant, Richard Littleton *medical educator*
Harbert, Guy Morley, Jr., *retired obstetrician, gynecologist*
Hillman, Bruce Jay *radiologist, researcher, consultant, educator*
Hostler, Sharon Lee *pediatrics educator, rehabilitation center executive*
Hunt, William B. *cardiopulmonary physician*
Jagger, Janine *epidemiologist*
Jane, John Anthony *neurosurgeon, educator*
Jones, Rayford Scott *surgeon, educator*
Kassell, Neal Frederic *neurosurgery educator*
Kattwinkel, John *physician, pediatrics educator, neonatologist*
Keats, Theodore Eliot *radiologist, educator*
Kelly, Thaddeus Elliott *medical geneticist*
Kitchin, James D., III, *obstetrician-gynecologist, educator*
Knaus, William A. *medical educator, researcher*
Larner, Joseph *pharmacology educator*
Lee, Jae Kyun *biomedical researcher, educator*
Mandell, Gerald Lee *internist, educator*
Marshall, John Crook *internal medicine educator, researcher*
McDuffie, Marcia Jensen *pediatrics educator, researcher*
Morgan, Raymond F. *plastic surgeon*
Muller, William Henry, Jr., *surgeon, educator*
Nolan, Stanton Peelle *surgeon, educator*
Owen, John Atkinson, Jr., *internist, educator*
Phillips, Lawrence H., II, *neurologist, educator*
Platts-Mills, Thomas Alexander E. *immunologist, educator, researcher*
Rehm, Patrice Koch *radiologist, educator*
Rein, Michael Frank *physician, medical educator*
Rowlingson, John Clyde *anesthesiologist, physician, educator*
Sarembock, Ian Joseph *internist*
Scheld, William Michael *internist, educator*
Schneider, Edward Martin *retired internist, medical educator*
Stevenson, Ian *psychiatrist, educator*
Teates, Charles David *radiologist, educator*
Thorner, Michael Oliver *medical educator*
Tillack, Thomas Warner *pathologist, educator*
Villar-Palasi, Carlos *pharmacology educator*
Wallace, Karl Kenneth, Jr., *physician, radiologist*
Weary, Peyton Edwin *retired medical educator*

Chesapeake
Kovalcik, Paul Jerome *surgeon*
Montag, Thomas W. *gynecologist, oncologist*

Crozet
Detmer, Don Eugene *health management and policy researcher, medical educator, surgeon*

Culpeper
Broman, George Ellis, Jr., *retired surgeon*

Fairfax
Dettinger, Garth Bryant *surgeon, physician, retired air force officer, county health officer*
Fisher, Linda Alice *physician*
Johnson, Clarion Ellis *physician*
Robert, Nicholas James *hematolgist, oncologist*
Rubinstein, Mark Isaac *physician*
Schulman, Joseph Daniel *physician, health company administrator, medical geneticist, reproductive biologist, educator*
Snyder, Roger Alan *physician, neurologist*
Stage, Thomas Benton *psychiatrist*

Falls Church
Cooper, James Nelson *medical educator*
Elliott, Virginia F. Harrison *retired anatomist, publisher, educator, investment advisor, kinesiologist, philanthropist*
Evans, Peter Yoshio *ophthalmologist, educator*
Golomb, Herbert Stanley *dermatologist*
Inglefield, Joseph T., Jr., *allergist, immunologist, pediatrician*
Kurtzke, John Francis, Sr., *neurologist, epidemiologist*
Malek, M. Mike *medical association administrator*
McCullough, William Lawrence *medical readiness consultant*
Scott, Hugh Patrick *physician, naval officer*
Travis, Tracy Leigh *emergency physician*
Wise, Thomas Nathan *psychiatrist*

Gainesville
Lee, Won Jay *radiologist*

Hampton
Brown, Loretta Ann Port *physician, geneticist*

Keswick
Rowe, William Joseph *internist*

Leesburg
Mitchell, Russell Harry *dermatologist*

Lexington
DeSilvey, Dennis Lee *cardiologist, educator, university administrator*

Lynchburg
Cunniff, Suzanne *surgical technician*
Lane, Richard Allan *preventive medicine physician, educator*

Marion
Armbrister, Douglas Kenley *surgeon*

Mc Lean
Laning, Robert Comegys *retired physician, former naval officer*
Wallace, Robert Bruce *retired surgeon*
Wright, William Evan *physician, consultant*

Mechanicsville
Lordi, William Michael *psychiatrist, child psychiatrist*

Midlothian
Friedel, Robert Oliver *physician*
O'Shanick, Gregory John *physician, medical association administrator*

Monterey
Tabatznik, Bernard *retired cardiologist*

Nellysford
Wood, Maurice *medical educator*

Newport News
Forbes, Sarah Elizabeth *gynecologist, real estate corporation officer*
Wargo, Lovetta Lynn *medical educator, occupational therapist, writer*

Norfolk
Andrews, William Cooke *physician*
Archer, Robert Patrick *psychologist, educator*
Evett, Russell Dougherty *internist, educator*
Faulconer, Robert Jamieson *pathologist, educator*
Jenson, Hal Brockbank *physician*
Kagan, Harvey J. *pediatrician*
Kreger, David Lawrence *gastroenterologist*
Lester, Richard Garrison *radiologist, educator*
Oehninger, Sergio C. *endocrinologist, obstetrician, gynecologist*
Oelberg, David George *neonatologist, educator, researcher*
Rohn, Reuben David *pediatric educator and administrator*
Schneider, Daniel Scott *pediatric cardiologist*
Stallings, Valerie A. *physician, state agency administrator*
Terzis, Julia Kallipolitou *plastic surgeon*
Wolcott, Hugh Dixon *obstetrics and gynecology educator*

North Garden
Moses, Hamilton, III, *academic neurologist, management consultant, hospital executive*

Norton
Vest, Gayle Southworth *obstetrician, gynecologist*

Petersburg
Ende, Milton *internist*

Portsmouth
Dunbar, Robert Paul, Jr., *orthopaedic surgeon, military officer*
O'Malley, Timothy Patrick *otolaryngologist*
Wolf, Jeffrey Stephen *physician*

Richmond
Atkinson, Richard Lee, Jr., *internal medicine educator*
Ayres, Stephen McClintock *physician, educator*
Balster, Robert Louis *drug abuse expert*
Bates, Hampton Robert, Jr., *pathologist*
Blumberg, Michael Zangwill *allergist*
Bodurtha, Joanne Norma *genetics educator*
DeLorenzo, Robert John *neurologist, molecular neuroscientist*
Dunn, Leo James *obstetrician, educator, gynecologist, educator*
Fierro, Marcella Farinelli *forensic pathologist*
Gilliam, F. Roosevelt *cardiologist, surgeon*
Ginder, Gordon Dean *physician, educator*
Howell, Talmadge Rudolph *radiologist*
Kaplowitz, Lisa Glauser *physician, educator*
Kendler, Kenneth S. *medical educator*
Kunos, George *pharmacologist*
Lawrence, Walter, Jr., *surgeon, educator*
Mauck, Henry Page, Jr., *medical and pediatrics educator*
Merrell, Ronald Clifton *surgeon, educator*
Mollen, Edward Leigh *pediatrician, allergist, clinical immunologist*
Mullinax, Perry Franklin *rheumatologist, allergist, immunologist*
Neufeld, Jacob A. *pediatrician, physiatrist, physical medicine and rehabilitation*
Osgood, Nancy Jean *medical educator, writer*
Owen, Duncan Shaw, Jr., *internist, educator*
Richardson, David Walthall *cardiologist, educator, consultant*
Sirica, Alphonse Eugene *pathology educator*
Snead, Thomas G. *healthcare executive*
Solan, Stuart Miley *physician*
Szakal, Andras Kalman *immunologist, anatomist, educator*
Tunner, William Sams *urological surgeon*
Turner, Elaine S. *allergist, immunologist*
Vijayaraman, Pugazhendhi *medical educator*
Walton, G. Clifford *family practice physician*
Ward, John Wesley *retired pharmacologist*
Wenzel, Richard Putnam *internist*
Wilkinson, David Stanley *pathologist, consultant, researcher, educator, physician*
Woolf, Steven H. *medical educator, researcher, preventive medicine physician*

Roanoke
Hutcheson, Jack Robert *hematologist, medical oncologist*
Litwiller, Roger W. *anesthesiologist, medical association executive*

Roseland
Stemmler, Edward Joseph *physician, retired association executive, retired academic dean*

Salem
Kim, Kye Young *psychiatrist*

Staunton
Lossing, Wallace William *inventor, minister*

Sterling
Jaffe, Russell Merritt *pathologist, research director*

Suffolk
Carroll, George Joseph *pathologist, educator*

Syria
Altaffer, Lawrence F., III, *retired physician, artist*

Vienna
Schwartz, Richard Harvey *pediatrician*

Virginia Beach
Carlston, John A. *allergist*
McDaniel, David Henry *physician*
Onsanit, Tawachai *physician*

Ware Neck
Tabb, Waller Crockett *retired allergist, retired immunologist*

White Stone
Duer, Ellen Ann Dagon *anesthesiologist, general practitioner*

Williamsburg
Connell, Alastair McCrae *physician*
Davis, Richard Bradley *internal medicine, pathology educator, physician*
Dhillon, Avtar Singh *psychiatrist*
Jacoby, William Jerome, Jr., *internist, retired military officer*
Maloney, Milford Charles *retired internal medicine educator*
Schwartz, Miles Joseph *cardiologist*
Steinsmith, William *internist, research scientist*

Winchester
Bechamps, Gerald Joseph *surgeon*
Creasy, Richard Alan *anesthesiologist*
Helentjaris, Diane *physician, medical association administrator*
Isenhower, Nelson Nolan *anesthesiologist*

Yorktown
Ray, Charles Dean *neurosurgeon, spine surgeon, bioengineer, inventor*

WASHINGTON

Auburn
Nazaire, Michel Harry *physician*
Sata, Lindbergh Saburo *psychiatrist, educator*

Bellevue
Brockenbrough, Edwin Chamberlayne *surgeon*
Hackett, Carol Ann Hedden *physician*
Lipton, Judith Eve *psychiatrist*
Phillips, Zaiga Alksnis *pediatrician*
Whatmore, George Bernard *physician, scientist, clinical neurophysiologist*

Bellingham
Howe, Warren Billings *physician*
James, Helen Ann *plastic surgeon*
Lau, Roy Esme *surgeon*

Centralia
Miller, James McCalmont *pediatrician*

Clarkston
Chinchinian, Harry *pathologist, educator*

Clyde Hill
Condon, Robert Edward *surgeon, educator, consultant*

Coupeville
Mayhew, Eric George *medical researcher, educator*

Edmonds
Bray, Ronald Eugene *obstetrician/gynecologist*
Yoon, Jay Myoung *oncologist, hematologist, internist*

Ellensburg
Sand, John Halvdan *obstetrician, gynecologist*

Everett
Smith, Thomas J. *surgeon, educator*
Valentine, Mark Conrad *dermatologist*

Friday Harbor
Geyman, John Payne *physician, educator*

Gig Harbor
Earley, Laurence Elliott *retired medical educator*

Issaquah
Barchet, Stephen *obstetrician, gynecologist, retired military officer*

Kent
Brannen, George Elsdon *surgeon*
O'Bara, Kenneth J. *physician*

Kirkland
Barto, Deborah Ann *physician*
Dundas, Dennis Franklin *plastic surgeon*
Dunn, Jeffrey Edward *neurologist*

Lynden
Hibbs, Clair M. *retired pathologist*

Mercer Island
Coe, Robert Campbell *retired surgeon*
Elgee, Neil Johnson *retired internist, educator, retired endocrinologist, educator*
Haviland, James West *physician, educator*

Olympia
Fisher, Nancy Louise *pediatrician, medical geneticist, former nurse*
Smith, Sherwood Paul *plastic surgeon*

Pullman
Robison, Linda M. *epidemiologist, medical researcher*

Richland
Bair, William J. *retired radiation biologist*
Mushen, Robert Linton *ophthalmologist, consultant*

Seattle
Aldea, Gabriel S. *cardiothoracic surgeon, educator*
Ansell, Julian S. *physician, retired urology educator*
Appelbaum, Frederick Ray *oncologist*
Auer, Nancy Jane *emergency physician, medical association administrator*
Bergman, Abraham *pediatrician*
Berkowitz, Bobbie *medical educator*
Blake-Inada, Louis Michael *cardiologist, researcher*
Boguski, Mark S. *medical association administrator*
Bornstein, Paul *medical educator, biochemist*
Bowden, Douglas McHose *neuropsychiatric scientist, educator, research center administrator*
Buck, Linda B. *physician, medical educator*
Catterall, William A. *pharmacology, neurobiology educator*
Chatard, Peter Ralph Noel, Jr., *aesthetic plastic surgeon*
Clarren, Sterling Keith *pediatrician*
Couser, William Griffith *medical educator, academic administrator, nephrologist*
Cullen, Bruce F. *anesthesiologist*
Dale, David C. *physician, medical educator*
Dawson, Patricia Lucille *surgeon*
Day, Robert Winsor *preventive medicine physician, researcher*
Dunner, David Louis *medical educator*
Ellis, Georgiana Kehr *internist*
Eschbach, Joseph Wetherill *nephrology educator*
Eyre, David R. *orthopedics educator*
Fine, James Stephen *physician*
Gayle, Helene D. *public health physician*
Giblett, Eloise Rosalie *retired hematologist*
Given, Douglass Bruce *physician*
Goodkin, Robert *neurologist, surgeon, educator*
Grayston, J. Thomas *medical and public health educator*
Groudine, Mark T. *oncologist*
Guntheroth, Warren Gaden *pediatrician, educator*
Guralnick, Michael J. *medical research administrator*
Hazzard, William Russell *geriatrician, educator*
Heimfeld, Shelly *hematologist, researcher, immunologist, researcher*
Henderson, Maureen McGrath *medical educator*
Henney, Christopher Scot *immunologist*
Holmes, King Kennard *medical educator*
Hornbein, Thomas Frederic *anesthesiologist*
Hudson, Leonard Dean *physician*
Kahn, Steven Emanuel *medical educator*
Kalina, Robert Edward *ophthalmologist, educator*
Karl, Helen Weist *pediatric anesthesia and pain management educator, researcher*
Kimball, Harry Raymond *medical educator, former medical association executive*
Klebanoff, Seymour Joseph *medical educator*
Kraft, George Howard *physician, educator*
Krohn, Kenneth Albert *radiology educator*
Larrabee, Wayne Fox, Jr., *facial plastic surgeon*
Larson, Eric B. *medical educator, director*
Loeser, John David *neurosurgeon, educator*
Lynn, Anne Marie *anesthesiologist, pediatrician*
Maier, Ronald Vitt *surgeon*
Mankoff, David Abraham *nuclear medicine physician*
Martin, George M. *pathologist, gerontologist, educator*
Martin, Thomas R. *medical educator, medical association administrator*
Matsen, Frederick Albert, III, *orthopedic educator*
Moore, Daniel Charles *retired anesthesiologist*
Motulsky, Arno Gunther *internist, geneticist, educator*
Nelp, Wil B. *physician, medical educator*
Nelson, James Alonzo *radiologist, educator*
Nicholls, Stephen Charles *surgeon, educator*
O'Brien, Kevin D. *medical educator*
Orcutt, James Craig *ophthalmologist*
Pagon, Roberta Anderson *pediatrics educator*
Palmer, Jerry Philip *medical educator, researcher, internist*
Petersdorf, Robert George *physician, medical educator, academic administrator*
Phillips, William Robert *physician*
Plorde, James Joseph *physician, educator*
Porte, Daniel, Jr., *physician, educator, health facility administrator*
Ravenholt, Reimert Thorolf *epidemiologist, researcher*
Ritchie, James L. *cardiologist*
Rivara, Frederick Peter *pediatrician, educator*
Robertson, William Osborne *physician*
Rosenblatt, Roger Alan *physician, educator*
Rosse, Cornelius *medical educator*
Routt, Milton Lee (Chip) *orthopedic trauma surgeon, educator*
Sale, George Edgar *pathologist*
Saneto, Russell Patrick *pediatric neurologist, epileptologist, neurobiologist*
Schimmelbusch, Werner Helmut *psychiatrist*
Shapiro, Gail Greenberg *pediatric allergy educator*
Shepard, Thomas Hill *physician, educator*
Simkin, Peter Anthony *internist, educator*
Stanford, Janet Lee *physician, epidemiologist*
Stenchever, Morton Albert *obstetrician, gynecologist*
Su, Judy Ya Hwa Lin *pharmacologist*
Swanson, Phillip Dean *neurologist*
Teitz, Carol *orthopedist, surgeon, educator*
Thomas, Edward Donnall *internist, hematologist, retired medical educator*
Todaro, George Joseph *pathologist, researcher*
Tucker, Gary Jay *psychiatrist, educator*
Waldhausen, John Henry Trescher *pediatric surgeon, educator*
Weiss, Noel S. *epidemiologist*
Welk, Richard Andrew *plastic surgeon*
Yue, Agnes Kau-Wah *otolaryngologist*
Zager, Richard A. *medical educator, researcher*

Selah
Markin, Karl Edward *obstetrician/gynecologist*

Shoreline
Merendino, K. Alvin *surgical educator*
Risse, Guenter Bernhard *physician, historian, educator*

Spokane
Cohen, Arnold Norman *gastroenterologist*
Demakas, John James *neurosurgeon*
Gibson, Melvin Roy *pharmacology educator*
Lee, Hi Young *family physician, acupuncturist*
Mielke, Clarence Harold, Jr., *hematologist*

Tacoma
Cuevas, Eduardo Samaniego *internist*
Hori, Kiyoaky *retired anesthesiologist*
Rahe, Richard Henry *psychiatrist, educator*
Verhey, Joseph William *psychiatrist, educator*
Wagonfeld, James B. *gastroenterologist*

University Place
Pliskow, Vita Sari *anesthesiologist*

Vashon
Vallarta, Josefina M. *retired child neurologist*

Walla Walla
Chaidarun, Sushela Songtanin *endocrinologist, researcher*
Johnson, Robert Arnold *physician, cardiologist, poet*

Wenatchee
Gotthold, William Eugene *emergency physician*
Knecht, Ben Harrold *surgeon*

WEST VIRGINIA

Beckley
Hooper, William Dale *surgeon*

Bridgeport
Gorby, William Guy *anesthesiologist*

Charleston
Boland, James Pius *surgeon, educator*
Pfister, Alfred Karl *internist, educator*

Clarksburg
de la Pena, Cordell Amado *pathologist*
Ona-Sarino, Milagros Felix *pathologist*
Sarino, Edgardo Formantes *radiologist, physician*

Huntington
Cocke, William Marvin, Jr., *plastic surgeon, educator*
Darby, H. Darrel *podiatric surgeon*
Molina, Rafael Evencio *urologist*
Morabito, Rocco Anthony *urologist*
Mufson, Maurice Albert *infectious diseases physician, educator*
Nerhood, Robert Clarke *obstetrician and gynecologist*
Sypher, Blake *medical educator*

Kingwood
Moyers, Sylvia Dean *retired medical librarian*

Martinsburg
Malin, Howard Gerald *podiatrist*

Morgantown
Albrink, Margaret Joralemon *medical educator*
Bang, Ki Moon *epidemiologist, educator*
Chisholm, Lionel Donald John *ophthalmologist*
Dawood, Mohamed Yusoff *obstetrician, gynecologist*
Ducatman, Alan Marc *physician*
Emery, Sanford Emil *orthopedic surgeon*
Fleming, William Wright, Jr., *pharmacology educator*
Glover, Douglas Dennis *obstetrics, gynecology and pharmacology educator*
Hill, Ronald Charles *surgeon, educator*
Hilloowala, Rumy A. *retired anatomist and anthropologist*
Iammarino, Richard Michael *pathologist, student support services director*
Jabbour, Nabil Milad *ophthalmologist*
Li, Qingdi Quentin *physician, research scientist, medical educator*
Martin, James Douglas *neurologist*
Murray, Gordon Franklin *medical educator*
Poland, Alan Paul *oncology educator*
Reed, Eddie *pharmacologist*
Riggs, Jack Edward *neurologist, educator*
Sikora, Rosanna Dawn *emergency physician, educator*

Ronceverte
Hooper, Anne Dodge *pathologist, educator*

Wheeling
Heceta, Estherbelle Aguilar *anesthesiologist*

WISCONSIN

Appleton
Boren, Clark Henry, Jr., *general and vascular surgeon*
Luther, Thomas William *retired dermatologist*

Brookfield
Hardman, Harold Francis *pharmacology educator*

Drummond
Kingdon, Henry Shannon *retired internist, biochemist, science administrator*

Eagle River
Agre, James Courtland *physical medicine and rehabilitation*

Fond Du Lac
Lambert, Eugene Kent *oncologist, hematologist*
Treffert, Darold Allen *psychiatrist, author, hospital director*

Green Bay
Pukel, Clifford Stuart *physician*

Hales Corners
Kuwayama, S. Paul *physician, immunologist, allergist*

Hartford
Babbitt, Donald Patrick *radiologist*

Janesville
Gianitsos, Anestis Nicholas *surgeon*
Sturm, Christopher Douglas *neurosurgeon*

La Crosse
Newcomer, Kermit Lee *retired internist, kidney specialist*
Rooney, Brenda Louise *epidemiologist, researcher*
Smith, Martin Jay *physician, biomedical research scientist*
Webster, Stephen Burtis *dermatologist, educator*

Lake Geneva
Petersen, Edward Schmidt *retired physician*

Madison
Albanese, Mark Alan *health sciences educator*
Albert, Daniel Myron *ophthalmologist, educator*
Bajad Sunil, Uttamrao *pharmacologist, researcher*
Boutwell, Roswell Knight *oncology educator*
Brooks, Benjamin Rix *neurologist, educator*
Burgess, Richard Ray *oncology educator, molecular biology researcher, biotechnology consultant*
Cohen, Marcus *allergist, immunologist*
Cripps, Derek J. *dermatologist, educator*
DeMets, David L. *medical educator, biomedical researcher*
Dodson, Vernon Nathan *preventive medicine physician, educator*
Fahien, Leonard August *physician, educator*
Farrell, Philip M. *dean, physician, educator, researcher*
Ford, Charles Nathaniel *otolaryngologist, educator*
Glassroth, Jeffrey *internist, educator*
Graziano, Frank Michael *medical educator, researcher*
Guillery, Rainer Walter *anatomy educator*
Hartmann, Henrik Anton *medical educator*
Haughton, Victor Mellet *physician, educator*
Hecht, Rudolph C. *physician, educator*
Iskandar, Bermans Jamil *pediatric neurosurgeon*
Javid, Manucher J. *retired neurosurgery educator*
Jefferson, James Walter *psychiatry educator*
Johnson, Maryl Rae *cardiologist*
Karofsky, Peter Stuart *pediatrician, medical educator*
Laessig, Ronald Harold *preventive medicine and pathology educator, state official*
Leavitt, Lewis A. *pediatrician, medical educator*
Lemanske, Robert F., Jr., *allergist, immunologist*
MacKinney, Archie Allen, Jr., *physician*
Maki, Dennis G. *medical educator, researcher, clinician*
Malter, James Samuel *pathologist, educator*
Myers, Franklin Lewis, II, *ophthalmologist*
Niederhuber, John Edward *surgical oncologist and molecular immunologist, university educator and administrator*
Nordby, Eugene Jorgen *orthopedic surgeon*
Peters, Henry Augustus *neuropsychiatrist*
Pitot, Henry Clement, III, *pathologist, educator*
Reizner, George Terry *medical educator*
Reynolds, Ernest West *retired internist, educator*
Roberts, Leigh Milton *psychiatrist*
Roberts, Richard Guy *physician, educator*
Robins, H(enry) Ian *medical oncologist*

Scarborough, John Samuel *pharmacy, medicine and ancient history educator*
Selvaggi, Suzanne Marie *pathologist, educator*
Sobkowicz, Hanna Maria *neurology researcher*
Sondel, Paul Mark *pediatric oncologist, educator*
Sonnedecker, Glenn Allen *pharmaceutical historian, pharmaceutical educator*
Urban, Frank Henry *retired dermatologist, state legislator*
Valdivia, Hector Horacio *medical educator*
Walker, Duard Lee *medical educator*
Wenger, Ronald David *surgeon*
Whiffen, James Douglass *surgeon, educator*
Wilson, Pamela Aird *physician*
Zografi, George *pharmacologist, educator*

Manitowoc
Trader, Joseph Edgar *orthopedic surgeon*

Marshfield
Myers, William Osgood *thoracic and cardiovascular surgeon*
Vidaillet, Humberto J., Jr., *physician, researcher*
Yale, Steven Howard *internist*

Menomonee Falls
Fisher, Robert Henri *physician*

Mequon
Cheema, Mohammad Aslam *retired cardiothoracic surgeon, community leader*
Krausen, Anthony Sharnik *plastic surgeon*
Terry, Leon Cass *neurologist, educator*

Middleton
Gilson, Warren E. *medical inventor*

Milwaukee
Atlee, John Light *physician, consultant*
Dhore, Jay Narayan *psychiatrist*
Carballo, Fernando Anthony *gastroenterologist, hepatologist*
Chan, Carlyle Hung-lun *psychiatrist, educator*
Cohen, Steven Howard *allergist, immunologist, educator*
Cooper, Richard Alan *hematologist, health policy analyst, dean*
De Lia, Julian Emilio *obstetrician, educator, gynecologist*
Esterly, Nancy Burton *physician*
Feinsilver, Donald Lee *psychiatry educator*
Fink, Jordan Norman *physician, educator*
Foldy, Seth Leonard *physician*
Gonnering, Russell Stephen *ophthalmic plastic surgeon*
Harris, Gerald Jay *ophthalmologist, educator*
Hosenpud, Jeffrey *cardiovascular physician*
Hur, Su-Ryong *physician, anesthesiologist*
Kampine, John P. *anesthesiology and physiology educator*
Kochar, Mahendr Singh *physician, educator, administrator, scientist, writer, consultant*
Larson, David Lee *surgeon*
Miller, Edward Carl William *physician*
Moffie, H. Steven *psychiatrist*
Montgomery, Robert Renwick *medical association administrator, educator*
Namdari, Bahram *surgeon*
Oldham, Keith T. *surgeon*
Olinger, Gordon Nordell *surgeon*
Pagel, Paul Stanley *anesthesiologist*
Port, Steven Charles *cardiologist, educator*
Schultz, Richard Otto *ophthalmologist, educator*
Shetty, Kaup Rajmohan *endocrinologist, educator*
Tector, Alfred J. *cardiothoracic surgeon*
Telford, Gordon Laing *surgeon, educator*
Towne, Jonathan Baker *vascular surgeon*
Wackym, Phillip Ashley *surgeon, researcher, otolaryngologist*
Yancey, Kim Bruce *dermatology researcher*
Youker, James Edward *radiologist*

Onalaska
Waite, Lawrence Wesley *osteopathic physician, educator*

Oshkosh
Cooper, Janelle Lunette *neurologist, educator*

Pewaukee
Kloehn, Ralph Anthony *plastic surgeon*

Racine
Stewart, Richard Donald *internist, educator, writer*

Sheboygan
Gore, Donald Ray *orthopedic surgeon*

Stevens Point
Huncharek, Michael Stephen *oncologist*

Sturgeon Bay
Greaves, Alison Ash *retired physician*

Waukesha
Kloss, Raymond *psychiatrist*

Wauwatosa
Hollister, Winston Ned *pathologist*

WYOMING

Buffalo
Fehir, Kim Michele *oncologist, hematologist*

Casper
Bennion, Scott Desmond *physician*

Cheyenne
Flick, William Fredrick *surgeon*

Laramie
Kelley, Robert Otis *medical science educator*
Berger, David *surgeon*

TERRITORIES OF THE UNITED STATES

GUAM

Hagatna
Espaldon, Ernesto Mercader *plastic surgeon, former senator*

Tamuning
Landstrom, Jerone T. *surgeon*

PUERTO RICO

Bayamon
Juarbe, Charles *otolaryngologist, head and neck surgeon*

Mayaguez
Sahai, Hardeo *medical statistics educator*

Ponce
Cummings, Luis Emilio *anesthesiologist, consultant*
Sala, Luis Francisco *surgeon, educator*

San Juan
Bonilla-Felix, Melvin A. *pediatrician, educator*
Cruz-Korchin, Norma I. *plastic surgeon*
Maldonado, Norman I. *physician, educator*

CANADA

ALBERTA

Calgary
Lederis, Karolis Paul (Karl Lederis) *pharmacologist, educator, researcher*
Leung, Alexander Kwok-Chu *pediatrician*
Smith, Eldon *cardiologist, physiologist, educator*

Edmonton
Miller, Jack David R. *radiologist, physician, educator*

BRITISH COLUMBIA

Vancouver
Baird, Patricia Ann *physician, educator*
Doyle, Patrick John *otolaryngologist, department chairman*
Eaves, Allen Charles Edward *hematologist, medical agency administrator*
Friedman, Sydney M. *anatomy educator, medical researcher*
Hardwick, David Francis *pathologist*
Ling, Victor *oncologist, educator*
McGeer, Edith Graef *neurological science educator*
Mizgala, Henry F. *physician, consultant, retired medical educator*
Roy, Chunilal *psychiatrist*
Sorensen, Poul Henrik Bredahl *physician, research scientist, pathologist*
Sutter, Morley Carman *medical scientist*
Tingle, Aubrey James *pediatric immunologist, research administrator*

MANITOBA

Winnipeg
Angel, Aubie *endocrinologist, academic administrator*
Friesen, Henry George *endocrinologist, educator*
Haworth, James Chilton *pediatrics educator*
Naimark, Arnold *medical educator, physiologist, internist*
Persaud, Trivedi Vidhya Nandan *anatomy educator, researcher, consultant*
Schacter, Brent Allan *oncologist, health facility administrator*

NEW BRUNSWICK

Fredericton
Hanson, Dana W. *dermatologist*

NOVA SCOTIA

Halifax
Casson, Alan Graham *thoracic surgeon, researcher*
Chowdhury, Dhiman *physician, consultant*
Langley, George Ross *medical educator*
Tonks, Robert Stanley *pharmacology and therapeutics educator, former university dean*

Mahone Bay
Collins, John Alfred *retired obstetrician-gynecologist, educator*

ONTARIO

Barry's Bay
Horoszewicz, Juliusz Stanislaw *oncologist, cancer researcher, laboratory administrator*

Cambridge
Brown, Gregory Michael *psychiatrist, educator, researcher*

Hamilton
Bienenstock, John *pathologist, educator, health facility administrator*
Roland, Charles Gordon *physician, medical historian, educator*

Kingston
Kaufman, Nathan *retired pathologist, educator*
Low, James A. *physician*

London
Marotta, Joseph Thomas *medical educator*
McWhinney, Ian Renwick *physician, educator*

Manotick
Osmond, Dennis Gordon *medical educator, researcher*

Ottawa
Chance, Graham Wilfrid *retired pediatrician, emeritus educator*
de Bold, Adolfo J. *pathology and physiology educator, research scientist*
Hagen, Paul Beo *physician, medical scientist*
Hurteau, Gilles David *retired obstetrician, gynecologist, educator, dean*
Jackson, W. Bruce *ophthalmology educator, researcher*
Lavoie, Lionel A. *physician, health science association administrator*
McDonald, John W. *internist*
Vassilyadi, Michael *pediatric neurosurgeon*

Sault Sainte Marie
Banerjee, Samarendranath *orthopedic surgeon*

Toronto
Broder, Irvin *physician, educator*
Bruce, William Robert *physician, educator*
Eisenberg, Howard Edward *physician, psychotherapist, consultant, educator, author*
Farkas, Leslie Gabriel *plastic surgeon*
Kalow, Werner *pharmacologist, toxicologist*
Langer, Bernard *medical association administrator*
Lindsay, William Kerr *surgeon*
Mc Culloch, Ernest Armstrong *internist, educator*
Neligan, Peter C. *plastic surgeon*
Nesbitt, Lloyd Ivan *podiatrist*
Ogilvie, Richard Ian *clinical pharmacologist*
San, Nguyen Duy *psychiatrist, educator*
Sole, Michael Joseph *cardiologist*
Till, James Edgar *medical educator, researcher*
Turner, Robert Edward *psychiatrist, educator*
Volpé, Robert *endocrinologist, researcher, educator*

Windsor
Ferguson, John Duncan *medical research educator*

QUEBEC

Montpellier
Poirier, Louis Joseph *neurology educator*

Montreal
Burgess, John Herbert *cardiologist, educator*
Clermont, Yves Wilfrid *anatomy educator, researcher*
Cruess, Richard Leigh *orthopedic surgeon, dean*
Feindel, William Howard *neurosurgeon, consultant*
Freeman, Carolyn Ruth *radiation oncologist*
Genest, Jacques *nephrologist, clinical scientist, administrator*
Gold, Phil *immunologist, educator, researcher*
Goldbloom, Victor Charles *pediatrician*
Goltzman, David *endocrinologist, educator, researcher*
Jones, Barbara Ellen *neuroscientist, educator*
Kramer, Michael Stuart *pediatric epidemiologist*
Leblond, Charles Philippe *anatomy educator, researcher*
Mac Lean, Lloyd Douglas *surgeon*
Mulder, David S. *cardiovascular surgeon*
Nadeau, Reginald Antoine *medical educator*
Nattel, Stanley *cardiologist, research scientist*
Ohayon, Maurice M. *research center administrator, psychiatrist*
Pasternac, André *cardiologist, educator*
Scriver, Charles Robert *medical researcher, human geneticist*
Snell, Linda S. *physician, medical educator*

Verdun
Gauthier, Serge Gaston *neurologist*

SASKATCHEWAN

Saskatoon
Popkin, David Richard *obstetrician, health science administrator*

Montreal
Becklake, Margaret Rigsby *epidemiologist, educator*
Ducharme, Francine Carole *nursing educator, researcher*

Sillery
Dalens, Bernard Jacques *pediatric anesthesiologist*

ARGENTINA

Buenos Aires
Diodato, Luis Hector *physician, researcher*
Montes, Leopoldo Feliciano *dermatologist, educator*

AUSTRALIA

Nedlands
Oxnard, Charles Ernest *anatomist, anthropologist, human biologist, educator*

Parkville
Azer, Samy Aziz *gastroenterologist, medical educator*
Denton, Derek Ashworth *medical researcher, medical scientist*
Metcalf, Donald *biomedical researcher*

Townsville, Queensland
Ho, Yik Hong *colon and rectal surgeon*

Vic
DeWitt, Dawn E. *medical educator, dean*

ENGLAND

Birmingham
Browne, Roger Michael *oral pathology educator, consultant*

London
Rutter, Michael Llewellyn *child psychiatry educator*
Vane, John Robert *pharmacologist*

Teddington
Roberts, Melville Parker *neurosurgeon, neuroanatomist, educator*

FINLAND

Helsinki
Liewendahl, Bo Kristian *pathologist, nuclear medicine physician*

Tampere
Pöntinen, Pekka Juhani *anesthesiologist, consultant*

FRANCE

Chartres
Benoit, Jean-Pierre Robert *retired pneumologist, consultant*

Neuilly-sur-Seine
Hewes, Thomas Francis *physician*

Paris
Dausset, Jean *immunologist*
Gontier, Jean Roger *medicine and physiology educator*
Levy, David Alfred *immunology educator, physician, scientist*

GERMANY

Bremen
Fahle, Manfred *ophthalmology researcher*

Halle
Schmoll, Hans Joachim *internal medicine, hematology, oncology educator*

Lübeck
Arnold, Hans Richard *neurosurgeon*

Mannheim
Henn, Fritz Albert *psychiatrist*

Tübingen
Nüsslein-Volhard, Christiane *medical researcher*

Wuppertal
Schubert, Guenther Erich *pathologist*

HUNGARY

Budapest
Pentelényi, Thomas John *neurosurgeon*

ISRAEL

Givatayim
Kornel, Ludwig *medical educator, physician, scientist*

JAPAN

Gummaken
Okada, Ryozo *educator, clinician and researcher*

Nagoya
Maeda, Kenji *medical educator*

Okayama
Morooka, Hiroshi *neurosurgeon*
Okada, Shigeru *pathology educator*

Okazaki
Ebashi, Setsuro *scientist, educator*

Ota-ku
Sano, Keiji *neurosurgeon, educator*

Saitama
Hozumi, Motoo *medical educator, researcher*

Sapporo
Nakagawa, Koji *endocrinologist, educator*

Tochigi
Honma, Koichi *pathologist, researcher*
Hyodo, Haruo *radiologist, educator*

Tokorozawa
Nakamura, Hiroshi *urology educator*

Tokyo
Fujimoto, Junichiro *pathologist*
Sakuta, Manabu *neurologist, educator*

Toyama
Sumiyoshi, Tomiki *psychiatrist, researcher*

Yokohama
Kaneko, Yoshihiro *cardiologist, researcher*

LEBANON

Beirut
Khatib, Rustom Atfat *gynecologist, researcher, endocrinologist, consultant, economist*

NETHERLANDS

Maastricht
Van Praag, Herman Meir *psychiatrist, educator, researcher*

POLAND

Warsaw
Pluta, Ryszard *neuropathologist, educator*

REPUBLIC OF KOREA

Dalseo-Ku Daegu
Park, Soong-Kook *internist, researcher*

RUSSIA

Moscow
Zubritsky, Alexander Nickolaevich *pathologist*

SAUDI ARABIA

Riyadh
Ismail, Nuhad *medical educator*

SINGAPORE

Singapore
Kuznetsov, Vladimir A. *biomedical researcher, computational biologist*

SLOVENIA

Maribor
Strojnik, Tadej *neurosurgeon, researcher*

SPAIN

Pamplona
Masdeu, Jose Cruz *neurologist, medical school administrator*

SWEDEN

Göteborg
Norrby, Klas Carl Vilhelm *pathology educator*

Stockholm
Ekman, Peter Erik *urologist, educator*
Iverius, Per-Henrik *physician, biochemist, educator*

SWITZERLAND

Zurich
Siegenthaler, Walter Ernst *internal medicine educator*
Zinkernagel, Rolf Martin *immunology educator*

TAIWAN

Kaohsiung
Wang, Gwo Jaw *orthopaedic surgery educator*

Taichung
Ou, Yen-Chuan *urologist*

Taipei
Ho, Low-Tone *medical educator*

TANZANIA

Moshi
Pomfret, David B. *medical educator, internist*

ADDRESS UNPUBLISHED

Abdullaev, Yalchin *neuroscientist, physician, educator*
Abildskov, J. A. *cardiologist, educator*
Achauer, Bruce Michael *plastic surgeon*
Achord, James Lee *retired gastroenterologist, educator*
Adair, Stefan Rene *plastic surgeon*
Adams, Christine Beate Lieber *psychiatrist, educator*
Adams, James Thomas *surgeon*
Adamson, John William *hematologist*
Adzick, Nick Scott *surgeon, pediatric surgery educator*
Aldrich, Franklin Dalton *medical researcher, consultant*
Alexander, George L. *radiologist*
Alexander, John Stone *retired radiologist*
Alfaro, Felix Benjamin *retired physician*
Allen, Joseph H. *retired radiologist, educator*
Allums, James A. *retired surgeon*
Altekruse, Joan Morrissey *retired preventive medicine educator*
Altman, Adele Rosenhain *radiologist*
Altshuler, Kenneth Z. *psychiatrist, educator*
Amis, Edward Stephen, Jr., *physician, retired naval officer*
Andela, Valentine Bisangena *medical researcher*
Anderson, Gary William *physician*
Anderson, George Kenneth *physician, foundation executive, retired air force officer*
Anderson, Geraldine Louise *medical researcher*
Anderson, Kathryn D. *surgeon*
Anderson, Richard McLemore *internist*
Andreoli, Thomas Eugene *physician*
Angel, Armando Carlos *rheumatologist, internist*
Appenzeller, Otto *neurologist, researcher*
Applebaum, Edward Leon *otolaryngologist, educator*
Arenson, Nathan *retired radiologist*
Argiris, Athanassios *oncologist, researcher*
Armaly, Mansour F(arid) *ophthalmologist, educator*
Badgley, Theodore McBride *psychiatrist, neurologist*
Baerg, Richard Henry *podiatrist, surgeon*
Bailey, Joselyn Elizabeth *physician*
Baird, William David *retired anesthesiologist*
Baker, Augustus L., Jr., *retired surgeon*
Balch, Henry H. *retired surgeon, educator*
Bales, Gertrude A. *retired otolaryngologist*
Ball, Carroll Raybourne *anatomist, medical educator, researcher*
Ball, Russell Allen *pathologist*
Ballas, Zuhair Khamis *physician*
Baney, Richard Neil *physician, internist*
Banke, Kathryn Kohler *epidemiologist*
Barbo, Dorothy Marie *obstetrician, gynecologist, educator*
Bardeguez-Brown, Arlene D. *obstetrician, gynecologist, educator*
Bardin, Clyde Wayne *biomedical researcher*
Baron, Jeffrey *retired pharmacologist*
Barrett, George C. *retired radiologist*
Barrett, Robert Todd *retired surgeon*
Barricks, Michael Eli *retinal surgeon*
Barron, Bruce Albrecht *physician, educator, medical researcher*
Bartlett, Eugene Fred *retired surgeon*
Basmajian, John Varoujan *medical scientist, educator, physician*
Batalden, Paul Bennett *pediatrician, educator*
Baum, Jules Leonard *ophthalmologist, educator*
Baxter, John Darling *internist, endocrinologist, educator, health facility administrator*
Bayes, Beverley Joan *retired pediatrician*
Beattie, George Chapin *retired orthopaedic surgeon*
Beck, Gustav Julius *retired pulmonologist, allergist, immunologist*
Becker, Bruce Carl, II, *physician, educator, health facility administrator*
Becker, Kyra J. *neurologist, educator*
Beckett, Victoria Ling *physician*
Beckson, Mace *psychiatrist*
Bednoff, Stuart Leon *obstetrician, gynecologist, educator*
Benfield, John Richard *surgeon, educator*
Bennett, Edward Virdell, Jr., *surgeon*
Berenson, Abbey Belina *gynecologist, educator, researcher*
Berg, Alfred Oren *epidemiology and family practice medicine educator*
Berger, Samuel Martin *physician*
Berglund, Robin G. *child psychiatrist, former corporate executive*
Bergquist, Sandra Lee *medical and legal consultant*
Berkley, Mary Corner *neurologist*
Berlin, Fred Saul *psychiatrist, educator*
Bernstein, Jay *pathologist, researcher, educator*
Bhat, Ram J. *anesthesiologist*
Biebuyck, Julien Francois *medical educator, administrator*
Biemuller, Martha Lydia *retired obstetrician-gynecologist*
Billion, John Joseph *orthopedic surgeon, former state representative*
Black, Keith Lanier *neurosurgeon, educator*
Blancato, Louis Sebastian *anesthesiologist*
Blazina, Janice Fay *transfusion medicine physician*
Blodgett, David William *preventive medicine physician*
Bloom, Eugene Charles *gastroenterologist, educator*
Blount, Benroe Wayne *physician*
Boal, Danielle K. *radiologist, educator*
Boggs, Charles Harmon, Jr., *retired surgeon*
Boling, Eldon Avery *physician*
Bond, Meredith *medical educator*
Bonn, Ethel May *psychiatrist, educator*
Boone, Charles W. *physician, pathologist*
Boone, Stephen Christopher *retired neurosurgeon*
Bowles, L. Thompson *retired medical association administrator*
Boyson, William Albert *retired obstetrician, gynecologist*
Bozzette, Samuel Anthony *physician, researcher*
Bragonier, John Robert *obstetrician-gynecologist*
Brandon, Kathryn Elizabeth Beck *pediatrician*
Braude, Robert Michael *retired medical library administrator*
Brent, Robert Leonard *radiology and pediatrics educator*
Brewer, Timothy Francis, III, *retired cardiologist*
Bristow, William Harvey, Jr., *psychiatrist*
Brohammer, Richard Frederic *psychiatrist*
Brown, Eli Matthew *anesthesiologist, department chairman*
Brown, James Gaston *retired obstetrician, gynecologist*
Brown, James W. *gastroenterologist*
Brown, Robert Charles *retired radiologist*
Browne, Thomas Reed *neurologist, researcher, educator*
Bruce, David Lionel *retired anesthesiologist, educator*
Bubenik, Oldrich Venceslas *surgeon, oncologist*
Bubrick, Melvin Phillip *surgeon*
Buchan, Ronald Forbes *internal and preventive medicine physician*
Bucove, Arnold David *psychiatrist*
Budoff, Penny Wise *retired physician, author, researcher*
Buhain, Wilfrido Javier *medical educator*
Buist, Neil Robertson MacKenzie *medical educator, medical administrator*
Burket, John McVey *retired dermatologist*
Burns, Rosalie Annette *retired neurologist, educator*
Burson, G. Timothy *neurosurgeon*
Butchko, Harriett Hays *physician*
Butler, Douglas John *physician*
Bynes, Frank Howard, Jr., *physician*
Cabell, Ben B. *retired pediatrician, naval officer*
Callahan, Daniel Joseph *surgeon, consultant*
Calmenson, Marvin *retired surgeon*
Calvert, William Preston *radiologist*
Campbell, Andrew William *immunotoxicology physician*
Caplice, Noel M. *cardiologist, researcher*
Carpenter, William T., Jr., *psychiatry and pharmacology educator*
Carrison, Dale Mitchell *emergency medicine physician*
Carswell, Jane Triplett *retired family physician*
Cartnick, Edward Nathaniel *obstetrician-gynecologist*
Cassady, James Robert *oncologist, educator*
Cassell, Eric Jonathan *physician*
Castro, Maria Graciela *medical educator, geneticist, researcher*
Cates, Willard *medical association administrator*
Chafkin, Rita M. *dermatologist*
Chaikof, Elliot Lorne *vascular surgeon*
Chaves-Carballo, Enrique *neuropediatrician*
Cheah, Keong-Chye *psychiatrist, educator*
Chen, Kuen Hai *physician*
Cherenzia, Bradley James *retired radiologist, consultant*
Chernoff, Amoz Immanuel *hematologist, consultant*
Chiariello, Mario *surgeon*
Chorpenning, Frank Winslow *immunology educator, researcher*
Chretien, Jane Henkel *internist*
Christenson, William Newcome *retired occupational and internal medicine physician*
Clausen, Jerry Lee *psychiatrist*
Cleaver, James Edward *radiologist, educator*
Clemendor, Anthony Arnold *obstetrician, gynecologist, educator*
Clemetson, Charles Alan Blake *physician*
Cline, Carolyn Joan *plastic and reconstructive surgeon*
Coe, Rodney Michael *medical educator*
Cohen, David John *cardiothoracic surgeon*
Collins, Allen Howard *psychiatrist*
Colomb, Camille Marie *anesthesiologist*
Colonnier, Marc Leopold *neuroanatomist, educator*
Connolly, Neville K. *surgeon, educator*
Connor, Daniel F. *child and adolescent psychiatrist, researcher*
Convery, Fredrick Richard *retired surgeon, orthopedist*
Conway, Gene Farris *cardiologist*
Coppolillo, Henry Peter *psychiatrist*
Corwin, William *psychiatrist*
Couture, Jean G. *retired surgeon, educator*
Covi, Lino *psychiatrist, educator*
Covintree, George E. *retired anesthesiologist*
Cowan, Robert Jenkins *retired radiologist, medical educator*
Craighead, John Edward *pathology educator*
Crino, Marjanne Helen *anesthesiologist*
Cronce, Paul Calvin *retired dermatologist*
Cross, Harold Dick *physician*
Cubbin, Catherine *social epidemiologist*
Culligan, Patrick John *obstetrician, urogynecologist, surgeon, researcher*
Culpepper, Larry *family medicine educator*
Dadabhoy, Zerin P. *anesthesiologist*
Dag-Ellams, Idris *neurosurgeon*
Dailey, Thomas Hammond *retired surgeon*
Danse, Ilene Homnick Raisfeld *physician, educator, toxicologist*
Date, Elaine Satomi *physiatrist, educator*
Davidson, Mayer B. *medical educator, researcher*
Davis, Lowell Livingston *cardiovascular surgeon*
Davis, Mary Helen *psychiatrist, psychoanalyst, educator*
Dawson, Peter John *pathologist, educator*
Degann, Sona Irene *obstetrician, gynecologist, educator*
de la Piedra, Jorge *orthopedic surgeon*
De Lorenzo, Robert Allan *emergency physician*
de Lorimier, Alfred Alexandre *retired physician, pediatric surgeon, medical educator*
DePalma, Ralph George *surgeon, educator*
De Vita, Michael Richard *obstetrician-gynecologist*
DeVita, Vincent Theodore, Jr., *oncologist*
Dews, P(eter) B(ooth) *medical scientist, educator*
Dhara, Venkata Ramana *physician, educator*
Dickes, Robert *psychiatrist*
Dickson, James Francis, III, *surgeon*
Diddle, Albert W. *obstetrician, gynecologist*
Diehl, Louis F. *hematologist*
Diener, Erwin *immunologist*
Dimancescu, Mihai D. *neurosurgeon, researcher, educator*
Ding, Jinwen *biomedical researcher*
DiPersio, John F. *oncologist*
Dito, William Robert *pathology educator*
Dmochowski, Jan Rafal *surgeon, researcher*
Dodge, R(alph) Edward, Jr., *physician*
Doherty, Peter Charles *immunologist*
Dolev, Jacqueline *physician, researcher*
Donley, Deedra Ann *medical educator*
Doraiswamy, P(udugramam) Murali *psychiatrist, educator, researcher, neuroscientist*
Dos, Serge Jacques *surgeon, physiology researcher*
Dowsett, Peter John *retired obstetrician, gynecologist*
Drake, Michael V. *ophthalmologist, educator, dean*
Drance, Stephen Michael *ophthalmologist, educator*
Draper, Edgar *psychiatrist*
Drews, Robert Carrel *retired physician*
Dryman, Amy *epidemiologist*
Dubin, Howard Victor *dermatologist*
Dugan, Charles Clark *physician, surgeon*
Dumont, Allan Eliot *retired physician, educator*
Durant, John Ridgeway *retired oncologist, health facility administrator, consultant*
Durell, Jack *psychiatrist*
Duvall, Gene Robert *radiologist*
Dyar, Kathryn Wilkin *pediatrician*
Dyck, George *psychiatry educator*
Dziewanowska, Zofia Elizabeth *neuropsychiatrist, pharmaceutical executive, researcher, educator*
Eaton, Merrill Thomas *psychiatrist, educator*
Edelson, Marshall *retired psychiatry educator, psychoanalyst*
Edmondson, Robert Campbell *retired hematologist, oncologist, internal medicine educator*
Edwards, Bruce George *retired ophthalmologist, naval officer*
Edwards, E. Stephen *retired pediatrician*
Edwards, Ephraim Zeno *retired anesthesiologist*
Edwards, Larry David *internist, educator, dean*
Eisenstat, Theodore Ellis *colon and rectal surgeon, educator*
Eisinger, Robert Peter *nephrologist, educator*
Elgart, Mervyn L. *retired dermatologist, educator*
Elias, Alan *physician, educator*
Ellis, Lawrence Dobson *internist, educator*
Engle, Howard A. *retired pediatrician*
Epps, Charles Harry, Jr., *retired orthopaedic surgery educator*
Esser, James Mark *cardiovascular and interventional radiologist*
Estes, Edward Harvey, Jr., *medical educator*
Etzel, Ruth Ann *pediatrician, epidemiologist, educator*
Evarts, Charles McCollister *orthopaedic surgeon*
Fanos, Kathleen Hilaire *osteopathic physician, podiatrist*
Faris, James Vannoy *interventional cardiologist, cardiology educator, hospital executive*
Fariss, Bruce Lindsay *endocrinologist, consultant*
Feinstein, Robert P. *dermatologist*
Felgar, Raymond E(ugene) *pathologist, medical educator*
Ferguson, Earl Wilson *cardiologist, medical executive, telemedicine consultant*
Ferguson, Emmet Fewell, Jr., *surgeon*
Ferstenfeld, Julian Erwin *internist, educator*
Figueroa, Roberto Andres *psychiatrist, researcher*
Fischer, A(lbert) Alan *family physician*
Fischer, David Seymour *internist, consultant*
Fishman, Glenn I. *medical educator*
Fishman, Lawrence Martin *endocrinologist*
Fitch, Frank Wesley *pathologist educator, immunologist, educator, administrator*
Fleishman, Philip Robert *internist*
Flick, Arnold L. *retired physician, community activist*
Fomon, Samuel Joseph *pediatrician, educator*
Forno, Karin Ida *physician, educator*
Fralinger, Jack Bruce *surgeon*
Frawley, Thomas Francis *retired internist, medical educator*
Fried, Floyd Alan *urologist*
Fristoe, Macalyne *speech-language pathologist, psychologist, educator, writer*
Frohman, Larry Philip *neuro-ophthalmologist*
Frost, J. Ormond *otolaryngologist, educator*
Furlow, Thomas William, Jr., *neurologist*
Furnas, David William *plastic surgeon, educator*
Gable, Karen Elaine *health science educator*
Gahagan, Thomas Gail *obstetrician, gynecologist*
Gahlinger, Paul Maria *occupational medicine physician, educator*
Galan, Vincent *anesthesiologist*
Galbraith, William Bruce *internist, educator*
Gangarosa, Raymond Eugene *epidemiologist, electrical engineer*
Garcia, Alexander *orthopedic surgeon*
Gardner, John Howland, III, *neurologist*
Garrett, Marshall Lee *anesthesiologist, educator*
Gartner, Lawrence Mitchel *pediatrician, medical college educator*
Gathright, John Byron, Jr., *colon and rectal surgeon, educator*
Gay, Hannah Berry *physician, educator*
Gaylin, Willard *physician, educator*
Geiger, Albert J., Jr., *retired radiologist*
Gelberg, Lillian *family medicine physician, educator*
Gemell, Nicholas I. *retired radiologist*
Genieser, Nancy Branom *radiologist*
Gewitz, Michael Harold *pediatrician*
Gherardi, Gherardo Joseph *pathologist*
Gibson, Milton Eugene *cardiologist*
Gilchrist, Gerald Seymour *pediatric hematologist, oncologist, educator*
Gill, Thomas James, III, *physician, educator*
Gillespie, Gary Don *physician*
Gillett, Richard Clark, Jr., *physician, educator, health facility administrator*
Glasauer, Franz Ernst *neurosurgeon*
Glaser, Robert Joy *retired internist, foundation administrator*
Glass, Dorothea Daniels *physiatrist, educator*
Glassman, Lawrence S. *plastic surgeon*
Gleason, Stephen Charles *physician*
Glimcher, Laurie H. *immunology educator*
Goffman, Thomas Edward *radiation oncologist, researcher*
Gold, Judith Hammerling *psychiatrist*
Goldberg, Burton David *pathologist, researcher, educator*
Goldberg, Mark Arthur *neurologist*
Goldberg, Michael Ellis *neurologist, neuroscientist*
Golden, Gerald Samuel *retired national medical board executive*
Goldmann, Morton Aaron *cardiologist, educator*
Goldstein, Avram *pharmacology educator*
Goldstein, Dora Benedict *pharmacologist, educator*
Goldstein, Naomi *retired psychiatrist*
Goodfellow, Robin Irene *surgeon*
Goodwin, Andrew Wirt, II, *radiologist*
Gottfried, Eugene Leslie *physician, educator*
Graham, David G. *preventive medicine physician, psychiatrist*
Graham, James Herbert *retired dermatologist*
Gray, Mary Jane *retired obstetrician, gynecologist*
Graziani, Leonard Joseph *pediatric neurologist, researcher*
Green, Louis Harry *retired surgeon*
Greenberg, Carolyn Phyllis *anesthesiologist, educator*
Greene, Alan Guyer *retired radiologist*
Greene, Donald Richard *dermatologist, educator*
Greenfield, Val Shea *ophthalmologist*
Greenstein, Robert *retired radiologist*
Gregory, Daniel Hayes *gastroenterologist*
Grendell, James Henry *medical educator*
Grenitz, Robert *retired obstetrician-gynecologist*
Griffen, Ward O., Jr., *surgeon, educator, medical board executive*
Griffith, B(ezaleel) Herold *physician, educator, plastic surgeon*
Griner, Paul Francis *physician*
Gross, Ruth Taubenhaus *former pediatrician*
Grossman, Joyce Renee *pediatrician, internist*
Gulbrandsen, Patricia Hughes *physician*
Gupta, Krishan Lal *physician, medical educator*
Gupta, Narendra Kumar *physician, educator*
Gupta, Ritesh *cardiologist, researcher*
Guyer, Bernard *maternal and child health educator*
Haggerty, Robert Johns *pediatrician, educator*
Haithcock, William Dana, Jr., *physician*
Halliday, William Ross *retired physician, speleologist, writer*
Hammel, Ernest Martin *medical educator, academic administrator*
Hance, Darwood B. *radiologist*
Hanna, Duke Ellsworth *neurological surgeon*
Hansell, John Royer *retired pathologist*
Hardaway, Robert Morris, III, *retired surgeon, educator, military officer*

PROFESSIONAL INDEX 5709 HEALTHCARE: MEDICINE

Hardman, Joel Griffeth *retired pharmacologist*
Harrigan, Rosanne Carol *medical educator*
Harrington, John Tolan *medical educator, internist, nephrologist, dean emeritus*
Harris, John H., Jr., *radiologist*
Harrison, Harold Henry, Sr., *physician, scientist, educator*
Harrop, Daniel Smith, III, *psychiatrist*
Hart, Cecil William Joseph *otolaryngologist, surgeon*
Hartmann, William Herman *retired pathologist, adminstrator*
Harvey, Birt *retired pediatrician, educator*
Hathaway, David Roger *physician, medical educator, scientist*
Hawthorne, Douglas D. *medical association administrator*
H'Doubler, Francis Todd, Jr., *surgeon*
Healy, Bernadine P. *physician, educator, federal agency administrator, organization executive*
Helfand, Arthur E. *podiatrist*
Hellerstein, David Joel *psychiatrist, researcher, writer*
Henderson, Melford J. *epidemiologist, molecular biologist, chemist*
Hendren, Robert Lee *psychiatrist, educator*
Heptinstall, Robert Hodgson *physician*
Herman, Martin Neal *neurologist, educator*
Herrera, Guillermo Antonio *pathologist, educator, researcher*
Herzberger, Eugene E. *retired neurosurgeon*
Higginbotham, Edith Arleane *radiologist, researcher*
Hill, C. Thomas, Jr., *radiologist*
Himes, John Harter *medical researcher, educator*
Hirose, Teruo Terry *surgeon, educator*
Hoeprich, Paul Daniel *physician educator*
Hogness, John Rusten *internist, educator, academic administrator*
Holland, Robert Campbell *anatomist, educator*
Hollenberg, Norman Kenneth *medical educator*
Hollis, Richard Shelton *retired obstetrician-gynecologist*
Holsgrove, Gareth John *medical association administrator*
Holtzman, Robert Neil Nehemiah *neurosurgeon, neurologist*
Hood, William Boyd, Jr., *cardiologist, educator*
Horner, George Marlin *retired obstetrician-gynecologist*
Horswill, C. Weir *retired obstetrician-gynecologist, photographer*
Hoskins, John Howard *urologist, educator*
Howard, Terry Thomas *obstetrician, gynecologist*
Howards, Stuart S. *urologist, educator*
Howell, Joel DuBose *internist, educator*
Howell, Julius Ammons *retired plastic surgeon*
Hricak, Hedvig *radiologist*
Huang, Russel Charles *surgeon, medical researcher*
Huggins, Charles Edward *obstetrician, gynecologist, educator*
Hughes-Ayanru, Grace *retired geriatrician*
Hunt, Oliver Raymond, Jr., *thoracic and cardiovascular surgeon*
Hunter, Daniel Clyde, Jr., *retired surgeon, educator*
Hurd, Suzanne Sheldon *retired federal agency health science director*
Hutcheon, Duncan Elliot *physician, educator*
Huth, Thomas Joseph *retired surgeon*
Ianchulev, Tsontcho Alexandrov *ophthalmologist, researcher*
Irish, Thomas Judson *retired plastic surgeon*
Irwin, Peter John *orthopaedic surgeon*
Iserson, Kenneth Victor *emergency medicine educator, bioethicist, author*
Izenstark, Joseph Louis *retired radiologist, physician, educator*
Jackson, David Huntsman *retired cardiologist*
Jacobey, John Arthur, III, *surgeon, educator*
Jacobson, Eugene Donald *medical educator, administrator, researcher*
Jalba, Mihai Sergiu *epidemiologist*
Janicak, Philip Gregory *psychiatry educator, researcher*
Janowitz, Henry David *gastroenterologist, researcher, medical educator*
Jarvik, Gail Pairitz *medical geneticist*
Jefferies, William McKendree *internist, educator*
Jeresaty, Robert Michel *cardiologist, educator*
Johnson, Arthur Ingram *obstetrician and gynecologist*
Johnson, David Porter *infectious diseases physician*
Johnson, Fernly Eldo *surgeon*
Johnson, Leonard Morris *retired pediatric surgeon*
Johnson, William G. *neurologist, educator*
Jones, Amelia Susan *retired anesthesiologist*
Jones, Billy Ernest *dermatology educator*
Jones, Walton Linton *internist, former government official*
Jordan, Deovina Nasis *administrative nurse*
Joshi, Pratibha C. *immunologist, researcher*
Judge, Nancy Elizabeth *obstetrician, gynecologist*
Judge, Rajinder *psychiatrist*
Jung, Rodney C. *internist, academic administrator*
Juskenas, Nellie K. *retired anesthesiologist*
Kantor, Harvey Sherwin *retired medical educator*
Kao, Simon C. *radiologist, educator*
Kaplan, Gabriela Diana *radiologist*
Karpinos, Robert Douglas *anesthesiologist*
Kasimis, Basil S. *oncologist*
Kaufman, Stephen Lawrence *radiologist, educator*
Keane, James R. *neurologist*
Keill, Stuart Langdon *psychiatrist*
Keller, Ben Robert, Jr., *gynecologist*
Kelley, Patrick Alan *neurologist, educator*
Kelly, John H., Jr., *epidemiologist, lifestyle and preventive medicine specialist*
Kendall, Harry Ovid *internist*
Kerr, Harry Davidson *emergency physician*
Kettelkamp, Donald Benjamin *retired orthopedic surgeon, eductor*
Khan, Arfa *radiologist, educator*
Kiesel, Ilmar Otto *retired radiologist*
Kim-Farley, Robert James *epidemiologist, educator*
Kinley, Christine T. *certified physician assistant*
Kinzie, Jeannie Jones *radiation oncologist, nuclear medicine physician*
Kirila, Carol Elizabeth *osteopathic physician, internist*
Kirkpatrick, Garland Penn *retired pediatrician*
Kitt, Walter *psychiatrist*
Kivikoski, Asko Ilmari *retired obstetrician, gynecologist*
Klitzman, Robert Lloyd *psychiatrist, writer*
Knapp, Howard Raymond *internist, clinical pharmacologist*
Knecht, Charles Lewis, III, *retired radiologist*
Knobloch, Ferdinand J. *psychiatrist, educator*
Kohrman, Arthur Fisher *pediatrics educator*
Kolff, Willem Johan *retired internist, medical educator*
Koreman, Dorothy Goldstein *physician, dermatologist*
Kraut, Joel Arthur *ophthalmologist*
Kreider, Clement Horst, Jr., *neurosurgeon*
Krizan, Kelly Joe *physician, leather craftsman*
Krop, Stephen *retired pharmacologist*
Kumar, Sanjaya *epidemiologist, biostatistician*
Kundel, Harold Louis *radiologist, educator*
Kunz, Alexandra Cavitt *physician, anthropologist, researcher*
Kurnick, Nathaniel Bertrand *retired oncologist-hematologist*
Kushwaha, Sudhir Singh *internist, cardiologist, educator*
Kwik-Kostek, Christine Irene *physician, retired military officer, medical officer*
Kydd, William *former medical association administrator*
Kyger, Edgar Ross *surgeon, educator*
La Bagnara, James, Jr., *otolaryngologist, educator*
Lai, Eric Pong Shing *family physician, educator*
Lake, Carol Lee *anesthesiologist, physician executive, educator*
Langfitt, Thomas William *neurosurgeon, foundation administrator*
Larar, Gerald N. *physician, research scientist*
Larson, Richard Smith *pathologist, researcher*
Larson, Roger Keith *physician, writer*
Lauderdale, Vance, Jr., *anesthesiologist*
Laupus, William Edward *physician, educator*
Lauterbach, Edward Charles *psychiatric educator*
LaVelle, Arthur *anatomy educator*
Lawless, Michael Rhodes *pediatrics educator*
Lawrence, Christine *physician*
Lawrence, David Long *radiologist*
Layton, Robert Glenn *radiologist*
Le Cocq, Frank *retired obstetrician/gynecologist*
Leidy, John William, Jr., *endocrinologist, educator*
Leman, Craig Billings *surgeon*
Leo, Michael Charles *emergency physician, surgeon, educator*
Levin, Alan Scott *pathologist, allergist, immunologist, lawyer*
Levin, Jack *physician, educator, biomedical investigator*
Lewers, Donald Theodore *nephrologist, internist*
Lewin, Marion Ein *consultant, physician, former medical association administrator*
Lifton, Robert Jay *psychiatrist, author*
Lim, Shun Ping *cardiologist, educator*
Lincicome, David Richard *biomedical and animal scientist*
Linz, Anthony James *osteopathic physician, consultant, educator*
Lipton, Glenn E. *orthopaedic surgeon*
Livezey, Mark Douglas *physician*
Lohmann, George Young, Jr., *neurosurgeon, hospital executive, international business executive, artist*
Loomis, Salora Dale *psychiatrist*
Looney, Gerald Lee *medical educator, administrator*
Loschen, Earl Lee *psychiatrist, educator*
Loube, Samuel Dennis *physician*
Lourenco, Ruy Valentim *physician, educator*
Luchansky, Edward *obstetrician-gynecologist, educator*
Ludwig, Stephen *pediatrics and emergency medicine educator*
Luhrs, Caro Elise *internal medicine physician, administrator, educator*
Lutz, Lawrence Joseph *family practice physician*
Macleod, Angus *retired internist*
MacLeod, Gordon C. *surgeon*
Maguire, James Harvey *physician*
Maioriello, Richard Patrick *retired otolaryngologist*
Mala, Theodore Anthony *physician, consultant*
Malach, Monte *physician*
Malloy, Craig Riggs *physician, educator*
Malone, Richard P. *psychiatrist*
Mannino, J(oseph) Robert *medical educator*
Marcdante, Karen Jean *medical educator*
Margolis, Harold Stephen *epidemiologist*
Markham, Charles Henry *neurologist*
Markham, Fred William, Jr., *medical educator*
Marko, Marlene *psychiatrist*
Markoe, Arnold Michael *radiation oncologist*
Maron, Arthur *pediatrician, medical administrator*
Marshall, Barry James *gastroenterologist*
Martin, Sarah *medical researcher*
Martinez-Maldonado, Manuel *medical service administrator, internist, nephrologist*
Martino, Silvana *osteopath, medical oncologist*
Mascola, Richard F. *former medical association administrator*
Massey, Robert Unruh *internist, educator, dean*
Materson, Richard Stephen *physician, educator*
Mates, Susan Onthank *physician, medical educator, writer, violinist*
Mathelier, Amedee C. *obstetrician-gynecologist*
Mathewson, John Jacob *emergency and family practice physician*
Mathias, Mervin A. *retired surgeon*
Matthews, George Robert *retired radiologist*
Matzke, Jay *internist*
May, Robert M. *retired obstetrician, gynecologist, educator*
McCarthy-Allen, Mary Frances *medical foundation administrator, not-for-profit fundraiser, consultant*
McCormick, Kenneth L. *pediatrics educator, researcher*
McCullough, David L. *urologist*
McDonald, Sandra Ann *surgical pathologist*
McEwen, Bruce S. *neuroendocrinology educator*
McGrath, Mary Helena *plastic surgeon, educator*
McGuire, Hunter Holmes, Jr., *retired surgeon, educator*
McKee, Janath deBin *medical researcher*
Meilman, Edward *physician*
Mellins, Harry Zachary *radiologist, educator*
Mendels, Joseph *psychiatrist, educator*
Mengel, Charles Edmund *physician, medical educator*
Mensah, George A. *medical association administrator, educator*
Mercado, Mary Gonzales *cardiologist*
Mereschak, Volmar A. *retired obstetrician-gynecologist*
Meyer, Greg Charles *psychiatrist*
Mikklesen, Edwin Jens *psychiatrist*
Miller, Anthony Bernard *physician, medical researcher*
Miller, Ross Hays *retired neurosurgeon*
Millikan, Clark Harold *physician*
Milnor, William Robert *physician*
Milstone, Leonard Matthew *physician, educator, researcher*
Mirin, Steven Martin *psychiatrist*
Mitchell, William Marvin *pathology educator*
Modisher, Melvin Wayne *obstetrician/gynecologist, educator*
Mohaideen, A. Hassan *surgeon, healthcare executive*
Molbegott, Lester Philip *anesthesiologist*
Montgomery, John Richard *pediatrician, educator*
Moore, Emily Allyn *pharmacologist*
Moossy, John *neuropathologist, neurologist, consultant*
Moran, Gregory John *emergency medicine physician, educator*
More, Jay *neurosurgeon*
Morgan, Stanley Charles *plastic and reconstructive surgeon*
Moser, Robert Lawrence *pathologist, health facility administrator*
Mostowycz, Leonidas *radiologist*
Motto, Jerome Arthur *psychiatry educator*
Mountain, Clifton Fletcher *surgeon, educator*
Mueller, Charles Barber *surgeon, educator*
Mulcahy, Gabriel M. *pathologist*
Munger, Bryce Leon *physician, educator*
Munster, Andrew Michael *surgeon, educator*
Murphey, Sheila Ann *infectious diseases physician, educator, researcher*
Myerowitz, P(aul) David *cardiac surgeon, educator*
Nadler, Sigmond Harold *physician, surgeon*
Nealis, James Garry Thomas, III, *pediatric neurologist, educator, author*
Nelson, Christopher Grant *dermatologist*
Nelson, Luther Sullivan *radiologist*
Nelson, Nancy Eleanor *pediatrician, educator*
Nelson, William Rankin *surgeon, educator*
Newman, Andrew *physician*
Nguyen, D.O., Tuan H. *cosmetic surgeon, general surgeon*
Nicholls, Richard Aurelius *obstetrician, gynecologist*
Niculescu, Florin Ioan *immunology and rheumatology researcher, educator*
Nieto, Juan Manuel *emergency medicine physician*
Nochlin-Soto, David *neuropathologist*
Nora, James Jackson *physician, writer, educator*
Norrid, Henry Gail *osteopathic physician and surgeon, researcher, educator, healthcare facility administrator*
Novack, Alvin John *physician*
Novack, Tevor D. *surgeon, consultant*
Odell, William Douglas *physician, educator, research scientist*
O'Gorman, Maurice R.G. *medical researcher*
Ogunyemi, Omolola Ijeoma *medical educator*
Olds, Jacqueline *psychiatrist, educator*
O'Leary, Denis Joseph *retired physician, insurance company executive*
O'Leary, Dennis Sophian *medical organization executive*
O'Leary, John Clarence *retired radiologist*
Onuigbo, Macaulay Amechi *physician, nephrologist, transplant physician*
Osment, Lamar Sutton *retired dermatologist, educator*
Packard, John Mallory *physician*
Paino, Javier E. *physician*
Painter, Robert Lowell *surgeon, educator*
Pantojas-Concepcion, Carlos A. *rheumatologist*
Parker, Brent Mershon *retired medical educator, internist, cardiologist*
Parker, Gerald William *internist, health facility administrator, retired military officer*
Parker, John William *retired pathology educator, investigator*
Parmley, Van Samuel *retired anesthesiologist*
Parsons, Harry Glenwood *retired surgeon*
Pascale, Jane Fay *pathologist*
Pastorek, Norman Joseph *facial plastic surgeon*
Patchin, Rebecca J. *anesthesiologist, educator, administrator*
Patterson, James Willis *pathology and dermatology educator*
Patterson, Joseph Flanner, Jr., *surgeon, anesthesiologist*
Pauly, John Edward *anatomist, educator*
Pederson, William Christopher *plastic surgeon*
Pedini, Egle Damijonaitis *radiologist*
Pedini, Kenneth *radiologist*
Peixoto Neto, Jose Ulysses *internist, researcher*
Pelletier, Louis Conrad *surgeon, educator, health facility administrator*
Pendergrass, Henry Pancoast *radiologist, nuclear medicine physician*
Penso, Christine Arety *obstetrician-gynecologist*
Perez, Dianne M. *medical researcher*
Perlmutter, David H. *physician, educator*
Persaud, Andrea Nandini *dermatologist*
Pesch, LeRoy Allen *physician, educator, health and hospital consultant, business executive*
Pesola, Gene Raymond *physician, educator*
Peszke, Michael Alfred *psychiatrist, writer*
Peterson, Ann Sullivan *physician, health care consultant*
Petryshyn, Walter Alexis *otolaryngologist*
Petz, Thomas Joseph *internist*
Pfister, Howard Frederick Carl *retired surgeon*
Philippon, Marc Joseph *orthopaedic surgeon*
Phillips, Robert Derrick *psychiatrist*
Pinsker, Walter *retired allergist, immunologist*
Pirro, Alfred Anthony, Jr., *physician*
Plourd, David M. *medical educator*
Podell, Robert Mann *obstetrician-gynecologist*
Pohorecky-Dolinsky, Larissa Alexandra *pharmacologist*
Poker, Nathan *retired radiologist*
Poppers, Paul Jules *anesthesiologist, educator*
Portnoy, Harold David *neurologist, surgeon*
Prange, Hilmar Walter *neurology educator*
Price, James Melford *retired physician, researcher*
Pritts, Elizabeth Anna *medical educator*
Propst, Michael Truman *pathologist*
Prusiner, Stanley Ben *neurology and biochemistry educator, researcher*
Punukollu, Gopi Krishna *cardiologist*
Qiao, Guilin *pharmacologist, medical researcher*
Quetglas, Moll Juan *plastic and maxillofacial surgeon*
Rachlin, William Selig *retired surgeon*
Rafiq, Azhar *medical educator, researcher*
Raichle, Marcus Edward *radiology, neurology educator*
Rako, Susan *psychiatrist, author*
Ram, Chitta Venkata *physician*
Ramirez-Rivera, Jose *physician*
Randolph, Judson Graves *pediatric surgeon*
Ranney, Helen Margaret *retired internist, hematologist, educator*
Rapp, Lynn Blair *obstetrician-gynecologist, educator*
Rasmussen, Howard *retired medical educator*
Raza, Asim *psychiatrist*
Rebhun, Joseph *allergist, immunologist, medical educator*
Regan, Frederic Dennis *cardiologist*
Reid, Orien *former medical association administrator*
Reingold, Arthur Lawrence *epidemiologist, educator*
Ren, Xing Jian *physician*
Rewcastle, Neill Barry *neuropathology educator*
Rich, Norman Minner *surgeon*
Richmond, Julius Benjamin *retired pediatrician, health policy educator*
Riddle, Mark Alan *child psychiatrist*
Riehle, Robert Arthur, Jr., *medical director, surgeon*
Rifkind, Richard Allen *physician*
Rigg, Charles Andrew *retired pediatrician*
Riker, William Kay *pharmacologist, educator*
Ris, Howard Clinton, Jr., *nonprofit public policy organization administrator*
Roberts, Alan Silverman *orthopedic surgeon*
Roberts, Albert Dee *internist*
Robinson, Nathaniel David, Jr., *physician, consultant*
Robson, Martin Cecil *surgery educator, plastic surgeon*
Rodgers, James Beall *surgeon*
Rodgers, Lawrence Rodney *internist, educator*
Rollins, Arlen Jeffery *osteopathic physician*
Roman, Stanford Augustus, Jr., *medical educator, dean*
Ronen-Zlotnik, Ela S. *cardiologist, writer*
Rosemberg, Eugenia *physician, educator, medical research administrator*
Rosen, Paul Peter *pathologist*
Rosenblum, Mindy Fleischer *pediatrician*
Rowley, William Robert *retired surgeon*
Rubin, Alan *physician*
Rubin, Robert Joseph *internist, consultant*
Rui, Hallgeir *cancer researcher*
Ruoho, Arnold Eino *pharmacology educator*
Russell, Douglas Campbell *cardiologist*
Russo, Jose *pathologist*
Ryan, Robert John *endocrinology educator and researcher*
Sacha, Robert Frank *osteopathic physician*
Salazar, Omar Mauricio *radiation oncologist, educator*
Samuels, Barry Ivan *radiologist, medical educator*
Sanders, Aaron Perry *radiation biophysics educator*
Sanfelippo, Peter Michael *cardiac, thoracic and vascular surgeon*
Santos, Arthur Magno *thoracic cardiovascular surgeon*
Saravolatz, Louis Donald *epidemiologist, physician educator*
Saraya, Nusshy *physician, education educator*
Sargent, William Winston *retired anesthesiologist*
Sarkar, Siddhartha *pathologist*
Sawczuk, Ihor S. *urologist*
Say, Carlos C. *physician, surgeon*
Scavone, Edmond *retired surgeon*
Schaefer, Heinrich C. *retired anesthesiologist*
Schauf, Victoria *pediatrician, educator, infectious diseases consultant*
Scher, Jordan Mayer *physician, psychiatrist, drug abuse specialist*
Schick, Paul K. *hematologist*
Schmidt, Sheila Elizabeth *physician, writer*
Schneck, Stuart Austin *retired neurologist, educator*
Schneider, Calvin *physician*
Schneider, Jan *retired obstetrics and gynecology educator*
Schooley, Robert T. *medical educator*
Schulman, Harold *obstetrician, gynecologist, perinatologist*
Schutt, Allan Jackson *retired medical oncologist*
Schwartz, Walter Richard *obstetrician/gynecologist, retired*
Sciammarella, Maria Graciela *internist, cardiologist*
Searcy, Ashburn Pidcock, Sr., *anesthesiologist*
Secor, Harold Edwin *retired obstetrician/gynecologist*
Sedlacek, Richard Leo *retired surgeon*
Seltser, Raymond *epidemiologist, educator*
Sever, John Louis *medical researcher, educator*
Sewell, Robert Dalton *pediatrician*
Shah, Nandlal Chimanlal *retired physiatrist*
Shane, John Marder *endocrinologist*
Shashidharan, Kalathil Kungatty *emergency physician, internist*
Shaw, Ronald Ahrend *physician, educator*
Shayman, James Alan *nephrologist, educator*
Sheard, Charles, III, *dermatologist*
Sher, Leo *psychiatrist*
Sherman, John Foord *biomedical consultant*
Sherman, Joseph Owen *pediatric surgeon*
Shetty, Mulki Radhakrishna *retired oncologist, consultant*
Shick, John Earl *retired radiologist*
Shorter, Nicholas Andrew *pediatric surgeon*
Shumacker, Harris B., Jr., *retired surgeon, educator, author*
Shuster, Frederick *retired internist, gastroenterologist*
Siddiqi, Javed *neurosurgeon*
Siemens, Albert J. *medical association administrator*
Siffert, Robert Spencer *orthopedic surgeon*
Sifontes, Jose E. *pediatrics educator*
Sigell, Leonard Trittack *pharmacologist, educator*
Sigmon, J. Lewis, Jr., *medical educator*
Silver, Malcolm David *pathologist, educator*
Silverstein, Martin Elliot *surgeon, consultant, writer*
Simmons, Geoffrey Stuart *physician*
Skolnick, Lawrence *neonatologist, medical administrator*
Slavit, David Hal *otolaryngologist*
Small, Joyce Graham *psychiatrist, educator*
Smith, Duret S. *physician, medical educator*
Smith, Hugh Elmore *retired obstetrician and gynecologist*
Smith, Martin Henry *retired pediatrician*

Smith, Martin Lane *biomedical researcher*
Smith, Stuart Lyon *psychiatrist, corporate executive*
Smith, Thomas Hunter *ophthalmologist, ophthalmic plastic and orbital surgeon*
Smyth, Nicholas Patrick Dillon *surgeon*
Snyderman, Ralph *medical educator, physician*
Sobin, Leslie Howard *pathologist, educator*
Sohn, Rayna Mayer *medical analyst, researcher, legal analyst*
Soltero-Harrington, Luis Rubén *retired surgeon, educator*
Sonders, Lawrence J. *obstetrician, gynecologist*
Sontag, James Mitchell *cancer researcher*
Sopher, Aviva Bracha *physician*
Sourial, Alfy Saif *surgeon*
Spackman, Thomas James *radiologist*
Speir, William Arthur, Jr., *critical care physician*
Spitzer, Walter Oswald *epidemiologist, educator*
Starr, Arnold *neurologist, educator*
Stein, Anthony C. *medical educator, researcher*
Stein, Bennett Mueller *neurosurgeon*
Stein, Paul David *cardiologist*
Steinman, Theodore Irving *nephrologist, educator*
Stollerman, Gene Howard *physician, educator*
Stone, James Robert *surgeon*
Stonnington, Henry Herbert *physician, medical executive, educator*
Strain, James Ellsworth *pediatrician, retired association administrator*
Strandberg, John David *comparative pathologist*
Strongin, Jonathan David *physician*
Sullivan, Colleen Anne *anesthesiologist, educator*
Summers, David Stewart *neurologist, consultant*
Suprun, Harry Zvi *pathologist*
Svensson, Lars Georg *cardiovascular and thoracic surgeon*
Swenson, James Reed *physician, educator*
Swiecicki, Martin *retired neurosurgeon*
Tagiuri, Consuelo Keller *child psychiatrist, educator*
Tank, Gerhard Willi *obstetrician and gynecologist*
Taren, James Arthur *neurosurgeon, educator*
Taylor, Peyton Troy, Jr., *gynecologic oncologist, educator*
Tegtmeier, Ronald Eugene *physician, surgeon*
Tepper, Lloyd Barton *preventive medicine physician, educator*
Thorsen, Marie Kristin *radiologist, educator*
Tiefenbrun, Jonathan *surgeon*
Tolliche, Charles R. *physician*
Tranquada, Robert Ernest *internist, educator*
Troost, Bradley Todd *neurologist, educator*
Tropez-Sims, Susanne *pediatrician, educator*
Tropp, Rory *emergency medicine physician*
Trumbull, William Ernest *retired surgeon, educator*
Truschke, Edward F. *retired medical association administrator*
Turk, Richard Errington *retired psychiatrist*
Turrill, Fred Lovejoy *surgeon*
Tykocinski, Mark L. *molecular immunologist, gene therapist*
Tyler, Carl Walter, Jr., *retired physician, health research administrator*
Udvarhelyi, George Bela *neurosurgery educator emeritus, cultural affairs administrator*
Ullman, Joel Clarke *obstetrician/gynecologist*
Vachher, Prehlad Singh *psychiatrist*
Valentine, William Newton *physician, educator*
Van Brunt, Edmund Ewing *physician*
Van Heertum, Ronald Lanny *physician*
Van Naarden Braun, Kim *epidemiologist*
Van Stone, William Webb *psychiatrist*
Vickers, Stanley *biochemical pharmacologist*
Vittetoe, Marie Clare *retired clinical laboratory science educator*
Volkman, Alvin *retired physician, research scientist, educator*
Vydareny, Kay Herzog *radiologist, medical educator*
Wachob, Tom Webb, Jr., *retired obstetrician-gynecologist*
Wade, David Stuart *surgeon*
Walker, James Steven *osteopath, emergency physician*
Wallace, Edwin Ruthven, IV, *psychiatrist, neuropsychiatrist psychotherapist*
Wang, Allan Xu Hui *physician*
Wang, Nancy *pathologist, educator*
Wang, Qin *medical educator*
Warheit, Peter S. *anesthesiologist*
Wasmuth, Carl Erwin *physician, lawyer*
Watanabe, Kyoichi A(loysius) *chemist, researcher, pharmacology educator*
Waters, William Carter, III, *retired internist, educator*
Watring, Watson Glenn *retired gynecologic oncologist, educator*
Watson, Donald Charles *cardiothoracic surgeon, educator*
Weber, Alvin Julian, III, *radiologist*
Weiden, Paul Lincoln *cancer researcher, oncologist, educator*
Weigensberg, Irving Joseph *radiation oncologist*
Weil, Richard, III, *surgeon, medical educator*
Weimann, Robert Bruce *retired surgeon*
Weir, Bryce Keith Alexander *neurosurgeon, neurologist, educator*
Weiss, Steven Gary *physician*
Wenkert, Deborah *pediatric rheumatologist, researcher*
West, Gregory Alan *physician*
White, Augustus Aaron, III, *orthopedic surgeon*
White, Kerr Lachlan *retired hygiene and tropical medicine physician, medical educator, foundation administrator*
White, Richard Thomas *radiologist*
Whitman, Gregory Theodore *neurologist*
Whitsell, John Crawford, II, *general surgeon*
Wilhelm, Morton *retired surgery educator*
Wilk, Ronald *physician*
Wilkinson, Grant Robert *pharmacology educator*
Williams, John Zigler *anesthesiologist*
Williams, Robert Leon *psychiatrist, neurologist, educator*
Wilmore, Douglas Wayne *surgeon, educator*
Wilson, Mary Elizabeth *epidemiologist, physician, educator*
Wishnick, Marcia Margolis *pediatrician, geneticist, educator*
Wittmann, Dietmar H. *surgery educator*
Worner, Theresa Marie *internist, educator*
Worrell, Richard Vernon *orthopedic surgeon, college dean, dean*
Wyngaarden, James Barnes *physician*
Yacoub, Jean *cardiologist*
Yalam, Arnold Robert *allergist, immunologist, consultant*
Yamamoto, Joe *psychiatrist, educator*
Yarchoan, Robert *clinical immunologist, researcher*
Yarington, Charles Thomas, Jr., *surgeon, educator, health facility administrator*
Yielding, K. Lemone *physician*
Yodaiken, Ralph E. *pathologist, occupational medicine physician, educator*
Yollick, Bernard Lawrence *otolaryngologist, surgeon*
Yood, Harold Stanley *retired internist*
Youmans, Julian Ray *neurosurgeon, educator*
Young, Grace May-En *pediatrician, educator*
Young, Marvin Richard *dermatologist, educator*
Youngstrom, Paul Clarence *anesthesiologist*
Zacarías, Fernando R. K. *physician*
Zapp, John S. *retired medical association administrator*
Zawacki, Bruce Edwin *surgeon, educator, ethicist*
Zeine, Rana R. *pathologist, research scientist*
Zimmerman, David Alan *cardiologist*
Zumwalt, Ross Eugene *forensic pathologist, educator*

HUMANITIES: LIBERAL STUDIES

UNITED STATES

ALABAMA

Auburn
Amacher, Richard Earl *literature educator*
Gerber, Larry George *historian, educator*
Harrell, David Edwin, Jr., *history professor*
Littleton, Taylor Dowe *humanities educator*
Morrow, Patrick David *English educator*
Noe, Kenneth William *historian, educator*

Auburn University
Lewis, Walter David *historian, educator*

Birmingham
Allen, Lee Norcross *historian, educator*
Burden, Cedric Jerome, Sr., *English educator*
Carter, William Causey *language educator*
Conley, Carolyn Alta *historian, educator*
Hamilton, Virginia Van der Veer *historian, educator*
Morton, Marilyn Miller *retired genealogy and history educator, lecturer, researcher, travel executive, director*
Tent, James Foster *historian*

Huntsville
Bounds, Sarah Etheline *historian*
Dunar, Andrew J. *historian, educator*
Hughes, Kaylene *historian, educator*

Jacksonville
Spector, Daniel Earl *historian, educator*

Lillian
Burnette, Ollen Lawrence, Jr., *historian*

Livingston
Schellhammer, Richard Charles *historian*

Loachapoka
Schafer, Elizabeth Diane *historian, writer*

Mobile
Gandy, Maurice Edward *English language educator, writer*
Hamner, Eugenie Lambert *English educator*
Kargleder, Charles Leonard *language educator*
Steadman, John Marcellus, III, *English educator*

Montgomery
Aleinikov, Andrei Grigoryevich *scientist, researcher, educator, consultant*
Cornett, Lloyd Harvey, Jr., *retired historian*
Gerard, William Blake *literature educator*
Gribben, Alan *English language educator, research consultant*
Napier, Cameron Mayson Freeman *historic preservationist*

Normal
Kearns, Nancy J. *language educator*

Ramer
Napier, John Hawkins, III, *historian*

Talladega
Jeffers, Trellie Lee James *language educator, dean*

Troy
McPherson, Milton Monroe *history professor*
Mitchell, Norma Taylor *history professor*

Tuscaloosa
Beito, David Timothy *humanities educator*
Crowley, John W(illiam) *English language educator*
Delpar, Helen *historian*
De Souza, Ismenia Sales *language educator*
Freyer, Tony Allan *historian, educator*
Hocutt, Max Oliver *retired philosophy educator*
Janiga-Perkins, Constance Gabrielle *language educator*
Shabazz, Amilcar *historian, humanities educator*

ALASKA

Anchorage
Kim, Taesoo *language educator*

Fairbanks
Cole, Terrence M. *historian, educator*

Juneau
Ruotsala, James Alfred *historian, writer*

ARIZONA

Apache Junction
Bracken, Harry McFarland *philosophy educator*
Ransom, Evelyn Naill *language educator, linguist*

Davis Monthan AFB
Miller, Charles Wallace *historian, environmental geologist, educator*

Gilbert
Stabler, Scott Lawrence *historian, educator*

Green Valley
Brewington, Arthur William *retired English language educator*

Kingman
Jones, Barbara Christine *linguist, creative arts designer, educator*

Phoenix
Drnjevic, Jonathan Mark *language educator*
Leiby, John Severn *historian, educator*
Rister, Gene Arnold *humanities educator*

Scottsdale
Donaldson, Scott *English language educator, writer*
Land, George A. *philosopher, writer, educator, consultant, speaker*

Sun City
Oppenheimer, Max, Jr., *foreign language educator, consultant*

Surprise
Clark, Lloyd *historian, writer, educator*

Tempe
Adelson, Roger Dean *history educator, editor, historian*
Brack, O. M., Jr., *English language educator*
García, Peter Joseph *humanities educator*
Garzon, Amalia *Spanish educator, translator*
Green, Monica H. *history professor*
Honegger, Gitta *language educator*
Iverson, Peter James *historian, educator*
Lockard, Joseph Franklin *literature educator, writer*
MacKinnon, Stephen R. *Asian studies administrator, educator*
Ruiz, Vicki Lynn *history professor, department chairman*
Tillman, Hoyt Cleveland *historian, educator, writer*
Tohe, Laura *English educator*
Wetsel, William David *literature educator*
Wong, Timothy C. *language and literature educator*

Tucson
Adjarian, Maude Madeleine *literature educator, researcher*
Birkinbine, John, II, *philatelist*
Boyle, Christopher George *English educator, counselor*
Dinnerstein, Leonard *historian, educator*
Herrnstadt, Richard Lawrence *American literature educator*
Jones, William Randolph *history educator*
Kaliher, Michael Dennis *historian, librarian*
Kellogg, Frederick *historian*
Mixon, Billie Louise *language educator*
Schulz, Renate Adele *German studies and second language acquisition educator*
Sheldon, Richard Neil *retired historian*
Zepeda, Ofelia *linguist, educator*

ARKANSAS

Arkadelphia
Graves, John William *historian*
Trofimova, Irina (Irene) Alexeevna *language educator*

Conway
Brodman, James William *historian, educator*
Ziegler, John Alan *historian, political scientist, educator*

Fayetteville
Levine, Daniel Blank *classical studies educator*

Jonesboro
Elkins, Francis Clark *history educator, university official*

Little Rock
Ferguson, John Lewis *state historian*
Lewis, Johanna Miller *historian, educator*

Malvern
Schultz, Marvin E. *historian, educator*

Mena
Eddleman, Floyd Eugene *retired English language educator*

Monticello
Babin, Claude Hunter *history professor*

Paragould
Cox, Loretta C. *language educator*

Siloam Springs
Roby, Warren B. *humanities educator*

State University
Darwin, John Scott *language educator*
Lott, Rick *language educator, poet*
Milner, Clyde A., II, *historian*
Schichler, Robert Lawrence *English language educator*

CALIFORNIA

Arcadia
Yen, Wen-Hsiung *language and music professional, educator*

Atherton
Bales, Royal Eugene *philosophy educator*

Bakersfield
Burns, Sarah Chloe *historian, educator*
Kegley, Jacquelyn Ann *philosophy educator*
Peterson, Pamela Carmelle *English language educator*
Schmidt, Joanne (Josephine Anne Schmidt) *language educator*

Berkeley
Ahrendt, Rebekah Susannah *language educator, musician*
Alter, Robert Bernard *comparative literature educator, critic*
Anderson, William Scovil *classics educator*
Bloom, Robert *language professional educator*
Booth, Stephen Walter *English language educator*
Costa, Gustavo *Italian studies scholar*
Gallagher, M. Catherine *English literature educator*
Herr, Richard *history professor*
Hull, Glynda *language educator*
Karlinsky, Simon *language educator, writer*
Kerman, Joseph Wilfred *musicologist, critic*
Lichterman, Martin *history professor*
Litwack, Leon Frank *historian, educator*
Long, Anthony Arthur *classics educator*
Middlekauff, Robert Lawrence *history educator, administrator*
Muscatine, Charles *English educator, author*
Nagler, Michael Nicholas *peace and conflict studies educator*
Rauch, Irmengard *linguist, educator*
Rex, Walter Edwin, III, *humanities educator*
Selz, Peter Howard *art historian, educator*
Shannon, Thomas Frederic *German language educator*
Sloane, Thomas O. *speech educator*
Wakeman, Frederic Evans, Jr., *historian, educator*
Wilson, W(illiam) Daniel *language professional, educator*
Zwerdling, Alex *English educator*

Beverly Hills
Heefner, Reginald Lee *linguist, entertainer, author*
Novak, Maximillian Erwin *retired language educator*

Cambria
Salaverria, Helena Clara *retired language educator*

Carmel
Chung, Kyung Cho *Korean specialist, educator, writer*

Chico
Shahid-García, María de Lourdes *foreign language educator*

Claremont
Ackerman, Gerald Martin *art historian, consultant*
Atlas, Jay David *philosopher, consultant, linguist*
Burns, Richard Dean *history educator, publisher, writer*
Davis, Nathaniel *humanities educator*
Goodrich, Norma Lorre (Mrs. John H. Howard) *French and comparative literature educator*
Kucheman, Clark Arthur *philosophy and religious studies educator*
McKirahan, Richard Duncan *classics and philosophy educator*
Moss, Myra Ellen (Myra Moss Rolle) *philosophy educator*
Neumann, Harry *philosophy educator*
Pinney, Thomas Clive *retired English language educator*
Shimkhada, Deepak *art historian*
Sontag, Frederick Earl *philosophy educator*
Ulitin, Vladimir Gregor *retired Russian language and literature educator*
Wheeler, Geraldine Hartshorn *historian, writer*
Woodress, James Leslie, Jr., *English language educator*
Young, Howard Thomas *foreign language educator*

Compton
Maradiaga Kieffer-Aanonsen, Nora Ludmila *language educator*

Culver City
Clodius, Albert Howard *history educator*

Cupertino
McCormick, Yumi *language educator, translator*
Tice, Bradley Scott *humanities educator*

Davis
Bernd, Clifford Albrecht *language educator*
Brower, Daniel Roberts *historian, educator, writer*
Druzhnikov, Yuri Ilya *literature educator, writer*
Hoffman, Michael Jerome *humanities educator, educator*
Traill, David Angus *classics educator*
Waddington, Raymond Bruce, Jr., *English language educator*
Williamson, Alan Bacher *English literature educator, poet, writer*
Willis, Frank Roy *history educator*

Del Mar
Johnson, Mary Evans *musicologist, musician*
Marx, Michael William *language educator, writer*

El Cerrito
Kuo, Ping-chia *historian, educator*

Emeryville
Reuter, William Charles *historian, educator*

Fallbrook
Tanner, John Douglas, Jr., *retired history educator, writer*

Fountain Valley
Crecelius, Daniel Neil *history professor*
Le, Vinh Tu *language educator, translator*

Fresno
Bundy-DeSoto, Teresa Mari *language educator, vocalist*

PROFESSIONAL INDEX 5711 HUMANITIES: LIBERAL STUDIES

Chang, Sidney H. (Sidney H. Chang) *history professor*
Genini, Ronald Walter *retired history educator, historian*
Kouymjian, Dickran *art historian, Orientalist, educator*
Kuhn, Rose Marie *language educator*

Fullerton
Carrithers, Joseph Edward *English composition and literature educator*
Elliott-Scheinberg, Wendy *history professor, genealogist*

Glendale
de Grassi, Leonard *art historian, educator*
Renner, Marguerite *history educator*

Grass Valley
Gillett, Annette Damron *retired speech and forensics educator*

Hayward
Gleason, Ken Bell *historian, educator, journalist*
Hammond, Marian Corleene *retired literature educator*

Hemet
Culverwell, Albert Henry *historian*

Huntington Beach
Winterowd, Walter Ross *English educator*

Irvine
Boyd, Carolyn Patricia *history professor*
Hine, Robert Van Norden, Jr., *historian, educator*
Hubert, Judd David *language educator*
Kluger, Ruth *German language educator, editor*
Lillyman, William John *German language educator, academic administrator*

La Jolla
Falk, Julia S. *linguist, educator, dean*
Langacker, Ronald Wayne *linguistics educator*
McDonald, Marianne *classicist*
Miyoshi, Masao *literature educator, writer*
Newmark, Leonard Daniel *linguistics educator*
Olafson, Frederick Arlan *philosophy educator*
Oreskes, Naomi *science historian*
Wright, Andrew *English literature educator*

La Verne
Marcus, Kenneth Hearne *historian, educator*

Laguna Niguel
Teitelbaum, Harry *English educator*

Livermore
Hiskes, Dolores G. *language educator*

Long Beach
Beebe, Sandra E. *retired English language educator, artist, writer*
Binkiewicz, Donna *historian, educator*
Nguyen, Huong Tran *English language professional, federal agency official*
Tang, Paul Chi Lung *philosophy educator*
Yousef, Fathi Salaama *communication studies educator, management consultant*

Los Altos
Nivison, David Shepherd *Chinese and philosophy educator*

Los Angeles
Alkon, Paul Kent *English language educator*
Allen, Michael John Bridgman *English educator*
Alpers, Edward Alter *history professor*
Bahr, Ehrhard *Germanic languages and literature educator*
Bartchy, S(tuart) Scott *history educator, researcher*
Boime, Albert Isaac *art history educator*
Bradshaw, Murray Charles *musicologist, educator*
Burns, Robert Ignatius *historian, educator, clergyman*
Caram, Eve La Salle *English educator, writer*
Cohen, S(tephen) Marshall *philosophy educator*
Darby, Joanne Tyndale (Jaye Darby) *arts and humanities educator*
Dumitrescu, Domnita *Spanish language educator, researcher*
Dyck, Andrew Roy *philologist, educator*
Hines, Thomas Spight *historian, educator, architecture critic*
Hovannisian, Richard G. *Armenian and Near East history educator*
Hsu, Kylie *language educator, researcher, linguist*
Hundley, Norris Cecil, Jr., *history educator*
Keenan, Edward L. *linguist, educator*
Kelly, Henry Ansgar *English language educator*
Kolve, V. A. *English literature educator*
Lagier, Christophe Philippe *language educator*
Laird, David *humanities educator emeritus*
Lattimore, Steven *classicist professor*
Levine, Philip *classics educator*
Lionnet, Francoise *French and comparative literature educator*
Mellor, Ronald John *history professor*
Nakanishi, Don Toshiaki *Asian American studies educator, writer*
Newhall, Eric Luther *American literature educator*
Ochs, Elinor *linguistics educator*
Rouse, Richard Hunter *historian, educator*
Schaefer, William David *English language educator*
Schutz, John Adolph *historian, educator, former university dean*
Schwartz, Leon *foreign language educator*
See, Carolyn *English language educator, novelist, book critic*
Seip, Terry Lee *history professor*
Shideler, Ross Patrick *foreign language and comparative literature educator, writer, translator, poet*
Smith, Bruce R. *English language educator*
Stockwell, Robert Paul *linguist, educator*
Tritle, Lawrence Alan *history educator*
Troy, Nancy J. *art history educator*
Weber, Eugen *historian, educator, writer*
White, Christopher Todd *language educator*
White, Kelvin Lewis *historian, researcher*
Wohl, Robert *historian, educator*
Wortham, Thomas Richard *English language educator*

Malibu
Marshall, Donald Glenn *English language and literature educator*
Tippens, Darryl Lee *literature educator, writer*

Marina
Madsen, Roy I., Jr., *language educator*

Merced
Elliott, Gordon Jefferson *retired English language educator*

Modesto
Miller, Raymond Elmo *speech educator*

Monterey
Astore, William Joseph *historian, dean*
de la Vega Montalvo, Guido Enrique *language educator, consultant*
Franke, Jack Emil *foreign language educator*
Peet, Phyllis Irene *women's studies educator*

Newport Beach
Brown, Giles Tyler *history educator, lecturer*
Mc Culloch, Samuel Clyde *history professor*

Northridge
Chen, Joseph Tao *historian, educator*
Koistinen, Paul Abraham Carl *historian, educator*

Oakland
Berry, Kathleen A. *English language educator*
Mayers, Eugene David *retired philosopher, educator*

Orange
Cumiford, William Lloyd *historian, educator, curator*
Martin, Mike W. *philosophy educator*

Oxnard
Hill, Alice Lorraine *history, genealogy and social researcher, educator*

Pacific Palisades
Garwood, Victor Paul *retired speech communication educator, audiologist*

Palmdale
Kilanowski, Dana Marcotte *historian, writer, filmmaker, archaeologist*

Palo Alto
Mommsen, Katharina *retired German language and literature educator*
Walker, Carolyn Peyton *English language educator*

Pasadena
Elliot, David Clephan *historian, educator*
Kousser, J(oseph) Morgan *history educator*
Parr, James Allan *literature professor*

Pebble Beach
Dallmann, William Charles *speech educator, writer*

Piedmont
Putter, Irving *French language educator*

Pittsburg
Kaiper, Donald Dixon *historian, educator*

Pleasant Hill
Ashby, Denise Stewart *speech educator, communication consultant*

Pleasanton
Heizer, Ruth Bradfute *philosophy educator*

Pomona
Cranston, John Welch *historian, educator*
Evans, William McKee *historian, educator*

Portola Valley
Carnochan, Walter Bliss *retired humanities educator*

Rancho Dominguez
Corominas, Juan M. *language educator, priest*

Rancho Santa Fe
Ruiz, Ramon Eduardo *history professor*

Riverside
Elliott, Emory Bernard *English language educator, educational administrator*
Fagundo, Ana Maria *creative writing and Spanish literature educator*
Grimm, Reinhold *humanities educator*
Jackson, Marguerite Faye Thurston *rhetoric and intercultural communications and language educator*
Ross, Delmer Gerrard *historian, educator*
Yount, Gwendolyn Audrey *humanities educator*

Rohnert Park
Shinagawa, Larry Hatime *American studies educator*

Sacramento
Avendaño, Fausto *language educator, writer*
Bradshaw, Merlin E. *language educator*
Carr, Gerald Francis *German educator*
Meindl, Robert James *English language educator, poet*

Saint Helena
Yates, Donald Alfred *retired literature educator*

San Bernardino
Ruml, Treadwell *English language educator*

San Diego
Alcosser, Sandra Beth *English language educator, writer*
Amstadt, Nancy Hollis *retired language educator*
bar-Lev, Zev *linguist, educator*
Brandes, Raymond Stewart *history educator*
Cobbs Hoffman, Elizabeth Anne *history educator*
Crocitti, John Joseph *historian, educator*
Davies, Thomas Mockett, Jr., *history educator*
Dunlop, Marianne *retired English as second language educator*
Peterson, Richard Hermann *retired history educator*
Sasaran, Laura Jeanne *humanities educator*
Scott, Bonnie Kime *English literature and cultural educator*
Swank, William George *historian, writer*
Vanderbilt, Kermit *English language educator*
Wawrytko, Sandra Ann *humanities educator*
Wilson, Jerry Clark *language educator*

San Francisco
Bardsley, Kay *historian, archivist, dance professional*
Costa-Zalessow, Natalia *foreign language educator*
Dennehy, Raymond Leo *philosopher, educator*
Dolan, Brian Patrick *humanities educator*
Hansen, Carol Louise *English language educator*
Henderson, Horace Edward *World War II historian, peace advocate*
Kelley, Michael Garhart Roosevelt *historian, educator, writer*
Langton, Daniel Joseph *English, writing educator, poet*
Lin, Robert Kwanhwan *language educator, consultant*
McGuire, William Albert *humanities educator*
Needleman, Jacob *philosophy educator, writer*
Satin, Joseph *language professional, university administrator*

San Juan Capistrano
Carlson, Lawrence Arvid *retired English language educator, real estate agent*

San Luis Obispo
LaScola, Russell A. *philosophy educator*
Lynch, Joseph James *philosophy educator*

San Marcos
Baringer, Sandra Kay *literature educator*

San Marino
Rolle, Andrew *historian, writer*
Travis, Albert Hartman *retired ancient language educator*
Zall, Paul Maxwell *retired English language educator, consultant*

Santa Barbara
Avalle-Arce, Juan Bautista *Spanish language educator*
Brownlee, Wilson Elliot, Jr., *history educator*
Chafe, Wallace LeSeur *linguist, educator*
Collins, Robert Oakley *history professor*
Crawford, Donald Wesley *philosophy educator, university official*
Del Chiaro, Mario Aldo *art historian, archeologist, etruscologist, educator*
Fingarette, Herbert *philosopher, educator*
Göllner, Marie Louise *musicologist, retired educator*
Gutierrez-Jones, Carl Scott *English educator*
Helgerson, Richard *English literature educator*
Hsu, Immanuel Chung Yueh *history professor*
Kuczynski, John-Michael Maxime *humanities educator, writer*
Mahlendorf, Ursula Renate *literature educator*
McGee, James Sears *historian, educator*
Renehan, Robert Francis Xavier *Greek and Latin educator*
Rose, Mark Allen *humanities educator*
Russell, Jeffrey Burton *historian, educator*
Wilkins, Burleigh Taylor *philosophy educator*

Santa Clara
laGuardia, Dolores *literature educator, writer, communications executive, educational association administrator*
Le, Son Minh *philosophy educator*
Maxwell, Kathleen Elizabeth *art historian*

Santa Cruz
Beecher, Jonathan French *history professor*
Catlos, Brian Aivars *historian, writer*
Ritscher, Lee A *literature educator*
Stevens, Stanley David *historian, researcher, retired librarian, archivist*
Suckiel, Ellen Kappy *philosophy educator*

Santa Monica
Aghabegian, Diana E. Bortnowsky *English language educator, publisher*

Santa Rosa
Aman, Reinhold Albert *philologist, publisher*

Santee
Peters, Raymond Eugene *historian, writer*

Saratoga
Cisneros, Rebecca G. *language educator*

Seaside
Anderson, David Louis *history educator*

Sherman Oaks
Howe, Daniel Walker *historian, educator*

Stanford
Baker, Keith Michael *history professor*
Chrissochoidis, Ilias *musicologist*
Dekker, George Gilbert *literature educator, literary scholar, writer*
Dunlop, John Barrett *foreign language educator, research institution scholar*
Duus, Peter *retired history educator*
Eitner, Lorenz Edwin Alfred *art historian, educator*
Felstiner, John *literature educator, translator*
Fleishman, Lazar *literature educator*
Fredrickson, George Marsh *history professor*
Gelpi, Albert Joseph *English educator, literary critic*
Greene, Roland *literature educator*
Gumbrecht, Hans Ulrich *literary criticism educator*
Kennedy, David Michael *historian, educator*
Loftis, John, Jr., (John Clyde Loftis Jr.) *English language educator*
Lohnes, Walter F. W. *German language and literature educator*
Moravcsik, Julius Matthew *philosophy educator*
Newman-Gordon, Pauline *French language and literature educator*
Perloff, Marjorie Gabrielle *English and comparative literature educator*
Plebuch, Tobias *musicologist*
Polhemus, Robert M. *language educator*
Robinson, Paul Arnold *historian, educator, writer*
Sheehan, James John *historian, educator*
Stansky, Peter David Lyman *historian*
Traugott, Elizabeth Closs *linguist, educator, researcher*

Stockton
Fung, Rosaline Lee *language educator*
Limbaugh, Ronald Hadley *retired history educator, history center director*

Thousand Oaks
Reaves, Michaela Crawford *history educator*

Torrance
Anderson, Marilyn Wheeler *English language educator*
Imbarus, Aura *language educator, consultant*

Ukiah
Lohrli, Anne *retired English language educator, writer*

Vallejo
Brown, Earl Kent *historian, clergyman*
Landauer, Elvie Ann Whitney *humanities educator, writer*

Van Nuys
Zucker, Alfred John *English language educator, academic administrator*

Woodland Hills
Siever-Henderson, Patricia *history university educator*

Yucaipa
Lardy, Leonard Anthony *English educator*

COLORADO

Boulder
Barchilon, Jacques *foreign language educator, researcher, writer*
Bickman, Martin *literature educator, writer*
Engel, Barbara Alpern *history professor*
Gonzalez-del-Valle, Luis Tomas *Spanish language educator*
Jurafsky, Daniel *linguist*
Limerick, Patricia Nelson *history professor*
Menn, Lise *linguistics educator*
Rood, David S. *linguistics educator*

Centennial
Morley, Judy Mattivi *historian, educator, preservation consultant*

Colorado Springs
Blackburn, Alexander Lambert *author, English literature educator*
Cramer, Owen Carver *classics educator*
Hallenbeck, Kenneth Luster *retired numismatist*
Hill, Christopher Vaughan *historian, educator*
Reinitz, Neale Robert *retired literature educator*
Stavig, Mark Luther *English language educator*
Tucker, Frank Hammond *history professor*

Denver
Conroy, Mary Elizabeth *history professor*
Fasel, Ida *English language educator, writer*
Frederick, Robert Allen *history educator*
Howard, W. Scott *language educator*
Hughes, J(ohnson) Donald *history educator, editor*
Johnson, Geraldine Esch *language specialist*
Pfnister, Allan Orel *humanities educator*
Ronning, Charlotte Jean *foreign language educator*
Storey, Brit Allan *historian*
Wetzel, Jodi (Joy Lynn Wetzel) *history and women's studies educator*

Dolores
Kreyche, Gerald Francis *retired philosophy educator*

Fort Collins
Collet, Vicki S. *literature educator*
McComb, David Glendinning *history educator*
Rollin, Bernard Elliot *philosophy educator, consultant*
Tremblay, William Andrew *English language educator, writer*

Golden
Eckley, Wilton Earl, Jr., *humanities educator, educator*

Greeley
Knott, Alexander Waller *historian, educator*
Worley, Lloyd Douglas *English language educator*

Lakewood
Woodruff, Kathryn Elaine *English language educator*

Palisade
Fay, Abbott Eastman *history educator*

Pueblo
Farwell, Hermon Waldo, Jr., *parliamentarian, educator, former speech communication educator*

U S A F Academy
Neiberg, Michael Scott *history professor*

Westminster
Bocock, Scott Gregory *historian*

Woodland Park
Mason, David James *English language educator*

CONNECTICUT

Clinton
Gilman, Frances M. *genealogist, librarian*

Colebrook
McNeill, William Hardy *retired history educator, writer*

East Granby
Scanlon, Lawrence Eugene *English language educator*

Enfield
Folmsbee, Patricia Hurley *reading and language arts consultant*

Essex
Hieatt, Allen Kent *language professional, educator*
Hieatt, Constance Bartlett *English language educator*

Fairfield
Levitt, Jesse *retired foreign language educator*
Mascia, Mark Joseph *language educator*
Newton, Lisa Haenlein *philosopher, educator*

Farmington
Higgins-Biddle, John Charles *humanities educator, consultant*
Reeves, John Drummond *English language professional, writer*

Greenwich
Wiener, Malcolm Hewitt *historian, writer*

Guilford
Colish, Marcia Lillian *history professor*

Hamden
Culler, Arthur Dwight *English language educator*
McClellan, Edwin *Japanese literature educator*
Mintz, Max M. *historian*
Pelikan, Jaroslav Jan *history professor*
Quirk, Ronald Joseph *language educator*

Hartford
Decker, Robert Owen *history educator, clergyman*
Gastmann, Albert Lodewijk *retired political science and language educator, writer*
Humphreys, Karen Lynne *language educator*

Ivoryton
Osborne, John Walter *historian, educator, author*

Meriden
Chiarenza, Frank John *English language educator*

Middletown
Buel, Richard Van Wyck, Jr., *history educator, writer, editor*
Gillmor, Charles Stewart *history and science educator, researcher*
Heimann-Hast, Sybil Dorothea *language arts and literature educator*
Meyer, Priscilla Ann *Russian language and literature educator*
Miel, Jan *humanities educator*
Pomper, Philip *history educator*
Reed, Joseph Wayne *American studies educator, artist*
Shapiro, Norman Richard *Romance languages and literatures educator*
Shields, David Brandon *historian, educator*
Wensinger, Arthur Stevens *language and literature educator, writer, translator*
Winston, Krishna *foreign language professional*

New Britain
Emeagwali, Gloria Thomas *humanities educator*
Heitner, John A. (Jack Heitner) *English language educator, writer*
Leeds, Barry Howard *English language educator*

New Haven
Abramson, Arthur Seymour *linguistics educator, researcher*
Bloom, Harold *humanities educator, writer*
Blum, John Morton *historian, educator*
Borroff, Marie *English language educator*
Brisman, Leslie *English language educator*
Bynum, Terrell Ward *humanities educator, consultant*
Erlich, Victor *Slavic languages educator*
Frank, Roberta *English language educator*
Freedman, Paul Harris *historian, educator*
Gilbert, Creighton Eddy *art historian*
Glier, Ingeborg Johanna *German language and literature educator*
Goffart, Walter André *history professor*
Greene, Liliane *French language and literature educator, editor*
Hallo, William Wolfgang *literature and language professor, writer*
Harries, Karsten *philosophy educator, researcher*
Hartman, Geoffrey H. *language professional, educator*
Hersey, George Leonard *retired art history educator*
Hollander, John *humanities educator, poet*
Holquist, James Michael *Russian and comparative literature educator*
Hyman, Paula E(llen) *history professor*
Insler, Stanley *philologist, educator*
Kagan, Donald *historian, educator*
Kennedy, Paul Michael *history professor*
Kevles, Daniel Jerome *history educator, writer*
Langer, Lawrence Lee *English educator, writer*
Lord, George deForest *English educator*
MacMullen, Ramsay *retired history educator*
Marcus, Ruth Barcan *philosopher, educator, writer, lecturer*
Pollitt, Jerome Jordan *art history educator*
Prown, Jules David *art historian educator*
Quaglia, Jordano *language educator, writer*
Rawson, Claude Julien *English educator*
Robinson, Fred Colson *English language educator*
Smith, John Edwin *philosophy educator*
Totman, Conrad Davis *history professor*
Underdown, David Edward *historian, educator*
Wandycz, Piotr Stefan *history educator*
Yeazell, Ruth Bernard *English language educator*

New London
Bombaci, Nancy Margaret *literature educator*

North Haven
Bennett, Harry Louis *history educator*

Old Lyme
Willauer, George Jacob *English literature educator*

Orange
Davis, David Brion *historian, educator*

Salisbury
Kilner, Ursula Blanche *genealogist, educator, writer*

Southbury
Bria, Susan S. *retired language educator, writer*

Stamford
Anderson, Susan Leigh *philosophy educator*

Storrs Mansfield
Brown, Richard David *history educator*
Coons, Ronald Edward *historian, educator*
Gross, Robert Alan *history professor*
Reed, Howard Alexander *historian, educator*
Troyer, John Gordon *philosopher, educator*

Trumbull
Allen, Richard Stanley (Dick Allen) *English language educator, author*

Washington
Leab, Daniel Joseph *history professor*

West Hartford
Collins, Alma Jones *English educator, writer*

Willimantic
Lacey, James Francis *American studies educator*
Meznar, Joan Ellen *historian, educator*

Windsor
Auten, Arthur Herbert *history educator*

Woodbridge
Dupré, Louis *retired philosopher, educator*
Kleiner, Diana Elizabeth Edelman *art history educator, administrator*

Woodstock
Susla, Jeffrey Jonathan *English language educator*

DELAWARE

Newark
Brown, Robert Fath *philosopher, educator*
Coulet du Gard, Donna M. *language educator*
Day, Robert Androus *English language educator, former library director, editor, publisher*
Halio, Jay Leon *language professional, educator*
Homer, William Innes *art history educator, art expert, author*
Isaacs, Diane Scharfeld *English educator*
Lathrop, Thomas Albert *language educator*
Lemay, J(oseph) A(lberic) Leo *American literature educator*
Steiner, Roger Jacob *linguistics educator, writer, researcher*
Tolles, Bryant Franklin, Jr., *history and art history educator*
Venezky, Richard Lawrence *English language educator*
Weintraub, Stanley *arts and humanities educator, writer*
Wolters, Raymond *historian, educator*

Wilmington
Kneavel, Ann Callanan *humanities educator, communications consultant*

DISTRICT OF COLUMBIA

Washington
Albrecht, Kathe Hicks *art historian, visual resources manager*
Bader, William Banks *historian, foundation executive, former corporate executive*
Bedini, Silvio A. *historian, author*
Beisner, Robert Lee *historian*
Bennett, Betty T. *English literature educator, university dean, writer*
Berkowitz, Edward David *historian*
Bernhardt, Barbara Izabela *language educator, writer*
Billington, James Hadley *historian, librarian*
Breitman, Richard David *historian, educator, writer*
Broun, Elizabeth *art historian, museum administrator*
Carone, Gabriela Roxana *philosophy educator, dancer*
Caws, Peter James *philosopher, educator*
Cheney, Lynne V. *humanities educator, writer*
Cua, Antonio S. *philosopher, educator*
Davidson, Dan Eugene *Russian language and area scholar, academic administrator*
Dougherty, Jude Patrick *philosophy educator, dean*
Dudley, William Sheldon *historian*
Farr, Judith Banzer *writer, literature educator*
Ferretti, Maddalena Funiciello *humanities educator*
Frost, Molly Spitzer *Chinese culture educator*
Gibert, Stephen P. *government educator, defense consultant*
Graves-Roman, Patricia Ann *educator, researcher, writer*
Hammond, William Michael *historian, educator*
Hawke, Paul Henry *historian*
Heelan, Patrick Aidan *philosophy educator*
Howland, Nina Davis *historian*
Howland, Richard Hubbard *architectural historian*
Kalb, Marvin *public policy and government educator*
Kapsch, Robert James *engineering and architectural historian*
Kazin, Michael *history educator, writer*
Kreidler, Charles W(illiam) *linguist, educator*
Kreinheder, Hazel Fuller *genealogist, historian*
Ladjevardi, Habib *historian*
Langer, Erick Detlef *historian, educator*
Lichtman, Allan Jay *historian, educator, consultant*
Lightfoot, David William *linguistics educator*
Livingston, Robert Gerald *historian, journalist*
Long, Pamela Olivia *historian*
Marr, Phebe Ann *retired historian, educator*
McAleavey, David *English educator*
McAuliffe, Jane Dammen *religious studies and Islamic studies educator*
McCartin, Joseph Anthony *historian, educator*
McKelvey, Virginia Maude *language educator*
McPherson, Alan L. *history professor*
Miller, Jeanne-Marie Anderson (Mrs. Nathan J. Miller) *English language educator, academic administrator*
Morris, Marcia A. *language educator*
Mujica, Barbara Louise *language educator, writer*
Neiditch, H. Michael *historian*
Newsom, Jon W. *musicologist*
Park, Alice Mary Crandall *genealogist*
Pope, Nancy *historian, curator*
Rand, Harry Zvi *art historian, poet*
Reagon, Bernice Johnson *cultural historian, educator, curator, singer, composer*
Ritchie, Donald A. *historian*
Robb, James Willis *Romance languages educator*
Roberts, Jeanne Addison *retired literature educator*
Rosenblatt, Jason Philip *English language educator*
Salamon, Linda Bradley *English literature educator*
Schneider, Cynthia Perrin *art historian, educator*
Scott, Gary Thomas *historian*
Severino, Roberto *foreign language educator, academic administration executive*
Sherman, Nancy *philosophy educator*
Simko, Jan *English, foreign language and literature educator*
Spector, Ronald H. *historian, educator*
Stone, Florence Smith *film festival executive, consultant*
Taylor, Estelle Wormley *English educator, dean*
Taylor, Henry Splawn *literature educator, poet, writer*
Vaslef, Irene *historian, librarian*
Veatch, Robert Marlin *philosophy educator, medical ethics researcher*
Vining, Margaret Simmons *historian, curator*
Voll, John Obert *history professor*
Wagstaff, Grayson *musicologist, educator*
Wippel, John Francis *philosophy educator*
Witek, John W. *history professor*
Wood, Mary Louise *humanities educator*

FLORIDA

Aventura
Cantor, Norman Frank *history educator, writer*

Beverly Hills
Larsen, Erik *art history educator*

Boca Raton
Collins, Robert Arnold *English language educator*
Frazer, Heather Turner *historian, educator*

Bradenton
Bateman, John Jay *classics educator*
Dickie, George Thomas *philosopher, educator*
Stewart, Priscilla Ann Mabie *art historian, educator*

Cooper City
Maugere, Dannis Paul *historian, educator*

Coral Gables
Pitcher, Jonathan Michael *language educator, researcher*

Davie
Ganson, Barbara Anne *history professor*

Daytona Beach
Buckelew, Richard Allan *historian, educator*
Carmona, José Antonio *Spanish language educator, English language educator*
Harrison, William D. *humanities educator*

Fort Lauderdale
Austin, John Norman *classics educator*
van der Veur, Paul W. *humanities educator*

Fort Myers
Fite, Gilbert Courtland *historian, educator, retired*
Harman, Joyce Elizabeth *humanities educator*

Gainesville
Brown, William Samuel, Jr., *communication sciences and disorders educator*
Calin, William *literature educator*
Der-Houssikian, Haig *linguistics educator*
Ginway, Mary Elizabeth *language educator*
Hartigan, Karelisa Dorothy *classics educator*
Kushner, David Zakeri *musicologist*
Needell, Jeffrey David *historian, educator*
Proctor, Samuel *history educator*
Schmeling, Gareth *classics educator*
Zieger, Robert Harman *history educator, historian*

Jacksonville
Courtwright, David Todd *history educator, author*
Stanton, Robert John, Jr., *English language educator*

Key Biscayne
Ross, Marilyn J. *English and communications educator*

Lake Worth
Wilson, William J. *English language educator*

Lutz
Currey, Cecil Barr *history professor*

Marathon
Wiecha, Joseph Augustine *linguist, educator*

Melbourne
Jones, Elaine Hancock *humanities educator*

Miami
Blanton, Jerry Cain *literature educator, writer, editor*
Lifshitz, Felice *historian, educator*
Lorenzo, Guadalupe *language educator, department chairman*
Mendoza De Arce, Daniel Leonel *retired humanities educator*
Neu, Charles Eric *historian, educator*
Patrouch, Joseph Francis *history professor*
Ruggiero, Guido *historian, educator*
Welch, Judy Ann *language educator*
Zayas-Bazan, Eduardo *foreign language educator*

Mount Dora
Anderson, Chester Grant *English educator*

Mulberry
Bowman, Hazel Lois *retired English language educator*

Naples
Kinder, Suzanne Fonay Wemple *historian, educator*
Nodes, Daniel Joseph *humanities educator, researcher*

North Port
Seiler, Charlotte Woody *retired educator*

Ocala
Vazquez, Debra Allen *literature educator*

Okeechobee
Egolf, James Edward *history educator, secondary school educator*

Oldsmar
Thompson, Mack Eugene *history educator*

Orlando
Caldero-Figueroa, Ana Jhanilca *language educator*
Gallagher, Shaun Andrew *philosophy educator, writer*
Moriarty, Michael Eugene *retired humanities educator*
Murphrey, Elizabeth Hobgood *history educator, librarian*
Pauley, Bruce Frederick *history professor*
Velez, Diana *historian, educator*

Ormond Beach
Cunsolo, Ronald S. *historian, educator*

Palm Beach
Gaudieri, Alexander V. J. *art historian, consultant, museum director*

Panama City
McWhorter, Susan Carol *English language educator*

Pensacola
Arnold, Barry Raynor *philosophy educator, medical ethicist, clergyman, counselor*
Broxton, Randall *historian, educator*
Maddock, Lawrence Hill *retired language educator*
Sprouse, James Richardson *literature educator*

Port Charlotte
Winters, Stanley B. *history educator, writer, civic activist*

Port Richey
Long, Michael Eldon *government and history educator*

Saint Augustine
Parker, Susan Richbourg *historian, consultant*

Saint Leo
Astolfi, Douglas M. *history professor*

Saint Petersburg
Walker, Brigitte Maria *translator, linguistic consultant*

Sarasota
Benowitz, June Melby *historian, educator*
Dungy, Kathryn R. *humanities educator*
Jacobson, Jeanne McKee *humanities educator, writer*
Lengyel, Alfonz *art history, archeology and museology educator*
Snyder, Lee Daniel *historian, educator*
Taplin, Winn Lowell *historian, retired senior intelligence operations officer*

Tallahassee
Bartlett, Richard Adams *retired history professor*
Bucuvalas, Tina *folklorist*
Davis, Bertram Hylton *retired English educator*
Dorn, Charles Meeker *art education educator*
Edwards, Leigh Holladay *literature educator*
Golden, Leon *classicist, educator*
Halpern, Paul G. *history educator*
Harper, George Mills *English language educator*
Laird, Doris Anne Marley *humanities educator, musician*
Marincola, John *classics educator*
Mele, Alfred R. *philosophy educator*
Moore, Dennis Duane *English educator*
Rogers, William Warren *historian, educator, publishing executive, writer*

Tampa
Anton, John Peter *philosopher, educator*
Brewer, Priscilla Joan *historian, educator*
Kasum, Michael *humanities educator, writer*
Perry, James Frederic *philosophy educator, writer*
Preto-Rodas, Richard A. *retired foreign language educator*
Turner, Stephen Park *philosopher, sociologist, educator*

Titusville
Jackson, Philip Irving *literature educator, writer*

Umatilla
Balandran, Stella Varona *interpreter, lyricist, composer, writer*

Winter Park
Benedict, Dorothy Jones *genealogist, researcher*
Mason, Aimee Hunnicutt Romberger *retired philosophy and humanities educator*
Seymour, Thaddeus *English educator*
Wilson, Robley Conant, Jr., *English educator, editor, author*

GEORGIA

Americus
Isaacs, Harold *history professor*

Andersonville
Boyles, Frederick Holdren *historian*

Athens
Balashov, Yuri V. *philosophy educator*
Gómez-Martinez, José Luis *Spanish language professional, researcher*
Kretzschmar, William Addison, Jr., *English language educator*
Mamatey, Victor Samuel *history educator*
Miller, Ronald Baxter *English language educator, writer*
Moore, Rayburn Sabatzky *American literature educator*
Spence, Sarah *comparatist educator*
Thomas, Emory M. *history professor*
Troutt Powell, Eve *historian, educator*

Atlanta
Benario, Herbert William *classicist, educator*
Burns, Thomas Samuel *history professor*
Chafee, Ingrid Roberta Hoover Coleman *retired language educator*
Chow, Rey *literature educator*
Crimmins, Timothy James *history professor*
Dobranski, Stephen Bitonti *literature educator*
Garrow, David Jeffries *historian, author*
Hallen, Barry *philosopher, educator*
Hartle, Robert Wyman *retired foreign language and literature educator*
Judovitz, Dalia *literature educator*
Kuntz, Marion Lucile Leathers *classicist, educator, historian*
Manley, Frank *retired English language educator, writer*
Risjord, Mark Winden *humanities educator*
Rojas, Carlos *Spanish literature educator*
Sheftall, Beverly Guy *women's studies educator*

Augusta
Dyer, James Harold, Jr., *language educator*
Griswold, Sara Y. *language educator*
Muntz, Ernest Gordon *historian, educator*

Barnesville
Horn, Jason G. *English educator*

Carrollton
Doxey, Wiliam Sanford, Jr., *retired language educator, writer*
Steely, Melvin T. *language educator*

Cochran
Ricks, John Addison, III, *history professor*

College Park
Payne, Harry Charles *historian, educator*

Dalton
Hutcheson, John Ambrose, Jr., *history professor*

Decatur
Dillingham, William Byron *literature educator, author*

Dublin
Claxton, Harriett Maroy Jones *language educator*

Dunwoody
Duvall, Marjorie L. *English and foreign language educator*

Ellenwood
Bauman, Mark Keith *historian, educator*

Kennesaw
Ribeiro, Lucia C. *language educator*

Macon
Huffman, Joan Brewer *history professor*
Young-Zook, Monica M. *language educator*

Madison
Aldridge, John Watson *English language educator, author*

Marietta
Rainey, Kenneth Tyler *English language educator*

Moultrie
Johnson, Edith Scott *English educator, writing consultant*

Mount Berry
Shiffman, Daniel Steven *literature educator*

Rome
Carper, N. Gordon *historian, educator*

Saint Simons
Spivey, Ted Ray *English educator*

Valdosta
Santas, Aristotelis *philosophy educator, massage therapist*

HAWAII

Hilo
Kinney, Jeanne Kawelolani *English studies educator, writer*

Honolulu
Aung-Thwin, Michael Arthur *history educator*
Bender, Byron Wilbur *linguistics educator*
Dyen, Isidore *linguistic scientist, educator*
Fujita, James Hiroshi *history educator*
Hoffmann, Kathryn Ann *humanities educator*
Jordan, Amos Azariah, Jr., *foreign affairs educator, retired military officer*
Kozok, Uli *language educator*
Ota, Katsuhiro Justin *language educator*
Peterson, Barbara Ann Bennett *history educator, television personality*
Rapson, Richard L. *history professor*
Rath, Richard Cullen *history professor*
Rehg, Kenneth Lee *linguistics educator*
Schweizer, Niklaus R. *German educator*
Seidensticker, Edward George *Japanese language and literature educator*
Stephan, John Jason *historian, educator*
Varley, Herbert Paul *Japanese language and cultural history educator*

Kaneohe
Nagtalon-Miller, Helen Rosete *humanities educator*

IDAHO

Boise
Steiner, Stanley F. *literature educator*

Caldwell
Rember, John V. *literature educator*

Jerome
Akers, Sharron Loella *language educator*
Ricketts, Virginia Lee *historian, researcher*

Moscow
Clanton, Orval Gene *historian, educator*
Greever, Janet Groff *history educator*
Harris, Robert Dalton *history educator, researcher, writer*
Lecompte, Janet *historian, writer*

Pocatello
Nickisch, Craig Wendell *language professional, educator*
Smith, Evelyn Elaine *language educator*

ILLINOIS

Bloomington
Brakebill, Tina Stewart *historian, writer*

Carbondale
Gilbert, Glenn Gordon *linguistics educator*
Griffiths, Brett Megan *English educator, writer*
Hahn, Lewis Edwin *philosopher, retired educator*
Hahn, Robert Alan *philosophy educator*
Lanigan, Richard Leo, Jr., *humanities educator, writer, editor*
Lawson, Richard Alan *literature educator, photographer*
Wiesen, S. Jonathan *historian, educator*

Carterville
Hale, Stan J. *humanities educator*
Montaño, Edgar J. *language educator*

Champaign
Douglas, George Halsey *literature educator, educator*
Koenker, Diane P. *history professor*
McGlathery, James Melville *foreign language educator*
Ratner, Lorman Alfred *history professor*
Smith, Ralph Alexander *cultural and educational policy educator*
Wheeler, Richard Paul *English educator, dean*

Chicago
Alexander, Michael Charles *historian, educator*
Aronson, Howard Isaac *linguist, educator*
Berk, Harlan Joseph *numismatist, writer, antiquarian*
Bevington, David Martin *English literature educator*
Biggs, Robert Dale *Near Eastern studies educator*
Booth, Wayne Clayson *English literature and rhetoric educator, author*
Bregoli-Russo, Mauda Rita *language educator*
Brekus, Catherine Anne *historian*
Brinkman, John Anthony *historian, educator*
Cohen, Ted *philosopher, educator*
Cullen, Charles Thomas *historian, librarian*
Davis, Michael Stuart *philosopher, educator*
De Armas, Frederick Alfred *foreign language educator*
Debus, Allen George *history educator*
Dembowski, Peter Florian *foreign language educator*
Edelstein, Teri J. *art history educator, art administrator, small business owner*
Elshtain, Jean Bethke *social and political ethics educator*
Emad, Parvis *philosophy educator*
Eslinger, Ellen Therese *historian*
Fasolt, Constantin *history professor*
Gannon, Sister Ann Ida *retired philosophy educator, former college administrator*
Gardiner, Judith Kegan *English language and women's studies educator*
Geyer, Michael *history professor*
Gilbert, Bentley Brinkerhoff *retired history professor, retired historian*
Golb, Norman *historian, writer*
Gossett, Philip *musicologist*
Grant, Robert McQueen *humanities educator*
Gray, Hanna Holborn *history educator*
Gross, Hanns *history professor*
Haley, George *Romance languages educator*
Harris, Neil *historian, educator*
Hellie, Richard *Russian history educator, researcher*
Hillocks, George, Jr., *English educator, researcher, consultant*
Holli, Melvin George *history educator*
Ingham, Norman William *Russian literature educator, genealogist*
Kaegi, Walter Emil *Byzantine history education educator*
Karanikas, Alexander *English language educator, author, actor*
Keenan, James George *classics educator*
Kolb, Gwin Jackson *language professional, educator*
Lawler, James Ronald *French language educator*
Lewis, Russell Lamar *historian, museum administrator*
Liebenow, Franklin Eastburn, Jr., *English literature educator*
Manning, Sylvia *English studies educator*
Najita, Tetsuo *history educator*
Nakamura, Kimiko *language educator*
Nashat, Guity *historian, education educator, researcher*
Nussbaum, Martha Craven *philosophy and classics educator*
Odishoo, Sarah A. *English language educator*
Remini, Robert Vincent *historian*
Riess, Steven Allan *historian, educator*
Romano-Magner, Patricia R. *English studies educator, researcher*
Rosenheim, Edward Weil *English educator*
Roy, David Tod *Chinese literature educator*
Saller, Richard Paul *classics educator*
Shaughnessy, Edward Louis *Chinese language educator*
Shen, Virginia Shiang-lan *Spanish and Chinese language educator*
Singleton, Gregory Holmes *historian, educator*
Sljivic-Simsic, Biljana B. *Slavic and Baltic languages educator*
Smith, Daniel Scott *history educator, historian*
Sochen, June *history professor*
Tang, Chenxi *literature educator*
Thaden, Edward Carl *history professor*
Thurner, Arthur W. *historian, educator*
Trumpener, Katie *literature educator*
Vertreace-Doody, Martha Modena *English educator, poet*
Wexman, Virginia Wright *English language educator*

Cicero
Nitzarim, Yoel David *language educator*

Dekalb
Baker, William *British literature educator*
Vande Creek, Drew Evan *historian, educator*

Elgin
Duffy, John Lewis *retired Latin, English and reading educator*

Evanston
Kalantzis, George *historian, educator*
McCurry, Stephanie *historian, educator*
Paden, William D. *French literature educator*
Reiss, Lenore Ann *language educator, retired secondary school educator*
Sheridan, James Edward *history professor*
Sundquist, Eric John *American studies educator*
Ver Steeg, Clarence Lester *historian, educator*
Weil, Irwin *language educator*
Wills, Garry *historian*
Wright, John *classics educator*

Glen Ellyn
Fox, Jeffrey Harrison *language educator*

Kankakee
Edwards, Richard Claire *retired speech educator*

Lake Bluff
Sweetser, Marie-Odile Gauny *retired foreign language educator*

Lake Forest
Beiriger, Eugene Edward *historian, educator, dean*

Lincolnwood
Hull, Elizabeth Anne *retired English language educator*

Macomb
Hallwas, John Edward *English language educator*
Jelatis, Virginia G. *historian, educator*
Morelli, Mario Frank *philosophy educator*
Spencer, Donald Spurgeon *historian, academic administrator*

Mount Vernon
Hall, Sharon Gay *retired language educator, artist*

Naperville
Shoemaker, Robert Willoughby *historian, educator*

Normal
Hesse, Douglas Dean *English educator*
Shields, John Charles *American studies and African American studies and literature educator*

Northbrook
Stamper, James M. *retired English language educator*
Young, Susan Jean *music specialist*

Oglesby
Charry, Stephen Walter *historian, educator*

Orland Park
Russell, Edward Francis *humanities educator, social sciences educator*

Palatine
Keres, Karen Lynne *English language educator*

Rockford
Berry, Wes *literature educator*
Hoshaw, Lloyd *retired historian, educator*

Rolling Meadows
Strongin, Bonnie Lynn *English language educator*

Romeoville
Lifka, Mary Lauranne *history professor*

Seymour
Carringer, Robert *English language and film educator*

Springfield
Bannister, Dan Wesley *retired historian*
Temple, Wayne Calhoun *historian, writer*

Urbana
Accad, Evelyne *language educator*
Aldridge, Alfred Owen *English language educator*
Arnstein, Walter Leonard *historian, educator*
Baym, Nina *English educator*
Bérubé, Michael *literature educator*
Haile, H. G. *German language and literature educator*
Hendrick, George *retired English language educator*
Hitchins, Keith Arnold *historian, educator*
Hoxie, Frederick Eugene *history professor*
Kim, Chin-Woo *linguist, educator*
Love, Joseph L. *history educator, former cultural studies center administrator*
McKay, John Patrick *history educator*
Solberg, Winton Udell *history educator*
Sousa, Ronald Wayne *foreign language educator*
Talbot, Emile Joseph *French language educator*
Toby, Ronald Paul *historian*
Watts, Emily Stipes *English language educator*

Westchester
Masterson, John Patrick *retired English language educator*

INDIANA

Angola
Zimmerman, James Allen *historian, educator*

Bloomington
Anderson, Judith Helena *English language educator*
Assensoh, Akwasi Bretuo *historian, educator*
Bernhardt-Kabisch, Ernest Karl-Heinz *English and comparative literature educator*
Buelow, George John *musicologist, educator*
Choksy, Jamsheed Kairshasp *historian, religious scholar, language professional, humanities educator*
Dunn, Jon Michael *informatics educator, dean*
Edgerton, William B. *foreign language educator*
Eisenberg, Paul David *philosophy educator*
Franks, Steven Laurence *linguist, educator*
Hanson, Karen *philosopher, educator*
Johnson, Owen Verne *historian, educator*
Juergens, George Ivar *history professor*
Knudsen, Laura Georgia *linguist*
Lebano, Edoardo Antonio *foreign language educator*
Lloyd, Rosemary *language educator*
Martins, Heitor Miranda *foreign language educator*
McCluskey, John Asberry, Jr., *literature educator, writer*
Mickel, Emanuel John *foreign language educator*
Nordloh, David Joseph *English language educator*
Ransel, David Lorimer *history professor*
Rosenberg, Samuel Nathan *French and Italian language educator*
Senchuk, Dennis M. *philosopher, educator*
Sinor, Denis *Orientalist, educator*
Valdman, Albert *language and linguistics educator*
Walbridge, John *foreign language educator*

Carmel
Sukapdjo, Wilma Irene *language educator*

Crawfordsville
Barnes, James John *history educator*

East Chicago
Riddle, Jared Matthew *English educator, actor*

Fort Wayne
Miller, Dawn L. *literature educator*
Scheetz, Sister Mary JoEllen *English language educator*

Gary
Kern, Paul Bentley *historian, educator*

Greencastle
Dittmer, John Avery *history professor*
Spicer, Harold Otis *retired English language educator, communications educator*
Weiss, Robert Orr *speech educator*

Huntington
Michelson, Paul E. *historian, educator*

Indianapolis
Baetzhold, Howard George *English language educator*
Beyer, Werner William *retired English educator*
Davis, Kenneth Wayne *English language educator, business communication consultant*
Hamilton, Sharon J. *literature educator, dean, writer*
Houser, Nathan *philosopher, educator*
Krasean, Thomas Karl *historian*
Mason, Thomas Alexander *historian, educator, author*
Plater, William Marmaduke *English language educator, academic administrator*

Kokomo
Cameron, Ann M. *language educator*

Muncie
Hayashi, Tetsumaro *retired literature educator, writer, editor*
Hozeski, Bruce William *English language and literature educator*

Nashville
Wills, Katherine V. Tsiopos *English language educator*

Newburgh
Belleau, Leisa A. *English educator*

Notre Dame
Appleby, R(obert) Scott *history educator*
Doody, Margaret Anne *English language educator*
Dubreil, Sebastien *language educator*
Gernes, Sonia Grace *literature educator, writer*
Lanzinger, Klaus *language educator*
Matthias, John Edward *English literature educator*
McInerny, Ralph Matthew *philosopher, educator, writer*
Quinn, Philip Lawrence *philosophy educator*
Rosenberg, Charles Michael *art historian, educator*

South Bend
Cook, Pamela Margaret *French educator*
van Inwagen, Peter Jan *philosophy educator*
Vasta, Edward *humanities educator*

Terre Haute
Baker, Ronald Lee *English educator*
Carmony, Marvin Dale *retired linguist, educator*
De Marr, Mary Jean *English language educator*
Pickett, William Beatty *history educator*

Valparaiso
Peters, Howard Nevin *foreign language educator*

Vincennes
Rogers, John Headley *literature and language professor*

West Lafayette
Bertolet, Rodney Jay *philosophy educator*
Contreni, John Joseph, Jr., *humanities educator, educator*
Mc Bride, William Leon *philosopher, educator*
Mork, Gordon Robert *historian, educator*
Saunders, James Robert *English educator*
Woodman, Harold David *historian, educator*

IOWA

Ames
Avalos, Hector Ignacio *language educator*
Cravens, Hamilton *history educator*
Maxwell-Dial, Eleanore *foreign language educator*
Mitchell, Jacqueline Keaton *English language educator*
Nostwich, Theodore Daniel *literature educator, researcher*
Zimmerman, Zora Devrnja *comparative literature and folklore educator*

Avoca
Hardisty, William Lee *English language educator*

Cedar Falls
Clohesy, William Warren *philosopher, educator*
Olsen-Dunbar, Jessica Ida *sign language educator*

Cedar Rapids
Lemos, John Paul *philosopher, educator*

Decorah
Christianson, John Robert *historian, educator*

Dubuque
Perry, E. Eugene *communication educator*

Fairfield
Aubrey, Bryan *educator, writer, editor*

Grinnell
Kintner, Philip L. *history professor*
Michaels, Jennifer Tonks *foreign language educator*
Smith, Don Alan *history professor*

Iowa City
Addis, Laird Clark, Jr., *philosopher, educator, musician*
Aspel, Paulene Violette *retired language educator*
Coolidge, Archibald Cary, Jr., *English language educator, literature researcher*
Dettmer, Helena R. *classics educator*
DiPardo, Anne *English language and education educator*
Ertl, Wolfgang *German language and literature educator*
Folsom, Lowell Edwin *language educator*
Fumerton, Richard Anthony *philosopher, educator*
Gelfand, Lawrence Emerson *historian, educator*
Goldstein, Jonathan Amos *retired ancient history and classics educator*
Green, Peter Morris *classics educator, writer, translator*
Hawley, Ellis Wayne *historian, educator*
Mentzer, Raymond Albert *religious history educator*
Mills, Margaret H. *language educator*
Nash, Jan R. Olive *historian, consultant*
Raeburn, John Hay *English language educator*
Scullion, Rosemarie *literature educator*
Solbrig, Ingeborg Hildegard *literature educator, writer*
Trank, Douglas Monty *rhetoric and speech communications educator*

Pella
Chia, Ning *history educator*
Den Adel, Raymond Lee *classics educator*

Sioux City
Nichols, Roger Sabin *genealogist, retired school counselor*

Storm Lake
Richey, Scott H *language educator*

KANSAS

Atchison
Lane, Elizabeth Ann *genealogist, researcher*

Chanute
Dillard, Dean Innes *English language educator, academic administrator*

Dighton
Stanley, Ellen May *historian, consultant*

El Dorado
Jenkinson, John Stephen *literature educator*

Fort Leavenworth
Rafuse, Ethan Sepp *historian, educator*

Hays
Duffy, Cheryl Hofstetter *language educator*

Lawrence
Baron, Frank *language educator*
Brundage, James Arthur *historian, educator*
Debicki, Andrew Peter *foreign language educator*
Dick, Ernst S. *retired German language educator*
Eldredge, Charles Child, III, *art history educator*
Farmer, Frank *language educator*
Gunn, James E. *English language educator*
Harvey, Douglas Scott *historian, educator*
Karcz, Andrzej *literature educator*
Kuznesof, Elizabeth Anne *history educator*
Li, Chu-Tsing *art history educator*
Pasco, Allan Humphrey *literature educator*
Saul, Norman Eugene *history educator*
Schoeck, Richard J(oseph) *English and humanities scholar, poet*
Spires, Robert Cecil *foreign language educator*
Tuttle, William McCullough, Jr., *history professor*
Woelfel, James Warren *philosophy and humanities educator*
Worth, George John *English literature educator*

Manhattan
Higham, Robin *historian, editor, publisher*
Machor, James Lawrence *language educator*

Mcpherson
Entz, Gary R. *historian, educator*

Newton
Sprunger, Keith L. *history educator*

Pittsburg
Viney, Donald Wayne *philosophy educator*

Prairie Village
Goheen, Ellen Rozanne *art historian*

Topeka
Averill, Thomas Fox *writer, educator*

KENTUCKY

Bowling Green
Minton, John Dean *historian, educator*

Covington
Cimprich, John Vincent *history educator*

Elsmere
Miller, Jackie Dean, I, *genealogist, historian*

Georgetown
Klotter, James C. *historian, educator*

Harrodsburg
Bradshaw, Phyllis Bowman *historian, historic site staff member*

Lexington
Coffman, Edward McKenzie *retired history professor*
Warth, Robert Douglas *history educator*

Louisville
Ford, Gordon Buell, Jr., *literature educator, writer*
Theiss, Gena Lee *genealogist, researcher*

Murray
Whisenhunt, Donald Wayne *history educator*

Owensboro
West, William Robert *history educator*

Richmond
Huch, Ronald Kind *historian, educator*

Southgate
Glenn, Jerry Hosmer, Jr., *retired language educator*

Wilmore
Kuhn, Anne Naomi Wicker (Mrs. Harold B. Kuhn) *foreign language educator*

LOUISIANA

Baton Rouge
Arceneaux, William *historian, educator, educational association administrator*
Cooper, William James, Jr., *history professor*
Culbert, David Holbrook *historian, educator, editor, writer*
Doty, Gresdna Ann *theatre historian, educator*
Hardy, John Edward *English language educator, author*
Olney, James *English language educator*
Ramirez, Arnulfo Gonzalez *language educator, linguist*
Ricapito, Joseph Virgil (Giuseppe Ricapito) *Spanish, Italian and comparative literature educator*
Sasek, Gloria Burns *English language and literature educator*
Smith, David Jeddie *American literature educator*
Wheeler, Otis Bullard *retired English educator and university official*

Hammond
Thorburn, James Alexander *retired humanities educator*

Lafayette
Raffel, Burton Nathan *retired educator, poet, writer, translator*

Leesville
Norman, Paralee Frances *English language educator, researcher*

Natchitoches
Smith, Jeffrey Robert *historian, educator*
Wells, Carol McConnell *genealogist, retired archivist*

New Orleans
Barton, Fredrick Preston *English language educator, administrator*
Bischof, Günter Josef *history professor*
Brumfield, William Craft *Slavic studies educator, photographer, writer*
Cook, Bernard Anthony *historian, educator*
Hasselbach, Karlheinz *literature educator*
Holditch, William Kenneth *American literature educator*
Kilroy, James Francis *humanities educator*
Luza, Radomir Vaclav *historian, educator*
Paolini, Gilberto *literature and science educator*
Pastorek, Marcia Jambu *language educator, writer*
Pindle, Arthur Jackson, Jr., *philosopher, researcher*
Poesch, Jessie Jean *art historian*
Reck, Andrew Joseph *philosopher, retired educator*
Roberts, Louise Nisbet *philosopher, educator*
Schalow, Frank Hickey *philosopher, educator*
Thompson, Annie Laura (Anne) *foreign language educator*
Werner, Robin A. *humanities educator*

Pineville
Howell, Thomas *history professor*

Ruston
Dodge Robbins, Dorothy Ellin *English educator*
Halliburton, Lloyd *Romance philology educator*

Shreveport
Jarzabek, Mary G. *language educator*

MAINE

Bar Harbor
Carpenter, William Morton *English educator, writer*

Biddeford
Bolle, Kees Willem *history professor*
Rothermel, Dan *humanities educator*

Brunswick
Hodge, James Lee *German language educator*
Martin, Harold Clark *humanities educator*

Bucksport
Ives, Edward Dawson *folklore educator*

Castine
Berleant, Arnold *philosopher*

Dresden
Turco, Lewis Putnam *English educator*

Hollis
Milardo, Margaret Powers *language educator*

Orono
See, Scott William *history professor*
Segal, Howard Paul *history educator*

Portland
Louden, Robert Burton *philosopher, educator*
Schwanauer, Francis *philosopher, educator*

Rockport
Goodwin, Doris Helen Kearns *historian*

Sanford
Allan, Jonathan David *autograph dealer, pop culture historian*

Scarborough
Hayden, Lisa C. *interpreter, translator, language educator, writer*
Sadik, Marvin Sherwood *art consultant, former museum director*

Waterville
Bassett, Charles Walker *English language educator*
Moroni, Mario *humanities educator*

West Boothbay Harbor
Marshall, Howard Lowen *musicologist, retired music educator*

MARYLAND

Annapolis
Lucas, George Ramsdell, Jr., *philosophy educator*
Yee, Cordell D.K. *liberal arts educator, historian*

Baltimore
Achinstein, Peter Jacob *philosopher, educator*
Baldwin, John Wesley *history professor*
Burke, Colin Bradley *retired historian*
Cacossa, Anthony Alexander *Romance languages educator*
Chapelle, Suzanne Ellery Greene *history professor*
Cohen, Warren I. *history professor*
Cooper, Jerrold Stephen *historian, educator*
Davidson, Roger, Jr., *historian, educator*
Frey, Ruth Lazetta *historian, educator*
Irwin, John Thomas *humanities educator*
Jeffries, John Worthington *historian, educator*
Johnson, Michael Paul *history educator*
Kessler, Herbert Leon *art historian, educator, university administrator*
Kurth, Lieselotte *foreign language educator*
Lidtke, Vernon LeRoy *history educator*
Roller, Matthew Benedict *classics educator*
Schneewind, Jerome Borges *philosophy educator*
Skinner, Daniel Thomas *language educator*
Varga, Nicholas *historian, archivist, retired educator*
Ziff, Larzer *English language educator*

Bel Air
Lu, David John *historian, writer*

Bethesda
Benson, Elizabeth Polk *art specialist*
Child-Olmsted, Gisèle Alexandra *retired language educator*
Duncan, Francis *historian, retired government official*
Gray, James Gordon, Jr., *speech educator*
Highfill, Philip Henry, Jr., *retired language educator*
Reed, Berenice Anne *art historian, artist, government official*
van der Linden, Frank Morris *historian*

Betterton
Kohl, Benjamin Gibbs *historian, educator*

Bowie
Sterling, Richard Leroy *English and foreign language educator*

Catonsville
Loerke, William Carl *art history educator*

Chevy Chase
Cline, Ruth Eleanor Harwood *translator*
Fern, Alan Maxwell *art historian, retired museum director*

College Park
Brush, Stephen George *historian, educator*
Collins, Merle *English and comparative literature educator*
De Lorenzo, William E. *foreign language educator*
Dopp, Bonnie Jo *musicologist, school librarian*
Hallett, Judith Peller *classical studies educator*
(Thompson) Knill, April Michele *historian, educator*
Levinson, Jerrold *humanities educator*
Olson, Keith Waldemar *history educator*
Oster, Rose Marie Gunhild *foreign language professional, educator*
Pasch, Alan *philosopher, educator*
Spear, Richard Edmund *art history educator*
Struna, Nancy L. *social historian and American studies educator*
Weart, Spencer Richard *historian*

Columbia
Marshall, Linda Murphy *linguist, government official*

Frostburg
Clulee, Nicholas Harkins *history professor*

Gaithersburg
Wang, Josephine Jung-Shan *language educator, translator*

Greenbelt
Scott-Childress, Reynolds Johnson *historian, educator*
Suid, Lawrence H. *historian, writer*

Hyattsville
Bloomfield, Maxwell Herron, III, *retired history and law educator*
Golden, Marita *English language educator, foundation executive*
Rodgers, Mary Columbro *literature educator, writer, academic administrator*

Lusby
Eshelman, Ralph Ellsworth *maritime historian, vertebrate paleontologist, cultural resource consultant*

Mitchellville
Embree, Ainslie Thomas *history educator*
Heald, Morrell *humanities educator*

Rockville
Cantelon, Philip Louis *historian*
Hewlett, Richard Greening *historian*
Kaplan, Lawrence Samuel *historian, educator*
Kinnane, Adrian *historian*

Salisbury
Jennings, Louis Brown *retired humanities educator*

Severna Park
Schick, Edgar Brehob *German literature educator*

Silver Spring
Borkovec, Vera Z. *Russian studies educator*
Calinger, Ronald Steve *historian*
Cole, Wayne Stanley *historian, educator*
luDoherty, William Thomas, Jr., *historian, retired educator*
Pacuska, Alison Brandi *Russian studies professional*
Papas, Irene Kalandros *English language educator, poet, writer*

Sparks
Suarez-Murias, Marguerite C. *retired language educator, retired literature educator*

Stevenson
North, Percy *art historian, educator*

Towson
Baker, Jean Harvey *history professor*
Harriss, Clarinda *language educator, poet*
Hirschmann, Edwin A. *historian, educator*
Pineo, Ronn *historian, educator*
Propst, M. Teresa Carson *historian*

Tracys Landing
Smith, Elbert Benjamin *historian, educator*

MASSACHUSETTS

Amesbury
Labaree, Benjamin Woods *history professor*

Amherst
Alexander, Alison F. *communication educator*
Baker, Lynne Rudder *philosophy educator*
Bezucha, Robert Joseph *history educator*
Clark, Carol Canda *art historian, educator*
Cohen, Alvin P. *language educator*
Gettier, Edmund Lee, III, *retired humanities educator*
Gibson, Walker *retired English language educator, poet, writer*
Greene, Theodore Phinney *historian, educator*
Kinney, Arthur Frederick *literary history educator, writer, editor*
Klement, Kevin Charles *humanities educator*
Oates, Stephen Baery *retired history educator*
Partee, Barbara Hall *linguist, educator*
Sinha, Manisha *historian, educator*
Taubman, Jane Andelman *Russian literature educator*
Taylor, Robert Edward *foreign language educator*
Wideman, John Edgar *English literature educator, novelist*
Wier, Dara *poet, English language educator*
Wolff, Robert Paul *philosophy educator*
Wyman, David Sword *historian, educator*

Arlington
Brooke, John L. *history professor*

Auburndale
Lindgren, Charlotte Holt *English language educator*

Belmont
Cavarnos, Constantine Peter *philosopher, writer*
Dohanian, Diran Kavork *art historian, educator*

Norberg, Arthur Lawrence, Jr., *historian, physicist, educator*
Pazandak, Carol Hendrickson *liberal arts educator*
Phillips, William David *history educator*
Ross, Donald, Jr., *English language educator, university administrator*
Sarles, Harvey B. *humanities educator*
Seidel, Robert Wayne *science historian, educator*
Tracy, James Donald *historian, educator*
Weiss, Gerhard Hans *German language educator*
Zou, Zhen *English and Chinese educator, translator and critic, computer technologist*

Moorhead
Buckley, Joan N. *English educator*
Coomber, James Elwood *English language educator*
Glasrud, Clarence Arthur *English educator*
Morrison, Barbara Sheffield *Japanese translator and interpreter, consultant, educator*

Northfield
Clark, Clifford Edward, Jr., *history professor*
Kutulas, Judy A. *historian, educator*
Soule, George Alan *literature educator, writer*
Yandell, Cathy Marleen *language educator*
Zelliot, Eleanor Mae *history educator*

Red Wing
Fritz, Henry Eugene *historian, educator*

Rochester
Robbins, Thomas Landau *humanities researcher*

Roseville
Gross, Alan Gerald *rhetoric educator*

Saint Cloud
Falk, Armand Elroy *retired English educator, writer*
Hofsommer, Donovan Lowell *history professor*
Mullins, Jeffrey Alan *historian, educator*

Saint Paul
Glancy, Helen Diane *literature educator*
Mather, Richard Burroughs *retired Chinese language and literature educator*
McDougal, Stuart Yeatman *comparative literature educator, author*
Monson, Dianne Lynn *literacy educator*
Nielsen, Suzanne Ruth *literature educator, writer*
Stewart, James Brewer *historian, writer, college administrator*
Weiner, Carl Dorian *historian*

Vadnais Heights
Polakiewicz, Leonard Anthony *foreign language and literature educator*

Virginia
Helland, Carol Jean *literature educator*

Winona
Ni, Ting *historian, educator*

MISSISSIPPI

Bay Saint Louis
Woodward, Ralph Lee, Jr., *historian, educator*

Cleveland
Boschert, Thomas Neville *historian, educator*

Clinton
Bigelow, Martha Mitchell *retired historian*

Columbus
Burger, Michael *humanities educator*

Gulfport
Swetman, Glenn Robert *English language educator, poet*

Hattiesburg
Escobar, Luz Marina *language educator*
Scarborough, William Kauffman *historian, educator*

Itta Bena
Hudspeth, Harvey Gresham *history professor*

Jackson
McLemore-Wheeler, Linda M. *literature educator*

Magnolia
Coney, Elaine Marie *English and foreign languages educator*

Senatobia
Banham, Sandra Rodgers *language educator*

Sumrall
Downey, James Cecil *retired music and humanities educator*

University
Hall, J(ames) R(obert) *English educator*
Jordan, Winthrop Donaldson *historian, educator*
Kiger, Joseph Charles *history professor*
Landon, Michael de Laval *historian, educator*
Miller, Brian Craig *historian, educator*

MISSOURI

Bolivar
Padgett, Thomas Eugene *language educator*

Columbia
Bien, Joseph Julius *philosophy educator*
Goodrich, James William *retired historian, association executive*
Lazzaro-Weis, Carol Marie *foreign languages educator*
Looser, Devoney Kay *English literature educator*
Mullen, Edward John, Jr., *Spanish language educator*
Nauert, Charles Garfield *history educator*
Overby, Osmund Rudolf *art historian, educator*
Schwartz, Richard Brenton *English language educator, dean, writer*
Strickland, Arvarh Eunice *history professor*
Timberlake, Charles Edward *history educator*
Vallentyne, Peter Lloyd *philosophy educator*
Zguta, Russell *history professor*

Florissant
Ashhurst, Anna Wayne *foreign language educator*

Joplin
Karmanova, Tatiana Victorovna *language educator*
Merriam, Allen Hayes *speech communication educator*

Kansas City
Ashworth, William B., Jr., *historian, educator*
Hoffmann, Donald *architectural historian*

Kirksville
Engber, Cheryl Ann *language educator, linguist*
Hanley, Mark Young *historian, educator, researcher*

Lees Summit
Himes, Brian David *reading educator*
Parker, Deborah A. *language educator, translator*

Marshall
Wildt, Katherine Ann *literature educator, writer, educator*

Poplar Bluff
Rivetti, Andrew Francis *language educator, department chairman*

Rolla
Christensen, Lawrence O. *historian, educator*

Saint Charles
Heidenreich, Donald Edward, Jr., *historian, educator*

Saint Joseph
Chelline, Warren Herman *language educator, minister*

Saint Louis
Arendt, Brian Bernard *historian, educator*
Barmann, Lawrence Francis *retired history educator*
Critchlow, Donald Thomas *history educator*
Herbert, Kevin Barry John *classics educator*
Hulsebosch, Daniel Joseph *historian, educator*
Madden, Thomas F. *medieval history eductor, author*
Mc Namee, Maurice Basil *English language educator*
Pautrot, Jean-Louis Jacques *literature and language professor*
Perry, Lewis Curtis *historian, educator*
Ruland, Richard Eugene *English and American literature educator, critic, literary historian*
Sale, Merritt *classicist, comparatist, educator*
Schwarz, Egon *humanities and German language educator, writer, literary critic*
Shea, Daniel Bartholomew, Jr., *English language educator, actor*
Sigala, Stephanie Childs *art historian, librarian*
van den Berg, Sara Jane *English educator*
Weixlmann, Joseph Norman, Jr., *English educator, provost*
Wellman, Carl Pierce *philosophy educator*
Witt, Michael John *history educator, priest*

Salem
Wood, Thomas Wesley *humanities educator, editor*

Springfield
Burgess, Ruth Lenora Vassar *speech and language educator*
Easley, June Ellen Price *genealogist*
Giglio, James Nicholas *humanities educator, writer*
Piston, William Garrett *historian, educator*
Sailors, Pamela Rene' *philosophy educator*
Sheng, Michael M. *historian, educator*

Warrensburg
Foley, William Edward *retired historian*

Washington
Gregory, Ralph J. *historian, curator*

MONTANA

Billings
DeRosier, Arthur Henry, Jr., *historian*
Jensen, Theodore W. *language educator*

Butte
Reardon, Stephen James, Jr., *retired English speech educator*

Miles City
Sleight, Garth Hessen *language educator, dean*

Missoula
Drake, Richard Regis *historian, educator*
Eglin, John Arthur *historian, educator*
Kittredge, William Alfred *humanities educator*
Wigfied-Phillip, Ruth Genivea *genealogist, author, researcher*

NEBRASKA

Kearney
Young, Ann Elizabeth O'Quinn *historian, educator*

Lincoln
Leinieks, Valdis *classicist, educator*
Rawley, James Albert *history professor*
Sawyer, Robert McLaran *history educator*
Stover, John Ford *railroad historian, educator*

North Platte
Wohler, Ruth *humanities educator*

Omaha
Brock, Stephen L. *supervisor international languages, consultant*
Gershovich, Moshe *historian, educator*
Horning, Ross Charles, Jr., *historian, educator*
Maher, Susan Marguerite *language educator*
Nielsen, Fredrick Henry *historian, educator*
Okhamafe, Imafedia *English literature and philosophy educator*
Skau, Michael W. *English educator*

NEVADA

Las Vegas
Donaghy, Henry James *English literature educator, academic administrator*
Hickey, David C. *art historian*
Tanenhaus, David Spinoza *historian, educator*

North Las Vegas
Miller, Eleanor *English language and literature educator*

NEW HAMPSHIRE

Berlin
May, William Francis *ethicist, educator*

Concord
Folch-Pi, Willa Babcock *romance language educator*

Derry
Holmes, Richard Dale *history consultant*

Durham
Gold, Janet Nowakowski *Spanish language educator*
Hapgood, Robert Derry *English educator*
Simic, Charles *English language educator, poet*
Wheeler, Douglas Lanphier *history educator, writer*

Freedom
Kucera, Henry *linguistics educator*

Hanover
Bien, Peter Adolph *English language educator, author*
Cook, William Wilbert *English language educator*
Daniell, Jere Rogers, II, *retired history educator, consultant, public lecturer*
Doney, Willis Frederick *philosophy educator*
Garthwaite, Gene Ralph *historian, educator*
Gert, Bernard *philosopher, educator*
Higgins, Lynn Anthony *humanities educator, writer*
Kremer, Richard Lynn *historian, educator*
Mansell, Darrel Lee, Jr., *English educator*
Oxenhandler, Neal *language educator, writer*
Russell, Robert Hilton *Romance languages and literature educator*
Scher, Steven Paul *literature educator*
Scherr, Barry Paul *foreign language educator*
Sheldon, Richard Robert *Russian language and literature educator*
Shewmaker, Kenneth Earl *history professor*
Wood, Charles Tuttle *history educator*

Keene
Crocker, Matthew Hallowell *historian, educator, writer, researcher*

Manchester
Paradis, Wilfrid H. *retired historian*

Meredith
Heald, Bruce Day *English and music educator, historian*

Mount Sunapee
Marashio, Paul William *humanities educator*

Nashua
Phelps, Bonnie Noreen *language educator, secondary school educator*

Plymouth
Rolph, Matthew G. J. *literature and language professor, consultant*

Portsmouth
Harter, Hugh Anthony *foreign language educator*

Rindge
Lupinin, Nickolas *history educator, editor, publisher*

NEW JERSEY

Avon By The Sea
Potter, Emma Josephine Hill *language educator*

Belle Mead
Brown, Elizabeth Schmeck *fashion historian*

Bridgewater
Mc Cormick, Richard Patrick *history professor*

Califon
Alvarez, Jaime *language educator, poet*

Camden
Showalter, English, Jr., *French language educator*

Cape May
Lassner, Franz George *retired history professor, archivist*
Turner, Almon Richard *retired art historian, educator*

Cranford
Russell, John Joseph *English educator*

Demarest
Brody, Saul Nathaniel *retired English literature educator*

Edison
Kushinsky, Jeanne Alice *humanities educator*

Glassboro
Wang, Q. Edward *history professor*

Hackensack
Fatemi, Saeid *language educator, writer, researcher*

Hewitt
Mollenkott, Virginia Ramey *English literature and language educator, author, guest lecturer*

Highland Lakes
Kiraly, Bèla Kàlmàn *retired history educator, Hungarian army officer*

Hightstown
Martin, David George *historian, Latin educator, author*

Jersey City
Coreil, Raymond Clyde *English educator*
D'Ambra, Eve *art historian*
Jennings, Sister Vivien *English language educator*
Winner, David Dario *humanities educator, writer*
Yaworsky, Bohdan *criminal justice educator, consultant*

Lawrenceville
Iorio, Dominick Anthony *philosophy educator, dean*
Maxwell, Max Anthony *language educator*
Stroh, Guy Weston *philosophy educator*

Lodi
McParland, Robert Patrick *English educator, writer*

Madison
Leavell, John Perry, Jr., *historian, educator*

Mahwah
Christopher, Robert *literature and language professor, researcher*
Weinberg, Sydney Stahl *historian*

Mays Landing
Benner, Richard Byron *philosophy educator*

Montclair
Pastor, Peter *history professor*
Stertz, Stephen Allen *historian, educator*

Morristown
Fredericks, Robert Joseph *language company executive*
Gorrell, Nancy S. *English language educator*

New Brunswick
Bahun, Sanja *literature educator, researcher*
Chambers, John Whiteclay, II, *history professor*
Fishbein, Leslie Ellen *humanities educator*
Gillette, William *historian, educator*
Goffen, Rona *art historian, educator*
Grob, Gerald N. *historian, educator*
Hartman, Mary S. *historian, educator*
Jenkins, Reese V. *historian, educator*
Kelley, Donald Reed *historian*
Levine, George Lewis *English language educator, literature critic*
Marder, Tod A. *art historian, educator*
O'Neill, William Lawrence *history professor*
Reed, James Wesley *social historian, educator*
Smith, Bonnie Gene *historian, educator*
Stich, Stephen Peter *philosophy educator*
Tu, Ching-I *humanities educator, researcher*
Zatlin, Phyllis *Spanish language educator, translator*

Newark
Diner, Steven Jay *history professor*
Franklin, H. Bruce *language educator, writer*
Schweizer, Karl Wolfgang *historian, educator, author*
Varzegar, Minoo *literature educator, reading specialist*

Paramus
Mahoney, Joseph Francis *historian, educator*

Pomona
Mench, Fred Charles *classics educator*

Pompton Plains
Meyer, Chester F. *language educator, writer*

Princeton
Aarsleff, Hans *linguistics educator*
Bermann, Sandra Lekas *English language educator*
Bowersock, Glen Warren *historian, educator*
Brombert, Victor Henri *literature educator, author*
Brown, Leon Carl *history educator*
Cooper, John Madison *philosophy educator*
Corngold, Stanley Alan *German and comparative literature educator, writer*
Curschmann, Michael Johann Hendrik *retired German language and literature educator*
Ermolaev, Herman Sergei *Slavic languages educator*
Gallo, Ruben *Latin American literature educator, art critic*
Gillispie, Charles Coulston *history of science educator*
Goheen, Robert Francis *classicist, educator, former ambassador*
Grafton, Anthony Thomas *history professor*
Habicht, Christian Herbert *history professor*
Harman, Gilbert Helms *philosophy educator*
Hollander, Robert B., Jr., *Romance languages educator*
Hynes, Samuel *English language educator, author*
Jordan, William Chester *history educator*
Knoepflmacher, Ulrich Camillus *literature educator*
Lewis, Bernard *Near Eastern studies educator*
Mackey, Louis Henry *philosophy educator*
Marks, John Henry *Near Eastern studies educator*
Mc Pherson, James Munro *history professor*
Moote, A. Lloyd *history professor*
Moynahan, Julian Lane *English language educator, author*
Nehamas, Alexander *philosophy educator*
Painter, Nell Irvin *historian, educator, writer*
Paret, Peter *historian*
Rabb, Theodore K. *historian, educator*
Rigolot, François *French literature educator, literary critic*
Robertson, David Allan, Jr., *English educator*
Schofield, Robert E(dwin) *history educator, academic administrator*
Schorske, Carl Emil *historian, educator*
Shimizu, Yoshiaki *art historian, department chairman*

PROFESSIONAL INDEX 5717 HUMANITIES: LIBERAL STUDIES

Showalter, Elaine *humanities educator*
Silbergeld, Jerome Leslie *art historian, educator*
West, Cornel *humanities educator, writer*
White, Morton Gabriel *philosopher, historian*
Wightman, Ludmilla G. Popova *language educator, foreign educator, translator*
Ziolkowski, Theodore Joseph *comparative literature educator*

Ridgewood
Hinckley, Deborah Clark *language services professional*

Stewartsville
Busch, Beverly Gail *English language educator, literature educator, instructional resource center administrator*

Teaneck
Fjordbotten, Alf Lee *language educator*
Gordon, Lois G. *English language educator*
Rudy, Willis *historian*
Wiener, Joel Howard *historian, educator*

Toms River
Bosley, Karen Lee *English and journalism educator*
Chopyk, Dan Bohdan *language educator, poet*

Trenton
George, Emery Edward *foreign language and studies educator, writer*

Upper Montclair
Adarkar, Aditya *humanities educator*
Valdez del Alamo, Elizabeth *art historian, educator*
Vega, Carlos B. *language educator, writer*

Wayne
Nalle, Sara Tilghman *historian, educator*
Rogoff, Paula Drimmer *English and foreign language educator*

West Long Branch
Dvoichenko-Markov, Demetrius *history educator*

West Paterson
Miller, Gail Wood *literature educator, consultant*

Westfield
Hull, Kathleen Ann *humanities educator*
McDevitt, Brian Peter *history professor, educational consultant*

Whiting
Kelsey, George E. *language educator*

NEW MEXICO

Albuquerque
Duke, Rachele Marongiu *language educator*
Gish, Robert Franklin *English language educator, writer*
Graham, Timothy Charles *historian, director*
Hutton, Paul Andrew *history educator, writer*
Lind, Levi Robert *classics educator, writer*
Peña, Juan José *interpreter*
Szasz, Ferenc M. *historian, educator*

Las Cruces
Dasenbrock, Reed Way *literature educator*
Flores, William Vincent *Latin American studies educator*

Las Vegas
Simpson, Dorothy Audrey *retired speech educator*

Pomona
Lubenow, William Cornelius *historian, educator*

Santa Fe
Gaustad, Edwin Scott *historian, educator*
Lehmberg, Stanford Eugene *historian, educator*
Maehl, William Henry *historian, university administrator, educational consultant*

Taos
Bolls, Imogene Lamb *English language educator, poet*

NEW YORK

Albany
Barker-Benfield, Graham John *historian*
Berman, Jeffrey *language educator*
Colombí-Monguió, Alicia de *foreign language educator, poet*
Donovan, Robert Alan *English educator*
Howell, Robert Charles *philosopher, educator*
Kecskes, Istvan *linguist, educator*
Kekes, John *philosopher, educator*
Martland, T(homas) R(odolphe) *philosophy educator*
Olmstead, Lucinda Sue *English professor*
Reese, William Lewis *philosophy educator*
Refai, Shahid *history professor*
Schneider, Duane Bernard *English literature educator*
Staley, Harry Charles *retired literature educator, poet*

Altamont
Armstrong, Agnes Rose Fingerlin *musicologist*

Amherst
Kurtz, Paul *philosopher, educator, writer, publisher*

Bayport
Mohanty, Christine Ann *retired language educator, actress*

Bayside
Low, Frederick Emerson *English educator*

Binghamton
Gaddis Rose, Marilyn *literature educator, translator*
Sklar, Kathryn Kish *historian, educator*
Stein, George Henry *historian, educator, administrator*

Brockport
Dabbagh, Mahmoud *language educator, researcher*
Leslie, William Bruce *history professor*
Owen, Karen Ann *historian, educator*

Bronx
Bowers, Francis Robert *literature educator*
Bullaro, Grace Russo *literature, film and foreign language educator, speaker, book reviewer*
Cammarata, Joan Frances *Spanish language and literature educator*
Dimler, George Richard *German language educator, editor*
Elenko, Stuart S. *historian, educator*
Hallett, Charles Arthur, Jr., *English and humanities educator*
Hermalyn, Gary Douglas *historian, educator*
Marún, Gioconda *Spanish language educator*
Ryan, James Daniel *history professor*
Spatt, Hartley Steven *humanities educator*
Ultan, Lloyd *historian, educator*
Valgemae, Mardi *English educator*
Wosk, Julie *humanities educator*

Bronxville
Peters, Sarah Whitaker *art historian, writer, lecturer*
Pollin, Burton Ralph *English educator*

Brooklyn
Barran, Thomas Paul *language educator*
Berger, David *history professor*
Blasi, Alberto *Romance languages educator, writer*
Buttaro, Lucia *language educator, consultant*
Everdell, William Romeyn *humanities educator, historian*
Flam, Jack Donald *art historian, educator*
Forsberg, Suzanne *humanities educator, humanities speaker*
Galgan, Gerald Joseph *philosopher, educator*
Gisolfi, Diana (Diana Gisolfi Pechukas) *art history educator*
Jaffe, Louise *English language educator, creative writer*
King, Margaret Leah *history professor*
Lobron, Barbara L. *speech educator, writer, editor, photographer*
Spector, Robert Donald *language professional, educator*
Thacher, Barbara Auchincloss *history educator*
Witherspoon, Maria Bernarda Pena *bilingual educator*

Brookville
Maillet, Lucienne *humanities educator*

Buffalo
Doyno, Victor Anthony *literature educator*
Dumitru, Magdalena Lucia *linguist, educator*
Grol, Regina *literature educator, translator*
Hare, Peter Hewitt *philosophy educator*
Iggers, Georg Gerson *history professor*
LaHood, Marvin John *English educator*
Merini, Rafika *foreign language, cultures and literatures educator*
Milligan, John Drane *historian, educator*
Payne, Frances Anne *literature educator, researcher*
Peradotto, John Joseph *classics educator, editor*
Riepe, Dale Maurice *philosopher, writer, illustrator, educator, Asian art dealer*
Robinson, Zan Dale *language educator, writer*
Siedlecki, Peter Anthony *English language and literature educator*
Twagilimana, Aimable *English educator, writer*
Williams, Lillian Serece *historian, social studies educator*
Yu, Jiyuan *philosopher, educator*

Canton
Goldberg, Rita Maria *foreign language educator*

Churchville
Clarke, Stephan Paul *retired language educator, retired writer*

Clifton Park
Monguió, Luis *Spanish language educator*

Clinton
Rabinowitz, Peter J. *literature educator, music critic*

Cornwall On Hudson
Rosenof, Theodore Dimon *historian, educator*

Cortland
Anderson, Donna Kay *musicologist, educator*
Nagel, Mechthild Euphrosyne *philosopher, educator, sociologist*

Delmar
Schwarz, Louise A. *band director*

Dobbs Ferry
Medoff, Richard Brad *speech educator*
Poian, Edward Licio *historian*

East Hampton
Bromley, Bruce Ditmas *language educator, writer*

Elmira
Shephard, Robert Parrish *historian, educator*

Fairport
Carlton, Charles Merritt *linguistics educator*
Graham, Susette Ryan *retired English educator*
Rueckert, William Howe *literature educator, writer*

Flushing
Bird, Thomas Edward *foreign language and literature educator*
Lonigan, Paul Raymond *language professional, educator*
Rabassa, Gregory *Romance languages educator, translator, poet*
Ranald, Margaret Loftus *English literature educator, author*
Tytell, John *humanities educator, writer*

Forest Hills
Kra, Pauline Skornicki *French language educator*

Fredonia
Goetz, Thomas Henry Paul *French literature educator*

Reiff, Daniel D. *art history educator*

Fresh Meadows
Duckett, Lila Wheeler *retired language educator, writer*

Garden City
Garner, Richard Keith *classicist, educator*
Jenkins, Kenneth Vincent *literature educator, writer*
Korshak, Yvonne *art historian*
Seyfried, Vincent F. *historian*
Shneidman, J. Lee *historian, educator*

Gardiner
Mabee, Carleton *historian, educator*

Geneseo
Edgar, William John *philosophy educator*
Gouvernet, Gerard Raoul *language educator*

Getzville
Saveth, Edward Norman *history educator*

Greenvale
Brier, Robert M *Egyptologist, educator, documentary presenter*
Dircks, Phyllis Toal *English language educator*

Guilderland
Berger, Morris Isaiah *humanities educator*

Hamilton
Busch, Briton Cooper *historian, educator*
Godwin, Joscelyn *humanities educator, writer*
Knuth, Deborah Jane *English and women's studies educator*
Pinchin, Jane *literature educator*
Soderberg, Dale LeRoy *English language educator, drama director, producer*
Staley, Lynn *English educator*

Hastings On Hudson
Del Duca, Rita *language educator*

Hempstead
Couser, G(riffith) Thomas *literature educator*
McPhee, Martha *literature educator*

Hicksville
Mund, Lorraine G. *English studies educator, writer*

Hillsdale
Parmet, Herbert Samuel *historian, writer*

Hudson
Lyons, Rosemary *language educator*

Huntington
Dircks, Richard Joseph *English language educator, writer*

Hurleyville
Hilfstein, Erna *science historian, educator*

Ithaca
Abrams, Meyer Howard *English language educator*
Bailey, Lee Worth *philosophy and religion educator*
Colby-Hall, Alice Mary *Romance studies educator*
Eddy, Donald Davis *English language educator*
Groos, Arthur Bernhard, Jr., *German studies educator, music educator*
Harris, Robert Lee, Jr., *history professor*
Hohendahl, Peter Uwe *German language and literature educator*
Hutcheson, Richard Ervin *philosophy educator, academic administrator*
Kammen, Michael *historian, educator*
Koschmann, J. Victor *history educator, academic program director*
Kronik, John William *Romance studies educator*
LaCapra, Dominick Charles *historian, educator*
LaFeber, Walter Frederick *history educator, author*
McConkey, James Rodney *English educator, writer*
McMillin, Scott *language educator*
Norton, Mary Beth *history educator, writer*
Porte, Joel Miles *English educator*
Radice, Mark A. *musicologist*
Radzinowicz, Mary Ann *language educator*
Schwarz, Daniel Roger *English and American literature educator*

Jamaica
Coppa, Frank John *historian, educator*
Ekbatani, Glayol *language educator, director, writer*
Harmond, Richard Peter *historian, educator*
Kinkley, Jeffrey C. *historian*
Mentz, Steven Roger *language educator*
Parmet, Robert David *historian, educator*

Jericho
Astuto, Philip Louis *retired Spanish educator*

Johnson City
Bernardo, Aldo Sisto *retired foreign language educator*

Kings Park
Fay, Thomas A. *philosopher, educator*

Kings Point
Greenwald, Richard Alan *history professor*

Loudonville
Boisvert, Raymond Donat *philosopher, educator*
Fiore, Peter Amadeus *English educator, clergy*

Middle Village
Walter, John Frederick *historical researcher, genealogist*

Monsey
Erickson, Barbara Martha *historian, writer*

Moravia
Dienhoffer, Margaret Quigley *historian, educator*

Mount Kisco
Dore, Anita Wilkes *English language educator*

New Paltz
Hathaway, Richard Dean *retired language educator*

Roper, Louis H. *historian, educator*

New Rochelle
Fitch, Nancy Elizabeth *historian, educator*
Kraman, Cynthia *humanities educator*
Schleifer, James Thomas *history professor*

New York
Aching, Gerard *language educator*
Allentuck, Marcia Epstein *English language and art history educator*
Apter, Emily *language educator*
Arac, Jonathan *English language educator*
Ashbery, John Lawrence *language educator, poet, playwright, art critic*
Baker, Paul Raymond *history educator*
Bell, James Brugler *historian, writer*
Bender, Thomas *history and humanities educator, writer*
Berghahn, Volker Rolf *history professor*
Bertram, Paul Benjamin *English language educator*
Birns, Nicholas Boe *literature educator, editor*
Bishop, Thomas Walter *French language and literature educator*
Blatner, Barbara Ann *literature educator*
Bonfante, Larissa *classics educator*
Boudreau, A. Allan *historian, writer, educator*
Boyd, Frances Armstrong *language educator, writer*
Brilliant, Richard *art history educator*
Brooks, Jerome Bernard *English and Afro-American literature educator*
Brown, Jonathan *art historian, fine arts educator*
Brush, Craig Balcombe *retired French language and computer educator*
Bulliet, Richard Williams *history educator, novelist*
Burbank, Jane Richardson *language educator*
Cahn, Steven Mark *philosopher, educator*
Castronovo, David *humanities educator, writer*
Cavallo, Jo Ann *Italian language educator*
Caws, Mary Ann *French language and comparative literature educator, critic*
Cohen, Morton Norton *English educator, writer*
Compagnon, Antoine Marcel *French language educator*
Cook, Blanche Wiesen *history educator, journalist*
Couchman, Jeffrey G. *literature educator, writer*
Czerwinski, Edward Joseph *foreign language educator*
Danisi, John J. *philosopher, educator*
Datema, Jessica Venning *humanities educator*
Davenport, John J. *philosopher, educator*
Deak, Istvan *historian, educator*
Dickey, Eleanor *humanities educator*
Dorris, George Edward *historian, educator, editor, author*
Driver, Martha Westcott *English language educator, writer, researcher*
Duberman, Martin *historian, educator*
Eckman, Lester Samuel *humanities educator*
Eisler, Colin Tobias *art historian, curator*
Ferrante, Joan Marguerite *language educator, literature educator, writer*
Foner, Eric *historian, educator*
Frank, Elizabeth *literature educator, writer*
Freedberg, David Adrian *art educator, historian*
Freedman, (Moses) Maurice *historian, researcher*
Freeman, James Beaumont *philosophy educator*
Frey, Julia Bloch *French language educator, art historian educator*
Friedman, Sanford *literature educator, writer*
Gay, Peter *history educator, author*
Gerdts, William Henry *art history educator*
Ginter, Valerian Alexius *urban historian, educator*
Gluck, Carol *history professor*
Gordon-Reed, Annette *historian, law educator*
Greenberg, Henry J. *historian*
Gromada, Thaddeus V. *historian, academic administrator*
Harris, Frederick John *foreign language and literature educator*
Harris, Katherine Safford *speech and hearing educator*
Harris, William Vernon *history educator*
Hartman, Joan Edna *English educator*
Harvey, Donald Joseph *historian, educator*
Heffner, Richard Douglas *historian, educator, communications consultant, television producer*
Hendin, Josephine Gattuso *language educator, writer*
Hill, May Brawley *art historian*
Hoeflin, Ronald Kent *philosopher, writer*
Hornbostel, Paula Rand *art historian*
Howe, Florence *English educator, writer*
Hussey, Mark Francis *English language educator*
Izzo, Francesco *musicologist*
Jackson, Kenneth Terry *historian, administrator*
Johnston, Ruth D. *English literature educator, women's studies educator, film studies educator*
Kaiser, Walter *English language educator*
Karsen, Sonja Petra *retired American-Hispanic literature educator*
Kastan, David Scott *literature educator, writer*
Kaur, Harminder *language educator*
Kerz, Louise *historian*
Krinsky, Carol Herselle *art history educator*
Kroeber, Karl *English language educator*
Lamont, Rosette Clementine *Romance languages educator, theatre journalist, translator*
LaRue, Jan (Pieters) (Adrian LaRue) *musicologist, educator, writer*
Leibowitz, Herbert Akiba *English language educator, author*
Lencek, Rado Ludovik *Slavic languages educator*
Lewyn, Ann Salfeld *retired English as a second language educator*
Lodge, Kirsten *language educator*
London, Herbert Ira *humanities educator, institute executive*
Low, Anthony *English language educator*
Malin, Irving *English literature educator, literary critic*
Markowitz, Gerald E. *historian, educator*
May, Gita *language educator, literature educator*
Mayerson, Philip *classics educator*
Maynard, John Rogers *English educator*
Maysilles, Elizabeth *speech communication professional, educator*
Meisel, Martin *English and comparative literature educator*
Meisel, Perry *English educator*
Menand, Louis *literature educator*
Middendorf, John Harlan *English literature educator*
Middlebrook, Diane Wood *English language educator, writer*

Miller, Nancy K. *literature educator*
Miller, Walter James *English and humanities educator, writer*
Mintz, Samuel Isaiah *English language educator, writer*
Mirrer, Louise *language educator, consultant*
Myers, Gerald E. *humanities educator*
Nafisi, Azar *humanities educator*
Olson, Roberta Jeanne Marie *art historian, author, educator, curator*
Paxton, Robert Owen *historian, educator*
Perna, Michael Lewis *language educator*
Phillips, Louis J. *humanities educator, writer*
Plottel, Jeanine Parisier *foreign language educator*
Poirier, Richard *literary critic, educator, editor*
Posner, Donald *art historian, educator*
Quinn, Alice Freeman *literature educator*
Quiñones Keber, Eloise *art historian, educator*
Rabassa, Clementine Christos *humanities educator, translator*
Ragusa, Olga Maria *retired Italian language educator*
Randall, Francis Ballard *historian, educator, writer*
Ravitch, Diane Silvers *historian, educator, author, government official*
Raymond, Dorothy Sarnoff *communications consultant, former actress and singer*
Reiman, Donald Henry *English language educator*
Reynolds, Donald Martin *art historian, foundation administrator, educator*
Rheins, Carl Jeffrey *historian, director*
Richtman, Jack *French language educator*
Rivera-Valdés, Sonia *humanities educator*
Robertson, Andrew Whitmore *historian*
Roos, Jane Mayo *art history educator*
Rosand, David *art history educator*
Rosenberg, John David *English educator, literary critic*
Rosenblum, Robert *art historian, educator*
Rosengarten, Frank *retired language educator, retired literature educator, writer*
Rosner, David *history educator*
Rothman, David J. *history and medical educator*
Rowen, Ruth Halle *musicologist, educator*
Salemi, Joseph Salvatore *classics and humanities educator, poet, writer*
Saloman, Ora Frishberg *musicologist, educator*
Salvesen, Magda Abercromby *art historian, garden historian*
Sandler, Lucy Freeman *art history educator*
Scheindlin, Raymond Paul *Hebrew literature educator, translator*
Seigel, Jerrold Edward *historian, writer*
Selig, Karl-Ludwig *language and literature educator*
Shearier, Stephen James *language educator*
Stade, George Gustav *humanities educator*
Steinberg, Leo *art historian, educator*
Steiner, Richard C. *semitic linguist, educator*
Stephens, Gary Ralph *American literature and journalism educator*
Stern, Fritz Richard *historian, educator*
Stimpson, Catharine Rosalind *English language educator, writer*
Subirats, Eduardo *language educator*
Tanselle, George Thomas *English language educator, foundation executive*
Taran, Leonardo *classicist, educator*
Tusiani, Joseph *foreign language educator, author*
Umeh, Marie Arlene *English language educator*
Unger, Irwin *historian, educator*
Unger, Peter Kenneth *philosophy educator*
Valenstein, Suzanne Gebhart *art historian*
Waldhorn, Arthur *literature educator, researcher, scriptwriter*
Walker, Robert Harris *historian, writer, editor*
Walkowitz, Daniel Jay *historian, filmmaker, educator*
Wasser, Henry *retired American literature and sociology educator*
Weil-Garris Brandt, Kathleen (Kathleen Brandt) *art historian*
Weinberg, H. Barbara *art historian, educator, curator*
Willett Bird, Susan *public and motivational speaker*
Wixom, William David *art historian, museum administrator, educator*
Wortman, Richard S. *historian, educator*
Wyschogrod, Edith *philosophy educator*
Yerushalmi, Yosef Hayim *historian, educator*
Yurchenco, Henrietta Weiss *ethnomusicologist, writer*

Newburgh
Adams, Barbara *English language educator, poet, writer*

Niagara University
Northcutt, Wayne *history educator*

Oakdale
Mieczkowski, Yanek *history professor, writer*

Olean
Mazon, Margaret Fausold *language educator*

Oneonta
Malhotra, Ashok Kumar *philosophy educator*
Shrader, Douglas Wall, Jr., *philosophy educator*

Oswego
Bishop, Rand *retired humanities educator*
Smiley, Marilynn Jean *musicologist*

Oyster Bay
Gable, John Allen *historian, association executive, educator*

Pittsford
French, Henry Pierson, Jr., *historian, educator*

Plattsburgh
Lindgren, James Michael *historian, educator*
Torres-Padilla, Jose Luis *English educator*

Port Washington
Williams, George Leo *historian, landmark preservationist, educator*

Potsdam
Harder, Kelsie Brown *retired language professional, educator*
Lunt, Lora G. *international education educator, language educator*
Serio, John N. *language educator*
Skandera-Trombley, Laura Elise *language professional, English*

Poughkeepsie
Bartlett, Lynn Conant *English literature educator*
Daniels, Elizabeth Adams *English language educator*
Griffen, Clyde Chesterman *retired history educator*
Hytier, Adrienne Doris *French language educator*
Kelley, David Christopher *philosopher*
Merrell, James Hart *history educator*
Peck, H. Daniel *literature educator*
Rashid, Ismail O. D. *historian, educator*
Sharp, Ronald Alan *English literature educator, dean, author*

Queensbury
Cavaluzzi, Anthony David *English studies educator*

Riverdale
Diaz, Marlene Carmen *language educator*

Rochester
Aldersley, Stephanie Polowe *language educator*
Bauman, M. Garrett *English educator*
Chiarenza, Carl *art historian, critic, artist, educator*
Gordon, Dane Rex *philosophy educator, minister*
Hauser, William Barry *history educator, historian*
Herminghouse, Patricia Anne *foreign language educator*
Hollis, Susan Tower *history professor*
Johnson, Bruce Marvin *English language educator*
Zagorin, Perez *historian, educator*

Rockville Centre
Fitzgerald, Janet Anne *philosophy educator, academic administrator*

Saint Bonaventure
Godet-Calogeras, JeanFrançois *historian, educator*

Sanborn
Michalak, Janet Carol *childhood education educator, coordinator*

Saratoga Springs
McNairy, Kate *humanities educator*

Sayville
Lippman, Sharon Rochelle *art historian, art therapist, filmmaker*

Scarsdale
Graff, Henry Franklin *historian, educator*

Schenectady
Morris, John Selwyn *philosophy educator, college president emeritus*

Setauket
Simpson, Louis Aston Marantz *English educator, author*

Setaukey
Venkateswaran, Pramila *literature educator*

Slingerlands
Zacek, Joseph Frederick *history educator, international studies consultant, Central and East European culture and affairs specialist*

Snyder
Levine, George Richard *English language educator*

Sparkill
Lauture, Denize Lucien *language educator, writer*

Staten Island
Cooper, Sandi E. *history educator*
Cross, Ronald *musicologist, educator*
Holder, Calvin Beresford *history professor*

Stony Brook
Goldberg, Homer Beryl *English language educator*
Harris, Alice Carmichael *linguist, educator*
Ihde, Don *philosophy educator, university administrator*
Kuspit, Donald Burton *art historian, art critic, educator*
Levin, Richard Louis *language educator*
Mignone, Mario B. *Italian studies educator*
Semmel, Bernard *historian, educator*
Videbaek, Bente A. *humanities educator*

Syracuse
Alston, William Payne *philosophy educator*
Denise, Theodore Cullom *philosophy educator*
Field, Daniel *history educator*
Powell, James Matthew *history professor*
Shires, Linda M. *English educator, writer*
Sternlicht, Sanford *English and theater arts educator, writer*
Tatham, David Frederic *art historian, educator*
Waddy, Patricia A. *architectural history educator*

Tarrytown
Fazzino, Adis Louise *language educator*

Troy
Ahlers, Rolf Willi *philosopher, theologian*
Baecker, David Alan *humanities educator*

Utica
Wagner, Frederick Reese *retired language educator*

Vestal
Wagar, (Walter) Warren (Walter Wagar) *historian, educator*

Wantagh
Galvan, Max *humanities educator*

Williamsville
Drew, Fraser Bragg Robert *language educator*
Garton, Charles *classics educator*

Yonkers
Viola, Mary Jo *art history educator*

NORTH CAROLINA

Andrews
Fonda, Ronald Alan *epistemologist*

Asheville
Voigt, Ellen *literature educator*

Cary
Mata, Elizabeth Adams *language educator, land investor*

Chapel Hill
Browning, Christopher R. *historian, educator*
Davis, Sarah Irwin *retired English language educator*
Debreczeny, Paul *Slavic language educator, writer*
Eaton, Charles Edward *English language educator, author*
Feinberg, Lawrence Edward *language educator, researcher*
Flora, Joseph M(artin) *English language educator*
Grendler, Paul Frederick *history educator*
Handy, Rollo Leroy *philosopher, researcher*
Heninger, Simeon Kahn, Jr., *English language educator*
Hsiao, Li-Ling *philosopher, educator*
Illiano, Antonio *language educator, researcher*
Jones, Houston Gwynne *history professor*
Kohn, Richard H. *historian, educator*
Levine, Madeline Geltman *Slavic literatures educator, translator*
Ludington, Townsend *English and American studies educator*
Nelson, Philip Francis *musicology educator, consultant, choral conductor*
Pfaff, Richard William *historian, educator*
Rabil, Albert, Jr., *humanities educator*
Schier, Donald Stephen *language educator*
Smith, Sidney Rufus, Jr., *linguist, educator*
Stadter, Philip Austin *classicist, educator*
Stephens, Laurence David, Jr., *linguist, investor, oil industry executive*
Vogler, Frederick Wright *French language educator*
Williamson, Joel Rudolph *humanities educator*
Youngman, Paul A. *language educator*

Charlotte
Aliaga-Buchenau, Ana-Isabel *humanities educator*
Castro, Mary McDermott *language educator*
Myers, Robert Manson *English educator, author*

Creedmoor
Husketh, Alma Ormond *retired language educator*

Davidson
Barnes, Robin *historian, educator*

Durham
Budd, Louis John *English language educator*
Chafe, William Henry *history educator*
Colton, Joel *historian, educator*
Davis, Calvin De Armond *historian, educator*
Franklin, John Hope *historian, educator, author*
Holley, Irving Brinton, Jr., *historian, educator*
Lerner, Warren *historian, educator*
Oates, John Francis *classics educator*
Ogede, Ode *literature educator*
Preston, Richard Arthur *historian*
Richardson, Lawrence, Jr., *Latin language educator, archeologist*
Roland, Alex Frederick *history professor*
Sanford, David Hawley *philosophy educator*
Scott, Anne Byrd Firor *history professor*
Smith, Grover C(leveland) *English language educator*
Thompson, James Howard *historian, library administrator*
Thompson, John Herd *history professor*
Whitlow, Stacey Mataxis *English educator, university educator*
Williams, George Walton *English educator*

Efland
Weinberg, Gerhard Ludwig *history professor*

Elon
Troxler, Carole Watterson *historian, educator*

Fayetteville
Conley, Raymond Leslie *English language educator*
Murray, Peter Carlisle *historian, educator*

Fearrington Village
Boewe, Charles Ernsr *historian, educator*
Cell, Gillian Townsend *historian, educator*

Franklin
Johnson, Herbert Alan *history and law educator, lawyer, chaplain*

Graham
Stanberry, D(osi) Elaine *English literature educator, writer*

Greensboro
Almeida, José Agustín *romance languages educator*
Bardolph, Richard *historian, educator*
Chappell, Fred Davis *English language educator, poet*
Ikegwu, Chinedum Emmanuel *literature educator*
Penninger, Frieda Elaine *retired English language educator*

Greenville
Runyan, Timothy Jack *historian, educator*

Hendersonville
Harris, James Braxton *retired humanities educator, freelance/self-employed writer*

High Point
McCaslin, Richard Bryan *history educator*

Jacksonville
Fischer, Violeta Pèrez Cubillas *Spanish literature and linguistics educator*
Kimball, Lynn Jerome *historian*

Laurinburg
Alexander, W. M. *philosophy educator*
Bayes, Ronald Homer *English language educator, author*

Maggie Valley
Pickard, John Benedict *English language educator*

New Bern
White, James Edward, III, *historian, educator*

Pleasant Garden
Kennett, Lee Boone, Jr., *historian, educator*

Raleigh
Belk, Leotis S. *language educator*
Katz, Steven Barry *language educator, writer*
Maldonado-DeOliveira, Débora *classicist, researcher*
Rhodes, Donald Robert *musicologist, retired electrical engineer*

Salisbury
Vance, Andrew Anderson, Jr., *humanities educator*
Vestal, Katherine R. *language educator*

Wilmington
Graham, Otis Livingston, Jr., *history educator*
Lapaire, P. J. G. *language educator*

Winston Salem
Barnett, Richard Chambers *historian, educator*
Borwick, Susan Harden *musicologist, educator*
Margitić, Milorad R. *language educator, researcher*
Shapere, Dudley *philosophy educator*
Sigal, Gale *literature educator*

NORTH DAKOTA

Bismarck
Newborg, Gerald Gordon *state archives administrator*

Fargo
Anderson, Gerald Dwight *history educator*
Danbom, David Byers *history educator*

Grand Forks
Berger, Albert Isaac *historian, consultant*

Wahpeton
Reubish, Gary Richard *English language educator*

OHIO

Ada
Lomax, John Phillip *history professor*

Akron
Knepper, George W. *history educator*
McMahon, William Edward *philosophy educator*

Ashland
Jamieson, Duncan Robert *historian, educator*
Schmidt-Rinehart, Barbara Coe *Spanish language educator*

Athens
Alexander, Charles Comer *history educator, writer*
Bond, Zinny Sans *linguistics educator*
Borchert, Donald Marvin *philosopher, educator*
Crowl, Samuel Renninger *former university dean, english language educator*
Láscar, Amado José *language educator, writer*
Ping, Charles Jackson *philosophy educator, retired university president*
Torres, Daniel *literature educator*
Whealey, Lois Deimel *humanities scholar*

Berea
Kennelly, Laura Ballard *writer, educator*

Bluffton
Gundy, Jeffrey Gene *English educator*

Bowling Green
Browne, Ray Broadus *popular culture educator*
Lavezzi, John Charles *art history educator, archaeologist*

Brecksville
Pappas, Effie Vamis *language educator, finance educator, writer, poet, artist*

Chagrin Falls
Rawski, Conrad H(enry) *humanities educator, medievalist*

Cincinnati
Alexander, John Kurt *history educator*
Beaver, Daniel Roy *history professor*
Brod, Evelyn Fay *foreign language educator*
Ciani, Alfred Joseph *language professional, associate dean*
Harmon, Patrick *historian, sports commentator*
Lewis, Gene Dale *historian, educator*
Lynch, Timothy Patrick *historian, educator*
McNay, John T. *humanities educator*
Rosen, Roberta *philosophy educator*
Schrier, Arnold *historian, educator*

Cleveland
Benseler, David Price *foreign language educator*
Curnow, Kathy *art historian, educator*
Friedman, Barton Robert *English educator*
Greppin, John Aird Coutts *philologist, editor, educator*
Hammack, David Conrad *history professor*
Levin, Miriam R. *historian, educator*
Miller, Genevieve *retired medical historian*
Olivares-Cuhat, Gabriela Antonia *literature and language professor*
Salomon, Roger Blaine *English language educator*
Taylor, Margaret Wischmeyer *retired language educator*

Columbus
Anderson, Donald Kennedy, Jr., *English educator*
Babcock, Charles Luther *classics educator*
Battersby, James Lyons, Jr., *English language educator*

Beja, Morris *English literature educator*
Farr, Marcia Elizabeth *English and linguistics educator*
Hare, Robert Yates *music history educator*
Hoffmann, Charles Wesley *retired foreign language educator*
Jarvis, Gilbert Andrew *humanities educator, writer*
Kasulis, Thomas Patrick *humanities educator*
Kuhn, Albert Joseph *English educator*
Meier, Samuel Arthur, III, *historian, educator*
Peterson, Gale Eugene *historian*
Rule, John Corwin *history professor*
Scanlan, James Patrick *philosophy and Slavic studies educator*
Shikina, Seiji *educator, consultant*
Stephan, Alexander Friedrich *German language and literature educator*

Cuyahoga Falls
Walker, Suzannah Wolf *language educator*

Dayton
Darst, Betty Jane *historian, educator*
Harden, Oleta Elizabeth *English educator, university administrator*
Haritos, Mary J. *language educator, interpreter*
Martin, Herbert Woodward *English educator, poet*
McWhorter, Stanley Bruce *English educator, researcher*
Pacernick, Gary B. *literature educator, poet*
Pringle, Mary Beth *language educator, writer*
Vice, Roy Lee *history educator*

Delaware
Lewes, Ulle Erika *English educator*

Fremont
Gerlach, Murney *administrator, educator, historian*
Wethington, Norbert Anthony *medieval scholar*

Gambier
Shutt, Timothy Baker *humanities educator, writer*

Granville
Knobel, Dale Thomas *historian, educator, academic administrator*
Lisska, Anthony Joseph *humanities educator, philosopher*
Santoni, Ronald Ernest *philosophy educator*
Vogel, Steven Michael *philosopher, educator*

Kent
Beer, Barrett Lynn *historian*
Chism, Rebecca Lynn *language educator*
Hassler, Donald Mackey, II, *English language educator, writer*
Kasten, Wendy Christina *literacy educator, writer, consultant*
McCormick, Edgar Lindsley *language educator, writer*
Piccirillo, Linda Ann *literature educator*
Reid, S.W. *English educator*
Rick, Newton Marcus *literature and language professor, classicist*

Marietta
Wilbanks, Jan Joseph *retired philosopher*

Newark
Tebben, Joseph Richard *ancient language educator*

North Canton
Vazzano, Frank Paul *historian, educator*

Oberlin
Baumann, Roland M. *historian, archivist, consultant*
Collins, Martha *English language educator, writer*
Faber, Sebastiaan *humanities educator*

Oxford
Baird, Jay Warren *historian, educator*
Bauer, Steven Albert *English educator, writer*
Pratt, William Crouch, Jr., *English language educator, writer*
Yamauchi, Edwin Masao *history professor*

Painesville
McQuaid, Kim *historian, educator, writer*

Portsmouth
Mirabello, Mark Linden *history professor*

Sebring
Saffell, John Edgar *retired history educator*

Solon
Gallo, Donald Robert *retired English educator*

Springfield
Sweet, Robert T. *humanities educator*

Strongsville
Blumer, Frederick Elwin *retired philosophy educator*

Tiffin
Davison, Kenneth Edwin *American studies educator, genealogist*
Moore, Vincent D. *humanities educator, writer*

Toledo
Carney, Margaret Lou *historian, curator*
Glaab, Charles Nelson *historian, educator*
Smith, Robert Freeman *history educator*

West Farmington
Smith, Agnes Monroe *history professor*

Wilmington
Townsend, June H. *foreign language educator*

Wooster
Calhoun, Daniel Fairchild *history educator*
Linehan, Mary *historian, educator*

Yellow Springs
Fogarty, Robert Stephen *historian, educator, editor*

Youngstown
Bowers, Bege K. *English educator, academic administrator*

OKLAHOMA

Ada
Daniel, Arlie Verl *speech education educator*

Lawton
Follett, M. Paul *genealogist, librarian*

Norman
Brown, Sidney DeVere *history educator*
Fears, Jesse Rufus *historian, educator, academic dean*
Gilje, Paul Arn *history educator*
Green, Ronald Simonds *historian, educator*
Hengst, Herbert Randall *retired educator*
Leitch, Vincent Barry *literary and cultural studies educator*
Lowitt, Richard *history professor*
Savage, William Woodrow, Jr., *historian, consultant, social sciences educator*

Oklahoma City
Baker, Doug W. *history and humanities educator*
Bowlby, Leymond Ambrose *linguist, translator*
Holt, Karen Anita Young *English educator*
Todd, Joe Lee *historian*

Stillwater
Agnew, Theodore Lee, Jr., *historian, educator*
Fischer, LeRoy Henry *historian, educator*
Luebke, Neil Robert *philosophy educator*

Tahlequah
Agnew, Brad *history professor*

Tulsa
Faingold, Eduardo Daniel *language and linguistics educator, researcher*

OREGON

Aloha
Gorea, Lucia-Iosefina *English educator, writer, poet*

Ashland
Bornet, Vaughn Davis *former social science educator, research historian*
Levy, Leonard Williams *history professor, writer*
Morris, Daniel Robert *language educator*

Clackamas
Etulain, Richard Wayne *historian, educator*

Corvallis
Campbell, Courtney Scott *humanities educator*
Yu, Shiao-ling S. *humanities educator*

Dayton
McKaughan, Howard Paul *linguistics educator*

Eugene
Pascal, C(ecil) Bennett *classics educator*
Viles, Andrew Michael *English language educator*
Wickes, George *English literature educator, writer*

Forest Grove
Boersema, David Brian *philosopher, educator*

Madras
Ramsey, Jarold William *English language educator, author*

Medford
Frost, Orcutt William *historian, educator*

Monmouth
Balke, Frank H. *language educator, director*

Newberg
Corning, Caitlin *historian, educator*

Pendleton
Grover, Dorys C. *English educator*

Port Orford
Drinnon, Richard *retired history educator*

Portland
Eifler, Mark Anthony *historian, educator*
Faller, Thompson Mason *philosophy educator*
Karant-Nunn, Susan Catherine *history educator*
Rottschaefer, William Andrew *philosophy educator*
Sacks, David Harris *historian, humanities educator*
Schmidt, Stanley Eugene *retired speech educator*
Steele, William Donald *literature educator*
Steinman, Lisa Malinowski *English literature educator, writer*

Salem
Dmytryshyn, Basil *historian, educator*

Sutherlin
Rose, Sarah Elizabeth *genealogist, counselor, web site designer*

PENNSYLVANIA

Allentown
Huang, Guiyou *English studies educator, writer*

Annville
Tezanos-Pinto, Rosa *Hispanic American literature educator*

Ardmore
Gutwirth, Marcel Marc *French literature educator*

Bala Cynwyd
Dorwart, Bonnie Brice *historian, retired rheumatologist*
Murphey, Murray Griffin *history professor*

Bethlehem
Beidler, Peter Grant *English educator*
Lempa, Heikki Emil *historian, educator*
Radycki, Diane Josephine *art historian*
Roberts, Leonard Robert *English language educator, poet*

Smolansky, Oles M. *humanities educator*

Blakeslee
Albano, Patrick Marino *historian, educator, archivist*

Bloomsburg
Yenika-Agbaw, Vivian S. *English studies educator, researcher*

Bryn Mawr
Bolger, Stephen Garrett *retired English and American studies educator*
Dudden, Arthur Power *historian, educator*
Gaisser, Julia Haig *classics educator*
King, Willard Fahrenkamp (Mrs. Edmund Ludwig King) *Spanish language educator*
Krausz, Michael *philosopher, educator*
Lane, Barbara Miller (Barbara Miller-Lane) *humanities educator*
Lang, Mabel Louise *classics educator*
McCabe, Louise Beachboard *language educator*
Trout, Charles Hathaway *historian, educator*

Carlisle
Allan, George *retired philosophy educator*
Fox, Arturo Angel *Spanish language educator*
Shrader, Charles Reginald *historian*

Chambersburg
O'Connor, John Morris, III, *retired humanities educator*

Clarion
Frakes, Robert M. *humanities educator, writer*

Collegeville
Zwerling, Philip *language educator, playwright*

Dallastown
Morton, David K. *language educator*

Easton
Schlueter, June Mayer *English educator, author*

Elizabethtown
Gottfried, Paul Edward *humanities educator, editor*

Elkins Park
Davidson, Abraham Aba *art historian, educator, photographer*

Erie
Allshouse, Robert Harold *history educator*

Greensburg
Flórez-Estrada, Nancy B. *language educator*
Spurlock, John *history professor*

Greenville
Hall, Mary Theresa *literature educator*

Gwynedd
Bieber, Konrad Ferdinand *retired language educator*

Gwynedd Valley
Duclow, Donald Francis *philosophy educator, researcher*
McGarry, Lisa Coughlin *language educator*

Harrisburg
Khanzhina, Helen P. *English educator, translator*

Haverford
Brand, Charles Macy *history professor*
Jorden, Eleanor Harz *linguist, educator*

Havertown
Smith, Phillip Thurmond *historian, educator*

Hummelstown
Clouse, Jerry Allan *architectural historian*

Indiana
Cashdollar, Charles David *history educator*

Kittanning
Smits, Ronald Francis *English educator, poet*

Kutztown
Meyer, Susan Moon *speech language pathologist, educator*

Lancaster
Binkley, Luther John *philosophy educator*
Hall, Kimberly *language educator, consultant*
Steiner, Robert Lisle *retired language consultant*

Latrobe
Torisky, Eugene Vincent, Jr., *philosopher, educator*

Leesport
Jackson, Eric Allen *philatelist*

Lewisburg
Payne, Michael David *English language educator*

Lock Haven
Congdon, Howard Krebs *philosopher, clergyman, educator*
Story, Julie Ann *English educator*

Lumberville
Fallon, Robert Thomas *English language educator*

Lykens
Sultzbaugh, John Stephan *historian, educator*

Mansfield
Guenther, Karen *history professor*

Meadville
Helmreich, Jonathan Ernst *history professor*

Media
Ginsberg, Robert E. *philosophy educator, editor*
Sorkin, Adam J. *English educator*

Melrose Park
Rabinovitz, Nili *language educator, consultant*

Merion Station
Littell, Marcia Sachs *Holocaust and genocide studies educator*

Millersville
Miller, Steven Max *humanities educator*

Nazareth
Haynes, Thomas Morris *philosophy educator*

New Castle
Sands, Christine Louise *English educator*

New Freedom
Sedlak, Valerie Frances *retired English language educator, retired academic administrator*

New Wilmington
Martin, Russell *historian, educator*

Philadelphia
Crissey, Harrington E., Jr., *English as second language educator*
Davis, Allen Freeman *history educator, author*
Fusco, Richard *English literature educator*
Hahn, Steven *history professor, writer*
Hall, Marcia Brown *art historian, educator*
Hilty, James Walter *historian, educator, media consultant*
Kallberg, Jeffrey *musicologist*
Kerwood, Karl Joseph *historian, researcher*
Knauer, Georg Nicolaus *classical philologist*
Kusmer, Kenneth Leslie *historian, educator*
Logan, Marie-Rose van Stynvoort *literature educator, publishing executive, writer*
Lowry, Ralph James, Sr., *retired history educator*
Lucid, Robert Francis *English educator*
Matus-Mendoza, Mariadelaluz *language educator, sociologist*
Means, John Barkley *foreign language educator, association executive*
Morello, Celeste Anne *historian, criminologist*
Moss, Roger William *historian, writer, administrator*
Peters, Edward Murray *history professor*
Robson, Roy Raymond *historian, educator*
Salessi, Jorge *language educator, writer*
Sanchez, Sonia *English literature educator*
Schiffman, Harold Fosdick *Asian language educator*
Sebold, Russell Perry, III, *Romance languages educator, writer*
Seneca, Michael Joseph *historian*
Steinberg, Jonathan *historian*
Stevens, Rosemary A. *medicine and public health historian, artist*
Welch, Charles Edgar, Jr., *retired English language educator, writer*
Woodside, Lisa Nicole *humanities educator*

Phoenixville
Di Giacomo, Michael *historian, educator*

Pittsburgh
Andrews, George Reid *historian, educator*
Anthony, Edward Mason *linguistics educator*
Brett, Edward Tracy *historian, educator*
Buchanan, James Junkin *classics educator*
Clack, Jerry *classics educator*
Di Medio, Gregory Lawrence *writer, information systems specialist*
Gale, Robert Lee *retired American literature educator and critic*
Goldstein, Donald Maurice *historian, educator*
Hicks, Wendell Leon *history educator, publisher, political scientist*
Miller, David William *historian, educator*
Paulston, Christina Bratt *linguistics educator*
Rawski, Evelyn Sakakida *history professor*
Rescher, Nicholas *philosopher, author, educator*
Rimer, John Thomas *foreign language educator, academic administrator, writer, translator*
Sheon, Aaron *art historian, educator*
Tarr, Joel Arthur *history and public policy educator*
Udler, Rubin Yakovlevich *linguist*
Weingartner, Rudolph Herbert *philosophy educator*

Reading
Blessing, Tim H. *historian, educator*

Scranton
Bourcier, Richard Joseph *French language and literature educator*
Homer, Francis Xavier James *history professor*
Zaydon, Jemille Ann *language educator, communications educator*

Selinsgrove
Kolbert, Jack *foreign language educator, French literature educator, humanities educator*
Whitman, Jeffrey Paul *philosophy educator*

Sharon
Berland, Kevin Joel *literature educator*

Slippery Rock
Cobb, Larry Russell *ethics educator*

State College
Goldschmidt, Arthur Eduard, Jr., *history educator, author*
Redford, Donald Bruce *historian, archaeologist*
Robinett, Betty Wallace *linguist, educator*
Schmalstieg, William Riegel *retired Slavic languages educator*
Strauss, Susan Gayle *linguistics educator*

Swarthmore
Gelzer, David Georg *English educator, missionary*
Kitao, T. Kaori *art history educator*
Morgan, Kathryn Lawson *retired historian, educator*
North, Helen Florence *classicist, educator*
Ostwald, Martin *retired classicist*

University Park
Ebitz, David MacKinnon *art historian, educator, museum director*
Grosholz, Emily Rolfe *philosophy educator, poet*

Halsey, Martha Taliaferro *Spanish language educator*
Kadir, Djelal *literature educator, writer, translator, editor*
Lacy, Norris J. *literature educator*
Lima, Robert *Hispanic studies and comparative literature educator*
Naydan, Michael M. *foreign language educator*
Nielsen, Aldon Lynn *literature educator*
Rose, Paul Lawrence *history educator*
Savignon, Sandra J. *linguistics educator*
Wanner, Adrian J. *literature educator*

Upper Burrell
Coohill, Joseph *historian, educator*
Franco Gómez, María Angeles *language educator*

Villanova
Bergquist, James Manning *history professor*
DeLaura, David Joseph *English language educator*
Hunt, John Mortimer, Jr., *classical studies educator*
McDiarmid, Lucy *English educator, author*
Salmon, John Hearsey McMillan *historian, educator*
Scholz, Sally J. *philosopher, educator*

Wallingford
Purcell, Mary Hamilton *speech educator*

Wayne
Frye, Roland Mushat *literary historian, theologian*

West Chester
Gougher, Ronald Lee *foreign language educator and administrator*
Hardy, Charles Ashley, III, *historian, educator*
Heston, Thomas J. *historian, educator*
Hipple, Walter John *English language educator*
Myrsiades, Kostas Yannis *literature educator*

Wilkes Barre
Hepp, John Henry, IV, *historian, lawyer*
Krawczeniuk, Joseph Volodymyr *humanities educator*

York
Jackson, Renée Bernadette *English language educator*

RHODE ISLAND

Jamestown
Wright, Harrison Morris *historian, educator*

Kingston
Kim, Yong Choon *philosopher, theologian, educator*

Newport
Grassey, Thomas Brandt *humanities educator*
Haas, William Paul *humanities educator, former college president*

North Kingstown
Mellor, Kathy *National Teacher of the Year 2004, ESL educator*

Providence
Ackerman, Felicia *philosophy educator, writer*
Armstrong, Paul Bradford *English language educator, dean*
Bensmaia, Reda *French studies educator, researcher*
Bewes, Timothy Richard Thomas *language educator*
Blasing, Mutlu Konuk *English language educator*
Donovan, Bruce Elliot *classics educator, university dean*
Enteman, Willard Finley *philosophy educator*
Fornara, Charles William *historian, classicist, educator*
Gill, Mary Louise Glanville *educator of classics and philosophy*
Gleason, Abbott *history professor*
Gorn, Elliott Jacob *historian, educator, writer*
Green, Angel Yvonne *literature educator*
Harleman, Ann *English language educator, writer*
Kim, Jaegwon *philosophy educator*
Konstan, David *classics and comparative literature educator, researcher*
Lemons, James Stanley *history educator*
Lesko, Leonard Henry *Egyptologist, educator, publisher*
Putnam, Michael Courtney Jenkins *classics educator*
Raaflaub, Kurt Arnold *classics educator*
Rohr, Donald Gerard *history professor*
Schulz, Juergen *art history educator*
Sosa, Ernest *philosopher, educator*
Valente, Luiz Fernando *Portuguese and Brazilian studies and comparative literature educator*
Vorenberg, Michael *history educator*
Wood, Gordon Stewart *historian, educator*
Wrenn, James Joseph *East Asian studies educator*

Smithfield
Litoff, Judy Barrett *history professor*

South Kingstown
Fredriksen, John Conrad *historian, consultant*

SOUTH CAROLINA

Aiken
Sykes, Richard Nesbit *history professor, department chairman*

Bluffton
Brown, Dallas Coverdale, Jr., *retired army officer, retired history educator*

Charleston
Barrett, Michael Baker *historian, educator*
Coates, Timothy Joel *historian*
Knee, Stuart Eugene *historian, educator*

Clemson
Charney, Mark Jay *language educator*
Moran, Ronald Wesson *retired English educator, dean, writer*
Riley, Helene Maria Kastinger *Germanist*
Underwood, Richard Allan *English language educator*

Clinton
Skinner, James Lister, III, *English language educator*

Columbia
Ashley, Perry Johnathan *journalism educator*
Briggs, Ward Wright *classics educator*
Bruccoli, Matthew Joseph *English educator, publisher*
Bueno, Otavio Augusto *philosopher, educator*
Edgar, Walter Bellingrath *historian, educator*
Geckle, George Leo, III, *retired English language educator*
Kay, Carol McGinnis *literature educator*
Littlefield, Daniel Curtis *historian, educator, researcher*
Long, Eugene Thomas, III, *philosophy educator, administrator*
Power, James Tracy *historian*
Sproat, John Gerald *historian, educator*
Synnott, Marcia Graham *history professor*

Due West
Carlock, John Bruce, Jr., *English educator*

Florence
Chapman, Richard Norman *historian, academic administrator*
Kaufman, Victor Scott *historian, educator*

Greenville
Benson, Theodore Lloyd *history professor*
Matzko, John Austin *historian*

Greenwood
Brennan, Patrick Joseph *history professor*
Cushing, Sara Elizabeth *English language educator, writer*

Hilton Head Island
Knox, John, Jr., *philosopher, educator*
Male, Roy Raymond *English language educator*

Newberry
Davidson, Michael Raymond *historian, educator*

North Myrtle Beach
Damerst, William *English and humanities educator*

Okatie
Hardin, James Neal *German and comparative literature educator, publisher*

Orangeburg
Johnson, Alex Claudius *English language educator*
Jones, Marcus Earl *humanities educator*
McIver, Barbara Basore *language educator*

Spartanburg
Deku, Afrikadzata *international, French, English and Afrikan-centric Continental Afrikan scholar, researcher, publisher, writer, educator*

Union
Murphy, Peter Gregory *literature educator, writer*

SOUTH DAKOTA

Aberdeen
Johnson, Edna Scott *English language educator, volunteer*
Matta, William B. *language educator*

Brookings
Evans, David Allan *English educator*
Funchion, Michael F. *historian, educator*
Ryder, Mary Ruth *English language educator*

Sioux Falls
Carlson Aronson, Marilyn A. *English language and education educator*
Herman, Charles Wendell *history educator*
Huseboe, Arthur Robert *American literature educator*
Olson, Gary Duane *history educator*
Staggers, Kermit LeMoyne, II, *history and political science educator, state legislator, municipal official*
Zinz, David Albert *humanities educator*

Vermillion
Basile, Joseph Lawrence *humanities educator*
Haddad, Emily Anne *literature educator*

TENNESSEE

Big Sandy
Chastain, Kenneth Duane *retired foreign language educator*

Chattanooga
Royer, William A. *language educator*

Columbia
Curry, Beatrice Chesrown *retired English educator*

Cookeville
Brinker, William John *history educator, researcher*
Campana, Phillip Joseph *German language educator*
Hinton, Paula Katherine *historian, educator, historian, researcher*

Dayton
Cornelius, Richard Meredith *English language educator*
Gartman, Max Dillon *language educator, educator*

Jefferson City
Baumgardner, James Lewis *history professor*

Johnson City
Schneider, Valerie Lois *speech educator*

Kingsport
Wolfe, Margaret Ripley *historian, educator, consultant*

Knoxville
Brady, Patrick *French literature educator, writer*
Cutler, Everette Wayne *history educator*
Fisher, John Hurt *English language educator*
Ford, Harriet-Lynn *English educator*
Francisco, Dorman Edward *language educator, writer*
He, Donghui *language educator*

Martin
Norton, Dorotha Oliver *speech educator*

Mc Minnville
McGee, Chad Alan *historian, educator*

Memphis
Edwards, Gary Thomas *historian, educator*
Jolly, William Thomas *foreign language educator*
Stagg, Louis Charles *English language and literature educator*

Morristown
Conry, Ruth P *language educator*

Murfreesboro
McCash, June Hall *retired language educator*
McDaniel, Rhonda Louise *literature educator*
Rupprecht, Nancy Ellen *historian, educator*

Nashville
Beach, Margaret Smith *retired language educator*
Boorman, Howard Lyon *history professor*
Churchill, Larry Raymond *ethics educator*
Compton, John Joseph *philosophy educator*
Conkin, Paul Keith *history professor*
Cook, Ann Jennalie *English language educator*
Dickerson, Dennis Clark *history educator*
Girgus, Sam B. *English literature educator*
Hassel, Rudolph Christopher *English educator*
Luis, William *language educator*
Pfanner, Helmut Franz *German language educator*
Risko, Victoria J. *language educator*
Seligson, Mitchell A. *Latin American studies educator*
Sevin, Dieter Hermann *language and literature professional, educator*
Voegeli, Victor Jacque *history educator, dean*

Sewanee
Chitty, Elizabeth Nickinson (Mary Chitty) *university historian*
Williamson, Samuel Ruthven, Jr., *historian, emeritus university president*
Winton, Calhoun *literature educator*

Shiloh
Allen, Stacy Dale *historian, parks director*

TEXAS

Abilene
Bailey, Fred Arthur *history educator*
McWhiney, Grady *history educator*
Walker, Beatriz Alem *language educator*

Arlington
Green, George N. *historian, educator*
Ignagni, Joseph Anthony *humanities educator, associate dean*

Austin
Bordie, John George *linguistics educator*
Braybrooke, David *philosopher, educator*
Brown, Norman Donald *history professor*
Carleton, Don Edward *history center administrator, educator, writer*
Causey, Robert Louis *philosopher, educator, consultant*
Corredor, Mary B. *language educator, consultant, translator*
Cox, Patrick *historian, writer*
Divine, Robert Alexander *history professor*
Dulles, John Watson Foster *history professor*
Falola, Toyin *history professor*
Farrell, Edmund James *retired English language educator, writer*
Freeman, Robert Schofield *musicologist, educator, pianist*
Friedman, Alan Warren *humanities educator*
Galinsky, Gotthard Karl *classicist, educator*
Goines, Patrick L. *historian, educator*
Gould, Lewis Ludlow *historian, educator*
Graham, Don Ballew *literature educator, writer*
Harms, Robert Thomas *linguist, educator*
Hinojosa-Smith, Roland *language educator, writer*
Kibler, William Westcott *French language and literature educator*
Kroll, John Hennig *classicist, numismatist*
La Salle, Peter *English educator, writer*
Levack, Brian Paul *history professor*
Lockett, Landon Johnson *former linguistic educator, researcher*
Louis, William Roger *historian*
Middleton, Christopher *Germanic languages and literature educator*
Moag, Rodney Frank *language educator, country music singer*
Newburger, Caryn Lason *English educator*
Pells, Richard H. *historian, educator*
Ramon, Emilio *language educator*
Rich, John Martin *humanities educator, researcher*
Seung, Thomas Kaehao *philosophy educator*
Staley, Thomas Fabian *language professional, academic administrator*
Sutherland, William Owen Sheppard *English language educator*
Tyler, Ronnie Curtis *historian*
Velz, John William *literature educator*
Wadlington, Warwick Paul *English language educator*
Werbow, Stanley Newman *language educator*
Whitbread, Thomas Bacon *English educator, author*

Beaumont
Hawkins, Emma B. *humanities educator*
Janak, Robert Louis *foreign language educator*

Brownsville
Adams, William Leigh *history professor*
Soldan, Angelika *philosopher, political scientist, educator*

Brownwood
Hopp, Glenn *literature educator*

Bryan
Bryant, Keith Lynn, Jr., *history professor*

Canyon
Peddie, Ian A. *language educator*

College Station
Cannon, Garland *linguist, educator*
Dethloff, Henry Clay *historian, educator*
Dunlap, Thomas R. *historian, educator*
Ezell, Margaret J. *language educator*
Harner, James Lowell *English language educator*
Unterberger, Betty Miller *history educator, writer*

Commerce
Linck, Charles Edward, Jr., *English language educator*

Corpus Christi
Snouffer, Nancy Kendall *English and reading educator*
Wooster, Robert *history professor*

Dallas
Chawner, Lucia Martha *language educator*
Comini, Alessandra *art historian, educator*
Countryman, Edward Francis *historian, educator*
Davis, Daisy Sidney *history professor*
Essary, Andrew Charles *philosophy educator, financial analyst*
Griffin, Randall C. *art historian, educator*
Hunter, Robert Grams *retired English language educator*
Terry, Marshall Northway, Jr., *English language educator, author*

Denton
Kamman, William *historian, educator*
Kesterson, David Bert *English language educator*
Nik, Ninfa *language educator*
Preston, Thomas Ronald *English language educator, researcher*
Snapp, Harry Franklin *historian, educator*
White, Nora Lizabeth *language educator*

Edinburg
Cararas, Sandra A. *literature educator*

El Paso
Bailey, Kenneth Kyle *history educator*
Clement-Fouts, Shirley George *educational services executive*
Dailey, Maceo Crenshaw, Jr., *humanities educator*
Deutsch, Sandra McGee *historian, educator*
Lujan, Rosa Emma *bilingual specialist, trainer, consultant, assistant principal*
Müller, Gene Alan *historian, consultant*

Fort Worth
Bedford, David Allen *language educator*
Boller, Paul Franklin, Jr., *retired American history educator, writer*
Gilderhus, Mark Theodore *historian, educator*
Meckna, Michael *musicologist, educator*
Reuter, Frank Theodore *history educator*
Wilson, Evelyn M. *literature educator*

Georgetown
Crowley, Weldon Samuel *retired history educator*

Grapevine
Stack, George Joseph *philosopher, writer*

Harlingen
Martin, Leland Morris (Pappy Martin) *history educator*

Hawkins
Smialek, William *musicologist*

Houston
Belk, Joan Pardue *English educator*
Castañeda, James Agustín *language educator, golf coach*
Chance, Jane *English literature educator*
Clear, Rosemary Elaine *translator, court interpreter, consultant*
de Kanter, Ellen Ann *English and foreign language educator*
Drew, Katherine Fischer *history professor*
Ehrmann, Susanna *foreign language educator, writer, photographer*
Gabbard, Lucina Paquet *retired literature educator, actress*
Gruber, Ira Dempsey *historian, educator*
Haskell, Thomas Langdon *history educator*
Kanellos, Nicolás *language educator, liberal studies educator*
Lamb, Sydney MacDonald *linguistics and cognitive science educator*
Law, Ronnie *historian, educator*
Leiber, Justin *philosophy educator, writer*
Lowry, Montecue Judson *military historian*
Martin, James Kirby *historian, educator*
McEvoy-Jamil, Patricia Ann *English language educator*
Mc Fadden, Joseph Michael *history educator*
Minter, David Lee *English literature educator*
Olivares, Jaime Ramon *history professor, researcher*
Owino, Meshack *history professor*
Patten, Robert Lowry *English language educator*
Pryor, William Daniel Lee *humanities educator*
Sher, George Allen *philosophy educator*
Skura, Meredith Anne *English educator*
Thompson, Ewa M. *foreign language educator*
Tran, Qui-Phiet *English educator*
Urbina, Manuel, II, *legal research historian, history educator*
Vallbona, Rima-Gretel Rothe *retired foreign language educator, writer*

Huntsville
Raymond, Kay E. (Kay Engelmann Raymond) *Spanish language educator, consultant*

Ruffin, Paul Dean *English language educator*

Irving
Sommerfeldt, John Robert *historian, educator*

Keene
Jones, Steve *history professor*

Laredo
Engling, Ezra Samuel *Spanish and literature educator, researcher*
McBurnette-Arguelles, Shannon Heather *language educator*

Levelland
Job, Valerie Y'llise *language educator*

Lewisville
Guthrie, Brian Michael *linguist*

Lubbock
Ketner, Kenneth Laine *philosopher, educator*
Kuethe, Allan J. *historian, educator*
Sears, Edward L. *English language educator, real estate investor*

Mesquite
Davis, Vivian *English language educator*

Montgomery
Kelsey, Clyde Eastman, Jr., *philosophy and psychology educator*

Mount Pleasant
Vaughn, William Preston *historian, educator*

Odessa
Toruño, Rhina M. *Literature educator, researcher, writer*

Paris
Proctor, Richard Owen *historian, public health administrator, army officer*

Plano
Giron Vives, Ana *language educator*

Richardson
Redman, Timothy Paul *English language educator, author, chess federation administrator*
Sodeman, Nancy Elizabeth *retired literature educator*

Round Top
Lentz, Edwin Lamar *art historian*

Rusk
McMinn, J. B. *retired philosophy educator, composer*

San Antonio
Daniel, Marian Phillips *language educator, secondary school educator*
Dunn, James David *language educator*
Leighton, Albert Chester *history professor*
Mendoza, Louis G. *literature educator, researcher*
Miller, Frank Lubbock (Char), IV, *historian, educator*
Passty, Jeanette Nyda *English language educator, writer*
Rodriguez, Roberto Ashley *language educator*
Smith, Rebecca Lynn *language educator*
von Raffler-Engel, Walburga (Walburga Engel) *linguist, cross-cultural communications specialist, lecturer, writer*
Woodson, Linda Townley *English educator, writer*

San Marcos
Randolph, Robert Morrison *literature educator*
Schuler, Nico Stephan *musicologist*

Schertz
Ringenbach, Paul Thomas *historian, consultant*

Stafford
Rosenkranz, Linda *English educator*

Stephenville
Christopher, Joe Randell *English language educator*

Sugar Land
Lawrence, Lois Armes *retired language educator, writer*

Waco
Collmer, Robert George *English language educator*
Donnelly, Phillip Johnathan *literature educator*
Hunt, Maurice Arthur *English educator, researcher*

Wichita Falls
Bourland, D(elphus) David, Jr., *linguist, educator*

UTAH

Cedar City
Mills, James *language educator*

Logan
Jones, Norman Leslie *historian, consultant, writer*

Ogden
Matt, Susan J. *historian, educator*
Stokes, Jeffery David *Spanish language educator*

Orem
Clark, Bruce Budge *humanities educator*

Paradise
Bremer, Ronald Allan *genealogist, editor*

Provo
Forster, Merlin Henry *foreign languages educator, writer, researcher*
Fox, Frank Wayne *history professor*
Lyon, James Karl *German language educator*
Murphy, John Joseph *English literature educator, critic, editor*
Peer, Larry Howard *literature educator*
Skinner, Andrew Charles *history educator, religious writer*

Salt Lake City
Dole, Janice Gail Arnold *literacy educator*
Sillars, Malcolm Osgood *communication educator*
Thalos, Mariam G *philosopher, educator*

Tremonton
Eakle, Arlene Haslam *genealogist*

VERMONT

Bennington
Wang, Shunzhu *humanities educator, researcher, translator*

Burlington
Brandenburg, Richard George *management educator*
Daniels, Robert Vincent *history educator, former state senator*
Fogel, Daniel Mark *university president, English language and American literature educator, author*
Hall, Robert William *philosophy and religion educator*

Lyndonville
Toborg, Alfred *history professor*

Middlebury
Jacobs, Travis Beal *historian, educator*
Vail, Van Horn *German language educator*

Montpelier
Facos, James Francis *English language educator, author*

New Haven
Clifford, Deborah Pickman *historian*

Northfield
Telford, Kenneth Alderman *philosopher, humanities educator*

Shelburne
Weiger, John George *foreign language educator*

White River Junction
Madden, Edward Harry *philosopher, retired educator*

VIRGINIA

Alexandria
Duncan, Richard Ray *history professor*
Falk, Stanley Lawrence *historian, consultant*
Lathbury, Roger *English language educator*

Annandale
Brotton, Joyce Dupras *English language educator*
Hutcheon, Wallace Schoonmaker *historian, educator*

Arlington
Allard, Dean Conrad *historian, retired naval history center director*
Boylan, Michael A. *philosophy educator, writer*
French, Mary B. *editor, photographer, poet and former*
Latham, Ernest Hargreaves, Jr., *historian, educator*
Strelau, Renate *historical researcher, artist*
Thompson, Wayne Wray *historian*
Wilcox, Shirley Jean Langdon *genealogist*

Ashland
Inge, Milton Thomas *American literature and culture educator, author*

Blacksburg
Baumgartner, Frederic Joseph *history professor*
Doswald, Herman Kenneth *German language educator, academic administrator*
Fowler, Virginia C. *literature educator*

Charlottesville
Abbot, William Wright *history professor*
Arnold, Albert James *foreign language educator*
Battestin, Martin Carey *retired English language educator*
Brooks, Peter (Preston) *French and comparative literature educator, department chair, writer*
Cano-Ballesta, Juan *Spanish language educator*
Chase, Karen Susan *English literature educator*
Cherno, Melvin *humanities educator*
Crackel, Theodore Joseph *historian, consultant*
Cushman, Stephen Bigelow *English educator, writer*
Edson, Evelyn *history professor, writer*
Forbes, John Douglas *architectural and economic historian*
Garrett, George Palmer, Jr., *creative writing and English language educator, writer*
Gianniny, Omer Allan, Jr., *retired humanities educator*
Graebner, Norman Arthur *history educator*
Haberly, David Tristram *language educator*
Hirsch, Eric Donald, Jr., *English language educator, educational reformer*
Humphreys, Paul William *philosophy educator, consultant*
Kett, Joseph Francis *historian, educator*
Kraehe, Enno Edward *history professor*
Lane, Ann Judith *history and women's studies educator*
Lang, Cecil Yelverton *English language educator*
Langbaum, Robert Woodrow *English language educator, author*
Leffler, Melvyn P. *history professor*
Levenson, Jacob Clavner *English language educator*
Little, W(illia)m A(lfred) *foreign language educator, researcher*
Lott, Eric William *literature educator*
McGann, Jerome John *English language educator*
Megill, Allan D. *historian*
Midelfort, Hans Christian Erik *history professor*
Mikalson, Jon Dennis *classics educator*
Nohrnberg, James Carson *English language educator*
Oliver, Charles Montgomery *retired English educator*

Perkowski, Jan Louis *language, literature and folklore educator*
Peterson, Merrill Daniel *history educator*
Rini, Joel *language educator, linguist*
Rorty, Richard McKay *philosophy educator*
Rubin, David Lee *humanities educator, publisher*
Sedgwick, Alexander *historian, educator*
Shaw, Donald Leslie *Spanish language educator*
Spacks, Patricia Meyer *English educator*
Spearing, Anthony Colin *English literature educator*
Stocker, Arthur Frederick *classics educator*
Wright, Charles Penzel, Jr., *English language educator*
Zunz, Olivier Jean *history professor*

Chesapeake
Deloach, Deanna Latrice *language educator*

Christiansburg
Fu, I-Ping Phyllis *language educator, researcher*

Covesville
Williams, Patricia Anne *philosopher, writer*

Crozet
Owen, Sarah-Katharine *language educator*

Danville
Hayes, Jack Irby *historian, educator*

Emory
Roper, John Herbert *historian, educator*

Fairfax
Bailey, Helen McShane *historian*
King, James Cecil *Medievalist, educator*
Lavine, Thelma Zeno *philosophy educator*
Stearns, Peter Nathaniel *history professor*

Falls Church
Brown, Lorraine A. *literature educator*

Farmville
Hevener, Fillmer, Jr., *English language educator, writer, portrait artist*

Fort Lee
Sterling, Keir Brooks *historian, educator*

Fredericksburg
Dorman, John Frederick *genealogist*
Eslinger-Brown, Vanessa Pauline *humanities educator*
Pitts, Angela L. *humanities educator, researcher*

Glen Allen
Hinkle, Douglas Paddock *retired languages educator*

Hampden Sydney
Arieti, James Alexander *classics educator, writer*

Hardyville
White, Gordon Eliot *historian*

Harrisonburg
Alotta, Robert Ignatius *historian, educator, writer*
Geary, Robert Francis, Jr., *English educator*
Hyser, Raymond M. *humanities educator*

Lexington
Brooke, George Mercer, Jr., *historian, educator*
Simpson, Pamela Hemenway *art historian, educator*

Lorton
Charlston, Jeffery Allen *historian, artist*

Lynchburg
Carey, Charles William, Jr., *historian, educator*
Cornett, Robert Arnold *philosophy educator*
Partie, David John *language educator*

Mc Lean
Scribner, Sherlie Ann *language educator*

Newport News
Santoro, Anthony Richard *history professor*

Norfolk
Evans, Rod L. *philosophy educator*
Hirrel, Leo P. *historian, retired military officer*
Thompson, Thelma Barnaby *English educator, university dean*

North
Fang, Joong *philosopher, mathematician, educator*

Oakton
MacCracken, Thomas Gregg *musicologist*

Petersburg
Garrott, Carl Lee *foreign language educator*

Portsmouth
Paquette, William Arthur *historian, educator*

Radford
du Plessis, Eric *literature educator, language educator*

Richmond
Appiah, Joseph Yaw *historian, educator*
Baker, Julie Ann *language educator*
Bonfiglio, Thomas Paul *literature and linguistics educator*
Hall, James H(errick), Jr., *philosophy educator, writer*
Kirkpatrick, Peter Steven *foreign language educator*
Levit, Héloïse B. (Ginger Levit) *art historian, art dealer, art consultant, journalist*
Rilling, John Robert *history professor*
Thurber, Timothy Nels *historian, educator*
Ward, Harry Merrill *history professor*

Sweet Briar
Piepho, Lee (Edward Lee Piepho) *humanities educator*

Williamsburg
Ball, Donald L. *retired English language educator*
Chappell, Miles Linwood, Jr., *art history educator*

Crapol, Edward P. *history professor*
Dowling, John Clarkson *language educator*
Ely, Melvin Patrick *historian, writer, educator*
Esler, Anthony James *historian, novelist, educator*
Hoffman, Ronald *historical institute administrator, educator*
Landen, Robert Geran *retired historian, educator, university administrator*
McGiffert, Michael *retired history educator, editor*
Nettels, Elsa *English language educator*
Oakley, John Howard *humanities educator*
Wallach, Alan *art historian, educator*

Winchester
Hofstra, Warren Raymond *historian, educator*
Meschutt, David Randolph *historian, curator*
Tisinger, Catherine Anne *history and economics educator*

Woodbridge
Hood, Ronald Chalmers, III, *historian, writer*

Yorktown
Romjue, John Lawson *historian, writer*

WASHINGTON

Aberdeen
Murrell, Gary *historian, educator*

Bellingham
Kennedy, Kathleen Ann *historian, educator*
Murdock, Mary-Elizabeth *history educator*

Bothell
Watts, Linda Susan *humanities educator*

Burien
Burgess, Charles Orville *history professor*

Cheney
Smith, Grant William *English language educator, civic fundraiser*
Steiner, Henry-York *English language and literature educator*

Federal Way
Boling, Joseph Edward *numismatist, retired military officer*

Lake Forest Park
Adams, Hazard Simeon *English educator, writer*

Mercer Island
Dawn, Clarence Ernest *history educator*

Olympia
Bruce, Robert Vance *historian, educator*

Pullman
Swan, Susan Linda *history professor*

Seattle
Brandauer, Frederick Paul *Asian language educator*
Bultmann, William Arnold *historian, educator*
Coburn, Robert Craig *philosopher, educator*
Coldewey, John Christopher *English literature educator*
Ellison, Herbert Jay *historian, educator*
Fine, Arthur I. *philosopher, educator*
Gerstenberger, Donna Lorine *humanities educator*
Halmi, Nicholas *language educator*
Harmon, Daniel Patrick *classics educator*
Heer, Nicholas Lawson *Arabist and Islamist educator*
Hufbauer, Karl George *science historian*
Jones, Edward Louis *historian, educator*
Keyt, David *philosophy and classics educator*
Matchett, William H(enry) *English literature educator*
Nutting, Maureen Murphy *historian, educator*
Pressly, Thomas James *history professor*
Pyle, Kenneth Birger *historian, educator*
Snow-Smith, Joanne Inloes *art history educator*
Starbuck, Susan *literature educator, writer*
VanArsdel, Rosemary Thorstenson *English studies educator*
Ziadeh, Farhat J. *Middle Eastern studies educator*

Spokane
Carriker, Robert Charles *history professor*
Mohrlang, Roger Lloyd *philosopher, educator*
Stackelberg, John Roderick *history professor*

Walla Walla
Carlsen, James Caldwell *musicologist, educator*

Yakima
Meshke, George Lewis *drama and humanities educator*

WEST VIRGINIA

Charles Town
Na, Tsung Shun (Terry Na) *Chinese studies educator, writer*

Fairmont
Lach, Peter *humanities educator*

Morgantown
Blaydes, Sophia Boyatzies *English language educator*
Singer, Armand Edwards *foreign language educator*

Reedsville
Williford, Drury Fisher, Jr., *historical researcher, writer, editor*

WISCONSIN

Appleton
Chaney, William Albert *historian, educator*
Doeringer, Franklin M. *historian, educator*
Goldgar, Bertrand Alvin *literary historian, educator*
Myers, Rex Charles *history educator, retired college dean*

Ashland
Small, Michele Geslin *English studies and modern languages educator*

Chippewa Falls
Schmider, Mary Ellen Heian *American studies educator, academic administrator*

Delafield
Gulgowski, Paul William *German language, social science, and history educator*

Eau Claire
Pace, Joel Frederic *language educator, researcher*

Ferryville
Tedeschi, John Alfred *historian, librarian*

Hales Corners
McNally, Vincent Joseph *historian, educator*

Kenosha
Kummings, Donald Dale *English educator*

La Crosse
Judson, John Irving *retired English educator, poet, writer, editor*

Madison
Berg, William James *French language educator, writer, translator*
Berghahn, Klaus Leo *German and Jewish studies educator*
Bogue, Allan George *history educator*
Brandt, Deborah *English educator*
Brembeck, Winston Lamont *retired speech communication educator*
Bühnemann, Gudrun *humanities educator*
Ciplijauskaite, Birute *humanities educator*
Cronon, William *history educator*
Dubrow, Heather *English educator*
Fowler, Barbara Hughes *classics educator*
Frykenberg, Robert Eric *historian, educator*
Hutchison, Jane Campbell *art history educator, researcher*
Karpat, Kemal H. *historian, educator*
Kleinhenz, Christopher *foreign language educator, researcher*
Knowles, Richard Alan John *English language educator*
Kutler, Stanley Ira *history and law educator, author*
Leavitt, Judith Walzer *history of medicine educator*
Loewenstein, David *literature educator*
Magnan, Sally Sieloff *language educator*
Murray, Julia Killin *art history educator*
Powell, Barry Bruce *classicist, educator*
Rideout, Walter Bates *English educator*
Sewell, Richard Herbert *historian, educator*
Shaw, Joseph Thomas *Slavic languages educator*
Singer, Marcus George *philosopher, author, educator*
Vowles, Richard Beckman *literature educator*
Weinbrot, Howard David *English educator*

Menasha
Leahy, Stephen Michael *history educator*

Menomonie
Schuler, Robert Jordan *English educator, writer*

Middleton
O'Brien, James Aloysius *foreign language educator*

Milwaukee
Curtain, Helena Hambuch *foreign language specialist*
Davies Cordova, Sarah P. *language educator*
Gallop, Jane (Jane Anne Gallop) *women's studies educator, writer*
Lea, Filomena *English language educator, writer*
Marten, James Alan *historian, educator*
Prucha, Francis Paul *historian, priest*
Siegel, Kristi Ellen *English educator*
Siegel, Robert Harold *English literature educator, writer*
Swanson, Roy Arthur *classicist, educator*
Theis, Peter George *retired classics educator*
Theoharis, Athan George *history educator*
Waldbaum, Jane Cohn *art history educator*

Monona
Brandes, Stuart Dean *historian, educator*

Oshkosh
Grieb, Kenneth Joseph *historian, educator*

Superior
Feldman, Egal *historian, educator*

Wausau
Veninga, James Frank *humanities educator, editor, author*
Whitney, John Denison *English educator, writer*

WYOMING

Casper
Durham, Lynda Laurene *language educator*

Cody
Price, B. Byron *historian*

Laramie
Chisum, Emmett Dewain *historian, archeologist, researcher*
Hardy, Deborah Welles *history professor*
Nye, Eric W. *English language and literature educator*
Williams, Roger Lawrence *historian, educator*

Sheridan
Aguirre-Batty, Mercedes *Spanish and English language educator, literature educator, educator*

TERRITORIES OF THE UNITED STATES

PUERTO RICO

Ponce
López-Alvarez, Carmen A. *language educator*

San Juan
Ocasio-Melendez, Marcial Enrique *history professor*
Picó, Fernando *historian, educator*

CANADA

BRITISH COLUMBIA

Burnaby
Buitenhuis, Peter Martinus *language professional, educator*
Cogswell, Frederick William *English language educator, poet, editor, publisher*
Kitchen, John Martin *historian, educator*

Richmond
Durrant, Geoffrey Hugh *retired English language educator*

Sidney
Saddlemyer, Ann (Eleanor Saddlemyer) *humanities educator, critic, theater historian*

Vancouver
Batts, Michael Stanley *German language educator*
Bentley, Thomas Roy *English language educator, writer, consultant, professor emeritus*
Conway, John S. *history professor*
Nosco, Peter Erling *humanities educator, consultant*
Overmyer, Daniel Lee *Asian studies educator*
Pacheco-Ransanz, Arsenio *Hispanic and Italian studies educator*
Unger, Richard Watson *history professor*

MANITOBA

Winnipeg
Rozumnyj, Jaroslav *literature educator, researcher*

NEW BRUNSWICK

Saint John
Condon, Thomas Joseph *university historian*

NOVA SCOTIA

Halifax
Carrigan, David Owen *history educator*
Gray, James *English literature educator*

ONTARIO

Brampton
Paikeday, Thomas M. *lexicographer and linguistic consultant*

Hamilton
McKay, Alexander Gordon *classics educator*

Kingston
Akenson, Donald Harman *historian, educator*
Dick, Susan Marie *English language educator*

London
Collins, Thomas Joseph *English language educator*
Gerber, Douglas Earl *classics educator*
Groden, Michael Lewis *English literature educator*

Nepean
Kallmann, Helmut Max *music historian, retired music librarian*

North York
Adelman, Howard *philosophy educator*
Thomas, Clara McCandless *retired English language educator, biographer*

Ottawa
Dray, William Herbert *philosophy educator*
Jaenen, Cornelius John *history professor, consultant*
Staines, David McKenzie *English educator*

Toronto
Blewett, David Lambert *English literature educator*
Granatstein, Jack Lawrence *history professor*
Herren, Michael Wayne *classical studies educator*
Johnson, Robert Eugene *historian, academic administrator*
Millgate, Jane *language professional*
Millgate, Michael (Michael Henry Millgate) *retired English educator*
Morey, Carl Reginald *musicologist*
Skvorecky, Josef Vaclav *English literature educator, novelist*
Webster, Jill Rosemary *historian, educator*
Wevers, John William *retired Semitic languages educator*

Waterloo
Haworth, Lawrence Lindley *philosophy educator*
Suits, Bernard Herbert *philosophy educator*

PRINCE EDWARD ISLAND

Montague
Cregier, Don Mesick *historian, educator, researcher, consultant*

QUEBEC

Montreal
Beugnot, Bernard Andre Henri *French literature educator*
Duquette, Jean-Pierre *retired French language and literature educator*
Hoffmann, Peter Conrad Werner *history educator*

Kinsley, William Benton *literature educator, educator*
Morin, Yves-Charles *linguistics educator, researcher*
Ormsby, Eric Linn *educator, researcher, writer*
Silverthorne, Michael James *classics educator*

North Hatley
Jones, Douglas Gordon *retired literature educator*

Sainte-Foy
Murray, Warren James *philosophy educator*

SASKATCHEWAN

Regina
Cleveland, Ray LeRoy *history educator*

Flamborough, Ontario
Lee, Alvin A. *literary educator, scholar, author*

MEXICO

Mexico City
Leon-Portilla, Miguel *historian, educator*

AUSTRIA

Graz
Weisstein, Ulrich Werner *English literature educator*

BRAZIL

Canoas
Sluberski, Thomas Richard *international educator, journalist, theologian*

ENGLAND

Lane End Bucks
Blackton, Charles S(tuart) *history educator*

London
Elson, Sarah Lee *art historian and consultant*
Graubard, Stephen Richards *history educator, editor*
Lowenthal, David *historian, geographer*
Perkin, Harold James *retired social historian, educator*
Rubin, Patricia Lee *art historian*

Manchester
Briscoe, John *classical languages educator*

Oxford
Carey, John *English language educator, literary critic*

Storrington
Osborne, Stephen J. *philatelist*

FINLAND

Helsinki
Hamalainen, Pekka Kalevi *historian, educator*

FRANCE

Indre-et-Loire
Schom, Alan Morris *historian, educator*

Toulouse
Courtés, Joseph Jean-Marie *humanities educator, writer, semiotician*

Vence
Polk, William Roe *historian*

Villeneuve d'Ascq
Allain, Louis *literature educator, scientific advisor*

GERMANY

Hamburg
Ludwig, Walther *classical and neo-Latin studies educator*

Münster
Spevack, Marvin *English educator*

Nuremberg
Doerries, Reinhard René *modern history educator*

Stuttgart
Bettisch, Johann *linguist, researcher*

HONG KONG

Pokfulam
McNaughton, William Frank *translator, educator*

ITALY

Genova
Montanari, Franco *classicist, educator*

Padova
Shea, William Rene *historian, science philosopher, educator*

Pietrasanta
Bugliani, Ann C. *international studies educator*

Verona
Pozzo, Riccardo *philosophy educator*

JAPAN

Bunkyo
Kobayashi, Seiei *English literature educator*

Kanagawa
Fukatsu, Tanefusa *retired Chinese classics educator*

Kashiwara
Hori, Keiko *English literature educator*

Osaka
Ishihara, Tsuyoshi *humanities educator*

NETHERLANDS

Amsterdam
Kolko, Gabriel *historian, educator*

PORTUGAL

Coimbra
Holm, John Alexander *linguist, educator*

SCOTLAND

Cellardyke Fife
Roff, William Robert *history educator, writer*

Edinburgh
Carp, Benjamin Louis *historian*

Saint Andrews
Dover, Sir Kenneth James *retired Greek scholar*

Stirling
Lenman, Bruce Philip *historian, educator*

SINGAPORE

Singapore
McDonough, Richard Michael *philosophy educator*

SPAIN

Barcelona
Vidal, Mercè *art historian, education educator*

SWEDEN

Lerum
Borei, Sven Hans Emil *translator*

SWITZERLAND

Zurich
Burkert, Walter *Greek language educator, historian*

TAIWAN

Taichung
Lu, Shih-Peng *history educator*

THAILAND

Bangkok
Sammon, William Joseph *historian, consultant*

ADDRESS UNPUBLISHED

Adams, David Parrish *historian, epidemiologist, educator*
Adler, Raphael *educator emeritus, speech pathologist*
Alexander, Doris Muriel *humanities educator, writer*
Allen, Dianna *language educator*
Allmendinger, David Frederick, Jr., *history educator*
Alvarez, René Luis *historian, educator*
Anderson, Jerry Maynard *retired speech educator*
Anderson, Rhoda *language educator*
Andrade, Carolyn L. *foreign language educator*
Angell, Richard Bradshaw *philosophy educator*
Ansbro, John Joseph *philosopher, educator*
Aptekar, Sheldon I. *speech, theatre, and performing art educator*
Ashkenazi, Elliott Uriel *historian, lawyer*
Asner, Glen R. *historian*
Attebery, Louie Wayne *English language educator, folklorist*
Bache-Snyder, Kaye Elizabeth *humanities educator, journalist*
Bailey, Charles-James Nice *linguistics educator*
Bailey, David Roy Shackleton *classics educator*
Baker, Ronald James *English language educator, university administrator*
Balkan, Evan Lindsey *literature educator, writer*
Baron, Sabrina Alcorn *historian, educator*
Basnett, Margaret G. *reading and language arts educator, consultant*
Bates, Margaret P. *historian*
Baxter, Stephen Bartow *retired history educator*
Beale, Georgia Robison *historian, educator*
Becker, Lawrence Carlyle *philosopher, educator, writer*
Benivegna, Vito Nicholas *language educator*

Bercovitch, Sacvan English language professional, educator
Berkhofer, Robert Frederick, Jr., retired history educator
Berlin, Edward Alan musicologist, writer, retired application developer
Bermack, Elaine speech educator
Berry, Moulouk language educator
Beschloss, Michael historian, writer, commentator
Biles, Gloria C. historian, educator
Binns, Jane Camille humanities educator
Bitman, Clara language educator, writer
Blackbourn, David Gordon history professor
Blissett, William Frank English literature educator
Bok, Sissela philosopher, writer
Bolsterli, Margaret Jones English educator, farmer
Bosco, Frederick J. language and linguistics educator
Bosmajian, Haig Aram speech communication educator
Boyer, Dale Kenneth English educator
Brettell, Richard Robson art historian, museum consultant, educator
Brewster, Elizabeth Winifred English language educator, poet, novelist
Bridges, Leonard Hal retired history educator, writer
Bruce, Dickson Davies, Jr., history educator
Brunner, Kathleen Marie humanities educator
Bryant, Paul Thompson English language educator
Bucelli, Maria-Elena language educator
Buckner, Sally Beaver English educator, writer
Burchett, Michael Henry history professor
Burianek, Irmtraud Eve historian, writer
Burrill, Kathleen R. F. (Kathleen R. F. Griffin-Burrill) language educator
Bush, Sarah Lillian historian
Cachia, Pierre Jacques Middle East languages and culture educator, researcher
Caldwell, Louise Phinney historical researcher, community volunteer
Calleo, David Patrick history, political, economy and international relations educator
Carlo, Paula Wheeler historian, history professor, researcher
Carrillo, Elisa Anna history professor, consultant
Carroll, Rosemary Frances historian, educator, lawyer
Cawley, Joseph Douglas retired reading educator
Chambers, Marjorie Bell historian
Chandler, Alfred Dupont, Jr., historian, educator
Chandra, Pramod art history educator
Chesson, Michael Bedout history professor, writer
Chevalier, David Valentine language educator
Ciavarelli, Maria Elisa language educator
Clark, Eve Vivienne linguistics educator
Clogan, Paul Maurice English language and literature educator
Collins, Jean Katherine English educator
Condit, Doris Elizabeth retired historian
Connell, Charles Roy language educator
Courtenay, William James historian, educator
Courtney, Edward retired classics educator
Craver, Earlene historian, educator
Crawford, Richard musicology educator
Crider, Allen Billy English educator, novelist
Crimando, Thomas Ignatius history educator
Cruz, Jesus history professor
Cummings, Gerardo Tonatiuh literature educator, researcher
Cummins, Marsha Z. retired literature educator
Cunningham, William Francis, Jr., English language educator, university administrator
Dai, Yingcong historian, educator
Delaty, Simone retired language educator
Demenchonok, Edward Vasilevich philosopher, linguist, researcher, educator
Demharter, Cheryl Ann Marie foreign language educator, former administrator
Derbyshire, William Wadleigh language educator, translator
DeSando, John Anthony retired humanities educator, film critic
Dias, Kathleen R. foreign language educator
Djordjevic, Dimitrije historian, educator
Doebler, Bettie Anne language educator, researcher, writer
Draper, Timothy Dean historian, educator
Duhl, Olga Anna literature educator, researcher
Dunbar, Maurice Victor English language educator
Durek, Dorothy Mary retired English language educator
Dyson, Anne Haas English language educator
Eaton, James Alonza humanities educator
Eby, Cecil DeGrotte English language educator, writer
Eckstein, Jerome retired philosopher, educator
Edwards, Michelle Andrea language educator, consultant
Egenes, Thomas Arthur ancient language educator
Eisner, Sigmund retired English language educator
Ellis, John Martin German literature educator
Erickson, Stacy Lynn literature educator
Espenlaub, Margo Linn women's studies educator, writer, artist
Esterhammer, Angela literary theorist, educator
Feeney, Matthew Edward linguist, educator
Filler, Susan Melanie musicologist
Fisher, Anita Jeanne (Kit Fisher) language educator
Fishman, George Mayer historian, educator
Flint, John E. historian, educator
Florea, Luminita Dana musicologist, educator, translator
Fraga, Mike A. history professor, accountant
Friedman, Victor Allen linguist, educator
Froberg, Brent Malcolm classics educator
Fuentes, June Toretta language educator
Gaddis, John Lewis history professor
Gatewood, Willard Badgett, Jr., retired historian, writer
Geist, Kathe Sternbach art history, cinema and English educator, writer
Gellinek, Christian Johann language educator
Gerlach, Jeanne Elaine English language educator
Giesey, Ralph Edwin retired historian
Gillespie, Gerald Ernest Paul comparative literature educator, writer
Gillett, Mary Caperton military historian
Girard, Theresa Mary language educator
Gollin, Rita Kaplan English literature educator
Gonzalez-Vales, Luis Ernesto historian, educational administrator
Graham, Lanier art historian, curator, cultural planner
Grant, Linda Hess language educator
Greene, John Colton retired history educator
Grinnell, Helen Dunn musicologist, arts administrator
Gromen, Richard John historian, educator
Gross, Irena Gridzinska humanities educator
Gumpel, Liselotte retired language educator
Gunther, Vanessa Ann historian, registered nurse
Guo, Sheng Ming retired history educator
Gurnow, Michael Erwin literature and film educator
Gurspan, Susan Judith language educator
Gyles, Mary Francis retired history educator
Hamelin, Marcel historian, educator
Hanley, Wayne M. historian, educator
Hanshe, John musicologist, writer
Haring, Ellen Stone (Mrs. E. S. Haring) philosophy educator
Harrell, Steven Jeffrey lexicographer
Hart, Arthur Alvin historian, author
Hart, Robert Lee retired English educator
Haworth, Dale Keith art history educator, gallery director
Heatwole, John Lawrence historian, sculptor
Herbst, Jurgen history and education educator
Hermalyn, Doc historian, writer, publishing executive
Hills, John F. language educator
Hoart, Gladys Gallagher English language educator
Hoffman, Daniel (Gerard) literature educator, poet
Holloway, Charles Edward language educator
Howard, Michael Eliot historian, educator
Hughes, Thomas Parke history professor
Hunt, Murray Watson humanities educator
Hunter, J(ames) Paul English language educator, literary critic, historian
Hutcheon, Linda Ann English language educator
Iglesias, Maria Estrella language educator, writer
Irwin, Anna Mae English language educator
Ivry, Alfred Lyon philosophy educator, historian
Johnson, Clifton Herman historian, archivist, former research center director
Johnson, John Prescott philosophy educator
Johnson, Vernon Eugene history educator
Jones, Peter d'Alroy historian, writer, retired educator
Jones, Stacy language educator, writer
Jordan, Nicole T.N. historian, educator
Kaminsky, Alice Richkin retired English language educator
Kane, Patricia Lanegran language professional, educator
Kaplan, Robert B. linguistics educator, consultant, researcher
Karlstrom, Paul Johnson art historian
Kastor, Frank Sullivan English language educator
Kay, Aman B. language educator, translator
Kerney, Yolonda V. music historian
Kessler-Harris, Alice historian, educator
Kim, Marianne Weiss humanities educator
Kohler, Sheila M. humanities educator, writer
Kolb, Harold Hutchinson, Jr., English language educator
Kornweibel, Theodore, Jr., retired history professor
Kramer, Dale Vernon retired English language educator
Kravitz, Ellen King musicologist, educator
Kuperman, Michael Aron language educator, writer
Kyvig, David Edward historian, educator
Labor, Earle Gene English language educator
Ladd, Brian K. historian, writer
Lantzer, Jason Scott historian, educator
Laqueur, Walter history professor
Laurent, Pierre-Henri history professor
Lawson Donadio, Carolina Anna foreign language educator, translator
Lee, Corinne Adams retired English teacher
Lee, James Wade humanities educator, writer, actor
Lewis, Douglas art historian
Limeberry, John Wesley humanities educator
Lincoln, Harry B. musicologist
Lindboe, Berit Roberg language educator, literature educator
Lindsey, Roberta Lewise music researcher, historian
Lisio, Donald John historian, educator
Longenecker, Stephen Lewis historian, educator
Lopez, Lily Samaniego language educator
Loughran, James Newman philosophy educator, college administrator
Lowenthal, Constance art historian, consultant
Lozano, Alfredo language educator
Maehl, William Harvey historian, educator
Mahoney, John L. English literature educator
Mahoney, Michael Robert Taylor art historian, educator
Manuelian, Lucy Der art historian, educator, architecture educator
Mapp, Edward Charles speech educator
Marchant, JoAnn Reviczky English language educator, actress
Marion, Marjorie Anne English language educator, education consultant
Marshall, Benjamin Vaughan literature and language professor
Matthews, Riki retired language educator
McCormick, John Owen retired comparative literature educator
McDermott, Agnes Charlene Senape philosophy educator
McDonald, Forrest historian, educator
McGann, Lisa B. Napoli language educator
McMaster, Juliet Sylvia English language educator
Meintsma, Peter Evans history and political science educator
Merfeld, Audra L. language educator
Millikan, William labor historian
Miscella, Maria Diana humanities educator
Mollohan, Beth M. humanities educator
Molloy, Sylvia Latin American literature educator, writer
Monaco, Chris historian, writer, documentary filmmaker
Monas, Sidney retired history educator
Moody, Jennifer Joy language educator, history professor
Moore, Cyrus language educator
Morgan, Edmund Sears retired history professor
Morrill, Penny Chittim art historian
Morrissey, Charles Thomas historian, educator
Murillo, Marisela English educator
Murnion, William Edward philosopher
Murphy, Francis English language educator
Murphy, Robert James language educator, consultant
Nagel, Thomas philosopher, educator, lawyer, educator
Nelli, Humbert Steven historian, researcher, retired social studies educator
Nelson, Claudia B. literature educator, writer
Nephew, Julia Anne language educator
New, Thomas L. public affairs, consultant
Newman, Georgia A. literature educator
Nicholas, Lynn Holman historian, researcher, writer
Nochman, Lois Wood Kivi (Mrs. Marvin Nochman) retired educator
Noel, Melvina literature educator
Noor, Ronny language educator, writer
Novak, Barbara art history educator
Nugent, Helen Jean history educator
Nugent, Walter Terry King historian
O'Dell, Kimberly Jane historian, educator
Odenigbo, Innocent Chukwunwike linguist, consultant
O'Donnell, James Joseph classicist, educational administrator
Ogbar, Jeffrey Ogbonna Green history professor
Ogden, Benjamin language educator
Oinas, Felix J. retired Slavic language educator
Olson, James Clifton historian, university president
Olson, Paul Richard Spanish literature educator, editor
Orcutt, Christopher C. language educator
Ornatowski, Cezar Maria rhetoric and communication educator, consultant
Palmer, Marilyn Joan English composition educator
Palter, Robert Monroe humanities educator
Panzer, Mary Caroline historian, museum curator
Paschoud, François university educator
Peyser, Joseph Leonard history professor, writer, translator
Pflanze, Otto Paul history professor
Pickrel, Paul English educator
Polistena, Joyce Carol art historian, educator
Pridgen, Rufus Allen retired literature educator
Prout, Carl Wesley retired history educator
Quint Sehat, Arlene art history educator, curator, museum administrator
Rakove, Jack Norman history professor
Rann, Robert Kennedy humanities educator
Rappaport, Susan Elizabeth English language educator
Rebay, Luciano Italian literature educator, literary critic
Reh, Sheila Natkins humanities educator
Reiman, Richard A. historian, educator
Rezelman, David Alan historian, educator
Reznikov, Vladimir Lvovich historian, playwright
Riasanovsky, Nicholas Valentine retired historian, educator
Richards, David Gleyre German language educator
Richardson, Robert Dale, Jr., English language educator
Rickard, Ruth David retired history and political science educator
Rizkallah, Morris Z. translator
Roalofs, Linda A. language educator
Roberts, Philip John history educator, editor
Robinson, Harlow Loomis language educator, historian, writer
Robles-Cereceres, Oscar Fernando language educator, researcher, writer
Roemer, Kenneth Morrison English language educator
Rollins, Alfred Brooks, Jr., historian, educator
Rosenberg, David Alan military historian, educator
Ross, Carol Ruth holocaust educator
Rouman, John Christ classics educator
Ruoff, A. LaVonne Brown English language educator
Ruse, Joan Riehle genealogist
Ryan, Henry Butterfield historian, consultant
Ryan, Marleigh Grayer language educator
Saint-Jacques, Bernard linguistics educator
Salgado, Susana musicologist, researcher, consultant
Sanner, Kristin Noelle language educator
Sari, Mouna language educator
Sawai, Dahleen Emi language educator
Sayre, Robert Freeman English language educator
Schadow, Karen E. public speaking trainer/educator
Schlagel, Richard H. philosophy educator
Schmitz, Dennis Mathew English language educator
Schor, Laura Strumingher historian
Schwantes, Carlos Arnaldo history educator, consultant
Schweitzer, Christoph Eugen liberal studies educator
Scott, Jane Madeline language educator
Scott, Michael Coleman philosophy educator
Serdari, Thomaï historian, librarian
Sessions, Bettye Jean humanities educator
Sferrazza, Anthony Carl historian, writer
Shaeffer, John Nees historian, educator
Sheffey, Ruthe Garnet English and humanities educator, speaker
Sheldon, Kathleen Eddy historian
Shillingsburg, Miriam Jones English educator, academic administrator
Shirai, Yasuhiro linguistic educator
Silverman, Kenneth Eugene English educator, writer
Singer, Beth J. philosopher
Smith, Gerrit Bruce foreign language educator
Smither, Howard Elbert musicologist, educator
Smock, Raymond William historian
Solomon, Robert Charles philosopher, educator
Solomon-Arnold, Irene Lena language educator
Sorrentino, Gilbert English language educator, novelist, poet
Stendahl, Brita Kristina humanities educator, social studies educator
Sternbach, Nancy Saporta language educator, researcher
Stewart, Dorothy Mary Hanton literature and writing educator
Stoesen, Alexander Rudolph retired history educator
Stokstad, Marilyn Jane art history educator, curator
Stolarik, M. Mark history professor
Straulman, Ann Therese retired English language educator
Street, John Charles linguistics educator
Stringer, Mary Evelyn art historian, educator
Styne, Marlys Marshall retired English educator
Sullivan, Mary Rose English language educator
Sutton, Julia musicologist, dance historian
Sykes, Sam Jones French educator
Tall, Sonia Terry humanities educator, researcher
Tallet, Jorge Antonio philosopher, writer
Tamimi, Maher M. language educator
Tayler, Irene English literature educator
Tedesco, Paul Herbert humanities educator
Thackray, Arnold Wilfrid historian, foundation executive
Tong, Rosemarie medical humanities and philosophy educator, consultant and researcher
Topik, Steven Curtis historian, educator
Torres, Shelby Credle English educator
Toulmin, Stephen Edelston humanities educator
Trelease, Allen William historian, educator
Valencia, Margarita Spanish language educator
van der Marck, Jan art historian
Vera Negron, Sandra literature educator, translator
Walsh, Roger N. psychiatry, philosophy, anthropology and religious studies educator
Wasserstein, Bernard Mano Julius historian
Weathersby, Kathryn historian
Weaver, Charles Horace humanities educator
Weber, Heidi Amelia-Anne historian, educator
Weber, Ralph Edward history professor
Weddle, Laura Mildred Thomas retired language educator
Weisbuch, Robert Alan English educator
Wetzel, Heinz foreign language educator
Wheeler, Burton M. literature educator, higher education consultant, college dean
Whitburn, Merrill Duane English literature educator
White, Charles Sidney John retired humanities educator
Wiener, Jon history professor
Wills, John Elliot, Jr., history educator, writer
Wiltrout, Ann Elizabeth foreign language educator
Winkler, Scott Alber literature educator
Wiswall, Dorothy Roller language educator
Wolff, Cynthia Griffin humanities educator, author
Woodbridge, John Dunning history and church history educator
Worthington, Deborah Eckhardt language educator
Wright, Elizabeth Rebecca humanities educator
Wright, Josephine Rosa Beatrice musicologist, educator
Wruck, Erich-Oskar retired foreign language educator, administrator
Yannella, Donald literature and language professor
Yolton, John William philosopher, educator
Zaferson, William S. philosophy educator, publisher
Zimmerman, Lynn Diann language educator, literary forensic consultant
Zimmermann, Thomas Callander Price retired historian, educator

HUMANITIES: LIBRARIES

UNITED STATES

ALABAMA

Birmingham
Beard, Craig Wyeth librarian
Goggin, Margaret Enid (Knox) librarian, educator
Murrell, Susan DeBrecht librarian
Spence, Paul Herbert librarian
Stephens, Jerry Wayne librarian, library director

Huntsville
Mathews, Fred Leroy librarian
Mok, Wai Yin library and information scientist, educator

Jacksonville
Hubbard, William James library director

Montgomery
Shepard, Judith Bethea librarian

Orange Beach
Owens, Marsha library director

Tuscaloosa
Dalton, Margaret Stieg library and information sciences educator

ALASKA

Anchorage
Braund-Allen, Julianna Elise librarian
Rollins, Alden Milton documents librarian

Juneau
Schorr, Alan Edward librarian, publisher
Smith, George Vinal librarian

ARIZONA

Peoria
Bailey, Claudia Jean retired professor, librarian, artist

Phoenix
Roof, Sally Jean-Marie library and information scientist, educator
Wells, GladysAnn library director

Scottsdale
Dalton, Phyllis Irene library consultant

Sun City
Crisman, Mary Frances Borden librarian

Sun City West
Williams, William Harrison retired librarian

Tempe
Metros, Mary Teresa librarian

Tucson
Grams, Theodore Carl William librarian, educator
Laird, Wilbur David, Jr., bookseller, editor
Swerdlove, Dorothy Louise librarian, consultant
White, Herbert Spencer research library educator, university dean

Wolfe, William Jerome *librarian, English language educator*

ARKANSAS

Bella Vista
Medin, Alice Louise *librarian*

Fayetteville
Jones, Phillip John *librarian*

Little Rock
Mulkey, Jack Clarendon *library director*

Lonoke
Ross, Philip Rowland *retired library director*

Pine Bluff
Economos, Cora Matheny *librarian*

Quitman
Martindale, Carla Joy *retired librarian*

CALIFORNIA

Alhambra
Birch, Tobeylynn *librarian*

Altadena
Dutton, Pauline Mae *fine arts and reference librarian*

Aptos
Heron, David Winston *librarian*

Auburn
Sanborn, Dorothy Chappell *retired librarian*

Bakersfield
Duquette, Diane Rhea *library director*

Berkeley
Buckland, Michael Keeble *librarian, educator*
Harlan, Robert Dale *information studies educator, academic administrator*
Minudri, Regina Ursula *librarian, consultant*
Torykian, Joan Marie *archivist*

Beverly Hills
Ramser, Wanda Tene *library and information scientist, educator*

Carlsbad
Lange, Clifford E. *librarian*

Culver City
Chow, Judy *librarian, educator*

Cupertino
Fletcher, Homer Lee *librarian*

Davis
Sharrow, Marilyn Jane *library administrator*

El Cerrito
Kao, Yasuko Watanabe *retired library administrator*

Fremont
Wood, Linda May *librarian*

Fresno
Gorman, Michael Joseph *library director, educator*

Fullerton
Ayala, John L. *librarian, dean*

Glendale
Michelson, Lillian *librarian, researcher*

La Jolla
Mirsky, Phyllis Simon *librarian*

La Mesa
Freeland, Robert Frederick *retired librarian*

Lafayette
Morehouse, Valerie Jeanne *librarian*

Livermore
Love, Sandra Rae *information specialist*

Long Beach
Proust, Joycelyn Ann *retired librarian*
Strait, Viola Edwina Washington *librarian*

Los Angeles
Bates, Marcia Jeanne *information scientist educator*
Bergman, Emily Anne *librarian*
Chang, Henry C. *library administrator*
Cuadra, Carlos Albert *information scientist, management executive*
Helgeson, Duane Marcellus *retired librarian*
Richardson, John Vinson, Jr., *library and information science educator*
Shank, Russell *librarian, educator*
Strong, Gary Eugene *librarian*
Sutherland, Michael Cruise *librarian*

Los Gatos
Conaway, Margaret Grimes (Peggy Conaway) *library administrator*

Menlo Park
White, Cecil Ray *librarian, consultant*

Mission Hills
Weber, Francis Joseph *archivist, museum director*

Monterey
Reneker, Maxine Hohman *librarian*

Monterey Park
Wilson, Linda *librarian*

Mountain View
Di Muccio, Mary-Jo *retired librarian*

North Hollywood
Schlosser, Anne Griffin *librarian*

Oakland
Hafter, Ruth Anne *library director, educator*
Smith, Eldred Reid *library educator*
Woodbury, Marda Liggett *librarian, writer*
Zemens, Anna Jo C. *library director*

Pasadena
Harmsen, Tyrus George *librarian*

Placerville
Wickline, Marian Elizabeth *former corporate librarian*

Pollock Pines
Rickard, Margaret Lynn *retired library director*

Redlands
Burgess, Larry Eugene *library director, history educator*

Riverside
Auth, Judith *library director*

Sacramento
Gray, Walter P., III, *historian, archivist, consultant*
Killian, Richard M. *library director*
Starr, Kevin *librarian, educator*
Zhou, Jian-zhong (Joe) *librarian*

San Bernardino
Burgess, Michael *library director, writer*

San Diego
Sauer, David Andrew *librarian, technical writer*

San Francisco
Aldrich, Michael Ray *library curator, health educator*
Brechka, Frank Tilson *retired librarian, historian*
Cline, Fred Albert, Jr., *retired librarian, conservationist*
Futch, Dorothy Helen *librarian, paralegal*
Van Buskirk, James Edward *librarian, writer*

San Jose
Light, Jane Ellen *librarian*
Schmidt, Cyril James *librarian*
Woolls, Esther Blanche *library science educator*

San Juan Capistrano
Peterson, Fred McCrae *retired librarian*

San Marino
McDermott, Irene Elizabeth *librarian, columnist*
Robertson, Mary Louise *archivist, art historian*

Santa Ana
Adams, John M. *library director*

Santa Barbara
Keator, Carol Lynne *library director*
Pritchard, Sarah Margaret *library director*

Santa Clara
Hopkinson, Shirley Lois *library and information science educator*

Santa Monica
Borko, Harold *information scientist, psychologist, educator*

Santa Rosa
Pearson, Roger Lee *library director*
Rosaschi, Jim *librarian*

Saratoga
Chisholm, Margaret Elizabeth *retired library education administrator*

Sebastopol
Sabsay, David *library consultant*

Stanford
Derksen, Charlotte Ruth Meynink *librarian*
Gold, Anne Marie *library director*
Keller, Michael Alan *librarian, educator, musicologist*

Stockton
Foster, Colleen *library director*

Thousand Oaks
Brogden, Stephen Richard *library director*

Tujunga
Pozzo, Mary Lou *retired librarian, writer*

Ventura
Kreissman, Starrett *librarian*

Yorba Linda
Naulty, Susan Louise *archivist*

COLORADO

Aurora
Miller, Sarah Pearl *librarian*

Boulder
O'Brien, Elmer John *librarian, educator*

Colorado Springs
Budington, William Stone *retired librarian*

Denver
Ahern, Arleen Fleming *retired librarian*
Ashton, Rick James *librarian*
Garcia, June Marie *librarian*
Lance, Keith Curry *library and information scientist*
Smith, Sallye Wrye *librarian*
White, Joyce Louise *librarian*

Edwards
Chambers, Joan Louise *retired librarian, retired dean*

Fort Collins
Mc Clellan, William Monson *library administrator, retired*

Golden
Mathews, E. Anne Jones *library educator and administrator, consultant*

Lakewood
Knott, William Alan *library director, management and building consultant*

Pueblo
Cress, Cecile Colleen *retired librarian*

CONNECTICUT

Bloomfield
Thorpe, James *humanities researcher*

Cheshire
Walter, Kenneth Gaines *library director*

Chester
Harwood, Eleanor Cash *librarian*

Fairfield
Bryan, Barbara Day *retired librarian*

Hamden
Lucas, Doina C. *librarian*

Hartford
Kaimowitz, Jeffrey Hugh *librarian*
Wiggin, Kendall French *state librarian*

Mystic
Rogers, Brian Deane *librarian*

New Britain
Sohn, Jeanne *librarian*

New Haven
Clarie, Thomas Cashin, II, *librarian*
Nellhaus, Tobin *librarian, theater educator*
Oliver-Warren, Mary Elizabeth *retired library science educator*
Stahl, Nanette *librarian, biblicist*
Stuehrenberg, Paul Frederick *librarian*

Niantic
Morrill, Billie Alberta *librarian*

Old Greenwich
McCarthy, Kevin E. *library director, consultant*

Simsbury
Roberts, Celia Ann *librarian*

Southbury
Rorick, William Calvin *librarian, educator, portrait artist*

West Hartford
Gerjuoy, Herbert George *educator, psychologist, consultant, poet*

Wilton
Poundstone, Sally Hill *library director*

DELAWARE

Dover
Wetherall, Robert Shaw *librarian*

Wilmington
Williams, Richmond Dean *library appraiser, consultant*

DISTRICT OF COLUMBIA

Washington
Akunwafor, Daniel Dominic *librarian, educator*
Baum, Ingeborg Ruth *librarian*
Carlin, John William *archivist, former governor*
Carr, Timothy Bernard *librarian*
Chin, Cecilia Hui-Hsin *librarian*
Craig, Susan Lyons *library director*
Daffron, MaryEllen *librarian*
Emperado, Mercedes Lopez *librarian*
Gifford, Prosser *library administrator*
Haley, Roger Kendall *librarian*
Harlem, Susan Lynn *librarian*
Harness, Gregory C. *Senate librarian*
Hedges, Kamla King *library director*
Heiss, Harry Glen *archivist*
Jackson, Mary Ellen *librarian, consultant*
Kalfatovic, Martin Robert *librarian*
Knezo, Genevieve Johanna *science and technology policy researcher*
Lee, Hwa-Wei *librarian, educator, consultant*
Marcum, Deanna Bowling *library administrator*
Missar, Charles Donald *retired librarian*
Player, Thelma B. *librarian*
Preer, Jean Lyon *information science educator*
Renninger, Mary Karen *librarian*
Rovelstad, Mathilde V(erner) *library science educator*
Soapes, Thomas F. *archivist*
Thomas, Mary Augusta *library administrator*
Trimble, Kathleen Louise *library director*
Turtell, Neal Timothy *librarian*
Wand, Patricia Ann *librarian*
Wattenmaker, Richard Joel *archive director, art scholar*
Young, Peter Robert *librarian*

FLORIDA

Boca Raton
Ferrari, Roberto C. *librarian*

Clearwater
Glymph, Dianne Tyler *librarian*

Daytona Beach
Sigerson, Marjorie Lorraine *librarian*

Deland
Caccamise, Genevra Louise Ball (Mrs. Alfred E. Caccamise) *retired librarian*
Dinkins, Debora E. *librarian*

Destin
Deel, Frances Quinn *retired librarian*

Fort Lauderdale
Cannon, Robert Eugene *library director*
Hershenson, Miriam Hannah Ratner *librarian*
Riggs, Donald Eugene *librarian, university official*

Fort Walton Beach
Hill, Carol Koelling *library director*

Gainesville
Brown, Myra Suzanne *university librarian*
Willocks, Robert Max *retired librarian*

Gulfport
Bourke, Thomas Anthony *librarian, writer*

Haines City
Kirk, Sherwood *librarian*

Hernando
Park, Chung Il *retired librarian*

Lakeland
Reich, David Lee *library director*

Lantana
Wetherby, Ivor Lois *librarian*

Melbourne
Regis, Nina *librarian, educator*

Miami
Treyz, Joseph Henry *librarian*

Naples
Hainsworth, Melody May *information professional, researcher*
Hall, Beverly Barton *librarian*

Oakland Park
Kilpatrick, Clifton Wayne *book dealer*
Rosenthal, Susan Barbara *retired librarian*

Ocala
Frow, Richard G. *retired librarian*
Tesmer, Nancy Ann Stutler *retired librarian*

Orlando
Allison, Anne Marie *retired librarian*
Green, Joal Fekete Stafford *library media specialist*

Palm Harbor
Jones, Winona Nigels *retired library media specialist*

Panama City
Bankhead, Sheila Walsh *librarian*
Robbins, Dorothy Ann *librarian*

Pensacola
Bumgardner, Kathryn H. *retired librarian*
Demars, Bonnie Macon *librarian*

Pompano Beach
Bethel, Marilyn Joyce *librarian*

Port Charlotte
Donovan, William Alan *retired librarian*

Saint Petersburg
Kent, Allen *library and information sciences educator*

Sarasota
Brandhorst, Wesley Theodore *retired information scientist*
De Gennaro, Richard *retired library director, library advisor*
Hummel, Dana D. Mallett *librarian*
Retzer, Mary Elizabeth Helm *retired librarian*
Straight, Elsie Hosking *retired art librarian, sculptor*

Tallahassee
Hunt, Mary Alice *library science educator*
Jordan, Tracey Alys *librarian*
Mason, Marilyn Gell *library administrator, writer, consultant*
Summers, Frank William *retired librarian*
Thompson, Jean Tanner *retired librarian*

Tampa
Harkness, Mary Lou *librarian*
Maiers, Michael Albert *librarian*

University Park
Compain, Rita *librarian*

West Palm Beach
Terwillegar, Jane Cusack *librarian, educator*

Winter Park
Rogers, Rutherford David *librarian*

GEORGIA

Athens
Donovan, James M. *librarian, anthropologist*

Atlanta
Brown, Lorene B(yron) *retired library educator, educational administrator*
Drake, Miriam Anna *librarian, educator, writer*
Flagg Davis, Vivian Annette *librarian, researcher, public policy consultant*
McCannon, Tricia Ann *multi-media specialist, writer, photographer, educator*
Roberts, Edward Graham *librarian*
Robison, Carolyn Love *retired librarian*

Wallace, Gladys Baldwin *librarian*
Yates, Ella Gaines *library consultant*

Augusta
Rowland, Arthur Ray *librarian*

Carrollton
Goodson, Carol Faye *librarian*

Cleveland
Edwards, John Carver *retired archivist*

Fayetteville
Neal, Joan Burkes *librarian*

Marietta
Rogers, Gail Elizabeth *library director*

Rome
Stephens, Michael Thoryne *librarian*

Savannah
Ball, Ardella Patricia *library media educator*
Dickerson, Lon Richard *library administrator*

HAWAII

Honolulu
Lee, Pali Jae (Polly Jae Stead Lee) *retired librarian, writer*
Lowell, Virginia Lee *librarian*
Spencer, Caroline *retired library director*

Kahului
Tolliver, Dorothy *librarian*

Lihue
Stevens, Robert David *librarian, educator*

IDAHO

Moscow
Force, Ronald Wayne *librarian*

ILLINOIS

Alton
Fortado, Robert Joseph *librarian, educator*

Aurora
Christiansen, Raymond Stephan *librarian, educator*

Calumet City
Muñoz, Romeo Solano *audio visual curator*

Carbondale
Bauner, Ruth Elizabeth *library administrator, reference librarian*
Koch, Loretta Peterson *librarian, educator*

Carol Stream
O'Dell, Lynn Marie Luegge (Mrs. Norman D. O'Dell) *librarian*

Champaign
Rayward, Warden Boyd *librarian, educator*
Ruan, Lian Jin *library director*

Chicago
Bodi, Sonia Ellen *library director, educator*
Brown, Richard Holbrook *library director, historian, researcher*
Choldin, Marianna Tax *librarian, educator*
Davis, Mary Ellen K. *library director*
Dempsey, Mary A. *library commissioner, lawyer*
Funk, Carla Jean *library association executive*
Gerdes, Neil Wayne *library director, educator*
Hanrath, Linda Carol *librarian, archivist*
John, Nancy R. *librarian, writer*
Maloy, Frances *librarian*
Miletich, Ivo *library and information scientist, bibliographer, educator, linguist, literature research specialist*
Parr, Virginia Helen *retired librarian*
Shedlock, James *library director, consultant*
Sullivan, Peggy (Peggy Anne Sullivan) *librarian, consultant*
Tinerella, Vincent P. *librarian, protective services official*
Wastawy, Sohair F. *library dean, consultant*

Dekalb
Hamilton, David Arnold *retired librarian*

Evanston
Cates, Jo Ann *library administrator, writer*
Crawford, Susan *library director, writer*

Itasca
Rice, Peggy A. *librarian*

Jacksonville
Gallas, Martin Hans *librarian*

Joliet
Johnston, James Robert *library director*

Quincy
Tyer, Travis Earl *library consultant*

Riverside
Van Cura, Joyce Bennett *librarian*

Rochester
Petterchak, Janice A. *researcher, writer, editor*

Schaumburg
Adrianopoli, Barbara Catherine *librarian*

Sycamore
Young, Arthur Price *librarian, educator*

Urbana
Bennett, Scott Boyce *retired librarian*
Brichford, Maynard Jay *archivist*
O'Brien, Nancy Patricia *librarian, educator*

Shtohryn, Dmytro Michael *librarian, educator*
Watson, Paula D. *library administrator*
Woodard, Beth Stuckey *librarian, educator*

Wauconda
Kramer, Pamela Kostenko *librarian*

Wheaton
Thompson, Bert Allen *retired librarian*
Tucker, Beverly Sowers *information specialist*

Wheeling
Long, Sarah Ann *librarian*

INDIANA

Bloomington
Chitwood, Julius Richard *retired librarian*
Legler, April Arington *librarian, educator*
Rudolph, Lavere Christian *library director*
Studwell, William Emmett *librarian, writer*

Bluffton
Elliott, Barbara Jean *librarian*

Fort Wayne
Krull, Jeffrey Robert *library director*

Gary
King, Marcia *library director*

Indianapolis
Ewick, Ray (Charles Ray Ewick) *librarian*
Fischler, Barbara Brand *librarian*
Gnat, Raymond Earl *librarian*
Young, Philip Howard *library director*

Lafayette
McKowen, Dorothy Keeton *librarian, educator, consultant*
Mobley, Emily Ruth *library dean, educator*

Michigan City
Glossinger, Donald Leo *library director*

Muncie
Schaefer, Patricia *librarian*
Yeamans, George Thomas *librarian, educator*

Notre Dame
Hayes, Stephen Matthew *librarian*

Richmond
Kirk, Thomas Garrett, Jr., *librarian*

Saint Meinrad
Daly, Simeon *retired librarian*

West Lafayette
Andrews, Theodora Anne *retired librarian, educator*
Fosmire, Michael *librarian, educator*
Markee, Katherine Madigan *librarian, educator*
Mullins, James Lee *library administrator*
Nixon, Judith May *librarian*
Saunders, Elmo Stewart *librarian, historian*

IOWA

Cedar Rapids
Armitage, Thomas Edward *library director*
Renter, Lois Irene Hutson *librarian*

Des Moines
Isenstein, Laura *library director*
Runge, Kay Kretschmar *library director*

Grinnell
McKee, Christopher Fulton *librarian, historian, educator*

Iowa City
Bentz, Dale Monroe *librarian*
Huttner, Sidney Frederick *librarian*
Miller, Dwight Merrick *archivist, historian*

North Liberty
Crowner, Dee Kay *library administrator*

Prairie City
Buckingham, Betty Jo *library media consultant*

West Bend
Wuebker, Colleen Marie *retired librarian*

West Branch
Mather, Mildred Eunice *retired archivist*
Walch, Timothy George *library administrator*

KANSAS

Arkansas City
Bachman, Neal Kenyon *librarian*

Atchison
Donaldson, Penny LeeAnne *library director*
McDonald, Joseph Andrew *information services director, consultant, writer*

Enterprise
Wickman, John Edward *librarian, historian*

Lawrence
Crowe, William Joseph *librarian*

Pittsburg
Lee, Earl Wayne *library science educator*

Topeka
Johnson, Duane Fadinand *librarian*

KENTUCKY

Campbellsville
Burch, John Russell, Jr., *library director*

Danville
Pappas, Marjorie L. *library studies educator*

Hopkinsville
Satterwhite, Robert Lee *library director*

Lexington
Mason, Ellsworth Goodwin *librarian*
Sineath, Timothy Wayne *library educator, university dean*
Steensland, Ronald Paul *librarian*

Louisville
Deering, Ronald Franklin *librarian, minister*

Morehead
Besant, Larry Xon *librarian, administrator, consultant*

Wilmore
Pohl, Gunther Erich *retired library administrator*

LOUISIANA

Baton Rouge
Hayward, Olga Loretta Hines (Mrs. Samuel Ellsworth Hayward) *retired librarian*
Jaques, Thomas Francis *librarian*
Lane, Margaret Beynon Taylor *librarian*
Lusk, Glenna Rae Knight (Mrs. Edwin Bruce Lusk) *librarian*
Patterson, Charles Darold *librarian, educator*

Lafayette
Carstens, Jane Ellen *retired library science educator*
Turner, I. Bruce *archivist*

Monroe
Smith, Donald Raymond *librarian*

New Orleans
Khaton, Sabrina Roslyn *librarian, accountant*
McReynolds, Rosalee *librarian*
Skinner, Robert Earle *librarian, writer*
Somers, Sally West *librarian*

Schriever
Shaffer, Margaret Minor *retired library director*

Shreveport
Pelton, James Rodger *librarian*
Wood, Julienne Louise *librarian, historian*

MAINE

Augusta
Norman, Melora Ranney *library director, educator*

Bangor
Rea, Ann W. *librarian*

Camden
Cagle, William Rea *librarian*
Moran, Elizabeth Ames *library director*

Orono
Risberg, Erica Lynn *archivist, film producer*

Waterville
Muehlner, Suanne Wilson *library director*

Westbrook
Parks, George Richard *retired librarian*

MARYLAND

Annapolis
Papenfuse, Edward Carl, Jr., *archivist, state official*
Werking, Richard Hume *librarian, historian, academic administrator*
Williams, J. Linda *librarian*

Baltimore
Allen, Norma Ann *librarian, educator*
Bradley, Wanda Louise *librarian*
Harris, Reginald Mervyn, Jr., *librarian, writer*
Hayden, Carla Diane *library director, educator*
Magnuson, Nancy *librarian*
McAdam, Paul Edward *retired library administrator*
Mc Cabe, Gerard Benedict *retired library administrator*

Beltsville
Andre, Pamela Q. J. *library director*

Bethesda
Humphreys, Betsy L. *librarian*
Knachel, Philip Atherton *librarian*
Lindberg, Donald Allan Bror *library administrator, pathologist, educator*
Tilley, Carolyn Bittner *technical information specialist*
Yang, Key Paik *librarian, archivist*

California
Avram, Henriette Davidson *librarian, government official*

Chestertown
Rather, Lucia Porcher Johnson *library administrator*

Chevy Chase
Basa, Enikö Molnár *librarian*

College Park
Lowell, Howard Parsons *archivist, federal agency administrator*
Wasserman, Paul *library and information science educator*

Columbia
Gruhl, Andrea Morris *librarian*

Gaithersburg
Bernstein, Steven *librarian, writer*

Germantown
Lewis, Robert John Cornelius Koons *retired library director*

Greenbelt
Hogensen, Margaret Hiner *librarian, consultant*
Moore, Virginia Bradley *librarian*

Potomac
Broderick, John Caruthers *retired librarian, educator*

Rockville
Henderson, Harriet *librarian*
Kohlhorst, Gail Lewis *librarian*

Salisbury
House, Charletta *librarian*
Wolter, John Amadeus *librarian, government official*

Silver Spring
Null, Elisabeth Higgins *librarian, writer*

Takoma Park
von Hake, Margaret Joan *librarian*

Towson
Fish, James Henry *library director*
Tull, Willis Clayton, Jr., *librarian*

MASSACHUSETTS

Amherst
Bridegam, Willis Edward, Jr., *retired librarian*

Arlington
Hamilton, Malcolm Cowan *retired librarian, editor, indexer, personnel professional*

Boston
Armstrong, Rodney *librarian*
Chen, Ching-chih *information science educator, consultant*
Desnoyers, Megan Floyd *archivist, educator*
Kominis, Katherine Elizabeth *librarian*
Kowal, Ruth Elizabeth *library administrator*
Margolis, Bernard Allen *library administrator*
Trinkaus-Randall, Gregor *librarian, archivist, preservation administrator*
von Fettweis, Yvonne Caché *archivist, historian*
Wendorf, Richard Harold *library director, scholar*

Cambridge
Bourneuf, Henri Joseph, Jr., *librarian*
Cole, Heather Ellen *librarian*
Flannery, Susan Marie *library administrator*
Gerratt, Bradley Scott *public administrator*
Stoddard, Roger Eliot *librarian*

Carlisle
Hedden, Heather Behn *information specialist*

Carver
Neubauer, Richard A. *library science educator, consultant*

Chestnut Hill
Yavarkovsky, Jerome Harold *library director*

Fall River
Sullivan, Ruth Anne *librarian*

Lexington
Davis, Barbara M(ae) *librarian*
Freitag, Wolfgang Martin *librarian, educator*

Lowell
Karr, Ronald Dale *librarian, historian*

Marstons Mills
Martin, Susan Katherine *librarian*

Natick
Rendell, Kenneth William *rare and historical documents dealer, consultant*

Newton
Glick-Weil, Kathy *library director*

Northampton
Piccinino, Rocco Michael *librarian*

Sheffield
Young, Susan Babson *retired library director*

Springfield
Utley, F. Knowlton *library director, educator*

Waltham
Hahn, Bessie King *library administrator, lecturer*
Preve, Roberta Jean *librarian, researcher*

Worcester
Dunlap, Ellen S. *library administrator*
McCorison, Marcus Allen *librarian, cultural organization administrator*

MICHIGAN

Allendale
Beasecker, Robert Francis *librarian, archivist*
Murray, Diane Elizabeth *librarian*

Ann Arbor
Beaubien, Anne Kathleen *librarian*
Dougherty, Richard Martin *library and information science educator*
Dunlap, Connie *librarian*
Gordon, Anitra *librarian*

Detroit
Field, Judith Judy *librarian*
Spyers-Duran, Peter *librarian, educator*

East Lansing
Chapin, Richard Earl *retired librarian*
Sowards, Steven Wesley *librarian*

Farmington Hills
Papai, Beverly Daffern *library director*

Garden City
Elmouchi, Joan Leslie *library director*

Grosse Pointe
Casey, Genevieve M(ary) *librarian, educator*

Holt
Smith, Betty W. *librarian*

Kalamazoo
Grotzinger, Laurel Ann *librarian, educator*

Lansing
Gomoll, Matilde I. *multi-media specialist*
Johnson, Veronica Ann Wilkerson *library director*

Owosso
Uptigrove, Kenneth R. *library administrator*

Plymouth
Berry, Charlene Helen *librarian, musician*
deBear, Richard Stephen *library planning consultant*

Port Huron
Miller, Theresa L. *library director*
Wu, Harry Pao-Tung *retired librarian*

Redford
Karpinski, Huberta Elaine *library trustee*

Saint Clair Shores
Woodford, Arthur MacKinnon *library director, historian*

MINNESOTA

Chisago City
Miller, Robert Carl *retired library director*

Duluth
Pearce, Donald Joslin *retired librarian*

Minneapolis
Asp, William George *librarian*
Johnson, Donald Clay *librarian, curator*
Johnson, Margaret Ann (Peggy) *library administrator*
Kukla, Edward Richard *rare books & special collections librarian*
Ostrem, Walter Martin *librarian, educator, consultant*
Shaughnessy, Thomas William *retired librarian*

Rochester
Key, Jack Dayton *librarian*

Roseville
Miller, Suzanne Marie *state librarian*

Saint Paul
Brudvig, Glenn Lowell *retired library director*
Fogerty, James Edward *archivist, state official*
Wagner, Mary Margaret *library and information science educator*
Zietlow, Ruth Ann *reference librarian*

Saint Peter
Haeuser, Michael John *library administrator*

Zumbrota
Post, Diana Constance *retired librarian*

MISSISSIPPI

Alcorn State
Yu, May Huang *librarian, educator, real estate agent*

Itta Bena
Henderson, Robbye Robinson *library director*

Jackson
Smith, Sharman Bridges *state librarian*

MISSOURI

Canton
Howe, Sandra Jo *library director*

Chesterfield
Landram, Christina Louella *librarian*

Columbia
Alexander, Martha Sue *retired librarian*
Almony, Robert Allen, Jr., *librarian, businessman*

Greenwood
Zeller, Marilynn Kay *retired librarian*

Hannibal
Andresen, Julie Ann Dothager *librarian*

Jefferson City
Croteau, Shelly Jeanne *archivist, educator*
Parker, Sara Ann *librarian, consultant*

Kansas City
Bradbury, Daniel Joseph *library administrator*
Miller, William Charles *theological librarian, educator*
Sheldon, Ted Preston *library dean*
Spalding, Helen H. *library director*

Lake Lotawana
Zobrist, Benedict Karl *library director, historian*

Parkville
Schultis, Gail Ann *library director*

Pleasant Valley
Nelson, Freda Nell Hein *librarian*

Portageville
Dial, Marshall Reece *library director*

Saint Louis
Guenther, Charles John *librarian, writer*
Holt, Glen Edward *library administrator*
Holt, Leslie Edmonds *librarian*
Lauenstein, Ann Gail *librarian*

Springfield
Busch, Annie *library director*

Warrensburg
Jurkowski, Odin Lech *librarian, educator*

MONTANA

Billings
Cochran, William Michael *librarian*

Bozeman
Kempcke, Ken *librarian*

Forsyth
Heser, Cheryl J. *library director*

Helena
Fitzpatrick, Lois Ann *library administrator*
Schlesinger, Deborah Lee *librarian*
Strege, Karen *library director*

NEBRASKA

Hastings
Yost, Dee Renee *librarian, educator*

Lincoln
Connor, Carol J. *library director*
Wagner, Rod *library director*

NEVADA

Carson City
Jones, Sara Sue Fisher *librarian*
Rocha, Guy Louis *archivist, historian*

Hawthorne
Pierce, Mildred Louise *librarian*

Las Vegas
Gray, Phyllis Anne *librarian*
Grosshans, Merilyn La Vonne *retired librarian*
Honsa, Vlasta *retired librarian*
McNeal, Betty Jean *librarian, writer*
Ramsey, Inez Linn *librarian, educator*
Reed, Ellen Beth *librarian*

Reno
Ross, Robert Donald *library director*

NEW HAMPSHIRE

Berlin
Doherty, Katherine Mann *librarian, writer*

Exeter
Thomas, Jacquelyn May *librarian*

Goffstown
Wajenberg, Arnold Sherman *retired librarian, educator*

Hampton
Morton, Donald John *librarian*

Hanover
Otto, Margaret Amelia *librarian*

NEW JERSEY

Brielle
McIntyre, Elizabeth Jones *retired multi-media specialist, educator*

Budd Lake
Hilbert, Rita L. *librarian*

Caldwell
Randall, Lynn Ellen *librarian*

Camden
Maxymuk, John Michael *librarian, writer*

Emerson
Hannon, Patricia Ann *library director*

Ewing
Meola, Marc *librarian*

Fort Lee
Altomara, Rita Ecke *library director, writer*

Glassboro
Martin, Marilyn Joan *library director*

Haledon
Dougherty, June Eileen *librarian*

Hoboken
Widdicombe, Richard Palmer *librarian*

Hopewell
Baeckler, Virginia Van Wynen *librarian*

Jersey City
Patterson, Grace Limerick *library director*

Laurel Springs
Cleveland, Susan Elizabeth *library administrator, researcher*

Lawrenceville
Congleton, Robert J. *librarian, educator, archivist*

Leonia
Berliner, Barbara *retired librarian, consultant*

Linden
Purves, Dennis Patrick *librarian*

Livingston
Sikora, Barbara Jean *library director*

Lodi
Karetzky, Joanne Louise *librarian*
Karetzky, Stephen *library director, educator, researcher*

Manalapan
Saretzky, Gary D. *archivist*

Monmouth Junction
Lawton, Deborah Simmons *library director, educational media specialist*

New Brunswick
Turock, Betty Jane *library and information science educator*

Newark
Tenney, Barbara Ann *librarian, director*

Princeton
Fox, Mary Ann Williams *librarian*
George, Mary Wiedenbeck *reference librarian, educator*

Princeton Junction
Butorac, Frank George *librarian, educator*

Rockaway
Kelsey, Ann Lee *library administrator*

Sewell
Wright, William Cook *archivist, historian, researcher*

South Orange
Bao, Xue-Ming *librarian, educator*

Succasunna
Romance, Mary C. *library director*

Trenton
Lockhart, Tina Marie *librarian*
Russell, Joyce Anne Rogers *librarian*

Union
Darden, Barbara S. *library director*

Wayne
Pardo, Janette M. *archivist, librarian*

West Caldwell
Sze, Melanie Chia-Yu *librarian*

NEW MEXICO

Albuquerque
Freeman, Patricia Elizabeth *multi-media specialist, educational consultant*
Snell, Patricia Poldervaart *librarian, consultant*

Carlsbad
Regan Gossage, Muriel *librarian*

Deming
Becker-Klicker, Margaret Chan *library director*

Farmington
Mathers, Margaret *reference librarian, archivist*

Los Alamos
Sayre, Edward Charles *librarian, consultant*

Santa Fe
Myers, R. David *library director, dean*
Wakashige, Benjamin Taka *librarian*

NEW YORK

Albany
Aceto, Vincent John *librarian, educator*
Merbler, Candace Anne *librarian*
Paulson, Peter John *librarian, publishing company executive*
Shubert, Joseph Francis *librarian*
Wilber, Roger Alan *library supervisor, writer*

Amherst
Bobinski, Mary Form *library director*

Bayside
Ausubel, Hillel *librarian*

Beechhurst
Wingate, Constance Blandy *librarian*

Bellmore
Andrews, Charles Rolland *library administrator*

Brightwaters
Kavanagh, Eileen J. *librarian*

Bronx
Humphry, James, III, *librarian, publishing executive*
Lopez-Fitzsimmons, Bernadette Maria *librarian*

Brooklyn
Lehner-Quam, Alison Lynn *library administrator*
Moore, Jane Ross *librarian, educator*
Schneider, Adele Goldberg *librarian, educator*
Sharify, Nasser *educator, author, librarian*

Buffalo
Bobinski, George Sylvan *librarian, educator*
Stoss, Frederick Warren *librarian, educator*

Corona
Jackson, Andrew Preston *library director*

Dryden
Slocum, Robert Bigney *retired librarian*

Edmeston
Blackman, Dorothy F. *library director*

Glens Falls
Mitscherlich Reynolds, A. Christine *conservator*

Hempstead
Glassman, Paul *library administrator, architecture educator*

Ithaca
Finch, C. Herbert *retired archivist, library administrator, historian*
Perry, Margaret *librarian, writer*

Jamaica
Drobnicki, John Arthur *librarian, educator*

Kings Point
Billy, George John *library director*

Lewiston
Newlin, Lyman Wilbur *bookseller, consultant*

Manhattan
Khalil, Mounir A. *librarian, educator*

Massapequa
Kappenberg, Marilyn Kascius *library director*

Mineola
Hammer, Deborah Marie *librarian, paralegal*

Monroe
Gocek, Matilda Arkenbout (Mrs. John A. Gocek) *librarian*

Mount Vernon
Griffith, Katherine Scott *librarian*

New Hartford
Anthony, Donald Charles *librarian, educator*

New York
Belliveau, Gerard Joseph, Jr., *librarian*
Berger, Pearl *library director*
Berner, Andrew Jay *library director, writer*
Boziwick, George E. *music librarian, composer, curator*
Brewer, Karen *librarian*
Browar, Lisa Muriel *librarian*
Cohen, Selma *reference librarian, researcher*
Edelman, Hendrik *library and information science educator*
Fedunok, Suzanne *librarian*
Fletcher, Harry George, III, *library director*
Gossage, Wayne *library director, management consultant, entrepreneur, executive recruiter*
Hewitt, Vivian Ann Davidson (Mrs. John Hamilton Hewitt Jr.) *retired librarian*
Kagan, Ilse Echt *research librarian, village historian*
Kasinec, Edward Joseph *library administrator*
Kent, Susan *library director, consultant*
LeClerc, Paul *library director*
Little, Robert David *library science educator*
LoSchiavo, Linda Bosco *library director*
Lowe, Ida Brandwayn *library administrator, systems administrator*
Lubetski, Edith Esther *librarian*
Mackey, Patricia Elaine *university librarian*
Margalith, Helen Margaret *retired librarian*
McKeever, Kent *library director, law librarian*
Meyerhoff, Erich *librarian, administrator*
Miller, Barbara Kenton *retired librarian*
Moreno, Barry *historian, writer*
Palmer, Robert Baylis *librarian*
Pierce, Charles Eliot, Jr., *library director, educator*
Rachow, Louis A(ugust) *librarian*
Root, Nina J. *librarian, writer*
Rosenthal, Faigi *librarian*
Rubinstein, Ernest *librarian, educator*
Slawsky, Donna Susan *librarian, singer*
Sullivan, Larry Edward *librarian*
Swan, Philip George *librarian, educator, artist*
Vilchez, Ricardo S. *library supervisor*
Whittingham, Charles Arthur *publisher, library administrator*

Oneonta
Johnson, Richard David *retired librarian*
Potter, Janet L. *university librarian, administrator*

Orchard Park
Greenwood, Audrey Gates *retired librarian*

Piermont
Brechtel, Unda Jurka *library director*

Poughkeepsie
Van Zanten, Frank Veldhuyzen *retired library system director*

Rexford
Nitecki, Joseph Zbigniew *librarian*

Rochester
Buff, Iva Moore *librarian, musicologist*
Swanton, Susan Irene *retired library director*

Roslyn
Siahpoosh, Farideh Tamaddon *librarian*

Scarborough
Stigall, Phyllis Graham *retired librarian*

Somers
Lane, David Oliver *retired librarian*

Staten Island
Auh, Yang John *librarian, educational administrator*
Black, Lawrence *librarian*

Stony Brook
Cook, Jeannine Salvo *librarian, consultant*

Syracuse
Abbott, George Lindell *librarian*
Luft, Eric v.d. *librarian, educator, publisher*
Stam, David Harry *librarian*

Tarrytown
Bowen, Christopher Edward *library director*

Tuxedo Park
Friedman, Rodger *antiquarian bookseller, consultant*

West Point
Watson, Georgianna *librarian*

White Plains
Manville, Stewart Roebling *archivist*
Scott-Williams, Wendy Lee *information technology specialist*

Williamsville
Cloudsley, Donald Hugh *library administrator*

NORTH CAROLINA

Asheville
Boyce, Emily Stewart *retired library and information science educator*

Chapel Hill
Kilgour, Frederick Gridley *librarian, educator*
Moran, Barbara Burns *librarian, educator*

Charlotte
Sintz, Edward Francis *librarian*
Welch, Jeanie Maxine *librarian*

Cove City
Hawkins, Elinor Dixon (Mrs. Carroll Woodard Hawkins) *retired librarian*

Davidson
Jones, Arthur Edwin, Jr., *library administrator, English and American literature educator*
Park, Leland Madison *librarian*

Durham
Canada, Mary Whitfield *retired librarian*
Holley, Edward Gailon *library science educator, former university dean*

Elizabeth City
Ballou, Leonard Ross *archivist, educator*

Fayetteville
Ross, Bernadette Marie-Teresa *librarian*

Greensboro
Kovacs, Beatrice *library studies educator*
Langstaff, Eleanor Marguerite *retired library science educator*

Hillsborough
Stephens, Brenda Wilson *librarian*

Murfreesboro
Muller, William Albert, III, *retired library director*

New Bern
White, Rhea Amelia *information scientist, consciousness researcher*

Raleigh
Littleton, Isaac Thomas, III, *retired university library administrator, consultant*
Moore, Thomas Lloyd *librarian*

Washington
Timour, John Arnold *retired librarian*

Winston Salem
Sutton, Lynn Sorensen *librarian*

Winton
Williams, Sue Darden *library director*

NORTH DAKOTA

Bismarck
Ott, Doris Ann *librarian*

Mayville
Karaim, Betty June *retired librarian*

OHIO

Ada
Herr, Sharon Marie *librarian*

Akron
Rebenack, John Henry *retired librarian*

Alliance
Clem, Harriet Frances *library director*

Bluffton
Dudley, Durand Stowell *librarian*

Bowerston
Spencer, Dawn Joyce *librarian, educator*

Bowling Green
Singer, Carol Ann *librarian, researcher*

Cadiz
Thompson, Sandra Lee *library administrator*

Cincinnati
Bellingham, Roger Gerry *librian, researcher, consultant*
Bestehorn, Ute Wiltrud *retired librarian*
Brestel, Mary Beth *librarian*
Everson, Jean Watkins Dolores *librarian, media consultant, educator*
Schutzius, Lucy Jean *retired librarian*
Zafren, Herbert Cecil *librarian, educator*

Cleveland
Gardner, Richard Kent *retired librarian, educator, consultant*

Columbus
Branscomb, Lewis Capers, Jr., *retired librarian, educator*
Sawyers, Elizabeth Joan *librarian, administrator*
Studer, William Joseph *library educator*

Dayton
Klinck, Cynthia Anne *library director*
Wyllie, Stanley Clarke *retired librarian*

Delaware
Schlichting, Catherine Fletcher Nicholson *librarian, educator*

Dublin
Baker, Mary Evelyn *retired librarian*
Meyer, Betty Jane *former librarian*

East Cleveland
Linderman, Eric Graham *librarian*

East Palestine
Rohrbaugh, Lisa Anne *librarian*

Elmore
Huizenga, Georgiana R. *public library director, storyteller*

Elyria
Bonnell-Mihalis, Pamela Gay *library director*

Hubbard
Trucksis, Theresa A. *retired library director*

Mentor
Jurewicz, Lynn *library director*

Middleburg Heights
Maciuszko, Kathleen Lynn *librarian, educator*

Middletown
Schaefer, Patricia Ann *retired librarian*

Mount Healthy
Scheffel, Kenneth Paul *retired archivist*

Oberlin
English, Ray *library administrator*
Greenberg, Eva Mueller *librarian*

Oregon
Poad, Flora Virginia *retired librarian and educator, retired elementary school educator*

Pemberville
King, Laura Jane *librarian, genealogist*

Portsmouth
Cain, Beverly Lynn *library director*

Tiffin
Hillmer, Margaret Patricia *library director*

Wickliffe
Fisher, Nancy DeButts *library director*

Wooster
Hickey, Damon Douglas *library director*

OKLAHOMA

Hodgen
Brower, Janice Kathleen *library technician*

Midwest City
McDowell, Cassandra *multi-media specialist*

Norman
Carroll, Frances Laverne *librarian, educator*
Kemp, Betty Ruth *retired librarian*
Lester, June *library information studies educator*
Sherman, Mary Angus *public library administrator*
Southwell, Kristina Lynn *archivist, librarian*

Welling
Varner, Joyce Ehrhardt *retired librarian*

OREGON

Albany
White, Diane O'Donnell *retired librarian*

Astoria
Foster, Michael William *librarian*

Beaverton
Pond, Patricia Brown *library science educator, university administrator*

Corvallis
Landers, Teresa Price *librarian*

Eugene
Edwards, Ralph M. *librarian*

Gold Hill
Barron, (Richard) Neil *librarian*

Keizer
Kenyon, Carleton Weller *librarian*

Portland
Baughman, Pauline Clara *librarian*
Browne, Joseph Peter *retired librarian*
Cooper, Ginnie *library director*
Eshelman, William Robert *librarian, editor*

Roseburg
Cook, Sybilla Avery *school library consultant*

Salem
Turnbaugh, Roy Carroll *archivist*

Wilsonville
Humphrey, Lois Ellen *librarian*

PENNSYLVANIA

Allentown
Sacks, Patricia Ann *librarian, consultant*

Audubon
Tanis, James Robert *library director, history educator, clergyman*

Beaver Falls
Focer-Richards, Linda Jean *library director*
Miller, Albert Jay *retired library director*

Bloomsburg
Vann, John Daniel, III, *library consultant, historian*

Bryn Mawr
Fletcher, Marjorie Amos *librarian*

Butler
Day, Margaret Ann *research librarian, information specialist*

Carlisle
Song, Yongyi *librarian*

Clarion
Miller, Andrea Lynn *library science educator*

Corsica
Elza, Betty Ann *retired librarian*

Cranberry Township
Lorenz, John George *librarian, consultant*

Doylestown
Wolfinger, Audrey Jane *retired librarian*

Greensburg
Duck, Patricia Mary *librarian*

Harrisburg
Emerick, John L. *library director*

New Holland
Fanus, Pauline Rife *librarian*

Philadelphia
Arnold, Lee *library director, archivist*
Bogis, Nana Eileen *librarian*

Pittsburgh
Josey, E(lonnie) J(Unius) *librarian, educator, former state administrator*
Minnigh, Joel Douglas *library director*
Willard, Louis Charles *librarian*

Punxsutawney
Dinsmore, Roberta Joan Maier *library director*

State College
Forth, Stuart *librarian*

University Park
Eaton, Nancy Ruth Linton *librarian, dean*
Joyce, William Leonard *librarian*

Wayne
Garrison, Guy Grady *librarian, educator*

West Chester
Schoelkopf, R. Gerald *archivist, librarian*

Wilkes Barre
Mech, Terrence Francis *library director*

Yardley
Du Bois, Paul Zinkhan *library consultant, book dealer*
Soultoukis, Donna Zoccola *library director*

RHODE ISLAND

Bristol
McMullen, Susan Taylor *librarian*

Coventry
Schweinsburg, Jane Duberg *librarian*

Kingston
Caldwell, Naomi Rachel *library and information scientist, educator*
Rathemacher, Andrée Jessica *librarian*

Middletown
Ottaviano, Doris Baginski *librarian*

Providence
Hamerly, Michael T. *librarian, historian*
Hunt, Cheryl North *librarian*
Kramer, Ilse Elisabeth *rare book bibliographer*

Warwick
Charette, Sharon Juliette *library administrator*

SOUTH CAROLINA

Aiken
Isaacs-Bright, Susan Virginia Kirkpatrick *research librarian, public speaker, advocate*

Bluffton
Cann, Sharon Lee *retired health science librarian*

Charleston
Buvinger, Jan *library director*

Clemson
Boykin, Joseph Floyd, Jr., *librarian*

Columbia
Duggan, Carol Cook *research director*

Griffin, Mary Frances *retired library media consultant*
Helsley, Alexia Jones *archivist*
Rawlinson, Helen Ann *librarian*
Toombs, Kenneth Eldridge *librarian*
Warren, Charles David *library administrator*
Willis, Paul Allen *librarian*
Zimmerman, Nancy Picciano *library science educator*

Georgetown
Bazemore, Trudy McConnell *librarian*

Greenville
Belk, F. Norman *librarian*

Orangeburg
Byers, Keith Thomas *librarian, educator*
Caldwell, Rossie Juanita Brower *retired library service educator*

SOUTH DAKOTA

Brookings
Marquardt, Steve Robert *library director*

Freeman
Koller, Berneda Joleen *library administrator*

Sioux Falls
Thompson, Ronelle Kay Hildebrandt *library director*

TENNESSEE

Chattanooga
McFarland, Jane Elizabeth *librarian*

Collegedale
Bennett, Peggy Elizabeth *librarian, library director, educator*

Greeneville
Smith, Myron John, Jr., *librarian, author*

Knoxville
Felder-Hoehne, Felicia Harris *librarian*
Watson, Patricia L. *library director*

Lebanon
Burns, George Franklin *archivist, retired English language educator*

Maryville
Tabor, Curtis Harold, Jr., *librarian, minister*

Memphis
Drescher, Judith Altman *library director*
Park, Elizabeth Haskell *librarian, educator*
Pourciau, Lester John, Jr., *retired librarian*
Wallis, Carlton Lamar *librarian*

Millington
Weatherford, Donna P. *library director, educator*

Murfreesboro
Marshall, John David *retired librarian, author*

Nashville
Gleaves, Edwin Sheffield *librarian*
Lyle, Virginia Reavis *retired archivist, genealogist*
Stewart, David Marshall *librarian*

Oak Ridge
McNeilly, Kathy Eden *librarian, library director*

Sewanee
Camp, Thomas Edward *retired librarian*
Dunkly, James Warren *theological librarian*
Watson, Gail H. *retired librarian*

Sparta
Young, Olivia Knowles *retired librarian*

TEXAS

Abilene
Specht, Alice Wilson *university libraries dean*
Tucker, John Mark *librarian, educator*

Aledo
Rowe, Sheryl Ann *librarian*

Austin
Billings, Harold Wayne *library director, editor*
Branch, Brenda Sue *library director*
Burson, Betsy Lee *librarian*
Davis, Donald Gordon, Jr., *librarian, educator, historian*
Felsted, Carla Martindell *librarian, writer, editor*
Gracy, David Bergen, II, *archivist, information science educator, writer*
Jackson, William Vernon *library science and Latin American studies educator*
Morrow, Sandra Kay *librarian*
Oram, Robert W. *library administrator*
Payne, John Ross *rare books, archives and photographs appraisal consulting company executive, library science educator*
Smith, Dorothy Brand *retired librarian*

Brownsville
Ferrier, Douglas M. *librarian*

Brownwood
Weeks, Patsy Ann Landry *librarian, educator*

Canyon Lake
Bowden, Virginia Massey *librarian*

Cedar Hill
Hickman, Traphene Parramore *retired library director, storyteller, library and library building consultant*

Cedar Park
Lam, Pauline Poha *library director*

Coldspring
Bunch, Robert Craig *librarian*

College Station
Wilson, Don Whitman *retired archivist, historian*

Dallas
Bockstruck, Lloyd DeWitt *librarian*
Ibach, Robert Daniel, Jr., *library director*
Salazar, Ramiro S. *library administrator*

Denton
Snapp, Elizabeth *librarian, educator*
Swigger, Keith *library and information scientist, educator*

El Paso
Gardner, Kerry Ann *librarian*

Fort Worth
Allmand, Linda F(aith) *retired library director*
Ard, Harold Jacob *library administrator*
de Tonnancour, Paul Roger Godefroy *library administrator*
Li, Richard T. *retired library director, secondary school educator*

Georgetown
Ramsey, Margie *librarian*

Grand Prairie
Ritterhouse, Kathy Lee *librarian*

Houston
Henington, David Mead *library director*
Holliday, Barbara Joyce *reference librarian, minister*
Hornak, Anna Frances *library administrator*
Radoff, Leonard Irving *librarian, consultant*
Russell, John Francis *retired librarian*
Scarbrough, Sara Eunice *librarian, archivist, consultant*
Witmer, John Richard *librarian*

Huntsville
Hickey, Lady Jane *librarian, minister*
Hoffmann, Frank William *library science educator, writer*

Irving
Parch, Grace Dolores *librarian*
Whisennand, Cynthia Simmons *librarian*

Lubbock
Verrone, Richard Burks *archivist, educator*
Wood, Richard Courtney *library director, educator*

Lufkin
Harmon, Jacqueline Baas *librarian, infosystems specialist*

Marshall
Magrill, Rose Mary *library director*

Mc Camey
Farley, Gail Conley *retired librarian*

Mcallen
McGee, William Howard John *librarian, administrator*

Montgomery
Smith, John Brewster *library administrator*

Palestine
Williams, Franklin Cadmus, Jr., *bibliographer*

Round Rock
Ricklefs, Dale Lynne *library director*

San Angelo
Chatfield, Mary Van Abshoven *librarian*

San Antonio
Brewster, Olive Nesbitt *retired librarian*
Hood, Sandra Dale *librarian*
Jones, Daniel Hare *librarian, consultant*
Kozuch, Julianna Bernadette *librarian, educator, consultant*
Lussky, Warren Alfred *librarian, educator, consultant*
Nance, Betty Love *librarian*
Newton, Virginia *archivist, historian, librarian*
Odom, Marjorie Mildred Morgan *retired librarian*
Ridder, Linda Gayle *librarian*

Sherman
Hardesty, Larry Lynn *librarian*

Tyler
Albertson, Christopher Adam *librarian*
Cleveland, Mary Louise *librarian, media specialist*
Green, Douglas Alvin *retired library director*

UTAH

Orem
Hall, Blaine Hill *retired librarian*

Provo
Jensen, Richard Dennis *librarian*

Salt Lake City
Owen, Amy *library director*

VERMONT

Essex Junction
Pillsbury, Penelope DeLaire *library director*

VIRGINIA

Alexandria
Berger, Patricia Wilson *retired librarian*
Brooks, Philip Coolidge, Jr., *archivist, curator, historian*
Cross, Dorothy Abigail *retired librarian*

Gernand, Bradley Elton *library manager, archivist*
Gray, Dorothy Louise Allman Pollet *librarian*
O'Brien, Patrick Michael *library administrator*

Arlington
Stone, Stuart Lee Morrison *librarian, language educator*

Assawoman
Holley, Pamela Spencer *retired librarian*

Castleton
Hahn, James Maglorie *former librarian, farmer*

Charlottesville
Berkeley, Edmund, Jr., *retired archivist, educator*
Berkeley, Francis Lewis, Jr., *retired archivist*

Chesapeake
Stillman, Margaret D. *library director*

Falls Church
Yoshimura, Yoshiko *librarian*

Farmville
Boyer, Calvin James *librarian*

Harrisonburg
Gill, Gerald Lawson *librarian*

Lexington
Gaines, James Edwin, Jr., *retired librarian*
Krantz, Linda Law *librarian*
Leach, Maurice Derby, Jr., *librarian, educator*

Norfolk
Shaw, Michael Evan *librarian*

Poquoson
Tai, Elizabeth Shi-Jue Lee *library director*

Rapidan
Grimm, Ben Emmet *former library director and consultant*

Richmond
Coalter, Milton J., Jr., *library director, educator*
Kozlowski, Ronald Stephan *retired librarian*
Treadway, Sandra Gioia *library director*

Roanoke
Cirasunda, Esther Bond *librarian*

Springfield
Doran, Doris Jeanne *librarian*

Virginia Beach
Sims, Martha J. *library director*

Williamsburg
Gough, Carolyn Harley *library director*
Moorman, John A. *librarian*

Winchester
Hughes, Donna Jean *librarian*

Woodbridge
Andrews, Michael William *librarian, information specialist*

WASHINGTON

Centralia
Meany, Philip Augustus *library director*

Ellensburg
Kline, Celeste Marie *librarian*

Maple Valley
Willson, David Allen *retired reference librarian, writer*

Olympia
Hutchins, Diane Elizabeth Rider *librarian*
Zussy, Nancy Louise *librarian*

Port Townsend
Hiatt, Peter *retired librarian studies educator*

Pullman
Zlatos, Christy *librarian*

Seattle
Bishop, Virginia Wakeman *retired librarian, retired humanities educator*
Blase, Nancy Gross *librarian*
Boylan, Merle Nelson *librarian, educator*
Fidel, Raya *library science educator*
Kruse, Paul Robert *retired librarian, educator*
Pearl, Nancy Linn *librarian*
Stroup, Elizabeth Faye *librarian*
Wilson, Lizabeth Anne *library director*

Spokane
Bender, Betty Wion *librarian*
Wirt, Michael James *library director*

Walla Walla
Yaple, Henry Mack *librarian*

WEST VIRGINIA

Glenville
Tubesing, Richard Lee *library director*

Morgantown
Pyles, Rodney Allen *archivist, county official*

Shepherdstown
Elliott, Jean Ann *librarian emeritus*

WISCONSIN

Eau Claire
Cox, Christopher *librarian*
Tiefel, Virginia May *librarian*

Franklin
Roark, Barbara Ann *librarian*

Madison
Bunge, Charles Albert *library science educator*
Christensen, Marguerite Alice *librarian*
Korenic, Lynette Marie *librarian*
Scherdin, Mary Jane Liskovec *retired librarian, information professional, researcher*

Menomonie
Lueder, Dianne Carol *library director*

Milwaukee
Blasinski, Clare Marie *librarian*
Gagliani, William Dennis *librarian*
Huston, Kathleen Marie *library administrator*
Valance, Marsha Jeanne *library director, story teller*

River Falls
Montgomery, Karen E. *library and information scientist*

Sheboygan Falls
Potter, Calvin J. *retired library director*

Thiensville
Roselle, William Charles *librarian*

WYOMING

Casper
Cottam, Keith M. *librarian, educator, administrator*

Cheyenne
Boughton, Lesley D. *library director*
Cuckow, Elizabeth Lena *librarian*

TERRITORIES OF THE UNITED STATES

AMERICAN SAMOA

Pago Pago
Fung-Chen-Pen, Emma Talauna Solaita *librarian, program director*

CANADA

ALBERTA

Calgary
MacDonald, Alan Hugh *librarian, university administrator*

Lethbridge
Rand, Duncan Dawson *retired librarian*

BRITISH COLUMBIA

North Vancouver
Ellis, Sarah Elizabeth *librarian*

Vancouver
Aalto, Madeleine *library director*
Piternick, Anne Brearley *librarian, educator*
Rothstein, Samuel *librarian, educator*

Victoria
Richards, Vincent Philip Haslewood *retired librarian*

NOVA SCOTIA

Bedford
Birdsall, William Forest *retired librarian*

Dartmouth
Horrocks, Norman *librarian, educator, editor*

Halifax
Dykstra Lynch, Mary Elizabeth *library and information science educator*

ONTARIO

Guelph
Land, Reginald Brian *library administrator*

Hamilton
Brackney, William Henry *archivist, historian*

Ottawa
Scott, Marianne Florence *retired librarian, educator*
Sylvestre, Jean Guy *former national librarian*
Wallot, Jean-Pierre *archivist, historian*

Scarborough
Bassnett, Peter James *retired librarian*

Toronto
Bryant, Josephine Harriet *library executive*
Moore, Carole Irene *librarian*
Packer, Katherine Helen *retired library educator*

QUEBEC

Laval
Adrian, Donna Jean *retired librarian*

Montreal
Large, John Andrew *library and information service educator*

Sainte-Foy
Bonnelly, Claude *library director*

SASKATCHEWAN

Saskatoon
Kennedy, Marjorie Ellen *librarian*

BAHRAIN

Manama
Sarhan, Mansoor Mohamed *library director*

CHINA

Beijing
Ren, Jiyu *library director*

CZECH REPUBLIC

Prague
Kalkus, Stanley *librarian, administrator, consultant*
Turková, Helga *library director*

DENMARK

Copenhagen
Larsen, Poul Steen *library educator*

ENGLAND

Barnston Wirral
Scragg, Thomas William *librarian, historical researcher, solicitor*

Oxford
Vaisey, David George *librarian, archivist*

FRANCE

Biarritz
Friedman, Richard Everett *librarian*

Lyon
Bazin, Patrick *library director*

GERMANY

Cologne
Neisser, Horst *library director*

Greifswald
Knöppel, Hans-Armin *librarian*

Lübeck
Fligge, Jörg *librarian, library director*

Stuttgart
Geh, Hans-Peter *retired library director, consultant*

GUATEMALA

Antigua
Rodgers, Frank *librarian*

HUNGARY

Budapest
Poprády, Géza *librarian*

KAZAKHSTAN

Almaty
Sadykova, Vera Philippovna *librarian, educator*

LATVIA

Riga
Buholte, Agnese *library director*

LITHUANIA

Vilnius
Butkevičiené, Birute *librarian*

MALDIVES

Male
Habeeb, Habeeba Hussain *librarian*

RUSSIA

Novocherkassk
Kiyanitza, Lubov Denisovna *library director*

SCOTLAND

Edinburgh
Matheson, Ann *librarian, writer*

SERBIA AND MONTENEGRO

Novi Sad
Vuksanović, Miro *library director, writer*

SWEDEN

Stockholm
Lidman, Tomas Erik *national archivist*

SWITZERLAND

Bern
Jauslin, Jean-Frédéric *library director*

Geneva
Jacquesson, Alain L. *librarian*

ADDRESS UNPUBLISHED

Adkins, Thomas Samuel *library director*
Anderson, Herschel Vincent *retired librarian*
Anderson, Mary Jane *public library consultant*
Anderson, Rachael Keller *retired library administrator*
Ariens, Karla Rae *library director*
Baker, Zachary Moshe *librarian*
Battin, Patricia Meyer *librarian*
Bino, Marial Desolyn *librarian, educator*
Blackburn, Joy Martin *librarian*
Bowen, Jean *retired librarian, consultant*
Brady, Jean Stein *retired librarian*
Brawner, Lee Basil *retired librarian, consultant*
Brooks Shoemaker, Virginia Lee *librarian*
Brown, Darmae Judd *librarian*
Brown, Elizabeth Eleanor *retired librarian*
Bruch, Virginia Irene Sullivan *librarian, writer*
Bulow, Jack Faye *retired library director*
Burton-Miskell, Helen *retired librarian*
Callard, Carole Crawford *librarian, educator*
Campbell, Henry Cummings *librarian*
Carter, Yvonne Breaux *retired librarian*
Clement, Hope Elizabeth Anna *retired librarian*
Clement, Yvonne Madeline *librarian*
Cochran, Carolyn *library director*
Crahan, Elizabeth Schmidt *librarian*
Crenshaw, Tena Lula *librarian*
Curley, Elmer Frank *librarian*
DeFato, Joan *retired librarian*
DeMita, Geraldine *librarian*
Dickinson, Donald Charles *library science educator*
Dietze, Joachim *librarian*
Dillon-McHugh, Cathleen Theresa *librarian, consultant, editor*
Domzella, Janet *retired library director*
Dyson, Allan Judge *retired librarian*
Edmonds, Anne Carey *librarian*
Elder, Mary Louise *librarian*
Else, Carolyn Joan *retired library director*
Elwood-Akers, Virginia Edythe *retired librarian, archivist*
Erickson, Alan Eric *librarian*
Estes, Elaine Rose Graham *retired librarian*
Euster, Joanne Reed *retired librarian*
Fasick, Adele Mongan *information services consultant*
Fawcett, John Thomas *archivist*
Flinner, Beatrice Jeffreys Allayaud *retired library and media sciences educator*
Ford, Barbara Jean *library studies educator*
Fout, Mary Jane *librarian, educator*
Fox, Carol Jean *librarian*
Frank, Lawrence James *library director*
Frantz, Ray William, Jr., *retired librarian*
Funk, Vicki Jane *librarian*
Gaertner, Donell John *retired library director*
Gatch, Milton McCormick, Jr., *library administrator, clergyman, educator*
Giebel, Miriam Catherine *librarian, genealogist*
Gold, Leonard Singer *librarian, translator*
Gould, Martha Bernice *retired librarian*
Greenberg, Hinda Feige *library director*
Gregor, Dorothy Deborah *retired librarian*
Gudmundsson, Finnbogi *library administrator*
Gundersheimer, Werner Leonard *library director*
Guthrie, Tara Sonali *librarian, music educator, soprano*
Hangen, Terra *librarian, writer*
Heanue, Anne Allen *retired librarian*
Hebert, Mary Olivia *retired librarian*
Herold, Jeffrey Roy Martin *retired library director*
Hill, Norma Louise *librarian*
Hoch, Ivo *former library director*
Hoke, Sheila Wilder *retired librarian*
Howard, Joseph Harvey *retired librarian*
Hughes, Sue Margaret *retired librarian*
Hutchins, Mary Louise *retired library director*
Irwin, Mildred Lorine Warrick *library consultant, civic worker*
Jackson, Eugene Bernard *librarian, educator*
Johnson, Wayne Harold *librarian*
Kalana, David Sterling *director of information systems*
Kallenberg, John Kenneth *retired librarian*
Kaser, David *retired librarian, educator, consultant*
Kendall, Charles Terry *librarian*
Kesseler, Matthew John *librarian*
Kirkland, Starr Melanie *librarian, writer*
Kiser, Nagiko Sato *retired librarian*
Kistler, John Michael *librarian, writer*
Klatt, Melvin John *library consultant*
Larson, Larry *retired librarian*
Lathrop, Ann *retired librarian, educator*
Lee, Harrison Hon *naval architecture librarian, consultant*
Lenix-Hooker, Catherine Jeanette *librarian*
Lesiak, Karen Ann *librarian*
Lewis, Emanuel Raymond *historian, psychologist, retired librarian*
Lindgren, William Dale *librarian*
Lovelace, Julianne *former library director*
Lucker, Jay K. *library science consultant*
Maltby, Florence Helen *library science educator*
McBurney, Margot B. *librarian*
McDonald-UmBayemake, Linda *librarian, rehabilitation counselor*
McDougall, Donald Blake *retired government official, librarian*
McGowan, Ian Duncan *retired librarian*
Metz, T(heodore) John *librarian, educator*
Miller, Alan Jay *rare book dealer, author*
Miller, Charles Edmond *retired library administrator*
Miller, Jacqueline Winslow *library director*
Miller, Marilyn Lea *library science educator*
Morgan, Jane Hale *retired library director*
Mountz, Louise Carson Smith *retired librarian*
Muñoz-Solá, Haydeé Socorro *library administrator*
Patterson, Robert Hudson *research library consultant*
Pitman, LaVern Frank *librarian*
Poole, Eva Duraine *librarian*
Pruter, Robert Douglas *librarian*
Repp, Joan Mercedes *retired librarian*
Rhoads, James Berton *archivist, former government official, consultant, educator*
Roberts, Judith Marie *librarian, educator*
Rockman, Ilene Frances *librarian, educator, editor*
Rouse, Roscoe, Jr., *librarian, educator*
Ruddick, Patsy Ruth *retired librarian*
Runkle, Martin Davey *library director*
Rusaw, Sally Ellen *librarian*
Sadler, Graham Hydrick *library administrator*
Sager, Donald Jack *librarian, consultant, former publisher*
Schewe, Donald Bruce *archivist, library director*
Scoles, Clyde Sheldon *library director*
Scott, Alice Holly *retired librarian*
Scott, Catherine Dorothy *librarian, information consultant*
Settles, Jeanne Dobson *librarian*
Shickley, Margaret S. *librarian*
Siefert-Kazanjian, Donna *corporate librarian*
Slavens, Thomas Paul *library science educator*
Smith, Barbara Jeanne *retired librarian*
Smith, Ruby Lucille *retired librarian*
Spaulding, Frank Henry *librarian*
Sprince, Leila Joy *librarian*
Stableford, Karen P. *library and information scientist*
Stavely, Keith Williams Fitzgerald *librarian*
Stewart, Dorothy K. *librarian*
Stone, Glenda Lee *librarian, genealogist*
Stubbs, Kendon Lee *retired librarian*
Summers, Lorraine Dey Schaeffer *retired librarian*
Suput, Ray Radoslav *librarian*
Sweetland, Loraine Fern *librarian, educator*
Teeple, Fiona Diane *librarian, lawyer*
Thiele, Gloria Day *retired librarian, small business owner*
Thorn, Rosemary Kost *former librarian*
Trezza, Alphonse Fiore *librarian, educator*
Triipan, Maive *library director*
Tu, Susan *retired librarian*
Turner, Brenda Gale *librarian, educator*
Turner, Marguerite Rose Cowles *library administrator*
VanMeter, Vandelia L. *retired director*
Van Orden, Phyllis Jeanne *librarian, educator*
Vickery, Byrdean Eyvonne Hughes (Mrs. Charles Everett Vickery Jr.) *retired library services administrator*
Wang, Chen-ku *retired library director*
Wartluft, David Jonathan *retired librarian, minister*
Weaver, Barbara Frances *librarian, consultant*
Wertsman, Vladimir Filip *librarian, information specialist, author, translator*
Whitmore, Menandra M. *librarian*
Wilkins, Barratt (George Wilkins) *librarian*
Williams, John Troy *librarian, educator*
Williams, Mildred Jane *librarian*
Williams, Richard Clarence *retired librarian*
Wilson, C. Daniel, Jr., *library director*
Wilson, Patricia Potter *library science and reading educator, educational and library consultant*
Wingate, Bettye Faye *librarian, educator*
Wolf, Cynthia Tribelhorn *librarian, library educator*
Woodrum, Patricia Ann *librarian*
Woods, Phyllis Michalik *librarian*
Wynar, Bohdan Stephen *librarian, writer, editor*
Yiotis, Gayle *archivist, researcher, anthropologist, writer*
Zack, Daniel Gerard *retired library director*

HUMANITIES: MUSEUMS

UNITED STATES

ALABAMA

Anniston
Bragg, Cheryl *museum director*

Birmingham
Trechsel, Gail *museum director*

Huntsville
Baldaia, Peter *curator*
Bass, Clayton *museum director*

Mc Calla
Kes, Vicki *museum director*

Mobile
Richelson, Paul William *curator*

Montgomery
Johnson, Mark Matthew *museum administrator*

Tuscaloosa
Diehl, Richard A. *museum director*

ALASKA

Fairbanks
Jonaitis, Aldona Claire *museum administrator, art historian*

Juneau
Daughhetee, Mark *curator, photographer*

ARIZONA

Bisbee
Gustavson, Carrie *museum director*

Flagstaff
Wolf, Arthur Henry *museum administrator*

Green Valley
Lusk, Harlan Gilbert *national park superintendent, business executive*

Phoenix
Ballinger, James K. *art museum executive*
Grinell, Sheila *museum director*

Portal
Zweifel, Richard George *curator*

Tempe
Zeitlin, Marilyn Audrey *museum director*

Tucson
Daley, Richard Halbert *museum director*
King, James Edward *retired museum director, consultant*
Rufe, Laurie J. *museum director*

CALIFORNIA

Arcata
Bailey, Stephen Fairchild *retired museum director, ornithologist*
Zielinski, Melissa L. *museum director*

Bakersfield
Enriquez, Carola Rupert *museum director*

Berkeley
Benedict, Burton *retired museum director, anthropology educator*
Consey, Kevin Edward *museum administrator*
Day, Lucille Lang *museum administrator, educator, writer*
Efimova, Alla *curator*

Bodega Bay
Cohen, Daniel Morris *museum administrator, marine biology researcher*

Burlingame
Stofflet, Mary Kirk *museum curator, writer*

Carmel Valley
Wolfe, Maurice Raymond *retired museum director, educator*

Carson
Zimmerer, Kathy Louise *university art gallery director*

Costa Mesa
Labbe, Armand Joseph *curator, anthropologist*

Fresno
Monaghan, Kathleen M. *art museum director*

La Jolla
Armstrong, Elizabeth Neilson *curator*
Beebe, Mary Livingstone *curator*
Davies, Hugh Marlais *museum director*

Long Beach
Glenn, Constance White *art museum director, educator, consultant*
Nelson, Harold Bernhard *museum director*

Los Angeles
Barron, Stephanie *curator*
Byrnes, James Bernard *museum director, consultant*
Fontenote-Jamerson, Belinda *museum director*
Gribbon, Deborah *museum director*
Hirano, Irene Ann Yasutake *museum director*
Holo, Selma Reuben *museum director, educator*
Hopkins, Henry Tyler *museum director, art educator*
Philbin, Ann M. *art facility director*
Powell, James Lawrence *museum director*
Rich, Andrea Louise *museum administrator*
Strick, Jeremy *curator*
Walsh, John *museum director*

Malibu
Zakian, Michael *museum director*

Mill Valley
Fuller, Glenn R. *park ranger*

Moraga
Silcox, Frances Eleanor *museum and exhibits planning consultant*

Newport Beach
Vine, Naomi *museum administrator*

Northridge
Lewis, Louise Miller *gallery director, art history educator*

Rancho Palos Verdes
Yassin, Robert Alan *museum administrator, curator*

Redding
Peterson, Robyn Gayle *museum curator*

Redlands
Griesemer, Allan David *retired museum director*

Riverside
Warren, Katherine Virginia *art gallery director*

Sacramento
Mette, Joseph P. *museum director and park facilities superintendent*

San Carlos
Schumacher, Henry Jerold *museum administrator, former career officer, business executive*

San Diego
Atkinson, D. Scott *curator*
Hager, Michael W. *museum director*
Longenecker, Martha W. *museum director*
Petersen, Martin Eugene *curator*

San Francisco
Leviton, Alan Edward *curator*
O'Neill, Brian *national recreation area administrator*
Parker, Harry S., III, *museum director*
Rinder, Lawrence R. *curator*
Ross, David A. *art museum director*
Sano, Emily Joy *museum director*

San Jose
Norberg, Deborah Dorsey *museum administrator*

Santa Barbara
Karpeles, David *museum director*
Kelm, Bonnie G. *art museum director, educator*

Santa Clara
Schapp, Rebecca Maria *museum director*

Santa Monica
Gabriel, Jeanette Hanisee *curator, art historian*

Stockton
Hepper, Iona Lydia *retired gallery owner*

The Sea Ranch
Baas, Jacquelynn *museum consultant, art historian*

Watsonville
Hernandez, Jo Farb *music director, consultant*

Yosemite National Park
Forgang, David M. *curator*

COLORADO

Boulder
Danilov, Victor Joseph *museum administrator, educator, consultant, writer*
Meier, Thomas Joseph *museum director, author*

Colorado Springs
LeMieux, Linda Dailey *museum director*

Cripple Creek
Swanson, Erik Christian *museum director*

Denver
Decatur, Raylene *former museum director*
Maytham, Thomas Northrup *art and museum consultant*
Sharp, Lewis I. *museum director*

Erie
Plehaty, Phyllis Juliette *curator*

CONNECTICUT

Hartford
Sellers, Kate M. *art museum director*

New Haven
Burger, Richard L. *museum director*
Hickey, Leo J(oseph) *museum curator, educator*
Meyers, Amy *museum director*
Yellis, Kenneth *museum administrator*

Storrs Mansfield
Censky, Ellen Joan *curator, biologist*

West Hartford
Faude, Wilson Hinsdale *museum director, consultant*

Weston
Daniel, James *curator, writer*
Oliver, Sandra *art dealer, painter*

DELAWARE

Wilmington
Blankenship, Roy *conservator, artist, writer*

DISTRICT OF COLUMBIA

Washington
Allman, William G. *curator*
Archambault, JoAllyn *museum administrator, anthropologist*
Blair, Thomas Delano *museum administrator*
Bloomfield, Sara J. *museum director*
Bretzfelder, Deborah May *retired museum staff member*
Buhler, Leslie Lynn *museum director*
Carr, Carolyn Kinder *deputy director and chief curator*
Dailey, John Revell *museum administrator, former career officer*
Demetrion, James Thomas *art museum director*
Duckworth, Walter Donald *museum executive, entomologist*
Dwyer Southern, Kathy *museum administrator*
Erwin, Douglas Hamilton *museum director, paleobiologist*
Escallon, Ana Maria *museum director, writer, curator*
Fauntleroy, Carma Cecil *arts administration executive*
Fitzhugh, William *curator*
Hand, John Oliver *museum curator*
Harvey, Eleanor Jones *museum curator*
Hoffmann, Robert Shaw *museum administrator, educator*
Ketchum, James Roe *curator*
Kornicker, Louis Sampson *museum curator*
Kurin, Richard *museum program director*
Larson, Judy L. *museum director, curator*
Legro, Patrice *museum director*
Levy, David Corcos *museum director*
McCracken, Ursula E. *museum director*
Neufeld, Michael John *curator, historian*
Noe, Adrianne *museum administrator*

Patton, Sharon F. *museum director*
Selin, Nina Evvie *philanthropist*
Small, Lawrence M. *museum executive*
Solinger, Janet W. *museum executive*
Sopher, Vicki Elaine *museum curator*
Stevenson, Frances Kellogg *museum program director*
Stevenson, Nancy Nelson *museum executive*
Ucko, David Alan *museum consultant*
Weil, Stephen Edward *retired museum official*
West, W. Richard *museum director*
Withuhn, William Lawrence *museum director, railroad economics and management consultant*
Wolanin, Barbara Ann Boese *art curator, art historian*

FLORIDA

Boca Raton
Kaye, Carole *museum director and curator*

Daytona Beach
Libby, Gary Russell *museum director emeritus, writer*

Fort Lauderdale
Cavendish, Kim L. Maher *museum administrator*

Gainesville
Dickinson, Joshua Clifton, Jr., *museum director, educator*
Emery, Kitty Frances *curator, educator*
Willumson, Glenn Gardner *curator, art historian*
Wing, Elizabeth Schwarz *museum curator, educator*

Jacksonville
Dundon, Margo Elaine *museum director*
Schlageter, Robert William *museum administrator*

Miami
Morgan, Dahlia *museum director, art educator*

Miami Beach
Camber, Diane Woolfe *museum director*

Naples
Brown, Alan Marshall, Jr., *art dealer, curator, art appraiser*

Niceville
Valdés, Karen W. *art gallery director, educator*

Orlando
Morrisey, Marena Grant *art museum administrator*

Saint Petersburg
Connelly, David O'Brien *art museum administrator, journalist*

Sarasota
Graham, Douglass of Montrose *museum curator, banker, artist, poet*
Wetenhall, John *museum director*

Tallahassee
Palladino-Craig, Allys *museum director*

Tampa
Kass, Emily *art museum administrator*

Vero Beach
Gedeon, Lucinda Heyel *museum director*

West Palm Beach
Orr-Cahall, Christina *art museum director, art historian*

GEORGIA

Athens
Manoguerra, Paul Andrew *curator*

Atlanta
Anderson, Maxwell L. *former museum director*
Bibb, Daniel Roland *antique painting restorer and conservator*
Davis, Eleanor Kay *museum administrator*
King, Linda Orr *museum director, consultant*
Vigtel, Gudmund *museum director emeritus*

Macon
Oliver, Katherine C. *museum director*

Roswell
Forbes, John Ripley *museum executive, educator, naturalist*

HAWAII

Honolulu
Billings, Kathy *national monument administrator* •
Klobe, Tom *art gallery director*

Kaneohe
Lagoria, Georgianna Marie *curator, writer, editor, visual art consultant*

Lihue
Lovell, Carol *museum director*

Mililani
Magee, Donald Edward *retired national park service administrator*

IDAHO

Coeur D Alene
Dahlgren, Dorothy *museum director*

Inkom
Jackson, Allen Keith *retired museum administrator*

ILLINOIS

Aurora
Mir, Ronen *museum director*

Bloomington
Bridges, Roger Dean *historical agency administrator*

Bolingbrook
Madori, Jan *art gallery director*

Carbondale
Whitlock, John Joseph *museum director*

Chicago
Balzekas, Stanley, Jr., *museum director*
Fitzpatrick, Robert John *museum director*
Flynn, John J. *museum curator*
Heltne, Paul Gregory *research scholar*
Kamyszew, Christopher D. *museum curator, executive educator, art consultant*
Knappenberger, Paul Henry, Jr., *science museum director*
Kubida, Judith Ann *museum administrator*
Mc Carter, John Wilbur, Jr., *museum executive*
Mosena, David R. *museum administrator*
Nordland, Gerald *art museum administrator, historian, consultant*
Weisberg, Lois *arts administrator, city official*
Wood, James Nowell *museum director and executive*
Wright, Antoinette D. *museum administrator*

Olympia Fields
MacMaster, Daniel Miller *retired museum official*

Schaumburg
Narkiewicz-Laine, Christian K. Gf. *museum director, painter, poet*

Springfield
Hallmark, Donald Parker *museum director, lecturer*
Mc Millan, R(obert) Bruce *museum executive, anthropologist*
Wynn, Nan L. *historic site administrator*

INDIANA

Bloomington
Calinescu, Adriana Gabriela *museum curator, art historian*

Evansville
Streetman, John William, III, *museum official*

Fort Wayne
Watkinson, Patricia Grieve *museum director*

Indianapolis
Cilella, Salvatore George, Jr., *museum director*
Gantz, Richard Alan *museum administrator*

Rochester
Willard, Shirley Ann Ogle *museum director, editor, historian*

IOWA

Iowa City
Smothers, Ann Elizabeth *museum director*

KANSAS

Larned
Linderer, Steve *historic site executive*

KENTUCKY

Louisville
Becker, Gail Roselyn *museum director*
Bentley, James Robert *association curator, historian, genealogist*

LOUISIANA

Baton Rouge
Gikas, Carol Sommerfeldt *museum director*

Lafayette
Henderson, Mary Stanley *museum director, writer*

New Orleans
Bullard, Edgar John, III, *museum director*
Casellas, Joachim *art gallery executive*
Fagaly, William Arthur *curator*
Smith, Geraldine *historic site administrator*
Wheat, Robert E. *museum director*

MAINE

Hancock
Silvestro, Clement Mario *museum director, historian*

Kennebunk
Escalet, Frank Diaz *art gallery owner, artist, educator*

MARYLAND

Baltimore
Bolger, Doreen *museum director*
Fiori, Dennis A. *museum director*

Clinton
Whittington, Ralph Edward *curator, librarian*

College Park
Quick, Edward Raymond *museum director, educator, curator*

Edgewater
Simons, Ross B. *environmental center director*

Hyattsville
Shestack, Alan *museum administrator*

Landover
Grasselli, Margaret Morgan *curator*

Mitchellville
Marsh, Caryl Amsterdam *museum exhibitions curator, psychologist, advisor*

MASSACHUSETTS

Acton
Gilpin, Deborah J. *museum administrator*

Babson Park
Palmerio, Elvira Castano *art gallery director, art historian*

Boston
Cronin, Bonnie Kathryn Lamb *museum director*
Curran, Emily Katherine *museum director*
Emerson, Anne Devereux *museum administrator*
Freed, Rita Evelyn *curator, Egyptologist, educator*
Hawley, Anne *museum director*
Hills, Patricia Gorton Schulze *curator*
Howlett, D(onald) Roger *art gallery executive, art historian*
Medvedow, Jill *museum director*
Rogers, Malcolm Austin *museum director, art historian*
Vermeule, Cornelius Clarkson, III, *museum curator*
Washburn, Bradford (Henry B. Washburn Jr.) *museum administrator, cartographer, photographer*
Wu, Tung *curator, art historian, art educator, artist*
Zannieri, Nina *museum director*

Cambridge
Cohn, Marjorie Benedict *curator, art historian, educator*
Gaskell, Ivan George Alexander De Wend *art museum curator*
Kennedy, Roger George *museum director, park service executive*
Slive, Seymour *museum director, fine arts educator*
Watson, Rubie *museum director*

Fitchburg
Jareckie, Stephen Barlow *museum curator*

Jamaica Plain
Zahn, Carl Frederick *museum publications director, designer, photographer*

Lexington
Ott, John Harlow *museum administrator*

Lincoln
Elias, Daniel *art gallery owner*

Milton
Randall, Lilian Maria Charlotte *museum curator*

Nantucket
Carr, James Revell *museum executive, curator*

Northampton
Fabing, Suzannah *museum director*

Southfield
Melvin, Ronald McKnight *retired museum director*

Springfield
Carvalho, Joseph, III, *museum and library executive*
Muhlberger, Richard Charles *former museum administrator, writer, educator*

Waltham
Arena, Albert A. *museum director*

Watertown
Fairbanks, Jonathan Leo *museum curator*

Williamstown
Conforti, Michael Peter *museum director, art historian*

Worcester
Welu, James A. *art museum director*

MICHIGAN

Ann Arbor
Bailey, Reeve Maclaren *museum curator*

Chelsea
Sawyer, Charles Henry *art educator, art museum director emeritus*

Detroit
Beal, Graham William John *museum director*
Darr, Alan Phipps *curator, historian*
Parrish, Maurice Drue *museum executive*
Peck, William Henry *museum curator, art historian, archaeologist, author, lecturer*

East Lansing
Bandes, Susan Jane *museum director, educator*
Dewhurst, Charles Kurt *museum director, cultural administrator, curator, folklorist, English language educator*

Grand Rapids
Frankforter, Weldon DeLoss *retired museum administrator*

Kalamazoo
Norris, Richard Patrick *museum director, historian, educator*

MINNESOTA

Minneapolis
King, Lyndel Irene Saunders *art museum director*

Saint Paul
Peterson, James Lincoln *museum executive*
White, William Thomas *curator, historian, educator*

MISSISSIPPI

Vicksburg
Joyner, Elizabeth *curator*

Washington
Branyan, Cheryl Munyer *museum administrator, consultant*

MISSOURI

Ballwin
Pallozola, Christine *non-profit administrator*

Florissant
Luebke, Martin Frederick *retired curator, retired private school educator*

Kansas City
McKenna, George LaVerne *art museum curator*
Scott, Deborah Emont *curator*

Rolla
Combs, Robert Kimbal *museum director*

Saint Joseph
Chilcote, Gary M. *museum director, reporter*

Saint Louis
Burke, James Donald *museum administrator*

Springfield
Berger, Jerry Allen *museum director*

MONTANA

Billings
Lorenz, Marianne *curator*

Crow Agency
Deernose, Kitty *curator*

Missoula
Brown, Robert Munro *museum director*
Millin, Laura Jeanne *museum director*

NEBRASKA

Boys Town
Lynch, Thomas Joseph *museum and historic house manager*

Lincoln
Wallis, Deborah *curator*

NEVADA

Baker
Mills, Rebecca *national park administrator*

Elko
Seymour, Lisa *museum director*

Las Vegas
Gillespie, Marilyn *museum administrator*
Le Blanc, Suzanne *museum director*
Lewis, Oli Parepa *curator*

NEW HAMPSHIRE

Newmarket
Ellis, David Wertz *retired museum director*

Portsmouth
Nylander, Jane Louise *museum director, lecturer, writer*

NEW JERSEY

Ho Ho Kus
Ciannella, Joeen Moore *museum director*

Holmdel
Smith, Sibley Judson, Jr., *historic site administrator, educator*

Morristown
Miller, Steven H. *museum director*

Newark
Price, Mary Sue Sweeney *museum director*
Reynolds, Valrae *museum curator*

NEW MEXICO

Albuquerque
Walch, Peter Sanborn *museum director, publisher*

Placitas
Smith, Richard Bowen *retired national park superintendent*

Santa Fe
Enyeart, James L. *museum director*
Fisher, Nora Caldwell *retired curator, photographer, researcher, writer*
Wilson, Thomas *museum director*

Silver City
Bettison, Cynthia Ann *museum director, archaeologist*

Taos
Tisdale, Shelby Jo-Anne *museum director, consultant*
Witt, David L. *curator, writer*

NEW YORK

Albany
Miles, Christine Marie *museum director*

Blue Mountain Lake
Day, Jacqueline Frances *museum director*

Brooklyn
Enseki, Carol *museum director*
Ferber, Linda S. *museum curator*
Lehman, Arnold Lester *museum official, art historian*
Shubert, Gabrielle S. *museum executive director*

Buffalo
Bayles, Jennifer Lucene *museum program director, educator*
Schultz, Douglas George *art museum director*

Cold Spring Harbor
MacKay, Robert Battin *museum director*

Corning
Spillman, Jane Shadel *curator, researcher, writer*
Whitehouse, David Bryn *museum director*

Hamilton
Moynihan, William J. *museum executive*

Hyde Park
Hunt, Mark Alan *museum director*

Katonah
Simpson, William Kelly *curator, Egyptologist, educator*

Long Island City
Heiss, Alanna *museum director*

New York
Arnot, Andrew H. *art gallery director*
Baragwanath, Albert Kingsmill *curator, writer*
Barnett, Vivian Endicott *curator*
Basquin, Mary Smyth (Kit Basquin) *museum administrator*
Bothmer, Dietrich Felix von *museum curator, archaeologist*
Brotman, Stuart Neil *museum administrator*
Bull, David *fine art conservator*
Carneiro, Robert Leonard *curator, anthropologist*
Carpenter, James Michael *curator*
Cohen, Mildred Thaler *art gallery director*
Cracraft, Joel *curator*
de Montebello, Philippe Lannes *museum administrator*
Desai, Vishakha N. *museum director, professional society administrator*
de Zegher, Catherine *museum director, curator*
Draper, James David *art museum curator*
Dunne, Linda *museum administrator*
Faunce, Sarah Cushing *former museum curator*
Freed, Stanley Arthur *retired museum curator*
Futter, Ellen Victoria *museum administrator*
Glimcher, Arnold B. *art gallery executive*
Globus, Dorothy Twining *museum director*
Govan, Michael *museum director*
Gumpert, Lynn *gallery director*
Gund, Agnes *former art museum administrator*
Haskell, Barbara *curator*
Hoffman, Nancy *art gallery director*
Hotchner, Holly *curator, museum director, conservator*
Hoving, Thomas *museum and cultural affairs consultant, author*
Howat, John Keith *retired museum executive*
Ilse-Neuman, Ursula *curator*
Ives, Colta Feller *museum curator, educator*
Kallir, Jane Katherine *art gallery director, author*
Kardon, Janet *museum director, curator, educator*
Kind, Phyllis *art gallery owner*
Kleeblatt, Norman L. *museum curator*
Kramer, Linda Konheim *curator, art historian*
Krens, Thomas *museum director*
Kuchta, Ronald Andrew *art museum director, magazine editor, curator*
Kujawski, Elizabeth Szancer *art curator, consultant*
Lerner, Martin *museum curator*
Levai, Pierre Alexandre *art gallery executive*
Leven, Ann Ruth *museum financial officer*
Levine, Louis D. *museum director, archaeologist*
Libin, Laurence Elliot *museum official*
Lowry, Glenn David *art museum director*
Lust, Herbert Cohnfeldt, II, *art gallery owner*
Martin, Mary Anne *art gallery owner*
Mc Shine, Kynaston Leigh *curator*
Mertens, Joan R. *museum curator, art historian*
Messer, Thomas Maria *museum director*
Murdock, Robert Mead *curator*
O'Brien, Catherine Louise *museum administrator*
Oldenburg, Richard Erik *auction house executive*
Pesner, Carole Manishin *art gallery owner*
Platnick, Norman I. *curator, entomologist*
Rosenbaum, Joan Hannah *museum director*
Sachs, Samuel, II, *museum director*
Simon, Ronald Charles *curator*
Stiassny, Melanie L.J. *curator*
Storr, Robert *curator, art educator*
Sutton, Karen E. *administrator*
Tobach, Ethel *retired curator*
Toll, Barbara Elizabeth *art gallery director*
Trippi, Peter *museum director*
Tyson, Neil DeGrasse *museum director*
Wardropper, Ian Bruce *museum curator, educator*
Weinberg, Adam D. *museum director*
Willis, Carol *museum director*
Wright, Gwendolyn *art center director, writer, educator*
Zugazagoitia, Julian *museum director*

Ossining
Cadge, William Fleming *art director, photographer*

Rochester
Bannon, Anthony Leo *museum director*
Holcomb, Grant, III, *museum director*

Sands Point
Olian, JoAnne Constance *curator, art historian*

Southampton
Lerner, Abram *retired museum director, artist*

Stuyvesant
Tripp, Susan Gerwe *museum director*

Syracuse
Skoler, Celia Rebecca *retired art gallery director*
Trop, Sandra *museum administrator*

Tupper Lake
Welsh, Peter Corbett *museum consultant, historian*

Utica
Schweizer, Paul Douglas *museum director*

Wantagh
Smits, Edward John *museum consultant*

Waterford
Gold, James Paul *museum director*

Willsboro
Gillilland, Thomas *art gallery director*

NORTH CAROLINA

Charlotte
Boggs, Willene Graythen *property manager, oil and gas broker, consultant*
Nicholson, Freda Hyams *museum executive, medical educator*

Pinehurst
Broadhurst, Judith Buck *art gallery owner*

Raleigh
Kuhler, Renaldo Gillet *retired museum official, scientific illustrator*
Wheeler, Lawrence Jefferson *art museum director*

Salisbury
Shalkop, Robert Leroy *retired museum director*

Winston Salem
Rauschenberg, Bradford Lee *museum researcher*
Whittington, Stephen Lunn *museum director*

OHIO

Akron
Kahan, Mitchell Douglas *art museum director*

Athens
Ahrens, Kent *museum director, art historian*

Cincinnati
Brown, Daniel *art consultant*
Crew, Spencer *museum administrator*
Desmarais, Charles Joseph *museum director, writer, editor*
Rigaud, Edwin Joseph *museum administrator*
Rogers, Millard Foster, Jr., *art museum director emeritus*
Rub, Timothy F. *museum director*
Timpano, Anne *museum director, art historian*
Weston, Phyllis Jean *art gallery director*

Cleveland
Reid, Katharine Lee *museum director*

Dayton
Meister, Mark Jay *museum director, professional society administrator*
Nyerges, Alexander Lee *museum director*

Kirtland
Johnston, Stanley Howard, Jr., *rare books curator, bibliographer*

Mentor
Miller, Frances Suzanne *historic site curator*

University Heights
Cook, Alexander Burns *museum curator, artist, educator*

Youngstown
Ruffer, David Gray *museum director, former college president*

OREGON

Milwaukie
Eichinger, Marilynne Hildegarde *museum administrator*

Portland
Jenkins, Donald John *museum administrator*
Taylor, J(ocelyn) Mary *museum administrator, zoologist, educator*

PENNSYLVANIA

Altoona
Moffitt, Charles William *art gallery director*

Chadds Ford
Duff, James Henry *museum director, environmental administrator*

Erie
Vanco, John L. *art museum director*

Fort Washington
Wint, Dennis Michael *museum director*

Harrisburg
Franco, Barbara Alice *museum director*
Mahey, John Andrew *retired museum director*

Merion Station
Camp, Kimberly N. *museum administrator, artist*

Philadelphia
Bantel, Linda Mae *former museum curator, consultant*
Carter, John Swain *museum administrator, consultant*
d'Harnoncourt, Anne *museum director, museum administrator*
Fisher, Wesley Andrew *museum director*
Gould, Claudia *museum director*
Hough, Melissa Ellen *curator, museum director*
Kolb, Nancy Dwyer *museum director*
McNamara, Kevin John *museum administrator*
Rouse, Terrie S. *museum administrator*
Shoemaker, Innis Howe *art museum curator*
Turner, Evan Hopkins *retired art museum director*

Pittsburgh
Dawson, Mary Ruth *curator, educator*
DeWalt, Bill *museum director*
King, Elaine A. *curator, art historian, critic*
Werner, Jane *museum administrator*

Reading
Dietrich, Bruce Leinbach *planetarium and museum administrator, astronomer, educator*

Strasburg
Lindsay, George Carroll *former museum director*

University Park
Muhlert, Jan Keene *art museum director*

Villanova
Scott, Robert Montgomery *museum executive, lawyer*

RHODE ISLAND

Newport
Coxe, Trudy *museum administrator, former state official*
Tinney, Harle Hope Hanson *museum administrator, owner*

Providence
Fishman, Bernard Philip *museum director*

Saunderstown
Leavitt, Thomas Whittlesey *retired museum director, educator*

SOUTH CAROLINA

Bishopville
Cox, Janson L. *museum administrator*

Camden
Craig, Joanna Burbank *historic site director*

Chesnee
Saunders, J. Farrell *historic site director*

Greenville
Davis, Joan Carroll *retired museum director*

Mount Pleasant
Macdonald, Robert Rigg, Jr., *retired museum director*

Pawleys Island
Noble, Joseph Veach *fine arts administrator*
Tarbox, Gurdon Lucius, Jr., *retired museum executive*

Walterboro
Drain, Danny *museum director*

TENNESSEE

Crossville
Elam, Leslie Albert *retired museum administrator*

Greeneville
Corey, Mark *historic site director*

Memphis
Czestochowski, Joseph Stephen *museum administrator*

TEXAS

Austin
Friis-Hansen, Dana *museum director*
Johnson, Eileen *curator, educator, commissioner*
Theriot, Edward C. *museum director*

El Paso
Sipiora, Leonard Paul *retired museum director, art appraiser*

Fort Worth
Auping, Michael G. *curator*

Fredericksburg
Manhart, Marcia Y(ockey) *art museum director*

Glen Rose
Blankenship, Jenny Mary *museum administrator*

Houston
Bowron, Edgar Peters *art museum curator, administrator*
Helfenstein, Josef *museum director*
Latimer, Roy Truett *museum executive*
Lee, Janie C. *curator*
Marzio, Peter Cort *museum director*
Mayo, Marti *museum director, curator*
Tucker, Anne Wilkes *curator, photography historian and critic, lecturer*

Irving
Piqué, Fernando Rafael *international art dealer, artist*

San Antonio
Chiego, William J. *museum director*
Endresen, Lisa Castro *curator*
Jansen-Brown, Angelika Charlotte *art museum director, independent curator*

UTAH

Hurricane
Adams, Margaret Bernice *retired museum official*

Salt Lake City
George, Sarah B. *museum director*
Oakes, Claudia *museum administrator*

VERMONT

Manchester
Kouwenhoven, Gerrit Wolphertsen *retired museum director*

Montpelier
Dumville, John P. *historic site director*

Shaftsbury
Williams, Robert Joseph *museum director, educator*

VIRGINIA

Alexandria
Gaynor, Margaret Cryor *program director*
Lundeberg, Philip Karl Boraas *curator, historian*
Patterson, Lillian Stanton *curator*

Charlottesville
Hartz, Jill *museum director*
Linden, Peppy G. *museum director*
O'Shaughnessy, Andrew Jackson *historic site research director, education educator*

Falls Church
Phillips, Laughlin *art museum chairman emeritus, former magazine editor*

Fredericksburg
Foster, Vonita White *museum director*

Lexington
Lynn, Michael A. *historic site director*

Lynchburg
Elson, James Martin *retired historic foundation director*

Mount Vernon
Rees, James Conway, IV, *historic site administrator*

Natural Bridge
Watkins, Angela Marie *museum administrator, writer*

Onancock
Verrill, John Howard *museum director*

Roanoke
Fitzgerald, Mary Eileen *museum program director*
Taubman, Jenny *museum program director*

Sterling
Friedheim, Jerry Warden *museum consultant*

Tazewell
Weeks, Ross Leonard, Jr., *museum executive*

Williamsburg
Christison, Muriel Branham *retired art museum director, fine arts educator*

WASHINGTON

Bellevue
Douglas, Diane Miriam *museum director*
Warren, James Ronald *retired museum director, writer, columnist*

Bellingham
Clark-Langager, Sarah Ann *curator, director, university official*
Livesay, Thomas Andrew *museum administrator, lecturer*

Redmond
Sobey, Edwin J. C. *museum director, oceanographer, consultant*

Seattle
Bufano, Ralph A. *museum executive*
Garfield, Leonard *museum director*
Shirley, Donna *museum director, former aerospace engineer*

Spokane
Mobley, Karen Ruth *art gallery director*

Tacoma
Callan, Josi Irene *museum director*

Wenatchee
Williams, Keith Roy *museum director*

WISCONSIN

Madison
Garver, Thomas Haskell *curator, art consultant, writer*
Westphal, Klaus Wilhelm *university museum director*

Milwaukee
Temmer, James Donald *museum director*

WYOMING

Cheyenne
Wilson-McKee, Marie *museum director*

CANADA

ALBERTA

Canmore
Janes, Robert Roy *museum executive, archaeologist, museum consultant, editor*

BRITISH COLUMBIA

Victoria
Finlay, James Campbell *retired museum director*
Segger, Martin Joseph *museum director, art history educator*

NEW BRUNSWICK

Fredericton
Lumsden, Ian Gordon *art gallery director*

NEWFOUNDLAND

Saint John's
Grattan, Patricia Elizabeth *retired art gallery director*

ONTARIO

London
Poole, Nancy Geddes *art gallery curator*

Ottawa
McAvity, John Gillis *museum director, association executive, museologist*

QUEBEC

Montreal
Brisebois, Marcel *museum director*

ENGLAND

London
Cuno, James *art museum director*

FRANCE

Paris
Rosenberg, Pierre Max *museum director*

ADDRESS UNPUBLISHED

Abbott, Rebecca Phillips *museum director, art consultant, photographer*
Armstrong, Thomas Newton, III, *art and garden specialist*
Beach, Milo C. *former art museum director*
Belkov, Meredith Ann *landmark administrator*
Bishop, Budd Harris *retired museum administrator, artist*
Brown, Suzanne Wiley *museum director*
Buck, Robert Treat, Jr., *gallery director, former museum director, educator*
Castile, Rand (Jesse Randolph III) *retired museum director*
Cikovsky, Nicolai, Jr., *retired curator, art history educator*
Coke, Frank Van Deren *museum director, photographer*
Deutsch, James I. *curator*
Deutschman, Louise Tolliver *curator*
DuBois, Alan Beekman *art museum curator*
Ebie, William D. *retired museum director*
Emery, Alan Roy *museum executive, business executive*
Fri, Robert Wheeler *museum director*
Friedman, Martin *museum director, arts adviser*
Glad, Suzanne Lockley *retired museum director*
Graves, Sid Foster, Jr., *retired library and museum director*
Grossman, Cissy *curator, art historian, art exhibit designer, Judaica connoisseur, appraiser*
Harrington, Beverly *museum director*
Hayes, Charles Franklin, III, *museum research consultant*
Hellmers, Norman Donald *retired historic site director*
Houlihan, Patrick Thomas *museum director*
Jacobowitz, Ellen Sue *museum curator, museum and temple administrator*
Kahn, James Steven *retired museum director*
Knowles, Elizabeth Pringle *museum director*
Lane, John Rodger *art museum director*
Lutts, Ralph Herbert *scholar, educator, museum administrator*
Mercuri, Joan B. *museum administrator*
Metcalf, William Edwards *educator, museum curator*
Millard, Charles Warren, III, *museum director, writer*
Monkman, Betty Claire *curator*
Mulryan, Lenore Hoag *art curator, author*
Naeve, Milo Merle *curator, director*
Nasgaard, Roald *museum curator*
Newsome, Steven Cameron *former museum director*
Nickles, Shelley Kaplan *curator, educator*
Pal, Pratapaditya *curator*
Perrot, Paul Norman *museum director*
Pilgrim, Dianne Hauserman *retired museum director*
Porter, Daniel Reed, III, *museum director*
Powell, Earl Alexander, III, *art museum director*
Prakapas, Eugene Joseph *art gallery director*
Radice, Anne-Imelda *museum director*
Reuther, Ronald Theodore *museum director*
Robertson, Charles James *museum director emeritus*
Rouse, Terrie Suzitte *former museum director*
Russell, Helen Diane *retired museum curator, educator*
Ryskamp, Charles Andrew *museum executive, educator*
Schneider, Janet M. *arts administrator, curator, painter*
Sennema, David Carl *museum and arts administration consultant*
Shimoda, Jerry Yasutaka *retired national historic park manager*
Siano, Mary Ann *art gallery director*
Skotheim, Robert Allen *retired college and museum administrator*
Skramstad, Harold Kenneth, Jr., *museum consultant*
Smith, Marjorie Aileen Matthews *museum director*
Steadman, David Wilton *retired museum official, church deacon*
Stearns, Robert Leland *curator*
Stewart, Robert Gordon *former museum curator*
Stuart, Joseph Martin *art museum administrator*
Summerfield, John Robert *textile curator*
Thyzel, Tim *curator, artist, educator*
Vail, Mary Barbara *publicist*
Walker, Roslyn Adele *retired museum director*
Way, Jacob Edson, III, *museum director, realtor*
Wieser, Siegfried *planetarium executive director*
Wolfe, Townsend Durant, III, *retired art museum director, curator*

INDUSTRY: MANUFACTURING
See also **FINANCE: FINANCIAL SERVICES**

UNITED STATES

ALABAMA

Albertville
Rice, Fuhrman D. (Runt Rice) *retired paper company executive*

Birmingham
Bailey, Kelly Frank *occupational health company executive*
Bennett, J. Claude *pharmaceutical executive*
Bennett, Joe Claude *pharmaceutical executive*
Carman, Thomas W. *health services company executive*
Chrencik, Frank *chemical company executive*
Cohen-DeMarco, Gale Maureen *pharmaceutical executive*
Crawford, Mac *health and medical products executive*
Daniel, Kenneth Rule *former iron and steel manufacturing company executive*
Dickerson, James H., Jr., *health products executive*
Furnas, Howard Earl *business executive*
Gorrie, Miller *construction executive*
Hall, Robert Alan *construction company executive*
Harbert, Bill Lebold *retired construction corporation executive*
James, Donald M. *construction materials executive*
Khan, Ejaz A. *chemicals executive, controller*
McMahon, John J., Jr., *metal processing company executive*
Neal, Phil Hudson, Jr., *manufacturing executive*
Richey, Van L. *steel company executive*
Sklenar, Herbert Anthony *industrial products manufacturing company executive*
Smith, Clyde M. *engineering and construction executive*
Styslinger, Lee Joseph, Jr., *manufacturing executive*
Tanner, Anthony J. *healthcare services corporation executive*
Tomkins, Mark E. *manufacturing executive*

Dothan
Marks, Marilyn *trailer company executive*
Palko, Lorri M. *automotive company executive*

Huntsville
King, Olin B. *electronics systems company executive*
Sapp, A. Eugene, Jr., *former electronics executive*

Madison
Stone, Frank Bruce *contractor*

Montgomery
Taylor, Watson Robbins *construction company executive*

Muscle Shoals
Roy, Amit H. *agricultural executive*

Opelika
Jenkins, Richard Lee *manufacturing executive*

Prattville
Lambert, Meg Stringer *construction executive, architect, interior designer*

Roanoke
Terry, Roy D. *apparel manufacturing company executive*

Tuscaloosa
Fowler, Conrad Murphree *retired manufacturing company executive*

ALASKA

Big Lake
DeLoach, Robert Edgar *corporate executive*

Haines
Kaufman, David Graham *construction executive*

Juneau
Smith, Charles Anthony *business executive*

ARIZONA

Carefree
Alexander, Judd Harris *retired paper company executive*
Garr, Carl Robert *manufacturing executive*

Chandler
Elliott, Lee Ann *company executive, former government official*
Joyce, Kenneth Thomas *electronics company executive*
McGinnis, Robert William *electronics company executive*

Flagstaff
Roe, Richard C. *industry consultant, former home furnishings manufacturing executive*

Gilbert
Earnhardt, Hal J., III, *automotive executive*
Stroble-Thompson, Colette Mary Houle *plastering and stucco company executive*

Glendale
Hamilton, Darded Cole *plastics company executive*

Laveen
Wade, Tyra V. *manufacturing executive*

Mesa
DeRosa, Francis Dominic *chemical company executive*
Luth, William Clair *retired research manager*

Paradise Valley
McKennon, Keith Robert *chemical company executive*

Patagonia
Bonner, Herbert Dwight *construction management educator*

Peoria
Cook, Mary Margaret *steamfitter, educator*

Phoenix
Bryant, Andrew *electronics executive*
Carter, Ronald Martin, Sr., *pharmaceutical company executive*
Crane, Ross *electronics executive*
Dewane, John Richard *retired manufacturing company executive, consultant, business owner*
Franke, William Augustus *corporate executive*
Fraser, Martin *automobile parts executive*
Gallagher, Philip *electronics executive*
Giedt, Bruce Alan *paper company executive*
Giltner, Phil *food distributing executive*
Jenkins, Maynard *automotive executive*
Jewett, Patrick *electronics executive*
Kamins, Edward *electronics executive*
Kitzman, Jerry Matson *pharmaceutical executive*
Klepinger, John William *trailer manufacturing company executive*
Mardian, Daniel *construction company director*
Martensen, Barbara *electronics executive*
Miller, Janice *electronics executive*
Motsenbocker, Rex Alan *construction company executive*
Peru, Ramiro G. *metal products executive*
Rapier, David *electronics executive*
Stegmayer, Joseph Henry *housing industry executive*
Thompson, Herbert Ernest *tool and die company executive*
Tsang, Raymond *electronics executive*
Vallee, Roy *electronics company executive*
White, Edward Allen *electronics company executive*

Prescott
Parkhurst, Charles Lloyd *electronics company executive*

Scottsdale
Freedman, Stanley Marvin *manufacturing executive*
Gans, Eugene Howard *cosmetic and pharmaceutical company executive, consultant*
Grenell, James Henry *retired manufacturing company executive*
Howard, William Gates, Jr., *electronics company executive*
Jesky, T. J. *pharmaceutical products executive*
Lloyd, Eugene Walter *retired construction company executive*
Rethore, Bernard Gabriel *retired manufacturing and mining company executive*
Walsh, Edward Joseph *toiletries and food company executive*

Sedona
Bell, Robert Matthew *pharmaceutical company consultant*

Surprise
Lazar, Max Seymour *retired pharmaceutical company executive*

Tempe
Penley, Larry Edward *management educator*

Tolleson
Etchart, Mike *agricultural products company executive*

Tucson
Acker, Loren Calvin *medical instrument company executive*
Finley, Dorothy Hunt *beverage distribution company executive*
Francesconi, Louise L. *electronics executive*
Leonard, Michael A. *retired automotive executive*
Meeker, Robert Eldon *retired manufacturing company executive*

ARKANSAS

Berryville
Prpich, Michael Frank *food company manager*

El Dorado
Nelson, Jerry R. *food company executive*

Fort Smith
Boreham, Roland Stanford, Jr., *electric motor company executive*

Hot Springs National Park
Schroeder, Donald Perry *retired food products company executive*

Leachville
Adams, Eddie *textiles executive*

Little Rock
Hickingbotham, Frank D. *food product executive*
McCoy, Stuart Sherman *manufacturing executive*
Shell, Robert J. *construction executive*

North Little Rock
Givens, John Kenneth *manufacturing executive*

Siloam Springs
McMennamy, Roger Neal *automotive executive*

Springdale
Baker, Mike *food products executive*
Baledge, Les R. *food products executive, lawyer*
Beach, Jean Mrha *food products executive*
Dunn, Jeri R. *food products executive*
Hankins, Steven G. *food company executive*
Huett, Greg *food products executive*
Igli, Kevin J. *food products executive*
Leatherby, Dennis *food products executive*
Lee, Greg W. *food company executive*
Pless, Rodney S. *food products executive*
Rose, Kenneth L. *food products executive*
Schaffer, Archie, III, *food products executive*
Tyson, Donald John *food company executive*
Tyson, John H. *food products executive*
Van Bebber, David L. *food products executive*

Stuttgart
Bell, Richard Eugene *grain and food company executive*

CALIFORNIA

Agoura Hills
Currie, Malcolm Roderick *aerospace and automotive executive, scientist*

Alameda
Monahan, John *medical products executive*

Alamo
Liggett, Lawrence Melvin *vacuum equipment manufacturing company executive*

Aliso Viejo
Trivelpiece, Craig Evan *computer electronics executive*

Anaheim
Baumgartner, Anton Edward *automotive sales professional*
Halligan, Joseph William *snack food industry executive*

Atherton
Goodman, Sam Richard *electronics company executive*
Hogan, Clarence Lester *retired electronics executive*

Bakersfield
Akers, Tom, Jr., *cotton broker, consultant*
Grimm, Bob *food products executive*
Lundquist, Gene Alan *cotton company executive*
Thomason, Scott *automobile executive*

Belmont
Endriz, John Guiry *retired electronics executive*

Berkeley
Barkin, Ronald S. *medical products executive*
Castello, John L. *pharmaceutical executive*
Dina, Dino *medical company executive*
Janney, Daniel S. *health products executive*

Beverly Hills
Leong, Margaret *construction executive*
Willson, James Douglas *aerospace executive*
Winthrop, John *wines and spirits company executive*

Bishop
Naso, Valerie Joan *automotive dealership executive, travel company operator*

Burbank
Joseff, Joan Castle *manufacturing executive*
Raulinaitis, Pranas Algis *electronics executive, consultant*

Burlingame
McGraw, Benjamin F., III, *biotechnology executive*
Mhatra, Nagesh *health products executive*

Calabasas
Cohen, William *construction executive*
Iacobellis, Sam Frank *retired aerospace company executive*
Laney, Michael L. *manufacturing executive*
Milne, Gordon A. *construction executive, mortgage company executive*

Camarillo
Boskovich, George, Jr., *food products executive*
Weiss, Carl *aerospace company executive*

Carlsbad
Aschenbrenner, Frank Aloysious *former diversified manufacturing company executive*
Carlo, Dennis J. *biotechnology company executive*
Crooke, Stanley Thomas *pharmaceutical executive*

PROFESSIONAL INDEX 5733 INDUSTRY: MANUFACTURING

Glavin, James B. *biotechnology executive*
Hammes, Michael Noel *automotive company executive*
Robb, Robert *biotechnology company executive*
Turner, Lyle C. *biotechnology company executive*

Carmel
Alich, John Arthur, Jr., *manufacturing executive*

Carmel Valley
Kasson, James Matthews *electronics executive*

Carmichael
Rich, Albert Clark *solar energy manufacturing executive*

Carson
Bensussen, Gale *health products company executive*

Castro Valley
Thorburn, Lisa A. *acoustical consulting company executive*

Chatsworth
Bhartia, Prakash *defense research management executive, researcher, educator*

City Of Commerce
Johnson, Keith Liddell *chemical company executive*

City Of Industry
Perry, William Joseph *food processing company executive*

Coachella
Barker, Douglas P. *food products executive*

Colton
Smith, Phillip J. *food products executive*

Colusa
Carter, Jane Foster *agricultural products executive*

Concord
Thompson, Jeremiah Beiseker *international medical business executive, sinologist*

Corona
Chao, Allen Y. *pharmaceutical executive*
Weisemann, Claus *pharmaceutical executive*

Corona Del Mar
Wolf, Karl Everett *aerospace and communications corporation executive*

Coronado
Dalton, Matt *retired foundry executive*
Sack, Edgar Albert *electronics company executive*

Costa Mesa
Alexiou, James *electronics executive*
Brady, John Patrick, Jr., *electronics educator, consultant*
Hazewinkel, Van *manufacturing executive*
Lerner, Sandy *cosmetics executive*
Mohajer, Dineh *cosmetics company executive*
Panic, Milan *pharmaceutical and health products company executive*
Scarborough, Stephen J. *construction executive*
Svendsen, Arthur E. *construction executive*
Thierstein, Hans *biotechnology company executive*

Coto De Caza
Bezar, Gilbert Edward *retired aerospace company executive, volunteer*

Culver City
Leve, Alan Donald *electronic materials manufacturing company owner, executive*

Cupertino
Mathias, Leslie Michael *electronic manufacturing company executive*

Cypress
Bowlus, Brad A. *health care company executive*
Garrett, Sharon *health services company executive*
Konowiecki, Joseph S. *health care company executive*
Scott, Gregory W. *health care company executive*

Davis
Bennett, Alan B. *research and development company executive, educator*

Delano
Caratan, Anton G. *food products executive*
Caratan, George *food products executive*

Dublin
Mettinger, Karl Lennart *pharmaceutical executive*
Rubinfeld, Joseph *biotechnology company executive*
Whetten, John D. *food products executive*

El Segundo
Eckert, Robert A. *manufacturing executive*
Kelble, Jack R. *electronics executive*
Manchester, Craig *construction executive*
Rosenfield, Gene *construction executive*

Emeryville
McEachern, Alexander *electronics company executive*
Moran, Mark *medical products executive*
Pien, Howard *pharmaceutical executive*

Escalon
Barton, Gerald Lee *farming company executive*

Fair Oaks
Chernev, Melvin *retired beverage company executive*

Foster City
Bischofberger, Norbert W. *medical products company executive*
Inouye, Michael K. *medical products company executive*
Martin, John C. *medical products executive*
Rudolph, John *construction executive*

Fremont
Chan, Fred S.L. *electronics company executive*
Chuang, Kevin *electronics manufacturing executive*
Ciffone, Donald *electronics company executive*
Conlisk, Raimon L. *high technology management consulting executive*
Guire, Ronald W. *electronics company executive*
Huang, Robert *electronics manufacturing executive*
Korn, Laurence *health products executive*
Lehrer, Steven *health products executive*
Rice, Donald B. *biotechnology company executive*
Rich, William E. *biotechnology executive*
Rugge, Henry Ferdinand *medical products executive*
Rusch, Thomas William *manufacturing executive*
Shah, Ajay *electronics company executive*
Wolf, Hans Abraham *retired pharmaceutical company executive*
Zimmer, George *men's apparel executive*

Fresno
Baloian, Edward *food products executive*
Baloian, Timothy *food products executive*
Emigh, Mike *agricultural products company executive*

Fullerton
Garrett, Scott T. *medical products executive*
Miller, Arnold *electronics executive*
Wareham, John L. *electronics executive*
Wareham, John P. *medical products executive*

Gardena
Kanner, Edwin Benjamin *electrical manufacturing company executive*
Morton, James Carnes, Jr., *automotive executive*

Hayward
Glaze, Thomas A. *biotechnology company executive*
Greetham, Elizabeth M. *health products executive*
Minzner, Dean Frederick *aviation company executive*
Pinckert, Warren, II, *pharmaceutical executive*
Pouletty, Philippe *health products executive*
Russell, Norman J.W. *biotechnology company executive*
Santi, Daniel V. *biotechnology company executive*
Taylor, Craig C. *biotechnology company executive*
Van Wart, Harold E. *biotechnology company executive*

Hillsborough
Keller, John Francis *retired wine company executive, former mayor*

Hollywood
Parks, Robert Myers *appliance manufacturing company executive*

Huntington Beach
Kovach, Ronald *footwear manufacturing executive*
Licata, Paul James *health products executive*

Indio
Bailey, Higgins D. *health products executive*
Tachovsky, Thomas G. *medical company executive*
York, Douglas Arthur *manufacturing and construction company executive*

Irvine
Allnut, Robert I. *pharmaceutical executive*
Alspach, Philip Halliday *manufacturing executive*
Anido, Vincente *biotechnology company executive*
Broadhurst, Norman Neil *food products executive*
Click, James H. *automotive executive*
Copeland, Lawrence R. *construction company executive*
Cortney, Michael C. *construction executive, civil engineer*
Halvorsen, Clay A. *construction executive*
McNeil, Robert G. *biotechnology company executive*
Mussallem, Michael A. *healthcare company executive*
Mussey, Joseph Arthur *health and medical product executive*
Olson, Gene L. *food products executive*
Pyott, David Edmund Ian *pharmaceutical executive*
Shrotriya, Rajesh C. *medical company executive*
Simmon, Vincent Fowler *biotechnology executive*
Wetterau, Mark S. *food products/distributor executive*

Jackson
Halvorson, William *former automotive executive*

La Jolla
Drake, Hudson Billings *aerospace and electronics company executive*
Elander, Richard Paul *consultant, retired pharmaceutical executive*
Geckler, Richard Delph *metal products company executive, retired*
Stevens, Paul Irving *manufacturing executive*
Todd, Harry Williams *aircraft propulsion system company executive*

La Puente
Hitchcock, Frederick E. "Fritz", Jr., *automotive company executive*

Lafayette
Lewis, Sheldon Noah *technology consultant*

Laguna Beach
Wong, Wallace *medical supplies company executive, real estate investor*

Laguna Hills
Rossiter, Bryant William *chemistry consultant*

Laguna Niguel
Ricci, Robert Ronald *manufacturing executive*

Lake Forest
Haggerty, Charles A. *retired electronics executive*

Lake View Terrace
Mann, Alfred *pharmaceutical executive*

Larkspur
Price, Tom *automotive sales executive*

Livingston
Carter, Paul *food products executive*
Fox, Robert August *food company executive*

Lodi
Elkins, Carl *food products executive*

Lompoc
Bongiorno, James William *electronics company executive*

Long Beach
Berenato, Joseph C. *manufacturing executive*
Heiser, James S. *manufacturing executive*

Los Altos
Beer, Clara Louise Johnson *retired electronics executive*

Los Angeles
Adler, Fred Peter *retired electronics company executive*
Ash, Roy Lawrence *business executive*
Atchley, Raymond Deval *technology company executive*
Campion, Robert Thomas *manufacturing executive*
Davidson, Robert C., Jr., *manufacturing executive*
dePaolis, Potito Umberto *food company executive*
Emanuele, R.M. *pharmaceutical executive*
Gerstell, A. Frederick *aggregates, asphalt and concrete manufacturing executive*
Hutchins, Joan Morthland *manufacturing executive, farmer*
Irani, Ray R. *oil, gas and chemical company executive*
Karatz, Bruce E. *construction executive*
Mager, Artur *retired aerospace company executive, consultant*
Mall, William John, Jr., *aerospace executive, retired Air Force general*
Marciano, Maurice *apparel executive*
Palevsky, Max *industrialist*
Perkins, William Clinton *manufacturing executive*
Ramer, Lawrence Jerome *corporation executive*
Rodstein, Richard M. *apparel executive*
Segil, Larraine Diane *materials company executive*
Spindler, Paul *corporate executive, consultant*
Tamkin, S. Jerome *business executive, consultant*
Ziering, Michael *medical products executive*

Lynwood
Nelson, Maurice S., Jr., *metal products company executive*

Malibu
Dankanyin, Robert John *international business executive*

Mariposa
Sutherland, Gail Russell *retired industrial equipment manufacturing company executive*

Mckinleyville
Thueson, David Orel *pharmaceutical executive, researcher, writer, educator*

Menlo Park
Barkas, Alexander E. *biotechnology company executive*
Belaroff, Joseph K. *pharmaceutical executive*
Bremser, George, Jr., *electronics company executive*
Carlson, Curtis R. *electronics research industry executive*
Jackson, Jeanne Pellegren *apparel executive*
Kalinske, Thomas J. *education, video game and toy company executive*
Kamin, William Stephen *food company executive, photographer*
Kashnow, Richard A. *electronics executive*
Okkarma, Thomas B. *biotechnology company executive*
Saifer, Mark Gary Pierce *pharmaceutical executive*
Wilson, James N. *health products executive*

Milpitas
Cannon, Michael R. *electronics executive*
Everett, David *electronics executive*
Granchelli, Ralph S. *company executive*
Gray, Bruce *computer and electronics company executive*
Lin Chien, Chester *electronics executive*
London, Craig *electronics executive*
Moore, George W. *electronics executive*
O'Connor, Kevin *electronics executive*
Onetto, Marc *manufacturing executive*
Patel, Kiran *manufacturing executive*
Roddick, David Bruce *construction company executive*
Rollinson, Frederick (Rick), III, *manufacturing executive*
Stephens, Bob *electronic executive*
Swanson, Robert H. Jr. *electronics executive*
Tang, Joe *electronics executive*
Wang, Susan S. *manufacturing executive*
Zohouri, Saeed *electronics company executive*

Mission Viejo
Faley, Robert Lawrence *retired instruments company executive*

Modesto
Riesenbeck, Ronald *supermarket executive*
Youga, Tony *winery executive*

Montecito
Meghreblian, Robert Vartan *manufacturing executive, physicist*

Monterey
Hanlon, James Allison *confectionery company executive*
Meyers, Gerald A. *metal products executive*

Mountain View
Clarke, C. Boyd *medical products executive*
Kisner, Daniel *electronics executive*
Perry, Michael S. *biotechnology company executive*
Reidel, Art *health products executive*

Napa
Eissmann, Walter James *consulting company executive*

Wahl, Howard Wayne *retired construction company executive, engineer*

Newark
Mueller, Nancy *food products executive*

Newport Beach
Bennett, Bruce W. *construction company executive, civil engineer*
Crean, John C. *retired housing and recreational vehicles manufacturing company executive*
Johnson, William Stanley *metal distribution company executive*
Jones, Roger Wayne *electronics executive*
Lyon, William *builder*
Rogers, Robert Reed *manufacturing executive*

Norco
Eisen, Hilda *food products executive*

North Hills
Boeckmann, Herbert F., II, *automotive executive*

Novato
Price, Frederic D. *pharmaceutical executive*

Oakland
Andrasick, James Stephen *diversified company executive*
Cronk, William F., III, *food products executive*
Heinrich, Daniel J. *chemicals executive*
Kahn, Timothy F. *food products company executive*
Koplin, Donald Leroy *health products executive, consumer advocate*
Matschullat, Robert W. *chemicals executive*
Rogers, T. Gary *food products company executive*
Saunders, Ward Bishop, Jr., *retired aluminum company executive*

Orange
Dimick, Neil Francis *medical products wholesale executive*
Hamann, Dennis *food products executive*
Kaempen, Charles Edward *manufacturing executive*

Oxnard
Gill, David *food products executive*
Kavli, Fred *retired manufacturing executive, retired engineering executive*

Palm Desert
Epstein, Marvin Morris *retired construction company executive*

Palm Springs
Brain, Jesse *manufacturing executive*

Palo Alto
Balzhiser, Richard Earl *research and development company executive*
Couder, Alain *personal computer manufacturing company executive*
DeLustro, Frank Anthony *biomedical company executive, research immunologist*
Friedman, Paul A. *biotechnology company executive*
Goff, Harry Russell *retired manufacturing company executive*
Kincaid, Judith Wells *electronics company executive*
Kung, Frank F. *biotechnology and life sciences investor, venture capitalist*
Lange, Louis G. *health products executive*
Mcglynn, Martin M *biotechnology company executive*
Schwartz, John J. *biotechnology company executive*
Staprans, Armand *electronics executive*
Whitfield, Roy A. *pharmaceutical executive*
Wick, Michael M. *biotechnology executive*
Winfield, Roy A. *pharmaceutical company executive*

Palos Verdes Estates
Mackenbach, Frederick W. *welding products manufacturing company executive*

Palos Verdes Peninsula
Grant, Robert Ulysses *retired manufacturing company executive*
Leone, William Charles *retired manufacturing executive*
Pfund, Edward Theodore, Jr., *electronics company executive*
Thomas, Hayward *manufacturing executive*
Wilson, Theodore Henry *retired electronics company executive, aerospace engineer*

Pasadena
Bishop, Robert Calvin *pharmaceutical company executive*
Marlen, James S. *chemical, plastics and building materials manufacturing company executive*
McNulty, James F. *engineering, construction company executive*
Neal, Philip Mark *diversified manufacturing executive*
O'Bryant, Daniel R. *manufacturing executive*
Tollenaere, Lawrence Robert *retired industrial products company executive*
Watson, Noel G. *construction executive*

Pico Rivera
Collanton, Greg *manufacturing executive, controller*
Cowan, Richard *manufacturing executive*

Playa Del Rey
Mishelevich, David Jacob *medical company executive, consultant*

Pleasanton
Bond, David F. *food products executive*
Ching, David T. *food products executive*
Gordon, Robert A. *food products executive*
Magelitz, Larry L. *construction company executive*
Weiss, Robert Stephen *medical manufacturing company financial executive*

Pomona
Brown, Ronald G. *automotive company executive*
Hogarty, Charles J. *automotive executive*

Portola Valley
Purl, O. Thomas *retired electronics company executive*

Poway
Barnhart, Douglas Edward *construction company executive*

Prather
Coren, Lance Scott *consulting firm executive*

Rancho Dominguez
Janura, Jan Arol *apparel manufacturing executive*

Rancho Mirage
Greenbaum, James Richard *liquor distributing company executive, real estate developer*

Rancho Murieta
Irelan, Robert Withers *retired metal products executive*

Rancho Santa Fe
Jordan, Charles Morrell *retired automotive designer*
Step, Eugene Lee *retired pharmaceutical company executive*

Redding
Emerson, Red *lumber company executive*
Emmerson, Archie Aldis (Red Emmerson) *sawmill owner*
Emmerson, Mark *paper/lumber company executive*

Redlands
Skomal, Edward Nelson *aerospace company executive, electromagnetic environments consultant*

Redondo Beach
Dockstader, Jack Lee *retired electronics executive*
Kagiwada, Reynold Shigeru *electronics executive*

Redwood City
Hanf, Michael W. *construction executive*
Hawkins, Trip *electronics company executive*
Howard, Russell J. *biotechnology company executive*
Matthews, William *health products executive*
Nosler, Peter Cole *construction company executive*
Selick, Howard E. (Barry Selick) *biotechnology executive*
Simon, Nicholas J., III, *medical products executive*
Wang, Chen Chi *electronics company, real estate, finance company, investment services, and international trade executive*
Williams, Duston *electronics company executive*

Rescue
Ackerly, Wendy Saunders *construction company executive*

Richmond
Cohen, Abraham Ezekiel *retired health care company executive*
Freiman, Paul E. *pharmaceutical company executive*
Lanphier, Edward O., II, *medical company executive*
Renton, Hollings C. *health products executive*

Riverside
Caudill, Edward B. *automotive executive*
Chamberlain, Willard Thomas *retired metals company executive*
Kummer, Glenn F. *retired manufacturing executive*
Plowman, Boyd R. *automotive executive*

Rocklin
Tal, Jacob *electronics executive*

Ross
Nicholson, William Joseph *forest products consultant*

Sacramento
Aldrich, Thomas Albert *former brewing executive, consultant*
Baccigaluppi, Roger John *agricultural company executive*
Lucchetti, David J. *manufacturing executive*
Mack, Edward Gibson *retired business executive*
Venosdel, Daniel Paul *agricultural association administrator*

Salinas
Drever, Mark *food products executive*
Esquivel, Joe G. *food products executive*
Esquivel, Mary *agricultural products company executive*
Taylor, Steven Bruce *agriculture company executive*

San Anselmo
Chiaverini, John Edward *construction company executive*

San Carlos
Gutow, Bernard Sidney *packaging manufacturing company executive*

San Clemente
Clark, Earnest Hubert, Jr., *tool company executive*
Steinberg, Howard *chemical company executive, consultant*

San Diego
Birndorf, Howard C. *health products executive*
Bronn, Mark R. *pharmaceutical executive*
Chiplin, John *medical company executive*
Colella, Samuel D. *biotechnology executive*
Cook, Joseph C., Jr., *pharmaceutical executive*
Dahlberg, Kenneth C. *manufacturing executive*
Darmstandler, Harry Max *real estate executive, retired air force officer*
Duddles, Charles Weller *food company executive*
Earl, Christopher D. *health products executive*
Engle, Steven B. *biotechnology company executive*
Flatley, Jay T. *biotechnology company executive*
Greene, Howard E., Jr., *pharmaceutical executive*
Hacksell, Uli *pharmaceutical executive*
Hixson, Harry F., Jr., *health products executive*
Ingle, M(orton) Blakeman *chemicals executive*
Iversen, Leslie Lars *pharmaceutical executive*
Jennings, Jackie *construction executive, contractor*
Johnson, M. Ross *pharmaceutical executive*
Knuth, Dean Leslie *research and development company executive, golf consultant, writer*
Kranzler, Jay D. *pharmaceutical executive*
Lewis, Alan James *pharmaceutical executive, pharmacologist*
Lief, Jack *pharmaceutical executive*
Loria, Emile *medical company executive*
Lyons, Gary A. *medical company executive*
Maier, Paul Victor *pharmaceutical executive*
McNamara, Kevin Michael *floorcovering company executive*
Moos, Walter Hamilton *pharmaceutical company executive*
Nassif, Thomas Anthony *business executive, former ambassador*
Pigliucci, Riccardo *pharmaceutical executive*
Price, Robert E. *manufacturing executive*
Proehl, Gerald T. *pharmaceutical executive*
Pyatt, Kedar Davis, Jr., *research and development company executive*
Quadros, Paul D. *health products executive*
Rastetter, Wiliam H. *biotechnology company executive*
Ray, Gene Wells *industrial executive*
Reich, Jack W. *health products executive*
Rice, Clare I. *electronics company executive*
Robinson, David E. *pharmaceuticals executive*
Rodríguez-Figueroa, R. Vilmarie *pharmaceutical executive*
Rohn, William R. *biotechnology company executive*
Roth, Duane J. *pharmaceutical executive*
Roth, Theodore D. *pharmaceutical executive*
Samant, Vijay B. *biotechnology company executive*
Schuhsler, Helmut *biotechnology company executive*
Shawver, Laura K. *biotechnology company executive*
Sobol, Robert E. *medical company executive*
Spanos, Alexander Gus *construction company owner, professional sports team owner*
Stevens, William C., Jr., *pharmaceutical executive*
Thomas, Robert McGuffey *automotive executive, educator*
Tidwell, Geoffrey Morgan *medical company executive*
White, Vance R.(Randy) *medical company executive*
Wierenga, Wendell D. *biotechnology company executive*
Woods, Randall E. *pharmaceutical executive*

San Francisco
Bergen, David M. *apparel executive*
Blatt, Lawrence M. *pharmaceutical company executive*
Broadway, Nancy Ruth *landscape design and construction company executive, consultant, model and actress*
Campbell, Jeffrey C. *pharmaceutical executive*
Gillette, James R. *construction executive*
Grubb, David H. *construction company executive*
Haas, Peter E., Sr., *apparel company executive*
Haas, Robert Douglas *apparel manufacturing company executive*
Hammergren, John H. *pharmaceutical executive*
Hawkins, Richard *pharmaceutical and cosmetics company executive*
Hill, Emma *apparel executive*
Horner, George F. *biotechnology company executive*
Jewett, George Frederick, Jr., *forest products company executive*
Julian, Paul C. *health products executive*
Keogh, Keith *food company executive*
Mahoney, David L. *former pharmaceutical wholesale and healthcare management company executive*
Marcus, Robert *aluminum company executive*
Marineau, Philip Albert *apparel executive*
Merrill, Harvie Martin *manufacturing executive, director*
Meyers, David L. *food products executive*
Ming, Jenny J. *retail apparel company executive*
Moreno, Albert F. *apparel executive, lawyer*
Morris-Tyndall, Lucy *construction executive*
Newman, Francis A. *medical device company executive*
Owen, Marc *health products executive*
Proctor, Georganne C. *company executive*
Pulido, Mark A. *pharmaceutical and cosmetics company executive*
Sadow, Harvey S. *health care company executive*
Seelenfreund, Alan *retired pharmaceutical company executive*
Shackley, Douglas John *fire alarm company executive*
Smith, Cheryl T. *pharmaceutical executive, public relations executive*
Tompkins, Susie *apparel company executive, creative director*
Tully, Herbert Bullard *chemical manufacturing executive*
Turek, Paul John, III, *construction executive*
Wolford, Richard *food products executive*
Zellerbach, William Joseph *retired paper company executive*

San Jose
Ackel, Rick R. *electronics manufacturing executive*
Bell, W. Donald *electronics company executive*
Carrekea, James *electronics company executive*
Cartwright, Peter *electronics company executive*
Chizen, Bruce *electronics executive*
Crawford, Curtis J. *computer and electronics company executive*
Fry, David *electronics executive*
Fry, John *electronics executive*
Furr, Randy W. *electronics manufacturing executive*
Hill, Richard S. *manufacturing executive*
Kissner, Charles D. *electrical company executive*
Madrid, Don *electronics executive*
Marks, Michael E. *electronics company executive*
Perlegos, George *electronic executive*
Rosendin, Raymond Joseph *electrical contracting company executive*
Schroeder, Kenneth L. *electronics executive*
Schroeder, William John *electronics executive*
Simon, Ralph E. *electronics executive*
Sola, Jure *electronics executive*
Steinberg, Charles Allan *electronics manufacturing company executive*
Straus, Jozef *manufacturing executive*
Wozniak, Curtis S. *electronics company executive*
Zafiropoulo, Arthur *electronics executive*

San Luis Obispo
Sullivan, Thomas James *retired manufacturing company executive*

San Mateo
Graham, Howard Holmes *financial executive*
Halperin, Robert Milton *retired electrical machinery company executive*
Hoops, Alan R. *health care company executive*
Sellers, Donald R. *biotechnology company executive*

San Rafael
Neuburger, Karen *apparel executive*
Parker, Pam *apparel manufacturing company executive*

San Ramon
Bruns, George H. *electronics executive*

Sanger
Albertson, David *food products executive*

Santa Ana
Phanstiel, Howard G. *managed health care company executive*
Washburn, Lawrence Robert *manufacturing executive*

Santa Barbara
Barber, Jerry Randel *medical device company executive*
Coffin, Dwight Clay *retired grain company executive*
Mai, David E. *biotechnology company executive*
Potter, David Samuel *former automotive company executive*
Prindle, William Roscoe *retired glass company executive*
Zaleski, James Vincent *electronics executive*

Santa Clara
Barrett, Craig R. *electronics company executive*
Barrett, Ronald W. *biopharmaceutical executive*
Burkett, Marvin D. *personal computer manufacturing company executive*
Dorchak, Glenda *electronics company executive*
Elkus, Richard J., Jr., *electronics company executive*
Faggin, Federico *electronics executive*
Grove, Andrew S. *electronics company executive*
Halla, Brian L. *electronics company executive*
Huang, Jen-Hsun *electronics executive*
Larson, William *electrical company executive*
Lee, Jimmy S.M. *electronic executive*
Moore, Gordon E. *electronics company executive*
Murray, Patricia *electronics company executive*
Otellini, Paul S. *electronics company executive*
Plewman, Patrick *health products executive*

Santa Fe Springs
Lovatt, Arthur Kingsbury, Jr., *manufacturing executive*

Santa Maria
Ardantz, Henri *agricultural products executive*
Ferini, Robert Pat *agricultural products company executive*

Santa Monica
Bush, William Glenn *manufacturing company executive, engineer*
Hardin, Wayne *automotive executive*

Santa Paula
Dillard, Michael L. *food products company executive*

Santa Rosa
Ogg, Robert Danforth *corporate executive*

Saratoga
Dalton, Peter John *electronics executive*
Houston, Joseph Brantley, Jr., *optical instrument company executive*

Sherman Oaks
Little, Carole *women's apparel company executive*
Reiner, Thomas Karl *manufacturing executive*

Simi Valley
Mow, William *apparel executive*

Solana Beach
Brody, Arthur *industrial executive*
Derbes, Daniel William *manufacturing executive*

Soquel
Goodman, Charles Schaffner, Jr., *food product executive, consultant*

South San Francisco
Desmond-Hellmann, Susan *medical products manufacturing executive*
Gower, James M. *biotechnology company executive*
Hull, Cordell William *business executive*
Lieberburg, Ivan *pharmaceutical executive*
Lindsay, Ronald M. *research and development company executive*
Potter, Myrtle S. *research and development company executive*
Scangos, George A. *medical company executive*
Walker, John P. *pharmaceutical executive*
Young, James W. *biotechnology company executive*

Stanford
Miller, William Frederick *research company executive, educator, business consultant*

Sun Valley
Kamins, Philip E. *diversified manufacturing company executive*

Sunnyvale
Bowman, A. Blaine *electronics company executive*
Gutshall, Thomas L. *clinical diagnostics company executive*
Keegan, Joseph D *medical company executive*
Lewis, John Clark, Jr., *retired manufacturing company executive*
Love, Ted W. *biotechnology company executive*
McCollam, Craig A. *manufacturing executive*
Miller, Richard A. *health products executive*
Ng, Betty *electronics executive*
Smith, Lonnie Max *diversified industries executive*
Thompson, Andrew *medical products executive*
Yancey, Gary *electronics company executive*

Tarzana
Firestone, Morton H. *business management executive*

Thousand Oaks
Falberg, Kathryn E. *pharmaceutical executive*
Morrow, George J. *pharmaceutical company executive*
Nanula, Richard *health products executive*
Rosenblatt, Alice F. *health products executive*
Sharer, Kevin W. *healthcare products company executive*

Torrance
Amemiya, Koichi *motor vehicle company executive*
Funo, Yukitoshi *automotive executive*
Kishita, Kazutaka *adhesive company executive, chemist*
Mann, Michael Martin *electronics company executive*

Turlock
Arias, Joe *agricultural products company executive*

Tustin
Hester, Norman Eric *chemical company technical executive, chemist*
Legere, Edward J. *health products executive*
Schectman, Stephen Barry *pharmaceutical executive*

Ukiah
Newell, Barbara Ann *coatings company executive*

Union City
Cross, Elizabeth *apparel manufacturing company executive*

Upland
Goodman, John M. *construction executive*

Valencia
House, David L. *electronics components company executive*

Vallejo
Womack, Thomas Houston *manufacturing executive*

Valley Center
Andersen, Robert *health products, business executive*

Van Nuys
Iacocca, Lee (Lido Anthony Iacocca) *former automotive manufacturing executive, venture capitalist*

Villa Park
Hawe, David Lee *manufacturing consultant, venture capitalist*

Walnut
Humphreys, Roy *construction executive*
Shea, John F. *construction executive, contractor*
Shontere, James G. *construction executive*

Walnut Creek
Hamlin, Kenneth Eldred, Jr., *retired pharmaceutical company executive*
Shastid, Jon Barton *wine company executive*

Watsonville
Costanzo, Patrick M. *construction executive*
Franich, Steven *automotive company executive*
Repass, Randy *electrical company executive*

West Sacramento
D'Arezzo, Dave *food products executive*

Westlake Village
Colburn, Keith W. *electronics executive*
DeLorenzo, David A. *food products executive*
Lullo, Thomas A. *electronics executive*
Nichols, Steven *apparel executive*
Powlick, George *shoe and clothing manufacturing executive*

Wilmington
Hamai, James Yutaka *business executive*

Woodland Hills
Brann, Alton Joseph *manufacturing executive*
Brown, Michael R. *former defense industry executive*
Dreier, R. Chad *construction and mortgage company executive*
Gellert, Jay M. *health and medical products executive*
Morishita, Akihiko *trading company executive*

Woodside
Gates, Milo Sedgwick *retired construction company executive*

COLORADO

Arvada
Holden, George Fredric *brewing company executive, public policy specialist, writer*

Boulder
Clark, Melvin Eugene *chemical company executive*
Demos, Steven *food products executive*
Kenney, Belinda Jill Forseman *technology company executive*
Lefkoff, Kyle *pharmaceutical executive*
Mancino, John Gregory *software company executive*
Robin, Howard W. *biotechnology company executive*

Breckenridge
Ehrhorn, Richard William *electronics company executive*

Broomfield
Hoover, R. David *packaging company executive*

Colorado Springs
Cimino, Jay *automotive company executive*
Stevenson, Bruce Warren *food products executive, researcher*

Columbine Valley
Plusk, Ronald Frank *manufacturing executive*

Denver
Childs, John David *retired computer hardware and services company executive*
Gates, Charles Cassius *rubber company executive*
Harmsen, Dorothy *food products executive*
Klump, Ron *food products executive*
Leprino, James G. *food products executive*
Livingston, Johnston Redmond *manufacturing executive*
Marcum, Walter Phillip *manufacturing executive*
Martin, J. Landis *manufacturing company executive, lawyer*
Mizel, Larry A. *housing construction company executive*
Perlmutter, Leonard Michael *concrete construction company executive*
Reidy, Mike *food products executive*
Shaffer, Oren George *former manufacturing company executive*
Shreve, Theodore Norris *construction company executive*
Weil, Jack Baum *clothing manufacturing company executive*

Englewood
Chavez, Lloyd G. *automotive executive*
Gertz, David Lee *homebuilding company executive*
Mahoney, Gerald Francis *manufacturing executive*
Reese, Monte Nelson *agricultural association executive*

Fort Collins
Watz, Martin Charles *brewery consultant*

Golden
Coors, Jeffrey H. *technology manufacturing executive*
Coors, Peter Hanson *brewery company executive*
Kiely, W. Leo, III, *brewery company executive*
Wolf, Timothy Van de Wint *food products company executive*

Greeley
Carrico, Stephen J. *construction company executive*
James, Philip J. *agricultural products executive*
Morgensen, Jerry Lynn *construction company executive*
Simons, John S. *food products executive*

Greenwood Village
Appel, Joel *household cleaner manufacturing executive*
McVey, Larry *household cleaner manufacturing executive*

Jefferson
Maatsch, Deborah Joan *manufacturing executive*

Lakewood
Rosa, Fredric David *construction company executive*

Littleton
Battilega, John A. *research and development company executive*
Dixon, Terry *automotive executive*

Lone Tree
Bauer, Randy Mark *management training firm executive*

Longmont
Breuer, Werner Alfred *retired plastics company executive*
Marcy, Charles Frederick *food company executive*

Monument
Karasa, Norman Lukas *home builder, developer, geologist*

Snowmass Village
Mattis, Louis Price *pharmaceutical and consumer products company executive*

Westminster
Freytag, J. Williams *medical company executive*
Hoffman, Stephen J. *pharmaceutical executive*
Michael, Hart E. *pharmaceutical executive*

CONNECTICUT

Bloomfield
Coburn, Richard Joseph *company executive, electrical engineer*
Garneau, Robert M. *aerospace and industrial products manufacturer*
Kaman, Charles Huron *diversified technologies corporation executive*

Branford
Begley, Richard F. *medical products executive*
Rothberg, Jonathan M. *medical products executive*

Bridgeport
Semple, Cecil Snowdon *retired manufacturing company executive*

Bristol
Barnes, Carlyle Fuller *manufacturing executive*
Barnes, Wallace *manufacturing executive*

Cheshire
Bell, Leonard *pharmaceutical executive*
Keiser, David Wharton *biotechnology executive*

Danbury
Baker, Leonard Morton *manufacturing executive*
Lichtenberger, H(orst) William *chemical company executive*
Reilley, Dennis H. *chemicals executive*
Sawyer, James S. *manufacturing executive*
Soviero, Joseph C. *chemical company executive*

Darien
Dordelman, William Forsyth *food company executive*
Sprole, Frank Arnott *retired pharmaceutical executive, lawyer*
Ziegler, William, III, *diversified industry executive*

East Hartford
Cassidy, John Francis, Jr., *industrial technology executive*

Fairfield
Beccalli, Ferdinando *manufacturing executive*
Calhoun, David L. *manufacturing executive*
Daley, Pamela *diversified services, technology and manufacturing company executive*
Fash, Victoria R. *healthcare company executive*
Immelt, Jeffrey R. *diversified technology and services company executive*
Krenicki, John, Jr., *manufacturing executive*
Levine, Stanley Walter *chemical company executive*
McLaughlin, John Richardson *electric motor company executive*
Reeves, Edmund Hoffman, III, *food products executive*
Sherin, Keith S. *electrical manufacturing company executive*
Sutphen, Harold Amerman, Jr., *retired paper company executive*

Greenwich
Cameron, Dort *electronics executive*
Case, Richard Paul *electronics executive*
Dettmer, Robert Gerhart *retired beverage company executive*
Farbish, Alfred B. *waterproofing materials executive*
Higgins, Shaun Brian *beverage company executive*
Kelly, David Austin *investment counselor*
Ostberg, A. Peter *food products/retail groceries executive*
Ritter, John C. *manufacturing executive*
Van Dijk, Frits *food products executive*
von der Heyden, Karl Mueller *retired manufacturing executive*

Hartford
Cardillo, Michael *health executive*
Hermann, Robert Jay *consultant, former manufacturing company engineering executive*

Madison
Golembeski, Jerome John *wire and cable company executive*

Middlebury
Calarco, Vincent Anthony *specialty chemicals company executive*
Fickenscher, Gerald H. *chemicals company executive*
Galie, Louis Michael *electronics company executive*
Wood, R. L. (Bob Wood) *chemicals executive*

Naugatuck
Flannery, Joseph Patrick *manufacturing executive, director*

New Canaan
Burns, Ivan Alfred *grocery products and industrial company executive*
Johnston, Douglas Frederick *industrial holding company executive*
Sachs, John Peter *carbon company executive*

New London
Kopchinski, Anita Francine *pharmaceutical executive*
Williams, Derek, Jr., *pharmaceutical professional*

Newtown
Farrell, Edgar Henry *building components manufacturing executive, lawyer*

North Branford
Ingram, George *business executive*
Mead, Lawrence Myers, Jr., *retired aerospace executive*

Norwalk
Griffin, Donald Wayne *retired diversified chemical company executive*
Harris, Holton Edwin *plastics machinery manufacturing executive*
MacInnis, Frank T. *construction executive, securities trader, holding company executive*
Ruggiero, Anthony William *chemical company executive*

Orange
Randall, Arthur Raymond *building contractor*

Plainfield
O'Connell, Francis V(incent) *textile printing company executive*

Plainville
Glassman, Gerald Seymour *metal finishing company executive*

Ridgefield
Casey, Gerard William *retired food products company executive, lawyer*
Knortz, Herbert Charles *retired conglomerate company executive*
Levine, Paul Michael *paper industry executive, consultant*

Riverside
Deering, Allan Brooks *retired soft drink company executive*

Somers
Blake, Stewart Prestley *retired ice cream company executive*

South Kent
Samartini, James Rogers *retired appliance company executive*

South Windsor
van Dokkum, Jan *manufacturing executive*

Southport
Gryka, George Edwin *chemical company executive*
Wheeler, Wilmot Fitch, Jr., *diversified manufacturing company executive*

Stamford
Amen, Robert M. *paper company executive*
Anderson, Susan Stuebing *business equipment company executive*
Balduino, Michael J. *paper company executive*
Buehler, William Frank *manufacturing executive*
Burston, Richard Mervin *business executive*
Buzzard, James A. *manufacturing executive*
Caldwell, Philip *retired automobile manufacturing company executive, retired financial services company executive*
Dammerman, Dennis Dean *diversified technology and services company executive*
Dillon, John T. *retired paper company executive*
Evans, Robert Sheldon *manufacturing executive, director*
Filter, E. Margie *business equipment manufacturing executive*
Friedman, Michael *pharmaceutical executive*
Gantos, LeRoy Douglas *retail clothing executive*
Gross, Ronald Martin *forest products executive*
Harper, Arthur H. *manufacturing executive*
Hicks, Wayland R. *electronic business equipment executive*
Hogan, Frank W., III, *manufacturing executive*
Hollander, Milton Bernard *corporate executive*
Horrigan, D. Gregory *packaging products executive*
Kingsley, John McCall, Jr., *manufacturing executive*
Lennard, Gerald *metal products executive*
Lesko, Newland A. *paper company executive*
Liddell, Chris R. *paper company executive*
Maarbjerg, Mary Penzold *office equipment company executive*
Motroni, Hector John *manufacturing executive*
Munera, Gerard Emmanuel *manufacturing executive*
Nevans, Roy Norman *food products executive, producer*
Olson, Richard E. *paper company executive*
Parker, Jack Steele *retired manufacturing company executive*
Phillips, Richard B. *paper company executive*
Reichenstein, Murray L. *electronics executive*
Romeril, Barry D. *office equipment company executive*
Silver, R. Philip *metal products executive*
Smith, J. Gordon *automotive executive*
Stoveken, James E., Jr., *paper packaging and chemical company executive*
Thomas, Dennis *paper company executive, former government official*
Udell, Howard R. *pharmaceutical executive*

Thomaston
Mühlanger, Erich *ski manufacturing company executive*

Wallingford
Jia, Weitao *dental products executive, researcher*
Lacourciere, William J. *pharmaceutical executive*

Waterbury
Luedke, Frederick Lee *manufacturing executive*

West Hartford
Doran, James Martin *retired food products company executive*
Raffay, Stephen Joseph *manufacturing executive, director*

Westport
Defeo, Ronald M. *machinery manufacturing executive*
Hedge, Arthur Joseph, Jr., *corporate executive*
McKane, David Bennett *business executive*
Widman, Phillip C. *machinery manufacturing executive*

Wilton
Kenton, James Alan *healthcare products executive*
Winger, Dennis L. *health products executive*

DELAWARE

Milford
Konowitz, Herbert Henry *textile company executive*

Montchanin
Olney, Robert C. *diversified products manufacturing executive*

Newark
Carroll, Charles E. *electronics executive*
Giacco, Alexander Fortunatus *chemical industry executive*
Gore, Genevieve Walton *manufacturing executive*
Gore, Robert W. *electronics executive*
Molz, Robert Joseph *manufacturing executive*

Rockland
Rubin, Alan A. *pharmaceutical and biotechnology consultant*

Wilmington
Borel, James Calvin *chemical company executive*
Cason, Roger Lee *retired chemical company executive, educator, consultant*
Connelly, Thomas M., Jr., *pharmaceutical executive*
Corbo, Vincent J. *textiles executive*
Donnelly, Edward J., Jr., *pharmaceutical executive*
Floyd, Israel J. *chemicals executive*
Frywald, J. Erik *agricultural products executive*
Gibson, Joseph Whitton, Jr., *retired chemical company executive*
Goodmanson, Richard R. *chemicals executive*
Gulyas, Diane H. *manufacturing executive*
Hodgson, John C. *manufacturing executive*
Holliday, Charles O., Jr., *chemical company executive*
Holtzman, Arnold Harold *chemical company executive*
Johnson, W. Donald *research and development company executive*
Krol, John A. *retired diversified chemicals executive*
Kullman, Ellen J. *manufacturing executive*
Landgraf, Kurt M. *chemicals executive*
Lassen, John Kai *development company executive*
Lewis, George Withrow *business executive*
Lukach, Carl Andrew *retired chemicals executive*
MacCormack, George F. *pharmaceutical executive*
McLeer, Laureen Dorothy *drug development and pharmaceutical professional*
Pfeiffer, Gary M. *chemical company executive*
Rose, Selwyn H. *chemical company executive*
Townsend, P(reston) Coleman *agricultural business executive*
Uffner, Michael S. *automotive executive*
Wells, James Robert *pharmaceutical company executive*

DISTRICT OF COLUMBIA

Washington
Buto, Kathleen A. *health products executive*
Collamore, Thomas Jones *corporate executive*
Culp, H. Lawrence *manufacturing executive*
Davis, Lance Alan *research and development executive, metallurgical engineer*
Fink, Richard H. *manufacturing executive*
Griffin, Robert Thomas *automotive company executive*
Grossi, Ralph Edward *agricultural conservation organization executive, farmer, rancher*
Halperin, Jerome Arthur *pharmaceutical executive*
Howell, Mary L. *diversified company executive*
Kelly, Marguerite Stehli *fashion executive, consultant*
Misner, Robert David *electronic warfare and magnetic recording consultant, electro-mechanical company executive*
Money, Arthur Lewis *electronics executive*
Moore, Robert Madison *food products executive, lawyer*
Persinger, Del Louis *pharmaceutical company executive*
Rales, Mitchell P. *automotive parts company executive*
Rales, Steven M. *automotive parts company executive*
Shepherd, Alan J. *construction executive, management consultant*
Sherman, George M. *manufacturing executive*
Slater, Doris Ernestine Wilke *business executive*
Thompson, Richard Leon *pharmaceutical company executive, lawyer*
Tomita, Kazuo (Joe) *automotive executive*
West, Douglas M. *automotive executive*

FLORIDA

Amelia Island
Adelman, Robert Paul *retired construction company executive, lawyer*
Ash, Frederick Melvin *retired manufacturing company executive*

Anna Maria
Kaiser, Albert Farr *diversified corporation executive*

Boca Raton
Feld, Joseph *construction executive*
Fournet, Ronald A. *electronics executive*
Judovits, Martin *textiles executive*
O'Donnell, Joseph Michael *electronics executive*
Wyatt, James Luther *drapery hardware company executive*

Bonita Springs
Sargent, Charles Lee *manufacturing executive*

Boynton Beach
Jensen, Reuben Rolland *former automotive company executive*

Bradenton
Howe, Carroll Victor *construction equipment company executive*
Price, Edgar Hilleary, Jr., *business consultant*

Brooksville
Pylipow, Stanley Ross *retired manufacturing company executive*

Cape Coral
McKinley, James Frank, Jr., *retired manufacturing executive*
Stuart, Robert *container manufacturing executive*

Clearwater
Brady, Sheila Ann *manufacturing executive*
Kiehl, E. Robert *manufacturing executive, consultant*
Smith, Marion Pafford *avionics company executive, retired*

Coconut Grove
Nahmad, Albert H. *manufacturing executive, United States federal commissioner*

Coral Gables
Burini, Sonia Montes de Oca *apparel manufacturing and public relations executive*
Potamkin, Alan *automotive company executive*
Yusko, Dave *automotive executive*

Deerfield Beach
Brown, Colin *automotive executive*

Delray Beach
Case, Manning Eugene, Jr., *retired food products executive*
Fitzpatrick, David J. *electronics executive*
Goldenberg, George *retired pharmaceutical company executive*
Goldstein, Barry J. *former home improvement center manufacturing executive*
Heit, Ivan *packaging equipment company executive*
Himmelright, Robert John, Jr., *rubber company executive*
Jacobson, Herbert Leonard *licensing executive*
Mayer, Marilyn Gooder *steel company executive*
Saffer, Alfred *retired chemical company executive*

Dunedin
Tweedy, Robert Hugh *retired equipment company executive*

Flagler Beach
Stockton, Anderson Berrian *electronics company executive, consultant, genealogist*

Fort Lauderdale
Berrard, S.R. *automotive executive, waste management administrator*

Hudson, Harris W. *automobile dealership executive*
Jackson, Michael J. *automotive retail company executive*
Karsner, Michael S. *industrial company executive*
Levy, Michael *electronic manufacturing company executive*
MacInnes, Donald A. *automotive executive*
Monaghan, Craig Thomas *automotive executive*
Morse, Edward J. *automotive executive*
Peltzer, Douglas Lea *semiconductor device manufacturing company executive*

Fort Myers
O'Dell, William Francis *retired business executive, writer*
Schultz, Gerald Alfred (Jerry Schultz) *retired chemicals executive*
Wendeborn, Richard Donald *retired manufacturing company executive*

Fort Pierce
Moore, Jo Ella *construction executive*

Gainesville
Lin, Steve T. *technology executive*

Hallandale
Glaubinger, Lawrence David *retired manufacturing company executive*

Heathrow
Darbelnet, Robert Louis *automobile association executive*

Hialeah
Engler, Eva Kay *dental and veterinary products company executive*

Hobe Sound
Casey, Edward Paul *manufacturing executive*
Craig, David Jeoffrey *retired manufacturing company executive*
McChristian, Joseph Alexander *international business executive*

Hollywood
Schwartz, Joseph *retired container company executive*
Spencer, Richard Thomas, III, *healthcare industry executive*

Holmes Beach
Rose, Dennis Norman *manufacturing executive*

Homestead
Willner, Eugene Burton *food and liquor company executive*

Indian River Shores
Wiegner, Edward Alex *multi-industry executive*

Islamorada
Gates, Richard Daniel *retired manufacturing company executive*

Jacksonville
Jackson, Julian Ellis *food company executive*
Mahaffy, Telfair *safety scientist*
McKinney, James Clayton *electronics executive, electrical engineer*
Nutter, Wallace Lee *paper manufacturing executive*
O'Connor, R. D. *retired health care executive*
Sheehan, John R. *food products executive*
Smith, David A. *medical services executive*
Welch, Philip Burland *electronics and office products company executive*

Jupiter
De George, Lawrence Joseph *diversified company executive*
Feinberg, Herbert *apparel, real estate, video and beverage executive*
Garfinkel, Harmon Mark *retired specialty chemicals company executive*

Key Largo
Davidson, Thomas Noel *metal products executive*

Lady Lake
Morse, Gary H. *construction executive*

Lakeland
Hatten, William Seward *manufacturing executive*
Mutz, Oscar Ulysses *manufacturing and distribution executive*

Leesburg
Talley, William Giles, Jr., *manufacturing executive*

Longwood
St. John, John *food company executive*
Zahn, Richard Gregory *construction executive*

Lutz
Fritzsche, R(obert) Wayne *corporate executive*

Marco Island
Guerrant, David Edward *retired food company executive*

Melbourne
Buescher, Howard *construction executive*
Buescher, Keith *construction executive*
Bush, Norman *research and development executive*

Merritt Island
Deardoff, R. Bruce *automotive executive*

Miami
Borkan, William Noah *retired biomedical electronics company executive, entrepreneur, inventor*
Braman, Norman *automotive executive, sports team executive*
Frigo, James Peter Paul *industrial hardware company executive*
Frost, Philip *pharmaceutical executive, dermatologist*
Sherman, Beatrice Ettinger *business executive*
Theodoli, Katrin *manufacturing executive*
Thornburg, Frederick Fletcher *diversified business executive, lawyer*

Naples
Baldwin, Ralph Belknap *retired manufacturing company executive, astronomer*
Berger, Charles Martin *retired lawn and garden company executive*
Butler, Frederick George *retired drug company executive*
Dykstra, David Allen *corporate executive*
Flaten, Alfred N. *retired food and consumer products executive*
Gade, Marvin Francis *retired paper company executive*
Laidig, William Rupert *retired paper company executive*
LaRusso, Anthony Carl *company executive, educator*
McDonell, Horace George, Jr., *instrument company executive*
Sharpe, Robert Francis *equipment manufacturing company executive*
Slayton, John Arthur *electric motor manufacturing executive*
Vanderslice, Thomas Aquinas *electronics executive*
von Arx, Dolph William *food products executive*
Williams, Edson Poe *retired automotive company executive*

New Port Richey
Lake, Victor Hugo *former manufacturing company executive*
Sebring, Marjorie Marie Allison *former home furnishings company executive*
Vajk, Hugo *manufacturing executive*

New Smyrna Beach
Skove, Thomas Malcolm *retired manufacturing company financial executive*

Niceville
Litke, Donald Paul *aquisition executive, retired military officer*

North Palm Beach
Hood, Edward Exum, Jr., *retired electrical manufacturing company executive*
Hushing, William Collins *retired corporate executive*

Ocean Ridge
Grabner, George John *manufacturing executive*

Orlando
Brownlee, Thomas Marshall *manufacturing executive*
Cates, Harold Thomas *aircraft and electronics company executive*
Cawthon, Frank H. *retired construction company executive*
Elliott, E.J. *manufacturing executive*
Morini, Angelo Sylvester *food company executive*
Pierce, Jerry Earl *business executive*
Smyth, Joseph Vincent *manufacturing executive*
Whitworth, Hall Baker *forest products company executive*

Osprey
Petrik, Gerd *pharmaceutical executive*

Palatka
Svetlik, Robert Wayne *contractor, writer*

Palm Beach
Habicht, Frank Henry *retired industrial executive*

Palm Beach Gardens
Keppler, William Edmund *multinational company executive*
Staub, W. Arthur *health care products executive*

Palm City
Conklin, George Melville *retired food products executive*
Derrickson, William Borden *manufacturing executive*
Wishart, Ronald Sinclair *retired chemical company executive*

Palm Harbor
Bennett, John Joseph *professional services company executive*

Pensacola
Jones, Harry Gordon *electronics company executive*

Ponte Vedra Beach
Elston, William Steger *food products company executive*
Langford, Dean Ted *lighting and precision materials company executive*

Punta Gorda
Koll, Richard Leroy *retired chemical company executive*
Ling, Chung-Mei *retired pharmaceutical company executive*

Reddick
Corwin, Joyce Elizabeth Stedman *construction company executive*

Royal Palm Beach
Perez, Jorge Luis *retired manufacturing executive*

Saint Petersburg
Dimas, Marilyn J. *health resources executive*
Joyce, Walter Joseph *retired electronics company executive*
Lewis, Chris A. *manufacturing executive*
Main, Timothy L. *electronics executive*
Mills, William Harold, Jr., *construction company executive*
Mondello, Mark T. *manufacturing executive*
Morean, William D. *manufacturing executive*
Naimoli, Vincent Joseph *diversified operating and holding company executive*

Sarasota
Berkoff, Charles Edward *pharmaceutical executive*
Daoust, Donald Roger *pharmaceutical and toiletries company executive, microbiologist*
Hoffman, Oscar Allen *retired forest products company executive*
James, C. Shelton *electronics company executive*
Kane, Stanley Bruce *food products executive*
Miranda, Carlos Sa *food products company executive*
Mullane, John Francis *pharmaceutical company executive*
Roth, James Frank *manufacturing company executive, chemist*
Slocum, Donald Hillman *product development executive*
Venit, William Bennett *electrical products company executive, consultant*
West, Bob *pharmaceutical executive*

South Florida
Hoffman, Randy Michael *automotive executive*

Spring Hill
Martin, Gary J. *retired business executive, mayor*

Stuart
Jaffe, Jeff Hugh *retired food products executive*
Leibson, Irving *retired industrial executive*
McKenna, Sidney F. *retired technical company executive*

Summerfield
McNulty, Carrell Stewart, Jr., *retired manufacturing company executive, architect*

Sunrise
Bainton, Donald J. *diversified manufacturing company executive*

Tamarac
Auletta, Joan Miglorisi *construction company executive, mortgage and insurance broker*

Tampa
Avery, Paul E. *food products executive*
Borreca, John Peter *building materials manufacturing executive*
Brown, Troy Anderson, Jr., *retired electrical distributing company executive*
DeFosset, Don *manufacturing executive*
Flom, Edward Leonard *retired steel company executive*
Hyatt, Kenneth E(rnest) *diversified manufacturing executive*
Johnson, Thomas S. *electronics executive*
MacDonald, John L. *chemical company executive*
McGriff, Cheryl Renee *medical products executive*
McKinney, Patricia J. *automobile company executive*
Merritt, Robert S. *food products executive*
Ohrt, William F. *manufacturing executive*
VanButsel, Michael R. *real estate broker, builder and developer*

Tequesta
Peterson, James Robert *retired writing instrument manufacturing executive*
Seal, John S., Jr., *manufacturing executive, consultant*

Venice
Lanford, Luke Dean *retired electronics company executive*

Vero Beach
Allik, Michael *diversified industry executive*
Cartwright, Alton Stuart *electrical manufacturing company executive*
Janicki, Robert Stephen *retired pharmaceutical executive*
Reed, Sherman Kennedy *chemical consultant*
Standish, John Spencer *textile manufacturing company executive*
Wilcox, Harry Wilbur, Jr., *retired corporate executive*

Village Of Golf
Boer, F. Peter *chemical company executive*

Wesley Chapel
Revelle, Donald Gene *manufacturing and health care company executive, consultant*

West Palm Beach
Jenkins, Ruben Lee *retired chemical company executive, lawyer*
Sander, Dorothy E. *manufacturing executive*
Vecellio, Leo Arthur, Jr., *construction company executive*

Weston
Staneart, Larry William *technology company marketing executive*

Winter Park
Farris, Michael R. *pharmaceutical executive*
Hughes, David Henry *manufacturing executive*
Kincaid, Rodney Lyle *construction company executive*
Kost, Wayne L. *manufacturing executive*

GEORGIA

Alpharetta
Brands, James Edwin *medical products executive*
Deitrich, Wayne H. *manufacturing executive*
Le Hetet, Jean-Pierre *paper company executive*
Roberts, Paul C. *paper company executive*
Thomas, Robert L. *retired manufacturing company executive*
Thompson, Peter J. *manufacturing executive*

Athens
Eberhart, William Coile *apparel repair specialist, writer*

Atlanta
Abrams, Edward Marvin *construction company executive*
Allan, Alexander R.C. (Sandy Allan) *food products executive*
Anderson, Ray C. *carpet company executive*
Bekkers, John *food products company executive*
Blount, Ben B., Jr., *administration and finance executive*
Bostic, James E., Jr., *paper company executive*
Brantley, L. Wayne *apparel executive*
Burandt, Michael Charles *lumber company executive, paper company executive, chemicals executive, consumer products company executive*
Casey, John M. *metal products executive*
Chestnut, James E. *beverage company executive*
Correll, Alston Dayton, Jr., (Pete Correll) *forest products company executive*
Cummings, Alexander B., Jr., *food products executive*
Daft, Douglas N. *food products executive*
Dallas, H. James *textiles executive*
Davis, Marvin Arnold *manufacturing executive*
Dayton, Harry F. *manufacturing executive*
DeMoura, Brian L. *textile manufacturing company executive*
DeRodes, Robert P. *manufacturing executive*
Donovan, Dennis *manufacturing executive*
Downs, John H., Jr., *food products executive*
Dunn, Jeffrey T. *food products executive*
Eaton, J. Stephen *healthcare company executive*
Ergas, Jean-Pierre Maurice *packaging company executive*
Fayard, Gary P. *food products executive*
Findley, Norman P. *food products executive*
Gallagher, Thomas C. *diversified manufacturing executive*
Gray, Robert F. *food products executive*
Hayford, Warren J. *metal products executive*
Hendrix, Daniel T. *textile manufacturing company executive*
Heyer, Steven J. *food products executive*
Huff, Danny W. *paper products executive*
Isdell, Edward Neville *food products executive*
Johnston, Summerfield K., Jr., *food products executive*
Johnston, Summerfield K., III, *food products executive*
Jones, Ingrid Saunders *food products executive*
Kline, Lowry F. *food products executive, lawyer*
Klinger, Steven J. *paper company executive*
Liebmann, Seymour W. *construction executive, consultant*
Love, Gay McLawhorn *manufacturing executive*
Lund, Victor L. *healthcare company executive*
Mannelly, Patrick J. *food products executive*
Marchese, Richard B. *manufacturing executive*
Marr, Daniel G. *food products executive*
Martinez, Ricardo *research and development company executive*
McCarthy, Ian J. *construction executive*
McKenna, Robert E. *automotive parts company executive*
Mellett, Edwin R. *soft drink executive*
Millikan, James Rolens *cleaning service executive, musician, composer, fitness consultant*
Milton, James W. *metal products executive*
Minnick, Mary E. *food products executive*
Mohan, Kshitij *healthcare company executive*
Morgan, John K. *chemicals executive, electronics executive*
Murphy, James Jeffrey *electronics executive*
Murphy, Kenyon W. *electronics executive, chemicals executive*
Nagel, Vernon J. *chemicals executive, electronics executive*
Nie, Zenon Stanley *manufacturing executive*
Nix, Jerry W. *automotive executive*
Palmer, Vicki R. *food products executive*
Parker, John R., Jr., *food products executive, lawyer*
Paterson, David J. *paper company executive*
Paul, Ronald L. *paper company executive*
Prince, Larry L. *automotive parts and supplies company executive*
Reiniche, Dominique *food products executive*
Reith, Carl Joseph *apparel industry executive*
Reyes, Jose Octavio *food products executive*
Russell, Terry *construction executive*
Schmitt, Edward A. *manufacturing executive*
Seretean, Martin B. (Bud Seretean) *carpet manufacturing company executive*
Single, Thomas E. *paper company executive*
Stirrup, John T. *metal products executive*
Tilley, Tana Marie *pharmaceutical executive*
Walker, John H. *textile manufacturing company executive*
Ware, Carl *bottling company executive*
Whitener, Gordon D. *textile manufacturing company executive*
Wurtz, George W., III, *paper company executive*

Austell
Robinson, Russell M. *manufacturing executive*

Ball Ground
Tucker, Robert Dennard *health care products executive*

Baxley
Reddy, Yenamala Ramachandra *metal processing executive*

Bogart
Hill, Ronald L. *automotive company executive*

Braselton
Copper, James Robert *manufacturing executive*

Brunswick
Iannicelli, Joseph *chemical company executive, consultant*

Calhoun
Bernstein, Phillip *crafts company executive*
Kilbride, William B. *textiles executive*
Kolb, David L. *carpet company executive*
Lorberbaum, Jeffrey S. *textiles executive*
Procopid, Frank A. *manufacturing executive*
Swift, John D. *manufacturing executive*
Thornton, H Monte *textiles executive*

Carrollton
Richards, Roy, Jr., *wire and cable manufacturing company executive*

Chickamauga
Chill, Leonard *chemicals executive*
Dana, Joseph F. *manufacturing executive*
Sinicropi, Joseph *manufacturing executive*

Columbus
Feldner, Ronald A. *automotive executive*
Heard, William T. *automotive executive*

Leebern, Donald M., Jr., *distilled beverage executive*
Murray, James J. *textiles executive*
Ogle, D. Clark *textiles executive*

Conyers
Burman, Marsha Linkwald *lighting manufacturing executive, manpower development professional*
Mc Clung, Jim Hill *light manufacturing company executive*

Dalton
Hollingsworth, Bayard *manufacturing executive*
Shaheen, Shaheen Azeez *textile executive*
Shaw, Robert E. *carpeting company executive*
Swanson, Larry *manufacturing executive*

Duluth
Beck, Andrew H. *farm equipment manufacturing executive*
Brody, Aaron Leo *food and packaging consultant*
Hillstead, Richard Averill *product development executive*
Ratliff, Robert J. *farm equipment manufacturing executive*

Evans
Karangu, David M. *automobile company executive*

Experiment
Reeves, Alan M. *automotive company executive*

Fort Valley
Maddox, Richard *manufacturing executive*

Fortson
Schmitt, Ralph George *manufacturing executive*

Kennesaw
Anderson, Steven Goodwin *medical products executive*
McSwain, Ron *textiles executive*

Lagrange
Malone, Thomas J. *textile company executive*

Lilburn
Baranco, Gregory T. *automobile dealership executive*

Marietta
Blount, Daniel J. *lumber company executive*
Gannon, Tom *paper company executive*
Humphrey, Stephen M. *paperboard company executive*
Lewis, William Headley, Jr., *manufacturing executive*
McGahan, Martin J. *health products executive*

Moultrie
Vereen, William Jerome *uniform manufacturing company executive*

Norcross
Adams, Kenneth Francis *automobile maufacturing company executive*
Balkcom, James R., Jr., *manufacturing executive*
Dobson, Terry *medical services company executive*
Moreno, Veronica *food products executive*
Rubright, James Alfred *paperboard and packaging company executive*
Szlam, Aleksander *manufacturing executive*
Thompson, Keith J. *medical services company executive*
Tufano, Charles C. *paper company executive*

Rome
Sellers, Jimmie *construction executive*

Roswell
Diercks, Chester William, Jr., *capital goods manufacturing company executive*
Krobot, Thomas C. *construction executive*

Savannah
Cartledge, Raymond Eugene *retired paper company executive*
Gillespie, Daniel Curtis, Sr., *retired non-profit company executive, consultant*
Granger, Harvey, Jr., *retired manufacturing company executive*
Hammond, C.F. *automotive executive*
Horan, Tom *automotive executive*
O'Brien, George Aloysius, Jr., *paper company executive*
Peer, George Joseph *metals company executive*
Spitz, Seymour James, Jr., *retired fragrance company executive*
Sprague, William Wallace, Jr., *retired food company executive*

Sea Island
Mc Swiney, James Wilmer *retired pulp and paper manufacturing company executive*

Smyrna
Tabron, Wendy *paper company executive*

Thomasville
Flowers, Langdon Strong *foods company executive*
Mc Mullian, Amos Ryals *food company executive*

Tucker
Franklin, Carol D. *electronics company executive*

West Point
Andrews, Gerald Bruce, Sr., *retired textile executive*
Glover, Clifford Clarke *retired construction company executive*

HAWAII

Hilo
Buyers, John William Amerman *agribusiness and specialty foods company executive*

Honolulu
Couch, John Charles *retired diversified company executive*
Finney, John Edgar, III, *food products executive*
Hughes, Robert Harrison *former agricultural products executive*
Schuler, James K. *construction executive*
Usui, Leslie Raymond *retired clothing executive*

Kaneohe
Vincent, Thomas James *retired manufacturing company executive*

Princeville
Forth, Kevin Bernard *beverage distributing industry consultant*

IDAHO

Boise
Appleton, Steven R. *electronics executive*
Cleary, Edward William *retired diversified forest products company executve*
Crumley, Theodore *paper lumber company executive*
Elg, Annette *food products executive*
Harad, George Jay *manufacturing executive*
Hlobik, Lawrence S. *agricultural products executive*
Johnston, Lawrence R. *food products executive*
Markuson, Richard K. *former pharmaceutical association executive*
Mogensen, Dennis *agricultural products company executive*
Parks, Roger *food products executive*
Simplot, Scott R. *diversified food products company executive*
Stover, Wilbur G., Jr., *manufacturing executive*
Washington, Dennis R. *contracting company executive*

Hayden Lake
Wogsland, James Willard *retired heavy machinery manufacturing executive*

Salmon
Snook, Quinton *construction company executive*

ILLINOIS

Abbott Park
Amundson, Joy A. *pharmaceutical and health products executive*
Aruffo, Alejandro *pharmaceutical executive*
Begley, Christopher B. *pharmaceutical executive*
Brown, Thomas D. *pharmaceutical executive*
Dempsey, William G. *pharmaceutical executive*
Flynn, Gary L. *pharmaceutical executive*
Freyman, Thomas C. *pharmaceutical executive*
Gonzalez, Richard A. *pharmaceutical executive*
Leiden, Jeffrey Marc M. *pharmaceutical executive, molecular biologist*
Lussen, John Frederick *pharmaceutical laboratory executive*
Nemmers, Joseph M., Jr., *pharmaceutical executive*
Wascoe, Thomas M. *pharmaceutical executive*
White, Miles D. *pharmaceutical company executive*
Wyatt, Lance B. *pharmaceutical executive*

Argonne
Goldman, Arthur Joseph *retired research and development company executive*

Arlington Heights
Church, Herbert Stephen, Jr., *retired construction company executive*
Johnson, Margaret H. *welding company executive*
Li, Norman N. *chemicals executive*

Aurora
Noglows, William P. *electronics executive*

Barrington
Furst, Warren Arthur *retired holding company executive*
Nadig, Gerald George *manufacturing executive*
Schwan, Howard W. *manufacturing executive*

Bedford Park
Courtney, David W. *chemical company executive*

Broadview
Pang, Joshua Keun-Uk *trade company executive*

Chester
Welge, Donald Edward *food manufacturing executive*

Chicago
Adelson, Lawrence Seth *electronics executive, lawyer*
Angelo, Jim *construction company executive*
Barnes, Brenda C. *food and apparel executive*
Begel, Thomas M. *manufacturing executive*
Borenstine, Alvin Jerome *search company executive*
Brake, Cecil Clifford *retired diversified manufacturing executive*
Bryan, John Henry *food and consumer products company executive*
Bueche, Wendell Francis *agricultural products company executive*
Burdiss, James E. *paper company executive*
Carr, Jeffrey W. *manufacturing executive*
Chaden, Lee A. *food products executive*
Chiappetta, Robert A. *manufacturing executive*
Clarke, Richard Stewart *security company executive*
Clevenger, Penelope *food products executive*
Cline, William Chambers *automotive executive*
Conant, Howard Rosset *steel company executive*
Cooper, Charles Gilbert *toiletries and cosmetics company executive*
Cotter, Daniel A. *diversified company executive*
Covalt, Robert Byron *chemicals executive*
Crown, Lester *manufacturing executive*
Crown, William H. *manufacturing executive*
Curran, Raymond M. *paper-based packaging company executive*
deKool, L.M. (Theo) *food products executive*
DiStasio, Richard P. *manufacturing executive*
Drexler, Richard Allan *manufacturing executive*
Ellis, Christopher L. *manufacturing executive*
Ferguson, Diana S. *food products executive*
Freidheim, Cyrus F., Jr., *fruit company executive*
Gamoran, Reuben *candy company executive*
Gidwitz, Gerald *retired hair care company executive*
Giesen, Richard Allyn *manufacturing executive*
Goetschel, Arthur W. *industrial manufacturing executive*
Gordon, Ellen Rubin *candy company executive*
Heisley, Michael E., Sr., *manufacturing executive*
Holland, Eugene, Jr., *lumber company executive*
Hunt, Craig A. *paper company executive*
Jamieson, James M. *manufacturing executive*
Jezuit, Leslie James *manufacturing executive*
Kalina, John *auto parts company executive*
Kampouris, Emmanuel Andrew *retired corporate executive*
Koeliner, Laurette *manufacturing executive, human resources specialist*
Kopriva, Robert S. *food products executive*
Lazarus, Steven *technology company exective*
Little, William G. *manufacturing executive*
Lockwood, Frank James *manufacturing executive*
Manganello, Timothy M. *auto parts company executive*
McKee, Keith Earl *manufacturing technology executive*
McMillan, C. Steven *consumer packaged goods company executive*
McMillan, Cary D. *food products executive*
McQuillen, James Francis *electronics executive*
Miglin, Marilyn *cosmetics executive*
Montgomery, Gary B. *manufacturing executive*
Moore, Patrick J. *paper company executive*
Murphy, Michael Emmett *retired food company executive*
Netherland, Joseph H. *manufacturing executive*
Nichol, Norman J. *manufacturing executive*
Nichols, John Doane *diversified manufacturing corporation executive*
Novich, Neil S. *metals distribution company executive*
Niihn, Adriaan *food products executive*
Owen, Clarence B. *construction materials manufacturing executive*
Parrish, Overton Burgin, Jr., *pharmaceutical corporation executive*
Patel, Homi Burjor *apparel company executive*
Reum, W. Robert *manufacturing executive*
Rosenberg, Gary Aron *real estate development executive, lawyer*
Rubin, Stephen D. *food products executive*
Sanderman, Maurice *construction company executive*
Sippey, Roger Boyd *corporate executive*
Skyes, Gregory *food products executive*
Sprieser, Judith A. *food products company executive*
Stack, Stephen S. *manufacturing executive*
Steinfeld, Manfred *furniture manufacturing executive*
Stoklosa, Gregory A. *paper company executive*
Stone, Alan *container company executive*
Stotler, Edith Ann *retired grain company executive, financial planner*
Sykes, Gregory *food products executive*
Taylor-Williams, Bonnie Jean *cosmetics executive*
Tryloff, Robin S. *food products executive*
Velasquez, Arthur *food products executive*
Walsh, Mathew M. *construction executive*
Waters, Ronald V., III, *candy company executive*
Wellington, Robert Hall *manufacturing executive, director*
Williams, Richard Lucas, III, *electronics company executive, lawyer*
Wolfert, Frederick E. (Rick Wolfert) *healthcare financial services company executive*
Wrigley, William, Jr., *candy company executive*
Zeid, Philip L. *metal recycling executive*
Zerbe, Darell *metal products executive*

Crystal Lake
Althoff, J(ames) L. *construction company executive*
Anderson, Lyle Arthur *retired manufacturing company executive*
Booth, David Layton *retired chemicals executive*

Decatur
Andreas, G(lenn) Allen, Jr., *agricultural company executive*
Batchelder, Lewis W. *grain company executive*
Kraft, Burnell D. *agricultural products company executive*
Madding, Claudia *agricultural products executive*
McNamara, John D. *food products executive*
Mills, Steven R. *food products executive*
Preiksaitis, Raymond V. *food products executive*
Schmalz, Douglas J. *agricultural company executive*

Deer Park
Buchanan, Richard Kent *electronics company executive*

Deerfield
Anderson, Timothy *pharmaceutical executive*
Beard, Eric A. *pharmaceutical executive*
Del Salto, Carlos *pharmaceutical executive*
Drohan, David F. *medical products company executive*
Graham, William B. *pharmaceutical company executive*
Parkinson, Robert L., Jr., *medical products executive, health facility administrator*
Rucci, Anthony Joseph *health care products and services executive*
Zywicki, Robert Albert *retired electrical distribution company executive*

Dekalb
Bickner, Bruce *food products executive*
Troyer, Alvah Forrest *agriculture executive, plant breeder*

Des Plaines
Frank, James S. *automotive executive*
Koford, Stuart Keith *electronics executive*
O'Dwyer, Mary Ann *automotive executive*
Pearson, Ford G. *automotive executive*

Downers Grove
Grinter, Donald W. *metal processing executive*
Stevenson, Judy G. *instrument manufacturing executive*

Effingham
Bonutti, Boris Paul *medical company executive*

Elgin
Bassoul, Selim A. *food products executive*

Elk Grove Village
Field, Larry *paper company executive*

Elmhurst
Duchossois, Richard Louis *manufacturing executive, racetrack executive*
Fealy, Robert S. *manufacturing executive*

Evanston
Menke, Allen Carl *industrial corporation executive*

Forest Park
Thomas, Alan *candy company executive*

Frankfort
Burhoe, Brian Walter *automotive service executive*

Franklin Park
Caruso, Fred *plastics manufacturing company executive*
Dean, Howard M., Jr., *food company executive*
Greisinger, James *food products executive*
Simpson, Michael *metals service center executive*

Freeport
McDonough, John J. *household products company executive*
Sovey, William Pierre *manufacturing executive*

Glen Ellyn
Cvengros, Joseph Michael *manufacturing company executive*

Glenview
Blase, Anthony Idomeneus *retired electronics executive, writer, poet*
Farrell, W. James *metal products manufacturing company executive*
Gillis, Marvin Bob *retired chemical executive, consultant*
Hickey, John Thomas *retired electronics company executive*
Hudnut, Stewart Skinner *manufacturing executive, lawyer*
Kinney, Jon C. *metal products executive*
Ptak, Frank Stanley *manufacturing executive*
Ringler, James M. *cookware company executive*
Salamoun, Peter V. *retired manufacturing executive*
Smith, Harold B. *manufacturing executive*

Gurnee
Reinhoudt, Johannes Feike *pharmaceutical industry executive*

Highland Park
Rudo, Milton *retired manufacturing company executive, consultant*

Hoffman Estates
Nicholas, Arthur Soterios *manufacturing executive*

Huntley
Plunkett, Melba Kathleen *manufacturing executive*

Inverness
Matsushima, Akira Paul *international company executive*

Itasca
Boler, John M. *manufacturing executive*
Fellowes, James *manufacturing executive*
Garratt, Reginald George *electronics executive*
Ladner, Kathleen Floyd-Teniya *business services executive*

Joliet
Schmitz, Edward Henry *retired distribution company executive*

Kenilworth
Weiner, Joel David *retired consumer packaged goods products executive*

La Grange
Rancourt, John Herbert *retired pharmaceutical company executive, marine engineer*

Lake Forest
Buckley, George W. *sporting goods executive*
Campbell, Andrew *manufacturing executive*
Carroll, Barry Joseph *manufacturing and real estate executive*
Clark, Wesley M. *manufacturing executive*
Donovan, Timothy R. *automotive executive*
Dreimann, Leonhard *manufacturing executive*
Fowler, Robert Edward, Jr., *former agricultural products company executive*
Frissora, Mark P. *automotive parts manufacturing company executive*
Hadad, Sam *food products distribution executive*
Hamilton, Peter Bannerman *manufacturing executive, lawyer*
Hammar, Lester Everett *retired manufacturing executive*
Haser, William H. *automotive executive*
Hodgson, Thomas Richard *retired healthcare company executive*
Keyser, Richard Lee *distribution company executive*
Larson, Peter N. *manufacturing executive*
Leemputte, Peter G. *manufacturing executive*
McGinley, Jack L. *healthcare company executive*
O'Mara, Thomas Patrick *manufacturing executive*
Reyes, M. Jude *food products distribution executive*
Romans, Donald Bishop *corporate executive*
Trammell, Kenneth R. *automotive executive*

Lanark
Abbott, David Henry *manufacturing executive*

Libertyville
Burrows, Brian William *research and development manufacturing executive*

Lincolnshire
Simes, Stephen Mark *pharmaceutical products executive*
Wesley, Norman H. *metal products executive*

Lisle
King, J. Joseph *electronics executive*
Krehbiel, Frederick August, II, *electronics company executive*

Loves Park
Gloyd, Lawrence Eugene *retired diversified manufacturing company executive*

Matteson
Johnson, Eric G. *food products company executive*

Mc Gaw Park
Kesman, Anthony K. *medical products executive*

Melrose Park
Bernick, Howard Barry *manufacturing executive*
Cernugel, William John *consumer products and special retail executive*
Douglas, Kenneth Jay *food products executive*
Lavin, Bernice E. *cosmetics executive*
Umans, Alvin Robert *manufacturing executive*
Van Helden, Pete *food products executive*
Wechter, Clari Ann *manufacturing executive*

Moline
Becherer, Hans Walter *retired agricultural equipment executive*
Jones, Nathan Jerome *farm machinery manufacturing company executive*
Lane, Robert W. *farm equipment manufacturing executive*

Mount Sterling
Tracy, Patrick F. *food products executive*

Mundelein
Mills, James Stephen *medical supply company executive*
Raviv, Gabriel *medical products executive*

Naperville
Dunning, Richard L. *health products executive*
Katai, Andrew Andras *chemical company executive*
Rao, Prasad *electronics executive*
Ryan, Joan *food company executive*
Smetana, Mark *food products executive*
Wake, Richard W. *food products executive*
Wake, Thomas G. *food products executive*

Niles
Abinion, Emir C. *automotive executive*
Herb, Marvin J. *food products executive*

Northbrook
Green, David *manufacturing executive*

Northfield
Brown, A. Demetrius *metal products executive*
Carlin, Donald Walter *retired food products executive, consultant*
Hadley, Stanton Thomas *manufacturing and marketing company executive, lawyer*
Holden, Betsy D. *food products company executive*
Knight, James Atwood *manufacturing executive*
Smeds, Edward William *retired food company executive*
Sneed, Paula Ann *food products executive*
Stepan, Frank Quinn *chemical company executive*

Oak Brook
Armario, Jose *restaurant executive*
Conley, Michael L. *food products executive*
Kanzler, Michael W. *manufacturing executive*
Kirshnan, Raama *electronics executive*
Onstead, R. Randall, Jr., *food products executive*
Roberts, Michael J. *food products executive*
Skinner, Jim *food products executive*
Smyth, Russell P. *food products executive*
Thompson, Don *food products executive*
Whaley, Marvin *food products executive*

Oak Park
Dong, Hanmin *forest products executive*

Olympia Fields
Delano, Jimmy Gboyega *business executive, accountant*

Orland Park
Kahn, Jan Edward *manufacturing executive*

Palos Park
Nelson, Lawrence Evan *business consultant*

Peoria
Baumgartner, Vito H. *manufacturing executive*
McPheeters, F. Lynn *manufacturing executive*
Oberhelman, Douglas R. *tractor company executive*
Owens, James W. *manufacturing executive*
Shaheen, Gerald L. *manufacturing executive*
Thompson, Richard L. *manufacturing executive*
Thorstenson, Terry N. *construction equipment company executive*

Prospect Heights
Byrne, Michael Joseph *manufacturing executive*

Quincy
Cornell, Helen W. *manufacturing executive*

Rockford
Bippus, David Paul *manufacturing executive*
O'Donnell, William David *retired construction firm executive*

Rolling Meadows
Cash, Alan Sherwin *electronics assembly specialist*
Hill, David K., Jr., *construction executive*

Rosemont
Isenberg, Howard Lee *manufacturing executive*
Meinert, John Raymond *investment banker, clothing manufacturing and retailing executive*

Saint Charles
Fishbune, Robert *food products executive*
Stone, John McWilliams, Jr., *electronics executive*
Wolski, L.G. *heavy manufacturing executive*

Schaumburg
Anderson, Scott A. *electronics executive*
Brown, Greg *electronics executive*
Canavan, Patrick J. *electronics executive*
Delaney, Gene *electronics executive*
Desai, Samir T. *electronics executive*
Galvin, Robert W. *electronics executive*
Moloney, Daniel M. *electronics executive*
Nemcek, Adrian R. *electronics executive*
Richter, Glenn *manufacturing executive*
Shlapak, Fred *electronics executive*
Soderberg, Leif G. *electronics company executive*
Soon-Shiong, Patrick *pharmaceutical executive*
Zander, Edward *electronics executive*

Tinley Park
Leeson, Janet Caroline Tollefson *cake specialties company executive*

Vernon Hills
Kaplan, Edward L. *electronics executive*

Warrenville
Horne, John R. *farm equipment company executive*
Lannert, Robert Cornelius *manufacturing executive*
Lennes, Gregory *manufacturing and financing company executive*

Waukegan
Cherry, Peter Ballard *electrical products corporation executive*

Westmont
DuBose, Michael T. *manufacturing executive*
Kuhn, Robert Mitchell *retired rubber company executive*

Wheeling
Rogers, Richard F. *construction company executive, architect, engineer*

Wilmette
Coughlan, Gary Patrick *pharmaceutical company executive*
Pearlman, Jerry Kent *electronics company executive*

Winnetka
Burt, Robert Norcross *retired diversified manufacturing company executive*
Gavin, James John, Jr., *diversified company executive*
Hartman, Robert S. *retired paper company executive*
Kennedy, George Danner *chemical company executive*
Puth, John Wells *consulting company executive*
Weldon, Theodore Tefft, Jr., *manufacturing executive*

Wood Dale
Storch, David *manufacturing executive*

Woodridge
Stall, Alan David *packaging company executive*

INDIANA

Anderson
Carrell, Terry Eugene *manufacturing executive*
Snyder, Thomas J. *automotive company executive*

Batesville
Hillenbrand, Daniel A. *manufacturing executive*
Sorenson, Scott K. *manufacturing executive*

Bluffton
Lawson, William Hogan, III, *electrical motor manufacturing executive*

Brownstown
Robertson, Joseph Edmond *grain processing company executive*
Robertson, Richard Robert *grain milling executive*

Carmel
Shoup, Charles Samuel, Jr., *chemicals and materials executive*
Walsh, John Charles *metallurgical company executive*

Columbus
Engelking, Ellen Melinda *textiles executive, manufacturing executive, real estate broker*
Henderson, James Alan *former engine company executive*
Loughrey, F. Joseph *manufacturing executive*
Miller, Joseph Irwin *automotive manufacturing company executive*

Elkhart
Holtz, Glenn Edward *band instrument manufacturing executive*
Kloska, Ronald Frank *manufacturing executive*
Martin, Rex *manufacturing executive*
Mathias, Margaret Grossman *manufacturing company executive, leasing company executive*
Mischke, Frederick Charles *retired manufacturing executive*

Evansville
Koch, Robert Louis, II, *manufacturing company executive, mechanical engineer*
Muehlbauer, James Herman *manufacturing executive*

Fort Wayne
Burns, Thagrus Asher *manufacturing company executive, former life insurance company executive*
Marine, Clyde Lockwood *agricultural business consultant*
Rifkin, Leonard *metals company executive*

Goshen
Davis, Cole (Coleman Davis III) *recreational vehicle manufacturing executive*

Granger
Miller, Callix Edwin *manufacturing executive, consultant*

Greenfield
Powdrill, Gary Leo *production operations manager*

Indianapolis
Atkins, Steven *construction executive, contractor*
Bindley, William Edward *pharmaceutical executive*
Brauer, Keith E. *medical products executive*
Breier, Alan *pharmaceutical executive*
Burks, Keith W. *pharmaceutical executive*
Dollens, Ronald W. *pharmaceuticals company executive*
Fischer, A. Charles *pharmaceutical executive*
Franson, Timothy Raymond *pharmaceutical executive, epidemiologist*
Golden, Charles Edward *pharmaceutical company executive*
Goodman, Dwight *manufacturing executive*
Hunt, Robert Chester *construction company executive*
Hunt, Robert G. *construction company executive*
King, J. B. *medical device company executive, lawyer*
Kirkham, James Alvin *manufacturing executive*
Lacy, Andre Balz *industrial executive*
Lewis, Jeff *construction company executive*
Long, William Allan *retired forest products company executive*
Lorell, Beverly H. *medical products executive*
Mays, William G. *chemical company executive*
McConnell, William F., Jr., *medical products executive*
Mc Farland, H. Richard *food company executive*
Peribere, Jerome A. *agricultural products executive*
Ramadan, Nabih M. *pharmaceutical company official, educator*
Risdon, Michael Paul *manufacturing executive*
Salentine, Thomas James *pharmaceutical company executive*
Scheumann, John B. *construction executive*
SerVaas, Beurt Richard *manufacturing executive*
Smith, Donald Archie *religion business executive, consultant*
Taurel, Sidney *pharmaceutical executive*

Jasper
Thyen, James C. *furniture company executive*

Lafayette
Meyer, Brud Richard *retired pharmaceutical company executive*

Middlebury
Corson, Thomas Harold *manufacturing executive*
Guequierre, John Phillip *manufacturing executive*

Mishawaka
Altman, Arnold David *manufacturing executive*
Kapson, Jordan *automotive executive*
Merryman, George *automotive executive*
Rubenstein, Pamela Silver *manufacturing executive*
Silver, Neil Marvin *manufacturing executive*

Muncie
Fisher, John Wesley *manufacturing executive, director*
Smith, Van P. *holding company executive*

Munster
Corsiglia, Robert Joseph *electrical construction company executive*

Nappanee
Shea, James F. *manufacturing executive*

Portage
Popp, Joseph Bruce *manufacturing executive*

Rosemont
Reyes, J. Christopher *food products distribution executive*

Seymour
Rust, Lois *food company executive*

Washington
Graham, David Bolden *food products executive*

Yorktown
Bryja, Frank Joseph *food distribution executive*

Zionsville
Grimm, Kay L. *agricultural products executive*

IOWA

Ames
Abbott, David L. *agricultural products executive*

Ankeny
Scott, Beverly Jeanne *contractor, writer*
Wirtz, Eli J. *convenience stores executive*

Boone
Beckwith, F. William *food products executive*

Cedar Rapids
Erickson, Lawrence A. (Larry Erickson) *electronics executive*
Jones, Clayton M. *computer and electronics company executive*

Davenport
Bannick, Janice Carol *automotive dealerships executive*
Juckem, Wilfred Philip *manufacturing executive*

Dubuque
Crahan, Jack Bertsch *retired manufacturing company executive*
Gansen, Ronald E. *lumber company executive*
McDonald, Robert Delos *manufacturing executive*
Tully, Thomas Alois *building materials executive, consultant, educator*

Humboldt
Dodgen, John N. *manufacturing executive*

Muscatine
Michaels, Jack D. *office furniture manufacturing executive*

Newton
Moore, George C. *manufacturing executive*
Ward, Lloyd D. *appliance company executive*

Okoboji
Pearson, Gerald Leon *food company executive*

Red Oak
Stoner, Leonard D. *automotive parts company executive*

Saint Ansgar
Kleinworth, Edward J. *agricultural company executive*

Springville
Nyquist, John Davis *retired radio manufacturing company executive*

Toddville
Hazeltine, Gerald Lester *food products executive*

West Des Moines
Briggs, John C. *food products executive*
Pomerantz, Marvin Alvin *manufacturing executive*

KANSAS

Abilene
Britt, Ronald leroy *retired manufacturing company executive*

Hutchinson
Dick, Harold Latham *manufacturing executive*

Kansas City
Baker, Clarence Albert, Sr., *structural steel construction company executive*

Leavenworth
Arneson, George Stephen *manufacturing executive, management consultant*

Lenexa
Ascher, James John *pharmaceutical executive*
Barr, William Crawford *manufacturing executive*

Paola
Krum, Jack Kern *food products executive*

Salina
Cosco, John Anthony *health care executive, educator, consultant, author*

Scott City
Duff, Craig *agricultural products executive*

Shawnee Mission
Barger, Donald Gordon, Jr., *automotive products company executive*
Gamet, Donald Max *appliance company executive*

Topeka
Etzel, Timothy *manufacturing executive*
Stroud, Jacqueline Lucille *medical supply company executive*

Wichita
Johnson, George Taylor *training and manufacturing executive*
Meyer, Russell William, Jr., *aircraft company executive*
Nienke, Steven A. *construction company executive*
Schuster, James Edward *aircraft manufacturing executive*

KENTUCKY

Bellevue
Carpenter, Woodrow Wilson *enamel company executive, ceramic engineer*

Bowling Green
Ahmed, S. Basheer *research company executive, educator*
Holland, John Ben *clothing manufacturing company executive*

Covington
D'Antoni, David J. *chemicals executive*
O'Brien, James J. *manufacturing executive*
Quin, Joseph Marvin *chemicals executive*

Erlanger
Cuneo, Dennis Clifford *automotive company executive*
Niimi, Atsushi *automotive executive*

Fort Mitchell
Drees, David G. *construction executive*
Drees, Ralph *construction executive*

Franklin
David, Phillip J. *biotechnology company executive*

Georgetown
Convis, Gary L. *automotive executive*

Greenville
Walters, Sue Fox *business executive, accountant*

Lexington
Chowdhury, Dipak K. *pharmaceutical executive, researcher*
Gornik, Kathy *electronics executive*
Gray, Lois Howard *construction company executive*
Holland, Robert, Jr., *food products executive*

Louisville
Bujake, John Edward, Jr., *beverage company executive*
Drazin, Avrum I. *manufacturing executive*
Dreher, Donald Dean *furniture manufacturing executive*
Heiden, Charles Kenneth *metal products executive, consultant, retired military officer*
Jones, David Allen *health benefits company executive*
Lego, Paul Edward *retired corporation executive*
Mountz, Wade *retired health service management executive*

Allegan
Kupstas, Corrine Lynn *manufacturing executive*

Ann Arbor
Caveney, William John *former pharmaceutical company executive, lawyer*
Cole, David Edward *automotive executive, educator*
Decaire, John *electronics executive, aerospace engineer*
Decker, Raymond Frank *technology transfer executive, metal products executive, scientist*
Eberbach, Steven John *retired electronics company executive*
Herzig, David Jacob *retired pharmaceutical company executive, consultant*
Musich, Shirley Ann *research and development company executive*
Penske, Roger S. *manufacturing and transportation executive*

Auburn Hills
Davidson, William M. *manufacturing executive, professional sports team executive*
Farrar, Stephen Prescott *glass products manufacturing executive*
Gerson, Ralph Joseph *corporate executive*
LaSorda, Thomas W. *automotive executive*
Sidlik, Thomas W. *automotive executive*
Trebing, David Martin *automotive executive*
Valade, Gary C. *automobile company executive*

Battle Creek
Bryant, John A. *food products executive*
Gutierrez, Carlos M. *grocery manufacturing company executive*
Mackay, A.D. David *food products executive*
Pilnick, Gary H. *food products executive*
Shei, H. Ray *food products executive*

Benton Harbor
Brown, Mark E. *manufacturing executive*
Fettig, Jeff M. *manufacturing executive*
Periquito, Paulo F.M.O. *manufacturing executive*
Thieneman, Michael D. *manufacturing executive*
Todman, Michael A. *manufacturing executive*

Beulah
Edwards, Wallace Winfield *retired automotive executive*

Birmingham
Foxen, Richard William *manufacturing executive*

Bloomfield Hills
DiFeo, Samuel X. *automotive executive*
Dugas, Richard J., Jr., *construction executive*
Frey, Stuart Macklin *automobile manufacturing company executive*
Hagenlocker, Edward E. *retired automobile company executive*
Mullens, Delbert W. *automotive executive*
O'Brien, Mark J. *real estate/residential construction executive*
Pulte, William J. *construction executive*

Bloomfield Village
Maxwell, Jack Erwin *manufacturing executive*

Brooklyn
Vischer, Harold Harry *manufacturing executive*

Burt
Wolverton, Thomas Frank *automotive company supervisor*

Cass City
Althaver, Lambert Ewing *manufacturing executive*

Dearborn
Barton, Robert H., III, *automotive executive*
Booker, W. Wayne *former automotive executive*
Brown, Thomas K. *automotive executive*
Buckingham, Lorie *automotive executive*
Chatterjee, Anjan *automotive executive*
Corlett, Ed *automotive executive*
Fields, Mark *automotive executive*
Ford, William Clay *automotive company executive, professional sports team executive*
Ford, William Clay, Jr., (Bill Ford) *automotive executive*
Fox, Stacy *automotive executive*
Johnston, Michael Francis *auto parts company executive*
Krygier, Roman J. *automotive executive*
Leclair, Don R., Jr., *automotive executive*
Lundy, J(oseph) Edward *retired automobile company executive*
Marcin, Robert H. *automotive executive*
Mays, J.C. *automotive executive*
Mohan Iyengar, Raj *automotive executive, researcher*
O'Connor, James G. *auto company executive*
Pacheco, Susan *automotive executive*
Parry-Jones, Richard *automotive executive*
Pestillo, Peter John *auto parts company executive, lawyer*
Petrauskas, Helen O. *automobile manufacturing company executive*
Rintamaki, John M. *automotive executive*
Ross, Dennis E. *automotive executive*
Scheele, Nicholas V. *automotive executive*
Smith, Gregory C. *automotive executive*
Thursfield, David W. *automotive executive*
Wagner, Terrance Carl *automotive executive*
Zimmerman, Martin B. *automotive executive*

Detroit
Aguirre, Pamela Ann *manufacturing executive*
Anderson, Bo I. *automotive executive*
Augustsson, Peter *automotive executive*
Barclay, Kathleen S. *automotive executive*
Browning, Jonathan *automotive executive*
Burns, Lawrence D. *automotive executive*
Burns, Michael J. *automotive executive*
Buttermore, John R. *automotive executive*
Cherry, Wayne K. *automotive executive*
Clarke, Troy A. *automotive executive*
Cole, Kenneth W. *automotive executive*
Dauch, Richard E. *automobile manufacturing company executive*
Demant, Hans Henrich *automotive executive*
Devine, John Martin *automotive company executive*
Elias, Arturo *automotive executive*
Elson, Gerald *automotive executive*
Forster, Carl-Peter *automotive executive*
Gerosa, Peter R. *automotive executive*
Gillum, Roderick D. *v.p. corporate responsibility and diversity*
Grimaldi, Michael J. *automotive executive*
Happel, R. William *automotive executive*
Henderson, Frederick A. *automotive executive*
Henry, William Lockwood *former food products executive, brewery executive*
Herberger, Douglas J. *automotive executive*
Hogan, Mark T. *automotive executive*
Hughes, Louis Ralph *automotive executive*
Kantrowitz, Jean *health products executive*
Koerner, Edward C. *automotive executive*
Kurnick, Robert H., Jr., *automotive executive, lawyer*
Levy, Edward Charles, Jr., *manufacturing executive*
Losh, J. Michael *automotive company executive*
Lowery, Elizabeth *automotive executive*
Lutz, Robert Anthony *automotive company executive*
Murtaugh, Phillip F. *automotive executive*
Patel, Homi K. *automotive executive*
Pickard, William Frank *plastics company executive*
Queen, James E. *automotive executive*
Rakolta, John, Jr., *construction executive*
Robinson, Joel D. *manufacturing executive*
Sears, Kent T. *automotive executive*
Smith, John Francis, Jr., *retired automobile company executive*
Soave, Anthony *manufacturing executive*
Spielman, Joseph D. *automotive executive*
Stephens, Thomas G. *automotive executive*
Szygenda, Ralph J. *automotive executive*
Wagoner, G. Richard, Jr., *automotive company executive*
Wale, Kevin E. *automotive executive*
Welburn, Edward T. *automotive executive*
Wieland, Gualterio *automotive executive*
Wiemels, James R. *automotive executive*
Williams, Kevin W. *automotive executive*
Young, Ray G. *automotive executive*

Farmington
Badawy, Aly Ahmed *automotive parts manufacturing company executive*

Ferndale
Dodd, Geralda *metal products executive*

Fraser
Butler, James E. *automotive executive*
Winget, Larry J., Sr., *automotive industry executive*

Grand Haven
Sabolcik, Gene *manufacturing executive*

Grand Rapids
Baker, Hollis MacLure *furniture manufacturing company executive*
Dykstra, William Dwight *business executive, consultant*
Hackett, James P. *manufacturing executive*
Keane, James P. *manufacturing executive*
Pew, Robert Cunningham, II, *office equipment manufacturing company executive*
Rougier-Chapman, Alwyn Spencer Douglas *furniture manufacturing company executive*
Woodrick, Robert *food products executive*

Grosse Pointe
Wilkinson, Warren Scripps *manufacturing executive*

Grosse Pointe Farms
Obolensky, Marilyn Wall (Mrs. Serge Obolensky) *metals company executive*
Valk, Robert Earl *corporate executive*

Holland
Haworth, Gerrard Wendell *office furniture manufacturing company executive*
Haworth, Richard G. *office furniture manufacturer*
Krasa, Robert *manufacturing executive*
Kreuze, Calvin *office products company executive*

Houghton
Utt, Glenn S., Jr., *medical products executive*

Jackson
Kelly, Robert Vincent, Jr., *metal company executive*

Kalamazoo
Bergy, Dean H. *health products executive*
Brown, John Wilford *health products executive*
Hubbard, William Neill, Jr., *retired pharmaceutical executive*
Hudson, Roy Davage *retired pharmaceutical executive*
Jones, Eugene Gordon *pharmaceutical company executive*
Markin, David Robert *motor company executive*
Meisenhelder, Robert John, II, *pharmaceutical company executive*
Moe, James Burton *pharmaceutical company executive*
Parfet, Donald Reid *pharmaceutical executive*

Lansing
Stowers, Mark David *chemicals executive*

Livonia
Cantie, Joseph S. *automotive executive*
Drouin, Joe *automotive executive*
Lunn, Steve *automotive executive*
Plant, John Charles *automotive equipment company executive*

Madison Heights
Kafarski, Mitchell I. *chemical processing company executive*

Mason
Myers, William *food container manufacturing executive*
Thayer, Bruce Allen *automotive executive, artist*

Midland
Allemang, Arnold A. *chemicals executive*
Bader, Kathleen M. *chemicals executive*
Carbone, Anthony J. *chemicals executive*
Gross, Richard M. *chemicals executive*
Hampton, Leroy *retired chemical company executive*
Hazleton, Richard A. *chemicals executive*
Kepler, David E., II, *chemicals executive*
Kreinberg, Romeo *chemicals executive*
Liveris, Andrew N. *chemicals executive*
Manetta, Richard *chemicals executive*
McMaster, Lee P. *chemicals executive*
Reinhard, Joao Pedro *chemicals company executive*
Schmidt, William C. *retired chemicals executive*
Stavropoulos, William S. *chemical executive*
Walthie, T. H. *chemicals executive*
Washington, Lawrence J., Jr., *chemicals executive*
Wood, Robert L. *chemicals executive*

Monroe
Darrow, Kurt L.
Kiser, Gerald L. *furniture company executive*

Muskegon
Blystone, John B. *manufacturing executive*
Turner, Peter Merrick *retired manufacturing company executive*

Northville
Clawson, Curtis J. *manufacturing executive*
Clemens, Michael Terrence *furniture manufacturing representative*
Yost, James A. *manufacturing executive*

Novi
Ligocki, Kathleen A. *auto parts company executive*
Mallak, James A. *auto parts company executive*

Okemos
Dowley, Joel Edward *manufacturing executive, lawyer*

Owosso
Guthrie, Carlton L. *automotive manufacturing company executive*

Plymouth
Leuliette, Timothy D. *automotive executive*
Massey, Donald E. *automotive executive*
Vlcek, Donald Joseph, Jr., *food distribution company executive, consultant, business author, executive coach*

Portage
MacMillan, Stephen P. *health products executive*

Rochester Hills
Akeel, Hadi Abu *robotics executive*
Bovee, David R. *automotive executive*
Denton, Lawrence A. *automotive executive*

Romeo
Stryker, James William *retired automotive executive, former military officer*

Rose Township
Fleming, Kathryn Alice *retired automotive executive*

Royal Oak
Cook, Noel Robert *manufacturing executive*

Saginaw
Remenar, Robert J. *automotive executive*

Saint Joseph
King, George Raleigh *retired manufacturing executive*

Saline
Macher, Frank E. *automotive executive*

Saranac
Herbrucks, Stephen *food products executive*

Southfield
DelGrosso, Douglas G. *manufacturing executive*
Gouldey, Glenn Charles *manufacturing executive*
Lynch, George Michael *auto parts manufacturing executive*
Maibach, Ben C., III, *construction company executive*
McClure, Charles G. *automotive executive*
Ponka, Lawrence John *automotive executive*
Rossiter, Robert E. *interior auto parts manufacturing executive*
Shilts, Nancy S. *automotive executive, lawyer*
Snell, Richard A. *equipment manufacturing company executive*
Stebbins, Donald J. *car parts manufacturing company executive*
Tupper, Leon F. *manufacturing executive*
Wajsgras, David C. *manufacturing executive*
Way, Kenneth L. *motor vehicle seat manufacturing company executive*
Wisne, Lawrence A. *metal products executive*

Taylor
Manoogian, Richard Alexander *manufacturing executive*
Rosowski, Robert Bernard *manufacturing executive*

Tecumseh
Herrick, Kenneth Gilbert *manufacturing executive*
Herrick, Todd W. *manufacturing executive*

Traverse City
Parsons, John Thoren *manufacturing executive*

Troy
Acton, David L(awrence) *automobile company executive*
Arle, John P. *electronics executive*
Barth, Volker J. *electronics executive*
Battenberg, J. T., III, *automotive company executive*
Bertrand, James A. *electronics executive*
Bickmeyer, Robert A. *retired automotive executive*
Blahnik, John G. *electronics executive*
Buschmann, Siegfried *manufacturing executive*
Butler, Kevin M. *electronics executive*
Corace, Joseph Russell *automotive executive*
Dawes, Alan S. *automotive company executive*
Elder, Irma *retail automotive executive*
Given, Kerry Wade *plastics industry executive*
Hachey, Guy C. *electronics executive*
Handleman, David *audio products company executive*
Healy, Karen *automotive executive*
Janak, Peter Harold *automotive company executive*
Lorenz, Mark C. *automotive executive*
Martin, Raymond Bruce *plumbing equipment manufacturing company executive*
Nelson, R. David *electronics executive*
O'Neal, Rodney *automotive executive*
Ordonez, Francisco A. (Frank) *automotive executive*
Owens, Jeffrey J. *electronics executive*
Pasricha, Atul *automotive executive*
Runkle, Donald L. *electronics executive*
Sharf, Stephan *automotive company executive*
Sheehan, John D. *automotive executive*
Sloan, Hugh Walter, Jr., *automotive executive*
Walker, Bette *automotive executive*
Weber, Mark R. *electronics executive*
Whitson, James P. *automotive executive*
Williams, David Perry *manufacturing executive*
Wohleen, David B. *electronics executive*
Yost, Larry D. *automotive executive*

Warren
Ableson, Donald William *automobile industry executive*
Mahone, Barbara Jean *automotive company executive*

Washington
Gothard, Donald Lee *retired auto company executive*

Whitehall
Squier, David Louis *manufacturing executive*

Ypsilanti
Edwards, Gerald *plastics company executive*

Zeeland
Bauer, Fred T. *technology products executive*
Nickels, Elizabeth Anne *office furniture manufacturing executive*
Volkema, Michael A. *office furniture manufacturer*

MINNESOTA

Austin
Johnson, Joel W. *food products executive*
McCoy, Michael J. *food products company executive*

Bayport
Garofalo, Donald R. *window manufacturing executive*
Humphrey, James E. *manufacturing executive*
Johnson, Michael O. *window manufacturing executive*

Bloomington
Sherman, Patsy O'Connell *retired technical development administrator, chemist*

Brooklyn Park
Rogers, David *apparel executive*

Eagan
Clemens, T. Pat *manufacturing executive*

Eden Prairie
Henningsen, Peter, Jr., *diversified industry executive*

Edina
Brown, Charles Eugene *retired electronics company executive*
Sampson, John Eugene *consulting company executive*

Fairmont
Rosen, Thomas J. *food and agricultural products executive*

Golden Valley
Hogan, Randall J. *manufacturing executive, electronics executive*

Hamel
Tiller, Thomas C. *manufacturing executive*

Hopkins
Rappaport, Gary Burton *defense equipment executive*

Inver Grove Heights
Johnson, John D. *grain company executive*
Schmitz, John *grain company executive*

Lindstrom
Messin, Marlene Ann *plastics company executive*

Loretto
Veit, Gae *construction executive*

Marshall
Beadle, John M. *food products executive*
Burr, Tracy L. *food products executive*
Herrmann, Dan *food products executive*
Miller, Donald *food products executive*
Pippin, M. Lenny *food products executive*

Mendota Heights
Frechette, Peter Loren *dental products executive*

Minneapolis
Bastiaens, F. Guillaume *food products executive*
Bonsignore, Michael Robert *former electronics and computer company executive*
Buhrmaster, Robert C. *manufacturing executive*
Collins, Arthur D., Jr., *medical products executive*
Curler, Jeffrey H. *packaging manufacturing executive*
Demeritt, Stephen R. *food products executive*
Dimond, Robert B. *food products executive*
Durkin, G. Michael *food products executive*
Ferrari, Giannantonio *electronics executive*
Findorff, Robert Lewis *retired air filtration equipment company executive*
Goldberger, Robert D. *food products company executive*
Hale, Roger Loucks *manufacturing executive, director*

Jacobs, Irwin Lawrence *diversified corporate executive*
Keiser, Kenneth E. *food products executive*
Lawrence, James A. *food products executive*
MacMillan, Whitney *food products and import/export company executive*
Micek, Ernest S. *former food products executive*
Mortenson, M. A., Jr., *construction executive*
Page, Gregory R. *food products executive*
Raisbeck, David W. *food products executive*
Reyelts, Paul C. *chemical company executive*
Roe, John H. *manufacturing executive*
Rompala, Richard M. *chemical company executive*
Spoor, William Howard *food company executive*
Stranghoener, Larry W. *manufacturing executive*
Sullivan, Austin Padraic, II, *diversified food company executive*
Van Dyke, William Grant *manufacturing executive*
Walsh, Paul S. *food products executive*
Wulf, Gene C. *manufacturing executive*
Wurtele, Christopher Angus *paint and coatings company executive*

Minnetonka
Byom, John E. *food company executive*
Fink, Richard *uniform company executive*
Leach, Michael *financial executive*
Moberly, Thomas *uniform company executive*
Moore, Terry L. *financial executive*

Minnetonka Mills
Hemsley, Stephen J. *healthcare company executive*

Moorhead
Stenerson, John Gorden *lumber and building materials executive*

Oakdale
Maekawa, Koji Ogura *technology company administrator*

Plymouth
Kahler, Herbert Frederick *diversified business executive*

Rochester
Mayr, James Jerome *fertilizer company executive*
Wood, Michael B. *chief executive officer, president*

Saint Paul
Campbell, Patrick D. *manufacturing executive*
Critzer, Susan L. *health products company executive*
DeSimone, Livio Diego *retired diversified manufacturing company executive*
Gherty, John E. *food products and agricultural products company executive*
Ihlenfeld, Jay V. *manufacturing executive*
Johnston, Manley Roderick *research and development company executive, chemist*
Knudson, Mark Bradley *medical corporation executive, venture capitalist*
Landwehr, Steven J. *manufacturing executive*
Laptewicz, Joseph E., Jr., *medical products executive*
Mahan, James T. *manufacturing executive*
McNerney, Walter James (Jim McNerney) *manufacturing executive*
Nozari, Moe S. *manufacturing executive*
Palensky, Frederick J. *manufacturing executive*
Powell, David W. *manufacturing executive*
Reich, Charles *manufacturing executive, research scientist*
Sauer, Brad T. *manufacturing executive, mechanical engineer*
Schuman, Allan L. *chemical company executive*
Stake, James B. *manufacturing executive*
Stroucken, Albert P.L. *chemical company executive*
Thulin, Inge G. *manufacturing executive*
Vierling, H. Philip *medical device company executive*
Wiens, Harold J. *electronics executive*

Stillwater
Delaney, John Charles *pharmaceutical company executive*

Wayzata
Blodgett, Frank Caleb *retired food company executive*
Hoffman, Gene D. *food company executive, consultant*
Johnson, Sankey Anton *manufacturing executive*
Luthringshauser, Daniel Rene *manufacturing executive*
Staley, Warren R. *agricultural products and diversified services company executive*
Swanson, Donald Frederick *retired food company executive*

MISSISSIPPI

Hattiesburg
Chain, Bobby Lee *electrical contractor, former mayor*

Jackson
Black, David R. *grocery company executive*
Johnson, Ronald E. *grocery company executive*
Julian, Michael *grocery company executive*

MISSOURI

Carthage
Flanigan, Matthew C. *manufacturing executive*
Wright, Felix E. *manufacturing executive*

Centralia
Everhart, James Gray *retired manufacturing executive*

Chesterfield
Carpenter, Will Dockery *chemical company executive*
Malvern, Donald *retired aircraft manufacturing company executive*

Excelsior Springs
Schroeder, Horst Wilhelm *food products executive*

Fulton
Backer, William Earnest *food products executive*

Grain Valley
Olsson, Björn Eskil *railroad supply company executive*

Granby
Haase, Dixie Carol *retired manufacturing worker, writer*

Kansas City
Bartlett, Paul Dana, Jr., *agribusiness executive*
Bass, Lee Marshall *food products company executive*
Belle, Gerald *pharmaceutical executive*
Berkley, Eugene Bertram (Bert Berkley) *envelope company executive*
Campbell, Terry M. *food products executive*
Dees, Stephen Phillip *agricultural finance executive, lawyer*
Dunn, Terrence P. *manufacturing executive*
Johnson, Richard Dean *pharmaceutical consultant, educator*
Kafoure, Michael D. *food products executive*
O'Dell, Jane *automotive company executive*
Sullivan, Charles A. *food products executive*
Terry, Robert Brooks *food products executive, lawyer*
Yarick, Paul E. *food products executive*

Lees Summit
Henley, Joseph Oliver *manufacturing executive*

Maryland Heights
Lowenberg, David A. *pharmaceutical executive*
Steward, David L. *technology company executive*
Tenholder, Edward J. *pharmaceutical executive*
Toan, Barrett A. *health products executive*

Naylor
Seratt, Rodger Calvin *manufacturing executive*

Saint Charles
Pundmann, Ed John, Jr., *automotive company executive*

Saint Louis
Abelov, Stephen Lawrence *uniform clothing company executive, consultant*
Adams, Albert Willie, Jr., *lubrication company executive*
Armstrong, J. Hord, III, *pharmaceutical company executive*
Baker, W. Randolph *brewery executive*
Beare, Gene Kerwin *electric company executive*
Berges, James G. *electric and electronic products executive*
Browde, Anatole *electronics company executive, consultant*
Brown, JoBeth Goode *food products executive, lawyer*
Busch, August Adolphus, III, *brewery executive*
Clausen, Robert A. *chemicals executive*
Clemens, Robert *instruments executive*
Crews, Terrell *agricultural products executive*
Cunningham, Charles Baker, III, *manufacturing executive*
Dill, Charles Anthony *manufacturing and computer company executive*
Donald, Arnold W. *food products executive*
Elsesser, James R. *food products company executive*
Farr, David N. *electronics executive*
Fox, Sam *manufacturing executive*
Galvin, Walter J. *electrical equipment manufacturing executive*
Gupta, Surendra Kumar *chemicals executive*
Hirsch, Raymond Robert *chemical company executive, lawyer*
Holman, C. Ray *medical products executive*
Howard, David P. *manufacturing executive*
Hunter, John C., III, *chemicals executive*
Jacob, John Edward *corporate executive, communications executive*
Kaestner, John Thomas *beverage company executive*
Keyes, Marion Alvah, IV, *manufacturing executive*
Knight, Charles Field *electrical equipment manufacturing company executive*
Kummer, Fred S. *construction company executive*
Lambright, Stephen Kirk *brewing company executive, lawyer*
McCarter, James Philip *biotechnology company executive, researcher*
McCarthy, Michael M. *construction executive*
McCoole, Robert F. *construction company executive*
McDonnell, Sanford Noyes *aircraft company executive*
McGinnis, W. Patrick *diversified company executive*
McKenna, William John *textile products executive*
Monroe, Thomas Edward *industrial corporation executive*
Peters, Charles A *electronics executive*
Posgay, Betty Marie *medical equipment company executive, artist*
Purnell, John H. *beverage company executive*
Reynolds, Robert A., Jr., *electric distributor executive*
Scherer, George F. *construction executive*
Shanahan, Michael Francis *retired manufacturing executive, former hockey team executive*
Shapiro, Robert B. *former food products manufacturing executive*
Sortwell, Christopher T. *food products executive*
Stokes, Patrick T. *brewery company executive*
Suter, Albert Edward *manufacturing executive*
Swain, David O. *manufacturing executive*
Swank, Darryl *agricultural products executive*
Wilson, Martin D. *pharmaceutical executive*
Winter, William Earl *retired beverage company executive*
Zwikelmaier, Kurt E. *pharmaceutical executive*

Springfield
Wooten, Rosalie *automotive company executive*

Webster Groves
Conerly, Richard Pugh *retired corporation executive*

Wentzville
Cowger, Gary L. *automotive executive*

MONTANA

Big Sky
Ryan, Raymond D. *retired steel company executive, insurance and marketing firm executive*

Stevensville
Derrick, William Dennis *retired physical plant administrator, consultant*

NEBRASKA

Lincoln
Fisher, Calvin David *food manufacturing company executive*
Tinstman, Dale Clinton *food products company consultant*

Lindsay
Parker, Gary Dean *manufacturing executive*

Omaha
Barber, Roger L. *grain marketing company executive*
Bolding, Jay D. *food products executive*
Bradbury, Doug *construction company executive*
Bragg, Russell J. *food products executive*
Gerhardt, Kenneth W. *retired agricultural products executive*
Goslee, Dwight J. *agricultural products executive*
Jantz, Kenneth M. *construction executive*
Johnson, Owen C. *food products executive*
Linville, Randal L. *agricultural company executive*
Nogg, Donald Irwin *retired paper distribution executive, population researcher*
Norton, Robert R., Jr., *former food products executive*
Regan, Timothy James *grain company executive*
Rohde, Bruce C. *food company executive, lawyer*
Scott, Walter, Jr., *construction company executive*
Stinson, Kenneth E. *construction and mining company executive*
Walter, Michael D. *food products executive*

NEVADA

Boulder City
Fisher, Paul Cary *writing supplies company executive*

Carson City
Burns, Dan W. *manufacturing executive*

Genoa
Goode, John Martin *manufacturing executive*

Henderson
Fiore, Nicholas Francis *special components and materials company executive*
Moon, David A. *manufacturing executive*

Hendersonville
Niemeyer, Erin Janice *pharmaceutical sales consultant, journalist, editor*

Incline Village
Strack, Harold Arthur *retired electronics company executive, retired air force officer, planner, analyst, author, musician*
Tedford, Jack Nowlan, III, *construction executive, small business owner*
Yount, George Stuart *paper company executive*

Las Vegas
Albanese, Thomas *food industry executive, consultant*
Barr, Wallace R. *electronics executive*
Jakopec, Carl Thomas *pharmaceutical company executive*
Jones, Fletcher, Jr., *automotive company executive*
Manley, Edward Harry, Jr., *food products executive*
Opfer, Neil David *construction educator, consultant*
Regazzi, John Henry *retired electronic distributor executive*
Root, Alan Charles *diversified manufacturing company executive*
Swanson, Kurt *metal fabricating company executive*

Reno
Jacobson, Raymond Earl *electronics company entrepreneur and executive*

Sparks
Kramer, Gordon Edward *manufacturing executive*

NEW HAMPSHIRE

Bennington
Verney, Richard Greville *paper company executive*

Concord
Slusser, Eugene Alvin *electronics manufacturing executive*

Hampton
Clark, Kevin P. *medical products executive*
Della Penta, David T. *medical products executive*
Meister, Paul M. *medical products executive*
Montrone, Paul Michael *scientific instruments company executive*
Russell, Richard R. *industrial executive*

Lisbon
Trelfa, Richard Thomas *paper company executive*

Meredith
Hatch, Frederick Tasker *chemicals consultant*

Milford
Morison, John Hopkins *casting manufacturing company executive*

Nashua
Egan, John Frederick *retired electronics executive*
Gregg, Hugh *former cabinet manufacturing company executive, former governor New Hampshire*

New Castle
Baker, Robert I. *manufacturing executive*
Rauh, John David *manufacturing executive*

New London
Condict, Edgar Rhodes *medical electronics, aviation instrument manufacturing and medical health care executive, inventor, mediator, pastor*

North Hampton
Taylor, Donald *retired manufacturing company executive*
White, Ralph Paul *automotive executive, consultant*

Portsmouth
Breen, Edward D. *manufacturing executive*
Kozlowski, L. Dennis (Dennis Kozlowski) *manufacturing executive*

Rochester
Shean, Timothy Joseph *manufacturing executive*

Salem
Bitter, Frank Gordon *manufacturing executive*

Winchester
MacKay, Neil Duncan *plastics company executive*

NEW JERSEY

Avenel
Sansone, Paul J. *automotive executive*

Barnegat
Bronkowski, Mark John *textiles executive, real estate agent*

Basking Ridge
Conklin, Donald Ransford *retired pharmaceutical company executive*
Fotiades, George L. *pharmaceutical executive*
Munch, Douglas Francis *pharmaceutical and health industry consultant*
Tamarelli, Alan Wayne *venture captial executive*

Berkeley Heights
Connell, Grover *food company executive*

Bloomfield
Shogen, Kuslima *pharmaceutical executive*

Boonton
Cappeline, Gary Anthoney *chemical company executive*

Bound Brook
Gould, Donald Everett *retired chemical company executive, consultant*

Bridgeton
Howell, James Burt, III, *retired agricultural products company sales consultant*

Bridgewater
Kennedy, James Andrew *chemical company executive*

Buena
Woitach, Paul *health products executive*

Califon
Clarke, Frank Henderson *retired chemical company executive, scientist*

Camden
Conant, Douglas R. *food products executive*
Johnson, David Willis *former food products executive*
Morrison, Dale F. *food company executive*

Carlstadt
Levy, Stuart S. *apparel company executive*

Carteret
Volla, Steven L. *food products executive*

Clinton
Hansen, Arthur Magne *engineering and manufacturing executive*

Cranford
Mullen, Edward K. *paper company executive*

Deepwater
Baillie, Joan M. *chemical company official, biology educator*

Denville
Minter, Jerry Burnett *electronic component company executive, engineer*

East Hanover
Bess, Alan L. *pharmaceutical executive, physician*
Dodsworth, Roy W. *pharmaceutical company executive*
Harshman, Richard R. *manufacturing executive*
Raymond, Pawlicki *pharmaceutical executive*

East Rutherford
Glassell, Claes *health products executive*
Mack, James A. *health products executive*

Eatontown
DeGiglio, Michael A. *food products executive*
Hollander, Kenneth S. *food products executive*
Ryan, David J. *food products executive*

Edison
Alexander, John Charles *pharmaceutical company executive, physician*
Samek, Edward Lasker *service company executive*

Elmwood Park
Wygod, Martin J. *pharmaceuticals executive*

Englewood Cliffs
Dash, Barry Harold *pharmaceutical company executive*
Feuerstein, Herbert *food company executive*

Kastory, Bernard H. *food products executive*
Neis, Arnold Hayward *pharmaceutical company executive*
Shoemate, Charles R. *former food company executive*

Fairfield
Stein, Robert Alan *electronics company executive*

Fairview
Anton, Harvey *textile company executive*

Farmingdale
Schluter, Peter Mueller *electronics company executive*

Flemington
Post, Richard Henry *pharmaceuticals executive*

Florham Park
Abramson, Clarence Allen *pharmaceutical company executive, lawyer*

Fort Lee
Smith, Jeffrey E. *pharmaceutical executive*

Fort Monmouth
Schwering, Felix Karl *electronics engineer, researcher*
Thornton, Clarence Gould *electronics engineering executive*

Franklin Lakes
Castellini, Clateo *retired medical technology company executive*
Considine, John *pharmaceutical company executive*
Friedman, Martin Burton *chemical company executive*

Freehold
Shapiro, Michael *supermarket corporate officer*

Glen Gardner
Epstein, Edward Joseph *textile company executive*

Hainesport
Sylk, Leonard Allen *housing company executive, real estate developer*

Highlands
Hansen, Christian Andreas, Jr., *plastics and chemical company executive*

Hillsborough
Kenyhercz, Thomas Michael *pharmaceutical company executive*

Holmdel
Kogelnik, Herwig Werner *electronics company executive*

Hopatcong
Reese, Harry Edwin, Jr., *electronics executive*

Hope
McDonald, John Joseph *electronics executive*

Iselin
Clarke, David H. *industrial products executive*
Goodwin, Billy W. *manufacturing executive*
Perry, Barry W. *manufacturing executive*
Smith, Orin Robert *chemical company executive*

Jersey City
O'Dea, William Patrick *research and development company executive*
Perhach, James Lawrence *pharmaceutical company executive*
Pietrini, Andrew Gabriel *automotive aftermarket executive*

Kendall Park
Hershenov, Bernard Zion *electronics research and development company executive*

Kenilworth
Bertolini, Robert J. *pharmaceutical executive*
Cesan, Raul *pharmaceutical company executive*
Hassan, Fred *pharmaceutical executive*
Pickett, Cecil *pharmaceutical executive*
Wyszomierski, Jack L. *pharmaceutical executive*

Kinnelon
Klaas, Nicholas Paul *management and technical consultant*

Kirkwood Voorhees
Cohen, Mark N. *business executive*

Linden
Covino, Charles Peter *chemicals executive*

Little Silver
Brennan, William Joseph *manufacturing executive*

Livingston
Candido, A. Michael *contracting company executive, real estate manager*

Madison
Essner, Robert Alan *pharmaceutical executive*
Luciano, Robert Peter *pharmaceutical company executive*
Mahady, Joseph M. *former pharmacy products company executive*
Martin, Kenneth J. *pharmaceutical executive*
Olivier, David M. *pharmaceutical company executive*
Stafford, John Rogers *pharmaceutical and household products company executive*

Mahwah
Gerstein, David Brown *hardware manufacturing company executive, professional basketball team executive*

Maplewood
Zoss, Abraham Oscar *chemical company executive*

Marlboro
Miller, Duane King *health and beauty care company executive*

Matawan
Amato, Vincent Vito *business executive*

Medford
Keele, Lyndon Alan *electronics executive*

Montvale
Corrado, Fred *food company executive*
Roob, Richard *manufacturing executive*
Scullion, Tony *pharmaceutical executive*
Unterbeck, Axel Joachim *pharmaceutical executive, director*

Moorestown
Springer, Douglas Hyde *retired food company executive, lawyer*

Morris Plains
Goodes, Melvin Russell *retired manufacturing company executive*
Larini, Ernest J. *former pharmaceuticals company executive*
Otani, Mike *optical company executive*

Morristown
Cameron, Nicholas Allen *diversified corporation executive*
Cote, David M. *diversified technology and manufacturing company executive*
Gilligan, Kevin *manufacturing executive*
Herman, Robert Lewis *cork company executive*
Kirby, Fred Morgan, II, *corporation executive*
Pawelec, William John *retired electronics company executive*
Pokelwaldt, Robert N. *former manufacturing company executive*
Sperber, Martin *pharmaceutical company executive, pharmacist*
WilliamS, Joseph Dalton *pharmaceutical company executive*

Mountain Lakes
O'Gara, Barbara Ann *soap company executive*

New Brunswick
Darretta, Robert J. *pharmaceutical executive*
Fine, Roger Seth *pharmaceutical executive, lawyer*
Gussin, Robert Zalmon *retired healthcare company executive*
Haines, William Joseph *retired pharmaceutical executive*
Heisen, JoAnn Heffernan *health care company executive*
Larsen, Ralph S(tanley) *retired pharmaceutical executive*
Lenehan, James T. *pharmaceutical executive*
Liao, Mei-June *biopharmaceutical company executive*
Poon, Christine A. *pharmaceutical executive*
Weldon, William C. *pharmaceutical executive*

New Providence
Chatterji, Debajyoti *retired manufacturing company executive, educator*
McCaffrey, Robert Henry, Jr., *retired manufacturing company executive*

North Brunswick
Bern, Ronald Lawrence *consulting company executive*
Ghosh, Alok *pharmaceutical executive*

Northvale
Di Mino, André Anthony *manufacturing executive, consultant*
Mittleberg, Eric Michael *pharmaceutical executive*

Nutley
English, Robert Joseph *electronic corporation executive*
Seyffarth, Linda Jean Wilcox *corporate executive*

Ocean City
Juliana, James Nicholas *ordnance company executive*

Paramus
Forman, Beth Rosalyne *specialty food trade executive*
Maclin, Ernest *biomedical diagnostics company executive*

Park Ridge
Koch, Craig R. *automobile rental and leasing company executive*

Parsippany
Kirkman, James A. *food products executive*
Mazur, Leonard L. *pharmaceutical company executive*
Newman, Mark S. *electronics company executive*
Schneider, Richard A. *electronics company executive*

Peapack
Rothwell, Timothy Gordon *pharmaceutical company executive*

Pennsauken
Coppola, K.T. *automotive executive*
Honickman, Harold *food manufacturing company executive*
Wilkinson, Walter *soft drink bottling company executive*

Piscataway
D'Aloia, G(iambattista) Peter *corporate executive*

Pompton Plains
Shrem, Charles Joseph *metals corporation executive*

Princeton
Campbell, Robert Emmett *retired health products executive, medical association administrator*
Cavanaugh, James Henry *medical corporate executive, former government official*
Dovey, Brian Hugh *health care products company executive, venture capitalist*

Drakeman, Lisa N. *biotechnology company executive*
Goldblatt, Barry Lance *manufacturing executive*
Kuebler, Christopher Allen *pharmaceutical executive*
Mario, Ernest *pharmaceutical company executive*
Minton, Dwight Church *manufacturing executive*
Mollica, Joseph A. *pharmaceutical executive*
Olsen, Gregory H. *fiber optic manufacturing executive, researcher*
Petrin, Jurij *pharmaceutical company executive*
Sapoff, Meyer *retired electronics executive*
Villafranca, Joseph J. *pharmaceutical executive, chemistry educator*
Wildnauer, Richard Harry *pharmaceutical executive*
Winn, Paul T. *electronics executive*

Red Bank
Sorsby, James Larry *home building company executive*

Ridgefield
Riggs, Rory B. *pharmaceutical executive*

Ridgewood
Healey, Frank Henry *retired research executive*

Rochelle Park
Schapiro, Jerome Bentley *chemicals executive*

Saddle Brook
Kelsey, David *manufacturing executive*

Saddle River
McClelland, William Craig *paper company executive*

Salem
Seabrook, John Martin *retired food products executive, chemical engineer*

Secaucus
Liao, Paul Foo-Hung *electronics executive*

Somerset
Aronson, Louis Vincent, II, *manufacturing executive*
Jones, Andrew William *pharmaceutical executive*

South Hackensack
Cohen, Brett I. *health products executive*

South Plainfield
Hunsinger, Doyle J. *electronics executive*

Springfield
Toresco, Donald *automotive executive*

Summit
Lindars, Laurence Edward *retired health care products executive*
Longfield, William Herman *health care company executive*
Young, Diane Caroline *pharmaceutical executive*
Zachary, Louis George *chemical company consultant*

Teaneck
Feinberg, Robert S. *plastics company executive, marketing professional*
Mirza, Muhammad Zubair *medical products executive, engineering consultant, inventor, product development company executive, researcher*

Teterboro
Adams, James Mills *retired chemicals executive*

Trenton
Roshon, George Kenneth *manufacturing executive*

Union
Franklin, William George *manufacturing executive*

Vincentown
Foster, David Ramsey *soap company executive*

Warren
Jackson, John Wyant *medical products executive*

Wayne
Bebele, John *manufacturing executive*
Heyman, Samuel J. *building materials manufacturing company executive*
Jeffrey, Robert George, Jr., *industrial company executive*

West Orange
Eisenberg, R. Neal *restoration company executive*

Westfield
McLean, Vincent Ronald *former manufacturing company financial executive*

Westwood
Black, Theodore Halsey *retired manufacturing company executive*

Whitehouse Station
Anstice, David W. *pharmaceutical executive*
Avedon, Marcia J. *pharmaceutical executive*
Bell, Paul R. *pharmaceutical executive*
Bossidy, Lawrence Arthur *former industrial manufacturing executive*
Clark, Richard T. *pharmaceutical executive*
Frazier, Kenneth C. *pharmaceutical executive*
Gilmartin, Raymond V. *pharmaceutical company executive*
Kelley, Bernard J. *pharmaceutical executive*
Lewent, Judy Carol *pharmaceutical executive*
McGlynn, Margaret G. *pharmaceutical executive*
McGuire, John Lawrence *pharmaceutical executive*
Wold Olsen, Per *pharmaceutical executive*
Yarno, Wendy *pharmaceutical executive*

Woodcliff Lake
Henkel, Herbert Ludwig *manufacturing executive*
Perrella, James Elbert *former manufacturing company executive*

Wyckoff
Brown, James Joseph *manufacturing executive*

NEW MEXICO

Albuquerque
Collins, Julie *healthcare organization executive*
Friberg, George Joseph *electronics company executive, entrepreneur*
Korman, Nathaniel Irving *research and development company executive*
Orona, Ernest Joseph *real estate and construction company executive*
Pohl, Elizabeth *contracting company executive*
Turner, Andrew L. *healthcare management company executive*
Woltil, Robert D. *healthcare management company executive*

Estancia
Swenka, Arthur John *retired food products executive*

Placitas
Golleher, George *food company executive*

Rio Rancho
Isenberg, Abraham Charles *shoe manufacturing company executive*

Roswell
Armstrong, Billie Bert *retired highway contractor*

Sandia Park
Wilczynski, Janusz S. *packaging technology executive, retired physicist*

Santa Fe
Odell, John H. *construction executive*

NEW YORK

Albany
D'Ambra, Thomas E. *pharmaceutical executive*
Heshmat, Hooshang *manufacturing executive*
Kuhla, Donald E. *chemicals executive*
Naumann, Hans J. *manufacturing executive*
Waldek, David P. *pharmaceutical executive*

Amityville
Soloway, Richard Lewis *electronic manufacturing company executive*

Bangall
Swanson, David Heath *agricultural company executive*

Batavia
Bidlack, Jerald Dean *manufacturing executive*

Bohemia
Hausman, Howard *electronics executive*
Rudolph, Scott *pharmaceutical executive*

Brooklyn
Hood, Ernest Alva, Sr., *pharmaceutical company executive*
Luterman, Gerald *electronics company executive*
Oussani, James John *stapling company executive*
Rutsky, Lester *retired textiles executive, writer*
Zisser, Martin Shepherd *fur apparel manufacturer, investor, trader*

Buffalo
Gisel, Bill *food products executive*
Lipke, Brian J. *metal products executive*
Rich, Robert E., Sr., *frozen foods company executive*
Starks, Fred William *chemicals executive*
Trego, Charles R., Jr., *food products company executive*

Callicoon
Kurtz, Joel *construction company executive*

Canandaigua
Sands, Richard E. *food products executive*

Clifton Park
Scher, Robert Sander *instrument design company executive*

Cooperstown
Tilton, Webster, Jr., *contractor*

Corning
Behm, Forrest Edwin *glass manufacturing company executive*
Ecklin, Robert Luther *materials company executive*
Houghton, James Richardson *glass manufacturing company executive*
Miller, Joseph A. *chemicals executive*

Cross River
Lang, Robert Mays, Jr., *manufacturing executive*

Derby
Goodell, Joseph Edward *manufacturing executive*

East Amherst
Watson, Stewart Charles *construction company executive*

East Aurora
Hawk, George Wayne *retired electronics company executive*

East Hampton
Karp, Harvey Lawrence *metal products manufacturing company executive*

East Meadow
Cymbler, Murray Joel *corporate professional*

East Northport
Kehoe, Thomas J. *food products executive*

Elmira
Van den Blink, Nelson Mooers *light industrial manufacturing executive*

Van Hornesville
Durham, Ormonde George, III, *manufacturing executive*

Webster
Duke, Charles Bryan *electronics executive, physicist, educator*

White Plains
Fowler, James D., Jr., *leadership executive*
Giuliano, Louis J. *industrial manufacturing company executive*
Greene, Leonard Michael *aerospace manufacturing executive, institute executive*
Krasne, Charles A. *food products executive*
Loranger, Steven R. *industrial manufacturing company executive*
McAuliffe, John C. *health/medical products executive*

Whitestone
Bodinger, William *health, medical products executive*
Rahr, Stewart *health medical products executive*

Williston Park
Segel, J. Norman *garment manufacturing company executive*

Woodbury
Guttenplan, Harold Esau *retired food company executive*

Yonkers
Holtz, Gilbert Joseph *steel company executive*

Youngstown
Alpert, Norman *chemical company executive*

NORTH CAROLINA

Asheville
Coli, Guido John *chemical company executive*
Vander Voort, Dale Gilbert *textile company executive*

Beaufort
Cullman, Hugh *retired tobacco company executive*

Belmont
Stowe, Robert Lee, III, *textile company executive*

Blowing Rock
Barnebey, Kenneth Alan *food company executive*

Burlington
Elingburg, Wesley R. *health products executive*
Flagg, Raymond Osbourn *retired biology executive*
MacMahon, Thomas P. *healthcare company executive*
Novak, Richard L. *health products executive*

Cary
Alstadt, Donald Martin *business executive*
Bogdanovich, Alexander *manufacturing executive*

Chapel Hill
Drutz, David Jules *biotechnology executive*

Charlotte
Aycock, Hugh David *steel manufacturing company executive*
Browning, Peter Crane *packaging company executive*
Burner, David L. *aerospace services company executive*
D'Angelo, Peter R. *electronics company executive*
DiMicco, Daniel R. *manufacturing executive*
Faison, Henry *electronics executive*
Ford, Steven J. *manufacturing executive*
Harrison, J. Frank, Jr., *soft drink company executive*
Huzl, James Frank *automotive executive*
Lea, Scott Carter *retired packaging company executive*
McKinnish, Richmond D. *manufacturing executive*
Moore, James L., Jr., *beverage company executive*
Munn, Stephen P. *manufacturing executive*
Nelson, Thomas C. *manufacturing executive*
O'Leary, Patrick J. *manufacturing executive*
Parmelle, William *light manufacturing executive*
Peacock, A(lvin) Ward *textile company executive*
Perkins, Jim C. *automotive executive*
Priestley, G. T. Eric *manufacturing executive*
Rathke, Dieter B. *construction company executive*
Siegel, Samuel *metals company executive*
Smith, O. Bruton *automotive company executive*
Spangler, Clemmie Dixon, Jr., *construction company executive*
Squires, James Ralph *development company executive*
Sulg, Madis *corporation executive, entrepreneur*
Walker, Kenneth Dale *automotive service company executive*

Durham
Althaus, David Steven *consultant*
Gillings, Dennis B. *medical products executive*

Elon
Powell, William Council, Sr., *service company executive*

Fayetteville
Richardson, Emilie White *manufacturing company executive, investment company executive, lecturer*

Flat Rock
Demartini, Robert John *textiles executive, entrepreneur*

Garner
Spencer, Thomas Melvin, III, *soft drink company executive*

Gastonia
Kimbrell, Willard Duke *textile company executive*
Lawson, William David, III, *retired cotton company executive*

Greensboro
Cummings, Candace S. *apparel company executive*
Daggett, Duane D. *house manufacturing executive*
Englar, John David *textile company executive, lawyer*
Hayes, Charles A. *mill company executive*
Korb, William Brown, Jr., *retired manufacturing executive*
McDonald, Mackey J. *apparel company executive*
Parke, Brian *textile company executive*
Shearer, Robert K. *apparel executive*
Staab, Thomas Robert *consumer product company financial executive*

Hertford
Johnson, Donald Lee *retired agricultural materials processing company executive*

Hickory
Nye, John Robert *furniture company executive, transportation consultant*
Shuford, Harley Ferguson, Jr., *furniture manufacturing executive*

High Point
Cole, Alan D. *manufacturing executive*
Fenn, Ormon William, Jr., *furniture company executive*
Hoffman, Ronald J. *light manufacturing executive*
Marsden, Lawrence Albert *retired textile company executive*

Jefferson
Van Arnam, Mark Stephen *manufacturing executive*

Kernersville
Dudley, Joe L. *cosmetic company executive*

Mount Airy
Woltz, Howard Osler, Jr., *steel and wire products company executive*

North Wilkesboro
Stone, Larry Dean *management executive*

Pinehurst
O'Neill, John Joseph, Jr., *business consultant, former chemical company executive*

Raleigh
Henry, Janice K. *construction materials company executive*
Kuykendall, William *automotive executive*
Prior, William Allen *electronics company executive*
Sloan, O. Temple, Jr., *automotive equipment executive*
Zelnak, Stephen P., Jr., *construction materials company executive*

Research Triangle Park
Bierman, James L. *contract research organization executive*
Framil, Armando Ramon *business developer*
Hamner, Charles *biotechnology company executive*
Ingram, Robert A. *pharmaceutical executive*
Niedel, James Edward *pharmaceuticals executive*
Russell, John S. *contract research organization executive*
Ward, Eric R. *agricultural products executive*

Rocky Mount
Stubbs, Will, Jr., *pharmaceutical company manager*

Rural Hall
Wager, Michael *manufacturing executive*

Sanford
Kilmartin, Joseph Francis, Jr., *business executive, consultant*

Shelby
Perry, Stephen Clayton *manufacturing executive*
Tichenor, Charles Beckham, II, *food and beverage executive*

Statesville
Stelzner, Paul Burke *textile company executive*

Trinity
Jones, Ronald *manufacturing executive*

Weldon
Barringer, Paul Brandon, II, *lumber company executive*

Wilkesboro
Niblock, Robert *home improvement warehouse executive*

Wilmington
Thompson, Donald Charles *electronics company executive, former coast guard officer*

Winston Salem
Blixt, Charles A. *tobacco company executive*
Hanes, Ralph Philip, Jr., *former textiles executive, arts patron, cattle farmer networker*
Lapiejko, Kenneth J. *tobacco company executive*
Livengood, Scott A. *food products executive*
Maselli, John Anthony *food products company executive*
Schindler, Andrew J. *tobacco company executive*
Sticht, J. Paul *retired food products and tobacco company executive*
Tate, John William *food products executive*
Wallace, Roanne *hosiery company executive*
Woodford, Duane Hugh *aerospace equipment manufacturing company executive, electrical engineer*

OHIO

Akron
Gibara, Samir G. *tire manufacturing executive*
Hackbirth, David William *aluminum company executive*
Kaufman, Donald Leroy *building products executive*
Keegan, Robert J. *manufacturing executive*
Snider, George Runyon, Jr., *franchising company executive*
Tieken, Robert W. *tire manufacturing company executive*
Tyrrell, Thomas Neil *former metal processing executive*

Avon Lake
Kent, Deborah *automotive executive*
Patient, William F. *chemicals executive*

Beachwood
Weatherhead, Albert John, III, *business executive*

Bellville
Hooker, James Todd *manufacturing executive*

Berea
Soppelsa, John Joseph *decal manufacturing company executive*

Canton
Ewing, David Charles *automobile dealership executive*
Griffith, James W. *manufacturing executive*
O'Dell, Walden Wesley *manufacturing executive*
Timken, W. Robert, Jr., *manufacturing executive*

Chagrin Falls
Brophy, Jere Hall *manufacturing executive*
Callahan, Francis Joseph *manufacturing executive*
Heckman, Henry Trevennen Shick *retired metal products executive*

Cincinnati
Aguirre, Fernando *food products executive*
Anderson, Jerry William, Jr., *technical and business consulting executive, educator*
Byrnes, Bruce L. *manufacturing executive*
Christensen, Paul Walter, Jr., *gear manufacturing company executive*
Clark, R. Kerry *manufacturing executive*
Coombe, V. Anderson *retired valve manufacturing company executive*
Daley, Clayton Carl, Jr., *cosmetics company executive*
Farmer, Richard T. *uniform rental and sales executive*
Farmer, Scott D. *apparel executive*
Fulmer, Michael Clifford *food company administrator*
Gale, William C. *apparel executive*
Heschel, Michael S. *retail food products executive*
Jones, Daniel W. *construction executive*
Kaune, James Edward *ship repair company executive, former naval officer*
Kendle, Candace *pharmaceutical executive*
Laney, Sandra Eileen *service company executive*
Leyda, James Perkins *small business consultant, retired pharmaceutical company executive*
Meyer, Daniel Joseph *machinery company executive*
Pichler, Joseph Anton *food products executive*
Rishel, James Burton *manufacturing executive, director*
Ruthman, Thomas Robert *manufacturing executive*
Schlotman, J. Michael *food products executive*
Shepherd, Elsbeth Weichsel *supply chain consultant*
Smale, John Gray *diversified industry executive*
Stern, Joseph Smith, Jr., *former footwear manufacturing company executive*
Thompson, Morley Punshon *textile company executive*

Cleveland
Butler, William E. *retired manufacturing company executive*
Collins, Duane E. *manufacturing executive*
Connor, Christopher M. *textiles executive*
Cutler, Alexander MacDonald *manufacturing executive*
Decker, John William *metal products executive*
Hamilton, William Milton *retired manufacturing executive*
Hardis, Stephen Roger *retired manufacturing company executive*
Hiemstra, Michael J. *manufacturing executive*
Holmes, Arthur S. *manufacturing executive*
Ivy, Conway Gayle *paint company executive*
Jameson, J(ames) Larry *chemical company executive*
Luke, Randall Dan *retired tire and rubber company executive, lawyer*
Mac Laren, David Sergeant *manufacturing corporation executive, inventor*
Mandel, Jack N. *manufacturing executive*
McFadden, John Volney *retired manufacturing company executive*
Miller, Carl George *automotive parts manufacturing executive*
Moll, Curtis E. *manufacturing executive*
Mooney, James P. *chemicals executive*
Parker, Patrick Streeter *manufacturing executive*
Ratner, Albert B. *building products company executive, land developer*
Reid, James Sims, Jr., *former automobile parts manufacturer*
Ryder, Robert P.
Van Aken, William J. *construction executive*
Washkewicz, Donald E. *manufacturing executive*
Weiss, Jeffrey M.
Weiss, Morry *greeting card company executive*
Weiss, Zev

Columbus
Carter, William H. *chemicals executive*
Cottingham, Richard Sumner *paper company executive*
Daab-Krzykowski, Andre *pharmaceutical and nutritional manufacturing company administrator*
Eaton, Michael Christopher *contractor*
Evans, Daniel E. *manufacturing and restaurant chain company executive*
Kidder, C. Robert *food products executive*
Knilans, Michael Jerome *supermarkets executive*
Kohrt, Carl Fredrick *research and development company executive*
Lazar, Theodore Aaron *retired manufacturing company executive, lawyer*
McConnell, John Henderson *metal and plastic products manufacturing executive, professional sports team executive*
Morrison, Craig O. *chemicals executive*
Radkoski, Donald J. *food products company executive*
Ricart, Fred *automotive company executive*
Schottenstein, Irving E. *construction company executive*
Schottenstein, Robert H. *construction executive*
Solso, Theodore M. *manufacturing executive*
Wigington, Ronald Lee *retired chemical information services executive*
Wolf, J. Steven (John Steven Wolf) *construction executive, land developer*
Yenkin, Bernard Kalman *coatings and resins company executive*

Cuyahoga Falls
Cevetillo-Tuccillo, Gerri Marie *manufacturing executive*

Dayton
Bray, William Otis, IV, *diversified electronics company executive*
Ciccarelli, John A. *manufacturing executive*
Diggs, Matthew O'Brien, Jr., *air conditioning and refrigeration manufacturing executive*
Duval, Daniel Webster *manufacturing executive*
Harlan, Norman Ralph *construction executive*
Hurd, Mark V. *manufacturing executive*
Kerley, James J. *manufacturing executive*
Ladehoff, Leo William *metal products manufacturing executive*
Mathile, Clayton Lee *pet food company executive*
McIlroy, Alan F. *manufacturing executive*
Shuey, John Henry *diversified products company executive*

Delaware
Eells, William Hastings *retired automobile company executive*
Huml, Donald Scott *manufacturing executive*

Dublin
Borror, Donald A. *construction company executive*
Borror, Douglas G. *construction company executive*
Davids, Jody *pharmaceutical and medical supply executive*
Lamp, Benson J. *tractor company executive*
Millar, James F. *pharmaceutical executive*
Miller, Richard J. *wholesale pharmaceutical distribution company executive*

Elyria
Mixon, Aaron Malachi, III, *medical products executive*
Spitzer, Alan *automotive executive*

Findlay
Dattilo, Thomas A. *diversified corporation executive*
Stephens, D. Richard *manufacturing executive*
Weaver, Philip G. *tire company executive*

Gates Mills
Veale, Tinkham, II, *former chemical company executive, engineer*

Greenville
Buchy, Jim *food products executive*

Grove City
Lok, Silmond Ray *pharmaceutical executive*

Hamilton
Epp, Mary Elizabeth *technologies consultant*

Hilliard
Baker, John *electronics executive*
Koehler, Jim *electronics executive*

Jackson Center
Thompson, Wade Francis Bruce *manufacturing executive*

Lakewood
Cochran, Earl Vernon *retired manufacturing company executive*

Lima
Pranses, Anthony Louis *retired electric company executive, organization executive*

Malvern
Witosky, Gary J. *manufacturing company executive*

Mansfield
Gorman, James Carvill *pump manufacturing company executive*

Mason
Wilson, Frederic Sandford *pharmaceutical company executive*

Maumee
Anderson, Richard Paul *agricultural company executive*

Mayfield Heights
Rankin, Alfred Marshall, Jr., *manufacturing executive*

Medina
Matejka, Robert *chemicals executive*
Smith, Richey *manufacturing executive*
Sullivan, Frank C. *manufacturing executive*
Sullivan, Thomas Christopher *coatings company executive*

Mentor
Callsen, Christian Edward *medical device company executive*
Sanford, Bill R. *medical products executive*

Middletown
Jenkins, Robert H. *steel company executive*

Milan
Henry, Joseph Patrick *chemical company executive*

Milford
Donahue, John Lawrence, Jr., *paper company executive*
Klosterman, Albert Leonard *technical development business executive, mechanical engineer*

New Albany
Jeffries, Michael S. *apparel executive*

New Bremen
Dicke, James Frederick, II, *manufacturing executive*

North Canton
Geswein, Gregory T. *electronic company executive*
Lynham, C(harles) Richard *manufacturing executive*

North Ridgeville
Stewart, Arden Ruth *automotive aftermarket manufacturing executive*

Orrville
Kamp, Philip *food products executive*
Mackus, Eloise L. *food products company executive*
Smucker, Richard K. *food company executive*
Smucker, Timothy P. *food company executive*

Perrysburg
King, John Joseph *manufacturing executive*

Powell
Arnold, A. Joel *pharmaceuticals company executive*
White, George Washington *automotive consultant*

Randolph
Pecano, Donald Carl *automotive manufacturing executive*

Reynoldsburg
Woodward, Greta Charmaine *construction company executive, rental and investment property manager*

Richfield
Anthony, Leonard Morris *steel company administrator, consultant*
Mott, Rodney *metal products executive*

Rocky River
Kamm, Christian Philip *manufacturing company executive, writer, investment company executive*
Shaffer, Clarence F. *retired electronics executive*

Shaker Heights
Unger, Paul A. *packaging and international affairs specialist*

Sidney
Evans, Eric Charles *management executive*

Solon
Bayman, James L. *electronics executive*
Rosica, Gabriel Adam *manufacturing executive, electrical engineer*

Tipp City
Tighe-Moore, Barbara Jeanne *electronics executive*

Toledo
Brown, David T. *manufacturing executive*
Carroll, William J. *automotive executive*
DeBacker, Michael L. *automotive executive, lawyer*
Hiner, Glen Harold, Jr., *materials company executive*
Lemieux, Joseph Henry *manufacturing executive*
Norton, Patrick H. *manufacturing executive*
Richter, Robert C. *automotive executive*
Romanoff, Milford Martin *retired building contractor*
Thaman, Michael H. *building material systems executive*
Van Hooser, David *retired manufacturing executive*

Warren
Spencer, James A. *automotive executive*

Westerville
Krueger-Horn, Cheryl *apparel executive*

Westlake
Hellman, Peter Stuart *technical manufacturing executive*

Wickliffe
Cooley, Charles P. *chemicals executive*
Hambrick, James L. *chemicals executive*

Youngstown
Marks, Esther L. *metals company executive*
Powers, Paul J. *manufacturing executive*

OKLAHOMA

Bristow
Primeaux, Henry, III, *automotive executive, author, speaker*

Norman
Casey, Rebecca Powell *apparel executive*

Oklahoma City
Batenic, Mark K. *manufacturing executive*
Clonts, George Gary *packaging company executive*
Hageman, Dale *alternative staffing company executive*
Pilcher, Gregory F. *manufacturing executive*
Rider, Neal J. *food wholesale executive*
Turner, Eugene Andrew *manufacturing executive*

Tulsa
Hildebrand, Steven B. *automobile rental company executive*
Marshall-Chapman, Paula *food products executive*
Narwold, Lewis Lammers, Jr., *paper products manufacturer*
Thomas, Robert Eggleston *retired corporate executive*

Wilburton
Pate, Thomas Lowell *manufacturing executive*

OREGON

Ashland
Meese, Celia Edwards *pharmaceutical company executive*

Beaverton
Blair, Donald W. *shoe manufacturing company executive*
Carter, James C. *apparel executive, lawyer*
Clarke, Thomas E. *apparel executive*
Dinh, Thin Van *electronics specialist*
Harold, Robert *apparel executive*
Knight, Philip H(ampson) *apparel executive*
Meyer, Jerome J. *diversified technology company executive*
Vancil, Bernard K. *research and development company executive, physicist*
Wills, Richard H. *electronics manufacturing executive*

Bend
Babcock, Walter Christian, Jr., *membrane company executive*

Eugene
Chaney, James Alan *construction company executive*
Woolley, Donna Pearl *lumber company executive*

Forest Grove
Coleman, Deborah Ann *electronics company executive*

Hillsboro
Barnes, Keith Lee *electronics executive*

Klamath Falls
Hoggarth, Karen *lumber company executive*
Wendt, Roderick C. *manufacturing executive*

Medford
Heimann, M.L. "Dick" *auto dealership executive*

Odell
Garcia, David *agricultural products executive*
Girardelli, Ronald K. *food products executive*

Portland
Boyle, Gertrude *sportswear company executive*
Cassard, Christopher D. *lumber company executive*
Donegan, Mark *metal products executive*
Drinkward, Cecil W. *construction company executive*
Flowerree, Robert Edmund *retired forest products company executive*
Larsson, William Dean *manufacturing executive*
Leineweber, Peter Anthony *forest products company executive*
McCormick, William Charles *manufacturing executive*
Pamplin, Robert Boisseau, Sr., *retired textile manufacturing executive*
Pamplin, Robert Boisseau, Jr., *manufacturing company executive, minister, writer*
Russell, Marjorie Rose *manufacturing executive*
Stott, Peter Walter *forest products company executive*
Swindells, William, Jr., *lumber and paper company executive*
Thurston, George R. *lumber company executive*
Whitsell, Helen Jo *lumber executive*

Roseburg
Ford, Allyn *manufacturing executive*

Salem
Donais, Gerald Alan *manufacturing executive*

Woodburn
Preece, Scott *food products executive*

PENNSYLVANIA

Allentown
Baker, Dexter Farrington *manufacturing executive, director*
Jones, John P., III, *chemicals executive*
Lovett, John Robert *retired chemical company executive*
Samuels, Abram *stage equipment manufacturing company executive*

Allison Park
Backus, John King *former chemical company research administrator*

Altoona
Sheetz, Joseph S. *retail grocery executive*
Yohn, Sharon A. *manufacturing executive*

Ambler
Zane, William Anthony *chemicals executive*

Avondale
Friel, Daniel Denwood, Sr., *manufacturing executive*

Bala Cynwyd
Driscoll, Edward Carroll *construction management firm executive*
Furlong, Edward V., Jr., *paper company executive*
Mardy, Michael John *food products executive*

Beaver Falls
Jannuzi, Eugene Fredric *manufacturing executive*

Bedford
Fries, Raymond Sebastian *manufacturing executive*

Belle Vernon
Wapiennik, Carl Francis *manufacturing firm executive, planetarium and science institute executive*

Bensalem
Bern, Dorrit J. *apparel company executive*
Orleans, Jeffrey P. *construction executive*

Berwyn
Burch, John Walter *mining equipment company executive*
Silverman, Stanley Wayne *chemical company executive*

Bethlehem
Barnette, Curtis Handley *steel company executive, lawyer*
Dunham, Duane R. *steel company executive*
Hartmann, Robert Elliott *manufacturing company executive, retired*
Marsh, Robert Harry *chemical company executive*

Blue Bell
McAdam, Will *electronics consultant*

Brackenridge
Bozzone, Robert P. *steel company executive*

Bradford
Rice, Lester *electronics company executive*

Bristol
Kimmel, Sidney *apparel company executive*

Camp Hill
Rugen, Karen *manufacturing executive, corporate communications specialist*
Twomey, Kevin *pharmaceutical executive*

Canonsburg
Coury, Robert J. *pharmaceutical executive*
Puskar, Milan *pharmaceuticals executive*

Central City
Brown, Robert Alan *retired construction materials company executive*

Chambersburg
Rumler, Robert Hoke *agricultural consultant, retired association executive*

Clarks Summit
Alperin, Irwin Ephraim *clothing company executive*

Collegeville
Graeff, David Wayne *maintenance executive, consultant*
Kun, Kenneth A. *business executive*
Ruffolo, Robert R. *research and development company executive*

Conshohocken
Lotman, Herbert *food processing executive*
Naples, Ronald James *manufacturing executive*
Spaeth, Karl Henry *retired chemical company executive, lawyer*

Cranberry Township
Hogberg, Carl Gustav *retired steel company executive*

Denver
Milner, Charles Fremont, Jr., *manufacturing executive*

East Stroudsburg
Bishop, Gerald Iveson *pharmaceutical executive*

Easton
Stipe, Edwin, III, *mechanical contracting company executive*
Sun, Robert Zu Jei *manufacturing company executive, inventor*

Eighty Four
Capone, Alphonse William *retired industrial executive*
Magerko, Maggie Hardy *lumber company executive*
Wallach, Dan *lumber company executive*

Emmaus
Adcock, Albert Eugene (Gene) *night vision equipment company executive*
Bowers, Klaus D(ieter) *retired electronics research development company executive*

Erie
Begley, Charlene *electronics executive*
Duval, Albert Frank *paper company executive*
Renkis, Alan Ilmars *plastics formulating company executive*

Exton
Aungst, Bruce Jeffrey *pharmaceutical company scientist*
de Rosen, Michel *pharmaceutical company executive*
Dorsey, Jeremiah Edmund *pharmaceutical company executive*

Fort Washington
Bajpai, Sanjay Kumar *strategic healthcare marketing, economics executive*

Gap
Beiler, Anne F. *food company executive*

Gilbertsville
Poste, George Henry *pharmaceutical company executive*

Glassport
Coslov, I. Michael *manufacturing executive*

Greentown
Askins, Wallace Boyd *manufacturing executive*
Forcheskie, Carl S. *former apparel company executive*

Greenville
Stuver, Francis Edward *former railway car company executive*

Hanover
Kline, Donald *food company executive*

Harleysville
Hendricks, Tim *construction company executive*

Harrisburg
Marley, James Earl *former manufacturing company executive*
Urkiel, William Stanley *diversified company executive*

Hatboro
Cuozzo, James Richard *paper converting machinery manufacturing executive*

Haverford
Talucci, Samuel James *retired chemical company executive*

Hershey
Cerminara, Frank *food products executive*
Davis, George F. *food products executive*
Lenny, Richard Herbert *food products executive, marketing professional*
Viviano, Joseph P. *food products executive*
Wolfe, Kenneth L. *food products manufacturing executive*

Hollidaysburg
Bloom, Lawrence Stephen *retired clothing company executive*

Horsham
Perdue, Franklin P. *retired poultry/agricultural products executive*

Jenkintown
Reese, Francis Edward *retired chemical company executive, consultant*

Johnstown
Sheehan, Edward James *technical consultant, former government official*

Kennett Square
May, Harold Edward *chemical company executive*

King Of Prussia
Wachs, David V. *retired apparel executive*

Lancaster
Dodge, Arthur Byron, Jr., *business executive, marketing professional*
High, S. Dale *diversified company executive*
Liddell, W. Kirk *specialty contracting company executive*
Lockhart, Michael D. *building materials company executive*
Lorch, George A. *manufacturing executive*
Smith, Thomas Clair *retired manufacturing company executive*

Large
Dick, Douglas Patrick *construction company executive*

Latrobe
Tambakeras, Markos I. *machine tool manufacturer*

Lebanon
McMindes, Roy James *aggregate company executive*
Paul, Herman Louis, Jr., *valve manufacturing company executive*

Levittown
Henshaw, Jonathan Cook *retired manufacturing executive*

Ligonier
Pilz, Alfred Norman *manufacturing executive*

Lyon Station
Breidegam, DeLight Edgar, Jr., *battery company executive*

Malvern
Espe, Matthew J. *manufacturing executive*
Forese, James John *business machine company executive*
James, George L. *healthcare manufacturing executive*
Stetson, John Batterson, IV, *construction executive*

Marion Center
Purdy, David Lawrence *medical products executive*

Mc Murray
Langenberg, Frederick Charles *business executive*

Meadville
Hoover, Lynn E. *manufacturing executive*

Media
Resnick, Stewart Allen *diversified company executive*

Mohnton
Bowers, Richard Philip *manufacturing executive*

Newtown
Ross, Edwin William *rubber company executive*

Newtown Square
Benenson, James, Jr., *manufacturer*

North Wales
Sheares, Bradley T. *pharmaceutical executive*

Paoli
Blankley, Walter Elwood *manufacturing executive*

Peach Glen
Carey, Dean Lavere *fruit canning company executive*

Philadelphia
Avery, William Joseph *packaging manufacturing company executive*
Azoulay, Bernard *chemicals company executive*
Carter, William A. *pharmaceuticals executive, medical educator*
Conway, John W. *manufacturing executive*
Croisetiere, Jacques M. *chemicals executive*
Eckenrode, William J. *former manufacturing executive*
Edwards, Barry R. *pharmaceutical executive*
Fitzpatrick, J. Michael *chemicals executive*
Garnier, Jean-Pierre *pharmaceutical executive*
Gruneich, Jeffrey Alan *biotechnology executive*
Gupta, Rajiv Lochan *chemical company executive*
Harper, Edwin Leland *manufacturing executive*

Katherine, Robert Andrew *chemical company executive*
Kiefer, J. Richard, Jr., *retired corporate executive*
Klein, Robert *retired manufacturing executive*
Leonard, William *food services company executive*
Liberati, Maria Theresa *fashion production company executive*
Lien, Eric L. *pharmaceutical executive*
Llewellyn, J. Bruce *food products executive*
Mee, Michael F. *retired pharmaceutical executive*
O'Brien, James Jerome *construction management consultant*
Potamkin, Robert *automotive executive*
Rastogi, Anil Kumar *medical device manufacturer, executive*
Rutherford, Alan *manufacturing executive*
Sohn, Catherine Angell *pharmaceutical executive, pharmacist*
Sutherland, L. Frederick *food company executive*
Yoh, Harold L., III, *company executive*

Pipersville
McNutt, Richard Hunt *manufacturing executive*

Pittsburgh
Agnew, Franklin Ernest, III, *former food company executive*
Belda, Alain J. P. *metal products executive*
Berkman, Louis *steel company executive*
Bunch, Charles E. *manufacturing executive*
Burnham, Donald Clemens *manufacturing executive*
Classon, Rolf Allan *pharmaceutical company executive*
Dick, David E. *construction company executive*
Edelman, Harry Rollings, III, *engineering and construction company executive*
Frank, Alan I W *manufacturing executive*
Harrison, Eric Jay *construction executive, consultant*
Harshman, Richard J. *metal products executive*
Hassey, L. Patrick *metal products executive*
Heilman, Marlin Stephen *medical products executive*
Horowitz, Carole Spiegel *landscape contractor*
Huntington, James Cantine, Jr., *equipment manufacturing company executive*
Johnson, William R. *food products executive*
LeBoeuf, Raymond Walter *manufacturing executive*
Minnaugh, Mark J *food products/retail grocery executive*
Paul, Robert Arthur *steel company executive*
Pinto, Joseph Gamini *manufacturing executive*
Simmons, Richard P. *retired steel company executive*
Stein, Laura *food products executive*
Thomas, W(illiam) Bruce *retired steel, oil, gas company executive*
Turnbull, Gordon·Keith *metal company executive, metallurgical engineer*
Turner, Walter W. *manufacturing executive*
Usher, Thomas James *steel executive, energy executive*
Van Oss, Stephen A. *electronics executive*
Wehmeier, Helge H. *pharmaceutical executive*
Winkleback, Arthur *food products executive*

Plymouth Meeting
Black, Jeffrey P. *manufacturing executive*
Black, Lennox K. *manufacturing executive*
Sickler, John J. *manufacturing executive*

Portland
Hutton, William Michael *manufacturing executive*

Reading
Cardy, Robert Willard *speciality steel company executive*
Ehlerman, Paul Michael *motorcycle and recreational batteries manufacturing company executive*
Miller, Marlin J., Jr., *pharmaceutical executive*

Royersford
Bothe, Marie *automotive executive*

Saint Davids
Smalley, Christopher Joseph *pharmaceutical company professional*

Sewickley
Bouchard, James Paul *steel manufacturing and planning executive*
Thorbecke, Willem Henry *international company executive, consultant*

Shady Grove
Bust, Jeffry D. *manufacturing executive*

Shippensburg
Collier, Duaine Alden *manufacturing and distribution company executive*
Luhrs, H. Ric *toy manufacturing company executive*

Souderton
Delp, R. Lee *meat packing company executive*

Spring City
Blanchard, Norman Harris *retired pharmaceutical executive*

Spring House
Payn, Clyde Francis *technology company executive, consultant*

State College
Byrom, Fletcher Lauman *chemical manufacturing company executive*
Carnes, James Edward *technology executive*
Huck, John Lloyd *pharmaceutical executive*

Sunbury
Mills, William R. *food products executive*

Swarthmore
Kaufman, Antoinette D. *business services company executive*

Unionville
Forney, Robert Clyde *retired chemical industry executive*

Valley Forge
Dachowski, Peter Richard *manufacturing executive*

Hilyard, James Emerson *manufacturing executive*

Verona
Lauterbach, Robert Emil *steel company executive*

Wallingford
Peabody, William Tyler, Jr., *retired paper manufacturing company executive*

Warminster
Hull, Lewis Woodruff *manufacturing executive*

Washington
Kastelic, Robert Frank *aerospace company executive*

Wayne
Agersborg, Helmer Pareli K. *pharmaceutical company executive, researcher*
Curry, Thomas James *retired manufacturers representative*
Karlson, Lawrence Carl *technological products company executive*
Wilson, James Lawrence *retired chemical company executive*
Yost, R. David *pharmaceutical executive*

Waynesboro
Benchoff, James Martin *manufacturing executive*

West Chester
Baldino, Frank *biopharmaceutical executive*
Blake, Paul *pharmaceutical executive*
Boruch, John N. *electronics company executive*
Buchi, J. Kevin *pharmaceutical executive*
Gadsby, Robin Edward *chemical company executive*
Heaps, Marvin Dale *retired food services company executive*
Kim, James Joo-Jin *electronics company executive*

West Point
Choi, Dennis W. *pharmaceutical executive, neurologist, educator*
Kim, Peter Sungbai *pharmaceutical executive, educator, research and development company executive*
Scolnick, Edward Mark *pharmaceutical executive*
Shahinfar, Shahnaz *pharmaceutical executive, nephrologist*

Wexford
Foster, Donald Lee *manufacturing executive, consultant*

Wyomissing
Beaver, Howard Oscar, Jr., *retired alloys manufacturing company executive*

Yardley
U'Prichard, David C. *pharmaceutical executive*

York
Jellison, William R. *medical supply company executive*
Kunkle, Gerald K. *medical supply company executive*
Myers, C. David *manufacturing executive*
Young, Michael R. *manufacturing executive*

RHODE ISLAND

Kingston
Muir, Donald M. *electronics company executive*

North Kingstown
Novich, Bruce Eric *chemicals executive*
Sharpe, Henry Dexter, Jr., *retired manufacturing company executive*

Pawtucket
Bifulco, Frank *toy company executive*
Goldner, Brian *toy company executive*
Holt, Richard B. *toy company executive*
Huebner, Chuck *toy manufacturing executive*
Romanzi, Kenneth *toy manufacturing executive*
Trueb, Martin R. *toy company executive*
Wilson, E. David *toy company executive*

Providence
Alderman, Ken *construction company executive*
Bready, Richard Lawrence *manufacturing executive*
Choquette, Paul Joseph, Jr., *construction company executive*
Gilbane, Thomas F., Jr., *building company executive*
Hardymon, James Franklin *retired diversified products company executive*
Reed, Cynthia S. *manufacturing executive*

West Kingston
Dowdell, Rodger Birtwell, Sr., *electronics company executive*

West Warwick
Galkin, Robert Theodore *company executive*

Woonsocket
Rickard, David B. *food company executive*
Sgarro, Douglas A. *pharmaceutical executive, lawyer*

SOUTH CAROLINA

Camden
Daniels, John Hancock *agricultural products company executive*

Charleston
Addlestone, Nathan Sidney *metals company executive*
Clawson, Harry Quintard Moore *retired business executive*
Geentiens, Gaston Petrus, Jr., *former construction management consultant company executive*
Harding, Enoch, Jr., *clothing executive*
Mahoney, John Joseph *business executive, educator*
Martin, Roblee Boettcher *retired cement manufacturing executive*
Thompson, W(ilmer) Leigh *pharmaceutical company executive, physician, pharmacologist*

Clemson
Petzel, Florence Eloise *textiles educator*

Clinton
Cornelson, George Henry, IV, *retired textile company executive*

Columbia
Lolas, Anthony Joseph, Sr., *health and environmental business executive*
Robinson, Robert Earl *chemicals executive*
Sumwalt, Robert Llewellyn, Jr., *retired construction company executive*

Denmark
Dolezal, Dale Francis *truck manufacturing company executive*

Fort Mill
Bowles, Crandall Close *textiles executive*
Cooper, Marvin D. *paper company executive*
Kutcher, Kenneth E. *manufacturing executive*

Greenville
Bauknight, Clarence Brock *consultant*
Klasing, John Christoph *manufacturing executive*
Maffucci, David G. *paper company executive*
Nemirow, Arnold Myles *manufacturing executive*
Newman, R. Donald *paper company executive*
Pribanic, Gerald J. *manufacturing executive*
Prochaska, Bobby J. *apparel executive*
Varin, Roger Robert *textile executive*

Greenwood
Self, W. M. *textile company executive*

Hartsville
Coker, Charles Westfield *diversified manufacturing company executive*
Hupfer, Charles J. *manufacturing executive*

Hilton Head Island
Cunningham, William Henry *retired food products executive*
Harty, James D. *former manufacturing company executive*
Lauer, Clinton Dillman *automotive executive*
Lewis, Gene Evans *retired medical equipment company executive*
Love, Richard Emerson *retired equipment manufacturing company executive*
Mersereau, Hiram Stipe *wood products company consultant*
Pritchard, Dalton Harold *retired electronics research engineer*
Rulis, Raymond Joseph *manufacturing company executive, consultant*
Russell, Allen Stevenson *retired aluminum company executive*

Laurens
Bost, John Rowan *retired manufacturing executive, engineer*

Mauldin
Martin, Sharon D. *automotive executive*

Murrells Inlet
Wollman, June Rose *clothing executive*

Newry
Scott, Ronald S. *construction executive*

North Charleston
Zucker, Jerry *chemical manufacturing executive*

Orangeburg
Kent, Harry Ross *construction executive, lay worker*

Round O
Leonard, Guy Meyers, Jr., *international holding company executive*

Simpsonville
Maguire, D. E. *electronics executive*

Spartanburg
Allen, G. Ashley *chemicals executive*
Dent, Frederick Baily *former mill executive, former ambassador, former secretary of commerce*
Milliken, Roger *textile company executive*

SOUTH DAKOTA

Dakota Dunes
Bond, Richard L. *food products executive*
Leman, Eugene D. *meat industry executive*
Lochner, James V. *food products executive*
Peterson, Robert L. *meat processing executive*

North Sioux City
Shipley, Larry *food products executive*

Rapid City
Daughenbaugh, Randall Jay *retired chemical company executive, consultant*

Sioux Falls
Christensen, David Allen *manufacturing executive*
Reynolds, Leo Thomas *electronics company executive*
Rosenthal, Joel *manufacturing executive*

TENNESSEE

Ashland City
Lindahl, Herbert Winfred *appliance manufacturing executive*

Bartlett
Huffman, Delton Cleon, Jr., *pharmacy association executive*

Brentwood
Cash, W. Larry *health products executive*
Smith, Wayne Thomas *healthcare company executive*

Bristol
Gregory, John M. *pharmaceutical executive*
Markison, Brian *pharmaceutical executive*

Chattanooga
Fry, William N., IV, *textiles executive*
St. Goar, Herbert *retired food corporation executive*

Collegedale
McKee, Ellsworth R. *food products executive*
McKee, Jack *food products executive*

Cordova
Dean, Jimmy *meat processing company executive, entertainer*

Crossville
Lawrence, Ralph Waldo *manufacturing executive*

Dandridge
Comer, Evan Philip *manufacturing executive*

Franklin
Andrews, William Frederick *manufacturing executive*

Kingsport
Coover, Harry Wesley *manufacturing executive*
Deavenport, Earnest W., Jr., *chemical executive*
Ferguson, J. Brian *chemicals executive*
Head, William Iverson, Sr., *retired chemical company executive*
Lorraine, Richard *chemicals executive*

Knoxville
Faires, Ross Norbert *manufacturing executive*
Martin, James Robert *identification company executive*
Stringfield, Hezz, Jr., *contractor, financial consultant*

Lebanon
Evins, Dan W. *food products executive*

Maryville
Clayton, Kevin T. *mobile home manufacturer*

Memphis
Baioni, Louis *textiles executive*
Brafford, H. Wayne *paper company executive*
Cannon, Robert Emmet *consumer products manufacturing company executive*
Dunnigan, T. Kevin *electrical and electronics manufacturing company executive*
Gestrich, Thomas E. *paper company executive*
Greiner, Charles H. *paper company executive*
Herbert, Paul *paper company executive*
Lee, Theresa K. *chemicals executive*
Levy, Robert Halle *apparel executive, writer*
Mantey, Elmer Martin *food company executive*

Nashville
Crawford, Edwin Mac *pharmaceutical executive*
Elsea, Gene *apparel executive, state legislator*
Fitzgerald, Edmund Bacon *electronics industry executive*
Harris, Ben T. *apparel manufacturing and retail executive*
Harris, J(acob) George *healthcare company executive*
Hofstead, James Warner *laundry machinery company executive, lawyer*
Livingston, Robert A. *brewing company executive*
Mizell, Andrew Hooper, III, *concrete company executive*
Wire, William Shidaker, II, *retired apparel and footwear manufacturing company executive*

Oak Ridge
Poutsma, Marvin L. *chemical research administrator*

Spring Hill
Trudell, Cynthia *automotive executive*

TEXAS

Addison
Anderson, Jack Roy *health care company executive*
Holl, David *cosmetics company executive*
Rogers, Richard Raymond *cosmetics company executive*

Alamo
Pritchett, Thomas Ronald *retired metal and chemical company executive*

Allen
Warren, Rita Simpson *manufacturing executive*

Amarillo
Attebury, William Hugh *construction company executive*

Arlington
Beckwitt, Richard *construction executive*
Horton, Donald R. *construction executive*
LeMaster, Dale *construction executive*
Mansen, Steven Robert *manufacturing executive*
Mc Keen, Chester M., Jr., *retired business executive*
Tomnitz, Donald J. *construction executive*

Austin
Cindrich, Nick *medical products company executive*
Culp, Joe C(arl) *electronics executive*
Hackett, Donald W. *health/medical products executive*
Hitt, Chris *food products company executive*
Inman, Bobby Ray *former electronics executive, investor, educator*
Maar, Rosina *medical organization executive*
Mackey, John P. *food company executive*
Rotunda, Joseph Louis *retail and service company executive*
Smith, Craig *medical company executive*
Sonnonstine, Terry James *research executive specialty chemicals company*
Sullivan, Jerry Stephen *electronics company executive*

Thompson, Larry Flack *nanotechnology and semiconductor process company executive*
Van Buren, William Benjamin, III, *retired pharmaceutical company executive*
Vykukal, Eugene Lawrence *wholesale drug company executive*
Zaccaro, John F. *health/medical products executive*

Baytown
Hébert, Malcolm Charles *contractor, designer*

Beaumont
Allen, Eugene R. *construction executive*

Boerne
Richmond, James Ellis *retired restaurant company executive*

Bonham
Sarantakos, Lynell Moss *agricultural products executive*

Bryan
Lusas, Edmund William *food processing research executive*

Carrollton
Heath, Jinger L. *cosmetics executive*
Hulbert, Paul William, Jr., *paper, lumber company executive*

Celina
Willard, Jane *grain company executive*

College Station
Kainthla, Ramesh Chand *manufacturing executive*
Palen, Joseph William *chemical process research company executive*

Coppell
McCally, Charles Richard *construction company executive, consultant, mathematician, educator*
Williams, Gretchen Minyard *food store executive*

Corpus Christi
Kane, Sam *meat company executive*

Dallas
Barnes, Robert Vertreese, Jr., *masonry contractor executive*
Bradford, William Edward *oil field equipment manufacturing company executive*
Bucy, J. Fred, Jr., *retired electronics company executive*
Calado, Miguel Maria *food company executive*
Day, Maurice Jerome *automobile parts distributing company executive*
Dunn, Robert *food products executive*
Echols, Leldon E. *construction executive*
Engles, Gregg L. *food company executive*
Ethridge, Joseph Alfred *manufacturing executive (heavy)*
Fino, Arthur F. *food products executive*
Forward, Gordon E. *former manufacturing executive*
Fromberg, Barry A. *food products executive*
Fulsham, Rawles *manufacturing executive*
Gafford, Ronald J. *construction executive*
Gifford, Porter William *retired construction materials manufacturing company executive*
Gold, Christina A. *cosmetics company executive*
Guerin, Dean Patrick *executive*
Hegi, Frederick B., Jr., *mobile home manufacturing executive*
Hirsch, Laurence Eliot *construction executive, mortgage banker*
Horn, Charles L. *construction supplies manufacturing executive*
Hubach, Joseph F. *electronics executive*
Jancauskas, Don *business executive*
Keown, Michael H. *food products executive*
Klein, Ronald H. *food products executive*
Korba, Robert W. *manufacturing executive*
Kostas, Evans *manufacturing executive*
LaRovere, Ralph *manufacturing executive*
Leedom, John Nesbett *distribution company executive, state senator*
Lovvorn, Holly *bottling manufacturing executive*
Lowe, Jack, Jr., *manufacturing executive*
March, Kevin P. *electronics executive*
Margerison, Richard Wayne *diversified industrial company executive*
Murphy, John Joseph *manufacturing executive*
Nishi, Yoshio *electronics executive, laboratory administrator*
Olson, Cory M. *food products executive*
Pearce, Ronald *retired cosmetic company executive*
Quinn, David W. *building company executive*
Roach, John D. *building products company executive*
Robertson, Beverly Carruth *retired steel company executive*
Rosson, Glenn Richard *building products and furniture company executive*
Sammons, Elaine D. *manufacturing executive*
Sanders, Rodger *construction executive*
Schenkel, Pete *food company executive*
Sherman, Floyd F. *construction executive*
Sleeman, Donald George *construction executive, contractor*
Solomon, William Tarver *general construction company executive*
Templeton, Richard K. *electronics company executive*
Tinklepaugh, William C. *food products executive*
Turner, Jim L. *bottler manufacturing executive*
Tyson, Lisa N. *food products executive*
White, Tom Willingham *private investor*
Wilson, Lawrence Alexander *construction company executive*
Wyant, Clyde W., Jr., *manufacturing executive*
Zeilstra, Donald J. *research and development company executive*
Zumwalt, Richard Dowling *flour mill executive*

Denton
Brown, John Fred *steel company executive*

Diboll
Harbordt, Charles Michael *forest products executive*

El Paso
Hunt, M.L. *construction executive*

Farmers Branch
Armand, Susanne Marie *pharmaceutical products executive*

Fort Mc Kavett
Stokes, Charles Eugene, Jr., *wool merchant, textile executive*

Fort Worth
Arena, M. Scott *retired pharmaceutical company executive*
Corbusier, Drue *apparel and home furnishings executive*
Curts, Harold Layne *construction executive*
Kemp, Thomas Joseph *retired electronics executive*
Pearce, Betty McMurray *retired manufacturing executive*
Roland, Billy Ray *electronics company executive*
Thornton, Charles Victor *metals executive*
Vanhaecke, Erwin S. F. *pharmaceutical executive*
Williamson, Philip *apparel executive*

Garland
Brumit, Jo Ann *sheet metal manufacturing executive*
Keebaugh, Michael D. *electronics executive*

Georgetown
Gerding, Thomas Graham *medical products executive*

Granbury
Adams, Christopher Steve, Jr., *retired defense electronics corporation executive, former air force officer*

Houston
Allspach, Eugene R. *chemicals executive*
Austin, Harry Guiden *engineering and construction company executive*
Bonner, David Calhoun *chemical company executive*
Boren, William Meredith *manufacturing executive*
Cameron, William Duncan *plastics company executive*
Carrig, Kenneth J. *food products executive*
Caskey, Charles Thomas *biotechnology executive, biology and genetics educator*
Cizik, Robert *manufacturing executive, director*
Clyburn, Rose Mary Reed *construction materials company executive*
Cotros, Charles H. *food products company executive*
Curtiss, Jeff *industrial company executive, lawyer*
DeNicola, T. Kevin *chemicals executive*
Dodson, D. Keith *engineering and construction company executive*
Gelb, Morris *chemical company executive*
Goff, Robert Burnside *retired food company executive*
Goodman, John B. *heating/air conditioning manufacturing executive*
Gruen, Frank *automotive industry executive*
Hafner, Joseph A., Jr., *food company executive*
Hartsfield, Henry Warren, Jr., *electronics executive, retired astronaut*
Heimbinder, Isaac *construction company executive, lawyer*
Hinchliffe, Stephen F., Jr., *chemicals executive*
Hollingsworth, B.B., Jr., *automotive executive*
Hubert, Jean-Luc *chemicals executive*
Hurwitz, Charles Edwin *manufacturing executive*
Hynes, Thomas N. (Toby Hynes) *automotive company executive*
Jacobson, Charles Allen *aerospace company executive*
Lankford, Thomas E. *food service company executive*
Lukens, Max L. *manufacturing company executive*
Mason, Chip *retired automotive executive*
McCleskey, Jerry Michael *retired chemical company executive*
McGuyer, Frank *construction executive*
Menscher, Barnet Gary *steel company executive*
Munisteri, Joseph George *construction executive*
Murray, Frank *former heating, air conditioning manufacturing executive*
Nichols, Michael Cooper *food products executive, lawyer*
Parks, David R. *heating/air conditioning manufacturing executive*
Pefanis, Harry *manufacturing executive*
Pendergrass, Glen *construction executive*
Perry, Robert (Bob Perry) *construction executive*
Pognonec, Yves Maurice *steel products executive*
Pulliam, Larry G. *food products executive*
Riedel, Alan Ellis *retired manufacturing company executive, lawyer*
Riley, Harold John, Jr., *manufacturing executive*
Rock, Douglas Lawrence *manufacturing executive*
Salinas, Martha F. *manufacturing executive*
Schnieders, Richard J. *food products executive*
Schumacher, Diane Kosmach *manufacturing executive, lawyer*
Schwartz, Paul N. *manufacturing executive*
Seegmiller, Ray Reuben *manufacturing executive*
Siess, Charles P., Jr., *manufacturing executive*
Snowden, Bernice Rives *former construction company executive*
Stubblefield, John K., Jr., *food products company executive*
Temple, Robert Winfield *chemical company executive*
Thompson, Scott L. *automotive executive*
Thompson-Draper, Cheryl L. *electronics executive, real estate executive*
Waggoner, James Virgil *chemicals company executive*
Waycaster, Bill *chemical company executive*
Wiater, Richard M. *manufacturing executive*
Wilson, Carl Weldon, Jr., *construction company executive, civil engineer*
Wnuk, Wade Joseph *manufacturing and service company executive*
Wuensche, Vernon Edgar *construction company executive*

Irving
Donehower, John W. *retired paper company executive*
Falk, Thomas J. *paper company executive*
Henry, Mitch *health products executive*
Larson, William B. *metal products executive*
Seifert, Kathi P. *manufacturing executive*

Kaufman
Teagle, David Bryan *manufacturing executive*

Longview
Mann, Jack Matthewson *bottling company executive*

Lufkin
Smith, Douglas V. *manufacturing executive, heavy*

Mansfield
Siméus, Dumas M. *food products executive*

Mc Kinney
Schottlaender, Colin *electronics executive*
Strickland, Jeffery *medical products executive*

Montgomery
Steed, Theresa Jean *manufacturing executive*

Pasadena
Chan, Philip S. *medical products executive*
Gross, Cynthia Sue *petrochemicals manufacturing executive*

Pittsburg
Cogdill, Richard A. *food products executive*
Goolsby, O. B., Jr., *food products executive*
Pilgrim, Lonnie (Bo Pilgrim) *poultry production company executive*

Plano
Bain, Travis Whitsett, II, *manufacturing and retail executive*
Bru, Abelardo E. *food products executive*
Cumming, Marilee *apparel company executive*
Hardy, Tom Charles, Jr., *medical equipment company*
McCraw, Michael K. *construction executive*
Naor, Daniel *food products executive*

Richardson
Goodspeed, Linda A. *manufacturing executive*
Richards, Frederick Francis, Jr., *manufacturing executive, consultant*
Schjerven, Robert E. *manufacturing executive*
Smith, Richard A. *manufacturing executive*

Richmond
Barratt, Cynthia Louise *pharmaceutical company executive*

Rockwall
Fisher, Gene Jordan *retired chemical company executive*

San Antonio
Anderson, Charles Edward, Jr., *research and development executive*
Bagley, William Evan *application technology specialist*
Brouillard, John C. *grocery company executive*
Cisneros, Henry G. *homebuilding executive, broadcast executive, former federal official*
Cloud, Bruce Benjamin, Sr., *construction company executive*
Ebrom, Charles *contracting executive*
McCombs, Red *automotive sales executive*
Torres, Arthuro G. *toy company executive*
Williams, Thomas Eugene *pediatric hematologist-oncologist, pharmaceutical executive*
Zachry, Henry Bartell, Jr., *construction executive*

Santa Fe
Lambert, Willie Lee Bell *mobile equipment company owner, educator*

Seguin
Robinson, Ronald Alan *manufacturing executive*

Sugar Land
Chapko, Stephen J. *electronics executive*
Fedrick, Lonnie M. *construction executive*
Olson, Larry D. *electronics executive*

The Woodlands
Blickwede, Donald Johnson *retired steel company executive*

Tyler
Smith, Howard Thompson *manufacturing executive*

Webster
Johnson, Keith H. *pharmaceutical executive*

Whitewright
Burg, John Parker *signal processing executive*

Zephyr
Lancaster, Carroll Townes, Jr., *business executive*

UTAH

Heber City
Day, Gerald W. *wholesale grocery company executive*

Logan
Wheeler, Dolores *food products executive*

Ogden
Nickerson, Guy Robert *lumber company executive*

Orem
Segelman, Alvin Burton *pharmaceutical executive, researcher, scientist, health science consultant, educator*

Provo
Newitt, Jay *construction management educator*

Salt Lake City
Anderson, Joseph Andrew, Jr., *retired apparel company executive, retail consultant*
Esplin, J. Kimo *chemical company executive*
Frank, Thomas *design, construction and management executive*
Hembree, James D. *retired chemical company executive*
Horan, John J. *pharmaceutical company executive*
Huntsman, Jon Meade *chemical company executive*
Huntsman, Peter R. *chemicals executive*
Jackson, Hunter *health products executive*
Motter, Thomas Franklin *medical products executive*
Norton, Delmar Lynn *candy company executive*
Steiner, Richard Russell *textile & apparel company executive*
Stitley, James Walter, Jr., *food manufacturing executive*

Sandy
Clark, Jeffrey Raphiel *research and development company executive*

Vineyard
Cannon, Joseph A. *steel products company executive, political party official*

West Jordan
Bland, Dorothy Ann *construction executive, real estate agent*

VERMONT

Arlington
Nowicki, George Lucian *retired chemical company executive*

Bennington
Killen, Carroll Gorden *electronics company executive*

Brattleboro
Cohen, Richard B. *grocery company executive*
Gross, Mark *food products executive*
Hamlin, William *grocery company executive*

Brownsville
Olderman, Gerald *retired medical device company executive*

Burlington
Pizzagalli, Angelo *construction company executive*

Pittsfield
Wacker, Susan Regina *creative design director*

Shelburne
Robert, Elisabeth B. *toy company executive*

South Burlington
Cohen, Bennett R. (Ben Cohen) *food products executive*
Pizzagalli, James *construction executive*

South Pomfret
Oatway, Francis Carlyle *corporate executive*

VIRGINIA

Alexandria
Crundwell, Duncan James *electronics executive*
Stempler, Jack Leon *government and aerospace company executive*
Wynn, Robert E. *electronics executive, retired career officer*

Arlington
Cocolis, Peter Konstantine *business development executive*
Cox, Henry *research engineer*
Culligan, Thomas M. *electronics executive*
Danjczek, David William *manufacturing executive*
Gracey, James Steele *corporate director, retired coast guard officer, consultant*
Guirguis, Raouf Albert *health science executive*
Howlett, Clifford Theodore, Jr., (Kip Howlett) *chemicals executive*
Rabbitt, Linda *construction executive*
Racette, Nancy Kelly *development company executive, consultant*
Woollen, Edmund *electronics executive*

Ashburn
Cuteri, Frank R., Jr., *automotive executive*

Charlottesville
Rader, Louis T. *corporation executive, educator*

Danville
Harker, Brian *tobacco company executive*

Deltaville
Koedel, John Gilbert, Jr., *retired metal products executive*

Dulles
Persavich, Warren Dale *diversified manufacturing company executive*

Edinburg
Rhodes, Stephen Michael *poultry company executive*

Fairfax
Stringfellow, Charles *automotive executive*

Glen Allen
Fife, William Franklin *retired drug company executive*
Minor, George Gilmer, III, *drug and hospital supply company executive*
Murphey, Robert Stafford *pharmaceutical executive*
Stokely, John E. *food distribution executive*

Harrisonburg
McCurdy, Donna T. *food products company executive*

Heathsville
Winkel, Raymond Norman *aerospace industry consultant, avionics manufacturing executive, retired naval officer*

Herndon
Guerreri, Carl Natale *electronic company executive*

Kilmarnock
Moore, William Black, Jr., *retired aluminum company executive*

Lynchburg
Denham, Paul Raymond *construction executive*

Manassas
Geerdes, James D(ivine) *chemical company executive*
Heimendinger, Larry Martin *computer software manufacturing company executive*
Parrish, Frank Jennings *retired food products executive*

Marion
Grinstead, Paul Lee *materials company official*

Mc Lean
Barnes, R.E. *food products executive*
Dempsey, James Raymon *industrial executive*
Hoogendoorn, Benno *food products executive*
Mars, Forrest E., Jr., *candy company executive*
Mars, Jacqueline Badger *food products executive*
Mars, John Franklin *candy company executive*
Schar, Dwight C. *construction company executive*
Steiner, Jeffrey Josef *industrial manufacturing company executive*

Mechanicsville
Hinkle, Barton Leslie *retired electronics company executive*

Newport News
Banks, Charles Augustus, III, *manufacturing executive*
Fricks, William Peavy *shipbuilding company executive*

Norfolk
Dennison, Stanley Scott *retired forest products company executive, consultant*

Petersburg
Wilson, John Robert, Jr., *pharmaceutical and chemical company executive*

Portsmouth
Mintz, Susan Ashinoff *apparel manufacturing company executive*

Reston
Even, Bryan J. *electronics executive*
Picard, Dennis J. *retired electronics company executive*

Richmond
Blumberg, Peter Steven *manufacturing executive*
Bunzl, Rudolph Hans *retired manufacturing executive*
Gottwald, Bruce Cobb *chemical company executive*
Gottwald, Floyd Dewey, Jr., *chemical company executive*
Gray, C. Michael *food products executive*
Helwig, Arthur Woods *retired chemical company executive*
Pauley, Stanley Frank *manufacturing executive*
Peterson, H(arry) William *chemicals executive, consultant*
Ritter, Robert T. *diversified company executive*
Rogers, James Edward *paper company executive*
Sheehan, Jeremiah J. *former metal company executive*
Slotnick, Robert D *food products executive*
Walker, Charles B. *chemicals company executive*
Watts, Robert Glenn *retired pharmaceutical executive*

Roanoke
Gray, Jeffrey T. *automotive executive*
Smith, Donald G. *metal products executive*
Wade, Jimmie L. *automotive executive*
Waldron, Karen *development, construction, and management company executive*
Willis, Gordon *construction executive*

Smithfield
Baxter, Raoul *meat packing company executive*
Luter, Joseph Williamson, III, *meat packing and processing company executive*

Springfield
Franklin, Jude Eric *electronics executive*

Sterling
Thompson, Warren M. *food franchise executive*

Suffolk
Birdsong, George Yancy *manufacturing executive*
Sorensen, Carl Edward *company executive*

Vienna
de Bearn, Gaston, XIV, *pharmaceutical company executive, consultant*

Virginia Beach
Hamilton, George Henry, Jr., *energy consultant*

Winchester
Holland, James Tulley *retired plastic products company executive*
Jolly, Bruce Dwight *manufacturing executive*

Yorktown
Gross, Leroy *retired sugar company executive*

WASHINGTON

Anacortes
Randolph, Carl Lowell *chemical company executive*

Belfair
Hager, Robert Worth *retired aerospace company executive*

Bellevue
Hovind, David J. *manufacturing executive*
Nowik, Dorothy Adam *medical equipment company executive*
Pigott, Charles McGee *transportation equipment manufacturing executive*
Pigott, Mark C. *automotive executive*
Tembreull, Michael A. *automotive executive*

Bellingham
Haggen, Donald E. *food products executive*
Henley, Dale C. *grocery company executive*
Kapcsandy, Louis Endre *building construction and manufacturing executive, chemical engineering consultant*

Bothell
Craves, Frederick B. *health products executive*
Fell, H. Perry *biotechnology company executive*
Gerber, William G. *medical company executive*
Stein, Michael A. *pharmaceutical executive*
Wilds, Daniel O. *health products executive*

Camano Island
Clowes, Garth Anthony *electronics executive, consultant*

Clinton
Holtby, Kenneth Fraser *retired manufacturing executive*

Coupeville
Thom, Richard David *retired aerospace executive*

Eastsound
Anders, William Alison *aerospace and defense manufacturing executive*

Federal Way
Corbin, William R. *wood products executive*
Hanson, Richard E. *paper company executive*
Hogans, Mack L. *paper company executive*
Keller, James R. *manufacturing executive*
McDade, Sandy D. *manufacturing executive*
Onustock, Michael R. *manufacturing executive*
Rogel, Steven R. *forest products company executive*
Taylor, Jack P. *lumber company executive*

Hoquiam
Lamb, Isabelle Smith *manufacturing executive*

Issaquah
Massick, James William *heavy equipment manufacturing company executive*
Wainwright, Paul Edward Blech *construction company executive*

Kent
Goo, Abraham Meu Sen *retired aircraft company executive*
Hebeler, Henry Koester *retired aerospace and electronics executive*

Kirkland
Witte, Peggy *metal products executive*

Lake Stevens
Durden, Rome L. *aircraft manufacturing company executive*

Lakewood
Cook, Anne Welsh *lumber company executive*

Longview
Wollenberg, Richard Peter *paper manufacturing company executive*

Manson
Stager, Donald K. *retired construction company executive*

Maple Valley
Brown, Thomas Andrew *retired aircraft/weaponry manufacturing executive*

Medina
Meeker, Milton Shy *manufacturing executive*

Mercer Island
Gould, Alvin R. *international business executive*

Mill Creek
Stelzer, Gustav R. *retired automotive executive*

Naches
Assink, Nellie Grace *agricultural executive*

Oak Harbor
Daugherty, Kenneth Earl *research company executive, educator*

Renton
Greenwood, Loren *toy manufacturing executive*
Huck, Larry Ralph *manufacturing executive, sales consultant*

Seattle
Albrecht, Richard Raymond *retired airplane manufacturing executive, lawyer*
Behnke, Carl Gilbert *beverage franchise executive*
Bundrant, Charles H. *food products executive*
Carter, Bruce L.A. *biotechnology company executive*
Casey, M. Michael *food products executive*
Cook, Jeremy Curnock *biotechnology executive*
Duncan, Steven Merle *construction company manager, philosophy educator*
Farrington-Hopf, Susan Kay *plumbing and heating contractor*
Friend, Stephen H. *biotechnology company executive*
Gillis, Steven *biotechnology company executive*
Lincoln, Howard *manufacturing company and sports team executive*
Link, Max E. *health products executive*
Parker, H. Stewart *biotechnology company executive*
Pollnow, C. *lumber company executive*
Puckett, Allen Weare *health care information systems executive*
Schoenfeld, Walter Edwin *manufacturing executive*
Smith, Orin C. *food products executive*

Spokane
Hiller, Stanley, Jr., *manufacturing executive*
Siegel, Louis Pendleton *forest products executive*
Tarr, Gregory L. *health and medical products company executive*

Tacoma
Hutchings, George Henry *food company executive*
Weyerhaeuser, George H., Jr., *paper manufacturing company executive*

Tukwila
Harnish, John J. *manufacturing executive*

Vancouver
Hammann, Gregg C. *fitness equipment executive*

Wenatchee
Birdsall, Brian *food products executive*
Chandler, Allen *food products executive*

Yakima
Long, David R. *food products executive*

WEST VIRGINIA

Charleston
Wehrle, Henry Bernard, III, *electrical supply company executive*

Redmond
Hylbert, Paul *construction executive*

WISCONSIN

Appleton
Barlow, F(rank) John *mechanical contracting company executive*
Boldt, Oscar Charles *construction company executive*
Grayson, David S. *paper company executive*
Spiegelberg, Harry Lester *retired paper products company executive*

Bowler
Maas, Duane Harris *distilling company executive*

Brookfield
Vitek, Richard Kenneth *retired scientific instrument company executive*

Cedarburg
Schaefer, Gordon Emory *food products executive*

Clintonville
Simpson, Vinson Raleigh *manufacturing executive, director*

Eau Claire
Cohen, Maryjo R. *manufacturing executive*
Cohen, Melvin Samuel *manufacturing executive*
Rasmussen, Earl R *lumber company and home improvement retail executive*

Fort Atkinson
Jones, Alan Porter, Jr., *food manufacturing executive*

Germantown
Dohmen, John F. *pharmaceutical executive*

Green Bay
Ferguson, Larry P. *food products executive*
Kress, William F. *manufacturing executive*
Kuehne, Carl W. *food products executive*
Liddy, Brian *food products executive*
Liegel, Craig A. *meat packing company executive*
Marsh, Miles L. *paper company executive*

Ixonia
Peebles, Allene Kay *manufactured housing company executive*

Kenosha
Emma, Edward C. *apparel executive*

Kohler
Cheney, Jeffrey Paul *manufacturing executive*
Kohler, Herbert Vollrath, Jr., *diversified manufacturing company executive*
Wells, Richard A. *manufacturing executive*

La Crosse
Drazkowski, Mark *food products executive*
Gelatt, Charles Daniel *manufacturing executive*

Madison
Macfarlane, Alastair Iain Robert *manufacturing executive*
Shain, Irving *retired chemical company executive and university chancellor*

Marathon
Menzner, Donald *food products executive*

Markesan
Chamberlain, Robert Glenn *retired tool manfacturing executive*

Mequon
Dohmen, Frederick Hoeger *retired pharmaceutical executive*

Merrill
Bierman, Jane *wood products company executive*

Milwaukee
Barnes, W. Michael *electronics executive*
Barth, John M. *manufacturing executive*
Beals, Vaughn Le Roy, Jr., *retired motorcycle manufacturing executive*
Bishop, Charles Joseph *manufacturing executive*
Bleustein, Jeffrey L. *automotive executive*
Carter, Valerie *food products executive*
Colbert, Virgis W. *food products executive*
Daniels-Carter, Valerie *food franchise executive*
Davis, Don H., Jr., *multi-industry high-technology company executive*
Grade, Jeffery T. *manufacturing executive*
Hoffman, Robert Butler *ministry industry executive*
Hudson, Katherine Mary *manufacturing executive*
Jacobs, Bruce E. *metal products executive*
Karst, Darren W. *food products executive*
Keyes, James Henry *manufacturing executive*
Koss, John Charles *consumer electronics products manufacturing company executive*
Marringa, Jacques Louis *manufacturing executive*
Parker, Charles Walter, Jr., *consultant, retired equipment company executive*
Roell, Stephen A. *manufacturing executive*
Shiely, John Stephen *manufacturing executive, lawyer*
Sterner, Frank Maurice *industrial executive*
Ziemer, James L. *automotive executive*

Mount Horeb
Barry, Jonathan B. *chemicals executive, communications executive*

Neenah
Bergstrom, Dedric Waldemar *retired paper company executive*

Oshkosh
Drebus, Richard William *pharmaceutical company executive*

Pleasant Prairie
Morrone, Frank *electronic manufacturing executive*

Racine
Campbell, Edward Joseph *retired machinery company executive*
Konz, Gerald Keith *retired manufacturing company executive*
McCollum, W. Lee *chemical company executive*
Perez, William D. *chemical company executive*
Rosso, Jean-Pierre *electronics executive*
Wambold, Richard Lawrence *manufacturing executive*

South Milwaukee
Kitzke, Eugene David *research and development company executive*

Sturtevant
Bailey, Michael J. *manufacturing executive*
Lawton, Gregory E. *manufacturing executive*

Sussex
Losee, John Frederick, Jr., *manufacturing executive*
Stromberg, Gregory *printing ink company executive*

Waterloo
Burke, Richard A. *manufacturing executive*

Waukesha
Hogan, Joseph M. *medical products executive*

West Bend
Darrow, Russe M. *automotive executive*
Gehl, William D. *manufacturing executive*

Wisconsin Rapids
Engelhardt, LeRoy A. *retired paper company executive*
Gottschalk, Guy *agricultural products executive*

WYOMING

Jackson
Furrer, John Rudolf *retired manufacturing executive*
Gordon, Stephen Maurice *manufacturing company executive, rancher*

Wilson
Harrell, Samuel Macy *agribusiness executive*

TERRITORIES OF THE UNITED STATES

GUAM

Tamuning
Yingling, Gerald Phillip *business executive*

PUERTO RICO

Dorado
Spector, Michael Joseph *agribusiness executive*

Juncos
Caraballo, Jose *pharmaceutical executive*

CANADA

ALBERTA

Calgary
Holman, J(ohn) Leonard *retired manufacturing corporation executive*

Edmonton
Stollery, Robert *construction company executive*

BRITISH COLUMBIA

North Vancouver
Gibbs, David George *retired food processing company executive*

Vancouver
Hastings, Paul J. *pharmaceutical executive*

Victoria
Fuller, James Chester Eedy *retired chemical company executive*

MANITOBA

Winnipeg
MacKenzie, George Allan *medical products executive*

NEW BRUNSWICK

Fredericton
Grotterod, Knut *retired paper company executive*

NOVA SCOTIA

Stellarton
Sobey, David Frank *food company executive*

ONTARIO

Aurora
Lanthier, Ronald Ross *retired manufacturing company executive*

Burlington
Bullock, James R. *company executive*
McMulkin, Francis John *retired steel company executive*

Cambridge
Turnbull, Robert Scott *retired manufacturing executive*
White, Joseph Charles *manufacturing and retailing company executive*

Don Mills
Hyde, Michael Arthur *consultant, retired chemical company executive*

Hamilton
Hantho, Chuck *retired metal products executive*

Markham
Burns, H(erbert) Michael *corporate director*

Mississauga
Colcleugh, David W. *chemical company executive*
Kennedy, John W. *health products executive*

Nepean
Chudobiak, Walter James *electronics company executive, electronic engineer*

Newmarket
Walker, Donald J. *automotive systems company executive*

Ottawa
Beare-Rogers, Joyce Louise *former research executive*
Goodine, Isaac Thomas *development executive, educator*

Toronto
Connell, Philip Francis *food industry executive*
Dale, Robert Gordon *business executive*
Detlefsen, Michael E. *food products executive*
Eagles, Stuart Ernest *business executive*
Lennox, R. Ian *health products executive*
Lewitt, Wilfred G. *health products executive*
Macdonald, Donald Stovel *corporate director*
Polistuk, Eugene V. *electronics manufacturing services executive*
Wleugel, John Peter *manufacturing executive*

QUEBEC

Montreal
Ferguson, Michael John *electronics and communications educator*
Herling, Michael *steel company executive*
Ivanier, Paul *steel products manufacturing company executive*
Molson, Eric H. *brewery company executive*
Plourde, Gerard *company executive*
Redfern, John D. *manufacturing executive*
Rolland, Lucien Gilbert *paper company executive, director*

SASKATCHEWAN

Regina
Phillips, Roger *retired steel company executive*

Montreal
O'Neill, Daniel J. *brewery company executive*

MEXICO

Mexico City
Rosenkranz, George *chemical company executive*
Vargas Legaspi, Juan *manufacturing executive*

AUSTRALIA

Sydney
Selley, Michael L. *pharmaceutical company executive*

THE BAHAMAS

Nassau
Dingman, Michael David *industrial company executive, international investor*

BRAZIL

Sao Paulo
Reigrod, Robert Hull *manufacturing executive*

CAMEROON

Yaoundé
Provencher-Kambour, Frances *business development advisor*

CHINA

Shanghai
Jackson, Robert Keith *retired manufacturing executive*

ENGLAND

Beckenham Kent
Lader, Malcolm Harold *pharmaceutical consultant*

London
Baird, Dugald Euan *automotive executive*
Barnevik, Percy Nils *electrical company executive*

Milton Keynes
Throdahl, Mark Crandall *medical technology company executive*

Surrey
Vere Hodge, Richard Anthony *pharmaceutical executive, consultant*

FINLAND

Tampere
Andriano, Kirk Patrick *pharmaceutical executive*

FRANCE

Nanterre
Payri, Joel *pharmaceutical marketing executive*

Paris
Collomb, Bertrand Pierre *cement company executive*
Lecerf, Olivier Maurice Marie *construction company executive*

GERMANY

Schleusingen-Gethles
Frank, Dieter *retired chemicals executive*

GREECE

Athens
Larounis, George Philip *manufacturing executive, director*

JAPAN

Kanagawa
Hoshino, Yoshiro *industrial technology critic*

Tokyo
Baba, Isamu *construction company executive*
Ohga, Norio *retired electronics executive*
Saba, Shoichi *manufacturing executive, director*
Wakumoto, Yoshihiko *electronics company executive, grants executive*

Toyota
Toyoda, Shoichiro *automobile company executive*

PHILIPPINES

Manila
Tiuman, Erich Lim *textile company executive*

SPAIN

Madrid
Feltenstein, Harry David, Jr., *chemical executive*

SWEDEN

Stockholm
Westerberg, Lars *automotive safety systems company executive*

SWITZERLAND

Basel
Martelet, Francois R. *pharmaceutical executive*

TAIWAN

Taipei
Chuang, Yii-Der *retired business executive amd diplomat*

VENEZUELA

Caracas
Salas, Randall Nouel *automotive company executive*

ADDRESS UNPUBLISHED

Aall, Christian Bergengren *software company executive*
Acerra, Michele (Mike Acerra) *engineering and construction company executive*
Adams, William White *retired manufacturing company executive*
Alford, Becky Dianne *food products executive*
Alig, Frank Douglas Stalnaker *retired construction company executive*
Allaire, Paul Arthur *former office equipment company executive*
Altschuler, Samuel *retired electronics company executive*
Ammon, R. Theodore *food products executive*
Amstutz, Daniel Gordon *international agriculture industry consultant, government official, retired federal agency administrator*
Anderer, Joseph Henry *textile company executive*
Anderson, Joseph Norman *executive consultant, former food company executive, former college president*
Andersson, Craig Remington *retired chemical company executive*
Andreas, Dwayne Orville *agricultural products executive*
Archibald, Nolan D. *household and industrial products company executive*
Aronowitz, Jack Leon *biotechnology and diagnostic manufacturing company executive, consultant*
Aschauer, Charles Joseph, Jr., *retired health products executive, corporate director*
Ashton, Harris John *business executive*
Asmussen, Nils Wirenfeldt *pharmaceutical executive*
Asplin, Edward William *retired packaging company executive*
Asura, John F. *paper company executive*
Atchison, Joseph Edward *pulp and paper industry consultant*
Azarnoff, Daniel Lester *pharmaceutical company consultant*
Barca, George Gino *winery executive, financial investor*
Barkley, Donald *manufacturing executive*
Barna, Peter *chemical company financial executive*
Barth, David Keck *distribution industry consultant*
Batts, Warren Leighton *retired diversified industry executive*
Bauman, Robert Patten *diversified company executive*
Bayly, George V. *manufacturing executive*
Beadle, John Grant *retired manufacturing company executive*
Beck, Albert *manufacturing executive*
Beebe, Stephen A. *agricultural products company executive*
Beighey, Lawrence Jerome *packaging company executive*
Bennett, Carrie *retired chemical company executive*
Bennett, Richard Thomas *manufacturing executive*
Bergman, Janet Eisenstein *food industry executive*
Bergmann, Donald Gerald *pharmaceutical company executive*
Bernsen, Harold John *manufacturing executive*
Bernthal, Harold George *healthcare company executive*
Berry, Robert Vaughan *retired electrical manufacturing company executive*
Beutler, Arthur Julius *manufacturing executive*
Bevington, Edmund Milton *electrical machinery manufacturing company executive*
Bible, Geoffrey Cyril *former tobacco company executive*
Bierwirth, John Cocks *retired manufacturing executive*
Biggers, William Joseph *retired manufacturing company executive*
Biggs, Arthur Edward *retired chemical manufacturing company executive*
Bixby, Harold Glenn *manufacturing executive, director*
Blanchard, Richard Frederick *construction executive*
Blum, Betty Ann *footwear company executive*
Bollenbacher, Herbert Kenneth *steel company official*
Borgnine, Tova *cosmetics executive*
Boyer, Robert Allan *business executive*
Boyle, R. Emmett *metal products executive*
Boyle, Tim *apparel executive*
Boylston, Benjamin Calvin *retired steel company executive*
Brancato, Leo John *manufacturing executive*
Braude, Edwin Simon *manufacturing executive*
Brewer, Richard B. *biotechnology company executive*
Bridenbaugh, Peter Reese *industrial research executive*
Brooker, Robert Elton, Jr., *retired manufacturing company executive*
Brown, Jerry Milford *medical company executive*
Bruggeman, Terrance *biotechnology company executive*
Buettner, Michael Lewis *healthcare manufacturing executive*
Bull, Bergen Ira *retired equipment manufacturing company executive*
Bullock, Francis Jeremiah *retired pharmaceutical research executive*
Burkart, Walter Mark *retired manufacturing company executive*
Burns, Ward *textile company executive*
Busch, J. Herbert *electrical contractor, writer*
Butcher, Jack Robert (Jack Risin) *manufacturing executive, film producer, actor*
Butler, Jack Fairchild *semiconductors company executive*
Cabaret, Joseph Ronald *retired defense company executive*
Calcaterra, Edward Lee *construction company executive*
Calvert, James Francis *manufacturing company executive, retired admiral*
Campbell, Richard Alden *electronics company executive*
Candlish, Malcolm *manufacturing executive*
Carpenter, Myron Arthur *manufacturing executive*
Carroll, Charles A. *manufacturing executive*
Carver, Juanita Ash *plastic company executive*
Casey, Michael D. *biotechnology company executive*
Cassidy, James Mark *construction company executive*
Castaldi, David Lawrence *healthcare company executive*
Castor, Jon Stuart *electronics company executive*
Chen, Di *electro-optic company executive, consultant*
Chihorek, John Paul *electronics company executive*
Chmielinski, Edward Alexander *retired electronics company executive*
Chu, James *electronics executive*
Cicolani, Angelo George *research and development company executive, operating engineer*
Clark, Darwin Edward *retired automotive executive*
Closset, Gerard Paul *forest products consultant*
Clouston, Ross Neal *retired food and related products company executive*
Cook, Richard Kelsey *aerospace industry executive*
Cooper, Norton J. (Sky Cooper) *liquor, wine and food company executive*
Coors, William K. *retired brewery executive*
Costello, James Joseph *retired electrical manufacturing company executive*
Cotting, James Charles *manufacturing executive, director*
Couch, John D. *health products executive*
Cox, John Francis *retired cosmetic company executive*
Cox, Wilford Donald *retired food company executive*
Craft, Edmund Coleman *retired automotive parts manufacturing company executive*
Crawford, James Dee *chemical distribution executive*
Crawford, William David *office equipment company executive*
Cull, Robert Robinette *electric products manufacturing company executive*
Culwell, Charles Louis *retired manufacturing company executive*
Curtis, Arnold Bennett *retired lumber company executive*
Cutter, David Lee *pharmaceutical company executive*
D'Agostino, Stephen Ignatius *bottling company executive*
Daly, William James *retired health industry distributing company executive*
D'Andrade, Hugh A(lfred) *retired pharmaceutical company executive, lawyer*
Danziger, Glenn Norman *former chemical sales company executive*
Darrow, William Richard *retired pharmaceutical company executive, consultant*
Davis, Darrell L. *automotive executive*
DeBruce, Paul *agricultural food products company executive*
Dennehy, Leisa Jeanotta *pharmaceutical executive*
Derrick, Bill *contracting company executive*
Deutsche, Kirsten Hansen *pharmaceutical company executive*
Devine, Donald C. *manufacturing executive*
de Vink, Lodewijk J. R. *healthcare consultant, former consumer pharmaceutical products company executive*
Dicciani, Nance Katherine *chemical company executive, chemical engineer*
Dickerson, Gary E. *former electronics executive*
Diener, Royce *retired health products executive*
Dinkel, John George *automotive executive, consultant*
Dohrmann, Russell William *manufacturing executive*
Donahue, Richard King *athletic apparel executive, lawyer*
Doran, Charles Edward *textile manufacturing executive*
Doyle, Irene Elizabeth *electronic sales executive, nurse*
Dragon, William, Jr., *footwear and apparel company executive*
Dressler, David Charles *retired aerospace company executive*
Drew, Walter Harlow *retired paper industry executive*
Duhaime, Nina Lee *business research and development*
Durr, Robert Joseph *construction firm executive, mechanical engineer*
Dyer, Natalie Mary *health products company executive, physician*
Earle, Arthur Percival *textile company executive, airport executive*
Edwards, Traci Van Arsdale *drug company official*
Elverum, Gerard William, Jr., *retired electronic and diversified company executive*
Ely, Paul C., Jr., *electronics company executive*
Engels, Lawrence Arthur *retired metals company executive*
Engibous, Thomas James *electronics company executive*
Erdeljac, Daniel Joseph *retired manufacturing company executive*
Essig, Mark G. *steel products company executive*
Evans, Thomas E. *autoparts company executive*
Eyngorn, Isaak Ykovlevich *electronics executive*
Fein, Seymour Howard *pharmaceutical executive*
Finlay, Robert Derek *food company executive*
Flanzraich, Neil William *pharmaceutical company executive, lawyer*
Flitcraft, Richard Kirby, II, *former chemical company executive*
Fluharty, David Arthur *automotive executive, statistician, consultant*
Flynn, Robert James *electronic commerce executive*
Fogg, Richard Lloyd *food products company executive*
Ford, Jerry Lee *service company executive*
Francisco, Wayne *automotive executive*
Freeman, Frank V. *manufacturing executive*
French, Clarence Levi, Jr., *retired shipbuilding company executive*
French, Harold Stanley *food company executive*
Frieling, Gerald Harvey, Jr., *specialty steel company executive*
Frisco, Louis Joseph *retired materials science company executive, electrical engineer*
Fritz, Rene Eugene, Jr., *manufacturing executive*
Fuente, David I. *office supply manufacturing executive*
Gassaway, William Brooks *retired manufacturing executive, writer*
Gifford, John Irving *retired agricultural equipment company executive*
Gillespie, Robert James *former manufacturing company executive*
Gilmour, Allan Dana *automotive company executive*

Giordano, Richard Vincent (Sir Richard Vincent Giordano) *chemicals executive*
Goldberg, Lee Winicki *furniture company executive*
Goodale, Toni Krissel *development consultant*
Gordon, Richard M. Erik *private investor, educator*
Gorman, Joseph Tolle *automotive parts manufacturing executive*
Gottlander, Robert Jan Lars *dental company executive*
Graber, William Raymond *former pharmaceutical executive*
Graham, Wallace Karl *chemical company executive*
Gray, Richard Alexander, Jr., *retired chemical company executive*
Greaser, Constance Udean *retired automotive industry executive*
Greenberg, Jack M. *former food products executive*
Griffin, Mark W. *paper company executive*
Grove, Richard Charles *retired power tool company executive*
Guiliano, Francis James *office products manufacturing company executive*
Gulcher, Robert Harry *aircraft company executive*
Gurney, Daniel Sexton *race car manufacturing company executive, racing team executive*
Haas, Frederick Carl *retired paper and chemical company executive*
Haberkorn, Judith R. *former manufacturing executive*
Haeberle, William Leroy *corporate director, business educator, entrepreneur*
Hake, Ralph F. *appliance manufacturing executive*
Hakimoglu, Ayhan *electronics company executive*
Halle, Bruce T. *automotive products company executive*
Hamister, Donald Bruce *retired electronics company executive*
Hammond, Robert Lee *retired feed company executive*
Harari, Guy *chemicals executive*
Harbert, Charles Armon *medicinal chemist*
Harper, Charles Michel *food company executive*
Harrell, Henry Howze *tobacco company executive*
Hartmann, George Herman *retired manufacturing company executive*
Hartwick, Thomas Stanley *technical management consultant*
Hausman, Arthur Herbert *electronics company executive*
Hayes, John Patrick *retired manufacturing company executive*
Heckel, John Louis (Jack Heckel) *aerospace company executive*
Heilmann, Christian Flemming *manufacturing executive*
Heininger, S(amuel) Allen *retired chemical company executive*
Heller, Ronald Gary *manufacturing company executive, lawyer*
Henning, George Thomas, Jr., *steel company executive*
Herbert, Gavin Shearer *health care products company executive*
Herman, Rayna S. *pharmaceutical consultant*
Herzfeld, Siegfried *manufacturing executive, consultant*
Heybach, John Peter *food products executive, information technology executive*
Hiatt, Arnold *shoe manufacturer, importer, retailer*
Hind, Harry William *pharmaceutical company executive*
Hines, Anthony Loring *automotive executive*
Hirsch, Horst Eberhard *business consultant*
Hoch, Orion Lindel *corporate executive*
Hochfeld, William Sidney *construction executive, consultant*
Holder, Richard Gibson *retired metal products executive*
Holmes, David Richard *computer and business forms company executive*
Holten, John V. *former food products/retail grocery executive*
Honse, Robert W. *agricultural company executive*
Hook, Jerry B. *pharmaceutical consultant*
Hornak, Thomas *retired electronics company executive*
Hsu, Gerald C. *electrical company executive*
Hudson, Franklin Donald *diversified company executive, consultant*
Hudson, William Jeffrey, Jr., *manufacturing executive*
Hume, Frederick Raymond *electronics company executive*
Hunt, V. William (Bill) *automotive supplier executive*
Hurd, Richard Nelson *pharmaceutical company executive*
Hushen, John Wallace *manufacturing executive*
Ivanchenko, Lauren Margaret Dowd *pharmaceutical executive*
Ivester, Melvin Douglas *retired beverage company executive*
Ix, Robert Edward *food company executive*
Jackson, Robbi Jo *agricultural products executive, lawyer*
Jackson, Robert Howard *food company executive, scientist*
Jaffe, Marvin Eugene *pharmaceutical company executive, neurologist*
Jenkins, Becki Eunice *medical products executive, writer*
Jenkins, Royal Gregory *manufacturing executive*
Johnson, Irving Stanley *pharmaceutical company executive, scientist*
Johnstone, John William, Jr., *retired chemical company executive*
Jones, Christine Massey *retired furniture company executive*
Jones, Robert Henry *automotive distribution executive*
Joyce, William Robert *textile machinery company executive*
Judelson, David N. *company executive*
Keeler, James Leonard *food products company executive*
Keen, Constantine *retired manufacturing company executive*
Keith, Brian Thomas *automobile executive*
Kelley, James *automotive sales executive*
Kelley, Thomas William *automotive sales executive*
Kelly, Anthony Odrian *flooring manufacturing company executive*
Kerber, Ronald Lee *industrial corporation executive*
Kern, Irving John *retired food company executive*
Kerr, Michael D. *construction company executive*
Kerstetter, Michael James *retired manufacturing company executive*
Khilnani, Vinod M. *manufacturing executive*
Killhour, William Gherky *paper company executive*
Killian, William Paul *industrial corporate executive*
King, Susan Bennett *retired glass company executive*
Kiselik, Paul Howard *manufacturing executive*
Klaehne, Eberhard O W *pharmaceutical executive, chemist*
Knight, Herbert Borwell *manufacturing executive*
Kogan, Richard J. *former pharmaceutical company executive*
Kraemer, Harry M. Jansen, Jr., *medical products executive*
Krause, Werner William *plastics company executive*
Kronschnabel, Robert James *retired manufacturing company executive*
Krupp, James Arthur Gustave *manufacturing executive, consultant*
Kulik, Rosalyn Franta *food company executive, consultant*
Kung, Patrick Chung-Shu *biotechnology executive*
Labrecque, Richard Joseph *retired industrial executive*
Lala, Dominick Joseph *manufacturing executive*
Landsberger, Kurt *scientific and medical products executive*
Lane, William W. *electronics executive*
Langbo, Arnold Gordon *former food company executive*
Langer, Dennis Henry *pharmaceutical company executive*
Langford, Walter Martin *retired greeting card and gift wrap manufacturing executive*
Laurenzo, Vincent Dennis *industrial management company executive*
LeBlanc, Leonard Joseph *electronics company executive*
Leff, Joseph Norman *yarn manufacturing company executive*
Lehman, John F., Jr., *industrialist*
Leopold, Ray *electronics executive*
Levaux, Hugh Pierre *pharmaceutical executive, consultant*
Leveille, Gilbert Antonio *food products executive*
Lew, Roger Alan *manufacturing executive*
Lewis, Arthur Dee *corporation executive*
Lewis, John D. *textile company executive*
Lewis, Martin R. *paper company executive, consultant*
Lewis, Rita Hoffman *plastic products manufacturing company executive*
Liebler, Arthur C. *automotive executive*
Liffers, William Albert *retired chemical company executive*
Linde, Ronald Keith *corporate executive, private investor*
Lindsay, James Wiley *retired agricultural company executive*
Lippincott, Philip Edward *retired paper products company executive*
Little, Freed Sebastian *retired petroleum equipment manufacturing company executive*
Lohman, Gordon Russell *retired manufacturing executive*
Lorenz, Ronald Theodore *manufacturing executive*
Lowden, John L. *retired corporate executive*
Lucas, William Ray *aerospace consultant*
Luke, David Lincoln, III, *retired paper company executive*
Lydon, Nicholas B. (Nick Lydon) *pharmaceutical executive, researcher*
Lynch, Charles Andrew *chemical industry consultant*
MacAvoy, Thomas Coleman *manufacturing executive, educator*
Madden, Richard Blaine *forest products executive*
Mahanes, David James, Jr., *retired distillery executive*
Malsack, James Thomas *retired manufacturing company executive*
Manchester, Kenneth Edward *electronics executive, consultant*
Mandel, Lewis Richard *retired pharmaceutical executive, consultant*
Mangapit, Conrado, Jr., *manufacturing executive*
Mangold, John Frederic *manufacturing company executive, former naval officer*
Marcy, Alvin Newell *contractor*
Marrington, Bernard Harvey *retired automotive company executive*
Martin, Albert Charles *manufacturing executive, lawyer*
Martin, Robert D. *former hospital executive*
Mason, Frank Henry, III, *automobile company executive, leasing company executive*
Mattoli, Agostino Marron *international business projects advisor*
Maughan, Rex *natural healthcare products company executive*
Maxwell, Jerome Eugene *corporate executive*
Mays, Betty Jean *retired automotive executive*
McClelland, George Duncan *business executive*
McColman, William Ernest *construction company executive*
McCracken, Edward R. *electronics executive*
McCurdy, Larry Wayne *automotive parts company executive*
McDade, Mark *biotechnology company executive*
McDonald, William Henry *financial executive*
Mc Donough, Richard Doyle *retired paper company executive*
McGillivray, Donald Dean *seed company executive, agronomist*
McGuinn, Edwin J. *chemicals executive*
Mehiel, Dennis *paper and packaging company executive*
Meilan, Celia *food products executive*
Merrick, George Boesch *aerospace company executive*
Messmore, David William *construction executive, former psychologist*
Miles, John Frederick *retired manufacturing company executive*
Miller, Harold Edward *retired manufacturing conglomerate executive, consultant*
Mills, Charles S. *healthcare supplies and products company executive*
Moore, John Ronald *manufacturing executive*
Moore, Kent *grocery company executive*
Moore, Malcolm Frederick *manufacturing executive*
Moore, Vernon Lee *retired food products executive, agriculturist, consultant*
Morgenstein, William *shoe company executive*
Morris, Albert Jerome *medical company executive*
Morris, G. Ronald *industrial executive*
Mortimer, John H. *home heating equipment manufacturing executive*
Mott, Stewart Rawlings *business executive, political activist*
Mudd, Sidney Peter *former beverage company executive*
Mueller, Robert Louis *business executive*
Mukamal, David Samier *sign manufacturing company executive*
Nalin, David Robert *retired pharmaceutical executive*
Nasser, Jacques *automotive executive*
Neff, Jack Kenneth *apparel manufacturing company executive*
Nelson, Glen David *medical products executive, physician*
Nesheim, Robert Olaf *retired food products executive*
Noe, Elnora (Ellie Noe) *retired chemicals executive*
Nord, Eric Thomas *retired manufacturing executive*
Nordlund, Donald Elmer *manufacturing executive, lawyer*
Novak, Alan Lee *retired pharmaceutical company executive*
Oaks, Maurice David *retired pharmaceutical company executive*
O'Donnell, Kevin *retired metal products executive*
Oelman, Robert Schantz *retired manufacturing executive*
Oesterling, Thomas Ovid *retired pharmaceutical executive*
Ordal, Caspar Reuben *business executive*
Ostberg, Henry Dean *corporate executive*
Ostby, Ronald *retired dairy and food products company executive*
Oster, Lewis Henry *manufacturing executive, engineering consultant*
Owens, Charles Vincent, Jr., *pharmaceutical executive, consultant*
Pace, George W. *food products company executive*
Padilla, James Jerome *automobile executive*
Palumbo, Daniel P. *former food products executive*
Parker, George *retired pen manufacturing company executive*
Parker, Michael D. *chemicals executive*
Peapples, George Alan *retired automotive executive*
Pearce, Paul Francis *retired aerospace electronics company executive*
Peck, Daniel Farnum *chemical company executive*
Pedhirney, Gayland *food products company executive*
Pepper, J. Stanley *construction company executive*
Perosch, Tony Anthony George *corporate executive, consul*
Petersen-Frey, Roland *manufacturing executive*
Peterson, Carl Eric *metals company executive, banker*
Peterson, Robert Austin *manufacturing company executive retired*
Petok, Samuel *retired manufacturing company executive*
Phinizy, Robert Burchall *electronics company executive*
Potts, Gerald Neal *manufacturing executive*
Powell, Thomas Edward, III, *biological supply company executive, physician*
Preston, Seymour Stotler, III, *chemicals executive*
Pruis, John J. *business executive*
Qualls, Robert L. *manufacturing executive, banker, former state official, educator*
Queen, Arthur Jerome *glass company executive*
Rao, Rama Krishna R. *pharmaceutical company executive*
Ray, Amrit *pharmaceuticals strategist, company executive*
Reavis, Hubert Gray, Jr., *retired metal products executive*
Regan, Paul Jerome, Jr., *manufacturing company executive, consultant*
Regelbrugge, Roger Rafael *steel company executive*
Reid-Anderson, James *diagnostic equipment company executive*
Renne, Paul F. *retired food products executive*
Rhodes, Peter Edward *label company executive*
Richard, Edward H. *manufacturing company executive, former municipal government official*
Richman, Paul *semiconductor industry executive, educator*
Richman, Peter *electronics executive*
Riklis, Meshulam *manufacturing and retail executive*
Rivera, Richard Edwin *former restaurant chain executive*
Roath, Stephen D. *retired pharmaceutical company executive*
Robbins, Ray C. *retired manufacturing executive*
Roesner, Peter Lowell *manufacturing executive*
Rogers, Gary L. *former diversified technology and services company executive*
Rooke, David Lee *retired chemical company executive*
Roorda, John Francis, Jr., *business consultant*
Roper, John Lonsdale, III, *shipyard executive*
Rosenberg, Rudy *chemical company executive*
Rothman, Deanna *electroplating company executive*
Roudane, Charles *metal and plastic products company executive*
Rubin, Irvin I. *plastics company executive*
Rubinovitz, Samuel *diversified manufacturing company executive*
Rudy, Raymond Bruce, Jr., *retired food company executive*
Rukeyser, Robert James *manufacturing executive*
Ryan, George William *manufacturing executive*
Rymar, Julian W. *manufacturing executive, director*
Sabo, Richard Steven *electrical company executive*
St. John, Bill Dean *diversified equipment and services company executive*
Salathe, John, Jr., *retired manufacturing executive*
Saliba, Jacob *manufacturing executive*
Salvador, Richard Anthony *pharmaceutical executive*
Samper, Joseph Phillip *retired photographic products company executive*
Samuel, George *healthcare information company executive*
Sanders, Wayne R. *paper products manufacturing executive*
Sauder, Maynard *manufacturing executive*
Saute, Robert Emile *drug and cosmetic consultant*
Savin, Ronald Richard *chemicals executive*
Scheele, Paul Drake *former hospital supply corporate executive*
Schlensker, Gary Chris *landscaping company executive*
Schwartz, Samuel *retired chemical company executive, business consultant*
Serenbetz, Robert *financial planner, retired manufacturing executive*
Shapira, David S. *food products/retail grocery executive*
Sharkey, Leonard Arthur *automobile company executive*
Sharp, William J. *manufacturing executive*
Shea, Bernard Charles *retired pharmaceutical company executive*
Shepherd, Mark, Jr., *retired electronics company executive*
Sherwin, Stephen A. *health products executive*
Shuster, Robert G. *electronics company executive, consultant*
Siegel, Jack Morton *retired biotechnology company executive*
Silver, George *metal trading and processing company executive*
Simeral, William Goodrich *retired chemical company executive*
Sissel, George Allen *manufacturing executive, lawyer, engineer*
Smith, Frederick Coe *retired manufacturing executive*
Smith, Goff *industrial equipment manufacturing executive*
Smith, Robert Hugh *former engineering construction company executive*
Smith, Rodney *retired electronics executive*
Solloway, C. Robert *retired forest products company executive*
Somers, Louis Robert *retired food company executive*
Sommer, Howard Ellsworth *textile executive*
Southerland, S. Duane *manufacturing executive*
Spliethoff, William Ludwig *chemical company executive*
Starr, Leon *retired chemical research company executive*
Steck, Warren Franklin *retired chemical company executive, biochemist*
Steffensen, Dwight A. *former medical products and data processing services executive*
Stempel, Robert C. *automobile manufacturing company executive*
Stern, Arthur Paul *electronics company executive*
Stewart, Joseph Turner, Jr., *retired pharmaceutical company executive*
Stewart, Peter Beaufort *retired beverage company executive*
Stiritz, William P. *food company executive*
Stott, Don S. *precious metals products executive*
Stratton, Robert *retired electronics executive*
Sudarsky, Jerry M. *industrialist*
Sullivan, Eugene John Joseph *manufacturing executive, director*
Sullivan, G. Craig *household products executive*
Szydlowski, Ralph *retired die maker, formability consultant*
Tallett, Elizabeth Edith *biopharmaceutical company executive*
Talley, Robert Morrell *aerospace company executive*
Tane, Susan Jaffe *retired manufacturing company executive*
Tannenberg, Dieter E. A. *retired manufacturing company executive*
Taylor, Robert Morgan *electronics executive*
Temple, Joseph George, Jr., *retired pharmaceutical executive, retired chemicals executive*
Templin, Kenneth Elwood *paper company executive*
Teplow, Theodore Herzl *retired valve company executive*
Thomas, Tom *retired plastics company executive*
Thompson, Ralph Newell *former chemical corporation executive*
Thorp, Benjamin A., III, *retired paper company executive*
Tinstman, Robert Allen *former construction company executive*
Torbica, Zeljko Marko *construction executive, educator*
Toupin, Harold Ovid *retired chemical company executive*
Trice, William Henry *paper company executive*
Tutor, Ronald N. *construction company executive*
Tuttle, William G(ilbert) T(ownsend), Jr., *research executive, retired military officer*
Uffelman, Malcolm Rucj *electronics company executive, electrical engineer*
Vallner, Joseph J. *medical products executive*
Van Tassel, James Henry *retired electronics executive*
Verderber, Joseph Anthony *capital equipment company executive*
Verfaillie, Hendrik A. *food products company executive*
Verma, Devesh *pharmaceutical executive, researcher*
Vitt, David Aaron *medical manufacturing company executive*
Volkhardt, John Malcolm *food company executive*
Wallman, Richard F. *electronics company executive*
Ward, Thomas *food products executive*
Wardrop, Richard M., Jr., *former steel holding company executive*
Warner, Walter D. *corporate executive, director*
Wasson, James Walter *aircraft electronics manufacturing company executive*
Watkins, Dean Allen *electronics executive, educator*
Wavle, James Edward, Jr., *pharmaceutical company executive, lawyer*
Weaver, William Charles *retired industrial executive*
Wechsler, Sergio *automotive executive, consultant*
Weiss, Max Tibor *retired aerospace company executive*
Weiswasser, Stephen *electronics manufacturing executive*
Welch, Oliver Wendell *retired pharmaceutical executive*
Wenstrup, H. Daniel *chemical company executive*
West, Kenneth Irwin *automotive executive*
Wharton, Thomas William *medical products executive*
White, Bertram Milton *chemicals executive*
White, Gerald Andrew *retired chemical company executive*
Whitwam, David Ray *appliance manufacturing company executive*
Wiesen, Donald Guy *retired diversified manufacturing company executive*

PROFESSIONAL INDEX 5751 INDUSTRY: SERVICE

Wiley, Carl Ross *timber company executive*
Willauer, Whiting Russell *retired manufacturing executive, systems engineer*
Williams, Carolyn Elizabeth *manufacturing executive*
Williams, Dorothy Standridge *soft drink company official, civic worker*
Williamson, Robert F. *health products executive*
Wilson, Delano Dee *consultant*
Winkler, Joseph Conrad *former recreational products manufacturing executive*
Witcher, Daniel Dougherty *retired pharmaceutical company executive*
Witt, Hugh Ernest *technology consultant*
Wolff, Brian Richard *metal products executive*
Wollert, Gerald Dale *retired food company executive, investor*
Wright, Linda Jean *manufacturing executive*
Yoh, Harold Lionel, Jr., *retired engineering, construction and management company executive*
Yontz, Kenneth Fredric *medical and chemical company executive*
Young, Jay Maitland *healthcare communications consultant*
Young, John Alan *electronics company executive*
Yuen, Henry C. *former consumer electronics manufacturing company executi*
Zajac, John *semiconductor equipment company executive*
Zapapas, James Richard *pharmaceutical company executive*
Zeffren, Eugene *toiletries company executive*
Zehnder, Frederick John *retired automotive executive*

INDUSTRY: SERVICE

UNITED STATES

ALABAMA

Auburn
Zallen, Harold *corporate executive, scientist, former university official*

Birmingham
Agee, Claudia *clerk, receptionist, tax consultant*
Bruno, Ronald G. *food service executive*
Chew, E. Byron *management consultant, educator*
Floyd, John Alex, Jr., *marketing executive, editor, horticulturist*
Harris, Aaron *management consultant*
Luckie, Robert Ervin, Jr., *advertising executive*
Morros, Stephen Vincent *marketing professional, educator*
Parker, John Malcolm *management and financial consultant*
Poe, Frank *convention center administrator*
Spahn, James Francis *marketing professional*
Stitt, Frank *food service executive*
Tonkery, Dan *Internet company executive*

Columbiana
Armistead, William Cole, Jr., *marketing professional*

Dadeville
Barnes, Ben Blair *computer company executive, electrical engineer*

Fairhope
Hart, Eric Mullins *consumer products company executive*

Gadsden
Grimm, James R. (Ronald Grimm) *multi-industry executive*

Huntsville
Gray, Ronald W. *business executive*
McIntyre-Ivy, Joan Carol *data processing executive*
Meadlock, James W. *computer graphics company executive*
Plunkett, Sara L. *communications company executive*

Hurtsboro
Bouilliant-Linet, Francis Jacques *global management consultant*

Montgomery
Calhoun, Gregory B. *retail food and beverage company executive*
Dillon, Jean Katherine *executive secretary, small business owner*
Holifield, Leonard Cleve *security firm executive, educator*
Murkett, Philip Tillotson *human resource executive*
Schloss, Samuel Leopold, Jr., *retired food service executive, consultant*

Selma
Price, Tina S. *administrative assistant*

Tuskegee Institute
Madison, Willie Clarence *park administrator*

ALASKA

Anchorage
Brady, Carl Franklin *retired aircraft charter company executive*
Porcaro, Michael Francis *advertising agency executive*
Shively, John Terry *business executive*

Fairbanks
Helfferich, Merritt Randolph *industry and education consultant*
Thompson, Daniel Emerson *vending machine service company executive*

Juneau
Elton, Kim Steven *state legislator, pollster*

ARIZONA

Cave Creek
O'Reilly, Thomas Eugene *retired human resources consultant*

Chandler
Brunello-McCay, Rosanne *sales executive*
Eckstat, Arthur Gene *consultant*
Goyer, Robert Stanton *communication educator*

Flagstaff
Bolin, Richard Luddington *industrial development consultant*
Evans, Ronald Allen *lodging chain executive*

Fountain Hills
Lacy, Herman Edgar *management consultant*

Mesa
Gottry, Steven Roger *communications executive, author, screenwriter*
Johnson, Doug *advertising and public relations executive*
Murphy, Edward Francis *sales executive*
Tindle, Charles Dwight Wood *broadcasting company executive*

Paradise Valley
Day, Richard Putnam *marketing, strategic planning and employee benefits consultant, arbitrator*
Hazard, Robert Culver, Jr., *hotel executive*
Joaquim, Richard Ralph *hotel executive*
Swanson, Robert Killen *management consultant*

Peoria
Gould, Dorothy Mae *executive secretary, soprano*
Schindler, William Stanley *retired public relations executive, consultant*

Phoenix
Armstrong, Nelson William, Jr., *gaming company executive*
Bergamo, Ron *marketing executive*
Church, Steve *communications executive*
Curcio, Christopher Frank *recreation director*
Drain, Albert Sterling *business management consultant*
Feldberg, Harley *marketing professional*
Gall, Donald Alan *data processing executive*
Hamada, Richard *computer company executive*
Horner, Harry Charles, Jr., *sales executive, theatrical and film consultant*
LaValle, Jennifer Suzette *marketing communications specialist, consultant*
Newman, Lois Mae *marketing executive*
Rubeli, Paul E. *gaming company executive*
Smith, George *marketing professional*
Snell, Richard *holding company executive*
Teets, John William *retired diversified company executive*

Prescott
Stuart, Spencer Raymond *management consultant*

Rio Verde
Scott, Louis Edward *advertising agency executive*

Scottsdale
Baum, Herbert Merrill *consumer products company executive*
Blinder, Martin S. *business consultant, art dealer*
Carter, Carla Cifelli *management consultant*
Grier, James Edward *hotel executive, lawyer*
Gwinn, Mary Dolores *business developer, philosopher, writer*
Highet, Mac *travel company executive*
Lavenson, Susan Barker *hotel corporate executive, consultant*
La Vista, Frank William *author, educator, speaker*
Lillestol, Jane Brush *development consultant*
MacKinnon, Sally Anne *retired fast food company executive*
Maggard, Woodrow Wilson, Jr., *management consultant*
Quigley, Jerome Harold *management consultant*
Schmitz, Shirley Gertrude *marketing and sales executive*
Slager, Donald W. *waste management executive*
Travers, Paul *company executive*
Van Brunt, Gary T. *consumer products company executive*
Van Weelden, Thomas H. *waste industry company executive*

Sedona
McLeod, Lorna A. *personnel director*
Wolfe, Al *marketing and advertising consultant*

Sierra Vista
Bowen, Harry Ernest *management consultant*

Sun City West
Berkenkamp, Fred Julius *management consultant*
Forti, Lenore Steimle *business consultant*
Stevens, George Richard *business consultant, public policy commentator*

Tempe
Huntsman, Edward *business consultant, marketing executive*
Jefferson, Myra LaVerne Tull *sales executive*
Meehan, Robert Henry *human resources executive, electronics company executive, business educator*
Sackton, Frank Joseph *public affairs educator*
Williams, James Eugene *management consultant*
Yazzie, Aaron Franklin *events laborer*

Tubac
Assunto, Richard Anthony *human resources specialist*

Tucson
Barton, Stanley Faulkner *management consultant*
Cooper, Corinne *communications consultant, lawyer*
Eberhardt, Marty Lampert *botanical garden administrator*
Horne, William McHenry *management educator*
Jones, Frank Wyman *management consultant, mechanical engineer*
Lewis, Wilbur H. *educational management consultant*
Poelstra, Edward M. *management consultant*
Reinius, Michele Reed *executive recruiter*
Rose, Hugh *management consultant*
Vaillancourt, Allison M *human resources specialist*
Walker, Ronald Hugh *retired management consultant*
Willert, Sister St. Joan *health care corporation executive*
Williams, Alan Keiser *management consultant*
Wise, Evan M. *management consultant*

ARKANSAS

Bentonville
Higham, Paul H. *marketing professional*

Conway
Hatcher, Joe Branch *management consultant*
Kline, Rodger S. *marketing professional*

Fayetteville
Edmark, David Stanley *communications director*

Fort Smith
Pendergrass, Ewell Dean *communications executive*

Jonesboro
Tims, Robert Austin *data processing official, pilot*

Little Rock
Cox, Frank *advertising executive*
Gardner, Jeffrey R. *communications executive*
Ingram, Dale *consumer products company executive*
McCaleb, Annette Watts *executive secretary*

Pine Bluff
Long, Edward Arlo *business consultant, retired manufacturing company executive*

Roland
Frazer, Randy *parks and recreation director*

CALIFORNIA

Agoura Hills
Gressak, Anthony Raymond, Jr., *sales executive*
Meyler, Nicholas James *management consultant*
Powers, J. D., III, *marketing executive*
Schmidt, Frank Broaker *executive recruiter*

Alameda
Potash, Jeremy Warner *public relations executive*

Alamo
Shiffer, James David *retired utility executive, consultant*
Whalen, John Sydney *management consultant*

Alhambra
Knighton, Barbara McLeod *occupational health specialist, risk specialist*

Aliso Viejo
Hawkins, Gregory J. *consumer products company executive*
Otero-Smart, Ingrid Amarillys *advertising executive*
Rollans, James O. *service company executive*

Alpine
Cole, George Arthur *marketing professional*

Anaheim
Kallay, Michael Frank, II, *medical devices company official*
Latham, Chad J. *management consultant*

Anaheim Hills
Warring, Jerome Thomas *management consultant*

Atherton
Phipps, Allen Mayhew *management consultant*

Avila Beach
McLaren, Archie Campbell, Jr., *marketing executive*

Baldwin Park
Snyder, Esther *food service executive*

Berkeley
Chamberlain, Bob *computer company executive*
Edwards, Susan M. *hotel executive*
Rippe, Lynn E. *contract administrator*
Thomas, Lisa *food service executive*
Waters, Alice *executive chef, restaurant owner, writer*
Wilton, Peter Campbell *marketing educator*

Beverly Hills
Bollenbach, Stephen Frasier *hotel executive*
Cantor, Alan Bruce *management consultant, computer software engineer*
David, Clive *event planning executive*
Hart, Matthew J. *hotel/recreation executive*
Hilton, Barron *hotel executive*
Kingsley, Patricia *public relations executive*
La Forgia, Robert M. *hotel executive*
Nyman, Michael S. *marketing executive*
Olman, Maryellen *human resources administrator*
Riess, Gordon Sanderson *management consultant*
Shepard, Kathryn Irene *public relations executive*
Toffel, Alvin Eugene *corporate executive, business and governmental consultant*
Yard, Sherry *chef*
Zarem, Abe Mordecai *management consulting executive*

Blue Jay
Gourley, James Walter, III, *management consultant*

Burbank
Cohen, Valerie A. *entertainment company executive*
Cook, Richard W. *motion picture company executive*
Frank, Amélie Lorraine *marketing professional*
Mooney, Andrew P. *consumer products company executive*
Sklar, Martin A. *recreational facility executive*
Stainton, David *recreational facility executive*
Thomas-Graham, Pamela *communications executive*

Calabasas
Stark, Martin J. *management consultant*

Camarillo
Cobb, Roy Lampkin, Jr., *retired computer sciences corporation executive*
Cobb, Shirley Ann Dodson *public relations consultant, journalist*

Cambria
Morse, Richard Jay *human resources specialist, consultant*

Campbell
Roberts, George P. *computer company executive*

Carlsbad
Conway, Daniel Edward *management consultant*
Craig, Jenny *weight management executive*
Mitchell, Thomas Edward, Jr., *communications cabling executive*
Wilson, Donald Grey *management consultant*

Carmel
Creighton, John Wallis, Jr., *novelist, publisher, former management educator, consultant*
Evans, Charlotte Mortimer *communications consultant, writer*
Lockton, David Ballard *business executive*
Smith, Gordon Paul *management consultant*

Carpinteria
Lopker, Pamela *technology industry executive*

Castaic
La Cava, Donald Leon *communications executive*

Chico
Hanton, E. Michael *public and personnel relations consultant*

Chino Hills
Burge, Willard, Jr., *software company executive*

Citrus Heights
Osaki, Mark Stephen *writer, development administrator*

Compton
Beauchamp, Patrick L. *distributing company executive*
Janeway, Barbara *public relations executive*

Corona
Rankin, Alex C. *management executive*

Corona Del Mar
O'Brien, John William, Jr., *investment management consultant, finance educator*
Terrell, A. John *retired university telecommunications director*

Costa Mesa
Cox, Fred B. *software company executive*
Gimple, W. Thomas *sales executive*

Crestline
Merrill, Steven William *research and development executive*

Culver City
Boonshaft, Hope Judith *public affairs executive*
Dutt, Birendra *research specialist*
Holt, Dennis F. *media buying company executive*
Lenk, Edward C. (Toby) *Internet company executive*

Cupertino
Cook, Timothy D. *computer company executive*
Dalrymple, Cheryl *retired computer company executive*
Devlin, Mike *software company executive*
Flynn, Ralph Melvin, Jr., *sales executive, marketing consultant*
Geddes, Barbara Sheryl *communications executive, consultant*
Hall, Brenda *human resources executive*
Heinen, Nancy R. *computer company executive*

Dana Point
Fabricant, Jill Diane *technology company executive*

Desert Hot Springs
Fulton, Norman Robert *credit manager*

Dublin
Chen, John S. *computer company executive*

El Cajon
Silverberg, Lewis Henry *legal consultant*

El Segundo
Bell, George F. *computer company executive*
Bernstein, Harvey N. *computer company executive*
Brown, Lorraine Ann *event coordinator, minister, hypnotist, therapeutic touch practitioner*
Cofoni, Paul M. *computer company executive*
Cordner, Tom *advertising executive*
DeBuck, Donald *computer company executive*
Farr, Kevin M. *consumer products executive*
Fisk, Hayward D. *computer company executive*
Honeycutt, Van B. *computer company executive*
Katz, Lew *advertising executive*
Laphen, Michael W. *computer company executive*
Level, Leon Jules *computer company executive*
McQuillin, Richard Ross *management consultant*
Tucker, Paul Thomas *computer company executive*

Emeryville
Jobs, Steven Paul *computer company executive*
Smith, Christopher Allen *technology company executive, finance professional*

Encino
Greenberg, Allan *advertising and marketing research consultant*
Laba, Marvin *management consultant*
Saginor, Sidney V. *management consultant*

Escondido
Mogul, Leslie Anne *business development and marketing consultant*

Foster City
Lutvak, Mark Allen *computer company executive*
McHenry, Julie *communications executive*
Miller, Jon Philip *marketing and business development professional, pharmaceutical executive*
Shaheen, George T. *management consultant*
Wilson, Lerry *public relations executive*

Fountain Valley
Berman, Steven Richard *computer company executive*

Fremont
Bagley, James W. *research company executive*
Hackworth, Michael L. *electronics company executive*
Lankford, James E. *food service executive*
Liang, Marcel *corporate executive*
Parikh, Mihir *consumer products company executive*
Saraf, Dilip Govind *career and management consultant*
Schauer, Ronald L. *executive*
Tantra, Muljadi *corporate marketing professional*

Fresno
Ganulin, Judy *public relations professional*

Fullerton
Sowder, Kathleen Adams *marketing executive*

Glendale
Altman, Steven *financial consulting company executive*
Dohring, Doug *marketing executive*
Dohring, Laurie *marketing executive*
Misa, Kenneth Franklin *management consultant*

Granada Hills
O'Connor, Betty Lou *hotel executive, food service executive*

Granite Bay
Holtz, Sara *marketing consultant*
Reisman, Judith Ann Gelernter *media communications executive, educator*

Half Moon Bay
Fennell, Diane Marie *marketing professional, process engineer*
Hinthorn, Micky Terzagian *volunteer, retired*

Hemet
Holley, Robert William *sales executive, minister*

Hillsborough
Westerfield, Putney *management consulting executive*

Huntington Beach
Fajardo, Frederick Joseph *public relations executive*

Indian Wells
Kelley, John Paul *communications consultant*

Indio
Garra, Raymond Hamilton, II, *marketing executive*

Irvine
Alcone, Matt *advertising executive*
Baab, Carlton *advertising executive*
Davis, William W., Sr., *computer company executive*
Leber, Mike *advertising executive*
Lightburn, Jeffrey Caldwell *corporate communications executive*
Madden, James Cooper, V, *management consultant*
Oliver, Travis *advertising agency executive*
Paine, David M. *public relations executive*
Seller, Gregory Erol *marketing executive, writer, consultant*
West, Robert Lee, Jr., *marketing professional*

Jackson
Halvorson, Frank Elsworth *sales executive*

Kentfield
Edgar, James Macmillan, Jr., *management consultant*

La Habra
Chase, Cochrane *advertising agency executive*

La Jolla
Bardwick, Judith Marcia *management consultant*
Kent, Paula *public relations, marketing and management consultant, lecturer*

La Quinta
Peden, Lynn Ellen *marketing executive*

Laguna Beach
Arnold, John David *management counselor, catalyst*
Taylor, James Walter *business and management educator*

Laguna Hills
Miller, Eldon Earl *corporate business publications consultant, retired manufacturing company executive*

Laguna Niguel
Greenberg, Lenore *public relations professional*

Lake Forest
Earhart, Donald Marion *management consultant, health care company executive*
Hopp, Terry A. *computer company executive*

Landers
Dougherty, Raleigh Gordon *manufacturer representative*

Larkspur
Amico, Charles William *management consultant*
Dellar, Michael D. *restaurant owner, hospitality industry consultant*
Ogden, Bradley M. *chef, restaurateur*

Livermore
Tripodes, James G. *nuclear safety and environmental regulatory affairs professional*

Long Beach
Aldrich, David Lawrence *public relations executive*
Brown, Roxanne (Jerene Roxanne Brown) *sales executive*
Halili, Antonio Marquez *facilities maintenance mechanic*
Sosoka, John Richard *consulting firm executive, engineer*
Young, Robert Edward *computer company executive*

Los Angeles
Anderson, Herbert W. *consumer products company executive*
Bakeman, Carol Ann *travel manager, singer*
Barnett, Marilyn *advertising agency executive*
Bender, Dean *public relations executive*
Berman, Geoffrey Louis *management company executive*
Bianchi, Carisa *advertising company executive*
Bloch, Paul *public relations executive*
Bohle, Sue *public relations executive*
Bremond, Duane Benjamin *marketing professional*
Burghdorf, Roger *business executive*
Burkle, Ronald W. *former food service executive, business investor*
Cecere, Domenico *homebuilding company executive*
Chang, Edward H. *computer company executive*
Clow, Lee *advertising agency executive*
Crosby, Peter Alan *management consultant*
Dallmeyer, Robert Frederick *exhibitions executive*
Engoron, Edward David *food service consultant, television and radio broadcaster*
Farrell, Joseph *movie market analyst, producer, entertainment research company executive, writer, sculptor, designer*
Ferry, Richard Michael *executive search firm executive*
Fils, Elliott *advertising executive*
Fishman, Arnie *marketing executive, consultant, film producer*
Frank, Lillian Gorman *human resources executive, psychologist, management consultant*
Georgesco, Victor *printing company executive*
Giffin, Margaret Ethel (Peggy Giffin) *management consultant*
Gottfried, Ira Sidney *management consulting executive*
Hale, Kaycee *research marketing professional*
Hansen, Alexander E. *advertising agency executive*
Hartsough, Gayla Anne Kraetsch *management consultant*
Hateley, J. Michael *human resources executive*
Helper, Lee *strategic business marketing and marketing communications consultant*
Hickman, Charles Wallace *Internet executive*
Hill, Dennis Guiton *consulting company executive*
Hirsh, Cynthia *food service executive*
Hofert, Jack *consulting company executive, lawyer*
Honig, Steven C. *public relations executive*
Hunt, Dennis *public relations executive*
Hutton, Fiona S. *communications executive*
Irving, Jack Howard *technical consultant*
Irwin-Hentschel, Noël *travel company executive*
Jacobs, Alicia Melvina *account executive*
Kleiman, Evan *chef*
Kline, Richard Stephen *public relations executive*
Knox, Gertie R. *company executive, accountant*
Lagasse, Emeril *chef*
Leahy, T. Liam *business development, technology investor*
LeMaster, Susan M. *marketing executive, writer*
Levine, Michael *public relations executive, writer, talk show host*
Litewka, Albert Bernard *communications and publishing company executive*
Logan, Nancy Jane *broadcast sales and marketing executive*
Mamer, John William *business educator*
Marshall-Daniels, Meryl *communications executive, mediator*
Mathias, Alice Irene *business management consultant*
Miller, Bruce *advertising executive*
Mracky, Ronald Sydney *marketing and media executive, tourism consultant*
Murray, Alice Pearl *data processing company executive*
Nadler, Gerald *management consultant, educator*
Peel, Mark *chef, restaurant owner*
Pondel, Roger S. *public relations executive*
Popek, Gerald John *computer software company executive, educator*
Proper, Mary *advertising executive*
Puck, Wolfgang *executive chef*
Quinn, Tom *communications executive*
Resnick, Lynda *business executive*
Rice, Regina Kelly *marketing executive*
Rogers, Ronald *public relations executive*
Sackman, Dave *marketing executive*
Santiago, Mike *communications executive*
Schultz, Louis Michael *advertising agency executive*
Silverman, Bruce Gary *advertising executive*
Silverton, Nancy *food service executive*
Sood, Ashish *marketing professional*
Splichal, Joachim *chef, restaurant owner*
Sylvester, Richard Russell *economist, management executive*
Tardio, Thomas A. *public relations executive*
Tatum, Jackie *former parks and recreation manager, municipal official*
Tomash, Erwin *retired computer equipment company executive*
Wade, Michael Robert Alexander *marketing specialist*
Williams, Carlton L. *communications executive*
Winkler, Howard Leslie *business, finance, government relations consultant*
Zelikow, Howard Monroe *management and financial consultant*

Malibu
Smith, Yvonne Smart *advertising executive*
Tellem, Susan Mary *public relations executive*

Manhattan Beach
Deutsch, Barry Joseph *consulting and management development company executive*

Marina Del Rey
Gold, Carol Sapin *international management consultant, speaker*
Haddad, Edmonde Alex *public affairs executive*

Martinez
Tetrault, Jeanne L. *building inspector*

Menlo Park
Alsop, Stewart *communications executive*
Creswell, Donald Creston *business executive*
Doerr, John *communications executive*
Karel, Steven *human resources specialist*
Kurtzig, Sandra L. *software company executive*
Kvamme, Mark D. *marketing professional*
Middleton, Teresa Muir *Internet company executive, researcher*
Saffo, Paul *communications executive*
Waddell, M. Keith *human resources specialist*

Mill Valley
Gianturco, Paola *communications consulting company executive*

Millbrae
Mank, Edward Warren *marketing professional*

Milpitas
Corrigan, Wilfred J. *computer company executive*
Levy, Kenneth *executive*
Park, Chong S. *computer company executive*
Rabbat, Guy *electronics company executive, inventor*
Tufano, Paul J *computer company executive*
Yansouni, Cyril J. *computer company executive*

Monrovia
Jalbert, Janelle Jennifer *executive recruiter, secondary school educator*
Jemelian, John Nazar *management consultant*

Monte Nido
Brandewie, Richard Anthony *laser and optics consultant*

Monterey
Shultz, Jeanne Marie *training director, workforce improvement analyst*

Moraga
Haag, Carol Ann Gunderson *marketing professional, consultant, hotel executive*

Morgan Hill
McGuire, Thomas Roger *distribution company executive*

Mountain View
Barksdale, James Love *communications company executive*
Belluzzo, Richard E. *former computer company executive*
Bennett, Stephen M. *computer company executive*
de Geus, Aart J. *computer software company executive*
Dixit, Anindya *business executive and information technology strategy consultant*
Drexler, Jerome *technology company executive*
East, John *computer company executive*
Edsell, Patrick L. *computer company executive*
Garlick, Larry *executive*
Koo, George Ping Shan *business consultant*
Kordestani, Omid *Internet company executive*
Otus, Simone *public relations executive*
Polese, Kim *software company executive*
Qureishi, A. Salam *computer software and services company executive*

Napa
Brough, Bruce Alvin *public relations executive, communications executive*

Newbury Park
Stadler, Katherine Loy *advertising sales executive*

Newport Beach
Cable, Wade H. *executive*
de Garcia, Lucia *marketing professional*
Di Massa, Ernani Vincenzo, Jr., *broadcast executive, television producer, writer*
Gellman, Gloria Gae Seeburger Schick *marketing professional*
Shonk, Albert Davenport, Jr., *advertising executive*

North Hollywood
Wadsworth, Steve *recreational facility executive*

Novato
Fraser, Margot *consumer products company executive*

Oakland
Crane, Robert Meredith *health care executive*
DiStefano, Tony E. *communications executive*
Ejabat, Mory *communications executive*
Johnston, Gerald E. *manufacturing company executive*
Warrick, Brooke *marketing executive*
Williams, Carol H. *advertising executive*

Oceanside
Peckham, Donald *computer company executive*

Orange
Kelley, Robert Paul, Jr., *management consultation executive*
Scherman, Carol E. *human resources professional*

Orinda
Woolsey, David Arthur *leasing and commercial company executive*

Pacific Palisades
Humphreys, Robert Lee *advertising executive*
Kalis, Murray *advertising agency executive, writer*

Palm Desert
Kern, Paul Alfred *advertising executive, consultant, realtor, financial analyst*
Miller, Donald Ross *management consultant*
West, Hugh Sterling *aircraft leasing company executive*

Palm Springs
Arnold, Stanley Norman *manufacturing consultant*
Underwood, Thomas Woodbrook *communications company executive*

Palo Alto
Barnholt, Edward W. *computer company executive*
Blackmore, Peter *computer company executive*
Colligan, John C. (Bud Colligan) *multimedia company executive*
Coughran, William M., Jr., *management consultant, researcher*
Dunn, Debra L. *computer company executive*
Estrin, Judith *computer company executive*
Fiorina, Carleton S. (Carly Fiorina) *computer company executive*
Hecht, Lee *software company executive*
Johnson, Allison *corporate communications specialist*
Joshi, Vyomesh *computer company executive*
Lampman, Richard H. *computer company executive*
Lehman, Michael Evans *computer company executive*
McKinney, Harry Webb *computer company executive*
Murray, Dave *marketing professional, editor*
Neale-May, Donovan *marketing professional*
Nelson-Walker, Roberta *management software company executive*
Rehman, Saifur *web site design company executive*
Robinson, Shane V. *computer company executive*
Seethaler, William Charles *international business executive, consultant*
Stephens, Bess *computer company executive*
Sullivan, Patrick Henry *management consultant*
Ticknor, Carolyn M. *computer company executive*
Waller, Peter William *public relations executive*
Wayman, Robert Paul *computer company executive*
Willem, Karen J. *business software company financial executive*
Winkler, Michael *computer company executive*
Zitzner, Duane E. *computer company executive*

Paradise
Bernstein, Elizabeth Ann *retired executive secretary*

Pasadena
Caine, Stephen Howard *data processing executive*
Caldwell, Kim A. *company executive*
Drutchas, Gerrick Gilbert (Baron Khabarovsky) *investigator*
Kaplan, Gary *executive recruiter*
Nackel, John George *technology executive*
Pleasants, John *online services company executive*
Stevens, Roy W. *sales and marketing executive*
Suh, Jung Sook Ky *management consultant, educator*
Watkins, John Francis *management consultant*

Paso Robles
Boxer, Jerome Harvey *computer and management consultant, vintner, accountant*

Petaluma
Guadarrama, Belinda *computer company executive*
Immel, Barbara K. *management consultant*

Playa Del Rey
Weir, Alexander, Jr., *utility consultant, inventor*

Pleasanton
Burd, Steven A. *food service executive*
Conway, Craig A. *computer software executive*
Jackson, Lawrence *food service executive*
Parker, Kevin T. *computer company executive*
Payack, Paul JJ *marketing executive*
Smith, Gary *marketing executive*

Poway
Bradley, R. Todd *computer company executive*
Inouye, Wayne Ryo *computer company executive*
Phillips, Steve *computer company executive*
Robino, David J. *computer company executive*
Sherwood, Rod(erick), III, *computer company executive*
Waitt, Theodore W. *computer company executive*

Rancho Mirage
Abel, Michael L. *marketing executive*

Rancho Palos Verdes
Rubenstein, Leonard Samuel *communications executive, ceramist, painter, photographer*

Rancho Santa Fe
Best, Jacob Hilmer, Jr., *retired hotel chain executive*
Bow, Stephen Tyler, Jr., *management consultant*
LaBonté, C(larence) Joseph *financial and marketing executive*
Matthews, Leonard Sarver *advertising and marketing executive*

Rancho Santa Margarita
Newton, Michelle Marie *sales executive*

Redding
Lawrence, Marjorie Diane Long *computer company executive, consultant*

Redwood City
Bell, George *media executive*
Bloom, Gary L. *database company executive*
Cooperman, Daniel *computer company executive, lawyer*
Ellison, Lawrence J. *computer company executive*
Henley, Jeffrey O. *computer software company executive*
Johnson, James Harding *advertising executive*
Katz, Safra *computer company executive*
Lane, Raymond J. *software systems consulting company executive*
Phillips, Charles *computer company executive*
Probst, Lawrence F., III, *computer company executive*
Sharpnack, Rayona *management consultant*
You, Harry L. *computer company executive*

Richmond
Robles, Eliodoro Gonzales *consulting company executive, educator*

Riverbank
Cooley, Stacy Raelyn *administrative assistant*

West Hollywood
Einstein, Clifford Jay *advertising executive*
Goin, Suzanne *food company executive, chef*
Hodal, Melanie *public relations executive*
Morris, Brian *advertising executive*

West Sacramento
Lloyd, Sharon *marketing professional*

Westlake Village
Murdock, David H. *diversified company executive*
Smyth, Glen Miller *management consultant*
Troxell, Lucy Davis *management consultant*

Whittier
Guerrero, Donna Marie *sales executive*

Woodland
Spisak, John Francis *environmental company executive*

Woodland Hills
Colby, David C. *healthcare management company executive*
Ennis, Thomas Michael *management consultant*
Randall, Craig *financial and business management consultant, accountant, computer specialist*
Stahlecker, Barbara Jean *marketing professional, consultant*

Woodside
Arthur, Greer Martin *maritime container leasing firm executive*

Yountville
Keller, Thomas A. *chef*

COLORADO

Allenspark
Newman, Dean Gordon *business consultant*

Aspen
Jennings, Richard Milburn *resort developer*

Aurora
Reitan, Harold Theodore *management consultant*

Black Hawk
Jones, Linda May *tour guide, writer*

Boulder
Burns, Daniel Hobart *management consultant*
Conway, Robert Edward *corporate executive*
Eldridge, Thomas Engle *restaurant executive*
Jerritts, Stephen G. *management consultant*

Brighton
Wagner, Samuel Albin Mar *records management executive, educator*

Broomfield
Crowe, James Quell *communications executive*
Woodard, Donald Marvin *marketing professional*

Colorado Springs
Fagin, Barry Steven *computer science educator, writer*
Fortune, James Michael *computer support manager*
Gardner, Donald Gene *management consultant, educator*
Yanney, Patrick Steven *human resources specialist*

Denver
Allen, Barry K. *communications executive, human resources specialist*
Allen, Richard *computer software executive*
Baer, Rich *communications executive, lawyer*
Blatter, Frank Edward *travel agency executive*
Browne, Spencer Ivan *mortgage company executive, internet executive*
Clinch, Nicholas Bayard, III, *business executive*
Cox, Louis Anthony, Jr., *telecommunications executive*
Cruciotti, Augie *communications executive*
Dunham, Joan Roberts *administrative assistant*
Engels, Patricia A. *communications executive*
Holtz, Clifford S. *communications executive*
Hughes, Bradley Richard *business executive*
Johnson, Harold Earl *human resources specialist*
Johnston, Gwinavere Adams *public relations consultant*
Karsh, Philip Howard *advertising executive*
Kurtz, Maxine *personnel consultant, lawyer*
Lazarus, Steven S. *management consultant, marketing consultant*
Lundy, Barbara Jean *training executive*
Lutsky, Sheldon Jay *financial and marketing consultant, writer*
Lytle, Gary R. *communications executive*
Mackinnon, Peggy Louise *public relations executive*
McVaney, C. Edward *computer software executive*
Murdock, Pamela Ervilla *travel and advertising company executive*
Myhren, Trygve Edward *communications company executive*
Neumeyer, Zachary T. *hotel executive*
Perington, Philip *management investment company executive*
Stockton, Kevin W. *insurance and investment professional*
Taylor, Julia Fisher *communications executive*
Taylor, Teresa *communications executive*
Walker, Joan H. *marketing and communications executive*

Durango
Foster, James Henry *advertising and public relations executive*

Englewood
Baratta, Robert M. *holding company executive*
Bennett, Robert R. *communications executive*
Campbell, Michael L. *recreational facility executive*
Cooper, Steven Jon *healthcare management consultant, educator*
Jones, Glenn Robert *cable systems executive*
Lambert, Shirley Anne *marketing professional, publisher*
Miles, Amy E. *recreational facility executive*

Neiser, Brent Allen *foundation executive, public affairs and personal finance consultant, speaker*

Fort Garland
Moullette, John Brinkley *retired corporate trainer, consultant*

Fraser
Hibbs, John David *computer company executive, electrical engineer, small business owner*

Golden
Fleener, Terry Noel *marketing professional*
Payton, Roger *logistics company executive*

Greeley
Miller, Diane Wilmarth *retired human resources director*

Greenwood Village
Benson, Robert Craig, III, *business consultant*

Lakewood
Martinen, John A. *travel company executive*
Walton, Roger Alan *public relations executive, mediator, writer*

Littleton
Dugan, Michael T. *communications executive*
Fisher, Louis McLane, Jr., *management consultant*
Inzano, Karen Lee *advertising agency executive*
McDonnell, Michael R. *communications executive*
Schomp, Lisa Juliana *automotive industry executive*

Louisville
Adams, Eula L. *data storage executive*
Martin, Patrick J. *technology company executive*
Sontag, Peter Michael *travel management company executive*

Loveland
Hach-Darrow, Kathryn *water testing company executive*

Monument
De Francesco, John Blaze, Jr., *public relations consultant, artist, writer*

Niwot
Farrington, Helen Agnes *personnel director*

Northglenn
Peters, LeRoy Richard *materials management consulting company executive*

Pagosa Springs
Howard, Carole Margaret Munroe *retired public relations executive*

Parker
Jankura, Donald Eugene *hotel executive, educator*
Lark-Noonan, M. Ann *management consultant, strategic planner, naturalist*

Pueblo
Stevens, Jill Winifred *project expediter*

Snowmass Village
Strand, Curt Robert *hotel executive*

Sterling
Jones, Laurie Ganong *sales and marketing executive*

Westminster
Shirai, Scott *communications executive*

CONNECTICUT

Bloomfield
Handel, Morton Emanuel *management consultation executive*

Bristol
LaGanga, Donna Brandeis *sales and marketing executive, management/educational administrator*

Cos Cob
Murphy, Robert Blair *management consulting company executive*

Danbury
Mann, Richard O. *public relations consulting company executive*

Darien
Chyung, Chi Han *management consultant*
Cronk, Leonard *management consultant*
Kobak, James Benedict *management consultant*
Morano, Gerard John *marketing executive*
Welsh, John Francis *retired advertising executive*

East Haddam
Clarke, Cordelia Kay Knight Mazuy *management consultant, artist*
Clarke, Logan, Jr., *management consultant*

Easton
Constantinople, Alexandra *communications executive*

Essex
Thompson, George Lee *consulting and retailing company executive*

Fairfield
Booth, George Keefer *financial service executive*
Comstock, Elizabeth J. *marketing executive*
Hergenhan, Joyce *public relations executive*
Jeffe, Robert Allan *diversities technology and services company executive*
Johnsen, Walter Craig *security firm executive*
Luther, David Byron *management consultant*
Orris-Modugno, Michele Marie *public relations, marketing and advertising consultant*
Reiner, Gary M. *diversified technology and services company executive*
Rice, John G. *diversified technology and services executive*

Weissman, Robert Evan *information services company executive*

Farmington
Keiler, Richard W. *advertising executive*

Glastonbury
Andrews, Bryant Aylesworth *software company executive*

Greenwich
Ball, John Fleming *advertising and film production executive*
Bara, Jean Marc *finance and communications executive, artist*
Broadhurst, Austin, Jr., *executive recruiter*
Carmichael, William Daniel *consultant, educator*
Davidson, Thomas Maxwell *international management company executive*
Donley, James Walton *management consultant*
Gérin, Jean-Louis *chef, restaurant owner*
Harrington, Robert Dudley, Jr., *retired printing company executive*
Jacobs, Bradley S. *rental company executive*
Lewis, Audrey Gersh *financial marketing, public relations, strategic communications consultant*
Milne, John N. *rental company executive*
Paulson, Paul Joseph *advertising executive*
Perless, Ellen *advertising executive*
Rizzo, Raymond S. *advertising executive*
Roberts, James Carl *communications executive, engineer*
Schlafly, Hubert Joseph, Jr., *communications executive*
Srere, Benson M. *communications company executive, consultant*
Whitmore, George Merle, Jr., *management consulting company executive*

Hartford
Bucknall, William L., Jr., *human resources professional*
Faruolo, Edward A. *marketing professional*
Krapek, Karl J. *telecommunications company professional*
McMahon, John E. *marketing analyst*
Whaley, Charles Henry, IV, *communications company executive*

Kent
Friedman, Frances *public relations executive*

Lakeville
Levy, Ira Howard *marketing professional, real estate developer*

Middlebury
Turcotte, Glenn W. *electrical products company executive*

Milford
Ferguson, Richard A. *communications executive*

New Britain
Loree, James M. *consumer products company executive*
Lundgren, John F. *consumer products company executive, bank executive*

New Canaan
Jakacki, Diane Katherine *multimedia entertainment company executive*
Kamerschen, Robert Jerome *consumer products executive, investor*
McCreight, John A. *management consultant*
Mc Mennamin, George Barry *advertising agency executive*
Means, David Hammond *retired advertising executive*
Ward, Richard Vance, Jr., *management executive*
White, Richard Booth *management consultant*

New Haven
Rae, Douglas Whiting *management educator*
Singer, Jon Douglas *receptionist, writer*

Newtown
Coates, John Peter *technical executive*
Cole, Richard John *marketing executive*
Goodwick, David Lee *advertising executive*

Norwalk
Allen, Robert *communications company executive*
Czajkowski-Barrett, Karen Angela *human resources specialist*
Gold, Richard N. *management consultant*
Mundt, Barry Maynard *management consultant*
Nightingale, William Joslyn *management consultant*
O'Connell, Gerlad M. *communications executive*
Pagano, Michael Pro *advertising executive*
Yeosock, Michael Michael *funeral director, civil engineer*

Old Saybrook
Phillips, William E. *advertising agency executive*

Redding
McClure, Grover Benjamin *management consultant*
Stack, J. William, Jr., *management consultant*

Ridgefield
Hancock, Ellen Marie *communications executive*
Lodewick, Philip Hughes *equipment leasing company executive*
Mulchahey, Terry S. *human resources executive, management consultant*
Priest, Alexia Z. *purchasing agent*
Swartout, Torin Sherwin Roberts *logistics executive, transportation consultant*

Riverside
Geismar, Richard Lee *communications executive*
MacDonald, Gordon Chalmers *management consultant*
McSpadden, Peter Ford *retired advertising agency executive*

Salisbury
Block, Zenas *management consultant, educator*

Shelton
Coverdale, Watson Shallcross, Jr., *communications executive*

Kantrowitz, Jonathan Daniel *educational publishing and services company executive, lawyer*

Sherman
Cohn, Jane Shapiro *public relations executive*

South Windsor
Cheshire, Michael J. *factory automation systems and software executive*
Streeter, Lincoln Howard *retired sales executive*

Southbury
Faga, Anthony, Jr., *sales operations professional*
Leonard, John Harry *advertising executive*
Welton, Sharon Marie *food service executive*

Southport
Savage, Robert Heath *advertising executive*

Stamford
Allocca, Antoinette *computer company executive*
Brannigan, Michael D. *sales executive*
Burns, Ursula *printing company executive*
Candland, Catherine C. *human resources executive*
Collins, Joseph Jameson *communications executive*
Daleo, Robert *communications executive*
Dell, Warren Frank, II, *management consultant*
Di Maria, Valerie Theresa *public relations executive*
Dolan, Thomas J. *consumer products company executive*
Everhart, Judd *public relations executive*
Fernandez, Manual A. *information technology consulting executive*
Firestone, James A. *consumer products company executive*
Fleisher, Michael D. *information technology consulting executive*
Forster, Paul H. *executive recruiter*
Gallaire, Hervé Jean *executive*
Hatch, Gilbert J. *consumer products company executive*
Kerr, Ian *public relations executive*
Light, (Marvin) Lawrence *advertising agency executive*
MacDonald, Michael C. *consumer products company executive*
McGarry, Diane E. *marketing professional*
McKean, Thomas B. *company executive*
Miller, Wilbur Hobart *management consultant*
Mulcahy, Anne Marie *printing company executive*
Paolillo, Regina M. *information technology consulting executive*
Pascual, Carlos *marketing professional*
Pollock, M. Duncan *advertising executive*
Rizzuto, Leandro Peter *consumer products company executive*
Silver, Charles Morton *communications company executive*
Steenburgh, Frank D. *consumer products company executive*
Stern, Arlene Helen *human resources specialist*
Stern, Brian E. *consumer products company executive*

Washington
Nussbaum, Paul A. *retired hospitality executive*

Waterbury
Vignola, Andrew Michael, Sr., *systems management executive*

Waterford
Hinkle, Janet *project leader*
Walsh, Peter Joseph *marketing professional*

West Hartford
Glasser, Joseph *manufacturing and marketing executive*
Karotkin, Rose A. *marketing professional*
Pressman, Thane A. *consumer products executive*

Weston
Murray, Thomas J. *advertising executive*

Westport
Aasen, Lawrence Obert *public relations executive*
Blau, Barry *marketing professional, financial consultant*
Gallagher, Michael Robert *consumer products company executive*
Kurz, Mitchell Howard *marketing communications executive*
Levien, Roger Eli *strategy and innovation consultant*
McFarland, Richard M. *executive recruiting consultant*
Schriever, Fred Martin *management consultant, financial investor*

Wilton
Bishop, William Wade *advertising executive*
Caravatt, Paul Joseph, Jr., *communications company executive*
Farley, James Parker *retired advertising agency executive*
Frank, Robert Allen *advertising executive*
McCracken, Douglas M. *consultant company executive*
Mitchell, Richard Boyle *security consultant*
Nickel, Albert George *advertising agency executive*
Weiland, Juliette Marie *public relations executive, freelance writer and photographer, freelance photographer, writer*

Woodbridge
Alvine, Robert *industrialist, entrepreneur, philanthropist*

Woodbury
Peck, Carole *food service executive*

Woodstock
Boote, Alfred Shepard *marketing researcher, educator*

DELAWARE

Milford
Bergmann, William J. *personnel director*

Millsboro
Carter, William Allen *sales executive, insurance company executive*

Newark
Silva, Luis M. *marketing professional*

Wilmington
Dao, Thuy Dinh *personal care industry executive*
Mobley, Stacey J. *consumer products company executive*
Rogerson, Craig Allan *manufacturing executive*
Shipley, Samuel Lynn *advertising and public relations executive*

Wyoming
Bailey, Kay Wood *management consultant*

DISTRICT OF COLUMBIA

Washington
Adams, A. John Bertrand *public affairs consultant*
Akey, Steven John *public relations executive*
Alexander, Clifford L., Jr., *management consultant, lawyer, former secretary of army*
Allen, Richard Vincent *international business consultant, policy advisor*
Allnutt, Robert Frederick *management consultant, corporate director*
Alloway, Robert Malcombe *computer consulting executive*
Barrett, Laurence Irwin *public relations executive, writer*
Becraft, Carolyn Howland *communications executive*
Bell, Jeanne Viner *public relations counselor*
Berman, Ellen Sue *energy and telecommunications executive, theatre producer*
Brown, Jeanette L. *environmental protection administrator*
Buscaino, Mark *forestry program administrator*
Cafritz, Peggy Cooper *communications executive*
Carey, Wilhelmina Cole *management consultant*
Cashion, Ann *food service executive*
Champlin, Steven M. *management consultant*
Clay, Don Richard *environmental consulting firm executive*
Cohen, Perry D. *management consultant*
Coin, Sheila Regan *organization and management development consultant*
Coltman, Edward Jeremiah *communication executive*
Conley, Jeff *company executive*
Cook, Frances D. *international business consultant*
Coons, Barbara Lynn *public relations executive, librarian*
Cope, Jeannette Naylor *executive search consultant*
Cornish, Danté Anthony *employee development specialist*
Corso, John Anthony *management consultant, educator*
Cressy, Peter Hollon *association executive, university chancellor, retired naval officer*
Culley-Foster, Anthony Robert *international business consultant*
Dach, Leslie Alan *public relations company executive*
Davis, Rex Darwin *business consultant*
Dawson, Mimi Weyforth, Sr., *public policy consultant*
Denysyk, Bohdan *international consultant*
DeVaul, Diane D. *policy director*
Dolan, Kay Frances *human resources administrator*
Ducat, Suzanne Basha *television producer, communications specialist*
Dugoff, Howard Jay *business consultant*
Eckles, Susan *former management executive*
Farrell, Richard T. *human resources administrator*
Fields, Stuart Howard *labor relations specialist*
Fuller, Edwin Daniel *hotel executive*
Garvey, Jane *public relations executive*
Gest, Kathryn Waters *public affairs professional*
Grant, Carl N. *communications and sales executive*
Gray, Todd *food service executive*
Griffin, Kelly Ann *public relations executive, consultant*
Gross, Patrick Walter *management consultant*
Guzda, Henry Peter *industrial relations specialist*
Hager, Susan Kulka *public relations executive*
Hannaford, Peter Dor *public relations executive, writer*
Hasselmo, Ann Hayes Die *executive recruiter, consultant, psychologist, educator, retired academic administrator*
Havlicek, Franklin J. *communications executive*
Herrett, Richard Allison *agricultural research institute administrator*
Hezir, Joseph S. *energy and environmental company executive*
Higgins, James Henry, III, *marketing executive*
Higgins, Kathryn O'Leary *consulting firm executive*
Hoffmann, Melane Kinney *marketing and public relations executive, writer*
Howard, Jack *labor relations consultant*
Howe, Fisher *management consultant, former government official*
Huberman, Benjamin *technology consultant*
Huggins, James Bernard *corporate executive*
Kaludis, George *management consultant, book company executive, educator*
Kingsley, Mary Lee *marketing professional*
Kinkead, Bob *food service executive*
Kleeschulte, Charles A. *communications director*
Kraus, Margery *management consultant, communications company executive*
Lasko, Joel *company executive*
Lattimore, Patricia *administration and management administrator*
Leibach, Dale William *government relations and public affairs executive*
Levinson, Nanette Segal *international relations educator, administrator*
Lewis, Jordan David *charity organization director, author, international speaker, educator*
Lisboa-Farrow, Elizabeth Oliver *public and government relations consultant*
Lubic, Benita Joan Alk *travel executive*
Majak, Roger *administration executive*
Manatos, Andrew E. *public relations executive*
Mansfield, Edward Patrick, Jr., *advertising executive*
Marriott, John Willard, Jr., *lodging and senior living executive*

Marriott, Richard Edwin *hotel and contract services executive*
Marumoto, William Hideo *management consultant*
Mayer, Susan *telecommunications company executive*
McBride, Jonathan Evans *executive search consultant*
McInerney, Joseph Aloysius *hotel executive*
Mederos, Carolina Luisa *public policy consultant*
Miceli, Marcia P. *management consultant, educator*
Miller, Robert Allen *hotel executive*
Millian, Kenneth Young *public policy consultant*
Moe, Ronald Chesney *public administration researcher, consultant*
Moore, Bob Stahly *communications executive*
Morris, Robert Crane *management training executive*
Norman, William Stanley *travel and tourism executive*
Novak, Vicki Ann *human resources specialist*
O'Brien, Morgan Edward *communications executive, lawyer*
O'Brien, Richard Francis *advertising agency association executive*
Palumbo, Benjamin Lewis *public affairs consulting company executive*
Pastan, Peter *chef, restaurant owner*
Patrick, Janet Cline *personnel company executive*
Payne, Michael Lee *association management executive*
Pedersen, Wesley Niels M. *public relations and public affairs executive*
Petrou, David Michael *marketing and communications executive*
Pfeiffer, Leonard, IV, *executive recruiter, consultant*
Pines, Wayne Lloyd *public relations executive*
Pouillon, Nora Emanuela *food service executive*
Pucie, Charles R., Jr., *public affairs executive*
Pyle, Robert Noble *government relations executive*
Rainey, Jean Osgood *public relations executive*
Reed, Travis Dean *public relations executive*
Rice, Lois Dickson *former computer company executive*
Ridley, Keith Alexander, IV, *funeral director*
Rosebush, James Scott *marketing professional, international management and public affairs consultant, former government official*
Rotunda, Donald Theodore *public relations consultant*
Sasso, John *advertising and public strategies executive*
Schriever, Bernard Adolph *management consultant*
Seats, Peggy Chisolm *marketing executive*
Sharples, Ruth Lissak *communications executive*
Shaw, William J. *hotel facility executive*
Shear, Natalie Pickus *conference and event management executive*
Silverman, Marcia *public relations executive*
Simon, Rosalyn McCord *public relations executive*
Sisco, Joseph John *management consultant, corporation director, educator, government official*
Skolfield, Melissa T. *public relations executive, government official*
Slagle, Larry B. *human resources specialist*
Smulkstys, Inga *operations and management executive*
Sorenson, Arne M. *hotel executive*
Stauffer, Thomas George *retired hotel executive*
Sterling, Charlotte B. *hotel executive*
Stewart, Roy J. *communications executive*
Sunderlin, Charles Eugene *consultant*
Swain, Susan Marie *communications executive*
Tanham, George Kilpatrick *retired research company executive*
Tate, Sheila Burke *public relations executive*
Taylor, Sandra E. *public relations executive*
Timmons, William Evan *corporate executive*
Trowbridge, Alexander Buel, Jr., *business consultant*
Tychan, Terrence J. *grants and acquisitions administrator*
Umpleby, Stuart Anspach *management consultant, educator*
Van Allen, Barbara Martz *marketing professional*
Vickery, Raymond Ezekiel, Jr., *international business consultant, lawyer*
Villarreal, June Patricia *sales consultant*
Vondracek, M. Jon *communications executive*
Vose, Kathryn Kahler *marketing and communication executive*
Walcott, John L. *communications executive*
Walker, Savannah T. *retired executive assistant, legislative assistant*
Watters, Susan J. *communications executive*
Wertheim, Mitzi Mallina *technology company executive*
White, Evelyn *human resources administrator*
Whittlesey, Judith Holloway *public relations executive*
Yrizarry, Magda N. *communications executive*
Yulish, Charles Barry *public relations executive*
Zimmerman, Carole Lee *public relations professional*

FLORIDA

Arcadia
White, Will Walter, III, *public relations consultant, writer*

Bartow
Jackson, Elijah, Jr., *communication executive*

Bascom
Hart, James Whitfield, Jr., *retired corporate public affairs executive, lawyer*

Boca Grande
Winterer, Victoria Thompson *hospitality executive*

Boca Raton
Beck, Louis S. *hotel executive*
Breakstone, Robert Albert *consumer products, e-commerce, information technology and consulting executive*
Dorfman, Allen Bernard *international management consultant*
Dunhill, Robert *advertising direct mail executive*
Finegold, Ronald *computer services executive*
Frank, William Edward, Jr., *executive recruitment company executive*

Katz, Richard Jon *marketing and advertising company executive*
Langbort, Polly *retired advertising executive*
Levin, Marlene *human resources executive, educator*
Miller, Tonya Alicia *training and development specialist, management consultant*
Monroe, William Lewis *human resources executive*
Rosner, M. Norton *business systems and financial services company executive*
Schechterman, Lawrence *private chef, business consultant*
Tanner, Travis *travel executive*
Turner, Lisa Phillips *human resources executive*
Yoder, Patricia Doherty *public relations executive*

Bonita Springs
Hauserman, Jacquita Knight *management consultant*

Bradenton
Blanchard, Leonard Albert *educator, consultant, writer*
Houston, Stanley Dunsmore *retired public relations executive*
Robinson, Hugh R. *retired marketing executive*
Wolf, John Michael *adult education seminar consultant*

Cape Coral
Milaski, John Joseph *business transformation industry consultant*

Casselberry
Pantuso, Vincent Joseph *food service consultant*

Celebration
O'Neal, Kathleen Len *communications executive, writer, management speaker, financial consultant*

Clearwater
Bazzone, Theresa (Terry) A. *sales executive*
Cano, Néstor *computer company executive*
Chisholm, William DeWayne *retired contract manager*
Hallam, Arlita Warrick *quality of life administrator*
Hamilton, Lawrence White *human resources executive*
Howells, Jeffrey P. *computer company executive*
Levy, Elio *marketing professional*
Raymund, Steven A. *computer company executive*
Scarne, John *game company executive*

Clearwater Beach
Strenski, James B. *retired communications executive*

Coconut Grove
Taylor, J(ames) Bennett *management consultant*
Turkel, Bruce *advertising executive*

Coral Gables
Aitken, Anne E. *computer company executive*
Buchsbaum, Karen Fuson *public relations executive, consultant*
Cole, Todd Godwin *management consultant transportation*
Hertz, Arthur Herman *communications executive*
Lomonosoff, James Marc *marketing professional*
Scandura, Teresa Anne *management educator*
Van Aken, Norman *chef*

Daytona Beach
Furstman, Shirley Elise Daddow *retired executive secretary*

Deerfield Beach
Moran, James M. *automotive sales executive*

Deland
Hodges, Brian W. *consumer products company executive*

Delray Beach
Charyk, Joseph Vincent *retired satellite telecommunications executive*
Ehrlich, Geraldine Elizabeth *management consultant*
Nelson, Bruce *consumer products company executive*
Randall, Priscilla Richmond *retired travel company executive*
Teisch, Morton *management consultant*

Deltona
Zagnoli, Roland Candiano *management and marketing consultant, pharmacist*

Dunedin
Metcalf, Robert John Elmer *industrial consultant*
Whiting, Susan D. *marketing professional*

Fort Lauderdale
Baruch, Eduard *management consultant*
Boles, Eric Paul *staffing company executive*
Cantwell, John Walsh *advertising executive*
Castillo, Carmen *staffing company executive*
Cordesman, Michael J. *waste management administrator*
Costello, John H., III, *business and marketing executive*
Danzig, William Harold *marketing executive*
Fine, Howard Alan *management consultant*
Hallman, Cinda A. *management consultant*
Jotcham, Thomas Denis *marketing communications consultant*
Kjellmark, Eric W., Jr., *management consultant, opera company director*
Knight, Kenneth Vincent *leisure company executive, entrepreneur, venture capitalist*
Koch, Katherine Rose *communications executive*
Krause, Roy G. *management consultant*
Marcy, Raymond *staffing and consulting company executive*
O'Connor, James E. *waste management executive*
Olen, Milton William, Jr., *marketing executive*
Smith, Mark W. *management consultant*
Zimmerman, Jordan *marketing professional*

Fort Myers
Antonic, James Paul *international marketing consultant*
Fromm, Winfield Eric *retired corporate executive, engineering consultant and investor*
Fulker, Edmund Norman *management consultant*

Goyak, Elizabeth Fairbairn *retired public relations executive*
Waites, William Ernest *advertising executive*

Fort Pierce
Thoma, Richard William *chemical safety and waste management consultant*

Gainesville
Siegel, Robert James *communications executive*
Swait, Joffre Dan, Jr., *marketing professional, educator*

Greenacres
Valliere, Flora Lee *law firm official*

Hobe Sound
Gold, Kenneth R. *computer software consulting executive*

Hollywood
Angstrom, Wayne Raymond *communications executive*
Cowan, Irving *real estate owner, developer*
Ladin, Eugene *communications company executive*
Poirier, Robert J. *floral company executive*

Hutchinson Island
Wegman, Harold Hugh *management consultant*

Indian Rocks Beach
Sullivan, Paul William *communications specialist*

Islamorada
Sieber, Dawn *food service executive*

Jacksonville
Bodkin, Ruby Pate *corporate executive, real estate broker, educator*
Broughton, Carolyn Miles *multimedia executive, public relations executive*
Davis, A. Dano *grocery store chain executive*
Dewan, Derek E. *staffing services executive*
Fahner, Harold Thomas *marketing executive*
Jones, Herman Otto, Jr., *corporate professional*
Maxwell, W(ilbur) Richard *retired management consultant*
Prussin, Jeffrey A. *management consultant*
Rowland, Allen R. *grocery company executive*
Schramm, Bernard Charles, Jr., *retired advertising agency executive*
Sederbaum, William

Jacksonville Beach
Saltzman, Irene Cameron *consumer products company executive*

Jensen Beach
Carney, Robert Arthur *restaurant executive*

Jupiter
Gerson, Irwin Conrad *advertising executive*

Key Biscayne
Duffy, Earl Gavin *hotel executive*
Evans, Peter Kenneth *advertising executive*

Key Largo
Chevins, Anthony Charles *retired advertising agency executive*

Lady Lake
Langevin, Thomas Harvey *higher education consultant*

Lake Buena Vista
Rasulo, James A. *parks director*

Lake Suzy
Ogan, Russell Griffith *business executive, retired air force officer*

Lake Worth
Gorman, Marcie Sothern *personal care industry executive*
Saffir, Leonard *public relations executive*

Lakeland
Jenkins, Howard M. *supermarket executive*
Meads, Walter Frederick *communications executive, consultant, writer*
Phillips, David P. *grocery company executive*
Rhodes, Jim *human resources professional*
Siedle, Robert Douglas *management consultant*
Waugaman, Richard William *sales executive*

Land O Lakes
O'Connell, Carmela Digristina *appraisal executive, consultant*

Largo
May, Andrew *technology company executive*
Ray, Roger Buchanan *retired communications executive, lawyer*

Longboat Key
Schoenberg, Lawrence Joseph *computer services company executive*
Winfree, Charles Van *management consultant*

Longwood
Bernabei, Raymond *management consultant*
Faller, Donald E. *marketing and operations executive*
Walters, Philip Raymond *foundation executive*

Lutz
Miller, Bonnie Sewell *marketing professional, writer*

Maitland
Kaplan, Judith Helene *company executive*

Mary Esther
McTyeire, Robert Adams *sound company executive*

Melbourne
Farmer, Phillip W. *communications executive*
Koenig, Harold Paul *management consultant, ecologist, evangelist, writer*

Lance, Howard L. *communications executive, industrial engineer*
Shaikh, Muzaffar Abid *management science educator*

Melbourne Beach
Harrington, Peter Tyrus *emergency management company executive, public relations consultant, author, photographer*
Harris, Jack Howard, II, *consulting firm executive*

Miami
Amos, Betty Giles *restaurant company executive, accountant*
Arison, Micky *cruise line company executive, sports team executive*
Bessette, Diane J. *homebuilding company executive*
Brenneman, Gregory D. *food service executive*
Buehler, Martin *hotel executive*
Conover, Pamela C. *cruise line executive*
Corbi, Lana *communications executive*
Cubas, Jose M(anuel) *advertising agency executive*
Dasburg, John Harold *restaurant executive*
Dye, H. Michael *marketing professional*
Fromkin, Ava Lynda *management consultant, healthcare risk management services*
Haar, Ana Maria Fernández *advertising and public relations executive*
Henderson, Gene M. *marketing professional*
Herbits, Stephen Edward *management consultant*
Hunter, Leland Clair, Jr., *management consultant*
LeBow, Bennett S. *communications executive*
Lefton, Donald E. *hotel executive*
Mustelier, Alina Olga *travel consultant, music educator*
Neuman, Susan Catherine *public relations and marketing consultant*
Nixon, David Patrick *public relations executive*
Paresky, Linda K. *travel company executive, educator*
Pogede, Alexander *consulting company executive*
Porter, Charles King *advertising executive*
Portland, Charles Denis *publishing executive*
Sanchez, Fausto H. *advertising agency executive*
Schwartz, Gerald *public relations and fundraising agency executive*
Strul, Gene M. *communications executive, former television news director*
Tuzel, Tulin *food service executive*
Valdes, Juan Carlos *marketing executive*
Warren, Mark Edward *cruise line executive, lawyer*
Weiser, Sherwood Manuel *hotel and corporation executive, lawyer*

Miami Beach
Sharlach, Jeffrey *public relations executive*

Naples
Ayres, John E., Jr., *hotel executive*
Berman, Robert S. *marketing consultant*
Bileydi, Sumer *advertising agency executive*
Borel, Richard Wilson *communications executive, consultant*
Censits, Richard John *retired business executive*
Franco, Anthony M. *public relations executive*
Gilman, John Richard, Jr., *retired management consultant, sculptor*
Kozitka, Richard Eugene *retired consumer products company executive*
Marshall, Charles *communications company executive*
Mehaffey, John Allen *marketing, newspaper management and advertising executive*
Moore, Mechlin Dongan *communications executive, marketing consultant*
Weeks, Lee *hotel executive*

New Port Richey
Rhodes, Eric Foster *employee relations consultant, writer*

North Fort Myers
Bayuk Sr., Thomas M. *restaurant owner, writer*
Gray, Carlos Gibson *restaurateur, agricultural products supplier, entertainer, producer*

North Miami
Roslow, Sydney *marketing educator*

Ocala
Niblock, Lee *recreation director*
Sostilio, Robert Francis *office equipment marketing consultant*
Sundstrom, Harold Walter *public relations executive*

Ocoee
Smith, Stephen F. *food service executive*

Oldsmar
Brunner, George Matthew *management consultant, former business executive*

Orange City
Schaeffer, Barbara Hamilton *retired rental leasing company executive, writer*

Orlando
Connolly, Joseph Francis, II, *educational executive, government consultant*
Dawson, Leslie Naryne *quality assurance professional*
Dimopoulos, Linda J. *food service executive*
Langton, Bryan D. *hotel executive*
Lee, Joe R. *food service executive*
Mahoney, Mary *hotel executive*
Maldonado, Graziano *management consultant, educator*
Smetheram, Herbert Edwin *management consultant*
Weiss, Al *hotel executive*
Yesawich, Peter Charles *advertising executive*

Osprey
Cochran, David MacDuffie *management consultant*

Oviedo
Millstein, Herbert Sydney *management consultant*

Palm Beach
Flanagan, Joseph Patrick *advertising executive*
Karp, Richard M. *advertising and communication executive*
Leone, Paul N. *hotel executive*
Rumbough, Stanley Maddox, Jr., *industrialist*
Tiefel, William Reginald *hotel company executive*

Palm Beach Gardens
Druck, Kalman Breschel *public relations counselor*
Mendelson, Richard Donald *former communications company executive*
Van Allen, Veronica Elaine *marketing and public relations professional*
Yackira, Michael William *power company executive*

Pembroke Pines
Grahm, Charles Morton *retired sales executive*

Pinellas Park
Mente, Ronald F. *consulting company executive*

Pompano Beach
Brands, Robert Franciscus *business executive*
Calevas, Harry Powell *management consultant*
Liakos, James Christ *business manager*

Ponte Vedra Beach
Gold, Keith Dean *advertising and design executive*
Leek, Jay Wilbur *management consultant*
Linnen, Thomas Francis *international strategic management consulting firm executive*

Port Charlotte
Reynolds, Helen Elizabeth *management services consultant*

Port Saint Lucie
Diltz, Jerry Dwaine *computer science educator, consultant*

Saint Augustine
Preysz, Louis Robert Fonss, III, *management consultant, educator*

Saint Cloud
Ortiz, Anthony *hotel executive*

Saint Petersburg
Butcher-Towzey, David *public relations executive*
DeLorenzo, David Joseph *retired public relations executive*
Greer, Tommy D. *marketing professional*
Kubiet, Leo Lawrence *newspaper advertising and marketing executive*
Williams, Yvonne G. *corporate trainer*

Sanibel
Brodbeck, William Jan *marketing consultant, speaker*

Santa Rosa Beach
Rees, Lane Charles *industrial relations consultant*

Sarasota
Beck, Robert Alfred *hotel administration educator*
Feder, Allan Appel *management executive, consultant*
Fendrick, Alan Burton *retired advertising executive*
Gittelson, Bernard *public relations consultant, author, lecturer*
Halladay, Laurie Ann *public relations consultant, former franchise executive*
Huff, Russell Joseph *public relations and publishing executive*
Kelly, John Love *public relations executive*
Landis, Edgar David *business consultant*
Lee, Nancy Ranck *management consultant*
Mattran, Donald Albert *management consultant, educator*
McDonald, Peggy Ann Stimmel *retired automobile company official*
Neeley, Delmar George *mediator, pastoral counselor*
Schlegel, John Frederick *management consultant, speaker*
Shulman, Arthur *communications executive*
Simon, Joseph Patrick *food services executive*
Stickler, Daniel Lee *health care management consultant*

Seffner
Seaman, Jeffrey *consumer products company executive*

Seminole
Evans, Thomas Passmore *management consultant*

Singer Island
Tremain, Alan *hotel executive*

Stuart
Donohue, Edith M. *human resources specialist, educator*
Perron, Brandon Alan *private investigator, director*
Riordan, James Quentin *retired company executive*

Sunny Isles Beach
Edelcup, Norman Scott *management and financial consultant*

Sunrise
Sorensen, Allan Chresten *service company executive*

Tallahassee
Cronin, Jerome Joseph, Jr., *marketing educator, consultant*
Finley-Hervey, Joycelyn Alexandria *management consultant, educator*
Morgante, John-Paul *human resources specialist*
Penson, Edward Martin *management consulting company executive*

Tampa
Callen, David H. *hotel executive*
Chaves, Wanda Vanessa *management consultant, educator*
Cunningham, Kathleen Ann *human resources specialist*
Dunkel, David L. *personnel firm executive*
Heuer, Martin *temporary services executive*
Jones, Vaughn Paul *construction marketing executive*
Kaylor, Jefferson Daniel, Jr., *business development professional*
Mangiapane, Joseph Arthur *consulting company executive, applied mechanics consultant*
Moltzon, Richard Francis *operations executive*
Ortinau, David Joseph *marketing specialist, educator*
Silver, Paul Robert *marketing executive, consultant*
West, Benjamin B. *advertising executive*

Tarpon Springs
Crismond, Linda Fry *public relations executive*

Tavares
Gross, Paul Allan *health service executive*

Venice
Harrington, John Vincent *retired communications company executive, engineer, educator*
Kater, Victor Ricardo *marketing professional, writer, economist*

Vero Beach
Binney, Jan Jarrell *publishing executive*
Fisher, Andrew *management consultant*
Leonsis, Ted *media executive*
McNamara, John J(oseph) *advertising executive, writer*
Menk, Carl William *executive search company executive*
Nesbit, Robert Grover *management consultant*
Nichols, Carl Wheeler *retired advertising agency executive*
Spivak, Alvin A. *retired public relations executive*

Wellington
Fitch, Mary Killeen *human resources specialist*
Lane, Brian M. *management executive*

West Palm Beach
Darter, Jeffrey Allen *data processing professional*
Fisher, Fenimore *business development consultant*
Johnson, Samira El-Chehabi *marketing professional*
King, Robert Howard *marketing professional*
Lacey, John William Charles *management consultant*
Ronan, William John *management consultant*
Stauderman, Bruce Ford *writer, advertising executive*

Weston
Barnes, William Douglas *advertising executive*

Winter Haven
Cover, Norman Bernard *retired electronic data processing administrator*

Winter Park
Powers, Ronald George *management consultant*
Safian, Shelley Carole *advertising executive*

GEORGIA

Acworth
Perry, Randall A. *business executive*

Albany
Robinson, J. Mack *communications executive*

Alpharetta
Braxton, Jerry W. *communications executive*
Esher, Brian Richard *chief executive officer*
Malloy, William G. *entertainment company executive*
Minner, Thomas O. *marketing executive*
Troop, Paul Melvin *public relations executive, journalist*

Athens
Thomas, Howard Lamar *chef, consultant, writer*

Atlanta
Allred, Jeffrey A. *communications executive*
Anderson, Al H., Jr., *communications executive*
Ashley, John Bryan *software executive, management consultant*
Baker, Jerry Herbert *executive search consultant*
Barnard, Patricia A. *human resources specialist*
Bennett, Dick *advertising executive*
Beres, Mary Elizabeth *management educator, religious leader*
Betty, Charles Garry (Garry Betty) *Internet company executive*
Bradshaw, Rod Eric *personnel consultant*
Braswell, Cruse C., Jr., *public relations executive*
Brewer, Charles M. *communications executive*
Brothers, June Esternaux Scott *forest products company vice president*
Brown-Olmstead, Amanda *public relations executive*
Buoch, William Thomas *corporate executive*
Burge, William Lee *retired business information executive*
Chapman, Thomas F. *communications executive*
Chartier, Kirk Lee Freund *business services executive*
Chasen, Sylvan Herbert *computer applications consultant, investment advisor*
Clement, William A., Jr., *computer company executive*
Cohn, Bob *public relations executive*
Collins, Douglas C. *hotel executive*
Cooper, Simon F. *hotel executive*
Cooper, Thomas Luther *retired printing company executive*
Crackett, Delores *womens bureau administrator*
Danielson, Gilbert Lawrence *consumer products company executive*
Darden, Claibourne Henry, Jr., *marketing research professional*
Dodson, Daniel, Jr., *advertising executive*
Dramis, Francis A., Jr., *communications company executive*
Duffey, Lee *communications company executive*
Dzvonik, Michael D. *advertising executive*
Easterly, David Eugene *communications executive*
Ehrlich, Jeffrey *data processing company executive*
Farley, Charles P. *public relations executive*
Fine, Frederick L. *computer company executive, health products executive*
Fletcher, Andy *marketing professional*
Fote, Charles T. *computer company executive*
Fredo, Peter W. *public relations executive*
Fuqua, John Brooks *retired consumer products and services company executive*
Gelardi, Robert Charles *trade association executive, consultant*
Gergel, Mark A. *communications executive*
Goldstein, Burton Benjamin, Jr., *communications executive*
Goldston, Nathaniel R., III, *food services company executive*
Goodwin, George Evans *public relations executive*
Greene, Warren *advertising executive*
Grzedzinski, Edward *data processing executive*
Hammill, Dick *advertising and marketing executive*
Harrison, Clifford *chef, small business owner*
Healy, Maureen *marketing executive*
Hoffman, Fred L. *human resources specialist*
Howell, Hilton Hatchett, Jr., *business executive*
Johnson, Jeff *marketing professional*
Jones, Boland T. *communications executive*
Kelly, Carol White *company executive*
Kent, Philip *communications executive*
Kline, J. Peter *hotel executive*
Kuhn, Brent *advertising executive*
Lee, Robert *hotel executive*
Levy, Rich *advertising executive*
Lnenicka, Wade Sheridan *purchasing official, councilman*
Locklin, Paul G. *executive*
Logsdon, James M. *information systems executive*
Love, Dennis M. *consumer products company executive*
Mahan, James S. *communications company executive*
Malhotra, Naresh Kumar *management educator*
Marano, Thomas J. *marketing professional*
Massey, Charles Knox, Jr., *advertising agency executive*
Matlock, Kent *advertising executive, public relations executive*
McChesney, Michael C. *computer network security company executive*
McKenzie, Kay Branch *public relations executive*
McNeil, Robert L., Jr., *marketing professional*
McQuary, Michael S. *Internet company executive*
Mecke, William Moyn *public affairs consultant*
Nardelli, Robert L. *consumer home products executive*
Oliver, Thomas *hotel executive*
Osorio, Claudio E. *computer company executive*
Overstreet, Jim *former public relations executive*
Payne, William P. *communications executive*
Perlman, Richard E. *medical software company executive*
Phillips, John *communications executive*
Quatrano, Anne *chef, restaurant owner*
Raper, Charles Albert *retired management consultant*
Reising, Juliet M. *information systems executive*
Robbins, James O. *communications executive*
Ryan, J. Bruce *healthcare management consulting executive*
Schulze, Horst H. *hotel company executive*
Schussel, Robert *beverage distributing executive*
Seeger, Guenter Otto *chef*
Seigel, Richard M. *consumer products company executive*
Shaftman, Fredrick Krisch *telephone communications executive, lawyer*
Smith, Sidney L. *advertising executive*
Soderberg, Bo S. *marketing executive*
Stormont, Richard Mansfield *hotel executive*
Summerlin, Glenn Wood *retired advertising executive*
Timm-Brock, Barbara *chief product officer*
Tomaszewski, Richard Paul *market representation executive*
Tuggle, Clyde Cebron *communications editor, beverage company executive*
Umphenour, Russell V., Jr., *food services executive*
Van Houten, G. David *food service executive*
Verrill, F. Glenn *advertising executive*
Vollkommer, Michael T. *credit reporting company executive*
Ward, Jackie M. *computer company executive*
Watkins, Sydney Lynn *sales executive*
Weidman, Sheila *marketing professional*
Whealy, Michael Thomas *data processing company executive, lawyer*
White, Ronald Leon *financial management consultant*
Wiglesworth, Michael Bland *advertising executive*
Wilson, Alexandra M. *communications executive*
Winograd, Audrey Lesser *retired advertising executive*

Buford
Greene, William L. *marketing professional, consultant*

Carrollton
Thorn, Stuart Wallace *marketing and financial executive*

Cedartown
Garner, Robby Glen *software research executive, roboticist*

Cumming
Willadsen, Michael Chris *marketing professional, sales executive*

Dawsonville
Jorgensen, Alfred H. *retired data processing executive, retired telecommunications industry executive*

Duluth
Hunter, Douglas Lee *ministry executive, former elevator executive*
McCullough, Robert *management consultant, information technology executive*

Evans
Welsh, Michael Louis *business executive*

Folkston
Wangsness, Genna Stead *hotel executive, innkeeper*

Gainesville
Davis, Connie Waters *public relations executive, marketing professional*

Griffin
Marshall, Allen Wright, III, *communications executive, financial consultant*

Kennesaw
Roebuck, Deborah Mae Britt *management consultant, educator*

Lawrenceville
Elleby, Gail *management consultant*

Marietta
Martin, Sherlonda S. *personnel director*
Smith, Baker Armstrong *management executive, lawyer*
Smith, Beverly Ann Evans *management consultant, small business owner*
Spann, George William *management consultant*

Mcdonough
Dunlap, Donald Kelder *rental company executive*

Mount Berry
Dhir, Krishna Swaroop *business administration educator*

Norcross
Bowman, Jerry W. *recruiting company executive*
Cramer, James Perry *management strategist, architectural author, educator*
Dumont, William K. *business communications management executive*
Galfas, Timothy, II, *franchising and turnaround administrator*
Koscik, Ella M. *management and technology company executive*
Penninger, Samuel A., Jr., *consumer products company executive*
Plumb, Russell H. *business company executive*
Strange, J. Leland *computer company executive*
Tenoso, Harold J. *consumer products company executive*
Tito, James P. *software company executive*

Oakwood
Jondahl, Terri Elise *importing and distribution company executive*

Oxford
Stamps, George Moreland *communications consultant, facsimile pioneer*

Peachtree City
Barrell, Dawn Holman *marketing specialist*

Pine Mountain
Callaway, Howard Hollis *business executive*

Roswell
Hill, Donald Dee *management consultant, lecturer, writer*
Rogers, Richard Hilton *hotel consultant, broker*

Saint Simons Island
Sullivan, Barbara Boyle *management consultant*

Savannah
Otter, John Martin, III, *retired television advertising consultant*
Sheehy, Barry Maurice *management consultant*

Smyrna
Davenport, Glenn A. *management executive*
Michels, Frances G. *management company executive*

Stone Mountain
Branscome, Curtis *parks and recreation director*

Thomasville
Turner, Marta Jones *public affairs professional*

Tucker
Broucek, William Samuel *printing plant executive*
Brown, Betsy S. *hotel executive*
Diamond, Gerald *holding company executive*
Guimbellot, Bobby E. *hotel executive*
Risner, Ray D. *computer company executive*

HAWAII

Honolulu
Devenot, David Charles *human resources specialist*
Hartley, Michael J. *online travel executive*
Kelley, Richard Roy *hotel executive*
Keogh, Richard John *firearms and explosives consultant*
Leyden, Michael Joseph, II, (Lei Jie Ming) *international business executive, educator, author*
Miyamoto, Craig Toyoki *public relations executive*
Niles, Geddes Leroy *private investigator*
O'Neill, Charles Kelly *marketing executive, former advertising agency executive*
Singer, Hersh *marketing executive*
Smales, Fred Benson *corporate executive*
Sorenson, Perry *resort facility executive*
Tatibouet, Andre Stephan *condominium and resort management firm executive*
Yamato, Kei C. *international business consultant*

Kapaau
Ralston, Joanne Smoot *public relations executive*

Waipahu
Look, Pauwilo *creative media developer, architecture marketer*

IDAHO

American Falls
Newlin, L. Max *parks and recreation director*

Bellevue
Pearson, Robert Greenlees *writing services company executive*

Boise
Eastland, Larry L. *entertainment and theme park development executive*
Foster, S. Thomas, Jr., *department chairman, quality management educator, consultant, writer*
Gellert, Edward Bradford *advertising agency executive*
Luthy, John Frederick *management consultant*
Sullivan, James Kirk *management consultant*
Thornton, Felicia *food service executive, corporate financial executive*

Idaho Falls
Barbe, Betty Catherine *marketing professional, retired financial analyst*
Gregory, Nelson Bruce *retired motel owner, retired naval officer*
Planchon, Harry Peter, Jr., *research development manager*

Kamiah
Mills, Carol Margaret *business consultant, public relations consultant*

Ketchum
Ziebarth, Robert Charles *management consultant*

Post Falls
Grassi, James Edward *Christian ministry executive director*

ILLINOIS

Addison
Christopher, Doris K. *consumer products company executive*
McDonald, David Eugene *transportation operator*

Aledo
Prosser, Wesley Lewis *advertising and public relations executive*

Alton
Burgess, Robert Ronald *human resources executive*
Cellini, William F. *hotel executive*

Arlington Heights
Fields, Sara A. *travel company executive*
Holtz, Michael P. *hotel executive*
Payne, Thomas H. *market research company executive*

Barrington
Lee, Catherine M. *business owner, educator*
Mathis, Jack David *advertising executive, consultant*
Murphy, Robert *executive search consultant*
Ross, Frank Howard, III, *management consultant*
Stephens, Norval Blair, Jr., *marketing consultant*
Sweet, Charles Wheeler *retired executive recruiter*

Bartlett
Robinson, Lois Hart *retired public relations executive*

Batavia
Brown, Gerald Curtis *retired army officer, engineering executive*

Bloomingdale
Flaherty, John Joseph *quality assurance company executive*
Wolande, Charles Sanford *former computer company executive*

Bolingbrook
Sheehan, James Patrick *printing company executive, former media company executive*
Stoelting, Curtis W. *consumer products company executive*

Broadview
Lazar, Jill Sue *home healthcare company executive*

Burr Ridge
Bottom, Dale Coyle *management consultant*
Zaccone, Suzanne Maria *sales executive*

Calumet City
Kovach, Joseph William *management consultant, psychologist, educator*

Carbondale
Jugenheimer, Donald Wayne *advertising and communications educator, university administrator*

Carol Stream
Gale, Neil Jan *Internet company executive, computer scientist, consultant*

Champaign
Moore, Jerry Jay *sales executive, retired archaeologist*

Chicago
Akins, Cindy S. *human resources professional*
Allen, Belle *management consulting firm executive, communications executive*
Amberg, Thomas L. *public relations executive*
Andrica, John Dean *management consultant*
Aubriot, Eric *chef*
Bacevicius, John Anthony, V, (John Bace) *research executive*
Bailey, Robert, Jr., *advertising executive*
Baker, Mark *food service executive*
Barry, Richard A. *public relations executive*
Bayless, Rick *chef*
Bensinger, Peter Benjamin *consulting firm executive*
Berman, Cheryl R. *advertising company executive*
Bernatowicz, Frank Allen *management consultant, expert witness*
Be Sant, Craig *marketing executive*
Bess, Ronald W. *advertising executive*
Beugen, Joan Beth *communications company executive*
Bishop, Mary Oltman *retired advertising executive*
Blackwell, Robert, Jr., *consulting firm executive*
Blackwell, Robert D., Sr., *consulting firm executive*
Bonaparte, William *communications company executive*
Borg, Frank *hotel executive*
Boyda, Debora *advertising executive*
Brandt, William Arthur, Jr., *consulting executive*
Brown, Jeremy Earle *advertising executive*
Burack, Elmer Howard *management educator*
Cardoso, Aldo *marketing professional*
Cary, Arlene D. *retired hotel company sales executive*
Cass, Edward Roberts (Peter Cass) *hotel and travel marketing professional*
Castorino, Sue *communications executive*
Chipparoni, Guy *communications company executive*
Chorengel, Bernd *international hotel corporation executive*
Conidi, Daniel Joseph *private investigation agency executive*
Corbett, Frank Joseph *advertising executive*
Cornell, Rob *hotel executive*
Cox, Allan James *management consultant*
Dammeyer, Rodney Foster *distribution company executive*
Deli, Anne Tynion *marketing executive*
Diederichs, Janet Wood *public relations executive*
Digangi, Al *marketing executive*
Doetsch, Virginia Lamb *former advertising executive, writer*
Donnelley, James Russell *printing company executive*
Draft, Howard Craig *advertising executive*
Edelman, Daniel Joseph *public relations executive*
Eibl, Clement *management consulting firm executive*
Fisher, Eugene *marketing professional*
Fisher, Lawrence Edgar *market research executive, anthropologist*
FitzSimons, Dennis Joseph *broadcasting and publishing executive*
Foster, James Reuben *travel company executive*
Fox, Suzy *management consultant, educator*
Frankel, Bernard *advertising executive*
Frazier, Anthony Vincent Earl *addictions, small business, and technology specialist*
Friedman, Marla Lee *human resources specialist, marketing professional*
Furcon, John Edward *management and organizational consultant*
Furth, Yvonne *advertising executive*
Gand, Gayle *chef*
Gardner, Howard Alan *travel company executive, writer, editor*
Gerber, Phillip *advertising executive*
Gilbert, David R. *public relations executive*
Glasser, James J. *leasing company executive, retired*
Goldring, Norman Max *advertising executive*
Golin, Alvin *public relations company executive*
Gray, Dawn Plambeck *work-family consultant*
Green, RuthAnn *marketing and management consultant*
Haffner, Charles Christian, III, *retired printing company executive*
Hansen, Carl R. *management consultant*
Harkna, Eric *advertising executive*
Hartman, Laura Beth Pincus *management consultant, writer, academic administrator*
Haupt, Roger A. *advertising executive*
Hayden, Harrold Harrison *information company executive*
Healy, Sondra Anita *consumer products company executive*
Hofrichter, David Alan *management consultant*
Hollis, Donald Roger *management consultant*
Husting, Peter Marden *advertising consultant*
Kloster, Carol Good *book and magazine distribution company*
Klues, Jack *communications executive*
Kobs, James Fred *direct marketing consultant*
Koernig, Stephen K. *marketing professional, educator*
Kornick, Michael *chef*
Krivkovich, Peter George *advertising executive*
Kubo, Gary Michael *advertising executive*
LaVelle, Avis *consulting firm executive*
Lee, Michael *leasing company executive, real estate company executive*
Leigh, Sherren *communications executive, editor, publisher*
Levine, Keith F. *marketing executive*
Levy, Deborah *security company executive*
Lewis, Evelyn *management consultant*
Lieberman, Pamela Forbes *consumer products company executive*
Lowry, James Hamilton *management consultant*
Lucas, Gregory *market researcher*
Mack, Jim *advertising executive*
Mackiewicz, Laura *advertising agency executive*
MacWilliams, Diane *communications executive*
Maczulski, Margaret Louise *event marketing professional, meeting manager*
Martinez, Josemaria Espino *computer services administrator*
McCallister, Richard Anthony *business consulting company executive*
McCann, Renetta *advertising executive*
McConnell, E. Hoy, II, *advertising/public policy executive*
McCullough, Richard Lawrence *advertising agency executive*
Melamed, Leo *global consulting firm executive*
Menendez, Marcelino Eulogio (Marc Menendez) *marketing professional*
Miller, Bernard Joseph, Jr., *advertising executive*
Miller, Ellen *advertising executive*
Mitchell, Lee Mark *communications executive, investment fund manager, lawyer*
Morley, Michael B. *public relations executive*
Moster, Mary Clare *public relations executive*
Nelson, Harry Donald *telecommunications executive*
O'Shea, Lynne Edeen *management consultant, educator*
Paul, Ronald Neale *management consultant*
Petrillo, Nancy *public relations executive*
Pincus, Theodore Henry *public relations executive*
Plank, Betsy (Mrs. Sherman V. Rosenfield) *public relations counsel*
Plotkin, Manuel D. *management consultant, educator, former corporate executive and government official*
Pope, Lena Elizabeth *human resources specialist*
Posner, Kathy Robin *communications executive*
Prather, Susan Lynn *public relations executive*
Pritzker, Thomas Jay *hotel business executive*
Provus, Barbara Lee *executive search consultant*
Rabin, Joseph Harry *marketing research company executive*
Raphaelson, Joel *retired advertising agency executive*
Reid, Daniel James *public relations executive*
Reitman, Jerry Irving *advertising agency executive*
Rooney, Phillip Bernard *service company executive*
Rosenthal, Albert Jay *advertising agency executive*
Schneider, Wesley Clair *marketing communications company executive*
Segal, Mindy *chef*
Senior, Richard John Lane *textile rental service executive*
Shimokubo, Janice Teruko *marketing professional*
Shirley, Virginia Lee *advertising executive*
Silich, Greg *advertising executive*
Singer, Emel *staffing industry executive*
Singer, Martin H. *Internet company executive*
Sive, Rebecca Anne *public affairs company executive*
Skala, Gary Dennis *management consultant*
Smeekes, Frank *executive recruiter, consultant*
Smith, Scott Clybourn *media company executive*
Sotelino, Gabino *chef*
Soto, Ramona *training specialist*
Stenger, Sarah *chef*
Sterling, John *consulting firm executive*
Stern, Carl William, Jr., *management consultant*
Stith, Mary Beth (Rae) *marketing professional for graphic design*
Strubel, Ella Doyle *advertising executive, public relations executive*
Struggles, John Edward *management consultant*
Talbot, Pamela *public relations executive*
Taylor, Collette *public relations executive*
Teichner, Lester *management consulting executive*
Thompson, Jayne Carr *public relations and communications executive, lawyer*
Toback, Paul A. *recreational facility executive*
Tramonto, Rick *chef*
Tribbett, Charles *executive recruiter*
Tripp, Marian Barlow Loofe *retired public relations executive*
Trotter, Charlie *chef*
Tyson, Kirk W. M. *management consultant*
Van Den Hende, Fred J(oseph) *human resources executive*
Vilim, Nancy Catherine *advertising agency executive*
Walters, Lawrence Charles *advertising executive*
Weinfurter, Daniel Joseph *business services executive*
Wiecek, Barbara Harriet *advertising executive*
Williams, Martha *consumer products company executive, entrepreneur*
Wolf, Linda S. *advertising executive*
Wooldridge, Patrice Marie *marketing professional, personal trainer*
Zhang, Zhukai *Internet company executive, consultant*

Crete
Langer, Steven *human resources management consultant and industrial psychologist*

Darien
Friedrich, Charles William *corporate executive*

Decatur
Blake, William Henry *credit and public relations consultant*

Deerfield
Eastham, Dennis Michael *advertising executive*
Gater, Chris *advertising executive*
Huff, Gayle Compton *advertising and marketing executive*
Simon, Marc *communications executive*
Strubel, Richard Perry *Internet company executive*

Des Plaines
Baerenklau, Alan H. *hotel executive*
Cronin, Kathleen Anne *executive search consultant*
Drake, Ann M. *consumer products company executive*
Dvorak, Kathleen S. *business products company executive*
Gochnauer, Richard Wallis *consumer products company executive*
Le Menager, Lois M. *incentive merchandise and travel company executive*
Mueller, Kurt M. *hotel executive*
Santisteban, Joseph Henry *human resources specialist*

Downers Grove
Ames, Sandra Patience *sales executive*
Bielefeldt, Catherine C. *sales executive*
Clement, Paul Platts, Jr., *performance technologist, educator*
Norton, Robert L. *consumer products company executive*
Pollard, C. William *environmental services administrator*
Pollard, C(harles) William *diversified services company executive*
Schwemm, John Butler *printing company executive, lawyer*
Soenen, Michael J. *flower company executive*
Veluchamy, Pethinaidu *marketing executive*
Ward, Jonathan P. *service company executive*

Dundee
Carlini, James *management consultant*

Edwardsville
Dietrich, Suzanne Claire *instructional designer, communications consultant*

Elgin
Rogers, Carleton Carson, Jr., *trade show and convention executive*

Elmhurst
Choyke, Phyllis May Ford (Mrs. Arthur Davis Choyke Jr.) *management executive, editor, poet*
Duarte, Gloria *chef*

Evanston
Blair, Virginia Ann *public relations executive*
Kotler, Philip *marketing educator, consultant, writer*
Larson, Paul William *public relations executive*
Robbins, Henry Zane *public relations and marketing executive*
Tornabene, Russell C. *communications executive*

Flossmoor
Crum, James Francis *waste recycling company executive*

Freeport
Galli, Joseph, Jr., *consumer products company executive*

Galena
Fullmer, Paul *public relations counselor*

Geneseo
Crisp, Sandra Sue *procurement analyst*

Geneva
Montgomery, Joel Robert *communications executive, consultant*
Xagas, Steven George James *diversified employment services firm executive*

Glen Ellyn
Parkhurst, Edwin Wallace, Jr., *healthcare management consultant*
Schmidt, Karen Lee *marketing professional, sales executive*

Glencoe
Cole, Kathleen Ann *advertising executive, retired social worker*
Isaacs, Roger David *public relations executive*
Niefeld, Jaye Sutter *advertising executive*

Glenview
Franklin, Lynne *business communications consultant, writer*
Grubbs, Robert W. *computer services company executive*
Kaplan, Steven M. *advertising executive*
Turner, Lee *travel company executive*

Glenwood
Latta, Brent *consumer products company executive*

Gurnee
Schoenfeld, Howard Allen *management consultant, lawyer*
Weber, James Stuart *management educator*

Highland Park
Axelrod, Leah Joy *tour company executive*
Bakalar, John Stephen *printing and publishing company executive*
Cohen, Burton David *franchising executive, lawyer*
Harris, Thomas L. *public relations executive*
Hattis, Albert Daniel *business executive, journalist*

Hinsdale
Amsler, Jana *chef*
Whitney, William Elliot, Jr., *advertising agency executive*

Hoffman Estates
Lee, Gregory *human resources specialist*
Marino, Nancy A. *marketing professional*
Martinez, Arthur C. *retail company executive*
Rooney, John Edward *communications company executive*

Hudson
Mills, Lois Jean *design company executive, retired education educator, aide*

Kenilworth
Steingraber, Frederick George *management consultant*

Lake Bluff
Fryburger, Vernon Ray, Jr., *advertising and marketing educator*
Griem, John Michael *management consultant*
Scott, Karen Bondurant *consumer catalog company executive*

Lake Forest
Bramhall, Robert Richard *management consultant*
Carter, Donald Patton *retired advertising executive*
Chieger, Kathryn Jean *recreation company executive*
Crawford, Robert W., Jr., *furniture rental company executive*
Davidson, Richard Alan *data communications company executive*
Fromm, Henry Gordon *retired manufacturing and marketing executive*
Goldstein, Marsha Feder *tour company executive*
Hecker, Lawrence Harris *industrial hygienist*
Johnson, Richard Darrell *management consultant*
Kenly, Granger Farwell *marketing consultant, college official*
Miller, Mark C. *waste management administrator*
Mohr, Roger John *advertising agency executive*
Reich, Victoria J. *consumer products company executive*

Libertyville
Conklin, Mara Loraine *public relations executive*
Ritson, Scott Campbell *management consultant*
Tullman, Glen *management consultant*
Voss, Joan Sarah *administrative assistant, writer*

Lincolnshire
DeCanniere, Dan *human resources executive*
Hebda, Lawrence John *data processing executive, consultant*
Omtvedt, Craig P. *consumer products executive*
Roche, Mark A. *consumer products company executive, lawyer*

Lincolnwood
Donovan, John Vincent *consulting company executive*
Grant, Paul Bernard *industrial relations educator, arbitrator*
Lebedow, Aaron Louis *consulting company executive*
Roemer, James Paul *data processing executive, writer*

Lisle
Sotir, Mark *automotive rental executive*

Litchfield
Mark, Wayne Michael *technical education marketing professional*
Talley, Hayward Leroy *communications executive*

Melrose Park
Bernick, Carol Lavin *consumer products company executive*

Moline
Schwiebert, Deborah Johnson *marketing executive*

Morton Grove
Smolyansky, Julie *consumer products company executive*

Mount Prospect
Sayers, Gale *computer company executive, retired professional football player*

Mundelein
Meehan, Jean Marie Ross *human resources, occupational health and safety management consultant*

Naperville
Bell, Bradley J. *water treatment company executive*
Ford, Ralph A. *moving and relocation company executive*
Fritz, Roger Jay *management consultant*
Fuhrer, Larry *management consultant, management educator, finance company executive*
Koch, William Joseph *public relations executive*
Modery, Richard Gillman *marketing and sales executive*
Snyder, Anthony Edward *communications executive*

Niles
Beton, John Allen *communications company executive*
Kelly, John *advertising executive*
Weisbach, Lou *advertising executive*

North Aurora
Hoover, Lola Mae *retired communications company executive*

Northbrook
Clarey, John Robert *executive search consultant*
Crockett, Joan M. *human resources executive*
Di Spigno, Guy Joseph *international management consultant, industrial psychologist*
Ehrenberg, Maureen *management consultant*
Ross, Debra Benita *jewelry designer, marketing executive*
Sudbrink, Jane Marie *sales and marketing executive*
Wajer, Ronald Edward *management consultant*

Oak Brook
Alvarez, Ralph *food service executive*
Babrowski, Claire Harbeck *fast food chain executive*
Bell, Charles H. *food service executive*
Crump-Caine, Lynn *food service executive*
DeLorey, John Alfred *printing company executive*
Fenton, Tim *food service executive*
Fields, Janice L. *food service executive*
Glenn, J. Thomas *consumer products company executive*
Nelson, Robert Eddinger *retired management consultant*
Paull, Matthew H. *food service executive*
Quinlan, Michael Robert *fast food franchise company executive*
Turner, Fred L. *retired fast food company executive*
Wigginton, Adam *marketing professional*

Oak Park
Ankrum, Dennis R. *industrial ergonomist, consultant*
Cannon, Patrick Francis *public relations executive*
Devereux, Timothy Edward *advertising executive*

Oakbrook Terrace
Hegenderfer, Jonita Susan *public relations executive*
Singhal, Vivek Kumar *management consultant*

Palatine
Medin, Lowell Ansgard *management executive*
Ramunno, Thomas Paul *management consultant*

Park Forest
Orr, Marcia *child development researcher, child care consultant*

Park Ridge
Campbell, Dorothy May *management consultant*
Williams, Sandra Lynn *management consultant*

Peoria Heights
Taylor, Kathy Deanne *marketing executive, consultant*

Plainfield
Hofer, Thomas W. *landscape company executive*

Prarie Grove
Kruper, John Gerald (Jack Kruper) *sales and marketing executive*

Prospect Heights
Lynch, William Thomas, Jr., *advertising agency executive*

River Forest
Hamper, Robert Joseph *marketing executive*

Riverwoods
Del Tiempo, Sandra Kay *sales executive*

Rockford
Morrissey, Mary F. (Fran) *human resource consulting company executive*

Rolling Meadows
Cain, R. Wayne *sales, finance and leasing company executive*

Rosemont
Blake, Norman Perkins, Jr., *computer company executive*
Small, Richard Donald *travel company executive*

Saint Charles
Benjamin, Lawrence *food service executive*
Griffin, Sheila MB *strategic marketing excutive*

Schaumburg
Bhatia, Viresh *computer company executive*
Growney, Robert L. *communications company professional*
Guimond, Richard Joseph *communications executive*
Hill, Raymond Joseph *packaging company executive*
Metty, Theresa M. *communications executive*
Sandler, Norman *communications executive*
Stabej, Rudolph John *computer consultant*
Turlik, Iwona *communication executive*
Warrior, Padmasree *communications executive*
Zafirovski, Mike S. *communications executive*

Skokie
Karp, Gary *marketing and public relations executive*
Sperzel, George E., Jr., *former personal care industry executive*
Wallace, Rick *marketing professional*

Springfield
Stroh, Raymond Eugene *retired personnel executive*
Whitaker, Victoria Manuela Katz *publisher, public relations executive, educator, consultant*

Sugar Grove
Carella, J(oseph) Dino *printing company executive*

Vernon Hills
Claassen, W(alter) Marshall *employment company executive*
Edwardson, John Albert *security firm executive*
Krasny, Michael P. *computer company executive*

Villa Park
Camp, Jeffery Mark *Web specialist, military officer*

Warrenville
Slavin, Thomas John *industrial hygienist, director*

Westchester
Anderson, Carol Lee *communications executive*
Faulkner, Robert Lloyd *advertising executive, graphics designer*

Western Springs
Frommelt, Jeffrey James *management consulting firm executive*
Reggio, Vito Anthony *management consultant*

Wheaton
Long, Charles Franklin *retired corporate communications executive*
Mellott, Robert Vernon *retired advertising executive*

Willowbrook
Foley, Joseph Lawrence *sales executive*
Mathisen-Reid, Rhoda Sharon *international communications consultant*

Wilmette
Chiaro, A. William *management consultant*

Winnetka
Bro, William Price *communications executive*
Hermann, Edward Robert *health engineer, educator, writer, consultant, hygieologist*
Kahn, Paul Frederick *executive search company executive*
Thomas, John Thieme *management consultant*

Woodridge
O'Connor, William Michael *search company executive*

INDIANA

Auburn
Kempf, Jane Elmira *marketing executive*

Bloomington
Hanks, Lawrence Julius, Sr., *management consultant, researcher*
Patterson, James Milton *marketing specialist, educator*

Columbus
Tucker, Thomas Randall *public relations executive*

Corydon
Walker, James Harper *retired security firm executive, writer*

Evansville
Hampel, Robert Edward *advertising executive*

Fort Wayne
Schweickart, Jim *advertising executive, broadcast executive, consultant*

Gary
Prettyman, Wendy Pettit *management company executive*

Greenwood
Saint-Pierre, Michael Robert *funeral director, consultant*

Huntertown
Becker, Cheri A(nn) *marketing professional, business consultant*

Indianapolis
Clary, Keith Uhl *retired employee relations executive*
Gilman, Alan B. *restaurant company executive*
Goldstein, Paul Robert *management company executive, consultant*
Hancock, Joan Herrin *retired executive search company executive*
Kirkpatrick, Robert Hugh *communications executive*
Meyer, Fred William, Jr., *memorial parks executive*
Miniear, J. Dederick *software company executive, consultant*
Nyhart, Eldon Howard *employee benefits consultant, lawyer*
Poinsette, Donald Eugene *business executive, value management consultant*

Rati, Robert Dean *data processing executive*
Santini, Gino *marketing professional*
Simmons, Roberta Johnson *public relations firm executive*
Slaymaker, Gene Arthur *public relations executive*
Smith, Carson Clay *business executive*
Walker, Frank Dilling *market research executive*

Liberty
Pringle, Lewis Gordon *marketing professional, educator*

Merrillville
White, Dean *advertising executive*

Monroeville
Ray, Annette D. *executive secretary*

Muncie
Barber, Earl Eugene *management consultant*
Kuratko, Donald F. *entrepreneur, educator, consultant*
Norris, Tracy Hopkins *retired public relations executive*

Notre Dame
Conlon, Edward J. *management educator*

Santa Claus
Edwards, James Dallas, III, *consulting company executive*

Valparaiso
Blaschke, Lawrence Raymond *electronic security services professional*
Schlender, William Elmer *management sciences educator*

West Lafayette
Brey, Eric Trent *hospitality and tourism educator*
Schendel, Dan Eldon *management consultant, business educator*

IOWA

Ames
Bonomi, Ferne Gater *public relations executive*

Ankeny
Lamberti, Donald *convenience store executive*
Lynn, Robert William *strategic planning consultant*

Cedar Falls
Mitra, Atul *management consultant, educator*

Cedar Rapids
Nebergall, Donald Charles *management consultant*
Stepp, Waylon Gene *management consultant, retired municipal official*
Stolte, Larry Gene *marketing executive, former computer and publishing company executive*
Vanderpool, Ward Melvin *management and marketing consultant*
Weber, Frederick Edwin *management recruiter*
Wiese, Daniel Edward *marketing and communications researcher*

Davenport
Monty, Mitchell *landscape company executive*

Fairfield
Hawthorne, Timothy Robert *direct response advertising and communications company executive*
Kelly, Thomas *advertising executive*

George
Symens, Maxine Brinkert Tanner *retired marketing professional*

Kellogg
Anderson, Dale C. *state agency professional, travel consultant*

Milford
Fontaine, Sue (Jeane Fontaine) *public relations professional*

Spencer
Maranell, Debra Jean *human resources specialist, quality assurance professional, insurance agent*

West Des Moines
Marshall, Russell Frank *consulting company executive*

KANSAS

Colby
Baldwin, Irene S. *corporate executive, real estate investor*

Junction City
Werts, Merrill Harmon *retired management consultant*

Kansas City
Olofson, Tom William *computer executive*

Lawrence
Burke, Paul E., Jr., *governmental relations consultant*
Mackenzie, Kenneth Donald *management consultant, educator*

Leawood
Joslin, Janine Elizabeth *preservation consultant*

New Century
Huber, Dennis G. *communications executive*

Olathe
Graham, James C. *food service executive*

Overland Park
Campbell, Harry *communications executive*
Fuller, Michael B. *communications executive*
Gerke, Thomas A. *communications executive*

Hodge, Ralph J. *communications executive*
Javadi, Yousef B. *communications executive*
Kissinger, Jim *communications executive*
McEvoy, Thomas J. *communications executive*
Meyer, John P. *communications executive*
Molz, Philip Jack *management consultant*
Murphy, Thomas E. *communications executive*
Stout, Michael W. *communications executive*

Pittsburg
Trent, Darrell M. *academic and corporate executive*

Shawnee Mission
Hill, Lloyd L. *food service executive*
Mealman, Glenn *corporate marketing executive*
Putman, Dale Cornelius *management consultant, lawyer*

Topeka
Franklin, Benjamin Barnum *dinner club executive*
Sipes, Karen Kay *communications executive*
Vidricksen, Ben Eugene *food service executive, state legislator*

Wichita
Herr, Peter Helmut Friederich *sales executive*
Johnson, Steven M. *food service executive*
Menefee, Frederick Lewis *advertising executive*

Winfield
Dolsen, David Horton *mortician*

KENTUCKY

Albany
Smith, Eugenia Sewell *funeral home executive*

Ashland
Carter, David Edward *communications executive, director*

Bowling Green
Garrison, Geneva *retired administrative assistant*

Covington
Surber, David Francis *public relations executive, consultant, television producer, journalist*

Crestwood
Snow, Edwin Fawcett *management consultant*

Hopkinsville
Neville, Thomas Lee *food service company executive*

Lexington
Blanchard, Richard Emile, Sr., *retired management services executive, consultant*
Curlander, Paul Joseph *computer company executive*
Millard, James Kemper *marketing executive*
Scharlatt, Harold *management company executive*

Louisville
Bridgeman, Ulysses, Jr., *food service executive*
Brown, Owsley, II, *diversified consumer products company executive*
Campbell, Christian L. *restaurant company executive*
Columbus, Shanna S. *advertising executive*
Decker, Jack Neal *production executive*
Deno, David *restaurant executive*
Doran, Vincent Francis *economic development executive*
French, Michael Bruce *marketing executive*
Lewis, Aylwin B. *food service executive*
Novak, David C. *restaurant company executive*
Oh, Christopher J. *advertising executive*
Pearson, Andrall Edwin *food service executive*
Power, David M. *advertising executive*
Power, Michael L. *advertising executive*
Rawley, Charles E., III, *food service executive*
Wagner, James Miller *funeral director*
Wesley, Stephen Burton *training professional*

Murray
Glass, Mary Jean *quality assurance professional*

LOUISIANA

Baton Rouge
Finney, Clifton Donald *publishing executive*
Hewitt, Maureen Gilgore *scholarly book publishing executive*

Belle Chasse
Yandle, Sylvester Elwood, II, *sales executive*

Hammond
Richardson, Thaddeus Maurice *funeral director*

Lafayette
Sides, Larry Eugene *advertising executive*

Lake Charles
Premeaux, Shane Richard *marketing educator*

Mandeville
Klein, Bernard Joseph *management specialist*

Many
Dutton, Frank Elroy *data processing executive, writer*

Metairie
Doody, Barbara Pettett *computer specialist*
Feran, Russell G. *sales executive*
Gereighty, Andrea Saunders *polling company executive, poet*
Grimm, John Lloyd *marketing professional*
Nix, Linda Anne Bean *public relations executive*
Schwegmann, Melinda *supermarket executive, former state official*

New Orleans
Allerton, William, III, *public relations executive*
Brennan, Lally *food service executive*
Cook, Victor Joseph, Jr., *marketing educator, consultant*
Crumley, Martha Ann *company executive*
Johnson, Arnold Ray *public relations executive*
Kearney, Anne *chef*
Matthews, Brenda J. *human resources specialist*
Menutis, Jamie *training services executive, writer*
Prudhomme, Paul *chef, restaurant owner*
Simmons, Norbert A. *entertainment company executive*
Spicer, Susan *food service executive*
Tahir, Mary Elizabeth (Liz Tahir) *marketing professional, consultant, speaker, writer*
Williams, Ronald David *telecommunications executive*

Pineville
Cummings, Karen Sue *retired corrections classification administrator*

Ruston
Hudnall, Jarrett, Jr., *management and marketing educator*

Shreveport
Johnson, Kristen A. *public relations executive, not-for-profit fundraiser*
Sandifer, Kevin Wayne *archival services executive*
Wright, Marie Beulah Battey *retired advertising executive*

MAINE

Augusta
Jacobson, James Lamma, Jr., *data processing company executive*
Roberts, Donald Albert *advertising, public relations, marketing and media consultant*

Brooklin
Schmidt, Klaus Dieter *management consultant, university administrator, marketing and management educator*

Cape Neddick
Ksypka, Helen *organizational consultant*

Center Lovell
Adams, Herbert Ryan *management consultant, retired minister*

Ellsworth
Becker, Ray Everett *management consultant*

Falmouth
Kendrick, Peter Murray *communications executive, investor*
Winton, Linda *international trainer and consultant*

Hollis Center
Kaake, Norman Bradford *quality assurance professional*

Portland
Bride, John W. *communications executive, entrepreneur*
Burgess, Meredith Nancy Strang *advertising agency executive*
Rogers, Richard Mead *food service executive*

South Portland
Fetteroll, Eugene Carl, Jr., *human resources professional*

Sumner
Rudd, David William *management consultant, chemical engineer, consultant*

Westbrook
Lee, Shepard *automobile dealership owner*

Whitefield
Marden, Kenneth Allen *advertising executive*

MARYLAND

Annapolis
Branand, Claire Diane *advertising executive, writer*
Crosby, Ralph Wolf *communications executive*
DiPentima, Renato Anthony *systems executive*
Jefferson, Ralph Harvey *international affairs consultant*
Martino, Peter Dominic *financial software company executive, real estate developer, real estate broker, federal agency administrator, consultant*
Miller, Patricia A. *training services executive*

Baldwin
Decker, James Ludlow *management consultant*

Baltimore
Brotman, Phyllis Block *advertising and public relations executive*
Cosner, David Dale, Sr., *plastics industry executive, marketing executive*
Digges, Edward S(imms) *business management consultant*
Dodge, Calvert Renaul *education and training executive, author, educator*
Eisner, Henry Wolfgang *advertising agency executive*
Friedman, Maria Andre *public relations executive*
Howes, James Guerdon *communications company executive*
Hug, Richard Ernest *environmental company executive*
Kim, Lillian G. Lee *retired administrative assistant*
Laric, Michael Victor *marketing professional, management consultant*
Lowenthal, Henry *retired greeting card company executive*
Moloney, Herbert W., III, *advertising executive*
Pollard, Shirley *employment training director, community services administrator, consultant*
Robinson, Brooks Calbert, Jr., *former professional baseball player, TV commentator, business consultant*
Robinson, Florine Samantha *marketing executive*
Roland, Donald Edward *advertising executive*
Rolland, Donald F. *printing company executive*
Talbot, Donald Roy *consulting services executive*
Williams, Roy L. *public relations executive, advocate*

Beltsville
Brown, Louis M., Jr., *computer company executive*
Miller, Ted Robert *policy analyst*
Quirk, Frank Joseph *management consulting company executive*
Ritz, David M. *photographic retail company executive*

Bethesda
Bennett, Marcus C. *company executive*
Cody, Thomas Gerald *management consultant, writer*
Craig, Douglas Warren *professional services industry executive*
Cutting, Mary Dorothea *audio and audio-visual communications company executive*
Deane, Leon *retired company executive*
Durek, Thomas Andrew *computer company executive*
Johnson, Eugene Clare *data processing company executive*
Johnson, Thomas Dale *management consultant*
McClure, Brooks *management consultant*
Mc Gurn, Barrett *communications executive, writer*
Miller, Judith Wolfe Cohen *consultant*
Mukunda, Ram *communications executive*
Nassetta, Christopher J. *hotel facility executive*
Shellow, Robert *management service company executive, consultant*
Southwick, Paul *retired public relations executive*
Swartz, Gordon *management consultant*
Terragno, Paul James *information industry executive*
Walter, W. Edward *hotel executive, corporate financial executive*
Wolfe, William J. *management consultant*

Bozman
Wyatt, Wilson Watkins, Jr., *management and public affairs executive, writer*

Cambridge
Burke, Gerard Patrick *business executive, lawyer*
Spahr, Elizabeth *environmental services administrator*

Chestertown
Docksteader, Karen Kemp *marketing professional*
Schreiber, Harry, Jr., *management consultant*

Chevy Chase
Ashe, Aaron Matthew *sales professional*
Baruch, Jordan Jay *management consultant*
Broide, Mace Irwin *retired public affairs consultant*
Michaelis, Michael *management and technical consultant*

Clinton
Brooks, Pauline C. *computer and networking services company executive*

Cockeysville Hunt Valley
Whitehurst, William Wilfred, Jr., *management consultant*

Columbia
Madison, Anne Conway *public relations and marketing professional*
Morice, William Daniel *business and tax counselor*
Singerman, Phillip A. *corporate executive*

Easton
U'Ren, Marie Rita *travel company executive, pre-school educator*

Elkridge
Zheng, Wenxin *fiber optic communication specialist*

Elkton
Jasinski-Caldwell, Mary L. *company executive*

Forest Hill
McIntosh, L(orne) William *marketing executive*

Fort Washington
Bradley, Melvin LeRoy *communications company executive*
Satterthwaite, George, II, *security firm executive*
Simpson, Raven C. *administrative assistant*

Frederick
Boyd, Joseph Aubrey *communications company executive*

Gaithersburg
Carey, John Edward *information services executive*
Ehrlich, Clifford John *Internet company executive*
Kress, Jill Clancy *human resources professional, consultant*
Landel, Michel *food service and management company executive*
Wohl, Ronald H. *management consultant, writing and editorial expert*

Germantown
Isaacson, Elaine Marie *sales and training agent*
Isbister, James David *pharmaceutical business executive*

Glen Arm
Lotz, George Michael *retired computer graphics executive, graphic designer, photographer*

Greenbelt
Fontaine, Kathleen Sturey *policy analyst*

Hunt Valley
Deieso, Donald Allan *environmental goods and services executive*

Jessup
Fox, Dawne Marie *safety scientist*

Kensington
Hum, Vance York *technology consulting executive*

Lanham Seabrook
Klein, Stephen *recreational fee-based club executive*
Liggins, Alfred C., III, *broadcasting company executive*
Plotnick, Stanley D. *recreational fee-based club executive*

Marydel
Neil, Fred Applestein *public relations executive*

Mitchellville
Akridge, Paul Bai *business consultant*

Montgomery Village
Molloy, Angela Margaret *advertising, marketing, and public relations executive*

Myersville
Patrick, Georgia O'Brien Lakaytis *communications executive*

Oakland
Cavarocchi, Nicholas Guy *public relations executive*

Ocean City
Phillips, Shirley Flowers *food service executive*

Owings Mills
Uleau, Thomas F. *corporate executive*

Potomac
Benton, Kay Myers *sales executive*
Fink, Daniel Julien *management consultant*
Foley, Joseph Patrick *public relations executive*
Medin, A. Louis *computer company executive*
Orski, C. Kenneth *consulting company executive, lawyer, publisher*
Owen, Harrison Hollingsworth *management consultant*
Rhode, Alfred Shimon *business consultant, finance educator*
Shirvinski, Adam John *management consultant*

Reisterstown
Donaho, John Albert *consultant*

Riverdale
Bernard, Cathy S. *management corporation executive*
Gonzalez Arias, Victor Hugo *management executive*

Rockville
Bainum, Stewart William, Jr., *health care and lodging company executive*
MacArthur, Diana Taylor *advanced technology executive*
Rourke, Bradley Kevin *public affairs executive*
Schneider, Steven L. *information company executive*
Smith, Mark Alan *management consultant*
Watson, Jerome Roland *marketing professional, researcher*

Severna Park
Humphreys Troy, Patricia *communications executive*

Shady Side
Devine, Donald J. *management and political consultant*

Silver Spring
Altschul, B J *public relations counselor*
Compton, Mary Beatrice Brown (Mrs. Ralph Theodore Compton) *public relations executive, writer*
Cunningham, Keith Allen, II, *computer services company executive*
Fields, Daisy Bresley *human resources specialist, writer*
Hubbell, Katherine Jean *retired marketing professional*
Kenner, Mary Ellen *marketing and communications executive*
Landry, Donald J. *hotel executive*
Ledsinger, Charles A. *hotel executive*
Perlmutter, Jerome Herbert *communications specialist*
Raphael, Coleman *business consultant*
Saunders, George Wendell *management consultant, retired government official*
Shih-Carducci, Joan Chia-mo *cooking educator, biochemist, medical technologist, author, writer*

Sparks
Rallo, James Gilbert *management company executive*

Stevensville
Barrett, John Anthony *publishing and printing company financial executive*

Sudlersville
Covington, Donald Kingsley, Jr., *plywood sales executive*

Timonium
Deise, Martin Van *management consultant*

Towson
Passano, E. Magruder, Jr., *strategic planning consultant*

Upper Marlboro
Symlar, Jesse Lee *executive*

West Bethesda
Vogelgesang, Sandra Louise *business executive, writer, consultant*

West River
Pratt, Katherine Merrick *environmental consulting company executive*

White Hall
Buhite, Thomas Jesse, Sr., *employee benefits consultant*

MASSACHUSETTS

Acton
Munson, Lawrence Shipley *management consultant*

Andover
Hasegawa, Tomohiro *marketing manager*

Ayer
Bloom, Edwin John, Jr., *retired human resources consultant*

Bedford
Daltas, Arthur John *management consultant, software services manager*
Webber, Howard Rodney *computer company executive*

Belchertown
Burstein, Michael Clifford *management consultant*
Marsh, Brian Richard *management executive, playwright, educator, clergyman*

Belmont
Bingham, George Walter Chandler *retired sales executive*
Klein, Martin Samuel *management consulting executive*
McGaw, Bridger E. *management consultant*

Beverly
Barger, Richard Wilson *hotel executive*
Ozzie, Ray *Internet company executive*

Billerica
Wacker-Brawley, Margaret *communications executive*

Bolton
Leighton, Charles Milton *retired specialty consumer products executive*

Boston
Andrews, Kenneth Richmond *business administration educator*
Argyropoulos, Ursula *food service executive*
Arnold, David John *marketing educator, consultant*
Berger, Jerome Morris *communications executive*
Berliner, Harvey P. *sales executive*
Berman, Lisa *advertising executive*
Bertino, Fred *advertising executive*
Brodeur, John *public relations executive*
Bronner, Michael *advertising executive, education assistance company executive*
Buchin, Stanley Ira *management consultant, finance educator*
Clarke, Terence Michael *public relations and advertising executive*
Coady, Nicole *food service executive*
Cone, Carol Lynn *public relations executive*
Connors, Jack, Jr., *advertising executive*
Connors, John Michael, Jr., *advertising agency executive*
Copithorne, David A. *public relations executive*
Cornwall, Deborah Joyce *consulting firm executive, management consultant*
Coutermarsh, Eva Marina *personnel executive*
Coville, Andrea *public relations executive*
Cutter, Curtis Carly *consulting company executive*
DeGraan, Edward F. *consumer products company executive*
Domini, Amy Lee *trustee*
Dowd, Peter Jerome *public relations executive*
Eskandarian, Edward *advertising agency executive*
Finucane, Anne M. *communications and marketing executive*
FitzGerald, Maura *public relations executive*
Gadiesh, Orit *management consulting executive*
Gasson, David S. *communications executive*
Ghirardi, James *communications executive*
Gray, Carla *marketing professional*
Hallagan, Robert E. *management consultant*
Hamersley, Gordon *food service executive*
Hardy, Victoria Elizabeth *management educator*
Hayes, Andrew Wallace, II, *consumer products company executive*
Hunter, Durant Adams *executive search company executive*
Hurd, J. Nicholas *executive recruiting consultant, former banker*
Judson, Arnold Sidney *management consultant*
Kaplan, Steven F. *business management executive*
Kelly, Francis J., III, *global marketing company president and COO*
Kenny, David *internet professional services executive*
Kilts, James M. *consumer products company executive*
Lawner, Ron *advertising executive*
Levy, Stephen Raymond *high technology company executive*
Luongo, C. Paul *public relations executive*
Lynch, Barbara *chef, restaurant owner*
McClelland, Frank *chef, restaurant owner*
McGovern, Patrick J. *communications executive*
Merullo-Boaz, Lisa Helen *marketing and fundraising executive*
Metcalfe, Robert M. *communications executive*
Oringer, Kenneth *chef, restaurant owner*
Pantano, Dick *advertising executive*
Porter, Michael E. *competitive strategy educator*
Pytka, Stephen Milton *office equipment executive*
Regis, Susan *food service executive*
Rimpel, Auguste Eugene, Jr., *management and technical consulting executive*
Rosen, David Michael *public relations administrator, public affairs consultant*
Sander, Alison Bishop *international consultant*
Saunders, Donald Leslie *hotel owner, real estate investor*
Schlow, Michael *food service executive*
Schneider, Joan *public relations company owner*
Shapiro, Eli *business consultant, educator, economist*
Shire, Lydia *food service executive*
Swaysland, Janet *advertising executive*
Tarantino, Louis Gerald *business executive, consultant, lawyer*
Tyszkowski, Robert *business executive*
Weber, Larry *public relations executive*
Wu, Guofa Felix *computer company executive*

Brookline
Martel, Lisa *food service executive*

Brookline Village
Frankenthaler, Stan *food service executive*

Burlington
Coffin, George Jarvis, III, *advertising executive*
Reeve, Pamela *communications executive*

Cambridge
Adams, Jody *chef, restaurant owner*
Altshuler, David T. *software company executive*
de Monteiro, Nadsa *chef*
Flaschen, David Jenkin Steward *venture capitalist*
Johnson, Steve *chef, restaurant owner*
Kelly, John Francis *company executive*
Kilpatrick, Maureen *food service executive*
Knickrehm, Glenn Allen *management executive*
Lauzier, Marijean *public relations executive*
Lydon, Amanda *chef*
Manzi, Jim P. *computer software company executive*
McBride, Robert Albert *training services executive*
Paicopolos, Ernest Michael *public opinion research company executive*
Rowley, Geoffrey Herbert *management consultant*
Sapienza, Tony *public relations executive*
Schlesinger, Chris *food service executive*
Shine, Daniel Joseph, Jr., *management consultant*
Sortun, Ana *food service executive*
Thompson, Doreen *public relations executive*
White, Jasper *food service executive*
Zollar, Alfred *computer company executive*

Canton
Pitts, Virginia M. *human resources executive*

Centerville
Shapiro, Harvey *journalist, writer, lyricist*

Charlestown
Wetherell, David S. *communications executive*

Chatham
Escalante, Judson Robert *business consultant*

Chelmsford
Fulks, Robert Grady *computer company executive*

Chestnut Hill
Ayas, Karen *management consultant, educator*
O'Block, Robert Paul *management consultant*
Rosensaft, Lester Jay *management consultant, lawyer, consultant*

Concord
Davies, Michael A. M. *management consultant*
Emerson, Richard B. *marketing company executive*
Ghosh, Partha S. *management consultant*

Danvers
Wilkes, Brent Ames *management consultant*

Dedham
Magner, Jerome Allen *entertainment company executive*
Redstone, Sumner Murray *entertainment company executive, lawyer*

Dorchester
Daniels, Richard J. *communications executive*

Dover
Bonis, Laszlo Joseph *business executive, scientist*
Mehta, Narinder Kumar *marketing executive*

Duxbury
Albritton, William Hoyle *training and consulting executive, lecturer, writer*
Erickson, Phyllis Traver *marketing executive*

Fall River
Washburn, Stewart Putnam *management consultant*

Falmouth
Nolan, Edmund Francis *management consultant*

Framingham
Bloom, Ted *communications executive*
Carrigan, Robert *technology media company executive*
Donovan, R. Michael *management consultant*
Hillman, Carol Barbara *communications executive, consultant*
Wulf, Sharon Ann *management consultant*

Gloucester
Hausman, William Ray *fund raising and management consultant*
Marolda, Anthony Joseph *management consulting company executive*
Means, Rosaline *business executive, business educator*

Hingham
Macchia, David Alan *management consultant*

Housatonic
Gilder, George Franklin *communications executive, writer*

Lexington
Brick, Donald Bernard *software company executive*
Fray, Lionel Louis *management consultant*
Hurd, Philip Justin *executive search consultant*
Peden, Keith J. *human resources specialist*
Piano, Phyllis J. *communications executive*
Spero, Rand Kevin *management consultant*

Longmeadow
Locklin, Wilbert Edwin *management consultant*

Malden
Jiang, Yong Ping *research scientist*

Marblehead
Phillips, Peter Lawrence *communications executive*

Marlborough
Illson, James Elias *management consultant*

Medway
Saenger, Bruce Walter *consulting firm executive*

Melrose
McLennan, Bernice Claire *human resources professional*

Needham
Grasso, James Anthony *public relations executive, educator*

New Bedford
Soares, Carl Lionel *quality assurance professional, metrologist*

Newton
Benner, Mary Wright *event planner*
Meador, Charles Lawrence *management and systems consultant, educator*

North Attleboro
Zani, Frederick Caesar *retired corporate consultant*

North Reading
Day, Ronald Elwin *consulting executive*

Norton
Holden, William *food service executive*

Norwell
Case, David Knowlton *management consultant*

Norwood
Fishman, Jerald G. *semiconductor executive*

Oak Bluffs
Lamb, Robert *industrial executive*

Peabody
Bierman, George William *technical consulting executive, food technologist*
Finch, Rogers Burton *association management consultant*
Gordon, Bernard M. *computer company executive*

Pittsfield
Glazer, Michael L. *consumer products company executive*
Wenner, Gene Charles *arts management executive*

Quincy
Hall, John Raymond, Jr., *fire protection executive*
Levin, Robert Joseph *retail grocery chain store executive*
Young, Richard William *corporate director*

Randolph
Boers, Celia Ann *public relations executive*
Huntington, Robert Howard *business management executive*

Rehoboth
Spooner, Russell Edward *retired printing company executive*

Rockport
Wiberg, Lars-Erik *occupational compatibility consultant*

Sheffield
Velmans, Loet Abraham *retired public relations executive*

Sherborn
Hancock, William Frank, Jr., *management consultant*

South Hadley
Colino, Richard Ralph *communications consultant*

Springfield
Ervin, Billy Maxwell *management consultant*
Vincensi, Avis A. *sales executive, medical educator*

Stow
Langenwalter, Gary Allan *manufacturing and management consulting company executive*

Tewksbury
Foley, Sylvester Robert, III, *human resources specialist, retired military officer*

Waban
Portuondo, Jose Francisco *management consultant*
Rossolimo, Alexander Nicholas *management consultant, business executive, corporate director*

Wakefield
Brady, Patrick *advertising executive*

Walpole
Coleman, John Joseph *telephone company executive*

Waltham
Buchholz, William James *communications executive, educator*
Pocock, J. Michael *consumer products company executive*
Schwartz, Paula Mae *communications company executive*
Schwartz, Steven Mark *marketing executive*
Turillo, Michael Joseph, Jr., *management consultant*

Wayland
Blair, John *consultant*

Wellesley
Heisler, Elwood Douglas *hotel executive*
Mitchell, Donald Wayne *management consultant, investment manager, lawyer, writer*
Tierney, Thomas J. *social entrepreneur*

Wellesley Hills
Coco, Samuel Barbin *venture consultant*

Wenham
Johnson, Alan B. *advertising executive*

West Chatham
Rhinesmith, Stephen Headley *management consultant*

Westford
Endyke, Debra Joan *data communications marketing professional*

Weston
Goldstein, Arthur Louis *retired water purification company executive*
Stambaugh, Armstrong A., Jr., *restaurant and hotel executive*

Westport
Norcross, Alvin Watt *retired personnel administrator, consultant*

Westwood
Daley, Charles Mike *consumer products company executive*

Williamstown
Driscoll, Genevieve Bosson (Jeanne Bosson Driscoll) *management and organization development consultant*
Sprague, John Louis *management consultant*

Wilmington
D'Alene, Alixandria Frances *human resources professional*

Winchester
Ferrera, Arthur Rocco *food distribution company executive*

Woburn
Mehra, Raman Kumar *aerospace and defense technology executive, automation and control engineering researcher*
Paul, Lois *public relations company executive*

Worcester
Camougis, George *health, safety and environmental consultant*
Candib, Murray A. *business executive, retail management consultant*

Yarmouth Port
Mitchell, Garry *management consultant, writer*

MICHIGAN

Ada
Brenner, David H. *marketing executive*
Lyall, Lynn *consumer products company executive*
Van Andel, Jay *direct selling company executive*
Van Andel, Steve Alan *consumer products company executive*

Ann Arbor
Agno, John G. *management consultant*
Bachelder, Cheryl Anne *marketing professional*
Belcher, Louis David *marketing and operations executive, former mayor*
Brandon, David A. *food service executive/restaurant manager*
Bryant, Barbara Everitt *academic researcher, market research consultant, former federal agency administrator*
Flint, H. Howard, II, *printing company executive*
Gannon, Michael J. *printing company executive*
Lindsay, June Campbell McKee *communications executive*
Martin, Claude Raymond, Jr., *marketing consultant, educator*
McGinn, Terence James *business consultant, minister*
Nikoui, Hossein Reza *quality assurance professional*
Oliver, Marguerite Bertoni *food service executive*
Silverman, Harry J. *pizza delivery company executive*

Auburn Hills
MacDonald, John *marketing executive*

Birmingham
Wagner, Bruce Stanley *marketing professional*

Bloomfield Hills
Abel Horowitz, Michelle Susan *advertising executive*
Adams, Charles Francis *advertising executive, real estate company executive*
Berline, James H. *advertising executive, public relations executive*
Bithell, Thomas Charles *human resources specialist, insurance consultant*
Czarnecki, Walter P. *truck rental company executive*
Sandy, William Haskell *training and communication systems executive*
Weil, John William *technology management consultant*

Canton
Wickus, James D. *food service executive*

Charlotte
Young, Everett J. *management consultant, agricultural economist*

Comstock Park
Harris, R(ichard) Steven *data processing executive, consultant, educator*

Dearborn
Ardisana, Beth *communications company executive*
Byars, Leisa *marketing professional, automotive executive*

Detroit
Barden, Don H. *communications executive*
Demos, Dave *marketing executive*
Engelhardt, Regina *cosmetologist, artist, small business owner*
Guarascio, Philip *advertising executive*
Harris, Steven Jay *public relations executive*
Ilitch, Denise *food services executive*
McCracken, Caron Francis *information technology consultant*
McWhorter, Sharon Louise *business executive, inventor, consultant*
Middlebrook, John G. *marketing executive, advertising executive*
Ponder, Dan *public relations executive*
Rosenau, Pete *public relations executive*
Schweitzer, Peter *advertising agency executive*
Sufalko, Dynah Naomi Juliette *marketing professional*
Tallet, Margaret Anne *theatre executive*
Wilson, Henry Arthur, Jr., *management consultant*

East Lansing
La Ferle, Carrie *advertising executive, educator*

Miracle, Gordon Eldon *advertising educator*
Torto, Christopher *communications executive*
Wilson, R. Dale *marketing educator, consultant*

Farmington
Dixson, J. B. *communications executive*

Farmington Hills
Bassett, Tina *communications executive*
Benedict, Elise *moving company executive*
Yagahashi, Takashi *chef*

Flushing
Bain, William David *electronics systems technician, writer*

Grand Rapids
Baker, Frank C. (Buzz Baker) *advertising executive*
Bruyn, Kimberly Ann *public relations executive, consultant*
Glinski, Timothy P. *computer company executive*
Gordon, Dan *food service executive*
Mbah, Chris H.N. *business educator*
Messner, James W. *advertising executive*
Plakmeyer, Steve *food service executive*
Portelli, Vincent George *business executive, consultant*
Purchase-Owens, Francena *human resources specialist, educator*
Sadler, David G(ary) *management executive*
Seyferth, Virginia M. *public relations executive*
Smith, Bill *advertising and marketing executive*
Spaulding, Dan *public relations executive*
Zimmerman, John *public relations executive*

Grosse Pointe
Blevins, William Edward *management consultant*

Grosse Pointe Park
Krebs, William Hoyt *industrial hygienist, health science association administrator*

Grosse Pointe Shores
Caldwell, John Thomas, Jr., *communications executive*

Grosse Pointe Woods
Cusmano, J. Joyce *public relations executive*

Hastings
Jones, Kensinger *advertising executive*

Holland
Mc Gurk, James Henry *consultant company executive*

Kalamazoo
Gilchrist, James A. *communication educator*
Lawrence, William Joseph, Jr., *retired corporate executive*

Keego Harbor
Gee, Sharon Lynn *funeral director, educator*

Lincoln Park
Kissel, Kevin Karl *warehouse manager, freelance/self-employed writer*

Livonia
Barfield, Jon E. *employment company executive*
Chowdhury, Subir *business executive, author, researcher*
Maibach, Ben C., Jr., *service executive*

Lupton
Scott, George Alfred *advertising executive, writer*

Madison Heights
Woodruff, Jane *sales executive*

Marquette
Pesola, William Ernest *restaurant management executive*

Midland
Maneri, Remo R. *management consultant*
Sosville, Dick *sales and marketing executive*

Novi
Kinsey, Charles John *industrial auctioneer, consultant, cattle breeder, farmer*

Port Sanilac
Birdsall, Arthur Anthony *management consultant*

Rochester Hills
Pfister, Karl Anton *industrial company executive*

Rockford
Knape, Herbert Fritz *business executive*

Royal Oak
Stanalajczo, Greg Charles *computer and technology company executive*

Saint Ignace
Dodson, Bruce J. *funeral director*

Southfield
Amladi, Prasad Ganesh *management consulting executive, health care consultant, researcher*
Caponigro, Jeffrey Ralph *public relations counselor*
Hudson, Cheryl L. *communications executive*
Jackson, Michael B. *service company executive*
Jackson, William Gene *computer company executive*
Kalter, Alan *advertising agency executive*
Koch, Albert Acheson *management consultant*

Southgate
Kohn, Julieanne *travel agent*

Taylor
Barry, Alan H. *consumer products company executive*
Wadhams, Timothy *consumer products company executive*

Traverse City
Bagley, Colleen *marketing executive*

Troy
Adderley, Terence E. *personnel director*
Baker, Ernest Waldo, Jr., *advertising executive*
Harrison, Christine Delane *company executive*
Hill, Richard A. *advertising executive*
Lorencz, Mary *public relations executive*
McLaren, Karen Lynn *advertising executive*
Meyers, Christine Laine *marketing and media executive, consultant*
White, Tommi A. *human resources firm executive*

Walled Lake
Gillespie, J. Martin *sales and distribution company executive*

Warren
Gervason, Robert J *advertising executive*
Gilbert, Suzanne Harris *advertising executive*
Hopp, Anthony James *advertising agency executive*
Zoubareff, Kathy Olga *administrative assistant*

West Bloomfield
Lewis, Harold Allen *childcare company executive*
Smith, Nancy Hohendorf *retired sales and marketing executive*

White Cloud
De Haan-Puls, Joyce Elaine *sales account representative, educator*

MINNESOTA

Austin
Budd, Jim *communications manager*

Bemidji
Nohner, Allen M. *corporate communications specialist*

Bloomington
Jeffries, Mary *public relations executive*
Miller, Kevin Robert *employee benefit consultant*
Norris, William C. *retired computer systems executive*

Chaska
Knapp, Peggy Durda *international company administrator*

Eden Prairie
Cervilla, Constance Marlene *marketing consultant*
Erickson, Kim *consumer products company executive*
Harmel, Paul *photography company executive*
Johnson, Howard Arthur, Jr., *corporate executive, operations analyst, financial officer*
Petersen, Maureen Jeanette Miller *management information consultant, former nurse*
Verdoorn, D.R. (Sid) *food service executive*

Edina
Burdick, Lou Brum *public relations executive*

Farmington
Wurdeman, Lew Edward *Internet company executive, consultant*

Hastings
Avent, Sharon L. Hoffman *manufacturing company executive*

Lake Crystal
Pawlitschek, Donald Paul *business consultant*

Mahtomedi
Brainerd, Richard Charles *human resources executive, consultant, educator*

Mankato
Schreier, Bradley *sales executive, marketing executive*
Taylor, Glen A. *printing, direct mail and technology company executive, professional sports team executive*

Minneapolis
Agyenkwah, Kennedy Seth *communications executive*
Beardsley, John Ray *public relations firm executive*
Bergeson, James *advertising executive*
Bird, Dick *sign painter*
Bonner, Brigid Ann *marketing professional*
Bonneville, Katherine Ann *human resources specialist, consultant*
Cameron, Patricia *advertising executive*
Casey, Lynn M. *public relations executive*
Courtney, Eugene Whitmal *computer company executive*
Diemand, Kim Eugene *human resources executive*
Doherty, Valerie *employment services professional, lawyer*
Dunlap, William DeWayne, Jr., *advertising agency executive*
Eich, Susan *public relations executive*
Eickhoff, John R. *information services company executive*
Fallon, Patrick R. *advertising executive*
Gage, Edwin C., III, (Skip Gage) *travel and marketing services executive*
Gavin, Sara *public relations executive*
Johnson, Lola Norine *retired advertising and public relations executive, educator*
Koutsky, Dean Roger *advertising executive*
Lenzmeier, Allen U. *consumer products company executive*
Liszt, Howard Paul *advertising executive*
Lynch, Leland T. *advertising executive*
Mouser, Les *advertising executive*
Nelson, Marilyn C. *hotel executive, travel company executive, food service executive, marketing professional*
Perlman, Lawrence *retired business executive, corporate director, consultant*
Pohlad, Robert C. *consumer products company executive*
Roth, Thomas *marketing executive*
Sanger, Stephen W. *consumer products company executive*
Schultz, Louis Edwin *management consultant*
Spong, Douglas K. *public relations executive*
Stage, Brian *hotel executive*
Sullivan, Michael Patrick *food service executive*
Tandon, Rajiv *training company executive*
Tunheim, Kathryn H. *public relations executive*
Turner, Ronald L. *information services executive*
Veblen, Thomas Clayton *management consultant*
Viault, Raymond G. *food company executive*
Westbrook, Bill *advertising executive*
Wickesberg, Albert Klumb *retired management educator*
Yourzak, Robert Joseph *management consultant, engineer, educator*
Zimmermann, Robert Laurence *marketing professional*

Minnetonka
Bissell, Brent John *advertising and direct marketing executive*
Cross, Bonham E(lwood) *retired newspaper account executive*
Curtis, C. *hotel executive*
Gillies, Donald Richard *marketing and advertising consultant, educator*
Kostka, Ronald Wayne *marketing consultant*
Schmidt, Russel Alan, II, *sales executive*

New Brighton
Grieman, John Joseph *communications executive*

New Hope
Olson, Clifford Larry *management consultant, entrepreneur*

North Mankato
Kozitza, William *printing company executive*

North Oaks
Blaha, Verle Dennis *golf course executive, electrical engineer*

Oakdale
Cederburg, Barbara M. *printing company executive*
Monahan, William T. *computer company executive*

Pequot Lakes
Gray, Allen (Ernest Bungaard) *radio executive*

Plymouth
Redgrave, Martyn Robert *hotel, food service executive*

Richfield
Schuett, Carol Ann *travel industry business analyst*

Rochester
Hiniker, LuAnn *management consultant, educator, researcher, grants consultant*
Nevling, Harry Reed *human resources consultant*

Saint Cloud
Gangopadhyay, Partha *management consultant*

Saint Louis Park
Wikman, Michael Raymond *advertising executive*

Saint Paul
Axelrod, Leonard *management consultant*
Baker, Douglas M., Jr., *service industry executive*
Boehnen, David Leo *food service executive, lawyer*
Brooks, Phillip *advertising executive*
Feinberg, David Erwin *publishing company executive*
Forshay, Steven R. *marketing professional, consultant*
Fritze, Steven L. *service industry executive*
Hill, James Stanley *computer consulting company executive*

Wayzata
Schoen, Charles Judd *service executive*
Waldera, Wayne Eugene *crisis management specialist*

Willmar
Norling, Rayburn *food service executive*

Woodbury
Fiedler, Robert Max *management consultant*

MISSISSIPPI

Bay Saint Louis
Torguson, Marlin F. *entertainment company executive*

Biloxi
Culberson, Gary Michael *hotel manager*
Love, James Sanford, III, *communications executive*

Carriere
Woodmansee, Glenn Edward *employee relations executive*

Columbus
Holt, Robert Ezel *data processing executive*
Labensky, Sarah Ross *culinary educator*

Jackson
Molpus, Dick H. *management company executive*
Patterson, Chan *food service executive*
Walker, Earl *food service executive*

Olive Branch
Frischenmeyer, Michael Leo *sales executive*

Ridgeland
Lewis, Larry Lisle *human resources specialist company executive*

Sumrall
Hudson, Mary Kay *business executive*

University
Potts, Marjorie *executive secretary, systems support specialist*

MISSOURI

Ballwin
Macauley, Edward C. *retired company executive*

Cape Girardeau
Smallwood, Glenn Walter, Jr., *utility marketing management executive*

Carthage
Workman, Leatta Ardyce *management consultant*

Clayton
Davis, William Albert *theme park director*
Vecchiotti, Robert Anthony *management and organizational consultant*

Fenton
Kienker, James W. *marketing executive*
Lipovsky, Robert P. *marketing executive*
Maritz, W. Stephen *marketing professional, service executive*

Golden City
Howard, Joanne Frances *marketing executive, researcher, funeral director*

Independence
Evans, Margaret Ann *human resources administrator, business owner*

Kansas City
Adams, Beverly Josephine *data processing specialist*
Baker, Ronald Phillip *service company executive*
Bartlett, Sherie *printing company executive*
Courson, Marna B.P. *public relations executive*
Dillingham, John Allen *marketing professional*
Druten, Robert S. *greeting card company executive*
Grossman, Jerome Barnett *retired service firm executive*
Hall, Donald Joyce, Sr., *greeting card company executive*
Hall, Donald Joyce, Jr., *consumer products company executive*
Kovac, F. Peter *advertising executive*
Kuhn, Whitey *advertising executive*
McElwreath, Sally Chin *corporate communications executive*
O'Shields, Charlie *marketing professional*
Robertson, Leon H. *management consultant, educator*
Smiley, David Bruce *administrative director*
Stevens, Jane *advertising executive*
Stowers, James W., III, *data processing executive*
Warakomski, Alphonse Walter Joseph, Jr., *sales executive, marketing professional*
Wittenborn, Dale *advertising executive*
Woodson, Stephen William *collection agency executive*

Lake Saint Louis
Dommermuth, William Peter *marketing consultant, educator*

Liberty
McCaslin, W.C. *products and packaging executive*

Monett
Henry, Michael E. *computer company executive*

North Kansas City
Davis, Michael Leonard *private investigator, consultant*

O Fallon
Ractliffe, Robert Edward George *management executive*

Raymore
Mehl, Donald Edward *retired marketing professional*

Saint Charles
Kelly, James Joseph *printing company executive*
Wagner, Mary Ann *human resources executive*
Wittmeyer, Richard Arthur *management consulting company executive*

Saint Louis
Adams, W. Randolph, Jr., *management consultant*
Anderson, Halvor *corporate officer*
Arnold, John Edward *marketing executive, consultant, financial planner*
Bateman, Sharon Louise *public relations executive*
Bellville, Margaret (Maggie Bellville) *communications executive*
Burgess, William Patrick *management consultant*
Davis, Irvin *advertising, public relations, broadcast executive*
Drury, Charles Louis, Jr., *hotel executive*
Epner, Steven Arthur *computer consultant*
Ferguson, Gary Warren *retired public relations executive*
Fosher, Donald Hobart *marketing professional, inventor*
Graham, John Dalby *public relations executive*
Handelman, Alice Samuels *public relations professional, writer*
Kennedy, Craig *rental company executive*
Kent, Jerald L. *communications company executive*
Khoury, George Gilbert *printing company executive, baseball association executive*
Lents, Peggy Iglauer *marketing professional*
Loynd, Richard Birkett *consumer products company executive*
Lyons, Gordon *marketing executive*
Musial, Stan(ley) (Frank Musial) *hotel and restaurant executive, former baseball team executive, former baseball player*
Provost, Cheryl Louise Winters *account executive*
Riley, Michael Robert *marketing and business development executive*
Rosen, Fred *travel company executive*
Schnuck, Scott C. *grocery store executive*
Shevitz, Mark H. *sales promotion and marketing executive*
Sibbald, John Ristow *management consultant*
Stork, Donald Arthur *advertising executive*
Taylor, Andrew C. *rental and leasing company executive*
Taylor, Jack C. *rental and leasing company executive*
Tyler, William Howard, Jr., *advertising executive, educator*

Vandiver, Donna *public relations executive*
Van Luven, William Robert *management consultant*
Waterbury, Jackson DeWitt *retired marketing executive*

Springfield
Hammons, John Q. *hotel executive*
Noble, Robert B. *advertising executive*
Witherspoon, John Thomas *water resources consultant*

Warrenton
Dapron, Elmer Joseph, Jr., *communications executive*

MONTANA

Belgrade
Aveson, Martha Caralyn *pharmaceutical company executive*

Helena
Waterman, Mignon Redfield *public relations executive, state legislator*

Kalispell
Gualandris, Fabio Luigi *company executive*

NEBRASKA

Bellevue
Jackson, Alan William *consulting company executive, educator*

Lincoln
Hays, Michael D. *research company executive*

Omaha
Brailey, Susan Louise *quality analyst, educator*
Caggiano, Joseph *advertising executive*
Clifton, James K. *market research company executive*
Eggers, James Wesley *executive search consultant*
Frazier, Chet June *advertising agency executive*
Gupta, Vinod *business lists company executive*
O'Donnell, James P. *food service executive*
Phares, Lynn Levisay *public relations communications executive*
Roskens, Ronald William *international business consultant*
Stubblefield, Robert F. *travel agency executive*

NEVADA

Henderson
Bruno, Cathy Eileen *management consultant, former state official, social sciences educator*
Cohan, George Sheldon *advertising and public relations executive*
Goldstein, Morris *retired entertainment company executive*
Klink, Karin Elizabeth *medical communications company executive, writer*
Roll, Irwin Clifford (Win Roll) *advertising, marketing and publishing executive*

Incline Village
Moore, Patricia Ann *medical technology investor, consultant*

Las Vegas
Adelson, Sheldon G. *hotel executive*
Arce, Phillip William *hotel and casino executive*
Atwood, Charles L. *recreational facility executive*
Basile, Richard Emanuel *retired management consultant, educator*
Beagles, Dorothy Boetticher *office administrator, homeopathic consultant*
Blau, Elizabeth Anne *restaurant executive*
Bolt, J. *communications executive*
Boyle, Carolyn Moore *public relations executive, marketing communications manager*
Collis, Kay Lynn *sales executive*
Connolly, Owen Robert *sales and business consultant*
Crevelt, Dwight Eugene *computer company executive*
Deasy, Jacqueline Hildegard *management consultant*
Ensign, Michael S. *resort company executive*
Gallagher, Thomas Edmund *hotel executive, lawyer*
Goodwin, Nancy Lee *corporate executive*
Griesche, Robert Price *hospital purchasing executive*
Hardie, George Graham *casino executive*
Jacobs, Gary N. *hotel executive, lawyer*
Landau, Ellis *gaming company executive*
Lanni, J(oseph) Terrence *hotel corporation executive*
Litman, Brian David *communications executive*
Loveman, Gary W. *gaming company executive*
Marmann, Sigrid *software development company executive*
Mataseje, Veronica Julia *sales executive*
Murren, James Joseph *recreational facility executive, hotel executive*
Neilsen, Craig H. *hotel executive*
Rowe, Carl Osborn *business consultant*
Satre, Philip Glen *casino entertainment executive, lawyer*
Schaeffer, Glenn William *casino corporate financial executive*
Shively, Judith Carolyn (Judy Shively) *contract administrator*
Sorrell, Michael E. *consulting company executive, hospitality executive*
Springer, Christine Gibbs *management consultant, business owner, educator*
Stanley, Tim *recreational facility executive*
Stark, S. Daniel, Jr., *gaming industry executive*
Thill, John Val *communications professional, writer, consultant*
Wade, Daniel M. *recreational facility executive, hotel executive*
Welter, William Michael *marketing and advertising executive*
Wilmott, Timothy J. *recreational facility executive*
Wynn, Stephen A. *hotel, entertainment facility executive*

Reno
Adams, Kenneth Robert *gaming analyst, writer, consultant, historian*
Chase, Shelley Lynne *management consultant*
Ford, Victoria *retired public relations executive, writer, oral historian*
Munro, Roderick Anthony *business improvement coach*
Perry, Anthony Frank *entertainment company executive, printing company executive, graphic designer*
Sklar, Louise Margaret *computer company executive*
Zadra, Sharon Kay *business development professional*

NEW HAMPSHIRE

Bedford
Hall, Pamela S. *environmental consulting firm executive*
Steadman, David Rosslyn Ayton *business executive, corporate director*

Center Harbor
Shaw, Robert William, Jr., *management consultant, venture capitalist*

Concord
Roberts, George Bernard, Jr., *management and government relations consultant, former state legislator*

Deering
Spitzer, Morton Edward *management consultant*

Fitzwilliam
Schott, John Robert *international consultant, educator*

Litchfield
Darlington, David William *management consultant*

Londonderry
Osen, Gregory Alan *water conditioning company executive*

Manchester
Colby, George Vincent, III, *logistics executive*
Cusson-Cail, Kathleen *consulting company executive*
Stimpson, Patricia *software company executive*

Merrimack
Gallup, Patricia *computer company executive*

Munsonville
Lyon, Ronald Edward *management consultant, computer consultant*

Nashua
Garbacz, Gerald George *information services company executive*
Hargreaves, David William *communications company executive*
Piper, Linda Ammann *staffing services executive*
Seidel, Carl William *business executive, consultant*

New London
Gepfert, Alan Harry *management consultant, business educator, author*
Zuehlke, Richard William *technical communications consultant, writer*

Peterborough
Day, John Sidney *management sciences educator*

Portsmouth
Akridge, William David *hotel management company executive*
Greene, Douglas Edward *hotel executive*
Waterhouse, Trenton Dean *marketing director*

Rochester
Kramer, Sherri Marcelle *gemologist, jeweler*
Patel, Piyush Hirjibhai *communications executive*

Rye
MacRury, King *management counselor*

Somersworth
Gow, Linda Yvonne Carignan Cherwin *travel executive*

Walpole
Hunter, Barbara Way *public relations consultant*

Waterville Valley
Grimes, Howard Ray *management consultant*

West Lebanon
Lawton, Jacqueline Agnes *retired communications company executive, management consultant*

NEW JERSEY

Allendale
Bisanzo, Mark Thomas *sales executive*
Petersen, Martin Ross *public affairs executive*

Allenhurst
Hinson, Robert William *advertising executive, consultant*

Atlantic City
Oswell, Audrey S. *casino executive*

Avenel
Segal, Barry *company executive*

Basking Ridge
Buist, Richardson *retired corporate executive, retired banker*
McGuire, Garry K., Sr., *communications executive*
Whelan, Mary Kathleen *marketing professional, consultant*

Bedminster
Eslambolchi, Hossein *communications executive*

Hart, Terry Jonathan *communications executive*
Horton, Thomas W. *telecommunications executive*
Polumbo, John *communications executive*
Weaver, Constance *communications executive*
Zeglis, John D. *communications executive, lawyer*

Belmar
Rasmussen, Mark William *restaurant owner and chef*

Bernardsville
Dixon, Richard Wayne *retired communications company executive*

Bloomfield
Kreie, Richard James *retired advertising executive*

Boonton
Bona, Frederick Emil *public relations executive*
Bridges, Beryl Clarke *marketing executive*

Branchburg
Hulse, Robert Douglas *high technology executive*

Brick
Roache, Patrick Michael, Jr., *management consultant*

Bridgewater
Sethi, Shyam Sunder *management consultant*
Skidmore, James Albert, Jr., *management, computer technology and engineering services company executive*

Brookside
Fairchild, Samuel Wilson *professional services company executive, former federal agency administrator*

Butler
Ward, Robert Allen, Jr., *advertising executive*

Caldwell
Chatlos, William Edward *management consultant*

Califon
Fouillade, Jean-Paul Eric *management consultant*

Camden
Gans, Samuel Myer *temporary employment service executive*

Carteret
Neff, Richard B. *consumer products company executive*
Vitrano, Frank *supermarket executive*

Cedar Grove
Carlozzi, Catherine L. *corporate communications consultant, writer*

Cherry Hill
Matthiessen, Robert E. *business executive*
Sax, Robert Edward *food service equipment company executive*

Clifton
Bronkesh, Annette Cylia *public relations executive*

Cranford
Halleck, George Thomas *marketing professional*
Von Zuben, Fred G. *corporate executive*

Delran
Gilbert, Harry Ephraim, Jr., *retired hotel executive*

East Rutherford
Blate, Alissa *advertising executive*
Kempner, Michael W. *public relations executive*
Maresca, Robert A. *broadcasting and advertising executive*

Edison
Currie, Robert *communications executive*

Elizabeth
Mogensen, Charles Ray, Jr., *food service administrator*

Englewood
Fay, Toni Georgette *communications executive*

Englewood Cliffs
Henderson, Mary R. (Nina) *food/consumer products executive*

Ewing
McCarty, John Albert *advertising and marketing educator, consultant*

Fairfield
Petrocelli, A. F. *hotel executive*

Far Hills
Alexandre, Kristin Kuhns *public relations executive, writer*

Florham Park
Fischer, Pamela Shadel *public relations executive*
Naimark, George Modell *marketing and management consultant*
Negi, Devendra S. *communications services company administrator*
Russell, Jesse E. *communications executive*

Franklin Lakes
Mattie, Jeanne Marie *public relations and communications consultant*
Williams, Edward David *consulting executive*

Gladstone
Close, Donald Pembroke *management consultant*

Glen Ridge
Agnew, Peter Tomlin *employee benefit consultant*

Glen Rock
Davis, Alison B. *management consultant executive*

Green Brook
Bohanan, David John *management consultant*

Hackensack
Dexheimer, Larry William *advertising agency executive*

Hackettstown
Van Campen, Stephen Bernard *executive recruiter, consultant*

Haddonfield
Bauer, Raymond Gale *sales professional*

Hamilton
Gideon, Richard Walter *broadcasting management consultant*

Hampton
Yates, Michael Francis *management consultant*

Hoboken
Bostwick, Randell A. *retired retail food company executive*
Fassoulis, Satiris Galahad *communications company executive*

Holmdel
Hudson, Wendy Joy *software manager*
Meyer, Robert Alan *consultant*
Polinsky, Joseph Thomas *recruiting and training consultant*

Jersey City
Ascolese, Michael J. *corporate communications executive*
Dupey, Michele Mary *communications specialist*

Kearny
Antunes, Daniel L. *sales consultant, camera operator*

Kenilworth
Johnson Velazco, Nancy Ruth *marketing professional*

Lawrenceville
Adams, Christine Hanson *advertising executive*
Coleman, Wade Hampton, III, *management consultant, mechanical engineer, former banker*
Cox, Teri P. *public relations executive*
Weaver, Charles Lyndell, Jr., *institutional and manufacturing facilities administrator, management and marketing systems consultant*

Leonia
Pinsdorf, Marion Kathryn *business executive, educator, author*

Liberty Corner
Schneider, Steven L. *company executive*

Lindenwold
Jackson, Yocontalie Ann *entertainment company executive*

Little Silver
Morrison, James Frederick *management consultant*

Livingston
Brody, Martin *food service company executive*
Guerra, Mary Louise *human resources executive*

Madison
Byrd, Stephen Fred *human resource consultant*
O'Brien, Mary Devon *communications executive, consultant*
Siegel, George Henry *international business development consultant*
Weiner, Lowell B. *corporate communications executive*

Mahwah
Eisner, Susan Pamela *communications executive, management consultant, educator*
Gibbons, Robert Philip *management consultant, director*

Margate City
Stoolman, Herbert Leonard *public relations executive*

Marlton
Farnath, Dorothy Whitmyer *recruitment company executive*
Farwell, Nancy Larraine *public relations executive*
Klein, Anne Sceia *public relations executive*
Klein, Gerhart Leopold *public relations executive*
McCullen, Michael John *retired advertising executive*

Mendham
Hambleton, George Blow Elliott *retired management consultant*

Metuchen
Rakov, Barbara Streem *marketing executive*

Mine Hill
Nadeau, Michael Joseph *staff assistant*

Monroe Township
Cushman, Helen Merle Baker *retired management consultant*

Montclair
Barnard, Kurt *retail trend/consumer spending forecaster, publisher*
Dubrow, Marsha Ann *management consultant, musicologist*
Harvey, Richard Dudley *marketing consultant*
Tintle, Carmel Joseph *public relations executive*

Montvale
Cervantez, Michelle *marketing professional*
Olson, Frank Albert *car rental company executive*

Moorestown
Delano-Condax, Kate (Kate Delano-Condax Decker) *marketing and public relations executive*

Morris Plains
Gulfo, Adele Madelyn *pharmaceutical marketing executive*

Morristown
Bailye, John E. *software company executive*
Haselmann, John Philip *management consultant*
McConnell, John Howard *personnel management consultant, writer*
Musa, John Davis *computer and infosystems executive, software reliability engineering researcher and expert, independent consultant, educator*
Porter, James T. *computer company executive*
Robson, George T., Sr., *computer company executive*
Savage, R. Bruce *computer company executive*
Weidenkopf, Thomas W. *human resources specialist*

Mountainside
Lipton, Bronna Jane *marketing communications executive*

Murray Hill
D'Amelio, Frank Anthony *communications company executive*

New Brunswick
Burke, James Edward *consumer products company executive*
Doorley, John *public relations executive, educator*
Livingston, Lee Franklin *real estate and finance consultant*
Wilson, Robert Nathan *health care company executive*

New Providence
Doescher, William Frederick *communications executive*
Keane, Brian Teagan *software development company executive*
Netravali, Arun N. *communications executive*
Russo, Patricia F. *communications executive*
Stanzione, Daniel C. *communications company executive*
Verwaayen, Ben J.M. *communications company executive*

New Vernon
Perdunn, Richard Francis *management consultant*

Newark
Lassiter, Teri Elizabeth *environmental safety manager, educator*
Lederman, Peter (Bernd) *environmental services executive, consultant, educator*
Passantino, Benjamin Arthur *business/marketing executive*

Oldwick
Griggs, Stephen L. *management consultant*

Paramus
Fader, Seymour Jeremiah *management and engineering consulting company executive*

Park Ridge
Kennedy, Brian James *marketing executive*

Parlin
Khan, Sajid A. *management consultant*

Parsippany
Belmonte, Steven Joseph *hotel chain executive*
Ferguson, Thomas George *retired healthcare advertising agency executive*
Specht, Dennis *company executive*
Weller, Robert N(orman) *hotel executive*

Paterson
Waitts, James Robert *marketing professional*

Pennington
Bertone, Thomas Lee *management consultant*
Spitzer, T. Quinn *management consultant company executive*

Pilesgrove
Mohrfeld, Richard Gentel *marketing professional*

Piscataway
Wing, Michael James *telecommunications executive*

Plainsboro
Devine, Hugh James, Jr., *marketing executive, consultant*
Spiegel, Phyllis *public relations consultant, journalist*

Princeton
Basáñez, Miguel Ebergenyi *opinion pollster, political science educator*
Connelly, John F. *communications executive*
Craigie, James R. *consumer products company executive, former sports equipment apparel company executive*
Evslin, Tom *internet telephone service executive*
Flanagan, Theresa *quality assurance professional*
Hillier, James *technology management executive, researcher*
Hollander, Lawrence Jay *marketing executive*
Kornhauser, Henry *advertising executive*
Makadok, Stanley *management consultant*
Morris, Mac Glenn *advertising bureau executive*
Narayanan, Vadake K. *management educator, consultant*
O'Neill, Harry William *survey research company executive*
Rogula, James Leroy *consumer products company executive*
Tomson, Jon Scott *business professional*
Williams, Brown F *media services company executive*

Randolph
Charm, Joel Barry *management consultant*
Chen, Kevin S. *corporate executive, consultant, educator*

Red Bank
Reinhart, Peter Sargent *corporate executive, lawyer*

Ridgewood
Sommer, Robert George *public relations executive*
Warner, John Edward *advertising executive*

River Edge
Jones, Thomas Owen *computer industry executive*

Rivervale
LaGreca, Thomas Richard *flooring company executive, lawyer*

Rockaway
Gebauer, Kurt Manfred *management executive*

Rockleigh
Siracusano, Louis H. *communications company executive*

Roseland
Butler, Gary C. *computer company executive*
Haviland, Richard John *data processing company executive*
Taub, Henry *retired computer services company executive*
Weinbach, Arthur Frederic *computer company executive*

Rutherford
Tortorello, Nicholas John *public opinion and market research company executive*

Saddle River
Roes, Nicholas A. *communications executive*

Scotch Plains
Johnsen, Karen Kennedy *marketing professional*
Margiotta, Joseph M. *printing company executive*

Short Hills
Schaefer, Charles James, III, *advertising agency executive, consultant*
Spector, Shelly *company executive*

Skillman
Gauff, Susan Tyrrell *marketing and human resources executive*

Somers Point
Hughes, David Robert *gaming company executive*

Somerset
Wallfesh, Henry Maurice *business communications company executive, editor, writer*

Somerville
Dobrinsky, Susan Elizabeth *human resources director*

Spring Lake
Ernst, John Louis *management consultant*

Summit
Fuess, Billings Sibley, Jr., *advertising executive*
Pace, Leonard *retired management consultant*
Weinstein, Stephen Brant *communications executive, researcher, writer*

Teaneck
Allen, Brenda Joyce *management consultant, editor-in-chief*
Coburn, Gordon *Internet company executive*
Connola, Donald Pascal, Jr., *management consultant*
Lafer, Fred Seymour *data processing company executive*

Three Bridges
Lawrence, Gerald Graham *management consultant*

Toms River
Kanarkowski, Edward Joseph *data processing company executive*
Schockaert, Barbara Ann *marketing professional*

Towaco
Stern, Richard Henry *advertising executive*

Trenton
Barclay, Warren M. *human resources specialist, researcher*
Robinson, Susan Mittleman *data processing executive*

Ventnor City
Bolton, Kenneth Albert *management consultant*

Verona
Greenwald, Robert *public relations executive*

Voorhees
Rowello, Robert John *communications executive*

Warren
Blass, Walter Paul *consultant, management educator*
DiPietro, Ralph Anthony *marketing and management consultant, educator*
Kozberg, Ronald Paul *health and human services administrator*

Watchung
Grey, Ruthann E. *communications specialist, management consultant*

West Caldwell
Dixon, Jo-Ann Conte *management consultant*

West Long Branch
Kovacs, Aimee *conference speaker, minister*

West Milford
Ferguson, Harley Robert *service company executive*

West Orange
Bogstahl, Deborah Marcelle *marketing professional, consultant*
Kyle, Corinne Silverman *management consultant*

Westfield
Mazzarese, Michael Louis *executive coach, consultant*

Whitehouse
Shelton, Craig *food service executive*

Whiting
Parker, John Osmyn *management consultant*

Woodcliff Lake
Bablin, Mark Edward *security administrator, mortgage consultant*

Wyckoff
Lavery, Daniel P. *management consultant*

NEW MEXICO

Albuquerque
Barker, Lynn M. *business executive*
Blewett, Kenneth K. *business executive*
Dunlap, Sam Bathurst *personnel consulting firm executive*
Gardner, Lenann McGookey *management consultant*
Hayo, George Edward *management consultant*
Leach, Richard Maxwell, Jr., (Max Leach Jr.) *corporate professional*
Lohrding, Ronald K. *business executive*
Myers, Carol McClary *retired sales administrator, editor*
Ofte, Donald *business executive*
Oppedahl, Phillip Edward *computer company executive*
O'Toole, Robert John, II, *telemarketing consultant*
Wellborn, Charles Ivey *science and technology business consultant*
Westwood, Albert Ronald Clifton *management consultant, researcher*

Corrales
Foryst, Carole *computer electronics executive*

Los Alamos
Kloepper, David Alan *retired management consultant*
Petrini, Fabrizio *computer science researcher*

Moriarty
Haver, Jurgen F. *marketing consultant*

Placitas
Reade, Lewis Pollock *business executive, retired diplomat, engineer*

Sandia Park
Greenwell, Ronald Everett *communications executive*

Santa Fe
Brandt, Richard Paul *communications and entertainment company executive*
Brown, Norman Wesley *retired advertising agency executive*
Mercer, James Lee *management consultant*
Merrin, Seymour *computer marketing company executive*
Miller, Dwight Richard *professional hair care industry executive, cosmetologist, consultant*
Peat, Randall Dean *defense analysis company executive, retired air force officer*
Robinson, Richard Gary *management consultant, accountant*

Silver City
Cox, Robert Gene *management consultant*

Taos
Brown, David Warfield *management educator*

NEW YORK

Albany
Lustenader, Barbara Diane *human resources specialist*
Schalit, Robert Edward *advertising executive*

Amherst
Cohen, Herman Nathan *private investigator*
Nickell, Joe *paranormal expert*

Annandale On Hudson
Darrow, Emily M. *public relations executive, writer*

Armonk
Bolduc, Ernest Joseph *association management consultant, not-for-profit developer, consultant*
Iwata, Jon C. *computer company executive*
Joyce, John R. *computer company executive*
Kohnstamm, Abby E. *marketing executive*
Loughridge, Mark *computer company executive*
Maine, Douglas L. *computer company executive*
Ward, Stephen M., Jr., *computer company executive*

Averill Park
Traver, Robert William, Sr., *management consultant, writer, engineer*

Bainbridge
Compton, John Robinson *retired rake company executive*

Beacon
Metz, Ferdinand *chef, educator, academic administrator*

Bedford
Husted, William Armstrong *sales executive*

Bedford Corners
Greene, Jesse J., Jr., *former computer company executive*

Bellmore
Brown, Earle Palmer *advertising agency executive*

Bellport
Hendrie, Elaine *public relations executive*

Berlin
Pelz, Caroline Duncombe *retired educational administrator*

Bethpage
Dolan, James L *communications executive*
Janczak, Andrew Anthony *executive*

Binghamton
Yammarino, Francis Joseph *management consultant, educator*

Briarcliff Manor
Driver, Sharon Humphreys *marketing executive*
Read, John Conyers *non-profit management*

Bronx
Aronowitz, Julian *management consultant*
Capodilupo, Jeanne Hatton *public relations executive*
Hudson, Frederick Bernard *management consultant*
Samuels, Leslie Eugene *marketing and management consultant*

Bronxville
Ellinghaus, William Maurice *communications executive*

Brooklyn
Allison, Mary Ann *consulting company executive, author, speaker*
Brooks, Peter *computer company executive, application developer*
Chandan, Jit S. *management consultant, educator*
Greenwood, Monique *innkeeper, writer, restaurant owner*
Isaacson, Arline Levine *food association administrator*
Korolev, Anatoly Y. *management consultant*
Logan, Paula M. *entertainment company executive, accountant*
Ortega, Maria A. *security firm executive, educator*
Reichel, Walter Emil *advertising executive*
Reisler, Helen Barbara *public relations executive*
Roche, John Edward *educator, human resources consultant*
Smith, John W(esley), Jr., *data processing executive, consultant*

Buffalo
Fryer, Appleton *publisher, sales executive, lecturer, diplomat*
Goralski, Donald John *public relations executive, counselor*
Halt, James George *advertising executive, graphic designer*
Moran, Charles *consumer products company executive*
Sobolewski, Timothy Richard *marketing executive*

Carmel
Iglehart, Patricia Ann *business development and communications executive*

Cheektowaga
Mruk, Eugene Robert *retired marketing professional, urban planner*

Chester
Mackerodt, Fred *public relations specialist*

Claverack
Barrett, William Gary *advertising and marketing executive*

Cold Spring
Milner, Debbi Elissa *computer company executive*
Milner, John *computer company executive*

Corning
Loose, John W. *sales company executive*
Weeks, Wendell P. *opto-electronics executive*

Croton On Hudson
Eswein, Bruce James, II, *human resources specialist*
Plotch, Walter *management consultant, fund raising counselor*

Cutchogue
Gibson, Pamela *business development consultant, audio director*

Delmar
Button, Rena Pritsker *public affairs executive*

Dobbs Ferry
Kalvin-Stiefel, Judy *public relations executive*

East Garden City
Bákér, J. A., II, *executive management advisor and consultant, architect, financial engineer*

East Hampton
Mencher, Stuart Alan *sales and marketing executive*

East Meadow
Fuchs, Jerome Herbert *management consultant*

Elmira
Laux, Edward J. *advertising executive*

Elmont
Butera, Ann Michele *consulting company executive*

Far Rockaway
Epstein, Samuel Abraham *sales executive*

Findley Lake
Gundersen, Allison Maureen *management consultant*

Flushing
Andrews, Phillip *public relations executive*

Forest Hills
Torrence-Thompson, Juanita Lee *public relations executive*
Van Westering, James Francis *management consultant, educator*

Fort Drum
Hilferty, Bryan Carey *public relations specialist*

Fredonia
Krohn, Franklin Bernard *marketing specialist, educator*

Garden City
Conlon, Thomas James *marketing executive*
Crom, James Oliver *professional training company executive*
Doucette, Mary-Alyce *computer company executive*

Glen Cove
Fajors, Nique *computer company executive, application developer*

Glen Head
Conway, David Antony *management executive, marketing professional*

Great Neck
Friedland, Louis N. *retired communications executive*
Schwartz, Alan Paul *corporate executive*

Hancock
DeLuca, Ronald *former advertising agency executive, consultant*

Harrison
Wilson, William James *marketing professional*

Hartsdale
Goodman, Stanley Leonard *advertising executive*
Greenawalt, Peggy Freed Tomarkin *advertising executive*
Pell, Arthur Robert *human resources specialist, consultant, author*

Hastings On Hudson
Cooper, Doris Jean *market research executive*

Hempstead
Evans, Joel Raymond *marketing educator, consultant*
Kruh, Louis *advertising executive, lawyer*

Holliswood
Greenblatt, Fred Harold *data processing consultant*

Honeoye Falls
Hillabrandt, Larry Lee *service industry executive*
VanAuken, Alan Bradley *management consultant*

Huntington
Seidman, Glenn Elliott *sales executive, marketing professional*

Hurley
Smith, Lewis Motter, Jr., *retired advertising and direct marketing executive*

Hyde Park
Ryan, L. Timothy *chef, educator, academic administrator*

Ilion
Nemyier, Margaret Gertrude *sales executive*

Islandia
Clarke, Jeff *computer company executive*
Gupta, Yogesh *computer company executive*
Robinson, Douglas *computer company executive*

Ithaca
Park, Roy Hampton, Jr., *advertising executive*

Jamaica
Jawin, Ann Juliano *human resource specialist*

Jericho
Rosen, Robert Arnold *management company executive, real estate investor*

Lake Luzerne
Goldstein, Manfred *retired consultant*

Lake Placid
Lussi, Caroline Frances Draper *resort executive*

Lake Success
Rickin, Sheila Anne *personnel professional*
Uchida, Kinya *consumer products company executive*

Lancaster
Neumaier, Gerhard John *environment consulting company executive*

Larchmont
Folter, Roland *book historian, rare books company executive, bibliographer*
Greenwald, Carol Schiro *professional services marketing research executive*
Moody, Kathryn Currier *communications executive, educator*
Plumez, Jean Paul *advertising agency executive, consultant*
Wielgus, Charles Joseph *information services company executive*

Latham
Schwartz, Robert William *management consultant*

Lewiston
Askins, Nancy Ellen Paulsen *training and organizational development professional*

Loudonville
Burstein, Sharon Ann *corporate communications specialist, designer*

Malverne
Freund, Richard L. *communications company executive, consultant, lawyer*

Mamaroneck
Smith, Douglas LaRue *marketing executive*

Manlius
Harriff, Suzanna Elizabeth (Bahner) *advertising consultant*

Melville
Blechschmidt, Edward Allan *data processing executive*
Krusos, Denis Angelo *communications company executive*
Lieberman, Carol *healthcare marketing communications consultant*
Ponzi Kay, Marylou *human resources specialist*

Merrick
Baron, Theodore *retired public relations executive*

Middle Island
Andrews, Gaylen *measurable response public relations expert*
Linick, Andrew S. *direct marketing expert*

Mount Kisco
Novak, Gregory *marketing professional*

Mount Vernon
Chagula, Paul Machiya *technology company executive, trade consultant*

New City
Giambalvo, Vincent *training services executive*

New Paltz
Nyquist, Thomas Eugene *consulting business executive*

New Rochelle
Miller, Rita *personnel consultant, diecasting company executive*

New York
Abernathy, James Logan *public relations executive*
Agisim, Philip *advertising and marketing company executive*
Ahrens, Thomas H. *production company executive*
Aiello, Stephen *public relations executive*
Alafouzo, Antonia *marketing and business strategy professional*
Alexander, Roy *public relations executive, editor, author*
Allen, Alice *communications and marketing executive*
Alschuler, Steven *public relations executive, communications consultant, writer, political consultant*
Altschuler, Marjorie *advertising executive*
Anders, Brenda Michelle *communications professional*
Anderson, Arthur Allan *management consultant*
Anderson, Gavin *business executive*
Andolsen, Alan Anthony *management consultant*
Antonuccio, Joseph Albert *management consultant*
Appel, Gloria *advertising executive*
Applebaum, Stuart S. *public relations executive*
Ardai, Charles E. *online services executive*
Arlow, Arnold Jack *advertising executive, artist*
Aronson, Donald Eric *professional services firms consultant, tax consultant*
Aronstam, Neil Lee *media marketing firm executive*
Axelrod, Norman N(athan) *optical technical planning and technology application consultant*
Axelson, Linda Rae *event planning specialist*
Axthelm, Nancy *advertising executive*
Bacher, Judith St. George *executive search consultant*
Bachrach, Nancy *advertising executive*
Baker, Stephen *advertising executive, author*
Baldwin, C. Stephen *human resources specialist*
Barnes, Arthur Roosevelt *advertising executive*
Baron, Sheri *advertising agency executive*
Barrett, Herbert *artists management executive*
Bartlett, Thomas Foster *management consultant*
Barton, Richard N. *computer company executive*
Barton, Thomas Heisler *management consultant*
Bartow, Diane Grace *marketing and sales executive*
Baruch, Ralph M. *communications executive*
Bastianich, Lidia Matticchio *chef, food service executive*
Batali, Mario *chef*
Bauman, Susan *communications executive*
Becker, Susan Kaplan *management and marketing communication consultant, educator*
Beckwith, Rodney Fisk *management consulting firm executive*
Beecher, William Manuel *management consultant*
Beinecke, William Sperry *corporate executive*
Bell, David Arthur *advertising agency executive*
Bell, Thomas Devereaux, Jr., *communications company executive*
Bellanger, Florian *food service executive, educator*
Bellows, Howard Arthur, Jr., *marketing research executive*
Berenson, Robert Leonard *advertising agency executive*
Bergen, John Donald *communications, public affairs executive*
Berlin, Andrew Mark *advertising agency executive*
Bernard, David George *retired management consultant*
Bernardin, Thomas L. *advertising executive*
Bernbach, John Lincoln *corporate strategies and investment executive*
Biederman, Barron Zachary (Barry Biederman) *advertising agency executive*
Bishop, Susan Katharine *executive search company executive*
Bishopric, Susan Ehrlich *public relations executive*
Blamer, Steven W. *advertising executive*
Blinder, Abe Lionel *management consultant*
Bloomgarden, Kathy Finn *public relations executive*
Boice, Craig Kendall *management consultant*
Bostock, Roy Jackson *advertising agency executive*
Boulud, Daniel *chef, restaurant owner*
Bradstock, John *advertising executive*
Brady, Adelaide Burks *public relations agency executive, giftware catalog executive*
Braz, Evandro Freitas *management consultant*
Brewster, Daniel Baugh, Jr., *communications executive*
Brisman, Jennifer *event planning executive*
Brooks, Gary *management consultant*
Brooks, Timothy H. *media executive*
Brown, Arnold *management consultant*
Brown, Hobson, Jr., *executive recruiting consultant*
Bruzs, Boris Olgerd *retired management consultant*
Burger, Chester *retired management consultant*
Burke, David *corporate chef, executive chef*
Burkhardt, Ronald Robert *advertising executive*
Burns, Kevin J. *computer software services executive*
Burson, Harold *public relations executive, director*
Burstell, Ed *personal care industry executive*
Burton, Peggy *advertising and marketing executive*
Busquet, Anne M. *Internet company executive*
Cage, Jack Hays *executive search consultant*
Cairns, Anne Marie *public relations executive*
Calabrese, Rosalie Sue *management consultant, writer*
Cameron, Ewen *advertising executive*
Capozzi, Lou *public relations executive*
Carey, Thomas Hilton *advertising agency executive*
Carmellini, Andrew *food service executive*
Carro, Carl Rafael *executive search consultant*
Carter, Carolyn Houchin *advertising agency executive*
Case, Stephen M. *media and entertainment company executive*
Casella, Jim *marketing professional*
Casey, Barbara Jeanne *marketing professional*
Cavanagh, Richard Edward *research association executive*
Chajet, Clive *brand and corporate image consultant*
Chandler, Robert Leslie *public relations executive*
Chang, Ling Wei *consulting services executive*
Cheney, Richard Eugene *public relations executive, psychoanalyst*
Chess, William *public relations executive*
Chodorow, Jeffrey *restaurant owner*
Clarke, Frank William *communication executive*
Cohen, Brian S. *public relations executive*
Conlin, Kelly P. *communications executive*
Cook, Ian M. *consumer products company executive*
Corbin, Herbert Leonard *public relations executive, director*
Corman, Judith *corporate communications specialist*
Cory, Christopher Thayer *communications executive*
Coster, Peter *management consulting firm executive*
Coyne, Nancy Carol *advertising executive*
Critchlow, Paul *communication and public affairs executive*
Culligan, John William *retired corporate executive*
Cuti, Anthony J. *consumer products company executive*
Cutler, Laurel *advertising agency executive*
Daniel, David Ronald *management consultant*
Danielides, Joannie C. *public relations executive*
Davidson, Donald William *advertising executive*
DeBow, Jay Howard Camden *public relations executive*
DeBow, Thomas Joseph, Jr., *advertising executive*
Delano, Lester Almy, Jr., *advertising executive*
de Margitay, Gedeon *acquisitions and management consultant*
Derfner, Carol Ann *management consultant, fundraising counsel*
DeSimone, Glenn J. *advertising executive*
Deuser, Jane *marketing professional*
Deutsch, Donny *advertising executive*
DeVard, Jerri *marketing professional*
Devitre, Dinyar S. *consumer products company executive, corporate financial executive*
de Vries, Madeline *public relations executive*
Diamond, Harris *corporate communications executive, lawyer*
Dimling, John Arthur *marketing executive*
DiSpirito, Rocco *restaurant owner, chef*
Doerfler, Ronald John *communications company executive*
Dolan, Michael *advertising agency executive*
Dolan, Regina A. *security firm executive*
Donaldson, John Cecil, Jr., *consumer products company executive*
Dooner, John Joseph, Jr., *advertising executive*
Drobis, David R. *retired public relations company executive*
Dru, Jean-Marie Paul *advertising executive*
Ducasse, Alain *food service executive*
Dugan, Lynn *communications company executive*
Duke, Robin Chandler Tippett *retired public relations executive*
Dunne, Diane C. *marketing professional*
Dunst, Laurence David *advertising executive*
Edelman, Richard Winston *public relations executive*
Edson, Andrew Stephen *public relations executive*
Eisler, Susan Krawetz *advertising executive*
Elkes, Terrence Allen *communications executive*
Elliott, John, Jr., *advertising agency executive*
Emanuel, Myron *corporate communications specialist, consultant*
Emerson, Andi (Mrs. Andi Emerson Weeks) *sales and advertising executive*
Engelman, Irwin *media marketing company executive*
Evans, Alfred Lee, Jr., *advertising executive*
Exposito, Daisy *advertising executive*
Fairbairn, Ursula Farrell *human resources executive*
Falk, Edgar Alan *public relations consulting executive, writer*
Faraone, Teri *public relations executive*
Farinelli, Jean L. *public relations executive*
Faris, George N. *management consultant*
Feigin, Barbara Sommer *marketing consultant*
Feintuch, Henry Philip *public relations executive*
Feldman, Robert C. *public relations executive*
Fenwick, Lex *communications executive*
Fernandes, Jeanne Mary *human resource administrator*
Feskoe, Gaffney Jon *management consultant*
Fili-Krushel, Patricia *media company executive*
Fine, Jo Renée *management executive*
Finn, David *public relations company executive, artist*
Finn, Peter *public relations executive*
Fisher, Gary Alan *marketing professional*
Flaherty, Tina Santi *corporate communications executive, writer*
Flaum, Sander Allen *advertising and marketing executive*
Flay, Bobby *food service executive*
Fleischman, Barbara Greenberg *public relations consultant*
Fletcher, Mary Lee *retired marketing professional*
Fluhr, Howard *consulting firm executive*
Folta, Carl D. *communications executive*
Ford, John Charles *communications executive*
Forman, Leonard P. *media company executive*
Foxworth, Jo *advertising agency executive*
Frank, Peter Bruce *management consultant, accountant*
Freeman, Michael J. *inventor, professor, author, corporate executive*
Fudge, Ann Marie *advertising executive*
Gardiner, E. Nicholas P. *executive search executive*
Gardner, Ralph David *advertising executive*
Garfinkel, Lee *advertising agency executive*
Geier, Philip Henry, Jr., *advertising executive*
Geller, Robert James *advertising agency executive*
Gerard-Sharp, Monica Fleur *communications executive*
Gilbert, Rose Bennett *communications company executive*
Gilburne, Miles R. *communications executive*
Ginsburg, Sigmund G. *management and executive search consultant*
Gitelson, Susan Aurelia *business executive, civic leader*
Glatt, Mitchell Steven *consumer products company executive*
Gold, Mari S. *public relations executive*
Goldschmidt, Charles *advertising agency executive*
Goldsmith, Clifford Henry *former tobacco company executive*
Goldsmith, Gary L. *advertising executive*
Goldstein, Gary Sanford *executive recruiter*
Goldstein, Richard A. *consumer products company executive*
Goldstone, Steven F. *consumer products company executive*
Gomez, Francis Dean *corporate executive, former foreign service officer*
Gordon, Leslie Peyton *executive recruiting consultant*
Gottlieb, Jerrold Howard *advertising executive*
Graves, Hillary *marketing professional*
Greeley, Sean McGovern *sales executive*
Greenberg, David I. *consumer products company executive*
Greenberg, Jeffrey W. *professional services company executive*
Greene, Adele S. *management consultant*
Greenland, Leo *advertising executive*
Groberg, James Jay *information sciences company executive*
Grossman, Jack *advertising agency executive*
Grossman, James A. *public relations executive*
Gumbinner, Paul S. *advertising and executive recruitment agency executive*
Guskov, Sergey *security firm executive*
Hammond, Lou Rena Charlotte *public relations executive*
Hart, Karen Ann *advertising executive*
Hatheway, John Harris *advertising agency executive*
Hearn, David *advertising executive*
Heekin, James Robson, III, *advertising executive*
Heinzerling, Larry Edward *communications executive*
Helmsley, Leona Mindy *hotel executive*
Hemsing, Josephine Claudia *public relations executive*
Herbert, Marilynne *public relations executive, freelance photographer*
Hock, Morton *entertainment advertising executive*
Hoog, Thomas W. *public relations executive*
Hooper, Ian (John Derek Glass) *marketing communications executive*
Hudes, Nana Brenda *marketing professional*
Hutsaliuk, Yarema *public relations executive, military officer*
Ilson, Bernard *public relations executive*
Jabbur, Ramzi J. *management consultant*
Jackson, James Lewis Perdue, II, *entertainment company executive*
Jacobsen, Sally *communications executive*
Jacoby, Robert Harold *management consulting executive*
James, Robert Leo *advertising agency executive*
Jean-Baptiste, Tricia *public relations executive*
Johnson, John William, Jr., *executive recruiter*
Johnson, Verdia E. *marketing professional*
Jonas, Gilbert *public relations and fund raising executive*
Josell, Jessica (Jessica Wechsler) *public relations executive*
Josephs, Ray *public relations and advertising executive, writer, international relations consultant*
Judge, Jerry *business executive*
Just, Gemma Rivoli *retired advertising executive*
Kaess, Ken *advertising executive*
Kahn, Alan J. *book distribution executive*
Kang, Eliot *advertising executive*
Kapner, Lori *marketing professional*
Karalekas, George Steven *advertising agency executive, political consultant*
Karp, Martin Everett *management consultant*
Katz, Marcia *public relations company executive*
Keenan, Michael Edgar *marketing professional*
Kelly, J. Michael *communications executive*
Kelly, Peter *communications executive*
Kelmenson, Leo-Arthur *advertising executive*
Kenny, Roger Michael *executive search consultant, writer*
Kieren, Thomas Henry *management consultant*
Kinser, Richard Edward *management consultant*
Kinsolving, Charles McIlvaine, Jr., *marketing executive*
Koenig, Jerome *newspaper advertising executive, actor, poet*
Kohut, John Walter *corporate executive*
Komisarjevsky, Christopher P.A. *public relations executive*
Kotcher, Raymond Lowell *public relations executive*
Kotuk, Andrea Mikotajuk *public relations executive, writer*
Kraus, Norma Jean *human resources executive*
Kraushar, Jonathan Pollack *communications and media consultant*
Kreisberg, Neil Ivan *advertising executive*
Kreston, Martin Howard *advertising, marketing, public relations, and publishing executive*
Krinsky, Robert Daniel *consulting firm executive*
Krukowski, Jan *communications executive*
Kucic, Joseph *management consultant, industrial engineer, network engineer, information security specialist*
Kugelman, Stephanie *advertising executive*
Kuperman, Robert Ian *advertising agency executive*
Kyriakou, Linda Grace *communications executive*
Lamont, Lee *music management executive*
Land, Irene Stokvis *marketing executive*
Lang, George *restaurateur*
Langton, Cleve Swanson *advertising executive*
LaNicca Albanese, Ellen *public relations executive*

Russo, Joseph Maria *public affairs executive*

Tallman
Strasser, Joel A. *public relations executive, engineer, executive producer*

Tappan
Fox, Muriel *retired public relations executive*

Tarrytown
Kirsch, Abigail *culinary productions executive*

Thornwood
Bassett, Lawrence C *management consultant*

Tuckahoe
Brecher, Bernd *management consultant*

Victor
Van Bortel, Mary Catherine *sales executive*

West Hempstead
DeGroff, Dale *food service executive*

West Nyack
Hilpert, Dale W. *retail shoe company executive*
Oppenheim, Robert *beauty industry executive*

Westbury
McCann, James F. *consumer products company executive*

Westhampton Beach
Maas, Jane Brown *advertising executive*

White Plains
Adkins, Rodney *computer company executive*
Allen, Ralph Dean *diversified company corporate executive*
Brown, Ronald C. *hotel executive*
Colwell, Howard Otis *advertising executive*
Cotter, Robert F. *hotel executive*
Denham, Paul *technology sales and marketing executive*
Lukaszewski, James Edmund *communications executive*
Salameh, Samer Fadi *communications executive*
Sternlicht, Barry Stuart *hotel executive*
Sussberg, Milton Joel *marketing professional*

Whitesboro
Bulman, William Patrick *data processing executive*

Williamsville
Truell, George Foster *management consultant*

Woodbury
Berezin, Evelyn *management consultant*

Woodhaven
Bolster, Jacqueline Neben (Mrs. John A. Bolster) *communications consultant*

Yaphank
Ahern, John James *software company executive*

Yonkers
Colabella, George Michael *management, fund raising consultant*
Miller, Karl A. *management counselor*
Wen, Sheree *computer company executive*

Yorktown Heights
Agerwala, Tilak Krishna Mahesh *computer company executive*
Rosenblatt, Stephen Paul *marketing and sales promotion company executive*

NORTH CAROLINA

Arden
Baker, Kerry Allen *management consultant*

Asheboro
Boone, Harvey Claxton *quality assurance professional, writer*

Asheville
Dunn, Shari *public relations executive*

Beaufort
Burgard, Ralph *cultural and education planner*

Canton
Dixon, Shirley Juanita *retired restaurant owner*

Cary
Craig, Harold Kent *mechanical contracting executive, systems analyst*
Sail, John *computer company executive*
Siporin, David *human resources specialist*
Taylor, James Francis *marketing professional*
Wait, George William *sales executive*

Chapel Hill
Hunt, Katrina Weisner *marketing professional*
Jerdee, Thomas Harlan *business administration educator, organization psychology researcher and consultant*
Passaro, Paul Charles *business executive*

Charlotte
Burke, Steven Charles *healthcare administration executive*
Carroll, David M. *communications professional*
Cleghorn, John Michael *communications executive*
Doherty, Barbara Whitehurst *chemical purchasing manager*
Eppes, Thomas Evans *advertising executive, public relations executive*
Ignozzi, Bryan K. *management consultant*
Kincaid, Steven Randall *marketing professional*
Lisenby, Terry S. *waste management executive*
Lyerly, Elaine Myrick *advertising executive*
Mascavage, Joseph Peter *training executive*
Ogirri, Dennis Arekpita *educator, political/business management consultant*
Osteen, Louis *chef*
Price, Charles R., Jr., *advertising executive*
Rivenbark, Jan Meredith *business consultant*

Wood, Donald Craig *retired marketing professional*

Clayton
Silberman, H. Lee *public relations executive, editorial consultant*

Clinton
Fetterman, Annabelle L. *packing company executive*

Denver
McIntosh, Anita Jane *retired administrative assistant*

Durham
Amaldoss, Wilfred *marketing educator*
Barker, Karen *restaurant owner, chef*
Ladd, Marcia Lee *medical equipment and supplies company executive*
Lieberman, Rochelle Phyllis *relocation company executive*
Otterbourg, Robert Kenneth *public relations consultant, writer*

Fayetteville
Baker, Samuel Garrard *advertising agency executive*
Watt, Katherine Ann *administrative assistant*

Flat Rock
Childress, Richard Thomas *management consultant*

Granite Falls
Speas, Charles Stuart *human resources consultant, entrepreneur*

Greensboro
Allen, Jesse Owen, III, *organizational behavior specialist*
Beahm, Roger *advertising executive*
Coyne, William P. *advertising executive*
Dillon, Terri L. *consulting firm executive*
Formo, Brenda Terrell *travel company executive*
Sanders, William Eugene *marketing executive*
Spears, Alexander White, III, *tobacco company executive*
Stone, Theresa M. *communications executive*

Greenville
Finkelday, John Paul *retail sales executive*

Hampstead
Walters, Sherwood George *management consultant, educator*

Harrisburg
Edwards, Larry Cecil *management consultant*

Hertford
McClung, Kenneth Austin, Jr., *training executive, performance consultant*

Hickory
George, Boyd Lee *consumer products company executive*
Knedlik, Ronald W. *retail grocery distributing executive*

High Point
Winn, Walter Garnett, Jr., *marketing strategist, advertising executive*

Hillsborough
Eustice, Russell Clifford *consulting company executive, academic director*

Kitty Hawk
Berger, Tina *hotel executive*

Mooresville
Pond, Dale C. *company executive*

Morrisville
Wing, Vanette *sales executive, consultant*

New Bern
Naumann, William Carl *consumer products company executive*

North Wilkesboro
Parsons, Irene Adelaide *management consultant*

Pilot Mountain
Daoud, Abraham Joseph, IV, *funeral director, former police officer*

Pinehurst
Gilmore, Voit *travel executive*
Mc Dannald, Clyde Elliott, Jr., *management consultation company executive*

Pittsboro
Squire, Alexander *management consultant*

Raleigh
Cornish, Thelbert Bernard, Jr., *internet service provider executive*
Doherty, Robert Cunningham *retired advertising executive*
Eberly, Harry Landis *retired communications company executive*
Hansen, Patricia Sellers *personal services executive*
Karmanos, Peter, Jr., *computer software company executive, professional sports team executive*
Leak, Robert Edwards *economic development consultant*
Merrell, W. M. *advertising executive*

Research Triangle Park
Sumney, Larry W. *research company executive*

Rocky Mount
Walker, Betsy Ellen *consulting and systems integration company executive*

Roxboro
Hollingsworth, Brenda Jackson *employment consultant*

Sanford
Sodini, Peter J. *food service executive*

Sapphire
Christy, Audrey Meyer *public relations consultant*

Southern Pines
Owings, Malcolm William *retired management consultant*

Supply
Jacobs, Richard Alan *management consultant*
Pollard, Joseph Augustine *advertising and public relations consultant*

Vass
Glassman, Edward *public relations management creativity consultant*

Weaverville
Parsons, Vinson Adair *retired computer software company executive*

Wilkesboro
Steed, John David *consumer products company executive*
Stone, Steven M. *consumer products company executive*

Wilmington
Maness, Eleanor Palmer *research analyst*

Wilson
Dean, Thomas A. *research laboratory executive*

Winston Salem
Evans, Lisbeth *business networking executive, political party official*
Griswold, George *marketing, advertising and public relations executive*
Gunzenhauser, Gerard Ralph, Jr., *management consultant, investor*
Ivey, Susan M. *tobacco company executive*
Johnston, James Wesley *retired business executive*
Kaufman, Charlotte S. *communications executive*

NORTH DAKOTA

Fargo
Tharaldson, Gary Dean *hotel developer and owner*

OHIO

Akron
Crawford, Robert John *credit company executive*
Glomski, Edward Earl *sales executive*
Hochschwender, Herman Karl *international consultant*
Jasso, William Gattis *public relations executive*
Meeker, David Anthony *public relations executive*
Molinari, Marco *marketing executive*
Sonnecken, Edwin Herbert *management consultant*

Bowling Green
Chauhan, D. S. *human resources specialist, educator*
Sloma, Robert J. *business process consultant*
Varney, Glenn Herbert *management educator*

Canton
Suarez, Benjamin *consumer products company executive*

Chagrin Falls
Fisher, Will Stratton *illumination consultant*
Stevenson, Thomas Herbert *management consultant, writer, executive coach*

Cincinnati
Andrews, John Wayne *retired marketing professional*
Arnold, Susan E. *consumer products company executive*
Artzt, Edwin Lewis *consumer products company executive*
Brown, Dale Patrick *retired advertising executive*
Brunner, Gordon F(rancis) *household products company executive*
Campbell, Audrey Leigh *communications professional*
Carraher, Charles Jacob, Jr., *professional speaker*
deCavel, Jean-Robert *chef*
Dillon, David Brian *retail grocery executive*
Goodman, Phyllis L. *public relations executive*
Hawkins, Lawrence Charles *management consultant, educator*
Henretta, Deb *consumer products company executive*
Hicks, Irle Raymond *retail food chain executive*
Howe, John Kingman *manufacturing, sales and marketing executive*
Hutton, Edward Luke *diversified public corporation executive*
Kernan, Jerome Bernard *retired marketing educator, researcher*
Klein, Charles Henle *lithographing company executive*
Kollstedt, Paula Lubke *communications executive, writer*
Lafley, Alan G. *consumer products company executive*
Liss, Herbert Myron *communications educator*
Lockhart, John Mallery *management consultant*
Maier, Jack C. *food products company executive*
Moore, John Edward *marketing professional, freelance writer*
Morris, Margaret Elizabeth *marketing professional*
Orr, James Francis *marketing and information services executive*
Otto, Charlotte R. *consumer products company executive*
Pryor, Jerry Dennis *corporate professional*
Rolls, Steven George *communications executive*
Shanks, Earl *marketing professional*
Shipley, Tony L(ee) *software company executive*
Stolley, Alexander *advertising executive*
Zaring, Allen G. *homebuilding company executive*

Cleveland
Byron, Rita Ellen Cooney *travel executive, publisher, real estate agent, civic leader, photojournalist, writer*

Crawford, Edward E. *consumer products company executive*
Danco, Léon Antoine *management consultant, educator*
DeGroote, Michael G. *management consulting company executive*
Dunbar, Mary Asmundson *communications executive, investor and public relations consultant*
Eaton, Henry Felix *public relations executive*
Fountain, Ronald Glenn *management consultant, finance/marketing executive, management educator*
Graham, John W. *advertising executive*
Griffith, Mary H. *corporate communications executive*
Henry, Edward Frank *computer accounting service executive*
Johnson, John Frank *professional recruitment executive*
Mabee, Keith V. *communications/investor relations executive*
Marcus, Donald Howard *advertising executive*
Perkovic, Robert Branko *retired international management consultant*
Pucko, Diane Bowles *public relations executive*
Roop, James John *public relations executive*
Somers, K(arl) Brent *consumer products company executive*
Stashower, David L. *advertising executive*
Stewart, Jack M. *management consulting firm executive*
Taw, Dudley Joseph *sales executive, director*
Thompson, Stephen Arthur *sales consultant*

Columbus
Alban, Roger Charles *small business consultant*
Burke, Kenneth Andrew *advertising executive*
Curtin, Michael Francis *printing company executive, publisher*
Jacobs, Alexis A. *automobile company executive*
Kerner, Joseph Frank, Jr., *management consultant, educator*
Lefavre, Hadia *human resources executive*
Mahoney, Kimberly Lynne *event and facility executive*
McClain, Thomas Emerson *communications executive*
Milenthal, David *advertising executive*
Reardon, Nancy Anne *human resource executive*
Ress, Charles William *management consultant*
Sullivan, Ernest Lee *human resources director*
Tipton, Clyde Raymond, Jr., *communications and resources development consultant*
Varga, Steven Carl *human resources professional*
Zambito, John R. *executive search firm executive*

Dayton
Pasupuleti, Venumadhav *business executive, consultant*
Riley, David Richard *management consultant, retired military officer*
Tatar, Jerome F. *business products executive*

Dublin
Anderson, Kerrii B. *food service executive*
Miller, Charles *business management market research consultant*
Schuessler, John T. *food service executive*
Smith, K(ermit) Wayne *computer company executive*
Thomas, R. David *food services company executive*
Watkins, Carole S. *human resources specialist, health facility administrator*
Wilkins, Jeffrey M. *commputer company executive*

Eastlake
Wheeler, Melanie Elaine *administrative assistant, realtor*

Elyria
Patton, Thomas James *sales and marketing executive*

Fostoria
Howard, Kathleen *computer company executive*

Gahanna
Breen, John Wakefield *personnel services company executive*

Gates Mills
Abbott, James Samuel, III, *marketing executive*
Reitman, Robert Stanley *business consultant, nonprofit agency advisor*

Germantown
Lansaw, Charles Ray *rendering industry executive*

Grove City
Hosler, Elizabeth *management consultant*

Holland
Sacksteder, Thomas Michael *corporate executive, entrepreneur, writer*

Hudson
Wilfong, Brenda Ann *telecommunications executive*

Kent
Bissler, Richard Thomas *mortician*

Lancaster
Katlic, John Edward *management consultant*
Phillips, Edward John *consulting firm executive*

Loveland
Peters, Thomas J *management consultant, writer*

Mansfield
Granter, Sharon Savoy *restaurateur, caterer*
Pesec, David John *data systems executive*

Marion
Fassler, Crystal G. *marketing consultant*

Maumee
Kimble, James A. *management consultant, accountant*
Konopinski, Virgil James *industrial hygienist, consultant*

PROFESSIONAL INDEX 5767 INDUSTRY: SERVICE

Mayfield Heights
Newman, Joseph Herzl *advertising consultant*

Medina
Balest, Victor Rudolph *sales executive*
Williams, Paul C(hester) *consultant*

Miamisburg
Peppel, Michael E. *computer company executive*
Thompson, Holley Marker *lawyer, marketing professional*

Middletown
Turpin, Richard E. *sales executive*

Napoleon
Frame, Lawrence Milven, Jr., *inventor*

New Albany
Duggan, Thomas Patrick *management consultant*

Perrysburg
Kovacik, Neal Stephen *hotel and restaurant executive*
Loeffler, William Robert *quality productivity delivery specialist, engineering educator*

Plain City
Kinman, Gary *landscape company executive*

Powell
Lee, Robert J. Y. *marketing professional*

Reynoldsburg
Stevens, Kenneth T. *personal care industry executive*

Rocky River
Hosek, John Jude *planning organization executive*

Salem
Fehr, Kenneth Manbeck *retired computer systems company executive*

Springfield
Henning, William Clifford *cemetery consulting company executive*

Stow
Fatchet, Jo A. *private investigator*

Sylvania
Ring, Herbert Everett *management executive*
White, Alan Edward *computer company executive*

Tipp City
Taylor, Robert Homer *quality assurance professional, pilot*

Toledo
Block, Allan James *communications executive*
Meier, John F. *consumer products company executive*
Vicary, William Charles, Jr., *director sales and marketing*

Warren
Chapman, Willie Dean *sales executive*

West Chester
End, William Thomas *business executive*

Westerville
Keller, Kenneth Christen *advertising executive*

Westlake
Doane, Tim *travel company executive*
George, James W. *travel company executive*
Kuhn, Edwin P. *travel company executive*

Wooster
Schmitt, Wolf Rudolf *consumer products executive*

Worthington
Bender, Bob *advertising executive*

Xenia
Nutter, Zoe Dell Lantis *retired public relations executive*

Youngstown
Estrin, Melvyn J. *computer products company executive*

OKLAHOMA

Cleveland
Henry, Kathleen Marie *marketing executive*

Edmond
Edwards, Jon Brian *food service executive*

Lawton
Hooper, Roy B. *lobbyist, consultant*

Monkey Island
Vanatta, Chester B. *retired business executive, educator*

Norman
Madden, Glenda Gail *sales professional*

Oklahoma City
Ackerman, Raymond Basil *advertising agency executive*
Binning, Gene Barton *computer company executive*
Blackwell, John Adrian, Jr., *computer company executive*
Carballo, Bernard A. *computer technology company executive*
Crow, Charles Delmar *human resources manager, consultant*
Grupe, Robert Charles *corporate training consultant*
LaMotte, Janet Allison *retired management specialist*
Winchester, Susan *human resources specialist, state representative*

Tahlequah
Hare, Jerry Wayne *communications executive*

Tulsa
Abagnale, Frank William, Jr., *document security company executive*
Crouch, Gary Clinton *financial management company executive, accountant*
Gentry, Bern Leon, Sr., *minority consulting company executive*
Vetal, Bradley S. *service company executive*

OREGON

Astoria
Holcom, Floyd Everett *international business consultant*

Beaverton
Fisher, K. Kimball *human resources specialist, consultant*
Stewart, Kirk T. *public relations executive*

Bend
Wonser, Michael Dean *retired public affairs director, art history educator*

Canby
Flinn, Roberta Jeanne *management, computer applications consultant*

Eugene
Chambers, Carolyn Silva *communications company executive*
Miner, John Burnham *industrial relations educator, writer*

Forest Grove
Carson, William Morris *manpower planning and development advisor*

Hillsboro
Dyess, Kirby A. *computer company executive*

Jacksonville
Hennion, Reeve Lawrence *communications executive*

Lake Oswego
Edstrom, Pam *public relations executive*
Parrick, Gerald Hathaway *communications and marketing executive*
Zorkin, Melissa Waggener *public relations executive*

Mcminnville
Naylor-Jackson, Jerry *public relations consultant, retired, entertainer, broadcaster*

Newberg
Austin, Joan D. *personal care industry executive*

Portland
Bosch, Samuel Henry *computer company executive*
Boulot, Philippe *chef*
Conkling, Roger Linton *management consultant, business administration educator, retired utilities executive*
Denhart, Gun *direct mail order company executive*
Fenner, Peter David *communications executive*
Griggs, Gail *former marketing executive*
Kupel, Frederick John *business services executive*
Martin, Lucy Z. *public relations executive*
Perotto, Gregory Todd *public relations professional*
Richards, Robert Charles *management consultant*
Rotzien, Frederick William, III, *marketing executive*
Service, William W. *restaurant company executive*
Smith, Russell Wesley *management and computer applications consultant, organizational development trainer*
Stevens, Curtis *consumer products company executive*
Suwyn, Mark A. *building products executive*
VanSickle, Sharon Dee *public relations executive*
Wieden, Dan G. *advertising executive*

Salem
Benson, Steven Donald *sheet metal research and marketing executive, sheet metal mechanic, programmer, author*
Benton, Jack Mitchell *management consultant*

Shady Cove
Meyers, Sharon May *sales executive*

Tualatin
Alley, Allen H. *semiconductor company executive*
Bouchard, Jeffrey B. *semiconductor company executive*
Fleischmann, Marc W. *semiconductor company executive*
Greenberg, Robert Y. *semiconductor company executive*
Hick, Kenneth William *marketing company executive*
Olsen, Hans H. *semiconductor company executive*
West, Michael G. *semiconductor company executive*
Yavorsky, William D. *semiconductor company executive*

PENNSYLVANIA

Bensalem
Gretz, Karl Frederick *management training consultant, writer*

Berwyn
Guenther, George Carpenter *travel company executive, retired*

Bethel Park
Willard, John Gerard *consultant, author, lecturer*

Bethlehem
Penny, Roger Pratt *management executive*

Blue Bell
Carrow, John C. *computer company executive*
Ostroff, Nat S. *communications executive*
Rose, Kenneth L. *business executive*
Weinbach, Lawrence Allen *computer company executive*

Brentwood
Swanson, Fred A. *retired communications designer, councilman*

Bryn Mawr
Peters, Douglas Scott *health care executive*
Wheeler, Grace R. *retired market researcher*

Buckingham
Altier, William John *management consultant*

Camp Hill
Crist, Christine Myers *consulting executive*

Chadds Ford
Martin, David Warren *management consultant*
Sanford, Richard D. *computer company executive*

Chambersburg
Furr, Quint Eugene *marketing executive*
Neilson, Winthrop Cunningham, III, *communications executive, financial communications consultant, photographer*

Cranberry Township
Patten, Charles Anthony *management consultant, retired manufacturing company executive, author, publisher*

Dallas
Fiegelman, Richard Paul *sales consultant, freelance writer*

East Earl
Jonassen, Gaylord D. *computer company executive, new products and market development*

Easton
Schwab, Mark *marketing executive*

Erie
Lund, Edwin Harrison *business accounting systems executive*
Ryan, James Thomas *organizational consultant, business owner*

Exton
Stuart, John E. *Internet company executive*

Freeport
Chvala, Kathleen Ann *customer service supervisor*

Gettysburg
Hallberg, Budd Jaye *management consulting firm executive*

Harrisburg
Moritz, Milton Edward *security consultant*

Harrison City
Langer, Alois *communications executive*

Havertown
Somach, S. Dennis *communications executive*

Hazleton
Colangelo, Rocco, Jr., *sales executive*

Huntingdon Valley
Vollum, Robert Boone *management consultant*

Ivyland
Thorne, John Watson, III, *advertising and marketing executive*

Kennett Square
Fish, Robert H. *long term care industry executive*
Hennes, Robert Taft *former management consultant, investment executive*

King Of Prussia
Clauson, Sharyn Ferne *consulting company executive, educator*
Marcus, Stephen Cecil *former printing company executive*
Szabo, Joseph Laszlo *management consultant*

Lafayette Hill
Duncalfe Holt, Lucinda Bromwyn *marketing executive*
Green, Raymond Ferguson St. John *marketing and advertising executive*

Lancaster
Kelly, Robert Lynn *advertising agency executive*
Taylor, Ann *human resources specialist, educator*
Veitch, Boyer Lewis *printing company executive*

Lebanon
Moss, Richard Spencer *communications executive*

Lewisburg
Rote, Nelle Fairchild Hefty *management consultant*
Warner-Mills, Susan *organizational and community development consultant*

Malvern
Everhart, Rodney Lee *software industry executive*
Herring, Raymond Mark *marketing professional, researcher*

Manns Choice
Braendel, Douglas Arthur *hotel executive*

Mars
Seltzer, Mitchell Sherman *hotel executive*

Mechanicsburg
Stone, Thomas Richardson *management consultant*

Media
Garvin, Florence Ward *management consultant*

Merion Station
Mayer, Charles Arthur *management consultant, musician*

Montgomeryville
Schmidt, William Max *management consultant, business executive*

Montoursville
Morrison, Michael Christopher *advertising executive*

Mountainhome
Buttz, Charles William *outdoor advertising executive*

New Cumberland
Loux, Jonathan Dale *business development consultant*

New Hope
Thomsen, Thomas Richard *retired communications company executive*

Nottingham
White, Richard Edmund *marketing executive*

Palmyra
Moseley, Marc Robards *sales executive*

Philadelphia
Adawi, Nadia Sharon *energy cooperative executive*
Armstrong, C. Michael *communications company executive*
Backstrom, C. Stephen *communications executive*
Ballou, Roger H. *travel company executive*
Banse, Amy L. *communications executive, lawyer*
Barnett, Samuel Treutlen *international company executive*
Barrett, James Edward, Jr., *management consultant*
Binswanger, David R. *business executive*
Block, Arthur R. *communications executive*
Burke, Stephen B. *communications executive*
Coblitz, Mark A. *communications executive*
Coulson, Zoe Elizabeth *retired consumer marketing executive*
Di Benedetto, C. Anthony *marketing educator*
Dooner, Marlene S. *communications executive*
Dordelman, William E. *communications executive*
Dougherty Buchholz, Karen *communications executive*
Dua, Kamal *communications executive*
Feninger, Claude *industry management services company executive*
Finney, Graham Stanley *management consultant*
Friedman, Polly *public relations executive, marketing professional*
Gatti, Leonard J. *communications executive*
Glazier, Eric James *management consultant*
Greene, Hans *facilities administrator*
Hemphill, John Lindsay, III, *administrative assistant*
Jordan, Clifford Henry *management consultant*
Lacroix, Jean-Marie *executive chef*
Leschly, Jan *consumer products company executive*
Mallon, Charles J. *management consultant executive*
Mazzafro, Joseph D. *international adoption agency executive, web designer*
Meyer Weisgerber, Martha Lindsey *account executive*
Mikalauskas, Kenneth *communications executive*
Oliva, Terence Anthony *marketing educator*
Pacifico, Kerry T. *corporate executive*
Pernot, Guillermo *chef, restaurant owner*
Pick, Robert S. *communications executive*
Pinola, Richard J. *management consultant*
Presser, Janice *business executive*
Roberts, Brian L. *communications executive*
Roberts, Ralph Joel *telecommunications executive, cable broadcast executive*
Salva, Lawrence J. *communications executive*
Smith, Lawrence S. *communications executive*
Stewart, Marvin Lewis *human resources professional*
Stowell, Linda *communications executive*
Tuan, Kailin *management consultant, educator*
Whelan, Daniel J. *communications company executive*

Phoenixville
Brundage, Russell Archibald *retired data processing executive*

Pittsburgh
Arbutina, Petra *advertising executive*
Bender, Charles Christian *retail home center executive*
Burger, Herbert Francis *advertising agency executive*
Dempsey, Jerry Edward *retired service company executive*
Fisher, James Aiken *industrial marketing consultant*
Genge, William Harrison *advertising executive, writer*
Kilkeary, Kevin P. *hospitality executive*
Neel, John Dodd *cemetery executive*
O'Hare, Virginia Lewis *human resources administrator*
Paugh, Patricia Lou *business consultant*
Peterman, Donna Cole *communications executive*
Rathke, Sheila Wells *strategic and marketing consultant*
Reichblum, Audrey Rosenthal *public relations executive, publishing executive*
Richardson, J. William *hotel executive*
Wang, Guangmiao *business executive, consultant*
Ziskind, Deborah Ziskind *public relations and legal marketing executive*

Port Royal
Wert, Jonathan Maxwell, II, *management consultant*

Quakertown
Emory, Thomas Mercer, Jr., *data communications equipment manufacturing executive*

Radnor
Marland, Alkis Joseph *leasing company executive, computer scientist, educator, financial planner*
Paier, Adolf Arthur *computer software and services company executive*
Thompson, Pamela Padwick *public relations executive*

Reading
Dersh, Rhoda E. *management consultant, business executive*

Kraras, Gust C. *hotel executive*

Ridley Park
Walls, William Walton, Jr., *management consultant*

Royersford
Rhoads, Michael Dennis *sales executive*

Rydal
Boreen, Henry Isaac *computer company executive*

Sewickley
Woody, Carol Clayman *data processing executive*

Shippensburg
Stone, Susan Ridgaway *marketing educator*

Solebury
Gart, Herbert Steven *communications executive, producer*

Southampton
Mitchell, William F. *environmental company executive*

Southeastern
Rassbach, Herbert David *marketing executive*

State College
Subler, Edward Pierre *advertising executive*

Steelton
Zimmerman, Connie Ann *public administrator*

Sunbury
Rich, Norman S. *food service executive*
Weis, Robert Freeman *supermarket company executive*

Swarthmore
Krizek, Edwin John *marketing professional*

Tannersville
Moore, James Alfred *ski company executive, lawyer*

University Park
Grewal, Rajdeep *marketing professional, educator*

Valley Forge
Campman, Christopher Kuller *consulting company executive*
LaBoon, Lawrence Joseph *human resources consultant*

Wallingford
Medina, Harold Raymond, III, *marketing executive*

Warminster
Brenner, Rena Claudy *communications executive*

Warrendale
Cooper, Eric *multimedia executive, consultant*
Gaetano, Joy M. *human resources executive*

Warrington
Shaw, Milton Herbert *conglomerate executive*

Washington Crossing
Clevenger, Roy Edward *credit and collections manager*

Wayne
Carroll, Robert W. *retired business executive*
Conde, Cristobal I. *computer company executive*
Mann, James L. *computer company executive*

West Chester
Briggs, Douglas D. *communications executive*
Czako, Alan H. *human resources specialist, benefits compensation analyst*
Dunlop, Edward Arthur *computer company executive*
Hanna, Colin Arthur *county official, management and computer consultant*
Hanson, Diane Charske *management consultant*
Meystel, Michael A. *Internet executive*
Murray, Lawrence *management consultant*
Rizzo, Joyce A. *environmental services executive*
Robertson, William L. *environmental services executive*

West Conshohocken
Mullen, Eileen Anne *human resources executive*

Willow Grove
Asplundh, Christopher B. *tree service company executive*
Dwyer, Joseph P. *lumber executive*
Schiffman, Louis F. *management consultant*

Wynnewood
Belinger, Harry Robert *retired business executive*

Yardley
Huret, Barry S. *marketing professional, consultant*
Minter, Philip Clayton *retired communications company executive*
Newsom, Carolyn Cardall *management consultant*
Weaver, William Clair, Jr., (Mike Weaver) *human resources development executive*

York
Amos, Stuart R. *corporate executive*
Horn, Russell Eugene, Jr., *business executive*
Livingston, Pamela A. *corporate image and marketing management consultant*

RHODE ISLAND

Barrington
Mihaly, Eugene Bramer *corporate executive, consultant, writer, educator*

East Greenwich
Rockett, Thomas J. *retired management consultant*

Jamestown
DiStefano, Gregory John *marketing professional*

North Kingstown
Kullberg, Gary Walter *advertising agency executive*

Pawtucket
Charness, Wayne Samuel *public relations executive*
DeWerth, Gordon Henry *management consultant*
Hargreaves, David R. *toy company executive*
Hassenfeld, Alan Geoffrey *consumer products company executive*
Verrecchia, Alfred Joseph *toy company executive*

Providence
Allio, Robert John *management consultant, educator*
Baar, James A. *public relations and corporate communications executive, author, consultant, internet publisher, software developer*
Butler, John D. *human resources executive*
D'Andrea, Vincent Charles *postal clerk*
Snibbe, Patricia Miscall *advertising executive*
Whiting, Brian Christopher *hospitality consultant*

Wakefield
Doody, Agnes G. *communications educator, management and communication consultant*

West Greenwich
Turner, W. Bruce *computer company executive*

SOUTH CAROLINA

Aiken
Coble, Paul Ishler *advertising agency executive*

Bluffton
Reuben, Alvin Bernard *communications and entertainment executive*

Charleston
Ballard, Mary Melinda *financial communications and marketing/advertising executive, consumer advocate*
De Wolff, Louis *management consultant*
Dupree, Nathalie *chef, television personality, writer*
Litvin, Stephen W. *management consultant, educator*
Waggoner, Robert *chef*

Columbia
Barnum, William Douglas *retired communications company executive*
Chernoff, Marvin *advertising executive*
Ede, Fred Okotchy *marketing educator*
Fischer, Robert Andrew *computer executive*
Gasque, Harrison (Allard Harrison Gasque) *security firm executive*
Grimball, Caroline Gordon *retail sales professional*
Hull, Rodney L. *advertising executive*
Krantz, Palmer Eric, III, *parks and recreation director*
Silver, Rick *marketing professional*

Greenville
Blackwell, Larry G. *computer company executive*
Callahan, Ralph Wilson, Jr., *advertising agency executive*
Estevez, C. Alex *computer company executive*
Fitzgerald, Eugene Francis *management consultant*
Townes, Bobby Joe *travel agency executive*

Hartsville
Cecil, Allan *corporate communications executive*
Hill, Frank Trent, Jr., *packaging company executive*

Hilton Head Island
Estrin, Deborah Perry *human resources executive*
Martin, Donald James *marketing professional*
McKeldin, William Evans *management consultant*
Patton, Joseph Donald, Jr., *management consultant*
Woodrum, Robert Lee *executive search consultant*

Lake Wylie
Buggie, Frederick Denman *management consultant*
Butler, Carol King *advertising executive*
Sanford, James Kenneth *public relations executive*

Mauldin
Looper-Wilson, Leah Marie *human resources specialist, controller, interior designer*

Mount Pleasant
Hill, Larkin Payne *real estate company operations administrator*

Pawleys Island
Grubb, William Francis Xavier *consumer software executive, marketing executive*

Prosperity
Jennings, Wirt Holman, Jr., *retired marketing executive*

Seabrook Island
Call, Lawrence Michael *consumer products company executive*

Seneca
Strong-Tidman, Virginia Adele *marketing professional*

Spartanburg
Dillard, Richard *director of public affairs*
Hutchinson, Ronald B. *restaurant executive*

Sullivans Island
Norton, Fran *recreation director*

TENNESSEE

Bartlett
Wallace, William Brian *sales executive*

Chattanooga
Knight, Ralph H. *consumer products company executive*
Meyer, Roger Arnold *management consultant, writer*

Cleveland
Rhodes, Arthur Delano *benefits administrator*

Gallatin
Bradley, Nolen Eugene, Jr., *retired personnel executive, educator*
Ellis, Joseph Newlin *retired distribution company executive*

Gatlinburg
Flanagan, Judy *special events professional, entertainment and marketing specialist, professional public speaker*

Germantown
Arendall, Charles Steven *management consultant, educator*
Murray, James Alan *urban and environmental consultant, investor*

Knoxville
Anderson, Charles, Jr., *printing/publishing company executive*
Campbell, John *printing/publishing company executive*
Campbell, Michael *entertainment industry executive*
Cornish, Jeff *petroleum sales executive*
Horne, Douglas A. *diversified companies executive*
Morton, Mike *consumer products executive*
Nesbit, Sandi Michelle *personnel director*
Sansom, William B. *consumer products executive*

Lebanon
Davis, Julie Kramer *communications executive*
Woodhouse, Michael A. *restaurant holdings company executive*

Madison
Cage, Allie M. *communications executive*
Hadley, John Livingston, V, *management executive, writer*

Memphis
Abston, Dunbar, Jr., *management executive*
Archer, Ward, Jr., *advertising executive*
Blake, Norman *hotel executive*
Edwards, Doris Porter *computer specialist*
Jallepalli, Raji *food service executive*
Krieger, Robert Lee, Jr., *human resource/management consultant, educator, writer, travel/meeting planner, political analyst, internet marketing consultant*
Malmo, John *advertising executive*
Mann, Donald Cameron *record company executive*
Williams, Russ *marketing professional*

Nashville
Allbritton, Cliff *personal and organizational consultant*
Brett, John Brendan, Jr., *corporate advertising and public relations executive*
Brown, Tony Ersic *record company executive*
Cawthon, William Connell *operations management consultant*
Chamberlain, David M. *consumer products company executive*
Dobbs, George Albert *funeral director, embalmer*
Dye, Hank *public relations executive*
Dysart, Benjamin Clay, III, *consultant, conservationist, engineer*
Evans, Franklin Bachelder *marketing educator emeritus*
Ferguson, John D. *prison management administrator*
Hillenmeyer, Henry Reiling, Jr., *restaurant company executive*
James, Kay Louise *management consultant, healthcare executive*
Lawrence, Thomas Patterson *public relations executive*
McNeely, Mark *marketing professional, journalist*
Meredith, Owen Nichols *public relations executive, genealogist*
Mitchell, Robert W. *diversified company executive*
Moore, William Grover, Jr., *management consultant, retired military officer*
Shipley Biddy, Shelia *artist management executive*
Van Mol, Louis John, Jr., *public relations executive*

Oak Ridge
Hudson, Sheila Donnette *waste management administrator*
Rupert, David Roy *human resources manager*

Shelbyville
Nelson, Clara Singleton *human resources consultant*

Tullahoma
Gossick, Lee Van *consultant, executive, retired air force officer*

TEXAS

Addison
Grote, Dick (Richard Charles Grote) *management consultant, educator, author, radio commentator*
Thomas, Philip Robinson *management consulting company executive*

Allen
Battat, Emile A. *management executive*

Amarillo
Stubben, Dolus Jane (D. J. Stubben) *advertising executive*
Turks, Hildegard Maria (Hildegard Maria Chronis) *retired security investigator, writer*

Arlington
English, Marlene Cabral *management consultant*
Harris, Vera Evelyn *human resources specialist*
Sawyer, Dolores *motel chain executive*
Spears, Georgann Wimbish *marketing executive*

Austin
Barrientos, Gonzalo *advertising executive, public relations executive, state legislator*
Belle-Isle, David Richard *organization and management consultant*
Bush, Neil *business executive*
Carona, John J. *management consultant, state legislator*
Casey, James Francis *management consultant*
Curle, Robin Lea *computer software industry executive*
Decaro, Angelo Anthony, Jr., *data processing executive*
Drongowski, Steve *advertising executive*
Gurasich, Stephen William, Jr., *advertising executive*
Hammer, Katherine Gonet *software company executive*
Hart, Roderick P. *communications educator, researcher, author*
Huber, John Charles *creativity researcher*
Jorgeson, Brent Wilson *management executive*
Knapp, Mark Lane *communication educator, consultant*
Laine, Katie Myers *communications consultant, executive coach*
Lambiase, Vincent A. *consumer products company executive*
Lenoir, Gloria Cisneros *consultant, educator*
Lindsay, Jon *business consultant, state legislator*
Lundgren, Clara Eloise *public affairs administrator, journalist*
Pate, Jacqueline Hail *retired data processing company executive*
Pearson, Jim Berry, Jr., *human resources specialist*
Peters, Gregory A. *technology company executive*
Sober, Debra Evonne *environmental services administrator*
Spence, Roy Milam, Jr., *advertising executive*
Trabulsi, Judy *advertising and marketing executive*
Vande Hey, James Michael *corporate executive, former air force officer*
Walls, Carl Edward, Jr., *food service executive*
Wooley, John C. *food service executive*
York, Candace A. *marketing professional, writer*
Young, Joan Crawford *advertising executive*

Bedford
Champney, Raymond Joseph *advertising and marketing executive, consultant*
Horvat, Vashti *online marketing consultant*
Owens, Merle Wayne *executive search consultant*

Bellaire
Streeter, Kevin D. *management consultant*

Cedar Park
Duke, Carol Michiels *personal care industry executive*

Cleveland
Rice, J. Andrew *management consultant, tree farmer*

College Station
Conole, Richard Clement *management consultant*
Gunn, Clare Alward *travel consultant, writer, retired educator*
Hise, Richard Todd *marketing professional, educator, consultant*

Colleyville
Bush, Holly Newsom *management consultant*
Self, Mark Edward *communications consultant*

Corpus Christi
Boyle, Dennis Joseph, III, *computer company executive*
DuVall, Lorraine *recreation center owner*
Stanford, Jane Herring *management consultant and educator, author*

Dallas
Aars, Rallin James *executive management, business development, marketing, communications, strategic planning, consultant*
Alvey, David Lynn *advertising executive, artist, curator, poet*
Azcarraga, Gaston *hotel executive*
Blinn, Mark A. *consumer products company executive*
Bowman, Kenneth Howard *sales executive, marketing professional*
Brierley, Harold M. *advertising executive*
Brinker, Norman E. *restaurant company executive*
Brooks, Douglas H. *food service executive*
Bryant, L. Gerald *management consultant*
Bushey, Marilyn *communications executive*
Carl, Robert E. *retired marketing company executive*
Chimbel, Bob *advertising executive*
Crusemann, F(rederick) Ross *advertising agency official*
Dalton, Harry Jirou, Jr., (Jerry Dalton) *public relations executive*
Davis, John F., III, *travel company executive*
Dawson, Edward Joseph *merger and acquisition executive*
Dedman, Robert Henry *sales executive*
Dieste, Tony *marketing professional*
Dillon, Donald Ward *management consultant*
Dozier, David Charles, Jr., *marketing public relations and advertising executive*
Dykeman, Alice Marie *public relations executive*
Edwards, Barry *leasing company executive*
Edwards, Warren D. *computer company executive*
Ellis, June B. *human resource consultant*
England, Julie Spicer *computer company executive*
Frank, Paula Feldman *business executive*
Gossen, Emmett Joseph, Jr., *motel chain executive, lawyer*
Govil, Manish Kumar *customer service administrator*
Grimes, David Lynn *communications company executive*
Harmel, Warren *marketing professional*
Head, Mark Davies *human resources and employee benefits services executive, consultant*
Heydrick, Linda Carol *consulting company executive, editor*
Horchow, S(amuel) Roger *marketing consultant*
Hunt, Caroline Rose *hotel executive*
Janzen, Howard E. *communications executive*
Kelly, Timothy E. *communications executive*
King, Mark *computer company executive*
Kleisner, Frederick J. *hotel executive*
Kusin, Gary M. *consumer products company executive*
Lane, Alvin Huey, Jr., *management consultant*
Langdale, Mark *hotel executive*

Leven, Stephen H. *human resources professional*
Levenson, Stanley Richard *public relations and advertising executive*
Liskow, Frederic Cullen (Ric) *printing company executive*
Love, Sammie L. *administrative assistant, writer*
Maritz, Philip F. (Flip Maritz) *hotel executive*
Metzner, Richard *advertising executive*
Mong, Robert William, Jr., *media executive*
Murphy, Randall Kent *management consultant*
O'Shea, Karen *public relations executive*
Pace, Carolina Jolliff *communications executive*
Pearson, Robert Lawrence *executive recruiter*
Rich, Jeffrey A. *computer company executive*
Richards, Stanford Harvey *advertising agency executive, design studio executive*
Sidu, Sanjiv *computer software executive*
Snead, Richard Thomas *restaurant company executive*
Sonsteby, Charles M. *food service executive*
Spiegel, Lawrence Howard *advertising executive*
Stern, Andrew Milton *public relations executive*
Vanderveld, John, Jr., *international business development specialist*
Von Kennel, Gary Phillip *marketing company executive*
Waters, Rollie O. *management consultant*
Weinkauf, William Carl *communications executive*
Westberry, David M. *executive search consultant*
Williams, Sterling L. *computer software executive*
Wilson, Catherine Cooper (Kitty Wilson) *communications executive, writer*
Wiss, Marvin J. *public relations executive, consultant*
Wyly, Charles Joseph, Jr., *corporate executive*
Zeitlin, Laurie *printing company executive*

Del Rio
Garrett, James William *computer company executive*
Prather, Gerald Luther *management consultant, retired air force officer, judge*

Denton
Siefkin, William Charles *investor, marketing/sales executive, consultant*

Dripping Springs
Nicholas, Nickie Lee *retired industrial hygienist*

Duncanville
Jenkins, Tony Dean *salesman*

El Paso
Cassidy, Richard Thomas *hotel executive, defense industry consultant, retired army officer*
Deerman, Ruth Gillett *sales executive*
Roberts, Ernst Edward *marketing consultant*

Fort Worth
Appel, Bernard Sidney *marketing consultant, former electronic company executive*
Bradshaw, James Edward (Jim Bradshaw) *consultant*
Browning, Tyson R. *management consultant*
Davis, Carol Lyn *administrative assistant*
Johnson, J. Mitchell *communications executive*
Pratt, Jack E., Sr., *hotel executive*
Ray, Paul Richard, Jr., *executive recruiter, consultant*
Shannon, Larry Redding *public relations executive*

Fredericksburg
Arnold, George Lawrence *retired advertising company executive*
Benedict, Mark J. *government analyst, marketing executive, lawyer, real estate investment consultant*

Frisco
Hawk, Phillip Michael *service corporation executive*
Migdol, Marvin Jacob *public relations and marketing executive, consultant*

Garland
Basham, Lloyd Moman *manufacturing service company executive*

Greenville
Brown, Harley Mitchell *retired computer company executive, writer*

Heath
Hargrave, Robert Warren *retired hair styling salon chain executive*

Highland Village
Lawrence, William Clarence *business executive, lawyer, mediator, politician*

Houston
Accardi, Larry J. *food service executive*
Anderson, William, Jr., (William Albion Anderson Jr.) *consultant*
Bazelides, Diane *public relations executive*
Billick, L. Larkin *marketing executive*
Blackburn, Sadie Gwin Allen *business executive*
Carlberg, W. Charles *advertising executive*
Combs, Janet Louise *sales and advertising company executive*
Drummond, Kirk G. *food service executive*
Ellis, Raymond Clinton, Jr., *hotel executive, educator*
Flato, William Roeder, Jr., *software development company executive*
Foote, Jill *management consultant, educator, investment banker*
Goings, Austin Nelson *sales executive*
Helland, George Archibald, Jr., *management consultant, manufacturing executive, former government official*
Herrington, James Benjamin, Jr., *job recruiting executive*
Holmes, Roscette Yvonne Lewis *organizational development and training consultant*
Ifft, Lewis George, III, *company administrator*
Jeanneret, Paul Richard *management consultant*
Jenkins, William E. *business executive*
Jones, Sonia Josephine *advertising executive*
Keating, Tim *chef*
Kors, R. Paul *search company executive*
Leth, Steven A. *management consultant*
Mampre, Virginia Elizabeth *communications executive*
Mark, Rebecca P. *environmental services administrator*
Marshall, Gregory K. *food service executive*
Mauck, William M., Jr., *retired executive recruiter, small business owner*
Mayo, Carolyn *marketing professional, public relations executive*
McCollam, Marion Andrus *consulting firm executive, educator*
McKim, Paul Arthur *management consultant, retired petroleum executive*
Morabito, Philip A. *public relations executive*
Murdy, William F. *diversified services executive*
Myers, A. Maurice *waste management executive*
Myers, James Clark *advertising and public relations executive*
Myers, Norman Allan *marketing professional*
Nacknouck, James Dominic *management executive*
O'Brient, David Warren *sales executive, consultant*
O'Donnell, Lawrence, III, *waste management executive*
Rieke, Ronald Alfred *computer company executive*
Roberts, Paul *chef*
Sill, Gerald de Schrenck *hotel executive*
Smith, Claire *chef*
Solymosy, Edmond Sigmond Albert *international marketing executive, retired army officer*
Steiner, David P. *waste management executive*
Stephens, Sidney Dee *human resources specialist, retired chemical manufacturing company executive*
Tilney, Elizabeth A. *marketing executive*
Vollmer, Helen *public relations executive*
Watson, Max P., Jr., *computer software company executive*
Yuen, Benson Bolden *airline management consultant, software executive*

Huntsville
Smyth, Joseph Philip *travel industry executive*
Stowe, Charles Robinson Beecher *management consultant, educator, lawyer*

Hurst
Bishara, Amin Tawadros *management and consulting firm executive, technical services executive*

Irving
Anderson, Greg R. *communications company executive*
Appel, John C. *communications company executive*
Caldwell, James D. *hospitality company executive*
Dinicola, Robert *retired consumer products company executive*
Duffy, Dan *computer company executive*
Forte, Mary L. *consumer products company executive*
Gibson, Colvin Donald *human resources specialist*
Gretzinger, Ralph Edwin, III, *management consultant*
Jorns, Steven D. *hotel executive*
Levy, Lester A. *sanitation company executive*
McClain, Dennis Douglas *advertising executive*
Munger, Sharon *market research firm executive*
Nugent, John Hilliard *communications executive*
Wicks, William Withington *retired public relations executive*

Junction
Evans, Jo Burt *communications executive, rancher*

Keller
Patterson, Ronald R(oy) *management consultant*

Kingwood
Chamoun-Nicolas, Habib *business development consultant*

Laredo
Kohl, John Preston *management educator*
Lakshmana, Viswanath *computer and information systems executive*

Leander
Merriman, Chrisann *marketing professional*

Lubbock
Davis, Alvin G. *company executive*
Fontenot, Andrea Dean *communications executive*

Plano
Adams, Barney *consumer products company executive*
Alberthal, Lester M., Jr., *retired information processing services executive*
Casavantes, Rita *defense electronics and engineering professional*
Collumb, Peter John *communications company executive*
Davis, Gary L. *human resources professional*
Davis, Robert D. *rental company executive*
Dougherty, F(rancis) Kelly *data processing executive*
Fadel, Mitchell E. *rental company executive*
Flores, Marion Thomas *advertising executive*
Hatfield, Darl P. *consumer products company executive*
Korst, Christopher A. *rental company executive*
Norwood, Cecilia Stubbs *communications executive*
Scott, Terry Lee *communications company executive*
Sivinski, Tina M. *human resources specialist*
Speese, Mark E. *rental company executive*

Port Arthur
Munoz, Andrea Lee *human resources specialist*

Richardson
Chlamtac, Imrich *computer company executive, educator*
Sperrin, Graham Frederick *marketing professional*

Rockwall
Bush, Larry Don *communications company administrator*
Wiorkowski, Gabrielle Kay *database consultant*

Round Rock
Bell, Paul D. *computer company executive*
Crawford, Kim *computer company executive*
Dell, Michael S. *computer company executive*
Goodman, Kim *marketing professional, computer company executive*
Hudson, Michel Colette *management consultant*
Marengi, Joseph Alexander *computer company executive*
Mott, Randall D. *computer company executive*
Rollins, Kevin B. *computer company executive*
Schneider, James M. *computer company executive*
Vanderslide, James T. *computer company executive*
Wahl, William Bryan *marketing professional, real estate officer*

San Angelo
Coe, Robert Stanford *retired management educator*

San Antonio
Bromley, Ernest W. *communications executive*
Butt, Charles Clarence *food service executive*
Caldwell, Royce S. *communications executive*
Carr, Cassandra Colvin *communications company executive*
Ellis, James D. *communications executive, lawyer*
Foster, Charles F. *communications executive*
Franklin, Larry Daniel *communications company executive*
Garcia, Henry Frank *supply management and project management consultant and trainer*
Holmes, Parris H., Jr., *information services professional*
Kehl, Randall Herman *executive, consultant, lawyer*
Keirnan, Donald E. *communications executive*
Labenz-Hough, Marlene *dispute resolution professional*
Mays, Mark Pitman *communication company executive*
Mills, Linda S. *public relations executive*
Montemayor, Carlos Rene *advertising agency executive*
Moya, Francisco Saez *consumer products company executive*
Nava, Carmen P. *communications executive*
Pliego-Stout, Patricia *travel company executive*
Shirley, Graham Edward *management executive*
Stephenson, Randall *communications executive*
Whitesell, Stephen Ernest *parks and recreation director*
Wilkins, Ray *communications executive*

San Marcos
Moore, Patsy Sites *food service consultant*
Wilson, Vicki Lynn *executive secretary, administrative assistant*

Southlake
Elliott, Dennis Dawson *communications executive*
Gilliland, Michael S. *travel company executive*
Kelly, Carol A. *travel company executive*
Schwarte, David A. *travel company executive*
Sorge, Karen Lee *commercial printing company executive, consultant*

Spring
Ciancimino, Joseph Andrew *data processing executive*
Cooley, Andrew Lyman *corporation executive, former army officer*
Maxfield, Mary Constance *management consultant*
Treasure-Terrell, Suzanne Marie *marketing and sales professional, writer, poet, lyricist*

Spring Branch
Barban, Arnold Melvin *advertising educator*
Fasano, Anthony John *marketing consultant*

Stephenville
Moore, Linda Kathleen *personnel agency executive*

Sugar Land
Preng, David Edward *management consultant*

The Woodlands
Glenn, Gerald Marvin *marketing, engineering and construction executive*
Jack, Nancy Rayford *supplemental resource company executive, consultant*
Morrison, Scott David *management consultant, small business owner*

Trophy Club
Caffee, Virginia Maureen *executive assistant*
Haerer, Deane Norman *marketing and public relations executive*
Holley, Cyrus Helmer *management consulting service executive*

Tyler
Resnik, Linda Ilene *marketing and information executive, publisher, consultant, writer*

Willis
Snider, Robert Larry *management consultant*

UTAH

Logan
Drozdeck, Steven Richard *management consultant*

Orem
Morey, Robert Hardy *communications executive*
Sawyer, Thomas Edgar *management consultant*

Park City
Milner, Harold William *hotel executive*
Weight, Alec Charles *retired management consultant*

Provo
Bartlett, Leonard Lee *retired communications educator, retired advertising agency executive*
Konecny-Costa, Jennifer *computer company executive*
Nelson, Stewart *computer company executive*

Salt Lake City
Carrell, Stewart *computer company executive*
Davis, Gene *public relations professional, state legislator*
Davis, Loyd Evan *defense industry marketing professional*
Elkins, Glen Ray *retired service company executive*
Howell, Kevin L. *hotel executive*
Howell, Scott Newell *computer company executive, state legislator*
Hutcherson, Christopher Alfred *marketing, recruiting and educational fundraising executive*
Jensen, Rodney H. *hotel executive*
Johnson, Jon L. *advertising executive*
Maher, David L. *drug store company executive*
Williams, J. Richard *service executive, real estate executive*

Sandy
Skidmore, Joyce Thorum *public relations and communication executive*

South Jordan
Wirthlin, Richard Bitner *research strategist*

VERMONT

Brattleboro
Cosgrove, Bryan *emergency planner*

Burlington
Allen, Bill *food service executive, writer*
Dominy, Garrett L. *business consulting company executive*

East Montpelier
Christiansen, Andrew P. *internet consulting business executive*

Essex Junction
Sweetser, Gene Gillman *quality assurance professional, state legislator*

Lower Waterford
Burnham, Patricia White *consultant, advocate, writer, business executive*

Ludlow
Mueller, Diane *hotel executive*

Middlebury
Benoit, Philip Grosvenor *communications executive, educator, writer*

Montpelier
Fitzhugh, William Wyvill, Jr., *printing company executive*
Klein, Tony *public relations executive, state representative*

Newfane
Farber, Lillian *retired photography equipment company executive*

North Clarendon
Hays, John C. *sales executive, marketing professional*

Norwich
Stevenson, Josiah, IV, *management consultant*

Stowe
Fiddler Nichols, Barbara Dillow *sales and marketing professional*
Marron, Richard C. *hotel executive, state representative*

Waitsfield
Hiscock, Richard Carson *marine safety investigator*
Parrish, Thomas Kirkpatrick, III, *marketing consultant*

Wilmington
Little, Thomas Mayer *public relations executive*

Woodstock
Hoyt, Coleman Eilliams *postal consultant*
Matlins, Stuart M. *management consultant, publisher*

VIRGINIA

Abingdon
Smith, Jack C. *supermarket executive*

Alexandria
Ancell, Robert Manning *leadership organization executive*
Ashford, John Edward *communications executive*
Carleson, Robert Bazil *public policy consultant*
Devantier, Paul W. *communications executive, broadcaster, administrator*
Foster, Robert Francis *communications executive*
Frommer, Lawrence Julian *retired travel company executive*
Harris, David Ford *management consultant, retired government official*
Harris, Lillian Irene *marketing professional*
James, Carol Lee *communications executive*
Johnston, Richard M. *communications executive*
Lantz, Phillip Edward *security firm executive, consultant*
Laurent, Lawrence Bell *communications executive, former journalist*
Lightner, Candace Lynne *nonprofit management consultant, advocate*
Luna, Patricia Adele *marketing executive*
McMillan, Charles William *consulting company executive*
Moran, Donald Will *consulting company executive*
Nelson, David Leonard *process management systems company executive*
Newton, Hugh C. *public relations executive*
Nodeen, Janey Price *company executive*
Paulson, Gwen O. Gampel *government relations consultant*
Pitzer, Jack Todd *purchasing agent, consultant, purchasing agent, educator*
Rogers, Paul A'Court *management consulting executive*
Saunders, Steven R. *corporate communications specialist*
Simmons, Richard De Lacey *mass media executive*
Stone, Ann Elizabeth *marketing agency executive, consultant*
Verburg, Edwin Arnold *management consultant*
Widner, Ralph Randolph *retired civic executive*

Wilding, James Anthony *airport administrator*

Annandale
Gioconda, Thomas F. *government services and construction company executive, retired military officer*
Jarvis, Elbert, II, (Jay Jarvis) *employee benefits specialist*
Khim, Jay Wook *high technology systems integration executive*

Arlington
Beaty, James Thomas *retired buyer*
Erwin, Frank William *personnel research and publishing executive*
Gallagher, Anne Porter *communications executive*
Gianturco, Delio E. *management consultant, educator, author*
Gunderson, Steve Craig *consultant, former congressman*
Hewitt, Thomas F. *hotel executive*
Kanter, L. Erick *public relations executive*
McCaslin, David E. *hotel executive*
McFarland, Walter Gerard *management consultant*
McGinn, Daniel G. *public relations executive*
Metz, Craig Huseman *business executive*
Potvin, William Tracey *management consultant*
Rabaut, Thomas W. *defense industry executive*
Rosenthal, Robert M. *automotive sales executive*
Samburg, A. Gene *security company executive*
Shaker, William Haygood *marketing professional, public policy reformer*
Whetsell, Paul W. *hotel executive*
Widener, Peri Ann *business development executive*
Zorthian, Barry *communications executive*

Ashburn
Trent, Grace Chen *communications executive*

Blacksburg
Weaver, Pamela Ann *hospitality research professional*

Burgess
Burch, Michael Ira *public relations executive, former government official*

Centreville
Tobin, Robert Edwin *regional director*

Chantilly
Anderson, Maynard Carlyle *national and international security executive*
Watkins, Felix Scott *printing company executive*
Welles, Judith *public affairs executive*

Charlottesville
Brown, Holmes *public affairs executive*
Colley, John Leonard, Jr., *educator, author, management consultant*
Haigh, Robert William *business administration educator*
MacIlwaine, Mary Jarratt *public relations executive*
Wolcott, John Winthrop, III, *retired corporate executive*

Chesterfield
Nixon, Samuel Anthony, Jr., *state legislator, information services executive*

Danville
Owen, Claude Bernard, Jr., *tobacco company executive*

Dulles
Miller, Jonathan F. *Internet company executive*

Fairfax
Arnold, Paul N. *business services company executive*
Baker, Daniel Richard *computer company executive, consultant*
Bersoff, Edward H. *information systems company executive*
Brands, Paul A. *management consultant*
Kieffer, Jarold Alan *publications company executive, writer*
Merrick, Phillip *technology company executive*
Pan, Elizabeth Lim *information systems company executive*
Saverot, Pierre-Michel *nuclear waste management company executive*
Stafford, Earl W. *technology executive*
Steventon, Robert Wesley *marketing executive*
Witek, James Eugene *retired public relations executive*

Fairfax Station
Bloomer, William Arthur *retired security industry executive*

Falls Church
Ashkin, Ronald Evan *international executive*
Bingman, Charles Franklin *public administration executive and educator*
Miller, Mary Jeannette *office management specialist*
Nashman, Alvin Eli *computer company executive*
Orkand, Donald Saul *management consultant*
Plevyak, Thomas Joseph *communications executive*

Fredericksburg
Geary, Patrick Joseph *security administrator, writer*
Hickman, Margaret Capellini *advertising executive*

Free Union
Horowitz, Barry Martin *systems research and engineering company executive*

Front Royal
Bonzagni, Vincent Francis *lawyer, program administrator, analyst, researcher*

Glasgow
Riegel, Kurt Wetherhold *environmental protection executive*

Great Falls
Bachner, John Philip *business consultant*

Hampton
Drummond, James Everman *defense technology transfer consultant, former army officer*

White, Debra Saunders *technology executive*

Hardy
Harriett, Rebecca *park director*

Herndon
Childers, Charles *communications executive*
Frazier, Paul Ignatius *marketing professional*
Gilbert, Douglas Brainerd *management executive*
White, Matthew C. *advertising executive*

Keswick
Woods, Reginald Foster *management consulting executive*

Kilmarnock
Ibañez, Alvaro *patent design company executive, artist*

Lake Ridge
Ingrassia, Anthony Frank *human resource specialist*

Lightfoot
Morris, Robert Louis *management consultant*

Manassas
Colgan, Charles Joseph *corporate professional, state legislator*

Mc Lean
Adler, Larry *marketing professional*
Capone, Lucien, Jr., *management consultant, former naval officer*
Casciano, John P. *executive*
Estren, Mark James *business and media consultant, TV producer, author*
Gangemi, Gaetano Tommaso, Sr., *computer company executive*
Jayne, Edward Randolph, II, *executive search consultant*
Kolombatovic, Vadja Vadim *retired management consulting company executive*
Moeller, Robert Charles (Bud Moeller) *management consultant*
Olson, Walter Justus, Jr., *management consultant*
Paschall, Lee McQuerter *retired communications consultant*
Rose, Susan Porter *consultant*
Shrader, Ralph W. *management consultant*
Smith, Esther Thomas *communications executive*
Watson, Jerry Carroll *advertising executive*
Webber, Diana L. *management consultant executive, engineering educator*
Welch, Jasper Arthur, Jr., *security company executive, consultant*
Williams, Earle Carter *retired professional services company executive*

Middleburg
McNichols, Gerald Robert *consulting company executive*

Midlothian
Wadsworth, Robert David *advertising agency executive*

Moneta
Ulmer, Walter Francis, Jr., *consultant, former army officer*

Newport News
Behlmar, Cindy Lee *business manager, consultant, speaker*

Norfolk
Bland, Gilbert Tyrone *food service executive*
Blount, Robert Haddock *corporate executive, retired naval officer*

Oak Hill
Okay, John Louis *management consultant*

Potomac Falls
Merna, Gerald Francis *advertising executive, retired military officer*

Reston
Clark, Katherine Karen *software company executive*
Dietrich, Dawn *software company executive*
Dussek, Steven P. *communications executive*
Easton, Glenn Hanson, Jr., *management and insurance consultant, federal official, naval officer*
Ewell, Dena Lynette *administrative management executive*
Fernandez, Raul J. *data processing executive*
Fitzpatrick, Patrick C. *data processing executive*
Foster, William Anthony *management consultant, educator*
Johnson, Thea Jean *internet and intranet security service provider*
Mowbray, Robert Norman *natural resource management consultant, forest ecologist*
Phillippi, Elmer Joseph, Jr., *data communications consultant*
Posey, Ada Louise *human resources specialist*
Salisbury, Alan Blanchard *information systems executive*
Sarreals, Sonia *data processing consultant*
Schick, Michael William *public relations executive*
Schleede, Glenn Roy *energy market and policy consultant*
Stone, Lawrence D. *software company executive*

Richmond
Bohannon, Sarah Virginia *personnel professional*
Braeckmans, Paul *advertising executive*
Dan, Michael T. *diversified services firm executive*
Huntsinger, Jerald E. *advertising executive*
Jacobs, Harry Milburn, Jr., *advertising executive*
Johnson, Johnny F. *marketing professional*
Joynes, Barbara Cole *marketing executive*
King, Allen B. *tobacco company executive*
Maneker, Deanna Marie *advertising executive*
Moyne, Yves M. *water treatment executive*
Raper, Mark Irvin *public relations executive*
Roper, Hartwell H. *tobacco company executive*
Sneed, Jimmy *chef, restaurant owner*

Saint Thomas
Greiner, Kenneth Donald, Jr., *management consultant*

Springfield
Bruen, John Dermot *management consultant*
Edwards-LeBoeuf, Renee Camille *public relations professional, logistics engineer*
Fedewa, Lawrence John *management consulting firm executive, entrepreneur*

Sterling
Schrader, William L. *communications executive*

Vienna
Armistead, William Spencer *communications executive*
Brandel, Ralph Edward *management consultant*
Gardenier, Turkan Kumbaraci *statistical company executive, researcher*
Hale, Thomas Morgan *professional services executive*
Koons, James E. *management consultant*
Sheinbaum, Gilbert Harold *international management consultant*
Ulvila, Jacob Walter *management consultant*
Van Stavoren, William David *consultant, retired government official*
Walker, Edward Keith, Jr., *retired management consultant, retired military officer*

Virginia Beach
Alexander, William Powell *business advisor*
Burgess, Marvin Franklin *human resources, management specialist, consultant*
Dixon, John Spencer *international executive*
Hilgers, John Jack William *management and transportation consultant*
Isaacs, Frederick Wilson *management consultant*
Picache, Josefina Reyes *travel service company executive, marriage counselor*
Tarbutton, Lloyd T. *franchise consultant*
Wick, Robert Thomas *retired supermarket executive*

Washington
Lynch, Reinhardt *chef, restaurant owner*

Washingtons Birthplace
Donahue, John Joseph *park and recreation director*

Waterford
Hallberg, Parker Franklin *environmental company executive*

Waynesboro
Layman, J. Allen *communications executive*
Quarforth, James S. *communications executive*

Williamsburg
Ackerman, Lennis Campbell *retired management consultant*
Hoving, John Hannes Forester *consulting firm executive*

Winchester
Bonometti, Robert John *technology management and strategy executive*
Engelage, James Roland *management consultant*
Gaither, George Manney *marketing consultant*

Wintergreen
Omohundro, William Addison *research marketing executive*

Woodbridge
Holman, Karen Marie Anderson *purchasing agent*
Locigno, Paul Robert *public affairs executive*

WASHINGTON

Bainbridge Island
Marsh, Donald Reppert *holding company executive*

Bellevue
Davis, Stephen B. *Internet company executive, lawyer*
Hall, Eleanor Williams *public relations executive*
Myhrvold, Nathan *technology executive*
O'Byrne, Michael *management consultant*
Pool, David *software executive*
Pritt, Frank W. *computer company executive*

Bothell
Hawthorne, Nan Louise *Internet resources consultant, web site designer, writer*

Des Moines
Brandmeir, Christopher Lee *hotel and tourism management educator*

Ephrata
Randolph, Kevin Howard *marketing executive*

Federal Way
Dooley, James H. *product company executive*
Muzyka-McGuire, Amy *marketing professional, nutrition consultant*
Rogel, Edward P. *corporate human resources executive*

Gig Harbor
Holmberg, Branton Kieth *management consultant*

Kent
Cheung, John B. *research and development executive*

Lacey
Breytspraak, John, Jr., *management consultant*

Malaga
Nanto, Roxanna Lynn *marketing professional, management consultant*

Medina
Dagnon, James Bernard *human resources executive*

Mercer Island
Dykstra, David Charles *management executive, consultant, accountant, author, educator*

Oak Harbor
Meaux, Alan Douglas *retired facilities technician, sculptor*

Olympia
Adkins, Ben Frank *management and engineering consultant*
Marcelynas, Richard Chadwick *management consultant*
Weese, Bruce Eric *sales executive*

Pullman
Gursoy, Dogan *hospitality and tourism educator, researcher*

Redmond
Ambrose, Adele D. *communications executive*
Ballmer, Steven A. *software company executive*
Caouette, David Paul *public relations executive*
Chakrin, Lewis M. *consumer products company executive*
Dahan, Andre *consumer products company executive*
Gyani, Mohan *communications company executive*
Hague, William W. *consumer products company executive*
Herbold, Robert J. *software company executive*
Johnson, Robert H. *communications executive*
Keith, Michael G. *consumer products company executive*
Landis, Gregory P. *consumer products company executive*
Lappenbusch, Richard W. *software company official*
Martinez, Maria *computer software company executive*
Marvin, D. Jane *consumer products company executive*
Mathews, Mich *computer company executive*
Nelson, Roderick D. *communications executive*
Roderick, Jordan M. *communications executive*
Sievert, G. Michael *marketing professional*
Slemons, Gregory L. *communications executive*

Seattle
Bezos, Jeffrey P. *multimedia executive*
Bianco, James A. *research and development executive*
Burns, Michael Joseph *operations and sales-marketing executive*
Dederer, Michael Eugene *public relations company executive*
Duryee, David Anthony *management consultant*
Eastham, John D. *business executive*
Elgin, Ron Alan *advertising executive*
Eller, Marlin *security firm executive*
Evans, Robert Vincent *sales and marketing executive*
Gerwick-Brodeur, Madeline Carol *marketing and timing professional*
Gist, Marilyn Elaine *organizational behavior and human resource management educator*
Glaser, Robert *communications company executive*
Hopson, Andy *public relations executive*
Hough, John Dennis *public relations executive*
Johnson, LuAn *disaster management consultant*
Komen, Richard B. *food service executive*
Kraft, Elaine Joy *community relations and communications official*
MacDonald, Andrew Stephen *management consulting firm executive*
McNab, Susan Elizabeth *human resources executive*
McReynolds, Neil Lawrence *management consultant*
Miyata, Keijiro *culinary arts educator*
Pizzorno, Joseph Egidio, Jr., *business executive*
Reis, Jean Stevenson *administrative secretary*
Stumbles, James Rubidge Washington *security firm executive*
von Bargen, Sally *stock image photography company executive*
Walker, Douglas *computer developement company executive*

Shoreline
Hutton, Winfield Travis *management consultant, educator*

Snoqualmie
Giuliani, David *personal care products company executive*
Stull, Mike *personal care industry executive*

Spokane
Geraghty, John Vincent *public relations consultant*
Moe, Orville Leroy *racetrack executive*
Storey, Francis Harold *business consultant, retired bank executive*
Tsutakawa, Edward Masao *management consultant*
Woodard, Alva Abe *business consultant*

Tacoma
Bartlett, Norma Thyra *retired administrative assistant*
Hudson, Edward Voyle *linen supply company executive*
Taylor, Peter van Voorhees *advertising and public relations consultant*

Vancouver
Hixon, Robin Ray *food service executive, writer*
Kodis, Mary Caroline *marketing consultant*
Ogden, Valeria Munson *management consultant, state representative*

Walla Walla
Potts, Charles Aaron *management executive, writer, publishing executive*

Wenatchee
Elwell, H. Terry *marketing professional, educator*

WEST VIRGINIA

Ansted
Shriver, Thomas L. *park director*

Charleston
Isabella, Mark Douglas *management consultant*
Offutt, Rebecca Sue *business and sales executive*

Davisville
Huber, Clayton Lloyd *marketing professional, engineer, construction executive*

Gallipolis Ferry
Brown, Nancy Jane *human resources specialist*

Harpers Ferry
Carlstrom, Terry R. *park administrator*

Huntington
Reynolds, Marshall Truman *printing company executive*

Morgantown
Blakeman, Robyn L. *advertising executive, educator*
Doney, Brent Clifford *industrial hygienist, public health service officer*

Parkersburg
Fahlgren, H(erbert) Smoot *advertising executive*

Summit Point
Taylor, Harold Allen, Jr., *industrial mineral-speciality metals marketing consultant*

Triadelphia
McCullough, John Phillip *management consultant, educator*

White Sulphur Springs
Kleisner, Ted. J. *hotel executive*

WISCONSIN

Appleton
Hasselbacher, Darlene M. *human resources executive*
McManus, John Francis *association executive, writer*
Underhill, Robert Alan *consumer products company executive*

Brookfield
Bader, Ronald L. *advertising executive*
Dillon, Donald F. *data processing executive*
Jensen, Kenneth R. *data processing executive*
Muma, Leslie M. *data processing executive*
Nickerson, Greg *public relations executive*
Saam, Robert Harry *human resources specialist, consultant*
Welnetz, David Charles *human resources executive*

Darien
Miller, Malcolm Henry *manufacturing sales executive, real estate developer*

Dodgeville
Eisenberg, Lee B. *communications executive, author*

Eau Claire
Leary, Robin Janell *executive secretary, municipal official*

Fond Du Lac
Ingle, Sud Ranganath *management consultant*

Glendale
Foran, David John *public relations consultant*

Green Bay
Bender, Brian *consumer products executive*

Hartford
Fowler, John *printing company executive*

Hartland
Peterson, Louis Robert *retired consumer products company executive*

Janesville
Roth, Sarah Eve *occupational safety professional*

Jefferson
Lochow, H. John *computer company executive*
Morgan, Gaylin F. *public relations consultant*
Myers, Gary *public relations executive*

Kohler
Kohler, Laura E. *human resources executive*

Lake Geneva
Weed, Edward Reilly *marketing executive*

Madison
Bishop, Carolyn Benkert *public relations counselor*
Dunham, Michael Herman *human services executive*
Henderson, Arvis Burl *data processing executive, biochemist*
Knapstein, Michael *advertising executive*
Kuzuhara, Loren Wyatt *management consultant, educator*
Piper, Odessa *chef*
Smith, Gary W.H. *retired sales executive*
Stites, Susan Kay *writer, human resources consultant*

Menasha
Streeter, Stephanie Anne *printing company executive*

Mequon
Elias, Paul S. *retired marketing executive*

Middleton
Lee, Leslie Warren *marketing executive, public speaker*

Milwaukee
Arbit, Bruce *direct marketing executive, consultant*
Colbert, Virgis William *brewery company executive*
Counsell, Paul S. *former advertising executive, counselor*
Davidson, Rick *staffing company executive*
Davis, Susan F. *human resources specialist*
Fromstein, Mitchell S. *retired office services company executive*
Hueneke, Terry A. *temporary services company executive*
Hunter, Victor Lee *marketing executive, consultant*
Joerres, Jeffrey A. *staffing company executive*
Joseph, Jules K. *retired public relations executive*
Kerr, Dorothy Marie Burmeister *marketing executive, consultant*

King, Frederic *health services management executive, educator*
Laughlin, Steven L. *advertising executive*
Manning, Kenneth Paul *technologies company executive*
Marcus, Stephen Howard *hospitality and entertainment company executive*
Quadracci, Thomas A. *printing company executive*
Randall, William Seymour *leasing company executive*
Sayles, Ronald Lyle *computer executive*
van Handel, Michael J. *staffing company executive*

Oshkosh
Siepmann, James Patrick *research company executive, retired physician*

Racine
Elliott, Dale Frederick *marketing professional*
Johnson-Leipold, Helen P. *outdoor recreation company executive*
Klein, Gabriella Sonja *retired communications executive*

Waterford
Karraker, Louis Rendleman *retired corporate executive*

Wausau
Wadzinski, Mary Beth *administrative assistant*

Weyauwega
Hanneman, Elaine Esther *salesperson*

Wisconsin Rapids
Knuteson, Miles Gene *advertising executive*

WYOMING

Alpine
Cittone, Henry Aron *hotel and restaurant management educator*

Wilson
Fritz, Jack Wayne *communications and marketing company executive*

TERRITORIES OF THE UNITED STATES

GUAM

Hagatna
Sablan, David J. *marketing professional, political organization worker*

PUERTO RICO

Guaynabo
de Cacho, Graciela Eleta *marketing executive*

San Juan
Roldan, Ulises *sales and marketing executive*

VIRGIN ISLANDS

Christiansted
Mann, Lynne Marie *executive administrative assistant*

Saint Thomas
O'Bryan, James A. *communications specialist, political organization administrator*

MILITARY ADDRESSES OF THE UNITED STATES

EUROPE

APO
Simpson, Sandra Kay *logistics management specialist*

CANADA

ALBERTA

Calgary
Hume, James Borden *corporate professional, foundation executive*
Manz, Calvin Kim *technology sector entrepreneur*

Edmonton
McKenna, Patrick James *management consultant*

Sherwood Park
Machuca, Carlos R. *management consultant*

BRITISH COLUMBIA

Vancouver
Campbell, Bruce Alan *corporate and executive coach*
Cormier, Jean G. *communications company executive*
Saywell, William George Gabriel *business development and management consultant*

Victoria
Nuttall, Richard Norris *management consultant, physician*

West Vancouver
Rae, Barbara Joyce *former employee placement company executive*

MANITOBA

Winnipeg
Asper, Leonard *communications executive*

NOVA SCOTIA

Halifax
Gratwick, John *management consulting executive, writer, consultant*

North Sydney
Nickerson, Jerry Edgar Alan *business executive*

ONTARIO

Brampton
Plastina, Frank *communications executive*

Freelton
Sonnenberg, Hardy *data processing company research and development executive, engineer*

Gloucester
Boisvert, Laurier Joseph *communications executive*

Kanata
Smith, Don *communications executive*

Markham
Ho, Kwok Yuen *data processing executive*

Mississauga
Bricel, Mark Leon *marketing executive*
Farrell, Craig *hotel executive*
Melnyk, Eugene N. *private investigator*
Thibault, J(oseph) Laurent *service company executive*

Niagara-on-the-Lake
Nielsen-Jones, Ian Richard *lottery and gaming executive, business operations consultant*

North York
Denham, Frederick Ronald *management consultant*

Ottawa
Courtois, Bernard Andre *communications executive*
Ouellet, André *business executive*

Saint Catharines
Bergevin, V. Réal *customer relationship management executive*

Toronto
Bandeen, Robert Angus *management consultant*
Carder, Paul Charles *retired advertising executive*
Curlook, Walter *management consultant*
Fatt, William R. *hospitality company executive*
Fierheller, George Alfred *corporate director*
Gregor, Tibor Philip *retired management consultant*
Jacob, Ellis *entertainment company executive*
Nesbitt, Mark *management consultant*
Pinto, Maxwell Salustiano *management consultant*
Rogers, Edward Samuel *communications company executive*
Seiersen, Nicholas Steen *management consultant*
Sharp, Isadore *hotel facility executive*
Viner, Peter *communications executive*

QUEBEC

Eastman
Emond, Lionel Joseph *management consultant*

Leclercville
Morin, Pierre Jean *retired management consultant, social services administrator*

Montreal
Beauregard, Luc *public relations executive*
Neveu, Jean *printing company executive*
Sirois, Charles *communications executive*
Wood, Dennis *communications executive*

Mount Royal
Chauvette, Claude R. *building materials company administrator*

Saint-Faustin-Lac-Carre
Des Marais, Pierre, II, *communications holding company executive*

Oakville
Jelinek, John Joseph *public relations executive*

Richmond
Cordoba, Mike *food service executive*

MEXICO

Mexico City
Nicholas, Ronald Wayde *business consultant*

Monterrey
Amores, Jose E. *cultural director*

AUSTRALIA

Brisbane
Edwards, Sir Llewellyn Roy *company executive*

Melbourne
Bellin, Howard *management consultant company executive*

North Sydney
Scott, Brian Walter *management consultant*

Woollahra
Palmerlee, April Wahlestedt *management consultant*

AUSTRIA

Vienna
Sindelka, Josef *postal service and telecommunications administrator*

BELGIUM

Brussels
Rossi, Pierre Marie *management consultant*

CHINA

Beijing
Yizhong, Li *business executive*

DENMARK

Copenhagen
Jiménez-Beltran, Domingo *executive*

Hoersholm
Sørensen, Erik *international company executive*

Odense
Keldmann, Erik Christian Vilhelm *innovation company executive*

EGYPT

Cairo
Fahmy, Ibrahim Mounir *hotel executive*

ENGLAND

Canterbury
Holwell, Peter *management consultant*

Cheshunt Hertfordshire
Leahy, Sir Terry *marketing professional, food products executive*

Letchworth
Everitt-Newton, Katherine Evelyn *international management consultant*

London
Davis, Ian *management consulting firm executive*
Habgood, Anthony John *corporate executive*
Hanson, Lord James Edward *industrialist*
Leaf, Robert Stephen *public relations executive*
Nelson, Walter Henry *communications consultant, author*
Nicholson, Geoffrey William Greer *management consultant*
Nordberg, Donald *communications executive*
Oliver, Jamie *chef, television personality*

Stroud
Robinson, John Beckwith *development management consultant*

Surrey
Weston, Sir John (Sir Philip John Weston) *company non-executive director, retired diplomat*

FRANCE

Paris
Courtaud, Bernard Jean-Jacques *human resource consulting executive*
Marcus, Claude *advertising executive*
Rouvillois, Philippe *research and development executive*
Unwin, Geoff *consulting company executive*

Suresnes
de Pouzilhac, Alain Duplessis *advertising executive*

GERMANY

Düsseldorf
Schulz, Ekkehard *business executive*
Simson, Wilhelm *company executive*

Essen
Albrecht, Theo *business executive*

Frankfurt
Neukirchen, Kajo *industry executive*

Munich
Miller, Gerald Milton, II, *management consultant*

Neu Isenburg
Hoare-Temple, Piers Howard *building maintenance executive*

Obertshausen
Albrecht, Karl *automotive and household plastic parts executive*

HONG KONG

Hong Kong
Hanrahan, Paul Thaddeus *marketing executive*

Pisanko, Henry Jonathan *command and control communications company executive*

ISRAEL

Rehovot

Zipori-Beckenstein, Pninit *business administration educator, researcher*

JAPAN

Choyoda-ku

Sakoda, Futoshi *executive*

Nagoya

Takeyama, Eizo *company executive*

Shinagawa

Ando, Kunitake *consumer products company executive*

Tokyo

Hakoshima, Shin-ichi *business executive*
Kobayashi, Susumu *computer company executive*
Miura, Akio *quality assurance management professional*

NETHERLANDS

Leiden

Dornbush, K. Terry *former ambassador, consulting company executive, educator*

NORWAY

Oslo

Heyerdahl, Jens P. *business executive*

PHILIPPINES

Dumaguete City

Galli, Darrell Joseph *retired management consultant*

PORTUGAL

Lisbon

Palmer, John N. *communications executive*

SINGAPORE

Singapore

Amelio, William J. *computer company executive*

SPAIN

Costa Den Blanes Mallorca

Polad, Farhang *company director*

SWEDEN

Göteborg

Johansson, Lennart Valdemar *Swedish industrialist*

Stockholm

Gyll, John Sören *company executive*
Johnson, Antonia Axson *corporate executive*

SWITZERLAND

Prilly

Domeniconi, Reto *business executive*

TURKEY

Ankara

Camlibel, Dizdar *marketing professional, advertising consultant*

ADDRESS UNPUBLISHED

Ackerley, Barry *communications executive*
Adkinson, Brian Lee *manufacturing company executive*
Aggarwal, Lalit K. *company executive, educator*
Alagem, Beny *computer company executive*
Aliperti, Clifford J. *advertising specialist, writer*
Allan, James S. *sales professional*
Allen, Bennie Carnel *employee relations specialist*
Allen, Paul G. *computer company executive, professional sports team executive*
Allmon, Michael W, Sr., *sales executive*
Amatangelo, Nicholas S. *retired financial printing and document management services executive, business educator*
Amparado, Keith D. *communications company executive*
Anand, Sanjay *training services executive, consultant, entrepreneur, educator*
Anderegg, Karen Klok *business executive*
Annunziata, Robert *fiber optics company executive*
Appell, Louise Sophia *consulting company executive*
Armstrong Squall, Paula Estelle *executive secretary*
Arnheim, Louise A. *communications executive*
Arnold, Jeffrey *Internet company executive*
Aruza, Albert Francis *consulting firm executive*
Asensi, Gustavo *advertising executive, cinematographer*
Augustine, Hilton H., Jr., *computer company executive*
Autolitano, Astrid *consumer products executive*
Avery, Stephen G. Brodie *marketing professional, consultant, sales executive*
Bahbah, Bishara Assad *marketing company executive*
Bainbridge, Dona Bardelli *marketing professional*
Ballard, Marion Scattergood *software development professional*
Bamberger, Gerald Francis *plastics marketing consultant*
Barad, Jill Elikann *family products company executive*
Barger, William James *management consultant, educator*
Barnes, Wesley Edward *energy and environmental executive*
Barnett, Elizabeth Hale *organizational consultant*
Barr, Michael Charles *management consultant, lawyer*
Barrett, Paulette Singer *public relations executive*
Barron, Peggy Pennisi *management consultant*
Bartlett, David *management consultant*
Bauer, Barbara Ann *marketing consultant*
Baxter, Barbara Morgan *Internet service provider executive, educator*
Beasley, Barbara Starin *sales executive, marketing professional*
Becker, Robert A. *advertising executive*
Bell, Jacqueline Michelle *marketing professional, public relations executive*
Bennett, Saul *public relations agency executive*
Benney, Douglas Mabley *direct marketing executive, consultant*
Berger, Frank Stanley *management executive*
Bergstein, Stanley Francis *horse racing executive*
Berman-Hammer, Susan *public relations executive*
Berra, Robert Louis *human resources consultant*
Bey, Joan S. *retired public information specialist, writer*
Binder, Amy Finn *public relations company executive*
Birk, John R. *management consultant*
Bisconti, Ann Stouffer *public opinion research company executive*
Black, Kris Susan Lynn *marketing company executive, speaker, author, poet*
Blacker, Harriet *public relations executive*
Blaine, Davis Robert *investment banker, valuation consultant executive*
Blake, John Edward *retired car rental company executive*
Blanchard, Townsend Eugene *retired service companies executive*
Bloustein, Peter Edward *entertainment management consultant, producer*
Blum, Bradley D. *former food service executive*
Boehlke, William Fredrick *public relations executive, consultant*
Booth, Bonnie Nelson *human resources consultant*
Booth, Margaret A(nn) *communications company executive*
Borges, William, III, *management consultant*
Botkin, Monty Lane *computer company executive*
Bowes, Henry Edward *retired communications executive*
Braddock, Richard S. *internet company executive*
Bramucci, Raymond L. *employment and training executive*
Breakstone, Kay Louise *public relations executive*
Brennan, Donna Lesley *public relations company executive*
Bridges-Kemp, Leslie LaVerne *administrative assistant*
Britt, Rebecca Fae *communications executive*
Broderson, Thelma Sylvia *marketing professional*
Broedling, Laurie Adele *human resources consultant, psychologist, educator*
Browne, Ann April *purchasing manager*
Brugger, Janet Harley *management consultant*
Bryant, Carla *management consultant, finance educator*
Buck, Earl Wayne *private investigator, motel owner*
Buck, Linda Dee *executive recruiting company executive*
Burgdoerfer, Jerry J. *marketing and distribution executive*
Burge, John Wesley, Jr., *management consultant*
Burnett, Iris Jacobson *corporate communications specialist*
Burnham, J. V. *retired sales executive*
Burton, Robert Gene *printing and publishing executive*
Butler, Robert Leonard *retired sales executive*
Butler, Robert Thomas *retired advertising executive*
Butts, Carol Henderson *human resources specialist, consultant*
Caine, Raymond William, Jr., *retired public relations executive*
Callan, John Garling *management consultant*
Cameron, Daniel Forrest *communications executive*
Camper, John Saxton *public relations and marketing executive*
Cappello, Eve *speaker, trainer, author*
Carlson, Kenneth George *data processing executive*
Carpenter, Candice *writer, former media executive*
Carpenter-Mason, Beverly Nadine *quality assurance professional, medical/surgical nurse*
Carter, Jaine M(arie) *human resources specialist, director*
Cartwright, Phillip August *management consultant*
Casadesus, Penelope Ann *advertising executive, film producer*
Cearley, Michael A. *communications executive, writer*
Cecil, Alex Thomson *travel executive*
Chamberlain, William Edwin, Jr., *management consultant*
Chaput, Eugene Michael *advertising executive*
Charles, Lyn Ellen *marketing executive, commercial artist, photograph*
Chaseman, Joel *communications consultant*
Cheser, Raymond Norris, III, *healthcare company executive*
Chill, Myrtle N. *advertising copywriter, promoter*
Chin, Janet Sau-Ying *data processing executive, consultant*
Chlebowski, John Francis, Jr., *leasing company executive*
Choueifati, Antoine (Tony Choueifati) *computer company executive*
Chrisanthopoulos, Peter *advertising executive*
Christian, Lori Coffelt *marketing professional*
Christianson, Philip D. *employee benefits executive*
Christopher, Richard Scott *public relations and advertising executive, editor*
Ciccarelli, Chick *marketing professional*
Cicero, J. Deborah *management consultant*
Citron, Richard Ira *management consultant*
Clarizio, Josephine Delores *corporate services executive, former manufacturing and engineering company executive, foundation executive*
Clark, Mark David *public relations consultant*
Clemmons, Evelyn Yvonne *administrative assistant*
Cobb, John Cecil, Jr., (Jack Cobb) *communications specialist and executive*
Cochetti, Roger James *international communications and internet company executive*
Cogdell, Evelyn Denise *administrative assistant, writer*
Coleman, Claire Kohn *public relations executive*
Coleman, Jacquelyn Lynzetta *public relations executive*
Collins, Douglas Patrick, Jr., *communications company executive, television producer*
Collins, Frank Charles, Jr., *industrial and service quality specialist*
Collins, Richard Stratton (Dick Collins) *retired public relations executive*
Collins, Russell Ambrose *retired advertising executive, creative director*
Connaughton, David Michael *management consultant*
Connell, Carol Matheson *corporate strategist, consultant*
Connell, Shirley Hudgins *public relations professional*
Cook, Jane Hampton *communications consultant*
Corle, Frederic William, II, *marketing professional*
Cortese, Richard Anthony *computer company executive*
Corwell, Ann Elizabeth *public relations executive*
Cramb, Charles W. *consumer products company executive*
Crawford, William Walsh *retired consumer products company executive*
Criswell, Kimberly Ann *executive coach, communications consultant, performing artist*
Croft, Kathryn Delaine *business executive, consultant*
Cruver, Suzanne Lee *communications executive, writer*
Crystal, Jonathan Andrew *executive recruiter*
Cunningham, Andrea Lee *public relations executive*
Curry, Carlton E. *corporate executive, city councilman*
Cutler, Norman Barry *funeral service executive*
Dancer, Peter L *quality assurance professional*
Dangoor, David Ezra Ramsi *consumer goods company executive*
Darien, Steven Martin *management consulting company executive*
DaVerne, Steven Richard *advertising director, artist, illustrator, behavior analyst*
Davis, Joseph Samuel *marketing executive, consultant*
Davis, William L. *publishing company executive*
Dayton, Sky *communications company executive*
Deacon, David Emmerson *business executive*
Decker, Gilbert Felton *consultant*
Derzai, Matthew *retired telecommunications company executive*
De Sofi, Oliver Julius *data processing executive*
DeVore, Kimberly K. *business executive*
deWilde, David Michael *management consultant, retired executive recruiter, lawyer, financial services executive*
Diamond, Susan Zee *management consultant*
DiDomenico, Mauro, Jr., *communication executive*
Diehl, Stephen Anthony *human resources consultant*
Dirvin, Gerald Vincent *retired consumer products company executive*
Doan, Mary Frances *advertising executive*
Dodson, Daniel, Sr., *advertising executive*
Dolgow, Allan Bentley *management consultant*
Dolich, Andrew Bruce *sports marketing executive*
Dolman, John Phillips, Jr., (Tim Dolman) *communications company executive*
Dorn, Norman Philip *management consulting firm executive*
Doud, Wallace C. *retired information systems executive*
Douglas, Victoria Jean *marketing professional, communications executive, educator*
Douty, Lucy Evelyn *sales and marketing executive*
Dow, Peter Anthony *advertising agency executive*
Dozier, Eleanor Cameron *computer company executive, writer*
Dreyer, John W. *print and graphics equipment executive*
Droullard, Steven Maurice *jewelry company executive*
Druckenmiller, Robert Thompson *public relations executive*
Dudley, Craig James *retired executive recruiter*
Dudley, Elizabeth Hymer *retired security executive, community volunteer*
Duffy, Martin Edward *management consultant, economist*
Duke, William Edward *public affairs executive*
Dunn, Frank A. *former communications executive*
Dunsky, Menahem *retired advertising agency executive, communications consultant, painter*
Dwan, Dennis Edwin *broadcast executive, photographer*
Easton, Charles Clement, Jr., *corporate executive*
Echols, Mary Evelyn *motivational speaker, writer*
Ecton, Donna R. *business executive*
Eddy, David Maxon *health policy and management advisor*
Eggleston, G(eorge) Dudley *management consultant, publisher*
Elix, Douglas Thorne *computer company executive*
Ellig, Bruce Robert *personnel director*
Emerling, Carol G(reenbaum) *consultant*
Emerson, Daniel Everett *retired communications company executive*
Erb, Richard Louis Lundin *resort and hotel executive*
Escobar, Anthony *marketing professional, consultant*
Evans, John Vaughan *communications satellite executive, physicist*
Evans, Pamela R. *sales and marketing executive*
Everett, Carl Nicholas *management consulting executive*
Everett, Elbert Kyle *marketing executive, consultant*
Faletra, Robert *technology company executive*
Faron, Fay Cheryl *private investigator, writer*
Farr, Mel *automotive sales executive, former professional football player*
Fay, Conner Martindale *retired business executive*
Feiner, Ava Sophia *public affairs and management consultant, economist*
Feld, Carole Leslie *marketing executive*
Feller, Robert William Andrew *baseball team public relations executive, retired baseball player*
Fernández, Alberto Antonio *security professional*
Fickinger, Wayne Joseph *communications executive*
Finkel, David *advertising executive*
Fischer, Angela Brown *business executive, civic volunteer*
Fischer, Russell Leonard *public relations executive*
Fischmar, Richard Mayer *resort executive, financial consultant*
Fleisher, Gary Mitchell *employment industry and management consulting executive*
Flickinger, Harry Harner *organization and business executive, management consultant*
Foote, William Chapin *business executive*
Forester, Jean Martha Brouillette *innkeeper, retired librarian, educator*
Foronda, Barbara Elaine *professional organizer, writer*
Forrester, Jay Wright *management specialist, educator*
Fox-Clarkson, Anne C. *computer company executive*
Francis, Philip Hamilton *management consultant*
Franke, John Charles *retired human resources executive*
Fredman, Mimi Ungar Coppersmith *advertising and publishing executive*
Fulchino, Paul Edward *management consultant*
Gabriel, Ethel Mary *entertainment executive*
Galbraith, Nanette Elaine Gerks *forensic and management sciences company executive*
Gambrell, Luck Flanders *corporate executive*
Garahan, Peter Thomas *software company executive*
Gardner, Cornelius John *sales executive*
Gardner, Meredith Lee *communication consultant*
Geary, Wendy Hewson *business manager, rancher*
Gendell, Gerald Stanleigh *retired public affairs executive*
George, William Douglas, Jr., *retired consumer products company executive*
Georgescu, Peter Andrew *retired advertising executive*
Gerlach, Douglas Eldon *financial writer, Internet developer*
Geschke, Charles M. *computer company executive*
Gibbon, Tim *communications executive*
Giddings, Helen *personnel management executive*
Gilford, Leon *business executive and consultant*
Gillice, Sondra Jupin (Mrs. Gardner Russell Brown) *sales and marketing executive*
Glacel, Barbara Pate *management consultant*
Glass, Kenneth Edward *management consultant*
Gleaves, Leon Rogers *marketing and sales executive*
Goldberg, Victor Joel *retired data processing company executive*
Golden, Bryan *management consultant, writer*
Goldfarb, Muriel Bernice *marketing consultant, advertising consultant*
Goldman, Alfred Emmanuel *marketing research consultant*
Goldman, Joseph Elias *retired advertising executive*
Goldschmidt, Peter Graham *physician executive, business development consultant*
Goldsmith, Jeff Charles *management consultant*
Goll, Stephen E. *telecommunications executive*
Gorsline, Stephen Paul *security specialist*
Gorup, Gregory James *marketing executive*
Gottlieb, Alan Merril *advertising, fundraising and broadcasting executive, writer*
Goyan, Jere Edwin *business executive, former university dean*
Grace, Marcia Bell *advertising executive*
Greathead, Roger J. *marketing professional*
Green, Howard Alan *management consultant, educator*
Greene, Alvin *service company executive, management consultant*
Grimes-Frederick, Dorothea D. *communications executive*
Gross, Laura Ann *marketing and communications professional, acupuncturist, herbalist*
Gross, Rosalie-Ethelyn *secretary*
Growick, Philip *advertising executive*
Grubb, Donald Hartman *paper industry company executive*
Gschwind, Donald *management and engineering consultant*
Gugel, Craig Thomas *advertising and strategic research executive*
Guhr, Daniel Johannes *management consultant*
Gumpert, Gustav *public relations executive*
Gunderson, Ted Lee *security consultant*
Gurwitch, Arnold Andrew *communications executive*
Haegele, John Ernest *business executive*
Hagel, John, III, *management consultant*
Hall, Adrienne A. *international marketing executive, venture capitalist consultant*
Hall, Hansel Crimiel *communications executive*
Halloran, Daniel Edward *personnel executive*
Hamilton, Joe *communications company executive*
Hamilton, Judith Hall *computer company executive*
Hamilton, Thomas Michael *marketing executive*
Hamlin, Sonya B. *communications specialist*
Hamm, Vernon Louis, Jr., *management and financial consultant*
Hapka, Catherine M. *Internet executive*
Harden, Mary Louise *human resources consultant, real estate broker, real estate appraiser*
Hargadon, Bernard Joseph, Jr., *retired consumer goods company executive*
Harlan, Kathleen Troy (Kay Harlan) *management consultant*
Harlan, Raymond Carter *retired military officer, communication executive, writer, educator, investigator*
Harold, Tom *advertising executive*
Harr, Lucy Loraine *public relations executive*
Harris, David Philip *crisis management executive*
Harris, Denise Michelle *advertising account executive*
Harris, Deondriea Cantrice *customer service administrator*
Harris, Louis *public opinion analyst, columnist*
Harris, Paul Smith *human resources professional*
Harris, Robert Norman *advertising and communications educator*

Sommers, William Paul *management consultant, research and development institute executive, think-tank executive*
Southern, Larry Gilmer *explosive safety specialist*
Souveroff, Vernon William, Jr., *business executive*
Speakes, Larry Melvin *public relations executive, writer*
Spears, Donald Edward *management consultant*
Speer, Richard John *security consultant*
Spellman, Douglas Toby *advertising executive*
Spirn, Michele Sobel *communications professional, writer*
Spivak, Joan Carol *healthcare communications specialist*
Splichal, Christine *restaurant owner*
Spoor, James Edward *human resources executive, entrepreneur*
Sproat, Kezia Vanmeter *communications executive, writer*
Stark, Diana *public relations executive*
Starkweather, Frederick Thomas *retired data processing executive*
Stengel, Ronald Francis *management consultant*
Stenitzer, George Ignatius *corporate communications executive*
Stepanski, Anthony Francis, Jr., *computer software company executive*
Stevens, Berton Louis, Jr., *data processing manager*
Stewart, Arthur Irving, III, (Art Stewart) *management consultant*
Stewart, Richard Alfred *business executive*
Stiles, Virginia Ford *data processing executive, poet*
Stillman, Richard Joseph *retired army officer, consultant, publisher, writer*
Stocker, Gregg *quality assurance professional, writer*
Stone, James Howard *management consultant*
Stover, Kenneth Alan *sales executive*
Strasser, Gabor *management consultant*
Strength, Janis Grace *management executive, educator*
Strifler, Stanley *former business solutions executive*
Stults, Walter Black *management consultant, former trade organization executive*
Sturges, John Siebrand *management consultant*
Sueltz, Patricia C. *computer company executive*
Suissa, David *advertising executive*
Sullivan, John Louis, Jr., *retired search company executive*
Sutherland, Maria T. *marketing professional, communications executive*
Szabo, Yurika Lin *marketing executive, advertising executive*
Taplett, Lloyd Melvin *human resources specialist, consultant*
Tarr, Curtis W. *business executive*
Taylor, Volney *retired information company executive*
Temerlin, Liener *advertising agency executive*
Tenney, Frank Putnam *marketing executive*
Terry, Elizabeth Hudson *personal care industry executive, realtor*
Terry, Kay Adell *marketing executive*
Tesarek, Dennis George *retired business consultant, writer, educator*
Tew, E. James, Jr., *management services company executive*
Thomas, Joe Carroll *retired human resources director*
Thompson, Craig Snover *corporate communications executive*
Thompson, Pamela *marketing executive*
Thongsak, Vajeeprasee Thomas *business planning executive*
Thorn, Brian Earl *Internet company executive*
Thrall, Richard Cameron, Jr., *broadcasting executive*
Tipton, Gary Lee *retired services company executive*
Tocci, Neil Michael *marketing and corporate communications executive, educator*
Todd, Edward William *marketing professional*
Toevs, Alden Louis *management consultant, researcher*
Togerson, John Dennis *retired computer software company executive*
Trani, John M. *former consumer products company executive*
Transou, Lynda Lou *advertising art administrator*
Traxler, Eva Maria *marketing professional*
Tribus, Myron *retired quality counselor, engineer, educator*
Triplett, Arlene Ann *management consultant*
Tritter, Richard Paul *strategic planning, safety and risk management consulting executive*
Trudeau, James Briane *communications executive*
Tuft, Mary Ann *executive search firm executive*
Turkel, Stanley *hotel consultant, management executive*
Turner, William Cochrane *international management consultant*
Uvena, Frank John *retired printing company executive, lawyer*
Vallerand, Philippe Georges *sales executive*
Van Dine, Alan Charles *advertising agency executive, writer*
Van Nevel, J. Paul *communications executive*
Verdier, Quentin Roosevelt *human resources consultant*
Vidovich, Mark A. *paper products executive*
Vogel, William Dickerman *financial services executive*
Waage, Sissel *environmental services administrator*
Wadley, M. Richard *consumer products executive*
Walker, Gloria Lee *training services executive*
Walker, R. Tracy *retired personnel director*
Wall, Carolyn Raimondi *communications executive*
Wallace, Guy William *management consultant*
Wallington, Patricia McDevitt *computer company executive*
Walsh, William Albert *management consultant, former naval officer*
Walters, Matthew Paul *recreational facility executive, consultant*
Ware, Robert K. *Internet company executive, researcher, web programmer*
Watson, H. Mitchell, Jr., *business software company executive*
Watts, Karen Southall *management consultant*
Weathersby, George Byron *business executive*
Webb, Doris McIntosh *human resources specialist*
Webb, William Timothy *mobile communications professional*
Weber, Kenneth J. *hotel executive*
Wehling, Robert Louis *retired household products company executive*
Weiner, Richard *public relations executive*
Weiner, Sharon Rose *public relations executive*
Weinstein, Marta *packaging services company executive*
Weismantel, Gregory Nelson *management consultant and software executive*
Weiss, Jerry Kenneth *sales executive, consultant, marketing professional*
Wells, Victor Hugh, Jr., *retired advertising agency executive*
Wentz, Jeffrey Lee *information systems executive*
Westheimer, Ruth Welling *retired management consultant*
Weston, Josh S. *retired data processing company executive*
Weston, Saundra Olivia (Saundra Laidlaw) *quality assurance professional, minister*
Weyl, Tom F. *advertising executive*
Wheaton, M. Gene *investigator, consultant*
Whelan, James Robert *communications executive, international trade and investment consultant, author, educator, mining executive*
Whisenhunt, Livia L. *marketing executive*
Whyte, Bruce Lincoln *management executive, marketing professional*
Wicks, David O., Jr., *communications executive*
Wiginton, Jay Spencer *sales executive*
Williams, Alfred Blythe *retired management consultant*
Williams, John Charles, II, *data processing executive*
Williams, Louis Clair, Jr., *public relations executive*
Willig, Karl Victor *computer firm executive*
Wimpress, Gordon Duncan, Jr., *corporate consultant, foundation executive*
Woerner, Louise *hotel executive*
Wolf, William Martin *computer company executive, consultant*
Worth, Gary James *communications executive*
Yadrick, Robert Martin *occupational analyst*
Yarrington, George A. *retired public relations executive, advertising executive, writer*
Yee, Nancy W. *travel consultant*
Yocam, Delbert Wayne *retired software products company executive*
York, Theodore Robert *retired consulting company executive*
Youst, David Bennett *career development educator*
Zaghloul, Dina Amal *quality assurance professional, consultant*
Zanes, George William *management, marketing, human resources consultant*
Zeien, Alfred M. *former consumer products company executive*
Zeller, Joseph Paul *advertising executive*
Ziegler, James L. *marketing executive*
Zinnen, Robert Oliver *general management executive*

INDUSTRY: TRADE

UNITED STATES

ALABAMA

Albertville
Patterson, Jeffery Allen *business owner*

Birmingham
Blair, Ludie Mae Riley *retired furniture company executive*
George, Frank Wade *small business owner, antiquarian book dealer*
Martin, R. Brad *retail executive*
Pizitz, Richard Alan *retail and real estate group executive*

Hoover
Lathem, Gina Cooley *small business owner*

Mobile
Gordon, James Oliver *small business owner, chiropractor*
Jones, Joseph Seymour *small business owner, poet*

Talladega
Weaver, Robert Cooper *small business owner, volunteer*

Tuscaloosa
Blackburn, John Leslie *small business owner*

ALASKA

Anchorage
Schnell, Roger Thomas *small business owner, retired state official*

Denali National Park
Swenson, Richard Allen *business owner, animal trainer*

ARIZONA

Anthem
Palenque, Stephanie Maher *small business owner, writer, book indexer*

Carefree
Howell, William Robert *retail company executive*

Cave Creek
Boat, Ronald Allen *business executive*

Chandler
Anderson, Darl *retail executive*
Basha, Edward N., Jr., *grocery chain owner*
Fowler, Reggie *retail executive*

Glendale
Lack, Larry Henry *small business owner*

Goodyear
McBride, Janet Marie *small business owner*

Lake Montezuma
Loveland, John Bigelow *small business owner*

Phoenix
DuMoulin, Diana Cristaudo *small business owner, writer, musician*

ARKANSAS

Bentonville
Connolly, Robert *retail executive*
Coughlin, Thomas Martin *wholesale goods company executive*
Degn, Doug *retail executive*
Dible, David D. *retail executive*
Dillman, Linda *retail executive*
Duke, Michael *retail executive*
Fitzsimmons, J. Jay *retail executive*
Ford, Rollin *retail executive*
Glass, David D. *retail executive, professional sports team executive*
Harris, Don S. *retail executive*
Haworth, Jim H. *retail executive*
Herkert, Craig R. *retail executive*
McMillon, Doug *retail executive*
Menzer, John *department store executive*
Menzner, John B. *retail executive*
Schoewe, Thomas M. *retail executive*
Scott, Lee (Harold Lee Scott Jr.) *retail executive*
Spragg, Gregg *retail executive*
Swanson, Celia *retail executive*
Turner, Kevin *retail executive*
Walton, S. Robson *discount department store chain executive*

Little Rock
Dillard, William, II, *department store chain executive*
Freeman, James I. *retail department store company executive*

CALIFORNIA

Anaheim
Brownhill, H. Bud *small business owner, canine behavior therapist*

Arcadia
Stangeland, Roger Earl *retail chain store executive*

Beverly Hills
Schwartz, Stephan Andrew *entrepreneur, writer*

Bodega Bay
Freeman, Donna Cook *small business owner*

Carmel
Aurner, Robert Ray, II, *retail executive*

Cathedral City
Jackman, Robert Alan *retail executive*

Chino Hills
Teng, Chen *import/export company executive, wholesale distribution executive*

City Of Commerce
Lynch, Martin Andrew *retail company executive*
Martin, Richard J. *food wholesale executive*
Plamann, Alfred A. *wholesale distribution executive*

Colton
Brown, Jack H. *supermarket company executive*

Concord
Mitchell, Carol Denise *small business owner, writer*

Escondido
Young, Gladys *business owner*

Fremont
Liang, Christine *import company executive*

Fresno
Winslow, Norman Eldon *business executive*

Glendale
Hughes, B. Wayne *retail executive*

Harbor City
Briese, Leonard Arden *inventor*

Hat Creek
Shepard, David Haspel *film restoration specialist*

Hollywood
Lore, Linda *retail executive*

Janesville
Lathrop, Lawrence Erwin, Jr., *retired business owner, retired state forest ranger*

LaPuente
Rojo De Santos, Anita *shop owner, writer*

Lake Forest
Massengill, Matthew H. *retail company executive*
Milligan, Steve *retail executive*
Shakeel, Arif *retail executive*

Long Beach
Wyse, Matthew F. *small business owner*

Los Angeles
Hawley, Philip Metschan *retired retail executive, consultant*
Roeder, Richard Kenneth *business owner, lawyer*
Sinay, Joseph *retail executive*
Williams, Theodore Earle *retired industrial distribution company executive*
Wylie, Pamela Jane *writer, producer, consultant, small business owner*

Los Osos
Just, Faye Jordan *antique restoration company executive*

Millbrae
Chow, Eileen Siu-Ha *computer retailing, investment company executive*

Modesto
Piccinini, Robert M. *grocery store chain executive*

Newark
Balmuth, Michael A. *retail executive*
Ferber, Norman Alan *retail executive*
Peters, James C. *retail executive*

Newport Coast
Pavony, William H. *retail executive, consultant*

Northridge
Orenstein, Michael (Ian Orenstein) *philatelic dealer, columnist*

Nuevo
Wagner, Cheri J. *business owner*

Oakland
Michael, Gary G. *retired retail supermarket and drug chain executive, university administrator*

Oceanside
Bell, Sharon Kaye *small business owner*

Orange
Underwood, Vernon O., Jr., *grocery stores executive*

Orinda
Somerset, Harold Richard *retail executive*

Oroville
Likley, Katherine *retired retail executive, writer*

Pacific Palisades
Diehl, Richard Kurth *retail business consultant*

Palm Desert
Vander Naald Egenes, Joan Elizabeth *small business owner, educator*

Palm Springs
Wiesner, John Joseph *retail chain store executive*

Palos Verdes Peninsula
Slayden, James Bragdon *retired department store executive*

Pleasanton
Everette, Bruce L. *retail executive*
Renda, Larree M. *retail executive*

Rancho Cucamonga
Merino, Akindotun *small business owner, consultant*

Redding
Streiff, Arlyne Bastunas *business owner, educator*

Redlands
Sagmeister, Edward Frank *retired military officer, business owner*

Riverside
Anderson, Jolene Slover *small business owner, publishing executive, consultant*

San Diego
Saito, Frank Kiyoji *import and export firm executive*
Stein, Franklin Joseph *import/export company executive*

San Francisco
Fisher, Donald G. *casual apparel chain stores executive*
Folkman, David H. *retail, wholesale and consumer products consultant*
Graw, LeRoy Harry *purchasing and contract management company executive*
Gust, Anne Baldwin *retail apparel company executive*
Lester, W. Howard *retail executive*
McCollam, Sharon L. *retail executive*
Pollitt, Byron H. *retail executive*
Pressler, Paul S. *retail executive*
Sage-Gavin, Eva Marie *retail executive*
Tasooji, Michael B. *retail executive*
Ullman, Myron Edward, III, *retail executive*

South San Francisco
Korman, Leo *wholesale distribution executive*
Mertens, Lynne G. *retail executive*

Thousand Oaks
Calborn, Keith W. *wholesale distribution executive*

Venice
Fracassi, Philip D. *bookstore retailer, publisher*

Walnut Creek
Bryant, Warren F. *retail executive*
Dreiling, Richard *retail executive*
Laddon, Michael M *retail executive*

West Sacramento
Coyne, William J. *retail executive*
Searson, Dee *retail products executive*
Solomon, Russell M. *retail products executive*
Teel, James E. *supermarket and drug store retail executive*
Teel, Joyce Raley *retail executive*

Westminster
Nguyen, Duoc Tan *small business owner*

Woodland Hills
Weider, Joseph *wholesale distribution executive*

COLORADO

Arvada
Glodava, Mila Garcia *entrepreneur, educator, consultant*

Aurora
Onyeuku, Alfred Eme *small business owner, consultant*
Reynolds, Robert Harrison *retired export company executive*

Boulder
Meyer, Andrea Peroutka *small business owner*

Broomfield
King, Robert *retail company executive*

Colorado Springs
Noyes, Richard Hall *bookseller*

Delta
Lowell, Lauretta Jane *craftsperson, poet*

Denver
Cashman, Michael Richard *small business owner*
Maul, Carol Elaine *small business owner*
Oakes, Terry Louis *retail clothing store executive*
Vigil, Jeffrey L. *infant and child products manufacturing executive*

Englewood
Lubetkin, Alvin Nat *sporting goods retail company executive*
Oshman, Marilyn *retail executive*

Littleton
Hickman, Marjorie Anderson *small business owner*

Loveland
Rodman, Alpine C. *arts and crafts company executive, photographer*
Rodman, Sue A. *wholesale company executive, artist, writer*

CONNECTICUT

Avon
Kling, Phradie (Phradie Kling Gold) *small business owner, educator*

Cheshire
Bozzuto, Michael Adam *wholesale grocery company executive*

Fairfield
Futterman, Jack *retail executive*
Wexler, Herbert Ira *retail company executive*

Greenwich
Rudy, Kathleen Vermeulen *small business owner*

New Britain
Darius, Franklin Alexander, Jr., (Chip Darius) *safety consultant, educator*

New London
Johnson, Diana Atwood *business owner, innkeeper*

Norwalk
Bennett, Carl *retired discount department store executive*

Norwich
Buddington, Olive Joyce *shop owner, retired education educator*

Shelton
York, Jerome B. *computer retail executive*

Stamford
Gilman, Kenneth B. *retail executive*
Hollinger, Morton *small business owner, artist*

DISTRICT OF COLUMBIA

Washington
Chalkley, Jacqueline Ann *retail company executive*
DeBusk, F. Amanda *export administration executive*
Hocker, John Robert *technical operations executive*
McGraw, Lavinia Morgan *retired retail executive*
Pelavin, Diane Christine *small business owner*
Smith, Jack Carl *foreign trade consultant*
Smith, Marie F. *small business owner, writer*
Tetelman, Alice Fran *small business owner*
Wurtzel, Alan Leon *retail company executive*

FLORIDA

Boca Raton
Galin, Tad, Sr., *home business owner*
Jamkus, Tom *wholesale distribution executive*
Ricciardi, Salvatore *wholesale distribution executive*
Rutner, Alan *wholesale grocery executive*

Bradenton
Beall, Robert Matthews, II, *retail chain executive*
Rutstein, Stanley Harold *apparel retailing company executive*

Clearwater
Henderson, Janet Lynn *small business owner*
Hoornstra, Edward H. *retail company executive*
Maxwell, Richard Anthony *retail executive*
Turley, Stewart *retired retail company executive*

Deerfield Beach
Foster, James R. *former wholesale distribution auto executive*

Delray Beach
Brown, Charles E. *retail executive*
Campbell, Cynthia *retail executive*
Carter-Miller, Jocelyn *retail executive*
Colley, Gerald (Jerry) E. *retail executive*
Crosson, Jay *retail executive*
Friend, Miriam Ruth *personnel company executive*
Holifield, Mark *retail executive*
Luechtefeld, Monica *retail executive*

Morrison, Patricia B. *retail executive*
van Kaldekerken, Rolf *retail executive*

Fort Lauderdale
Boire, Ron *retail executive*
Drury, John R. *retail executive*
Dwors, Robert F. *retail executive*
Evans, James D., Jr., *retail executive*
Ferrando, Jonathan P. *retail executive*
Gordon, Marc *retail executive*
London, Michael *retail executive*
Loos, John Thompson *business owner*
Maroone, Michael E. *car and truck sales executive*
Schoonover, Philip *retail executive*
Walden, John *retail executive*
Wojcik, Cass *decorative supply company executive, former city official*

Fort Myers
Colgate, Doris Eleanor *sailing school owner and administrator*
Moore, Spencer Roneal *retired business owner, accounts receivable funder*

Gainesville
Hollien, Patricia Ann *small business owner, researcher*
McClellan, Richard Augustus *retired small business owner*
Silas, Nancy *small business owner*

Highland Beach
Frager, Albert S. *retired retail food company executive*

Jacksonville
Constantini, JoAnn M. *small business owner, systems administrator, consultant*
Lazaran, Frank *retail executive*
McCook, Richard Paul *grocery chain financial executive*
Stein, Jay *retail executive*
Tolford, Frank Stefan *bookstore executive*

Key West
Murphy, S(usan) (Jane Murphy) *small business owner*

Lakeland
Luther, George Albert *truck brokerage executive*

Longboat Key
Goldsmith, Jack Landman *former retail company executive*

Medley
Delgado, Orlando *import company executive*

Merritt Island
Smith, David Edward *small business owner, aerospace engineer, aerospace scientist*

Miami
Barragan, Hugo *retail executive*
Chaplin, Harvey *wine and liquor wholesale executive*
Ferrari, Leonardo *small business owner*
Risi, Louis James, Jr., *business executive*

Miami Beach
Rawl, Arthur Julian (Lord of Cursons) *retail executive, accountant, consultant, author*

Miramar
Catalano, Carl Philip *small business owner*

Naples
Ludwig, Richard Joseph *small business owner*
McCarthy, Joseph Harold *consultant, former retail food company executive*
White, Warren Wurtele *retired retailing executive*

Orlando
Morgan, Thomas I. *retail executive*

Palm Beach
Black, Leonard Julius *retail store consultant*

Parrish
Corey, Kay Janis *business owner, designer, nurse*

Saint Augustine
Bishop, Claire DeArment *small business owner, former librarian*

Saint Petersburg
Erman, Aila *small business owner*
Nunn, Margaret Baker *owner boutique*

Saint Petersburg Beach
Bradshaw, John Robert Covington, III, *internet service company executive*

Sarasota
Meyer, B. Fred *small business executive, home designer and builder, product designer*

Tampa
Davis, Blondell Gilliam *business manager, evangelist, artist, author, poet*
Fasola, Alfred F., Jr., *retail sporting goods executive*
Keller, Shari Ann *small business owner*

Winter Park
Kindlund, Newton Carlton *retail executive*

GEORGIA

Alpharetta
Greene, Melinda Jean *retail maintenance analyst*
Watts, William David *corporate executive, business owner*

Appling
Jones, Nancy Steed *small business owner*

Atlanta
Blake, Francis Stanton *retail executive, lawyer*
Davis, Jay M. *wholesale distribution executive*
Gibson, Wayne *retail executive*

Griffin, Ron *retail executive*
Kalafut, George Wendell *distribution company executive, retired naval officer*
Lennie, Bill *retail executive*
Marcus, Bernard *retired retail executive*
Martineau, Lynn *retail executive*
Menear, Craig *retail executive*
Mercer, Larry *retail executive*
Rice, Troy *retail executive*
Ridley, Clarence Haverty *retail executive*
Shannon, Patrick S. *retail executive*
Weeks, Helen Ballard *retail executive*
Wilson, Faye *retail executive*
Wolf, Charles A. *retail camera and photographic supplies executive*

Dalton
Saul, Julian *retail executive*

Decatur
Murray, Raymond Lee *retired clothing designer, writer*
Solomon, Hilda Pearl *wholesale executive*

Dunwoody
Maddox, Jerry Aven *retired catalog management executive*

Kennesaw
Leahey, Thomas P. *retail floor covering company executive*
Nassar, A.J. *retail executive*

Macon
Davis, Anita Yvonne *small business owner, writer*

Marietta
Short-Mayfield, Patricia Ahlene *business owner*

Norcross
Sellers, Mark S. *retail executive*

Savannah
Stinn, Bradley J. *jewelry retailer*

Social Circle
Penland, John Thomas *retired import and export and development companies executive*

Tunnel Hill
McNelley, Judy Anne *small business owner*

IDAHO

Boise
Btler, Robert C. *retail executive*
Cefalo, Romeo R. *retail executive*
Dunst, Robert J., Jr., *retail executive*
Gabriel, Clarence J. *retail executive*
Herbert, Kathy *retail executive*
Long, William D. *grocery store executive*
Lynch, Peter L. *supermarket/drug store executive*
Piva, Gary *retail grocery executive*
Stablein, Lawrence A. *retail executive*
Tripp, Kevin *retail executive*

Post Falls
Wheeler, Theodore K., Jr., *small business owner*

ILLINOIS

Bensenville
Leach, Donald Paul *small business owner*

Bloomingdale
Kovanda, Gary *computer wholesale distributing executive*

Burr Ridge
Jones, Shirley Joyce *small business owner, fashion designer*

Chicago
Bozic, Michael C. *retail company executive*
Dowling, Doris Anderson *business owner, educator, consultant*
Field, Marshall *retail executive*
Gall, Betty Bluebaum *retired office services company executive*
Gin, Sue Ling *retail executive*
Hoye, Donald J. *hardware distribution company executive*
Hunt, Holly *small business owner*
Lund, Bruce Donald *small business executive*
Patinkin, Hugh M. *retail executive*
Paup, Thomas *retail department store executive*
Puican, Michael *small business owner, poet*
Robins, Joel *import/export company executive*
Tomaino, Joseph Carmine *former retail executive, former postal inspector*
Vrablik, Edward Robert *import/export company executive*
Ziegler, Ann E. *retail executive*

Deerfield
Bernauer, David W. *retail company executive*
Rein, Jeffrey A. *retail executive*
Rudolphsen, William M. *retail executive*

Glen Ellyn
Baloun, John Charles *wholesale grocery company executive, retired*

Glencoe
Nebenzahl, Kenneth *rare book and map dealer, author*

Glenview
Letham, Dennis J. *wholesale company executive*
Mc Nitt, Willard Charles *business executive*

Hoffman Estates
Bousquette, Janine M. *retail executive*
Boyer, Jeffrey N. *former retail executive*
Cosby, Mark S *retail executive*
Good, Mark *retail executive*
Gorey, Thomas C. *retail executive*
Heideman, Lyle *retail executive*
Kelly, Gerald F *retail executive*

Lacy, Alan Jasper *retail executive*
LaPorta, Sara *retail executive*
Meads, Mindy *merchandising and design executive*
Post, Jerry T *retail executive*
White, William, III, *retail executive*

Lake Forest
Loux, P. Ogden *distribution company executive*
Stirling, Ellen Adair *retail executive*

Lincolnshire
Knopik, Robert *retail executive, consultant*

Morton Grove
McKenna, Andrew James *paper distribution and printing company executive, baseball club executive*

Oak Brook
Hodnik, David F. *retail company executive*
Jones, Jeffrey W. *retail executive*

Palatine
Cesario, Robert Charles *franchise executive, consultant*

Plainfield
Bennett-Hammerberg, Janie Marie *small business owner, writer, consultant, administrative assistant*

River Grove
Litzsinger, Richard Mark *retail executive*
Stanton, Kathryn *retail bookstores/educational products and services executive*
Traut, Christopher D. *educational materials distribution executive*

Round Lake
Laskowski, Richard E. *retail hardware company executive*

Saint Charles
LaHood, Julie Ann *small business owner*
Liska, Margaret Naylor *retired small business owner*

Skokie
Van Gelder, Marc Christiaan *retail executive*

Wheeling
Ochsner, Othon Henry, II, *importer, restaurant critic*
Schulman, Alan Michael *small business owner*

INDIANA

Bicknell
Risley, Gregory Byron *furniture company executive, interior designer*

Bloomington
Stephens, Jay Martin *business owner*

Elkhart
Drexler, Rudy Matthew, Jr., *professional law enforcement dog trainer*

Fort Wayne
Cast, Anita Hursh *small business owner*
Cummings, William Robert, Jr., *business executive*
Curtis, Douglas Homer *small business owner*

Indianapolis
LaCrosse, James *retail executive*
Norwalk, Kelli Curran *retail executive, entrepreneur*
Pyle, R. Michael *wholesale distribution executive, educator*

Jasper
Newman, Leonard Jay *retail jewel merchant, gemologist*

Kendallville
Martin, Daniel Francis *small business owner*

IOWA

Ankeny
Lamb, Ronald M. *convenience stores executive*

Boone
Cramer, Robert *retail executive*

Cedar Rapids
Baldwin, George Koehler *retired retail executive*

Davenport
Sievert, Mary Elizabeth *small business owner, retired secondary school educator*

West Des Moines
Pearson, Ronald Dale *retail food stores corporation executive*
Wheeler, Mike *retail food store corporate executive*

West Union
Rivera, Shawna Colleen *small business owner*

KANSAS

Kansas City
Baska, James Louis *wholesale grocery company executive*
Carolan, Douglas *wholesale company executive*

Neodesha
James, Charles (Chuck) Edward *small business owner, writer*

Shawnee Mission
Moeller, Laura Lee *former retail executive, library consultant*

Topeka
Cantrell, Duane L. *retail executive*
Douglass, Steven J. *retail executive*
Porzig, Ullrich E. *retail executive*

Wichita
Gates, Walter Edward *small business owner*
Trombold, Walter Stevenson *supply company executive*

KENTUCKY

Bowling Green
Gipson, Jim *wholesale distribution executive*

Hebron
Howell, Joseph Toy *company owner*

Lexington
Jones, Bonnie Quantrell *automobile dealer*

Winchester
Book, John Kenneth (Kenny Book) *retail store owner*

LOUISIANA

Coushatta
Wiggins, Mary Ann Wise *small business owner, educator*

Shreveport
Dickson, Markham Allen *wholesale company executive*

MAINE

Freeport
Gorman, Leon A. *mail order company executive*
Sidar, Thomas Wilson *retail executive*

Kennebunk
Ward, Nina Gillson *jewelry store executive*

Portland
Farrington, Hugh G. *wholesale food and retail drug company executive*
Massaua, John Roger *retail executive*
Stanley, Eliot Hungerford *small business owner, writer, lawyer*

Sedgwick
Donnell, William Ray *small business owner, communications executive*

MARYLAND

Annapolis
Manos, Pete Lazaros *supermarket executive*

Baltimore
Cain, Marcena Jean Beesley *retail executive*
Kotter, Laurie Marie *small business owner, music educator*
Stein, Bernard Alvin *business consultant*

Cockeysville Hunt Valley
Roeder Vaughan, Mimi *small business owner*

Forest Hill
Klein, Shirley Snyderman *retail executive*

Potomac
Carper, Fern Gayle *small business owner, writer*
Shapiro, Richard Gerald *retired department store executive, consultant*

Riva
Barto, Bradley Edward *small business owner, educator*

MASSACHUSETTS

Auburn
Baker, David Arthur *small business owner, manufacturer*

Boston
DeAmicis, Susan McNair *small business owner*
Pivirotto, Richard Roy *former retail executive*
Rosenberg, Manuel *retail company executive*

Canton
Bentas, Lily Haseotes *retail executive*
Brenner, Harry J. *retail executive*
Palihnich, Nicholas Joseph, Jr., *retail executive*
Reichman, Joel H. *retail executive*
Watchmaker, Kenneth *retail executive*

Framingham
Anderson, Basil L. *retail executive*
Doody, Joseph G. *retail executive*
English, Edmond *retail company executive*
Feldberg, Sumner Lee *retired retail company executive*
Hoyt, Susan *retail stores executive*
Lesser, Richard G. *retail apparel company executive*
Mahoney, John J. *office supply company executive*
Parneros, Demos *retail executive*
Sargent, Ronald L. *retail office and business products executive*
VanWoerkom, Jack *retail executive, lawyer*
Vassalluzzo, Joseph S. *retail company executive*

Holyoke
Radner, Sidney Hollis *retired rug company executive*

Lawrence
Barbagallo, Joseph C. *small business owner*

Medfield
McQuillen, Jeremiah Joseph *distribution executive*

Natick
Forward, Frank *wholesale distribution executive*
Sen, Laura J. *wholesale distribution executive*
Wedge, Michael T. *wholesale distribution executive*
Zarkin, Herbert J. *retail company executive*

Pittsfield
Feldman, Robert J. *retail executive*

Quincy
Conley, Olga L. *retail executive*
Cooke, Gordon R. *retail executive*
Cooke, Gordon Richard *retail executive*

Winchendon
Holohan, Jane Patricia *shop owner, writer*

MICHIGAN

Ann Arbor
Josefowicz, Gregory P. *retail executive*

Bad Axe
Sullivan, James Gerald *small business owner*

Birmingham
Glassman, Eric I. *retail executive*

Bloomfield Hills
Robinson, Jack Albert *retail executive*

Detroit
McGee, Sherry *retail executive*
Tushman, J. Lawrence *wholesale distribution executive*
Washington, Lantz H. *small business owner*

Grand Rapids
DeLapa, Judith Anne *business owner*
Kolk, Fritz D. *retail executive*
Meijer, Douglas *retail company executive*
Meijer, Hank *retail company executive*
Meijer, Mark *retail executive*
Sturken, Craig *retail executive*
Walsh, James *retail supermarket executive*

Grosse Pointe Farms
Allen, Lee Harrison *industrial consultant, wholesale company executive*

Hudsonville
DeHoop, Troy Timothy *small business owner*

Jackson
Mills, P. Gerald *retail executive*

Lansing
LaHaine, Gilbert Eugene *retail lumber company executive*

Naubinway
Beaudoin, Robert Lawrence *small business owner*

Pontiac
Bowman, Kone J *small business owner, financial analyst*

Redford
Barnaby, Alan *retail executive*

Rochester
Conaway, Charles C. *former retail company executive*

Southfield
Bledsoe, Laurita *small business owner, publisher*
Primo, Joan Erwina *retail and real estate consulting business owner*

Troy
Austin, Karen *retail executive*
Criancamilli, Andrew A. *retail executive*
Crowley, William C. *retail executive*
Day, Julian C. *retail executive*
Kelly, Janet G. *retail executive*
Lueken, Harold W. *retail executive*
Strome, Stephen *distribution company executive*

MINNESOTA

Eden Prairie
Engel, Susan E. *retail executive*
Jackson, Darren Richard *retail company executive*
Knous, Pamela K. *wholesale distribution executive*
Noddle, Jeffrey *retail and food distribution executive*
Wright, Michael William *wholesale distribution and retail executive*

Edina
Emmerich, Karol Denise *foundation executive, daylily hybridizer, former retail executive*
Froemming, Herbert Dean *retired retail executive*

Excelsior
Beeler, Donald Daryl *retired retail executive*

Minneapolis
Ahlers, Linda L. *retail executive*
Francis, Michael R. *retail executive*
Hale, James Thomas *retail executive, lawyer*
Lindahl, Dennis *retail executive*
Mammel, Russell Norman *retired food distribution company executive*
Marshall, Ron *retail executive*
Paulu, Frances Brown *retired international center administrator*
Schulze, Richard M. *retail electronics company executive*
Scovanner, Douglas *retail company executive*
Stephenson, Vivian M. *former retail executive*
Storch, Gerald L. *retail executive*
Trestman, Frank D. *distribution company executive, director*
Tuzcu, Ertugrul *retail executive*
Ulrich, Robert J. *retail executive*
Woodrow, Kennth B. *retail company executive*

Minnetonka
DiGeso, Amy *mail order company executive*
Kriegel, David L. *retail executive*

Richfield
Anderson, Bradbury H. *retail executive*

Linton, Michael Alan *retail company executive*

Saint Paul
Johnson, Lynn *liquor company wholesaler*
Nash, Nicholas David *retail executive*

Shakopee
Shore, Leann Marie *small business owner, occupational therapist*

Walker
Collins, Thomas William *caterer, consultant*

MISSISSIPPI

Clarksdale
Levingston, Jon Stuart *retail executive*

MISSOURI

Charleston
Cassell, Lucille Richardson *small business owner*

Chesterfield
Ross, E. Earl *small business owner*

Creve Coeur
Kemper, Christina *small business owner, respiratory therapist, elementary school educator*

Cuba
Work, Bruce Van Syoc *business consultant*

Eureka
Zimmers, Vivian Eleanor *development and administrative consultant*

Kansas City
Baker, Sharlynn Ruth *livery and limousine service owner*
Barron, Millard E. *retail executive*
Stueck, William Noble *small business owner*

Kingsville
Stimac, John Anthony *small business owner, poet, cartoonist, inventor*

Lebanon
Louderback, Kevin Wayne *business owner*

Maryland Heights
Marcus, John *wholesale distribution executive*

O Fallon
Wood, Leslie Ann *retail administrator*

Overland
Clark, Maxine *retail executive*

Saint Louis
Bennet, Richard W., III, *retail executive*
Berger, Wayne C. *retail executive*
Bridgewater, Bernard Adolphus, Jr., *retired footwear company executive, consultant*
Capps, W. Lee, III, *retail executive*
Dunham, John L. *retail company executive*
Edison, Bernard Alan *retired retail apparel company executive*
Fingleton, Thomas D. *retail executive*
Hinshaw, Juanita *electric distributor executive*
Kahn, Eugene S. *department store chain executive*
Loeb, Jerome Thomas *retail executive*
McNamara, William P. *retail executive*
Newman, Andrew Edison *restaurant executive*
Novak, Camille *small business owner, consultant*
Schnuck, Craig D. *grocery store company executive*
Schnuck, Todd Robert *grocery store company executive*
Skinner, Robert C., Jr., *retail executive*
Upbin, Hal J. *consumer products executive*

Saint Peters
Van Lokeren, Mary Ann Krey *beer wholesaler executive*

NEBRASKA

Omaha
Shaw, Raymond Arthur *retail manager*

NEVADA

Henderson
Fehr, Gregory Paris *marketing and distribution company executive*

Las Vegas
Marcovitz, Leonard Edward *retail executive*

Reno
Weber, Michael Mathew *small business owner*

NEW HAMPSHIRE

Concord
Katsakiores, Phyllis May *small business owner, city councilor*

Conway
Blodgett, Julian Robert *small business owner*

Keene
Lichtenstein, Sally (Ali) Tucker *small business owner, writer, educator*

Manchester
Bramante, Fredrick J., Jr., *retail executive*
Poloian, Lynda Gamans *retailing educator*

New Castle
Friese, George Ralph *retail executive*

New London
Thoma, Kurt Michael *business owner*

North Salem
Stone, Robert Eldred *small business owner, museum director*

Rochester
Coviello, Robert Frank *retail executive*

NEW JERSEY

Burlington
Nesci, Mark A. *retail executive*

Carteret
Donald, James L. *supermarket executive*
Scott, Eileen Rose *retail executive*

Clifton
Axelrod, Norman *retail company executive*
Giles, William (Bill) T. *retail executive*

Colts Neck
Mauro, Anthony Peter *small business owner*

East Orange
Teetsell, Janice Marie Newman *business owner, lawyer*

Elizabeth
Gellert, George Geza *food importing company executive*

Freehold
Foster, Eric Harold, Jr., *retail executive*
Saker, Joseph J. *supermarket company executive*

Hoboken
Schultz, Kenneth Carl *antiques dealer*

Jersey City
Pasternak, Kenneth D. *trading company executive*

Livingston
Piscopo, Phil *wholesale distribution executive*

Mahwah
Inserra, Lawrence R. *retail executive*

Montclair
Murphy, Betty Jagoda *small business owner*

Montvale
Ulrich, Robert Gardner *retail food chain executive, lawyer*
Wood, James *supermarket executive*

Neptune
Harran, Susan R. *small business owner, writer*

New Milford
Walsh, Joseph Michael *magazine distribution executive*

North Bergen
Karp, Roberta S. *wholesale apparel and accessories executive*
Slatner, Thomas Allen *bookseller*

Paterson
Papageorgis, Jack *small business owner*

Pennington
Donnelly, Gerard Kevin *marketing and retail executive*

Plainfield
DeFreitas, Douglas Davis *small business owner*

Princeton
Bergman, Victoria Besterman *small business owner, consultant*
Campbell, Mildred Corum *business owner, nurse*
Hochschwender, Karl Albert *international trade and government relations consultant*
Szaban, Marilyn C. *small business owner*

Secaucus
Syms, Marcy *retail executive*

Union
Eisenberg, Warren *retail executive*
Feinstein, Leonard *retail executive*
Temares, Steven H. *retail executive*

Verona
Brightman, Robert Lloyd *importer, textile company executive, consultant*

Wayne
Arthur, Ray *retail executive*
Arthur, Raymond L. *retail toy and game company executive*
Barbour, John *retail executive*
Brockett, Francesca L. *retail executive*
Derby, Deborah *retail executive*
Feldt, James E. *retail executive*
Holohan, John *retail executive*
Kay, Christopher K. *retail executive*
Kornblum, Warren *retail executive*
Markee, Richard L. *retail executive*
Wahle, Elliott *retail executive*

Whippany
Curwin, Ronald *home equipment stores executive*

Wilkesboro
Jennings, Perry G. *retail executive*
Kasberger, John L. *retail executive*

NEW MEXICO

Carlsbad
Queen, Dorothy *distribution company executive*

Ruidoso
McIntosh, Cathleen Anne *small business owner, educator*

Tijeras
Sholtis, Joseph Arnold, Jr., *business owner, nuclear and aerospace engineer, consultant*

NEW YORK

Appleton
Singer, Thomas Kenyon *international business consultant, fruit grower*

Bellport
Regalmuto, Nancy Marie *small business owner, psychic consultant, therapist*

Binghamton
Bochnovich, John Andrew *small business owner*

Bronx
Kramer, Eleanor *retired real estate broker, tax practitioner, financial consultant*
Lyons, Maxine Evadney *small business owner, poet*

Brooklyn
Magliocco, John *wholesale distribution executive*
Petersen, Richard John *small business owner, educator*
Zelin, Jerome *retired retail executive*

Farmingdale
Lobel, Sharon *retail executive*

Katonah
Levine, Pamela Gail *business owner*

Melville
Leno, Sam R. *retail executive*

New York
Abrahamsen, Abel *wholesale and retail import company executive*
Bacon, Chantal *retail executive*
Becker, Isidore A. *business executive*
Brown, Andreas Le *book store and art gallery executive*
Caputo, Lucio *trade company executive*
Catsimatidis, John Andreas *retail chain executive, airline executive*
Chaney, Gerald M. *retail executive*
Chung, Chia Mou (Charles Chung) *former Oriental art business owner*
Donohue, Margaret Anne *retail company executive*
Drexler, Millard S. *retail executive*
Farah, Roger *retail company executive*
Fernandez, James *retail products executive*
Finkelstein, Edward Sydney *department store executive*
Friedman, Rachelle *music retail executive*
Isogai, Masaharu *international business consultant, former women's apparel executive*
Kaplan, Ira *import/export company executive*
Kettaneh, Anthony C. *small business owner, consultant*
Kowalski, Michael J. *retail executive*
Lombardi, Joseph J. *retail executive*
Lundgren, Terry J. *retail executive*
Matthews, Norman Stuart *department store executive*
Mello, Dawn *retail executive*
Michelson, Gertrude Geraldine *retired retail company executive*
Mondlin, Marvin *retail executive, antiquarian book dealer*
Quinn, James E. *retail products executive*
Quint, Ira *retail executive*
Riggio, Stephen *book store chain executive*
Sadove, Stephen Irving *retail executive*
Schiller, Justin Galland *antiquarian bookseller, researcher, editor*
, *retail executive*
Sherman, Jeffrey Barry *retail executive*
Spivak, Stuart *retail executive*
Stanton, Ronald P. *export company executive*
Stern, Madeleine Bettina *rare books dealer, author*
Tendler, David *international trade company executive*
Toulantis, Marie *retail executive*
Trammell, Joseph Emanuel *small business owner, media consultant*
Washburn, Joan Thomas *business owner, art gallery director*
Weiner, Edward G. *export company executive*
Wilson, Fred *retail executive*

Rochester
McCurdy, Gilbert Geier *retired retailer*
Wegman, Daniel R. *retail executive*

Ronkonkoma
Nussdorf, Glenn *distribution executive*

Rye
Francis, Charles Gordon *business executive, writer*

Stony Brook
Grudens, Richard William *retail executive, writer*

Suffern
Jaffe, Elliot Stanley *retail executive*

NORTH CAROLINA

Black Mountain
Ingle, Robert P. *retail groceries company executive*
Lanning, James W. *retail executive*
Tudor, Brenda S. *retail company executive*

Charlotte
Alexander, R. David *retail executive*
Belk, Irwin *retail executive*
Belk, John Montgomery *retired retail executive*
Belk, John R. *retail executive*
Gambrell, Sarah Belk *retail executive*
Gross, Edward H. *wholesale distributing executive*
Kelly, R. James *retail executive*
Levine, Howard R. *retail executive*
Walton, Bill R. *retail executive*

Fayetteville
Shaffer, Denny Richard *small business owner*

Greensboro
Goulder, Gerald Polster *retail executive, management consultant, lawyer*
Orlowsky, Martin L. *executive manager*

Henderson
Bush, Jack Eugene *retail executive*

Highlands
Shaffner, Randolph Preston *shop owner, educator, writer, publisher*

Kinston
Peede, Wayne Carroll *small business owner*

Mooresville
Black, Kenneth W., Jr., *retail executive*

North Wilkesboro
Wessling, Gregory Jay *retail executive*
Whiddon, Thomas E. *retail executive*

Rocky Mount
Kowalk, Jeffrey M. *wholesale distribution executive*
Wordsworth, Jerry L. *wholesale distribution executive*

Salisbury
Candler, Faxon David *small business owner*

Sanford
Kelly, Daniel J. *retail executive*

Spindale
Howard, Elizabeth Ann Blanton *courier service executive*

Wilkesboro
Anderson, Theresa A. *retail executive*
Bridgeford, Gregory M. *retail executive*
Brown, Michael K. *retail executive*
Canter, Charles W. (Nick) *retail executive*
Croom, Marshall A. *retail executive*
Gfeller, Robert J., Jr., *retail executive*
Herring, A. Lee *retail executive*
Hull, Robert F., Jr., *retail executive*
McCanless, Ross W. *retail executive*
Shelton, David E. *retail executive*
Sowder, Eric D. *retail executive*

Wilson
Atkinson, Ann Lennette *mortician*

NORTH DAKOTA

Fargo
McWilliams, Carey Scott *small business owner, writer*

Minot
Welstad, Kirk *small business owner*

OHIO

Bexley
Unverferth, Barbara Patten *small business owner*

Cincinnati
Clark, David W. *retail executive*
Cole, Tom *retail executive*
Grove, Janet E. *retail executive*
Hodge, Robert Joseph *retail executive*
Hoguet, David Dilworth *rental furniture executive*
Hoguet, Karen M. *retail department store executive*
Javosky, Rudolph V. *retail executive*
Kronick, Susan D. *retail executive*
McGeorge, Don W. *retail executive*
Tysoe, Ronald W. *retail executive*
Tysor, Ronald W. *retail executive*
Zimmerman, James M. *retail company executive*

Cleveland
Anderson, Warren *distribution company executive*
Crosby, Fred McClellan *retail home and office furnishings executive*
Hennessy, Sean P. *retail executive*
Stone, Harry H. *retail executive*

Columbus
Biresi, Mark A. *retail executive*
Faber, Timothy *retail executive*
Finkelman, Daniel P. *retail executive*
Hailey, V. Ann *retail executive*
Holman-Rao, Marie *retail executive*
Holtz, Diane *retail executive*
Kaufman, Barry D. *retail executive*
Kelley, William G. *retail stores executive*
Ketteler, Thomas R. *retail executive*
Killion, Theo *retail executive*
LaHowchic, Nicholas John *retail specialty company executive*
Potter, Michael J. *retail stores executive*
Razek, Edward G. *retail executive*
Ricart, Rhett C. *retail automotive executive*
Ricker, Jon *retail executive*
Schlesinger, Leonard Arthur *retail executive*
Soll, Bruce A. *retail executive*
Thompson, David W. *retail executive*
Travis, Tracey Thomas *retail executive*
Turney, Sharon Jester *retail executive*
Wexner, Leslie Herbert *retail executive*

Dayton
Jenefsky, Jack *wholesale company executive*
Petrick, Joseph Anthony *small business owner, management consultant, educator*
Rose, Stuart *retail executive*

Dublin
Walter, Robert D. *wholesale pharmaceutical distribution executive*

Fairlawn
Brubaker, Karen Sue *small business owner*

Hudson
Duchon, Roseann Marie *small business owner, consultant*

Milford
Conover, Nellie Coburn *retired retail furniture company executive*

New Albany
Riley, Susan Jean *retail executive*

Newark
Black, Boyd Carson *small business owner*

Pickerington
Callander, Kay Eileen Paisley *business owner, retired education educator, writer*

Reynoldsburg
Fiske, Neil *retail executive*
Nichols, Grace A. *retail executive*

Shaker Heights
Feuer, Michael *office products superstore executive*
Killeen, Michael F. *retail executive*

Youngstown
Catoline-Ackerman, Pauline Dessie *small business owner*

OKLAHOMA

Oklahoma City
Davis, Emery Stephen *wholesale food company executive*
Hansen, Mark S. *food marketing and distribution company executive*
Williams, Richard Donald *retired wholesale food company executive*

OREGON

Bend
Nosler, Robert Amos *sports company executive*

Burns
Timms, Eugene Dale *wholesale business owner, state senator*

Junction City
Stong, John Elliott *retail music and electronic company executive*

Medford
De Boer, Sydney B. *auto dealership executive*

Portland
Lilly, Elizabeth Giles *small business owner*
Tomjack, T.J. *wholesale distribution executive*

Prineville
Wick, Philip *wholesale distribution executive*

Salem
Winters, Jackie F. *small business owner, foundation administrator*

Seaside
Doolittle, Trudy Ann *small business owner, application developer, consultant*

PENNSYLVANIA

Altoona
Kaufman, Harry *retail executive*
Sheetz, Stanton R. *grocery retail executive*

Bala Cynwyd
Armani, Aida Mary *small business executive*

Berwyn
Fry, Clarence Herbert *retired retail executive*

Bristol
Boneparth, Peter *retail executive*

Camp Hill
Beasley, Ed *retail executive*
Cardinale, Gerald P. *retail executive*
Davis, Don P. *retail executive*
deBruin, Jerry Mark *retail executive*
Gerson, Elliot S. *lawyer, retail company executive*
Hall, Christopher S. *retail executive*
Keough, Philip J., IV, *retail executive*
Learish, John *retail executive*
Lester, Wilson A., Jr., *retail executive*
Lovett, Keith W *retail executive*
Mastrian, James P. *retail executive*
Miller, Robert G. *drug store chain company executive*
Panzer, Mark *retail executive*
Sammons, Mary F. *retail executive*
Sari, Robert *retail executive*
Shirtliff, Bryan *retail executive*
Standley, John *drug retail company executive*
Todd, Murray *retail executive*

Eighty Four
Hardy, Joseph A., Sr., *wholesale distribution executive*

Erie
Hagen, Thomas Bailey *business owner, former state official, retired insurance company executive*

Glenside
Frudakis, Rosalie *small business owner*

Hawley
Kanzer, Larry *small business owner, food service director*

Media
Chambers, Ed *convenience store executive*
Wood, Richard D., Jr., *retail executive*

Philadelphia
Babich, George, Jr., *retail executive*
Korman, Bernard J. *retail executive*
Lyons, Lewis *retail executive*
Ranick, Marvin *retail sales executive*
Stevenson, Lawrence N. *retail executive*

Pittsburgh
McAnally, David F. *distribution company executive*

Reading
Boscov, Albert *retail executive*

Shamokin Dam
Matter, Harry H. *retired wholesale business executive, reflexologist*

Shiremanstown
Nesbit, William Terry *small business owner, consultant*

Williamsport
Largen, Joseph *retailer, furniture manufacturer, book wholesaler*

Wormleysburg
Grass, Alexander *retail company executive*

RHODE ISLAND

Block Island
Connolly, Violette M. *small business owner*

Providence
Killeen, Johanne *small business owner*

Woonsocket
Bodine, Chris W. *retail executive*
Ferdinandi, V. Michael *retail executive*
Merlo, Larry J. *retail executive*
Ryan, Thomas M. *drug store chain executive*
Solberg, Larry D. *retail executive*

SOUTH CAROLINA

Lexington
Kennedy, Sandra Elaine *small business owner*

Yemassee
Olendorf, William Carr, Jr., *small business owner*

TENNESSEE

Goodlettsville
Shaffer, Donald S. *retail executive*

Hermitage
Reid, Donna Joyce *small business owner*

Jefferson City
Trent, Wendell Campbell *business owner*

Johnson City
Ice, Billie Oberta *retail executive*

Knoxville
Harris, Charles Edgar *retired wholesale distribution company executive*
Krauter, Lana Cain *retail executive*
Walker, W. Jack *retired small business owner*

La Vergne
Daniel, William Donnie *video game distribution executive*

Memphis
Odland, Steve *retail executive*
Wright Carrier, J. T. *business owner*

Nashville
Ingram, John *wholesale distribution executive*
Turner, Cal, Jr., *discount stores executive*
Zibart, Michael Alan *wholesale book company executive*
Zimmerman, Raymond *retail chain executive*

TEXAS

Allen
Mitchell, Ralph *wholesale distribution executive*

Amarillo
Marmaduke, John H. *retail executive*

Argyle
Merritt, Joe Frank *industrial supply executive*

Austin
Girling, Robert George William, III, *business owner*
Wilson, Margaret Scarbrough *retail executive*

Bastrop
Reaves, Melvin Junior *retired small business owner*

Beaumont
Alter, Nelson Tobias *jewelry retailer and wholesaler*

Boerne
Morton, Michael Ray *retail company consultant*

Bryan
Smith, Elouise Beard *restaurant owner*

Corpus Christi
Finley, George Alvin, III, *wholesale executive*

Dallas
Augur, Marilyn Hussman *distribution executive*
Bracken, Frank D. *retail executive*
Castagna, Vanessa J. *retail executive*
Glazer, Bennett J. *wholesale distribution executive*
Glazer, Robert S. *wholesale distribution executive*
Haggar, J. M., III, *retail executive*
Hallam, Robert G. *wholesale distribution executive*
Halpin, James *former retail computer stores executive*
Matthews, Clark J(io), II, *retail executive, lawyer, retired*
McDougall, Ronald Alexander *restaurant executive*

Mondry, Lawrence N. *retail sales professional*
Moneypenny, Edward William *retail executive*
Oesterreicher, James E. *former department stores executive*
Stone, Donald James *retired retail executive*
Tansky, Burton *department store executive*

El Paso
Miller, Deane Guynes *salon and cosmetic studio owner*

Elmendorf
Teague, Mary Elizabeth *small business owner*

Fort Worth
Edmondson, David J. *retail executive*
Follit, Evelyn V. *retail executive*
Girouard, Marvin J. *retail executive*
Michero, William Henderson *retired retail trade executive*
Newman, Michael D. *retail executive*
Roach, John Vinson, II, *retail company executive*
Roberts, Leonard H. *retail executive*
Thompson, Carson R. *retail and manufacturing company executive*

Gainesville
Brooks, Jerry Robert *small business owner*

Horseshoe Bay
Simpson, H. Richard (Dick Simpson) *retailer*

Houston
Barricklo, Jack Nelson *small business owner*
Calbert, Mike *retail executive*
Castillo, Josephine *small business owner, educator*
Castleberry, Michael Dan *grocery supply company financial executive*
Gaucher, Jane Heyck *retail executive*
Levit, Max *wholesale distribution executive, food service executive*
Levit, Milton *grocery supply company executive*
MacAvery, Tristan Alexander (Tristan Black Wolf) *small business owner, writer, actor*
Nelson, James *wholesale food distribution executive*
Spitler, Kenneth F. *wholesale distribution executive*
Texas, Sam Fayad *small business owner, political activist*
Wike, D. Elaine *small business owner*
Woodhouse, John Frederick *food distribution company executive*
Zaleski, Linda C. *retail executive*

Irving
Buthman, Mark A. *retail executive*
Greer, C. Scott *retail executive*
Ritchie-Ramirez, Judy *small business owner, artist*
Rouleau, R. Michael *retail executive*
Wyly, Sam *retail executive*

Kingwood
Spartz, Alice Anne Lenore *retired retail executive*

Lewisville
Willmott, Peter Sherman *retail executive*

Longview
McKinley, Jimmie Joe *business executive*

Lubbock
Willingham, Mary Maxine *fashion retailer*

Mc Kinney
Fairman, Jarrett Sylvester *retail company executive*

Plano
Cavanaugh, Robert B. *department store executive*
Harris, Wayne *retail executive*
Layton, Mark C. *wholesale distribution executive*
McKay, Donald A. *retail company executive*
Neppl, Walter Joseph *retired retail store executive*
Powell, James R. *wholesale distribution executive*
Questrom, Allen I. *retail executive*
Raish, Stephen E *retail executive*

Round Mountain
McReynolds, Mary Maureen *small business owner*

San Antonio
Brouillard, John Charles *retail company executive*
Lopez, M. Edward *small business owner*

Seabrook
Spears, James Grady *small business owner*

Sulphur Springs
Law, Kerry W. *wholesale executive*
McKenzie, Michael K. *wholesale company executive*

Terrell
Wolfe, Tracey Dianne *distributing company executive*

Texarkana
Floyd, Stacy Y. *retail executive*
Hubbard, Sonia Y. *retail executive*

Tyler
Brookshire, Bruce G. *retail grocery store executive*
Edwards, D. M. *retail, wholesale distribution and commercial real estate investment executive*
Massey, Marvin S., Jr., *grocery retail executive*
Triplett, Preston *retail food company executive*

Waxahachie
Johnson, Ronald Kay *retail company executive*

Wimberley
Ellis, John *small business owner*
Franklin, Sue Morgan *small business owner, educator*

UTAH

Logan
Watterson, Scott *home fitness equipment manufacturer*

Salt Lake City
Fields, Debbi *cookie franchise executive*
Miller, Lorraine *business owner*

VERMONT

Brattleboro
Albertian, Edward *wholesale distribution executive*
Harris, Reuben *wholesale distribution executive*
Wright, Ron *retail executive*

Colchester
Lawton, Lorilee Ann *fire sprinkler contractor company owner, accountant*

Vergennes
Grant, Edwin Randolph *retail executive, manufacturing executive*

VIRGINIA

Alexandria
Elkins, Dan *small business owner, educator*

Arlington
Scarborough, Robert Henry, Jr., *enterpreneur*

Bristol
McGlothlin, James W. *wholesale distribution executive*

Bristow
Schrock, Simon *retail executive*

Chantilly
Tobin, Robert G. *supermarket chain executive*

Charlottesville
Lupton, Mary Hosmer *retired small business owner*

Chesapeake
Brock, Macon F., Sr., *retail company executive*
Coble, Frederick Charles *discount retail executive*
Sasser, Robert *retail buyer*

Fairfax
Bohan, Gloria *travel retail executive*
Pugh, Arthur James (Jay Pugh) *retired department store executive, consultant*
Rogers, William Fenna, Jr., *supermarket executive, management consultant*

Mc Lean
Vandemark, Robert Goodyear *retired retail company executive*

Nellysford
Pfaltz, Katharine *small business owner, writer*

Norfolk
DeVenny, Lillian Nickell *trophy company executive*

Occoquan
Nemecek, Albert Duncan, Jr., *retail company executive, investment banker, management consultant*

Purcellville
Sharples, Winston Singleton *automobile importer and distributor*

Richmond
Austin-Stephens, Ann-Marie *retail executive*
Bowman, Dennis J. *retail computer executive*
Cannon, W. Stephen *retail executive, lawyer*
Casini, Jane Sloan *wholesale distribution executive*
Chalifoux, Michael T. *retail electronics company executive*
Dias, Fiona P. *retail executive*
Dunn, Philip J. *retail executive, treasurer, controller*
Foss, Michael E. *retail executive*
Froman, John W. *retail executive*
Harvey, Ollie Marie *small business owner, not-for-profit developer*
Luo, Shawn Haisheng *retail company executive*
Maguire, Kim D. *retail executive*
McCollough, W. Alan *electronics retail executive*
Mierenfeld, Gary M. *retail executive*
Ukrop, James E. *retail executive*
Wells, Jeffrey S. *retail executive, human resources specialist*

Salem
Brand, Edward Cabell *retail executive*

Staunton
Hammaker, Paul M. *retail executive, business educator, author*

Upperville
Powell Gebhard, Joy Lee (Bok Sin Lee) *small business owner*

Vienna
Edwards, Phillip Milton *retired import-export company executive*

Williamsburg
Cauthen, Charles Edward, Jr., *retail executive, business consultant*

WASHINGTON

Bellingham
Cole, Craig W. *grocery chain executive*

Issaquah
Brotman, Jeffrey H. *variety stores executive*
Galanti, Richard A. *wholesale business executive*
Sinegal, James D. *wholesale distribution executive*

Mercer Island
Sanford, Kenneth Richard *small business owner*

Monroe
Kirwan, Katharyn race (Mrs. Gerald Bourke Kirwan Jr.) *retail executive*

Redmond
Brakken, William *home improvement retail executive*

Seattle
Bridge, Herbert Marvin *jewelry executive*
Cottle, Gail Ann *retail executive*
Fix, Wilbur James *department store executive*
Leale, Olivia Mason *import marketing company executive*
Nordstrom, Blake W. *retail executive*
Nordstrom, Bruce A. *department store executive*
Nordstrom, John N. *department store executive*
Stearns, Susan Tracey *lighting design company executive, lawyer*
Stewart, Thomas J. *wholesale distribution executive*

Spokane
Chamberlain, Barbara Kaye *small business owner, communications executive*
Krueger, Larry Eugene *import/export company executive, lawyer*
Leighton, Jack Richard *small business owner, former educator*
Sines, Randy Dwain *business executive*

Yakima
Newland, Ruth Laura *small business owner*

WEST VIRGINIA

Martinsburg
Ayers, Anne Louise *small business owner, consultant, counselor*

WISCONSIN

Arcadia
Wanek, Todd *retail executive*

Beloit
Hendricks, Kenneth *wholesale distribution executive*
Story, Kendra *wholesale distribution executive*

Bowler
Bartholomaus, Brett William *small business owner*

Eau Claire
Helland, Mark Duane *small business owner*
Menard, John R., Jr., *home improvement retail executive*

Glendale
Bosomworth, Paul A, *small business owner, ceramics engineer*

Green Bay
Duncan, Sam K. *retail executive*
Eugster, Jack Wilson *retail executive*
Lynch, Matthew J. *retail executive*

Menomonee Falls
Blanc, Caryn *retail executive*
Kellogg, William S. *retail executive*
Mansell, Kevin B. *retail executive*
McDonald, Wesley S. *retail executive*
Meier, Arlene *retail executive*
Montgomery, R. Lawrence *department store chain executive*
Vasques, Gary *retail executive, marketing professional*

Milwaukee
Mariano, Robert A. *retail executive*

Wausau
Builer, Dorothy Marion *business owner*

WYOMING

Jackson
Law, Clarene Alta *small business owner, state legislator*

CANADA

ALBERTA

Calgary
Slater, Gary *retail executive*

MANITOBA

Winnipeg
Cohen, Albert Diamond *retail executive*

QUEBEC

Montreal
Toutant, Sylvain *retail executive*

MEXICO

Mexico City
Kim, Earnest Jae-Hyun *import and export company executive*

CHINA

Shanghai
Chueh, Chun Fei *import/export company executive*

ADDRESS UNPUBLISHED

Adamson, James B. *retail executive*
Aved, Barry *retail executive, consultant*
Baker, Edward Kevin *retail executive*
Barlow, John Leon *retired retail executive*
Bates, Dena Beth *shop owner*
Beavers, Karen Marjorie *small business owner*
Binder, Madeline Dotti *retail executive*
Blum, Gerald Henry *department store executive*
Bravo, Rose Marie *retail executive*
Burris, Lauren Bayleran *business owner*
Chevalier, Paul Edward *retired retail executive, lawyer*
Church, Bryan P. *business owner, educator*
Colgate, Stephen *small business owner*
Compton, Harold F. *former retail executive*
Cope, Kenneth Wayne *chain store executive*
Copps, Michael William *former retail and wholesale company executive*
Cox, Joy Dean *small business owner*
Crowley, Jerome Joseph, Jr., *retired retail executive*
Day, John Denton *retired company executive, cattle and horse rancher, breeder, trainer, wrangler, actor, educator*
DeVivo, Ange *retired small business owner*
Dobson, Melanie Beroth *small business owner, public relations executive*
Dominick, Kathleen Marilyn *small business owner, consultant*
Duffy, Harry Arthur *violin expert and dealer*
Dworin, Micki (Maxine Dworin) *automobile dealership executive*
Edwards, Patrick Ross *former retail company executive, lawyer, management consultant*
Ettore, Joseph R. *discount department store chain executive*
Evans, Robert George, Jr., *retail and mail order executive*
Eyler, John H., Jr., *retail toy and game company executive*
Farr, Ivanne Estelle *small business owner, consultant, artist, sculptor*
Feuer, Marshall Zev *import/export company executive*
Fields, Douglas Philip *building supply wholesale company executive*
Fields, Leo *former jewelry company executive, investor*
Finnigan, Robert Emmet *retired small business owner*
Fortgang, Charles *wholesale distribution executive*
Gagen, J. Wilfrid *business owner, marketing and public relations executive, consultant*
Galvao, Louis Alberto *import and export corporation executive, consultant*
Genuardi, Charles A. *former retail executive*
Geoffroy, Charles Henry *retired business executive*
Goldner, Sheldon Herbert *export-import company executive*
Goldstein, Alfred George *retail and consumer products executive*
Goldstein, Michael *retail executive*
Goldstein, Norman Ray *international trading company executive, consultant*
Goodman, Gail Busman *small business owner*
Gray, Deborah Mary *wine importer*
Haas, Edward Lee *business executive, consultant*
Hambrecht, Patricia G. *retail executive*
Hawk, Robert Dooley *wholesale grocery company executive*
Hirsch, Larry Joseph *retired retail executive, lawyer*
Holzkamp, Jane Strauss *business owner*
Jenkins, Charles H., Jr., *retail company executive*
Johnson, Dolores Estelle *retired small business owner*
Jourdan, Toni Christina *small business owner, actress, writer*
Kingsley, David H *small business owner*
Kipper, Barbara Levy *wholesale distribution executive*
Kogut, John Anthony *retail/wholesale executive*
Kopack, Pamela Lee (Pamela Lee MacMinn) *business services executive*
Kwasnick, Paul Jack *retail executive*
Lang, William Charles *financial executive*
Larrimore, Randall Walter *retired wholesale company executive*
Lehrer, Merrill Clark *retail sales consultant*
Lipsey, Joseph, Jr., *water bottling company executive, retail and wholesale corporation executive*
Lowry, Marilyn Jean *horticultural retail company executive*
Marcus, Lee Evan *small business owner, consultant, accountant*
Marshall, George Dwire *retired supermarket chain executive*
Martini, Robert Edward *wholesale pharmaceutical and medical supplies company executive*
McClendon, Irvin Lee, Sr., *business owner, writer, editor, proofreader, tutor*
McConnell, Jack B. *physican, retired corporate executive*
Meek, Forrest Burns *retired trading company executive*
Mench, John William *retail store executive, electrical engineer*
Metz, Steven William *small business owner*
Milstein, Monroe Gary *retail executive*
Moy, Audrey *retired retail buyer*
Nicholas, Lawrence Bruce *advisory company executive*
Nichols, David L. *retail executive*
Nishimura, Joseph Yo *retired retail executive, accountant*
Oppman, John Christopher *small business owner*
Orban, Kurt *foreign trade company executive*
Oxnam, Philip Linton *small business owner*
Paterson, Robert E. *trading stamp company executive*
Pearl, B. Michael *business owner*
Peterson, Coleman Hollis *former retail store executive*
Peterson, Gary J *retail executive*
Pham, Lara Bach-Vien *small business owner*
Quimby, Jeffrey Yorke *small business owner*
Ransome, Ernest Leslie, III, *retail company executive*
Raskin, Michael A. *retail company executive*
Raymond, Ural Wayne *retired retail executive*
Richards, Craig M. *wholesale distribution executive*
Ritchey, Samuel Donley, Jr., *retired retail store executive*
Roberts, Patricia Lee *small business owner, consultant*
Rodbell, Clyde Armand *retired distribution executive*

Rohner, Bonnie-Jean *small business owner, computer consultant*
Ruland, Mildred Ardelia *retail executive, retail buyer*
Runge, Donald Edward *food wholesale company executive*
Samson, Alvin *former distributing company executive, consultant*
Schwartz, Carolyn Lynn *retail executive, musician*
Schwartz, Mark *former retail executive*
Scott, Sylvia Jane *small business owner*
Segal, Robert S. *retail executive*
Sharp, Richard L. *retail company executive*
Snodgrass, Lynn *small business owner, former state legislator*
Spitzer, Matthew Lawrence *retired retail store executive*
Stemberg, Thomas George *retail office supply store executive*
Stettner, Jerald W. *retail drugs stores executive*
Stronach, Belinda *former retail executive*
Tate, Fran M. *small business owner*
Tielke, James Clemens *retail and manufacturing management consultant*
Toscano, Samuel, Jr., *wholesale distribution executive*
Trutter, John Thomas *consulting company executive*
Vernon, Carl Atlee, Jr., *retired wholesale food distributor executive*
Waddle, John Frederick *former retail chain executive*
Weiss, Michael Allen *retail executive*
Werries, E. Dean *food distribution company executive*
Winn, Herschel C. *retired retail electronics company executive*
Winter, Richard Samuel, Jr., *computer training company owner, writer*
Wolf, Chadwick Linwood *small business owner, firefighter*

INDUSTRY: TRANSPORTATION

UNITED STATES

ALABAMA

Abbeville
Anderson, Ruth T. *retired air traffic controller*

Birmingham
Brough, James A. *airport terminal executive*
Haworth, Michael Elliott, Jr., *aerospace company executive*

Gulf Shores
Wallace, John Loys *aviation services executive*

Huntsville
Bolte, James T. *transportation executive*
Tucker, Richard A. *airport terminal executive*

Meridianville
Oberhausen, Joyce Ann Wynn *aircraft company executive, artist*

ALASKA

Anchorage
Bowers, Paul D. *transportation company executive*
Sullivan, George Murray *transportation consultant, former mayor*
Williams, Eleanor Joyce *retired government air traffic control specialist*

ARIZONA

Bullhead City
Hicks, Norm *airport authority executive*

Goodyear
Borton, George Robert *retired airline captain*

Grand Canyon
Bryant, Leland Marshal *business and nonprofit executive*

Phoenix
Enzor, Gary R. *trucking executive*
Johnson, Robert D. *aerospace transportation executive*
Krietor, David *airport authority executive*
Moyes, Jerry C. *transportation executive*
Solomon, John Davis *aviation executive*

Prescott
Waldock, William David *aeronautical science and aviation safety educator*

Sun City West
Hartzog, Ira Barnes *aviation executive*

Tempe
Kerr, Derek J. *transportation executive*
Parker, W. Douglas *transportation executive*

Tucson
Burg, Walter A. *airport terminal executive*
Mercker, Mary Alice *aviation school administrator*

ARKANSAS

Bella Vista
Pogue, William Reid *former astronaut, foundation executive, business and aerospace consultant*

Fort Smith
Davidson, Robert *trucking executive*
Young, Robert A., III, *freight systems executive*

Harrison
Garrison, F. Sheridan *transportation executive*

Huntsville
Carr, Gerald Paul *former astronaut, retired business executive, former marine officer*

Little Rock
Schwartz, Deborah S. *airport manager*

Lowell
Garrison, Wayne *transportation executive*
Hunt, J. B. (Johnnie Bryan Hunt) *retired transportation executive*
Thompson, Kirk *transportation executive*
Walton, Jerry W. *trucking executive*

Pine Bluff
Seawell, William Thomas *former airline executive*

CALIFORNIA

Anaheim
Linhart, Eddie Gene *aerospace executive*

Edwards
Brand, Vance Devoe *astronaut*

El Segundo
McCarty, Shirley Carolyn *aerospace executive*
Musk, Elon *aerospace transportation executive*

Fremont
Smith, Bernald Stephen *retired airline pilot, aviation consultant*

Hawthorne
Hunt, Brian L. *program manager*

Hermosa Beach
Kokalj, James Edward *retired aerospace administrator*

Huntington Beach
Burson, Thomas Daniel *retired aerospace company executive*

Inyokern
Bass, Nancy Agnes *airport executive*

Irvine
Crowley, Daniel Francis, Jr., *transportation and logistics executive*
Lorimer, Mark W. *transportation company executive*

La Mesa
Hansen, Grant Lewis *retired aerospace and information systems executive*

La Palma
Knowles, Marie L. *transportation executive*

Long Beach
Myers, John Wescott *aviation executive*

Los Angeles
Bruce, William A. *airport executive*
Gasich, Welko Elton *retired aerospace executive, management consultant*
Kennard, Lydia H. *airport terminal executive*
Myers, Albert F. *aerospace executive*
Sugar, Ronald D. *aerospace executive*
Waugh, Richard B., Jr., *aircraft company executive, lawyer*
Welborne, John Howard *railway company executive, lawyer*

Malibu
Ensign, Richard Papworth *transportation executive*

Manhattan Beach
Williams, Emma *rail transportation executive*

Marina Del Rey
Gregg, Lucius Perry, Jr., *aerospace executive*

Mojave
Melvill, Michael W. *aircraft company executive, experimental test pilot*
Rutan, Richard Glenn (Dick Rutan) *aircraft company executive, aviator*
Yeager, Jeana *aviator*

Montecito
Coln, William Alexander, III, *retired pilot*

Newbury Park
Lindsey, Joanne M. *flight attendant, poet*

Oakland
Haskell, Arthur Jacob *retired steamship company executive*
Rhein, Timothy J. *retired transportation company executive*
Wade, Bill *airport executive*

Palo Alto
Berry, Robert Emanuel *aerospace company executive*
Moffitt, Donald Eugene *transportation company executive*
O'Brien, Raymond Francis *transportation executive*
Ratnathicam, Chutta *transportation executive*

Palos Verdes Estates
Smith, Stephen Randolph *aerospace executive*

Palos Verdes Peninsula
Rechtin, Eberhardt *retired aerospace executive, retired educator*
Slusser, Robert Wyman *aerospace company executive*

Pasadena
Hemann, Raymond Glenn *research company executive*

Pleasanton
Wu, Jia Hao *transportation executive, researcher, consultant*

Ramona
Hoffman, Wayne Melvin *retired airline official*

Richmond
Shladover, Steven Elliot *transportation research professional*

Riverside
Bielucke, Edward Anthony, III, *transportation executive, writer*

Sacramento
Hall, Terry L. *aerospace executive*
Wolfe, Robert A. *aerospace executive*

San Diego
Bowens, Thella *senior aviation director*
Reading, James Edward *transportation executive*

San Francisco
Anschutz, Philip F. *transportation executive, communications executive*
Brice, Charles Steven *airline executive*
Freitag, Peter Roy *transportation specialist*
Martin, John L. *airport executive*
Royer, Kathleen Rose *pilot*
Smartt, Bill *air courier company executive*
Waller, Stephen *air transportation executive*

San Jose
Stapleton, Beverly Cooper *aerospace company executive*
Tonseth, Ralph G. *airport executive*

San Luis Obispo
Williams, David Alexander *retired chief pilot*

San Mateo
Trabitz, Eugene Leonard *aerospace company executive*

Santa Ana
Bailey, Don Matthew *aerospace and electronics company executive*
Dean, William Evans *aerospace industry executive*

Saratoga
Reagan, Joseph Bernard *retired aerospace executive, management consultant*

Sherman Oaks
Caren, Robert Poston *aerospace company executive*

Solana Beach
Arledge, Charles Stone *former aerospace executive, entrepreneur*

Stockton
Biddle, Donald Ray *aerospace company executive*
DeAngelis, Dan *transportation executive*

Temecula
Steiling, Daniel Paul *retired railroad conductor, writer, geographer, educator*

Torrance
Esmond, Donald V. *transportation executive*
Illingworth, Davis (Dave), Jr., *transportation executive*
Press, James E. *transportation executive*
Yamamoto, Akimasa *transportation executive*

COLORADO

Colorado Springs
Pickett, David Franklin, Jr., *technology company executive*

Denver
Baumgartner, Bruce *airport terminal executive*
Davis, Jerry Ray *retired railroad company executive*
McMorris, Jerry *transportation company executive, sports team executive*
Meurlin, Keith W. *airport manager*

Golden
Lindsay, Nathan James *space systems consultant, retired military officer*

Littleton
Kleinknecht, Kenneth Samuel *retired aerospace company executive, former federal space agency official*

Trinidad
Potter, William Bartlett *business executive*

CONNECTICUT

Fairfield
Murphy, Eugene F. *retired aerospace, communications and electronics executive*

Greenwich
Roitsch, Paul Albert *pilot*

Hartford
David, George Alfred Lawrence *aerospace transportation executive*
Page, Stephen Franklin *aerospace transportation executive*

Newington
Robert, Kenneth J. *aviation administrator*

Stamford
Barker, James Rex *water transportation executive, director*
Tregurtha, Paul Richard *marine transportation company executive*

DISTRICT OF COLUMBIA

Washington
Altschul, Alfred Samuel *airline executive*
Boehler, Gabriel D. *aerospace company executive, educator*
Carlton, Bruce J. *transportation company executive*
Donovan, George Joseph *industry executive, consultant*
Downey, Mortimer Leo, III, *transportation executive*
Hallett, Carol Boyd *air transportation executive*
Hinson, David Russell *airline company executive, federal agency administrator*
Morgan, Ronald E. *retired federal air traffic director*
Potter, John E. *postal service executive*
Tranyham, David Francis *United States Government administrator*
von Kann, Clifton Ferdinand *aviation and space executive, software executive*
Warrington, George D. *rail transportation executive*
Willis, Kevin *airport administrator*

FLORIDA

Boca Raton
Borman, Frank *former astronaut, laser patent company executive*
Garelick, Martin *retired transportation executive*

Daytona Beach
Chabrian, Peggy *air transportation executive*
Miller, Sanford *car rental company executive*

Fort Lauderdale
Donaway, Carl D. *messenger service executive*
Kendall, James Robert *air transportation executive, consultant*
Sherry, William F. *airport executive*

Jacksonville
Aftoora, Patricia Joan *transportation executive*
Anderson, John Quentin *retired rail transportation executive*
Carpenter, Alvin Rauso *transportation executive*
Crowe, Jeffrey C. *transportation executive, federal agency administrator*
Gerkens, Henry H. *trucking executive*
LaRose, Robert C. *trucking executive*
Ward, Michael J. *rail transportation executive*

Miami
Dellapa, Gary J. *aviation consultant*
Fain, Richard David *cruise line executive*
Gittens, Angela *airport executive*
Greer, Raymond B. *transportation executive*
Higginbottom, Samuel Logan *retired aerospace company executive*
Leinbach, Tracy A. *transportation executive*
Romeo, Anthony C. *air transportation services executive*
Swienton, Gregory T. *transportation company executive*
Williams, Eric Joseph *transportation executive*

Montverde
Harris, Martin Harvey *aerospace company executive*

Naples
Myers, Robert Jay *retired aerospace company executive*

Orlando
Davis, H. Alan *retired airline captain, consultant*
Kilbourne, Krystal Hewett *retired rail transportation executive*
Pearlman, Louis Jay *aviation and entertainment company executive*
Van den Berg, Egerton *airport executive*

Palm Beach Gardens
Colussy, Dan Alfred *aviation executive*

Palm Harbor
Morgan, Albert George Leonard *retired airline pilot, writer*

Plantation
Fellows, John *delivery service executive*

Ponte Vedra Beach
Fiorentino, Thomas Martin *transportation executive, lawyer*
Hamilton, William Berry, Jr., *retired shipping company executive*
Spence, Richard Dee *retired rail transportation executive*

Royal Palm Beach
Zucker, Leonard Charles *trucking executive, rabbi*

Saint Cloud
Haines, Jr., Robert L. *air transportation management, consultant*

Sanibel
Hasselman, Richard B. *retired transportation company executive*

Satellite Beach
Loney, Mary Rose *former airport administrator, aviation industry consultant*

Stuart
Logan, Henry Vincent *transportation executive, consultant*

Tallahassee
Thagard, Norman E. *astronaut, physician, engineer, educator*

Tampa
Kelly, Robert Vincent, III, *transportation executive*
Miller, Louis E. *airport terminal executive, accountant*
Zell, Samuel *transportation leasing company executive*

Vero Beach
Ingwersen, Martin Lewis *water transportation executive*

Weeki Wachee
Luffsey, Walter Stith *air transportation executive, consultant*

GEORGIA

Alpharetta
Chatlen, Stanley Lee *logistics executive*
McCullough, Ross A., Jr., *delivery service executive*

Atlanta
Abney, David *delivery service executive*
Beystehner, John J. *transportation executive*
Colman, Robert L. *airline company executive*
Darden, Calvin *delivery service executive*
Decosta, Benjamin *airport executive*
Escarra, Vicki B. *airline company executive*
Eskew, Michael L. *package distribution company executive*
Grinstein, Gerald *transportation executive*
Hill, Allen E. *transportation services executive*
Kelly, James P. *delivery service executive*
McDevitt, John *delivery service executive*
Oppenlander, Robert *retired airline executive*
Palumbo, Michael J. *air transportation executive*
Robb, Curtis *air transportation executive*

Decatur
Rutland, Robert J. *transportation executive*

Duluth
O'Dell, Richard *trucking executive*

Macon
Hails, Robert Emmet *aerospace consultant, business executive, former air force officer*

Newnan
McBroom, Thomas William, Sr., *aviation consultant*

Roswell
Dolan, Dennis Joseph *airline pilot, lawyer*

Savannah
Graham, Patrick Samuel *air transportation executive*

Union City
Jones, Emanuel D. *transportation company executive*

HAWAII

Honolulu
Wilson, Charles Robert *port captain, harbor master*

IDAHO

Boise
Ilett, Frank, Jr., *trucking company executive, educator*

Idaho Falls
Thorsen, James Hugh *retired aviation director, retired airport manager*

ILLINOIS

AMF Ohare
Guyette, James M. *airline executive*

Arlington Heights
Hudson, Ronald Morgan *aviation planner*

Chicago
al-Chalabi, Suhail Abdul-Jabbar *transportation executive*
Apelbaum, Phyllis L. *delivery messenger service executive*
Barriger, John Walker, IV, *transportation executive*
Bell, James A. *aerospace transportation executive*
Burkhardt, Edward Arnold *railway executive*
De Leon, Rudy *aerospace transportation executive*
Dutta, Rono J. *air transportation executive*
Fischbach, Charles Peter *railway executive, consultant, lawyer, arbitrator, mediator*
Gibson, Roger *air transportation executive*
Heineman, Ben Walter *corporation executive*
Hullin, Tod Robert *aerospace transportation executive*
Koelliner, Laurette T. *aerospace transportation executive*
Nord, Henry J. *transportation executive*
Reed, John Shedd *former railway executive*
Sookik, Bonnie W. *air transportation executive*
Springer, Denis E. *former railroad executive*
Stonecipher, Harry Curtis *aerospace transportation executive*
Studdert, Andrew Paul *air transportation executive*
Tilton, Glenn F. *air transportation executive*

Deerfield
Karlin, Jerome B. *retail company executive*

Elk Grove Village
Brace, Frederic (Jake) F. *air transportation executive*
Hacker, Douglas A. *air transportation executive*

Hanover Park
Manton, William Jeffrey *operating engineer, fleet consultant*

Lake Barrington
Worrell, Sharyn Dianne *retired flight attendant*

Lansing
Ansary, Hanson Jaber *transportation and telecommunications executive*

Marion
Crane, Hugh Wingate *railroad executive*

Mount Vernon
Nicholson, Gerald Lee *airport administrator*

Naperville
Gannon, Jeffrey P. *trucking/relocation services executive*
Lake, Robert D. *transportation executive*

Oak Brook
Duerinck, Louis T. *retired railroad executive, attorney*
Veno, Ronald James, Jr., *travel industry executive*

Park Ridge
Carr, Gilbert Randle *retired railroad executive*

Warrenville
Ustian, Daniel C. *trucking executive*

Westmont
Kelley, Brian P. *transportation executive*
Rogers, James W. *trucking executive*

Wood Dale
Goodwin, James E. *retired air transportation executive*

INDIANA

Evansville
Shaffer, Michael L. *transportation company executive*

Griffith
Luetschwager, Mary Susan *transportation company professional*

Indianapolis
Mikelsons, J. George *air aerospace transportation executive*
Roberts, David *airport executive*
Wensits, David L. *aerospace executive*

Jeffersonville
Hagan, Michael Charles *transporation executive*

Princeton
Okamoto, Seizo *transportation executive*

IOWA

Des Moines
Kandris, Michael *trucking executive*

Fort Dodge
Smith, William G. *transportation executive*

Ottumwa
Downing, Darrell W. *aviation educator*

KANSAS

Overland Park
Zollars, William D. *freight company executive*

Shawnee Mission
Smith, Michael L. *transportation company executive*

Wichita
Bell, Baillis F. *airport terminal executive*
Rosendale, George William *aircraft company executive*

KENTUCKY

Franklin
Clark, James Benton *railroad industry consultant, former executive*

Louisville
Carranza, Jovita *delivery service executive*
Christopher, Ray Louis *pilot, journalist, author*
DeLong, James Clifford *air transportation executive*
Hayes, William Meredith *pilot, retired career officer*
Johnson, Charlie W. *transportation executive*

LOUISIANA

Kenner
Williams, Roy *airport terminal executive*

New Orleans
Amoss, W. James, Jr., *shipping company executive*
Cazayoux, Charles *airport executive*
Johnson, Peter Forbes *transportation executive, business owner*
Rathke, Dale Lawrence *retired aerospace executive, management consultant*

MAINE

Bangor
Hupp, Rebecca *airport terminal executive*

Nobleboro
Fisher, Allan Campbell *retired railway executive*

Rockland
Ziegelaar, Bob W. *transportation executive*

MARYLAND

Baltimore
Mathison, Theodore E. *retired air transportation executive*
Steele, George Peabody *retired marine transportation executive*

Bethesda
Coffman, Vance D. *aerospace company executive*
Coleman, Joseph Michael *truck lease and logistics consultant*

Hancock, Dain M. *aerospace transportation executive*
Kubasik, Christopher E. *aerospace transportation executive*
Marsh, G. Thomas *aerospace transportation executive*
O'Neill, Malcolm R. *aerospace executive*
Rymarcsuk, Jim Arthur *aerospace industry executive, consultant*
Smith, Albert E. *areonautics company professional*
Tellep, Daniel Michael *aerospace executive, mechanical engineer*
Tourino, Ralph Gene *aerospace transportation executive*

Chevy Chase
Farrell, Joseph Michael *steamship company executive*

Columbia
Gottfeld, Gunther Max *retired urban mass transit official, consultant*

Gibson Island
Forster, William Hull *aerospace executive, management consultant*

Preston
Suggs, Leo H. *transportation executive*

Rockville
Fthenakis, Emanuel John *diversified aerospace company executive*

MASSACHUSETTS

Boston
Doherty, Robert Francis, Jr., *aerospace and defense industry professional*
Klotz, Charles Rodger *shipping company and investment company executive*
Tocco, Stephen *former airport administrator*

Brookline
Frankel, Ernst Gabriel *shipping and aviation business executive, educator*

Cambridge
John, Richard Rodda *transportation executive*
Widnall, Sheila Evans *aeronautical educator, former secretary of the airforce, former university official*

Chatham
Bohman, Raynard Frederick, Jr., *transportation consultant, professional association administrator*

Concord
Smith, Eric Parkman *retired railroad executive*

Cotuit
Ballou, Kenneth Walter *retired business executive, university dean*

East Boston
Coy, Craig P. *airport terminal executive*

Lexington
Burnham, Daniel Patrick *aerospace transportation executive*

Marlborough
Birstein, Seymour Joseph *aerospace company executive*

North Billerica
Mellon, Timothy *transportation executive*

Stow
Shrader, William Whitney *radar consulting scientist*

Waltham
Neumann, Ed *human resource executive*

Woods Hole
Raskin, Fred Charles *transportation and utility holding company executive*

MICHIGAN

Ann Arbor
Bagian, James Philip *former astronaut, public health service officer, medical educator*
Drake, John Warren *aviation consultant*
Yamashina, Tadashi (George) *transportation executive*

Detroit
Feldhouse, Lynn *automotive company executive*
Newman, Andrea Fischer *air transportation executive*
Robinson, Lester W. *airport executive*

Grand Rapids
Auwers, Stanley John *motor carrier executive*

Waterford
Randall, Karl W. *aviation executive, lawyer*

MINNESOTA

Eagan
Felix, Cheryl A. *air transportation executive*
Han, Bernard L. *air transportation executive*
Steenland, Douglas *air transportation executive*

Eden Prairie
Lindbloom, Chad M. *transportation executive*
Radunz, Paul A. *transportation executive*
Wiehoff, John P. *trucking executive*

Minneapolis
Anderson, Tim *airport terminal executive*
Hamiel, Jeff *airport executive*
Harper, Donald Victor *retired transportation and logistics educator*
Nyrop, Donald William *airline executive*

Olson, James Richard *retired transportation executive*
Oppegaard, Grant E. *water transportation executive*

North Oaks
Engle, Donald Edward *retired railway executive, lawyer*

Saint Paul
Anderson, Richard H. *air transportation executive*

Warba
Currie, Earl James *transportation executive*

MISSISSIPPI

Jackson
Liles, William Jackson, III, *trucking company executive*

Pascagoula
Dur, Philip Alphonse *defense aerospace executive, retired naval officer*

Pass Christian
Clark, John Walter, Jr., *shipping company executive*

MISSOURI

Fenton
Baer, Robert J. *transportation company executive*
Ellington, Donald E. *transportation company executive*
McClure, Richard P. *transportation executive*
Stadler, Gerald P. *transportation executive*

Kansas City
Baisden, Eleanor Marguerite *retired airline compensation executive, consultant*
Monello, Joseph D. *financial asset management company executive*
Widmar, Russell C. *airport executive*

Lambert Airport
Griggs, Leonard LeRoy, Jr., *airport executive*

Saint Louis
Albaugh, James F. *aerospace transportation executive*
Ross, Donald *transportation executive*

Springfield
Moss, Elizabeth Lucille (Betty Moss) *retired transportation executive*

Tecumseh
Davis, Michael Chase *retired aerospace industry executive, retired military officer*

NEBRASKA

Omaha
Bowen, Brent *aviation educator*
Davidson, Richard K. *railroad company executive*
Evans, Ivor J. (Ike) *railroad executive*
Smithey, Donald Leon *airport authority director*
Young, James R. *railroad transportation executive*

NEVADA

Lake Tahoe
Sprague, Billy Michael *aerospace transportation executive*

Las Vegas
Walker, Randall H. *air transportation executive*

Reno
Klinefelter, Gary V. *transportation executive, insurance company executive*
Shoen, Edward Joseph *transportation and insurance companies executive*
White, Robert C. *air transportation executive*

Yerington
Burrowes, Robert Arthur *transportation consultant, travel-tour operator*

NEW HAMPSHIRE

Dover
Nelson, Michael Underhill *association executive*

Hancock
Baddour, Anne Bridge *pilot*

Keene
Perkins, Richard P. *pilot*

NEW JERSEY

Delanco
Muhlschlegel, Harry J. *transportation company executive*

Egg Harbor Township
Raftner, Thomas *airport terminal executive*

Elizabeth
Karlberg, John *transportation company executive*

Flemington
Kettler, Carl Frederick *airline executive*

Lebanon
Pollazzi, Roger G. *transportation executive*

Martinsville
Weiss, Allan Joseph *transport company executive, lawyer*

Wilcutt, Terence W. *astronaut*
Williams, David R. *astronaut*
Williams, Jeffrey N. *astronaut*
Williams, Sunita L. *astronaut*
Young, John Watts *astronaut*
Zamka, George D. *astronaut*

Irving
Plaskett, Thomas George *transportation company executive, corporate director*

Lindale
Carter, Thomas Smith, Jr., *retired rail transportation executive*

Roanoke
Steward, Jerry Wayne *air transportation executive, consultant*

San Antonio
Gonzalez, Efren *former airport executive*
Kutchins, Michael Joseph *aviation consultant, former airport executive*
Rush, W. Marvin *trucking executive*

UTAH

Bountiful
Clement, Walter Hough *retired railroad executive*

Dugway
Eshom-Smith, Corina May *air transportation executive*

North Salt Lake
Bouley, Joseph Richard *pilot*

Orem
Snow, Marlon O. *trucking executive, state agency administrator*

Saint George
Atkin, Jerry C. *air transportation executive*

Salt Lake City
England, Daniel Eugene *trucking executive*

VERMONT

Middlebury
Bergesen, Robert Nelson *transportation consultant*

Rutland
Boyle, Francis Joseph *transportation and energy company executive*

South Burlington
Hamilton, John J., Jr., *airport executive*

VIRGINIA

Alexandria
Coyne, James Kitchenman, III, *association executive, congressman, aviator*
Matthews, Sir Stuart *aviation industry executive*

Arlington
Ashby, N. Bruce *air transportation executive*
Baldanza, B. Ben *air transportation executive*
Beier, Anita P. *air transportation executive*
Chiames, Christopher L. *air transportation executive*
Cragin, Maureen Patricia *aerospace transportation executive, former federal agency administrator*
Crellin, Alan W. *air transportation executive*
Davis, David M. *air transportation executive*
Gangwal, Rakesh *airline executive*
Gault, Jeffrey Wayne *air transportation executive*
Glass, Jerrold A. *air transportation executive*
Harrington, George Fred *aviation consultant*
Lakefield, Bruce R. *air transportation executive*
Langstaff, David Hamilton *aerospace industry executive*
Mainwaring, Thomas Lloyd *management consultant, former motor freight company executive*
Prestifilippo, John *air transportation executive*
Serck-Hanssen, Eilif *air transportation executive*
Stokes, B. R. *retired transportation consultant*
Sweeney, Randall W. *aerospace transportation executive*
Wolf, Stephen M. *airline executive*

Catlett
Broderick, Anthony James *air transportation executive*

Chesterfield
Congdon, John Rhodes *transportation executive*

Dulles
Skeen, Kerry B. *airline executive*

Fairfax
Harrison, Robert Allen *retired aerospace executive*

Fairfax Station
Starry, Donn Albert *former aerospace company executive, former army officer*

Falls Church
Mancuso, Michael John *ship and submarine company executive*
Tether, Anthony John *aerospace executive*

Gainesville
Levell, Edward, Jr., *retired aiport executive*

Hampton
Daniels, Cindy Lou *space agency executive*

Herndon
O'Neill, James R. *aerospace transportation executive*
Rump, Kendall E. *air transportation executive*

Mc Lean
Checchi, Alfred A. *air transportation executive, financial consultant*

Newport News
Schievelbein, Thomas Clayton *shipyard executive, sales executive*
Smith, James Robert *airport terminal executive*

Norfolk
Cox, David A. *rail transportation executive*
Goode, David Ronald *transportation company executive*
McKinnon, Arnold Borden *retired transportation company executive*
Scott, Kenneth R. *transportation executive*
Tobias, Stephen C. *rail transportation executive*

Poquoson
Holloway, Paul Fayette *retired aerospace executive*

Reston
Crawford, Lawrence Robert *aviation and aerospace consultant*
Harris, Paul Lynwood *retired aerospace transportation executive*
Kreyling, Edward George, Jr., *railroad executive*

Richmond
Hanley, Patrick D. *trucking executive*
Kaczka, Jeff *trucking/relocation services executive*
Watkins, Hays Thomas *retired railroad executive*

Sterling
Thompson, David Walker *astronautics company executive*

Vienna
Beyer, Barbara Lynn *aviation consultant*
Rogers, Raymond Jesse *retired federal railroad associate administrator*

Williamsburg
Barausky, Kenneth P. *aerospace company executive*
Spitzer, Cary Redford *avionics consultant, electrical engineer*

WASHINGTON

Kent
Bangsund, Edward Lee *former aerospace company executive, consultant*

Kirkland
Clarkson, Lawrence William *air transportation executive*

Seattle
Ayer, William S. *air transportation executive*
Cella, John J. *freight company executive*
Cline, Robert Stanley *retired air freight company executive*
Kelley, John F. *retired airline executive*
Knox, Venerria L. *transportation executive*
Lindsey, Gina Marie *airport executive*
Rose, Peter J. *delivery service executive*
Schmidt, Peter Gustav *shipbuilding industry executive*
Smith, F. D. (Ricky Smith) *rail transporation executive*
Tilden, Bradley D. *air transportation executive*
Warner, John D. *aerospace company executive*

Spanaway
Loete, Steven Donald *pilot*

Vancouver
Robertson, Joel Thomas *railroad executive*

Vashon
Mantle, Peter John *aerospace executive, consultant*

WEST VIRGINIA

Huntington
Salyers, Larry G. *airport terminal executive*

WISCONSIN

Appleton
Petinga, Charles Michael *transportation executive*

Green Bay
Gannon, Thomas A. *trucking executive*
Lofgren, Christopher B. *trucking executive*

Milwaukee
Bateman, C. Barry *airport terminal executive*

WYOMING

Worland
Woods, Lawrence Milton *airline company executive*

TERRITORIES OF THE UNITED STATES

VIRGIN ISLANDS

St Thomas
Finch, Gordon A. *airport terminal executive*

CANADA

ALBERTA

Calgary
McCaig, Jeffrey James *transportation company executive*

Edmonton
Marcotte, Brian *transportation executive*

NOVA SCOTIA

Halifax
Oldfield, Karen *transportation executive*
Renouf, Harold Augustus *retired transportation executive*

ONTARIO

Brampton
Savoie, Leonard Norman *transportation company executive*

Ottawa
Coleman, John Morley *transportation engineering executive*

QUEBEC

Montreal
Tellier, Paul M. *railroad transportation executive*

Saint-Anne-Des-Lacs
Rochette, Louis *retired shipowner and shipbuilder*

Saint-Sauveur
Hanigan, Lawrence *retired railway executive*

AUSTRALIA

Springfield
Spalvins, Janis Gunars *steamship company executive*

DENMARK

Thisted
Nordqvist, Erik Askbo *shipping company executive*

ENGLAND

Harmondsworth
Marshall, Lord Colin (Lord Marshall of Knightsbridge) *airline executive*

London
Kallakis, Achilleas Michalis S. *shipping and real estate company executive*

SWITZERLAND

Geneva
Aaronson, Robert Jay *aviation executive*

ADDRESS UNPUBLISHED

Aldrin, Buzz *former astronaut, science consultant*
Allen, Charlie Lee *air transportation executive*
Ames, Donald Paul *retired aerospace company executive, researcher*
Barber, Theodore Francis *aircraft mechanics professional*
Barnhart, Larry Leroy *transportation executive*
Bergrun, Norman Riley *aerospace executive*
Blanchard, David Lawrence *aerospace executive, real estate developer, management consultant*
Bodden, Jane Ellen *retired airline reservations manager*
Brazier, Don Roland *retired railroad executive*
Brown, Donald Douglas *transportation company executive, retired air force officer, consultant*
Brown, Robert E. *transportation executive*
Brunson, Burlie Allen *aerospace transportation executive*
Burton, Raymond Charles, Jr., *retired transportation company executive*
Caine, Franklyn A. *aerospace transportation executive*
Carty, Donald J. *former airline company executive*
Collins, Eileen Marie *astronaut*
Compton, William F. *retired air transportation executive*
Condit, Philip Murray *former aerospace executive, engineer*
Cook, Stephen Champlin *shipping company executive*
Cooper, John Byrne, Jr., *airline pilot*
Crowder, Richard Morgan *pilot*
Culbertson, Philip Edgar, Sr., *aerospace company executive, consultant*
Dansby, Ronnie *transportation executive*
Delaney, Robert Vernon *logistics and transportation executive*
Dely, Steven *aerospace company executive*
Dewar, James McEwen *marketing, aerospace and defense executive, developing nations consultant*
Diaz, Alphonso Vincent *aerospace executive*
Donovan, Kathleen A. *water transportation executive, county official*
Ferreira, Jo Ann Jeanette Chanoux *time-definite transportation industry executive*
Ferrell, David Stanley *aerospace company executive*
Fish, Howard Math *aerospace transportation executive*
Gitner, Gerald L. *air transportation executive, investment banker*
Glennon, Harrison Randolph, Jr., *retired shipping company executive*
Goldstein, Bernard *transportation and casino gaming company executive*
Graebner, James Herbert *transportation executive*
Guinasso, Victor *delivery service executive*
Harp, Solomon, III, *former airport executive*
Hawkins, Willis Moore *aerospace and astronautical consultant*

Hedrick, Larry Willis *retired airport executive*
Heitz, Edward Fred *freight traffic consultant*
Johnson, Gregory Carl *pilot, astronaut, career officer*
Johnson, Robert *airport terminal executive*
Keenan, Anthony Lee *trucking company executive*
King, Edward William *retired transportation executive*
Koch, John Howard *retired air transportation executive, transportation engineer, consultant*
Kresa, Kent *retired aerospace executive*
Lesko, Harry Joseph *transportation company executive*
Lette, Daniel Ivan *pilot*
Lewis, Andrew Lindsay, Jr., (Drew Lewis) *former transportation and natural resources executive*
Lewis, Martin Edward *shipping company executive, foreign government concessionary*
Lorenzo, Francisco A. *airline companies executive*
Marshall, Charles Noble *rail transportation executive*
Masiello, Rocco Joseph *airlines and aerospace manufacturing executive*
Mast, Stewart Dale *retired airport manager*
Matthews, L. White, III, *railroad executive*
McCarthy, Paul Fenton *aerospace executive, former naval officer*
Miller, Paul David *aerospace executive*
Mitchell, Pamela Ann *airline pilot*
Mullin, Leo Francis *airline executive*
Musgrave, Story *astronaut, surgeon, pilot, physiologist, educator*
Parker, James Francis *former air transportation executive, lawyer*
Platt, Lewis Emmett *aerospace transportation executive*
Quade, Marshall Ross *transportation planner*
Quesnel, Gregory L. *transportation company executive*
Regalado, Raul L. *airport executive*
Renda, Dominic Phillip *airline executive*
Rivkind, Perry Abbot *federal railroad agency administrator*
Roberts, Linda *truck transportation services company executive*
Rose, James Turner *aerospace consultant*
Ruegg, Donald George *retired railway company executive*
Saleh, Brian Behrooz *aerospace executive*
Saubert, Walter E. (Wally Saubert) *trucking and transportation company executive*
Savitz, Maxine Lazarus *aerospace company executive*
Schaefer, C. Barry *railroad executive, lawyer, investment banker*
Sears, Michael M. *former aerospace transportation executive*
Seymour, Joseph John *air transportation executive*
Shockley, Edward Julian *retired aerospace company executive*
Smith, Russell Francis *transportation executive*
Snowden, Lawrence Fontaine *retired aircraft company executive, retired marine corps general officer*
Stevens, Robert J. *aerospace transportation executive*
Stromquist, Kenneth James, Jr., *pilot, retired military officer*
Swinburn, Charles *rail transportation executive*
Tague, John P *air transportation executive*
van Hoften, James Dougal Adrianus *business executive, former astronaut*
Vecci, Raymond Joseph *airline industry consultant*
Voss, Omer Gerald *truck company executive*
Wallace, F. Blake *aerospace executive, mechanical engineer*
Warner, Emily Hanrahan Howell *retired pilot, writer*
Washburn, Donald Arthur *transportation executive, investor*
Yeager, Phillip Charles *transportation company exeuctive*

INDUSTRY: UTILITIES, ENERGY, RESOURCES

UNITED STATES

ALABAMA

Birmingham
Drummond, Garry N. *mining company executive*
Franklin, H. Allen *electric company executive*
Harris, Elmer Beseler *electric utility executive*
Warren, William Michael, Jr., *utilities company executive*

Foley
St. John, Henry Sewell, Jr., *utility company executive*

Shoal Creek
Ahearn, John Francis, Jr., *retired oil and gas company executive*

ALASKA

Anchorage
Duncan, Ronald A. *telecommunications company executive*

Fairbanks
Beistline, Earl Hoover *mining consultant*

ARIZONA

Phoenix
Snider, Timothy R. *mining executive*
Wolfe, William Downing *nuclear energy industry executive*

Prescott
Bennett, Kenneth R. *oil company executive, state legislator*

Scottsdale
Baker, Jeffrey Charles *telecommunications executive*
Birkelbach, Albert Ottmar *retired oil company executive*
Holliger, Fred Lee *oil company executive*

Sedona
Dansby, John Walter *retired oil company executive*

Show Low
Pershing, Robert George *telecommunications company executive*

Sun City
Black, Robert Frederick *former oil company executive*

Tempe
Hickson, Robin Julian *mining company executive*

Tucson
Heller, Frederick *retired mining company executive*
Jamison, Harrison Clyde *retired oil company executive*
Kissinger, Karen G. *energy executive*
Peeler, Stuart Thorne *petroleum industry executive and independent oil operator*
Peters, Charles William *research and development company manager*

ARKANSAS

El Dorado
Deming, Claiborne P. *oil industry executive*
McNutt, Jack Wray *oil company executive*
Nolan, William C., Jr., *energy executive*
Watkins, Jerry West *retired oil company executive, lawyer*

Fayetteville
Scharlau, Charles Edward, III, *natural gas company executive*

Little Rock
Bemis, Michael B. *utility company executive*
Ford, Joe Thomas *telephone company executive, former state senator*
Ford, Scott T. *telecommunications company executive*
Frantz, Francis X. *telecommunications industry executive, lawyer*
Gardner, Kathleen D. *gas company executive, lawyer*
Orsini, Tom *retired telecommunications company executive*

CALIFORNIA

Anaheim
Fenton, Donald Mason *retired oil company executive*
Stegemeier, Richard Joseph *oil company executive*

Camarillo
MacAlister, Robert Stuart *oil industry executive, consultant*

Carmel
Hamilton, Lyman Critchfield, Jr., *telecommunications industry executive*

El Segundo
Dallas, Terry G. *gas industry executive*
Imle, John F., Jr., *oil company executive*
Williamson, Charles R. *energy company executive*

Elk Grove
Romano, Sheila June *telecommunications industry executive, artist, writer*

Folsom
Regan, William Joseph, Jr., *energy company executive*

Goleta
Specht, Gordon Dean *retired petroleum executive*

Hillsborough
Quigley, Philip J. *retired telecommunications industry executive*

Huntington Beach
Schaffner-Irvin, Kristen *oil executive*

Irvine
McDaniel, Thomas R. *utilities executive*
Shirilau, Mark Steven *utilities executive*

La Jolla
Rinaker, Samuel Mayo, Jr., *retired utilities executive*

La Mesa
Trujillo, Solomon D. *telecommunications executive*

La Palma
Thelander, Beverly *oil company executive*

Los Angeles
Chazen, Stephen I. *oil company executive*
Davis, Marvin *petroleum company executive, entrepreneur*
Foley, John V. *water company executive*
Glickman, David *telecommunications industry executive*
Laurance, Dale R. *oil company executive*
Mandles, Martinn H. *facility services company executive*
Van Horne, R. Richard *oil company executive*

Manteca
Talmage, Kenneth Kellogg *business executive*

Martinez
Meyer, Jarold Alan *oil company research executive*

Mill Valley
Premo, Paul Mark *oil company executive*

Monterey Park
Montag, David Moses *telecommunications industry executive*

Newport Coast
Swan, Peer Alden *public utility executive*

Oakland
Morris, Ronald Lew *oil and gas company executive*

Pacific Palisades
Klein, Joseph Mark *retired mining company executive*
Middleton, James Arthur *oil and gas company executive*
Mulryan, Henry Trist *mineral company executive, consultant*

Palo Alto
Glauthier, T. J. *non-profit executive*

Palos Verdes Peninsula
Christie, Hans Frederick *retired utility company subsidiaries executive, consultant*
Greenberg, Kate *telecommunications industry executive*

Pasadena
White Thomson, Ian leonard *retired mining executive*

Petaluma
Frederickson, Arman Frederick *minerals and petroleum company executive*

Redwood City
Woods, Jacqueline F. *telecommunications industry executive*

Riverside
Pratt, John Jackson *property manager, retired telephone installer*

Rosemead
Bryson, John E. *utilities company executive*
Craver, Theodore F., Sr., *utilites/energy executive*
Featherstone, Diane L. *utilities executive*
Fohrer, Alan J. *utilities company executive*
Foster, Robert G. *utilities executive*
Moody, Wesley C. *utilities executive*
Noonan, Thomas M. *utilities executive*
Parsky, Barbara *utilities executive*
Rosenblum, Richard Mark *utilities executive*
Ryder, Beverly *utilities executive*
Smith, Anthony L. *utilities executive*
Yazdi, Mahvash *utilities executive*

Sacramento
Wickland, J. Al, Jr., *petroleum product executive, real estate executive*

San Diego
Baum, Stephen L. *utilities company executive*
Roper, William Alford, Jr., *diversified technology services company executive*
Sulpizio, Richard *communications company executive*

San Francisco
Bonney, John Dennis *retired oil company executive*
Caccamo, Aldo M. *oil industry executive*
Darbee, Peter A. *electric power company executive*
Flittie, Clifford Gilliland *retired petroleum company executive*
Glynn, Robert D., Jr., *electric power and gas industry executive*
Klitten, Martin R. *oil industry executive*
Maddox, Lyndell E. *utilities company executive*
Matzke, Richard H. *oil industry executive*
Paul, Donald Lee *oil company executive, geophysicist*
Sullivan, James N. *retired oil industry executive*
Williams, Neville *international solar energy corporation executive*
Zaccaria, Adrian *utilities executive*

San Jose
Bodensteiner, Lisa M. *utilities executive, lawyer*
Chandler, Mark *telecommunications industry executive*
Curtis, Ann B. *utilities executive*
Macias, E. James *utilities executive*
Malis, Andrew Gary *telecommunications company executive*
Mason, Thomas R. *utilities executive*
Quon, Malcolm Yee *defence systems company executive*

San Mateo
Ginn, Sam L. *telephone company executive*

San Rafael
Latno, Arthur Clement, Jr., *telephone company executive*

San Ramon
Bethancourt, John E. *oil industry executive*
Derr, Kenneth T. *retired oil company executive*
Gass, John D. *oil industry executive*
Kirkland, George L. *oil industry executive*
Krattebol, David M. *oil industry executive*
Laidlaw, William Samuel Hugh *oil company executive*
McDonald, John W. *oil industry executive*
O'Reilly, David J. *oil company executive*
Robertson, Peter James *oil company executive*
Watson, John S. *oil company executive*
Wilcox, Raymond I. *oil industry executive*
Woertz, Patricia A. *petroleum industry executive*
Yarrington, Patricia *oil industry executive*
Zygocki, Rhonda I. *oil industry executive*

Santa Barbara
Casey, Mary A. *telecommunications company executive*
Enos, Kelly D. *telecommunications company financial executive*
Mc Duffie, Malcolm *oil company executive*

Santa Clara
Koomen, Cornelis Jan *telecommunications and electronics executive*

Santa Rosa
Hinch, Stephen Walter *telecommunications industry executive*

South Pasadena
Finnell, Michael Hartman *corporate executive*

Stanford
Brinegar, Claude Stout *retired oil company executive*

Templeton
Gandsey, Louis John *petroleum and environmental consultant*

Van Nuys
Farman, Richard Donald *energy company executive*

COLORADO

Boulder
Hill, Melvin James *retired oil company executive*

Broomfield
Patel, Sunit *telecommunications industry executive*

Centennial
Haley, John David *petroleum consulting company executive*

Colorado Springs
King, Peter Joseph, Jr., *retired gas company executive*

Denver
Anderson, Donald H. *gas industry executive*
Danos, Robert McClure *retired oil company executive*
Dyer, Edward James "Jim" *public utilities commissioner*
Hall, Larry Dean *business executive, lawyer*
Hansen, Bruce D. *mining executive*
Johnston, Van Robert *management educator*
Kruger, Paula *telecommunications industry executive*
Krysiak, William J. *gas industry executive*
Lassonde, Peirre *mining executive*
Macey, William Blackmore *oil company executive*
Murdy, Wayne William *mining company executive, financial officer*
Norman, John Edward *petroleum landman*
Notebaert, Richard C. *telecommunications industry executive*
Outlaw, Lanny F. *gas company executive*
Owens, Marvin Franklin, Jr., *oil company executive*
Ramji, Al-Noor *telecommunications industry executive*
Roellig, Mark D. *telecommunications industry executive, lawyer*
Spies, Allan *telecommunications executive*
Thompson, Lohren Matthew *oil company executive*
Trueblood, Harry Albert, Jr., *oil company executive*
Wilks, Lewis O. *telecommunications company executive*

Englewood
Malone, John C. *telecommunications executive*
Somers, Daniel E. *telecommunications industry executive*

Evergreen
McEldowney, Roland Conant *mining executive, photographer*

Golden
Matthews, Thomas Michael *former energy company executive*

Littleton
Fryt, Monte Stanislaus *petroleum company executive, speaker, advisor*
VanderLinden, Camilla Denice Dunn *telecommunications industry executive*

Loveland
Bierbaum, J. Armin *petroleum company executive, consultant*

CONNECTICUT

Berlin
Grise, Cheryl *electric power industry executive*
Shivery, Charles W. *utilities executive*

Darien
Smith, Elwin Earl *mining and oil company executive*

Fairfield
Campbell, James P. *utilities executive*
Conaty, William J. *electric power industry executive*
Woodburn, William A. *utilities executive*

Greenwich
Alonzo, Martin Vincent *mining and aluminum company executive, investor, financial consultant*
DeCrane, Alfred Charles, Jr., *petroleum company executive*
Kinnear, James Wesley, III, *retired petroleum company executive*
Nelson, Don Harris *gas and oil industry executive*
Schmidt, Herman J. *former oil company executive*
Tell, William Kirn, Jr., *retired oil company executive, lawyer*

Guilford
Morgan, Leon Alford *retired utility executive*

Hartford
Butler, Gregory B. *utilities executive*
Dixon, Robert F. *telecommunications executive*

Madison
Evans, Evan *petroleum executive*
Kay, Herbert *retired natural resources company executive*

New Britain
Opie, John D. *retired electric power industry executive*

New Canaan
McIvor, Donald Kenneth *retired petroleum company executive*

New Haven
Miglio, Daniel Joseph *retired telecommunications company executive*

Norwalk
Kabala, Stanley J. *telecommunications company executive*

Old Greenwich
Allen, Jefferson F. *oil company executive*
Hittle, Richard Howard *corporate executive, international affairs consultant*

Southport
Damson, Barrie Morton *oil and gas exploration company executive*

Stamford
Bijur, Peter I. *retired petroleum company executive*
Jacobson, Ishler *retired utility executive*
Mc Kinley, John Key *retired oil company executive*
Neal, A. Michael *utilities executive*
Nissen, David R. *utilities executive*

Westport
Nedom, H. Arthur *petroleum consultant*

DELAWARE

Newark
Connelly, Donald Preston *retired electric and gas utility company executive*

Wilmington
Cosgrove, Howard Edward, Jr., *utilities executive*
Graham, Barbara S. *electric power industry executive*

DISTRICT OF COLUMBIA

Washington
Boergers, David Paul *energy executive*
Bradshaw, Richard Eugene *government relations, energy and environment consultant*
Buchan, Douglas Charles *petroleum company executive, government official*
Davidson, Peter *telecommunications industry executive*
DeGraffenreidt, James H., Jr., *gas company executive*
Deland, Michael Reeves *energy executive*
Derrick, John Martin, Jr., *electric company executive*
Dominy, Charles E. (Chuck Dominy) *oil industry executive*
Felder, Richard Bruce *pipeline safety administrator*
Friedman, Gregory H. *energy administrator*
Hedlund, Charles John *oil company executive, conservationist*
Johns, Marie C. *telecommunications industry executive*
King, Gwendolyn S. *retired utility company executive, former federal official*
Kripowicz, Robert S. *energy administrator*
Largent, Steven Michael *telecommunications industry executive, former congressman, former professional football player*
McCollam, William, Jr., *utility company executive*
McGee, Robert Merrill *oil company executive*
Miller, Susan M. *telecommunications industry executive*
Modiano, Albert Louis *gas, oil industry executive*
Naughton, Lorraine Riffle *oil industry administrator*
Nelson, Larry Dean *telecommunications and computer systems company executive, consultant*
Paige, Hilliard Wegner *corporate director, consultant*
Rouse, James J. *oil industry executive*
Sterling, Christopher H. *telecommunications educator*
Thompson, William Reid *public utility executive, lawyer*
Wheeler, Thomas Edgar *former telecommunications executive*
Williams, Andrew W. *energy executive*
Wraase, Dennis Richard *utilities company executive, accountant*

FLORIDA

Belleair Beach
Ayers, Richard Wayne *electric power industry executive, writer, journalist*

Boca Raton
Gralla, Eugene *natural gas company executive*

Bradenton
Watkins, William, Jr., *electric power industry executive*

Deerfield Beach
Laser, Charles, Jr., *oil company executive*

Eustis
Welch, Jerry *oil company executive*

Fort Lauderdale
Sklar, Alexander *electric company executive*

Gainesville
Milbrath, Robert Henry *retired petroleum executive*

Jacksonville
Francis, James Delbert *oil company executive*

Juno Beach
Broadhead, James Lowell *electrical power industry executive*

Dewhurst, Moray P. *energy executive*

Key West
Evans, John Derby *telecommunications company executive*

Largo
Dolan, John E. *consultant, retired utility executive*
Loader, Jay Gordon *retired utility company executive*

Longwood
Cirello, John *utility and engineering company executive*

Marco Island
Meyer, Jon Howard *utility executive, consultant*

Miami
Eisenberg, David H. *telecommunications executive*
Weiser, Ralph Raphael *oil industry executive*

Naples
Johnson, Kenneth Oscar *oil company executive*
Johnson, Zane Quentin *retired petroleum company executive*
Marino, William Francis *telecommunications industry executive, consultant*
Rowe, Jack Field *retired electric utility executive*
Spetrino, Russell John *retired utility company executive, lawyer*

North Palm Beach
Hay, Lewis, III, *utilities company executive*

Palm Beach
Donnell, John Randolph *retired petroleum executive*

Palm Beach Gardens
Harnett, Joseph Durham *oil company executive*
Nielsen, Steven E. *telecommunications company executive*

Palm Coast
Farrell, Joseph Christopher *retired mining executive, services executive*

Ponte Vedra Beach
Green, Norman Kenneth *retired oil industry executive, former naval officer*
Wood, Quentin Eugene *oil company executive*

Saint Petersburg
Fleming, William Sloan *energy executive, computer company executive*
Korpan, Richard *energy executive*

Sarasota
Torrey, Richard Frank *utility executive*

Sun City Center
McGrath, John Francis *retired utilities executive*

Tallahassee
Laughlin, William Eugene *retired electric power industry executive*

Tampa
Leavengood, Victor Price *telephone company executive*

Vero Beach
Bennett, Jack Franklin *oil company executive*
Fitzgeorge, Harold James *former oil and gas company executive*

West Palm Beach
Diasio, Richard Leonard *power transmission executive, sports facility executive, race car manufacturer executive*
Kiely, Dan Ray *telecommunications and banking consultant*
Koch, William I. *energy company executive*

Winter Park
Spake, Ned Bernarr *energy company executive*

GEORGIA

Alpharetta
Heyman, John H. *energy executive*

Atlanta
Ackerman, F. Duane *telecommunication industry executive*
Adams, Rex M. *telecommunications executive*
Adams, Valencia I. *telecommunications industry executive*
Anderson, Richard A. *telecommunications industry executive*
Arroyo, F. Thaddeus *telecommunications industry executive*
Bolch, Carl Edward, Jr., *petroleum company executive, lawyer*
Boniface, Barry *telecommunications industry executive*
Bradley, Rickford D. *telecommunications industry executive*
Burns, M. Michele *energy executive, former air transportation executive*
Burns, Richard *telecommunications industry executive*
Carbonell, Joaquin R., III, *telecommunications industry executive*
Chilton, Horace Thomas *pipeline company executive*
Clift, W.E. *telecommunications industry executive*
Cowan, Keith O. *telecommunications industry executive*
Dahlberg, Alfred William *electric company executive*
Dowling, Kathy *telecommunications industry executive*
Droege, Mark E. *telecommunications industry executive*
Drummond, Jere A. *telecommunications company executive*
Dunn, Rebecca M. *telecommunications industry executive*
Dykes, Ronald Mitchell *telecommunications executive*

Frieson, Ronald E. *telecommunications industry executive*
Frost, Norman Cooper *retired telephone company executive*
Fuller, S(heri) Marce *energy executive*
Funderburg, Jan *telecommunications industry executive*
Greene, Margaret H. *telecommunications industry executive*
Griffin, Clayton Houstoun *retired power company engineer, lecturer*
Hallacy, Don *telecommunications industry executive*
Hamm, Stan(ley) (Charles Hamm) *former telecommunications company executive*
Harris, Isiah, Jr., *telecommunications industry executive*
Hayes, Jimmy W. *telecommunications company executive*
Latham, Deborah L. *energy marketing and services company executive*
Lee, Donna A. *telecommunications industry executive*
Lefar, Marc *telecommunications industry executive*
Lindner, Richard G. *telecommunications industry executive*
Odom, Rod D., Jr., *telecommunications industry executive*
Owen, Steven Keith *utilities executive*
Palmer, Ben M. *gas industry executive*
Pate, William *telecommunications industry executive*
Peon, Roberto *telecommunications industry executive*
Ramsey, Ira Clayton *retired pipeline company executive*
Ratcliffe, David M. *utilities executive*
Reynolds, Edgar L. *telecommunications industry executive*
Riley, J. Michael *energy executive*
Robie, Clarence W. *electric company executive*
Scobey, David W., Jr., *telecommunications industry executive*
Shannon, W. Patrick *telecommunications industry executive*
Sibbernsen, Richard *telecommunications industry executive*
Sigman, Stanley T. *telecommunications industry executive*
Smith, Elmer *telecommunications industry executive*
Wentworth, Lynn A. *telecommunications industry executive*
Westbrook, Larry *electric power industry executive*

Conyers
Kilkelly, Brian Holten *lighting company executive*

Gainesville
Leet, Richard Hale *oil company executive*

High Shoals
Bracewell, Gaynor Lee *hydro electric plant owner, developer*

Lawrenceville
McClure, David H. *utilities company analyst*

Norcross
Sharon, Thomas E. *science company executive*

Roswell
Burgess, John Frank *retired utilities executive*

Savannah
Gilbert, John B. *retired electric and power company official*

Smyrna
Dumbacher, Robert J. *gas company executive*

HAWAII

Honolulu
Clarke, Robert F. *utilities company executive*
Williams, Carl Harwell *utilities executive*

Kaneohe
Amioka, Wallace Shuzo *retired petroleum company executive*

Waikoloa
Calvert, Delbert William *retired energy executive*

IDAHO

Coeur D Alene
Wheeler, Dennis Earl *mining company executive, lawyer*

Idaho Falls
Newman, Stanley Ray *oil industry executive*

ILLINOIS

Argonne
Ban, Stephen Dennis *gas industry executive*
Mattas, Richard Frank *nuclear energy industry executive*

Arlington Heights
Morrow, George Lester *retired oil and gas executive*

Aurora
Fisher, Thomas Lee *gas company executive*

Barrington Hills
Perry, I. Chet *petroleum company executive*

Chicago
Brooker, Thomas Kimball *oil company executive*
Carlson, LeRoy Theodore, Jr., *telecommunications industry executive*
Clark, Frank M. *utilities executive*
Conrad, John R. *retired electric power industry executive*
Dunn, Christopher Joseph *telecommunications industry executive*
Gillis, Ruth Ann M. *electric company executive*

Gratz, Jay M. *steel company executive*
Henry, Brian C. *telephone company executive*
Morrow, Richard Martin *retired oil company executive*
Rogers, Desiree Glapion *utilities executive*
Rowe, John William *utilities executive*
Strobel, Pamela B. *energy executive*
Terry, Richard Edward *public utility holding company executive*

Flossmoor
Pierce, Shelby Crawford *management and oil industry consultant*

Hinsdale
Brandt, John Ashworth *fuel company executive*

Naperville
Birck, Michael John *telecommunications industry executive*
Gracey, Paul C., Jr., *utilities executive*
Hawley, Richard L. *utilities executive*
Prabhu, Krish Anant *telecommunications company executive, educator*

Oak Brook
Barnholt, Brandon K. *gas station/convenience store executive*
Harless, Katherine J. *telecommunications company executive*

Peoria
DuBois, Mark Benjamin *former utilities executive, educator*

Schaumburg
Lynch, Thomas J. *telecommunications industry executive*

Warrenville
Grote, Byron *gas industry executive*

West Frankfort
Williams, Joseph Scott *energy and natural resources company executive, city commissioner*

INDIANA

Columbus
Able, Warren Walter *natural resource company executive, physician*

Frankfort
Stonehill, Lloyd Herschel *gas industry executive, mechanical engineer*

Hammond
Schroer, Edmund Armin *retired utility company executive*

Indianapolis
Krueger, Betty Jane *telecommunications company executive*
Todd, Zane Grey *retired utilities executive*

Lawrenceburg
Dautel, Charles Shreve *retired mining company executive*

Merrillville
Neale, Gary Lee *utilities executive*

Plainfield
Harkness, Maurice Stephen *utility company executive*

IOWA

Des Moines
Abel, Gregory E. *utility company executive*
Sokol, David L. *energy services provider company executive*

KANSAS

Eskridge
Taylor, Russell Benton *mining executive*

Overland Park
Betts, Gene M. *telecommunications industry executive*
Forsee, Gary D. *telecommunications industry executive*
Garcia, John A. *telecommunications industry executive*
Hansen, Jim *telecommunications industry executive*
Lauer, Len J. *telecommunications industry executive*
Prout, William C. *telecommunications industry executive*
Strandjord, M. Jeannine *telecommunications industry executive*
Thomas, David P. *telecommunications industry executive*
Walker, Kathryn A. *telecommunications industry executive*

Pittsburg
Nettels, George Edward, Jr., *retired mining executive*

Shawnee Mission
Pressman, Ronald R. *utilities executive*

Topeka
Spencer, William Edwin *telephone company executive, engineer*
Wittig, David C. *energy executive*

Wichita
Cadman, Wilson Kennedy *retired utility company executive*
Feilmeier, Steve *energy executive*
Moeller, Joseph (Joe) W. *energy executive*
Varner, Sterling Verl *retired oil company executive*

KENTUCKY

Ashland
Luellen, Charles J. *retired oil company executive*
Tepper, Scott M. *mining executive*
Weaver, Carlton Davis *retired oil industry executive*
Yancey, Robert Earl, Jr., *retired oil company executive*

Covington
Brothers, John Alfred *retired oil company executive*

Crescent Springs
Chellgren, Paul Wilbur *industrial company executive*

Lexington
Boyd, James Robert *energy company executive*

Louisville
Hale, Roger W. *utilities company executive*
Ronald, Peter *utilities executive*
Royer, Robert Lewis *retired utility company executive*
Staffieri, Victor A. *energy company executive*
Trotter, Lloyd G. *electric power industry executive*

Paducah
Starkey, Russell Bruce, Jr., *energy executive*

LOUISIANA

Monroe
Ewing, R. Stewart *telecommunications company executive*
Fouts, James Fremont *mining company executive*
Post, Glen Fleming, III, *telecommunications executive*

New Orleans
Adkerson, Richard C. *mining executive*
Bachmann, Richard Arthur *oil company executive*
Hintz, Donald C. *energy executive*
Johnson, Mark J. *mining executive*
Leonard, J. Wayne *energy company executive*
Lind, Thomas Otto *barge transportation company executive*
Luft, Robert *energy executive*
Lupberger, Edwin Adolph *retired utility executive*
Moffett, James Robert *oil and gas company executive*
Murrish, Charles Howard *oil and gas exploration company executive, geologist*
Quirk, Kathleen L. *mining executive*
Sloan, Robert D. *energy executive*

Pineville
Nesbitt, Gregory Leon *utility executive, mechanical engineer*

MAINE

Augusta
Weil, Gordon Lee *energy executive, publishing executive*

Eliot
Tillinghast, John Avery *utilities executive*

Surry
Kilgore, John Edward, Jr., *former petroleum company executive*

Yarmouth
Haynes, Peter Lancaster *retired utility executive*

MARYLAND

Annapolis
Marienthal, George *telecommunications company executive*

Baltimore
Chagnoni, Kathleen *energy executive*
Ihrie, Robert *oil, gas and real estate company executive*
Owsley, Thomas L. *oil industry executive*
Poindexter, Christian Herndon *utility company executive*
Rosenberg, Frank Blaustein *petroleum company executive*
Rosenberg, Henry A., Jr., *petroleum executive*
Wheeler, John Ernest, Jr., *oil company executive*

Bethesda
Ikle, Doris Margret *energy executive*
McMurphy, Michael Allen *energy company executive, lawyer*
Olmsted, Jerauld Lockwood *telephone company executive*

Boyds
Love, Dana Francis Ignatius *telecommunications industry executive*

Glen Arm
Jackson, Theodore Marshall *retired oil company executive*

Hagerstown
Noia, Alan James *utility company executive*
Serkes, Jeffrey D. *energy executive*

Hughesville
Hilwig, Joseph Michael *electric company director*
Tudor, Thomas Rae *electric power industry executive*

Lanham Seabrook
Parker, William H., Jr., *telecommunications industry executive*

Lutherville Timonium
Bevis, Robert E. *retired oil company executive*

Rockville
Griffith, Jerry Dice *energy and management consultant*

PROFESSIONAL INDEX 5785 INDUSTRY: UTILITIES, ENERGY, RESOURCES

Silver Spring
Jacobs, George *broadcast engineering consulting company executive*

MASSACHUSETTS

Boston
Grimes, Calvin M., Jr., *oil industry executive*
Kennedy, Joseph Patrick, II, *utilities executive, former congressman*
May, Thomas J. *electric company executive*
Wright, Russell D. *electrical utility executive*

Centerville
Anderson, Gerald Edwin *utilities executive*
Scherer, Harold Nicholas, Jr., *electric utility company executive, engineer*

Chelsea
Kaneb, Gary R. *oil industry executive*
Kuhne, Alice *oil industry executive*

Danvers
Dolan, John Ralph *retired corporation executive*

Falmouth
McInnes, Donald Gordon *railroad executive*

Harwich Port
Staszesky, Francis Myron *independent energy consultant*

Melrose
Brown, Ronald Osborne *telecommunications and computer systems consultant*

Needham
Cogswell, John Heyland *retired telecommunications industry executive, financial consultant*

Waltham
McManmon, Thomas Arthur, Jr., *oil industry executive*
Messman, Jack L. *oil executive*
Slifka, Alfred A. *oil corporation executive*

Westborough
Bok, Joan Toland *utilities executive*
Young, Roger Austin *natural gas distribution company executive*

Westford
Decker, Michael B. *utilities executive*

MICHIGAN

Dearborn
Boulanger, Rodney Edmund *energy company executive*

Detroit
Beale, Susan M. *electric power industry executive*
Earley, Anthony Francis, Jr., *utilities company executive, lawyer*
Ewing, Stephen E. *natural gas company executive*
Redfield, Jean M. *electric power company executive*

Jackson
Fryling, Victor J. *energy company executive*
McCormick, William Thomas, Jr., *electric and gas company executive*
Webb, Thomas J. *utilities executive*
Whipple, Kenneth *utilities executive*

Saint Clair Shores
Glancy, Alfred Robinson, III, *retired public utility company executive*

Shelby Township
Fillbrook, Thomas George *telephone company executive*

MINNESOTA

Burnsville
O'Brien, Gerald James *utilities executive*

Eden Prairie
Emison, James Wade *petroleum company executive*

Fergus Falls
MacFarlane, John Charles *utility company executive*

Minneapolis
Brunetti, Wayne Henry *utilities executive*
Fowke, Benjamin G.S., III, *energy executive*
McIntyre, Edward J. *power company executive*

Minnetonka
Brown, Stephen S. *telecommunications industry executive*

Saint Paul
Estenson, Noel K. *refining and fertilizer company executive*
Robertson, Jerry Earl *retired manufacturing company executive*

MISSISSIPPI

Clinton
Roberts, Bert C., Jr., *telecommunications company executive*

Jackson
Busby, A. Patrick *gas, oil industry executive*
Kingsley, Oliver Dowling, Jr., *former energy company executive*
Lampton, Leslie B., Sr., *oil industry executive*
Waites, Robert Guinn *utilities executive*

MISSOURI

Clayton
Novelly, Paul Anthony *petrochemical and refining company executive*

Kansas City
Baker, John Russell *utilities executive*
Dobson, Rick *energy executive*
Green, Robert K. *energy executive*
Potter, George William, Jr., *mining executive*
Stamm, Keith G. *energy executive*
Wolf, Dale Joseph *utilities company executive*

Lebanon
Beavers, Roy Lackey *retired utility executive, essayist, activist*

Saint Louis
Alessandro, D. Beatty *electric power industry executive*
Baxter, Warner L. *energy executive*
Clark, Maura J. *oil, gas industry executive*
Kalkware, Kent D. *telecommunications professional*
Monser, Edward L. *electric power industry executive*
Mueller, Charles William *electric utility executive*
Navarre, Richard A. *mining executive*
O'Malley, Thomas D. *petroleum industry executive*
Quenon, Robert Hagerty *retired mining consultant and holding company executive*
Vogel, Carl E. *telecommunications industry executive*

Springfield
Jura, James J. *electric utility executive*

MONTANA

Billings
Nance, Robert Lewis *oil company executive*
Reed, Kenneth G. *petroleum company executive*

Butte
Burke, John James *utilities executive, lawyer*

Missoula
Brumit, Lawrence Edward, III, *oil field service company executive*

NEBRASKA

Hastings
Creigh, Thomas, Jr., *utilities executive*

Omaha
Crouse, Jerry K. *energy company executive*
Grewcock, Bruce E. *mining executive*
Hawks, Howard L. *energy executive*

NEVADA

Henderson
Trimble, Thomas James *retired utility company executive, lawyer*

Las Vegas
Grace, John William *electrical company executive*
Hughes, Nicholas Melvin *mining company executive*
Laub, William Murray *retired utility executive*

Reno
Brennan, Susan Mallick *utilities executive*
Busig, Rick Harold *mining executive*
Gundersen, Wayne Campbell *management consultant, oil and gas consultant*
Higgins, Walter M., III, *electric power industry executive*

Winnemucca
Hesse, Martha O. *gas industry executive*

NEW HAMPSHIRE

Portsmouth
Powers, Henry Martin, Jr., *oil industry executive*

NEW JERSEY

Basking Ridge
Collis, Sidney Robert *retired telephone company executive*
Matthews, Craig Gerard *energy company executive*
Peterson, Donald K. *telecommunications executive*

Bedminster
Dorman, David W. *telecommunications industry executive*
Hannigan, William J. *telecommunications industry executive*
Kean, John *utility company executive*
Strigl, Dennis F. *telecommunications industry executive*

Chatham
Sundberg, Carl-Erik Wilhelm *telecommunications executive, researcher*

East Brunswick
Grundman, Thomas K. *energy executive*

Edison
Citron, Jeffrey A. *telecommunications industry executive*

Florham Park
MacMillan, David Paul *retired oil company executive*

Fort Lee
Schiessler, Robert Walter *retired chemical and oil company executive*

Kirkwood Voorhees
Barr, J. James *company executive*
Wolf, Ellen C. *water company executive*

Maplewood
Joel, Amos Edward, Jr., *telecommunications consultant*

Morristown
Desch, Matthew J. *telecommunications industry executive*
Hafer, Frederick Douglass *utilities executive*

Murray Hill
Brewington, James *telecommunications industry executive*
Christy, Cindy *telecommunications industry executive*
Davidson, Janet G. *telecommunications industry executive*
Mejia, Jose A. *telecommunications industry executive*

New Providence
McGinn, Richard A. *telecommunications company executive*
O'Shea, William (Bill) T. *telecommunications industry executive*

Newark
Ferland, E. James *electric power industry executive*

Nutley
Mallard, Stephen Anthony *retired utility company executive*

Paulsboro
Wise, John James *retired oil company executive*

Peapack
Walsh, Philip Cornelius *retired mining executive*

Piscataway
Lewis, Peter A. *energy consultant*

Princeton
Farley, Edward Raymond, Jr., *mining and manufacturing company executive*
McCullough, John Price *retired oil company executive*
Mulhauser, Craig H. *energy executive*

Randolph
Rathore, Uma Pandey *utilities executive*

Red Bank
Chynoweth, Alan Gerald *retired telecommunications research executive, consultant*
Sullivan, Timothy Patrick *telecommunications company executive*

Union
Lewandowski, Andrew Anthony *utilities executive, consultant*

Watchung
Cohen, Melvin Irwin *retired communications systems and technology executive*

NEW MEXICO

Albuquerque
Long, Robert Leroy *retired utilities executive, consultant*

Corrales
Sageser, Kendall Wayne *mineral exploration executive*

Hobbs
Garey, Donald Lee *pipeline and oil company executive*

Roswell
Anderson, Donald Bernard *oil company executive*
Robinson, Mark Leighton *oil company executive, petroleum geologist, horse farm owner*

Santa Fe
Pickrell, Thomas Richard *retired oil company executive*

NEW YORK

Albany
Jasinski, Kenneth M. *energy executive*
von Schack, Wesley W. *energy services company executive*

Armonk
Engel, Joel Stanley *telecommunications executive*

Binghamton
Carrigg, James A. *retired utility company executive*

Bridgehampton
Enstine, Raymond Wilton, Jr., *propane gas company executive*

Brooklyn
Catell, Robert Barry *gas utility executive*
Nozzolillo, Anthony *utilities executive*

Fresh Meadows
Jackson, Rhonda *telecommunications professional, poet*

Greenvale
Cordaro, Matthew Charles *energy and utility executive, educator*

Irvington
Carey, Edward John *utilities executive*

Jericho
Fitteron, John Joseph *gas industry executive, real estate company executive*
Liebowitz, Leo *oil company executive*

Melville
Ostertag, Ronald A. *manufacturing company executive*

New Rochelle
Crawford, Susan Carol *administrative coordinator*

New York
Alpert, Warren *oil company executive, philanthropist*
Babbio, Lawrence T. *telecommunications industry executive*
Bardin, Mary Beth *telecommunications company executive*
Bartlett, Thomas A. *telecommunications industry executive*
Belfer, Robert Alexander *oil and gas company executive*
Benson, David H. *telecommunications industry executive*
Bisbee, Joyce Evelyn *retired utility company executive*
Boden, Katherine L. *utilities executive*
Brown, Edward James, Sr., *utilities executive*
D'Alessio, Frederick D. *telecommunications company executive*
Diercksen, John W. *telecommunications industry executive*
Douglas, Paul Wolff *retired mining executive*
Duffy, Simon *telecommunications industry executive*
Freilich, Joan Sherman *utilities executive*
Gelfand, Neal *oil company executive*
Gordon, Bruce *telecommunications industry executive*
Heitmann, William F. *telecommunications industry executive*
Hess, John B. *oil industry executive*
Lee, Charles Robert *telecommunications company executive*
Luce, Charles Franklin *former utilities executive, lawyer*
Lyons, John Matthew *telecommunications executive, broadcasting executive*
McGrath, Eugene R. *utility company executive*
Mooney, James F. *telecommunications industry executive*
Morse, Edward Lewis *petroleum industry executive*
Mossavar-Rahmani, Bijan *oil and gas company executive*
Noski, Charles H. *telecommunications executive*
Osborne, Richard de Jongh *mining and metals company executive*
Schreyer, John Y. *oil industry executive*
Seidenberg, Ivan G. *telecommunications company executive*
Silverman, Henry Richard *diversified business executive, lawyer*
Singer, Ezra D. *telecommunications industry executive*
Taaffe, Paul *utilities company executive*
Tauke, Thomas Joseph *telecommunications company executive, former congressman*
Warner, Rawleigh, Jr., *oil company executive*
Wegleitner, Mark A. *telecommunications industry executive*
Wrobel, Bruce J. *energy and utilities company executive*

Poughkeepsie
Mack, John Edward, III, *utility company executive*

Rye
Lawi, David Steven *utilities executive, merchant banker*

Schenectady
Robb, Walter Lee *retired electric company executive, management company executive*

Syosset
Vermylen, Paul Anthony, Jr., *oil company executive*

Syracuse
Davis, William E. *utilities executive*
Kerr, Darlene Dixon *electric power company executive*

Wappingers Falls
Nolan, John Thomas, Jr., *retired oil industry administrator*

White Plains
Araskog, Rand Vincent *former diversified telecommunications multinational company executive*
Underweiser, Irwin Philip *mining executive, lawyer*
Urbach, Michael H. *utilities/energy executive*

Whitestone
Bocchino, Frances Lucia *retired oil company official*

Williamsville
Ackerman, Philip Charles *utilities executive, lawyer*
Kennedy, Bernard Joseph *retired utility executive*

NORTH CAROLINA

Asheboro
Croom, John Henry, III, *utility company executive*

Black Mountain
Cody, Hiram Sedgwick, Jr., *retired telecommunications industry executive*

Cary
Buckler, Sheldon A. *technology company executive*

Charlotte
Anderson, Paul Milton *energy executive*
Ervine, Timothy DuWayne *utilities executive*
Evans, Robert B. *energy executive*
Fowler, Fred J. *energy executive*
Grigg, William Humphrey *utilities executive*
Ladd, Robert T. *energy executive*
McGee, Richard K. *energy executive*
Mogg, Jimmy W. *gas industry executive*
Mullinax, A. R. *energy executive*
O'Connor, Thomas C. *gas industry executive*
Osborne, Richard Jay *electric utility company executive*
Shaw, Ruth G. *energy company executive*

Durham
Fassett, John D. *retired utility executive, consultant*

Greensboro
Shelton, Ralph K. *fuel company executive*

Hendersonville
Haynes, John Mabin *retired utilities executive*

Raleigh
Cavanaugh, William, III, *electric utility company executive*
Clapp, Allen Linville *electric supply and communications utility consultant, mediator/arbitrator*
Harder, Glenn E. *utilities, energy company executive*
Johnson, William Dean *power company executive*
McGehee, Robert B. *energy executive*
Scott, Peter M. *utility company executive*
Smith, Sherwood Hubbard, Jr., *retired electric utilities executive*

Southern Shores
Kegel, William George *mining company executive*

Statesville
Grogan, David R. *work saver company executive*

Wilmington
Flohr, Daniel P. *telecommunications industry executive*

NORTH DAKOTA

Bismarck
Robinson, Warren Lowe *utilities executive*

OHIO

Akron
Alexander, Anthony J. *electric power industry executive*
Marsh, Richard H. *utilities company executive*
Vespoli, Leila L. *energy executive, lawyer*

Bannock
Gentile, Anthony *coal company executive*

Bexley
Maloney, Gerald P. *retired utilities executive*

Cincinnati
Aumiller, Wendy L. *utilities executive*
Braunstein, Mary *energy consulting company executive*
Bryant, John *utilities executive*
Cunningham, James Melvin *telecommunications executive*
Cyrus, Michael J. *electric power industry executive*
Duncan, R. Foster *utilities company executive*
Ehrnschwender, Arthur Robert *former utility company executive*
Esamann, Douglas F. *utilities executive*
Ficke, Gregory C. *utilities executive*
Foley, Cheryl M. *electric power industry executive*
Gaines, Bennett L. *utilities executive*
Grealis, William J. *energy executive*
Hale, J. Joseph, Jr., *utilities executive*
Janson, Julia S. *utilities executive*
Kiggen, James D. *telecommunications industry executive*
Murphy, Theodore R., II, *utilities executive*
Newton, Frederick J., III, *utilities executive*
Noonan, Sheila M. *energy consulting company executive*
Randolph, Jackson Harold *utility company executive*
Reising, Ronald *utilities executive*
Rogers, James Eugene *electric and gas utility executive*
Verhagen, Timothy *utilities executive*
Wozny, David *utilities executive*

Cleveland
Brinzo, John S. *mining executive*
Ginn, Robert Martin *retired utility company executive*
Leaks, Marna Hale *utilities executive*
Miller, John Robert *oil industry executive*
O'Neil, Thomas J. *mining company executive*

Columbus
Fayne, Henry W. *electric power industry executive*
Hagan, Thomas M. *electric power industry executive*
Koeppel, Holly *electric power industry executive*
Massey, Robert John *telecommunications executive*
Morris, Michael G. *utilities executive*
Powers, Robert P. *electric power industry executive*
Richard, Oliver, III, (Rick Richard) *energy company executive*
Shockley, Thomas V., III, *electric power industry executive*
Vassell, Gregory S. *electric utility consultant*

Dayton
Forster, Peter Hans *utility company executive*
Hill, Allen M. *public utility executive*
Lansaw, Judy W. *public utility executive*

Findlay
Yammine, Riad Nassif *retired oil company executive*

Painesville
Smith, William Robert *utility company executive*

Perrysburg
Williamson, John Pritchard *utilities executive*

South Charleston
Weatherby, Donald Alan *telecommunications industry executive, writer*

OKLAHOMA

Bartlesville
Allen, W. Wayne *retired oil industry executive*
Cox, Glenn Andrew, Jr., *petroleum company executive*
Mulva, James Joseph *oil company executive*
Silas, Cecil Jesse *retired petroleum company executive*

Enid
Ward, Llewellyn Orcutt, III, *oil company executive*

Jennings
Nixon, Arlie James *gas and oil company executive*

Oklahoma City
Bode, Denise Anne *petroleum association executive*
Campbell, David Gwynne *petroleum executive, geologist*
Corbett, Luke R. *energy executive*
Gustafson, William Gene *oil industry executive*
Harlan, Ross Edgar *retired utility company executive, writer, lecturer, consultant*
Hefner, William Johnson, Jr., (W. John Hefner Jr.) *oil and gas industry executive*
Kirkpatrick, John Elson *retired oil company executive, retired naval reserve officer*
Nichols, J. Larry *energy company executive, lawyer*
Peace, H. W., II, *oil company executive*
Strecker, Al *energy executive*
Wilkerson, Matha Ann *oil company executive*
Wohleber, Robert Michael *oil industry executive*

Ponca City
Leonard, Samuel Wallace *oil company and bank executive*

Seminole
Moran, Melvin Robert *oil industry executive*

Tulsa
Bailey, Keith E. *petroleum pipeline company executive*
Bender, James J. *oil industry executive*
Berlin, Steven Ritt *oil company executive*
Braumiller, Allen Spooner *oil and gas exploration company executive, geologist*
Cadieux, Chester *gas industry executive*
Carter, Terry *gas industry executive*
Chappel, Donald R. *petroleum pipeline company executive*
Dotson, George Stephen *drilling company executive*
Helmerich, Walter Hugo, III, *oil company executive*
Horkey, William Richard *retired diversified oil company executive*
Ingram, Charles Clark, Jr., *energy company executive*
Kneale, James C. *gas company executive*
Kronfeld, Edwin *natural gas company executive*
Kyle, David L. *gas industry executive*
Malcolm, Steven J. *petroleum pipeline company executive*
McCarthy, Jack D. *oil industry executive*
Warren, W. K., Jr., *oil industry executive*

OREGON

Beaverton
Timmins, Timothy A. *telecommunications industry executive*

Lincoln City
Morrow, James Thomas *energy executive*

Portland
Bacon, Vicky Lee *lighting services executive*
Frisbee, Don Calvin *retired utilities executive*
Reiten, Richard G. *natural gas industry executive*

Salem
Heine, Steven Robert *telecommunications industry executive, poet, writer*

PENNSYLVANIA

Allentown
Biggar, John R. *utilities energy executive*
Hecht, William F. *electric power industry executive*
Wagner, Harold A. *industrial gas and chemical company executive*

Allison Park
Sullivan, Neil Maxwell *oil and gas company executive*

Bryn Mawr
Braha, Thomas I. *business executive*

Camp Hill
Fazzolari, Salvatore D. *mining products executive*
Hathaway, Derek C. *mining products executive*

Coraopolis
Koepfinger, Joseph Leo *retired utilities executive*

Coudersport
Schleyer, William T. *cable company executive*

Ephrata
Sweigart, Anne B. *communications company executive*

Exton
Mauch, Robert Carl *energy executive*

Gladwyne
Patten, Lanny Ray *industrial gas industry executive*

Haverford
Olson, Robert Edward *coal mining executive*

Johnstown
Simmons, Elroy, Jr., *retired utility executive*

King Of Prussia
Greenberg, Lon Richard *energy company executive, lawyer*
Mendicino, Anthony J. *gas company executive*

New Hope
John, Francis D. *energy executive*

Philadelphia
Albertini, William Oliver *retired telecommunications industry executive*
Calman, Robert Frederick *mining executive*
Campbell, Robert H. *retired oil company executive*
Delaney, Terence (Terry) P. *gas industry executive*
Dingus, Michael H. *gas industry executive*
Drosdick, John Girard *oil company executive*
Fischer, Bruce G. *gas industry executive*
Fretz, Deborah McDermott *oil industry executive*
Hofmann, Thomas W. *petroleum company executive*
Krott, Joseph P. *gas industry executive, comptroller*
Kuritzkes, Michael S. *gas industry executive*
Maness, Joel H. *gas industry executive*
McNeill, Corbin Asahel, Jr., *utilities executive*
Mulé, Ann C. *oil industry executive*
Mulholland, Paul A. *gas industry executive*
Naku, Rolf D. *gas industry executive*
Owens, Robert W. *gas industry executive*

Pittsburgh
Bartley, Burnett Graham, Jr., *oil company and manufacturing executive*
Brown, Bobby R. *retired coal company executive*
Corcoran, Thomas A. *metals and mining company executive*
Gerber, Murry S. *utilities, gas, oil executive*
Marshall, David D. *electric utilities executive*
Murphy, John Nolan *mining executive, researcher, electrical engineer*
Porges, David L. *utilities, gas, oil executive*
Stirewalt, John Newman *coal company executive*
Wagner, Florence Zeleznik *telecommunications executive*

Presto
Moeller, Audrey Carolyn *retired energy company executive, corporate secretary*

Radnor
Castle, Joseph Lanktree, II, *energy company executive, consultant*

Wayne
Lefevre, Thomas Vernon *retired utility company executive, lawyer*

West Sunbury
Stewart, Mark Thomas *gas industry executive*

SOUTH CAROLINA

Columbia
Arthur, H. Thomas, II, *energy executive*
Gressette, Lawrence M., Jr., *utilities executive*
Marsh, Kevin B. *energy executive*
Timmerman, William B. *utilities executive, accountant*

Hilton Head Island
Simpson, John Wistar *energy consultant, former manufacturing company executive*

Murrells Inlet
Justice, Franklin Pierce, Jr., *oil company executive*

Myrtle Beach
Atkinson, Harold Witherspoon *utilities consultant, real estate broker*

Sheldon
Lowrie, William G. *former oil company executive*

SOUTH DAKOTA

Pierre
Dunn, James Bernard *mining company executive, state legislator*

Rapid City
Lien, Bruce Hawkins *minerals and oil company executive*

Sioux Falls
Hylland, Richard R. *utility company executive*
Lewis, Merle Dean *electric and gas utility executive*
Newell, Daniel K. *utilities company executive*

TENNESSEE

Chattanooga
Scalice, John A. *nuclear energy executive*

Knoxville
McCullough, Glenn L., Jr., *electric power industry executive*
Prosser, George T. *utilities executive*

Nashville
Adams, Kenneth Stanley, Jr., (Bud Adams) *energy company executive, football executive*
McCormick, Richard *retired telecommunications company executive*

TEXAS

Addison
Murray, Patrick M. *oilfield service company executive*
Pryor, Richard Walter *telecommunications executive, retired air force officer*

Austin
Anderson, Lynn D. *telecommunications industry executive*
Brigham, Ben M. *oil industry executive*
Deisler, Paul Frederick, Jr., *retired oil company executive*
Franklin, Robert Drury *oil company executive, lawyer*
Gibson, Jerry Leigh *oil company executive*
Haas, Joseph Marshall *petroleum consultant*
Larkam, Peter Howard *electric utility executive, entrepreneur*
Ogden, Steve *oil and gas company executive, state legislator*
Spagnolo, Mark F. *telecommunications industry executive*

Beaumont
Smith, Floyd Rodenback *retired utilities executive*

Breckenridge
Reaugh, Orland H. *oil industry executive*

Carrollton
Johnson, James L. *telecommunications industry executive*
Kaiser, Robert A. *telecommunications industry executive*
Parker, Terry S. *telecommunications industry executive*

Channelview
Gower, Bob G. *gas and oil industry executive*

Conroe
Mitchell, Robert James *petroleum company executive*

Corpus Christi
Benner, Richard Walter *oil company executive, geologist, engineer*
Haas, Paul Raymond *petroleum company executive*
Norman, Wyatt Thomas, III, *landman, consultant*
Paulson, Bernard Arthur *oil company executive, consultant*

Dallas
Barnes, John R. *petroleum company executive*
Best, Robert Wayne *gas transmission company executive, lawyer*
Brachman, Malcolm K. *oil company executive*
Bright, Harvey R. *petroleum corporation executive*
Brooks, Edgar R. (Dick Brooks) *utility company executive*
Brown, Lonnie *utility company executive*
Campbell, Kevin P. *oil industry executive*
Carson, Virginia Hill *oil and gas executive*
Farell, Dan *utilities executive*
Fielder, Charles Robert *oil industry executive*
Gaut, C. Christopher *gas company executive*
Gibbs, Jarrell H. *utilities executive*
Gratton, Patrick John Francis *oil company executive*
Harbin, John Pickens *oil well company executive*
Hunt, Ray L. *petroleum company executive*
Jennings, James Burnett *oil company executive*
Jones, Everett Riley, Jr., *oil company executive*
Mackenzie, Nanci *gas company executive*
Mandeville, Hubert Turner, Jr., *oil company executive*
McNally, Michael James *electric power industry executive*
Mitchell, A. Joe, Jr., *telecommunications industry executive*
Moore, Christopher Robertson Kinley *energy industry consultant*
Nevins, William J. *oil and gas brokerage executive, consultant*
Norsworthy, Lamar *petroleum company executive*
Nye, Erle Allen *electric power industry executive, lawyer*
Perry, George Wilson *oil and gas company executive*
Plummer, Paul James *energy executive*
Robillard, Donald F., Jr., *gas and oil industry executive*
Sentell, Susan B. *telecommunications company executive*
Sepuldadl, Lynn *utility company executive*
Sizer, Phillip Spelman *consultant, retired oil field services executive*
Slawter, John David, Jr., *oil company and manufacturing executive*
Smith, R. J., Jr., *oil company executive*
Thorne, Carl F. *gas industry executive*
Wilder, C. John *energy industry executive*
Wilson, Richard A. *oil/gas industry support services executive*
Winters, J(ohn) Otis *retired oil industry consultant*

El Paso
Shelton, Patricia A. *gas company executive*

Flower Mound
Cox, David Leon *telecommunications company executive*

Fort Worth
Armiger, Gene Gibbon *telecommunications executive, consultant*
Bass, Perry Richardson *oil company executive*
Boschetti, Philip J. *oil company executive*
Catacosinos, William James *utility company executive*
Hudson, Edward Randall, Jr., *gas and oil industry executive*
Hyde, Clarence Brodie, II, *oil company executive*
Moncrief, William Alvin, Jr., *oil and gas producer*

Fredericksburg
Malec, William Frank *utilities company executive*

Frisco
Ellison, Luther Frederick *oil company executive*
Larsen, David Wayne *telecommunications industry executive*
Mackenzie, John *retired oil industry executive*

Horseshoe Bay
Jorden, James Roy *oil company engineering executive, consultant*

Houston
Adkins, Albert G. *oil industry executive*
Ajello, James A. *energy executive*
Arledge, David A. *energy executive*
Armstrong, Greg L. *oil company executive*
Austin, H. Brent *electric power industry executive*
Barracano, Henry Ralph *retired oil company executive, consultant*
Barrow, Thomas Davies *oil and mining company executive*
Bartling, Phyllis McGinness *oil company executive*
Batchelder, E. L. (Gene) *oil industry executive*

Haskayne, Richard Francis *petroleum company executive*
Horton, William Russell *retired utility company executive*
Maier, Gerald James *corporate executive*
McKinnon, F(rancis) A(rthur) Richard *utilities executive*
Morgan, Gwyn *oil and gas executive*
O'Brien, David Peter *gas industry executive, lawyer*
Pourbaix, Alexander *energy executive*
Seaman, Daryl Kenneth *oil company executive*
Southern, Nancy C. *utilities executive*
Southern, Ronald D. *diversified corporation executive*
Swartout, Hank B. *oil and gas industry executive*
Wagner, Norman Ernest *corporate education executive*

Red Deer
Donald, Jack C. *corporate executive*

BRITISH COLUMBIA

Vancouver
Keevil, Norman B. *mining executive*

MANITOBA

Saint Andrews
Lang, Otto *retired gas industry executive, former Canadian cabinet minister*

Winnipeg
Burns, James William *business executive*

NOVA SCOTIA

Halifax
Mann, David *energy and services company executive*

ONTARIO

Brockville
Spalding, James Stuart *retired telecommunications company executive*

North York
Blundell, William Richard Charles *retired electric company executive*

Toronto
Chabot, Diane *telecommunications executive*
Clitheroe, Eleanor *utilities executive*
Hyland, Geoffrey Fyfe *energy service company executive*
Kerr, David Wylie *natural resource company executive*
Martin, Robert William *corporate director*
Munk, Peter *mining executive*
Osler, Gordon Peter *retired utility company executive*
Peterson, Robert B. *petroleum company executive*
Strong, Maurice Frederick *hydro-electric power company executive, former United Nations official*
Ward, Milton Hawkins *former mining company executive*
Wilson, Lynton Ronald *retired telecommunications company executive*

QUEBEC

Montreal
Caillé, André *public service company executive*
Cyr, J. V. Raymond *telecommunications industry executive*
Engen, D(onald) Travis *diversified telecommunications company executive*

EGYPT

Cairo
Abbas, Ali El-Sayed *oil company executive, researcher*

ENGLAND

London
Gillam, Sir Patrick *oil company executive, banker*
Greener, Anthony *telecommunications industry executive*

FRANCE

Paris
Mestrallet, Gérard *utilities executive, professional society administrator*

JAPAN

Yokohama
Ito, Noboru *electric power industry executive*

KYRGYZSTAN

Bishkek
Arne, Kenneth George *mining executive, mineral consultant*

NETHERLANDS

The Hague
Hodge, Susan *oil industry executive*
van Wachem, Lodewijk Christiaan *petroleum company executive*

ADDRESS UNPUBLISHED

Addy, Frederick Seale *retired oil company executive*
Anderson, Robert Orville *oil and gas company executive*
Andras, Oscar Sidney *oil company executive*
Arlidge, John Walter *retired utility company executive*
Arthur, John Morrison *retired utility executive*
Ataie, Ata Jennati *oil products marketing executive*
Barham, Charles Dewey, Jr., *electric utility executive, lawyer*
Barrack, William Sample, Jr., *petroleum company executive*
Baumgartner, John H. *refining and petroleum products company executive*
Benediktson, Stephan Vilberg *oil company executive*
Bernard, Betsy J. *former telecommunications industry executive*
Berry, William Willis *retired utility executive*
Bliss, Kevin James *oil industry executive, lawyer*
Bowlin, Michael Ray *retired oil company executive*
Brace, Robert P. *former electric power utility executive*
Browne, (Edmund) John Phillip *oil industry executive*
Bruce, James Edmund *retired utility company executive*
Bryan, James Lee *retired oil field service company executive*
Bumbery, Joseph Lawrence *diversified telecommunications company executive*
Burrow, Harold *former gas company executive*
Chelle, Robert Frederick *entrepreneurial leadership educator*
Chen, George Chi-Ming *energy company executive*
Childers, Charles Eugene *mining company executive*
Clark, Philip Raymond *nuclear utility executive, engineer*
Conger, Harry Milton *mining company executive*
Cookson, Albert Ernest *telephone and telegraph company executive*
Counsil, William Glenn *electric utility executive*
Curtis, Edward Joseph, Jr., *gas industry executive, management consultant*
Demere, Robert Houstoun, Jr., *oil company executive*
Dergarabedian, Paul *energy and environmental company executive*
Di Giovanni, Anthony *retired coal mining company executive*
Donahue, Donald Jordan *mining company executive*
Dragoumis, Paul *electric utility company executive*
Draper, E(rnest) Linn, Jr., *retired electric utility executive*
Driscoll, Garrett Bates *retired telecommunications executive*
English, Floyd Leroy *telecommunications company executive*
Esrey, William Todd *telecommunications company executive*
Estes, Jack Charles *oil service company executive, scientist*
Ewing, Wayne Turner *coal company executive*
Fagin, David Kyle *natural resources executive*
Finger, Harold B. *consultant*
Flickinger, Joe Arden *telecommunications educator*
Ford, Judith Ann Tudor *retired natural gas distribution company executive*
Forsgren, John H., Jr., *utilities company executive*
Fuller, Harry Laurance *retired oil company executive*
Gabel, Ronald Glen *telecommunications executive*
Gadomski, Robert Eugene *former chemical and industrial gas company executive*
Garberding, Larry Gilbert *retired utilities companies executive*
Gardiner, Hobart Clive *petroleum company executive*
Gerard, Roy Dupuy *retired oil company executive*
Green, Richard Calvin, Jr., *electric power and gas industry executive*
Greer, Carl Crawford *petroleum company executive*
Gurian, Mal *telecommunications executive*
Hall, Milton Reese *retired oil company executive*
Hamilton, Allan Corning *retired oil company executive*
Hammer, Harold Harlan *oil company financial executive*
Hancock, John Coulter *telecommunications company executive*
Harris, Howard Hunter *retired oil industry executive*
Heiney, John Weitzel *former utility executive*
Helton, Sandra Lynn *telecommunications industry executive*
Herron, Edwin Hunter, Jr., *energy consultant*
Hines, Andrew Hampton, Jr., *utilities executive*
Hogg, Karen Sue *retired telecommunications industry executive*
Houston, John R. *telecommunications industry executive*
Howard, James Joseph, III, *utility company executive*
Huffman, James Thomas William *oil exploration company executive*
Humke, Ramon Lyle *utilities executive*
Hurst, Leland Lyle *natural gas company executive*
Inglis, James *telecommunications company executive*
Isaacs, Jonathan William *oil company executive*
Jackson, Robert William *retired utility company executive*
Johnson, Curtis Lildon *drilling engineer*
Jordan, Pearl Oneta *telecommunications industry executive*
Kaculi, Xhemal T. *oil industry analysis engineer*
Kaufman, Raymond L. *energy company executive*
Kebblish, John Basil *retired coal company executive, consultant*
Kertz, Hubert Leonard *telephone company executive*
Kettel, Edward Joseph *oil company executive, retired*
King, William Collins *oil company executive*
Kirkby, Maurice Anthony *oil company executive*
Kloepfer, Clarence Victor *oil company executive*
Krempel, Roger Ernest *public works management consultant*
Kuehn, Ronald L., Jr., *natural resources company executive*
Laman, Jerry Thomas *mining company executive*
Leva, James Robert *retired electric utility company executive*
Lewis, Floyd Wallace *former electric utility executive*
Lilly, Edward Guerrant, Jr., *retired utility company executive*
Long, Alfred B. *former oil company executive, consultant*
Lortie, John William *solar research company executive*
Loveland, Eugene Franklin *retired petroleum executive*
Maher, Patrick Joseph *retired utility company executive*
Mayo, John Sullivan *telecommunications company executive*
Mc Carthy, Walter John, Jr., *retired utility executive*
McCready, Kenneth Frank *former electric utility executive*
McSweeny, William Francis *petroleum company executive, author*
Meek, Paul Derald *oil and chemical company executive*
Mohebbi, Afshin *former telecommunications industry executive*
Montgomery, Roy Delbert *retired gas utility company executive*
Morrell, Gene Paul *liquid terminal company executive, consultant*
Munsey, Virdell Everard, Jr., *retired utility executive*
Nicholson, Leland Ross *retired utilities company executive, energy consultant*
Nurenberg, David *retired oil company executive*
O'Connor, James John *retired utility company executive*
O'Hare, James Raymond *energy company executive*
Ormasa, John *retired utilities executive*
Osterhoff, James Marvin *retired telecommunications company executive*
Pack, Allen S. *retired coal company executive*
Perry, Kenneth Walter *retired integrated oil company executive*
Pierce, Lisa Margaret *telecommunications executive, product and market development manager, lecturer*
Portal, Gilbert Marcel Adrien *oil company executive*
Priory, Richard Baldwin *former electric power industry executive*
Raymond, Lee R. *oil company executive*
Rendu, Jean-Michel Marie *mining executive*
Roe, Thomas Coombe *former utility company executive*
Rogers, Justin Towner, Jr., *retired utility company executive*
Rue, Douglas Michael *technical application consultant*
St. Clair, Thomas McBryar *mining and manufacturing company executive*
Salerno, Frederic V. *retired telecommunications company executive*
Samuels, John Stockwell, III, *mining company executive, financier*
Sanders, Charles Franklin *management and engineering consultant*
Sant, Roger W. *energy executive*
Schenck, Jack Lee *retired electric utility executive*
Schenker, Leo *retired utility company executive*
Scott, Donahue *energy executive*
Scott, Isadore Meyer *former energy company executive*
Shattuck, Mayo Adams, III, *integrated utility executive*
Shoup, Andrew James, Jr., *retired oil company executive*
Shultz, Delray Franklin (Lucky Shultz) *business and management consultant, coach*
Smith, Paul Vergon, Jr., *retired gas industry executive*
Sprow, Frank Barker *oil company executive*
Stratman, Joseph Lee *retired petroleum refining company executive, consultant, chemical engineer*
Taylor, Gerald H. *telecommunications company executive*
Thomas, Kenneth Glyndwr *mining executive*
Thompson, Jack Edward *mining company executive*
Threet, Jack Curtis *oil company executive*
Travis, Vance Kenneth *petroleum business executive*
Tucker, H. Richard *oil company executive*
Tuer, David A. *petroleum industry executive*
Turner, Thomas Marshall *telecommunications executive, consultant*
Watson, George W. *energy executive*
Weaver, William Schildecker *retired electric power industry executive*
White, Martin Arthur *utilities company executive*
White, Willis Sheridan, Jr., *retired utilities company executive*
Wickstrom, Jon Alan *telecommunications executive, consultant*
Wilson, Walter Clinton *retired gas industry executive*
Wise, William Allen *energy company executive*
Witte, Merlin Michael *oil company executive*
Wood, Willis Bowne, Jr., *retired utilities executive*
Wright, Randolph Earle *retired petroleum company executive*

INFORMATION TECHNOLOGY
See also SCIENCE: MATHEMATICS AND COMPUTER SCIENCE

UNITED STATES

ALABAMA

Birmingham
Crump, Michael David *network technician*

Florence
Foote, Avon Edward *web developer/producer, communications educator*

Huntsville
Childs, Rand Hampton *information technology executive, consultant*

Tallassee
Baker, Barry Gorden *computer technician*

ARIZONA

Phoenix
Kossek, Sebastian Alexander *information technology executive*

Scottsdale
Friesen, Oris Dewayne *software engineer, historian*
Stott, Brian *software company executive, consultant*

Surprise
Jackson, Randy *information technology executive*

Tempe
Crown, Eric J. *information systems executive*
Crown, Timothy A. *computer technology company executive*
Laybourne, Stanley *computer technology company executive*
Smith, Branson M. *computer technology company executive*

Tucson
Donoghue, John Charles *application developer, consultant*
Fredericksen, Dick Hartman *retired computer programmer*

ARKANSAS

De Witt
Davenport, Heath Shane *information technology manager, educator*

CALIFORNIA

Alviso
Ramsay, Michael *information technology executive*

Anaheim
Davis, Robert L. *information technology executive*

Antelope
Nenov, Ivo P. *mathematical and software researcher*

Burlingame
Garnett, Katrina A. *information technology executive*

Calabasas
Sloan, Michael Dana *information systems specialist*

Corona Del Mar
Zabrodsky, Alexander *network technician*

Cupertino
Clyde, Robert Allan *computer software engineer*
Haskell, Barry Geoffry *computer company researcher*
Thompson, John W. *information technology executive*

Cypress
Cao, Dac-Buu *software engineer*

Danville
Bergsten, James Robert *computer technology architect*

Del Mar
Fricke, Martin Paul *science company executive*

Fair Oaks
Maskall, Martha Josephine *web site designer, publishing executive, health consultant*

Fremont
Sarkar, Arindam *information technology executive*
Tang, John *network technician, information scientist, educator*

Fullerton
Morton, Michael James *software engineer*

Glen Ellen
Hurlbert, Roger William *information service industry executive*

Granada Hills
Shoemaker, Harold Lloyd *infosystem specialist*

Irvine
Godfrey, Raymond Michael *information systems educator*
Smith, Vincent C. *information technology executive*

Long Beach
Loganbill, G. Bruce *logopedic pathologist*

Los Alamitos
Weinberger, Frank *information management consultant*

Los Angeles
Groppe, Laura *interactive software company executive*
Hwang, John Dzen *information systems educator*
Martin, Nanice S. *software company executive*

Lynwood
Legesse, Solomon *technology executive*

Martinez
Tong, Siu Wing *computer programmer*

Menlo Park
Zdeblick, Mark James *information technology executive*

Milpitas
Hawkins, Jeff *information technology executive*
Levinson, Marina *information technology executive*
Treichel, Helmuth W.A. *technology executive*

Monterey
Hennessy, Robert Thomas *information technology executive*

Monterey Park
Tsao, Gus *information technology executive*

Mountain View
Brin, Sergey *information technology executive*
Page, Larry *information technology executive*
Schmidt, Eric Emerson *information technology executive*
Sclavos, Stratton *information technology executive*

Oakland
Wills, John Arthur *computer programmer, analyst*

Palo Alto
Denzel, Nora *information technology executive*
Greene, Diane *information technology executive*
Mayo, Robert N. *computer science researcher*

Pleasanton
Bergquist, Rick *software company executive*
Caldwell, Nanci *software company executive*
Dubois, Guy *software company executive*
Gregoire, Michael P. *software company executive*
Gupta, Ram *software company executive*
Wilmington, W. Phillip *software company executive*

Poway
Kubilus, Norbert John *information technology executive*
Turner, David G. *information technology executive*

Rancho Palos Verdes
Savage, Terry Richard *information systems executive*

Redwood City
Davidson, Mary Ann *information technology executive*
Hagart-Alexander, Claud *software engineer*
Mattrick, Don A. *interactive entertainment software company executive*
Rohde, James Vincent *software systems company executive*
Smith, Nancy L. *information technology executive*

San Bruno
Hariton, Lorraine Jill *information technology executive*

San Diego
Backes, Jack Abraham *retired application developer*
Goldstein, Mark Kingston Levin *information technology executive, researcher*
Kronewitter, Frank Dell *software engineer, researcher*
Stapleton, Michael *information technology executive*
Sutton, Keith H. *information technology executive*
Tom, Lawrence *technology executive*

San Francisco
Kapor, Mitchell David *software developer, foundation executive*
Keeney, Ralph Lyons *decision and risk analyst, educator*
Penn, Lee *information technology consultant, journalist*
Pure, Pamela *information technology executive*
Reid, Rob *information technology executive*
Ryan, Dennis *information technology executive*
Ryan, Sean *information technology executive*
Salmi, Mika *information technology executive*
Valeskie-Hamner, Gail Yvonne *information systems specialist*

San Jose
Chambers, John Thomas *computer systems network executive*
Chuang, Alfred *information technology executive*
Halloran, Mike *software company executive, music publishing executive*
Melvin, Vincent P. *information technology executive*
Morgridge, John P. *computer systems network executive*
Powell, Dennis *computer systems network executive*
Sauvageau, Yvon *application developer*
Scheinman, A. Daniel *computer system networks executive*
Ulmer, David *information technology executive*
Whitman, Margaret C. (Meg Whitman) *internet company executive*

San Mateo
Brzozowsky, Keith William *software consultant*
Grecsek, Matthew Thomas *software developer*
Lawrie, J. Michael *software company executive*
Siebel, Thomas M. *software company executive*

San Ramon
Moore, Justin Edward *information technology executive*
Schofield, James Roy *computer programmer*

Santa Ana
Abramo, Guy P. *information technology executive*
Flastrup, Asger *information technology executive*
Foster, Kent B. *information technology executive*
Koppen, Hans T. *information technology executive*
Murai, Kevin *information technology executive*
Spierkel, Gregory M. *information technology executive*

Santa Barbara
Boehm, Eric Hartzell *information management executive*

Santa Clara
Chen, Deanford Frederick *software engineer*
Moore, Bruce *information technology executive*
Weigle, Peggy *information technology executive*

Santa Cruz
Lindquist, Claude S. *technical consultant and executive, educator, researcher*

Sausalito
Jeffrey, Francis *software developer, forecaster, bioethicist*

Scotts Valley
Janssen, James Robert *consulting software engineer*

Sunnyvale
Andreessen, Marc *software company executive, internet innovator*
Calderoni, Robert M. *software company executive*
Cambou, Bertrand *information technology executive*
Edwards, William T. (Billy Edwards) *information technology executive*
Kriens, Scott G. *information technology executive*
McCoy, Thomas *information technology executive*
Meyer, Derrick R. *information technology executive*
Morris, Iain *information technology executive*
Perdikou, Kim *information technology executive*
Ruiz, Hector *information technology executive*
Sindu, Pradeep *information technology executive*
Sohn, Young K. *information technology executive*

Thousand Oaks
Dayem, Hassan *information technology executive*

Tustin
Maeschen, David Michael *software engineer*

Walnut Creek
Arnold, William Thomas *software developer, chemist*

West Sacramento
Wilson, Eric F.G. *information technology executive*

Westlake Village
Gibson, John Robert *software engineer*
Wester, Aaron Micah *web production manager, consultant*

COLORADO

Broomfield
O'Hara, Kevin J. *information technology executive*

Colorado Springs
Fahey, Henry Martin *information technology executive*

Denver
Thompson, Joseph Paul *retired systems administrator*

Fort Collins
Lameiro, Gerard Francis *corporate strategist*

Greenwood Village
Battista, Guy *information technology executive*

Lakewood
Siska, Robert John *software engineer*

Littleton
Marion, John Martin *information technology educator*

Louisville
Kocol, Robert S. *information technology executive*
Maddock, Jerome Torrence *information services specialist*

CONNECTICUT

Danbury
Fuller, Cassandra Miller *applications specialist*
Williamson, Brian David *information systems executive, consultant*

Enfield
Oliver, Bruce Lawrence *retired information systems specialist, educator*

Greenwich
Lipner, William E. *information systems executive*

Kent
Peck, Darryl *software company executive*

Mashantucket
Yale, John Paul *computer systems developer*

Stamford
Peterson, Karen L. *information technology manager*
Tierney, Patrick John *information services executive*

Westport
Frese, Edward Scheer, Jr., (Ted Frese) *information technology executive, consultant*

Windsor
Stone, William Charles *software executive, consultant*

DELAWARE

Newark
Godwin, Ralph Edward *retired computer operator*

DISTRICT OF COLUMBIA

Washington
Brailer, David J. *health information technology executive*
Choudhury, Raj Deo *information technology manager*
Day, Melvin Sherman *information and telecommunications company executive*
Golden, James Leslie *information technology executive*
Gregory, John Forrest *information technology specialist, librarian*
Hungate, Joseph Irvin, III, *information technology executive*
Leslie, Donald S. *information technology manager*
McCaleb, Margaret Anne Sheehan *application developer*
McConnell, Bruce William *information technology executive*
Nguyen, Alex Thinh *internet company executive, aerospace engineer, consultant*
Rausch, Howard *information service executive*
Rose, George Andrew *software developer, information systems specialist*
Vaughan, Kenneth Edward *application developer*

FLORIDA

Alachua
Neubauer, Hugo Duane, Jr., *computer network engineer*

Altamonte Springs
Frankel, Andrew Joel *management and information technology consultant*

Clearwater
Dannewitz, Charles V. *information technology executive*
Duerst, Andreas *information technology executive*
Gass, Andy *information technology executive*
Hunter, William J. *information technology executive*
Osbourn, Joseph A. *information technology executive*
Saydun, Yuda *information technology executive*
Todd, William K., Jr., *information technology executive*
Trepani, Joseph B. *information technology executive*
Youna, Gerard *information technology executive*

Fort Pierce
Hurley, William Joseph *retired information technology executive*

Jacksonville
Chambers, Jack Allen *educator*
Salem, Karen E. *information technology executive*

Lake Mary
Bodden, M. David *computer professional, consultant*

Melbourne
Hughes, Edwin Lawson *retired information technology executive*

Miami
Watson, Doug *information technology executive*
Zito, Judi *information technology executive*

Miami Shores
Deeb, Khaled Kevin *information technology educator*

Orlando
Andrew, Brian J. *information technology company executive*
Henry, Christopher Joel *software consultant*
Steward, Sherry Ann *information technology executive, educator*

Ormond Beach
Burke, Marguerite Jodi Larcombe *application developer, consultant*

Pensacola
Gamblin, William Basil, Jr., *application developer, writer, photographer*

Tallahassee
Mason, Robert McSpadden *technology management educator, consultant*

Tampa
Gill, Thomas Grandon *information technology executive, educator*
Wyman, Richard Thomas *information services consultant*

Venice
Kleinlein, Kathy Lynn *training and development executive*

GEORGIA

Alpharetta
Cook, Richard C. *application developer*
Desai, Hiren D. *software engineer*
Lademacher, Hartmut *computer software and services company executive*
McCormick, James K. *application developer*
Travers, James M. *application developer*

Atlanta
Coady, William Francis *information technology executive, consultant*
Coley, Barbara Yvonne *computer software consultant*
Ellis, U. Bertram, Jr., *internet services company executive*
Goldfarb, Eric Daniel *information technology executive, computer industry analyst*
Kirberger, Michael Patrick *application developer, researcher*
Kochengin, Sergey Alexandrovich *information technology consultant*
Morrison, Gregory Bernard *information systems specialist*
Odom, Steve *information technology executive*
Rink, Christopher Lee *information technology consultant, photographer*

Dublin
Watt, Dwight, Jr., (Arthur Dwight Watt Jr.) *computer programming and microcomputer specialist*

Kennesaw
Jenkins, Joyce Ann *information technology manager, educator*

Macon
Stewart, Jeffrey Vincent, III, *information technology educator*

Savannah
Palanca, Terilyn *software industry analyst*

Phillips, Robert L., Jr., *application developer, consultant*

HAWAII

Honolulu
Bossert, Philip Joseph *information systems executive*

Kihei
Wright, Thomas Parker *application developer*

ILLINOIS

Champaign
Chang, Kathy Kuhl *computer programmer, analyst*
Veasey, Byron Keith *information systems consultant*

Chicago
Buckley, Joseph Paul, III, *polygraph specialist*
Costin, J(oseph) Laurence, Jr., *information services executive*
Cox, Clifford Ernest *information systems consulting executive, former academic administrator*
Desouza, Kevin Clyde *application developer*
Drewry, June E. *information technology executive*
Dwyer, Dennis D. *information technology executive*
Kaplan, Jonathan H B *healthcare business transformation and information technology specialist*
Krawczyk, Eva *information systems analyst, educator*
Noonan, Jack *application developer*
Stark, Henry *technology educator*

Effingham
Franklin, William Price *computer programmer*

Libertyville
Shen, Xiaohui *application developer, researcher*

Lincolnwood
Johansson, Nils A. *information services executive*

Northfield
Pratt, Murray Lester *collaborative commerce specialist*

Rockford
Duck, Vaughn Michael *software company executive*

Rosemont
Grosso, James Alan *information technology executive*

Schaumburg
Sikora, Sheryl L. *application developer*

Vernon Hills
Halitsky, Steve *application developer, researcher*
Klein, Barbara A. *information technology executive*
Leahy, Christine A. *information technology executive*

Woodridge
Puthenpurakal, Joseph Mathew *information technology executive*

INDIANA

Bloomington
Dunning, Jeremy David *application developer, dean, educator*

Indianapolis
Afshar, Nader *application developer*
Lowe, Mary Katherine *technology company executive, writer*
Niederberger, Jane *information technology executive*

Lowell
Elkins, Jeni L. McIntosh *webmaster*

Spencer
Young, Frederic Hisgin *information systems executive, data processing consultant*

IOWA

Waverly
Brunkhorst, Robert John *computer programmer, analyst*

KANSAS

Manhattan
Streeter, John Willis *information systems manager*

Overland Park
Leonard, Markus Dayle *software systems engineer*

Topeka
Freden, Sharon Elsie Christman *state education official*

MARYLAND

Annapolis
Hill, Kennard F. *computing systems company executive*

Baltimore
Park, Mary Woodfill *information consultant*

Bethesda
White, Jeannette Lee *information technology executive*

Columbia
Kendrick, John Lawrence *software engineer*

Gaithersburg
Hoferek, Mary Judith *information systems specialist, educator*
Yuan, Jian *network technician, researcher, engineering educator*

Hanover
Chiarella, Donald Joseph Gray *information systems specialist, educator*

Hyattsville
Asongu, Januarius Jingwa *information technology executive*
Bender, Howard Jeffrey *software engineering consultant*
Fortson-Rivers, Tina E. (Thomasena Elizabeth Fortson-Rivers) *information technology specialist*

Rockville
Gibson, William M. *technology company executive*
Nevin, Joseph Francis *computer systems engineer*

Suitland
Basinger, William Daniel *computer programmer*

Takoma Park
Meijer, Miriam Claude *information technology executive, historian*
Rice, Rick Blackburn *computer programmer, systems analyst*

MASSACHUSETTS

Beverly
Smith, Derek Armand *information technology executive*

Boston
Lane, Kathy S. *information technology executive, consumer products company executive*
Stallman, Richard Matthew *software developer*
White, Jan Tuttle (Mrs. Benjamin Winthrop White) *information technology executive*

Brockton
Jellows, Tracy Patrick *application developer*

Cambridge
Gagliardi, Ugo Oscar *systems software architect, educator*
Greenberg, Jerry A. *information technology executive*
Khakifirooz, Ali *information technology researcher*
Moore, J. Stuart *information technology executive*
Sterbenz, James Philip Guenther *computer network scientist*

Chicopee
Pace, Eston A. *systems administrator*

Duxbury
Zachmann, William Francis *computer and communications industry market research company executive*

Foxboro
Martin, Peter Gerard *marketing infosystems specialist, consultant, secondary school educator*

Gardner
Yablonski, Michael Edward *application developer*

Gloucester
Knupp, Ralph *information technology executive*

Needham
Reed, David Patrick *infosystems specialist*

Sudbury
McCree, Paul William, Jr., *systems design and engineering company executive*

Westford
Selesky, Donald Bryant *software developer*

MICHIGAN

Canton
Csaszar, Peter *software engineer*

Detroit
Stern, Myles Steven *information technology educator, consultant*

Flint
Bever, Timothy Michael *systems software engineer*

Grand Rapids
Becker, Robert Joseph *database consultant, computer science specialist, database software developer and educator*

Midland
Duncan, Christopher *information technology executive*

MINNESOTA

Eden Prairie
Borlik, Robert W. *information technology executive*

Minneapolis
Krause, Timothy Gilbert *web site manager*

MISSISSIPPI

Laurel
Ruth, Edward Keith *information systems specialist, management consultant*

MISSOURI

Hazelwood
Burleski, Joseph Anthony, Jr., *information technology executive*

Kansas City
Mazza-Deblauwe, Tania Sue *software engineer, technology educator*
Patterson, Neal L. *information systems company executive*

O Fallon
Raeuchle, John Steven *application developer*

Rolla
Datz, Israel Mortimer *information systems specialist*

Saint Louis
Elliott, Susan Spoehrer *information technology executive*
Ottinger, Maurice Armand *software engineer, educator*

NEVADA

Las Vegas
Komm, Kermit Matthew *software engineer*
Marcella, Joseph *information system administrator*
Mizer, Richard Anthony *technology company executive*

North Las Vegas
Folden, Norman C. (Skip Folden) *information systems executive, consultant*

Reno
Matthews, Thomas J. *game company executive*
Mullarkey, Maureen T. *game company executive*
Ragavan, Anpalaki Jeyabalasinkham *software developer, researcher*

NEW HAMPSHIRE

Franconia
Schaffer, David Edwin *retired management systems executive*

Nashua
Smith, Thomas Raymond, III, *software engineer*

New Hampton
Taylor, Kenneth Richard *information technology executive, consultant*

Weare
White, Karen Ruth Jones *information systems executive*

NEW JERSEY

Basking Ridge
Samuelson, Cynthia *information technology executive*

Cherry Hill
Schelm, Roger Leonard *information systems specialist*

Fairfield
Grant, Daniel Gordon *information services company executive*

Florham Park
Begeja, Lee *inventive researcher*

Hackettstown
Fremon, Richard C. *retired infosystems specialist*

Hoboken
Besser, Ronald *information technology educator*

Livingston
Burns, Edward Charles *infosystems specialist*

Madison
Shelby, Bryan Rohrer *information systems management consultant*

Morristown
Bockian, James Bernard *computer systems executive, writer*

Mount Laurel
Li, Pearl Nei-Chien Chu *technology company executive*

Murray Hill
Bruch, Ruth E. *information technology executive*
Ritchie, Dennis M. *software engineer*

Newark
Nash, Alicia *computer programmer, physicist*

Piscataway
Kenney, Mary R. *software engineer*
Kiddie, Thomas James *application developer, educator*

Rochelle Park
Olzerowicz, Sharon *information technology executive*

Roseland
Graham, Patricia *information technology executive*

Smithville
Bergeron, Robert Francis, Jr., (Terry Bergeron) *software engineer*

Somerset
Bess, Leon *application developer, consultant, systems analyst*
Lee, Thai Theresa *information technology executive*

South Orange
Long, Philip Lee *information systems executive*

Sparta
Guida, Pat *information broker, literature chemist*

Teaneck
Mahadeva, Kumar *information technology executive*

NEW MEXICO

Albuquerque
McBride, Teresa *information systems specialist*

Kirtland Afb
Anderson, Christine Marlene *software engineer*

Las Cruces
Kilmer, Neal Harold *application developer*

NEW YORK

Albany
Gaddy, Sheila Mae *application developer, geriatrics nurse, writer, volunteer*

Armonk
Gerstner, Louis Vincent, Jr., *retired information technology executive*
Harreld, James Bruce *information technology executive*

Ballston Lake
McCann, Chris (Christian David McCann) *application developer, educator*

Brooklyn
Davis, William Terry *software engineer, technology manager*
Doucette, David Robert *computer systems company executive*
Fowler, John Dale, Jr., *biotechnology management consultant, private equity investor*
Gilmore, Jennifer A.W. *computer specialist, educator*

Buffalo
Axlerod, Harvey Steven *application developer*

Cazenovia
Carlson, William Clifford *retired defense company executive, retired naval officer*

Corning
Flaws, James B. *technology executive*

Dundee
Pfendt, Henry George *retired information systems executive, management consultant*

East Amherst
Llop, Tobey Hooker *information technology executive*

East Setauket
Simons, James *technology company executive*

Glen Wild
Kaszas, William Joseph *technology educator*

Hicksville
Notaro, Anthony *application developer*
Yen, Henry Chin-Yuan *computer systems programmer, software engineer, consulting company executive*

Islandia
Cron, Kenneth D. *information technology executive*

Jamaica
Chropufka, Mark A. *information management specialist, poet*
Washington, William Thomas *technical manager, educator*

Johnstown
Prestopnik, Richard John *electronics and computer educator*

Larchmont
Wit, David Edmund *software company executive*

Maspeth
Heppa, Douglas Van *computer specialist*

Melville
Provenzano, Dominic *information specialist*
Settle, Mark *information technology executive*
Webber, Pamela D. *information technology executive*

New York
Burkhardt, Roger *information technology executive*
Garvin, Andrew Paul *information company executive, author, consultant*
Green-Dorsey, Jean Audrey *information technology executive*
Haddock, Robert Lynn *information services entrepreneur, writer*
Hedbring, Charles *computer consultant, writer*
Hopple, Richard Van Tromp, Jr., *internet media executive*
Kozik, Susan S. *information technology executive*
Mehlman, Lon Douglas *information technology specialist, investment banker, venture capitalist*
Morris, Stephen Burritt *marketing information executive*
O'Connor, Kevin *computer programing executive*
Powell, Timothy Wood *information executive, consultant*
Rodriguez, Julio *information technology executive*
Ross, Karen *information technology executive*
Waite, David Allen *software development executive*
Walsh, Annmarie Hauck *research firm executive*
Woods, Dan *information technology manager, consultant*
Wyn-Jones, Alun (William Wyn-Jones) *software developer, mathematician*

Owego
Zendle, Howard Mark *software development researcher*

Pittsford
Saini, Vasant Durgadas *computer software company executive*

Poughkeepsie
Bari, Paola *application developer*

Rochester
Ciolek, Nancy A. *information technology educator*
Georges, John Peter *information technology consultant*

Tarrytown
Kenney, Dion Patrick *information technology executive, entrepreneur*

Troy
Demertzoglou, Pindaro Epaminonda *systems administrator, education educator*

White Plains
Donofrio, Nick *information technology executive*
Horn, Paul M. *information technology executive, crystallographer*
Kelly, John E., III, *information technology executive*
MacDonald, J. Randall *information technology executive, human resources specialist*
Mills, Steven A. *information technology executive*
Moffat, Robert W., Jr., *information technology executive*
Palmisano, Samuel J. *information technology executive*
Williams, Edward W. *information technology executive*

Yorktown Heights
Winterton, Joseph Henry *computer software executive*

NORTH CAROLINA

Cary
Goodnight, James H. *software company executive*
Sall, John *information technology executive*

Chapel Hill
Smith, Janet Sue *systems specialist*

Charlotte
Maclean, Rhonda *information technology executive*

Cherokee
Parker, Joyce White *application developer, educator*

Raleigh
Szulik, Matthew J. *information technology executive*

Spindale
Odom, Kenneth James *information technology executive*

OHIO

Cincinnati
Fairobent, Douglas Kevin *computer programmer*
Govern, Maureen *information technology executive*

Cleveland
Gorney, John *information technology executive*

Columbus
Adams, Richard C. *information technology executive*
Brown, Rowland Chauncey Widrig *information systems, strategic planning and ethics consultant*
Taylor, Celianna Isley *information systems specialist*

Dayton
Siefert, David Michael *information technology executive, manufacturing executive*

Fairborn
Johansen, Mark Daniel *application developer*

Miamisburg
McLaughlin, Allan D. *information technology executive*

Upper Sandusky
Baker, Harrison Scott *computer consultant*

Westlake
Whitehouse, John Harlan, Jr., *systems software consultant, diagnostician*

Worthington
Trevor, Alexander Bruen *technology consultant*

OKLAHOMA

Ada
Baker, Judith Ann *retired computer technician*

Mustang
Laurent, Jerry Suzanna *technical communications specialist*

Norman
Chidambaram, Laku *information technology educator*

Tulsa
Davis, Lourie Irene Bell *computer education and information systems specialist*

OREGON

Beaverton
Cohen, Stuart F. *software development company executive*

Frei, Brent R. *computer software executive*
George, Stephan (Steve) Anthony *web site designer*
Goggin, John R. *software quality engineer*
Green, Thornton George *software engineer*
Gurspan, Mitchell Scott *technology architect, author*
Ha, Chong Wan *information technology executive*
Hans, Kamal Joseph *information technology executive, actor*
Hantman, Barry G. *software engineer*
Harris, Anthony Nathaniel *systems administrator*
Heck, Debra Upchurch *information technology, procurement professional*
Hudson, Carolyn Brauer *application developer, educator*
Hunter, Kenneth M. *business information systems educator*
Jaw, Andrew Chung-Shiang *software analyst*
Jennings, Kenneth W. *software engineer, All Time Jeopardy Champion*
Jones, Carleton Shaw *information systems company executive, lawyer*
Jones, Gwenyth Ellen *publishing information systems/technology executive*
Jordan, Michael Hugh *information technology executive*
Katragadda, Siddharth *application developer, writer*
Kelley, Mary Elizabeth (Mary LaGrone) *information technology executive*
Lau, Joanna T. *information technology executive*
Leven, Linda *application developer, writer, actress, model, artist*
Levy, Leslie Ann *application developer*
Mahmoud, Ahmed Mohamed *information technology executive*
Maruoka, Jo Ann Elizabeth *retired information systems manager*
Mbarika, Victor W. *information technology educator*
McCausland, Peter *technology company executive*
McConnell, Christopher F. *technology company administrator*
McMillan, Paul Jeffrey *application developer*
Mills, Kevin Lee *information technology researcher*
Minshall, Greg *computer programmer*
Morgan, M. Jane *computer systems consultant*
Morrison, Martin *computer systems analyst*
Mosher, Sue A. *computer consultant*
Mueller, Gary Alfred *software engineer*
Nason, Dolores Irene *computer company executive, social services administrator, eucharistic minister*
Nicols, Angela C. *software engineer, computer consultant*
Paolucci, Massimo *application developer, researcher*
Paul, Vivek *information technology executive*
Pelton, Walter Eugene *information technology executive, mathematician, physicist*
Person, Andrea Meredith *application developer*
Pierce, Charles Earl *software engineer, entrepreneur*
Ramirez, Edward Anthony *information technology manager*
Riccitiello, John S. *former interactive software/gaming executive, venture capitalist*
Roberts, George J. *information technology executive*
Roberts, Marie Dyer *retired computer systems specialist*
Rudnick, Ben *software professional, retail automotive executive*
Schneider, Sharon M. *systems administrator, information technologist*
Schramm, Geoffrey Saunders *webmaster*
Scott, Karen Elizabeth *information technology assistant*
Simmons, Scott Martin *information specialist*
Smith, Lyle Matthew *web producer, writer*
Spitzer, Craig M. *information technology executive*
Tarjan, Robert Wegg *retired information services executive, part-time math teacher*
Thomas, Donald Lee *construction technology educator*
Thompson, Kenneth *software engineer*
Treinavicz, Kathryn Mary *application developer*
Visocki, Nancy Gayle *information services consultant*
Yopconka, Natalie Ann Catherine *computer specialist, educator, business owner*
Zehring, Karen *information executive*

INTERNET *See* INFORMATION TECHNOLOGY

LAW: JUDICIAL ADMINISTRATION

UNITED STATES

ALABAMA

Albertville
Johnson, Clark Everette, Jr., *judge*

Ashland
Ingram, Kenneth Frank *retired state supreme court justice*

Birmingham
Acker, William Marsh, Jr., *federal judge*
Bennett, Thomas B. *federal judge*
Blackburn, Sharon Lovelace *federal judge*
Ferguson, Ralph Alton, Jr., (Sonny Ferguson) *circuit court judge*
Guin, Junius Foy, Jr., *federal judge*
Pointer, Sam Clyde, Jr., *retired federal judge, lawyer*

Fort Payne
Whitemire, Steve L. *judge*

Mobile
Butler, Charles Randolph, Jr., *federal judge*
Cox, Emmett Ripley *judge*
Howard, Alex T., Jr., *federal judge*
Milling, Bert William, Jr., *magistrate judge*
Pittman, Virgil *federal judge*

Montgomery
Black, Robert Coleman *judge, lawyer*
Brown, Jean Williams *state supreme court justice*
Carnes, Edward E. *federal judge*
De Ment, Ira *judge*
Dubina, Joel Fredrick *federal judge*
Godbold, John Cooper *judge*
Harwood, Robert Bernard, Jr., *state supreme court justice*
Hobbs, Truman McGill *federal judge*
Hooper, Perry Ollie *retired state supreme court judge*
Houston, James Gorman, Jr., *state supreme court justice*
Johnstone, Douglas Inge *state supreme court justice*
Lyons, Champ, Jr., *state supreme court justice*
Maddox, Alva Hugh *retired state supreme court justice*
McPherson, Vanzetta Penn *magistrate judge*
See, Harold Frend *judge, law educator*
Steele, Rodney Redfearn *judge*
Stuart, Lyn (Jacquelyn L. Stuart) *judge*
Thompson, Myron H. *federal judge*
Woodall, Thomas A. *state supreme court justice*

Tuscaloosa
England, John Henry, Jr., *judge*

ALASKA

Anchorage
Branson, Albert Harold (Harry Branson) *judge, educator*
Bryner, Alexander O. *state supreme court chief justice*
Eastaugh, Robert L. *state supreme court justice*
Fabe, Dana Anderson *state supreme court justice*
Singleton, James Keith *federal judge*
von der Heydt, James Arnold *federal judge*

Fairbanks
Kleinfeld, Andrew J. *federal judge*

Juneau
Carpeneti, Walter L. *judge*

ARIZONA

Phoenix
Anderson, Lawrence Ohaco *magistrate judge, lawyer*
Broomfield, Robert Cameron *federal judge*
Canby, William Cameron, Jr., *judge*
Carroll, Earl Hamblin *federal judge*
Gaines, Francis Pendleton, III, *judge*
Hurwitz, Andrew D. *judge*
Jones, Charles E. *chief justice supreme court*
Martone, Frederick J. *judge*
Mathis, Virginia *federal judge*
McClennen, Crane *judge*
McGregor, Ruth Van Roekel *state supreme court justice*
McNamee, Stephen M. *federal judge*
Myers, Robert David *judge*
Rosenblatt, Paul Gerhardt *judge*
Ryan, Michael D. *state supreme court justice*
Schroeder, Mary Murphy *federal judge*
Silver, Roslyn Olson *federal judge*
Silverman, Barry G. *federal judge*
Strand, Roger Gordon *federal judge*
Weisenburger, Theodore Maurice *retired judge, poet, educator, writer*
Winthrop, Lawrence Fredrick *judge*

Springerville
Geisler, Sherry Lynn *magistrate*

Tucson
Brammer, J. William, Jr., *judge, lawyer*
Browning, William Docker *federal judge*
Lacagnina, Michael Anthony *judge*
Marquez, Alfredo C. *federal judge*
Roll, John McCarthy *judge*
Zlaket, Thomas Andrew *attorney, former state supreme court chief justice*

ARKANSAS

Batesville
Harkey, John Norman *judge*

Conway
Hays, Steele *retired state supreme court judge*

El Dorado
Barnes, Harry Francis *federal judge*

Fayetteville
Hendren, Jimm Larry *federal judge*
Smith, Lavenski R. (Vence Smith) *federal judge*
Waters, H. Franklin *federal judge*

Little Rock
Arnold, Morris Sheppard *judge*
Arnold, Richard Sheppard *federal judge*
Corbin, Donald L. *state supreme court justice*
Dickey, Betty C. *judge*
Glaze, Thomas A. *state supreme court justice*
Hannah, Jim *state supreme court justice*
Imber, Annabelle Clinton *state supreme court justice*
Reasoner, Stephen M. *federal judge*
Roaf, Andree Layton *judge*
Stroud, John Fred, Jr., *judge*
Thornton, Ray *state supreme court justice, former congressman*
Wilson, William R., Jr., *judge*
Wright, Susan Webber *judge*

CALIFORNIA

Alameda
Bartalini, C. Richard *judge*

Chatsworth
Schwab, Howard Joel *judge*

Fresno
Coyle, Robert Everett *federal judge*
Wanger, Oliver Winston *federal judge*

Glendale
Early, Alexander Rieman, III, *judge*

Irvine
Curtis, Jesse William, Jr., *retired federal judge*

Long Beach
Tucker, Marcus Othello *judge*

Los Angeles
Alarcon, Arthur Lawrence *federal judge*
Armstrong, Orville *judge*
Baird, Lourdes G. *federal judge*
Bufford, Samuel Lawrence *federal judge*
Carroll, Ellen A. *judge, lawyer*
Chapman, Rosalyn M. *federal judge*
Chavez, Victor Edwin *judge*
Collins, Audrey B. *judge*
Curry, Daniel Arthur *judge*
Fischer, Dale Susan *judge*
Fleming, Macklin *judge, author*
Highberger, William Foster *lawyer*
Ito, Lance Allan *judge*
Johnson, Earl, Jr., *judge, author*
Kelleher, Robert Joseph *judge*
Manella, Nora M. *federal judge*
March, Kathleen Patricia *judge*
Marshall, Consuelo Bland *federal judge*
Mosk, Richard Mitchell *judge*
Norris, William Albert *retired judge*
Pfaelzer, Mariana R. *federal judge*
Rafeedie, Edward *senior federal judge*
Takasugi, Robert Mitsuhiro *federal judge*
Tevrizian, Dickran M., Jr., *judge*
Yager, Thomas C. *retired judge*

Mendocino
Masterson, William A. *retired judge*

Oakland
Armstrong, Saundra Brown *federal judge*
Jensen, D. Lowell *federal judge, lawyer, government official*
Newsome, Randall Jackson *judge*
Tchaikovsky, Leslie J. *federal judge*
Wilken, Claudia *judge*

Panorama City
Chen, Edward M. *judge*

Pasadena
Boochever, Robert *judge*
Fernandez, Ferdinand Francis *federal judge*
Fisher, Raymond Corley *judge*
Goodwin, Alfred Theodore *federal judge*
Hall, Cynthia Holcomb *federal judge*
Johnson, Barbara Jean *retired judge, lawyer*
Kozinski, Alex *federal judge*
Nelson, Dorothy Wright (Mrs. James F. Nelson) *federal judge*
Paez, Richard A. *federal judge*
Rymer, Pamela Ann *federal judge*
Tashima, Atsushi Wallace *federal judge*

Pauma Valley
Lewis, Gerald Jorgensen *judge*

Riverside
Holmes, Dallas Scott *judge, educator*
Phillips, Virginia A. *judge*
Timlin, Robert J. *judge*

Sacramento
Karlton, Lawrence K. *federal judge*
Levi, David F. *federal judge*
Schwartz, Milton Lewis *federal judge*
Van Camp, Brian Ralph *judge*

San Diego
Aaron, Cynthia G. *judge*
Bowie, Peter Wentworth *judge, educator*
Brewster, Rudi Milton *judge*
Burns, Larry Alan *judge*
Gonzalez, Irma Elsa *federal judge*
Harutunian, Albert T(heodore), III, *judge*
Huff, Marilyn L. *federal judge*
Jones, Napoleon A., Jr., *judge*
Keep, Judith N. *federal judge*
McKeown, Mary Margaret *federal judge*
Porter, Louisa S. *federal judge*
Rhoades, John Skylstead, Sr., *federal judge*
Thompson, David Renwick *federal judge*
Thompson, Gordon, Jr., *federal judge*
Turrentine, Howard Boyd *federal judge*
Wallace, J. Clifford *federal judge*

San Francisco
Baxter, Marvin Ray *state supreme court justice*
Bea, Carlos Tiburcio *federal judge*
Berzon, Marsha S. *federal judge*
Breall, Susan *judge*
Brown, Janice Rogers *state supreme court justice*
Browning, James Robert *federal judge*
Bybee, Jay Scott *federal judge, federal agency administrator*
Callahan, Consuelo Maria *federal judge*
Chesney, Maxine M. *judge*
Chin, Ming *state supreme court justice*
Conti, Samuel *federal judge*
Fletcher, William A. *federal judge, law educator*
George, Ronald M. *state supreme court chief justice*
Graber, Susan P. *federal judge*
Haerle, Paul Raymond *judge*
Illston, Susan Y. *federal judge*
James, Maria-Elena *federal judge*
Jarvis, Donald Bertram *judge*
Kennard, Joyce L. *judge*
Kolkey, Daniel Miles *former judge, lawyer*
Moreno, Carlos R. *state supreme court justice*
Noonan, John T., Jr., *federal judge, law educator*
Patel, Marilyn Hall *judge*
Robertson, Armand James, II, *judge*
Schwarzer, William W *federal judge*
Sneed, Joseph Tyree, III, *federal judge*
Walker, Vaughn R. *federal judge*
Wardlaw, Kim A.M. *federal judge*
Werdegar, Kathryn Mickle *state supreme court justice*
Zimmerman, Bernard *judge*

San Jose
Maloney, Patrick Raymond *retired judge*
Morgan, Marilyn *federal judge*
Stewart, Melinda Jane *judge*
Whyte, Ronald M. *judge*

San Marino
Mortimer, Wendell Reed, Jr., *judge*

Santa Ana
Barr, James Norman *federal judge*
Ferguson, Warren John *federal judge*
Stotler, Alicemarie Huber *federal judge*

Santa Barbara
Aldisert, Ruggero John *judge*

Santa Monica
Vega, Benjamin Urbizo *retired judge, television producer*

Sonoma
Herron, Ellen Patricia *retired judge*

Studio City
Gold, Arnold Henry *judge*

Woodland Hills
Lax, Kathleen Thompson *judge*
Mund, Geraldine *judge*
Pregerson, Harry *federal judge*

COLORADO

Denver
Abram, Donald Eugene *retired federal judge*
Bender, Michael Lee *judge*
Coan, Patricia A. *magistrate judge*
Coats, Nathan B. *state supreme court justice*
Ebel, David M. *federal judge*
Felter, Edwin Lester, Jr., *judge*
Figa, Phillip Sam *judge*
Hobbs, Gregory James, Jr., *state supreme court justice*
Kane, John Lawrence, Jr., *judge*
Keithley, Roger Lee *judge*
Kirshbaum, Howard M. *retired judge, arbiter*
Krieger, Marcia Smith *federal judge*
Lucero, Carlos *federal judge*
Martinez, Alex J. *state supreme court justice*
McWilliams, Robert Hugh *federal judge*
Miller, Walker David *judge*
Mullarkey, Mary J. *state supreme court chief justice*
Nottingham, Edward Willis, Jr., *federal judge*
Porfilio, John Carbone *federal judge*
Rice, Nancy E. *judge*
Rovira, Luis Dario *state supreme court justice*
Satter, Raymond Nathan *judge*
Swihart, Steven Taylor *judge*
Tymkovich, Timothy Michael *federal judge*
Weinshienk, Zita Leeson *federal judge*

Englewood
Erickson, William Hurt *retired state supreme court justice*

Fort Collins
Gandy, H. Conway *retired judge, state official*

Golden
Rodgers, Frederic Barker *judge*
Scott, Gregory Kellam *judge trial referee, former state supreme court justice, lawyer*

Hotchkiss
Ela, William MacHarg *judge, mediator, arbitrator*

Leadville
Watson, Jack Crozier *retired state supreme court justice*

CONNECTICUT

Bridgeport
Eginton, Warren William *federal judge*

Danbury
Yamin, Dianne Elizabeth *judge*

Guilford
Ross, Michael Frederick *magistrate, lawyer*

Hartford
Bieluch, William Charles *judge*
Borden, David M. *state supreme court justice*
Chatigny, Robert Neil *judge*
Droney, Christopher F. *judge*
Dupont, Antoinette Loiacono *judge*
Katz, Joette *state supreme court justice*
Killian, Robert Kenneth, Jr., *judge, lawyer*
Martinez, Donna F. *federal judge*
Newman, Jon O. *federal judge*
Norcott, Flemming L., Jr., *state supreme court justice*
Palmer, Richard N. *state supreme court justice*
Peters, Ellen Ash *judge, retired Supreme Court chief justice*
Schaller, Barry R. *judge*
Shea, David Michael *state supreme court justice*
Squatrito, Dominic J. *judge*
Sullivan, William J. *state supreme court justice*
Thompson, Alvin W. *judge*
Vertefeuille, Christine Siegrist *judge*
Wright, Douglass Brownell *retired judge, lawyer*
Zarella, Peter T. *state supreme court justice*

Milford
Upson, Thomas Fisher *judge, former state senator, lawyer*

New Britain
Meskill, Thomas J. *federal judge*

New Haven
Arterton, Janet Bond *federal judge*

Berdon, Robert Irwin *judge trial referee, retired state supreme court justice*
Burns, Ellen Bree *federal judge*
Cabranes, José Alberto *judge*
Calabresi, Guido *federal judge, law educator*
Dorsey, Peter Collins *federal judge*
Walker, John Mercer, Jr., *federal judge*
Winter, Ralph Karl, Jr., *federal judge*

New London
Santaniello, Angelo Gary *retired state supreme court justice*

Oxford
Marano, Richard Michael *judge*

Stamford
Callahan, Robert Jeremiah *retired judge, mediator*

Vernon Rockville
Purnell, Oliver James, III, *judge*

Waterbury
Goettel, Gerard Louis *federal judge*
McDonald, Francis Michael *judge trial referee, retired state supreme court justice*

DELAWARE

Dover
Steele, Myron Thomas *state supreme court chief justice*

Georgetown
Holland, Randy James *state supreme court justice*

Wilmington
Ambro, Thomas L. *federal judge*
Berger, Carolyn *state supreme court justice*
Jacobs, Jack Bernard *judge*
Latchum, James Levin *federal judge*
Robinson, Sue L(ewis) *federal judge*
Roth, Jane Richards *federal judge*
Schwartz, Murray Merle *federal judge*
Stapleton, Walter King *federal judge*

DISTRICT OF COLUMBIA

Washington
Archer, Glenn LeRoy, Jr., *federal judge*
Bacon, Sylvia *judge, law educator*
Bartnoff, Judith *judge*
Baskir, Lawrence M. *chief judge*
Bayly, John Henry, Jr., *judge*
Beghe, Renato *federal judge*
Belson, James Anthony *judge*
Berkley, Burton *federal judge*
Braden, Susan Gertrude *federal judge, lawyer, consultant*
Breyer, Stephen Gerald *United States supreme court justice*
Bryson, William Curtis *federal judge*
Burnett, Arthur Louis, Sr., *judge*
Chabot, Herbert L. *judge*
Chiechi, Carolyn Phyllis *federal judge*
Clevenger, Raymond Charles, III, *federal judge*
Cohen, Mary Ann *judge*
Couvillion, David Irvin *federal judge*
Cowen, Arnold Wilson *retired federal judge*
Crawford, Susan Jean *federal judge*
Dawson, Howard Athalone, Jr., *federal judge*
Edwards, Harry T. *federal judge*
Effron, Andrew S. *federal judge*
Farrell, Michael W. *state supreme court justice*
Ferren, John Maxwell *judge*
Flannery, Thomas Aquinas *federal judge*
Foley, Maurice Brian *federal judge*
Friedman, Daniel Mortimer *federal judge*
Gajarsa, Arthur J. *circuit court judge*
Gale, Joseph H. *federal judge*
Gallagher, George R. *retired judge*
Garland, Merrick Brian *federal judge*
Gerber, Joel *federal judge*
Gibson, Reginald Walker *federal judge*
Ginsburg, Douglas Howard *federal judge*
Ginsburg, Ruth Bader *United States Supreme Court justice*
Glickman, Stephen *state supreme court justice*
Goldberg, Stanley Joshua *federal judge*
Gonzales, Alberto R. *federal official, former state supreme court justice, former secretary of state*
Goodrich, George Herbert *judge*
Green, Joyce Hens *federal judge*
Henderson, Karen LeCraft *federal judge*
Hewitt, Emily Clark *judge, minister*
Holdaway, Ronald M. *retired federal judge*
Horn, Marian Blank *federal judge*
Ivers, Donald Louis *judge*
Jackson, Thomas Penfield *federal judge*
Jacobs, Julian I. *federal judge*
Kennedy, Anthony McLeod *United States supreme court justice*
Kessler, Gladys *federal judge*
King, Warren R. *judge*
Kline, Norman Douglas *federal judge*
Kollar-Kotelly, Colleen *federal judge*
Kramer, Kenneth Bentley *federal judge, former congressman*
Kroupa, Diane Lynn *federal judge*
Laro, David *judge*
Leon, Richard J. *federal judge*
Liberty, Arthur Andrew *judge*
Lourie, Alan David *federal judge*
Mack, Julia Cooper *retired judge*
Margolis, Lawrence Stanley *federal judge*
Marvel, L. Paige *judge*
Mayer, Haldane Robert *federal chief judge*
McGranery, Regina C. *judge*
Mencher, Bruce Stephan *judge*
Merow, James F. *federal judge*
Michel, Paul Redmond *federal judge*
Miller, Christine Odell Cook *judge*
Newman, Pauline *federal judge*
Oberdorfer, Louis F. *federal judge*
O'Connor, Sandra Day *United States Supreme Court Justice*
Parr, Carolyn Miller *federal judge*
Plager, S. Jay *judge*
Prost, Sharon *federal judge*
Queen, Evelyn E. Crawford *retired judge*
Rader, Randall Ray *federal judge*
Randolph, A(rthur) Raymond *federal judge*
Rehnquist, William Hubbs *United States supreme court chief justice*
Roberts, John Glover, Jr., *federal judge*
Robertson, James *judge*
Rogers, Judith W. *federal judge*
Rothstein, Barbara Jacobs *federal judge*
Ruiz, Vanessa *federal judge*
Ruwe, Robert P. *federal judge*
Scalia, Antonin *judge*
Schall, Alvin Anthony *federal judge*
Schwelb, Frank Ernest *appellate judge*
Sentelle, David Bryan *federal judge*
Simpson, Charles Reagan *retired judge*
Smith, Loren Allan *federal judge*
Smith, Roy Philip *judge*
Steadman, John Montague *appellate court judge*
Steinberg, Jonathan Robert *judge*
Stevens, John Paul *judge*
Sullivan, Eugene Raymond *judge*
Swift, Stephen Jensen *federal judge*
Sypolt, Diane Gilbert *federal judge*
Tatel, David Stephen *federal judge*
Terry, John Alfred *state supreme court judge*
Thomas, Clarence *United States supreme court justice*
Thornton, Michael B. *federal judge*
Turner, James Thomas *judge*
Urbina, Ricardo Manuel *judge*
Wagner, Annice McBryde *judge*
Wagner, Curtis Lee, Jr., *judge*
Wald, Patricia McGowan *retired federal judge*
Walton, Reggie Barnett *judge*
Washington, Eric T. *state supreme court justice*
Wells, Thomas B. *federal judge*
Williams, Mary Ellen Coster *judge*
Williams, Stephen Fain *federal judge*
Yoder, Ronnie A. *judge*

FLORIDA

Boca Raton
Bernstein, Edwin S. *judge*

Daytona Beach
Palmer, William D. *judge*

Deland
Sanders, Edwin Perry Bartley *judge*

Destin
Robinson, Wilkes Coleman *retired federal judge*

Fort Lauderdale
Gonzalez, Jose Alejandro, Jr., *federal judge*
Ray, Raymond B. *federal judge*
Seltzer, Barry S. *federal judge*
Zloch, William J. *federal judge*

Fort Myers
Schoonover, Jack Ronald *retired judge*
Shafer, Robert Tinsley, Jr., *judge*

Jacksonville
Black, Susan Harrell *federal judge*
Gooding, David Michael *judge*
Hill, James Clinkscales *federal judge*
Melton, Howell Webster, Sr., *federal judge*
Schlesinger, Harvey Erwin *judge*
Tjoflat, Gerald Bard *federal judge*

Longboat Key
Morse, Marvin Henry *retired judge*

Merritt Island
Johnson, Clarence Traylor, Jr., *state judge*

Miami
Barkett, Rosemary *federal judge*
Blake, Stanford *judge*
Davis, Edward Bertrand *retired federal judge, lawyer*
Friedman, Ronald Michael *judge*
Graham, Donald Lynn *federal judge*
Highsmith, Shelby *federal judge*
King, James Lawrence *federal judge*
Marcus, Stanley *federal judge*
Rosinek, Jeffrey *judge*
Seitz, Patricia Ann *federal judge*
Shevin, Robert Lewis *judge*
Siegel, Paul *judge*
Sorrentino, Charlene H. *federal judge*
Ungaro-Benages, Ursula Mancusi *federal judge*
Wilson, Thomas Strong, Jr., (Tam Wilson) *judge*

Naples
Gindin, William Howard *retired judge*

North Palm Beach
Siegendorf, Arden M. *judge*

Orlando
Conway, Anne Callaghan *federal judge*
Fawsett, Patricia Combs *federal judge*
Glazebrook, James Grinstead *judge*
Jennemann, Karen Sue *judge*
Thorpe, Janet Claire *judge*
Young, George Cressler *federal judge*

Saint Petersburg
Grube, Karl Bertram *judge*
Roney, Paul H(itch) *federal judge*

Tallahassee
Anstead, Harry Lee *state supreme court justice*
Bell, Kenneth B. *judge*
Cantero, Raoul G., III, *judge*
Grimes, Stephen Henry *retired state supreme court justice*
Harding, Major Best *former state supreme court chief justice*
Lewis, R. Fred *judge*
McCord, Guyte Pierce, Jr., *retired judge*
Pariente, Barbara J. *state supreme court chief justice*
Quince, Peggy A. *state supreme court justice*
Webster, Peter David *judge*
Wells, Charles Talley *state supreme court justice*

Tampa
Baynes, Thomas Edward, Jr., *judge, lawyer, educator*
Bucklew, Susan Cawthon *federal judge*
Dail, Joseph Garner, Jr., *judge*
Glenn, Paul M. *federal judge*
Jenkins, Elizabeth Ann *federal judge*
Kovachevich, Elizabeth Anne *judge*
Wilson, Charles Reginald *federal judge*

Viera
Rainwater, Tonya B. *judge*

West Palm Beach
Ryskamp, Kenneth Lee *federal judge*
Wroble, Arthur Gerard *judge*

Winter Park
Graham, Bruce Joseph *retired judge*

GEORGIA

Atlanta
Benham, Robert *state supreme court justice*
Bihary, Joyce *federal judge*
Birch, Stanley Francis, Jr., *federal judge*
Camp, Jack Tarpley, Jr., *judge*
Carley, George H. *judge*
Carnes, Julie Elizabeth *judge*
Deane, Richard Hunter, Jr., *lawyer, former federal judge*
Duffey, William Simon, Jr., *federal judge, lawyer*
Edmondson, James Larry *federal judge*
Evans, Orinda D. *federal judge*
Feldman, Joel Martin *magistrate judge*
Fletcher, Norman S. *state supreme court justice*
Forrester, J. Owen *federal judge*
Hatchett, Glenda A. *municipal judge*
Hines, Preston Harris *state supreme court justice*
Hull, Frank Mays *federal judge*
Hunstein, Carol *state supreme court justice*
Kravitch, Phyllis A. *federal judge*
Martin, Beverly *federal judge*
Murphy, Margaret Hackett *US bankruptcy judge*
O'Kelley, William Clark *federal judge*
Pryor, William Holcombe, Jr., *federal judge, former state attorney general*
Sears, Leah J. *state supreme court justice*
Thompson, Hugh P. *state supreme court justice*
Ward, Horace Taliaferro *federal judge*

Augusta
Bowen, Dudley Hollingsworth, Jr., *federal judge*

Brunswick
Alaimo, Anthony A. *federal judge*

Columbus
Laney, John Thomas, III, *federal judge*

Jeffersonville
Fitzpatrick, Duross *federal judge*

Lawrenceville
Iannazzone, Joseph Charles *judge*
Reeves, Gene *judge*

Macon
Anderson, Robert Lanier, III, *federal judge*
Hershner, Robert Franklin, Jr., *judge*
Owens, Wilbur Dawson, Jr., *federal judge*
Phillips, J(ohn) Taylor *judge*

Marietta
Smith, George Thornewell *retired state supreme court justice*

Newnan
Drake, W. Homer, Jr., *federal judge*

Rome
Murphy, Harold Loyd *federal judge*

Savannah
Edenfield, Berry Avant *federal judge*
Moore, William Theodore, Jr., *judge*

HAWAII

Honolulu
Acoba, Simeon Rivera, Jr., *state supreme court justice, educator*
Clifton, Richard Randall *federal judge*
Gillmor, Helen *federal judge*
Heen, Walter Meheula *retired judge, former political party executive*
Levinson, Steven Henry *state supreme court justice*
Moon, Ronald T. Y. *state supreme court chief justice*
Nakayama, Paula Aiko *state supreme court justice*
Watanabe, Corinne Kaoru Amemiya *judge, state official, lawyer*

IDAHO

Boise
Eismann, Daniel T. *state supreme court justice*
Kidwell, Wayne L. *state supreme court justice*
Lodge, Edward James *federal judge*
McDevitt, Charles Francis *retired state supreme court justice, lawyer*
Nelson, Thomas G. *federal judge*
Trott, Stephen Spangler *federal judge, musician*
Walters, Jesse Raymond, Jr., *state supreme court justice*
Winmill, B. Lynn *judge*

Idaho Falls
Shindurling, Jon J. *judge*

Twin Falls
Hohnhorst, John Charles *judge*

ILLINOIS

Barrington
Wynn, Thomas Joseph *judge, educator*

Benton
Foreman, James Louis *retired judge*
Gilbert, J. Phil *federal judge*

Chicago
Alesia, James H(enry) *judge*
Ashman, Martin C. *federal judge*
Aspen, Marvin Edward *federal judge*
Bauer, William Joseph *federal judge*
Bucklo, Elaine Edwards *United States district court judge*
Conlon, Suzanne B. *federal judge*
Cudahy, Richard D. *judge*
Easterbrook, Frank Hoover Hoover *federal judge*
Fairchild, Thomas E. *federal judge*
Fitzgerald, Thomas Robert *judge*
Flaum, Joel Martin *chief judge*
Funderburk, Raymond *judge*
Gottschall, Joan B. *judge*
Grady, John F. *federal judge*
Hart, William Thomas *federal judge*
Johnson, Glenn Thompson *retired judge*
Jones, Dorothy F. *judge*
Leighton, George Neves *retired federal judge*
Leinenweber, Harry D. *federal judge*
Manning, Blanche M. *federal judge*
Markey, Howard Thomas *retired law educator, former federal judge*
McMorrow, Mary Ann G. *state supreme court chief justice*
Miller, Benjamin K. *retired state supreme court justice*
Moran, James Byron *federal judge*
Nordberg, John Albert *federal judge*
Norgle, Charles Ronald, Sr., *federal judge*
Pallmeyer, Rebecca Ruth *judge*
Posner, Richard Allen *judge*
Rovner, Ilana Kara Diamond *federal judge*
Schmetterer, Jack Baer *federal judge*
Shadur, Milton Irving *judge*
Sonderby, Susan Pierson *federal judge*
Squires, John Henry *judge*
Sykes, Diane S. *federal judge, former state supreme court justice*
Williams, Ann Claire *federal judge*
Zagel, James Block *federal judge*

Danville
Garman, Rita B. *judge*

Downers Grove
McGarr, Frank James *retired federal judge, dispute resolution consultant*

East Saint Louis
Stiehl, William D. *federal judge*

Glenview
Tristano, Sandra *circuit court judge*

Homewood
Dietch, Henry Xerxes *judge*

Maple Park
Nickels, John L. *retired state supreme court justice*

Peoria
Heiple, James Dee *retired state supreme court justice*
Mihm, Michael Martin *federal judge*

Petersburg
Wood, Harlington, Jr., *federal judge*

Pontiac
Glennon, Charles Edward *retired judge, lawyer*

Rockford
Reinhard, Philip G. *federal judge*

Rolling Meadows
Roti, Thomas David *judge*

Springfield
Evans, Charles H. *federal judge*
Gramlich, Charles J. *judge*
Mills, Richard Henry *federal judge*
Rarick, Philip Joseph *judge*

Taylorville
Spears, Ronald Dean *judge*

Waukegan
Brady, Terrence Joseph *judge*

Wheaton
Leston, Patrick John *judge*
Thomas, Robert R. *state supreme court justice*

INDIANA

Boonville
Campbell, Edward Adolph *judge, electrical engineer*

Crown Point
Dywan, Jeffery Joseph *judge*

Evansville
Capshaw, Tommie Dean *judge*

Fort Wayne
Lee, William Charles *judge*

Indianapolis
Barker, Sarah Evans *judge*
Boehm, Theodore Reed *judge*
Dickson, Brent E(llis) *state supreme court justice*
Dillin, S. Hugh *federal judge*
Foster, Kennard P. *magistrate judge*
Givan, Richard Martin *retired judge*
Hamilton, David F. *judge*
McKinney, Larry J. *federal judge*
Metz, Anthony J., III, *federal judge*
Rucker, Robert D. *state supreme court justice*
Shepard, Randall Terry *state supreme court chief justice*

Shields, V. Sue *federal magistrate judge*
Sullivan, Frank, Jr., *state supreme court justice*

Kokomo
Stein, Eleanor Bankoff *judge*

Lafayette
Kanne, Michael Stephen *federal judge*

Lagrange
Brown, George E. *judge, educator*

South Bend
Manion, Daniel Anthony *federal judge*
Ripple, Kenneth Francis *federal judge*
Rodibaugh, Robert Kurtz *retired judge*
Sharp, Allen *federal judge*

IOWA

Algona
Andreasen, James Hallis *retired state supreme court judge*

Cedar Rapids
Hansen, David Rasmussen *federal judge*
Mc Manus, Edward Joseph *federal judge*
Melloy, Michael J. *federal judge*

Chariton
Stuart, William Corwin *judge*

Council Bluffs
Peterson, Richard William *retired judge, lawyer*

Des Moines
Bremer, Celeste F. *judge*
Carter, James H. *judge*
Colloton, Steven M. *federal judge*
Fagg, George Gardner *federal judge*
Harris, K. David *senior state supreme court justice*
Larson, Jerry Leroy *state supreme court justice*
Lavorato, Louis A. *state supreme court chief justice*
McGiverin, Arthur A. *former state supreme court chief justice*
Streit, Michael J. *state supreme court justice*
Ternus, Marsha K. *state supreme court justice*
Vietor, Harold Duane *federal judge*
Walters, Ross A. *federal judge*
Wolle, Charles Robert *judge*

Fort Dodge
Cady, Mark S. *state supreme court justice*

Ida Grove
Snell, Bruce M., Jr., *retired judge*

Osceola
Reynoldson, Walter Ward *retired judge, lawyer*

Sioux City
O'Brien, Donald Eugene *federal judge*

KANSAS

Kansas City
Lungstrum, John W. *federal judge*
VanBebber, George Thomas *federal judge*
Vratil, Kathryn Hoefer *federal judge*

Lawrence
Briscoe, Mary Beck *federal judge*
Six, Fred N. *retired state supreme court justice*

Topeka
Allegrucci, Donald Lee *state supreme court justice*
Cox, Joseph Lawrence *judge*
Crow, Sam Alfred *judge*
Davis, Robert Edward *state supreme court justice*
Gernon, Robert L. *judge*
Larson, Edward *retired state supreme court justice*
Luckert, Marla Jo *state supreme court justice*
Marquardt, Christel Elisabeth *judge*
McFarland, Kay Eleanor *state supreme court chief justice*
Nuss, Lawton R. *judge*
Robinson, Julie Ann *judge*
Rogers, Richard Dean *federal judge*

Wichita
Brown, Wesley Ernest *federal judge*

KENTUCKY

Bowling Green
Huddleston, Joseph Russell *judge*

Elizabethtown
Cooper, William S. *state supreme court justice*

Frankfort
Johnstone, Martin E. *state supreme court justice*
Lambert, Joseph Earl *state supreme court chief justice*
Wintersheimer, Donald Carl *state supreme court justice*

Lexington
Coffman, Jennifer Burcham *judge*
Forester, Karl S. *chief district court judge*
Keller, James *state supreme court justice*
Varellas, Sandra Motte *judge*

London
Siler, Eugene Edward, Jr., *federal judge*

Louisville
Boggs, Danny Julian *federal judge*
Heyburn, John Gilpin, II, *federal judge*
Martin, Boyce Ficklen, Jr., *federal judge*
Simpson, Charles R., III, *judge*
Strause, Randall Scott *judge*

Madisonville
Spain, Thomas B. *retired state supreme court justice*

Murray
Buckingham, David Cowan *judge*

Newport
Wehr, William James *judge*

Paducah
Graves, John William *state supreme court justice*
King, W. David *magistrate judge*

Prestonsburg
Stumbo, Janet Lynn *state supreme court justice*

Richmond
Chenault, James Stouffer *judge*

Wickliffe
Shadoan, William Lewis *judge*

LOUISIANA

Baton Rouge
Cole, Luther Francis *former state supreme court associate justice*
Noland, Christine A. *magistrate judge*
Parker, John Victor *federal judge*
Polozola, Frank Joseph *federal judge*
Riedlinger, Stephen C. *federal judge*

Lafayette
Davis, William Eugene *judge*
Duhe, John Malcolm, Jr., *federal judge*

Lake Charles
Trimble, James T., Jr., *federal judge*

Metairie
Schwartz, Charles, Jr., *federal judge*

New Orleans
Beer, Peter Hill *federal judge*
Berrigan, Helen Ginger *federal judge*
Brown, Jerry A. *federal bankruptcy judge*
Calogero, Pascal Frank, Jr., *judge*
Clement, Edith Brown *federal judge*
Dennis, James Leon *federal judge*
Duplantier, Adrian Guy *federal judge*
Duval, Stanwood Richardson, Jr., *judge*
Feldman, Martin L. C. *federal judge*
Johnson, Bernette J. *state supreme court justice*
Kimball, Catherine D. *state supreme court justice*
Knoll, Jeannette Theriot *state supreme court justice*
Livaudais, Marcel, Jr., *federal judge*
Mentz, Henry Alvan, Jr., *federal judge*
Pickering, Charles W., Sr., *federal judge*
Porteous, G. Thomas, Jr., *judge*
Sear, Morey Leonard *federal judge, educator*
Traylor, Chet D. *state supreme court justice*
Victory, Jeffrey Paul *state supreme court justice*
Weimer, John L. *state supreme court justice*
Wiener, Jacques Loeb, Jr., *judge*

Ponchatoula
Kuhn, James E. *judge*

Shreveport
Payne, Roy Steven *judge*
Stagg, Tom *federal judge*
Stewart, Carl E. *federal judge*

MAINE

Auburn
Clifford, Robert William *state supreme court justice*

Augusta
Calkins, Susan W. *state supreme court justice*
Dana, Howard H., Jr., *state supreme court justice*

Bangor
Rudman, Paul Lewis *judge*

Portland
Alexander, Donald G. *state supreme court justice*
Bradford, Carl O. *judge*
Carter, Gene *judge*
Coffin, Frank Morey *judge*
Glassman, Caroline Duby *state supreme court justice*
Hornby, David Brock *federal judge*
Lipez, Kermit V. *federal judge, former state supreme court justice*
McKusick, Vincent Lee *former state supreme court chief justice, lawyer, arbitrator, mediator*
Saufley, Leigh Ingalls *judge*
Wathen, Daniel Everett *former state supreme court chief justice*

Rockland
Collins, Samuel W., Jr., *judge*

MARYLAND

Accokeek
Beddow, Richard Harold *retired judge*

Annapolis
Battaglia, Lynne Ann *judge*
Cathell, Dale Roberts *judge*
Eldridge, John Cole *judge*

Baltimore
Bell, Robert M. *state supreme court justice*
Black, Walter Evan, Jr., *federal judge*
Blake, Catherine C. *judge*
Bredar, James Kelleher *judge*
Davis, Andre Maurice *judge, educator*
Derby, Ernest Stephen *federal judge*
Garbis, Marvin Joseph *judge*
Harvey, Alexander, II, *federal judge*
Holt-Stone, C. Yvonne *judge*
Karwacki, Robert Lee *former judge*
Legg, Benson Everett *federal judge*
Motz, Diana Gribbon *judge*
Motz, John Frederick *federal judge*
Niemeyer, Paul Victor *federal judge*
Rodowsky, Lawrence Francis *retired state judge*
Smalkin, Frederic N. *federal judge*
Smith, Carol E. *judge*

Bethesda
Harris, Stanley S. *retired judge, arbitrator, mediator*
Nejelski, Paul Arthur *retired judge, freelance writer*

Cambridge
Ames, George Robert, Jr., *judge*

Greenbelt
Chasanow, Deborah K. *federal judge*
Chasanow, Howard Stuart *retired judge, mediator*
Messitte, Peter Jo *judge*
Titus, Roger Warren *judge*

Olney
Northrop, Edward Skottowe *federal judge*

Rockville
Megan, Thomas Ignatius *retired judge*
Raker, Irma *judge*

Towson
Wilner, Alan M. *judge*

Upper Marlboro
Harrell, Glenn T., Jr., *judge*

MASSACHUSETTS

Boston
Boudin, Michael *federal judge*
Bowler, Marianne Bianca *federal judge*
Budd, Wayne A. *U.S. attorney*
Campbell, Levin Hicks *federal judge*
Collings, Robert Biddlecombe *judge*
Connolly, Thomas Edward *judge*
Cordy, Robert J. *judge*
Cowin, Judith Arnold *state supreme court judge*
Dreben, Raya Spiegel *judge*
Feeney, Joan N. *judge*
Gertner, Nancy *federal judge, educator*
Gorton, Nathaniel M. *federal judge*
Greaney, John M. *state supreme court justice*
Ireland, Roderick L. *state supreme court justice*
Keeton, Robert Ernest *federal judge*
Lasker, Morris E. *judge*
Lindsay, Reginald Carl *judge*
Lynch, Sandra Lea *federal judge*
Marshall, Margaret Hilary *state supreme court chief justice*
Saris, Patti Barbara *federal judge*
Skinner, Walter Jay *federal judge*
Sosman, Martha B. *state supreme court justice*
Spina, Francis X. *state supreme court judge*
Stahl, Norman H. *judge*
Stearns, Richard Gaylore *judge*
Tauro, Joseph Louis *federal judge*
Torruella, Juan R. *federal judge*
Wolf, Mark Lawrence *federal judge*
Woodlock, Douglas Preston *judge*
Young, William Glover *federal judge*
Zobel, Rya Weickert *federal judge*

Cambridge
Abrams, Ruth Ida *retired state supreme court justice*
Boorstein, Beverly Weinger *judge*
Kaplan, Benjamin *judge*

Harwich Port
Smith, Ralph Wesley, Jr., *retired federal judge*

Holyoke
Crampton Kamukala, Rebekah Jean *judge, educator*

Longmeadow
Keady, George Cregan, Jr., *judge*

Springfield
Neiman, Kenneth Paul *judge*
Ponsor, Michael Adrian *federal judge*

MICHIGAN

Ann Arbor
Guy, Ralph B., Jr., *federal judge*

Birmingham
Kaufman, Ira Gladstone *judge*

Detroit
Callahan, J(ohn) William (Bill Callahan) *judge*
Corrigan, Maura Denise *judge*
Duggan, Patrick James *federal judge*
Edmunds, Nancy Garlock *federal judge*
Feikens, John *federal judge*
Friedman, Bernard Alvin *federal judge*
Hood, Denise Page *federal judge*
Keith, Damon Jerome *federal judge*
Levin, Charles Leonard *state supreme court justice*
Mallett, Conrad LeRoy, Jr., *former state supreme court chief justice, hospital administrator*
Morgan, Virginia Mattison *magistrate judge*
O'Meara, John Corbett *federal judge*
Rosen, Gerald Ellis *federal judge*
Ryan, James Leo *federal judge*
Taylor, Anna Diggs *federal judge*
Teranes, Paul S. *county judge, mediator*
Woods, George Edward *judge*

Glen Arbor
Newblatt, Stewart Albert *federal judge*

Grand Rapids
Bell, Robert Holmes *district judge*
Brenneman, Hugh Warren, Jr., *judge*
Miles, Wendell A. *federal judge*
Quist, Gordon Jay *federal judge*
Stevenson, Jo Ann C. *federal bankruptcy judge*

Kalamazoo
Enslen, Richard Alan *federal judge*

Lansing
Cavanagh, Michael Francis *state supreme court justice*
Kelly, Marilyn *state supreme court justice*
Markman, Stephen J. *state supreme court justice*
McKeague, David William *judge*
Suhrheinrich, Richard Fred *federal judge*
Taylor, Clifford Woodworth *state supreme court justice*
Young, Robert P., Jr., *state supreme court justice*

Midland
Clulo, Paul Jacques *judge*
Ludington, Thomas Lamson *judge*

Port Huron
Keyes, Allen E. *judge*

Saint Clair Shores
Hausner, John Herman *retired judge*
Ryan, Harold Martin *judge*

Southfield
Graves, Ray Reynolds *retired judge*

Traverse City
Weaver, Elizabeth A. *state supreme court justice*

White Lake
Boyle, Patricia Jean *retired state supreme court justice*

MINNESOTA

Anoka
Quinn, R. Joseph *district judge*

Duluth
Heaney, Gerald William *federal judge*

Eden Prairie
Arthur, Lindsay Grier *retired judge, author, editor*

Lake Elmo
Tomljanovich, Esther M. *retired judge*

Minneapolis
Alton, Ann Leslie *judge, lawyer, educator*
Amdahl, Douglas Kenneth *retired state supreme court justice*
Davis, Michael J. *judge*
Doty, David Singleton *federal judge*
Lebedoff, Jonathan Galanter *federal judge*
Loken, James Burton *federal judge*
MacLaughlin, Harry Hunter *federal judge*
Montgomery, Ann D. *federal judge, educator*
Murphy, Diana E. *federal judge*
Neville, Cara Lee T. *judge*
Noel, Franklin Linwood *judge*
Rosenbaum, James Michael *judge*

Minnetonka
Rogers, James Devitt *judge*

Saint Paul
Alsop, Donald Douglas *federal judge*
Anderson, Paul Holden *state supreme court justice*
Anderson, Russell A. *state supreme court justice*
Blatz, Kathleen Anne *judge, state agency administrator, state legislator*
Gilbert, James H. *judge*
Hanson, Samuel Lee *judge*
Kyle, Richard House *federal judge*
Lay, Donald Pomeroy *federal judge*
Meyer, Helen M. *judge*
Page, Alan C. *state supreme court justice*
Renner, Robert George *federal judge*
Stringer, Edward Charles *judge, lawyer*
Willis, Bruce Donald *judge*

MISSISSIPPI

Aberdeen
Davidson, Glen Harris *federal judge*

Batesville
Carlson, George Clarence, Jr., *judge*

Gulfport
Roper, John Marlin, Sr., *federal magistrate judge*
Russell, Dan M., Jr., *federal judge*
Senter, Lyonel Thomas, Jr., *federal judge*

Jackson
Banks, Fred Lee, Jr., *lawyer, former state supreme court presiding justice*
Barksdale, Rhesa Hawkins *federal judge*
Cobb, Kay Beevers *state supreme court justice, former state senator*
Diaz, Oliver E., Jr., *state supreme court justice*
Easley, Charles D., Jr., *state supreme court justice*
Graves, James E. *state supreme court justice, educator*
Jolly, E. Grady *federal judge*
Lee, Tom Stewart *judge*
McRae, Charles R. (Chuck McCrae) *state supreme court justice*
Pittman, Edwin Lloyd *state supreme court chief justice*
Smith, James W., Jr., *state supreme court chief justice*
Sugg, Robert Perkins *former state supreme court justice*
Waller, William Lowe, Jr., *state supreme court justice*

Natchez
Bramlette, David C., III, *federal judge*

Oxford
Mills, Michael Paul *judge*

MISSOURI

Benton
Heckemeyer, Anthony Joseph *circuit court judge*

Cape Girardeau
Blanton, Lewis M. *federal judge*

Clayton
Farragut-Hemphill, Sandra *judge*

High Ridge
Karll, Jo Ann *retired judge, lawyer*

Jefferson City
Blackmar, Charles Blakey *state supreme court justice*
Knox, William Arthur *judge*
Limbaugh, Stephen Nathaniel, Jr., *state supreme court judge*
Price, William Ray, Jr., *state supreme court judge*
Stith, Laura Denvir *state supreme court justice*
Teitelman, Richard B. *state supreme court judge*
White, Ronnie L. *state supreme court justice*
Wolff, Michael A. *state supreme court judge*

Kansas City
Benton, William Duane *federal judge*
Bowman, Pasco Middleton, II, *judge*
Gaitan, Fernando J., Jr., *federal judge*
Gibson, John Robert *federal judge*
Laughrey, Nanette Kay *judge, federal*
Sachs, Howard F(rederic) *federal judge*
Whipple, Dean *federal judge*
Wright, Scott Olin *federal judge*

Saint Louis
Filippine, Edward Louis *federal judge*
Gaertner, Gary M., Sr., *judge*
Gruender, Raymond W. *federal judge, former prosecutor*
Hamilton, Jean Constance *judge*
Jackson, Carol E. *federal judge*
Limbaugh, Stephen Nathaniel *federal judge*
McMillian, Theodore *federal judge*
Medler, Mary Ann L. *federal judge*
Perry, Catherine D. *judge*
Seiler, James Elmer *judge*
Shaw, Charles Alexander *judge*
Stohr, Donald J. *federal judge*

Springfield
Holstein, John Charles *former state supreme court judge*
Parrish, John Edward *state appellate judge*

MONTANA

Billings
Fagg, Russell *judge, lawyer*
Thomas, Sidney R. *federal judge*

Circle
McDonough, Russell Charles *retired state supreme court justice*

Helena
Cotter, Patricia O'Brien *state supreme court justice*
Gray, Karla Marie *judge*
Harrison, John Conway *retired state supreme court justice*
Leaphart, W. William *state supreme court justice*
Nelson, James C *state supreme court justice*
Regnier, James *state supreme court justice*
Rice, Jim *state supreme court justice*

Polson
Turnage, Jean Allen *retired state supreme court chief justice*

NEBRASKA

Lincoln
Beam, Clarence Arlen *judge*
Connolly, William M. *state supreme court justice*
Gerrard, John M. *state supreme court justice*
Hastings, William Charles *retired state supreme court chief justice*
Hendry, John *state supreme court justice*
Kopf, Richard G. *federal judge*
McCormack, Michael *state supreme court justice*
Miller-Lerman, Lindsey *state supreme court justice*
Piester, David L(ee) *magistrate judge*
Stephan, Kenneth C. *judge*
Urbom, Warren Keith *federal judge*
Wright, John F. *judge*

Omaha
Grant, John Thomas *retired state supreme court justice*
Riley, William Jay *federal judge*
Ross, Donald Roe *federal judge*
Shanahan, Thomas M. *judge*
Strom, Lyle Elmer *judge*

NEVADA

Carson City
Agosti, Deborah Ann *state supreme court justice*
Gibbons, Mark *judge*
Maupin, A. William *state supreme court justice*
Rose, Robert Edgar *state supreme court justice*
Springer, Charles Edward *retired judge*

Las Vegas
Becker, Nancy Anne *state supreme court justice*
George, Lloyd D. *federal judge*
Johnston, Robert Jake *federal magistrate judge*
Mahan, James Cameron *judge*
Pro, Philip Martin *judge*
Rawlinson, Johnnie Blakeney *federal judge*
Steffen, Thomas Lee *retired judge, lawyer*

Reno
Brunetti, Melvin T. *federal judge*
Hagen, David Warner *judge*
Hug, Procter Ralph, Jr., *federal judge*
McKibben, Howard D. *federal judge*
Reed, Edward Cornelius, Jr., *federal judge*

NEW HAMPSHIRE

Concord
Barbadoro, Paul James *federal judge*
Brock, David Allen *state supreme court chief justice*
Broderick, John T., Jr., *state supreme court chief justice*
Dalianis, Linda Stewart *judge*
DiClerico, Joseph Anthony, Jr., *federal judge*
Duggan, James E., Jr., *state supreme court justice*
Howard, Jeffrey R. *federal judge*
McAuliffe, Steven James *federal judge*
Muirhead, James Russell *federal judge*
Nadeau, Joseph P. *state supreme court justice*

Rochester
Jones, Franklin Charles *judge*

NEW JERSEY

Atlantic City
Knight, Edward R. *judge, lawyer, educator, psychologist*

Camden
Brotman, Stanley Seymour *federal judge*
Irenas, Joseph Eron *judge, director*
Laskin, Lee B. *judge, lawyer, state senator*
Simandle, Jerome B. *federal judge*

Egg Harbor Township
Lashman, Shelley Bortin *retired judge*

Hackensack
Kestin, Howard H. *judge*
Stein, Gary S. *retired judge, lawyer*

Millburn
Kuttner, Bernard A. *judge*

Morristown
LaVecchia, Jaynee *state supreme court justice*

Newark
Ackerman, Harold A. *federal judge*
Alito, Samuel Anthony, Jr., *federal judge*
Barry, Maryanne Trump *federal judge*
Bissell, John W. *federal judge*
Debevoise, Dickinson Richards *federal judge*
Fuentes, Julio M. *federal judge*
Garth, Leonard I. *judge*
Greenaway, Joseph Anthony, Jr., *judge*
Hochberg, Faith S. *US district court judge*
Lechner, Alfred James, Jr., *judge*

Oceanport
D'Amico, John, Jr., *judge*

Red Bank
O'Hern, Daniel Joseph *retired state supreme court justice*

Somerville
Yurasko, Frank Noel *judge*

Trenton
Albin, Barry Todd *state supreme court justice*
Cooper, Mary Little *federal judge, former banking commissioner*
Cowen, Robert E. *federal judge*
Greenberg, Morton Ira *federal judge*
Long, Virginia *state supreme court justice*
Poritz, Deborah T. *state supreme court chief justice, former attorney general*
Thompson, Anne Elise *federal judge*
Wallace, John E. *judge*
Zazzali, James R. *state supreme court associate justice*

NEW MEXICO

Albuquerque
Black, Bruce D. *judge*
Conway, John E. *federal judge*
Hansen, Curtis LeRoy *federal judge*
Hartz, Harris L *federal judge*
Parker, James Aubrey *federal judge*

Santa Fe
Bosson, Richard Campbell *state supreme court justice*
Chavez, Edward L. *judge*
Kelly, Paul Joseph, Jr., *judge*
Maes, Petra Jimenez *state supreme court justice*
Minzner, Pamela Burgy *state supreme court justice*
Serna, Patricio *state supreme court justice*
Vazquez, Martha Alicia *judge*
Yalman, Ann *judge, lawyer*

Silver City
Hodges, Norman *retired district judge*

NEW YORK

Albany
Graffeo, Victoria A. *state appeals court judge*
Kaye, Judith Smith *state appeals court chief judge*
Meader, John Daniel *judge*
Miner, Roger Jeffrey *judge*
Read, Susan Phillips *state appeals court judge*

Binghamton
Peckham, Eugene Eliot *judge, lawyer*

Bronx
Bamberger, Phylis Skloot *judge*

Brooklyn
Amon, Carol Bagley *federal judge*
Bramwell, Henry *federal judge*
Duberstein, Conrad B. *federal judge*
Garaufis, Nicholas G. *district court judge*
Gershon, Nina *federal judge*
Glasser, Israel Leo *federal judge*
Korman, Edward R. *federal judge*
Raggi, Reena *circuit judge*
Reichbach, Gustin Lewis *state supreme court justice*
Ryan, Leonard Eames *judge*
Sifton, Charles Proctor *federal judge*
Trager, David G. *federal judge*
Weinstein, Jack Bertrand *federal judge*

Buffalo
Bucki, Carl Leo *judge*
Elfvin, John Thomas *federal judge*
Heckman, Carol E. *lawyer*
Pietruszka, Michael F. *judge*
Schroeder, Harold Kenneth, Jr., *US magistrate judge*
Skretny, William Marion *federal judge*

Central Islip
Bernstein, Stan *federal bankruptcy judge*
Boyle, E. Thomas *federal magistrate judge*
Cyganowski, Melanie L. *bankruptcy judge*
Eisenberg, Dorothy *federal judge*
Platt, Thomas Collier, Jr., *federal judge*
Seybert, Joanna *federal judge*
Spatt, Arthur Donald *federal judge*

Delhi
Becker, Carl Frederick *judge*

Garden City
Harwood, Stanley *retired judge, lawyer*

Huntington
Jones, Farrell *retired judge*

Kingston
Bradley, Vincent Gerard *judge*

New York
Aquilino, Thomas Joseph, Jr., *federal judge, law educator*
Baer, Harold, Jr., *judge*
Barzilay, Judith Morgenstern *federal judge*
Batts, Deborah A. *judge*
Berman, Richard Miles *judge*
Blinder, Albert Allan *judge*
Buchwald, Naomi Reice *judge*
Carman, Gregory Wright *federal judge*
Castel, P. Kevin *judge*
Cedarbaum, Miriam Goldman *federal judge*
Ciparick, Carmen Beauchamp *judge*
Cote, Denise Louise *federal judge*
Feinberg, Wilfred *judge*
Francis, James Clark, IV, *judge*
Freedman, Helen E. *justice*
Gerber, Robert Evan *judge*
Griesa, Thomas Poole *federal judge*
Gropper, Allan Louis *bankruptcy judge*
Haight, Charles Sherman, Jr., *federal judge*
Hall, Peter W. *federal judge, former proscutor*
Jacobs, Dennis *federal judge*
Jurow, George *judge*
Kaplan, Lewis A. *judge*
Katzmann, Robert Allen *federal judge*
Kearse, Amalya Lyle *federal judge*
Keenan, John Fontaine *judge*
Koeltl, John George *judge*
Kram, Shirley Wohl *federal judge*
Leisure, Peter Keeton *federal judge*
Leval, Pierre Nelson *federal judge*
Lowe, Mary Johnson *federal judge*
Martin, John Sherwood, Jr., *federal judge*
McLaughlin, Joseph Michael *federal judge, law educator*
Motley, Constance Baker (Mrs. Joel Wilson Motley) *federal judge, former city official*
Mukasey, Michael B. *federal judge*
Musgrave, R. Kenton *federal judge*
Owen, Richard *federal judge*
Patterson, Robert Porter, Jr., *federal judge*
Peck, Andrew Jay *federal judge*
Pogue, Donald Carl *federal judge*
Pooler, Rosemary S. *federal judge*
Preska, Loretta A. *federal judge*
Rakoff, Jed Saul *federal judge, author*
Restani, Jane A. *federal judge*
Sack, Robert David *judge, law educator*
Sand, Leonard B. *federal judge*
Sklar, Stanley Lawrence *judge*
Smith, George Bundy *state appeals court judge*
Smith, Robert Sherlock *judge*
Sotomayor, Sonia *federal judge*
Sprizzo, John Emilio *judge*
Straub, Chester John *judge*
Titone, Vito Joseph *former state court justice*
Tsoucalas, Nicholas *federal judge*
Wesley, Richard C. *federal judge*
Williams, Milton Lawrence *judge, educator*
Wood, Kimba M. *judge*

Penn Yan
Falvey, W(illiam) Patrick *judge*

Poughkeepsie
Dolan, Thomas Joseph *judge*
Rosenblatt, Albert Martin *state appeals court judge*

Rochester
Kehoe, L. Paul *state judge*
Larimer, David George *federal judge*
Siragusa, Charles J. *judge*
Telesca, Michael Anthony *federal judge*
Van Graafeiland, Ellsworth Alfred *federal judge*
Witmer, G. Robert *retired state supreme court justice*

Rome
Simons, Richard Duncan *lawyer, retired judge*

Sag Harbor
Pierce, Lawrence Warren *retired federal judge*

Schenectady
Levine, Howard Arnold *judge*

Smallwood
Golden, Elliott *judge*

Syracuse
McCurn, Neal Peters *federal judge*
Munson, Howard G. *federal judge*
Scullin, Frederick James, Jr., *judge*
Wells, Peter Nathaniel *judge, lawyer*

Utica
Cardamone, Richard J. *judge*

White Plains
Brieant, Charles La Monte *federal judge*
Carey, John *judge*
Conner, William Curtis *judge*
Hardin, Adlai Stevenson, Jr., *judge*
Nastasi, Aldo A. *judge*
Parker, Barrington D., Jr., *federal judge, lawyer*

NORTH CAROLINA

Asheville
Thornburg, Lacy Herman *federal judge*

Charlotte
Horn, Carl, III, *federal judge*
Mullen, Graham C. *federal judge*
Voorhees, Richard Lesley *federal judge*

Greensboro
Bullock, Frank William, Jr., *federal judge*
Frye, Henry E. *retired state supreme court chief justice*
Osteen, William L. *federal judge*
Tilley, Norwood Carlton, Jr., *federal judge*

Hendersonville
Franks, Stephen F. *retired judge*

Raleigh
Brady, Edward Thomas *judge*
Britt, W. Earl *federal judge*
Brown, James Joseph *judge*
Duncan, Allyson K. *federal judge*
Eagles, Sidney Smith, Jr., *judge*
Edmunds, Robert H., Jr., *state supreme court justice*
Lake, I. Beverly, Jr., *judge*
Martin, John Charles *judge*
Martin, Mark D. *state supreme court justice*
McGee, Linda Mace *judge, lawyer*
Orr, Robert F. *judge*
Parker, Sarah Elizabeth *state supreme court justice*
Wainwright, George *judge*
Webb, John *retired state supreme court justice*

Randleman
Jordan, Lillian B. *judge*

Wilmington
Fox, James Carroll *federal judge*

Winston Salem
Beaty, James Arthur, Jr., *federal judge*
Carruthers, Catharine *federal judge*
Eliason, Russell Allen *judge*

NORTH DAKOTA

Bismarck
Conmy, Patrick A. *federal judge*
Kapsner, Carol Ronning *state supreme court justice*
Maring, Mary Muehlen *state supreme court justice*
Neumann, William Allen *state supreme court justice*
Sandstrom, Dale Vernon *state supreme court justice*
VandeWalle, Gerald Wayne *state supreme court chief justice*
Van Sickle, Bruce Marion *federal judge*

Fargo
Bright, Myron H. *federal judge*
Bye, Kermit Edward *judge, lawyer*
Klein, Karen K. *federal judge*
Magill, Frank John *federal judge*

Minot
Kerian, Jon Robert *retired judge*

OHIO

Akron
Bell, Samuel H. *federal judge, educator*
Shea-Stonum, Marilyn *federal bankruptcy judge*

Bowling Green
Baird, James Abington *retired judge*

Cincinnati
Beckwith, Sandra Shank *judge*
Black, Robert L., Jr., *retired judge*
Clay, Eric L. *federal judge*
Cook, Deborah L. *judge, former state supreme court justice*
Dlott, Susan Judy *judge, lawyer*
Hopkins, Jeffrey P. *federal judge*
Jones, Nathaniel Raphael *retired federal judge*
Kennedy, Cornelia Groefsema *federal judge*
Nelson, David Aldrich *judge*
Nelson, Frederick Dickson *judge*
Painter, Mark Philip *judge*
Panioto, Ronald Angelo *judge*
Perlman, Burton *judge*
Rogers, John Marshall *judge, law educator*
Spiegel, S. Arthur *federal judge*
Sutton, Jeffrey S. *federal judge*
Weber, Herman Jacob *federal judge*

Circleville
Ammer, William *retired judge*
Long, Jan Michael *judge*

Cleveland
Aldrich, Ann *federal judge*
Burke, Lillian Walker *retired judge*
Gaughan, Patricia Anne *judge*
Hemann, Patricia A. *federal judge*
Manos, John M. *federal judge*
Markus, Richard M. *judge, mediator*
Matia, Paul Ramon *federal judge*
Moore, Karen Nelson *judge*
Oliver, Solomon, Jr., *judge*
O'Malley, Kathleen M. *federal judge*
Wells, Lesley *federal judge*

Columbus
Cole, Ransey Guy, Jr., *federal judge*
Douglas, Andrew *retired state supreme court justice*
Graham, James Lowell *federal judge*
Holschuh, John David *federal judge*
Mc Cormac, John Waverly *judge*
Miller, Nodine *judge*
Moyer, Thomas J. *state supreme court chief justice*

Norris, Alan Eugene *federal judge*
O'Connor, Maureen *judge*
Pfeifer, Paul E. *state supreme court justice*
Resnick, Alice Robie *judge*
Sargus, Edmund A., Jr., *judge*
Sellers, Barbara Jackson *federal judge*
Smith, George Curtis *judge*
Stratton, Evelyn Lundberg *judge*
Sweeney, Asher William *state supreme court justice*
Sweeney, Francis E. *state supreme court justice*

Dayton
Anderson, Charles Austin *judge*
Clark, William Alfred *federal judge*
Knapp, James Ian Keith *judge*
Petzold, John Paul *judge*

Kettering
Porter, Walter Arthur *retired judge*

Lima
Rogers, Richard Michael *judge*

Lucasville
Reno, Ottie Wayne *former judge*

Medina
Batchelder, Alice M. *federal judge*

Middletown
Powell, Stephen Walter *judge*

Sandusky
Stacey, James Allen *retired judge*

Toledo
Carr, James Gray *judge*
Katz, David Allan *federal judge*
Potter, John William *federal judge*

Warren
Nader, Robert Alexander *judge, lawyer*

Xenia
Wolaver, Stephen Arthur *judge*

OKLAHOMA

Atoka
Gabbard, Douglas, II, (James Gabbard) *judge*

Chandler
Foster, Robert Lawson *retired judge, deacon*

Lawton
Moore, Roy Dean *retired judge*

Norman
Trimble, Preston Albert *retired judge*

Oklahoma City
Alley, Wayne Edward *federal judge, retired army officer*
Cauthron, Robin J. *federal judge*
Hargrave, Rudolph *state supreme court chief justice*
Henry, Robert Harlan *federal judge, former attorney general*
Hodges, Ralph B. *state supreme court justice*
Holloway, William Judson, Jr., *federal judge*
Lavender, Robert Eugene *state supreme court justice*
Leonard, Timothy Dwight *judge*
Miles-La Grange, Vicki *judge*
Opala, Marian P(eter) *state supreme court justice*
Russell, David L. *federal judge*
Summers, Hardy *state supreme court justice*
Thompson, Ralph Gordon *federal judge*
Watt, Joseph Michael *state supreme court chief justice*
West, Lee Roy *federal judge*
Winchester, James R. *state supreme court justice*

Tulsa
Cook, Harold Dale *federal judge*
Goodman, Jerry L(ynn) *judge*
Holmes, Sven Erik *federal judge, educator*
Kern, Terry C. *judge*
Seymour, Stephanie Kulp *federal judge*
Taylor, Joe Clinton *judge*

OREGON

Eugene
Hogan, Michael R(obert) *judge*

Portland
Beatty, John Cabeen, Jr., *judge*
Dunn, Randall L. *federal judge*
Frye, Helen Jackson *federal judge*
Higdon, Polly Susanne *federal judge*
Jones, Robert Edward *federal judge*
Leavy, Edward *federal judge*
Marsh, Malcolm F. *federal judge*
O'Scannlain, Diarmuid Fionntain *federal judge*
Panner, Owen M. *federal judge*
Redden, James Anthony *federal judge*
Rosenblum, Ellen F. *judge*
Roth, Phillip Joseph *retired judge*
Skopil, Otto Richard, Jr., *federal judge*
Stewart, Janice Mae *federal judge*
Sullivan, Donal D. *federal bankruptcy judge*
Unis, Richard L. *judge*
Van Hoomissen, George Albert *state supreme court justice*

Salem
Balmer, Thomas Ancil *state supreme court justice*
Carson, Wallace Preston, Jr., *judge*
De Muniz, Paul J. *state supreme court justice*
Durham, Robert Donald, Jr., *state supreme court justice*
Linde, Hans Arthur *state supreme court justice*
Peterson, Edwin J. *retired judge, mediator, law educator*
Riggs, R. William *judge*

Sweet Home
Miller, Keith Allen *judge, lawyer*

PENNSYLVANIA

Allentown
Platt, William Henry *judge*

Bala Cynwyd
Beck, Phyllis Whitman *judge*

Devon
Lamb, William H. *state supreme court justices*

Duncansville
Smith, D. Brooks *federal judge*

East Lansdowne
Tolliver, Elkin, Jr., *judge*

Erie
Mencer, Glenn Everell *federal judge*

Harrisburg
Rambo, Sylvia H. *federal judge*
Saylor, Thomas G. *state supreme court justice*

Mechanicsburg
Eakin, J. Michael *judge*

Philadelphia
Bartle, Harvey, III, *federal judge*
Bechtle, Louis Charles *lawyer, retired federal judge*
Becker, Edward Roy *judge*
Buckwalter, Ronald Lawrence *federal judge*
Castille, Ronald D. *judge*
Chertoff, Michael *federal judge*
Coleman, Gerald Charles *judge, law educator*
Dalzell, Stewart *federal judge*
Diamond, Paul Steven *federal judge, lawyer, educator*
DuBois, Jan Ely *federal judge*
Fullam, John P. *federal judge*
Green, Clifford Scott *federal judge*
Joyner, J(ames) Curtis *judge*
Kelly, Robert F. *federal judge*
Ludwig, Edmund Vincent *federal judge*
McKee, Theodore A. *federal judge*
Newcomer, Clarence Charles *federal judge*
Nigro, Russell M. *state supreme court justice*
Nygaard, Richard Lowell *federal judge*
O'Neill, Thomas Newman, Jr., *federal judge*
Pollak, Louis Heilprin *judge, educator*
Reed, Lowell A., Jr., *federal judge*
Rendell, Marjorie O. *federal judge*
Robreno, Eduardo C. *federal judge*
Rueter, Thomas James *federal judge*
Scirica, Anthony Joseph *federal judge*
Shapiro, Norma Sondra Levy *federal judge*
Sigmund, Diane Weiss *judge*
Sloviter, Dolores Korman *federal judge*
Van Antwerpen, Franklin Stuart *federal judge*
Weiner, Charles R. *federal judge*
Welsh, Diane M. *federal judge*
Yohn, William H(endricks), Jr., *federal judge*

Pittsburgh
Ambrose, Donetta W. *federal judge*
Bloch, Alan Neil *federal judge*
Cappy, Ralph Joseph *judge*
Cohill, Maurice Blanchard, Jr., *federal judge*
Conti, Joy Flowers *judge*
Diamond, Gustave *federal judge*
Fisher, D. Michael *US Circuit Court judge*
Flaherty, John Paul, Jr., *retired judge*
Lee, Donald John *federal judge*
McCullough, M. Bruce *judge*
Ross, Eunice Latshaw *judge*
Sensenich, Ila Jeanne *judge*
Standish, William Lloyd *judge*
Weis, Joseph Francis, Jr., *federal judge*
Ziegler, Donald Emil *federal judge*

Scranton
Blewitt, Thomas Michael *chief federal magistrate judge*
Conaboy, Richard Paul *federal judge*
Nealon, William Joseph, Jr., *federal judge*
O'Malley, Carlon Martin *judge*
Vanaskie, Thomas Ignatius *judge*

Towanda
Mott, John C. *judge*

Washington
Mc Cune, Barron Patterson *retired federal judge*

West Chester
Griffith, Edward *judge*

West Conshohocken
Newman, Sandra Schultz *state supreme court justice*

Wilkes Barre
Rosenn, Max *federal judge*

Williamsport
McClure, James Focht, Jr., *federal judge*
Muir, Malcolm *federal judge*

RHODE ISLAND

Providence
Flaherty, Francis Xavier *judge*
Flanders, Robert G., Jr., *state supreme court justice*
Goldberg, Maureen McKenna *state supreme court justice*
Hagopian, Jacob *federal judge*
Harwood, Patricia L. *judge*
Lagueux, Ronald Rene *federal judge*
Lisi, Mary M. *federal judge*
Selya, Bruce Marshall *federal judge*
Torres, Ernest C. *federal judge*
Weisberger, Joseph Robert *retired judge*
Williams, Frank J. *judge, historian, writer*

SOUTH CAROLINA

Camden
Chapman, Robert Foster *judge*
Jacobs, Rolly Warren *judge*

Cameron
Ulmer, Jeanne Wilde *judge*

Charleston
Hawkins, Falcon Black, Jr., *federal judge*

Columbia
Bristow, Walter James, Jr., *retired judge*
Burnett, E. C., III, *state supreme court justice*
Currie, Cameron McGowan *federal judge*
Hamilton, Clyde Henry *judge*
Martin, John Randolph *judge*
Pleicones, Costa M. *state supreme court justice*
Shedd, Dennis W. *federal judge*
Toal, Jean Hoefer *state supreme court chief justice*

Georgetown
Walters, Alan Wayne *judge*

Greenville
Herlong, Henry Michael, Jr., *federal judge*
Traxler, William Byrd, Jr., *federal judge*
Wilkins, William Walter *federal judge*

Greenwood
Moore, James E. *state supreme court justice*

Marion
Waller, John Henry, Jr., *state supreme court justice*

Myrtle Beach
Harwell, David Walker *retired state supreme court chief justice*

Orangeburg
Finney, Ernest Adolphus, Jr., *retired state supreme court chief justice*

SOUTH DAKOTA

Deadwood
Johns, Timothy Robert *judge*

Pierre
Gilbertson, David *state supreme court justice*
Konenkamp, John K. *state supreme court justice*
Miller, Robert Arthur *former state supreme court chief justice*
Sabers, Richard Wayne *state supreme court justice*
Zinter, Steven L. *state supreme court justice*

Rapid City
Schreier, Karen Elizabeth *judge*

Sioux Falls
Meierhenry, Judith Knittel *judge, lawyer*
Piersol, Lawrence L. *federal judge*
Wollman, Roger Leland *federal judge*

TENNESSEE

Chattanooga
Barker, William M. *state supreme court justice*
Edgar, R(obert) Allan *federal judge*
Franks, Herschel Pickens *judge*

Greeneville
Hull, Thomas Gray *federal judge*
Parsons, Marcia Phillips *judge*

Jackson
Boswell, G(eorge) Harvey *federal judge*
Todd, James Dale *federal judge*

Knoxville
Anderson, Edward Riley *state supreme court justice*
Jarvis, James Howard, II, *judge*
Jordan, Robert Leon *judge*
Murrian, Robert Phillip *retired federal judge, educator*
Phillips, Thomas Wade *judge, lawyer*

Memphis
Donald, Bernice B. *judge*
Gibbons, Julia Smith *federal judge*
Gilman, Ronald Lee *federal judge*
Holder, Janice Marie *state supreme court justice*
Vescovo, Diane Kirkland *federal judge*

Nashville
Birch, Adolpho A., Jr., *state supreme court justice*
Brown, Joe Blackburn *judge*
Daughtrey, Martha Craig *federal judge*
Drowota, Frank F., III, *state supreme court chief justice*
Echols, Robert L. *federal judge*
Merritt, Gilbert Stroud *federal judge*
Nixon, John Trice *judge*
Trauger, Aleta Arthur *judge*
Wiseman, Thomas Anderton, Jr., *federal judge*

Newport
Porter, James Kenneth *retired judge*

Signal Mountain
Cooper, Robert Elbert *state supreme court justice*

TEXAS

Amarillo
Johnson, Philip Wayne *judge*
Robinson, Mary Lou *federal judge*

Angleton
Germany, Garvin Holt, Jr., *retired judge, lawyer*

Arlington
Wright, James Edward *judge*

Austin
Aboussie, Marilyn *retired state judge*
Benavides, Fortunato Pedro (Pete Benavides) *federal judge*
Garwood, William Lockhart *judge*
Gonzalez, Raul A. *retired state supreme court justice, lawyer*
Greenhill, Joe Robert *former chief justice state supreme court, lawyer*
Hecht, Nathan Lincoln *state supreme court justice*
Hudspeth, Harry Lee *federal judge*
Jefferson, Wallace B. *state supreme court justice*
Keller, Sharon Faye *judge*
Meyers, Lawrence Edward *state judge*
Miller, Charles E. (Chuck Miller) *judge*
Nowlin, James Robertson *federal judge*
O'Neill, Harriet *state supreme court justice*
Owen, Priscilla Richman *state supreme court justice*
Pitman, Robert L. *judge*
Pope, Andrew Jackson, Jr., (Jack Pope) *retired judge*
Ray, Cread L., Jr., *retired state supreme court justice*
Reavley, Thomas Morrow *federal judge*
Smith, Steven W. *judge*
Sparks, Sam *federal judge*
Spector, Rose *state supreme court justice*
Wainwright, Dale V. *judge*
Williams, Mary Pearl *judge*

Beaumont
Burgess, Don R. *judge*
Cobb, Howell *federal judge*

Bryan
Smith, Steven Lee *judge*

Corpus Christi
Head, Hayden Wilson, Jr., *judge*
Hunter, Jack E. *judge*
Jack, Janis Graham *judge*
Tagle, Hilda Gloria *former judge*

Dallas
Boyle, Jane J. *federal judge, lawyer*
Haynes, Catharina D. *judge*
Higginbotham, Patrick Errol *federal judge*
Lang-Miers, Elizabeth Ann *judge*
Lynn, Barbara Michele *judge*
McGuire, Robert C. *retired federal bankruptcy judge*
Price, Robert Eben *judge*
Robertson, Ted Zanderson *judge*
Sanders, Harold Barefoot, Jr., *judge*

Edinburg
Hinojosa, Federico Gustavo, Jr., *judge*

El Paso
Briones, David *judge*

Fort Worth
Hardy, Cheril S. *judge*
McBryde, John Henry *federal judge*
Means, Terry Robert *federal judge*
Sullivan, Frank W *judge*
Tillman, Massie Monroe *mediator, arbitrator, art gallery owner, retired federal judge*

Houston
Atlas, Nancy Friedman *judge*
Brown, Karen Kennedy *judge*
Bue, Carl Olaf, Jr., *retired federal judge*
Clark, Letitia Z. *federal judge*
DeMoss, Harold Raymond, Jr., *federal judge*
Gilmore, Vanessa D. *federal judge*
Hanks, George Carol, Jr., *state judge*
Harmon, Melinda Furche *federal judge*
Hittner, David *federal judge*
Hoyt, Kenneth M. *federal judge*
Hughes, Lynn Nettleton *federal judge*
Jones, Edith Hollan *federal judge*
King, Carolyn Dineen *federal judge*
Lake, Sim *federal judge*
Rosenthal, Lee H. *federal judge*
Smith, Jerry Edwin *federal judge*
Stacy, Frances H. *federal judge*
Werlein, Ewing, Jr., *federal judge*

Kaufman
Tygrett, Howard Volney, Jr., *judge, lawyer*

Laredo
Kazen, George Philip *federal judge*

Lockhart
McCormick, Michael Jerry *retired judge*

Mcallen
Hinojosa, Ricardo H. *federal judge*

Midland
Morrow, William Clarence *judge, lawyer, mediator*

Pampa
Cain, Donald Ezell *retired judge*

Richmond
Elliott, Brady Gifford *judge*

San Antonio
Furgeson, William Royal *federal judge*
Garza, Emilio M(iller) *federal judge*
Hardberger, Phillip Duane *judge, lawyer, journalist*
King, Ronald Baker *federal judge*
Nowak, Nancy Stein *judge*

Sherman
Brown, Paul Neeley *federal judge*

Temple
Clawson, James F., Jr., *judge, mediator, arbitrator*

Tyler
Guthrie, Judith K. *federal judge*
McKee, Harry W. *federal judge*
Steger, William Merritt *federal judge*

Victoria
Rainey, John David *federal judge*

UTAH

Provo
Harding, Ray Murray, Jr., *judge*
Schofield, Anthony Wayne *judge*

Salt Lake City
Anderson, Stephen Hale *federal judge*
Campbell, Tena *judge*
Clark, Glen Edward *judge*
Durham, Christine Meaders *state supreme court chief justice*
Durrant, Matthew B. *state supreme court justice*
Greene, John Thomas *judge*
Jenkins, Bruce Sterling *federal judge*
Mc Connell, Michael W. *judge, law educator*
McKay, Monroe Gunn *federal judge*
Murphy, Michael R. *federal judge*
Nehring, Ronald E. *judge*
Parrish, Jill Niederhauser *judge*
Rigtrup, Kenneth *state judge, arbitrator, mediator*
Sam, David *federal judge*
Wilkins, Michael Jon *state supreme court justice*

VERMONT

Brattleboro
Murtha, J. Garvan *federal judge*
Oakes, James L. *federal judge*

Montpelier
Dooley, John Augustine, III, *state supreme court justice*
Gibson, Ernest Willard, III, *retired state supreme court justice*
Johnson, Denise Reinka *state supreme court justice*
Skoglund, Marilyn *state supreme court justice*

Waterbury Center
Amestoy, Jeffrey Lee *state supreme court chief justice*

Woodstock
Billings, Franklin Swift, Jr., *federal judge*

VIRGINIA

Abingdon
Jones, James Parker *federal judge*
Widener, Hiram Emory, Jr., *judge*
Williams, Glen Morgan *federal judge*

Alexandria
Bostetter, Martin V. B., Jr., *bankruptcy court judge*
Brinkema, Leonie Milhomme *federal judge*
Ellis, Thomas Selby, III, *federal judge*
Luttig, J. Michael *federal judge*

Annandale
Armstrong, Henry Jere *retired judge*
Hollis, Daryl Joseph *judge*

Charlottesville
Crigler, B. Waugh *US magistrate judge*
Hogshire, Edward Leigh *judge*
Michael, James Harry, Jr., *federal judge*
Wilkinson, James Harvie, III, *federal judge*

Chesterfield
Davis, Bonnie Christell *judge*

Covington
Stephenson, Roscoe Bolar, Jr., *state supreme court justice*

Danville
Kiser, Jackson L. *federal judge*
Milam, Joseph Walton, Jr., *judge*

Fairfax
Williams, Marcus Doyle *judge*

Falls Church
Barton, Robert Leroy, Jr., *judge, educator*
Cooper, Jean Saralee *judge*
Mathon, Lauren R. *judge*

Fredericksburg
Brown, Harold Eugene *retired magistrate*

Lynchburg
Moon, Norman K. *judge*

Manassas
Van Broekhoven, Rollin Adrian *federal judge*

Norfolk
Adams, David Huntington *judge*
Bonney, Hal James, Jr., *federal judge*
Jackson, Raymond A. *federal judge*
Morgan, Henry Coke, Jr., *judge*
Prince, William Taliaferro *retired federal judge*
Smith, Rebecca Beach *federal judge*

Richmond
Agee, G. Steven *judge*
Carrico, Harry Lee *retired judge*
Compton, Asbury Christian *state supreme court justice*
Gregory, Roger Lee *federal judge*
Hassell, Leroy Rountree, Sr., *state supreme court chief justice*
Kinser, Cynthia D. *state supreme court justice*
Lacy, Elizabeth Bermingham *state supreme court justice*
Lemons, Donald W. *state supreme court justice*
Poff, Richard Harding *retired state supreme court justice*
Tice, Douglas Oscar, Jr., *federal bankruptcy judge*
Williams, Karen Johnson *federal judge*
Williams, Richard Leroy *federal judge*

Roanoke
Turk, James Clinton *federal judge*

Salem
Koontz, Lawrence L., Jr., *state supreme court justice*
Pearson, Henry Clyde *retired judge*

Staunton
Cochran, George Moffett *retired judge*

Stuart
Clark, Martin F(illmore), Jr., *judge*

Virginia Beach
Keenan, Barbara Milano *judge*

Warrenton
Anthony, Joan Caton *administrative judge*

WASHINGTON

Bellevue
Andersen, James A. *retired state supreme court justice*

Kent
McDermott, Richard Francis *judge*

Mercer Island
Noe, James Alva *retired judge*

Olympia
Alexander, Gerry L. *state supreme court chief justice*
Bridge, Bobbe J. *state supreme court justice*
Fairhurst, Mary E. *judge*
Guy, Richard P. *retired state supreme court justice*
Ireland, Faith *state supreme court justice*
Johnson, Charles William *state supreme court justice*
Madsen, Barbara A *state supreme court justice*
Owens, Susan *state supreme court justice*
Sanders, Richard Browning *judge*
Smith, Charles Z. *retired state supreme court justice*

Seattle
Beezer, Robert Renaut *federal judge*
Bladen, Edwin Mark *lawyer, judge*
Dimmick, Carolyn Reaber *federal judge*
Farris, Jerome *federal judge*
Fletcher, Betty Binns *federal judge*
Gould, Ronald Murray *federal judge*
Mc Govern, Walter T. *federal judge*
Overstreet, Karen A. *federal bankruptcy judge*
Tallman, Richard C. *federal judge, lawyer*
Weinberg, John Lee *federal judge*
Zilly, Thomas Samuel *federal judge*

Spokane
Imbrogno, Cynthia *magistrate judge*
Murphy, James Michael *retired judge, mediator, arbitrator*
Quackenbush, Justin Lowe *federal judge*
Van Sickle, Frederick L. *federal judge*
Whaley, Robert Hamilton *judge*
Williams, Patricia C. *federal judge*

Tacoma
Arnold, J. Kelley *US magistrate judge*
Bryan, Robert J. *federal judge*

Tukwila
Talmadge, Philip Albert *former state supreme court justice, former state senator*

Vancouver
Harris, Robert L(ee) *judge*

Yakima
McDonald, Alan Angus *federal judge*
Suko, Lonny Ray *judge*

WEST VIRGINIA

Beckley
Faber, David Alan *federal judge*

Charleston
Albright, Joseph P. *state supreme court justice*
Brewer, Lewis Gordon *judge, lawyer, educator*
Copenhaver, John Thomas, Jr., *federal judge*
Davis, Robin Jean *state supreme court justice*
Goodwin, Joseph Robert *judge*
King, Robert Bruce *federal judge*
Maynard, Elliott *state supreme court justice*
McGraw, Warren Randolph *state supreme court justice*
Michael, M. Blane *federal judge*
Stanley, Mary Elizabeth *judge*
Starcher, Larry Victor *state supreme court justice*

Clarksburg
Keeley, Irene Patricia Murphy *federal judge*

Elkins
Maxwell, Robert Earl *federal judge*

Martinsburg
Wilkes, Christopher Comas *judge*

Wheeling
Recht, Arthur *former state supreme court justice*

Williamson
Thornsbury, Michael *judge*

WISCONSIN

Appleton
Froehlich, Harold Vernon *judge, former congressman*

Madison
Bablitch, William A. *state supreme court justice*
Bartell, Angela Gina Baldi *judge*
Bradley, Ann Walsh *state supreme court justice*
Butler, Louis Bennett, Jr., *state supreme court justice*
Crabb, Barbara Brandriff *federal judge*
Crocker, Stephen L. *federal magistrate judge*
Crooks, N(eil) Patrick *state supreme court justice*
Heffernan, Nathan Stewart *retired state supreme court chief justice*
Martin, Robert David *judge, educator*
Prosser, David Thomas, Jr., *state supreme court justice, former state legislator*
Shabaz, John C. *judge*
Wilcox, Jon P. *state supreme court justice*

Milwaukee
Adelman, Lynn *federal judge*
Evans, Terence Thomas *federal judge*
Goodstein, Aaron E. *federal magistrate judge*
McGarity, Margaret Dee *federal judge*
Shapiro, James Edward *judge*
Stadtmueller, Joseph Peter *federal judge*

WYOMING

Casper
Downes, William F. *judge*

Cheyenne
Brimmer, Clarence Addison *federal judge*
Brorby, Wade *federal judge*
Golden, T. Michael *state supreme court justice*
Hill, William U. *state supreme court chief justice*
Kite, Marilyn S. *state supreme court justice, lawyer*
Lehman, Larry L. *state supreme court justice*
O'Brien, Terrence Leo *federal judge*
Schrader, Robert Wesley *judge*
Voigt, Barton R. *state supreme court justice*

Cody
Patrick, H. Hunter *judge*

TERRITORIES OF THE UNITED STATES

AMERICAN SAMOA

Pago Pago
Kruse, F. Michael *judge*
Richmond, Lyle L. *judge*

GUAM

Hagatna
Carbullido, F. Philip *judge*
Maraman, Katherine Ann *judge*
Siguenza, Peter Charles, Jr., *territory supreme court justice*
Tydingco-Gatewood, Frances Marie *judge*
Unpingco, John Walter Sablan *federal judge*

NORTHERN MARIANA ISLANDS

Saipan
Castro, Alexandro C. *judge*
Demapan, Miguel S. *judge*
Manglona, John A. *judge*
Munson, Alex Robert *judge*

PUERTO RICO

Hato Rey
Cerezo, Carmen Consuelo *judge*

San Juan
Acosta, Raymond Luis *federal judge*
Andréu-García, José Antonio *territory supreme court chief justice*
Casellas, Salvador E. *judge*
Corrada del Rio, Baltasar *supreme court justice*
Delgado-Colon, Aida M. *federal judge*
Dominguez, Daniel R. *judge*
Fusté, José Antonio *federal judge*
Fuster, Jaime B. *supreme court justice*
Gierbolini-Ortiz, Gilberto *federal judge*
Hernandez-Denton, Federico *supreme court justice*
Merly, Miriam Naveira *state supreme court justice*
Rebollo-Lopez, Francisco *state supreme court justice*
Rivera Perez, Efrain E. *state supreme court justice*

VIRGIN ISLANDS

Charlotte Amalie
Barnard, Geoffrey W. *magistrate judge*

Christiansted
Finch, Raymond Lawrence *chief judge*
Resnick, Jeffrey Lance *federal magistrate judge*

St Croix
Moore, Thomas Kail *magistrate district court judge*

CANADA

ALBERTA

Edmonton
Fraser, Catherine Anne *Canadian chief justice*
Stevenson, William Alexander *retired justice of Supreme Court of Canada*

NEW BRUNSWICK

Fredericton
Strange, Henry Hazen *judge*

Westfield
Logan, Rodman Emmason *retired jurist*

NOVA SCOTIA

Halifax
Glube, Constance Rachelle *Canadian chief justice*

ONTARIO

Bracebridge
Evans, John David Daniel *judge*

Ottawa
Heald, Darrel Verner *retired Canadian federal judge*
MacKay, William Andrew *judge*
Major, John Charles *judge*
Margeson, Theodore Earl *judge*
McLachlin, Beverley *Canadian supreme court chief justice*
Strayer, Barry Lee *federal judge*

Toronto
Boland, Janet Lang *judge*
Harris, Sydney Malcolm *retired judge*
McMurtry, R. Roy *chief justice*

QUEBEC

Montreal
Gold, Alan B. *former Canadian chief justice*
Rothman, Melvin L. *judge*

Quebec City
L'Heureux-Dubé, Claire *judge*

SASKATCHEWAN

Regina
Bayda, Edward Dmytro *judge*

Montreal
Bisson, Claude *retired chief justice of Quebec*
Gonthier, Charles Doherty *retired judge*

NETHERLANDS

Hague
Owada, Hisashi *judge*

The Hague
Aldrich, George Hoover *judge, arbitrator*
Allison, Richard Clark *judge*
Parra-Aranguren, Gonzalo *judge International Court of Justice*

ADDRESS UNPUBLISHED

Abrahamson, Shirley Schlanger *state supreme court chief justice*
Aiken, Ann L. *federal judge*
Albritton, William Harold, III, *federal judge*
Alexander, S. Allan *magistrate judge*
Arnold, W. H. (Dub Arnold) *former state supreme court chief justice*
Askey, William Hartman *US magistrate judge, lawyer*
Austin, John DeLong *judge*
Baca, Joseph Francis *retired judge*
Barliant, Ronald *federal judge*
Beck, Ronna Lee *judge*
Beisner, Ralph Andrew *judge*
Bellacosa, Joseph W. *retired state supreme court justice*
Bertelsman, William Odis *federal judge*
Boren, Roger W. *judge*
Boudreau, Daniel J. *state supreme court justice*
Boulden, Judith Ann *judge*
Brackett, Colquitt Prater, Jr., *judge, lawyer*
Breslin, Peg M. *judge*
Brett, Thomas Rutherford *federal judge*
Brightmire, Paul William *retired judge*
Brown, Michael John *retired judge*
Brown, Robert Laidlaw *state supreme court justice*
Buchanan, Theresa Carroll *judge*
Bush, Lynn Jeanne *judge*
Buttler, John Howland *retired judge, retired arbitrator*
Butzner, John Decker, Jr., *retired federal judge*
Callow, Keith McLean *judge*
Callow, William Grant *retired judge*
Campbell, John M. *judge*
Castagna, William John *federal judge*
Ceci, Louis J. *former state supreme court justice*
Clark, Leif Michael *federal judge*
Coffey, John Louis *judge*
Cohn, Avern Levin *district judge*
Colaianni, Joseph Vincent *judge*
Compton, Allen T. *retired state supreme court justice*
Cook, Julian Abele, Jr., *federal judge*
Cyr, Conrad Keefe *federal judge*
Daugherty, Frederick Alvin *federal judge*
Day, Roland Bernard *retired chief justice state supreme court*
Dela Cruz, Jose Santos *retired state supreme court justice*
Delucchi, Alfred Attilio *retired judge*
Eaton, Joe Oscar *federal judge*
Edwards, Ninian Murry *judge*
Engel, Albert Joseph *retired federal judge*
Enoch, Craig Trively *lawyer, former state supreme court justice*
Epstein, Judith Ann *judge*
Fahrnbruch, Dale E. *retired state supreme court justice*
Fay, Peter Thorp *federal judge*
Firestone, Nancy B. *federal judge*
Fisk, Merlin Edgar *judge*
Flynn, Peter Anthony *judge*
Freeman, Charles E. *state supreme court justice*
Gardner, Anne Lancaster *judge*
Gillette, W. Michael *state supreme court justice*
Goetz, Clarence Edward *retired judge, retired chief magistrate judge*
Goldstein, Debra Holly *judge*
Gorence, Patricia Josetta *judge*
Grant, Isabella Horton *retired judge*
Griffin, Robert Paul *former United States senator, state supreme court justice*
Hamblen, Lapsley Walker, Jr., *judge*
Hawkins, Michael Daly *federal judge*
Hellerstein, Alvin Kenneth *judge*
Hightower, Jack English *former state supreme court justice, congressman*
Hodge, Verne Antonio *retired chief judge*

Hogan, Thomas Francis *federal judge*
Howard, George, Jr., *federal judge*
Hunt, William E., Sr., *retired state supreme court justice*
Jenkins, Michael Grady *judge*
Joiner, Charles Wycliffe *judge*
Jones, Phyllis Gene *judge*
Kauger, Yvonne *state supreme court justice*
Kenworthy, William Eugene *judge*
Kilbride, Thomas L. *judge*
Krupansky, Blanche Ethel *retired judge*
Krupansky, Robert Bazil *federal judge*
Lancaster, Joan Ericksen *state supreme court justice*
Laycraft, James Herbert *retired judge*
Lee, Barbara A. *retired federal magistrate judge*
Lee, Dan M. *retired state supreme court chief justice*
Lemmon, Harry Thomas *retired state supreme court justice*
Linn, Richard *federal judge*
Lively, Pierce *federal judge*
Low, Harry William *judge*
Magnuson, Paul Arthur *federal judge*
Mai, Harold Leverne *retired judge*
Manglona, Ramona V. *judge, former state attorney general*
Matthews, Warren Wayne *state supreme court justice*
McCown, Hale *retired judge*
McKee, Roger Curtis *retired federal judge*
McRae, Robert Malcolm, Jr., *federal judge*
Metzner, Charles Miller *federal judge*
Moeller, James *retired state supreme court justice*
Moore, Roy S. *former state supreme court chief justice*
Muecke, Charles Andrew (Carl Muecke) *former federal judge*
Mydland, Gordon James *judge*
Nangle, John Francis *federal judge*
Nesbit, Phyllis Schneider *judge*
Neuman, Linda Kinney *retired state supreme court justice, lawyer*
Newbern, William David *retired state supreme court justice*
Newman, Theodore Roosevelt, Jr., *judge*
O'Connor, Michol *judge*
Papadakos, Nicholas Peter *retired state supreme court justice*
Payne, Mary Libby *retired judge*
Pokras, Sheila Frances *retired judge*
Porter, James Morris *retired judge*
Potter, Robert Daniel *federal judge*
Prado, Edward Charles *federal judge*
Prager, David *retired state supreme court chief justice*
Prather, Lenore Loving *former state supreme court chief justice*
Quillen, William Tatem *retired judge, lawyer, educator*
Rabin, Gilbert *judge, lawyer*
Ramil, Mario R. *retired state supreme court justice*
Reinhardt, Stephen Roy *federal judge*
Rice, Walter Herbert *federal judge*
Robart, James Louis *federal judge, lawyer*
Roszkowski, Stanley Julian *retired federal judge*
Schneider, Michael H. *federal judge*
Schroeder, Gerald Frank *state supreme court vice chief justice*
Schultz, Louis William *retired judge*
Senechal, Alice R. *federal judge, lawyer*
Shaw, Leander Jerry, Jr., *retired state supreme court justice*
Shearing, Miriam *state supreme court justice*
Sheedy, Patrick Thomas *judge*
Shubb, William Barnet *judge*
Silberman, Laurence Hirsch *federal judge*
Simms, Robert D. *former state supreme court justice*
Sinclair, Virgil Lee, Jr., *judge, writer*
Smith, Fern M. *judge*
Souter, David Hackett *United States Supreme Court justice*
Stahl, Madonna *retired judge*
Staker, Robert Jackson *judge*
Stanton, Louis Lee *federal judge*
Sweet, Robert Workman *federal judge*
Tacha, Deanell Reece *federal judge*
Thurmond, George Murat *judge*
Trout, Linda Copple *state supreme court chief justice*
Utter, Robert French *retired judge*
Verniero, Peter G. *former state supreme court justice*
Waldon, Alton Ronald, Jr., *judge*
Wellford, Harry Walker *retired federal judge*
White, Helene Nita *federal judge*
Wicker, Thomas Carey, Jr., *retired judge*
Williams, Spencer Mortimer *federal judge*
Wolin, Alfred M. *former federal judge*
Wood, Diane Pamela *judge*

LAW: LAW PRACTICE AND ADMINISTRATION

UNITED STATES

ALABAMA

Andalusia
Fuller, William Sidney *lawyer*

Anniston
Klinefelter, James Louis *lawyer*

Bay Minette
Granade, Fred King *lawyer*

Birmingham
Alford, Margie Searcy *lawyer, author*
Avant, Grady, Jr., *lawyer*
Baker, David Remember *lawyer*
Balch, Samuel Eason *lawyer*
Blan, Ollie Lionel, Jr., *retired lawyer*
Brown, Ephraim Taylor, Jr., *lawyer*
Carmody, Richard Patrick *lawyer*
Carruthers, Thomas Neely *lawyer*
Childs, Larry Brittain *lawyer*
Christian, Thomas William *lawyer*
Clark, William Northington *lawyer, retired military officer*
Coleman, Brittin Turner *lawyer*
Coleman, John James, III, *lawyer, educator*
Cook, Ralph D. *lawyer, retired state supreme court justice*
Cooper, Jerome A. *lawyer*
Cooper, N. Lee *lawyer*
DeGaris, Annesley Hodges *lawyer, educator*
Denson, William Frank, III, *lawyer*
Farley, Joseph McConnell *lawyer*
Feenker, Cherie Diane *law librarian*
Friend, Edward Malcolm, III, *lawyer, educator*
Gale, Fournier Joseph, III, *lawyer*
Garner, Robert Edward Lee *lawyer*
Givhan, Robert Marcus *lawyer*
Hagefstration, John E., Jr., *lawyer*
Hardin, Edward Lester, Jr., *lawyer*
Haskell, Wyatt Rushton *lawyer*
Hinton, James Forrest, Jr., *lawyer*
Howell, William Ashley, III, *lawyer*
Irons, William Lee *lawyer*
Johnson, Eric Heath *lawyer*
Johnson, Joseph H., Jr., *lawyer*
Kracke, Robert Russell *lawyer*
Lacy, Alexander Shelton *lawyer*
Langum, David John *law educator, historian*
Loder, Lee Wendell *lawyer*
Logan, J. Patrick *lawyer*
Long, Deborah Joyce *lawyer*
Long, Thad Gladden *lawyer*
Mc Millan, George Duncan Hastie, Jr., *lawyer, former state official*
McWhorter, Hobart Amory, Jr., *lawyer*
Mills, William Hayes *lawyer*
Molen, John Klauminzer *lawyer*
Nelson, Leonard John, III, *lawyer, educator*
North, James Little *lawyer*
Palmer, Robert Leslie *lawyer*
Redden, Lawrence Drew *lawyer*
Robin, Theodore Tydings, Jr., *lawyer, engineer, consultant*
Rogers, Ernest Mabry *lawyer*
Rotch, James E. *lawyer*
Rountree, Asa *lawyer*
Selfe, Edward Milton *lawyer*
Shanks, William Ennis, Jr., *lawyer*
Stabler, Lewis Vastine, Jr., *lawyer*
Stewart, Donald W. *lawyer*
Sullivan, Elizabeth B. *paralegal studies educator*
Todd, Judith F. *lawyer*
Trimmier, Charles Stephen, Jr., *lawyer*
Vinson, Laurence Duncan, Jr., *lawyer*
Weeks, Arthur Andrew *retired lawyer, law educator*
Wells, Huey Thomas, Jr., *lawyer*
Wilson, James Charles, Jr., *lawyer*
Wrinkle, John Newton *lawyer*
Yoder, Stephen Alan *lawyer*

Clanton
Jackson, John Hollis, Jr., *lawyer*

Dadeville
Oliver, John Percy, II, *lawyer, consultant*

Decatur
Belser, Howard McGriff, Jr., *lawyer*
Blackburn, John Gilmer *lawyer*
Caddell, John A. *lawyer*

Demopolis
Lloyd, Hugh Adams *lawyer*

Florala
Duplechin, D. James *lawyer*

Foley
Pfeifer, William Lee, Jr., *lawyer*

Huntsville
Durnya, Louis Richard *lawyer*
Gabig, Jerome S., Jr., *lawyer*
Huckaby, Gary Carlton *lawyer*
Richardson, Patrick William *lawyer*

Jasper
Thomas, Steven Allen *lawyer*

Mobile
Armbrecht, William Henry, III, *retired lawyer*
Baxley, Phillip Kent *lawyer*
Braswell, Louis Erskine *lawyer*
Campbell, Robert Craig, III, *lawyer, educator*
Finkbohner, George Wheeler, Jr., *lawyer*
Graddick, Charles Allen *lawyer*
Granade, Callie Virginia Smith S. *lawyer, federal district judge*
Harris, Benjamin Harte, Jr., *lawyer*
Helmsing, Frederick George *lawyer*
Holland, Lyman Faith, Jr., *lawyer*
Holmes, Broox Garrett *lawyer*
McCoy, Douglas Leon *lawyer*
Murchison, David Roderick *lawyer*
Peebles, E(mory) B(ush), III, *lawyer*
Pierce, Donald Fay *lawyer*
Quina, Marion Albert, Jr., *lawyer*
Roedder, William Chapman, Jr., *lawyer*
Vulevich, Edward, Jr., *prosecutor*
York, David P. *lawyer*

Montgomery
Byars, Walter Ryland, Jr., *lawyer*
Campbell, Maria Bouchelle *lawyer, consultant*
Canary, Leura *prosecutor*
Darby, Larry Eugene *lawyer*
Dees, Morris Seligman, Jr., *lawyer*
Ely, Robert Eugene *lawyer, author, educator*
Eubanks, Ronald W. *lawyer, broadcaster*
Gregory, William Stanley *lawyer*
Hamner, Reginald Turner *lawyer*
Hester, Douglas Benjamin *lawyer, federal official*
Kloess, Lawrence Herman, Jr., *retired lawyer*
Langford, Charles Douglas *lawyer*
Laurie, Robin Garrett *lawyer*
Lawson, Thomas Seay, Jr., *lawyer*
Leslie, Henry Arthur *lawyer, retired banker*
Lewis, Joseph Brady (Jay Lewis) *lawyer*
McFadden, Frank Hampton *lawyer, business executive, former judge*
Nachman, Merton Roland, Jr., *lawyer*
Prestwood, Alvin Tennyson *lawyer*
Salmon, Joseph Thaddeus *lawyer*
Smith, Maury Drane *lawyer*
Stevenson, Bryan Allen *lawyer*
Volz, Charles Harvie, Jr., *lawyer*
Wood, James Jerry *lawyer*

Opelika
Samford, Yetta Glenn, Jr., *lawyer, director*

Orange Beach
Adams, Daniel Fenton *law educator*

Owens Cross Roads
Williams, Lowell Craig *lawyer, employee relations executive*

Point Clear
Holt, Thaddeus *lawyer*

Sheffield
Hamby, Gene Malcolm, Jr., *lawyer*

Tuscaloosa
Cook, Camille Wright *retired law educator*
Filler, Daniel M. *law educator*
Hubbard, Perry *lawyer, educator*

Tuskegee
Gray, Fred David *lawyer*

ALASKA

Anchorage
Bond, Marc Douglas *lawyer*
Burgess, Timothy M. *prosecutor*
Butler, Rex Lamont *lawyer*
Cantor, James Elliot *lawyer*
Ealy, Jonathan Bruce *lawyer*
Ebell, C. Walter (Cecil Walter Ebell) *lawyer*
Greenstein, Marla Nan *lawyer*
Gruenberg, Max F., Jr., *lawyer*
Hayes, George Nicholas *lawyer*
Hughes, Mary Katherine *lawyer*
Linxwiler, James David *lawyer*
Metzger, Yale Hyder *lawyer, educator*
Oesting, David W. *lawyer*
Ostrovsky, Lawrence Zelig *lawyer*
Roberts, John Derham *lawyer*
Ross, Wayne Anthony *lawyer*
Rosston, Richard Mark *lawyer*
Walther, Dale Jay *lawyer*
Willard-Jones, Donna C. *lawyer*

Bethel
Cooke, Christopher Robert *former state judge, lawyer*

Fairbanks
Bodwell, Lori *lawyer*
Schendel, William Burnett *lawyer*

Juneau
Collins, Patricia A. *lawyer, judge*

Kodiak
Jamin, Matthew Daniel *lawyer, magistrate judge*

Nondalton
Gay, Sarah Elizabeth *lawyer*

Salcha
Rice, Julian Casavant *lawyer*

ARIZONA

Carefree
Putney, Mark William *lawyer, utilities executive*

Eloy
O'Leary, Thomas Michael *lawyer*

Flagstaff
Cowser, Danny Lee *lawyer, mental health specialist*

Grand Canyon
Breecher-Breen, Sheila Rae *lawyer*

Kingman
Basinger, Richard Lee *lawyer*
Hlavac, Dana Paul *lawyer, consultant*

Paradise Valley
Tubman, William Charles *lawyer*

Peoria
Engelhardt, Thomas Francis *lawyer, consultant*

Phoenix
Allen, Robert Eugene Barton *lawyer*
Alsentzer, William James, Jr., *lawyer*
Andersen, Ronald Meredith *lawyer*
Bain, C. Randall *lawyer*
Baker, William Dunlap *lawyer*
Bakker, Thomas Gordon *lawyer*
Begam, Robert George *lawyer*
Beggs, Harry Mark *lawyer*
Bivens, Donald Wayne *lawyer, judge*
Blanchard, Charles Alan *lawyer, former state senator*
Bodney, David Jeremy *lawyer*
Bouma, John Jacob *lawyer*
Brewer, Charles Moulton *lawyer*
Burke, Timothy John *lawyer*
Calderon, Ernest *lawyer*
Case, David Leon *lawyer*
Chanen, Steven Robert *lawyer*
Charlton, Paul *lawyer*
Coghill, William Thomas, Jr., *retired lawyer*
Cohen, Jon Stephan *lawyer*
Cole, George Thomas *lawyer*
Comus, Louis Francis, Jr., *lawyer*
Condo, James Robert *lawyer*
Conrad, John Regis *lawyer, engineering executive, consultant*
Cooledge, Richard Calvin *lawyer*
Coppersmith, Sam *lawyer*
Corson, Kimball Jay *lawyer*
Crockett, Clyll Webb *lawyer*
Curry, J. Stanton *lawyer, educator*
Davies, David George *lawyer, educator*
Dawson, John Joseph *lawyer*
Derdenger, Patrick *lawyer*
Derouin, James Gilbert *lawyer*
Dunipace, Ian Douglas *lawyer*
Ehmann, Anthony Valentine *lawyer*
Everett, James Joseph *lawyer*
Feder, Bruce *lawyer*
Feinstein, Allen Lewis *lawyer*
Flickinger, Don Jacob *patent agent*
Forshey, Timothy Allan *lawyer*
Gaffney, Donald Lee *lawyer*
Gallagher, Michael L. *lawyer*
Gilbert, Donald Roy *lawyer*
Gladner, Marc Stefan *lawyer*
Goldstein, Stuart Wolf *lawyer*
Gomez, David Frederick *lawyer*
Griller, Gordon Moore *legal association administrator*
Haga, David L. *lawyer*
Halpern, Barry David *lawyer*
Hammond, Larry Austin *lawyer*
Harrison, Mark Isaac *lawyer*
Hay, John Leonard *lawyer*
Hayden, William Robert *lawyer*
Henze, Tom *lawyer*
Hicks, William Albert, III, *lawyer*
Hirsch, Steven A. *lawyer*
Hoecker, Thomas Ralph *lawyer*
Howard, William Matthew *arbitrator, writer, lawyer*
Huntwork, James Roden *lawyer*
Inman, William Peter *lawyer*
Jacobson, Edward (Julian Edward Jacobson) *lawyer*
James, Charles E., Jr., *lawyer*
Jirauch, Charles W. *lawyer*
Johnston, Logan Truax, III, *lawyer*
Klahr, Gary Peter *retired lawyer*
Klausner, Jack Daniel *lawyer*
Klein, R. Kent *lawyer*
Knoller, Guy David *lawyer*
Koester, Berthold Karl *lawyer, law educator, retired honorary German consul*
Kurn, Neal *lawyer*
Lee, Richard H(arlo) *lawyer*
Levetown, Robert Alexander *lawyer*
Lubin, Stanley *lawyer*
Lundeen, Bradley Curtis *lawyer*
Martori, Joseph Peter *lawyer*
Mc Clennen, Louis *lawyer, educator*
McRae, Hamilton Eugene, III, *lawyer*
Merritt, Nancy-Jo *lawyer*
Mousel, Craig Lawrence *lawyer*
Olsen, Alfred Jon *lawyer*
Perry, Lee Rowan *retired lawyer*
Phillips, James Harold *lawyer*
Pietzsch, Michael Edward *lawyer*
Platt, Warren E. *lawyer*
Pogson, Stephen Walter *lawyer*
Rathwell, Peter John *lawyer*
Rose, Scott A. *lawyer*
Roush, Charles Dow *lawyer*
Rudolph, Gilbert Lawrence *lawyer*
Sanders, Barry R. *lawyer*
Savage, Stephen Michael *lawyer*
Sherk, Kenneth John *lawyer*
Silverman, Alan Henry *lawyer*
Smock, Timothy Robert *lawyer*
Storey, Norman C. *lawyer*
Swartz, Melvin Jay *lawyer, writer*
Tennen, Leslie Irwin *lawyer, consultant, inventor*
Thompson, Joel Erik *lawyer*
Thompson, Terence William *lawyer*
Udall, Calvin Hunt *lawyer*
Ulrich, Paul Graham *lawyer, writer, editor*
Van Haren, Peter *lawyer*
Walker, Richard K. *lawyer*
Wall, Donald Arthur *lawyer*
Wheeler, Steven M. *lawyer*
Whisler, James Steven *lawyer, mining and manufacturing executive*
Williams, Quinn Patrick *lawyer*
Wilmer, Charles Mark *lawyer*
Wolf, G. Van Velsor, Jr., *lawyer*

Prescott
Chamberlain, David Alanson *lawyer, consultant, writer*
Gose, Richard Vernie *lawyer*
Madden, Paul Robert *lawyer, director*

Scottsdale
Buri, Charles Edward *lawyer*
Casper, Eric Michael *lawyer*
Grant, Merwin Darwin *lawyer*
Hutchison, Stanley Philip *retired lawyer*
Krupp, Clarence William *lawyer, personnel and hospital administrator*
Lindgren, D(erbin) Kenneth, Jr., *retired lawyer*
Lowry, Edward Francis, Jr., *lawyer*
Marks, Merton Eleazer *lawyer, international arbitrator, mediator, consultant*
Nielsen, Greg Ross *lawyer*
Overgaard, Cordell Jersild *lawyer, business executive, director*
Roberts, Jean Reed *lawyer*
Smith, David Burnell *lawyer*
Titus, Jon Alan *lawyer*
Whittington, Thomas Lee *lawyer*

Sun City
Keesling, Karen Ruth *lawyer*
Treece, James Lyle *lawyer*

Surprise
Fennelly, Jane Corey *lawyer*

Tempe
Bender, Paul *lawyer, educator*
Ching, Anthony Bartholomew *lawyer, educator, consultant*
Fanning, Francis Gerard *lawyer*
Jennings, Marianne Moody *lawyer, educator*
Matheson, Alan Adams *law educator*
Moya, Patrick Robert *lawyer*
Schatzki, George *law educator*
Shimpock, Kathy Elizabeth *lawyer, writer*
Spritzer, Ralph Simon *lawyer, educator*

Tucson
Augello, William Joseph *lawyer*
Betteridge, Frances Carpenter *retired lawyer, mediator*
Blackman, Jeffrey William *lawyer*
Boswell, Susan G. *lawyer*
Eckhardt, August Gottlieb *retired law educator*

Feldman, Stanley George *lawyer*
Fortman, Marvin *law educator, consultant*
Froman, Sandra Sue *lawyer*
Gantz, David Alfred *lawyer, university official*
Gonzales, Richard Joseph *lawyer*
Heaphy, John Merrill *lawyer*
Isaak, G. Eugene *lawyer*
Jacobs, William Russell, II, *lawyer*
Jurkowitz, Daniel S. *lawyer, prosecutor, judge*
Kimble, William Earl *lawyer*
Kozolchyk, Boris *law educator, consultant*
Lesher, Stephen Harrison *lawyer*
Meehan, Michael Joseph *lawyer*
Morrow, James Franklin *lawyer*
Noonan, James C. *lawyer, mediator, arbitrator*
Osborne, John Edwards *lawyer*
Pace, Thomas M. *lawyer*
Samet, Dee-Dee *lawyer*
Schorr, S. L. *lawyer*
Simmons, Sarah R. *lawyer*
Staubitz, Arthur Frederick *lawyer, healthcare
    products company executive*
Strong, John William *lawyer, educator*
Sweeney, Joseph Dudley *law educator, political
    organization worker*
Tindall, Robert Emmett *lawyer, educator*
Treadwell-Rubin, Pamela A. *lawyer*

Yuma
Hossler, David Joseph *lawyer, law educator*
Hunt, Gerald Wallace *lawyer*

ARKANSAS

Bentonville
Hyde, Thomas D. *lawyer*
Mars, Tom *lawyer*

Cherokee Village
Burke, Richard Kitchens *lawyer, educator*

Conway
Johnson, James Douglas (Jim Johnson) *lawyer*

Crossett
Hubbell, Billy James *lawyer*

El Dorado
Wynne, William Joseph *lawyer*

Fayetteville
Bassett, Woodson William, Jr., *lawyer*
Epley, Lewis Everett, Jr., *lawyer*
Kester, Charles Melvin *lawyer*
Nance, Cynthia Eleanor *law educator*
Pearson, Charles Thomas, Jr., *lawyer, director*
Pettus, E. Lamar *lawyer*
Rhoads, Robert K. *lawyer, retail executive*
VanWinkle, John Ragan *lawyer*

Fort Smith
Cromwell, William M. *lawyer*
Daily, Thomas A. *lawyer*
Gean, Thomas C. *prosecutor*

Helena
Roscopf, Charles Buford *lawyer*

Hot Springs National Park
Schnipper, Don Martin *lawyer*

Jonesboro
Deacon, John C. *lawyer*
McNeill, Paul Deane *lawyer*

Little Rock
Anderson, Philip Sidney *lawyer*
Campbell, George Emerson *lawyer*
Cherry, Sandra Wilson *lawyer*
Cross, J. Bruce *lawyer*
Cummins, H. E. Bud, III, *lawyer*
Drummond, Winslow *lawyer*
Fitzhugh, Kathryn Corrothers *law librarian*
Fogleman, John Albert *lawyer, retired judge*
Gunter, Russell Allen *lawyer*
Hargis, David Michael *lawyer*
Haught, William Dixon *lawyer, writer*
Jennings, Alston *lawyer*
Julian, Jim Lee *lawyer*
Lipe, Linda Bon *lawyer*
May, Ronald Alan *lawyer*
Murphey, Arthur Gage, Jr., *law educator*
Nelson, Edward Sheffield *lawyer, retired utilities
    executive*
Ross, Robert Dwain *lawyer*
Sherman, William Farrar *lawyer, former state
    legislator*
Stockburger, Jean Dawson *lawyer*
Thomas, Thorp *retired lawyer*
Witherspoon, Carolyn Brack *lawyer*
Wright, Robert Ross, III, *law educator*

Malvern
Dodd, Jerry Lee *lawyer*

Marked Tree
Everett, Mike *lawyer*

Monticello
Ball, William Kenneth *lawyer*

North Little Rock
Patty, Claibourne Watkins, Jr., *lawyer*

Osceola
Wilson, Ralph Edwin *lawyer, justice*

Pine Bluff
Jones, John Harris *lawyer*
Strode, Joseph Arlin *lawyer*

Rogers
Myers, Dane Jacob *lawyer, podiatrist*

Searcy
Hughes, Thomas Morgan, III, *lawyer*

Springdale
Hudson, R. Read *lawyer, food products executive*

Warren
Claycomb, Hugh Murray *lawyer, author*

CALIFORNIA

Alameda
Stonehouse, James Adam *lawyer*

Alamo
Madden, Palmer Brown *lawyer*
Schreiber, John T. *lawyer*

Aliso Viejo
Fisher, Lawrence N. *lawyer, engineering company
    executive*

Arcadia
Gelber, Louise C(arp) *lawyer*

Atherton
Ferris, Robert Albert *lawyer, venture capitalist*

Auburn
Lyon, Bruce Arnold *lawyer, educator*

Bakersfield
Karcher, Steven Michael *lawyer*
Martin, George Francis *lawyer*
Tornstrom, Robert Ernest *lawyer, oil company
    executive*

Belvedere Tiburon
Bremer, William Richard *lawyer*
Buell, Edward Rick, II, *lawyer*

Berkeley
Barnes, Thomas G. *law educator*
Barton, Babette B. *lawyer, educator*
Berring, Robert Charles, Jr., *law educator, law
    librarian, former dean*
Buxbaum, Richard M. *law educator, lawyer*
Choper, Jesse Herbert *law educator, university dean*
De Goff, Victoria Joan *lawyer*
Eisenberg, Melvin A. *law educator*
Feeley, Malcolm McCollum *law educator, political
    scientist*
Frickey, Philip Paul *law educator*
Halbach, Edward Christian, Jr., *law educator*
Haley, George Patrick *lawyer*
McNulty, John Kent *lawyer, educator*
Messinger, Sheldon L(eopold) *law educator*
Mishkin, Paul J. *lawyer, educator*
Moran, Rachel *lawyer, educator*
Ogg, Wilson Reid *lawyer, retired judge, poet,
    publishing executive, educator*
Peterson, Andrea Lenore *law educator*
Post, Robert Charles *law educator*
Rappaport, Stuart Ramon *lawyer*
Reidhaar, Donald Laverne *lawyer*
Samuelson, Pamela Ann *law educator*
Scheiber, Harry N. *law educator*
Sorensen, Linda *lawyer*
Sparks, John Edward *lawyer*
Wolfram, Charles William *law educator*
Woodhouse, Thomas Edwin *lawyer*

Beverly Hills
Anderson, Kenneth Allen *lawyer, hotel executive*
Burns, Marvin Gerald *lawyer*
Factor, Max, III, *arbitrator, mediator*
Hogan, Steven L. *lawyer*
Horwin, Leonard *retired lawyer*
Isaacman, Alan L. *lawyer*
Jaffe, F. Filmore *lawyer, retired judge*
Juno, Cynthia *lawyer*
Kane, Paula *lawyer*
Karlin, Michael Jonathan Abraham *lawyer*
Kite, Richard Lloyd *lawyer, real estate development
    company executive*
Kleiner, Madeleine A. *lawyer*
Ramer, Bruce M. *lawyer*
Rosky, Burton Seymour *lawyer*
Russell, Irwin Emanuel *lawyer*
Schiff, Gunther Hans *lawyer*
Sherwood, Arthur Lawrence *lawyer*
Shire, Harold Raymond *law educator, writer*
Sobelle, Richard E. *lawyer*
Thompson, Richard Dickson *lawyer*
Warren, Steve *lawyer*

Bonita
Kline, Paul Conley *lawyer*

Brea
Churchill, James Allen *lawyer*

Burbank
Ajalat, Sol Peter *lawyer*
Braverman, Alan N. *lawyer*
Cunningham, Robert D. *lawyer*
Wise, Helena Sunny *lawyer*

Burlingame
Cotchett, Joseph Winters *lawyer, author*
Ocheltree, Richard Lawrence *lawyer, retired forest
    products company executive*

Calabasas
Grimwade, Richard Llewellyn *lawyer*

California City
Friedl, Rick *lawyer, former academic administrator*

Calimesa
McNulty, James Francis, Jr., *lawyer, consultant*

Campbell
Bass, Lewis *lawyer*
Beizer, Lance Kurt *lawyer*
Castello, Raymond Vincent *lawyer*

Capistrano Beach
Gregory, George G. *retired lawyer*

Carmel
Bengert, W. Raymond *lawyer, chemical engineer*
Robinson, John Minor *lawyer, retired business
    executive*

Carmichael
Halpenny, Diana Doris *lawyer*

Chatsworth
Klein, Jeffrey S. *lawyer, media executive*

Chico
Schweitzer, Sandra Lynn *lawyer, nurse*

Chino
Determan, John David *lawyer*
Van Wagner, Ellen *lawyer, law educator*

Claremont
Ansell, Edward Orin *lawyer*
Ferguson, Cleve Robert *lawyer, educator*
Hafif, Gregory Keith *lawyer*

Clovis
Ninnis, William Raymond, Jr., *lawyer*

Coalinga
Frame, Ted Ronald *lawyer*

Concord
Schwartz, Eric *lawyer*

Corona
Everett Nollkamper, Pamela Irene *legal
    management company executive, educator*

Corona Del Mar
Allen, Russell G. *lawyer*

Coronado
Betts, Barbara Lang *lawyer, rancher, realtor*
Heisner, John Richard *lawyer*

Costa Mesa
Anderson, Jon David *lawyer*
Caldwell, Courtney Lynn *lawyer, real estate
    consultant*
Currie, Robert Emil *lawyer*
Daniels, James Walter *lawyer*
Guilford, Andrew John *lawyer*
Hay, Howard Clinton *lawyer*
Jones, H(arold) Gilbert, Jr., *lawyer*
Marshall, Ellen Ruth *lawyer*
Phelps, Aaron K(ay) *lawyer*
Reich, Peter Lester *legal educator, legal and
    historical consultant*
Tanner, R. Marshall *lawyer*
Tennyson, Peter Joseph *lawyer*

Cotati
Robertson, William Abbott *arbitrator, mediator,
    lawyer*

Cupertino
Jelinch, Frank Anthony *lawyer*

Cypress
Olschwang, Alan Paul *lawyer*

Danville
Candland, D. Stuart *lawyer*

Darwin
Palazzo, Robert Paul *lawyer, accountant*

Davis
Bartosic, Florian *law educator, lawyer, arbitrator*
Feeney, Floyd Fulton *legal educator*
Imwinkelried, Edward John *law educator*
Wolk, Bruce Alan *law educator*
Wydick, Richard Crews *lawyer, educator*

Del Mar
Seitman, John Michael *arbitrator, mediator, lawyer*

East Palo Alto
Bates, William, III, *lawyer*
Furbush, David Malcolm *lawyer*
Lesser, Henry *lawyer*

El Segundo
Codon, Dennis P. *lawyer*
Gambaro, Ernest Umberto *lawyer, consultant,
    engineer*
Hunter, Larry Dean *lawyer*
Muhlbach, Robert Arthur *lawyer*
Pearce, Harry Jonathan *lawyer*
Willis, Judy Ann *lawyer*

Emeryville
Arguedas, Cristina C. *lawyer*
Howe, Drayton Ford, Jr., *lawyer*
Loving, Deborah June Pierre *lawyer, real estate
    broker*

Encinitas
Wigmore, John Grant *lawyer*

Encino
Lombardini, Carol Ann *lawyer*
Smith, Selma Moidel *lawyer, composer*

Escondido
Godone-Maresca, Lillian *lawyer*
Mayer, James Hock *mediator, lawyer*

Eureka
Clark, Dwight William *lawyer*

Fairfield
Haas, Richard *lawyer*

Fallbrook
Sorbello, Joseph Charles *retired lawyer*

Foster City
Jeffrey, John Orval *lawyer*
Lonnquist, George Eric *lawyer*

Fremont
Cummings, John Patrick *lawyer*

Fresno
Ewell, A. Ben, Jr., *lawyer, small business owner*
Jamison, Daniel Oliver *lawyer*
Lagle, John Franklin *lawyer*

Lambe, James Patrick *lawyer*
Little, Kevin Gerard *lawyer*
McGregor, John Joseph *lawyer*
Palmer, Samuel Copeland, III, *lawyer*

Fullerton
Bush, William Merritt *lawyer*
Frizell, Samuel *law educator*
Goldstein, Edward David *lawyer, former glass
    company executive*
Moerbeek, Stanley Leonard *lawyer*
Roberts, Mark Scott *lawyer*
Steinmeyer, Robert Jay *lawyer*

Glendale
Hoffman, Donald M. *lawyer*
Kazanjian, Phillip Carl *lawyer*
MacDonald, Kirk Stewart *lawyer*
Martinetti, Ronald Anthony *lawyer*
Scott, A. Timothy *lawyer, business executive*
Simpson, Allyson Bilich *lawyer*

Glendora
Chan, Daniel Chung-Yin *lawyer*

Gold River
Andrew, John Henry *lawyer, retail corporation
    executive, author*

Greenbrae
Bonapart, Alan David *lawyer*

Hacienda Heights
Wang, George K.F. *international lawyer*

Half Moon Bay
Lambert, Frederick William *lawyer, educator*

Hayward
Goodman, Louis J. *lawyer*
Smith, John Kerwin *lawyer*

Hollywood
Gould, Julian Saul *lawyer*

Huntington Beach
Cook, Debbie *lawyer, councilman*
Garrels, Sherry Ann *lawyer*
Jensen, Dennis Lowell *lawyer*
Nikas, Richard John *lawyer*

Hydesville
Shulman, Adley M. *lawyer, educator*

Imperial Beach
Merkin, William Leslie *retired lawyer*

Indian Wells
McDermott, Thomas John, Jr., *lawyer*

Indio
De Salva, Christopher Joseph *lawyer, consultant*

Irvine
Beard, Ronald Stratton *lawyer*
Black, William Rea *lawyer*
Clark, Karen Heath *lawyer*
Creatura, Mark Anthony *lawyer*
Hurst, Charles Wilson *lawyer*
Knobbe, Louis Joseph *lawyer, educator*
Pitcher, Thomas B. *lawyer*
Specter, Richard Bruce *lawyer*
Tachner, Leonard *lawyer*
Wertheim, Jay Philip *lawyer*
Wintrode, Ralph Charles *lawyer*

La Canada Flintridge
Costello, Francis William *lawyer*
Wallace, James Wendell *lawyer*

La Jolla
Buchholz, Debby *lawyer*
Kirchheimer, Arthur E(dward) *lawyer, business
    executive*
Wilkins, Floyd, Jr., *retired lawyer, consultant*
Wilson, Bonnie Jean *lawyer, educator, investor*
ZoBell, Karl *lawyer*

Lafayette
Davies, Paul Lewis, Jr., *retired lawyer*

Laguna Hills
Reinglass, Michelle Annette *lawyer*

Laguna Niguel
Cifarelli, Thomas Abitabile *lawyer*

Larkspur
Greenberg, Myron Silver *lawyer*
Ratner, David Louis *retired law educator*
Saxe, Steven Louis *lawyer*

Lompoc
Keller, Janice N. *lawyer, councilwoman*

Long Beach
Bursley, Kathleen A. *lawyer*
Calhoun, John R. *lawyer*
Deukmejian, George *lawyer, former governor*
Fuller, Jack Arthur *lawyer*
Haile, Lawrence Barclay *lawyer*
Helwick, Christine *lawyer*
Hennen, Thomas Waldo *lawyer*
Lodwick, Michael Wayne *lawyer*
Sinclitico, Dennis J. *lawyer*
Wise, George Edward *lawyer*

Los Alamitos
Nemirow, Lawrence H. *lawyer*

Los Altos
Weir, Robert H. *lawyer*

Los Angeles
Aaron, Benjamin *law educator, arbitrator*
Abrams, Norman *law educator, academic
    administrator*
Abramson, Leslie Hope *lawyer*
Adamek, Charles Andrew *lawyer*
Adams, Thomas Merritt *lawyer*
Adell, Hirsch *lawyer*

Adler, Erwin Ellery *lawyer*
Adler, Sara *arbitrator, mediator*
Allred, Gloria Rachel *lawyer*
Amkraut, David M.h. *lawyer, judge*
Anderson, Charles David *lawyer*
Angel, Arthur Ronald *lawyer, consultant*
Angelo, Christopher Edmond *lawyer, consultant*
Antin, Michael *lawyer*
Apfel, Gary *lawyer*
April, Rand Scott *lawyer*
Arkoz, David X. *lawyer*
Arnkra, Joe *legal administrator, writer*
Arnold, Dennis B. *lawyer*
Azad, Susan S. *lawyer*
Bakaly, Charles George, Jr., *lawyer, mediator*
Barrett, Jane Hayes *lawyer*
Barsky, Wayne Mitchell *lawyer*
Barton, Alan Joel *lawyer*
Baum, Michael Lin *lawyer*
Baumann, Richard Gordon *lawyer*
Baumgarten, Ronald Neal *lawyer*
Bender, Charles William *lawyer*
Bendix, Helen Irene *lawyer*
Bennett, Fred Gilbert *lawyer*
Bernacchi, Richard Lloyd *lawyer*
Bishop, Sidney Willard *lawyer*
Black, Donna Ruth *lawyer*
Blencowe, Paul Sherwood *lawyer, private investor*
Blendell, Elizabeth A. *lawyer*
Blumberg, Grace Ganz *law educator, lawyer*
Bodkin, Henry Grattan, Jr., *lawyer*
Bomes, Stephen D. *lawyer*
Bonesteel, Michael John *lawyer*
Boras, Kim *lawyer*
Bordy, Michael Jeffrey *lawyer*
Bortman, David *lawyer*
Bosl, Phillip L. *lawyer*
Boxer, Lester *lawyer*
Bradley, Lawrence D., Jr. *lawyer*
Branca, John Gregory *lawyer, consultant*
Braudrick, Arthur C., Jr., *lawyer*
Brault, Lisa J. *prosecutor*
Braun, David A(dlai) *lawyer*
Bressan, Paul Louis *lawyer*
Brian, Brad D. *lawyer*
Bringardner, John Michael *lawyer, clergyman*
Brittenham, Skip *lawyer*
Bryan, Karen Smith *lawyer*
Burch, Robert Dale *lawyer*
Burke, Robert Bertram *lawyer, political consultant, lobbyist*
Burke, Yvonne Watson Brathwaite (Mrs. William A. Burke) *lawyer*
Byrd, Christine Waterman Swent *lawyer*
Campbell, Jennifer Louise *lawyer*
Carlson, Robert Edwin *lawyer*
Carr, James Patrick *lawyer*
Carr, Willard Zeller, Jr., *lawyer*
Carrey, Neil *lawyer, educator*
Carroll, Raoul Lord *lawyer, investment banker*
Cartwright, Brian Grant *lawyer*
Castro, Leonard Edward *lawyer*
Chemerinsky, Erwin *law educator*
Chiate, Kenneth Reed *lawyer*
Christ, Roxanne E. *lawyer*
Christol, Carl Q(uimby) *lawyer, political science educator*
Chu, Morgan *lawyer*
Clark, R(ufus) Bradbury *lawyer, director*
Cleary, William Joseph, Jr., *lawyer*
Cochran, Johnnie L., Jr., *lawyer*
Cohen, Cynthia Marylyn *lawyer*
Cole, Curtis Allen *lawyer*
Coleman, Rexford Lee *lawyer, educator*
Collier, Charles Arthur, Jr., *lawyer*
Conn, David P. *lawyer*
Cook, Melanie K. *lawyer*
Cooley, Steve *prosecutor*
Copley, Ralph D., Jr., *lawyer*
Creim, William Benjamin *lawyer*
Dana, Lauren Elizabeth *lawyer*
Daniels, John Peter *lawyer*
Daniels, William Anthony *lawyer, writer*
Danielson, Walter George *lawyer*
Darby, G(eorge) Harrison *lawyer*
De Brier, Donald Paul *lawyer*
de Castro, Hugo Daniel *lawyer*
Delgadillo, Rockard J. (Rocky Delgadillo) *lawyer*
Demoff, Marvin Alan *lawyer*
Denham, Robert Edwin *lawyer, investment company executive*
Diamond, Stanley Jay *lawyer*
Dienes, Louis Robert *lawyer*
Dinel, Richard Henry *lawyer*
Donaldson, Michael Cleaves *lawyer*
Doran, Kenneth M. *lawyer*
Emanuel, William Joseph *lawyer*
English, Stephen Raymond *lawyer*
Etra, Donald *lawyer*
Fairbank, Robert Harold *lawyer*
Farmer, Robert Lindsay *lawyer*
Farrar, Stanley F. *lawyer*
Feigen, Brenda S. *lawyer, film producer, author*
Fein, Ronald Lawrence *lawyer*
Fenning, Lisa Hill *lawyer, mediator, former federal judge*
Fields, Bertram Harris *lawyer*
Fisher, Barry Alan *lawyer*
Fisher, Ruth E. *lawyer*
Fleer, Keith George *lawyer, former motion picture executive*
Follick, Edwin Duane *law educator, dean, chiropractor*
Fontaine, Valerie Anne *lawyer, legal search consultant*
Friedman, Alan E. *lawyer*
Gallo, Jon Joseph *lawyer*
Galton, Stephen Harold *lawyer*
Geragos, Mark J. *lawyer*
Gest, Howard David *lawyer*
Girardi, Thomas Vincent *lawyer*
Glushien, Morris P. *lawyer, arbitrator*
Goldman, Allan Bailey *lawyer*
Goldstein, Michael Gerald *lawyer, director*
Goodman, Max A. *lawyer, educator*
Gordon, David Eliot *lawyer*
Gorman, Joseph Gregory, Jr., *lawyer*
Gould, David *lawyer*
Green, Kenneth Norton *law educator*
Green, William Porter *lawyer*
Grobe, Charles Stephen *lawyer, accountant*
Gross, Ariela Julie *law educator*
Grush, Julius Sidney *lawyer*
Gurfein, Peter J. *lawyer*
Haakh, Gilbert Edward *lawyer*

Hahn, Elliott Julius *lawyer*
Halkett, Alan Neilson *lawyer*
Handzlik, Jan Lawrence *lawyer*
Hansell, Dean *lawyer*
Hanson, John J. *lawyer*
Hart, Larry Calvin *lawyer*
Havel, Richard W. *lawyer*
Hayutin, David Lionel *lawyer*
Heinke, Rex S. *lawyer*
Heller, Philip *lawyer*
Hemminger, Pamela Lynn *lawyer*
Henry, Carl Nolan *lawyer*
Hernandez, Antonia *lawyer*
Heyck, Theodore Daly *lawyer*
Heyler, Grover Ross *retired lawyer*
Hieronymus, Edward Whittlesey *lawyer*
Hight, B. Boyd *lawyer*
Holliday, Thomas Edgar *lawyer*
Holtzman, Robert Arthur *lawyer*
Hoye, Maria Pilar *lawyer*
Hudson, Jeffrey Reid *lawyer*
Hufstedler, Seth Martin *lawyer*
Hufstedler, Shirley Mount (Mrs. Seth M. Hufstedler) *lawyer, former federal judge*
Hyman, Milton Bernard *lawyer*
Hyman, Ursula H. *lawyer*
Iamele, Richard Thomas *law librarian*
Imre, Christina Joanne *lawyer*
Irwin, Philip Donnan *lawyer*
Jackson, Morton Barrows *lawyer*
Johnson, Jonathan Edwin, II, *lawyer*
Johnson, Philip Leslie *lawyer*
Jordan, Martha B. *lawyer*
Jordan, Robert Leon *lawyer, educator*
Kadison, Stuart Lynn *lawyer, educator, writer*
Kamine, Bernard S. *lawyer*
Kanoff, Mary Ellen *lawyer*
Karst, Kenneth Leslie *law educator*
Kelly, Pamela B. *lawyer*
Kenoff, Jay Stewart *lawyer*
Kiekhofer, William Henry *lawyer*
Kindel, James Horace, Jr., *lawyer*
King, Peter Nelson *lawyer*
Kirwan, Betty Jane Jane *lawyer*
Kirwan, R. DeWitt *lawyer*
Klinger, Marilyn Sydney *lawyer*
Krupka, Robert George *lawyer*
Kuechle, John Merrill *lawyer*
Kupietzky, Moshe J. *lawyer*
Lappen, Chester I. *lawyer*
Latham, Joseph Al, Jr., *lawyer*
Lauchengco, Jose Yujuico, Jr., *lawyer*
Lavin, Laurence Michael *lawyer*
Lawton, Eric *lawyer, photographer, visual artist, author*
Leibow, Ronald Louis *lawyer*
Lesser, Joan L. *lawyer*
Letwin, Leon *law educator*
Leung, Frankie Fook-Lun *lawyer*
Levenson, Laurie L. *law educator*
Levine, Meldon Edises *lawyer, former congressman*
Levine, Thomas Jeffrey Pello *lawyer*
Lewis, Cherie Sue *lawyer, English language and journalism educator*
Lindholm, Dwight Henry *lawyer*
Lipsig, Ethan *lawyer*
Litvack, Sanford Martin *lawyer*
Long, Gregory Alan *lawyer*
LoPucki, Lynn Michael *law educator*
Ludlam, James Edward *lawyer*
Lund, James Louis *lawyer*
Lynch, Patrick *lawyer*
MacLaughlin, Francis Joseph *lawyer*
Mancino, Douglas Michael *lawyer*
Marcus, Stephen Howard *lawyer*
Mason, Cheryl White *lawyer*
Mavis, Darrell *lawyer, educator*
May, Lawrence Edward *lawyer*
McAniff, Edward John *lawyer*
McKinzie, Carl Wayne *lawyer*
McLane, Frederick Berg *lawyer*
Medearis, Miller *lawyer*
Meisinger, Louis M. *lawyer*
Menes, Paul Ira *lawyer*
Mersel, Marjorie Kathryn Pedersen *lawyer*
Metzger, Robert Streicher *lawyer*
Meyer, Michael Edwin *lawyer*
Millard, Neal Steven *lawyer, educator*
Miller, Milton Allen *lawyer*
Mintz, Marshall Gary *lawyer*
Molleur, Richard Raymond *lawyer*
Moloney, Stephen Michael *lawyer*
Morgenthaler-Lever, Alisa *lawyer*
Moskowitz, Joel Steven *lawyer*
Neely, Sally Schultz *lawyer*
Neiter, Gerald Irving *lawyer*
Nelson, Grant Steel *lawyer, educator*
Neufeld, Timothy Lee *lawyer*
Newman, Michael Rodney *lawyer*
Nicholas, Frederick M. *lawyer*
Nicholas, William Richard *lawyer*
Niemeth, Charles Frederick *lawyer*
Nobumoto, Karen S. *prosecutor*
Nocas, Andrew James *lawyer*
Nochimson, David *lawyer*
Ochoa, Arthur J. *lawyer, hospital administrator*
O'Connell, Kevin *lawyer*
O'Donnell, Pierce Henry *lawyer*
Ohlgren, Joel R. *lawyer*
O'Leary, Prentice Lee *lawyer*
Oliver, Anthony Thomas, Jr., *lawyer*
Oliver, Dale Hugh *lawyer*
Olsen, Frances Elisabeth *law educator, theorist*
Olson, Ronald Leroy *lawyer*
Ordin, Andrea Sheridan *lawyer*
Owen, Michael Lee *lawyer*
Palmer, Pamela S. *lawyer*
Palmieri, Victor Henry *lawyer, business executive*
Pasich, Kirk Alan *lawyer*
Patterson, Charles Ernest *lawyer*
Peck, Austin H., Jr., *lawyer*
Perez, Edith R. *lawyer*
Perry, Ralph Barton, III, *lawyer*
Pesta, Ben W., II, *lawyer, writer*
Peters, Aulana Louise *lawyer, former government agency commissioner*
Phillips, Patricia Dominis *lawyer*
Pieper, Darold D. *lawyer*
Pircher, Leo Joseph *lawyer, director*
Poindexter, William Mersereau *lawyer*
Pollock, John Phleger *lawyer*
Porter, Verna Louise *lawyer*
Power, John Bruce *lawyer*
Presant, Sanford Calvin *lawyer, educator, writer, tax specialist*

Pruetz, Adrian Mary *lawyer*
Pugsley, Robert Adrian *law educator*
Rabinovitz, Joel *lawyer, educator*
Rae, Matthew Sanderson, Jr., *lawyer*
Raeder, Myrna Sharon *lawyer, educator*
Rath, Howard Grant, Jr., *lawyer*
Ray, Gilbert T. *lawyer*
Reed, Leland *lawyer*
Reeves, Barbara Ann *lawyer*
Renwick, Edward S. *lawyer*
Richardson, Arthur Wilhelm *lawyer*
Roberts, Virgil Patrick *lawyer, business executive*
Robertson, Hugh Duff *lawyer*
Rosenbaum, Mark Dale *lawyer*
Rosenthal, Sol *lawyer*
Rotell, Cynthia A. *lawyer*
Rothenberg, Alan I. *lawyer, professional sports association executive*
Ruhl, Mary B. *lawyer*
Rutter, Marshall Anthony *lawyer*
Salvaty, Benjamin Benedict *lawyer*
Samet, Jack I. *lawyer*
Saxe, Deborah Crandall *lawyer*
Schmidt, Karl A. *lawyer*
Schulman, Robert S. *lawyer*
Scott, Michael Dennis *lawyer*
Scoular, Robert Frank *lawyer*
Shacter, David Mervyn *lawyer*
Shanks, Patricia L. *lawyer*
Shapiro, Marvin Seymour *lawyer*
Shapiro, Robert *lawyer*
Sheehan, Lawrence James *lawyer*
Sherwood, Allen Joseph *retired lawyer*
Shortz, Richard Alan *lawyer*
Shultz, John David *lawyer*
Silbergeld, Arthur F. *lawyer*
Solis, Carlos *lawyer*
Spitzer, Matthew Laurence *law educator, dean*
Stamm, Alan *lawyer*
Starrett, Lucinda *lawyer*
Stephens, George Edward, Jr., *lawyer*
Stone, Lawrence Maurice *lawyer, educator*
Streiker, Susan L. *law librarian*
Strong, George Gordon, Jr., *litigation and management consultant*
Su, Julie *legal association administrator*
Talcott, Robert Marc *lawyer*
Tarr, Ralph William *lawyer, former federal government official*
Taylor, Minna *lawyer*
Teele, Cynthia Lombard *lawyer*
Tepper, R(obert) Bruce, Jr., *lawyer*
Thorpe, Douglas L. *lawyer*
Title, Gail Migdal *lawyer*
Tobisman, Stuart Paul *lawyer*
Treister, George Marvin *lawyer*
Treusch, Paul Ellsworth *law educator, lawyer*
Trygstad, Lawrence Benson *lawyer*
Ukropina, James R. *lawyer*
Valerio Barrad, Catherine M. *lawyer*
Van de Kamp, John Kalar *lawyer*
Vaughn, William Weaver *retired lawyer*
Vertun, Alan Stuart *lawyer*
Volpert, Richard Sidney *lawyer*
Von Eschen, Lisa A. *lawyer*
von Kalinowski, Julian Onesime *lawyer*
Wagner, Darryl William *lawyer*
Wallock, Terrence J. *lawyer*
Warren, John Sheldon *lawyer, educator*
Watson, Glenn Robert *lawyer*
Wayte, Alan (Paul Wayte) *lawyer*
Weatherup, Roy Garfield *lawyer*
Weinstock, Harold *lawyer*
Weiser, Frank Alan *lawyer*
Weiss, Walter Stanley *lawyer*
White, Robert Joel *lawyer*
Williams, Richard Thomas *lawyer*
Wilson, Donald Kenneth, Jr., *lawyer, publisher*
Wine, Mark Philip *lawyer*
Wolfen, Werner F. *lawyer*
Woodland, Irwin Francis *lawyer*
Wright, Kenneth Brooks *lawyer*
Yamaguchi, Colleen S. *lawyer*
Yang, Debra W. *lawyer*
Zelon, Laurie Dee *lawyer*
Ziffren, Kenneth *lawyer*

Lynwood

Sterling, Arthur James *legal assistant*

Malibu

de la Rocha, Raquelle *lawyer, educator, state agency administrator*

Manhattan Beach

Hallett, James M. *lawyer*

Marina Del Rey

Annotico, Richard Anthony *legal administrator, real estate investor*

Martinez

Williams, Charles Judson *lawyer, writer*

Menlo Park

Bader, W(illiam) Reece *lawyer*
Brest, Paul A. *law educator*
Coats, William Sloan, III, *lawyer*
Dyer, Charles Arnold *lawyer*
Gunderson, Robert Vernon, Jr., *lawyer*
Haslam, Robert Thomas, III, *lawyer*
Kaufman, Christopher Lee *lawyer*
Kelly, Daniel Grady, Jr., *lawyer*
Kirk, Cassius Lamb, Jr., *retired lawyer, investor*
Madison, James Raymond *lawyer*
Mendelson, Alan Charles *lawyer*
Taylor, Robert P. *lawyer*
Terman, Donna Lea *lawyer, foundation administrator*

Mill Valley

Hoffman, John Douglas *lawyer, mediator*
Nemir, Donald Philip *lawyer*
Selvig, Jettie Pierce *lawyer*

Millbrae

Lande, James Avra *lawyer*
Rosenthal, Herbert Marshall *lawyer*

Mission Viejo

Duringer, David Robert *lawyer*
Ruben, Audrey H. *lawyer, arbitrator, actress*
Ruben, Robert Joseph *lawyer*
Tuohey, Conrad Gravier *lawyer*

Modesto

Murphy, John Thomas *lawyer*

Monte Sereno

Allan, Lionel Manning *lawyer*

Monterey

Bomberger, Russell Branson *lawyer, writer*
Davis, Craig Alphin *lawyer, manufacturing company executive*
Fenton, Lewis Lowry *lawyer*
Haddad, Louis Nicholas *paralegal*

Moraga

Kilbourne, George William *lawyer*

Morgan Hill

Foster, John Robert *lawyer*

Mountain View

Pasahow, Lynn H(arold) *lawyer*

Napa

Kuntz, Charles Powers *lawyer*
Snow, Tower Charles, Jr., *lawyer*

Newport Beach

Adams, William George *lawyer*
Baskin, Scott David *lawyer*
Brown, Ernest Christopher *lawyer, engineer*
Cano, Kristin Maria *lawyer*
Carman, Ernest Day *lawyer*
Carmichael, David Richard *lawyer*
Jeffers, Michael Bogue *lawyer*
Lawless, William Burns *lawyer, retired judge, academic administrator*
Mallory, Frank Linus *lawyer*
Mandel, Maurice, II, *lawyer, educator, mediator*
Millar, Richard William, Jr., *lawyer*
Mortensen, Arvid LeGrande *lawyer*
Pepe, Stephen Phillip *lawyer*
Phillips, Layn R. *lawyer*
Schiff, Laurie *lawyer*
Schnapp, Roger Herbert *lawyer, consultant*
Schumacher, Stephen Joseph *lawyer, educator*
Wagner, John Leo *lawyer, former magistrate judge*
Weissbard, Samuel Held *lawyer*
Wentworth, Theodore Sumner *lawyer*

North Hollywood

Kreger, Melvin Joseph *lawyer*
Runquist, Lisa A. *lawyer*
Shapiro, Larry *lawyer, Internet company executive*

Northridge

Avsharian, Roupen *prosecutor, department chairman, educator*
Walcher, Alan Ernest *lawyer*

Oak Park

Vinson, William Theodore *lawyer, diversified corporation executive*

Oakland

Bacon, Robert Dale *lawyer*
Berry, Phillip Samuel *lawyer*
Bryant, Arthur H. *lawyer*
Deming, Willis Riley *lawyer*
Drexel, Baron Jerome *lawyer*
Holst, James E. *lawyer*
Johnson, Kenneth F. *lawyer*
Koch, Richard Phillips (Terry Koch) *lawyer*
McDonnell, John L., Jr., *lawyer*
Miller, Kirk Edward *lawyer, health foundation executive*
Miller, Thomas Robbins *lawyer, publisher*
Ong, George E. *lawyer*
Peters, Arnold Stevens *legal association administrator, mechanical engineer*
Quinby, William Albert *lawyer, arbitrator, mediator*
Reese, Charles Woodrow, Jr., *lawyer*
Roster, Michael *lawyer*
Shapiro, David W. *prosecutor*
Stromme, Gary L. *law librarian*
West, Natalie Elsa *lawyer*
Wood, James Michael *lawyer*

Oceanside

Sullivan, Patrick James *lawyer*

Ontario

Dunn, Donald Jack *law librarian, law educator, dean, lawyer*

Orange

Batchelor, James Kent *lawyer*
Doti, Frank John *law educator, consultant*
Sawdei, Milan A. *lawyer*

Orinda

Hetland, John Robert *lawyer, educator*

Oxnard

Hiepler, Mark O. *lawyer*

Pacific Palisades

Cale, Charles Griffin *lawyer, private investor*
Flattery, Thomas Long *lawyer, legal administrator*
Horowitz, Edward Jay *lawyer*
Jones, Edgar Allan, Jr., *law educator, arbitrator, lawyer*
Mendel, Dennis D. *lawyer*
Sevilla, Stanley *lawyer*
Verrone, Patric Miller *lawyer, writer*

Palm Desert

Bernhard, Herbert Ashley *lawyer*
Goldberg, Martin Stanford *retired lawyer*
Pierno, Anthony Robert *lawyer*

Palm Springs

Diodosio, Charles Joseph *lawyer*
Dupree, Stanley M. *lawyer*
FitzGerald, John Edward, III, *lawyer*
Kimberling, John Farrell *retired lawyer*

Palo Alto

Baron, Frederick David *lawyer*
Baskins, Ann O. *lawyer, computer company executive*
Baum, Brandon *lawyer, law educator*
Benton, Lee F. *lawyer*

Bradley, Donald Edward *lawyer*
Climan, Richard Elliot *lawyer*
Davidson, Gordon K. *lawyer*
Dwyer, John Charles *lawyer*
Faxon, Thomas Baker *retired lawyer*
Halluin, Albert Price *lawyer*
Heuman, Donna *lawyer*
Hinckley, Robert Craig *lawyer*
Jackson, Cynthia L. *lawyer*
Johnson, Craig W. *lawyer*
Laurie, Ronald Sheldon *lawyer*
Massey, Henry P., Jr., *lawyer*
McCall, Jennifer Jordan *lawyer*
Miller, Michael Patiky *lawyer*
Mosher, Roger L. *lawyer*
Nopar, Alan Scott *lawyer*
Nordlund, Donald Craig *lawyer*
Patten, Valerie Lynn *lawyer*
Patterson, Robert Edward *lawyer*
Phair, Joseph Baschon *lawyer*
Rinsky, Arthur C. *lawyer*
Shulman, Ron E. *lawyer*
Simon, James Lowell *lawyer*
Smith, Glenn A. *lawyer*
Sonsini, Larry W. *lawyer*
Spanner, Robert Alan *lawyer*
Sundheim, George (Duf) *lawyer, political organization worker*
Tanner, Douglas Alan *lawyer*
Tiffany, Joseph Raymond, II, *lawyer*
Trumbull, Terry Alan *energy and environmental consultant, lawyer*
Van Atta, David Murray *lawyer*
Wheeler, Raymond Louis *lawyer*

Palos Verdes Estates
Blackman, Lee L. *lawyer*
Brigden, Ann Schwartz *mediator, educator*
DeLuce, Richard David *lawyer*

Paramount
Hall, Howard Harry *lawyer*

Pasadena
Brenner, Anita Susan *lawyer*
Call, Merlin Wendell *lawyer*
Calleton, Theodore Edward *lawyer, educator*
D'Angelo, Robert William *lawyer*
Davis, Edmond Ray *lawyer*
Haight, James Theron *lawyer, corporate executive*
Hunt, Gordon *lawyer*
Koelzer, George Joseph *lawyer*
Logan, Francis Dummer *retired lawyer*
Mosher, Sally Ekenberg *lawyer, musician*
Mueth, Joseph Edward *lawyer*
Myers, R(alph) Chandler *lawyer*
Tanner, Dee Boshard *retired lawyer*
Weinman, Glenn Alan *lawyer*
Wyatt, Joseph Lucian, Jr., *lawyer, writer*
Yohalem, Harry Morton *lawyer*

Petaluma
Eller, Leslie Robert *lawyer*
Paul, Amy *lawyer*

Piedmont
Aderton, Jane Reynolds *lawyer*
Oser, Judi *lawyer, artist*

Pittsburg
Williscroft-Barcus, Beverly Ruth *lawyer*

Placentia
Evans, Winthrop Shattuck *retired lawyer*

Pleasanton
Opperwall, Stephen Gabriel *lawyer*
Ross, Michael Charles *lawyer*
Scott, G. Judson, Jr., *lawyer*
Staley, John Fredric *lawyer*

Point Richmond
Edginton, John Arthur *lawyer*

Portola Valley
Cooper, John Joseph *lawyer*
Nycum, Susan Hubbell *lawyer*

Rancho Mirage
Leydorf, Frederick Leroy *lawyer*
Reuben, Don Harold *lawyer*

Rancho Palos Verdes
Schimmenti, John Joseph *lawyer*
Swank, Damon Raynard *lawyer*

Rancho Santa Fe
Peterson, Nad A. *retired lawyer*
Woolley, Roger Swire *lawyer*

Rancho Santa Margarita
Curtis, John Joseph *lawyer, writer*

Redlands
Shimoff, Paul Martin *lawyer*

Redondo Beach
Oh, Angela E. *lawyer*

Redwood City
Bell, Frank Ouray, Jr., *lawyer*
Coddington, Clinton Hays *lawyer*
Mandel, Martin Louis *lawyer*
Millard, Richard Steven *lawyer*
Tight, Dexter Corwin *lawyer*
Verhoeven, Charles K. *lawyer*
Wilhelm, Robert Oscar *lawyer, civil engineer, developer*

Richmond
Dolberg, David Spencer *lawyer*
Jenkins, Everett Wilbur, Jr., *lawyer, author, historian*
Quenneville, Kathleen *lawyer*
Richards, Gerald Thomas *lawyer, consultant, educator, writer*

Riverside
Darling, Scott Edward *lawyer*
Marlatt, Michael James *lawyer*
Van Wagenen, Jeffrey Anthony *prosecutor, consultant*

Rolling Hills
Rumbaugh, Charles Earl *arbitrator, mediator, educator, lawyer, speaker*

Rosemead
Danner, Bryant Craig *lawyer*

Sacramento
Arkin, Michael Barry *lawyer, arbitrator, writer*
Bell, Wayne S. *lawyer, state agency official*
Blake, D. Steven *lawyer*
Bobrow, Susan Lukin *lawyer*
Brewer, Roy Edward *lawyer*
Brookman, Anthony Raymond *lawyer*
Burton, Randall James *lawyer*
Day, James McAdam, Jr., *lawyer*
Felderstein, Steven Howard *lawyer*
Foster, Douglas Taylor *lawyer, investor*
Friedman, Morton Lee *lawyer*
Gillan, Kayla J. *lawyer*
Goode, Barry Paul *lawyer*
Gray-Fuson, Joan Lorraine *lawyer*
Hendrickson, George M. *prosecutor*
Houpt, James Edward *lawyer*
Janigian, Bruce Jasper *lawyer, educator*
Keiner, Christian Mark *lawyer*
Lee, Michael Gregory *lawyer*
Malloy, Michael Patrick *law educator, consultant*
McGrath, William Arthur *arbitrator, mediator, lawyer*
Morgan-Prager, Karole *lawyer, publishing executive*
Owen, Allan Jacobs *lawyer*
Radford, R. S. *lawyer, law educator*
Robbins, Stephen J. M. *lawyer*
Root, Gerald Edward *legal administrator*
Scott, McGregor W. *lawyer*
Taylor, Walter Wallace *retired lawyer*
Ubaldi, Michael Vincent *lawyer*
Wile, Philip Hodges *law educator*
Zeff, Ophelia Hope *lawyer*

San Anselmo
Murphy, Barry Ames *lawyer*
Truett, Harold Joseph, III, (Tim Truett) *lawyer*

San Bernardino
Fullerton, Robert Victor *lawyer*
McNally, Sean Patrick *prosecutor*

San Carlos
Foster, Mark Edward *lawyer, consultant, international lobbyist*
Lee, John Jin *lawyer*

San Clemente
Fisher, Myron R. *lawyer*
Geyser, Lynne M. *lawyer, writer*

San Diego
Barton, Thomas Donald *lawyer, educator*
Bleiler, Charles Arthur *lawyer*
Boggs, William S. *lawyer*
Brierton, Cheryl Lynn *lawyer*
Brooks, John White *lawyer*
Brown, LaMar Bevan *lawyer*
Chatroo, Arthur Jay *lawyer*
Cogan, Mary Jo Gleber *lawyer*
Corbett, Luke Robinson *lawyer*
Damoose, George Lynn *lawyer*
Dorne, David J. *lawyer*
Dostart, Paul Joseph *lawyer, investor, director, entrepreneur*
Dumanis, Bonnie M. *prosecutor*
Dyer, Charles Richard *law librarian, law educator*
Eger, John Mitchell *lawyer, educator*
Eigner, William Whitling *lawyer*
Fagan, Peter Ledford *lawyer, naval officer*
Fauchier, Dan R(ay) *mediator, arbitrator, educator, construction management consultant,*
Friedman, Gary E. *lawyer*
Greenwood, Richard Hopson *lawyer, minister*
Guinn, Stanley Willis *lawyer*
Heidrich, Robert Wesley *lawyer*
Herring, Charles David *lawyer, educator*
Higgs, Craig DeWitt *lawyer*
Hofflund, Paul *lawyer*
Kelly, Karla Rosemarie *lawyer*
Klinedinst, John David *lawyer*
Kuntz, William Richard, Jr., *lawyer*
Lam, Carol C. *lawyer*
Lathrop, Mitchell Lee *lawyer*
LeBeau, Charles Paul *lawyer*
Lerach, William S. *lawyer*
McClellan, Craig Rene *lawyer*
McGinnis, Robert E. *lawyer*
Mebane, Julie Shaffer *lawyer*
Mittermiller, James Joseph *lawyer*
Morris, Grant Harold *law educator*
Noziska, Charles Brant *lawyer*
Partida, Gilbert A. *lawyer*
Payne, Margaret Anne *lawyer*
Pugh, Richard Crawford *lawyer, educator*
Rehmus, Charles Martin *law educator, arbitrator*
Reif, Louis Raymond *lawyer, utilities executive*
Roseman, Charles Sanford *lawyer*
Ross, Terry D. *lawyer*
St. George, William Ross *lawyer, retired naval officer, consultant*
Samuelson, Derrick William *lawyer*
Santee, Dale William *lawyer, air force officer*
Schoville, Dennis A(rnold) *lawyer*
Seidenwurm, Richard Lewis *lawyer*
Shapiro, Philip Alan *lawyer*
Shearer, William Kennedy *lawyer, publisher*
Shippey, Sandra Lee *lawyer*
Smith, Steven Ray *law educator*
Snyder, David Richard *lawyer*
Sterrett, James Kelley, II, *lawyer*
Sullivan, Michelle Cornejo *lawyer*
Tragen, Irving Glenne *consultant*
Weaver, Michael James *lawyer*
Weidner, Lauren Finder *lawyer*
Wildenthal, Bryan Hobson, II, *law educator*
Wilson, Hugh Steven *lawyer*
Wolfe, Deborah Ann *lawyer*

San Francisco
Abbott, Barry Alexander *lawyer*
Acker, Frederick Wayne *lawyer*
Alexander, Robert C. *lawyer*
Alexis, Geraldine M. *lawyer*
Anderson, Edward Virgil *lawyer*
Arbuthnot, Robert Murray *lawyer*
Baker, Cameron *lawyer*
Barbagelata, Robert Dominic *lawyer*
Baxter, Ralph H., Jr., *lawyer*
Bleich, Jeffrey Laurence *lawyer, law educator*
Block, David Jeffrey *lawyer, investment manager*
Bondoc, Rommel *lawyer*
Borowsky, Philip *lawyer*
Bostwick, James Stephen *lawyer*
Bothwell, Anthony Peirson Xavier, Sr., *lawyer, educator*
Boutin, Peter Rucker *lawyer*
Boven, Douglas George *lawyer*
Bridges, Robert Lysle *retired lawyer*
Briscoe, John *lawyer*
Brown, Donald Wesley *lawyer*
Bruen, James A. *lawyer*
Buccieri, Shirley H. *lawyer*
Burden, James Ewers *lawyer*
Burns, Brian Patrick *lawyer*
Burt, Rick *lawyer*
Bushnell, Roderick Paul *lawyer*
Byers, Brett Douglas *lawyer, investment company executive*
Cabraser, Elizabeth Joan *lawyer*
Callan, Terrence A. *lawyer*
Callison, Russell James *lawyer*
Campbell, Scott Robert *lawyer, former food company executive*
Carrow, Robert Duane *lawyer, barrister*
Casey, Bernard J. *lawyer*
Cheatham, Robert William *lawyer*
Clopton, Karen Valentia *lawyer, president civil services commission*
Coffin, Judy Sue *lawyer*
Cohler, Charles B. *lawyer*
Cohn, Nathan *lawyer*
Coleman, Thomas Young *lawyer*
Coombe, George William, Jr., *lawyer, retired banker*
Corcoran, Maureen Elizabeth *lawyer*
Cowan, Stephen A. *lawyer*
Cranston, Mary B. *lawyer*
Crawford, Roy Edgington, III, *lawyer*
Crist, Paul Grant *lawyer*
Deane, Elaine *lawyer*
Dell, Robert Michael *lawyer*
DeMuro, Paul Robert *lawyer*
Diekmann, Gilmore Frederick, Jr., *lawyer*
Dryden, Robert Eugene *lawyer*
Duffy, Jan *law educator, lawyer*
Dunne, Kevin Joseph *lawyer*
Edwards, Robin Morse *lawyer*
Evers, William Dohrmann *lawyer*
Feller, Lloyd Harris *lawyer*
Fergus, Gary Scott *lawyer*
Finberg, James Michael *lawyer*
Finck, Kevin William *lawyer*
Fledderman, Harry L. *lawyer*
Fogel, Paul David *lawyer*
Fohrman, Burton H. *lawyer*
Foster, David Scott *lawyer*
Freeman, Tom M. *lawyer*
Freud, Nicholas S. *lawyer*
Friedman, K. Bruce *lawyer*
Friese, Robert Charles *lawyer*
Furth, Frederick Paul *lawyer*
Garvey, Joanne Marie *lawyer*
Gelhaus, Robert Joseph *lawyer, publisher*
Gibson, Virginia Lee *lawyer*
Glazer, Jack Henry *lawyer*
Gowdy, Franklin Brockway *lawyer*
Gresham, Zane Oliver *lawyer*
Guggenhime, Richard Johnson *lawyer*
Haas, Raymond P. *lawyer*
Hall, Paul J. *lawyer*
Hallinan, Terence *prosecutor*
Halloran, Michael James *lawyer*
Heilbron, David Michael *lawyer*
Henke, Dan *law educator*
Henson, Ray David *law educator, consultant*
Herrera, Dennis J. *lawyer*
Hilton, Stanley Goumas *lawyer, educator, writer*
Hinman, Harvey DeForest *lawyer*
Hisert, George A. *lawyer*
Hofmann, John Richard, Jr., *retired lawyer*
Holden, Frederick Douglass, Jr., *lawyer*
Homer, Barry Wayne *lawyer*
Howard, Carl *lawyer*
Hudner, Philip *lawyer, rancher*
Hudson, Mark Woodbridge *lawyer*
Hui, Helen Yuen Hing *lawyer*
James, David Lee *lawyer, international advisor, author*
Jones, Frances Mary *law librarian*
Kasanin, Mark Owen *lawyer*
Kelly, J. Michael *lawyer*
Kern, John McDougall *lawyer*
Knapp, Charles Lincoln *law educator*
Knebel, Jack Gillen *lawyer*
Koeppel, John A. *lawyer*
Kornblum, Guy Orville *lawyer*
Kuhl, Paul Beach *lawyer*
Lacovara, Michael *lawyer*
Ladar, Jerrold Morton *lawyer*
Lane, Fielding H. *lawyer*
Larson, John William *lawyer*
La Vine, Robert L. *lawyer*
Lee, Richard Diebold *law educator, legal publisher, consultant*
Leshy, John David *lawyer, legal educator, government official*
Livsey, Robert Callister *lawyer*
Lombardi, David Ennis, Jr., *lawyer, lecturer, mediator*
Lopes, James Louis *lawyer*
Lynch, Timothy Jeremiah-Mahoney *lawyer, educator, theologian, realtor, writer*
MacGowan, Eugenia *lawyer*
Maier, Peter Klaus *lawyer*
Mann, Bruce Alan *lawyer, bank executive, investment banker*
Manning, Jerome Alan *retired lawyer*
Marcus, Richard Leon *lawyer, educator*
Marshall, Raymond Charles *lawyer*
Martel, John Sheldon *lawyer, writer*
Mattes, Martin Anthony *lawyer*
Matthews, Philip Richard *lawyer*
McElhinny, Harold John *lawyer*
McKelvey, Judith Grant *lawyer, educator, university dean*
Mc Laughlin, Jerome Michael *lawyer, shipping company executive*
Meadows, John Frederick *lawyer*
Meyerson, Ivan D. *lawyer, holding company executive*
Miles, Donald F. *lawyer*
Miller, William Napier Cripps *lawyer*
Millstein, David J. *lawyer*
Minnick, Malcolm David *lawyer*
Mitchell, Bruce Tyson *lawyer*
Morrissey, John Carroll, Sr., *lawyer*
Murray, Kathleen Anne *lawyer*
Musfelt, Duane Clark *lawyer*
Odgers, Richard William *lawyer*
Offer, Stuart Jay *lawyer*
Okeke, Christian Nwachukwu *law educator*
Olson, Robert Howard *lawyer*
Palmer, Venrice Romito *lawyer, educator*
Penskar, Mark Howard *lawyer*
Petty, George Oliver *lawyer*
Philipsborn, John Timothy *lawyer, writer*
Phillips, Richard Myron *lawyer, educator*
Poole, Edward G. *attorney*
Poole, Gordon Leicester *lawyer*
Popofsky, Melvin Laurence *lawyer*
Radlo, Edward John *lawyer, mathematician*
Ragan, Charles Ransom *lawyer*
Reding, John Anthony *lawyer*
Reese, John Robert *lawyer*
Rembe, Toni *lawyer, director*
Renfrew, Charles Byron *lawyer*
Rice, Denis Timlin *lawyer*
Richards, Norman Blanchard *lawyer*
Richmond, Diana *lawyer*
Rogan, Richard A. *lawyer*
Rosch, John Thomas *lawyer*
Rose, Jordan Payman *lawyer*
Rosen, Sanford Jay *lawyer*
Rosenthal, Kenneth W. *lawyer*
Rossmann, Antonio *lawyer, educator*
Rowland, John Arthur *lawyer*
Russoniello, Joseph Pascal *lawyer*
Ryan, Kevin V. *lawyer*
Salomon, Darrell Joseph *lawyer*
Savage, Mark Randall *lawyer*
Schon, Steven Eliot *lawyer*
Seabolt, Richard L. *lawyer*
Seavey, William Arthur *lawyer, vintner*
Shapiro, Gary John *retired lawyer*
Shenk, George H. *lawyer*
Sherman, Martin Peter *lawyer*
Shiffman, Michael A. *lawyer*
Singer, Allen Morris *lawyer*
Siniscalco, Gary Richard *lawyer*
Smegal, Thomas Frank, Jr., *lawyer*
Smith, Kerry Clark *lawyer*
Smith, Robert Michael *lawyer, mediator, arbitrator*
Smoke, Richard Edwin *lawyer, investment advisor*
Soberon, Presentacion Zablan *state bar administrator*
Sochynsky, Yaroslav *lawyer, arbitrator, mediator*
Sparks, Thomas E., Jr., *lawyer*
Staring, Graydon Shaw *lawyer*
Steer, Reginald David *lawyer*
Stephens, Shand Scott *lawyer*
Stinnett, Terrance LLoyd *lawyer*
Stotter, Lawrence Henry *lawyer*
Stromberg, Ross Ernest *lawyer*
Studley, Jamienne Shayne *lawyer, educator*
Sugarman, Myron George *lawyer*
Sullivan, Robert Edward *lawyer*
Sullivan, William Francis *lawyer*
Sutton, John Paul *lawyer*
Taylor, William James (Zak Taylor) *lawyer*
Thomas, William Scott *lawyer*
Thompson, Robert Charles *lawyer*
Thornton, Charles Victor *lawyer*
Tobin, James Michael *lawyer*
Trautman, William Ellsworth *lawyer*
Traynor, John Michael *lawyer*
Truong, D. Hiep *lawyer*
Uilkema, John K. *lawyer*
Vazquez-Azpiri, A. James *lawyer*
Veaco, Kristina *lawyer*
Venning, Robert Stanley *lawyer*
Walsh, Francis Richard *law educator, lawyer, arbitrator*
Walsh, Joseph Richard *lawyer, bank executive*
Wang, William Kai-Sheng *law educator*
Warmer, Richard Craig *lawyer*
Weber, Arnold I. *lawyer*
Welborn, Caryl Bartelman *lawyer*
Wetmore, Keith Chidester *lawyer*
Whitehead, David Barry *lawyer*
Wild, Nelson Hopkins *lawyer*
Wilson, John Pasley *law educator*
Wingate, C. Keith *law educator*
Wood, Robert Warren *lawyer*
Woods, James Robert *lawyer*
Worthington, Bruce R. *lawyer*
Wyatt, Thomas Csaba *lawyer*
Wyle, Frederick S. *lawyer*
Young, Bryant Llewellyn *lawyer, business executive*
Young, Douglas Rea *lawyer*
Ziegler, R. W., Jr., *lawyer, consultant*
Ziering, William Mark *lawyer*

San Jose
Anstandig, Marshall W. *lawyer, publishing executive*
Bennion, David Jacobsen *lawyer*
Bohn, Robert Herbert *lawyer*
Clark, William Frederick *lawyer*
Cottle, Karen Olson *lawyer*
Denver, Thomas H. R. *lawyer*
Doyle, J. Richard *lawyer*
Gallo, Joan Rosenberg *lawyer*
Hannon, Timothy Patrick *lawyer, educator, judge*
Hernández, Fernando Vargas *lawyer*
Katzman, Richard Alan *lawyer, arbitrator*
Knapp, David William *lawyer, writer*
Kraw, George Martin *lawyer, essayist*
Kretchmer, Kathy L. *lawyer*
Kuklin, Susan Beverly *law librarian, lawyer*
McManis, James *lawyer*
Mitchell, David Walker *lawyer*
Naegele, Joseph Loyola, Sr., *lawyer*
Sauers, William Dale *lawyer, playwright*
Shannon, David M. *lawyer*
Stein, John C. *lawyer*
Stevenson, Karen *lawyer*
Stutzman, Thomas Chase, Sr., *lawyer*
Towery, James E. *lawyer*

San Juan Capistrano
Suzuki, Yasuhiko *retired law educator*

San Luis Obispo
Daly, John Paul *lawyer*

San Marcos
Berry, Dawn Bradley *writer, lawyer, jeweler*

San Marino
Cranston, Howard Stephen *lawyer, management consultant*
Galbraith, James Marshall *lawyer, business executive*
Tomich, Lillian *lawyer*

San Mateo
Chong, Rachelle B. *lawyer, federal communications commissioner*
Grill, Lawrence J. *lawyer, accountant, corporate/banking executive*
Kenney, William Fitzgerald *lawyer*
Monaco, Daniel Joseph *lawyer*
O'Reilly, Terence John *lawyer*
Slabach, Stephen Hall *lawyer*

San Pedro
Russell, Thomas Arthur *lawyer*

San Rafael
Chilvers, Robert Merritt *lawyer*
Drexler, Kenneth *lawyer*
Freitas, David Prince *lawyer*

San Ramon
Dennis, Patricia Diaz *lawyer*
James, Charles Albert *lawyer*
Welch, Thomas Andrew *international and domestic commercial arbitrator*

Santa Ana
Anderson, James E., Jr., *lawyer, information technology executive*
Andres, Eugen Charles *lawyer*
Callahan, Daniel J. *lawyer*
Capizzi, Michael Robert *prosecutor*
Chudzinski, Mark Adam *lawyer*
DeRoy, Craig I. *lawyer*
Dillard, John Martin *lawyer, pilot*
Frost, Winston Lyle *lawyer, educator*
Harley, Robison Dooling, Jr., *lawyer, educator*
Mei, Tom Y. K. *lawyer*
Mosich, Nicholas Joseph *lawyer*
Storer, Maryruth *law librarian*

Santa Barbara
Elliott, Warren G. *lawyer*
Falstrom, Kenneth Edward *lawyer*
Herman, James Edward *lawyer*
Israel, Barry John *lawyer*
Ledbetter, Michael Ray *lawyer*
McEwen, Willard Winfield, Jr., *lawyer, judge*
Pyle, Kurt H. *lawyer*
Reed, Frank Fremont, II, *retired lawyer*
Simpson, Curtis Chapman, III, *lawyer*
Sulzbach, Christi Rocovich *lawyer*

Santa Clara
Alexander, George Jonathon *law educator, former dean*
Blawie, James Louis *law educator*
Dunlap, F. Thomas, Jr., *lawyer, electronics executive*
Glancy, Dorothy Jean *lawyer, educator*

Santa Monica
Axe, Norman Gold *lawyer*
Boltz, Gerald Edmund *lawyer*
Bower, Allan Maxwell *lawyer*
Chaleff, Gerald Lawrence *lawyer*
Cooper, Jay Leslie *lawyer*
Fagen, Peter Kirk *lawyer*
Grossman, Marshall Bruce *lawyer*
Hinerfeld, Robert Elliot *lawyer*
Jones, William Allen *lawyer, entertainment company executive*
Kaplowitz, Karen (Jill) *lawyer, business consultant*
Kirkland, John C. *lawyer*
Levin, Marvin Eugene *lawyer*
Loo, Thomas S. *lawyer*
McMillan, M. Sean *lawyer*
Morgan, Kermit Johnson *lawyer*
Muller, Edward Robert *lawyer*
Preble, Laurence George *lawyer*
Prewoznik, Jerome Frank *lawyer*
Risman, Michael *lawyer, business executive, securities company executive, real estate developer*

Santa Rosa
Adams, Delphine Szyndrowski *lawyer*
Anderson, Edwin C., Jr. *lawyer*
Courteau, Girard Robert *retired prosecutor*
O'Connor, Paul Daniel *lawyer*

Sausalito
Berkman, William Roger *lawyer, army reserve officer*
Gordon, Robert Eugene *lawyer*
Klott, David Lee *lawyer*
Robertson, J. Martin *lawyer*

Selma
Janian, Paulette *lawyer*

Sherman Oaks
Crump, Gerald Franklin *retired lawyer*
Feldman, Phillip *lawyer*
Levin, Evanne Lynn *lawyer, educator*

Sonoma
Obninsky, Victor Peter *lawyer*

Stanford
Babcock, Barbara Allen *law educator, lawyer*
Barton, John Hays *law educator*
Cohen, William *law educator*
Ehrlich, Thomas *law educator*
Franklin, Marc Adam *law educator*
Friedman, Lawrence M. *law educator*
Goldstein, Paul *lawyer, educator*
Gould, William Benjamin, IV, *lawyer, educator, federal agency administrator*
Grossman, Claudio M. *lawyer*
Grundfest, Joseph Alexander *law educator, lawyer, economist*
Lemley, Mark Alan *law educator*
Lessig, Lawrence *law educator*
Mann, J. Keith *retired law educator, arbitrator*
Rhode, Deborah Lynn *law educator*
Sofaer, Abraham David *lawyer, educator, judge, consultant*
Williams, Howard Russell *lawyer, educator*

Stockton
Malm, Scott *lawyer*
Parish, William Henry *lawyer*
Taft, Perry Hazard *retired lawyer*

Studio City
Miller, Charles Maurice *lawyer*

Sunnyvale
McReynolds, Stephen Paul *lawyer*
Thornton, D. Whitney, II, *lawyer*
Zahrt, William Dietrich, II, *lawyer*

Tarzana
Gentile, Joseph F. *lawyer, educator*

Temecula
Rosenstein, Robert Bryce *lawyer, financial advisor*

Thousand Oaks
Geiser, Thomas Christopher *lawyer*
Odre, Steven M. *lawyer*
Trover, Ellen Lloyd *lawyer, rancher*
Williams, Henry Newton *retired lawyer*

Tiburon
McAmis, Edwin Earl *lawyer*
Widman, Gary Lee *lawyer, former government official*

Torrance
Bryan, Sharon Ann *lawyer*
Johnson, Einar William *lawyer*
Kaufman, Sanford Paul *lawyer*
Kohan, Betsy Burns *lawyer*
Moore, Christopher M. *lawyer*
Petillon, Lee Ritchey *lawyer*
Van Emburgh, Joanne *lawyer*

Tustin
Kraft, Henry Robert *lawyer*
Madory, Richard Eugene *lawyer*

Ukiah
Sager, Madeline Dean *lawyer*

Universal City
Golper, John Bruce *lawyer*
Peter, Arnold Philimon *lawyer, business executive*

Van Nuys
Arabian, Armand *retired arbitrator, mediator, lawyer*
McLain, Christopher M. *lawyer*
Schell, George Aaron *lawyer*

Ventura
Gartner, Harold Henry, III, *lawyer*

Victorville
Quadri, Fazle Rab *lawyer, government official*

Visalia
Crowe, Daniel Walston *lawyer*
Crowe, John T. *lawyer*
Hart, Timothy Ray *lawyer, dean*

Walnut
McKee, Catherine Lynch *law educator, lawyer*

Walnut Creek
Burnison, Boyd Edward *lawyer*
Curtin, Daniel Joseph, Jr., *lawyer*
De Benedictis, Dario *retired lawyer, retired arbitrator, retired mediator*
Derby, Steven Leo *lawyer*
Gardner, Trudi York *lawyer, insurance company executive*
Gill, Margaret Gaskins *lawyer*
Ginsburg, Gerald J. *lawyer, business executive*
Hanschen, Peter Walter *lawyer*
Horner, Clifford R. *lawyer*
Medak, Walter Hans *lawyer*
Nolan, David Charles *lawyer, arbitrator, mediator*
Ogilby, Barry Ray *lawyer*
Pagter, Carl Richard *lawyer*
Rainey, William Joel *lawyer*
Rathjen, Jon Laurence *lawyer, arbitrator, mediator*
Skaggs, Sanford Merle *lawyer*
Willson, Prentiss, Jr., *lawyer*

West Covina
Ebiner, Robert Maurice *lawyer*
McHale, Edward Robertson *retired lawyer*

Westlake Village
Carter, C. Michael *lawyer*
Hoefflin, Richard Michael *lawyer, judicial administrator*
Masry, Edward L. *lawyer*

Woodland Hills
Barrett, Robert Matthew *law educator, lawyer*
Even, Randolph M. *lawyer*
Glick, Earl A. *lawyer*
Johnson-Champ, Debra Sue *lawyer, educator, writer, artist*
Kaufman, Albert I. *lawyer*
Lin, Lawrence Shuh Liang *lawyer*
Rolin, Christopher Ernest *lawyer*
Schor, Suzi *lawyer, psychologist*
Westen, Brodie Curtis *lawyer*

COLORADO

Alamosa
Garcia, Castelar Medardo *lawyer*

Arvada
Johnson, Christian Kent *lawyer*
Kreis, Elizabeth Susan *lawyer*
Peck, Kenneth E. *lawyer*

Aurora
Hampton, Clyde Robert *lawyer, educator*
Katz, Michael Jeffery *lawyer*
Khanna, Kishanlal K. *lawyer, educator*
Stauffer, Scott William *lawyer, accountant*

Boulder
Bintliff, Barbara Ann *law educator, library director*
Deaktor, Darryl Barnett *lawyer*
Dubofsky, Jean Eberhart *lawyer, retired state supreme court justice*
Dumas, Jeffrey Mack *lawyer*
Echohawk, John Ernest *lawyer*
Fenster, Herbert Lawrence *lawyer*
Fiflis, Ted James *lawyer, educator*
Flowers, William Harold, Jr., *lawyer*
Getches, David Harding *law educator, state environmental executive, lawyer, dean*
Gray, William R. *lawyer*
Kerr, Baine Perkins, Jr., *lawyer, writer*
Madden, Alice Donnelly *lawyer*
Moses, Raphael Jacob *lawyer*
Porzak, Glenn E. *lawyer*
Ranniger, Leslie Jean *lawyer*
Steuben, Norton Leslie *lawyer, educator*
Underwood, Anthony Paul *lawyer*
Ward, Denitta Dawn *lawyer*
Wittemyer, John *lawyer*
Yuhnke, Robert E. *lawyer, educator, consultant*

Breckenridge
Fromm, Jeffery Bernard *lawyer*

Broomfield
Jonsen, Eric Richard *lawyer*
Stortz, Thomas C. *lawyer, communications executive*

Canon City
Fredrickson, Bryan Timothy *lawyer*

Centennial
Barnthouse, William Joseph *lawyer*

Colorado Springs
Adams, Deborah Rowland *lawyer*
Buell, Bruce Temple *lawyer*
Gaddis, Larry Roy *lawyer*
Kubida, William Joseph *lawyer*
McCready, Guy Michael *lawyer*
Sheffield, Alden Daniel, Jr., *lawyer*
Swanson, Victoria Clare Heldman *lawyer*
Wheeler, Stephen Frederick *legal administrator*

Delta
Wendt, John Arthur Frederic, Jr., *lawyer*

Denver
Asphaug, Rolf Gunnar *lawyer*
Austin, H(arry) Gregory *lawyer*
Babiniec, Dennis Henry *lawyer*
Bader, Gerald Louis, Jr., *lawyer*
Baer, Richard N. (Rich Baer) *lawyer*
Bain, Donald Knight *lawyer*
Belitz, Paul Edward *lawyer*
Benson, Robert Eugene *lawyer*
Benton, Auburn Edgar *lawyer*
Blair, Andrew Lane, Jr., *lawyer, educator*
Blitz, Stephen M. *lawyer*
Breeskin, Michael Wayne *lawyer*
Burke, Gay Ann Wolesensky *lawyer*
Butler, David *lawyer*
Byrne, Thomas J. *lawyer*
Cain, Douglas Mylchreest *lawyer*
Campbell, Leonard M. *lawyer*
Campbell, William J. *lawyer*
Carrigan, Jim R. *arbitrator, mediator, retired judge*
Cassidy, Samuel H. *lawyer, lieutenant governor, state legislator, humanities educator*
Cheroutes, Michael Louis *lawyer*
Cohen, Jeffrey *lawyer*
Conover, Frederic King *lawyer*
Cooper, Paul Douglas *lawyer*
Cope, Thomas Field *lawyer*
Copeland, Eugene Leroy *lawyer, writer*
Cox, William Vaughan *lawyer*
Davis, R. Steven *lawyer*
Dean, James Benwell *lawyer*
Devine, Sharon Jean *lawyer*
Dowdle, Patrick Dennis *lawyer*
Dunham, Stephen Sampson *lawyer*
Dunn, Randy Edwin *lawyer*
DuVivier, Katharine Keyes *lawyer, educator*
Featherstone, Bruce Alan *lawyer*
Gehres, James *retired lawyer*
George, Russell Lloyd *lawyer, former state legislator*
Gilbert, Alan Jay *lawyer, educator*
Grant, Patrick Alexander *lawyer, association executive*
Grissom, Garth Clyde *lawyer, director*
Haddon, Harold Alan *lawyer*
Harris, Dale Ray *lawyer*
Hautzinger, James Edward *lawyer*
Hawley, Robert Cross *lawyer*
Heiserman, Robert Gifford *lawyer*
Hendrix, Lynn Parker *lawyer*
Hensen, Stephen Jerome *lawyer*
Hoagland, Donald Wright *lawyer*
Hodges, Joseph Gilluly, Jr., *lawyer*
Hoffman, Daniel Steven *lawyer, law educator*
Holme, Howard Kelley *lawyer, executive*
Holme, Richard Phillips *lawyer*
Hopfenbeck, George Martin, Jr., *lawyer*
Houtsma, Peter C. *lawyer*
Imig, William Graff *lawyer, lobbyist*
Irwin, R. Robert *lawyer*
Jacobs, Paul Alan *lawyer*
Jones, Richard Michael *lawyer*
Kahn, Edwin Sam *lawyer*
Keatinge, Robert Reed *lawyer*
Keller, Glen Elven, Jr., *lawyer*
Kerwin, Mary Ann Collins *lawyer*
Kintzele, John Alfred *lawyer*
Krendl, Cathy Stricklin *lawyer*
Lamm, Richard Douglas *lawyer, former governor of Colorado*
Law, John Manning *retired lawyer*
Lerman, Eileen R. *lawyer*
Low, Andrew M. *lawyer*
Low, John Wayland *lawyer*
Lutz, John Shafroth *lawyer*
Mackey, Pamela Robillard *lawyer*
Maldonado, Kirk Francis *lawyer*
Marquess, Lawrence Wade *lawyer*
Martin, Dallas Rea *lawyer*
Martz, Clyde Ollen *lawyer, educator*
Matsukage, Fay Mariko *lawyer*
Mauro, Richard Frank *lawyer, investment manager*
McCabe, John L. *lawyer*
McConnell, Michael Theodore *lawyer*
McDonnell, Barbara *lawyer*
McGuane, Frank L., Jr., *lawyer*
McIntosh, Carolyn Leigh *lawyer*
McKenna, Frederick Gregory *lawyer, consultant*
McMichael, Donald Earl *lawyer*
Merker, Steven Joseph *lawyer*
Merritt, Jeralyn E. *lawyer*
Miller, Gale Timothy *lawyer*
Miller, Robert Nolen *lawyer*
Mitchem, Allen P. *lawyer*
Murane, William Edward *lawyer*
Newcom, Jennings Jay *lawyer*
O'Conner, Loretta Rae *lawyer*
O'Keefe, Edward Franklin *lawyer*
Olsen, M. Kent *lawyer, educator*
Pack, Stuart Harris *lawyer*
Palmer, David Gilbert *lawyer*
Pascoe, Donald Monte *lawyer*
Potter, Gary Thomas *lawyer*
Prochnow, James R. *lawyer*
Quiat, Gerald M. *lawyer*
Ray, Bruce David *lawyer, writer*
Rench, Stephen Charles *lawyer*
Rich, Robert Stephen *lawyer*
Roesler, John Bruce *lawyer*
Ruppert, John Lawrence *lawyer*
Samuels, Donald L. *lawyer*
Sattler, Bruce Weimer *lawyer*
Sayre, John Marshall *lawyer, former government official*
Seawell, Donald Ray *lawyer, publisher, arts center executive, producer*
Shepherd, John Frederic *lawyer*
Smith, Daniel Timothy *lawyer*
Smith, Laurie Hyson *lawyer*
Springer, Jeffrey Alan *lawyer*
Steefel, David Simon *lawyer*
Strenski, Robert Francis *lawyer*
Suthers, John William *prosecutor*
Tanabe, Charles Y. *lawyer*
Thomasch, Roger Paul *lawyer*
Tisdale, Douglas Michael *lawyer*
Truhlar, Robert J. *lawyer*
Ulrich, Theodore Albert *lawyer*
Walker, Timothy Blake *lawyer, educator*
Wedgle, Richard Jay *lawyer*
Wheeler, Malcolm Edward *lawyer, educator*
Williams, Andrea Irene *arbitrator, mediator, consultant*
Williams, Michael Anthony *lawyer*
Wohlgenant, Richard Glen *lawyer, director*
Woodward, Lester Ray *lawyer*
Wunnicke, Brooke *lawyer*
Yegge, Robert Bernard *law educator, dean*

Durango
Burnham, Bryson Payne *retired lawyer*

Englewood
DeMuth, Alan Cornelius *lawyer*
DeMuth, Laurence Wheeler, Jr., *lawyer, utilities executive*
Karstaedt, Arthur R., III, *lawyer*
Lidstone, Herrick Kenley, Jr., *lawyer*
Shannon, Malcolm Lloyd, Jr., *lawyer*
Spencer, Margaret Gilliam *lawyer*
Steinhauser, John William *retired lawyer*

Fort Collins
Carlson, Alan Douglas *lawyer*
Downey, Arthur Harold, Jr., *lawyer, mediator*
Hjelmfelt, David Charles *lawyer*
Johnson, Donald Edward, Jr., *lawyer*
Rogers, Garth Winfield *lawyer*

Frisco
Helmer, David Alan *lawyer*

Golden
Alberts, Celia Anne *lawyer*
Boumann, Robert Lyle *lawyer*
Eiberger, Carl Frederick *lawyer*
Kopel, David Benjamin *lawyer*
Phillipson, Donald E. *lawyer*

Grand Junction
Griff, Harry *lawyer*

Greeley
Conway, Rebecca Ann Koppes *lawyer*
Frey, Henry Charles *lawyer*

Greenwood Village
Aspinwall, David Charles *lawyer, insurance company executive*
Bain, James William *lawyer*
Dymond, Lewis Wandell *lawyer, mediator, educator*
Poe, Robert Alan *lawyer*
Ramsey, John Arthur *lawyer*

Lafayette
Manka, Ronald Eugene *lawyer*

Lakewood
Guyton, Samuel Percy *retired lawyer*
Humphrey, Charles Edward, Jr., *lawyer*
Isely, Henry Philip *association executive, integrative engineer, writer, educator*
McElwee, Dennis John *lawyer, former pharmaceutical company executive*
Meyer, Lynn Nix *lawyer*

Littleton
Meyer, Milton Edward, Jr., *lawyer, artist*
Perlman, B. Arthur *lawyer*

Lone Tree
Spelts, Richard John *lawyer*

Louisville
Kenney, Alan Adams *lawyer*

Morrison
Bowen, Peter Geoffrey *arbitrator, business educator*

Pagosa Springs
Kelly, Reid Browne *lawyer*

Parker
Greenberg, Morton Paul *lawyer, consultant, life settlement broker*

Placerville
Reagan, Harry Edwin, III, *lawyer*

Pueblo
Farley, Thomas T. *lawyer*
Humes, James Calhoun *lawyer, communications consultant, writer, educator*
Kogovsek, Daniel Charles *lawyer*
O'Callaghan, R.J. Patrick *lawyer*

Rocky Ford
Mendenhall, Harry Barton *lawyer*

Sedalia
Ewing, Robert Craig *lawyer, educator*

Westminster
Gaither, John Francis, Jr., *lawyer*

CONNECTICUT

Avon
Godbout, Arthur Richard, Jr., *lawyer*

Bethel
Medvecky, Thomas Edward *lawyer*

Bloomfield
Messemer, Glenn Matthew *lawyer*

Bridgeport
Bowen, Patrick Harvey *lawyer, consultant*
Graham, Kenneth Albert *lawyer*
Schrandt, Curtis Leon *lawyer, securities analyst, financial advisor*

Brookfield
Lewis, Edwin Leonard, III, *lawyer*
Secola, Joseph Paul *lawyer*

Brooklyn
Dune, Steve Charles *retired lawyer*

Danbury
Geoghan, Joseph Edward *former lawyer, chemical company executive*
Stichnoth, John A. *corporate lawyer*

Darien
Brown, James Shelly *lawyer*
Dale, Erwin Randolph *lawyer, author*
Himmelreich, David Baker *lawyer*
Prince, Kenneth Stephen *lawyer*

Derby
McEvoy, Sharlene Ann *law educator*

Fairfield
Caruso, Daniel F. *lawyer, judge, former state legislator*
Heineman, Benjamin Walter, Jr., *lawyer*

Farmington
Blechner, Barbara B. *law educator, consultant, lawyer*
Grafstein, Joel M. *lawyer*
Herzog, Brigitte *lawyer*
Wiechmann, Eric Watt *lawyer*

Greenwich
Bam, Foster *lawyer*
Berk, Alan S. *law firm executive*
Brandrup, Douglas Warren *lawyer*
Cantor, Samuel C. *lawyer, company executive*
Cantwell, Robert *lawyer*
Dederick, Ronald Osburn *lawyer*
Forrow, Brian Derek *lawyer*
Gelfman, Robert William *retired lawyer*
Lowenstein, Peter David *lawyer*
Lynch, William Redington *lawyer*
Mendenhall, John Ryan *retired lawyer, transportation executive*
More, Douglas McLochlan *lawyer*
Nimetz, Matthew *lawyer, investment company executive*
Pascarella, Henry William *lawyer*
Schoonmaker, Samuel Vail, III, *lawyer*
Selby, Leland Clay *lawyer*
Sexton, David Farrington *lawyer, investment banking executive*
Storms, Clifford Beekman *lawyer*
Stratton, Walter Love *lawyer*
Turner, Stephen Miller *lawyer, oil company executive*
Welt, Philip Stanley *lawyer, consultant*

Hamden
Loken, Gregory Arnold *law educator*
Margulies, Martin B. *lawyer, educator*

Hartford
Alfano, Charles Thomas, Sr., *lawyer*
Anthony, J(ulian) Danford, Jr., *lawyer*
Berall, Frank Stewart *lawyer*
Blumberg, Phillip Irvin *law educator*
Briskman, Louis Jacob *lawyer*
Buck, Gurdon Hall *lawyer, urban planner, mediator*
Cain, George Harvey *lawyer, business executive*
Caspar, George J., III, *lawyer*
Coyle, Michael Lee *lawyer*
Cullina, William Michael *lawyer*
Del Negro, John Thomas *lawyer*
Dempsey, Edward Joseph *lawyer*
Godfrey, Robert Douglas *lawyer*
Harkin, Ruth R. *lawyer*
Harrison, Thomas Flatley *lawyer*
Johnson, Dwight Alan *lawyer*
Kennedy, Jack Stanners *lawyer*
Klippel, Charles H *lawyer, insurance company executive*
Knickerbocker, Robert Platt, Jr., *lawyer*
Leonhardt, Clifton Andrew *lawyer, public official*
Lloyd, Alex *lawyer*
Lotstein, James Irving *lawyer*
Lyon, James Burroughs *lawyer*
McCarthy, Patrice Ann *lawyer*
Merriam, Dwight Haines *lawyer, land use planner*
Metzler, Robert J., II, *lawyer*
Middlebrook, Stephen Beach *lawyer*
Morawetz, Thomas H. *law educator*
Murtha, John Stephen *lawyer*
Nimirowski, Ramona Furphy *legal administrator*
Nolan, John Blanchard *lawyer*
Oakes, Dennis *lawyer, insurance company executive*
O'Donnell, Edward Francis, Jr., *lawyer*
Orth, Paul William *retired lawyer*
Pepe, Louis Robert *lawyer, educator*
Pinney, Sidney Dillingham, Jr., *lawyer*
Richter, Donald Paul *lawyer*
Ryan, David Thomas *lawyer*
Schroth, Peter W(Illiam) *lawyer, management and law educator*
See, Edmund M. *lawyer*
Sorokin, Ethel Silver *lawyer*
Space, Theodore Maxwell *lawyer*
Stravalle-Schmidt, Ann Roberta *lawyer*
Strohmenger, Thomas C *lawyer*
Sussman, Mark Richard *lawyer*
Tancredi, James J. *lawyer*
Taylor, Allan Bert *lawyer*
Trachsel, William Henry *corporate lawyer*
Voigt, Richard *lawyer*
Weinberger, Steven *lawyer, educator*
Wolin, Neal Steven *lawyer*
Wolman, Martin *lawyer*
Young, Dona Davis Gagliano *lawyer*

Lakeville
Cook, Charles David *international lawyer, arbitrator, consultant*
Jones, Ronald David *lawyer*

Litchfield
Fiederowicz, Walter Michael *lawyer*

Madison
Clendenen, William Herbert, Jr., *lawyer*
Scully, Roger Tehan, II, *lawyer*

Manchester
Jacobs, Ronald *prosecutor*

Meriden
Luby, Thomas Stewart *lawyer*

Milford
Benedosso, Anthony Nechols *lawyer*
Berchem, Robert Lee, Sr., *lawyer*
Broughel, Andrew Joseph *lawyer*
Sagarin, J. Daniel *lawyer*

Monroe
Hyman, Andrew Theodore *patent lawyer, physicist*

Mystic
Palmer, Richard Crist *lawyer*

New Britain
Hogan, John W., Jr., *lawyer*
Tedford, Deborah J. *lawyer*

New Canaan
Steinmetz, Richard Bird, Jr., *lawyer*

New Haven
Ayres, Ian *law educator*
Belt, David Levin *lawyer*
Birnbaum, Irwin Morton *lawyer*
Carty, Paul Vernon *lawyer*
Clark, Elias *law educator*
Cohen, Morris Leo *retired law librarian and educator*
Danaher, John Anthony, III, *prosecutor*
Days, Drew S., III, *lawyer, law educator*
De Lio, Anthony Peter *lawyer*
Donnelly, Robert L. *lawyer, corporation executive*
Donohue, John Joseph *law educator*
Duke, Steven Barry *law educator*
Ellickson, Robert Chester *law educator*
Freed, Daniel Josef *law educator*
Gastwirth, Donald Edward *lawyer, literary agent*
Geisler, Thomas Milton, Jr., *lawyer*
Gewirtz, Paul D. *lawyer, legal educator*
Gildea, Brian Michael *lawyer*
Goldstein, Abraham Samuel *lawyer, educator*
Greenfield, James Robert *lawyer*
Hansmann, Henry Baethke *law educator*
Johnstone, Quintin *law educator*
Kauffman, Stephen Blair *law librarian, educator*
Knag, Paul Everett *lawyer*
Langbein, John Harriss *lawyer, educator*
Macey, Jonathan R. *law educator*
O'Connor, Kevin James *lawyer*
Priest, George L. *law educator*
Reisman, William M. *lawyer, educator*
Robinson, Dorothy K. *lawyer*
Rose-Ackerman, Susan *law and political economy educator*
Schloss, Irving Steven *lawyer*
Simon, John Gerald *law educator*
Wagoner, Walter Dray, Jr., *lawyer*

New London
Asselin, John Thomas *lawyer*
Reardon, Robert Ignatius, Jr., *lawyer*

New Milford
Edmondson, John Richard *lawyer, pharmaceutical manufacturing company executive*

Norfolk
Jessup, Philip Caryl, Jr., *retired lawyer*

North Stonington
Svengalis, Kendall Frayne *law librarian, educator, publishing executive*

Norwalk
Cammaker, Sheldon Ira *lawyer*
Jacobs, Mark Randolph *lawyer*
Raikes, Charles FitzGerald *retired lawyer*

Redding
Gooch, Anthony Cushing *retired lawyer*
Russell, Allan David *lawyer*

Ridgefield
Foster, Julie Irene *lawyer*
Fricke, Richard John *lawyer*
Geloso-Barone, Rosalia A. *lawyer*

Roxbury
Friedman, John Maxwell, Jr., *lawyer*
Knutson, David Harry *retired lawyer, banker*

Shelton
Asija, S(atya) Pal *lawyer*

Simsbury
Main, Philip David *lawyer, probate judge*

Southbury
Auerbach, Ernest Sigmund *lawyer, company executive, writer*
Heitler, George *lawyer*

Southport
Sanetti, Stephen Louis *lawyer*

Stamford
Apfelbaum, Marc *lawyer*
Barreca, Christopher Anthony *lawyer*
Burgess, Lynne A *lawyer*
Cacace, Michael Joseph *lawyer*
Critelli, Michael J. *lawyer, manufacturing executive*
Dupont, Ralph Paul *lawyer, educator*
Gold, Steven Michael *lawyer*
Hubschman, Henry A. *lawyer*
Livolsi, Frank William, Jr., *lawyer*
Margolis, Emanuel *lawyer, educator*
Mayes, Michele Coleman *lawyer*
McClave, Wilkes, III, *lawyer, business executive*
Merritt, William Alfred, Jr., *retired lawyer, real estate company executive*
Nichols, Ralph Arthur *lawyer*
Perle, Eugene Gabriel *lawyer*
Rose, Richard Loomis *lawyer*
Shanman, James Alan *lawyer*
Sherman, Michael *lawyer*
Skidd, Thomas Patrick, Jr., *lawyer*
Speziale, John Albert *lawyer*
Staab, Diane D. *lawyer*
Stapleton, James Francis *lawyer*
Teitell, Conrad Laurence *lawyer, author*
Walsh, David James *lawyer*
Williamson, Keith Harvey *lawyer*
Willkie, Wendell Lewis, II, *lawyer*

Stonington
Van Rees, Cornelius S. *lawyer*

Storrs Mansfield
Tucker, Edwin Wallace *law educator*

Stratford
DiCicco, Margaret C. *lawyer*
O'Rourke, James Louis *lawyer*

Trumbull
Czajkowski, Frank Henry *lawyer*
Williams, Ronald Doherty *lawyer*

Washington
Fishman, Mitchell Steven *lawyer*

Waterbury
Dost, Mark W. *lawyer*

Waterford
Pavetti, Francis James *lawyer*

West Hartford
Dowling, Vincent John *retired lawyer*
Elliot, Ralph Gregory *lawyer*
Lynch, Karen Renzulli *lawyer*

Weston
Aibel, Howard J. *arbitrator, mediator*
Cohen, Fred Howard *lawyer, investment company executive*
Murray, Stephen James *lawyer*
Tavrow, Richard Lawrence *lawyer, corporate executive*

Westport
Amschler, James Ralph *lawyer, relocation company executive, consultant*
Barton, James Miller *lawyer, international business consultant*
Carr, Cynthia *lawyer*
Cramer, Allan P. *lawyer*
Daw, Harold John *lawyer, director*
Grodd, Leslie Eric *lawyer*
Paul, Roland Arthur *lawyer*
Razzano, Pasquale Angelo *lawyer*
Sheiman, Ronald Lee *lawyer*
Spitzer, Vlad Gerard *lawyer*

Wethersfield
Terk, Glenn Thomas *lawyer*

Wilton
Adams, Thomas Tilley *lawyer*
Duke, Robert Dominick *lawyer*
Healy, James Casey *lawyer*
Slater, Ralph Evan *lawyer*

Windsor
Morelli, Carmen *lawyer*

Winsted
Finch, Frank Herschel, Jr., *lawyer*

DELAWARE

Dover
Denn, Matthew P. *lawyer*
Ennis, Bruce Clifford *retired lawyer*
Stone, F. L. Peter *lawyer*
Twilley, Joshua Marion *lawyer*

Greenville
Long, Linda Ann *lawyer*

Newark
Elson, Charles Myer *law educator*
McCann, Richard Stephen *lawyer*
Welsh, Paul Patrick *retired lawyer*

Wilmington
Bader, John Merwin *lawyer*
Baumann, Julian Henry, Jr., *lawyer*
Biondi, O. Francis *lawyer*
Blumenfeld, Jack Barry *lawyer*
Boardman, William Penniman *lawyer, banker*
Carpenter, Edmund Nelson, II, *retired lawyer*
Connolly, Colm F. *prosecutor*
Devine, Donn *lawyer, genealogist, former city official*
Erisman, James A. *lawyer*
Fenton, Wendell *lawyer*
Finkelstein, Jesse Adam *lawyer*
Freeh, Louis Joseph *lawyer*
Gamble, Donald Geoffrey Bidmead *lawyer*
Goldstein, Jack Charles *lawyer*
Green, James Samuel *lawyer*
Hannigan, Patricia C. *prosecutor*
Herdeg, John Andrew *lawyer*
Jewell, George Benson *lawyer, educator, minister*
Johnston, William David *lawyer*
Julian, J. R. *lawyer*
Kelleher, Daniel Francis *lawyer*
Kirk, Richard Dillon *lawyer*
Kirkpatrick, Andrew Booth, Jr., *lawyer*
Klayman, Barry Martin *lawyer*
Kristol, Daniel Marvin *lawyer*
Magee, Thomas Hugh *lawyer*
McDowell, Charles S. *lawyer*
Parsons, Donald Francis *lawyer*
Pazuniak, George *lawyer*
Rodgers, Stephen John *lawyer, physician, consultant*
Rothschild, Steven James *lawyer*
Rudge, Howard J. *corporate lawyer*
Semple, James William *lawyer*
Sheridan, John Robert *lawyer*
Sleet, Gregory M. *lawyer, judge*
Smith, Craig Bennett *lawyer*
Sullivan, Lawrence Matthew *lawyer*
Tigani, Bruce William *lawyer*
Waisanen, Christine M. *lawyer, writer*
Ward, Rodman, Jr., *lawyer, director*
Whitney, Douglas Edgar, Sr., *lawyer*
Wier, Richard Royal, Jr., *lawyer*

DISTRICT OF COLUMBIA

Washington
Aaronson, David Ernest *law educator, lawyer*
Abbott, Alden Francis *lawyer, government official, educator*
Abeles, Charles Calvert *retired lawyer*
Acheson, David Campion *lawyer, author, policy analyst*
Ackerson, Nels J(ohn) *lawyer*
Adams, Roger C. *lawyer*
Adamson, Terrence Burdett *lawyer*
Adler, Howard, Jr., *lawyer*
Adler, Howard Bruce *lawyer*
Agrast, Mark David *lawyer*
Aisenberg, Irwin Morton *lawyer*
Alexander, Clifford Joseph *lawyer*
Alexander, Donald Crichton *lawyer*
Allard, Nicholas W. *lawyer*
Allen, William Hayes *lawyer, educator*
Alvarez, Scott G. *lawyer*
Amron, Cory M. *lawyer*
Andersen, Robert Michael *lawyer*
Anderson, Frederick Randolph, Jr., *lawyer, law educator*
Andrew, Joseph Jerald *lawyer*
Andrews, Mark Joseph *lawyer*
Anthony, Stephen Pierce *lawyer*
Apple, James Glenn *lawyer, educator*
Aron, Mark G. *lawyer, transportation executive*
Ashton, Richard M. *federal lawyer*
Atwood, James R. *lawyer*
Aufhauser, David D. *lawyer, former federal agency administrator*
Augustyn, Noel James *lawyer*
Avil, Richard Daniel, Jr., *lawyer*
Axelrod, Jonathan Gans *lawyer*
Ayer, Donald Belton *lawyer*
Babby, Lon S. *lawyer*
Bachman, Kenneth Leroy, Jr., *lawyer*
Baer, William J. *lawyer*
Banzhaf, John F., III, *legal association administrator, lawyer*
Baran, Jan Witold *lawyer, educator*
Bardin, David J. *lawyer*
Barnes, Donald Michael *lawyer*
Barnes, Mark James *lawyer*
Barnes, Michael Darr *lawyer, think tank executive*
Barnett, Robert Bruce *lawyer, educator*
Barr, Michael Blanton *lawyer*
Barrie, John Paul *lawyer, educator*
Barron, Jerome Aure *law educator*
Barron, Myra Hymovich *lawyer*
Barshefsky, Charlene *lawyer, former diplomat*
Barusch, Ronald Charles *lawyer*
Basseches, Robert Treinis *lawyer*
Batla, Raymond John, Jr., *lawyer*
Bebchick, Leonard Norman *lawyer*
Becker, Grace Chung *lawyer*
Beckwith, Edward Jay *lawyer*
Beers, Donald Osborne *lawyer*
Beizer, Robert A. *lawyer*
Bell, Stephen Robert *lawyer*
Beller, Herbert N. *lawyer*
Bellinger, Edgar Thomson *lawyer*
Bello, Judith Hippler *lawyer, trade association administrator*
Belman, Murray Joel *lawyer*
Bennett, Alexander Elliot *lawyer*
Bennett, Robert Stephen *lawyer*
Beresford, Douglas Lincoln *lawyer*
Bergner, Jane Cohen *lawyer*
Berl, Joseph M. *lawyer*
Berman, Marshall Fox *lawyer*
Berner, Frederic George, Jr., *lawyer*
Bernhard, Berl *lawyer*
Bernstein, Mitchell Harris *lawyer*
Berz, David Richard *lawyer*
Best, Judah *lawyer*
Bickwit, Leonard, Jr., *lawyer*
Biddle, Timothy Maurice *lawyer*
Bierman, James Norman *lawyer*
Billauer, Barbara Pfeffer *lawyer, educator*
Bingaman, Anne K. *lawyer*
Birnkrant, Henry Joseph *lawyer*
Black, Stephen Franklin *lawyer*
Blair, Robert Allen *business executive, lawyer*
Blair, William McCormick, Jr., *lawyer*
Blake, Jonathan Dewey *lawyer*
Blazek-White, Doris *lawyer*
Bleakley, Peter Kimberley *lawyer*
Bliss, Donald Tiffany, Jr., *lawyer*
Bloch, Richard Isaac *labor arbitrator*

Bloch, Stuart Marshall lawyer
Bloch, Susan Low law educator
Boehm, Steven Bruce lawyer
Bogard, Lawrence Joseph lawyer
Boggs, George Trenholm lawyer
Boggs, Thomas Hale, Jr., lawyer, director
Boland, Christopher Thomas, II, lawyer
Bondareff, Joan M. retired government official, lawyer
Bonvillian, William Boone lawyer
Born, Brooksley Elizabeth lawyer
Borsari, George Robert, Jr., lawyer, broadcaster
Boskey, Bennett lawyer
Boyd, Stephen Mather arbitrator, mediator, lawyer
Braceras, Jennifer C. lawyer
Bradley, Leigh A. government official, lawyer
Braverman, Burt Alan lawyer
Bredhoff, Elliot lawyer
Bregman, Arthur Randolph lawyer, educator
Brenner, Janet Maybin Walker lawyer
Briggs, Alan Leonard lawyer
Brockway, David Hunt lawyer
Bromwich, Michael Ray lawyer
Bronstein, Alvin J. lawyer
Brown, Charles Freeman, II, lawyer
Brown, David Nelson lawyer
Brown, Donald Arthur lawyer
Brown, George Leslie legislative affairs and business development consultant, former manufacturing company executive, former lieutenant governor
Brown, Preston lawyer
Brown, Richard L. lawyer
Brown, Thomas Philip, III, lawyer
Browne, Richard Cullen lawyer
Brown Weiss, Edith law educator
Bruce, E(stel) Edward lawyer
Brunsvold, Brian Garrett lawyer, educator
Brustein, Michael Labe lawyer
Bryson, Jeffrey T. lawyer
Buc, Nancy Lillian lawyer
Bucholtz, Harold Ronald lawyer
Buckley, Jeremiah Stephen lawyer
Buffon, Charles Edward lawyer
Burack, Michael Leonard lawyer
Burchill, William Roberts, Jr., lawyer
Burka, Robert Alan lawyer
Burke, Beverly J. lawyer, energy executive
Burns, Stephen Gilbert lawyer
Burt, Jeffrey Amsterdam lawyer
Busby, David lawyer
Buscemi, Peter lawyer
Bushmiller, Ann E. lawyer
Butler, Michael Francis lawyer
Calamaro, Raymond Stuart lawyer
Calderwood, James Albert lawyer
Campbell, James Sargent lawyer
Canfield, Edward Francis lawyer, business executive
Cantor, Herbert I. lawyer
Caplin, Mortimer Maxwell lawyer, educator
Carey, Sarah Collins lawyer
Carneal, George Upshur lawyer
Carney, Robert Thomas lawyer
Caro, Luisa lawyer
Carome, Patrick Joseph lawyer
Carpenter, Sheila Jane lawyer
Carr, Lawrence Edward, Jr., lawyer
Carroll, J. Speed lawyer, consultant, financial executive
Carrow, Milton Michael law educator
Carter, Barry Edward lawyer, educator, administrator
Carter, William Joseph lawyer
Cashen, Henry Christopher, II, lawyer, former government official
Casserly, James Lund lawyer
Cassidy, Robert Charles, Jr., lawyer
Cavanagh, Rita A. lawyer, educator
Chabot, Elliot Charles lawyer
Chabot, Philip Louis, Jr., lawyer
Chameides, Steven B. lawyer
Chanin, Leah Farb law library administrator, lawyer, consultant, law educator
Chanin, Michael Henry lawyer
Chanin, Robert Howard lawyer
Cho, Sung Yoon law librarian
Chopko, Mark E. lawyer
Christaldi, Brian lawyer
Christian, Betty Jo lawyer
Christian, Ernest Silsbee, Jr., lawyer
Cicconi, James William lawyer
Clagett, Brice McAdoo lawyer, writer, genealogist
Clark, LeRoy D. legal educator, lawyer
Cobb, Calvin Hayes, Jr., lawyer
Cobb, Ty lawyer
Cobbs, Louise Bertram lawyer
Coerper, Milo George lawyer, priest
Coffield, Shirley Ann lawyer, educator
Cohen, Edward Barth lawyer
Cohen, Louis Richard lawyer
Cohen, Nelson Craig lawyer
Cohen, Sheldon Stanley lawyer
Cohn, Sherman Louis lawyer, educator
Cole, John Pope, Jr., lawyer
Cole, Robert Theodore lawyer
Coleman, William Thaddeus, Jr., lawyer
Collins, Bruce Dennis lawyer
Collins, Daniel Francis lawyer
Collins, John Timothy lawyer
Collinson, Dale Stanley lawyer
Colson, Earl Morton lawyer, educator
Columbus, R. Timothy lawyer
Comstock, Robert Francis lawyer
Condrell, William Kenneth lawyer
Cook, Harry Clayton, Jr., lawyer
Cook, Michael Harry lawyer
Cooper, Alan Samuel lawyer, educator
Cooper, Clement Theodore lawyer
Cooper, Jacqueline Gerson lawyer
Cooper, Richard Melvyn lawyer
Cope, John R(obert) lawyer
Cortese, Alfred William, Jr., lawyer, consultant
Coulter, Ann lawyer, author
Coursen, Christopher Dennison lawyer
Cox, Kenneth Allen lawyer, communications consultant
Craft, Robert Homan, Jr., lawyer
Craig, Gregory Bestor lawyer, government official
Crosby, William Duncan, Jr., lawyer
Crumlish, Joseph Dougherty lawyer
Crump, John lawyer
Culvahouse, Arthur Boggess, Jr., lawyer
Cummings, Frank lawyer
Cutler, Lloyd Norton lawyer
Cymrot, Mark Alan lawyer
Cys, Richard L. lawyer
Czarra, Edgar F., Jr., lawyer
Daddario, Emilio Quincy retired lawyer
Dalley, George Albert lawyer, consultant
Danas, Andrew Michael lawyer
Daniels, Diana M. lawyer
Davidson, Daniel Ira lawyer
Davidson, Daniel Morton lawyer
Davidson, Tom William lawyer
Davies, Charles R. lawyer
Day, James MacDonald lawyer, educator
deKieffer, Donald Eulette lawyer
de Leon, Sylvia A. lawyer
Dembling, Paul Gerald lawyer, former government official
Denger, Michael Louis lawyer
Denison, Mary Boney lawyer
Derrick, Butler Carson, Jr., lawyer, former congressman
Determan, Sara-Ann lawyer
Devall, James Lee lawyer
Dicello, Francis P. lawyer
Dickson, Constance Pierce law librarian
Dickstein, Sidney lawyer
Diercks, Walter Elmer lawyer
Dillon-Ridgley, Dianne Granville mediator, consultant, association executive
Dinan, Donald Robert lawyer
Dinh, Viet D. law educator
Disheroon, Fred Russell lawyer
Docter, Charles Alfred lawyer, former state legislator
Dolan, Michael William lawyer
Dole, Robert J. lawyer, former senator
Dolin, Mitchell f. lawyer
Donegan, Charles Edward lawyer, educator
Donohoe, Charles Richard general patent counsel
Doolittle, Jesse William, Jr., lawyer
Dorsen, David M(ilton) lawyer
Dotson, Donald L. lawyer
Dowley, Joseph Kyran lawyer, member congressional staff
Downs, Clark Evans lawyer
Dreisbach, Daniel Livingstone lawyer, educator
Drinan, Robert Frederick lawyer, former congressman, educator, clergyman
Dunn, Loretta Lynn lawyer
Dunner, Donald Robert lawyer
Durney, Michael Cavalier lawyer
Duvall, John Edward law librarian
Dwyer, Maureen E. lawyer
Dye, Rebecca Feemster legislative counsel
Dye, Stuart S. lawyer
Dyk, Timothy Belcher federal judge, educator
Eastment, Thomas James lawyer
Easton, John Jay, Jr., lawyer
Edson, Charles Louis lawyer, educator
Efros, Ellen Ann lawyer
Ehrenhaft, Peter David lawyer
Eisenberg, Meyer lawyer
Elcano, Mary S. lawyer
Ellicott, John LeMoyne lawyer
Elmer, Brian Christian lawyer
Elrod, Eugene Richard lawyer
Epstein, Gary Marvin lawyer
Evans, Robert David legal association executive
Everett, Ralph Bernard lawyer
Ewing, Ky Pepper, Jr., lawyer
Fahrenkopf, Frank Joseph, Jr., lawyer
Fairbanks, Richard Monroe, III, lawyer, former ambassador at large
Faley, R. Scott (Richard Scott Faley) lawyer
Falk, James Harvey, Sr., lawyer
Farabow, Ford Franklin, Jr., lawyer
Faust, Marcus G. lawyer
Fedders, John Michael lawyer
Feffer, Gerald Alan lawyer
Feinberg, Kenneth Roy lawyer, law educator
Feldhaus, Stephen Martin lawyer
Feldman, Clarice Rochelle lawyer
Feldman, Mark B. lawyer
Feldman, Roger David lawyer
Fels, Nicholas Wolff lawyer
Ferrand, Louis George lawyer
Ferrara, Ralph C. lawyer
Fielding, Fred Fisher lawyer
Fields, Wendy Lynn lawyer
Finkel, Eugene Jay lawyer
Finston, Susan Kling lawyer
Firestone, Charles Morton lawyer, educator
Fishburne, Benjamin P., III, lawyer
Fisher, Benjamin Chatburn lawyer
Fitzpatrick, James Franklin lawyer
Flannery, Ellen Joanne lawyer
Fleischaker, Marc L. lawyer
Flood, John Joseph lawyer
Forester, John Gordon, Jr., lawyer
Forrest, Herbert Emerson lawyer
Fortuno, Victor M. lawyer
Foscarinis, Maria lawyer
Foster, C(harles) Allen lawyer
Fowler, J. Edward lawyer
Fowler, Tillie Kidd lawyer
Fox, Sarah lawyer
Frank, Richard Asher lawyer, health products executive
Frank, Theodore David lawyer
Freedman, Jay Weil lawyer
Frisby, Herbert Russell lawyer
Frost, Edmund Bowen lawyer
Gable, Edward Brennan, Jr., lawyer
Garrett, Theodore Louis lawyer
Garrish, Theodore John lawyer
Gaskell, Judith Ann law librarian
Gati, Toby T. international advisor
Geller, Kenneth Steven lawyer
Gellhorn, Ernest Albert Eugene lawyer
Geltman, Edward Alan lawyer
Geniesse, Robert John lawyer
George, Joey Russell lawyer
Gerson, Stuart Michael lawyer
Gibbs, Lawrence Blair lawyer
Gideon, Kenneth Wayne lawyer
Gilfoyle, Nathalie Floyd Preston lawyer
Gilmore, James Stuart, III, lawyer, former governor
Ginsburg, Charles David lawyer
Ginsburg, Martin David lawyer, educator
Glancz, Ronald Robert lawyer
Glasgow, Norman Milton lawyer
Glick, Leslie Alan lawyer
Glover, Jere Walton lawyer
Glynn, Marilyn lawyer
Goelzer, Daniel Lee lawyer
Gold, Peter Frederick lawyer
Goldberg, Jolande Elisabeth law librarian, lawyer
Goldberg, Seth A. lawyer
Goldschmid, Harvey Jerome law educator
Goldsmith, Willis Jay lawyer
Goldstein, Frank Robert lawyer
Goldstein, Michael B. lawyer
Goldsten, Robert Emanuel lawyer, investor
Goodman, Alfred Nelson lawyer
Gorelick, Jamie Shona lawyer
Gorinson, Stanley M. lawyer
Gorrell, J. Warren, Jr., lawyer
Graham, Thomas, Jr., lawyer
Graham, Thomas Richard lawyer
Gray, Clayland Boyden lawyer
Green, Donald Hugh lawyer
Green, Thomas Charles lawyer
Greenberger, I. Michael lawyer
Greenwald, John Doyle lawyer
Grenier, Edward Joseph, Jr., lawyer
Gribbon, Daniel McNamara lawyer
Grier, Phillip Michael lawyer, former association executive
Gross, Roberta Lee inspector general
Grossman, Joanne Barbara lawyer
Gulland, Eugene D. lawyer
Gurulé, Jimmy legal educator, federal agency administrator
Gutman, Harry Largman lawyer, educator
Guttman, Egon law educator
Haines, Terry L. lawyer, consultant
Halvorson, Newman Thorbus, Jr., lawyer
Hansen, Mark Charles lawyer
Harbour, Pamela Jones lawyer
Harman, William Boys, Jr., lawyer
Harrington, Anthony Stephen lawyer, diplomat
Harris, Don Victor, Jr., lawyer
Harris, Jeffrey lawyer
Harris, Scott Blake lawyer
Harris, Steven Brown lawyer
Harrison, Donald lawyer
Harrison, Earl David lawyer, real estate company officer
Harrison, Marion Edwyn lawyer
Hart, Christopher Alvin lawyer
Hassett, Joseph Mark lawyer
Hausfeld, Michael D. lawyer
Haynes, R. Michael lawyer
Haynes, William J(ames), II, lawyer
Haythe, Winston McDonald lawyer, educator, consultant, real estate investor
Hebert, Jay Howell lawyer
Heckman, Jerome Harold lawyer
Heenan, Michael Terence lawyer
Heffernan, James Vincent lawyer
Hefter, Laurence Roy lawyer
Heller, Jack Isaac lawyer
Heller, John Roderick, III, lawyer, business executive
Henderson, Douglas Boyd lawyer
Henderson, Thomas Henry, Jr., lawyer, legal association executive
Henke, Michael John lawyer, educator
Hennessy, Ellen Anne lawyer, benefits compensation analyst, educator
Herrera, Jessica Rae lawyer, educator
Herzstein, Robert Erwin lawyer
Hewitt, Paul Buck lawyer
Hiatt, Johnathan P. lawyer, labor union administrator
Hickey, Bruce William lawyer
Hiestand, O.S., Jr., lawyer
Higuchi, Shirley A. lawyer
Hill, Eleanor Jean lawyer
Hills, Carla Anderson lawyer, former federal official
Hills, Roderick M. lawyer, former government official
Hirschhorn, Eric Leonard lawyer
Hobbs, J. Timothy, Sr., lawyer
Hobelman, Carl Donald lawyer
Hobson, James Richmond lawyer
Hoffinger, Adam Steven lawyer
Hoffman, Joel Elihu lawyer
Ho-Gonzalez, William lawyer
Hollis, Sheila Slocum lawyer
Hopson, Mark D. lawyer
Horahan, Edward Bernard, III, lawyer
Horlick, Gary Norman lawyer, legal educator
Horn, Charles M. lawyer
Horn, Donald Herbert lawyer
Horne, Michael Stewart lawyer
House, W(illiam) Michael lawyer
Houseman, Alan William lawyer
Howard, Roscoe Conklin, Jr., lawyer, educator
Huberman, Richard Lee lawyer
Huddleson, Edwin Emmett, III, lawyer
Huge, Harry lawyer
Hughes, Marija Matich law librarian
Hugler, Edward Charles lawyer, federal and state government
Hunnicutt, Charles Alvin lawyer
Husband, Phillip Lyle lawyer
Hutt, Peter Barton lawyer
Hyman, Lester Samuel lawyer
Inman, Harry Ansel lawyer
Ireland, Oliver lawyer
Isbell, David Bradford lawyer, educator
Israelite, David M. prosecutor
Ives, Stephen Bradshaw, Jr., retired lawyer
Jackson, James Kinsey lawyer
Jacobsen, Raymond Alfred, Jr., lawyer
Jacobson, David Edward lawyer
Jacobson, Richard Lee lawyer, educator
Jamar, Steven Dwight law educator
Jensen, Paul Rolf lawyer, real estate investor
Johnson, David Raymond lawyer
Johnson, Oliver Thomas, Jr., lawyer
Johnson, Philip McBride lawyer
Jones, Aidan Drexel lawyer
Jones, George Washington, Jr., lawyer
Jones, Kelsey A. law educator, law administrator
Jones, Mary Gardiner lawyer, educator, consumer interest organization executive
Jordan, Jon Byron lawyer
Jordan, Robert Elijah, III, lawyer
Joseph, Daniel Mordecai lawyer
Journey, Drexel Dahlke lawyer
Kabel, Robert James lawyer
Kafka, Gerald Andrew lawyer
Kahn, Edwin Leonard lawyer
Kaplan, Elaine D. lawyer
Kaplan, Gilbert B. lawyer
Kappler, Ann M. lawyer, finance company executive
Kass, Benny Lee lawyer
Kaswell, Stuart Joel lawyer
Katz, Deborah A. lawyer
Katz, John W. lawyer, state official
Katz, Sherman E. lawyer
Katzen, Sally lawyer, educator
Kaufman, Thomas Frederick lawyer, legal educator
Keeney, John C. lawyer
Keeney, John Christopher, Jr., lawyer
Keightley, James J. lawyer
Keir, David Sherwood lawyer
Kelly, William Charles, Jr., lawyer
Kendall, David E. lawyer
Kennard, Mary Elizabeth lawyer
Kennard, William Earl former lawyer
Kennedy, Jerry Wayne lawyer
Kent, Alan Heywood lawyer
Kerr, Stuart H. lawyer, think tank executive
Kessler, Judd Lewis lawyer
Kiddoo, Jean Lynn lawyer
Kies, Kenneth J. lawyer
Kiko, Philip George lawyer
King, Patricia Ann law educator
Kingham, Richard Frank lawyer
Kirsch, Laurence Stephen lawyer
Kissel, Peter Charles lawyer
Kittrie, Nicholas international lawyer, writer
Klarfeld, Peter James lawyer
Klawiter, Donald Casimir lawyer
Klee, Ann R. lawyer
Klein, Michael Roger lawyer, business executive
Knapp, George M. lawyer
Knapp, Rosalind Ann lawyer
Knauer, Leon Thomas lawyer
Knebel, John Albert lawyer, former government official
Koch, Kathleen Day lawyer
Korth, Fritz-Alan lawyer
Kosarin, Jonathan Henry lawyer, consultant
Kovacic, William Evan law educator
Kovacs, William Lawrence lawyer
Kramer, Andrew Michael lawyer
Kramer, William David lawyer
Kramm, Deborah Lucille lawyer
Krasnow, Erwin Gilbert lawyer
Kriesberg, Simeon M. lawyer
Kroener, William Frederick, III, lawyer
Kronstein, Werner J lawyer
Krump, Gary Joseph lawyer, judge
Kuder, Armin Ulrich lawyer
Kyhos, Thomas Flynn lawyer
Lackey, Michael E., Jr., lawyer, educator
Lambert, Jeremiah Daniel lawyer, educator
Lambert, Steven Charles lawyer
Lamm, Carolyn Beth lawyer
Lanam, Linda Lee lawyer
Landfield, Richard lawyer
Lane, Bruce Stuart lawyer
Lane, John Dennis lawyer
Lapidus, Lawrence Searle lawyer
Laporte, Gerald Joseph Sylvestre lawyer
Larroca, Raymond G. lawyer
Laster, Gail W. lawyer
Latham, Patricia Horan lawyer
Latham, Peter Samuel lawyer
Latham, Weldon Hurd lawyer
Latimer, Allie B. retired lawyer
Laughlin, James Harold, Jr., lawyer
Lautrup, Greer Olsen lawyer
Lavelle, Joseph P. lawyer
Lavine, Henry Wolfe lawyer
Lawler, William E., III, lawyer
Lazarus, Arthur, Jr., retired lawyer
Lazarus, Kenneth Anthony lawyer
Leary, Mary Lou prosecutor
Legro, Stanley Wayne environmental lawyer
Leibold, Arthur William, Jr., lawyer
Leonard, Will Ernest, Jr., lawyer
Lessenco, Gilbert Barry lawyer
Lettow, Charles Frederick lawyer
Levin, Edward M. law consultant
Levin, Edward Ross lawyer
Levine, Henry David lawyer
Levinson, Lawrence Edward lawyer, corporation executive
Levy, Mark Irving lawyer
Lewis, David John lawyer
Lewis, Eleanor Roberts lawyer
Lewis, Glenn C. lawyer
Lewis, Guy A. prosecutor
Lewis, Lorraine general counsel
Lewis, William Henry, Jr., lawyer
Lewis, Wilma Antoinette lawyer, former prosecutor and federal agency admin
Lichtenstein, Elissa Charlene legal association executive
Liebman, Ronald Stanley lawyer
Liedquist, Robert Eric lawyer
Lifschitz, Judah lawyer
Lindsey, Seth Mark lawyer, federal agency administrator
Linowitz, Sol Myron lawyer
Lipstein, Robert A. lawyer
Livingston, Bob (Robert Linlithgow Livingston Jr.) lawyer, former congressman
Loots, James Mason lawyer
Lopatin, Alan G. lawyer
Lott, Cindy M. lawyer
Lowe, Randall Brian lawyer
Lubic, Robert Bennett lawyer, arbitrator, law educator
Luce, Gregory M. lawyer
Lupo, Raphael V. lawyer
Lybecker, Martin Earl lawyer
Lyons, Dennis Gerald lawyer
MacBeth, Angus lawyer
Macdonald, David Robert lawyer, fund administrator
MacDougall, Gordon Pier lawyer
Macleod, John Amend lawyer
Madden, Murdaugh Stuart lawyer
Madden, Thomas James lawyer, educator
Maechling, Charles, Jr., lawyer, diplomat, educator, writer
Magielnicki, Robert L. lawyer
Maginnis, John C., III, lawyer
Mahar, Ellen Patricia law librarian
Majev, Howard Rudolph lawyer
Malone, William Robert lawyer
Manatt, Charles Taylor lawyer
Mann, Donegan lawyer
Mann, Lawrence Moses lawyer
Manning, Michael J. lawyer
Manson, Joseph Lloyd, III, lawyer
Manwell, John Parker, II, lawyer
Mapes, William Rodgers, Jr., lawyer
Marans, J. Eugene lawyer
Marcin, Peter R. lawyer, real estate broker
Marcuss, Stanley Joseph lawyer

FLORIDA

Alachua

Altamonte Springs

Aventura

Bartow

Bascom

Boca Raton

Bonita Springs
Dignan, Thomas Gregory, Jr., *lawyer*
Olander, Ray Gunnar *retired lawyer*

Boynton Beach
Hermann, Philip J. *lawyer*
Sutter, William Paul *lawyer*

Bradenton
Brenner, Frank *lawyer*
Groseclose, Lynn Hunter *lawyer*
LaForest, Lana Jean *lawyer*
Padgett, Gail Blanchard *lawyer*
St. Paul, Alexandra De La Vergne *lawyer*
Thomas, Ella Cooper *lawyer*

Brandon
Curry, Clifton Conrad, Jr., *lawyer*

Brooksville
Brown, James Milton *law educator*

Cape Coral
Parrett, Sherman O. *lawyer*

Celebration
Schroeder, James White *retired lawyer*

Clearwater
Borja, Mary Ellen Murphy *lawyer*
Coleman, Jeffrey Peters *lawyer*
Dougall-Sides, Leslie K. *lawyer*
Fine, A(rthur) Kenneth *lawyer*
Hogan, Elwood *lawyer*
McCormack, John Robert *lawyer*
Pope, Fred Wallace, Jr., *lawyer*
Sandefer, G(eorge) Larry *lawyer*
Tragos, George Euripedes *lawyer*
Weidemeyer, Carleton Lloyd *lawyer*
Zschau, Julius James *lawyer*

Coconut Creek
Sheehy, Frances Diane *lawyer*

Coral Gables
Anthony, Andrew John *lawyer*
Bolton, David *lawyer, educator*
Dady, Robert Edward *lawyer*
David, George A. *lawyer*
Fournaris, Theodore James *lawyer*
Gonzalez, Ervin Amado *lawyer*
Hall, Miles Lewis, Jr., *lawyer*
Hirschhorn, Joel *lawyer*
Hoffman, Carl H. *lawyer*
McGrane, Miles A., III, *lawyer*
Moreno, Fernando *lawyer, educator*
Moss, Ambler Holmes, Jr., *lawyer, former
ambassador*
Olazabal, Ann Morales *business law educator*
Paul, Robert *lawyer*
Simpson, Russell Gordon *lawyer, former mayor,
not-for-profit developer, consultant*

Dade City
Brennan, Thomas Emmett *lawyer*

Daytona Beach
Barker, Robert Osborne (Bob Barker) *educator,
mediator*
Harris, Christy Franklin *lawyer*
Neitzke, Eric Karl *lawyer*

Deerfield Beach
Caso, Dawn Marie *lawyer, consultant, law educator*

Deland
McCann, Greg *law educator, consultant*

Delray Beach
Armstrong, Jack Gilliland *lawyer*
Fannin, David Cecil *lawyer*
Larry, R. Heath *lawyer, director*
Reichart, Stuart Richard *lawyer*
Silberman, Charlotte Schatzberg *retired lawyer,
artist*

Fort Lauderdale
Benjamin, James Scott *lawyer*
Bogenschutz, J. David *lawyer*
Brawer, Marc Harris *lawyer*
Bunnell, George Eli *lawyer*
Bustamante, Nestor *lawyer*
Cane, Marilyn Blumberg *lawyer, educator*
Clubb, Bruce Edwin *retired lawyer*
Cole, James Otis *lawyer*
Dressler, Robert A. *lawyer*
Fanizza, Joanne *lawyer*
Gardner, Russell Menese *lawyer*
Glantz, Wendy Newman *lawyer*
Goldberg, Alan Joel *lawyer*
Gore, George Henry *lawyer*
Haliczer, James Solomon *lawyer*
Harbaugh, Joseph Delbert *legal educator, consultant*
Hargrove, John Russell *lawyer*
Hess, George Franklin, II, *lawyer*
Hester, Julia A. *lawyer*
Hirsch, Jeffrey Allan *lawyer*
Jarvis, Robert Mark *law educator*
Joseph, Paul R *law educator*
Kelly, John Patrick *lawyer*
Kreizinger, Loreen I. *lawyer*
Kubler, Frank Lawrence *lawyer*
Lataif, Lawrence P. *lawyer*
Leighton, James H. *law educator, department
chairman*
Meeks, William Herman, III, *lawyer*
Mintz, Joel Alan *law educator*
Nyce, John Daniel *lawyer*
Oltman, John Harold *patent lawyer*
Richmond, Gail Levin *law educator*
Russell, Terrence Joseph *lawyer*
Sale, David Todd *lawyer*
Sanders, Dale R. *lawyer*
Schreiber, Alan Hickman *lawyer*
Sherman, Richard Allen, Sr., *lawyer*
Strickland, Wilton L. *lawyer*
Tacher, Robert Frederick *lawyer*
Turner, Hugh Joseph, Jr., *lawyer*
Wich, Donald Anthony, Jr., *lawyer*

Fort Myers
Colasurd, Richard Michael *lawyer*

Consilio, Barbara Ann *legal administrator,
management consultant*
Kiernan, Edwin A., Jr., *lawyer, corporation
executive*
Medvecky, Robert Stephen *lawyer*
Miller, William Charles *lawyer*
O'Donnell, Bernard Joseph, Jr., *lawyer*
Peterson, Rodney Delos *retired mediator, economist*
Rubinstein, Alan Jay *lawyer*

Fort Pierce
Conklin, Howard Lawrence *lawyer*
Sneed, Richard Durwood, Jr., *lawyer*

Gainesville
Boyes, Patrice Flinchbaugh *lawyer*
Criser, Marshall M. *lawyer, retired university
president*
Gordon, Michael Wallace *law educator*
Israel, Jerold Harvey *law educator*
Maurer, Virginia Gallaher *law educator*
McMahon, Martin James, Jr., *law educator,
consultant*
Van Alstyne, W. Scott, Jr., *lawyer, educator*
Weyrauch, Walter Otto *law educator*

Gulf Breeze
Burr, Timothy Fuller *lawyer*

Gulfport
Allen, John Thomas, Jr., *lawyer*
Cox, Nicholas Bernard *law educator*
Jackson, Nicholas Miller *lawyer, researcher*

Haines City
Mc Dougall, Dugald Stewart *retired lawyer*

Hallandale
Engel, Tala *lawyer*

Hialeah
Gross, Richard Wilson *lawyer*

Hobe Sound
Markoe, Frank, Jr., *lawyer, business and hospital
executive*

Hollywood
Korthals, Candace Durbin *lawyer*
Rogovin, Lawrence H. *lawyer*
Russell, Antonette Patrice *lawyer*
Tannen, Ricki Lewis *lawyer, psychologist, educator*

Indian Harbor Beach
Tasker, Molly Jean *lawyer*

Jacksonville
Ansbacher, Barry Barnett *lawyer*
Appel, Laurence B. *lawyer, retail executive*
Beytagh, Francis Xavier, Jr., *law educator*
Boyer, Tyrie Alvis *lawyer*
Braddock, Donald Layton *lawyer, accountant, real
estate broker, investor*
Bradford, Dana Gibson, II, *lawyer*
Bryan, Joseph Shepard, Jr., *lawyer*
Bullock, Bruce Stanley *lawyer*
Callender, John Francis *lawyer*
Coker, Howard Coleman *lawyer*
Commander, Charles Edward *lawyer, real estate
consultant*
Crawford, John Richard *lawyer*
Farmer, Guy Otto, II, *lawyer*
Fawbush, Andrew Jackson *lawyer*
Ferguson, Thomas Crooks *lawyer*
Gabel, George DeSaussure, Jr., *lawyer*
Getman, Willard Etheridge *lawyer, arbitrator,
mediator*
Halverson, Steven Thomas *lawyer, construction
executive*
Hill, Debra S. *lawyer*
Houser, John Edward *lawyer*
Kaunitz, Karen Rose Koppel *retired lawyer*
Kelso, Linda Yayoi *lawyer*
Kent, John Bradford *lawyer*
Lee, Lewis Swift *lawyer*
Legler, Mitchell Wooten *lawyer*
Liles, Rutledge Richardson *lawyer*
McBurney, Charles Walker, Jr., *lawyer*
McWilliams, John Lawrence, III, *lawyer*
Milton, Joseph Payne *lawyer*
Moseley, James Francis *lawyer*
Rinaman, James Curtis, Jr., *lawyer*
Schupp, Robert Warren *law educator*
Siegel, Edward *lawyer*
Thomas, Archibald Johns, III, *lawyer*
Thrasher, John *lawyer, former state legislator*
Wallis, Donald Wills *lawyer*
Weaver, Dianne Jay *lawyer*
White, Edward Alfred *lawyer*
Wirtz, Gregg Lee *lawyer*
Zahra, Ellis E. *lawyer*

Jacksonville Beach
Mahorner, James M. *lawyer*

Jasper
McCormick, John Hoyle *lawyer*

Jensen Beach
Stuart, Harold Cutliff *lawyer, business executive*

Jupiter
Brophy, Gilbert Thomas *lawyer*
Click, David Forrest *lawyer, investment advisor*
del Russo, Alessandra Luini *retired law educator*

Key Biscayne
Pearson, John Edward *lawyer*
Stephens, William Theodore *lawyer, business
executive*

Key Largo
Mattson, James Stewart *lawyer, environmental
scientist, educator*

Key West
Eden, Nathan E. *lawyer*
MacDougall, Peter *lawyer*

Lake Placid
Roberts, William B. *lawyer, business executive*

Lake Wales
Adams, Paul Winfrey *lawyer, business executive*
Wales, Gwynne Huntington *retired lawyer*

Lake Worth
Dembicer, Edwin Herbert *retired lawyer*

Lakeland
Cooper, James Russell *retired law educator*
Kittleson, Henry Marshall *lawyer*
Koren, Edward Franz *lawyer*
Wendel, John Fredric *lawyer, professional sports
consultant*

Largo
Fedor, Allan John *lawyer*
Trevena, John Harry *lawyer*

Lauderdale By The Sea
Yonkman, Fredrick Albers *lawyer, management
consultant*

Lecanto
Corsi, Philip Donald *lawyer*
Goss, Richard Henry *lawyer*

Leesburg
Austin, Robert Eugene, Jr., *lawyer*
Fechtel, Vincent John *legal administrator*

Longboat Key
Freeman, Richard Merrell *lawyer, corporate
director*

Longwood
Cordes, Alexander Charles *lawyer*
Dicks, Jack William *lawyer, magazine publisher,
investment advisor*
Hernandez, H(ermes) Manuel *lawyer*
Tomasulo, Virginia Merrills *retired lawyer*

Maitland
Rajtar, Steven Allen *lawyer*
Sharett, Alan Richard *lawyer, environmental and
disability litigator, mediator and arbitrator, law
educator*

Marco Island
Boardman, Harold Frederick, Jr., *lawyer, retired
corporate executive*

Melbourne
Ballantyne, Richard Lee *lawyer*
Brown, Seymour R. *lawyer*
Cacciatore, S. Sammy *lawyer*
Stack, Charles Rickman *lawyer*

Miami
Alvarez, Cesar L. *lawyer*
Amarilios, John Alexander *lawyer, real estate
consultant*
Anderson, Terence James *law educator*
Arbuz, Joseph Robert *lawyer*
Aronovitz, Tod *lawyer*
Astigarraga, Jose I(gnacio) *lawyer*
Baena, Scott Louis *lawyer*
Baker, Thomas Eugene *law educator*
Bartelstone, Ted Henry *lawyer*
Baumberger, Charles Henry *lawyer*
Becerra, Robert John *lawyer*
Beckham, Walter Hull, Jr., *lawyer, educator*
Berger, Steven R. *lawyer, state official*
Berley, David Richard *lawyer*
Berman, Bruce Judson *lawyer*
Black, Roy *lawyer*
Blumberg, Edward Robert *lawyer*
Border, James Robert *lawyer, accountant*
Bronis, Stephen Jay *lawyer*
Burnett, Henry *lawyer*
Campos-Orrego, Nora Patricia *lawyer, consultant*
Cardenas, Alberto R. *lawyer*
Carnesoltas, Ana-Maria *lawyer*
Castillo, Angel, Jr., *lawyer*
Clarke, Mercer Kaye *lawyer*
Coffey, Kendall Brindley *lawyer*
Cohen, Jeffrey Michael *lawyer*
Cohn, Don Stephen *lawyer*
Connor, Terence Gregory *lawyer*
Critchlow, Richard H. *lawyer*
Darmody, Stephen Jerome *lawyer*
DeMaria, Joseph Angelo *lawyer*
Dominik, Jack Edward *lawyer*
DuFresne, Elizabeth Jamison *lawyer*
Eaton, Joel Douglas *lawyer*
Elliot, Cameron Robert *lawyer*
Evans, Thomas William *lawyer*
Ferrell, Milton Morgan, Jr., *lawyer*
Fleit, Martin *lawyer*
Fleming, Joseph Z. *lawyer*
Friedman, Richard Nathan *lawyer*
Garrett, Richard G. *lawyer*
Glickman, Fred Elliott *lawyer*
Gong, Edmond Joseph *lawyer*
Gragg, Karl Lawrence *lawyer*
Greenberg, Stewart Gary *lawyer*
Greenleaf, Walter Franklin *lawyer*
Greer, Alan Graham *lawyer*
Grossman, Robert Louis *lawyer*
Hall, Adam Stuart *lawyer*
Hall, Andrew Clifford *lawyer*
Halsey, Douglas Martin *lawyer*
Hartz, Steven Edward Marshall *lawyer, educator*
Hector, Louis Julius *lawyer*
Herron, James Michael *retired lawyer*
Hoffman, Larry J. *lawyer*
Hogg, Jesse Stephen *lawyer*
Houlihan, Gerald John *lawyer*
Hrinak, Donna Jean *lawyer, former ambassador*
Hudson, Robert Franklin, Jr., *lawyer*
Imperato, Joseph John *lawyer, composer*
Jacobson, Bernard *lawyer*
Jimenez, Marcos Daniel *lawyer*
Johnston, Philip Connelly *lawyer*
Katz, Lawrence Sheldon *lawyer*
Klock, Joseph Peter, Jr., *lawyer*
Korchin, Judith Miriam *lawyer*
Kuker, Alan Michael *lawyer*
Lampen, Richard Jay *lawyer, investment banker,
securities trader*
Landy, Burton Aaron *lawyer*
Levine, Robert Jeffrey *lawyer*
Lipcon, Charles Roy *lawyer*
Lipoff, Norman Harold *lawyer*

Long, Maxine Master *lawyer*
Louis, Paul Adolph *lawyer*
Maher, Stephen Trivett *lawyer, educator*
Matthews, Douglas Eugene *lawyer, educator,
consultant*
Mehta, Eileen Rose *lawyer*
Miller, James M. *lawyer*
Miller Udell, Bronwyn *lawyer*
Milstein, Richard Craig *lawyer*
Morgan, Charles Oxford, Jr., *lawyer*
Morton, Richard *lawyer, financial consultant*
Mudd, John Philip *lawyer*
Munn, Janet Teresa *lawyer*
Murphy, Timothy James *lawyer*
Nachwalter, Michael *lawyer*
Nagin, Stephen Elias *lawyer, educator*
Nuernberg, William R(ichard) *lawyer*
O'Connor, Kathleen Mary *lawyer*
O'Meara, Vicki A. *lawyer*
Payne, R.W., Jr., *lawyer*
Pena, Guillermo Enrique *lawyer*
Perwin, Jean Shapiro *lawyer*
Pratt, John Patrick *lawyer*
Quentel, Albert Drew *lawyer*
Rickard, Lisa Ann *lawyer*
Rogers, Harvey Delano *lawyer*
Ruffner, Charles Louis *lawyer*
Rundle, Katherine Fernandez *state's attorney*
Sacher, Barton Stuart *lawyer*
Scheer, Mark Jeffrey *lawyer*
Schuette, Charles A. *lawyer*
Scott, Thomas Emerson, Jr., *lawyer, former
prosecutor*
Silber, Norman Jules *lawyer*
Skolnick, S. Harold *lawyer*
Stanley, Sherry A. *lawyer*
Stansell, Leland Edwin, Jr., *lawyer, mediator,
educator*
Steinberg, Marty *lawyer*
Stokes, Paul Mason *lawyer*
Thornton, John William, Sr., *lawyer*
Touby, Kathleen Anita *lawyer*
Vento, M. Thérèse *lawyer*
Walters, David McLean *lawyer*
Walton, Rodney Earl *lawyer*
Weiner, Lawrence *lawyer*
Weinger, Steven Murray *lawyer*
Weinstein, Alan Edward *lawyer*
Weinstein, Andrew H. *lawyer*
Welbaum, R(ome) Earl *lawyer*
Wing, James David *lawyer*
Wiseheart, Malcolm Boyd, Jr., *lawyer*
Wright, Blandin James *lawyer*
Zack, Stephen Neil *lawyer*

Miami Beach
Freedman, Monroe Henry *lawyer, educator,
columnist*

Miami Gardens
Ersek, Gregory Joseph Mark *lawyer, business
administrator*
Light, Alfred Robert *lawyer, political scientist,
educator*

Miami Lakes
Cohen, Ronald J. *lawyer*

Naples
Anderson, John Thomas *lawyer*
Blumenthal, Ronnie *lawyer*
Bruce, Jackson Martin, Jr., *lawyer*
Buckley, Frederick Jean *lawyer*
Cardillo, John Pollara *lawyer*
Crehan, Joseph Edward *lawyer*
Doub, William Offutt *lawyer*
Ericson, Roger Delwin *lawyer, forest resource
company executive*
Fultz, Robert Edward *lawyer*
McCaffrey, Judith Elizabeth *lawyer*
McSwiney, Charles Ronald *lawyer*
Norton, Elizabeth Wychgel *lawyer*
Petersen, David L. *lawyer*
Schauer, Wilbert Edward, Jr., *lawyer, manufacturing
executive*
Smith, Numa Lamar, Jr., *lawyer*
Snyder, Marion Gene *lawyer, former congressman*
Spanton, William Floyd *lawyer, consultant*
Strauss, Jerome Manfred *lawyer, banker*
Westman, Carl Edward *lawyer*

New Port Richey
Focht, Theodore Harold *lawyer, educator*

New Smyrna Beach
Dunagan, Walter Benton *lawyer, educator*

North Miami
Dellagloria, John Castle *city attorney, educator*

North Palm Beach
Coyle, Dennis Patrick *lawyer*

Orlando
Abbott, Charles Warren *lawyer*
Ahlers, Glen-Peter, Sr., *law library director,
educator, consultant*
Blackford, Robert Newton *lawyer, director*
Blaher, Neal Jonathan *lawyer*
Capouano, Albert D. *lawyer*
Christiansen, Patrick T. *lawyer*
deBeaubien, Hugo H. *lawyer*
Eagan, William Leon *lawyer*
Frey, Louis, Jr., *lawyer, federal and state
government official*
Handley, Leon Hunter *lawyer*
Henry, William Oscar Eugene *lawyer*
Jontz, Jeffry Robert *lawyer*
Kelaher, James Peirce *lawyer*
Lefkowitz, Ivan Martin *lawyer*
Leonhardt, Frederick Wayne *lawyer*
Losey, Ralph Colby *lawyer*
Lowndes, John Foy *lawyer*
Mock, Frank Mackenzie *lawyer*
Mooney, Thomas Robert *lawyer*
Motes, Carl Dalton *lawyer*
Murrell, Robert George *lawyer*
Nadeau, Robert Bertrand, Jr., *lawyer*
Neal, Thomas Frederick *lawyer*
Neff, A. Guy *lawyer*
Pierce, John Gerald (Jerry Pierce) *lawyer*
Ragland, Robert Allen *lawyer*
Reed, John Alton *lawyer*
Reinhart, Richard Paul *lawyer*

Sheaffer, William Jay *lawyer*
Shives, Paula J *lawyer*
Sims, Roger W. *lawyer*
Skambis, Christopher Charles, Jr., *lawyer*
Snively, Stephen Wayne *lawyer*
Subin, Eli Harold *lawyer*
Weiss, Christopher John *lawyer*
Yates, Leighton Delevan, Jr., *lawyer*

Palatka
Baldwin, Allen Adail *lawyer, writer*

Palm Beach
Adler, Frederick Richard *lawyer, financier*
Canary, Nancy Halliday *lawyer*
Crawford, Sandra Kay *lawyer*
Devins, Robert Sylvester *retired lawyer*
Loring, Arthur *lawyer, diversified financial services company executive*
Parker, Ellis Jackson, III, *lawyer, broadcaster*
Rauch, George Washington *lawyer, director*

Palm Beach Gardens
Auerbach, Paul Ira *lawyer*
Kahn, David Miller *lawyer, educator*

Palm Coast
Duncan, Donald William *lawyer*
Patz, Edward Frank *retired lawyer*

Palm Harbor
Rezanka, Thomas W. *lawyer*
Summers-Powell, Alan *lawyer*

Panama City
Fensom, James B. *lawyer*

Panama City Beach
Patterson, Christopher Nida *lawyer*

Pembroke Pines
Granata, Linda M. *lawyer*

Pensacola
Bozeman, Frank Carmack *lawyer*
Geeker, Nicholas Peter *lawyer, judge*
Levin, Fredric Gerson *lawyer*
McKenzie, James Franklin *lawyer*
Moulton, Wilbur Wright, Jr., *lawyer*
Soloway, Daniel Mark *lawyer*
Windham, John Franklin *lawyer, educator*

Pineland
Donlon, William James *retired lawyer*

Plant City
Buchman, Kenneth William *lawyer*
Sparkman, Steven Leonard *lawyer*

Plantation
Sperry, Martin Jay *lawyer*
Stone, Marc J. *lawyer*

Polk City
Closen, Michael Lee *retired law educator*

Pompano Beach
Ephraim, Charles *lawyer*
Gude, Nancy Carlson *lawyer*
Hasenauer, Judith Anne *lawyer*
Kory, Marianne Greene *lawyer*
Service, John Gregory *law educator*
Shulmister, M(orris) Ross *lawyer*
Szilassy, Sandor *retired lawyer, library director, educator*

Ponte Vedra Beach
Kuhn, Bowie K. *lawyer, former professional baseball commissioner, consultant*
Saltmarsh, Sara Elizabeth *lawyer*

Port Saint Lucie
Lambert, George Robert *lawyer, realtor*

Punta Gorda
Montano, Arthur *lawyer*

Saint Augustine
Ansbacher, Sidney Franklyn *lawyer*
Brady, James Joseph *labor arbitrator*

Saint Petersburg
Armstrong, Kenneth *lawyer*
Bairstow, Frances Kanevsky *arbitrator, mediator, educator*
Battaglia, Anthony Sylvester *lawyer*
Carrere, Charles Scott *law educator, judge*
Escarraz, Enrique, III, *lawyer*
Georges, Richard Martin *lawyer, educator*
Glass, Roy Leonard *lawyer*
Harrell, Roy G., Jr., *lawyer*
Henniger, David Thomas *lawyer*
Hudkins, John W. *lawyer*
Hungate, Mark Edward *lawyer*
Jacob, Bruce Robert *law educator*
Keane, Michael J. *lawyer*
Kiefner, John Robert, Jr., *lawyer, educator*
Lang, Joseph Hagedorn *lawyer*
Mann, Sam Henry, Jr., *lawyer*
McKeown, H. Mary *lawyer, law educator*
Moody, Lizabeth Ann *lawyer, educator*
Ross, Howard Philip *lawyer*
Woodard, Joseph Lamar *law librarian, law educator*

Saint Petersburg Beach
Garnett, Stanley Iredale, II, *lawyer, utility company executive*
Milham, Julee Lynn *lawyer, arbitrator, mediator*

Sanibel
Rothschild, Donald Phillip *retired lawyer, arbitrator*

Sarasota
Christopher, William Garth *lawyer*
Clarke, Garvey Elliott *lawyer*
Ehrlich, Bernard Herbert *lawyer, association executive*
Garland, Richard Roger *lawyer*
Gladding, Nicholas C. *lawyer*
Greenfield, Bruce Harold *lawyer, merchant banker*
Greenfield, Robert Kauffman *retired lawyer*
Hull, J(ames) Richard *retired lawyer, business executive*
Janney, Oliver James *lawyer, plastics and semiconductor company executive*
Kimbrough, Robert Averyt *lawyer*
Partoyan, Garo Arakel *lawyer*
Raimi, Burton Louis *lawyer*
Salomone, William Gerald *lawyer*
Wadsworth, Dyer Seymour *retired lawyer*

Sebring
McCollum, James Fountain *lawyer*
Weimer, Peter Dwight *retired mediator, lawyer, corporate executive*

Shalimar
Chesser, David Michael *lawyer*

South Miami
Keedy, Christian David *lawyer*

Stuart
Gary, Willie E. *lawyer*

Sun City Center
Fuller, Samuel Ashby *retired lawyer, mining company executive*

Tallahassee
Alderman, Silvia Morell *lawyer*
Aurell, John Karl *lawyer*
Barnett, Martha Walters *lawyer*
Boyd, Joseph Arthur, Jr., *lawyer*
Carson, Leonard Allen *lawyer*
Cummings, Frederic Alan *lawyer*
Curtin, Lawrence N. *lawyer*
Dariotis, Terrence Theodore *lawyer*
DeFoor, J. Allison, II, *lawyer*
Ervin, Robert Marvin *lawyer*
Gievers, Karen A. *lawyer*
Griffith, Elwin Jabez *lawyer, university administrator*
Holcomb, Lyle Donald, Jr., *retired lawyer*
Kerns, David Vincent *lawyer*
Kirwin, Thomas F. *prosecutor*
Kitchen, E.C. Deeno *lawyer*
Levine, A. Kenneth *lawyer*
Miller, Gregory R. *lawyer*
Miller, Morris Henry *lawyer*
Minnick, Bruce Alexander *lawyer*
Phipps, Benjamin Kimball, II, *lawyer*
Reid, Sue Titus *law educator*
Rodriguez, Raquel *lawyer*
Saunders, Ron *lawyer, former state legislator*
Schroeder, Edwin Maher *law educator*
Teson, Fernando Roberto *law educator, consultant*
Zaiser, Kent Ames *lawyer*

Tampa
Albritton, Arthur Dallas *lawyer*
Arcuri, Shirley Copeland *lawyer*
Barton, Bernard Alan, Jr., *lawyer*
Blacklidge, Raymond Mark *lawyer*
Blue, James Monroe *lawyer*
Boos, Robert Walter, II, *lawyer*
Brown, Enola T. *lawyer*
Campbell, Richard Bruce *lawyer*
Christian, Terry Clifton *lawyer*
Corcoran, Clement Timothy, III, *lawyer, retired judge*
Cunningham, Anthony Willard *lawyer*
Davis, Richard Earl *lawyer*
Doliner, Nathaniel Lee *lawyer*
Ellwanger, Thomas John *lawyer*
Fraley, F. Ronald *lawyer*
Gifford, Donald Arthur *lawyer*
Gilbert, Leonard Harold *lawyer*
Gonzalez, Joe Manuel *lawyer*
Gordon, Jeffrey (Jack Gordon) *lawyer*
Grammig, Robert James *lawyer*
Hardy, Paul Duane *lawyer*
Humphries, J. Bob *lawyer*
Huneycutt, Alice Ruth *lawyer*
Jamieson, Michael Lawrence *lawyer*
Jones, John Arthur *lawyer*
Kelly, Thomas Paine, Jr., *lawyer*
Knopik, Christopher Scott *lawyer*
MacDonald, Thomas Cook, Jr., *lawyer, mediator*
Martin, Gary Wayne *lawyer*
McAdams, John Pope *lawyer*
McBride, William Howard, Jr., *lawyer*
McDevitt, Sheila Marie *lawyer, energy company executive*
McKay, Richard James *lawyer*
Munoz, Shane Thomas *lawyer*
Murphy, James Burton, Jr., *lawyer*
Murray, John Michael *lawyer*
Oehler, Richard Dale *lawyer*
Olson, John Karl *lawyer*
Pellett, Jon Michael *lawyer*
Perez, Paul Ignatius *lawyer*
Petrila, John Philip *health law educator*
Rardon, Larry L. *lawyer*
Rasmussen, Robert Carl *lawyer*
Roberson, Bruce Heerdt *lawyer*
Robinson, John William, IV, *lawyer*
Rosenkranz, Stanley William *lawyer*
Schwenke, Roger Dean *lawyer*
Smith, William Reece, Jr., *lawyer*
Somers, Clifford Louis *lawyer*
Stallings, Norman (Charles Norman Stallings) *lawyer*
Stalnaker, Lance Kuebler *lawyer*
Stiles, Mary Ann *lawyer, author, lobbyist*
Tanzer, Jed Samuel *lawyer, financial consultant*
Thomas, Gregg Darrow *lawyer*
Thomas, Wayne Lee *lawyer*
Vogt, Martha Diane *lawyer*
Wagner, Frederick William (Bill Wagner) *lawyer*
Waller, Edward Martin, Jr., *lawyer*
Whatley, Jacqueline Beltram *lawyer*
Yerrid, C. Steven *lawyer*
Young, Gwynne A. *lawyer*

Venice
Brott, Irving Deerin, Jr., *lawyer, judge*
Miller, Allan John *lawyer*

Vero Beach
Ahrensfeld, Thomas Frederick *retired lawyer*
Case, Douglas Manning *lawyer*
Gordon, William Stout *lawyer*
Kenrich, John Lewis *retired lawyer*

Wellington
Beck, Jan Scott *lawyer*

West Palm Beach
Beall, Kenneth Sutter, Jr., *lawyer*
Beasley, James W., Jr., *lawyer*
Brams, Jeffrey Brent *lawyer*
Chopin, L. Frank *lawyer*
Chopin, Susan Gardiner *lawyer*
Clark, David William *lawyer, councilman*
Conrad, Bette Anne Kester *lawyer, writer, minister*
Damsel, Charles H., Jr., *lawyer*
Farina, John *lawyer*
Goetz, Cecelia Helen *lawyer, retired judge*
Grogan, Robert Harris *lawyer*
Hill, Thomas William, Jr., *lawyer, educator*
Kamen, Michael Andrew *lawyer*
Laing, Robert Scott *lawyer*
Layman, David Michael *lawyer*
Montgomery, Robert Morel, Jr., *lawyer*
Moore, George Crawford Jackson *lawyer*
Mrachek, Lorin Louis *lawyer*
Orlovsky, Donald Albert *lawyer*
Rosen, Marvin Shelby *lawyer*
Royce, Raymond Watson *lawyer, rancher, citrus grower, invester*
Scarola, John *lawyer*
Smith, David Shiverick *lawyer, former ambassador*
Vilchez, Victoria Anne *lawyer*

Weston
Cornell, G(eorge) Ware, Jr., *lawyer*
Kniskern, Joseph Warren *lawyer*

Winter Park
Builder, J. Lindsay, Jr., *lawyer*
Godbold, Gene Hamilton *lawyer*
Hadley, Ralph Vincent, III, *lawyer*
Heinle, Richard Alan *lawyer*
Helms, Roger D. *lawyer*
Johnson, Kraig Nelson *lawyer, arbitrator, mediator*
Wagner, Lynn Edward *lawyer*

GEORGIA

Alpharetta
Bettis, Barry Phillip *lawyer*

Athens
Beaird, James Ralph *law educator, dean*
Carlson, Ronald Lee *lawyer, educator*
Chaffin, Verner Franklin *lawyer, educator*
Ellington, Charles Ronald *lawyer, educator*
Hellerstein, Walter *lawyer*
Houser, Ronald Edward *lawyer, arbitrator, mediator*
Huszagh, Fredrick Wickett *lawyer, educator, information management company executive*
Kurtz, Paul Michael *law educator*
Larson, Edward John *law educator, lawyer, historian*
Puckett, Elizabeth Ann *law librarian, law educator*
Sachs, Margaret V. *law educator*
Tolley, Edward Donald *lawyer*

Atlanta
Abbott, Herschel Lee, Jr., *lawyer*
Abernathy, Thomas Edwards, IV, *lawyer*
Albert, Ross Alan *lawyer*
Alexander, Kent B. *lawyer*
Alexander, Miles Jordan *lawyer*
Altman, Robert *lawyer*
Anderson, Peter Joseph *lawyer*
Arthur, Thomas Carlton *law educator*
Bankoff, Joseph R. *lawyer*
Barker, Clayton Robert, III, *lawyer*
Barkoff, Rupert Mitchell *lawyer*
Barnett, Preston B. *lawyer, communications executive*
Barr, Robert Laurence, Jr., *lawyer*
Barwick, William D. *lawyer*
Beckham, Walter Hull, III, *lawyer*
Bernstein, Deena Robin *lawyer*
Billington, Barry E. *lawyer*
Bird, Wendell Raleigh *lawyer*
Blackburn, William Stanley *lawyer*
Blackstock, Jerry B. *lawyer*
Blank, A(ndrew) Russell *lawyer*
Bloodworth, Albert William Franklin *lawyer*
Bondurant, Emmet Jopling, II, *lawyer*
Booth, Gordon Dean, Jr., *lawyer*
Bowling, Daniel S., III, *lawyer*
Bradley, Phillip Alden *lawyer*
Branch, Thomas Broughton, III, *lawyer*
Bratton, James Henry, Jr., *lawyer*
Byrne, Granville Bland, III, *lawyer*
Cadenhead, Alfred Paul *lawyer*
Capron, John M. *lawyer*
Carson, Christopher Leonard *lawyer*
Cavin, Kristine Smith *lawyer*
Chilivis, Nickolas Peter *lawyer*
Chisholm, Tommy *lawyer, utilities executive*
Clarke, Thomas Hal *lawyer*
Cobb, Charles Kenche, Jr., *lawyer, real estate broker*
Cohen, Ezra Harry *lawyer*
Cohen, George Leon *lawyer*
Cohen, N. Jerold *lawyer*
Collins, Donnell Jawan *lawyer*
Collins, Steven M. *lawyer*
Crews, William Edwin *lawyer*
Croft, Terrence Lee *lawyer*
Curtis, Philip Kerry *lawyer*
Cutshaw, Kenneth Andrew *lawyer*
Davis, E(dward) Marcus *lawyer*
Davis, Frank Tradewell, Jr., *lawyer*
Denny, Richard Alden, Jr., *retired lawyer*
Despriet, John G. *lawyer*
Doyle, Michael A. *lawyer*
Draper, Stephen Elliot *lawyer, engineer*
Driver, Walter W., Jr., *lawyer*
Durrett, James Frazer, Jr., *retired lawyer*
Eckl, William Wray *lawyer*
Edwards, Stephen Allen *lawyer*
Egan, Michael Joseph *retired lawyer, state legislator*
Eidson, James Anthony *lawyer*
Eisner, Rebecca Suzanne *lawyer*
Epstein, David Gustav *lawyer*
Etheridge, Jack Paul *arbitrator, mediator, former judge*
Farnham, Clayton Henson *lawyer*
Felton, Jule Wimberly, Jr., *lawyer*
Fernandez, Frank L. *lawyer, retail executive*
Fleming, Julian Denver, Jr., *lawyer*
Forbes, Theodore McCoy, Jr., *arbitrator, mediator, retired lawyer*
Foreman, Edward Rawson *retired lawyer*
Fortin, Raymond D. *lawyer*
Franklin, Charles Scothern *lawyer*
Gambrell, David Henry *lawyer*
Genberg, Ira *lawyer*
Girth, Marjorie Louisa *lawyer, educator*
Glaser, Arthur Henry *lawyer, mediator*
Goldstein, Elliott *lawyer, director*
González, Carlos A. *lawyer*
Gonzalez-Pita, J. Alberto *lawyer*
Grant, Walter Matthews *lawyer, corporate executive*
Greenblatt, Edward Lande *lawyer*
Greer, Bernard Lewis, Jr., *lawyer*
Groton, James Purnell *lawyer, arbitrator*
Harkey, Robert Shelton *retired lawyer*
Harness, William Walter *lawyer*
Hasson, James Keith, Jr., *lawyer, law educator*
Hawks, Barrett Kingsbury *lawyer*
Hay, Peter Heinrich *law educator*
Hayworth, Andrea Elizabeth *lawyer*
Heady, Eugene Joseph *lawyer*
Hendrick, David Richard *lawyer*
Hendricks, Nathan VanMeter, III, *lawyer*
Henson, Howard Kirk *lawyer*
Herrin, Barry Scott *lawyer, writer*
Hinchey, John William *lawyer*
Hoff, Gerhardt Michael *lawyer, insurance company executive*
Hoffman, Michael William *lawyer, accountant*
Hopkins, John David *lawyer*
Howard, Harry Clay *lawyer*
Howell, Arthur *lawyer*
Hunter, Forrest Walker *lawyer*
Ide, Roy William, III, *lawyer*
Isaf, Fred Thomas *lawyer*
Izard, John *lawyer*
Janney, Donald Wayne *lawyer*
Jenkins, Albert Felton, Jr., *lawyer*
Jones, Frank Cater *retired lawyer*
Jones, Glower Whitehead *lawyer*
Katz, Joel Abraham *lawyer, music consultant*
Kelley, James Francis *lawyer*
Kessler, Richard Paul, Jr., *lawyer*
Khoury, Kenneth F. *lawyer*
Kilgore, Cada T., III, *lawyer*
Killingsworth, Vernon Scott *technology lawyer*
Killorin, Robert Ware *lawyer*
Kinzer, William Luther *lawyer*
Kitchens, William H. *lawyer*
Klamon, Lawrence Paine *lawyer*
Knowles, Marjorie Fine *lawyer, educator, dean*
Lamon, Harry Vincent, Jr., *lawyer, director*
Landau, Michael B. *law educator, musician, writer*
Landon, James Henry *lawyer*
Lanier, George H. *lawyer*
Leonard, David Morse *lawyer*
Lester, Charles Turner, Jr., *lawyer*
Linkous, William Joseph, Jr., *lawyer*
Lipshutz, Robert Jerome *lawyer, former government official*
Lower, Robert Cassel *lawyer, educator*
Manning, Clarence Bond *lawyer*
Marshall, John Treutlen *lawyer, educator*
Marvin, Charles Arthur *law educator*
McAlpin, Kirk Martin *lawyer*
McMahon, Teri Lynn *lawyer*
McNeill, Thomas Ray *lawyer*
Meltz, David Barry *law educator*
Miller, Douglas L. *lawyer*
Mobley, John Homer, II, *lawyer*
Moeling, Walter Goos, IV, *lawyer*
Morgan, Charles Russell *lawyer*
Mull, Gale W. *lawyer*
Muller, William Manning *corporate lawyer*
Myers, Johnnie Dumas *law educator*
Oakley, Mary Ann Bryant *lawyer*
O'Callaghan, William Lawrence, Jr., *lawyer*
Ordover, Abraham Philip *lawyer, mediator*
Ortiz, Jay Richard Gentry *lawyer*
Owen, Robert Hubert *lawyer, former real estate broker*
Parker, Wilmer, III, *lawyer, educator*
Patterson, William Robert *retired lawyer*
Phillips, Barry *lawyer*
Piassick, Joel Bernard *lawyer*
Pike, Larry Samuel *lawyer*
Pilcher, James Brownie *lawyer*
Pless, Laurance Davidson *lawyer*
Podgor, Ellen Sue *law educator*
Price, Elizabeth Anne *lawyer*
Raby, Kenneth Alan *lawyer, retired army officer*
Reed, Glen Alfred *lawyer*
Remar, Robert Boyle *lawyer*
Rhodes, Thomas Willard *lawyer*
Rogers, C. B. *lawyer*
Savell, Edward Lupo *lawyer*
Schock, Robert Christopher *lawyer*
Schroder, Jack Spalding, Jr., *lawyer*
Schulte, Jeffrey Lewis *lawyer*
Shapiro, George Howard *retired lawyer*
Sibley, James Malcolm *retired lawyer*
Silverstein, Leonard A. *lawyer*
Smith, Alexander Wyly, Jr., *lawyer*
Smith, Jeffrey Carlin *lawyer*
Smith, Jeffrey Michael *lawyer*
Smith, Lawrence A. *lawyer*
Smith, Sidney Oslin, Jr., *lawyer*
Smith, Walton Napier *lawyer*
Stallings, Ronald Denis *lawyer*
Stamps, Thomas Paty *lawyer, consultant*
Stephenson, Mason Williams *lawyer*
Stokes, James Sewell *lawyer*
Sullivan, Terrance Charles *lawyer*
Swift, Frank Meador *lawyer*
Tanenbaum, Allan Jay *lawyer*
Tanner, W(alter) Rhett *lawyer*
Taylor, George Kimbrough, Jr., *lawyer*
Taylor, Roger Dale *lawyer*
Taylor, Virginia S. *lawyer*
Thrower, Randolph William *lawyer*
Varner, Chilton Davis *lawyer*
Vaughn, Michael S. *law educator*
Volentine, Richard J., Jr., *lawyer*
Wakefield, Stephen Alan *lawyer*
Walsh, W. Terence *lawyer*
Washington, Tanya Monique *law educator*
Webb, J. David *lawyer*
Wellon, Robert G. *lawyer*
Williams, Neil, Jr., *lawyer*
Wilson, James Hargrove, Jr., *lawyer*
Womack, Mary Pauline *lawyer*

Wood, L. Lin, Jr., *lawyer*
Worley, David *lawyer*
Wright, Frederick Lewis, II, *lawyer*
Wright, Peter Meldrim *lawyer*
Zell, Glenn *lawyer*
Zink, Charles Talbott *lawyer*

Augusta
Booth, Edmund A., Jr., *prosecutor*
Lee, Lansing Burrows, Jr., *lawyer, corporate executive*
Miller, Alfred Montague *lawyer*

Canton
Hasty, William Grady, Jr., *lawyer*

Carrollton
Tisinger, David Harvey *lawyer*

College Park
Stokes, Arch *lawyer, writer*

Columbus
Brinkley, Jack Thomas *lawyer, former congressman*
Johnson, Walter Frank, Jr., *lawyer*
McGlamry, Max Reginald *lawyer*
Page, William Marion *lawyer*
Patrick, James Duvall, Jr., *lawyer*
Poydasheff, Robert Stephen *lawyer*
Wooten, Joel Orba, Jr., *lawyer*

Decatur
Murphy, Deborah Jane *lawyer*

Douglas
Hayes, Dewey *lawyer*
Hayes, Dewey Norman, Jr., *lawyer*

Dublin
Greene, Jule Blounte *lawyer*

Duluth
Sloan, Donnie Robert, Jr., *lawyer*
Tewes, R. Scott *lawyer*

Dunwoody
Callison, James W. *retired lawyer, consultant, airline executive*

East Point
Rattray, James Bailey *lawyer*

Ellabell
Lee, Frederick Drexel *lawyer*

Gainesville
Hester, Francis Bartow, III, (Frank Hester) *lawyer*
Schuder, Raymond Francis *lawyer*

Hamilton
Byrd, Gary Ellis *lawyer*

Jasper
Marger, Edwin *lawyer*

Lawrenceville
Henson, Gene Ethridge *retired legal administrator, interior designer*

Leesburg
Myers, David Wayne *legal assistant*

Macon
Brown, Stephen Phillip *judge*
Ennis, Edgar William, Jr., *lawyer*
Robinson, W. Lee *lawyer*
Snow, Cubbedge, Jr., *lawyer*
Wiggins, James L. *lawyer*
Wood, Frank Maxwell *lawyer*
Woody, Thomas Clifton, II, *assistant district attorney*

Madison
DuBose, Charles Wilson *lawyer*

Marietta
Bentley, Fred Douglas, Sr., *lawyer*
Clay, Charles Commander (Chuck Clay) *lawyer, former state senator*
Dalziel, Charles Meredith, Jr., *lawyer*
Nowland, James Ferrell *lawyer*

Metter
Doremus, Ogden *lawyer*

Moultrie
Collum, Rick Daniel *lawyer*

Newnan
Franklin, Bruce Walter *lawyer*

Norcross
Anderson, Albert Sydney, III, *lawyer*
Caldwell, Claud Reid *lawyer*
Hahn, Stanley Robert, Jr., *lawyer, financial executive*

Perry
Geiger, James Norman *lawyer*

Roswell
Baker, Anita Diane *lawyer*
England, John Melvin *lawyer, clergyman*
Roland, Raymond William *lawyer, mediator*

Saint Marys
Smith, Charles Courtland, Jr., *lawyer, state legislator*

Savannah
Bowman, Catherine McKenzie *lawyer*
Dickey, David Herschel *lawyer, accountant*
Dixon, Harry D., Jr., (Donnie Dixon) *former prosecutor*
Forbes, Morton Gerald *lawyer*
Friedman, Julian Richard *lawyer*
Kitchings, Alton Dwith *lawyer*
McCracken, Eugene Luke *lawyer*
Rawson, William Robert *lawyer, retired manufacturing company executive*
Searcy, William Nelson *lawyer, director*

Thompson, Richard S. *lawyer*

Sea Island
Revoile, Charles Patrick *lawyer*

Sky Valley
Wilkinson, Albert Mims, Jr., *lawyer*

Smyrna
Seigler, Michael Edward *lawyer, librarian*

Statesboro
Classens, Michael John *lawyer*
Franklin, James Burke *lawyer*
Stone, Ralph Kenny *lawyer*

Stone Mountain
Le, Chi-Dinh *law educator, writer*

Summerville
Connelly, Lewis Branch Sutton *lawyer*

Swainsboro
Cadle, Jerry Neal *lawyer*

Tifton
Reinhardt, George Robert *lawyer*

Tucker
Sturges, Lynn H. *lawyer, sociologist*

Valdosta
Copeland, Roy Wilson *lawyer*
Dodd, Roger J. *lawyer*
Edwards, Edith Martha *lawyer*
Sinnott, John Patrick *lawyer, educator*

Watkinsville
Wright, Robert Joseph *lawyer*

Winder
McLemore, Michael Kerr *lawyer, minister*

HAWAII

Hilo
Chong, Clayton Elliott *lawyer*

Honolulu
Adams, Jo-Ann Marie *lawyer, actress*
Akiba, Lorraine Hiroko *lawyer*
Archer, Richard Joseph *lawyer*
Asai-Sato, Carol Yuki *lawyer*
Bloede, Victor Carl *lawyer, academic executive*
Boas, Frank *retired lawyer*
Callies, David Lee *lawyer, educator*
Cassiday, Benjamin Buckles, III, *lawyer*
Char, Vernon Fook Leong *lawyer*
Ching, Wesley H. H. *lawyer*
Chuck, Walter G(oonsun) *lawyer, director*
Chun-Hoon, Lowell Koon Ying *lawyer*
Cowan, Stuart Marshall *lawyer*
Crosier, Douglas A. *lawyer*
Deaver, Phillip Lester *lawyer*
Devens, Paul *lawyer*
Dodd, William Horace *lawyer*
Edmunds, John Sanford *lawyer*
Faust, Anne Sonia *lawyer*
Fukumoto, Leslie Satsuki *lawyer*
Gay, E(mil) Laurence *lawyer*
Gelber, Don Jeffrey *lawyer*
Gerson, Mervyn Stuart *lawyer*
Gierlach, David J. *lawyer*
Godbey, Robert Carson *lawyer*
Hazlett, Mark A. *lawyer*
Heller, Ronald Ian *lawyer*
Hipp, Kenneth Byron *lawyer*
Iwai, Wilfred Kiyoshi *lawyer*
Katayama, Robert Nobuichi *lawyer*
Kawachika, James Akio *lawyer*
Kemper, Edward Crawford *lawyer*
Keppeler, Herbert Karl Bruss *lawyer*
Lacy, John R. *lawyer*
Lee, Dale W. *lawyer*
Lilly, Michael Alexander *lawyer, writer*
Louie, David Mark *lawyer*
Marrack, Alexander Case *lawyer*
Mau-Shimizu, Patricia Ann *lawyer*
McShane, Rosemary *lawyer*
Miller, Richard Sherwin *law educator*
Miyasaki, Shuichi *lawyer*
Moore, Ernest Carroll, III, *lawyer*
Moroney, Michael John *lawyer*
Nakata, Gary Kenji *lawyer*
Okinaga, Lawrence Shoji *lawyer*
Plum, William J. *lawyer*
Portnoy, Jeffrey Steven *lawyer*
Quinn, William Francis *lawyer, director*
Reber, David James *lawyer*
Sato, Glenn Kenji *lawyer*
Schnack, Harold Clifford *retired lawyer*
Schweigert, Jack *lawyer*
Shigetomi, Keith Shigeo *lawyer*
Taira, Darryl M. *lawyer*
Turbin, Richard *lawyer*
Weight, Michael Anthony *lawyer, former judge*
Woo, Vernon Ying-Tsai *lawyer, real estate developer, judge*

Kailua Kona
Zola, Michael S. *lawyer*

Kapolei
Zabanal, Eduardo Olegario *lawyer*

Kihei
Burns, Richard Gordon *retired lawyer, writer, consultant*

Kula
Maloney, Michael Patrick *lawyer, mediator, arbitrator*
Richardson, Robert Allen *retired lawyer, educator*
Rohlfing, Frederick William *lawyer, political consultant, retired judge*

Paia
Baybayan, Ronald Alan *lawyer*

IDAHO

Boise
Clark, Merlyn Wesley *lawyer*
Doolittle, Michael Jim *lawyer*
Dryden, William George *lawyer*
Erickson, Robert Stanley *lawyer*
Geston, Mark Symington *lawyer*
Hanks, Stephen Grant *lawyer, construction executive*
Holleran, John W. *lawyer*
Leroy, David Henry *lawyer, state and federal official*
Longeteig, Iver J. *lawyer*
McGown, John, Jr., *lawyer*
Meyer, Christopher Hawkins *lawyer*
Minnich, Diane Kay *legal association administrator*
Moss, Thomas E. *prosecutor*
Myers, William Gerry Gerry, III, *lawyer*
Park, William Anthony (Tony Park) *lawyer*
Schild, Raymond Douglas *lawyer*
Shurtliff, Marvin Karl *lawyer*
Silak, Cathy R. *lawyer, former state supreme court justice*
Sims, John R. *lawyer*
Thomas, Eugene C. *lawyer*
Uranga, Jean R. *lawyer*
VanHole, William Remi *lawyer*
Wetherell, Michael E. *lawyer*

Caldwell
Kerrick, David Ellsworth *lawyer*

Eagle
Richardson, Betty H. *lawyer, former prosecutor*

Hailey
Hogue, Terry Glynn *lawyer*
Youngblood, Deborah Sue *lawyer, speech pathology/audiology services professional*

Idaho Falls
Hart, Stephen Strong *lawyer*
Ohman, John Michael *lawyer*

Kamiah
Mills, Lawrence *lawyer, business and transportation consultant*

Ketchum
Holland, Robert James *retired lawyer*

Lewiston
Aherin, Darrel William *lawyer*
Tait, John Reid *lawyer*

Moscow
Greene, Timothy Geddes *lawyer*

Pocatello
Nye, W. Marcus W. *lawyer*

Twin Falls
Berry, L. Clyel *lawyer*
Sudweeks, Jay Dean *lawyer*

ILLINOIS

Alton
Struif, L. James *lawyer*
Talbert, Hugh Mathis *lawyer*

Arlington Heights
Biestek, John Paul *lawyer*
Giampietro, Wayne Bruce *lawyer*
Kroll, Steven L. *lawyer*
Tucker, Bowen Hayward *lawyer*

Aurora
Lowe, Ralph Edward *lawyer*

Barrington
Lee, William Marshall *lawyer*
Wyatt, James Frank, Jr., *lawyer*

Bedford Park
Cascino, Anthony Elmo, Jr., *lawyer, insurance executive*

Belleville
Bauman, John Duane *lawyer*
Gossage, Roza *lawyer, educator*
Heiligenstein, Christian Enric *lawyer*
Hess, Frederick J. *lawyer*
Ripplinger, George Raymond, Jr., *lawyer*

Bloomington
Bragg, Michael Ellis *lawyer, insurance company executive*
Deneen, Daniel Guy *lawyer*
Eckols, Thomas Aud *lawyer, educator*
McHugh, Donald P. *lawyer*
Sullivan, Laura Patricia *lawyer, insurance company executive*

Bourbonnais
McClure, Thomas Edward *lawyer*

Bridgeview
Marcello, Frank F. *lawyer, educator, writer*

Buffalo Grove
Robins, Martin B. *lawyer*
Ward, Michael W. *lawyer*

Burr Ridge
Brennan, James Joseph *lawyer, banking and financial services executive*

Calumet City
Scullion, Annette Murphy *lawyer, educator*

Carbondale
Clemons, John Robert *lawyer*
Lee, Mark Richard *lawyer, educator*
Schroeder, William Arthur *law educator*

Carrollton
Strickland, Hugh Alfred *lawyer*

Champaign
Boyle, Francis Anthony *law educator*
Cribbet, John Edward *law educator, former university chancellor*
Gunsalus, Carolyn Kristina *law educator, consultant*
Hurd, Heidi M. *law educator, humanities educator, dean*
Kindt, John Warren *lawyer, educator, consultant*
Krause, Harry Dieter *law educator*
Maggs, Peter Blount *lawyer, educator*
Mamer, Stuart Mies *lawyer*
Mc Cord, John Harrison *lawyer, educator*
Miller, Harold Arthur *lawyer*
Nowak, John E. *law educator*
Painter, Richard William *law educator*

Charleston
Gano, Kenneth Redman, Jr., *lawyer*

Chicago
Abell, David Robert *lawyer*
Abrams, Lee Norman *lawyer*
Acker, Frederick George *lawyer*
Adducci, James Dominick *lawyer*
Adelman, Stanley Joseph *lawyer*
Adelman, Steven Herbert *lawyer*
Alberts, Barry S. *lawyer*
Allen, Henry Sermones, Jr., *lawyer*
Allen, Julie O'Donnell *lawyer*
Allen, Ronald Jay *law educator*
Allen, Thomas Draper *lawyer*
Alschuler, Albert W. *law educator*
Amend, James Michael *lawyer*
Anderson, J. Trent *lawyer*
Anderson, Kimball Richard *lawyer*
Angst, Gerald L. *lawyer*
Anthony, Michael Francis *lawyer*
Antonio, Douglas John *lawyer*
Anvaripour, M. A. *lawyer*
Appel, Nina Schick *law educator, dean, academic administrator*
Armstrong, Edwin Richard *lawyer, publisher, editor*
Aronson, Virginia L. L. *lawyer*
Athas, Gus James *lawyer*
Auerbach, Marshall Jay *lawyer*
Avery, Robert Dean *lawyer*
Badel, Julie *lawyer*
Baer, John Richard Frederick *lawyer*
Bailey, Robert Short *lawyer*
Bain, Douglas G. *lawyer, air transportation executive*
Baird, Douglas Gordon *law educator, dean*
Baker, Bruce Jay *lawyer*
Baker, James Edward Sproul *retired lawyer*
Baker, Pamela *lawyer*
Baldwin, Shaun McParland *lawyer*
Banoff, Sheldon Irwin *lawyer*
Bardgett, John E. *lawyer*
Barker, William Thomas *lawyer*
Barnett, William A. *lawyer*
Barr, John Robert *retired lawyer*
Barron, Harold Sheldon *lawyer*
Barron, Howard Robert *lawyer*
Bart, Susan T. *lawyer*
Bartlit, Fred Holcomb, Jr., *lawyer, educator*
Baruch, Hurd *lawyer*
Bashwiner, Steven Lacelle *lawyer*
Baugher, Peter V. *lawyer*
Becker, Theodore Michaelson *lawyer*
Beem, Jack Darrel *lawyer*
Bellows, Laurel Gordon *lawyer*
Benak, James Donald *lawyer*
Bennett, Robert William *law educator*
Berens, Mark Harry *lawyer*
Berenzweig, Jack Charles *lawyer*
Berger, Robert Michael *lawyer*
Berkoff, Mark Andrew *lawyer*
Bernardini, Charles *lawyer, former alderman*
Berner, Robert Lee, Jr., *lawyer*
Bernick, David M. *lawyer*
Berning, Larry D. *lawyer*
Bernstein, Charles Bernard *lawyer*
Berolzheimer, Karl *lawyer*
Bertagnolli, Leslie A. *lawyer*
Biebel, Paul Philip, Jr., *lawyer*
Bierig, Jack R. *lawyer, educator*
Bitner, John Howard *lawyer*
Bixby, Frank Lyman *lawyer*
Blatt, Richard Lee *lawyer*
Block, Neal Jay *lawyer*
Blount, Michael Eugene *lawyer*
Blume, Paul Chiappe *lawyer*
Boehnen, Daniel A. *lawyer*
Boggs, Catherine J. *lawyer*
Boies, Wilber H. *lawyer*
Bomchill, Fern Cheryl *lawyer*
Boocock, Stephen William *lawyer*
Bowe, William J(ohn) *lawyer*
Bowen, Stephen Stewart *lawyer*
Bramnik, Robert Paul *lawyer*
Brice, Roger Thomas *lawyer*
Bridgman, Thomas Francis *retired lawyer*
Brizzolara, Charles Anthony *lawyer, director*
Bro, Ruth Hill *lawyer*
Brogan, Lisa S. *lawyer*
Brown, Alan Crawford *lawyer*
Brown, Donald James, Jr., *lawyer*
Brown, Gregory K. *lawyer*
Bulger, Brian Wegg *lawyer*
Bunge, Jonathan Gunn *lawyer*
Burgdoerfer, Jerry *lawyer*
Burke, John Michael *lawyer*
Burke, Michelle C. *lawyer*
Burke, Thomas Joseph, Jr., *lawyer*
Burke, William Joseph *lawyer*
Burns, Terrence Michael *lawyer*
Busey, Roxane C. *lawyer*
Butler, John William *lawyer*
Carlin, Dennis J. *lawyer*
Carlson, Walter Carl *lawyer*
Carr, Walter Stanley *lawyer*
Carren, Jeffrey P. *lawyer*
Carroll, William Kenneth *law educator, psychologist, theologian*
Cassel, Douglass Watts, Jr., *lawyer, educator, journalist*
Chandler, Kent, Jr., *lawyer*
Cheely, Daniel Joseph *lawyer*
Chefitz, Joel Gerald *lawyer*
Chemers, Robert Marc *lawyer*
Cherney, James Alan *lawyer*
Cherry, Daniel Ronald *lawyer*
Chester, Mark Vincent *lawyer*
Chestnut, John William *lawyer*
Chiles, Stephen Michael *lawyer*

Sullivan, Marcia Waite *lawyer*
Sullivan, Thomas Patrick *lawyer*
Sumners, Pamela Lauren *lawyer*
Sundvall, Sheila A. *lawyer*
Sunstein, Cass Robert *law educator*
Suskin, Howard Steven *lawyer*
Sussman, Arthur Melvin *law educator, foundation administrator*
Sweeney, James Raymond *lawyer*
Sweet, Allan Jay *lawyer*
Swibel, Steven Warren *lawyer*
Swiger, Elinor Porter *lawyer*
Sykes, Alan O'Neil *lawyer, educator*
Tabin, Julius *patent lawyer, physicist*
Taren, Jeffrey Lynn *lawyer*
Tarun, Robert Walter *lawyer*
Tetzlaff, Theodore R. *lawyer*
Theis, William Harold *lawyer, educator*
Theobald, Edward Robert *lawyer*
Thomas, Frederick Bradley *lawyer*
Thomas, Stephen Paul *lawyer*
Thompson, James Robert, Jr., *lawyer, former governor*
Thompson, Michael *lawyer*
Thomson, George Ronald *lawyer, educator*
Tinaglia, Michael Lee *lawyer*
Tobin, Craig Daniel *lawyer*
Tobin, Thomas F. *lawyer*
Toohey, James Kevin *lawyer*
Trapp, James McCreery *lawyer*
Trienens, Howard Joseph *lawyer*
Trost, Eileen Bannon *lawyer*
Truskowski, John Budd *lawyer*
Tryban, Esther Elizabeth *lawyer*
Turow, Scott F. *lawyer, writer*
Ungaretti, Richard Anthony *lawyer*
Van Demark, Ruth Elaine *lawyer*
Van Tine, Matthew Eric *lawyer*
Veverka, Donald John *lawyer*
Vojcanin, Sava Alexander *lawyer*
Vranicar, Michael Gregory *lawyer*
Vree, Roger Allen *lawyer*
Wade, Edwin Lee *author, lawyer*
Wahlen, Edwin Alfred *lawyer*
Waintroob, Andrea Ruth *lawyer*
Wander, Herbert Stanton *lawyer*
Wanke, Ronald Lee *lawyer*
Weaver, Timothy Allan *lawyer*
Webb, Dan K. *lawyer*
Weber, Susan A. *lawyer*
Webster, David Macpherson *lawyer*
Weigle, Maurice S. *lawyer*
Weil, Andrew Lawrence *lawyer*
Weinkopf, Friedrich J. *lawyer*
Weissman, Michael Lewis *lawyer*
Weldon-Linne, Madeleine Marie *lawyer*
Welsh, Kelly Raymond *lawyer, former telecommunications company executive*
Wesley, William Matthew *lawyer*
Wexler, Richard Lewis *lawyer*
Whalen, Wayne W. *lawyer*
White, Linda Diane *lawyer*
Wiggins, Charles Henry, Jr., *lawyer*
Wilcox, Mark Dean *lawyer*
Wildman, Max Edward *lawyer, director*
Willian, Clyde Franklin *lawyer*
Wilson, Roger Goodwin *lawyer*
Wise, William Jerrard *lawyer*
Witcoff, Sheldon William *lawyer*
Wood, Allison Lorraine *lawyer*
Wright, Judith Margaret *law librarian, educator, dean*
Zabel, Sheldon Alter *lawyer, law educator*
Zemm, Sandra Phyllis *lawyer*
Zenner, Sheldon Toby *lawyer*
Zhao, Jia *lawyer*
Zimmerman, Kent M. *lawyer*
Zolno, Mark S. *lawyer*
Zoub, Burton Irving *lawyer*

Chicago Heights
Cifelli, John Louis *lawyer*

Cicero
Paprocki, Thomas John *lawyer, priest*

Crete
Teykl, James Stephen *lawyer*

Crystal Lake
Shank, William O. *lawyer*

Decatur
Byers, Franklin Hays, II, *lawyer*
Dunn, John Francis *lawyer, state representative*
Reising, Richard P. *lawyer*
Smith, David James *corporate lawyer*
Vigneri, Joseph William *lawyer*

Deerfield
Birmingham, William Joseph *retired lawyer*
Dawson, Suzanne Stockus *lawyer*
Oettinger, Julian Alan *lawyer, pharmaceutical executive*
Scott, Theodore R. *lawyer*
Vollen, Robert Jay *lawyer*

Dekalb
Tucker, Watson Billopp *lawyer*

Des Plaines
Brodl, Raymond Frank *lawyer, former lumber company executive*
Meyer, Susan M. *lawyer*

Downers Grove
Myers, Daniel N. *lawyer, association executive*

East Alton
Clark, Mark Jeffrey *paralegal, researcher*

Edwardsville
Rikli, Donald Carl *lawyer*

Elgin
Akemann, David R. *lawyer*
Carbary, Jonathan Leigh *lawyer*
Golden, Loren S. *lawyer*

Evanston
Creamer, Robert Allan *lawyer*
Morrison, John Horton *lawyer*
Rosic, George Steve *lawyer*
Salem, Richard Allen *mediator*
Schulte, Bruce John *lawyer*
Witwer, Samuel Weiler, Jr., *lawyer*

Franklin Park
Blanchard, Eric Alan *lawyer*

Galesburg
Mustain, Douglas Dee *lawyer*

Geneseo
Brown, Mabel Welton *lawyer*

Geneva
Landmeier, Allen Lee *lawyer*
Tyler, Lloyd John *retired lawyer*

Genoa
Cromley, Jon Lowell *lawyer*

Gillespie
Verticchio, Rick *lawyer*

Glen Ellyn
Conti, Lee Ann *lawyer*
Hudson, Dennis Lee *lawyer, retired government official, arbitrator, educator*
Sandrok, Richard William *lawyer*
Ulrich, Werner *patent lawyer*

Glenview
Berkman, Michael G. *lawyer, chemical consultant*
Knox, James Edwin *lawyer*
Marmet, Gottlieb John *lawyer*
Miller, Edward Boone *lawyer*

Hanover
Bleveans, John *lawyer*

Highland Park
Gash, Lauren Beth *lawyer, state legislator*
Karol, Nathaniel H. *lawyer, consultant*
Lippe, Melvin Karl *lawyer*
Nelson, Richard David *lawyer*
Ruder, David Sturtevant *lawyer, educator, government official*
Schindel, Donald Marvin *retired lawyer*

Hinsdale
Farrug, Eugene Joseph, Sr., *retired lawyer*
Hetke, Richard Louis *lawyer*

Hoffman Estates
Zopp, Andrea Lynne *lawyer, retail executive*

Joliet
Lenard, George Dean *lawyer*

Kenilworth
Feng, Paul Yen-Hsiung *lawyer, chemist*
McKittrick, William Wood *lawyer*
Milnikel, Robert Saxon *lawyer*
Weaver, Clifford Lee *retired lawyer, winery owner*

La Grange
Kerr, Alexander Duncan, Jr., *lawyer*

La Salle
McClintock, Thomas Lee *lawyer*

Lafox
Seils, William George *lawyer*

Lake Bluff
Burns, Kenneth Jones, Jr., *lawyer, consultant*
Kennedy, John Foran *retired lawyer*

Lake Forest
Covington, George Morse *lawyer*
Edwards, Christine Annette *retired lawyer, securities firm executive*
Emerson, William Harry *lawyer, retired, oil company executive*
Francois, William Armand *lawyer*
Niemann, William Lovekamp *lawyer*
Palmer, Ann Therese Darin *lawyer*
Sikorovsky, Eugene Frank *retired lawyer*

Lake Zurich
Scott, John Joseph *lawyer*

Lansing
Hill, Philip *retired lawyer*

Lemont
Young, Robert Bruce *lawyer*

Lewistown
Davis, William C., Jr., *lawyer*

Lincolnshire
Bartlett, Robert William *lawyer*
Para, Gerard Albert *lawyer, real estate broker, consultant*

Lincolnwood
Ghezzi, Sheryl Rae *lawyer, real estate broker*
Salit, Gary *lawyer*
Zaremski, Miles Jay *lawyer*

Lisle
Butt, Edward Thomas, Jr., *lawyer*

Long Grove
Davis, Britton Anthony *retired lawyer*
Fisher, Joy Deborah *lawyer*
Obert, Paul Richard *lawyer, manufacturing executive*

Macomb
Bracey, Willie Earl *lawyer, university program director*

Marengo
Franks, Herbert Hoover *lawyer*

Mattoon
Corn, Stephen Leslie *lawyer*
Horsley, Jack Everett *lawyer, writer*

Mc Gaw Park
Feather, William L. *corporate lawyer*

Mokena
Sangmeister, George Edward *lawyer, consultant, former congressman*

Moline
Cottrell, Frank Stewart *former lawyer, manufacturing executive*
Jenkins, James Robert *lawyer, chemicals executive*
Schwiebert, Mark William *lawyer, mayor*

Mount Carmel
Rhine, John E. *lawyer*

Mount Vernon
Harvey, Morris Lane *lawyer*

Naperville
Fawell, Harris W. *lawyer, former congressman*
Fenech, Joseph Charles *lawyer*
Larson, Mark Edward, Jr., *lawyer, educator, financial advisor*
Nortell, Bruce *lawyer*
Strobel, Russ M. *lawyer*
Tibble, Douglas Clair *lawyer*

Niles
Sassan, Dennis Donald *lawyer*

Normal
Bender, Paul Edward *lawyer*
Kethineni, Sesha Rajani *criminal justice professor*
Rochelle, Victor Cleanthus *lawyer*

North Aurora
Cole, Sarah *law enforcement librarian*

North Chicago
de Lasa, José M. *lawyer*

Northbrook
Bohlender, Hugh Darrow *lawyer*
Lapin, Harvey I. *lawyer*
Rosemarin, Carey Stephen *lawyer*
Sernett, Richard Patrick *lawyer*
Stewart, Charles Leslie *lawyer*
Teichner, Bruce A. *lawyer*
Wallace, Harry Leland *lawyer*

Oak Brook
Barnes, Karen Kay *lawyer*
Bennett, Margaret Airola *lawyer*
Congalton, Susan Tichenor *lawyer*
Hollins, Mitchell Leslie *lawyer*
Santona, Gloria *lawyer*

Oak Park
Schubert, Blake H. *lawyer*
Sengpiehl, Paul Marvin *lawyer, former state official*

Oakbrook Terrace
Weiland, Mark Bradley *corporate lawyer*

Olympia Fields
Nuding, Doris Leona *law librarian, legal assistant, researcher*

Oswego
May, Frank Brendan, Jr., *lawyer*

Palatine
Pinderski, Jerome Wilbert, Jr., *lawyer*
Victor, Michael Gary *lawyer, physician*
Wardell, John Watson *lawyer*
Zamarin, Ronald George *lawyer*

Palos Hills
McInerney, Noreen Linda *lawyer*

Park Forest
Goodrich, John Bernard *lawyer, consultant*

Park Ridge
Hegarty, Mary Frances *lawyer*
LaRue, Paul Hubert *retired lawyer*
Schmidt, Wayne Walter *law association executive*
Wasko, Steven E. *lawyer*

Peoria
Allen, Lyle Wallace *lawyer*
Buda, James B. *lawyer, manufacturing executive*
Coletta, Ralph John *retired lawyer*
Parsons, Richard Hugo *lawyer*
Tomlin, James Milton *lawyer*

Prospect Heights
Leopold, Mark F. *lawyer*

River Forest
Li, Tze-chung *lawyer, educator*

Riverwoods
Ford, Michael W. *lawyer*
Yarrington, Hugh *corporate lawyer, communications company executive*

Rock Island
Ciaccio, Karin McLaughlin *lawyer*
Wallace, Franklin Sherwood *lawyer, director*

Rockford
Johnson, Thomas Stuart *lawyer*
Reno, Roger *lawyer*

Rosemont
Nichols, Robert Hastings *lawyer*

Schaumburg
Lawson, A. Peter *lawyer*

Schiller Park
Congalton, Christopher William *lawyer*

South Holland
Wolf, Wayne Lowell *criminal justice educator, researcher*

Springfield
Abbott, Randall (Lee Abbott) *lawyer*
Burns, James B. *prosecutor*
Cullen, Mark Kenneth *lawyer*
Dodge, James William *lawyer, educator*
Duggan, Timothy E. *lawyer*
Kerr, Gary Enrico *lawyer, educator*
Malany, Le Grand Lynn *lawyer, engineer, bank executive*
Mathewson, Mark Stuart *lawyer, editor*
Miller, Jan Paul *lawyer*
Morse, Saul Julian *lawyer*
O'Brien, Dennis Sean *lawyer*
Van Meter, Abram DeBois *lawyer, retired banker*
Walbaum, Robert C. *lawyer*

Taylorville
Austin, Daniel William *lawyer*

Toledo
Prather, William C., III, *lawyer, writer*

Urbana
Balbach, Stanley Byron *lawyer*
Fitz-Gerald, Roger Miller *lawyer*
Thies, Richard Leon *lawyer, director*
Webber, Carl Maddra *lawyer*

Vernon Hills
Richards, Alan Edward *lawyer*

Warrenville
Boardman, Robert A. *lawyer*
Johnson, Douglas Wells *lawyer*

Watseka
Tungate, James Lester *lawyer*

Wauconda
Malik, Thomas Warren *lawyer*

Waukegan
Hall, Albert L. *retired lawyer*
Henrick, Michael Francis *lawyer*
Leibowitz, David Perry *lawyer*

Western Springs
Hanson, Heidi Elizabeth *lawyer*
Rhoads, Paul Kelly *lawyer*
Shannon, Peter Michael, Jr., *lawyer*

Wheaton
Cunningham, William Francis *lawyer*
DaRosa, Ronald Anthony *lawyer*
Didzerekis, Paul Patrick *lawyer*
Stein, Lawrence A. *lawyer*

Willowbrook
Walton, Stanley Anthony, III, *lawyer*

Wilmette
Atkinson, Jeff John Frederick *law educator, lawyer, writer*
Browder, William Bayard *corporation executive, lawyer*
Frick, Robert Hathaway *retired lawyer*
Geller, William Alan *criminal justice researcher, police and public safety consultant*
Lieberman, Eugene *lawyer*

Winnetka
Crowe, Robert William *lawyer, mediator*
Fawcett, Dwight Winter *retired lawyer*
Greenblatt, Ray Harris *lawyer*
Hales, Daniel B. *lawyer*
Krucks, William Norman *lawyer*
McWhirter, Bruce J. *retired lawyer*

Woodstock
Ackley, Robert O. *lawyer*

INDIANA

Beech Grove
Brown, Richard Lawrence *lawyer*

Bloomington
Aman, Alfred Charles, Jr., *law educator*
Mallor, Andrew C. *lawyer*
Robel, Lauren *law educator*
Ryan, Marianne Elizabeth *lawyer*
Shreve, Gene Russell *law educator*

Carmel
Capehart, Craig Earl *lawyer*

Columbus
Crump, Francis Jefferson, III, *lawyer*
Harrison, Patrick Woods *lawyer*

Crown Point
Back, Michael Wayne *lawyer*

Danville
Baldwin, Jeffrey Kenton *lawyer, educator*
Baldwin, Patricia Ann *lawyer*

Dyer
Van Bokkelen, Joseph Scott *prosecutor*

Elkhart
Treckelo, Richard M. *lawyer*

Evansville
Bodkin, Robert Thomas *lawyer*
Clouse, John Daniel *lawyer*
Harrison, Joseph Heavrin *lawyer*
Miller, Daniel Raymond *prosecutor*
Reed, Helen Skuggedal *law librarian, musician*

Fort Wayne
Cain, Tim J. *lawyer*
Colvin, Sherrill William *lawyer*
Lebamoff, Ivan Argire *lawyer*
Pope, Mark Andrew *lawyer, university administrator*
Roby, Daniel Arthur *lawyer*
Shoaff, Thomas Mitchell *lawyer*
Smith, Maxwell Paul *retired lawyer*
Tourkow, Joshua Isaac *lawyer*

Cooper, Richard Earl *lawyer*
Cowan, Frederic Joseph *lawyer*
Crutcher, Michael Bayard *lawyer*
Davidson, Gordon Byron *lawyer*
Dudley, George Ellsworth *lawyer*
Duffy, Martin Patrick *lawyer*
Eschels, Philip C. *lawyer*
Ethridge, Larry Clayton *lawyer*
Faller, Rhoda *lawyer*
Fassler, Charles *lawyer*
Ferguson, Jo McCown *lawyer*
Fuchs, Olivia Anne Morris *lawyer*
Gilman, Sheldon Glenn *lawyer*
Gorman, Chris *lawyer*
Guethlein, William O. *lawyer*
Juber, David L. *prosecutor*
Klotter, John Charles *retired legal educator*
Lanier, Philip M. *lawyer*
Lavelle, Charles Joseph *lawyer*
Lay, Norvie Lee *law educator*
Lyndrup, Peggy B. *lawyer*
Maggiolo, Allison Joseph *lawyer*
Mellen, Francis Joseph, Jr., *lawyer*
Northern, Richard *lawyer*
Osborn, John Simcoe, Jr., *lawyer*
Palmer, Larry Isaac *lawyer, educator*
Partin, C. Fred *lawyer*
Pedley, Lawrence Lindsay *lawyer*
Pelfrey, D. Patton *lawyer*
Reed, D. Gary *lawyer*
Reed, John Squires, II, *lawyer*
Renau, Donald Irwin *lawyer*
Rose, Charles Alexander *lawyer*
Rothstein, Mark Alan *health law and bioethics educator*
Runyon, Keith Leslie *lawyer, newspaper editor*
Silverthorn, Robert Sterner, Jr., *lawyer*
Skees, William Leonard, Jr., *lawyer*
Spalding, Catherine *lawyer*
Talbott, Ben Johnson, Jr., *lawyer*
Troutman, J. Gregory *lawyer*
Vish, Donald H. *lawyer, pension fund administrator*
Welsh, Sir Alfred John *lawyer, international advisor*
Willenbrink, Rose Ann *lawyer*

Munfordville
Craddock, John Durrett, III, *lawyer*
Lang, George Edward *lawyer*

Newport
Siverd, Robert Joseph *lawyer*

Owensboro
Stevenson, John W. *lawyer*

Scottsville
Secrest, James Seaton, Sr., *lawyer*

Shelbyville
Igleheart, Ted Lewis *lawyer*

Somerset
Prather, John Gideon *lawyer*

LOUISIANA

Alexandria
Gist, Howard Battle, Jr., *lawyer*

Baton Rouge
Anderson, Lawrence Robert, Jr., *lawyer*
Bayard, Alton Ernest, III, *lawyer*
Blackman, John Calhoun, IV, *lawyer*
Dugas, David Roy *lawyer*
Hymel, L(ezin) J(oseph) *lawyer, former prosecutor*
Johnson, Joseph Clayton, Jr., *lawyer*
Leonard, Paul Haralson *retired lawyer*
Pugh, George Willard *law educator*
Richards, Marta Alison *lawyer*
Riddick, Winston Wade, Sr., *lawyer*
Rubin, Michael Harry *lawyer, educator*
Seaver, Jeffrey Mark, Sr., *lawyer*
Taylor, John McKowen *lawyer*
Unglesby, Lewis O. *lawyer*
Wittenbrink, Jeffrey Scott *lawyer*

Cheneyville
Ewin, Gordon Overton *retired lawyer, farmer*

Covington
Looney, James Holland *lawyer*
Rice, Winston Edward *lawyer*

Destrehan
Griffith, Steven Franklin, Sr., *lawyer, real estate title insurance agent and investor*

Franklin
McClelland, James Ray *lawyer*

Jefferson
Conino, Joseph Aloysius *lawyer*

Kaplan
LeMoine, Frank Eugene *lawyer, judge*

Kenner
Valvo, Barbara-Ann *lawyer, surgeon*

La Place
Cicet, Donald James *lawyer*

Lafayette
Angers, Winston Thomas *lawyer*
Davidson, James Joseph, III, *lawyer*
Goforth, William H. *lawyer*
Judice, Marc Wayne *lawyer*
Pate, James Lavert *lawyer*
Saloom, Kaliste Joseph, Jr., *lawyer, retired judge*
Theall, Susan Lorna *lawyer*

Lake Charles
McLeod, William Lasater, Jr., *lawyer, former judge and state legislator*
Sanchez, Walter Marshall *lawyer*
Veron, J. Michael *lawyer, writer*

Leesville
Smith, Simeon Christie, III, *lawyer, judge*

Mandeville
Christian, John Catlett, Jr., *lawyer*
Cressy, David Sarrat *lawyer*

Marksville
Riddle, Charles Addison, III, *district attorney, former state legislator*

Metairie
Album, Jerald Lewis *lawyer*
Dean, Bruce Campbell *lawyer*
Hardy, Ashton Richard *lawyer*
McMahon, Robert Albert, Jr., *lawyer*

Monroe
Sartor, Daniel Ryan, Jr., *lawyer*

New Orleans
Abaunza, Donald Richard *lawyer*
Abbott, Hirschel Theron, Jr., *lawyer*
Acomb, Robert Bailey, Jr., *lawyer, educator*
Allen, Frank Clinton, Jr., *lawyer, chemical engineer*
Alsobrook, Henry Bernis, Jr., *lawyer*
Ates, J. Robert *lawyer*
Babst, James A. *lawyer*
Barham, Mack Elwin *lawyer, educator*
Barry, Francis Julian, Jr., *lawyer*
Beahm, Franklin D. *lawyer*
Beck, William Harold, Jr., *lawyer*
Benjamin, Edward Bernard, Jr., *lawyer*
Bieck, Robert Barton, Jr., *lawyer*
Bronfin, Fred *lawyer*
Cheatwood, Roy Clifton *lawyer*
Ciolino, Dane Stephen *law educator*
Claverie, Philip deVilliers *lawyer*
Coleman, James Julian *lawyer*
Coleman, James Julian, Jr., *lawyer, industrialist, real estate executive*
Combe, John Clifford, Jr., *lawyer*
Correro, Anthony James, III, *lawyer*
Crusto, Mitchell Ferdinand *lawyer, educator, consultant*
Denegre, George *lawyer*
Dittman, Stevan Craig *lawyer*
Eckstein, Michael Lehman *lawyer*
Falgoust, Dean Thomas *lawyer, accountant*
Fendler, Sherman Gene *lawyer*
Force, Robert *law educator*
Forman, William Harper, Jr., *lawyer*
Friedman, Joel William *law educator*
Gay, Esmond Phelps *lawyer*
Gertler, Meyer H. *lawyer*
Getten, Thomas Frank *lawyer*
Goins, Richard Anthony *lawyer, educator*
Guidry, Susan Gail *lawyer*
Healy, George William, III, *lawyer, mediator*
Hearn, Sharon Sklamba *lawyer*
Henderson, Helena Naughton *legal association administrator*
Hoffman, Donald Alfred *lawyer*
Jones, Philip Kirkpatrick, Jr., *lawyer*
Jordan, Eddie J. *lawyer, former prosecutor*
Judell, Harold Benn *lawyer*
Katz, Morton Howard *lawyer*
Kemp, James Bradley, Jr., *lawyer*
Kern, Clifford Harold, Jr., *retired lawyer*
King, Rebecca J. *lawyer, consultant*
Lee, Wayne J. *lawyer*
Lemann, Thomas Berthelot *lawyer*
Letten, James *prosecutor*
Lovett, William Anthony *law and economics educator*
Lowe, Robert Charles *lawyer*
Maloney, Marilyn C. *lawyer*
Marcus, Bernard *lawyer, consultant*
Martinez, Judy Perry *lawyer*
McGlone, Michael Anthony *lawyer*
McMillan, Lee Richards, II, *lawyer*
Miller, Gary H. *lawyer*
Mintz, Albert *lawyer*
Molony, Michael Janssens, Jr., *lawyer, arbitrator, mediator*
Neff, Carole Cukell *lawyer*
Nehrbass, Seth Martin *patent lawyer*
Osakwe, Christopher *lawyer, educator*
Ostendorf, Lance Stephen *lawyer, educator, financial consultant*
Palmer, Vernon Valentine *law educator*
Pearce, John Y. *lawyer*
Pugh, William Whitmell Hill, III, *lawyer*
Redmann, John William *lawyer, consultant*
Rodriguez, Antonio Jose *lawyer*
Rosen, Charles, II, *lawyer*
Rosen, William Warren *lawyer*
Sessions, Cicero Columbus *retired lawyer*
Simon, H(uey) Paul *lawyer*
Sinor, Howard Earl, Jr., *lawyer*
Snyder, Charles Aubrey *lawyer*
Stapp, Dan Ernest *retired lawyer, utilities executive*
Sutterfield, James Ray *lawyer*
Thomas, Joseph Winand *lawyer*
Title, Peter Stephen *lawyer*
Vance, Robert Patrick *lawyer*
Vaudry, J. William, Jr., *lawyer*
Wax, George Louis *lawyer*
Wegmann, Cynthia Anne *lawyer*
Weinmann, John Giffen *lawyer, diplomat*
Weiss, Kenneth Andrew *lawyer, law educator*
Willems, Constance Charles *lawyer*
Wolfe, Richard Peel *lawyer*
Wright, William Everard, Jr., *lawyer*

Shreveport
Achee, Roland Joseph *lawyer*
Bryant, J(ames) Bruce *lawyer*
Carmody, Arthur Roderick, Jr., *lawyer, director*
Chastain, Merritt Banning, Jr., *lawyer*
Cox, John Thomas, Jr., *lawyer*
Feldman, Larry, Jr., *lawyer*
Goodman, Robert Uhle *lawyer*
Halliburton, John Robert *lawyer*
Hardtner, Quintin Theodore, III, *lawyer*
Hetherwick, Gilbert Lewis *lawyer*
Nelson, Ralph Stanley *lawyer*
Perlman, Jerald Lee *lawyer*
Smith, Brian David *lawyer, educator*
Washington, Donald W. *prosecutor*
Woodman, Walter James *lawyer*

Slidell
SSingletary, Alvin D. *lawyer*

MAINE

Augusta
Wilkinson, Lester F., Jr., *lawyer*

Brunswick
Owen, H. Martyn *retired lawyer*

Camden
Sanford, John Joseph *lawyer, director*

Castine
Wiswall, Frank Lawrence, Jr., *lawyer, educator*

Georgetown
Chapin, Richard *arbitrator, consultant*

Orrs Island
Nelson, Robert Louis *lawyer*

Portland
Berry, Henry Newhall, III, *lawyer*
Burns, George F. *lawyer*
Courtney, Ann M. *lawyer*
Graffam, Ward Irving *lawyer*
Harvey, Charles Albert, Jr., *lawyer*
Hunt, David Evans *lawyer*
Ingalls, Everett Palmer, III, *lawyer*
Lancaster, Ralph Ivan, Jr., *lawyer*
Rundlett, Ellsworth Turner, III, *lawyer*
Silsby, Paula *prosecutor*
Smith, William Charles *lawyer*
Stauffer, Eric P. *lawyer*
Thompson, Peter L. *lawyer*
White, Jeffrey Munroe *lawyer*
Zarr, Melvyn *lawyer, law educator*

Raymond
Coughlan, Patrick Campbell *lawyer, mediator*

Saco
Prescott, Dana E. *lawyer*

Skowhegan
Youney, John William *lawyer*

Tenants Harbor
Bates, John Cecil, Jr., *lawyer*

Waterville
Sandy, Robert Edward, Jr., *lawyer*

Wells
Carleton, Joseph George, Jr., *lawyer, state legislator*

Yarmouth
Webster, Peter Bridgman *lawyer*

York
Berlew, Frank Kingston *lawyer*

MARYLAND

Abingdon
Wolf, Martin Eugene *lawyer, educator*

Annapolis
Ferris, William Michael *lawyer*
Klein, Robert Dale *lawyer*
Levitan, Laurence *lawyer, former state senator*
Lillard, John Franklin, III, *lawyer*
Lucas, Steven Mitchell *lawyer*
Michaelson, Benjamin, Jr., *lawyer, director*
Perkins, Roger Allan *lawyer*

Arnold
Green, John Cawley *lawyer*

Ashton
Whelan, Roger Michael *lawyer, educator*

Baltimore
Applefeld, Laurie S. *lawyer*
Archibald, James Kenway *lawyer*
Arnick, John Stephen *lawyer, legislator*
Ayres, Jeffrey Peabody *lawyer*
Bair, Robert Rippel *lawyer*
Baker, William Parr *lawyer*
Bartlett, James Wilson, III, *lawyer*
Berlage, Jan Ingham *lawyer*
Blakeslee, Wesley Daniel *lawyer, consultant*
Blanton, Edward Lee, Jr., *lawyer*
Bogen, David Skillen *law educator*
Bowen, Lowell Reed *lawyer*
Burch, Francis Boucher, Jr., *lawyer*
Carbine, James Edmond *lawyer*
Carey, Anthony Morris *lawyer*
Carlin, Paul Victor *legal association executive*
Chaplin, Peggy Louie *lawyer*
Chernow, Jeffrey Scott *lawyer, educator, writer*
Chiu, Hungdah *lawyer, legal educator*
Civiletti, Benjamin R. *lawyer, former United States attorney general*
Cole, Emried Dargan, Jr., *lawyer*
Cook, Bryson Leitch *lawyer*
Coppel, Lawrence David *lawyer*
Crowe, Thomas Leonard *lawyer*
Curran, Robert Bruce *lawyer*
De Shields-Minnis, Tarra Ramit *lawyer*
Devan, Deborah Hunt *lawyer*
DeVries, Donald Lawson, Jr., *lawyer*
DiBiagio, Thomas M. *prosecutor*
Doory, Ann Marie *lawyer, legislator*
Ellin, Marvin *lawyer*
Erwin, H. Robert *lawyer*
Evans, Nolly Seymour *lawyer*
Eveleth, Janet Stidman *law association administrator*
Fax, Charles Samuel *lawyer*
Feder, David L. *lawyer*
Fenton, Charles E. *lawyer*
Ferro, Elizabeth Krams *lawyer*
Fisher, Morton Poe, Jr., *lawyer*
Gately, Mark Donohue *lawyer*
Goldman, Brian Arthur *lawyer, accountant*
Gray, Frank Truan *lawyer*
Gray, Oscar Shalom *lawyer*
Grieb, Elizabeth *lawyer*
Hafets, Richard Jay *lawyer*
Haines, Thomas W. W. *lawyer*
Hansen, Christopher Agnew *lawyer*
Herschman, Jeffrey D. *lawyer*
Hirsh, Theodore William *lawyer*
Hochberg, Bayard Zabdial *lawyer*
Honemann, Daniel Henry *lawyer*
Hopps, Raymond, Jr., *lawyer, film producer*
Howard, John Vincent, Jr., *lawyer*
Howell, Harley Thomas *lawyer*
Johnson, Harry Sterling *lawyer*
Johnston, Edward Allan *lawyer*
Johnston, George W. *lawyer*
Jones, John Martin, Jr., *lawyer*
Kandel, Nelson Robert *lawyer*
Katz, Laurence M. *legal educator*
Kramer, Paul R. *lawyer*
Levin, Edward Jesse *lawyer*
Levine, Richard E. *lawyer*
Liebmann, George W(illiam) *lawyer*
Lundy, Audie Lee, Jr., *lawyer*
McClung, A(lexander) Keith, Jr., *retired lawyer*
McPherson, Donald Paxton, III, *lawyer*
McWilliams, John Michael *lawyer*
Melvin, Norman Cecil *lawyer*
Messina, Bonnie Lynn *lawyer*
Milio, Louis Romolo *retired law educator, social worker*
Miller, Decatur Howard *lawyer*
Mogol, Alan Jay *lawyer*
Moser, M(artin) Peter *lawyer*
Orman, Leonard Arnold *lawyer*
Pappas, George Frank *lawyer*
Peacock, James Daniel *lawyer*
Plant, Albin MacDonough *lawyer*
Plummer, Risque Wilson *retired lawyer*
Pokempner, Joseph Kres *lawyer*
Pollak, Joanne E. *lawyer*
Pollak, Mark *lawyer*
Radding, Andrew *lawyer*
Reno, Russell Ronald, Jr., *lawyer*
Reynolds, William Leroy *lawyer, educator*
Robinson, Zelig *lawyer*
Rosenthal, William J. *lawyer*
Sack, Sylvan Hanan *lawyer*
Schochor, Jonathan *lawyer, educator*
Scriggins, Larry Palmer *lawyer, director*
Sfekas, Stephen James *lawyer, educator*
Shapiro, Harry Dean *lawyer*
Short, Alexander Campbell *lawyer*
Speed, Leslie Bokee *lawyer*
Stalfort, John Arthur *lawyer*
Stewart, C(ornelius) Van Leuven *lawyer*
Stiller, Shale David *lawyer, educator*
Summers, Thomas Carey *lawyer*
Sykes, Melvin Julius *lawyer*
Walker, Irving Edward *lawyer*
Walter, Harold M. *lawyer*
Wasserman, Richard Leo *lawyer*
White, Pamela Janice *lawyer*
Whitman, Marland Hamilton, Jr., *lawyer*
Wilson, Thomas Matthew, III, *lawyer*
Winn, James Julius, Jr., *lawyer*
Zinkham, W. Robert *lawyer*

Bethesda
Baird, Bruce Allen *lawyer*
Bason, George F., Jr., *lawyer*
Bauersfeld, Carl Frederick *lawyer*
Beatty, Richard Scrivener *retired lawyer*
Calvert, Gordon Lee *retired legal association executive*
Daniels, Michael Paul *lawyer*
Deckelbaum, Nelson *lawyer*
Eisen, Eric Anshel *lawyer*
English, William deShay *lawyer, director*
Eule, Norman Louis *lawyer*
Feuerstein, Donald Martin *lawyer*
Frosh, Brian Esten *lawyer, state senator*
Goodwin, Robert Cronin *lawyer*
Gottlieb, Jonathan W. *lawyer*
Hannan, Myles *lawyer, banker*
Hewes, Laurence Ilsley, III, *lawyer, management, development, legal consultant*
Huebner, Emily Zug *judicial administrator*
Menaker, Frank H., Jr., *lawyer*
Nelson, William Eugene *lawyer*
Pipkin, James Harold, Jr., *lawyer*
Rosenberg, Mark Louis *lawyer*
Rosengren, Paul Gregory *lawyer*
Ross, William Warfield *lawyer*
Ryan, Joseph *lawyer*
Saloschin, Robert L. *lawyer*
Schifter, Richard *lawyer*
Schimel, Richard E. *lawyer*
Schoem, Alan Howard *lawyer*
Silver, David *lawyer*
Weinberger, Alan David *lawyer*

Cabin John
Capo, Rafael V. *lawyer*

Cambridge
Jenkins, Robert Rowe *lawyer*

Catonsville
Hubbard, Herbert Hendrix *lawyer*
Zumbrun, Alvin John Thomas *law and criminology educator*

Chevy Chase
Bruder, George Frederick *lawyer*
Gildenhorn, Joseph Bernard *lawyer, businessman, former diplomat*
Ketcham, Orman Weston *lawyer, former judge*
Klain, Ronald Alan *lawyer*
Mackall, Laidler Bowie *lawyer*
Meyerson, Christopher Cortlandt *lawyer*
Pierson, W. DeVier *lawyer*
Sagawa, Shirley Sachi *lawyer*
Toy, Charles David *lawyer*

College Park
Feinstein, Frederick Lee *lawyer*
Yoho, Billy Lee *lawyer*

Columbia
Jacobs, William Michael *lawyer*
Maseritz, Guy B. *lawyer*
Siegel, David Burton *lawyer*
Ulman, Louis Jay *lawyer*

Comus
Choukas-Bradley, James Richard *lawyer*

Crownsville
Irish, Leon Eugene *lawyer, educator, non-profit organization executive*

Derwood
Mylonakis, Stamatios Gregory *patent agent, polymer science consultant*
Wong, Richard Lee *lawyer*

Easton
Ikenberry, Henry Cephas, Jr., *lawyer*
Maffitt, James Strawbridge *lawyer*

Elkton
Scott, Doris Petersen *lawyer*

Ellicott City
Pairo, Preston Abercrombie, Jr., *lawyer*

Fort Washington
Alexander, Gary R. *lawyer, state legislator, lobbyist*

Frederick
Borison, Scott Craig *lawyer*
Duncan, Stephen Mack *lawyer*
Hogan, Ilona Modly *lawyer*

Fruitland
Woods, William Ellis *lawyer, pharmacist, association executive*

Gaithersburg
McCann, Joseph Leo *lawyer, former government official*
McDowell, Donna Schultz *lawyer, educator*
Sherer, Samuel Ayers *lawyer, urban planning consultant*

Galena
Jolly, Charles Nelson *lawyer, pharmaceutical company executive*

Glen Burnie
Smith, John Stanley *lawyer, arbitrator, mediator*

Glyndon
Renbaum, Barry Jeffrey *lawyer*

Greenbelt
Billingsley, Lance W. *lawyer*
Brugger, George Albert *lawyer*
Greenwald, Andrew Eric *lawyer*
Jackley, Michael Dano *lawyer*
Jascourt, Hugh D. *lawyer, arbitrator, mediator*

Hagerstown
Berkson, Jacob Benjamin *lawyer, writer*

Hyattsville
Rummel, Edgar Ferrand *retired lawyer*

Kensington
Dauster, William Gary *lawyer, economist*
Mathias, Joseph Marshall *lawyer, judge*

Linthicum
Burns, Michael William *lawyer former state legislator*

Lutherville
Freeland, Charles *lawyer, accountant*

North Potomac
Lehman, Leonard *retired lawyer, consultant*

Parkville
Hill, Milton King, Jr., *retired lawyer*

Patuxent River
Fitzhugh, David Michael *lawyer*

Potomac
Chandler, James Phillip *law educator*
Feldman, Myer *lawyer*
Hall, William Darlington *lawyer*
Meyer, Lawrence George *lawyer*
Peter, Phillips Smith *lawyer*
Redding, Robert Ellsworth *lawyer*
Troffkin, Howard Julian *lawyer, diversified company executive*

Prince Frederick
Reynolds, Christopher John *lawyer*

Rock Hall
Cowperthwait, Lindley Murray *lawyer*

Rockville
Barkley, Brian Evan *lawyer, political consultant*
Berryman, Richard Byron *lawyer*
Boetticher, Helene *lawyer*
Bolle, Robert L. *lawyer, administrator*
Cheston, Sheila Carol *lawyer*
Cyr, Karen D. *lawyer*
Daisley, William Prescott *lawyer*
De Jong, David Samuel *lawyer, educator*
Donnally, Robert Andrew *lawyer*
Friedman, Greg Stuart *lawyer, investment advisor*
Frye, Roland Mushat, Jr., *lawyer*
Gordon, Joan Irma *lawyer*
Gordon, Michael Robert *lawyer, state legislator*
Grozbean, Stuart Harvey *lawyer*
Kadish, Richard L. *lawyer*
Karp, Ronald Alvin *lawyer*
Katz, Steven Martin *lawyer, accountant*
Kerxton, Alan Smith *lawyer*
Pensinger, John Lynn *lawyer*
Rachanow, Gerald Marvin *lawyer, pharmacist*
Thompson, James Lee *lawyer*
Van Grack, Steven *lawyer*
Viertel, George Joseph *lawyer, arbitrator, mediator, consulting engineer*
Zaphiriou, George Aristotle *lawyer, educator*

Saint Michaels
Brown, Omer Forrest, II, *lawyer*

Salisbury
Clarke, Wm. A. Lee, III, *lawyer*

Silver Spring
Bernard, Hugh Y(ancey), Jr., *law educator, librarian*
Craig, Paul Max, Jr., *retired lawyer*
Davis, Richmond T.P. *lawyer*
Kramer, Gerson Balfour *lawyer*
Sterling, Eric Edward *lawyer, legal policy advocate*

Towson
Carney, Bradford George Yost *lawyer, educator*
Lutz, Randall Matthew *lawyer*
McIntire, T. Bryan *lawyer, councilman*
Proctor, Kenneth Donald *lawyer*
Putzel, Constance Kellner *lawyer*

Upper Marlboro
Morrison, Anne Deinlein *law librarian*
Platt, Steven Irving *lawyer, judge*

Westminster
Dulany, William Bevard *lawyer*
Staples, Lyle Newton *lawyer*

Wheaton
Kirchman, Eric Hans *lawyer*

White Plains
Robinson, Scharn *lawyer, author, researcher*

MASSACHUSETTS

Amherst
Howland, Richard Moulton *retired lawyer*

Arlington
Keshian, Richard *lawyer*

Ashfield
Pepyne, Edward Walter *lawyer, psychologist, former educator*

Auburndale
Bernard, Michael Mark *lawyer, city planning consultant*

Barnstable
Perry, Blair Lane *lawyer*

Bedford
Driscoll, Kimberlee Marie *lawyer*
Wieand, Jeffrey Scott *lawyer*

Belmont
Greer, Gordon Bruce *retired lawyer, writer*
Simpson, Russell Avington *retired law firm administrator*

Boston
Abbott, William Saunders *lawyer*
Abraham, Nicholas Albert *lawyer, real estate developer*
Abrams, Roger Ian *law educator, arbitrator*
Adler, Sidney W. *lawyer*
Aresty, Jeffrey M. *lawyer*
Auerbach, Joseph *former lawyer, law educator*
Bae, Frank S. H. *law educator, law library administrator*
Bangs, Will Johnston *lawyer*
Berman, Mark Niles *lawyer*
Bernhard, Alexander Alfred *lawyer*
Berry, Janis Marie *lawyer*
Bines, Harvey Ernest *lawyer, educator, writer*
Bloch, Donald Martin *lawyer*
Bodoff, Joseph Samuel Uberman *lawyer*
Bohnen, Michael J. *lawyer*
Bok, John Fairfield *retired lawyer*
Bonifaz, John Cristopher *lawyer*
Bornheimer, Allen Millard *lawyer*
Brody, Richard Eric *lawyer*
Brountas, Paul Peter *lawyer*
Brown, Michael Robert *lawyer*
Buchanan, Robert McLeod *lawyer*
Burleigh, Lewis Albert *lawyer*
Burns, Thomas David *lawyer*
Burr, Francis Hardon *lawyer*
Carpenter, Robert Brent *lawyer*
Carr, Stephen W. *lawyer*
Carter, T(homas) Barton *law educator*
Cogan, John Francis, Jr., *lawyer*
Cohn, Andrew Howard *lawyer*
Conley, Daniel F. *prosecutor*
Craver, James Bernard *lawyer*
Cronin, Philip Mark *lawyer*
Curley, Robert Ambrose, Jr., *lawyer*
Daley, Paul Patrick *lawyer*
Dando, A. Jeffrey *lawyer, consultant*
Daynard, Richard Alan *law educator*
Delaney, John White *lawyer*
de Rham, Casimir, Jr., *lawyer*
Deutsch, Stephen B. *lawyer*
DiCara, Lawrence S. *lawyer*
Dillon, James Joseph *lawyer*
Dineen, John K. *lawyer*
Donahue, Charlotte Mary *lawyer*
Duffy, James Francis, III, *lawyer*
Ehrlich, M. Gordon *lawyer*
Elfman, Eric Michael *lawyer*
Ellis, Douglass N., Jr., *lawyer*
Ellis, Fredric Lee *lawyer*
Engel, David Lewis *lawyer*
Epstein, Elaine May *lawyer*
Eurich, Richard Rex *lawyer*
Feisel, Lyle Dean *lawyer*
Felter, John Kenneth *lawyer*
Finn, Terrence M. *lawyer*
Fischer, Eric Robert *lawyer, educator*
Floor, Richard Earl *lawyer*
Fortier, Albert Mark, Jr., *lawyer*
Fox, Francis Haney *lawyer*
Fraser, Robert Burchmore *lawyer*
Friedman, David Samuel *lawyer*
Galvin, Robert J. *lawyer*
Garcia, Adolfo Ramon *lawyer*
Gargiulo, Andrea W. *lawyer*
Gaudreau, Russell A., Jr., *lawyer, educator*
Gelb, Richard Mark *lawyer*
Giso, Frank, III, *lawyer*
Glosband, Daniel Martin *lawyer*
Gonson, S. Donald *lawyer*
Goodman, Louis Allan *lawyer*
Gossels, Claus Peter Rolf *lawyer*
Greco, Michael S. *lawyer*
Haddad, Ernest Mudarri *lawyer*
Haley, Paul Richard *lawyer, state legislator*
Hall, David *law educator, dean, department chairman*
Hall, Henry Lyon, Jr., *lawyer*
Halström, Frederic Norman *lawyer*
Harrington, John Michael, Jr., *lawyer*
Hawkey, G. Michael *lawyer, real estate investor and developer*
Hayes, Robert Francis *lawyer*
Hieken, Charles *lawyer*
Hinchey, Edward Thomas *lawyer*
Hrones, Stephen Baylis *lawyer, educator*
Huang, Thomas Weishing *lawyer*
Hunter, Floyd Dore *lawyer*
Jones, Sheldon Atwell *lawyer*
Jordan, Alexander Joseph, Jr., *lawyer*
Kalkstein, Joshua Adam *lawyer*
Kanin, Dennis Roy *lawyer*
Kassler, Haskell A. *lawyer*
Katzmann, Gary Stephen *lawyer*
Kavanaugh, James Francis, Jr., *lawyer*
Keating, Michael Burns *lawyer, educator*
Kehoe, William Francis *lawyer*
Keller, Stanley *lawyer*
Kidder, George Howell *lawyer*
Kindregan, Charles Peter *law educator*
King, William Bruce *retired lawyer*
Kirchick, William Dean *lawyer*
Klipp, Todd Lamont Causey *lawyer*
Kopelman, Leonard *lawyer*
Koutoujian, Peter John *lawyer*
Kozik, K. *lawyer*
Lamb, Kevin Thomas *lawyer*
Last, Michael P. *lawyer*
Lee, Paul W. *lawyer*
Lewis, Scott P. *lawyer*
Licata, Arthur Frank *lawyer*
Litwin, Paul Jeffrey *lawyer*
Loeser, Hans Ferdinand *lawyer*
Looney, William Francis, Jr., *lawyer*
Lukey, Joan A. *lawyer*
Lynch, Francis Charles *lawyer*
Lyons, Paul Vincent *lawyer*
Malt, Ronald Bradford *lawyer*
Martin, Stanley Allen *lawyer*
McKenzie, Elizabeth McDaniel *law librarian*
McKittrick, Neil Vincent *lawyer*
McMahon, Thomas John *law educator*
Menoyo, Eric Felix *lawyer*
Mercer, Richard James *lawyer*
Merrill, Stephen *lawyer, consultant, former governor*
Meserve, William George *lawyer*
Mikels, Richard Eliot *lawyer*
Milstein, Richard Sherman *lawyer*
Moncreiff, Robert P. *lawyer*
Mooney, Michael Edward *lawyer*
Moriarty, George Marshall *lawyer*
Muldoon, Robert Joseph, Jr., *lawyer*
Norris, Charles Head *prosecutor, manufacturing executive*
Norstrand, Hans Peter *lawyer, real estate public official, municipal official*
Novack, Kenneth Joseph *lawyer*
Nutt, Robert L. *lawyer, educator*
O'Donnell, Thomas Lawrence Patrick *lawyer*
O'Neill, Philip Daniel, Jr., *lawyer, educator*
Packenham, Richard Daniel *lawyer*
Park, William Wynnewood *law educator*
Parker, Christopher William *lawyer*
Partan, Daniel Gordon *lawyer, educator*
Patterson, John de la Roche, Jr., *lawyer*
Pechilis, William John *lawyer*
Perera, Lawrence Thacher *lawyer*
Perkins, John Allen *lawyer*
Pomeroy, Robert Corttis *lawyer*
Popeo, R. Robert *lawyer*
Poss, Stephen Daniel *lawyer*
Ragalevsky, Stanley Victor *lawyer*
Raish, David Langdon *lawyer*
Reardon, Frank Emond *lawyer*
Reardon, James G. *lawyer*
Richmond, Alice Elenor *lawyer*
Ritt, Roger Merrill *lawyer*
Rivlin, Rachel *lawyer*
Rodman, John Slater *lawyer*
Ryan, Allan Andrew, Jr., *lawyer, author, lecturer*
Sargeant, Ernest James *lawyer, educator*
Sawyer, William C. *lawyer*
Schlichtmann, Jan R. *lawyer*
Sears, John Winthrop *lawyer*
Segal, Phyllis Nichamoff *mediator*
Shapiro, Sandra *lawyer*
Skrine, Bruce E. *retired lawyer*
Smith, Edwin Eric *lawyer*
Smith, Perry Marshall *lawyer*
Smith, Philip Jones *lawyer*
Soden, Richard Allan *lawyer*
Solet, Maxwell David *lawyer*
Sonnenschein, Adam *lawyer*
Southard, William G. *lawyer*
Southgate, Richard W. *lawyer, director*
Southworth, William Walter *lawyer, title insurance company executive*
Spelfogel, Scott David *lawyer*
Spiess, Gary A. *lawyer*
Steinberg, Laura *lawyer*
Stern, Donald Kenneth *lawyer*
Storey, James Moorfield *lawyer*
Sugarman, Paul Ronald *lawyer, educator, academic administrator*
Sullivan, Michael J. *prosecutor*
Surkin, Elliot Mark *lawyer*
Swaim, C. Hall *lawyer*
Swope, Jeffrey Peyton *lawyer*
Taylor, Thomas William *lawyer*
Thibeault, George Walter *lawyer*
Todaro, Elisabeth M. *lawyer*
Touster, Saul *law educator*
Tuchmann, Robert *lawyer*
Van, Peter *lawyer*
Vance, Verne Widney, Jr., *retired lawyer*
Vaughan, Herbert Wiley *retired lawyer*
Weaver, Paul David *lawyer*
Weiner, Stephen Mark *lawyer*
Weitzel, John Patterson *lawyer*
Wellington, Carol Strong *law librarian*
Weltman, David Lee *lawyer*
Whitlock, John L. *lawyer*
Whitters, James Payton, III, *lawyer, university administrator*
Wild, Victor Allyn *prosecutor, educator*
Willard, Richard Kennon *lawyer*
Woodburn, Ralph Robert, Jr., *lawyer*
Young, Raymond Henry *lawyer*
Zack, Arnold Marshall *lawyer, mediator, arbitrator*

Braintree
Riccio, Frank Joseph *lawyer, educator*

Brighton
Garber, Paul William *lawyer*

Brookline
Ellis, Sharon Henderson *arbitrator, mediator*
Lerman, Herbert S. *lawyer*

Cambridge
Alevizos, Susan Bamberger *lawyer, santouri player, author*
Alevizos, Theodore G. *lawyer, singer, author*
Andrews, William Dorey *law educator, lawyer*
Bartholet, Elizabeth *law educator*
Bellamy, Werten F. W., Jr., *lawyer*
Bok, Derek *law educator, former university president*
Coglianese, Cary *lawyer, educator*
Crawford, Linda Sibery *lawyer, educator*
Dershowitz, Alan Morton *lawyer, educator*
Downey, Richard Ralph *lawyer, accountant, management consultant*
Edley, Christopher F., Jr., *law educator*
Fisher, Roger Dummer *lawyer, educator, negotiation expert*
Frug, Gerald E. *law educator*
Glendon, Mary Ann *law educator*
Hostage, John Brayne Arthur *law librarian*
Kagan, Elena *law educator*
Kaplow, Louis *law educator*
Kaufman, Andrew Lee *law educator*
Martin, Harry S., III, *law educator, law librarian*
Miller, Arthur Raphael *law educator*
Patton, Bruce M. *law educator, management consultant*
Sander, Frank Ernest Arnold *law educator*
Schauer, Frederick Franklin *law educator*
Steiner, Henry Jacob *law and human rights educator*
Stone, Alan Abraham *law and psychiatry educator, psychiatrist*
Ta, Tai Van *lawyer, researcher*
Tribe, Laurence Henry *lawyer, educator*
Vagts, Detlev Frederick *law educator*
von Mehren, Arthur Taylor *lawyer, educator*
Warren, Alvin Clifford, Jr., *lawyer*
Warren, Elizabeth *law educator*
Weiler, Paul Cronin *law educator*
Westfall, David *lawyer, educator*
Zittrain, Jonathan L. *law educator*

Chatham
Popkin, Alice Brandeis *lawyer*

Chestnut Hill
Batchelder, Samuel Lawrence, Jr., *retired corporate lawyer*

Concord
Bander, Edward Julius *law librarian emeritus, lawyer*

Dennis Port
Singer, Myer R(ichard) *lawyer*

Dover
Edwards, Carl Norman *lawyer*

Florence
Park, Beverly Goodman *lawyer*
Platt, Rutherford Hayes *lawyer, educator, geographer, consultant*

Framingham
Curry, Thomas Francis *lawyer*
Kriegsman, Edward Michael *lawyer*
Meltzer, Jay H. *lawyer, retail executive*
Vrabel, Joseph P. *lawyer*

Gloucester
Birchfield, John Kermit, Jr., *lawyer*

Hinsdale
Rutiger, Paul *lawyer, educator*

Holden
Price, Robert DeMille *lawyer*

Hyannis
Segersten, Robert Hagy *lawyer, investment banker*

Ipswich
Getchell, Charles Willard, Jr., *lawyer, publisher*

Lexington
Burkett, Bradford Charles *lawyer*
Hines, Edward Francis, Jr., *lawyer*

Lincoln
Gnichtel, William Van Orden *lawyer*
Lufkin, Martha B.G. *lawyer, legal writer*
Schwartz, Edward Arthur *lawyer*

Longmeadow
Quinn, Andrew Peter, Jr., *lawyer, insurance executive retired*

Lowell
Burke, William Joseph *law educator, lawyer*
Curtis, James Theodore *lawyer*
Maille, Brenda Patricia *lawyer*
Martin, William Francis, Jr., *lawyer*

Lynnfield
McGivney, John Joseph *lawyer*

Marblehead
Page, George Alfred, Jr., *lawyer*

Marion
Worley, Robert William, Jr., *retired lawyer*

Medford
Berman, David *lawyer, poet*
Salacuse, Jeswald William *lawyer, educator*

Methuen
DiFruscia, Anthony R. *lawyer, real estate executive*

Nantucket
Schultz, Franklin M. *retired law educator*

Natick
Goglia, Charles A., Jr., *lawyer*
Grassia, Thomas Charles *lawyer, writer*
Marr, David E. *lawyer*
Sandman, Paul William *lawyer*

Needham
Cox, Gilbert W., Jr., *lawyer*

New Bedford
Hurwitz, Barrett Alan *lawyer*

Newburyport
Connolly, James Thomas *lawyer*

Newton
Appleman, Lawrence Joel *lawyer, engineer*
Baron, Charles Hillel *lawyer, educator*
Coquillette, Daniel Robert *lawyer, educator*
Frankenheim, Samuel *retired lawyer*
Glazer, Donald Wayne *lawyer, business executive, educator*
Goldweitz, Julie *lawyer*
Horbaczewski, Henry Zygmunt *lawyer, publishing executive*
Huber, Richard Gregory *lawyer, educator*
Lane, Newton Alexander *retired lawyer*
Metzer, Patricia Ann *lawyer*
Peterson, Osler Leopold *lawyer*
Walker, Paul Howard *retired lawyer*

Newton Center
Snyder, John Gorvers *lawyer*
Soifer, Aviam *law educator, dean*

Northampton
Hastings, Wilmot Reed *lawyer, writer*
Miles, Harry Lehman *lawyer, educator*

Norwell
Mullare, T(homas) Kenwood, Jr., *lawyer*

Norwood
Singer, Paula Noyes *lawyer, software company executive*

Pittsfield
Doyle, Anthony Peter *lawyer*
Green, Nathaniel Kimball *lawyer*

Quincy
Hayes, Mary Dianne Wixted *lawyer*

Randolph
Johnson, Laurence Michael *lawyer*

Rockport
Ambrogi, Robert James *arbitrator*

Salem
Griffin, Thomas McLean *retired lawyer*
Hayes, John Charles *lawyer*
Moran, Philip David *lawyer*

South Boston
Burnstein, Daniel *lawyer*

Springfield
Cohen, Andrew Jay *lawyer*
Dibble, Francis Daniel, Jr., *lawyer*
Fein, Sherman Edward *lawyer, psychologist*
Goldstein, Anne Brenda *law educator*
Maidman, Stephen Paul *lawyer*
Miller, J(ohn) Wesley, III, *lawyer*
Nicolai, Paul Peter *lawyer*
Oldershaw, Louis Frederick *retired lawyer*
Santopietro, Albert Robert *lawyer*
Susse, Sandra Slone *lawyer*
Sweeney, Kevin Michael *lawyer*
Weiss, Ronald Phillip *lawyer*

Stoughton
Gabovitch, Steven Alan *lawyer, accountant*
George, Arthur Charles *lawyer*
Schepps, Victoria Hayward *lawyer*

Stow
Golder, Leonard Howard *lawyer, writer*

Truro
Chaplin, Ansel Burt *lawyer*
Friedman, Edward David *lawyer, arbitrator*

Wakefield
Courtenay, Lisa A. *paralegal, foundation administrator*

Waltham
Dickie, Robert Benjamin *lawyer, consultant, educator*
Dulchinos, Peter *lawyer*
Hester, Patrick Joseph *lawyer*
Lenzen, Glenn Howard, Jr., *lawyer*
Lichtenstein, Stephen David *law educator*
Stephens, Jay B. *lawyer, manufacturing executive*

Watertown
Karaian, Norma Maksoodian *lawyer*

Wayland
Norris, Melvin *lawyer*

Wellesley
Shea, Megan Carroll *lawyer, law educator*
Silberman, Robert A. S. *lawyer*
Wong, Bella Toy Funnd *lawyer*

West Chatham
Rowley, Glenn Harry *lawyer*

West Falmouth
Carlson, David Bret *lawyer*

West Springfield
Ely, John P. *lawyer*

Weston
Bateman, Thomas Robert *lawyer*
Lashman, L. Edward *arbitrator, mediator, consultant*
Thomas, Roger Meriwether *lawyer*

Weymouth
Fitzsimmons, B. Joseph, Jr., *lawyer*

Winchester
Bigelow, Robert P. *lawyer, arbitrator, mediator, journalist*

Windsor
Leaf, Martin Norman *lawyer*

Winthrop
Brown, Patricia Irene *retired law librarian, lawyer*

Worcester
Baldiga, Joseph Hilding *lawyer*
Bernstein, William Elliott *lawyer*
Cowan, Fairman Chaffee *lawyer*
Donnelly, James Corcoran, Jr., *lawyer*
Feener, Donald Edward *lawyer*
Fox, Douglas Lee *lawyer*
Lougee, David Louis *lawyer*
Moschos, Michael Christos *lawyer*
Silver, Marvin S. *lawyer*
Van Nostrand, Richard Charles *lawyer*

Yarmouth Port
Paquin, Thomas Christopher *lawyer*

MICHIGAN

Ada
Mc Callum, Charles Edward *lawyer*

Albion
Horstman, Allen *law educator*
Moore, David Gregory *lawyer*

Ann Arbor
Allen, Layman Edward *law educator, research scientist*
Barr, Michael S. *law educator*
Bilyeau, Amy Marie *law librarian*
Britton, Clarold Lawrence *lawyer, consultant*
Browder, Olin Lorraine *legal educator*
Buesser, Anthony Carpenter *lawyer*
Cooper, Edward Hayes *lawyer, educator*
DeVine, Edmond Francis *lawyer*
Dew, Thomas Edward *lawyer*
Dobranski, Bernard *law educator*
Duquette, Donald Norman *law educator*
Eggertsen, John Hale *lawyer*
Ellmann, Douglas Stanley *lawyer*
Frankena, Karl R. *lawyer*
Hertz, Dawn Leslie *lawyer*
Joscelyn, Kent B(uckley) *lawyer*
Kahn, Douglas Allen *legal educator*
Kamisar, Yale *lawyer, educator*
Krier, James Edward *law educator, writer*
Leary, Margaret *law librarian, library director*
Lempert, Richard Owen *lawyer, educator*
Lowenstein, Joan Holly *lawyer*
MacKinnon, Catharine Alice *lawyer, law educator, legal scholar, writer*
Reed, John Wesley *lawyer, educator*
St. Antoine, Theodore Joseph *retired law educator, arbitrator*
Schneider, Carl Edward *law educator*
Siedel, George John, III, *law educator*
Stevenson, Robert Bruce *lawyer*
Vining, Joseph (George Joseph Vining) *law educator*
Waggoner, Lawrence William *law educator*
Walsh, James Joseph *lawyer*
White, James Boyd *law educator*

Auburn Hills
O'Brien, William J., III, *lawyer*

Battle Creek
Kelly, Janet Langford *lawyer*
Markey, James Kevin *lawyer*

Bay City
Greve, Guy Robert *lawyer*

Beverly Hills
Hertzberg, David Gordon *retired lawyer*

Bingham Farms
Banas, C(hristine) Leslie *lawyer*
Baumkel, Mark S. *lawyer*
Berman, Leonard Keith *lawyer*
Burstein, Richard Joel *lawyer*
Larky, Sheldon Glen *lawyer*
Shaevsky, Mark *lawyer*

Birmingham
Elsman, James Leonard, Jr., *lawyer*
Harms, Steven Alan *lawyer*
Kienbaum, Thomas Gerd *lawyer*
Lesser, Margo Rogers *legal consultant*
Robinson, Marietta S. *lawyer*
Sweeney, Thomas Frederick *lawyer*
Wells, Steven Wayne *lawyer*

Bloomfield
Kanter, Alan Michael *lawyer*

Bloomfield Hills
Baker, Robert Edward *lawyer, retired financial corporation executive*
Birnkrant, Sherwin Maurice *lawyer*
Callow, Thomas Edward *lawyer*
Charla, Leonard Francis *lawyer*
Clippert, Charles Frederick *lawyer*
Cunningham, Gary H. *lawyer*
Dawson, Stephen Everette *lawyer*
Googasian, George Ara *lawyer*
Gornbein, Henry Seidel *lawyer*
Hertz, Howard *lawyer*
Janover, Robert H. *lawyer*
Kasischke, Louis Walter *lawyer*
Kirk, John MacGregor *lawyer*
Ledwidge, Patrick Joseph *lawyer*
Lehman, Richard Leroy *lawyer*
LoPrete, James Hugh *lawyer*
Martin, J(oseph) Patrick *lawyer, judge*
McCuen, John Francis, Jr., *lawyer*
McGarry, Alexander Banting *lawyer*
Meyer, George Herbert *lawyer*
Morganroth, Fred *lawyer*
Nern, Christopher Carl *lawyer*
Norris, John Hart *lawyer, director*
Rader, Ralph Terrance *lawyer*
Simon, Evelyn *lawyer*
Snyder, George Edward *lawyer*
Solomon, Mark Raymond *lawyer, educator*
Stewart, Michael B. *lawyer, mechanical and aerospace engineer*
Stoller, John R. *lawyer*
Williams, Walter Joseph *lawyer*
Yamin, Joseph Francis *lawyer, counselor*

Brighton
Gardella, Robert Christopher *lawyer*

Burton
Breczinski, Michael Joseph *lawyer*

Charlevoix
Telgenhof, Allen Ray *lawyer*

Dearborn
Kahn, Mark Leo *arbitrator, educator*
Taub, Robert Allan *lawyer*

Detroit
Adams, James Charles *lawyer*
Andreoff, Christopher Andon *lawyer*
Babcock, Charles Witten, Jr., *lawyer*
Beyer, Daniel G. *lawyer*
Brady, Edmund Matthew, Jr., *lawyer*
Brand, George Edward, Jr., *lawyer*
Brustad, Orin Daniel *lawyer*
Calkins, Stephen *lawyer, law educator*
Candler, James Nall, Jr., *lawyer*
Cohen, Norton Jacob *lawyer*
Collier, James Warren *lawyer*
Collins, Jeffrey G. *lawyer*
Connor, Laurence Davis *lawyer, director*
Cothorn, John Arthur *lawyer*
Darlow, Julia Donovan *lawyer*
Deason, Herold McClure *lawyer*
Driker, Eugene *lawyer*
Dunn, William Bradley *lawyer*
Everingham, James Theodore *lawyer*
Faison, W. Mack *lawyer*
Fromm, Frederick Andrew, Jr., *lawyer*
Gershel, Alan M. *prosecutor*
Gottschalk, Thomas A. *lawyer*
Green, Saul A. *lawyer*
Gushee, Richard Bordley *lawyer*
Hall, Elliott Sawyer *lawyer*
Hampton, Verne Churchill, II, *lawyer*
Hoops, Frederick Kurre *lawyer*
Howbert, Edgar Charles *lawyer*
Humphries, James Nathan *lawyer*
Jacobs, John Patrick *lawyer*
James, Phyllis A. *lawyer*
Krsul, John Aloysius, Jr., *lawyer*
Labadie, Dwight Daniel *lawyer*
Lamborn, LeRoy Leslie *law educator*
Lawrence, John Kidder *lawyer*
Leuchtman, Stephen Nathan *lawyer*
Lockman, Stuart M. *lawyer*
Mahoney, Joan *law educator*
Mamat, Frank Trustick *lawyer*
Maurer, David Leo *lawyer*
McKim, Samuel John, III, *lawyer*
Mengel, Christopher Emile *lawyer, educator*
Miller, George DeWitt, Jr., *lawyer*
Mitseff, Carl *lawyer*
Myers, Rodman Nathaniel *lawyer*
Nadeau, Steven C. *lawyer*
Peters, John Douglas *lawyer, artist*
Rogers, Hon Paulletto *researcher, writer*
Saxton, William Marvin *lawyer*
Schwartz, Alan E. *lawyer, director*
Scott, John Edward Smith *lawyer*
Sedler, Robert Allen *law educator*
Semple, Lloyd Ashby *lawyer*
Shannon, Margaret Anne *lawyer*
Shapiro, Michael Bruce *lawyer*
Smith, James Albert *lawyer*
Sparrow, Herbert George, III, *lawyer, educator*
Tarnacki, Duane L. *lawyer*
Thelen, Bruce Cyril *lawyer*
Thomas, Russell Joseph, Jr., *lawyer*
Thoms, David Moore *lawyer*
Thurber, Peter Palms *lawyer*
Timm, Roger K. *lawyer*
Turner, Reginald Maurice, Jr., *lawyer*
Volz, William Harry *law educator, administrator*
Weinberg, Jonathan T. *law educator*
White, Katherine E. *law educator*
Wise, John Augustus *lawyer, director*
Wittlinger, Timothy David *lawyer*
Wu, Frank H. *law educator, journalist*
Wyrick, Jermaine Albert *lawyer*
Zalman, Marvin *law educator*
Zuckerman, Richard Engle *lawyer, law educator*

Dexter
Millman, Jode Susan *lawyer, writer*

East Lansing
Essa, Daniel F. *lawyer*
Johnson, Clark Cumings *lawyer, educator, department chairman*
Lashbrooke, Elvin Carroll, Jr., *law educator, consultant*
Revelos, Constantine Nicholas *law educator, writer*
White, James Alfred *lawyer*
Wilkinson, William Sherwood *lawyer*

Farmington
Gordon, Arnold Mark *lawyer*
McFarland, Robert Edwin *lawyer*

Farmington Hills
Brodhead, William McNulty *lawyer, former congressman*
Fenton, Robert Leonard *lawyer, literary agent, movie producer, writer*
Meyer, Philip Gilbert *lawyer*

Flint
Gernstein, Stanley B. *lawyer*

Frankfort
Gerberding, Miles Carston *lawyer*

Grand Rapids
Bair, Joel Evan *lawyer*
Barnes, Thomas John *lawyer*
Birkbeck, A.J. Koerts *lawyer*
Bradshaw, Conrad Allan *lawyer*
Brinkmeyer, Scott S. *lawyer*
Chiara, Margaret-Mary *United States attorney*
Curtin, Timothy John *lawyer*
Davis, Henry Barnard, Jr., *lawyer*
Drew, Stephen Richard *lawyer*
Harris, Richard W. *law educator, lawyer, accountant*
Marshall, J. Stephen *lawyer*
Mears, Patrick Edward *lawyer*
Mitchell, James Albee *lawyer*
Neckers, Bruce Warren *lawyer*
Titley, Larry J. *lawyer*
Van Haren, W(illiam) Michael *lawyer*
Van Oostenburg, Paul Gary *lawyer*

Greenville
Mullendore, James Myers *lawyer*
Palmer, Richard Douglas *lawyer*

Grosse Pointe
Barrows, Ronald Thomas *lawyer*
Behringer, Samuel Joseph, Jr., *lawyer*
Goss, James William *lawyer*
Pytell, Robert Henry *retired lawyer, former judge*

Grosse Pointe Farms
Axe, John Randolph *lawyer, finance company executive*

Grosse Pointe Park
Centner, Charles William *lawyer, educator*
Mogk, John Edward *law educator, association executive, consultant*

Grosse Pointe Woods
Prather, Kenneth Earl *lawyer*

Harbor Springs
Lampert, Charles E. *lawyer*
Smith, Wayne Richard *lawyer*

Highland
Bullard, Willis Clare, Jr., *lawyer*

Holt
Legere Jr, Henry J. *lawyer*

Howell
Parker, Robert Ernser *lawyer*

Inkster
Bullock, Steven Carl *lawyer*

Ionia
Palmer, Charles A. *lawyer, educator*

Ishpeming
Steward, James Brian *lawyer, pharmacist*

Jackson
Smith, Stanton Kinnie, Jr., *lawyer*

Kalamazoo
Bauhof, James Francis *lawyer*
Bus, Roger Jay *lawyer*
Enslen, Pamela Chapman *lawyer*
Gordon, Edgar George *retired lawyer*
Hilboldt, James Sonnemann *lawyer, investment advisor*
Morris, Christopher David *lawyer*

Lansing
Baker, Frederick Milton, Jr., *lawyer*
Brewer, Mark Courtland *lawyer*
Coey, David Conrad *lawyer*
Devaney, Dennis Martin *lawyer, educator*
Ewert, Quentin Albert *lawyer, consultant*
Fitzgerald, John Warner *law educator*
Foster, Joe C., Jr., *lawyer*
Kelley, Frank Joseph *lawyer, former state attorney general*
Linder, Iris Kay *lawyer*
Marvin, David Edward Shreve *lawyer*
Rasmusson, Thomas Elmo *lawyer*
Rooney, John Philip *law educator*
Stockmeyer, Norman Otto *law educator, consultant*
Warren, Joseph Addison, III, *law and history educator*

Lincoln Park
Zelenak, Edward Michael *lawyer, musician*

Livonia
Bialosky, David L. *lawyer, automotive executive*
Hoffman, Barry Paul *lawyer*

Marquette
Osstyn, Randolph Beier *lawyer*

Midland
Scriven, John G. *retired lawyer, chemical company executive*

Monroe
Lipford, Rocque Edward *lawyer, corporate executive*

Mount Clemens
Brumbaugh, George Edwin, Jr., *lawyer*

Mount Pleasant
Lynch, John Joseph *lawyer*

Muskegon
Kara, Paul Mark *corporate executive*
Kolenic, Anthony James, Jr., *lawyer, educator*
McKendry, John H., Jr., *lawyer, educator*
Nehra, Gerald Peter *lawyer*

Niles
Pasula, Angela Marie *lawyer*

Northville
Leavitt, Martin Jack *lawyer*

Plymouth
Longhofer, Ronald Stephen *lawyer*

Rapid City
Ring, Ronald Herman *lawyer*

Romeo
Clark, Mark Lee *lawyer*

Royal Oak
Monnich, John Robert *lawyer*

Saginaw
Martin, Walter *retired lawyer*

Saint Clair Shores
Joslyn, Robert Bruce *lawyer*
Stevens, Clark Valentine *lawyer*

Saline
Anderson, Austin Gothard *lawyer, consultant, academic administrator*
Harbour, Nancy Caine *lawyer*

Shelby
Burrows, Jay Edward *lawyer*

South Haven
Waxman, Sheldon Robert *lawyer*

Southfield
Adelman, Martin Jerome *law educator*
Dawson, Dennis Ray *lawyer, manufacturing executive*
DeLong, Donald Alan *lawyer*
Fieger, Geoffrey Nels *lawyer*
Hanket, Mark John *lawyer*
Hotelling, Harold *law and economics educator*
Jacobs, John E. *lawyer*
Leib, Jeffrey M. *lawyer*
McClow, Roger James *labor lawyer*
Ritchie, Alexander Buchan *lawyer*
Sullivan, Robert Emmet, Jr., *lawyer*
Targan, Holli Hart *lawyer*
Thurswell, Gerald Elliott *lawyer*
Toll, Sheldon Samuel *lawyer*
Turner, Lee Irwin *lawyer*
Winzenreid, James Ernest *lawyer, entrepreneur*

Sterling Heights
Novak, Joseph Anthony *law librarian*

Taylor
Leekley, John Robert *lawyer*

Three Rivers
Warnock, William Reid *lawyer*

Traverse City
Dettmer, Michael Hayes *lawyer, former prosecutor*
Gillman, Michael Joseph *lawyer*
Quandt, Joseph Edward *lawyer, educator*
Quick, Albert Thomas *lawyer, educator*

Troy
Alterman, Irwin Michael *lawyer*
Baker, Vernon G., II, *lawyer*
Cantor, Bernard Jack *lawyer*
Gelder, John William *lawyer*
Haron, David Lawrence *lawyer*
Kruse, John Alphonse *lawyer*
LaDuke, Nancie *lawyer, corporate executive*
May, Alan Alfred *lawyer*
Morgan, Michael Vincent *lawyer*
Nolte, Henry R., Jr., *lawyer, former automobile company executive*
Robinson, Logan Gilmore *lawyer*
Schmidt, Michael Francis *lawyer*
Thurber, John Alexander *lawyer*
Webster, Robert Byron *lawyer*

Warren
Bridenstine, Louis Henry, Jr., *lawyer*

Waterford
Hall, Terrence Lyon *lawyer*

West Bloomfield
Darke, Richard Francis *lawyer*
Gullen, Christopher Roy *lawyer*

Ypsilanti
Barr, John Monte *lawyer*
McLain, Dennis O. *lawyer*

MINNESOTA

Anoka
Goodell, Robert D. *lawyer, educator*

Austin
Schneider, Mahlon C. *lawyer*

Bemidji
Kief, Paul Allan *lawyer*

Bloomington
Boedigheimer, Robert David *lawyer*
Broeker, John Milton *lawyer*
Grinnell, Joseph Fox *lawyer*
Mooty, John William *lawyer*

Brainerd
O'Hara, William Desmond, Jr., *lawyer*

Chatfield
Opat, Matthew John *lawyer*

Crosby
Barnum, Charles Earl, III, *lawyer*

Duluth
Balmer, James Walter *lawyer*
Burns, Richard Ramsey *lawyer*

Eagan
Todd, John Joseph *lawyer*

Eden Prairie
Carlson, Jeffrey *lawyer*
Friederichs, Norman Paul *lawyer*
Nilles, John Michael *lawyer*

Edina
Burk, Robert S. *lawyer*
Neff, Fred Leonard *lawyer*

Fergus Falls
Bigwood, Robert William *lawyer*

Forest Lake
Rachie, Cyrus *retired lawyer*

Fridley
Savelkoul, Donald Charles *retired lawyer*

Golden Valley
Schlichting, William Henry *lawyer, writer*

Hallock
Malm, Roger Charles *lawyer*

Hawley
Baer, Zenas *lawyer*

Hopkins
Hunter, Donald Forrest *lawyer*

Kenyon
Peterson, Franklin Delano *lawyer*

Little Canada
Hardman, James Charles *lawyer, motor carrier executive*

Marine On Saint Croix
Haynsworth, Harry Jay, IV, *lawyer, educator*

Marshall
Paskach, David M. *lawyer, food products executive*

Medford
Paschke, Jerry Bryan *lawyer*

Minneapolis
Al, Marc Andre *lawyer*
Allers, Marlene Elaine *legal administrator*
Anderson, Alan Marshall *lawyer*
Anderson, Eric Scott *lawyer*
Ayling, Corey John *lawyer*
Baillie, James Leonard *lawyer*
Bearmon, Lee *lawyer*
Berens, William Joseph *lawyer*
Berg, Thomas Kenneth *lawyer*
Bergerson, David Raymond *lawyer*
Bernhardson, Ivy Schutz *lawyer*
Bland, J(ohn) Richard *lawyer*
Borger, John Philip *lawyer*
Breimayer, Joseph Frederick *patent lawyer*
Bress, Michael E. *retired lawyer*
Brink, David Ryrie *lawyer*
Bruner, Philip Lane *lawyer*
Buratti, Dennis P. *lawyer*
Burns, Robert Arthur *lawyer*
Busdicker, Gordon G. *retired lawyer*
Carlson, Thomas David *lawyer*
Ciresi, Michael Vincent *lawyer*
Clary, Bradley G. *lawyer, educator*
Cole, Phillip Allen *lawyer*
Comstock, Rebecca Ann *lawyer*
Conn, Gordon Brainard, Jr., *lawyer*
DiPietro, Mark Joseph *lawyer*
Eck, George Gregory *lawyer*
Erstad, Leon Robert *lawyer*
Faricy, John Hartnett, Jr., *lawyer*
Feuss, Linda Anne Upsall *lawyer*
Finzen, Bruce Arthur *lawyer*
Flom, Gerald Trossen *lawyer*
Forneris, Jeanne M. *lawyer*
French, John Dwyer *lawyer*
Garon, Philip Stephen *lawyer*
Garton, Thomas William *lawyer*
Gill, Richard Lawrence *lawyer*
Gordon, Corey Lee *lawyer*
Gordon, John Bennett *lawyer*
Gottschalk, Stephen Elmer *lawyer*
Greener, Ralph Bertram *lawyer*
Griffith, G. Larry *lawyer*
Grodsky, Jamie Anne *law educator*
Hagglund, Clarence Edward *lawyer, publishing company owner*
Hanson, Bruce Eugene *lawyer*
Hanson, Kent Bryan *lawyer*
Hart, Buster Clarence *lawyer*
Hayward, Edward Joseph *lawyer*
Heffelfinger, Thomas Backer *lawyer*
Heiberg, Robert Alan *lawyer*
Hektner, Candice Elaine *lawyer*
Hendrixson, Peter S. *lawyer*
Henson, Robert Frank *lawyer*
Hibbs, John Stanley *lawyer*
Hippee, William H., Jr., *lawyer*
Hobbins, Robert Leo *lawyer*
Homolka, Daniel Michael *lawyer*
Howland, Joan Sidney *law librarian, educator*
Jackson, Renee Leone *lawyer*
Jarboe, Mark Alan *lawyer*
Johannsen, Marc Alan *lawyer*
Johnson, Alex Moore *lawyer, educator*
Johnson, Gary M. *lawyer*
Jones, B. Todd *lawyer, former prosecutor*
Kantor, David *lawyer*
Kaplan, Sheldon *lawyer, director*
Kelly, A. David *lawyer*
Keppel, William James *lawyer, educator, writer*
Kirtley, Jane Elizabeth *law educator*
Klaas, Paul Barry *lawyer*
Koneck, John Michael *lawyer*
Lach, Susan Marie *lawyer*
Lareau, Richard George *lawyer*
Lazar, Raymond Michael *lawyer, educator*
Lebedoff, David M. *lawyer, writer*
Lillehaug, David Lee *lawyer*
Lueck, Martin R. *lawyer*
Magnuson, Roger James *lawyer*
Manning, William Henry *lawyer*
Marshall, Siri Swenson *lawyer*
Martin, Phillip Hammond *lawyer*
McGuire, Timothy James *lawyer, editor, columnist*
McGunnigle, George Francis *judge*
Meller, Robert Louis, Jr., *lawyer*
Mellum, Gale Robert *lawyer*
Meshbesher, Ronald I. *lawyer*
Nelson, Gary Michael *lawyer*
Nelson, Richard Arthur *lawyer*
Nelson, Steven Craig *lawyer*

Novak, Leslie Howard *lawyer*
O'Neill, Brian Boru *lawyer*
Palmer, Brian Eugene *lawyer*
Palmer, Deborah Jean *lawyer*
Peterson, Mark Bradley *lawyer*
Peterson, William George *lawyer*
Platt, Nina *law librarian*
Pluimer, Edward J. *lawyer*
Potuznik, Charles Laddy *lawyer*
Pratte, Robert John *lawyer*
Price, Joseph Michael *lawyer*
Radmer, Michael John *lawyer, educator*
Reilly, George *lawyer*
Rein, Stanley Michael *lawyer*
Reinhart, Robert Rountree, Jr., *lawyer*
Reister, Raymond Alex *retired lawyer*
Reuter, James William *lawyer*
Rockwell, Winthrop Adams *lawyer*
Roe, Roger Rolland, Jr., *lawyer*
Rothenberg, Elliot Calvin *lawyer, author*
Sacks, Allen Irving *lawyer*
Safley, James Robert *lawyer*
Schermer, Judith Kahn *lawyer*
Schneider, Elaine Carol *lawyer, researcher, writer*
Schnell, Robert Lee, Jr., *lawyer*
Schnobrich, Roger William *lawyer*
Schoettle, Ferdinand P. *lawyer, educator*
Shnider, Bruce Jay *lawyer*
Silver, Alan Irving *lawyer*
Silverman, Robert Joseph *lawyer*
Sippel, William Leroy *lawyer*
Sisk, Gregory Charles *lawyer, educator*
Skare, Robert Martin *lawyer, director*
Smith, Curtis David *lawyer*
Sortland, Paul Allan *lawyer*
Stageberg, Roger V. *lawyer*
Stern, Leo G. *lawyer*
Struthers, Margo S. *lawyer*
Struyk, Robert John *lawyer*
Sullivan, E. Thomas *law educator*
Symonds, Terri Lee *law educator*
Thorson, Steven Greg *lawyer*
Trucano, Michael *lawyer*
Vander Molen, Thomas Dale *lawyer*
Ventres, Judith Martin *lawyer*
Wahoske, Michael James *lawyer*
Whelpley, Dennis Porter *lawyer*
Wicks, John R. *lawyer*
Windhorst, John William, Jr., *lawyer*
Witort, Janet Lee *lawyer*
Yost, Gerald B. *lawyer*
Younger, Judith Tess *law educator*

Minnetonka
Carpenter, Norman Roblee *retired lawyer*
Freeman, Gerald Russell *lawyer*
Heckt, Melvin Dean *lawyer*
Lubben, David J. *lawyer*
Van Brunt, William A. *lawyer, business executive*

Moorhead
Miller, Keith Lloyd *lawyer*

Owatonna
Aune, Debra Bjurquist *lawyer*

Pipestone
Scott, William Paul *lawyer*

Plymouth
Saville, Derric James *lawyer*

Rochester
Lantz, William Charles *lawyer*
Orwoll, Gregg S.K. *lawyer*
Somsen, Henry Northrop *retired lawyer*

Saint Cloud
Carpenter, Kevin Starr *lawyer*

Saint Paul
Allison, John Robert *lawyer*
Bastian, Gary Warren *judge*
Carruthers, Philip Charles *lawyer, public official*
Daly, Joseph Leo *law educator*
Dordell, Timothy Paul *lawyer*
Finley, Joseph Michael *lawyer*
Fisk, Martin H. *lawyer*
Galvin, Michael John, Jr., *lawyer*
Gehan, Mark William *lawyer*
Geis, Jerome Arthur *lawyer, legal educator*
Hansen, Eric Peter *lawyer*
Hansen, Robyn L. *lawyer*
Johnson, Paul Oren *lawyer*
Jones, C. Paul *lawyer, educator*
Kirwin, Kenneth Francis *law educator*
Larson, David Allen *law educator*
Lebedoff, Randy Miller *lawyer*
Leighton, Robert Joseph *lawyer*
McNeely, John J. *lawyer*
Micallef, Joseph Stephen *retired lawyer*
O'Leary, Daniel Brian *lawyer, educator*
Seymour, McNeil Vernam *lawyer*
Sheahan, Michael John *lawyer*
Trojack, John Edward *lawyer*
Ziegler, Richard Ferdinand *lawyer*

Shakopee
McCloud, Samuel Alfred *lawyer*

South Saint Paul
Pugh, Thomas Wilfred *lawyer*

Stillwater
Hutchinson, Michael Clark *lawyer*

Wayzata
Alton, Howard Robert, Jr., *lawyer, real estate and food company executive*
Johnson, Eugene Laurence *lawyer*
Reutiman, Robert William, Jr., *lawyer*

Winona
Brosnahan, Roger Paul *lawyer*

Woodbury
Spencer, David James *lawyer*

MISSISSIPPI

Bay Saint Louis
Bernstein, Joseph *lawyer*

Bay Springs
Shoemaker, Bobby Lynn *lawyer*

Biloxi
Dornan, Donald C., Jr., *lawyer*

Clarksdale
Connell, Edward Peacock, Sr., *lawyer*

Cleveland
Alexander, William Brooks *lawyer, former state senator*

Diamondhead
Reddien, Charles Henry, II, *lawyer, diversified financial services company executive, consultant*

Flowood
Wilson, William Roberts, Jr., (Bob Wilson) *lawyer, apparel executive*

Greenville
Martin, Andrew Ayers *lawyer, physician, educator*

Greenwood
Deaton, Charles Milton *lawyer*

Gulfport
Harral, John Menteith *lawyer*
Owen, Joe Sam *lawyer*

Hattiesburg
Adelman, Michael Schwartz *lawyer*
Lawrence, Charles Edward, Jr., *lawyer, judge*

Hernando
Brown, William A. *lawyer, mediator, financial planner*

Jackson
Burch, Donald Victor *lawyer*
Chatham, Lloyd Reeve *lawyer*
Chinn, Mark Allan *lawyer*
Corlew, John Gordon *lawyer*
Fillingane, Joey *lawyer, state representative*
Fuselier, Louis Alfred *lawyer*
Hafter, Jerome Charles *lawyer*
Harkins, Patrick Nicholas, III, *lawyer*
Henegan, John C(lark) *lawyer*
Houston, Jamie Giles, III, *lawyer, accountant*
Howell, Joel Walter, III, *lawyer*
Hughes, Byron William *lawyer, oil exploration company executive*
Hutchison, Mark Stevenson *lawyer*
Johnson, Mark Wayne *lawyer*
King, Robert Wilson *lawyer*
Lampton, Dunn O. *prosecutor*
Langford, James Jerry *lawyer*
Moize, Jerry Dee *lawyer, government official*
O'Mara, James Wright *lawyer*
Peden, James Alton, Jr., *lawyer*
Purdy, William Richard *lawyer*
Ray, H. M. *lawyer*
Roberts, Richard C., III, *lawyer*
Scanlon, Pat H. *lawyer*
Shinn, Clinton Wesley *lawyer*
Stubblefield, J(oseph) Stephen *lawyer*
Travis, Jay A., III, *lawyer*
Walker, John Leonard *lawyer*
West, Carol Catherine *law educator*

Madison
Obert, Keith David *lawyer*

New Albany
Sumners, Lester Furr *lawyer*

Ocean Springs
Luckey, Alwyn Hall *lawyer*

Olive Branch
Carnall, George Hursey, II, *lawyer, business executive*

Oxford
Greenlee, Jim Ming *prosecutor*
Rayburn, S. T. *lawyer*

Southaven
Taylor, Ronald Louis *lawyer*

Starkville
Yoste, Charles Todd *lawyer*

Tupelo
Bush, Fred Marshall, Jr., *lawyer*
Clayton, Claude F., Jr., *lawyer*
Moffett, T(er... K(ay) *lawyer*

Tylertown
Mord, Irving Conrad, II, *lawyer*

Vicksburg
Mazzeo-Merkle, Linda Lou *legal administrator*

MISSOURI

Ballwin
Winning, John Patrick *lawyer*

Cape Girardeau
McManaman, Kenneth Charles *lawyer*

Cassville
Melton, Emory Leon *lawyer, state legislator, publisher*

Chesterfield
Denneen, John Paul *lawyer*
Fagerberg, Roger Richard *lawyer*
Hier, Marshall David *lawyer*

Clayton
Komen, Leonard *lawyer*
Mohrman, Henry J(oe), Jr., *lawyer, investment manager*
Tremayne, Eric Flory *lawyer*

Columbia
Bunn, Ronald Freeze *lawyer, academic administrator*
Harter, Philip J. *lawyer, educator*
Mays, William Gay, II, *lawyer, real estate developer*
Peth, Howard Allen *lawyer, educator*
Phillips, Walter Ray *lawyer, educator*
Schwabe, John Bennett, II, *lawyer*
Turley, J. William *lawyer*
Welliver, Warren Dee *lawyer, retired state supreme court justice*
Westbrook, James Edwin *lawyer, educator*
Whitman, Dale Alan *lawyer, law educator*

Farmington
Pratte, Geoffrey Lynn *lawyer, arbitrator*

Hannibal
Riggs, Louis *lawyer, columnist*
Terrell, James Daniel *lawyer*

Hillsboro
Howald, John William *lawyer*

Independence
Cady, Elwyn Loomis, Jr., *medico legal consultant, educator*
Lashley, Curtis Dale *lawyer*
Minton, Kent W. *lawyer*

Jefferson City
Baker, Wade Franklin *retired state bar executive*
Bartlett, Alex *lawyer*
Deutsch, James Bernard *lawyer*
Doerhoff, Dale Charles *lawyer*
Lanning, Linda Lee *lawyer*
Tettlebaum, Harvey M. *lawyer*

Joplin
Scott, Robert Haywood, Jr., *lawyer*

Kansas City
Bacon, Jennifer Gille *lawyer*
Beck, William G. *lawyer*
Becker, Thomas Bain *lawyer*
Beckett, Theodore Charles *lawyer*
Beckett, Theodore Cornwall *lawyer*
Beihl, Frederick *lawyer*
Bellmann, Thomas Richard *lawyer*
Bevan, Robert Lewis *lawyer*
Boggs, James Dotson *lawyer*
Bradshaw, Jean Paul, II, *lawyer*
Brake, Timothy L. *lawyer*
Brous, Thomas Richard *lawyer*
Bryant, Richard Todd *lawyer*
Canfield, Robert Cleo *lawyer*
Clark, Charles Edward *arbitrator*
Clarke, Milton Charles *lawyer*
Clegg, Karen Kohler *lawyer*
Crawford, Howard Allen *lawyer*
Cross, William Dennis *lawyer*
Davis, John Charles *lawyer*
Deacy, Thomas Edward, Jr., *lawyer*
Dicus, Stephen Howard *lawyer*
Doan, Kirk Hugh *lawyer*
Egan, Charles Joseph, Jr., *lawyer, consumer products company executive*
Eldridge, Truman Kermit, Jr., *lawyer*
Foster, Mark Stephen *lawyer*
Frantze, David Wayne *lawyer*
Gorman, Gerald Warner *lawyer*
Graves, Todd Peterson *prosecutor*
Hill, Stephen L., Jr., *lawyer, former prosecutor*
Hindman, Larrie C. *lawyer*
Hubbell, Ernest *lawyer*
Johnson, Mark Eugene *lawyer*
Kaplan, Harvey L. *lawyer*
Kilroy, John Muir *lawyer*
King, Richard Allen *lawyer*
Langworthy, Robert Burton *lawyer*
Levings, Theresa Lawrence *lawyer*
Lindsey, David Hosford *lawyer*
Litan, Robert Eli *lawyer, economist*
Lolli, Don R(ay) *lawyer*
Lombardi, Cornelius Ennis, Jr., *lawyer*
Margolin, Abraham Eugene *lawyer, director*
McManus, James William *lawyer*
Milton, Chad Earl *lawyer*
Minnick, David Michael *lawyer*
Moore, Stephen James *lawyer*
Mordy, James Calvin *lawyer*
Newsom, James Thomas *lawyer*
Northrip, Robert Earl *lawyer*
Owens, Dennis James Campbell *lawyer*
Parker, Marietta *prosecutor*
Pelofsky, Joel *lawyer*
Pemberton, Bradley Powell *lawyer*
Plax, Karen Ann *lawyer*
Popper, Robert *law educator, former dean*
Price, James Tucker *lawyer*
Robb, Gary Charles *lawyer*
Sampson, William Roth *lawyer*
Scarritt, Richard Winn *lawyer*
Setzler, Edward Allan *lawyer*
Shaw, John W. *lawyer*
Shughart, Donald Louis *retired lawyer*
Siro, Rik Neal *lawyer*
Small, Stephen Bradley *lawyer*
Smithson, Lowell Lee *lawyer*
Spalty, Edward Robert *lawyer*
Spencer, Richard Henry *lawyer*
Stoup, Arthur Harry *lawyer*
Toll, Perry Mark *lawyer, educator*
Tyler, John Edward, III, *lawyer*
Vandever, William Dirk *lawyer*
Van Dyke, Thomas Wesley *lawyer*
Vering, John Albert *lawyer*
Viani, James Laurence *lawyer*
Vleisides, Gregory William *lawyer*
Whittaker, Judith Ann Cameron *lawyer*
Willy, Thomas Ralph *lawyer*
Wirken, James Charles *lawyer*
Wolf, Jerome Thomas *lawyer*
Wrobley, Ralph Gene *lawyer*
Wyrsch, James Robert *lawyer, educator, writer*

Lake Saint Louis
Callahan, Robert John, Jr., *lawyer, arbitrator*

Lexington
Giorza, John C. *lawyer*

Liberty
Sayles, Cathy A. *lawyer*

Manchester
Forsman, Alpheus Edwin *retired lawyer*

Maryland Heights
Cooper, Richard Alan *lawyer*

Maryville
McLaughlin, James Patrick *lawyer, educator*

Mount Vernon
Stemmons, Randee Smith *lawyer*

Saint Charles
Zerr, Richard Kevin *lawyer*

Saint Joseph
Davis, Lance Barrow *lawyer, municipal judge*
Kranitz, Theodore Mitchell *lawyer*

Saint Louis
Appleton, R. O., Jr., *lawyer*
Arnold, Fred English *lawyer*
Arnold, John Fox *lawyer*
Atwood, Hollye Stolz *lawyer*
Aylward, Ronald Lee *lawyer*
Babington, Charles Martin, III, *lawyer*
Babler, Wayne E. *lawyer, retired utilities executive*
Bailey, R(obert) Greg *lawyer*
Baker, Nannette A. *lawyer, city official*
Banks, Eric Kendall *lawyer*
Banstetter, Robert J. *lawyer*
Baum, Gordon Lee *lawyer, non-profit organization administrator*
Becker, David Mandel *law educator, author, consultant*
Berger, John Torrey, Jr., *lawyer*
Biesterfeld, Craig Stewart *lawyer*
Blanke, Richard Brian *lawyer*
Bloom, Allen Jerry *lawyer*
Bobak, Mark T. *lawyer*
Boggs, Beth Clemens *lawyer*
Bonacorsi, Mary Catherine *lawyer*
Boudreau, Thomas M. *lawyer*
Breece, Robert William, Jr., *lawyer*
Brickey, Kathleen Fitzgerald *law educator*
Brickler, John Weise *lawyer*
Brown, Paul Sherman *lawyer*
Brownlee, Robert Hammel *lawyer*
Bruning, Anthony Steven *lawyer*
Bryan, Henry C(lark), Jr., *retired lawyer*
Burke, Thomas Michael *lawyer*
Carp, Larry *lawyer*
Carr, Gary Thomas *lawyer*
Charlson, Alan Edward *lawyer, retail executive*
Clear, John Michael *lawyer*
Conran, Joseph Palmer *lawyer*
Cornfeld, Dave Louis *lawyer*
Corrigan, William M. *lawyer*
Covington, Ann K. *lawyer, former state supreme court justice*
Cullen, James D. *lawyer*
DeWoskin, Alan Ellis *lawyer*
Dorwart, Donald Bruce *lawyer*
Dougherty, Alfred Franklin, Jr., *lawyer*
Dowd, Edward L., Jr., *lawyer, former prosecutor*
Duesenberg, Richard William *lawyer*
Elbert, Charles Steiner *lawyer*
Elliott, Howard, Jr., *lawyer, gas distribution company executive*
Ellis, Dorsey Daniel, Jr., *lawyer, educator*
Evans, Lawrence E. *lawyer, educator*
Falk, William James *lawyer*
Farnam, Thomas Campbell *lawyer, educator*
Fessenden, Ann T. *law librarian*
Fisher, Harry *lawyer, theologian, writer*
Fogle, James Lee *lawyer*
Gerard, Jules Bernard *law educator*
Gillis, John Lamb, Jr., *lawyer*
Gilster, Peter Stuart *lawyer*
Goebel, John J. *lawyer*
Goldstein, Steven *lawyer*
Goodman, Harold S. *lawyer*
Gray, Charles Elmer *lawyer, rancher, investor*
Grebel, Lawrence Bovard *lawyer*
Green, Dennis Joseph *lawyer*
Greenley, Beverly Jane *lawyer, educator*
Guerri, William Grant *lawyer*
Gullborg, Peter William *lawyer*
Gunn, Michael Peter *lawyer*
Haar, Robert Theodore *lawyer*
Hansen, Charles *lawyer*
Harris, Harvey Alan *lawyer*
Harris, Whitney Robson *lawyer, educator, military officer, philanthropist*
Hays, Ruth *lawyer*
Hetlage, Robert Owen *lawyer*
Hiles, Bradley Stephen *lawyer*
Inkley, John James, Jr., *lawyer*
Jackson, Rebecca R. *lawyer*
Jaudes, Richard Edward *lawyer*
Johnson, E. Perry *lawyer*
Keller, Juan Dane *lawyer*
Klobasa, John Anthony *lawyer*
Kortenhof, Joseph Michael *lawyer, educator*
Kuhlmann, Fred Mark *lawyer, business executive*
Lane, Frank Joseph, Jr., *lawyer*
Lause, Michael Francis *lawyer*
Lebowitz, Albert *lawyer, writer*
Lieberman, Edward Jay *lawyer*
Lowenhaupt, Charles Abraham *lawyer*
Luberda, George Joseph *lawyer, educator*
Lucchesi, Lionel Louis *lawyer*
Lucy, Robert Meredith *lawyer*
Mandelstamm, Jerome Robert *lawyer*
Massey, Raymond Lee *lawyer*
McCarter, Charles Chase *lawyer*
McDaniel, James Edwin *lawyer*
McKinnis, Michael B. *lawyer*
Meisel, George Vincent *lawyer*
Merrill, Charles Eugene *lawyer*
Metcalfe, Walter Lee, Jr., *lawyer*
Michenfelder, Albert A. *lawyer*
Mohan, John J. *lawyer*
Moore, McPherson Dorsett *lawyer*
Mulligan, Michael Dennis *lawyer*
Needham, Carol Ann *lawyer, educator*
Neville, James Morton *retired lawyer, consumer products company executive*
Newman, Charles A. *lawyer*
Newman, Joan Meskiel *lawyer*
Noel, Edwin Lawrence *lawyer*
O'Keefe, Michael Daniel *lawyer*
Olson, Robert Grant *lawyer*
O'Malley, Kevin Francis *lawyer, writer, educator*

Ortbals, Gerald Ray *lawyer*
Palans, Lloyd Alex *lawyer*
Peper, Christian Baird *lawyer*
Perotti, Rose Norma *lawyer*
Phoenix, G. Keith *lawyer*
Pickle, Robert Douglas *lawyer, apparel executive*
Poscover, Maury B. *lawyer*
Rabbitt, Daniel Thomas, Jr., *lawyer*
Redd, Charles Appleton *lawyer*
Riddle, Veryl Lee *lawyer*
Riggio, Nicholas Jospeh, Sr., *lawyer*
Ringkamp, Stephen H. *lawyer, educator*
Ritter, Robert Forcier *lawyer*
Ritterskamp, Douglas Dolvin *lawyer*
Rose, Albert Schoenburg *lawyer, educator*
Rubenstein, Jerome Max *lawyer*
Sale, Llewellyn, III, *lawyer*
Sant, John Talbot *lawyer*
Schoene, Kathleen Snyder *lawyer*
Sestric, Anthony James *lawyer*
Shaw, Curt *lawyer, communications executive*
Shaw, Curtis S *lawyer*
Sherby, Kathleen Reilly *lawyer*
Smith, Arthur Lee *lawyer*
Sneeringer, Stephen Geddes *lawyer*
Sobol, Lawrence Raymond *lawyer*
Stewart, Allan Forbes *lawyer*
Suhre, Walter Anthony, Jr., *retired lawyer, brewery executive*
Teasdale, Kenneth Fulbright *lawyer*
Tierney, Michael Edward *lawyer*
Turcotte, John Arthur, Jr., *lawyer*
Virtel, James John *lawyer*
Walsh, Thomas Charles *lawyer*
Webb Anderson, JoAnn Marie *lawyer, community advocate*
Weiss, Charles Andrew *lawyer*
Wilson, Margaret Bush *lawyer*
Withers, W. Wayne *lawyer*
Woodruff, Bruce Emery *lawyer*
Young, Marvin Oscar *lawyer*

Salem
Hall, Glenn Allen *lawyer, state representative*

Springfield
Baxter-Smith, Gregory John *lawyer*
Crites, Richard Don *lawyer*
Hulston, John Kenton *lawyer, director*
McDonald, William Henry *lawyer*
Sherwood, Devon Fredrick *lawyer*

Stockton
Hammons, Brian Kent *lawyer, business executive*

Town And Country
Heller, Annette Patsy Seigel *lawyer*

Warrensburg
Young, Mary Ann *lawyer*

MONTANA

Billings
Baugh, Gary Todd *lawyer*
Beiswanger, Gary Lee *lawyer*
Dalthorp, George Carrol *lawyer*
Gallinger, Lorraine D. *prosecutor*
Mercer, William W. *prosecutor*
Mitchell, Laura Ann *lawyer*
Murphy, Gregory Gerard *lawyer*
Thompson, James William *lawyer*
Toole, Bruce Ryan *retired lawyer*
Towe, Thomas Edward *lawyer*

Bozeman
Conover, Richard Corrill *lawyer*
Frohnmayer, John Edward *lawyer, legal scholar, ethicist, writer*
Nelson, Steven Dwayne *lawyer*
Wylie, Paul Richter, Jr., *lawyer*

Butte
Carlson, Robert M. *lawyer*
Peterson, John Leonard *lawyer, judge*

Cameron
Van Doren, Emerson Barclay *mediator*

Columbia Falls
Chisholm, Dean D. *lawyer*

Dillon
Suenram, Andy *lawyer*

Great Falls
Doherty, Steve *lawyer, former state legislator*
Gray, Orville *lawyer*
Hartelius, Channing Julius *lawyer*

Helena
Meadows, Judith Adams *law librarian, educator*

Kalispell
Lerner, Alan Jay *lawyer*

Missoula
Bowman, Jean Louise *lawyer, civic worker*
George, Alexander Andrew *lawyer*
Molloy, Donald William *lawyer*
Morales, Julio K. *lawyer*
Sullivan, Robert John *lawyer*
Willey, Charles Wayne *lawyer*

Whitehall
Bernard, Donald Ray *law educator, international business counselor*

NEBRASKA

Bellevue
Schroeder, Van Ace *lawyer*

Columbus
Schumacher, Paul Maynard *lawyer*

Crete
Panec, William Joseph *lawyer*

Fremont
Line, William Gunderson *lawyer*

Grand Island
Ahlschwede, Earl David *lawyer*

Lincoln
Alexis, Carl Odman *lawyer, earth scientist*
Atwood, Raymond Percival, Jr., *lawyer*
Frobom, LeAnn Larson *lawyer*
Guthery, John M. *lawyer*
Harnsberger, Richard Stephen *law educator*
Hayes, Jason William *lawyer, law educator*
Hewitt, James Watt *retired lawyer*
Johnson, Douglas Blaikie *lawyer*
Leiter, Richard Allen *law librarian, law educator*
Lichty, Warren Dewey, Jr., *lawyer*
Lyons, William Harry *law educator*
Ogle, Robbin Sue *criminal justice educator*
Perlman, Harvey Stuart *lawyer, educator*
Rembolt, James Earl *lawyer*
Rowe, David Winfield *lawyer*
Schizas, Jennifer Anne *law association administrator*
Smith, Richard Wendell *lawyer*
Zink, Walter Earl, II, *lawyer*

North Platte
Kay, Stephen William *lawyer*

Omaha
Achelpohl, Steven Edward *lawyer, political organization worker*
Barrett, Frank Joseph *lawyer, former insurance company executive*
Belian, Julia *law educator*
Brownrigg, John Clinton *lawyer*
Caporale, D. Nick *lawyer*
Dolan, James Vincent *lawyer*
Fairbanks, Charles F. *law educator*
Fitzgerald, James Patrick *lawyer*
Forbes, Franklin Sim *lawyer, educator*
Gleason, James Mullaney *lawyer, insurance executive*
Grant, John P. *lawyer*
Heavican, Michael G. *prosecutor*
Jansen, James Steven *lawyer*
Jenkins, Melvin Lemuel *lawyer*
Kelly, Robert Quaine *retired law librarian, educator*
Krutter, Forrest Nathan *lawyer*
Lamson, William Maxwell, Jr., *lawyer*
Longo, Amy L. *lawyer*
McCusker, Thomas J. *lawyer, insurance company executive*
Monaghan, Thomas Justin *former prosecutor*
O'Connor, Robert Edward, Jr., *lawyer*
Schropp, Tobin *lawyer*
Stenberg, Donald B. *lawyer*
von Bernuth, Carl W. *lawyer, diversified corporation executive*
Vosburg, Bruce David *lawyer*
Welch, James Douglas *lawyer, engineer*
Wells, Roger W. *lawyer, food products executive*

Valentine
O'Kief, W. Gerald *lawyer*

NEVADA

Las Vegas
Arum, Robert *lawyer, sports events promoter*
Bersi, Ann *lawyer*
Bogden, Daniel G. *prosecutor*
Bridges, B. Ried *lawyer*
Brown, Joseph Wentling *lawyer*
Bryan, Richard H. *lawyer, educator, former senator*
Chesnut, Carol Fitting *lawyer*
Curran, William P. *lawyer*
DeLury, Bernard Edward, Jr., *lawyer*
Eskin, Jeffrey Laurence *lawyer*
Faiss, Robert Dean *lawyer*
Goldberg, Aubrey *lawyer*
Goodwin, John Robert *lawyer, law educator, author*
Gross, Marvin Samuel *lawyer*
Gubler, John Gray *lawyer*
Hilbrecht, Norman Ty *lawyer*
Hill, Judith Deegan *retired lawyer*
Kirsch, Lynn *lawyer*
Landreth, Kathryn E. *lawyer*
Leleu, Jonathan Paul *lawyer*
Lovell, Carl Erwin, Jr., *lawyer*
Lukens, John Patrick *lawyer*
Mansfield, Lorraine J. *lawyer*
Miller, Robert Joseph *lawyer, former governor*
Nasky, H(arold) Gregory *lawyer*
Palmer, William Berry, II, *lawyer*
Schreiber, David M. *lawyer, judge*
Sklar, Alan Curtis *lawyer*
Solomon, Jack Avrum, Jr., *lawyer, automotive distributor, art dealer*
Stoberski, Michael Edward *lawyer*
Sturman, Glorida J. *lawyer*
Warren, Susan Carol *legal assistant, clerk, writer*
Wilson, Joseph Morris, III, *lawyer*

Reno
Flanagan, Norman Patrick *lawyer*
Fletcher, Douglas Charles *lawyer*
Guild, Clark Joseph, Jr., *lawyer*
Hibbs, Loyal Robert *lawyer*
Hill, Earl McColl *lawyer*
Hunterton, C. Stanley *lawyer*
Johnson, David D. *lawyer, game company executive*
Kent, Stephen Smiley *lawyer*
Marshall, Robert William *lawyer, rancher*
Pagni, Albert Frank *lawyer*
Robison, Kent Richard *lawyer*
Stumpf, Felix Franklin *law educator*
Walther, Steven T. *lawyer*

Sun Valley
Mumm, Christopher Eric *lawyer, county government official*

NEW HAMPSHIRE

Center Sandwich
Kilbourn, William Douglas, Jr., *law educator*

Concord
Chamberlain, Douglas Reginald *lawyer*
Chapman, William Lansing *lawyer*
Hilliard, Russell F. *lawyer*
Ilodcs, Paul William *lawyer, recording industry executive*
McLaughlin, Philip T. *lawyer, former state attorney general*
Potter, Fred Leon *lawyer, insurance company executive, consultant*
Rath, Thomas David *lawyer, former state attorney general*
Rines, Robert Harvey *lawyer, educator, composer*

Dover
Catalfo, Alfred, Jr. (Alfio Catalfo) *lawyer*

East Sullivan
Hoffman, John Ernest, Jr., *retired lawyer*

Hampton
DuChene, Todd Michael *lawyer*

Hanover
Gardner, Peter Jaglom *lawyer, publishing executive*
Lundquist, Weyman Ivan *lawyer*
Prager, Susan Westerberg *law educator, provost*

Hollis
Lumbard, Eliot Howland *lawyer, educator*

Hopkinton
Mekeel, Robert K. *lawyer*

Keene
Bell, Ernest Lorne, III, *retired lawyer*

Laconia
Martin, Willard Gordon, Jr., *lawyer*
Mitchell, Walter Louis, III, *lawyer*

Lebanon
Baker, William Arnold *lawyer*
Trunzo, Thomas Harold, Jr., *lawyer*

Littleton
Merritt, Thomas Butler *lawyer*

Lyme
Carmichael, Donald Scott *lawyer, business executive*

Manchester
Bussiere, Emile R. *lawyer*
Harvell, Michael Cleland *lawyer*
Hutchins, Peter Edward *lawyer*
Middleton, Jack Baer *lawyer*
Monson, John Rudolph *lawyer*
Nixon, David L. *lawyer*
Richards, Thomas H. *lawyer, arbitrator*
Stebbins, Henry Blanchard *lawyer*
Zachos, Kimon Stephen *lawyer*

Nashua
Hanson, Arnold Philip *retired lawyer*
Jette, Ernest Arthur *lawyer*

New Durham
Uttal, Susan *legal administrator*

New London
Baldwin, William Howard *lawyer, retired foundation executive*
Merwin, John David *retired lawyer, former governor*

Newport
Stamatakis, Carol Marie *lawyer, former state legislator*

Orford
Martin, Allen *retired lawyer*

Plainfield
Brown, Judith Olans *lawyer, educator*

Plymouth
Sawyer, Leonard Sylvester *retired lawyer*

Portsmouth
Abelson, Elias *lawyer*
Doleac, Charles Bartholomew *lawyer*
Lytton, William Bryan *lawyer*
Mason, J. William L. *lawyer*
Tober, Stephen Lloyd *lawyer*
Volk, Kenneth Hohne *lawyer*
Watson, Thomas Roger *lawyer*

Salem
Jones, Michael Earl *lawyer*

West Lebanon
Isaacs, Robert Charles *retired lawyer*

Windham
George, Kimberly Ann *lawyer*

NEW JERSEY

Allendale
Morris, Edward William, Jr., *lawyer*

Asbury Park
Rosenbloom, Norma Frisch *lawyer*

Atlantic City
Jacobson, Carole Renee *lawyer, educator*
Zlotnick, Norman Lee *lawyer*

Barnegat Light
Gibbs, Frederick Winfield *lawyer, communications company executive*

Bayonne
Olsen, Mary Ann *lawyer*

Belle Mead
Gladstone, Robert Albert *lawyer*

Bloomfield
Lordi, Katherine Mary *lawyer*
Weisert, Kent Albert Frederick *lawyer*

Boonton
Massler, Howard Arnold *lawyer*

Bridgewater
Ball, Owen Keith, Jr., *lawyer*
Dahling, Gerald Vernon *lawyer*
Feingold, Mark Howard *lawyer*
Linett, David *lawyer*

Budd Lake
Webb, John Gibbon, III, *lawyer*

Burlington
Domzalski, Kenneth Stanley *lawyer*
Tang, Paul C. *lawyer*

Caldwell
Castano, Gregory Joseph *lawyer*

Camden
Feinman, Jay Murray *law educator*
Furey, John J. *lawyer*
Kaden, Ellen Oran *lawyer, consumer products company executive*
Pomorski, Stanislaw *lawyer, educator*

Cape May Court House
Fineberg, Robert Alan *lawyer*

Carteret
Strassler, Marc A. *corporate lawyer*

Chatham
Jacobs, Andrew Robert *lawyer*
Warm, Elliot L. *lawyer*
Zegas, Alan Lee *lawyer*

Cherry Hill
Adler, John Herbert *lawyer, state legislator*
Garrigle, William Aloysius *lawyer*
Jozwiak, Steven Jay *lawyer*
Kole, Janet Stephanie *lawyer, writer, photographer*
Korin, Joel Benjamin *lawyer, educator*
Liebman, Emmanuel *lawyer*
Myers, Daniel William, II, *lawyer*
Rabil, Mitchell Joseph *lawyer*
Rose, Joel Alan *legal consultant*
Tomar, William *lawyer*

Chester
Pfaffenroth, Peter Albert *lawyer*

Clark
Barr, Jon-Henry *lawyer*

Cliffside Park
Swann, Barbara *lawyer*

Clifton
Feinstein, Miles Roger *lawyer*
Goldberger, Alan Steven *lawyer*
Lieb, L. Robert *lawyer*
Malamud, Alexander *lawyer, consultant*
Palma, Nicholas James *lawyer*

Collingswood
Martin, Burchard V. *lawyer*

Cranbury
Iatesta, John Michael *lawyer*

Cranford
McCreedy, Edwin James *lawyer*
Messing, Sara Virginia Drick *lawyer*

East Brunswick
Applebaum, Charles *lawyer*
Burns, Barbara *lawyer*

East Hanover
Davidson, Anne Stowell *lawyer*

Edgewater
Virelli, Louis James, Jr., *lawyer*

Edison
Behr, Omri M. *lawyer*
Vercammen, Kenneth Albert *lawyer, prosecutor*
Zhao, Jiwei *lawyer*

Englewood Cliffs
Cohen, Philip Gary *lawyer*
Heller, Hanes Ayres *lawyer*

Fairfield
Connell, William Terrence *lawyer, judge*

Flemington
Buchsbaum, Peter A. *lawyer*
Lenagh, Thomas Hugh *lawyer, financial advisor*
Miller, Louis H. *lawyer*
Sozansky, Michael William, Jr., *lawyer*

Florham Park
Calabrese, Arnold J. *lawyer*
Chase, Eric Lewis *lawyer*
Duquette, David Joseph, Jr., *lawyer, investor*
Hardin, William Downer *retired lawyer*
Kandravy, John *lawyer*
Laulicht, Murray Jack *lawyer*
Nittoly, Paul Gerard *lawyer*
O'Connell, Daniel F. *lawyer*
Reid, Charles Adams, III, *lawyer*
Witman, Leonard Joel *lawyer*

Fort Lee
Cox, Melvin Monroe *lawyer*

Freehold
Lijoi, Peter Bruno *lawyer*

Garfield
Herpst, Robert Dix *lawyer, optics and materials technology executive*

Glassboro
Jiao, Allan Y. *law educator*

Glen Ridge
Connolly, Joseph Thomas *lawyer, judge*

Glen Rock
Britcher, E. Drew *lawyer*

Greenwich
Lane, Mark *lawyer, educator, writer*

Hackensack
Bronson, Meridith J. *lawyer*
Caminiti, Donald Angelo *lawyer*
Greenberg, Steven Morey *lawyer*
Mullin, Patrick Allen *lawyer*
Navatta, Anna Paula *lawyer*
Peterson, Linda Ellen *lawyer*
Pollinger, William Joshua *lawyer*
Spiegel, Linda F. *lawyer*
Strull, James Richard *lawyer*
Vort, Robert A. *lawyer*

Hackettstown
Alper, Michael F. *lawyer, political consultant*
Kobert, Joel A. *lawyer*
Mulligan, Elinor Patterson *lawyer*

Haddonfield
Ewan, David E. *lawyer*
Iavicoli, Mario Anthony *lawyer*

Ho Ho Kus
Bryan, Thomas Lynn *lawyer, educator*

Hoboken
Sommers, George R. *lawyer*

Iselin
Barre, Steven Craig *lawyer*
Dornbusch, Arthur A., II, *lawyer*

Jersey City
McFadden, Rosemary Theresa *lawyer, financial services executive*
Nevins, Arthur Gerard, Jr., *lawyer*
Signorile, Vincent Anthony *lawyer*

Kearny
Dunne, Frederick R., Jr., *lawyer*

Kendall Park
Fisch, Joseph *lawyer*

Kenilworth
Connors, Joseph Conlin *lawyer, pharmaceutical executive*
Hoffman, John Fletcher *lawyer*

Keyport
Colmant, Andrew Robert *lawyer*

Lakewood
Bielory, Abraham Melvin *lawyer, financial executive*

Lawrenceville
Stark, Albert Maxwell *lawyer*

Liberty Corner
Apruzzese, Vincent John *lawyer*

Little Silver
Schmidt, Daniel Edward, IV, *lawyer, commercial arbitrator*

Livingston
Harris, Brian Craig *lawyer*
Klein, Peter Martin *lawyer, retired transportation company executive*
Nagel, Bruce H. *lawyer*
Rosenberg, Paul I. *lawyer*
Sukoneck, Ira David *lawyer*

Madison
Guigon, John V. *corporate lawyer*
McGrath, Joseph Patrick *lawyer*
Stein, Lawrence V *lawyer*

Mahwah
Bear, Larry Alan *retired lawyer, educator*

Manalapan
Stone, Fred Michael *lawyer*

Maplewood
Joseph, Susan B. *lawyer*

Marlton
Shabel, Norman *lawyer*

Mc Afee
Fogel, Richard *lawyer, educator*

Mendham
Tramutola, Joseph Louis *lawyer, educator*

Metuchen
Frizell, David J. *lawyer*

Millburn
Grosman, Alan M. *lawyer*
Madden, Edward George, Jr., *lawyer*

Milltown
Haws, Robert John *lawyer*

Montclair
Conrad, David Williams *lawyer*
Gutman, Richard Martin *lawyer*
Ward, Roger Coursen *lawyer*

Morris Plains
Johnson, Gregory L. *lawyer*
Mellinger, Louis Philip *lawyer*
Pluciennik, Thomas Casimir *lawyer, former assistant county prosecutor*

Morristown
Aspero, Benedict Vincent *lawyer*
Barba, Julius William *lawyer*
Berkley, Peter Lee *lawyer*
Bernstein, Jan Lenore *lawyer*
Bromberg, Myron James *lawyer*

Clemente, Mark Andrew *lawyer*
Gillen, James Robert *lawyer, insurance company executive*
Handler, Lauren E. *lawyer*
Herzberg, Peter Jay *lawyer*
Huettner, Richard Alfred *lawyer*
Humick, Thomas Charles Campbell *lawyer*
Hyland, William Francis *lawyer*
Jolles, Ira Hervey *lawyer*
Korf, Gene Robert *lawyer*
Kreindler, Peter Michael *lawyer*
Newman, John Merle *lawyer*
O'Grady, Dennis Joseph *lawyer*
Pellecchia, John Michael *lawyer*
Pollock, Stewart Glasson *lawyer, former state supreme court justice*
Rose, Robert Gordon *lawyer*
Sherman, Sandra Brown *lawyer*
Sperling, Joy Harmon *lawyer*
Stanton, Patrick Michael *lawyer*

Mountain Lakes
Daniel, Royal Thomas, III, *lawyer, engineer, accountant*

Mountainside
Helander, Robert Charles *lawyer*

New Brunswick
Birbauer, Richard Frank *lawyer*
Scott, David Rodick *lawyer, legal educator*
Yorke, Marianne *lawyer, real estate executive*

New Providence
Bernstein, Nadia J. *lawyer*
Cooper, R. John, III, *lawyer*
McCarthy, G. Daniel *lawyer*
Rawson, Richard J. *corporate lawyer*

New Vernon
Kushen, Allan Stanford *retired lawyer*

Newark
Askin, Frank *law educator*
Bizub, Johanna Catherine *law librarian*
Blumrosen, Alfred William *law educator*
Brescher, John B., Jr., *lawyer*
Christie, Christopher James *lawyer*
Corbin Walker, Karol *lawyer*
Costenbader, Charles Michael *lawyer*
Cummis, Clive Sanford *lawyer*
Day, Edward Francis, Jr., *lawyer*
Dee, Francis X. *lawyer*
Defeis, Elizabeth Frances *law educator, lawyer*
Del Tufo, Robert J. *lawyer, former US attorney, former state attorney general*
Eittreim, Richard MacNutt *lawyer*
English, Nicholas Conover *lawyer*
Freilich, Irvin Mayer *lawyer*
Gauster, Stephen Wilhelm *lawyer, corporate financial executive*
Haring, Eugene Miller *lawyer*
Hill, Richard Warren *lawyer*
Karp, Donald Mathew *lawyer, banker*
Kott, David Russell *lawyer*
Levine, Benjamin *lawyer*
Liftin, John Matthew M. *lawyer*
Maderer, William. F. *lawyer*
McGuire, William B(enedict) *lawyer*
Medvin, Alan York *lawyer*
Milita, Martin Joseph *lawyer*
Neuer, Philip David *lawyer, real estate consultant*
Paul, James Caverly Newlin *law educator, retired dean*
Radin, Steven S. *lawyer*
Reich, Laurence *lawyer*
Reilly, William Thomas *lawyer*
Robertson, William Withers *lawyer*
Slavitt, Ben J. *lawyer*
Storch, Susan Borowski *lawyer*
Tischman, Michael Bernard *lawyer*
Wyer, James Ingersoll *lawyer*
Zuckerman, Herbert Lawrence *lawyer*

Newton
Cox, William Martin *lawyer, educator*
Morgenstern, Robert Terence *lawyer*

Oakhurst
Widman, Douglas Jack *lawyer*

Ocean
Brown, Sanford Donald *lawyer*

Ocean City
Kyriazis, Arthur John (Athanasios Ioannis Kyriazis) *lawyer, biotechnologist*

Old Bridge
Downs, Thomas Edward, IV, *lawyer*

Oradell
Blakeslee, Edward Eaton *lawyer, insurance executive*
Mavroudis, John M. *lawyer*

Paramus
Blue, Catherine Anne *lawyer*
Gilbert, Stephen Alan *lawyer, organization executive*
Levy, Joseph *lawyer*

Parsippany
Deones, Jack E. *lawyer, business executive*
Gallagher, Jerome Francis, Jr., *lawyer*
Kallmann, Stanley Walter *lawyer*
Markus, Allan Lewis *lawyer*

Paterson
Mussano, Theodore Anthony *court services supervisor*

Pennington
Kozlowski, Thomas Joseph, Jr., *lawyer, trust company executive*

Piscataway
Lee, Barbara Anne *law educator, dean*
Smith, Bob *lawyer, state senator, educator*

Pitman
Cloues, Edward Blanchard, II, *lawyer*

Plainfield
Bober, Joanne L. *lawyer*

Pleasantville
Sinderbrand, David I. *lawyer*

Point Pleasant Beach
Herr, Philip Michael *lawyer, accountant*

Princeton
Ackourey, Peter Paul *lawyer*
Anderson, Ellis Bernard *retired lawyer, pharmaceutical company executive*
Beidler, Marsha Wolf *lawyer*
Bergman, Edward Jonathan *lawyer, educator*
Durst, Robert Joseph, II, *lawyer*
Greenman, Jane Friedlieb *lawyer, human resources executive*
Grossman, Allen Neil *lawyer*
Hill, James Scott *lawyer*
Karpoff, Michael Steven *lawyer*
Katzenbach, Nicholas deBelleville *lawyer*
Kenny, Robert *lawyer*
Miller, Richard Mark *lawyer*
Plevy, Arthur L. *lawyer*
Rose, Edith Sprung *retired lawyer*
Shaver, Philip Alcott *lawyer*
Stern, Bruce H. *lawyer*
Szwalbenest, Benedykt Jan *lawyer*
Theroux, William Gerard *lawyer*
Ufford, Charles Wilbur, Jr., *lawyer*

Princeton Junction
DiSciullo, Alan Michael *lawyer*

Rahway
Reldan, Robert Ronald *law educator, psychological consultant, poet*

Ramsey
Weber, Walter Winfield, Jr., *lawyer, director*

Randolph
Scheneck, Carol Ann *lawyer, educator*

Red Bank
Anderson, James Francis *lawyer*
Auerbach, Philip Gary *lawyer*
Hempstead, George H., III, *lawyer, diversified company executive*
Michaelson, Peter Lee *lawyer*
Neff, Robert Carey *lawyer*
Waldman, Daniel M. *lawyer*
Warshaw, Michael Thomas *lawyer*

Ridgewood
Harris, Micalyn Shafer *lawyer, educator, arbitrator, consultant, mediator*
Seigel, Jan Kearney *lawyer*
Trocano, Russell Peter *lawyer*

River Vale
Clemen, John Douglas *lawyer*

Rockaway
Bruno, Anthony D. *lawyer*

Roseland
Bennett, John K. *lawyer*
Besser, Albert Gordon *lawyer*
Danzis, Colin Michael *lawyer*
Eakeley, Douglas Scott *lawyer*
Eichler, Burton Lawrence *lawyer*
Foster, M. Joan *lawyer*
Hayden, Joseph A., Jr., *lawyer*
Levithan, Allen B. *lawyer*
Lowenstein, Alan Victor *lawyer*
McMahon, Edward Richard *lawyer*
Ploscowe, Stephen Allen *lawyer*
Positan, Wayne John *lawyer*
Schenkler, Bernard *lawyer*
Smith, Wendy Hope *lawyer*
Stern, Herbert Jay *lawyer*
Tarino, Gary Edward *lawyer*
Vanderbilt, Arthur T., II, *lawyer*
Wells, Theodore V., Jr., *lawyer*
Wovsaniker, Alan *lawyer, educator*

Roselle
Budanitsky, Sander *lawyer*

Saddle Brook
Pearlman, Peter Steven *lawyer*

Sayreville
Corman, Randy *lawyer*

Scotch Plains
Klock, John Henry *lawyer*
Kraus, Robert H. *lawyer*
Shaw, Alan *lawyer, corporate executive*

Secaucus
Fitzpatrick, Harold Francis *lawyer*
Goldstein, Ira J. *lawyer*

Ship Bottom
Shackleton, Richard James *lawyer, director*

Short Hills
Fast, Kenneth H. *lawyer*
Hazlehurst, Robert Purviance, Jr., *lawyer*
Marshall, John Patrick *lawyer*
Schirmeister, Charles F. *retired lawyer*
Siegfried, David Charles *retired lawyer*

Shrewsbury
Hopkins, Charles Peter, II, *lawyer*

Somers Point
Beakley, Robert Paul *lawyer*

Somerville
Dreier, William Alan *lawyer*
Hutcheon, Peter David *lawyer*
Ligorano, Michael Kenneth *lawyer*
O'Brian, Harold Samuel *lawyer*
Sponzilli, Edward George *lawyer*

South Orange
Delo, Ellen Sanderson *lawyer*

South Plainfield
Santoro, Frank Anthony *lawyer*

Sparta
McMeen, Elmer Ellsworth, III, *retired lawyer, guitarist*

Spring Lake
Pandolfe, John Thomas, Jr., *lawyer*

Springfield
Mytelka, Arnold Krieger *lawyer*

Summit
Caming, H. W. William *lawyer, consultant*
Cooper, John Weeks *lawyer*
Kenyon, Edward Tipton *lawyer*
Macioce, Frank Michael *lawyer, financial services company executive*
Pfaltz, Hugo Menzel, Jr., *lawyer*
Saffer, Judith Mack *lawyer*
Stone, Frank Bush *lawyer*
Woller, James Alan *lawyer*

Teaneck
Kaplan, Howard M(ark) *lawyer*
Shen, Michael *lawyer*

Tenafly
Spike, Michele Kahn *lawyer*

Toms River
Berman, Michael Barry *lawyer*

Trenton
Bigham, William J. *lawyer*
Caldwell, Wesley Stuart, III, *lawyer, lobbyist*
DeCotiis, Michael R. *lawyer*
Doherty, Robert Christopher *lawyer*
Jones, Dale Edwin *public defender*
Sterns, Joel Henry *lawyer*

Union
Bottitta, Joseph Anthony *lawyer*
Mark, Michael David *lawyer*
Suplee, Katherine Ann *lawyer*
Yoskowitz, Marlene *lawyer, educator*

Union City
Stier, Edwin H. *lawyer*

Ventnor City
Campbell, Thomas Douglas *lawyer, consultant*

Vineland
O'Neill, Joseph Dean *lawyer*

Voorhees
Suflas, Steven William *lawyer*

Wall
Nucciarone, A. Patrick *lawyer*

Warren
DiFrancesco, Donald T. *lawyer*
Jacobson, Gary Steven *lawyer*

Wayne
Fiedler, Laurie W. *lawyer*
Gelman, Jon Leonard *lawyer*
Harrington, Kevin Paul *lawyer*

West Orange
Cuozzi, William Francis, Jr., *lawyer*
Goldberg, Leonard Marvin *lawyer*
Gordon, Michael *lawyer*
Jordan, Leo John *lawyer*
Laves, Benjamin Samuel *lawyer*
McKinney, John Adams, Jr., *lawyer*
Richmond, Harold Nicholas *lawyer*

Westfield
Bobis, Daniel Harold *lawyer*

Westmont
Martin, Burchard Samuel *lawyer*

Whippany
Meola, Janice Grace *lawyer*

Willingboro
Tarver, Margaret Leggett *retired lawyer, forensic scientist*

Woodbridge
Barcan, Stephen Emanuel *lawyer*
Estis, Dennis Arnold *lawyer*

Woodcliff Lake
Falcon, Raymond Jesus, Jr., *lawyer*
Nachtigal, Patricia *lawyer*
Phillips, John C. *lawyer*

NEW MEXICO

Albuquerque
Bardacke, Paul Gregory *lawyer, former attorney general*
Beach, Arthur O'Neal *lawyer*
Bova, Vincent Arthur, Jr., *lawyer, consultant, photographer*
Cargo, David Francis *lawyer*
Chávez, Carmela Bernadette *lawyer, consultant*
Chavez, Martin Joseph *lawyer, mayor*
Farmer, Terry D(wayne) *lawyer*
Fish, Paul Mathew *lawyer*
Hart, Frederick Michael *law educator*
Iglesias, David Claudio *prosecutor*
Keleher, Michael Lawrence *lawyer*
Lawit, John Walter *lawyer*
Long, Stephen Carrel Mike *lawyer*
Loubet, Jeffrey W. *lawyer*
Moore, Charles Loyd *lawyer*
Moughan, Peter Richard, Jr., *lawyer*
O'Brien, Daniel J. *lawyer*
Paster, Janice Dubinsky *lawyer, former state legislator*
Ramo, Roberta Cooper *lawyer*
Rivera, Rhonda Rae *law professor, legal scholary lawyer, artibrator*
Roehl, Jerrald J. *lawyer*
Salazar, John Paul *lawyer*
Schuler, Alison Kay *lawyer*
Sisk, Daniel Arthur *lawyer*
Thornton, J. Duke *lawyer*
Tinnin, Robert Priest, Jr., *lawyer*
Weeth, George Wright *lawyer*

Bayard
Foy, Thomas Paul *lawyer, retired state legislator, retired bank executive*

Carlsbad
Byers, Matthew T(odd) *lawyer, educator*

Chama
McElhaney, James Willson *lawyer, educator, author, trial consultant*

Clovis
Skarda, Lynell Griffith *lawyer, banker*

Farmington
Moeller, Floyd Douglas *lawyer*
Morgan, Jack M. *lawyer*
Titus, Victor Allen *lawyer*

Las Cruces
Lindley, Jearl Ray *lawyer*
Lutz, William Lan *lawyer*
Murphy, Michael Terrence *lawyer*
Neumann, Rita Nunez *lawyer*
Winfree, Latham Thomas *law educator*

Placitas
Schoen, Stevan Jay *lawyer*

Roswell
Haines, Thomas David, Jr., *lawyer*
Kraft, Richard Lee *lawyer*
Nibert, Gregory James *lawyer*

Santa Fe
Abeles, Richard Alan *lawyer*
Brannen, Jeffrey Richard *lawyer*
Burton, John Paul (Jack Burton) *lawyer*
Carpenter, Richard Norris *retired lawyer*
Casey, Patrick Anthony *lawyer*
Coffield, Conrad Eugene *lawyer*
Cohen, Saul *lawyer*
Culbert, Peter V. *lawyer*
Dodds, Robert James, III, *lawyer*
Hickey, John Miller *lawyer*
Huffaker, Gregory Dorian, Jr., *lawyer*
Justice, Jack Burton *retired lawyer, writer*
McClaugherty, Joe L. *lawyer, educator*
Moll, Deborah Adelaide *lawyer*
Pound, John Bennett *lawyer*
Schwarz, Michael *lawyer*
Wolford, Richard Howard *lawyer*

Santa Rosa
Alcott, Colin C. *prosecutor*

Santa Teresa
McDonald, Charles Edward *lawyer*

Seneca
Monroe, Kendyl Kurth *retired lawyer*

Taos
Boles, David LaVelle *lawyer*

NEW YORK

Albany
Alessi, Robert Joseph *lawyer, real estate developer, pharmacist*
Baum, Joseph Thomas *lawyer*
Catalano, Jane Donna *lawyer*
Devine, Eugene Peter *lawyer*
Doherty, Glen Patrick *lawyer*
Dulin, Thomas N. *lawyer*
Fein, Scott Norris *lawyer*
Koff, Howard Michael *lawyer*
Laird, Edward DeHart, Jr., *lawyer*
Platkin, Richard M. *lawyer*
Powers, John Kieran *lawyer*
Provorny, Frederick Alan *lawyer, educator*
Scott, William Proctor, III, *lawyer*
Standard, Kenneth G. *lawyer*
Wallender, Michael Todd *lawyer*

Amagansett
Frankl, Kenneth Richard *retired lawyer*
Zychick, Joel David *lawyer*

Amherst
Pajak, David Joseph *lawyer, consultant*

Ardsley On Hudson
Stein, Milton Michael *lawyer*

Armonk
Boies, David *lawyer*
Lineen, Edward M. *lawyer, information technology executive*
Lowell, Stanley Herbert *retired lawyer*
Quinn, James W. *lawyer*
Wolff, Kurt Jakob *lawyer, director*

Astoria
Ghosal, Dino *lawyer, educator, social worker*

Atlantic Beach
Lore, Martin Maxwell *lawyer*

Babylon
Hennelly, Edmund Paul *lawyer, oil company executive*

Ballston Spa
Brown, Ifigenia Theodore *lawyer*

Bayside
Bernstein, Barry S. *lawyer*

Bedford
Atkins, Ronald Raymond *lawyer*

Bellerose
Dornagon, Mandy M. *lawyer*

Bethpage
Sanna, Richard Jeffrey *lawyer*

Binghamton
Anderson, Warren Mattice *lawyer*
Axtell, Clayton Morgan, Jr., *lawyer*
Gates, Gregory Ansel *lawyer*
Gerhart, Eugene Clifton *lawyer*
Gouldin, David Millen *lawyer*
Thompson, Carlton Frederick *lawyer*

Bridgehampton
Cummings, Richard M. *law educator, consultant, writer*

Bronx
Balka, Sigmund Ronell *lawyer*
Cornfield, Melvin *lawyer, university institute director*

Bronxville
Cutler, Kenneth Burnett *lawyer, investment company executive*
Falvey, Patrick Joseph *lawyer*
Fuller, David Otis, Jr., *lawyer*
Hagendorn, William H. *lawyer*

Brooklyn
Barabash, Claire *lawyer, special education administrator, psychologist*
Diamond, Murray J. *lawyer*
Kamins, Barry Michael *lawyer*
Karmel, Roberta Segal *lawyer, educator*
Maslow, Aaron D. *lawyer*
Mauskopf, Roslynn R. *prosecutor*
Onken, George Marcellus *retired lawyer*
Raskind, Leo Joseph *law educator*
Schussler, Theodore *lawyer, physician, educator, consultant*
Taylor, Shannon *lawyer, not-for-profit developer*
Vinegrad, Alan *prosecutor*

Buffalo
Barber, Janice Ann *lawyer*
Battle, Michael A. *lawyer*
Brydges, Thomas Eugene *lawyer*
Day, Donald Sheldon *lawyer*
Doren, Robert Alan *lawyer*
Freedman, Maryann Saccomando *lawyer*
Gardner, Arnold Burton *lawyer*
Gentile, Carmen James *lawyer*
Glanville, Robert Edward *lawyer*
Goldberg, Neil A. *lawyer*
Grasser, George Robert *lawyer, real estate consultant*
Greene, Robert Michael *lawyer*
Halpern, Ralph Lawrence *lawyer*
Hayes, David Ralph *lawyer*
Hayes, J. Michael *lawyer*
Headrick, Thomas Edward *lawyer, educator*
Herdzik, Arthur Alan *lawyer*
Jasen, Matthew Joseph *lawyer, state justice*
Kristoff, Karl W. *lawyer*
Manning, Kenneth Alan *lawyer*
Mattar, Lawrence Joseph *lawyer*
Mucci, Gary Louis *lawyer*
Newman, Stephen Michael *lawyer*
O'Donnell, Denise Ellen *lawyer*
Odza, Randall M. *lawyer*
O'Loughlin, Sandra S. *lawyer*
Pearson, Paul David *lawyer, arbitrator, mediator*
Rachlin, Lauren David *lawyer*
Runfola, Ross Thomas *lawyer, educator, writer, journalist, poet*
Salisbury, Eugene W. *lawyer, justice*
Segalla, Thomas Francis *lawyer*
Sherwood, Arthur Morley *lawyer*
Toohey, Philip S. *lawyer*
Wisbaum, Wayne David *lawyer*

Canaan
Pennell, William Brooke *lawyer*

Carle Place
Mulhern, Edwin Joseph *lawyer*

Carmel
Laporte, Cloyd, Jr., *lawyer, retired manufacturing executive*

Cazenovia
Shattuck, George Clement *retired lawyer*

Cedarhurst
Taubenfeld, Harry Samuel *lawyer*

Chestnut Ridge
Burns, Richard Owen *lawyer*

Clifton Park
Healy, Joseph Robert *lawyer*
Hilts, Earl T. *lawyer, government official, educator*

Cold Spring Harbor
Wallin, James Peter *lawyer*

Commack
Steindler, Walter G. *retired lawyer*

Corning
Becraft, Charles D., Jr., *lawyer*
Ughetta, William Casper *lawyer, manufacturing executive, director*

Cortland
Taylor, Leland Baridon *lawyer*

Croton On Hudson
Hoffman, Paul Shafer *lawyer*

Delhi
Hartmann, James M. *lawyer*

Delmar
Eldridge, Douglas Alan *lawyer*
Everett, James W., Jr., *lawyer*

Depew
Saleh, David John *lawyer*

Champion, Sara Stewart *lawyer*
Chapman, Shelley C. *lawyer*
Chapnick, David B. *lawyer*
Chappell, John Charles *lawyer*
Chase, Oscar G(ottfried) *law educator, consultant, author*
Chasey, Jacqueline *lawyer*
Chazen, Hartley James *lawyer*
Checkman, Neil Bruce *lawyer*
Chell, Beverly C. *lawyer, media company executive*
Chen, Wesley *lawyer*
Chiang, Yung Frank *law educator*
Chiarchiaro, Frank John *lawyer*
Chilstrom, Robert Meade *lawyer*
Chin, Sylvia Fung *lawyer*
Christensen, Henry, III, *lawyer*
Christy, Arthur Hill *lawyer*
Chromow, Sheri P. *lawyer*
Clapman, Peter Carlyle *lawyer, insurance company executive*
Clark, Carolyn Cochran *lawyer*
Clark, Celia Rue *lawyer*
Clark, Jonathan Montgomery *lawyer*
Clark, Merrell Edward, Jr., *lawyer*
Clary, Richard Wayland *lawyer*
Cliff, Walter Conway *lawyer*
Cobb, Peter Z. *lawyer*
Coffee, John Collins, Jr., *legal educator*
Cohen, Edmund Stephen *lawyer*
Cohen, Henry Rodgin *lawyer*
Cohen, Joshua Robert *lawyer*
Cohen, Robert Stephan *lawyer*
Cole, Charles Dewey, Jr., *lawyer*
Cole, Lewis George *lawyer*
Coleman, Jerome P. *lawyer*
Coll, John Peter, Jr., *lawyer*
Collins, J. Barclay, II, *lawyer, oil industry executive*
Collins, Wayne Dale *lawyer*
Conboy, Kenneth *lawyer, former federal judge*
Connolly, Kevin Jude *lawyer*
Connors, Peter J. *lawyer*
Conrad, Winthrop Brown, Jr., *lawyer*
Constantine, Jan Friedman *lawyer*
Conston, Henry Siegismund *lawyer*
Cook, Michael Lewis *lawyer*
Cooney, John Patrick, Jr., *lawyer*
Cooper, Michael Anthony *lawyer*
Cooper, Stephen Herbert *lawyer*
Corbin, Sol Neil *lawyer*
Cornell, John Robert *lawyer*
Cornish, Kelley A. *lawyer*
Costikyan, Edward N. *lawyer*
Cotter, James Michael *lawyer*
Cotton, Richard *lawyer*
Cowan, Wallace Edgar *lawyer*
Cowen, Edward S. *lawyer, consultant*
Cowen, Robert Nathan *lawyer*
Craft, Randal Robert, Jr., *lawyer*
Cramer, Edward Morton *lawyer, music company executive*
Crane, Benjamin Field *lawyer*
Crane, Roger Ryan, Jr., *lawyer*
Cranney, Marilyn Kanrek *lawyer*
Crary, Miner Dunham, Jr., *lawyer*
Crean, Peter Thomas *lawyer*
Creel, Thomas Leonard *lawyer*
Creenan, Katherine Heras *lawyer*
Critchlow, Charles Howard *lawyer*
Crough, Maureen M. *lawyer*
Crowell, Kenneth E. *lawyer, chemical engineer*
Cubitto, Robert J. *lawyer*
Cuiffo, Frank Wayne *lawyer*
Cuneo, Donald Lane *lawyer, educator*
Cunha, Mark Geoffrey *lawyer*
Cuomo, Mario Matthew *lawyer, former governor*
Curci-Gonzalez, Lucy *law librarian*
Curtis, Frank R. *lawyer*
Curtis, Susan Grace *lawyer*
Curtis, Susan M. *lawyer*
Czepiel, Lori Anne *lawyer*
Dallas, William Moffit, Jr., *lawyer*
Damashek, Philip Michael *lawyer*
D'Amato, Alfonse M. *lawyer, former senator*
Dankin, Peter Alfred *lawyer*
Dannhauser, Stephen J. *lawyer*
Dansky, Ira M. *lawyer*
Darrell, Norris, Jr., *lawyer*
Darrow, Jill E(llen) *lawyer*
David, Reuben *lawyer*
Davidson, George Allan *lawyer*
Davidson, Robert Bruce *lawyer*
Davis, Evan Anderson *lawyer*
Davis, Michael Steven *lawyer*
Davis, Richard Joel *lawyer, former government official*
Davis, Richard Ralph *lawyer*
Dean, Robert Stuart *lawyer*
Debo, Vincent Joseph *lawyer, director, manufacturing executive*
DeCarlo, Donald Thomas *lawyer, insurance company executive*
De Natale, Andrew Peter *lawyer*
DeNiro, Mary Lyn S. *lawyer*
Derzaw, Richard Lawrence *lawyer*
de Saint Phalle, Pierre Claude *lawyer*
De Sear, Edward Marshall *lawyer*
Dessen, Stanley Benjamin *lawyer, cosmetics company executive*
Detjen, David Wheeler *lawyer*
Diamant, Aviva F. *lawyer*
Diamond, Bernard Robin *lawyer*
Diamond, Stanley *lawyer*
DiBlasi, Gandolfo Vincent *lawyer*
Dichter, Barry Joel *lawyer*
Dies, George A. *lawyer*
Diskant, Gregory L. *lawyer*
Donahue, Anne de la Blanchetai *lawyer*
Donald, Norman Henderson, III, *lawyer*
Donovan, Richard Edward *lawyer*
Dopf, Glenn William *lawyer*
Dorkey, Charles E., III, *lawyer*
Dorsen, Norman *lawyer, educator*
Douchkess, George *retired lawyer*
Douglas, James McCrystal *lawyer*
Doyle, Joseph Anthony *retired lawyer*
Doyle, Paul Francis *lawyer*
Drebsky, Dennis Jay *lawyer*
Dreizen, Alison M. *lawyer*
Dresner, Byron *lawyer*
Dressel, Henry Francis *retired lawyer*
Dubin, James Michael *lawyer*
Duffy, Edmund Charles *lawyer*
Duffy, W. Leslie *lawyer*
Dundas, Philip Blair, Jr., *lawyer*
Dunham, Christopher Cooper *lawyer*
Dunham, Corydon Bushell *lawyer, broadcasting executive*
Dunham, Wolcott Balestier, Jr., *lawyer*
Dunn, M(orris) Douglas *lawyer*
Dunne, Gerard Francis *lawyer*
Dworkin, Ronald Myles *legal educator*
Eakins, William Shannon *lawyer*
Earle, Victor Montagne, III, *lawyer*
Easton, Reed W. *lawyer, law educator*
Edelbaum, Philip R. *lawyer*
Edelman, Paul Sterling *lawyer*
Edelson, Gilbert Seymour *lawyer*
Ehrenkranz, Joel S. *lawyer*
Einhorn, David Allen *lawyer*
Einstein, Steven Henry *investment banker, lawyer, accountant*
Eiseman, Neal Martin *lawyer*
Eisert, Edward Gaver *lawyer*
Eisgruber, Christopher L. *law educator*
Elsen, Sheldon Howard *lawyer*
Engel, Ralph Manuel *lawyer*
Entwistle, Andrew John *lawyer, consultant*
Epling, Richard Louis *lawyer*
Epstein, Jeremy G. *lawyer*
Epstein, Melvin *lawyer*
Epstein, Michael Alan *lawyer*
Ericson, Robert Walter *lawyer*
Estes, Richard Martin *lawyer*
Estreicher, Samuel *lawyer, educator*
Ettinger, John Riche *lawyer*
Evans, Douglas Hayward *lawyer*
Evans, John Thomas *lawyer*
Evans, Martin Frederic *lawyer*
Evarts, William Maxwell, Jr., *lawyer*
Faber, Peter Lewis *lawyer*
Fabricant, Robert Edmund *lawyer*
Fagen, Leslie Gordon *lawyer*
Fales, Haliburton, II, *lawyer*
Farber, Donald Clifford *lawyer, educator*
Farnsworth, Edward Allan *lawyer, educator*
Fasman, Zachary Dean *lawyer*
Fass, Peter Michael *lawyer, educator*
Faulkner, Walter Thomas *lawyer, director*
Feder, Arthur A. *lawyer, business executive*
Feder, Saul E. *lawyer*
Feerick, John David *law educator*
Feiman, Ronald Mark *lawyer*
Feintuch, Richard David *lawyer*
Feit, Glenn M. *lawyer*
Feldberg, Michael Svetkey *lawyer*
Felder, Myrna *lawyer*
Felder, Raoul Lionel *lawyer*
Feldman, Franklin *lawyer, printmaker*
Feldman, Mark *lawyer*
Feldman, Noah *law educator*
Feltenstein, Martha *lawyer*
Fenster, Marvin *lawyer, department store executive*
Fensterstock, Blair Courtney *lawyer*
Filler, Ronald Howard *lawyer*
Finch, Edward Ridley, Jr., *lawyer, diplomat, writer, educator*
Fink, Robert Steven *lawyer, writer, educator*
Finkelstein, Allen Lewis *lawyer*
Finkelstein, Bernard *lawyer*
Finkelstein, Ira Allen *lawyer*
Finkelstein, Nancy R. *lawyer*
Finkelstein, Stuart M. *lawyer*
Finnerty, Joseph Gregory, III, *lawyer*
Fiorilla, John Leopoldo *lawyer, investment company executive*
First, Harry *law educator*
Fishbein, Peter Melvin *lawyer*
Fisher, Ann Bailen *lawyer*
Fisher, Robert I. *lawyer*
Fishman, Ellen Beth *lawyer*
Fishman, Fred Norman *lawyer*
Fiske, Robert Bishop, Jr., *lawyer*
Fitzpatrick, Joseph Mark *lawyer*
Flanagan, Deborah Mary *lawyer*
Fleischer, Arthur, Jr., *lawyer*
Fleischman, Edward Hirsh *lawyer, consultant*
Fleischman, Keith Martin *lawyer*
Fletcher, Anthony L. *lawyer*
Flint, George Squire *lawyer*
Flom, Joseph Harold *lawyer, director*
Fodor, Susanna Serena *lawyer*
Fogelman, Martin *lawyer, law educator*
Folkenflik, Max *lawyer*
Foncillas, Ignacio *lawyer*
Forger, Alexander Darrow *lawyer*
Forstadt, Joseph Lawrence *lawyer*
Fortenbaugh, Samuel Byrod, III, *lawyer*
Foster, David Lee *lawyer*
Fox, Donald Thomas *lawyer*
Franck, Thomas Martin *law educator*
Frank, Lloyd *lawyer, retired chemical company executive*
Frankel, Sandor *lawyer, author*
Franklin, Blake Timothy *lawyer*
Frazza, George S. *lawyer, business executive*
Fredericks, Wesley Charles, Jr., *lawyer*
Fredericks, William Curtis *lawyer*
Freedman, Gerald M. *lawyer*
Freeman, David John *lawyer*
Freilicher, Morton *lawyer, educator*
French, John, III, *lawyer, director*
Freund, Fred A. *retired lawyer*
Frey, Andrew Lewis *lawyer*
Freyer, Dana Hartman *lawyer*
Fricklas, Michael David *lawyer*
Fried, Arthur *lawyer*
Fried, Burton Theodore *lawyer*
Fried, Donald David *lawyer*
Friedlander, Jeffrey D. *lawyer*
Friedman, Alan Roy *lawyer*
Friedman, Bart *lawyer*
Friedman, Samuel Selig *lawyer*
Friedman, Victor Stanley *lawyer*
Friedman, Wilbur Harvey *lawyer*
Frisch, Harry David *lawyer, consultant, investment company executive*
Frommer, William S. *lawyer*
Frost, William Lee *lawyer*
Fry, Morton Harrison, II, *lawyer*
Fuzesi, Stephen, Jr., *lawyer, communications executive*
Gabay, Donald *lawyer*
Galant, Herbert Lewis *lawyer*
Gallagher, Brian John *lawyer*
Gamboni, Ciro Anthony *lawyer*
Gambro, Michael S. *lawyer*
Gans, Walter Gideon *lawyer*
Ganz, David L. *lawyer*
Ganz, Howard Laurence *lawyer*
Garcia, Angela G. *lawyer*
Garfinkel, Barry Herbert *lawyer*
Garfunkel, Alan J. *lawyer*
Garland, Sylvia Dillof *lawyer*
Garson, Gary Wayne *lawyer*
Garvey, Richard Anthony *retired lawyer*
Gassel, Philip Michael *lawyer*
Gay, Faith E. *lawyer, educator*
Gelb, Judith Anne *lawyer*
Gelfman, Peter Trustman *lawyer*
Geltzer, Robert Lawrence *lawyer, former retail executive, arbitrator, mediator*
Genova, Diane Melisano *lawyer*
Gerard, Whitney Ian *lawyer*
Getnick, Neil Victor *lawyer*
Gibbs, Lippman Martin *lawyer*
Gibson, William S. *lawyer*
Gifford, William C. *lawyer, educator*
Gill, E. Ann *lawyer*
Gillers, Stephen *law educator, university official*
Gillespie, George Joseph, III, *lawyer*
Gitter, Max *lawyer*
Glekel, Jeffrey Ives *lawyer*
Glickstein, Steven *lawyer*
Goetz, Maurice Harold *lawyer*
Gold, Simeon *lawyer*
Gold, Stuart Walter *lawyer*
Goldberg, David *lawyer, law educator*
Goldberg, Jay *lawyer*
Golden, Arthur F. *lawyer*
Goldfein, Shepard *lawyer*
Goldman, Charles Norton *retired corporate lawyer*
Goldman, Lawrence Saul *lawyer*
Goldman, Louis Budwig *lawyer*
Goldman, Marvin Gerald *lawyer*
Goldstein, Charles Arthur *lawyer*
Goldstein, Eugene E. *lawyer*
Goldstein, Howard Sheldon *lawyer*
Goldstein, Howard Warren *lawyer*
Goldstein, Marcia Landweber *lawyer*
Goldstein, Sandra Cara *lawyer*
Golick, Toby *law educator, legal services administrator*
Goodale, James Campbell *lawyer, media executive, television producer/host*
Goodfriend, Herbert Jay *lawyer*
Goodhartz, Gerald *law librarian*
Goodman, Gary A. *lawyer*
Goodridge, Allan D. *lawyer*
Goodwillie, Eugene William, Jr., *lawyer*
Goott, Alan F(ranklin) *lawyer*
Gordon, Michael Mackin *lawyer*
Gordon, Stephen Louis *lawyer*
Gottesman, A(rthur) Edward *lawyer*
Gotthoffer, Lance *lawyer*
Gotts, Ilene Knable *lawyer*
Grad, Frank Paul *law educator, lawyer*
Graff, George Leonard *lawyer*
Graham, Jul Eliot *lawyer, educator*
Graham, Philip L., Jr., *lawyer*
Granoff, Gary Charles *lawyer, investment company executive*
Grassi, Joseph F. *lawyer, mediator, arbitrator*
Green, Alvin *lawyer, consultant*
Green, Jonathan David *lawyer*
Green, Robert S. *lawyer*
Greenawalt, Robert Kent *lawyer, law educator*
Greenawalt, William Sloan *lawyer*
Greenbaum, Maurice Coleman *lawyer*
Greenberg, Daniel Herbert *lawyer*
Greenberg, Gary Howard *lawyer*
Greenberg, Ira George *lawyer*
Greenberg, Jack *lawyer, law educator*
Greenberg, Philip Alan *lawyer*
Greenberger, Howard Leroy *lawyer, educator*
Greene, Bernard Harold *lawyer*
Greenman, Frederick F., Jr., *lawyer*
Greenman, Paula S. *lawyer*
Greenspon, Robert Alan *lawyer*
Greer, Allen Curtis, II, *lawyer, investment management executive*
Greilsheimer, James Gans *lawyer*
Grew, Robert Ralph *retired lawyer*
Gross, Karen Charal *lawyer*
Gross, Steven Ross *lawyer*
Grossman, Dan Steven *lawyer*
Grosz, Morton Eric *lawyer*
Grubin, Sharon E. *lawyer*
Grubman, Allen J. *lawyer*
Gruen, Michael Stephan *lawyer*
Gruson, Michael *lawyer*
Guedry, James Walter *lawyer, retired paper corporation executive*
Guggenheim, Martin Franklin *law educator, lawyer*
Gupta, Paul R. *lawyer*
Gurfein, Richard Alan *lawyer*
Gustafson, Albert Katsuaki *lawyer, engineer*
Habian, Bruce George *lawyer*
Hackett, Kevin R. *lawyer*
Haig, Robert Leighton *lawyer*
Haims, Bruce David *lawyer*
Haje, Peter Robert *lawyer*
Halberstam, Malvina *law educator, lawyer*
Halket, Thomas D(aniel) *lawyer*
Halliday, Joseph William *lawyer*
Halperin, Richard E. *lawyer, holding company executive*
Hamburg, Charles Bruce *lawyer*
Hamel, Rodolphe *retired lawyer, pharmaceutical executive*
Hamm, David Bernard *lawyer*
Handelsman, Lawrence Marc *lawyer*
Handler, Arthur M. *lawyer*
Hanson, Jean Elizabeth *lawyer*
Harbison, James Wesley, Jr., *lawyer*
Harley, Colin Emile *lawyer*
Harlow, Ruth *lawyer*
Harnik, Hans *lawyer*
Harper, Emery Walter *lawyer*
Harper, Gerard Edward *lawyer*
Harris, Joel B. (Joel Bruce Harris) *lawyer*
Harrison, S. David *lawyer*
Hart, Joseph Thomas Campbell *lawyer*
Hart, Robert M. *lawyer*
Hartmann, Carl Joseph *lawyer, consultant*
Hartnick, Alan Jay *lawyer, law educator*
Hartzell, Andrew Cornelius, Jr., *retired lawyer*
Hassan, Ibne *lawyer, diplomat, political philosopher, international strategist*
Hauser, Rita Eleanore Abrams *lawyer*
Hawke, Roger Jewett *lawyer*
Hayden, Raymond Paul *lawyer*
Hayes, Gerald Joseph *lawyer*
Hayman, Linda C. *lawyer*
Head, Elizabeth *lawyer*
Healy, Harold Harris, Jr., *lawyer*
Healy, Nicholas Joseph *lawyer, educator*
Hearn, George Henry *lawyer, steamship corporate executive*
Heftler, Thomas E. *lawyer*
Heineman, Andrew David *retired lawyer*
Heisler, Stanley Dean *lawyer*
Heitner, Kenneth Howard *lawyer*
Heleniak, David William *lawyer, educator*
Hellenbrand, Samuel Henry *lawyer*
Henderson, Donald Bernard, Jr., *lawyer*
Hendry, Andrew Delaney *lawyer, consumer products company executive*
Henkel, David Seabury *retired lawyer*
Henkin, Louis *lawyer, law educator*
Henry, Sally McDonald *lawyer*
Herbst, Todd L. *lawyer*
Herlihy, Edward D. *lawyer*
Herman, Kenneth Beaumont *lawyer*
Herold, Karl Guenter *lawyer*
Hersh, Robert Michael *lawyer, insurance company executive*
Hershcopf, Gerald Thea *lawyer*
Herz, Andrew Lee *lawyer*
Herzeca, Lois Friedman *lawyer*
Hiden, Robert Battaile, Jr., *lawyer*
Higgs, John H. *lawyer*
Hill, Alfred *lawyer, educator*
Hirsch, Barry *lawyer*
Hirsch, Jerome S. *lawyer*
Hirschfeld, Michael *lawyer*
Hirshfield, Stuart *lawyer*
Hirshowitz, Melvin Stephen *lawyer*
Hodes, Robert Bernard *lawyer*
Hoffman, David Nathaniel *lawyer*
Hoffman, Mathew *lawyer*
Hoffmann, Brian *lawyer*
Hoffmann, Elinor R. *lawyer*
Holley, Steven Lyon *lawyer*
Hollyer, A(rthur) Rene *lawyer*
Holman, Bud George *lawyer*
Holsenbeck, G(eorge) Penn *lawyer*
Holtzman, Elizabeth *lawyer*
Holtzmann, Howard Marshall *lawyer, judge*
Hooker, Wade Stuart, Jr., *lawyer*
Horowitz, Raymond J. *lawyer, director*
Horwitz, Ethan *lawyer*
Howe, Richard Rives *lawyer*
Hritz, George F. *lawyer*
Hruska, Alan J. *lawyer*
Huck, L. Francis *lawyer*
Hudspeth, Stephen Mason *lawyer*
Huffman, Richard Lee *lawyer*
Hughes, Kevin Peter *lawyer*
Huhs, John I. *international lawyer*
Hulbert, Richard Woodward *lawyer*
Hull, Philip Glasgow *lawyer*
Hupper, John Roscoe *retired lawyer*
Hurlock, James Bickford *retired lawyer*
Huttner, Constance S. *lawyer*
Hyde, David Rowley *lawyer*
Hyman, Jerome Elliot *lawyer*
Hynes, Patricia Mary *lawyer*
Iannuzzi, John Nicholas *lawyer, author, educator*
Immergut, Mel M. *lawyer*
Ingram, Samuel William, Jr., *lawyer*
Insel, Michael S. *lawyer*
Intriligator, Marc Steven *lawyer*
Isaacson, Allen Ira *lawyer*
Iseman, Joseph Seeman *lawyer*
Isquith, Fred Taylor *lawyer*
Issler, Harry *lawyer*
Itzkoff, Norman Jay *lawyer*
Ivanick, Carol W. Trencher *lawyer*
Jackson, Thomas Gene *lawyer*
Jacob, Edwin J. *lawyer*
Jacobs, Arnold Stephen *lawyer*
Jacobs, Paul *lawyer*
Jacobs, Robert Alan *lawyer*
Jacobson, Jerold Dennis *lawyer*
Jaffe, Alan Steven *lawyer*
Jaffe, Mark M. *lawyer*
Janklow, Morton Lloyd *lawyer, literary agent*
Janowitz, James Arnold *lawyer*
Jasper, Seymour *lawyer*
Jassy, Everett Lewis *lawyer*
Jerome, John James *lawyer*
Jeydel, Richard K. *lawyer*
Jiménez, Emilio *corporate lawyer*
Jinnett, Robert Jefferson *lawyer*
Jock, Paul F., II, *lawyer*
Joffe, Robert David *lawyer*
Johnson, Jeh Charles *lawyer*
Jones, Douglas Wiley *lawyer*
Jordan, Vernon Eulion, Jr., *lawyer, former association official*
Joseph, Ellen R. *lawyer*
Joseph, Gregory Paul *lawyer*
Joseph, Leonard *lawyer*
Josephson, William Howard *lawyer*
Juceam, Robert E. *lawyer*
Kaden, Lewis B. *law educator, lawyer*
Kafin, Robert Joseph *lawyer*
Kahn, Alan Edwin *lawyer*
Kahn, Anthony F. *lawyer*
Kailas, Leo George *lawyer*
Kalikow, Richard R. *lawyer*
Kalish, Arthur *lawyer*
Kalish, Myron *lawyer*
Kallen, Laurel Lynn *prosecutor*
Kambour, Annaliese Spofford *lawyer, media company executive*
Kamin, Sherwin *lawyer*
Kaminsky, Arthur Charles *lawyer*
Kandel, William Lloyd *lawyer, mediator, arbitrator, educator, writer*
Kane, Alice Theresa *lawyer*
Kanrek, Victoria Jane *lawyer*
Kanter, Carl Irwin *retired lawyer*
Kanter, Stacy J. *lawyer*
Kaplan, Carl Eliot *lawyer*
Kaplan, Mark Norman *lawyer*
Kaplan, Susan *lawyer*
Kaplen, Michael V. *lawyer*
Karasz, Peter *lawyer*
Karatz, William Warren *lawyer*
Karls, John Spencer *lawyer, accountant*
Kartiganer, Joseph *retired lawyer*
Kasowitz, Marc Elliot *lawyer*
Kassebaum, John Philip *lawyer*
Katsh, Salem Michael *lawyer*
Katsoris, Constantine Nicholas *lawyer, consultant*
Katz, Jerome Charles *lawyer*
Katz, Robert James *lawyer*
Katz, Ronald Scott *lawyer*
Kaufman, Arthur Stephen *lawyer*

Schwartz, Barry Fredric *lawyer, diversified holding company executive*
Schwartz, Carol Vivian *lawyer*
Schwartz, Herbert Frederick *lawyer*
Schwartz, Marvin *lawyer*
Schwartz, Renee Gerstler *lawyer*
Schwartz, William *lawyer, educator*
Schwind, Michael Angelo *law educator*
Sederbaum, Arthur David *lawyer*
Seidel, Selvyn *lawyer, educator*
Seidler, B(ernard) Alan *lawyer*
Seifert, Thomas Lloyd *lawyer*
Seiff, Eric A. *lawyer*
Seitelman, Mark Elias *lawyer*
Seligman, Frederick *lawyer*
Seltzer, Richard C. *lawyer*
Senzel, Martin Lee *lawyer*
Serbaroli, Francis J. *lawyer, educator, writer*
Serchuk, Ivan *lawyer*
Serota, James Ian *lawyer*
Setrakian, Berge *lawyer*
Seward, George Chester *lawyer*
Seymour, Everett Hedden, Jr., *lawyer*
Shainwald, Sybil *lawyer*
Shapiro, Isaac *lawyer*
Shapiro, Steven R. *legal association administrator*
Shargel, Gerald L. *lawyer*
Sharpe, Robert Francis, Jr., *lawyer*
Shaw, Theodore M. *legal association administrator*
Shea, Edward Emmett *lawyer, educator, author*
Shea, James William *lawyer*
Shechtman, Ronald H. *lawyer*
Sheehan, Robert C. *lawyer*
Shenker, Joseph C. *lawyer*
Shepard, Robert M. *lawyer, investment banker, engineer*
Shepherd, John Michael *lawyer*
Shields, Craig M. *lawyer*
Shientag, Florence Perlow *lawyer*
Shinkle, John Thomas *lawyer*
Shorter, James Russell, Jr., *lawyer*
Shoss, Cynthia Renée *lawyer*
Shyer, John D. *lawyer*
Sidamon-Eristoff, Constantine *lawyer*
Siegel, Jeffrey Norton *lawyer*
Siegel, Stanley *lawyer, educator*
Siffert, John Sand *lawyer, educator, writer*
Sigmond, Carol Ann *lawyer*
Silberberg, Richard Howard *lawyer*
Silkenat, James Robert *lawyer*
Siller, Stephen I. *lawyer*
Silverberg, Michael Joel *lawyer*
Silverman, Arthur Charles *lawyer*
Silverman, Leon *lawyer*
Silverman, Moses *lawyer*
Simmons, Peter Lawrence *lawyer*
Simone, Joseph R. *lawyer*
Simons, Albert, III, *lawyer*
Sinsheimer, Warren Jack *lawyer*
Siskind, Arthur *lawyer, director*
Siskind, Donald Henry *lawyer*
Skigen, Patricia Sue *lawyer*
Skirnick, Robert Andrew *lawyer*
Skolnick, Jerome H. *law educator*
Sladkus, Harvey Ira *lawyer*
Slotnick, Barry Ivan *lawyer*
Small, Jonathan Andrew *lawyer*
Smalley, David Vincent *lawyer*
Smith, Bradley Youle *lawyer*
Smith, Edward Paul, Jr., *lawyer*
Smith, James Walker *lawyer*
Smith, Robert Everett *lawyer*
Smith, Thomas A. *lawyer, investment company executive*
Smith, Thomas Ramsaur, Jr., *lawyer*
Smith, Vincent Milton *lawyer, designer, Feng Shui lecturer, consultant, writer*
Smoak, Evan L. *lawyer*
Snow, Charles *lawyer*
Sokoloff, Audrey L. *lawyer*
Solomon, Stephen L. *lawyer*
Sorkin, Ira Lee *lawyer*
Sorkin, Laurence Truman *lawyer*
Sorter, George Hans *accounting and law educator, consultant*
Sovern, Michael Ira *law educator*
Soyster, Margaret Blair *lawyer*
Spanbock, Maurice Samuel *lawyer*
Spatt, Robert Edward *lawyer*
Spear, Harvey M. *lawyer*
Spelfogel, Evan J. *lawyer, educator*
Sperling, Allan George *lawyer*
Spiegel, Jerrold Bruce *lawyer*
Spillane, Dennis Kevin *lawyer*
Squire, Walter Charles *lawyer*
Staffaroni, Robert J. *lawyer*
Stamm, Charles H. *lawyer*
Starer, Brian Douglas *lawyer*
Stark, Robert J. *lawyer*
Stathis, Nicholas John *lawyer*
Stecher, Esta E. *lawyer, investment company executive*
Stein, Stephen William *lawyer*
Steinberg, Howard Eli *lawyer, diversified financial services company executive*
Stephenson, Alan Clements *lawyer*
Stern, Peter R. *lawyer*
Sternman, Joel W. *lawyer*
Steuer, Richard Marc *lawyer*
Stever, Donald Winfred *lawyer*
Stewart, Richard Burleson *law educator*
Stoll, Neal Richard *lawyer*
Stone, David Philip *lawyer*
Stone, Merrill Brent *lawyer*
Stratakis, Christ *lawyer*
Strauss, Gary Joseph *lawyer*
Strauss, Peter L(ester) *law educator*
Strickon, Harvey Alan *lawyer*
Strom, Milton Gary *lawyer*
Strossen, Nadine *legal association administrator, law educator*
Strum, Jay Gerson *lawyer*
Struve, Guy Miller *lawyer*
Stuart, Alice Melissa *lawyer*
Stumer, Mark Bradley *lawyer, business consultant, restaurateur*
Sturman, Deborah Muscha *lawyer, columnist*
Sugarman, Irwin J. *lawyer*
Sugarman, Robert Gary *lawyer*
Sullivan, Irene A. *lawyer*
Sun, Jeffrey C. *legal educator*
Sussman, Alexander Ralph *lawyer*
Sutherland, Susan J. *lawyer*
Swardenski, Jay Gordon *lawyer*
Sweeney, Thomas Joseph, Jr., *lawyer*
Swire, James Bennett *lawyer*
Tancredi, Laurence Richard *law and psychiatry educator, physician*
Tarnoff, Jerome *lawyer*
Taylor, Willard B. *lawyer*
Tehan, John Bashir *lawyer*
Teich, Howard Bernard *lawyer, activist, public affairs specialist*
Teiman, Richard B. *lawyer*
Telsey, Suzanne Lisa *lawyer*
Teplen, Philip H. *lawyer*
Terrell, J. Anthony *lawyer*
Terry, Frederick Arthur, Jr., *lawyer*
Terry, James Joseph, Jr., *lawyer*
Testa, Michael Harold *lawyer*
Thackeray, Jonathan E. *lawyer*
Thalacker, Arbie Robert *lawyer, director*
Thomas, Jeremiah Lindsay, III, *lawyer*
Thomas, Robert Morton, Jr., *lawyer*
Thompson, Loran Tyson *lawyer*
Thoyer, Judith Reinhardt *lawyer*
Thurston, Sally A. *lawyer*
Tiano, Linda V. *lawyer*
Tilewick, Robert *lawyer*
Tillinghast, David Rollhaus *lawyer*
Todd, Ronald Gary *lawyer*
Toumey, Donald Joseph *lawyer*
Tract, Marc Mitchell *lawyer*
Tramontine, John Orlando *retired lawyer*
Traverso, Anthony A. *lawyer*
Treadway, James Curran Erik Corbett *lawyer, investment company executive, former government official*
Tritter, Daniel F. *lawyer, writer*
Tulchin, David Bruce *lawyer*
Turner, E. Deane *lawyer*
Underberg, Mark Alan *lawyer*
Uram, Gerald Robert *lawyer*
Urowsky, Richard J. *lawyer*
Vachss, Andrew Henry *lawyer, writer, juvenile justice and child abuse consultant*
Valente, Peter Charles *lawyer*
Vanni, Robert John *lawyer*
Varet, Michael A. *lawyer*
Vassallo, Edward E. *lawyer*
Vassil, John Charles *lawyer*
Veasey, Eugene Norman *lawyer, retired state supreme court chief justice*
Vega, Matias Alfonso *lawyer*
Vernon, Darryl Mitchell *lawyer*
Versfelt, David Scott *lawyer*
Victor, A. Paul *lawyer*
Viener, John D. *lawyer*
Vig, Vernon Edward *lawyer*
Viktora, Richard Emil *lawyer*
Vitkowsky, Vincent Joseph *lawyer*
Vittor, Kenneth Mark *lawyer*
Vladeck, Judith Pomarlen *lawyer*
Vogel, Howard Stanley *lawyer*
von Mehren, Robert Brandt *retired lawyer*
Vrancik, Barbara A. *lawyer*
Wachsman, Harvey Frederick *lawyer, neurosurgeon*
Wachtel, Norman Jay *lawyer*
Wagner, Barry J. *lawyer*
Wailand, George *lawyer*
Wainwright, Carroll Livingston, Jr., *lawyer*
Waks, Jay Warren *lawyer*
Wald, Bernard Joseph *lawyer*
Walden, Janet C. *lawyer*
Waldman, Seymour Morton *lawyer*
Wall, Charles R. *lawyer*
Wall, Duane *lawyer*
Wallace, Nora Ann *lawyer*
Wallace, Walter C. *lawyer, government official*
Wallach, Eric Jean *lawyer*
Wallance, Gregory J. *lawyer*
Walpin, Gerald *lawyer*
Wang, Albert Huai-En *lawyer*
Ward, Sarah M. *lawyer*
Warden, John L. *lawyer*
Warren, William Bradford *lawyer*
Warshauer, Irene C. *lawyer*
Washburn, David Thacher *lawyer*
Watanabe, Roy Noboru *lawyer*
Watson, Richard Allen *lawyer*
Watson, Solomon Brown, IV, *lawyer, business executive*
Watts, David Eide *lawyer*
Weiksner, Sandra S. *lawyer*
Weiler, Joseph *law educator*
Weinberg, Herschel Mayer *lawyer*
Weinberger, Harold Paul *lawyer*
Weiner, Andrew Jay *lawyer*
Weiner, Earl David *lawyer*
Weiner, Stephen Arthur *lawyer*
Weingarten, Rhonda *lawyer*
Weinrich, Johnathan Edward *lawyer*
Weinschel, Alan Jay *lawyer*
Weinstock, Leonard *lawyer*
Weisbrod, Carl *lawyer, public official*
Weiss, Jonathan Arthur *lawyer*
Weiss, Lawrence N. *lawyer*
Weiss, Melvyn I. *lawyer*
Weitz, Harvey *lawyer, educator*
Weld, Jonathan Minot *lawyer*
Wellington, Harry Hillel *lawyer, educator*
Wender, Ira Tensard *lawyer*
Werner, Robert L. *lawyer, consultant*
Wesely, Edwin Joseph *lawyer*
West, Stephen Kingsbury *lawyer, director*
Wexelbaum, Michael *lawyer*
White, Harry Edward, Jr., *lawyer*
White, John Patrick *lawyer*
Whitmer, Frederick Lee *lawyer*
Whoriskey, Robert Donald *lawyer*
Wiegley, Roger Douglas *lawyer*
Wilcox, John Caven *lawyer, corporate consultant*
Wildes, Leon *lawyer, educator*
Wilkinson, John Hart *lawyer*
Will, Alfred Joseph *lawyer*
Williamson, Douglas Franklin, Jr., *lawyer*
Willis, William Ervin *lawyer*
Wilson, Paul Holliday, Jr., *lawyer*
Windels, Paul, Jr., *lawyer*
Winfield, Richard Neill *lawyer*
Wing, John Russell *lawyer*
Winslade, Thomas Edwin *lawyer*
Winterer, Philip Steele *lawyer*
Wise, Aaron Noah *lawyer*
Witkin, Eric Douglas *lawyer*
Witmeyer, John Jacob, III, *lawyer*
Witzel, Steven M. *lawyer*
Wohl, Frank Harold *lawyer*
Wolfe, James Ronald *lawyer*
Wolff, Jesse David *lawyer*
Wolff, Margaret Louise *lawyer*
Wolkoff, Eugene Arnold *lawyer*
Wollan, Eugene *lawyer*
Wollman, Eric *lawyer*
Wolson, Craig Alan *lawyer*
Wood, David Clarence *lawyer*
Wood, Joshua Warren, III, *lawyer, alternative dispute resolution executive*
Worenklein, Jacob Joshua *lawyer*
Wray, Cecil, Jr., *lawyer*
Wrubel, Barbara *lawyer, educator, former editor*
Wu, Robin Chi Ching *lawyer*
Wulf, Melvin Lawrence *lawyer*
Wyckoff, E. Lisk, Jr., *lawyer*
Yamin, Michael Geoffrey *lawyer*
Yelenick, Mary Therese *lawyer*
Yerman, Fredric Warren *lawyer*
Yodowitz, Edward Jay *lawyer*
Young, Alice *lawyer*
Young, John Edward *lawyer*
Young, William F. *legal educator*
Younger, Stephen P. *lawyer*
Youngwood, Alfred Donald *lawyer*
Zaitzeff, Roger Michael *lawyer*
Zammit, Joseph Paul *lawyer*
Zauderer, Mark Carl *lawyer*
Zedrosser, Joseph John *lawyer*
Zerin, Steven David *lawyer*
Ziegler, Henry Steinway *lawyer*
Ziegler, John Augustus, Jr., *lawyer*
Zifchak, William C. *lawyer*
Zimand, Harvey Folks *lawyer*
Zimmett, Mark Paul *lawyer, educator*
Zissu, Michael Jerome *lawyer*
Zissu, Roger L. *lawyer*
Zivin, Norman H. *lawyer*
Zoogman, Nicholas Jay *lawyer*
Zornow, David M. *lawyer*
Zuckerman, Paul Herbert *lawyer*
Zukerman, Michael *lawyer*

Newark
Reid, James Edward *lawyer*

Newburgh
Liberth, Richard Francis *lawyer*
Zeisel, Laura *lawyer, educator, environmental council*

Niagara Falls
Anton, Ronald David *lawyer*
Berrigan, Patrick Joseph *lawyer*

Niagara University
Ireland, Timothy O *criminal justice educator*

Niskayuna
Sokolow, Lloyd Bruce *lawyer, psychotherapist*

Nyack
Cember, M. Nathan *lawyer, speaker*

Old Chatham
Severs, Charles A., III, *lawyer*

Olean
Heyer, John Henry, II, *lawyer*

Oneida
Matthews, William Doty *lawyer, consumer products manufacturing company executive*

Orangeburg
Rivet, Diana Wittmer *lawyer, developer*

Orchard Park
Sullivan, Mortimer Allen, Jr., *lawyer*

Oswego
Greene, Stephen Craig *lawyer*

Oyster Bay
Bernstein, Jacob *lawyer*
Ott, Gilbert Russell, Jr., *lawyer*
Robinson, Edward T., III, *lawyer*

Patchogue
Esteve, Edward V. *lawyer*

Pearl River
Meyer, Irwin Stephan *lawyer, accountant*
Riley, James Kevin *lawyer*

Pittsford
Braunsdorf, Paul Raymond *lawyer*
George, Richard Neill *retired lawyer*
Hampson, Thomas Meredith *lawyer*
Hartman, James Matthew *lawyer*
Scutt, Robert Carl *lawyer*
Snyder, Donald Edward *corporate executive*
Stonehill, Eric *lawyer*
Turri, Joseph A. *lawyer*

Pomona
Fisch, Edith L. *lawyer*

Port Washington
Herz, Arnold D. *lawyer*
Lingelbach, Albert Lane *lawyer*
Mayer, Renee G. *lawyer*
Ullman, Leo Solomon *lawyer*

Poughkeepsie
Ostertag, Robert Louis *lawyer*
Shatz, Phillip *lawyer*
Taphorn, Joseph Bernard *lawyer*
Teal, Arabella W. *lawyer, former state attorney general*

Purchase
Andrews, David Ralph *lawyer*
Gioffre, Bruno Joseph *lawyer*
Hanft, Noah Jonathan *lawyer*
Kelly, Edmund Joseph *lawyer, bank executive, investment banker*
McKenna, Matthew Morgan *lawyer*
Wallach, Ira David *lawyer, business executive*

Rensselaerville
Fletcher, Raymond Russwald, Jr., *lawyer*

Rhinebeck
Melley, Steven Michael *lawyer*

Riverhead
Maggipinto, V. Anthony *lawyer*

Rochester
Affronti, Francis Christopher *lawyer*
Brovitz, Richard Stuart *lawyer*
Buckley, Michael Francis *lawyer*
Clement, Thomas Earl *retired lawyer*
Clifford, Eugene Thomas *lawyer*
Colby, William Michael *lawyer*
Dolin, Lonny H. *lawyer*
Evans, Eric Alan *lawyer*
Geiger, Alexander *lawyer*
Goldman, Joel J. *retired lawyer*
Gootnick, Margery Fischbein *lawyer*
Hallenbeck, Alfred M. *lawyer*
Hanford, M. Shae *lawyer*
Harris, Wayne Manley *lawyer*
Harter, Ralph Millard Peter *lawyer, educator*
Kurland, Harold Arthur *lawyer*
Lundback, Staffan Bengt Gunnar *lawyer*
Mayka, Stephen Paul *lawyer*
McCrory, John Brooks *retired lawyer*
Moore, James Conklin *lawyer*
Morris, James E. *lawyer, judge, educator*
Morrison, Patrice B. *lawyer*
Ornt, Jeanine Arden *lawyer*
Palermo, Anthony Robert *lawyer*
Paley, Gerald Larry *lawyer*
Payment, Kenneth Arnold *lawyer*
Robfogel, Susan Salitan *lawyer*
Rosenbaum, Richard Merrill *lawyer*
Rosenhouse, Michael Allan *lawyer, editorial consultant*
Schumacher, Jon Lee *lawyer*
Stewart, Sue S. *lawyer*
Swett, Albert Hersey *retired lawyer, business executive, consultant*
Trevett, Thomas Neil *lawyer*
Van Graafeiland, Gary P. *lawyer*
Vick, Paul Ashton *lawyer*
Vigdor, Justin Leonard *lawyer*
Waite, Stephen Holden *lawyer*
Wild, Robert Warren *lawyer*
Witmer, George Robert, Jr., *lawyer*
Young, Deborah Schwind *lawyer*

Rye
Dixon, Paul Edward *lawyer, metal products and manufacturing company executive*
Lobl, Herbert Max *lawyer, writer*
Roberts, Thomas Alba *lawyer*

Salamanca
Brady, Thomas Carl *lawyer*

Sands Point
Busner, Philip H. *retired lawyer, judge*

Scarsdale
Angel, Dennis *lawyer*
Beuchert, Edward William *lawyer*
Ellis, James Henry *lawyer, management consultant*
Hoffman, Richard M. *lawyer*
Macchia, Vincent Michael *lawyer*
O'Brien, Edward Ignatius *private investor, corporation director*
Sabadie, Francisca Alejandra *lawyer, interpreter, translator*
Van Gundy, Gregory Frank *retired lawyer*

Schenectady
Cullen, Kathleen Joy *lawyer*
Levine, Sanford Harold *lawyer*

Schoharie
Duncombe, Raynor Bailey *lawyer*

Scottsville
Williams, Henry Ward, Jr., *lawyer, writer*

Smithtown
Dowis, Lenore *lawyer*
Goodman, Richard Shalem *lawyer, orthopedic surgeon*
Spellman, Thomas Joseph, Jr., *lawyer*

Somers
Lemke, Judith A. *lawyer*

South Richmond Hill
Goldsmith, Michael Lawrence *lawyer*

South Salem
Cowles, Frederick Oliver *lawyer*

Southampton
Lopez, David *lawyer*

Spring Valley
Barr, Harvey Stephen *lawyer*

Staten Island
Howard, Davis Jonathan *lawyer, educator, writer*
Humphries, Edward Francis *lawyer*
Landron, Michel John *lawyer*

Stony Point
Diederich, Michael David, Jr., *lawyer*

Suffern
Stack, Daniel *lawyer, financial consultant*

Syosset
Bermas, Stephen *lawyer*

Syracuse
Ackerman, Kenneth Edward *lawyer, educator*
Bodow, Wayne R. *lawyer*
Brickwedde, Richard James *lawyer*
Bullock, Stephen C. *lawyer*
Butler, John Edward *lawyer*
Day, Christian C. *lawyer, educator, department chairman*
DiLorenzo, Louis Patrick *lawyer*
Engel, Richard Lee *lawyer, educator*
Fiske, Jordan Jay *lawyer, retired prosecutor*
Fitzpatrick, James David *lawyer*
Gaal, John *lawyer*

Gerber, Edward F. *retired lawyer*
Hancock, Stewart F., Jr., *law educator, judge*
Hayes, David Michael *lawyer*
Herzog, Peter Emilius *retired legal educator*
Hildebrandt, George Frederick *lawyer*
Hole, Richard Douglas *lawyer*
King, Bernard T. *lawyer*
McGuire, George R. *lawyer, educator*
O'Connor, Michael E. *lawyer*
Pinsky, Roy David *lawyer*
Rivette, Francis Robert *lawyer*
Rosenthal, Alan *lawyer*
Shulman, Barry Martin *lawyer*
Suddaby, Glenn T. *lawyer*
Traylor, Robert Arthur *lawyer*
Williams, Samuel Robert *lawyer*
Zimmerman, Golda *lawyer, educator*

Tarrytown
Harrison, Michael *lawyer*

Troy
Finkel, Sanford Norman *lawyer*
Frost, Jerome Kenneth *lawyer*
Jones, E. Stewart, Jr., *lawyer*

Uniondale
Cassidy, David Michael *lawyer*
Gracin, Hank *lawyer*
Lemle, Robert Spencer *lawyer*
Meng, M. Kathryn *lawyer*
Pratt, George Cheney *law educator, retired federal judge*

Valley Stream
Isaacs, Leonard Bernard *lawyer*
Levine, Marilyn Markovich *lawyer, arbitrator*

Vestal
McGuire, John Thomas *lawyer, educator*

Wappingers Falls
Haynes, Paul R. *lawyer*

Warsaw
Cook, Charlotte Smallwood *lawyer*

Waterford
Glavin, A. Rita Chandellier (Mrs. James Henry Glavin III) *lawyer*
Glavin, James Henry, III, *lawyer*
Novotny, F. Douglas *lawyer*

Watertown
Militello, Samuel Philip *lawyer*

West Harrison
Johnson, Craig Edward *lawyer*

West Point
Stock, Margaret Deborah *lawyer*

Westbury
Boes, Lawrence William *lawyer*

White Plains
Alin, Robert David *lawyer*
Berlin, Alan Daniel *lawyer, international energy and legal consultant*
Bodnar, Peter O. *lawyer*
Carlisle, Jay Charles, II, *lawyer, educator*
Carlucci, Joseph P. *lawyer*
D'Aloise, Lawrence T., Jr., *lawyer*
Doyle, Dennis T. *lawyer*
Feder, Robert *lawyer*
Feldman, Jerome Ira *lawyer, patent development executive*
Fleming, Robert Burke *law educator, lawyer*
Friedman, Stephen J *lawyer*
Gjertsen, O. Gerard *lawyer*
Greenspan, Leon Joseph *lawyer*
Halpern, Philip Morgan *lawyer*
Jacobson, Sandra W. *lawyer*
Kurzman, Robert Graham *lawyer, educator*
Levine, Steven Jon *lawyer*
Madden, M. Stuart *lawyer*
Maffeo, Vincent Anthony *lawyer, executive*
Munneke, Gary Arthur *law educator, consultant*
Nesci, Vincent Peter *lawyer*
Newman, Marie Stefanini *law librarian, educator*
Null, William Seth *lawyer*
Payson, Martin F. *lawyer*
Pitegoff, Thomas Michael *lawyer*
Pollak, Martin Marshall *lawyer, training company executive*
Robinson, Nicholas Adams *lawyer, educator*
Rosenberg, Michael *lawyer*
Rosner, Jonathan Levi *lawyer*
Silverberg, Steven Mark *lawyer*
Sloan, F(rank) Blaine *law educator*

Wolcott
Bartlett, Cody Blake *lawyer, educator*

Woodbury
Mangia, Angelo James *lawyer*

Woodmere
Raab, Ira Jerry *lawyer, judge*

Yonkers
Connors, James Patrick *lawyer*

NORTH CAROLINA

Arden
Seagle, J. Harold *lawyer*

Asheboro
Bunch, W(alter) Edward *lawyer*
Burton, Bernard Ottway *lawyer*

Asheville
Bissette, Winston Louis, Jr., *lawyer, mayor*
Chidnese, Patrick N. *retired lawyer*
Cogburn, Max Oliver *lawyer*
Davis, Roy Walton, Jr., *lawyer*
Dillard, John Robert *lawyer*
Frue, William Calhoun *lawyer*
Hamilton, Jackson Douglas *lawyer*
Hyde, Herbert Lee *lawyer*
Johnston, John Devereaux, Jr., *retired law educator*
Lavelle, Brian Francis David *lawyer*
Wilson, Thomas Douglas, Jr., *lawyer*

Banner Elk
Bernstein, Mark R. *retired lawyer*

Beaufort
Tilghman, Carl Lewis *lawyer*

Blowing Rock
Corlett, Edward Stanley, III, *retired lawyer*

Buies Creek
Davis, Ferd Leary, Jr., *law educator, lawyer, consultant*
Whichard, Willis Padgett *law educator, retired state supreme court justice*

Burlington
Slayton, John Howard *lawyer, trust company executive*

Carthage
Lapping, Sherwod Foster *lawyer*

Cary
Cromer, Charles Lemuel *lawyer, state legislator*
Montgomery, Charles Harvey *lawyer*

Chapel Hill
Boyarsky, Saul *lawyer, forensic urologist, physiologist, educator*
Broun, Kenneth Stanley *lawyer, educator*
Brower, David John *lawyer, urban planner, educator*
Campbell, William Aubrey *law educator*
Daye, Charles Edward *law educator*
Ferrell, Joseph Stevens *law educator*
Freedman, Irving Melvin *lawyer*
Gressman, Eugene *lawyer*
Hardin, Paul, III, *law educator*
Haskell, Paul Gershon *retired law educator*
Lawrence, David Michael *lawyer, educator*
Lilley, Albert Frederick *retired lawyer*
Loeb, Ben Fohl, Jr., *retired law educator*
Southern, Robert Allen *lawyer*
Wegner, Judith Welch *law educator, former dean*

Charlotte
Ayscue, Edwin Osborne, Jr., *lawyer*
Beddow, John Warren *lawyer*
Belthoff, Richard Charles, Jr., *lawyer*
Brackett, Martin Luther, Jr., *lawyer*
Bragg, Ellis Meredith, Jr., *lawyer*
Buckley, Charles Robinson, III, *lawyer*
Calloway, Mark T. *lawyer, former prosecutor*
Campbell, Clair Gilliland *lawyer*
Chambers, Julius LeVonne *lawyer*
Conrad, Robert J. *prosecutor*
Cowell, Marion Aubrey, Jr., *lawyer*
Cramer, Robert W. *lawyer*
Culbreth, James Harold, Jr., *lawyer*
Dagenhart, Larry Jones *lawyer*
Davis, William Maxie, Jr., *lawyer*
Dunn, Jackson Thomas, Jr., *lawyer, legal educator*
Erdman, David Williams *lawyer*
Eve, Robert Michael, Jr., *lawyer*
Gage, Gaston Hemphill *lawyer*
Hanna, George Verner, III, *lawyer*
Kearney, Christopher J. *lawyer*
Loughridge, John Halsted, Jr., *lawyer*
McBryde, Neill Gregory *lawyer*
McGill, John Knox *lawyer*
Monge, Jay Parry *lawyer*
Orsbon, Richard Anthony *lawyer*
Polking, Paul J. *lawyer*
Pruden, James Norfleet, III, *lawyer*
Raper, William Cranford *lawyer*
Robinson, Russell Marable, II, *lawyer*
Taylor, David Brooke *lawyer, banker*
Thigpen, Richard Elton, Jr., *lawyer*
Thompson, Sydnor, Jr., (Charles William Sydnor Thompson Jr.) *lawyer, mediator, arbitrator*
Treanor, Mark C. *lawyer, diversified financial services company executive*
Van Allen, William Kent *lawyer*
Van Alstyne, Vance Brownell *arbitration management consultant*
Van Hoy, Philip Marshall *lawyer*
Vinroot, Richard Allen *lawyer, mayor*
Walker, Clarence Wesley *lawyer*
Wood, William McBrayer *lawyer*
Woolard, William Leon *lawyer, electrical distributing company executive*
Wyrsch, Martha B. *lawyer*

Cherokee
Martin, Harry Corpening *lawyer, retired state supreme court justice*

Cherryville
Huffstetler, Palmer Eugene *lawyer*

Cullowhee
Wilson, LeVon Edward *law educator, lawyer*

Dunn
Pope, Wiley Jackson *lawyer, small business owner*

Durham
Bartlett, Katharine Tiffany *law educator*
Buchanan, Phillip Hoge *lawyer, foundation executive, educator, academic administrator*
Carrington, Paul DeWitt *lawyer, educator*
Christie, George Custis *lawyer, educator, author*
Conner, James Leon, II, *lawyer, arbitrator, mediator*
Cox, James D. *law educator*
Demott, Deborah Ann *lawyer, educator*
Holder, Angela Roddey *lawyer, educator*
Horowitz, Donald Leonard *lawyer, educator, researcher, political scientist, arbitrator*
Jenkins, Richard Erik *patent lawyer*
Markham, Charles Buchanan *retired lawyer*
Maxwell, Richard Callender *retired lawyer, educator*
McCusker, Paul Donald *lawyer, educator*
McMahon, John Alexander *law educator*
Mosteller, Robert P. *law educator*
Poole, Robert Steven *lawyer, writer*
Robertson, Horace Bascomb, Jr., *retired law educator*
Rowe, Thomas Dudley, Jr., *law educator*
Schwarcz, Steven Lance *law educator, lawyer*
Sloan, Maceo Kennedy *lawyer, investment company executive*

Elizabeth City
Riley, John Frederick *lawyer*

Elkin
Gillespie, James Davis *lawyer*

Fairview
Rhynedance, Harold Dexter, Jr., *lawyer, consultant*

Fayetteville
Mitchell, Ronnie Monroe *lawyer, educator*
Rand, Anthony Eden *lawyer*
Redding, Bobbie Newman *lawyer*
Ruppe, Arthur Maxwell *retired lawyer*
Townsend, William Jackson *lawyer*

Fort Bragg
Gordon, David Stott *lawyer*

Gastonia
Stott, Grady Bernell *lawyer*

Goldsboro
Hine, John Charles *lawyer*

Greensboro
Clark, David McKenzie *lawyer*
Davis, Herbert Owen *lawyer*
Floyd, Jack William *lawyer*
Gumbiner, Kenneth Jay *lawyer*
Hunter, Bynum Merritt *lawyer*
Lloyd, Robert Blackwell, Jr., *lawyer*
Melvin, Charles Edward, Jr., *lawyer*
Schell, Braxton *lawyer*
Smith, Lanty L(loyd) *lawyer, business executive*
Swan, George Steven *law educator*
Wagoner, Anna Mills *prosecutor*

Greenville
Burti, Christopher Louis *lawyer*
Dixon, Phillip Ray, Sr., *lawyer*
Stevens, David Boyette *law educator*

Hendersonville
Howell, George Washington *lawyer, consultant*

High Point
Baker, Walter Wray, Jr., *lawyer*
McAllister, Kenneth Wayne *lawyer*
Sheahan, Robert Emmett *lawyer, consultant*

Jamestown
Schmitt, William Allen *lawyer*

Kitty Hawk
Tucker, Don Eugene *retired lawyer*

Kure Beach
O'Keefe, Raymond Peter *lawyer, educator*

Leland
Barnhardt, Zeb Elonzo, Jr., *lawyer*

Lenoir
Flaherty, David Thomas, Jr., *lawyer*

Marion
Burgin, Charles Edward *lawyer*

Morganton
Simpson, Daniel Reid *lawyer, mediator*

Murphy
Bata, Rudolph Andrew, Jr., *lawyer*

New Bern
Davis, James Lee *lawyer*
Overholt, Hugh Robert *lawyer, retired army officer*

Newton
Cutchin, John Franks *lawyer*

North Wilkesboro
Warden, William C. *lawyer*

Pittsboro
Hubbard, Thomas Edwin (Tim Hubbard) *lawyer*

Raleigh
Blackburn, James B., III, *lawyer*
Carlton, Alfred Pershing, Jr., *lawyer*
Carter, Jean Gordon *lawyer*
Case, Charles Dixon *lawyer*
Currin, Samuel Thomas *lawyer, former judge*
Dannelly, William David *lawyer*
Davis, Egbert Lawrence, III, *lawyer*
Dean, Christine Witcover *lawyer*
Dixon, Wright Tracy, Jr., *retired lawyer*
Dorsett, James K., III, *lawyer*
Edwards, Charles Archibald *lawyer*
Ellis, Lester Neal, Jr., *lawyer*
Ellis, Richard W. *lawyer*
Glass, Fred Stephen *lawyer*
Graham, William Edgar, Jr., *lawyer, retired utility company executive*
Hall, John Thomas *lawyer, educator*
Hargrove, Wade Hampton *lawyer*
Hoon, Peggy Ellen *lawyer, librarian*
Hunt, James Baxter, Jr., *lawyer, former governor*
Jernigan, John Lee *lawyer*
Jordan, John Richard, Jr., *lawyer*
Joyner, Walton Kitchin *lawyer*
Kapp, Michael Keith *lawyer*
Kirk-Duggan, Michael Allan *retired law, economics and computer sciences educator*
Lambe, Catherine van de Velde *law librarian*
Maupin, Armistead Jones *lawyer*
McCormick, Thomas A., Jr., *city attorney*
Millberg, John C. *lawyer*
Mitchell, Burley Bayard, Jr., *lawyer*
Mitchell, Henry Allen, Jr., *lawyer, insurance company executive*
Neely, Charles B., Jr., *lawyer*
Parker, John Hill *lawyer*
Pinnix, John Lawrence *lawyer*
Powell, Durwood Royce *lawyer*
Ragsdale, George Robinson *lawyer*
Roach, Wesley Linville *lawyer, insurance executive*
Suhr, Paul Augustine *lawyer*
Taylor, Raymond Mason *lawyer, former government official, educator*
Thomas, Jason Selig *lawyer*
Trott, William Macnider *lawyer*
Wetsch, Laura Johnson *lawyer*
Whitney, Frank D. *prosecutor*
Wicker, Dennis A. *lawyer*
Wilson, Donald Hurst, III, *mediator, biopharmaceutical industry executive*

Rocky Mount
Zipf, Robert Eugene, Jr., *legal medicine consultant, pathologist*

Sanford
Raisig, Paul Jones, Jr., *lawyer*

Tarboro
Hopkins, Grover Prevatte *lawyer*

Tryon
McDermott, Renée R(assler) *lawyer*

Washington
Rader, Steven Palmer *lawyer*

Wilmington
Dixon, Daniel Roberts, Jr., *retired tax lawyer*
Jones, Lucian Cox *lawyer*
McCauley, Cleyburn Lycurgus *lawyer*
Medlock, Donald Larson *lawyer*

Winston Salem
Adams, Alfred Gray *lawyer*
Barnhill, Henry Grady, Jr., *lawyer*
Blynn, Guy Marc *lawyer*
Davis, Linwood Layfield *lawyer*
Foy, Herbert Miles, III, *lawyer, educator*
Gitter, Allan Reinhold *lawyer*
Graham, William Thomas *lawyer*
Greason, Murray Crossley, Jr., *lawyer*
Gunter, Michael Donwell *lawyer*
Holton, Walter Clinton, Jr., *lawyer*
Humphrey, Dudley *lawyer*
Kelly, James Howard, Jr., *lawyer*
Leonard, R. Michael *lawyer*
Maready, William Frank *lawyer*
Murphy, Frank *lawyer*
Osborn, Malcolm Everett *lawyer*
Ray, Michael Edwin *lawyer*
Robinson, Edward Norwood *lawyer*
Roemer, Henry Conrad, Jr., *lawyer*
Ross, Charles Thomas *lawyer*
Sandridge, William Pendleton, Jr., *lawyer*
Schollander, Wendell Leslie, Jr., *lawyer*
Sharpe, Keith Yount *retired lawyer*
Steele, Thomas McKnight *law educator*
Stockton, Ralph Madison, Jr., *lawyer*
Vaughn, Robert Candler, Jr., *lawyer*
Walker, George Kontz *law educator*
Womble, William Fletcher *lawyer*

NORTH DAKOTA

Bismarck
Edin, Charles Thomas *lawyer*
Klemin, Lawrence R. *lawyer*
Loble, Lester Henry, II, *lawyer, business executive*
Murry, Charles Emerson *lawyer, official*
Snyder, Robert John *lawyer*
Strutz, William A. *lawyer*

Fargo
Amlund, Curtis Arthur *law educator*
Crothers, Daniel J. *lawyer*
Holman, Maureen *lawyer*
Unhjem, Michael Bruce *lawyer*
Wrigley, Drew H. *lawyer*

Mandan
Bair, Bruce B. *lawyer*

Minot
Armstrong, Phillip Dale *lawyer*
Lee, Gary *lawyer*

OHIO

Ada
Fenton, Howard Nathan, III, *lawyer, educator*

Akron
Aynes, Richard L(ee) *law educator*
Bonsky, Jack Alan *lawyer*
Cahoon, Peter Thomas *lawyer*
Cherpas, Christopher Theodore *lawyer*
Chrisant, Rosemarie Kathryn *law library administrator*
Fisher, James Lee *lawyer*
Harvie, Crawford Thomas *lawyer*
Holloway, Donald Phillip *lawyer*
Lee, Brant Thomas *lawyer, federal official, educator*
Lombardi, Frederick McKean *lawyer*
Rooney, George Willard *lawyer*
Trotter, Thomas Robert *lawyer*
Wolfe, John Leslie *lawyer*

Athens
Bridgewater, Erle Henry *lawyer*
Lavelle, William Ambrose *lawyer, judge*
Yanity, Joseph Blair, Jr., *lawyer*

Aurora
Berry, Dean Lester *lawyer*

Beachwood
Pinkas, Robert Paul *lawyer, venture capitalist*

Brecksville
McBride, Judith Bliss *lawyer, educator, writer*

Bucyrus
Neff, Robert Clark, Sr., *lawyer*

Canfield
Hill, Thomas Allen *lawyer*

Canton
Barnhart, Gene *lawyer*
Ergazos, John William *lawyer*
Mokodean, Michael John *lawyer, accountant*

Celina
Myers, Daniel *lawyer*

Centerville
Giffen, Daniel Harris *lawyer, educator*

Chesterland
Kancelbaum, Joshua Jacob *lawyer*

Chillicothe
Boulger, William Charles *lawyer*

Cincinnati
Acheson, Edwin R., Jr., *lawyer*
Adams, Edmund John *lawyer*
Anderson, James Milton *lawyer*
Anderson, William Hopple *lawyer*
Anthony, Thomas Dale *lawyer*
Bahlman, William Thorne, Jr., *retired lawyer*
Bibus, Thomas William *lawyer*
Bissinger, Mark Christian *lawyer*
Black, Stephen L. *lawyer*
Broderick, Dennis John *lawyer, retail executive*
Bromberg, Robert Sheldon *lawyer*
Buechner, Robert William *lawyer, educator*
Burke, Timothy Michael *lawyer, educator*
Calico, Paul B. *lawyer*
Carr, George Francis, Jr., *lawyer*
Chesley, Stanley Morris *lawyer*
Christenson, Gordon A. *law educator*
Cissell, James Charles *lawyer*
Cody, Thomas Gerald *lawyer*
Daugherty, Kendra Lea *lawyer*
Dehner, Joseph Julnes *lawyer*
DeLong, Deborah *lawyer*
Donnelly, Thomas Christian *lawyer, athletic director*
Dornette, W(illiam) Stuart *lawyer, educator*
Elleman, Lawrence Robert *lawyer*
Evans, James E. *lawyer*
Faller, Susan Grogan *lawyer*
Finan, Richard H. *lawyer*
Fink, Jerold Albert *lawyer*
Frantz, Robert Wesley *lawyer*
Freedman, William Mark *lawyer, educator*
Friedman, Penny *lawyer*
Garfinkel, Jane E. *lawyer*
Gettler, Benjamin *lawyer, manufacturing executive*
Halpert, Douglas Joshua *lawyer*
Hardy, William Robinson *lawyer*
Harris, Irving *lawyer*
Heldman, James Gardner *lawyer*
Heldman, Paul W. *lawyer, food service executive*
Henderson, Stephen Paul *lawyer*
Hermanies, John Hans *retired lawyer*
Hill, Thomas Clark *lawyer*
Hoffheimer, Daniel Joseph *lawyer*
Holschuh, John David, Jr., *lawyer*
Johnson, James J. *lawyer*
Kelley, John Joseph, Jr., *lawyer*
Kiel, Frederick Orin *lawyer*
Kordons, Uldis *lawyer*
Lawrence, James Kaufman Lebensburger *lawyer*
Lawson, Kenneth L. *lawyer*
Lesick, John Richard *retired lawyer, consultant*
Levin, Debbe Ann *lawyer*
Lindberg, Charles David *lawyer*
Manley, Robert Edward *lawyer, economist*
Manly, Marc Edward *lawyer*
Mann, David Scott *lawyer*
Mara, Timothy Gerald *lawyer*
Marks, Edward G. *lawyer*
Martineau, Robert John *law educator*
Maxwell, Robert Wallace, II, *lawyer*
McClain, William Andrew *lawyer*
McDowell, John Eugene *lawyer*
Meranus, Leonard Stanley *lawyer*
Meyers, Karen Diane *lawyer, educator, corporate officer*
Meyers, Pamela Sue *lawyer*
Nechemias, Stephen Murray *lawyer*
Neumark, Michael Harry *lawyer*
O'Reilly, James Thomas *lawyer, educator, author*
Parker, R. Joseph *lawyer*
Petrie, Bruce Inglis *lawyer*
Porter, Robert Carl, Jr., *lawyer*
Reichert, David *lawyer*
Rich, Robert Edward *lawyer*
Rose, Donald McGregor *retired lawyer*
Rubin, Robert Samuel *lawyer*
Schuck, Thomas Robert *lawyer, farmer*
Schwab, Nelson, Jr., *lawyer*
Silbersack, Mark Louis *lawyer*
Sims, Victor Dwayne *lawyer*
Smith, Sheila Marie *lawyer*
Stanton, Jeanne Frances *retired lawyer*
Strauss, William Victor *lawyer*
Swigert, James Mack *lawyer*
Tobias, Charles Harrison, Jr., *lawyer*
Tobias, Paul Henry *lawyer*
Trauth, Joseph Louis, Jr., *lawyer*
Turpening, Patricia Eileen Keller *law librarian*
Vander Laan, Mark Alan *lawyer*
Vogel, Cedric Wakelee *lawyer*
Wales, Ross Elliot *lawyer*
Watts, Barbara Gayle *law academic administrator*
Weeks, Steven Wiley *lawyer*
White, Alfred Kenneth, Jr., *lawyer*
Woodside, Frank C., III, *lawyer, educator, physician*

Cleveland
Adamo, Kenneth R. *lawyer*
Andrews, Oakley V. *lawyer*
Ashmus, Keith Allen *lawyer*
Austin, Arthur Donald, II, *lawyer, educator*
Bacon, Brett Kermit *lawyer*
Bates, Walter Alan *retired lawyer*
Baughman, R(obert) Patrick *lawyer*
Berger, Sanford Jason *lawyer, securities dealer, real estate broker*
Berick, James Herschel *lawyer*
Braverman, Herbert Leslie *lawyer*
Bravo, Kenneth Allan *lawyer*
Brennan, Maureen *lawyer*
Brown, Bruce Andrew *lawyer*
Brucken, Robert Matthew *lawyer*
Burge, David Alan *patent lawyer, writer*
Burke, Kathleen B. B. *lawyer*
Cairns, James Donald *lawyer*
Calfee, John Beverly *retired lawyer*
Callahan, Thomas James *lawyer*
Carrick, Kathleen Michele *law librarian*
Carter, Daniel Paul *lawyer, educator*
Clarke, Charles Fenton *lawyer*
Collin, Thomas James *lawyer*
Coquillette, William Hollis *lawyer*
Crehore, Charles Aaron *lawyer*
Cudak, Gail Linda *lawyer*
Currivan, John Daniel *lawyer*
Cyphert, Michael A. *lawyer*
Dampeer, John Lyell *retired lawyer*
Dauscher, Raymond G. *lawyer*
Domiano, Joseph Charles *lawyer*
Drinko, John Deaver *lawyer*
Duncan, Ed Eugene *lawyer*
Dunlap, Jeffrey Scott *lawyer*
Dunn, George J. *lawyer, oil company executive*
Duvin, Robert Phillip *lawyer*
Eklund, Claudia Rieth *lawyer*
Fabens, Andrew Lawrie, III, *lawyer*
Falsgraf, William Wendell *retired lawyer*
Fay, Regan Joseph *lawyer*
Fischer, Michelle K. *lawyer*
Fisher, Thomas Edward *lawyer*
Fletcher, Robert *retired lawyer, horologist*
Foster, Dennis James *legal recruiting services executive*
Freimuth, Marc William *lawyer*
Friedman, Harold Edward *lawyer*
Glaser, Robert Edward *lawyer*
Goins, Frances Floriano *lawyer*
Gold, Gerald Seymour *lawyer*
Goldfarb, Bernard Sanford *lawyer*
Goler, Michael David *lawyer*
Grossman, Theodore Martin *lawyer*
Haiman, Irwin Sanford *lawyer*
Hardy, Michael Lynn *lawyer*
Henes, Samuel Ernst *lawyer*
Hochman, Kenneth George *lawyer*
Hoerner, Robert Jack *lawyer*
Hollington, Richard Rings, Jr., *lawyer*
Horvitz, Michael John *lawyer*
Jacobs, Leslie William *lawyer*
Jaffe, Donald Nolan *lawyer*
Janke, Ronald Robert *lawyer*
Jorgenson, Mary Ann *lawyer*
Kahrl, Robert Conley *lawyer*
Karp, Marvin Louis *lawyer*
Katcher, Richard *lawyer*
Katz, Lewis Robert *law educator*
Kelly, Dennis Michael *lawyer*
Kilbane, Thomas Stanton *lawyer*
Koblenz, N(orman) Herschel *lawyer*
Kramer, Edward George *lawyer*
Kramer, Eugene Leo *lawyer*
Kurit, Neil *lawyer*
Lawniczak, James Michael *lawyer*
Lazar, Kathy Pittak *lawyer*
Lazzaro, S. Robert E. *lawyer*
Lease, Robert K. *lawyer*
Leavitt, Jeffrey Stuart *lawyer*
Leiken, Earl Murray *lawyer*
Lennox, Heather *lawyer*
Leukart, Barbara J. J. *lawyer*
Lewis, John Bruce *lawyer*
Lowe, James Allison *lawyer, educator*
Maher, Edward Joseph *lawyer*
Maloney, Mary D. *lawyer*
Markey, Robert Guy *lawyer*
Marting, Michael G. *lawyer*
Mason, Thomas Albert *lawyer*
Mast, Bernadette Mihalic *lawyer*
McAndrews, James Patrick *lawyer*
Mc Cartan, Patrick Francis *lawyer*
McCarthy, Mark Francis *lawyer*
McLaughlin, Patrick Michael *lawyer*
Mehlman, Maxwell Jonathan *law educator*
Meyer, G. Christopher *lawyer*
Millisor, Kenneth Ray *lawyer*
Millstone, David Jeffrey *lawyer*
Moore, Kenneth Cameron *lawyer*
Newman, John M., Jr., *lawyer*
Norman, Forrest Alonzo *lawyer*
Ollinger, W. James *lawyer*
Pace, Stanley Dan *lawyer*
Pearlman, Samuel Segel *lawyer, educator*
Perris, Terrence George *lawyer*
Podboy, Alvin Michael, Jr., *law library director, lawyer*
Pollock, R. Jeffrey *lawyer*
Putka, Andrew Charles *lawyer*
Rains, M. Neal *lawyer*
Rapp, Robert Neil *lawyer*
Rauzi, Harold Ray *lawyer, respiratory therapist*
Rawson, Rachel L. *lawyer*
Reppert, Richard Levi *lawyer*
Rickert, Jeanne Martin M. *lawyer*
Roberts-Mamone, Lisa A. *lawyer*
Rosenbaum, Jacob I. *lawyer*
Ross, Harold Anthony *lawyer*
Ruf, H(arold) William, Jr., *retired lawyer, corporation executive*
Sawyer, Raymond Terry *lawyer, consultant, theater producer*
Schiller, James Joseph *lawyer*
Shapiro, Fred David *lawyer*
Sharpe, Calvin William *law educator, arbitrator*
Sicherman, Marvin Allen *lawyer*
Skulina, Thomas Raymond *lawyer*
Slinger, Michael Jeffery *law library director*
Smith, Barbara Jean *lawyer*
Sogg, Wilton Sherman *lawyer*
Solomon, Randall Lee *lawyer*
Spero, Keith Erwin *lawyer, educator*
Stanley, Hugh Monroe, Jr., *lawyer*
Stellato, Louis Eugene *lawyer*
Strauch, John L. *lawyer*
Strauss, David J. *lawyer*
Striefsky, Linda A(nn) *lawyer*
Strimbu, Victor, Jr., *lawyer*
Stuhan, Richard George *lawyer*
Stuhldreher, George William *lawyer*
Summers, William Lawrence *lawyer*
Swartzbaugh, Marc L. *lawyer*
Szaller, James Francis *lawyer*
Taft, Seth Chase *retired lawyer*
Thimmig, Diana M. *lawyer*
Toohey, Brian Frederick *lawyer*
Toomajian, William Martin *lawyer*
Trapp, Mary Jane *lawyer*
Utrata, Carl Ignatius *corporate counsel, corporate executive*
Vergon, Frederick Porter, Jr., *lawyer*
von Mehren, George M. *lawyer*
Waldeck, John Walter, Jr., *lawyer*
Wallach, Mark Irwin *lawyer*
Watson, Richard Thomas *lawyer*
Weaver, Robin Geoffrey *lawyer, educator*
Weber, Robert Carl *lawyer*
Weiler, Jeffry Louis *lawyer*
Weinberger, Peter Henry *lawyer*
Werber, Stephen Jay *lawyer, educator*
White, Gregory A. *lawyer*
Whitney, Richard Buckner *lawyer*
Withers, Carl Raymond *lawyer*
Young, James Edward *lawyer*
Zambie, Allan John *lawyer*

Columbus
Adams, John Marshall *lawyer*
Anderson, Jon Mac *lawyer, educator*
Bailey, Daniel Allen *lawyer*
Barnes, Wallace Ray *retired lawyer*
Bell, Albert Jerome *lawyer*
Berndt, Ellen German *lawyer*
Binning, J. Boyd *lawyer*
Blackburn, John D(avid) *legal educator, lawyer*
Bonini, James *federal court official*
Bowen, John Wesley Edward, IV, *lawyer*
Bridgman, G(eorge) Ross *lawyer*
Brooks, Richard Dickinson *lawyer*
Brown, Herbert Russell *lawyer, writer*
Brubaker, Robert Loring *lawyer*
Buchenroth, Stephen Richard *lawyer*
Burchfield, James Ralph *lawyer*
Campbell, Joel Roderick *lawyer*
Carnahan, John Anderson *lawyer*
Carpenter, Michael H. *lawyer*
Chester, John Jonas *lawyer, educator*
Cox, Paul L. *lawyer*
Cross, Jeffrey D. *lawyer, electric power industry executive*
Crowder, Marjorie Briggs *lawyer*
Cvetanovich, Dan L. *lawyer*
Di Lorenzo, John Florio, Jr., *retired lawyer (corporate)*
Dowd, Andrew Joseph *lawyer, utility company executive*
Draper, Gerald Linden *lawyer*
Fahey, Richard Paul *lawyer*
Fay, Terrence Michael *lawyer*
Federle, Katherine Hunt *lawyer*
Fisher, Lloyd Edison, Jr., *lawyer*
Frasier, Ralph Kennedy *lawyer, investment banker*
Fried, Samuel *lawyer*
Frye, Richard Arthur *lawyer*
Fu, Paul Shan *law librarian, consultant*
Geary, William Lee *lawyer*
Gibson, Rick J. *lawyer*
Goulder, Diane Kessler *lawyer*
Graff, Douglas Eric *lawyer*
Greek, Darold I. *lawyer*
Gross, James Howard *lawyer*
Gutfeld, Norman E. *lawyer*
Hardymon, David Wayne *lawyer*
Harwood, Sandra Stabile *lawyer, state representative*
Hatler, Patricia Ruth *lawyer*
Hollenbaugh, H(enry) Ritchey *lawyer*
Hutson, Jeffrey Woodward *lawyer*
Jackson, Janet Elizabeth *city attorney, association executive*
Johnson, Mark Alan *lawyer*
Kasouf, Joseph Chickery *lawyer, consultant*
Katz, Janyce C(harlene) *lawyer*
Kemp, Daniel Warren *lawyer*
Ketcham, Richard Scott *lawyer*
King, G. Roger *lawyer*
Koblentz, Robert Alan *lawyer*
Kuehnle, Kenton Lee *lawyer*
Kurtz, Charles Jewett, III, *lawyer*
La Cour, Louis Bernard *retired lawyer*
Larzelere, Kathy Lynn Heckler *paralegal*
Lehman, Harry Jac *lawyer*
Lippe, Jerry Leonard *lawyer*
Long, Thomas Leslie *lawyer*
Mann, William Craig *lawyer*
Markus, Kent Richard *lawyer*
McConnaughey, George Carlton, Jr., *retired lawyer*
McCutchan, Gordon Eugene *retired lawyer, insurance company executive*
McDermott, Kevin R. *lawyer*
McKenna, Alvin James *lawyer*
McMahon, John Patrick *retired lawyer*
McNealey, J. Jeffrey *lawyer, corporate executive*
Mencer, Jetta *lawyer*
Miller, Terry Morrow *lawyer*
Minor, Robert Allen *lawyer*
Mirman, Joel Harvey *lawyer*
Moloney, Thomas E. *lawyer*
Mone, Robert Paul *lawyer*
Morgan, Dennis Richard *lawyer*
Moul, William Charles *lawyer*
Murphy, Earl Finbar *law educator*
Oman, Richard Heer *lawyer*
O'Shaughnessy, Christopher T. *lawyer*
Petricoff, M. Howard *lawyer, educator*
Phillips, James Edgar *lawyer*
Quigley, John Bernard *law educator*
Radnor, Alan T. *lawyer*
Ramey, Denny L. *bar association executive director*
Ray, Frank Allen *lawyer*
Reasoner, Willis Irl, III, *lawyer*
Rector, Susan Darnell *lawyer*
Robinson, Barry R. *lawyer*
Robol, Richard Thomas *lawyer*
Rose, Michael Dean *lawyer, educator*
Ryan, Joseph W., Jr., *lawyer*
Schrag, Edward A., Jr., *lawyer*
Selcer, David Mark *lawyer*
Sidman, Robert John *lawyer*
Sites, Richard Loren *lawyer, educator*
Sowald, Beatrice Kronick *lawyer*
Stern, Geoffrey *lawyer, disciplinary counsel*
Stinehart, Roger Ray *lawyer*
Sully, Ira Bennett *lawyer*
Swetnam, Daniel Richard *lawyer*
Taft, Sheldon Ashley *lawyer*
Taggart, Thomas Michael *lawyer*
Tait, Robert E. *lawyer*
Tannous, Robert Joseph *lawyer*
Tarpy, Thomas Michael *lawyer*
Taylor, Joel Sanford *retired lawyer*
Thomas, Duke Winston *lawyer*
Todd, William Michael *lawyer*
Treneff, Craig Paul *lawyer*
Tripp, Thomas Neal *lawyer, political consultant*
Turano, David A. *lawyer*
Warner, Charles Collins *lawyer*
Whipps, Edward Franklin *lawyer*
Wightman, Alec *lawyer*
Willcox, Roderick Harrison *lawyer*
Yeazel, Keith Arthur *lawyer*

Cuyahoga Falls
Jones, John Frank *retired lawyer*

Dayton
Chernesky, Richard John *lawyer*
Farquhar, Robert Nichols *lawyer*
Gottschlich, Gary William *lawyer*
Hadley, Robert James *lawyer*
Heyman, Ralph Edmond *lawyer*
Hitter, Joseph Ira *lawyer*
Hoak, Jonathan S. *lawyer*
Holz, Michael Harold *lawyer*
Jenks, Thomas Edward *lawyer*
Johnson, C. Terry *lawyer*
Krygowski, Walter John *lawyer*
Lockhart, Gregory Gordon *prosecutor*
Macklin, Crofford Johnson, Jr., *lawyer*
Posey, Terry Wayne *lawyer*
Rambo, James Edmondson *lawyer*
Rapp, Gerald Duane *lawyer, manufacturing executive*
Rogers, Richard Hunter *lawyer, business executive*
Saul, Irving Isaac *lawyer*
Taronji, Jaime, Jr., *lawyer*
Vaughn, Noel Wyandt *lawyer*

Delaware
Martin, Stephen David *lawyer*

Dublin
Bennett, George H., Jr., *lawyer, healthcare company executive*
Lane, James Edward *retired lawyer, consultant*
Maloon, Jerry L. *trial lawyer, physician, medico legal consultant*
Sheffer, Brent Alan *lawyer*
Tenuta, Luigia *lawyer*
Williams, Paul Stratton *lawyer*

Eastlake
Balester, Vivian Shelton *legal research consultant, retired lawyer*

Eaton
Thomas, James William *lawyer*

Fairfield
Grove, Jack Frederick *lawyer, educator*

Findlay
Hackenberg, David Alan *lawyer*
Kline, James Edward *lawyer*

Franklin
Ruppert, Rupert Earl *lawyer, political consultant*

Girard
Denney, James Allen *lawyer*

Hilliard
Cooper, Almeta E. *lawyer, medical association administrator*

Howard
Lee, William Johnson *lawyer*

Hudson
Elliott, Frances Carano *lawyer, educator*

Independence
Kola, Arthur Anthony *lawyer*

Ironton
Allen, Craig Adams *lawyer, director*

Jefferson
Geary, Michael Philip *lawyer*

Lakewood
Baxter, Howard H. *retired lawyer*

Lancaster
Libert, Donald Joseph *lawyer*

Lebanon
Baldwin, James Edward *lawyer, city administrator*

Lima
Robenalt, John Alton *lawyer*

Lorain
Mumford, Beverly Jean *paralegal*

Marietta
Fields, William Albert *lawyer*
Huck, Daniel N. *lawyer, educator*

Marion
Frericks, Timothy Matthew *lawyer*

Marysville
Hamilton, Robert Otte *lawyer*

Massillon
Netzly, Dwight H. *lawyer*

Maumee
Marsh, Benjamin Franklin *lawyer*
McBride, Beverly Jean *lawyer*
Tuschman, James Marshall *lawyer*

Mechanicsburg
Saxbe, William Bart *lawyer, former government official*

Medina
Arnold, Alanna S. Welling *lawyer, mediator*
Ballard, John Stuart *retired educator, former mayor, former lawyer*

Mentor
Driggs, Charles Mulford *lawyer*

Miamisburg
Andreozzi, Louis Joseph *lawyer*
Byrd, James Everett *lawyer*

Middletown
Bailey, William Rufus *lawyer, corporation executive*
Rathman, William Ernest *retired lawyer, minister*

Milford Center
McDonald, Alan Thomas *lawyer*

Mount Vernon
Rose, Kim Matthew *lawyer, educator*
Turner, Harry Edward *lawyer*

Newark
Hite, David L. *lawyer*
Mantonya, John Butcher *lawyer*
Meyer, Christopher Richard *lawyer*

North Canton
Dettinger, Warren Walter *lawyer*

Oxford
Brown, Edward Maurice *retired lawyer, business executive*

Painesville
Aveni, Anthony Joseph *lawyer, educator*
Dean, J. Thomas *lawyer*

Perrysburg
Spitzer, John Brumback *lawyer*

Portsmouth
Gerlach, Franklin Theodore *lawyer*
Horr, William Henry *retired lawyer*

Ravenna
Nolfi, Edward Anthony *lawyer*

Reynoldsburg
Cochran, Shirley Ann *mediator*

Saint Marys
Huber, William Evan *lawyer*

Sandusky
Bailey, K. Ronald *lawyer*

Seaman
Young, Vernon Lewis *lawyer*

Shaker Heights
Ekelman, Daniel Louis *lawyer*
Messinger, Donald Hathaway *lawyer*

South Russell
Preston, Robert Bruce *retired lawyer*

Springfield
Browne, William Bitner *lawyer*
Harkins, Daniel Conger *lawyer*
Lagos, James Harry *lawyer*

Toledo
Anspach, Robert Michael *lawyer*
Baker, Richard Southworth *lawyer*
Brown, Charles Earl *lawyer*
Dalrymple, Thomas Lawrence *retired lawyer*
Dane, Stephen Mark *lawyer*
Doner, Gary William *lawyer*
Gouttiere, John P. *lawyer*
Hilbert, John Warren, II, *lawyer*
Jackson, Reginald Sherman, Jr., *lawyer, educator*
Machin, Barbara E. *lawyer*
Majdalani, Brenda J. *prosecutor, educator*
O'Connell, Maurice Daniel *lawyer*
Pletz, Thomas Gregory *lawyer*
St. Clair, Donald David *lawyer*
Ward, David A. *corporate lawyer*
Webb, Thomas Irwin, Jr., *lawyer, director*
Wicklund, David Wayne *lawyer*
Witherell, Dennis Patrick *lawyer*

Warren
Letson, William Normand *lawyer*
McGeough, Robert Saunders *lawyer*
Rossi, Anthony Gerald *lawyer*
Vigorito, Philip Michael *lawyer*

Westerville
Westervelt, Charles Ephraim, Jr., *lawyer*
Young, Sheldon Mike *lawyer, author*

Westlake
Donahue, Charles Bertrand, II, *lawyer*

Wickliffe
Kidder, Fred Dockstater *lawyer*

Wilmington
Schutt, Walter Eugene *lawyer*

Wooster
Johnston, John Clifford, Jr., *lawyer*
Kennedy, Charles Allen *lawyer*

Xenia
Chappars, Timothy Stephen *lawyer*

Youngstown
Blair, Richard Bryson *lawyer*
Carlin, Clair Myron *lawyer*
Jeren, John Anthony, Jr., *lawyer*
Matune, Frank Joseph *lawyer*
Nadler, Myron Jay *lawyer, director*
Roth, Daniel Benjamin *lawyer, business executive*
Rupeka, Robert W. *court administrator*

Zanesville
Micheli, Frank James *lawyer*

OKLAHOMA

Alva
Mitchell, Allan Edwin *lawyer*

Bartlesville
Roff, Alan Lee *lawyer, consultant*

Broken Arrow
Frieze, H(arold) Delbert *lawyer*
Stewart, Murray Baker *retired lawyer*

Chandler
Swanson, Robert Lee *lawyer*

Edmond
Lester, Andrew William *lawyer*
Loving, Susan Brimer *lawyer, former state official*

Enid
Jones, Stephen *lawyer*

Guthrie
Davis, Frank Wayne *lawyer*

Guymon
Wood, Donald Euriah *lawyer*

Mcalester
Cornish, Richard Pool *lawyer*
Neal, Charles D., Jr., *lawyer*

Muskogee
Robinson, Adelbert Carl *lawyer, judge*
Sperling, Sheldon J. *prosecutor*

Norman
Fairbanks, Robert Alvin *lawyer*
Petersen, Catherine Holland *lawyer*
Winchell, Michael George *lawyer*

Oklahoma City
Allen, Robert Dee *lawyer*
Askins, Jari *lawyer, department chairman, state representative*
Bailey, Burck *lawyer*
Barth, J. Edward *lawyer, shareholder*
Boston, William Clayton *lawyer*
Brooks, Norma Newton *legal assistant*
Burget, Mark Edward *lawyer*
Cantrell, Charles L. *lawyer, educator*
Coats, Andrew Montgomery *lawyer, former mayor, dean*
Cook, Gayle Freeman *lawyer*
Court, Leonard *lawyer, educator*
Cunningham, Stanley Lloyd *lawyer*
Derrick, Gary Wayne *lawyer*
Durland, Jack Raymond *retired lawyer*
Elder, James Carl *lawyer*
Fenton, Elliott Clayton *lawyer*
Hanna, Terry Ross *lawyer, small business owner*
Hemry, Jerome Eldon *lawyer*
Johnson, Robert Max *lawyer*
Kenney, John Arthur *lawyer*
Kline, David Adam *lawyer, educator, writer*
Lambird, Mona Salyer *lawyer*
Legg, William Jefferson *lawyer*
Ligon, Duke R *lawyer*
Mather, Stephanie June *lawyer*
McCampbell, Robert Garner *prosecutor*
Moler, Edward Harold *lawyer*
Nelon, Robert Dale *lawyer*
Nesbitt, Charles Rudolph *lawyer, energy consultant*
Pain, Betsy M. *lawyer*
Paul, William George *lawyer*
Ross, William Jarboe *lawyer*
Ryan, Patrick M. *lawyer*
Steinhorn, Irwin Harry *lawyer, educator, corporate executive*
Stringer, L. E. (Dean Stringer) *retired lawyer*
Todd, Janet Stapleton *law librarian*
Tompkins, Raymond Edgar *lawyer*
Walsh, Lawrence Edward *lawyer*
Wood, Paula Davidson *lawyer*
Zevnik-Sawatzky, Donna Dee *retired litigation coordinator*
Zuhdi, Nabil (Bill Zuhdi) *lawyer, litigator, consultant, producer*

Pawnee
Towery, Curtis Kent *lawyer*

Ponca City
Northcutt, Clarence Dewey *lawyer*
Raley, John W., Jr., *lawyer*

Pryor
Stinson, Marion Dennis *lawyer, land use planner, judge*

Sapulpa
Gardner, Dale Ray *lawyer*

Seminole
Elsener, G. Dale *lawyer*

Stillwater
Fischer, Richard Samuel *lawyer*

Tinker AFB
Livingston, Douglas Mark *lawyer*

Tulsa
Arrington, John Leslie, Jr., *lawyer*
Balman, Steven K. *lawyer*
Belsky, Martin Henry *law educator, lawyer*
Biolchini, Robert Fredrick *lawyer*
Bowman, David Wesley *lawyer*
Bryant, Hubert Hale *lawyer*
Clark, Gary Carl *lawyer*
Clark, Joseph Francis, Jr., *lawyer*
Cooper, Richard Casey *lawyer*
Crawford, B. *lawyer*
Davenport, Gerald Bruce *lawyer*
Eagleton, Edward John *lawyer*
Eldridge, Richard Mark *lawyer*
Engel, David Wayne *lawyer, federal official*
Farrell, John L., Jr., *lawyer, business executive*
Frey, Martin Alan *lawyer, educator*
Gaberino, John Anthony, Jr., *lawyer*
Gotwals, Charles Place, Jr., *lawyer*
Hatfield, Jack Kenton *lawyer, accountant*
Howard, Gene Claude *lawyer, retired state senator*
Huffman, Robert Allen, Jr., *lawyer*
Imel, John Michael *lawyer*
Johnson, Cornelius Raymond *assistant city attorney*
Kihle, Donald Arthur *lawyer*
Luthey, Graydon Dean, Jr., *lawyer, educator*
Marlar, Donald Floyd *lawyer*
Medina, J. Michael *lawyer, educator*
O'Meilia, David E. *lawyer*
Raynolds, William F., II, *lawyer*
Slicker, Frederick Kent *lawyer*
Sneed, James Lynde *lawyer*
Steltzlen, Janelle Hicks *lawyer*
Strecker, David Eugene *lawyer*

Vinita
Johnston, Oscar Black, III, *lawyer*

Yukon
Hixson, Wendell Mark *lawyer*

OREGON

Astoria
Haskell, Donald McMillan *lawyer*

Brookings
Hinton, Floyd *lawyer*
Maxwell, William Stirling *retired lawyer*

Canby
Drummond, Gerard Kasper *lawyer, retired minerals company executive*

Central Point
Ingraham, Laura *lawyer, political commentator*
Richardson, Dennis Michael *lawyer, educator*

Coquille
Lounsbury, Steven Richard *lawyer*

Corvallis
Achterman, Gail Louise *lawyer*

Eugene
Aldave, Barbara Bader *law educator, lawyer*
DuPriest, Douglas Millhollen *lawyer*
Horn, John Harold *lawyer*
Kirkpatrick, Laird Clifford *law educator*
Lowry, Robert Dudley *lawyer*
Mumford, William Porter, II, *retired lawyer*
Scoles, Eugene Francis *law educator, lawyer*

Grants Pass
Baker, Lindi L. *lawyer*
Sloan, William Marshall *lawyer*

Lake Oswego
Byczynski, Edward Frank *lawyer, financial executive*
Kuntz, Joel Dubois *lawyer*
Rasmussen, Richard Robert *lawyer*

Lincoln City
Arant, Eugene Wesley *lawyer*

Medford
Carter, William G. *lawyer*
Deatherage, William Vernon *lawyer*
O'Connor, Karl William (Goodyear Johnson) *lawyer*

Oregon City
McFarland, Carol Anne *lawyer*

Pendleton
Rew, Lawrence Boyd *lawyer*

Portland
Abrams, Marc *lawyer, state political party executive*
Abravanel, Allan Ray *lawyer*
Anderson, Herbert Hatfield *lawyer, farmer*
Anderson, Mark Alexander *lawyer*
Arthur, Michael Elbert *lawyer, financial advisor*
Backlar, Byron *lawyer*
Bauman, Frank Anthony *retired lawyer*
Bernstine, Daniel O'Neal *law educator, university president*
Birmingham, Patrick Michael *lawyer*
Boly, Jeffrey Elwyn *retired lawyer*
Bovarnick, Paul Simon *lawyer*
Brenneman, Delbert Jay *lawyer*
Cable, John Franklin *lawyer*
Canaday, Richard A. *lawyer*
Chevis, Cheryl Ann *lawyer*
Crowell, John B., Jr., *lawyer, former government official*
DeChaine, Dean Dennis *lawyer*
Deering, Thomas Phillips *retired lawyer*
Dotten, Michael Chester *lawyer*
Eakin, Margaretta Morgan *lawyer*
English, Stephen Francis *lawyer*
Feuerstein, Howard M. *lawyer*
Foley, Ridgway Knight, Jr., *lawyer, writer*
Franzke, Richard Albert *lawyer*
Glasgow, Robert Efrom *lawyer*
Grossmann, Ronald Stanyer *lawyer*
Hanlon, Michael Gregory *lawyer*
Hanna, Harry Mitchell *lawyer*
Harnden, Edwin A. *lawyer*
Harrell, Gary Paul *lawyer*
Hart, John Edward *lawyer*
Helmer, M(artha) Christie *lawyer*
Hergenhan, Kenneth William *lawyer*
Hirshon, Robert Edward *lawyer*
Holman, Donald Reid *retired lawyer*
Houser, Douglas Guy *lawyer*
Hribernick, Paul R. *lawyer*
Huffman, James Lloyd *law educator*
Jarvis, Peter R. *lawyer*
Johansen, Judith A. *lawyer*
Johnston, David Frederick *lawyer*
Jolles, Bernard *lawyer*
Josephson, Richard Carl *lawyer*
Kanter, Stephen *law educator, dean*
Kennedy, Jack Leland *lawyer*
Kester, Randall Blair *lawyer*
Krahmer, Donald Leroy, Jr., *lawyer*
Livingston, Louis Bayer *lawyer*
Love, William Edward *lawyer*
Lusky, John Anderson *lawyer*
Maloney, Robert E., Jr., *lawyer*
Matarazzo, Harris Starr *lawyer*
Miller, William Richey, Jr., *lawyer*
Moore, Thomas Scott *lawyer*
Mosman, Michael W. *prosecutor*
Mowe, Gregory Robert *lawyer*
Noonan, William Donald *lawyer, physician*
Olson, Kristine *prosecutor*
Paulus, Norma Jean Petersen *lawyer*
Pratt, Scott Owen *lawyer*
Purcell, John F. *lawyer*
Richardson, Campbell *retired lawyer*
Richter, Peter Christian *lawyer*
Rosen, Steven O. *lawyer*
Ryan, John Duncan *lawyer*
Sand, Thomas Charles *lawyer*
Savage, John William *lawyer*
Schuster, Philip Frederick, II, *lawyer, writer, law educator*
Seaman, Robert E., III, *lawyer*
Shinn, Michael Robert *lawyer*
Simpson, Robert Glenn *lawyer*
Stephens, Donald L., Jr., *lawyer*
Stewart, Milton Roy *lawyer*
Stone, Richard James *lawyer*
Sullivan, Edward Joseph *lawyer, educator*
Van Valkenburg, Edgar Walter *lawyer*
Waggoner, James Clyde *lawyer*
Weaver, Delbert Allen *lawyer*
Westwood, James Nicholson *lawyer*
White, Douglas James, Jr., *lawyer*
Williamson, Charles Ready, III, *lawyer*
Wilson, Owen Meredith, Jr., *lawyer*
Wood, Marcus Andrew *lawyer*
Wyse, William Walker *lawyer, real estate executive*
Zalutsky, Morton Herman *lawyer*

Salem
Bailey, Henry John, III, *retired lawyer, educator*
Breen, Richard F., Jr., *law librarian, lawyer, educator*
Clark, David Scott *law educator, consultant*
Haselton, Rick Thomas *lawyer*
Mannix, Kevin Leese *lawyer, political organization executive*
Nafziger, James Albert Richmond *lawyer, educator*

Tigard
Lowry, David Burton *lawyer*

Zigzag
Rieke, Forrest Neill *lawyer*

PENNSYLVANIA

Aliquippa
D'Agostino, Richard Daniel *lawyer*

Allentown
Altemose, Mark Kenneth *lawyer*
Brown, Robert Wayne *lawyer*
Hauck, Jeffrey Peter Artorius Martel *lawyer, protective services official*
Holt, Leon Conrad, Jr., *lawyer, business executive*
McGinley, Paul Anthony, Jr., *lawyer*
Moyer, Michael Edward *lawyer*
Nagel, Edward McCaul *lawyer, former utilities executive*
Zamborsky, Donald A. *lawyer*

Allison Park
Herrington, John David, III, *lawyer, director*
Ries, William Campbell *lawyer*

Ambler
Glassmoyer, Thomas Parvin *lawyer*

Ardmore
Narin, Stephen B. *lawyer*

Bala Cynwyd
Cades, Stewart Russell *lawyer, communications company executive*
Garrity, Vincent Francis, Jr., *lawyer*
Odell, Herbert *lawyer*
Schwartz, Jeffrey Byron *lawyer*
Wiener, Thomas Eli *lawyer*

Beaver
Petrush, John Joseph *lawyer*

Berwyn
Markle, John, Jr., *lawyer*
Wood, Thomas E. *lawyer*

Bethlehem
Hemphill, Meredith, Jr., *retired lawyer*
Spry, Donald Francis, II, *lawyer*

Blue Bell
Elliott, John Michael *lawyer*
Siedzikowski, Henry Francis *lawyer*
Sundheim, Nancy Straus *lawyer*
Swansen, Samuel Theodore *lawyer*
Teklits, Joseph Anthony *lawyer*

Bridgeville
Irvine, Peter Bennington *clergyman*

Bryn Mawr
Frick, Benjamin Charles *lawyer*
Leto, Francis Joseph *lawyer, educator*
Mezvinsky, Edward M. *lawyer*
Phillips, Stephen S. *lawyer*

Camp Hill
Mackin, Charles Philip, Jr., *lawyer*

Chadds Ford
Cohen, Felix Asher *lawyer*
Gordon, William Edmund, Jr., *lawyer*
Lamonaca, Joseph Michael *lawyer, pilot*

Clarks Summit
Beemer, John Barry *lawyer*

Conshohocken
Bramson, Robert Sherman *lawyer*
Nowak, Gregory Joseph *lawyer, educator*

Doylestown
Elliott, Richard Howard *lawyer*

Du Bois
Blakley, Benjamin Spencer, III, *lawyer*

East Stroudsburg
Upright, Kirby Grant *lawyer*

Edinboro
Travis, Grant Carner *lawyer*

Elkins Park
Shmukler, Stanford *lawyer*

Erie
Cullen, James Donald *lawyer*
Van Gorder, Jan Reid *lawyer, insurance company executive*

Etters
Steps, Barbara Jill *lawyer*

Exton
Hedges, Donald Walton *lawyer*
Teti, Louis N. *lawyer*

Fayetteville
Molitor, Graham Thomas Tate *lawyer*

Feasterville Trevose
Osterhout, Richard Cadwallader *lawyer*

Fort Washington
Moulton, Hugh Geoffrey *lawyer, retired business executive*

Frackville
Domalakes, Paul George *lawyer*

Gettysburg
Smith, Emory Clark *lawyer, financial advisor*

Gladwyne
Acton, David *lawyer*
Booth, Harold Waverly *lawyer, finance and investment company executive*

Glenside
Goldberg, Steven Selig *education law educator*
Mermelstein, Jules Joshua *lawyer, township commissioner*

Greensburg
Belden, H. Reginald, Jr., *lawyer*
Gounley, Dennis Joseph *lawyer*
Heubel, William Bernard *lawyer, international contract consultant*

Grove City
McBride, Milford Lawrence, Jr., *lawyer*

Harrisburg
Cline, Andrew Haley *lawyer*
Cooper, Jeffrey *lawyer*
Diehm, James Warren *lawyer, educator*
Gale, Randall Glenn *lawyer*
Golden, Thomas M. *lawyer*
Gornish, Gerald *lawyer*
Hanson, Robert DeLolle *lawyer*
Howett, John Charles, Jr., *lawyer*
Kane, Yvette *lawyer, judge*
Kelly, Robert Edward, Jr., *lawyer*
Klein, Michael D. *lawyer*
Kury, Franklin Leo *lawyer*
Lappas, Spero Thomas *lawyer*
Long, Robert Howard, Jr., *lawyer*
Miller, Leslie Anne *lawyer*
Nauman, Spencer Gilbert, Jr., *lawyer, director*
Sheldon, J. Michael *lawyer, educator*
Sullivan, John Cornelius, Jr., *lawyer*
Tyler, Brian Joseph *lawyer*
Van Zile, Philip Taylor, III, *lawyer, educator*
Warshaw, Allen Charles *lawyer*
West, James Joseph *lawyer*

Hatboro
Nicholson, Bruce Allen *lawyer*

Haverford
Stiller, Jennifer Anne *lawyer*
Stroud, James Stanley *retired lawyer*

Hazleton
Schiavo, Pasco Louis *lawyer*

Hershey
Reese, Robert M. *retired lawyer*

Horsham
Best, Franklin Luther, Jr., *lawyer*

Huntingdon Valley
Forman, Howard Irving *lawyer, former government official*
Kaufman, David Joseph *lawyer*
Toll, Robert Irwin *lawyer, real estate developer*

Jenkintown
Dickstein, Joan Borteck *arbitrator, conflict management consultant*
Robbins, Jack Winton *lawyer*
Worthington, Sandra Boulton *lawyer*

Jersey Shore
Flayhart, Martin Albert *lawyer*

Johnstown
Glosser, William Louis *lawyer*

Jones Mills
Fish, Paul Waring *lawyer*

Kennett Square
Bainbridge, John Seaman *retired law school administrator, law educator, lawyer*
Partnoy, Ronald Allen *lawyer*

King Of Prussia
Boles, Donald Michael *lawyer*
Gadsden, Christopher Henry *lawyer, educator*
Schneider, Pam Horvitz *lawyer*

Kingston
Shaffer, Charles Alan *lawyer*

Lake Harmony
Polansky, Larry Paul *court administrator, consultant*

Lancaster
Hall, Thomas Wayne *lawyer*
Lewis, Alvin Bower, Jr., *lawyer*
Minney, Michael Jay *lawyer*
Nast, Dianne Martha *lawyer*
Pyfer, John Frederick, Jr., *lawyer*
Roda, Joseph Francis *lawyer*
Zimmerman, D(onald) Patrick *lawyer*

Langhorne
Hillje, Barbara Brown *lawyer*

Lansdale
Sultanik, Jeffrey Ted *lawyer*

Lemoyne
Stewart, Richard Williams *lawyer*

Lewisburg
Knight, Louise Osborn *lawyer*

Mc Keesport
Kessler, Steven Fisher *lawyer*

Mc Murray
Brzustowicz, John Cinq-Mars *lawyer*

Meadville
Barrett, Bruce Alan *lawyer*

Media
Berman, Bernard Mayer *lawyer*
Blake, David Gordon *lawyer*
Durham, James W. *lawyer*
Emerson, Sterling Jonathan *lawyer*
Ewing, Robert Clark *lawyer*
Garrison, Susan Kay *lawyer*
Rubin, Arnold E. *lawyer*

Mendenhall
Reinert, Norbert Frederick *patent lawyer, retired chemical company executive*

Monroeville
Cohen, Laura *lawyer*

Moon Township
Alstadt, Lynn Jeffery *lawyer*
Lipson, Barry J. *lawyer, columnist*

Morrisville
Heefner, William Frederick *lawyer*

Mount Gretna
Warshaw, Roberta Sue *lawyer*

Natrona Heights
Maleski, Cynthia Maria *lawyer*

New Buffalo
Cramer, John McNaight *lawyer*

New Castle
Manolis, James William *lawyer*

New Kensington
Wallace, Henry Jared, Jr., *lawyer*

Newtown
Kardos, Mel D. *lawyer, educator*
Zicherman, David L. *lawyer, educator, financial consultant*

Newtown Square
Bower, Ward Alan *management consultant, lawyer*

Norristown
Aman, George Matthias, III, *lawyer*
Britt, Earl Thomas *lawyer*
Gold-Bikin, Lynne Z. *lawyer*
Rees, Thomas Dynevor *lawyer*
Rounick, Jack A. *lawyer, company executive*
Scheffler, Stuart Jay *lawyer*

Orefield
Dimmich, Jeffrey Robert *lawyer*

Philadelphia
Abramowitz, Robert Leslie *lawyer*
Adamany, David Walter *law and political science educator*
Adams, Arlin Marvin *lawyer, arbitrator, mediator, retired judge*
Anders, Jerrold P. *lawyer*
Asher, Steven Alan *lawyer*
Auerbach, Sheryl Lynn *lawyer*
Auten, David Charles *lawyer*
Baccini, Laurance Ellis *lawyer*
Bachman, Arthur *lawyer*
Barrett, John J(ames), Jr., *lawyer*
Bartolomeo, Paul Joseph, Jr., *lawyer*
Beasley, James Edwin *lawyer*
Berger, David *lawyer*
Berger, Harold *lawyer, electrical engineer*
Berger, Lawrence Howard *lawyer*
Berkley, Emily Carolan *lawyer*
Berkman, Richard Lyle *lawyer*
Bershad, Jack R. *retired lawyer*
Bildersee, Robert Alan *lawyer*
Binder, David Franklin *lawyer, writer*
Black, Allen Decatur *lawyer*
Boggia, Eugene Stephen *lawyer*
Bogutz, Jerome Edwin *lawyer, educator*
Boss, Amelia Helen *law educator, lawyer*
Bradshaw, William Elbert *lawyer*
Bressler, Barry E. *lawyer*
Brown, Stephen D. *lawyer*
Brown, William Hill, III, *lawyer*
Browne, Stanhope Stryker *lawyer*
Buccino, Ernest John, Jr., *lawyer*
Burbank, Stephen Bradner *law educator*
Calvert, Jay H., Jr., *lawyer*
Cannon, John, III, *lawyer*
Carnecchia, Baldo M., Jr., *lawyer*
Carroll, Mark Thomas *lawyer*
Carson, Timothy Joseph *lawyer*
Casper, Charles B. *lawyer*
Cherken, Harry Sarkis, Jr., *lawyer*
Child, John Sowden, Jr., *lawyer*
Chimples, George *lawyer*
Clark, John Arthur *lawyer*
Clark, William H., Jr., *lawyer*
Cohen, David Louis *lawyer*
Coleman, Robert J. *lawyer*
Colli, Bart Joseph *lawyer*
Collings, Robert L. *lawyer*
Comisky, Hope A. *lawyer*
Connor, Joseph Patrick, III, *lawyer*
Cooney, J(ohn) Gordon, Jr., *lawyer*
Cox, Roger Frazier *lawyer*
Coyne, Charles Cole *lawyer*
Cozen, Stephen Allen *lawyer*
Cramer, Harold *lawyer*
Damsgaard, Kell Marsh *lawyer*
Davis, Alan Jay *lawyer*
Davis, C. VanLeer, III, *lawyer*
DeBunda, Salvatore Michael *lawyer*
Del Raso, Joseph Vincent *lawyer*
Devlin, John Gerard *lawyer, author*
Diaz, Nelson *lawyer*
Dichter, Mark S. *lawyer*
Dilks, Park Bankert, Jr., *lawyer*
Donohue, James J. *lawyer*
Donohue, John Patrick *lawyer*
Doran, William Michael *lawyer*
Dorfman, John Charles *lawyer*
Dragon, Albert *lawyer*
Drake, William Frank, Jr., *lawyer*
Dubin, Leonard *lawyer*
Dubin, Stephen Victor *lawyer*
Dworetzky, Joseph Anthony *lawyer, city official*
Efstratiades, Anastasius *lawyer*
Esser, Carl Eric *lawyer*
Ewald, William Bragg, III, *law educator, philosopher, educator*
Fader, Henry Conrad *lawyer*
Fala, Herman C. *lawyer*
Farley, Barbara L. *lawyer*
Feirson, Steven B. *lawyer*
Fickler, Arlene *lawyer*
Fiebach, H. Robert *lawyer*
Fineman, S. David *lawyer*
Finkelstein, Joseph Simon *lawyer*
Fitts, Michael Andrew *law educator, dean*
Flanagan, Joseph Patrick, Jr., *lawyer*
Fox, Reeder Rodman *lawyer*
Foxman, Stephen Mark *lawyer*
Frank, Barry H. *lawyer*
Frank, George Andrew *lawyer*
Frank, Harvey *lawyer, author*
Freedman, Robert Louis *lawyer*
Gadon, Steven Franklin *lawyer*
Garcia, Rudolph *lawyer*
Genkin, Barry Howard *lawyer*
George, Paul M. *law librarian, library director*
German, Edward Cecil *lawyer*
Gerstenhber, Murray *law educator, mathematics professor*
Gilberg, Kenneth Roy *lawyer*
Gittis, Howard *lawyer*
Glanton, Richard H. *lawyer*
Goldberg, Joseph *lawyer*
Goldberg, Marvin Allen *lawyer, business consultant*
Goldberg, Richard Robert *lawyer*
Goldstein, William Marks *lawyer*
Goodman, Stephen Murry *lawyer*
Gordesky, Morton *lawyer*
Gordon, George G. *lawyer*
Gough, John Francis *lawyer*
Grady, Thomas Michael *lawyer*
Grant, M. Duncan *lawyer*
Grayson, Zachary Louis *lawyer*
Grove, David Lavan *lawyer*
Grunfeld, David I. *lawyer*
Haley, Vincent Peter *lawyer*
Hangley, William Thomas *lawyer*
Harkins, John Graham, Jr., *lawyer*
Harmelin, Stephen Joseph *lawyer*
Harris, Judith E. *lawyer*
Harvey, Gregory Merrill *lawyer*
Haviland, Bancroft Dawley *lawyer*
Heinzen, Bernard George *lawyer*
Henrich, William Joseph, Jr., *lawyer*
Hickok, D. Alicia *lawyer*
Hottensen, Margaret M. *lawyer*
Hoyle, Lawrence Truman, Jr., *lawyer*
Hunter, James Austen, Jr., *lawyer*
Jellinek, Miles Andrew *lawyer*
Jones, Robert Jeffries *lawyer*
Jurewicz, Richard Michael *lawyer*
Kaier, Edward John *lawyer*
Keene, John Clark *lawyer, educator*
Kessler, Alan Craig *lawyer*
Klasko, Herbert Ronald *lawyer, law educator, writer*
Klein, Howard Bruce *lawyer, law educator*
Kline, Thomas Richard *lawyer*
Kolsby, Herbert F. *lawyer, educator*
Kopp, Charles Gilbert *lawyer*
Kormes, John Winston *lawyer*
Krzyzanowski, Richard L. *lawyer, corporate executive*
LaCheen, Stephen Robert *lawyer*
Ledwith, John Francis *lawyer*
Leech, Noyes Elwood *lawyer, educator*
Leonard, Thomas *lawyer*
Levin, Murray Simon *lawyer*
Levy, Dale Penneys *lawyer*
Lewis, John Hardy, Jr., *lawyer*
Libonati, Michael Ernest *law educator, writer*
Lichtenstein, Robert Jay *lawyer*
Lillie, Charisse Ranielle *lawyer, educator*
Lipman, Frederick D. *lawyer, writer, law educator*
Lombard, John James, Jr., *lawyer, writer*
Lonergan, Robert A. *lawyer*
Lotman, Arline Jolles *lawyer*
Loveless, George Group *retired lawyer*
Lowery, William Herbert *lawyer*
Lucian, John *lawyer*
Madva, Stephen Alan *lawyer*
Magargee, W(illiam) Scott, III, *lawyer*
Magaziner, Fred Thomas *lawyer*
Mann, Theodore R. *lawyer*
Mannino, Edward Francis *lawyer, educator*
Marino, Donald C. *lawyer*
Mason, Theodore W. *lawyer*
Mattoon, Peter Mills *lawyer*
Maxey, David Walker *lawyer*
McCausland, Margaret A. *lawyer, educator*
McHugh, James Joseph *lawyer*
McKeever, John Eugene *lawyer*
McKenzie, James W. *lawyer*
McMichael, Lawrence Grover *lawyer*
McQuiston, Robert Earl *lawyer*
Meehan, Patrick L. *prosecutor*
Meigs, John Forsyth *lawyer*
Messa, Joseph Louis, Jr., *lawyer*
Meyers, Howard L. *lawyer*
Milbourne, Walter Robertson *lawyer*
Miller, Henry Franklin *lawyer*
Milone, Francis Michael *lawyer*
Minisi, Anthony S. *lawyer*
Mirabello, Francis Joseph *lawyer*
Moses, Bonnie Smith *lawyer, educator*
Moss, Arthur Henshey *lawyer*
Mullinix, Edward Wingate *lawyer*
Murphy, William Patrick *lawyer, editor, writer*
Nocella, Richard J. *lawyer*
O'Brien, William Jerome, II, *lawyer*
Ominsky, Alan Jay *lawyer, medical educator*
Ominsky, Harris *lawyer*
O'Reilly, Timothy Patrick *lawyer*
Oswald, Stanton S. *lawyer*
Packer, Rekha Desai *lawyer*
Pagliaro, James Domenic *lawyer*
Palmer, Richard Ware *lawyer*
Panzer, Mitchell Emanuel *lawyer*
Parry, William DeWitt *lawyer*
Phelan, John M. *lawyer*
Pokotilow, Manny David *lawyer, educator*
Pollack, Michael *lawyer*
Posner, Edward Martin *lawyer*
Poul, Franklin *lawyer*
Powell, Walter Hecht *retired labor arbitrator*
Price, Robert Stanley *lawyer*
Promislo, Daniel *lawyer*
Rabinowitz, Samuel Nathan *lawyer*
Rachofsky, David J. *lawyer*
Rackow, Julian Paul *lawyer*
Rainone, Michael Carmine *lawyer*
Ramsey, Natalie D. *lawyer*
Reed, Michael Haywood *lawyer*
Reich, Abraham Charles *lawyer*
Reiss, John Barlow *lawyer*
Reiter, Joseph Henry *lawyer, retired judge*
Reitz, Curtis Randall *lawyer, educator*
Rhodes, Alice Graham *lawyer*
Roberts, Carl Geoffrey *lawyer*
Root, Stanley William, Jr., *lawyer, retired*
Rosenberg, Howell K. *lawyer*
Rosenbleeth, Richard M. *lawyer*
Rosenstein, James Alfred *lawyer, mediator, negotiation facilitator*
Ross, Daniel R. *lawyer*
Ross, Murray Louis *lawyer, business executive*
Samuel, Ralph David *lawyer*
Satinsky, Barnett *lawyer*
Schaub, Harry Carl *lawyer*
Scher, Howard Dennis *lawyer*
Schneider, Richard Graham *lawyer*
Schorling, William Harrison *lawyer*
Schwartz, Robert M. *lawyer*
Segal, Robert Martin *lawyer*
Seidel, Arthur Harris *lawyer*
Shapiro, Raymond L. *lawyer*
Sheils, Denis Francis *lawyer*
Shestack, Jerome Joseph *lawyer*
Siegel, Bernard Louis *lawyer*
Sigmond, Richard Brian *lawyer*
Simkanich, John Joseph *lawyer, civil engineer*
Sloane, Richard *lawyer*
Smith, John Francis, III, *lawyer*
Solano, Carl Anthony *lawyer*
Sonnenfeld, Marc Jay *lawyer*
Spaeth, Edmund Benjamin, Jr., *retired lawyer, retired law educator, former judge*
Spector, Martin Wolf *lawyer, business executive*
Spolan, Harmon Samuel *lawyer*
Steinberg, Robert Philip *lawyer*
Stern, Joan Naomi *lawyer*
Stewart, Robert Forrest, Jr., *lawyer*
Strasbaugh, Wayne Ralph *lawyer*
Strickler, Matthew M. *lawyer*
Stuntebeck, Clinton A. *lawyer*
Subak, John Thomas *lawyer*
Summers, Clyde Wilson *law educator*
Temin, Michael Lehman *lawyer*
Thomas, Lowell Shumway, Jr., *lawyer*
Tiger, Ira Paul *retired lawyer*
Vaira, Peter Francis *lawyer*
Warner, Theodore Kugler, Jr., *lawyer*
Weil, Jeffrey George *lawyer*
Whiteside, William Anthony, Jr., *retired lawyer*
Whitman, Jules Isidoré *lawyer*
Wiener, Ronald Martin *lawyer*
Wild, Richard P. *lawyer*
Wilf, Frederic Marshal *lawyer*
Wilson, Rhonda Hill *lawyer*
Wittels, Barnaby Caesar *lawyer, writer*
Wolf, Robert B. *lawyer*
Wolff, Deborah H(orowitz) *lawyer*
Wright, Minturn Tatum, III, *retired lawyer*
Wrobleski, Jeanne Pauline *lawyer*
Young, Andrew Brodbeck *lawyer*
Young, Roma Skeen *lawyer*
Zuckerman, Brian D. *lawyer*

Pipersville
Sigety, Charles Edward *lawyer, consultant, family business consultant*

Pittsburgh
Aronson, Mark Berne *retired lawyer, advocate*
Artz, John Curtis *lawyer*
Basinski, Anthony Joseph *lawyer*
Bleier, Michael E. *lawyer*
Blenko, Walter John, Jr., *lawyer*
Blum, Eva Tansky *lawyer*
Bochicchio, Vito Salvatore *lawyer*
Bonessa, Dennis R. *lawyer*
Boswell, William Paret *lawyer*
Brand, Ronald Alvah *lawyer*
Brown, David Ronald *lawyer*
Brown, James Benton *lawyer*
Buchanan, Mary Beth *prosecutor*
Candris, Laura A. *lawyer*
Cheever, George Martin *lawyer*
Cohen, Henry C. *lawyer*
Colen, Frederick Haas *lawyer*
Coney, Aims C., Jr., *lawyer, labor-management negotiator*
Connors, Eugene Kenneth *lawyer, educator*
Cooper, Thomas Louis *lawyer*
Corbett, Thomas Wingett, Jr., *lawyer*
Cowan, Barton Zalman *lawyer*
Cusick, Daniel Francis *lawyer*
Daniel, Robert Michael *lawyer*
Davenport, Ronald Ross, Jr., *lawyer*
Davis, Lewis U., Jr., *lawyer*
DeForest, Walter Pattison, III, *lawyer*
Demmler, John Henry *retired lawyer*
Denys, Sylvia *lawyer, researcher*
Donnelly, Thomas Joseph *lawyer, director*
Doty, Robert Walter *lawyer*
Ehrenwerth, David Harry *lawyer*
Evans, Bruce Dwight *lawyer*
Fishman, Craig L. *lawyer*

Flatley, Lawrence Edward *lawyer*
Flinn, Michael James *lawyer*
Fort, James Tomlinson *lawyer*
Frank, Ronald William *lawyer*
Frolik, Lawrence Anton *law educator, lawyer, consultant*
Geeseman, Robert George *lawyer*
Gold, Harold Arthur *lawyer*
Goldberg, Mark Joel *lawyer*
Hardie, James Hiller *lawyer*
Hartman, Ronald G. *lawyer*
Harty, James Quinn *lawyer*
Hellman, Arthur David *law educator, consultant*
Hershey, Dale *lawyer, educator*
Hershey, Nathan *lawyer, educator*
Hill, John Howard *retired lawyer*
Hitt, Leo N. *lawyer, educator*
Hollinshead, Earl Darnell, Jr., *lawyer*
Hull, John Daniel, IV, *lawyer*
Hurnyak, Christina Kaiser *lawyer*
Johnson, Barbara Elizabeth *lawyer*
Johnson, Robert Alan *lawyer*
Jones, Craig Ward *lawyer*
Jordan, Gregory B. *lawyer*
Kabala, Edward John *lawyer, corporate executive*
Kelly, Linda L. *prosecutor*
Kenrick, Charles William *lawyer*
Ketter, David Lee *lawyer*
Klett, Edwin L. *lawyer*
Leech, Jeffrey James *lawyer*
Leibowitz, Marvin *lawyer*
Litman, Roslyn Margolis *lawyer*
Lynch, Victor K. *lawyer*
Lyncheski, John E. *lawyer*
McCartney, Robert Charles *retired lawyer*
McConomy, James Herbert *lawyer*
McGinley, John Regis, Jr., *lawyer*
McGough, Walter Thomas, Jr., *lawyer*
McLaughlin, John Sherman *lawyer*
Meisel, Alan *law educator*
Mulvihill, Keithley D. *lawyer*
Murdoch, David Armor *lawyer*
Mutterperl, William Charles *lawyer, corporate financial executive*
Newlin, William Rankin *lawyer*
Nordenberg, Mark Alan *law educator, academic administrator*
Norris, James Harold *lawyer*
Nute, Leslie F. *lawyer*
Ober, Russell John, Jr., *lawyer*
O'Connor, Edward Gearing *lawyer*
Olson, Stephen M(ichael) *lawyer*
Orsatti, Ernest Benjamin *lawyer*
Phillips, Larry Edward *lawyer*
Picadio, Anthony Peter *lawyer*
Plowman, Jack Wesley *lawyer*
Post, Peter David *lawyer*
Powderly, William H., III, *lawyer*
Prosperi, Louis Anthony *lawyer*
Pushinsky, Jon *lawyer*
Randolph, Robert DeWitt *lawyer*
Reed, W. Franklin *lawyer*
Restivo, James John, Jr., *lawyer*
Ritchey, Patrick William *lawyer*
Roman, Andrew Michael *lawyer, educator*
Rosenberger, Bryan David *lawyer*
Sandman, Dan D. *lawyer*
Scheinholtz, Leonard Louis *lawyer*
Schwendeman, Paul William *lawyer*
Sherry, John Sebastian *lawyer*
Shuman, Joseph Duff *lawyer*
Silverman, Arnold Barry *lawyer*
Springer, Eric Winston *lawyer, director*
Stepanian, Steven Arvid, II, *lawyer, financial consultant*
Strader, James David *lawyer*
Stroyd, Arthur Heister *lawyer*
Sweeney, Clayton Anthony *lawyer, business executive*
Symons, Edward Leonard, Jr., *law educator, investment adviser*
Tarasi, Louis Michael, Jr., *lawyer*
Thieman, Frederick W. *lawyer*
Thomas, Richard Irwin *lawyer*
Thompson, Thomas Martin *lawyer*
Thurman, Andrew Edward *lawyer*
Tungate, David E. *lawyer, educator*
Turner, Harry Woodruff *lawyer*
Ubinger, John W., Jr., *lawyer*
Ummer, James Walter *lawyer*
Van Kirk, Thomas L. *lawyer*
Vater, Charles J. *lawyer*
Veeder, Peter Greig *lawyer*
Walton, Jon David *lawyer*
Weil, Andrew L. *retired lawyer*
Whitehead, Paul *lawyer, labor union administrator*
Wiley, S. Donald *lawyer, food products executive*
Wilkinson, James Allan *lawyer, healthcare executive*
Williams, Stephen Edward *corporate lawyer*
Yorsz, Stanley *lawyer*
Zittrain, Lester Eugene *lawyer*

Plymouth Meeting
Carbine, Sharon *lawyer, corporation executive*
Kranzdorf, Norman M(elvin) *lawyer, real estate executive*

Pottsville
Jones, Joseph Hayward *lawyer*

Radnor
Nofer, George Hancock *lawyer*

Reading
Eshelman, David Richard *lawyer*
Kline, Sidney DeLong, Jr., *lawyer*
Linton, Jack Arthur *lawyer*
Rothermel, Daniel Krott *lawyer, holding company executive*

Rockledge
Blessing, Maribeth *lawyer, educator, mediator, arbitrator*

Royersford
Chance, Steven Kent *lawyer*

Scranton
Burke, Henry Patrick *lawyer*
Friedrichs, David O. *legal educator*
Haggerty, James Joseph *lawyer*
Marino, Thomas A. *lawyer*

Solebury
Cross, Robert William *lawyer, venture capital executive*
Valentine, H. Jeffrey *legal association executive*

Somerset
Carroll, William Richard *lawyer*

Souderton
Marden, Jack Mortimer *lawyer*

Spring City
Mayerson, Hy *lawyer*

Spring House
Rosoff, William A. *lawyer, executive*

Springfield
Maclay, Donald Merle *retired lawyer*

State College
Engle, Jill Callahan *law educator*
Myers, Barry Lee *lawyer*
Nollau, Lee Gordon *lawyer*

Stroudsburg
Jacobson, Gilbert H. *lawyer, director*

Sunbury
Fernsler, John Paul *lawyer*

Swarthmore
Elman, Gerry Jay *lawyer*

Uniontown
Coldren, Ira Burdette, Jr., *lawyer*

Villanova
Bersoff, Donald Neil *lawyer, psychologist*
Maule, James Edward *law educator, lawyer*
Zearfoss, Herbert Keyser *retired lawyer*

Warren
Ristau, Mark Moody *lawyer, petroleum consultant*

Warrendale
Richards, John Thomas, Jr., *lawyer*

Washington
Allison, Jonathan *retired lawyer*
Lerner, William C. *lawyer*
Posner, David S. *lawyer*
Richman, Stephen I. *lawyer*
Schwarz, Frederick A.O., Jr., *lawyer*

Washington Crossing
Sloca, Steven Lane *lawyer*

Wayne
Spiess, F. Harry, Jr., *lawyer*
Wilson, Bruce Brighton *lawyer, retired transportation executive*

West Chester
Ewing, Joseph Neff, Jr., *retired lawyer*
Kaufman, Daniel J. *lawyer*

West Conshohocken
Teillon, Louis Pierre, Jr., *lawyer*

Wexford
Micale, Frank Jude *lawyer*

White Oak
Pribanic, Victor Hunter *lawyer*

Wilkes Barre
Morgan, Dennis Keith *lawyer*
O'Donnell, Catherine Rose *lawyer*

Williamsport
Ertel, Allen Edward *lawyer, former congressman*

Womelsdorf
Worley, Jane Ludwig *lawyer*

Yardley
Hamberg, Gilbert Lee *lawyer*

York
Hoffmeyer, William Frederick *lawyer, educator*
Perry, Ronald *lawyer*

Youngstown
Love, George H., Jr., *lawyer*

RHODE ISLAND

Barrington
Soutter, Thomas Douglas *retired lawyer*

Bristol
Berman, Garrett L. *eyewitness and jury educator*
Bogus, Carl Thomas *law educator*
Kent, Robert Brydon *law educator*

Cranston
Ferguson, Christine C. *lawyer, state agency administrator*
Mansolillo, Charles Ronald *lawyer*
Simonian, John S. *lawyer*

East Greenwich
Dence, Edward William, Jr., *lawyer, banker*

Hope Valley
Walker, Howard Ernest *lawyer*

Jamestown
Parks, Albert Lauriston *lawyer*

Little Compton
Caron, Wilfred Rene *retired lawyer*

Newport
McConnell, David Kelso *lawyer*

Pawtucket
Belliveau, Kathrin Pagonis *lawyer*

Providence
Berkelhammer, Robert Bruce *lawyer*
Carlotti, Stephen Jon *lawyer*
Clifford, Sidney, Jr., *lawyer, judge*
Conley, Patrick T. *lawyer, writer, historian*
Courage, Thomas Roberts *lawyer*
Curran, Joseph Patrick *lawyer*
Demopulos, Harold William *lawyer*
DiMonte, Vincent A. *lawyer*
Donnelly, Kevin William *lawyer*
Farrell, Margaret Dawson *lawyer*
Fogarty, Edward Michael *lawyer*
Gale, Edwin John *judge*
Gasbarro, Pasco, Jr., *lawyer*
Johnson, Vahe Duncan *lawyer*
Jones, Lauren Evans *lawyer*
Kacir, Barbara Brattin *lawyer*
Kean, John Vaughan *retired lawyer*
Kraemer, Michael Frederick *lawyer*
Licht, Richard A. *lawyer*
Lipsey, Howard Irwin *law educator, justice, lawyer*
Long, Beverly Glenn *retired lawyer*
Long, Nicholas Trott *lawyer*
McCann, Gail Elizabeth *lawyer*
McElroy, Michael Robert *lawyer*
McIntyre, Jerry L. *lawyer*
Mulhearn, Christopher Michael *lawyer*
Olsen, Hans Peter *lawyer*
Roney, John M. *lawyer*
Salter, Lester Herbert *lawyer*
Sherman, Deming Eliot *lawyer*
Smith, Robert Ellis *lawyer, journalist*
Staples, Richard Farnsworth *lawyer*
Tobin, Bentley *lawyer*

Scituate
Gorham, Bradford *lawyer*

Wakefield
Hart, Kenneth Nelson *lawyer*

Warwick
Goldman, Steven Jason *lawyer, accountant, consultant*
Knowles, Charles Timothy *lawyer, state legislator, military officer, educator*
Reilly, John B. *lawyer*
Riffkin, Mitchell Sanford *lawyer*
St. Pierre, Michael A. *lawyer*

West Warwick
Bottella, Tammy Ann *lawyer*
Pollock, Bruce Gerald *lawyer*

Westerly
Nardone, William Andrew *lawyer*
Panciera, Richard Conner *lawyer*

Woonsocket
Lankowsky, Zenon P. *lawyer*
Roszkowski, Joseph John *lawyer*

SOUTH CAROLINA

Aiken
Amabile, John Louis *lawyer*
Pearce, Richard Lee *lawyer*
Rudnick, Irene Krugman *lawyer, former state legislator, educator*

Beaufort
Harvey, William Brantley, Jr., *lawyer, former lieutenant governor*

Bishopville
Jennings, Jacob Hill *lawyer, director*

Charleston
Branham, C. Michael *lawyer*
Cannon, Hugh *lawyer*
Donnem, Roland William *retired lawyer, real estate owner, developer*
Dulles, Frederick Hendrik *lawyer*
Farr, Charles Sims *lawyer*
Freer, Robert Elliott, Jr., *lawyer*
Kahn, Ellis Irvin *lawyer*
Lader, Philip *lawyer, academic administrator, diplomat*
Leath, William Jefferson, Jr., *lawyer*
Patrick, Charles William, Jr., *lawyer*
Robinson, Neil Cibley, Jr., *lawyer*
Rosen, Richard S. *lawyer*

Clemson
Cox, Headley Morris, Jr., *lawyer, educator*

Columbia
Arvay, Nancy Joan *lawyer*
Bernstein, Barry Joel *lawyer*
Blanton, Hoover Clarence *lawyer*
Brown, Robert Charles *lawyer*
Buchanan, William Jennings *lawyer, judge*
Burnette, Mary Malissa *lawyer*
Cotty, William Frank (Bill Cotty) *lawyer, state legislator*
Crystal, Nathan Maxwell *law educator, consultant*
Day, Richard Earl *lawyer, educator*
Felix, Robert Louis *law educator*
Finkel, Gerald Michael *lawyer*
Gibbes, William Holman *lawyer*
Gray, Elizabeth Van Doren *lawyer*
Handel, Richard Craig *lawyer*
Harpootlian, Richard Ara *lawyer*
Harvey, Jonathan Matthew *lawyer*
Johnson, Lawrence Wilbur, Jr., *lawyer*
Jones, Hartwell Kelley, Jr., *lawyer*
Matthews, Steve Allen *lawyer*
McCullough, Ralph Clayton, II, *lawyer, educator*
McLeod, Walton James *lawyer, state legislator*
Morrison, Stephen George *lawyer*
Nexsen, Julian Jacobs *lawyer*
Pollard, William Albert *lawyer*
Powell, Burnele Venable *dean*
Roberts, Pamela J. *lawyer*
Strom, J. Preston, Jr., *lawyer*
Swerling, Jack Bruce *lawyer*
Tate, Harold Simmons, Jr., *lawyer*
Thurmond, J. Strom, Jr., *lawyer*
Yarborough, Clinton Joseph *lawyer*

Conway
Martin, Gregory Keith *lawyer, mayor*

Georgetown
Moore, Albert Cunningham *lawyer, insurance company executive*

Greenville
Coates, William Alexander *lawyer*
Csontos, Alan Arthur *lawyer*
Dobson, Robert Albertus, III, *lawyer, volunteer*
Edwards, Harry LaFoy *lawyer*
Foulke, Edwin Gerhart, Jr., *lawyer*
Horton, James Wright *retired lawyer*
Hutson, Melvin Robert *lawyer*
Kappel, Matthew Jay *lawyer*
Massey, Raymond David *lawyer*
Mauldin, John Inglis *public defender*
McKinney, Ronald W. *lawyer*
Phillips, Joseph Brantley, Jr., *lawyer*
Riley, Richard Wilson *lawyer, former federal official*
Smoak, Lewis Tyson *lawyer*
Todd, John Dickerson, Jr., *retired lawyer*
Walters, Johnnie McKeiver *lawyer*
White, Daniel Bowman *lawyer*
Williams, Martha Garrison *lawyer*
Wyche, Cyril Thomas *lawyer*

Greenwood
Nexsen, Julian Jacobs, Jr., *lawyer*

Hartsville
DeLoach, Harris E(ugene), Jr., *lawyer, manufacturing executive*

Hemingway
Chandler, William Henry *lawyer*

Hilton Head Island
Becker, Karl Martin *lawyer*
Berry, Loren Curtis *retired lawyer, consultant*
Bethea, William Lamar, Jr., *lawyer*
Donohoe, James Day *lawyer*
Esposito, John Vincent *lawyer*
Hagoort, Thomas Henry *lawyer*
Scarminach, Charles Anthony *lawyer*

Irmo
Brown, Leonard Ashleigh (Smokey), Jr., *lawyer*

Johns Island
Carter, Mary Andrews *paralegal*

Kiawah Island
Coyle, Martin Adolphus, Jr., *lawyer, consultant*

Langley
Bell, Robert Morrall *lawyer*

Lexington
Lide, Vinton DeVane *lawyer*
Wilkins, Robert Pearce *lawyer*

Mount Pleasant
Hahn, H. Blair *lawyer*

Myrtle Beach
Breen, David Hart *lawyer*

Newberry
Partridge, William Franklin, Jr., *lawyer*

North Charleston
Wigger, Jarrel L. *lawyer*

North Myrtle Beach
Wheless, Albert Eugene *lawyer*

Rock Hill
Hardin, James Carlisle, III, *lawyer, educator*

Salem
Everett, C(harles) Curtis *retired lawyer*

Seneca
Sires, Norman Gruber, Jr., *lawyer*

Spartanburg
Dineen, Joseph Lawrence *legal compliance professional, consultant*
King, Henry Spencer, III, *lawyer*
Smith, William Douglas *lawyer*

Summerville
Hardee-Thomas, Marva A. *lawyer*

Walterboro
Cone, George Wallis *lawyer*

SOUTH DAKOTA

Belle Fourche
Day, Michael W. *lawyer*

Britton
Farrar, Frank Leroy *lawyer, former governor*

Dakota Dunes
Hagan, Sheila B. *corporate lawyer*

Fort Pierre
Poches, Charles, Jr., *lawyer*

Gregory
Johnson, Charles Rick *lawyer*

Pierre
Gerdes, David Alan *lawyer*
Johnson, Julie Marie *lawyer, lobbyist, judge*
Thompson, Charles Murray *lawyer*

Rapid City
Foye, Thomas Harold *lawyer*
Goodsell, G. Verne *lawyer*
Graslie, Thomas Eric *lawyer*
Hagg, Rexford A. *lawyer, former state legislatorr*

Sioux Falls
Hayes, Robert E. *lawyer*
Johnson, Richard Arlo *lawyer*
Luce, Michael Leigh *lawyer*
Marshall, Mark F. *lawyer*

McMahon, James E. *lawyer*
Prendergast, Terry Neill *lawyer*

Vermillion
Davidson, John Henry *legal educator*

TENNESSEE

Bolivar
Cary, Charles Muse *lawyer*

Brentwood
Brown, Bobby Wayne *lawyer, educator, accountant*
Martin, William Edwin *lawyer, business executive*
Mc Creary, James Franklin *lawyer, mediator*
Provine, John Calhoun *retired lawyer*
Schreiber, Kurt Gilbert *lawyer*

Chattanooga
Bahner, Thomas Maxfield *lawyer*
Bowen, Maurice Richard, Jr., *lawyer, director*
Campbell, Paul, III, *lawyer*
Gearhiser, Charles Josef *lawyer*
Mattice, Harry Sandlin, Jr., *prosecutor*
Moore, Hugh Jacob, Jr., *lawyer*
Morris, Buckner Stuart *lawyer*
Phillips, John Bomar *lawyer*

Collierville
Springfield, James Francis *retired lawyer, banker*

Columbia
Moore, Tom White, Jr., *lawyer*

Cookeville
Qualls, Steven Daniel *lawyer*

Dyersburg
Wilder, James Sampson, III, *lawyer, judge*

Etowah
Parker, Eugene LeRoy, III, *lawyer*

Fayetteville
Dickey, John Harwell *lawyer*

Franklin
Sutter, Lawrence A. *lawyer, educator*

Gatlinburg
Powell, Russell A. *lawyer*

Humboldt
Boyte, George Griffin *lawyer*

Johnson City
Epps, James Haws, III, *lawyer*

Jonesborough
Jenkins, Ronald Wayne *lawyer, engineer, mediator*

Kingsport
Boyd, Lon Vernon *lawyer, alderman*
Shine, David Bruce *lawyer*

Knoxville
Campbell, Robert Roe *lawyer*
Creekmore, David Dickason *lawyer, educator*
Dillard, W. Thomas *lawyer*
Gentry, Mack A. *lawyer*
Johnson, Steven Boyd *lawyer*
Kirkpatrick, Carl Kimmel *prosecutor*
Lucas, John Allen *lawyer*
Midkiff, Kimberly Ann *paralegal*
Ownby, Jere Franklin, III, *lawyer*
Rayson, Edwin Hope *lawyer*
Reeves, Pamela *lawyer*
Ritchie, Albert *lawyer*
Smartt, John Madison *lawyer*
Wheeler, John Watson *lawyer*
Worthington, Carole Yard Lynch *lawyer*

Lebanon
Blackstock, James Fielding *lawyer*
Rochelle, Robert Thomas *lawyer, former state legislator*

Mc Ewen
Williams, John Lee *lawyer*

Mc Minnville
Potter, Clement Dale *district attorney general*

Memphis
Allen, Newton Perkins *lawyer*
Broadhurst, Jerome Anthony *lawyer*
Carr, Oscar Clark, III, *lawyer*
Clark, Ross Bert, II, *lawyer*
Clippard, Richard F. *prosecutor*
Coleman, Veronica Freeman *prosecutor*
Cook, August Joseph *lawyer, accountant*
Dann, Alexander William, Jr., *lawyer*
deWitt, Charles Benjamin, III, *lawyer, educator*
Doggrell, Henry Patton *lawyer*
Friedman, Robert Michael *lawyer*
Gipson, Harvey Lofton *lawyer*
Hancock, Jonathan Cromwell *lawyer*
Harris, Terrell Lee *prosecutor*
Harvey, Albert C. *lawyer*
Hunt, Sean Antone *lawyer, civil engineer*
Jackson, Thomas Francis, III, *lawyer*
Jerry, Robert Howard, II, *law educator*
Ledbetter, Paul Mark *lawyer, writer*
Manire, James McDonnell *lawyer*
Masterson, Kenneth Rhodes *lawyer*
Matthews, Paul Aaron *lawyer*
Monypeny, David Murray *lawyer*
Noel, Randall Deane *lawyer*
Raines, Jim Neal *lawyer*
Rawlins, Donald Ray *lawyer*
Russell, James Franklin *lawyer*
Rutledge, Roger Keith *lawyer*
Schuler, Walter E. *lawyer*
Scroggs, Larry Kenneth *lawyer, state legislator*
Steinhauer, Gillian *lawyer*
Tate, Stonewall Shepherd *lawyer*
White, Nicholas L. *legal educator*
Winchester, Richard Lee, Jr., *lawyer*

Morristown
Murphy, Michael Cary *lawyer*

Murfreesboro
Heffington, Jack Grisham *lawyer, banker, insurance company executive, horse breeder*

Nashville
Bass, James Orin, Sr., *lawyer*
Belton, Robert *law educator*
Bloch, Frank Samuel *law educator*
Blumstein, James Franklin *law educator, lawyer, consultant*
Bostick, Charles Dent *retired lawyer, educator*
Camp, Randy Coleman *lawyer*
Cheek, James Howe, III, *lawyer, educator*
Cobb, Stephen A. *lawyer*
Cohen, William Mark *lawyer*
Conner, Lewis Homer, Jr., *lawyer*
Crutchfield, William Ward *lawyer, state legislator*
Day, John Arthur *lawyer*
DeLanis, James Alfred *lawyer*
Dixon, Carl Franklin *lawyer*
Edwards, Mark E. *healthcare company lawyer*
Ely, James Wallace, Jr., *law educator*
Gannon, John Sexton *lawyer, management consultant, arbitrator, mediator*
Gillmor, John Edward *lawyer*
Goggin, Wendy *prosecutor*
Hardin, Hal D. *lawyer, judge, former US attorney*
Hart, Richard Banner *lawyer*
Henry, Douglas *lawyer, state legislator*
Ledyard, Robins Heard *lawyer*
Lyon, Philip Kirkland *lawyer*
Madu, Leonard Ekwugha *lawyer, human rights advocate, columnist*
Maier, Harold Geistweit *law educator, lawyer*
Martin, Henry Alan *public defender*
May, Joseph Leserman (Jack May) *retired lawyer*
Mayden, Barbara Mendel *lawyer*
McDonald, Michael Eugene *lawyer, educator, clergyman*
Ramsaur, Allan Fields *lawyer, lobbyist*
Sanders, James F. *lawyer*
Sims, Wilson *lawyer*
Soderquist, Larry Dean *law educator, lawyer, consultant, writer*
Tarpley, John R. *lawyer*
Thomas, Randall Stuart *lawyer, educator*
Thomas, Robert Paige *lawyer*
Torrey, Claudia Olivia *lawyer*
Trautman, Herman Louis *lawyer, educator*
Trent, John Thomas, Jr., *lawyer*
Tuke, Robert Dudley *lawyer, educator*
Vines, James *lawyer*
Walkup, John Knox *lawyer*
Waterman, Robert A. *lawyer*
White, Bruce David *law and ethics educator, consultant*
Winstead, George Alvis *law librarian, biochemist, educator, consultant*
Yarbrough, Edward Meacham *lawyer*
Youngblood, Elaine Michele *lawyer*
Yuspeh, Alan Ralph *lawyer, healthcare company executive*

Newport
Myers, John William *lawyer*

Paris
Rose, Todd Alan *lawyer*

Powell
Hyman, Roger David *lawyer*

Sevierville
Waters, John B. *lawyer*

Signal Mountain
Anderson, Charles Hill *lawyer*
Ragan, Charles Oliver, Jr., *lawyer*

Soddy Daisy
Leitner, Paul Revere *lawyer*

South Pittsburg
Ables, Charles Robert *lawyer, judge*

Union City
Graham, Hardy Moore *lawyer*

Waverly
Peeler, William James *lawyer*

TEXAS

Abilene
Boone, Billy Warren *lawyer, judge*
Robinson, Vianei Lopez *lawyer*
Sartain, James Edward *lawyer*
Suttle, Stephen Hungate *lawyer*
Tomme, Curtis Rabon *lawyer*

Addison
Kneipper, Richard Keith *lawyer*
Lawson, Gary B. *lawyer*
Pommerening, Edwin Carlton *lawyer*

Amarillo
Cox, Roger Stephen *lawyer*
Madden, Wales Hendrix, Jr., *lawyer*
Smithee, John True *lawyer, state legislator*

Arlington
Dowdy, John Vernard, Jr., *lawyer, educator, arbitrator*
Jensen, John Robert *lawyer*
Pierson, Grey *lawyer*
Rosenberry, William Kenneth *lawyer, educator*

Austin
Allday, Martin Lewis *lawyer*
Anderson, David Arnold *law educator*
Ascher, Mark Louis *legal educator*
Baade, Hans Wolfgang *legal educator, law expert*
Baker, Mark Bruce *lawyer, educator*
Black, William Earl *lawyer*
Bobbitt, Philip Chase *writer, educator, public official*
Botsford, David L. *lawyer*
Cantú, Norma V. *law educator, former federal official*
Churgin, Michael Jay *law educator*
Clark, Pat English *lawyer*
Cook, J(ohn) Rowland *lawyer*
Coultas, Edward Owen *lawyer*
Cruz, Ted *lawyer*
Cunningham, Judy Marie *lawyer*
Davis, Robert Larry *lawyer*
Demond, Walter Eugene *lawyer*
Denius, Franklin Wofford *lawyer*
Donley, Dennis W. *lawyer*
Dougherty, John Chrysostom, III, *retired lawyer*
Dyer, Cromwell Adair, Jr., *lawyer, legal association administrator*
Fernandes, Edward F. *lawyer*
Fink, Vella Mary *lawyer*
Gangstad, John Erik *lawyer*
Gibbins, Bob *lawyer*
Godfrey, Cullen Michael *lawyer, academic administrator*
Goldstein, E. Ernest *lawyer, consultant*
Golemon, Ronald Kinnan *lawyer*
Graglia, Lino Anthony *lawyer, educator*
Graham, Seldon Bain, Jr., *lawyer, engineer*
Greene, John Joseph *lawyer*
Greig, Brian Strother *lawyer*
Hale, Louis Dewitt *lawyer*
Hamilton, Dagmar Strandberg *lawyer, educator*
Hardin, Dale Wayne *retired lawyer, federal official*
Harrison, Richard Wayne *lawyer*
Hazel, Joseph Patrick *retired law educator*
Heath, Claude Robert *lawyer*
Helman, Stephen Jody *lawyer*
Henderson, George Ervin *lawyer*
Jentz, Gaylord Adair *law educator*
Jones, Bill *lawyer*
Judson, Philip Livingston *lawyer*
Kerr, Stanley Munger *investigator, lawyer, educator, judge*
Kilgore, Gary Lynn *lawyer*
Lochridge, Lloyd Pampell, Jr., *lawyer*
McCullough, Frank Witcher, III, *lawyer*
McDaniel, Myra Atwell *lawyer, former state official*
Mersky, Roy Martin *law educator, librarian*
Moss, Bill Ralph *lawyer*
Moss, Logan Vansen *lawyer*
Mullenix, Linda Susan *lawyer, educator*
Osborne, Duncan Elliott *lawyer*
Otto, Byron Leonard *lawyer, state administrator*
Patman, Philip Franklin *lawyer*
Pena, Richard *lawyer*
Pirkey, Louis Thomas *lawyer*
Probus, Michael Maurice, Jr., *lawyer*
Roan, Forrest Calvin, Jr., *lawyer*
Schulze, Eric William *lawyer, legal publications editor, publisher*
Schuurman, Willem Gerhard *lawyer*
Schwartz, Aaron Robert *lawyer, former state legislator*
Schwartz, Leonard Jay *lawyer*
Shapiro, David L. *lawyer*
Smith, Lawrence Shannon *lawyer*
Spivey, Broadus Autry *lawyer*
Stephen, John Erle *lawyer, consultant*
Strauser, Robert Wayne *lawyer*
Stutts, William Floyd, Jr., *lawyer, educator*
Sullivan, Teresa Ann *law and sociology educator, academic administrator*
Sutton, John F., Jr., *law educator, dean, lawyer*
Temple, Larry Eugene *lawyer*
Thompson, G. Gaye *lawyer*
Weddington, Sarah Ragle *lawyer, educator, speaker, writer*
Weinberg, Louise *law educator, author*
Weinman, Daryl Gail *lawyer*
Weintraub, Russell Jay *lawyer, educator*
Wentworth, Earl Jeffrey *lawyer, realtor, state legislator*
West, Royce *lawyer, state legislator*
Westbrook, Jay Lawrence *law educator*
Whitehurst, William Oscar *lawyer*
Winters, Sam *lawyer*
Wise, Miguel David *lawyer*
Yudof, Mark George *law educator, university system chancellor*

Baytown
Chavez, John Anthony *lawyer*

Beaumont
Black, Robert Allen *lawyer*
Dowell, James Dale *lawyer*
Dryden, Woodson E. *lawyer*
Johnson, Leanne *lawyer*
Newton, John Wharton, III, *lawyer*
Orwig, Matthew Dane *lawyer*
Scofield, Louis M., Jr., *lawyer*

Bellaire
Hollrah, David *lawyer*
Jacobus, Charles Joseph *lawyer, title company executive, writer*
Lilienstern, O. Clayton *lawyer, educator*
Soffar, William Douglas *lawyer*

Bellville
Borgeson, Earl Charles *law librarian, educator*

Belton
Burrows, Jon Hanes *lawyer*

Borger
Edmonds, Thomas Leon *lawyer, management consultant*

Brenham
Moorman, Richard Hal, IV, *lawyer*

Brownsville
Fleming, Tommy Wayne *lawyer*
Weisfeld, Sheldon *lawyer*

Brownwood
Bell, William Woodward *lawyer*

Bryan
Miller, Thomas Eugene *lawyer, writer*
Strong, Stephen Andrew *lawyer*

Carrollton
Riggs, Arthur Jordy *retired lawyer*
Turner, Bruce Edward *lawyer*

Cat Spring
Conner, Warren Wesley *lawyer*

College Station
Carlton, Dean *lawyer*

Colleyville
Whittenberg, Ira Orville *lawyer*

Conroe
Bowersox, Thomas H. *lawyer*

Corpus Christi
Alberts, Harold *lawyer*
Branscomb, Harvie, Jr., *lawyer*
Coover, Ann E. *lawyer*
Davis, Martin Clay *lawyer, professor*
Leon, Rolando Luis *lawyer*
Stukenberg, Michael Wesley *lawyer*
Wood, James Allen *retired lawyer*

Dallas
Abney, Frederick Sherwood *lawyer*
Acker, Rodney *lawyer*
Ackerman, Deborah *lawyer*
Anderson, Barbara McComas *lawyer*
Anderson, E. Karl *lawyer*
Anglin, Michael Williams *lawyer*
Babcock, Charles Lynde, IV, *lawyer*
Baggett, Steven Ray *lawyer*
Baggett, W. Mike *lawyer*
Bangs, Nelson A. *lawyer*
Baron, Frederick M. *lawyer*
Beane, Jerry Lynn *lawyer*
Beuttenmuller, Rudolf William *lawyer*
Bickel, John W., II, *lawyer*
Birkeland, Bryan Collier *lawyer*
Blanchette, James Grady, Jr., *lawyer*
Bliss, Robert Harms *lawyer*
Bonesio, Woodrow Michael *lawyer*
Bradley, Jean Marie *lawyer*
Brady, Jack Edgar *lawyer*
Brin, Royal Henry, Jr., *lawyer*
Bumpas, Stuart Maryman *lawyer*
Burke, William Temple, Jr., *lawyer*
Burns, Sandra *lawyer, educator*
Busbee, Kline Daniel, Jr., *law educator, lawyer*
Carpenter, Gordon Russell *retired lawyer, banker*
Case, Thomas Louis *lawyer*
Chase, J. Scott *Lawyer (corporate)*
Clark, Robert Murel, Jr., *lawyer*
Cloutman, Edward Bradbury, III, *lawyer*
Coleman, Robert Winston *lawyer*
Conant, Allah B., Jr., *lawyer*
Copley, Edward Alvin *lawyer*
Cover, Kathi A. *lawyer*
Cowart, T(homas) David *lawyer*
Creel, Luther Edward, III, *lawyer*
Crichton, Thomas, IV, *lawyer*
Crotty, Robert Bell *lawyer*
Crowley, James Worthington *retired lawyer, business consultant, investor*
Curran, G. Michael *lawyer*
Daly, Gail M. *law librarian, educator*
Davis, Clarice McDonald *lawyer*
DelHomme, Beverly Ann *lawyer*
Demarest, Sylvia M. *lawyer*
Dicus, Brian George *lawyer*
Doke, Marshall J., Jr., *lawyer*
Dutton, Diana Cheryl *lawyer*
Dyess, Bobby Dale *lawyer*
Eaton, Michael William *lawyer, educator*
Elkins-Elliott, Kay *law educator*
Ellis, Alfred Wright (Al Ellis) *lawyer*
Ellis, James Alvis, Jr., *lawyer*
Emery, Herschell Gene *lawyer*
Everbach, Otto George *lawyer*
Fanning, Barry Hedges *lawyer*
Farquhar, Robert Michael *lawyer*
Feld, Alan David *lawyer*
Feldman, H. Larry *lawyer*
Fenner, Suzan Ellen *lawyer*
Fifield, William O. *lawyer*
Figari, Ernest Emil, Jr., *lawyer, educator*
Finston, Felicia A. *lawyer*
Flegle, Jim L. *lawyer*
Flood, Joan Moore *paralegal*
French, Joseph Jordan, Jr., *lawyer*
Freytag, Sharon Nelson *lawyer*
Frisbie, Curtis Lynn, Jr., *lawyer*
Galvin, Charles O'Neill *law educator*
Gardner, Stephen Henry *lawyer*
Garner, Bryan Andrew *law educator, consultant, writer*
Gilmore, Jerry Carl *lawyer*
Glancy, Walter John *lawyer*
Glendenning, Don Mark *lawyer*
Goodstein, Barnett Maurice *lawyer*
Goolsby, Michelle *lawyer, food products executive*
Gores, Christopher Merrel *lawyer*
Green, Jesse Joseph *lawyer*
Hackney, Hugh Edward *lawyer*
Hammond, Herbert J. *lawyer, arbitrator, mediator*
Hansen, Eugenia S. *lawyer*
Hartnett, Thomas Robert, III, *lawyer, author*
Hartnett, Will Ford *lawyer*
Hartt, Grover, III, *lawyer*
Haworth, Charles Ray *lawyer*
Henkel, Kathryn Gundy *lawyer*
Hennessy, Daniel Kraft *lawyer*
Henry, Vic Houston *lawyer*
Hicks, Marion Lawrence, Jr., (Larry Hicks) *lawyer*
Hill, Bill *prosecutor*
Hinshaw, Chester John *lawyer*
Hofmeister, Kent S. *lawyer*
Holmes, James Hill, III, *lawyer*
Honea, Floyd Franklin *lawyer*
Houser, Barbara J. *lawyer*
Huffman, Gregory Scott Combest *lawyer*
Hughes, Vester Thomas, Jr., *lawyer*
Jayson, Melinda Gayle *lawyer*
Jennings, Susan Jane *lawyer*
Jones, Lindy Don *lawyer*
Joplin, Julian Mike *lawyer*
Jordan, William Davis *lawyer*
Keithley, Bradford Gene *lawyer*
Kennedy, Marc J. *lawyer*
Kent, David Charles *lawyer*
Kinnebrew, Jackson Metcalfe *lawyer*
Kitner, David N. *lawyer*
Kobdish, George Charles *lawyer*
Kohl, Kathleen Allison Barnhart *lawyer*
Kuhn, Willis Evan, II, *lawyer, mediator*
Lacy, John Ford *retired lawyer*

Lan, Donald Paul, Jr., *lawyer*
Lastelick, Jerry *lawyer*
Levin, Hervey Phillip *lawyer, director*
Levin, Richard C. *lawyer*
Lowe, John Stanley *lawyer, educator*
Malorzo, Thomas Vincent *lawyer*
Mankoff, Ronald Morton *retired lawyer*
Maris, Stephen S. *lawyer, educator*
Martin, Boe Willis *lawyer*
Massman, Richard Allan *lawyer*
McAtee, David Ray *lawyer*
McCormack, William Arthur *lawyer*
McCurley, Carl Michael *lawyer*
McCurley, Mary Johanna *lawyer*
Mc Elhaney, John Hess *lawyer*
McGarry, Charles William *lawyer*
McGowan, Patrick Francis *lawyer*
McKnight, Joseph Webb *law educator, historian*
McLane, David Glenn *lawyer*
McNamara, Anne H. *lawyer, corporate executive*
McWilliams, Mike C. *lawyer*
Meyer, Ferdinand Charles, Jr., *lawyer*
Miers, Harriet E. *lawyer*
Mighell, Kenneth John *lawyer*
Miller, Stewart Ransom *lawyer*
Mills, Jerry Woodrow *lawyer*
Mondul, Donald David *patent lawyer*
Moore, Edward Warren *lawyer*
Mow, Robert Henry, Jr., *lawyer*
Mueller, Mark Christopher *lawyer*
Nelson, Elaine Edwards *lawyer*
Nelson, Keith Milton *lawyer*
Nichols, Henry Louis *lawyer*
Nolan, John Michael *lawyer*
Peterson, Edward Adrian *lawyer*
Peterson, Eric H. *lawyer, energy executive*
Pew, John Glenn, Jr., *lawyer*
Phelan, Robin Eric *lawyer*
Pingree, Bruce Douglas *lawyer*
Pleasant, James Scott *lawyer*
Portman, Glenn Arthur *lawyer*
Prather, Robert Charles, Sr., *lawyer*
Price, John Aley *lawyer*
Prothro, Jerry Robert *lawyer*
Pruessner, David Morgan *lawyer*
Purnell, Charles Giles *lawyer*
Purnell, Maurice Eugene, Jr., *lawyer*
Raggio, Louise Ballerstedt *lawyer*
Rasch, Stephen Christopher *lawyer*
Reid, Rust Endicott *lawyer*
Riddle, Michael Lee *lawyer*
Ringle, Brett Adelbert *lawyer, petroleum company executive*
Roberts, Harry Morris, Jr., *lawyer*
Robinson, Malcolm S. *lawyer*
Rodgers, John Hunter *lawyer*
Salazar, Steve *lawyer*
Schreiber, Sally Ann *lawyer*
See, Robert Fleming, Jr., *lawyer*
Selinger, Jerry Robin *lawyer*
Sloman, Marvin Sherk *lawyer*
Smith, Brian *lawyer*
Smith, Milton Clark, Jr., *lawyer*
Smith, Russell Bryan *lawyer*
Spears, Robert Fields *lawyer*
Stalcup, Joe Alan *lawyer, clergyman*
Steinberg, Lawrence Edward *lawyer*
Stephens, Richard H. *retired prosecutor*
Stockard, James Alfred *lawyer*
Storey, Charles Porter *lawyer*
Strauss, Robert Schwarz *lawyer, former ambassador*
Tarnay, Thomas N. *lawyer*
Thomson, Basil Henry, Jr., *lawyer, university general counsel*
True, Roy Joe *lawyer*
Tubb, James Clarence *lawyer*
Tucker, Laurey Dan *lawyer*
Veach, Robert Raymond, Jr., *lawyer*
Walkowiak, Vincent Steven *lawyer*
Wallace, Anderson, Jr., *lawyer, educator*
Westfall, Constance Courtney *lawyer*
Whitaker, Elizabeth *lawyer*
White, James Richard *lawyer*
Willingham, Clark Suttles *lawyer*
Wilson, Claude Raymond, Jr., *lawyer*
Young, Barney Thornton *lawyer*
Zisman, Barry Stuart *lawyer*

Denton
Chilton, Bradley Stewart *law educator*
Gabriel, Eberhard John *lawyer, bank executive*
Lawhon, John E., III, *lawyer, former county official*
Waage, Mervin Bernard *lawyer*

East Bernard
Boettcher, Armin Schlick *lawyer, banker*

El Paso
Dinsmoor, Robert Davidson *lawyer, judge*
Feuille, Richard Harlan *lawyer, director*
Gordon, Norman James *lawyer*
Leachman, Russell DeWitt *lawyer*
Marshall, Richard Treeger *lawyer*
Morton, Fred J. *lawyer*
Smith, Tad Randolph *lawyer*

Ennis
Swanson, Wallace Martin *lawyer*

Euless
Paran, Mark Lloyd *retired lawyer*

Farmersville
Seward, Richard Bevin *lawyer*

Flower Mound
Hunt, David Ford *lawyer*
Maddocks, Robert Allen *lawyer, manufacturing executive*

Fort Worth
Berenson, William Keith *lawyer*
Brender, Art *lawyer*
Brown, C. Harold *lawyer*
Brown, Richard Lee *lawyer, director*
Canas, Eduardo *lawyer*
Chalk, John Allen, Sr., *lawyer*
Collins, Whitfield James *lawyer*
Cottongame, W. Brice *lawyer*
Curry, Donald Robert *lawyer, oil company executive*
Dean, Beale *lawyer*
Dent, Edward Dwain *lawyer*
Elliott, Frank Wallace *lawyer, educator*
Hall, Randy Jarvis *lawyer*
Harcrow, E. Earl *lawyer*
Hart, John Clifton *lawyer*
Hill, Mark C. *lawyer*
Ingram, Denny Ouzts, Jr., *lawyer, educator*
Kelly, Dee J. *lawyer*
Kelly, Raymond Boone, III, *lawyer*
Langenheim, Roger Allen *lawyer*
Larimore, Tom L. *lawyer*
McConnell, Michael Arthur *lawyer*
Minton, Jerry Davis *lawyer, consultant, retired banker*
Munn, Cecil Edwin *lawyer*
Myers, Thomas Everett *lawyer*
Quinn, Francis Xavier *arbitrator, mediator, author, lecturer*
Shannon, Joe, Jr., *lawyer*
Sharpe, James Shelby *lawyer*
Simon, Roger Frank *law educator*
Tatum, Stephen Lyle *lawyer*
Tillman, Karen Sue *lawyer*
Watson, Robert Francis *lawyer*
Weekley, Frederick Clay, Jr., *lawyer*
West, Robert Grady *lawyer*

Gainesville
Stormer, Cindy Hodge *lawyer, educator*

Galveston
Caldwell, Garnett Ernest *lawyer*
Kilgore, Jeffrey Harper *lawyer*
O'Toole, Austin Martin *lawyer*

Garland
Hinton, Charles *lawyer*
Irby, Holt *lawyer*

Georgetown
Bryce, William Delf *lawyer*
Gattis, Dan Moore *lawyer, state representative, rancher*

Grapevine
Franks, Jon Michael *lawyer, mediator*

Hallettsville
Baber, Wilbur H., Jr., *lawyer*

Harlingen
Johnson, Orrin Wendell *lawyer*
Pope, William L. *lawyer, judge*

Heath
Kolodey, Fred James *lawyer*

Houston
Addison, Linda Leuchter *lawyer, writer, commentator, columnist*
Agosto, Benny, Jr., *lawyer*
Allender, John Roland *lawyer*
Amdur, Arthur R. *lawyer*
Anderson, Eric Severin *lawyer*
Anderson, Thomas Dunaway *retired lawyer*
Andrews, Sally S. *lawyer*
Atlas, Scott J. *lawyer*
Bachmann, Richard H. *lawyer*
Bargfrede, James Allen *lawyer*
Barnett, Edward William *lawyer*
Bech, Douglas York *lawyer, resort executive*
Beirne, Martin Douglas *lawyer*
Bellatti, Lawrence Lee *lawyer*
Berg, David Howard *lawyer*
Berner, Arthur Samuel *lawyer*
Bilger, Bruce R. *lawyer*
Blackshear, A. T., Jr., *lawyer*
Bland, John Lloyd *lawyer*
Bliss, Ronald Glenn *lawyer*
Bluestein, Edwin A., Jr., *lawyer*
Brann, Richard Roland *lawyer*
Bridges, David Manning *lawyer*
Brinson, Gay Creswell, Jr., *retired lawyer*
Brunson, John Soles *lawyer, investor*
Buckingham, Edwin John, III, *lawyer*
Burch, Voris Reagan *mediator, arbitrator, retired lawyer*
Burton, Joseph Randolph *lawyer*
Bux, William John *lawyer*
Cabello, J. David *retired lawyer*
Caddy, Michael Douglas *lawyer*
Callahan, Gerald William *lawyer, oil company executive*
Campbell, Bert Louis *lawyer, mediator, arbitrator*
Carmody, James Albert *lawyer*
Carr, Edward A. *lawyer*
Carroll, James Vincent, III, *lawyer*
Carstarphen, Edward Morgan, III, *lawyer*
Carter, John Francis, II, *lawyer*
Carter, John Loyd *lawyer*
Caudill, William Howard *lawyer*
Clarke, Robert Logan *lawyer*
Clore, Lawrence Hubert *lawyer*
Coghlan, Kelly Jack *lawyer*
Coleman, Lester L. *corporate lawyer*
Conlon, Michael William *lawyer*
Cook, Eugene Augustus *lawyer*
Cornelison, Albert Otto (Bert), Jr., *lawyer*
Cox, James Talley *lawyer*
Crocker, Samuel Sackett *lawyer*
Cunningham, Tom Alan *lawyer*
DeMent, James Alderson, Jr., *lawyer*
Devlin, Francis James *lawyer*
Dilg, Joseph Carl *lawyer*
Dillard, Stephen C. *lawyer*
Dinkins, Carol Eggert *lawyer*
Disher, David Alan *lawyer, consultant*
Douglas, James Matthew *law educator*
Douglass, John Jay *lawyer, educator*
Dula, Arthur McKee, III, *lawyer*
Dunlop, Fred Hurston *lawyer*
Dworsky, Clara Weiner *lawyer, former merchandise brokerage executive*
Dykes, Osborne Jefferson, III, *lawyer*
Eastin, Keith E. *lawyer*
Eckhardt, William Rudolf, III, *lawyer*
Engerrand, Kenneth G. *lawyer, educator*
Essmyer, Michael Martin *lawyer*
Eubank, J. Thomas *lawyer*
Ewen, Pamela Binnings *lawyer*
Farenthold, Frances Tarlton *lawyer*
Farnsworth, T. Brooke *lawyer*
Finch, Michael Paul *lawyer*
Forbes, Arthur Lee, III, *lawyer*
Foster, Charles Crawford *lawyer, educator*
Frels, Kelly *lawyer*
Frost, Charles Estes, Jr., *lawyer*
Fudge, Edward William *lawyer*
Fullenweider, Donn Charles *lawyer*
Gates, Stephen Frye *lawyer, oil industry executive*
Gibson, Rex Hilton *lawyer*
Gilbert, Keith Thomas *lawyer, consultant*
Gillmore, Kathleen Cory *lawyer*
Gissel, L. Henry, Jr., *lawyer*
Gonynor, Francis James *lawyer*
Gover, Alan Shore *lawyer*
Graebner, Carol F. *lawyer*
Graving, Richard John *law educator*
Grossberg, Marc Elias *lawyer*
Guest, Floyd Emory, Jr., *lawyer*
Gunter, Joseph Clifford, III, *lawyer*
Gutheinz, Joseph Richard, Jr., *lawyer, politician, investigative consultant, retired army officer and NASA official, educator, author*
Hall, Anthony W., Jr., *lawyer*
Hall, Charles Washington *lawyer*
Harper, Alfred John, II, *lawyer*
Harrington, Bruce Michael *lawyer, investor*
Harris, Warren Wayne *lawyer*
Harvin, David Tarleton *lawyer*
Haynes, Richard *lawyer*
Heeg, Peggy A. *lawyer, former gas industry executive*
Heinrich, Randall Wayne *lawyer*
Hlavinka, Paul Thomas *lawyer*
Holloway, Gordon Arthur *lawyer*
Hollyfield, John Scoggins *lawyer*
Holstead, John Burnham *retired lawyer*
Hope, Henry Welcker *lawyer*
Hoyt, Mont Powell *lawyer*
Hudson, Franklin *lawyer, real estate developer*
Hudspeth, Chalmers Mac *lawyer, educator*
Hull, Robert Joe *lawyer*
Irvin, Michael P. *lawyer*
Jamail, Joseph Dahr, Jr., *lawyer*
Jansen, Donald Orville *lawyer*
Jewell, George Hiram *lawyer*
Jones, Frank Griffith *lawyer*
Jordan, Charles Milton *lawyer*
Kaplan, Lee Landa *lawyer*
Kay, Joel Phillip *lawyer*
Keith, Susan S. *lawyer, business executive*
Kemp, Roland Connor *lawyer*
Ketchand, Robert Lee *lawyer*
Kirk, John Robert, Jr., *lawyer*
Koenig, Rodney Curtis *lawyer, rancher*
Kratochvil, L(ouis) Glen *lawyer*
Krebs, Arno William, Jr., *lawyer*
Kruse, Layne E. *lawyer*
Kurz, Thomas Patrick *lawyer*
LaBoon, Robert Bruce *lawyer*
Lacey, David Morgan *lawyer, school administrator*
Lackey, S. Allen *lawyer, petroleum company executive*
LaFuze, William L. *lawyer*
Lake, Kathleen Cooper *lawyer*
Lanier, W. Mark *lawyer*
Larkin, Lee Roy *retired lawyer*
Linden, William M. *lawyer*
Lopez, David Tiburcio *lawyer, educator, arbitrator, mediator*
Marston, Edgar Jean, III, *lawyer*
Martin, Jay Griffith *lawyer*
Martin, Paul Edward *lawyer*
Massad, Stephen Albert *lawyer*
Masters, Claude Bivin *lawyer*
McClure, Daniel M. *lawyer*
McDaniel, Jarrel Dave *lawyer*
McDonald, Donald C. *lawyer*
McFall, Donald Beury *lawyer*
McQuarrie, Claude Monroe, III, *lawyer*
Meek, Susan Bieber *lawyer, physician, mediator, consultant*
Menn, Stephen Edward *lawyer*
Moehlman, Michael Scott *lawyer*
Moncure, John Lewis *lawyer*
Morgan, Richard Greer *lawyer*
Morris, Carloss (William Morris) *lawyer, insurance company executive*
Murphy, Ewell Edward, Jr., *lawyer*
Nacol, Mae *lawyer*
Nations, Howard Lynn *lawyer*
Neslage, John Edward *lawyer*
Nolen, Roy Lemuel *retired lawyer*
Norman, Kenneth Glen *lawyer*
Nunnally, Knox Dillon *lawyer*
O'Brien, Eva Fromm *lawyer*
Oldham, Darius Dudley *lawyer*
Oldham, J. Thomas *lawyer, educator*
Osterberg, Edward Charles, Jr., *lawyer*
Perez, Jose Rafael, Jr., *lawyer*
Pinchak, Ann Simcha *lawyer*
Plaeger, Frederick Joseph, II, *lawyer*
Poitevent, Edward Butts, II, *lawyer*
Porter, Thomas William, III, *lawyer*
Pravel, Bernarr Roe *lawyer*
Prestridge, Pamela Adair *lawyer*
Pritchard, William Winther *lawyer, drilling company executive*
Pugsley, Frank Burruss *lawyer*
Raley, John Wesley, III, *lawyer*
Ray, Hugh Massey, Jr., *lawyer*
Reasoner, Harry Max *lawyer*
Robertson, James Woolsey *lawyer*
Rogers, Arthur Hamilton, III, *lawyer*
Rosenthal, Charles A., Jr., *prosecutor*
Rowland, Robert Alexander, III, *lawyer*
Rozzell, Scott Ellis *lawyer*
Rustay, Jennifer B. *lawyer*
Ryan, Vince *lawyer*
Salch, Steven Charles *lawyer, mediator, arbitrator*
Sales, James Bohus *lawyer*
Sapp, Walter William *lawyer, energy company executive*
Saunders, Charles Albert *lawyer*
Schechter, Arthur Louis *lawyer*
Scholin, Margo S. *lawyer*
Schwartz, Charles Walter *lawyer*
Schwartzel, Charles Boone *lawyer*
Schwind, William F., Jr., *lawyer, oil industry executive*
Scott, Ronald *lawyer*
Seale, Robert Arthur, Jr., *lawyer*
Sellingsloh, John S. *lawyer*
Serres, Gregory A. *prosecutor*
Shaddix, James W. *retired lawyer*
Shaddock, Carroll Sidney *lawyer*
Shead, William C. *lawyer*
Sheinfeld, Myron M. *lawyer, educator*
Shelby, Michael T. *lawyer*
Sheppard, Ben H., Jr., *lawyer*
Short, J. Lindsey, Jr., *lawyer*
Shurn, Peter Joseph, III, *lawyer*
Silva, Eugene Joseph *lawyer*
Simmons, Stephen Judson *lawyer*
Sing, William Bender *lawyer*
Smith, Alison Leigh *lawyer*
Smith, Walter John *lawyer*
Sonfield, Robert Leon, Jr., *lawyer*
Spalding, Andrew Freeman *lawyer*
Stewart, Pamela L. *lawyer*
Still, Charles Henry, Sr., *lawyer*
Stradley, William Jackson *lawyer*
Streng, William Paul *lawyer, educator*
Stryker, Steven Charles *lawyer*
Susman, Morton Lee *lawyer*
Susman, Stephen Daily *lawyer*
Sydow, Michael David *lawyer*
Szalkowski, Charles Conrad *lawyer*
Taheri, Marshall M. *lawyer, educator*
Tartt, Blake *lawyer*
Toedt, D(ell) C(harles), III, *lawyer*
Touchy, Deborah K.P. *lawyer, accountant*
Tripp, Karen Bryant *lawyer*
Van Fleet, George Allan *lawyer*
Varner, David Eugene *lawyer*
Vickery, Edward Downtain *lawyer*
Wagner, Leslie *lawyer*
Wall, Kenneth E., Jr., *lawyer*
Wallis, Olney Gray *lawyer*
Walls, Robert Hamilton, Jr., *lawyer*
Walton, Dan Gibson *lawyer*
Watson, John Allen *lawyer*
Webb, Jack M. *lawyer*
Weber, Fredric Alan *lawyer*
Weller, Philip Douglas *lawyer*
Wells, Benjamin Gladney *lawyer*
Wheelan, R(ichelieu) E(dward) *lawyer*
Wilde, Carlton D. *lawyer, director*
Wilde, William Key *lawyer*
Williamson, Peter David *lawyer*
Wilson, David Vandiver, II, *lawyer*
Worthington, William Albert, III, *lawyer*
Wray, Thomas Jefferson *lawyer*
Yetter, R. Paul *lawyer*
Yokubaitis, Roger T. *lawyer*
Zager, Steven Mark *lawyer*
Zeigler, Ann dePender *lawyer*

Humble
Harrison, Brooks Talton *law firm official*
Pickle, George Edward *lawyer*

Huntsville
Peck, Leonard Warren, Jr., *lawyer*

Ingram
Gambrell, James Bruton, III, *lawyer, educator*

Irving
Beach, Charles Addison *lawyer*
Beasley, Mark V. *lawyer*
Cunningham, Cathy Meyer *lawyer*
de Mars, Susan S. *lawyer, health products executive*
Duran, Lois Janine *lawyer*
Pitts, Joe W., III, (Chip Pitts) *lawyer, law educator*
Ryan, Robert Collins *lawyer*
Sullivan, Paul E. *lawyer, oil industry executive*

Kerrville
Parmley, Robert James *lawyer, consultant*

Kilgore
Rorschach, Richard Gordon *lawyer*

Lamesa
Saleh, John *lawyer*

Lindale
Jackson, Gary Dean *lawyer*

Little Elm
Middleton, Linda Jean Greathouse *lawyer*

Livingston
Meyer, Roberta *mediator, communication consultant*

Lockhart
Scudday, Roy George *lawyer*

Longview
Harrison, Guy Newell *lawyer*

Lubbock
Barnhill, Robert Edwin, III, *lawyer*
Brock, Ralph Haney *lawyer*
Crowson, James Lawrence *lawyer, financial company executive, academic administrator*
Purdom, Thomas James *lawyer*
Skillern, Frank Fletcher *law educator*

Mason
Johnson, Rufus Winfield *lawyer*
Wilkerson, James Neill *retired lawyer*

Mc Kinney
Dowdy, William Clarence, Jr., *retired lawyer*

Mcallen
Connors, Joseph Aloysius, III, *lawyer*

Midland
Estes, Andrew Harper *lawyer*
MacDonald, Leland Lloyd *lawyer*
Taylor, Nicholas C. *lawyer, state agency administrator, energy executive*

Missouri City
Hodges, Jot Holiver, Jr., *retired lawyer, business executive*

Orange
Dugas, Louis, Jr., *lawyer*

Pearland
Powell, John S., III, *lawyer, writer*

Plano
Altabef, Peter Anthony *lawyer*
Blachly, Jack Lee *lawyer*
Friedlander, D. Gilbert *lawyer*
Hemingway, Richard William *law educator*
Levine, Harold *lawyer*
Lotter, Charles Robert *lawyer, retail executive*

Pottsboro
Thomas, Ann Van Wynen *law educator*

Richardson
Conkel, Robert Dale *lawyer, pension consultant*
DeBusk, Manuel Conrad *lawyer, business executive*
Ellwanger, J. David *lawyer*
Martin, Richard Kelley *lawyer*
Olson, Dennis Oliver *lawyer*
Smith, Mark P. *foundation executive*
Sowers, Wesley Hoyt *lawyer, management consultant*

Rockport
Benningfield, Carol Ann *lawyer*
Porter, Charles Raleigh, Jr., *retired lawyer*

Rockwall
Bruce, Dana Glenn *lawyer*

Round Rock
Green, Thomas B. *lawyer, computer company executive*

San Angelo
Carter, James Alfred *lawyer*
McLaughlin, John Mark *lawyer*
Moeller, Galen Ashley *lawyer*
Sutton, John Ewing *lawyer*

San Antonio
Armstrong, William Tucker, III, *lawyer*
Bayern, Arthur Herbert *lawyer*
Bennett, Steven Alan *lawyer*
Bettac, Robert Edward *lawyer*
Biery, Evelyn Hudson *lawyer*
Bramble, Ronald Lee *business and legal consultant*
Branton, James LaVoy *lawyer*
Case, Jeff Dean *lawyer*
Castleberry, James Newton, Jr., *retired law educator, dean*
de la Garza, Luis Adolfo *lawyer*
Emery, Nancy Beth *lawyer*
Goff, Colleen Mullen *lawyer*
Hardy, Harvey Louchard *retired lawyer*
Henry, Peter York *lawyer, mediator*
Johnson, Anne Stuckly *retired lawyer*
Macon, Jane Haun *lawyer*
Maloney, Marynell *lawyer*
Maloney, Pat, Sr., *lawyer*
Mathy, Pamela Ann *lawyer*
Millet, John Porath *lawyer*
Moynihan, John Bignell *retired lawyer*
Pfeiffer, Philip J. *lawyer*
Pipkin, Marvin Grady *lawyer*
Reams, Bernard Dinsmore, Jr., *lawyer, educator*
Reed, James C., Jr., *lawyer*
Reed, Susan D. *prosecutor*
Rodriguez, Xavier *lawyer*
Ross, James Ulric *lawyer, accountant, educator*
Ruttenberg, Frank Z. *lawyer*
Schlueter, David Arnold *law educator*
Schmutz, John Francis *lawyer*
Shearn, Michael Joseph *lawyer, arbitrator, mediator*
Spears, Sally *lawyer*
Steen, John Thomas, Jr., *lawyer*
Sutton, Johnny K. *lawyer*
Vazquez, Gilbert Falcon *lawyer*
Wallis, Ben Alton, Jr., *lawyer*
Weiner, Marcia Myra *judge*
Williamson, Deborah Daywood *lawyer*

San Marcos
Kyle, Henry Carper, III, *lawyer*
Parkin-Speer, Diane *English law educator*

Sealy
Stevens, Rhea Christina *lawyer*

Sherman
Freels, Jesse Saunders, Jr., *lawyer*

Southlake
Brunig, Robert Arthur *lawyer*

Spearman
Jarvis, Billy Britt *lawyer*

Spring
Farley, Andrew Newell *lawyer, consultant*
Hendricks, Randal Arlan *lawyer*

Stephenville
Batson, David Warren *lawyer*

Sugar Land
Hitchcock, Bion Earl *lawyer*

Temple
Cuba, Benjamin James *lawyer, mediator*
Pickle, Jerry Richard *lawyer*

The Woodlands
Hagerman, John David *lawyer*
Schlacks, Stephen Mark *lawyer*

Tyler
Ellis, Donald Lee *lawyer*
Patterson, Donald Ross *lawyer, educator*
Yeager, Ruth *lawyer*

Victoria
McKay, Robert Connally *lawyer*

Waco
Mc Swain, Angus Stewart, Jr., *retired law educator*
Morrison, Michael Dean *lawyer, law educator*
Ressler, Parke E(dward) *lawyer, accountant*
Smith, Cullen *lawyer*

Wichita Falls
Farris, Charlye Ola *lawyer*
Williams, Steven Mark *lawyer*

Wimberley
Brinsmade, Lyon Louis *retired lawyer*

Yoakum
Kvinta, Charles J. *lawyer*

UTAH

Logan
Honaker, Jimmie Joe *lawyer, ecologist*
Jenkins, James C. *lawyer*

Midvale
Dahl, Everett E. *lawyer*

Ogden
Mecham, Glenn Jefferson *lawyer, mayor*

Orem
Michell, Auriel Ibn *lawyer, writer*

Provo
Abbott, Charles Favour *lawyer*
Brown, Joseph William *retired patent agent*
Hill, Richard Lee *lawyer*

Saint George
Terry, Gary A. *lawyer, former trade association executive*

Salt Lake City
Adams, John A. *lawyer*
Adams, Joseph Keith *lawyer*
Anderson, Robert Monte *lawyer*
Atkin, Gary Eugene *lawyer*
Baldwin, John *legal association administrator, lawyer*
Barton, Paul J. *lawyer*
Barusch, Lawrence Roos *lawyer*
Baucom, Sidney George *lawyer*
Becker, Ralph Elihu, Jr., *lawyer, planner*
Beless, Rosemary June *lawyer*
Berman, Daniel Lewis *lawyer*
Bigler, Glade S. *lawyer*
Bushnell, Daniel S. *lawyer*
Castleton, David J. *lawyer*
Christensen, Patricia Anne Watkins *lawyer*
Christensen, Ray Richards *lawyer*
Clark, Scott H. *lawyer*
Cornaby, Kay Sterling *lawyer, former state senator*
Curtis, LeGrand R., Jr., *lawyer*
Dragoo, Denise Ann *lawyer*
Eklund, Carl Andrew *lawyer*
Gardiner, Lester Raymond, Jr., *lawyer*
Holbrook, Donald Benson *lawyer*
Humpherys, LeGrande Rich *lawyer*
Hunter, M(ilton) Reed, Jr., *lawyer*
Jensen, Dallin W. *lawyer*
Jones, Michael Frank *lawyer*
Kirkham, John Spencer *lawyer, director*
Lee, James B. *lawyer*
Lochhead, Robert Bruce *lawyer*
Mabey, Ralph R. *lawyer*
Manning, Brent V. *lawyer*
Mooney, Jerome Henri *lawyer*
Moore, Debra *lawyer*
Moore, James R. *lawyer*
Nydegger, Rick D. *lawyer*
Oaks, Dallin Harris *lawyer, church official*
Ockey, Ronald J. *lawyer*
Owen, Langdon Talbot, Jr., *lawyer*
Purser, Donald Joseph *lawyer*
Rasmussen, Thomas Val, Jr., *lawyer, small business owner*
Reeder, F. Robert *lawyer*
Schwendiman, Stephen Glenn *lawyer*
Scofield, David William *lawyer*
Shea, Patrick A. *lawyer, educator*
Sine, Wesley Franklin *lawyer*
Smith, Janet Hugie *lawyer*
Solano, Henry L. *lawyer*
Swinton, Jeffrey Cheever *lawyer*
Thompson, Neil Daniel *legal and genealogical researcher, retired lawyer*
Verhaaren, Harold Carl *lawyer*
Warner, Paul M. *prosecutor*
West, Stephen Allan *lawyer*
Wilde, Robert *lawyer*
Zimmer, Markus Bernhard *federal court administrator*
Zimmerman, Michael David *lawyer*

South Jordan
Larson, Bryan Alan *lawyer*

Springville
Ashworth, Brent Ferrin *lawyer*

Vernal
Judd, Dennis L. *lawyer*

VERMONT

Barre
Koch, Thomas Frederick *lawyer*

Brattleboro
McCarty, William Michael, Jr., *lawyer*
Reid, David G. *lawyer*

Burlington
Dinse, John Merrell *lawyer*
Frank, Joseph Elihu *lawyer*
Montroll, Andrew H. *lawyer, councilman*
Rendall, Donald James, Jr., *lawyer*
Wick, Hilton Addison *lawyer*

Castleton
Stafford, Robert Theodore *lawyer, former senator*

Colchester
Salmon, Thomas Paul *lawyer, academic administrator*

Concord
Norsworthy, Elizabeth Krassovsky *lawyer*

Essex Junction
Sweetser, Susan W. *lawyer, advocate, former state legislator*

Montpelier
Diamond, M. Jerome *lawyer, former state official*
Errecart, Joyce Hier *lawyer*
Guild, Alden *retired lawyer*
Saxman, Anna Esther *lawyer*
Valerio, Matthew F. *lawyer*

Rutland
Taylor, A. Jeffry *lawyer*

Shelburne
Canfield, Andrew Trotter *lawyer, writer*

South Burlington
Adams, Charles Jairus *lawyer*

South Royalton
Wroth, L(awrence) Kinvin *lawyer, educator*

Stowe
Anderson, Rudolph J., Jr., *lawyer*
Whiteman, Joseph David *retired lawyer, manufacturing company executive*

Warren
Raphael, Albert Ash, Jr., *retired lawyer*

White River Junction
Davis, Emily S. *lawyer*

VIRGINIA

Abingdon
Brownlee, John L. *prosecutor*
McElroy, Howard Chowning *lawyer*

Alexandria
Abell, Richard Bender (Richard Lon Welch) *lawyer, federal official*
Buechner, Jack W(illiam) *lawyer, government affairs consultant, educational association administrator*
Burch, John Thomas, Jr., *lawyer*
Carter, Richard Dennis *lawyer, educator*
Cauley, Michael A. *prosecutor*
Cottrell, James Ray *lawyer*
Dennison, Donald Lee *lawyer*
DiMuro, Bernard Joseph *lawyer*
Flater, Morris Eugene *lawyer*
Franklin, Jeanne F. *lawyer*
Gannon, Martin C. *lawyer*
Georges, Peter John *lawyer*
Goodman, Sherri Wasserman *lawyer*
Goolrick, Robert Mason *lawyer*
Greigg, Ronald Edwin *lawyer*
Higgins, Mary Celeste *lawyer, researcher*
Hirschkop, Philip Jay *lawyer, educator*
Holcomb, Richard Dennis *lawyer*
Huckabee, Harlow Maxwell *lawyer, writer*
Hussey, Ward MacLean *lawyer, former government official*
Kaplan, Richard Alan *government official*
Kopp, Eugene Paul *lawyer*
Kotlarchuk, Ihor O. E. *lawyer*
McDowell, Charles Eager *lawyer, retired military officer*
McGuire, Edward David, Jr., *lawyer*
McNulty, Paul J. *prosecutor*
Mossinghoff, Gerald Joseph *patent law expert, educator*
O'Connor, Charles P. *lawyer*
O'Hara, John Patrick *lawyer, accountant*
Paturis, E(mmanuel) Michael *lawyer*
Pyle, Howard *lawyer, consultant*
Straub, Peter Thornton *lawyer*
Sturtevant, Brereton *retired lawyer, former government official*
Swift, Stephen Christopher *lawyer*
Van Cleve, Ruth Gill *retired lawyer, government official*
Von Drehle, Ramon Arnold *lawyer*
Walkup, Charlotte Lloyd *lawyer*
Walkup, Homer Allen *lawyer, writer*
Wendel, Charles Allen *lawyer*
Wieder, Bruce Terrill *lawyer, electrical engineer*
Williams, John Edward *lawyer*

Amherst
Martin, Stephen Clarke *lawyer, mediator, arbitrator*

Annandale
Hovis, Robert Houston, III, *lawyer*

Arlington
Anthony, Robert Armstrong *lawyer, educator*
Barry, Lance Leonard *judge*
Brenner, Edgar H. *law administrator*
Burgess, David *lawyer*
Carbaugh, John Edward, Jr., *lawyer*
Cohen, Sheldon Irwin *lawyer*
Cragin, Charles Langmaid *lawyer*
Doyle, Gerard Francis *lawyer*
Drayton, William *social entrepreneur, lawyer, management consultant*
Fowler, David Lucas *corporate lawyer*
Fuller, Robert L(eander) *lawyer*
Gainer, Ronald Lee *lawyer*
Garnett, Griffin Taylor *lawyer, writer*
Green, Richard Alan *lawyer*
Hansen, Kenneth D. *lawyer, ophthalmologist*
Hansen, Orval *lawyer, former congressman, think tank executive*
Johnson, Charles Owen *retired lawyer*
Kelly, John James *lawyer*
Korman, James William *lawyer*
Krauss, Michael Ian *law educator*
Kuelbs, John Thomas *lawyer*
Lanier, Elizabeth K. *lawyer*
Litman, Richard Curtis *lawyer*
Malone, William Grady *retired lawyer*
McDermott, Francis Owen *retired lawyer*
Parker, Jeffrey Scott *law educator*
Rotunda, Ronald Daniel *law educator, consultant*
Scafetta, Joseph, Jr., *lawyer*
Schmidt, Paul Wickham *lawyer*
Schrier-Polak, Carol *lawyer*
Walker, Woodrow Wilson *retired lawyer, timber farmer, real estate investor*
Weinberg, Robert Lester *lawyer, law educator*
Wheeler, Barbara Monica *lawyer*

Blacksburg
Jensen, Walter Edward *lawyer, educator*

Blackstone
Allen, Jeffrey Rodgers *lawyer*

Burke
Hipfel, Steven J. *lawyer*

Centreville
Etters, Ronald Milton *lawyer, former government official*

Chantilly
Becker, James Richard *lawyer*
Helmer, Steven James *lawyer*

Charlottesville
Alford, Neill Herbert, Jr., *retired law educator*
Bonnie, Richard Jeffrey *law educator, lawyer, consultant*
Cannon, Jonathan Z. *lawyer, educator*
Chandler, Lawrence Bradford, Jr., *lawyer*
Cohen, Edwin Samuel *lawyer, educator*
Dooley, Michael P. *law educator*
Dunn, William Wyly *corporate lawyer*
Groiss, Fred George *lawyer*
Henderson, Stanley Dale *lawyer, educator*
Hodous, Robert Power *lawyer*
Howard, Arthur Ellsworth Dick *law educator*
Jeffries, John Calvin, Jr., *law educator*
Landess, Fred Stone *lawyer*
Martin, David Alan *law educator*
Meador, Daniel John *law educator*
Menefee, Samuel Pyeatt *lawyer, anthropologist*
Merrill, Richard Austin *lawyer*
Middleditch, Leigh Benjamin, Jr., *lawyer, educator*
Monahan, John T. *law educator, psychologist*
Moore, John Norton *lawyer, diplomat, educator*
O'Connell, Jeffrey *law educator*
Slaughter, Edward Ratliff, Jr., *lawyer*
Turner, Robert Foster *law educator, writer*
Wadlington, Walter James *law educator*
Wenger, Larry Bruce *law librarian, law educator*
White, George Edward *law educator, lawyer*
White, Thomas Raeburn, III, *law educator, consultant*
Whitehead, John Wayne *law educator, organization administrator, author*
Wyatt, Deborah Chasen *lawyer*

Chesapeake
Leftwich, James Asbury, Jr., *lawyer, entrepreneur*

Chester
Gray, Charles Robert *lawyer*

Danville
Conway, French Hoge *lawyer*
Regan, Michael Patrick *lawyer*
Talbott, Frank, III, *lawyer*

Earlysville
Grattan, George Gilmer, IV, *lawyer*

Edinburg
Cohen, Lewis Isaac *lawyer*

Fairfax
Anderson, David Lawrence *lawyer*
Appler, Thomas L. *lawyer*
Arnold, William McCauley *lawyer*
Arntson, Peter Andrew *lawyer*
Baird, Charles Bruce *lawyer, consultant*
Brown, Gary Wayne *lawyer*
Byrd Mische, Richard J. *lawyer*
Codding, Frederick Hayden *lawyer*
Downey, Richard Lawrence *lawyer*
Folk, Thomas Robert *lawyer*
Frieden, Jonathan David *lawyer*
Gillespie, Samuel H., III, *lawyer, oil company executive*
Hopson, Everett George *retired lawyer*
Keith, John A.C. *lawyer*
Mackall, Henry Clinton *lawyer*
Rust, John Howson, Jr., *lawyer, state legislator*
Sanderson, Douglas Jay *lawyer*
Schwartz, Philip *lawyer*

Fairfax Station
Bishop, Alfred Chilton, Jr., *lawyer*
Carver, George Allen, Jr., *retired lawyer*

Falls Church
Boehm, Kenneth *legal association administrator*
Brady, Rupert Joseph *retired lawyer*
Chabraja, Nicholas D. *lawyer*
Dewey-Balzhiser, Anne Elizabeth Marie *lawyer*
Diamond, Robert Michael *lawyer*
Flaherty, Peter *legal association administrator*
Golden, Wilson *lawyer*
Honigberg, Carol Crossman *lawyer*
Kirk, Dennis Dean *lawyer*
Lynn, Edward E. *corporate executive, lawyer*
Meserve, Richard Andrew *lawyer*
Perkins, Jack Edwin *lawyer*
Pischke, Vail W. *lawyer, Judge*
Savner, David A. *lawyer*
Thomas, William Griffith *lawyer*
Ward, Joe Henry, Jr., *retired lawyer*
Wood, John Martin *lawyer*

Fort Belvoir
Harms, John Kevin *lawyer*

Fort Eustis
Smail, Laurence Mitchell *lawyer, educator*

Franklin
Cobb, G. Elliott, Jr., *lawyer*

Fredericksburg
Dahnk, Jean Patricia *lawyer*

Front Royal
Napier, Douglas William *lawyer*

Galax
Kapp, John Paul *lawyer, physician, educator*

Glen Allen
Batzli, Terrence Raymond *lawyer*
Weaver, Mollie Little *lawyer*

Gloucester
Hicks, C. Flippo *lawyer*

Great Falls
Fisher, Bart Steven *lawyer, educator, investment banker*
Mitchell, Roy Shaw *lawyer*

Neidich, George Arthur *lawyer*
Preston, Charles George *lawyer*

Halifax
Greenbacker, John Everett *retired lawyer and naval officer*

Hampton
Nelson, Wallace Jay *patent attorney*
Smith, Stephen Mark *lawyer*

Harrisonburg
Wallinger, M(elvin) Bruce *lawyer*

Hayes
Casson, Richard Frederick *lawyer, travel bureau executive*
Phillips, Elizabeth Jason *lawyer, state agency administrator*

Haymarket
Frank, Jacob *lawyer*

Hopewell
Clark, Bruce Arlington, Jr., *lawyer*
Williams, C. James, III, (Jim Williams) *lawyer*

Hot Springs
Deeds, Robert Creigh *lawyer, state legislator*

Ivy
Wilcox, Harvey John *lawyer*

Keswick
Hawkins, Edward J. *retired lawyer*
Kunkel, David Nelson *lawyer*

Leesburg
Jacob, Walter Charles *lawyer*
Kelly, Lawrence Edward *lawyer, photographer*

Lexington
Jost, Timothy Stoltzfus *law educator*
Kirgis, Frederic Lee *law educator*
Wiant, Sarah Kirsten *law library administrator, educator, director*

Locust Grove
Grante, Jullian Irving *criminal justice consultant*
Huntsman, Lawrence Darrow *lawyer, director*

Lovettsville
Flannery, John Philip *lawyer*

Lynchburg
Healy, Joseph Francis, Jr., *lawyer, retired air transportation executive*
Packert, G(ayla) Beth *retired lawyer*
Wetzel, Robert Charles *lawyer*

Manakin Sabot
Bright, Craig Bartley *lawyer*

Manassas
Foote, John Holland *lawyer*

Martinsville
Frith, Douglas Kyle *retired lawyer*

Mason Neck
Brittigan, Robert Lee *retired lawyer*

Mc Lean
Alexander, Fred Calvin, Jr., *lawyer*
Aucutt, Ronald David *lawyer*
Boyd, Ralph F., Jr., *lawyer, former federal agency administrator*
Brady, Phillip Donley *lawyer*
Brown, Thomas Cartmel, Jr., *lawyer*
Byrnes, William Joseph *lawyer*
Chapple, Thomas Leslie *lawyer*
Church, Randolph Warner, Jr., *lawyer*
Condo, Joseph A. *lawyer*
Corson, J. Jay, IV, *lawyer*
Fritz, Thomas Vincent *business executive*
Gammon, James Alan *lawyer*
Halagao, Avelino Garabiles *lawyer*
Herge, J. Curtis *lawyer*
Hicks, C. Thomas, III, *lawyer*
Hoffmann, Martin Richard *lawyer*
Ingersoll, William Boley *lawyer, real estate developer*
Jackson, William Paul, Jr., *lawyer*
Kennedy, Cornelius Bryant *retired lawyer*
Kondracki, Edward John *lawyer*
LeSourd, Nancy Susan Oliver *lawyer, writer*
Marino, Michael Frank, III, *lawyer*
McCorkindale, Douglas Hamilton *lawyer, publishing executive*
Miller, Donald Eugene *lawyer*
Molineaux, Charles Borromeo *lawyer, arbitrator, columnist, poet*
Morris, James Malachy *lawyer*
Morse, Duane D(ale) *lawyer*
Murphy, Thomas Patrick *lawyer*
Noonan, Jean *lawyer*
Olson, William Jeffrey *lawyer*
Price, Ilene Rosenberg *lawyer*
Quinlan, J(oseph) Michael *lawyer*
Rawls, Charles Richardson *lawyer, government official*
Shapiro, Nelson Hirsh *lawyer*
Sparks, Robert Ronold, Jr., *lawyer*
Stump, John Sutton *retired lawyer*
Tansill, Frederick Joseph *lawyer*
Townsend, Christopher Gordon *lawyer*
Van Lare, Wendell John *lawyer*
Wall, Barbara Wartelle *lawyer*

Middleburg
Beddall, Thomas Henry *lawyer*

Midlothian
Shands, William Ridley, Jr., *lawyer*
Tuttle, Roger Lewis *lawyer, educator*

Montross
Monaco, Grace Powers *lawyer*

Nellysford
Sims, John Rogers, Jr., *lawyer*

Newport News
Cuthrell, Carl Edward *lawyer, educator, clergyman*
Kamp, Arthur Joseph, Jr., *lawyer*

Norfolk
Albert, Alan Dale *lawyer*
Baird, Edward Rouzie, Jr., *retired lawyer*
Bishop, Bruce Taylor *lawyer*
Clark, Morton Hutchinson *lawyer*
Corcoran, Andrew Patrick, Jr., *lawyer*
Davis, Terry Hunter, Jr., *lawyer*
Drescher, John Webb *lawyer*
Johnson, Thomas G., Jr., *lawyer*
Lawrence, Joe Gray, Jr., *lawyer*
Mayo, Alex T., Jr., *lawyer*
McCaa, James Cureton, III, *lawyer*
Parker, Richard Wilson *lawyer, retired rail transportation executive*
Pearson, John Yeardley, Jr., *lawyer*
Poston, Anita Owings *lawyer*
Rashkind, Alan Brody *lawyer*
Rephan, Jack *lawyer*
Russell, C. Edward, Jr., *lawyer*
Ryan, John M. *lawyer*
Ryan, Louis Farthing *lawyer*
Shannon, John Sanford *lawyer, retired railway executive*

Oakton
Duesenberg, Robert H. *retired lawyer*
Vernava, Anthony Michael *lawyer*

Orange
Thomas, Franklin A., III, *lawyer*

Petersburg
Everitt, Alice Lubin *labor arbitrator*
Shell, Louis Calvin *lawyer*
Spero, Morton Bertram *retired lawyer*

Portsmouth
Porter, J. Ridgely, III, *lawyer*

Pulaski
McCarthy, Thomas James, Jr., *lawyer*

Radford
Turk, James Clinton, Jr., *lawyer*

Reston
Bredehoft, Elaine Charlson *lawyer*
Butler, Katherine E. *lawyer*
Finkelstein, Jay Gary *lawyer*
Keler, Marianne Martha *lawyer*
Maitland, Guy Edison Clay *lawyer*
Platt, Leslie A. *lawyer*
Rau, Lee Arthur *lawyer*
Reicin, Eric David *lawyer*
Scharff, Joseph Laurent *lawyer*
Toole, John Harper *lawyer*
Walton, Edmund Lewis, Jr., *lawyer*

Richmond
Bagley, Philip Joseph, III, *lawyer*
Baliles, Gerald L. *lawyer, former governor*
Beales, Randolph A. *lawyer, former Attorney General*
Belcher, Dennis Irl *lawyer*
Booker, Lewis Thomas *lawyer*
Brasfield, Evans Booker *lawyer*
Brissette, Martha Blevins *lawyer*
Brooks, Robert Franklin, Sr., *lawyer*
Bryson, William Hamilton *law educator*
Buford, Robert Pegram *lawyer*
Burke, John K(irkland), Jr., *lawyer*
Burrus, Robert Lewis, Jr., *lawyer*
Burtch, Jack Willard, Jr., *lawyer*
Carrell, Daniel Allan *lawyer*
Carter, Joseph Carlyle, Jr., *lawyer*
Catlett, Richard H., Jr., *retired lawyer*
Chandler, Theodore Lindy, Jr., *lawyer*
Clinard, Robert Noel *lawyer*
Cohn, David Stephen *lawyer*
Cullen, Richard *lawyer, former state attorney general*
Cutchins, Clifford Armstrong, IV, *lawyer*
Dabney, H. Slayton, Jr., *lawyer*
Denny, Collins, III, *lawyer*
Dray, Mark S. *lawyer*
Edmonds, Thomas Andrew *legal association administrator*
Ellis, Andrew Jackson, Jr., *lawyer*
Flippen, Edward L. *lawyer*
Freeman, George Clemon, Jr., *lawyer*
Gary, Richard David *lawyer*
Goodpasture, Philip Henry *lawyer*
Graves, H. Brice *retired lawyer*
Grey, Robert J. *lawyer*
Hackney, Virginia Howitz *lawyer*
Hall, Stephen Charles *lawyer*
Hettrick, George Harrison *lawyer*
Horsley, Waller Holladay *lawyer*
Kearfott, Joseph Conrad *lawyer*
King, William H., Jr., *lawyer*
Landin, David Craig *lawyer*
Ledbetter, David Oscar *lawyer*
Levit, Jay J(oseph) *lawyer*
McClard, Jack Edward *lawyer*
McFarlane, Walter Alexander *lawyer, educator*
Merhige, Robert Reynold, Jr., *lawyer*
Mezzullo, Louis Albert *lawyer*
Millhiser, Thomas McNally *lawyer*
Milme, Patrick Joseph *retired lawyer*
Minardi, Richard A., Jr., *lawyer*
Moore, Thurston Roach *lawyer*
Patterson, Robert Hobson, Jr., *lawyer*
Pinckney, Charles Cotesworth *lawyer*
Pope, Robert Dean *lawyer*
Powell, Lewis Franklin, III, *lawyer*
Rainey, Gordon Fryer, Jr., *lawyer*
Redmond, David Dudley *lawyer*
Rigsby, Linda Flory *lawyer*
Robinson, John Victor *lawyer*
Rolfe, Robert Martin *lawyer*
Rubinstein, Phyllis M. *lawyer*
Rucker, Douglas Pendleton, Jr., *lawyer*
Rudlin, David Alan *lawyer*
Ryland, Walter H. *lawyer*
Sharer, John Daniel *lawyer*
Slater, Thomas Glascock, Jr., *lawyer*
Slaughter, Alexander Hoke *lawyer*
Smith, Julious Perry, Jr., *lawyer*
Smith, R. Gordon *lawyer*
Starke, Harold E., Jr., *lawyer*
Street, Walter Scott, III, *lawyer*
Strickland, William Jesse *lawyer*
Thomas, John Charles *lawyer, former state supreme court justice*
Thompson, Paul Michael *lawyer*
Thro, William Eugene *lawyer*
Troy, Anthony Francis *lawyer*
Walsh, William Arthur, Jr., *lawyer*
Warthen, Harry Justice, III, *lawyer*
White, Hugh Vernon, Jr., *lawyer*
Williams, Steven Robert *lawyer*
Witt, Walter Francis, Jr., *lawyer*
Wright, Wiley Reed, Jr., *lawyer, retired judge, mediator*

Roanoke
Bates, Harold Martin *lawyer*
Butler, Manley Caldwell *retired lawyer*
Effel, Laura *lawyer*
Fishwick, John Palmer *retired lawyer, retired railroad executive*
Glenn, Robert Eastwood *lawyer*
Glover, Harry Allen, Jr., *lawyer*
Hylton, Myles Talbert *lawyer*
Jennings, James Wilson, Jr., *lawyer*
Lemon, William Jacob *lawyer*
Marshall, Heman Alexander, III, *lawyer*
McGarry, Richard Lawrence *lawyer*
Steele, Anita Martin (Margaret Anne Martin) *law librarian, legal educator*
Thomson, Paul Rice, Jr., *lawyer*
Woodrum, Clifton A., III, *lawyer, former state legislator*

Salem
Griffith, H(oward) Morgan *lawyer*

Schley
McVey, Henry Hanna, III, *retired lawyer*

Spotsylvania
Manthei, Richard Dale *retired lawyer, health care company executive*
Pugh, Randall Scott *lawyer*

Springfield
Chappell, Milton Leroy *lawyer*
Englert, Roy Theodore *lawyer*
Long, Clarence Dickinson, III, *lawyer*

Sterling
Clegg, Roger Burton *lawyer*
McBarnette, Bruce Olvin *lawyer, corporate executive*

Suffolk
Young, Hubert Howell, Jr., *lawyer, real estate investor and developer*

Vienna
Gavin, Donald Glenn *lawyer, educator*
Hagberg, Chris Eric *lawyer*
Johnson, Richard Clark *lawyer*
Maiwurm, James John *lawyer*
Peltz, Paulette Beatrice *corporate lawyer*
Razzano, Frank Charles *lawyer*
Stearns, Frank Warren *lawyer*
Titus, Bruce Earl *lawyer*
Whitaker, Thomas Patrick *lawyer*

Virginia Beach
Dumville, S(amuel) Lawrence *lawyer*
Frantz, Thomas Richard *lawyer*
Harrell, Charles Lydon, Jr., *lawyer*
Jones, John Lou *retired arbitrator, rail transportation executive*
Pickett, Owen B. *lawyer, former congressman*
Savage, Toy Dixon, Jr., *lawyer*
Spitzli, Donald Hawkes, Jr., *lawyer*

Warrenton
Brooke, Edward William *lawyer, former senator*
Morrison, Paul A. *lawyer*

Waterford
Harris, Caspa, Jr., *lawyer, educator, association administrator*

White Stone
Ames, John Lewis *lawyer*

Williamsburg
Burdette, Robert Bruce *retired lawyer*
Church, Dale Walker *lawyer*
Geddy, Vernon Meredith, Jr., *lawyer*
Lund, Wendell Luther *retired lawyer*
Marcus, Paul *law educator*
Margolin, Robert Jeremy *lawyer*
Sullivan, Timothy Jackson *law educator, academic administrator*
Tortorice, Donald A. *law educator*

Winchester
Adams, Nate Lavinder, III, *lawyer*
Tisinger, Billy Joe *lawyer*

Woodstock
Walton, Morgan Lauck, III, *lawyer*

Wytheville
Baird, Thomas Bryan, Jr., *retired lawyer*

WASHINGTON

Bainbridge Island
Fischer, Thomas Covell *law educator, consultant, writer*

Bellevue
Andrews, Richard Lee *lawyer*
Hannah, Lawrence Burlison *lawyer*
Medved, Robert Allen *lawyer*
Morie, G. Glen *lawyer, manufacturing executive*
Pinney, Alesia L. *lawyer*
Sebris, Robert, Jr., *lawyer*
Sweeney, David Brian *lawyer*

Bellingham
Anderson, David Bowen *lawyer*
Packer, Mark Barry *lawyer, financial consultant, foundation official*
Raas, Daniel Alan *lawyer*

Centralia
Bates, Charles Walter *lawyer, human resources executive, politician*
Buzzard, Steven Ray *lawyer*
Wright, Daniel A. *lawyer*

Eastsound
Hoagland, Karl King, Jr., *lawyer*

Edmonds
Conom, Tom Peter *lawyer*

Everett
Fitzpatrick, Thomas Mark *lawyer*
Ostergaard, Joni Hammersla *lawyer*

Federal Way
Nance, John Joseph *lawyer, writer, air safety analyst, broadcaster, consultant*

Friday Harbor
Gonser, Thomas Howard *lawyer, former bar association executive*

Gig Harbor
Thompson, Ronald Edward *lawyer*

Hoquiam
Kessler, Keith Leon *lawyer*

Issaquah
Benoliel, Joel *lawyer*
Moch, Robert Gaston *retired lawyer*
Oles, Stuart Gregory *lawyer*

Kennewick
Hames, William Lester *lawyer*

Keyport
Treacy, Gerald Bernard, Jr., *lawyer*

Kirkland
Cowan, Douglas Leo *lawyer*
Spence, Michael Allan *lawyer*

Lynnwood
Bergstedt, Anders Spencer *lawyer*

Montesano
Stewart, James Malcom *lawyer*

Mount Vernon
Moser, C. Thomas *lawyer*

Newcastle
Erxleben, William Charles *lawyer, consultant*

Olympia
Roe, Charles Barnett *lawyer*
Walker, Francis Joseph *lawyer*
Welsh, John Beresford, Jr., *retired lawyer*
Williams, Wayne Leroy *lawyer*

Redmond
Neukom, William H. *lawyer*

Sammamish
Waitt, Robert Kenneth *lawyer*

Seattle
Alkire, John D. *lawyer, arbitrator, mediator*
Alsdorf, Robert Hermann *lawyer*
Anderson, Peter MacArthur *lawyer*
Andrews, J. David *lawyer*
Bailey, William Scherer *lawyer, educator*
Barnes, Susan Lewis *lawyer*
Berman, Steve William *lawyer, author*
Black, W. L. Rivers, III, *lawyer*
Blair, M. Wayne *lawyer*
Blom, Daniel Charles *lawyer, investor, retired insurance company executive*
Boeder, Thomas L. *lawyer*
Boggs, Paula Elaine *lawyer*
Boman, Marc Allen *lawyer*
Boxx, Karen Elizabeth *lawyer, educator*
Bridge, Jonathan Joseph *lawyer, retail executive*
Bringman, Joseph Edward *lawyer*
Bucklin, Mark Richard *lawyer*
Budigan, William Clay *lawyer, educator*
Burke, William Thomas *law educator, lawyer*
Cavanaugh, Michael Everett *lawyer, arbitrator, mediator*
Chapman, Fay L. *lawyer*
Claflin, Arthur Cary *lawyer*
Comfort, Robert Dennis *lawyer*
Cross, Bruce Michael *lawyer*
Davis, John MacDougall *lawyer*
DeVore, Paul Cameron *lawyer*
Dolan, Andrew Kevin *lawyer*
Elliott, Clifton Langsdale *lawyer*
Ellis, James Reed *retired lawyer*
Fisher, Jeffrey L. *lawyer*
Frost, Barbara Sherry *lawyer*
Gibbs, Nancy Patricia *lawyer*
Giles, Robert Edward, Jr., *lawyer*
Ginsberg, Phillip H(enry) *lawyer*
Gittinger, D. Wayne *lawyer*
Glover, Karen E. *lawyer*
Goeltz, Thomas A. *lawyer*
Gores, Thomas C. *lawyer*
Gorton, Slade *attorney, former senator*
Graham, Stephen Michael *lawyer*
Gray, Marvin Lee, Jr., *lawyer*
Greenan, Thomas J. *lawyer*
Greenfield, Ester Frances *lawyer*
Gustafson, Alice Fairleigh *lawyer*
Haman, Raymond William *lawyer*
Hamilton, Steven G. *lawyer*
Hazelton, Penny Ann *law librarian, educator*
Hendricks, Katherine *lawyer*
Hermsen, James R. *lawyer*
Hilpert, Edward Theodore, Jr., *lawyer*
Huston, John Charles *law educator*
Isaki, Lucy Power Slyngstad *lawyer*
Jaffe, Robert Stanley *lawyer*
Johnson, Bruce Edward Humble *lawyer*
Judson, C(harles) James (Jim Judson) *lawyer*
Kane, Alan Henry *lawyer*

Kane, Christopher *lawyer*
Kaplan, Barry Martin *lawyer*
Keegan, John E. *lawyer*
Klein, Otto George, III, *lawyer*
Koehler, Reginald Stafford, III, *lawyer*
Kuhrau, Edward W. *lawyer*
Lawless, Janine A. *lawyer*
Leitzell, Terry Lee *lawyer*
Lemly, Thomas Adger *lawyer*
Loftus, Thomas Daniel *lawyer*
Longfelder, Lawrence Lee *lawyer*
Losey, Beverley Brown *lawyer, nurse*
Lundgren, Gail M. *lawyer*
Maleng, Norm *prosecutor*
Manning, J. Richard *lawyer*
McCann, Richard Eugene *retired lawyer*
McCune, Philip Spear *lawyer*
McKay, John *lawyer*
McKinstry, Ronald E. *lawyer*
McLean, Dennis Edgar *lawyer*
Mines, Michael *lawyer*
Mussehl, Robert Clarence *lawyer*
Nellermoe, Leslie Carol *lawyer*
Niemi, Janice *retired lawyer, retired state legislator*
Oehler, Richard William *lawyer*
Olsen, Harold Fremont *lawyer*
Palmer, Douglas S., Jr., *lawyer*
Parks, Patricia Jean *lawyer*
Paul, Thomas Frank *lawyer*
Perey, Ron *lawyer*
Petrie, Gregory Steven *lawyer*
Pflaumer, Katrina C. *lawyer*
Price, John Richard *lawyer, law educator*
Pritchard, Llewelyn G. *lawyer*
Pym, Bruce Michael *lawyer*
Redman, Eric *lawyer*
Ritter, Daniel Benjamin *lawyer*
Rosen, Jon Howard *lawyer*
Ruddy, James W. *lawyer*
Russell, Robie George *lawyer*
Sandler, Michael David *lawyer*
Sayre, Matt Melvin Mathias *lawyer*
Scott, Brian David *lawyer*
Sherland, Barbara C. *lawyer*
Squires, William Randolph, III, *lawyer*
Starr, Isidore *law educator*
Stoebuck, William Brees *law educator*
Stokke, Diane Rees *lawyer*
Thorson, Lee A. *lawyer*
Tomlinson, John Randolph *lawyer*
Treiger, Irwin Louis *lawyer*
Tune, James Fulcher *lawyer*
Vestal, Josephine Burnet *lawyer*
Vogel, David Seth *lawyer*
Wagner, Patricia Hamm *lawyer*
Wagoner, David Everett *lawyer, arbitrator*
Wechsler, Mary Heyrman *lawyer*
White, Rebecca T. *lawyer*
White, Rick *lawyer, former congressman*
Whitson, Lish *lawyer*
Williams, J. Vernon *retired lawyer*
Williams, Rebecca Lynn *lawyer, nurse*
Wilson, L. Michelle *lawyer*
Wilson, Richard Randolph *lawyer*

Selah
Ring, Lucile Wiley *lawyer*

Silverdale
Fjelstad, Paul *lawyer, editor*

Spokane
Anderson, Robert Edward *lawyer*
Antonietti, Joan L(ynn) *lawyer*
Clarke, Judy *lawyer*
Clements, Theodore *lawyer, law educator, dean*
Harbaugh, Daniel Paul *lawyer*
Koegen, Roy Jerome *lawyer*
Kovacevich, Robert Eugene *lawyer*
Lineberger, Peter Saalfield *lawyer*
McDevitt, James A. *lawyer*
Weatherhead, Leslie R. *lawyer*

Tacoma
George, Nicholas *lawyer, entrepreneur*
Holt, William E. *lawyer*
Krueger, James A. *lawyer*
Lowenberg, Timothy Joseph *lawyer*
Mack, Robert E. *lawyer*
Miller, Judson Frederick *lawyer, former military officer*
Mungia, Salvador Alejo *lawyer*
Waldo, James Chandler *lawyer*

Tumwater
Edmondson, Frank Kelley, Jr., *lawyer, legal administrator*

Vancouver
Dodds, Michael Bruce *lawyer*
Karpinski, John Stanley *lawyer*

Walla Walla
Hayner, Herman Henry *lawyer*
Martin, John Hugh *lawyer, retired*

Yakima
Larson, Paul Martin *lawyer*
Tenney, Robert Carl *lawyer*
Wright, J(ames) Lawrence *lawyer*

WEST VIRGINIA

Beckley
Kennedy, David Tinsley *retired lawyer, labor arbitrator*

Charleston
Betts, Rebecca A. *lawyer*
Brown, James Knight *lawyer*
Callaghan, Dan O. *lawyer*
Chaney, Michael Thomas *lawyer*
Cline, Michael Robert *lawyer*
Dissen, James Hardiman *lawyer*
Heath, Mark E. *lawyer*
Lane, Charlotte *lawyer*
McCuskey, John F. *lawyer*
Neely, Richard *lawyer*
O'Connor, Otis Leslie *lawyer, director*
Robinson, E. Glenn *lawyer*
Rowe, Larry Linwell *lawyer*
Victorson, Michael Bruce *lawyer*
Warner, Karl K. *prosecutor*
Zak, Robert Joseph *lawyer*

Clarksburg
West, James C., Jr., *lawyer*

Fairmont
Aloi, Michael John *lawyer*
Stanton, George Patrick, Jr., *lawyer*

Fairview
Bunner, William Keck *lawyer*

Gassaway
Jones, Jeniver James *lawyer*

Huntington
Bagley, Charles Frank, III, *lawyer*
Underwood, Mark Forest *lawyer*

Lewisburg
Ford, Richard Edmond *lawyer*

Logan
Hrutkay, Lidella Wilson *lawyer, state legislator*

Martinsburg
Hill, Philip Bonner *lawyer*
Martin, Clarence Eugene, III, *lawyer*

Morgantown
Cleckley, Franklin D. *law educator*
Cohen, Richard Paul *lawyer*
Fisher, John Welton, II, *law educator, magistrate judge, university official*
Fusco, Andrew G. *lawyer*
Morris, William Otis, Jr., *lawyer, educator, writer*

Parkersburg
Keltner, Robert Earl *lawyer, researcher, business executive*
Richardson, William Berkley *lawyer*

Romney
Saville, Royce Blair *lawyer*

Summersville
Davis, Stephen Allen *lawyer*

Weirton
Fahey, William Thomas, II, *lawyer*

Weston
Oldaker, Bradley Russell *lawyer*

Wheeling
Bailey, John P. *lawyer*
Gardill, James Clark *lawyer*
Hill, Barry Morton *lawyer*
Johnston, Thomas E. *prosecutor*

WISCONSIN

Appleton
Chudacoff, Bruce Michael *lawyer*
Drescher, Kathleen Ebben *lawyer*
Drescher, Park Morris *lawyer*
Eno, Woodrow E. *lawyer*
Lorge, Robert Gerald Augustine *lawyer, real estate broker*

Casco
Richards, Steven George *lawyer*

Cedarburg
Hazelwood, John A. *lawyer*

Cross Plains
Atterbury, Lee Richard *lawyer*

Deerfield
Pappas, David Christopher *lawyer*

Delafield
Hausman, C. Michael *lawyer, judge*
McClure, Thomas James *lawyer*

Dodgeville
Boyer, Dennis Lee *lawyer, policy analyst, writer*

Eagle River
Kulzick, Ken Stafford *retired lawyer, travel writer*

Eau Claire
Frank, John LeRoy

Elkhorn
Eberhardt, Daniel Hugo *lawyer*
Sostarich, Mark Edward *lawyer*

Evansville
Decker, John Robert *lawyer*

Germantown
Ehlinger, Ralph Jerome *lawyer*

Green Bay
Burnett, Ralph George *lawyer*

Greendale
Vinent-Cantoral, Aida R. *mediator*

Hales Corners
Case, Karen Ann *lawyer*

Janesville
Steil, George Kenneth, Sr., *lawyer*

Kenosha
Higgins, John Patrick *lawyer, mediator, educator, lobbyist*

Kohler
Black, Natalie A. *lawyer*
Sheedy, Kathleen Ann *lawyer*

La Crosse
Klos, Jerome John *lawyer, director*
Nix, Edmund Alfred *lawyer*
Sleik, Thomas Scott *lawyer*

Lake Geneva
Braden, Berwyn Bartow *lawyer*

Lodi
Smith, Michael W. *lawyer*

Madison
Baldwin, Gordon Brewster *law educator, lawyer*
Baldwin, Janice Murphy *lawyer*
Barnhill, Charles Joseph, Jr., *lawyer*
Barnick, Helen *retired judicial clerk*
Bartell, Jeffrey Bruce *lawyer*
Bochert, Linda H. *lawyer*
Boller, Matthew Hubly *lawyer*
Braden, Betty Jane *legal association administrator*
Bremer, Howard Walter *lawyer, consultant*
Brewster, Francis Anthony *lawyer*
Bugge, Lawrence John *lawyer, educator*
Chandler, Richard Gates *lawyer*
Charo, Robin Alta *law educator*
Field, Henry Augustus, Jr., *lawyer*
Hanson, David James *lawyer*
Helstad, Orrin L. *lawyer, legal educator*
Hempe, A. Henry *lawyer, consultant, arbitrator*
Heymann, S. Richard *lawyer*
Hofeldt, John W. *lawyer*
Jones, James Edward, Jr., *retired law educator*
Kuehling, Robert Warren *lawyer, accountant*
Langer, Richard J. *lawyer*
Linstroth, Tod Brian *lawyer*
Long, Theodore James *lawyer*
MacDougall, Priscilla Ruth *lawyer*
McCallum, Laurie Riach *state government lawyer*
Mebane, David Cummins *lawyer*
Melli, Marygold Shire *law educator*
Mitby, John Chester *lawyer*
Mowris, Gerald William *lawyer*
Prange, Roy Leonard, Jr., *lawyer*
Ragatz, Thomas George *lawyer*
Steingass, Susan R. *lawyer*
Sweet, Howard A. *lawyer*
Temkin, Harvey L. *lawyer*
Van Hollen, J.B. *lawyer*
Vaughan, Michael Richard *lawyer*
Walsh, David Graves *lawyer*

Menomonee Falls
Dynek, Sigrid *corporate lawyer, retail executive*
Schepp, Richard D. *lawyer, retail executive*

Menomonie
Steans, Phillip Michael *lawyer*

Middleton
Berman, Ronald Charles *lawyer, accountant*
Nora, Wendy Alison *lawyer*

Milwaukee
Abraham, William John, Jr., *lawyer*
Babler, Wayne E., Jr., *lawyer*
Ballman, Patricia Kling *lawyer*
Bannen, Carol *information resources director*
Bannen, John Thomas *lawyer*
Berkoff, Marshall Richard *lawyer*
Biehl, Michael Melvin *lawyer, author*
Biller, Joel Wilson *lawyer, former foreign service officer*
Biskupic, Steven M. *lawyer*
Blain, Peter Charles *lawyer*
Bolger, T(homas) Michael *lawyer*
Bremer, John M. *lawyer*
Busch, John Arthur *lawyer*
Calise, William Joseph, Jr., *lawyer*
Cannon, David Joseph *lawyer*
Casey, John Alexander *lawyer*
Casper, Richard Henry *lawyer*
Chokey, James A. *lawyer*
Christiansen, Keith Allan *lawyer*
Clark, James Richard *lawyer*
Connolly, Gerald Edward *lawyer*
Daily, Frank J(erome) *lawyer*
Dallman, Robert Edward *lawyer*
Donovan, Michael Joseph *lawyer*
Duback, Steven Rahr *lawyer*
Ericson, James Donald *retired lawyer*
Florsheim, Richard Steven *lawyer*
Frauen, Kurt Herman *lawyer*
Frautschi, Timothy Clark *lawyer*
Friedman, James Dennis *lawyer*
Gaines, Irving David *lawyer*
Galanis, John William *lawyer*
Gallagher, Richard Sidney *lawyer*
Gefke, Henry Jerome *lawyer*
Gemignani, Joseph Adolph *lawyer*
Geske, Janine Patricia *law educator, former state supreme court justice*
Ghiardi, James Domenic *lawyer, educator*
Giese, Heiner *lawyer, real estate investor*
Goodkind, Conrad George *lawyer*
Graber, Richard William *lawyer, political organization worker*
Grenig, Jay Edward *law educator*
Haberman, F. William *lawyer*
Habush, Robert Lee *lawyer*
Harrington, John Timothy *retired lawyer*
Hase, David John *lawyer*
Hatch, Michael Ward *lawyer*
Hoefle, Paul Ryan *lawyer*
Hoffman, Nathaniel A. *lawyer*
Holz, Harry George *lawyer*
Huff, Marsha Elkins *lawyer*
Iding, Allan Earl *lawyer*
Johnson, James N. *lawyer*
Jost, Lawrence John *lawyer*
Kessler, Joan F. *lawyer*
Kircher, John Joseph *law educator*
Knight, George B. *lawyer*
Kringel, Jerome Howard *lawyer*
Krueger, Raymond Robert *lawyer*
Kubale, Bernard Stephen *lawyer*
Kurtz, Harvey A. *lawyer*
LaBudde, Roy Christian *lawyer*
Levine, Herbert *lawyer*
Levit, William Harold, Jr., *lawyer*
Lione, Gail Ann *lawyer*
Lueders, Wayne Richard *lawyer*
Lynch, Michael *lawyer, staffing company executive*
MacGregor, David Lee *lawyer*
Martin, Quinn William *lawyer*
Maynard, John Ralph *lawyer*
McGaffey, Jere D. *retired lawyer*
McSweeney, Maurice J. (Marc McSweeney) *lawyer*
Meldman, Robert Edward *lawyer*
Melin, Robert Arthur *lawyer*
Michelstetter, Stanley Hubert *lawyer*
O'Shaughnessy, James Patrick *lawyer*
Phillips, Thomas John *lawyer*
Pindyck, Bruce Eben *lawyer, corporate executive*
Pollen, Raymond James *lawyer*
Richman, Stephen Erik *lawyer*
Rintelman, Donald Brian *lawyer*
Ryan, Patrick Michael *lawyer*
Salustro, Larry J. *lawyer*
Santelle, James Lewis *prosecutor*
Schnur, Robert Arnold *lawyer*
Scrivner, Thomas William *lawyer*
Shapiro, Robyn Sue *lawyer, educator*
Shriner, Thomas L., Jr., *lawyer*
Smith, David Bruce *lawyer*
Sturm, William Charles *lawyer*
Surridge, Stephen Zehring *lawyer, writer*
Terschan, Frank Robert *lawyer*
Titley, Robert L. *lawyer*
Trebon, Lawrence Alan *lawyer*
Trecek, Timothy Scott *lawyer*
Van Grunsven, Paul Robert *lawyer*
Walmer, Edwin Fitch *lawyer*
Wiley, Edwin Packard *retired lawyer*
Will, Trevor Jonathan *lawyer*
Williams, Clay Rule *lawyer*
Winsten, Saul Nathan *lawyer*

Minocqua
Lund, John Richard *lawyer, director*

Monroe
Kittelsen, Rodney Olin *lawyer*

Montello
Wissbaum, Donna Cacic *lawyer*

Mosinee
Hartz, Luetta Bertha *legal secretary*

Oak Creek
Giblin, Louis *lawyer*

Oshkosh
Kelly, John Martin *lawyer*

Phelps
Coccia, Michel Andre *retired lawyer*

Port Washington
Meyer, Raymond George, II, *lawyer*

Racine
Coates, Glenn Richard *lawyer*
Du Rocher, James Howard *lawyer*
Schoone, Adrian Paul *lawyer*
Smith, Stephen James *lawyer, director*
Wheaton, Douglas B. *lawyer*

Rhinelander
McEldowney, Todd Richard *lawyer*

Ripon
Prissel, Barbara Ann *paralegal, law educator*

River Falls
Zajac, Claire Marie *lawyer*

Stoughton
Wetzel, Volker Knoppke *law educator*

Sun Prairie
Berkenstadt, James Allan *lawyer*
Eustice, Francis Joseph *lawyer*

Union Grove
Stern, Walter Wolf, III, *lawyer*

Waukesha
Davis, J. Mac *lawyer, state judge*
Jastroch, Leonard Andrew *lawyer*

Wausau
Deffner, Roger L. *lawyer, investment counselor, chef*
Drengler, William Allan John *lawyer*
Grischke, Alan Edward *lawyer*
Kammer, Robert Arthur, Jr., *lawyer*
Molinaro, Thomas J. *lawyer*
Orr, San Watterson, Jr., *lawyer*

Wauwassa
O'Dess, Mary Abigail *lawyer*

Williams Bay
Tobin, Dennis Michael *lawyer*

WYOMING

Buffalo
Kirven, Timothy J. *lawyer*

Casper
Combs, W(illiam) Henry, III, *lawyer*
Durham, Harry Blaine, III, *lawyer*
Gray, Jan Charles *lawyer, business owner*
Hjelmstad, William David *lawyer*
Lowe, Robert Stanley *lawyer*
Reese, Thomas Frank *lawyer*
Sullivan, Michael John *lawyer, former ambassador*

Cheyenne
Carmichael, David H. *lawyer*
Freudenthal, Steven Franklin *lawyer, political organization chairman*
Hanes, John Grier *lawyer, state legislator*
Mackey, Terrence Wayne *lawyer*
Mc Clintock, Archie Glenn *lawyer*
Mead, Matthew Hansen *prosecutor*
Palma, Jack D. *lawyer*

Evanston
Combs, William L. *lawyer*

Gillette
Lubnau, Thomas Edwin, II, *lawyer*

Jackson
Schuster, Robert Parks *lawyer*

Shockey, Gary Lee *lawyer*
Spence, Gerald Leonard *lawyer, writer*

Laramie
Fulton, Jo Ann *lawyer*
Kinney, Lisa Frances *lawyer*
Selig, Joel Louis *lawyer, educator*

Riverton
Girard, Nettabell *lawyer*
Hursh, John R. *lawyer*

Sheridan
Lonabaugh, Ellsworth Eugene *retired lawyer*

Wheatland
Hunkins, Raymond Breedlove *lawyer, rancher*

TERRITORIES OF THE UNITED STATES

GUAM

Hagatna
Troutman, Charles Henry, III, *lawyer*

Tamuning
Aguigui, Ignacio Cruz *lawyer*

NORTHERN MARIANA ISLANDS

Saipan
Soll, Herbert D. *lawyer*

PUERTO RICO

Guaynabo
Lasa-Ferrer, Armando *lawyer*

Old San Juan
Weinstein-Bacal, Stuart Allen *lawyer, educator*

Ponce
Leon-Sotomayor, Jose Rafael *lawyer, engineer, educator*

San Juan
Garcia, Humberto Sigifredo *lawyer*
Gil, Guillermo *prosecutor*
Irizarry-Yunque, Carlos Juan *lawyer, educator*
Martinez-Munoz, Hector *lawyer*
Negron-Garcia, Antonio S. *law educator, former territory supreme court justice*
Pierluisi, Pedro R. *lawyer*
Rodriguez-Diaz, Juan E. *lawyer*

VIRGIN ISLANDS

Charlotte Amalie
Feuerzeig, Henry Louis *lawyer*

Christiansted
Bland, James Theodore, Jr., *lawyer*
Grey, Samuel T. *lawyer*

St Thomas
Carty, Amos W. *lawyer*
Nissman, David M. *lawyer*

MILITARY ADDRESSES OF THE UNITED STATES

EUROPE

APO
Kammerer, Kelly Christian *lawyer*

FPO
Blazewick, Robert B. *lawyer, educator, military officer*

CANADA

ALBERTA

Calgary
Chrétien, Jean (Joseph Jacques Jean Chrétien) *lawyer, former prime minister of Canada*
Lougheed, Peter *lawyer, former Canadian premier*

BRITISH COLUMBIA

Burnaby
Switlo, Janice Georgina Alice E. *barrister, solicitor, mediator, legal and business consultant, strategist*

Sooke
Howard, John Lindsay *lawyer, forest industry company executive*

Vancouver
Bonner, Robert William *lawyer, director*
Head, Ivan Leigh *law educator*
McEachern, Allan *lawyer*
Penikett, Antony David John *negotiator, writer, politician*
Peterson, Leslie Raymond *barrister*

Victoria
MacIsaac, Ronald Frances Thérès *lawyer*

MANITOBA

Winnipeg
Anderson, David Trevor *law educator*
Edwards, Clifford Henry Coad *law educator*
Schnoor, Jeffrey Arnold *lawyer*

NEW BRUNSWICK

Moncton
McKenna, Frank Joseph *lawyer*

Rothesay
Fairweather, Robert Gordon Lee *lawyer*

NOVA SCOTIA

Halifax
Dexter, Robert Paul *lawyer*
Mingo, James William Edgar *lawyer*

ONTARIO

Markham
Gulden, Simon *lawyer, investment/real estate development executive, business and legal consultant*

Ottawa
d'Aquino, Thomas *lawyer, entrepreneur, educator, strategist*
Dawson, Mary E. *lawyer*
Tassé, Roger *lawyer, former Canadian government official*
Urie, John James *lawyer, retired Canadian federal judge*

Thornhill
Lublinski, Michael *lawyer*

Toronto
Arthurs, Harry William *legal educator, former university president*
Barker, Bruce Crichlow *barrister, solicitor*
Chester, Robert Simon George *lawyer*
Davis, William Grenville *lawyer, former Canadian government official*
Dickens, Bernard Morris *law educator*
Dubin, Charles Leonard *lawyer*
Elliott, Roy Fraser *lawyer, holding and management company executive*
Farquharson, Gordon MacKay *lawyer, director*
Iacobucci, Frank *lawyer, educator, jurist*
McKeown, William Philip *lawyer*
Peterson, David Robert *lawyer, former Canadian government official*

QUEBEC

Chicoutimi
Cain, Michael Haney *lawyer*

Gatineau
Beaudoin, Gérald A(rmand) *lawyer, educator, senator*

Ile Perrot
Lalonde, Marc *lawyer, former Canadian government official*

Montreal
Kaufman, Donna S. *lawyer*
Lacoste, Paul *law educator, academic administrator*
Popovici, Adrian *law educator*
Pound, Richard William Duncan *lawyer, accountant*
Robb, James Alexander *lawyer*
Steinberg, Norman Michael *lawyer*
Tremblay, Andre Gabriel *lawyer*

Sainte-Foy
Normand, Robert *retired lawyer*

Sillery
Dinan, Robert Michael *lawyer*

Westmount
Fortier, L. Yves *barrister*

SASKATCHEWAN

Regina
MacKay, Harold Hugh *lawyer*

Saskatoon
Ish, Daniel Russell *law educator, academic administrator*

Kugaaruk
Rodnunsky, Sidney *lawyer, educator*

Ottawa
Easter, Arnold Wayne *solicitor*

Quebec City
LeMay, Jacques *lawyer*
Verge, Pierre *legal educator*

BELGIUM

Brussels
Barnum, John Wallace *lawyer*
Bustin, George Leo *lawyer*
Horton, Linda Rae *lawyer*

BELIZE

Belize City
Brown, Sir George Noel *chief justice*

CHINA

Hong Kong
Halperin, David Richard *lawyer*

DENMARK

Copenhagen
Elmer, Michael Bendik *legal administrator*

Odense
Lauritsen, Kaj Torben *retired lawyer, former association executive*

ENGLAND

Beverley
Edles, Gary Joel *lawyer*

Isle of Wight
Brown, John Robert *lawyer*

London
Albert, Robert Alan *lawyer*
Cole, Richard A. *retired lawyer*
Fabricant, Arthur E. *lawyer, corporate executive*
Glass, Douglas B. *lawyer*
Glazer, Barry David *lawyer*
Haubold, Samuel Allen *lawyer*
Hicks, J. Portis *lawyer*
Hudson, Manley O., Jr., *lawyer*
Miller, Scott D. *lawyer*
Montgomery, John Warwick (Baron of Kiltartan and Lord of Morris, Comte de St. Germain de Montgommery) *law educator, theologian*
Morrison, William David *lawyer*
Phocas, George John *international lawyer, business executive*
Quillen, Cecil Dyer, III, *lawyer*
Rolle, Martha Collins (Martha Traudt Collins) *lawyer*
Stern, Stephen Jeffrey *lawyer*
Stevens, Robert Bocking *lawyer, educator*
Thomas, Allen Lloyd *lawyer, private investor*
Zonana, Victor *lawyer, educator*

Sunbury-on-Thames
Lynch, John Edward, Jr., *lawyer*

Wiltshire
Sherwin, James Terry *lawyer*

FINLAND

Helsinki
Juhani, Erma *lawyer, former stock exchange executive*

FRANCE

Draguignan
Frame, Nancy Davis *lawyer*

Paris
Baum, Axel Helmuth *lawyer*
Bedjaoui, M. Mohammed *former judge International Court of Justice*
Landers, Steven E. *lawyer*
Rawlings, Boynton Mott *lawyer*
Reeves, Van Kirk *lawyer*
Salans, Carl Fredric *lawyer*

GERMANY

Frankfurt
Simitis, Spiros *legal educator*

Göttingen
Starck, Christian Walter *jurist*

HONG KONG

Hong Kong
Choo, Yeow Ming *lawyer*
O'Brien, Timothy James *lawyer*

INDONESIA

Jakarta
Hsi, Edward Yang *lawyer, industrialist, medical venture capitalist, political advisor*

IRELAND

Dublin
Calvani, Terry *lawyer*

ISRAEL

Jerusalem
Rosenne, Meir *lawyer, government agency administrator*

Tel Aviv
Gross, Joseph H. *lawyer, educator*

ITALY

Rome
McGurn, William Barrett, III, *lawyer*

JAPAN

Hachioji
Kojima, Takeshi *law educator, arbitrator, writer*

Tokyo
Ishizuka, Nobuhisa *lawyer*
Nakamura, Hideo *law educator*
Shirai, Shun *law educator, lawyer*

LUXEMBOURG

Kirchberg
Leger, Philippe *legal administrator*

NETHERLANDS

Amsterdam
Liem, Edwin T.H. *lawyer*

The Hague
Brower, Charles Nelson *lawyer, judge*
Buergenthal, Thomas *international judge, educator*
Higgins, Dame Rosalyn *judge of international court of justice*
Jiuyong, Shi *judge*
Kooijmans, Pieter Hendrik *judge International Court of Justice*
Koroma, Abdul G. *judge of international court of justice*
Rezek, Francisco *judge, former supreme court justice, educator*

NORWAY

Oslo
Fitzpatrick, Whitfield Westfeldt *lawyer*
Fleischer, Carl August *law educator, consultant*

PHILIPPINES

Manila
Sumida, Gerald Aquinas *lawyer*

POLAND

Cracow
Kasper, Horst Manfred *lawyer*

SCOTLAND

Edinburgh
Macneil, Ian Roderick *lawyer, educator*

Midlothian
Barnes, Joy Chappell *lawyer*

SIERRA LEONE

Freetown
Crane, David Michael *prosecutor, former judge advocate*

SOUTH AFRICA

Johannesburg
Tager, Louise Arlene *high court advocate*

Waterkloof
Aiello, James Andrew *lawyer*

SPAIN

Madrid
Herrero Rodriguez de Miñon, Miguel *former Spanish member of parliament, lawyer, international legal consultant*

SWEDEN

Lidingö
Crapon de Caprona, Count Noël François Marie *lawyer, retired United Nations official, historian*

SWITZERLAND

Chateau d'Oex
Berman, Joshua Mordecai *lawyer, manufacturing executive*

Fribourg
Gurley, Franklin Louis *lawyer, military historian*

Geneva
Capron, Alexander Morgan *lawyer, law educator, bioethicist*

TANZANIA

Arusha
Rapp, Stephen John *international prosecutor*

UNITED ARAB EMIRATES

Abu Dhabi
Taylor, Frederick William, Jr., (Fritz Taylor) *lawyer*

VENEZUELA

Caracas

Eljuri, Elisabeth *lawyer*

ADDRESS UNPUBLISHED

Abramson, Elliott Myron *law educator, researcher*
Adams, Thomas Lawrence *lawyer*
Adams, Thomas Lynch, Jr., *lawyer*
Adaniya, Kevin Seisho *lawyer*
Aikman, Albert Edward *lawyer*
Alberger, William Relph *lawyer, government official*
Albin, Barry G. *lawyer, rabbi*
Alexander, Richard Elmont *lawyer*
Alfred, Stephen Jay *retired lawyer*
Allen, Toni K. *lawyer*
Allred, Michael Sylvester *lawyer*
Alpern, Andrew *lawyer, architect, historian*
Amberg, Stanley Louis *lawyer*
Anderson, Alan Stewart *lawyer*
Anderson, Geoffrey Allen *retired lawyer*
Anderson, John Bayard *lawyer, educator, former congressman*
Ansley, Shepard Bryan *lawyer*
Archer, Dennis Wayne *lawyer, former mayor*
Areen, Judith Carol *law educator, dean*
Arnold, Jerome Gilbert *lawyer*
Ashe, Bernard Flemming *arbitrator, educator, lawyer*
Ashkin, Roberta Ellen *lawyer*
Assael, Michael *lawyer, accountant*
Attaway, Fritz Edward Edward *lawyer*
Atterbury, Robert Rennie, III, *retired lawyer*
Avallone, Anthony Francis *retired lawyer*
Babb, Frank Edward *lawyer, executive*
Bagley, Dennis Joseph *lawyer*
Bagley, William Thompson *lawyer*
Bailey, Brad Duane *lawyer*
Bailey, F(rancis) Lee *lawyer*
Bain, William Donald, Jr., *lawyer, chemical company executive*
Baker, Donald *lawyer, director*
Baker, James A. *lawyer, former state supreme court justice*
Baker, William Thompson, Jr., *lawyer*
Bakken, Gordon Morris *law educator*
Bakkensen, John Reser *lawyer*
Bales, John Foster, III, *retired lawyer*
Ball, James Herington *retired lawyer*
Bandy, Jack D. *lawyer*
Banks, Robert Sherwood *lawyer*
Barbee, Lloyd Augustus *lawyer*
Barlow, William Kyle *lawyer, state legislator*
Barr, Charles F. *lawyer, reinsurance company executive*
Basiszta, Martin Winston *lawyer*
Bateman, David Alfred *lawyer*
Baum, Stanley David *lawyer*
Bean, Bruce Winfield *lawyer*
Beauzay, Victor H(ilton) *lawyer*
Beck, Stuart Edwin *lawyer*
Beisner, John Herbert *lawyer*
Beldock, Myron *lawyer*
Bell, Haney Hardy, III, *lawyer*
Bell, Keith Whitman *lawyer*
Belleville, Philip Frederick *lawyer*
Ben-Veniste, Richard *lawyer*
Bergan, William Luke *lawyer*
Beringer, William Ernst *mediator, arbitrator, lawyer*
Berle, Peter Adolf Augustus *lawyer, media director*
Berman, Lori Beth *lawyer*
Berman, Richard Bruce *lawyer*
Bernstein, George L. *lawyer, accountant*
Bernstein, Merton Clay *law educator, lawyer, arbitrator*
Berrey, Robert Forrest *lawyer*
Berry, Robert Worth *lawyer, retired law educator, retired military officer*
Bersin, Alan Douglas *lawyer, school system administrator*
Besing, Ray Gilbert *lawyer, writer, lecturer*
Bettenhausen, Matthew Robert *lawyer*
Beukema, John Frederick *lawyer*
Bibik, Jacqueline Avis *lawyer*
Bierstedt, Peter Richard *lawyer, entertainment industry consultant*
Blackburn, Richard Wallace *lawyer*
Blatt, Harold Geller *lawyer*
Blazzard, Norse Novar *lawyer*
Bleicher, Samuel Abram *lawyer, government official*
Blewett, Robert Noall *lawyer*
Block, Dennis Jeffrey *lawyer*
Bloomer, Harold Franklin, Jr., *retired lawyer*
Bloomfield, David Charles *lawyer, educator, public and not-for-profit executive*
Blow, George *lawyer*
Blumenthal, William *lawyer*
Boesel, Milton Charles, Jr., *lawyer, business executive*
Boho, Dan L. *lawyer*
Boner, Eleanor Katz *lawyer*
Bonham-Yeaman, Doria *retired law educator*
Booher, Alice Ann *lawyer*
Boone, Richard Winston, Sr., *lawyer*
Booth, Robert Ward *lawyer*
Borenstein, Mark A. *lawyer*
Borenstein, Milton Conrad *lawyer, manufacturing executive*
Bork, Robert Heron *lawyer, author, educator, former federal judge*
Borowitz, Albert Ira *lawyer, author*
Bost, Thomas Glen *lawyer, educator*
Bouvier, Marshall Andre *lawyer*
Bovaird, Brendan Peter *lawyer*
Bower, Jean Ramsay *lawyer, writer*
Boyd, Thomas Marshall *lawyer*
Bradley, Amelia Jane *lawyer*
Brafford, William Charles *lawyer*
Branagan, James Joseph *lawyer*
Bransdorfer, Stephen Christie *retired lawyer*
Brantz, George Murray *retired lawyer*
Braun, Jerome Irwin *lawyer*
Brehl, James William *lawyer*
Brodhead, David Crawmer *lawyer*
Broughton, Phillip Charles *lawyer, director*
Brown, Charles Dodgson *lawyer*
Brown, J.E. "Buster" *lawyer, consultant*
Brown, Margaret deBeers *lawyer*
Bruess, Charles Edward *lawyer*
Buchbinder, Darrell Bruce *lawyer*
Buchmann, Alan Paul *lawyer*
Burkey, Lee Melville *lawyer*
Burris, Steven Michael *lawyer*
Butler, James Robertson, Jr., *lawyer*
Cacciatore, Ronald Keith *lawyer*
Calhoun-Senghor, Keith *lawyer*
Cambrice, Robert Louis *prosecutor*
Campbell, Frederick Hollister *retired lawyer, historian*
Campion, Thomas Francis *lawyer*
Canady, Charles Terrence *lawyer, former congressman*
Capps, James Leigh, II, *lawyer, reserve military career officer*
Cardinali, Albert John *lawyer*
Carey, Jana Howard *lawyer*
Carmack, Mildred Jean *retired lawyer*
Carpenter, Susan Karen *defender*
Carr, Jesse Metteau, III, *lawyer, engineering executive*
Carroll, Joseph J(ohn) *lawyer*
Carten, Francis Noel *lawyer*
Carter, Jeanne Wilmot *lawyer, publisher*
Casella, Peter F(iore) *patent and licensing executive*
Casey, Robert Reisch *lawyer*
Casillas, Mark *lawyer*
Casselman, William E., II, *lawyer*
Cassidy, John Harold *lawyer*
Castel, Jean Gabriel *lawyer*
Castro, Raul Hector *lawyer, former ambassador, former governor*
Catuzzi, J(erome) P(rimo), Jr., *lawyer*
Cazalas, Mary Rebecca Williams *lawyer, nurse*
Cermak, Josef Rudolf Cenek *lawyer, director*
Chamberlin, Michael Meade *lawyer*
Charles, Robert Bruce *lawyer*
Chave, Carolyn Margaret *arbitrator, retired lawyer*
Cheek, Michael Carroll *lawyer*
Cherovsky, Erwin Louis *lawyer, writer*
Chin, Kelvin Henry *business development director*
Chin, William Y. *law educator*
Christensen, Karen Kay *lawyer*
Clabaugh, Elmer Eugene, Jr., *retired lawyer*
Clark, Beverly Ann *lawyer*
Clark, Donald Otis *lawyer*
Clark, Robert Charles *law educator*
Clarke, Edward Owen, Jr., *lawyer*
Cobb, Miles Alan *retired lawyer*
Cobb, Sue McCourt *lawyer, educator*
Cohen, Anita Marilyn *retired lawyer*
Cohen, Jay Allen *lawyer, accountant*
Coleman, John Michael *lawyer, consumer products executive*
Coleman, Richard William *retired lawyer*
Coleman, Robert Lee *retired lawyer*
Colman, Richard Thomas *retired lawyer*
Colodny, Edwin Irving *lawyer, retired air transportation executive*
Cologne, Gordon Bennett *lawyer*
Colton, Sterling Don *lawyer, business executive, missionary*
Comfrey, Kathleen Marie *lawyer*
Comisky, Ian Michael *lawyer*
Condra, Allen Lee *retired lawyer, state official*
Connell, William D. *lawyer*
Connelly, Sharon Rudolph *lawyer*
Cook, Glen André *lawyer, military officer*
Cook, Quentin LaMar *lawyer, healthcare executive, church leader*
Cooper, Hal Dean *lawyer*
Corle, James Thomas *lawyer*
Coughlan, Kenneth L. *lawyer*
Cox, Chapman Beecher *retired lawyer, corporate financial executive*
Cox, Marshall *lawyer*
Crain, J. Lester, Jr., *corporate lawyer*
Crawford, Carol Tallman *law educator*
Crawford, Muriel Laura *lawyer, author, educator*
Cremins, James Smyth *political party official, lawyer*
Cronson, Robert Granville *lawyer*
Crook, Donald Martin *lawyer*
Cross, Elmo Garnett, Jr., *lawyer*
Crowe, James Joseph *lawyer*
Cumberland, William Edwin *lawyer*
Cunningham, Alice Welt *lawyer, educator*
Dandridge, LeNor *paralegal*
Datiles, J. Michelle *legal researcher*
David, Marilyn Hattie *lawyer, retired military officer*
D'Avignon, Roy Joseph *lawyer*
Davis, Clarence Clinton, Jr., *lawyer*
Davis, Earon Scott *massage and bodywork consultant, lawyer*
Davis, Frederick Benjamin *retired law educator*
Davis, Joanne Fatse *lawyer*
Davis, Roger Edwin *lawyer, retired discount chain executive*
Davis, Wanda Rose *lawyer*
Dean, Michael M. *lawyer*
Dees, C. Stanley *lawyer*
DeLaFuente, Charles *lawyer, educator, journalist*
Delgado Barrio, Francisco Javier *former president supreme court of Spain*
DeVylder, Edgar Paul, Jr., *lawyer*
Diamant, William *lawyer*
Diamond, Stuart *law educator, consultant*
DiBattiste, Carol A. *lawyer*
Dickson, Robert Lee *lawyer*
Dickstein, Michael Ethan *lawyer, arbitrator*
Diehl, Deborah Hilda *lawyer*
Dillon, Clifford Brien *retired lawyer*
DiMento, Carol A.G. *lawyer*
Dimitry, Theodore George *retired lawyer*
Dissen, Walter Charles *lawyer*
Dokurno, Anthony David *lawyer*
Dolan, Peter Brown *lawyer*
Dolph, Wilbert Emery *lawyer*
Dondanville, John Wallace *lawyer*
Dorrier, Lindsay Gordon, Jr., *lawyer*
Dowben, Carla Lurie *lawyer, educator*
Doyle, Austin Joseph *lawyer*
Drabkin, Murray *lawyer*
Drost, Marianne *lawyer*
Dryden, Mary Elizabeth *law librarian, writer, actress*
Dubuc, Carroll Edward *lawyer*
Dunfee, Thomas Wylie *law educator*
Dunn, Robert Lawrence *lawyer*
Dunn, Warren Howard *retired lawyer, brewery executive*
Durgin, Diane *arbitrator, lawyer, mediator*
Dutile, Fernand Neville *law educator*
Early, Bert Hylton *lawyer, consultant*
Easterling, Charles Armo *lawyer*
Eaton, Larry Ralph *lawyer*
Edwards, Daniel Paul *lawyer, educator*
Edwards, Priscilla Ann *paralegal, business owner*
Edwards, Richard Alan *retired lawyer*
Ehrlich, Stephen Richard *lawyer*
Eichhorn, Frederick Foltz, Jr., *retired lawyer*
Ellenberger, Jack Stuart *law librarian*
Ellis, Carolyn Terry *lawyer*
Embry, Stephen Creston *lawyer*
Engelhardt, John Hugo *lawyer, banker*
English, Charles Brand *retired lawyer*
Erlebacher, Arlene Cernik *retired lawyer*
Erlenborn, John Neal *lawyer, educator, former congressman*
Estes, Carl Lewis, II, *lawyer*
Ettinger, Joseph Alan *lawyer*
Eustis, Albert Anthony *lawyer, diversified industry corporate executive*
Everdell, William *retired lawyer*
Faber, Michael Warren *lawyer*
Famularo, Joseph L. *former prosecutor*
Fantino, Lisa Maria *lawyer, reporter*
Fanwick, Ernest *lawyer*
Farmakides, John Basil *lawyer*
Farmer, Cornelia Griffin *lawyer, consultant, hearings official*
Feazell, Thomas Lee *lawyer, business executive*
Feldkamp, John Calvin *lawyer, educational administrator*
Fellers, Rhonda Gay *lawyer*
Fellman, Gerry Louis *lawyer, arbitrator*
Ferguson, Bradford Lee *lawyer*
Ferraro, Geraldine Anne *lawyer, former congresswoman*
Fetzer, Mark Stephen *lawyer*
Field, Arthur Norman *lawyer*
Finelsen, Libbi June *lawyer*
Fiorito, Edward Gerald *lawyer*
Firestone, Bruce Michael *lawyer, educator*
Fischer, David Charles *lawyer*
Fiss, Owen M. *law educator*
Fitzsimmons, Ellen Marie *lawyer*
Flanary, Donald Herbert, Jr., *lawyer*
Flick, John Edmond *lawyer*
Flinn, Charles Gallagher *lawyer, priest*
Ford, George Burt *retired lawyer*
Forry, John Ingram *lawyer*
Fort, Denise Douglas *law educator, former state official*
Foster, Judith Christine *lawyer, writer*
Fowler, Donald Raymond *retired lawyer, educator*
Fowler, Flora Daun *retired lawyer*
Fox, Eleanor Mae Cohen *lawyer, educator, writer*
Fraidin, Stephen *lawyer*
Francis, Jerome Leslie *lawyer*
Frank, James Stuart *lawyer*
Frankel, James Burton *retired lawyer*
Franklin, Michael Harold *arbitrator, lawyer, consultant*
French, Daniel J. *former prosecutor*
Fried, Charles *law educator*
Friedlander, James Stuart *lawyer*
Friedman, Paul Richard *lawyer*
Frost, Sterling Newell *arbitrator, mediator, management consultant*
Furman, Howard *mediator, arbitrator, lawyer*
Futter, Victor *lawyer*
Gaberman, Harry *retired lawyer*
Gaines, Cherie Adelaide *lawyer*
Gamble, E. James *lawyer, accountant*
Garcia, Evaristo, Jr., *lawyer*
Gee, Robert Neil *law librarian*
Gershman, Gary Paul *law educator*
Getzendanner, Susan *lawyer, former federal judge*
Gibb, Roberta Louise *lawyer, artist*
Gilbert, Ronald Rhea *lawyer*
Gilden, Richard Henry *lawyer*
Gingold, Dennis Marc *lawyer*
Ginsberg, Ernest *lawyer, banker*
Giusti, William Roger *lawyer*
Gladden, Joseph Rhea, Jr., *lawyer*
Glaser, Patricia L. *lawyer*
Glasser, Ira Saul *civil liberties organization executive*
Gleeson, Paul Francis *retired lawyer*
Glosser, Jeffrey Mark *lawyer*
Gobel, John Henry *lawyer*
Gold, Martin Elliott *lawyer, educator*
Goldberg, Joel Henry *lawyer*
Goldberg, Michael Bradley *lawyer*
Goodman, Elizabeth Ann *retired lawyer*
Gorske, Robert H. *lawyer*
Gourvitz, Elliot Howard *lawyer*
Grab, Frederick Charles *lawyer*
Grace, Walter Charles *retired prosecutor*
Grayson, Edward Davis *lawyer, manufacturing executive*
Grech, David John *lawyer, writer*
Green, Carol H. *lawyer, educator, journalist*
Green, Carole L. *lawyer*
Greenberg, Harold *legal educator*
Greenberg, Ronald David *lawyer, law educator*
Greenebaum, Leonard Charles *retired lawyer*
Griffin, Campbell Arthur, Jr., *retired lawyer*
Gross, Richard Benjamin *lawyer*
Grutman, Jewel Humphrey *lawyer, writer*
Gudenberg, Harry Richard *arbitrator, mediator*
Gunger, Richard William *lawyer*
Gutman, Richard Edward *lawyer*
Guttentag, Joseph Harris *lawyer, educator*
Haber, Joel Abba *lawyer*
Hackel-Sims, Stella Bloomberg *lawyer, former government official*
Hackett, Robert John *lawyer*
Hackett, Wesley Phelps, Jr., *lawyer*
Hajek, Robert J., Sr., *lawyer, real estate broker, commodities broker, nursing home owner*
Haley, George Brock, Jr., *retired lawyer*
Hall, James Evan *lawyer*
Hall, Joan Torrens *lawyer*
Hall, John Hopkins *retired lawyer*
Halleck, Charles White *lawyer, photographer, former judge*
Halpern, James Bladen *lawyer*
Hammond, Glenn Barry, Sr., *lawyer, electrical engineer*
Hampton, Charles Edwin *lawyer, mathematician, computer programmer*
Handler, Harold Robert *lawyer*
Hannon, Gerard V. *lawyer*
Hansen, John Alton *lawyer*
Hanzlik, Rayburn DeMara *lawyer*
Harbus, Richard *arbitrator, mediator*
Hardy, Robert Paul *lawyer*
Hare, Frances Hutcheson, Jr., *lawyer, educator*
Harff, Charles Henry *lawyer, diversified industrial company executive, retired*
Harman, Wallace Patrick *lawyer*
Harnack, Don Steger *retired lawyer*
Harper, Conrad Kenneth *lawyer, former government official*
Harper, Harlan, Jr., *lawyer*
Harriman, John Howland *retired lawyer*
Harris, Janine Diane *lawyer*
Harris, Jay Stephen *lawyer, producer*
Harris, Richard Eugene Vassau *lawyer*
Harrison, Charles Maurice *lawyer, former communications company executive*
Harvey, Marc S(an) *lawyer, historian, law educator*
Hauver, Constance Longshore *lawyer*
Hayes, Byron Jackson, Jr., *retired lawyer*
Hazard, Geoffrey Cornell, Jr., *law educator*
Heard, James Henry *lawyer, educator*
Heath, Richard Eddy *lawyer*
Hedien, Colette Johnston *lawyer*
Heffron, Howard A. *lawyer*
Heider, Jon Vinton *retired lawyer, corporate executive*
Heins, Samuel David *lawyer*
Heise, John Irvin, Jr., *lawyer*
Helburn, Isadore B. *retired arbitrator, mediator, educator*
Helfer, Michael Stevens *lawyer, business executive*
Hennessy, Dean McDonald *lawyer, multinational corporation executive*
Henry, DeLysle Leon *lawyer*
Heppe, Karol Virginia *lawyer, educator*
Hermann, Donald Harold James *lawyer, educator*
Herring, Jerone Carson *retired lawyer, bank executive*
Herringer, Maryellen Cattani *lawyer*
Hershatter, Richard Lawrence *lawyer, writer*
Hester, Thomas Patrick *lawyer, business executive*
Heymann, Philip Benjamin *law educator, academic director*
Hickey, Timothy Andrew *lawyer*
Hilker, Walter Robert, Jr., *lawyer*
Hill, Harold Nelson, Jr., *lawyer*
Hoffman, Alan Craig *lawyer, consultant*
Hoffman, S. David *lawyer, engineer, educator, artist*
Holden, William Hoyt, Jr., *lawyer*
Holmes, Michael Gene *lawyer*
Holmes, Paul Kinloch, III, *former prosecutor*
Holt, Marjorie Sewell *lawyer, retired congresswoman*
Holtzschue, Karl Bressem *lawyer, author, educator*
Honeystein, Karl *lawyer, entertainment company executive*
Honnold, John Otis *law educator*
Hopkins, George Mathews Marks *retired patent lawyer, business executive*
Horwitz, Donald Paul *lawyer*
Hough, Thomas Henry Michael *retired lawyer, educator*
Howard, John Wayne *lawyer*
Howard, Nancy E. *lawyer*
Howell, Ally Windsor *lawyer, author, editor*
Howell, Donald Lee *lawyer*
Hoyle, William Vinton, Jr., *lawyer*
Hsu, Emilie Tien-Jung *lawyer*
Hudson, Eliot R. *lawyer*
Hulin, Frances C. *retired prosecutor*
Humphreys, Robert Russell *lawyer, consultant, arbitrator*
Hunt, Thomas Reed, Jr., *lawyer*
Hunter, Jack Duval *retired lawyer*
Hunter, Jack Duval, II, *lawyer*
Husney, Elliott Ronald *lawyer, financier*
Hvass, Sheryl Ramstad *lawyer*
Hybl, William Joseph *lawyer, foundation executive*
Hyde, Alan Litchfield *retired lawyer*
Idzik, Daniel Ronald *retired lawyer*
Ieyoub, Richard Phillip *lawyer, former state attorney general*
Iklé, Richard Adolph *lawyer*
Irvine, John Alexander *lawyer*
Isaacs, Michael Burton *lawyer*
Jackman, James David *lawyer*
Jackson, Raymond Sidney, Jr., *lawyer*
Jacobowitz, Harold Saul *lawyer*
James, Michael Andrew *lawyer*
Jameson, Paula Ann *retired lawyer*
Javits, Eric Moses *lawyer, diplomat*
Javits, Joshua Moses *lawyer*
Jekenewicz, Tricia A *legal assistant, writer*
Jennings, Thomas Parks *lawyer*
Jensen, Robert Trygve *retired lawyer*
Jespersen, Robert Randolph *legal consultant*
Joelson, Mark René *lawyer*
Johns, Warren LeRoi *retired lawyer*
Johnson, Edward Michael *lawyer, consultant*
Johnson, James Terence *lawyer, educator, minister*
Johnson, Richard Tenney *lawyer*
Johnson, Richard Wesley *lawyer*
Johnston, Joanne Spitznagel *lawyer, writing consultant*
Jones, Keith Alden *lawyer*
Jones, William Rex *law educator*
Jordan, Michelle Denise *lawyer*
Kallgren, Edward Eugene *lawyer*
Kantrowitz, Susan Lee *lawyer*
Kaplan, Helene Lois *lawyer*
Kapnick, Richard Bradshaw *lawyer*
Kaster, Laura A. *lawyer*
Katz, Melissa *plaintiff attorney*
Kaufman, James Jay *retired lawyer*
Kaye, Stuart Martin *lawyer*
Keaty, Robert Burke *lawyer, business consultant*
Keeling, J(ohn) Michael *lawyer, trade association executive*
Kelehear, Carole Marchbanks Spann *legal assistant*
Kelly, Anastasia Donovan *lawyer*
Kennedy, Harold Edward *lawyer*
Kennedy, Thomas J. *lawyer*
Kern, Jerome H. *lawyer*
Kerstetter, Wayne Arthur *law educator, lawyer*
Keys, Jerry Malcom *lawyer, educator*
Kienitz, LaDonna Trapp *lawyer, librarian, municipal official*
Kilbane, Catherine M. *lawyer*
Killeen, Michael John *lawyer*
Kimball, Spencer Levan *lawyer, educator*
King, Jack A. *lawyer*
King, James Forrest, Jr., *lawyer*
King, Robert Lucien *lawyer*
Kinser, Katherine Anne *lawyer*
Kinsolving, Augustus Blagden *lawyer*
Klafter, Cary Ira *lawyer*
Klaus, Charles *retired lawyer*
Klaus, William Robert *lawyer*
Kleiman, Bernard *lawyer*
Klein, Judah Baer *retired lawyer*

Williamson, Edwin Dargan *lawyer, former federal official*
Wilson, Bruce Duxbury *lawyer*
Wilson, Rhys Thaddeus *lawyer*
Winslow, F. Dana (Francis Dana Winslow) *judge, former record company owner*
Winslow, John Franklin *lawyer*
Winslow, Julian Dallas *retired lawyer, historian, writer*
Winthrop, Sherman *lawyer*
Wirtz, William Willard *lawyer*
Wise, Sandra Casber *lawyer*
Wittig, Raymond Shaffer *lawyer, intellectual property technology manager*
Wolf, Gary Wickert *retired lawyer*
Wolfson, Michael George *lawyer*
Wong-Diaz, Francisco Raimundo *lawyer, educator*
Wood, Robert Charles *lawyer, real estate developer*
Wooldridge, William Charles *lawyer*
Woolsey, John Munro, Jr., *retired lawyer*
Workman, Margaret Lee *lawyer*
Worrell, Stewart Phillip *lawyer, trust executive*
Wright, Robert Payton *lawyer*
Wruble, Bernhardt Karp *lawyer*
Wunsch, Kathryn Sutherland *retired lawyer*
Wyatt, Robert Lee, IV, *lawyer*
Wyshak, Lillian Worthing *lawyer*
Yarbro, Alan David *lawyer*
Yeager, Mark Leonard *lawyer*
York, Alexandra *lawyer*
Yoskowitz, Irving Benjamin *lawyer, merchant banker*
Young, John Hardin *lawyer, corporate executive*
Yurchuck, Roger Alexander *retired lawyer*
Zagorin, Janet Susan *legal firm administrator, marketing professional*
Ziegler, William Alexander *lawyer*
Zillman, Donald Norman *law educator, university official*
Zimmerman, Jean *lawyer*
Zoeller, Donald J. *lawyer*
Zohn, Martin Steven *lawyer*

MEDICINE *See* HEALTHCARE: MEDICINE

MILITARY

UNITED STATES

ALABAMA

Alexander City
Shuler, Ellie Givan, Jr., *retired military officer, military museum administrator*

Auburn
Tolbert, Clinton Jame *army officer, machinist*

Birmingham
Davis, Gwendolyn Louise *air force officer, English educator*

Enterprise
Garrett, Thomas W. *retired career officer*

Foley
Kingston, George Willis *retired naval officer, small business owner*

Huntsville
Urias, John M. *military officer, government agency administrator*
Williamson, Donald Ray *retired career Army officer*

Maxwell AFB
Lester, Richard I. *military educator*

Montgomery
Uzzell-Baggett, Karon Lynette *career officer*

Redstone Arsenal
Parlier, Greg H. *military officer, engineer*

Union Grove
Roberts, Lynn Novak *government employee*

ALASKA

Anchorage
Gamble, Patrick K. *retired military officer, rail transportation executive*

ARIZONA

Davis Monthan AFB
Foglesong, Robert H. *lieutenant general United States Air Force*
Woods, Sharhonda Michele *military officer*

Green Valley
Bennett, Bradley Frederick *retired military officer, science association director*

Phoenix
Lawlis, Patricia Kite *air force officer, computer consultant*

Prescott
Schaeffer, Reiner Horst *military officer, foreign language professional*

Scottsdale
Coffinger, Maralin Katharyne *retired career officer, consultant*

Sonoita
Hanson, Thor *retired health agency executive and naval officer*

Surprise
Lucchetti, Lynn L. *career officer*

Tucson
Bryan, Gordon Redman, Jr., *retired naval officer*
Wickham, John Adams, Jr., *retired army officer*

Yuma
Hudson, John Irvin *retired career officer*

ARKANSAS

Blytheville
Slowik, Richard Andrew *air force officer*

Mountain Home
Baker, Robert Leon *naval medical officer*

CALIFORNIA

Anaheim
O'Berry, Carl Gerald *former career officer, electrical engineer*

Arroyo Grande
Oseguera, Palma Marie *retired career officer*

Camp Pendleton
Prato, Kimberly *public affairs officer*

Carlsbad
Kauderer, Bernard Marvin *retired naval officer, consultant*

Chula Vista
Briggs, Franklin Henry *retired naval officer*
Worthington, George Rhodes *retired naval officer*

Coronado
Butcher, Bobby Gene *retired military officer*

El Segundo
Harper, David Taylor *civilian military employee*

Escondido
Briggs, Edward Samuel *naval officer*
Dotto, Peter Attilius *retired marine corps officer, defense consultant*

Folsom
Jefferds, William John *military advisor*

Healdsburg
Eade, George James *retired air force officer, research executive, defense consultant*

Long Beach
Higginson, John *retired career officer*

Los Alamitos
Dunne, Donald Redmond *military officer*

Los Altos Hills
Wheeler, Frank Knowles Blasdell *retired military officer, business consultant*

Monterey
Hoivik, Thomas Harry *military educator, international consultant*
Matthews, David Fort *career officer*
Schrady, David Alan *civilian military employee, educator*

Oxnard
Kirschbaum, Alan Ira *air force officer, systems integration specialist*

Palo Alto
Parker, James Wesley *former career naval officer, investment company executive*

Pasadena
Hunter, Milton *retired army officer*

Pebble Beach
Mauz, Henry Herrward, Jr., *retired naval officer*

Riverside
Czekanski, James P. *military officer*

San Diego
Contreras, Thomas J., Jr., *career officer*
Everett, Hobart Ray, Jr., *engineer, naval officer, consultant, researcher*
Koenig, Harold Martin *former United States Navy surgeon general*

San Marcos
Jones, William Henry *retired military officer*

Santa Barbara
Conley, Philip James, Jr., *retired air force officer*

Santa Maria
Everhart, Leon Eugene *retired career officer*
Roadarmel, Stanley Bruce *civilian military employee*

Santa Rosa
Andriano-Moore, Richard Count *retired military officer, secondary school educator, elementary school educator*
Bowen, James Thomas *career officer*

Saratoga
Henderson, William Darryl *army officer, writer*

Seaside
Gales, Samuel Joel *retired civilian military employee, counselor*

Travis AFB
Kelly, Christopher A. *brigadier general United States air force*

Vandenberg Afb
Hamel, Michael A. *career officer*

Windsor
Sparks, Bennett Sher *military officer*

COLORADO

Colorado Springs
Bowen, Clotilde Marion Dent *retired career officer, psychiatrist*
Delph, Kathleen Anne *foundation administrator, development director*
Drennan, Jerry M. *career officer*
Geraci, Richard V. *military officer, government agency administrator*
Meyerrose, Dale William *career officer*
Partridge, William J. *military officer, government agency administrator*
Skora, Wayne Philip *retired air force officer*

Denver
Avrit, Richard Calvin *defense consultant, career officer*
Charlip, Ralph Blair *military officer, health facility administrator*
Dugan, Michael Joseph *former career officer, health agency executive*

Durango
Fogleman, Ronald Robert *retired air force officer, consultant*

Englewood
Ahearn, Joseph August *military officer, civil engineer*

Falcon AFB
Dylewski, Gary R. *retired career officer*

Fort Collins
Roberts, Archibald Edward *retired career officer, writer*

Monument
Breckner, William John, Jr., *retired military officer*

Peterson AFB
Dekok, Roger Gregory *career officer*
Rees, Raymond F. *military officer*

Thornton
Thompson, Robert Frank, Jr., *career officer*

U S A F Academy
Krise, Thomas Warren *military officer, English language educator*

Woodland Park
Stewart, Robert Lee *retired career officer, astronaut*

CONNECTICUT

New London
Bald, Ronald James *military officer*

Niantic
Hunt, Francis Howard *retired navy laboratory official*

DELAWARE

Wilmington
Krulak, Charles Chandler *marine officer*

DISTRICT OF COLUMBIA

Bolling AFB
Dendinger, William J. *career officer, chaplain*

Fort Mcnair
Chilcoat, Richard Allen *army officer, university president*
Miller, David Allen *air force officer*

Pentagon
Adams, Ronald Emerson *army officer, federal agency administrator*

Washington
Aboul-Enein, Youssef H. *military officer*
Albright, Joseph William *army officer*
Barry, John L. *military officer*
Bath, Ronald J. *military officer*
Bedard, Emil R. *career officer*
Bowman, Frank Lee (Skip Bowman) *admiral and director naval nuclear propulsion*
Bradley, John A. *career military officer*
Brownlee, R. L. *civilian military employee*
Bussy, Carvel de *retired military officer, educator*
Campbell, James L. *military career officer*
Campbell, William H. *career officer*
Clark, Vernon E. *chief of US Naval Operations*
Cody, Richard A. *career military officer*
Collins, Thomas Hansen *coast guard officer*
Crawford, Hunt Dorn, Jr., *retired military officer, educator, diplomat*
Dawson, Howard W., Jr., *military officer*
DeMesme, Ruby Butler *civilian military executive*
Dils, Robert M. *military officer*
Dodgen, Larry J. *career officer*
Downie, Richard Duncan *military officer, government agency administrator*
Dyke, Charles William *retired army officer*
England, Gordon R. *civilian military employee*
Erdtmann, Frederick J. *military officer, medical association administrator*
Felman, Marc David *air force officer*
Fogelsong, Robert H. *military officer*
Froman, Veronica Zasadni *career officer*
Fuhrman, Russell L. *career officer*
Gibson, Christopher Patrick *military career officer*
Gibson, Emmitt E. *career officer*
Gill, Clair F. *military career officer*
Goodpaster, Andrew Jackson *retired military officer*
Gordon, John A. *career officer*
Greenert, Jonathan W. *career officer*
Hagee, Michael W. *commandant of the US Marine Corps*
Hazard, Roberta Louise *career officer*
Helmly, James R. *military officer*
Henningsen, Jacqueline Vincent *civilian military official*
Hobbins, William T. *career officer*
Hooper, John David *coast guard officer*
Howell, Deborah S. *career officer*
Huston, John Wilson *air force officer, historian*
Johnson, Hansford Tillman *civilian military employee*
Jones, Anthony Ray *military career officer*
Jumper, John Phillip *US Air Force Chief of Staff*
Keaney, Thomas Addis *strategic studies educator*
Keating, Timothy J. *career military officer*
Kellogg, Joseph K., Jr., *military career officer*
Kostelnik, Michael Charles *NASA administrator, retired air force officer*
Leaf, Howard Westley *retired military officer, official*
Lietzau, William Kendall *career officer, lawyer*
Marchand, Michael J. *military officer*
McGinn, Dennis Vincent *career officer*
Metcalf, Howard *military officer*
Metzger, James W. *military officer*
Mosely, Teed M. *career officer*
Nathman, John B. *career military officer*
Nutting, Wallace Hall *army officer*
Odom, William Eldridge *army officer, educator*
Ohle, David H. *military career officer*
Pace, Peter *military officer*
Paige, Kathleen K. *naval officer*
Pamerleau, Susan L. *career officer*
Pellegrino, Stephen Charles *civilian military employee*
Pionk, Jerome Lee *government official, association administrator*
Plewes, Thomas Jeffrey *military officer*
Potter, Lorraine K. *career military officer*
Rives, Jack L. *military officer*
Robison, Victor James, Jr., *retired military officer*
Roche, James G. *civilian military employee*
Romig, Thomas J. *military officer*
Schmitt, John K. *army officer*
Schoomaker, Peter J. *US Army Chief of Staff*
Schwartz, Norton A. *military officer*
Scott, Terry D. *military officer*
Scowcroft, Brent *retired air force officer, government official*
Shipway, John Francis *retired career officer*
Sinn, Jerry L. *army officer*
Stierle, Linda J. *military officer*
Strock, Carl A. *career military officer*
Swarthworth, Sharon T. *military officer*
Tilley, Jack L. *military officer*
Tornblom, Claudia L. *civilian military employee*
Tracey, Patricia A. *career officer*
Van Winkle, Hans A. *military officer*
Weaver, Christopher E. *naval officer*

FLORIDA

Celebration
Whelden, Craig B. *retired army officer*

Destin
Stansberry, James Wesley *air force officer*

Eglin AFB
Head, William Christopher *military officer, health care administrator*

Fernandina Beach
Rogers, Robert Burnett *naval officer*

Haines City
Clement, Robert William *retired air force officer*

Jacksonville
Carlson, Raymond Howard *retired military officer, prosecutor*
Delaney, Kevin Francis *retired naval officer, consulting firm executive*
Klain, David Richard *naval officer*
Lestage, Daniel Barfield *retired military officer, physician*
Surrency, Gary Lawrence *military officer, counselor, writer*

Lake Forest
Ross, Jimmy Douglas *retired military officer*

Longwood
Smyth, Joseph Patrick *retired naval officer, physician*

Lutz
Bedke, Ernest Alford *retired air force officer*

MacDill AFB
Barno, David W. *career military officer*
Cofer, Jonathan H. *career officer*

Melbourne
Hodges, Carroll Broadus *retired army officer*
Laposata, Joseph Samuel *army officer*
Simokaitis, Frank Joseph *air force officer, lawyer*

Melbourne Beach
Scanlon, Charles Francis *retired army officer, defense consultant, writer, publisher*

Miami
Clem, Ralph S. *career officer, educator*
Ramos-Moll, Ervin *career officer, federal agency administrator*

Naples
Delano, Victor *retired naval officer*
Slaff, Allan Paul *naval officer, university administrator, educator, entrepeneur*

Orlando
Bigum, Randall K. *retired military officer*
Bond, William L. *career officer*

Limpus, Charles Everett, III, *non-commissioned officer*

Oviedo
Parker, Harry Lee *retired army officer, counselor*

Palm Bay
Sheets, Fredrick Sidney *retired military officer, auditor*

Palm Beach Gardens
Giordano, Andrew Anthony *retired naval officer*

Panama City
Cox, Ron Dean *non-commissioned officer, educator, psychologist*

Sarasota
Cooper, William Ewing, Jr., *retired army officer*
Gauch, Eugene William, Jr., *retired air force officer*
Harvey, Donald Phillips *retired naval officer*
Heiser, Rolland Valentine *former army officer, foundation executive*

Tallahassee
Davis, Larry Michael *air force officer, healthcare manager, consultant*
Ervin, Charles Phifer, Jr., *retired military officer, education educator*

Tampa
Abizaid, John P. *career military officer*
Haggis, Arthur George, Jr., *retired military officer, educator, publisher*
Jackson, Dennis Kent *military career officer*
Matheny, Charles Woodburn, Jr., *former army officer, civil engineer, city official*

Tyndall AFB
Arnold, Larry Keith *major general United States Air Force*

West Palm Beach
Thomashow, Steven Roy *military officer, intelligence officer*

Windermere
Garner, Jay Montgomery *former career officer*

GEORGIA

Athens
Habiger, Eugene E. *retired career officer*

Atlanta
Donald, James E. *retired career officer, government agency executive*
Harrison, George Brooks *research engineer, retired career officer*
McGuinn, Michael Edward, III, *retired army officer*
Prendergast, Kenneth Lee Michael, Jr., *career officer*

Forest Park
Fisher, George Alexander, Jr., *lieutenant general United States Army*
Riggs, John M. *army officer*

Fort Mcpherson
Edwards, Warren Chappelle *military career officer*
Hendrix, John Walter *lieutenant general United States Army*
Piacentini, Nicholas A., Jr., *military officer*
Williamson, Kenneth N. *civilian military employee*

Fort Stewart
Webster, William G., Jr., *army officer*

Greensboro
Watts, Ronald Lester *retired military officer*

Jonesboro
Galvin, John Rogers *retired army officer, law educator*

Louisville
Hoover, John Elwood *former military officer, consultant, author, speaker on US military history*

Robins AFB
Batbie, John J., Jr., *military officer*
Haines, Dennis G. *military officer*
Whaley, Wallace W. *military officer*

Warner Robins
Nugteren, Cornelius *air force officer*

HAWAII

Camp H M Smith
Hailston, Earl B. *career officer*

Hickam AFB
Polk, Steven R. *military officer*

Honolulu
Hays, Ronald Jackson *career officer*

Kaneohe
Pimper, Elizabeth Marie *naval officer*

Waipahu
Reyes, Arturo Pacheco *civilian military employee*

ILLINOIS

Hoffman Estates
Pagonis, William Gus *retired army general*

Mattoon
Phipps, John Randolph *retired army officer*

O Fallon
Voellger, Gary A. *business consulting executive, retired air force officer*

Rockford
Borling, John Lorin *military officer*

Scott Air Force Base
Welser, William, III, *military officer*

Springfield
Herriford, Robert Levi, Sr., *army officer*

Sugar Grove
Durrenberger, William John *retired army general, educator, investor*

Taylor Ridge
Potthast, David Raymond *retired military officer, secondary school educator*

INDIANA

Indianapolis
Poel, Robert Walter *air force officer, physician*

IOWA

Burlington
Hutchins, Timothy Paul *military officer*

KANSAS

Fort Leavenworth
Riley, James Clifford *military career officer*

KENTUCKY

Fort Campbell
Clark, Robert T. *career officer*

LOUISIANA

New Orleans
Cotton, John G. *career military officer*
McCarthy, Dennis M. *military officer*

MAINE

Orrington
Snyder, Arnold Lee, Jr., *retired air force officer, research director*

MARYLAND

Aberdeen Proving Ground
Doesburg, John C. *military career officer*

Adelphi
Kendrick, Kerry *military officer*
Whitford, Dennis J. *military officer*

Annapolis
Finerty, Martin Joseph, Jr., *military officer, researcher, association management executive*
Katz, Douglas Jeffrey *retired naval officer, consultant*
Trost, Carlisle Albert Herman *retired naval officer*

Arnold
Williams, James Arthur *retired army officer, information systems company executive*

Baltimore
Michitsch, John F. *career officer*
Scales, Robert H., Jr., *retired army officer*

Bethesda
Daniel, Charles Dwelle, Jr., *consultant, retired army officer*
Griffith, Robert Dean *non-commissioned officer, nurse*
Hauck, Frederick Hamilton *retired military officer, retired astronaut, business executive*
Kem, Richard Samuel *retired army officer*
Less, Anthony Albert *retired naval officer*
Martin, Kathleen L. *military officer, hospital administrator*
Merchant, P. Glenn *military officer, physician*
Owen, Thomas Barron *retired naval officer, space company executive*
Schmidt, Raymond Paul *military officer, historian, diplomat*
Sizemore, R. Tom, III, *military officer, hospital administrator*
Zimble, James Allen *military officer, obstetrician, gynecologist, educator*

Burtonsville
Hudson, McKinley *army officer, retired zoo deputy director*

Fort George G Meade
Hayden, Michael V. *career officer, federal agency administrator*
Kera, Tiiu *career officer*

Fort Washington
Wooten, Ralph G. *career officer*

Lutherville Timonium
Sagerholm, James Alvin *retired naval officer*

Patuxent River
Conway, Frank P. *military officer, educator*

Silver Spring
Brog, David *consultant, former air force officer*
Oberst, Richard B. *military officer, hospital administrator*

Solomons
Dorsey, James Francis, Jr., *naval officer*

Trappe
Anderson, Andrew Herbert *retired army officer*

MASSACHUSETTS

Burlington
Dyer, Joseph Wendell *retired naval officer*

Cambridge
Hutchison, William Edward, Jr., *military officer, aerospace engineer, aerospace scientist*

Hanscom AFB
Johnson, Charles L., II, *military officer*

Lexington
Trainor, Bernard Edmund *retired military officer*

Natick
Miller, George David *retired military officer, not-for-profit executive*

North Oxford
Carney, Roger Francis Xavier *retired army officer*

Osterville
Schwarztrauber, Sayre Archie *former naval officer, maritime consultant*

Pittsfield
Watts, Dennis Lester *retired military officer*

MINNESOTA

Plymouth
Shadley, Robert D. *retired army officer*

MISSISSIPPI

Keesler AFB
Harrell, Elizabeth Ann *career officer*
Locker, Dan Lewis *career officer*

Pass Christian
McCardell, James Elton *retired naval officer*

MISSOURI

Chesterfield
Willis, Frank Edward *retired air force officer*

Florissant
Reese, Alferd George *retired army civilian logistics specialist*

Fort Leonard Wood
Ryder, Donald J. *military career officer*

Imperial
McGraw, Bryan Kelly *military officer*

Kansas City
Creighton, Neal *retired army officer*

Poplar Bluff
Young, William Webb *military officer, poet*

Saint Louis
Strevey, Tracy Elmer, Jr., *army officer, surgeon, physician executive*

NEBRASKA

Offutt A F B
Cartwright, James E. *career military officer*
Goslin, Thomas B. *career officer*
Hinson, Robert C. *career officer*
Mies, Richard W. *career officer*

NEW JERSEY

Moorestown
Apperson, Jack Alfonso *retired army officer, business executive*

Princeton
Unruh, Howard K., Jr., *military officer, university administrator*

South Orange
Collins, John W., Jr., *retired military officer, technologist, educator*

NEW MEXICO

Albuquerque
Flournoy, John Charles, Sr., *retired civilian military employee, retired military officer*

Kirtland Afb
Gideon, Francis C., Jr., *career officer*

Santa Fe
Sumner, Gordon, Jr., *retired military officer*

NEW YORK

Fort Drum
Miller, Thomas G. *career officer*

Hamburg
Markulis, Henryk John *career military officer*

Marcellus
Taylor, Robert Wilson *military officer, publishing executive*

New York
Dresser, Noreen Dean O'Hara *civilian army official, artist*
Prueher, Joseph W. *retired military officer, former ambassador*
Schwarzkopf, H. Norman *retired army officer, public speaker*

Plattsburgh
Davis, Harley Cleo *retired career officer*

Rome
Ferens, Daniel Vincent *civilian military employee*

Spring Valley
Steinberg, Milton *civilian military employee*

West Point
Boettner, Daisie Dawson *military officer, mechanical engineering educator*
Bozeman, Laura Beth *military officer, educator*

NORTH CAROLINA

Chapel Hill
Linville, Ray Pate *educational administrator, analyst, editor, writer*

Fort Bragg
Boykin, William G. *career officer*
Brown, Bryan D. *career officer*
McNeill, Dan K. *military career officer*
Ryneska, John Joseph *military career officer*

Hope Mills
Bergman, Mark *non-commissioned officer*

Pinehurst
Carroll, Kent Jean *retired naval officer*

Research Triangle Park
Sculley, Patrick David *retired army officer, science honor society director*

Southern Shores
Gould, Burnham Sylvester *retired military analyst*

Spring Hope
Hildreth, James Robert *retired air force officer*

OHIO

Beavercreek
Laine, Trevor Ian *military officer, engineer*

Cincinnati
Griffin, Robert H. *career officer*
Smittle, Nelson Dean *military analyst, artist*

Columbus
MacGhee, David F. *retired military officer, air transportation executive*
Saunders, Mary L. *career officer*

Dayton
Heil, Michael Lloyd *military officer, academic administrator*

Enon
Whitlock, David C. *retired military officer*

Tiffin
Einsel, David William, Jr., *retired army officer and consultant*

Wright Patterson Afb
Amend, Joseph H., III, *military officer*
Kelley, Joseph E. *career officer*
Paul, Richard R. *military officer*

OKLAHOMA

Edmond
Hopwood, Howard Hoppy Perry *military officer*

Oklahoma City
Reimer, Dennis J. *retired career military officer*

OREGON

Klamath Falls
Taylor, Gregory Alwin *coast guard officer, engineer*

PENNSYLVANIA

Bethlehem
Rokke, Ervin Jerome *college president*

Gettysburg
Coughenour, Kavin Luther *career officer, military historian*

Johnstown
Samples, Jerry Wayne *military officer, educator*

King Of Prussia
Gallis, John Nicholas *retired military officer, executive leadership training consultant*

Mechanicsburg
Derr, William James *retired non-commissioned officer*

Philadelphia
Dobbs, Stanley *military officer, information quality engineer*
Retz, William Andrew *retired naval officer*

Wayne
Long, Peter Avard Chipman *retired military officer*

RHODE ISLAND

Newport
Carpenter, Stanley Dean MacDonald *military officer, educator*

Portsmouth
Bergstrom, Albion Andrew *retired military officer, educator*

SOUTH CAROLINA

Bluffton
Pendley, William Tyler *naval officer, international relations educator*

Charleston
Grinalds, John Southy *military officer, academic administrator*
Watts, Claudius Elmer, III, *retired military officer*

Fort Jackson
Brinsfield, John Wesley *military officer, educator*

Hilton Head Island
Brown, Arthur Edmon, Jr., *retired army officer*

New Zion
Gibbons, Robert Butler, Jr., *retired military officer*

Newberry
Lander, James Albert *retired military officer, comptroller*

Seneca
Clausen, Hugh Joseph *retired army officer*

Sumter
Kellum, Donald Arthur *military officer*
Olsen, Thomas Richard, Sr., *air force officer*

Wedgefield
McLaurin, Hugh McFaddin, III, *military officer, historian consultant*

York
Blackwell, Paul Eugene, Sr., *army officer*

SOUTH DAKOTA

Rapid City
Sykora, Harold James *military officer*

TENNESSEE

Memphis
West, Christopher Eugene *military officer*

TEXAS

Austin
Howell, Jefferson Davis *career officer*
Meigs, Montgomery Cunningham, Jr., *retired military officer, educator*

Belton
Shoemaker, Robert Morin *retired army officer, county government official*

Bullard
Morley, William George *retired military officer, educator*

Castroville
Eyre, Pamela Catherine *retired career officer*

College Station
Carlton, Paul Kendall, Jr., *physician, retired air force officer*
Schunicht, Shannon Anthony *retired army officer, politician*

El Paso
Shapiro, Stephen Richard *retired air force officer, physician*

Fort Bliss
Yingling, John A. *military officer*

Fort Hood
Metz, Thomas Fredric *career military officer*
Odierno, Raymond T. *career military officer*

Fort Sam Houston
McFarren, Freddy E. *military career officer*
Moloff, Alan Lawrence *military officer, physician*
Peake, James Benjamin *military career officer*

Fort Worth
Lichtman, David Michael *military officer, health care administrator, orthopedist, educator*
Tanzi, David E. *military officer*

Georgetown
Graham, Charles Passmore *retired army officer*
Weyrauch, Paul Turney *retired army officer, retired principal*

Harker Heights
Hughes, William Foster *career officer, surgeon, obstetrician, gynecologist*

Kelly A F B
Bielowicz, Paul L. *career officer*

Lackland A F B
Dremsa, Theresa Lynn *military officer, researcher*
Farage, Michael N. *career officer*
Mabry, Earl W. *military officer*

Lubbock
Huffman, Walter B. *retired army officer, dean, law educator*

Mc Kinney
Perryman, Gerald F., Jr., *retired career officer, defense company executive*

Midlothian
Sibley, James Scarborough *career officer*

Plano
Edmonds, Albert J. *career officer*

Randolph A F B
Lamontagne, Donald A. *career officer*
Stinson, Nancy *military officer*

Randolph Afb
Ellis, Edward R. *career officer*

Sachse
Eichelberger, Charles Bell *retired career officer*

San Antonio
Clarke, Mary Elizabeth *retired career officer*
Detro, John Fitzgerald *military officer*
Kelling, George Horton *retired military officer*
Kline, John William *retired air force officer, management consultant*
Ryder, Gene Ed *retired United States Air Force training administrator*

San Marcos
Bullock, Jerry McKee *retired military officer, consultant, educator*

Santa Fe
Blount, James Robert *military career officer*

Sheppard AFB
Cook, Sharla J. *career officer*

The Woodlands
Jones, Lincoln, III, *army officer*

UTAH

Highland
Baum, Kerry Robert *retired military officer, director*

Hill AFB
Bergren, Scott C. *career officer*

Salt Lake City
McFerren, Carl Davis, II, *retired military officer, risk management consultant*

VERMONT

Burlington
Cram, Reginald Maurice *retired air force officer*

VIRGINIA

Alexandria
Adams, Ranald Trevor, Jr., *retired air force officer*
Bowman, Richard Carl *defense consultant, retired air force officer*
Brown, Frederic Joseph *army officer*
Burke, Kelly Howard *former air force officer, business executive, investor*
Curtin, Gary Lee *air force officer*
DeLuca, Anthony J. *civilian military employee*
Dunn, Bernard Daniel *former naval officer, consultant*
Fedorochko, William, Jr., *retired army officer, defense policy analyst*
Gatanas, Harry D. *career officer*
Jackson, Gary Lee *military analyst*
Kern, Paul John *career military officer*
Kroesen, Frederick James *retired army officer, consultant*
Larson, Charles Robert *naval officer*
Loren, Donald Patrick *naval officer*
Lyons, James Aloysius, Jr., *naval officer*
Seely, James Michael *defense consultant, retired naval officer, small business owner*
Simmons, Edwin Howard *marine corps officer, historian*
Smith, Larry G. *career military officer*
Wilson, Charles H. (Charles Harrison Wilson) *retired air force officer, financial planner, human resource development professional*

Arlington
Becton, Julius Wesley, Jr., *retired military officer*
Blum, H. Steven *military officer*
Carr, Kenneth Monroe *naval officer*
Coady, Philip James, Jr., *retired naval officer*
Costello, John *military officer*
Cosumano, Joseph *military officer, government agency administrator*
DeFilippi, George *retired air force officer*
Dietrick, Kevin M. *military officer*
Dubin, Henry C. *civilian military employee*
Flowers, Robert B. *retired military officer*
Forrester, Eugene Priest *retired military officer*
Graves, Ernest, Jr., *retired army officer, consultant, engineer*
Griffin, Paul, Jr., *navy officer, engineer, educator*
James, Daniel, III, *military officer*
Kelley, Paul Xavier *retired military officer*
Krusa-Dossin, Mary Ann *military officer*
Miller, Kenneth Gregory *retired air force officer*
Putnam, George W., Jr., *retired army officer*
Rogers, Alan Victor *former career officer*
Schultz, Roger C. *career officer*
Singstock, David John *military officer*

Ashburn
Weyman, Steven Aloysius *retired military officer*

Chesapeake
Picotte, Leonard Francis *naval officer*
Powers, Robert Lawrence *civilian military employee*

Dahlgren
Cryer, John *military officer, government agency administrator*
Steiner, Alan P. *military officer, government agency administrator*

Dulles
Glacel, Robert Allan *retired military career officer*

Fairfax
Johnson, Wallace *retired army officer*
Rosenkranz, Robert Bernard *military officer*
Tobin, Paul Edward, Jr., *naval officer*

Fairfax Station
Baer, Robert Jacob *retired military officer*

Falls Church
Gray, D'Wayne *retired marine corps officer*
Hill, Mack C. *career officer*
Randolph, Leonard McElroy, Jr., *career officer*

Fort Belvoir
Clark, Trudy H. *career officer*
Foley, David W. *career officer*
St. John, Adrian, II, *retired army officer*

Fort Monroe
Abrams, John N. *army officer*

Fort Myer
Hart, Herbert Michael *military officer*

Great Falls
Cowhill, William Joseph *retired naval officer, consultant*

Gum Spring
Dilworth, Robert Lexow *career military officer, educator*

Hampton
Crawford, Tommy F. *career officer*

Herndon
Montgomery, Hugh Everett, Jr., *civilian military executive*

Leesburg
McDonough, Joseph Corbett *former army officer, aviation consultant*

Lexington
Peay, J.H. Binford, III, *retired army officer*

Lynchburg
Snead, George Murrell, Jr., *army officer, scientist, consultant*

Mc Lean
Layman, Lawrence *naval officer*
Molino, Thomas Michael *retired military officer*
Oren, John Birdsell *retired coast guard officer*
Scott, Bruce K. *retired military officer*
Yarborough, William Glenn, Jr., *military officer, forest farmer, defense and international business executive*

Merrifield
Earner, William Anthony, Jr., *naval officer*

Millboro
Minetree, James Lawrence, III, *retired military officer, educator*

Norfolk
Berndt, Martin R. *career officer*
Burnette, Thomas N. *career officer*
Downey, Gary Neil *marine corps officer*
Fallon, William J. *career officer*
Kernan, William Frank *career officer*
Konetzni, Albert H., Jr., *career officer*
Kubic, Charles Richard *naval officer*
Reason, J. Paul *naval officer*
Train, Harry Depue, II, *retired naval officer*

Oakton
Frost, S. David *retired naval officer*
Strean, Bernard M. *retired naval officer*

Quantico
Harrington, Jeffrey Michael *military officer*
Howard, Patrick Gene *marine corps officer*
Sanftleben, Kurt Allen *career officer*

Reston
Brown, James Robert *retired air force officer*
Naylon, Michael Edward *retired army officer*
Seiberlich, Carl Joseph *retired naval officer*
Wilkinson, Edward Anderson, Jr., *retired military officer, manufacturing executive*

Rosslyn
McCarthy, Michael James *military intelligence officer*

Round Hill
Tice, Raphael Dean *army officer*

Spotsylvania
Haddock, Raymond Earl *career officer*
Orsini, Eric Andrew *army official*

Springfield
Roberts, Paul Franklin, II, *financial executive*
Watts, Helena Roselle *military analyst*

Vienna
Anderson, Earl E. *retired military officer, legal association administrator*
Chamberlin, Edward Robert *career officer, educator*
Chandler, Hubert Thomas *former army officer*
Jenkins, Robert Gordon *retired air force officer, technology executive, government executive*
Webb, William Loyd, Jr., *army officer*

White Stone
Wroth, James Melvin *retired military officer*

Woodbridge
Hollingsworth, Bobby G. *career officer*
Messerschmidt, William Harclerode *retired army noncommissioned officer, musician*

WASHINGTON

Anacortes
Higgins, Robert (Robert Walter Higgins) *career officer, physician*

Lynnwood
Jenes, Theodore George, Jr., *retired career officer*

Seattle
Ellison, Henry Phillips *military officer*

WYOMING

Fe Warren Afb
Neary, Thomas H. *career officer*

MILITARY ADDRESSES OF THE UNITED STATES

ATLANTIC

Fpo
Green, Kevin Patrick *career officer*
Stavridis, James George *military officer*

EUROPE

APO
Baptiste, Thomas L. *career officer*
Begert, William J. *lieutenant general United States Air Force*
Corley, John D. W. *military officer*
Ralston, Joseph W. *career officer*

FPO
Holmes, Michael L. *career officer*
Mullen, Michael G. *career military officer*

PACIFIC

Apo
Dunkle, Keith Allen *military officer*
Dunn, Michael M. *military officer*
Herrin, Mark Malachi *military officer*
Hester, Paul V. *career officer*
Timmerman, Thomas J. *military planner, operations analyst*

CANADA

ONTARIO

Ottawa
de Chastelain, A(lfred) John G(ardyne) D(rummond) *Canadian army officer, diplomat*
Henault, R. R. *military officer*

Stittsville
Tellier, Henri *retired Canadian military officer*

Winnipeg
Hodgkins, William F. *career officer*

GERMANY

Heidelburg
Sanchez, Ricardo S. *career military officer*
Wojdakowski, Walter *career military officer*
Yarvis, Jeffrey Scott *military officer, social worker*

INDONESIA

West Haven
Callison, Charles Stuart *retired foreign service officer, development economist*

ITALY

Aviano AB
Moorhead, Glen W. (Wally), III, *career officer*

ADDRESS UNPUBLISHED

Adams, Michael John *retired air force non-commissioned officer*
Adams, Patrick O. *career officer*
Aldridge, Donald O'Neal *military officer*
Anderson, Edgar Ratcliffe, Jr., *career officer, physician, health facility administrator*
Anderson, William Robert *career naval officer*
Astriab, Steven Michael *military officer*
Austin, Robert Clarke *naval officer*
Bankers, James *military officer*
Barber, James Alden *navy officer, educator*
Baril, Maurice *career officer*
Barnidge, Leroy, Jr., *military officer*
Barrett, Thomas J. *career military officer*
Bartrem, Duane Harvey *retired military officer, designer, building consultant*
Bauman, Richard Arnold *coast guard officer*
Baxter, Duby Yvonne *government official*
Bell, Burwell Baxter, III, *general United States Army*
Bender, Erwin Rader, Jr., *air force officer*
Blanchard, George Samuel *retired army officer*
Block, Emil Nathaniel, Jr., *retired air force officer*
Boutelle, Steven W. *army officer*
Brakebill, Jean Newton *career officer, nurse, educator*
Brown, Donna Marie *buyer, writer*
Buckley, Edward T., Jr., *career officer*
Buker, Robert Hutchinson, Sr., *army officer, thoracic surgeon*
Burfeindt, Douglas Glenn *civilian military official*
Cain, Eddie *retired military officer*
Casey, George William, Jr., *career military officer*
Chelberg, Robert Douglas *army officer*
Clark, Wesley K. *retired military officer*

Coolidge, Charles H., Jr., *career officer*
Cooper, William Thomas *retired air force officer, writer, educator*
Crowder, Henry Alvin *retired military officer*
Curran, John Mark *military career officer*
Davis, Dempsie Augustus *military officer, educator, financial planner*
Davis, Henry Jefferson, Jr., *former naval officer*
Doornink, Barbara *military officer*
Dozier, James Lee *former army officer*
Eberhart, Ralph E. *career officer*
Ellis, Larry R. *military officer*
Engel, Richard L. *career officer*
Ertwine, Dean R. *retired military officer*
Evans, Jack *city official*
Fargo, Thomas Boulton *career military officer*
Farmer, Kenneth, Jr., *military officer*
Fishburne, Lillian E. *career officer*
Fisher, Stephen Todd *retired military officer, healthcare consultant*
Fisher, Thomas Scott *army officer, broadcasting network executive*
Fitz-Enz, David G. *retired military officer, television producer*
Foote, Evelyn Patricia *retired military officer*
Fowler, Stephen Eugene *retired military officer, human resources executive*
Franks, Tommy Ray *retired army officer*
Galloway, William Rodney *military officer*
Gardner, Emerson N., Jr., *military officer*
Gerras, Stephen Joseph *military officer, psychologist*
Giambastiani, Edmund P., Jr., *military officer, federal agency administrator*
Gray, David Lawrence *retired air force officer*
Grechanik, Jeffrey *military officer*
Greeley, Jennifer Ann *military officer, educator*
Gregory, Frederick D. *career officer, space agency administrator*
Gunhus, Gaylord T. *military career officer*
Gunn, Lee Fredric *career officer*
Guthrie, Wallace Nessler, Jr., *naval officer*
Handy, John W. *air force officer*
Harper, Henry H. *retired military officer*
Harris, Marcelite Jordan *retired career officer*
Harvill, Brian Scott *military officer*
Hayes, Bernard M. *military officer, researcher*
Heckman, Gary Walter *military career officer*
Henry, Charles Howard *non-commissioned officer*
Hessert, Wilfred *retired military officer*
Hill, James T. *career officer*
Holland, Charles R. *military officer*
Horner, Charles Albert *retired air force officer*
Hostettler, Stephen John *naval officer*
Ivany, Robert Rudolph *military officer, historian*
Johnson, Joyce *retired military officer*
Johnson, Silas R., Jr., *consultant, retired air force officer*
Jones, David Charles *retired air force officer, former chairman Joint Chiefs of Staff*
Jones, James L., Jr., *military officer*
Judd, Christy Ann *USN instructor, statistical engineer*
Juskowiak, Terry Eugene *career military officer*
Keane, John Michael *retired military officer*
Keenan, Joseph Michael *military officer*
Keene-Burgess, Ruth Frances *military official*
Kelley, Larry Dale *retired army officer*
Kennedy, William F. *army reserve technician*
Kerrick, Donald L. *career officer*
Kerwin, Walter Thomas, Jr., *career officer, consultant*
Kojac, Jeffrey S. *military officer*
Kutyna, Donald Joseph *air force officer*
Lautenbacher, Conrad Charles, Jr., *naval officer, management consultant, federal government executive*
Lindquist, Michael Adrian *career military officer*
Lynch, Jessica *military officer*
Lyons, John W(inship) *retired government official, chemist, consultant*
Manganaro, Francis Ferdinand *naval officer*
Mangual, Jesus A. *army officer*
Marlow, Edward A. *former army officer*
Martin, James Victor, Jr., *foreign service officer, writer*
Mc Fadden, George Linus *retired army officer*
McKinnon, Daniel Wayne, Jr., *naval officer*
McLean, Craig Elliott *retired non-commissioned officer*
Moore, William Leroy, Jr., *career officer, physician*
Morgan, Thomas Rowland *retired marine corps officer*
Mullen, William Joseph, III, *military analyst, retired career officer*
Nabors, Robert L. *military officer*
Nelson, Ben, Jr., *retired air force officer*
Nelson, Richard A. *military career officer*
Oerding, James Bryan *military educator*
Olson, Phillip Roger *naval officer*
Otstott, Charles Paddock *retired military officer, information technology executive, consultant*
Palmer, Dave Richard *retired military officer, academic administrator*
Parent, Rodolphe Jean *Canadian air force officer, pilot*
Petraeus, David Howell *career military officer*
Pirie, Robert Burns, Jr., *defense analyst*
Price, Joseph Sterling *retired air force officer*
Price, Robert Ira *coast guard officer*
Radzik, Albin F. *military analyst, consultant*
Rhoades, M. Stephen *career officer*
Riddle, Wesley Allen *army officer, writer*
Robinson, David Brooks *retired naval officer*
Robinson, Ronald Gene *military contract negotiator, educator*
Rogers, Bernard William *military officer*
Rondeau, Ann E. *career officer*
Rubenstein, David Aaron *military officer, healthcare administrator*
Ryan, John R. *career officer*
Sanderson, James Richard *retired naval officer, planning and investment company consultant*
Sandstrom, James E. *military career officer*
Scholes, Edison Earl *army officer*
Shalikashvili, John Malchase *retired military career officer*
Shapiro, Sumner *retired naval officer*
Shaw, John Frederick *retired naval officer*
Sherrard, James E., III, *retired military officer*
Silliman, John Parks, Jr., *national guard officer, engineering consultant*
Simmons, Bettye H. *career officer*
Smith, Loretta Mae *civilian military officer*
Smith, Zannie O. *retired career officer*
Smoker, Roy Ellis *retired military officer*
Solomon, Billy K. *army officer*
Springer, Robert Dale *retired air force officer, consultant, lecturer*
Tarantino, David A., Jr., *military officer, emergency physician*
Taylor, James L. *naval officer*
Taylor, Wesley Bayard, Jr., *retired army officer*
Tregurtha, James David *retired career Navy officer, engineer*
Truckenbrodt, Yolanda Bernabe *retired air force officer, consultant*
Tuttle, Jerry Owen *retired naval officer, business executive*
Vessey, John William, Jr., *army officer*
Vincent, Hal Wellman *marine corps officer, investor*
von Kaenel, Howard J. *army officer*
Walden, Joseph Lawrence *career officer*
Wallace, Stewart S. *career military officer*
Weiss, Donald A. *naval officer*
Wetekam, Donald J. *career officer*
Wheeler, Albin Gray *retired military officer, retail executive, educator*
Wilcox, Brian James *military analyst*
Wilson, Frances C. *career military officer*
Yacavone, David William *military officer, consultant, researcher*
Yeosock, John John *army officer*
Zais, Mitchell M. *career military officer*
Zuick, Ernest Ronald, Jr., *career officer, advertising executive*

REAL ESTATE

UNITED STATES

ALABAMA

Arab
Hammond, Ralph Charles *real estate executive*

Birmingham
Copeland, Hunter Armstrong *retired real estate executive*

Montgomery
Cassels, Martha Beasley *realtor, developer*

ALASKA

Anchorage
Ballard, Kirsten Kay *environmentalist, writer*
Behrend, Donald Fraser *environmental educator, university administrator*
Faulkner, Sewell Ford *real estate executive*
Kelly, Maxine Ann *retired property developer*

Girdwood
Trautner, John James *real estate executive*

ARIZONA

Bullhead City
Jones, Vernon Quentin *surveyor*

Phoenix
Clements, John Robert *real estate professional*
De Michele, O. Mark *real estate company executive*
Lewis, Orme, Jr., *real estate company executive, land use adviser*
Sertich, Kelli Ann *land use planner*

Prescott
Anderson, Walter Lee *environmental educator, artist, photographer*

Scottsdale
Hadder, Donald Everett, Sr., *urban planner*
Hanneman, Le Roy C., Jr., *real estate executive*
Leonard, George Edmund *real estate, bank, high tech and consulting executive*

Sedona
Copeland, Suzanne Johnson *real estate executive*

Tempe
Jungbluth, Kirk E. *real estate appraiser*

Tucson
Best, Gary Thorman *commercial real estate broker*
Bodinson, Holt *conservationist*
Carman, Mary Ann *realtor, writer, retired medical/surgical nurse*
Lanham, Sandra *conservationist*
Lehrling, Terry James *real estate broker*
Longan, George Baker, III, *real estate company executive*
Tang, Esther Don *development consultant, retired social worker*

ARKANSAS

Blytheville
Baker, Carlene Poff *real estate agent, reporter*

Fayetteville
Jackson, Robert Lee *real estate agent*

Magnolia
Juniker, Anthony Michael *economic developer, consultant*

Rogers
Cooper, John Alfred, Jr., *community development company executive*

CALIFORNIA

Berkeley
Wachs, Martin *urban planning educator, author, consultant*

Beverly Hills
Bergman, Nancy Palm *real estate investment company executive*
Glazer, Guilford *real estate developer*
Seeger, Melinda Wayne *realtor*
Shapell, Nathan *financial and real estate executive*
Tamkin, Curtis Sloane *real estate development company executive*
Victor, Robert Eugene *real estate corporation executive, lawyer*

Big Sur
Cross, Robert Louis *realtor, landscape architect, land use planner, writer, real estate appraiser*

Campbell
Nicholson, Joseph Bruce *real estate developer*

Carmel
Didion, James J. *real estate company executive*

Chula Vista
Heise, Steven Anthony *surveyor, consultant*

Coronado
Stames, William Alexander *realtor, cost management executive*

Costa Mesa
Cohen, Stanley *commercial real estate developer*

Cupertino
Berg, Karl *real estate company executive*

El Segundo
Wirta, Raymond E. *real estate company executive*

Emeryville
Spadora, Hope Georgeanne *real estate company executive*

Fair Oaks
Papa, Michael Joseph *real estate broker*
Yarrigle, Charlene Sandra Shuey *realtor, investment advisor*

Foster City
Butcher, C. Preston *real estate company executive*

Fountain Valley
Smith, Marie Edmonds *real estate agent, property manager*

Fullerton
Ambrose, Henry Bartlett *real estate broker, writer*

Glendale
Gedjeyan, Hovannes John *real estate broker*

Granite Bay
Kemper, Dorla Dean Eaton (Dorla Dean Eaton) *real estate broker*

Grass Valley
Ozanich, Charles George *real estate broker*

Greenbrae
Burger, Eugene J. *property manager*
Burger, Stephen L. *real estate company executive*

Hermosa Beach
Williams, Jack Jeff *realtor, retired executive administrator*

Irvine
Chronley, James Andrew *real estate executive*
Stack, Geoffrey Lawrence *real estate developer*

La Jolla
Anthony, Harry Antoniades *city planner, architect, educator*
Foley, L(ewis) Michael *real estate executive*
Ripley, Stuart McKinnon *real estate consultant*

Laguna Beach
Hanauer, Joe Franklin *real estate executive*

Laguna Niguel
York, James Orison *real estate executive*

Long Beach
Davies, Grace Lucille *real estate educator*
Rosenberg, Jill *realtor, civic leader*

Los Alamitos
Spiegel, Marilyn Harriet *real estate executive*

Los Angeles
Coleman, Victor J. *real estate company executive*
Cushman, John C., III, *real estate company executive*
Davis, Richard S. *real estate company executive, corporate financial executive*
Furlotti, Alexander Amato *real estate development company executive*
Gilchrist, Richard Irwin *real estate developer*
Levy, Alan David *real estate executive*
Linsk, Michael Stephen *real estate executive*
Ross, Stan *real estate company executive*
Swartz, Roslyn Holt *real estate company executive*
White, Brett *real estate company executive*
Ziman, Richard S. *real estate company executive*

Lynwood
Dove, Donald Augustine *city planner, educator*

Manhattan Beach
Schoenfeld, Lawrence Jon *real estate developer, asset lender*

Marina Del Rey
Masotti, Louis Henry *real estate educator, consultant*

Mission Viejo
Harris, Ruby Lee *real estate agent*

Newport Beach
Bren, Donald L. *real estate company executive*
Fawcett, John Scott *real estate developer*
Kenney, William John, Jr., *real estate development executive*
Matteucci, Dominick Vincent *real estate developer*
Mink, Maxine Mock *real estate company executive*
Webb, H. Lawrence *real estate executive*

Oakland
Ostrander, Willis Frederick *real estate appraiser*

Oceanside
Munson, Lucille Marguerite (Mrs. Arthur E. Munson) *real estate broker*

Ontario
Ariss, David William, Sr., *real estate developer, consultant*
Previtti, James P. *real estate executive*

Palm Desert
DeMarco, Ralph John *real estate developer*

Palm Springs
Coffey, Nancy Ann *real estate broker*

Palmdale
Anderson, R(obert) Gregg *real estate company executive*

Palo Alto
McIntyre, Robert Wheeler *retired conservation organization executive*
Moore, Cassandra Chrones *real estate broker and policy analyst*
Wong, Y(ing) Wood *real estate investment company executive, real estate development company executive, venture capital investment company executive*

Pasadena
Crowley, John Crane *real estate developer*

Penn Valley
Nix, Barbara Lois *real estate broker*

Rancho Santa Fe
Dieffenbach, Otto Weaver, III, *real estate company executive*

Redondo Beach
Abernethy, Robert John *real estate developer*

Riverside
Oakes, Judy Dianne *real estate broker*

Sacramento
Lukenbill, Gregg *real estate developer, sports promoter*

San Bernardino
Willis, Harold Wendt, Sr., *real estate developer*

San Diego
Acosta, Gary E. *real estate company executive*
Davis, John Warren *real estate broker, contractor*
Klein, Saul D. *real estate company executive*
Mc Comic, Robert Barry *real estate development company executive, lawyer*
Oldham, Maxine Jernigan *real estate broker*

San Francisco
Bracken, Thomas Robert James *real estate investment executive*
Chicotel, Richard A. *real estate company executive*
Freund, Fredric S. *real estate broker, property manager*
Shannon, Glenn A. *real estate company executive*
Shorenstein, Walter Herbert *commercial real estate development company executive*

San Jose
Rothblatt, Donald Noah *urban and regional planner, educator*

San Marcos
Wingert, Hannelore Christiane *real estate agent, chemical company executive*

San Rafael
Roulac, Stephen E. *real estate consultant*

Santa Barbara
Charness, Gary *real estate broker, educator*
Smyth, Theodore Hilton *real estate developer*

Santa Cruz
Dilbeck, Charles Stevens, Jr., *real estate company executive*

Santa Rosa
Rabinowitsh, Steve *urban planner educator, city council member*

Seal Beach
Osgood, Frank William *urban and economic planner, writer*

Thousand Oaks
Gregory, Calvin *real estate investor*

Twain Harte
Kinsinger, Robert Earl *property company executive, educational consultant*

Upland
Lewis, Goldy Sarah *real estate developer, corporation executive*

Valencia
Cusamano, Gary M. *real estate executive*
Lee, Thomas L. *real estate executive*

Visalia
Nevin, David Wright *real estate broker, mortgage broker*

Vista
Cavanaugh, Kenneth Clinton *retired housing consultant*

Westlake Village
Long, W. Michael *real estate company executive*

Yorba Linda
Vilardi, Agnes Francine *real estate broker*

COLORADO

Aspen
Clauson, F.L. Stan, Jr., *city planner, consultant*

Aurora
Lochmiller, Kurtis L. *real estate entrepreneur*
Nolen, James Allen *property manager, writer*

Boulder
Stepanek, Joseph Edward *industrial development consultant*

Colorado Springs
Christensen, C. Lewis *real estate developer*

Commerce City
Hayes, James Anthony *city planner, business owner*

Denver
Mandarich, David D. *real estate corporation executive*

Englewood
Moran, Gregory Allan *real estate developer, real estate agent*

Fort Collins
Jensen, Margaret *real estate broker*
Shively, Robert William *urban planner*
Sprague, Amaris Jeanne *real estate broker*

Grand Junction
Nelson, Paul William *real estate broker*

Greenwood Village
Liniger, Dave *real estate company executive*

Littleton
Grant, Newell M. *real estate investment manager*

Louisville
Schonbrun, Michael K. *senior housing developer and operator*

Loveland
Harrison, Craig Donald *water rights broker, real estate and land use planner*

Monument
Boggs, Steven Eugene *real estate broker, lawyer*

Vail
Kelton, Arthur Marvin, Jr., *real estate developer*

Woody Creek
Jenkins, Robert Berryman *real estate developer*

CONNECTICUT

Bethel
Kurfehs, Harold Charles *real estate executive*

Bridgeport
Dexter, Gregory Warren *real estate and financial investor*
Schwartz, James Peter *real estate broker*

Greenwich
Badman, John, III, *real estate developer, architect*
Griggs, Nina M. *realtor*
Urstadt, Charles J. *real estate executive*

Hartford
Louargand, Marc Andrew *real estate executive, financial consultant*

New Haven
Alexander, Bruce Donald *real estate executive, educator*
Harrison, Henry Starin *real estate educator, entrepreneur*

North Haven
Pearce, Herbert Henry *real estate company executive*

Old Greenwich
Parris, Sally Nye *real estate agent*

Stamford
Koproski, Alexander Robert *real estate company executive*

DELAWARE

Dover
Taylor, Suzonne Berry Stewart *real estate broker*

Newark
Byrne, John Michael *energy and environmental policy educator, researcher*

Rehoboth Beach
Little, R. Donald *real estate entrepreneur*

Wilmington
Maley, Patricia Ann *preservation planner*

DISTRICT OF COLUMBIA

Washington
Anlian, Steven James *urban planner, consultant*
Blackwelder, Brent Francis *environmentalist*
Carr, Oliver T., Jr., *real estate company executive*
Carr, Thomas A. *real estate company executive*
Gelburd, Diane Elizabeth *conservationist*
Gibbons, Petch *real estate company executive*
Hawkins, Philip Linton *real estate executive*
Janes, William Sargent *real estate corporation executive*
Jones, Susan Dorfman *real estate broker, writer*
McGarry, W. David *real estate company executive*
Meyer, Alden Merrill *environmental association executive*
Oge, Margo Tsirigotis *environmentalist*
Stegman, Michael Allen *city and regional planning educator*
Stollman, Israel *city planner*
Stone, Roger David *environmentalist*
Train, Russell Errol *environmentalist*
Wallace Douglas, Jean *conservationist*
Wang, Kim *real estate broker, librarian*
Wheeler, Douglas Paul *conservationist, government official, lawyer*
Wilder, James Edward *resident manager*

FLORIDA

Boca Raton
Goray, Gerald Allen *real estate company executive, lawyer*
Innes-Brown, Georgette Meyer *real estate broker, insurance broker*
Siegel, Ned Lawrence *real estate developer*

Cedar Key
Starnes, Earl Maxwell *urban and regional planner, architect*

Clearwater
Dodge, Adriana *real estate investor, educator*

Coral Gables
Blumberg, Philip Flayderman *real estate developer*

Deland
Tedros, Theodore Zaki *real estate broker, appraiser, educator*

Dunedin
Krone, Norman Bernard *commercial real estate developer, lawyer*

Dunnellon
Sawick, Karen Ann *real estate agent*

Eagle Lake
McNeil, Edward Warren *real estate company executive*

Fort Lauderdale
Craib, Kenneth Bryden *resource development executive, physicist, economist*
Markos, Chris *retired real estate company executive*
Taylor, Ralph Orien, Jr., *real estate developer, investor*

Fort Myers
Courtney, James Edmond *real estate developer*

Gainesville
York, Vermelle Cardwell *real estate broker and developer*

Jacksonville
Aleschus, Justine Lawrence *retired real estate broker*
Clarkson, Charles Andrew *real estate investment executive*
Lovett, Radford Dow *marine terminal real estate and investment company executive*
Stein, Martin (Hap), Jr., *real estate company executive*
Stern, Steven Alan *sports development owner*

Jupiter
Welch, Martha Lynn *environmentalist, educator*

Lakeland
McKeel, Seth Douglas *real estate manager, commissioner*

Lantana
Weeks, Charles, Jr., *real estate executive, retired publishing company executive*

Longwood
Gasperoni, Emil, Sr., *realtor, developer*

Maitland
Vallee, Judith Delaney *environmentalist, writer, fundraiser*

Melbourne
Glindeman, Henry Peter, Jr., *real estate developer*
Michalski, Thomas Joseph *city planner, developer*

Miami
Bregman, Michael Evan *urban planner*
Glogower, Michael Howard *public housing senior functional specialist*
Miller, Stuart A. *real estate executive, lawyer*
Nestor Castellano, Brenda Diana *real estate company executive*
Raffel, Leroy B. *real estate development company executive*
Salvaneschi, Luigi *real estate and development executive, business educator*
Segal, Simon *real estate executive, finance company executive*
Stover, James Howard *retired real estate executive*
West, Macdonald *real estate executive*

Miami Beach
Garbe-Morillo, Patricia Ann *preservationist*

Naples
Dorio, Martin Matthew, Jr., *real estate company executive, investor*
Keller, Theodore G., Jr., *investment property owner and manager*
Llewellyn, Leonard Frank *real estate broker, investment company executive*
Stastny, John Anton *real estate executive*

Niceville
Rasmussen, Robert Dee *retired real estate appraiser*

North Miami Beach
Katzman, Chaim *real estate company executive, investment company executive*
Sipzner, Howard M. *real estate executive*
Valero, Doron *real estate executive*

Ocala
Booth, Jane Schuele *real estate company executive, real estate broker*

Ocean Ridge
Mueller, Gerry *realtor, investor, former internet executive*

Ormond Beach
Buonamano, Anthony F. *real estate agent, engineering company executive*

Palm Beach
Bagby, Martha L. Green *real estate holding company executive, writer, publishing executive*
Coudert, Dale Hokin *real estate executive, marketing consultant*
Dillard, Rodney Jefferson *real estate executive*
Klotsche, Charles Martin *real estate development company executive, photographer, writer, financial columnist*

Palm Beach Gardens
Bragdon, Clifford Richardson *city planner, educator*

Palm Coast
Barnes, Judith Ann *real estate executive*

Panama City
Navon, Robert *real estate investor, former book publisher*

Plantation
Weiss, David I. *land developer, business executive, lawyer*

Ponte Vedra Beach
Berry, Clare Gebert *real estate broker*

Safety Harbor
Crafton-Masterson, Adrienne *real estate company executive*

Saint Petersburg
Hurley, John Kenneth *real estate and merchant banking executive*
Rummel, Harold Edwin *real estate development and retail sales executive*

Saint Petersburg Beach
Hurley, Frank Thomas, Jr., *realtor*

Sarasota
Blomgren, Bruce Holmes *real estate developer, marina developer, consultant*
Close, Michael John *property manager, lawyer*
Levitt, Jaren *real estate corporation officer*

Sebring
Sherrick, Daniel Noah *real estate broker*

Tallahassee
Lisenby, Dorrece Edenfield *realtor*
Morgan, Constance Louise *real estate executive*
Tookes, James Nelson *real estate investment company executive*

Tampa
Gidel, Robert Hugh *real estate investor*
Kanstoroom, David Arnold *real estate developer, entrepreneur*
Purcell, Henry, III, *real estate developer*

Titusville
Morton, Craig Richard *real estate investor*

Vero Beach
Freeman, Donald Wilford *real estate developer, horse breeder*

Winter Park
Strawn, Frances Freeland *real estate executive*

GEORGIA

Alpharetta
Charania, Barkat *real estate consultant*
Cline, Stewart M. *real estate executive*
Weitz, John Jerome, Jr., *city planner*

Athens
Melton, Wayne Charles *real estate executive*

Atlanta
Adams, David Porterfield, III, *real estate appraiser*
Bell, Thomas D., Jr., *real estate company executive*
Comstock, Robert Donald, Jr., *real estate executive*
Cousins, Thomas G. *real estate company executive*
Cupp, Robert Erhard *land use planner, golf course architect*
Ficke, Bruce William *real estate executive*
Glover, John Trapnell *real estate executive*
Gregory (Greg), Henry D., Jr., *real estate company executive*
Hutcheson, John K. *real estate company executive*
Kerley, William J. *real estate corporation executive*
Nichols, Elizabeth Litterer *real estate developer*
Peterson, Bob *real estate company executive*
Raines, Tim D. *real estate corporation executive*
Russell, Herman Jerome *retired real estate developer company executive*
Simpson, Allan Boyd *real estate company executive*
Taylor, Scott *real estate company executive*
Terwilliger, J. Ronald *real estate company executive*
Wieland, John *real estate executive*
Wittner-Neiman, Sloane Phyllis Ann *realtor, writer, artist*
Wolbrink, James Francis *real estate investor*

Columbus
Bailey, Herta Luise *real estate broker*

Cumming
French, James Thomas *real estate broker*

Flovilla
Lamb, Deryle Jean *preservationist*

Folkston
Crumbley, Esther Helen Kendrick *retired real estate agent, retired secondary school educator, councilman*

Forsyth
Coleman, Steven Andrew *surveyor*

Macon
Jones, John Ellis *real estate broker*

Marietta
McAuley, Thomas H. *real estate executive*

Newnan
Barron, Thomas Willis *real estate broker*

Peachtree City
Clark, James Kermit, Jr., *real estate executive*

Stone Mountain
Malone, Embry *property manager, advocate*

Suwanee
Colgan, George Phillips *real estate developer, real estate analyst*

Toccoa
Maypole, John Floyd *real estate holding company executive*

Tucker
Roberts, Thomas Heym *city and regional planner, consultant*

HAWAII

Honolulu
Adcock, Betty-Lee *real estate company officer*
Jones, Pamela S. *real estate development executive*
Lighter, Eric Aaron *real estate and law enforcement software developer, consultant*
Walker, Margaret Smith *real estate company executive*

Kapolei
Wong, Edwina A. Lee *real estate broker*

Koloa
Cobb, Rowena Noelani Blake *real estate broker*

Princeville
Rowe-Maas, Betty Lu *real estate investor*

IDAHO

Boise
Banks, Robert K. *real estate executive, lawyer, food products executive*
Hegg, David Alan *real estate analyst*

Idaho Falls
Thorsen, Nancy Dain *real estate broker*

Troy
Hepler, Merlin Judson, Jr., *real estate broker*

ILLINOIS

Aurora
Stephens, Steve Arnold *real estate broker*

Champaign
Guttenberg, Albert Ziskind *planning educator*

Chicago
Amato, Isabella Antonia *real estate executive*
Berger, Miles Lee *land economist*
Bohn, Charlotte Galitz *retired real estate executive*
Branch, Ronald L. *real estate company executive*
Brennan, Michael *real estate company executive*
Bucksbaum, John *real estate development company executive*
Bucksbaum, Matthew *real estate investment trust company executive*
Callahan, Timothy T. *real estate company executive*
Campbell, Gavin Elliott *real estate investor and developer*
Chapman, Robert J. *real estate company executive*
Colleran, Michael *real estate company executive*
Daley, Vincent Raymond, Jr., *real estate company executive, consultant*
Daly, Patrick F. *real estate executive, architect*
Darchun, Lino Auksutis *real estate professional*
Duncan, Bruce W. *real estate company executive*
Eubanks-Pope, Sharon G. *real estate company executive, entrepreneur*
Field, Karen Ann (Karen Ann Schaffner) *real estate broker*
Fox, Leslie B. *real estate company executive*
Freibaum, Bernard *real estate development company executive*
Galowich, Ronald Howard *real estate investment executive, venture capitalist*
Geoga, Douglas Gerard *real estate developer, lawyer*
Gerber, John J. *real estate executive*
Glaze, Robert Howe *real estate executive*
Good, Sheldon Fred *realtor*
Havala, Michael J. *real estate company executive*
Heneghan, Thomas P. *real estate company executive*
Jarrett, Valerie Bowman *property management executive, stock exchange executive*
Julmy, Camille P. *real estate company executive*
Klebba, Raymond Allen *property manager*
Lapidus, Dennis *real estate developer*
Maduros, John *real estate company executive*
Matanky, James E. *real estate developer*
Michaels, Robert A. *real estate development company executive*
Morrill, R. Layne *real estate broker, executive, professional association administrator*
Neithercut, David J. *real estate executive*
Pacher, Nancy A. *real estate company executive*

Pappas, Philip James *real estate company executive*
Patterson, Jeffrey A. *real estate company executive*
Primo, Quintin E., III, *real estate company executive*
Reilly, Robert Frederick *valuation consultant*
Shaffer, Jack *real estate company executive*
Shidler, Jay H. *real estate company executive*
Smietana, Robert E. *real estate company executive*
Smith, Tom W. *surveyor, researcher*
Strohm, Bruce C. *real estate company executive*
Totlis, Gust John *retired title insurance company executive*
Travis, Dempsey Jerome *real estate company executive*
Winslow, Robert A. *real estate company executive*
Wirtz, William Wadsworth *real estate executive, professional sports team executive*

Darien
Skweres, Thomas A. *real estate company executive*

Dundee
Ulakovich, Ronald Stephen *real estate developer*

Edwardsville
Wentz, Charles Alvin, Jr., *environmentalist, chemical engineer*

Elgin
Karner-Breyer, Candice Michelle *real estate broker*

Glen Carbon
Ottwein, Merrill William George *real estate company executive, veterinarian*

Lake Zurich
Schultz, Carl Herbert *real estate management and development company executive*

Nashville
Cude, Thomas Bret *real estate broker*

Northbrook
Levy, Arnold S(tuart) *real estate company executive*
Metz, Adam S. *real estate executive*

Oak Brook
Fisher, Paul S. *real estate company executive*
Gates, John S., Jr., *real estate company executive*
Goodwin, Daniel L. *real estate company executive*
Mullen, Michael M. *real estate company executive*

Ottawa
Breipohl, Walter Eugene *real estate broker*

Palatine
Harbeck, William James *real estate executive, lawyer, international consultant*

Saint Charles
Urhausen, James Nicholas *real estate developer, construction executive*

Skokie
Alter, Michael *real estate company executive*

Westmont
Harten, Ann M. *relocation services executive*

INDIANA

Columbus
Shannon, Carolyn Jean *real estate company executive*

Elkhart
Vite, Frank Anthony *realtor*

Fort Wayne
Hirschy, Gordon Harold *real estate broker, auctioneer*

Greenwood
Tomlin, Jeanne Brannon *real estate broker, small business owner*

Indianapolis
Borns, Robert Aaron *real estate developer*
Cohoat, Matthew A. *real estate company executive*
Crosser, Richard H. *real estate company executive*
Frisch, Fred I. *real estate executive*
Hefner, Thomas L. *real estate company executive*
Jewett, John Rhodes *real estate executive*
Oklak, Dennis D. *real estate company executive*
Simon, David *real estate company officer*
Simon, Melvon *real estate company officer*
Sokolov, Richard Saul *real estate company executive*
Sterrett, Steven E. *real estate company officer*
Weeks, A. Ray *real estate company executive*

Jeffersonville
Reisert, Charles Edward, Jr., *real estate executive*

Lafayette
Shook, James Creighton *real estate executive*

Newburgh
Tierney, Gordon Paul *real estate broker, genealogist*

Terre Haute
Perry, Eston Lee *real estate and equipment leasing company executive*

IOWA

Cedar Rapids
Baermann, Donna Lee Roth *real estate property executive, retired insurance analyst*
Knepper, Eugene Arthur *realtor*

KANSAS

Overland Park
McChesney, Samuel Parker, III, *real estate executive*

Topeka
Barnett, Mary Lorene *real estate manager*

KENTUCKY

Bowling Green
Stewart, Harold Sanford *real estate investment and supply executive*

Covington
Fleischer-Rieveschl, Ellen Lee *real estate agent*

Fort Mitchell
Weiskittel, Ralph Joseph *retired real estate broker*

Frankfort
Collins, Hubert *real estate broker, state representative*

Lexington
Gable, Robert Elledy *real estate investment company executive*

Middlesboro
Daniel, Barbara Ann *realtor, advertising executive*

LOUISIANA

Baton Rouge
Skillman, Ernest Edward, Jr., *real estate sales and management executive*

Covington
Maurin, James E. *real estate executive*

Leesville
Thompson, Darlene Bennett *realtor, musician*

Monroe
Guy, William Achilles, Jr., (Rod Guy Jr.) *urban planner, economic development consultant*

New Orleans
Bell, Bryan *real estate and oil investment executive, educator*
Jones, Glenn Earle *property management executive*
Lupo, Robert Edward Smith *real estate developer and investor*

Shreveport
Robinson, Edna Earle *real estate company executive*

MAINE

Bangor
Foster, Walter Herbert, Jr., *real estate company executive*

Gardiner
Gosline, Norman Abbot *real estate appraiser, consultant*

Lincolnville
Williams, Robert Luther *city planning consultant*

Port Clyde
Duarte, Patricia M. *real estate and insurance broker*

MARYLAND

Annapolis
Wright, David Lawrence *realtor, real estate broker*

Baltimore
DeVito, Mathias Joseph *retired real estate executive*
Rosen, Michael Howard *real estate executive*

Bethesda
Clark, A. James *real estate company executive*
Kibbe, James William *real estate broker*
Klatzkin, Terri *real estate company executive*
Nussdorf, Lawrence C. *real estate/construction executive*
Sams, James Farid *real estate development company executive*

Cambridge
Miller, Robert Edvin *environmental education specialist, researcher, industrial hygienist*

Chevy Chase
Lee, Edward Brooke, Jr., *real estate executive, fund raiser*

College Park
Shen, Qing *urban planning educator, researcher*

Columbia
Deering, Anthony Wayne Marion *real estate developer*
Dreir, R. Chad *real estate executive*
McCuan, William Patrick *real estate company executive*
McGregor, Douglas A. *real estate company executive*
Millspaugh, Martin Laurence *real estate developer, urban development consultant*

Frederick
Whelihan, Alan Stuart *real estate developer, automotive executive*

Potomac
Eaves, Maria Perry *realtor*
Noonan, Patrick Francis *conservation executive*

Reisterstown
Bart, Polly Turner *real estate developer*

Salisbury
Nutter, David George *urban planner*

Silver Spring
Laughlin, Naomi Myers *realtor*
McCray, Lora *real estate developer*

Takoma Park
Urciolo, John Raphael, II, *real estate developer, real estate and finance educator*

Westminster
Erb, Betty Jane *retired real estate agent, activist*

MASSACHUSETTS

Amherst
Bentley, Richard Norcross *regional planner, writer, educator*
Larson, Joseph Stanley *environmentalist, educator*

Ayer
Holmes, Jean Louise *real estate investor, Holocaust scholar, educator*

Boston
Bailey, Peter Arthur *real estate executive*
Beal, Robert Lawrence *real estate executive*
Holland, James R. *real estate company officer*
Karman, James B. *real estate company executive*
Lovejoy, George Montgomery, Jr., *real estate company executive*
Lundgren, Richard John *real estate executive, city planner, preservationist*
Radloff, Robert Albert *real estate company executive*
Roberts, Sandra Brown *realty company executive*
Thomas, Carol Louise Joseph *community planning company executive*
Wiggleworth, Margaret *property manager*

Brockton
Compton, William Thomas *real estate investor*

Cambridge
Axelrod, Emily H. *urban planner*
de Marneffe, Barbara Rowe *historic preservationist*
Fleming, Ronald Lee *urban designer, arts administrator, preservation planner, environmental educator*
Spunt, Shepard Armin *real estate company executive, management and financial consultant*
Susskind, Lawrence Elliott *urban and environmental planner, educator, public dispute mediator*
Vigier, François Claude Denis *city planning educator*
Wood, Richard Robinson *real estate company executive*

East Bridgewater
Farrell, Sharon Elaine *retired real estate broker*

Fairhaven
Hotchkiss, Henry Washington *real estate broker and financial consultant*

Gloucester
Sallah, Majeed (Jim Sallah) *retired real estate developer*

Lexington
Frieden, Bernard Joel *urban studies educator*

Natick
Strauss, Harlee Sue *environmental consultant*

Newton
Nahigian, Robert John *real estate development broker*

Rockport
Johnson, Janet Lou *real estate company executive, writer*

Waltham
Nelson, Arthur Hunt *real estate company executive*

Whitinsville
O'Connell, Roberta M. *realtor*

Winchester
Blackham, Ann Rosemary (Mrs. J. W. Blackham) *realtor*

MICHIGAN

Ann Arbor
Clark, Thomas B., Sr., *real estate broker*
Surovell, Edward David *real estate company executive*

Bloomfield Hills
Grosfeld, James *real estate development company executive*
Halso, Robert *real estate company executive*
Taubman, Robert S. *real estate developer*

East Lansing
Anderton, James Franklin, IV, *real estate development executive*
Strauss, Eric James *urban planning educator, lawyer, consultant*

Grosse Ile
Smith, Veronica Latta *real estate corporation officer*

Grosse Pointe Shores
LaHood, Mary Anne *real estate investor*

Milford
McGhie, Michael *real estate company executive*

Saginaw
Cline, Thomas William *real estate leasing company executive, management consultant*

White Lake
Clyburn, Luther Linn *real estate broker, appraiser, ship captain*

MINNESOTA

Detroit Lakes
Remmen, Lawrence P. *city planner*

Duluth
Bowman, Roger Manwaring *real estate executive*

Minneapolis
Boelter, Philip Floyd *real estate company officer, mortgage company executive*
Bolan, Richard Stuart *urban planner, educator, researcher*
Hawkins, Paul E. *real estate company executive*
Kreiser, Frank David *real estate company executive*
Lucas, Margaret Exner *housing developer*
Stofer, Boyd B. *real estate company executive*
Stuebner, James Cloyd *real estate developer, contractor*

Minnetonka
Rauenhorst, Mark *property manager, real estate company executive*

North Oaks
McDonald, Malcolm Willis *retired real estate company executive*

MISSISSIPPI

Meridian
Church, George Millord *retired real estate company executive*

MISSOURI

Chesterfield
Morley, Harry Thomas, Jr., *real estate executive*

Columbia
Northway, Wanda I. *real estate company executive*

Gray Summit
Desloge, Christopher Davis, Sr., *real estate and merchant banking executive*

Holden
Martin, Laurabelle *real estate and farm land owner and manager*

Independence
Francis, Mary Frances Van Dyke *real estate executive, editor*

Ironton
Sebastian, Phylis Sue (Ingram) *real estate broker, antique appraiser*

Kansas City
Dumovich, Loretta *real estate and transportation company executive*
Esrey, Robert E. *real estate company executive*
Harris, R. Lee *real estate company executive*
Shutz, Byron Christopher *real estate executive*

Lake Saint Louis
Royal, William Henry *retired real estate developer, architect*

Saint Joseph
Rachow, Sharon Dianne *realtor*

Saint Louis
Burkhart, Mark *real estate company executive*
Lang, Danny Robert *planning consultant*
Marking, T(heodore) Joseph, Jr., *transportation and urban planner*
Meissner, Edwin Benjamin, Jr., *retired real estate broker*

Springfield
Aull, Elizabeth Berryman *real estate development executive*

Stockton
Jackson, Betty L. Deason *real estate developer*

MONTANA

Great Falls
Stevens, George Alexander *real estate broker*

NEVADA

Carson City
Empey, Gene F. *real estate executive*
Evangelatos, Gregory Gerasimos *city planner*

Las Vegas
Canarelli, Lawrence D. *real estate developer*
Lee, Theodore Bo *real estate developer*
Pulliam, Francine Sarno *real estate broker, real estate developer*

Reno
Coleman, James Scott *environmental research executive*

NEW HAMPSHIRE

Hinsdale
Smith, Edwin O. *real estate executive, state legislator*

Salem
Spero, Nora Mancini *realtor, writer*

NEW JERSEY

Atlantic Highlands
Hawley, Joseph B. *property management executive, educator*

Bedminster
Hudacsko, Dennis Wayne *urban planner*

Bound Brook
Chandler, Marguerite Nella *real estate corporation executive*

Chatham
Lax, Philip *land developer, space planner*

Cherry Hill
Copsetta, Norman George *real estate executive*

Cranford
Hersh, Mitchell E. *real estate company executive, director*
Jones, Timothy M. *real estate company executive*
Lefkowitz, Barry *real estate company executive*

Englewood Cliffs
Books, Roberta Paula *real estate finance executive*

Flemington
Salamon, Renay *real estate broker*

Florham Park
Gale, Stan *real estate company executive*
Yeager, Mark *real estate company executive*

Haworth
Strum, Brian J. *real estate executive*

Hightstown
Finn, Gerald C. *real estate company executive*
Finn, Jeffrey M. *real estate company executive*

Lakewood
Rode, Leif *retired real estate personal computer consultant*

Livingston
Marlow, Ian Michael *real estate company executive*

Morristown
Lieblich, Frederich *real estate consultant*

Parsippany
Becker, Robert *real estate company executive*

Princeton
Broad, Barbara Prentice *retired real estate agent*

Red Bank
Hovnanian, Ara K. *real estate developer*
Hovnanian, Kevork S. *real estate developer*

Saddle Brook
Roth, Steven *realty company executive*

Sea Girt
Cleary, Martin Joseph *real estate company executive*

Secaucus
Stern, Emanuel *real estate developer*

South Orange
Thonet, John A. *environmental planning and engineering consultant*

Upper Saddle River
Marron, Darlene Lorraine *real estate company executive*

NEW MEXICO

Albuquerque
Davis, Betty Bourbonia *real estate company executive*
Godfrey, Richard George *real estate appraiser, consultant*
Kohn, Emil *real estate broker*
Stahl, Jack Leland *real estate company executive*

Las Cruces
Parsley, Steven Dwayne *title company executive*

Mora
Hanks, Eugene Ralph *real estate developer, rancher, forester, retired military officer, investor*

NEW YORK

Bronx
Adinolfi, Vincent John *realtor, product designer*

Brooklyn
Stuckey, James P. *real estate company executive*

Canaan
Belknap, Michael H. P. *real estate developer*

Cedarhurst
Milk, Jared Marc *real estate company executive, writer*

Central Islip
McGowan, Harold *real estate developer, investor, scientist, author, philanthropist*

Corona
Maruca, Rita *real estate company executive, real estate broker*

Douglaston
Balbi, Kenneth Emilio *environmental specialist, researcher*

Dundee
Miller, Ronald K. *real estate broker, educator*

Elizabethtown
Houseal, Brian L. *conservationist*

Elma
Wirth, Sandra Lee *real estate company owner*

Elmsford
Raymond, George Marc *city planner, educator*

Goshen
Ward, William Francis, Jr., *real estate investment banker*

Ithaca
Colbert, Robert Reed, Jr., *real estate developer*

Larchmont
Levi, James Harry *real estate executive, investment banker*

Melville
Campofranco, Salvatore *real estate company executive*
Maturo, J. Michael *real estate company executive, corporate financial executive*
Rechler, Scott *real estate company executive*

Mount Vernon
Rossini, Joseph *contracting and development corporate executive*

New Hyde Park
Agin, Herbert *real estate company executive*
Cooper, Milton *real estate investment trust executive*
Flynn, Michael J. *real estate executive*
Henry, David B. *real estate company executive*
Pappagallo, Michael V. *realty company executive*

New York
Benenson, Edward Hartley *realty company executive*
Betts, Roland W. *real estate developer*
Boxer, Jason T. *title company executive*
Brown, Harry Joe (Harry Joe "Coco" Brown) *real estate developer*
Clark, Ric *real estate company executive*
Cohen, Irving Elias *real estate executive*
Cohen, Michael T. *real estate company executive*
Consolo, Faith Hope *real estate broker*
Corcoran, Barbara *real estate company executive*
Farley, Katherine G. *real estate company executive*
Fox-Freund, Barbara Susan *real estate company executive*
Freedman, Robert L. *real estate company executive*
Friedrich, Dennis H. *real estate company executive*
Furnary, Stephen J. *real estate company executive*
Garfield, Leslie Jerome *real estate executive*
Gochberg, Thomas *real estate investor, financial executive*
Goldenberg, Charles Lawrence *real estate company executive*
Gosin, Barry M. *real estate company executive*
Grau, Marcy Beinish *real estate broker, former investment banker*
Grossman, Charles *real estate company executive*
Gural, Jeffrey R. *real estate company executive*
Hemmerdinger, H. Dale *real estate executive*
Hernstadt, Judith Filenbaum *city planner, real estate executive, broadcasting executive*
Himmel, Leslie Wohlman *real estate manager*
Host, Stig *real estate company executive, oil company executive*
Howell, William Page *real estate company executive*
Kalikow, Peter Stephen *real estate developer, former newspaper owner, publisher*
Kendall Levine, Judy *real estate broker, interior designer, writer*
Kuhn, James D. *real estate company executive*
Laurie, Craig *real estate company executive*
Lavori, Nora *real estate executive, lawyer*
MacDonald, Scott *real estate company executive*
Marder, John G. *real estate investor, marketing consultant, corporate director, bison rancher*
Marshall, Alton Garwood *real estate counselor*
Mirante, Arthur J., II, *real estate company executive*
Mosler, Bruce E. *real estate company executive*
Newman, William *real estate executive*
Nolan, Christopher Aloysius, III, *real estate developer, architect*
Perry-Widney, Marilyn (Marilyn Perry) *international finance and real estate executive, television producer*
Petz, Edwin V. *real estate executive, lawyer*
Phillips, Karen A. *urban planner*
Rampe, Kevin M. *real estate developer*
Rose, Daniel *real estate company executive, consultant*
Rose, Elihu *real estate executive*
Ruben, Lawrence *real estate developer, building company executive, lawyer*
Rufrano, Glenn *real estate company executive*
Schlang, David *real estate company executive, lawyer*
Scott, Stanley DeForest *real estate executive, former lithography company executive*
Siderow, Neil *real estate company executive*
Siegel, Stephen *real estate company executive*
Silverstein, Larry A. *real estate developer*
Smith, Andrew Alfred, Jr., *urban planner*
Speyer, Jerry I. *real estate company executive*
Stacom, Darcy A. *real estate company executive*
Stein, Ellen Gail *executive manager*
Stern, Leonard Norman *real estate developer, former pet supply manufacturing company executive*
Streicker, John H. *real estate company executive*
Sullivan, Frank L., Jr., *real estate company executive*
Thomas, Violeta de los Angeles *real estate broker*
Tighe, Mary Ann *real estate company executive*
Tishman, John L. *realty and construction company executive*
Toote, Gloria E. A. *real estate developer, lawyer, columnist*
Urstadt, Charles Deane *real estate executive*
Weiss, Donald S. *real estate developer*
Wolf, Peter Michael *investment manager, writer*
Zuccotti, John Eugene *real estate company executive*

Pawling
Wood, Christopher L.J. *real estate executive*

Poughkeepsie
Gold, Burton *real estate developer*

Rochester
Pettinella, Edward *real estate company executive*

Walker, Michael Charles, Sr., *retirement services executive*

Rye
Feinberg, Norman Maurice *real estate company executive*

Stony Brook
Koppelman, Lee Edward *regional planner, educator*

Syracuse
De Long, Jacob Edward *real estate broker*
Whaley, Ross Samuel *environmentalist, educator*

Westchester
Kepcher, Carolyn *real estate company executive*

White Plains
McCarthy, John Robert *real estate company officer*

NORTH CAROLINA

Asheville
Sarai, Darshan Singh *environmentalist, entomologist*

Chapel Hill
Chapman, Robert Lee, III, *real estate developer*
Weiss, Shirley F. *urban and regional planner, economist, educator*

Charlotte
Cox, Linda Smoak *real estate broker*
Eski, John Robert *residential appraiser, real estate consultant*
Harris, John W. *real estate company executive*
Wiggins, Nancy Bowen *real estate broker, market research consultant*

Murphy
Pezzella, Jerry James, Jr., *investment and real estate executive*

Raleigh
Fritsch, Edward *real estate company executive*
Hunt, Kemp Neal *real estate company executive*
Willer, Edward Herman *real estate broker*

Statesville
Redman, William Walter, Jr., *realtor*

NORTH DAKOTA

Bismarck
Clairmont, William Edward *real estate developer*

OHIO

Akron
Peavy, Homer Louis, Jr., *real estate executive, accountant*

Amelia
Hayden, John W. *real estate company executive*

Beachwood
Jacobstein, David M. *real estate company executive*
Wolstein, Scott Alan *real estate company executive*

Cincinnati
Dunigan, Dennis Wayne *real estate executive*
Randman, Barry I. *real estate developer*
Schuler, Robert Leo *appraiser, consultant*

Cleveland
Gould, Bonnie M(arincic) *realtor*
Jacobs, Richard E. *real estate company executive, sports team owner*
Maier, Howard Robert *urban planner, government agency administrator*

Columbus
Coopersmith, Jeffrey Alan *real estate developer*
Glimcher, Herbert *real estate company executive*
Glimcher, Michael P. *real estate company executive*
Janik, Melinda A. *real estate company executive*

Dayton
Stout, Donald Everett *real estate developer, environmental preservationist*
Wertz, Kenneth Dean *real estate executive*

Dublin
Donnell, Jon M. *real estate executive*

Hebron
Slater, Wanda Marie Worth *property manager*

Hudson
Stec, John Zygmunt *real estate executive*

Richmond Heights
Friedman, Jeffrey I. *real estate company executive*

Shaker Heights
Solganik, Marvin *real estate executive*
Winter, John Alexander *realtor, real estate appraiser*

Shelby
Phelan, Martha Armstrong *realtor*

Toledo
Batt, Nick *property and investment executive*

Wilmington
Evans, Elizabeth Ann West *retired real estate agent*

Youngstown
Camacci, Michael A. *commercial real estate broker, development consultant*

OKLAHOMA

Oklahoma City
Bradford, Dennis Doyle *real estate broker, developer*
Mathews, Louise Robison *real estate broker, writer, historian*

Tulsa
Vincent, Carl G., Jr., *real estate portfolio manager*

Warr Acres
Phillips, Richard Carey *real estate executive*

OREGON

Gladstone
Beals, Herbert Kyle *community planner, historian, consultant*

Portland
Cogan, Arnold M. *planning consultant*
Packard, Robert Goodale, III, *urban planner*
Standring, James Douglas *real estate developer*

Springfield
Davis, George Donald *executive land use policy consultant*
Jennison, Brian (Lester) *environmental specialist*

PENNSYLVANIA

Allentown
Saab, Deanne Keltum *real estate appraiser, real estate broker*

Ardmore
Waetzman, Larry Samuel *planning company executive*

Blue Bell
Deschaine, Barbara Ralph *retired real estate broker*

Camp Hill
Kleiman, Richard *realtor*

Chadds Ford
Moore, Bruce E. *real estate company executive*

Downingtown
Hankowsky, William P. *real estate company executive*

Doylestown
Long, Ronald Alex *real estate and financial consultant, lawyer, educator*

Erie
Gottschalk, Frank Klaus *real estate company executive*

Huntingdon Valley
Barzilay, Zvi *real estate executive*

Indiana
Masilela, Calvin Onias *land use planner, educator*

Johnstown
Stevens, Terry L. *realty company executive*

Meadville
Cable, Mabel Elizabeth *urban planner, artist*

Philadelphia
Bacon, Edmund Norwood *city planner*
Binswanger, Frank G., Jr., *realty company executive*
Binswanger, John K. *real estate company executive*
Mellman, Leonard *real estate investor and advisor*
Mendelow, Clive G. *real estate company executive*
Peck, Robert McCracken *naturalist, science historian, writer*
Pew, Robert Anderson *retired real estate and equipment leasing corporation officer*
Plumer, Alvin H. (Bud) *realtor*
Rubin, George *real estate executive*
Rubin, Ronald *real estate executive*
Weller, Jonathan *real estate investment company executive*

Plymouth Meeting
Marr, Christopher P. *real estate company executive*

Somerset
Barkman, Annette Shaulis *real estate management executive*

Southeastern
Zlotolow-Stambler, Ernest *real estate executive, architectural executive*

West Chester
Knuth Fischer, Cynthia Strout *environmental consultant*

Willow Grove
Moore, Norma Jean *real estate broker*

RHODE ISLAND

Foster
Sawyer, Mildred Clementina *retired real estate agent*

Providence
Hitt, Mary Frances Lyster *environmentalist, deacon*

Wakefield
Morrison, Fred Beverly *real estate consultant*

Warwick
Lachapelle, Cleo Edward *retired real estate broker*

SOUTH CAROLINA

Charleston
Limehouse, Harry Bancroft, Jr., *real estate developer, transportation consultant*

Columbia
Sloan, Saundra Jennings *real estate company executive*

Donalds
Armstrong, Alfreda Juanita *real estate executive*

Easley
Spearman, Patsy Cordle *real estate broker*

Greenville
Shockley, Milton M., Jr., *real estate brokerage executive*

Hilton Head Island
Brown, Adolph Dupree *real estate developer*
Gruchacz, Robert S. *real estate executive*

Spartanburg
Carroll-Belenchia, Elizabeth *international corporate realtor*

SOUTH DAKOTA

Rapid City
Hamilton, Douglas Warren *real estate executive*

Sioux Falls
Kuhle, Shirley Jean *real estate appraiser*
Wilkes, Jeffrey Blaine *real estate appraiser*

TENNESSEE

Chattanooga
Foy, John N. *real estate company executive*
Lebovitz, Charles B. *real estate company executive*
Lebovitz, Stephen D. *property manager*

Elizabethton
Hardin, Gerald Larson *city planner and community developer, educator*

Kingsport
Bailey, William Henry *real estate appraiser*

Memphis
Edwards, Martin *real estate company executive*
Haizlip, Henry Hardin, Jr., *real estate consultant, former banker*

Nashville
Beck, Robert Beryl *real estate executive*
Boyer, James Floyd *land surveyor, state legislator*
Greer, Herschel Lynn, Jr., *real estate executive*

TEXAS

Addison
Cotter, Ka *real estate company executive*
Hinckley, Jim *real estate company executive*
Kimbler, Larry Bernard *real estate executive, accountant*
Ragusa, Elysia *real estate company executive*
Staubach, Roger Thomas *real estate executive, former professional football player*

Argyle
Stallings, Frank, Jr., *realtor, director*

Austin
Anderson, Mo *real estate company executive*
Keller, Gary *real estate company executive*
Stoll, William Hermann *real estate company executive*
Willis, Mark *real estate company executive*

Boerne
Daugherty, Linda Hagaman *real estate company executive*

Calvert
Alemán, Marthanne Payne *environmental planner, consultant*

Carrollton
Lucas, Jay R. *real estate company executive*

College Station
Jackson, Thomas O. *real estate appraiser, urban planner*

Dallas
Brown, Stephen Bryan *real estate editor*
Byrne, Tim *real estate company executive*
Crow, F. Trammell *real estate company executive*
Davis, Nancy *real estate company executive*
Doran, Mark Richard *real estate financial executive*
Duvall, William (Bill) C. *real estate company executive*
Eller, Timothy R. (Tim Eller) *real estate company executive, construction executive*
Ernest, Michael A. *real estate company executive*
Marlow, Patricia Bair Bond *realtor*
Miller, Geraldine (Tincy) *real estate company executive, educational association administrator*
Perot, H. Ross, Jr., *real estate developer, former sports team executive*
Pogue, A Mack *real estate company executive*
Sulentic, Robert E. *real estate company executive*
Weitzman, Herbert D. *real estate company executive*
Williams, J. McDonald *real estate development company executive*

El Paso
Hunt, Woody L. *real estate executive*
Keller, Robert M. *real estate broker*
Lyle, James Arthur *real estate broker*

Fort Worth
Alberts, Dennis H. *real estate company executive*
Goff, John C. *real estate company executive*

Galveston
McLeod, E. Douglas *real estate developer, lawyer*

Granbury
Almy, Earle Vaughn, Jr., (Buddy Almy) *real estate executive*

Hillsboro
McClendon, Fred Vernon *real estate professional, business consultant, equine and realty appraiser, financial consultant*

Houston
Alexander, Andrew M. *real estate investment company executive*
Alexander, Stanford *real estate investment company executive*
Campo, Richard J. *real estate company executive*
Debrovner, Martin *real estate company executive*
Duncan, Robert *real estate company executive*
Goldsmith, Billy Joe *real estate broker, rancher*
Gregory, William Roger *real estate company executive*
Hale, C. Robert, III, *real estate company executive*
Harding, Steve *real estate company executive*
Heard, Larry *real estate company executive*
Hines, Jeffrey C. *real estate executive*
Johnson, C. Hastings *real estate executive*
Kirk, Rick U. *real estate company executive*
Kollaer, Jim C. *real estate executive, architect*
Lanier, Robert C. (Bob Lanier) *real estate owner, developer, former mayor*
Leluer, Kenneth Eugene *economic consultant*
Meyer, Marjorie Jean *real estate manager*
Oden, Keith D. *real estate company executive*
Richter, Stephen C. *real estate company executive*
Ryan, Thomas L. *environmentalist*
Steen, Dennis M. *real estate company executive*
Strudler, Robert Jacob *real estate development executive*
Waltrip, Robert L. *environmentalist*

Irving
Stone, R. Dary *real estate executive*

Katy
Sadowski, Chester Philip, Jr., *real estate executive*

Lubbock
Wall, Betty Jane *real estate consultant*

Mico
Shockey, Thomas Edward *real estate executive, engineer*

Plano
Ford, H. Ross, III, *real estate company executive*
Hilton, Steven J. *real estate executive*
Landon, John R. *real estate executive*

Port Aransas
Turner, Elizabeth Adams Noble (Betty Turner) *real estate company executive*

Rowlett
Efrussy, Alan Maurice *urban planner*

San Antonio
Bryan, Richard Ray *retired real estate and construction executive*
Condos, Barbara Seale *real estate broker, developer, investor*
Sinkin, Fay Marie *environmentalist*
Williamson, Fletcher Phillips *real estate broker*

Temple
Moore, Joanna Elizabeth *real estate professional*

Waco
Rusling, Barbara N(eubert) *real estate broker*

UTAH

Midvale
Teerlink, J(oseph) Leland *real estate developer*

Park City
Corradini, Deedee *real estate company executive, former mayor*

Santa Clara
Tolbert, Beth Willden *real estate company executive, real estate broker*

VERMONT

Colchester
Sweeny, Arthur, III, *realtor*

Middlebury
Jenks-Jay, Nan *environmentalist educator*

Randolph
French, Patsy J. *property manager, state representative*

VIRGINIA

Alexandria
Blair, Bryce *real estate company executive*
Borum, Olin Henry *realtor, former government official*
Michael, Ann Dozier Marino *real estate broker*
Sargeant, Thomas *real estate company executive*

Annandale
Hollis, Linda Eardley *urban planning consultant*

Bristow
Mac Donald, Margaret Clark *retired real estate agent*

Chesterfield
Jacobson, Thomas Elton *suburban planner, county official*

Dumfries
Thrall, Eileen Fowler *real estate broker, government staff official*

Fairfax
Yeonas, George C. *real estate executive*

Lansdowne
Fujishiro, Katakazu Kenneth *retired urban and regional planner, engineer*

Mc Lean
Alberts, Henry Celler *real estate company executive*
McLean, Robert, III, *real estate company executive*
Nobil, James Howard, Jr., *real estate investor, developer, consultant, broker*
Talbot, Martha Hayne *conservationist, biologist*

Mechanicsville
Liggan, Joanne Dunkley *realtor*

Nellysford
McWane, Joyce Hobbs *title company executive*

Newport News
Goldberg, Stanley Irwin *real estate company executive*

Norfolk
Nusbaum, Alan B. *real estate executive*

Reston
Van Putten, Mark *environmentalist*

Richmond
Foster, Charles H. *real estate executive*
Girone, Joan Christine Cruse *realtor, former county official*
Plaisted, Harris Merrill, III, *real estate executive*
Tuck, Grayson Edwin *real estate agent, former natural gas transmission executive*

Virginia Beach
Divaris, Gerald S. *real estate executive*

WASHINGTON

Bellevue
Scott, John Lennox *real estate company executive*

Edmonds
Bell, Nancy Lee Hoyt *real estate investor, middle school educator, volunteer*

Federal Way
Fulton, Daniel S. *corporate real estate executive*

Oakville
Magnus, Lennea D. *community development planner*

Olympia
Hong, Rani Jenelle *real estate broker*

Renton
Kredlo, Thomas Andrew *real estate appraiser*

Seattle
Ecklund, Ralph Earl *property manager*
Eskelin, John Thurston *city planner*
Sander, Susan Berry *environmental planning engineering corporation executive*
Sasaki, Tsutomu (Tom Sasaki) *real estate company executive, international trading company executive, consultant*
Sauter, Michael Joseph *real estate company executive*
Wesley, Virginia Anne *real estate property manager*

Sequim
Jackson, Patrick Joseph *real estate company officer*

Spanaway
McKinnon, James Buckner *real estate sales executive, writer, researcher*

WEST VIRGINIA

Weirton
Diniaco, Gus G. *retired real estate appraiser*

WISCONSIN

Barron
Kurschner, David L. *realtor, small business owner*

Beaver Dam
Butterbrodt, John Ervin *real estate executive*

Belgium
Sullivan, Patricia W. (Terry Sullivan) *real estate trainer*

Lake Mills
Lazaris, Pamela Adriane *community planning and development consultant*

Madison
Malkasian, William *real estate company executive*
Mullins, Jerome Joseph *real estate developer, consulting engineer*
Ring, Gerald J. *real estate developer, insurance executive*
Vandell, Kerry Dean *real estate and urban economics educator*

Wauwatosa
Franke, Brent Douglas *real estate/insurance executive*
Barrere, Jamie Newton *real estate executive*

TERRITORIES OF THE UNITED STATES

PUERTO RICO

York
Kay, Jack Robert *real estate company executive*

VIRGIN ISLANDS

Saint Thomas
Meyers, Stuart Irwin *real estate developer*

St Thomas
de Jongh, John P., Jr., *real estate company executive*
Dudley, George H.T. *real estate company executive*
Williams, Wesley S., Jr., *real estate company executive*

CANADA

ALBERTA

Calgary
McEwen, Alexander Campbell *cadastral studies educator, former Canadian government official, land administration consultant*
Milavsky, Harold Phillip *real estate executive*

NOVA SCOTIA

Stellarton
Sobey, Donald Creighton Rae *real estate developer*

ONTARIO

Etobicoke
McIntyre, John George Wallace *real estate development and management consultant*

Newmarket
Wood, Neil Roderick *real estate development company executive*

Ottawa
Gordon, Steve *real estate executive*

Toronto
Arnell, Gordon Edwin *real estate development company executive*
Ballett, David Howard *property management executive*
Braithwaite, J. Lorne *real estate executive*
Carrothers, Gerald Arthur Patrick *environmental and city planning educator*
Dimma, William Andrew *real estate executive*
Farley, Tom *real estate company executive*

QUEBEC

Montreal
Gabbour, Iskandar *city and regional planning educator*

MEXICO

Garza Garcia
Gustafson, Eric William *real estate investor, wildlife habitat conservationist*

BULGARIA

Sofia
Exerowa, Dotchi Russeva *chemist, researcher*

ENGLAND

London
Hall, Sir Peter Geoffrey *urban and regional planning educator*

HONG KONG

Hong Kong
Kee, Lee Shau *real estate developer*

MONACO

Monte Carlo
Lovett, Laurence Dow *retired real estate and steamship executive*

SPAIN

Adeje
Grindley, Bruce Alan *real estate agency executive*

ADDRESS UNPUBLISHED

Aulbach, George Louis *retired real estate company executive*
Austin, Grant William *real estate appraiser*
Baiman, Gail *real estate broker*
Bartlett, Arthur Eugene *real estate company executive*
Bartolini, Bruce Anthony *real estate executive*
Beal, Merrill David *conservationist, museum director*
Bednarowski, Keith *construction, design and real estate executive*
Bergau, Frank Conrad *real estate, commercial and investment properties executive*
Berliner, Ruth Shirley *real estate company executive*
Bernhardt, Arthur Dieter *building industry executive, consultant*
Bonin, Paul Joseph *real estate and banking executive*

Broek, Howard Windolph *real estate executive*
Brooks, Michael Paul *retired urban planning educator*
Broughton, James Walter *real estate development executive, consultant*
Bryan, Mary Jo W. *realtor, artist, art educator*
Campbell, Jane Turner *retired realtor, retired secondary school educator, retired adult education educator*
Chase, J. Vincent *shopping center executive*
Chesler, Doris Adelle *real estate professional*
Clancy, John Patrick *real estate company executive*
Clark, Philip Hart *retired urban and regional planner*
Cohen, Stanley Alvin *land use planner*
Colton, Victor Robert *real estate developer, investor*
Corey, Kenneth Edward *urban planning and geography educator, researcher*
Corkran, Virginia B. *retired real estate agent*
Darlington, Hilda Walker *real estate company officer*
Dasso, Jerome Joseph *real estate educator*
Davis, Mary Byrd *conservationist, researcher*
DeBock, Ronald Gene *real estate company executive*
DeWitt, Sallie Lee *realtor*
Dickey, Robert Marvin (Rick Dickey) *property manager*
Dillon, Phillip Michael *real estate developer, construction executive*
Elkin, Norman *urban planner*
Ellett, Alan Sidney *real estate development company executive*
Ellis, William Ben *environmental educator, retired utility executive*
Engels, Beatrice Ann *retired real estate company executive, poet, artist*
Estrin, Richard William *real estate broker, retired newspaper editor*
Fino, Marie Georgette Keck *retired real estate broker*
Fischer, Michael Ludwig *environmental executive*
Fournier, Walter Frank *real estate executive*
Gasper, Ruth Eileen *real estate executive*
Gilbert, Frederick E. *development planner, Africanist, consultant*
Goddess, Lynn Barbara *commercial real estate broker*
Greenberg, Judith Ann *real estate developer*
Hakala, Karen Louise *retired real estate administrator*
Hedrich, Cleda Pollard *real estate broker, writer*
Hietala, Valerie Grace *realtor, environmentalist, educator*
Holleb, Doris B. *urban planner, economist*
House, Sherman August *conservationist, emergency medical technician*
Hufschmidt, Maynard Michael *resources planning educator*
Johnson, Kay Durbahn *real estate manager, consultant*
Kohn, Robert Samuel, Jr., *real estate investment consultant*
Kremer, Honor Frances (Noreen Kremer) *real estate broker, small business owner*
Lamy, M(ary) Rebecca *consultant, land developer, government official*
Lehman, Joan Alice *real estate executive*
Levine, Michael Joseph *economic development executive*
Lowenthal, Susan *realtor, artist*
MacNeill, James William *international environment management consultant*
Maguire, Robert Francis, III, *real estate investor*
Maier, Robert Henry *real estate executive*
Mariucci, Anne L. *real estate development company executive*
Mercurio, Renard Michael *real estate corporation executive*
Messenkopf, Eugene John *real estate developer and hotel executive*
Meyer, Daniel Kramer *real estate executive*
Michael, George T. *real estate manager*
Miranda, Daniel Frank *lawyer, real estate executive*
Mohamed, Joseph, Sr., *real estate broker, farmer*
Payne, Daniel Harold (Harold Payne) *real estate developer, small business owner*
Peacock, Christopher A. *former real estate company executive*
Pence, Jean Virginia (Jean Pence) *retired real estate broker*
Perkins, Charles Theodore *real estate developer, consultant*
Potter, J. Stewart *property manager*
Prentiss, Michael Vernon *urban planner*
Rassman, Joel H. *real estate company executive, accountant*
Rau, David Edward *financial and real estate consultant*
Reschke, Michael W. *real estate executive*
Ridloff, Richard *real estate investment advisor, lawyer, consultant*
Riss, Robert Bailey *real estate investor*
Ritchey, Camilla Collett *real estate executive*
Rosenfeld, Mark Kenneth *real estate developer*
Ross, Beverley Long *real estate broker*
Schneider, Rita Joyce *property management company executive, real estate broker, mortgage broker*
Smith, Robert J., Jr., *real estate executive*
Snook, Paul *real estate company executive*
Struhl, Stanley Frederick *real estate developer*
Sweeney, Gerard H. *real estate company executive*
Taubman, A. Alfred *real estate developer*
Trump, Donald John *real estate developer*
Voell, Richard Allen *retired private investor*
Wall, Jeff F. *urban planner*
Weekley, David *real estate developer*
Weiss, Scott Alan *commercial real estate consultant*
Williams, Phyllis Cutforth *retired realtor*
Woods, Sandra Kay *real estate executive*

RELIGION

UNITED STATES

ALABAMA

Andalusia
Patterson, Edwin *minister*

Birmingham
Foley, David E. *bishop*
Hull, William Edward *theology educator*
Loftin, Sister Mary Frances *religious organization administrator*
Roby, Jasper *bishop*
Scales, William Clinton, Sr., *minister, small business owner*
Zahl, Paul Francis Matthew *dean*

Cordova
Anthony, Yancey Lamar *minister*

Gadsden
Arnold, Don Carl *pastor, religious organization executive*

Greensboro
Massey, James Earl *clergyman, educator*

Hayden
King, Vickie Ruth *minister, shop owner*

Huntsville
Fargerson, Gordon Shawn *minister*

Mobile
Lipscomb, Oscar Hugh *archbishop*

Union Grove
Drew, Thomas Paul *chaplain*

ALASKA

Anchorage
Charles, George P. *religious studies educator*
Fleming, Carolyn Elizabeth *religious organization administrator, interior designer*

ARIZONA

Duncan
Ouzts, Eugene Thomas *minister, secondary education educator*

Green Valley
Pike, George Harold, Jr., *religious organization executive, clergyman*

Hereford
Seeland, Arthur David *bishop*

Phoenix
Kuzma, George Martin *retired bishop*
Olmsted, Thomas James *archbishop*
Whitlow, William La Fond *minister, theology school planter*

Scottsdale
Coutts, Lawrence Robert *publisher*
Kaufman, Jeffrey Allen *publisher*
Kilgore, L(eRoy) Wilson *minister*
Sapp, Donald Gene *retired minister*
Stines, Fred, Jr., *publisher*

Sun City
Cooper, Vivian M. *minister, writer*
Hamilton, Ronald Ray *minister*
Lapsley, James Norvell, Jr., *minister, pastoral theology educator*
Randall, Claire *church executive*

Tucson
Perret, Gary William *priest, educator*

ARKANSAS

Conway
Leffler, Jean Riise *religious organization administrator*

El Dorado
Lee, Vernon Roy *minister*

Little Rock
McKnight, William Edwin *minister*

Marion
Hughes, Michael Randolph *evangelist*

Siloam Springs
Lewis, Cecil Dwain *minister*

Subiaco
Pirrera, Aaron Charles *priest, headmaster*

CALIFORNIA

Acton
Butman, Harry Raymond *clergyman, writer*

Altadena
Willans, Jean Stone *bishop, religious organization executive*

Angwin
Maxwell, Donald Malcolm *clergyman, religious educator*

Azusa
Vest, R. Lamar *church administrator*

Bakersfield
Frazier, Jo Frances *religious organization administrator*
Zarra, Ernest Joseph, III, *educator, researcher*

Berkeley
Gall, Donald Arthur *minister*
Mudge, Lewis Seymour *theologian, educator, university dean*
Renz, Christopher David *priest*
Welch, Claude (Claude Raymond Welch) *theology educator*

Big Sur
Wong, Joseph H. *religious organization administrator, theology studies educator*

Burbank
Bower, Richard James *minister*

Camarillo
Ford, Paul Francis *theology studies educator, musician*

Castro Valley
Morrison, Glenn Leslie *minister*

Chino Hills
Nash, Sylvia Dotseth *consultant*

Claremont
Genung, Dan Baldwin *minister, writer*
Reynolds, Margaret Ann *minister, educator*
Sanders, James Alvin *minister, religious studies educator*

Clovis
Smith, William Clarke *clergyman*

Costa Mesa
Ratcliff, Donald Earl *minister, educator*
Williams, William Corey *theology educator, consultant*

Del Mar
Randall, Chandler Corydon *church rector*

Duarte
Driskill, James Lawrence *minister*
Probst, John Elwin *chaplain, minister*

El Cajon
Bazzi, Michael J. *priest, educator*

El Cerrito
Maxwell, John E. *priest, educator*

El Monte
Hwang, Tzu-Yang *minister*

Elk Grove
Vang, Timothy Teng *religious organization administrator*

Escondido
Linzey, Verna May *minister, writer*

Etna
Auxentios, *clergyman*

Fair Oaks
Davidson, Diane (Marie Davidson) *publisher*

Fountain Valley
Einstein, Stephen Jan *rabbi*

Fresno
Hunter, Tracy Alexander *priest*
O'Berg, Robert Myron *minister*
Steinbock, John Thomas *bishop*
Xiong, Tousu Saydangnmvang *minister*

Garden Grove
Schuller, Robert Harold *minister, writer*

Happy Camp
Black, Barbara Ann *publisher*

Irvine
Rachlis, Arnold Israel *rabbi, religion educator*
Reisman, Richard S. *publisher*

La Jolla
Freedman, David Noel *religious studies educator*
Waddy, Lawrence Heber *religious writer*

La Quinta
Mathre, Lawrence Gerhard *minister, federal agency administrator*

Laguna Hills
Wheatley, Melvin Ernest, Jr., *retired bishop*

Lake Forest
Kabilamany, Caleb K. *religious studies educator, civil engineer, consultant*

Lakewood
Carr, Firpo Wycoff *bible scholar, educator, writer*

Loma Linda
Lewis, Victor Wayne, I, *minister*

Long Beach
Lowentrout, Peter Murray *religious studies educator*

Los Alamitos
Booth, John Nicholls *minister, writer, photographer*

Los Angeles
Arzube, Juan Alfredo *bishop*
Berenbaum, Michael Gary *theology educator*
Boyd, Malcolm *minister, writer*
Breuer, Stephen Ernest *religious organization administrator*
Chedid, John G. *retired bishop*
Crossley, John Parshley, Jr., *religious studies educator, researcher, consultant*
Fitzgerald, Tikhon (Lee R. H. Fitzgerald) *bishop*
Freehling, Allen Isaac *rabbi*
Hudson, Christopher John *publisher*
Knight, Henry L. *minister*
Mahony, Roger Michael *archbishop*
Mc Pherson, Rolf Kennedy *clergyman, religious organization administrator*
O'Connor, Kevin Thomas *religious organization administrator*
Phillips, Keith Wendall *minister*
Pressman, Jacob *retired rabbi*
Raymond, Wilfred J. *priest, educator*
VanderWilt, Jeffrey T. *theology studies educator*
Williams, Ronald Dean *minister, religious organization administrator*

Los Gatos
Sawyer, Malcolm James, Jr., *religious studies educator*

Monterey Park
Szeto, Paul (Cheuk-Ching Szeto) *religious mission executive*

Oakland
Jakubowsky, Frank Raymond *religious writer*

Orange
Brown, Tod David *bishop*
Mc Farland, Norman Francis *bishop*

Palm Desert
Cedar, Paul Arnold *church executive, minister*
Dugan, Robert Perry, Jr., *retired minister, religious organization administrator*
Ponder, Catherine *clergywoman, author*
Stenhouse, Everett Ray *clergy administrator*

Palm Springs
Jones, Milton Wakefield *publisher*
Martin, Ann Bodenhamer *minister, writer*
Rupracht, William George *chaplain*

Palo Alto
Forbes, Alfred Dean *religious studies researcher*

Pasadena
Shuster, Marguerite *minister, educator*
Torres, Ralph Chon *minister*

Pittsburg
Schmalenberger, Jerry Lew *pastor, religious studies educator*

Pixely
Golden, Raymond Lee *retired theology studies educator, retired minister*

Portola Valley
Garsh, Thomas Burton *publisher*

Redding
Nicholas, David Robert *minister, college president*

Redlands
Huntley, William Barney *religious studies professor*

Reedley
Dick, Henry Henry *minister*

Sacramento
Cole, Glen David *minister*
Quinn, Francis A. *bishop*

San Bruno
Rozman, James D. *church administrator*

San Diego
Bauer, Judy Marie *minister*
Brom, Robert H. *bishop*
Cabrera, Quincy Rodolfo *minister, educator*
Downing, David Charles *retired minister*
Fleischmann, Paul *religious organization administrator, minister*
Hunt, Barnabas John *priest, religious organization administrator*
Jenson, Ronald Allen *religious executive, educator*
Lynberg, Terence Ellsworth *minister, education educator*
Owen-Towle, Carolyn Sheets *clergywoman*
Skelly, John Joshua *retired clergyman, fundraiser*

San Francisco
Brickner, David *religious organization administrator, consultant*
Brown, Amos Cleophilus *minister*
DuBose, Francis Marquis *clergyman*
Grohe, Linda Squires *dean*
Kelly, James Anthony *priest*
Kendall, Robert Daniel *priest, theology educator*
Levada, William Joseph *archbishop*
Reed, Robert Daniel *publisher*
Rosen, Moishe *religious organization founder*
Sparer, Malcolm Martin *rabbi*

San Jose
Chae, Yoon Kwon *minister, educator*
Es-Haq, Fereidoun *minister, marriage and family therapist*

San Juan Bautista
Fort, Robert Bradley *minister*

San Juan Capistrano
Warren, Rick Duane *minister, writer*

San Rafael
Trepp, Leo *rabbi*

Santa Barbara
Albanese, Catherine *religious studies educator*
Campbell, Robert Charles *minister, theology educator*
Friedland, Roger *religious studies educator, writer*

Santa Rosa
Walsh, Daniel Francis *bishop*

Santee
Morris, Henry Madison, III, *minister, speaker, writer, consultant*

Seaside
Stringer, Charles Columbus, Jr., *minister, protective services official, writer*

Solana Beach
Friedman, Maurice Stanley *religious educator*

Sonora
Chandler, E(dwin) Russell *clergyman, writer*

Thousand Oaks
Hudson, Barbara *religious writer, actor*

Turlock
Stensether, John Eldon *minister*

Tustin
Crouch, Paul Franklin *minister, religious organization administrator*

Upland
Jordan, Charles Wesley *retired bishop*

Vallejo
McGowan, Thomas Randolph *retired religious organization administrator*

West Hollywood
Eger, Denise Leese *rabbi*
Perry, Troy D. *clergyman, religious organization administrator*
Wilson, Nancy Linda *religious organization administrator*

COLORADO

Arvada
Howard, Barry Christopher *minister*
Pettit, Claud Martin *religious organization administrator*

Aurora
Nichols, Clyde Richard *minister, consumer products company executive*
Stifel, Frederick Benton *minister, biochemist, nutritionist*

Buena Vista
Goddard, Hazel Bryan *religious organization administrator*

Canon City
Williamson, Edward Henry *chaplain, army officer*

Colorado Springs
Freeman, J. P. Ladyhawk *vicar, underwater exploration, security and transportation executive, educator, fashion model, legislative advocate*
Hanifen, Richard Charles *retired bishop*
Johnson, Henry Fred *clergy*
Loux, Gordon Dale *company executive*
Pickle, Joseph Wesley, Jr., *religious studies educator*

Denver
Brownlee, Judith Marilyn *priestess, psychotherapist, psychic*
Burrell, Calvin Archie *minister*
Chaput, Charles J. *archbishop*
Sheeran, Michael John Leo *priest, college administrator*

Dillon
Follett, Robert John Richard *publisher*

Fort Collins
Chorpenning, H. R., III *minister*
Rolston, Holmes, III *theologian, educator, philosopher*

Lafayette
Short, Ray Everett *minister, sociology educator emeritus, author, lecturer*

Lakewood
Barger, Louise Baldwin *religious organization administrator*
Hickman, Ruth Virginia *Bible educator*

Northglenn
Winter, William Paul, Jr., *ministry director*

CONNECTICUT

Bridgeport
Black, Hillel Moses *publisher*
Lori, William E. *bishop*

East Hartford
Scholsky, Martin Joseph *priest*

Greenwich
Johnson, Herbert Michael *publisher*
Moore, John Plunkett Dennis *publisher*

Hamden
Forman, Charles William *religious studies educator*
Weinstein, Stanley *Buddhist studies educator*

Hartford
Cronin, Daniel Anthony *archbishop*

Macaluso, Christie A. *bishop*
Markham, Ian Stephen *theology studies educator, dean*
Petty, M. S. Marty *publisher*
Winter, Miriam Therese (Gloria Frances Winter) *nun, religious education educator*

Lyme
Bessie, Simon Michael *publisher*

Middletown
Crites, Stephen Decatur *religion educator*
Hoffmann, Leonard A *church administrator, director*
Rockwood, Irving E., Jr., *publisher*
Swain, James Barrett *pastor, education educator*

Monroe
Davis, Bobby J. *pastor, family therapist*

New Haven
Malherbe, Abraham Johannes, VI, *religion educator, writer*
Meeks, Wayne A. *religious studies educator*
Wilson, Robert Rutherford *religious studies educator*

Norwalk
Olmstead-Sawyer, Jeanette *pastor*

Norwich
Cote, Michael Richard *bishop*
Hart, Daniel Anthony *bishop*
Weinberg, Norbert *rabbi*

Plantsville
Roy, Ralph Lord *clergyman*

Ridgefield
Davie, Malcolm Henderson *minister, city official*

Shelton
Wham, William Neil *publisher*

Torrington
Drobena, Thomas John *minister, educator*

Wilton
Davis, Joel *publisher*
Steinfeld, Thomas Albert *retired publisher*

DELAWARE

Wilmington
Saltarelli, Michael A. *priest*

DISTRICT OF COLUMBIA

Washington
Allen, William Jere *minister*
Apostolos-Cappadona, Diane Pan *religion and art educator*
Baxter, Nathan Dwight *dean*
Burke, John *priest*
Di Lella, Alexander Anthony *biblical studies educator*
Dunn, James Milton *religious organization administrator*
Dunton, James Raynor *publisher*
Fitzmyer, Joseph Augustine *retired theology educator, priest*
Godsey, John Drew *minister, theology educator emeritus*
Harvey, Jane Hull *church administrator*
Height, Dorothy I. *association executive*
Hellwig, Monika Konrad *organization executive, theology educator*
Hickey, James Aloysius Cardinal *emeritus archbishop*
Hug, James Edwin *religious organization executive*
Irwin, Paul Garfield *minister, social services executive*
Maldonado, F. César *priest, educator*
Marrett, Michael McFarlene *chaplain*
McCarrick, Theodore Edgar Cardinal *archbishop*
McCrabb, Donald Raymond *pastoral field educator*
Mead, Christina Dykstra *church administrator*
Novak, Michael (Michael John Novak) *religion educator, author, editor*
O'Brien, Edwin Frederick *archbishop*
Pitts, Tyrone S. *reverend*
Romig, Edgar Dutcher *clergyman*
Roque, Francis Xavier *auxiliary bishop*
Ross, Robinette Davis *publisher*
Rowson, Richard Cavanagh *publisher*
Saperstein, Marc Eli *religious studies educator, rabbi*
Shearin, Morris Lee *minister*
Sullivan, John Fox *publisher*
Trisco, Robert Frederick *church historian, educator*
Wogaman, John Philip *retired minister and educator*

FLORIDA

Boca Raton
Agler, Richard Dean *rabbi*
Laine, Iris Ruth *minister, public relations/advertising executive*
Singer, Merle Elliot *rabbi*

Brandon
Halse, Frank Adams, Jr., *retired minister*

Carrollwood
O'Keefe, Fredrick Rea *bishop, consultant, educator, writer*

Cocoa
Fountain, Edwin Byrd *minister, educator, librarian, poet*

Coral Gables
Fitzgerald, John Thomas, Jr., *religious studies educator*

Crawfordville
Brumby, James Remley, III, (Knox Brumby) *retired priest*

Daytona Beach
Bronson, Oswald Perry, Sr., *religious organization administrator, clergyman*

Delray Beach
Wells, Mary Elizabeth Thompson *minister*

Fort Lauderdale
Beatty, Robert Clinton *religious studies educator*

Fort Pierce
Garment, Robert James *clergyman*

Jacksonville
Holliday, Patricia Ruth McKenzie *evangelist*
Mueller, Cherone *religious organization administrator, writer, minister*
Taylor, Robert M. *minister*

Melbourne
Krieger, Robert Edward *publisher*

Miami
Gudorf, Christine Ekhart *religious studies educator*
Harper, Kenneth Charles *clergyman*
Nash, Carol *minister, director*
Patterson, Rickey Lee *clergyman*

Miami Beach
Lehrman, Irving *rabbi*

Miami Shores
Favalora, John Clement *bishop*
Sunshine, Edward Robert *theology educator*

Naples
Salt, Alfred Lewis *priest*

Ocala
Massa, Conrad Harry *religious studies educator*
Woods, Mae *minister*

Orange Park
Bartholomew, John Niles *retired church administrator*

Orlando
O'Farrell, Mark Theodore *religious organization administrator*
Reyes, Jose Antonio, Sr., *minister*
Wenski, Thomas Gerard *bishop*

Palm Beach Gardens
McCall, Duke Kimbrough *clergyman*

Penney Farms
Muilenburg, John Powell *minister*

Pensacola
Mountcastle, William Wallace, Jr., *philosophy and religion educator*
Ricard, John H. *bishop, educator*

Pompano Beach
Corsello, Lily Joann *minister, counselor, educator*

Saint Augustine
McCarty, Doran Chester *religious organization administrator*
Rice, David Preston *minister*

Saint Petersburg
Lamar, William Fred *chaplain, educator*

Sarasota
Hilt, Thomas Harry *minister*
Jones, Tracey Kirk, Jr., *retired minister, educator*
Larsen, Lawrence Bernard, Jr., *priest, pastoral psychotherapist*
McFarlin, Diane Hooten *publisher*

Tallahassee
McBride, Donna Jannean *publisher*

Tampa
Banker, Jan Williams *minister, writer*

Tarpon Springs
Pittman, Roy Clinton, Jr., *neurosurgeon, lawyer, theologian, philospher*

Venice
Nevins, John J. *bishop*

Vero Beach
Beran, Denis Carl *publisher*

West Palm Beach
Johnson, Martin Allen *publisher, artist*
Nolan, Richard Thomas *clergyman, educator*
Westman, Steven Ronald *rabbi*

Yalaha
Searcy, Dorothy James *missionary*

GEORGIA

Albany
Revills, Isaiah *minister*

Alpharetta
McCullar, Michael D. *pastor*

Americus
Gonzalez, George G. *pastor*

Athens
Algeo, John Thomas *retired educator, association executive*
Slater, Thomas Bowie *minister, educator*
Spears, Louise Elizabeth *minister, secondary school educator*

Atlanta
Donoghue, John Francis *archbishop*
Graham, Matt Patrick *minister, librarian*
King, Barbara Lewis *minister, lecturer*
Patton, Laurie Louise *religious studies educator, writer*

Rosser, Essie *minister, counselor, marketing professional*
Skillrud, Harold Clayton *minister, retired bishop*
Stanley, Ronnie L., Jr., *theology educator, college dean, clergyman*
Westerhoff, John Henry, III, *clergyman, theologian, educator*

Augusta
Jones, Vernon Keith *minister, educator*
MacLeod, James L. *minister, finance company executive, art gallery owner*

Dacula
Murphree, Harold T. *retired minister*

Dahlonega
Newman, Thomas Daniel *minister, school administrator, archaeologist*

Decatur
Hagood, Thomas Richard, Jr., *minister, publisher*
Hale, Cynthia Lynette *religious organization administrator*

Lagrange
Cook, John Granger *religious studies educator, philosopher, educator*

Lawrenceville
Gericke, Paul William *minister, educator*

Macon
Franklin, Roosevelt *minister*
Staton, Cecil Pope, Jr., *religious and academic publisher, educator, broadcast executive*

Metter
Guido, Michael Anthony *evangelist*

Millen
Bray, Phillip Wayne *minister, writer*

Norcross
Granger, Philip Richard *minister*

Peachtree City
Dillard, George Stewart, III, *minister*
Yother, Michele *publisher*

Riverdale
Waters, John W. *minister, educator*

Savannah
Boland, John Kevin *bishop*

Stone Mountain
Dearfield, Rock *minister, parochial school administrator*

Tifton
Roberts, Curtis Creed *minister, writer*

Villa Rica
Hutto, John Robert, Jr., *pastor*

Woodstock
Collins, David Browning *religious institution administrator*

HAWAII

Honolulu
Merrifield, Donald Paul *hispanic ministries coordinator*
Strickland, John Arthur Van *minister*

Kahului
Domingo, Cora Maria Corazon Encarnacion *minister*

Kihei
Palusky, Alice *missionary, educator*

IDAHO

Nampa
Bowers, Curtis Ray, Jr., *chaplain*

ILLINOIS

Bartlett
Robinson, Jack Fay *clergyman*

Bartonville
Garrione, Robert Michael *clergy member*

Belleville
Gregory, Wilton D. *bishop*
Studer, Louis *priest, religious organization administrator*
Wittenbrink, Boniface Leo *priest*

Chicago
Almen, Lowell Gordon *church official*
Barbour, Claude Marie *minister, educator*
Baumhart, Raymond Charles *Roman Catholic church administrator*
Betz, Hans Dieter *theology educator*
Browning, Don Spencer *religious educator*
Brummel, Mark Joseph *religious organization administrator*
Bumbaugh, David Edward *religious studies educator, minister*
Carr, Anne Elizabeth *theology educator*
Doherty, Sister Barbara *religious institution administrator*
Doniger, Wendy *history of religions educator*
Farrakhan, Louis *religious leader*
George, Francis *archbishop*
Godfrey, Donal Charles *priest*
Hanson, Mark S. *bishop*
Harris, Mildred Clopton *clergy member, educator*
Hayes, Charles *religious organization executive, clergyman*
James, Marie Moody *clergywoman, musician, vocal music educator*

Jegen, Sister Carol Frances *religion educator*
Klauck, Hans-Josef *theology educator*
Kobler, John F. *priest, researcher*
Lathon, Sheraine *clergyman*
Lotocky, Innocent Hilarius *bishop*
Marshall, Cody *bishop*
McDonald, Theresa Beatrice Pierce (Mrs. Ollie McDonald) *church official, minister*
McGinn, Bernard John *religious educator*
Poethig, Eunice Blanchard *clergywoman*
Shafer, Eric Christopher *minister*
Simon, Mordecai *religious association administrator, clergyman*
Snyder, Graydon F. *religion educator*
Thurston, Stephen John *pastor*
Tipton, Margaret Ann *religious organization administrator, writer*
Walter, Charles Sebastian *Roman Catholic priest*
Yu, Anthony C. *religion and literature educator*

Decatur
Mittal, Sushil *religious studies educator*

Elgin
Reimer, Judy Mills *pastor, religious executive*

Elk Grove Village
Stein, David Timothy *minister*

Galva
Swatos, William Henry, Jr., *priest, sociologist*

Glenview
Braun, Eunice Hockspeier *religious order executive, author, lecturer*

Highland Park
Einisman, Myron Sachar *publisher*

Itasca
Constant, Anita Aurelia *publisher*

Jacksonville
Porter, Adam Lowry *religious studies educator*

Joliet
Imesch, Joseph Leopold *bishop*
Kaffer, Roger Louis *bishop*

Kankakee
Dalton, Ronnie Thomas *theology educator*

Lake Forest
Price, John Edward *religion educator*

Libertyville
Schroeder, W(illiam) Widick *religion educator*

Lincoln
Wilson, Robert Allen *religion educator*

Loves Park
Schlub, Teresa Rae *minister*

Moline
Johnson, Mary Lou *lay worker, educator*

Naperville
Raccah, Dominique Marcelle *publisher*
Worden, William Patrick *deacon*

Niles
Grace, John Joseph *retired priest*

O Fallon
Wilhelm, Phillip Eugene *church administrator, music educator*

Oak Park
Cary, William Sterling *retired church executive*
Gerson, Gary Stanford *rabbi*

Peoria
Parsons, Donald James *retired bishop*
Saxon, Randall Lee *pastor, author, educator*

River Forest
O'Meara, Thomas Franklin *priest, educator*

Riverside
Marty, Martin Emil *religion educator, editor*

Rock Island
Brandenburg, Sister M. Luka *nun, educator*

Rockford
Doran, Thomas George *bishop*
McClelland, Patricia G. *minister*

Rolling Meadows
Giese, Robert James *minister*

Savoy
Gauger, Randy Jay *minister*

South Holland
Perry, Joseph N. *bishop*

Springfield
Beckwith, Peter Hess *bishop*
Bell, John Perry *minister, religious organization administrator*
Ryan, Daniel Leo *bishop*

Villa Park
Pittelko, Roger Dean *clergyman, religious educator*

Wheaton
Gill, Kenneth Duane *minister, director*
Harris, Eleanor Lynne *religious studies educator, literature educator, minister, writer*
Pappas, Barbara Estelle *Biblical studies educator, author*

INDIANA

Anderson
Conrad, Harold August *retired religious pension board executive*

Kufeldt, George *biblical educator*
Lambert, Lloyd Laverne *minister*

Demotte
Huff, John David *church administrator*

Evansville
Hoy, George Philip *clergyman, county official*

Fishers
Christenson, Le Roy Howard *missions consultant*

Fort Wayne
Bunkowske, Eugene Walter *religious studies educator*
Mann, David William *minister*
Mather, George Ross *clergy member*
Shannon, Angela Lynn *minister*

Huntington
Fairchild, Mark Robin *theology studies educator*

Indianapolis
Bates, Gerald Earl *bishop emeritus*
Buechlein, Daniel Mark *archbishop*
Crow, Paul Abernathy, Jr., *retired minister*
Dickinson, Richard Donald Nye *clergyman, educator, theological seminary administrator*
French, Tarence Wade, Sr., *minister*
Hamm, Richard L. *church administrator*
Johnson, James P. *religious organization executive*
Marshall, Carolyn Ann M. *church official*
Page, Curtis Matthewson *minister*
Peterson, Erling Winston *religion educator*
Towne, Edgar Arthur *theologian, educator*
Watkins, Harold Robert *minister*
Woodring, DeWayne Stanley *religious organization administrator*

Jasper
Brenner, Raymond Anthony *priest*

Leo
Wright, Marsha Jane *pastor*

Marion
Brannon, Ronald Roy *retired minister*
Walker, Corean Jones *evangelist*

Noblesville
Wilson, Norman Glenn *church administrator, writer*

Notre Dame
Blantz, Thomas Edward *Roman Catholic priest, educator*
Hesburgh, Theodore Martin *clergyman, former university president*
Williams, Oliver Franklin *priest, educator*

Oakland City
Johnson, Ora J. *clergyman*

Plymouth
Fager, Everett Dean *minister*

South Bend
Reamer, Shirley Jean *minister*

Terre Haute
Chambers, Curtis Allen *clergyman, church communications executive*

Valparaiso
Becker, Matthew Lee *religious studies educator, minister*

Whiting
Finnegan, Eugene G. *religious studies educator*

Winona Lake
Ashman, Charles H. *retired minister*
Davis, John James *religion educator*
Julien, Thomas Theodore *religious denomination administrator*

IOWA

Ames
Baum, Robert M. *religious studies educator, researcher*

Cedar Falls
Lindberg, Duane R. *bishop, historian*

Decorah
Farwell, Elwin D. *minister, educational consultant*

Des Moines
Boyle, Bruce James *publisher*
Charron, Joseph L. *bishop*

Dubuque
Barta, James Omer *priest, psychology educator, church administrator*
Beck, Robert Raymond *priest*
Burkhart, John Ernest *minister, theology studies educator*
Hanus, Jerome George *archbishop*
Nessan, Craig Lee *minister, educator*

Grinnell
Mitchell, Orlan E. *clergyman, former college president*

Iowa City
Bozeman, Theodore D. *religion educator*
Clark, Dianne Elizabeth *religious studies and reading educator*
Forell, George Wolfgang *religion educator*

Mount Vernon
Molleur, Joseph *religious studies educator*

Orange City
Scorza, Sylvio Joseph *religion educator*

Sioux City
Mack, Thomas Russell *foundation administrator, management consultant*

Waterloo
Waters, Ronald W. *theology studies educator, church executive, pastor*

Waverly
Koob, Kathryn Loraine *religious studies educator*

KANSAS

Baxter Springs
Whiteley, Henry Howard *religious studies educator, minister*

Copeland
Birney, Walter Leroy *religious administrator*

Hillsboro
Miller, Douglas B. *theology studies educator*

Kansas City
Keleher, James P. *bishop*

Manhattan
Gillispie, Harold Leon *minister*

Prairie Village
Vogel, Arthur Anton *clergyman*

Salina
Fitzsimons, George Kinzie *bishop*

Shawnee Mission
Mandl, Herbert Jay *rabbi*

Topeka
Goetz, Roger Melvin *minister*

Wichita
McCrary, Larry Dale *minister, religious studies educator*

KENTUCKY

Boston
Rosenbaum, Stanley Ned *theology educator*

Covington
Hughes, William Anthony *retired bishop*

Crestwood
Roy, Elmon Harold *minister*

Elizabethtown
Phelps, Dennis Lane *minister, educator, author*

Frankfort
Sias, Mary *university executive*

Louisville
Boykin, Gladys *retired religious organization administrator*
Dale, Judy Ries *religious organization administrator, consultant*
Kelly, Thomas Cajetan *archbishop*
Reed, David Benson *bishop*
Zimmerman, Gideon K. *minister*

Owensboro
McRaith, John Jeremiah *bishop*

Paint Lick
Burton, Charles Lawrence *priest, small business owner*

Paris
Steffer, Robert Wesley *clergyman*

Pineville
Lucas, Roy Edward, Jr., *minister*
Whittaker, Bill Douglas *minister*

Stanford
Baughman, James Carson *minister, sports official*

Wilmore
Kinlaw, Dennis Franklin *clergyman, society executive*
Rader, Paul Alexander *minister, religious organization administrator*

Winchester
Hall, Bennett Freeman *minister*

LOUISIANA

Baton Rouge
Adams, Sharon Butler *minister, philosopher, researcher*
Koehler, Robert Brien *priest*
Phillabaum, Leslie Ervin *publisher*
Witcher, Robert Campbell, Sr., *bishop*

Boyce
Lewis, Patsy Joanne *religious studies educator, writer*

Columbia
McGee, Bruce D. *evangelist*

Crowley
Foreman, Alfred G. *theologian, philosopher*

Denham Springs
Cowart, Keith Bertrand *minister, educator*

Franklinton
Von Kanel, Danny Renard *minister, writer*

New Iberia
Henton, Willis Ryan *retired bishop*

New Orleans
Carter, James Clarence *pastor, educator*
Hughes, Alfred Clifton *archbishop*
Markuly, Mark Steven *religious studies educator*
Schulte, Francis B. *retired archbishop*

Shreveport
Friend, William Benedict *bishop*
Webb, Donald Arthur *minister*

Springhill
Morgan, Larry Ronald *minister*

Tioga
Brandow, Stephen Jon *priest*
Tenney, Tom Fred *bishop*

MAINE

Bridgton
Normann, Margaret Ella *deacon, educator*

Brooklin
Meserve, Mollie Ann *publisher*

Brooksville
Sutherland, Malcolm Read, Jr., *clergyman, educator*

Brunswick
Ault, James Mase *bishop*
Geoghegan, William Davidson *religion educator, minister*

Farmington
Reid, Jennifer Irene McPherran *religious studies educator*

Islesboro
Maes, John Leopold *theologian, psychologist, educator*

Manchester
Clark, Beth *minister*

Portland
Gerry, Joseph John *bishop*
Ives, Samuel Clifton *minister*

MARYLAND

Baltimore
Byron, William James *author, management educator, researcher, former university president*
Hicks, Sherman Gregory *pastor*
Mocko, George Paul *minister*
Robinson, Sally Shoemaker *lay associate*
Strickland, Marshall Hayward *bishop*
Zaiman, Joel Hirsh *rabbi*

Bethesda
Geyer, Alan Francis *theology educator, politics educator*
Zurkowski, Paul George *publisher*

Catonsville
Wynn, John Charles *clergyman, retired religion educator*

College Park
McNaughton, Kenneth John *publisher*

Columbia
Davis, Benjamin George *theologian, educator*

Elkridge
Byrd, Alicia D. *minister, sociologist*

Gaithersburg
Hall, Arthur Raymond, Jr., *retired minister*
Rupert, Hoover (Lynn Hoover Rupert) *minister, writer*

Hagerstown
Coffen, Richard Wayne *minister, editor*

La Plata
Mariya, Deborah Luethje *minister*

Marydel
LaBarge, Christopher W. *priest*

Mitchellville
Brubaker, Lauren Edgar *minister, educator*

Severn
Freeman, Joel Arthur *author, organizational cultural change facilitator*

Silver Spring
Beach, Bert Beverly *clergyman*
Cathey, Mary Ellen Jackson *religious studies educator*
Chery, Reginald *minister*
Herbers, Tod Arthur *publisher*
O'Meara, Noel P. *priest, religious organization administrator*
Paulsen, Jan *clergyman, church administrator*
Thompson, George Ralph *church administrator*
Ziegler, Gwendolyn Woods *minister, consultant*

Stevenson
Margalit, Shlomo *educator*

MASSACHUSETTS

Amherst
Wills, David Wood *minister, educator*

Andover
Simone, Joseph *clergyman, educator*

Auburn
Bachelder, Robert Stephen *minister*

Auburndale
Gulbrandsen, Natalie Webber *religious association administrator*

Berlin
Lohr, Harold Russell *retired bishop*

Boston
D'Avolio, Gerald Donald *religious organization administrator, lawyer*
Harris, Barbara C(lementine) *bishop*
Harris, Virginia *religious organization administrator, publisher*
Kessler, Diane Cooksey *religious organization administrator, minister*
Korff, Y. A. *grand rabbi*
Mason, Herbert Warren, Jr., *religion and history educator, author*
Rouner, Leroy Stephens *religious studies educator, philosophy educator*
Shaw, M. Thomas, III, *bishop*

Braintree
Robertson, Michael Swing *minister*

Brighton
Murphy, William F. *priest, monsignor, religion educator*
O'Malley, Sean Patrick *archbishop*

Brockton
Holland, David Vernon *minister*
Lightford, Melvin *minister*

Brookline
Samra, Nicholas James *bishop*
Skeete, Helen Watkins *minister, counselor*

Cambridge
Aitken, Ellen Bradshaw *religious studies educator*
Clifford, Richard John *religious studies educator*
Fiorenza, Francis P. *religion educator*
Gomes, Peter John *clergyman, educator*
Horn, Henry Eyster *retired minister*
Kaufman, Gordon Dester *theology educator*
Picardi, Gerard A. *publisher*
Schuessler Fiorenza, Elisabeth *theology educator*
Williams, Preston Noah *theology educator*

Chestnut Hill
Goizueta, Roberto Segundo *theology studies educator*
Helmick, Raymond Glen *priest, educator*
Mc Innes, William Charles *priest, academic administrator*

Dedham
Janson, Barbara Jean *publisher*
Spoolstra, Linda Carol *minister, educator, religious organization administrator*

Dorchester
Boles, John P. *bishop*

Haverhill
Korinow, Ira Lee *rabbi*

Leeds
Grenz, Linda L. *Episcopal priest*

Marlborough
Matera, Richard Ernest *retired minister*
Wolkovich-Valkavicius, William Lawrence *priest*

Mashpee
Payne, Paula Marie *minister*

Medford
O'Leary, David *priest, theologian, educator*

Methuen
McNaughton, William John *retired bishop*

New Bedford
Kellaway, Richard Allen *minister, art association administrator*

Newton
Tannenwald, Leslie Keiter *rabbi, justice of peace, educational administrator, chaplain*

North Grafton
Kosch, Philip Cobe *dean, veterinary medicine educator*

Northampton
Derr, Thomas Sieger *religion educator*
Donfried, Karl Paul *minister, theology educator*

Norton
Worthley, Harold Field *retired minister, educator*

Randolph
Whitaker, Arthur Luther *retired minister, psychologist*

South Hamilton
Ciampa, Roy Emilius *religious studies educator*

Springfield
McDonnell, Timothy Anthony *bishop*

Waltham
Delaney, Mary Anne *retired theology studies educator*

Wellesley
Hobbs, Edward Craig *religious studies educator*

Weston
Barry, William Anthony *priest, writer*
Oelgeschlager, Guenther Karl *publisher*

Westwood
Bier, Louis Henry Gustav *minister*

Williamstown
Eusden, John Dykstra *theology educator, minister*

Worcester
Clark, William Anthony *religious studies educator*
Parsons, Edwin Spencer *clergyman, educator*
Scanlon, Peter Joseph *priest*
Shannon, Thomas A. *religious studies educator*

MICHIGAN

Ann Arbor
Gomez, Luis Oscar *Asian and religious studies educator, clinical psychology educator*
Lightfoot, Albert J. *clergyman*
Mayes, Ila Laverne *minister*

Bloomfield Hills
Syme, Daniel Bailey *rabbi, institution executive*

Caro
Wright, Stephen Nathan *religious organization administrator*

Clarkston
Keough, James Gillman, Jr., *minister*

Dearborn
Hess, Margaret Johnston *religious writer, educator*

Detroit
Anderson, Moses B. *bishop*
Maida, Adam Joseph Cardinal *archbishop*
Mc Gehee, H(arry) Coleman, Jr., *bishop*
Silverman, Mark *publisher*
Vigneron, Allen Henry *theology studies educator, rector, auxiliary bishop*

Farmington
Penberthy, Stanley Josiah, Jr., *publisher*
Wine, Sherwin Theodore *rabbi*

Farmington Hills
Plaut, Jonathan Victor *rabbi*

Flint
Bonner, Darlene E. *minister, writer*

Gaylord
Cooney, Patrick Ronald *bishop*

Grand Rapids
Anderson, Roger Gordon *minister*
Beals, Paul Archer *religious studies educator*
DeVries, Robert K. *religious book publisher*
Hofman, Leonard John *minister*
Schwanda, Tom *religious studies educator*

Holland
Van Voorst, Robert E. *theology educator, minister*

Jackson
Popp, Nathaniel *archbishop*

Kalamazoo
Badra, Robert George *theology studies educator, humanities educator*

Lansing
Umfleet, Randy Gene *minister, music educator*

Livonia
Haggard, Joan Claire *church musician, piano instructor, accompanist, adjudicator*

Marquette
Burt, John Harris *bishop*

Northville
Davis, Lawrence Edward *church official*

Oak Park
Dill, Ellen Renée *minister, educator, writer*

Portage
Lee, Edward L. *retired bishop*

Roscommon
Mainprize, Donald Charles *minister, writer*

Southfield
Ibrahim, Ibrahim N. *bishop*
Willingham, Edward Bacon, Jr., *ecumenical minister, administrator*

Spring Arbor
Thompson, Stanley B. *church administrator*

Traverse City
Burton, Betty June *retired pastor*

Whitehall
Sirotko, Theodore Francis *priest, retired military officer*

MINNESOTA

Alexandria
Hultstrand, Donald Maynard *bishop*

Austin
Alcorn, Wallace Arthur *minister, writer*

Bloomington
Brokke, Catherine Juliet *mission executive*
Thomas, Margaret Jean *clergywoman, religious research consultant*

Collegeville
Rolfson, Helen C. *theology studies educator, translator*

Cottage Grove
Hudnut, Robert Kilborne *clergyman, author*

Crookston
Balke, Victor H. *bishop*

Duluth
Craig, Robert H. *theology studies educator*

Edina
Brown, Laurence David *retired bishop*
Putnam, Frederick Warren, Jr., *bishop*

Excelsior
Fenske, Jerald Allan *minister*
Parker, Robert Chauncey Humphrey *clergyman, publishing executive, psychic*

Fergus Falls
Overgaard, Robert Milton *retired religious organization administrator*

Grand Rapids
Merrill, Arthur Lewis *retired theology educator*

Inver Grove Heights
Koenig, Robert August *minister, educator*

Lake Elmo
Schultz, Clarence John *minister*

Mankato
Orvick, George Myron *church denomination executive, minister*
Purscell, Keith William *minister*

Minneapolis
Chemberlin, Peg *clergy, religious organization administrator*
Dyrud, Amos Oliver *minister, educator*
Hamel, William John *church administrator, minister*
Klemp, Harold *minister, writer*
Mason, Barbara Fountain *minister*
Miller, William Alvin *clergyman, author, lecturer*

Moorhead
Jacobson, Arland Dean *religion educator*

New Ulm
Nienstedt, John Clayton *priest, educator*

Northfield
Swanson, Stephen Olney *minister, retired English educator*

Preston
Schommer, Trudy Marie *pastoral minister, religion education*

Rochester
Rinden, David Lee *clergyman*

Rosemount
Aadland, Thomas Vernon *minister*

Roseville
McMillan, Mary Bigelow *retired minister, volunteer*

Saint Paul
Caneday, Ardel Bruce *religious studies educator, writer*
Flynn, Harry Joseph *bishop*
Haemig, Mary Jane *religious studies educator*
Hopper, David Henry *religion educator*
Mullin, James Albert *executive*

Savage
Soderquist, Ronald Bruce *minister, ministry consultant*

Woodbury
Woodruff, Ellen Louise *chaplain*

MISSISSIPPI

Bay Saint Louis
Fisher, Robert Bruce *priest*

Biloxi
Howze, Joseph Lawson Edward *retired bishop*

Clinton
Hensley, John Clark *religious organization administrator, minister*

Indianola
Matthews, David *clergyman*

Jackson
Gordon, Granville Hollis *church official*
Gray, Duncan Montgomery, Jr., *retired bishop*

Minter City
Mitchell, Patsy Malier *religious school founder and administrator*

Ocean Springs
Foster, William Silas, Jr., *retired minister*

MISSOURI

Ballwin
Ackerson, Charles Stanley *minister, social worker*

Bridgeton
Asma, Lawrence Francis *priest*

Cameron
Rose-Heim, William Bentley *minister, mediator, business owner, entrepreneur*

Charleston
Wallhausen, Mildred Carolyn *publisher*

Clayton
O'Donnell, Edward Joseph *bishop, former editor*

Excelsior Springs
Mitchell, Earl Wesley *clergyman*

Fayette
Keeling, Joe Keith *religion educator, college official and dean*

Florissant
Stormer, John Anthony *minister emeritus, author, publisher*

Hazelwood
Rose, Joseph Hugh *clergyman*
Urshan, Nathaniel Andrew *minister, church administrator*

Highlandville
Pruter, Karl Hugo *bishop*

Independence
Lindgren, A(lan) Bruce *church administrator*
Tyree, Alan Dean *clergyman*

Jefferson City
King, Robert Henry *minister, religious organization administrator, former education educator*

Joplin
Butler, Paul Thurman *retired religious studies educator*
Minor, Ronald Ray *minister*

Kansas City
Adams, Charles Geoffrey *minister, educator*
Cunningham, Paul George *minister*
Diehl, James Harvey *church administrator*
Finn, Robert W. *bishop*
Friedlander, Edward Robert *pathologist*
Gray, Helen Theresa Goit *religion editor*
Hebenstreit, Jean Estill Stark *religion educator, practitioner*
Hoyland, Janet Louise *clergywoman*
Knight, John Allan *clergyman, philosophy and religion educator*
Mutti, Albert Frederick *retired minister*
Petosa, Jason Joseph *publisher*
Wilder, Terry L. *religious studies educator*

Lees Summit
Mosley, Glenn Richard *religious organization administrator, minister*

Ozark
Thornton, Andrew John *minister*

Poplar Bluff
Black, Ronnie Delane *religious organization administrator, mayor*
Carr, Charles Louis *retired religious organization administrator*
Duncan, Leland Ray *retired mission administrator*

Raymore
Miller, William Lee, Jr., *minister*

Rush Hill
Scheffler, Lewis Francis *pastor, educator, research scientist*

Saint Louis
Brighton, Louis Andrew *religious studies educator*
Burke, Raymond L. *archbishop*
DaCorte, Allan Francis *priest, financial consultant and advisor*
Kieschnick, Gerald B. *religious organization administrator*
Mahsman, David Lawrence *religious publications editor*
McClain, Curtis Keith, Jr., *religious studies educator, minister*
Merrell, James Lee *religious editor, clergyman*
Naumann, Joseph F. *bishop*
O'Keefe, Martin D. *priest, philosopher, educator, classicist*
Reese, Martha Grace *minister, lawyer*
Shreckhise, Robert Lynn *minister, theology studies educator*
Wiley, Gregory Robert *publisher*
Wilke, LeRoy *church administrator*

Springfield
Baird, Robert Dean *mission director*
Bertrand, Rabekah Pickett *religious studies educator*
Haltom, Michael Fred *religious studies educator, military officer*
Trask, Thomas Edward *religious organization administrator*

MONTANA

Bigfork
Shea, Donald William *priest, retired military officer*

Helena
Jones, Charles Irving *bishop*

Kalispell
Vickers, Lee Louise *minister*

NEBRASKA

Grand Island
Mc Namara, Lawrence J. *bishop*
Zichek, Melvin Eddie *retired minister*

Lincoln
Bruskewitz, Fabian W. *bishop*
Wiersbe, Warren Wendell *clergyman, author, lecturer*

Omaha
Curtiss, Elden F. *bishop*
Harmless, J. William *theologian, educator*

Papillion
Zuerlein, Damian Joseph *priest*

NEVADA

Carson City
Convis, Charles Lester *publisher*
Deterding, Paul E. *pastor*
Traylor, William Robert *publisher*

Las Vegas
Bishop, Leo Kenneth *clergyman, educator*

Reno
Apassa, Cyril Omo-Osagie *clergyman, educator*
Chrystal, William George *minister*
Savoy, Douglas Eugene *bishop, religious studies educator, explorer, author*
Straling, Phillip Francis *bishop*
Walrath, Harry Rienzi *retired minister*

Weld, Roger Bowen *retired religious organization administrator*

Sparks
Pryor, Eric Jon *minister, writer*

NEW HAMPSHIRE

Center Sandwich
Booty, John Everitt *emeritus educator*

Concord
Robinson, V. Gene (The Right Reverend V. Gene Robinson) *bishop*

Hanover
Green, Ronald Michael *ethics and religious studies educator*
Hemphill, Margaret Ayars *priest, artist*

Jaffrey
Van Ness, Patricia Wood *religious studies educator, consultant, author*

Loudon
Moore, Beatrice *religious organization administrator*

Manchester
Christian, Francis Joseph *bishop*
McCormack, John Brendan *bishop*

North Hampton
Osenton, Thomas George *publisher*

West Chesterfield
Garinger, Louis Daniel *religion educator*

NEW JERSEY

Caldwell
Campbell, Sister Maura *theology and philosophy educator*

Chatham
Marconi, Dominic Anthony *retired bishop*

Cherry Hill
Bryan, Henry Collier *clergyman, retired secondary school educator*

Clinton
Moore, Alma Donst *writer, lyricist*

Cranbury
Yoseloff, Thomas *publisher*

Denville
Tartaglia, Richard V. *priest*

Eatontown
Priesand, Sally Jane *rabbi*

Edison
Roskoski, John *religious studies educator, coach*

Englewood
Saliba, Philip E. *archbishop*

Fort Lee
Sherry, Paul Henry *minister, religious organization administrator*

Freehold
Jawidzik, Edward Mark *priest*

Hightstown
Hull, Gretchen Gaebelein *lay worker, writer, lecturer*

Jersey City
Ashley, Willard Walden C., Sr., *minister*
Katz, Colleen *publisher*

Lakewood
Levovitz, Pesach Zechariah *rabbi*

Little Falls
Glasser, Lynn Schreiber *publisher*

Madison
Ariarajah, S. Wesley *educator, former clergyman, church administrator*
Farias, Joseph G. *priest, consultant*
Yrigoyen, Charles, Jr., *church denomination executive*

Mahwah
Padovano, Anthony Thomas *theologian, educator, literature educator*

Marlton
Clemens, David Allen *minister*

Medford
Hogan, Thomas Harlan *publisher*

Metuchen
Demkovitz, Russell Bernard *deacon, ceremetary director*

Morris Plains
Spong, John Shelby *retired bishop*

Neptune
Collins, Robert T. *publisher*
Manuel, Sandra Lorraine *minister*

New Brunswick
Bowden, Henry Warner *religion educator*
Johnson, James Turner *theology studies educator*

Newark
Howard, M(oses) William, Jr., *minister*
Johnson, Evelyn *minister, educator*
Myers, John Joseph *bishop*

Newfield
Hartman, Jeffrey Edward *pastor*

Paterson
Ramos, Peter *religious studies educator, minister*

Piscataway
Wasserman, Marlie P(arker) *publisher*

Point Pleasant
Marjanczyk, Joseph Anicetus *priest*

Pomona
Constantelos, Demetrios John *priest, educator*

Princeton
Allen, Diogenes *clergyman, philosophy educator*
Armstrong, Richard Stoll *minister, educator, writer, poet*
Belshaw, George Phelps Mellick *bishop*
Griffith, Ruth Marie *religious studies educator*
Metzger, Bruce Manning *clergyman, educator*
Miller, Patrick Dwight, Jr., *religion educator, minister*
Stackhouse, Max Lynn *religious studies educator*
West, Charles Converse *retired theologian*

Ridgewood
Kiernan, Richard Francis *publisher*

Rutherford
Gerety, Peter Leo *archbishop*

South River
Jackiewicz, Frederick Waclaw *priest*

Teaneck
Meno, John Peter *chorepiscopus*

Toms River
Donaldson, Marcia Jean *lay worker*

Trenton
Old, Hughes Oliphant *research theologian, clergyman*

Union City
Younan, Joseph *bishop*

Warren
Wildrick, Kenyon Jones *minister*

Watchung
Miller, John Ronald *minister*

West Milford
Stelpstra, William John *minister*

West Paterson
Pataki, Andrew *bishop*

Willingboro
Bass, Joseph Oscar *minister*

Woodbury
Doughty, A. Glenn *minister*

NEW MEXICO

Moriarty
Moonwalker, Tu *minister, counselor, artist*

Portales
Overton, Edwin Dean *campus minister, educator*

White Sands Missile Range
Linzey, James Franklin *minister, military officer, vocalist*

NEW YORK

Adams Center
Hood, Thomas Gregory *minister*

Albany
Bowen, Mary Lu *ecumenical administrator*
Hubbard, Howard James *bishop*

Angola
Green, Gerard Leo *priest, educator*

Baldwin Place
Kurian, George Thomas *publisher*

Brainard
Isaksen, Robert L. *retired bishop*

Bronx
Canavan, Francis *priest, educator*
Dulles, Avery *cardinal, theologian*
Fahey, Charles Joseph *priest, gerontology educator*
Hennessy, Thomas Christopher *clergyman, educator, retired university dean*
Hunt, George William *priest, magazine editor*
Kelly, George Anthony *clergyman, author, educator*
Parker, Everett Carlton *clergyman*

Bronxville
L'Huillier, Peter *archbishop*

Brooklyn
Al-Hafeez, Humza *minister, editor*
Catanello, Ignatius Anthony *bishop*
DiMarzio, Nicholas Anthony *bishop*
Garrison, Maurice Allen Martin *missionary, minister*
Hausman, Jill Susan *rabbi, cantor, vocalist, lyricist, poet, composer*
Pasciuto, Joseph Doria *priest*
Sorscher, Marvin Loeb *religious studies educator, rabbi*
Staggers, Mary E. *minister*

Buffalo
Small, William C. *religious organization administrator*

Cambridge
Kriss, Gary W(ayne) *Episcopal priest*

Canton
O'Connor, Daniel William *retired religious studies and classical languages educator*

Centerport
McQueeney, Henry Martin, Sr., *publisher*
Stevens, Martin Brian *publisher*

Chautauqua
Campbell, Joan Brown *religious organization executive*

Corning
Davis, Francis Raymond *priest*

Coxsackie
Moyna, John Lawrence *priest*

Douglaston
Valero, René Arnold *clergyman*

Elma
Virkler, Mark William *religious educator*

Elmhurst
Cush, John Patrick *priest, theology studies educator*

Garrison
Egan, Daniel Francis *priest*

Glen Cove
Costa, Thomas Charles *priest*

Glen Head
Huber, Don Lawrence *publisher*

Granville
Ranney, Daniel Anthony *minister, language educator*

Hawthorne
Scheffler, Eckart Arthur *publisher*

Hempstead
Zagano, Phyllis *religious studies educator*

Hicksville
Batule, Robert John *priest, writer*

Hollis
Stephens, B. Consuela *minister, consultant*

Kingston
Tsirpanlis, Constantine N. *theology, philosophy, classics and history educator*

Lakemont
Brothers, Fletcher Arnold *minister, religious organization founder, director*

Larchmont
Rainier, Robert Paul *publisher, consultant*

Mechanicville
Rhodes, Alan Charles *minister*

Middle Village
Kolatch, Alfred Jacob *publisher*

Millbrook
Lindsley, James Elliott *minister, writer*

Minetto
Sivers, Richard Henry *minister, writer*

Mount Vernon
Moore, W. Darin *minister*

New York
Anderson, Fred Richard *minister, writer*
Balter, Bernice *religious organization administrator*
Baranski, Joan Sullivan *publisher*
Begell, William *publisher*
Berner, Mary *publisher*
Bretton-Granatoor, Gary Martin *rabbi*
Caine, Edward Peter *religious organization administrator*
Church, Frank Forrester *minister, author, columnist*
Cone, James Hal *theologian, educator, author*
Conlon, Peggy Eileen *publisher*
Demetrios, (Demetrios Trakatellis) *archbishop*
Doherty, Thomas *publisher*
Driver, Tom Faw *theologian, writer, justice/peace advocate, photographer*
Forbes, Christopher (Kip Forbes) *publisher*
Friedman, Herbert A. *rabbi, educator, fund raising executive*
Friedman, J. Roger *publisher*
Gage, Robert Clifford *minister*
Geer, John Farr *retired religious organization administrator*
Germano, William Paul *publisher*
Giniger, Kenneth Seeman *publisher*
Ginsberg, Hersh Meier *rabbi, religious organization executive*
Griswold, Frank Tracy, III, *bishop*
Habecker, Eugene Brubaker *religious association executive*
Harvey, O.S.F.S., John F *priest, theologian, educator*
Hertzberg, Arthur *rabbi, educator*
Hirsch, Roseann Conte *publisher*
Holmes, Miriam H. *publisher*
Isay, Jane Franzblau *publisher*
Kartsev, Vladimir Petrovich *publisher*
Kern, William Bliem, Jr., *minister*
Kraemer, David C. *theology educator*
Laurus, (Laurus Skurla) *archbishop*
Leonard, Richard Davis *minister*
McGeady, Sister Mary Rose *retired religious organization administrator*
Meyer, Sheldon *publisher*
Mironovich, Alex *publisher*
Molho, Emanuel *publisher*
Morris, Clayton Leslie *priest*
Murdoch, (Keith) Rupert *publisher*
Nadich, Judah *rabbi*
Ochs, Carol Rebecca *theologian, philosophy and religion educator*
O'Keefe, Vincent Thomas *clergyman, educational administrator*

Oshin, Diane *publisher*
Paro, Jeff *publisher*
Perry, David *priest*
Platzner, Linda *publisher*
Powers, Edward Alton *minister, educator*
Reidy, Carolyn Kroll *publisher*
Rosenberg, Ellen Y. *religious association administrator*
Ross, Norman Alan *publisher*
Roth, Sol *rabbi*
Rusch, William Graham *religious organization administrator*
Schorsch, Ismar *clergyman, Jewish history educator*
Sharpton, Alfred Charles, Jr., *minister, political activist*
Shriver, Donald Woods, Jr., *theology educator*
Siegel, Morton Kallos *religious organization administrator, educational administrator*
Simpson, Mary Michael *priest, psychotherapist*
Sohl, Joyce Darlene *religious organization administrator*
Stolper, Pinchas Aryeh *religious organization executive, rabbi*
Talley, Truman Macdonald *publisher*
Tannenbaum, Bernice Salpeter *national religious organization executive*
Thurman, Robert *philosophy, religious studies educator*
Truesdell, Walter George *minister, librarian*
Tucker, Alan David *publisher*
Twiname, John Dean *minister, human services administrator*
von Knorring, Henrik Johan *publisher*
Ware, Alberta *minister, educator*
Weinreb, Tzvi Hersh *religious organization administrator, rabbi*
Welsh, Donald Emory *publisher*
Whiteman, Douglas E. *publisher*
Wiener, Marvin S. *rabbi, editor, executive*
Wolnek, Stephen S. *religious organization administrator*
Yoffie, Erich H. *religious organization administrator*
Yu, Andrew *minister*
Zanetti, Richard Joseph *publisher*
Zeldin, Richard Packer *publisher*

Newport
Wilson, Eldon Ray *minister*

Niskayuna
Nichols, Albert Myron *retired minister*

Nyack
Mann, Kenneth Walker *retired minister, psychologist*

Ogdensburg
Cunningham, Robert Joseph *bishop*

Pawling
Peale, Ruth Stafford (Mrs. Norman Vincent Peale) *religious leader*

Pleasantville
Hundersmarck, Lawrence F. *theology studies educator*

Poughkeepsie
Glasse, John Howell *retired philosophy and theology educator*
Harmelink, Herman, III, *minister, writer, religious studies educator*

Rochester
Clark, Matthew Harvey *bishop*
Elliott, Ralph H. *educator*
Goodell, Gary Lloyd *minister, educator*
Gripe, Alan Gordon *minister*
Lacey, Dorothy Ellen *theology studies educator, religious organization administrator*
Portanova, Carolyn Amick *religious organization administrator*
Webster, Gordon Visscher, Jr., *minister*

Scarsdale
Johnson, William Alexander *clergyman, philosophy educator*
Rubenstein, Jacob Samuel *rabbi*

Setauket
Card, Richard Abbott *religious institute executive, educator*

Spencertown
Lieber, Charles Donald *publisher*

Spring Valley
Stedge-Fowler, Joyce *retired clergywoman*

Syosset
Theodosius, *retired leader of the Orthodox Church in America*

Syracuse
Costello, Thomas Joseph *bishop*
Harrison, Frank J. *retired bishop*
Lang, James Patrick *priest*
Moynihan, James M. *bishop*
Wiggins, James Bryan *religion educator*

Troy
Phelan, Thomas *clergyman, academic administrator, educator*

Unionville
Kemnitz, Thomas Milton *publisher*

Weedsport
Kinch, Christopher Peter *priest*

Westbury
De Pauw, Gommar Albert *priest, educator*

Williamsville
Jones, Robert Alfred *retired clergyman*

Wolcott
Searle, Robert Ferguson *minister*

Yonkers
Gunner, Murray *religious organization administrator*

Youngstown
Lamb, Charles F. *educator, retired minister*

NORTH CAROLINA

Asheboro
Clark, Lawrence James *minister*

Asheville
Sims, Bennett Jones *minister, educator*

Belmont
Baumstein, Paschal M. *priest*

Brevard
Flory, Margaret Martha *retired religious organization administrator*

Cary
Slaatte, Howard Alexander *minister, philosophy educator*
Taylor, David Wyatt Aiken *retired clergyman*

Chapel Hill
Chang, Kuk Won *theology educator, researcher, pastor*
Dixon, John Wesley, Jr., *retired religion and art educator*

Charlotte
Curlin, William G. *bishop*
Freeman, Sidney Lee *minister*
Graham, William Franklin (William Franklin Graham) *evangelist*
Gregory, Jeannette T. *publisher, writer*
Grigg, Eddie Garman *minister, educator*
Helton, Max Edward *minister, consultant, religious organization executive*
McKay-Wilkinson, Julie Ann *minister, marriage and family therapist*
Oliver, John William Posegate *minister*
Walker, Jewett Lynius *clergyman, church official*

Concord
Robinson, Harold Oscar *clergyman, educator*

Dunn
Davis, Dolly *religious organization administrator*
Heath, Preston *clergy member, religious organization administrator*

Durham
Dorn, Louis Otto *retired minister*
Lilly, James Edward *minister, entrepreneur*
Meyers, Carol Lyons *religion, history and archaeology educator*
Meyers, Eric Mark *religion educator*
Smith, Harmon Lee, Jr., *clergyman, moral theology educator*
Steinmetz, David Curtis *religious studies educator*
Westbrook, Don Arlen *minister*

Fletcher
Tolbert, Gary J. *minister*

Garner
Henderson, Shirley Elizabeth *minister*

Greensboro
Dziordz, Walter Michael *priest*

Greenville
Jackson, Bobby Rand *minister*

Hendersonville
Trexler, Edgar Ray *minister, editor*

Lake Junaluska
Tullis, Edward Lewis *retired bishop*

Lillington
McClain, Gregory David *chaplin*

Monroe
Kyle, John Emery *mission executive*

Raleigh
Buchanan, Ray Allen *clergyman*
Lolley, William Randall *minister*

Reidsville
Hart, Richard Wesley *religious organization administrator, pastor*

Robbins
Mac Kenzie, James Donald *clergyman*

Salisbury
Bamberg-Revis, Ethel M. *minister, educator*

Snow Hill
Stevens, JoAnn A. *textile, political leader, author, minister*

Stedman
Taylor, David *clergy member, religious administrator*

Taylorsville
Ross, David Edmond *church official*

Trenton
Dillahunty, George Robert *minister*

Wake Forest
Boozer, John Elbert *priest, minister*

Warsaw
Blackmore, James Herrall *clergyman, educator, author*

Waynesville
Hale, Joe (Joseph Rice) *church organization executive*
Stokes, Mack Boyd (Marion Boyd Stokes) *bishop*

Weaverville
Edwards, Otis Carl, Jr., *theology educator*

Wilmington
Conser, Walter Hurley, Jr., *religion and philosophy educator*
Stokes, John Lemacks, II, *clergyman, retired university official*

Winston Salem
Capps, Richard Henry *retired minister*
Harrelson, Walter Joseph *minister, religion educator emeritus*
Ludolf, Marilyn Marie Keaton *lay worker*
Mendez, John *minister*
Rights, Graham Henry *retired minister*
Spach, Jule Christian *church executive*
Winn, Albert Curry *clergyman*

NORTH DAKOTA

Fargo
Foss, Richard John *bishop*
Sullivan, James Stephen *retired bishop*

Minot AFB
Luckett, Byron Edward, Jr., *chaplain, career officer*

OHIO

Ashland
Hawk, L. Daniel *minister, religious studies educator*
Watson, JoAnn Ford *theology studies educator*

Athens
Morgans, Bob D. *minister*

Canton
Mann, John Martin *minister*

Chesterland
Ruble, Bernard Roy *minister, labor relations and human resources consultant, educator*

Cincinnati
Adams, Mendle Eugene *minister*
Anderson, Joan Balyeat *religion educator, minister*
Harrington, Jeremy Thomas *priest, publishing executive*
O'Donnell, Robert Patrick *priest*
Pilarczyk, Daniel Edward *archbishop*
Sallquist, Gary Ardin *minister, non-profit executive*
Skavlem, Melissa Kline *publisher*
Zola, Gary Phillip *rabbi, historian, religious educational administrator*

Clayton
Stutzman, L. Lee *pastor*

Cleveland
Abrams, Sylvia Fleck *religious studies educator*
Battle, Hilary Howard *minister, educator*
Borchert, Catherine Glennan *minister*
Bouie, Oliver D. *minister*
Buhrow, William Carl *religious organization administrator*
Guffey, Edith Ann *religious organization administrator*
Pilla, Anthony Michael *bishop*
Quinlan, Eileen *nun, literature educator*
Williams, Arthur Benjamin, Jr., *bishop*

Columbus
Darling, George Curtis *minister, administrator*
Donovan, Dennis Dale *priest*
Walls, James Douglas *minister*

Dayton
Leigh, Gloria Lorraine *retired religious studies educator*

Euclid
Obloy, Leonard Gerard *priest*

Findlay
Fry, Charles George *theologian, educator*
Wilkin, Richard Edwin *clergyman, religious organization executive*

London
Hughes, Clyde Matthew *religious denomination executive*

Loveland
Grimmet, Alex J. *clergyman, school administrator, elementary and secondary education educator*

Mansfield
Whitmer, Eugene Roger *minister, retired secondary school educator*

Miamisburg
Brewster, Charles Edward *writer, engineer*

Saint Marys
Ball, Judy Kay *minister*

Sebring
Doty, James Edward *pastor, psychologist*

Steubenville
Scanlan, Michael *priest, academic administrator*
Sheldon, Gilbert Ignatius *clergyman*

Westerville
Schultz, Arthur LeRoy *clergyman, educator*

Wickliffe
Pevec, Anthony Edward *bishop*

Worthington
Browning, Robert Lynn *educator, clergyman*

OKLAHOMA

Bartlesville
Sweem, Billy Don *minister*

Bethany
Leggett, James Daniel *bishop*

Oklahoma City
Beltran, Eusebius Joseph *archbishop*
Clayton, Lawrence Otto *minister, writer, educator, alcohol and drug counselor*
Hampton, Carol McDonald *priest, educator, historian*
Niccum, Larry Curt *minister, educator*
Ridley, Betty Ann *religous educator, lay worker*

Shawnee
Wilks, Thomas Milton *religious studies educator, minister*

Texhoma
Jackson, Paul Howard *minister*

Tulsa
Cox, William Jackson *retired bishop*
Gottschalk, Sister Mary Therese *nun, hospital administrator*
Osborn, La Donna Carol *clergywoman*
Rex, Lonnie Royce *religious organization administrator*
Roberts, Oral (Granville Oral Roberts) *clergyman*
Sotak, John Joseph *priest, educator*

Vinita
Wright, Jo Anne *Episcopal priest*

OREGON

Corvallis
Dennis, John Davison *minister*
McCarthy, William Robert *minister*

Dallas
Calkins, Loren Gene *religious organization administrator, pastor*

Eugene
Sanders, Jack Thomas *religious studies educator*

Medford
Hellemose, Aage *minister*

Newberg
Tsohantaridis, Timotheos *minister, religion educator*

Portland
Langrock, Karl Frederick *former academic administrator*
Richards, Herbert East *minister emeritus, commentator*

Salem
Muntz, J(ohn) Richard *clergyman*

Turner
Ratzlaff, Ruben Menno *religion educator, minister*

PENNSYLVANIA

Akron
Livingston, Margery Elsie *missionary, clinical psychologist*

Allentown
Cullen, Edward Peter *bishop*
Revak, Francis Charles *priest, educator*

Annville
Robbins, Jeffrey W. *theologian, philosopher*

Beaver Falls
Watt, Johnathan Mark *religious studies educator*

Bensalem
Bevan, Norman Edward *religious organization executive*

Bethlehem
Caldwell, Douglas W. *clergyman*
Steffen, Lloyd Howard *minister, religion educator*
Weissler, Chava (Lenore) *religious studies educator*

Beyer
Cornell, William Harvey *clergyman*

Bradford
Cox, J. Arthur *minister*

Camp Hill
Johnston, Thomas McElree, Jr., *retired church administrator*

Chambersburg
Reber, Calvin Henry *theological studies educator, minister*
Yeun, Paul Lorenzo *minister*

Clarion
Grejda, Gail Fulton *dean*

Clinton
Talbot, Mary Lee *minister*

Coatesville
Green, Norman Marston, Jr., *retired minister*

Cranberry Township
Tiller, Olive Marie *retired church worker*

Drexel Hill
Thompson, William David *minister, homiletics educator*

Elizabethtown
Brown, Dale Weaver *clergyman, theologian, educator*

Erie
Murphy, Michael Joseph *retired bishop*
Rowley, Robert Deane, Jr., *bishop*
Trautman, Donald W. *bishop*

Glenside
McCartney, Dan G. *theology studies educator, musician*

Gwynedd
LeFevre, Perry Deyo *minister, theology educator*

Harrisburg
Dattilo, Nicholas C. *bishop*
Farrington, Debra Kelli *publisher, writer*

Hatfield
Taylor, Alan Charles *chaplain, counselor, researcher*

Haverford
Kee, Howard Clark *religion educator*

Huntingdon
Durnbaugh, Donald Floyd *church history educator, researcher*

Jim Thorpe
Umbehocker, Kenneth Sheldon *priest*

Johnstown
Miloro, Protopresbter Frank *church official, religious studies educator*
Nicholas, (Richard G. Smisko) *bishop*
Smisko, Nicholas Richard *bishop, educator*

Lancaster
Glick, Garland Wayne *retired theological seminary president*

Lansdale
Rothenberger, Jack Renninger *clergyman*

Lewisburg
Jump, Chester Jackson, Jr., *clergyman, church official*

Lititz
Haines, Ronald H. *retired bishop*

Malvern
Brighton, Ruth Louise *lay worker, educator*

Perkasie
Lang, Susan Marie *minister*

Philadelphia
Bartlett, Allen Lyman, Jr., *retired bishop*
Bracey, Cookie Frances Lee *minister*
Burch, Francis Floyd *clergyman*
Krych, Margaret A *religious organization administrator, educator*
Marple, Dorothy Jane *retired church executive*
Poythress, Vern Sheridan *religion educator, minister*
Rigali, Justin F. *archbishop*
Sulyk, Stephen *retired archbishop*
Trulear, Harold Dean *minister, theological educator, social researcher*
Wengert, Timothy *church history educator, clergyman*

Pittsburgh
Bashore, George Willis *retired bishop*
Brauner, Ronald Allan *religion educator*
Holder, Gerald D., Jr., *dean*
Koedel, Robert Craig *minister, historian, educator*
Maximos, Metropolitan (Maximos Demetrios Aghiorgoussis) *bishop, metropolitan*
McCoid, Donald James *bishop*
Mc Dowell, John B. *bishop*
Mina, John Louis (Ivan Minea) *religious studies educator, archivist*
Schaub, Marilyn McNamara *religion educator*
Shaffer, Terry George *pastor*
Slusser, Michael *theology studies educator, department chairman, priest*
Zeolla, Kim Anne *minister*

Quarryville
Harris, Robert Laird *minister, theology educator emeritus*

Rydal
Black, Thomas Donald *retired religious organization administrator*

Saint Peters
Detterline, Milton E., Jr., *minister*

Scranton
De Celles, Charles Edouard *theologian, educator*
Dougherty, John Martin *bishop*
Timlin, James Clifford *bishop*

Selinsgrove
Thomforde, Christopher Meredith *minister*

Sewickley
Newell, Byron Bruce, Jr., *pastor*

Souderton
Lapp, James Merrill *clergyman, marriage and family therapist*

South Canaan
Herman, *archbishop, head of Orthodox Church in America*

State College
Brotzman, Harry, Jr., *minister*

Sunbury
Ely, Donald J(ean) *retired clergyman, secondary school educator*

Swarthmore
Frost, Jerry William *religion and history educator, library administrator*

Tylersport
Raub, Donald Wilmer *minister, author*

Valley Forge
Harvey, Carole (Kate Harvey) *minister, church official*
Medley, Alex Roy *executive minister*
Weaver, Peter David *bishop, religious organization administrator*
Wright-Riggins, Aidsand F., III, *religious organization executive*

Waynesboro
Coles, Robert Nelson, Sr., *religious organization administrator*

Waynesburg
Visser, Richard Edgar *minister*

Wynnewood
Russell, Horace Orlando *theology studies educator*
Sider, Ronald J. *theology educator, author*
Wachs, Saul Philip *Jewish education educator*

RHODE ISLAND

East Providence
Spina, Douglas John *priest, educator*

Lincoln
Barlow, August Ralph, Jr., *minister*

Middletown
Demy, Timothy James *military chaplain*

Providence
Frerichs, Ernest Sunley *religious studies educator*
Mulvee, Robert Edward *bishop*
Olyan, Saul Mitchell *religious studies educator*

SOUTH CAROLINA

Anderson
Sustar, T. David *religious organization administrator*

Chapin
Branham, Mack Carison, Jr., *retired theological seminary educator, minister*

Charleston
Donehue, John Douglas *interdenominational ministries executive*
Salmon, Edward Lloyd, Jr., *bishop*

Columbia
Adams, John Hurst *bishop*

Elgin
Belton, Sheila Jan *minister, writer*

Greenville
Bell, Robert Daniel *religious studies educator*

Leesville
Crumley, James Robert, Jr., *retired clergyman*

Spartanburg
Bullard, John Moore *religion educator, church musician*
Fogartie, James Eugene *retired clergyman*

Taylors
Smith, Morton Howison *religious organization administrator, educator*
Vaughn, John Carroll *minister, educator*

White Rock
Aull, James Stroud *retired bishop*

Winnsboro
McCants, Clyde Taft *retired clergyman*

SOUTH DAKOTA

Sioux Falls
Carlson, Robert James *bishop*
Cowles, Ronald Eugene *church administrator*

TENNESSEE

Antioch
Worthington, Melvin Leroy *minister, writer*

Brentwood
Stephens, Shirley Lynne *writer, editor*

Chattanooga
Haden, Benjamin *minister, retired publishing executive, broadcast executive*
Hodge, Raymond Douglas *minister*
Mohney, Nell Webb *religion educator, speaker, author*
Ragon, Robert Ronald *clergyman*

Clarksville
Maynard, Terrell Dennis *minister*
Reaves, Barry Reco *minister*

Cleveland
Baker, Michael Lyndon *minister*
Taylor, William Al *church administrator*
Walker, Donald Murray *minister*

East Ridge
Collins, Joda Lee *minister*

Germantown
Allison, Beverly Gray *seminary president, evangelism educator*
Floyd, John David *theology educator, minister*

Knoxville
Prince, Matthew Sperry *religious organization executive*

La Follette
Eads, Ora Wilbert *clergyman, church official*

Loudon
Hallstrand, Sarah Laymon *denomination executive*
Jones, Robert Gean *religion educator*
Puckett, Robert Marion *clergyman*

Memphis
Magrill, Joe Richard, Jr., *religious organization administrator, minister*

McKenzie, Steven L. *theology studies educator, writer*
Steib, James Terry *bishop*
Todd, Virgil Holcomb *clergyman, religion educator*
Walker, Randolph Meade *minister*

Murfreesboro
Walker, David Ellis, Jr., *educator, minister, consultant*

Nashville
Bigham, Wanda Durrett *religious organization administrator*
Chapman, Morris Hines *denominational executive*
Collins, Joyce P. *minister, librarian, educator*
Draper, James Thomas, Jr., (Jimmy Draper) *clergyman*
Hall, Richard Clyde, Jr., *retired religious educational administrator*
Kmiec, Edward Urban *bishop*
Land, Richard Dale *minister, religious organization administrator*
Moss, Carl Michael *minister, religious studies educator*
TeSelle, Eugene Arthur, Jr., *religion educator*

Sewanee
Gessell, John Maurice *minister, educator*
Hughes, Robert Davis, III, *theology studies educator*
Lytle, Guy Fitch, III, *priest, educator, dean*
Parsley, Henry Nutt, Jr., *bishop, academic administrator*

Signal Mountain
Hall, Thor *religion educator*

Springfield
Fagan, A. Rudolph *minister*

TEXAS

Alice
Tetlie, Harold *priest*

Amarillo
DeVaughn, Michael Richard *minister, administrator*
Klein, Jerry Lee, Sr., *religion educator, minister*

Arlington
Lingerfelt, B. Eugene, Jr., *minister*

Austin
Hitchcock, Joanna *publisher*
Jinkins, Wm. Michael *theology studies educator*
Wahlberg, Philip Lawrence *former bishop*

Brownsville
Fitzpatrick, John J. *bishop*
Pena, Raymundo Joseph *bishop*

Channelview
Graves, Thurman B. *minister, counselor*

Cleburne
Bushor, Mark Eldon *pastor, writer, consultant*

Corpus Christi
Fleischer, Daniel *minister, religious organization administrator*

Dallas
Blue, J(ohn) Ronald *evangelical mission executive*
Carnes, Joseph Sydney *clergyman*
Daves, Don Michael *minister*
Esqueda, Octavio Javier *religious studies educator*
Galante, Joseph A. *bishop*
Grahmann, Charles V. *bishop*
Gross, Harriet P. Marcus *religious studies and writing educator*
Kirby, James Edmund, Jr., *theology educator*
Lang, James Devore, Jr., *ministry executive*
Lovin, Robin Warren *clergy member, educator*
Pauley, Shirley Stewart *religious organization executive*
Pinson, William Meredith, Jr., *pastor, writer, administrator*
Turknett, James C. *minister*
Valentine, Foy Dan *clergyman*
Wiles, Charles Preston *minister*

Fort Worth
Garrett, James Leo, Jr., *theology educator*
Gilbert, James Cayce *minister*
Lawson, Carole Jean *religious educator, author, poet*
Patterson, Paige *church administrator, former seminary president*
Rogers, Charles Ray *minister, religious organization administrator*
Teegarden, Kenneth Leroy *clergyman*

Grand Prairie
Fickling, Karl Frederick *church consultant, educator*

Houston
Arnold, James Phillip *religious studies educator, history educator*
Beard, Dennis Alton *pastor*
Ellis, Walter Leon *minister*
Fiorenza, Joseph A. *bishop*
Joyce, James Daniel *clergyman*
Karff, Samuel Egal *rabbi*
Killion, Vida Frazier *minister, writer*
Mattox, Ethel Odessa *writer*
Montgomery, Cleothus *minister*
Nielsen, Niels Christian, Jr., *theology educator*
Sampson, Franklin Delano *minister*
Shiu, Bingiee *religious studies educator*
Sit, Hong Chan *minister*
Stephens, Carson Wade *minister*

Jacksonville
Blaylock, James Carl *clergyman, librarian*

Kerrville
Jordan, Sam Latron *minister, mediator*
Williams, William Henry, II, *publisher*

Kingwood
Barkley, Bronson Lee *minister*

Lubbock
Blevins, Stanley Nance *minister, educator*
Neyland, Malcolm *priest*

Mcallen
Sutton, William Blaylock *pastor*

Odessa
Pugh, Jessie Truman *minister*

Plano
Miller, Ken Leroy *religious studies educator, consultant, writer*

Richardson
Lowe, J. Allen *minister*
Williams, James Francis, Jr., *religious organization administrator*

San Antonio
Fecher, Vincent John *priest*
Jones, Oscar Calvin *minister, dean*
Leies, John Alex *theology educator, clergyman*
Mc Allister, Gerald Nicholas *retired bishop, clergyman*
Rankin, John Karl *retired minister, retired theology studies educator*

Schulenburg
Clark, I. E. *publisher*

Spring
Hunt, T(homas) W(ebb) *retired religion educator*

Temple
Beyer, Richard J. *priest, writer*

Texarkana
Cross, Irvie Keil *religious organization executive*

The Woodlands
Machle, Edward Johnstone *theology educator, retired*
Sudbury, John Dean *religious foundation executive, petroleum chemist*

Tyler
Corrada del Rio, Alvaro *bishop*

Victoria
Fellhauer, David E. *bishop*

Waco
Flanders, Henry Jackson, Jr., *religious studies educator*
Talbert, Charles Harold *religion educator*

Waxahachie
Tschoepe, Thomas *retired bishop*

UTAH

Ogden
Harrington, Mary Evelina Paulson (Polly Harrington) *religious journalist, writer, educator*

Salt Lake City
Bateman, Merrill Joseph *church administrator*
Eyring, Henry Bennion *bishop*
Hinckley, Gordon B. *religious organization administrator*
Holland, Jeffrey R. *religious organization administrator*
Monson, Thomas Spencer *religious organization administrator, former publishing company executive*
Niederauer, George H. *bishop*
Packer, Boyd K. *church official*
Perry, L. Tom *religious organization administrator, merchant*
Scott, Richard G. *religious organization administrator*
Smith, Eldred Gee *church leader*
Wirthlin, Joseph B. *religious organization administrator*

VERMONT

Brattleboro
Hawkes, Mary Newgeon *retired minister, educator*

Burlington
Angell, Kenneth Anthony *bishop*

Middlebury
Ferm, Robert Livingston *religion educator*

Northfield
Wick, William Shinn *clergyman, chaplain*

Pawlet
Buechner, Carl Frederick *minister, author*

Quechee
Wood, R. Stewart, Jr., *retired bishop*

White River Junction
Rutter, Frances Tompson *publisher*

Wolcott
Fisher, Neal Floyd *religious organization administrator*

VIRGINIA

Amissville
Coutu, Charles Arthur *deacon*

Arlington
Kane, Annette Pieslak *religious organization executive*

Ashland
Tuell, Steven Shawn *religious studies educator, minister*

Blacksburg
Grover, Norman LaMotte *theologian, philosopher*

Chantilly
Chrzanowski, Leye Jeannette *publisher*

Charlottesville
Childress, James Franklin *theology and medical educator*
Finley, Robert Van Eaton *minister*
Scott, Nathan Alexander, Jr., *minister, literary critic, religious educator*
Unsworth, Richard Preston *minister, educator, school administrator*

Emory
Kellogg, Frederic Richard *religious studies educator*

Falls Church
Bankson, Marjory Zoet *former religious association administrator*
Benton, Nicholas Frederick *publisher*
Lotz, Denton *minister, church official*

Fredericksburg
Bailey, Amos Purnell *clergyman, syndicated columnist, author*

Front Royal
Andes, Larry Dale *minister*

Glen Allen
Anderson, James Frederick *clergyman*

Hampton
Smith, Sr., Jackie Wayne *minister*

Harrisonburg
Burkholder, Owen Eugene *religious organization administrator*
Pannell, Richard Anthony *religious organization administrator*

King George
Agnew, Christopher Mack *minister, historian*

Lynchburg
Brindle, Wayne Allan *religious studies educator*
Falwell, Jerry L. *minister*

Lyndhurst
Dieter, Melvin Easterday *retired minister, educator*

Martinsville
Plonk, William McGuire *retired minister*
Shackleford, William Alton, Sr., *minister*

Mechanicsville
Gerrish, Brian Albert *theologian, educator, minister*

Midlothian
Hanes-Stevens, LaVerne E. *minister, social services administrator*

Mineral
Speer, Jack Atkeson *publisher*

Oakton
Terzian, Grace Paine *publisher*

Penn Laird
Wise, Charles Conrad, Jr., *educator, past government official, author*

Radford
McNeil, Ramsey English *religious studies educator*

Richmond
Barton, Jonathan Miller *clergyman*
Dombalis, Constantine Nicholas *minister, writer*
Hicks, Douglas A. *religious studies educator, minister*
Lee, Peter James *bishop*
Moore, John Sterling, Jr., *retired minister*
Robertson, LaVerne *minister*

Suffolk
Sweat, Carl Leondus, Jr., *minister, educator*

Vienna
Burr, Ronald Edwin *publisher*

Virginia Beach
Christy, Larry Todd *publisher*
Taylor, Lewis Jerome, Jr., *retired priest*
Williams, J(ohn) Rodman *theologian, educator, clergyman*

Williamsburg
Holmes, David Lynn *religion educator*

Woodbridge
Townsend, Kenneth Ross *retired priest*

Yorktown
Wood, James Edward, Jr., *religion educator, author*

WASHINGTON

Arlington
Kell, Lyle Nicholas *retired minister, retired real estate broker*

Bellevue
Berkley, James Donald *clergyman*

Bothell
Wirt, Sherwood Eliot *minister, writer*

Des Moines
Andrews, William F. *minister*
Tuell, Jack Marvin *retired bishop*

Issaquah
Berto, Deborah Lynn *publisher*

Langley
Le Roy, Robert Powell *retired minister, educator, writer*

Prosser
Cooper, Lynn Dale *retired minister, retired navy chaplain*

Seattle
Burrows, Elizabeth MacDonald *religious organization executive, educator*
Fluke, Lyla Schram (Mrs. John M. Fluke Sr.) *publisher*
Robb, John Wesley *religion educator*
Szeto, Hung *publisher*

Spokane
Edwards, James Robert *minister, religious educator*
Lee, Richard Francis James *evangelical clergyman, media consultant, lawyer*

Tacoma
Peterson, Thomas Charles *minister, pastoral counselor and therapist*
Wiegman, Eugene William *minister, former college administrator*

Tukwila
Robinson, Howard Arthur, Jr., *minister*

University Place
Seiber, Richard Allan *retired minister*

Vancouver
Congdon, Roger Douglass *theology educator, minister*
Crews, William Odell, Jr., *religious organization administrator*

WEST VIRGINIA

Beckley
Rehbein, Edward Andrew *minister, geologist, consultant*

Charleston
Leasor, Jane *religion and philosophy educator, musician*
Scott, Olof Henderson, Jr., *priest*

Harpers Ferry
Lupoli, John *minister, photographer*

Morgantown
Hudson, David M. *minister*

Pennsboro
Poling, Kermit William *minister*

Wheeling
Thurston, Bonnie Bowman *religious educator, minister, poet*

WISCONSIN

Cottage Grove
Baird, Robert Dahlen *retired theology studies educator*
Zingaro, John Charles *minister*

Green Bay
Banks, Robert J. *bishop*
Geisendorfer, James Vernon *religious writer, researcher*

Iola
Mishler, Clifford Leslie *publisher*

Madison
Cohen, Charles Lloyd *history and religious studies educator*
Fitchen, Allen Nelson *publisher*
Fox, Michael Vass *Hebrew educator*
Little, George Daniel *clergyman*
Thomas, J. Mark *sociology educator, research fellow, minister*

Milwaukee
Hirsch, June Schaut *chaplain*
McCann, Margaret Ann *sister, educator*
Schaefer, Jame *religious studies educator*
Stubbe, Ray William *minister, writer*
Weakland, Rembert G. *retired archbishop*

Nashotah
Munday, Robert Stevenson *priest, academic administrator*

Oshkosh
Barwig, Regis Norbert James *priest*

Sturgeon Bay
Van Duyse, Francis Donald (Fritz Van) *publisher*

Wisconsin Rapids
Parker, Arnold John *minister*

WYOMING

Cheyenne
Hart, Joseph H. *bishop emeritus*

TERRITORIES OF THE UNITED STATES

AMERICAN SAMOA

Pago Pago
Weitzel, John Quinn *bishop*

FEDERATED STATES OF MICRONESIA

Chuuk
Samo, Amando *bishop*

GUAM

Agana Heights
Apuron, Anthony Sablan *archbishop*

PUERTO RICO

San Juan
Aponte Martinez, Luis Cardinal *archbishop emeritus*
Gonzalez, Roberto O. *bishop*

CANADA

ALBERTA

Edmonton
Mac Neil, Joseph Neil *archbishop*

BRITISH COLUMBIA

Prince George
Kerr, Nancy Karolyn *pastor, mental health services professional*

Victoria
Hollis, Reginald *archbishop*

MANITOBA

Churchill
Rouleau, Reynald *bishop*

NEWFOUNDLAND

Corner Brook
Payne, Sidney Stewart *retired archbishop*

ONTARIO

Brampton
Bastian, Donald Noel *retired bishop*

Cambridge
MacBain, William Halley *minister, theology educator, seminary chancellor*

Kitchener
Winger, Roger Elson *retired church administrator*

London
Hooper, Wayne Nelson *clergy member*

Ottawa
Macklem, Michael Kirkpatrick *publisher*
Ryan, William Francis *priest*
Squire, Anne Marguerite *religious leader*

Pickering
Irwin, John Wesley *publisher*

Sault Sainte Marie
Ferris, Ronald Curry *bishop*

Scarborough
Mikloshazy, Attila *bishop*

Thorold
O'Mara, John Aloysius *retired bishop*

Toronto
Finlay, Terence Edward *retired archbishop*
Jay, Charles Douglas *religion educator, college administrator, clergyman*
McWilliam, Joanne Elizabeth *retired religion educator*
Novak, David *Judaic studies educator, rabbi*
Plaut, Wolf Gunther *minister, author*

Waterloo
Van Seters, John *retired biblical literature educator*

Windsor
La Rocque, Eugene Philippe *bishop emeritus*

QUEBEC

Beauharnois
Lebel, Robert *bishop*

Chicoutimi
Couture, Jean Guy *bishop*

Outremont
Derderian, Hovnan *church official*

Rimouski
Blanchet, Bertrand *archbishop*

Rouyn
Hamelin, Jean-Guy *bishop*

Westmount
Coolidge, Robert Tytus *deacon, historian, educator*

SASKATCHEWAN

Saskatoon
Jacobson, Sverre Theodore *retired minister*

Montreal
Hutchison, Andrew Sandford *archbishop*
Turcotte, Jean-Claude Cardinal *archbishop*

Quebec City
Stavert, Alexander Bruce *bishop*

MEXICO

Aguascalientes
Godinez Flores, Ramon *bishop*

Guadalajara
Sandoval Iñiguez, Juan Cardinal *archbishop*

Mexico City
Rivera Carrera, Norberto Cardinal *archbishop*

San Nicolas
Suarez Rivera, Adolfo Antonio Cardinal *retired archbishop*

THE BAHAMAS

Nassau
Harrison, Johnnie Sheppard *religious organization administrator*

BELGIUM

Brussels
Jadot, Jean Lambert Octave *clergyman*

BRAZIL

Rio de Janeiro
Sales, Eugenio de Araujo Cardinal *archbishop emeritus*

CHILE

Talca
McNamee, Sister Catherine *theology studies educator*

ENGLAND

London
Hornyak, Eugene Augustine *bishop*
Hunsberger, Alice Chandler *religion educator, human rights activist, scholar*

Tunbridge Wells
Howden, Frank Newton *Episcopal priest, humanities educator*

INDIA

Kerala
Devi, Amritanandamayi (Sri Mata Amritanandamayi Devi) *spiritual advisor*

IRAN

Tehran
Mardinkha, Khnania, IV, *church administrator*

ITALY

Rome
Baum, William Wakefield Cardinal *archbishop emeritus*
Billy, Dennis Joseph *priest*
Kolvenbach, Peter Hans *priest, religious order superior*

Vatican City
Foley, John Patrick *archbishop*
Stafford, James Francis *cardinal*
Szoka, Edmund Casimir Cardinal *archbishop*

JAPAN

Kyoto
Zikmund, Barbara Brown *minister, church history educator*

SOUTH AFRICA

Cape Town
Tutu, Desmond Mpilo *archbishop emeritus*

VATICAN CITY

Vatican City
John Paul, His Holiness Pope, II, (Karol Jozef Wojtyla) *Bishop of Rome*
Stafford, J. Francis Cardinal *archbishop*

ADDRESS UNPUBLISHED

Abrahamson, Karen K. *theologian, editor*
Aitken, Robert Baker *religious studies educator, writer*
Allison, Andrew Marvin *church administrator*

Ambrozic, Aloysius Cardinal (His Eminence Aloysius Cardinal Ambrozic) *cardinal*
Anderson, John Firth *retired religious organization administrator, retired librarian*
Anjulis, Stanley Joseph *retired church administrator*
Armstrong, (Arthur) James (Arthur Armstrong) *minister, educator, consultant, writer*
Aronson, Jason *publisher*
Baehr, Theodore *religious organization administrator, communications executive*
Banks, Deirdre Margaret *retired church organization administrator*
Barker, Verlyn Lloyd *retired minister, educator*
Barré, Lloyd Milton *retired religion educator, researcher, writer*
Barreda, José D. *minister, religious organization administrator*
Bayne, David Cowan *priest, legal scholar, law educator*
Bechtol, Larry Owen *pastor*
Beldon, Sanford T. *publisher*
Bender, Ross Thomas *minister*
Be Vier, William A. *religious studies educator*
Bevilacqua, Cardinal Anthony Joseph *archbishop emeritus*
Bodey, Richard Allen *minister, educator*
Bosco, Anthony Gerard *bishop*
Bothwell, John Charles *retired archbishop*
Broadwater, James E. *publisher*
Brooks, Babert Vincent *publisher*
Buckley, Michael J. *theology educator*
Cacciavillan, Agostino *cardinal*
Capon, Edwin Gould *church organization administrator, clergyman*
Capper, Daniel Stuart, Jr., *religious studies educator*
Case, Michael Lawrence *theology studies educator, minister*
Castle, Howard Blaine *retired religious organization administrator*
Chewning, Richard Carter *retired religious business ethics educator*
Christopher, Sharon A. Brown *bishop*
Clement, John Edward Strausz *retired minister, retired religious organization administrator*
Clymer, Wayne Kenton *bishop*
Cobb, John Boswell, Jr., *clergyman, educator*
Cole, Clifford Adair *clergyman*
Corbett, Gordon Leroy *minister*
Crabtree, Davida Foy *minister*
Craddock, Elaine *religious studies educator*
Craig, Judith *bishop*
Dawes, Leslie Dawn *minister, small business owner*
Dipko, Thomas Earl *retired minister, national church executive*
Douglass, Jane Dempsey *theology educator*
Dudick, Michael Joseph *retired bishop*
Duecker, Robert Sheldon *retired bishop*
Ebacher, Roger *archbishop*
Egan, Edward M. *cardinal*
English-Anderson, San Dei *minister*
Epp, Eldon Jay *religion educator*
Erickson, James Huston *clergyman, physician*
Estep, John Hayes *religious organization administrator, clergyman*
Ewing, Elisabeth Anne Rooney *priest*
Ewing, James E. *priest*
Farley, Benjamin Wirt *religious studies educator, writer*
Fazio, Evelyn M. *publisher*
Ferguson, Whitworth, III, *pastor*
Finnegan, Sara Anne (Sara F. Lycett) *publisher*
Flores, Patrick F. *retired archbishop*
Forst, Marion Francis *bishop*
Frankson-Kendrick, Sarah Jane *publisher*
Fry, Hedy *member of parliament*
Fullard, Henrietta *minister*
Gemignani, Michael Caesar *clergyman, retired educator*
Gerstner, Jonathan Neil *religious studies educator*
Gessel, Gerald Emery *minister*
Gralla, Milton *publisher*
Grant, Leonard Tydings *clergyman*
Gregory, Myra May *religious organization administrator, educator*
Griffin, James Anthony *bishop*
Guccione, Robert Charles Josep *publisher*
Gutmann, Reinhart Bruno *clergyman, social worker*
Hagelstein, Robert Philip *publisher*
Haines, Lee Mark, Jr., *religious denomination administrator*
Hambige, Douglas Walter *archbishop*
Hammond, Charles Ainley *clergyman*
Harris, Nicholas George *publisher*
Harris, Rogers Sanders *bishop*
Haryono, Ignatius Wibisono *writer*
Hernandez, Ramon Robert *retired clergyman and librarian*
Holle, Reginald Henry *retired bishop*
Hughes, Edward T. *retired bishop*
Hummel, Gene Maywood *retired bishop*
Huras, William David *retired bishop*
Hurley, Francis T. *retired archbishop*
Huron, Roderick Eugene *minister, writer*
Hurst, Kenneth Thurston *publisher*
Huyler, Jean Wiley *minister*
Jaeger, James Gordon *minister, librarian*
Jarrell, Charles Michael *bishop*
Jiler, William Laurence *publisher*
Johnson, Gordon Gilbert *religion educator, minister*
Johnson, Jennie *chaplain, social worker*
Jones, William Augustus, Jr., *retired bishop*
Joslin, David Bruce *bishop*
Kari, Daven Michael *religious studies educator*
Keeler, William H. *archbishop*
Kelley, Edward Allen *publisher*
Kellogg, David *publisher*
Kempski, Ralph Aloisius *bishop*
Kidd, James Lambert *retired minister*
Knott, Claudette Yvonne Clark *religious studies educator*
Krause, Edward Charles *priest, educator*
Kucera, Daniel William *retired bishop*
Landes, George Miller *biblical studies educator*
Lansdale, H. Parker *minister, historian, non-profit administrator*
Law, Bernard Francis Cardinal *retired archbishop*
Lazor, Theodosius (His Beatitude Metropolitan Theodosius) *retired archbishop*
Leavy, Herbert Theodore *publisher*
Light, Arthur Heath *bishop*
Lindstrom, Donald Fredrick, Jr., *priest, counselor, consultant*
Lohmuller, Martin Nicholas *retired bishop*
Loppnow, Milo Alvin *clergyman, former church official*

Luetkehoelter, Gottlieb Werner (Lee Luetkehoelter) *retired bishop, clergyman*
Lugenbeel, Edward Elmer *publisher*
Mackey, Jeffrey Allen *priest*
Maginnis, Robert P. *bishop*
Maloney, Pamela *minister*
Martino, Joseph F. *bishop*
McClellan, Larry Allen *minister, educator*
McClinton, Wendell C. *religious organization administrator*
McClurg, Patricia A. *minister*
McCoy, Gordon R. *minister*
McKee, Adele Dieckmann *retired church music director, educator*
McKelway, Alexander Jeffrey *religion studies educator*
McKinley, Ellen Bacon *priest*
Mc Kinney, Joseph Crescent *retired bishop*
McMaster, Belle Miller *religious organization administrator*
McQuilkin, John Robertson *religion educator, academic administrator, writer*
Meade, Kenneth Albert *retired minister*
Melczek, Dale J. *bishop*
Melvin, Billy Alfred *clergyman*
Milhouse, Paul William *bishop*
Miller, Mary Hotchkiss *lay worker*
Miller, Vernon Dallace *minister*
Milligan, Sister Mary *theology educator, religious consultant*
Mischke, Carl Herbert *retired religious association executive*
Morris, Marie Schuessler *dean*
Muckerman, Norman James *priest, writer*
Mulder, Edwin George *retired minister, church official*
Mullan, Donald William *archbishop*
Norgren, William Andrew *retired religious denomination administrator*
Nottingham, William Jesse *retired church mission executive, minister*
Nunn, Charles Burgess *religious organization executive*
Nusim, Roberta *publisher*
Nwokoye, Patrick Ikechukwu *priest, researcher*
Nycklemoe, Glenn Winston *bishop*
Oden, William Bryant *bishop, educator*
Ogden, Maurice B. *retired minister, writer*
Oh, Mark Edward *minister*
Ortiz, Angel Vicente *church administrator*
Osborne, James Alfred *religious organization administrator*
Ostaszewski, Alyce Vitella *religion educator*
Osvath, Ludovic Lajos *minister*
Palms, Roger Curtis *educator, editor, clergyman*
Pasternak, Patricia A. *writer, freelance/self-employed newswriter*
Peace, John T. *religious studies educator*
Peck, Paul Lachlan *minister*
Plomp, Teunis (Tony Plomp) *minister*
Post, Avery Denison *retired church official*
Post, Stephen Garrard *theologian, philosopher, educator*
Poteat, James Donald *retired diaconal minister, retired military officer*
Powell, Donald David *religious studies educator*
Preus, David Walter *bishop, minister*
Probasco, Calvin Henry Charles *clergyman, college administrator*
Reilly, Daniel Patrick *retired bishop*
Reynolds, Lewis Dayton *pastor*
Righter, Walter Cameron *bishop*
Ritchings, Frances Anne *priest*
Ruof, Richard Alan *minister, poet, writer*
Salatka, Charles Alexander *retired archbishop*
Sanfilippo, Mary Helena *nun*
Scantlan, George William *minister*
Scharlemann, Robert Paul *religious studies educator, clergyman*
Scherch, Richard Otto *minister, consultant*
Schmitt, Howard Stanley *minister*
Schuelke, John Paul *religious organization administrator*
Seale, James Millard *retired religious organization administrator, clergyman*
Shaw, Robert Eugene *retired minister, administrator*
Shotwell, Malcolm Green *retired minister*
Sider, Harvey Ray *retired minister, religious organization administrator*
Singletary, Patricia Ann *minister*
Sloyan, Gerard Stephen *religious studies educator, priest*
Smith, D(aisy) Mullett *publisher*
Solano, Julio Rafael *priest, educator*
Spake, Kluane *minister, writer*
Sparks, William Sheral *retired seminary librarian*
Stanley, Myrtle Brooks *minister, educational and religious consultant*
Stendahl, Krister *retired bishop*
Storey, Gregory Dean *publisher, editor*
Thompson, Eugene Mayne *retired minister*
Thompson, Richard Lloyd *retired pastor*
Thottupuram, Kurian Cherian *priest, college director, educator*
Troxel, Ronald Lewis *religious studies educator*
Truehill, Marshall, Jr., *minister*
Vachon, Louis-Albert Cardinal *archbishop*
Van Dyck, Nicholas Booraem *minister, foundation official*
Vasko, Peter Theodore Frederick *priest*
Vlazny, John George *bishop*
Waltz, Alan Kent *clergyman, denominational executive*
Wantland, William Charles *retired bishop, lawyer*
Weaver, Gail Elaine *religious organization administrator, tax specialist, consultant*
Weber, Gloria Richie *retired minister, retired state legislator*
Weihmuller, Patricia Ann *retired minister, artist*
Weinhauer, William Gillette *retired bishop*
Weinkauf, Mary Louise Stanley *clergywoman*
Weiss, Daniel Edwin *minister, educator*
White, Lerrill James *clinical pastoral educator*
Williams, Ervin Eugene *religious organization administrator*
Wills, Charles Francis *former church executive, retired career officer*
Wilson, Lois M. *minister*
Wilson, Warren Samuel *clergyman, bishop*
Winslow, David Allen *chaplain, retired naval officer*
Wisehart, Mary Ruth *retired religious organization administrator*
Wold, Margaret Barth *religion educator, author*
Wolford, Kathryn Frances *religious organization executive*
Woods, J. P. *religious organization administrator*
Wooten, Cecil Aaron *retired religious organization administrator*
Wooten, Joan Hedrich *minister*
Ziegler, Earl Keller *minister*

SCIENCE: LIFE SCIENCE

UNITED STATES

ALABAMA

Auburn
Ball, Donald Maury *agronomist, consultant*
Brewer, Jesse Wayne *entomologist, educator*
Guertal, Elizabeth Anderson *agronomist, educator*
Klesius, Phillip Harry *microbiologist, researcher*
Zhang, Daowei *forest economist, researcher, educator*

Auburn University
Fadamiro, Henry Y. *science educator, researcher*

Birmingham
Davenport, Horace Willard *physiologist, science educator*
Finley, Sara Crews *medical geneticist, educator*
Friedlander, Michael J. *neuroscientist, animal physiologist, medical educator*
Marchase, Richard Banfield *cell biologist, educator*
Michalek, Suzanne M. *biology professor*
Page, John Gardner *toxicologist, research scientist, director*
Rouse, John Wilson, Jr., *technology consultant*
Schafer, James Arthur *physiologist*

Decatur
O'Brien, Richard Alan *research scientist*

Huntsville
Bearden, Thomas Eugene *research scientist, researcher*
Dimmock, John Oliver *physics educator*
Gillani, Noor V. *atmospheric scientist, researcher, educator*

Mobile
Blackburn, Dale Aaron *science educator*
French, Elizabeth Irene *biology professor, violinist*
Taylor, Aubrey Elmo *physiologist, educator*

Montgomery
Sass, Neil Leslie *toxicologist*

Talladega
Schwinghamer, Mary Denise *veterinarian*

Tuscaloosa
Darden, William Howard, Jr., *biology professor*

Tuskegee Institute
Datiri, Benjamin Chumang *soil and environmental scientist*

ALASKA

Anchorage
Maki, Alan Walter *biologist, environmental scientist*
Nielsen, Jennifer Lee *molecular ecologist, researcher*
Parker, Walter Bruce *arctic research specialist, consultant*

Fairbanks
Kessel, Brina *ornithologist, educator, researcher*
Schamel, Douglas L. *science educator, researcher*

Juneau
Shepard, Beatrice L. *retired microbiologist, historian*

Soldotna
Franzmann, Albert Wilhelm *wildlife veterinarian, consultant*

ARIZONA

Bisbee
Behney, Charles Augustus, Jr., *veterinarian*
Milton, John P. *ecologist, educator, author, photographer*

Flagstaff
Cortner, Hanna Joan *research scientist, educator*
Hammond, Howard David *retired botanist, editor*
Price, Peter Wilfrid *ecology educator, researcher*
Putnam, William Lowell *science association administrator*
Slobodchikoff, Constantine Nicholas *biologist, educator*

Glendale
Jordan, Melanie Alison *research scientist, educator*

Phoenix
Bolin, Vernon Spencer *microbiologist, consultant*
DelParigi, Angelo *research scientist*
Kimball, Bruce Arnold *soil scientist*
Papp, Harry *science association administrator*
Wall, Gerard W. *physiologist, researcher*

Scottsdale
Northey, William Thomas *microbiologist, educator*

Surprise
Veigel, Jon Michael *science administrator*

Tempe
Amin, Omar Mohamed *parasitologist*
Lohr, Dennis E. *research scientist, education educator*

Tucson
Acker, Robert Flint *microbiologist*
Boyse, Edward Arthur *microbiologist, medical researcher*
Brusca, Richard Charles *biologist, researcher, educator*
Chapman, Reginald Frederick *entomologist*
Erickson, Robert Porter *genetics researcher, educator, clinician*
Fritts, Harold Clark *dendrochronology educator, researcher*
Ganguly, Jibamitra *science educator*
Gerba, Charles Peter *microbiologist, educator*
Green, Robert Scott *biotechnology company executive*
Hildebrand, John G(rant) *neurobiologist, educator*
Hull, Herbert Mitchell *plant physiologist, researcher*
Jeter, Wayburn Stewart *retired microbiology educator, microbiologist*
Kaszniak, Alfred Wayne *neuropsychologist*
Lai, LiWen *molecular geneticist, educator*
McCormick, Floyd Guy, Jr., *agricultural educator, college administrator*
Neuman, Shlomo P. *hydrology educator*
Shannon, Robert Rennie *optical sciences center administrator, educator*
Strausfeld, Nicholas James *neurobiology and evolutionary biology researcher, educator*

Wikieup
Brattstrom, Bayard Holmes *biology professor*

ARKANSAS

Cherokee Village
Hollingsworth, John Alexander *retired science and mathematics educator, writer, consultant*

Fayetteville
Brown, Connell Jean *retired animal science educator*
Kellogg, David Wayne *agriculture educator, researcher*
Morris, Justin Roy *food scientist, consultant, enologist, research director, science administrator*
Musacchia, X(avier) J(oseph) *physiology and biophysics educator*
Musick, Gerald Joe *retired entomology educator*
Riggs, Robert Dale *plant pathology and nematology educator*
Steele, Kenneth Franklin, Jr., *science educator*

Hermitage
Heilman, Thomas Lewis *science educator*

Jefferson
Casciano, Daniel Anthony *biologist, educator*
Schwetz, Bernard Anthony *toxicologist*

Little Rock
Hinson, Jack Allsbrook *research toxicologist, educator*
McSwain, Byrdie Engle *laboratory scientist, immunohematologist*

Monticello
Cain, Michael Dean *research forester*

CALIFORNIA

Alameda
Luther, John Stafford *biology professor, consultant*

Albany
Schwimmer, Sigmund *food enzymologist*

Atherton
Starr, Chauncey *research institute executive*

Berkeley
Baldwin, Bruce Gregg *botany educator, researcher*
Barrett, Reginald Haughton *biology professor, wildlife management educator*
Bissell, Mina J. *research laboratory administrator, biochemist*
Brenner, Sydney *molecular biologist, researcher*
Burnside, Mary Beth *biology professor, researcher*
Casida, John Edward *entomology educator*
Chapela, Ignacio H. *biologist, researcher*
Cline, Thomas Warren *geneticist, educator*
Freeling, Michael Richard *genetics educator, researcher*
Harris, Eva *molecular biology educator*
Hazen, Terry Clyde *microbial ecologist, educator*
Johnson, Ned Keith *ornithologist, educator*
Levine, Mark David *science administrator, director*
Levine, Michael Steven *science educator*
Lidicker, William Zander, Jr., *zoologist, educator*
Martin, G. Steven *biochemist, educator*
Meyer, Barbara Jean *science educator*
Narasimhan, Thiruppudaimarudhur Narayanaiyer *science educator, research scientist*
Portnoy, Daniel *microbiology educator*
Quail, Peter Hugh *biologist, educator*
Quinn, Nigel William Trevelyan *scientist, engineer*
Rajkumar, Lakshmanaswamy *biologist, researcher*
Schachman, Howard Kapnek *molecular biologist, educator*
Schekman, Randy W. *molecular biology administrator, biochemist*
Shank, Charles Vernon *science administrator, educator*
Sposito, Garrison *soil scientist, educator, reseacher*
Teeguarden, Dennis Earl *forest economist, educator*
Wake, David Burton *biology professor*
Wake, Marvalee Hendricks *biology professor*
Yund, Mary Alice *biotechnology consultant*

Beverly Hills
Smith, Marilyn Noeltner *retired science educator*

Bodega Bay
Clegg, James Standish *physiologist, biochemist, educator*
Hand, Cadet Hammond, Jr., *marine biologist, educator*

Cardiff
Cowan, William Maxwell *neurobiologist*

Carlsbad
Hale, David Fredrick *biotechnology executive*

Carmel
Epel, David *biologist, educator*
Pasten, Laura Jean *veterinarian*

Chico
Ediger, Robert Ike *botanist, educator*
Kistner, David Harold *biology professor*

Cupertino
Cheeseman, Douglas Taylor, Jr., *wildlife tour executive, photographer, educator*

Davis
Addicott, Fredrick Taylor *botanist*
Ardans, Alexander Andrew *veterinarian, laboratory director, educator*
Ateh, Comfort Muyang *science educator, researcher*
Barbour, Michael G(eorge) *botany educator, ecological consultant*
Barthold, Stephen W. *veterinarian*
Baskin, Ronald Joseph *cell biologist, physiologist, biophysicist educator, dean*
Colvin, Harry Walter, Jr., *physiology educator*
Epstein, Emanuel *plant physiologist*
Frankel, Edwin N. *food scientist, educator*
Freedland, Richard Allan *retired biologist, educator*
German, Bruce J. *science educator, science administrator*
Gifford, Ernest Milton *biologist, educator*
Gottlieb, Leslie *geneticist, educator*
Gubler, Walter Douglas *plant pathologist, educator*
Hastings, Alan *environmental biology educator*
Hendrickx, Andrew George *research physiologist*
Hess, Charles Edward *environmental horticulture educator*
Hope, Hakon *research scientist*
Horwitz, Barbara Ann *physiologist, educator, consultant*
Hristova, Krassimira Radoykova *microbiologist, researcher*
Jones, Edward George *neuroscience professor*
Kado, Clarence Isao *molecular biologist*
Kester, Dale Emmert *pomologist, educator*
Kofranek, Anton Miles *floriculturist, educator*
Kuhl, Tonya L. *science educator*
Lucas, William John *science educator*
Meyer, Margaret Eleanor *microbiologist, educator*
Moyle, Peter Briggs *fisheries and biology educator*
Murphy, Frederick Augustus *virologist, researcher*
Murphy, Terence Martin *biology professor*
Qualset, Calvin O. *plant genetics and agronomy educator*
Rappaport, Lawrence *plant physiology and horticulture educator*
Rhode, Edward Albert *veterinary medicine educator, veterinary cardiologist*
Rost, Thomas Lowell *plant biology educator*
Roth, John Roger *geneticist, biology educator*
Schoener, Thomas William *zoology educator, researcher*
Sillman, Arnold Joel *physiologist, educator*
Stewart, James Ian *agricultural water scientist, cropping system developer, consultant*
Tang, Feng *research scientist*
Van Alfen, Neal K. *plant pathologist*
Watt, Kenneth Edmund Ferguson *zoology educator*

Del Mar
Farquhar, Marilyn Gist *cell biologist, pathologist, educator*

Duarte
Vaughn, James English, Jr., *neurobiologist*

El Segundo
Seymour, Scott *science administrator*

Emeryville
Choi, Doo-Sup *molecular biologist*
Houghton, Michael *geneticist*

Escondido
de la Torre, Jack Carlos *clinical neuroscientist*

Fallbrook
Loeber, Thomas Stanton *retired biologist*

Foster City
Goldenstein, Lissa A. *biotechnology company executive*

Fremont
White, Raymond Leslie *geneticist*

Fullerton
Dickson, Kathryn *science educator*

Garden Grove
Gandhi, Manish P. *microbiologist*

Gilroy
Barham, Warren Sandusky *horticulturist*

Hayward
Opp, Susan *science educator, researcher*

Healdsburg
Vedros, Neylan Anthony *microbiologist, educator*

Hopland
Jones, Milton Bennion *retired agronomist, educator*

Irvine
Ayala, Francisco José *geneticist, educator*
Demetrescu, Mihai Constantin *research scientist, educator, computer company executive*
Lenhoff, Howard Maer *biological sciences educator, academic administrator, activist*
Stanbridge, Eric John *biology professor*
Steward, Oswald *neuroscience educator, researcher*

Kensington
Stent, Gunther Siegmund *molecular biologist, educator*

La Jolla
Alvariño De Leira, Angeles (Angeles Alvariño) *biologist, oceanographer*
Baldridge, Kim *science educator*

Golden
Zunger, Alex *research scientist*

Highlands Ranch
Brierley, James Alan *biohydrometallurgy consultant*

Lakewood
Bettinghaus, Erwin Paul *research scientist*

Littleton
Vail, Charles Daniel *veterinarian, consultant*

Longmont
Dierks, Richard Ernest *veterinarian, educational administrator*

CONNECTICUT

Branford
Gordon, John Charles *forestry educator*

East Glastonbury
Smith, David Clark *research scientist*

Farmington
Bronner, Felix *physiologist, biophysicist, educator, painter*
Klobutcher, Lawrence Anthony *biologist, educator*
Rothfield, Lawrence I. *microbiology educator*

Groton
Huang, Liang Hsiung *microbiologist*

Hamden
Adair, Eleanor Reed *environmental biologist*
Smith, David Martyn *retired forestry educator*

Hartford
Wolf, Barry *genetics, pediatric educator*

Madison
Kilbourne, Edwin Dennis *virologist, educator*
Stevenson, Robert Edwin *microbiologist, consultant*

Middletown
Zito, Christopher Richard *molecular biologist, biochemist*

Mystic
Ballard, Robert Duane *marine geologist*

New Britain
Parikh, Nimmi Chandra *Physics educator*

New Haven
Altman, Sidney *biology professor*
Anderson, John Fredric *science administrator, entomologist, researcher*
Aronson, Peter Samuel *physiologist, researcher*
Brown, Thomas Huntington *neuroscientist*
Brunson, Kenneth Wayne *cancer biologist*
Chandler, William Knox *physiologist*
Ciuparu, Dragos Mihael *research scientist, educator*
Cohen, Lawrence Baruch *neurobiologist, educator*
Cresswell, Peter *immunobiologist, educator*
DuBois, Arthur Brooks *physiologist, educator*
Flavell, Richard *science educator, department chairman*
Galston, Arthur William *biology professor*
Graedel, Thomas Eldon *industrial ecology educator, researcher*
Pollard, Thomas Dean *cell biologist, educator*
Rakic, Pasko *neuroscientist, educator*
Redmond, Donald Eugene, Jr., *neuroscientist, educator*
Ruddle, Nancy Hartman *microbiology educator, microbiologist, researcher*
Slayman, Carolyn Walch *geneticist, educator*
Summers, William Cofield *science educator*
Waggoner, Paul Edward *agricultural scientist*

New London
Tassinari, Melissa Sherman *toxicologist*

Norwalk
Post, Gerald Steven *veterinarian*

Old Greenwich
DeOrchis, Frankie Juanita *forester, writer*

Southport
Hill, David Lawrence *research corporation executive*

Storrs Mansfield
Laufer, Hans *developmental biologist, educator*
Marcus, Philip Irving *virology educator, researcher*
Slater, James Alexander *entomologist, educator*

West Simsbury
Morest, Donald Kent *neuroscientist, educator*

Westport
Altman, Lawrence Gene *biologist, educator*

DELAWARE

Dover
Broderick, Cyril Emery, Sr., *plant physiologist, educator*
Peiffer, Randel Aaron *agricultural sciences educator, researcher*

Greenville
Schroeder, Herman Elbert *scientific consultant*

Lewes
Carriker, Melbourne Romaine *retired marine biologist*

Newark
Campbell, Linzy Leon *molecular biology researcher, educator*
DeLorme, Michael *toxicologist, researcher*
Fattah, Abbas *research scientist*
Harik, Vasyl Michael *research scientist*

Wilmington
Darko, Denis F. *research scientist, educator, physician*
Hartzell, Charles R. *research administrator, biochemist, cell biologist*
Van Dyk, Tina Kangas *microbiologist, researcher*
Waritz, Richard Stefan *toxicologist, researcher*

DISTRICT OF COLUMBIA

Washington
Affronti, Lewis Francis, Sr., *microbiologist, educator*
Ampy, Franklin Roosevelt *zoologist, educator*
Anderson, Donald Morgan *entomologist, researcher*
Apple, Martin Allen *science executive, scientist, educator*
Banks, Richard Charles *ornithologist*
Batdorf, Lynn Robert *horticulturist*
Bellanti, Joseph A. *microbiologist, educator*
Berg, Patricia Elene *molecular biologist*
Bernthal, Frederick Michael *association executive*
Boright, John Phillips *science administrator*
Briscuso, Raymond J. *biotechnologist*
Brown, Lester Russell *research institute executive*
Carhart, Homer W(alter) *retired research scientist*
Case, Larry D. *agricultural education specialist*
Challinor, David *retired scientist*
Chamot, Dennis *research organization executive*
Chapman, George Bunker *biology professor*
Coleman, Bernell *physiologist, educator*
Colglazier, E. William *science academy administrator, physicist*
Corell, Robert Walden *science administrator, educator*
Creedon, Jeremiah F. *aeronautical research laboratory administrator*
Dantzler, Andrew Alan *science administrator*
Davis, Donald Ray *entomologist*
Davis, Randy Lee *soil scientist*
De Fabo, Edward Charles *photobiology and photoimmunology, research scientist, educator*
DeGiovanni-Donnelly, Rosalie Frances *biology researcher, educator*
Didion, Catherine Jay *science association administrator*
Dombeck, Michael Paul *fisheries biologist*
Duckett, Catherine Natalia *entomologist, educator*
Elias, Thomas Sam *botanist, author*
Feldbaum, Carl *biotechnologist*
Feulner, Edwin J., Jr., *research foundation executive*
Hammonds, Timothy Merrill *association executive, economist*
Harding, Fann *health scientist, administrator*
Harter, Donald Harry *neurologist, medical educator*
Henkin, Robert Irwin *neurobiologist, internal medicine, nutrition and neurology educator, scientific products company executive, taste and smell disease physician*
Henry, Thomas Joseph *research entomologist*
Hope, William Duane *zoologist, curator*
Huang, Yiau-Min *entomologist, researcher*
Huntress, Wesley Theodore, Jr., *scientist*
Jones, Kerri-Ann *director scientific organization*
Kapetanakos, Christos Anastasios *science administrator, physics educator*
Kass, Leon Richard *science educator*
Kennedy, Eugene Richard *microbiologist, university dean*
Kleiman, Devra Gail *zoologist, zoological park research scientist*
Krombein, Karl vonVorse *entomologist*
Kuntner, Matjaz *evolutionary biologist*
McEwen, Gerald Noah, Jr., *bio-scientist executive*
Meyers, Wayne Marvin *microbiologist*
Miller, Alan Stanley *ecology center administrator, law educator*
Mkhize, Siphiwe Felix *agriculturist, diplomat*
Nabholz, Joseph Vincent *biologist, ecologist*
Nicolson, Dan H. *plant taxonomist*
Nightingale, Elena Ottolenghi *geneticist, pediatrician, academic administrator, educator*
Perez-Gelabert, Daniel Ernesto *biologist*
Preer, James Randolph *science educator*
Pyke, Thomas Nicholas, Jr., *government science and engineering administrator*
Ridenour, Amy Moritz *research center administrator*
Ritter, Donald Lawrence *environmental policy institute executive*
Schad, Theodore MacNeeve *science research administrator, civil engineer, consultant*
Schram, Susan Gale *agriculturist, consultant*
Schultz, Todd R. *science administrator*
Simpson, Michael Marcial *science specialist, consultant*
Southerland, Derrick Theodore *microbiologist*
Spelman, Lucy H. *zoological park administrator*
Tidball, M. Elizabeth Peters *physiologist, educator*
Tingus, Steven James *physiologist researcher, educator, policymaker*
Todhunter, John Anthony *toxicologist, consultant*
Torrey, Barbara Boyle *research council administrator*
Wasshausen, Dieter Carl *systematic botanist*
Watkins, Shirley Robinson *agriculture department administrator*
West, Robert MacLellan *science educator, consultant*
Wilf, Peter Daniel *paleobiologist*

FLORIDA

Apopka
Lobinske, Richard John *entomologist*

Boca Raton
Furman, Mark Evan *neuroscientist*
Samuels, William Mason *physiology association executive*

Bradenton
Anderson, Herbert G. *marine biologist, researcher*
Diana, John Nicholas *physiologist*
Rechcigl, Jack Edward *soil and environmental sciences educator*

Brandon
Jurch, George R., Jr., *retired science educator*

Coral Gables
Lucà-Moretti, Maurizio *research scientist, nutrition researcher*
Schaiberger, George Elmer *microbiologist educator*

Coral Springs
Bolene, Rosalie Steele (Margaret Bolene) *bacteriologist, volunteer*

Daytona Beach
Duma, Richard Joseph *microbiologist, educator, pathologist, researcher, physician*
Scott, John Brooks *retired research institute executive*

Deerfield Beach
Gambino, S(alvatore) Raymond *medical laboratory executive, educator*

Delray Beach
Chavin, Walter *biological science educator and researcher*

Destin
Giadrosich, Donald Louis *research scientist, retired electrical engineer*

Fort Lauderdale
Fitzpatrick, George E. *research scientist, educator*

Fort Pierce
Rice, Mary Esther *biologist*

Gainesville
Besch, Emerson Louis *physiology educator, past academic administrator*
Bonzongo, Jean-Claude Justin *science educator*
Burridge, Michael John *veterinarian, educator, research director*
Cantliffe, Daniel James *horticulture educator*
Cha, Seunghee *molecular biologist, dentist*
Chan, Edward K.L. *biology professor, researcher*
Conrad, Joseph Henry *animal nutrition educator*
Cuda, James Paul *entomologist, educator*
Dilcher, David Leonard *paleobotany educator, research scholar*
Drummond, Willa Hendricks *physiology and medical educator*
Drury, Kenneth Clayton *biological scientist*
Dunn, William A., Jr., *cell biologist, educator*
Grobman, Arnold Brams *retired biology educator and academic administrator*
Grobman, Hulda Gross (Mrs. Arnold B. Grobman) *retired health sciences educator*
Gutekunst, Richard Ralph *microbiology educator*
Hall, David Walter *botanist, consultant*
Himes, James Albert *retired veterinary medicine educator*
Holbrook, Karen Ann *biology educator, researcher, dean*
Hoy, Marjorie Ann *entomology educator*
Jones, Richard Lamar *entomology educator*
Li, Qin-Bao *biological scientist, laboratory manager*
Mariani, Christopher Leonard *veterinarian, educator*
Mead, Frank Waldreth *taxonomic entomologist*
Nguyen, Ru *entomologist*
Nicoletti, Paul Lee *retired veterinarian, educator*
Oberlander, Herbert *retired physiologist*
Popenoe, Hugh Llywelyn *soils educator*
Purcifull, Dan Elwood *plant virologist, educator*
Quesenberry, Kenneth Hays *agronomy educator*
Schelske, Claire L. *limnologist, educator*
Schmidt-Nielsen, Bodil Mimi (Mrs. Roger G. Chagnon) *physiologist, educator*
Seale, James Lawrence, Jr., *agricultural economics educator, international trade researcher*
Teixeira, Arthur Alves *food engineer, educator, consultant*
Vierck, Charles John, Jr., *neuroscience educator, scientist*
Wilcox, Charles Julian *geneticist, educator*
Yamamoto, Janet Kazuko *science educator*

Gulf Breeze
Menzer, Robert Everett *toxicologist, educator*
Wickramasekera, Ian Edward *psychophysiologist, psychology educator*

Hallandale
Tasker, John Baker *veterinary medical educator, college dean*

Hobe Sound
Hand, Peter James *neurobiologist, educator*

Hollywood
Matasa, Claude George *researcher, science administrator, educator*

Homestead
Dong, Quan *ecologist, educator*
Roberts, Larry Spurgeon *biological science educator, zoologist*

Jacksonville
Bodkin, Lawrence Edward *essayist, research development company executive, gemologist, inventor, writer*

Lake Alfred
Kender, Walter John *horticulturist, educator*

Lakeland
Pospichal, Marcie W. *neuroscientist, psychologist, educator*

Largo
Mandelker, Lester *veterinarian*

Margate
Franks, Allen P. *research institute executive, educator*

Melbourne
Helmstetter, Charles Edward *microbiologist*
Storrs, Eleanor Emerett *research institute consultant*

Miami
Abraham, William Michael *physiologist, educator*
Buchwald, Peter Sandor *science association director*
Kohen, Elil *science educator*
Ling, Jian *research scientist, consultant*
Muench, Karl Hugo *clinical geneticist*
Noziere, Barbara *science educator, researcher*

New Port Richey
Day, Peter Rodney *geneticist, educator*

Orlando
Dubey, Vinod Shanker *microbiologist, biochemist, researcher*

Palm City
Boss, Manley Leon *plant physiologist*

Palm Coast
Bullard, Ervin Trowbridge *horticulturist*

Port Saint Lucie
Austin, Philip *research scientist*

Punta Gorda
Beever, James William, III, *biologist*

Ramrod Key
Clark, John Russell *marine biologist*

Ruskin
Briscoe, Anne M. *retired scientist, educator*

Saint Augustine
Flemister, Launcelot Johnson *physiologist, educator*
Xue, Rui-De *entomologist*

Saint Petersburg
Byrd, Isaac Burlin *retired biologist*
D'Elia, Christopher Francis *marine biologist, educator*
Mueller, O. Thomas *molecular geneticist, pediatrics educator*

Sarasota
Clark, Eugenie *zoologist, educator*
Mahadevan, Kumar *marine laboratory administrator, researcher*
Seibert, Russell Jacob *botanist, research associate*

Stuart
Robinson, Michael Hill *retired zoological park director, biologist*

Sun City Center
Rubin, Robert Jay *toxicologist*

Tallahassee
Abele, Lawrence Gordon *biology professor, dean, academic administrator*
James, Frances Crews *retired zoology educator*
Onokpise, Oghenekome Ukrakpo *agronomist, educator, forest geneticist, agroforester*

Tampa
Germroth, Peter *biologist, educator*
Hickman, Hugh V. *science educator, researcher*
Jove, Richard *molecular biologist*
Ketcham, Beverly Lynn *biologist, educator*
Lim, Daniel Van *microbiology educator*

Tequesta
Larson, Edythe K. *science educator*

Venice
Barnhart, Charles Elmer *animal sciences educator*

Winter Haven
Grierson, William *retired agricultural educator*

Winter Park
Fluno, John Arthur *entomologist, consultant*

GEORGIA

Alpharetta
Balows, Albert *microbiologist, educator*
Rettig, Terry *veterinarian, wildlife consultant, construction contractor*

Athens
Albersheim, Peter *biology professor*
Avise, John Charles *geneticist, educator*
Dickerson, Harry Wilson, Jr., *veterinary microbiologist, educator*
Giles, Norman Henry *geneticist, science educator*
Gray, Elmer William *entomologist, consultant*
Jurat-Fuentes, Juan Luis *entomologist, researcher*
Maier, Robert J. *microbiologist, educator*
Meyer, Judy L. *science educator, director*
Meyers, Joseph Michael *biologist, researcher*
Plummer, Gayther L(ynn) *ecologist, climatologist, researcher*
Shockley, Floyd Wayne *research scientist*
Shotts, Emmett Booker, Jr., *microbiology educator, researcher*
Tyler, David Earl *veterinary medical educator*

Atlanta
Chai, Xin-Sheng, Sr., *research scientist*
Circeo, Louis Joseph, Jr., *research scientist, civil engineer*
Clifton, David Samuel, Jr., *research executive, economist*
Compans, Richard W. *microbiology educator*
Dowdle, Walter Reid *microbiologist, medical center administrator*
Facklam, Richard R. *microbiologist, director scientific organization*
Fowler, Bruce Andrew *toxicologist, researcher, public health service officer*
Glass, Roger I. *virologist*
Gunn, Robert Burns *physiology educator*
Jeffery, Geoffrey Marron *medical parasitologist*
Jiang, Baoming *scientist*
Marder, Seth Richard *science educator, small business owner*
McQueen, David Vincent *research scientist*
Shur, Barry David *cell biologist, researcher*
Spitznagel, John Keith *microbiologist, immunologist, physician*

Vesper, Hubert Walter *food scientist, researcher*
Warren, Stephen Theodore *human geneticist, educator*

Augusta
Baker, Carleton Harold *physiology educator*
Hayes, John Thompson *biology professor, academic administrator*
Inscho, Edward William *physiology educator*
Kutlar, Ferdane *genetics educator, researcher*
Yu, Robert Kuan-jen *biochemistry educator*

Bowden
Sulzer, Alexander Jackson *retired research microbiologist, educator*

Columbus
Riggsby, Ernest Duward *science educator, educational consultant*

Decatur
Cavallaro, Joseph John *retired microbiologist*

Duluth
Johnston, William David *biotechnology executive*

Dunwoody
La Motte, Louis Cossitt, Jr., *medical scientist, consultant*

Griffin
Beuchat, Larry R. *food scientist, educator*
Doyle, Michael Patrick *microbiologist, educator, director*
Shuman, Larry Myers *soil chemist*

Macon
Volpe, Erminio Peter *biologist, educator*

Martinez
Chaudhary, Shaukat Ali *ecologist, plant taxonomist*

Newton
Blood, Elizabeth R. *research scientist*

Norcross
Dibb, David Walter *research association administrator*
Wagner, Robert Earl *retired agronomist*

Savannah
Eaves, George Newton *lecturer, consultant, research administrator*

Tifton
Burton, Glenn Willard *geneticist*
Ruberson, John Russell *entomology educator*

Waleska
Robertson, Eddie B. *biologist, educator*

HAWAII

Ewa Beach
Chock, Alvin Keali'i *retired botanist*

Hawaii National Park
Camp, Richard J. *ecologist, statistician, researcher*

Honolulu
Carson, Hampton Lawrence *geneticist, educator*
Easton, Emmett Richard *entomologist, zoologist, researcher, academic administrator*
Fok, Agnes Kwan *retired cell biologist, educator*
Fujioka, Roger Sadao *microbiologist, researcher*
Gubler, Duane J. *research scientist, educator, virologist*
Kamemoto, Fred Isamu *retired zoologist*
Kay, Elizabeth Alison *zoology educator*
Mandel, Morton *molecular biologist*
Sagawa, Yoneo *horticulturist, educator*
Sether, Diane M. *research scientist*
Turner, Fred, Jr., *soil scientist, consultant*
Wright, Mark G. *entomologist*

Kalaheo
Cox, Paul Alan *ethnobotanist, educator*

IDAHO

Moscow
Roberts, Lorin Watson *botanist, educator*

Sun Valley
Ring, Terry William *company executive, environmentalist*

Twin Falls
Burton, Lawrence DeVere *agriculturist, educator*

ILLINOIS

Argonne
Allain, Jean Paul *research scientist*
Grunder, Hermann A. *science administrator*
Schriesheim, Alan *research administrator*

Berwyn
Parker, Alan John *veterinary neurologist, educator, researcher*

Bridgeview
Parmer, Dan Gerald *veterinarian*

Brookfield
Rabb, George Bernard *zoologist, conservationist*

Burr Ridge
Rosenberg, Robert Brinkmann *technology organization executive*

Carbondale
Achenbach, Laurie A. *science educator*
Burr, Brooks Milo *zoology educator*
Renzaglia, Karen A. *biologist, educator*

Champaign
Batzli, George Oliver *ecology educator*
Crnekovic, Victoria Estefania *biologist, educator*
Levin, Geoffrey Arthur *botanist*
Ridlen, Samuel Franklin *agriculture educator*

Chicago
Allampallam, Krishnan *biotechnology consultant*
Beattie, Ted Arthur *zoological gardens and aquarium administrator*
Bell, Kevin J. *zoological park administrator*
Chakrabarty, Ananda Mohan *microbiologist*
Chauhan, Neelima B. *neuroscientist, researcher*
Cohen, Edward Philip *microbiology and immunology educator, physician*
Davidson, Richard Laurence *geneticist, educator*
De, Devasmita *research aquarist*
Desjardins, Claude *physiologist, dean*
Fisher, Lester Emil *zoo administrator*
Fukui, Yoshio *biology professor*
Gassman, Merrill Loren *biologist, educator*
Greenberg, Bernard *entomologist, educator*
Houk, James Charles *physiologist, educator*
Kocka, Frank Edward *retired microbiologist*
Kopec, John William *research scientist*
Li, Wen-Hsiung *geneticist*
Lindquist, Susan Lee *biology and microbiology educator*
Mateles, Richard Isaac *biotechnologist*
McClintock, Martha K. *biologist, educator*
Mullins, Obera *retired microbiologist*
Olopade, Olufunmilayo Falusi *oncologist, geneticist, educator*
Park, Thomas Joseph *biology researcher, educator*
Parks, Joan H. *research scientist, educator*
Rempfer, Dietmar *research scientist, consultant*
Roizman, Bernard *virologist, educator*
Sivananthan, Sivalingam *science educator*
Solaro, Ross John *physiologist, biophysicist*
Storb, Ursula Beate *molecular genetics and cell biology educator*
Straus, Lorna Puttkammer *biology professor*
Thompson, Steven *zoological park administrator*
Webb, Emily *retired plant morphologist*

Dekalb
Zar, Jerrold H(oward) *biologist, statistician*

Downers Grove
Brekke, Stewart Ernest *retired chemistry and physics educator*

Evanston
Dallos, Peter John *neurobiologist, educator*
Mason, Thomas Oliver *materials science and engineering educator, researcher*
Novales, Ronald Richards *zoologist, educator*
Wu, Tai Te *biological sciences and engineering educator*

Glendale Heights
Pimental, Patricia Ann *neuropsychologist, consulting company executive, author*

Glenview
Kinigakis, Panagiotis *research scientist, engineer, inventor, author*

Hinsdale
Pawley, Ray Lynn *retired zoological park consultant, real estate developer*

Lisle
Smith, Jared Russell William *research executive, research scientist, consultant, poet*
Ware, George Henry *botanist*

Macomb
Barclay, Martha Jane *science educator, research scientist*

Maywood
Cera, Lee Marie *veterinarian*
Zlobin, Andrew *molecular biologist, virologist*

Normal
Brown, Lauren Evans *zoologist, researcher, educator*

North Chicago
Albach, Richard Allen *microbiology educator*
Yoon, Ji-Won *virology, immunology and diabetes educator, research administrator*

Northbrook
King, Robert Charles *biologist, educator*
Storhoff, James Justin *scientist*

Oak Brook
Ding, Jianchi *embryologist, researcher*

Peoria
Kurtzman, Cletus Paul *microbiologist, researcher*

River Grove
Gardner, Sandi B. *biology professor*

Savoy
Sinclair, James Burton *retired plant pathology educator, consultant*

Skokie
Bell, Rosonald Renae *toxicologist*

Springfield
Munyer, Edward A. *zoologist*

Urbana
Banwart, Wayne Lee *agronomy, environmental science educator*
Berenbaum, May Roberta *entomology educator*
Bullo, Francesco *science educator*
Chow, Poo *wood technologist, scientist*
Crang, Richard Francis Earl *plant and cell biologist, research center administrator*
Cronan, Jr., John Emerson *microbiologist*
Dziuk, Philip John *animal scientist educator*
Endress, Anton G. *horticulturist, educator*
Frazzetta, Thomas Henry *evolutionary biologist, functional morphologist, educator*
Heath, James Edward *retired physiology educator*
Heichel, Gary Harold *agronomist, educator*
Hoeft, Robert Gene *agriculture educator*
Holt, Donald A. *agronomist, consultant, researcher, retired academic administrator*
Mc Glamery, Marshal Dean *crop scientist, weed science educator*
Meyer, Richard Charles *microbiologist, educator*
Nanney, David Ledbetter *geneticist, educator*
Portis, Archie Ray, Jr., *plant physiologist, agronomy educator*
Ridgway, Marcella Davies *veterinarian*
Robinson, Gene Ezia *biologist, educator*
Seigler, David Stanley *botanist, educator, chemist*
Splittstoesser, Walter Emil *plant physiologist*
Weaver, John H *research scientist, educator*
Whitt, Gregory Sidney *evolution educator*

Wheaton
Page, L. Kristen *biologist, educator*

INDIANA

Bloomington
Clevenger, Sarah *botanist, computer consultant*
DeVoe, Robert Donald *visual physiologist*
Gest, Howard *microbiologist, educator*
Hammel, Harold Theodore *physiology and biophysics educator, researcher*
Heiser, Charles Bixler, Jr., *botany educator*
Hites, Ronald Atlee *environmental science educator, chemist*
Ketterson, Ellen D. *biologist, educator*
Nolan, Val, Jr., *biologist, lawyer*
Ruesink, Albert William *biologist, plant sciences educator*
Steinmetz, Joseph Edward *neuroscience and psychology educator*
Weinberg, Eugene David *microbiologist, educator*

Carmel
Rott, Stephen Ross *biologist, educator*

Chesterton
Wiemann, Marion Russell, Jr., (Baron of Camster) *biologist*

Evansville
Price, Charles Lee *science educator*

Greenfield
Wolff, Ronald Keith *toxicologist, researcher*

Hammond
Gealt, Michael A. *environmental microbiologist, educator*

Hobart
Seeley, Mark *agronomist*

Indianapolis
Cliff, Johnnie Marie *mathematics and chemistry educator*
Damush, Teresa Marie *research scientist*
Fibiger, Hans Christian *science administrator*
Jones, Robert Brooke *microbiologist, educator, associate dean*
Ochs, Sidney *neurophysiology educator*
Rhoades, Rodney Allen *physiologist, educator*
Storhoff, Diana Carmack *research scientist*
Wu, Min *cell biologist, researcher, educator*

Lafayette
Achgill, Ralph Kenneth *retired research scientist*
Harris, Donald Wayne *research scientist*
Hasegawa, Paul M. *horticulturist, educator*
Nicholson, Ralph Lester *botanist, educator*

Lanesville
Cleveland, Peggy Rose Richey *cytotechnologist*

Marion
Goff, Albert Michael *entomologist, educator*

Muncie
Amschler, Denise H. *health science educator*
Hendrix, Jon Richard *biology professor*
Henzlik, Raymond Eugene *zoophysiologist, educator*
Mertens, Thomas Robert *biology professor*
Wise, Charles Davidson *science educator*

Notre Dame
Burns, Peter C. *science educator, engineering educator*
Jensen, Richard Jorg *biologist, educator*
Pollard, Morris *microbiologist, educator*

West Lafayette
Albright, Jack Lawrence *animal science and veterinary educator*
Amstutz, Harold Emerson *veterinarian, educator*
Cassens, Daniel Lee *forester, educator*
Diekman, Mark A. *animal science educator*
Duerstock, Bradley S. *neurobiologist, researcher*
Hoxie, Robert Prynne *retired entomologist*
Hunt, Michael O'Leary *wood science and engineering educator*
Janick, Jules *horticultural scientist, educator*
Le Master, Dennis Clyde *natural resource economics and policy educator*
Mason, Sally Kay Frost *biology professor, provost, dean*
McFee, William Warren *soil scientist*
Ohm, Herbert Willis *agronomy educator*
Ortman, Eldon E. *entomologist, educator*
Pittendrigh, Barry Robert *entomology professor*
Sherman, Louis Allen *biology professor, department chairman*
Stob, Martin *physiology educator*
White, Joe Lloyd *soil scientist, educator*

IOWA

Ames
Anderson, Lloyd Lee *animal science educator*
Beran, George Wesley *veterinary microbiology educator*
Bolin, Steven Robert *veterinarian researcher*
Cheville, Norman Frederick *veterinary pathologist, dean*
Freeman, Albert E. *agricultural science educator, dairy cattle geneticist*
Greve, John Henry *veterinary parasitologist, educator*
Hallauer, Arnel Roy *geneticist*
Hatfield, Jerry Lee *plant physiologist, biometeorologist*
Johnson, Lawrence Alan *cereal technologist, educator, administrator*
Karlen, Douglas Lawrence *soil scientist*
Lee, Seong-Jae *research scientist*
Mengeling, William Lloyd *retired veterinarian, virologist*
Mertins, James Walter *entomologist*
Moon, Harley William *veterinarian*
Moore, Kenneth James *agronomy educator, scientist*
O'Berry, Phillip Aaron *veterinarian*
Ross, Richard Francis *veterinarian, microbiologist, educator, dean*
Seaton, Vaughn Allen *retired veterinary pathology educator*
Stalheim, Ole Henry V. *veterinarian, educator*
Thompson, Louis Milton *agronomy educator, scientist*
Ugurlu, Ozan *research scientist*
Voss, Regis Dale *agronomist, educator*
Willham, Richard Lewis *animal science educator*

Belle Plaine
Danker, Thomas Nathan *agronomist*

Des Moines
Rosen, Matthew Stephen *botanist, consultant*

Grinnell
Campbell, David George *ecologist, researcher, author*
Walker, Waldo Sylvester *biologist, educator, academic administrator*

Iowa City
Cruden, Robert William *botany educator*
Gibson, David Thomas *microbiology educator*
Hausler, William John, Jr., *microbiologist, educator, public health service officer*
Hell, Johannes Wilhelm *neuroscientist, researcher*
Husted, Russell Forest *research scientist*
Kessel, Richard Glen *zoology educator*
Koontz, Frank P. *microbiology educator, research administrator*
Lee, John D. *science educator*
Lim, Ramon (Khe-Siong Lim) *neuroscience educator, researcher*
Maxson, Linda Ellen *biologist, educator*
Pessin, Jeffrey E. *physiology educator*
Stay, Barbara *zoologist, educator*
Wunder, Charles C(ooper) *physiology and biophysics educator, gravitational biologist*

Johnston
Duvick, Donald Nelson *plant breeder*

KANSAS

Emporia
Sundberg, Marshall David *biology professor*

Hays
Coyne, Patrick Ivan *physiological ecologist*

Kansas City
Cheney, Paul D. *physiologist, educator*
Doull, John *toxicologist, pharmacologist*
Greenwald, Gilbert Saul *physiologist*

Lansing
Rawlings, Gregory Owen *science educator, consultant*

Lawrence
Armitage, Kenneth Barclay *biology and ecology professor*
Bovee, Eugene Cleveland *protozoologist, emeritus educator*
Byers, George William *retired entomology educator*
Downing, David *science administrator*
Johnston, Richard Fourness *biologist, educator*
Lane, Meredith Anne *botany educator, museum curator*
Lichtwardt, Robert William *mycologist*
Shankel, Delbert Merrill *microbiologist, biologist, educator*

Manhattan
Chakrabarti, Seemanti *entomologist, researcher*
Erickson, Howard Hugh *veterinarian, physiology educator*
Haub, Mark D. *exercise physiologist*
Kirkham, M. B. *plant physiologist, educator*
Mengel, David Bruce *agronomy and soil science educator*
Posler, Gerry Lynn *agronomist, educator*

Neosho Falls
Bader, Robert Smith *biology, zoology educator and researcher*

Overland Park
Goetz, Kenneth Lee *cardiovascular physiologist, research consultant, writer*

Parsons
Lomas, Lyle Wayne *agricultural research administrator, educator*

Topeka
Mara, John Lawrence *retired veterinarian, consultant*

KENTUCKY

Cynthiana
Bandurski, Bruce Lord *retired ecological and environmental scientist*

Highland Heights
Staneck, Joseph L. *microbiologist, science administrator*

Lexington
Frye, Wilbur Wayne *retired soil science educator, researcher, administrator*
Goodman, Norman Loyal *microbiologist, educator*
Hopper, Kevin R. *biologist*
Humphries, Asa Alan, Jr., *biologist, educator, dean*
Lodder, Robert A. *science educator*
Mitchell, George Ernest, Jr., *animal scientist, educator*
Reed, Michael Robert *agricultural economist*
Sekulic, Dusan P. *science educator, researcher*
Timoney, Peter Joseph *veterinarian, virologist, educator, consultant*
Wekstein, David Robert *physiology educator, researcher*

Louisville
Brittian, Kenneth Ray *research scientist*
Egilmez, Nejat K. *science educator*
Harris, Patrick Donald *physiology educator*
Lominadze, David *physiologist, researcher*

Prestonsburg
Pridham, Thomas Grenville *retired research microbiologist*

Richmond
Branson, Branley Allan *biology professor*

LOUISIANA

Baton Rouge
Besch, Everett Dickman *veterinarian, university dean and educator emeritus*
Burns, Paul Yoder *forester, educator*
Chapman, Russell Leonard *botany educator*
Hansel, William *biology professor*
Head, Jonathan Frederick *cell biologist*
Martin, Freddie Anthony *agronomist, educator*
Patrick, William Hardy, Jr., *wetland biogeochemist, educator, laboratory director*
Pollock, David Daniel *biologist, educator, research scientist*

Chauvin
Sammarco, Paul William *ecologist, researcher*

Covington
Gerone, Peter John *microbiologist, research institute administrator*

Eunice
Randall Joubert, Lorrie Boullion *science educator*

New Orleans
Beard, Elizabeth Letitia *physiologist, educator*
Fingerman, Milton *biologist, educator*
Ivens, Mary Sue *microbiologist, mycologist*
Levitzky, Michael Gordon *physiology educator, researcher*
Lingle, Sarah Elizabeth *research scientist*
Mitchell, Kenneth D. *physiologist, educator*
Morales-Ramos, Juan Alfredo *entomologist, researcher*
Navar, Luis Gabriel *physiology educator, researcher*
Orihel, Thomas Charles *parasitology educator, research scientist*
Pedersen, Pedie *physiology educator*
Rajasekaran, Kanniah *agricultural biotechnologist, researcher*
Superneau, Duane William *geneticist, physician*
Welden, Arthur Luna *biology professor*
Whidden, Stanley John *physiologist, physician*

Ruston
White, James C. *science educator, consultant*

Shreveport
Jamison, Richard Melvin *virologist, educator*

MAINE

Bar Harbor
Leiter, Edward Henry *cell biologist, researcher*
Paigen, Kenneth *geneticist, science administrator*

Damariscotta
Fuller, Melvin Stuart *botany educator*

Mount Desert
Crawford, Richard Bradway *biologist, biochemist, educator*

Orono
Chute, Harold LeRoy *veterinary pathologist, former chemical company executive*
Ellis, William Grenville, Jr., *marine biologist, educator*

Sangerville
Harris, Norman Edwin *food scientist, consultant*

Waterville
Fleming, James Rodger *science historian, educator*

MARYLAND

Aberdeen Proving Ground
Stuebing, Edward Willis *research scientist*

Baltimore
Agnew, William S. *physiology educator*
Beachy, Philip Arden *molecular biology educator*
Bhardwaj, Anish *neuroscientist, medical educator*
Brady, Joseph Vincent *behavioral biologist, educator*
Broda-Hydorn, Susan *entomologist*
Brown, Donald David *biology professor*
Clements, Janice *science educator*
Dawson, Valina L. *science educator*
Desiderio, Stephen *molecular biology educator*
DeTolla, Louis James *research scientist and veterinarian*
Fitzgerald, Robert Schaefer *physiologist, educator*
Gall, Joseph Grafton *biologist, researcher, educator*
Gallo, Robert Charles *research scientist*
Goldberg, Alan Marvin *toxicologist, educator*
Greider, Carol Widney *molecular biology educator*
Habermann, Helen Margaret *plant physiologist, educator*
Hansen, Barbara Caleen *physiologist, science educator*
Huganir, Richard Lewis *neuroscientist, educator, researcher*
Kirsch, Thorsten *cell biologist, educator*
Littlefield, John Walley *geneticist, cell biologist, pediatrician*
Massof, Robert William *neuroscientist, educator*
McKusick, Victor Almon *geneticist, educator, physician*
Permutt, Solbert *physiologist, physician*
Redfield, Robert R. *virologist, medical educator*
Sack, George Henry, Jr., *molecular geneticist*
Seydoux, Geraldine *molecular biologist*
Sidransky, David *molecular biologist*
Stewart, Doris Mae *biology professor*
Suskind, Sigmund Richard *microbiology educator*
Tamminga, Carol Ann *neuroscientist*
Trpis, Milan *vector biologist, scientist, educator*
Uhl, George R. *science administrator*

Beltsville
Collins, Anita Marguerite *research geneticist*
Murrell, Kenneth Darwin *microbiologist, parasitologist*
Palm, Mary Egdahl *mycologist*
Schneider, Edwin Kahn *research scientist*
Shropshire, Ashaki Djenaba-Serwaa *microbiologist*
Stolwijk, Jan Adrianus Jozef *physiologist, biophysicist*

Bethesda
Bennink, Jack Richard *microbiologist, researcher*
Berzofsky, Jay A. *science administrator*
Bodine, David Monroe, IV, *genetic and molecular biologist*
Brady, Roscoe Owen *neurogeneticist, educator*
Brinley, F(loyd) J(ohn), Jr., *health science executive, physician*
Broder, Christopher Charles *microbiologist*
Burg, Maurice Benjamin *physiologist, internist*
Burns, Drusilla Lorene *microbiologist*
Candotti, Fabio *geneticist*
Chan, Wai-Yee *geneticist, educator*
Chen, Liping *molecular biologist, researcher, biochemist*
Dheenadhayalan, Veerabadran *biologist, researcher*
Di Paolo, Joseph Amedeo *geneticist*
Dorr, Ann Pierce *science educator*
Dwyer, Dennis Michael *microbiologist*
Ehrenfeld, Ellie (Elvera Ehrenfeld) *biologist, researcher*
Francomano, Clair Ann *geneticist*
Frank, Martin *physiology educator, health scientist, association executive*
Galperin, Michael Y. *microbiologist*
Gerfen, Charles R. *science administrator*
Gershengorn, Marvin C *research scientist, director*
Gray, Paulette Styles *biologist*
Greenberg, Judith Horovitz *genetics and developmental biology administrator*
Grisham, Joe Wheeler *cell biologist, educator*
Gruber, Jack *virologist, cancer research program administrator, medical researcher*
Guttman, Helene Nathan *biomedical research consultant, transpersonal counselor, regression therapist*
Hardy, John *research scientist, science administrator*
Hausman, Steven Jack *health science administrator*
Hodgdon, Harry Edward *association executive, wildlife biologist*
Hsu, S. Dana *biologist*
Jackson, Michael John *retired physiologist, association executive*
Kallioniemi, Olli Pekka *geneticist, researcher*
Lai, Zhennan *research scientist*
Lorber, Mortimer *retired physiology educator*
Moss, Bernard *virologist, researcher*
Nash, Howard Allen *geneticist, researcher*
Ochej, Helen Wanda *biologist, researcher, information scientist*
Optican, Lance Michael *research scientist*
Pakaluk, Debra Lorraine Behm *science educator, community service coordinator*
Petralia, Ronald Sebastian *entomologist, neurobiologist*
Potter, Michael *genetics researcher, medical researcher*
Purcell, Robert Harry *virologist, researcher*
Robinson, David Mason *cell physiologist*
Rubin, Gerald Mayer *molecular biologist, biochemistry educator*
Ryan, Kevin William *virologist, researcher, science educator, clinical research administrator*
Salmoiraghi, Gian Carlo *physiologist, educator*
Schlom, Jeffrey Bert *research scientist*
Sewell, Rodney milton *biologist*
Shulman, Lawrence Edward *biomedical research administrator, rheumatologist*
Sokoloff, Louis *physiologist, neuroscientist*
Ungerleider, Leslie G. *neuroscientist*
Webster, Henry de Forest *neuroscientist*
Wolpert-DeFilippes, Mary K. *science administrator*
Wurtz, Robert Henry *neuroscientist*
Yamada, Kenneth Manao *cell biologist*
Zierdt, Charles Henry *microbiologist*

Chevy Chase
Choppin, Purnell Whittington *research administrator, virology researcher, educator*
Kandel, Eric Richard *neuroscience educator*
Van Akkeren, Lorraine Sue *research assistant*

College Park
Cooper, Chester Lawrence *research administrator*
Diener, Theodor Otto *plant pathologist, researcher*
Fanning, Delvin Seymour *soil science educator*
Gantt, Elisabeth *plant biology educator, researcher*
Izaurralde, Roberto César *science educator, researcher*
Jeffery, William Richard *developmental biology educator, researcher*
Miller, Raymond Jarvis *agronomy educator*
O'Connor, John Dennis *biology professor*
Popper, Arthur N. *biology professor*
Weiner, Ronald Martin *microbiology and cell biology educator, research scientist*

Columbia
Davis, Guy Donald *research scientist*
Keeton, Morris Teuton *research scholar*

Derwood
Kusterer, Thomas *project administrator*
Vaughn, Steven D. *veterinary administrator*

Edgewater
Kushlan, James A. *biologist, research administrator, author, educator*

Frederick
Jenkins, Nancy A. *research scientist*
Knisely, Ralph Franklin *retired microbiologist*

Gaithersburg
Aiuto, Russell *science education consultant*
Baum, Howard Richard *research scientist*
Powell, Lura J. *science association administrator*

Garrett Park
Baldwin, Calvin Benham, Jr., *retired medical research administrator*

Germantown
Iqbal, Zafar *biochemist, neurochemist*
Norcross, Marvin Augustus *veterinarian, retired government agency official*

Greenbelt
Comiso, Josefino Cacas *research scientist*
Middleton, Elizabeth McPhee *research scientist*
Thomas, Lindsey Kay, Jr., *research ecology biologist, educator, consultant*

Jefferson
Beall, James Robert *toxicologist, consultant*

Kensington
Jackson, William David *research executive*

Laurel
Rorie, Conrad Jonathan *scientist, naval officer*

Monkton
Mountcastle, Vernon Benjamin *neurophysiologist*

Potomac
Brewer, Nathan Ronald *veterinarian, consultant*
Khachaturian, Zaven Setrak *neuroscientist*
Yufik, Yan Mark *director research development*

Rockville
Beer, Janusz Zygmunt *radiation and photo biologist, scientist*
Carter, Kenneth Charles *geneticist*
Crawford, Lester Mills, Jr., *veterinarian*
Eisen, Jonathan A. *research scientist*
Fleischmann, Robert D. *research scientist*
Fraser, Claire M. *research scientist, science administrator*
Gail, Mitchell H. *science foundation executive*
Gluckstein, Fritz Paul *veterinarian, biomedical information specialist*
Gougé, Susan Cornelia Jones *microbiologist*
Henricson, Beth Ellen *microbiologist*
Kirkness, Ewen F. *research scientist*
Lee, Norman H. *research scientist*
Leef, James Lewis *biology professor, immunology research executive, immunologist, director*
Mertz, Walter *retired government research executive*
Mummaneni, Padmaja *research scientist, educator*
Nene, Vishvanath *research scientist*
Nierman, William C. *research scientist*
Poljak, Roberto J(uan) *research director, biotechnology educator*
Pospisil, George Curtis *human research educator*
Rosen, Saul Woolf *research scientist, health facility administrator*
Salzberg, Steven *research scientist*
Stangel, Ivan *biomaterials scientist, educator*
Sundlof, Stephen Frederick *veterinary administrator*
Venter, J. Craig *science foundation director, geneticist*
Welsch, Federico *cancer researcher*
White, Owen *research scientist*

Salisbury
DiGiovanna, Augustine Gaspar *biologist, educator*
Moultrie, Fred *geneticist, researcher*

Silver Spring
Brandt, Carl David *research virologist*
Corwin, Jeff *biologist, anthropologist, television host*
Erk, Frank Chris *biologist, educator*
Kant, Gloria Jean *retired neuroscientist, researcher*

Stevensville
Lain, David Cornelius *health scientist, researcher*

Towson
Shah, Shirish Kalyanbhai *computer science, chemistry and environmental science educator*

MASSACHUSETTS

Amherst
Dolan, Michael Francis *science educator*
Hepler, Peter K. *biologist, educator*
Litsky, Bertha Yanis *microbiologist, artist*
Margulis, Lynn (Lynn Alexander) *evolutionist, educator*
Palmer, John Derry *physiology educator*
Palser, Barbara F. *botany researcher, retired educator*
Webley, Wilmore Christopher *microbiologist, researcher*
Xing, Baoshan *science educator*
Zimmermann, Robert A. *molecular biologist, science educator*

Andover
Appleby, David *biotechnologist*

Belmont
Todtenkopf, Mark Steven *neuroscientist*

Beverly
Roberts, Richard John *molecular biologist, consultant, research director*

Boston
Beinfeld, Margery Cohen *neurobiology educator*
Broitman, Selwyn Arthur *microbiologist, educator*
Carradini, Lawrence *comparative biologist, science administrator*
Carvalho, John Joseph, IV, *molecular geneticist, philosopher of science*
Chattopadhyay, Naibedya *physiologist, educator, researcher*
El-Baz, Farouk *science administrator, educator*
Essex, Myron Elmer *microbiology and virology educator*
Evgenov, Oleg V. *medical scientist*
Foote, Warren Edgar *neuroscientist, psychologist, educator*
Gimbrone, Michael Anthony, Jr., *research scientist, pathologist, educator*
Green, Howard *biologist, educator*
Greenberg, Michael *neuroscientist, educator*
Haseltine, William Alan *virology educator*
Hochschild, Ann *molecular biologist*
Hu, Jianming *virologist, molecular biologist*
Hubel, David Hunter *physiologist, science educator*
Kahn, C. Ronald *research laboratory administrator*
Kaminer, Benjamin *physician, educator*
Kravitz, Edward Arthur *neuroscientist*
Kwan, Paul W. *science educator*
Leder, Philip *geneticist, educator*
Leeman, Susan Epstein *neuroscientist, educator*
Levy, Stuart B. *molecular biology, genetics educator, research administrator*
Lewis, Kim *microbiologist*
Liu, Xiaoqing *molecular biologist, biochemist*
Mathis, Diane *cell biologist, educator*
Mekalanos, John J. *microbiology educator*
Morton, Cynthia C. *geneticist*
Myers, Richard Hepworth *medical geneticist, educator*
Nadler, Lee M. *research scientist*
Ratner, Marcia *research scientist*
Shatz, Carla J. *biology professor*
Sidman, Richard Leon *neuroscientist, educator*
Sonenshein, Abraham Lincoln *microbiology educator*
Szostak, Jack William *molecular biologist, educator*
Tabin, Clifford S. *geneticist, educator*
Tosteson, Daniel Charles *physiologist, medical school dean emeritus*
Turner, Raymond Edward *science educator, researcher, administrator*

Brookline
Zhang, Xin *science educator*

Cambridge
Arkhipova, Irina R. *biologist*
Barnett, David Philip *horticulturist*
Bazzaz, Fakhri A. *plant biology educator, administrator*
Beckwith, Jonathan Roger *geneticist*
Branton, Daniel *biology professor*
Dowling, John Elliott *biology professor*
Erikson, Raymond Leo *biology professor*
Forman, Richard T. T. *ecology educator*
Fox, Maurice Sanford *molecular biologist, educator*
Gilbert, Walter *molecular biologist, educator*
Goldberg, Ray Allan *agriculturist, educator*
Hartl, Daniel Lee *genetics educator*
Hastings, John Woodland *biologist, educator*
Hopkins, Nancy H. *biology professor*
Horvitz, Howard Robert *biology professor, researcher*
Hubbard, Ruth *biology professor*
Hynes, Richard Olding *biology researcher, educator*
Jaenisch, Rudolf *biologist, educator*
Kanwisher, Nancy G. *neuroscientist*
Knoll, Andrew Herbert T. *biology professor*
Lander, Eric Steven *geneticist, molecular biologist, mathematician, director*
Levi, Herbert Walter *biologist, educator*
Magasanik, Boris *microbiology educator*
Maniatis, Thomas Peter *molecular biology educator*
Marcus, Richard Sargon *research scientist*
Mayr, Ernst *retired zoologist, philosopher*
Melton, Douglas A. *molecular and cell biology educator*
Mickelson, Claudia Ann *biosafety officer, scientist*
Miller, Earl K. *neuroscientist, educator*
Montana, Enrico Sakai *research scientist*
Pardue, Mary-Lou *biology professor*
Pfister, Donald Henry *biology professor*
Pierce, Naomi Ellen *biology professor, researcher*
Prinn, Ronald G. *atmospheric science educator*
Rich, Alexander *molecular biologist, educator*
Rogers, Stephen G. *biotechnologist*
Shieber, Stuart Merrill *natural sciences educator*
Tannenbaum, Steven Robert *toxicologist, chemist*
Tonegawa, Susumu *biology professor*
Torriani-Gorini, Annamaria *microbiologist, educator*
Villa-Komaroff, Lydia *molecular biologist, educator, university official*
Wilson, Edward Osborne *biologist, educator, writer*
Young, Richard Allen *molecular biologist, educator*

Charlestown
Bush, Ashley Ian *neuroscientist, psychiatrist*
Moskowitz, Michael Arthur *neuroscientist, neurologist*
Valera, Eve Marie *neuroscientist*

Chestnut Hill
Ting, Yu-chen *science educator, researcher*

Falmouth
Milkman, Roger Dawson *genetics educator, molecular evolution researcher*

Framingham
Goldman, Ralph Frederick *research physiologist, educator*

Holliston
Prosser, Robert Arthur *retired research scientist*

Hopkinton
Gielo-Perczak, Krystyna *research scientist*

Jamaica Plain
Parris, Thomas Martin *research scientist, consultant*

Lexington
Drouilhet, Paul Raymond, Jr., *science laboratory director, electrical engineer*

Fillios, Louis Charles *retired science educator*
Gibbs, Martin *biologist, educator*

Lincoln
Payne, Roger Searle *zoology researcher and administrator, conservationist*

Natick
Lachica, R(eynato) Victor *microbiologist*
Sahatjian, Ronald Alexander *science foundation executive*

New Bedford
Buff, Eugene *geneticist, researcher*
Smietana, Walter *educational research director*

North Grafton
Schwartz, Anthony *veterinary surgeon, educator*

Norwood
Pence, Robert Dudley *biomedical research administrator, hospital administrator*

Shrewsbury
Baguisi, Alexander *embryologist*

South Hadley
Bledzki, Leszek Andrzej *limnologist, researcher*
Townsend, Jane Kaltenbach *biologist, educator*

Southborough
Madras, Bertha Kalifon *neuroscientist, educator, consultant*

Waltham
Galinat, Walton Clarence *research scientist*
Symosek, Peter Frank *research scientist*

West Falmouth
Vaccaro, Ralph Francis *marine biologist*

Westborough
Kodenkandath, Thomas A. *research scientist*
Nichols, Guy Warren *retired institute executive, utilities executive*

Weston
Marshall, Jean McElroy *physiologist*

Williamstown
Lee, Arthur Virgil, III, *biotechnology company executive*

Woods Hole
Loewenstein, Werner Randolph *physiologist, biophysicist, educator*
Woodwell, George Masters *ecology research director, lecturer*

Worcester
Bagshaw, Joseph Charles *molecular biologist, educator*
Engle, Linda Jane *molecular biologist*
Harnois, Marion C. *toxicologist, consultant*
Kennedy, Linda Mann *neuroscience educator, researcher*
Leonard, Thomas J. *biologist, department chairman*
Mendenhall, Harlan Vincent *research surgeon*

MICHIGAN

Allendale
Baker-Clark, Charles Allen *food scientist, educator*

Ann Arbor
Akil, Huda *neuroscientist, educator, researcher*
Beeton, Alfred Merle *laboratory director, limnologist, biologist, educator, environmentalist*
Brouhard, Gary John *research scientist, web site designer*
Clewell, Don B. *microbial geneticist, educator*
Cochran, Kenneth William *toxicologist*
Dawson, William Ryan *zoology educator*
Drach, John Charles *research scientist, educator*
Easter, Stephen Sherman, Jr., *biology professor*
Edwards, Paul N. *science educator*
Faulkner, John Arthur *physiologist, educator*
Gelehrter, Thomas David *medical and genetics educator, physician*
Ginsburg, David *human genetics educator, researcher*
Hartung, Rolf *environmental toxicology educator, researcher, consultant*
Hawkins, Joseph Elmer, Jr., *retired acoustic physiologist, medical educator*
Kaufman, Peter Bishop *biological sciences educator*
Kostyo, Jack Lawrence *physiology educator*
Kothary, Piyush C. *research scientist*
Ling, Song *research scientist*
Lomax, Margaret Irene *molecular biologist*
Lowe, John Burton *molecular biologist, educator, pathologist*
Moore, Thomas Edwin *biologist, educator, museum director*
Mourou, Gerard A. *research administrator*
Neidhardt, Frederick Carl *microbiologist, educator*
Petty, Elizabeth Marie *geneticist*
Richardson, Rudy James *toxicology and neurosciences educator*
Sarabandi, Kamal *science administrator*
Shappirio, David Gordon *biologist, educator*
Sloat, Barbara Furin *cell biologist, educator*
Stoermer, Eugene Filmore *biologist, educator*
Whitehouse, Frank, Jr., *microbiologist, educator*
Williams, John Andrew *physiology educator, consultant*
Woods, James H. *research scientist, consultant*

Bloomfield Hills
Miller, Dorothy Anne Smith *retired cytogenetics educator*

Detroit
Beierwaltes, William Howard *physiologist, educator*
Edwards, Brian Francis Peregrine *science educator*
Jammalamadaka, Papa Rao *molecular biologist*
Joiner, Michael Charles *radation biologist, researcher*
Krawetz, Stephen Andrew *molecular medicine and genetics scientist*
Lerner, Stephen Alexander *microbiologist, physician, educator*
Novak, Raymond Francis *environmental health/toxicology research institute director, pharmacology educator*
Soltanian-Zadeh, Hamid *research scientist, educator*
Van Dyke, Daniel L. *geneticist*
Wheater, Michelle Kurpakus *biologist, educator*

East Lansing
Bromley, Stephen C. *zoology educator*
Bukovac, Martin John *horticulturist, educator*
Dennis, Frank George, Jr., *retired horticulture educator*
Fluck, Michele M(arguerite) *biology professor*
Gerhardt, Philipp *microbiologist, educator*
Hackel, Emanuel *science educator*
Kende, Hans Janos *plant physiology educator*
Li, Shu-Guang *science educator*
McMeekin, Dorothy *botany, plant pathology educator*
Nelson, Ronald Harvey *animal science educator, researcher*
Petrides, George Athan *ecologist, educator*
Root-Bernstein, Robert Scott *biologist, educator*
Thomashow, Michael F. *microbiologist, educator*
Tiedje, James Michael *microbiologist, educator, ecologist*
Zeikus, J. Gregory *microbiologist, educator*

Edwardsburg
Floyd, Alton David *cell biologist, consultant*

Flint
Wigston, David Lawrence *biologist, dean*

Grand Rapids
Carlotti, Ronald John *food scientist*
Vande Woude, George Franklin *molecular biologist, cancer researcher*

Hickory Corners
Lauff, George Howard *biologist*

Highland Park
Crittenden, Mary Lynne *science educator*

Houghton
Pennington, Wayne D. *science educator*

Kalamazoo
Kujawski, Daniel *science educator*
Marshall, Vincent de Paul *industrial microbiologist, researcher*

Lansing
Nsofor, Leslie Monagolum *food scientist, researcher*

Midland
Brodeur, Julie Celine *marine biologist*
Bus, James Stanley *toxicologist*
Davidson, John Hunter *agriculturist*

Onsted
Freeman, Fred Wesley *forester, educator*

Petoskey
Nicholson, William Noel *clinical neuropsychologist*

Rochester Hills
Unakar, Nalin Jayantilal *biological sciences educator*

Rockford
Irish, Diana Maria *wildlife rehabilitation agent*

Royal Oak
Kagan, Ron *zoological park administrator*

Warren
Cheng, Yang-Tse *research scientist, materials scientist, physicist*

Ypsilanti
Caswell, Herbert Hall, Jr., *retired biology educator*

MINNESOTA

Chaska
Kwak, Seung-Keon *research scientist*

Detroit Lakes
Johansson, John Thomas *retired science educator*

Duluth
Heller, Lois Jane *physiologist, educator, researcher*
Johnson, Arthur Gilbert *microbiology educator*

Mapleton
John, Hugo Herman *natural resources educator*

Marcell
Aldrich, Richard John *agronomist, educator*

Minneapolis
Dworkin, Martin *microbiologist, educator*
Gorham, Eville *ecologist, biogeochemist, educator*
Gudmundson, Barbara Rohrke *ecologist*
Haase, Ashley Thomson *microbiology educator, researcher*
Hill, Tessa *president non profit environmental group*
Johnson, Kenneth Harvey *veterinary pathologist*
Opitz, Donald L *science educator*
Rahman, Yueh-Erh *biologist*
Serstock, Doris Shay *retired microbiologist, educator, civic worker*
Sinha, Akhouri A. *geneticist, researcher, cell biologist, educator*
Watson, Dennis Wallace *microbiology educator, scientist*

Moorhead
Gee, Robert LeRoy *agriculturist, dairy farmer*

Morris
Ordway, Ellen *biologist, educator, entomologist, researcher*

Rochester
Maher, L. James, III, *molecular biologist*
Shepherd, John Thompson *physiologist*

Roseville
Marten, Gordon Cornelius *research agronomist, educator, federal agency administrator*
Ucko, Franz *research scientist, consultant, writer*

Saint Joseph
Kirick, Daniel John *agronomist*

Saint Louis Park
Frestedt, Joy Louise *science administrator*

Saint Paul
Barnwell, Franklin Hershel *zoology educator*
Busch, Robert Henry *geneticist, researcher*
Cheng, H(wei) H(sien) *soil scientist, agronomic and environmental science educator*
Davis, Margaret Bryan *paleoecology researcher, educator*
Diesch, Stanley La Verne *veterinarian, educator*
Ehlke, Nancy Jo *agronomist*
Ek, Alan Ryan *forester, educator*
Feeney, Daniel Arthur *veterinary radiologist*
Kommedahl, Thor *plant pathology educator*
Labuza, Theodore Peter *food science educator*
Leonard, Kurt John *plant pathologist, retired university program director*
May, Georgiana *biologist, educator*
McKinnell, Robert Gilmore *retired zoology, genetics and cell biology educator*
Phillips, Ronald Lewis *plant geneticist, educator*
Roy, Robert Russell *toxicologist*
Stadelmann, Eduard Joseph *plant physiologist, educator, researcher*
Wendt, Hans W. *life scientist*
Wilson, Michael John *biologist, educator*

MISSISSIPPI

Jackson
Mosley, Jessie Bryant *retired science educator*

Lorman
Panicker, Girish Kumar *agricultural scientist, consultant*

Mississippi State
Jenkins, Johnie Norton *research geneticist, research administrator*
Reddy, Kambham Raja *plant physiology educator*
Thomson, John U. *veterinarian, dean*

Oxford
Duke, Stephen Oscar *physiologist, research scientist, educator*
Rego, Cesar *science educator, researcher*

Stoneville
Hamel, Paul Bernard *ornithologist, researcher*
Meadows, James Steven *forester*
Ranney, Carleton David *retired plant pathology researcher, administrator*

University
Keiser, Edmund Davis, Jr., *biologist, educator*

MISSOURI

Chesterfield
Graham, Donald James *food technologist*
Lala, Deepak S. *research scientist*
Williams, Luther Steward *research scientist*

Columbia
Blevins, Dale Glenn *agronomy educator*
Brown, Olen Ray *medical microbiology and toxicology expert witness, researcher, educator, consultant, writer*
Eisenstark, Abraham *research director, microbiologist*
Finkelstein, Richard Alan *retired microbiology educator, consultant*
Ignoffo, Carlo Michael *insect pathologist-virologist*
Kornegay, Joe Neal *dean, veterinary educator, veterinary neurologist*
Kremer, Robert John *microbiologist, educator*
Mitchell, Roger Lowry *retired agronomy educator*
Morehouse, Lawrence Glen *veterinarian, educator, academic administrator*
Munson, Richard Howard *horticulturist*
Nichols, Leland M. *retired microbiologist, counter-bioterrorism researcher*
Poehlmann, Carl John *agronomist, researcher*
Roberts, R. Michael *animal scientist, biochemist, educator*
Tyler, Jeff Wayne *veterinarian, researcher*
Vogt, Albert Ralph *forester, educator, program director*
Yanders, Armon Frederick *biological sciences educator, research administrator*
Youmans, William Barton *retired physiologist*

Eureka
Lindsey, Susan Lyndaker *zoologist*

Jefferson City
Reidinger, Russell Frederick, Jr., *fish and wildlife scientist*

Kansas City
Hagsten, Ib *animal scientist, livestock consultant*
Krumlauf, Robert Eugene *neuroscientist, educator*
Peters, Ralph Irwin, Jr., *biology professor, researcher*
Reichard, Larry A. *biologist, educator*
Sauer, Brian *molecular geneticist, researcher*
Spigarelli, James L. *science administrator*

Kirksville
Peterson, Donald Fred *physiologist, educator*

Mountain Grove
Waldstein, Daniel Eric *science educator*

Saint Louis
Agrawal, Harish Chandra *neurobiologist, researcher, educator*
Allen, Garland Edward *biology professor, science historian*
Bourne, Carol Elizabeth Mulligan *biology professor, phycologist*
Curran, Michael Walter *management scientist*
Curtiss, Roy, III, *biology professor*
Fraley, Robert T. *biotechnologist*
Goodenough, Ursula Wiltshire *cell biologist, researcher, educator*
Grant, Hugh *biotechnology company executive*
Green, Maurice *molecular biologist, educator, virologist*
Hoessle, Charles Herman *zoo director*
Hultgren, Scott J. *microbiologist educator*
Laskowski, Leonard Francis, Jr., *microbiologist*
Mumm, Steven Robert *geneticist, educator*
Murray, Patrick Robert *microbiologist, educator*
Petersen, Steven E. *neuroscientist, educator, health facility administrator*
Raven, Peter Hamilton *botanical garden director, botany educator*
Saleem, Kadharbatcha S *neurobiologist, research scientist*
Schaal, Barbara Anna *evolutionary biologist, educator*
Schlesinger, Milton J. *virology educator, researcher*
Sutter, Jane Elizabeth *science educator, writer, lecturer, conservationist*
Templeton, Alan Robert *biology professor*
Weck, Margaret A. *science educator*
Wold, William Sydney *molecular biology educator*
Woolsey, Thomas Allen *neurobiologist*
Zhu, Xin Liang *molecular biologist, researcher*

Wentzville
Garrett, Dwayne Everett *veterinary clinic executive*

West Plains
Wilcoxson, Roy Dell *plant pathologist, researcher, educator*

Windyville
Condron, Barbara O'Guinn *metaphysics educator, school administrator, publisher*

MONTANA

Bozeman
Costerton, John William Fisher *microbiologist*
Patten, Duncan Theunissen *ecologist educator*
Todd, Kenneth S., Jr., *parasitologist, educator*

Hamilton
Garon, Claude Francis *laboratory administrator, researcher*
Hadlow, William *retired veterinarian, pathologist*

Havre
Clouse, Vickie Rae *biologist, paleontologist, educator*

Helena
Johnson, John Philip *geneticist, researcher*

Missoula
Gibson, Kenneth E. *entomologist*
Thomas, Jack Ward *wildlife biologist*

Moccasin
Chen, Chengci *science educator, research scientist*

NEBRASKA

Lincoln
Francis, Charles Andrew *agronomy educator, consultant*
Genoways, Hugh Howard *systematic biologist, educator*
Hanway, Donald Grant *retired agronomist, educator*
Kamil, Alan C. *biology professor*
Massengale, Martin Andrew *agronomist, university president*
Taylor, Stephen Lloyd *food toxicologist, educator, food scientist*
Van Etten, James *plant pathologist, educator*
Vidaver, Anne Marie *plant pathology educator*

Omaha
Badeer, Henry Sarkis *physiology educator*
Carson, Steven Douglas *science educator, biomedical researcher*
Dvornyk, Volodymyr *research geneticist*
Rogan, Eleanor Groeniger *cancer researcher, educator*
Simmons, Lee Guyton, Jr., *zoological park director*

NEVADA

Las Vegas
Alexander, John Bradfield *scientist, retired army officer*
Capanna, Albert Howard *neurosurgeon, neuroscientist, lawyer*

Minden
Petchenev, Alex *scientist*

North Las Vegas
Blizard, Susan Kennedy *biology professor*

Reno
Bohmont, Dale Wendell *agricultural consultant*
Gifford, Gerald Frederic *retired science educator*
Redmond, Kelly Thomas *climatologist*
Smith, Aaron *retired research director, clinical psychologist*

NEW HAMPSHIRE

Center Harbor
Smith, William Hulse *forestry and environmental studies educator*

Concord
Hartman, Sally P. *toxicologist*

Durham
Golinski, Jan Victor *history of science educator*
Pistole, Thomas Gordon *microbiology educator, researcher*

Hanover
Gilbert, John Jouett *aquatic ecologist, educator*
Spiegel, Evelyn Sclufer *biology professor*
Spiegel, Melvin *retired biology educator*

Lebanon
Munck, Allan Ulf *physiologist, educator*
Ou, Lo-Chang *physiology educator*

Lyme
Swan, Henry *forester, consultant*

Sanbornton
Weiant, Elizabeth Abbott *retired biology educator*

Silver Lake
Pallone, Adrian Joseph *research scientist*

NEW JERSEY

Allentown
Huang, Wenlin *scientist, researcher*

Basking Ridge
Riesenberger, John Richard *science administrator*

Caldwell
Choi, Sook Chong Yoo *physiologist, educator*

Cranford
Jenssen, Warren Donald *microbiologist, consultant*

East Brunswick
Dombrowski, Anne Wesseling *retired microbiologist, researcher*

East Hanover
Nemecek, Georgina Marie *molecular pharmacologist*

Edison
Menoutis, James Vassillios *research scientist*

Hamburg
Buist, Jean Mackerley *veterinarian*

Highland Park
Feuerwerker, Elie *biologist, educator*

Highlands
Psuty, Norbert Phillip *marine sciences educator*

Hoboken
Abel, Robert Berger *science administrator*
Yevick, George Johannus *scientist*

Holmdel
Zhang, Xuemei *reliability scientist*

Hopatcong
Oken, Robert *neuroscientist, researcher, consultant*

Jersey City
Singer, Howard Jack *biology professor, researcher*

Kenilworth
Pickett, Cecil Bruce *cell biologist*

Kinnelon
Richardson, Joseph Blancet *retired science educator, educational consultant*

Lakewood
Witman, Edward Paul *philosophy educator*

Lebanon
Frascella, Daniel William, Jr., *scientist*

Madison
Demain, Arnold Lester *microbiologist, educator*

Marlton
Sidelsky, Patricia Loney *science educator*

Medford
Martin, Joseph Vinson *neuroscientist, educator*

Montclair
Chinard, Francis Pierre *physiologist, consultant physician*

Moorestown
Kalidindi, Surya Raju *science educator*

Mount Arlington
Cohen, Irving David *science administrator*

Murray Hill
Ng, Hock Min *research scientist*

New Brunswick
Chikindas, Michael L. *science educator*
Datta, Prasun *molecular biologist*
Ehrenfeld, David William *biology professor, writer*
Funk, Cyril Reed, Jr., *agronomist, educator*
Lachance, Paul Albert *food science educator, clergyman*
Mainelis, Gediminas *research scientist, educator*
Maramorosch, Karl *virologist, educator*
Pramer, David *microbiologist, educator, research administrator*
Raskin, Ilya *biology professor*
Tedrow, John Charles Fremont *soils educator*
Totten, Lisa Ann *science educator*
Vayda, Andrew P. *human ecology and anthropology educator*
Wang, Yanxin *research scientist*

New Bruswick
Kjer, Karl Morgan *biologist*

Newark
Ledeen, Robert Wagner *neurochemist, educator*
Parrott, Andrew Myles *research scientist*
Vatner, Stephen F. *physiologist, researcher, research scientist*
Weis, Judith Shulman *biology professor*

Piscataway
Browning, Edward Tracy *neurobiologist, pharmacologist*
Denhardt, David Tilton *molecular and cell biology educator*
Douglas, Michael Ronald *science educator*
Essien, Francine B. *biologist, educator*
Liu, Alice Y. C. *biology professor*
Messing, Joachim Wilhelm *molecular biology educator*
Quinn, Christopher Cardinal *neurobiologist, educator*
Wang, Tsuey Tang *science educator, venture capitalist*

Plainfield
Frost, David *former biology educator, medical editor, consultant*

Port Norris
Canzonier, Walter Jude *shellfish aquaculturist*

Princeton
Altmann, Jeanne *zoologist, educator*
Altmann, Stuart Allen *biologist, educator*
Ballou, Janice Donelon *research director*
Bassler, Bonnie *molecular biologist*
Drakeman, Donald Lee *biotechnology company executive, lawyer*
Gould, Elizabeth *neuroscientist, educator*
Grant, Peter Raymond *biologist, researcher, educator*
Grigger, Jane Elizabeth *earth science educator, photographer*
Jacobs, William Paul *botanist, educator*
Shenk, Thomas Eugene *molecular biology educator, academic administrator*
Wieschaus, Eric F. *molecular biologist, educator*
Witkin, Evelyn Maisel *retired geneticist*

Rahway
Reynolds, Glenn Franklin *medicinal research scientist*

Red Bank
Fred, Rogers Murray, III, *veterinary oncologist*

Shrewsbury
Westerman, Liane Marie *research scientist executive*

Stanton
Kille, John William, Jr., *toxicology and biomedical product consultant*

Stratford
Li, David Wan-Cheng *cell biologist*

Toms River
Kudryasheva, Aleksandra A. *scientist, researcher, educator*

West Trenton
Tessler, Steven *ecologist, data processing executive*

Wyckoff
Cropper, Susan Peggy *veterinarian*

NEW MEXICO

Albuquerque
Bear, David George *cell biologist, educator*
Cheng, Yung Sung *research scientist*
Henderson, Rogene Faulkner *toxicologist, researcher*
Hsi, David Ching Heng *plant pathologist and geneticist, educator*
Mauderly, Joe Lloyd *pulmonary toxicologist*
Muggenburg, Bruce Al *veterinary physiologist*
Raybourn, Elaine Marie *research scientist*

Alto
Thrasher, Jack Dwayne *toxicologist, researcher, consultant*

Las Cruces
Cooch, F. Graham *ecologist, educator, ecologist, researcher*
McElyea, Ulysses, Jr., *veterinarian*
Schemnitz, Sanford David *wildlife biology educator*
Sengupta-Gopalan, Champa *research scientist, educator*
Tonn, Robert James *retired entomologist*

Los Alamos
Canavan, Gregory H. *science educator*
Gregg, Charles Thornton *research company executive*
Nanos, George Peter, Jr., *science administrator, military officer, physicist*
Wallace, Terry Charles, Sr., *retired technical administrator, researcher*

Santa Fe
Guthrie, Catherine S. (Catherine S. Nicholson-Guthrie) *retired research scientist*
Harding, Marie *ecological executive, artist*
Smith, Philip Meek *science policy consultant, writer*

NEW YORK

Albany
Burger, Harold Alan *virologist*
Hitchcock, Karen Ruth *biology professor, dean, academic administrator*
Rieder, Conly LeRoy *cell biologist, consultant*
Stevens, Roy W. *microbiologist, researcher*
Stewart, Margaret McBride *biology professor, researcher*
Yu, Jiang W. *research scientist*

Amherst
Edsberg, Laura E. *research scientist, consultant*

Annandale
Cutler, Robert W. *biologist, educator*

Baldwin
Lister, Bruce Alcott *food scientist, consultant*

Bronx
Adinolfi, Marion Darlyne *research scientist*
Bennett, Michael Vander Laan *neuroscience educator*
Conway, William Gaylord *zoologist, zoo director, conservationist*
Dong, Feng *molecular biologist*
Goodrich, James Tait *neuroscientist, neurosurgeon*
Long, Gregory R. *botanic garden administrator*
Mukherjee, Asit Baran *geneticist, educator*
Schaller, George Beals *zoologist*
Waelsch, Salome Gluecksohn *geneticist, educator*

Bronxville
Hutchison, Dorris Jeannette *retired microbiologist, educator*

Brooklyn
Altura, Burton Myron *physiologist, educator*
Carswell, Lois Malakoff *botanical gardens executive, consultant*
Gabriel, Mordecai Lionel *biologist, educator*
Gootman, Phyllis Myrna *physiology, neuroscience and biophysics educator*
Lipson, Steven Mark *applied virologist, microbiologist, educator*
List, Bobye Goodman *science foundation director*
Schiffman, Gerald *microbiologist, educator*
Vassalle, Mario *physiologist*
Zuk, Judith *botanic garden administrator*

Buffalo
Duax, William Leo *biological researcher*
Tomasi, Thomas B. *cell biologist, administrator*

Burnt Hills
DeVries, Robert Charles *scientist, researcher, consultant*

Cheektowaga
Keem, Michael Dennis *veterinarian*

Cobleskill
Ingels, Jack Edward *horticulture educator*

Cold Spring Harbor
Honey, Sangeet *molecular biologist*
Kidner, Catherine Anne *biologist*
Watson, James Dewey *molecular biologist, educator*

Cooperstown
Harman, Willard Nelson *malacologist, educator*

Corning
Pindel, David Lee *biologist, educator*

East Aurora
Sand, Seaward Alwyn *geneticist, researcher*

Farmingdale
Madeska, Valerie Gay *research scientist*

Flushing
Commoner, Barry *biologist, educator*

Fredonia
Benton, Allen Haydon *biology professor*
Brown, William Douglas *biology professor*

Garden City
Podwall, Kathryn Stanley *biology professor*

Geneva
Nault, Brian A. *entomologist, researcher, education educator*
Siebert, Karl Joseph *food science educator, consultant*

Great Neck
Puttlitz, Donald Herbert *medical microbiologist*

Hamilton
Shen, Quang *science educator*

Hastings On Hudson
Cornwell, Anne Chritake *neuropsychologist, scientist, educator, researcher*

Hawthorne
Darzynkiewicz, Zbigniew D. *research scientist*

Hempstead
Cassidy, David C. *science educator, historian*
Hastings, Harold Morris *science educator*

Homer
Gustafson, John Alfred *biology professor*

Ithaca
Alexander, Martin *microbiologist, educator*
Chiang, Huai Chang *entomologist, educator*
Davies, Peter John *plant physiology educator, researcher*
Earle, Elizabeth Deutsch *biology professor*
Eisner, Thomas *biologist, educator*
Fick, Gary Warren *agronomy educator, forage crops researcher*
Foote, Robert Hutchinson *animal physiology educator*
Ghiorse, William Cushing *microbiology educator, editor*
Gillett, James Warren *ecotoxicology educator*
Hairston, Nelson George, Jr., *ecologist, educator*
Henry, Susan Armstrong *biology professor, dean*
Hudler, George *plant pathologist, educator*
Jagendorf, André Tridon *plant physiologist*
Kallfelz, Francis A. *veterinary medicine educator*
Kennedy, Wilbert Keith, Sr., *agronomy educator, retired university official*
Kingsbury, John Merriam *botanist, educator*
Korf, Richard Paul *mycology educator*
Kramer, John Paul *entomologist, educator*
Lengemann, Frederick William *physiology educator, scientist*
Leopold, A. Carl *plant physiologist*
Mai, William Frederick *plant nematologist, educator*
Mortlock, Robert Paul *microbiologist, educator*
Nasrallah, June *plant pathologist, department chairman*
Novak, Joseph Donald *science educator, knowledge studies specialist*
Pimentel, David *entomologist, educator*
Poppensiek, George Charles *veterinary scientist, educator*
Schlafer, Donald Hughes *veterinary pathologist*
Seeley, John George *horticulture educator*
Walcott, Charles *neurobiology and behavior educator*
Wasserman, Robert Harold *biology professor*
Welch, Ross Maynard *plant physiologist, researcher, educator*
Wootton, John Francis *physiology educator*

Jamaica
Gillespie, Marc E. *molecular biologist, educator*

Larchmont
Sklarew, Robert Jay *biomedical research educator, consultant*

Levittown
Stalter, Richard B. *biology professor, researcher*

Loudonville
LaRow, Edward J. *biologist, educator*

Millbrook
Likens, Gene Elden *biology and ecology educator, administrator*

New Hyde Park
Isenberg, Henry David *microbiology educator*

New Rochelle
Beardsley, Robert Eugene *microbiologist, educator*

New York
Auer, Manfred Stefan *structural biologist, biochemist*
Bhattacharya, Satyajit *research scientist*
Blobel, Günter *cell biologist, educator*
Bock, Walter Joseph *zoology educator*
Caesar, Godfrey Wrensford *biologist, educator*
Calame, Kathryn Lee *microbiologist, educator*
Catanzaro, Daniel Frank *molecular biologist, educator*
Chaganti, Raju S. *geneticist, educator, researcher*
Chua, Nam-Hai *plant molecular biologist, educator*
Cohen, David Harris *neurobiology educator, university official*
Cohen, Joel Ephraim *biologist, educator, demographer*
Cranefield, Paul Frederic *physiology educator, physician, scientist*
Dales, Samuel *microbiologist, virologist, educator*
Dandashi, S. Alexander-Levy *operations research scientist, consultant, corporate and government advisor*
Darnell, James Edwin, Jr., *molecular biologist, educator*
Desnick, Robert John *human geneticist*
Despommier, Dickson Donald *microbiology educator, parasitologist*
Eckhardt, Laurel Ann *biologist, researcher, educator*
Feldman, Samuel Mitchell *neuroscientist, educator*
Fuchs, Elaine V. *molecular biologist, educator*
Giampietro, Philip Francis *clinical geneticist, pediatrics educator*
Godson, Godfrey Nigel *molecular geneticist, educator*
Grafstein, Bernice *physiology and neuroscience educator, researcher*
Greengard, Paul *neuroscientist, educator*
Hirschhorn, Rochelle *genetics educator*
Hu, Chuan *cell biologist*
Hudspeth, Albert James *biomedical researcher, educator*
Kelly, Thomas Jesse, Jr., *molecular biologist*
Leaman, Leonard S., Jr., *science educator*
Lederberg, Joshua *geneticist, educator*
Llinás, Rodolfo Riascos *neuroscientist, researcher*
Maas, Werner Karl *microbiology educator*
MacKinnon, Roderick *neuroscientist, educator*
MacNamara, Brian Scott *veterinarian, law educator*
Massague, Joan *science educator*
Mombaerts, Peter *biology professor*
Moore, John P. *microbiologist, immunologist, medical educator*
Moroz, Pavel Emanuel *research scientist*
Morse, Stephen Scott *virologist, epidemiologist, immunologist, educator*
Moy, Richard L. *virologist*
Osgood, Richard Magee, Jr., *electrical engineering educator, research administrator*
Pietruski, John Michael, Jr., *biotechnology company executive, pharmaceuticals executive*
Pollack, Robert Elliot *biologist, educator, author*
Prives, Carol *biologist, educator*
Ribary, Urs *neuroscientist, researcher, educator*
Rice, Charles M. *virologist, educator*
Rothman, James Edward *cell biologist, educator*
Rozen, Jerome George, Jr., *research entomologist, museum curator and research administrator*
Rubinstein, Ellis Marc *science association director*
Rybin, Vitalyi Olegovich *research scientist*
Sabatini, David Domingo *cell biologist, biochemist*
Sastry, Srin *scientist, researcher, educator*
Saunders, Sylvia Christie *biologist, educator*
Segal, Sheldon Jerome *biologist, educator, foundation administrator*
Seyedi, Nahid *physiologist, researcher*
She, Qing-Bai *biologist, researcher*
Sheetz, Michael Patrick *cell biology educator*
Shelanski, Michael L. *cell biologist, educator*
Stirling, Alexandra Lucero *science administrator, writer*
Stotzky, Guenther *microbiologist, educator*
Stutman, Leonard Jay *research scientist, cardiologist*
Sultzer, Barnet Martin *microbiology and immunology researcher*
Tierno, Philip Mario, Jr., *microbiologist, educator, researcher*
Todd, Andrew Christian *research scientist, consultant*
Trager, William *biology professor*
Wharton, Danny Carroll *zoo biologist*

Wiesel, Torsten Nils *neurobiologist, educator*
Windhager, Erich Ernst *physiologist, educator*
Yeung, Wei-Jun Jean *research scientist*
Young, Michael Warren *geneticist, educator*
Zinder, Norton David *genetics educator, university dean*

Owego
Kemp, Eugene Thomas *retired veterinarian*

Palisades
Huang, Huei-Ping *research scientist*

Pearl River
Bigelis, Ramunas *research scientist*

Pittsford
Coleman, Paul David *neurobiology researcher, educator*

Potsdam
Zhang, Tianxi *research scientist, researcher*

Purchase
Ehrman, Lee *geneticist, educator*

Riverhead
Kent, Robert John *marine biologist*

Rochester
Chang, Chawnshang *science educator, laboratory administrator*
Clarkson, Thomas William *toxicologist, educator*
Doty, Robert William *neurophysiologist, educator*
Frisina, Robert Dana *sensory neuroscientist, educator*
Lawton, Kathy G. *biology professor*
Mosmann, Tim *microbiologist, educator, immunologist*
Rodgers, Suzanne Hooker *ergonomics consultant, physiologist*
Weiss, Bernard *toxicology educator*

Scarsdale
Rivlin, Richard Saul *physiologist, educator*

Setauket
Doering, Charles Henry *research scientist, educator, editor, publisher*

Southold
Callis, Jerry Jackson *veterinarian*

Stanfordville
Tetor, David R. *agriculturist, consultant*

Stone Ridge
Terpening, Donald Lester *science educator, medical technologist*

Stony Brook
Akella, Umasundari Srivenkata *research scholar*
Lennarz, William Joseph *research biologist, educator*
Rohlf, F. James *biometrician, educator*
Semyonov, Oleg G. *research scientist*

Syracuse
Dunham, Philip Bigelow *biology professor, physiologist*
Turner, Christopher Edward *cell biology educator*
Verrillo, Ronald Thomas *neuroscience educator, researcher*

Troy
Berg, Daniel *science and technology educator*
Ehrlich, Henry Lutz *biology professor*
Lvov, Yuri Victorovich *science educator*
Rumyantsev, Sergey L. *research scientist, educator*

Upton
Chaudhari, Praveen *science administrator, materials physicist*
Paul, Peter *science administrator*

Utica
Antzelevitch, Charles *research center executive*

Valhalla
Chung, Fung-Lung *cancer research scientist*

White Plains
Peyton, Donald Leon *retired standards association executive*
Smith, Gerard Peter *neuroscientist*

Woodbury
Kantarci, Sibel *geneticist*

Yorktown Heights
Cai, Jin *research scientist, electrical engineer*
Lu, Yingdong *research scientist*
Wynne, James *research scientist*

NORTH CAROLINA

Asheboro
Jones, David M. *zoological park administrator*

Asheville
Parresol, Bernard Ross *research biometrician, statistician*

Beaufort
Ramus, Joseph S. *marine biologist*

Brevard
Glesener, Robert Richard *biologist, educator, researcher*

Chapel Hill
Andrews, Richard Nigel Lyon *public policy educator, environmental studies administrator*
Feduccia, J. Alan *biologist, educator*
Hackenbrock, Charles R. *cell biologist, educator*
Judd, Burke Haycock *geneticist*
Lundblad, Roger Lauren *biotechnology consultant*
Mueller, Nancy Schneider *retired biology educator*
Redinbo, Matthew R. *science educator, researcher*
Smithies, Oliver *geneticist, educator*
Straley, Joseph Ward *retired molecular spectrascopist, retired science educator*
Stumpf, Walter Erich *cell biology educator, researcher*
Warren, Donald William *physiology educator, dentistry educator*
Weiss, Charles Manuel *environmental biologist*
Wetzel, Robert George *botany educator*

Charlotte
Ruiz, Macedonio *entomologist*
Schneider, Stanley Scott *biology professor*

Clayton
Branch, Stacy *veterinarian, educator*

Durham
Blum, Jacob Joseph *physiologist, educator*
Bolognesi, Dani Paul *virologist, educator*
Cook-Deegan, Robert Mullan *science and health policy analyst, physician*
Cullen, Bryan Richard *microbiologist, educator*
Gillham, Nicholas Wright *geneticist, educator*
Hogan, Brigid L. *molecular biologist*
Keene, Jack Donald *molecular genetics and microbiology educator*
Livingstone, Daniel Archibald *zoology educator*
Mushak, Paul *toxicologist, consultant*
Nadadur, Srikanth S *molecular biologist*
Naylor, Aubrey Willard *botany educator*
Pearsall, Samuel Haff, III, *landscape ecologist, geographer, foundation administrator*
Purves, Dale *neurobiology research educator*
Raetz, Christian R. H. *biochemistry educator*
Reller, L. Barth *medical microbiologist, infectious diseases physician, educator*
Richardson, Stephen Giles *biotechnology company executive*
Rouse, Doris Jane *physiologist, research administrator*
Schmidt-Nielsen, Knut *physiologist, educator*
Somjen, George Gustav *physiologist*
Strittermatter, Warren J. *science educator, health science association administrator*

Gastonia
Flynn, Duane James *entomologist*

Greensboro
O'Brien, William John *ecology researcher*

Greenville
Meggs, William Joel *toxicologist, allergist, emergency physician, educator*
Thurber, Robert Eugene *physiologist, researcher*
Wiley, John Edwin *cytogeneticist*

Hendersonville
Brittain, James Edward *science and technology educator, researcher*

Kitty Hawk
Sjoerdsma, Albert *research institute executive*

Raleigh
Aronson, Arthur Lawrence *retired veterinarian, toxicologist, educator, pharmacologist*
Barefoot, Aldos Cortez, Jr., *forester, educator*
Benson, D(avid) Michael *plant pathologist*
Burkholder, Joann M. *botany educator*
Colpetzer, Keith Edward *entomologist, consultant*
Cook, Maurice Gayle *soil science educator, consultant*
Cooper, Arthur Wells *ecologist, educator*
Davey, Charles Bingham *soil science educator*
Dunphy, Edward James *crop science extension specialist*
Foegeding, Edward A. *food scientist, educator*
Goodman, Major Merlin *botanical sciences educator*
Gordon, Morris Aaron *medical mycologist, microbiologist*
Hardin, James W. *botanist, herbarium curator, educator*
Havlin, John Leroy *soil scientist, educator*
Hodgson, Ernest *toxicology educator*
Huber, Steven C. *plant physiologist, educator*
Klaenhammer, Todd R. *microbiologist, educator*
McDowell, Robert E. *animal science educator*
Moreland, Donald Edwin *plant physiologist*
Roberts, John Douglas *veterinarian, educator*
Stuber, Charles William *genetics educator, researcher*
Timothy, David Harry *retired biology educator*
Triantaphyllou, H. H. *plant pathologist*

Research Triangle Park
Bond, Enriqueta Carter *science administrator*
Fought, Lorianne *plant pathologist*
Haynes, Victoria F. *science administrator*
Mumford, Stephen Douglas *research scientist*

Washington
Heck, Henry D'Arcy *retired toxicologist, consultant*

Wilmington
Roer, Robert David *physiologist, educator*

Winston Salem
Cheng, Heng-Jie *physician scientist*
Ganz, Charles *laboratory executive*
Gmeiner, William Henry *science educator*
Laxminarayana, Dama *geneticist, researcher, educator*
Pandres, Dave, Jr., *science educator, researcher*
Rautaharju, Pentti Matti *research scientist, educator*

NORTH DAKOTA

Bisbee
Keller, Michelle R. *science educator, secondary education educator*

Fargo
Schmidt, Claude Henri *retired research administrator*

OHIO

Akron
Chung, Benjamin T. F. *science educator*
Millman, Irving *microbiologist, educator, retired inventor*

Ashland
Rueger, Daniel Scott *horticulture educator*

Avon Lake
Zurcher, Vickie Lee *geneticist*

Bowling Green
Clark, Eloise Elizabeth *biologist, educator*

Cincinnati
Etges, Frank Joseph *parasitology educator*
Horseman, Nelson Douglas *molecular and cellular physiology educator*
Monaco, John J. *molecular genetics research educator*
Nebert, Daniel Walter *molecular geneticist, research administrator*
Saal, Howard Max *clinical geneticist, pediatrician, educator*
Safferman, Robert Samuel *microbiologist, researcher*
Schaefer, Frank William, III, *microbiologist, researcher*
Schiff, Gilbert Martin *virologist, microbiologist, medical educator*
Sperelakis, Nicholas, Sr., *physiology and biophysics educator, researcher*
Sunagawa, Masanori *physiologist, researcher*

Cleveland
Blackwell, John *science educator*
Buck, Matthias *science educator*
Dell'Osso, Louis Frank *neuroscience educator*
Herrup, Karl *neurobiologist*
Jacobs, Michael Roy *microbiologist, researcher*
Perry, George *neuroscientist, educator*
Suri, Jasjit S. *research scientist*
Taylor, Steve Henry *zoologist*

Columbus
Boerner, Ralph E. J. *forest soil ecologist, plant biology educator*
Capen, Charles Chabert *veterinary pathology educator*
Cheesman, Kerry Lee *education educator, researcher*
Disinger, John Franklin *natural resources educator*
Fawcett, Sherwood Luther *research laboratory executive*
Floyd, Gary Leon *plant cell biologist*
Fry, Donald Lewis *physiologist, educator*
Glaser, Ronald *microbiology educator, scientist*
Kapral, Frank Albert *medical microbiology and immunology educator*
Melling, Jack *biotechnologist, director*
Peterle, Tony John *zoologist, educator*
Piggrem, Gary Wayne *science educator, writer*
Reeve, John Newton *molecular biology and microbiology educator*
Robinson, David Milton *microbiologist*
Roth, Robert Earl *environmental educator*
Shetlar, David John *entomologist, educator, research scientist*
Snyder, Susan Leach *science educator, writer*
Stansbery, David Honor *ecologist, malacologist*
Triplehorn, Charles A. *entomology educator, insects curator*
Westman, Judith Ann *clinical geneticist*
Wood, Jackie Dale *physiologist, educator, researcher*
Zartman, David Lester *animal sciences educator, researcher*

Dayton
Isaacson, Milton Stanley (Jim Isaacson) *research and development company executive, engineer*
Sudkamp, Thomas *science educator*

Delaware
Iverson, Louis Robert *research ecologist*

Granville
Haubrich, Robert Rice *biology professor*

Kent
Cooperrider, Tom S. *retired botanist, educator*
Dutta, Hiran Moyee *biologist, educator*
House-Soremekun, Bessie *political science educator*

Oberlin
Luck, Dennis Noel *biologist, educator, researcher*

Oxford
Eshbaugh, W(illiam) Hardy *botanist, educator*
Rypstra, Ann *zoology educator*

Portsmouth
Burns, Eugene Hugh, Jr., *biology professor*

Powell
Borin, Gerald W. *zoological park administrator*

Springfield
Hobbs, Horton Holcombe, III, *biology professor*
Ryu, Kyoo-Hai Lee *physiologist*

Toledo
Chakraborty, Joana *physiologist, educator, science administrator*

Wooster
Ferree, David Curtis *horticultural researcher*
Madden, Laurence Vincent *plant pathology educator*
Saif, Linda J. *animal scientist*

Wyoming
Cooley, William Edward *research scientist, consultant*

Yellow Springs
Webb, Paul *physiologist, educator, researcher, consultant*

OKLAHOMA

Durant
Rice, Stanley Arthur *biology professor*

El Reno
Slagell-Gossen, Reonna Richele *science educator, researcher*

Lane
Edelson, Jonathan Victor *entomologist, educator*

Langston
Mallik, Muhammad Abdul-Bari *soil microbiologist*

Norman
Carpenter, Charles Congden *zoologist, educator*
Hutchison, Victor Hobbs *biologist, educator*

Oklahoma City
Branch, John Curtis *biology professor, lawyer*
Dubowski, Kurt Max *toxicologist, educator, consultant*
Gonzalez, Larry Paul *research scientist, medical educator*

Pawhuska
Strahm, Samuel Edward *veterinarian*

Ponca City
Wann, Laymond Doyle *retired petroleum research scientist*

Sand Springs
Quinn, Art Jay *veterinarian, retired educator*

Stillwater
Confer, Anthony Wayne *veterinary pathologist, educator*
Ewing, Sidney Alton *veterinary medical educator, parasitologist*
Gilliland, Stanley Eugene *dairy-food microbiology educator*
Grischkowsky, Daniel Richard *research scientist, educator*
Langwig, John Edward *retired wood science educator*
Lorenz, Michael Duane *veterinary medicine educator, dean*
Lynch, Thomas Bernard *science educator*
Pagilla, Prabhakar Reddy *science educator, consultant*
Royer, Tom A. *entomologist, educator*

Tulsa
Korstad, John Edward *biology professor*

OREGON

Ashland
Christianson, Roger Gordon *biology professor, department chairman*

Beaverton
Liu, Kevin H. *research scientist, software architect*

Bend
Collins, Sally Duke *forest service manager*
Crampton, George Harris *neuroscientist, retired military officer*

Corvallis
Castle, Emery Neal *agricultural and resource economist, educator*
Chambers, Kenton Lee *botany educator*
Dougherty, William G. *microbiologist, educator*
Frakes, Rodney Vance *plant geneticist, educator*
Loper, Joyce E. *plant pathologist, educator*
Lubchenco, Jane *marine biologist, educator*
Morita, Richard Yukio *microbiology and oceanography educator*
Pinkerton, John N. *plant pathologist*
Poinar, George Orlo, Jr., *insect pathologist and paleontologist, educator*
Rose, Robert William, Jr., (Robin Rose) *forest regeneration scientist, educator*
Westwood, Melvin Neil *horticulturist, pomologist*

Eugene
Castenholz, Richard William *ecologist, researcher, educator*
Matthews, Brian W. *molecular biology educator*

Hillsboro
Matlock, John Hudson *science administrator, materials engineer*

Klamath Falls
Dow, Martha Anne *biology professor*

Pendleton
Klepper, Elizabeth Lee *physiologist*

Portland
Barmack, Neal Herbert *neuroscientist*
Gillette, Richard Gareth *neurophysiology educator, researcher*
Hagenstein, William David *forester, consultant*
Kirschner, Marc Alan *neuroscientist*
Kolmes, Steven Albert *biologist, educator*
Seil, Fredrick John *retired neuroscientist*

Salem
Erickson, Ray Charles *retired wildlife biologist*

Talent
MacMillen, Richard Edward *biological sciences educator, researcher*

Yachats
Gerdemann, James Wessel *plant pathologist, educator*

PENNSYLVANIA

Allentown
Oplinger, Carl Spadt *biology professor*

Andalusia
Ewalt, Jacquelyn Marie *biologist*

Annville
Verhoek, Susan Elizabeth *botany educator*

Bala Cynwyd
Corliss, John Ozro *zoology educator*

Doylestown
Marino, Paul Michael *science education educator*
Mishler, John Milton (Yochanan Menashsheh ben Shaul) *natural sciences educator, administrator, artist*

Durham
de Limantour, Clarice Barr *food scientist*

Easton
Fried, Bernard *parasitologist, biology educator*

Edinboro
Miller, G(erson) H(arry) *research institute director, mathematician, computer scientist, chemist*
Snyder, Donald Benjamin *biology professor*
Thomas, Paul Milton *retired science educator*

Elizabethtown
Coren, Jonathon Silow *science educator, researcher*

Elizabethville
Romberger, John Albert *scientist, historian*

Exton
Hidalgo, Ismael J. *pharmaceutical scientist*

Gettysburg
Hendrix, Sherman Samuel *biology professor, researcher*

Gladwyne
Allen, Theresa Ohotnicky *neurobiologist, consultant*

Haverford
DiBerardino, Marie Antoinette *developmental biologist, educator*
Erickson, Ralph O. *botany educator*

Hershey
Hopper, Anita Klein *molecular genetics educator*
Norgren, Ralph *neuroscientist*
Undar, Akif *research scientist, biomedical engineer, educator*

Holland
Umbreit, Wayne William *bacteriologist, educator*

Indiana
Farag, Waleed E *science educator*

Jenkintown
Purcell, James Michael *science educator*

Kennett Square
Fussell, Catharine Pugh *biological researcher*
Poppenga, Robert H. *veterinary toxicology educator*

Lansdale
Elliott, Arthur Y. *microbiologist, administrator*

Lewisburg
Sojka, Gary Allan *biologist, educator, academic administrator*

Media
Brobeck, John Raymond *physiology educator*

Narberth
Nathanson, Neal *virologist, epidemiologist, educator*

Philadelphia
Adler, Martin William *neuropharmacologist*
Alcock, Charles Roger *science educator*
Armstrong, Clay *physiology educator*
Assoian, Richard Kenneth *molecular biologist, educator*
Beauchamp, Gary Keith *physiologist*
Brinster, Ralph Lawrence *biologist, educator*
Cashmore, Anthony *biologist, educator*
Cox, Robert Harold *physiology educator*
Davies, Helen C. *microbiology educator*
Doms, Robert W. *science educator*
Eisenstein, Toby K. *microbiology educator*
Fisher, Aron Baer *physiology and medicine educator*
Furth, John Jacob *molecular biologist, pathologist, educator*
Giger, Urs *veterinarian, educator*
Hammond, Benjamin Franklin *microbiologist, educator*
Hoskins, Alexander L. (Pete Hoskins) *zoological park administrator*
Hua, Xianxin *cell and cancer biology educator*
Jaynes, James B. *geneticist, educator*
Kaji, Akira *microbiology scientist, educator*
Koprowski, Hilary *microbiologist, educator*
Lambertsen, Christian James *environmental physiologist, physician, educator*
Meyer, Paul William *arboretum director, horticulturist*
Okere, Chuma Onyeaghala *neuroscientist*
Patrick, Ruth (Mrs. Ruth Hodge Van Dusen) *limnologist, diatom taxonomist, educator*
Pepe, Frank A. *cell and developmental biology educator*
Rubin, Benjamin Arnold *microbiologist, immunologist, medical educator, researcher*
Sanger, Joseph William *cell biologist*
Schaedler, Russell William *microbiologist, physician, educator*
Schneider, Adele Sandra *clinical geneticist*
Schwartz, Arthur Gerald *microbiology educator*
Shockman, Gerald David *microbiologist, educator*
Silvers, Willys Kent *geneticist*
Skalka, Anna Marie *molecular biologist*
Van Bockstaele, Elisabeth Jeanne *neuroscientist, researcher*
Young, Robert Crabill *medical researcher, science facility administrator, internist*

Pipersville
Erickson, Edward Leonard *biotechnology company executive, administrator*

Pitcairn
Rose, Robert Didier *neurophysiologist*

Pittsburgh
Cruz, Robyn Flaum *research scientist, clinician*
Edmonds, Mary Patricia *biological sciences educator*
Ehrlich, Garth David *molecular biologist*
Feingold, David Sidney *microbiology educator*
Harrold, Ronald Thomas *research scientist*
Jones, Elizabeth Winifred *biology professor*
Kamboh, M. Ilyas *geneticist*
Kiger, Robert William *botanist, science historian, educator*
LaJohn, Lawrence Anthony *research scientist*
Marazita, Mary Louise *genetics researcher*
Moore, Robert Yates *neuroscience educator*
Partanen, Carl Richard *biology professor*
Taylor, D. Lansing *cell biology educator*
Willke, Theodore Lawrence *research facility director*

Slippery Rock
Kefeli, Valentin Ilich *biologist, botanist, educator, researcher*

State College
Cowen, Barrett Stickney *microbiology educator*
Hettche, L. Raymond *research director*
Madjid, A. Hamid *retired science educator*

Swarthmore
Gilbert, Scott Frederick *biologist, educator, author*

University Park
Bollag, Jean-Marc *soil biochemistry educator, consultant*
Buskirk, Elsworth Robert *physiologist, educator*
Fedoroff, Nina Vsevolod *research scientist, consultant, educator*
Fowler, H(oratio) Seymour *retired science educator*
Gnana Asir, Viji *plant pathologist*
Nei, Masatoshi *biology professor*
Stern, Robert Morris *gastrointestinal psychophysiology researcher, psychology educator*
Stinson, Richard Floyd *retired horticulturist, educator*
Wolfe, Douglas E. *science educator, researcher*
Zatsiorsky, Vladimir Moiseevich (Michailovich) *biomechanics educator, researcher*

Wallingford
Severdia, Anthony George *chemistry researcher*

Wayne
Krutsick, Robert Stanley *retired science center executive*
Thelen, Edmund *research executive*

West Point
Hilleman, Maurice Ralph *virus research scientist*
Manning, Barton Harley *neuroscientist*
Schaffner, Carolyn Marie *research administrator, biologist*

Wilkes Barre
Hayes, Wilbur Frank *retired biology educator*
Ogren, Robert Edward *biologist, educator*

Wynnewood
Prendergast, George C. *cancer biologist, researcher*
Rubin, Leonard Sidney *physiologist, educator, researcher*

RHODE ISLAND

Cranston
Mruk, Charles Karzimer *agronomist*
Vavala, Domenic Anthony *medical scientist, retired military officer*

Kingston
Goos, Roger Delmon *mycologist*
Harrison, Robert William *zoologist, educator*
Hufnagel, Linda Ann *biology professor, researcher*
Markin, Karen Mary *research scientist, journalist*

Newport
Koch, Robert Michael *research scientist, consultant, educator*

North Scituate
Dupree, Thomas Andrew *forester, state official*

Providence
Dickersin, Kay *researcher, educator*
Dowben, Robert Morris *physiologist, researcher*
Gerbi, Susan Alexandra *biology professor*
Schmitt, Johanna Marie *plant population biologist, educator*
Takao, Motoharu *physiologist*
Wood, Craig Breckinridge *paleobiologist, natural science educator*

SOUTH CAROLINA

Aiken
Bertsch, Paul M. *ecologist, director*
Punshon, Tracy *research scientist*
Wood, Susan *applied technology center executive*

Charleston
Forsythe, Dennis M. *biology professor*
Kalivas, Peter W. *physiologist, educator, department chairman*
Ogretmen, Besim *science educator, molecular biologist, researcher*
Yu, Shan Ping *neuroscientist, educator*

Clemson
Birrenkott, Glenn P., Jr., *poultry science educator*
Caldwell, Judith *horticultural educator*
Straka, Thomas James *forester, educator*

Columbia
Dawson, Wallace Douglas, Jr., *geneticist*
Gaevski, Mikhail Erikovich *research scientist*
Hughes, Austin Leland *biological sciences educator*
Rhoades, Donald Scott *zoo and botanical park curator, biology professor*
Watabe, Norimitsu *biology and marine science educator*

Easley
Spearman, David Hagood *veterinarian*

Goose Creek
Marks, Melvin Paul *entomologist, consultant*

Hilton Head Island
Adams, William Hensley *ecologist, educator*
Lefer, Allan Mark *physiologist*

North Myrtle Beach
Maloney, Terry *horticulturist, educator*

Prosperity
Long, William McMurray *physiology educator*

Rock Hill
Mitchell, Paula Levin *biology professor, editor*

Simpsonville
Pratt, Harry Davis *retired entomologist*

Spartanburg
Leonard, Walter Raymond *retired biology educator*

SOUTH DAKOTA

Brookings
Catangui, Michael Aguilar *entomologist, researcher*

Volga
Moldenhauer, William Calvin *soil scientist*

TENNESSEE

Gatlinburg
Cave, Kent R. *national park ranger*

Johnson City
Rasch, Ellen Myrberg *cell biology educator*

Kingsport
Ogbonnaya, Chuks Alfred *entomologist, agronomist, environmentalist*

Knoxville
Anderson, Ilse Janell *clinical geneticist*
Caponetti, James Dante *botany educator*
Creasia, Donald Anthony *toxicologist, researcher*
Draughon, Frances Ann *microbiology educator*
Mazur, Peter *cell physiologist, cryobiologist*
Mc Hargue, Carl Jack *research laboratory administrator*
White, David Cleaveland *microbial ecologist, environmental toxicologist*

Maryville
Hall, Marion Trufant *botany educator, arboretum director*

Memphis
Curran, Thomas *molecular biologist, educator*
Freeman, Bob A. *retired microbiology educator, retired dean*
Hofmann, Polly A. *physiologist, science educator*
Howe, Martha Morgan *microbiologist, educator*
Leffler, Charles William *physiology and pediatrics educator*
Van Middlesworth, Lester *physiology, biophysics and medicine educator*
Webster, Robert G. *virologist, educator*

Nashville
Auerbach, Stanley Irving *ecologist, environmental scientist, educator*
Fischer, Charlotte Froese *research scientist, educator*
Granner, Daryl Kitley *physiology and medicine educator*
Haines, Jonathan L. *science educator*
Orgebin-Crist, Marie-Claire *biology professor, department chairman*
Phillips, John A(tlas), III, *geneticist, educator*
Pincus, Theodore *microbiologist, rheumatologist, educator*
Shneyder, Artyom V. *science educator, researcher*

Oak Ridge
Phillips, Debra Helen *soil scientist, researcher*
Xu, Ying *computational biologist*

Sewanee
Yeatman, Harry Clay *biologist, educator*

Smithville
Vaughn, Eulalia Cobb *retired science educator, mathematician*

TEXAS

Amarillo
Cummins, Joseph M. *biotechnology company executive*

Austin
Biesele, John Julius *biologist, educator*
Drummond Borg, Lesley Margaret *clinical geneticist*
Fryxell, Greta Albrecht *marine botany educator, oceanographer*
Grant, Verne Edwin *biology professor*
Hubbs, Clark *zoologist, researcher*
Jacobson, Antone Gardner *zoology educator*
Kronz, Frederick Mark *science educator*
Patterson, Donald Eugene *research scientist*
Simpson, Beryl Brintnall *botany educator*
Sutton, Harry Eldon *geneticist, educator*
Thornton, Joseph Scott *research institute executive, materials scientist*
Turner, Billie Lee *botanist, educator*

Bandera
Bartley, William Call *science administrator*

Bogata
Marris, Roy O. *agriculturist, consultant*

Brownwood
Simmons, Marsha Thrift *science and reading educator, musician*

Bryan
Milford, Murray Hudson *retired soil science educator*

Cedar Park
Albin, Leslie Owens *biology professor*

Cibolo
Newsom, Melvin Max *retired research company executive*

College Station
Armstrong, Robert Beall *physiologist, educator*
Bazer, Fuller Warren *science educator, researcher*
Beaver, Bonnie Veryle *veterinarian, educator*
Black, Samuel Harold *microbiology and immunology educator*
Borlaug, Norman Ernest *agricultural scientist*
Brown, Robert Dale *wildlife science educator, department head*
Dees, William Leslie *veterinary medicine educator*
Drees, Bastiaan Meijer *entomologist*
Granger, Harris Joseph *physiologist, educator*
Hall, Timothy Couzens *biology professor, consultant*
Ibragimov, Akif *research scientist, educator*
Kohel, Russell James *geneticist*
McCallum, Roderick Eugene *dean, microbiologist*
McCrady, James David *veterinarian, educator*
Neill, William Harold, Jr., *biological science educator, researcher*
Nobles, Maria Morgun *soil scientist, researcher*
Safe, Stephen H. *science educator*
Storey, J. Benton *horticulturist, educator*
Turner, Nancy Delane *nutritionist, educator, researcher*

Corpus Christi
Berkebile, Charles Alan *geology educator, hydrogeology researcher*

Corsicana
Carroll, Ray Dean, Sr., *veterinarian*

Dallas
Bates, Barry Leon *biology professor*
Brown, Michael Stuart *geneticist, educator, science administrator*
Daly, David Michael *neuroscientist, computer scientist, information technology executive*
Kalchev, George Dimitrov *research scientist*
Kern, Janet Kinnear *neuroscientist*
McKnight, Steven Lanier *molecular biologist*
Olson, Eric N. *molecular biologist, educator*
Read, James Carroll *geneticist educator*
Reinert, James A. *entomology educator*
Sudhof, Thomas Christian *molecular genetics educator, neuroscientist*
Vanatta, John Crothers, III, *physiologist, physician, educator*
Vitetta, Ellen S. *microbiologist educator, immunologist*

Denton
Crawford, Gladys Pauline *microbiologist, educator*
Marshall, David Douglas *science educator*
Ver Duin, D'Arlene K. *research scientist*

Diboll
Fisher, Richard Forrest *research scientist, department chairman*

Fort Worth
Manning, Walter Scott, Jr., *veterinarian*

Galveston
Budelmann, Bernd Ulrich *zoologist, educator*
Frederickson, Christopher John *neuroscientist*
Horning, Markus *marine biologist, educator, researcher*
Santschi, Peter Hans *marine sciences educator*
Willis, William Darrell, Jr., *neurophysiologist, educator*
Würsig, Bernd Gerhard *marine biology educator*
Zimmerman, Roger Joseph *fishery biologist*

Georgetown
Girvin, Eb Carl *biology professor*

Hempstead
Propst, Catherine Lamb *biotechnology company executive*

Houston
Baughn, Robert Elroy *microbiology educator*
Brown, Jack Harold Upton *physiologist, biomedical engineer, academic administrator*
Butel, Janet Susan *research scientist, virology educator*
Byrne, John H. *neuroscientist, department chairman*
Chiao, Paul J. *molecular biologist, educator*
DeBakey, Lois *science communications educator, editor, writer*
DeBakey, Selma *science communications educator, writer, editor, lecturer*
Dronamraju, Krishna Rao *geneticist*
Durham, Susan K. *research scientist*
Eaton, Kimberly Napoli *medical scientist, academic administrator*
Fox, George Edward *molecular biology educator*
Jurtshuk, Peter, Jr., *microbiologist, educator*
Mendoza-Londono, Roberto *geneticist, pediatrician*
Nelson, David Loren *geneticist, educator*
Radomski, Marek Witold *science educator*
Sass, Ronald Lewis *biology and chemistry educator*
Schull, William J. *geneticist, educator*
Schultz, Stanley George *physiologist, educator, dean*
Steele, James Harlan *former public health veterinarian, educator*
Strong, Louise Connally *geneticist*
Wiley, Pamela Michelle *science educator, writer*

Xu, Xiaochun *biologist, researcher*
Zhang, Chunlong *environmental educator*
Zhou, Juhua *molecular biologist*

Hunt
Price, Donald Albert *veterinarian, consultant*

Lubbock
Hentges, David John *microbiology educator*
Jackson, Raymond Carl *cytogeneticist*
Skoog, Gerald Duane *science educator*
Wendt, Charles William *soil physicist, educator*

Mcallen
Saenz, Velma Lisa *plant protection and quarantine officer*

Pearland
Shurtleff, Malcolm C. *plant pathologist, consultant, educator, extension specialist*

Plano
MacAlpine, Michelle Lewis *neuroscientist*

Port Aransas
Schake, Lowell Martin *animal science educator*

Richardson
Gray, Donald Melvin *molecular and cell biology educator*
Laseter, John Luther *clinical and forensic toxicologist*
Lin, Zhiang *science educator*
Wood, Joseph George *neurobiologist, educator*

Round Rock
Schneider, Dennis Ray *microbiology educator and executive*

San Antonio
Burch, James Leo *science research institute executive*
Clamann, York H. *biologist, educator*
Corrigan, Helen González *retired cytologist*
Gates, Mahlon Eugene *applied research executive, former government official, former army officer*
Irving, George Washington, III, *veterinarian, research director, small business executive*
Kittle, Joseph S. *science administrator, consultant*
Martinez, Joe Louis, Jr., *neurobiologist, educator*
McComas, David John *science administrator, space physicist*
McIntosh, Dennis Keith *veterinarian, consultant*
Webb, James Taylor *physiologist, pilot*
Zoghby, Jeriad Marcus *lead analytical specialist, consultant*

San Marcos
McLean, Robert James Cameron *microbiologist, educator*

Uvalde
Ramsey, Frank Allen *veterinarian, retired army officer*

Waco
Hillis, William Daniel *biology professor*
Wivagg, Daniel Edwin *biology educator, editor*

Warda
Kunze, George William *retired soil scientist*

UTAH

Cedar City
Mayron, Lewis Walter *clinical ecology consultant*

Ephraim
Blauer, A. Clyde *microbiologist, educator, botanist*

Genola
Newcomb, Helene E *retired research scientist*

Logan
McNeal, Lyle Glen *science educator, rancher, consultant*
Rashid, Kamal A. *university administrator, research educator*
Rasmussen, Harry Paul *horticulture and landscape educator*
Shultz, Leila McReynolds *botanist, educator*
Sidwell, Robert William *virologist, educator*

Orem
Harper, Kimball Taylor *ecologist, educator*

Providence
Vest, Hyrum Grant, Jr., *retired horticultural sciences educator*

Provo
Blake, George Rowland *soil science educator, water resources research administrator*
Crookston, R. Kent *agronomy educator*
McArthur, Eldon Durant *geneticist, researcher*
Smith, H(oward) Duane *zoology educator*
Woodbury, Dixon John *physiologist, educator, research scientist*

Salt Lake City
Capecchi, Mario Renato *genetics educator*
Johnson, Stephen Charles *exercise physiology and sport science educator*
Planelles, Vicente *molecular biologist*
Salisbury, Frank Boyer *plant physiologist, educator, author*

Springville
Bybee, Paul Joseph *zoologist, educator, paleontologist, biologist*

VERMONT

Brattleboro
Ames, Adelbert, III, *neurophysiologist, educator*

Burlington
Bartlett, Richmond Jay *soil chemistry educator, researcher*
Bramley, Andrew John *animal science educator*
Gouli, Svetlana Yurievna *microbiologist, researcher*
Gouli, Vladimir Vasilievich *entomologist*
Kindstedt, Paul Stephen *food science educator*

Charlotte
Melby, Edward Carlos, Jr., *veterinarian*

Greensboro
Hill, Lewis Reuben *horticulturist, nursery owner, author*

Middlebury
Meakin, John David *retired university research executive, educator*

Morrisville
Lechevalier, Hubert Arthur *microbiology educator*
Lechevalier, Mary Pfeil *retired microbiologist, educator*

Norwich
Naumann, Robert Bruno Alexander *chemistry and physics educator*

Waterbury
Travis, Randall Howard *retired physiologist, retired endocrinologist*

VIRGINIA

Alexandria
Woolley, Mary Elizabeth *research administrator*

Amissville
Hunter, Beverly Claire *research scientist, educator*

Arlington
Bawa, Raj *science educator, biodefense specialist, nanotechnology expert, biotechnology firm executive*
Bridgewater, Albert Louis *retired science foundation administrator*
Glaser, Gerard *science administrator*
Haq, Bilal Ul *national science foundation program director, researcher*
Harris, William James, Jr., *research administrator, educator*
Held, Joe Roger *retired veterinarian*
Junker, Bobby Ray *research and development executive, physicist*
Morse, Larry Eugene *botanist, conservationist*
O'Neill, Brian *research organization administrator*
Ordway, Frederick Ira, III, *science educator, consultant, researcher, writer*
Richtol, Herbert Harold *science foundation consultant*
Werbos, Paul John *neural net research director*

Blacksburg
Burkhart, Harold Eugene *forestry educator*
Cowles, Joe Richard *biology professor*
De Datta, Surajit Kumar *soil scientist, agronomist, educator*
Gwazdauskas, Francis Charles *animal science educator, dairy scientist*
Kabir, Firoz *wood technologist, researcher*
Kelly, James Michael *plant and soil scientist*
McKenna, James Richard *agronomy educator*

Chantilly
Srivastava, Kailash Chandra *microbiologist*

Charlottesville
Allis, C. David *science educator*
Block, Gene David *biologist, educator, science administrator*
Garrett, Reginald Hooker *biology professor, researcher*
Kadner, Robert Joseph *microbiology educator*
Menaker, Michael *biology professor, department chairman*
Perez-Reyes, Edward *molecular physiologist*
Tuttle, Jeremy Ballou *neurobiologist*
Wright, Theodore Robert Fairbank *biologist, educator*

Cobbs Creek
Crum, John Kistler *non-profit consultant*

Dulles
Elias, Antonio L. *science administrator*

Fairfax
Geller, Harold Arthur *earth and space sciences executive, educator*
Hanson, Robin Dale *science educator*
Soyfer, Valery Nikolayevich *geneticist, biophysicist*

Falls Church
Hart, C(harles) W(illard), Jr., *zoologist, curator*
Simpson, John Arol *retired government executive, physicist*

Front Royal
Douglas, J(ocelyn) Fielding *toxicologist, consultant*

Galax
Dunson, William Albert *biology professor, ecological consultant*

Hampton
Freeman, Delma C., Jr., *science association director*

Haymarket
Katz, Alan Charles *toxicologist*

Keswick
Rafajko, Robert Richard *medical research company executive*

Manakin Sabot
Bayliss, John Temple *retired science educator, retired energy executive*

Manassas
Isbister, Jenefir Diane Wilkinson *microbiologist, researcher, educator, consultant*
Jong, Shung-Chang *mycologist*

Mc Lean
Cardwell, Thomas Augusta, III, *research scientist, retired career officer, executive*
Layson, William McIntyre *retired research consulting company executive*
Talbot, Lee Merriam *ecologist, educator, foundation administrator*

Midlothian
Wang, Buqian *materials research scientist*

Newport News
Harris, Charles George *research scientist, consultant*

Norfolk
Colberg-Ochs, Sheri Renee *physiologist, educator*

Richmond
Boadle-Biber, Margaret Clare *physiology educator*

Staunton
Cook, Clarence Edgar *research facility scientist*

Suffolk
Phipps, Patrick Michael *plant pathology educator*

Virginia Beach
Rodriguez-Rodriguez, Pedro Pablo *retired veterinarian*

Williamsburg
Griffith, Melvin Eugene *entomologist, public health official*
Guastaferro, Angelo *space science administrator, consultant*

WASHINGTON

Bellingham
Ross, June Rosa Pitt *biologist, educator*

Edmonds
Paul, Ronald Stanley *research institute executive*

Kennewick
Cobb, William Thompson *environmental and agricultural consultant*

Long Beach
West, Douglas Xavier *retired science educator*

Olympia
Heilenday, Frank Tod *science educator*

Prosser
Proebsting, Edward Louis, Jr., *retired research horticulturist*

Pullman
Edwards, Charles Gould *food scientist, educator, microbiologist, chemist*
Henson, James Bond *veterinary pathologist*
Hosick, Howard Lawrence *cell biology educator, academic administrator*
Thomashow, Linda Suzanne *microbiologist*

Richland
Bian, Randy Xindi *research scientist*
Chikalla, Thomas David *retired science facility administrator*
Lin, Yuehe *research scientist*

Seattle
Bassingthwaighte, James Bucklin *physiologist, educator, medical researcher*
Boersma, P. Dee *marine biologist, educator*
Brownstein, Barbara Lavin *geneticist, educator, university official*
Daniel, Thomas L. *zoology educator*
Disteche, Christine M. *geneticist*
Gottschling, Daniel E. *molecular research biologist*
Hartwell, Leland Harrison (lee hartwell) *geneticist, educator*
Hellström, Karl Erik *science educator, researcher*
Hendrickson, Anita Elizabeth *biology professor*
Hille, Bertil *physiology educator*
Hohmann, John G. *neurobiologist*
Hood, Leroy Edward *molecular biologist, educator*
Karr, James Richard *ecologist, educator, research director*
King, Mary-Claire *geneticist, educator*
Kirby, Ronald Eugene *fish and wildlife research administrator*
Klausner, Richard D. *cell biologist, researcher*
Kruckeberg, Arthur Rice *botanist, educator*
Kuhl, Patricia K. *science educator, educator*
Nester, Eugene William *microbiology educator*
Ning, Xue-Han (Hsueh-Han Ning) *physiologist, researcher*
Olstad, Roger Gale *science educator*
Reed, Steven I. *science association director*
Riddiford, Lynn Moorhead *zoologist, educator*
Schiffrin, Milton Julius *physiologist*
Smith, Orville Auverne *physiology educator*
Stahl, David A. *microbiologist, educator*
Tews, Leonard L. *retired science educator, poet*
Woods, James Sterrett *toxicologist*
Wott, John Arthur *arboretum and botanical garden executive, horticulture educator*

Sedro-Woolley
Rochefort, Regina Marie *ecologist, botanist*

Sequim
Pearson, Walter Howard *marine biologist, researcher*

Silverdale
Tozer, William Evans *entomologist, educator*

Wapato
Arthurs, Steven Paul *entomologist, researcher*

Wenatchee
Elfving, Don C. *horticulturist, educator*
Schrader, Lawrence Edwin *plant physiologist, educator*

WEST VIRGINIA

Buckhannon
McCormick, Rodger John *biologist, educator, minister*

Charleston
Bhasin, Madan Mohan *research scientist*
Gillespie, William Harry *forestry executive, geology educator*

Clarksburg
Walmsley, James Naylor *hydroponic farming executive*

Kearneysville
Biggs, Alan Richard *plant pathologist, educator*

Morgantown
Amrine, James Wesley, Jr., *entomologist, educator*
Cochrane, Robert Lowe *biologist*
Gladfelter, Wilbert Eugene *physiology educator*
Nath, Joginder *genetics and biology educator, researcher*
O'Callaghan, James Patrick *neuroscientist*

WISCONSIN

Cottage Grove
Lund, Daryl Bert *food science educator*

Kenosha
Li, Zhaohui *science educator*

Madison
Beyer-Mears, Annette *physiologist*
Borisy, Gary G. *molecular biology educator*
Brock, Thomas Dale *microbiology educator*
Burkholder, Wendell Eugene *retired entomology educator, researcher*
Buss, Daryl Dean *veterinarian, dean*
De Foliart, Gene Ray *retired entomologist, researcher, educator*
Dolan, Terrence Raymond *neurophysiology educator*
Easterday, Bernard Carlyle *veterinary medicine educator*
Ensign, Jerald C. *bacteriology educator*
Evert, Ray Franklin *botany educator*
Greaser, Marion Lewis *science educator*
Greenspan, Daniel S. *molecular biologist, educator*
Hagedorn, Donald James *phytopathologist, educator, agricultural consultant*
Hopen, Herbert John *horticulture educator*
Iltis, Hugh Hellmut *plant taxonomist-evolutionist, educator, environmental advocate*
Jackson, Marion Leroy *agronomist, soil scientist*
Jeanne, Robert Lawrence *entomologist, educator*
Kaesberg, Paul Joseph *virology researcher*
Kemnitz, Joseph William *physiologist, researcher*
Kimble, Judith E. *molecular biologist, cell biologist*
Lillesand, Thomas Martin *remote sensing educator*
Mandrekar, Michelle Nelson *research scientist*
Marrett, Cora B. *science educator*
Miller, Paul Dean *breeding consultant, geneticist, educator*
Moss, Richard L. *physiology educator*
Newcomb, Eldon Henry *retired botany educator*
Olson, Norman Fredrick *food science educator*
Pella, Milton Orville *retired science educator*
Peterson, David Maurice *plant physiologist, research leader*
Rankin, Scott Anthony *food scientist, researcher*
Ris, Hans *zoologist, educator*
Rueckert, Roland Rudyard *retired virologist, educator*
Sharkey, Thomas David *botanist, educator*
Sheffield, Lewis Glosson *physiologist*
Susman, Millard *geneticist, educator*
Szybalski, Waclaw *geneticist, educator*
Zedler, Joy Buswell *ecological sciences educator*

Middleton
Horsch, Robert B. *biotechnologist*

Milwaukee
Boese, Gil Karyle *cultural organization executive*
Cowley, Allen Wilson, Jr., *physiologist*
Ignacio, Reinere John Dy *research scientist*
Penz, Carla Maria *biologist, researcher*
Rhead, William James *biochemical geneticist*
Schumann, Gail L. *plant pathologist, educator*

Oshkosh
Balzar, Tammy J. *research scientist*

Sheboygan
Strysick, Michael Otto *terrestrial ecologist, physicist, microbiologist*

TERRITORIES OF THE UNITED STATES

GUAM

Mangilao
Lobban, Christopher Simon *science educator*

PUERTO RICO

Aguadilla
Gómez-Jiménez, Carlos *science educator, microbiologist, geneticist*

Ponce
Matta, Jaime L *research scientist, educator*
Moura, Jose *wine consultant*

San Juan
Fernández-Coll, Fred *microbiologist, food technology laboratory director*
Hillyer, George V. *microbiologist, educator, medical researcher*
Lugo, Ariel E. *ecologist, botanist, federal agency administrator*

Pluke, Richard William Hay *entomologist, researcher*

CANADA

ALBERTA

Calgary
Jones, Geoffrey Melvill *physiology research educator*

Edmonton
Christian, Ralph Gordon *agricultural research and animal health consultant*
Cossins, Edwin Albert *biology professor, academic administrator*

BRITISH COLUMBIA

Burnaby
Borden, John Harvey *entomologist, educator*

Sidney
Bigelow, Margaret Elizabeth Barr (M.E. Barr) *mycology educator*
Kendrick, William Bryce *biology professor, writer, publisher, consultant, editor*
Mann, Cedric Robert *retired institute administrator, oceanographer*

Vancouver
Blair, Robert *animal science administrator, educator, researcher*
Hoar, William Stewart *zoologist, educator*
Jones, David Robert *zoology educator*
Lindsey, Casimir Charles *zoologist, educator*
Maclachlan, Gordon Alistair *biology professor, researcher*
Mc Lean, Donald Millis *microbiology and pathology educator, physician*
Newman, Murray Arthur *aquarium administrator*
Phillips, Anthony George *neurobiology researcher*
Phillips, John Edward *zoologist, educator*
Rennie, Paul Steven *research scientist*
Shaw, Michael *biologist, educator*
Wellington, William George *entomologist, ecologist, educator*

Victoria
Turpin, David Howard *biologist, educator*

West Vancouver
Donaldson, Edward Mossop *research scientist, aquaculture consultant*

MANITOBA

Winnipeg
Alfa, Michelle Josephine *microbiologist, educator*
Suzuki, Isamu *microbiology educator, researcher*

NOVA SCOTIA

Dartmouth
Mann, Kenneth Henry *marine ecologist*

Halifax
Hall, Brian Keith *biology educator, author, scientist*

ONTARIO

Bowmanville
Evans, Essi H. *research scientist*

Deep River
Newcombe, Howard Borden *biologist, consultant*

Downsview
Forer, Arthur H. *biology professor, researcher, editor*

Greely
Lister, Earle Edward *retired animal science consultant*

Guelph
Beveridge, Terrance James *microbiology educator, researcher*
Bewley, John Derek *botany researcher, educator*
Jorgensen, Erik *forest pathologist, educator, consultant*
Kasha, Kenneth John *agriculturist, educator*

Kingston
Leggett, William C. *biology professor, academic administrator*
Smallman, Beverley N. *retired biology professor*
Wyatt, Gerard Robert *biology professor, researcher*

London
Kang, Chil-Yong *virology, immunology educator*
Lala, Peeyush Kanti *research scientist, educator*
Locke, Michael *zoology educator*

North York
Davey, Kenneth George *biologist, university official*
Regan, David *brain researcher*

Ottawa
Baum, Bernard Rene *research scientist*
Carty, Arthur John *science policy advisor, research administrator*
Francis, Charles MacKenzie *wildlife biologist*
Hughes, Stanley John *mycologist*
Perry, Malcolm Blythe *biologist, researcher*
Sells, Bruce Howard *biomedical sciences educator*
Storey, Kenneth Bruce *biology professor*

Peterborough
Davis, Gordon Richard Fuerst *retired biologist, translator*

Hutchinson, Thomas Cuthbert *ecology and environmental educator*

Scarborough
White, Calvin John *zoo executive, zoological association executive, financial manager*

Stittsville
MacLeod, Robert Angus *microbiology educator, researcher*

Toronto
Carlen, Peter Louis *neuroscientist, educator, science administrator, researcher*
Liversage, Richard Albert *cell biologist, educator*
MacLennan, David Herman *research scientist, educator*
Masui, Yoshio *zoology educator*
Moens, Peter B. *biology researcher and educator*
Stadelman, William Ralph *chemical institution executive*
Tobe, Stephen Solomon *zoology educator*

Waterloo
Hynes, Hugh Bernard Noel *biologist, educator*
Warner, Barry Gregory *ecologist, educator*

QUEBEC

Laval
Talbot, Pierre Joseph *microbiologist, researcher*

Montreal
Aguayo, Alberto Juan *neuroscientist*
Carroll, Robert Lynn *biology professor, vertebrate paleontologist, museum curator, paleontologist, curator*
Chang, Thomas Ming Swi *medical scientist, biotechnologist*
Dansereau, Pierre *ecologist*
Diksic, Mirko *research scientist, educator*
Gibbs, Sarah Preble *biologist, educator*
Jolicoeur, Paul *molecular biologist*
Milic-Emili, Joseph *physiologist, educator*

Sainte Anne de Bellevue
Grant, William Frederick *geneticist, educator*

Sherbrooke
Bourget, Edwin Robert *marine ecologist, educator*

SASKATCHEWAN

Regina
Sonntag, Bernard H. *retired agrologist, public service executive*

Saskatoon
Babiuk, Lorne Alan *virologist, immunologist, research administrator*
Huang, Pan Ming *soil science educator*
Kartha, Kutty Krishnan *plant pathologist*
Shokeir, Mohamed Hassan Kamel *medical geneticist, educator*

Quebec City
Potvin, Pierre *physiologist, educator*

Saint Jean-Sur-Richelieu
Trudel, Marc J. *botanist, educator*

Ville Saint Laurent
Braquet, Pierre G. *science educator, health science association administrator*

AUSTRALIA

Randwick
Hall, Peter Francis *physiologist*

Southport
Buckley, Ralf Christopher *research scientist*

BELGIUM

Antwerp
Snyders, Dirk Johan *electrophysiologist, biophysicist, educator*

Oost-Vlaanderen
Stroobandt, Dirk Rudy *research scientist, educator*

CROATIA

Zagreb
Štambuk, Nikola *research scientist*

CZECH REPUBLIC

Prague
Bubeník, Jan *cancer researcher, biology educator*

ENGLAND

Cambridge
Huxley, Sir Andrew (Sir Andrew Fielding Huxley) *physiologist, educator*
Klug, Aaron *molecular biologist*
Sanger, Frederick *retired molecular biologist*

Kent Cranbrook
Hattersley-Smith, Geoffrey Francis *retired government research scientist*

Leeds
Phillips, Oliver *tropical forest ecologist*

London
Morris, Desmond (John) *zoologist, writer, artist*

Oxford
Gowans, Sir James Learmonth *science administrator, immunologist*

FRANCE

Gif-sur-Yvette
Duplessy, Jean Claude *research scientist*

Noisy le Grand
Le Quéré, Jean François Marie *scientific instrumentation researcher*

Orsay
Fiszer-Szafarz, Berta (Berta Safars) *research scientist, researcher*

Paris
Jacob, François *biologist, educator*
Kourilsky, François Michel *research scientist*
Montagnier, Luc Antoine *virologist*
Raharinaivo, André Léon *research executive, educator*

GERMANY

Düsseldorf
Stuhl, Oskar Paul *scientific and regulatory consultant*

Stuttgart
von Klitzing, Klaus *research facility administrator, physicist*

Würzburg
Hölldobler, Berthold Karl *zoologist*

HONG KONG

Hong Kong
Tsui, Lap-Chee *molecular genetics educator*

Kowloon
Kung, Shain-dow *molecular biologist, academic administrator*
Randall, David John *physiologist, zoologist, educator*

INDIA

New Delhi
Narain, Prem *agricultural scientist, educator, researcher*
Srivastava, Radhey Shyam *research scientist, researcher*

Ranchi
Srivastava, Vishnu Chandra *agronomy educator*

ISRAEL

Karkur
Hillel, Daniel *soil physics and hydrology educator, researcher, consultant*

Rehovot
Sachs, Leo *geneticist, educator*

Rosh-Pina
Gophen, Moshe *research scientist*

ITALY

Naples
Tarro, Giulio *virologist*

Rome
Levi-Montalcini, Rita *neurobiologist, researcher*

JAPAN

Tokyo
Arai, Toshihiko *retired microbiology and immunology educator*
Ishii, Akira *medical parasitologist, malariologist, allergologist*
Ogawa, Seiji *research scientist, biophysicist*

LEBANON

Beirut
Toufeili, Imad *science educator*

NEW ZEALAND

Palmerston North
Krone, Cheryl A. *research scientist, consultant*

NORWAY

Kjeller
Maeland, Arnulf Julius *research scientist*

PAKISTAN

Faisalabad Punjab
Siddique, Muhammad *poultry pathobiologist*

POLAND

Warsaw
Koscielak, Jerzy *scientist, science administrator*

REPUBLIC OF KOREA

Daejon
Jeong, Hawoong *science educator*

SWEDEN

Uppsala
Carr, Andrew *zoologist*

SWITZERLAND

Basel
Arber, Werner *microbiologist*
Gehring, Walter Jakob *biology and genetics educator*

Zurich
Wüthrich, Kurt *molecular biologist, biophysical chemist, educator*

TAIWAN

Taichung
Wilson, Thomas Woodrow, III, *research scientist, consultant*

VENEZUELA

Caracas
Nassar, Jafet M. *plant animal specialist, researcher*

ADDRESS UNPUBLISHED

Able, Kenneth Paul *biology professor*
Adamson, Dan Klinglesmith *retired science association executive*
Ahearne, John Francis *scientific research administrator, researcher*
Ahrens, Franklin Alfred *veterinary pharmacology educator*
Aikens, Martha Brunette *national park service administrator*
Alexander, Edward Russell *retired disease research administrator, educator*
Alfano, Robert R. *science educator, engineering educator*
Allen, Barry W. *research scientist, writer*
Allen, Charles T *entomologist*
Allen, Lew, Jr., *laboratory executive, former air force officer*
Anderson, William Carl *association executive, environmental engineer, consultant*
Andrews, Richard Vincent *physiologist, educator*
Arnott, Howard Joseph *biology professor, dean*
Arya, Vikram *research scientist*
Atkin, J Myron *science educator*
Baker, Joseph Roderick, III, *aviculturist*
Bansil, Arun *research scientist*
Barabino, William Albert *science and technology researcher, inventor*
Barlow, John Sutton *neurophysiologist, electroencephalographer, lexicographer*
Barnard, Donald Roy *medical and veterinary entomologist*
Barnes, Robert F *agronomist*
Barnes-Kempton, Isabel Janet *microbiology educator, college dean*
Barrett, Izadore *retired fisheries research administrator*
Becherer, Richard Joseph *science administrator, physicist*
Beggs, William H. *microbiologist, researcher*
Bernard, Richard Lawson *retired geneticist, educator*
Bers, Donald Martin *physiology educator*
Bertram, Melissa C. *agricultural research scientist*
Bick, Katherine Livingstone *neurobiologist, international liaison, consultant*
Bidwell, Roger Grafton Shelford *biologist, educator*
Bishop, William Peter *science administrator, management consultant, rancher, consultant*
Blanchard, David Joseph *research scientist*
Block, Barbara Ann *biology professor*
Blum, Samuel *retired research scientist*
Bonner, John Tyler *biology professor*
Bottone, Edward Joseph *microbiologist, educator*
Boyette, Lisa Wynn *retired research scientist*
Boyle, Tatiana Gennadievna *research scientist*
Bremner, John McColl *agronomy and biochemistry educator*
Brenchley, Jean Elnora *microbiologist, researcher, science administrator*
Brown, Jeannette Elizabeth *retired science educator*
Browne, Frederick Douglas *physiologist, educator*
Browne, John Charles *retired physics researcher, former national research laboratory executive*
Bryant, Donald Ashley *molecular biologist*
Bullock, Theodore Holmes *biologist, educator*
Burkes, Lionel Seaton *science educator, writer, researcher*
Burns, Denver P. *forestry research administrator*
Calabrese, Anthony *retired marine biologist*
Caldwell, Elwood Fleming *food scientist, educator*
Cameron, Roy Eugene *scientist*
Cardwell, Kitty Frances *agricultural science administrator*
Carter, David LaVere *soil scientist, researcher, consultant*
Cheng, Yue *molecular geneticist, pathologist*
Choi, Man-Yeon *entomologist, researcher*
Clayton, David A(lvin) *biology professor*
Cockerham, Lorris G. *radiation toxicologist*
Colwell, Rita Rossi *microbiologist, former federal agency administrator, medical educator*

Conover, Lloyd Hillyard *retired pharmaceutical research scientist and executive*
Creech, John Lewis *retired scientist, consultant*
D'Alesandro, Philip Anthony *parasitologist, immunologist, retired medical educator*
Davis, J. Michael *environmental health scientist*
Decker, Walter Johns *toxicologist*
Deshefy, Gregory Scott *ecologist, environmentalist*
Detweiler, David Kenneth *veterinary physiologist, educator*
Deviney, Marvin Lee, Jr., *research institute scientist, program manager*
Doman, Elvira *retired science administrator*
Dugan, Patrick Raymond *microbiologist, university dean*
Durham, Thena Monts *microbiologist, researcher, management executive*
Edwards, Charles *neuroscientist, educator*
Ellner, Paul Daniel *microbiologist*
Elson, Hannah Friedman *biologist, researcher*
Eno, Amos Stewart *natural resource foundation administrator*
Eugster, Albrecht Konrad *veterinarian, laboratory director, emeritus*
Evans, Charles Wayne, II, *biologist, researcher*
Farber, Neal Mark *biotech executive, molecular biologist*
Farkas, Daniel Frederick *food science and technology educator*
Feir, Dorothy Jean *entomologist, physiologist, educator*
Feldman, Jack L. *neurobiology educator*
Fisher, Dale Dunbar *animal scientist, dairy nutritionist*
Flemming, David Paul *biologist*
Fotopoulos, Sophia Stathopoulos *medical research scientist, administrator*
Fox, Michael Wilson *veterinarian, bioethicist, animal behaviorist*
Foy, Charles Daley *retired soil scientist*
Freeman, Arthur *veterinarian, retired association administrator*
Gabor-Hotchkiss, Magda *research scientist, librarian*
Gage, Patrick (Leonard Patrick Gage) *biotech/pharmaceutical consultant*
Garruto, Ralph Michael *biomedical anthropologist, educator, biologist, neuroscientist*
Gay, William Ingalls *veterinarian, health science administrator*
Gift, James Joseph *aquatic toxicologist*
Glick, J. Leslie *bio and information technology entrepreneur*
Goeddel, David V. *science research facility executive, biochemist*
Goldstein, Walter Elliott *biotechnology executive*
Goodwin, Richard Hale *botany educator*
Gordis, Enoch *retired science administrator, internist*
Green, Bennett Donald *biotechnologist*
Greenman, David Lewis *retired physiologist, toxicologist*
Guo, ZengKui *research scientist*
Hale, Wesley Raymond *research scientist, chemical engineer*
Hall, Barry G. *evolutionary biologist*
Hamdy, Mostafa Kamal *microbiologist, educator*
Han, Qiwen *research scientist*
Harlin, Marilyn Miler *marine botany educator, researcher, consultant*
Harriman, Philip Darling *geneticist, science foundation executive*
Hauptmann, Randal Mark *biotechnologist*
Hayakawa, Kan-Ichi *retired food science educator*
Heinicke, Ralph Martin *consultant*
Hemmingsen, Barbara Bruff *retired microbiologist*
Henriquez, Jilcia *research scientist*
Herman, Richard J. *marine life administrator*
Herz, Michael Joseph *marine environmental scientist*
Hess, Dori L. *science educator*
Hildebrand, Verna Lee *human ecology educator*
Howard-Peebles, Patricia N. *clinical cytogeneticist*
Hyvonen, Sami Rikhard *research scientist*
Iacono, James Michael *research center administrator, nutrition educator*
Inouye, David William *biology professor*
Kamrin, Michael Arnold *toxicology educator*
Karp, Gerald Charles *biologist, educator, writer*
Keith, Jerry M. *molecular biologist*
Kennedy, Charles *retired neuroscientist, retired medical educator*
Kerr, Janet Spence *physiologist, pharmacologist, researcher*
Kim, Charles Wesley *microbiology educator*
Kim, Seon-Young *microbiologist, researcher*
Kirsteuer, Ernst Karl Eberhart *biologist, curator*
Kittleson, Mark Douglas *veterinary cardiologist, veterinary medicine educator*
Kolb, James A. *science association director, writer*
Koller, Loren D. *veterinary medicine educator*
Kornguth, Steven Edward *biologist*
Kumako, Kuami Mawunyo *agricultural scientist*
Lafever, Howard Nelson *plant breeder, geneticist, educator*
Langdale, Noah Noel, Jr., *research educator, former university president*
Langer, Glenn Arthur *cellular physiologist, educator*
Layne, James Nathaniel *vertebrate biologist*
Leath, Kenneth Thomas *research plant pathologist, educator, agricultural consultant*
Lee, Henry C. *forensic scientist*
Leng, Yongsheng *research scientist*
Leventhal, Ruth *retired parasitology educator, university official*
Levine, Arnold Jay *molecular biology educator*
Lewis, Brian Kreglow *retired physiologist, computer scientist*
Li, Qing'an *scientist, researcher*
Liu, Jianhua *molecular biologist, researcher*
London, Jan *food scientist, writer*
Lynch, Harry James *retired biologist*
Lynch, John Thomas *retired science foundation administrator, physicist*
Magee, John Francis *research company executive*
Mahoney, Michael J. *science administrator, educator*
Mannari, Rajan Krishnamachary *biotechnologist, researcher*
Mark, Hon Fong Louie *cytogeneticist, researcher*
Maroni, Donna Farolino *biologist, researcher*
Martino, Joseph Paul *research scientist, researcher*
Maslansky, Carol Jeanne *toxicologist*
Massaro, Linda P. *science foundation executive*
Maunder, Addison Bruce *agronomic research company executive*
McCann, Peter Paul *biology researcher, educator*
McClellan, Roger Orville *toxicologist*
McGraw, Donald Jesse *biologist, science historian, writer*
McShefferty, John *retired research company executive, consultant*
Menn, Julius Joel *scientist*
Menzies, Carl Stephen *agricultural research administrator, ruminant nutritionist*
Metzler, Ruth Horton *genealogical educator*
Michaelis, Elias K. *neurochemist*
Miller, Louis Howard *biologist, researcher*
Miller, Patrick William *research administrator, educator*
Mitchell, John Laurin Amos *biological science educator*
Moore, J Strother *science educator, researcher*
Moss, Thomas Henry *science association administrator*
Mudavanhu, Blessing *research scientist*
Murarka, Shyam Prasad *science and engineering educator, administrator*
Murray, Joseph James, Jr., *zoologist*
Nath, Shyamal K. *research scientist*
Neaves, William Barlow *cell biologist, educator*
Orr, H. Allen *biologist, critic*
Ostlind, Dan A. *retired parasitologist*
Oswald, Robert Bernard *retired science administrator, nuclear engineer*
Paganelli, Charles Victor *physiologist, educator*
Palade, George Emil *research scientist, educator*
Parsons, Patrick Jeremy *research scientist, science educator*
Peaslee, Margaret Mae Hermanek *zoology educator*
Peter, Richard Ector *zoology educator*
Pettit, Ghery DeWitt *retired veterinary medicine educator*
Phillis, John Whitfield *physiologist, educator*
Pinter, Gabriel George *physiology educator*
Plotkin, Stanley Alan *virologist*
Polley, Richard Donald *microbiologist, inorganics and polymer chemist*
Punzo, Fred *science educator*
Purcell, Karen Anne *veterinarian*
Raisys, Vidmantas A. *toxicology educator, clinical chemist*
Roeller, Herbert Alfred *biology and medical scientist, educator*
Rogers, Jack David *plant pathologist, educator*
Rose, Michael Robertson *evolutionary biology educator, consultant*
Ross, Jeffrey Alan *research biologist*
Rothman, Frank George *biology professor, academic administrator, biochemical genetics researcher, geneticist*
Russell, Liane Brauch *retired geneticist*
Saalfeld, Fred Erich *science educator, researcher*
Salkind, Michael Jay *science administrator, metallurgical engineer*
Salthe, Stanley Norman *retired theoretical biology educator*
Sattler, Rolf *retired plant morphologist, educator*
Schaechter, Moselio *microbiology educator*
Scherer, James R. *research scientist*
Scheuerle, Angela Elizabeth *geneticist*
Schlub, Robert Louis *plant pathologist, educator*
Schwab, John Harris *microbiology and immunology educator*
Schwartz, William Lewis *retired veterinary pathologist*
Sehlaoui, Abdelilah Salim *science educator, researcher*
Seshadri, Arathi H. *research scientist, educator*
Setser, Carole Sue *retired food science educator*
Shahied, Ishak I. *science educator*
Shands, Gail Maxine *environmental scientist*
Shils, Maurice Edward *physiologist, educator, research scientist*
Simon, Melvin I. *molecular biologist, educator*
Simpson, Frederick James *retired research administrator*
Sjostrand, Fritiof Stig *biologist, educator*
Smeltzer, Debra Jean *botanist*
Smith, Hamilton Othanel *molecular biologist, educator*
Snow, Joel Alan *research director*
Sokal, Robert Reuven *biology professor, writer*
Soper, James Herbert *botanist, curator*
Southwick, Charles Henry *zoologist, educator*
Sponsler, George Curtis, III, *research administrator, lawyer*
Stark, Nellie May *forester, ecologist, educator*
Stavroulakis, Anthea Merrie *biology professor*
Stickle, David Walter *microbiologist*
Stickney, Robert Roy *fisheries educator*
Suri, Roland Erwin *neuroscientist*
Suthers, Hannah Louise Bonsey *biologist, consultant*
Talmage, David Wilson *microbiology and medical educator, physician, former university administrator*
Tanaka, Kay *genetics educator*
Tandler, Bernard *cell biology educator*
Taylor, Roy Lewis *botanist, educator*
Taylor, Welton Ivan *microbiologist, consultant, food scientist*
Thomas, Adrian Wesley *research scientist, director, retired science educator*
Thomas, Teresa Ann *microbiologist, educator*
Thomson, Keith Stewart *biologist, author*
Ullman, Edwin Fisher *biotechnology consultant*
Unger, Paul Walter *retired soil scientist*
Urban, Misty Rae *research scientist*
Vaughan, John Charles, III, *horticultural products executive*
Vincent, James Louis *biotechnology company executive*
Wasserman, Gerald Steward *psychobiology educator*
Weber, Lavern John *retired marine science administrator, educator*
Wei, Qingyi *cancer research educator*
Weller, Milton Webster *wetland ecologist, educator*
Williams, George Christopher *biologist, ecology and evolution educator*
Willson, Mary Frances *ecology researcher, educator*
Witte, Owen Neil *microbiologist, molecular biologist, educator*
Woo, Savio Lau Ching *molecular medical geneticist*
Yang, Xiangzhong *research scientist, administrator, educator*
Young, Judith Anne *animal conservationist*
Yu, Jun *biologist*
Yunis, Jorge Jose *anatomy, pathology, and microbiology educator*
Zhang, Lin *research scientist, educator*
Zhang, Liping *research scientist*
Zhang, Zhongjian *research scientist*
Zhao, Guang-Quan *developmental reproductive biologist, researcher*
Zhiyou, Wen *research scientist*
Zhou, Cheng Ji *neuroscientist*
Zhu, Yong *research scientist*
Zwislocki, Jozef John *neuroscience educator, researcher*

SCIENCE: MATHEMATICS AND COMPUTER SCIENCE *See also* INFORMATION TECHNOLOGY

UNITED STATES

ALABAMA

Athens
Hodson, Roy Goode, Jr., *retired logistician*

Auburn
Govil, Narendra Kumar *mathematics professor*

Birmingham
Gfeller, Lisa Anne *computer systems analyst*
Jones, Warren Thomas *computer science educator*
Peeples, William Dewey, Jr., *mathematics professor*
Reilly, Kevin Denis *computer scientist, educator*
Wheeler, Ruric E. *mathematics professor*
Whigham, Mark Anthony *computer scientist*

Florence
Johnson, Johnny Ray *mathematics professor*

Huntsville
Freas, George Wilson, II, *computer consultant*
McAuley, Van Alfon *aerospace mathematician*
Pruitt, Alice Fay *mathematician, engineer*
Zutaut, Steven Eric *systems analyst, application developer*

Mobile
Bertagnolli-Comstock, Amanda K. *mathematician, educator*
McCleery, Winston Theodore *computer consulting company executive*

Montgomery
Kim, Ki Hang *mathematician*

Pelham
Turner, Malcolm Elijah *biomathematician, educator*

Tuscaloosa
Aziz, Nasrullah *mathematician, educator*
Mysore, Shrikanth Bhaskar *operations research specialist*

ARIZONA

Fountain Hills
Israel, Robert Allan *statistician*

Phoenix
Doto, Irene Louise *statistician*
Pillalamarri, Seshasayi *computer scientist and engineer, researcher*

Scottsdale
Drake, Albert Estern *retired statistics educator, farming administrator*

Tempe
Smith, Harvey Alvin *mathematics educator, consultant*
Yau, Stephen Sik-sang *computer science and engineering educator, computer scientist, researcher*

Tucson
Myers, Donald Earl *mathematics professor*
Willoughby, Stephen Schuyler *mathematics professor*

ARKANSAS

Arkadelphia
Worth, Fred *mathematician, educator*

Batesville
Carius, Robert Wilhelm *mathematics and science educator, retired naval officer*

Conway
Spatz, Kenneth Chris(topher), Jr., *statistics educator*

Fayetteville
Khavinson, Dmitry *mathematician, educator*

Little Rock
Chiang, Chia-Chu *computer scientist, educator*
Townsend, James Willis *computer scientist*
Yarberry, Lonnie Stephen *information scientist, director*

Magnolia
Avard, Joseph L. *mathematician, educator*

Mountain Home
Preis, Christy Charlene *mathematics professor*

Russellville
Finan, Marcel Bassil *mathematics educator, researcher*

CALIFORNIA

Arcadia
Seitz, Charles Lewis *computer scientist and engineer*

Bakersfield
Fiedler, Joseph Robert *mathematician, educator*

Berkeley
Arveson, William Barnes *mathematics professor*
Bajcsy, Ruzena Kucerova *computer science educator*
Bergman, George Mark *mathematician, educator*
Bickel, Peter John *statistician, educator*
Borcherds, Richard Ewen *mathematics professor*
Chern, Shiing-Shen *mathematics professor*
Chorin, Alexandre Joel *mathematician, educator*
Cooper, Michael David *information scientist, educator*
Cooper, William Secord *information science educator*
Freedman, David Amiel *statistics educator, consultant*
Graham, Susan Lois *computer science educator, consultant*
Hyman, Edward Jay *forensic psychologist, cognitive and information scientist, consultant, educator, television news commentator*
Jones, Vaughan Frederick Randal *mathematician, educator*
Kaplansky, Irving *mathematician, educator, research institute director*
Karp, Richard Manning *computer sciences educator*
Minkus, Jerome Bernard *mathematician, educator*
Pham, Quang Xuan *statistics educator*
Ratner, Marina *mathematician, educator, researcher*
Séquin, Carlo H. *computer science educator*
Vojta, Paul Alan *mathematics professor*
Wahl, Bernt Rainer *mathematician, writer, application developer*
Wolf, Joseph Albert *mathematician, educator*

Brea
Painchaud, Phillip Andre *metrologist*

Carlsbad
Halberg, Charles John August, Jr., *mathematics professor*

Carson
Suchenek, Marek Andrzej *computer science educator*

Claremont
Henriksen, Melvin *mathematician, educator*
Myhre, Janet *mathematician, educator*

Concord
Fuld, Fred, III, *computer consultant, financial consultant*

Costa Mesa
DeMille, Dianne Lynne *mathematics educator, administrator*

Davis
Fannjiang, Albert *mathematician, educator*
Mulase, Motohico *mathematics professor*
Thurston, William Paul *mathematician*
Wegelin, Jacob Andreas *statistician*

Elk Grove
McDavid, Douglas Warren *executive research consultant*

Escondido
Ziegler, James Russell *computer consultant*

Gilroy
McCarty, Robert Clarke *mathematician*

Hayward
Duncan, Doris Gottschalk *information systems educator*
Merris, Russell L. *mathematician, educator*
Roby, Tom *mathematician, educator*
Sabharwal, Ranjit Singh *mathematician*

Irvine
Hoffman, Donald David *cognitive and computer science educator*
Kaneda, Masayoshi *mathematics educator, researcher*
Kobsa, Alfred *computer scientist, educator*
Lathrop, Richard Harold *computer science educator*
Saari, Donald Gene *mathematician, economist*
Shen, Ba-Zhong *mathematician, computer scientist*
Wan, Frederic Yui-Ming *mathematician, educator*

La Honda
Henderson, D. Austin *computer scientist*

La Jolla
Bunch, James Raymond *mathematician, educator*
Burgin, George Hans *computer scientist, educator*
Graham, Ronald Lewis *mathematician*
Halkin, Hubert *mathematics educator, research mathematician*
Martin, James John, Jr., *retired consulting research firm executive, systems analyst*
Rajasekar, Arcot *computer scientist*
Rosen, Judah Ben *computer scientist*
Rosenblatt, Murray *mathematics professor*
Terras, Audrey Anne *mathematics professor*
Wulbert, Daniel Eliot *mathematician, educator*
Zyroff, Ellen Slotoroff *information scientist, classicist, educator*

Livermore
Fodor, Imola Katalin *mathematician, researcher*
Haga, Enoch John *computer educator, author*

Long Beach
Schroeder, Arnold Leon *mathematics professor*
Wollmer, Richard Dietrich *statistics and operations research educator*

Los Angeles
Alexander, Kenneth Sidney *mathematician, educator*

Bekey, George Albert *computer scientist, educator, engineer*
Boehm, Barry William *computer science educator*
Dabrowska, Dorota Maria *statistician, educator*
Delaney, Matthew Sylvester *mathematics professor, academic administrator*
Golomb, Solomon Wolf *mathematician, electrical engineer, educator, university official*
Gordon, Basil *mathematician, educator*
Greenberger, Martin *biotechnologist, information scientist, educator*
Jacobsen, Laren *programmer, analyst*
Jones, Gerald Paul *software educator*
Kalaba, Robert Edwin *applied mathematician*
Lototsky, Sergey *mathematician, educator*
Palmer, Roger Cain *information scientist*
Pearl, Judea *computer scientist, educator*
Petak, William John *systems management educator*
Port, Sidney Charles *mathematician, educator*
Sherman, Jimmie Lee *mathematician, educator*
Tartakovsky, Alexander G. *mathematician, educator*
Verona, Andrei *mathematician, educator*
Waterman, Michael Spencer *mathematics educator, biology educator*

Los Gatos
Rissanen, Jorma Johannes *computer scientist*

Marina Del Rey
Neuman, Clifford *computer scientist, educator*

Menlo Park
Bourne, Charles Percy *information scientist, educator*
Mulgaonkar, Prasanna G. *computer scientist*
Neumann, Peter Gabriel *computer scientist*

Monterey
Denning, Peter James *computer scientist, engineer*
Gaver, Donald Paul *mathematics professor, consultant*

Moss Landing
Lange, Lester Henry *mathematics professor*

Oakland
Givant, Steven Roger *mathematician, computer scientist, educator*
Henkin, Leon Albert *mathematician, educator*
Zelmanowitz, Julius Martin *mathematics educator, university administrator*

Pacific Palisades
Griver, Jeanette A *human factors scientist, consultant*

Palo Alto
Kay, Alan C. *computer scientist*
Keller, Arthur Michael *computer science researcher*

Paradise
Barr, Donald Roy *statistics and operations research educator, statistician*

Pasadena
Borodin, Alexei *mathematician*
Fast, Henryk *mathematician, educator*
Franklin, Joel Nicholas *mathematician, educator*
Gref, Lynn G. *mathematician*
Keller, Herbert Bishop *mathematics professor*
Pelletier, Sandra Maureen *mathematician, educator*
Saffman, Philip G. *mathematician, educator*

Perris
Tankersley, Michael Leonard (Mujahide Abdullah Rafi Rashid) *computer systems administrator*

Playa Vista
Noh, Jun-yong *computer scientist, researcher*

Pomona
Agvanian, Youri *mathematician, educator, physicist*

Portola Valley
Kuo, Franklin F. *computer scientist, electrical engineer*

Riverside
McClanahan, Michael Nelson *systems analyst*
Ratliff, Louis Jackson, Jr., *mathematics professor*
Schaible, Siegfried *mathematician, educator*

Rowland Heights
Cordova, John Michael *mathematician, educator*
Cruz, Wilfredo Vargas *software safety and reliability consultant*

Sacramento
Norman, Ben Eric *mathematician, educator*
Speed, Cynthia Agnes *retired mathematics educator*

San Diego
Calabrese, Philip George *mathematician, researcher, small business owner*
Hales, Alfred Washington *mathematics educator, consultant*
Loper, Warren Edward *computer scientist*
McLeod, Douglas Bailey *mathematician, educator*
Mestechkin, Mikhail Markovich *math physicist*
Reese, Michael *mathematics professor*
Tsybakov, Boris Solomon *information theory and communication networks researcher, educator*
Van Tassel, Lowell Thomas *mathematics professor*
Velo, Ani Piro *mathematician, educator*

San Francisco
Cruse, Allan Baird *mathematician, computer scientist, educator*
Kao, John Sterling *mathematician, educator*
Lu, Ying *statistician, educator*
Shvidler, Mark Joseph *mathematician*

San Jose
Ho, Chungwu *mathematician, educator*
Togasaki, Shinobu *computer scientist*
Zhai, Shumin *computer scientist*

San Marino
Lashley, Virginia Stephenson Hughes *retired computer science educator*

San Rafael
Barker, Celeste Arlette *computer scientist*

Santa Ana
Re Velle, Jack B(oyer) *statistician, consultant*

Santa Barbara
Johnsen, Eugene Carlyle *mathematician, educator*
Marcus, Marvin *mathematician, educator*
Minc, Henryk *mathematics professor*
Newman, Morris *mathematician, educator*
Simons, Stephen *mathematics educator, researcher*

Santa Clara
Gosling, James *computer scientist, web programmer*
Halmos, Paul Richard *mathematician, educator*
Klosinski, Leonard Frank *mathematics professor*
Smith, Stephen Allen *mathematician, educator*
Tran, Nicholas Q. *computer scientist, educator*

Santa Cruz
Huskey, Harry Douglas *information and computer science educator*
Stormes, John Max *instructional systems developer*

Santa Monica
Sun, Li *statistician*
Ware, Willis Howard *computer scientist*

Santa Rosa
Wiggins, Patricia Ann *computer systems analyst, state legislator*

Sebastopol
Wall, Larry *computer scientist, web programmer*

Simi Valley
Loomis, Jennifer MacKenzie *information technology consultant*

South San Francisco
Exuzides, Alex *statistician, researcher*

Stanford
Anderson, Theodore Wilbur *statistics educator*
Brown, Byron William, Jr., *biostatistician, educator*
Cohen, Paul Joseph *mathematician*
Dantzig, George Bernard *applied mathematics educator*
Efron, Bradley *mathematics professor*
Eliashberg, Yakov *mathematician, educator*
Feigenbaum, Edward Albert *computer science educator*
Karlin, Samuel *mathematics educator, researcher*
Keller, Joseph Bishop *mathematician, educator*
Knuth, Donald Ervin *computer sciences educator*
Levy, Doron *mathematics professor*
McCarthy, John *computer scientist, educator*
Moses, Lincoln E. *statistician, educator*
Olkin, Ingram *statistician, educator*
Schoen, Richard Melvin *mathematics educator, researcher*
Ullman, Jeffrey David *computer scientist, educator*
Whittemore, Alice *biostatistician*

Sunnyvale
Frank, Jeremy D. *computer scientist*

Temecula
May, Brian Thomas *mathematician, educator*

Thousand Oaks
Sladek, Lyle Virgil *mathematician, educator*

Torrance
Kerstiens, Gene J. *mathemagenician, consultant*

Tustin
Abu-Mostafa, Ayman Said *computer consultant*

Westlake Village
Munson, John Backus *computer systems consultant, retired computer engineering company executive*

Woodland Hills
Stratton, Gregory Alexander *computer specialist, administrator, mayor*

Yorba Linda
Sperling, Scott Edward *software consultant, Bible expositor*

COLORADO

Boulder
Beylkin, Gregory *mathematician*
Cai, Xiao-Chuan *computer science educator*
Glover, Fred William *mathematical optimization, artificial intelligence and optimization research director, educator*
Monarchi, David Edward *management scientist, information scientist, educator*
Mycielski, Jan *mathematician, educator*
Uhrik, Carl Thomas *computer scientist, educator*

Colorado Springs
Simmons, George Finlay *retired mathematics professor*

Denver
Mendez, Celestino Galo *mathematics professor*
Talman, Louis A. *mathematician*

Fort Collins
Estep, Donald Joseph *mathematician, educator*
Loy, Ivan *mathematician, educator*
Mielke, Paul William, Jr., *statistician, consultant*

Littleton
Riley, Mary Jane *computer scientist*

Woodland Park
Olson, Warren Kinley *operations research analyst, engineer, physicist*
Trench, William Frederick *mathematician, educator*

CONNECTICUT

Ansonia
Kerpa, Gary J. *computer science consultant*

Broad Brook
Johnston, Robert Everett *information management executive*

Cheshire
Tufte, Edward Rolf *writer, publisher, statistics educator*

Fairfield
Eigel, Edwin George, Jr., *mathematics educator, retired university president*
Shaffer, Dorothy Browne *retired mathematician, educator*

Hartford
Swyers, Donald G. *information scientist*
Younessi, Houman *computer science educator*

Manchester
Sears, Sandra Lee *computer consultant*

Middletown
Comfort, William Wistar *mathematics professor*
Grothendieck, Alexandre *retired mathematician*

New Britain
O'Connell, Brian Michael *computer scientist, educator*

New Haven
Coifman, Ronald R. *mathematician, educator*
Fischer, Michael John *computer science educator*
Howe, Roger Evans *mathematician, educator*
Mandelbrot, Benoit B. *mathematician, scientist, educator*
Margulis, Gregory A. *mathematics educator, researcher*
Martinsson, Per-Gunnar Johan *mathematician, mechanical engineer*
Massey, William S. *mathematician, educator*
Mostow, George Daniel *mathematics professor*
Orszag, Steven Alan *applied mathematician, educator*
Zelmanov, Efim Isaakovich *mathematician, educator*

Quaker Hill
Zhang, Yao *statistician*

Ridgefield
Roy, Tapon *statistician, researcher*

Stamford
Frank, Laura Jean *computer scientist*
Mersereau, Stephen Crocker *electronic commerce executive*
Rogan, Stephen Joseph *software implementation consultant*

Storrs Mansfield
Abikoff, William *mathematician, educator*

Waterbury
Rosa, Domenico *mathematics professor*

West Haven
Kyriakides, Tassos Constantino *biostatistician*

Wilton
Brown, James Thompson, Jr., *computer information scientist, logistics specialist*

DELAWARE

Newark
Colton, David Lem *mathematician, educator*
Stark, Robert Martin *mathematician, civil engineer, educator*

Wilmington
Shevchuck, Harry *retired image systems consultant*
Smeck, William H. *computer scientist*
Wachtel, Howard K. *mathematician, educator*

DISTRICT OF COLUMBIA

Washington
Chiazze, Leonard, Jr., *biostatistician, epidemiologist, educator*
Cohen, Michael Paul *statistician*
Coles, Bertha Sharon Giles *visual information specialist*
Crawford, Natalie Wilson *applied mathematician*
Davis, Peter P. *statistician*
Feil, Michael Bruce *statistician*
Gillman, Daniel W. *information scientist*
Goldfield, Edwin David *statistician*
Goldhaber, Jacob Kopel *retired mathematician, educator*
Gray, Mary Wheat *statistician, lawyer*
Hedges, Harry George *retired computer scientist, educator*
Hunter, Ronald V. *administrator*
Kotz, Samuel *statistician, educator, translator, editor*
Loosbrock, Carol Marie *information management professional*
Lutterodt, Clement H. *mathematician, educator*
MacDonald, Purificacion O. *statistician, researcher*
Mani, Inderjeet *computer scientist, educator*
Mann, Charles Roy *statistician*
Raphael, Louise Arakelian *mathematician, educator*
Ryan, David Alan *computer specialist*
Saworotnow, Parfeny Pavlovich *mathematician, educator*
Shaw, William Frederick *statistician*
Viehe, Karl William *mathematics educator, lawyer, investment banker*
Wulf, William Allan *computer information scientist, educator, federal agency administrator*

FLORIDA

Bonita Springs
Powell, Robert Ellis *mathematics educator, college dean*

Boynton Beach
Sanderson, Jerome Alan *retired statistician, accountant*
Waterman, Daniel *mathematician, educator*

Coral Gables
Howard, Bernard Eufinger *mathematics and computer science educator*

Daytona Beach
Pagan Ortiz, Alex Omar *computer systems analyst, educator*
Seenith, Sivasundaram *mathematician, educator*

Delray Beach
Beckman, Frank Samuel *computer science educator, researcher*
Hegstrom, William Jean *retired mathematics professor*
Mavrides, Gregory *computer scientist, psychoanalyst, computer engineer, computer company executive*

Dunedin
Klingbiel, Paul Herman *retired information scientist*

Fort Lauderdale
Littman, Marlyn Kemper *information scientist, educator*

Gainesville
Bona, Miklos *mathematician, educator*
Cenzer, Douglas Alfred *mathematician, educator*
Chaovalitwongse, Wanpracha *mathematician, researcher*
Dinculeanu, Nicolae *mathematician, educator*
Emch, Gerard Gustav *mathematics and physics educator*
Mukherjee, Bhramar *statistician, educator*
Schneider, Markus *computer scientist, researcher*
Tiep, Pham Huu *mathematician, educator*
Weinrich, Brian Erwin *mathematician, computer scientist*

Highland Beach
Schor, Stanley Sidney *mathematical sciences educator*

Jacksonville
Cole, Linda Sue *grant and program planner, computer software professional*
Robinson, Christine Marie *mathematics educator*

Lake Buena Vista
Bill, Theodore Theoron *technology consultant*

Lakeland
Jelsovsky, Daniel Douglas *mathematician, educator*

Largo
Camara, Vincent Antonin Reginald *mathematician, educator, statistician, researcher*

Melbourne
Agarwal, Ravi P. *mathematician, educator*
Lakshmikantham, Vangipuram *mathematics professor*

Miami
Chen, Shu-Ching *computer science educator*
Dimitriou, Dolores Ennis *computer consultant*
Edward, Julian Kevin *mathematician, educator*

Milton
McKinney, George Harris, Jr., *training systems analyst*

North Miami Beach
Su, Hui Fang Huang *mathematician, educator*

Ocala
Alexis, Noel Richard *mathematician, educator*

Orlando
Deo, Narsingh *computer scientist, educator*
Ismail, Mourad El-Houssieny *mathematician, educator, researcher*
Lisetti, Christine Laetitia *computer scientist, educator*
Marinescu, Dan Cristian *computer sciences educator, consultant*

Palm Harbor
Williams, Thomas Arthur *biomedical computing consultant, psychiatrist*

Panama City
Dang, Hai *geographic information system specialist*

Punta Gorda
Smith, Charles Edwin *computer science educator*

Riviera Beach
Berliner, Hans Jack *retired computer science educator*

Saint Augustine
Jurgens, Julie Graham *mathematics professor*

Saint Petersburg
Berg, Lee R. *computer consultant*
Fishman, Mark Brian *computer scientist, educator*
Schrader, Daryl Lynn *mathematician, educator*
White, June Miller *mathematics professor, educational consultant*

Tallahassee
Conaway, Charles William *information scientist, educator*
George, Joey F. *computer science educator*
Gilmer, Robert *mathematics professor*
Hunter, Christopher *retired mathematics educator*
Nichols, Eugene Douglas *mathematics professor*
Porter, Rhonda Catina *mathematician, educator*

Tampa
Dion, Charles J. *statistician*

Lopez, Ruben *information scientist*
Roop, Mitchell A. *information scientist*

Winter Park
Swan, Richard Gordon *retired mathematics educator*

GEORGIA

Americus
Yemelyanov, Alexander M. *mathematician, educator*

Athens
Bargmann, Rolf Erwin *computer scientist, educator*
Lynch, James Walter *mathematician, educator*
Wang, Shuzhou *mathematician, educator, research scientist*

Atlanta
Ames, William Francis *mathematician, educator*
Bruckman, Amy Susan *computer scientist, educator*
Ellison, Earl Otto *computer scientist*
Foley, James David *computer science educator, consultant*
Goodman, Seymour Evan *computer science and international studies educator, researcher, consultant*
Hale, Jack K. *mathematics educator, research center administrator*
Halloran, M. Elizabeth *statistician, educator*
He, Hongyu *mathematician, educator*
King, K(imberly) N(elson) *computer science educator*
Mickens, Ronald Elbert *applied mathematician, physics educator*
Oliker, Vladimir *mathematician, educator*
Pu, Calton *computer scientist*
Wilding, Diane *computer scientist, consultant*

Augusta
Christensen, David William *mathematician, engineer*
Craig, Cynthia Mae *mathematics professor*
Thiruvaiyaru, Dharma S. *mathematics and statistics educator, consultant, researcher*

Brunswick
Mihal, Sandra Powell *systems analyst*

Lovejoy
Onukwuli, Francis Osita *computer scientist, secondary education educator, mathematician*

Milledgeville
DeVries, David John *mathematician, educator*

Rome
Tapia, Martha Luisa *mathematics professor*

Savannah
John, Selena Latricia *systems analyst*

Statesboro
Damelin, Steven Benjamin *mathematician, educator*
Humphrey, Patricia Buslee *statistician, researcher*
Kaymakcalan, Billur *mathematician, educator*

HAWAII

Hilo
Gersting, Judith Lee *computer scientist, educator, researcher*
Li, Shuguang *mathematics professor, researcher*

Honolulu
Swanson, Richard William *retired statistician*

IDAHO

Moscow
Goetschel, Roy Hartzell, Jr., *mathematician, researcher*
Shafii, Bahman *statistician, educator, researcher*

Rexburg
Harris, Ann Marie *mathematician, educator*

ILLINOIS

Argonne
Plaskacz, Edward John *computational scientist, engineer*

Aurora
Butler, Patricia E. *mathematician, educator*

Belleville
Hedges, Patrick Armand *information technology, communications and computer systems security specialist*

Carbondale
Neuman, Edward George *mathematician, educator*

Carrollton
McAdams, H. T. *statistician, researcher*

Champaign
Adawi, Omar *mathematician, physicist, educator*
Philipp, Walter Viktor *mathematician, educator*
Turquette, Atwell Rufus *logician*
Wasserman, Stanley *statistician, educator*

Charleston
Gordon, Yevgeniy I. *mathematician, educator*

Chicago
Ash, J. Marshall *mathematician, educator*
Bona, Jerry Lloyd *mathematician, educator*
Dardai, Shahid Moinuddin *computer science educator*
Drinfeld, Vladimir Gershonovich *mathematician, educator*
Dukic, Vanja *mathematician, educator*
Dupont, Todd F. *mathematics and computer science educator*
Gibbons, Robert D. *biostatistics educator*
Gillet, Henri Antoine Denis Ciaran *mathematician, educator*
Hanson, Floyd Bliss *mathematician*
Kirkpatrick, Anne Saunders *systems analyst*
Kwembe, Tor Anthony *mathematical educator, researcher*
Larson, Nancy Celeste *computer systems manager*
Madansky, Albert *statistics educator*
Morris, Ashley *information scientist, educator*
O'Donnell, Michael James *computer scientist*
Ong, Michael King *mathematician, educator, bank executive*
Sclove, Stanley Louis *statistics educator*
Sistla, Aravinda Prasad *computer scientist, educator*
Stigler, Stephen Mack *statistician, educator*
Tangora, Martin Charles *mathematician, educator*
Thisted, Ronald Aaron *statistician, educator, consultant*
Tsai, Jingpha (Jeffrey Tsai) *computer scientist, educator*
Wirszup, Izaak *mathematician, educator*
Yee, Wai Gen *computer scientist, educator*
Yoshida, Hiroyuki *mathematician, computer scientist, educator, medical science educator*
Zimmer, Robert J. *mathematician*

Dekalb
Ewell, John Albert, III, *mathematician, educator*

Evanston
Bellow, Alexandra *mathematician, educator*
Chen, Gui-Qiang *mathematician, educator, researcher*
Davis, Stephen Howard *applied mathematics educator*
Devinatz, Allen *retired mathematician, mathematics educator*
Heitsch, James Lawrence *mathematician, educator*
Ionescu Tulcea, Cassius *research mathematician, educator*
Jerome, Joseph Walter *mathematics professor*
Matkowsky, Bernard Judah *applied mathematician, educator*
Olmstead, William Edward *mathematics professor*
Schank, Roger Carl *computer science and psychology educator*
Severini, Thomas Alan *statistician and educator*
Tanner, Martin Abba *statistics and human oncology educator*

Glen Ellyn
Rogers, Teri Ellen *mathematician, educator*

Godfrey
McDaniels, John Louis *retired mathematics educator*

La Grange Park
Butler, Margaret Kampschaefer *retired computer scientist*

Naperville
Fleming, Norman Patrick *information scientist*

Normal
Vanden Eynden, Charles Lawrence *mathematician, educator*

O Fallon
Bjerkaas, Carlton Lee *technology services company executive*

Palatine
Bender, Virginia Best *computer scientist, educator*

Peoria
Szeto, George *mathematician, educator*

Springfield
Patton, Mary Knox *mathematician, educator*

University Park
Hakala, Reino William *mathematician, educator*

Urbana
Carroll, Robert Wayne *mathematics professor*
D'Angelo, John Philip *mathematician*
Fossum, Robert Merle *mathematician, educator*
Henson, C. Ward *mathematician, educator*
Jockusch, Carl Groos, Jr., *mathematics professor*
Knight, Frank Bardsley *mathematics professor*
Liebman, Judith Rae Stenzel *operations research educator*
Schupp, Paul Eugene *mathematician, educator*
Sullivan, John Matthew *mathematician, educator*
Tondeur, Philippe Maurice *mathematician, educator*
Williams, Martha Ethelyn *information science educator*
Wong, Martin D.F. *computer scientist, educator*

Westchester
Pavelka, Elaine Blanche *mathematics professor*

Wood Dale
Yumoto, Futoshi *statistician, researcher*

INDIANA

Bloomington
Hara, Noriko *information scientist, educator*
Houswerth, Elizabeth Ann *mathematics professor*
McRobbie, Michael Alexander *computer scientist, researcher, academic administrator*
Mostafa, Javed *information scientist, educator*
Prosser, Franklin Pierce *computer scientist*
Purdom, Paul Walton, Jr., *computer scientist*
Puri, Madan Lal *mathematics professor*
Temam, Roger M. *mathematician, educator*

Evansville
Kimberling, Clark Hershall *mathematics educator, small business owner*

Fort Wayne
Beineke, Lowell Wayne *mathematics professor*
Dragnev, Peter D. *mathematician, educator*
Romary, Thomas Gerald *mathematician, educator, writer*

Gary
Hozo, Iztok *mathematician, educator*

Greencastle
Anderson, John Robert *retired mathematics educator*

Huntington
Eggleton, Patrick J. *mathematician, educator*

Indianapolis
Becker, Karla Lynn *systems analyst*
Yovits, Marshall Clinton *computer and information science educator, university dean*

Lafayette
de Branges de Bourcia, Louis *mathematics professor*
Drazin, Michael Peter *mathematician, researcher*

Muncie
Ali, Mir Masoom *statistician, educator*

Notre Dame
Bass, Steven Craig *computer science educator*
Faybusovich, Leonid *mathematician, educator*
Pollak, Barth *mathematics professor*
Sommese, Andrew John *mathematics professor*
Stoll, Wilhelm *mathematics professor*

West Lafayette
Abhyankar, Shreeram S. *mathematics and industrial engineering educator*
Feng, Zhilan J *mathematician, educator*

Winona Lake
Dilling, Richard A. *mathematician, educator*

IOWA

Ames
Bibi, Tauqir *mathematician, educator, researcher*
Dahiya, Rajbir Singh *mathematics educator, researcher*
David, Herbert Aron *statistician, educator*
Fuller, Wayne Arthur *statistics educator*
Isaacson, Dean Leroy *statistician*
Weber, Eric Scott *mathematician, educator*
Willis, Jerry Weldon *computer systems educator, writer*

Cedar Falls
Wirth, David Eugene *software designer, consultant*

Des Moines
Munson, Jay Donald *statistician*

Grinnell
Adelberg, Arnold Melvin *mathematics educator, researcher*

Iowa City
Broffitt, James Drake *statistics and actuarial science educator*
Hethcote, Herbert Wayne *mathematician, educator*
Hogg, Robert Vincent, Jr., *mathematical statistician, educator*
Johnson, Eugene Walter *mathematician, educator*
Jorgensen, Palle E.T. *mathematician, educator*
Robertson, Timothy Joel *statistician, educator*

KANSAS

Arkansas City
Nichols, Gregory A. *mathematician, educator*

Atchison
Fellin, Jo Ann *mathematics professor*

Lawrence
Himmelberg, Charles John, III, *mathematics educator, researcher*
Van Vleck, Fred Scott *mathematician, educator, researcher*
Wallace, Victor Lew *computer science educator*

Manhattan
Higgins, James Jacob *statistics educator*

Overland Park
Appelbaum, Elizabeth Berman (Elizabeth Berman) *mathematician*

Pittsburg
Jayawardhana, Ananda Amarasekara *statistician, educator*

Shawnee Mission
Flora, Jairus Dale, Jr., *statistician*

Wichita
Acker, Andrew French, III, *mathematics educator, researcher*
Bagai, Rajiv *computer science educator*
Chopra, Dharam Vir *statistician, educator*
Palmer, Ada Margaret *systems analyst, consultant*

KENTUCKY

Lexington
Cui, Chengwu *imaging scientist, researcher*
Manivannan, Dakshnamoorthy *computer scientist, educator*

Louisville
Brantley, William Albert *information architect, consultant*
Greaver, Joanne Hutchins *mathematics educator, author*
Hoye, Robert Earl *systems science educator*

Owensboro
Mowers, Kathy A. *mathematics professor*

LOUISIANA

Baton Rouge
Chen, Jianhua *computer science educator, researcher*
Durresi, Arjan *computer science educator*
Kovacs, Mihaly *mathematician, researcher*
Oxley, James Grieve *mathematics professor*

Hammond
Brown, Robert Carl *mathematician, educator*

Lafayette
Cain, Judith Sharp *mathematics educator and consultant*

New Orleans
Birtel, Frank Thomas *mathematician, philosopher, educator*
Dauns, John *mathematician, educator*
Gokcen, Ibrahim *computer science researcher*
Harvey, John Grover *mathematics professor, information scientist*
Thomson, Jessica Lee *biostatistician, educator, consultant, researcher*
Yang, DaGang *mathematician, educator*

Shreveport
Brandl, Mary-Katherine *mathematics professor*

MAINE

Blue Hill
Papert, Seymour Aubrey *mathematician, educator, writer*

Orono
Bradley, David Michael *mathematician, educator*

Palermo
Anderson, Alfred Oliver *mathematician, consultant*

Yarmouth
Grover, Mark Donald *computer scientist*

MARYLAND

Adamstown
Tidball, Charles Stanley *computer scientist, educator*

Adelphi
Kirwan, William English, II, *mathematics educator, university official, academic administrator*

Annapolis
Crawford, Carol Gloria *mathematician, educator*
Sheppard, John Wilbur *computer research scientist*

Baltimore
Arsham, Hossein *operations research analyst*
Bausell, R. Barker, Jr., *research methodology educator*
Boardman, John Michael *mathematician, educator*
Kosaraju, S. Rao *computer science educator, researcher*
Lidtke, Doris Keefe *retired computer science educator*
Masson, Gerald M. *computer science educator*
Potra, Florian Alexander *mathematics professor*
Rosenberg, Edwin Harold *systems analyst*
Seidman, Thomas Israel *mathematics professor*
Shiffman, Bernard *mathematician, educator*
Wierman, John Charles *mathematician, educator*

Bethesda
Chartrand, Robert Lee *information scientist*
Lillard, Mark Hill, III, *computer consulting executive, former air force officer*
Moriyama, Iwao Milton *statistician, consultant*
Moshman, Jack *statistical consultant*
Smith, Kent Ashton *scientific and technical information executive*
Weiss, George Herbert *mathematician, consultant*
Zheng, Gang *mathematician, statistician, researcher*

College Park
Antman, Stuart Sheldon *mathematician, educator*
Edgeman, Rick Lee *statistics educator, consultant*
Hendler, James Alexander *computer science educator, consultant*
Lucas, Henry Cameron, Jr., *information systems educator, writer, consultant*
Miller, Raymond Edward *computer science educator*
Minker, Jack *computer scientist, educator*
Olver, Frank William John *research mathematician*
Rosenfeld, Azriel *computer science educator, consultant*
Shneiderman, Ben Abraham *computer science educator, writer*
White, Marilyn Domas *information science educator*
Yorke, James Alan *chaos mathematician*
Youssef, Moustafa Amin *computer scientist, researcher*
Zelkowitz, Marvin Victor *computer science educator*

Columbia
Gregorie, Corazon Arzalem *operations supervisor*

Eldersburg
Spohn, William Gideon, Jr., *mathematician, retired musician*

Fort George G Meade
Schmitt, Robert Lee *computer scientist*

Gaithersburg
Carasso, Alfred Sam *mathematician*
Hultquist, Micki M. *biostatistician*
Rosenblatt, Joan Raup *mathematical statistician*

Hunt Valley
Igusa, Jun-Ichi *mathematician, educator*

Hyattsville
Embody, Daniel Robert *biometrician*
Gonzalez, Joe Fred, Jr., *mathematical statistician, educator*

Shimizu, Iris M. *statistician, consultant*

Lexington Park
Jackameit, Kevin Charles *information scientist*

Linthicum Heights
Tietz, Dietmar Juergen *website engineer, scientist*

Madison
Hoffman, Kenneth Myron *mathematician, educator*

Potomac
Crowson, Henry Lawrence *mathematician, educator*
Frieder, Gideon *computer science and engineering educator*
Medin, Julia Adele *mathematics educator, researcher*
Navarro, Joseph Anthony *statistician, consultant*

Rockville
Brasoveanu, Dan *systems analyst*
Kalton, Graham *survey statistician*
Pennello, Gene Anthony *statistician*
Rashid, Mushfiqur M *statistician*
Tracy, LaRee Ann *statistician, medical researcher*
Waksberg, Joseph *statistical company executive, researcher*

Silver Spring
Chacko, George Kuttickal *systems science educator, consultant*
Sammet, Jean E. *computer scientist*
Sirken, Monroe Gilbert *statistician*
Weiss, Leonard *mathematician, consultant*

Simpsonville
Bluher, Gregory *computer scientist, mathematician*

Towson
Coughlin, James Patrick *mathematician, educator*
Lazar, Jonathan Kumin *computer scientist, educator*

Washington
Bevan, William Charles *systems analyst*

MASSACHUSETTS

Acton
Smith, Raoul Normand *computer science educator*

Amherst
Hayes, David Ryan *mathematics professor*
Jeneralczuk, Joanna Maria *mathematician, educator*
Velleman, Daniel Jon *mathematics professor*

Belmont
Reynolds, William Francis *mathematics professor*

Boston
Berkey, Dennis D. *mathematics professor*
D'Agostino, Ralph Benedict *mathematician, statistician, educator, consultant*
Falb, Peter Lawrence *mathematician, educator, investment company executive*
Gilmore, Maurice Eugene *mathematics professor*
Nam, Byung-Ho *statistician, educator*
Ramoni, Marco F. *computer scientist*
Rand, William Medden *biostatistics educator*
Schoenfeld, David Alan *statistician, educator*
Schribman, Shelley Iris *database engineer, consultant*
Xi, Hongwei *computer scientist, educator*
Zelen, Marvin *statistics educator*

Cambridge
Bartee, Thomas Creson *computer scientist, educator*
Bott, Raoul *mathematician, educator*
Chow, Shein-Chung *statistician, researcher*
Dennis, Jack Bonnell *computer scientist, educator*
Dudley, Richard Mansfield *mathematician, educator*
Gleason, Andrew Mattei *retired mathematician, educator*
Greenspan, Harvey Philip *applied mathematician, educator*
Grosz, Barbara Jean *computer science educator*
Helgason, Sigurdur *mathematician, educator*
Horn, Berthold Klaus Paul *computer scientist, engineering educator*
Kac, Victor G. *mathematician, educator*
Kazhdan, David *mathematician, educator*
Light, Richard Jay *statistician, educator*
Lipson, Pamela *information scientist*
Lynch, Nancy Ann *computer scientist, educator*
Mackey, George Whitelaw *mathematician, educator*
Mazur, Barry Charles *mathematician*
McMullen, Curtis T. *mathematics professor*
Meng, Xiao-Li *statistician*
Moses, Joel *computer scientist, educator*
Mosteller, Frederick *mathematical statistician, educator*
Oettinger, Anthony Gervin *mathematician, educator*
Orlin, James Berger *mathematician, management scientist, educator*
Pak, Igor *mathematician, educator*
Roberts, Edward Baer *technology management educator*
Roberts, Nancy *computer educator*
Rockart, John Fralick *information systems researcher*
Rubin, Donald Bruce *statistician, educator, research company executive*
Singer, Isadore Manuel *mathematician, educator*
Stanley, Richard P. *mathematics professor*
Toomre, Alar *applied mathematician, theoretical astronomer*
Vadhan, Salil Pravin *computer scientist, educator*
Valiant, Leslie Gabriel *computer scientist, educator*
Yau, Shing-Tung *mathematics professor*

Chelmsford
Barlas, Julie Sandall *computer scientist, former librarian*

Duxbury
Thrasher, Dianne Elizabeth *mathematics educator, computer consultant*

East Falmouth
Howard, Louis Norberg *former mathematics educator*

Framingham
Feldman, Susan Eleanor *technology analyst*
Yonda, Alfred William *mathematician*

Lexington
Kelly, Kevin A. *mathematician, educator*
Schafer, Alice Turner *retired mathematics educator*

Lincoln
LeGates, John Crews Boulton *information scientist*

Medford
Jacob, Robert Joseph Kassel *computer scientist, educator*

Newton Center
Williamson, Susan *mathematician, educator*

North Andover
Kurzweil, Raymond C. *computer scientist, entrepreneur*

North Dartmouth
Hegedus, Stephen John *mathematician, educator, researcher*

Northampton
Robinson, John Alan *logic and computer science educator*

Scituate
Ekstrom, John Edward *mathematician, educator*

Shrewsbury
Fondurulia, Julie A. *computer scientist*

Waltham
Brown, Edgar Henry, Jr., *mathematician, educator*

Watertown
Stoddard, Anne Maher *biostatistician, researcher, educator*

Westborough
Crosby, Thomas W. *computer scientist*

Westfield
Buckmore, Alvah Clarence, Jr., *computer scientist, ballistician*

Weston
Berwick, Robert Cregar *computer science educator*

Westport Point
Fanning, William Henry, Jr., *computer specialist*

Winchester
Dalton, Robert Edgar *retired mathematician, computer scientist*

Worcester
Fehribach, Joseph David *mathematician, educator*
Malone, Joseph James *mathematics educator, researcher*

MICHIGAN

Ann Arbor
Becker, Mark Paul Paul *statistics and sociology educator, consultant*
Beutler, Frederick Joseph *information scientist*
Conway, Lynn *computer scientist, electrical engineer, educator*
Gehring, Frederick William *mathematician, educator*
Hill, Bruce Marvin *statistician, scientist, educator*
Kalbfleisch, John David *statistics educator*
Leabo, Dick A. *retired statistics educator*
Reeves, Daniel Martin *computer scientist*

Auburn Hills
Neumann, Charles Henry *mathematician, educator*

Bellevue
Hamel, Louis Reginald *systems analysis consultant*

Big Rapids
Siddikov, Bakhodirzhon *mathematician, educator*
Tymes, Nathaniel, Jr., *statistician, educator*

Bloomfield Hills
Greenwood, Frank *information scientist, educator*

Dearborn
Brown, James Ward *mathematician, educator, author*

Detroit
Dwyer, John M. *mathematician, statistician, computer scientist*
Gunasekera, Thilak Wijenayaka *mathematician, educator*
Kahn, Steven Marshall *mathematics professor*
Mordukhovich, Boris Sholimovich *mathematician, educator, researcher*
Morrison, Gary Ray *instructional technology educator, researcher*
Rajlich, Vaclav Thomas *computer science educator, researcher, consultant*
Schreiber, Bertram Manuel *mathematics professor*
Spansky, Robert Alan *retired computer systems analyst*

East Lansing
Hilbert, Virginia Lois *computer consultant and training executive*
Li, Tien-Yien *mathematics professor*
McCarthy, John David *mathematician, educator*
Stapleton, James Hall *statistician, educator*
Weng, Juyang John *computer science educator, researcher*

Farmington
Ginsberg, Myron *computer scientist*

Flint
McCartin, Brian James *mathematician, educator*

Kalamazoo
Yang, Li *computer scientist, educator*

Livonia
Schwartz, Randy Ken *mathematician, educator*

Mount Pleasant
Lee, Carl *statistician, educator*

North Muskegon
Lynch, Robert Emmett *mathematics educator*

Novi
Chow, Chi-Ming *retired mathematics educator*

Saline
Cornell, Richard Garth *biostatistics educator*

Southfield
Bindschadler, David E. *mathematician, department chairman, application developer*

Warren
Johnson, Leonard Gustave *research mathematician, consultant*

West Bloomfield
Miller, Nancy Ellen *computer consultant*

Ypsilanti
Farah, Badie Naiem *computer information systems educator, consultant*

MINNESOTA

Bloomington
Jensen, Richard Allen *mathematician, educator*

Mankato
Hopkins, Layne Victor *computer science educator*
Rahman, Mezbahur *statistics educator*

Minneapolis
Arnold, Douglas Norman *mathematician*
Bingham, Christopher *statistics educator*
Brasket, Curt Justin *systems analyst, chess player*
Garfield, Joan Barbara *statistics educator*
Lipovetsky, Stan (Stanislav Lipovetsky) *statistician, mathematician*
Markus, Lawrence *retired mathematics educator*
Nitsche, Johannes Carl Christian *mathematics professor*
Serrin, James Burton *mathematics professor*
Warner, William Hamer *applied mathematician*

Moorhead
Heuer, Gerald Arthur *mathematician, educator*

Moose Lake
DeVillion, Kevin John *computer systems administrator, consultant*

Northfield
Appleyard, David Frank *mathematics and computer science educator*
Steen, Lynn Arthur *mathematician, educator*

Saint Charles
Van Norman, Willis Roger *retired computer systems researcher, consultant*

Saint Cloud
Olagunju, Amos Omotayo *computer science educator, consultant*

Saint Paul
Geisser, Seymour *statistics educator*

Shakopee
Qiu, Peihua *statistician, educator, statistician, researcher*

MISSISSIPPI

Alcorn
Hawkins, Sidney Taylor *mathematician, educator*

Corinth
Brooks, Jo Anne *mathematician, educator*

Long Beach
Miller, James Edward *computer scientist, educator*

Mississippi State
Qian, Chuanxi *mathematics professor*

MISSOURI

Cape Girardeau
Bruening, James Theodore *mathematician, educator*

Columbia
Beem, John Kelly *retired mathematician, educator*
Flournoy, Nancy *statistician, educator*

Ferguson
Pescarino, Richard Angelo *mathematician, educator*

Joplin
Cassens, Patrick *mathematician, educator*

Kansas City
Delaware, Richard Raymond *mathematician, educator*
Noe, James Kirby *computer consultant*

Rolla
Bekker, Miron Boris *mathematician, educator*
Charatonik, Wlodzimierz Jan *mathematician*
Grimm, Louis John *mathematician, educator*
Ingram, William Thomas, III, *mathematics professor*
Zobrist, George Winston *computer scientist, educator*

Saint Louis
Baernstein, Albert, II, *mathematician, educator*
Boothby, William Munger *retired mathematics professor*
Ding, Hongming *mathematician, educator*
Pollack, Seymour Victor *computer science educator*
Wilson, Edward Nathan *mathematician, educator*

Trenton
Pushkarsky, Louis Paul *retired mathematics educator*

MONTANA

Dillon
Thompson, Edward Otis *mathematician, educator*

NEBRASKA

Kearney
Fredrickson, Scott Alfred *instructional technology educator, consultant*

Lincoln
Harris, Bernard *statistician, mathematician, educator*
Iyengar, Srikanth B *mathematician, educator*
Wiegand, Sylvia Margaret *mathematician, educator*

Omaha
Chen, Zhengxin *computer scientist*
Jiang, Hong *information scientist*
Wilhelmi, Cynthia Joy *information technology professional, consultant*

NEVADA

Incline Village
Bixby, Robert Eugene *computer, mathematics educator*

Las Vegas
Berghel, Hal L. *computer science educator, columnist, author, consultant*
Blattner, Meera McCuaig *computer science educator*
Lima, Donald Roger *retired computer programmer*

Reno
Kleinfeld, Erwin *mathematician, educator*

NEW HAMPSHIRE

Hanover
Baumgartner, James Earl *mathematics educator*
Kurtz, Thomas Eugene *mathematics professor*

Nashua
An, Ning *computer scientist, researcher*

NEW JERSEY

Chatham
White, Benjamin Steven *mathematician, researcher*

Cherry Hill
Levin, Joshua Zev *computer scientist, consultant, transportation engineer*

Clifton
Minkoff, John *applied mathematics, signal processing, and engineering educator*

Cranford
Petryshyn, Wolodymyr V. *retired mathematician*

Edison
Miniere, Michael Anthony *mathematician, educator*

Florham Park
Shor, Peter W. *mathematician, researcher*

Highlands
Dann, Emily *mathematics professor*

Jersey City
Liu, Kejian *biostatistician*
Poiani, Eileen Louise *mathematics educator, college administrator, higher education planner*

Kenilworth
Abreu, Paula Cristina *statistician, researcher*

Lakewood
Houle, Joseph E. *mathematics professor*

Maplewood
Slepian, David *mathematician, communications engineer*

Matawan
Campbell, Earl Duncan *computer consultant*

Middletown
Kogan, Yaakov *mathematician, researcher*

Montclair
Koeller, Andreas *computer scientist, educator*

Mount Laurel
Huttner, Louise Ann *mathematician, educator*

Neshanic Station
Muckenhoupt, Benjamin *retired mathematics educator*

New Brunswick
Bahri, Abbas *mathematician, educator*
Kahn, Jeffry *mathematics professor*
Kantor, Paul *information scientist, educator*
Kruskal, Martin David *mathematical physicist, astrophysicist*

Kulikowski, Casimir Alexander *computer science and engineering educator*
Saracevic, Tefko *information science educator*
Scanlon, Jane Cronin *mathematics professor*
Strawderman, William E. *statistics educator*
Weibel, Charles Alexander *mathematician*

New Providence
Wright, Margaret Hagen *computer scientist, administrator*

Newark
Miura, Robert Mitsuru *mathematician, researcher, educator*

Oradell
Tong, Hing *mathematician, educator*

Piscataway
Lepowsky, James *mathematician, educator*
Reiley, T. Phillip *systems analyst, consultant*
Roberts, Fred Stephen *mathematician, educator*
Taft, Earl Jay *mathematics professor*

Princeton
Bombieri, Enrico *mathematician, educator*
Bourgain, Jean *mathematician*
Browder, William *mathematician, educator*
Chang, Sun-Yung Alice *mathematics professor*
Chazelle, Bernard *computer science educator*
Deligne, Pierre René *mathematician*
Fefferman, Charles Louis *mathematics professor*
Goddard, Peter *academic administrator, mathematical physicist,*
Gunning, Robert Clifford *mathematician, educator*
Haberman, Shelby Joel *statistician, educator*
Khutoryansky, Naum M. *mathematician, educator*
Kobayashi, Hisashi *computer scientist, dean*
Kohn, Joseph John *mathematician, educator*
Langlands, Robert Phelan *mathematician, educator*
Mihram, George Arthur *mathematician*
Nash, John Forbes, Jr., *research mathematician*
Selberg, Atle *retired mathematician*
Seymour, Paul Douglas *mathematician, educator*
Shimura, Goro *mathematician, educator*
Sinharay, Sandip *statistician, researcher*
Voevodsky, Vladimir *mathematician*
Wiles, Andrew J. *mathematician, educator*
Zhao, Wenyi *systems analyst*

Princeton Junction
Wu, Huan-ter *statistician*

Ridgefield Park
Litwinowicz, Anthony *information specialist, researcher*

Rivervale
Posamentier, Alfred Steven *mathematics educator, university administrator*

Short Hills
Loren, Allan Z. *business information company executive*

Somerset
Becker, Phyllis *systems analyst*

Somerville
Alfred, Siham A. *mathematician, educator*

Teaneck
Zwass, Vladimir *computer science and information systems educator*

Union
Emanouilidis, Emanuel Vasilios *computer scientist, educator*

Weehawken
Metallo, Frances Rosebell *mathematics professor*

West Orange
Ko, Chia-Wen *biostatistician, researcher*

Westwood
Badalamenti, Anthony Francis *mathematician, researcher*

Willingboro
Ingerman, Peter Zilahy *systems analyst, consultant*

Yardville
Zweig, Steven Frederick *statistician*

NEW MEXICO

Albuquerque
Bell, Stoughton *computer scientist, mathematician, educator*
Day, David Minot *mathematician, researcher*
Haley, Richard Edward, Jr., *computer scientist*
Ihde, Mary Katherine *retired mathematics educator*
Jones, Rondall Eugene *mathematician*

Laguna
Reichmann, Péter Iván *mathematics professor*

Las Cruces
Selden, Annie *mathematics professor*

Los Alamos
Stoopes, Gary Robert *technical consultant, geoscientist*

Los Lunas
Robinson, Mary Reid *mathematics professor*

Santa Fe
Kellner, Richard George *mathematician, computer scientist*

Tome
Koopmans, Lambert Herman *retired mathematician*

NEW YORK

Albany
Lenart, Cristian Paul *mathematician, educator*
Rosenkrantz, Daniel J. *computer science educator*

Amherst
Kang, Cong X. *mathematician, educator*

Aurora
Shilepsky, Arnold Charles *mathematics educator, computer consultant*

Binghamton
Geer, James Francis *mathematics professor*
Hilton, Peter John *mathematician, educator*
Klir, George Jiri *systems science educator*
Zaslavsky, Thomas *mathematics professor*

Bronx
Keen, Linda *mathematician, educator*
Koranyi, Adam *mathematics professor*
Rose, Israel Harold *mathematics professor*
Seltzer, William *statistician, social researcher, former international organization director*

Brooklyn
Lutwak, Erwin *mathematician, educator*
Menil, Violeta Cruz *mathematician, educator, consultant*
Pennisten, John William *computer scientist, actuary, linguist*
Schoutens, Hans *mathematician, educator*
Weill, Georges Gustave *mathematics educator*

Buffalo
Coburn, Lewis Alan *mathematics professor*
Hauptman, Herbert Aaron *mathematician, educator, researcher*
Penniman, W. David *information scientist, educator, consultant*
Piech, Margaret Ann *mathematics professor*
Priore, Roger L. *biostatistics educator, consultant*
Seitz, Mary Lee *mathematics professor*
Shapiro, Stuart Charles *computer scientist, educator*
Wiesenberg, Russel John *statistician*

Central Islip
Loughlin, Timothy Arthur *mathematics professor*

Chappaqua
Glazer, Richard Basil *university program director*

Clinton
Redfield, Robert Horace *mathematician, educator*

Dix Hills
Guram, Gurpal Singh *mathematician, educator*

Farmingdale
Chrysafi, Loucas Andrew *mathematician, educator*

Flushing
Mendelson, Elliott *mathematician, educator*

Geneseo
Lin, Rong *computer scientist, educator*

Hamburg
O'Day, John Ignatius *retired computer science educator*

Hamilton
Tucker, Thomas William *mathematics professor*

Hawthorne
Dan, Asit *computer scientist, research scientist*

Hempstead
Greenwell, Raymond N. *mathematician, educator, writer*

Hicksville
Whitlock, Prentice Earle *retired mathematics educator, clergyman*

Ithaca
Billera, Louis J(oseph) *mathematics professor*
Bramble, James Henry *mathematician, educator*
Dynkin, Eugene B. *mathematics professor*
Earle, Clifford John, Jr., *mathematician*
Hartmanis, Juris *computer scientist, educator*
Hopcroft, John Edward *computer scientist*
Morgenstern, Matthew *computer scientist*
Nerode, Anil *mathematician, educator*
Shore, Richard Arnold *mathematics professor*
Trotter, Leslie Earl *operations research educator, consultant*

Kenmore
Kenny, John Edward *computer analyst*

Kingston
Shaffer, Sheila Weekes *mathematics educator*

Liverpool
Allen, David Charles *computer science educator*

Long Island
Berry, Andrew Jonathan *mathematician, educator*

New York
Agwu, Nkechi Madonna *mathematics professor*
Aschoff, Lawrence Michael (Mick Aschoff) *computer information scientist*
Barquero, Pedro B. *mathematician, researcher*
Chichilnisky, Graciela *mathematician, educator, economist, writer*
Christ, Lily Esther Shih *mathematics educator*
Derman, Cyrus *mathematical statistician*
Dobelis, Miervaldis Christian *systems designer*
Edwards, Harold Mortimer *mathematics professor*
Frankel, Martin Richard *statistician, educator, consultant*
Garabedian, Paul Roesel *mathematics professor*
Gardella, Francis John *mathematics professor*
Gomory, Ralph Edward *mathematician, manufacturing company executive, foundation executive*
Gross, Jonathan Light *computer scientist, mathematician, educator*
Habib, Ibrahim Wahby *computer networks engineer, educator, consultant*
Hoppensteadt, Frank Charles *educator, mathematician, university administrator*
Kavalerchik, Boris Yakovlevich *information technology developer, researcher*
Krol, Marina *computer scientist, researcher*
Kurnow, Ernest *statistician, educator*
Lax, Peter David *mathematician, educator*
Lipan, Howard Kenneth *information and technology consultant*
Lo, Shaw-Hwa *statistician, educator*
Morawetz, Cathleen Synge *mathematician*
Moyne, John Abel *computer scientist, linguist, educator*
Nirenberg, Louis *mathematician, educator*
Paik, Myunghee Cho *statistician, educator*
Pierre, Dwight Anthony *mathematician, educator*
Sarkar, Indra Neil *medical informatician*
Saul, Mark E. *mathematics educator, consultant*
Schulzrinne, Henning G. *computer science educator*
Sellers, Peter Hoadley *mathematician, educator*
Shasha, Dennis Elliott *computer scientist, author*
Shim, Sang-Yeun *mathematician, researcher*
Sohmer, Bernard *mathematics educator, administrator*
Traub, J(oseph) F(rederick) *computer scientist, educator*
Widlund, Olof Bertil *computer science educator*

Oneonta
Kazas, Angeliki *mathematician, educator*
Sweet, Norman Byron *mathematician, educator*

Orangeburg
Siegel, Carole Ethel *mathematician*

Pittsford
Hollingsworth, Jack Waring *mathematics and computer science educator*

Potsdam
Alhakim, Abbas Mahdi *statistician, educator*

Rexford
Habetler, George Joseph *retired mathematics educator*

Rhinebeck
Scherr, Allan Lee *computer scientist, executive, consultant*

Riverdale
Bencsáth, Katalin A. *mathematician*

Rochester
Angel, Allen Robert *mathematics educator, author, consultant*
Raimi, Ralph Alexis *mathematics professor*
Simon, William *biomathematician, educator*
Zhao, Hongwei *biostatistician*

Stillwater
O'Connor, Abigail Elizabeth *mathematician, educator, science educator*

Stony Brook
Ahn, Hongshik *statistician, educator*
Anderson, Michael Thomas *mathematics researcher, educator*
Glimm, James Gilbert *mathematician, educator*
Laspina, Peter Joseph *computer resource educator*
Lawson, H(erbert) Blaine, Jr., *mathematician, educator*
Michelsohn, Marie-Louise *mathematician, educator*
Milnor, John Willard *mathematician*
Tewarson, Reginald Prabhakar *retired mathematics educator, consultant*
Tucker, Alan Curtiss *mathematics professor*

Syracuse
Church, Philip Throop *retired mathematics professor*
Graver, Jack Edward *mathematics professor*
Hale, Karen Suzanne *mathematics professor*
Hansen, Per Brinch *computer scientist, researcher*
Hsu, Lifang *statistician, department chairman*
Malhotra, Yogesh *former computer scientist, management educator, corporate and national consultant, entrepreneur, former computer engineer*
Pardee, Otway O'Meara *computer scientist, educator*

Tarrytown
Maun, Mary Ellen *computer consultant*

Troy
Szymanski, Boleslaw Karol *computer scientist, educator, entrepreneur*

Upton
Ma, Yeming *statistician, medical researcher*

Valley Stream
De Mita, Francis Anthony *mathematics professor*

West Hempstead
Guggenheimer, Heinrich Walter *mathematician, educator*

Westbury
Sandler, Gerald Howard *computer science educator, company executive*

White Plains
Chen, Shuang *computer science professional*
Heo, Moonseong *statistician, researcher*
Machover, Carl *computer graphics consultant*

Williamsville
Berner, Robert Frank *managerial statistics educator, administrator*
Brown, Stephen Ira *philosophy educator*

Yorktown Heights
Auslander, Marc Alan *computer scientist*
d'Heurle, François Max *research scientist, engineering educator*
Hoffman, Alan Jerome *mathematician, educator*
Lei, Hui *computer scientist*
Neti, Chalapathy *computer scientist, researcher*
Saon, George A. *computer scientist, researcher*

NORTH CAROLINA

Archdale
O'Hara, Karen Ann *mathematician, educator*

Asheville
Codd, Richard Trent, Jr., *computer scientist, educator*

Cape Carteret
Mullikin, Thomas Wilson *mathematics professor*

Chapel Hill
Brooks, Frederick Phillips, Jr., *computer scientist, educator*
Brown, Keith John *computer applications analyst*
Coulter, Elizabeth Jackson *biostatistician, educator*

Charlotte
″awczak, Janusz *mathematician, educator*

Cullowhee
Willis, Ralph Houston *mathematics professor*

Durham
Edelsbrunner, Herbert *computer scientist, mathematician*
Johnson, Kristina M. *technology director*
Sowa, Artur *mathematician, researcher*

Greensboro
Posey, Eldon Eugene *mathematician, educator*
Tang, Guoqing *mathematics professor*

Murfreesboro
Obuchowska, Wieslawa Teresa *mathematician, educator*

Raleigh
Bakalov, Bojko *mathematician*
Chou, Wushow *computer scientist, educator*
Kang, Min *mathematician, educator*
Nelson, Larry A. *statistics educator, consultant*
Pao, Chia-Ven *mathematics professor*

Research Triangle Park
Krishen, Alok *biostatistician*

Salisbury
Sullivan, Sharon Lee *mathematician, educator*

Southport
Johnston, Dennis Roy *computer systems integrator*

West Jefferson
Merrion, Arthur Benjamin *mathematics professor, tree farmer*

OHIO

Akron
Wortham, James Calvin *retired mathematics educator*

Alliance
Zwilling, Michael Louis *mathematician, educator*

Athens
Wen, Shih-Liang *mathematics professor*

Berea
Little, Richard Allen *mathematics and computer science educator*

Canton
Kasturiarachi, Aloysius Bathi *mathematician, educator, researcher*

Cincinnati
Banagl, Markus *mathematician*
Dumas, H. Scott *mathematician, educator*
Flick, Thomas Michael *mathematics educator, educational administrator*
Kim, Sung Eun *statistician, educator*
Semon, Warren Lloyd *retired computer sciences educator*

Cleveland
Butler, Christopher David *mathematics professor*
Cirincione, Ross Joseph *mathematician, educator*
Clark, Robert Arthur *mathematician, educator*
Flynn, James O'Donnell *statistician, educator*
Goffman, William *mathematician, educator*
Szarek, Stanislaw Jerzy *mathematics professor*
Waren, Allan David *computer information scientist, educator*
Woyczynski, Wojbor Andrzej *mathematician, educator*

Columbus
Chandrasekaran, Balakrishnan *computer and information science educator*
Dull, Clifford John *religious groups analyst*
Friedman, Avner *mathematician, educator*
Muller, Mervin Edgar *computer scientist, statistician, educator*
Wang, Deliang *computer scientist, educator*
Zweben, Stuart Harvey *information scientist, educator*

Dayton
Khalimsky, Efim *mathematics and computer science educator*

Granville
Bonar, Daniel Donald *mathematics professor*
Kretchmar, R. Matthew *computer science educator*

Grove City
Kimethu, Susan Wanja *computer specialist, database manager*

Kent
Bansal, Arvind Kumar *computer scientist, educator*
Reed, Beverly Marie *mathematician, educator*
Rollick, Mary Beth *mathematician, educator*
Varga, Richard Steven *mathematics professor*

Lakeside Marblehead
Garrow, Robert Joseph, Jr., *mathematician, educator*

Mansfield
Gregory, Thomas Bradford *mathematics professor*

Mason
Chesley, Ann Marie *systems analyst*

Rockford
Thompson, Robert Douglas *computer science educator, banker, consultant*

Vermilion
Vance, Elbridge Putnam *mathematics educator*

Warren
He, Min *mathematics professor*

Wilberforce
Hargraves, William Frederick, II, *mathematics and computer science educator*

Wooster
Geiser, Robert Neil *computer scientist*
Hales, Raleigh Stanton, Jr., *mathematics professor, academic administrator*

Youngstown
Smotzer, Thomas David *mathematician*

OKLAHOMA

Edmond
Loman, Mary LaVerne *retired mathematics educator*

Norman
Apanasov, Boris N. *mathematics professor, researcher*
Bethel, Joann D. *computer programmer, analyst*
Dickey, Leonid Alexander *mathematician, educator*
Lakshmivarahan, Sivaramakrishnan *computer science educator*
Munteanu, Laura *mathematician, educator*
Provine, Lorraine *retired mathematics educator*

Stillwater
Payton, Mark Edward *statistician, educator*
Pritsker, Igor *mathematics professor*

Tahlequah
Diamantopoulos, John C.D. *mathematician, educator*

Tulsa
Dimiceli, Vincent Edward *mathematician, educator*
Lang, Andrew Stuart Ian Donald *mathematician, consultant*
Sowell, Debra Ann Olson *mathematician, educator, academic administrator*

OREGON

Ashland
Backus, John *computer scientist*

Beaverton
Hall, Howard Pickering *engineering and mathematics educator*

Corvallis
Parks, Harold Raymond *mathematician, educator*
Shiue, Wen-Tsong *electrical and computer scientist, educator*

Eugene
Kennevan, Walter James *computer science educator*

Hillsboro
Daim, Tugrul Unsal *technology management specialist, educator*
Ferguson, James Clarke *mathematician, algorithmist*
Pixley, Carl Preston *mathematician*

Oregon City
Baratto, Stefan *mathematics professor*

Portland
Ahuja, Jagdish Chand *mathematics professor*
Daescu, Dacian N. *mathematics professor*
Lambert, Richard William *retired mathematics professor*

Tualatin
Brown, Robert Wallace *retired mathematics educator*

PENNSYLVANIA

Aston
DiMarco, David *mathematician, educator*

Bethlehem
Ghosh, Bhaskar Kumar *statistics educator, researcher*
Schattschneider, Doris Jean *retired mathematics educator*
Styer, Jane M. *computer consultant*

Bryn Mawr
Ackoff, Russell Lincoln *systems sciences educator*

Coatesville
Burton, Mary Louise Himes *computer specialist*

Easton
Traldi, Lorenzo *mathematician, educator*

Hollidaysburg
Deskevich, Paul *mathematics professor*

Indiana
Shim, Leem Seop *computer scinetist, educator, researcher*

Johnstown
Danchanko, Marilyn A. *mathematics professor*

King Of Prussia
Yan, Ying *statistician, researcher*

Kutztown
Pirmot, Thomas L. *mathematician, educator*

Laureldale
Rozzi, Christine M. *mathematician, educator*

Manheim
Soltys, Stephen Robert *mathematician, educator*

Meadville
Cable, Charles Allen *mathematician*

Philadelphia
Alsardary, Salar *mathematician, educator*
Banerji, Ranan Bihari *mathematics and computer science educator*
Cowles, Roger E. *computer consultant*
de Cani, John Stapley *statistician, educator*
Ehrenpreis, Leon *mathematician, educator, rabbi*
Fernholz, Luisa Turrin *statistician, educator*
Freyd, Peter John *mathematician, computer scientist, educator*
Garfield, Eugene *information scientist, author, publisher*
Iglewicz, Boris *statistician, educator*
Kadison, Richard Vincent *mathematician, educator*
Knopp, Marvin Isadore *mathematics professor*
Mode, Charles J. *mathematician, educator*
Porter, Gerald Joseph *mathematician, educator*
Roth, Marilyn Dorothy *information scientist*
Scedrov, Andre *mathematics and computer science researcher, educator*
Shatz, Stephen Sidney *mathematician, educator*
Smith, Woollcott *statistician, educator*
White, Howard D. *information science educator*

Pittsburgh
Balas, Egon *applied mathematician, educator*
Bocea, Marian *mathematician*
Buchanan, Bruce G. *computer scientist, educator*
Caginalp, Gunduz *mathematician, educator, researcher*
Carbo, Toni (Toni Carbo Bearman) *information scientist, educator*
Chrysanthis, Panos Kypros *computer science educator, researcher*
Cravens, Gary Dean *informaticist, physician*
Druzdzel, Marek Jozef *researcher and educator*
Gurtin, Morton Edward *mathematics professor*
Kass, Robert Eben *statistician, educator*
Kemerer, Chris F. *information scientist, educator*
Kraut, Robert E. *computer studies educator*
Lehoczky, John Paul *statistics educator*
Noll, Walter *mathematics professor*

Reading
Rochowicz, John Anthony, Jr., *mathematician, mathematics and physics educator*

Rydal
Bacon, George Hughes, Jr., *retired systems analyst*

Schnecksville
Schillow, Ned William *mathematics educator*

Swarthmore
Kelemen, Charles F. *computer science educator*

Tobyhanna
Lapidus, Arnold *mathematician, educator*

University Park
Andrews, George Eyre *mathematics professor*
Antle, Charles Edward *statistics educator*
Barlow, Jesse Louis *computer scientist, educator*
Waterhouse, William Charles *mathematics professor*

Villanova
Beck, Robert Edward *computer scientist, educator*

Wallingford
Morrison, Donald Franklin *statistician, educator*

Washington
Forrest, Robert Gilliland *mathematics professor*

RHODE ISLAND

Kingston
Beauregard, Raymond A. *mathematician, educator*

Providence
Dafermos, Constantine Michael *applied mathematics educator*
Davis, Philip J. *mathematician*
Ewing, John Harwood *mathematics professor, department chairman*
Fleming, Wendell Helms *mathematician, educator*
Freiberger, Walter Frederick *mathematics professor, actuarial science consultant*
Jin, Ya *mathematics researcher*
Kushner, Harold Joseph *mathematics professor*
Mumford, David Bryant *mathematics professor*
Savage, John Edmund *computer science educator, researcher*
Shu, Chi-Wang *mathematics educator, researcher*
Silverman, Joseph Hillel *mathematics professor*

SOUTH CAROLINA

Aiken
Li, Rao *mathematician, computer scientist*

Charleston
Hoel, David Gerhard *statistician, scientist, educator*

Clemson
Brawley, Joel Vincent *mathematician, educator*

Orangeburg
Bozinovski, Stevo *computer science educator, researcher*

Viswanath, Guttalu Ramachandra Rao *mathematics educator, consultant, researcher*

Pendleton
Marshall, Gerald Lee *mathematician, educator*

Spartanburg
Codespoti, Daniel Joseph *retired computer scientist*
Hilton, Theodore Craig *computer scientist, Internet company executive*

Summerville
Diamond, Michael Shawn *science and math educator, computer consultant*

SOUTH DAKOTA

Vermillion
Lio, Yuhlong *mathematician, educator*

TENNESSEE

Brownsville
Kalin, Robert *retired mathematics educator*

Collegedale
Moore, Robert Crumley *mathematician, educator*

Jackson
Dawson, C. Bryan *mathematician*

Johnson City
Hong, Don *mathematician, educator*

Knoxville
Schaefer, Philip William *mathematics educator, researcher*
Tenopir, Carol *information science educator*

Martin
Petty, James Alan *mathematics educator, consultant*

Memphis
Schelp, Richard Herbert *mathematics professor*
Xiong, Xiaoping *statistician, researcher*

Nashville
Beauchamp, John Jones *mathematician, educator*
Cooil, Bruce Kimo *mathematical statistician, statistics educator*
Dupont, William Dudley *biostatistician, educator*
Fischer, Patrick Carl *computer scientist, retired educator*
Jonsson, Bjarni *mathematician, educator*
McCowan, Otis Blakely *mathematics professor*
Rowan, William Hamilton, Jr., *computer science educator*
Saff, Edward Barry *mathematics professor*
Williams, Marsha Rhea *computer scientist, educator, researcher, consultant*

Oak Ridge
Hartley, Dean S., III, *operations research specialist*
Raridon, Richard Jay *computer specialist*

TEXAS

Abilene
Retzer, Kenneth Albert *mathematics professor, entrepreneur*

Arlington
Greenspan, Donald *mathematician, educator*
Han, Chien-Pai *statistics educator*
Kojouharov, Hristo Venelinov *mathematician, educator, mathematician, researcher*

Austin
Clark, Charles T(aliferro) *retired business statistics educator*
Garner, Harvey Louis *computer scientist, consultant, electrical engineering educator*
Gillman, Leonard *mathematician, educator*
Jones, William Richard *database administrator*
Lam, Simon Shin-Sing *computer science educator*
Novak, Gordon S., Jr., *computer scientist, educator*
Pickett, Sandra *information scientist*
Seifoullaev, Roustam Kafar *mathematician, programmer*
Turney, James Edward *computer scientist*
Uhlenbeck, Karen Keskulla *mathematician, educator*
Voges, Linda Kay *mathematics educator, telecommunications engineer*
Williamson, Hugh Jackson *statistician*

Beaumont
Chiou, Paul C.J. *statistician, educator*

Brenham
Zientek, Linda Reichwein *mathematician, educator*

Brownsville
Yi, Taeil *mathematician, educator*
Zdansky, Janice Cecelia *mathematician*

College Station
Ewing, Richard Edward *mathematics, chemical and petroleum engineering educator*
Zheng, Qi *statistician, biomathematician*

Dallas
Ajaev, Vladimir S. *mathematician, educator*
Barr, Richard Stuart *computer science and management science educator*
Chen, Zhangxin John *mathematics professor*

Denton
Garcia, Oscar Nicolas *computer science educator*
Grigorieva, Ellina *mathematics professor, researcher*
Mauldin, Richard Daniel *mathematics professor*
Renka, Robert Joseph *computer science educator, consultant*

El Paso
Foged, Leslie Owen *mathematician, educator*

Quevedo, Hector Adolf *operations research specialist, environmental scientist*
Tchoshanov, Mourat Ashirovich *mathematician, educator*

Fort Hood
Scott, Karen Lou *systems analyst*

Fort Worth
Doran, Robert Stuart *mathematician, educator*
Fan, Peng *mathematician*
Sullenberger, Ara Broocks *mathematics professor*

Galveston
Robertson, Paul Francis *mathematician, educator*

Houston
Crutchfield, Robert Alan *computer scientist, minister*
Gardner, Everette Shaw, Jr., *information sciences educator, consultant, author*
Glowinski, Roland *mathematics professor*
Golubitsky, Martin Aaron *mathematician, educator*
Johnson, Olin Glynn *computer science educator*
Kakadiaris, Ioannis *computer science educator*
Liles, Clifton Roy *software designer*
Ma, Jingjing *mathematician*
Martinez, Lori Anne Brubaker *mathematician, educator*
Miller, Charles Rickie *thermal and fluid systems analyst, engineering manager*
Scott, David Warren *statistics educator*
Wang, Chao-Cheng *mathematician, engineer*
Westberry, John Elliott *mathematics professor*
Wright, Clark Phillips *computer systems specialist*

Irving
Anderson, Michael Curtis *computer industry analyst*
Conger, Sue Ann *computer information systems educator*

Kingsville
Cecil, David Rolf *mathematician, educator*
Morey, Philip Stockton, Jr., *mathematics professor*

Lewisville
Ferguson, R. Neil *computer systems consultant*

Lubbock
Conover, William Jay *statistics educator*
Seshaiyer, Padmanabhan *mathematician, educator*

Mesquite
Sepulvado, Joseph Michael *computer information scientist*

New Caney
Hayes, Ann Carson *computer services executive*

Richardson
Constantinescu, Tiberiu *mathematician*
Easttom, Chuck *computer scientist, educator*
Hennessey, Audrey Kathleen *computer researcher, educator*
Odushkin, Taras *mathematician*

Round Rock
Khalid, Humayun *computer scientist, consultant*

San Antonio
Estep, Myrna Lynne *systems analyst, philosophy educator*
Grigoryan, Artyom Mkrtichi *mathematician*
Hall, Douglas Lee *computer science educator*
Le, Dung *mathmatics educator, researcher*
Tian, Qi *computer science educator*
Traylor, Donald Reginald *mathematics educator*

San Marcos
Keller, Thomas Michael *mathematician, educator*

Temple
Rajab, Mohammad Hasan *biostatistician, educator*

Tyler
Bailey, Nan Hutchins *mathematician, educator*

Waco
Henderson, Johnny *mathematician, educator*
Odell, Patrick Lowry *mathematics professor*
Walbesser, Henry Herman *computer science educator*

Whitehouse
Cavanaugh, Charles Davis *computer scientist, educator*

UTAH

Orem
Moore, Hal G. *mathematician, educator*

Provo
Ivie, Evan Leon *computer science educator*

Salt Lake City
Cherkaev, Andrej Vsevolodovich *mathematician, educator*
Horn, Susan Dadakis *statistics educator*

VERMONT

Burlington
Aleong, John *statistician, educator*

North Bennington
Adler, Irving *mathematician*

Norwich
Snapper, Ernst *mathematics professor*

VIRGINIA

Alexandria
Chen, Fen *mathematician, educator, researcher*
Perchik, Benjamin Ivan *operations research analyst*

Tichenor, Charles Beckham, III, *operations research analyst*

Arlington
Golladay, Mary Jean *statistician*
Osterholz, John Louis *information administrator*
Perry, Walter Leo *information scientist, operations research specialist*
Suh, Jinwoo *computer scientist*

Blacksburg
Good, Irving John *statistics educator, mathematician, philosopher of science*
Sandu, Adrian *mathematician, computer scientist, educator*

Charlottesville
Rosenblum, Marvin *mathematics educator*
Rovnyak, James *mathematician, educator*
Tang, Jinshan *computer scientist, researcher*

Clifton
Hoffman, Karla Leigh *mathematician, educator*

Dahlgren
Adams, Michelle Leigh *computer scientist*

Fairfax
Mulvaney, Mary Frederica *systems analyst*
Nefissi, Sami *mathematician, educator*
Sauer, Timothy DuWayne *mathematician, educator*
Sullivan, Keith Montgomery *operations research specialist*

Falls Church
Flory, Robert Mikesell *computer systems analyst, personnel management specialist*

Farmville
Rowland, Rhonda Stockton *mathematician, educator*

Fort Belvoir
Clema, Joe Kotouc *computer scientist*
Raymond, George Edward, Jr. (Chip Raymond) *operations research analyst*

Fredericksburg
Hajek, Otomar *mathematician, educator*

Hampton
Verma, Arun K. *mathematician, educator*

Heathsville
Stubbs, Susan Conklin *retired statistician*

Herndon
Douglass, Robert Joseph, Jr., *computer scientist*
Hermansen, John Christian *computational linguist*
Hollis, Katherine Mary *information scientist, consultant*

Leesburg
Hetzel, Alice M. *statistician, researcher*

Lexington
Tierney, Michael John *mathematics and computer science educator*

Lynchburg
Terzic, Petar *mathematician, educator*

Manakin Sabot
Thompson, Walter David, Jr., *systems analyst*

Middleburg
Tucker, John Richard *mathematician, educator, writer, researcher*

Newport News
Summerville, Richard M. *mathematician, academic administrator*

Norfolk
Adam, John Anthony *mathematician, educator*
Kaneko, Hideaki *mathematics professor*
Maly, Kurt John *computer science educator*

Petersburg
Perdue, Diana S. *mathematician, educator*

Reston
Wetsch, John Robert *information systems specialist*

Richmond
Charlesworth, Arthur Thomas *mathematics and computer science educator*
Owens, Arne Wesley *systems analyst*

Springfield
Leake, Charles Robert *systems analyst, educator*

Sterling
Heberling, Timothy Alan *information scientist*
Martin, Roger John *computer scientist*

Sweet Briar
Wassell, Stephen Robert *mathematics educator, researcher*

Vienna
Gardenier, John Stark *statistician, research ethicist, lecturer, writer*

Warrenton
Gullace, Marlene Frances *information engineer, systems analyst, consultant*

Williamsburg
Rodman, Leiba *mathematician*
Zhang, Xiaodong *computer scientist, educator, researcher*

Wise
Grable, Dillon Ross *computer scientist, educator, music educator*

WASHINGTON

Eastsound
de Boor, Carl *mathematician*

Ellensburg
Comstock, Dale Robert *mathematics professor*

Federal Way
Cunningham, John Randolph *project manager*

Kenmore
Sobolewski, John Stephen *computer scientist, consultant*

Kennewick
Cochran, James Alan *mathematics professor, department chairman*

Kent
Personette, Louise Metzger (Sister Mary Roger Metzger) *mathematics educator*

Pullman
Ahn, Sung Keuk *statistician, educator*
Kallaher, Michael Joseph *mathematics professor*

Redmond
Chayes, Jennifer Tour *mathematical physicist, educator*
Freedman, Michael Hartley *mathematician, educator*
Kimmich, Jon Bradford *computer science program executive*
Lomet, David Bruce *computer scientist*

Seattle
Breslow, Norman Edward *biostatistics educator, researcher*
Gillispie, Steven Brian *systems analyst, researcher*
Klee, Victor La Rue *mathematician, educator*
Kumar, Subodha *information scientist, educator*
Lee, John Marshall *mathematics professor*
Michael, Ernest Arthur *mathematics professor*
Murray, James Dickson *mathematical biology educator*
Nijenhuis, Albert *mathematician, educator*
O'Malley, Robert Edmund, Jr., *mathematics professor*
Pyke, Ronald *mathematics professor*
Scroggie, Wayne Lee *computer scientist, management consultant*
Segal, Jack *mathematics professor*
Urban, Nicole D. *biostatistician*

Tacoma
Burns, Robin C(arol) *mathematics theoretician, accountant*

White Salmon
Verry, William Robert *retired mathematics researcher*

Yakima
Jongeward, George Ronald *retired systems analyst*

WEST VIRGINIA

Glenville
Ellis, Mark Lee *mathematician, educator*

Institute
Zaman, Naveed *mathematician, educator*

Morgantown
De Vore, Paul Warren *technology educator*
Hensel, Robin Ann Morgan *mathematics and computer science educator*

WISCONSIN

Green Bay
Conley, William Cleland *statistician, educator*

La Crosse
Maresh, Richard Joseph *mathematics professor*
Matchett, Andrew James *mathematics professor*

Madison
Askey, Richard Allen *mathematics educator*
Beck, Anatole *mathematician, educator*
Draper, Norman Richard *statistician, educator*
Johnson, Millard Wallace, Jr., *mathematics and engineering educator*
Johnson, Richard Arnold *statistics educator, consultant*
Malkus, David Starr *mathematician*
Mau, Bob *statistician*
Mitchell, Julie Carol *mathematician, educator, biochemist, educator*
Ney, Peter Ernest *mathematician, educator*
Ono, Ken *mathematician, educator*
Parter, Seymour Victor *computer science and mathematics educator*
Robinson, Stephen Michael *applied mathematician, educator*
Ron, Amos *computer scientist, educator, mathematician*

Milwaukee
Reynolds, Barbara E. *mathematics professor*
Teply, Mark Lawrence *mathematics professor*

Sun Prairie
Terhune, Karen Marie *mathematics, secondary school educator*

Whitefish Bay
Pustejovsky, Susan F. *mathematics educator*

Whitewater
Baica, Malvina Florica *mathematics educator*

WYOMING

Laramie
Shader, Bryan Lynn *mathematics professor*
Spears, Diana Faye *computer scientist*

TERRITORIES OF THE UNITED STATES

PUERTO RICO

Mayaguez
Collins, Dennis Glenn *mathematics professor*

San Juan
Janwa, Heera Lal *mathematician, educator*
Pasnicu, Cornel *mathematician, educator*
Teleman, Silviu *mathematician, educator*

CANADA

ALBERTA

Edmonton
Davis, Wayne Alton *computer science educator*

BRITISH COLUMBIA

Vancouver
Boyd, David William *mathematician, educator*
Clark, Colin Whitcomb *mathematics professor*
Feldman, Joel Shalom *mathematician*
Granirer, Edmond Ernest *mathematician, educator*
Sion, Maurice *mathematics professor*

Victoria
Manning, Eric *computer science and engineering educator, university dean, researcher*
Meadow, Charles *information scientist, consultant*

NOVA SCOTIA

Halifax
Fillmore, Peter Arthur *mathematician, educator*

ONTARIO

Chatham
Shakhmundes, Lev *mathematician*

Kingston
Campbell, L(ouis) Lorne *mathematics professor*

London
Bauer, Michael Anthony *computer scientist, educator*
Borwein, David *mathematics professor*

Mississauga
Al-Nachawati, Hicham Mustapha *statistician*

Ottawa
Csörgö, Miklós *mathematics and statistics educator*
Dawson, Donald Andrew *mathematics educator, researcher*
Dlab, Vlastimil *mathematics educator, researcher*
Fellegi, Ivan Peter *statistician*

Toronto
Cook, Stephen Arthur *mathematics and computer science educator*
Friedlander, John Benjamin *mathematician, educator*
Gotlieb, Calvin Carl *computer scientist, educator*
Rooney, Paul George *mathematics professor*

Waterloo
Aczél, János Dezsö *mathematician*
Gladwell, Graham Maurice Leslie *mathematician, civil engineering educator*
Paldus, Josef *mathematics professor*
Sprott, David Arthur *statistics and psychology educator*

QUEBEC

Montreal
Dubuc, Serge *mathematics professor*
Maag, Urs Richard *statistics educator*
Moser, William Oscar Jules *mathematics professor*
Romanov, Volodymyr Alexeevich *computer science educator, researcher*
Suen, Ching Yee *computer scientist and educator, researcher*

Quebec City
Theodorescu, Radu Amza Serban *mathematician, educator*

SASKATCHEWAN

Regina
Symes, Lawrence Richard *computer science educator, university dean*

AUSTRALIA

Canberra
Gani, Joseph Mark *statistics educator, administrator, researcher*

CHINA

Changchun Jilin
Bi, Shuwei *management information systems educator*

CZECH REPUBLIC

Prague
Jech, Thomas J. *mathematics professor*

ENGLAND

Leicester
Harijan, Ram *technology transfer researcher*

London
Ralston, Anthony *computer scientist, mathematician, educator*

FRANCE

Paris
Serre, Jean-Pierre *mathematician, scholar*
Yuechiming, Roger Yue Yuen Shing *mathematics professor*

GERMANY

Bremen
Wells, Raymond O'Neil, Jr., *mathematics educator, researcher*

HONG KONG

South Horizons
Chen, Concordia Chao *mathematician*

HUNGARY

Szeged
Nyúl, László G. *mathematician, educator, researcher*

JAPAN

Ichihara
Kuma, Hisao *information systems educator*

Sapporo
Asari, Eikichi *information sciences educator, researcher*

Tokyo
Eto, Hajime *information scientist, educator*

LEBANON

Beirut
Habre, Samer S *mathematician, educator*

RUSSIA

Moscow
Novikov, Sergei Petrovitch *mathematician*

SCOTLAND

Edinburgh
Atiyah, Sir Michael Francis *mathematician*

ADDRESS UNPUBLISHED

Aaron, Bud *systems analyst*
Abbey, Scott Gerson *computer information scientist*
Agnihothri, Saligrama R. *mathematics professor*
Ambainis, Andris *computer scientist*
Anderson, Jacqueline Annette *computer specialist*
Aprilakis, Anna *mathematics professor*
Arden, Bruce Wesley *retired computer scientist, retired engineering educator*
Bailar, Barbara Ann *retired statistician*
Barrett, Lida Kittrell *mathematics professor*
Basch, Reva *information services company executive*
Belinsky, Rachel *mathematician, educator*
Benson, Donald Charles *mathematician, educator*
Berndt, Markus *mathematician*
Berra, P. Bruce *computer educator*
Binkley, Timothy *computer graphics educator*
Blcher, Frauke Maria *mathematician, educator*
Boardman, Elizabeth Drake *computer science educator*
Bobbitt, James Lyle *computer programmer, systems analyst*
Bowlby, Richard Eric *retired computer systems analyst*
Box, George Edward Pelham *statistics educator*
Bright-Hollomon, Crystal *operations research specialist*
Browder, Felix Earl *mathematician, educator*
Brown, Alton Raymond *mathematician, researcher*
Caldwell, Cindy Sue *mathematician, educator*
Cameron, Kirk MacGregor Drummond *statistician*
Campbell, Sharon Milligan *mathematician, educator*
Case, Colleen Mae *computer scientist, educator*
Champine, George A. *computer scientist*
Chen, Tar Timothy *biostatistician*
Chow, Timothy Yi-Chung *mathematician, systems engineer*
Cintron, Virginia *information scientist*
Cline, Melissa Suzanne *computer scientist*
Conn, Richard Lee *computer scientist, educator*
Covin, Carol Louise *computer consultant*
Croog, Roslyn Zeporah *chief systems engineer*
Damien, Paul *mathematician, writer*
Davis, Marjorie Ann *program analyst*
Diagana, Toka *mathematician, researcher*

Dixon, Diane Marie *statistician*
Efird, Jimmy Thomas *statistician*
Eklof, Paul C. *mathematician, educator*
Elam, Fred Eldon *retired career army officer*
Elliott, David LeRoy *mathematician, educator, engineering educator*
Erickson, Robert *computer science educator*
Ezell, Margaret Prather *information systems executive*
Farid, Farid O. *mathematics professor*
Fidler, Mark T. *mathematician, educator, writer*
Fisher, Gordon McCrea *mathematician, educator*
Fleming, James Edward, Jr. *information scientist, educator*
Flores, Alfinio *mathematician, educator*
Fraser, Ailana Margaret *mathematician, educator*
Freitag, Harlow *retired computer scientist and corporate executive*
Garland, Howard *mathematician, educator*
Gelfand, Israel Moseevich *mathematician, biologist*
Gerson, Donald Jerome *computer scientist, consultant*
Gessaman, Margaret Palmer *mathematician, educator, retired dean*
Gifford, Marjorie Fitting *mathematician, educator, consultant*
Gnanadesikan, Ramanathan *retired statistics educator, researcher*
Goldberg, Samuel *retired mathematician, foundation officer*
Goldman, Benjamin Allen *statistician, writer*
Gonye, Zsuzsanna *mathematician, educator*
Gorenstein, Samuel *retired mathematician, educator*
Gosciewski, Robert Louis *logistician*
Grasserbauer, Doris *computer scientist, mathematician, educator*
Greever, Margaret Quarles *retired mathematics educator*
Griffiths, Phillip A. *mathematician, former academic administrator*
Halberstam, Heini *mathematics professor*
Hamblen, John Wesley *computer scientist, genealogist*
Hardie, Michael Howard *mathematician, educator*
Hardy, Michael John *statistician, educator*
Harris, Theodore Edward *mathematician, educator*
Hetyei, Gabor *mathematician, educator*
Hinton, Norman Wayne *retired information services executive*
Holford, Theodore Richard *biostatistician, educator*
Holland, Burt S. *statistics educator, consultant*
Holland, Michael James *computer services administrator*
Holland, Richard A. *retired statistician*
Holmes, Calvin Virgil *mathematician, educator*
Hornback, Joseph Hope *mathematics professor*
House, Stephen Eugene *information systems consultant*
Hunte, Beryl Eleanor *mathematics educator, consultant*
Husain, Taqdir *mathematics professor*
Jiang, Tao *mathematician, educator*
Johnstone, Iain Murray *statistician, educator, consultant*
Jones, Anita Katherine *computer scientist, educator*
Kadota, Takashi Theodore *mathematician, electrical engineer*
Karnaugh, Maurice *computer scientist, educator*
Kasami, Tadao *information science educator*
King, Amy Cathryne Patterson *retired mathematics educator, researcher*
Kirshbaum, Jon Alan *information systems consultant, retired educational administrator*
Kister, James Milton *retired mathematician, educator*
Krantz, Steven George *mathematics educator, writer*
Kushner, Todd Roger *computer scientist, software engineer*
Lampson, Butler Wright *computer scientist*
Landau, Susan *computer scientist*
Lane, Adelaide Irene *computer systems specialist, researcher*
Lange, Frederick Edward, Jr., *computer information systems architect*
Larson, Janice Talley *computer science programmer*
Latham, Charlotte *mathematics professor*
Lee, Dong Hoon *mathematician, educator*
Lerner, Vladimir Semion *computer scientist, educator*
Leuschke, Graham J. *mathematician, educator*
Li, Xiaojie *statistician*
Liu, Xiaoqing Frank *computer scientist, educator*
Liu, Yong *computer scientist, researcher*
Low, Emmet Francis, Jr., *mathematics educator*
MacLane, Saunders *mathematician, educator*
Manika, John Francis *computer systems educator, computer information systems analyst*
March, Michael F. *propulsion systems analyst, consultant*
Massad, Jordan Elias *mathematician*
Mattson, Harold Frazyer, Jr., *mathematics professor*
McKellips, Terral Lane *mathematics educator, university administrator*
Mell, William Eric *mathematician*
Miller, Allen Richard *retired mathematician*
Neller, Todd W. *computer science educator*
Neusel, Mara Dicle *mathematician, educator*
Newbury, Kirsten Rae *computer scientist, educator*
Nguyen, Dong *computer scientist, researcher, education educator*
Norman, E. Gladys *retired business computer educator, consultant*
Norton, Robert Michael *mathematician, educator, statistician*
Nuzzo, Anthony Gerald *services executive*
Nyberg, Stanley Eric *cognitive scientist*
Pollock, Karen Anne *computer analyst*
Porter, Hayden Samuel *computer science educator*
Qi, Xiujuan *mathematician, educator*
Riffenburgh, Robert Harry *biostatistician, researcher*
Ritter, Jack Charles *mathematician, computer graphics designer*
Robold, Alice Ilene *retired mathematician, educator*
Roitman, Judith *mathematician, educator*
Romano, Nicholas Charles *information scientist, educator*
Sa, Ping *statistician, educator*
Sahinalp, Suleyman Cenk *computer scientist*
Sapariuc, Ioan *mathematician, researcher*
Scheirer, Curry M *metrologist*
Schuiski, Larry Leroy *information scientist, consultant*
Seidman, Stephen Benjamin *dean, computer science educator*

Shaffer, Judy Ann *educator, data processing professional*
Shier, Gloria Bulan *mathematics professor*
Sills, Richard Reynolds *scientist, educator*
Sloane, Neil James Alexander *mathematician, researcher*
Soifer, Jed Joshua *mathematics and science educator*
Spinrad, Robert Joseph *computer scientist*
Stanard, Christopher Leon *statistician*
Suppes, Patrick *philosophy, statistics, psychology educator*
Tan, Hui Qian *computer science and civil engineering educator*
Thomas, Tarquin Craig *computer scientist, writer*
Tobiassen, Barbara Sue *systems analyst consultant, educator, Peace Corps volunteer*
Troy, William C. *mathematician, educator*
Tyrl, Paul *mathematics educator, researcher, consultant*
Vasily, John Timothy *information systems executive, state government official*
Vinson, Beth W. *systems analyst, web site designer*
Wadleigh, Kevin Richard *mathematician*
Ward, Jacqueline Selma Sklar *mathematician, educator*
Watkins, Ann Esther *mathematics professor*
Welna, Cecilia *retired mathematics educator*
Winder, Robert Owen *mathematician, computer engineer, geophysicist*
Winkelnkemper, Horst Elmar *mathematician, educator*
Wolfram, David Anthony *computer scientist*
Wozniak, Stephen Gary *computer scientist, philanthropist*
Wren, Stephen Corey *mathematician, inventor*
Wu, Margaret Anne *computer scientist, educator*
Yackel, James William *mathematician, academic administrator*
Yates, Gwendolyn Draper *mathematician, educator*
Yeadon, Tammy Pamela *information specialist*
Zeilberger, Doron *researcher, mathematics educator*
Zhang, Shu *statistician*
Zierler, Neal *retired mathematician*

SCIENCE: PHYSICAL SCIENCE

UNITED STATES

ALABAMA

Auburn
Neely, William Charles *chemistry educator, consultant, research scientist*
Park, Minseo *physicist, educator*
Samoylova, Tatiana I. *biochemist, researcher*

Birmingham
Krishna, N(epalli) Rama *biochemist*
Miyagawa, Ichiro *physicist*
Moran, Mary Shanks *hydrogeologist*
Raisch, Kevin Paul *research scientist, educator*
Robinson, Edward Lee *retired physics educator, consultant*
Vyazovkin, Sergey *chemist, educator*

Daphne
Baugh, Charles Milton *biochemistry educator, college dean*

Dothan
Mocker, Hans Walter *physicist*

Enterprise
Stagliano, James Joseph *physical science educator, scientist*

Gordo
McKnight, William Baldwin *physics educator*

Huntsville
Allan, Barry David *research chemist, government official*
Brandon, Walter Wiley, Jr., *retired physicist, retired aerospace engineer*
Cornatzer, William Eugene *retired biochemistry educator*
Costes, Nicholas Constantine *aerospace technologist, educator, retired government official*
Dahm, Werner K. *aerodynamicist*
Decher, Rudolf *physicist, researcher*
Ho, Joseph Xiaomin *aerospace scientist*
Norman, Ralph Louis *physicist, consultant*
Paciesas, William Simon *astrophysicist, educator*
Parnell, Thomas Alfred *physicist*
Smith, Robert Earl *space scientist*
Stuhlinger, Ernst *physicist*
Vaughan, William Walton *atmospheric scientist*
Wright, John Collins *retired chemistry educator*

Normal
Edwards, Matthew E. *physicist, educator*

Tuscaloosa
Cava, Michael Patrick *chemist, educator*
LaMoreaux, Philip Elmer *geologist, hydrogeologist, consultant*
Mancini, Ernest Anthony *geologist, educator, researcher*
Vincent, John Bertram *chemist, educator*

ALASKA

Anchorage
Sells, Colin David *meteorologist*

Fairbanks
Duffy, Lawrence Kevin *biochemist, educator*
Fathauer, Theodore Frederick *meteorologist*
Lingle, Craig Stanley *glaciologist, educator*
Nagabhushana, Nagendra *materials scientist, educator*
Roederer, Juan Gualterio *physics educator*
Wackerbauer, Renate Anna *physicist*
Weller, Gunter Ernst *geophysics educator*

Zhang, Xiangdong *research scientist, educator*

ARIZONA

Amado
Criswell, Stephen *astronomer*

Flagstaff
Millis, Robert Lowell *astronomer, science observatory director*
Shoemaker, Carolyn Spellman *planetary astronomer*
Titus, Timothy Neal *aerospace scientist, military officer*

Green Valley
Dingle, Albert Nelson *meteorology educator*

Litchfield Park
McKeighen, Ronald Eugene *physicist*

Mesa
Dorland, Elizabeth M. *chemistry professor*
Pierce, Byron James *research scientist*

Oracle
Garmany, Catharine Doremus *astronomer*

Peoria
McMahon, Maribeth Lovette *physicist*

Phoenix
Allen, John Rybolt L. *chemist, biochemist*
Everett, Paul Marvin *physicist*

Rio Rico
Lowell, J(ames) David *geological consultant, cattle rancher*

Scottsdale
Hockmuth, Joseph Frank *physicist, psychotherapist*
Kinsinger, Jack Burl *chemist, educator*
Molever, Keith *chemist, consumer products company executive*

Sierra Vista
Ponder, Herman *geologist*

Tempe
Blankenship, Robert Eugene *biochemistry educator*
Buseck, Peter R. *geochemistry educator*
Chung, Young Sir *materials scientist*
Cowley, John Maxwell *physics educator*
Glick, Milton Don *chemist, university administrator*
Goronkin, Herbert *physicist*
Herald, Cherry Lou *research educator, research director*
Juvet, Richard Spalding, Jr., *chemistry professor*
Mahajan, Subhash *electronic materials educator*
McKelvy, Michael John *materials chemist, research scientist*
Moore, Carleton Bryant *geochemistry educator*
Pettit, George Robert *chemist, educator, cancer researcher*
Picraux, Samuel Thomas *applied science and physics researcher*
Smith, David John *physicist, researcher*
Starrfield, Sumner Grosby *astrophysics educator, researcher*
Theodore, David *research scientist*
Winicov, Ilga Butelis *biochemist, educator*

Tucson
Angel, James Roger Prior *astronomer*
Barrett, Bruce Richard *physics educator*
Basford, Robert Eugene *retired biochemistry educator, researcher*
Bloembergen, Nicolaas *physicist, researcher*
Broadfoot, Albert Lyle *physicist*
Cameron, Alastair Graham Walter *astrophysicist, educator*
Crawford, David L. *astronomer*
Davis, George Herbert *geologist, educator*
Davis, Stanley Nelson *hydrologist, educator*
Dessler, Alexander Jack *astrophysicist, educator*
De Young, David Spencer *astrophysicist, educator*
Dunn, Floyd *biophysics and biomedical engeering educator*
Girardeau, Marvin Denham *physics educator*
Green, Richard Frederick *astronomer*
Gruhl, James *energy scientist, artist*
Gutsche, Carl David *chemistry professor*
Hall, Henry Kingston, Jr., *chemistry professor*
Harrison, Edward Robert *physicist, educator, science administrator*
Hay, Richard Le Roy *geology educator*
Haynes, Caleb Vance, Jr., *geology and archaeology educator*
Hays, James Fred *geologist, educator*
Hill, Henry Allen *physicist, researcher*
Hubbard, William Bogel *planetary sciences educator*
Hunten, Donald Mount *planetary scientist, educator*
Jefferies, John Trevor *astrophysicist, observatory administrator*
Kamilli, Robert Joseph *geologist*
Karkoschka, Erich *planetary science researcher, writer*
Kennicutt, Robert Charles, Jr., *astronomer*
Kessler, John Otto *physicist, researcher*
Lamb, Willis Eugene, Jr., *physicist, researcher*
Law, John Harold *biochemistry educator*
Magee, Wayne Edward *biochemistry educator, researcher*
Morrison, Roger Barron *geologist*
Mould, Jeremy Richard *astronomer*
Neugebauer, Marcia *physicist, administrator*
Pacholczyk, Andrzej Grzegorz *astrophysicist*
Parmenter, Robert Haley *physics educator*
Prewitt, Charles Thompson *geochemist*
Roemer, Elizabeth *astronomer, educator*
Schaefer, John Paul *chemist*
Scotti, James Vernon *astronomer*
Sprague, Ann Louise *space scientist*
Stein, Daniel L. *physicist, educator*
Strittmatter, Peter Albert *astronomer, educator*
Tifft, William Grant *astronomer, educator*
Wang, Wei *physicist, researcher*
Whitaker, Ewen Adair *retired astronomer*
Willott, Elizabeth *biochemist, educator, ecologist, researcher*
Wolff, Sidney Carne *astronomer, observatory administrator*

ARKANSAS

Bella Vista
Johnson, A(lyn) William *chemistry educator, writer, researcher, consultant*
Sautter, Chester Arthur *physicist, educator*

Little Rock
Braithwaite, Wilfred John *physics educator*
Darsey, Jerome Anthony (Jerry Darsey) *chemistry professor, consultant*
Sharma, Rajesh *research scientist*

Palmer
Knight, William R. *research scientist, educator*

Pine Bluff
Perschbacher, Peter Wesley *environmental scientist, educator*
Walker, Richard Brian *chemistry professor*

CALIFORNIA

Albany
Eastwood, DeLyle *chemist*

Alhambra
Im, Jaemo *research scientist*

Apple Valley
Mays, George Walter, Jr., *educational technology educator, consultant, tutor*

Atascadero
Ogier, Walter Thomas *retired physics educator*

Atherton
Coleman, Robert Griffin *geology educator*
Fried, John H. *chemist*
Gill, Stephen Paschall *retired physicist, mathematician*
Levinthal, Elliott Charles *physicist, researcher*

Auburn
Hess, Patrick Henry *chemist, researcher*

Azusa
Kostoulas, Ioannis Georgiou *physicist*

Bayside
Cocks, George Gosson *retired chemical microscopy educator*

Bellflower
Martin, Melissa Carol *radiological physicist*

Berkeley
Attwood, David Thomas *physicist, researcher*
Bartlett, Neil *chemist, emeritus educator*
Benson, Sally M. *atmospheric scientist*
Bergman, Robert George *chemist, educator*
Bertozzi, Carolyn R. *chemistry professor*
Bolt, Bruce Alan *seismologist*
Bragg, Robert Henry *physicist, researcher*
Bustamante, Carlos J. *biophysicist, educator*
Carmichael, Ian Stuart Edward *geologist, educator*
Cerny, Joseph, III, *chemistry educator, scientific laboratory administrator, university dean and official*
Chamberlain, Owen *nuclear physicist*
Chamberlin, Michael John *biochemistry educator*
Chew, Geoffrey Foucar *physicist*
Clarke, John *physics educator*
Diamond, Richard Martin *nuclear chemist*
Dietrich, William E. *geophysicist, educator*
Fleming, Graham Richard *chemistry educator*
Fowler, Thomas Kenneth *physicist*
Fréchet, Jean Marie Joseph *chemistry professor*
Gaillard, Mary Katharine *physics educator*
Glaser, Donald Arthur *physicist*
Goldhaber, Gerson *physicist, researcher*
Hahn, Erwin Louis *physicist, researcher*
Hang, Bo *biochemist*
Hoffman, Darleane Christian *chemistry professor*
Jackson, J(ohn) David *physicist, researcher*
Jeanloz, Raymond *geophysicist, educator*
Johnston, Harold S(ledge) *chemistry professor*
Kerth, Leroy T. *physics educator*
Kirz, Janos *physicist*
Klinman, Judith Pollock *biochemist, educator*
Koshland, Daniel Edward, Jr., *biochemist, educator*
Kurtzman, Ralph Harold *biochemist, researcher, consultant*
Langridge, Robert *biophysicist, educator*
Leopold, Luna Bergere *geology educator*
Lester, William Alexander, Jr., *chemist, educator*
Linn, Stuart Michael *biochemist, educator*
Lipps, Jere Henry *paleontology educator*
Louie, Steven Gwon Sheng *physics educator, researcher*
Lu, Adolph *physicist, educator*
Ma, Chung-Pei Michelle *astronomer, educator*
Mandelstam, Stanley *physicist*
Marletta, Michael A. *biochemistry educator, researcher, protein chemist*
McKee, Christopher Fulton *physicist, astronomer, educator*
Miller, William Hughes *theoretical chemist, educator*
Murayama, Hitoshi *physicist, educator*
Phillips, Norman Edgar *chemistry professor*
Pines, Alexander *chemistry educator, researcher, consultant*
Rasmussen, John Oscar *nuclear research scientist*
Raymond, Kenneth Norman *chemistry educator, research chemist*
Richardson, John David *physicist*
Ritchie, Robert Oliver *materials science educator*
Sessler, Andrew Marienhoff *physicist*
Shen, Yuen-Ron *physics educator*
Shugart, Howard Alan *physicist, researcher*
Smith, Kirk Robert *environmental health sciences educator, researcher*
Spieler, Helmuth *physicist*
Spinrad, Hyron *astronomer*
Steiner, Herbert Max *physics educator*
Strauss, Herbert Leopold *chemistry professor*
Streitwieser, Andrew, Jr., *chemistry professor*
Tanner, Lee E. *retired materials scientist, photographer, writer, curator*

Thompson, Anthony Wayne *metallurgist, educator, consultant*
Tjian, Robert Tse Nan *biochemistry educator, biology researcher, virology researcher*
Townes, Charles Hard *physics educator*
Trilling, George Henry *physicist, researcher*
Valentine, James William *paleobiology educator, writer*
Weber, Eicke Richard *physicist*

Burbank
Razouk, Rashad Elias *retired chemistry educator*

Burlingame
Hubbard, Gregory Scott *physicist*

California City
Paiva, Clifford Anthony *physicist, consultant*

Canyon Lake
Schilling, Frederick Augustus, Jr., *geologist, consultant*

Carlsbad
Lu, Taijin *physical chemist, researcher*
Smith, Warren James *optical scientist, consultant, lecturer, author*

Carmel
Vagnini, Livio Lee *chemist, forensic consultant*

Carpinteria
Fisher, John Crocker *physicist*

Castaic
Holmes, Dale Arthur *optics scientist*

China Lake
Bennett, Jean Louise McPherson *physicist, research scientist*

Chula Vista
Smith, Peggy O'Doniel *retired physicist*

Claremont
Eagleton, Robert Don *physics educator*
Hansch, Corwin Herman *chemistry professor*
Helliwell, Thomas McCaffree *physicist, researcher*
Oxtoby, David William *college president, chemistry educator*

Concord
Hearst, John Eugene *chemistry educator, researcher, consultant*

Corona Del Mar
Britten, Roy John *biophysicist*

Costa Mesa
Lattanzio, Stephen Paul *astronomy educator*

Crescent City
Carter, Neville Louis *geophysicist, educator*

Dana Point
Parker, John Marchbank *consulting geologist*

Davis
Burri, Betty Jane *research chemist*
Cahill, Thomas Andrew *physicist, researcher*
Conn, Eric Edward *plant biochemist*
Day, Howard Wilman *geology educator*
Jungerman, John Albert *physics educator*
Liu, Gang-Yu *chemist, educator*
Mukherjee, Amiya K. *metallurgy and materials science educator*
Nash, Charles Presley *chemistry professor*
Shackelford, James Floyd *materials science educator, researcher*
Stumpf, Paul Karl *biochemistry educator emeritus*
Troy, Frederic Arthur, II, *medical biochemistry educator*
Turcotte, Donald Lawson *geophysical sciences educator*
Volman, David Herschel *chemistry professor*
Zhou, Xinzhang *materials scientist, ceramist*

Duarte
Yoshida, Akira *biochemist*

El Cerrito
Alpen, Edward Lewis *biophysicist, educator*

El Granada
Heere, Karen R. *astrophysicist*

Emeryville
Gombocz, Erich Alfred *biochemist*
Masri, Merle Sid *biochemist, consultant*

Encinitas
Payne, James Richard *environmental chemist*

Encino
Hawthorne, Marion Frederick *chemistry professor*
Phelps, Michael Edward *biophysics educator*

Escondido
Tomomatsu, Hideo *chemist*

Foster City
Hotz, Henry Palmer *retired physicist*
Zaidi, Iqbal Mehdi *biochemist, scientist*

Fountain Valley
Armstrong, Jeffrey Lee *oceanographer*
Davis, Jeremy Matthew *chemist*

Fremont
Fang, Xiangyu *materials scientist*
Zhao, Mingjun *physicist, research scientist*

Fresno
Kauffman, George Bernard *chemistry professor*
Stetson, Robert Francis *retired metallurgist*

Fullerton
Khakoo, Murtadha Abdulrasul *physicist, educator, research scientist, consultant*
Shapiro, Mark Howard *physicist, educator, academic dean, consultant*

Wan, Julia Chang *retired science educator*
Woyski, Margaret Skillman *retired geology educator*

Glen Ellen
Berkland, James Omer *geologist*

Glendale
Kazarian, Poghos F. *physicist, researcher, educator*

Hemet
Berger, Lev Isaac *physicist, researcher*

Hollister
Smith, George Larry *analytical and environmental chemist*
Spencer, Douglas Lloyd *chemist, manufacturing executive*

Irvine
Aswad, Dana William *biochemist, educator*
Bander, Myron *physics educator, university dean*
Bystritskii, Vitaly Mikhailovich *physicist, researcher*
Cho, Zang Hee *physics educator*
Clark, Bruce Robert *geologist, consultant*
Dzyaloshinskii, Igor Ekhielievich *physicist*
Maradudin, Alexei A. *physics educator*
McLaughlin, Calvin Sturgis *biochemistry educator*
Nalcioglu, Orhan *physics educator, radiological sciences educator*
Nowick, Arthur Stanley *metallurgy and materials science educator*
Overman, Larry Eugene *chemistry educator*
Phalen, Robert Franklynn *environmental scientist*
Rowland, Frank Sherwood *chemistry professor*
Rynn, Nathan *physics educator, consultant*
Ufimtsev, Pyotr Yakovlevich *physicist, electrical engineer, educator*
Wallis, Richard Fisher *physicist, researcher*
White, Stephen Halley *biophysicist, educator*
Zhu, Peter C. *chemist*

Kensington
Appelman, Evan Hugh *retired chemist*
Connick, Robert Elwell *retired chemistry educator*

La Canada Flintridge
Baines, Kevin Hays *planetary scientist, astronomer*

La Jolla
Andre, Michael Paul *physicist, educator*
Arnold, James Richard *chemist, educator*
Asmus, John Fredrich *physicist*
Backus, George Edward *theoretical geophysicist*
Berger, Wolfgang H. *oceanographer, marine geologist*
Boger, Dale L. *chemistry professor*
Buckingham, Michael John *oceanography educator*
Burbidge, E. Margaret *astronomer, educator*
Burbidge, Geoffrey *astrophysicist, educator*
Case, Kenneth Myron *physics educator*
Cox, Charles Shipley *oceanography researcher, educator*
Dixon, Jack Edward *biological chemistry educator, consultant*
Driscoll, Charles Frederick *physics educator*
Edelman, Gerald Maurice *biochemist, neuroscientist, educator*
Engvall, Eva *biochemist*
Fisher, Frederick Hendrick *oceanographer emeritus*
Geiduschek, E(rnest) Peter *biophysics and molecular biology educator*
Gilbert, James Freeman *geophysics educator*
Itano, Harvey Akio *biochemistry educator*
Janda, Kim D. *chemist, educator*
Kadonaga, James Takuro *biochemist*
Keeling, Charles David *oceanography educator*
Kitada, Shinichi *biochemist*
Kolodner, Richard David *biochemist, educator*
Lal, Devendra *nuclear geophysics educator*
Lauer, James Lothar *physicist, researcher*
Lindenberg, Katja *chemistry professor*
McCammon, James Andrew *chemistry professor*
McIlwain, Carl Edwin *physicist*
Munk, Walter Heinrich *geophysics educator*
Nicolaou, K. C. *chemistry professor*
O'Neil, Thomas Michael *physicist, researcher*
Patton, Stuart *biochemist, educator*
Rebek, Julius, Jr., *chemistry educator, consultant*
Ride, Sally Kristen *physics educator, scientist, former astronaut*
Rotenberg, Manuel *physics educator*
Sclater, John George *geophysics educator*
Sham, Lu Jeu *physics educator*
Sharpless, K. Barry *chemist, educator*
Shor, George G., Jr., *geophysicist, oceanographic administrator, engineer*
Shuler, Kurt Egon *chemist, educator*
Sinha, Sunil Kumar *physicist*
Somerville, Richard Chapin James *atmospheric scientist, educator*
Spiess, Fred Noel *oceanographer, educator*
Stone, William Ross *research and development company executive, physicist*
Taylor, Susan Serota *biochemistry researcher*
Thiemens, Mark H. *chemistry professor*
Tietz, Norbert Wolfgang *clinical chemistry educator, administrator*
Tsien, Roger Yonchien *chemist, cell biologist*
Vale, Wylie W. *biochemist*
Van Lint, Victor Anton Jacobus *physicist*
Verma, Inder M. *biochemist*
Watson, Kenneth Marshall *physics educator*
Wolynes, Peter Guy *chemistry researcher, educator*
York, Herbert Frank *physics educator, government official*

La Verne
Hwang, Cordelia Jong *chemist*

Laguna Beach
Benford, Gregory Albert *physicist, writer*
Castro, Charles Edward *chemist, consultant*

Lancaster
Kiersch, George Alfred *geological consultant, retired educator*

Livermore
Alder, Berni Julian *physicist, researcher*
Glenzer, Siegfried Heinz *physicist, educator, researcher*

Holzrichter, John F. *physicist*
Hooper, Edwin Bickford *physicist*
Kidder, Ray Edward *physicist, consultant*
Kirkwood, Robert Keith *applied physicist*
Lambert, Michael Allen *physicist*
Lassila, David H. *materials scientist, researcher*
Leith, Cecil Eldon, Jr., *retired physicist*
Max, Claire Ellen *physicist*
Mirkarimi, Paul B. *materials scientist, researcher*
Nuckolls, John Hopkins *physicist, researcher*
Santer, Benjamin *atmospheric scientist, meteorologist*
Schock, Robert Norman *geophysicist*
Spiller, Eberhard Adolf *physicist, researcher*
Tarter, Curtis Bruce *physicist, science administrator*
Weber, Stephen Vance *physics researcher, astrophysicist*
Weyhenmeyer, Constanze Elisabeth *environmental scientist, researcher*

Loma Linda
Slattery, Charles Wilbur *biochemistry educator*

Long Beach
Bauer, Roger Duane *chemistry educator, science consultant*
Hu, Chi Yu *physicist, educator*
McGaughey, Charles Gilbert *retired research biochemist*
Mezyk, Stephen *chemist, educator*

Los Altos
Fraknoi, Andrew *astronomy educator, astronomical society executive*
Hahn, Harold Thomas *physical chemist, chemical engineer*

Los Angeles
Adamson, Arthur Wilson *chemistry educator*
Anderson, W. French *biochemist, physician*
Benson, Sidney William *chemistry researcher*
Bhaumik, Mani Lal *physicist*
Billig, Franklin Anthony *chemist*
Boyer, Paul D. *biochemist, educator*
Braginsky, Stanislav Iosifovich *physicist, geophysicist, researcher*
Carter, Emily Ann *physical chemist, researcher, educator*
Chen, Francis F. *physics and engineering educator*
Christophe, Caloz *research scientist*
Clarke, Steven Gerard *chemistry professor*
Coleman, Charles Clyde *physicist, educator*
Coleman, Paul Jerome, Jr., *physicist, researcher*
Cornwall, John Michael *physics educator, consultant, researcher*
Coroniti, Ferdinand Vincent *physics educator, consultant*
Dows, David Alan *chemistry professor*
Dunn, Arnold Samuel *biochemistry educator*
Dunn, Bruce Sidney *materials science educator*
Fischer, Alfred George *geology educator*
Foote, Christopher Spencer *chemist, educator*
Fulco, Armand John *biochemist*
Ganas, Perry Spiros *physicist*
Ghil, Michael *atmospheric scientist, geophysicist*
Houk, Kendall Newcomb *chemistry professor*
Igo, George Jerome *physics educator*
Jaffe, Sigmund *chemist, educator*
Jordan, Thomas Hillman *geophysicist, educator*
Kaplan, Isaac Raymond *chemistry professor*
Kassner, Michael Ernest *materials science educator, researcher*
Kedes, Laurence H. *biochemistry educator, physician, researcher*
Kivelson, Margaret Galland *physicist*
Knopoff, Leon *geophysics educator*
Kobe, Lan *medical physicist*
Koga, Rokutaro (Rocky Koga) *physicist*
Krupp, Edwin Charles *astronomer*
Levine, Raphael David *chemistry professor*
Lieber, Michael Randall *biochemist, educator*
Maki, Kazumi *physicist, researcher*
Markland, Francis Swaby, Jr., *biochemist, educator*
McLean, Ian Small *astronomer, physics educator*
Neelin, J. David *meteorologist, educator*
Neufeld, Elizabeth Fondal *biochemist, educator*
Nimni, Marcel Ephraim *biochemistry educator*
Olah, George Andrew *chemist, educator*
Paulson, Donald Robert *chemistry professor*
Reiss, Howard *chemistry professor*
Roberts, Sidney *biological chemist*
Scott, Robert Lane *chemist, educator*
Shapiro, Isadore *materials scientist, consultant*
Shvetsov, Alexander Anatolievich *biochemist, researcher*
Smith, Emil L. *biochemist, educator*
Smith, William Ray *retired biophysicist, retired engineer*
Stanton, Robert James, Jr., *geologist, educator*
Stellwagen, Robert Harwood *biochemistry educator*
Thorne, Richard Mansergh *physicist*
Trimble, Stanley Wayne *hydrology and geography educator*
Tsao, Jennie Ching-I *research scientist, educator*
Tu, King-Ning *materials scientist, educator*
Vidale, John Emilio *geologist*
Walker, Raymond John *physicist*
Whitten, Charles Alexander, Jr., *physics educator*
Woodruff, Fay *paleoceanographer, geological researcher*
Wudl, Fred *chemistry professor*
Yanai, Michio *atmospheric scientist*
Yang, Henry S. (Hong Yang) *metallurgist, materials engineer*
Ye, Hengchun *meteorologist, educator*

Los Gatos
Foy, Wade Hampton *retired research scientist*

Los Osos
Topp, Alphonso Axel, Jr., *environmental scientist, consultant*

Malibu
Liu, David Shiao-Kung *physical scientist*
Pepper, David M. *physicist, educator, writer, inventor*

Marina
Shane, William Whitney *astronomer*

Mckinleyville
Peithman, Roscoe Edward *physicist, educator*

Menlo Park
Allison, Anthony Clifford *research scientist, consultant*
Boyarski, Adam Michael *physicist*
Bukry, John David *geologist*
Bynum, Gretchen Luepke *geologist*
Coward, David Hand *physicist, researcher*
Drell, Sidney David *physicist, researcher*
Funkhouser, Lawrence William *retired geologist*
Holzer, Thomas Lequear *geologist*
Kuwabara, James Shigeru *research hydrologist*
Lachenbruch, Arthur Herold *geophysicist, researcher*
McGarr, Arthur Francis *geophysicist*
Penzias, Arno Allan *astrophysicist, technology consultant, research scientist, information systems specialist*
Richter, Burton *physicist, educator*
Taylor, Richard Edward *physicist, researcher*

Mill Valley
Meyers, Robert Allen *chemist, publisher*

Milpitas
Evans, Susan A. *chemist*

Modesto
Morrison, Robert Lee *physical scientist*

Moffett Field
Bakes, Emma *astrophysicist*
Lissauer, Jack Jonathan *astronomy educator*
Pendleton, Yvonne *astrophysicist*
Whiting, Ellis Eugene *retired research scientist*

Monrovia
Andary, Thomas Joseph *biochemist, researcher*

Montecito
Wheelon, Albert Dewell *physicist*

Monterey
Shull, Harrison *chemist, educator*

Morgan Hill
O'Handley, Douglas Alexander *retired astronomer*

Moss Landing
Brewer, Peter George *ocean geochemist*
Clague, David A. *geologist*

Mountain View
Yan, Qing *bioinformatics scientist*

Murrieta
Lake, Bruce Meno *applied physicist*

Napa
Chung, Dae Hyun *retired geophysicist*

Newbury Park
Fenton, Dennis Michael *research scientist*

Newport Beach
Kolyer, John McNaughton *materials specialist, chemist*

Northridge
Smathers, James Burton *medical physicist, educator*
Stampke, Stuart Reh *physicist, researcher*

Novato
Hanahan, Donald James *biochemist, educator*

Oakland
Ames, Bruce N(athan) *biochemist and molecular biology educator, department chairman*
Brust, David *physicist*
Carwell, Hattie Virginia *health physicist*
Finkle, Bernard J. *biochemist, researcher*
Linford, Rulon Kesler *retired physicist, engineer*
Steele, Richard Donald *researcher, linguist, physicist*

Orange
Talbott, George Robert *physicist, mathematician, educator*

Orinda
Heftmann, Erich *biochemist*
Mikalow, Alfred Alexander, II, *deep sea diver, marine surveyor, marine diving consultant*

Palo Alto
Andersen, Torben Brender *optical researcher, astronomer, software engineer*
Arnold Quinn, Helen Rhoda *physicist*
Aschwanden, Markus Josef *astrophysicist*
Cohen, Karl Paley *nuclear energy consultant*
Cutler, Leonard Samuel *physicist*
Dabbagh, Karim *research scientist*
Eng, Lawrence Fook *biochemistry educator, neurochemist*
Ernst, Wallace Gary *geology educator*
Flory, Curt Alan *research physicist*
Huberman, Bernardo A *physicist*
Loewenstein, Walter Bernard *nuclear power technologist*
Perl, Martin Lewis *physicist, educator, chemical engineer*
Saxena, Arjun Nath *physicist*
Schulz, Michael *physicist*
Skoog, Douglas Arvid *retired chemistry educator, writer*
Taimuty, Samuel Isaac *physicist*
Tucker, Brian *seismologist*
Varney, Robert Nathan *retired physicist, researcher*

Palos Verdes Estates
Paulikas, George Algis *retired physicist*

Pasadena
Ahrens, Thomas J. *geophysicist*
Albee, Arden Leroy *geologist, educator*
Allen, Clarence Roderic *geologist, educator*
Anderson, Don Lynn *geophysicist*
Barnes, Charles Andrew *physicist, researcher*
Baskin, John Spencer *physicist*
Beauchamp, Jesse Lee (Jack Beauchamp) *chemistry professor*
Bejczy, Antal Károly *research scientist, research facility administrator*

Bugga, Ratnakumar Venkata *electrochemist, researcher*
Buratti, Bonnie J. *aerospace scientist*
Chahine, Moustafa Toufic *atmospheric scientist*
Chan, Sunney Ignatius *chemist, educator*
Cooray, Asantha Roshan *astrophysicist, researcher*
Dervan, Peter Brendan *chemistry educator*
Dressler, Alan Michael *astronomer*
Ellis, Richard Salisbury *astronomer, educator*
Ferber, Robert Rudolf *physics researcher, educator, science administrator*
Frautschi, Steven Clark *physicist, researcher*
Freedman, Wendy Laurel *astronomer, educator*
Fu, Lee-Lueng *oceanographer*
Goldreich, Peter Martin *astrophysics and planetary physics educator*
Gray, Harry Barkus *chemistry professor*
Gurnis, Michael Christopher *geological sciences educator*
Heindl, Clifford Joseph *physicist, researcher*
Helin, Eleanor Francis *astronomer, geologist*
Hitlin, David George *physicist, researcher*
Janssen, Michael Allen *astronomer*
Jun, Insoo *nuclear scientist, researcher*
Kahle, Anne B. *geophysicist*
Lewis, Nathan Saul *chemistry professor*
Liepmann, Hans Wolfgang *physicist, researcher*
Lopes, Rosaly Mutel Crocce *astronomer, planetary geologist*
Marcus, Rudolph Arthur *chemist, educator*
Mc Koy, Basil Vincent Charles *theoretical chemist, educator*
Neugebauer, Gerry *retired astrophysicist, educator*
Oemler, Augustus, Jr., *astronomer, educator*
Parilis, Edward S. *physicist, researcher, consultant*
Politzer, Hugh David *physicist, educator*
Preskill, John Phillip *physics educator*
Roberts, John D. *chemist, educator*
Sackmann, Inge-Juliana *astrophysicist*
Sandage, Allan Rex *astronomer*
Sanders, Gary Hilton *physicist*
Sargent, Wallace Leslie William *astronomer, educator*
Schmidt, Maarten *astronomy educator*
Schwarz, John Henry *theoretical physicist, educator*
Sekanina, Zdenek *astronomer*
Smith, Edward John *geophysicist, physicist*
Spilker, Linda Joyce *aerospace scientist*
Stone, Edward C. *physicist, researcher*
Thorne, Kip Stephen *physicist, researcher*
Tombrello, Thomas Anthony, Jr., *physics educator, consultant*
Vogt, Rochus Eugen *physicist, researcher*
Wasserburg, Gerald Joseph *geology and geophysics educator*
Webster, Christopher R. *chemist, physicist, research scientist*
Wennberg, Paul *chemist*
Yeomans, Donald Keith *astronomer*
Zewail, Ahmed Hassan *chemistry and physics educator, editor, consultant*

Pleasanton
Bjorkholm, John Ernst *retired physicist*
Denavit, Jacques *retired physicist*
Stallings, Charles Henry *retired physicist*

Point Mugu
Fisk, Charles John *meteorologist, researcher, consultant*

Pomona
Aurilia, Antonio *physicist, researcher*
Bidlack, Wayne Ross *nutritional biochemist, toxicologist, food scientist*

Ramona
Yoldas, Bulent Erturk *materials scientist, educator*

Rancho Palos Verdes
Smirnov, Alexei Vladimirovich *research scientist, consultant*

Rancho Santa Fe
Creutz, Edward Chester *physicist, museum consultant*

Redondo Beach
Ball, William Paul *physicist, engineer*
Contescu, Cristian Ion *chemist, researcher*
Foster, John Stuart, Jr., *physicist, former defense industry executive*
Mulvey, Gerald John *meteorologist*

Ridgecrest
Bennett, Harold Earl *physicist, optics researcher*

Riverside
Atkinson, Roger *chemist, educator, science administrator*
Green, Harry Western, II, *geology-geophysics educator*
Rabenstein, Dallas Leroy *chemistry professor*
Zaera, Francisco *chemistry professor, consultant*

Rohnert Park
Trowbridge, Dale Brian *chemistry professor*

Sacramento
Peterson, Roy Martin, Jr., *environmental scientist*
Purdy, James Aaron *medical physics educator*
Rosenfeld, Arthur H. *physics educator, research director*

San Carlos
Dafforn, Geoffrey Alan *biochemist*

San Clemente
Wolfram, Thomas *physicist, educator*

San Diego
Balakin, Konstantin V. *chemist, researcher*
Bussard, Robert William *physicist*
Cantor, Charles Robert *biochemistry educator*
Chou, Kuo-Chen *biophysical chemist*
Cobble, James Wikle *chemistry professor*
Gastil, Russell Gordon *geologist, educator*
Haener, Juan A. *physicist*
L'Annunziata, Michael Frank *chemist, consultant, nuclear scientist*
Lao, Lang Li *nuclear fusion research physicist*
Pecsok, Robert Louis *chemist, educator*
Pincus, Howard J. *geologist, engineer, educator*
Robbins, Eleanora Iberall *biogeologist, researcher*
Shneour, Elie Alexis *biophysicist, researcher, historian*
Timoshchuk, Victor Arkadyevich *research scientist*

San Francisco
Batterman, Boris William *physicist, educator, academic director*
Burlingame, Alma Lyman *chemist, educator*
Cassman, Marvin *biochemist*
Cluff, Lloyd Sterling *earthquake geologist*
Dickinson, Wade *physicist, oil and gas company executive, educator*
Dill, Kenneth Austin *pharmaceutical chemistry educator*
Goldstein, David Baird *energy program director, physicist*
Grodsky, Gerold Morton *biochemistry educator*
Highsmith, Stefan *biochemistry educator*
James, Thomas Larry *chemistry professor*
Kelly, Regis Baker *biochemistry educator, biophysics educator*
Mandra, York T. *geology educator*
Marshall, Grayson William, Jr., *biomaterials scientist, health sciences educator*
Martin, David William, Jr., *biomedical research company executive, educator*
Marzke, Ronald Oscar *physics and astronomy educator*
Nguyen, Ann Cac Khue *pharmaceutical and medicinal chemist*

San Jose
Bandic, Zvonimir Z *physicist, researcher, electrical engineer*
Castellano, Joseph Anthony *retired chemist, management consulting firm executive*
Eigler, Donald Mark *physicist*
Forster, Julian *physicist, consultant*
Gruber, John Balsbaugh *physics educator, university administrator*
Hawker, Craig J. *research scientist*
Hoyt, Roger Franklin *physicist*
Mate, Charles Mathew *physicist*
Neptune, John Addison *retired chemistry educator, consultant*
Parkin, Stuart Stephen Papworth *materials scientist*
Winters, Harold Franklin *physicist*

San Luis Obispo
Grismore, Roger *physics educator, researcher*
Hafemeister, David Walter *physicist*

San Mateo
Holmes, John Richard *physicist, researcher*

San Pedro
Plutchak, Noel Bernard *meteorologist, management consultant*
Simmons, William *physicist, retired aerospace research executive*

San Rafael
Pomerantz, Martin Arthur *astronomer, educator*

San Ramon
Su, George Shenghui (Sheng-Hui Su) *chemist, medical researcher, educator*

Santa Ana
Kropp, William Rudolph *physicist*

Santa Barbara
Ahlers, Guenter *physicist, researcher*
Atwater, Tanya Maria *marine geophysicist, educator*
Bowers, Michael Thomas *chemistry professor*
Bruice, Thomas C. *chemist, educator*
Crowell, John C(hambers) *geology educator, researcher*
Dudziak, Walter Francis *physicist*
Dunne, Thomas *geology educator*
Ford, Peter C. *chemistry professor*
Heeger, Alan Jay *physicist, educator*
Hubbard, Arthur Thornton *chemistry educator, electro-surface chemist*
Kennedy, John Harvey *chemistry professor*
Kohn, Walter *educator, physicist*
Langer, James Stephen *physicist, researcher*
Luyendyk, Bruce Peter *geophysicist, educator, institution administrator*
Macdonald, Ken Craig *geophysicist*
Martzen, Philip D. *physicist, software developer*
Meinel, Aden Baker *optics scientist*
Morse, Daniel E. *biochemistry educator, science administrator*
Moskovits, Martin *chemist, educator, dean*
Pilgeram, Laurence Oscar *biochemist*
Stucky, Galen D. *chemist, biochemist, educator*
White, Robert Stephen *physics educator*
Yankwich, Peter Ewald *chemistry educator*

Santa Clara
Gozani, Tsahi *nuclear physicist*
Lee, Chan-Yun *physicist, process engineer, educator*

Santa Cruz
Brown, George Stephen *physics educator*
Bunnett, Joseph Frederick *chemist, educator*
Epps, Harland Warren *astronomy educator, optical design consultant*
Faber, Sandra Moore *astronomer, educator*
Fan, Guangwei *seismologist*
Flatté, Stanley Martin *physicist, researcher*
Hill, Terrell Leslie *chemist, biophysicist*
Knittle, Elise *geophysicist, educator*
Kraft, Robert Paul *astronomer, educator*
Lay, Thorne *geosciences educator*
Osterbrock, Donald E(dward) *astronomy educator*
Sands, Matthew Linzee *physicist, researcher*
Silver, Mary Wilcox *oceanography educator*
Wipke, W. Todd *chemistry professor*
Wu, Ru-Shan *geophysicist*

Santa Maria
Ellis, Emory Leon *former biochemist*

Santa Monica
Intriligator, Devrie Shapiro *physicist*
Park, Edward Cahill, Jr., *retired physicist*
Shipbaugh, Calvin LeRoy *physicist*

Shingle Springs
Sorensen, Raymond Andrew *physics educator*

Solana Beach
Agnew, Harold Melvin *physicist*

Stanford
Allen, Matthew Arnold *physicist*
Baldwin, Robert Lesh *biochemist, educator*
Berg, Paul *biochemist, educator*
Bienenstock, Arthur Irwin *physicist, educator, federal official*
Blandford, Roger David *astronomy educator*
Brauman, John I. *chemist, educator*
Bube, Richard Howard *materials scientist, educator*
Byer, Robert Louis *applied physics educator, university dean*
Collman, James Paddock *chemistry professor*
Dorfan, Jonathan Mannie *physicist, researcher*
Flinn, Paul Anthony *materials scientist*
Harbaugh, John Warvelle *geologist, educator*
Harrison, Walter Ashley *physicist, researcher*
Herring, William Conyers *physicist, emeritus educator*
Kallosh, Renata *physics educator*
Kapitulnik, Aharon *physicist, educator*
Kornberg, Arthur *biochemist, educator*
Kornberg, Roger David *biochemist, structural biologist*
Kovach, Robert Louis *geophysics educator*
Laughlin, Robert B. *physics educator*
Lehman, I(srael) Robert *biochemist, educator*
Little, William Arthur *physicist, researcher*
Matson, Pamela Anne *environmental scientist, science educator*
McConnell, Harden Marsden *biophysical chemistry researcher, chemistry educator*
Osheroff, Douglas Dean *educator, physicist, researcher*
Ross, John *physical chemist, educator*
Schneider, Stephen Henry *climatologist, environmental policy analyst, researcher*
Stryer, Lubert *biochemist, educator*
Sturrock, Peter Andrew *space science and astrophysics educator*
Taube, Henry *chemistry professor*
Thompson, George Albert *geophysics educator*
Trost, Barry Martin *chemist, educator*
Wagoner, Robert Vernon *astrophysicist, educator*
Walt, Martin *physicist, consulting educator*
Wang, Suwen *physicist, researcher*
Wender, Paul Anthony *chemistry professor*
Wojcicki, Stanley George *physicist, researcher*
Zare, Richard Neil *chemistry professor*

Sunnyvale
Chang, William Zhi-Ming
Holmes, Richard Brooks *mathematical physicist*
Wu, Yider *semiconductor scientist, researcher*

Sunol
Snetsinger, Kenneth George *retired mineralogist*

Thousand Oaks
Sherman, Gerald *nuclear physicist, financial estate adviser, financial company executive*

Toluca Lake
Litwack, Gerald *biochemistry researcher, educator, administrator*

Torrance
Lieberman, Robert Arthur *physicist*
Rogers, Howard H. *retired chemist*

Tustin
Clauson, Gary Lewis *chemist*

Valencia
Levy, Ezra Cesar *aerospace scientist, real estate broker*

Walnut Creek
Wu, Tse Cheng *research chemist*

Woodland Hills
Monteau, Norman Keith *gemologist*

Woodside
Ashley, Holt *aerospace scientist, educator*
Klein, August Stone *retired physicist*

COLORADO

Aurora
Grace, William Pershing *petroleum geologist, real estate developer*
Hodges, Robert Stanley *biochemist, educator, researcher in biotechnology*

Boulder
Albritton, Daniel Lee *atmospheric scientist*
Araujo-Pradere, Eduardo A. *geophysicist, researcher*
Bartlett, David Farnham *physics educator*
Begelman, Mitchell Craig *astrophysicist, educator, writer*
Budd, David A. *geologist, educator*
Chappell, Charles Franklin *meteorologist, consultant*
Conti, Peter Selby *astronomy educator*
Cooper, John *physicist, educator*
Cornell, Eric Allin *physics educator*
Cristol, Stanley Jerome *chemistry professor*
Cziczo, Daniel James *research scientist, educator*
Dudhia, Jimy *atmospheric scientist*
Dunn, Gordon Harold *physicist, researcher*
Ferguson, Eldon Earl *retired physicist*
Fleming, Rex James *meteorologist*
Garstang, Roy Henry *astrophysicist, educator*
Gossard, Earl Everett *physicist*
Hermann, Allen Max *physics educator*
Hofmann, David John *atmospheric science researcher, educator*
Hogg, David Clarence *physicist*
Holzer, Thomas E. *physicist*
Jin, Deborah *physicist, educator*
Joselyn, Jo Ann *space scientist*
Kabos, Pavel J.D. *physicist*
Kapteyn, Henry Cornelius *physics and engineering educator*
Kellogg, William Welch *meteorologist, researcher*
Kessinger, Cathy Jeanne *meteorologist, researcher*
King, Edward Louis *retired chemistry educator*
Kisslinger, Carl *geophysicist, educator*
Lally, Vincent Edward *atmospheric scientist*
LeMone, Margaret Anne *atmospheric scientist*
Lineberger, William Carl *chemistry educator*
Low, Boon Chye *physicist*
MacDonald, Alexander Edward *meteorologist*
Mahanthappa, Kalyana Thipperudraiah *physicist, researcher*
Mahlman, Jerry David *climate and atmospheric scientist*
Malde, Harold Edwin *retired federal government geologist*
Pankove, Jacques Isaac *physicist, researcher*
Randa, James Paul *physicist, electrical engineer*
Roellig, Leonard Oscar *physics educator*
Schneider, Nicholas McCord *planetary scientist, educator, textbook author*
Smith, Joel B. *environmental analyst*
Smythe, William Rodman *physicist, researcher*
Snow, Theodore Peck *astrophysics educator*
Tatarskii, Valerian Il'Ich *physics researcher*
Tolbert, Bert Mills *biochemist, educator*
Tolbert, Margaret A. *geochemistry educator*
Trenberth, Kevin Edward *atmospheric scientist*
Truce, William Everett *chemist, educator*
Washington, Warren Morton *meteorologist*
Wieman, Carl E. *physics educator*
Ye, Jun *physicist, researcher*

Brighton
Rinkenberger, Richard Krug *physical scientist, geologist, consultant*

Colorado Springs
Bowers, Larry Donald *chemistry and pathology educator*
Corry, Charles Elmo *geophysicist, not-for-profit developer*
Hoffman, John Raleigh *physicist*
Redding, Rogers Walker *physics educator, university official*
Rogers, Steven Ray *physicist*
Schwartz, Donald *chemistry professor*
Stahl, Philip Anthony *physics educator*

Denver
Bufe, Charles Glenn *geophysicist, researcher*
Cobban, William Aubrey *paleontologist*
Eaton, Gareth Richard *chemistry educator, university dean*
Fails, Thomas Glenn *geologist*
Gries, Robbie Rice *geologist, gas and petroleum company executive*
Hetzel, Fredrick William *biophysicist, educator*
Johnson, Walter Earl *geophysicist*
Klipping, Robert Samuel *geophysicist*
Landon, Susan Melinda *petroleum geologist*
Mullineaux, Donal Ray *geologist*
Neumann, Herschel *physics educator*
Smith, Dwight Morrell *chemistry professor, academic administrator*
Weihaupt, John George *geosciences educator, scientist, university administrator*

Dillon
Roder, Hans Martin *retired physicist, consultant*

Evergreen
Haun, John Daniel *petroleum geologist, educator*
Heyl, Allen Van, Jr., *geologist*

Fort Collins
Bamburg, James Robert *biochemistry educator*
Bernstein, Elliot Roy *chemistry professor*
Gadaleta, Sabino *research scientist*
Johnson, Robert Britten *geology educator*
Kohli, Sandeep *materials scientist, researcher*
Meyers, Albert Irving *emeritus chemistry educator*
Patton, Carl Elliott *physics educator*
Vonder Haar, Thomas H. *meteorology educator*

Golden
Duke, Michael B. *aerospace scientist*
Hamilton, Warren Bell *geologist, researcher, geophysicist, educator*
Krauss, George *metallurgist*
Speer, John Gordon *metallurgist, educator, materials scientist, educator*
Trefny, John Ulric *college president*
Weimer, Robert Jay *geology educator, energy consultant, civic leader*
Zhong, Dalong *materials scientist, consultant*

Grand Junction
Rutz, Richard Frederick *physicist, researcher*

Highlands Ranch
Krinsky, Fredda S. *clinical chemist, consultant*

Lafayette
McNeill, William *environmental scientist*

Lakewood
Bailey, Zelda Chapman *hydrologist*
Hansen, Richard Olaf *geophysicist, educator*
Quinn, John Michael *physicist, geophysicist*

Littleton
Harney, Patricia Rae *environmental scientist, nuclear energy industry executive*
Paull, Richard Allen *geologist, educator*

Ridgway
Lathrop, Kaye Don *nuclear scientist, educator*

CONNECTICUT

Bethel
Cheh, Huk Yuk *electrochemist, battery company executive*
Schetky, Laurence McDonald *metallurgist, researcher*

Bloomfield
Ivey, Elizabeth S. *retired physicist, educator*

Bridgeport
Chih, Chung-Ying *physicist, consultant*
Reed, Charles Eli *retired chemist, chemical engineer*

Clinton
Panayotov, Christo Angelov *research scientist, consultant*

Farmington
Goodson, Richard Carle, Jr., *chemist*
Osborn, Mary Jane Merten *biochemist, educator*
Spencer, Richard Paul *biochemist, educator, physician*

Groton
Harwood, Harold James, Jr., *biochemist*
Swindell, Archie Calhoun, Jr., *research biochemist, statistician*
Wallach, Morton L. *scientist*

Guilford
Engelman, Donald Max *molecular biophysics and biochemistry educator*
Handschumacher, Robert Edmund *biochemistry educator*

Ledyard
Chiang, Albert Chinfa *polymer chemist*

Manchester
Galasso, Francis Salvatore *materials scientist*

Middletown
De Rocco, Andrew Gabriel *physicist, educator*
Ettre, Leslie Stephen *chemist*
Fry, Albert Joseph *chemistry professor*

New Britain
Baskerville, Charles Alexander *geologist, educator*
Dimmick, Charles William *geology educator*

New Haven
Adair, Robert Kemp *physicist, educator*
Baltay, Charles *physicist, educator*
Berson, Jerome Abraham *chemistry professor*
Bromley, David Allan *physicist, engineer, educator*
Casten, Richard Francis *physicist*
Chupka, William Andrew *chemical physicist, educator*
Herzenberg, Arvid *physicist, researcher*
Klein, Martin Jesse *physicist, educator, science historian*
Marchesi, Vincent T. *biochemist, educator*
Reed, Mark Arthur *educator, researcher*
Richards, Frederic Middlebrook *biochemist, educator*
Sandweiss, Jack *physicist, researcher*
Shulman, Robert Gerson *biophysics educator*
Slayman, Clifford Leroy *biophysicist, educator*
Sofia, Sabatino *astronomy educator*
Steitz, Joan Argetsinger *biochemistry educator*
Tully, John Charles *research chemical physicist*
Turekian, Karl Karekin *geochemistry educator*
Wasserman, Harry Hershal *chemistry professor*
Zamfir, Nicolae Victor *physicist, researcher*
Zeller, Michael Edward *physicist, researcher*

New London
Kavarnos, George James *research chemist*

New Milford
Fabricand, Burton Paul *physicist, researcher*

Pawcatuck
Ravdel, Boris *electrochemist, researcher*

Ridgefield
Matteo, Martha R. *biochemist*

Rocky Hill
Chu, Hsien-Kun *chemist, researcher*

Stamford
Chang, Ted T. *chemist*
Colthup, Norman Bertram *retired spectroscopist*

Stonington
Mantz, Arlan W. *physics educator*

Storrs Mansfield
Bartram, Ralph Herbert *physicist*
Devereux, Owen Francis *retired metallurgy educator*
Klemens, Paul Gustav *physicist, researcher*
Marcus, Harris Leon *materials science educator*
Reifsnider, Kenneth Leonard *metallurgist, educator*

Tolland
Feller, Winthrop Bruce *physycist, executive*

Wallingford
Romine, Jeffrey Lee *chemist*

Waterford
Johnson, Gary William *environmental scientist, consultant*

West Hartford
Markham, Claire Agnes (M. Clare Markham) *retired chemistry educator, consultant*

West Haven
Onton, Ann Louise Reuther *chemist*

Westport
Smith, Peter Wolfgang *physicist, artist*

Woodbury
Skinner, Brian John *geologist, educator*

DELAWARE

Dover
Wasfi, Sadiq Hassan *chemistry professor*

New Castle
Bellenger, George Collier, Jr., *physics educator*

Newark
Burmeister, John Luther *chemistry professor, consultant*
Gantzer, Mary Lou *research chemist*
Hutton, David Glenn *environmental scientist, consultant, chemical engineer*
Murray, Richard Bennett *physics educator*
Ness, Norman Frederick *astrophysicist, educator, administrator*
Theopold, Klaus Hellmut *chemistry professor*

Wilmington
Crittenden, Eugene Dwight, Jr., *chemical company executive*
Jezl, Barbara Ann *retired chemist, automation consultant*
Kissa, Erik *retired chemist, consultant*
Kwolek, Stephanie Louise *chemist, researcher*
Marcali, Jean Gregory *retired chemist*
McCoy, Verl Eugene, Jr., *physical chemist, consultant*
Memeger, Wesley, Jr., *retired chemist, painter*
Parshall, George William *chemist, researcher*
Saye, JoAnne M. *research scientist, pharmacologist*
Smook, Malcolm Andrew *chemist, chemical company executive*

DISTRICT OF COLUMBIA

Washington
Alexander, Joseph Kunkle, Jr., *physicist*
Andreadis, Tim D. *physicist, researcher*
Armstrong, Spence M. *aerospace technology administrator*
Baker, D. James *oceanographic and atmospheric administrator*
Beall, James Howard *physicist, educator*
Berendzen, Richard *astronomer, educator, author*
Bierly, Eugene Wendell *meteorologist, science administrator*
Brown, Louis *physicist, researcher*
Campbell, Bruce *geologist*
Cheetham, Alan Herbert *paleontologist*
Córdova, France Anne-Dominic *astrophysics scientist, administrator*
Crumbling, Deana Marie *environmental scientist*
Davidson, Eugene Abraham *biochemist, educator, academic administrator*
Deschamps, Jeffrey R. *chemist, researcher*
Donohue, Joyce Morrissey *biochemist, toxicologist, dietician, educator*
Dutro, John Thomas, Jr., *geologist, paleontologist*
Dymond, Kenneth F. *physicist, researcher*
Eghbal, Morad *geologist, lawyer*
El Khadem, Hassan Saad *chemistry educator, researcher*
Fainberg, Anthony *physicist*
Fogleman, Guy Carroll *physicist, mathematician, educator*
Forbes, Nancy Anne *physicist, writer*
Friedberg, Felix *biochemist, educator*
Galloway, Eilene Marie *space and astronautics consultant*
Giacconi, Riccardo *astrophysicist, educator*
Girard, James Emery *chemistry professor*
Goff, James Franklin *physicist, consultant*
Goldstein, Allan Leonard *biochemist, educator*
Hallgren, Richard Edwin *meteorologist*
Harwit, Martin Otto *astrophysicist, writer, educator, museum director*
Heineman, Heinz *chemist*
Heinemann, Heinz *chemist, educator, researcher, consultant*
Holloway, John Thomas *physicist, consultant*
Johnston, Kenneth John *astronomer, scientific director naval observatory*
Karle, Isabella L. *chemist*
Karle, Jerome *physicist, researcher*
Kimble, Melinda Louise *environmental administrator*
Klein, Philipp Hillel *electronic materials consultant*
Knopman, Debra Sara *environmental scientist, director, hydrologist, policy analyst*
Lash, Jonathan *non-profit environment/development executive*
Ledley, Robert Steven *biophysicist*
Lehman, Donald Richard *physicist, educator, academic administrator*
Lehmberg, Robert Henry *research physicist*
Liu, Xiao *physicist, researcher*
Logsdon, John Mortimer, III, *aerospace analyst, physics professor*
Loyevsky, Mark Michael *biochemist, researcher*
Lozansky, Edward Dmitry *physicist, consultant, writer*
Mandula, Jeffrey Ellis *physicist*
Mao, Ho-kwang *geophysicist, educator*
Marlay, Robert Charles *physicist, engineer*
Meijer, Paul Herman Ernst *educator, physicist*
Morehouse, David Frank *geologist*
Ohring, George *meteorologist*
Oliver, William Albert, Jr., *paleontologist, researcher*
Orbach, Raymond Lee *physicist, researcher*
Pardavi-Horvath, Martha Maria *physicist, educator*
Pascu, Dan *astronomer*
Pojeta, John, Jr., *geologist, researcher*
Pope, Michael Thor *chemistry professor*
Press, Frank *geophysicist*
Roscher, Nina Matheny *chemistry professor*
Rosenberg, Jerome David *physicist*
Ross, Malcolm *minerals consultant*
Sayre, Edward Vale *chemist*
Shamim, Mah Talat *chemist*
Shanny, Ramy *physicist*
Shuler, James Mannie *health physicist*
Siegel, Frederic Richard *geology educator*
Singer, Maxine Frank *retired biochemist, scientific institute executive*
Solomon, Sean Carl *geophysicist, lab administrator*
Soulen, Robert John *physicist*
Spilhaus, Athelstan Frederick, Jr., *oceanographer, association executive*
Stanley, Jean-Daniel *geological oceanographer*
Uberall, Herbert Michael Stefan *physicist, researcher*
White, Robert Mayer *meteorologist*
Willard, Matthew Ashe *materials scientist, researcher*
Yochelson, Ellis L(eon) *paleontologist*
Youtcheff, John Sheldon *physicist*

FLORIDA

Alachua
Schneider, Richard T(heodore) *optics research executive, engineer*

Altamonte Springs
Sepulveda, Nicasio *hydrologist, researcher*

Boca Raton
Resnick, Robert *physicist, researcher*
Rosenkranz, Herbert S. *public health educator*
Ross, Fred Michael *organic chemist*
Weissbach, Herbert *biochemist, researcher*
Wiesenfeld, John Richard *chemistry professor*

Bonita Springs
Brown, Theodore Lawrence *chemistry professor*

Bradenton
Compton, Charles Daniel *chemistry professor*

Cape Coral
West, John Merle *retired physicist, nuclear consultant*

Coral Gables
Criss, Cecil M. *chemistry professor*
Einspruch, Norman Gerald *physicist, engineering educator*
Glaser, Luis *biochemistry educator*
Leblanc, Roger Maurice *chemistry professor*
Van Vliet, Carolyne Marina *physicist, researcher*

Dade City
Burdick, Glenn Arthur *physicist, engineering educator*

Dania
Dodge, Richard Eugene *oceanographer, educator, marine life administrator*

Delray Beach
Solon, Leonard R(aymond) *retired physicist, educator, consultant*
Zarwyn, Berthold *physical scientist*

Fort Myers
Horecker, Bernard Leonard *retired biochemistry educator*
Missimer, Thomas Michael *geologist*
Sheline, Raymond K. *nuclear chemistry educator*

Gainesville
Cabrera-Trujillo, Remigio *research scientist, physicist*
Cousins, Robert John *nutritional biochemist, educator*
Davis, George Kelso *nutrition biochemist, educator*
Fan, Z. Hugh *chemist, biomedical engineer*
Hanrahan, Robert Joseph *chemist, educator*
Hanson, Harold Palmer *physicist, government official, editor, academic administrator*
Heo, Young-Woo *research scientist*
Katritzky, Alan Roy *chemistry professor*
Mareci, Thomas Harold *biophysicist, educator*
Micha, David Allan *chemistry and physics educator*
Mitselmakher, Guenakh *physics educator, researcher*
Opdyke, Neil Donald *geology educator*
Pop, Emil *research chemist*
Sabin, John Rogers *physics educator*
Singley, John Edward, Jr., *retired environmental scientist, consultant*
Sisler, Harry Hall *retired chemistry professor*
Trickey, Samuel Baldwin *physics educator, researcher, university administrator*
Yost, Richard Alan *chemistry professor*

Gonzalez
Plischke, Le Moyne Wilfred *research chemist*

Hialeah Gardens
Tuninskaya, Galina M. *chemist, consultant*

Jacksonville
Beattie, Donald A. *energy scientist, consultant*

Jupiter
Jacobson, Jerry Irving *biophysicist, theoretical physicist*

Key West
Trammell, Herbert Eugene *physicist, laboratory executive*

Lakeland
McFarlin, Richard Francis *retired industrial chemist, researcher*

Lantana
Balis, Moses Earl *biochemist, educator*

Longboat Key
Stapleton, Harvey James *physics educator*

Lutz
Koff, Fred William *retired research chemist*

Melbourne
Babich, Michael Wayne *chemistry educator, educational administrator*
Nelson, Gordon Leigh *chemist, educator*

Miami
Fine, Rana Arnold *chemical and physical oceanographer*
Freire, Jose A. *physicist, writer*
Hirschberg, Joseph Gustav *educator, physicist*
Li, Qi *research scientist, consultant*
Mares-Guia, Marcos Luiz *biochemist, consultant*
Mooers, Christopher Northrup Kennard *physical oceanographer, educator*
Ostlund, H. Gote *atmospheric and marine scientist, educator*

Mount Dora
Foote, Nathan Maxted *retired physical science educator*

Naples
Leitner, Alfred *mathematical physicist, educator, educational film producer*
Marcuvitz, Nathan *electrophysics educator*

Ocala
Fredericks, William John *chemistry professor*

Orlando
Baker, Peter Mitchell *laser scientist, educator*
Blue, Joseph Edward *physicist*
Efthimiou, Costas John *physicist, educator, physicist, researcher*
Llewellyn, Ralph Alvin *physics educator*
Ting, Robert Yen-ying *physicist*

Ormond Beach
Kanfer, Julian Norman *biochemist, educator*

Palm Beach Gardens
Furda, Ivan *chemist, consultant*
Levitt, George *retired chemist*

Palmetto Bay
Nakashima, Tadayoshi *retired biochemist, researcher*

Pensacola
Steinhoff, Raymond O(akley) *consulting geologist*

Punta Gorda
Fullman, Robert Louis *metallurgy consultant*

Saint Petersburg
Hallock-Muller, Pamela *oceanography educator, biogeologist, researcher*
Hsu, Tsong Han *chemist, researcher*
Rydstrom, Carlton Lionel *chemist, chemicals consultant*

Sanford
Dickison, Alexander Kane *physical science educator*

Sarasota
Kerker, Milton *chemistry professor*
Pierce, Richard Harry *oceanographer*

Tallahassee
Choppin, Gregory Robert *chemistry professor*
Gleeson, Thomas Alexander *retired meteorologist*
Herndon, Roy Clifford *physicist*
Kemper, Kirby Wayne *physics educator*
Kromhout, Robert Andrew *physics professor*
Loper, David Eric *geophysicist, mathematician*
Mandelkern, Leo *biophysics and chemistry educator*
Marshall, Alan George *chemistry and biochemistry educator*
Pfeffer, Richard Lawrence *meteorology and geophysics educator*
Plendl, Hans S. *retired physicist, editor*
Rikvold, Per Arne *physics researcher and educator*
Robson, Donald *physics educator*
Schrieffer, John Robert *physics educator, science administrator*
Zou, Xiaolei *meteorologist, educator*

Tampa
Binford, Jesse Stone, Jr., *chemistry professor*
Johnson, Anthony O'Leary (Andy Johnson) *meteorologist, consultant*
Jones, William Denver *physicist, researcher*
Martin, Dean Frederick *chemist, educator*
Szonntagh, Eugene L. *chemical engineer, chemist, hygienist, educator, archaeometrist, musicologist, organist, historian*
Zhu, Yiliang *research scientist, educator*

Venice
Feldmann, Edward George *pharmaceutical chemist, pharmacologist*
Peterson, Francis *physicist, educator*

West Palm Beach
Arzoumanidis, Gregory G. *chemist*

GEORGIA

Athens
Black, Clanton Candler, Jr., *biochemistry educator, researcher*
Black, Marsha C. *environmental scientist*
Chu, Chung Kwang *medicinal chemistry educator*
Darvill, Alan G. *biochemist, plant biologist, educator*
Johnson, Michael Kenneth *chemistry professor*
Loux, Nicholas Thomas *chemist, researcher*
Schaefer, Henry Frederick, III, *chemistry professor*

Atlanta
Allison, Stuart Anthony *chemistry educator, researcher*
Cramer, Howard Ross *geologist, environmental consultant*
Dennison, Daniel Bassel *chemist*
Dickinson, Robert Earl *atmospheric scientist, educator*
Finkelstein, David Ritz *physicist, educator, consultant*
Flannery, M. Raymond *physicist, researcher*
Fox, Ronald Forrest *physics educator*
Gimmestad, Gary Gene *physicist, researcher*
Iacobucci, Guillermo Arturo *chemist*
Jastrow, Robert *physicist, educator*
Johnson, Ronald Carl *chemistry professor*
Kahn, Bernd *radiochemist, educator*
Lin, Ming-Chang *physical chemistry educator, researcher*
Long, Leland Timothy *geophysicist educator, seismologist*
Massey, Walter Eugene *physicist, science foundation administrator*
Msezane, Alfred Zakele *physics educator*
Snyder, Robert Lyman *materials scientist, educator*
Strekowski, Lucjan *chemistry professor*
Wong, Ching-Ping *chemist, materials scientist, engineer, educator*

Carrollton
Swamy-Mruthinti, Satyanarayana *biochemist, developmental biologist*

Duluth
Bridges, Alan Lynn *physicist, computer scientist, systems software engineer*

Hull
Melton, Charles Estel *retired physicist, educator*

Lithonia
Baxter, Gene Francis *chemical researcher, consultant*

Marietta
Berryhill, Henry Lee, Jr., *geologist, researcher*

Milledgeville
McGinnis, Michael Boyd *chemistry professor*

Peachtree City
Roobol, Norman Richard *industrial coatings consultant, educator*

Savannah
Sanders, James Grady *biogeochemist*
Simonaitis, Richard Ambrose *chemist*
Walter, Paul Hermann Lawrence *chemistry professor*
Windom, Herbert Lynn *oceanographer, environmental scientist*

Stone Mountain
Reichert, Leo Edmund, Jr., *biochemist, endocrinologist*

HAWAII

Camp H M Smith
Surface, Stephen Walter *water treatment chemist, environmental protection specialist*

Hawaii National Park
Swanson, Donald Alan *geologist*

Hilo
Binder, Philippe-Michel *physicist, educator*
Fisher, Robert Scott *astronomer*

Honolulu
Hawke, Bernard Ray *planetary scientist*
Ihrig, Judson La Moure *chemist*
Karl, David Michael *oceanographer, educator*
Keil, Klaus *geology educator, consultant*
Khan, Mohammad Asad *geophysicist, educator, former energy minister and senator of Pakistan*
Mader, Charles Lavern *chemist*
Raleigh, Cecil Baring *geophysicist*
Rosendal, Hans Erik *meteorologist*
Wills-Toro, Luis Alberto *physicist, mathematician*

IDAHO

Boise
Punnoose, Alex *physics educator*
Szerbiak, Robert Bruce *geophysicist, researcher*

Idaho Falls
Boring, Ronald Laurids *research scientist*

Moscow
Machleidt, Ruprecht *physicist*
Miller, Maynard Malcolm *geologist, educator, research institute director, explorer, legislator*
Patankar, Sunil Narayan *research scientist*
Renfrew, Malcolm MacKenzie *chemist, educator*
Shreeve, Jean'ne Marie *chemist, educator*

Pocatello
Gesell, Thomas Frederick *physicist, educator*

ILLINOIS

Argonne
Ahmad, Irshad *physicist, nuclear chemist*
Crabtree, George *physicist*
Derrick, Malcolm *physicist*
Katz, Joseph Jacob *retired chemist, educator*
Koetzle, Thomas Frederick *chemist, researcher*
Kukhtin, Alexander V. *chemist*
Lawson, Robert Davis *theoretical nuclear physicist*
Marshall, Christopher L. *research scientist, chemist*
Perlow, Gilbert J(erome) *physicist, editor*
Peshkin, Murray *physicist*
Sabau, Carmen Sybile *chemist*

Arlington Heights
Lewin, Seymour Zalman *chemistry professor, consultant*
Smith, Norman Obed *physical chemist, educator*

Batavia
Balbekov, Valeri I. *physicist, researcher*
Bardeen, William Allan *research physicist*
Chrisman, Bruce Lowell *physicist, administrator*
Jonckheere, Alan Mathew *physicist*
Raja, Rajendran *physicist*
Tollestrup, Alvin Virgil *physicist*
Witherell, Michael S. *physicist, educator*
Yeh, Gong Ping (G.P.) *physicist*

Burr Ridge
Vasiliauskas, Edmund *retired chemistry professor*

Champaign
Balbach, Harold Edward *environmental scientist*
Buschbach, Thomas Charles *geologist, consultant*
Cartwright, Keros *hydrogeologist, researcher*
Gross, David Lee *geologist*
Hager, Lowell Paul *biochemistry educator*
Herzog, Beverly Leah *hydrogeologist*
Krug, Edward Charles *environmental scientist*
Slichter, Charles Pence *physicist, researcher*
Wolfram, Stephen *physicist, computer company executive*

Chicago
Beckers, Jacques Maurice *astrophysicist*
Blumberg, Avrom Aaron *physical chemistry educator*
Bongolan-Walsh, Vena Pearl *research scientist*
Chambers, Donald Arthur *biochemistry and molecular medicine educator*
Clayton, Robert Norman *chemist, educator*
Cronin, James Watson *physicist, researcher*
Dutta, Mitra *physicist, educator*
Eastman, Dean Eric *physicist, researcher*
Erber, Thomas *physics educator*
Freed, Karl Frederick *chemistry professor*
Giger, Maryellen Lissak *medical physicist*
Gislason, Eric Arni *chemistry professor*
Gomer, Robert *chemistry professor*
Halpern, Jack *chemist, educator*
Harvey, Ronald Gilbert *research chemist*
Hildebrand, Roger Henry *astrophysicist, physicist*
Iqbal, Zafar Mohd *cancer researcher, biochemist, pharmacologist, toxicologist, consultant, molecular biologist*
Kleppa, Ole J. *chemistry professor*
Kouvel, James Spyros *physicist, researcher*
Krawetz, Arthur Altshuler *chemist, science administrator*
Levy, Donald Harris *chemistry professor*
Liao, Shutsung *biochemist, molecular oncologist*
Makinen, Marvin William *biophysicist, educator*
Mintzer, David *physics educator*
Nagel, Sidney Robert *physics educator*
Nambu, Yoichiro *physics educator*
Oehme, Reinhard *physicist, researcher*
Oka, Takeshi *physicist, chemist, astronomer, educator*
Olsen, Edward John *geologist, educator, curator*
Palmer, Patrick Edward *radio astronomer, educator*
Platzman, George William *geophysicist, educator*
Reiffel, Leonard *physicist, medical physicist, scientific consultant*
Rosner, Jonathan Lincoln *physicist, researcher*
Rosner, Robert *astrophysicist, educator*
Sager, William Frederick *retired chemistry educator*
Steiner, Donald Frederick *biochemist, physician, educator*
Stroscio, Michael Anthony *physicist, researcher*
Truran, James Wellington, Jr., *astrophysicist, educator*
Turner, Michael Stanley *astrophysics educator, researcher*
Warren, Glenn James *environmental scientist*

Dekalb
Rossing, Thomas D. *physics educator*

Downers Grove
Feinstein, Robert Norman *retired biochemist*
Hubbard, Lincoln Beals *medical physicist, consultant*
Shen, Sin-Yan *physicist, conductor, acoustics specialist, music director*

Elk Grove Village
Jan, Chwu-Ching Hwang *environmental chemistry consultant*

Evanston
Allred, Albert Louis *chemistry professor*
Basolo, Fred *chemistry professor*
Chang, R. P. H. *materials science educator*
Ibers, James Arthur *chemist, educator*
Lambert, Joseph Buckley *chemistry professor*
Margoliash, Emanuel *biochemist, educator*
Meshii, Masahiro *materials science educator*
Mirkin, Chad A. *chemistry professor*
Moore, C. Bradley *chemistry professor*
Oakes, Robert James *physics educator*
Rosenzweig, Amy *biochemist, educator*
Sachtler, Wolfgang Max Hugo *chemistry professor*
Schluter, Robert Arvel *physicist*
Seidman, David N(athaniel) *materials science and engineering educator*
Silverman, Richard Bruce *chemist, educator, biochemist*
Ulmer, Melville Paul *physics and astronomy educator*
Walter, Robert Irving *chemistry professor*
Weertman, Johannes *materials science educator*
Weertman, Julia Randall *materials science and engineering educator*
Wessels, Bruce W. *materials scientist, educator*

Glen Ellyn
Mooring, F. Paul *physics editor*

Glenview
Rorig, Kurt Joachim *chemist, research director*

Grayslake
Barrington, Leonard Barry *chemist, educator, writer*

Hinsdale
Kaminsky, Manfred Stephan *physicist*

Homewood
Parker, Eugene Newman *retired physicist, educator*

Lake Forest
Weston, Arthur Walter *chemist, scientific and business executive*

Lemont
Cho, Yanglai *physicist*

Libertyville
Korenev, Sergey Alexandrovich *physicist*

Lincolnwood
Bezkorovainy, Anatoly *medical educator, biochemist*

Lisle
Staab, Thomas Eugene *chemist*

Lombard
McCoy, Jeanie Shearer *analytical chemist, consultant*

Maywood
Bermes, Edward William, Jr., *biochemist, educator*
Schultz, Richard Michael *biochemistry educator, researcher*

Mount Carmel
Fornoff, Frank J(unior) *retired chemistry educator, consultant*

Naperville
Joyce, William H. *chemist*
Sellers, Gregory Jude *physicist*
Sherren, Anne Terry *chemistry professor*

North Chicago
Loga, Sanda *physicist, researcher*

Northfield
Shabica, Charles Wright *geologist, earth science educator*

Oak Park
Fanta, Paul Edward *chemist, educator*

Peoria
Chamberlain, Joseph Miles *astronomer, educator*
Fanta, George Frederick *chemist, researcher*
Nielsen, Harald Christian *retired chemist, researcher*
Reith, Maarten Edward A. *neurochemist*

Rock Island
Anderson, Richard Charles *geology educator*
Hammer, William Roy *paleontologist, educator*
Sundelius, Harold W. *geology educator*

Rockford
Walhout, Justine Simon *chemistry professor*

Skokie
Hamer, Martin *retired chemist*

Urbana
Beak, Peter Andrew *chemistry professor*
Birnbaum, Howard Kent *materials science educator*
Crofts, Antony Richard *biochemistry and biophysics educator*
Ehrlich, Gert *science educator, researcher*
Forbes, Richard Mather *biochemistry educator*
Ginsberg, Donald Maurice *physicist, researcher*
Goldwasser, Edwin Leo *physicist*
Govindjee, *biophysics, biochemistry, and biology educator*
Greene, Laura Helen *physicist*
Gruebele, Martin *chemistry, physics, and biophysics educator*
Hou, Xiaoqiang *mineralogist*
Iben, Icko, Jr., *astrophysicist, educator*
Jackson, Edwin Atlee *physicist, educator*
Jonas, Jiri *chemist, educator*
Kieffer, Susan Werner *geologist, educator, media consultant*
Kirkpatrick, R(obert) James *geology educator*
Klein, Miles Vincent *physics educator*
Lauterbur, Paul C(hristian) *chemistry professor*
Makri, Nancy *chemistry educator*
Mapother, Dillon Edward *physicist, academic administrator*
Rebeiz, Constantin A. *plant biochemist, educator, lab administrator*
Salamon, Myron Ben *physicist, educator, dean*
Satterthwaite, Cameron B. *physics educator*
Simon, Jack Aaron *geologist, former state official*
Snyder, Lewis Emil *astrophysicist, educator*
Suslick, Kenneth Sanders *chemistry professor*
Switzer, Robert Lee *biochemistry educator*

Wilmette
Klotz, Irving Myron *chemist, educator*
Rocek, Jan *chemist, educator*

INDIANA

Bloomington
Cameron, John M. *nuclear scientist, educator, science administrator*
Day, Harry Gilbert *nutritional biochemist, consultant*
Easton, Susan Dawn *biochemist, educator*
Edmondson, Frank Kelley *retired astronomer*
Finkelstein, David Barry *geologist, researcher*
Hattin, Donald Edward *geologist, educator*
Hendry, Archibald Wagstaff *physics educator*
Kauffman, Erle Galen *geologist, paleontologist*
Letsinger, Robert Lewis *chemistry professor*
Peters, Dennis Gail *chemist*
Pollock, Robert Elwood *nuclear scientist*
Schaich, William L. *physics educator*
Smith, Ronald Thomas *environmental scientist*

Chesterton
Crewe, Albert Victor *physicist, artist, business executive*

East Chicago
Valia, Hardarshan S. *research scientist*

Elkhart
Free, Helen Murray *chemist, consultant*

Fort Wayne
Stevenson, Kenneth Lee *chemist, educator*

Indianapolis
Aprison, Morris Herman *retired biochemist, experimental and theoretical neurobiologist, emeritus educator*
Fife, Wilmer Krafft *chemistry professor*
Lau, Pauline Young *chemist*
Malik, David Joseph *chemist, educator*
Mirsky, Arthur *geologist, department chairman*
Zheng, Qi-Huang *chemist, educator*

Lafayette
Brewster, James Henry *retired chemistry educator*
Brown, Herbert Charles *chemistry professor*
Feuer, Henry *retired chemist*
Loeffler, Frank Joseph *physicist, educator*
Porile, Norbert Thomas *chemistry professor*
Whistler, Roy Lester *chemist, educator, industrialist*

Madison
Tatera, James Frank *chemist, process analysis specialist*

Muncie
Harris, Joseph McAllister *retired chemist*

New Albany
Crump, Claudia *geography educator*

Notre Dame
Burns, Peter Carman *geologist, educator*
Feigl, Dorothy Marie *chemistry educator, university official*
Huber, Paul William *biochemistry educator, researcher*
Meisel, Dan *chemist*
Mobashery, Shahriar *chemist*
Schuler, Robert Hugo *chemist, educator*
Shephard, William Danks *physicist, educator*
Trozzolo, Anthony Marion *chemistry professor*

Terre Haute
Guthrie, Frank Albert *chemistry professor*

West Lafayette
Adelman, Steven Allen *theoretical physical chemist, chemistry educator*
Barnes, Virgil Everett, II, *physics educator*
Cooks, R(obert) Graham *chemist, educator*
Cramer, William Anthony *biochemistry and biophysics researcher, educator*
Hanks, Alan R. *chemistry professor*
Judd, William Robert *engineering geologist, educator*
Laskowski, Michael, Jr., *chemist, educator*
Lipschutz, Michael Elazar *chemistry educator, consultant, researcher*
McMillin, David Robert *chemistry professor*
Mohtar, Rabi H. *hydrologist*
Morrison, Harry *chemistry professor*
Negishi, Ei-ichi *chemistry professor*
Overhauser, Albert Warner *physicist*
Rossmann, Michael George *biochemist, educator*

IOWA

Ames
Armstrong, Daniel Wayne *chemist, educator*
Barton, Thomas Jackson *chemistry professor, researcher*
Bowen, George Hamilton, Jr., *astrophysicist, educator*
Clem, John Richard *physicist, educator*
Gordon, Mark S. *chemist, educator*
Horowitz, Jack *biochemistry educator*
Jacobson, Robert Andrew *chemistry professor*
Lo, Chester C.H. *research scientist*
Smith, John Francis *materials science educator*
Tabatabai, M. Ali *chemist, biochemist*
Yeung, Edward Szeshing *chemist*

Cedar Falls
Koob, Robert Duane *chemistry educator, educational administrator*

Cedar Rapids
Bahadur, Birendra *display specialist, liquid crystal researcher*

Des Moines
Bartschat, Klaus Richard Wilhelm *physics educator*

Grinnell
Swartz, James Edward *chemistry educator, dean, university administrator*

Iowa City
Baker, Richard Graves *geology educator, palynologist*
Burton, Donald Joseph *chemistry professor*
Campbell, Kevin Peter *physiology and biophysics educator, researcher*
Conway, Thomas William *biochemist, educator*
Donelson, John Everett *biochemistry educator, molecular biologist*
Linhardt, Robert John J *medicinal chemistry educator*
Montgomery, Rex *biochemist, educator*
Plapp, Bryce Vernon *biochemistry educator*
Van Allen, James Alfred *physicist, researcher*

Le Mars
Rebstock, Theodore Lynn *chemist, educator, retired research scientist*

North Liberty
Glenister, Brian Frederick *geologist, educator*

Spencer
Lemke, Alan James *environmental specialist*

Spirit Lake
Brett, George Wendell *former geologist, philatelist*

West Des Moines
Lynch, David William *physicist, retired educator*

KANSAS

Clay Center
Churchill, Thomas John *broadcast meteorologist*

Kansas City
Noelken, Milton Edward *biochemistry educator, researcher*

Lawrence
Ammar, Raymond George *physicist, researcher*
Angino, Ernest Edward *retired geology and engineering educator*
Brady, Lawrence Lee *geologist*
Dreschhoff, Gisela Auguste Marie *physicist, researcher*
Enos, Paul *geologist, educator*
Gerhard, Lee Clarence *geologist, educator*
Harmony, Marlin Dale *chemistry professor*
Landgrebe, John Allan *chemistry professor*
Merriam, Daniel F(rancis) *geologist*
Mitscher, Lester Allen *chemist, educator*

Manhattan
Fateley, William Gene *chemist, educator, inventor, administrator*
Jiang, Hongxing *physics educator, researcher*

Overland Park
Ostby, Frederick Paul, Jr., *meteorologist, retired government official, science administrator*

Shawnee Mission
Billings, Patricia Jean *inventor*

Topeka
Barton, Janice Sweeny *chemistry educator*

Strominger, Jack Leonard *biochemist*
Walsh, Christopher Thomas *biochemist, department chairman*
Wang, Jian *physical chemist, researcher*
White, Morris Francis *biochemistry educator*
Zimmerman, George Ogurek *physicist, researcher*

Bourne
Fantozzi, Peggy Ryone *geologist, environmental planner*

Brighton
Fischer, Irene Kaminka *geodesist, researcher, retired mathematician*

Brookfield
Anderson, Theodore Robert *physicist, small business owner*

Brookline
Basu, Soumendra Nath *materials scientist, educator*
Workman, Jerome James, Jr., *chemist*

Byfield
Yesair, David Wayne *biochemist*

Cambridge
Alberty, Robert Arnold *chemistry professor*
Anderson, James Gilbert *chemistry professor*
Arkani-Hamed, Nima *physicist*
Barger, James Edwin *physicist*
Benedek, George Bernard *physicist, researcher*
Biemann, Klaus *chemistry professor*
Blout, Elkan Rogers *biological chemistry educator, university dean*
Bradt, Hale Van Dorn *physicist, x-ray astronomer, educator*
Branscomb, Lewis McAdory *physicist, researcher*
Burchfiel, Burrell Clark *geology educator*
Burke, Bernard Flood *physicist, educator*
Canizares, Claude Roger *astrophysicist, educator*
Ceyer, Sylvia T. *chemistry professor*
Chisholm, Sallie Watson *biological oceanography educator, researcher*
Clark, George Whipple *physics educator*
Cohn, Daniel Ross *physicist*
Coleman, Sidney Richard *physicist, researcher*
Corey, Elias James *chemistry professor*
Dalgarno, Alexander *astronomy educator*
Doty, Paul Mead *biochemist, educator, arms control specialist*
Dresselhaus, Mildred Spiewak *physics and engineering educator*
Eagar, Thomas Waddy *metallurgist, educator*
Evans, David A(lbert) *chemistry educator*
Evans, James Brian *geophysics educator*
Feld, Michael Stephen *physics educator*
Field, George Brooks *theoretical astrophysicist*
Field, Robert Warren *chemistry professor*
Foner, Simon *research physicist*
French, Anthony Philip *physicist, educator*
Frey, Frederick August *geochemistry researcher, educator*
Friedman, Jerome Isaac *physics educator, researcher*
Friend, Cynthia M. *chemist, educator*
Garrelick, Joel Marc *acoustical scientist, consultant*
Geller, Margaret Joan *astrophysicist, educator*
Georgi, Howard *physics educator*
Gingerich, Owen Jay *astronomer, educator*
Goldstone, Jeffrey *physicist, educator*
Greene, Frederick D., II, *chemistry professor*
Grindlay, Jonathan Ellis *astrophysics educator*
Grove, Timothy Lynn *geology educator*
Guth, Alan Harvey *physicist, researcher*
Halperin, Bertrand Israel *physics educator*
Hau, Lene *physicist, optics scientist*
Herschbach, Dudley Robert *chemistry professor*
Hewitt, Jacqueline N. *astronomy educator*
Hoffman, Paul Felix *geologist, educator*
Holdren, John Paul *energy and resource educator, researcher, author, consultant*
Holm, Richard Hadley *chemist, educator*
Holton, Gerald *physicist, science historian*
Houtchens, Robert Austin, Jr., *biochemist*
Hu, Haijun *atmospheric scientist, electrical engineer*
Huang, Kerson *physics educator*
Huchra, John Peter *astronomer, educator*
Jackiw, Roman *physicist, researcher*
Jaffe, Arthur Michael *physicist, mathematician, educator*
Joss, Paul Christopher *astrophysicist, atmospheric physicist, educator*
Kamentsky, Louis Aaron *biophysicist*
Keck, James Collyer *physicist, researcher*
Ketterle, Wolfgang *physics educator*
Khorana, Har Gobind *chemist, educator*
King, Ronold Wyeth Percival *physics educator*
Kistiakowsky, Vera *physics researcher, educator*
Klemperer, William *chemistry professor*
Knowles, Jeremy Randall *chemist, educator*
Kurtz, Michael Julian *astronomer, computer scientist*
Langmuir, Charles Herbert *geology educator*
Lindzen, Richard Siegmund *meteorologist, educator*
Lippard, Stephen James *chemist, educator*
Lipscomb, William Nunn, Jr., *physical chemistry educator*
Livingston, James Duane *physicist, researcher*
Lomon, Earle Leonard *physicist, educator, consultant*
Low, Francis Eugene *physics educator*
Lyon, Richard Harold *physicist, educator*
Marsden, Brian Geoffrey *astronomer*
Martin, Paul Cecil *physicist, researcher*
Meselson, Matthew Stanley *biochemist, educator*
Milner, Richard Gerard *physicist*
Molina, Mario Jose *physical chemist, educator*
Moran, James Michael, Jr., *astronomer, educator*
Narayan, Ramesh *astronomy educator*
Nelson, David Robert *physics educator*
Newell, Reginald Edward *physics educator*
Olbert, Stanislaw *physicist*
Oppenheim, Irwin *chemical physicist, educator*
Paul, William *physicist, researcher*
Petersen, Ulrich *geology educator*
Pettengill, Gordon H(emenway) *physicist, researcher*
Pritchard, David Edward *physics educator*
Ramsey, Norman F. *physicist, researcher*
Raymo, Maureen Elizabeth *geologist, researcher*
Redwine, Robert Page *physicist, researcher*
Rice, James Robert *engineering scientist, geophysicist*
Rose, Robert Michael *materials science and engineering educator*
Rubin, Lawrence Gilbert *physicist, laboratory manager*
Schechter, Paul *physicist, educator*
Schrock, Richard Royce *chemistry educator*
Seyferth, Dietmar *chemist, educator*
Shapiro, Irwin Ira *physicist, researcher*
Silbey, Robert James *chemistry educator, researcher, consultant*
Solomon, Arthur Kaskel *biophysics educator*
Spaepen, Frans August *applied physics researcher, educator*
Steadman, Stephen Geoffrey *physicist*
Steinfeld, Jeffrey Irwin *chemistry educator, consultant, writer*
Strandberg, Malcom Woodrow Pershing *physicist*
Stubbe, JoAnne *chemistry professor*
Thaddeus, Patrick *physicist, researcher*
Ting, Samuel Chao Chung *physicist, researcher*
Tinkham, Michael *physicist, researcher*
Verdine, Gregory Lawrence *chemist, educator*
Vessot, Robert Frederick Charles *physicist, researcher*
Wang, James Chuo *biochemistry and molecular biology educator*
Waugh, John Stewart *chemist, educator*
Weinberg, Robert Allan *biochemist, educator*
Westheimer, Frank Henry *chemist, educator*
Whitesides, George McClelland *chemistry professor*
Wilczek, Frank Anthony *physics educator*
Wilson, Robert Woodrow *radio astronomer*
Wood, John Armstead *planetary scientist, geological sciences educator*
Xie, Xiaoliang Sunney *chemist, educator*

Charlestown
Cheng, Leo Ling *biophysicist, researcher*

Chestnut Hill
Auld, David Stuart *biochemist, educator*
Fourkas, John T. *chemistry educator*

Chilmark
Lazarus, David *physicist, researcher*

Concord
Plummer, William Torsch *optical physicist*

Cotuit
Miller, Robert Charles *retired physicist*

East Orleans
Romey, William Dowden *geologist, educator*

Falmouth
Adelman, William J., Jr., *biophysicist*
Goody, Richard Mead *geophysicist*

Gloucester
Socolow, Arthur Abraham *geologist*

Hanscom AFB
Mailloux, Robert Joseph *physicist*

Ipswich
Herrmann, Robert Lawrence *biochemist, educator*

Lexington
Buchanan, John Machlin *biochemistry educator*
Champion, Kenneth Stanley Warner *physicist*
Dionne, Gerald Francis *research physicist, educator, consultant*
Nash, Leonard Kollender *retired chemistry professor*
Silverman, Sam Mendel *physicist, lawyer*
Steiner, John William *retired biophysicist*
Wang, Chi Hua *chemist, education educator*
Williamson, Richard Cardinal *physicist*

Lowell
Kannenberg, Lloyd Chambers *physicist, researcher*
Suplinskas, Raymond Joseph *materials scientist*

Medford
Cavallaro, Mary Caroline *retired physics educator*
Gunther, Leon *physicist, educator*
Schneps, Jack *physics educator*

Medway
Arthur, Wallace *physicist, educator*

Needham
Holt, Stephen S. *astrophysicist*

Newton
Aronow, Saul *radiological physicist, consultant*
Dunlap, William Crawford *physicist*
Jeanloz, Roger William *biochemist, educator*
Lichtin, Norman Nahum *chemistry professor*

North Andover
Shenai-Khatkhate, Deodatta Vinayak *chemical researcher*

North Dartmouth
Dowd, John Peter *physics educator*

Pittsfield
Wheelock, Kenneth Steven *chemist*

Roxbury
Simons, Elizabeth R(eiman) *biochemist, educator*

Salem
Brown, Walter Redvers John *physicist*

Shrewsbury
Nixon, Eugene Ray *chemist, educator*

South Hadley
Bergen, Robert Ludlum, Jr., *retired materials scientist*
Campbell, Mary Kathryn *chemistry professor*
Leal, Joseph Rogers *chemist*
Williamson, Kenneth Lee *chemistry professor*

Springfield
Smist, Julianne Marie *chemist, educator*

Waltham
Deser, Stanley *physicist, researcher*
Epstein, Irving Robert *chemistry professor*
Foxman, Bruce Mayer *chemist, educator*
Lees, Marjorie Berman *biochemist, neuroscientist*
Petsko, Gregory Anthony *chemistry and biochemistry scientist educator*
Snider, Barry B. *organic chemist*
Zhabotinsky, Anatol Markovitch *biophysicist, educator*

Watertown
Lin, Juchui Ray (Ju-Chui Lin) *polymer scientist*

Wayland
Brynjolfsson, Ari *nuclear physicist*
Clark, Melville, Jr., *physicist, electrical engineer*
Prabakaran, Daniel *biochemist, researcher*

Wellesley
Charpie, Robert Alan *physicist, researcher*
Kato, Walter Yoneo *physicist*
Snitzer, Elias *physicist*

Westford
Salah, Joseph Elias *research scientist, educator*

Weston
Lin, Alice Lee Lan *physicist, researcher, educator*
Wang, Chia Ping *physicist, researcher*

Williamstown
Markgraf, J(ohn) Hodge *chemist, educator*
Park, David Allen *physicist, researcher*
Pasachoff, Jay Myron *astronomer, educator*
Wobus, Reinhard Arthur *geologist, educator*

Winchester
Milburn, Richard Henry *physics educator*

Woods Hole
Berggren, William Alfred *geologist, research micropaleontologist, educator*
Cohen, Seymour Stanley *biochemist, educator*
Fenwick, Judith L. *oceanographer, researcher*
Gagosian, Robert B. *chemist, educator*
Hart, Stanley Robert *geochemist, educator*
Steele, John Hyslop *marine scientist, oceanographic institute administrator*
Uchupi, Elazar *geologist, researcher*

Worcester
Pavlik, James William *chemistry professor*

Yarmouth Port
Darby, Joseph Branch, Jr., *retired metallurgist, retired federal agency administrator*
LeBaron, Francis Newton *biochemistry educator*

MICHIGAN

Albion
Green, David William *chemist, educator*
Taylor, Lawrence Dow *geologist, educator*

Ann Arbor
Agranoff, Bernard William *biochemist, educator*
Akerlof, Carl William *physics educator*
Ashe, Arthur James, III, *chemistry professor*
Atreya, Sushil Kumar *planetary-space science educator, astrophysicist*
Bartell, Lawrence Sims *chemist, educator*
Coward, James Kenderdine *chemist*
Dekker, Eugene Earl *biochemistry educator*
Donahue, Thomas Michael *physics educator*
Duff, Michael James *physicist*
Farrand, William Richard *geology educator*
Filisko, Frank Edward *physicist, researcher*
Fisk, Lennard Ayres *physicist, researcher*
Freese, Katherine *physicist, researcher*
Griffin, Henry Claude *chemistry professor*
Haddock, Fred(erick) T(heodore), Jr., *retired astronomer*
Hagel, William Carl *metallurgical consultant*
Jiang, Wenhui *materials scientist*
Jones, Lawrence William *retired educator, physicist*
Kesler, Stephen Edward *economic geology educator*
Killeen, Timothy L. *aerospace scientist, research administrator*
Krisch, Alan David *physics educator*
Ludwig, Martha *biochemist, educator*
Massey, Vincent *biochemist, educator*
Mazzeo, Anthony R. *chemist*
Morris, Michael David *chemistry professor*
Murnane, Margaret Mary *engineering and physics educator*
Neal, Homer Alfred *physics educator, researcher, university administrator*
Nordman, Christer Eric *chemistry professor*
Nriagu, Jerome Okon *environmental geochemist*
Parkinson, William Charles *physicist, researcher*
Pollack, Henry Nathan *geophysics educator*
Robertson, Richard Earl *physical chemist, educator*
Roe, Byron Paul *physics educator*
Roush, William R. *chemistry educator*
Schacht, Jochen Heinrich *biochemistry educator*
Sun, Kai *materials scientist, research scientist*
Van der Voo, Rob *geophysicist*
Veltman, Martinus J.G. *retired physics educator*
Walter, Lynn M. *geologist, educator*
Zhang, Youxue *geology educator*

Belleville
Wilson, David James *chemistry researcher, educator*

Big Rapids
Mathison, Ian William *chemistry professor, dean, consultant*

Birmingham
Smith, George Wolfram *physicist, researcher*

Chassell
Spain, James Dorris, Jr., *biochemist, educator*

Chelsea
Crane, Horace Richard *physicist, researcher*

Detroit
Drescher, Dennis George *biochemist, researcher*
Frade, Peter Daniel *chemist, educator, administrator*
Gupta, Suraj Narayan *physicist, researcher*
Oliver, John Preston *chemistry professor, dean*
Svoboda, Mary Beth *health physicist, environmental science educator*

East Lansing
Abolins, Maris Arvids *physics researcher and educator*
Austin, Sam M. *physics educator*
Benenson, Walter *nuclear physics educator*
Blosser, Henry Gabriel *physicist*
Burnett, Jean Bullard (Mrs. James R. Burnett) *biochemist, educator*
Case, Eldon Darrel *materials science educator*
Cross, Aureal Theophilus *geology and botany educator*
Dye, James Louis *chemistry professor*
Gelbke, Claus-Konrad *nuclear physics educator*
Harrison, Michael Jay *physicist, researcher*
Pollack, Gerald Leslie *physicist, researcher*
Preiss, Jack *biochemistry educator*
Spence, Robert Dean *physics educator*
Stein, Robert Foster *astrophysicist, educator*

Farmington Hills
Chapman, Gilbert Bryant *physicist*
Theodore, Ares Nicholas *research chemist*

Highland
Brown, Ray Kent *biochemist, physician, educator*

Kalamazoo
Greenfield, John Charles *bio-organic chemist*

Leland
Small, Hamish *chemist*

Marquette
Donovan, David William *physics professor, researcher*

Midland
Chao, Marshall *chemist*
Dorman, Linneaus Cuthbert *retired chemist*

Mount Pleasant
Dietrich, Richard Vincent *geologist, educator*

Niles
Chmiel, Chester T. *chemist, consultant*

Northville
Bohm, Henry Victor *physicist*

Rochester
Ovshinsky, Stanford Robert *physicist, inventor, energy executive, information company executive*
Xia, Yang *physicist, educator*

Rochester Hills
Fritzsche, Hellmut *physics educator*

Romulus
Yussouff, Mohammed *retired physicist, educator*

Sears
McCullough, Willard G. *retired biochemist*

Shelby Township
Heremans, Joseph Pierre *physicist*

Warren
Deak, Charles Karol *chemist*
Gaarenstroom, Stephen William *chemist*
Herbst, Jan Francis *physicist, researcher*

West Bloomfield
Harwood, Julius J. *metallurgist, educator*

Ypsilanti
Barnes, James Milton *physics and astronomy educator*

MINNESOTA

Apple Valley
Brown, Francis William *chemist, consultant*

Austin
Schmid, Harald Heinrich Otto *biochemistry educator, academic director*

Bloomington
Bekrenev, Anatoliy *physicist*

Duluth
Rapp, George Robert (Rip Rapp) *geology and archeology educator*
Zhdankin, Viktor Vladimirovich *chemistry professor*

Lake Elmo
Vivona, Daniel Nicholas *chemist*

Lakeville
Phinney, William Charles *retired geologist*

Mahtomedi
Holmen, Reynold Algott Emanuel *chemist*

Minneapolis
Ackerman, Eugene *biophysics educator*
Berg, Stanton Oneal *firearms and ballistics consultant*
Carr, Peter William *chemistry professor*
Goldman, Allen Marshall *physics educator*
Halley, James Woods *physics educator*
Heller, Kenneth Jeffrey *physicist*
Hogenkamp, Henricus Petrus Cornelis *biochemistry researcher, biochemistry educator*
Kuhi, Leonard Vello *astronomer, university administrator*
Portoghese, Philip Salvatore *medicinal chemist, educator*
Rubens, Sidney Michel *physicist, technical advisor*
Truhlar, Donald Gene *chemist, educator*
Vainshtein, Arkady *physics educator*
Victora, Randall Harry *physicist, researcher*
Wright, Herbert E(dgar), Jr., *geologist*

Minnetonka
Stokes, Robert James *retired materials scientist*

Moorhead
Strong, Judith Ann *chemist, educator*

Northfield
Casper, Barry Michael *physics educator*
Cederberg, James *physics educator*
Fick, Herbert J. *chemist, consultant*
Henrickson, Eiler Leonard *retired geologist, educator*
Wickramasekara, Sujeev *physicist, educator*

Saint Paul
Hobbie, Russell Klyver *physics educator*
Newmark, Richard Alan *chemist*
Perry, James Alfred *environmental scientist, consultant, science educator, department chairman*
Prager, Stephen *chemistry professor*
Schwartz, Albert Truman *chemistry professor*

MISSISSIPPI

Bay Saint Louis
Hurlburt, Harley Ernest *ocean modeling and prediction scientist*
Lewando, Alfred Gerard, Jr., *oceanographer*
Rondeau, Clement Robert *petroleum geologist*

Hattiesburg
Nanda, Ajaya Kumar *chemist, educator*

Jackson
Smith, Edgar Eugene *biochemist, university administrator*

Olive Branch
Farr, Walter Evans *chemist, chemical engineer*

Stennis Space Center
Chin-Bing, Stanley Arthur *physicist, educator*
Fleischer, Peter *research geologist, oceanographer, educator*

University
Breazeale, Mack Alfred *physics educator*
Tschumper, Gregory Scott *chemist, educator*

MISSOURI

Chesterfield
Fujiwara, Hideji *chemist, researcher*
Sikorski, James Alan *research chemist*

Clinton
Kelsay, David Roland *chemist*

Columbia
Chen, Shi-Jie *biophysicist*
Decker, Wayne Leroy *meteorologist, educator*
Eerkens, Jeff W. *nuclear scientist, educator, laser engineer*
Gehrke, Charles William *biochemistry educator*
Katti, Kattesh V. *biochemist, educator, research scientist*
Kuznetsov, Oleg A. *biophysicist*
Plummer, Patricia Lynne Moore *chemistry and physics educator*
Randall, Linda Lea *biochemist, educator*
Sun, Albert Yung-Kwang *biochemistry and neurochemistry educator*
Weisman, Gary Andrew *biochemist*
Wixom, Robert Llewellyn *biochemistry educator*

Creve Coeur
Bockserman, Robert Julian *chemist*

Ferguson
Chubb, Charles Ray *physicist, researcher*

Independence
Lemon, Leslie Roy *radar meteorologist*

Kansas City
Cheng, Kuang Lu *chemist, educator*
Ching, Wai Yim *physics educator, researcher*
Durig, James Robert *chemistry professor*
Parizek, Eldon Joseph *geologist, educator, dean*
Rost, William Joseph *chemist*
Wilkinson, Ralph Russell *biochemistry educator, toxicologist*

Kirksville
Festa, Roger Reginald *chemist, educator*

Lees Summit
Hubbard, Harold Mead *energy and environmental scientist, consultant*

Rolla
Adawi, Ibrahim Hasan *physics educator*
Alexander, Ralph William, Jr., *physics educator*
Mc Farland, Robert Harold *physicist, researcher*
Trueblood, Max Blair *physicist, educator*

Saint Louis
Ackers, Gary Keith *biophysical chemistry educator, researcher*
Agarwal, Ramesh Kumar *aeronautical scientist, researcher, educator*
Bender, Carl Martin *physics educator, consultant*
Burgess, James Harland *physics educator, researcher*
Fitzpatrick, Susan *biochemist, neurologist, foundation executive*
Frieden, Carl *biochemist, educator*
Friedlander, Michael Wulf *physicist, researcher*
Gokel, George William *organic chemist, educator*
Gross, Michael Lawrence *chemistry professor*
Handel, Peter H. *physics educator*
Hawkins, Pamela Leigh Huffman *biochemist*
Huynh, Quang Khai *biochemist*
Israel, Martin Henry *astrophysicist, educator, academic administrator*
Macias, Edward S. *chemistry educator, university official and dean*
Miller, James Gegan *research scientist, physics educator*
Murray, Robert Wallace *chemistry professor*
Schilling, James Stanford *physicist, educator*
Sly, William S. *biochemist, educator*
Wrighton, Mark Stephen *chemistry professor*

Springfield
Thompson, Clifton C. *retired chemistry educator, university administrator*

Warrensburg
Stalick, Wayne M. *chemistry educator, law firm consultant*

Willow Springs
Jordan, Gilbert Fred *geophysicist, physicist*

MONTANA

Bozeman
Drobizhev, Mikhail Anatolievich *physicist*
Grieco, Paul Anthony *chemistry professor*
Hiscock, William A. *physicist, educator*
Horner, John Robert *paleontologist, researcher*

Columbia Falls
Spade-Shenker, George Lawrence (George Shenker) *scientist*

Dayton
von Volborth, Alexis *geochemist, geological engineering educator*

Kalispell
Freiberg, Robert Jerry *laser physicist, engineer, technology administrator, consultant*

Livingston
Wright, Richard Kirk *physicist, materials researcher, physiologist, consultant*

Missoula
DeGraw, Joseph Irving, Jr., *chemist, consultant*
Osterheld, R(obert) Keith *chemistry professor*

Monarch
Baker, David Warren *earth scientist*

NEBRASKA

Kearney
Wubbels, Gene Gerald *chemistry professor*

Lincoln
Jones, Lee Bennett *chemist, educator, university official*
Spreitzer, Robert Joseph *biochemist, educator*
Yoder, Bruce Alan *chemist*

Omaha
Bergt, Gregory Paul *chemist, consultant*
Zepf, Thomas Herman *physics educator, researcher*

NEVADA

Carson City
Crawford, John Edward *geologist, scientist*

Henderson
Holloway, Robert Wester *radiochemist*
Pellock, John David *chemist, educator*
Trivelpiece, Alvin William *physicist, educator, consultant*

Las Vegas
Broca, Laurent Antoine *aerospace scientist*

Reno
Price, Jonathan G. *geologist*
Sladek, Ronald John *physics educator*
Taranik, James Vladimir *geologist, educator*

Sparks
Bonham, Harold Florian *research geologist, consultant*

NEW HAMPSHIRE

Durham
Stubbs, Jeffrey Matthew *research scientist*

Glen
Zager, Ronald I. *chemist, consultant*

Grantham
Grimley, Robert Thomas *chemistry professor*

Hanover
Curphey, Thomas John *chemist, researcher*
Kantrowitz, Arthur *physicist, researcher, educator*
Montgomery, David Campbell *physicist, researcher*
Stockmayer, Walter H(ugo) *chemistry professor*
Wegner, Gary Alan *astronomer*

Jaffrey
Walling, Cheves Thomson *chemistry professor*

Salem
Simmons, Marvin Gene *geophysics educator*

NEW JERSEY

Annandale
Gorbaty, Martin Leo *chemist, researcher*

Basking Ridge
Morgan, Samuel P(ope) *physicist, applied mathematician*

Belleville
Berenfeld, Mark M. *chemist*

Berkeley Heights
Geusic, Joseph Edward Edward *physicist*
Mac Rae, Alfred Urquhart *physicist, electrical engineer*

Bogota
Condon, Francis Edward *retired chemistry educator*

Bridgewater
Albrechtsen, Adrian Edysel *metallurgist, consultant*

Caldwell
Surmatis, Joseph D. *retired chemist*

Camden
Beck, David Paul *biochemist*

Cliffside Park
Ginos, James Zissis *retired research chemist*

Columbia
Timcenko, Lydia Teodora *biochemist, chemist*

Demarest
Ruderman, Warren *chemist*

East Brunswick
Wagman, Gerald Howard *retired biochemist*

East Hanover
Edelson, Edward Harold *research chemist*

Freehold
Kwon, Joon Taek *retired chemistry researcher*

Glassboro
Mosto, Patricia *environmental scientist, educator*

Highland Park
Brudner, Harvey Jerome *physicist*

Hightstown
Shoemaker, Frank Crawford *retired physicist*

Hoboken
Bose, Ajay Kumar *chemistry professor*
Eide, Hans A. *physicist, educator*
Schmidt, George *physicist, educator*

Holmdel
Gordon, James Power *optics scientist*
Kaminow, Ivan Paul *physicist*
Mollenauer, Linn Frederick *retired physicist*

Jackson
Arminas, Scott Arnold *chemist, poet, writer*

Jersey City
Fan, Chonglun *materials scientist, researcher*
Koster, Emlyn Howard *geologist, educator*

Kenilworth
Korfmacher, Walter Averill *chemist, researcher*
Pramanik, Birendra Nath *research executive*

Lakewood
Karol, Frederick John *industrial chemist*

Lambertville
Beyea, Jan Edgar *physicist*

Lawrenceville
Brill, Michael Henry *physicist, vision scientist, editor*
Sheats, John Eugene *chemistry professor*

Leonia
Kurtz, Anthony David *physicist*

Livingston
Green, Richard *research scientist, consultant*

Madison
Carter, Ashley Hale *physicist, educator*

Manahawkin
Logan, Ralph Andre *physicist*

Manasquan
Pond, Thomas Alexander *physics educator, university official*

Maplewood
Johnson, Dewey, Jr., *retired biochemist*
Tatyrek, Alfred Frank *consultant, materials and environmental engineer, analytical and research chemist*

Mendham
Dombrowski, Robert Theodore *materials scientist and information architect*

Middletown
Iannone, Patrick Paul *optics scientist, researcher*
Lundgren, Carl William, Jr., *physicist*

Milltown
Sacharow, Stanley *chemist, consultant, writer*

Morris Plains
Capellos, Chris Spiridon *chemist*

Morristown
Baughman, Ray Henry *materials scientist*

Neptune
Aguiar, Adam Martin *chemist, educator*

New Brunswick
Pandey, Ramesh Chandra *chemist, chemicals executive*
Robock, Alan *meteorology educator*
Rosen, Robert Thomas *analytical and food chemist*
Strauss, Ulrich Paul *chemist, educator*

New Providence
Glass, Alastair Malcolm *physicist, research director*
Lanzerotti, Louis John *physicist*
Matthews, Manyalibo Joseph *physicist, researcher*
Murray, Cherry Ann *physicist, researcher*
Sivco, Deborah Lee *research materials scientist*
van Dover, Robert Bruce *physicist*
White, Alice Elizabeth *physicist, researcher*

Newark
Goode, Philip Ranson *astrophysicist, physics educator*
Iqbal, Zafar *physicist*
Spruch, Grace Marmor *physics educator*

North Plainfield
Thomas, Lewis *physicist, researcher*

Nutley
Hung, Frank Chien-Hsin *chemist, researcher*
Kong, Norman *chemist*

Oldwick
Sinfelt, John Henry *chemist*
Van Doren, Shaun Clark *chemist, former mayer, city official*

Paulsboro
Langley, Michael Lee *chemist*

Piscataway
Cohen, Morrel Herman *physicist, biologist, educator*
Devlin, Thomas Joseph *physicist*
Fecko, Mariusz Andrzej *research scientist*
Goldin, Gerald Alan *physicist, educator*
Idol, James Daniel, Jr., *chemist, educator, inventor, consultant*
Kear, Bernard Henry *materials scientist, consultant*
Klein, Lisa Carol *materials scientist, educator*
Kotliar, B. Gabriel *physics educator*
Leath, Paul Larry *physicist, educator, former university official*
Lebowitz, Joel Louis *mathematical physicist, educator*
Lindenfeld, Peter *physics educator*
Manowitz, Paul *biochemist, researcher, educator*
Polefka, Thomas Gregory *biochemist*
Reinberg, Danny *biochemist, educator*
Robbins, Allen Bishop *physics educator*
Yacowitz, Harold *biochemist, nutritionist*
Zimmermann, Frank Martin *physicist, surface scientist, educator*

Pomona
Paul, Edward *chemistry professor*
Sharon, Yitzhak Yaakov *physicist, researcher*

Port Murray
Kunzler, John Eugene *physicist*

Princeton
Adler, Stephen Louis *physicist*
Alexe, Gabriela *research scientist*
Anderson, Philip W. *physicist*
Arunasalam, Vickramasingam (Willie) *retired physicist*
Bahcall, John Norris *astrophysicist*
Bonini, William Emory *geophysics educator*
Brinkman, William Frank *physicist, research executive*
Bryan, Kirk, Jr., *research meteorologist, research oceanographer*
Christman, Edward Arthur *physicist*
Davidson, Ronald Crosby *physicist, researcher*
Dyson, Freeman John *physicist, educator*
Fisch, Nathaniel Joseph *physicist*
Fitch, Val Logsdon *physics educator*
Florey, Klaus Georg *chemist, pharmaceutical consultant*
Grisham, Larry Richard *physicist*
Groves, John Taylor, III, *chemist, educator*
Hulse, Russell Alan *physicist*
Huse, David A. *physicist, educator*
Hut, Piet *astrophysics educator*
Jenkins, Edward Beynon *research astronomer*
Kauzmann, Walter Joseph *chemistry professor*
Lehmann, Kevin *chemist, educator*
Lieb, Elliott Hershel *physicist, mathematician, educator*
Long, Frank Wesley, Jr., *chemist*
Manabe, Syukuro *climatologist*
Morgan, William Jason *geophysics educator*
Ondetti, Miguel Angel *chemist, consultant*
Oppenheimer, Michael *physicist*
Ostriker, Jeremiah Paul *astrophysicist, educator*
Ramaprasad, Kackadasam Raghavachar *physical chemist*
Royce, Barrie Saunders Hart *physicist, researcher*
Rutherford, Paul Harding *physicist*
Sabb, Annmarie Louise *chemist, researcher*
Seiberg, Nathan *physics educator*
Sterzer, Fred *research physicist*
Stillinger, Frank Henry *chemist, educator*
Taylor, Edward Curtis *chemistry professor*
Taylor, Joseph Hooton, Jr., *radio astronomer*
Torquato, Salvatore *materials science and chemistry educator*
Tremaine, Scott Duncan *astrophysicist*
Van Houten, Franklyn Bosworth *geologist, educator*
Wheeler, John Archibald *physicist, educator*
Wightman, Arthur Strong *physicist, researcher*
Witten, Edward *mathematical physicist*

Rahway
Garcia, Maria Luisa *biochemist, researcher*
Kaczorowski, Gregory John *biochemist, researcher, science administrator*

Somerset
Eggleton, Benjamin John *physics researcher*

South Hackensack
Stier, Roger Edwin *chemist, researcher*

Springfield
Panish, Morton B. *retired physical chemist*

Stirling
Walsh, Peter Joseph *physics educator*

Summit
Burbank, Robinson Derry *crystallographer*
Phillips, James Charles *physicist, researcher*
Rosensweig, Ronald Ellis *scientist consultant*
Vandenberg, Joka Maria *physicist, researcher*
Wissbrun, Kurt Falke *chemist, consultant*

Teaneck
Fajans, Jack *physics educator*

Union
Zois, Constantine Nicholas Athanasios *meteorology educator*

Wall
Leupold, Herbert August *physicist*

Wayne
Kardan, Mahmoud *chemist, educator*

West Caldwell
Piel, Emil J. *retired science and engineering educator*

Woodbury
Nace, Donald M. *retired chemist*

NEW MEXICO

Albuquerque
Beckel, Charles Leroy *physicist, educator*
Duncan, Irma Wagner *retired biochemist, museum educator*
Gander, John Edward *biochemistry educator*
Garland, James Wilson, Jr., *retired physics educator*
Harrison, Charles Wagner, Jr., *applied physicist*
Leeper, Ramon Joe *physicist*
Loftfield, Robert Berner *biochemistry educator*
Papyrin, Anatolii Nikiforovich *physicist, researcher*
Renschler, Clifford L. *chemist*
Robinson, Charles Paul *nuclear physicist, diplomat, business executive*
Romig, Alton Dale, Jr., *materials scientist, educator*
Taylor, Douglas John *materials scientist, researcher, materials engineer*
Van Devender, J. Pace *physical scientist, management consultant*

Carlsbad
Paviet-Hartmann, Patricia *chemist, researcher*

Kirtland Afb
Alejandro, Steven B. *physicist*
Baum, Carl Edward *electromagnetic theorist*
Degnan, James Henry *physicist*

Las Cruces
Richardson, Albert Edward *chemistry educator, consultant, researcher*

Los Alamos
Brown, Lowell Severt *physicist, researcher*
Clausen, Bjørn *materials scientist, researcher*
Engelhardt, Albert George *physicist*
Gibson, Benjamin Franklin *physicist*
Grilly, Edward Rogers *physicist*
Judd, O'Dean P. *physicist*
Keepin, George Robert, Jr., *physicist*
King, Jerry Wayne *research chemist*
Lu, Ningping *environmental chemist*
Lyman, John L. *chemist, researcher*
Makaruk, Hanna Ewa *theoretical physicist*
Maloy, Stuart *materials scientist, engineer*
Masunov, Artem *theoretical chemist, researcher*
Mead, William Charles *physicist*
Michaudon, André Francisque *physicist*
Mihalas, Dimitri Manuel *astrophysicist, educator*
Mitchell, Terence Edward *materials scientist*
Morales, Reynaldo *physicist*
Nieto, Michael Martin *theoretical physicist*
Nix, James Rayford *nuclear physicist, consultant*
Press, William Henry *astrophysicist, computer scientist*
Ramirez, Arthur P. *physicist*
Rosen, Louis *physicist*
Selden, Robert Wentworth *physicist, science advisor*
Sharp, David Howland *physicist*
Smith, James Lawrence *research physicist*
Snell, Charles Murrell *physicist, astrophysicist*
Thompson, Joe D. *physicist*
Venhaus, Thomas J. *physicist*
Wahl, Arthur Charles *retired chemistry educator*
Wallstrom, Timothy C. *physicist*
Wingo, Robert Matthew *chemist, chemical engineer*
WoldeGabriel, Giday *research geologist*
Zhang, Dongxiao *research scientist*

Los Lunas
Seiler, Fritz Arnold *physicist*

Mayhill
Pastor, Stephen Daniel *chemistry educator, researcher, consultant*

Placitas
Long, Timothy Scott *chemist, consultant*

Santa Fe
Cowan, George Arthur *chemist, bank executive, director*
Fisher, Robert Alan *laser physicist*
Gell-Mann, Murray *theoretical physicist, educator*
Giovanielli, Damon Vincent *physicist, consulting company executive*
Jones, Walter Harrison *chemist, educator*
Kropschot, Richard Henry *retired physicist, science laboratory administrator*
Leibowitz, Jack Richard *physicist, educator*
Lynn, John Eric *nuclear physics research consultant*
Romanowski, Thomas Andrew *physics educator*
Sayre, William O. *geologist, educator*
Stalker, James Raghi *meteorologist, environmental services administrator*
White, David Hywel *physics educator*

Socorro
Cardenas, Meinhard Bayani Ramos *hydrologist*
Scholle, Peter Allen *geologist, researcher*

Sunspot
Keil, Stephen Lesley *astrophysicist*

NEW YORK

Albany
Fakundiny, Robert Harry *geologist, educator, consultant*
Iyer, Seema *chemist*
Kim, Jai Soo *retired physicist*
Qi, Zhigang *materials scientist, chemist*
Rej, Robert *biochemist*
Schneider, Allan Stanford *biochemistry, neuroscience and pharmacology educator, biomedical research scientist*

Alfred
Pye, Lenwood David *materials science educator, researcher, consultant*
Wang, Xingwu *physics educator*

Alfred Station
Condrate, Robert Adam, Sr., *spectroscopy educator*

Amherst
Ismail, Abu Zafar Mohamed *physics educator, researcher, consultant*

Big Flats
Keck, Donald Bruce *physicist*

Binghamton
Coates, Donald Robert *geology educator, scientist*
Eisch, John Joseph *chemist, educator, writer, consultant*
Naslund, Howard Richard *geological science educator*
Nelson, Charles A. *physicist, educator*
Whittingham, M(ichael) Stanley *chemist*

Brewster
Blyakhman, Yefim Moisei *chemist, researcher*

Bronx
Friedman, Joel M. *biophysicist, educator*
Yalow, Rosalyn Sussman *nobel laureate, biophysicist*

Brookhaven
Kouts, Herbert John Cecil *retired physicist*

Brooklyn
Armenakas, Anthony Emmanuel *aerospace educator*
Castleman, Louis Samuel *metallurgist, educator*
Charton, Marvin *chemist, educator*
Choudhury, Deo Chand *physicist, researcher*
Eirich, Frederick Roland *chemist, educator*
Fleyshman, Bentsion *physicist, researcher, retired mathematician*
Franco, Victor *theoretical physics educator*
Friedman, Gerald Manfred *geologist, educator*
Izmailov, Alexander F. *physicist, mathematician, researcher*
Jivetin, Alexander *geophysicist, educator*
Karan, Hiroko Ito *organic chemistry educator*
Ma, Tsu Sheng *chemist, educator, consultant*
Mashkevich, Stefan Vladimirovich *physicist, researcher, computer scientist*
Mook, Sarah *retired chemist*
Rokhvarger, Anatoly Efim *materials science and ceramic technology scientist*
Shcherbakova, Estella *chemist, mathematician, educator*
Shedrinsky, Alexander Mikchail *chemistry professor, conservator, consultant*
Tamir, Theodor *electrophysics researcher, educator*
Weil, Edward David *chemistry researcher, consultant, educator*

Buffalo
Amborski, Leonard Edward *retired chemist*
Anbar, Michael *biophysics educator*
Baier, Robert Edward *chemist, educator*
Bardos, Thomas Joseph *chemist, educator*
Chiewanichakorn, Methee *research scientist*
Coppens, Philip *chemist*
Jain, Piyare Lal *physics educator*
Patel, Mulchand Shambhubhai *biochemist, researcher*
Reitan, Paul Hartman *geologist, educator*
Treanor, Charles Edward *scientist*
Tritsch, George Leopold *biochemist, educator, retired biomedical researcher*
Wang, Jui Hsin *biochemistry educator*

Canandaigua
Lowther, Frank Eugene *research physicist*

Chestnut Ridge
Huntoon, Robert Brian *chemist, food industry consultant*

Clinton
Ring, James Walter *physics educator*

Corning
Miller, Roger Allen *physicist*
Sala, Martin Andrew *biophysicist, inventor*
Stookey, Stanley Donald *chemist*
Visovsky, Nick John *research scientist*

Delmar
Matuszek, John Michael, Jr., *environmental scientist, educator, consultant*

East Hampton
Garrett, Charles Geoffrey Blythe *physicist, consultant*

Farmingdale
Nolan, Peter John *physics educator*

Flushing
Engel, Robert *chemist, educator, dean*
Finks, Robert Melvin *paleontologist, educator*
Goldman, Norman Lewis *chemistry professor*
Speidel, David Harold *geology educator*

Fredonia
Berkley, John L. *geology educator, meteoriticist*

Freeport
Pullman, Maynard Edward *biochemist*

Geneva
Roelofs, Wendell Lee *biochemistry educator, consultant*

Hannacroix
Schwebler, Stephen *retired chemist*

Hempstead
Wolff, Manfred Paul (Fred Paul Wolff) *geologist, educator, environmental scientist, consultant*
Zajac, Alfred *physicist, researcher*

Ithaca
Bassett, William Akers *geologist, educator, retired*
Bauer, Simon Harvey *chemistry professor*
Bauman, Dale Elton *nutritional biochemistry educator*
Berkelman, Karl *physics educator*
Bethe, Hans Albrecht *physicist, researcher*
Burns, Joseph Arthur *planetary science educator*
Craighead, Harold G. *physics educator*
Freed, Jack Herschel *chemist, educator*
Gierasch, Peter Jay *astronomy educator*
Ginsparg, Paul *physicist*
Goldsmith, Paul Felix *physics and astronomy educator*
Gottfried, Kurt *physicist, researcher*
Hart, Edward Walter *physicist*
Hess, George Paul *biochemist, educator*
Hoffmann, Roald *chemist, educator*
Holcomb, Donald Frank *physicist, academic administrator*
Isakovic, Abdel *physicist, researcher*
Kinoshita, Toichiro *physicist*
Lee, David Morris *physics educator*
Lee, Stephen *chemist, educator*
Liboff, Richard Lawrence *physicist, researcher*
Lumley, John Leask *physicist, researcher*
McMurry, John Edward *chemistry professor*
Mermin, N. David *physicist, researcher, writer*
Oliver, Jack Ertle *geophysicist, educator*
Pohl, Robert Otto *physics educator*
Richardson, Robert Coleman *physics educator, researcher*
Salpeter, Edwin Ernest *physical sciences educator*
Scheraga, Harold Abraham *physical chemistry educator*
Squyres, Steven Weldon *astronomy educator, planetary geology researcher*
Terzian, Yervant *astronomy and astrophysics educator*
Teukolsky, Saul *physicist, educator*
Widom, Benjamin *chemistry professor*
York, James Wesley, Jr., *theoretical physicist, educator*

Jamaica
Greenberg, Jacob *biochemist, educator, consultant*
Lengyel, István *chemist, educator*
Sun, Siao Fang *chemistry professor*

Latham
Lvovsky, Yuri *physicist, engineer*

Lewiston
Dexter, Theodore Henry *chemist*

Manlius
Brophy, Mary O'Reilly *environmental scientist*
Martonosi, Anthony Nicholas *biochemistry educator, researcher*

Melville
Damadian, Raymond Vahan *biophysicist*

New Rochelle
Margolin, Harold *metallurgical educator*

New York
Allison, Michael David *space scientist, astronomy educator*
Amols, Howard Ira *medical physicist*
Baker, William Oliver *retired research chemist*
Bederson, Benjamin *physicist, researcher*
Berne, Bruce J. *chemistry professor*
Birman, Joseph Leon *physics educator*
Bornmann, William Gerard *organic chemist*
Borowitz, Sidney *retired physics educator*
Boskey, Adele Ludin *biochemistry educator, researcher*
Breslow, Ronald Charles *chemist, educator*
Campbell, George, Jr., *physicist, administrator*
Chan, Siu-Wai *materials science educator*
Cheng, Chuen Yan *biochemist, educator*
Chevray, Rene *physics educator*
Cohen, Ezechiel Godert David *physicist, researcher*
Courant, Ernest David *physicist, educator*
Cross, George Alan Martin *biochemistry educator, researcher*
Danishefsky, Samuel J. *chemistry professor*
de Duve, Christian René *chemist, educator*
Demler, Frederick Russel *minerals economist, commodities broker*
Edelman, Isidore Samuel *biochemist, medical educator*
Eisenthal, Kenneth B. *physical chemistry educator*
Erlanger, Bernard Ferdinand *biochemist, educator*
Fraenkel, George Kessler *chemistry professor*
Goulianos, Konstantin *physics educator*
Haines, Thomas Henry *biochemist, educator, researcher*
Hajjar, David Phillip *biochemist, educator*
Hansen, James E. *physicist, meteorologist, federal agency administrator*
Harris, Cyril Manton *physicist, engineering and architecture educator, consulting acoustical engineer*
Hendrickson, Wayne A(rthur) *biochemist, educator*
Hoffert, Martin Irving *applied science educator*
Hoffman, Linda M. *chemist, educator*
Huang, Limin *chemist, researcher*
Kaku, Michio *theoretical nuclear physicist, educator*
Katsoyannis, Panayotis George *biochemist, educator*
Katz, Thomas J. *chemistry educator*
Khuri, Nicola Najib *physicist, researcher*
Krasna, Alvin Isaac *biochemist, educator*
Kuo, John Tsungfen *geophysicist, educator, researcher*
Lee, Tsung-Dao *physicist, researcher*
Lief, Eugene Paul *medical physicist*
Liu, Charles *astrophysicist*
Lubell, Michael Stephen *physicist, researcher, physics educator*
Mac Low, Mordecai-Mark *astrophysicist*
McKay, Kenneth Gardiner *physicist, electronics company executive*
Merrifield, Robert Bruce *biochemist, educator*
Mezei, Mihaly *chemist*
Middleton, David *physicist, applied mathematician, educator*
Nakanishi, Koji *chemistry educator, research institute administrator*
Newell, Norman Dennis *paleontologist, geologist, museum curator, educator*
Nickoloff, Edward Lee *radiology physicist*
Norell, Mark Allen *paleontology educator*
Oppenheimer, Ben R. *research scientist*
Oreskes, Irwin *biochemistry educator*
Pechukas, Philip *chemistry professor*
Percus, Jerome Kenneth *physicist, researcher*
Peskin, Charles *physicist, researcher*
Pinczuk, Aron *physicist*
Pokotilov, Andriy *physicist*
Ptashne, Mark Steven *biochemistry educator*
Rampino, Michael Robert *earth and environmental science educator*
Rhodes, Yorke E(dward) *organic chemist, educator*
Robinson, Enders Anthony *geophysicist, educator, writer*
Roeder, Robert Gayle *biochemist, molecular biologist, educator*
Russell, Charlotte Sananes *biochemistry educator, researcher*
Sarachik, Myriam Paula Morgenstein *physics educator*
Schwartz, Melvin *physics educator, laboratory administrator*
Scott, Willard Herman *meteorologist, newscaster*
Seeman, Nadrian Charles *chemistry professor*
Sidran, Miriam *retired physics educator, researcher*
Simon, Eric Jacob *neurochemist, educator*
Soter, Steven *research scientist*
Spielman, Andrew Ian *biochemist*
Srivastava, Shekhar *research scientist*
Stork, Gilbert *chemistry educator, investigator*
Störmer, Horst Ludwig *physicist*
Stroke, Hinko Henry *physicist, researcher*
tBreslow, Esther May Greenberg *biochemistry educator, researcher*
Turro, Nicholas John *chemistry professor*
Verdol, Joseph Arthur *chemist*
Wearne, Susan L *mathematical biology research scientist*
Werthamer, Nathan Richard *physicist*

Niagara Falls
Bharadwaj, Prem Datta *physics educator*
Knowles, Richard Norris *chemist*

Niskayuna
Edelheit, Lewis S. *research physicist*
Kambour, Roger Peabody *retired polymer physical chemist, researcher*
Katz, Samuel *geophysics educator*
White, Frederick Andrew *physics educator, physicist*

Northport
Allocca, John Anthony *medical research scientist*

Oneonta
Hickey, Francis Roger *physicist, researcher*
Horner, Carl Matthew *chemistry professor*
Merilan, Michael Preston *astrophysicist, educator, dean*

Orangeburg
Lajtha, Abel *biochemist*

Palisades
Broecker, Wallace S. *geophysics educator*
Cane, Mark Alan *oceanography and climate researcher*
Gordon, Arnold L. *oceanographer*
Hayes, Dennis Edward *geophysicist, educator*
Kellogg, Herbert Humphrey *metallurgist, educator*
Kent, Dennis V. *paleomagnetist, educator, researcher*
Nedimovic, Mladen *geophysicist*
Richards, Paul Granston *geophysics educator, seismologist*

Patchogue
Marr, Robert Bruce *physicist, researcher*

Pearl River
Barringer, William Charles *retired chemist*
Doedée, Marijo *chemist*

Peru
Dawson, James Clifford *environmental science educator, geologist*

Pittsford
Goldstein, David Arthur *biophysicist, educator*
Simon, Albert *physicist, engineer, educator*

Pomona
Gletsos, Constantine *chemist*

Potsdam
Fendler, Janos Hugo *chemistry professor*
Hopke, Philip Karl *chemical engineering educator, atmospheric scientist*
Islam, Muhammad Azadul *physicist, educator, researcher*
Mackay, Raymond Arthur *chemist*
Matijevic, Egon *chemistry professor*
Privman, Vladimir *physics educator*
Sokolov, Igor *physicist, researcher*

Poughkeepsie
Beck, Curt Werner *chemist, educator*
Deiters, Sister Joan Adele *psychoanalyst, nun, chemistry educator*
Lang, William Warner *physicist*
Pliskin, William Aaron *physicist*

Ridge
Blume, Martin *physicist*

Rochester
Basavappa, Ravi *biophysical scientist, educator*
Bigelow, Nicholas Pierre *physicist, researcher*
Boeckman, Robert Kenneth, Jr., *chemistry educator, organic chemistry researcher*
Buff, Frank Paul *chemist, educator*
Cain, B(urton) Edward *chemistry professor*
Conwell, Esther Marly *physicist, researcher*
Duarte, Francisco Javier *physicist, researcher*
Ferbel, Thomas *physics educator, physicist*
Gates, Marshall DeMotte, Jr., *chemistry educator*
Kampmeier, Jack August Carlos *chemist, educator*
Kende, Andrew Steven *chemist, educator*

Knauer, James Philip *physicist*
Knox, Robert Seiple *physicist, researcher*
La Celle, Paul Louis *biophysics educator*
Lever, O. William, Jr., *chemist*
Li, James Chen Min *materials science educator*
Makous, Walter Leon *visual scientist, educator*
Melissinos, Adrian Constantin *physicist, researcher*
Salamone, Joseph Charles *polymer chemistry educator*
Saunders, William Hundley, Jr., *retired chemist, educator*
Sherman, Fred *biochemist, educator*
Thomas, John Howard *astrophysicist, engineer, educator*
Thorndike, Edward Harmon *physicist*

Roslyn
Stein, Theodore Anthony *biochemist, educator*

Rouses Point
Weierstall, Richard Paul *retired pharmaceutical chemist*

Saint James
Bigeleisen, Jacob *chemist, educator*

Scarborough
Wittcoff, Harold Aaron *chemist*

Scarsdale
Porosoff, Harold *chemist, research and development director*

Schenectady
Frost, Robert Edwin *chemistry professor*
Philip, A. G. Davis *astronomer, editor, educator*

Sherburne
Dodd, Jack Gordon, Jr., *physicist, researcher*

South Setauket
Friedlander, Gerhart *nuclear chemist*

Southold
Bachrach, Howard L. *biochemist*

Spencerport
Vizy, Kalman Nicholas *research physicist, educator*

Staten Island
Yang, Song-Yu *research biochemist*

Stony Brook
Alexander, John Macmillan, Jr., *chemistry professor*
Asryan, Levon V. *physicist, electrical engineer, researcher*
Bokuniewicz, Henry Joseph *oceanography educator*
Bonner, Francis Truesdale *chemist, educator, university dean*
Brown, Gerald Edward *physicist, researcher*
Chen, JiuHua *physicist, geophysicist, educator*
Friedman, Harold Leo *chemistry professor*
Geller, Marvin Alan *meteorology educator, researcher*
Ojima, Iwao *chemistry educator*
Shrock, Robert E. *physicist, educator, research scientist*
Swanson, Robert Lawrence *oceanographer, academic program administrator*
Wurster, Charles Frederick *environmental scientist, educator*
Yang, Chen Ning *physicist, educator*

Syracuse
Baldwin, John Edwin *chemistry educator*
Birge, Robert Richards *chemistry professor*
Honig, Arnold *physics professor, researcher*
Levy, H. Richard *biochemistry educator*
Muller, Ernest H. *geology educator*
Prucha, John James *geologist, educator*
Sage, Martin Lee *chemistry professor*
Smith, Kenneth Judson, Jr., *chemist, theoretician, educator*

Troy
Ferris, James Peter *chemist, educator*
Giaever, Ivar *physicist*
Krause, Sonja *chemistry professor*
Levinger, Joseph Solomon *physicist, researcher*
Medicus, Heinrich Adolf *physicist, researcher*
Sperber, Daniel *physicist*
Willis, John Patrick *chemist*

Upton
Ben-Zvi, Ilan *physicist, educator*
Bond, Peter Danford *physicist*
Fowler, Joanna S. *chemist*
Goldhaber, Maurice *physicist, researcher*
Hendrie, Joseph Mallam *physicist, nuclear engineer, government official*
Lindenbaum, S(eymour) J(oseph) *physicist*
Lowenstein, Derek Irving *physicist*
Meinhold, Charles Boyd *health physicist*
Ozaki, Satoshi *physicist*
Ruggiero, Alessandro G. *physicist, researcher*
Samios, Nicholas Peter *physicist*
Setlow, Jane Kellock *biophysicist*
Setlow, Richard Burton *biophysicist, researcher*
Sutin, Norman *chemistry educator, scientist*
Tannenbaum, Michael J(ay) *physicist*

Webster
Zhang, Shengliang *materials scientist, physicist*

Wellsville
Van Tyne, Arthur Morris *geologist*

White Plains
Surpris, Joseph W. *research scientist*

Yorktown Heights
Avouris, Phaedon *chemical physicist*
Fowler, Alan Bicksler *retired physicist*
Keyes, Robert W. *physicist, researcher*
Kim, Hyungjun *materials scientist, researcher*
Lang, Norton David *physicist*
Sorokin, Peter Pitirimovich *physicist, researcher*
Tersoff, Jerry David *physicist*
Wu, Chai Wah *research scientist*

NORTH CAROLINA

Asheville
Easterling, David Royer *climatologist*
Haggard, William Henry *meteorologist*
Kessler, Donald Joe *research scientist, physicist, consultant*
Meyerson, Seymour *retired chemist*

Beaufort
Bonaventura, Celia Jean *biochemist, researcher*

Cary
Kung, Pang-Jen *materials scientist, electrical engineer*

Chapel Hill
Bursey, Maurice M. *chemistry professor*
Dolan, Louise Ann *physicist*
Eliel, Ernest Ludwig *chemist, educator*
Forman, Donald T. *biochemist, educator*
Frampton, Paul Howard *physics researcher, educator*
Irene, Eugene Arthur *physical chemistry and materials science educator, researcher*
Kim, Chong Soong *aerosol science and inhalation technology researcher*
Lee, Kuo-Hsiung *medicinal chemistry educator*
Ligett, Waldo Buford *chemist*
Macdonald, James Ross *physicist, researcher*
Merzbacher, Eugen *physicist, researcher*
Mitchell, Earl Nelson *physicist, researcher*
Neumann, Andrew Conrad *geological oceanography educator*
Parr, Robert Ghormley *chemistry professor*
Pedersen, Lee G. *chemistry educator*
Rogers, John James William *geology educator*
Shelton, Robert Neal *physics educator, researcher*
Slifkin, Lawrence Myer *physics educator*
Tsui, Frank *physicist, educator*
Wolfenden, Richard Vance *biochemistry educator*

Charlotte
Phambu, Nsoki *physical chemist, researcher*

Durham
Fridovich, Irwin *biochemistry educator*
Hammes, Gordon G. *chemistry professor*
Han, Moo-Young *physicist, educator*
Hobbs, Marcus Edwin *retired chemistry educator*
Jaszczak, Ronald Jack *physicist, researcher, consultant*
Joklik, Wolfgang Karl *biochemist, virologist, educator*
Meyer, Horst *physics educator*
Modrich, Paul L. *biochemistry educator*
Pearsall, George Wilbur *materials scientist, mechanical engineer, educator, consultant*
Perkins, Ronald Dee *geologist, educator*
Peterson, Max Rupert, Jr., *chemist, researcher*
Quinn, Jarus William *physicist, former association executive*
Roberson, Nathan Russell *physicist, researcher*
Smith, Peter *chemist, educator, consultant*
Walker, William D. *physicist, educator, researcher*
Walter, Richard Lawrence *physicist, researcher*

Fayetteville
Resnick, Paul R. *research chemist*

Greensboro
Clark, Clifton Bob *physicist*
Hageseth, Gaylord Terrence *physicist, educator*

Hendersonville
Saby, John Sanford *physicist, consultant*

Linwood
Barnes, Melver Raymond *retired chemist*

Pinehurst
Huizenga, John Robert *nuclear chemist, educator*

Raleigh
Aspnes, David Erik *physicist, researcher*
Bernholc, Jerzy *physicist, educator*
Cuculo, John A. *chemist, educator*
Cuomo, Jerome John *materials scientist*
Deihl, Susan Galyen *historic preservationist*
Mitchell, Gary Earl *physicist, researcher*
Oraefo, Johnny Ndubuisi *geologist, corporation executive, consultant*
Osteryoung, Janet Gretchen *chemistry professor*
Senzel, Alan Joseph *analytical chemistry consultant, music critic*
Sheng, Quan *chemist*
Swaisgood, Harold Everett *biochemist, educator*
Whitten, Jerry Lynn *chemistry professor*

Research Triangle Park
Fisher, Robert Perry *health effects scientist*
Pouliot, George A. *physical scientist, researcher*
Reynolds, Peter James *physicist*
Selkirk, James Kirkwood *biochemist, researcher*
Wani, Mansukhlal Chhaganlal *chemist*

Stella
Quin, Louis DuBose *chemist, educator*

Tryon
Mellberg, James Richard *dental research chemist*

Washington
Blackwell, F. Oris *environmental scientist, educator*

Wilmington
Bissette, Samuel Delk *astronomer, artist, financial executive*
Cooper, William James *chemist*
Kelley, Patricia Hagelin *geology educator*

Winston Salem
Mokrasch, Lewis Carl *neurochemist, educator*
Rodgman, Alan *chemist, consultant*

NORTH DAKOTA

Fargo
Tallman, Dennis Earl *chemistry professor, research scientist*
Wagner, Alexander Johannes *physicist, educator*

Grand Forks
Hoffmann, Mark R. *physical chemist, educator*
Jacobs, Francis Albin *biochemist, educator*
Nordlie, Robert Conrad *biochemistry educator*

OHIO

Akron
Gent, Alan Neville *physicist, researcher*
Kennedy, Joseph Paul *chemist, researcher*
Sahoo, Sangrama Kesari *physical chemist, researcher*

Athens
Dewald, Howard Dean *chemistry educator, researcher*

Beavercreek
Gupta, Vijay Kumar *retired chemistry professor*

Centerburg
Reynolds, Don William *geologist*

Chardon
Uscheek, David Petrovich *retired chemist*

Cincinnati
Alexander, John J. *chemistry professor*
Bobst, Albert *chemistry professor*
Briskin, Madeleine *paleo-oceanographer, paleoclimatologist, micropaleontologist*
Federle, Thomas W. *environmental scientist, microbiologist*
Francis, Marion David *consulting chemist*
Goodman, Bernard *physics educator*
Iroh, Jude Onwuegbu *chemistry professor*
Jensen, Elwood Vernon *biochemist*
Kawahara, Fred Katsumi *research chemist*
Meal, Larie *chemistry educator, researcher, consultant*
Merchant, Mylon Eugene *physicist, engineer*
Mukerjee, Debdas *environmental health scientist, educator*
Putnam, Frank William *biochemistry and immunology educator*
Relyea, Carl Miller *retired hydrologist*
Schaefer, Dale W. *physicist, researcher, administrator*
Sullivan, James F. *physicist, researcher*
Utegulov, Zhandos N. *research scientist*
Witten, Louis *physics educator*

Cleveland
Bidelman, William Pendry *astronomer, educator*
Brown, Robert William *physics educator, physicist*
Carey, Paul Richard *biophysicist*
Chamis, Christos Constantinos *aerospace scientist, educator*
Deissler, Robert George *fluid dynamicist, researcher*
Dowell, Michael Brendan *chemist*
Hanson, Richard Winfield *biochemist, educator*
Huterer, Dragon *physicist*
Klopman, Gilles *chemistry professor*
Koenig, Jack L. *chemist, educator*
Kowalski, Kenneth Lawrence *physicist, researcher*
Krieger, Irvin Mitchell *chemistry professor, consultant*
Landau, Bernard Robert *biochemistry educator, physician*
Lando, Jerome Burton *macromolecular science educator*
Mawardi, Osman Kamel *plasma physicist*
Rogers, Charles Edwin *physical chemistry educator*
Schuele, Donald Edward *physics educator*
Slobozhanin, Lev Arkadievich *fluid mechanics researcher*
Zhang, Nengli *thermophysics scientist*
Zhu, Dongming *materials scientist*

Columbus
Adelson, Edward *physicist, educator, musician*
Behrman, Edward Joseph *biochemistry educator*
Bergstrom, Stig Magnus *geology educator*
Chisholm, Malcolm Harold *chemistry professor*
Corbato, Charles Edward *geology educator*
Cornwell, David George *biochemist, educator*
Daehn, Glenn Steven *materials scientist*
Elliot, David Hawksley *geologist, educator*
Faure, Gunter *geology educator*
Firestone, Richard Francis *chemistry professor*
Foland, Kenneth A. *geological sciences educator*
Goodridge, Alan Gardner *research biochemist, educator*
Ling, Ta-Yung *physicist*
Madia, William Juul *chemist*
Mayer, Victor James *geologist, educator*
Mehta, Kamal Deep *biochemistry educator, molecular biology educator*
Milford, Frederick John *retired research company executive*
Min, David B. *chemist, educator, research scientist*
Newsom, Gerald Higley *astronomy educator*
Preobrazhensky, Alexander Anatoliyevich *biochemist*
Reibel, Kurt *physicist, researcher*
Relle, Ferenc Matyas *chemist*
Soloway, Albert Herman *medicinal chemist*
Sullivan, Kathryn D. *geologist, former astronaut*
Wali, Mohan Kishen *environmental science and natural resources educator*
Wilkins, John Warren *physics educator*
Wojcicki, Andrew Adalbert *chemist, educator*

Copley
Hayasi, Nisiki *physicist, applied mathematician, business executive, inventor*

Dayton
Battino, Rubin *retired chemistry professor*
Emrick, Donald Day *chemist, consultant*
Nielsen, Philip Edward *physicist, research manager*
Patton, Steven Todd *research physicist*

Fairborn
Workman, John Mitchell *chemist*

Hamilton
Cantrell, Joseph Sires *chemistry professor*

Kent
Myers, R(alph) Thomas *chemist, educator*

Kettering
Clark, Leland Charles, Jr., *biochemist, medical products executive*

Mansfield
Gibson, David Mark *biochemist, educator*

Marietta
Jache, Albert William *retired chemistry educator, scientist*
Putnam, Robert Ervin *chemist, consultant*

Middletown
Marine, Susan Sonchik *analytical chemist, educator*

New Albany
Williams, James Case *metallurgist*

Norwalk
Germann, Richard P(aul) *consultant, pharmaceutical company chemist, executive*

Norwood
Jones, Robert W. *health physics and radiochemistry consultant*

Oberlin
Carlton, Terry Scott *chemist, educator*
Singer, Leonard S. *chemist, research scientist, consultant*
Warner, Robert Edson *physics educator*
Weinstock, Robert *physics educator*

Oxford
Cox, James Allan *chemistry professor*
Gordon, Gilbert *chemist, educator*
Macklin, Philip Alan *physics educator*
Yang, Kewu *chemist*

Sheffield Village
Herdendorf, Charles Edward, III, *oceanographer, limnologist, consultant*

Stow
Kim, Kwang-Jea *research scientist, polymer engineer*

Toledo
Ivanov, Alexander V. *biochemist, researcher*
Miroshnichenko, Anatoly S. *astronomer, researcher*

Walton Hills
Elliott, Stanley B. *chemist, researcher*

West Chester
Mack, Mark Philip *chemical company executive*

Wickliffe
Dunn, Horton, Jr., *organic chemist*
Krause, Marjorie N. *biochemist*

Wright Patterson Afb
Fernelius, Nils Conard *physicist*
Garscadden, Alan *physicist*

Yellow Springs
Spokane, Robert Bruce *biophysical chemist*

Youngstown
Zitto, Richard Joseph *physics educator*

OKLAHOMA

Ada
Stafford, Donald Gene *chemistry professor*

Bartlesville
Dwiggins, Claudius William, Jr., *chemist*
Hogan, John Paul *chemistry researcher, consultant*

Lawton
Nalley, Elizabeth Ann *chemistry professor*

Norman
Bluestein, Howard Bruce *meteorology educator*
Cowan, John James *physicist, educator, astronomer, educator*
Houser, Robert P., Jr., *chemist, educator*
Kessler, Edwin *meteorology educator, consultant*
Lamb, Peter James *meteorology educator, researcher, consultant*
Magarian, Robert Armen *medicinal chemist, researcher, educator, author, inventor*
Pigott, John Dowling *geologist, geophysicist, geochemist, educator, consultant*

Oklahoma City
Alaupovic, Petar *biochemist, educator*
England, Gary Alan *television meteorologist*
Johnson, B(ruce) Connor *biochemist, educator, consultant*
Troutman, George William *geologist, petroleum geological advisor*
Weigel, Paul Henry *biochemistry educator, researcher, consultant*
Zhao, Wei (Wayne) *materials scientist, researcher, transmission electron microscopist*
Zhu, Hua *biochemist, researcher*

Skiatook
Harwell, Kenneth E. *chemist, researcher, consultant*

Stillwater
Berlin, Kenneth Darrell *chemistry educator, consultant, researcher*
Melcher, Ulrich Karl *biochemistry educator*
Sherman, Robert Lee, Jr., *chemist, educator*
Wicksted, James Peter *physicist, educator, research scientist*

Tulsa
Blais, Roger Nathaniel *physics educator*
Busch, Daniel Adolph *geologist, educator*

OREGON

Ashland
Addicott, Warren Oliver *retired geologist, educator*

Espinoza, Edgard O'Niel *forensic chemist*
Goddard, Kenneth William *forensic scientist, writer*
Grover, James Robb *chemist, editor*

Beaverton
Wang, Baoliang (Bob Wang) *applications scientist, researcher*

Corvallis
Baird, William McKenzie *chemical carcinogenesis researcher, biochemistry educator*
Dalrymple, Gary Brent *research geologist*
Drake, Charles Whitney *physicist*
Huyer, Adriana *oceanographer, educator*
Karplus, Paul Andrew *biochemistry educator*
Mathews, Christopher King *biochemist, educator*
McKinney, William Mark *retired geology educator*
Sleight, Arthur William *chemist, educator*
Van Holde, Kensal Edward *biochemistry educator*
Whanger, Philip Daniel *biochemistry educator and researcher, nutrition educator*
Yeats, Robert Sheppard *geologist, educator*

Dallas
White, Donald Harvey *physics educator emeritus*

Eugene
Crasemann, Bernd *physicist, researcher*
Csonka, Paul L. *theoretical physicist, educator*
Donnelly, Russell James *physicist, researcher*
Griffith, Osbie Hayes *chemistry professor*
Mazo, Robert Marc *retired chemistry educator*
Retallack, Gregory John *geologist, educator*
Schellman, John A. *chemistry professor*
von Hippel, Peter Hans *chemistry educator, molecular biology researcher*
Youngquist, Walter Lewellyn *geologist, consultant*

Lincoln City
Daves, Glenn Doyle, Jr., *science educator, chemist, researcher*

Portland
Claycomb, Cecil Keith *biochemist, educator*
Hammond, George Simms *chemist, consultant*
Lincoln, Sandra Eleanor *chemistry professor*
Pearson, David Petri *chemist*
Quigley, Thomas *research scientist*
Viator, John A. *biomedical physicist, military officer*
Weeks, Wilford Frank *retired geophysics educator, glaciologist*

Salem
Gillette, P. Roger *physicist, systems engineer*

PENNSYLVANIA

Abington
Schuster, Ingeborg Ida *chemistry professor*

Alcoa Center
Ray, Siba Prasad *materials scientist, ceramics scientist*

Allentown
Goldey, James Mearns *retired physicist*
Orphanides, Gus George *licensing executive*
Pinschmidt, Robert Krantz, Jr., *chemist, researcher*

Berwyn
Devlin, Thomas McKeown *biochemist, educator*

Bethlehem
Alhadeff, Jack Abraham *biochemist, educator*
Ghadiali, Samir N. *research scientist, educator*
Heindel, Ned Duane *chemistry professor*
Herman, Richard Gerald *research chemist, consultant, educator*
Kanofsky, Alvin Sheldon *physics educator*
Lyman, Charles Edson *materials scientist, educator*
Smyth, Donald Morgan *chemical educator, researcher*

Blue Bell
Wilson, H(arold) Fred(erick) *chemist, research scientist*

Bryn Mawr
Crawford, Maria Luisa Buse *geology educator*

Carlisle
Laws, Kenneth L. *physics educator, author*
Long, Howard Charles *physics educator emeritus*

Chadds Ford
Webster, Owen Wright *chemist*

Danville
Chan, Yiumo *biochemist*

Doylestown
Brink, Frank, Jr., *biophysicist, former educator*

Feasterville
Dickstein, Jack *chemist*

Gladwyne
Fenichel, Richard Lee *retired biochemist*

Gouldsboro
Nass, Leonard Ira *chemist, consultant*

Harrisburg
Stanley, Edward Alexander *geologist, forensic scientist, technical and academic administrator*

Haverford
Roelofs, Lyle Dean *physicist, researcher*

Hazleton
Miller, David Emanuel *physics educator, researcher*

Huntingdon
Trexler, John Peter *retired geology educator, researcher*

Huntingdon Valley
Godfrey, John Carl *medicinal chemist*

Johnstown
Brice, William Riley *geology educator, planetary science educator*

Kennett Square
Lippincott, Sarah Lee *astronomer, graphologist*

Lehman
Felty, Wayne Lee *chemist, educator*

Lincoln University
Williams, Willie, Jr., *physicist, researcher*

Media
Voltz, Sterling Ernest *physical chemist, researcher*

Mount Joy
Lodde, Gordon Maynard *health physics consultant*

New Hope
Rodwell, John Dennis *biochemist*

Newtown
Long, Harry (On-Yuen Eng) *chemist, science and technology executive, consultant*

Norristown
Whittington, Cathy Dee *chemist*

Oakdale
Wang, Chuan-Bao *chemist, research scientist*

Philadelphia
Ajzenberg-Selove, Fay *physicist, researcher*
Chance, Britton *biophysics and physical chemistry educator emeritus*
Childress, Scott Julius *medicinal chemist*
Cohn, Mildred *biochemist, educator*
Dalton, David Robert *chemistry professor*
Davis, Raymond, Jr., *physical chemistry researcher*
Dutton, P(eter) Leslie *biochemist, educator*
Dymicky, Michael *retired chemist*
Fitts, Donald Dennis *chemist, educator*
Frankel, Sherman *physicist, educator*
Glusker, Jenny Pickworth *chemist*
Gogotsi, Yury *materials science educator*
Hameka, Hendrik Frederik *chemist, educator*
Hirschmann, Ralph Franz *chemist*
Hossain, Murshed *physicist, researcher*
Kachur, Alexander Victor *chemist*
Kricka, Larry J. *chemistry professor*
Kritchevsky, David *biochemist, educator*
Langacker, Paul George *physics educator*
Levitt, Israel Monroe *retired astronomer*
Liebman, Paul Arno *biophysicist, educator*
MacDiarmid, Alan Graham *metallurgist, educator*
Malamud, Daniel *biochemistry educator*
Marinelli, Joseph Marcello *aerospace advisor*
Noordergraaf, Abraham *biophysics educator*
Scandura, Joseph Michael *cognitive scientist, software engineer*
Shen, Benjamin Shih-Ping *scientist, engineer, educator*
Vitek, Vaclav *materials scientist*
Wales, Walter D. *physicist, researcher*

Pittsburgh
Asher, Sanford Abraham *chemist, educator*
Berry, Guy Curtis *polymer science educator, researcher*
Biondi, Manfred Anthony *physicist, researcher*
Carr, Walter James, Jr., *research physicist, consultant*
Cassidy, William Arthur *geology and planetary science educator*
Choyke, Wolfgang Justus *physicist*
Cohen, Bernard Leonard *physicist, researcher*
Coltman, John Wesley *physicist*
Emmerich, Werner Sigmund *physicist, educator*
Feller, Robert Livingston *chemist, art conservation scientist*
Fetkovich, John G. *physics educator*
Gerjuoy, Edward *physicist, lawyer*
Griffiths, Robert Budington *physics educator*
Itkin, Ivan *nuclear scientist, applied mathematician*
Klein-Seetharaman, Judith *biochemist*
Kuksenok, Olga *physicist, researcher*
Kumta, Prashant Nagesh *materials science educator, engineering educator, consultant*
Laughlin, David Eugene *materials science educator, metallurgical consultant*
Leney, George Willard *retired consulting engineer*
Maher, James Vincent, Jr., *physics educator*
Massalski, Thaddeus Bronislaw *materials scientist, educator*
Matyjaszewski, Krzysztof *chemist, educator*
Nagle, John Frederick *physicist*
Page, Lorne Albert *physicist, researcher*
Plazek, Donald John *materials scientist, educator*
Rosenberg, Jerome Laib *chemist, educator*
Ruddy, Francis (Frank) Henry *nuclear physicist*
Sashin, Donald *pet physicist, radiological physicist, educator*
Sekerka, Robert Floyd *physics educator, scientist*
Shapiro, Zalman Mordecai *chemist, consultant*
White, Robert Marshall *physicist, government official, educator*
Yates, John Thomas, Jr., *chemistry educator, research director*
Young, Hugh David *physics educator, writer, organist*

Pottstown
Hergert, Herbert Lawrence *consultant*

Rosemount
Berliner, Ernst *retired chemistry professor*

Saint Marys
Sorg, David Joseph *materials physicist*

Scranton
Marx, David Earl *chemistry professor, consultant*

South Park
Lotze, Barbara *retired physicist*

Spring House
Hann, William Mathis *chemist, researcher*

State College
Garrett, Steven Lurie *physicist*
German, Randall Michael *materials engineering educator, consultant*
Ginoza, William *former biophysics educator*
Roy, Della Martin *materials science educator, researcher*
Schmalz, Robert Fowler *geology educator*

Swarthmore
Bilaniuk, Oleksa Myron *physicist, researcher*
Pasternack, Robert Francis *chemistry professor*

University Park
Allcock, Harry R. *chemistry professor*
Badding, John Victor *chemistry professor*
Barnes, Hubert Lloyd *geochemistry educator*
Benkovic, Stephen James *chemist*
Blackadar, Alfred Kimball *meteorologist, educator*
Cahir, John Joseph *meteorologist, educational administrator*
Castleman, Albert Welford, Jr., *physical chemist, educator*
Collins, John Clements *physicist, researcher*
Dutton, John Altnow *meteorologist, educator*
Garrison, Barbara Jane *chemistry professor*
Hosler, Charles Luther, Jr., *meteorologist, educator*
Howell, Benjamin Franklin, Jr., *geophysicist, educator*
Jackman, Lloyd Miles *chemistry professor*
Kasting, James Fraser *research meteorologist, physicist*
Liu, Zi-Kui *materials science and engineering educator*
Ma, Xiaoliang *research scientist*
Mahan, Gerald Dennis *physics educator, researcher*
Mészáros, Peter Istvan *astrophysicist, researcher, astronomy educator*
Ross, A. Catharine *biochemist, educator*
Roy, Rustum *interdisciplinary educator, materials researcher*
Song, Chunshan *chemist, chemical engineer, educator*
White, William Blaine *geochemist, researcher*
Winograd, Nicholas *chemist*

Valley Forge
Erb, Robert Allan *physical scientist*

Villanova
Edwards, John Ralph *retired chemist, educator*
Phares, Alain Joseph *physicist, researcher*

Wayne
Kauffman, Joel Mervin *chemistry educator, researcher, consultant*

Waynesburg
Maguire, Mildred May *chemistry educator, magnetic resonance researcher*

West Point
Farber, Leonid *materials scientist*

Wexford
Bossart, Paul Nathaniel, Jr., *geologist, geophysicist, consultant*

Willow Grove
Sundar, Veeraraghavan V. *materials scientist*

Wyndmoor
Fishman, Marshall Lewis *chemist*
Marmer, William N. *chemist, researcher*
Pfeffer, Philip Elliot *biophysicist*

Wynnewood
Rosen, Gerald Harris *physicist, consultant, educator*

Yardley
Yee, David *chemist*

RHODE ISLAND

East Greenwich
Carlson, Shawn Eric *physicist*

Kingston
Nixon, Scott West *oceanography science educator*

Narragansett
Pilson, Michael Edward Quinton *oceanography educator*

Newport
Galivan, John Henry *biochemist, educator, public health officer, research administrator*

Providence
Avery, Donald Hills *metallurgist, educator, ethnographer*
Briant, Clyde Leonard *metallurgist, educator*
Carpenter, Gene Blakely *crystallography and chemistry educator*
Cooper, Leon N. *physicist, researcher*
Dahlberg, Albert Edward *biochemistry educator*
Elbaum, Charles *physicist, educator, researcher*
Gerritsen, Hendrik Jurjen *physics educator, researcher*
Lanou, Robert Eugene, Jr., *physicist, researcher*
Levin, Frank S. *physicist, researcher*
Pieters, Carle McGetchin *geology educator, planetary scientist, researcher*
Stratt, Richard Mark *chemistry researcher, educator*
Tauc, Jan *physics educator*
Widgoff, Mildred *physicist, researcher*

Wakefield
Moore, George Emerson, Jr., *geologist, educator*

SOUTH CAROLINA

Aiken
Dickson, Paul Wesley, Jr., *physicist*

Anderson
Elzerman, Alan William *environmental chemistry educator*

Clemson
Beyerlein, Adolph Louis *retired chemist, educator*
Clayton, Donald Delbert *astrophysicist, nuclear physicist, educator*
Krause, Lois Ruth Breur *chemistry educator*

Columbia
Farber, Emmanuel *pathology and biochemistry educator*
Nagpal, Madan Lal *biochemist, educator, researcher*
Profeta, Salvatore, Jr., *chemist*
Secor, Donald Terry, Jr., *geologist, educator*
Shafer, John Milton *hydrologist, consultant, software developer*
Tarakji, Ahmad Houssam *research scientist, electrical engineer*

Johns Island
Norton, Norman James *retired exploration geologist, educator*

Mount Pleasant
Thordarson, William *retired hydrogeologist*

SOUTH DAKOTA

Rapid City
Smith, Paul Letton, Jr., *geophysicist*

Sioux Falls
Viste, Arlen Ellard *chemistry professor*

Spearfish
Erickson, Richard Ames *physicist, emeritus educator*

TENNESSEE

Brentwood
Heiser, Arnold Melvin *astronomer*

Clinton
Hutchens, Gail R. *chemist*

Cookeville
Kumar, Krishna *retired physics educator*

Fayetteville
Wolfhard, Hans Georg *research scientist*

Greenback
Weeks, Robert Andrew *materials science researcher, educator*

Johnson City
Kasmai, Hamid Saleh *chemistry educator, researcher, consultant*

Knoxville
Alexeff, Igor *physicist, electrical engineer, educator emeritus*
Gentry, Robert Vance *physicist, researcher, writer*
Ghosh, Narendra Nath *research scientist*
Grossbeck, Martin Lester *metallurgist*
Nayak, Subhadarshi *research scientist*
Renshaw, Amanda Frances *retired physicist, nuclear engineer*
Schweitzer, George Keene *chemistry professor*
Song, Ping *research scientist, educator*
Williams, Thomas Ffrancon *chemist, educator*
Wunderlich, Bernhard *physical chemistry educator*

Memphis
Crane, Laura Jane *retired chemist*
Desiderio, Dominic Morse, Jr., *chemistry and neurochemistry educator*
Fain, John Nicholas *biochemistry educator*
Jernigan, Howard Maxwell, Jr., *biochemistry educator, researcher*
Lasslo, Andrew *medicinal chemist, educator*
Mishra, Sanjay R *physicist*

Nashville
Bayuzick, Robert J. *materials scientist, educator*
Chappell, Charles Richard *space scientist*
Chytil, Frank *biochemist*
Cunningham, Leon William *biochemist, educator*
Dettbarn, Wolf-Dietrich *neurochemist, pharmacologist, educator*
Feldman, Leonard Cecil *physicist*
Fort, Tomlinson *chemist, chemical engineering educator*
Hamilton, Joseph Hants, Jr., *physicist, researcher*
Hercules, David Michael *chemistry professor, consultant*
Inagami, Tadashi *biochemistry educator*
Lukehart, Charles Martin *chemistry professor*
Roos, Charles Edwin *physicist*
Silberman, Enrique *physics researcher and administrator*
Surowiec, Andrew Julius *biophysicist, researcher*
Wert, James Junior *materials scientist, educator*

Oak Ridge
Borie, Bernard Simon, Jr., *retired physicist, educator*
Carlsmith, Roger Snedden *chemistry and energy conservation researcher*
Dickens, Justin Kirk *nuclear physicist*
George, Easo Pulinthitta *materials scientist, educator*
Hartman, Frederick Cooper *biochemist, researcher*
Hu, Zhiyu *research scientist, educator*
Kosacki, Igor *physicist, educator*
Krause, Manfred Otto *physicist*
Larson, Bennett Charles *solid state physicist, researcher*
Maienschein, Fred *retired physicist*
Manly, William Donald *metallurgist*
Mullins, David Roy *chemist, researcher*
Paranthaman, Mariappan Parans *research scientist*
Plasil, Franz *physicist*
Postma, Herman *physicist, consultant*
Protopopescu, Vladimir Alexandru *research scientist, educator*
Shishlo, Andrei Petrovich *physicist, researcher*
Watson, Evelyn Egner *radiation scientist*
Weinberg, Alvin Martin *physicist*
Xu, Yongli *research scientist*
Young, Jack Phillip *chemist*
Zucker, Alexander *physicist, administrator*

Signal Mountain
Howe, Lyman Harold, III, *chemist, researcher*

TEXAS

Arlington
Kirk, Wiley Price, Jr., *physics and electrical engineering educator*
Shanmugam, Ganapathy *geologist, researcher*
Smith, Charles Isaac *geology educator*
Willoughby, Sarah-Margaret C. *chemist, educator, chemical engineer, consultant*

Austin
Bard, Allen Joseph *chemist, educator*
Bash, Frank Ness *astronomer, educator*
Bengtson, Roger Dean *physicist, department chairman*
Boggs, James Ernest *chemistry professor*
Clark, Roy Thomas, Jr., *retired chemistry professor, academic administrator*
DeWitt-Morette, Cécile *physicist*
Duncombe, Raynor Lockwood *astronomer*
Erskine, James Lorenzo *physics educator*
Fisher, William Lawrence *geologist, educator*
Folk, Robert Louis *geologist, educator*
Folkers, Karl August *chemistry professor*
Fonken, Gerhard Joseph *retired chemistry educator, academic administrator*
Gentle, Kenneth William *physicist*
Griffy, Thomas Alan *physics educator*
Hazeltine, Richard Deimel *physics educator, university institute director*
Hilburn, John Charles *geologist, geophysicist*
Hurley, Laurence Harold *medicinal chemistry educator*
Lagow, Richard James *chemistry professor*
Mark, Hans Michael *physicist, government official*
Martin, Stephen F. *chemist, educator, researcher*
Maxwell, Arthur Eugene *oceanographer, marine geophysicist, educator*
Mear, Charles Eugene *geologist, consultant*
Mooney, John Bradford, Jr., *oceanographer, engineer, consultant*
Phillips, Joseph Daniel *geophysicist, oceanographer*
Reed, Lester James *biochemist, educator*
Stewart, Kent Kallam *analytical biochemistry educator*
Tatham, Robert Haines *geophysicist, educator*
Udagawa, Takeshi *physicist, researcher*
Wheeler, John Craig *astrophysicist, writer*
White, John Michael *chemistry educator*
Williams, Calvit Herndon *retired chemist*
Willson, C. Grant *chemistry educator, engineering educator*
Yu, Roger Hong *physics educator*
Zeng, Hongliu Henry *geophysicist, geologist*
Ziegler, Daniel Martin *chemistry professor*

Baytown
Waddell, Walter Harvey *chemist*

Beaumont
Bahrim, Cristian *physicist, educator*

Carrollton
Wang, Peter Zhenming *physicist*

College Station
Arnowitt, Richard Lewis *physics educator, researcher*
Berg, Robert Raymond *geologist, educator*
Conway, Dwight Colbur *chemistry professor*
Cotton, Frank Albert *chemist, educator*
Darensbourg, Marcetta York *chemistry professor*
Eaton, Gordon Pryor *geologist, consultant*
Goodman, David Wayne *research chemist, educator*
Hardy, John Christopher *physicist, researcher*
Laane, Jaan *chemistry professor*
McIntyre, John Armin *physics educator*
Mohamed, Ahmed A. *chemist, researcher*
Nachman, Ronald James *research chemist*
Natowitz, Joseph B. *chemistry educator, research administrator*
O'Connor, Rod *chemist, consultant, inventor*
Prescott, John Mack *biochemist, retired university administrator*
Reid, Robert Osborne *oceanographer*
Scott, Alastair Ian *chemistry professor*
Wild, James Robert *biochemistry and genetics educator*

Conroe
Nachman, Joseph Frank *retired metallurgical consultant*

Dallas
Brooks, James Elwood *geologist, educator*
Estabrook, Ronald Winfield *chemistry professor*
Frank, Steven Neil *chemist*
Gibbs, James Alanson *geologist*
Marshall, John Harris, Jr., *geologist, oil company executive*
Ray, Bradley Stephen *petroleum geologist*
Ries, Edward Richard *petroleum geologist, consultant*
Sharp, William Wheeler *geologist*
Singer, Robert W. *metallurgist, company executive officer*
Tucker, J. Walter, Jr., *steel manufacturing executive*
Wheeler, Edward Norwood *chemical consultant*
Woolley, Bryan (Lowell Bryan Woolley) *author, journalist*

Denton
Chang, Yongbin *physicist*
Smith, H. Morgan *environmental scientist, educator*

Edinburg
Hannan, Mohammad A. *physicist, researcher*

El Paso
Bang, John Jongchun *environmental scientist, researcher*

Fort Worth
Bailey, James Stephen *scientist*
Caldwell, Billy Ray *geologist*
Quarles, Carroll Adair, Jr., *physicist, researcher*
Reinecke, Manfred G. *chemistry professor*
Webb, Theodore Stratton, Jr., *aerospace scientist, consultant*

Galveston
Balaban, Alexandru T. *chemistry educator, researcher*
Gorenstein, David G. *chemistry and biochemistry educator*
Kurosky, Alexander *biochemist, educator*
Schoenbucher, Bruce *health physicist*

Houston
Abbey, George W. S. *space center executive*
Adams, W. Wade *research scientist*
Anderson, Richard Carl *geophysical exploration company executive*
Askew, William Earl *chemist, educator*
Baker, Stephen Denio *physics educator*
Bally, Albert W. *retired petroleum geologist, geology educator*
Black, David Charles *astrophysicist*
Bonner, Billy Edward *physics educator*
Brandt, I. Marvin *chemist, engineer*
Brotzen, Franz Richard *materials scientist, educator*
Burke, Kevin Charles Antony *geologist*
Chu, Paul Ching-Wu *physicist, educator*
Chu, Wei-Kan *physicist, researcher*
Curl, Robert Floyd, Jr., *chemistry professor*
Freeman, John Clinton *meteorologist, oceanographer*
Freeman, John W. *astrophysicist, educator*
Gibson, Everett Kay, Jr., *space scientist, geochemist*
Goloby, George William, Jr., *environmental scientist, editor*
Hackerman, Norman *chemist, academic administrator*
Halbouty, Michel Thomas *geologist, petroleum engineer, petroleum operator*
Hoffman, Ronald Bruce *biophysicist, life scientist, consultant*
Hor, Pei Herng *physicist, educator*
Hulet, Randall Gardner *physics educator*
Hursan, Gabor *geophysicist*
Hussain, Moinuddin Syed *geologist, engineer, consultant*
Kinsey, James Lloyd *chemist, educator*
Kit, Saul *biochemist, educator*
Kochi, Jay Kazuo *chemist, educator*
Kolla, Venkatarathnam *geologist, consultant*
Kouri, Donald Jack *chemist, educator*
Lane, Neal Francis *physics educator, former government official*
Levy, Eugene Howard *planetary sciences educator, researcher*
Lewis, Edward Sheldon *chemistry professor*
Liang, Edison Parktak *astrophysicist, educator, researcher*
Liu, Lumei *chemistry researcher*
Lucid, Shannon W. *biochemist, astronaut*
Mackwell, Stephen Joseph *geophysicist, educator*
Martirosyan, Karen *research scientist*
Matthews, Kathleen Shive *biochemistry educator*
McCleary, Henry Glen *geophysicist*
Mendelson, Robert Allen *polymer scientist, rheologist*
Meng, Ru-Ling *research scientist*
Nemphos, Speros P. *chemist, consultant*
Nordlander, Peter Jan Arne *physics educator, researcher*
Reiff, Patricia Hofer *space physicist, educator*
Reso, Anthony *geologist, educator, earth resources economist*
Scuseria, Gustavo Enrique *theoretical chemist*
Sercombe, William John *geologist*
Slaugh, Lynn H. *chemist*
Smalley, Richard Errett *chemistry and physics educator, researcher*
Talwani, Manik *geophysicist, educator*
Vilas, Faith *aerospace scientist*
Viswanathan, Gopalakrishnan *metallurgist, researcher*
Wei, Ying *chemist*
Weinstein, Roy *physics educator, researcher*
Wilson, Thomas Leon *physicist, researcher*
Yang, Chao Yuh *chemistry professor, medical educator*

Humble
Brinkley, Charles Alexander *geologist*

Irving
Hendrickson, Constance Marie McRight *chemist, consultant*
Holdar, Robert Martin *chemist*

Kerrville
Shaw, Alan Bosworth *geologist, paleontologist*
Sparks, Don Bertrand *retired geophysicist*

Kingsville
Chang, Ni-Bin *environmental pollution control educator*

Lubbock
Adamcik, Joe Alfred *retired chemistry educator, retired attorney*
Everse, Johannes *biochemist, researcher*
Laing, Malcolm Brian *geologist, consultant*
Viatchenko-Karpinski, Serge *biophysicist, researcher*

Midland
Berner, Leo De Witte, Jr., *retired oceanographer*
Hord, John Alan *geological engineer*

New Braunfels
Wilson, James Lee *retired geology educator, consultant*

Pasadena
Root, M. Belinda *chemist*

Richardson
Manton, William Inwood *geologist, educator*
Rutford, Robert Hoxie *geologist, educator*

Rowlett
Patterson, Edward Palmer *retired physical scientist*

San Antonio
Anderson, Brooks Doran, II, *geologist, consultant*
Budalur, Thyagarajan Subbanarayan *chemistry professor*
Burton, Russell Rohan *aerospace scientist, researcher*
Cragnolino, Gustavo Adolfo *research scientist*
Denny, John Bernard *biochemist, educator*
Dinwiddie, Cynthia L. *geologist*
Lyle, Robert Edward *chemist*
Markwell, Dick R(obert) *retired chemist*
Masters, Bettie Sue Siler *biochemist, educator*
Pensado, Osvaldo *research scientist*
Rafelson, Max Emanuel, Jr., *biochemist, medical school administrator*
Sablik, Martin John *research physicist*
Synek, Miroslav *physicist, chemist, world affairs independent consultant, researcher*

Southlake
Herrmann, Debra McGuire *chemist, educator*

Stafford
Odegard, Mark Erie *geophysicist, consultant*

Sugar Land
Downs, Hartley H., III, *chemist*
Huston, Daniel Cliff *geophysicist*

The Woodlands
Westmoreland, Thomas Delbert, Jr., *chemist*

Uvalde
Graham, Robert Albert *research physicist*

Waco
Cleaver, Gerald Bryan *physicist, researcher*
Hassell, Clinton Alton *chemist, educator*
Pedrotti, Leno Stephano *physics educator*

UTAH

American Fork
Zhou, Bing-Nan *chemist, educator*

Brigham City
Hepworth, John Leonard *chemist, researcher*

Dugway
Phan, Richard Man *chemist*

Holladay
O'Halloran, Thomas Alphonsus, Jr., *physicist, researcher*

Logan
Aust, Steven Douglas *biochemistry, biotechnology and toxicology educator*
Schunk, Robert Walter *space physics research administrator*

North Logan
Sunderland, Norman Ray (Norm Sunderland) *health physicist, nuclear engineer educator*

Provo
Cheney, Brigham Vernon *physical chemist, consultant*
Henderson, Douglas James *physicist, chemist, researcher*
Izatt, Reed M. *chemistry researcher*

Salt Lake City
Anspaugh, Lynn Richard *research biophysicist*
Dick, Bertram Gale, Jr., *physics educator*
Efros, Alexei L. *physics educator, researcher*
Foltz, Rodger Lowell *chemistry educator, mass spectroscopist*
Gortatowski, Melvin Jerome *retired chemist*
Kim, Sung Wan *chemistry professor*
Miller, Jan Dean *metallurgy educator*
Olson, Ferron Allred *metallurgist, educator*
Parry, Robert Walter *chemistry professor*
Poulter, Charles Dale *chemist, educator, consultant*
Stang, Peter John *organic chemist*
Straight, Richard Coleman *photobiologist, natural philosopher*
Taylor, Philip Craig *physics educator*
Velick, Sidney Frederick *research biochemist, educator*
Zhdanov, Michael Semenovich *geophysicist, educator*

VERMONT

Burlington
Nyborg, Wesley Lemars *physics educator*
Weed, Lawrence L. *biochemist*
Zhou, Xu *research scientist, educator*

Middlebury
Winkler, Paul Frank, Jr., *astrophysicist, educator*

Shelburne
White, William North *chemistry professor*

Thetford
Hoagland, Mahlon *biochemist, educator*

VIRGINIA

Alexandria
Brenner, Alfred Ephraim *physicist*
Campbell, Francis James *retired chemist*
Carter, William Harold, Sr., *physicist, researcher, electrical engineer*
Gutsch, William Anthony, Jr., *astronomer*
Krebs, Martha *physicist, federal science agency administrator*
Masterson, Kleber Sanlin, Jr., *physicist*
Milling, Marcus Eugene, Sr., *geologist*
Muir, Warren Roger *chemist, executive*
Romney, Carl F. *seismologist*
Toulmin, Priestley *retired geologist*
Willis, Clifford Leon *geologist*
Zook, Theresa Fuetterer *gemologist, consultant*

Annandale
Matuszko, Anthony Joseph *research chemist, administrator*
Raab, Harry Frederick, Jr., *retired physicist*

Arlington
Cavanaugh, Margaret Anne *chemist*
Chubb, Talbot Albert *physicist, consultant*
Debney, George C. *mathematical physicist*
Dorman, Craig Emery *oceanographer, academic administrator*
Ensminger, Luther Glenn *chemist, consultant*
Erb, Karl Albert *physicist, government official*
Gergely, Tomas *astronomer*
Goldberg, Marvin *physicist*
Lean, Judith *physicist, researcher*
Leinen, Margaret Sandra *oceanographic researcher*
Matthews, Allan Freeman *geologist*
Schwartz, Lyle Howard *materials scientist, science administrator*
Van Horn, Hugh M. *physicist, astronomer, educator*
Whitcomb, James Hall *geophysicist, foundation administrator*
Wodarczyk, Francis John *chemist*
Zirkind, Ralph *physicist, educator*

Blacksburg
Graybeal, Jack Daniel *chemist, educator*

Chantilly
deMonsabert, Winston Russel *chemist, consultant*

Charlottesville
Biltonen, Rodney Lincoln *biochemist and pharmacology educator*
Bloomfield, Louis Aub *physicist, researcher*
Carter, William Walton *physicist, researcher*
Chevalier, Roger Alan *astronomy educator, consultant*
Fredrick, Laurence William *astronomer, educator*
Gallagher, Thomas Francis *physicist*
Gaskin, Felicia *biochemist, educator*
Good, Richard Standish *geologist*
Grimes, Russell Newell *chemistry educator, inorganic chemist*
Hornberger, George Milton *environmental science educator*
Howe, James Maxwell *materials scientist, educator*
Kuhlmann-Wilsdorf, Doris *materials scientist, educator*
Lo, Fred Kwok Yung *astronomer*
Lo, Kwok-Yung *astronomer, educator, researcher*
Martin, Robert Bruce *chemistry professor*
Meem, James Lawrence, Jr., *nuclear scientist*
Pate, Brooks *chemist*
Sarazin, Craig Leigh *astronomer*
Shen, Tsung Ying *medicinal chemistry educator*
Thornton, Kathryn C. *physicist, astronaut*
Vanden Bout, Paul Adrian *astronomer, physicist, educator*

Clifton
Brooks, Matthew Wayne *agrichemical regulatory chemist, consultant*

Dahlgren
Bressler, Barry Lee *theoretical physicist, systems analyst*
Holt, William Henry *physicist, researcher*
Walters, Robert Ancil *physicist, mathematician*

Fairfax
Morowitz, Harold Joseph *biophysicist, educator*
Xing, Guang-Qian *aerospace scientist*

Falls Church
Akkara, Joseph Augustine *chemist, educator*
Benson, William Edward (Barnes) *geologist*
Spindel, William *retired chemist, consultant*

Floyd
Clemens, Donald Faull *chemistry professor*

Gainesville
Steger, Edward Herman *chemist*

Hampden Sydney
Joyner, Weyland Thomas *physicist, educator, business consultant*
Porterfield, William Wendell *chemist, educator*

Hampton
Hongyu, Liu *atmospheric scientist*
Jin, Zhonghai *physicist*
Tripathi, Ram Kishore *physicist, researcher*
Yamakov, Vesselin Ivanov *aerospace scientist, researcher*

Harrisonburg
Baker, George Harold, III, *physicist*

Hartfield
Johnson, Carl Randolph *chemist, educator*

Herndon
Crossfield, Albert Scott *aeronautical science consultant, pilot*

Lexington
Spencer, Edgar Winston *geology educator*

Lynchburg
McClenon, John Raymond *retired chemistry educator*
Morgan, Evan *retired chemist*

Mc Lean
Braddock, Joseph Vincent *physicist*
Doyle, Frederick Joseph *retired government research scientist*
Gifford, Franklin Andrew, Jr., *meteorologist, consultant*
Theon, John Speridon *meteorologist, researcher*

Midlothian
Cruse, Robert Ridgely *retired research chemist*

Monroe
Pettus, William G. *retired nuclear scientist, research scientist*

Norfolk
Noginov, Mikhail A. *physicist, researcher, educator*

Petersburg
Brown, Jack D(elbert) *chemist, researcher*
Stronach, Carey Elliott *physicist, researcher*

Reston
Groat, Charles George *geologist, science administrator*
Hirsch, Robert Maurice *hydrologist*
Kramish, Arnold *physicist, historian, author*
Naeser, Nancy Dearien *geologist, researcher*
Peck, Dallas Lynn *retired geologist*
Wang, Jin *research scientist*

Richmond
Fenn, John Bennett *chemist, educator*
Gipson, Jeffery *chemistry professor*
Lilly, Arnys Clifton, Jr., *physicist*
White, Morris Fred, Jr., *physicist*

Roanoke
Al-Zubaidi, Amer Aziz *physicist, researcher*

Vienna
Bhide, Manohar Gopal *nuclear scientist, educator*
Kitchens, Clarence Wesley, Jr., *technology administrator*
Wiesnet, Donald Richard *retired hydrologist*

Williamsburg
Goodwin, Bruce Kesseli *retired geology educator, researcher*
Kossler, William John *physics educator*
Starnes, William Herbert, Jr., *chemist, educator*

Winchester
Ludwig, George Harry *retired physicist, electrical engineer*

WASHINGTON

Bellevue
Benveniste, Jacob *retired physicist*

Bellingham
Brakke, Myron Kendall *retired research chemist, educator*
Cox, David Jackson *biochemistry educator*
Nelson, George Driver *astronomy and education educator, former astronaut*

Bonney Lake
Wang, Lin *physicist, computer science educator, computer software consultant*

Camano Island
O'Connor, Thomas Edward *petroleum geologist, management consultant*

Camas
Valanis, Kirk Christian *theoretical mechanics researcher, educator*

Eastsound
Fowles, George Richard *physicist, researcher*

Edmonds
Galster, Richard W. *engineering geologist*

Everett
Brown, Frederick Calvin *physicist, researcher*

Federal Way
Ma, Zhenkui *remote sensing applications scientist, consultant*

Friday Harbor
Agosta, William Carleton *chemist, educator*

Kent
Popova, Olga K *geologist, researcher*

Lakewood
Kanarowski, Stanley Martin *chemist, government official*

Lynden
Harshman, Dale Richard *physicist*

Lynnwood
Olsen, Kenneth Harold *geophysicist, astrophysicist*

Manchester
Fearon, Lee Charles *chemist*

Olympia
Bloomquist, Rodney Gordon *geologist*

Pullman
Banas, Emil Mike *physicist, researcher*
Hipps, Kerry Wayne *chemistry educator, research scientist*
Ryan, Clarence Augustine, Jr., *biochemistry educator*

Redmond
Borgs, Christian H. *mathematical physicist*

Richland
Bevelacqua, Joseph John *physicist, researcher*
Bush, Spencer Harrison *metallurgist, consultant*
Dunning, Thom H., Jr., *environmental molecular science executive*
Elderkin, Charles Edwin *retired meteorologist*
Hrma, Pavel *materials scientist, educator*
Jacobsen, Gerald Bernhardt *biochemist*
Moore, Emmett Burris, Jr., *physical chemist, educator*
Onishi, Yasuo *environmental researcher*

Seattle
Alger, Glenn M. *meteorologist*
Andersen, Niels Hjorth *chemistry professor, consultant, biophysicist, researcher*
Baum, William Alvin *astronomer, educator*
Bernard, Eddie Nolan *oceanographer*
Borden, Weston Thatcher *chemistry professor*
Brown, Craig William *physical chemist*
Brown, Robert Alan *atmospheric science educator, research scientist*
Brownlee, Donald Eugene, II, *astronomer, educator*
Christian, Gary Dale *chemistry professor*
Creager, Joe Scott *geology and oceanography educator*
Dale, Beverly A. *biochemist, researcher*
Dalton, Larry Raymond *chemistry educator, researcher, consultant*
Davidson, Ernest Roy *chemist, educator*
Dehmelt, Hans Georg *physicist, educator*
Deming, Jody Wheeler *oceanography educator*
El-Moslimany, Ann Paxton *paleoecologist, educator, writer*
Engel, Thomas *chemistry professor*
Erdmann, Joachim Christian *physicist*
Evans, Bernard William *geologist, educator*
Fischer, Edmond Henri *biochemistry educator*
Fischer, Fred Walter *physicist, engineer, educator*
Gates, R. Jordan *meteorologist*
Gordon, Milton Paul *biochemist, educator*
Halver, John Emil *nutritional biochemist*
Heath, George Ross *oceanographer*
Henley, Ernest Mark *physics educator, university dean emeritus*
Ingalls, Robert Lynn *physicist, researcher*
Kells, Lyman F. *astrophysicist, generalist*
King, Ivan Robert *astronomy educator*
Krebs, Edwin Gerhard *biochemistry educator*
Kwiram, Alvin L. *physical chemistry educator, university official*
Lord, Jere Johns *retired physics educator*
Lubatti, Henry Joseph *physicist, researcher*
Malins, Donald Clive *biochemistry, researcher*
Mulally, Alan R. *aerospace company executive*
Olmstead, Marjorie Ann *physics educator*
Porter, Stephen Cummings *geologist, educator*
Rabinovitch, Benton Seymour *chemist, educator emeritus*
Reinhardt, William Parker *chemical physicist, educator*
Robertson, Robert Graham Hamish *physicist*
Stern, Edward Abraham *physics educator*
Stolov, Walter Charles *medicine physicist, physiatrist, educator*
Szkody, Paula *astronomy educator, researcher*
Thouless, David James *retired physicist, educator*
Walsh, Kenneth Andrew *biochemist*
Wilets, Lawrence *physics educator*
Yuan, Chun *physicist, educator*

Silverdale
Walske, M(ax) Carl, Jr., *physicist*

Spokane
Crosby, Glenn Arthur *chemistry professor*
Hilst, Glenn Rudolph *environmental research administrator, research scientist*

Tacoma
Wolf, Frederick George *environmental scientist, administrator*

WEST VIRGINIA

Charleston
Dasher, George Roy *geologist*
Galya, Thomas Andrew *geologist*

Fairmont
Swiger, Elizabeth Davis *chemist, educator*

Keyser
Falkowski, Theresa Gae *chemistry professor*

Morgantown
Beattie, Diana Scott *biochemistry educator*
Butcher, Fred R. *biochemistry educator, university administrator*
Seehra, Mohindar Singh *physics educator, researcher*

WISCONSIN

Appleton
Lokensgard, Jerrold Paul *chemist, educator, organic chemist*

Eau Claire
Dusk, Brooke *meteorologist*
McEllistrem, Marcus T. *chemistry professor, semiconductor materials researcher*
Whitfield, Scott Burwick *physics educator*

Greenville
Zhao, Rongguo *chemist*

Kenosha
Kolb, Vera M. *chemist, educator*

La Crosse
Rozelle, Lee Theodore *physical chemist, researcher*

Madison
Anderson, Louis Wilmer, Jr., *physicist, researcher*
Balantekin, Akif Baha *physicist, educator*
Banfield, Jillian *mineralogist, geomicrobiologist, educator*
Barger, Vernon Duane *physicist, educator*
Bentley, Charles Raymond *geophysics educator*
Botez, Dan *physicist*
Burris, Robert Harza *biochemist, educator*
Cassinelli, Joseph Patrick *astronomy educator*
Christensen, Nikolas Ivan *geophysicist, educator*
Churchwell, Edward Bruce *astronomer, educator*
Clay, Clarence Samuel *acoustical oceanographer*
Cleland, W(illiam) Wallace *biochemistry educator*
Code, Arthur Dodd *astrophysics educator*
Connors, Kenneth Antonio *retired chemistry educator*
Coppersmith, Susan Nan *physicist*
Craddock, Campbell (John Campbell Craddock) *geologist, educator*
Curtiss, Charles Francis *chemist, educator*
DeWerd, Larry Albert *medical physicist, educator*
Dott, Robert Henry, Jr., *geologist, educator*
Ediger, Mark D. *chemistry educator*
Ellis, Arthur Baron *chemist, educator*
Farrar, Thomas C. *chemist, educator*
Frey, Perry A. *biochemistry educator*
Greenler, Robert George *physics educator, researcher*
Himpsel, Franz Josef *physicist, researcher*
Hokin, Lowell Edward *biochemist, educator*
Houghton, David Drew *meteorologist, educator*
Kiessling, Laura Lee *chemist, researcher*
Lagally, Max Gunter *physics educator*
Lardy, Henry A(rnold) *biochemistry educator*
Lawler, James Edward *physics educator*
Lin, Chun Chia *research physicist, educator*
Maher, Louis James, Jr., *geologist, educator*
Morton, Stephen Dana *chemist, consultant*
Mukerjee, Pasupati *chemistry professor*
Pray, Lloyd Charles *geologist, educator*
Rich, Daniel Hulbert *chemistry professor*
Scherer, Victor Richard *physicist, computer scientist, consultant, musician*
Sih, Charles John *pharmaceutical chemistry educator*
Skinner, James Lauriston *chemist, educator*
Suttie, John Weston *biochemist*
Symon, Keith Randolph *physics educator, consultant*
Tomé, Wolfgang Axel *physicist, researcher, educator*
Trubetskoy, Vladimir Sergeevich *polymer chemist*
Valley, John Williams *geology educator, researcher*
Vaughan, Worth Edward *chemistry professor*
Zimmerman, Howard Elliot *chemist, educator*

Milwaukee
Aita, Carolyn Rubin *materials scientist*
Bader, Alfred Robert *chemist*
Baker, John Edward *cardiac biochemist, educator*
Burch, Thaddeus Joseph, Jr., *physics educator, clergyman*
Buss, Daniel Frank *environmental scientist*
Griffith, Owen Wendell *biochemistry educator*
Haworth, Daniel Thomas *chemistry professor*
Hendee, William Richard *medical physics educator, university official, radiologist*
Janda, Lubomir Miro *organic chemist*
Karkheck, John Peter *physics educator, researcher*
Saldin, Dilano Kerzaman *physicist, educator*
Severson, Sally *meteorologist*
Sosnovsky, George *chemist, educator*

Oregon
Draeger, Norman Arthur *physical chemist, surface scientist*

Racine
Isenberg, Norbert *chemist, educator*

Stoughton
Huber, David Lawrence *physicist, researcher*

Washington Island
Raup, David Malcolm *paleontology educator*

Waukesha
Kocharian, Armen *physicist*

Williams Bay
Hobbs, Lewis Mankin *astronomer*

WYOMING

Big Horn
Schultz, Harry Pershing *chemistry researcher, retired educator*

Casper
Ptasynski, Harry *geologist, oil industry executive*
Wold, John Schiller *geologist, former congressman*

Kelly
Knowles, William S. *retired chemist*

Laramie
Frost, Carol D. *geology educator*
Grandy, Walter Thomas, Jr., *physicist, researcher*
Meyer, Edmond Gerald *energy and natural resources educator, resources scientist, entrepreneur, former chemistry educator, university administrator*

Story
Bredehoeft, John Dallas *geologist*

TERRITORIES OF THE UNITED STATES

PUERTO RICO

Angeles
Avila, Carlos Alberto *physics researcher, inventor*

Mayaguez
Meléndez, Enrique *chemist, educator*

Vega Alta
Matos, Cruz Alfonso *environmental consultant*

CANADA

ALBERTA

Calgary
Campbell, Finley Alexander *geologist, consultant*
Mossop, Grant Dilworth *geologist, researcher*
Walker, Roger Geoffrey *geology educator, consultant*

Drumheller
Currie, Philip John *research paleontologist, museum curator*

Edmonton
Gough, Denis Ian *geophysics educator*
Harris, Walter Edgar *chemistry professor*
Kay, Cyril Max *biochemist, educator*
Rutter, Nathaniel Westlund *geologist, educator*
Stelck, Charles Richard *geology educator*

BRITISH COLUMBIA

Burnaby
Wainwright, David Stanley *intellectual property professional*

Lions Bay
Bartholomew, Gilbert Alfred *retired physicist*

Penticton
Chapman, John Donald *research biophysicist*

Sidney
Petrie, William *physicist, researcher*
van den Bergh, Sidney *astronomer*

Vancouver
Bloom, Myer *physicist, researcher*
Hardy, Walter Newbold *physics professor, researcher*
Russell, Richard Doncaster *geophysicist, educator, geoscientist*
Sinclair, Alastair James *geology educator*
Vogt, Erich Wolfgang *physicist, academic administrator*

Victoria
Batten, Alan Henry *astronomer*
Best, Melvyn Edward *geophysicist*
Hutchings, John Barrie *astronomer, researcher*
Israel, Werner *physics educator*
Leffek, Kenneth Thomas *retired chemist, educator*
Morton, Donald Charles *astronomer*
Stetson, Peter Brailey *astronomer*
Wiles, David McKeen *chemist*

West Vancouver
Wynne-Edwards, Hugh Robert *geologist, educator, entrepreneur*

MANITOBA

Winnipeg
Ferguson, Robert Bury *mineralogy educator*
Mantsch, Henry Horst *chemistry educator*
Schaefer, Theodore Peter *chemistry educator, retired*
Smith, Ian Cormack Palmer *biophysicist*

NEWFOUNDLAND

Saint John's
Gibbons, Rex Vincent *geologist*
Rochester, Michael Grant *geophysics educator*

NOVA SCOTIA

Dartmouth
Elliott, James A. *oceanographer, researcher*

Halifax
Dahn, Jeff Raymond *physics educator*
Hiltz, Arnold Aubrey *retired chemist*
Jones, William Ernest *chemistry professor*

Tatamagouche
Roach, Margot Ruth *retired biophysicist, educator*

ONTARIO

Brampton
Hu, Qiang *research scientist, educator, engineer*

Collingwood
Morley, Lawrence Whitaker *geophysicist, remote sensing consultant*

Deep River
Davies, John Arthur *physics and engineering educator, scientist*
Milton, John Charles Douglas *nuclear physicist, researcher*

Guelph
Dickinson, William Trevor *hydrologist, educator*
Karl, Gabriel *physics educator*

Hamilton
Datars, William Ross *physicist, researcher*
Garland, William James *engineering physics educator*
Gillespie, Ronald James *chemistry educator, researcher, writer*
Jonasson, Ralph George *research chemist*
Spenser, Ian Daniel *chemist educator*
Sprung, Donald Whitfield Loyal *physics educator*

Harrow
Saha, Uttam Kumar *environmental scientist, researcher*

Kingston
Ewan, George Thomson *physicist, researcher*
Spencer, John Hedley *biochemistry educator*
Stewart, Alec Thompson *physicist, educator*
Szarek, Walter Anthony *chemist, educator*

London
Bancroft, George Michael *chemical physicist, educator*
Dreimanis, Aleksis *emeritus geology educator*
Fyfe, William Sefton *geochemist, educator*
Stewart, Harold Brown *biochemist*
Stillman, Martin J. *physical science research administrator, bioinorganic chemist*

Manotick
Hobson, George Donale *retired geophysicist*

Ottawa
Alper, Howard *chemistry professor*
Andrew, Bryan Haydn *astronomer*
Halliday, Ian *astronomer*
Harington, Charles Richard *vertebrate paleontologist*
Himms-Hagen, Jean Margaret *biochemist, educator*
Holmes, John Leonard *chemistry professor*
Ingold, Keith Usherwood *chemist, educator*
Kates, Morris *biochemist, educator*

Ramsay, Donald Allan *physical chemist*
Redhead, Paul Aveling *physicist*
Schneider, William George *chemist, research consultant*
St-Onge, Denis Alderic *geologist, research scientist*
Veizer, Ján *geology educator*
Whitehead, J. Rennie *science consultant*

Richmond Hill
Garrison, Robert Frederick *astronomer, educator*

Toronto
Armstrong, Robin Louis *physics educator*
Bohme, Diethard Kurt *chemistry professor*
Bond, John Richard *astrophysicist*
Brook, Adrian Gibbs *chemistry professor*
Dunlop, David John *geophysics educator, researcher*
Goldberg, David Meyer *biochemistry educator*
Hofmann, Theo *biochemist, educator*
Kresge, Alexander Jerry *chemistry professor*
Litherland, Albert Edward *physics educator*
Norris, Geoffrey *geology educator, consultant*
Packham, Marian Aitchison *biochemistry educator*
Polanyi, John Charles *chemist, educator*
Pritchard, Huw Owen *chemist, educator*
Shepherd, Gordon Greeley *space physics educator, researcher*
Stoicheff, Boris Peter *physicist, researcher*

Waterloo
Morgan, Alan Vivian *geologist, educator*
Wen, Geyi *applied physics educator*

Windsor
Thibert, Roger Joseph *clinical chemist, educator*

QUEBEC

Montreal
Barrette, Jean *physicist, researcher*
Das Gupta, Subal *physics educator, researcher*
de Takacsy, Nicholas Benedict *physicist, researcher*
Eisenberg, Adi *chemist*
Johnstone, Rose Mamelak (Mrs. Douglas Johnstone) *biochemistry educator*
Leroy, Claude *physics educator, researcher*
Michaud, Georges Joseph *astrophysics educator*
Mysak, Lawrence Alexander *oceanographer, climatologist, mathematician, educator*
Perlin, Arthur Saul *chemistry professor*
Podgorsak, Ervin B. *medical physicist, educator, administrator*
Solomon, Samuel *biochemistry educator, administrator*
Sourkes, Theodore Lionel *biochemistry educator*
Taras, Paul *physicist, researcher*
Whitehead, Michael Anthony *chemistry professor*

Outremont
Levesque, Rene Jules Albert *retired physicist*

Pointe Claire
Bolker, Henry Irving *retired chemist, research institute director, educator*

Pointe-Claire
Bachynski, Morrel Paul *physicist*

Sherbrooke
Tremblay, André-Marie *physicist*

SASKATCHEWAN

Saskatoon
Hirose, Akira *physics educator, researcher*

Edmonton
Ostroverkhova, Oksana *physicist*

Laval
Baroudy, Bahige Mourad *biochemist, researcher*

Quebec City
Page, Michel *biochemist, researcher*

Sherbrooke
Deslongchamps, Pierre *chemistry professor*

MEXICO

Cuernavaca
Bolivar Zapata, Francisco *biochemist*

AUSTRALIA

Canberra
Taylor, Stuart Ross *geochemist, author*

Wembley
Koslow, Julian Anthony *oceanographer, research scientist*

AUSTRIA

Vienna
Pohl, Adolf Leopold *clinical chemist, quality assurance consultant*

BELGIUM

Liège
Mosora-Stan, Florentina Ioana *physics educator*

BRAZIL

Sorocaba
Martins, Nelson *physics educator*

CHINA

Shanghai
Langford, Roland Everett *environmental scientist, safety engineer, writer*

COTE D'IVOIRE

Abidjan
Obrou, Kouadio Olivier *physics professor, researcher*

CZECH REPUBLIC

Prague
Čejka, Jiří *chemist, researcher*

DENMARK

Copenhagen
Mottelson, Ben R. *physicist*
Pethick, Christopher John *physicist*

ENGLAND

Bedfordshire
Gelman, Leonid Moiseevich *scientist, vibroacoustician, educator*

Brighton
Kroto, Harold Walter *chemistry researcher, educator*

Cambridge
Buckingham, Amyand David *chemistry professor*
Edwards, Sir Samuel Frederick *physicist, researcher*
Hawking, Stephen W. *astrophysicist, mathematician*
Rees, Martin John *astronomy educator*

Falmer
Cornforth, Sir John Warcup *chemist*

London
Koonin, Steven Elliot *physicist, educator*
Scott, Raymond Peter William *chemistry research educator, writer*

Nottingham
Krasnov, Kirill *physicist, researcher*

FRANCE

Creteil
Renoux, André *physicist, researcher*

Orsay
Friedel, Jacques *physics educator*

Paris
Boccara, Nino *physicist*
de Gennes, Pierre-Gilles *physicist, educator*
Lehn, Jean-Marie Pierre *chemistry professor*
Lucas, Georges *physicist, researcher*

Villefranche-sur-Mer
Legendre, Louis *oceanographer, educator, research scientist*

GEORGIA

Tbilisi
Bibilashvili, Tamar *physicist, educator*

GERMANY

Frankfurt
Michel, Hartmut *biochemist*

Garching
Fischer, Ernst Otto *chemist, educator*
Mössbauer, Rudolf Ludwig *physicist, researcher*

Göttingen
Eigen, Manfred *physicist*
Sheldrick, George Michael *chemistry educator, crystallographer*

Munich
Huber, Robert *biochemist, educator*

Stuttgart
Cardona, Manuel *physics educator*

ISRAEL

Ra ananna
Hayon, Elie M. *chemist, educator*

Rehovot
Sharon, Nathan *biochemist*

Tel Aviv
Jortner, Joshua *physical chemistry scientist, educator*

ITALY

Frascati
Haegi, Marcel *physicist*

JAPAN

Gyoda
Shibasaki, Yoshio *chemistry educator, researcher*

Higashi-Hiroshima
Suzuki, Nobutaka *chemistry professor*

Nagoya
Kaneyoshi, Takahito *physicist, educator*

Okayama
Ubuka, Toshihiko *biochemist, educator, academic administrator*

Osaka
Ikeda, Kazuyosi *physicist, poet*

Shimizu
Uyeda, Seiya *geophysics educator*

Shinjuku
Shimada, Haruo *physical chemistry educator*

Tokyo
Esaki, Leo *physicist, foundation executive, university president*
Fuketa, Toyojiro *physicist*
Iida, Shuichi *physicist, educator*
Sakurada, Yutaka *chemist*

Toyama
Ishii, Yoshinori *environmental science educator*
Taketomi, Susamu *physicist, researcher*

MALAYSIA

Petaling Jaya
Wong, Kuok-Shoong Daniel *research scientist*

NETHERLANDS

Utrecht
't Hooft, Gerardus *physicist, researcher*

REPUBLIC OF KOREA

An San
Lee, Dohyung *aeronautics research scientist*

RUSSIA

Moscow
Ginzburg, Vitaly Lazarevich *physicist*
Goldanskii, Vitalii Iosifovich *chemist, physicist*

SWEDEN

Stockholm
Hallberg, Bengt O. *systems strategy director, fiber optic specialist*
Peskov, Vladimir Dmitrievich *physicist, educator, consultant*

Österskär
Bolin, Bert Richard Johannes *atmospheric physicist, research meteorologist*

SWITZERLAND

Geneva
Charpak, Georges *physicist, nuclear scientist*
Steinberger, Jack *physicist, researcher*

Wollerau
Rohrer, Heinrich *physicist*

Zurich
Binnig, Gerd Karl *physicist, educator*
Ernst, Richard Robert *chemist, educator*
Eschenmoser, Albert *chemist*

TAIWAN

Taipei
Lee, Yuan Tseh *chemistry professor*

ADDRESS UNPUBLISHED

Abdaladze, Merabi *physicist*
Ahmad, Moghisuddin *chemist, researcher*
Ahmad, Salahuddin *nuclear scientist*
Alexander, Thomas G. *chemist, researcher*
Alpher, Ralph Asher *physicist, educator*
Ancker-Johnson, Betsy *physicist, engineer, retired automotive company executive*
Anders, Edward *chemist, educator*
Andersen, Roy Stuart *physicist*
Armstrong, Donald *biochemistry, pathophysiology educator*
Atlas, David *meteorologist, research scientist*
Bai, Chuanyong *nuclear scientist*
Baker, Daniel Neil *physicist*
Baldwin, George Curriden *physicist, researcher*
Bandeen, William Reid *retired meteorologist*
Barr, John Baldwin *chemist, research scientist*
Bauer, Henry Hermann *chemistry and science educator*
Baur, Werner Heinz *mineralogist, educator*
Becchetti, Frederick Daniel, Jr., *physicist, researcher*
Behrendt, John Charles *geophysicist researcher, writer*
Behrens, James William *physicist, administrator, author*
Bellini, Francesco *chemist*
Benjamin, Arlin James *physicist*
Bennett, William Ralph, Jr., *physicist, researcher*
Bernfeld, Peter Harry William *retired biochemist*
Bersin, Richard Lewis *physicist, plasma process technologist*
Berthold, John William, III, *physicist*
Bhattramakki, Dinakar *research scientist*
Biederman, Edwin Williams, Jr., *retired geologist*
Bigelow, Charles Cross *retired biochemist, retired university administrator*
Bikales, Norbert M. *chemist, science administrator*
Bodanszky, Miklos *chemist, educator*
Boschmann, Erwin *chemistry professor*
Bostrom, Carl Otto *physicist, laboratory director emeritus*
Boyer, Herbert Wayne *retired biochemist*
Bradbeer, Clive *biochemistry and microbiology educator, research scientist*
Braden, Charles Hosea *physicist, university administrator*
Breitenberger, Ernst *scientist, educator*
Bretthauer, Erich Walter *chemist, educator*
Brown, Barbara S. *environmental scientist*
Brown, Rhonda Rochelle *chemist, health facility administrator, lawyer*
Bunyan, Ellen Lackey Spotz *retired chemist*
Butler, Orton Carmichael *climatologist*
Calvert, Jack George *atmospheric chemist, educator*
Cane, David E. *chemistry professor*
Capasso, Federico *physicist*
Cardman, Lawrence Santo *physics educator, research administrator*
Carney, Nancy Ann *research scientist*
Carroll, Harvey Franklin *retired chemistry and nutrition educator*
Carton, Robert John *retired environmental scientist*
Cathou, Renata Egone *chemist, consultant*
Chadsey, Harold A. *astronomer*
Chang, Clarence Dayton *retired chemist*
Chemla, Daniel S. *physics educator*
Cheng, Baolian *physicist*
Chin, Mian *research scientist*
Chizmeshya, Andrew Vincent George *physicist, research scientist*
Chow, Jimmy Tai-Nin *chemist*
Christoffersen, Ralph Earl *chemist, researcher*
Chu, Steven *physics educator*
Church, Eugene Lent *physicist, consulting scientist*
Cohen, Philip *retired hydrogeologist*
Cohen, Stanley *biochemistry educator*
Colby, Frank Gerhardt *scientific consultant*
Compton, W. Dale *physicist, researcher, engineer*
Conrath, Barney Jay *astrophysicist*
Cooper, Austin Morris *chemist, chemical engineer, consultant, researcher*
Cox, James Carl, Jr., *chemist, researcher, lexicographer, consultant*
Cox, Robert Hames *chemist, scientific consultant*
Crabtree, Robert Howard *chemistry professor, consultant*
Craven, Stephen M. *retired research chemist*
Critoph, Eugene *retired physicist, nuclear research company executive*
Crutzen, Paul Josef *research meteorologist, chemist*
Cuatrecasas, Pedro Martin *research biochemist, pharmaceutical executive*
Cusanovich, Michael Anthony *biochemist*
Dale, Wesley John *chemistry professor*
Daniels, William Burton *retired physicist, educator*
Dash, Sanford Mark *aerospace scientist*
Day, Richard Allen *chemistry professor*
Deisenhofer, Johann *biochemistry educator, researcher*
De Loach, Bernard Collins, Jr., *retired physicist*
Denton, Medona Bonner *research chemistry educator*
de Planque, E. Gail *physicist*
Deryuga, Vyacheslav O. *nuclear physicist, computer scientist, consultant*
Detert, Miriam Anne *chemical analyst*
Dickinson, William Richard *retired geologist*
Dickman, Robert S. *aerospace consultant, retired career officer*
Diehl, Harry Alfred *chemist, genealogist*
Dixon, Gordon Henry *biochemist, educator*
Donath, Fred Arthur *geologist, geophysicist*
Dossena, Tiziano Thomas *environmental scientist*
Dow, Garnett McCormick *geoscientist*
Dubin, Daniel Herschel Eli *physicist, educator*
Ebisuzaki, Yukiko *retired chemistry educator*
Edwards, Helen Thom *physicist*
Einhorn, Martin B. *physics educator*
English, Bruce Vaughan *environmental consultant*
Esquivel, Agerico Liwag *retired research physicist*
Ewen, H.I. *physicist*
Farmer, Crofton Bernard *atmospheric physicist*
Feldmann, Frank Neil *chemistry professor*
Fey, Willard *global environmental researcher, educator*
Flor, Loy Lorenz *retired chemist, corrosion engineer, consultant*
Flores, George Anthony *physicist, researcher*
Flynn, George William *chemistry educator, researcher*
Ford, Kenneth William *physicist*
Fox, John David *educator, physicist*
Fradkin, David Milton *physicist, researcher*
Franz, John E. *bio-organic chemist, researcher*
Franz, Judy R. *physics educator*
Frauenfelder, Hans *physicist, researcher*
Friedlander, Charles Douglas (Chuck Friedlander) *space consultant*
Gabel, Connie *chemist, educator*
Gardner, Wilford Robert *physicist, researcher*
Garwin, Richard Lawrence *physicist*
Gedevanishvili, Shalva *materials scientist, researcher*
Gelboin, Harry Victor *biochemistry educator, researcher*
Geller, Seymour *retired educator, researcher*
Gervay, Joseph Edmund *chemist, researcher, retired research scientist*
Gilinsky, Victor *physicist*
Glashow, Sheldon Lee *physicist, researcher*
Goldberger, Marvin Leonard *physicist, researcher*
Golden, David Edward *physicist*
Goldstein, Irving Solomon *chemistry professor, consultant*
Gordon, William Edwin *physicist, educator, electrical engineer, academic administrator*
Gorski, Waldemar *chemist, educator*
Gottesman, Stephen Thancy *astronomy educator, researcher*
Grady, Lee Timothy *pharmaceutical chemist*

Greaves, William Webster *chemist, patent analyst, community liaison*
Griesé, John William, III, *astronomer, educator, advocate*
Grimes, James Gordon *geologist*
Gummel, Hermann Karl *retired physicist, laboratory administrator*
Gunter, William Dayle, Jr., *physicist, consultant*
Guo, Xiaofeng *physicist*
Hagemier, Herman Frederick *chemist*
Halpern, Alvin Michael *retired physicist, educator, consultant*
Hardy, Ralph W. F. *biochemist, biotechnology executive*
Haslett, Jared Wooddell *physicist, researcher*
Heeschen, David Sutphin *astronomer, educator*
Heller, Adam *chemist, researcher*
Hereford, Frank Loucks, Jr., *physicist, researcher*
Hermann, Robert Bell *physical chemist, consultant*
Herzfeld, Charles Maria *physicist, educator*
Hinkley, Everett David, Jr., *physicist*
Ho, Chih-Ming *physicist, researcher*
Hoeg, Donald Francis *chemist, consultant, former research and development executive*
Hoffleit, Ellen Dorrit *astronomer*
Hogen-Esch, Thieo E. *chemistry professor*
Holmes, Jerry Dell *retired chemist*
Holtzberg, Frederic *retired chemist*
Horton, Robert Carlton *geologist*
Hosang, Robert Michael *research scientist*
Howard, Robert Franklin *observatory administrator, astronomer*
Hulet, Ervin Kenneth *retired nuclear chemist*
Hunter, James Edward *chemist, consultant*
Ignatiev, Alex *physics researcher*
Imhof, Joseph M. *chemist, researcher*
Ingle, James Chesney, Jr., *geology educator*
Inlow, Rush Osborne *chemist*
Johnson, Arthur William, Jr., *retired planetarium executive*
Johnson, Charles Leslie *aerospace physicist, consultant*
Johnson, David Wilfred, Jr., *ceramic scientist, researcher*
Johnson, Francis Severin *physicist*
Jones, Thornton Keith *research chemist*
Jordan, Robert Reed *geologist, educator*
Jordan, Thomas Fredrick *physics educator*
Kamanu, Uchemadu Chee *chemist*
Kasprzak, Lucian Alexander *physicist, researcher, technical manager, materials scientist*
Kasten, Janice Haas *chemist, writer*
Kastner, Marc Aaron *physics educator*
Keith, Carl D. *retired chemist*
Kelsey, Donald Ross *chemist*
Kennel, Charles Frederick *physics educator, government official, academic administrator*
Kerr, Donald MacLean, Jr., *physicist*
Klema, Ernest Donald *nuclear physicist, educator*
Klute, Allan Aloys *retired physicist, retired economist*
Knight, Patricia Marie *medical device researcher, consultant*
Knudsen, William Claire *geophysicist, researcher*
Korn, Jessica Susan *research scientist, educator*
Kraichnan, Robert Harry *physicist, consultant*
Krakower, Terri Jan *biochemist, researcher*
Kraus, Naomi *retired biochemistry educator*
Kravitz, Rubin *chemist*
Kumar, Kaplesh *materials scientist*
Kustin, Kenneth *chemist*
Lackner, Klaus Stephan *physicist*
Langerak, Esley Oren *retired research chemist*
Laporte, Leo Frederic *earth sciences educator, paleontologist*
Leachtenauer, Jon Clark *optical scientist*
LeBlond, Paul Henri *oceanographer, educator*
Lederman, Leon Max *physicist, researcher*
Lehmann, (A) Spencer *retired chemist, retired chemical engineer*
Levenson, Marc David *optics and lasers specialist, scientist, editor*
Lightman, Alan Paige *writer, physicist, educator*
Lin, Chenchy Jeffrey *research scientist*
Lippincott, James Andrew *biochemistry and biological sciences educator*
Loach, Paul Allen *biochemist, biophysicist, educator*
Lopez Garcia, Diego *researcher*
Los, Marinus *retired agrochemical researcher*
Lu, Zhiming *hydrologist*
Lukacs, Michael Edward *electro-optics researcher*
Luntz, Benjamin F. *physicist, educator, writer*
Lurix, Paul Leslie, Jr., *chemist*
Maddin, Robert *metallurgist, educator*
Maglich, Bogdan Castle *physicist*
Maling, George Croswell, Jr., *physicist*
Maltsev, Nikolai Elyseevich *research scientist*
March, Jacqueline Front *retired chemist*
Marcuse, Dietrich *retired physicist*
Marinetti, Guido V. *biochemistry educator*
Mashnik, Stepan G. *physicist*
Mataré, Herbert F. *physicist, consultant*
Mattoo, Autar K. *biochemist*
Mayo, Dana Walker *chemistry professor*
McCormick, Donald Bruce *retired biochemist, educator*
McTague, John Paul *materials scientist, educator, chemist, researcher*
Melvin, Peter Joseph *astrophysicist, educator*
Mendelson, Sol *physical science educator, consultant*
Metz, Werner Adam *physicist*
Meunier, Vincent *physicist*
Miller, Phillip Edward *environmental scientist*
Mislow, Kurt Martin *chemist, educator*
Moeck, Peter *crystallographer, materials scientist*
Monroe, Frederick Fales *geologist, oceanographer*
Mukerjee, Shaibal *environmental scientist*
Mullis, Kary Banks *biochemist*
Nacht, Sergio *biochemist*
Nemec, Josef *retired organic chemist, researcher*
Neumark, Gertrude Fanny *materials science educator*
Nevill, William Albert *chemistry professor*
Newton, Roger Gerhard *educator, physicist*
Nirenberg, Marshall Warren *biochemist*
Nobles, Laurence Hewit *retired geology educator*
Ogliaruso, Michael Anthony *retired chemist, educator, actor*
Oort, Abraham Hans *meteorologist, researcher, educator*
Orttung, William Herbert *chemistry professor*
Pall-Pallant, Teri *paleontologist, inventor, behavioral scientist, design engineer, advertising agency executive*
Panofsky, Wolfgang Kurt Hermann *physicist, researcher*
Parr, Albert Clarence *physicist*
Patchett, Arthur Allan *medicinal chemist, pharmaceutical executive*
Pearson, Ralph Gottfrid *chemistry professor*
Peiris, Suhithi Mahesica *research chemist*
Petersen, Arne Joaquin *chemist*
Portis, Alan Mark *physicist, researcher*
Pound, Robert Vivian *physics educator*
Pradzynski, Andrzej Henryk *chemist*
Price, Clifford Warren *retired metallurgist, researcher*
Price, Paul Buford *physicist, researcher*
Proctor, Richard J. *geologist, consultant*
Pytlinski, Jerzy Teodor *physicist, educator, research administrator*
Pytte, Agnar *physicist, retired academic administrator*
Qutub, Musa Yacub *hydrogeologist, educator, consultant*
Rabó, Jule Anthony *chemical researcher, consultant*
Read, Virginia Hall *retired biochemistry educator*
Reichmanis, Elsa *chemist*
Rhyne, James Jennings *condensed matter physicist*
Rice, Stuart Alan *chemist, educator*
Richards, Paul Linford *physics educator, researcher*
Richardson, Charles Clifton *biochemist, educator*
Richart, Douglas Stephen *retired chemist*
Roberts, Thomas George *retired physicist*
Robertson, John Archibald Law *nuclear scientist*
Robinson, Bruce Butler *physicist*
Roman, Nancy Grace *astronomer, consultant*
Rose, Marian Henrietta *physics researcher*
Rose, William Kenneth *astronomer, educator*
Rosenberg, Eli Ira *physicist, educator*
Rosenkilde, Carl Edward *retired physicist*
Ross, Alberta Barkley *retired chemist*
Roys, John E. *chemist*
Rubin, Vera Cooper *astronomer, researcher*
Ruedenberg, Klaus *theoretical chemist, educator*
Rybczyk, Joseph Anthony *physicist, researcher, writer*
Satinover, Jeffrey B. *physicist, psychiatrist, writer*
Savukov, Igor M. *physicist, researcher*
Sayre, David *physicist*
Schelar, Virginia Mae *chemistry consultant*
Schepartz, Alanna *biochemist, educator*
Schonhorn, Harold *chemist, researcher*
Schutz, Donald Frank *geochemist, environmental corporate executive*
Schwartz, Shirley E. *chemist, researcher*
Scott, T. Gordon *chemistry and math educator, writer*
Scully, Marlan Orvil *physics educator*
Sedor, Frank A. *chemist*
Sharon, Timothy Michael *physicist*
Sheinin, Rose *biochemist, educator*
Shi, Xiangyang *research scientist*
Shirley, David Arthur *chemistry educator, science administrator*
Simpson, Gerald D. *research scientist, consultant, educator*
Simpson, Robert Homer *meteorologist, consultant*
Singer, S(iegfried) Fred *geophysicist, educator*
Sink, John Davis *chemist, clergyperson*
Smith, Charles Haddon *geoscientist, consultant*
Snell, Esmond Emerson *biochemist*
Sobolev, Alexandre Andreevich *physicist*
Solomon, Susan *chemist, scientist*
Song, Xuedong *chemist*
Speier, John Leo, Jr., *retired chemist*
Spejewski, Eugene Henry *physicist, researcher*
Spencer, David Anthony *geologist, researcher*
Squibb, Samuel Dexter *chemistry professor*
Srinivasan, Rangaswamy *chemical physicist*
Stavrev, Krassimir K. *chemist, researcher*
Sternberg, Jeffrey *research manager*
Stevenson, Paul Michael *physics professor, researcher*
Stief, Louis John *chemist*
Straus, Leon Stephan *physicist*
Strouth, Baron Howard Steven *geologist, mining engineer*
Stubbs, Gerald *biochemist, educator*
Sullivan, Nicholas G. *science educator, speleologist*
Sultan, Cornel *research scientist, consultant*
Sun, Zuo *research scientist, consultant*
Sunderman, Duane Neuman *chemist, research institute executive*
Symchowicz, Samson *retired biochemist*
Tan, Guolong *research scientist*
Taylor, Kathleen (Christine Taylor) *physical chemist, researcher*
Taylor, Ronald Charles *retired meteorologist*
Tedford, Charles Franklin *biophysicist*
Thompson, Mary Eileen *chemistry professor*
Tipler, Frank Jennings, III, *physicist*
Tsigelny, Igor *research scientist*
Tucker, Dennis Stephen *materials scientist*
Tuul, Johannes *physics educator, researcher*
Umemoto, Teruo *chemist, researcher, chemicals executive*
Upgren, Arthur Reinhold, Jr., *astronomer, educator, writer*
Urry, Grant Wayne *retired chemistry educator*
Van Dalen, Gordon John *physicist, educator*
van der Meer, Simon *physicist*
Vanderwalker, Diane Mary *materials scientist*
Vanier, Jacques *physicist*
Veronis, George *geophysicist, educator*
Villforth, John Carl *engineer, health physicist*
Vinet, Luc *physicist*
Vo, Nghia Van *materials scientist, electrical engineer*
Vook, Frederick Ludwig *physicist, consultant*
Wahl, Floyd Michael *geologist*
Wald, Francine Joy Weintraub (Mrs. Bernard J. Wald) *physicist, academic administrator*
Wall, Frederick Theodore *retired chemistry educator*
Wallace, Jane House *retired geologist*
Wallace, Robert Earl *geologist*
Warshawsky, Isidore *physicist, consultant*
Wattenberg, Albert *physicist, researcher*
Weinberg, Steven *physics educator*
Weinreb, Michael Philip *physicist*
Weisburger, Elizabeth Kreiser *retired chemist*
Weisz, Paul B(urg) *physicist, researcher, chemical engineer*
Wetherill, George West *geophysicist, planetary scientist*
Wheeler, John Oliver *geologist*
Wiener, Russell Warren *environmental scientist, researcher*
Wilson, Kenneth Geddes *physics research administrator*
Wolff, Manfred Ernst *medicinal chemist, pharmaceutical company executive*
Wolff, Peter Adalbert *physicist, researcher*
Woo, Jonathan C. G. *chemist, portfolio manager, management consultant*
Woodruff, Truman O(wen) *physicist, emeritus educator*
Wroblowa, Halina Stefania *electrochemist*
Wyrtki, Klaus *oceanography educator*
Xiang, Hui *biochemist, researcher*
Yates, David John C. *chemist, researcher*
Yearian, Mason Russell *retired physicist*
Yeliseev, Alexei Arkadievich *biochemist, researcher*
Younathan, Janet N. *chemist*
Zaffaroni, Alejandro C. *biochemist, medical research company executive*
Zakim, David *biochemist*
Zaleski, Jan Franciszek *biochemist*
Zimm, Bruno Hasbrouck *physical chemistry educator*
Ziolo, Ronald F. *research scientist, educator, academic administrator, writer*

SOCIAL SCIENCE

UNITED STATES

ALABAMA

Auburn
Seroka, James Henry *social sciences educator, university administrator*
Whitten, David Owen *economics professor*

Birmingham
Bradley, Laurence Alan *psychologist*
Cockerham, William Carl *sociologist, educator*
Morrisey, Michael A. *health economics educator*
Nunn, Grady Harrison *political science educator emeritus*
Ramey, Craig T. *psychology educator*
Schwebel, David Charles *psychologist, educator*
Taub, Edward *psychology researcher*

Dothan
Wright, Burton *sociologist*

Duncanville
Prescott, Perry Don *psychology educator, counselor*

Fort Rucker
Stewart, John Edward *psychologist, researcher*

Hartselle
Slate, Joe Hutson *psychologist, educator*

Huntsville
Traylor, Orba Forest *economist, lawyer, educator*

Jacksonville
Dunaway, Carolyn Bennett *retired sociology educator*

Montevallo
McChesney, Robert Michael, Sr., *political science educator*

Montgomery
Wendzel, Robert Leroy *political science educator*

Pell City
Passey, George Edward *psychology educator*

Tuscaloosa
Baklanoff, Eric Nicholas *economist, educator*
Cramer, Dale Lewis *retired economics educator*
Fish, Mary Martha *economics professor*

ALASKA

Anchorage
Ippolito, Maria F. *psychologist, educator*
Obermeyer, Theresa Nangle *sociology educator*
Suddock, Frances Suter Thorson *grief educator, writer*
Wood, Darryl Scott *criminologist, educator*

ARIZONA

Flagstaff
Cothran, Dan Allen *political scientist, educator*
McDonald, Craydon Dean *psychologist*
Smith, Zachary Alden *political science and public administration educator*

Gila Bend
Barnes, William Wayne *geographer, writer*

Glendale
Haran, Robert Emmet *political scientist*
Howell, Llewellyn Donald *management educator*
Mathis, F. John *economist, educator*

Phoenix
Cheifetz, Lorna Gale *psychologist*

Sacaton
Stephenson, Larry Kirk *stategic planner, geography educator*

Scottsdale
Braun, Stephen Hughes *psychologist*
Dean, Leslie Alan (Cap Dean) *economist, consultant*
Kizziar, Janet Wright *psychologist, writer, lecturer*
O'Brien, John Conway *economist, educator, writer*

Sierra Vista
Lutes, Todd Oakley *political science educator*

Sun City West
Nordin, John Algot *economist, educator*

Tempe
Alisky, Marvin Howard *political science educator*
Gordon, Leonard *retired sociology educator*
Haygood, Robert Collins *industrial psychologist, educator, consultant*
Johanson, Donald Carl *physical anthropologist*
Knox, Robert Lee *economics professor*
Montero, Darrel Martin *social worker, sociologist, educator*
Prescott, Edward C. *economist, educator*
Simon, Sheldon Weiss *political science educator*
Strom, Robert Duane *psychologist, educator*
Uttal, William R(eichenstein) *psychology and engineering educator, research scientist*
Weigend, Guido Gustav *geographer, educator*

Tucson
Axinn, George Harold *rural sociology educator*
Batterbury, Simon Peregrine John *geographer, educator*
Bechtel, Robert Bernard *social sciences educator, consultant*
Berliner, David Charles *psychologist*
Block, Michael Kent *economics and law educator, public policy association executive, former government official, consultant*
Brainerd, Charles J(on) *experimental psychologist, applied mathematician, educator*
Breiger, Ronald Louis *social sciences educator*
Clarke, James Weston *political science educator, writer*
Fontana, Bernard Lee *retired anthropologist, writer, consultant*
Ingram, Helen Moyer *political science educator*
Kay, Margarita *retired social sciences educator, retired nursing educator*
Larwood, Laurie *psychologist*
Longacre, William Atlas *anthropology educator*
Marshall, Robert Herman *economics professor*
Reitan, Ralph Meldahl *clinical neuropsychologist, former educator*
Smith, David Wayne *psychologist, educator*
Smith, Kenneth Rodger *university dean, economics educator*
Snyder, Richard Gerald *research scientist, administrator, educator, consultant*
Soren, David *archaeologist, educator, writer*
Stini, William Arthur *anthropologist, educator*
Stubblefield, Thomas Mason *agricultural economist, educator*
Thompson, Raymond Harris *retired anthropologist, educator*
Underwood, Jane Hainline Hammons *anthropologist, educator*
Vincent, Thomas Lange *political science professor*
Volgy, Thomas John *political science educator, organization official*
Wahlke, John Charles *political science educator*

West Sedona
Eggert, Robert John, Sr., *economist*

Yuma
Norton, Dunbar Sutton *economic developer*

ARKANSAS

Fayetteville
Mc Gimsey, Charles Robert, III, *anthropologist*
Purvis, Hoyt Hughes *political scientist, academic administrator, educator*
Studer, Patricia S. *psychologist*

Hot Springs National Park
Plummer, Jack Moore *psychologist*

Little Rock
Briscoe, David Lloyd *academic sociologist, educator*
Kaza, Greg John *economist, educator*
Ledbetter, Calvin Reville, Jr., (Cal Ledbetter) *political science educator, university dean, former legislator*

Pine Bluff
Engle, Carole Ruth *aquaculture economics educator*
Tai, Chong-Soo Stephen *political scientist, educator*

Scott
Rolingson, Martha *research archeologist*

Siloam Springs
Oliver, Gary Jackson *psychologist, educator*

CALIFORNIA

Alameda
Boyer, Ford Sylvester *relationship consultant, minister*

Anaheim
Gobar, Alfred Julian *retired economic consultant, educator*

Arcata
Bowker, Lee Harrington *sociologist, educator, writer*
Emenhiser, JeDon Allen *political science educator, academic administrator*

Bakersfield
Singer, George Milton *clinical psychologist*

Barstow
Nyborg, Kenneth Wayne *retired social sciences educator, small business owner*

Benicia
Nelson, Elmer Kingsholm, Jr., (Kim Nelson) *educator, writer, mediator, consultant*

Berkeley
Adelman, Irma Glicman *economics professor*

Akerlof, George Arthur *economics professor*
Alhadeff, David Albert *economics professor*
Auerbach, Alan Jeffrey *economist, educator*
Baumrind, Diana *research psychologist*
Bellah, Robert Neelly *sociologist, educator*
Berck, Peter *agricultural economics educator*
Brandes, Stanley Howard *anthropology educator, writer*
Breslauer, George William *political science educator*
Cheit, Earl Frank *economist, educator*
Colson, Elizabeth Florence *anthropologist*
Ervin-Tripp, Susan Moore *psychology professor*
Foster, George McClelland, Jr., *anthropologist, educator*
Freedman, Mervin Burton *psychologist, educator*
Glenn, Evelyn Nakano *social sciences educator*
Hafter, Ervin R. *psychology educator*
Hout, Michael *sociologist, educator*
Howell, Francis Clark *paleo-anthropologist*
Hu, Teh-wei *economics professor*
Ivry, Richard *psychology educator*
Jensen, Arthur Robert *psychology educator*
Joyce, Rosemary Alexandria *anthropology educator*
Judge, George Garrett *economics professor*
Kirch, Patrick Vinton *anthropology educator, archaeologist*
Lambert, Nadine Murphy *psychologist, educator*
Landau, Martin *political science educator*
Lee, Ronald Demos *demographer, economist, educator*
Letiche, John Marion *economist, educator*
Luker, Kristin *sociology educator*
Maisel, Sherman Joseph *economist, educator*
Maslach, Christina *psychology educator*
McFadden, Daniel Little *economist, educator*
Muir, William Ker, Jr., *political science educator*
Nader, Laura *anthropology educator*
Quigley, John Michael *economist, educator*
Ranney, Austin (Joseph Ranney) *political science educator*
Rausser, Gordon C(lyde) *agricultural and resource economics educator*
Reich, Michael *economics professor*
Rosenzweig, Mark Richard *psychology educator*
Scotchmer, Suzanne Andersen *economics professor*
Shannon, Chris *economics professor*
Smolensky, Eugene *economics professor*
Stewart, Patricia Rhodes *former clinical psychologist, researcher*
Sulloway, Frank Jones *social sciences educator, historian*
Swope, Alan Joseph *psychologist, educator*
Varian, Hal Ronald *economics professor*
Williamson, Oliver Eaton *economics and law educator*
Zysman, John Adler *political scientist, educator*

Beverly Hills
Yaryan, Ruby Bell *psychologist*

Bonita
Deane, Debbe *psychologist, journalist, editor, consultant*

Burlingame
Schwantes, Robert Sidney *international relations executive*

Canoga Park
Hawes, Bess Lomax *retired anthropologist*

Carlsbad
Fikes, Jay Courtney *anthropology educator, art dealer*
Somit, Albert *political educator*

Carmichael
Hellmuth, William Frederick *economics professor*

Carpinteria
Schmidhauser, John Richard *political science educator*
Wheeler, John Harvey *political scientist, writer*

Carson
Palmer, Beverly Blazey *psychologist, educator*

Chico
Loker, William Meverell *anthropologist, educator*
McNall, Scott Grant *sociologist, educator, academic administrator*
Schmidt, Diane Ellen *political scientist*
Smith, Valene Smith *anthropologist, educator*
Spear, Paul Stanley *psychology educator, musician*

Claremont
Albaum, Jean Stirling *psychologist, educator*
Borcherding, Thomas Earl *economist*
Csikszentmihalyi, Mihaly *psychology educator*
Filson, Darren *economics professor, consultant*
Halpern, Diane F. *psychology educator, professional association executive*
Lasswell, Marcia Lee *psychologist, educator*
Leeb, Charles Samuel *clinical psychologist*
Likens, James Dean *economics professor*
Rossum, Ralph Arthur *political science educator*

Corona Del Mar
Hinderaker, Ivan *political science educator*

Culver City
Friedland, David L. *industrial and organizational psychologist*
Maltzman, Irving Myron *psychology educator*

Danville
Phelps, Orme Wheelock *economics educator emeritus*

Davis
Cohen, Lawrence Edward *sociology educator, criminologist*
Groth, Alexander Jacob *political science educator*
Krubitzer, Leah *psychology educator, neuroscientist*
Mason, William A(lvin) *psychologist, educator, researcher*
McHenry, Henry Malcolm *anthropologist, educator*
Musolf, Lloyd Daryl *political science educator, institute administrator*
Owings, Donald Henry *psychology educator*
Rothchild, Donald Sylvester *political science educator*

Simonton, Dean Keith *psychology educator*
Skinner, G(eorge) William *anthropologist, educator*
Smith, Michael Peter *social science educator, researcher*
Spindler, George Dearborn *anthropologist, educator, writer, editor*

Del Mar
Boynton, Robert Merrill *retired psychology educator*

El Cerrito
Conti, Isabella *psychologist, consultant*

Escondido
Damsbo, Ann Marie *psychologist*

Fairfield
Stevenson, James D(onald), Jr., *psychologist, counselor*

Foster City
Thomlinson, Ralph *demographer, educator*

Fremont
Feinberg, Richard Alan *clinical psychologist*
Nguyen, Sam (Van Nguyen) *economist, researcher*

Fresno
Dackawich, S. John *sociology educator*
Joseph, James William *political scientist, educator, political analyst*
O'Connor, Kevin John *psychologist, educator*

Fullerton
de Rios, Marlene Dobkin *medical anthropologist, educator*
Hershey, Gerald Lee *psychologist, educator*
Kaisch, Kenneth Burton *psychologist, priest*

Glendale
Shahshahani, Ahmad *economics professor*

Glendora
Cerullo, Rudy Michael, II, *psychology, theology educator, minister*

Goleta
Frech, Harry Edward, III, *economics educator, consultant*
Zuk, Gerald Harvey *psychologist, consultant*

Granada Hills
Aller, Wayne Kendall *psychology educator, researcher, computer education company executive, property manager*

Granite Bay
Hartmann, Frederick Howard *political science educator emeritus*

Guerneville
Mannino, J. Davis *psychologist, educator, author*

Hayward
Jun, Jong Sup *public administration educator*
Meyer, Ann Jane *human development educator*
Reevy-Manning, Gretchen Maria *psychology educator*
Staudohar, Paul David *economics professor, labor arbitrator*
Whalen, Thomas Earl *psychology educator*

Healdsburg
Glad, Joan Bourne *retired clinical psychologist, educator*

Hemet
Levine, Elaine Prado *psychologist, music educator, artist*

Hermosa Beach
Wickwire, Patricia Joanne Nellor *psychologist, educator*

Highland
Miller, R. Warburton *psychologist, farmer*

Hollywood
Fisher, Joel Marshall *political scientist, legal consultant, educator*

Huntington Beach
Martin, Wilfred Wesley Finny *psychologist, property owner and manager*

Irvine
Bean, Frank D(awson) *sociology and demography educator*
Burton, Michael Ladd *anthropology educator*
Danziger, James Norris *political science educator*
Huff, C(larence) Ronald *public policy and criminology educator*
Lave, Charles Arthur *economics professor*
Luce, R(obert) Duncan *psychology educator*
Margolis, Julius *economist, educator*
Mc Gaugh, James Lafayette *psychobiologist*
Monroe, Kristen Renwick *political scientist, educator*
Schonfeld, William Rost *political science educator, researcher*
Sperling, George *cognitive scientist, educator*
White, Douglas Richie *anthropology educator*

Kenwood
Podboy, John Watts *clinical, forensic psychologist*

La Jolla
Cain, William Stanley *experimental psychologist, educator, researcher*
Coburn, Marjorie Foster *psychologist, educator*
Cowhey, Peter Francis *international relations educator, consultant*
Crawford, Vincent Paul *economist, educator*
Erie, Steven Philip *political science educator*
Fantino, Edmund *psychology educator*
Farson, Richard Evans *psychologist*
Fowler, Raymond Dalton *psychologist, educator*
Granger, Clive William John *economist, educator*
Harris, Philip Robert *management and space psychologist*

Kaplan, Robert Malcolm *health researcher, educator*
Lane, Sylvia *economist, educator*
Machina, Mark Joseph *economist*
Madsen, Richard Paul *sociology educator, writer*
Mandler, George *psychologist, educator*
Mandler, Jean Matter *psychologist, educator*
Pratt, George Janes, Jr., *psychologist, author*
Schneider, Benjamin *psychology educator, consultant*
Sobel, Joel Kenneth *economist*
Spiro, Melford Elliot *anthropology educator*
Starr, Ross Marc *economist, educator*
Timmermann, Allan Gilling *economics professor*
Weiner, Ferne *psychologist*
White, Michelle Jo *economics professor*

Laguna Beach
Bent, Alan Edward *political science educator, administrator*
Dale, Leon Andrew *economist, educator*

Laguna Niguel
Freeland, Darryl Creighton *psychologist, educator*

Lake Arrowhead
Beckman, James Wallace Bim *economist, marketing professional, educator*

Lancaster
Ellsworth, Richard German *psychologist*
Fluckey, Allison Evans *psychology professor*
Kottraba, Carin *psychologist*

Larkspur
Saxton, Lloyd *psychologist, writer*

Loma Linda
Betancourt, Hector Mainhard *psychology scientist, educator*

Long Beach
Fiebert, Martin Stephen *psychology educator, psychologist*
Hershberger, Scott Laurence *psychologist, educator, statistician, researcher*

Los Angeles
Allen, William Richard *retired economist*
Alvarez, Rodolfo *sociology educator, consultant*
Anawalt, Patricia Rieff *anthropologist, researcher*
Bennett, Charles Franklin, Jr., *biogeographer, educator*
Black, Sandra Eilene *economist, educator*
Brubaker, William Rogers *sociology educator*
Cerrell, Joseph Robert *political scientist, public relations consultant*
Chambers, Mortimer Hardin, Jr., *retired history educator*
Champagne, Duane Willard *sociology educator*
Cheeseboro, Margrit *economics educator*
Clark, Burton Robert *sociologist, educator*
Clark, William Arthur V. *geographer*
Coombs, Robert Holman *behavioral scientist, medical educator, therapist, writer*
Currie, Janet M. *economics professor*
Darby, Michael Rucker *economist, educator*
Dawson, Adam *private investigator*
Dekmejian, Richard Hrair *political science educator*
Dosamantes-Beaudry, Irma *psychology educator*
Edgerton, Robert Breckenridge *anthropologist, educator*
Ellickson, Bryan Carl *economics professor*
Fanselow, Michael Scott *psychology educator*
Forness, Steven Robert *educational psychologist*
Frank, Gelya *anthropologist, educator*
Friedland, Lilli *psychologist, consultant*
Goldberg, Herb *psychologist, educator*
Goldschmidt, Walter Rochs *anthropologist, educator*
Goldstein, Michael Saul *sociologist*
Harberger, Arnold Carl *economist, educator*
Hirsch, Werner Zvi *economist, educator*
Intriligator, Michael David *economist, educator*
Jansson, Bruce Stevenson *social sciences educator, researcher*
Kandal, Terry R. *sociology educator, consultant*
Kelley, Harold Harding *psychology educator*
Klein, Benjamin *economics educator, consultant*
La Force, James Clayburn, Jr., *economist, educator*
Lapatin, Kenneth D.S. *archaeologist, art historian*
Leijonhufvud, Axel Stig Bengt *economics professor*
Lesser, Ian O. *foreign affairs expert*
Light, Ivan Hubert *sociology educator*
Lowenthal, Abraham Frederic *international relations educator*
MacLeod, William Bentley *economics and law educator*
Malamuth, Neil Moshe *psychology and communication educator*
Maquet, Jacques Jerome Pierre *anthropologist, writer*
McCombs, Jeffrey Scott *economist, educator*
McGraw, Phillip C. *psychologist, television personality*
Messner, Michael A. *sociologist, educator*
Michael, William Burton *psychologist, educator*
Montoya, Velma *economist, policy consultant*
Morgner, Aurelius *economist, educator*
Nelson, Howard Joseph *geographer, educator*
Orme, Antony Ronald *geography educator*
Phinney, Jean Swift *psychology educator*
Raven, Bertram H(erbert) *psychology educator*
Roy, William Glenn *sociology educator*
Sandler, Todd Michael *economist, political scientist, educator*
Sapra, Sunil K. *economics professor*
Sears, David O'Keefe *psychology educator*
Shieh, John Ting-chung *economics professor, department chairman*
Shneidman, Edwin S. *psychologist, educator, thanatologist, suicidologist*
Sklar, Richard Lawrence *political science educator*
Sorenson, Olav *sociologist, finance educator*
Strack, Stephen Naylor *psychologist*
Taylor, Shelley E. *psychology researcher and educator*
Thompson, Richard Frederick *psychologist, neuroscientist, educator*
Totten, George Oakley, III, *political science educator*
Turner, Ralph Herbert *sociologist, educator*
Watson, Sharon Gitin *psychologist*
Wilcox, Rand Roger *psychology educator*

Wittrock, Merlin Carl *educational psychologist*
Wong, James Bok *economist, engineer, technologist*
Wood, Nancy Elizabeth *psychologist, educator*
Zeitlin, Maurice *sociology educator, writer*
Zucker, Lynne Goodman *sociology educator, consultant*

Madera
Glynn, James A. *sociology educator, author*

Mendocino
Bilas, Richard A. *economist*

Menlo Park
Clair, Theodore Nat *educational psychologist*
Keeley, Michael Clark *economist*
Lindzey, Gardner *psychologist, educator*
Tiet, Quyen Q. *clinical psychologist, researcher*
Vane, Sylvia Brakke *anthropologist, writer, publishing executive, researcher*

Mill Valley
Harner, Michael James *anthropologist, educator, author*

Modesto
Berry, John Charles *clinical psychologist, educational administrator*

Moffett Field
Clearwater, Yvonne A. *psychologist*
Cohen, Malcolm Martin *psychologist, researcher*
Mallis, Melissa Mercedes *research psychologist*

Monterey
Boger, Dan Calvin *economics professor, consultant*
Reese, William Albert, III, *psychologist, clinical neuropsychologist*

Monterey Park
Amezcua, Charlie Anthony *social science counselor*

Moraga
Hansen, George Eric *political scientist, educator*

Newport Beach
Lawson, Thomas Cheney *fraud examiner*
Whittemore, Paul Baxter *psychologist*

Northridge
Mitchell, Rie Rogers *psychologist, counselor, educator*
Reagan, Janet Thompson *psychologist, educator*

Novato
Bugental, James Frederick Thomas *retired psychologist, educator*
Criswell, Eleanor Camp *psychologist*

Oakland
Anderson, Robert Thomas *anthropologist, researcher, physician*
De Vos, George Alphonse *psychologist, anthropologist*
Farrell, Kenneth Royden *economist*
Nathan, Laura E. *sociology educator*
Neeley, Beverly Evon *sociologist, consultant*
Theroux, David Jon *economist, educator, research and development company executive*

Oceanside
Hertweck, E. Romayne *psychology educator*

Orange
Booth, Donald Richard *economist, educator*

Orinda
Amoroso, Richard Louis *cosmologist, educator*

Pacific Grove
Haider, Paul Randall *psychology consultant*

Pacific Palisades
Hoffenberg, Marvin *retired political science educator, consultant*
Katz, George Gershon *psychologist*
Longaker, Richard Pancoast *political science educator emeritus*

Palo Alto
Beutler, Larry Edward *psychology educator*
Botcheva, Luba *psychologist, researcher*
Brown, H. William *urban economist, private banker*
Calvin, Allen David *psychologist, educator*
Hammett, Benjamin Cowles *psychologist*
Moos, Rudolf H. *psychologist, researcher*
Rosaldo, Renato Ignacio, Jr., *cultural anthropology educator*
Scitovsky, Anne Aickelin *economist, researcher*

Pasadena
Horner, Althea Jane *psychologist*
Munger, Edwin Stanton *political geography educator*
Scudder, Thayer *anthropologist, educator*

Pleasant Hill
Richard, Robert Carter *psychologist*

Pomona
Garrity, Rodman Fox *psychologist, educator*

Portola Valley
Piaget, Gerald Warren *psychologist, educator*
Ward, Robert Edward *retired political science educator and university administrator*

Rancho Palos Verdes
Loether, Herman John *sociologist, educator*

Rancho Santa Margarita
Aguilera, Donna Conant *psychologist, researcher*

Redondo Beach
McWilliams, Margaret Ann *home economics educator, author*

Redwood City
Alexander, Theron *behavioral scientist, psychologist, writer*

Riverside
Calfee, Robert Chilton *psychologist, educational researcher*
Carpenter, Mark Warren *social sciences educator*
Griffin, Keith Broadwell *retired economics educator*
Petrinovich, Lewis Franklin *psychology educator*
Rosenthal, Robert *psychology educator*
Taylor, R. Ervin, Jr., *archaeologist*
Turk, Austin Theodore *sociology educator*
Ullah, Aman *economist, educator*
Warren, David Hardy *psychology educator*

Rohnert Park
Byrne, Noel Thomas *sociologist, educator*
Leeder, Elaine *sociologist, educator, writer*
Rosin, R. Thomas *anthropologist, educator*

Rolling Hills Estates
Castor, Wilbur (Webb) Wright *futurist, writer, consultant, playwright, actor*

Sacramento
Behrman, Bruce Ward *social sciences educator*
Bruce, Thomas Edward *psychology educator, thanatologist*
Chu, Judy May *psychology educator, city official*
Kawamoto, Walter *family life research and service executive*
Majesty, Melvin Sidney *psychologist, consultant*
Newland, Chester Albert *public administration educator*
Post, August Alan *economist, artist*
Sherwood, Robert Petersen *retired sociology educator*
Yang, Yung Y. *economics educator, consultant*

San Bernardino
Maul, Terry Lee *psychologist, educator*
Turpin, Joseph Ovila *counselor, educator*

San Clemente
Ditty, Marilyn Louise *gerontologist, educator*

San Diego
Blade, Melinda Kim *archaeologist, educator, research scientist*
Del Castillo, Adelaida Rebecca *social sciences educator, researcher*
Edwards, Darrel *psychologist*
Emerick, Robert Earl *retired sociologist, educator*
Gazell, James Albert *public administration educator*
Getis, Arthur *geography educator*
Heer, David Macalpine *sociology educator*
Hoston, Germaine Annette *political science educator*
Lewis, Shirley Jeane *psychotherapist, educator*
Litrownik, Alan Jay *psychologist, educator*
Madhavan, Murugappa Chettiar *economics educator, international consultant*
McKeown, Michael Eugene *psychologist, consultant*
Ojeda, Norma *social sciences educator, researcher*
Paupp, Terrence Edward *research associate, educator*
Shedroff, Sharon D. *psychologist, researcher, anthropologist, consultant*
Stoessinger, John George *political science educator*
Storer, Norman William *sociologist, educator*
Trembley, Mark Michel *geographer, educator*
Van Kirk, Jaye Frances *psychology educator*
Weeks, John Robert *geographer, sociology educator*

San Francisco
Adler, Nancy Elinor *psychologist, educator*
Butz, Otto William *political science educator*
Chou, Erwin C. *economist*
Cirese, Robert Charles *economist, real estate investment counselor*
Crittenden, Mary Rita *clinical psychology educator*
Estes, Carroll Lynn *sociologist, educator*
Fox, Patrick John *sociology educator*
Gemello, John Michael *economics educator, consultant, academic administrator*
Hawthorne, Mark R. *investigator, educator*
Hudson, Darril *political scientist, educator*
Krippner, Stanley Curtis *psychologist*
Luft, Harold S. *health economist*
Marston, Michael *urban economist, asset management executive*
Moser, R. Kevin *clinical psychologist, educator*
Rice, Dorothy Pechman (Mrs. John Donald Rice) *medical economist*
Rubin, Seth Isaiah *psychologist*
Schneider, Kirk J. *psychologist, writer*
Sedway, Lynn Massel *real estate economist*
Smith, Robert Charles *political science educator, researcher*
van den Daele, Leland Douglas *psychology educator, psychological measurement company executive*
Warner, Rollin Miles, Jr., *economics educator, real estate broker*
Wells, Gertrude Beverly *psychologist*

San Jose
Cedolini, Anthony John *psychologist*
McDowell, Jennifer *sociologist, composer, playwright, publisher*
Pellegrini, Robert J. *psychology educator*
Voth, Alden H. *political science educator*
Wiens, Beverly Jo *psychology professor*

San Luis Obispo
Fairbanks, William Louis, II, *anthropologist, educator*
Geringer, John Michael *economist, educator*

San Rafael
Hoyt, Michael F. *psychologist, writer*
Tosti, Donald Thomas *psychologist, consultant*

San Ramon
Kalicki, Jan H. *economist, political scientist*

Santa Barbara
Aigner, Dennis John *economics educator, consultant*
Bohn, Henning *economist, educator*
Collins, Fuji *clinical psychologist*
Comanor, William S. *economist, educator*
Davidson, Roger H(arry) *political scientist, educator*
Erasmus, Charles John *anthropologist, educator*
Glasgow, Garrett Edwin *political science educator*
Gravitz, Herbert L. *clinical psychologist, writer*
Jochim, Michael Allan *archaeologist*
Mack, Judith Cole Schrim *retired political scientist*
Mayer, Richard Edwin *psychology educator*
Robinson, William I. *sociologist*
Sherman, Alan Robert *psychologist, educator*
Steigerwald, Douglas Gardiner *economics professor*

Santa Clara
Field, Alexander James *economics professor, dean*

Santa Cruz
Males, Michael Arnold *sociologist, educator, writer, consultant*
Pettigrew, Thomas Fraser *social psychologist, educator*
Resneck-Sannes, Helen *psychologist*
Roby, Pamela Ann *sociologist, educator*
Smith, M(ahlon) Brewster *retired psychologist, educator*
Tharp, Roland George *psychology professor*

Santa Monica
Berres, Frances Brandes *clinical psychologist*
Ellickson, Phyllis Lynn *political scientist*
Russell, Marlou *psychologist*
Smith, James Patrick *economist*
Wolf, Charles, Jr., *economist, educator*

Seaside
Mendoza, Ruben G. *anthropologist, educator, archaeologist*
Segall, Daniel Owen *psychologist, researcher*

Somerset
Carr, Les *psychologist, educator*

Sonora
Clarke, Paula Katherine *anthropology educator, sociology educator*

Stanford
Amemiya, Takeshi *economist, statistician*
Arrow, Kenneth Joseph *economist, educator*
Bandura, Albert *psychologist, educator*
Brody, Richard Alan *political science educator, researcher*
Bueno de Mesquita, Bruce James *political science educator*
Bunzel, John Harvey *political science educator, researcher*
Carlsmith, James Merrill *psychologist, educator*
Damon, William Van Buren *developmental psychologist, educator, writer*
Enthoven, Alain Charles *economist, educator*
Ferguson, James *anthropologist, educator*
Friedman, Milton *retired economist*
Fuchs, Victor Robert *economist, educator*
Gage, Nathaniel Lees *psychologist, educator*
George, Alexander Lawrence *political scientist, educator*
Hickman, Bert George, Jr., *economist, educator*
Howell, James Edwin *economist, educator*
Huntington, Hillard Griswold *economist*
Inkeles, Alex *sociology educator*
Klein, Richard G. *anthropologist, educator*
Krumboltz, John Dwight *psychologist, educator*
Kurz, Mordecai *economics professor*
Lazear, Edward Paul *economics and labor relations educator, researcher*
Lepper, Mark Roger *psychology educator*
Lewis, John Wilson *political science educator*
Maccoby, Eleanor Emmons *psychology educator*
March, James Gardner *social scientist, educator*
Martin, Joanne *social sciences educator*
McAdam, Douglas John *sociologist, educator, director*
Mc Lure, Charles E., Jr., *economist, consultant*
Noll, Roger Gordon *economist, educator*
Padilla, Amado M. *psychologist, adult education educator*
Ricardo-Campbell, Rita *economist, educator*
Roberts, Donald John *economics and business educator, consultant*
Scott, W. Richard *retired sociologist, educator*
Scott, W(illiam) Richard *sociology educator*
Van Horne, James Carter *economist, educator*
Wacziarg, Romain Thomas *social sciences educator*
Zajonc, Robert B(oleslaw) *psychology educator*

Sylmar
Yguado, Alex Rocco *economics professor*

Tiburon
Barron-Druckrey, Eleanor *psychologist*

Trabuco Canyon
Addy, Jo Alison Phears *economist*

Turlock
Ahlem, Lloyd Harold *psychologist*

Ventura
Bowles, Walter Donald *economist, educator*
Naurath, David Allison *engineering psychologist, researcher*

Victorville
Dilliard, Maxine K. *retired school psychologist*

Visalia
Daniels, Madeline Marie *forensic psychologist, educator, author*

Walnut Creek
Keith, Bruce Edgar *political analyst, genealogist*

Woodland Hills
Holland, Kathleen *political science educator*

COLORADO

Arvada
Yamamoto, Kaoru *retired psychology and education educator*

Aspen
Manosevitz, Martin *psychologist*

Boulder
Adler, Patricia Ann *sociologist, educator*
Beer, Francis Anthony *political science educator*
Borysenko, Joan *psychologist, biologist*
Bourne, Lyle Eugene, Jr., *psychology educator*
Greenberg, Edward Seymour *political science educator, writer*
Healy, Alice Fenvessy *psychology educator, researcher*
Hubbard, Eleanor A. *sociologist, educator*
Jessor, Richard *psychologist, educator*
Kintsch, Walter *psychology educator, director*
Menken, Jane Ava *demographer, educator*
Neinas, Charles Merrill *economist, consultant, sports association executive*
Walker, Deward Edgar, Jr., *anthropologist, educator*
White, Gilbert F(owler) *geographer, educator*

Centennial
Milliken, John Gordon *research economist*

Colorado Springs
Brooks, Glenn Ellis *political science educator, educational administrator*
Farrer, Claire Anne Rafferty *anthropologist, educator, folklorist*
Standing Bear, Zugguelgeres Galafach *criminologist, forensic scientist, educator*

Denver
Adelman, Jonathan Reuben *political science educator, consultant*
Britz, John Dominic, II, *political scientist, consultant*
Conger, John Janeway *psychologist, educator*
Curl, Layton Seth *psychologist, consultant, educator*
Kestenbaum, Richard *psychologist*
Nelson, Sarah Milledge *archaeology educator*
Piland, Neill Finnes *health services economist, researcher*
Piper, Steven Lee *economist*
Snyder, Charles Royce *sociologist, educator*
Winters, Richard Allen *mineral economist*
Zimet, Carl Norman *psychologist, educator*

Durango
Zeller, Christopher Lee *archaeologist, preservationist*

Fort Collins
Bennett, Thomas LeRoy, Jr., *clinical neuropsychology educator*
Butki, Brian David *psychologist, educator*
Eitzen, David Stanley *sociologist, educator*
Moorcroft, William Herbert *retired bio-psychologist, educator, researcher*
Nobe, Kenneth Charles *international agricultural and water resource economics consultant*
Ozawa, Terutomo *economics educator, consultant*
Suinn, Richard Michael *psychologist*

Golden
Petrick, Alfred, Jr., *mineral economics educator, consultant*

Grand Junction
Bacon, Phillip *geographer, author, consultant*
Morton, Louis George *retired social sciences educator*

Greeley
Kelsey, Michael Loyal *geography educator*
Woody, William Douglas *social sciences educator, researcher*

Greenwood Village
Hendrick, Hal Wilmans *human factors educator*

Lafayette
Conrad, Kelley Allen *industrial and organizational psychologist*

Lakewood
Kulkarni, Kishore Ganesh *economics educator, consultant*

Littleton
Cabell, Elizabeth Arlisse *psychologist*
Lohman, Loretta Cecelia *social scientist, consultant*

Loveland
Ahmann, John Stanley *retired psychologist*
Walker, Laurie Shannon *psychologist, counselor*

Nederland
Sutton, Philip D. (Philip Dietrich Sutton) *psychologist, educator*

Pine
Jones, David Milton *economist, educator*

Pueblo
Keller, Robert L. *criminologist, educator*
Mo, Suchoon *psychology educator*
Vega, Jose Guadalupe *neuropsychologist, clinical professional*

CONNECTICUT

Barkhamsted
Stokes, Susan *political science educator*

Bloomfield
Scheuch, Richard *economist, educator*

Bridgeport
Maloney, Maureen Murphy *social sciences educator*

Brookfield
Stern, Michael Lawrence *psychologist, educator*

Cromwell
Günther-Stirn, Dagmar Dorothea *retired social sciences educator*

Danbury
Tolor, Alexander *psychologist, educator*

Fairfield
Kleine, Herman *economist*
Timmermann, Sandra *educational gerontologist, communication specialist*

Greenwich
Clark, Harry Warren *public policy consultant*

Guilford
Chatt, Allen Barrett *psychologist, neuroscientist*

Hartford
Curran, Ward Schenk *economist, educator*
Gunderson, Gerald Axel *economics educator, administrator*

Higganum
de Brigard, Emilie *anthropologist, consultant*

Killingworth
Kilby, Peter *economics educator*

Middlebury
Phillips, Walter Mills, III, *psychologist, educator*

Middletown
Barber, William Joseph *educator, economist*
Blume, Ginger (Elaine Blume) *psychologist*
Crenshaw, Martha *political science educator*
Harris, Dale Benner *psychologist, educator*
Miller, Richard Alan *economist, educator*
Scheibe, Karl Edward *psychology educator*
Wasch, William Karl *gerontologist, consultant*

Milford
Haigh, Charles *criminal justice educator*
Schwartz, Richard Edward Derecktor *retired sociologist, educator*

Naugatuck
Suscovich, David J. *neuropsychologist, marriage and family therapist*

New Britain
Chavarro, Adolfo *psychology professor, researcher*

New Haven
Bell, Wendell *sociologist, educator, futurist*
Blatt, Sidney Jules *psychology educator and investigator, psychoanalyst*
Brainard, William Crittenden *economist, educator, university official*
Brantl, Sister Charlesmarie *economics professor*
Brownell, Kelly David *psychologist, educator*
Coe, Michael Douglas *anthropologist, educator*
Conklin, Harold Colyer *anthropologist, educator*
Crakes, Gary Michael *economics professor*
Ember, Carol R. *anthropology educator, author*
Ember, Melvin Lawrence *anthropologist, educator*
Erikson, Kai *sociologist, educator*
Errington, James Joseph *anthropology educator*
Evenson, Robert Eugene *economist, educator*
Fang, Hanming *economist, educator*
Green, Donald Philip *political scientist, educator*
Jackson, Shirley Ann *sociology educator*
Kazdin, Alan E. *psychology educator*
LaPalombara, Joseph *political science and industrial management educator*
Marks, Lawrence Edward *psychologist, educator*
Marmor, Theodore Richard *political science and public management educator*
Mayhew, David Raymond *political science educator*
McGuire, William James *social psychology educator*
Peck, Merton Joseph *economist, educator*
Phillips, Peter Charles Bonest *economist, educator, researcher*
Pospisil, Leopold Jaroslav *anthropology and law educator*
Ranis, Gustav *economist, educator*
Reynolds, Lloyd George *economist, educator*
Rouse, Irving *anthropologist, emeritus educator*
Russett, Bruce Martin *political science educator*
Scarf, Herbert Eli *economics educator*
Schultz, T. Paul *economics professor*
Shubik, Martin *economics professor*
Sternberg, Robert Jeffrey *psychology educator, researcher*
Stevens, Joseph Charles *psychology educator*
Sutterlin, James Smyrl *political science educator, researcher*
Westerfield, Holt Bradford *political scientist, educator*
Zigler, Edward Frank *psychologist, educator*

New London
Chrisler, Joan C. *psychologist, educator*
Winter, Jerry Alan *sociology educator*

North Haven
Dahl, Robert Alan *political science educator*
Mahl, George Franklin *psychoanalyst, psychologist, educator*

Norwalk
Rosado, Rodolfo Jose *psychologist, educator*

Old Lyme
Johnson, James Myron *psychologist, educator*

Sharon
Mesniaeff, Gregory *economist, securities analyst*

Southbury
Atwood, Edward Charles *economist, educator*

Stamford
Grossman, Sanford Jay *economics professor*
Robins, Robert Sidwar *political science educator, administrator*
Teeters, Nancy Hays *economist, director*

Storrs
Miceli, Thomas Joseph *economist, educator*

Voluntown
Thevenet, Patricia Confrey *social studies educator*

Wallingford
Cline, John Carroll *clinical psychologist*

West Hartford
Farnen, Russell Francis *political scientist, educator*

Weston
Gerber, Frances Joyce *retired early childhood educator*

Willimantic
Danforth, Jeffrey Scott *psychologist, educator*

DELAWARE

Dover
Hoff, Samuel Boyer *political scientist, educator*

Lewes
Chapman, Janet Carter Goodrich (Mrs. John William Chapman) *economist, educator*

Newark
Abrams, Burton A. *economics professor*
Bilinsky, Yaroslav *political scientist*
Brams, Marvin Robert *economist, mental health counselor, interfaith minister*
Bunkše, Edmunds Valdemārs *geographer, educator, consultant*
DiRenzo, Gordon James *sociologist, psychologist, educator*
Garland, Howard *psychology educator*
Graham, Frances Keesler (Mrs. David Tredway Graham) *psychologist, educator*
Mangone, Gerard J. *international and maritime law educator*
Raffel, Jeffrey Allen *urban affairs educator*
Tannian, Francis Xavier *economist, educator*

Wilmington
Kneavel, Thomas Charles, Jr., *psychologist, educator*

DISTRICT OF COLUMBIA

Washington
Aaron, Henry J. *economist*
Aaron, Henry Jacob *economics professor*
Abler, Ronald Francis *geography educator*
Abraham, Katharine Gail *economics professor*
Albanese, Jay Samuel *criminologist, educator*
Arend, Anthony Clark *international relations educator*
Aring, Monika Kosmahl *education economist, consultant, researcher*
Aschheim, Joseph *economist, educator*
Åslund, Anders *economist*
Baer, Michael Alan *political scientist, educator*
Bartlett, Bruce Reeves *economist, columnist*
Barton, Jean Marie *psychologist, educator*
Becker, Mary Louise *political scientist*
Bergmann, Barbara Rose *economics professor*
Bergsten, C. Fred *economist*
Besen, Stanley Martin *economist*
Bhattacharya, Rina *economist*
Birdsall, Nancy *economist*
Blair, Bruce G. *policy analyst*
Bloch, Farrell Edward *economist, writer*
Bluth, B. J. (Elizabeth Jean Catherine Bluth) *sociologist, aerospace technologist*
Bolino, August Constantino *economics professor*
Brimmer, Andrew Felton *economist, consultant*
Bruck, Nicholas *economist, educator*
Brzezinski, Zbigniew *political science educator, author*
Buckberg, Albert *retired economist*
Burtless, Gary Thomas *economist, consultant*
Calder, Kent Eyring *political science educator, diplomat*
Caldwell, Willard E. *psychologist, educator*
Carliner, Michael Simon *economist, association executive*
Carpenter, Ted Galen *political scientist*
Carro, Cecilia *political scientist, researcher*
Chang, Won *economist*
Checchi, Vincent Victor *retired economist*
Cline, William Richard *economist, educator*
Cole, Daniel Gerard *geographer, information scientist, cartographer*
Collins, Eileen Louise *economist*
Corbet, Richard Hugh *trade policy specialist, writer*
Cordella, Tito *economist*
Craig, John Tucker *economist, consultant*
Crocker, William Henry *ethnologist, researcher*
Crowe, William James, Jr., *educator, international consultant*
Danziger, Raphael *political scientist, researcher*
Davis, Shelton Harold *social anthropologist*
Day, Lincoln Hubert *demographer, educator*
Dillon, Wilton Sterling *anthropologist, foundation administrator*
Dizard, Wilson Paul, Jr., *international affairs consultant, educator*
Dollar, David Richard *economist*
Downs, Anthony *urban economist, real estate consultant*
Eads, George Curtis *economic consultant*
Elliott, Kimberly Ann *economist*
English, Richard Allyn *sociologist, social work educator*
Ershler, William Baldwin *biogerontologist, educator*
Etzioni, Amitai *sociologist, educator*
Falcoff, Mark *Latin American specialist*
Faux, Jeff (Geoffrey Peter Faux) *economist, writer*
Feshbach, Murray *demographer, educator*
Feuer, Marvin C. *political scientist, educator*
Franco, Robert *economist*
Frank, Isaiah *economist, educator*
Froehle, Bryan Thomas *sociologist, director*
Gallo, Anthony Ernest *playwright, economist*
Genia, Vicky *psychologist*
Gillingham, Robert Fenton *economist, consultant*
Godson, Roy Simon *political scientist, think tank executive*
Gonzalez-Hermosillo, Brenda *economist, researcher*
Goode, Richard Benjamin *economist, educator*
Gordon, Lincoln *political economist*
Gorte, Ross William *economist, researcher*
Gramlich, Edward Martin *public policy, economics educator, federal agency administrator*
Grapin, Jacqueline G. *economist*
Gravitz, Melvin A *psychologist, consultant*
Greenberg, Milton *political scientist, educator*
Haaga, John Gregory *demographer*
Hall, George Robert *economist*
Halperin, Morton H. *political scientist*
Hartmann, Heidi Irmgard Victoria *economist, research organization executive*
Helms, Robert Brake *economist, research director*
Hess, Stephen *political scientist, author*
Hrung, Warren *economist*
Hudson, Michael Craig *political science educator*
Hufbauer, Gary Clyde *economist, lawyer, educator*
Hughes, Kent Higgon *economist*
Jacobson, Allen Howard *economist*
Jaspersen, Frederick Zarr *economist*
Joyner, Christopher Clayton *international relations educator*
Kanaan, Oussama *economist*
Kemp, Geoffrey Thomas Howard *international affairs specialist*
Kendrick, John Whitefield *economist, educator, consultant*
Kennedy, Muriel *psychologist, consultant, educator*
Kilpatrick, Henry Edward *economist, educator, consultant*
Kirkpatrick, Jeane Duane Jordan *political scientist, government official*
Kohn, Donald L. *economist, federal agency administrator*
Krulfeld, Ruth Marilyn *anthropologist, educator*
Kuh, Charlotte Virginia *economist*
Kvint, Vladimir Lev *economist, mining engineer, finance educator*
Kybal, Elba Gómez del Rey *economist, non-profit organization executive*
Laden, Ben Ellis *economist, writer*
Lardy, Nicholas Richard *economist, educator*
LeoGrande, William Mark *political science educator, writer*
Lieber, Robert James *political science educator, writer*
Littig, Lawrence William *psychologist, educator*
Madian, Alan Leonard *economist, management consultant*
Makalou, Oumar *economic advisor*
Manchester, Paul Brunson *economist*
Mann, Thomas Edward *political scientist*
Marcuss, Rosemary Daly *economist*
Martinez, Herminia S. *economist, banker*
Marx, Paul Louis *economist*
Maudlin, Robert V. *economics and government affairs consultant*
McGinnies, Elliott Morse *psychologist, educator*
Meggers, Betty Jane *anthropologist, researcher*
Melanson, Richard Allen *political science educator*
Mellor, John Williams *economist, policy consultant firm executive*
Millar, James Robert *economist, educator, university official*
Miller, James Clifford, III, *economist*
Miller, Margery *psychologist, speech pathologist, mental health educator, administrator*
Minarik, Joseph John *economist, researcher*
Mistral, Jacques *economist*
Morgan, Bruce Ray *international consultant*
Muldrow, Tressie Wright *psychologist*
Muller, Steven *international studies educator, academic administrator*
Munnell, Alicia Haydock *economist*
Nagorski, Zygmunt *political scientist, writer*
Nash, John Davidson, Jr., *economist*
Ndegwa, Stephen N. *political scientist, educator*
Nelsen, Hart Michael *sociologist, educator*
Newman, Monroe *retired economist, educator*
Niskanen, William Arthur, Jr., *economist, think-tank executive*
O'Connor, Karen *political science educator, researcher, writer*
Offutt, Susan Elizabeth *economist*
Ooms, Van Doorn *economist*
Orszag, Jonathan Marc *economist, consultant*
Orszag, Peter Richard *economist*
Ortner, Donald J. *biological anthropologist, educator*
Oweiss, Ibrahim Mohamed *economist, educator*
Ozer, Martha Ross *psychologist, counselor*
Paci, Pierella *economist*
Pasternack, Robert Harry *school psychologist*
Pasurka, Carl A., Jr., *economist*
Penner, Rudolph Gerhard *economist, educator*
Perito, Robert Michael *political scientist*
Perry, George Lewis *research economist, consultant*
Phillips, Karen Borlaug *economist, railroad industry executive*
Phillips, Susan Meredith *financial economist, university administrator*
Pickenpaugh, Thomas Edward *archaeologist, anthropologist*
Pirchner, Herman, Jr., *foreign policy specialist*
Popkin, Joel *economist, consultant*
Prestowitz, Clyde Vincent *economist, researcher*
Quintanilla-Villanueva, Rosalinda *economist*
Randall, Robert L(ee) *ecological economist*
Rao, Vijayendra *economist*
Raslear, Thomas Gregory *psychologist*
Ravenal, Earl Cedric *international relations educator, author*
Reining, Priscilla Copeland *anthropologist*
Reischauer, Robert D. *research organization executive*
Relyea, Harold Clarence *political scientist*
Ridley, Stanley Eugene *clinical psychologist, consultant*
Roberts, Markley *economist, educator*
Roberts, Walter Ronald *political science educator, former government official*
Rodriguez, Rita Maria *economist*
Roett, Riordan *political science educator, consultant*
Rosenau, James Nathan *political scientist, author*
Rosenberg, Joel Barry *government economist*
Ryn, Claes Gösta *political science educator, author, research institute administrator*
Sawhill, Isabel Van Devanter *economist*
Scheffman, David Theodore *economist, management educator, consultant*
Schlesinger, James Rodney *economist*
Schley, Wayne Arthur *political consultant*
Schmukler, Sergio L. *economist*
Scholl, Kathleen Kay *economist*
Shambaugh, David Leigh *political scientist, educator, writer*
Shapiro, Robert Jacob *economic affairs executive*
Sharma, Martha Bridges *geography educator*
Sibley, Lynn M. *anthropologist, educator*
Silverman, Lester Paul *economist, energy industry consultant*
Simes, Dimitri Konstantin *international affairs expert and educator*
Snyder, Jed C. *foreign affairs specialist*
Solomon, Elinor Harris *economics professor*
Solomon, Richard Harvey *political scientist*
Squires, Gregory Douglas *sociologist, educator*
Stanford, Dennis Joe *archaeologist, museum curator*
Steinberg, David Isaac *social sciences educator, consultant*
Stelzer, Irwin Mark *economist*
Stent, Angela E. *political scientist, educator, director*
Stephenson, Sherry Madeline *trade economist*
Sterner, Michael Edmund *international affairs consultant*
Stone, Russell A. *sociology educator*
Struelens, Michel Maurice Joseph Georges *political science educator, foreign affairs consultant*
Sunley, Emil McKee *economist*
Sweeney, Richard James *economics educator*
Thurber, James A. *political scientist, educator*
Timmer, Charles Peter *agricultural and development economist*
Turner, John Andrew *economist*
VandenBos, Gary Roger *psychologist, publisher*
Warren, Steven F. *psychologist, educator*
Weinhold, Linda Lillian *psychologist, researcher*
Weintraub, Sidney *economist, educator*
White, John Kenneth *politics educator*
White, Roger Stuart *economist*
Whitehurst, Grover Jay *federal official, psychologist and educator*
Wilensky, Gail Roggin *economist, researcher*
Williamson, John *economist*
Willner, Ann Ruth *political scientist, educator*
Willner, Dorothy *anthropologist, educator*
Wilson, Ewen Maclellan *economist*
Wolf, Alfred Clarence *retired economist*
Wood, Bernard Anthony *anthropology educator*

FLORIDA

Aventura
Krop, Lois Pulver *psychologist*

Bal Harbour
Bond, Alma Halbert *psychoanalyst, author*

Boca Raton
Tata, Robert Joseph *retired geographer, educator*

Boynton Beach
Mittel, John J. *economist, corporate executive*
Vella, Fred John *social studies educator*

Bradenton
Merrick, Janna Carol *political scientist, educator*

Brandon
Mussenden, Gerald *psychologist*

Cape Coral
Shuman, Carolyn Rae (Thorburn) *psychologist, columnist, writer, nurse*

Clearwater
Peterson, James Robert *engineering psychologist*

Cocoa
McLendon, Dorothy *school psychologist*

Coral Gables
Mundy, Peter *psychology educator*
Schwartztol, Holly Wechsler *psychologist*

Davie
Morris, Joseph Raymond *business and economics educator*

Daytona Beach
Frederick-Recascino, Christina Marie *psychologist, educator*
Patterson, Roger Lewis *psychologist*

Deland
Wood, Richard Harvey, Jr., *economics professor*

Dunedin
O'Dea, J. David *psychologist, educator*

Estero
Routh, Donald K(ent) *psychology educator*

Fort Lauderdale
Azrin, Nathan Harold *psychologist, educator*
Bartelstone, Rona Sue *gerontologist*
Collins, Ronald William *psychologist, educator*
Costa, Robin Leueen *psychologist, counselor*
Maxwell, Sara Elizabeth *psychologist, educator, speech pathologist, director*

Fort Myers
Smith, Paul Frederick *economist, former educator*
Sprinkel, Beryl Wayne *economist, consultant*

Gainesville
Albarracín, Dolores *psychologist, educator*
Bernard, H. Russell *anthropologist, educator, editor*
Dewsbury, Donald Allen *psychology historian, comparative psychologist*
Doty, Leilani *geriatric neuropsychologist, administrator*
Milanich, Jerald Thomas *archaeologist, museum curator*
Mills, Teheran L. (Terry Mills) *sociology educator*
Moore, John Hartwell *anthropology educator, consultant*
Schlenker, Barry Richard *psychologist, educator, researcher*
Shih, Chuan-kang *anthropologist*
Thiele, Leslie Paul *political science educator*
von Mering, Otto Oswald *anthropology educator*
Wagner, Eric Armin *sociology educator*
Wass, Hannelore Lina *educational psychology educator*

Hobe Sound
Snook, Stover Hoffman *social sciences educator, researcher*

Hollywood
Foreman, Edwin Francis *economist, real estate broker*
Sundel, Martin *psychologist, educator, management consultant*
Valdes, Jacqueline Chehebar *psychologist, consultant, researcher*

Jacksonville
Cason, Fred Lee *political scientist, educator*
Ejimofor, Cornelius Ogu *political scientist, educator*
Libby, Ronald Theodore *political science educator, consultant, researcher*
Urbina, Susana Patricia *psychology educator, consultant*

Lake City
McMahon, Sean Howard *social studies educator*

Lakeland
Ratliff, Charles Edward, Jr., *economics professor*

Largo
Ellis, Susan Gottenberg *psychologist*

Maitland
Blackburn, John Oliver *economist, consultant*
Von Hilsheimer, George Edwin, III, *neuropsychologist*

Miami
Anbarci, Nejat Mehmet *economist, educator*
Bravo, Irene Maria *psychologist, educator*
Burnett, Keitha Denise *social studies educator*
Escotet, Miguel-Angel *psychologist, educator*
Fine, Jeffrey Louis *psychologist, writer, researcher, lecturer*
Finley, Gordon Ellis *psychology educator*
Griffith, Daniel Alva *geography educator*
Humphries, Joan Ropes *psychologist, educator*
Huysman, Arlene Weiss *psychologist, educator, writer*
Kanet, Roger Edward *political science educator*
Koncsol, Stephen Wayne *psychologist, educator*
Rosenbaum, Allan *public administration educator, academic administrator, international governance advisor*
Rosenberg, Mark B. *political science educator, university official*
Russell, Elbert Winslow *neuropsychologist*
Salazar-Carrillo, Jorge *economics professor*
Weagraff, Patrick James *psychology educator, writer*

Ocala
Grissom, Robert Jesse, Sr., *criminal justice educator*

Orlando
Jerome, Christian Joseph *psychologist, researcher*
Kennedy, Robert Samuel *experimental psychologist, consultant*
Renk, Kimberly Dawn *social sciences educator*

Palm Bay
Seifer, Ronald Leslie *psychologist*

Palm Beach
Amling, Frederick *economist, educator, investment advisor*

Palm Harbor
Padberg, Daniel Ivan *agricultural economics educator, researcher*

Panama City
Caiazzo, Tom A *political scientist, educator*
Roberts, Paul Craig, III, *economics educator, author, columnist*

Pensacola
Davis, Wesley D. *psychologist, educator*
Kernstock, Elwyn Nicholas *political science educator, author*
Killian, Lewis Martin *sociology educator*

Plantation
Appel, Antoinette Ruth *neuropsychologist*

Pompano Beach
Gilchrist, William Risque, Jr., *economist*

Ponte Vedra Beach
Moore, David Graham *sociologist, educator*
Wu, Hsiu Kwang *economist, educator*

Port Charlotte
Von Holden, Martin Harvey *psychologist*

Port Richey
Mueller, Lois M. *psychologist*

Port Saint Lucie
Augelli, John Pat *geographer, educator, writer, consultant, rancher*

Saint Augustine
Henderson, Hazel *economist, writer, lecturer*
Kiehlbauch, John B *psychologist*

Saint Petersburg
Baker, Victoria Jean *anthropology educator*
Price-Smith, Andrew Thomas *social sciences educator, consultant*

Sanibel
Crown, David Allan *criminologist, educator*

Sarasota
Coufoudakis, Van *political science educator*
Cramer, Stanley Howard *psychology educator, author*
Gordon, Sanford Daniel *economics professor*
Hamberg, Daniel *economist, educator*
Masters, John Christopher *psychologist, educator, writer*
Ruva, Christine Lorraine *psychologist, educator*
Serrie, Hendrick *retired anthropology and international business educator*

Sparr
Tovi, Murray *futurist, research scientist*

Stuart
Dimbath, Merle F. *economic consultant, business educator*

Summerland Key
Muth, John Fraser *economics professor*

Sun City Center
Hall, John Fry *retired psychologist*
Leonard, William Norris *economist, educator*

Tallahassee
Cobbe, James Hamilton *economics professor*
Guy, Mary Ellen Johnston *political science educator*
Holcombe, Randall Gregory *economics professor*
Hull, Elaine Mangelsdorf *psychology educator*
Johnson, Benjamin F., VI, *economist, consultant*
Joiner, Thomas *psychology educator*
Laird, William Everette, Jr., *economics educator, administrator*
Martin, Leisa Ann *social sciences educator*
Moore, Kurt Richard *anthropologist, fundraiser, investor*
Nam, Charles Benjamin *demographer, sociologist, educator, writer*
Roady, Elston Edward (Steve) *political scientist, educator*
Standley-Burt, Nancy Vilma *retired psychologist, educator*
Zirps, Fotena Anatolia *psychologist, researcher*

Tampa
Brady, Kathleen Deming *psychologist, occupational therapist, educator*
DeSalvo, Joseph Salvatore *economics educator, researcher*
Donchin, Emanuel *psychologist, educator*
Ernst, Roger *international studies educator, consultant*
Genshaft, Judy Lynn *psychologist, educator*
Heide, Kathleen Margaret *criminology educator, psychotherapist*
Kimmel, Ellen Bishop *psychologist, educator*
MacManus, Susan Ann *political science educator, researcher*
Piper, John Richard *political science educator*
Spielberger, Charles Donald *psychology educator, behiovial medicine, clinical and health psychologist*
Vanden, Harry Edwin *political science educator*
Weiner, Irving Bernard *psychologist*

Tequesta
Swets, John Arthur *psychologist, researcher*

Venice
Delaney, Robert Finley *columnist, political sociologist, lecturer*
Gooding, Charles Thomas *psychology educator, retired college provost*

West Palm Beach
Dye, Thomas Roy *political science educator*
Gold, Bela *economist, educator*
McCluskey, Neil Gerard *gerontologist, educator, literary agent*

GEORGIA

Albany
Stallworth, Charles Derotha, Jr., *psychologist*

Alpharetta
Marsella, Anthony Joseph *psychologist, educator*

Athens
Allsbrook, Ogden Olmstead, Jr., *retired economics educator*
Bertsch, Gary Kenneth *political scientist, educator*
Clute, Robert Eugene *political and social science educator*
Dunn, Delmer Delano *political science educator*
Fincher, Cameron Lane *psychology professor*
Garbin, Albeno Patrick *sociology educator*
Kamerschen, David Roy *economist, educator*
Mustard, David Brendan MacDougal *economist, educator*
Nichols, William Curtis *psychologist, family therapist, consultant*
O'Toole, Laurence Joseph *public administration and policy educator, researcher*
Pollack, Robert Harvey *psychology educator*
Tesser, Abraham *social psychologist*

Atlanta
Bahl, Roy Winford *economist, educator, consultant*
Bailey, Michael Stewart *political science educator*
Endicott, John Edgar *international relations educator*
Garland, LaRetta Matthews *psychologist, educator, nursing educator*
Kerr, Nancy Helen *psychology educator*
Knapp, Charles Boynton *economist, educator, former university president*
Littrell, Jill *social sciences educator*
Muth, Richard Ferris *economics professor*
Paredes, James Anthony *anthropologist, educator*
Payne, Maxwell Carr, Jr., *retired psychology educator*
Reese, Cynthia Dene *psychologist, educator, quality assurance professional, risk management consultant*
Rubin, Paul Harold *economist*
Snarey, John Robert *psychologist, researcher, medical educator*
Stephan, Paula Elizabeth *economics educator, university official*
Thursby, Jerry Gilbert *economics educator, consultant*
Tillman, Mary Norman *urban affairs consultant*
Wald, Michael Leonard *economist*

Augusta
Davis, Catherine Lucy *psychologist, diabetes researcher*

Barnesville
Terry, Pamela Mays *psychology educator*

Blackshear
Walker, Thomas Michael *school psychologist*

Carrollton
Aanstoos, Christopher Michael *psychology educator*
Cao, Li *social studies educator, educator*
Clark, Janet Eileen *political scientist, educator*

Columbus
Kerr, Allen Stewart *retired psychologist*
McFarland, Samuel P., Jr., *psychologist*

Decatur
Beran, Michael James *research psychologist, primatologist*
Lucius, Randall H. *psychologist*

Evans
Zachert, Virginia *psychologist, educator*

Gainesville
Ferriss, Abbott Lamoyne *sociology educator emeritus*

Kennesaw
Karcher, Barbara Correnti *sociologist, educator*
Li, Chien-pin *political scientist, educator*

Lawrenceville
Reuter, Helen Hyde *psychologist*

Macon
Craig, Kern William *political science educator*
Lewis, Sandra Combs *research psychologist, writer*
Murdoch, Bernard Constantine *psychology educator*

Marietta
Dudley, Gary Edward *clinical psychologist*

Oxford
Cody, William Bermond *political science educator*

Rome
Black, Suzanne Watkins DuPuy *psychology educator*
Granrose, Cherlyn Sue *psychologist, educator, medical researcher*
Johnson, Alberta Clark *psychology educator*

Roswell
Klein, John Jacob *retired economist*

Savannah
Rozantine, Gayle Stubbs *clinical psychologist*

Statesboro
Freeman, Robert Noble *psychology educator*
Henry, Nicholas Llewellyn *public administration educator*
Lloyd, Margaret Ann *psychologist, educator*
Pino, Nathan Willett *criminologist, educator, sociologist*

Stockbridge
Grimes, Richard Allen *economics professor*

Suwanee
Swanson, David H(enry) *consultant, retired economist, educator*

Toccoa Falls
Allison, Norman Ernest, Jr., *anthropologist, educator*

HAWAII

Hilo
Dixon, Paul William *psychology educator*

Holualoa
Scarr, Sandra Wood *retired psychology educator, researcher*

Honolulu
Bitterman, Morton Edward *psychologist, educator*
Cho, Lee-Jay *social scientist, demographer*
Fullmer, Daniel Warren *former psychologist, educator*
Ishikawa-Fullmer, Janet Satomi *psychologist, educator*
Kennedy, Reneau Charlene Ufford *forensic psychologist, consultant*
Kumar, Raj *psychologist, hypnotherapist*
Nordyke, Eleanor Cole *population researcher, public health nurse*
Paige, Glenn Durland *political scientist, educator*
Pedersen, Paul Bodholdt *psychologist, educator*
Perkinson, Robert Reps *social studies educator*
Riggs, Fred Warren *political science educator*
Shay, Roshani Cari *political science educator*
Spencer, James H. *social sciences educator, consultant*
Stamper, Ewa Szumotalska *psychologist*
Steinemann, Namji Kim *social studies educator*

IDAHO

Boise
Overgaard, Willard Michele *retired political scientist, jurisprudent*
Slaughter, Richard Arthur *political scientist, economist, educator*

Sandpoint
Glock, Charles Young *sociologist, writer*

Sun Valley
Stewart, John Todd *economist, consultant*

ILLINOIS

Arlington Heights
Griffin, Jean Latz *political strategist, writer*
Tongue, William Walter *economics and business consultant, educator*

Barrington
Chung, Joseph Sang-hoon *economics professor*

Barrington Hills
Wood, Andrée Robitaille *archaeologist, researcher*

Belvidere
Mc Nelly, Frederick Wright, Jr., *psychologist*

Carbondale
Benford, Robert Dee *sociology educator, editor*
Karau, Steven James *social psychologist, researcher*
Trescott, Paul Barton *economics professor*

Champaign
Arnould, Richard Julius *economist, educator, consultant, dean*
Cho, In-Koo *economist, educator*
Davis, James Henry *retired psychology educator*
Due, John Fitzgerald *economist, educator emeritus*
Dulany, Donelson Edwin, Jr., *psychology educator*
Eriksen, Charles Walter *psychologist, educator*
Farmer, Helen Sweeney *psychology educator*
Kanfer, Frederick H. *psychologist, educator*
Miller, Gregory Allen *psychology educator*
Scott, Anna Marie Porter Wall *sociology educator*
Yannelis, Nicholas C. *economist, educator*

Charleston
Havey, J. Michael *psychologist, educator*

Chicago
Aliber, Robert Z. *economist, educator*
Allen, Danielle *political scientist, educator*
Altman, Edward G. *retired psychologist, educator*
Baum, Bernard Helmut *sociologist, educator*
Becker, Gary Stanley *economist, educator*
Bertenthal, Bennett Ira *psychologist, educator*
Bidwell, Charles Edward *sociologist, educator*
Block, Richard L. *sociologist, criminologist, educator*
Boyer, John William *history educator, dean*
Coase, Ronald Harry *economist, educator*
Cohler, Bertram Joseph *social sciences educator, clinical psychologist*
Cropsey, Joseph *political science educator*
Cruthird, Robert Lee *sociology educator*
Dust, Margaret Cecile *psychology educator*
Fernandez, James *anthropology educator*
Fogel, Robert William *economist, educator, historian*
Freeman, Leslie Gordon *anthropologist, educator*
Freeman, Susan Tax *anthropologist, educator, culinary historian*
Friedrich, Paul *anthropologist, linguist, poet*
Genetski, Robert James *economist*
Gibson, McGuire *archaeologist, educator*
Ginsburg, Norton Sydney *retired geographer*
Gittins, Anthony J. *anthropologist, theology studies educator*
Gould, John Philip *economist, educator*
Harrow, Martin *psychologist, educator*
Hebel, Doris A. *astrologer*
Heckman, James Joseph *economist, econometrician, educator*
Hollis-Sawyer, Lisa Ann *psychologist, gerontologist, researcher*
Johnson, Janet Helen *Egyptology educator*
Kaplan, Morton A. *political science and philosophy educator*
Kennedy, Eugene Cullen *psychology educator, writer*
Larson, Allan Louis *political scientist, educator, lay church worker*
Laumann, Edward Otto *sociology educator*
Lincoln, Bruce Kenneth *anthropology, classics and history of religions educator*
Lipson, Charles Henry *political scientist, educator*
Liu, Ben-chieh *economist*
Lucas, Robert Emerson, Jr., *economist, educator*
McNeill, G. David *psycholinguist, educator*
Mikesell, Marvin Wray *geography educator*
Miller, Oscar *economics professor*
Moretti, Robert James *psychologist, educator*
Morewitz, Stephen John *behavioral scientist, consultant, educator*
Mugnaini, Enrico *neuroscience educator*
Myerson, Roger Bruce *economist, game theorist, educator*
Nicholas, Ralph Wallace W. *anthropologist, educator*
Peltzman, Sam *economics professor*
Pugh, Roderick Wellington *retired psychologist*
Rosen, Ellen Freda *psychologist, educator*
Rosen, George *economist, educator*
Sanders, Jacquelyn Seevak *psychologist, educator*
Simons, Helen *school psychologist, psychotherapist, educator*
Smith, Raymond Thomas *anthropology educator*
Smith, Stan Vladimir *economist, financial service company executive*
Stocking, George Ward, Jr., *anthropology educator*
Stolzenberg, Ross Mark *sociology educator*
Stover, Leon (Eugene Stover) *anthropology educator, writer, critic*
Taub, Richard Paul *social sciences educator*
Telser, Lester Greenspan *educator, economist*
Thomas, Joseph Erumappettical *psychologist*
Thompson, John H. *social science research executive*
Upshaw, Harry Stephan *psychology educator*
Walberg, Herbert John *psychologist, educator, consultant*
Wiser, James Louis *political science educator*
Zagar, Robert John *psychologist, researcher*
Zellner, Arnold *economics and statistics educator*

Darien
Klassek, Christine Paulette *behavioral scientist*

Deerfield
Halpin, Mary Elizabeth *psychologist*

Dekalb
McSpadden, Lettie *political science educator*
Rembusch, Joseph John *psychologist, management consulting company executive*
Slotsve, George Aaron *economist, educator, consultant*
Wang, Fahui *geographer*

Downers Grove
Feeney, Don Joseph, Jr., *psychologist*

Edwardsville
Browne, Dallas *anthropologist, educator*

DeGarmo, Denise Kay *political scientist, educator*
Ferguson, Eva Dreikurs *psychologist, educator, researcher, author*
Lin, Steven An-Yhi *economics educator, consultant*

Evanston
Braeutigam, Ronald Ray *economics professor*
Canes-Wrone, Brandice *political scientist, educator*
Fine, Gary Alan *sociology educator*
Gordon, Robert James *economics professor*
Horowitz, Joel Lawrence *economics educator, consultant*
Hurter, Arthur Patrick *economist, educator*
Irons, William George *anthropology educator*
Mills, Edwin Smith *economics professor*
Mineka, Susan *psychology educator*
Moskos, Charles C. *sociology educator*
Shanas, Ethel *sociology educator*
Sweet, Jerry James *clinical psychologist*
Weisbrod, Burton Allen *economist, educator*

Galesburg
Breitborde, Lawrence Bart *anthropologist, educator*

Glen Ellyn
Frateschi, Lawrence Jan *economist, statistician, educator*

Glencoe
Warren, Elizabeth Curran *retired political science educator*

Hinsdale
Dederick, Robert Gogan *economist*

Huntley
Saporta, Jack *psychologist, educator*

Joliet
Holmgren, Myron Roger *social sciences educator*

Lemont
Santini, Danilo John *energy economist, urban systems engineer*

Macomb
Walzer, Norman Charles *economics professor*

Maryville
Stark, Patricia Ann *psychologist*

Naperville
Cowlishaw, Mary Lou *government educator*
Kelley, Karl Neal *psychology educator*

Oak Brook
Curt, Carol Lynn *psychologist, consultant*

Rockford
Clodius, Robert LeRoy *retired economist*

Saint Charles
Osowiec, Darlene Ann *clinical psychologist, educator, consultant*

Springfield
Gregg, Phillip Martin *political scientist, educator*
Phillips, John Robert *political scientist, educator*
Reyman, Jonathan Eric *archaeologist, anthropologist, researcher*
Wehrle, Leroy Snyder *economist, educator*

Urbana
Arends-Kuenning, Mary Paula *economics professor, consultant*
Bruner, Edward M. *anthropology educator*
Carmen, Ira Harris *political scientist, educator*
Ferber, Marianne Abeles *economics professor*
Gabriel, Michael *psychology educator*
Giles, Eugene *anthropology educator*
Gove, Samuel Kimball *political science educator*
Lüschen, Günther Rudolf Friedo *sociology educator*
Nettl, Bruno *anthropology and musicology educator*
Powers, Elizabeth T. *economist*
Resek, Robert William *economist*
Rich, Robert F. *law and political science educator*
Sprague, Robert L. *retired psychologist*
Thompson, Robert Lee *agricultural economist, educator*
Yu, George Tzuchiao *political science educator*

Western Springs
Zamora, Marjorie Dixon *retired political science educator*

Wheaton
Allen, Henry Lee *sociology educator, consultant*

Wilmette
Schloss, Nathan *retired economist*
Walker, Ronald Edward *psychologist, educator*

Winnetka
Krueger, Deborah A. Blake *school psychologist, consultant*

INDIANA

Bloomington
Alex-Assensoh, Yvette Marie *political scientist*
Atwood, Christopher Pratt *social studies professor*
Baye, Michael Roy *economics professor*
Becker, Robert Allen *economist, educator*
Brehm, Sharon Stephens *psychology educator, university administrator*
Caldwell, Lynton Keith *social scientist, educator*
Conrad, Geoffrey Wentworth *archaeologist, educator*
Estes, William Kaye *psychologist, educator*
Goldstone, Robert L. *psychologist, educator*
Guth, Sherman Leon (S. Lee Guth) *psychologist, educator*
Hofstadter, Douglas Richard *cognitive scientist, educator, writer*
Ingersoll, Gary Michael *educational psychologist*
Mikesell, John L. *economics professor*
Moran, Emilio Federico *anthropology and ecology educator*
Nosofsky, Robert M. *psychology educator*
Ostrom, Elinor *political science educator, researcher*

PROFESSIONAL INDEX 5889 SOCIAL SCIENCE

Ostrom, Vincent A(lfred) *political science educator*
Patrick, John Joseph *social sciences educator*
Peebles, Christopher Spalding *anthropologist, educator, dean, academic administrator*
Reingold, David Ami *sociologist, educator*
Risinger, C. Frederick *social studies educator*
St. John, Edward P. *social sciences educator*
Saunders, W(arren) Phillip, Jr., *economics educator, consultant, author*
Timberlake, William David *psychology educator*
von Furstenberg, George Michael *economics educator, researcher*

Carmel
Rychlak, Joseph Frank *psychology educator, theoretician*

Columbus
Williams, Robert Joseph *behavioral health services executive, psychologist*

Fort Wayne
Lutz, James Michael *political scientist, educator, writer*

Franklin
Launey, George Volney, III, *economics professor*

Gary
Poulard, Jean Victor *political scientist, educator*

Granger
Craypo, Charles *labor economics educator*

Greencastle
Ross, Scott R. *psychologist, educator*

Greenwood
Waldkoetter, Raymond Oliver *psychologist, consultant*

Hanover
Calkins, Ralph Nelson *economics professor*

Indianapolis
Fastenau, Philip S. *neuropsychologist, educator*
Featherstonaugh, Henry Gordon *psychologist, health facility administrator*
Krauss, John Landers *public policy, urban affairs consultant, mediator, arbitrator*
Labsvirs, Janis *economist, educator*
Sachs, Stephen Mark *political scientist, consultant*

Kokomo
Wysong, Earl Edward *sociologist, educator*

Lafayette
Hardin, Lowell Stewart *retired economics educator*
Schönemann, Peter Hans *psychology educator*
Schweickert, Richard Justus *psychologist, educator*

Madison
Rawson, Harve E. *psychologist, writer*

Muncie
Bogg, Richard Allan *sociologist, educator*
Cheng, Chu Yuan *economics professor*
Meyer, Fred Albert, Jr., *political science educator*
Swartz, B(enjamin) K(insell), Jr., *archaeologist, educator*

Notre Dame
Arnold, Peri Ethan *political scientist*
Bartell, Ernest *economist, educator, priest*
Despres, Leo Arthur *sociology and anthropology educator, academic administrator*
Dowty, Alan Kent *political scientist, educator*
Ghilarducci, M. Teresa *economist, educator*
Hallinan, Maureen Theresa *sociologist, educator*
Mainwaring, Scott Patterson *political scientist, educator*
McElroy, Jerome Lathrop *economics professor*
Mirowski, Philip Edward *economics professor*
Moore, Kenneth E. *anthropologist, educator, writer*
Swartz, Thomas R. *economist, educator*
Valenzuela, Julio Samuel *sociologist, educator*
Weigert, Andrew Joseph *sociology educator*
Welch, Michael R. *sociologist, educator*

Richmond
Veramallay, Ashton Isardatt *economist, educator*

Ridgeville
Church, Jay Kay *psychologist, educator*

Terre Haute
Conway, Lucian Gideon, III, *social sciences educator*
Kukral, Michael Andrew *geographer, educator*

Trafalgar
Montgomery, Steven Charles *psychologist, minister*

West Lafayette
Cicirelli, Victor George *psychologist*
Connor, John Murray *agricultural economics educator*
Farris, Paul Leonard *agricultural economist*
Feld, Scott Lauren *sociologist, political scientist*
Gruen, Gerald Elmer *psychologist, educator*
Horwich, George *economist, educator*
Kadiyala, Koteswara Rao *econometrics educator*
Knudsen, Dean DeWayne *sociology educator*
Kovenock, Daniel J. *economist, educator*
Perrucci, Robert *sociologist, educator*
Swensen, Clifford Henrik, Jr., *psychologist, educator*
Weidenaar, Dennis Jay *economics professor*
Weinstein, Michael Alan *political science educator*

IOWA

Ames
Brown, Frederick Gramm *psychology educator*
Fox, Karl August *economist, eco-behavioral scientist*
Orazem, Peter Francis *economics professor*
Quirmbach, Herman Charles *economics professor*
Roskey, Carol Boyd *social studies educator, dean, director*
Tesfatsion, Leigh S. *economics educator, consultant*

Cedar Falls
DeSoto, M. Catherine *biological psychologist*
Gilgen, Albert Rudolph *psychologist, educator*

Clive
Miller, Kenneth Edward *sociologist, educator*

Coggon
Hammer, Robert Eugene *psychologist*

Des Moines
Demorest, Allan Frederick *retired psychologist*

Dubuque
Jorgensen, Gerald Thomas *psychologist, educator, lawyer*

Fayette
Barker, Richard Alexander *organizational psychologist*

Grinnell
Moyer, H. Wayne *political science educator*

Iowa City
Albrecht, William Price *economist, educator, government official*
Barkan, Joel David *political science educator, consultant*
Forsythe, Robert Elliott *economics professor*
Geweke, John Frederick *economics professor*
Hudson, John Boswell *sociologist, educator*
Kim, Chong Lim *political science educator*
Loewenberg, Gerhard *political science educator*
Nathan, Peter E. *psychologist, educator*
Shannon, Lyle William *sociology educator*
Siebert, Calvin D. *economist, educator*
Suls, Jerry M. *psychologist, educator*
Wasserman, Edward Arnold *psychology educator*

Mount Vernon
Ruppel, Howard James, Jr., *sociologist, sexologist, educator*

Nevada
Bivens, Gordon Ellsworth *economist, educator*

Oskaloosa
Porter, David Lindsey *history and political science educator, author*

KANSAS

El Dorado
Stone, Duane Snyder *school psychologist, clergyman*

Fort Leavenworth
Alvarez, Jeffrey L. *psychologist, researcher*

Garden City
Thomas, Gregory Hall *psychology professor*

Hays
Levy, Patricia Anne *social sciences educator*

Hutchinson
Rosenblad, Helen Viola *social services coordinator*

Kansas City
Penick, Elizabeth C. *psychologist*
Twillman, Robert Keith *psychologist*

Lawrence
Barnett, William Arnold *economics professor*
Harvey, Mark Austin *political scientist, educator, political scientist, consultant*
Heller, Francis H(oward) *law and political science educator emeritus*
Rosenbloom, Joshua Levi *economist, educator*
Schroeder, Stephen Robert *psychology researcher*
Shaffer, Harry George *economics professor*
Shulenburger, David Edwin *economics educator, university official*

Manhattan
Babcock, Michael Ward *economics professor*
Hoyt, Kenneth Boyd *educational psychology educator*
Murray, John Patrick *psychologist, educator, researcher*
Roper, Donna C. *archaeologist*
Thomas, Lloyd Brewster *economics professor*
Wallis, Robert Ray *psychologist*

Ottawa
Brady, Gordon Leonard, Jr., *economist*

Overland Park
Burger, Henry G. *vocabulary scientist, anthropologist, publisher*
FitzGerald, Thomas Joe *psychologist*

Saint John
Robinson, Alexander Jacob *clinical psychologist*

Shawnee Mission
Gaar, Marilyn Audrey Wiegraffe *political scientist, educator, property manager*

Topeka
Cann, Steven J. *political science educator*

Wichita
Clark, Susan Matthews *psychologist*
Ericson, David Frank *political scientist, educator*
Kahn, Melvin A. *political science educator*

Winfield
Schul, Bill Dean *psychological administrator, author*

KENTUCKY

Bowling Green
Cangemi, Joseph Peter *psychologist, consultant, educator*
Cravens, Raymond Lewis *retired political science educator*

Campbellsville
Chowning, John E. *political scientist, educator, minister*

Corbin
Doby, John Thomas *social psychologist*

Covington
Giesbrecht, Martin Gerhard *retired economics educator, clarinetist*

Highland Heights
Donnelly, Sharlotte K. B. Neely *anthropology educator, author*

Independence
Hopgood, James F. *anthropologist, educator*

Lexington
Gallagher, Eugene Bennett *sociologist, medical educator*
Hall, Harry H. *agricultural economics educator*
Hochstrasser, Donald Lee *cultural anthropologist, community health and public administrator*
Hultman, Charles William *economics professor*
Stempel, John Dallas *international studies educator*
Stilwell, William Earle, III, *psychology educator, retired military officer*
Straus, Robert *behavioral sciences educator*
Wildasin, David E(arl) *economics educator*
Worell, Judith P. *psychologist, educator*
Zentall, Thomas R. *psychologist, educator*

Louisville
Edgell, Stephen Edward *psychology educator, statistical consultant*
Stanton, M(orris) Duncan *psychologist, researcher, dean*
Welsh, Douglas Lee *psychologist, researcher*
Ziegler, Charles Edward *political science educator, department chairman*

Madisonville
Baldwin, Kathryn Leigh *psychologist, educator, consultant*

Morehead
Miller, Green Russell *economist, educator*

Pikeville
Cade, Nancy Jean *history and political science educator*

Prestonsburg
Mc Aninch, Robert Danford *philosophy and government affairs educator*

Richmond
Engle, Fred Allen, Jr., *economics professor, writer*

LOUISIANA

Alexandria
Thevenot, Maude Travis *retired home economist*

Baton Rouge
Beard, Thomas Rex *economics professor*
Cramer, Gail Latimer *economist*
Daniel, Ross Preston, III, *economist, educator*
Riopelle, Arthur Jean *psychologist*

Chalmette
Bayham, Michael Robert, Jr., *political consultant*

Lafayette
Dur, Philip Francis *political scientist, educator, retired foreign service officer*

Lake Charles
Middleton, George, Jr., *clinical child psychologist*
Weeber, Stan C. *sociologist, educator*

Metairie
Falco, Maria Josephine *political scientist, academic administrator*
Wood, Jonathan Stuart *economist, educator*

Monroe
Bulot, James John *gerontologist, educator*
Fouts, Elizabeth Browne *psychologist, metals company executive*

Natchitoches
Nagel, Paul B. *geography and social studies educator*

New Orleans
Andrews, E. Wyllys *archaeologist, educator*
Balée, William L. *anthropology educator*
Boudreaux, Kenneth Justin *economics and finance educator, consultant*
Bricker, Harvey Miller *anthropology educator*
Bricker, Victoria Reifler *anthropology educator*
Freudenberger, Herman *retired economics educator*
Jacobsen, Thomas Warren *retired archaeologist, educator, freelance journalist*
Kadowtiz, Philip J. *social sciences educator*
Langston, Thomas Samuel *political science educator*
Moely, Barbara E. *psychology researcher, educator*
Olson, Richard David *psychology educator*
O'Neal, Edgar Carl *psychology educator*
Paradise, Louis Vincent *educational psychology educator, university official*
Wallace, Julian Craig *psychology educator, researcher*

Oakdale
Bellah, Lisa Danielle *psychologist, educator*

Pineville
Thrasher, Fay C. *clinical psychologist*

Ruston
Sale, Tom S., III, *financial economist*

Shreveport
Joiner, Gary Dillard *cartographer, history educator, author*
Pederson, William David *political scientist, educator*
Staats, Thomas Elwyn *neuropsychologist*

MAINE

Augusta
Nickerson, John Mitchell *political science educator*

Bath
Stoudt, Howard Webster *biological anthropologist, human factors specialist, consultant*

Brunswick
Crandall, Elizabeth Walbert *home economics educator*
Fitzgerald, John Michael *economist, educator*
Fuchs, Alfred Herman *psychologist, educator*
Morgan, Richard Ernest *political scientist, educator*
Riley, Matilda White (Mrs. John W. Riley Jr.) *sociologist*

Falmouth
Pierce, Philip Sargent *clinical psychologist*

Farmington
Melcher, James Patrick *political scientist, educator*

Islesboro
Caplow, Theodore *sociologist, educator*

Kittery Point
Howells, William White *anthropology educator*

Lewiston
Dennison, Gerard Francis *economic analyst*
Kessler, Mark Allen *political scientist, educator*

Lisbon Falls
Raskin, Michael Neil *psychologist, writer*

Orono
Cohn, Steven Frederick *sociology educator, consultant*
Devino, William Stanley *economist, educator*
Goldstone, Sanford *psychology educator*
Martindale, Colin Eugene *psychology educator, author*

Portland
O'Brien, John Matthew *psychologist, educator*

Sanford
Will, Jerrie Ann *psychologist*

Sidney
Tietenberg, Thomas *economist, department chairman*

Waterville
Gemery, Henry Albert *economics professor*
Gilkes, Cheryl Louise Townsend *sociologist, educator, minister*
Yeterian, Edward Harry *psychologist, educator, administrator*

MARYLAND

Annapolis
Brann, Eva Toni Helene *archaeology educator*
Connolly, Janet Elizabeth *retired sociologist and criminal justice educator*
Reich, Merrill Drury *intelligence consultant, writer*

Baltimore
Anderson, Gerard Fenton *economist, university program administrator*
Ball, Gregory Francis *biological psychology educator*
Barnow, Burt S. *economist*
Bright, Margaret *sociologist*
Catania, A(nthony) Charles *psychology educator*
Christ, Carl Finley *economist, educator*
Cooper, Joseph *political scientist, educator*
Davis, Carole Joan *psychologist, consultant*
Desoto, Clinton Burgel *psychologist, educator*
Dickey, George Edward *water resources consultant, economics educator*
Dietze, Gottfried *political science educator*
Entwisle, Doris Roberts *sociology educator*
Ginsberg, Benjamin *political science educator*
Green, Bert Franklin, Jr., *psychologist*
Groenheim, Henri Arnold *psychologist, consultant*
Hollwitz, John Charles *educational administrator, consultant*
Howard, J. Woodford, Jr., *political science educator*
Jamison, Kay *psychologist*
Karni, Edi *economics professor*
Maccini, Louis John *economic educator*
Melick, Clifford Francis *sociologist, researcher*
Money, John William *retired psychologist, educator*
Radin, Beryl Avis *public administration and policy educator*
Rose, Hugh *retired economics educator*
Salamon, Lester Milton *political science educator*
Stanley, Julian Cecil, Jr., *psychology educator*
Wolman, M. Gordon *geography educator*
Yantis, Steven George *psychology educator*
Young, Hobart Peyton *economist, mathematician, educator*

Bethesda
Bailey, Eric Jon *medical anthropologist, health scientist administrator*
Banik, Sambhu Nath *psychologist*
Cleary, Robert Edward *government and public affairs educator*
Cuerdon, Timothy *psychologist*
de Vries, Margaret Garritsen *economist*
Dommen, Arthur John *agricultural economist, historian*
Duncan, Constance Catharine *psychologist, educator, researcher*
Fischetti, Michael *public administration educator, arbitrator*
Gordon, Harold W. *psychologist*

Haugan, Gertrude M. *clinical psychologist*
Holland, Robert Carl *economist*
Jamison, Dean Tecumseh *economist*
Krantz, David S. *medical psychology educator, researcher*
Lamb, Michael E. *psychology researcher*
Lystad, Mary Hanemann (Mrs. Robert Lystad) *sociologist, writer*
Mirsky, Allan Franklin *psychologist, researcher*
Mishkin, Mortimer *neuropsychologist*
Reiser, Brian Sydney *economist, statistician*
Reynolds, Robert Joel *economist, consultant*
Ruttenberg, Ruth A. *economist*
Solomon, Robert *economist*
Striner, Herbert Edward *economics educator*
Taylor, William Jesse, Jr., *international studies educator, research corporation president*
Wechsler, Andrew Robert *international economic consultant*

Bowie
Bushnell, David Sherman *psychologist, consultant*
Yager, Joseph Arthur, Jr., *economist*

Charlotte Hall
Brown, Ira Hugo *psychologist, educator*

Chestertown
Littlefield, Lauren Montenegro *psychologist, educator*
Wendel, Richard Frederick *economist, educator, consultant*

Chevy Chase
Alexander, Arthur Jacob *economist*
Cody, Peter Malcolm *economist, development, management consultant*
Emery, Robert Firestone *economist, educator*
Greene, Kay C. *psychologist, author*
Guenther, Kenneth Allen *economist, consultant*
Linowes, David Francis *political economist, educator, corporate executive*
Norwood, Bernard *economist*
Norwood, Janet Lippe *economist*
Opper, Barbara Negri *financial economist*
Sapin, Burton Malcolm *political science educator, foreign policy analyst*
Teitel, Simon *economist, educator*

College Park
Dill, Bonnie Thornton *sociology educator*
Ernstein, Julie H. *archaeologist, educator, researcher*
Gaylin, Ned L. *psychology educator*
Goode, B. Erich *sociologist, educator, retired criminologist*
Hill, Clara Edith *psychology educator*
Just, Richard Eugene *agricultural and resource economics educator consultant*
Leitenberg, Milton *political scientist, researcher*
Lichtenberg, Erik Russell *economics professor*
Marshall, Monty Glenn *political research scientist, consultant*
Nerlove, Marc Leon *economics professor*
Olson, Charles Eric *economist*
Piper, Don Courtney *political scientist, educator*
Presser, Harriet Betty *sociology educator*
Presser, Stanley *sociology educator*
Quester, George Herman *political science educator*
Schelling, Thomas Crombie *economist, educator*
Segal, David Robert *sociology educator*
Sigall, Harold Fred *psychology educator*
Sorenson, Georgia Lynn Jones *political scientist, educator*
Tismaneanu, Vladimir *political science educator, researcher*

Columbia
Bell, James Edward *psychologist, educator*
May, John Raymond *clinical psychologist*

Cumberland
Heckert, Paul Charles *sociologist, educator*

Davidsonville
Blaxall, Martha Ossoff *economist*

Ellicott City
Robison, Susan Miller *psychologist, speaker, consultant*
Webster, Sharon B. *economist*

Fort Washington
McCafferty, James Arthur *sociologist*

Gaithersburg
George, Kathryn Elaine *economist, financial writer*
Ross, Sherman *psychologist, educator*

Hagerstown
Ward, Spring Tina *history and political science educator*

Lanham
McClain, George Nelson *economist, lawyer*

Laurel
McConnaughey, James Walter *economist*

Leonardtown
Donely, George Anthony Thomas, III, *economist, consultant*

Lutherville
Eisenberg, Joseph Martin *psychologist, consultant*

Lutherville Timonium
Muuss, Rolf Eduard *retired psychologist, author*

Mc Henry
Kelly, Robert William *economist*

Mechanicsville
Rands, Robert Lawrence *archaeologist*

Mitchellville
Blasier, Cole *political scientist, educator*
Henle, Peter *retired economic consultant, arbitrator*

Potomac
Jones, Sidney Lewis *economist, researcher, educator*
Kling, William *economist, retired foreign service officer*
Oh, John Kie-Chiang *political science educator, university official*
Reichley, A. James *political scientist*
Rotberg, Iris Comens *social scientist*
Vadus, Gloria A. *scientific document examiner*
Walker, Charls Edward *economist, consultant*
Wonnacott, Paul *retired economics professor*
Young, Lih Ying H. *economist, consultant, advocate*

Rockville
Kurzman, Harold Philip *transportation economist, consultant*
Niewiaroski, Trudi Osmers (Gertrude Niewiaroski) *social studies educator*
Wang, Kung-Lee *economics consultant*
Wilson, James J. *public administration consultant*

Royal Oak
Israel, Lesley Lowe *retired political consultant*

Salisbury
Losonczy, Marta Elizabeth *psychologist, educator*
Wu, Ying *economics educator, researcher*

Silver Spring
Ahmad, Mirza Muzaffar *economic advisor*
Alexander, Herbert E. *political scientist*
Blankenheimer, Bernard *economics consultant*
Burcroff, Richard Tomkinson, II, *economist*
Glickman, Albert Seymour *psychologist, educator*
Goodall, Jane *ethologist*
Hsueh, Chun-tu *political scientist, historian, foundation executive*
Katz, Pearl *anthropologist, public health analyst*
Mohr, Christina *retired economist*
Moon, Marilyn Lee *economist*
Oswald, Rudolph A. *economist*
Rayburn, Carole Ann (Mary Aida Rayburn) *psychologist, researcher, writer, consultant*

Temple Hills
Day, Mary Jane Thomas *cartographer*
Smith, Irving *gerontologist*

Towson
Zweback, Stanley *psychologist, educator*

Westminster
Medina, Janet Gail *school psychologist, educator*

Wheaton
Ghosh, Arun Kumar *economics, social sciences and accounting educator*

MASSACHUSETTS

Acton
Evans, Robert, Jr., *economics professor*

Agawam
Sylvester, John Andrew *social studies educator*

Amherst
Aizen, Icek *psychology professor, consultant*
Alfange, Dean, Jr., *political science educator*
Averill, James Reed *psychology educator*
Benson, Lucy Wilson *political and diplomatic consultant*
Berger, Seymour Maurice *social psychologist*
Bickford, John H. *psychologist, educator*
Blass, Elliott M. *psychologist, educator*
Folbre, Nancy *economics professor*
Klare, Michael Thomas *social science educator, program director*
Mc Donagh, Edward Charles *sociologist, university administrator*
Strickland, Bonnie Ruth *psychologist, educator*
Taubman, William Chase *political science educator, writer*
Woodbury, Richard Benjamin *anthropologist, educator*

Andover
Arce, Pedro L. *economic development executive, banker*

Belmont
Feldstein, Kathleen Foley *economist, consultant*
Heyman, Gene Morris *research psychologist, educator*
Kargman (Witkin), Marie *marriage counselor, consultant*
Killgore, William Dale (Scott), Jr., *neuropsychologist*
Levendusky, Philip George *psychologist, education administrator*

Berkley
Murtagh, Michael Paul *psychologist*

Boston
Appley, Mortimer Herbert *psychologist, university president emeritus*
Berger, Harvey Robert *psychologist*
Cleary, Paul David *sociomedical educator*
Connor, Walter Downing *political scientist, educator, researcher*
Dentler, Robert Arnold *sociologist, educator*
Ellis, Randall Poor *economist, educator*
Farmer, Paul Edward *medical anthropologist*
Gamst, Frederick Charles *social anthropologist*
Garrett, Gerald R. *sociology educator, criminologist, consultant*
Gleason, Jean Berko *psychology educator*
Greenwood, Joen Elizabeth *economist, consultant*
Grossman, Frances Kaplan *psychologist*
Hammond, Norman David Curle *archaeology educator, researcher*
Infante, Isa Maria *political scientist, educator*
Leffert, James Steven *psychologist*
Manning, Peter Kirby *sociologist educator*
McGuire, Thomas G. *economist, educator, mental health services professional, researcher*
Merton, Robert C. *economist, educator*
Newhouse, Joseph Paul *economist, educator*
Nichols, Albert L. *economic consultant*
Nolan, Cathal J. *political scientist, educator, historian*
Palmer, David Scott *political scientist, educator*
Plotkin, Irving H(erman) *economist, consultant*
Ra'anan, Uri (Heinz Felix Frischwasser) *international politics educator*
Rossell, Christine Hamilton *political science educator*
Roth, Alvin Eliot *economics educator*
Salinger, Michael Alvin *economist, educator*
Sanders, Irwin Taylor *sociology educator*
Waksler, Frances Chaput *sociologist, educator*
Watanabe, Paul Yashihiko *political scientist, educator*
Woerner, Frederick Frank *international relations educator*
Yeager, Peter Cleary *sociologist, educator*

Brockton
O'Brien, John Steininger *clinical psychologist*
O'Farrell, Timothy James *psychologist, educator*

Brookline
Cromwell, Adelaide M. *sociology educator*

Burlington
Halvorson, Peter Chase *social studies educator*

Cambridge
Alt, James Edward *political science educator*
Bailyn, Lotte *psychology and management educator*
Bane, Mary Jo *political science educator*
Bator, Francis Michel *economist, educator*
Berndt, Ernst Rudolf *economist, educator*
Blackmer, Donald Laurence Morton *political scientist*
Borjas, George J(esus) *economics professor*
Caramazza, Alfonso *psychology educator*
Caves, Richard Earl *economist, educator*
Champion, Hale (Charles Hale Champion) *political science educator, former public official*
Chandra, Satish *psychologist*
Cooper, Richard Newell *economist, educator*
Dominguez, Jorge Ignacio *government educator*
Eckaus, Richard Samuel *economist, educator*
Ellwood, David Tabor *public policy educator*
Feldstein, Martin Stuart *economist, educator*
Fisher, Franklin Marvin *economist*
Friedman, Benjamin Morton *economics professor*
Frisch, Rose Epstein *population sciences researcher*
Galbraith, John Kenneth *retired economist*
Gardner, Howard Earl *psychologist, educator, writer*
George, Kenneth Martin *anthropology educator*
Gibbs, Brian J. *behavioral scientist, educator, consultant*
Gilligan, Carol *psychologist, writer*
Goldin, Claudia Dale *economics educator*
Goldman, Marshall Irwin *economist, educator*
Hausman, Jerry Allen *economics educator, consultant*
Hersch, Joni *economist, educator*
Herzlinger, Regina *economist, educator*
Hoffmann, Inge Schneier *psychologist, educator*
Jacoby, Henry Donnan *economist, educator*
Jencks, Christopher Sandys *public policy educator*
Johnson, Willard Raymond *political science educator, consultant*
Jorgenson, Dale Weldeau *economist, educator*
Joskow, Paul Lewis *economist, educator*
Juma, Calestous *international development educator*
Kagan, Jerome *psychologist, educator*
Katz, Lawrence Francis *economics professor*
Kaysen, Carl *economics professor*
Kelman, Herbert Chanoch *psychology educator*
Keniston, Kenneth *psychologist, educator*
Kennedy, Stephen Dandridge *economist, researcher*
Keyfitz, Nathan *sociologist, demographer, educator*
Kleinman, Arthur Michael *medical anthropologist, psychiatrist, educator*
Kosslyn, Stephen M. *psychologist educator*
Kremer, Michael *economist, educator*
Lamberg-Karlovsky, Clifford Charles *anthropologist, archaeologist*
Langer, Ellen Jane *psychologist, educator, writer, artist*
LeVine, Robert Alan *anthropology educator, researcher*
Lieberson, Stanley *sociologist, educator*
Linsky, Marty *public policy educator, consultant*
Maass, Arthur *political science and environmental studies educator*
Maher, Brendan Arnold *psychology educator, editor*
Mankiw, Nicholas Gregory *economics professor, federal agency administrator*
Marder, William David *health economist*
Meyer, John Robert *economist, educator*
Mitten, David Gordon *classical archaeologist*
Moore, Mark Harrison *criminal justice and public policy educator*
Moore, Sally Falk *anthropology educator*
Patterson, Orlando *sociologist*
Perkins, Dwight Heald *economics professor*
Pfaltzgraff, Robert Louis, Jr., *political scientist, educator*
Pinker, Steven A. *cognitive scientist, educator*
Poterba, James Michael *economist, educator*
Rathjens, George William *political scientist, educator*
Rogoff, Kenneth Saul *economics professor*
Rosovsky, Henry *economist, educator*
Ruggie, John Gerard *political science educator, diplomat*
Samuelson, Paul Anthony *economist, educator*
Sapolsky, Harvey Morton *political scientist, educator*
Sen, Amartya Kumar *economist, educator*
Siegel, Abraham J. *economics educator, academic administrator*
Skocpol, Theda Ruth *sociology and political science educator*
Skolnikoff, Eugene B. *political science educator*
Solow, Robert Merton *economist, educator*
Stager, Lawrence E. *archaeologist, educator*
Temin, Peter *economist, educator*
Treitel, Corinna *social studies educator*
Verba, Sidney *political scientist, educator*
Vogel, Ezra F. *sociology educator*
Willie, Charles Vert *sociology educator*
Wilson, William Julius *sociology educator*
Yip, Winnie *health economics educator*
Zeckhauser, Richard Jay *economist, educator*
Zeidenstein, George *population educator*
Zinberg, Dorothy Shore *science policy educator*

Charlestown
Lasko, Natasha B. *psychologist*

Chestnut Hill
Carfora, John Michael *economics educator, academic administrator*
Smith, David Horton *retired social sciences educator*
Williamson, John Butler *sociology educator*
Wolfe, Alan *political science educator, writer*

Concord
Codere, Helen Frances *anthropologist, educator, university dean*

Dorchester
Berg, John Conrad *political science educator*

Framingham
West, Doe *bioethicist, social justice activist, researcher*

Gloucester
McCarl, Henry Newton *economics and geology consultant, venture capitalist*

Haydenville
Shallcross, Doris Jane *creative behavioral educator*

Ipswich
Jennings, Frederic Beach, Jr., *economist, saltwater flyfishing guide*

Lexington
Bernardi, John Lawrence, Jr., *economic historian, educator, consultant*
Collins, Allan Meakin *cognitive scientist, psychologist, educator*
Gutheim, Allen Herman *economist*
Horowitz, Morris A. *retired economics educator*
Jordan, Judith Victoria *clinical psychologist, educator*
Manganello, James Angelo *psychologist*
Ronchi, Donald M. *psychologist, educator*
Washburn, Barbara Polk *cartographer, researcher, explorer*

Lowell
Pyle, Jean L. *economist, consultant, educator*

Marblehead
Speller, Kerstin G. Rinta *psychologist*

Medford
Ambady, Nalini *social psychologist, educator, researcher*
Conklin, John Evan *sociology educator*
DeBold, Joseph Francis *psychology educator*
Elkind, David *psychology educator*
Goodwin, Neva R. *economist*
Granott, Nira *psychology researcher*
Luria, Zella Hurwitz *psychology educator*
Miczek, Klaus Alexander *psychology educator*
Thompson, David *economist, researcher*

Montague
Kohler, Heinz *economics professor*

Nantucket
Sangree, Walter Hinchman *social anthropologist, educator*

Needham
Boulding, Elise Marie *sociologist, educator*
Glaser, Daniel *sociologist, educator*

New Town
Carton, Lonnie Caming *educational psychologist*

Newton
Holbik, Karel *economics professor*

Newton Center
Cousineau, Madeleine *sociologist, educator*

North Adams
Sabot, Richard Henry *economics educator, researcher, investor, entrepreneur*

North Andover
Wessel, Harry *political scientist, educator, director*

North Dartmouth
Barrow, Clyde Wayne *political scientist, educator*
Magrass, Yale Robert *sociology educator, writer*

Northampton
Lehmann, Phyllis Williams *archaeologist, educator*
Rose, Peter Isaac *sociologist, writer*
Zimbalist, Andrew S. *economist, educator*

Orleans
Rappaport, Margaret M.W.E. *psychologist, physician, writer, pilot, consultant*

Quincy
Johnson, Norine Goode *psychologist, educator*
Spangler, Arthur Stephenson, Jr., *psychologist*

Rockport
Harries, James Theodore *psychologist*

Salem
Higgins, Gina O'Connell *psychologist, writer*

Scituate
Reynolds, Paul Davidson *social sciences educator*

Shelburne Falls
Collard, Roberta R. *emeritus educator, researcher*

Shrewsbury
Lucas, Sandra J. *psychologist*

Siasconset
Emerson, Alice Frey *political scientist, educator emerita*

South Hadley
Tatum, Beverly Daniel *psychology and education educator*

Springfield
Agonafer, Mulugeta Gabriel *political scientist, educator*
Smolowitz, Ira Ephraim *finance educator, academic dean*

Stoughton
Gallant, George William *political scientist*

Waban
Hewlett-Kierstead, Nancy Carrick *psychologist, educator*

Waltham
Altman, Stuart Harold *economist, educator*
Domar, Alice Diane *psychologist, educator*
Hansen, Karen Vyonne *sociology educator*
McCulloch, Rachel *economics researcher, educator*
Sekuler, Robert William *psychologist, educator*
Shepard, Donald Sloane *public policy research educator*
Zebrowitz, Leslie Ann *psychology educator*

Wellesley
Bishop, Robert Lyle *economist, educator*
Eilts, Hermann Frederick *international relations educator, former diplomat*
Giddon, Donald B(ernard) *psychologist, educator*
Miller, Linda B. *political scientist*
Morant, Ricardo Bernardino *psychology educator*
Stettner, Edward A. *political science educator*

Westborough
Staffier, Pamela Moorman *psychologist*
Tobias, Lester Lee *psychological consultant*

Weston
Kraft, Gerald *economist*

Williamstown
Bolton, Roger Edwin *economist, educator*
Crider, Andrew Blake *psychologist*
Fuller, Renee Nuni *psychologist, educational publisher*
Hill, Catharine B. *economics professor, provost*
Kassin, Saul *psychology educator*
Sheahan, John Bernard *economist, educator*
Solomon, Paul Robert *neuropsychologist, educator*

Worcester
Ainlay, Stephen Charles *academic administrator*
Lidz, Charles Wilmanns *sociologist*
Mathisen, Howard *psychologist, minister*
Ross, Robert Jon Sanford *sociology educator*
Turner, Billie Lee, II, *geography educator*
Upshur, Carole Christofk *psychologist, educator*
Wilkes, John M. *sociologist*

MICHIGAN

Adrian
Weathers, Milledge Wright *retired economics educator*

Ann Arbor
Apperson, Jean *psychologist*
Arlinghaus, Sandra Judith Lach *mathematical geographer, educator*
Berent, Stanley *psychologist, educator, researcher, consultant*
Bishop, Elizabeth Shreve *psychologist*
Brown, Donald Robert *psychology educator*
Campbell, John Creighton *political science educator*
Cohen, Malcolm Stuart *economist, business executive*
Converse, Philip Ernest *social science educator*
Eccles, Jacquelynne S. *psychology educator*
Featherman, David Lee *social science research executive*
Freedman, Ronald *sociology educator*
Frey, William H. *demographer, educator*
Fusfeld, Daniel Roland *economist*
Gomberg, Edith S. *psychologist, educator*
Gruppen, Larry Dale *psychologist, educational researcher*
Haefner, Don Paul *retired psychology educator*
Hagen, John William *psychology educator*
House, James Stephen *sociological social psychologist, educator*
Howrey, Eugene Philip *economics educator, consultant*
Inglehart, Ronald Franklin *political science educator*
Jackson, James Sidney *psychology educator*
Johnston, Lloyd Douglas *social scientist*
Kahn, Robert L(ouis) *psychologist, educator*
Kingdon, John Wells *political science educator*
Kmenta, Jan *economics professor*
Lupia, Arthur W. *political science educator*
Manis, Melvin *psychologist, educator*
Markovits, Andrei Steven *political science educator*
Mc Cracken, Paul Winston *retired economist, business educator*
McKeachie, Wilbert James *psychologist, educator*
Mitchell, Edward John *economist, retired educator*
Mizruchi, Mark Sheldon *sociology and business administration educator*
Moholy-Nagy, Hattula *archaeologist*
Mueggler, Erik *anthropologist, educator*
Ono, Hiromi *sociologist, researcher*
Paige, Jeffery Mayland *sociologist, educator*
Parsons, Jeffrey Robinson *anthropologist, educator*
Pedley, John Griffiths *archaeologist, educator*
Quintyn, Conrad Bezekiah *anthropologist, educator*
Shapiro, Matthew David *economist, educator*
Stafford, Frank P. *economist, educator*
Stafford, Frank Peter, Jr., *economics educator, consultant*
Stein, Howard *economics professor*
Steiner, Peter Otto *economics educator, dean*
Stevenson, Harold William *psychology educator*
Thornton, Arland *sociologist, educator*
Waltz, Susan *international relations educator*
Whitman, Marina Von Neumann *economist, educator*
Williams, David R. *sociologist, educator, senior research scientist*
Williams, Melvin Donald *anthropologist, educator*
Woronoff, Israel *former psychology educator*
Zucker, Robert A(lpert) *psychologist*

Auburn Hills
Etefia, Florence Victoria *school psychologist*

Big Rapids
Roy, Donald H. *political scientist, educator*

Bloomfield Hills
Sugrue, Dennis Patrick *clinical psychologist*

Canton
Schulz, Karen Alice *psychologist, medical psychotherapist, medical and vocational case manager*

Detroit
Cantoni, Louis Joseph *psychologist, poet, sculptor*
Fleming, George Robert *psychologist*
Goodman, Allen Charles *economist, educator*
Hunter Iii, Hansen French *political scientist, consultant*
MacDonald, Douglas Andrew *psychologist, educator*
Marx, Thomas George *economist*
McArthur, Steven Francis *psychologist, educator*
Smith, Bradley William *criminal justice educator*
Trix, Frances *linguistic anthropologist, consultant*

East Lansing
Abeles, Norman *psychologist, educator*
Abramson, Paul Robert *political scientist, educator*
Baillie, Richard Thomas *economist, educator*
Ballbach, Philip Thornton *political consultant, investor*
Busch, Lawrence Michael *sociologist, researcher*
Crewe, Nancy Moe *psychologist and educator*
Dow, Steven Benjamin *social studies educator*
Finifter, Ada Weintraub *political scientist, educator*
Gass, Gertrude Zemon *psychologist, researcher*
Ilgen, Daniel Richard *psychology educator*
Koo, Anthony Ying Chang *economist, educator*
Kreinin, Mordecha Eliahu *economics professor*
Ladenson, Mark Lawrence *economist, educator*
Liedholm, Carl Edward *economics professor*
Manderscheid, Lester Vincent *agricultural economics educator*
Menchik, Paul Leonard *economist, educator*
Press, Charles *retired political science educator*
Strassmann, W. Paul *economics professor*
Winder, Clarence Leland *psychologist, educator*
Woodbury, Stephen Abbott *economics educator*

Grand Rapids
Kooistra, William Henry *clinical psychologist*
Monsma, Stephen Vos *political scientist, educator*
Tiemstra, John Peter *economics professor*
Yamazaki, Makoto *economics professor*

Holland
Holmes, Jack Edward *political science educator*

Howell
Rohrabacher, Janet Hammond *geneologist, archivist*

Kalamazoo
Mc Allister, Lester Belden *economics professor*
Pratt, Helen Diann *clinical psychologist, educator*

Mount Pleasant
Browne, William P. *political science educator*
Thayer, Frederick Clifton *public policy educator*

Northport
Thomas, Philip Stanley *economist, educator*

Novi
Sobczak, Judy Marie *clinical psychologist*

Okemos
Berkman, Claire Fleet *psychologist*
Solo, Robert Alexander *economist, educator*

Petoskey
Ketcham, Warren Andrew *psychologist, educator*

Port Huron
Moss, Carl Arthur *psychologist*

Portage
Gardner-Bonneau, Daryle Jean *human factors engineering scientist, consultant*

Rochester Hills
Minton, Henry Lee *psychology educator*

Saint Clair Shores
Vogel, Sally Thomas *psychologist, social worker, educator*

Saline
Hansen, Janice Elizabeth *psychologist*

Sault Sainte Marie
Johnson, Gary Robert *political scientist*

Southfield
Birdsong, Emil Ardell *clinical psychologist*
Gregory, Karl Dwight *economist, educator, consultant*
Ross, Dale Garand *therapist, programming consultant, speaker, writer*
Thimotheose, Kadakampallil George *psychologist*
Weiner, Karen Colby (Karen Lynn Colby) *psychologist, lawyer*

University Center
Dykhuizen, C. Jeffrey *child development psychologist, educator*
Hill, Alan Gordon *sociologist, educator*
Hoerneman, Calvin A., Jr., *economics professor*

Ypsilanti
Friedman, Monroe *psychologist, educator*
Weinstein, Jay A. *social science educator, researcher*

MINNESOTA

Duluth
Bower, John Richard Fenn *archaeologist, educator*
Mehrotra, Chandra *psychology professor, dean*

Edina
Gottesman, Irving Isadore *psychology educator*

Forest Lake
Marchese, Ronald Thomas *ancient history and archaeology educator*

Mankato
Friend, Donald Agar *geographer, geomorphologist, educator*
Widner, Robert Lee, Jr., *psychologist, educator*

Marshall
Joo, Hee-Jong *criminology educator*

Minneapolis
Adams, John Stephen *geography educator*
Bancroft, Ann E. *polar explorer*
Berscheid, Ellen S. *psychology educator, writer, researcher*
Chipman, John Somerset *economist, educator*
Frank, Kerry Dean *psychology educator, consultant*
Hansen, Jo-Ida Charlotte *psychology educator, researcher*
Holt, Robert Theodore *political scientist, dean, educator*
Hurwicz, Leonid *economist, educator*
Jeffrey-Smith, Lilli Ann *biofeedback specialist, educator, administrator*
Johnson, David Wolcott *psychologist, educator*
Knoke, David Harmon *sociology educator*
Kudrle, Robert Thomas *economist, educator*
Lewis, Stephen Richmond, Jr., *economist, educator*
Nightingale, Edmund Joseph *clinical psychologist, educator*
Ostrom, Don *political science educator*
Porter, Philip Wayland *geography educator*
Reiss, Ira Leonard *retired sociology educator, writer*
Rogers, William Cecil *political science educator, consultant*
Schreiner, John Christian *economics consultant, software publisher*
Schwartzberg, Joseph Emanuel
Scoville, James Griffin *economics professor*
Shively, William Phillips *political scientist, educator*
Strommen, Merton Peter *research psychologist, clergyman*
Ward, David Allen *sociology educator*
Ysseldyke, James Edward *psychology educator, dean*

Moorhead
Noblitt, Harding Coolidge *political scientist, educator*
Trainor, John Felix *retired economics educator*

Morris
Joo, Seung-Ho *political scientist, educator*

Northfield
Clark, William Hartley *political science educator*

Saint Cloud
Frank, Stephen Ira *political science educator*
Leppman, Elizabeth Jane *geographer, educator*
Prout, Robert Stephen *higher education consultant, law enforcement consultant*
Ward, Edward Anthony *economist, educator*

Saint Paul
Dahl, Reynold Paul *applied economics educator*
Jessup, Paul Frederick *financial economist, educator*
Johnson, Badri Nahvi *sociology educator, real estate company officer*
Mabry, Paul Davis *psychobiologist, educator, researcher*
Malecki, Edward Stanley, Jr., *political science educator*
Rossmann, Jack Eugene *psychology educator*
Ruttan, Vernon Wesley *agricultural economist, educator*
Schultz, David A. *political science educator, editor, writer, lawyer*
Swenson, Tami Charlotte *research analyst*
Zimmerman, Larry John *anthropologist, educator*

Saint Peter
Hilbert, Richard Andrew *sociologist, educator*
Mc Rostie, Clair Neil *economics professor*

Winona
Holm, Joy Alice *psychology educator, goldsmith, artist, art educator*

MISSISSIPPI

Biloxi
Cox, Albert Harrington, Jr., *economist*
Crumbaugh, James Charles *psychologist*

Blue Mountain
Cockrell, Thomas D. *social sciences educator*

Forest
Park, James Wallace *economics professor*

Hattiesburg
Burrus, John N(ewell) *sociology educator*
Davis, Charles Raymond *political scientist, educator*

Jackson
Otieno, Tabitha Nyaboke *social sciences educator, researcher*
Thaw, Andrew Kurt *psychologist, educator, research scientist*

Mississippi State
Clynch, Edward John *political science educator, researcher*
Cosby, Arthur G. *social sciences educator*

Ridgeland
O'Neill, Paul John *retired psychology educator*

Tupelo
Witty, Thomas Ezekiel, III, *psychologist, researcher*

MISSOURI

Bolivar
Brown, Autry *psychology educator, clergyman*
Hood, Michael Lee *psychologist, clinical researcher, educator*

Cape Girardeau
Rhodes, Joel Paul *social studies educator*

Columbia
Bank, Barbara J. *sociology educator*
Biddle, Bruce Jesse *social psychologist, educator*
Dolliver, Robert Henry *psychology educator*
Eastman, Harold Dwight *retired social studies educator, journalist*
LoPiccolo, Joseph *psychologist, educator, author*
Ratti, Ronald Andrew *economics professor*
Rowlett, Ralph Morgan *archaeologist, educator*
Salter, Christopher Lord *geography educator*

Grandview
Justesen, Don Robert *psychologist*

Half Way
Graves, Jerrell Loren *demographic studies researcher*

Hollister
Herron, Gayle Ann *forensic psychologist, mental health consultant, psychotherapist, health facility administrator, columnist*

Kansas City
Eddy, William Bahret *psychology educator, university dean*
Graham, Charles *research psychologist*
Lubin, Bernard *psychologist, educator*
Nagle, Jean Susan Karabacz *sociologist, psychologist*
Roosa, Jan Bertorotta *clinical psychologist*
Schrum, Janice Lynn *social sciences educator*

Kirksville
McDuff, Elaine Marie *sociologist, educator*

Maryville
Kharadia, Virabhai Chelabhai *economist, educator, researcher*

Saint Joseph
Boor, Myron Vernon *psychologist, educator*

Saint Louis
Beck, Lois Grant *anthropologist, educator, author*
Browman, David L(udvig) *archaeologist*
Entessar, Tahmineh *political scientist, educator*
Epstein, Lee Joan *political science educator*
Kling, Merle *political scientist, university official*
Leguey-Feilleux, Jean-Robert *political scientist, educator*
Leven, Charles Louis *economics professor*
Le Vine, Victor Theodore *political science educator*
Lindsey, Linda Lee *sociology educator*
Miller, Gary J. *political economist*
North, Douglass Cecil *economist, educator*
Nygard, Paul David *social sciences educator*
O'Connell, Daniel Craig *psychology educator*
Rosenzweig, Saul *psychologist, educator, administrator*
Salisbury, Robert Holt *political science educator*
Schmid, Frank Andreas *economist*
Smith, Richard Jay *anthropologist, orthodontist, educator*
Storandt, Martha *psychologist*
Thompson, Vetta Lynn Sanders *psychologist, educator*
Virgo, John Michael *economist, researcher, educator*
Voss, K. Dirk *social sciences educator, researcher*
Watson, Patty Jo *anthropology educator*
Weidenbaum, Murray Lew *economist, educator*
Welch, Patrick James *economics educator, author, consultant*
Williams, Mary Alice Baldwin *retired home economist, volunteer consultant*
Witherspoon, William *investment economist*

Springfield
Jones, Robert Gordon *psychology educator, councilman*
Stone, Allan David *economics professor*
Tempelmeyer, Teresa Catlin *psychologist, social sciences educator, researcher*
Van Cleave, William Robert *international relations educator*

Warrensburg
Fernquist, Robert *sociology educator*

MONTANA

Bozeman
Duffié, Mary Katharine *anthropologist, researcher, educator*
Gray, Philip Howard *former psychologist, writer, educator*

Helena
Lowney, Jeremiah *sociologist, educator, priest*
Seiler, Karen Peake *organizational psychologist*

Missoula
Grieves, Forest Leslie *political science educator*
Lopach, James Joseph *political science educator*
Russell, Bruce Alan, Sr., *social scientist, educator*
Watkins, John Goodrich *psychologist, educator*
Wollersheim, Janet Puccinelli *psychology educator*

NEBRASKA

Alliance
Haefele, Edwin Theodore *political theorist, consultant*

Grand Island
Buettner, Anne Yu Ramona Wing-mui *psychologist*

Harrison
Knudson, Ruthann *environmental consultant*

Kearney
Harrold, Francis Bernard, Jr., *anthropology educator*

Lincoln
Anderson, John Edwin *economics professor, consultant*
Bodvarsson, Orn Bodvar *economist, educator*
Deegan, Mary Jo *sociology educator*
MacPhee, Craig Robert *economist, educator*
McCutcheon, Allan Lee *sociology educator*
Ottoson, Howard Warren *economist, retired academic administrator*
Peterson, Wallace Carroll, Sr., *economics professor*
Rohren, Brenda Marie Anderson *therapist, educator*
Stoddard, Robert H. *geography educator*

Omaha
Allen, Robert Francis *economist, educator*
Bartle, John R. *social sciences educator*
Clark, Terry Dee *political scientist, educator*
Diamond, Arthur Mansfield, Jr., *economics professor*
Justice, Bob Joe *corporate development executive*
Louisa, Angelo Joseph *social studies educator, researcher*
North, Terry Claire *clinical psychologist*

NEVADA

Ely
Alderman, Minnis Amelia *psychologist, educator, small business owner*

Incline Village
Jones, Robert Alonzo *economist*

Las Vegas
Bowers, Michael Wayne *political science educator, writer*
Cole, Ann Harriet *psychologist, consultant*
de Rocher, Denise D. *social sciences educator, language educator*
Goldstein, Steven Edward *psychologist*
Goodall, Leonard Edwin *public administration educator*
Jelen, Ted G. *political scientist*
Mortillaro, Louis Francis *psychologist*
Weeks, Gerald *psychology educator*

Reno
Cargill, Thomas Frank *economist, educator*
Chapman, Samuel Greeley *political science educator, criminologist*
Cummings, Nicholas Andrew *psychologist*
Fruzzetti, Alan E. *psychologist, educator*
Haynes, Gary Anthony *archaeologist*
Leland, Joy Hanson *retired anthropologist, alcohol research specialist*
Lemire, David Stephen *school psychologist, educator*
Webster, Michael Anderson *experimental psychologist*

Zephyr Cove
Hudzinski, Leonard Gerard *social sciences educator, researcher*

NEW HAMPSHIRE

Bedford
Collins, Diana Josephine *psychologist*

Concord
Rogers, Katherine Diane *political consultant, commissioner*

Durham
Boy, Angelo V. *psychologist, educator*
Gumprecht, Blake *geographer, educator*
Kendall-Tackett, Kathleen Ann *researcher, health psychologist*
Palmer, Stuart Hunter *sociology educator*
Scharff, Robert Caesar *social sciences educator, writer, humanities educator*
Woodward, Robert Simpson, IV, *economics professor*

Francestown
Foster, Margery Somers *economics professor*

Goffstown
Oktavec, Eileen M. *anthropologist, artist*

Hanover
Baldwin, William Lee *retired economics professor*
Bower, Richard Stuart *economist, educator*
Demko, George Joseph *geographer*
Endicott, Kirk Michael *anthropologist, educator*
Fischel, William Alan *economics professor*
Hall, Raymond *sociology educator*
Kleck, Robert Eldon *psychology educator*
Lyons, Gene Martin *political scientist, educator*
Masters, Roger Davis *government and neurotoxicology educator*
Riggs, Lorrin Andrews *psychologist, educator*
Rutter, Jeremy Bentham *archaeologist, educator*
Starzinger, Vincent Evans *political scientist, educator*
Welsch, Robert Louis *anthropologist, curator*

Henniker
Braiterman, Thea Gilda *economics educator, state legislator, selectman*

Hooksett
Clamp, Christina A. *sociology educator*

Hudson
Dumond, Robert Wilfred *clinical mental health consultant, lay pastoral worker*

Keene
Alvarez, Kristin Jones *geographer, educator*
Baldwin, Peter Arthur *psychologist, educator, author, minister*

Hackett, John Thomas *retired economist*

Lebanon
Emery, Virginia Olga Beattie *psychologist, researcher*

Nashua
Flynn, William Berchman, Jr., *psychology educator, clinical psychologist*

Portsmouth
Cole-McCrea, Candace *social sciences educator*

NEW JERSEY

Belle Mead
Moevs, Maria Teresa Marabini *archaeologist*

Belmar
De Santo, Donald James *psychologist, educational administrator*

Camden
Harrison, Russell Sage *political science educator, consultant*
Van Til, Jon *sociology educator*
Worrall, John Dennis *economics educator, consultant, writer*
Yamada, Tetsuji *health economist, educator*

Cranbury
Hawver, Dennis A. *psychological consultant*

Cranford
Herz, Sylvia Beatrice *clinical and community psychologist*

Denville
Breed, Ria *anthropologist*

Dover
Seadler, Stephen Edward *social scientist, philosopher, writer*

East Orange
Wolff, Derish Michael *economist, company executive*

Eastampton
Haws, Elizabeth Anne *education administrator, school psychologist*

Englewood Cliffs
Farrell, Patricia Ann *psychologist, educator, writer*

Flemington
Jackson, Ryno Marshall *forensic psychologist, consultant*

Florham Park
Brodkin, Adele Ruth Meyer *psychologist*

Fort Lee
Kofman, Mikhail *economist, engineering executive*

Hackensack
Schwartz, Mildred Anne *retired sociologist*

Hasbrouck Heights
Perham, Roy Gates, III, *industrial psychologist*

Jackson
Leveson, Irving Frederick *economist*
Turner, Pamela *psychologist*

Jersey City
Hordon, Harris Eugene *economics professor*

Lakewood
Levine, Stephen M. *psychologist, educator*

Livingston
Friedman, Merton Hirsch *retired psychologist, educator*

Lodi
Guillory, Ann Verrett *psychologist, educator*

Lyndhurst
Bunda, Stephen Myron *political advisor, counselor, lawyer, classical philosopher*

Madison
Friedenfels, Roxanne M. *sociologist, educator*
Koppl, Roger Glenn *economist, educator*
Reader, Jonathan Whittier *sociology educator, consultant*

Manahawkin
Pulz, Gary Edward *psychologist*

Milltown
Sacharow, Beverly *gerontologist*

Montvale
Baba, Thomas Frank *corporate economist, economics educator*

Mount Laurel
Burnham, Lem *psychologist, think-tank executive*

Mountain Lakes
Loomis, Rebecca C. *psychology educator*

New Brunswick
Alexander, Robert Jackson *economist, educator*
Dutta, Manoranjan *economics professor*
Glasser, Paul Harold *sociologist, educator, social worker, university administrator*
Glickman, Norman Jay *economist, urban policy analyst*
Hassett, Afton Luevano *psychologist, educator*
Killingsworth, Mark R. *economics educator, consultant*
Leventhal, Howard *health psychology educator, researcher*
Mandel, Ruth Blumenstock *politics educator, educational association administrator, researcher*
Mechanic, David *social sciences educator*

Midlarsky, Manus Issachar *political scientist, educator*
Nordstrom, Karl Fredrik *geographer, educator*
Pallone, Nathaniel John *psychologist, educator*
Reock, Ernest C., Jr., *retired government services educator, academic director*
Rhodes, Edward Joseph *national security specialist, political scientist*
Rockoff, Hugh Touff *economist, educator*
Rosenberg, Seymour *psychologist, educator*
Russell, Louise Bennett *economist, educator*
Tiger, Lionel *social scientist, anthropology consultant*
Toby, Jackson *sociologist, educator*

New Providence
Roth, Robert Howard *psychologist*

Newark
Adler, Freda Schaffer (Mrs. G. O. W. Mueller) *criminologist, educator*
Carroll, John Douglas *mathematical and statistical psychologist*
Cheng, Mei-Fang *psychobiology educator, neuroethology researcher, biologist*
Ferguson, R. Brian *anthropologist, educator*
Ferguson, Yale Hicks *political scientist, educator*
Hiltz, Starr Roxanne *sociologist, educator, computer scientist, writer, lecturer, consultant*
Pagán, Gilberto, Jr., *clinical psychologist*

Oakland
Guller, Irving Bernard *forensic, clinical psychologist, consultant*

Paramus
Lieberman, Charles *economist, money manager*

Parsippany
Rappaport, Alan Fred *clinical psychologist*

Paterson
Paulhus, Thomas A. *social studies educator*

Piscataway
McCrady, Barbara Sachs *psychologist, educator*
Peterson, Donald Robert *psychologist, educator, university administrator*
Riss, Richard Michael *research economist, church history educator*
Schwebel, Milton *psychologist, educator*
Waxman, Chaim I. *sociology educator, researcher*
West, Mark Otto *sociology educator*
White, Helene R. *sociologist, educator*

Port Elizabeth
Ficcaglia, Leslie M. *psychologist, portrait artist*

Princeton
Barlow, Walter Greenwood *public opinion analyst, management consultant*
Blackman, Sue Anne Batey *economics researcher*
Blinder, Alan Stuart *economist, educator*
Bogan, Elizabeth Chapin *economist, educator*
Bogucki, Peter Ignatius *archaeologist*
Chow, Gregory Chi-Chong *economist, educator*
Coffey, Joseph Irving *international affairs educator*
Cook, Michael Allan *social sciences educator*
Cooper, Joel *psychology educator*
Doig, Jameson Wallace *political science educator*
Fried, Eleanor Reingold *psychologist, educator*
Friedberg, Aaron Louis *political science educator*
Geertz, Clifford James *anthropology educator*
Gilpin, Robert George, Jr., *political science educator*
Girgus, Joan Stern *psychologist, university administrator*
Glucksberg, Sam *psychology educator*
Gordenker, Leon *political sciences educator*
Greenstein, Fred Irwin *political science educator*
Gross, Charles Gordon *psychology educator, neuroscientist*
Haxby, James Van Loan *psychologist, educator*
Hirschman, Albert Otto *political economist, educator*
Hitz, Frederick Porter *public and international affairs educator*
Hoebel, Bartley Gore *psychology educator*
Kahneman, Daniel *psychology educator*
Kateb, George Anthony *political science educator*
Kenen, Peter Bain *economist, educator*
Krugman, Paul Robin *economics professor*
Kuenne, Robert Eugene *economics professor*
Lazarus, Arnold Allan *psychologist, educator*
Malkiel, Burton Gordon *economist, educator*
Manning, Winton Howard *psychologist, educational administrator*
Maskin, Eric Stark *economics professor*
Miller, George Armitage *psychologist, educator*
Parry, Scott Brink *psychologist*
Reinhardt, Uwe Ernst *economist, educator*
Rosenthal, Howard Lewis *political science educator*
Rozman, Gilbert Friedell *sociologist, educator*
Shear, Ione Mylonas *archaeologist*
Shear, Theodore Leslie, Jr., *archaeologist, educator*
Spence, Donald Pond *psychologist, psychoanalyst*
Starr, Paul Elliot *sociologist, writer, editor, educator*
Tienda, Marta *demographer, educator*
Trussell, James *economist, educator, dean*
Tucker, Joshua Aaron *political scientist*
Westoff, Charles Francis *demographer, educator*
Willig, Robert Daniel *economics professor*
Willingham, Warren Willcox *psychologist, testing service executive*

Red Bank
McWhinney, Madeline H. (Mrs. John Denny Dale) *economist, director*

Saddle River
Lasser, Gail Maria *psychologist, educator*

Scotch Plains
Hallard, Wayne Bruce *retired economist*

Somerset
Dahbany, Avivah *psychologist, educator*
Lichtig, Leo Kenneth *health economist*

Springfield
Shilling, A. Gary *economic consultant, investment advisor*

Sussex
MacMurren, Harold Henry, Jr., *psychologist, lawyer*

Teaneck
Brudner, Helen Gross *social sciences educator*
Cassimatis, Peter John *economics professor*
McGrath, Robert Edward *psychology educator*

Tenafly
Blank, Marion Sue *psychologist, educator*

Titusville
Bhattacharjya, Ashoke Sanjoy *economist, researcher*

Trenton
McGowan, Joan Yuhas *development researcher*

Union
Kim, Youn-Suk Ernest *economist, educator*
Sigmon, Scott B. *psychologist*

Verona
Aronow, Edward *psychologist, educator*

Wayne
Principe, Michael Luis *political science educator*
Salny, Abbie Feinstein *psychologist*
Sheffield, Carole Jean *political science educator*

Westwood
Fabrikant, Craig Steven *psychologist*

Whitehouse Station
Hunsche, Elke Greta Irma *economist*

NEW MEXICO

Albuquerque
Baker, Arnold Barry *economist*
Baker, Chester Bird *agricultural economics educator*
Basso, Keith Hamilton *cultural anthropologist, linguist, educator*
Burris, Beverly Hudeck *sociology educator*
Condie, Carol Joy *anthropologist, research facility administrator*
Davidge, K. Genevieve *clinical social worker*
Elliott, Charles Harold *clinical psychologist*
Harris, Fred R. *political scientist, educator, retired senator*
Heady, Ferrel *retired political science educator*
May, Philip Alan *sociology educator*
Raish, Carol Brooks *anthropologist, archaeologist*
Schwerin, Karl Henry *anthropology educator, researcher*
Stuart, David Edward *anthropologist, writer, educator*
Wynne, Louis *psychologist*

Bayard
Lopez, Linda Carol *social sciences educator*

Corrales
Adams, James Frederick *psychologist, educational administrator*

El Prado
Young, Jon Nathan *archaeologist*

Kirtland Afb
Tritten, James John *national security educator*

Las Cruces
Roscoe, Stanley Nelson *psychologist, aeronautical engineer*

Las Vegas
Riley, Carroll Lavern *anthropology educator*

Los Alamos
Masse, William Bruce *archaeologist*
Thompson, Lois Jean Heidke Ore *psychologist*

Santa Fe
Anderson, Darrell Edward *psychologist, educator*
Kingman, Elizabeth Yelm *anthropologist*
Noble, Merrill Emmett *retired psychology educator, psychologist*
Perry, Nancy Estelle *psychologist*
Williams, Stephen *anthropologist, educator*

NEW YORK

Albany
Alba, Richard Denis *sociologist, educator*
Capaldi, Elizabeth Ann Deutsch *psychological sciences educator*
Cruz, José Edgardo *political science educator*
Jiha, Jacques *economist*
Smith, Michael Ernest *archaeologist, educator*
Thompson, Frank Joseph *political science educator*
Zimmerman, Joseph Francis *political scientist, educator*

Alfred
Greil, Arthur Lawrence *sociology educator*

Amherst
Aurbach, Herbert Alexander *sociology educator*
Brown, Murray *economist, educator*
Wiesenberg, Jacqueline Leonardi *social sciences educator*

Annandale On Hudson
Papadimitriou, Dimitri Basil *economist, educator, academic administrator*

Averill Park
Haines, Walter Wells *retired economics educator*

Bellport
Moeller, Mary Ella *retired home economist, educator, radio commentator*

Binghamton
Isaacson, Robert Lee *psychology educator, researcher*

James, Gary Douglas *biological anthropologist, educator, researcher*
Levis, Donald James *psychologist, educator*
Polachek, Solomon William *economist, educator*
Ziemski, Connie Marie *social studies educator*

Bronx
Bauman, Laurie Julia *sociologist, researcher*
Burton, Leslie Anne *psychologist*
Busch-Rossnagel, Nancy Ann *psychology educator, university dean*
Fishman, Joshua Aaron *sociolinguist, educator*
Hooker, Olivia J. *psychologist, educator*
Regan, Richard Joseph *political science professor, writer*

Bronxville
Mills, Nicolaus *American studies educator, writer*

Brooklyn
Bloom, Howard Kenneth *paleopsychologist, writer*
Isacoff, Mark *psychologist*
James, Milton Garnet *economist*
Jean-Louis, Girardin *psychologist, educator, researcher*
LaFont, Suzanne *anthropologist, educator*
Martinez-Pons, Manuel *psychologist, educator*
Nye, William Roger *psychologist*
Reinisch, June Machover *psychologist, educator*
Szenberg, Michael *economics educator, editor, consultant*
Torras, Mariano *economist, educator*
Varma, Ranbir *economics professor*

Brookville
Kusukawa, Akira *demographer, educator*

Buffalo
Boot, John C.G. *economist, educator*
Delaney, Tim *sociologist, educator*
Ehrlich, Isaac *economist, educator, department chairman*
Floss, Frederick George *economics and finance educator, consultant*
Frone, Michael R. *psychologist, researcher*
Gort, Michael *economics professor*
Hetzner, Donald Raymund *social studies educator, forensic social scientist*
Holmes, James M. *social studies educator, economist*
Lamb, Charles Moody *political scientist, educator*
Tedlock, Barbara Helen *anthropologist, educator, academic administrator*

Castile
Krolikowski, Gary E. *social sciences educator*

Clayton
Schmidt, Karl M., Jr., *political science educator*

Clinton
Raybeck, Douglas *anthropologist, educator*

Conesus
Dadrian, Vahakn Norair *sociology educator*

Cooperstown
Fenton, William Nelson *anthropologist, anthropology educator emeritus*

De Witt
Pearl, Harvey *rehabilitation psychologist*

Delhi
Van Brunt, Arthur Hoffman (Peter) *economist, educator*

Dobbs Ferry
Culhane, Hind Rassam *psychologist, educator, film historian*
Kraetzer, Mary C. *sociologist, educator, consultant*
Perelle, Ira B. *psychologist, educator*
Sutton, Francis Xavier *social scientist, consultant*

East Meadow
Albert, Gerald *clinical psychologist*

Feura Bush
Byrne, Donn Erwin *psychologist, educator*

Flushing
Goh, David Shuh-Jen *psychology educator*
Hacker, Andrew *political science educator*
Lakah, Jacqueline Rabbat *political scientist, consultant*
Li, Hongzhi *Falun Dafa founder, author*
Pellitteri, John Steven *psychologist, therapist, educator*

Forest Hills
Bertolini, Joseph Clifford *political scientist, educator*
Ustayev, Rakhim *psychologist*

Fredonia
Klonsky, Bruce Gary *psychology professor*

Garden City
Koenig, Louis William *political science educator, author*
Ohrenstein, Roman Abraham *economics educator, economist, rabbi*

Garrison
Murray, Thomas Henry *bioethics educator, writer*

Geneseo
Battersby, Harold Ronald *retired anthropologist, archaeologist, linguist*
Olczak, Paul Vincent *psychology educator*

Geneva
Lurie, Daphne *clinical psychologist, lecturer, educator*

Great Neck
Joskow, Jules *economic research company executive*
Minkoff, Jack *retired economics educator*

Greenport
Watts, Harold Wesley *economist, educator*

Greenvale
Zwicker, Charles *economist, educator, accountant, consultant*

Hamilton
Blum, Lester *economics professor*
Dovidio, John Francis *psychology educator*
Haines, Michael Robert *economist, educator*

Hampton Bays
Baker, Donald Gene *social sciences educator*

Hartsdale
Stein, Michael David *psychologist*

Hempstead
Block, Jules Richard *retired psychologist, educator, university official*
Salzinger, Kurt *psychology educator*
Wattel, Harold Louis *economics professor*

Hewlett
Salamon, Michael Jacob *psychologist, health care and psychology educator, media consultant*

Huletts Landing
Kapusinski, Albert Thomas *economist, educator*

Ithaca
Ascher, Robert *anthropologist, educator, archaeologist, film producer*
Assie-Lumumba, N'Dri T. *Africana studies educator*
Beneria, Lourdes *economist, educator*
Bensel, Richard Franklin *political science educator*
Briggs, Vernon Mason, Jr., *economics professor*
Chapman, Lewis Duane *economist*
Darlington, Richard Benjamin *psychology educator*
Easley, David *economics professor*
Ehrenberg, Ronald Gordon *economist, educator*
Fireside, Harvey Francis *political scientist, educator*
Heckathorn, Douglas D. *sociologist, educator, epidemiologist*
Jarrow, Robert Alan *economics and finance educator, consultant*
Kahn, Alfred Edward *economist, educator, government official*
Kennedy, Kenneth Adrian Raine *biological anthropologist, forensic anthropologist*
LaDue, Eddy Lorain *economist, educator*
Lowi, Theodore J(ay) *political science educator*
Lyons, Thomas Patrick *economics professor*
Pelto, Gretel H. *nutritional anthropologist, educator*
Pinstrup-Andersen, Per *economist, educator*
Rader, Nancy Louise de Villiers *psychology educator, consultant*
Rosen, Bernard Carl *sociologist, social psychologist, educator*
Shell, Karl *economist*
Smith, Robert John *anthropology educator*
Stycos, Joseph Mayone *retired demographer, educator*
Thorbecke, Erik *economics professor*
Tomek, William Goodrich *agricultural economist*
Waldman, Michael *economist, educator*

Jamaica
Gesualdi, Louis J. *social sciences educator*
Lees, Francis *economics professor*

Johnstown
DiNitto, Andrew Joseph *political scientist, educator*

Katonah
Wenglowski, Gary Martin *economist*

Larchmont
Siegel, Nathaniel Harold *sociology educator*

Levittown
Elliott, Franklyn *psychologist*
Juszczak, Nicholas Mauro *psychology educator*

Liberty
Green, Harold Martin *social science writer*

Lincolndale
Joerger, Jay Herman *psychologist, entrepreneur*

Liverpool
Egan, Marsha Christine *school psychologist*

Mamaroneck
Scheidlinger, Saul *psychologist*

Mexico
Sade, Donald Stone *anthropology educator*

Middle Village
Schiffman, Jacquelyn Linda *psychologist, consultant, artist*

Millbrook
Flexner, Kurt Fisher *economist, educator*

Mount Kisco
Schwarz, Wolfgang *psychologist*

Mount Vernon
Cammarosano, Joseph Raphael *economist, educator*

New City
Wechman, Robert Joseph *economist, educator*

New Paltz
Neuman, Joel H. *psychologist, educator*
Schnell, George Adam *geographer, educator*

New Rochelle
Berlage, Gai Ingham *sociologist, educator*
Golub, Sharon Bramson *psychologist, educator*

New York
Andersen, Marianne Singer *clinical psychologist*
Andersen, Susan Marie *psychologist, educator*
Andreassi, John Lawrence *psychologist, educator*
Angelo, Larian *economist*
Anspach, Ernst *economist, lawyer*
Arther, Richard Oberlin *polygraphist, educator*
Baldwin, David Allen *political science educator*
Bardach, Joan Lucile *clinical psychologist*
Barron, Susan *clinical psychologist*
Bartolini, Leonardo *economist*
Betts, Richard Kevin *political science educator*
Blechner, Mark Jacob *psychologist, educator*
Boodey, Cecil Webster, Jr., *political science educator*
Boorstein, Laurence *economist, educator*
Bowen, William Gordon *economist, educator, foundation administrator*
Bowers, Patricia Eleanor Fritz *economist*
Braham, Randolph Lewis *political science educator*
Brams, Steven John *political scientist, educator, game theorist*
Brooks-Gunn, Jeanne *psychologist*
Browne, Joy *psychologist, radio personality*
Buchholz, Ester Schaler *psychologist*
Buck, Louise Zierdt *psychologist*
Butler, Robert Neil *gerontologist, psychiatrist, writer, educator*
Caraley, Demetrios James *political scientist, educator, writer*
Carey, Alida Livingston *political scientist, writer, reporter*
Chamberlain, Neil Cornelius Wolverton *economist, emeritus educator*
Charney, Craig Russell *pollster, political scientist*
Chelstrom, Marilyn Ann *political education consultant*
Clamar, Aphrodite J. *psychologist*
Cochrane, James Louis *economist*
Cohen, Michael *psychologist*
Cohen, Stephen Frand *political scientist, historian, educator, author, broadcaster*
Comitas, Lambros *anthropologist, educator*
Connelly, Joan Breton *archaeologist*
Dalton, Dennis Gilmore *political science educator*
del Cerro, Gerardo *sociologist, researcher*
deMause, Lloyd *psychohistorian*
Demeny, Paul George *demographer, researcher*
Denoon, David Baugh Holden *economist, educator, consultant*
Domowitz, Ian *economics professor*
Dowling, Edward Thomas *economics professor*
Duke, Anthony Drexel *sociologist, educator, philanthropist*
Edinger, Lewis Joachim *political science educator*
Edwards, Franklin R. *economist, educator, consultant*
Edwards, Linda Nasif *economics professor*
Elinson, Jack *sociology educator*
Ellis, Albert *clinical psychologist, educator, author*
Engler, Robert *political science educator, author*
Epstein, Cynthia Fuchs *sociology educator, writer*
Fancher, Edwin Crawford *psychologist, educator*
Felgran, Steven David *economist, educator*
Finger, Seymour Maxwell *political science educator, former ambassador*
Flannelly, Kevin J. *psychologist, research analyst*
Foley, Duncan Karl *economist, educator*
Fox, Richard Gabriel *anthropologist, educator*
Franklin, Julian Harold *political science educator*
Freidenbergs, Ingrid *psychologist*
Freund, William Curt *economist, educator*
Frost, Ellen Elizabeth *psychologist*
Galanter, Eugene *psychologist, educator*
Gans, Herbert J. *sociologist, educator*
Gianaris, Nicholas Vasil *economics professor*
Glass, David Carter *psychology educator*
Glickman, Michael Richard *social studies educator*
Goldberger, Leo *psychologist, educator*
Goldman, George David *psychologist, psychoanalyst*
Goss, Mary E. Weber *sociology educator*
Greene Oster, Selmaree *medical anthropologist, researcher*
Griffin, Anne *political scientist, educator*
Gross, Alan Ellis *psychologist, educator, researcher, mediator, consultant*
Gross, Feliks *sociologist, educator, writer*
Grossman, Michael *economics professor*
Gullo, Stephen Pernice *psychologist, corporate executive*
Habachy, Suzan Salwa Saba *development economist, non profit administrator*
Haber, Pierre-Claude *psychologist*
Halper, Thomas *political science educator*
Hammer, Emanuel Frederick *clinical psychologist, psychoanalyst*
Harkavy-Friedman, Jill Martine *psychologist*
Heal, Geoffrey Martin *economics and business educator*
Heilbroner, Robert Louis *economist, writer*
Heilbrun, James *economist, educator*
Helmreich, William Benno *sociology educator, consultant*
Heyde, Martha Bennett (Mrs. Ernest R. Heyde) *psychologist*
Heydebrand, Wolf Von *sociology educator*
Higgins, E. Tory *psychology educator, research scientist*
Hoffman, Martin Leon *psychology educator*
Holloway, Ralph Leslie *anthropology educator*
Hormats, Robert David *economist, investment banker*
Hoxter, Curtis Joseph *international economic advisor, public relations executive*
Ivanovitch, Michael S. *economist*
Jacoby, Jacob *consumer psychology educator*
Jasso, Guillermina *sociologist, educator*
Jervis, Robert *political science educator*
Jordan, Theresa Joan *psychologist, educator*
Kandel, Denise Bystryn *sociologist*
Kaplan, Lawrence Jay *economist, educator*
Karl, Kurt Erskine *economist*
Kavaler-Adler, Susan *clinical psychologist, psychoanalyst*
Kavesh, Robert A. *economist, educator*
Kazemi, Farhad *political scientist, educator*
Krauss, Herbert Harris *psychologist*
Kurzweil, Edith *sociology educator, editor*
Laibman, David *economist, educator*
Lazarcik, Gregor *educator, financial research company executive, economist*
Lefkowitz, Joel M. *psychologist, educator*
Lehman, Edward William *sociology educator, researcher*
Lentner, Howard Henry *political scientist*
Lew, Jacob *public administration educator*
Lichtblau, John H. *economist*
Lieberman, Robert C(harles) *political scientist*
Lipsey, Robert Edward *economist, educator*
Lothian, James Robert *economist, educator*
Low, Setha Marilyn *anthropology and psychology educator, consultant*
Magee-Egan, Pauline Cecilia *psychology and management educator*
Maldonado-Bear, Rita Marinita *economist, educator*
Marlin, John Tepper *economist, writer, consultant*
Martin, Linda Gaye *demographer, economist*
Marty, Alvin Leonard *economist, educator*
McCarthy, Jonathan Paul *economist*
Mc Cullough, J. Lee *industrial psychologist*
Meyer-Bahlburg, Heino F.L. *psychology educator*
Mincer, Jacob *economics educator*
Molz, Redmond Kathleen *public administration educator*
Moskowitz, Arnold X. *economist, strategist, educator*
Mroz, John Edwin *political scientist*
Muller, Charlotte Feldman *economist, educator*
Mundell, Robert Alexander *economist, educator*
Murphy, Austin de la Salle *economist, educator, banker*
Nadiri, M. Ishaq *economics educator, researcher, lecturer, consultant*
Nakamura, James I. *economics educator*
Netzer, Dick *economics professor*
O'Neill, June Ellenoff *economist*
Papalia, Diane Ellen *human development educator*
Patrick, Hugh Talbot *economist, educator*
Peck, Fred Neil *economist, educator*
Persell, Caroline Hodges *sociologist, educator, author, researcher, consultant*
Petchesky, Rosalind Pollack *political scientist, educator, social sciences educator*
Pitcavage, Mark Thomas *political scientist, writer, historian*
Piven, Frances Fox *political scientist, educator*
Psomiades, Harry John *political science educator*
Pye, Gordon Bruce *economist*
Quackenbush, Margery Clouser *psychoanalyst, administrator*
Radner, Roy *economist, educator, researcher*
Rao, Sethuramiah Lakshminarayana *demographer, United Nations official*
Riss, Eric *psychologist*
Rivlin, Benjamin *political science educator*
Robinson, Daniel N. *psychology and philosophy educator*
Rosenthal, Gert *economist*
Ross, Jeffrey Allan *political scientist, educator*
Sachs, Jeffrey David *economist, educator*
Sands, Harry *psychologist, health administrator, researcher*
Sbaity-Kassem, Fatima Hasan *political economist, researcher*
Scanlon, Rosemary *economist*
Scelsa, Joseph Vincent *sociologist, educator, university executive*
Schneier, Edward Vincent *political science educator*
Schotter, Andrew Roye *economics educator, consultant*
Schupbach, Rosa Lechner *retired economist*
Schwab, George David *social science educator, author*
Schwartz, Anna Jacobson *economic historian*
Scott, Nancy Ellen *psychologist*
Sheldon, Eleanor Harriet Bernert *sociologist, writer*
Sherry, George Leon *political science educator*
Silver, Morris *economist, educator*
Simon, Jacqueline Albert *political scientist, journalist*
Skinner, Elliott Percival *anthropology educator*
Small, George LeRoy *geographer, educator*
Smithson, Charles Wayne *economist, consultant*
Solecki, R. Stefan *anthropologist, educator*
Stiglitz, Joseph Eugene *economist, educator*
Suraci, Patrick Joseph *clinical psychologist*
Sylla, Richard Eugene *economics professor*
Tallmer, Margot Sallop *psychologist, psychoanalyst, gerontologist*
Taylor, Lance Jerome *economics professor*
Tepper, Lynn Marsha *gerontology educator*
Terris, Lillian Dick *psychologist, association executive*
Tester, Leonard Wayne *psychology educator*
Todaro, Michael Paul *economics educator, consultant*
Velayo, Richard Soriano *psychologist, educator, researcher*
Vitz, Paul Clayton *psychologist, educator*
Walter, Ingo *economics professor*
Weiss, Samuel Abraham *psychologist, psychoanalyst*
Wellisz, Stanislaw *economics professor*
Westheimer, Ruth Siegel (Karola Westheimer) *psychologist, television personality*
Wexler, Nancy Sabin *clinical neuropsychology educator*
White, Lawrence J. *economics professor*
Wolff, Edward Nathan *economist, educator*
Wolman, William *economist, journalist, broadcaster*
Zawistowski, Stephen Louis *psychologist, educator*

Niagara University
Osberg, Timothy Michael *psychologist, educator, researcher*

Niskayuna
Wright, Theodore Paul, Jr., *political science educator*

North Woodmere
Aviles, Alice Alers *psychologist*

Oneonta
vom Saal, Walter *psychology educator*

Oswego
Gordon, Norman Botnick *psychology educator*

Palisades
Miller, Roberta Balstad *social scientist*

Pleasant Valley
Marshall, Natalie Junemann *economics professor*

Pleasantville
Katen, Joan Alice *political scientist, educator*

Port Washington
Schneider, Greta *economist, speaker, author, real estate investor*

Potsdam
Atesoglu, H. Sonmez *economist, educator*
Wickman, Peter M. *sociologist, educator*

Poughkeepsie
Johnson, M(aurice) Glen *political science educator*
Moon, Seungsook *sociologist, educator*
Trumbetta, Susan L. *psychology educator*

Purchase
Newton, Esther Mary *anthropologist, educator*
Ryan, Edward W. *economics professor*

Queens
Kreisler, Rochelle *psychologist*
Singh, Ronald *social sciences educator, researcher*

Queens Village
Chowdhury, Mohammed Shamsul *economics professor*

Rochester
Bluhm, William Theodore *political scientist, educator*
Buckingham, Barbara Rae *social studies educator*
Deci, Edward Lewis *psychologist, educator*
DuBrin, Andrew John *behavioral sciences, management educator, writer*
Elliot, Andrew J. *psychology professor*
Fenno, Richard Francis, Jr., *political scientist, educator*
Freeman, Leslie Jean *neuropsychologist, researcher*
Hopkins, Thomas Duvall *economics professor*
Jones, Ronald Winthrop *economics professor*
Laties, Victor Gregory *psychology educator*
Levy, Harold David *psycholinguist*
Long, John Broaddus, Jr., *economist, educator*
Mc Kenzie, Lionel Wilfred *economist, educator*
Phelps, Charles Elliott *economics professor, director*
Plosser, Charles Irving *economist, educator*
Regenstreif, S(amuel) Peter *political scientist, educator*
Steamer, Robert Julius *political science educator*
Vernarelli, Michael Joseph *economics educator, consultant*
Zax, Melvin *psychologist, educator*

Rockville Centre
Lewittes, Don Jordan *clinical psychologist*

Rye Brook
Aquino, Joseph Mario *clinical psychologist*

Sanborn
Gerbasi, Kathleen Carrese *psychologist, educator*

Scarborough
Parks, Robert Henry *consulting economist, educator*

Scarsdale
Cohen, Irwin *economist*

Schenectady
Board, Joseph Breckinridge, Jr., *political scientist, educator*
Sharlet, Robert *political science educator, researcher*

Slingerlands
Bragle, George W. *criminal justice educator*

Somers
Trzasko, Joseph Anthony *psychologist, educator*

Staten Island
Meltzer, Yale Leon *economist, educator*

Stony Brook
Carr, Edward Gary *psychology educator*
Goodman, Norman *sociologist, researcher*
Grim, Patrick Neal *philosopher, logician, educator*
Leakey, Richard Erskine *paleoanthropologist, museum director*
Neuberger, Egon *economics professor*
Schneider, Mark *political science educator*
Stolzberg, Mark Elliott *psychologist*
Stone, Elizabeth Cecilia *anthropology educator*
Tanur, Judith Mark *sociologist, educator*
Travis, Martin Bice *political scientist, educator*

Syracuse
Birkhead, Guthrie Sweeney, Jr., *political scientist, university dean*
Braungart, Margaret Mitchell *psychology and bioethics educator*
Braungart, Richard Gottfried *sociology and international relations educator*
Fiske, Sandra Rappaport *psychologist, educator*
Frohock, Fred Manuel *political science educator*
Jensen, Robert Granville *geography educator, university dean*
Kriesberg, Louis *sociologist, educator*
Mazur, Allan Carl *sociologist, engineer, educator*
Meinig, Donald William *geography educator*
Monmonier, Mark *geographer, graphics educator, essayist*
Sprafkin, Robert Peter *psychologist, educator*
Wilkinson, Louise Cherry *psychology educator, dean*
Zito, George Vincent *sociologist, sociology educator*

Tarrytown
Lawry, John D. *psychologist, educator*
Weiner, Max *educational psychology educator*

Troy
Brazil, Harold Edmund *political science educator*
Layne, Linda Louise *cultural anthropologist, educator*
Schechter, Stephen L. *political scientist*

Warwick
Kaminsky, Anatol *educator, writer*

West Point
Keith, Bruce Edward *sociologist*

White Plains
Bloom, Adam I. *psychologist*
Kaushik, Surendra Kumar *economist*
Rapp, Richard Tilden *economist, consultant*

Whitestone
Caputo, Daniel Vincent *psychologist*

Williamstown
Frank, Joshua M. *economist, think-tank executive*

Woodbury
Agresti, Miriam Monell *psychologist*

Woodstock
Lieberman, Josefa Nina *psychologist, educator, writer*

Yonkers
Lupiani, Donald Anthony *psychologist*
Monegro, Francisco *psychology educator, alternative medicine consultant*
Varma, Baidya Nath *sociologist, broadcaster, poet*

NORTH CAROLINA

Asheville
Dickens, Charles Henderson *retired social scientist, consultant*

Biltmore Forest
Sgro, Joseph Anthony *retired psychologist, educator*

Black Mountain
Proctor, Jesse Harris, Jr., *political science educator*

Boone
Jones, Dan Lewis *psychologist*
Keefe, Susan Emley *anthropology educator*

Cashiers
O'Connell, Edward James, Jr., *psychology educator, computer applications and data analysis consultant*

Chapel Hill
Baker, Paul Thornell *anthropology educator*
Barbarin, Oscar Anthony *psychologist*
Baroff, George Stanley *psychologist, educator*
Black, Stanley Warren, III, *economics professor*
Boyarsky, Rose Eisman *psychologist*
Brown, Frank *social science educator*
Dahlstrom, William Grant *psychologist, educator*
Fieleke, Norman Siegfried *economist, educator*
Fox, Ronald Ernest *psychologist*
Friedman, James Winstein *economist, educator*
Gottlieb, Gilbert *psychobiologist, educator*
Graham, George Adams *political scientist, emeritus educator*
Gray, Virginia Hickman *political science educator*
Gray-Little, Bernadette *psychologist, educator*
Hartlyn, Jonathan *political scientist, educator*
Huber, Evelyne *political science educator*
Ingram, James Carlton *economist, educator*
Jones, Lyle Vincent *psychologist, educator*
Latané, Bibb *social psychologist*
Ornstein, Peter Arnold *psychologist, educator*
Pfouts, Ralph William *economist, consultant*
Rindfuss, Ronald Richard *sociology educator*
Salemi, Michael Kerry *economist, educator*
Schoultz, Lars *political scientist, educator*
Smith, James Finley *economist, educator*
Snyder, Glenn Herald *political science educator, writer*
Stenberg, Carl W., III, *public administration educator, dean*
Steponaitis, Vincas Petras *archaeologist, anthropologist, educator*
Treml, Vladimir Guy *economist, educator*
Wasik, Barbara Hanna *psychologist, educator*
Weinstein, Sidney *neuropsychologist*
Wilson, Glenn *economist, educator*
Wright, Deil Spencer *political science educator*

Charlotte
Brandon, William Pew, Jr., *social sciences educator*
Combs, Cindy Culbreth *social sciences educator, consultant*
Dorin, Dennis Daniel *political science educator, researcher*
Goolkasian, Paula A. *psychologist, educator*
Harver, Andrew Robert *psychology educator*
Neel, Richard Eugene *economics and business educator*
Webster, Murray Alexander, Jr., *sociologist, educator*

Clemmons
Church, Avery Grenfell *retired anthropology educator, poet*

Davidson
Ross, Clark Grant *economics professor*

Durham
Aldrich, John Herbert *political science educator*
Blumenthal, James A. *psychologist, researcher*
Boguslavsky, George William *psychologist, educator*
Bollerslev, Tim Peter *economics professor*
Braibanti, Ralph John *political scientist, educator*
Burmeister, Edwin *economics educator*
Conklin, George Henry *sociologist, educator*
Cook, Philip Jackson *economist, educator*
Elliot, Jeffrey M. *political science educator, author*
Flippen, Brenda Jane *psychology professor, consultant*
Gillespie, Michael Allen *political science and philosophy educator, writer*
Gittler, Joseph Bertram *sociology educator*
Guseh, James Sawalla *public administration educator*
Holsti, Ole Rudolf *political scientist, educator*
Kelley, Allen Charles *economist, educator*
Keohane, Robert Owen *political scientist, educator*
Land, Kenneth Carl *sociology educator, demographer, statistician, consultant*
Lockhead, Gregory Roger *psychology educator*
McClain, Paula Denice *political scientist, educator*
Mickiewicz, Ellen Propper *political and social science educator*
Robins, Clive Justin *psychology educator, researcher, psychotherapist*
Simons, Elwyn LaVerne *physical anthropologist, primatologist, paleontologist, educator*
Sloan, Frank Allen *economist, educator*
Staddon, John Eric Rayner *psychology, zoology, neurobiology educator*
Surwit, Richard Samuel *psychology educator*
Talley, Joseph Eugene *psychologist*
Tiryakian, Edward Ashod *sociology educator*

Franklin
Earhart, Eileen Magie *retired child and family life educator*

Greensboro
Chandler, Austin Grace *psychologist*
Gill, Diane Louise *psychology educator, university official*
Goldman, Bert Arthur *psychologist, educator*
Helms-VanStone, Mary Wallace *anthropology educator*
Newell, Charles Ansel, Jr., *social studies educator*
Prysby, Charles Lee *political science educator*
Shelton, David Howard *economics professor*
Zopf, Paul Edward, Jr., *sociologist*

High Point
Corey, James William *political scientist, educator*

Hillsborough
Goodwin, Craufurd David *economics professor*

Jacksonville
Guyer, Charles Grayson, II, *psychologist*

Kinston
Adams, Tj *behavioral specialist, writer, evangelist*

Newport
Rettie, Dwight Fay *retired political science educator, writer*

Pembroke
King, Beverly Rae *developmental psychologist*

Pittsboro
Doenges, Byron Frederick *economist, educator, former government official*
Richardson, Richard Judson *retired political science educator*

Raleigh
Allen, Steven Glen *economics and business educator*
Corder, Billie Farmer *clinical psychologist, artist*
Fearn, Robert Morcom *economics professor, finance educator, consultant*
Flath, David Joseph *economist, educator*
Hayes, Charles Austin *economic development executive, consultant*
Hiday, Virginia Aldigé *sociologist educator*
Imade, Lucky Osagie *political scientist, educator*
Johnson, Charles Lavon, Jr., *clinical neuropsychologist, consultant*
Newman, Slater Edmund *psychologist, educator*

Wilmington
Bomhan, Ruth Walker *social studies educator*
Puente, Antonio E. *psychologist, educator, scientist*

Winston Salem
Karnes, Lucia Rooney *psychologist*
King, Arthur Thomas *economics educator, retired air force officer*
Soares, Joseph Arlie *sociologist, educator*
Twiggs, Dennis Glenn *psychologist, writer*

NORTH DAKOTA

Fargo
Riley, Thomas Joseph *anthropologist, educational administrator*

Grand Forks
Russell, Sue Ann *clinical psychologist*
Tyler, John Duke *psychologist, educator*

Minot
Ellis, Lee *social sciences educator*

OHIO

Akron
Coyne, Thomas Joseph *economist, finance educator*
Franck, Ardath Amond *psychologist, educator*
Prosnick, Kevin Paul *psychologist, researcher*
Sterns, Harvey Leonard *psychologist, gerontologist*
Su, Dongwei *economist, educator*

Ashland
Ford, Lucille Garber *economist, educator*

Athens
Lancaster, Lynne Chapman *archaeologist, education educator*
Stump, Earl Spencer *psychologist*
Vedder, Richard Kent *economics professor*

Beachwood
Curran, Audrey Harwell *psychologist, educator*
Wolf, Milton Albert *economist, former ambassador, investor*

Bluffton
Friesen, Ronald Lee *economics educator*

Bowling Green
Berger, Bonnie G. *sport psychologist, educator*
Guion, Robert Morgan *psychologist, educator*
Hakel, Milton Daniel, Jr., *psychology educator, consultant, publisher*
McCaghy, Charles Henry *sociology educator*
Merriam, John Goodwin *political scientist, educator*

Centerville
Kauffold, Ruth Elizabeth *clinical psychologist*

Cincinnati
Bieliauskas, Vytautas Joseph *psychologist, educator*
Bishop, George Franklin *political scientist, educator*
Bluestein, Venus Weller *retired psychologist, educator*
Dember, William Norton *retired psychologist, educator*
Howison, Joan L. *geographer, writer*

Cleveland
Bate, Brian R. *retired psychologist*
Beall, Cynthia *anthropologist, educator*
Binstock, Robert Henry *public policy educator, writer, lecturer*
Carlsson, Bo Axel Vilhelm *economics professor*
Carrol, Edward Nicholas *psychologist*
Deal, William Thomas *school psychologist*
Grundy, Kenneth William *political science educator*
Kilbane, Sally Conway *economics professor*
Kolb, David Allen *psychology educator*
Manos, Peter John *social studies educator, theater director, writer, actor*
Mayland, Kenneth Theodore *economist*
McHale, Vincent Edward *political science educator*
Miller, Sandra A. Caramela *gerontologist, educator*
Myers, Eddie Earl *clinical psychologist*
Sibley, Willis Elbridge *anthropology educator, consultant*

Columbus
Alger, Chadwick Fairfax *political scientist, educator*
Baird, Leonard Lynn *social scientist, educator, researcher, editor*
Beck, Paul Allen *political science educator*
Ellingson, Jill Evelyn *psychologist, educator*
Evans, Paul Dale *economist, educator*
Gilliom, Morris Eugene *social studies and global educator*
Herson, Lawrence J.R. *social sciences educator, consultant*
Johnson, Neal Frederick *psychological scientist, educator*
Kagel, John Henry *economist, researcher*
Kessel, John Howard *political scientist, educator*
Kiecolt-Glaser, Janice Kay *psychologist*
Lee, Lung-fei *economist, educator*
Lundstedt, Sven Bertil *behavioral and social scientist, educator*
Lynn, Arthur Dellert, Jr., *economist, educator*
Marilley, Suzanne Marie *political scientist, educator*
Millett, Stephen Malcolm *futurist, consultant, historian*
Mueller, John Ernest *political science educator, dance critic and historian*
Namboodiri, Krishnan *sociology educator*
Naylor, James Charles *psychologist, educator*
Osipow, Samuel Herman *psychology educator*
Reichwein, Jeffrey Charles *archaeologist*
Reiss, Steven *psychology educator*
Sporleder, Thomas Lynn *economist, researcher*
Tuckman, Bruce Wayne *educational psychologist, educator, researcher*
Tybout, Richard Alton *economics professor*
Viezer, Timothy Wayne *economist, investment company executive*
Weisberg, Herbert Frank *political science educator*

Findlay
Peters, Milton Eugene *educational psychologist*

Hamilton
New, Rosetta Holbrock *home economics educator, nutrition consultant*

Hudson
Sorgi, Mercedes Prieto *psychologist*

Kent
Feinberg, Richard *anthropologist, educator*
Neal-Barnett, Angela Marie *psychology educator*
Pino, Julio Cesar *social studies educator, writer*

Lima
Roller, Duane Williamson *archaeologist, educator*

Louisville
Faigley, Joseph Raymond *social studies educator*

Lyndhurst
Dellas, Marie C. *retired psychology educator, consultant*

Mansfield
Burke, Victor Lee *sociologist, educator*
Hussain, Nayyer *economics professor*

Moreland Hills
Tolchinsky, Paul Dean *organization design psychologist*

Oberlin
Brown, John Lott *psychology professor*
Friedman, William John *psychology educator*
Kruks, Sonia R. *social sciences educator, researcher*
Miller, Judith Beinstein *psychology professor*
Taylor, Richard Wirth *political science educator*

Oxford
Barilleaux, Ryan J. *politcal science educator*
Bergen, Doris *psychologist, educator*
DeLue, Steven Muller *political scientist, educator*
Rejai, Mostafa *political science educator*

Pepper Pike
Alexander-Haynes, Sandra *psychologist, educator*

Powell
Spangler, Edra Mildred *clinical psychologist*

Ravenna
Benshoff-Ludick, Dixie Lee *psychologist, educator*

Sardinia
Evans, C(aroline) Sue *social sciences educator*

Shaker Heights
Ludwig, L(owell) Mark *social science educator*

Stow
Kalkhoff, William Webster *sociologist, educator*

The Plains
Klare, George Roger *psychology educator*

Tiffin
Gridley, Mark Charles *psychologist*

Toledo
Al-Marayati, Abid A. *political science educator*

Davis, David Howard *political science educator*
Heintz, Carolinea Cabaniss *retired home economics educator*
Jan, George Pokung *political science educator*
Metress, Seamus P. *anthropology educator, Irish studies researcher*
Mihura, Joni L. *psychologist, educator*
Mohler, Terence John *psychologist*

University Heights
Carrington, Gary *psychologist*
Eslinger, Kenneth Nelson *social sciences educator*

Wadsworth
Pipitone, Phyllis L. *psychologist, educator, author*

Westerville
Washington, La Trice M. *social studies educator*

Wilberforce
Anyalewechi, Patrick Okechukwu *psychology educator*

Wright Patterson Afb
Boff, Kenneth Richard *engineering research psychologist*

Youngstown
Binning, William Charles *political scientist, educator*
Mehra, Jagdish *economics professor*
Sweeney, Christopher John *psychology educator, consultant*
Usip, Ebenge Efetia *economics professor*

Zanesville
Shatz, Mark Allen *psychologist, educator*
Workman, James E. *retired school psychologist*

OKLAHOMA

Durant
Kennedy, Elizabeth Carol *psychologist, educator*

Edmond
Necco, E(dna) Joanne *school psychologist*
Smock, Donald Joe *governmental liaison, political consultant*

Goodwell
Duren, Brad L. *social studies educator*

Norman
Affleck, Marilyn *retired sociology educator*
Bell, Robert Eugene *anthropologist educator*
Henderson, George *educational sociologist, educator*
Kondonassis, Alexander John *economist, educator*
Logue, Dennis Emhardt *financial economics educator, consultant, dean*

Oklahoma City
Allbright, Karan Elizabeth *psychologist, consultant*
Craig, George Dennis *economics educator, consultant*
Lovallo, William Robert *psychologist, educator, researcher*
Morgan, Catherine Marie *psychologist, writer*
Prinzo, O. Veronika *engineering research psychologist*
Rundell, Orvis Herman, Jr., *psychologist, educator*
Schroeder, David J. Dean *psychologist*

Stillwater
Darcy, Robert Emmett *political scientist, educator, statistician*
Moomaw, Ronald Lee *economics professor*
Poole, Richard William *economics professor*
Rickman, Dan Scott *economics professor*
Steindl, Frank George *economist, educator*

Tulsa
Brian, Tom J. *psychologist, director*
Brooker, Timothy Douglas *social studies educator*

OREGON

Corvallis
Clinton, Richard Lee *international relations educator*
Gillis, John Simon *psychologist, educator*
Harter, Lafayette George, Jr., *retired economics educator*

Eugene
Davis, Richard Malone *economics professor*
Freyd, Jennifer Joy *psychology educator*
Gwartney, Patricia Anne *sociology educator*
Khang, Chulsoon *economics professor*
Littman, Richard Anton *psychologist, educator*
Lukacs, John Robert *anthropologist, educator*
Mikesell, Raymond Frech *economics professor*
Peterson, Donna Rae *gerontologist*

Fairview
Blodgett, Forrest Clinton *economics professor*

Florence
Marble, Duane Francis *geography educator, researcher*

Lake Oswego
Tammen, Ronald *international politics educator*

Newberg
Adams, Wayne Verdun *pediatric psychologist, educator*

Pendleton
Reeder, Clinton Bruce *economist, public policy consultant, farmer*

Portland
Cookson, Peter Willis, Jr., *sociologist, writer*
Davis, James Allan *gerontologist, educator*
Matarazzo, Joseph Dominic *psychologist, educator*
Matarazzo, Ruth Gadbois *psychologist, educator*
Wiens, Arthur Nicholai *psychology educator*

Salem
Thompson, George Frederick, Jr., *public management educator*
Warnath, Maxine Ammer *organizational psychologist, mediator*

Sandy
Silvey, Murl L. *psychologist*

PENNSYLVANIA

Abington
Schwartz, Lita Linzef *psychologist, educator*

Allentown
Dolan, Michael John *psychologist*
Graham, Kenneth Robert *psychologist, educator*

Annville
Cullari, Salvatore Santino *clinical psychologist, educator, writer*

Bartonsville
Cashion, Deena Dianne *social studies educator, pastor*

Bethlehem
Aronson, Jay Richard *economics educator, researcher, academic administrator*
Frankel, Barbara Brown *cultural anthropologist*
Hagar, Susan Mack *school psychologist, school counselor*
Heath, Douglas Edwin *geography educator*
Scheirer, William Kenneth *economist, consultant*
Schwartz, Eli *economics educator, writer*
Smolansky, Bettie Moretz *sociology educator*
Wittreich, Warren James *psychologist, consultant*

Bloomsburg
Holloway, Sybil Lymorise *psychologist, writer*
Tloczynski, Joseph *psychology professor, researcher*

Bridgeville
Moore, Daniel Edmund *psychologist, educator, retired educational administrator*

Bryn Mawr
Anderson, Eric Edward *psycholgist, consultant, director*
Hoffman, Howard Stanley *experimental psychologist, educator*
Littell, Julia Harrington *social sciences educator*
Porter, Judith Deborah Revitch *sociologist*

Carlisle
Biddle, Tami Davis *social studies educator*
Jacobs, Norman G(abriel) *sociologist, educator*
Jones, Oliver Hastings *consulting economist*

Coopersburg
Bednar, Charles Sokol *political scientist, educator*

Coudersport
Kysor, Daniel Francis *psychologist*

Cranberry Township
Fitzpatrick, Robert *psychologist*

Doylestown
Ginsberg, Barry Gavrille *psychologist, marriage and family therapist, consultant, trainer*

East Stroudsburg
Crotty, Patricia McGee *political science educator*

Easton
Kincaid, John *political science educator, editor*
Murphy, Bruce Allen *government and law educator, author*

Erie
Adovasio, J. M. *anthropologist, archeologist, educator*
Ayrault, Evelyn West *psychologist, writer*
Bennett, Charles Andrew *economics professor, department chairman*

Exton
Ma, Jinpeng *economics and business educator*

Fairless Hills
Rosella, John Daniel *clinical psychologist, educator*

Friendsville
Babb, Harold *psychologist, educator*

Gettysburg
Plischke, Elmer *political science educator*
Schein, Virginia Ellen *psychologist, editor*

Greensburg
Ramm, Douglas Robert *psychologist*

Grove City
Campbell, George Van Pelt *sociology and religion educator*

Haverford
de Laguna, Frederica *anthropology educator emeritus, writer, publisher*
Glickman, Harvey *retired social sciences educator*
Northrup, Herbert Roof *economist, business executive*

Immaculata
Rondinaro, Peter Dominick *social sciences educator, psychologist*

Indiana
Garvin, C(larence) Alexander, Jr., *economics professor*
Mc Cauley, R. Paul *criminologist, educator*
Miller, Vincent Paul, Jr., *geography and regional planning educator*
Stern, T. Noel *political scientist, educator*
Tobin, Lois Moore *retired home economist, educator*
Walker, Donald Anthony *economist, educator*

Kelton
Gulick, Walter Lawrence *psychologist, former college president*

Kutztown
Dougherty, Percy H. *geographer, educator, politician, planner*

Lancaster
Stephenson, Donald Grier, Jr., *political science professor*
Wenger, Jay Lamar *psychology educator*

Lewisburg
Bannon, George *retired economics educator, department chairman*
Candland, Douglas Keith *psychology professor*

Lincoln University
Nwachuku, Levi Akalazu *social sciences and behavioral studies educator*

Lock Haven
Forbes, Edward John, III, *developmental psychologist, educator*

Loretto
Melusky, Joseph Anthony *political science professor, department chairman*

Meadville
Adams, Earl William, Jr., *economics professor*

Media
Cimbala, Stephen Joseph *political science educator*
Gordon, Lisa Diane *psychologist*

Milford
Rosenblum, Jeffrey Ira *consulting economist*

Newtown
Richard, James Thomas *retired psychologist, educator*

Norristown
Gaber, Robert *psychologist*

Philadelphia
Behrman, Jere Richard *economics professor*
Berg, Ivar Elis, Jr., *social science educator*
Cass, David *economist, educator*
Clark, John J. *economist, finance educator*
Coché, Judith *psychologist, educator*
Coraza, Mary Catherine *psychologist*
Cunningham, Jacqueline Lemmé *psychologist, educator, researcher*
Diebold, Francis X. *economist, educator*
Dinges, David F. *psychology and psychiatry educator*
Donaldson, Thomas *ethicist, educator*
Erdmann, James Bernard *educational psychologist*
Evan, William Martin *sociologist, educator*
Fox, Renée Claire *sociology educator*
Frankel, Francine Ruth *political science educator*
Furstenberg, Frank F. *social studies educator*
Gelles, Richard James *sociology and psychology educator, academic administrator*
Goodenough, Ward Hunt *anthropologist, educator*
Hall, Charles P(otter), Jr., *economics professor*
Harvey, John Adriance *psychology and pharmacology educator, researcher, consultant*
Jeon, Bang Nam *economist, researcher*
Katsenelinboigen, Aron Josef *economist*
Katz, Elihu *sociologist, communications educator*
Kettl, Donald Francis *political science educator*
Klausner, Samuel Zundel *sociologist, educator*
Klein, Lawrence Robert *economist, educator*
Logue, John J(oseph) *psychologist*
LoSciuto, Leonard Anthony *psychologist, educator*
Meyer, Marshall Warner *management and sociology educator*
Michael, Henry N. *geographer, anthropologist*
Miller, Ronald Eugene *regional science educator*
Nachmias, Jacob *psychologist, educator*
Orne, Emily Carota *psychologist, researcher*
Orr, Nancy A. *educational psychologist*
Phelps, Charlotte DeMonte *retired economics educator*
Preston, Samuel Hulse *demographer*
Price, R. Arlen *psychology and psychiatry educator*
Raff, Daniel Martin Gorodetsky *economist, economic and business historian, educator*
Rescorla, Robert Arthur *psychology educator*
Richards, Virginia M. *psychologist*
Rima, Ingrid Hahne *economics professor*
Rosenberg, Robert Allen *psychologist, educator, optometrist*
Sabloff, Jeremy Arac *archaeologist*
Seligman, Martin E.P. *psychologist, educator*
Sherman, Lawrence William *criminologist*
Shure, Myrna Beth *psychologist, educator*
Simon, Anita *psychologist*
Sloan, Denise May *psychology educator*
Summers, Anita Arrow *public policy and management educator*
Summers, Robert *economics professor*
Tokar, Bette Lewis *economics professor*
Wadden, Thomas Anthony *psychologist, educator*
Wallace, Anthony Francis Clarke *anthropologist, educator*
Zuckerman, Marvin *psychologist*

Pittsburgh
Barry, Herbert, III, *psychologist, educator*
Blumstein, Alfred *urban and public affairs educator*
Bobrow, Davis Bernard *public policy educator*
Brustein, William Irving *sociology educator*
Cagney, William Robert *psychologist*
Curry, Nancy Ellen *psychologist, psychoanalyst, educator*
Davis, Otto Anderson *economics professor*
Dawes, Robyn Mason *psychology educator*
Drennan, Robert D. *archeology educator, researcher*
Eaton, Joseph W. *sociology educator*
Fararo, Thomas John *sociologist, educator*
Fischhoff, Baruch *psychologist, educator*
Ginsburg, Mark Barry *comparative sociology of education educator*
Hammond, Paul Young *political scientist, educator*
Holzner, Burkart *sociologist, educator*
Kenkel, James Lawrence *economics professor*
Lave, Judith Rice *economics professor*
McCallum, Bennett Tarlton *economist, educator*

Meltzer, Allan H. *economist, educator*
Moore, Omar Khayyam *experimental sociologist*
Ogul, Morris Samuel *political science educator, consultant*
Park, Inuck *economist, researcher*
Perlman, Mark *economist, educator*
Perloff, Robert *psychologist, educator*
Resnick, Lauren B. *psychology educator*
Schorr-Ribera, Hilda Keren *psychologist*
Strauss, Robert Philip *economics professor*
Sussna, Edward *economist, educator*

Radnor
Rosnow, Ralph Leon *psychology researcher and educator*

Rydal
Heebner, Albert Gilbert *economist, educator, bank executive*

Scranton
Cannon, J. Timothy *psychology educator, neuroscientist*
Giunta, Agatino John *economist, educator*
Parente, William Joseph *political science educator*
Sebastianelli, Carl Thomas *clinical psychologist*
Yamanouchi-Rynn, Midori *social sciences educator*

Selinsgrove
Lopez, Andrea Michelle *political scientist, educator*

Shippensburg
Bej, Emil *economics educator, researcher, journalist*
France, Olin Kenneth, Jr., *psychologist*

Spring Grove
Butler, Raymond Archibald *cartographer*

State College
Schaie, K(laus) Warner *human development and psychology educator*
Wyand, Martin Judd *economics educator, retired military officer*

Swarthmore
Hollister, Robinson Gill, Jr., *economics professor*
Hopkins, Raymond Frederick *political science educator*
Keith, Jennie *anthropology educator and administrator, writer*
Marecek, Jeanne *psychologist, educator*
Pryor, Frederic L. *economist, educator*

University Park
Cougevan, Katie Pilgeram *psychologist*
Firebaugh, Glenn Allen *sociology educator*
Friedman, Robert Sidney *political science educator*
Humphrey, Craig Reed *social studies educator*
Klein, Philip Alexander *economist*
Newsome, Lee Ann *anthropologist, educator*
Ray, William Jackson *psychologist*
Walker, Alan C. *anthropologist, educator*

Valley Forge
Guttentag, Jack Mark *economist, educator*

Villanova
Johannes, John Roland *political science educator, academic administrator*
Lesch, Ann Mosely *political scientist, educator*

Wallingford
Scherer, Frederic Michael *economics professor*

Wayne
MacNeal, Edward Arthur *economic consultant*
Stayton, William Ralph *psychologist, educator*

West Chester
Green, Andrew Wilson *economist, educator, lawyer*
Zlotowski, Martin *psychologist*

Wilkes Barre
Baldino, Thomas Joseph *political scientist, educator*

Wynnewood
Phillips, Almarin *economics educator, consultant*

Yardley
Brick, John *biological psychologist, educator, researcher*

York
McMillan, Wendell Marlin *economist*

RHODE ISLAND

Barrington
Paolino, Ronald Mario *clinical psychologist, consultant, psychopharmacologist, pharmacist*

Kingston
Burkett, John Philip *economics professor*
Collyer, Charles Edmund *psychologist, educator*
Cunnigen, Donald *sociologist, educator*
Molloy, David Scott, Jr., *labor relations educator*
Newman, Barbara Miller *psychologist, educator*
Prochaska, James O. *psychologist, educator*
Turnbaugh, William Arthur *archaeologist, educator*

Newport
Brown, David William *economist, educator, consultant*

Peace Dale
Brennan, Noel-Anne Gerson *anthropologist, educator, writer*

Providence
Anderson, James Alfred *psychology educator*
Anton, Thomas Julius *political science and public policy educator, consultant*
Boisvert, Charles Miga *psychologist, educator*
Feldman, Allan Maurice *economist*
Goldscheider, Frances K. *sociologist, educator*
Goldstein, Sidney *sociology educator, demographer*
Goodman, Elliot Raymond *political scientist, educator*
Goulder, Caroljean Hempstead *retired psychologist, consultant*

Grossman, Herschel I. *economics professor*
Heath, Dwight Braley *anthropologist, educator*
Holloway, Robert Ross *archaeologist, educator*
Jones, Ferdinand Taylor, Jr., *psychologist, educator*
Kates, Robert William *geographer, educator*
Liu, Jianhong *sociologist, educator*
Marsh, Robert Mortimer *sociologist, educator*
Modell, John *social sciences educator*
Riordan, Cornelius *sociology educator, writer, consultant*
Rueschemeyer, Marilyn Schattner *sociology educator*
Shapiro, Ronald Gary *psychologist*
Siqueland, Einar *psychology educator*
Stein, Jerome Leon *economist, educator*
Stultz, Newell Maynard *retired political science educator*
Wetle, Terrie Fox *gerontologist, educator, dean*

Smithfield
Morahan-Martin, Janet May *psychologist, educator*

Wakefield
Newman, Philip Robert *psychologist*

SOUTH CAROLINA

Abbeville
Cellura, A(ngele) Raymond *psychologist*

Charleston
Bowman, Daniel Oliver *retired psychologist*
Kimmel, Herbert David *psychology educator*
Moore, William Vincent *political science educator*
Quinn, E. Moore *linguistic anthropology educator*
Sharpe, Kathryn Moye *psychologist*
Smedley, Charles Vincent *sociology educator*

Clemson
Melton, Gary Bentley *psychology and law educator*
Tamura, Robert *economics professor, consultant*

Columbia
Akhavi, Shahrough *political science professor*
Cohn, Elchanan *economics professor*
Davis, Keith Eugene *psychologist, educator, consultant*
Kiker, Billy Frazier *economics professor*
Logan, Sandra Jean *retired economics and business educator*
Markovsky, Barry Neil *sociology educator*
Martin, Robert William *econometrician*
Powell, Donald Ashmore *clinical research psychologist*
Rippeteau, Bruce Estes *archaeologist, administrator*
Starr, Harvey *political scientist, educator*
Weber, Lynn *sociology educator*
Wilder, Ronald Parker *economics professor*
Wood, Oliver Gillan, Jr., *economist, educator*

Fort Mill
Park, John *finance, investment consultant*

Greenville
Abrams, Douglas Carl *social studies educator*
Trevillian, Wallace Dabney *retired economics professor, retired dean*

Spartanburg
McAbee, Thomas Allen *psychologist*
Reid, Alliston King *psychology educator, researcher*

SOUTH DAKOTA

Aberdeen
Hedges, Mark Stephen *clinical psychologist*

Brookings
Gilbert, Howard Alden *retired economics professor*
Tolle, Gordon J. *political science educator*

Canton
Perkinson, Robert Ronald *psychologist, consultant*

Keystone
Wagner, Mary Kathryn *sociology educator, former state legislator*

Kyle
White Buffalo, Charles Dean *social studies educator, consultant*

Sioux Falls
Williams, W. Vail *psychologist*

Vermillion
Clem, Alan Leland *retired political scientist, educator*
Schweinle, Amy *psychologist, educator*
Wang, X. T. (Xiaotian Wang) *psychologist, educator*

TENNESSEE

Chattanooga
Guo, Zibin *medical anthropologist*
Rabin, Alan A. *economics professor*
Wilson, Richard Lee *political science educator*

Germantown
Depperschmidt, Thomas Orlando *economist, consultant*

Kingsport
Everett, Michael David *economist, educator*

Knoxville
Blanton, Priscilla White *social sciences educator, psychologist, researcher*
Bruce, Donald James *economics educator*
Harris, Diana Koffman *sociologist, educator*
Stephens, Otis Hammond, Jr., *political science and law educator*
Verplanck, William Samuel *psychologist, educator*

Memphis
Ashley, Aaron Lee *psychologist, educator*
Forde, David Robert *social sciences educator, criminologist, researcher*
Harkins, John Edward *social studies educator, historian*
Johnson, Johnny *research psychologist, consultant*
Jones, Effie L. *social sciences educator*
Kemme, David Michael *economics professor*
Papachristou, Patricia Towne *economics professor*
Pohlmann, Marcus D. *political science educator*
Rubin, Rose Mohr *economics professor*
Sherman, Janann Margaret *history educator, writer*

Murfreesboro
Breault, Kevin D. *sociology educator, research scientist*
Littlepage, Glenn E. *social psychology educator*
Zietz, Joachim *economics professor*

Nashville
Benbow, Camilla Persson *psychology educator, researcher*
Blair, Margaret Mendenhall *research economist, consultant, law educator*
Chait, Andrea Melinda *school psychologist*
Conley, John P. *economist, educator*
Cornfield, Daniel Benjamin *sociology educator*
Fulmer, Douglas Alan *political consultant, journalist*
Graham, George J., Jr., *political scientist, educator*
Guinsburg, Philip Fried *alcohol and substance abuse counselor*
Hargrove, Erwin Charles, Jr., *political science educator*
Havens, Murray Clark *political scientist, educator*
Joyner, John Wesley *psychologist, educator*
Kaas, Jon H. *psychology educator*
Lazar, Irving *psychologist*
McCarty, Richard Charles *psychology educator, university dean*
Russell, Clifford Springer *economics and public policy educator*
Schall, Jeffrey D. *psychology educator*
Schoggen, Phil H(oward) *psychologist, educator*
Strupp, Hans Hermann *psychologist, educator*
Westfield, Fred M. *economics professor*
Young, Tommie Morton *social psychology educator, writer*

Newport
Branam, Linda Gail *psychologist, educator*

TEXAS

Abilene
Bridges, Julian Curtis *sociologist educator, department head*

Alpine
Sechrest, Larry J. *economist, educator*

Amarillo
Ayad, Joseph Magdy *retired psychologist*

Arlington
Cole, Richard Louis *political scientist, educator*
Ramsey, Charles Eugene *sociologist, educator*

Austin
Blake, Robert Rogers *psychologist, behavioral science company executive*
Blodgett, Warren Terrell *public affairs educator*
Buchanan, Bruce, II, *political science educator*
Burnham, Walter Dean *political science educator*
Buss, David Michael *psychology educator*
Drake, Stephen Douglas *psychologist, health facility administrator*
Dusansky, Richard *economist, educator*
Ekland-Olson, Sheldon *sociology educator, dean*
Epstein, Jeremiah Fain *anthropologist, educator*
Firey, Walter Irving, Jr., *retired sociologist, educator*
Glade, William Patton, Jr., *economics professor*
Glenn, Norval Dwight *sociologist, educator*
Griffin, Alan Nash *psychologist*
Hamermesh, Daniel Selim *economics professor*
Hansen, Niles Maurice *economics professor*
Hester, Thomas Roy *anthropologist, educator*
Hirsch, Michael Lee *social studies educator, mayor*
Holtzman, Wayne Harold *psychologist, educator*
Holz, Robert Kenneth *retired geography educator*
Huff, David L. *geography educator*
Huston, Ted Laird *psychology educator*
Iscoe, Ira *psychology educator*
Jordan-Bychkov, Terry Gilbert *geography educator*
Keith, Timothy Zook *psychology educator*
Kendrick, David Andrew *economist, educator*
Lariviere, Richard Wilfred *university administrator, educator, consultant*
Loehlin, John Clinton *psychologist, educator*
Lopreato, Joseph *evolutionary sociologist, writer*
Mc Donald, Stephen Lee *economics professor*
McFadden, Dennis *experimental psychology educator*
Meston, Cindy M(ay) *psychologist, educator*
Pingree, Dianne *sociologist, educator, psychotherapist*
Reid, Jackson Brock *psychologist, educator*
Roach, James Robert *retired political science educator*
Rostow, Elspeth Davies *political science educator*
Schmandt, Jurgen A. *public affairs educator*
Schmitt, Karl Michael *retired political scientist*
Smith, Alfred Goud *anthropologist, educator*
Speed, Shannon Eleanora *anthropologist, educator*
Stinchcombe, Maxwell B. *economist, educator*
Walter, Virginia Lee *psychologist, educator*
Warr, Eric Mark *sociologist, educator*

Beaumont
Nguyen, Nhung Thanh *psychologist, educator*

Bellaire
Mayo, Clyde Calvin *psychologist, educator*

Brooks AFB
Caldwell, John Alvis, Jr., *experimental psychologist*
Patterson, John C. *clinical psychology researcher*

Bryan
Branson, Robert Earl *marketing economist*

Canyon
Thoman, Roy Edward *political scientist, educator*
Welch, Reed Lynn *political scientist, educator*

College Station
Arnold, J(ames) Barto, III, *marine archaeologist*
Bass, George Fletcher *retired archaeology educator*
Bessler, David A *economist*
Bond, Jon Roy *political science educator*
Edwards, George Charles, III, *political science educator, writer*
Furubotn, Eirik Grundtvig *economics professor*
Greenhut, Melvin Leonard *economist, educator*
Jansen, Dennis William *economics educator, consultant*
Knutson, Ronald Dale *economist, educator, academic administrator*
Meier, Kenneth John *political scientist*
Moroney, John Rodgers *economist, educator*
Nederman, Cary Joseph *political scientist, director*
Saving, Thomas Robert *economics educator, consultant*
Steffy, John Richard *nautical archaeologist, educator*
Van Riper, Paul Pritchard *political science educator*

Corpus Christi
Cutlip, Randall Brower *retired psychologist, university president emeritus*
Long, Ralph Stewart *clinical psychologist*
Rios, Jo Marie *political science educator*

Dallas
Betts, Dianne Connally *economist, educator*
Cochran, Kendall Pinney *economics professor*
Cochran, Mona Sheinfeld *economics educator, consultant*
Free, Mary Moore *biological and medical anthropologist*
Gibby, Mabel Enid Kunce *psychologist*
Gruben, William Charles *economist, writer*
Humphreys, Jean Surratt *social sciences educator*
Kemper, Robert Van *anthropologist, educator, minister*
Murphy, John Carter *economics professor*

Denton
Belfiglio, Valentine John *political science educator, pharmacist, consultant*
Leung, Paul *psychologist, rehabilitation educator*
Newell, Charldean *public administration educator*

El Paso
Fullerton, Thomas Mankin, Jr., *economist*
Penley, Julie Anne *psychologist, educator*

Euless
Mabry, Philip T. *political consultant*

Fort Worth
Dees, Sandra Kay Martin *psychologist, research scientist*
Durham, Floyd Wesley, Jr., *economist, educator*
Jackson, Donald Wilson *political science educator, lawyer*
Mullendore, Walter Edward *retired economist*
Simpson, Dennis Dwayne *psychologist, educator*

Galveston
Barratt, Ernest Stoelting *psychologist, educator*
Fisher, Seymour *psychologist, educator*
Markides, Kyriakos Socrates *gerontology educator*

Georgetown
Neville, Gwen Kennedy *anthropology educator*

Houston
Aday, Luann *social science educator*
Allen, Jon G. *psychologist*
Brito, Dagobert Llanos *economics professor*
Bryant, John Bradbury *economics educator, consultant*
Callender, Norma Anne *psychology educator, counselor*
Cloninger, Dale Owen *finance and economics educator*
Coker, Sally Jo (Bozeman) *sociology educator*
Condit, Linda Faulkner *economist*
Cuthbertson, Gilbert Morris *political science educator*
Davidson, Chandler *sociologist, educator*
Foster, Dale Warren *political scientist, educator, management consultant, real estate broker, accountant*
Grossett, Deborah Lou *psychologist, consultant*
Hartgrove-Freile, Janice Lynn *psychologist, educator, writer*
Haymond, Paula J. *psychologist, diagnostician, hypnotherapist*
Justice, Blair (David Blair Justice) *psychology educator, writer*
Kershaw, Carol Jean *psychologist*
Knight, Jennifer Lynn *psychologist, researcher*
Lachar, David *psychologist, educator*
Lewis, Lisa *psychologist, administrator*
Martin, Randi Christine *psychology educator*
Martin, William C. *sociology educator, writer*
Miller, Janel Howell *psychologist*
Rosin, Lindsay Zweig *clinical psychologist*
Sickles, Robin C. *economics and statistics educator, consultant*
White, Nancy Elizabeth *psychologist, artist*

Kingsville
Harun, Syed Mahbub *economist, educator, economist, researcher*

Lubbock
Gilliam, John Charles *economist, educator*
Willingham, Welborn Iefer *psychologist, educator*

Mcallen
Rebuelta, Avelino Luis *public administration educator*

Midland
Sherpa, Fran Magruder *geography educator, animal scientist, small business owner*

North Zulch
Fleming, Jon Hugh *psychology educator, business executive, educational consultant*

Olney
Timmons, Gordon David *economics professor, farmer*

Post
Earl, Lewis Harold *economics and management consultant, lawyer*

Prairie View
French, Laurence Armand *social science educator, psychology educator*
Prestage, Jewel Limar *political science educator*

Richardson
Andrews, Melinda Wilson *human development researcher*
Berry, Brian Joe Lobley *geographer, political economist, urban planner*
Faria, Joao Ricardo *economist, educator*
Holmes, Jennifer Smith *political scientist, educator*

San Angelo
Butler, Michael Ward *economics professor*
Schell, Kraig Lee *psychologist, educator*

San Antonio
Bellows, Thomas John *political scientist, educator*
Breit, William *economist, educator, writer*
Brooks, Franklin Ramon *psychologist, army officer*
Furino, Antonio *economist, educator*
Gambitta, Richard Anthony *political science educator*
Garb, Howard Neil *clinical psychologist, educator*
Hazuda, Helen Pauline *sociologist, educator*
McDonald, James H. *anthropologist, educator*
Ribble, Ronald George *retired psychologist, educator, writer*
Rogers, William *psychologist, behavior specialist, writer, lecturer, journalist*
Spiro, Herbert John *political scientist, politician, educator, ambassador*
Spraggins, Johnnie David *social studies educator*
Truett, Lila Flory *economics professor*

San Marcos
Boehm, Richard Glennon *geography educator, writer*

Sherman
Parker, Harry John *retired psychologist, educator*

Stafford
Krenek, Mary Louise *political scientist, researcher, historian*

Sugar Land
Harribance, Sean Lalsingh *parapsychologist*

Tyler
Martin, William Allen *sociology educator*
Pandey, Vivek K. *finance educator, researcher*

Waco
Sharp, Ronald Arvell *sociology educator*

Weatherford
Buckner-Reitman, Joyce *psychologist, educator*

UTAH

Bountiful
Mangum, Garth Leroy *economist, educator*

Logan
Fifield, Marvin G. *psychologist, educator*
Roberts, Richard N. *psychologist*

North Salt Lake
Barden, Robert Christopher *lawyer, psychologist, educator, legislative analyst, speaker, writer*

Provo
Ballif-Spanvill, Bonnie *psychologist, educator*
Creer, Thomas Laselle *psychologist, educator*
Fry, Earl Howard *political scientist, educator*
Hill, Edward Jeffrey *family life educator*
Kunz, Phillip Ray *sociologist, educator*
Porter, Blaine Robert Milton *sociology and psychology educator*
Slife, Brent Donald *psychologist, educator, author*
Snow, Karl Nelson, Jr., *public management educator, university administrator, former state senator*
Wilson, Ramon B. *retired economics professor*

Salt Lake City
Benjamin, Lorna Smith *psychologist*
Huefner, Robert P. *political science educator*
Korbanka, Juergen Erich *psychologist, educator*
Kumpfer, Karol Linda *research psychologist*
Weigel, Richard George *psychologist, educator*

Sandy
Park, William Laird *agricultural economics educator, consultant, college associate dean*
Smith, Willard Grant *psychologist*

South Jordan
Rowley, Maxine Lewis *home economics and consumer educator, writer*

VERMONT

Barre
Black, Percy *psychology educator*

Brandon
Farnsworth, Frank Albert *retired economics educator*

Brattleboro
Kotkov, Benjamin *clinical psychologist*

Burlington
Berkowitz, Stephen David *sociologist, educator*
Cutler, Stephen Joel *sociologist, educator*
Dinitz, Jeffrey H. *mathematics educator*
Hilberg, Raul *political science educator*
Lawson, Robert Bernard *psychology educator*

PROFESSIONAL INDEX 5897 SOCIAL SCIENCE

Mintz, Beth Ann *sociology educator*
Sampson, Samuel Franklin *sociology educator*
Stout, Neil Ralph *retired history educator*
Visser, Thomas Durant *social studies educator, writer*

Charlotte
Naylor, Thomas Herbert *economist, educator, consultant*

Middlebury
Colander, David Charles *economist, educator*
Lamberti, Marjorie *retired social studies educator*
Robison, Olin Clyde *political science educator, former college president*

Norwich
Foster, Michael Kirk *anthropologist, linguist*

Shelburne
Smallwood, Franklin *political science educator*

VIRGINIA

Alexandria
Carvalho, Julie Ann *psychologist*
Hinkle, Wade P. *political scientist*
Johnson, Edgar McCarthy *psychologist*
Krueger, Gerald Peter *psychologist*
Lytle, Michael Allen *criminologist, consultant*
Matalin, Mary *political consultant*
Parsons, Henry McIlvaine *psychologist*
Reinl, Harry Charles *economist*
Sitilides, John *government relations executive, policy analyst*

Arlington
Angell, Wayne D. *economist, banker*
Bradburn, Norman M. *behavioral science educator*
Chipman, Susan Elizabeth *psychologist, researcher*
Clare, Kenneth Guilford *economist, consultant*
Clump, Michael Aden *psychologist, educator*
Coats, Warren L., Jr., *economist*
Cobble, Steven Bruce *political consultant, strategist*
Coleman, Rodney Albert *government affairs consultant*
Davis, Lynn Etheridge *political scientist, educator*
Fuchs, Roland John *geography educator, university science official*
Gramm, Wendy Lee *economics educator, former government official*
Gunn, Joseph Ridgeway, III, *consulting economist*
Howenstine, E. Jay *housing economist*
Kerns, Wilmer Lee *social science researcher*
McClelland, Harold Franklin *economics professor*
Siddayao, Corazón Morales *economist, educator, consultant*
Sundquist, James Lloyd *retired political scientist*
Taddesse, Samuel *economist, consultant*
Tullock, Gordon *economics professor*
Tyler, Robert R. *psychologist, consultant*
Weidemann, Celia Jean *social scientist, management consultant, financial consultant*

Blacksburg
Bryant, Clifton Dow *sociologist, educator*
Jannuzi, F. Tomasson *economics professor*
Schnitzer, Martin Colby *economist, educator*
Taylor, Charles Lewis *political science educator*

Bluemont
Kobetz, Richard William *criminologist, consultant*

Burke
Bermant, Gordon *psychologist, lawyer, consultant, writer*

Charlottesville
Abraham, Henry Julian *political science educator*
Elzinga, Kenneth Gerald *economics professor*
Epstein, William *experimental psychologist*
Feigert, Frank Brook *retired political science educator, writer*
Handler, Jerome Sidney *anthropology educator*
Henry, Laurin Luther *public affairs educator*
Hymes, Dell Hathaway *anthropologist, educator*
Kiewra, Gustave Paul *psychologist, educator*
McLaren, John Edward *economics professor*
Meiburg, Charles Owen *business administration educator*
Olsen, Edgar Oliver *economics professor*
Perdue, Charles L., Jr., *social sciences educator, language educator*
Rhoads, Steven Eric *political science educator*
Sykes, Gresham M'Cready *sociologist, educator, artist*
Wagner, Roy *anthropology educator, researcher*
Whitaker, John King *economics professor*

Eastville
Williams, Ida Jones *consumer and home economics educator, writer*

Fairfax
Barth, Michael Carl *economist*
Bennett, James Thomas *economics professor*
Boneau, C. Alan *psychology educator, researcher*
Buchanan, James McGill *economist, educator*
Dennis, Rutledge M. *sociology educator, researcher*
Druckman, Daniel *social sciences educator, consultant, researcher*
Francis, Walton Joseph *economist*
Goldstone, Jack Andrew *sociologist*
Kash, Don Eldon *political science educator*
Kitsantas, Anastasia *educational psychologist*
Lehman, Elyse Brauch *psychologist, educator*
Machado, Carolyn Frances *political consultant*
Pfiffner, James Price *political science educator*
Pruitt, Dean Garner *psychologist, educator*
Rowley, Charles Kershaw *economics professor*
Smith, Vernon Lomax *economist, researcher*
Steele, Howard Loucks *economic development consultant, author*
Tolchin, Susan Jane *public administration educator, writer*
Travis, Toni-Michelle C. *political analyst, educator*
Wagner, Richard E. *economist, educator*
Williams, Thomas Rhys *anthropologist, educator*

Fairfax Station
Sielicki-Korczak, Boris Zdzislaw *political educator, investigative consultant*

Falls Church
Calkins, Susannah Eby *retired economist*
Cazan, Matthew John *political science educator*
Clizbe, John Anthony *psychologist, organization administrator*
Green, James Wyche *sociologist, anthropologist, psychotherapist*
Weiss, Armand Berl *economist, association management executive*

Farmville
Dorrill, William Franklin *political scientist, educator*

Ferrum
Reilly, Kevin Patrick *psychology educator*

Fredericksburg
Crippen, Timothy Alan *sociology educator*
Rampersad, Peggy A. Snellings *sociologist, consultant*
Sisk, Fred Dean *retired cartographer*

Hampton
Burgess, Gary Thomas *social studies educator, consultant*

Harrisonburg
Franctort, Alfred John, Jr., *economics professor*
Ivory, Ming Marie *political scientist*
Rosser, John Barkley, Jr., *economics professor*

Lexington
Elmes, David Gordon *psychologist, educator*
Jarrard, Leonard Everett *psychologist, educator*
John, Lewis George *political science educator*
Kassens, Alice Louise *economist, educator*
Phillips, Charles Franklin, Jr., *retired economist*
Winfrey, John Crawford *economist, educator*

Lynchburg
Duff, Ernest Arthur *political scientist, educator*
Morland, John Kenneth *sociology and anthropology educator*
Whittemore, Linda Genevieve *clinical psychologist*

Mc Lean
Auerbach, Anita L. *clinical psychologist*
Hjort, Howard Warren *consultant, economist*
Johnson, Omotunde Evan George *economist*
Kohli, Harinder S. *business executive, development economist*
Lee, Daniel Kuhn *economist*
Stevens, Richard Gordon *political scientist, educator*
Whitehead, Clay Thomas *economist*
Zakheim, Dov Solomon *economist, government official*

Midlothian
Stringham, Luther Winters *economist, administrator*

Norfolk
LeFever, Gretchen B. *clinical psychologist, educator*

Oakton
Zhang, Ming *policy analyst*

Palmyra
Chapin, Suzanne Phillips *retired psychologist*

Purcellville
Grow, Robert Theodore *economist, association executive*

Quantico
Harmon, Christopher C. *international relations educator, writer*

Reston
Payne, Roger Lee *geographer*

Richmond
Allen, Ann Salathe *social studies educator, researcher*
Campbell, Thomas Corwith, Jr., *economics professor*
Coogle, Constance L. *gerontology educator, researcher*
Geary, David Patrick *criminal justice educator, consultant, writer*
Kenzer, Robert Charles *social studies educator*
Leary, David Edward *psychologist, educator*
Murdoch-Kitt, Norma Hood *clinical psychologist*
Palen, J(oseph) John *sociology educator*
Parham, Iris Ann *gerontology educator*
Snellings, Eleanor Craig *retired economics educator*
Wight, Jonathan B. *economist, educator*

Round Hill
Gunberg, Edwin Woodrow, Jr., *counseling psychologist, consultant, researcher*

Salem
Weiss, Gregory Lee *sociology educator*

Sperryville
Armor, David J. *sociologist*

Springfield
Chatelier, Paul Richard *aviation psychologist*

Sterling
Blum, John Curtis *agricultural economist*
Cleveland, Harlan *political scientist, public affairs executive*

Sweet Briar
Shea, Brent Mack *social sciences educator*

Virginia Beach
Harter, John J. *economic analyst*

Warrenton
Malmgren, Harald Bernard *economist*

Williamsburg
Johnston, Robert Atkinson *psychologist, educator*
Smith, Roger Winston *political theorist, educator*

WASHINGTON

Bellevue
Reinleitner, Katherine Mindlin *psychologist, foundation administrator*

Bellingham
Burdge, Rabel James *sociology educator*
Lippman, Louis Grombacher *psychology educator*

Des Moines
Ortmeyer, Carl Edward *retired demographer*

Ellensburg
Jacobs, Robert Cooper *political scientist, consultant*

Friday Harbor
MacGinitie, Walter Harold *psychologist, educator*

Hansville
Blalock, Ann Bonar *evaluation researcher*

Kirkland
Goldman, Ralph Morris *political science educator*

La Conner
Knopf, Kenyon Alfred *economist, educator*

Lacey
Price, David Harold *anthropologist, educator*

Mercer Island
Page, Ellis Batten *psychologist, educator*

Mount Vernon
Garcia, John *psychologist, educator*

Olympia
Gilbert, Jorge *sociologist, educator, consul*

Port Angeles
Osborne, Richard Hazelet *anthropology and medical genetics educator*
Sonnenfeld, Joseph *geographer, researcher*

Pullman
Dillman, Donald Andrew *sociologist, educator, survey methodologist*
McSweeney, Frances Kaye *psychology educator*
Rosa, Eugene Anthony *sociologist, environmental scientist, educator*
Warner, Dennis Allan *psychology educator*

Redmond
Kirilova, Svetlana Nikolova *psychologist, consultant*
Pagulayan, Randy Jay *psychologist*

Richland
Roop, Joseph McLeod *economist*
Sonnenfeld, David Allan *sociologist*

Seattle
Beyers, William Bjorn *geography educator*
Borgatta, Edgar F. *social psychologist, educator*
Brammer, Lawrence Martin *psychology educator*
Chirot, Daniel *sociology and international studies educator*
Donovan, Dennis Michael *psychologist, researcher*
Ellings, Richard James *political and economic research institution executive*
Fiedler, Fred Edward *organizational psychology educator, consultant*
Graham, James Christopher *psychologist, consultant*
Gross, Edward *retired sociologist*
Hechter, Michael Norman *sociologist*
Hirschman, Charles, Jr., *sociologist, educator*
Huber, Vandra Lee *businesss educator, consultant*
Hy, Lê Xuân *psychologist, educator*
Narver, John Colin *business administration educator emeritus*
Olson, David John *political science educator*
Patrick, Donald Lee *social scientist, health services researcher*
Schall, Lawrence Delano *economics educator, consultant*
Schwartz, Pepper Judith *sociologist, educator*
Startz, Richard *economist*
Turnovsky, Stephen John *economics professor*
van den Berghe, Pierre Louis *sociologist*
Vitiello, Michael V. *gerontologist, educator*
West, John Garrett *political scientist, educator*

Sequim
Guilmet, George Michael *cultural anthropologist, educator*
Mc Hugh, Margaret Ann Gloe *retired psychologist*

Spokane
Novak, Terry Lee *public administration educator*

Tacoma
Porter, Karen Ann *anthropologist, educator*
Schauss, Alexander George *psychologist, biomedical researcher*
West, Carolyn Marie *psychologist, educator, writer*

University Place
Bourgaize, Robert G. *economist*

Vancouver
Archer, Stephen Hunt *economist, educator*
Craven, James Michael *economist, educator*

Walla Walla
Belay, Halefom *economist, educator*

WEST VIRGINIA

Bethany
Cooey, William Randolph *economics professor*

Charleston
Brookshire, Michael L. *forensic economist, economics educator*

Fairmont
Fulda, Michael *political scientist, educator, space policy researcher*

Harpers Ferry
Boucher, Wayne Irving *policy analyst*

Morgantown
Bell, Lewis Clay *economics educator, government administrator*
Colyer, Dale Keith *agricultural economics educator*
D'Souza, Gerard Eugene *economist, educator*
Kim, Hong Nack *political science educator*
Peterson, Sophia *international studies educator*
Witt, Tom *economics researcher, educator*

Parsons
Burns, Robert Alan *economic developer, educator*

West Liberty
Forrester, James Ronald *political science professor*

WISCONSIN

Appleton
Alger, Daniel Richard *economist*

Bayside
Kaufman, Harvey Isidore *neuropsychology consultant*

Beloit
Davis, Harry Rex *political science educator*
Green, William *archaeologist*
Kreider, Leonard Emil *economics professor*

Brookfield
Zander, Gaillienne Glashow *psychologist*

Cascade
Baumann, Carol Edler *retired political scientist*

Eau Claire
Davidson, John Kenneth, Sr., *sociologist, educator, researcher, writer, consultant*
Dick, Raymond Dale *psychology educator*
Hugo, Miriam Jeanne *counseling psychologist, educator*

Fennimore
Croft, Candace Ann *psychology educator, academic administrator*

Green Bay
Kraft, Michael Eugene *political science educator*

Kenosha
Beyer, Sylvia *social psychologist*
Cyr, Arthur I. *political science and economics educator*

La Crosse
Morehouse, Richard Edward *psychology educator*

Madison
Andreano, Ralph Louis *economist, educator*
Baldwin, Robert Edward *economics professor*
Bennett, Kenneth Alan *retired biological anthropologist*
Bloch, Peter Conrad *economist, educator*
Brock, William Allen, III, *economist, educator*
Chapman, Loren J. *psychology educator*
Cohen, Bernard Cecil *political scientist, educator*
Culbertson, Frances Mitchell *psychology educator*
Enright, Robert D. *social sciences educator*
Goldberger, Arthur Stanley *economics professor*
Graf, Truman Frederick *agricultural economist, educator*
Haller, Archibald Orben *sociologist, educator*
Hansen, W. Lee *economics professor*
Kluender, Keith R. *psychology educator*
Luening, Robert Adami *agricultural economics educator emeritus*
Morgan, Theodore *economist*
Mueller, Willard Fritz *economics professor*
Nichols, Donald Arthur *economist, educator*
Owens, Robert George *psychologist, researcher*
Rice, Joy Katharine *psychologist, educational policy studies and women's studies educator*
Robinson, Arthur Howard *geography educator*
Schmidt, John Richard *agricultural economics educator*
Scholz, John Karl *economist, educator*
Slesinger, Doris Peyser *sociology educator*
Strier, Karen Barbara *anthropologist, educator*
Thiesenhusen, William Charles *agricultural economist, educator*
Weimer, David Leo *political science educator*
Wilson, Franklin D. *sociology educator*
Wolfe, Barbara L. *economics educator, researcher*
Young, Merwin Crawford *political science educator*

Menasha
Peter, Gregory A. *sociology educator*
Taheri, Abbas Ali *economist, educator*

Middleton
Dorner, Peter Paul *retired economist, educator*
Taylor, Fannie Turnbull *social education and arts administration educator*

Milwaukee
Bibby, John Franklin *political science educator, writer*
Perlman, Richard Wilfred *economist, educator*
Quereshi, Mohammed Younus *psychology educator, consultant*
Warren, Richard M. *experimental psychologist, educator*
Wolfe, Christopher *political science educator*

Oshkosh
Gruberg, Martin *political science educator*

Washburn
Stewart, John Miller *behavioral scientist, psychobiologist, educator*

Waukesha
Graham, George Andrew, Jr., *psychologist, consultant*

Whitefish Bay
Hawkins, Brett William *political science educator*

Whitewater
Laurent, Jerome King *economics professor*

WYOMING

Laramie
Allen, John Logan *geographer, department chairman*
Chai, Winberg *political science educator*
Crocker, Thomas Dunstan *economics professor*
Gill, George Wilhelm *anthropologist*
Shaffer, Sherrill Lynn *economist*

Powell
Brophy, Dennis Richard *psychology and philosophy educator, administrator, clergyman*

Wilson
Breitenbach, Mary Louise McGraw *psychologist, chemical dependency counselor*
Divita, James J. *retired social studies educator, writer, researcher*
Helser, Marilyn A. *business educator*

TERRITORIES OF THE UNITED STATES

GUAM

Mangilao
Iverson, Thomas John *economist, educator*

PUERTO RICO

Hormigueros
Acosta, Ursula *psychologist*

CANADA

ALBERTA

Calgary
Sinclair, Brian Robert *psychologist, architect, educator*
Stebbins, Robert Alan *sociology educator*

Edmonton
Freeman, Milton Malcolm Roland *anthropology educator*
Krotki, Karol Jozef *sociology educator, demographer*

Saint Albert
Randhawa, Bikkar Singh *psychologist, educator*

BRITISH COLUMBIA

Burnaby
Brantingham, Paul Jeffrey *criminology educator*
Copes, Parzival *economist, researcher*
Kimura, Doreen *psychology educator, researcher*

Vancouver
Aberle, David Friend *anthropologist, educator*
Cynader, Max Sigmund *psychology, physiology and brain research educator, researcher*
Feaver, George Arthur *political science educator*
Holsti, Kalevi Jacque *political scientist, educator*
Jones, Lawrence Donald *economics professor*
Kesselman, Jonathan Rhys *economics educator, public policy researcher*
Laponce, Jean Antoine *political scientist, educator*
Marchak, Maureen Patricia *anthropology and sociology educator*
Nemetz, Peter Newman *economics researcher, policy analysis educator*
Olsen, Inger Anna *retired psychologist*
Robinson, John Lewis *geography educator*
Shearer, Ronald Alexander *economics professor*
Slaymaker, Olav *geography educator*
Suedfeld, Peter *psychologist, educator*
Tees, Richard Chisholm *psychology educator, researcher*
Walker, Michael Angus *economist, director*

NEW BRUNSWICK

Fredericton
Kenyon, Gary Michael *gerontology educator, researcher*

NOVA SCOTIA

Chester Basin
Parr-Johnston, Elizabeth *economy and policy consultant*

Halifax
Lenzer, Irmingard Isolde *psychology educator*
Stairs, Denis Winfield *political science educator*

ONTARIO

Hamilton
George, Peter James *economist, educator*
Ryan, Ellen Bouchard *psychology educator, gerontologist*

Kingston
Kaliski, Stephan Felix *economics professor*
MacKinnon, James Gordon *economist, educator*
Meisel, John *political scientist*

London
Laidler, David Ernest William *economics professor*
Wonnacott, Ronald Johnston *economics professor*

Niagara-on-the-Lake
Olley, Robert Edward *economist, educator*

North York
Flock, Howard *psychology educator*

Ottawa
Brooks, David Barry *resource economist*
Dagum, Camilo *economist, educator*
Griller, David *economics and technology consultant*

Saint Catharines
Stevenson, Garth *social sciences educator*

Toronto
Bird, Richard Miller *economics professor*
Carr, Jack Leslie *economics educator, economic consultant*
DeWitt, David B. *political scientist, educator, political organization worker*
Dobson, Wendy Kathleen *economics professor*
Ferguson, Kingsley George *retired psychologist*
Goldfarb, Martin *sociologist, researcher*
Grayson, Albert Kirk *Near Eastern studies educator*
Helleiner, Gerald Karl *economics professor*
Munro, John Henry Alexander *economics educator, writer*
Pratt, Robert Cranford *political scientist, educator*
Rapoport, Anatol *peace studies educator, mathematical biologist*
Rose, Jeffrey Raymond *economist, educator, negotiator*
Smith, Lawrence Berk *economist, educator*

Waterloo
Fallding, Harold Joseph *sociology educator*
Nelson, J. Gordon *geography educator*
Vogel-Sprott, Muriel Doris *psychology educator, researcher*

Windsor
Auld, Frank *psychologist, educator*

QUEBEC

Montreal
Brecher, Irving *economics professor*
Brecher, Michael *political science educator*
Dufour, Jean-Marie *economics researcher, educator*
Ikawa-Smith, Fumiko *anthropologist, educator*
Matziorinis, Kenneth N. *economist*
Melzack, Ronald *psychology educator*
Milner, Brenda Atkinson Langford *neuropsychologist*
Nayar, Baldev Raj *political science educator*
Normandeau, Andre Gabriel *criminologist, educator*
Raynauld, Andre *economist, educator*
Stewart, Jane *psychology educator*
Szabo, Denis *criminologist, educator*
Trigger, Bruce Graham *anthropology educator*
Vaillancourt, Jean-Guy *sociology researcher and educator*
Waller, Harold Myron *political science educator*

Quebec City
Belanger, Gerard *economics professor*
Tremblay, Marc Adélard *anthropologist, educator*

MEXICO

Mexico City
Gonzalez-Sanchez, Enrique *economist*

Puebla
Creuheras, Santiago *social scientist*

ARGENTINA

Buenos Aires
Berardi, Jorge Enrique *economist*
Lopez-Murphy, Ricardo Hipolito *economist*

AUSTRALIA

Sydney
Blakely, Edward James *economics professor*

Victoria Armadale
Neil, Sandra Eilleen Silverberg *psychologist*

AUSTRIA

Graz
Prisching, Manfred *sociology educator*

BELGIUM

Brussels
Prodi, Romano *economist, educator, researcher, former prime minister of Italy, international commission executive*

BRAZIL

Rio de Janeiro
Resende, Marcelo *economist, educator*

CHINA

Beijing
Banister, Judith *demographer, educator*

DENMARK

Copenhagen
Olgaard, Anders *economics professor*

Gentofte
Egsmose, Ragna Kopp *cultural sociologist, researcher*

EGYPT

Cairo
Sullivan, Earl Le Roy *political science educator, academic administrator*

ENGLAND

Aldwych London
O'Brien, Patrick Karl *economic history educator*

Cambridge
Mirrlees, Sir James Alexander *economics professor*
Renfrew, Andrew Colin (Lord Renfrew of Kaimsthorn) *archaeologist, academic administrator*
Richard, Alison Fettes *anthropology educator*

Durham
Spooner, Frank Clyffurde *economic history educator*

Guildford
Bulmer, Martin *sociologist, educator*

London
Dahrendorf, Lord Ralf Gustav *social scientist, educator*
Douglas, Mary Tew *anthropology and humanities educator*
Foldes, Lucien Paul *economics professor*
Junz, Helen B. *economist*
Kuper, Adam Jonathan *anthropologist, educator*
Portes, Richard David *economics professor*
Shaw, Timothy Milton *political science educator*
Steele, Howard L. *psychology educator*

Oxford
Halsey, Albert Henry *sociologist*
Mattli, Walter *political scientist, educator*
Nolan, James Lawry, Jr., *sociologist*
Varese, Federico *political science educator*

York
Williams, Alan Harold *economics professor*

ESTONIA

Tallinn
Köörna, Arno *economist, educator*

FRANCE

Guyancourt
Dubar, Claude Roger *sociologist*

Paris
Allais, Maurice Felix *economist*
Fitoussi, Jean-Paul Samuel *economist, educator*
Kouyaté, Lansana *economist, federal official, diplomat*
Memmi, Albert *sociologist, educator*

GERMANY

Berlin
Blankart, Charles Beat *economics professor*
Weiss, Dieter Waldemar *economics educator, consultant*

Bochum
Folkers, Cay *economics professor*

Bonn
Albach, Horst *economist*
Krelle, Wilhelm Ernst *emeritus economics educator*
Selten, Reinhard *retired economist, educator*

Frankfurt
Glatzer, Wolfgang P. W. *sociology educator*

Göttingen
Achtenhagen, Frank *economics professor*

Hamburg
Holler, Manfred Joseph *economics professor*

Munich
Reimann, Helga Luise *sociologist*
Whetten, Lawrence L. *international relations educator*

Siegen
Buhr, Walter Heinrich Wilhelm *economics professor*

GREECE

Athens
Kalamotousakis, George John *economist, merchant banker, educator*

HONG KONG

Hong Kong
Lau, Lawrence Juen-Yee *economics educator, consultant*

Kowloon
Qiu, Larry Dongxiao *economics professor*
Wu, Xiaogang *social sciences educator, researcher*

HUNGARY

Budapest
Forgó, Ferenc *economics professor*
Simai, Mihaly *economics and business educator*

ISRAEL

Arad
Hollander, Samuel *economist, educator*

Beer Sheva
Hare, A(lexander) Paul *sociology educator*

Metar
Lithwick, Norman Harvey *economics professor*

ITALY

Pisa
Settis, Salvatore *archaeologist, art historian*

Rome
Gros-Pietro, Gian Maria *economics professor*
Scognamiglio, Carlo *economics and finance educator, Italian government senator*
Westley, John Richard *economist*

JAPAN

Ibaraki
Kawano, Toshiaki *retired economics educator*

Mie
Isshiki, Masayuki *sociologist, educator, dean*

Nagoya
Kajitani, Motohisa *sociology educator*

Sakai
Fujita, Sei *political economist, educator*

Tokyo
Fukushima, Kiyohiko *economist*
Gyohten, Toyoo *economist*
Iinuma, Hiroichi *international economics and trade educator, researcher*
Lo, Fu-chen *economist, educator, ambassador*
Maki, Atsushi *economics professor*
Miyazaki, Koichi *economics professor*
Nishiyama, Chiaki *economist, educator*
Van Ginkel, Johannes Auguste *geographer, educator*

Yokohama
Kuroda, Yasumasa *political science educator, researcher*

MALTA

Valletta
Bonello, Michael C. *economist*

NIGERIA

Ijebu Ode
Adedeji, Adebayo *economist, former government official*

PHILIPPINES

Makati
Thompson, Willard Scott (W. Scott Thompson) *social sciences educator*

REPUBLIC OF KOREA

Kwangju
Kim, Kyou Yung *economist, educator*
Lee, Jung-Koo *economist, educator*

Seoul
Ahn, Choong Yong *economics professor*

Suwon
Lee, Tong Hun *economics professor*

RUSSIA

Moscow
Saltykov, Boris Georgievich *economist, politician*

SINGAPORE

Singapore
Pelizzo, Riccardo *political scientist*

SPAIN

Castellon
Georgantzis, Nikolaos *economist*

SRI LANKA

Colombo
Munasinghe, Mohan *development economist*
Spain, James William *political scientist, writer, investor*

SWITZERLAND

Geneva
Sidjanski, Dusan *economist, educator*

TAIWAN

Taichung
Yen, Gili *economics researcher*

THAILAND

Bangkok
Kornell, Ronald Frank *economist*

UKRAINE

Mariupol
Vasiljev, Alexander Valerjovich *metallurgical engineer, economist*

ADDRESS UNPUBLISHED

Adams, Robert McCormick *anthropologist, educator*
Agnew, Robert *retired psychologist, poet*
Ahmed, Syed Z. *anthropologist*
Akutagawa, Donald *psychologist, educator*
Alker, Hayward Rose *political scientist, educator*
Alkov, Robert Adolf *retired psychologist*
Allen, Bruce Templeton *retired economics professor*
Allen, Leatrice Delorice *psychologist*
Allen, William Sheridan *retired social sciences educator*
Alpher, Victor Seth *consultant, clinical psychologist*
Altman, Irwin *psychology educator*
Anderson, Bernard E. *economist*
Anderson, James George *sociologist, educator*
Anderson, Odin Waldemar *sociologist, educator*
Andrain, Charles Franklin *political science educator*
Arditti, Fred D. *economist, educator*
Athanasiou, Robert Byron *retired physician, psychologist*
Axilrod, Stephen Harvey *global economic consultant, economist*
Azman, Rosiana Lynne *psychologist, educator*
Baba, Marietta Lynn *business anthropologist, university administrator*
Baldwin, Sidney *retired political science professor*
Barber, Clarence Lyle *economics educator*
Barnes, Samuel Henry *political scientist, educator*
Barrios, Luis *psychologist, educator, priest*
Bateson, Mary Catherine *anthropology educator emerita*
Beal, Wanda Elnora *psychologist, writer, artist*
Beck, Colleen Marguerite *archaeologist*
Bergin, Allen Eric *clinical psychologist, educator*
Bert, Clara Virginia *retired home economics educator, school system administrator*
Blank, Rebecca Margaret *economist*
Blaszczynski, Andre Boguslaw *economist, educator*
Bluestone, Barry Alan *economics professor, educator*
Bohannan, Paul James *anthropologist, writer, former university administrator*
Bohn, Marsha J. *anthropologist, researcher*
Bonnell, Victoria Eileen *sociologist, educator*
Bourguignon, Erika Eichhorn *anthropologist, educator*
Bourque, Susan Carolyn *political scientist*
Bowman, Larry Wayne *investigator, English and criminal justice educator*
Brandl, John Edward *public affairs educator*
Bredfeldt, John Creighton *economist, financial analyst, retired military officer*
Briggs, Philip James *political science educator, author, lecturer, reviewer*
Brint, Steven Gregory *sociologist, educator*
Buchin, Jean *psychologist, educator*
Buck, Jane Louise *psychology educator*
Burns, Joseph M. *economist*
Caine, Eric Russell *social sciences educator*
Canjar, Patricia McWade *psychologist*
Cantril, Albert H(adley) *public opinion analyst*
Carliner, Geoffrey Owen *economist, director*
Carlsen, Mary Baird *clinical psychologist*
Carlson, Gustav Gunnar *anthropology educator*
Carlson, Janet Frances *psychologist, educator*
Carlson, Roger David *psychologist, clergyman, educator*
Carpentieri, Sarah C. *neuropsychologist, researcher, clinical psychologist*
Casper, Julie Ann *geographer, writer*
Cattell, Heather Birkett *psychologist*
Chao, Ruth *psychologist, researcher*
Chapman, Hope Horan *psychologist*
Chapman, Richard LeRoy *retired public policy researcher*
Chatterji, Angana P. *anthropologist*
Christian, James Wayne *economist*
Clark, Caleb Morgan *political scientist, educator*
Clark, Jere Walton *economics educator, researcher*
Cochran, John P. *economics professor*
Cohen, Jerome *psychology educator, electrophysiologist*
Collier, William Gayle *psychology educator, researcher*
Collins, Harker *economist, manufacturing executive, publisher, marketing, financial, business and legal consultant*
Colosimo, Mary Lynn Sukurs *psychology educator*
Cotten, Annie Laura *psychologist, educator*
Cox, Gary Walter *political science educator*
Crawford, Edward E. *retired psychologist*
Crozier, Prudence Slitor *economist*
Cutting, Laurie E. *psychology educator, researcher*
Daniel, Coldwell, III, *economist, educator*
Daniels, Arlene Kaplan *sociology educator*
Danielsen, Albert Leroy *economics educator, energy and utilities consultant*
Dawkins, Marva Phyllis *psychologist, educator*
Dean, Edwin Robinson *economist, educator, consultant*
Debreu, Gerard *economics and mathematics educator*
Demma, Joe *political scientist, consultant*
Denevan, William Maxfield *geographer, historical ecologist*
DeVaris, Jeannette Mary *psychologist*
Dewald, William Guenthner *economist*
d'Heurle, Adma Jeha *psychology educator*
Dobriansky, Lev Eugene *economist, educator, diplomat*
Dole, Arthur Alexander *psychology educator*
Donaldson, Loraine *economics professor*
Dowd, Morgan Daniel *political science educator*
Dowen, Robert Lynn *international affairs analyst and political consultant, editor, writer*
Drummond, Dorothy Weitz *geography education consultant, educator, author*
Dwyer, Gerald Paul, Jr., *economist, bank executive*
Dzindolet, Mary Teresa *psychology educator*
Earle, Timothy Keese *anthropology educator*
Ebert, Viola Roth *neuropsychologist, entrepreneur*
Edwards, Ward Dennis *psychology and industrial engineering educator*
Egnor, Joanne McClellan *psychology educator*
Eikleberry, Carol *psychologist, writer*
Elgin, Gita *psychologist*
Engel, Bernard Theodore *psychologist, educator*
England, Paula Suzanne *sociologist, educator*
Ericson, Phyllis Jane *psychologist, psychotherapist, consultant*
Eron, Leonard David *psychology educator*
Everly, George Stotelmyer, Jr., *psychologist, psychophysiologist, educator, mathematician*
Farmer, Christopher J. *political scientist, writer*
Fels, Rendigs *economist, educator*
Finberg, Bonny *psychologist, writer*
Finnberg, Elaine Agnes *psychologist, editor*
Folds-Bennett, Trisha Helen *psychologist, educator*
Fontes, Patricia J. *educational psychologist*
Foreman, Kelly Marie *anthropologist, music educator*
Foster, Carol Elise *psychologist, writer*
Franklin, Margery Bodansky *psychology educator, researcher*
Fred-Mensah, Ben Kwame *international development educator, consultant*
Freilich, Morris *anthropologist, educator*
Freshman, Brenda Lee *psychologist, educator, psychologist, researcher*
Friedman, Martin Philip *applied behavior sciences specialist, education educator*
Fromlet, K. Hubert *banking economist*
Frost, Ellen Louise *political economist*
Funseth, Robert Lloyd Eric Martin *international consultant, lecturer, retired senior foreign service officer, foundation administrator*
Gardner, Bruce Lynn *agricultural economist*
Gardner, Marvin Allen, Jr., *pastoral and clinical psychologist*
Garzarelli, Elaine Marie *economist*
Gay, David Edward Ryan *economist*
Geake, Raymond Robert *psychologist*
Geckil, Ilhan Kubilay *economist, consultant*
Geertz, Hildred Storey *anthropology educator*
Genis, Alice Singer *psychologist*
Glendening, Terry Sky *psychologist*
Goldston, Stephen Eugene *community psychologist, educator, consultant*
Graham, Norma Van Surdam *psychologist, educator*
Greeley, Andrew Moran *sociologist, writer*
Greenberg, Ira Arthur *psychologist*
Greenwood, Janet Kae Daly *psychologist, educational administrator, marketing professional*
Gunczler, Jeannette *economist, writer*
Haber, Ralph Norman *psychology consultant, researcher, educator*
Hahn, Frank Horace *economics professor*
Haining, Jeane *psychologist*
Hall, Ella Taylor *clinical school psychologist*
Hall, Jay *social psychologist*
Hamilton, Jack Richard *former social psychologist*
Hanks, Gary Arlin *psychology educator*
Hanushek, Eric Alan *economics professor*
Harshbarger, Richard B. *retired economics educator*
Hartzell, Irene Janofsky *psychologist*
Harvey, James Cardwell *political science educator, consultant*
Haywood, H(erbert) Carl(ton) *psychologist, educator*
Hefferan, Colien Joan *economist*
Helfgott, Roy B. *economist, educator*
Henderson, Karen Sue *psychologist*
Hewitt, Benjamin Attmore *psychologist, consultant*
Hiler, Monica Jean *reading and sociology educator*
Hilliard, Sam Bowers *geography educator*
Hires, William Leland *psychologist, consultant*
Hirsh-Pasek, Kathryn Ann *psychology educator*
Hodge, David R. *social science researcher*
Hodgson, Dorothy L. *social studies educator*
Holmes, Paul Luther *political scientist, educational consultant*
Hughes, Ann Hightower *retired economist, international trade consultant*
Hume, Susan Rachel *finance and economics educator*
Humphrey, Kathryn Long *school psychologist, writer*
Ichiishi, Tatsuro *economics and mathematics educator*
Igbineweka, Andrew Osabuohien *public administration, political science educator*
Isaacs, Kenneth S(idney) *psychoanalyst, educator*
Jacobsen, Diane DeMell *business executive and foreign policy specialist*
James, Estelle *economist, educator*
Jett, Stephen Clinton *geography and textiles educator, researcher*
Johnson, Albert Wesley *professor emeritus*
Johnson, Daniel Milo *sociology educator, university dean*
Johnson, J(anet) Susan *psychologist*
Jordan, Robert Smith *political science educator*
Kahana, Eva Frost *sociology educator*
Kaliski, Mary *psychologist*
Kalu, Kalu Ndukwe *political scientist, educator*
Karczmar, Mieczyslaw *economist*
Karson, Samuel *psychologist, educator*
Kaslow, Florence Whiteman *psychologist, educator, family business consultant*
Kendrick, Budd Leroy *psychologist*
Kennedy, Marla Catherine *psychologist*
Kennedy-Minott, Rodney *international relations educator, former ambassador*
Kenyon, Daphne Anne *economics professor*
Keyes, Margaret Naumann *home economics educator*
Khavari, Khalil Akhtar *psychology educator*
Kiesler, Charles Adolphus *psychologist, academic administrator*
King, Rosalyn Mercita *social sciences educator, researcher*
Kirkpatrick, James Joseph *psychologist*
Kohan, Dennis Lynn *international trade educator, consultant*
Koo, Shou-Eng *economics professor*
Korey, John L. *political scientist, educator*
Kostere, Kim Martin *psychologist, consultant*
Kovacs, Malcolm *sociology educator, religious studies educator*
Kreps, Juanita Morris *economics educator, former government official*
Landon, William J. *retired intelligence officer*
Lanzillotti, Robert Franklin *economist, educator*
Lasky, Richard Donald *psychoanalyst, educator*
Laws, Eric Laban *psychologist, educator*
LeBlanc, Hugh Linus *political science educator, consultant*
Lee, Won-Chan *psychometrician*
Leff, Walli F. *psychologist, writer*
Lewis, Charles Leonard *psychologist*
Lewis, Robert Turner *former psychologist*
Lichtenberg, Byron K. *futurist, manufacturing executive, space flight consultant, pilot*
Lief, Thomas Parrish *sociologist, educator*
Lindsey, Lawrence Benjamin *economist*
Linz, Gerhard David *psychologist, consultant*
Lipsey, Richard George *economist, educator*
Lipsitt, Lewis Paeff *psychology educator*
Liu, Ruth Xiaoru *criminologist, educator*
Locke, Edwin Allen, III, *retired psychologist, educator*
Loftus, Elizabeth F. *psychology educator*
Lonergan, Thomas Francis, III, *criminal justice consultant*
Ludden, John Franklin *retired financial economist*
Lueptow, Lloyd Benjamin *retired sociology educator*
MacDougall, Sir Donald (Sir George Donald Alastair MacDougall) *economist*
MacLennan, Beryce Winifred *psychologist*
Maehr, Martin Louis *psychology educator*
Mair, Charles *social studies educator*
Marcus, Edward *economist, educator*
Mark, Jonathan Greenfield *political scientist, educator, writer*
Markovich, Patricia Helen *economist*
Marti, Gerardo *sociologist, educator, minister*
Marvick, Elizabeth Wirth *retired political scientist*
Marx, Gary T. *sociologist, writer*
Masakowski, Yvonne Rose *psychologist, researcher*
Massa, Salvatore Peter *psychologist*
Matema, Zsun-nee Kimball (Annette K. Miller) *social sciences educator*
Matheny, Adam Pence, Jr., *child psychologist, educator, consultant, researcher*
McArthur, John William *economist, researcher*
McCall, Madhavi Michael *social sciences educator*
McCann, Lee I. *psychology educator*
Mc Clellan, Catharine *anthropologist, educator*
McDougal, Marie Patricia *retired educator, freelance writer and editor*
McGough, Duane Theodore *economist, consultant, retired government official*
McGreevy, Mary Sharron *former psychology educator*
Menaker, Shirley Ann Lasch *psychology educator, academic administrator*
Mesa-Lago, Carmelo *economist, educator*
Meyerovitz, Fayona Brenda *psychologist, consultant*
Migue, Jean Luc *economics professor*
Moore, John Runyan *agricultural and resource economics educator*
Morris, Dolores Orinskia *psychologist, psychoanalyst*
Morris, Jane Elizabeth *home economics educator*
Muhn, Judy Ann *psychologist, trainer, genealogist*
Murphy, Evelyn Frances *economist*
Mutalipassi, Louis Richard *psychologist, educator*
Nadolski, Dora J. *social sciences educator, researcher*
Naples, Caesar Joseph *law and public policy educator, lawyer, consultant*
Natani, Kirmach *forensic psychologist*
Newborn, Jud *anthropologist, writer, curator, educator, historian*
Nierenberg, Norman *urban land economist, retired state official*
Noll, Richard Dean, Jr., *psychologist, educator, historian*
Norman, Donald Arthur *cognitive scientist*
O'Brien, John Wilfrid *economist, emeritus university president, educator*
Olson, William Clinton *anthologist, international affairs administrator*
O'Neal, Harriet Roberts *psychologist, psycholegal consultant*
Ouimette, Paige *psychologist, researcher*
Pace, Charles Robert *psychologist, educator*
Pannell, Clifton Wyndham *geography educator, writer*
Paravastu, Swamy *economist, researcher*
Pattanaik, Prasanta Kumar *economics professor*
Patterson, James E. *economist, author, speaker*
Patterson, Samuel C. *political science educator*
Pearson, Richard Joseph *archaeologist, educator*
Pedersen, Knud George *economics educator, academic administrator*
Pérez-Monforti, Jessica L. *social sciences educator, researcher*
Peters, Kristen Michele *psychologist, researcher*
Phelps, Gerry Charlotte *economist, minister*
Pollack, Gerald Alexander *economist, government official*
Pomerantz, James Robert *psychology educator, academic administrator*
Power, Mary Susan *political scientist, educator*
Pracht, Drenda Kay *psychologist*
Premack, David *psychologist*
Prewitt, Kenneth *political science educator, foundation executive*
Prothro, Edwin Terry *psychologist educator*
Randall, Richard Rainier *geographer*
Raphaelson, Arnold Herbert *economist educator*
Reed, Diane Marie *psychologist*
Reese, Hayne Waring *psychologist, educator*
Reich, Otto Juan *political analyst, business consultant*
Reider, Richard Gary *geographer, educator*
Renfro, William Leonard *futurist, lawyer, inventor, entrepreneur*
Revankar, Nagesh Subray *economics professor*
Revere, Virginia Lehr *clinical psychologist*
Reynolds, Clark Winton *economist, educator*
Richards, Ruth *psychiatrist, educational psychologist*
Richmond, Anthony Henry *sociologist, emeritus educator*
Rickel, Annette Urso *psychology and psychiatry researcher, educator*
Riecken, Henry William *psychologist, research director*
Risley, Todd Robert *psychologist, educator*
Roberts, Ray Crouse, Jr., *retired economics educator*
Robinson, James Arthur *policy scientist*
Robinson, Marguerite Stern *anthropologist, educator, consultant*
Robinson, Marshall Alan *economics educator, foundation executive*
Roche de Coppens, Peter George *sociologist, educator*
Rosen, Lawrence *anthropologist, educator*
Rosen, Theodore Howard *psychologist, consultant*
Ross, William Dee, Jr., *economist*
Rossi, Peter Henry *sociology educator*
Ruback, Richard Barry *psychologist, educator*
Rubenzer, Steven James *forensic psychologist*
Rubin, Zick *psychology educator, lawyer, writer*
Rubner, Michael *international relations educator, university administrator*
Ruchelman, Leonard Isadore *urban studies and public administration educator*
Ruderman, Armand Peter *health economics educator, consultant, volunteer*
Santana, Niurka Maribel *psychologist, educator*
Santuzzi, Alecia Marie *psychologist, educator, researcher*
Sargent, Thomas Andrew *retired political science educator*
Schaler, Jeffrey Alfred *psychologist, educator*
Schlichting, Kimberly Sue *psychologist, educator, health facility administrator*
Schmandt-Besserat, Denise *archaeologist, educator*
Schmidt, Harvey Martin *economic forecaster, educator, financial consultant*
Schmidt, Martha Bubeck *social sciences educator*
Sebastian, Peter *international affairs consultant, former ambassador*
Shakow, Alexander *economist, government official*
Shapiro, Leo J. *social researcher*
Sharpe, William Forsyth *economics professor*
Shepard, Roger Newland *psychologist, educator*
Shepp, Bryan Eugene *psychologist, educator*
Simon, Norma Plavnick *psychologist*
Sims, Kent Otway *economist*
Sinai, Allen Leo *economist, educator*
Sisley, Emily Lucretia *retired psychologist, medical writer*
Smason, Ivan *psychologist, writer*
Smelser, Neil Joseph *sociologist*
Smith, V. Kerry *economics professor*
Smith, Vme Edom (Verna Mae Edom Smith) *sociology educator, freelance writer, photographer*
Sonderegger, Theo Brown *psychology educator*
Souzdaltsev, Igor Nikolayevich *economist*
Spelke, Elizabeth Shilin *psychology educator*
Stallone, Thomas Michael Kearney *clinical psychologist*
Steffen, Konrad *geography educator*
Stephen, Michael *psychologist*
Stewart, Charles Todd, Jr., *retired economist*
Striker, Cecil Leopold *archaeologist, educator*
Studness, Charles Michael *economist*
Stufano, Thomas Joseph *criminologist, author, inventor*
Stumpf, Heinrich J. *psychometrician, research consultant*
Sumner, William Marvin *anthropology and archaeology educator*
Swaner-Smoot, Paula Margetts *clinical psychologist*
Swanstrom, Thomas Evan *economist*
Swartz, Jon David *psychologist, educator*
Swiger, Mark *social studies educator*
Taranto, Maria Antoinette *psychology researcher and educator*
Tarrance, Vernon Lance, Jr., *public opinion research executive*
Tartaro, Christine *criminologist, educator*
Taylor, Charles Henry *psychoanalyst, educator*
Tenopyr, Mary Louise Welsh (Mrs. Joseph Tenopyr) *psychologist*
Ter Horst, Jerald Franklin *public affairs counsel*
Textor, Robert Bayard *cultural anthropology writer, consultant, educator*
Thiessen, Delbert Duane *psychologist*
Thompson, Alan Eric *economics professor*
Tonello-Stuart, Enrica Maria *political economist*
Tremblay, Richard Ernest *psychology educator*
Tripp, Aili Mari *political science educator*
van de Zilver, Peter A.L. *economist, business executive*
Van Dyk, Frederick Theodore *political scientist, writer*
Veseth, Michael Aaron *economics professor*
Vlachos, Peter George *economics professor*
Volcker, Paul A. *economist*
Volkmann, Frances Cooper *psychologist, educator*
Walker, Clarence Eugene *psychology educator*
Wallerstein, Judith Saretsky *psychologist, researcher*
Ward, Albert Eugene *archaeologist, ethnohistorian, research center executive*
Ward, Jeannette Poole *retired psychologist, educator*
Warne, William Robert *economist*
Waud, Roger Neil *economist, educator*
Weber, Mary Ellen Healy *economist*
Weil, Rolf Alfred *economist, university president emeritus*
Weissenburger, David Allen *psychologist, educator, consultant*
Werner-Jacobsen, Emmy Elisabeth *developmental psychologist*
White, Larry D. *retired political science educator*
Wilcox, Diane Marie *educational psychologist, software designer*
Wilkinson, Doris *medical sociology educator*

Wolfe, Gregory Baker *international relations educator*
Wonders, William Clare *geography educator*
Wood, Robert Coldwell *political scientist*
Woodcock, Richard Wesley *educational psychologist*

Wright, James David *sociology educator, writer*
Wrong, Dennis Hume *sociologist, educator*
Yale (Yeleyenide-Yale), Melpomene Fotine *anthropologist, archaeologist, art historian, conservator, researcher*

Yost, William Albert *psychology educator, hearing researcher*
Zavala, Albert *research psychologist*
Zeigler, L(uther) Harmon *political science educator*

Zimet, Lloyd *sport psychologist, health planner, educator*
Zuckerman, Harriet *sociologist, educator*
Zuiches, James Joseph *sociologist, educator*